RadioTimes
GUIDE TO
FILMS
2017

Edited by the Radio Times Film Unit
IMMEDIATE MEDIA COMPANY LTD

Published by Immediate Media Company London Ltd Vineyard House 44 Brook Green London W6 7BT
ISBN 13 978-0-9929364-3-3
First published in the United Kingdom 2000
Seventeenth edition published in the United Kingdom 2016
Copyright © 2016 Immediate Media Company London Ltd

Managing Director, *Radio Times* Group Kathy Day
Editorial Director Ben Preston
Publisher Richard Campbell
Senior Production Co-ordinator Steve Calver
Head of Retail Jessica Batten
Cover design by Jacob Howard/Marlene Diaz Ellinghaus
Cover picture credits Kobal; Allstar; Walt Disney Company Ltd; Universal Pictures
Cover picture research by Rachel Young
Text design by Ben Cracknell Studios
Additional text design by Ranjika De Silva
Typesetting by David Lewis XML Associates Ltd
Printed in the UK by CPI Clowes Ltd, Beccles

Contents

How to use this guide

Welcome to the 2017 edition of the *Radio Times Guide to Films*. With a grand total of 24,039 films filling 1,712 pages, this 17th edition of the *Guide* is the most comprehensive ever.

Of the 504 new entries (films that have never appeared in any *Radio Times Guide to Films*), many were released in UK cinemas during the past 12 months; some were shown on TV; others became available on DVD/Blu-ray or download. For instance, early Ealing drama *Painted Boats*, which unlike their well-known comedies reflects the studio's documentary work during the war, has recently made its way to TV – and it's the 21st film by *Fish Called Wanda* director Charles Crichton to feature in the Guide (see page 957).

From a British stalwart to perhaps the most famous director of modern times... Steven Spielberg is turning 70, and to celebrate the occasion, one of his greatest creations – *ET the Extra-Terrestrial* – is flying majestically across our cover.

In 2010, *ET* was voted by thousands of *Radio Times* readers as your favourite family film of all time. And, along with his creator, the lonely little alien is also celebrating a birthday, his 35th.

As always, we aim to be the most up-to-date guide on the market, thanks to the advance work of our reviewers.

You will find a large number of reviews for movies that hadn't yet made it to cinemas in the UK at the time of going to press, and in excess of 90 previews, clearly signposted, of major films that were not available for review prior to our deadline – Wolverine himself, Hugh Jackman, will be in fine voice as PT Barnum in musical *The Greatest Showman on Earth* and fresh from starring with Jackman as the most British of heroes, Eddie the Eagle, Taron Egerton will be heading off on a new Kingsman adventure.

If you have any recommendations or changes that you'd like us to incorporate in the next edition of the *Radio Times Guide to Films*, please get in touch – this year, I would particularly like to thank Brian Rees for his contributions to the indexes. All your suggestions are invaluable and we would be delighted to hear your comments. You can write to us at: *Radio Times Guide to Films*, Immediate Media Company Ltd, Vineyard House, 44 Brook Green, London W6 7BT; or email us at films@radiotimes.com.

SUE ROBINSON, EDITOR

100 LANDMARK FILMS

First identified in the 2007 edition of the *Guide*, these 100 key influential films are flagged in the A to Z pages by a tinted marker above each title. The films have been earmarked for Landmark status as pivotal works whose impact is still felt for reasons of artistic and stylistic innovation, as watersheds in content and technique, and as key films of their time. They are easy to find as you browse through the section, and an explanation of each choice is included to complement the review.

TITLES

Films are listed under the titles by which we consider them to be best known in the UK and these titles are shown as they appear on screen. While many foreign-language movies are listed under their English title, others are listed under their original title, especially if they are particularly famous or were released theatrically or on DVD/video under that title.

Alternative titles If you cannot find the film you are looking for in the main A-Z section, refer to the appendix of alternative titles at the back of the book. You should find a cross-reference to the film you're seeking there. The alternative title appendix is not a complete index of all the alternative titles and/or foreign-language titles by which a film might be known – it is a selective appendix, designed to help you find the film you're looking for.

Alphabetisation Titles are listed alphabetically, ignoring definite and indefinite articles (a, an, the, including foreign-language articles such as le, la, les, das, il, el), place names being the exception, eg Los Angeles. Titles are also listed alphabetically by word, with initials counting as an individual word. For example, *Back to the Future* comes before *Backdraft*; *LA Confidential* before *Labyrinth*. Punctuation, such as apostrophes and colons, is also ignored. A hyphen equals a space (ie *Life-Size* comes before *Life Stinks*, not after it). Some film series have been re-ordered to reflect their chronology – *Harry Potter and the Philosopher's Stone* now comes before *Harry Potter and the Chamber of Secrets*, while *Die Hard with a Vengeance* precedes *Die Hard 4.0*.

STAR RATINGS

The star rating assigned to a film reflects the opinion of the reviewer. Many older films may be considered "difficult" (*The Battleship Potemkin*) or offensive (Leni Riefenstahl's *Triumph of the Will*) by today's audiences but will still have a high star rating because of their importance and/or their technical excellence.

The star ratings also help rank a movie within its genre. For example, a TV movie may be granted five stars in comparison to other TV movies (*The Autobiography of Miss Jane Pittman* versus *Danielle Steel's No Greater Love*); but you wouldn't compare it to *Citizen Kane*. Action film *The Fast and the Furious* rates four stars when compared to *Delta Force 2*, but you wouldn't compare it to *Kiss Me Kate*.

And within each star rating (since we don't give half stars), there may be a band of quality, some two-star movies being better than others. (The handful of "lost" films and previews included in this guide have no star rating, as either no prints exist or none was available prior to our deadline.)

Times change, perspectives change and, on occasion, so do our star ratings, as we are constantly reassessing and updating our entries. As a guideline, the star ratings mean:

★ poor
★★ could be worse
★★★ worth watching
★★★★ very good
★★★★★ outstanding

Films with only one star are probably so bad that most viewers wouldn't want to waste a couple of hours of their time on such efforts, yet some may be hilarious as only a one-star film can be. Those that have two will have some points of merit and a number of faults, but may appeal to fans of a certain actor or genre, or as a moderately watchable or undemanding time-waster.

Granting three stars means that, although a film is not without flaws, the positives outweigh the negatives. Films that have four stars are beyond being just watchable – within their genre, they're special, even if with a few flaws. Those films granted five stars are the outstanding, brilliant few. In fact, there are only 878 in our guide – only 3.6 per cent of the total.

BBFC CERTIFICATES

Where possible we give the current BBFC (British Board of Film Classification) DVD/Blu-ray certificate. For post-1982 films not released on DVD/Blu-ray or video in the UK, we list the original cinema certificate. Definitions of current certificates appear at the foot of each page in the A-Z section of the guide.

We haven't included older cinema certificates (X, AA, A), since expectations of content have changed so these are no longer a useful guide. Back in 1953 *Abbott and Costello Meet Dr Jekyll and Mr Hyde* was rated X, but has been granted a PG certificate on DVD. However, if a film was given a U certificate pre-1982, this is listed because it remains a good indication of a film's content.

In 2002, the BBFC introduced the 12A certificate for cinema only. This is listed where no DVD/Blu-ray/video certificate exists.

Note: there is no certificate for foreign-language films, made-for-TV movies and others that have not received a cinema/video/DVD/Blu-ray release in the UK. Those that received a limited theatrical release may only have been certificated by the local authority in the release area. This local authority certificate will not be listed.

GENRE

These are set by our editorial team to give you some indication of the type of film, as a guide only. See also the notes regarding the Appendix of Five-Star and Four-Star Films.

YEAR

Wherever possible, this is the copyright year of the film, not the year in which it was released. When we have been unable to confirm a copyright year, we have used the year of production; if that cannot be confirmed, we have used the year of first release.

COLOUR

This refers to the original colour of the film, ie the colour in which it was made: black and white, colour, tinted, sepia or a combination of these. Films that were originally made in black and white but now exist in colourised versions will still be listed as "BW", ie black and white.

RUNNING TIME
Where there is a certificate, the running time relates to that certificate: that is, a video/DVD/Blu-ray running time if the film is/was available on one of those media in the UK, or the theatrical running time if not. For some obscure films, it may not be possible to give a running time. In the case of a few silent films, we may only have been able to obtain information regarding the number of reels, so again no running time is listed.

COUNTRY OF ORIGIN
The country, or countries, of origin is determined by which country/countries financed the film, not where it was made.

UK – United Kingdom	Egy – Egypt	P Ric – Puerto Rico
US – United States	Est – Estonia	Pak – Pakistan
Afg – Afghanistan	Fin – Finland	Pan – Panama
Alg – Algeria	Fr – France	Phil – Philippines
Arg – Argentina	Ger – Germany (pre-1945, post-1990)	Pol – Poland
Arm – Armenia	Gr – Greece	Por – Portugal
Aus – Australia	HK – Hong Kong	Rom – Romania
Ban – Bangladesh	Hun – Hungary	Rus – Russia (pre-1922, post-1996)
Bel – Belgium	Ice – Iceland	S Afr – South Africa
Bol – Bolivia	Ind – India	S Kor – South Korea
Bra – Brazil	Ire – Republic of Ireland	Sen – Senegal
Bul – Bulgaria		Ser – Serbia
Camb – Cambodia	Is – Israel	Sing – Singapore
Can – Canada	It – Italy	Sp – Spain
Cay – Cayman Is	Iv C – Ivory Coast	Sri L – Sri Lanka
Chi – China	Jam – Jamaica	Swe – Sweden
Chil – Chile	Jpn – Japan	Swi – Switzerland
Col – Colombia	Kaz – Kazakhstan	Tai – Taiwan
Cos R – Costa Rica	Ken – Kenya	Thai – Thailand
Cro – Croatia	Leb – Lebanon	Tun – Tunisia
Cub – Cuba	Lith – Lithuania	Tur – Turkey
Cur – Curaçao	Lux – Luxembourg	USSR – Soviet Union (1922–96)
Cyp – Cyprus	Mac – Macedonia	
Cz – Czechoslovakia (up to 1993)	Mex – Mexico	Ukr – Ukraine
Cz Rep – Czech Republic (1993 and onwards)	Mor – Morocco	Urug – Uruguay
	NZ – New Zealand	Ven – Venezuela
	Nep – Nepal	Viet – Vietnam
Den – Denmark	Neth – Netherlands	W Ger – West Germany (1945–90)
E Ger – East Germany (1945–90)	Nic – Nicaragua	
	Nig – Nigeria	Yug – Yugoslavia
Ecu – Ecuador	Nor – Norway	Zim – Zimbabwe

REVIEWS
These have been written by our team of reviewers (for more details, see page 6), and the opinions expressed in them are their own, based on their expertise and critical judgement. If an alternative version of a film is available, such as a director's cut, it will be noted here.

LANGUAGE INFORMATION
If we have been able to confirm whether a film is available in subtitled or dubbed versions, we have specified. If we have been unable to confirm this information, or if different versions of a film may be available, we have given the language of the film only (ie "German", rather than "German +subtitles" or "German dubbed").

FAMILY VIEWING
Where available and appropriate, we have included a content warning at the end of the review. Where no advice as to the film's suitability has been given, please be guided by the BBFC certificate and the content of the review itself. For those films without a certificate, the reviewers' comments should give an indication of the content of the movie.

DVD AND BLU-RAY AVAILABILITY
DVD = available on DVD (Region 2)
Blu-ray = available on Blu-ray
The information is correct at the time of going to press and is

based on availability in the UK. DVD availability means that, at some point, the film was released – however, it may not currently be on a distributor's list. If you're looking for a particular title, it's also worth trying the on-demand services online – for more details, go to: www.radiotimes.com/usingondemand. Only those films that have a valid BBFC certificate are flagged by us as being available.

CAST LIST
For each film, we have included a selected cast list of actors followed by the characters they play (where known). Famous people, when playing themselves in a film, appear with no character name. Generally, documentaries include minimal cast.

Some actors are occasionally credited in different ways on different films. For example, early in his career, Charles Bronson used his real surname and was credited as Charles Buchinski. In these cases, we have printed the actor's name as he/she was credited on that film, followed in square brackets by the name under which that actor is listed in our index: eg Charles Buchinski [Charles Bronson].

A number – eg (1), (2) – after a person's name is an indicator that there is another person of the same name on our database.

In the case of animated films, the actor credited to a character is providing the voice only.

CREDITS
Each entry includes a director credit and a writer credit. In a small number of cases, we were unable to confirm the writer credit, and so none appears. In some cases we have given additional names of those who have contributed to a screenplay, such as the person responsible for the adaptation or for additional dialogue. There may also be credits for cinematography, music, costume design, art direction and others. These have been included if the reviewer has singled out this aspect of a film for special commendation, or if it received an award.

DIRECTORS' AND ACTORS' INDEXES
These are indexes to the films of the actors and directors that appear in this book, not complete filmographies. If an actor does not appear in the cast list for a film in the A–Z, then that film will not appear after the actor's name in the index. And if an actor or director has only one film listed in the A–Z, his or her name has not been included in the index.

Index entries also include years of birth and death, which we have included where known, and regularly update. These have been exhaustively researched by contributing editor David Parkinson, who explains: "Dates are the most disputed item in film history. When the vanity of stars and the duplicity of studio publicity machines are taken into account, it becomes almost impossible to be 100 per cent accurate. Each has been checked against five reputable sources, and a majority decision made."

APPENDIX OF ALTERNATIVE TITLES
This is not a complete index of all alternative and foreign-language titles by which a film might be known – it is a selective appendix, designed to help you find the film you're looking for.

APPENDIX OF AWARDS
International awards covered are the British Academy Film Awards ("Baftas"), Academy Awards ("Oscars"), Golden Globe Awards (from the Hollywood Foreign Press Association), and those of the Cannes and Berlin film festivals. Categories in the appendix are: best film, best foreign-language film, best director, best actor, best actress, best supporting actor, best supporting actress and best screenplay. For the Academy Awards, Baftas and Golden Globes, the year of the award relates to the year of the eligible films, not of the event. For Cannes and Berlin, it is the year of the event. For the Baftas and the Oscars we have included winners and nominees; for others, winners only.

APPENDIX OF FIVE-STAR AND FOUR-STAR FILMS
This includes all our five- and four-star films, listed by genre, with UK DVD and Blu-ray availability. The headings under which the films are found are determined by the genre given in the individual entries in the A–Z. Those films that have multiple genres will appear several times in the appendix. *The English Patient* (1996), for example, appears three times in the appendix: under "War", "Romance" and "Drama".

Contributing reviewers

DAVID PARKINSON (DP) has been reviewing for *Radio Times* since 1995. Specialising in foreign-language films, he is also a contributing editor on *Empire*. He writes for several websites in Britain and the US, and has published numerous books, including *A History of Film* and *100 Ideas that Changed Film*.

ANDREW COLLINS (AC) has been the film editor of *Radio Times* since 2001. On BBC Radio 4, he presented *Back Row* and still contributes to *The Film Programme* and *Front Row*. A former editor of *Empire*, he also co-hosted ITV's *Collins & Maconie's Movie Club* with Stuart Maconie and reviews films for BBC News.

DAVE ALDRIDGE (DA) is a former editor of *Film Review* magazine. He is a regular contributor on film and DVD topics on national and local radio, as well as to *Radio Times* and other entertainment magazines.

BRIAN BAXTER (BB) has devoted his career exclusively to film. A former programmer for the National Film Theatre, he was Films Editor for BBC1 and 2. He has worked as a journalist since his teens, and is a regular contributor to *The Guardian*.

RONALD BERGAN (RB) has lectured on literature, theatre and film. A regular contributor to *The Guardian*, his numerous books on cinema include biographies of the Coen Brothers, Sergei Eisenstein, Jean Renoir, Dustin Hoffman and Katharine Hepburn.

JO BERRY (JB) has written about film for publications including *Empire*, *eve*, *Maxim*, *Sight & Sound*, *The Guardian* and the *Daily Express*. She is author of *The Ultimate DVD Easter Egg Guide*, *Chick Flicks* (with Angie Errigo) and *The Parents' Guide to Kids' Movies*.

JASON CARO (JC) is a devotee of sci-fi, fantasy and thrillers, and has been a regular contributor to *Film Review* magazine as well as several specialist science-fiction publications.

ALLEN EYLES (AE) is a film historian whose many books include studies of stars such as James Stewart, and surveys of the major UK cinema circuits. He founded the magazine *Focus on Film*, is a former editor of *Films and Filming* and currently edits *Picture House*.

JOHN FERGUSON (JF) has edited DVD/video magazines in the UK, Australia and New Zealand, including *Video Home Entertainment* and the Melbourne-based *Screen Print*. He is currently editor of *Stack*, a monthly magazine covering DVD, games and music.

DICK FIDDY (DF) is a freelance writer/researcher, and a TV consultant for the BFI. He has worked on various archive shows including *The A to Z of TV* and *TV Heaven* (both for C4) and was contributing editor on the *Radio Times Guide to TV Comedy*.

SLOAN FREER (SF) is an arts journalist and film critic with a passion for leftfield cinema. She has contributed to publications including *The Observer*, *Q*, *Total Film*, *Metro*, *Kerrang!* and *Bizarre*.

LORIEN HAYNES (LH) is a celebrity interviewer, film reviewer and broadcaster, who writes for *Harper's Bazaar*, *Red*, *The Mail on Sunday*, *The Sunday Telegraph*, *She* and *Little White Lies*. She is currently living and screen-writing in LA.

TOM HUTCHINSON (TH), who sadly died in August 2005, contributed film reviews to *Radio Times* for a decade, and also wrote for *The Sunday Telegraph* and *The Mail on Sunday*. A broadcaster for both radio and film, he also worked with director J Lee Thompson on several scripts, and wrote books on Marilyn Monroe and his friend Rod Steiger.

ALAN JONES (AJ) has reviewed fantasy, horror and sci-fi movies for *Radio Times* since 1995. He has written numerous genre programmes for television, is the author of *The Rough Guide to Horror Movies* and *Profondo Argento*, and is a co-director of Film4 FrightFest.

ROBYN KARNEY (RK) is a former critic and interviewer for *Empire* magazine. Her books include *The Foreign Film Guide* with Ronald Bergan, *A Star Danced: the Life of Audrey Hepburn* and *A Singular Man: Burt Lancaster*.

KAREN KRIZANOVICH (KK) is a writer/broadcaster for Radio 4, CNN, *Newsnight*, *Cosmopolitan*, *Empire* and the *Guardian* film blog among others. She also has an MBA in Film Finance.

STELLA PAPAMICHAEL (SP) is a freelance journalist who has reviewed films since her teens. She has contributed to the BBC Film Network, and *Digital Spy* among other publications.

BRIAN PENDREIGH (BP) writes for various publications, including *The Times*. Previously he was cinema editor on *The Scotsman* and contributing editor of *Hotdog* magazine. His books include *The Pocket Scottish Movie Book* (2002) and *The Man in the Seventh Row: The Movie Lover's Novel* (2011).

JAMIE RUSSELL (JR) is an author and screenwriter, whose work has appeared in the *Sunday Times*, the *Guardian*, *Total Film*, *Sight & Sound* and *FHM* among others. He has written books on horror, war cinema and William S Burroughs.

ROBERT SELLERS (RS) is an established freelance writer and the author of a number of film biographies, as well as *Very Naughty Boys – the Inside Story of HandMade Films*.

TONY SLOMAN (TS) is a producer, editor and writer. His credits include *Radio On*, *Cross of Iron*, *Chitty Chitty Bang Bang* and cult TV series *The Prisoner*. He is also a lecturer and broadcaster, served for ten years as a governor of the BFI and is a life member of Bafta.

ADAM SMITH (AS) is *Empire's* Senior Writer and has also written about movies for *Q*, *GQ*, *FHM*, *Arena*, *The Observer* and *The Independent*. He is a regular contributor to Radio 4's *Front Row*.

ADDITIONAL REVIEWERS

Omar Ahmed (OA), Keith Bailey (KB), Lucy Barrick (LB), Mark Braxton (MB), David Brown (DvB), David Butcher (DB), Maj Canton (MC), John Carroll (JnC), Stephen Carty (SC), David Crawford (DC), Gill Crawford (GC), Joe Cunningham (JoC), Emma Daly (ED), Geoff Ellis (GE), Angie Errigo (AME), Huw Fullerton (HF), John Fogarty (JwF), Leslie Felperin (LF), Narinder Flora (NF), Michael Fox (MF), Peter Freedman (PF), Ian Freer (IF), Rupert Frost (RF), Nick Funnell (NPF), John Gammon (JG), Sue George (SG), Alison Graham (AG), Kieran Grant (KG), Scott Hamilton/Chris Holland (ST), Sue Heal (SH), Stephen Hughes (StH), Sophie Ivan (SI), Trevor Johnston (TJ), Frances Lass (FL), James Luxford (JL), David McGillivray (DM), Stuart Manning (SM), Caroline Martin (CM), John Marriott (JM), Dan Meier (DnM), Steve Morrissey (SvM), Gareth Moses (GM), Patrick Mulkern (PM), Sam Oliver (SaO), David Oppedisano (DO), Terry Payne (TrP), Chris Pearson (CLP), Rebecca Pike (ReP), Colin Prior (CP), Jane Rackham (JnR), Richard Rees (RR), Anna Richards (AR), Gary Rose (GR), Simon Rose (SR), Jessica Schuster (JS), Jack Seale (JkS), Emma Simmonds (EAS), Alexia Skinitis (AlS), Neil Smith (NS), Terry Staunton (TeS), Susannah Straughan (SS), Emma Sturgess (ES), Kate Sullivan (KS), Adrian Turner (AT), Tom Vallance (TV), Claire Webb (CW), Damon Wise (DW)

Editorial team

Edited by Sue Robinson (SuR)
Contributing editors Andrew Collins, Kilmeny Fane-Saunders (KFS), David Parkinson
Radio Times Film Unit Jeremy Aspinall (JA), Sean Cronin (SeC), Tom Folley (TF), Jamie Healy (JH), Tony Peters (TP)
Database designed by Mark Ginns

Sources
Certain data published under licence from Baseline II Inc.
Certain data published under licence from the British Board of Film Classification.
Some material is verified from the Motion Picture Guide, published by Cinebooks, New York, with kind permission.

A-Z of films

ABC Africa ★★★★
Documentary   2001 · Iran/Fr · Colour · 85min

Invited by the UN to study the work of the Uganda Women's Effort to Save Orphans, director Abbas Kiarostami went to the country to scout locations but ended up shooting the footage for the documentary on digital video. Once more he was working with children, but for the first time it was outside his homeland and using an unfamiliar format. Nevertheless, Iran's foremost film-maker has succeeded in finding reasons for optimism among the nearly two million orphans left helpless by the ravages of war and Aids. An unsentimental view full of remarkable resilience and compassion. DP English, Farsi +subtitles.

■ Dir Abbas Kiarostami · Cinematographer Seifollah Samadian

ABCD ★★★
Drama   1999 · US · Colour · 105min

With its acronymic title translating as "American-Born Confused Dashi", this is an assured insight into the problems facing Indians resident in the States. Krutin Patel's debut feature hones in on the human drama, but there's also plenty of wry humour at the expense of traditionalists and progressives, as a 20-something and his sister try to live their own lives without alienating their interventionist mother (Madhur Jaffrey). DP

Madhur Jaffrey Anju · Faran Tahir Raj · Sheetal Sheth Nina · Aasif Mandvi Ashok · David Ari Brian ■ Dir Krutin Patel · Scr James McManus, Krutin Patel, from a story by Patel

The ABCs of Death ★★★ 18
Horror anthology   2012 · US · Colour · 124min

The producers of this bold project were certainly taking a risk when they asked 26 directors from across the globe to make a short film about death according to a letter assigned to them. Inevitably, the quality across this alphabet of doom is patchy, varying as much as the subject matter, but gore is not necessarily the prime mover in many of the segments. Indeed the better ones have an interesting story to tell. For instance, in Unearthed, British director Ben Wheatley offers his unique slant on a vampire hunt. The whole may not add up to the sum of its parts, but at least it has a few choice gems to show for its ambition. JA English, French, Japanese, Spanish +subtitles. Violence, swearing, drug abuse, sex scenes, nudity. DVD BD

■ Dir Nacho Vigalondo, Adrián García Bogliano, Ernesto Díaz Espinoza, Marcel Sarmiento, Angela Bettis, Noboru Iguchi, Andrew Traucki, Thomas Cappelen Malling, Jorge Michel Grau, Yudai Yamaguchi, Anders Morgenthaler, Timo Tjahjanto, Ti West, Banjong Pisanthanakun, Hélène Cattet, Bruno Forzani, Simon Rumley, Adam Wingard, Srdjan Spasojevic, Jake West, Lee Hardcastle, Ben Wheatley, Kaare Andrews, Jon Schnepp, Xavier Gens, Jason Eisener, Yoshihiro Nishimura

LANDMARK FILM
Jean-Luc Godard's Paris locale and groovy technique influences future movie-makers

A Bout de Souffle ★★★★★ PG
Drama   1959 · Fr · BW · 86min

Inspired by Gun Crazy, Joseph H Lewis's B-movie film noir, and made with the assistance of François Truffaut and Claude Chabrol, this is the keystone of the French New Wave. A homage to such fatalistic heroes as Jean Gabin and Humphrey Bogart, Jean-Luc Godard's masterpiece employs just about every cinematic trick associated with the nouvelle vague: location shooting, direct sound, hand-held footage (masterfully shot by Raoul Coutard), jump cuts, in-jokes and visual tributes to master film-makers. Jean-Paul Belmondo is superbly shambolic as the petty thief whose brief dalliance with American newspaper vendor Jean Seberg precipitates his demise. The film's influence is incalculable. DP French +subtitles. DVD BD

Jean-Paul Belmondo Michel Poiccard/Laszlo Kovacs · Jean Seberg Patricia Franchini · Van Doude Journalist · Daniel Boulanger Police Inspector · Henri-Jacques Huet Antonio Berrutti · Liliane Robin Minouche · Claude Mansard Claudius Mansard · Roger Hanin Carl Zombach · Jean-Pierre Melville Parvulesco · Richard Balducci Tolmatchoff · Jean-Luc Godard Informer ■ Dir Jean-Luc Godard · Scr Jean-Luc Godard, from a story by François Truffaut · Cinematographer Raoul Coutard

A-Haunting We Will Go ★★ U
Comedy   1942 · US · BW · 63min

This is the second of the five indifferent pictures Laurel and Hardy made for 20th Century-Fox in the early 1940s. As the script was written while they were on tour, Laurel was denied the opportunity to add some much needed comic genius to this tiresome tale of crooks and coffins. Mediocre. DP

Stan Laurel Stan · Oliver Hardy Ollie · Harry A Jansen Dante the magician · Sheila Ryan Margo · John Shelton Tommy White · Don Costello (1) Doc Lake · Elisha Cook Jr Frank Lucas ■ Dir Alfred Werker · Scr Lou Breslow, from a story by Breslow, Stanley Rauh

AI: Artificial Intelligence ★★★★ 12
Science-fiction fantasy drama   2001 · US · Colour · 139min

Steven Spielberg's ambitious, dark-toned fable takes the story of Pinocchio, gives it a daring twist and decks it out with terrific special effects. Haley Joel Osment (The Sixth Sense) plays an android child, programmed to love and allocated to a couple whose own critically ill son has been cryogenically frozen. When the real son is healed, the robot boy is left to fend for himself in a brutal world that doesn't want him. In a difficult role, Osment proves once again what a fine young actor he is, while Jude Law gives a showy performance as his guide-cum-protector. This is by far the director's bleakest work and Osment's desperate quest to become a "real" boy and win back the love of his human mother is a disturbing one. KFS DVD BD

Haley Joel Osment David · Jude Law Gigolo Joe · Frances O'Connor Monica Swinton · Brendan Gleeson Lord Johnson-Johnson · Sam Robards Henry Swinton · William Hurt Prof Hobby (the Visionary) · Jake Thomas Martin Swinton · Ben Kingsley Specialist · Robin Williams Dr Know · Meryl Streep Blue mecha ■ Dir Steven Spielberg · Scr Steven Spielberg, from a story by Ian Watson, from the short story Supertoys Last All Summer Long by Brian W Aldiss

A la Place du Coeur ★★ 15
Romantic drama   1998 · Fr · Colour · 107min

Robert Guédiguian's follow-up to his acclaimed breakthrough picture, Marius et Jeannette, came as a surprise to many. Yet, for all its good intentions and the committed naturalism of the performances, this slice-of-life tale, about a white teenager (Laure Raoust) who embarks on an affair with a jailed young black (Alexandre Ogou), rings hollow. DP French +subtitles. Swearing, nudity, sexual references.

Ariane Ascaride Marianne · Christine Brücher Francine · Jean-Pierre Darroussin Joel · Gérard Meylan Franck · Alexandre Ogou Bébé · Laure Raoust Clim ■ Dir Robert Guédiguian · Scr Jean-Louis Milesi, Robert Guédiguian, from the novel If Beale Street Could Talk by James Baldwin

A Ma Soeur! ★★ 18
Drama   2001 · Fr/It/Sp · Colour · 81min

Anaïs Reboux impresses as the grumpily plump 12-year-old envying glamorous Roxane Mesquida's fling with student Libero De Rienzo. This would have been a fascinating insight into corrupted innocence had Catherine Breillat concentrated on the shock of watching their graphically depicted sexual encounters in the sisters' shared holiday bedroom. But she concludes proceedings with a brutal incident of such calculated sensationalism that it devalues all that has gone before. DP French, Italian +subtitles. DVD

Anaïs Reboux Anaïs · Roxane Mesquida Elena · Libero De Rienzo Fernando · Arsinée Khanjian Mother · Romain Goupil Father ■ Dir/Scr Catherine Breillat

A Nous la Liberté ★★★ U
Satire   1931 · Fr · BW · 83min

Director René Clair's classic satire on modern life tells of an escaped convict who ends up running a gramophone factory and is then blackmailed by his cell-mate. Both end up as vagabonds. Made during the Depression, it chimed with audiences at the time who loved its mixture of music, comedy and radical politics. Clair's imagery of mass production with human automatons, led to the film being banned by the left-wing government of Hungary and the right-wing government of Portugal. It was also the inspiration for Chaplin's Modern Times, and when Clair's producer wanted to take out a legal action for plagiarism, the director refused, saying he felt flattered. AT French +subtitles. DVD

Henri Marchand Emile · Raymond Cordy Louis · Rolla France Jeanne · Paul Olivier Paul Imaque · Shelly Jacques Paul · André Michaud Foreman · Germaine Aussey Maud · Alexandre D'Arcy [Alex D'Arcy] Gigolo ■ Dir/Scr René Clair

A Propos de Nice ★★★★ U
Silent experimental documentary   1930 · Fr · BW · 26min

At a time when documentarists across Europe were making "city symphonies", the French director Jean Vigo produced this delightful Riviera rhapsody. Vigo was one of the great screen poets, but the inspiration for this playful portrait clearly comes from the montage experiments of cinematographer Boris Kaufman's older brother, Dziga Vertov, the Polish director of the hugely influential Man with a Movie Camera. Brilliantly using transitions and parallel cutting, Vigo throws in some superb sequences, such as the sunbather turning into a skeleton and promenaders becoming strutting animals. Most famously, he employed a series of dissolves to strip a woman, a scene that was originally cut by British censors. DP

■ Dir/Scr Jean Vigo · Cinematographer Boris Kaufman

ATM ★ 15
Horror   2012 · US/Can · Colour · 86min

Another entry in the sparsely populated "confined space" genre (Phone Booth, Elevator), this inexcusably illogical chiller is written by Christopher Sparling who scripted the far superior Buried. On the way home from a Christmas party, three co-workers stop for cash at a remote ATM and get trapped there by a hooded psycho. The thin cat-and-mouse thrills deflate under the director's insecure hand, with the three leads clearly as non-plussed as the viewer. AJ Violence.

Brian Geraghty David Hargrove · Alice Eve Emily Brandt · Josh Peck Corey Thompson ■ Dir David Brooks (3) · Scr Chris Sparling

The A-Team ★★★
Action adventure   1983 · US · Colour · 100min

Pilot for the dumb, fun 1980s show about a quartet of fugitive ex-soldiers: George Peppard (brainy), Mr T (brawny) and Tim Dunigan (charming, replaced by Dirk Benedict in the series) who come to the aid of the little guys. A comic book blend of The Magnificent Seven and Mission: Impossible, the likeable vigilantes help the villagers of a small Mexican town stand-up against bandidos. Military experience and some dreadful disguises help win the day in an entertainingly implausible kind of way. JC

George Peppard Colonel John "Hannibal" Smith · Dwight Schultz Murdock · Mr T BA Baracus · Tim Dunigan Templeton (Face Man) · Melinda Culea Amy Allen · Bill Lucking [William Lucking] Colonel Lynch ■ Dir Rod Holcomb · Scr Stephen J Cannell, Frank Lupo

The A-Team ★★ 12
Action adventure   2010 · US/UK · Colour · 113min

In this big-screen remake of the popular 1980s TV series, Col "Hannibal" Smith (Liam Neeson) and his crack squad of covert operatives are wrongfully jailed during a mission to steal back printing plates capable of flooding the world with millions of counterfeit US dollars. The movie frequently doffs its cap to the original, but is too brash and loud to retain any of its charm, and director Joe Carnahan piles on the explosions and gunfights with a heavy hand. TeS Some violence, brief swearing. DVD BD

Liam Neeson Col John "Hannibal" Smith · Bradley Cooper Lt Templeton "Faceman" Peck · Jessica Biel Capt Charissa Sosa · Quinton "Rampage" Jackson Sgt BA Baracus · Sharlto Copley Capt HM "Howlin' Mad" Murdock · Patrick Wilson Lynch · Dirk Benedict Pensacola prisoner Milt · Dwight Schultz German doctor 1 ■ Dir Joe Carnahan · Scr Joe Carnahan, Skip Woods, Brian Bloom, from the TV series by Stephen J Cannell, Frank Lupo

AVP: Alien vs Predator ★★★ 15
Science-fiction action thriller   2004 · US/UK/Cz Rep/Can/Ger · Colour · 96min

In director Paul WS Anderson's sometimes inspired melding of two sci-fi horror franchises, an expedition heads for Antarctica after billionaire Lance Henriksen discovers a pyramid under the ice. This proves to be the venue for a Predator v Alien smackdown, with the expedition's crew as the warm-up. The characterisation is nonexistent, but Sanaa Lathan shines during the thrilling finale. This guilty pleasure is all about slime-covered face-offs between monster-movie icons, and that's where Anderson really delivers. AJ Violence. DVD BD

Sanaa Lathan Alexa Woods · Raoul Bova Sebastian De Rosa · Ewen Bremner Graeme Miller · Colin Salmon Maxwell Stafford · Lance Henriksen Charles Bishop Weyland · Tommy Flanagan Mark Verheiden ■ Dir Paul WS Anderson [Paul Anderson (1)] · Scr Paul WS Anderson, from a story by Anderson, Dan O'Bannon, Ronald Shusett, from characters by O'Bannon, Shusett, and from those created by Jim & John Thomas

AVPR: Aliens vs Predator Requiem ★★ 15
Science-fiction action thriller   2007 · US · Colour · 89min

There's not much Aliens vs Predator in this confusing and tension-free addition to the dual monster franchise. Following on from 2004's AVP: Alien vs Predator, a spaceship carrying a hybrid "Predalien" and several face-huggers crashes near a small Colorado town and a battle-weary veteran Predator is dispatched to deal with the mayhem. Co-directors Colin and Greg Strause are renowned for their visual effects work on films like 300 and 4: Rise of the Silver Surfer. But everything here feels overdone – this unscary trudge through the sci-fi horror conventions has all been done better before. AJ Violence, swearing. DVD BD

Steven Pasquale Dallas · Reiko Aylesworth Kelly · John Ortiz (1) Morales · Johnny Lewis Ricky · Ariel Gade Molly · Kristen Hager Jesse ■ Dir The Brothers Strause [Colin Strause], The Brothers Strause [Greg Strause] · Scr Shane Salerno, from characters by Dan O'Bannon, Ronald Shusett, and from those created by Jim and John Thomas

AWOL ★★ 18
Action thriller   1990 · US · Colour · 103min

Although Jean-Claude Van Damme gawps blankly, at least his director Sheldon Lettich knows how to move the action along in this mildly efficient thriller. Balancing most of the tale between the sentimental, the risible and the hysterically overacted, Van Damme provides volleys of well-crafted fisticuffs, and brings a certain humanity to his punch-drunk protagonist, a French legionnaire who's deserted to the States. JM Violence, swearing, nudity. *DVD*

Jean-Claude Van Damme *Lyon Gaultier* • Harrison Page *Joshua* • Deborah Rennard *Cynthia* • Lisa Pelikan *Helene* • Ashley Johnson *Nicole* • Brian Thompson *Russell* • Voyo *Sergeant Hartog* • Michel Qissi *Moustafa* ■ *Dir* Sheldon Lettich • *Scr* Sheldon Lettich, Jean-Claude Van Damme, RN Warren, from a story by Van Damme

Aaaaaaaah! ★ 18
Horror comedy   2015 · UK · Colour · 79min

This brainchild of writer/director Steve Oram (*Sightseers*) has no dialogue, just grunts, groans and guttural sounds. What passes for a plot sees an alpha male (Oram) in a battle for supremacy with a community led by Julian Rhind-Tutt and Toyah Willcox. Pythonesque comic genius, or a movie take on *The Emperor's New Clothes*? Public opinion will tend towards the latter. DA Violence, sex scenes, nudity. *DVD* *BL*

Julian Barratt *Jupiter* • Lucy Honigman *Denise* • Tom Meeten *Keith* • Steve Oram *Smith* • Toyah Willcox *Barabara* • Noel Fielding *Carl* ■ *Dir/Scr* Steve Oram

Aaron Loves Angela ★★★
Romantic action drama
1975 · US · Colour · 99min

The son of one of African-American cinema's leading pioneers, Gordon Parks Jr was best known for *Superfly* when he took this unexpected detour from hard-hitting blaxploitation. Set in Harlem, its combination of star-crossed romance, gang rivalry and urban deprivation invites comparisons with *West Side Story*, especially as the girl is a Puerto Rican. But the focus isn't restricted to Irene Cara and her black beau, Kevin Hooks, as the director adds coarse comedy, the music of José Feliciano and uncompromising action to the explosive mixture. DP

Kevin Hooks *Aaron* • Irene Cara *Angela* • Moses Gunn *Ike* • Robert Hooks *Beau* • Ernestine Jackson *Cleo* • Leon Pinkney *Willie* ■ *Dir* Gordon Parks Jr • *Scr* Gerald Sanford

ABBA the Movie ★★★ U
Music documentary drama
1977 · Swe/Aus · Colour · 96min

This visual record of the Swedish superstars' 1977 Australian tour shows why they were billed as the most popular group in the world and became the pinnacle of kitsch glam. There is a story, involving a journalist desperate to secure an interview with the band, but really it's just an excuse to hear every major hit, from *Waterloo* to *Dancing Queen*. Sing along and say, "Thank you for the music." AJ *DVD* *BL*

Robert Hughes *Ashley* • Tom Oliver *Bodyguard/Bartender/Taxi driver* • Bruce Barry *Radio station manager* • Stig Anderson *Manager* • Anni-Frid Lyngstad • Benny Andersson • Bjorn Ulvaeus • Agnetha Faltskog ■ *Dir/Scr* Lasse Hallström

Abbott and Costello in Society ★★
Comedy   1944 · US · BW · 75min

This very average Abbott and Costello flick relies too much on slapstick gags which don't seem as funny today as they did during the war. The same can be said for the plot, which has Bud and Lou as two dumb plumbers who gatecrash a posh weekend party. There's some charming fluff involving 1940s vocalist Marion Hutton (Betty's sister) as a taxi driver with the hots for Kirby Grant. Substantial footage from the WC Fields classic *Never Give a Sucker an Even Break* was hijacked to boost the production values of the chase sequences. TS

Bud Abbott *Eddie Harrington* • Lou Costello *Albert Mansfield* • Marion Hutton *Elsie Hammerdingle* • Kirby Grant *Peter Evans* • Margaret Irving *Mrs Roger Winthrop* • Ann Gillis *Gloria Winthrop* • Arthur Treacher *Pipps* •

Thomas Gomez *Drexel* ■ *Dir* Jean Yarbrough • *Scr* John Grant, Edmund L Hartmann, Hal Fimberg, Sid Fields, Clyde Bruckman, from a story by Hugh Wedlock Jr, Howard Snyder

Abbott and Costello in Hollywood ★★ U
Comedy   1945 · US · BW · 82min

This typical Abbott and Costello vehicle offers some interesting behind-the-scenes glimpses of MGM at work; the film also includes guest appearances by the likes of Lucille Ball, Jackie "Butch" Jenkins and director Robert Z Leonard. The plot has Bud and Lou as a barber and shoeshine boy respectively, attempting to be Hollywood agents, though it's just a peg on which to hang a series of comic routines. TS

Bud Abbott *Buzz Kurtis* • Lou Costello *Abercrombie* • Frances Rafferty *Claire Warren* • Robert Stanton [Bob Haymes] *Jeff Parker* • Jean Porter *Ruthie* • Warner Anderson *Norman Royce* • Mike Mazurki *Klondike Pete* ■ *Dir* S Sylvan Simon • *Scr* Nat Perrin, Lou Breslow

Abbott and Costello Meet Frankenstein ★★★ PG
Comedy   1948 · US · BW · 79min

Bud and Lou often just weren't funny enough by themselves. So Universal set up a series of confrontations from the horror films that had been such a success for the studio in the 1930s. This was one of the naively funniest, with the boys delivering crates to a wax museum (of course), unaware that their consignment contains Count Dracula and Frankenstein's monster. Bela Lugosi and Lon Chaney Jr as the Wolf Man play it straight enough to be naturally comic, so the real comedians end up as stooges. TH

Bud Abbott *Chick* • Lou Costello *Wilbur* • Lon Chaney Jr *Lawrence Talbot/the Wolf Man* • Bela Lugosi *Dracula* • Glenn Strange *The Monster* • Lenore Aubert *Sandra Mornay* • Jane Randolph *Joan Raymond* • Frank Ferguson *Mr McDougal* • Charles Bradstreet *Dr Steven* ■ *Dir* Charles T Barton [Charles Barton] • *Scr* Robert Lees, Frederic I Rinaldo, John Grant, from the novel *Frankenstein* by Mary Shelley

Abbott and Costello Meet the Killer, Boris Karloff ★★ PG
Comedy mystery   1949 · US · BW · 80min

This sort of title really should have caught on. Picture, if you will, "Bill & Ted Meet the Terminator, Arnold Schwarzenegger". The only snag is that Boris Karloff is not the killer. In fact, he's scarcely in the movie at all, although his charlatan swami does have the best scenes, notably the one in which he urges the mesmerised Lou Costello to top himself. The rest of this wobbly whodunnit revolves around bellboy Lou being scared out of his ample skin by clues that have vanished before hotel detective Bud Abbott lays eyes on them. DP

Bud Abbott *Casey Edwards* • Lou Costello *Freddie Phillips* • Boris Karloff *Swami Talpur* • Lenore Aubert *Angela Gordon* • Gar Moore *Jeff Wilson* ■ *Dir* Charles T Barton [Charles Barton] • *Scr* Hugh Wedlock Jr, John Grant, Howard Snyder

Abbott and Costello in the Foreign Legion ★★ U
Comedy   1950 · US · BW · 76min

Between meeting Dracula and the Invisible Man, Abbott and Costello took time out to cavort on existing sets on Universal's backlot, but they could well have done with some scriptwriting help. The duo were also beginning to show their age physically, and Lou in particular was starting to look a little grotesque in this comedy that plays like a Bing-and-Bob reject. TS

Bud Abbott *Jonesy* • Lou Costello *Lou Hotchkiss* • Patricia Medina *Nicole* • Walter Slezak *Axmann* • Douglass Dumbrille *Hamud El Khalid* ■ *Dir* Charles Lamont • *Scr* Leonard Stern, John Grant, Martin Ragaway, from a story by DD Beauchamp

Abbott and Costello Meet the Invisible Man ★★ U
Comedy   1951 · US · BW · 78min

Bungling private eyes Bud and Lou are hired by boxer Arthur Franz to get him off a murder rap in this acceptable time-passer. There is a modicum of mystery beneath the thin layer of comedy, and the highlight is a boxing bout in which Bud gets an invisible hand to hold off the champ. DP

Bud Abbott *Bud Alexander* • Lou Costello *Lou Francis* • Nancy Guild *Helen Gray* • Arthur Franz *Tommy Nelson* • Adele Jergens *Boots Marsden* • Sheldon Leonard *Morgan* • William Frawley *Detective Roberts* • Gavin Muir *Dr Philip Gray* ■ *Dir* Charles Lamont • *Scr* Robert Lees, Frederic I Rinaldo, John Grant, from the novel *The Invisible Man* by HG Wells

Abbott and Costello Meet Captain Kidd ★★ U
Comedy   1952 · US · Colour · 70min

In this rare colour outing for Bud and Lou, they are shanghaied by pirate Charles Laughton in his race for buried loot with Hillary Brooke's Anne Bonney. Slapsticking way below even their usual standard, the boys are as much use on the treasure hunt as a map without an X, while Laughton shamelessly spoofs his performance as Captain Bligh in the 1935 version of *Mutiny on the Bounty*. DP

Bud Abbott *Rocky Stonebridge* • Lou Costello *Oliver "Puddin' Head" Johnson* • Charles Laughton *Captain Kidd* • Hillary Brooke *Captain Bonney* • Fran Warren *Lady Jane* • Bill Shirley *Bruce Martingale* • Leif Erickson *Morgan* ■ *Dir* Charles Lamont • *Scr* Howard Dimsdale, John Grant

Abbott and Costello Go to Mars ★ U
Comedy   1953 · US · BW · 73min

Having run out of exotic backgrounds on Earth, the duo board a spaceship and think they've landed on Mars when they're in the middle of the New Orleans Mardi Gras. Hijacked by a couple of bank robbers, they escape to Venus, which is populated solely by former Miss Universe contestants under Mari Blanchard as Queen Allura. The stars' comic inventiveness was at a standstill and the tired routines won't have improved with age. AE

Bud Abbott *Lester* • Lou Costello *Orville* • Robert Paige *Dr Wilson* • Mari Blanchard *Allura* • Martha Hyer *Janie* • Horace McMahon *Mugsy* • Anita Ekberg *Venusian woman* ■ *Dir* Charles Lamont • *Scr* DD Beauchamp, John Grant, from a story by Howard Christie, Beauchamp

Abbott and Costello Meet Dr Jekyll and Mr Hyde ★★★ PG
Comedy   1953 · US · BW · 73min

It sounds like the double date from hell, but this is one of Bud and Lou's livelier outings. The boys play a couple of sacked cops who hope to impress Inspector Reginald Denny by capturing the monster that is terrorising London. There are even a couple of laughs in the wax museum and rooftop chase scenes, although the romance between Helen Wescott and Craig Stevens slows things down a touch. Boris Karloff juicily hams up the roles of the mad scientist and his alter ego, making Jekyll seem every bit as sinister as Hyde. DP

Bud Abbott *Slim* • Lou Costello *Tubby* • Boris Karloff *Dr Jekyll/Mr Hyde* • Helen Westcott *Vicky Edwards* • Craig Stevens *Bruce Adams* • Reginald Denny *Inspector* ■ *Dir* Charles Lamont • *Scr* Lee Loeb, John Grant, from the novel *The Strange Case of Dr Jekyll and Mr Hyde* by Robert Louis Stevenson

Abbott and Costello Meet the Keystone Cops ★★ U
Comedy   1955 · US · BW · 75min

Intimidating Bud and slaphappy Lou are sold a run-down film studio in the early days of Hollywood, though they turn out to be better stuntmen than producers. Inept timing stifles the gags, but the chase finale is up there with the best of the original

Keystones. However, the real interest lies in a guest appearance from comedy giant Mack Sennett. TH

Bud Abbott *Harry Pierce* • Lou Costello *Willie Piper* • Fred Clark *Joseph Gorman/Sergei Trumanoff* • Lynn Bari *Leota Van Cleef* • Frank Wilcox *Snavely* • Maxie Rosenbloom *Hinds* • Henry Kulky *Brakeman* • Sam Flint *Conductor* • Mack Sennett ■ *Dir* Charles Lamont • *Scr* John Grant, from a story by Lee Cobb

Abbott and Costello Meet the Mummy ★ U
Comedy   1955 · US · BW · 76min

Abbott and Costello ended 15 years at Universal with this dismal low-budget attempt to excavate some humour from a story of buried treasure in Egypt. Having run through the rest of the studio's horror gallery earlier, Bud and Lou now stir up the Mummy (here played by minor actor Eddie Parker) who's a rather lifeless figure compared to the likes of Dracula and the Wolf Man. At least character actress Marie Windsor brings waspish authority to her role of villainess. AE

Bud Abbott *Peter* • Lou Costello *Freddie* • Marie Windsor *Madame Rontru* • Michael Ansara *Charlie* • Dan Seymour *Josef* • Kurt Katch *Dr Zomer* • Richard Karlan *Hetsut* • Richard Deacon *Semu* • Eddie Parker *Klaris, the mummy* ■ *Dir* Charles Lamont • *Scr* John Grant, from a story by Lee Loeb

The Abdication ★★
Historical drama   1974 · UK · Colour · 100min

Liv Ullmann steps into Garbo's shoes by playing Queen Christina, who abdicates the Swedish throne and heads for Rome, wanting to be accepted as a Catholic and undergoing a searching inquisition from Cardinal Peter Finch. Having already played Pope Joan and fresh from *Lost Horizon*, Ullmann looks as if she's about to break into a schmaltzy song. Anthony Harvey directs, presumably in the hope of turning this piece of stodge into another *Lion in Winter*. AT

Peter Finch *Cardinal Azzolino* • Liv Ullmann *Queen Christina* • Cyril Cusack *Oxenstierna* • Graham Crowden *Cardinal Barberini* • Michael Dunn *The Dwarf* • Lewis Fiander *Father Dominic* • Kathleen Byron *Queen Mother* • James Faulkner *Magnus* • Ania Marson *Ebba Sparre* ■ *Dir* Anthony Harvey • *Scr* Ruth Wolff, from her play

Abducted ★★
Thriller   2007 · Can · Colour · 89min

In this watchable tale, unscrupulous prison warden Eric Breker attempts to further his political career by manipulating an unjustly sentenced inmate (Andrew Walker) into kidnapping Breker's wife. A pedestrian script and cheap visuals initially hamstring the action, but solid acting from Sarah Wynter as the increasingly willing abductee adds an emotional dimension that sets the film up for a stronger second half. SF

Sarah Wynter *Melanie Stone* • Andrew Walker [Andrew Kevin Walker] *Jack Carlson* • Eric Breker *Tom Stone* • Carl Marotte *John Delaney* • Ellen Dubin *Stephanie Baker* ■ *Dir* Richard Roy • *Scr* Laurie Horowitz

Abduction ★★ 12
Action thriller   2011 · US · Colour · 101min

Rebellious teen Nathan (Taylor Lautner) goes on the run from enemy agents who want his father's file of assassins, in director John Singleton's lacklustre thriller. It's a run-of-the-mill game of cat and mouse, peppered with underwhelming chase sequences and a flimsy plot. *Twilight* fans may swoon at Lautner's bare chest and brooding, but he's upstaged at every turn by crime lord Michael Nyqvist, while Alfred Molina and Sigourney Weaver sleepwalk through their supporting roles as ambiguous CIA operatives. TeS Violence, some swearing. *DVD* *BL*

Taylor Lautner *Nathan* • Lily Collins *Karen* • Alfred Molina *Frank Burton* • Jason Isaacs *Kevin* • Maria Bello *Mara* • Sigourney Weaver *Dr Bennett* • Michael Nyqvist *Kozlow* ■ *Dir* John Singleton • *Scr* Shawn Christensen

A

The Abduction Club ★★★ 🔞12
Period adventure
2002 · UK/Fr/Ire/Ger · Colour · 92min

This romp has a pleasingly anachronistic undertone that prevents it from feeling like a Sunday evening serial. Set in 18th-century Ireland, when second sons were wont to kidnap heiresses in order to persuade them to marry, Stefan Schwartz's boisterous adventure is soon slowed by stereotypical characters and clichéd dialogue. However, Daniel Lapaine and Matthew Rhys are dashing as the headstrong suitors seeking to keep spirited sisters Sophia Myles and Alice Evans out of the clutches of cad Liam Cunningham. DP **DVD**

Daniel Lapaine *Byrne* · Matthew Rhys *Strang* · Sophia Myles *Anne Kennedy* · Alice Evans *Catharine Kennedy* · Edward Woodward *Lord Fermoy* · Liam Cunningham *John Power* · Patrick Malahide *Sir Myles* ■ *Dir* Stefan Schwartz · *Scr* Bill Britten, Richard Crawford

Abel ★★★★ 15
Drama
2010 · Mex · Colour · 78min

An intuitive performance by nine-year-old actor Christopher Ruíz-Esparza helps Mexican star Diego Luna's affectionate directorial debut over its more melodramatic moments. Returning from a psychiatric institution for the first time since his father left to work in the States, Abel stuns his mother and siblings by imposing a strict regime on the household that amusingly benefits them all. Luna makes fine use of the shabby interiors to prevent the film from turning into a twee fairy tale, keeping the focus firmly on the decline of family values. DP Spanish +subtitles. Swearing. **DVD**

Christopher Ruíz-Esparza *Abel* · Gerardo Ruíz-Esparza *Paúl* · José María Yazpik *Anselmo* · Karina Gidi *Cecilia* · Geraldine Alejandra *Selene* ■ *Dir* Diego Luna · *Scr* Diego Luna, Augusto Mendoza · *Production Designer* Brigitte Broch

Aberdeen ★★★
Drama
2000 · UK/Nor/Swe · Colour · 113min

Hingeing on a volatile relationship between father and daughter, this is a road trip where the journey is essentially emotional, with Lena Headey and Stellan Skarsgård both excellent as the pair. Sent to Oslo with orders to bring her alcoholic father back to Aberdeen, Headey scuppers what should have been a straightforward trip with a bout of lounge-rage at Oslo airport and they are forbidden a flight. Fuelled by alcohol (Skarsgård), coke (Headey) and anger (both), it's touch and go whether they'll make it without concussing each other with their hefty emotional baggage. LH

Stellan Skarsgård *Tomas* · Lena Headey *Kaisa* · Ian Hart *Clive* · Charlotte Rampling *Helen* · Louise Goodall *Nurse* · Jason Hetherington *Perkins* ■ *Dir* Hans Petter Moland · *Scr* Kristin Amundsen, Hans Petter Moland, from a story by Lars Bill Lundholm

Abhijan ★★★ 🅟🅖
Drama
1962 · Ind · BW · 145min

This was the closest cinema pioneer Satyajit Ray ever came to making a mainstream melodrama and even then he only assumed the reins of this dramatisation after Bijoy Chatterjee (who was a personal friend) suffered a crisis of confidence after a single day's shooting. Soumitra Chatterjee reveals a darker side as a cab driver who falls among smugglers after losing his job and finds himself torn between a Catholic schoolteacher (Ruma Guha Thakurta) and a prostitute (Bollywood superstar Waheeda Rehman). DP Bengali +subtitles. **DVD**

Soumitra Chatterjee *Narsingh* · Waheeda Rehman *Gulabi* · Ruma Guha Thakurta *Neeli* · Gyanesh Mukherjee *Joseph* · Charuprakash Ghosh *Sukhanram* · Robi Ghosh *Rama* ■ *Dir* Satyajit Ray · *Scr* Satyajit Ray, from the novel by Tarashankar Bannerjee

Abie's Irish Rose ★★ 🅤
Silent comedy
1928 · US · BW · 108min

This is a maudlin silent version of Anne Nichols's hit Broadway play about an Irish girl who marries a Jewish boy and starts up a feud between their two families. Directed by Victor Fleming, who would make *Gone with the Wind* a decade later, the film was mightily berated by the *New Yorker*, whose critic, the waspish Dorothy Parker, wrote: "They gave me the best view... they put me behind a post." TH

Jean Hersholt *Solomon Levy* · Charles Rogers *Abie Levy* · Nancy Carroll *Rosemary Murphy* · J Farrell MacDonald *Patrick Murphy* · Bernard Gorcey *Isaac Cohen* · Ida Kramer *Mrs Isaac Cohen* · Nick Cogley *Father Whalen* · Camillus Pretal *Rabbi Jacob Samuels* ■ *Dir* Victor Fleming · *Scr* Julian Johnson, Herman Mankiewicz, from the play by Anne Nichols

Abie's Irish Rose ★★ 🅤
Comedy
1946 · US · BW · 96min

Eighteen years after Victor Fleming's silent version, this tale of a Jewish boy and an Irish girl who fall in love seems even more dumb and sluggish in this mawkish makeover from producer Bing Crosby and director Edward Sutherland. Joanne Dru, Richard Norris and Michael Chekhov head the cast, while the screenplay is by the original playwright, Anne Nichols – not that it helps, though. TH

Joanne Dru *Rosemary* · Richard Norris *Abie* · Michael Chekhov *Solomon Levy* · JM Kerrigan *Patrick Murphy* · George E Stone *Isaac Cohen* · Vera Gordon *Mrs Cohen* · Emory Parnell *Father Whalen* · Art Baker *Rabbi Samuels* · Eric Blore *Hotel manager* ■ *Dir* Edward Sutherland [A Edward Sutherland] · *Scr* Anne Nichols, from her play · *Producer* Bing Crosby

Abigail's Party ★★★★★★ 🅟🅖
Satirical comedy drama
1977 · UK · Colour · 102min

Director Mike Leigh's quintessential probe into the stiff British middle classes cuts a scalpel-sharp swathe through 1970s social mores and pretensions. Alison Steadman gives a masterful portrayal as Beverly, the hostess with the mostest, who invites some neighbours over for drinks and then proceeds to needle and cajole them with insensitive remarks. The tension rises as Beverly plays Demis Roussos songs and emasculates her snob workaholic husband with obnoxious glee. Although painful, agonising and ultimately depressing, this fascinating portrait of suburban angst is a bittersweet yet still hilarious masterpiece of manners and seething emotions. AJ **DVD**

Alison Steadman *Beverly* · Tim Stern *Laurence* · Janine Duvitski *Angela* · John Salthouse *Tony* · Harriet Reynolds *Susan* ■ *Dir* Mike Leigh · *Scr* Mike Leigh, from his play

Abilene Town ★★★ 🅟🅖
Western
1945 · US · BW · 89min

Randolph Scott made virtually nothing but westerns after the Second World War and in this early example he's the marshal of Abilene, the town where the cattle drives end. Bringing prosperity as well as trouble, the rowdy cowboys dare to disturb the church service with their six-gun salute to Ann Dvorak's singing in the local saloon. It's a lively stew of rather familiar confrontations, with a spirited Rhonda Fleming as the grocer's daughter who tries to keep Scott from doing what a man has to do. AE **DVD**

Randolph Scott *Dan Mitchell* · Ann Dvorak *Rita* · Edgar Buchanan *Bravo Trimble* · Rhonda Fleming *Sherry Balder* · Lloyd Bridges *Henry Dreiser* · Helen Boice *Big Annie* · Howard Freeman *Ed Balder* · Richard Hale *Charlie Fair* · Jack Lambert *Jet Younger* ■ *Dir* Edwin L Marin · *Scr* Harold Shumate, from the novel *Trail Town* by Ernest Haycox

Ab-normal Beauty ★★★ 🔞18
Psychological horror thriller
2004 · HK · Colour · 97min

Embellishing visually stunning chills with an art house hue, Oxide Pang's polished feature explores the unconventional ideology of beauty in horror. With atmospheric nods to the work of controversial still-life artist Joel-Peter Witkin, the film charts the psychological and physical decline of a female art student (Race Wong) who becomes obsessed with death after photographing a horrific car crash. For the first hour, it's fascinating and provocative. But the film then moves onto more familiar horror ground with the introduction of a sadistic serial-killer subplot. SF Cantonese +subtitles. Violence. **DVD**

Race Wong *Jiney* · Rosanne Wong *Jas* · Anson Leung *Anson* · Michelle Mee *Jiney's mum* ■ *Dir* Oxide Pang · *Scr* Oxide Pang, Pak Sing Pang

The Abominable Dr Phibes ★★★★ 15
Horror
1971 · UK · Colour · 93min

Vincent Price's role as an ex-vaudevillian madman living in a secret underground mechanical world is his only self-originated monster and is superbly tailored for the horror maestro. Phibes is a deformed maniac with a florid sense of style and an inclination to ham, who concocts a divinely ingenious revenge, gruesomely inspired by ancient plagues, on the surgeons he holds responsible for the death of his wife. Full of gaudy Art Deco excess, surprise charm and sardonic violence, this deadpan send-up is a classy delight. Originally billed with the tagline "Love means never having to say you're ugly"! Price reprised the role the following year in *Dr Phibes Rises Again*. AJ Violence. **DVD** **Blu**

Vincent Price *Dr Anton Phibes* · Joseph Cotten *Dr Vesalius* · Hugh Griffith *Rabbi* · Terry-Thomas *Dr Longstreet* · Virginia North *Vulnavia* · Aubrey Woods *Goldsmith* · Susan Travers *Nurse Allan* · Alex Scott (1) *Dr Hargreaves* · Peter Gilmore *Dr Kitaj* · Edward Burnham *Dr Dunwoody* · Peter Jeffrey *Inspector Trout* · Maurice Kaufman *Dr Whitcombe* ■ *Dir* Robert Fuest · *Scr* James Whiton, William Goldstein

The Abominable Snowman ★★★ 🅟🅖
Horror
1957 · UK · BW · 86min

Based on Nigel (*Quatermass*) Kneale's television play, this subtle Hammer horror follows two men with opposing views who go on a Yeti expedition to the Himalayas. Gunrunner Forrest Tucker plans to capture and exploit the legendary creature, while botanist Peter Cushing thinks research is more important. The man-beast turns out to have a surprise for both in this gripping slice of monster macabre. Tensely directed by Val Guest, the film uses eerie claustrophobia to convey a taut paranoid atmosphere that makes you overlook the fakeness of the studio-built mountains. AJ **DVD**

Forrest Tucker *Tom Friend* · Peter Cushing *Dr John Rollason* · Maureen Connell *Helen Rollason* · Richard Wattis *Peter Fox* · Robert Brown *Ed Shelley* · Michael Brill *Andrew McNee* ■ *Dir* Val Guest · *Scr* Nigel Kneale, from his TV play

Abouna ★★★ 🅟🅖
Drama
2002 · Chad/Fr · Colour · 80min

Having considered the impressions of a returning exile in *Bye Bye Africa*, Mahamat-Saleh Haroun examines the plight of those left behind by migrant workers in this wry, occasionally tragic, but ultimately optimistic study of life on the Chad-Cameroon border. Dispelling the sub-Saharan cinematic myth of towns having a purely negative impact on families and communities, the film also dares to be gently critical of conditions in the strict Koranic school to which teenager Ahidjo Mahamat Moussa and his asthmatic younger brother Hamza Moctar Aguid are sent. DP Chad Arabic +subtitles. **DVD**

Ahidjo Mahamat Moussa *Tahir Brahim* · Hamza Moctar Aguid *Amine Brahim* · Zara Haroun *Achta Brahim* · Mounira Khalil *Mute girl* · Koulsy Lamko *Mr Brahim* · Garba Issa *Master* ■ *Dir/Scr* Mahamat-Saleh Haroun

About a Boy ★★★★ 🔞12
Romantic comedy drama
2002 · Ger/US/Fr/UK · Colour · 96min

Nick Hornby's answer to Bridget Jones gets to the big screen via a surprising source, with *American Pie* directors Chris and Paul Weitz at the helm. But, unlike the Americanised version of Hornby's *High Fidelity*, this movie remains on home turf. Hugh Grant is on excellent form as a 30-something, shallow singleton, who intends to use single-parent support groups to pick up women. One of his would-be conquests introduces him to troubled boy Nicholas Hoult and his suicidal mother Toni Collette. All goes surprisingly well until the confirmed bachelor falls for single mother Rachel Weisz, which puts a strain on their friendship. Funny and moving, this is an endearing examination of masculinity. LH **DVD** **Blu**

Hugh Grant *Will* · Toni Collette *Fiona* · Rachel Weisz *Rachel* · Nicholas Hoult *Marcus* · Isabel Brook *Angie* · Sharon Small *Christine* · Victoria Smurfit *Suzie* · Nicholas Hutchison *John* ■ *Dir* Chris Weitz, Paul Weitz · *Scr* Peter Hedges, Chris Weitz, Paul Weitz

About Adam ★★★ 15
Romantic comedy
2000 · Ire/UK/US · Colour · 92min

Stuart Townsend stars as the charming layabout who bewitches every member of an outwardly respectable family. Kate Hudson, Frances O'Connor, Charlotte Bradley and Alan Maher do well as the siblings who succumb to his charms. Writer/director Gerard Stembridge tones down the amorality of this sly social sitcom with some sparkling dialogue, and is greatly aided in the glossy telling of his tale by the willing cast and Bruno de Keyzer's attractive Dublin-based photography. DP Swearing. **DVD**

Stuart Townsend *Adam* · Frances O'Connor *Laura* · Charlotte Bradley *Alice* · Kate Hudson *Lucy Owens* · Alan Maher *David* · Tommy Tiernan *Simon* · Brendan Dempsey *Martin* · Cathleen Bradley *Karen* · Rosaleen Linehan *Peggy* · Roger Gregg *Professor McCormick* ■ *Dir/Scr* Gerard Stembridge

About Elly ★★★★ 🔞12A
Drama
2009 · Iran/Fr · Colour · 114min

This film from Iranian Asghar Farhadi (*Nader and Simin, a Separation*) is an arresting combination of high-tension domestic nightmare and thought-provoking moral debate. It's the story of an upscale Tehran couple who invite their young daughter's teacher, Elly (Taraneh Alidoosti), to join them and a group of friends on a weekend by the sea. However, little do they know what turmoil will erupt because of assumptions about Elly's marital availability. Farhadi never questions Islamic law itself – what's fascinating is that he puts the spotlight on the errors of judgement that individuals make when dealing with sensitive issues. TJ Farsi +subtitles. Some violence, swearing. **DVD**

Golshifteh Farahani *Sepideh* · Taraneh Alidoosti *Elly* · Shahab Hosseini *Ahmad* · Merila Zare'i *Shohreh* ■ *Dir/Scr* Asghar Farhadi

About Last Night... ★★★ 🔞18
Comedy drama
1986 · US · Colour · 102min

Rob Lowe and Demi Moore star in this 1980s look at the lifestyles and lovestyles of young city professionals. The film is based on David Mamet's play *Sexual Perversity in Chicago*, though you'd hardly know it, since it is a far slicker affair than Mamet would ever produce. Yet it does retain at least some of the playwright's insight and intelligence, while also providing its ration of entertainment. Lowe and Moore do well, although it is James Belushi, in an over-the-top supporting performance, who all but walks off with the show. PF Swearing, nudity. **DVD** **Blu**

Rob Lowe *Danny Martin* · Demi Moore *Debbie Sullivan* · James Belushi *Bernie Litko* · Elizabeth Perkins *Joan* · George DiCenzo *Mr Favio* · Michael Alldredge *Mother Malone* · Robin Thomas *Steve Carlson* · Donna Gibbons *Alex* ■ *Dir* Edward Zwick · *Scr* Tim Kazurinsky, Denise DeClue, from the play *Sexual Perversity in Chicago* by David Mamet

About Last Night ★★★ 15
Romantic comedy
2013 · US · Colour · 100min

After his broadly comic antics in *Ride Along*, Kevin Hart takes a stab at more sophisticated comedy and the delicate art of romance in a remake of the 1986 Rob Lowe/Demi Moore film. Director Steve Pink neatly blends comedy with drama in the tale of two LA couples, from their first meeting in a bar, through the ups and downs of their stormy relationships. Some might not appreciate the frank language and sexy tone, but this is a portrait of modern love in raw detail. **DA** Swearing, sex scenes, drug abuse, brief nudity.

Kevin Hart *Bernie* • Michael Ealy *Danny* • Regina Hall *Joan* • Joy Bryant *Debbie* ▪ *Dir* Steve Pink • *Scr* Leslye Headland, from the 1986 film, from the play *Sexual Perversity in Chicago* by David Mamet

About Mrs Leslie ★★U
Romantic drama 1954 · US · BW · 103min

This melodramatic tale tells the story in flashback of a couple of lovers who meet sporadically, spending time together once a year. Trouble is, he's the marvellously rugged Robert Ryan, and audiences may well wonder what on earth he sees in Shirley Booth. Distinguished film historian David Shipman called this "a very special film", but, despite the quality of the playing, this soap opera takes a lot of believing. **TS**

Shirley Booth *Mrs Vivien Leslie* • Robert Ryan *George Leslie* • Marjie Millar *Nadine Roland* • Alex Nicol *Ian McKay* • Sammy White *Harry Willey* • James Bell *Mr Poole* • Virginia Brissac *Mrs Poole* • Eileen Janssen [Eilene Janssen] *Pixie* ▪ *Dir* Daniel Mann • *Scr* Ketti Frings, Hal Kanter, from the novel by Vina Delmar

About Schmidt ★★★★15
Comedy drama 2002 · US · Colour · 120min

In director Alexander Payne's endearing tragicomedy, Jack Nicholson plays a man who feels disconnected from his own life, a mood brought on by forced retirement, the sudden death of his wife and his daughter's impending marriage to a man he regards as a loser. His road trip to her wedding is the start of a very offbeat journey, as a subdued Nicholson gets to grips with new beginnings. It's funnier than it sounds as the film's quirky approach to this late-life crisis is typified by Schmidt's hilarious outpouring of pent-up bitterness in his letters to a Tanzanian orphan he has sponsored. While this is not a movie of dramatic or comic peaks, the star's poignant performance extracts meaning from the smallest moments. **JC** Swearing. *DVD*

Jack Nicholson *Warren Schmidt* • Hope Davis *Jeannie* • Dermot Mulroney *Randall Hertzel* • Kathy Bates *Roberta Hertzel* • Len Cariou *Ray* • Howard Hesseman *Larry* • June Squibb *Helen Schmidt* • Harry Groener *John* ▪ *Dir* Alexander Payne • *Scr* Alexander Payne, Jim Taylor, from the novel by Louis Begley

About Time ★★★★12
Science-fiction romantic comedy
2013 · UK · Colour · 118min

The premise for Richard Curtis's film may at first seem like an absurd storyline more at home in *Doctor Who* (Curtis did in fact pen an episode in which the Time Lord met Van Gogh), but *About Time* does see a return to form for the writer/director. When Domhnall Gleeson discovers that he can travel back in time on his 21st birthday, he puts his new-found skill to use in the way most guys his age would – to get himself a girlfriend. But it isn't his love life that forms the most touching thread of this romantic comedy. Gleeson's relationship with dad Bill Nighy (played in typically bumbling fashion) is at the heart of a film that can stand tall against Curtis classics *Notting Hill* and *Four Weddings*. **AIS** Swearing, sexual references. *DVD* 🔵

Domhnall Gleeson *Tim* • Rachel McAdams *Mary* • Bill Nighy *Dad* • Tom Hollander *Harry* • Margot Robbie *Charlotte* • Lisa Eichhorn *Jean* ▪ *Dir/Scr* Richard Curtis

Above and Beyond ★
Second World War drama
1952 · US · BW · 122min

Robert Taylor is given the job of dropping the Bomb on Hiroshima while his amour, Eleanor Parker, is moved into an army camp for security reasons. Poor dear, she hasn't been told what hubby's up to. It's all quite pathetic, really, trivialising a major

historic event and patronising to women even in 1952. **AT**

Robert Taylor (1) *Col Paul Tibbets* • Eleanor Parker *Lucy Tibbets* • James Whitmore *Maj Uanna* • Larry Keating *Maj Gen Vernon C Brent* • Larry Gates *Capt Parsons* • Marilyn Erskine *Marge Bratton* • Stephen Dunne [Steve Dunne] *Maj Harry Bratton* • Robert Burton *Gen Samuel E Roberts* ▪ *Dir* Melvin Frank, Norman Panama • *Scr* Beirne Lay Jr, Frank Panama

Above Suspicion ★★★★
Spy drama 1943 · US · BW · 90min

Joan Crawford's presence is, for once, rather muted in this entertaining spy drama. Not only does she have to share star-billing with Fred MacMurray – they're honeymooning Americans caught up in espionage in pre-war Germany – but she also has to compete with the heel-clicking dynamism of Conrad Veidt and a marvellously villainous Basil Rathbone. So the star who could even upstage herself is considerably controlled, allowing the plot to gain proper prominence. The result is terrifically enjoyable escapism. **TH**

Joan Crawford *Frances Myles* • Fred MacMurray *Richard Myles* • Conrad Veidt *Hassert Seidel* • Basil Rathbone *Sig Von Aschenhausen* • Reginald Owen *Dr Mespelbrunn* • Richard Ainley *Peter Galt* • Cecil Cunningham *Countess* • Ann Shoemaker *Aunt Ellen* ▪ *Dir* Richard Thorpe • *Scr* Keith Winter, Melville Baker, Patricia Coleman, from the novel by Helen MacInnes

Above Suspicion ★★★18
Crime drama 1995 · US · Colour · 91min

Christopher Reeve plays a cop who is paralysed after a bungled drugs raid in this uncomfortable example of art imitating life – it was filmed about a year before the star's tragic horse-riding accident. Together with wife Kim Cattrall, he plots an intricate insurance scam, but things don't go according to plan. It's a classy straight-to-video thriller with an enjoyably convoluted plot, and director Steven Schachter handles the twists and turns with some skill. **JF**

Christopher Reeve *Dempsey* • Joe Mantegna *Rhinehart* • Kim Cattrall *Gail* • Edward Kerr *Nick* • Geoffrey Rivas *Enrique* • Finola Hughes *Iris* • William H Macy *Prosecutor (DA)* ▪ *Dir* Steven Schachter • *Scr* Jerry Lazarus, William H Macy, Steven Schachter

Above Suspicion ★★
Thriller 2000 · US · Colour · 99min

Annabella Sciorra begins to suspect that her building contractor husband Scott Bakula is a killer after he lies about a missed appointment. Surely a man who coaches his daughter's baseball team can't be a fugitive from justice? This tepid thriller rarely rouses you to care. **DP**

Scott Bakula *James Stockton* • Annabella Sciorra *Lisa Stockton* • Edward Asner *Thomas O'Claire* • George Dzundza *Stamos* ▪ *Dir/Scr* Stephen La Rocque

Above the Rim ★★15
Sports drama 1994 · US · Colour · 93min

Every hackneyed cliché is depressingly frog-marched before the camera in this sports-themed "gangsta ghetto" fare telling the tired tale of talented high school basketball player Duane Martin, torn between two friends on opposing sides of the law. One is drug-dealer Tupac Shakur who wants him playing on his tough inner-city team. The other is coach Leon, a former champion haunted by the death of his best friend. **AJ** *DVD*

Duane Martin *Kyle* • Leon *Shep* • Tupac Shakur *Birdie* • David Bailey *Rollins* • Tonya Pinkins *Mailika* • Marlon Wayans *Bugaloo* • Bernie Mac *Flip* ▪ *Dir* Jeff Pollack • *Scr* Jeff Pollack, Barry Michael Cooper, from a story by Pollack, Benny Medina

Above Us the Waves ★★U
Second World War drama
1955 · UK · BW · 95min

Having failed with torpedoes, John Mills and his rookie crew set out in midget submarines to try to sink the German battleship *Tirpitz* in this rather disappointing Second World War action adventure.

Riddled with stiff-upper-lipped stereotypes, this is one of those proud re-creations of an "against the odds" mission that were the staple of postwar British cinema. However, by opting to examine the cramped conditions of his characters rather than go overboard on their heroic exploits, director Ralph Thomas kills the pace of the picture. **DP** *DVD*

John Mills *Commander Frazer* • John Gregson *Lt Alec Duffy* • Donald Sinden *Lt Tom Corbett* • James Robertson-Justice *Admiral Ryder* • Michael Medwin *Smart* • James Kenney *Abercrombie* • OE Hasse *Tirpitz Captain* • William Russell *Ramsey* • Thomas Heathcote *Hutchins* • Lee Patterson *Cox* • Theodore Bikel *German officer* • Anthony Newley *X2 engineer* ▪ *Dir* Ralph Thomas • *Scr* Robin Estridge, from a story by CET Warren, James Benson

Abraham Lincoln ★★★U
Historical drama 1930 · US · Tinted · 92min

The last gasp of genius from the great silent film-maker, DW Griffith, this biopic of the American president has too much explanatory detail but boasts some remarkable visual set pieces. Written by Stephen Vincent Benet and Gerrit Lloyd, it stars Walter Huston as Lincoln and Una Merkel as his wife, and shows how the great man entered small-town politics before rising to the highest office in the land. Griffith was accused of racism in *The Birth of a Nation*; here, he shows a capacity for tolerance. **TH** *DVD*

Walter Huston *Abraham Lincoln* • Una Merkel *Ann Rutledge* • Kay Hammond *Mary Todd Lincoln* • E Alyn Warren *Stephen Douglas* • Hobart Bosworth *Gen Robert E Lee* • Fred Warren *Gen Ulysses S Grant* • Henry B Walthall *Col Marshall* • Frank Campeau *Gen Sheridan* ▪ *Dir* DW Griffith • *Scr* Stephen Vincent Benet, Gerrit Lloyd • *Cinematographer* Karl Struss

Abraham Lincoln: Vampire Hunter ★★★★15
Horror thriller 2012 · US · Colour · 100min

Who knew the 16th President of the United States was the scourge of the undead? Seth Grahame-Smith adapts his own novel for this action-packed story, brought to life by director Timur Bekmambetov. Benjamin Walker's likeable hero holds his own through the main vampire action and the anti-slavery subplot, however improbable it all becomes. Terrific supporting turns from Anthony Mackie and Dominic Cooper add spice to a wildly enjoyable yarn. **KK** Violence, swearing, a sex scene. *DVD* 🔵

Benjamin Walker *Abraham Lincoln* • Dominic Cooper *Henry Sturgess* • Anthony Mackie *William* • Mary Elizabeth Winstead *Mary Todd Lincoln* • Rufus Sewell *Adam* • Marton Csokas *Jack Armstrong* ▪ *Dir* Timur Bekmambetov • *Scr* Simon Kinberg, Seth Grahame-Smith, from Grahame-Smith's novel

Abraham Valley ★★★PG
Drama 1993 · Por/Fr/Swi · Colour · 188min

Manoel de Oliveira reworks Gustave Flaubert's *Madame Bovary* in this typically stylised outing. In translating the story to a wine-growing region of modern-day Portugal, novelist Augustina Bessa-Luis draws on her own acquaintances for inspiration. However, this is still very much the director's film, sprawling like an epic cinematic poem. As the lame adulteress whose amours scandalise her staid community, Leonor Silveira is deliciously dolorous, while Luís Miguel Cintra is doggedly decent as the doctor she marries. **DP** Portuguese +subtitles.

Mario Barroso *Narrator* • Leonor Silveira *Ema Cardeano* • Cecile Sanz de Alba *Young Ema* • Luís Miguel Cintra *Carlos Paiva* • Rui de Carvalho *Paulino Cardeano* ▪ *Dir* Manoel de Oliveira • *Scr* Manoel de Oliveira, from the novel *Vale Abraao* by Augustina Bessa-Luis

Abroad with Two Yanks ★★U
Comedy 1944 · US · BW · 81min

The two Yanks are lovable William Bendix and straight-up Dennis O'Keefe, and abroad is Australia, where the two marines find themselves competing for the attentions of

the same woman, Helen Walker. It's likeable, lightweight stuff, without much substance, given pace and comedic style by veteran Allan Dwan. **TS**

William Bendix *Biff Koraski* • Helen Walker *Joyce Stuart* • Dennis O'Keefe *Jeff Reardon* • John Loder *Cyril North* • George Cleveland *Roderick Stuart* • Janet Lambert *Alice* • James Flavin *Sergeant Wiggins* • Arthur Hunnicutt *Arkie* ▪ *Dir* Allan Dwan • *Scr* Charles Rogers, Wilkie Mahoney, Ted Sills

Absence of Malice ★★★PG
Drama 1981 · US · Colour · 111min

Miami reporter Sally Field defames honest businessman Paul Newman in this big-issue drama that is a watchable experience thanks to stalwart performances from the leading players. Sydney Pollack's direction is well focused and ex-newspaperman Kurt Luedtke's script makes all the right liberal noises as Sally Field's journalist is manipulated by government leaks about Newman's Mafia relatives. The standout, however, is Oscar-nominated, Melinda Dillon as Newman's frightened alibi. **TH** *DVD*

Paul Newman *Michael Gallagher* • Sally Field *Megan Carter* • Bob Balaban *Elliot Rosen* • Melinda Dillon *Teresa* • Luther Adler *Malderone* • Barry Primus *Waddell* • Josef Sommer *McAdam* • John Harkins *Davidek* ▪ *Dir* Sydney Pollack • *Scr* Kurt Luedtke

Absence of the Good ★★★15
Thriller 1999 · US · Colour · 94min

John Flynn is an underrated and largely unsung action director and here he brings his usual no-frills professionalism to a familiar but quietly satisfying serial killer thriller. Stephen Baldwin (nicely understated for once) is the cop recovering from the accidental death of his son who becomes obsessed with a killer who is leaving a trail of bodies behind him as he searches for his own perfect home. You'll guess the identity of the killer long before Baldwin does, but Flynn sustains a believable air of suspense throughout. **JF** *DVD*

Stephen Baldwin *Caleb Barnes* • Rob Knepper [Robert Knepper] *Glenn Dwyer* • Shawn Huff *Mary Barnes* • Tyne Daly *Marcia Lyons* • Allen Garfield *Lt Paul Taylor* ▪ *Dir* John Flynn • *Scr* James Reid

The Absent-Minded Professor ★★★U
Fantasy comedy 1961 · US · BW · 92min

This warm-hearted slice of Walt Disney-style Americana stars likeable Fred MacMurray as the inventor of flying rubber. Wicked Keenan Wynn wants to steal it, and that's about the nub of the flub. The image of the flubber-driven family car crossing the Moon so inspired a young Steven Spielberg that he copied it to provide the most potent shot in *ET*, and eventually used it as the logo of his company, Amblin. A sequel, *Son of Flubber*, followed, as did a TV remake and a big screen offering, *Flubber*, starring Robin Williams. **TS** *DVD*

Fred MacMurray *Professor Ned Brainard* • Nancy Olson *Betsy Carlisle* • Keenan Wynn *Alonzo Hawk* • Tommy Kirk *Bill Hawk* • Leon Ames *Rufus Daggett* • Elliott Reid *Shelby Ashton* • Edward Andrews *Defence Secretary* • Wally Brown *Coach Elkins* ▪ *Dir* Robert Stevenson • *Scr* Bill Walsh, from a story by Samuel W Taylor

The Absent One ★★★18
Crime mystery thriller
2014 · Den/Ger/Swe · Colour · 119min

This Danish policier brings another outing for Department Q, the over-worked Copenhagen detectives tackling a massive pile of cold cases first introduced in *The Keeper of Lost Causes*. This time the suicide of a retired country cop obsessed with proving the innocence of his convicted killer son sends world-weary Nikolaj Lie Kaas and trusty sidekick Fares Fares to re-open files from years earlier. This sequel is no world-beater – just a solid offering for genre fans. **TJ** In Danish, French. Violence.

Nikolaj Lie Kaas *Carl Morck* • Fares Fares *Assad* • Pilou Asbaek *Ditlev Pram* • David Dencik *Ulrik Dybbol* ■ *Dir* Mikkel Norgaard • *Scr* Rasmus Heisterberg, Nikolaj Arcel, from the novel *Disgrace* by Jussi Adler-Olsen

Absentia ★★★ 15

Horror thriller	2011 · US · Colour · 87min

Are the spooks for real or is the horror all in the mind? It's a well-worn path but here it delivers genuine scares on a micro-budget. Our very believable heroine is Courtney Bell, who's being pressured by a cop (Dave Levine) to have her husband declared legally dead, *in absentia*. She's pregnant with the cop's child, a complication that might explain the ghoulish nightmares she keeps having. An interesting, though remarkably restrained horror movie. SvM Swearing, brief violence. DVD BL

Courtney Bell *Tricia* • Katie Parker *Callie* • Dave Levine *Detective Mallory* • Morgan Peter Brown *Daniel Riley* ■ *Dir/Scr* Mike Flanagan

Absolute Beginners ★★ 15

Musical	1986 · UK · Colour · 102min

This is a dismal attempt to turn Colin MacInnes's cult novel about the birth of the teenage nation in Britain into an 1980s *Expresso Bongo* without the talents of Cliff Richard. Will fashion designer Patsy Kensit choose romance with trendy photographer Eddie O'Connell or toff couturier James Fox in this highly stylised view of 1950s pop culture and changing social mores? Songs by David Bowie, Ray Davies, Sade and the Style Council do help lighten the lively, if vacuous, load. AJ Some swearing. DVD BL

Eddie O'Connell *Colin Young* • Patsy Kensit *Crepe Suzette* • David Bowie *Vendice Partners* • James Fox *Henley of Mayfair* • Ray Davies *Arthur* • Mandy Rice-Davies *Mum* • Steven Berkoff *Fanatic* • Sade *Athene Duncannon* ■ *Dir* Julien Temple • *Scr* Richard Burridge, Christopher Wicking, Don MacPherson, Colin MacInnes, from the novel by Colin MacInnes

Absolute Power ★★★ 15

Crime drama	1996 · US · Colour · 116min

Clint Eastwood composes the music (with Lennie Niehaus), directs and stars in this well-paced tale of high-level corruption. Clint plays a master burglar who, while robbing a mansion, witnesses President Gene Hackman indulging in a sadistic sex act that leads to the death of a rich man's wife. Whitney and his estranged daughter (Laura Linney) must then stay one step ahead of the police and the president's men. Credibility is the main casualty of the piece, but William Goldman's taut script is well realised by thoughtful direction and the high-calibre cast. TH Violence, swearing, sex scenes. DVD BL

Clint Eastwood *Luther Whitney* • Gene Hackman *President Richmond* • Ed Harris *Seth Frank* • Laura Linney *Kate Whitney* • Scott Glenn *Bill Burton* • Dennis Haysbert *Tim Collin* • Judy Davis *Gloria Russell* • EG Marshall *Walter Sullivan* • Alison Eastwood *Art student* • Kimber Eastwood *White House tour guide* ■ *Dir* Clint Eastwood • *Scr* William Goldman, from the novel by David Baldacci

Absolutely Anything ★★ 12A

Science-fiction comedy adventure	
2015 · UK/US · Colour · 85min	

Terry Jones directs Simon Pegg as a man given the power to do absolutely anything by a group of aliens (Jones's Python pals). There's a sense that Jones didn't know where to go once the main premise was established, but Pegg does his best to make sense of the surreal madness, remaining likeable especially when next to a one-dimensional Kate Beckinsale. Animated segments offer some nostalgic interest to Python fans, but it's scant reward for a wish-fulfilment comedy that doesn't fulfil anyone's wishes. JL Some swearing, sexual references.

Simon Pegg *Neil Clarke* • Kate Beckinsale *Catherine* • Sanjeev Bhaskar *Ray* • Eddie Izzard *Headmaster* • Meera Syal *Fiona* • John Cleese *Chief alien* • Terry Gilliam *Nasty alien* • Terry Jones *Scientist alien* • Eric Idle *Salubrious Gat* •

Michael Palin *Kindly alien* • Joanna Lumley *Fenella* ■ *Dir* Terry Jones • *Scr* Terry Jones, Gavin Scott

Absolutely Fabulous: the Movie ★★★ 15

Comedy	2016 · UK · Colour · 90min

Nearly 25 years after their first series, sitcom socialites Eddy and Patsy get their own movie! Here, the shambolic pair (played as ever by Jennifer Saunders and Joanna Lumley) go on the run after being suspected of killing Kate Moss, and try to make a new life on the French Riviera. This unusual road movie hurries along at a fast pace, throwing in gags alongside the pair's unique perspective on everything from ageing to social media. With a dizzying mix of showbiz cameos and returning cast, Lumley and Saunders are having just as much fun as ever in what is basically a feature-length pay-off for loyal fans. JL Swearing, drug abuse. ■

Jennifer Saunders *Edina Monsoon* • Joanna Lumley *Patsy Stone* • Julia Sawalha *Saffy* • Jane Horrocks *Bubble* • June Whitfield *Mother* • Lulu • Emma Bunton • Celia Imrie *Claudia Bing* • Kathy Burke *Magda* ■ *Dir* Mandie Fletcher • *Scr* Jennifer Saunders

Absolution ★ 15

Thriller	1978 · UK · Colour · 91min

Lashings of Catholic guilt pervade this totally bonkers potboiler, with Richard Burton as the priest in a Catholic boarding school for boys whose protégé, Dominic Guard, runs away with hippy Billy Connolly and turns into a killer. Unlike red wine, the three years this movie spent on the shelf did not improve it. AT

Richard Burton *Father Goddard* • Dominic Guard *Benjie Stanfield* • Billy Connolly *Blakey* • Andrew Keir *Headmaster* • Dai Bradley [David Bradley (3)] *Arthur Dyson* • Willoughby Gray *Brigadier Walsh* • Preston Lockwood *Father Hibbert* • Brook Williams *Father Clarence* ■ *Dir* Anthony Page • *Scr* Anthony Shaffer

The Abyss ★★★ 15

Science-fiction thriller	
1989 · US · Colour · 133min	

James Cameron's bloated, sentimental epic was criticised on release, but it remains a fascinating folly. Ed Harris is the leader of an underwater team working for an oil company that is pressed into service to rescue the crew of a crippled submarine. Harris is great in a rare leading-man role and there is first-rate support from Mary Elizabeth Mastrantonio as his estranged partner. Cameron excels in cranking up the tension within the cramped quarters and the awe-inspiring effects deservedly won an Oscar. The added scenes in the Special Edition (a tense standoff between the superpowers) are a major improvement. JF Violence, swearing. DVD

Ed Harris *Bud Brigman* • Mary Elizabeth Mastrantonio *Lindsey Brigman* • Michael Biehn *Lieutenant Coffey* • Leo Burmester *Catfish De Vries* • Todd Graff *Alan "Hippy" Carnes* • John Bedford Lloyd *Jammer Willis* • JC Quinn *"Sonny" Dawson* • Kimberly Scott *Lisa "One Night" Standing* • Captain Kidd Brewer Jr *Lew Finler* • George Robert Klek *Wilhite* • Christopher Murphy *Schoenick* ■ *Dir/Scr* James Cameron • *Special Effects* Joe Unsinn, Joseph Viskocil

Las Acacias ★★★★★ 12

Road movie drama	
2011 · Arg/Sp · Colour · 82min	

A lonely trucker finds his life changing when he accepts a paying passenger in this character-driven road movie, winner of the Camera d'Or prize for the best first feature at Cannes in 2011. Gruff, taciturn Germán de Silva is initially not best pleased when he picks up Hebe Duarte as arranged, because bringing her baby daughter along isn't part of the bargain. Gradually, however, in the course of the journey, barriers are broken down and perspectives changed. The story unfolds at a steady pace with very little dialogue, but the performers seem to live out their roles in a way that almost goes beyond acting, so once it reels you in, this is

absolutely captivating. TJ Spanish, Guarani +subtitles. DVD SL

Germán de Silva *Rubén* • Hebe Duarte *Jacinta* • Nayra Calle Mamani *Anahí* ■ *Dir* Pablo Giorgelli • *Scr* Pablo Giorgelli, Salvador Roselli • *Cinematographer* Diego Poleri

Accattone ★★★★ 15

Drama	1961 · It · BW · 111min

Pier Paolo Pasolini made his directorial debut with this uncompromising study of life on the mean streets of Rome. Using a cast of actors drawn mostly from the city's slums, he manages to find a raw poetry in the dealings of the pimps, prostitutes and petty thieves who populate a world with which he was very familiar. Franco Citti brings an indolent charm to his portrayal of Accattone, a wastrel who's reluctant to work, yet insufficiently ruthless to live by crime. However, it's Pasolini's ability to re-create the teeming urban bustle, which he ironically counterpoints with the music of Bach, that gives this ultimately tragic tale its authenticity and power. DP Italian +subtitles. DVD BL

Franco Citti *Vittorio Accattone* • Franca Pasut *Stella* • Silvana Corsini *Maddalena* • Paolo Guidi *Ascenza* • Adriana Asti *Amore* • Renato Capogna *Renato* ■ *Dir/Scr* Pier Paolo Pasolini

Accent on Youth ★★★

Romance	1935 · US · BW · 77min

Paramount made two subsequent versions of Samson Raphaelson's hit Broadway comedy – *Mr Music* (1950) and *But Not for Me* (1959) – though neither had the sparkle of the first, directed with style by Wesley Ruggles (one of the original Keystone Kops). Sylvia Sidney escapes from her usual tragic roles to play a young secretary who falls for her middle-aged employer (the mellifluous-voiced Herbert Marshall). It is rather wordy, but fortunately most of those words are witty and crisply delivered. RB

Sylvia Sidney *Linda Brown* • Herbert Marshall *Steven Gaye* • Philip Reed *Dickie Reynolds* • Astrid Allwyn *Genevieve Lang* • Holmes Herbert *Frank Galloway* • Donald Meek *Orville* ■ *Dir* Wesley Ruggles • *Scr* Herbert Fields, Claude Binyon, from the play by Samson Raphaelson

Acceptance ★★

Comedy	2009 · US · Colour · 95min

Susan Coll's bestselling novel is the source for this engaging yet inconsistent comedy, in which Mae Whitman's struggle to write a college application essay causes emotional meltdown for the teen. Awkwardly mixing comedy and melodrama to emphasise its central message of accepting people for who they are, the tale starts off light-heartedly, but a desperation ensues that turns even enthusiastic mum Joan Cusack into a neurotic mess. A predictable ending restores everyone's equilibrium, but the solutions feel lame. SF

Mae Whitman *Taylor Rockefeller* • Joan Cusack *Nina Rockefeller* • Kiersten Warren *Grace* • Brigid Brannagh *Olivia* • Jonathan Keltz *"AP" Harry* ■ *Dir* Sanaa Hamri • *Scr* Suzette Couture, from the novel by Susan Coll

Accepted ★★★ 12

Comedy	2006 · US · Colour · 89min

The stresses of university admission are the target of this good-natured teen comedy. Justin Long plays a high-school slacker who is turned down by all his college choices. Instead of retiring to his bedroom to sulk, he enterprisingly creates a college with a decidedly unorthodox curriculum for himself and his fellow rejects. This entertaining nonsense is carried off with some aplomb by first-time director Steve Pink and his young cast. But it never quite reaches the heights of its obvious inspiration, John Hughes's classic *Ferris Bueller's Day Off*. Pink was screenwriter on John Cusack's *Grosse Pointe Blank* and *High Fidelity*; Ann Cusack (John's sister) plays Long's mum here. AS Swearing, sexual references, drug abuse. DVD

Justin Long *Bartleby Gaines* • Jonah Hill *Sherman Schrader* • Blake Lively *Monica* • Maria Thayer *Rory* • Anthony Heald *Dean Van Horne* •

Adam Herschman *Glen* • Ann Cusack *Diane Gaines* ■ *Dir* Steve Pink • *Scr* Adam Cooper, Bill Collage, Mark Perez, from a story by Perez

Accident ★★★★★ PG

Drama	1967 · UK · Colour · 101min

Shimmeringly photographed by Gerry Fisher, Oxford and its surrounding countryside have never looked as beautiful as in this delicious exercise in character assassination. Dirk Bogarde and Stanley Baker seize upon every opportunity presented in Harold Pinter's merciless script, as two Oxford dons become infatuated with the same student, and donnish civility only thinly veils the disappointment, lust and cruelty of unfulfilled middle age. Michael York, Delphine Seyrig and Vivien Merchant also give impeccable performances as those unfortunate enough to be caught up in Bogarde and Baker's mind games. Joseph Losey's relentless direction leaves the characters with few hiding places. Brilliant. DP DVD

Dirk Bogarde *Stephen* • Stanley Baker *Charley* • Jacqueline Sassard *Anna* • Delphine Seyrig *Francesca* • Alexander Knox *Provost* • Michael York *William* • Vivien Merchant *Rosalind* • Harold Pinter *Bell* • Ann Firbank *Laura* ■ *Dir* Joseph Losey • *Scr* Harold Pinter, from the novel by Nicholas Mosley • *Cinematographer* Gerry Fisher

Accidental Friendship ★★

Drama	2008 · Can · Colour · 95min

A homeless woman and a female police officer develop an unlikely bond in this manipulative true-story drama. *Grey's Anatomy* star Chandra Wilson brings poignant dignity to her role as the dispossessed dog lover whose dedication to her animals over herself attracts the benevolence of a big-hearted LA cop (Kathleen Munroe). Heartfelt performances and an overall air of authenticity mitigate some of the film's contrivances, resulting in a humbling and occasionally inspirational experience. SF

Chandra Wilson *Yvonne* • Kathleen Munroe *Tami* • Gabriel Hogan *Kevin* • Alison Sealy-Smith *Chris* • Ben Vereen *Wes* ■ *Dir* Don McBrearty • *Scr* Anna Sandor

Accidental Hero ★★★★ 15

Comedy drama	1992 · US · Colour · 113min

Another of Stephen Frears's box-office failures, this was originally released as *Hero* in the States. Clearly influenced by Billy Wilder's *Ace in the Hole*, Frears's film is seriously underrated, a drama about a plane crash in which Geena Davis's TV reporter is saved by a mystery Good Samaritan. We know it's Dustin Hoffman, but when Andy Garcia claims to be the "Angel of Flight 104" he's swept up in the media hysteria. Sometimes funny, often deeply cynical and pessimistic, it's a clever and brave picture. AT Swearing. DVD

Dustin Hoffman *Bernie Laplante* • Geena Davis *Gale Gayley* • Andy Garcia *John Bubber* • Joan Cusack *Evelyn* • Kevin J O'Connor *Chucky* • Maury Chaykin *Winston* • Stephen Tobolowsky *Wallace* • Christian Clemenson *Conklin* • Tom Arnold *Chick* • Warren Berlinger *Judge Goines* ■ *Dir* Stephen Frears • *Scr* David Webb Peoples, from a story by Laura Ziskin, Alvin Sergent, Peoples

The Accidental Husband ★★ 12

Romantic comedy	2008 · US · Colour · 86min

Uma Thurman plays a lovesick talk-show host in this laboured romantic comedy. As she prepares to get hitched to Colin Firth (doing his usual stiff-upper-lip routine), a gruff firefighter (Jeffrey Dean Morgan) worms his way into her affections. It's an unlikely match brought about by silly contrivances (including a faked marriage certificate) and a bit of banter that aims for witty and falls just short of banal. In all, there are very few laughs to be had and a good deal of wincing as co-producer Thurman resorts to pratfalls and severe head injury to get a chuckle. SP Brief swearing. DVD

Uma Thurman *Dr Emma Lloyd* • Colin Firth *Michael* • Jeffrey Dean Morgan *Patrick* • Sam Shepard *Wilder* • Isabella Rossellini *Mrs Bollenbecker* • Keir Dullea *Mr Bollenbecker* • Sarita Choudhury *Sunny* ■ *Dir* Griffin Dunne • *Scr* Mimi Hare, Clare Naylor, Bonnie Sikowitz

Accidental Love ★★ 15

Romantic comedy
2013 · US/UK · Colour · 96min

An accident with a nail gun leaves a small-town waitress (Jessica Biel) with a bolt in her brain, prompting bizarre personality swings, in this political satire-cum-farce. Originally filmed back in 2008 under the title *Nailed*, it was disowned by director David O Russell, who's credited here as Stephen Greene. The central thrust sees a thoroughly game Biel travel to Washington to seek a change in the healthcare laws, and the result is wildly uneven in its madcap wit, but it's bonkers enough to keep you watching. TJ Sexual references. DVD

Jessica Biel *Alice Eckle* • Jake Gyllenhaal *Howard Birdwell* • Catherine Keener *Rep Pam Hendrickson* • James Marsden *Scott* • Tracy Morgan *Keyshawn* ■ *Dir* Stephen Greene [David O Russell] • *Scr* Kristin Corc, Matthew Silverstein, Dave Jeser, from their story, based on Gore's novel *Sammy's Hill*

The Accidental Spy ★★ 12

Action adventure thriller
2001 · HK · Colour · 83min

Sports equipment salesman Jackie Chan becomes the pawn in a hunt for missing phials of ultra-addictive opium in this pedestrian action adventure. Notable for its horrendous dubbing, this is one of Chan's least exciting projects. Though there's no denying his amazing physical abilities, the plot is patchy, the obligatory slapstick inappropriate, and the fight sequences repetitive. SF Cantonese, Mandarin, Korean, Turkish, French dubbed. DVD BL

Jackie Chan *Buck Yuen* • Eric Tsang *Many Liu* • Vivian Hsu *Yong* • Wu Hsing-kuo *Mr Zen* • Alfred Cheung *Cheung* • Kim Min-jeong *Carmen Wong* • Anthony Rene Jones *Philip Ashley* ■ *Dir* Teddy Chen • *Scr* Ivy Ho

The Accidental Tourist ★★★★ PG

Comedy drama
1988 · US · Colour · 116min

This underrated story remains one of director Lawrence Kasdan's best films. William Hurt is wonderful as the travel writer whose life falls apart when his young son dies and his wife (Kathleen Turner) leaves him; an Oscar-winning Geena Davis plays the loopy dog trainer who helps him recover. While there are plenty of laughs along the way, an air of melancholy hangs over the piece as Kasdan movingly probes the emotions Hurt has buried. JF DVD

William Hurt *Macon Leary* • Kathleen Turner *Sarah Leary* • Geena Davis *Muriel Pritchett* • Amy Wright *Rose Leary* • Bill Pullman *Julian Edge* • Robert Gorman [Robert Hy Gorman] *Alexander Pritchett* • David Ogden Stiers *Porter Leary* • Ed Begley Jr *Charles Leary* • Bradley Mott *Mr Loomis* ■ *Dir* Lawrence Kasdan • *Scr* Frank Galati, Lawrence Kasdan, from the novel by Anne Tyler

The Accidental Witness ★★

Thriller
2006 · US · Colour · 90min

Being in the wrong place at the wrong time leaves aspiring Seattle lawyer Natasha Gregson Wagner the target for murder in this badly paced and unconvincing thriller from actor/film-maker Kristoffer Tabori (son of *Dirty Harry* director Don Siegel). Wagner's awful performance doesn't help, drawing attention to the weak plotting and almost total lack of atmosphere. Consequently, only the tense score makes the signposted climax interesting. SF

Natasha Gregson Wagner *Christine Sternwald* • Currie Graham *Victor Sandeman* • Aaron Pearl *Jeff Monroe* • Scott Hylands *Detective Bill Malone* ■ *Dir* Kristoffer Tabori • *Scr* Michael Rhodes

Acción Mutante ★★ 18

Science-fiction horror
1993 · Sp · Colour · 89min

Spanish director Alex de la Iglesia's debut feature begins in crackerjack comic-book style as members of a disabled terrorist group in 2012 kidnap a debutante's daughter and hold her to ransom on a distant mining planet. But, although gory, nasty and sexy in equal proportion, this Pedro Almodóvar-produced trash peters out into sci-fi on the verge of a nervous breakdown. AJ Spanish +subtitles.

Antonio Resines *Ramón Yarritu* • Alex Angulo *Alex* • Frédérique Feder *Patricia Orujo* • Fernando Guillén [Fernando Guillen-Cuervo] *Orujo* • Enrique San Francisco *Novio Ultrajado* ■ *Dir* Alex de la Iglesia • *Scr* Alex de la Iglesia, Jorge Guerricaechevarría

L'Accompagnatrice ★★★★ PG

Second World War drama
1992 · Fr · Colour · 111min

The Nazi occupation of France during the Second World War provides the backdrop for this compelling, but not always convincing, story of a young pianist who finds herself playing accompanist both on and off stage to her glamorous employer. François Truffaut's protégé Claude Miller has always excelled at directing young actresses and here he coaxes a bewitching performance from Romane Bohringer, who judges the differing shades of devotion, jealousy, timidity and regret to perfection. Elena Safonova has a ball as the singer torn between her collaborator husband and her Resistance hero lover. DP French +subtitles.

Richard Bohringer *Charles Brice* • Elena Safonova *Irène Brice* • Romane Bohringer *Sophie Vasseur* • Bernard Verley *Jacques Ceniat* • Samuel Labarthe *Jacques Fabert* • Nelly Borgeaud *Madame Vasseur* • Julien Rassam *Benoit Weizman* • Jean-Pierre Kohut Svelko *General Heller* • Claude Rich *Minister* ■ *Dir* Claude Miller • *Scr* Claude Miller, Luc Béraud, from the novel by Nina Berberova

According to Greta ★★ 15

Romantic drama
2009 · US · Colour · 88min

Hilary Duff nails adolescent obnoxiousness yet struggles to convey its emotional causes in this clichéd and lazy, coming-of-age melodrama. Ultra-cynical and generally unlikeable, she plays a rebellious and suicidal 17-year-old who's sent off for a straightening-out summer with her grandparents (an excellent if wasted Ellen Burstyn and Michael Murphy). Romance and simplistic life lessons predictably follow, but the meaty issues behind her poisonous personality are never explored with the depth and seriousness they deserve. SF Drug abuse. DVD

Hilary Duff *Greta* • Ellen Burstyn *Katherine* • Melissa Leo *Karen* • Michael Murphy (1) *Joseph* ■ *Dir* Nancy Bardawil • *Scr* Michael Gilvary

Account Rendered ★

Crime drama
1957 · UK · BW · 61min

Griffith Jones plays a city banker who is apparently knocked unconscious when his two-timing wife, Ursula Howells, is murdered. We've heard that one before, say the men from Scotland Yard, so it's up to the hapless Jones to prove his innocence. This substandard B-movie is notable only for an early screen appearance by Honor Blackman. AT

Honor Blackman *Sarah Hayward* • Griffith Jones *Robert Ainsworth* • Ursula Howells *Lucille Ainsworth* • Ewen Solon *Inspector Marshall* ■ *Dir* Peter Graham Scott • *Scr* Barbara S Harper, from the novel by Pamela Barrington

The Accountant

Drama
2016 · US · Colour · 128min

This is a preview – no prints were available to review as we went to press: Hardly the most exciting of titles. But add in a touch of *Rain Man* and a dash of organised crime and you may well have all the ingredients for a decent thriller. Ben Affleck stars as a maths savant who relates to numbers more than people and who plays a nice little

earner cooking the books for criminal gangs. But as the authorities start sniffing around, it looks like our hero's desire to get out will be his undoing. TP

Ben Affleck *Chris* • Anna Kendrick *Dana* • John Lithgow *Lamar Black* • JK Simmons *Ray King* • Jeffrey Tambor *Francis Silverberg* ■ *Dir* Gavin O'Connor • *Scr* Bill Dubuque

Accused ★★

Crime drama
1936 · UK · BW · 87min

In this backstage murder mystery, set in Paris, Douglas Fairbanks Jnr and Dolores Del Rio star as a married couple who perform one of those acts in which the man is tied to a revolving table and the woman throws knives at him. There's a whiff of adultery in the air, and the show's spiteful star (Florence Desmond) winds up with a dagger in her heart. It's a modestly enjoyable effort that features Googie Withers in a minor role. AT

Douglas Fairbanks Jr *Tony Seymour* • Dolores Del Rio *Gaby Seymour* • Florence Desmond *Yvette Delange* • Basil Sydney *Eugene Roget* • Athole Stewart *President of Court* • Cecil Humphreys *Prosecuting counsel* • Esme Percy *Morel* • Edward Rigby *Alphonse* • George Moore Marriott *Dubec* • Cyril Raymond *Guy Henry* • Googie Withers *Ninette* ■ *Dir* Thornton Freeland • *Scr* Zoe Akins, George Barraud

The Accused ★★★

Crime drama
1949 · US · BW · 100min

Loretta Young stars as the emotionally frigid professor of psychology who kills one of her students after he attempts to seduce her on a beach. Making the death look like a drowning accident, Young takes sleeping pills then heads for hospital where a serious case of flashback syndrome assails her, together with the cops and her lawyer. Hollywood was then at the height of its Freudian phase and you need to know what "cyclothymia" means to get the most out of this *noir*-like melodrama. AT

Loretta Young *Wilma Tuttle* • Robert Cummings *Warren Ford* • Wendell Corey *Lt Ted Dorgan* • Sam Jaffe *Dr Romley* • Douglas Dick *Bill Perry* • Suzanne Dalbert *Susan Duval* • George Spaulding *Dean Rhodes* • Sara Allgood *Mrs Conner* ■ *Dir* William Dieterle • *Scr* Ketti Frings, from the novel *Be Still, My Love* by June Truesdell

The Accused ★★★★ 18

Drama
1988 · US · Colour · 105min

Jodie Foster won her first best actress Oscar for her moving performance here as Sarah Tobias, the brash working-class waitress who is gang raped in a bar and then endures public scrutiny so her attackers and those who watched can be brought to justice. Jonathan Kaplan's controversial movie raised a storm of protest on its release from those who believed its content veered too close to gratuitous voyeurism – yes, the rape scene is explicit and integral to the plot. But both Foster and Kelly McGillis, as the crusading lawyer, are superb and the film raises some pointed questions about an emotive subject. JB Violence, nudity, swearing, drug abuse. DVD

Jodie Foster *Sarah Tobias* • Kelly McGillis *Kathryn Murphy* • Bernie Coulson *Kenneth Joyce* • Leo Rossi *Cliff "Scorpion" Albrecht* • Ann Hearn *Sally Fraser* • Carmen Argenziano *DA Paul Rudolph* • Steve Antin *Bob Joiner* • Tom O'Brien *Larry* • Peter Van Norden *Paulsen* ■ *Dir* Jonathan Kaplan • *Scr* Tom Topor

Accused at 17 ★★

Crime drama
2009 · US · Colour · 89min

High-schooler Nicole Gale Anderson learns big lessons about trust in this flimsy and cliché-packed crime tale that sees her framed for murdering a classmate by one of her best friends. Consequently, it's up to her tenacious mum (a robust Cynthia Gibb) to reveal how a mean girl-style revenge plan turned deadly. Skeletal plotting ensures Gibb achieves her goals with unconvincing ease while poor direction robs even the more dramatic events of any emotional impact. SF

Cynthia Gibb *Jacqui* • Nicole Gale Anderson *Bianca* • Janet Montgomery *Fallyn* ■ *Dir* Doug Campbell • *Scr* Christine Conradt

Accused of Murder ★★

Murder mystery
1956 · US · Colour · 73min

This poverty-stricken thriller features nightclub singer Vera Ralston as the prime suspect for the murder of shady lawyer Sidney Blackmer. Detective David Brian is convinced of her innocence, while his sergeant Lee Van Cleef thinks she's guilty. A have-it-both-ways ending is the nail in the coffin of this weakly scripted tale. RK

David Brian *Lt Roy Hargis* • Vera Ralston *Ilona Vance* • Sidney Blackmer *Hobart* • Virginia Grey *Sandra* • Warren Stevens *Stan* • Lee Van Cleef *Sgt Lackey* ■ *Dir* Joseph Kane • *Scr* WR Burnett, Bob Williams, from the novel *Vanity Row* by Burnett

Ace Eli and Rodger of the Skies ★★

Adventure
1973 · US · Colour · 92min

Stunt pilot Cliff Robertson teaches his son Eric Shea the tricks of his trade during the Roaring Twenties in this mediocre action adventure, notable for being based on a story by Steven Spielberg and for marking the screen debut of Broadway diva Bernadette Peters. Dogged by production problems and re-edited against director John Erman's wishes, it's only worth catching for the breathtaking aerial photography. AJ

Cliff Robertson *Eli* • Pamela Franklin *Shelby* • Eric Shea *Rodger* • Rosemary Murphy *Hannah* • Bernadette Peters *Allison* • Alice Ghostley *Sister Lite* • Kelly Jean Peters *Rachel* • Don Keefer *Mr Parsons* ■ *Dir* Bill Sampson [John Erman] • *Scr* Chips Rosen [Claudia Salter], from a story by Steven Spielberg • *Cinematographer* David M Walsh

Ace High ★★★ 15

Spaghetti western comedy
1968 · It · Colour · 116min

Eli Wallach is the nominal star of Giuseppe Colizzi's confidently directed spaghetti western – which is also known as *Four Gunmen of Ave Maria*, *Have Gun Will Travel* and *Revenge at El Paso*. However, aficionados will be drawn by the prospect of seeing one of the genre's most enduring double acts, Terence Hill and Bud Spencer. Blonde-haired Hill carries the plot as an outlaw called Cat Stevens, who escapes from a necktie party only to resume his life of crime while searching for the trio of drifters who landed him in jail in the first place. DP In English, Italian.

Eli Wallach *Cacopoulos* • Terence Hill *Cat Stevens* • Bud Spencer *Hutch Bessy* • Brock Peters *Thomas* • Kevin McCarthy *Drake* ■ *Dir/Scr* Giuseppe Colizzi

Ace in the Hole ★★★★★

Satirical drama
1951 · US · BW · 111min

"I've met some hard-boiled eggs in my time," says Jan Sterling to Kirk Douglas. "But you – you're 20 minutes!" Sterling's husband gets trapped in a cave; Douglas is the on-the-skids journalist who prolongs the man's agony while turning the accident into a major human interest story. Sterling co-operates with the scheme, making dough from the crowds who show up to watch the rescue operation. Few movies are as tough as this one, which is probably why it flopped at the box office – audiences don't like having their noses rubbed in their own dirt. However, it's one of Hollywood's great masterpieces, filled with Wilder's caustic wit and Douglas's trademark intensity. AT BL

Kirk Douglas *Chuck Tatum* • Jan Sterling *Lorraine* • Bob Arthur *Herbie Cook* • Porter Hall *Jacob Q Boot* • Frank Cady *Mr Federber* • Richard Benedict *Leo Minosa* • Ray Teal *Sheriff* • Lewis Martin *McCardle* • John Berkes *Papa Minosa* • Frances Dominguez *Mama Minosa* ■ *Dir* Billy Wilder • *Scr* Billy Wilder, Lesser Samuels, Walter Newman

Ace of Aces ★★★

First World War drama
1933 · US · BW · 75min

This is one of several powerful deglamourisations of war from the pen of John Monk Saunders, who served in the Army Air Corps and won an Oscar for the story of *The Dawn Patrol* (1930). Richard

A

Dix is the sculptor with pacifist leanings, goaded by his girlfriend (Elizabeth Allan) into becoming a First World War pilot. He turns into a cold-blooded ace of the air until a meeting with Allan in Paris leaves him disillusioned and resigned to his fate. Skilfully directed by J Walter Ruben, it may not be subtle but it still reverberates with feeling. AE

Richard Dix *Lt Rex Thorne* • Elizabeth Allan *Nancy Adams* • Ralph Bellamy *Major Blake* • Theodore Newton *Lt Foster Kelly* • Bill Cagney [William Cagney] *Lt Meeker* • Clarence Stroud *Lt Carroll Winstead* ■ *Dir* J Walter Ruben • *Scr* John Monk Saunders, HW Hanemann, from Saunders's story *Bird of Prey*

The Ace of Hearts ★★★
Silent crime drama   1921 · US · BW · 75min

The most celebrated of director Wallace Worsley's five collaborations with Lon Chaney was undoubtedly *The Hunchback of Notre Dame* (1923). But this is not without interest, even though the "Man of a Thousand Faces" takes something of a back seat, as waiter John Bowers allows sentiment to blunt his terrorist purpose. The introduction of the sinister assassination bureau is splendidly atmospheric, but the action becomes melodramatic once Bowers falls for co-conspirator Leatrice Joy. DP

Lon Chaney *Mr Farallone* • Leatrice Joy *Lilith* • John Bowers *Mr Forrest* • Hardee Kirkland *Mr Morgridge* • Raymond Hatton *The Menace* • Edwin N Wallock *Chemist* ■ *Dir* Wallace Worsley • *Scr* Ruth Wightman, from a story by Gouverneur Morris

Ace Ventura: Pet Detective ★★★★12
Comedy   1993 · US · Colour · 82min

Doctor Dolittle meets *The Crying Game* in the smash hit that made Jim Carrey an overnight comedy sensation. The rubber-faced star plays a bumbling, Hawaiian-shirted detective hired to find the kidnapped dolphin mascot of the Miami Dolphins football team. Your reaction to the film will largely depend on whether you find Carrey's distinctive style of extremely physical comedy – often compared to that of Jerry Lewis – stupidly hilarious or downright annoying. Tom Shadyac directs with anarchic energy and quirky imagination. AJ Swearing. *DVD*

Jim Carrey *Ace Ventura* • Courteney Cox *Melissa* • Sean Young *Lieutenant Lois Einhorn* • Tone Loc *Emilio* • Dan Marino • Noble Willingham *Riddle* • Troy Evans *Podacter* • Raynor Scheine *Woodstock* • Udo Kier *Camp* • Frank Adonis *Vinnie* • Tiny Ron *Roc* ■ *Dir* Tom Shadyac • *Scr* Jack Bernstein, Tom Shadyac, Jim Carrey, from a story by Bernstein

Ace Ventura: When Nature Calls ★★PG
Comedy   1995 · US · Colour · 88min

Jim Carrey's breakthrough hit *Ace Ventura: Pet Detective* exuded a barmy charm, but this silly sequel is often just plain irritating. For this adventure, Ace is off to Africa where he gets mixed up with warring tribes and the hunt for a rare bat. The slim plot is just the flimsiest of excuses for Carrey's wacky grimaces, while the slapstick is juvenile. JF Some violence, swearing. *DVD*

Jim Carrey *Ace Ventura* • Ian McNeice *Fulton Greenwall* • Simon Callow *Vincent Cadby* • Maynard Eziashi *Ouda* • Bob Gunton *Burton Quinn* • Sophie Okonedo *Princess* • Tommy Davidson *Tiny warrior* • Adewale [Adewale Akinnuoye-Agbaje] *Hitu* ■ *Dir/Scr* Steve Oedekerk

Aces and Eights ★★U
Western   1936 · US · BW · 55min

Poker fans will recognise the title immediately – the infamous "dead man's hand", held by Wild Bill Hickock as he was shot in the back and killed by gambler Jack McCall on the night of 2 August 1876 in Deadwood City. The estimable Tim McCoy is fine as the gambler trying to clear himself of murder. McCoy may defeat the villains, but not the programme filler plot and slim

production values of this run-of-the-mill western. TS

Tim McCoy *Gentleman Tim Madigan* • Luana Walters *Juanita Hernandez* • Rex Lease *Jose Hernandez* • Wheeler Oakman *Ace Morgan* • Charles Stevens *Capt Felipe* • Earl Hodgins [Earle Hodgins] *Marshal* ■ *Dir* Sam Newfield • *Scr* Arthur Durlan

Aces 'n' Eights ★★
Western   2008 · US · Colour · 80min

A taciturn Casper Van Dien broods his way through this fast-paced and dramatic homage to the spaghetti western. He plays a retired gunslinger who's forced to confront his brutal former gang to protect his ageing rancher boss (Ernest Borgnine) against an encroaching railroad company. Despite its predictability, this tale of corruption and revenge is consistently entertaining, compensating for a lack of imagination and occasional bursts of over-sentimentality and impressively well-drawn villains. SF

Casper Van Dien *Luke Rivers* • Bruce Boxleitner *DC Cracker* • Ernest Borgnine *Thurmond Prescott* • Jeff Kober *Tate* • Jack Noseworthy *Riley* • William Atherton *Howard* • Jake Thomas *Noah* ■ *Dir* Craig R Baxley • *Scr* Ronald M Cohen, Dennis Shryack

Aces High ★★★PG
First World War action drama   1976 · UK · Colour · 108min

Jack Gold's stout anti-war statement actually takes its cue from an early sound film, 1930's *Journey's End*, but transposes the action from the trenches to the skies. It is here that the film finds its conviction, in the form of dogfight sequences that succeed in being both thrilling and horrifying. Back at base, however, where eager First World War flier Peter Firth comes to understand the cynicism of his superior, Malcolm McDowell, events are not as well realised. JM *DVD* *Blu-ray*

Malcolm McDowell *Gresham* • Christopher Plummer *Sinclair* • Simon Ward *Crawford* • Peter Firth *Croft* • John Gielgud *Headmaster* • Trevor Howard *Lt Col Silkin* • Richard Johnson *Colonel Lyle* • Ray Milland *Brigadier Whale* ■ *Dir* Jack Gold • *Scr* Howard Barker, from the film *Journey's End* by James Whale, from the play by RC Sherriff

Aces: Iron Eagle III ★★15
Action adventure   1992 · US · Colour · 94min

A far cry from its predecessors, this was John Glen's first feature after directing five James Bond movies, and the sense of anticlimax is there for all to see. Yet this vaguely silly enterprise is not without its pleasures. Louis Gossett Jr returns as the USAF ace who recruits his pals in a flying circus to deliver a South American village from the clutches of a drug baron. The final *Iron Eagle* appeared in 1995. DP Swearing, violence. *DVD*

Louis Gossett Jr *Colonel Charles "Chappy" Sinclair* • Rachel McLish *Anna* • Christopher Cazenove *Palmer* • Sonny Chiba *Horikoshi* • Horst Buchholz *Leichman* • Paul Freeman *Kleiss* • Ray Mancini *Chico* ■ *Dir* John Glen • *Scr* Kevin Elders, from characters by Elders, Sidney J Furie

The Acid House ★★18
Drama   1998 · UK · Colour · 106min

This trio of very dark tales from Irvine Welsh's anthology has a great cast, but these stories are too wild, weird and unpleasant to appeal to anybody other than hard-core fans of Welsh's book. Although the stories – a downtrodden teen meets God and is transformed into a fly, nice guy suffers from the neighbour from hell, and an acid-taking clubber swaps bodies with a newborn baby – all offer dramatic potential, they seem more calculated to shock and offend with graphic sex and in-your-face nastiness than to actually entertain. JC *DVD*

Stephen McCole *Boab* • Maurice Roëves *God* • Garry Sweeney *Kev* ("The Granton Star Cause") • Jenny McCrindle *Evelyn* • Kevin McKidd *Johnny* • Ewen Bremner *Coco* • Martin Clunes *Rory* • Simon Weir *Tambo* • Alex Howden *Boab Snr* ■ *Dir* Paul McGuigan • *Scr* Irvine Welsh, from his short stories

Across 110th Street ★★18
Blaxploitation crime thriller   1972 · US · Colour · 97min

In New York, the demarcation line between squalor and style, war and peace, was always 110th Street. Below the line was Central Park, above it was Harlem and mayhem. Even if that isn't the case today, in this movie crooked cop Anthony Quinn has Harlem's racketeers to deal with. Director Barry Shear tries to be hard-edged and aim for realism, but doesn't always succeed. AT Swearing, violence. *DVD*

Anthony Quinn *Captain Frank Mattelli* • Yaphet Kotto *Detective Lieutenant Pope* • Anthony Franciosa *Nick D'Salvio* • Paul Benjamin *Jim Harris* • Ed Bernard *Joe Logart* • Richard Ward *Doc Johnson* • Norma Donaldson *Gloria Roberts* • Antonio Fargas *Henry J Jackson* ■ *Dir* Barry Shear • *Scr* Luther Davis, from Wally Ferris's novel

Across the Bridge ★★★★PG
Thriller   1957 · UK · BW · 99min

Rod Steiger takes on the ultimate scene-stealer – a small dog – and just about wins in this thriller, adapted from a Graham Greene story. Steiger plays a fraudster on the run who murders a man and assumes his identity, only to discover his victim is also a fugitive. His attempts to escape are further hampered when he becomes attached to the dead man's mangy mongrel. There was friction between director Ken Annakin and his star during production, but Steiger gives one of his best and most poignant performances here. TH *DVD*

Rod Steiger *Carl Schaffner* • David Knight *Johnny* • Marla Landi *Mary* • Noel Willman *Chief of Police* • Bernard Lee *Chief Inspector Hadden* • Bill Nagy *Paul Scarff* • Eric Pohlman [Eric Pohlmann] *Police Sergeant* ■ *Dir* Ken Annakin • *Scr* Guy Elmes, Denis Freeman, from a story by Graham Greene

Across the Great Divide ★★U
Period adventure   1977 · US · Colour · 96min

Following the success of *The Adventures of the Wilderness Family*, producer Arthur R Dubs and director Stewart Raffill returned to the Rocky Mountains for this old-fashioned rite-of-passage picture. As the orphans risking all to claim their estate in Salem, Oregan, Heather Rattray and Mark Edward Hall give spirited performances, although conman Robert F Logan hogs nearly all their scenes. For all its visual splendour, the film lacks a sense of period (it's set in 1876) and the perils faced by the trio are predictable and too easily overcome. DP

Robert Logan *Zachariah Coop* • Heather Rattray *Holly Smith* • Mark Edward Hall *Jason Smith* • George "Buck" Flower *Ben* • Hal Bokar *Sternface* ■ *Dir/Scr* Stewart Raffill • *Producer* Arthur R Dubs

Across the Pacific ★★★U
Spy drama   1942 · US · BW · 96min

The original script for this wartime melodrama, written in 1941, described a Japanese plan to attack Pearl Harbor and when that really happened the script was rewritten, set near the Panama Canal and peopled with sundry spies, adventurers and mystery women. Humphrey Bogart plays a spy ordered to keep tabs on Sydney Greenstreet. What happens is purely formulaic, and enjoyable only because of the interplay between Bogart, Greenstreet and Mary Astor. AT

Humphrey Bogart *Rick Leland* • Mary Astor *Alberta Marlow* • Sydney Greenstreet *Dr Lorenz* • Charles Halton *AV Smith* • Victor Sen Yung *Joe Totsuiko* • Roland Got *Sugi* ■ *Dir* John Huston • *Scr* Richard Macaulay, from the serial *Aloha Means Goodbye* by Robert Carson in *The Saturday Evening Post*

Across the Tracks ★★15
Drama   1990 · US · Colour · 96min

Brad Pitt got one of his first opportunities to star in this below-par tale of sibling rivalry. He plays a clean-cut running star who tries to save cynical brother Rick Schroder from drug peddling by

encouraging him to take up athletics. Few demands are made of Pitt's acting ability, as writer/director Sandy Tung's script is awash with clichéd situations and unconvincing sports sequences. DP Swearing, drug abuse.

Rick Schroder *Billy Maloney* • Brad Pitt *Joe Maloney* • Carrie Snodgress *Rosemary Maloney* • David Anthony Marshall *Louie* • Thomas Mikal Ford *Coach Walsh* • John Linton *Brad* • Cyril O'Reilly *Coach Ryder* • Jack McGee *Frank* ■ *Dir/Scr* Sandy Tung

Across the Universe ★★★12
Romantic musical drama   2007 · US · Colour · 127min

Blending 33 songs by the Beatles and all manner of visual tricks, director Julie Taymor (*Frida*) evokes a psychedelic 1960s vibe to tell a vibrant yet convoluted story of star-crossed lovers. In a nod to a couple of well-known Fab Four songs, British actor Jim Sturgess plays a Liverpudlian painter named Jude who heads to the US and falls for a free spirit called Lucy (Evan Rachel Wood). There are depictions of anti-war rallies and the faltering civil rights movement, but Taymor doesn't emphasise those themes so much as drown them out in colour and music. It's a veritable feast for the senses – just don't expect it to rock your world. SP Drug references, nudity, brief swearing. *DVD* *Blu-ray*

Evan Rachel Wood *Lucy* • Jim Sturgess *Jude* • Joe Anderson (1) *Max* • Dana Fuchs *Sadie* • Martin Luther McCoy [Martin Luther] *Jo-Jo* • TV Carpio *Prudence* • Eddie Izzard *Mr Kite* • Bono *Dr Robert* • Salma Hayek *Singing nurse* ■ *Dir* Julie Taymor • *Scr* Dick Clement, Ian La Frenais, from a story by Julie Taymor, Clement, La Frenais • *Cinematographer* Bruno Delbonnel

Across the Wide Missouri ★★★PG
Western adventure   1951 · US · Colour · 75min

After unfavourable previews, director William A Wellman's epic was hacked down to its current length. Narration was added, which only serves to diminish and simplify a movie of real grandeur. The use of Technicolor is exemplary, as vast landscapes are bloodied by the advance of "civilisation" in the shape of pioneers in the Rocky Mountains of the 1820s, and the score by David Raksin is outstanding. Clark Gable seems uncomfortably cast as real-life trapper Flint Mitchell, and the complex dialogue scenes with the native Americans severely hinder the plot's progression. TS *DVD*

Clark Gable *Flint Mitchell* • Ricardo Montalban *Ironshirt* • John Hodiak *Brecan* • Adolphe Menjou *Pierre* • Maria Elena Marques *Kamiah* • J Carrol Naish *Looking Glass* • Jack Holt *Bear Ghost* • Alan Napier *Captain Humberstone Lyon* • Howard Keel *Narrator* ■ *Dir* William Wellman [William A Wellman] • *Scr* Talbot Jennings, from a story by Jennings, Frank Cavett, from a novel by Bernard DeVoto • *Music* David Raksin • *Cinematographer* William C Mellor

The Act of Killing ★★★★★
Documentary   2012 · Den/Nor/UK/Ger/Fin/Swe/Neth/Pol · Colour · 122min

In Indonesia in 1965, thousands of men, women and children were slaughtered in an attempted military coup, yet the perpetrators never faced justice. To get to the heart of this spine-chilling story, director Joshua Oppenheimer asked some of the most notorious assassins to re-enact scenes from their past, in the style of a Hollywood movie. They seem oblivious to the idea that portraying real-life atrocities in this way is in gruesomely bad taste, showing how apparently rational men can delude themselves. This is uncomfortable but fascinating, using film as a hall of mirrors to reveal not just the faces, but the twisted souls, of murderers. DW Indonesian, English +subtitles. *DVD* *Blu-ray*

■ *Dir* Joshua Oppenheimer (2)

Act of Love ★★★
Drama   1953 · US · BW · 109min

Kirk Douglas took full advantage of the postwar tax breaks available to American actors working in Europe, and this intense adult romance is a prime example of his output during that period. Dany Robin plays the destitute girl bored GI Douglas falls for, while other cast members include Barbara Laage and a pretty youngster awaiting discovery called Brigitte Bardot. An intelligent, mature movie. **TS**

Kirk Douglas *Robert Teller* • Dany Robin *Lisa* • Barbara Laage *Nina* • Robert Strauss *Blackwood* • Gabrielle Dorziat *Adele* • Grégoire Aslan *Commissaire* • Marthe Mercadier *Young woman* • Brigitte Bardot *Mimi* ■ *Dir* Anatole Litvak • *Scr* Irwin Shaw, from the novel *The Girl on the Via Flaminia* by Alfred Hayes

Act of Love ★★★

Drama based on a true story
1980 · US · Colour · 104min

Ron Howard (Richie Cunningham in TV series *Happy Days* and now a director) gives a good account of himself in this TV movie, in which he is prosecuted for the mercy killing of his brother, a pre-*Diner* Mickey Rourke, after he is injured in a motorbike smash. Based on a true story, the film raises some interesting issues, but even though the verdict remains in doubt to the end, director Jud Taylor fails to wring the full drama out of the courtroom scenes. **DP**

Ron Howard *Leon Cybulkowski* • Robert Foxworth *Andrew Rose* • Mickey Rourke *Joseph Cybulkowski* • David Spielberg *Victor Burton* • Jacqueline Brookes *Eugenia Cybulkowski* • Mary Kay Place *Editor* ■ *Dir* Jud Taylor • *Scr* Michael de Guzman, from a book by Paige Mitchell

Act of the Heart ★★★

Religious drama   1970 · Can · Colour · 103min

An obsessive love affair within an obsessive religious faith lifts this Canadian movie out of the ordinary. while the acting elevates it even further. Country girl Geneviève Bujold falls desperately in love with priest Donald Sutherland when she goes to his urban parish to sing in the choir. The film is darker in hue than the surface gloss suggests, though non-religious audiences may wonder why everything is so intense. **TH**

Geneviève Bujold *Martha Hayes* • Donald Sutherland *Father Michael Ferrier* • Monique Leyrac *Johane Foss* • Bill Mitchell *Russell Foss* ■ *Dir/Scr* Paul Almond

Act of Valor ★★ 15

Military action adventure
2012 · US · Colour · 104min

A gushy love letter to America's elite special-ops force, the Navy SEALs. Filmed with the help and hardware of the US Navy, and featuring serving SEALs in supporting roles, this fictional tale tells of a pan-global SEALs bid to stop a squad of terrorist suicide bombers from infiltrating the US. The firefight scenes are undeniably terrific, but as a whole it's as dumb as they come. **DA** Violence, swearing. *DVD*

Roselyn Sanchez *Agent Lisa Morales* • Jason Cottle *Abu Shabal* • Alex Veadov *Christo* • Nestor Serrano *Walter Ross* ■ *Dir* Mike "Mouse" McCoy, Scott Waugh • *Scr* Kurt Johnstad

Act of Vengeance ★★★ 18

Drama based on a true story
1986 · Can/US · Colour · 87min

Charles Bronson, given the right material, can deliver beautifully understated performances. In this tough drama, he plays an honest union man running for office against the villainous incumbent Wilford Brimley. The star is ably supported by the likes of Ellen Burstyn, Hoyt Axton and a young Ellen Barkin, and the no-frills direction of *The Long Good Friday*'s John MacKenzie is quietly effective. Look out, too, for a pre-stardom appearance by Keanu Reeves. **JF**

Charles Bronson *Jock Yablonski* • Ellen Burstyn *Margaret Yablonski* • Wilford Brimley *Tony Boyle* • Hoyt Axton *Silhous Huddleston* • Robert Schenkkan *Paul Gilly* • Ellen Barkin *Annette Gilly* • Maury Chaykin *Claude Vealy* • Keanu Reeves *Buddy Palmer* ■ *Dir* John Mackenzie (1) • *Scr* Scott Spencer, from the book by Trevor Armbrister

Act of Violence ★★★

Film noir   1949 · US · BW · 82min

This fine *film noir* melodrama from MGM allows its talented young contract director Fred Zinnemann to flex his creative muscles. There's a great cast, including two of Hollywood's finest second league heavyweights, Robert Ryan and Van Heflin, the latter particularly good as an officer who, while he was a prisoner of war, betrayed his men. Ryan is his fellow prisoner who seeks revenge. Janet Leigh is wasted as Heflin's worried wife, but there's a remarkable performance from the redoubtable Mary Astor as a bar-room prostitute. A grim but satisfying movie. **TS**

Van Heflin *Frank R Enley* • Robert Ryan *Joe Parkson* • Janet Leigh *Edith Enley* • Mary Astor *Pat* • Phyllis Thaxter *Ann* • Berry Kroeger *Johnny* • Taylor Holmes *Gavery* • Harry Antrim *Fred* • Connie Gilchrist *Martha* ■ *Dir* Fred Zinnemann • *Scr* Robert L Richards

Act One ★

Biographical drama   1963 · US · BW · 110min

The autobiography of playwright Moss Hart who, with George S Kaufman, wrote some of the best comedies ever to come out of America makes an entertaining and fascinating read. This attempt to film it, however, is an abject failure. The movie doesn't find a way of translating Hart's genial account into a suitable narrative, leaving only a series of static scenes and a lot of name-dropping. **RK**

George Hamilton *Moss Hart* • Jason Robards Jr [Jason Robards] *George S Kaufman* • Jack Klugman *Joe Hyman* • Sam Levene *Richard Maxwell* • Ruth Ford *Beatrice Kaufman* • Eli Wallach *Warren Stone* • Joseph Leon *Max Siegel* • George Segal *Lester Sweyd* • Martin Wolfson *Mr Hart* ■ *Dir* Dore Schary • *Scr* Dore Schary, from the autobiography by Moss Hart

Action in Arabia ★★★ U

Spy drama   1944 · US · BW · 75min

Footage from Ernest B Schoedsack and Merian C Cooper's aborted 1933 biopic of Lawrence of Arabia adds some local colour to this otherwise anaemic spy thriller. The film provides a dashing showcase for George Sanders, playing an intrepid reporter who teams up with Virginia Bruce's plucky agent to prevent various Arab tribes rallying to the Nazi cause. It's efficiently directed by Leonide Moguy, but the movie is held together by Sanders's polished performance. **DP**

George Sanders *Gordon* • Virginia Bruce *Yvonne* • Lenore Aubert *Mouniran* • Gene Lockhart *Danesco* • Robert Armstrong *Reed* • HB Warner *Rashid* ■ *Dir* Leonide Moguy [Léonide Moguy] • *Scr* Philip MacDonald, Herbert J Biberman

Action in the North Atlantic ★★★

Second World War drama
1943 · US · BW · 127min

This flag-waver began as one of many Warner Bros short films designed to salute various aspects of the war effort - this time the merchant marine - but ended up a full-length feature. Humphrey Bogart and Raymond Massey play the courageous seamen who sail from the USA to Murmansk in the Soviet Union, dodging German U-boats and bombers all the way. Bogart and Massey make a convincing pair of heroes and the action sequences are impressive. **AT** In English, German.

Humphrey Bogart *Joe Rossi* • Raymond Massey *Captain Steve Jarvis* • Alan Hale *Boats O'Hara* • Julie Bishop *Pearl* • Ruth Gordon *Mrs Jarvis* • Sam Levene *Chips Abrams* • Dane Clark *Johnny Pulaski* ■ *Dir* Lloyd Bacon • *Scr* John Howard Lawson, from the novel by Guy Gilpatric

Action Jackson ★★★ 18

Action thriller   1988 · US · Colour · 91min

Rocky star Carl Weathers is smart Detroit cop Jericho "Action" Jackson (he's even got a Harvard law degree!) out to nail evil auto magnate Craig T Nelson in this loud *Commando* clone liberally dosed with outlandish explosions, huge car crashes and stylish shoot-outs. Illogical and

incomprehensible it may be most of the time, but the memorable high octane action more than makes up for its plot deficiencies. Featuring an early appearance by Sharon Stone. **AJ** Violence, nudity, sex scenes, swearing.

Carl Weathers *Jericho "Action" Jackson* • Craig T Nelson *Peter Dellaplane* • Vanity *Sydney Ash* • Sharon Stone *Patrice Dellaplane* • Thomas F Wilson *Officer Kornblau* • Bill Duke *Captain Armbruster* • Robert Davi *Tony Moretti* • Jack Thibeau *Detective Kotterwell* ■ *Dir* Craig R Baxley • *Scr* Robert Reneau

The Actors ★★ 15

Crime comedy
2003 · UK/Ire/US/Ger · Colour · 87min

Michael Caine plays a veteran stage performer tackling the part of Richard III in an amateurish Irish production. Comedian Dylan Moran is the protégé Caine persuades to take on fake identities in order to con a local gangster. Although Moran's character transformations are pulled off with reasonable credibility, writer/director Conor McPherson undermines these deceptions with inane plotting and one-dimensional characters. **JC** Swearing. *DVD*

Michael Caine *Anthony O'Malley* • Dylan Moran *Tom* • Michael Gambon *Barreller* • Lena Headey *Dolores Barreller* • Miranda Richardson *Mrs Magnani* • Michael McElhatton *Jock* • Aisling O'Sullivan *Rita* ■ *Dir* Conor McPherson • *Scr* Conor McPherson, from a story by Neil Jordan

Actors and Sin ★★★

Comedy drama   1952 · US · BW · 85min

Two featurettes, glued together: the first is about a grand actor who makes the suicide of his vain, hateful daughter look like murder. The second is a satire about a Hollywood agent who sells a script that everyone thinks is brilliant and turns out to be written by a nine-year-old. Ben Hecht puts all available cynicism into this project, but the second story is rivetingly weird as Hecht casts his own daughter as the moppet writer and her lack of acting ability is excruciatingly obvious. **AT**

Edward G Robinson *Maurice* • Marsha Hunt *Marcia* • Dan O'Herlihy *Alfred O'Shea* • Eddie Albert *Orlando Higgens* • Tracey Roberts *Miss Flannigan* • Jenny Hecht *Daisy Marcher* ■ *Dir/Scr* Ben Hecht

An Actor's Revenge ★★★★ PG

Drama   1963 · Jpn · Colour · 108min

Having starred in the 1935 version, veteran actor Kazuo Hasegawa reprises the dual role of Yukinojo the female impersonator and Yamitaro, the bandit who befriends him. Revelling in his scheme to destroy the triumvirate responsible for the suicide of his parents - he starts by seducing the daughter of one of the men - Hasegawa gives a performance of rare immersion and control. While remaining faithful to the original, director Kon Ichikawa creates a nice sense of nostalgia and irony by re-creating not only the conventions of Kabuki theatre, but also the look of Japanese painting and the films of the early sound era. **DP** Japanese +subtitles. *DVD*

Kazuo Hasegawa *Yamitaro/Yukinojo* • Fujiko Yamamoto *Ohatsu* • Ayako Wakao *Namiji* • Ganjiro Nakamura *Sansai Dobe* ■ *Dir* Kon Ichikawa • *Scr* Teinosuke Kinugasa, Daisuke Ito, Natto Wada

The Actress ★★★★ U

Biographical drama   1953 · US · BW · 90min

Keeping up with the Jones girl is some feat! As Ruth Jones, aspiring thespian and would-be star, Jean Simmons is an obstinate and headstrong teenager demanding her theatrical rights despite opposition from Spencer Tracy as her seafaring father. Every dad will have his day, but not for very long, in this endearing adaptation of actress Ruth Gordon's play about her Broadway-bound early days in a Massachusetts small town. Anthony Perkins makes a rather timid debut as Ruth's boyfriend, but it's Tracy's movie, although

Simmons does stand up to him remarkably well. **TH**

Spencer Tracy *Clinton Jones* • Jean Simmons *Ruth Gordon Jones* • Teresa Wright *Annie Jones* • Anthony Perkins *Fred Whitmarsh* • Ian Wolfe *Mr Bagley* • Kay Williams *Hazel Dawn* • Mary Wickes *Emma Glavey* • Norma Jean Nilsson *Anna* • Dawn Bender *Katherine* ■ *Dir* George Cukor • *Scr* Ruth Gordon, from her play *Years Ago*

The Actress ★★★

Period biographical drama
1992 · HK · Colour · 146min

Maggie Cheung won Berlin's best actress prize for her work in this Brechtian biopic of Ruan Ling Yu, the 1930s Chinese movie star who was driven to suicide at the age of 25 by press criticism of her relationship with a married man. It's an affecting performance, although it loses some of its impact through comparison with footage of the real Ruan in the silent clips with which director Stanley Kwan studs the action. There are also several interviews with friends and colleagues, whose testimony echoes Kwan's contention that this fragile icon was broken by a combination of celebrity and hypocrisy. **DP** Cantonese +subtitles.

Maggie Cheung Man Yuk [Maggie Cheung] *Ruan Ling Yu* • Tony Leung Ka-Fai [Tony Leung (1)] *Tsai Chu Shong* • Carina Lau *Lily Li* • Lawrence Ng *Chang Ta Min* • Lee Waise ■ *Dir* Stanley Kwan • *Scr* Chui Tai An-Ping

Actresses ★★★ 15

Drama   1996 · Sp · Colour · 87min

Intimacy and intensity are the bywords for Ventura Pons's adaptation of JM Benet I Jornet's acclaimed play about the encounters between an ambitious drama student and a legendary diva's favourite pupils. However, such is his emphasis on the mood and language of this essentially theatrical piece that Pons neglects the cinematic potential of the allusions to *Rashomon* and *All about Eve* that arise as the truth slowly emerges from the embittered trio's well-practised reminiscences. The performances, however, are impeccable. **DP** Catalan, Spanish +subtitles. Swearing.

Núria Espert *Gloria Marc* • Rosa Maria Sarda *Assumpta Roca* • Anna Lizaran *Maria Caminal* • Mercè Pons *Girl* ■ *Dir* Ventura Pons • *Scr* Ventura Pons, JM Benet I Jornet, from the play *ER* by Jornet

Acts of Godfrey ★★ 15

Black comedy drama   2011 · UK · Colour · 84min

The directorial debut of writer and musician Johnny Daukes is audacious, presented as it is entirely in rhyming couplets. However, not even the presence of Simon Callow (as the eponymous deity-cum-Greek chorus) and Harry Enfield (as a pitilessly ingratiating fraudster) can disguise the fact that the storyline - about a group of people attending a weekend sales seminar at a country hotel - leaves much to be desired. There are a few witty lines and Daukes also manages the odd visual flourish, but Shakespeare it's not. **DP** Swearing, sex scenes.

Simon Callow *Godfrey* • Harry Enfield *Malcolm* • Iain Robertson *Vic Timms* • Myfanwy Waring *Mary* • Celia Imrie *Helen McGann* • Jay Simpson *Phil* ■ *Dir/Scr* Johnny Daukes

Acts of Love ★★ 18

Romantic drama   1995 · US · Colour · 104min

It's hard to swallow Dennis Hopper as a shy teacher, married (unhappily) to Amy Irving, who lives on a farm with his sick mother (Julie Harris). The plot doesn't get any more credible when his character gets a new lease of life through an affair with a student (Amy Locane). Hopper lurches around with a limp, though that's nothing compared to Ed Jones's script. **TH** Swearing, sex scenes.

Dennis Hopper *Joseph Svenden* • Amy Irving *Rosealee Henson* • Amy Locane *Catherine Wheeler* • Julie Harris (2) *Joseph's other* • Gary Busey *Major Nathan Wheeler* • Hal Holbrook *Dr Evans* • Christopher Pettiet *Robert Henson* • Priscilla Pointer *Lily Henson* ■ *Dir* Bruno Barreto • *Scr* Ed Jones, from the novel *Farmer* by Jim Harrison

Ada ★★★
Drama   1961 · US · Colour · 108min

Susan Hayward stars as former prostitute Ada, the fiery wife of southern politician Dean Martin, in an MGM rags-to-riches tale. Wilfrid Hyde White is Martin's scheming political adviser, who threatens to expose Hayward's colourful past if she continues to appear at her husband's side. Martin Balsam is also effective as Martin's press agent. This mesmerising melodrama is directed with a knowing hand by Daniel Mann. TS

Susan Hayward *Ada* • Dean Martin *Bo Gillis* • Wilfrid Hyde White *Sylvester Marin* • Ralph Meeker *Colonel Yancey* • Martin Balsam *Steve Jackson* • Frank Maxwell *Ronnie Hallerton* • Connie Sawyer *Alice Sweet* • Ford Rainey *Speaker* • Charles Watts *Al Winslow* • Larry Gates *Joe Adams* ■ *Dir* Daniel Mann • *Scr* Arthur Sheekman, William Driskill, from the novel *Ada Dallas* by Wirt Williams

Adalen 31 ★★★
Period drama   1969 · Swe · Colour · 114min

Bo Widerberg has an eye for lyrical imagery, but such pictorialism seems out of place in the reconstruction of a key moment in Swedish labour history. The 1931 protracted strike by the paper mill workers in an isolated northern town resulted in five people being killed by panicked soldiers. The violence is all the more shocking for the beauty of the visuals. But while we know everything about the striker's son and the plant manager's pregnant daughter, we get little insight into the hardships suffered by their families. DP Swedish +subtitles.

Peter Schildt *Kjell Andersson* • Kerstin Tidelius *Kjell's mother* • Roland Hedlund *Harald Andersson* • Stefan Feierbach *Åke* • Martin Widerberg *Martin* • Marie De Geer *Anna* ■ *Dir/Scr* Bo Widerberg

Adam ★★★★ 15
Biographical drama   1983 · US · Colour · 91min

This moving and classy TV movie stars Daniel J Travanti and JoBeth Williams as parents who suffer the anguish of having their son kidnapped. In the hope of helping other families with missing children, the couple lobby Congress to give parents access to the FBI's national crime computer. Subtly and movingly performed, this is above average, and earned an Emmy nomination for outstanding drama. A weak sequel, *Adam: His Song Continues*, followed. JB

Daniel J Travanti *John Walsh* • JoBeth Williams *Reve Walsh* • Martha Scott *Gram Walsh* • Richard Masur *Jay Howell* • Paul Regina *Joe Walsh* • Mason Adams *Ray Mellette* ■ *Dir* Michael Tuchner • *Scr* Allan Leicht

Adam ★★★ 12
Romantic drama   2009 · US · Colour · 94min

The set-up (girl meets boy when she moves into his New York apartment block) must have been used dozens of times, but what makes this romantic drama different is that Adam (Hugh Dancy) has Asperger's syndrome, a form of autism. He's a skilled electrical engineer, but less skilled at social interaction. His new neighbour Beth (Rose Byrne) is a spoilt only child, but her heart is in the right place and she gently draws him out of his shell. The situations are sometimes a little too cute, the dialogue a little too neat, but just when you think that it's going to get too gooey, director/writer Max Mayer pulls back and, with the help of his likeable leads, charms his way out of the morass. BP Some swearing. *DVD*

Hugh Dancy *Adam Raki* • Rose Byrne *Beth Buchwald* • Frankie Faison *Harlan* • Mark Linn-Baker *Mr Klieber* • Amy Irving *Rebecca Buchwald* • Peter Gallagher *Marty Buchwald* ■ *Dir/Scr* Max Mayer

Adam and Evelyne ★★★
Romantic comedy   1949 · UK · BW · 82min

Stewart Granger and Jean Simmons, who married in real life a year later, first played opposite each other in this pleasing comedy (although they both appeared three years earlier in *Caesar and Cleopatra*). He's a professional gambler who pretends to work on the stock exchange; she's an orphan who thinks he's her father but soon learns differently. Jest, not incest, is the name of this game, exuberantly performed by its two stars. The only thing that lets it down is Harold French's stodgy direction. AT

Stewart Granger *Adam Black* • Jean Simmons *Evelyne Wallace* • Edwin Styles *Bill Murray* • Raymond Young *Roddy Black* • Helen Cherry *Moira* • Beatrice Varley *Mrs Parker* • Joan Swinstead *Molly* • Wilfrid Hyde White *Colonel Bradley* • Irene Handl *Manageress* • Dora Bryan *Store assistant* ■ *Dir* Harold French • *Scr* Noel Langley, Lesley Storm, George Barraud, Nicholas Phipps

Adam & Paul ★★★ 15
Comedy drama   2004 · Ire · Colour · 82min

Adam and Paul (played by screenwriter Mark O'Halloran and Tom Murphy) are two Dublin junkies. The story follows them over the course of a day as they pursue a fix, encountering en route friends, acquaintances and strangers, most of them hostile. Although watching the physical ravages of heroin withdrawal borders on the nauseating at times, the tone here is more quietly observant than judgemental. The script and direction extract considerable comedy out of the duo's picaresque adventures, which are spiked by moments of absurdity and tenderness. LF Swearing, drug abuse. *DVD*

Tom Murphy *Paul* • Mark O'Halloran *Adam* • Louise Lewis (2) *Janine* • Gary Egan *Georgie* • Deirdre Molloy *Marian* • Mary Murray *Orla* • Paul Roe *Wayne* ■ *Dir* Lenny Abrahamson • *Scr* Mark O'Halloran

Adam at 6 AM ★★★ 15
Drama   1970 · US · Colour · 90min

A young Michael Douglas overcomes miscasting with an acceptable performance as a West Coast professor in search of himself and a simpler life in rural America. The film, which offers neither a pulsating plot nor sparkling dialogue, flopped on its first outing. But it does have a certain offbeat appeal, as well as an authentic feel for its Missouri locations, and a strong performance by Joe Don Baker as the foreman of a crew of labourers who employs Douglas. PF

Michael Douglas (1) *Adam Gaines* • Lee Purcell *Jerri Jo Hopper* • Joe Don Baker *Harvey Gavin* • Charles Aidman *Mr Hopper* • Marge Redmond *Cleo* • Louise Latham *Mrs Hopper* • Grayson Hall *Inez Treadley* • Carolyn Conwell *Mavis* • Dana Elcar *Van* • Meg Foster *Joyce* ■ *Dir* Robert Scheerer • *Scr* Stephen Karpf, Elinor Karpf

Adam Had Four Sons ★★★
Melodrama   1941 · US · BW · 108min

In this powerful melodrama, Ingrid Bergman stars as a governess hired to look after Warner Baxter's family shortly before a family tragedy. There's a cracking turn from up-and-coming Susan Hayward as a girl you wouldn't want to bring home to your parents, but otherwise this would-be sincere drama suffers from serious undercasting. Bergman's star quality keeps you watching and caring. TS

Ingrid Bergman *Emilie Gallatin* • Warner Baxter *Adam Stoddard* • Susan Hayward *Hester* • Fay Wray *Molly Stoddard* • Helen Westley *Cousin Philippa* • Richard Denning *Jack Stoddard* • Johnny Downs *David Stoddard* • June Lockhart *Vance* ■ *Dir* Gregory Ratoff • *Scr* William Hurlbut, Michael Blankfort, from the novel *Legacy* by Charles Bonner

Adam Sandler's Eight Crazy Nights ★ 12
Animated musical comedy   2003 · US · Colour · 73min

Festive cartoon fun gets an adult flavour in this ill-conceived musical comedy. An inane combination of bad-taste humour, flat animation and puerile songs, it's little more than a crude vanity project for Adam Sandler. Co-writer/producer Sandler also voices the film's central characters. Escaping a yuletide prison sentence, Davey gets one last shot at redemption by performing community service as Whitey's assistant. The result is merely a torrent of scatological gags and juvenile sexual innuendo. SF *DVD*

Adam Sandler *Davey Stone/Whitey/Eleanor* • Austin Stout *Benjamin* • Kevin Nealon *Mayor* • Rob Schneider *Chinese waiter/Narrator* • Norm Crosby *Judge* • Jon Lovitz *Tom Baltezor* ■ *Dir* Seth Kearsley • *Scr* Brooks Arthur, Allen Covert, Brad Isaacs, Adam Sandler

Adam's Rib ★★★★★ U
Classic comedy   1949 · US · BW · 96min

This witty and sophisticated "battle of the sexes" comedy is a peerless joy. Tailor-made for Spencer Tracy and Katharine Hepburn, it gave the roles of a lifetime to an enduring partnership that first flourished on screen in the 1942 comedy *Woman of the Year*. They face each other as married lawyers on opposing sides in court, as Hepburn defends and Tracy prosecutes Judy Holliday. She almost puts the star couple in the shade as the dizzy blonde accused of a shooting involving her philandering husband Tom Ewell. Here the delightful Oscar-nominated screenplay by Ruth Gordon and Garson Kanin brings out the best in the talented stars, and the subtle direction of George Cukor shows him to be a master of his craft. The sexual politics of the piece are as relevant now as they were prescient then, and the movie stands as a glorious tribute to all involved. TS *DVD*

Spencer Tracy *Adam Bonner* • Katharine Hepburn *Amanda Bonner* • Judy Holliday *Doris Attinger* • Tom Ewell *Warren Attinger* • David Wayne *Kip Lurie* • Jean Hagen *Beryl Caighn* • Hope Emerson *Olympia La Pere* • Eve March *Grace* • Polly Moran *Mrs McGrath* • Clarence Kolb *Judge Reiser* ■ *Dir* George Cukor • *Scr* Ruth Gordon, Garson Kanin

Adam's Woman ★★
Period adventure   1970 · Aus · Colour · 116min

This well-intentioned adventure is compromised by the casting of Beau Bridges as an American sailor wrongly sentenced to transportation to the penal colony that is now known as Australia. Bridges is there to lure the American audience while alienating the British audience. John Mills appears briefly as the Governor. AT

Beau Bridges *Adam* • Jane Merrow *Bess* • James Booth *Dyson* • Andrew Keir *O'Shea* • Tracy Reed *Duchess* • Peter O'Shaughnessy *Barrett* • John Mills *Sir Philip* ■ *Dir* Philip Leacock • *Scr* Richard Fielder, from a story by Lowell Barrington

Adaptation. ★★★★ 15
Satirical comedy drama   2002 · US · Colour · 110min

Being John Malkovich director Spike Jonze again demonstrates his style and originality with this inventive comedy drama. Based on a screenplay by previous collaborator Charlie Kaufman (who credits his fictitious twin brother Donald as co-writer), the film takes the idea of life imitating art to new extremes. Instead of a straight adaptation of journalist Susan Orlean's non-fiction book *The Orchid Thief*, Jonze presents a surreal version of Kaufman turning the literary work into a screenplay. It's a dark, hilarious and visually intoxicating celluloid trip, made even more appealing by a riveting double turn from Nicolas Cage as both the creatively blocked Charlie and as Donald, who's an aspiring screenwriter of action blockbusters. But it's Meryl Streep who's the biggest revelation in this dazzling and vibrant movie. SF *DVD*

Nicolas Cage *Charlie Kaufman/Donald Kaufman* • Meryl Streep *Susan Orlean* • Chris Cooper *John Laroche* • Tilda Swinton *Valerie* • Cara Seymour *Amelia* • Brian Cox (1) *Robert McKee* • Judy Greer *Alice the waitress* • Maggie Gyllenhaal *Caroline* ■ *Dir* Spike Jonze • *Scr* Charlie Kaufman, Donald [Charlie] Kaufman, from the non-fiction book *The Orchid Thief* by Susan Orlean

The Addams Family ★★★★ PG
Comedy horror   1991 · US · Colour · 95min

Hollywood's plundering of classic TV series has produced its fair share of turkeys, but this is a glorious exception. This is partly owing to director Barry Sonnenfeld's wise decision to stick with the black humour of Charles Addams's original *New Yorker* cartoons and some inspired casting. Anjelica Huston and Raul Julia are note perfect as loving Morticia and Gomez, while Christopher Lloyd is equally born to play Fester. However, these stars are almost surpassed by the astonishingly agile Thing and by Christina Ricci's splendid performance as the young Wednesday. The plot – a confidence trickster (Lloyd) poses as Fester to steal the Addams fortune – is a tad contrived, but the result is a witty family comedy. JF Some violence, brief swearing. *DVD* Blu

Anjelica Huston *Morticia Addams* • Raul Julia *Gomez Addams* • Christopher Lloyd *Uncle Fester Addams/Gordon Craven* • Dan Hedaya *Tully Alford* • Elizabeth Wilson *Abigail Craven* • Judith Malina *Granny* • Carel Struycken *Lurch* • Christina Ricci *Wednesday Addams* • Jimmy Workman *Pugsley Addams* • Dana Ivey *Margaret Alford* • Paul Benedict *Judge Womack* ■ *Dir* Barry Sonnenfeld • *Scr* Caroline Thompson, Larry Wilson, from characters by Charles Addams

Addams Family Values ★★★★ PG
Comedy horror   1993 · US · Colour · 90min

This delightful follow-up to *The Addams Family* has a more expansive plot and is blessed with an even blacker vein of humour than the original. This time, Gomez and Morticia (Raul Julia and Anjelica Huston) have a new baby, much to the displeasure of their other children, while Fester has fallen under the spell of the youngster's new black widow nanny (Joan Cusack). Once again, the playing is faultless, but it is Christina Ricci who effortlessly steals the show, whether trying to bump off her new sibling or creating havoc at an all-American summer camp. The sets are wonderful, the cinematography exquisite and the direction exhilarating. JF Cartoonish violence, some swearing. *DVD*

Anjelica Huston *Morticia Addams* • Raul Julia *Gomez Addams* • Christopher Lloyd *Uncle Fester* • Joan Cusack *Debbie Jellinsky* • Christina Ricci *Wednesday Addams* • Carol Kane *Granny* • Jimmy Workman *Pugsley Addams* • Carel Struycken *Lurch* • Peter MacNicol *Gary Granger* • Christine Baranski *Becky Granger* ■ *Dir* Barry Sonnenfeld • *Scr* Paul Rudnick, from characters by Charles Addams

Addams Family Reunion ★ PG
Comedy horror   1998 · US · Colour · 87min

Even the Addams family themselves would be turning in their graves over this one. Carel Struycken aside, none of the original stars of the excellent first two films is back for this cheap TV-movie cash-in. Tim Curry and Daryl Hannah take on the Raul Julia and Anjelica Huston roles with enthusiasm, but they can't do anything with the unfunny, childish script. JF

Tim Curry *Gomez Addams* • Daryl Hannah *Morticia Addams* • Nicole Marie Fugere *Wednesday Addams* • Jerry Messing *Pugsley Addams* • Ray Walston *Walter* • Kevin McCarthy *Grandpa Addams* • Estelle Harris *Grandma Addams* • Carel Struycken *Lurch* • Ed Begley Jr *Phillip Adams* ■ *Dir* Dave Payne [Dave Payne] • *Scr* Scott Sandin, Rob Krechner, from characters by Charles Addams

Addicted to Fresno ★ 15
Comedy   2015 · US · Colour · 85min

A willing cast is subsumed by dross in this hugely disappointing comedy. The descent into mirthless mundanity begins when sex addict Judy Greer's latest conquest is accidentally killed in the hotel she cleans with sister Natasha Lyonne. The harder the performers try to make this grim mess work, the worse it gets, with the jokes about addiction, rape, murder, dementia and the Holocaust competing to see which can be both the most offensive and the least amusing. DP Sexual references, swearing, drug abuse.

Judy Greer *Shannon* • Natasha Lyonne *Martha* • Malcolm Barrett *Eric* • Jessica St Clair *Kristen* ■ *Dir* Jamie Babbit • *Scr* Karey Dornetto

Addicted to Love ★★★ 15
Romantic black comedy
1997 · US · Colour · 96min

In this surprisingly dark romantic comedy, the usually sweet Meg Ryan stars as a vengeful ex-girlfriend who spends her waking hours thinking up ways of making life hell for the man who dumped her (Tcheky Karyo). This involves teaming up with the more strait-laced Matthew Broderick, whose childhood sweetheart has dumped him for Meg's ex. A tale of love gone sour from actor-turned-director Griffin Dunne, this has an enjoyably acidic bite. JB Swearing, sex scenes, nudity. **DVD**

Meg Ryan *Maggie* · Matthew Broderick *Sam* · Kelly Preston *Linda Green* · Tcheky Karyo *Anton Depeaux* · Maureen Stapleton *Nana* · Nesbitt Blaisdell *Ed Green* · Remak Ramsay *Professor Wells* · Lee Wilkof *Carl* ■ *Dir* Griffin Dunne · *Scr* Robert Gordon

Addicted to Sheep ★★★ PG
Documentary   2015 · UK · Colour · 85min

This enchanting film makes for perfect entertainment, a celebration of tenant farmers Tom and Kay Hutchinson and their life breeding Swaledale sheep in the upper reaches of County Durham. They are a cheerful couple who love doing what they do, and they are joined by their three delightful children; each shares their parents' unsentimental, pragmatic approach to livestock. The Hutchinsons make paltry money, but that's never the point. Theirs is an enviable life. AG

■ *Dir* Magali Pettier

The Addiction ★★★ 18
Horror   1994 · US · BW · 78min

Shot in black and white for that Andy Warhol feel, Abel Ferrara's New Wave tale is his most idiosyncratic film to date. Lili Taylor is the New York University philosophy student-turned-vampire who spends as much time pondering the Nietzschean significance of her gory deeds as she does shooting up blood. Intriguing and stylish, if pretentiously over-intellectualised, the film is hard-hitting if you're in the right frame of mind and can cope with such arch dialogue as "Do you want an apology for ethical relativism?" AJ Violence, swearing, drug abuse. **DVD**

Lili Taylor *Kathleen Conklin* · Christopher Walken *Peina* · Annabella Sciorra *Casanova* · Edie Falco *Jean* · Paul Calderon *Professor* · Fredro Starr *Black* ■ *Dir* Abel Ferrara · *Scr* Nicholas St John

The Adding Machine ★★★
Fantasy drama   1969 · US/UK · Colour · 104min

This grim, symbolic fantasy was adapted from Elmer Rice's agitprop play of the 1920s. Milo O'Shea is Mr Zero, an oppressed office drudge who murders his boss, is executed and sent not to hell, but to a heavenly waiting area populated by other killers en route to a new life. Directed by Jerome Epstein, with luminous photography by Walter Lassally, it lacks the Expressionist edge that such an allegory needs, but there are some memorable performances. TH

Phyllis Diller *Mrs Zero* · Milo O'Shea *Zero* · Billie Whitelaw *Daisy* · Sydney Chaplin *Lieutenant Charles* · Julian Glover *Shrdlu* · Raymond Huntley *Smithers* · Phil Brown *Don* · Libby Morris *Ethel* · Hugh McDermott *Harry* ■ *Dir* Jerome Epstein · Paul Calderon · *Cinematographer* Walter Lassally

Adios, Sabata ★★★ 12
Spaghetti western   1970 · It · Colour · 101min

A lesser-known but still competent spaghetti western, this is a sequel to the 1969 film *Sabata*, which starred Lee Van Cleef. In 19th-century Mexico, Yul Brynner is the archetypal gunslinger supreme, who teams up with a band of Mexican revolutionaries planning to steal a shipment of gold. Quite an acceptable offering, with a few original touches added to the usual body count. PF Italian dubbed. **DVD**

Yul Brynner *Sabata* · Dean Reed *Ballantine* · Pedro Sanchez [Ignazio Spalla] *Escudo* · Gerard Herter *Colonel Skimmel* · Sal Borgese

Septiembre · Franco Fantasia *Ocano* · Gianni Rizzo *Folgen* · Salvatore Billa *Manuel* · Massimo Carocci *Juan* ■ *Dir* Frank Kramer [Gianfranco Parolini] · *Scr* Renato Izzo, Gianfranco Parolini

The Adjuster ★★★ 18
Drama   1991 · Can · Colour · 98min

Preoccupied with images and the way in which we perceive them, Atom Egoyan is one of the most intriguing directors working today. Elias Koteas and Arsinée Khanjian are perhaps the perfect Egoyan couple. He studies accident scenes and photographs to assess insurance claims, while she is a porn film censor. He sleeps with his clients, she secretly records the scenes she is paid to withhold from the public. Nothing is what it seems in this teasing film, in which the full picture is as likely to emerge in a close-up as it is in a long shot. DP Sex scenes, nudity. **DVD**

Elias Koteas *Noah Render* · Arsinée Khanjian *Hera Render* · Maury Chaykin *Bubba* · Gabrielle Rose *Mimi* · Jennifer Dale *Arianne* · David Hemblen *Bert* · Rose Sarkisyan *Seta* ■ *Dir/Scr* Atom Egoyan

The Adjustment Bureau ★★★ 12
Romantic science-fiction drama
2010 · US · Colour · 101min

Matt Damon is a senatorial candidate, Emily Blunt a promising dancer. Will fate keep them apart in this amalgam of love story and high-concept sci-fi thriller, the directorial debut of *Bourne Ultimatum* screenwriter George Nolfi? Originating from a 1954 short story by sci-fi maestro Philip K Dick, the ambitious and imaginative film struggles to explain some nagging inconsistencies. But Damon and Blunt have such obvious chemistry that we do start to believe the ripple effects from a single kiss could indeed change our future. TJ Swearing, a sex scene. **DVD**

Matt Damon *David Norris* · Emily Blunt *Elise Sellas* · Anthony Mackie *Harry Mitchell* · John Slattery *Richardson* · Terence Stamp *Thompson* ■ *Dir* George Nolfi · *Scr* George Nolfi, from the short story *Adjustment Team* by Philip K Dick

The Admirable Crichton ★★★ U
Comedy adventure   1957 · UK · Colour · 89min

This is an agreeably dated version of JM Barrie's play, about the butler to Lord Loam taking over as master when the family is shipwrecked. It's a splendid vehicle for Kenneth More's genial urbanity, though Cecil Parker, as the bemused peer, seems more in touch with early 20th-century times. Diane Cilento and Sally Ann Howes are the charmers vying for Crichton's impeccable affections. TH

Kenneth More *Crichton* · Diane Cilento *Tweeny* · Cecil Parker *Lord Loam* · Sally Ann Howes *Lady Mary* · Martita Hunt *Lady Brocklehurst* · Jack Watling *Treherne* · Peter Graves (1) *Brocklehurst* · Gerald Harper *Ernest* ■ *Dir* Lewis Gilbert · *Scr* Vernon Harris, from the play by JM Barrie

The Admiral Was a Lady ★★ U
Comedy   1950 · US · BW · 86min

This sometimes droll, but mostly dull, film attempts to make a comedy of sexual manners out of seafaring Wanda Hendrix's hold over four disparate but somewhat dissolute men. Hendrix is good fun and Edmond O'Brien is watchable as always, but, despite a decent cast that struggles vainly with the poor material, this one fails to ignite from reel one. SH

Edmond O'Brien *Jimmie Stevens* · Wanda Hendrix *Jean Madison* · Rudy Vallee *Peter Pettigrew* · Johnny Sands *Eddie* · Steve Brodie *Mike* · Richard Erdman *Ollie* · Hillary Brooke *Mrs Pettigrew* ■ *Dir* Albert S Rogell · *Scr* Sidney Salkow, John O'Dea

Admission ★★ 12
Comedy   2013 · US · Colour · 102min

Three years after *Date Night*, comedian Tina Fey finds time to venture back onto the big screen. This time, though, it hardly seems worth the bother. She plays an admissions officer at an Ivy League university, who gets all in a twist with her ethics and emotions when she discovers that one of the high-school students she must vet for entry could be the son she secretly gave up for adoption. Her performance is fine and there's quality support from Paul Rudd, but the movie eventually slips between the cracks of comedy and drama by trying to do too much. There are chuckles and moving moments, just not enough of them. DA Swearing, sexual references. **DVD** 🔵

Tina Fey *Portia Nathan* · Paul Rudd *John Pressman* · Michael Sheen *Mark* · Wallace Shawn *Clarence* ■ *Dir* Paul Weitz · *Scr* Karen Croner, from Jean Hanff Korelitz's novel

Adolf Hitler – My Part in His Downfall ★★★ PG
Biographical Second World War comedy
1972 · UK · Colour · 101min

Spike Milligan doesn't write the script or play himself in this adaptation of his bestselling wartime memoir; Johnny Byrne does the honours in the first department, while Jim Dale portrays the future Goon. (Milligan puts in an appearance as his own father.) It must have been a near impossible task to turn Milligan's priceless prose into a coherent movie, but this is a pretty fair effort that's bound to ring bells with anyone who survived basic training. The shifts between absurd comedy and sudden tragedy are neatly handled, and the supporting cast more than pass muster. DP **DVD**

Jim Dale *Spike Milligan* · Arthur Lowe *Major Drysdale* · Bill Maynard *Sergeant Ellis* · Windsor Davies *Sergeant Mackay* · Tony Selby *Bill* · Geoffrey Hughes *Larry* · Jim Norton *Pongo* · David Belcher *Smith* · Spike Milligan *Spike's father* · Pat Coombs *Spike's mother* ■ *Dir* Norman Cohen · *Scr* Johnny Byrne, from the memoir by Spike Milligan

Adoration ★★★ 15
Drama   2008 · Can/Fr · Colour · 101min

After his mainstream thriller *Where the Truth Lies*, director Atom Egoyan returns to a more familiar psychological landscape with this thoughtful drama. Devon Bostick plays a teenager who has never really recovered from the death of his mother and father. With the encouragement of his teacher (Arsinée Khanjian), he creates an alternative version of his life for a class assignment, based on a real-life case of a terrorist who tried to blow up a plane by planting a bomb in his girlfriend's luggage. However, things get out of hand when his fictional story spills out over the web and is taken to be fact. Although the film touches on very topical political issues, Egoyan explores his usual themes of family secrets, grief and how technology can distort reality. The plotting is a little contrived, not to mention convoluted, but the performances are exemplary. JF In English, French.

Arsinée Khanjian *Sabine* · Scott Speedman *Tom* · Rachel Blanchard *Rachel* · Noam Jenkins *Sami* · Devon Bostick *Simon* · Kenneth Welsh *Morris* ■ *Dir/Scr* Atom Egoyan

Adore ★★ 15
Drama   2013 · Fr/Aus · Colour · 106min

Naomi Watts and Robin Wright play sun-kissed Australian women of a certain age in a tale that titillates more than it illuminates, as they become involved with each other's teenage sons. Doris Lessing's original novella barely convinced, but this adaptation simplifies the dynamics further by reducing the young men (Xavier Samuel, James Frecheville) to peevish door-slammers. However, the beauty of the opulent New South Wales coast and the easy, credible performances of the two leads are compensations. SvM Swearing, sex scenes.

Naomi Watts *Lil* · Robin Wright *Roz* · Xavier Samuel *Ian* · James Frecheville *Tom* · Gary Sweet *Saul* ■ *Dir* Anne Fontaine · *Scr* Christopher Hampton, Anne Fontaine, from the novella *The Grandmothers* by Doris Lessing

Adrenalin: Fear the Rush ★★ 18
Science-fiction action thriller
1995 · US · Colour · 93min

Species babe Natasha Henstridge and *Highlander* star Christopher Lambert join forces as two cops on the trail of a plague-infected serial killer in a so-so effort scripted and directed by direct-to-video master Albert Pyun. The two photogenic stars add solid weight to the budget bravado. AJ Swearing, violence. **DVD**

Christopher Lambert [Christopher Lambert] *Lemieux* · Natasha Henstridge *Delon* · Norbert Weisser *Cuzo* · Elizabeth Barondes *Wocek* · Xavier Declie *Volker* · Craig Davis *Suspect* · Nicholas Guest *Rennard* · Andrew Divoff *Sterns* ■ *Dir/Scr* Albert Pyun

Adrift ★★ 15
Thriller   2006 · Ger/US · Colour · 90min

Released in certain territories as *Open Water 2*, this seems to have no real link to that ingenious feature beyond its similar premise. A group of friends holidaying on a yacht wind up bobbing around in the ocean with no way back on board. What character delineation there is is pretty superficial as the plot winds its way via the couples' mutual bickering to a deeply unsatisfactory dénouement. It may, however, mitigate the general tedium for some audiences that, because of one failed plan, the last third of the movie is performed in the nude. AS Swearing, nudity. **DVD**

Susan May Pratt *Amy* · Richard Speight Jr *James* · Niklaus Lange *Zach* · Ali Hillis *Lauren* · Cameron Richardson *Michelle* · Eric Dane *Dan* ■ *Dir* Hans Horn · *Scr* Adam Kreutner, Dave Mitchell · *Cinematographer* Bernhard Jasper

Adrift ★★★ 12
Coming-of-age drama
2009 · Bra · Colour · 97min

A family in crisis strays into deep emotional waters in this Brazilian drama. Vincent Cassel and his wife Debora Bloch have fallen out of love, and are spending one last seaside holiday with their three kids before separating. But the story really focuses on confused 14-year-old Laura Neiva, who discovers several skeletons in her parents' closet, and also becomes aware of the power her own budding sexuality has over boys. *Adrift* may not tell us anything new about the human condition, but it is beautifully shot and impeccably acted, especially by screen newcomer Neiva. DA Portuguese, French +subtitles. Swearing, sexual references. **DVD**

Vincent Cassel *Mathias* · Debora Bloch *Clarice* · Laura Neiva *Filipa* · Camila Belle *Angela* · Cauã Reymond *Barman* ■ *Dir/Scr* Heitor Dhalia

Adult Life Skills ★★★ 15
Comedy   2016 · UK · Colour · 96min

Expanding the Bafta-nominated short *Emotional Fusebox*, acclaimed editor Rachel Tunnard's feature debut employs a blend of comedy and melodrama to explore the emotional state of a 29-year-old (Jodie Whittaker) striving to reconcile the loss of a beloved twin brother with the need to get on with her own life. Beck Rainford's production design is outstanding and offers more insights into Whittaker's psyche than the irksome indie soundtrack, but the willing cast can't quite overcome the cloying sense of contrivance. DP Swearing.

Jodie Whittaker *Anna* · Ozzy Myers *Clint* · Brett Goldstein *Brendan* · Alice Lowe *Alice* · Lorraine Ashbourne *Marion* ■ *Dir/Scr* Rachel Tunnard

Adulthood ★★★ 15
Social drama   2008 · UK · Colour · 95min

Noel Clarke's sequel to *Kidulthood* is set six years after that first slice of west London teen turbulence. Sam (writer/director Clarke) has served his sentence for the killing of local rival Trife. Fresh out of prison, he has renounced violence, but violence has not renounced him. During his first 24 hours of freedom, Sam finds that plenty of Trife's friends are still eager to exact revenge. Clarke's employment of a flashier film style means that *Adulthood*, though

A

consistently watchable, is occasionally a little overdone. But this is still competent British film-making, and though it helps to have seen *Kidulthood*, it's not essential. DA Violence, swearing, sexual references, drug abuse. DVD BL

Noel Clarke *Sam Peel* • Adam Deacon *Jay* • Scarlett Alice Johnson *Lexi* • Jacob Anderson *Omen* • Ben "Plan B" Drew [Ben Drew] *Dabs* • Danny Dyer *Hayden* • Femi Oyeniran *Moony* ■ *Dir/Scr* Noel Clarke

Advance to the Rear ★★★

Comedy western   1964 · US · BW · 96min

This sweet-tempered send-up of Civil War heroics from *Destry Rides Again* director George Marshall has a company of Union misfits sent out of the reach of battle, but still managing to capture a rebel spy (Stella Stevens) and save a vast pay-out in gold. The situations are obvious, but Glenn Ford injects an amused authority into the action so the result is gentle satire that saddles up the usual clichés but for different reasons. TH

Glenn Ford *Captain Jared Heath* • Stella Stevens *Martha Lou* • Melvyn Douglas *Colonel Claude Brackenby* • Jim Backus *General Willoughby* • Joan Blondell *Jenny* ■ *Dir* George Marshall · *Scr* Samuel A Peeples, William Bowers, from the novel *The Company of Cowards* by Jack Schaefer

Adventure ★★

Adventure drama   1945 · US · BW · 128min

Clark Gable had famously gone off to fight in the Second World War and was decorated after flying bomb runs over Germany. But in 1945 he returned to Hollywood and made *Adventure*, giving MGM the dreamy advertising slogan, "Gable's back and Garson's got him!". But the movie, so anticipated, was a syrupy romance between a merchant sailor and a priggish bookworm. AT

Clark Gable *Harry Patterson* • Greer Garson *Emily Sears* • Joan Blondell *Helen Melohn* • Thomas Mitchell *Mudgin* • Tom Tully *Gus* • John Qualen *Model T* • Richard Haydn *Limo* ■ *Dir* Victor Fleming · *Scr* Frederick Hazlitt Brennan, Vincent Lawrence, from a novel by Clyde Brion Davis

An Adventure for Two ★★

Drama   1979 · Fr · Colour · 112min

This rarely seen feature is one of writer/ director Claude Lelouch's more puzzling offerings. So much of it seems to have been designed to vex the viewer, particularly in terms of its stuttering structure, its pernickety attention to minor detail and its often dubious incidents. Yet Lelouch makes arresting use of locations in both the US and Canada and draws credible performances from Jacques Dutronc and Catherine Deneuve as a runaway gangster and his hostage. DP French +subtitles.

Catherine Deneuve *Françoise* • Jacques Dutronc *Simon* • Jacques Villeret *Tonton* • Gerard Caillaud *Bliche* • Paul Preboist *Inspector Mimile* • Bernard Crommbey [Bernard Crombey] *Inspector Alain* • Gilberte Genait *Zézette* ■ *Dir/Scr* Claude Lelouch

Adventure in Baltimore ★★☉

Comedy   1949 · US · BW · 88min

This was a vehicle supposedly tailored for Shirley Temple, a Hollywood veteran at the age of 21, who retired from the screen soon after this movie was released. The tale of the independent girl who scandalises her home town with her paintings and feminist leanings sits awkwardly with Temple's frothy image. Robert Young appears as her father, a pastor who comes round to his daughter's point of view. TS

Robert Young (1) *Dr Sheldon* • Shirley Temple *Dinah Sheldon* • John Agar *Tom Wade* • Albert Sharpe *Mr Fletcher* • Josephine Hutchinson *Mrs Sheldon* • Charles Kemper *Mr Steuben* • Johnny Sands *Gene Sheldon* ■ *Dir* Richard Wallace · *Scr* Lionel Houser, from a story by Lesser Samuels, Christopher Isherwood

Adventure in the Hopfields ★★☉

Adventure drama   1954 · UK · BW · 60min

In days of yore, the poor folk of South London flocked to Kent and went hop-picking. But this adventure is no bucolic idyll. Made for the Children's Film Foundation, and starring popular child actor Mandy Miller, this exciting tale offers bullying, theft and a climactic lightning storm. A little piece of British social history from the future director of *The Towering Inferno*. AT

Mandy Miller (1) *Jenny Quin* • Mona Washbourne *Mrs McBain* • Hilda Fenemore *Mrs Quin* • Russell Waters *Mr Quin* • Melvyn Hayes *Reilly* • Harold Lang *Sam Hines* • Wallas Eaton *Postman* • Jane Asher ■ *Dir* John Guillermin · *Scr* John Cresswell, from the novel *The Hop Dog* by Nora Lavin, Molly Thorp

The Adventure of Sherlock Holmes' Smarter Brother ★★★ PG

Comedy   1975 · US/UK · Colour · 87min

Gene Wilder's directorial debut owes much to his slapdash, slapstick mentor Mel Brooks. Wilder also stars as a wonderfully supercilious Sigerson Holmes, taking over a blackmail case, involving Madeline Kahn and opera star Dom DeLuise, from his more famous brother Sherlock (Douglas Wilmer), and then becoming entangled with stolen state secrets. The best humour is very funny indeed, but, apart from that, the whimsy can be rather tiresome. TH Swearing. DVD

Gene Wilder *Sigerson Holmes* • Madeline Kahn *Jenny* • Marty Feldman *Orville Sacker* • Dom DeLuise *Gambetti* • Leo McKern *Moriarty* • Roy Kinnear *Moriarty's aide* • John Le Mesurier *Lord Redcliff* • Douglas Wilmer *Sherlock Holmes* • Thorley Walters *Dr Watson* ■ *Dir/Scr* Gene Wilder

Adventureland ★★★★ 15

Romantic comedy drama   2009 · US · Colour · 102min

It's the summer of 1987, and Jesse Eisenberg is working at an amusement park when the chance of romance arrives in the shape of Kristen Stewart. Although written and directed by *Superbad*'s Greg Mottola, he avoids teen gross-out antics. Eisenberg is suitably vulnerable while Stewart captures the silent suffering of adolescence brilliantly. It's a movie that has a warm, nostalgic glow even with *Rock Me Amadeus* on the soundtrack – and that's quite an achievement. JR Swearing, sexual references, drug abuse. DVD BL

Jesse Eisenberg *James Brennan* • Kristen Stewart *Em Lewin* • Ryan Reynolds *Mike Connell* • Martin Starr *Joel Schiffman* • Kristen Wiig *Paulette* • Bill Hader *Bobby* ■ *Dir/Scr* Greg Mottola

The Adventurers ★★☉

Adventure   1950 · UK · BW · 77min

This sturdy British would-be action drama set in South Africa is about the squabbling members of an expedition searching for a cache of diamonds. Jack Hawkins is cast against type as a villain, who enlists an unconvincing Dennis Price, a young Peter Hammond and Grégoire Aslan to help him recover the treasure. This could have been quite stirring if it hadn't been morbidly under-directed at a snail's pace by David MacDonald. TS

Jack Hawkins *Pieter Brandt* • Peter Hammond *Hendrik Von Thaal* • Dennis Price *Clive Hunter* • Grégoire Aslan *Dominic* • Charles Paton *Barman* • Siobhan McKenna *Anne Hunter* • Bernard Lee O'Connell ■ *Dir* David MacDonald · *Scr* Robert Westerby

The Adventurers ★★☉

Action adventure   1968 · Fr/It · Colour · 100min

The "adventurers" of the title are Alain Delon and Lino Ventura, whose partnership here was a huge European casting coup. Delon and Ventura play a daredevil and inventor respectively who team up for stunts involving fast cars and a plane they plan to fly under the Arc de Triomphe.

Joanna Shimkus briefly introduces a touch of *Jules et Jim* into the proceedings, before they become dominated by a race against the Mafia for hidden treasure. AT French dubbed.

Alain Delon *Manu* • Lino Ventura *Roland* • Joanna Shimkus *Letitia* ■ *Dir* Robert Enrico · *Scr* Robert Enrico, Pierre Pelegri, José Giovanni, from the novel *Les Aventuriers* by Giovanni

The Adventurers ★ 18

Action adventure   1970 · US · Colour · 163min

Lewis Gilbert directs this monumentally bad adaptation of Harold Robbins's potboiler about South American revolution, torrid sex and macho posturing. Bekim Fehmiu, a Yugoslavian actor whose career was deservedly short-lived, is at the top of a bewildering list of international stars. The film is a mishmash of orgies, violence, Freudian psychobabble and jet-set locations. AT

Bekim Fehmiu *Dax Xenos* • Alan Badel *Rojo* • Candice Bergen *Sue Ann Daley* • Ernest Borgnine *Fat Cat* • Leigh Taylor-Young *Amparo* • Fernando Rey *Jaime Xenox* • Charles Aznavour *Marcel Campion* • Olivia de Havilland *Deborah Hadley* • John Ireland *Mr Hadley* • Rossano Brazzi *Baron de Coyne* • Sydney Tafler *Colonel Gutierrez* • Peter Graves (1) *Trustee banker* • Jaclyn Smith *Belinda* • Lois Maxwell *Woman at fashion show* ■ *Dir* Lewis Gilbert · *Scr* Lewis Gilbert, Michael Hastings, from the novel by Harold Robbins

Adventures of a Plumber's Mate ★ 18

Sex comedy   1978 · UK · Colour · 84min

An example of the British blue-comedy boom of the 1970s, this tatty tale presents wife-beating as slapstick. Christopher Neil is unappealing as the hero, whose attempts to settle his debts bring him into contact with endless sex-starved women and gangster William Rushton. DP Swearing, sex scenes, nudity.

Christopher Neil *Sid South* • Arthur Mullard *Blackie* • Elaine Paige *Susie* • Anna Quayle *Loretta Proudfoot* ■ *Dir* Stanley Long · *Scr* Stephen D Frances, Aubrey Cash

Adventures of a Private Eye ★ 18

Sex comedy   1977 · UK · Colour · 92min

Following on from the surprisingly profitable *Adventures of a Taxi Driver*, this smutty romp sticks to the same formula. Christopher Neil, in the title role, strips at regular intervals to satisfy a blackmailer's demand that he sleep with every pretty girl he meets. Comic stalwarts aside, this is really no more than soft-core pulp. DP

Christopher Neil *Bob West* • Suzy Kendall *Laura Sutton* • Harry H Corbett *Sydney* • Liz Fraser *Violet* • Irene Handl *Miss Friggin* • Ian Lavender *Derek* • Jon Pertwee *Judd Blake* • Adrienne Posta *Lisa Moroni* • Anna Quayle *Medea* • William Rushton *Wilfred* • Diana Dors *Mrs Horne* ■ *Dir* Stanley Long · *Scr* Michael Armstrong

Adventures of a Taxi Driver ★★ 18

Sex comedy   1975 · UK · Colour · 86min

Back in the 1970s, smutty comedies such as this were the order of the day for comedy actors trying to break into movies. Barry Evans, who came to prominence in the *Doctor* TV series, plays a cabbie who moves away from his nagging family and enjoys a number of amorous encounters. JF Swearing, sex scenes, drug abuse, nudity.

Barry Evans *Joe North* • Judy Geeson *Nikki* • Adrienne Posta *Carol* • Diana Dors *Mrs North* • Liz Fraser *Maisie* • Ian Lavender *Ronald* • Robert Lindsay *Tom* • Henry McGee *Inspector Rogers* ■ *Dir* Stanley A Long [Stanley Long] · *Scr* Suzanne Mercer

The Adventures of Baron Munchausen ★★★★ PG

Fantasy adventure   1988 · UK/W Ger · Colour · 121min

John Neville plays the legendary liar to perfection in this sumptuous revision of the Rudolph Erich Raspe stories that gives a delicious contemporary relevance to the infamous baron's outlandish exploits.

Director Terry Gilliam's grandiose masterpiece visualises a warped world of chaotic Pythonesque extremes that extends from the Moon (with the lunar king played by Robin Williams) to Mount Etna (where Oliver Reed gives a brilliant performance) as the baron reunites his four fantastically talented friends to fight the Turkish army. It's an opulent odyssey that balances romance, comedy and thrills. AJ Violence, swearing, brief nudity. DVD BL

John Neville *Baron Munchausen* • Eric Idle *Desmond/Berthold* • Sarah Polley *Sally Salt* • Oliver Reed *Vulcan* • Charles McKeown *Rupert/ Adolphus* • Winston Dennis *Bill Albrecht* • Jack Purvis *Jeremy/Gustavus* • Valentina Cortese *Queen Ariadne/Violet* • Jonathan Pryce *Horatio Jackson* • Uma Thurman *Venus/Rose* • Bill Paterson *Henry Salt* • Peter Jeffrey *Sultan* • Alison Steadman *Daisy* • Sting *Heroic officer* • Robin Williams *King of the moon* ■ *Dir* Terry Gilliam · *Scr* Charles McKeown, Terry Gilliam, from the stories by Rudolph Erich Raspe

The Adventures of Barry McKenzie ★★★ 15

Comedy   1972 · Aus · Colour · 101min

This is a scrappy but often hilarious screen version of the *Private Eye* comic strip, with Barry Crocker escorting his Aunt Edna Everage through England's grottiest highways and dirtiest byways, and ending with Humphries "flashing his nasty" in front of Joan Bakewell on a late-night TV show. Words like "chunder" and "tubes of beer" entered the English language and frankly, possums, a lot of it is disgusting. There's a sequel, *Barry McKenzie Holds His Own*, followed two years later. AT DVD

Barry Crocker *Barry McKenzie* • Barry Humphries *Edna Everage/Hoot/Dr Meyer de Lamphrey* • Paul Bertram *Curly* • Dennis Price *Mr Gort* • Avice Landone *Mrs Gort* • Peter Cook *Dominic* • Mary Anne Severne *Lesley* • Dick Bentley *Detective* • Spike Milligan *Landlord* ■ *Dir* Bruce Beresford · *Scr* Bruce Beresford, Barry Humphries, from the comic strip *The Wonderful World of Barry McKenzie* by Humphries

The Adventures of Brer Rabbit ★★

Animated comedy   2006 · US · Colour · 71min

The mischievous bunny from the Uncle Remus folk tales gets a makeover in this flimsy but good-humoured animation. Danny Glover and Wanda Sykes are among the voice talents giving a street-smart flavour to the sanitised antics, as a contemporary youngster learns how to cope with her own family issues by hearing how trickster Brer Rabbit continually outwits his fellow animals. The patchwork structure makes it easily digestible for the under-sixes, who'll best appreciate the film's light-hearted morality lessons and colourful visuals. SF

Nick Cannon *Brer Rabbit* • Gary Anthony Williams *Brer Bear* • DL Hughley *Brer Fox* • Phil LaMarr *Brer Gator* • Wayne Brady *Brer Wolf* • Danny Glover *Brer Turtle* • Wanda Sykes *Sister Moon* ■ *Dir* Byron Vaughns · *Scr* John Loy, from characters by Joel Chandler Harris (uncredited)

The Adventures of Buckaroo Banzai across the 8th Dimension ★★ 12

Science-fiction comedy   1984 · US · Colour · 99min

Comic-book hero and rock star Banzai (Peter Weller) crashes his Jet Car through the eighth dimension and unwittingly opens a hole in time. Unless he and his weirdo team of Hong Kong Cavaliers close it, evil aliens will overrun the Earth. Far too clever and quirky for its own good, this esoteric cult movie is a wacky spaced-out oddity. An amazing cast tries to keep it all accessible but it degenerates into an impenetrable mess. AJ DVD BL CS

Peter Weller *Buckaroo Banzai* • John Lithgow *Dr Emilio Lizardo/Lord John Whorfin* • Ellen Barkin *Penny Priddy* • Jeff Goldblum *New Jersey* • Christopher Lloyd *John Bigboote* • Lewis Smith *Perfect Tommy* • Robert Ito *Professor Hikita* ■ *Dir* WD Richter · *Scr* Earl Mac Rauch

The Adventures of Bullwhip Griffin ★★★ U

Comedy adventure 1967 · US · Colour · 105min

This lively western spoof would have been even more entertaining if the mediocre songs had been dropped and director James Neilson had kept a tighter rein on the action. Roddy McDowall has a ball as the staid Boston butler who gains a reputation as a boxer after he unwillingly joins his young master, Bryan Russell, on the California gold rush. Karl Malden, who has stolen Richard Haydn's treasure map, relishes the chance to play a wicked master of disguise. DP

Roddy McDowall *Bullwhip Griffin* • Suzanne Pleshette *Arabella Flagg* • Karl Malden *Judge Higgins* • Harry Guardino *Sam Trimble* • Bryan Russell *Jack Flagg* • Richard Haydn *Quentin Bartlett* • Liam Redmond *Captain Swain* • Hermione Baddeley *Irene Chesney* • Cecil Kellaway *Mr Pemberton* ■ *Dir* James Neilson • *Scr* Lowell S Hawley, from the novel *By the Great Horn Spoon* by Sid Fleischman

Adventures of Captain Fabian ★★ PG

Adventure 1951 · US/Fr · BW · 100min

Although William Marshall was credited as director of this mediocre costume melodrama, the influence of his unbilled assistant, Robert Florey (a maverick whose credentials never quite matched his potential), is evident. Errol Flynn overdoes the dash as he delivers servant Micheline Presle from a murder charge and he's upstaged from both Vincent Price as a New Orleans fop and the ever-dependable Agnes Moorehead. DP

Errol Flynn *Captain Michael Fabian* • Micheline Presle *Lea Mariotte* • Vincent Price *George Brissac* • Agnes Moorehead *Aunt Jezebel* • Victor Francen *Henri Brissac* • Jim Gérald *Constable* ■ *Dir* William Marshall (1) • *Scr* Errol Flynn, from the novel *Fabulous Ann Madlock* by Robert Shannon

Adventures of Don Juan ★★★ PG

Period adventure 1948 · US · Colour · 110min

Errol Flynn's career was at a low ebb when Warner Bros gave him a shot at playing Don Juan. He attempts to revive the athleticism and charm of his 1930s swashbucklers, and credit must go to director Vincent Sherman, who tactfully photographs the star from angles that disguise the facial ravages of booze, drugs and women. Despite some fine swordplay, and decent acting from both damsel-in-distress Viveca Lindfors and arch-villain Robert Douglas, the film bombed in America, though it was a hit in Europe, where Flynn ended his career. AT

Errol Flynn *Don Juan* • Viveca Lindfors *Queen Margaret* • Robert Douglas *Duke de Lorca* • Alan Hale *Leporello* • Romney Brent *King Phillip III* • Ann Rutherford *Donna Elena* • Robert Warwick *Count De Polan* • Jerry Austin *Don Sebastian* ■ *Dir* Vincent Sherman • *Scr* George Oppenheimer, Harry Kurnitz, from a story by Herbert Dalmas

The Adventures of Elmo in Grouchland ★★★ U

Musical adventure 1999 · US · Colour · 70min

Sesame Street has always aimed to entertain adults while teaching children, though this big-screen adaptation - concerning Elmo the muppet chasing his runaway blanket to Grouchland and finding both under the thumb of the selfish Mr Huxley (Mandy Patinkin) - is almost exclusively aimed at the five-and-under crowd. What's left over for grown-ups is a few hilarious one-liners, and Bert and Ernie's pleasing appearances. KB **DVD**

Vanessa L Williams *Queen of Trash* • Mandy Patinkin *Huxley* • Kevin Clash *Elmo/Pestie/ Grouch jailer/Grouch cab driver* • Fran Brill *Zoe/ Pestie/Prairie Dawn* • Sonia Manzano *Maria* • Roscoe Orman *Gordon* • Stephanie D'Abruzzo *Grizzy/Pestie* ■ *Dir* Gary Halvorson • *Scr* Mitchell Kriegman, Joseph Mazzarino, from a story by Kriegman

The Adventures of Ford Fairlane ★★ 18

Action comedy 1990 · US · Colour · 97min

Controversial sexist comic Andrew Dice Clay crashed and burned in an awkward misstep from action director Renny Harlin. The over-hyped Clay plays a rock 'n' roll detective investigating the death of a heavy metal singer on stage in this crude adventure, big on empty spectacle but very low on honest laughs. AJ

Andrew Dice Clay *Ford Fairlane* • Wayne Newton *Julian Grendel* • Priscilla Presley *Colleen Sutton* • Morris Day *Don Cleveland* • Lauren Holly *Jazz* • Maddie Corman *Zuzu Petals* • Gilbert Gottfried *Johnny Crunch* • David Patrick Kelly *Sam* • Robert Englund *Smiley* ■ *Dir* Renny Harlin • *Scr* Daniel Waters, James Cappe, David Arnott, from characters by Rex Weiner

The Adventures of Gerard ★★

Historical adventure 1970 · UK/It/Swi · Colour · 91min

Based on the stories of Sir Arthur Conan Doyle, this free-spirited romp through the Napoleonic Wars might well puncture a few inflated ideas about military glory, but director Jerzy Skolimowski seems to have embarked on this campaign with little or no strategy. The jokes are haphazard, the acting veers between the astute and the theatrical, period detail is flouted and the battle scenes are more shambolic than satire intended. DP

Peter McEnery *Colonel Etienne Gerard* • Claudia Cardinale *Countess Teresa* • Eli Wallach *Napoleon* • Jack Hawkins *Millefleurs* • Mark Burns *Colonel Russell* • Norman Rossington *Sgt Papilette* • John Neville *Wellington* ■ *Dir* Jerzy Skolimowski • *Scr* HAL Craig, Henry Lester, Gene Gutowski, Jerzy Skolimowski, from the stories by Sir Arthur Conan Doyle

The Adventures of Huck Finn ★★★ PG

Adventure 1993 · US · Colour · 107min

With his wide eyes and refreshingly uncontrived manner, Elijah Wood gives a good account of himself in the title role in this Disney version of the Mark Twain classic, while escaped slave Jim is played with great finesse by Courtney B Vance. If writer/director Stephen Sommers occasionally soft-soaps and over-modernises in an attempt to connect with his audience, he still gets fine performances from a brutish Ron Perlman and the roguish duo of Jason Robards and Robbie Coltrane. DP **DVD**

Elijah Wood *Huck Finn* • Courtney B Vance *Jim* • Robbie Coltrane *The Duke* • Jason Robards *The King* • Ron Perlman *Pap Finn* • Dana Ivey *Widow Douglas* • Anne Heche *Mary Jane Wilks* • James Gammon *Deputy Hines* • Paxton Whitehead *Harvey Wilks* • Tom Aldredge *Dr Robinson* ■ *Dir* Stephen Sommers • *Scr* Stephen Sommers, from the novel by Mark Twain

The Adventures of Huckleberry Finn ★★★ U

Adventure 1939 · US · BW · 90min

This was a showcase for MGM's popular and versatile male star Mickey Rooney, who was Oscar-nominated the same year for *Babes in Arms*. Although lacking the lavish Technicolor of David O Selznick's earlier *The Adventures of Tom Sawyer*, this film does benefit from producer Joseph L Mankiewicz's insistence on filming on authentic river locations. The members of the cast look perfect, as if they had just stepped out of Mark Twain's pages, particularly Rex Ingram as Jim the slave and Elizabeth Risdon as the Widow Douglass. TS

Mickey Rooney *Huckleberry Finn* • Walter Connolly *The King* • William Frawley *The Duke* • Rex Ingram (2) *Jim* • Lynne Carver *Mary Jane* • Jo Ann Sayers *Susan* • Minor Watson *Captain Brandy* • Elisabeth Risdon *Widow Douglass* • Clara Blandick *Miss Watson* ■ *Dir* Richard Thorpe • *Scr* Hugo Butler, from the novel by Mark Twain

The Adventures of Huckleberry Finn ★★★ U

Adventure 1960 · US · Colour · 106min

For all its Mississippi locations, this version of the great Mark Twain novel doesn't sweep us along in the torrential way it should. Maybe Eddie Hodges, as the mischievous Huck, is too prim, or perhaps director Michael Curtiz cut too many of the book's grimmer aspects. It's still an enjoyable epic, however, with Tony Randall as a superbly roguish conman and lively cameos by Buster Keaton and Andy Devine. As the slave, former light heavyweight boxing world champion Archie Moore is a knockout. TH

Tony Randall *The King* • Eddie Hodges *Huckleberry Finn* • Archie Moore *Jim* • Patty McCormack *Joanna* • Neville Brand *Pap* • Mickey Shaughnessy *The Duke* • Judy Canova *Sheriff's wife* • Andy Devine *Mr Carmody* • Buster Keaton *Lion tamer* • John Carradine *Slave Catcher* • Dean Stanton [Harry Dean Stanton] *Slave Catcher* ■ *Dir* Michael Curtiz • *Scr* James Lee, from the novel by Mark Twain

The Adventures of Ichabod and Mr Toad ★★★ U

Animated adventure 1949 · US/UK · Colour · 65min

This Disney feature begins with a whimsical version of the Washington Irving story *The Legend of Sleepy Hollow*. The tale of put-upon schoolmaster Ichabod Crane is pleasingly told by Bing Crosby, but it's the adventures of Toad of Toad Hall that capture the imagination. Basil Rathbone provides the narration, while Toad is superbly voiced by Eric Blore, best known as the butler in many of the Rogers-Astaire musicals. DP

Bing Crosby *Narrator* • Basil Rathbone *Narrator* • Eric Blore *Mr Toad* ■ *Dir* Jack Kinney, Clyde Geronimi, James Algar • *Scr* Erdman Penner, Winston Hibler, Joe Rinaldi, Ted Sears, Homer Brightman, Harry Reeves, from the short story *The Legend of Sleepy Hollow* by Washington Irving and from the novel *The Wind in the Willows* by Kenneth Grahame

The Adventures of Marco Polo ★★ U

Historical adventure 1938 · US · BW · 99min

Gary Cooper is the most unlikely Marco Polo, but that didn't stop producer Samuel Goldwyn from casting him in this would-be tongue-in-cheek spectacular. Trouble is, it's not funny enough, nor at all spectacular, and, with cheesy art direction that cries out for Technicolor, the end result is both silly and dull. Also surprisingly dull is villain Basil Rathbone as Ahmed, his character not helped by director Archie Mayo's lack of imagination. Altogether a misfire, but Lana Turner fans should watch for her brief appearance as a handmaiden. TS

Gary Cooper *Marco Polo* • Sigrid Gurie *Princess Kukachin* • Basil Rathbone *Ahmed* • Ernest Truex *Binguccio* • George Barbier *Kublai Khan* • Binnie Barnes *Nazama* • Alan Hale *Kaidu* • Lana Turner *Maid* ■ *Dir* Archie Mayo • *Scr* Robert E Sherwood, from a story by NA Pogson

The Adventures of Mark Twain ★★★ U

Biographical drama 1944 · US · BW · 130min

Fredric March plays the title role in this competent biography of Samuel Clemens, alias Mark Twain, America's greatest humorist. Twain, of course, was the creator of Huckleberry Finn, Tom Sawyer and half the entries in any decent book of quotations. He also had an eventful life, which in turn makes an enjoyable film, despite a script which at times suggests that rumours of Twain's wit must have been greatly exaggerated. PF

Fredric March *Samuel Clemens/Mark Twain* • Alexis Smith *Olivia Langdon* • Donald Crisp *JB Pond* • Alan Hale *Steve Gillis* • C Aubrey Smith *Oxford Chancellor* • John Carradine *Bret Harte* • William Henry *Charles Langdon* • Robert Barrat *Horace E Bixby* ■ *Dir* Irving Rapper • *Scr* Alan LeMay, Harry Chandlee

The Adventures of Milo and Otis ★★★ U

Adventure 1986 · Jpn · Colour · 71min

Owing a huge debt to Disney's 1963 film *The Incredible Journey*, this Japanese live-action animal tale is far superior to the studio's own 1993 remake *Homeward Bound: the Incredible Journey*, as the cat and dog of the title don't "speak" for themselves, making their perilous exploits seem all the more thrilling. Dudley Moore might not have been everyone's choice as narrator, but his lively voiceover gives the action sequences a bit more bite and prevents the gentler moments lapsing into whimsy. DP

Dudley Moore *Narrator* ■ *Dir* Masanori Hata • *Scr* Mark Saltzman, from a story by Masanori Hata

The Adventures of Mowgli ★★★

Animated adventure 1967 · USSR/US · Colour · 89min

Originally released a year after Disney made box-office history with *The Jungle Book*, this 1967 Soviet version of Rudyard Kipling's popular classic was re-edited and re-voiced in 1996 for a new generation of cartoon fans. Charlton Heston narrates the story of the foundling who is raised by wolves before embarking upon a series of adventures with the animals of the jungle. As directed by R Davidov, the animation has none of Disney's cuteness, but it was a prestige project for the Soyuzmultfilm studios and the care taken is evident. DP Russian dubbed.

Charlton Heston *Narrator* • Sam Elliott *Kaa* • Dana Delany *Bagheera* • Ian Corlett *Mowgli* • Scott McNeil *Shere Khan* • Cam Lane *Baloo* ■ *Dir* Terry Klausen, R Davidov • *Scr* L Belokurov, with English adaptation by David Longworth, Cordell Wynne, Harry Kalensky, Allan Stanleigh, from the novel *The Jungle Book* by Rudyard Kipling

The Adventures of Pinocchio ★★ U

Fantasy adventure 1996 · UK/Fr/Ger/Cz Rep · Colour · 90min

Despite state-of-the-art digital technology and creatures from the Jim Henson workshop, this is a disappointing rendition of Carlo Collodi's enchanting morality tale. Martin Landau brings some melancholy gravitas to the proceedings as Geppetto the woodcarver, and Udo Kier is suitably sinister as the puppeteer who lures little boys to his terrifying theme park. Director Steve Barron overplays his hand, however, so the film feels like a glorified pantomime. DP **DVD**

Martin Landau *Geppetto* • Jonathan Taylor Thomas *Pinocchio* • Geneviève Bujold *Leona* • Udo Kier *Lorenzini* • Bebe Neuwirth *Felinet* • Rob Schneider *Volpe* • Corey Carrier *Lampwick* • Marcello Magni *Baker* • Dawn French *Baker's wife* • Griff Rhys Jones *Tino* • John Sessions *Schoolmaster* ■ *Dir* Steve Barron • *Scr* Sherry Mills, Steve Barron, Tom Benedek, Barry Berman, from the novel by Carlo Collodi

The Adventures of Priscilla, Queen of the Desert ★★★★ 15

Comedy drama 1994 · Aus · Colour · 98min

In this wondrously camp classic, director Stephan Elliott tosses the niceties of sexual politics out of the window of a speeding bus and sets about exposing the soft underbelly of the Australian male. Two drag queens and a transsexual travel across the outback in a dilapidated coach for a gig in that bastion of machismo, Alice Springs, en route finding themselves in all manner of hilarious fish-out-of-water situations. Ingeniously cast against type, Terence Stamp is a revelation as the hard-drinking transsexual. Brilliantly bitchy, fabulously photographed and wonderfully played, this frock opera addresses the issues with satirical accuracy and profound insight. DP Swearing. **DVD** **CS**

A

Terence Stamp *Bernadette* • Hugo Weaving *Tick/Mitzi* • Guy Pearce *Adam/Felicia* • Bill Hunter *Bob* • Sarah Chadwick *Marion* • Mark Holmes *Benjamin* • Julia Cortez *Cynthia* • Ken Radley *Frank* ■ *Dir/Scr* Stephan Elliott • *Cinematographer* Brian Breheny • *Costume Designers* Lizzy Gardiner, Tim Chappel

The Adventures of Robin Hood ★★★★★ U

Classic swashbuckling adventure
1938 · US · Colour · 101min

Shot in bright-as-a-button Technicolor, this swashbuckler is an action picture that still delights people of all ages. It was intended to star James Cagney, but seems tailor-made for Errol Flynn as Sherwood's noblest outlaw. Flynn woos Olivia de Havilland and crosses swords with Basil Rathbone and Claude Rains, while Erich Wolfgang Korngold's music goes brassily heraldic. A few weeks into production, studio boss Jack Warner thought the rushes lacked sparkle and replaced director William Keighley with Michael Curtiz. The result was a box-office smash and Oscars for the score, editing and interior decoration. AT *DVD*

Errol Flynn *Robin Hood* • Olivia de Havilland *Maid Marian* • Basil Rathbone *Sir Guy of Gisbourne* • Claude Rains *Prince John* • Patric Knowles *Will Scarlet* • Eugene Pallette *Friar Tuck* • Alan Hale *Little John* • Melville Cooper *High Sheriff of Nottingham* • Ian Hunter *King Richard* • Una O'Connor *Bess* ■ *Dir* Michael Curtiz, William Keighley • *Scr* Norman Reilly Raine, Seton I Miller, from ancient Robin Hood legends, the novel *Ivanhoe* by Sir Walter Scott, and the operetta *Robin Hood* by De Koven-Smith • *Cinematographers* Sol Polito, Tony Gaudio, W Howard Greene • *Music* Erich Wolfgang Korngold • *Art Director* Carl Jules Weyl

The Adventures of Robinson Crusoe ★★★★ U

Adventure 1952 · US · Colour · 89min

Considering what director Luis Buñuel did with *Wuthering Heights*, this is an astonishingly restrained adaptation of Daniel Defoe's classic castaway tale. Gone is the surrealism one expects of Buñuel, and in its place comes a heartfelt optimism about the strength of humanity. Dan O'Herlihy received an Oscar nomination for his portrayal of the privileged man who comes to a greater understanding of life through his unbearable isolation. The arrival of Friday (Jaime Fernandez), offers an even more strenuous test and he finds himself reverting to his old ways. DP In Spanish.

Dan O'Herlihy *Robinson Crusoe* • Jaime Fernandez *Man Friday* • Felipe da Alba *Captain Oberzo* • Chel Lopez *Bosun* • José Chavez *Mutineer* • Emilio Garibay *Mutineer* ■ *Dir* Luis Buñuel • *Scr* Luis Buñuel, Philip Ansell Roll [Hugo Butler], from the novel by Daniel Defoe

The Adventures of Rocky & Bullwinkle ★★★ U

Part-animated comedy
1999 · US/Ger · Colour · 87min

Robert De Niro plays a cartoon villain intent on world domination in this big-screen revival of the popular US children's series of the 1950s and 60s. Animated heroes Rocky (a squirrel) and Bullwinkle (a moose) are brought out of retirement to do battle with Fearless Leader (De Niro) and his associates (Rene Russo and Jason Alexander), who've been transformed into live-action baddies. It's all fast, fun and gloriously tongue-in-cheek. Their antics will please younger viewers, and De Niro gleefully sends himself up. DA *DVD*

Rene Russo *Natasha Fatale* • Jason Alexander *Boris Badenov* • Piper Perabo *Karen Sympathy* • Randy Quaid *Cappy von Trapment* • Robert De Niro *Fearless Leader* • June Foray *Rocket J "Rocky" Squirrel/Natasha/Narrator's mother* • Keith Scott *Bullwinkle J Moose/Fearless Leader/ Boris/Narrator* • Billy Crystal *Travelling mattress salesman* • Whoopi Goldberg *Judge* ■ *Dir* Des McAnuff • *Scr* Kenneth Lonergan, from characters by Jay Way

The Adventures of Sebastian Cole ★★★ 15

Comedy drama 1998 · US · Colour · 94min

Told mostly in flashback, Tod Williams's episodic debut turns the rites-of-passage picture on its head. Where else would you encounter a drunkenly irresponsible mother, a motorcycling sister and a fiercely Catholic stepfather who decides to have a sex-change operation? Yet, despite this determined kookiness, there's an almost Andy Hardy feel to the pep talks shared by tousle-haired Adrian Grenier and the bewigged Clark Gregg. Sufficiently confident to leave plot strands untied, this is an authentically fuzzy snapshot of a life in progress. DP

Adrian Grenier *Sebastian Cole* • Clark Gregg *Hark/Henrietta Cole* • Aleksa Palladino *Mary* • Margaret Colin *Joan Cole* • John Shea *Hartley* • Marni Lustig *Jessica* • Famke Janssen *Fiona* ■ *Dir/Scr* Tod Williams

The Adventures of Sharkboy and Lavagirl ★★ U

Fantasy action adventure
2005 · US · Colour · 88min

Robert Rodriguez's family adventure is all about the power of dreams, specifically those of a meek and bullied boy named Max (Cayden Boyd). Max retreats into his imagination only to discover that the titular superheroes of his fantasies have become real. Most of the film takes place in a CGI world of Max's imaginings, with rivers of milk, giant cookies and an actual brainstorm. The film certainly has an upbeat energy, but this could be a headache-inducing ride, with gaudy, brash art direction and uneven performances. GM *DVD* Sp

Taylor Lautner *Sharkboy* • Taylor Dooley *Lavagirl* • Cayden Boyd *Max* • George Lopez *Mr Electric/Tobor/Ice Guardian/Mr Electricidad* • David Arquette *Max's dad* • Kristin Davis *Max's mom* • Jacob Davich *Linus/Minus* ■ *Dir* Robert Rodriguez • *Scr* Robert Rodriguez, Marcel Rodriguez, from a story by Racer Rodriguez

The Adventures of Sherlock Holmes ★★★★ PG

Mystery 1939 · US · BW · 81min

Following *The Hound of the Baskervilles*, this second teaming of Basil Rathbone and Nigel Bruce as Holmes and Watson is one of the master detective's best screen cases. Borrowing from the stories of Sir Arthur Conan Doyle and the stage play by William Gillette, the film superbly re-creates the atmosphere of 221B Baker Street and Victorian London. Holmes never had a more devilish adversary than George Zucco as Moriarty. DP *DVD*

Basil Rathbone *Sherlock Holmes* • Nigel Bruce *Dr Watson* • Ida Lupino *Ann Brandon* • Alan Marshal *Jerrold Hunter* • Terry Kilburn *Billy* • George Zucco *Professor Moriarty* • Henry Stephenson *Sir Ronald Ramsgate* • EE Clive *Inspector Bristol* • Arthur Hohl *Bassick* • May Beatty *Mrs Jameson* ■ *Dir* Alfred Werker • *Scr* Edwin Blum, William Drake, from the play *Sherlock Holmes* by William Gillette, from the stories of Sir Arthur Conan Doyle

The Adventures of Tartu ★★

Second World War spy drama
1943 · UK · BW · 112min

In order to sabotage a Nazi nerve gas factory, Robert Donat goes undercover in Czechoslovakia as a Romanian ex-diplomat. Valerie Hobson is also undercover, though she's posing as a Nazi. Harold S Bucquet's film is solidly made and reasonably tense, but the casting of Donat can't help reminding viewers of the far superior *The Thirty-Nine Steps*. AT

Robert Donat *Captain Terence Stevenson* • Valerie Hobson *Maruschka* • Walter Rilla *Inspector Otto Vogel* • Glynis Johns *Paula Palacek* • Phyllis Morris *Anna Palacek* ■ *Dir* Harold S Bucquet • *Scr* Howard Emmet Rogers, John Lee Mahin, Miles Malleson, from a story by John C Higgins

The Adventures of the Wilderness Family ★★ U

Adventure 1975 · US · Colour · 98min

Echoes of *Swiss Family Robinson* reverberate around this encounter with the great outdoors, as an identically named family quits Los Angeles to set up home in the Colorado Rockies. However, the marauding wildlife, suspicious locals and unyielding flora soon prove as irksome as the crime and pollution they have left behind. Stewart Raffill makes the most of his breathtaking locations, but the survivalist angle is all too familiar. DP

Robert F Logan [Robert Logan] *Skip* • Susan Damante Shaw *Pat* • Hollye Holmes *Jenny* • Ham Larsen *Toby* ■ *Dir/Scr* Stewart Raffill

The Adventures of Tintin: the Secret of the Unicorn ★★★ PG

Animated action adventure
2011 · US/NZ/Bel · Colour · 102min

This much-anticipated adventure featuring the bequiffed boy reporter sees director Steven Spielberg use the motion-capture process for the first time. The tale of lost parchments and sunken treasure has its share of thrills and spills, but it doesn't do a great deal to make the juvenile hack's personality any more compelling. The occasional Spielberg touches remind us what a master the director is. But despite Jamie Bell's valiant voice contribution, it becomes increasingly difficult to care about our shiny-faced hero. Only Andy Serkis's boozy Captain Haddock and Snowy the hyper-intelligent mutt triumph over the deadening effect of the technology. AS Some violence. *DVD* Blu

Jamie Bell *Tintin* • Andy Serkis *Captain Haddock/Sir Francis Haddock* • Daniel Craig *Sakharine/Red Rackham* • Nick Frost *Thomson* • Simon Pegg *Thompson* • Toby Jones *Silk* • Mackenzie Crook *Ernie* ■ *Dir* Steven Spielberg • *Scr* Joe Cornish, Steven Moffat, Edgar Wright, from characters by Hergé • *Cinematographer* Janusz Kaminski • *Music* John Williams

The Adventures of Tom Sawyer ★★★★ U

Adventure 1938 · US · Colour · 90min

This superb David O Selznick production, made the year before he gave the world *Gone with the Wind*, remains the most entertaining, and most faithful, of all screen adaptations of Mark Twain's tale. The nightmare sequences in the caverns are brilliantly executed, and the use of early Technicolor particularly effective. The pace is fast, the running time taut and the casting impeccable: apart from the two decent boy leads, who could fail to warm to a period romp featuring Walter Brennan, May Robson and Victor Jory. TS *DVD*

Tommy Kelly *Tom Sawyer* • Jackie Moran *Huckleberry Finn* • Ann Gillis *Becky Thatcher* • May Robson *Aunt Polly* • Walter Brennan *Muff Potter* • Victor Jory *Injun Joe* • David Holt *Sid Sawyer* • Victor Kilian *Sheriff* • Nana Bryant *Mrs Thatcher* • Donald Meek *Superintendent* • Charles Richman *Judge Thatcher* ■ *Dir* Norman Taurog • *Scr* John VA Weaver, from the novel by Mark Twain

The Adventures of Tom Thumb and Thumbelina ★★ U

Animated musical adventure
2002 · US · Colour · 71min

Once upon a time, children would forgive the shoddy graphics and atrocious songs in a cheaply made animation such as this one because animals talked, there was plenty of slapstick and good triumphed over evil. Jennifer Love Hewitt sings sweetly as she laments being imprisoned by both a French carnival barker and the Mole King, but Elijah Wood is less than convincing as her hero. DP *DVD*

Jennifer Love Hewitt *Thumbelina* • Elijah Wood *Tom Thumb* • Alexandra Boyd *Bertha Beetle* • Peter Gallagher *Mole King* • Rachel Griffiths *Albertine* • Robert Guillaume *Ben* • Jane Leeves

Margaret Beetle • Esai Morales *Vergas Mouse* • Bebe Neuwirth *Thumbelina's mother* ■ *Dir* Glenn Chaika • *Scr* Willard Carroll

The Adversary ★★★

Drama 1970 · Ind · BW · 109min

Following his father's death, Dhritiman Chatterjee is forced to abandon his studies and find work to support his family, but cannot compete in the rat race. Satyajit Ray paints a perceptive portrait of an educated but listless character attempting to manage life in the stressful environment of Calcutta. The supporting characters are also incisively drawn in this sharply observed tale from India's master auteur that's at once amusing, poignant and bitter. RB Bengali +subtitles. *DVD*

Dhritiman Chatterjee *Siddhartha* • Krishna Bose *Sutapa* • Jaysree Roy *Keya* • Debraj Roy *Tunu* ■ *Dir* Satyajit Ray • *Scr* Satyajit Ray, from the novel *Pratidwandi* by Sunil Ganguly • *Music* Satyajit Ray

Advise and Consent ★★★★ PG

Political drama 1962 · US · BW · 132min

Otto Preminger's superb study of political shenanigans in Washington provides marvellous roles for Henry Fonda as the liberal politician that ailing president Franchot Tone wants to promote and Charles Laughton, in his last film, as the southern senator opposed to the appointment. This was all but unique among Hollywood movies of the time in using homosexuality as a plot device, and, although it may seem a little tame today, it was significant and shocking enough on its release. TS

Henry Fonda *Robert Leffingwell* • Charles Laughton *Sen Seabright "Seb" Cooley* • Don Murray *Sen Brigham Anderson* • Walter Pidgeon *Sen Bob Munson* • Peter Lawford *Sen Lafe Smith* • George Grizzard *Sen Fred Van Ackerman* • Gene Tierney *Dolly Harrison* • Franchot Tone *President* • Lew Ayres *Vice-President* • Burgess Meredith *Herbert Gelman* ■ *Dir* Otto Preminger • *Scr* Wendell Mayes, from the novel by Allen Drury

Ae Fond Kiss... ★★★ 15

Romantic drama
2004 · UK/Ger/It/Sp/Fr · Colour · 100min

In Ken Loach's surprisingly sexy modern variation on *Romeo and Juliet*, the star-crossed lovers are a Scots-Pakistani DJ (Atta Yaqub) and an Irish music teacher (Eva Birthistle) living in contemporary Glasgow. Yaqub's parents are planning a traditional arranged marriage for him, but he embarks on a relationship with Birthistle. Loach's film emerges as a touching modern love story that should reach beyond his usual audience. BP In English, Punjabi. Swearing, sex scenes. *DVD*

Atta Yaqub *Casim Khan* • Eva Birthistle *Roisin Hanlon* • Shamshad Akhatar *Sadia Khan* • Ghizala Avan *Rukhsana Khan* • Shabana Bakhsh *Tahara Khan* • Ahmad Riaz *Tariq Khan* • Gerard Kelly *Parish priest* ■ *Dir* Ken Loach • *Scr* Paul Laverty

Aeonflux ★★ 15

Science-fiction thriller
2005 · US · Colour · 89min

Based on the MTV animated series, this slick action adventure is set in the year 2415, when the survivors of a killer virus inhabit a hi-tech walled city. Here, acrobatic rebel agent Charlize Theron seeks vengeance for her sister's political murder and gets the opportunity when she's ordered to assassinate dictator Marton Csokas. While the original cartoon was tongue in cheek, Karyn Kusama's version takes itself too seriously and is hampered by an underdeveloped storyline and weak dialogue. SF Violence. *DVD* Blu

Charlize Theron *Aeon Flux* • Marton Csokas *Chairman Trevor Goodchild* • Jonny Lee Miller *Oren Goodchild* • Sophie Okonedo *Sithandra Freya* • Frances McDormand *Handler* • Pete Postlethwaite *Keeper* ■ *Dir* Karyn Kusama • *Scr* Phil Hay, Matt Manfredi, from the characters by Peter Chung

A

The Affair ★★ PG
Romantic drama 1973 · US · Colour · 70min

Made for American television, this trifling melodrama was shown theatrically in Europe, where its threadbare production values were painfully obvious. Nevertheless, this tale of a young woman disabled since childhood who finds romance with a sophisticated lawyer is given poignancy by the casting of Natalie Wood opposite her real-life husband, Robert Wagner. Director Gilbert Cates occasionally comes up with a few insights amid the tosh but Wagner's just not in Wood's league. **TS**

Natalie Wood *Courtney Patterson* · Robert Wagner *Marcus Simon* · Bruce Davison *Jamie Patterson* · Jamie Smith-Jackson *Jennifer* · Pat Harrington *Frank* ■ *Dir* Gilbert Cates · *Scr* Barbara Turner · *Producers* Aaron Spelling, Leonard Goldberg

Affair in Trinidad ★★★ PG
Spy drama 1952 · US · BW · 94min

Rita Hayworth and Glenn Ford, stars of *Gilda*, are re-united here for a spy drama set in a far-flung international Hollywood hotspot. The plot is some nonsense about spy rings, with Ford helping Hayworth find her husband's killer, but who cares when the stars strike such sparks from each other? Alexander Scourby makes an effective villain, and veteran director Vincent Sherman is in his element with this kind of material. Despite its flaws, this is highly entertaining, and Hayworth is simply ravishing in her return to the screen after a four-year break following her marriage to Prince Ali Khan. **TS DVD**

Rita Hayworth *Chris Emery* · Glenn Ford *Steve Emery* · Alexander Scourby *Max Fabian* · Valerie Bettis *Veronica* · Torin Thatcher *Inspector Smythe* · Howard Wendell *Anderson* ■ *Dir* Vincent Sherman · *Scr* Oscar Saul, James Gunn, from a story by Virginia Van Upp, Berne Giler

The Affair of the Necklace ★★ 12
Period romantic drama 2001 · US · Colour · 112min

Director Charles Shyer delivers a stodgy period drama, based on a true event that has since been credited as one of the contributory causes of the French Revolution. While that sounds potentially fascinating, the result is actually a turgid and woefully miscast mess, as Hilary Swank fails to look like a delicate French lady trying to regain her noble birthright by meddling in court intrigue. Equally out of their depth and looking far too 21st-century are Adrien Brody and Simon Baker as two of her fellow schemers. So it's left to Jonathan Pryce and Christopher Walken to inject some humour by camping it up. **JB DVD**

Hilary Swank *Jeanne de la Motte-Valois* · Jonathan Pryce *Cardinal Louis de Rohan* · Simon Baker (1) *Rétaux de Villette* · Adrien Brody *Nicolas de la Motte* · Brian Cox (1) *Baron de Breteuil* · Joely Richardson *Marie Antoinette* · Christopher Walken *Cagliostro* ■ *Dir* Charles Shyer · *Scr* John Sweet

An Affair to Remember ★★★★ U
Romantic drama 1957 · US · Colour · 109min

The incomparable Cary Grant is at his slickly arch and urbane best as a wealthy, idle womaniser who meets his match in self-contained, sassy Deborah Kerr aboard a luxury liner. Director Leo McCarey (who also made 1939's *Love Affair* on which this is based) dresses his sophisticated comedy of sexual manners in an atmosphere of rhinestone-encrusted dresses, impeccably pressed dinner suits and raised champagne glasses. The second half slips off the boil somewhat, but this remains a cinematic object lesson in the perfect rapier delivery of cut-and-thrust dialogue. **SH DVD Blu**

Cary Grant *Nickie Ferrante* · Deborah Kerr *Terry McKay* · Richard Denning *Kenneth* · Neva Patterson *Lois* · Cathleen Nesbitt *Grandmother* · Robert Q Lewis *Announcer* · Charles Watts *Hathaway* · Fortunio Bonanova *Courbet* ■

Dir Leo McCarey · *Scr* Delmer Daves, Donald Ogden Stewart (uncredited), Leo McCarey, from a story by McCarey, Mildred Cram

Affair with a Stranger ★★★ U
Romantic drama 1953 · US · BW · 86min

A well-cast Victor Mature and Jean Simmons play a warring couple who adopt a child as their union collapses in this lesson in how not to handle a disintegrating relationship. Director Roy Rowland brings out the best in the stars, who make this crazy premise credible. However, having set everything up, Rowland seems unsure about the direction his characters should take. **SH**

Jean Simmons *Carolyn Parker* · Victor Mature *Bill Blakeley* · Mary Jo Tarola *Dolly Murray* · Monica Lewis *Janet Boothe* · Jane Darwell *Ma Stanton* · Dabbs Greer *Happy Murray* · Wally Vernon *Joe* · Nicholas Joy *George Craig* ■ *Dir* Roy Rowland · *Scr* Richard Flournoy

Une Affaire de Femmes ★★★
Second World War drama 1988 · Fr · Colour · 110min

Isabelle Huppert won the best actress prize at the Venice film festival for her portrayal of a mother whose struggle to survive the Nazi Occupation brought her into conflict with the Vichy authorities. Before becoming the last woman in France to be guillotined, Marie Latour performs abortions with a detachment that causes many to label her a monster. But Claude Chabrol refuses to take sides, adopting Jean Renoir's famous maxim that everyone has their reasons, as he dispassionately reconstructs the bleak realities of the early 1940s. **DP** French +subtitles.

Isabelle Huppert *Marie* · François Cluzet *Paul* · Marie Trintignant *Lulu/Lucie* · Nils Tavernier *Lucien* ■ *Dir* Claude Chabrol · *Scr* Claude Chabrol, Colo Tavernier O'Hagan, from the novel by Francis Szpiner

Les Affaires Publiques ★★★
Comedy 1934 · Fr · BW · 25min

Robert Bresson made this short during his 20s, while he was in the thrall of René Clair and Charlie Chaplin. He later disowned this early work, and for many years it was thought to be lost until it was discovered and restored in the mid-1980s. Bresson rejected the term burlesque, preferring to call it a "crazy comedy". The film stars Beby the clown as the dictator in an imaginary country, and follows his not especially comic misadventures in a provincial town. It remains significant today only as the aberrant work of a future great director before he radicalised his life and art. **BB** French +subtitles.

Beby *Chancellor* · Andrée Servilanges *Princess* · Marcel Dalio *Sculptor/Fireman/Radio voice* · Gilles Margaritis *Chauffeur* ■ *Dir* Robert Bresson · *Scr* Robert Bresson, Andre Josset, Paul Weill

The Affairs of Annabel ★★★ U
Satire 1938 · US · BW · 67min

This good-natured, fast-moving semi-satire on the film industry features wacky Lucille Ball as a star and rueful, lovable Jack Oakie as her inept press agent, who's always cooking up stunts that don't work. The film was popular enough in its day to inspire a limp sequel, *Annabel Takes a Tour*, with the same cast but a different director. Lucille Ball would eventually derive personal satisfaction from buying RKO, the studio where she filmed this trifle, and renaming it Desilu, where *I Love Lucy* was recorded for posterity. **TS**

Lucille Ball *Annabel Allison* · Jack Oakie *Lanny Morgan* · Ruth Donnelly *Josephine* · Bradley Page *Webb* · Fritz Feld *Vladimir* · Thurston Hall *Major* · Elisabeth Risdon *Mrs Fletcher* · Granville Bates *Mr Fletcher* ■ *Dir* Ben Stoloff · *Scr* Bert Granet, Paul Yawitz, from a story by Charles Hoffman

The Affairs of Cellini ★★
Comedy 1934 · US · BW · 84min

Hopelessly dated, this saunter through a Hollywood Renaissance initially offers some pleasure, largely thanks to director Gregory La Cava's sense of fun. In the title role, a bearded Fredric March proves he was one of the few stars of the time who looked truly comfortable in costume, and a top-billed Constance Bennett and Oscar-nominated Frank Morgan are enjoyable enough to watch, but the farcical tone does become irritating. Quite saucy in its own pre-censorship way. **TS**

Constance Bennett *Duchess of Florence* · Fredric March *Benvenuto Cellini* · Frank Morgan *Alessandro, Duke of Florence* · Fay Wray *Angela* · Vince Barnett *Ascanio* · Jessie Ralph *Beatrice* · Louis Calhern *Ottaviano* · Lucille Ball *Lady-in-waiting* ■ *Dir* Gregory La Cava · *Scr* Bess Meredyth, from the play *The Firebrand* by Edwin Justus Mayer

The Affairs of Dobie Gillis ★★★ U
Musical comedy 1953 · US · Colour · 72min

It's youthful love at first sight when Debbie Reynolds and Bobby Van meet at the freshmen's get-together at Grainbelt College – motto: learn, learn, learn; work, work, work. She's there to do just that, he's there to have fun. True love faces numerous obstacles, especially Reynolds's tyrannical father, Hanley Stafford, in this good-natured and increasingly silly, semi-musical college caper. The appealing and talented Van dances up a storm, as do Reynolds, Bob Fosse before he became famous, and Barbara Ruick. **RK**

Debbie Reynolds *Pansy Hammer* · Bobby Van *Dobie Gillis* · Barbara Ruick *Lorna Ellingboe* · Bob Fosse *Charlie Trask* · Hanley Stafford *Mr Hammer* · Lurene Tuttle *Mrs Hammer* · Hans Conried *Professor Amos Pomfritt* · Charles Lane (2) *Professor Obispo* ■ *Dir* Don Weis · *Scr* Max Shulman

The Affairs of Martha ★★★ U
Comedy 1942 · US · BW · 66min

Although he would later become known for *films noirs*, heist thrillers and collaborations with his Greek wife Melina Mercouri, Jules Dassin directed several light entertainments in his early career. His second feature proved an admirable showcase for Marsha Hunt as the Swedish maid, who not only writes a pseudonymous account of her life with a society family, but also marries son-and-heir Richard Carlson after a drunken night out. The support cast is splendid, as is the literate screenplay. **DP**

Marsha Hunt *Martha Lindstrom* · Richard Carlson *Jeff Sommerfield* · Marjorie Main *Mrs McKissick* · Virginia Weidler *Miranda Sommerfield* · Spring Byington *Mrs Sophie Sommerfield* · Allyn Joslyn *Joel Archer* · Barry Nelson *Danny O'Brien* · Frances Drake *Sylvia Norwood* · Margaret Hamilton *Guinevere* ■ *Dir* Jules Dassin · *Scr* Isobel Lennart, Lee Gold

The Affairs of Susan ★★★
Comedy 1945 · US · BW · 109min

Actress Susan Darell, portrayed by a very effervescent Joan Fontaine, gets to reveal four different personae during a series of flashbacks at fiancé Walter Abel's bachelor party, where he has invited two other suitors plus Susan's previous husband, George Brent. This is a witty and classy Hal Wallis production, which rightly garnered an Oscar nomination for best original story. The real surprise is Fontaine, who proves what a capable actress she is, offering a charming and utterly beguiling star performance in an unfairly neglected comedy. **TS**

Joan Fontaine *Susan Darell* · George Brent *Roger Berton* · Dennis O'Keefe *Bill Anthony* · Don DeFore *Mike Ward* · Rita Johnson *Mona Kent* · Walter Abel *Richard Aiken* · Byron Barr *Chick* · Mary Field *Nancy* · Francis Pierlot *Uncle Jimmy* ■ *Dir* William A Seiter · *Scr* Laszlo Gorog, Richard Flournoy, Thomas Monroe, from a story by Gorog, Monroe

Affectionately Yours ★★
Comedy 1941 · US · BW · 87min

Top news correspondent Dennis Morgan rushes home from an overseas assignment to win back his wife Merle Oberon. Rita Hayworth appears as "the other woman", and she's the best thing in a supposed marital comedy that misfires in every direction. Ralph Bellamy is fine as a rival for Oberon's affections, but neither of the stars has the right personality or touch to rescue the weak material. **RK**

Merle Oberon *Sue Marberry* · Dennis Morgan *Richard "Rickey" Mayberry* · Rita Hayworth *Irene Malcolm* · Ralph Bellamy *Owen Wright* · George Tobias *Pasha* · James Gleason *Chester Phillips* · Hattie McDaniel *Cynthia* · Jerome Cowan *Cullen* · Alexis Smith *Guest* · Butterfly McQueen *Butterfly* ■ *Dir* Lloyd Bacon · *Scr* Edward Kaufman, from a story by Fanya Foss, Aleen Leslie

Affliction ★★★ 15
Drama 1997 · US · Colour · 109min

Part thriller, part examination of a man in midlife crisis, this is bleak but well-performed. Nick Nolte plays a traffic cop in a small New England town. When his friend Jim True returns from a hunting expedition claiming the businessman he took with him died from a self-inflicted wound, Nolte seeks an escape from his damning ex-wife by turning detective. His subsequent mental disintegration is both painful and powerful to watch. Too black to be mainstream, this is nevertheless a tour de force for Nolte, though it was James Coburn who won the Oscar for his portrayal of Nolte's abusive father. **LH** Swearing, violence. **DVD**

Nick Nolte *Wade Whitehouse* · Sissy Spacek *Margie Fogg* · James Coburn *Glen Whitehouse* · c Rolfe *Whitehouse* · Mary Beth Hurt *Lillian* · Jim True *Jack Hewitt* ■ *Dir* Paul Schrader · *Scr* Paul Schrader, from the novel by Russell Banks

Afghan Star ★★★
Documentary 2008 · UK/Afg · Colour · 88min

Afghanistan may still be a conflict zone, but, as this award-winning film shows, Afghans have adopted the TV talent show with at least as much enthusiasm as any other nationality since the Taliban's ban on singing and dancing was lifted in 2004. **DP** English, Pashtu, Dari +subtitles. **DVD**

■ *Dir* Havana Marking

Afraid of the Dark ★★★ 18
Psychological thriller 1991 · UK/Fr · Colour · 87min

The directorial debut of Mark Peploe, a regular scriptwriter for his brother-in-law Bernardo Bertolucci, this is an eerily effective exercise in suspense. The always watchable James Fox is a cop trying to protect his small son and his blind wife (Fanny Ardant) from the attentions of a neighbourhood psycho, who may be window cleaner and pornographer Paul McGann. It's a quirky blend of *Wait until Dark* and Michael Powell's shocker *Peeping Tom* that throws up as many surprises as it does artistic pretensions. **AT**

James Fox *Frank* · Fanny Ardant *Miriam* · Paul McGann *Tony Dalton* · Clare Holman *Rose* · Robert Stephens *Dan Burns* · Susan Woolridge *Lucy Trent* · Ben Keyworth *Lucas* ■ *Dir/Scr* Mark Peploe

L'Afrance ★★★ 15
Drama 2001 · Fr/Sen · Colour · 90min

Acclaimed on the festival circuit, Alain Gomis's debut feature is a charged, compassionate and uncompromising look at the realities facing sub-Saharan exiles in modern France. Torn between a desire to make a difference in his native Senegal and staying in Paris with girlfriend Delphine Zingg, Djolof Mbengue has to battle with the immigration authorities to extend the visa that will enable him to complete his studies. But while Gomis handles this personal history with tact, his primary focus is on the socio-economic pressures that drive so many young African men to endure dead-end jobs and prejudice. **DP** French +subtitles.

A

Djolof Mbengue *El Hadj* • Delphine Zingg *Myriam* • Samir Guesmi *Khalid* • Théophile Moussa Sowié *Demba* • Thierno Ndiaye Doss [Thierno Ndiaye] *Father* ■ *Dir* Alain Gomis • *Scr* Alain Gomis, Pierre Schöller, Marc Wels, Xavier Christiaens, Nathalie Stragier

Africa Screams ★★ U
Comedy 1949 · US · BW · 79min

Abbott and Costello find themselves at the mercy of rampaging lions, cheeky chimps and hostile locals when bookseller Bud persuades explorer Frank Buck that Lou is the big game hunter he needs for his safari. Using every convention of the *Tarzan* movies, this forgettable comedy is as dense as the jungle, with the biggest laughs being Lou's name (Stanley Livingston) and the scene in which he fights off a frisky kitten. DP *DVD*

Bud Abbott *Buzz Johnson* • Lou Costello *Stanley Livingston* • Hillary Brooke *Diana Emerson* • Max Baer *Boots* • Buddy Baer *Grappler* ■ *Dir* Charles Barton • *Scr* Earl Baldwin

Africa United ★★★ 12
Adventure comedy drama
2010 · UK/Rwanda/S Afr · Colour · 84min

In this appealing adventure story for older children, a talented Rwandan teenager has hopes of being selected by FIFA for the 2010 World Cup opening ceremony. But thanks to his bumbling fast-talking pal, the boys end up travelling to South Africa under their own steam. What follows is a portrait of Africa for 12-plus viewers, blending comedy and high jinks with the very real issues affecting the continent – including Aids, poverty and civil conflict. Amazingly, it works pretty well, thanks in no small part to delightful performances from footballing hopeful Roger Nsengiyumva and his motor-mouth "manager" Eriya Ndayambaje. TJ Violence, swearing, sexual references. *DVD*

Eriya Ndayambaje *Dudu* • Roger Nsengiyumva *Fabrice* • Sanyu Joanita Kintu *Beatrice* • Yves Dusenge *Foreman George* ■ *Dir* Debs Gardner-Paterson • *Scr* Rhidian Brook, from a story by Erix Kabera

African Cats ★★★ U
Wildlife documentary 2011 · US · Colour · 85min

In the wake of the remarkable achievements of David Attenborough and Disney's wildlife documentaries, which stretch back to the late 1940s, this most recent effort from Disney and Attenborough's sometime producer Alastair Fothergill takes superb footage of animals on the Masai Mara reserve in Kenya but wraps it up in a storyline that plays like a feline soap opera. The pride of lions is supposedly headed by Fang, though his role model seems to be the Cowardly Lion from *The Wizard of Oz*. Meanwhile, cheetah Sita is struggling to raise five little cubs on her own. The end product is very sentimental and deeply old-fashioned, but the footage of these spectacular animals in their natural habitat is breathtaking. BP

Patrick Stewart *Narrator* ■ *Dir* Alastair Fothergill, Keith Scholey

The African Queen ★★★★★ U
Classic romantic adventure
1951 · UK · Colour · 100min

What an inspired pairing! And to think, Charlie Allnutt and Rose Sayer were nearly played by David Niven and Bette Davis. Initially, all was not well between Katharine Hepburn and Humphrey Bogart – playing a prim missionary and the gin-drinking captain of a small riverboat – but from the moment she began basing her character on Eleanor Roosevelt, the elements fused into a unique screen chemistry, and a gentle humour began to seep into the action, as the pair conduct their own battle against invading Germans in Africa. With director John Huston distracted by extracurricular safaris, the location work was clearly a strain, but the discord and discomfort resulted in a classic, and a long overdue Oscar for Bogart. DP *DVD*

Humphrey Bogart *Charlie Allnutt* • Katharine Hepburn *Rose Sayer* • Robert Morley *Reverend Samuel Sayer* • Peter Bull *German Captain* • Theodore Bikel *German First Officer* • Walter Gotell *German Second Officer* • Gerald Onn *Petty Officer* ■ *Dir* John Huston • *Scr* James Agee, John Huston, from the novel by CS Forester • *Producer* SP Eagle [Sam Spiegel] • *Cinematographer* Jack Cardiff

Afro Saxons ★★
Documentary 2008 · UK · Colour · 84min

Rachel Wang and Mark Currie's documentary follows various hairdressers as they prepare for the annual Black Beauty Awards. However, few concessions are made to those not familiar with this highly competitive but rather insular world. Thai couple George and Apple Kosit (who only style Afro hair) are clearly compelling characters and the action perks up during their sojourn in Paris, but other characters are less interesting. There's some amusing cattiness during the awards ceremony itself, but otherwise this is strictly a salon speciality. DP

■ *Dir/Scr* Mark Currie, Rachel Wang

After Dark, My Sweet ★★★★ 18
Crime thriller 1990 · US · Colour · 111min

This bleak slice of pulp fiction has a brooding central performance from Jason Patric. He plays a washed-up former boxer who gets entangled in a kidnapping being planned by Bruce Dern and sultry Rachel Ward. Director James Foley resists the temptation to put his foot on the throttle and is content to coolly watch the characters as they become locked in a doomed dance of greed and betrayal. JF Violence, swearing, nudity, sex scenes, drug abuse.

Jason Patric *Kevin "Collie" Collins* • Rachel Ward *Fay Anderson* • Bruce Dern *Uncle Bud* • George Dickerson *Doc Goldman* • James Cotton *Charlie* • Corey Carrier *Jack* • Rocky Giordani *Bert* • Jeanie Moore *Nanny* ■ *Dir* James Foley • *Scr* Bob Redlin, from the novel by Jim Thompson

After Darkness ★★ 18
Psychological drama
1985 · UK/Swi · Colour · 104min

This never overcomes the flimsiness of its plot and the transparency of the principal protagonists. In delivering younger brother Julian Sands from an asylum, anthropologist John Hurt seems interested solely in helping him deal with the memory of his twin's death. When student Victoria Abril comes between them, however, it soon becomes clear which sibling is the more troubled. Haunting dreams and mysterious pronouncements litter the action, but the melodramatics aren't persuasive. DP *DVD*

John Hurt *Peter Huninger* • Julian Sands *Laurence Huninger* • Victoria Abril *Pascale* • Pamela Salem *Elisabeth Huninger* • William Jacques *Dr Coles* ■ *Dir/Scr* Dominique Othenin-Girard, Sergio Guerraz

After Earth ★★ 12
Science-fiction adventure
2013 · US · Colour · 95min

Will and Jaden Smith star here as father-and-son astronauts who crash-land on Earth 1,000 years after humanity has left the planet and must overcome the dangers of the now hostile terrain. Smith Sr wrote the story as the first part of a possible trilogy, and it's also clearly intended to elevate his son to star status. However, the plodding plot is told in unimaginative broad strokes, while Smith Jr's inexperience shows in the stilted delivery of his dialogue. Apart from the odd effective sequence, this is nothing but a by-the-numbers survival story peddling contrived emotion, glittering sets and repetitive CGI peril. AJ *DVD*

Will Smith *Cypher Raige* • Jaden Smith *Kitai Raige* • Sophie Okonedo *Faia Raige* • Zoë Isabella Kravitz [Zoë Kravitz] *Senshi Raige* • Glenn Morshower *Commander Velan* ■ *Dir* M Night Shyamalan • *Scr* Gary Whitta, M Night Shyamalan, from a story by Will Smith

After Hours ★★★★ 15
Black comedy 1985 · US · Colour · 93min

Griffin Dunne plays the angst-ridden everyman to manic perfection in this brilliantly original black comedy from director Martin Scorsese. In a spiralling tale of nightmarish persecution and paranoia, Dunne sees his date with unhinged Rosanna Arquette become a rollercoaster ride into urban hell. New York's SoHo district becomes a Kafkaesque labyrinth, populated by avant-garde crazies, bloodthirsty gangsters and flaky *Alice in Wonderland*-style headcases. It's weird, wonderful and wildly funny, and Scorsese won the best director prize at Cannes for his efforts. AJ Violence, swearing, nudity. *DVD* Blu-ray

Griffin Dunne *Paul Hackett* • Rosanna Arquette *Marcy Franklin* • Verna Bloom *June* • Thomas Chong [Tommy Chong] *Pepe* • Linda Fiorentino *Kiki* • Teri Garr *Julie* • John Heard *Tom the bartender* • Richard "Cheech" Marin *Neil* ■ *Dir* Martin Scorsese • *Scr* Joseph Minion • *Cinematographer* Michael Ballhaus

After Life ★★★★ PG
Fantasy drama 1998 · Jpn · Colour · 118min

Japanese director Hirokazu Koreeda's vision of heaven has an irresistible simplicity to match its subtle ingenuity. Set in a spartan transit camp, the action focuses on a celestial film unit as it tries to help various recently departed souls re-create the favourite memory that will be their sole solace in eternity. Beautifully acted by a cast that includes several non-professionals, this is a sublime celebration of life and the everyday joys that make it so worthwhile. DP Japanese +subtitles. Some swearing. *DVD*

Arata Takashi Mochizuki • Erika Oda *Shiori Satonaka* • Susumu Terajima *Satoru Kawashima* • Takashi Naito *Takuro Sugie* ■ *Dir/Scr* Hirokazu Koreeda

After.Life ★★★ 15
Horror thriller 2009 · US · Colour · 98min

Debuting director Agnieszka Wojtowicz-Vosloo keeps everyone guessing in this metaphysical mystery. It's never clear whether mortician Liam Neeson can communicate with the cadavers on his slab, and whether teacher Christina Ricci did perish in a car crash, or has been abducted and injected with a muscle-relaxing drug. The calculated vagueness and convoluted plot do begin to frustrate, along with the coy angles used to film Ricci's often naked body. Nevertheless, Neeson and Ricci achieve a quirky chemistry, while the climax is quietly effective. DP Swearing, nudity. *DVD* Blu-ray

Christina Ricci *Anna Taylor* • Liam Neeson *Eliot Deacon* • Justin Long *Paul* • Chandler Canterbury *Jack* • Celia Weston *Beatrice Taylor* • Josh Charles *Tom* ■ *Dir* Agnieszka Wojtowicz-Vosloo • *Scr* Agnieszka Wojtowicz-Vosloo, Paul Vosloo, Jakub Korolczuk

After Lucia ★★★ 15
Drama 2012 · Mex/Fr · Colour · 97min

Michel Franco follows up the impressive *Daniel & Ana* (2009) with another sickening exposé of Mexican attitudes to intimidation and violence. As much a treatise on grief as bullying, the story centres on a provincial teenager (Tessa Ia), who falls in with a clique of mean girls at her new school when she moves with her chef father (Hernán Mendoza) to Mexico City after the death of her mother. A gruelling saga, made all the more authentic by the terrifying classmates, played by Ia's real-life friends. DP Spanish +subtitles. Violence, swearing, a sex scene, drug abuse. *DVD*

Tessa Ia *Alejandra* • Hernán Mendoza *Roberto* • Gonzálo Vega Sisto *José* • Tamara Yazbek Bernal *Camila* ■ *Dir/Scr* Michel Franco

After Midnight ★★★ 18
Horror 1989 · US · Colour · 88min

This better-than-average horror anthology features three stories that provide a fourth climax. Each tale of terror is told by students on a "psychology of fear" course and involve a haunted mansion, killer dogs, mysterious phone calls (the best section) and zombies. Produced, written and directed by Ken and Jim Wheat (the genre's answer to the Coen brothers), the classic *Dead of Night* format is stirred up with some very convincing special effects to leave the viewer suitably shaken. AJ

Ramy Zeda *Professor Derek* • Jillian McWhirter *Allison* • Pamela Segall *Cheryl* • Nadine Van Der Velde *Joan* • Marc McClure *Kevin* • Marg Helgenberger *Alex* • Billy Ray Sharkey *Ray* ■ *Dir/Scr* Ken Wheat, Jim Wheat

After Midnight ★★
Drama 1990 · UK · Colour · 90min

This tale of a drunken Dublin hotel nightwatchman starts and ends reasonably well, but too much of what is served up in between is misjudged. Saeed Jaffrey turns in a mischievously maudlin performance as the writer whose reasons for abandoning his craft are a secret. However, while his crooked schemes are amusing enough, his treatment of receptionist Hayley Mills and a Chinese prostitute is every bit as objectionable as his racist rivalry with Egyptian night manager Vladek Sheybal. DP

Saeed Jaffrey *Jas* • Hayley Mills *Sally* • Vladek Sheybal *El-Alfi* • Dhirendra *Ranj* • Ian Dury • Maurice O'Donoghue • Patrick Condren ■ *Dir/Scr* Shani Grewal [Shani S Grewal]

After Midnight ★★★ 15
Romantic comedy 2003 · It · Colour · 87min

In this romantic triangle set in Turin's landmark Mole Antonelliana – home of the Museum of Cinema – Giorgio Pasotti is the timid museum caretaker who offers sanctuary to sassy fast-food worker Francesca Inaudi after she pours boiling fat on her boorish boss. Inaudi may be seduced by this repository of vintage exhibits and the clips from the Lumière-era shorts, but viewers may be underwhelmed by the *Jules et Jim*-style melodrama involving her boyfriend, car thief Fabio Troiano. But director Davide Ferrario makes atmospheric use of his surroundings and achieves some splendid digital-video effects. DP Italian +subtitles. Sex scenes. *DVD*

Giorgio Pasotti *Martino* • Francesca Inaudi *Amanda* • Fabio Troiano *"The Angel"* • Francesca Picozza *Barbara* • Silvio Orlando *The narrator* • Pietro Eandi *Martino's grandfather* • Andrea Romero *Fast food owner* • Giampiero Perone *Bruno the night watchman* ■ *Dir/Scr* Davide Ferrario

After Office Hours ★★★
Crime comedy drama 1935 · US · BW · 71min

Clark Gable stars as a newspaper man who, with the aid of his glamorous society-girl-cum-reporter (Constance Bennett) solves a murder. A solidly entertaining example of the then fashionable newsroom genre, when papers were papers and reporters played detective, it was written by Herman J Mankiewicz (later to script *Citizen Kane* with Orson Welles) and directed by one of the studio's slickest craftsmen, Robert Z Leonard. The result is a sparky, witty and fast-moving comedy melodrama. RK

Constance Bennett *Sharon Norwood* • Clark Gable *Jim Branch* • Stuart Erwin *Hank Parr* • Billie Burke *Mrs Norwood* • Harvey Stephens *Tommy Bannister* • Katherine Alexander *Mrs Patterson* • Hale Hamilton *Mr Patterson* • Henry Travers *Cap* ■ *Dir* Robert Z Leonard • *Scr* Herman J Mankiewicz, from a story by Laurence Stallings, Dale Van Every

After the Apocalypse ★★★★ 12A
Documentary 2010 · UK · Colour · 64min

Despite official denials, the Kremlin was fully aware that north-eastern Kazakhstan was inhabited when it tested over 450 atomic devices from 1949-89. As scientists play the blame game, locals are fighting for the right to have babies in the face of insistence that those suffering from chromosomal damage should be prevented from doing so. Exposing both government indifference and scientific arrogance, this deeply disconcerting documentary makes for relentlessly difficult viewing, yet there are still moments of poignancy and defiant optimism. DP Russian, Kazakh +subtitles. Swearing.

■ *Dir* Antony Butts

After the Fall ★★
Drama   2010 · US · Colour · 98min

Triumph-through-adversity dramas are rarely as underwhelming or contrived as this pedestrian TV movie about a paralysed 20-something's journey to recovery. Light on both plot and emotion, it sees bland equestrian competitor Jenna (*Desperate Housewives'* Andrea Bowen) having to learn to function again following a riding accident. What's missing is some skilful heart-tugging, replaced instead by clumsy faith references and simplistic messages of self-belief. SF

Andrea Bowen *Jenna Danville* • Greg Evigan *Phillip Danville* • Alicia Ziegler *Heather Banks* • Fiona Dourif *Annie* • Rick Malambri *Will Dutton* ■ *Dir* Bradford May • *Scr* Wayne Lemon

After the Fox ★★★ U
Comedy   1966 · US/UK/It · Colour · 101min

Peter Sellers stars as a heist-fumbling supercrook, a master of disguise but not of his criminal career, who breaks out of jail to handle the smuggling of loot and to save his film-starlet sister's honour. The pretence of conning police and villagers into landing stolen gold during a movie "shoot" is a hoot, but the script collapses because the writing styles of New Yorker Neil Simon and Italian Cesare Zavattini clash awkwardly. However, the best joke of all is Victor Mature as a fading beefcake star, sending up his own image. TH *DVD*

Peter Sellers *Aldo Vanucci* • Victor Mature *Tony Powell* • Britt Ekland *Gina Romantica* • Martin Balsam *Harry* • Akim Tamiroff *Okra* • Paolo Stoppa *Polio* • Tino Buazzeli *Siepi* • Mac Ronay *Carlo* ■ *Dir* Vittorio De Sica • *Scr* Neil Simon, Cesare Zavattini

After the Night ★★★ 15
Action drama   2013 · Swi/Por · Colour · 99min

Outsiders often offer the keenest insights into a place and here Swiss feature debutant Basil da Cunha certainly captures the unique atmosphere of Lisbon's rundown Reboleira district. The action follows the dreadlocked Sombra (non-actor Pedro Ferreira), who returns from prison to find a tight deadline on an outstanding debt to a gangster. Despite the meandering narrative and muddy photography, this is an intriguing snapshot of ghetto life that makes a virtue of its clichés, caricatures and contrivances. DP Creoles +subtitles. Swearing, some violence, drug abuse.

Pedro Ferreira *Sombra* • Joao Vega *Olos* • Nelson da Cruz Duarte Rodrigues *Nuvem* • Ana Clara Baptista de Melo Soares Barros *Clarinha* • Susana Maria Mendes da Costa *Tia do Sombra* • Jose Zeferino da Cruz *Dr Julio o Bruxo* ■ *Dir/Scr* Basil da Cunha

After the Rehearsal ★★★ 15
Drama   1984 · Swe · Colour · 70min

This chamber drama was originally filmed for television before finally receiving a theatrical release two years into Ingmar Bergman's "retirement". Dozing on a stage dressed for his production of the play, Erland Josephson has encounters with former mistress Ingrid Thulin and aspiring actress Lena Olin. It is Olin who hopes an affair will further her career, despite the revelation her mother once had an affair with the director. Sven Nykvist's tight angles intensify the intrigue, as we wonder how autobiographical Bergman's insights into art and emotion really are. While superbly acted and directed with disciplined economy, this is very much a minor Bergman work. DP Swedish +subtitles. *DVD*

Erland Josephson *Henrik Vogler* • Ingrid Thulin *Rakel Egerman* • Lena Olin *Anna Egerman* ■ *Dir/Scr* Ingmar Bergman • *Cinematographer* Sven Nykvist

After the Storm ★★ 12
Suspense thriller   2001 · US · Colour · 99min

A charismatic Benjamin Bratt stars as a beachcomber who grudgingly joins forces with Armand Assante to salvage the rich pickings of a yacht sunk during a vicious storm. The tropical setting is easy on the eye and Bratt and Mili Avital make a handsome couple. But after a decent opening section, the film gets bogged down by tedious plotting. Less static direction would have helped. JC *DVD*

Benjamin Bratt *Arno* • Armand Assante *Jean-Pierre* • Mili Avital *Conquina* • Simone-Elise Girard *Janine* • Steven Lang *Sgt Major Jim* • Nestor Serrano *Ortega* • Arthur J Nascarella [Arthur Nascarella] *Louie Gavotte* • Jennifer Beals *Mrs Gavotte* ■ *Dir* Guy Ferland • *Scr* AE Hotchner, from a short story by Ernest Hemingway

After the Sunset ★★★ 12
Crime caper   2004 · US · Colour · 93min

A jewel thief is tempted to come out of retirement in a pleasant Caribbean-set caper with Pierce Brosnan and Salma Hayek, plus Woody Harrelson as the FBI man on their trail. Director Brett Ratner offers perhaps more than enough tasteless jokes about suntan-oil application and scenes of Hayek in skimpy swimwear, but the cast's playfulness works within the predictable plot. KK Swearing, sexual references. *DVD*

Pierce Brosnan *Max Burdett* • Salma Hayek *Lola Cirillo* • Woody Harrelson *Stanley P Lloyd* • Don Cheadle *Henri Mooré* • Naomie Harris *Sophie St Vincent* • Chris Penn *Rowdy fan* • Mykelti Williamson *Agent Stafford* • Obba Babatundé [Obba Babatunde] *Zacharias* ■ *Dir* Brett Ratner • *Scr* Paul Zbyszewski, Craig Rosenberg, from a story by Zbyszewski

After the Thin Man ★★★ U
Detective comedy   1936 · US · BW · 107min

In this sequel to *The Thin Man*, William Powell, Myrna Loy and Asta the dog once more waltz through high society, solving three murders between cocktails and sharing bedroom scenes that put witty repartee before any hanky-panky. There's a minor twist with James Stewart playing a meek ex-lover, but it might seem far too slight and slow for modern audiences. This was, however, a big hit in 1936 and the stars still have a considerable amount of charm. *Another Thin Man* followed in 1939. AT *DVD*

William Powell *Nick Charles* • Myrna Loy *Nora Charles* • James Stewart *David Graham* • Elissa Landi *Selma Landis* • Joseph Calleia *Dancer* • Jessie Ralph *Aunt Katherine* • Alan Marshal *Robert* • Teddy Hart *Caspar* ■ *Dir* WS Van Dyke • *Scr* Frances Goodrich, Albert Hackett, from a story by Dashiell Hammett

After the Wedding ★★★ 15
Melodrama   2006 · Den/UK/Swe · Colour · 118min

Danish actor Mads Mikkelsen (*Casino Royale*) reunites with *Open Hearts* director Susanne Bier for this brazenly contrived yet compelling melodrama. Businessman Jorgen (Rolf Lassgard) offers aid worker Jacob (Mikkelsen) a large donation on the condition that he travels to Copenhagen to meet him. Jacob agrees and finds a seemingly spur-of-the-moment invitation throws up some unexpected revelations. Bier's measured direction makes the taciturn Jacob's entrapment by both the manipulative Jorgen and old flame Hélène (Sidse Babett Knudsen) all the more engrossing. DP Danish, Swedish, English, Hindi +subtitles. *DVD*

Mads Mikkelsen *Jacob* • Rolf Lassgard *Jorgen* • Sidse Babett Knudsen *Hélène* • Stine Fischer Christensen *Anna* • Christian Tafdrup *Christian* ■ *Dir* Susanne Bier • *Scr* Anders Thomas Jensen, from a story by Susanne Bier, Jensen

After Tonight ★★★
Romantic spy drama   1933 · US · BW · 69min

Two years after Dietrich and Garbo played exotic Great War spies in *Dishonored* and *Mata Hari*, Constance Bennett is the elusive K-14 in this sluggish but involving melodrama from prolific screenwriter Jane Murfin. Posing as a cabaret singer, a seamstress and a Red Cross nurse, Bennett leads the Austrians a merry dance as she smuggles secrets to her Russian contacts. The cheap-looking sets are at least shrouded in moody shadow, but there's a distinct lack of chemistry between Bennett and her leading man, Gilbert Roland. DP

Constance Bennett *Carla Vaniska* • Gilbert Roland *Capt Rudolph "Rudy" Ritter* • Edward Ellis *Maj Lieber* • Lucien Prival *Lt Erlich* • Dir George Archainbaud • *Scr* Jane Murfin, Albert Shelby Le Vino, Worthington Miner, from a story by Murfin

Afterglow ★★★★ 15
Drama   1997 · US · Colour · 109min

Writer/director Alan Rudolph here delivers a by-turns moving and funny tale of love, loss and relationships for which Julie Christie was nominated for an Oscar. She plays a former B-movie actress who embarks on an affair with a younger man in response to her philandering husband's (Nick Nolte) string of younger lovers. Lara Flynn Boyle and Jonny Lee Miller are the younger couple caught in their own web of adultery and lies, but the show truly belongs to the more seasoned stars, the mesmerising Nolte and Christie, whose performances will wrench your heart. JB Swearing, sexual situations, mild violence.

Nick Nolte *Lucky "Fix-It" Mann* • Julie Christie *Phyllis Mann* • Lara Flynn Boyle *Marianne Byron* • Jonny Lee Miller *Jeffrey Byron* • Jay Underwood *Donald Duncan* • Domini Blythe *Helene Pelletier* • Yves Corbeil *Bernard Omay* • Alan Fawcett *Count Falco/Jack Dana* ■ *Dir/Scr* Alan Rudolph

AfterLife ★★ 15
Drama   2003 · UK · Colour · 100min

In striving to be topical and controversial, debuting director Alison Peebles winds up being merely melodramatic in this dour slice of Scottish life. The film's agenda is established by journalist Kevin McKidd's visit to doctor James Laurenson to investigate his links to a Swiss euthanasia clinic. Thus, the revelation that McKidd's mother has ovarian cancer and that he will become responsible for his Down's syndrome sister comes as no surprise. The cast works hard, but Peebles's storytelling lacks finesse. DP *DVD*

Kevin McKidd *Kenny Brogan* • Lindsay Duncan *May Brogan* • Paula Sage *Roberta Brogan* • Shirley Henderson *Ruby* • James Laurenson *Professor George Wilkinshaw* ■ *Dir* Alison Peebles • *Scr* Andrea Gibb

Afternoon Delight ★★★ 18
Comedy drama   2013 · US · Colour · 93min

This raunchy and refreshingly honest indie focuses on young mother Kathryn Hahn, whose marriage is in a rut. After visiting a strip bar with her surly husband to put the zip back into their love life, Hahn meets teenage stripper Juno Temple and invites the young woman to work as her son's nanny. This can't end well, not least because the story takes some implausible turns. Nevertheless, writer/director Jill Soloway puts a lot of thought into her characters and creates a sexy, truthful comedy. DW Swearing, sex scenes. *DVD*

Kathryn Hahn *Rachel* • Juno Temple *McKenna* • Josh Radnor *Jeff* • Jane Lynch *Dr Lenore* • Jessica St Clair *Stephanie* ■ *Dir/Scr* Jill Soloway

Afterschool ★★★ 18
Drama   2008 · US/Fr · Colour · 106min

Writer/director Antonio Campos's audacious debut feature focuses on the nature of voyeurism and the ethics of image-making. Robert (Ezra Miller) is a student at a top East Coast prep school who seeks refuge from his isolation in the comic, tragic and pornographic clips he finds online. He joins the school video club and loses his virginity to Amy (Addison Timlin), only to become increasingly withdrawn after witnessing the agonising deaths of two twin sisters. Campos is clearly influenced by Gus Van Sant's *Elephant* and the work of Michael Haneke here, and if his film does have a tendency towards minimalist excess, that doesn't detract from it being an undeniably disconcerting piece of work. DP Swearing, sexual references. *DVD*

Ezra Miller *Robert* • Jeremy Allen White *Dave* • Emory Cohen *Trevor* • Rosemarie DeWitt *Ms Vogel* • Christopher McCann *Mr Ullman* • Michael Stuhlbarg *Mr Burke* ■ *Dir/Scr* Antonio Campos

Aftershock ★★★ 18
Disaster horror thriller   2012 · US/Chil · Colour · 87min

In this ambitious mix of disaster and horror, four tourists and their Chilean guides are dancing the night away in a crowded nightclub when a massive earthquake hits. Much of the action is cleverly re-created from real CCTV footage, with co-producer, co-writer and star Eli Roth bringing all his genre knowledge to deliver catastrophe and truly startling bloody shocks on a tight budget. The set-up is a tad overlong and leering exploitation does enter the frame during an extended rape scene, but, as a Roger Corman-style version of *The Impossible*, this is still effective and brutally entertaining. AJ English, Spanish +subtitles. Violence

Eli Roth *Gringo* • Andrea Osvart *Monica* • Ariel Levy *Ariel* • Natasha Yarovenko *Irina* • Nicolás Martinez *Pollo* ■ *Dir* Nicolás López • *Scr* Eli Roth, Guillermo Amoedo, Nicolás López

Against All Flags ★★★ PG
Adventure   1952 · US · Colour · 80min

Errol Flynn is on top late-career form as a British naval officer who gets involved with beautiful buccaneer Maureen O'Hara in a Madagascan pirate stronghold ruled over by the scowling Anthony Quinn. This rollicking costume adventure is generally good fun, with rich Technicolor giving O'Hara's red hair and green eyes an even greater lustre. Though the credited director is George Sherman, it is a little-known fact that Douglas Sirk actually undertook most of the work behind the camera. Remade as *The King's Pirate* with Doug McClure, using footage from this original. TS *DVD*

Errol Flynn *Brian Hawke* • Maureen O'Hara *Spitfire Stevens* • Anthony Quinn *Captain Roc Brasiliano* • Mildred Natwick *Miss MacGregor* • Alice Kelley *Princess Patma* • Robert Warwick *Captain Kidd* ■ *Dir* George Sherman • *Scr* Aeneas MacKenzie, Joseph Hoffman, from a story by MacKenzie

Against All Odds ★★★ 18
Thriller   1984 · US · Colour · 116min

This is a loose remake of the Robert Mitchum/Jane Greer *film noir* classic *Build My Gallows High*, with Jeff Bridges in the pay of, then on the run from, minor mobster James Woods. Greer herself appears as the mother of her original character, now played by Rachel Ward, and Richard Widmark, another familiar face from the *film noir* era, also features. Director Taylor Hackford maintains a moody atmosphere as the action takes in the streets of Los Angeles and the spectacular Mayan ruins of Mexico. AT Violence, sex scenes, drug abuse, nudity. *DVD*

Rachel Ward *Jessie Wyler* • Jeff Bridges *Terry Brogan* • James Woods *Jake Wise* • Alex Karras *Hank Sully* • Jane Greer *Mrs Wyler* • Richard Widmark *Ben Caxton* • Saul Rubinek *Steve Kirsch* • Swoosie Kurtz *Edie* • Dorian Harewood *Tommy* • Pat Corley *Ed Phillips* ■ *Dir* Taylor Hackford • *Scr* Eric Hughes, from the film and novel *Build My Gallows High* by Geoffrey Homes [Daniel Mainwaring]

Against Her Will ★★★ PG
Courtroom drama   1992 · US · Colour · 89min

Subtitled *An Incident in Baltimore*, this stars Walter Matthau, returning to the role he created so memorably in the 1990 TV movie *The Incident*, once again fighting bigotry in 1940s America. He plays an attorney who ruffles more than a few feathers when he takes up the case of a young woman from Greece who has been declared insane by the state government. As with the previous film, there's considerable charm in both the delightful playing of Matthau and the direction of veteran Delbert Mann. Another sequel,

Incident in a Small Town, followed in 1993. JF

Walter Matthau *Harmon Cobb* • Harry Morgan *Judge Stoddard Bell* • Susan Blakely *Billie Cobb* • Ariana Richards *Nancy* • Barton Heyman *Donald* ■ *Dir* Delbert Mann • *Scr* Michael Norell, James Norell

Against the Ropes ★★12
Biographical sports drama
2003 · US/Ger · Colour · 106min

The life story of boxing promoter Jackie Kallen emerges here as an uncertain, ragged mess, hampered by a simplistic script and a strangely unappealing performance from Meg Ryan. Despite the energy injected by Omar Epps as the wannabe champ and Tony Shalhoub's enthusiastic hamming as a sexist rival promoter, this remains a featherweight affair. AS Swearing. *DVD*

Meg Ryan *Jackie Kallen* • Omar Epps *Luther Shaw* • Tony Shalhoub *Sam LaRocca* • Tim Daly [Timothy Daly] *Gavin Reese* • Charles S Dutton *Felix Reynolds* • Kerry Washington *Renee* • Joe Cortese *Irving Abel* ■ *Dir* Charles S Dutton • *Scr* Cheryl Edwards

Against the Wall ★★★18
Prison drama based on a true story
1994 · US · Colour · 110min

The true story of the Attica prison break in the 1970s is turned into a trim, taut and suspenseful pseudo-documentary TV movie, thanks to John Frankenheimer's solid direction and great performances by Samuel L Jackson and Kyle MacLachlan. Taking the perspective of a rookie warden appalled by the awful treatment of prisoners in the facility, Frankenheimer accents the convicts' grievances by having the do-gooder held hostage by rioters. AJ *DVD*

Kyle MacLachlan *Michael Smith* • Samuel L Jackson *Jamaal* • Harry Dean Stanton *Hal* • Anne Heche *Sharon* • Clarence Williams III *Chaka* • Frederic Forrest *Weisbad* • Philip Bosco *Corrections Commissioner Russell Oswald* • Tom Bower *Ed* ■ *Dir* John Frankenheimer • *Scr* Ron Hutchinson

Against the Wind ★★★PG
Spy drama
1947 · UK · BW · 91min

The screenwriter of several classic Ealing comedies, TEB Clarke could turn his hand to several genres, as this tale of spy-school treachery, co-written with Michael Pertwee, proves. Paying tribute to the contribution of saboteurs to the war effort, the film owes a debt to the pseudo-documentary style of such Hollywood thrillers as *The House on 92nd Street*. Jack Warner and Simone Signoret stand out in a cast of dependable character actors, although they are slightly hampered by director Charles Crichton's preoccupation with authentic detail. DP *DVD*

Robert Beatty *Father Phillip* • Simone Signoret *Michele* • Jack Warner *Max Cronk* • Gordon Jackson *Johnny Duncan* • Paul Dupuis *Jacques Picquart* • Gisèle Préville *Julie* • John Slater *Emile Meyer* • James Robertson-Justice *Ackerman* ■ *Dir* Charles Crichton • *Scr* TEB Clarke, Michael Pertwee, from a story by J Elder Wills

Agatha ★★★PG
Drama
1978 · UK/US · Colour · 100min

Director Michael Apted's drama is based on a real-life incident in 1926 when crime novelist Agatha Christie disappeared, casting suspicion on her husband and sparking off a nationwide hunt. Vanessa Redgrave is fine as the redoubtable writer of whodunnits, but Dustin Hoffman is less successful as the American journalist on her trail, and his lack of stature in his scenes with Redgrave is often comical. Apted, meanwhile, ladles on the 1920s style, but loses his way when it comes to plot and suspense, though the overall result is entertaining enough. TH

Vanessa Redgrave *Agatha Christie* • Dustin Hoffman *Wally Stanton* • Timothy Dalton *Archie Christie* • Helen Morse *Evelyn* • Celia Gregory *Nancy Neele* • Tony Britton *William Collins* • Timothy West *Kenward* • Alan Badel *Lord Brackenbury* ■ *Dir* Michael Apted • *Scr* Kathleen Tynan, Arthur Hopcraft, from a story by Tynan

Agatha Christie's A Caribbean Mystery ★★PG
Murder mystery   1983 · US · Colour · 92min

Helen Hayes appears as Miss Marple in a mystery based on one of Agatha Christie's weaker whodunnits, in which the spinster sleuth investigates the death of an elderly major the morning after he revealed a sensational tale of greed and murder to her. Making the best of her miscasting, the 83-year-old Hayes still compares unfavourably with Margaret Rutherford and Joan Hickson, but this TV movie benefits from not having the all-star cast that spoils the guessing game in so many other Christie adaptations. DP

Helen Hayes *Miss Jane Marple* • Barnard Hughes *Mr Rafiel* • Jameson Parker *Tim Kendall* • Season Hubley *Molly Kendall* • Swoosie Kurtz *Ruth Walters* • Cassie Yates *Lucky Dyson* • Zakes Mokae *Captain Daventry* • Stephen Macht *Greg Dyson* ■ *Dir* Robert Michael Lewis • *Scr* Sue Grafton, Steven Humphrey, from the novel by Agatha Christie

Agatha Christie's Murder in Three Acts ★★★
Murder mystery   1986 · US · Colour · 100min

The action may have been shifted from the quiet English resort of Loomouth to Acapulco, but this is still just about recognisable as the novel *Three Act Tragedy*. With vicars and neurologists falling like flies, even Hercule Poirot isn't convinced foul play is afoot until he discovers the dangers of colourless nicotine. A splendid cast of suspects lines up for this TV movie, with Tony Curtis, Lisa Eichhorn and Emma Samms giving nothing away. Peter Ustinov engages the "little grey cells" in what isn't a classic Christie, but it should keep you guessing. DP

Peter Ustinov *Hercule Poirot* • Tony Curtis *Charles Cartwright* • Emma Samms *Jennifer "Egg" Eastman* • Jonathan Cecil *Hastings* • Fernando Allende *Ricardo Montoya* • Pedro Armendáriz Jr *Colonel Mateo* • Lisa Eichhorn *Cynthia Dayton* • Dana Elcar *Dr Walter Strange* ■ *Dir* Gary Nelson • *Scr* Scott Swanton, from the novel *Three Act Tragedy* by Agatha Christie

Agatha Christie's Murder Is Easy ★★PG
Murder mystery   1982 · US · Colour · 95min

What you get is precisely what you see – there are no hidden depths to plummet here in this conveyor-belt made-for-TV movie. Bill Bixby is a computer expert who finds himself caught up in murderous events beyond his ken, while there's a solid supporting cast, plus Lesley-Anne Down as co-star. Easy, undemanding entertainment. SH

Bill Bixby *Luke Williams* • Lesley-Anne Down *Bridget Conway* • Olivia de Havilland *Honoria Waynflete* • Helen Hayes *Lavinia Fullerton* • Patrick Allen *Major Horton* • Shane Briant *Dr Thomas* • Freddie Jones *Constable Reed* • Leigh Lawson *Jimmy Lorrimer* • Jonathan Pryce *Mr Ellsworthy* ■ *Dir* Claude Whatham • *Scr* Carmen Culver, from the novel *Easy to Kill* by Agatha Christie

Agatha Christie's Murder with Mirrors ★★★PG
Murder mystery   1985 · US/UK · Colour · 93min

Director Dick Lowry makes an efficient job of adapting the Queen of Crime's 1952 thriller, *They Do It with Mirrors*. Making her second appearance as Miss Marple, Helen Hayes brought down the curtain on a 75-year screen career by deducing which of the gallery of eccentrics, gathered at a rambling English mansion, intends bumping off John Mills's beloved wife, Bette Davis. Although not one of Christie's best mysteries, it's certainly one of the busiest with countless characters to keep track of and a rather contrived conclusion. DP

Helen Hayes *Miss Jane Marple* • Bette Davis *Carrie Louise* • John Mills *Lewis Serrocold* • Leo McKern *Inspector Curry* • Dorothy Tutin *Mildred* • Anton Rodgers *Dr Max Hargrove* • Frances de la Tour *Ms Bellaver* • Tim Roth *Edgar* ■ *Dir* Dick Lowry • *Scr* George Eckstein, from the novel *They Do It with Mirrors* by Agatha Christie

Agatha Christie's Sparkling Cyanide ★★PG
Murder mystery   1983 · US · Colour · 91min

One of the attractions for Agatha Christie's American fans is her essential Englishness, so it seems odd to transfer the action to Pasadena. With a couple of fatal toasts as its high points, the twisting plot will certainly keep you guessing. However, the tinkering with the original makes the mystery feel forced, and the resolution is not one of the author's best. DP

Anthony Andrews *Tony Browne* • Deborah Raffin *Iris Murdoch* • Pamela Bellwood *Ruth Lessing* • Nancy Marchand *Lucilla Drake* • Josef Sommer *George Barton* • David Huffman *Stephan Farraday* • Christine Belford *Rosemary Barton* • June Chadwick *Sandra Farraday* ■ *Dir* Robert Michael Lewis • *Scr* Robert Malcolm Young, Sue Grafton, Steven Humphrey, from the novel by Agatha Christie

L'Age d'Or ★★★★★15
Satire   1930 · Fr · BW · 62min

Having avowed that *Un Chien Andalou*, his previous collaboration with co-writer and surrealist artist Salvador Dali, meant nothing at all, Luis Buñuel declared that this second surrealist outing was "a desperate and passionate call to murder". He certainly got his wish, as the film caused riots when it premiered in Paris and was banned for 49 years at the insistence of the French fascists. Exploring the themes that would sustain his entire career, Buñuel mercilessly pillories the bourgeoisie, with virtually every scene touching on the conflict between sexual desire and religious and political repression. The satire is both erotic and hilarious and still has the power to provoke. DP French +subtitles. Violence, sexual references. *DVD*

Lya Lys *The woman* • Gaston Modot *The man* • Max Ernst *Bandit Chief* • Pierre Prévert *Péman, a bandit* ■ *Dir* Luis Buñuel • *Scr* Luis Buñuel, Salvador Dali • *Cinematographer* Albert Duverger

Age Isn't Everything ★★★
Comedy drama   1991 · US · Colour · 91min

A twist on the body-swap theme that was so popular in the 1980s has Jonathan Silverman as a disgruntled 25-year-old office worker who turns overnight into an octagenarian with a Yiddish accent. Thoroughly rattled, the young man in an old man's body goes to a host of doctors (including American health guru Dr Joyce Brothers) to see if the effects can be reversed. A strong cast of supporting players, whose faces will be familiar to you even if their names are not, make this dark if sometimes sentimental comedy a touch above the average. FL

Jonathan Silverman *Seymour* • Paul Sorvino *Max* • Rita Moreno *Rita* • Robert Prosky *Seymour's grandfather* • Rita Karin *Seymour's grandmother* • Dr Joyce Brothers ■ *Dir/Scr* Douglas Katz

The Age of Adaline ★★★12
Romantic fantasy drama
2015 · US · Colour · 107min

Hit by lightning in the 1930s, beautiful widow and mother Adaline Bowman (Blake Lively) stops ageing. To avoid suspicion, she changes name, job and location every ten years, but complications ensue when the wrinkle-free beauty falls for a tech entrepreneur. Although photogenic, Lively doesn't have the star power to keep us riveted, especially as the script makes so little of over a century of living. At least, Harrison Ford and Kathy Baker shine in support. KK Some sexual references. *DVD*

Blake Lively *Adaline Bowman* • Michiel Huisman *Ellis Jones* • Harrison Ford *William Jones* • Ellen Burstyn *Flemming* • Kathy Baker *Kathy Jones* • Amanda Crew *Kikki Jones* ■ *Dir* Lee Toland Krieger • *Scr* J Mills Goodloe, Salvador Paskowitz

Age of Consent ★★★15
Romantic drama   1969 · Aus · Colour · 95min

Michael Powell's final feature film is about an artist (James Mason) who runs out of inspiration and retreats to the Great Barrier Reef with his young model (Helen Mirren).

"The film was full of nudity," wrote Powell, "but it is a painter's nudity." Filmed mainly on Dunk Island (now a resort), it is undeniably beautiful and filled with engaging characters. AT *DVD*

James Mason *Bradley Morahan* • Helen Mirren *Cora* • Jack MacGowran *Nat Kelly* • Neva Carr-Glyn *Ma Ryan* • Andonia Katsaros *Isabel Marley* • Michael Boddy *Hendricks* • Harold Hopkins *Ted Farrell* • Clarissa Kaye *Meg* ■ *Dir* Michael Powell • *Scr* Peter Yeldham, from the novel by Norman Lindsay

Age of Heroes ★★★15
Second World War drama based on a true story
2011 · UK · Colour · 89min

The real-life exploits of James Bond creator Ian Fleming are the inspiration for this old-fashioned yet enjoyable wartime adventure. Sean Bean stars as Jones, who's ordered by intelligence officer Fleming (James D'Arcy) to destroy a Nazi communications post in occupied Norway. Bean and Danny Dyer (as a headstrong corporal released from military prison for the operation) butt heads in an engaging manner, and the icy locations are atmospheric, but a hurried ending brings it all to an underwhelming finish. DW Violence, swearing. *DVD* Blu

Sean Bean *Jones* • Izabella Miko *Jensen* • Danny Dyer *Rains* • James D'Arcy *Ian Fleming* • Sebastian Street *Colonel Archer* ■ *Dir* Adrian Vitoria • *Scr* Adrian Vitoria, Ed Scates

The Age of Innocence ★
Period romantic melodrama
1934 · US · BW · 71min

A rising young lawyer in late 19th-century New York falls in love with a woman in the throes of a divorce. Prevented from marrying her by high society's moral constraints, he marries someone else, but continues to see his true love. John Boles and Irene Dunne star in this bowdlerisation of Edith Wharton's famous novel, which is reduced to a small-scale and dreary melodrama under the first-time direction of Philip Moeller. RK

Irene Dunne *Countess Ellen Olenska* • John Boles *Newland Archer* • Lionel Atwill *Julius Beaufort* • Laura Hope Crews *Mrs Welland* • Helen Westley *Granny Mingott* • Julie Haydon *May Welland* • Herbert Yost *Mr Welland* • Theresa Maxwell Conover *Mrs Archer* ■ *Dir* Philip Moeller • *Scr* Sarah Y Mason, Victor Heerman, from the novel by Edith Wharton • *Music* Max Steiner

The Age of Innocence ★★★★U
Period romantic drama
1993 · US · Colour · 132min

Eyebrows were raised when Martin Scorsese announced he was going to adapt Edith Wharton's Pulitzer Prize-winning novel about polite New York society in the 1870s. Yet, influenced by *The Heiress* and *The Magnificent Ambersons*, this is a directorial triumph, with the camera unobtrusively accumulating the small details that help make the story of Newland Archer and the Countess Olenska so compelling. Credit must also go here to cinematographer Michael Ballhaus and production designer Dante Ferretti. Unfortunately, some of the cast, notably Winona Ryder, seem a little stiff; Daniel Day-Lewis and Michelle Pfeiffer, however, excel in conveying the conflict between their passion and their breeding. DP *DVD*

Daniel Day-Lewis *Newland Archer* • Michelle Pfeiffer *Ellen Olenska* • Winona Ryder *May Welland* • Alexis Smith *Louisa van der Luyden* • Geraldine Chaplin *Mrs Welland* • Mary Beth Hurt *Regina Beaufort* • Alec McCowen *Sillerton Jackson* • Richard E Grant *Larry Lefferts* • Miriam Margolyes *Mrs Mingott* • Robert Sean Leonard *Ted Archer* • Sian Phillips *Mrs Archer* • Joanne Woodward *Narrator* ■ *Dir* Martin Scorsese • *Scr* Jay Cocks, Martin Scorsese, from the novel by Edith Wharton

The Age of Stupid ★★★
Part-animated drama documentary
2008 · UK · Colour · 92min

It's the year 2055 and the last man alive (Pete Postlethwaite) is recording a farewell message from an Arctic archive that contains the priceless relics of a doomed species. Summoning up clips on a drag-and-display screen, he laments the ignorance and arrogance of post-millennial humanity, which ignored all the portents and warnings, and continued to consume itself out of existence. Director Franny Armstrong's (*McLibel*) bold drama documentary was filmed in six countries over three years, and her footage has been neatly shaped to seem like the work of diverse individuals. But the message is consistent throughout and Postlethwaite's world-weary fury avoids preaching. Sadly, it's hard to see how this finger-wagging from the future is going to prick the collective conscience of the world's political, commercial and industrial communities. DP *DVD*

Pete Postlethwaite *The archivist* ■
Dir/Scr Franny Armstrong

Age of the Dragons ★★12
Fantasy adventure
2010 · US/UK · Colour · 90min

It must have seemed like a good idea at the time: transform Herman Melville's classic *Moby Dick* into a story about dragons, with Ahab seeking vengeance on the winged beast that killed his family when he was young. It sounds full of promise, but the results are actually far from enticing. *Lethal Weapon* star Danny Glover doesn't put enough passion or menace into Ahab, while Vinnie Jones sleepwalks through his performance as Ahab's chief harpoonist and the CGI dragons vary wildly in quality. Disappointing. KK Violence, gore. *DVD*

Danny Glover *Ahab* · Vinnie Jones *Stubb* · Corey Sevier *Ishmael* · Sofia Pernas *Rachel* · Kepa Kruse [John Kepa Kruse] *Queequeg* · Larry Bagby [Larry Bagby III] *Flask* ■ *Dir* Ryan Little · *Scr* McKay Daines, from a story by Gil Aglaure, Anne Black, from the novel *Moby Dick, or The Whale* by Herman Melville

Age of Uprising: the Legend of Michael Kohlhaas ★★15
Historical drama 2013 · Fr/Ger · Colour · 121min

A powerful central performance and an atmospheric sense of period sadly do little for this bookish take on the tale of Michael Kollhaas, a real-life 16th-century folk hero whose exploits were fictionalised some centuries later by German author Heinrich von Kleist. Mads Mikkelsen brings a proud intensity to the role of Kollhass, but the slow pace soon drains away the drama. Action scenes are intermittent, and with little in the way of political intrigue, it's hard to care by the end of a long two hours for Kollhass and his really rather futile cause. DW In French. Violence, sex scenes

Mads Mikkelsen *Michael Kohlhaas* · Mélusine Mayance *Lisbeth* · Delphine Chuillot *Judith* · David Kross *Preacher* · Bruno Ganz *Governor* ■ *Dir* Arnaud des Pallières · *Scr* Christelle Berthevas, from a novella by Heinrich von Kleist

Agency ★★
Drama 1981 · Can · Colour · 94min

It is one of the tragedies of cinema that movie producers failed to find roles worthy of the great Robert Mitchum in his later years, when his craggy, sleepy-eyed features cried out for a decent film. Here the great Mitch plays a dodgy politician trying to corrupt the world by inserting subliminal messages in TV programmes. Directed by George Kaczender, this is a non-starter. TS

Robert Mitchum *Ted Quinn* · Lee Majors *Philip Morgan* · Valerie Perrine *Brenda Wilcox* · Saul Rubinek *Sam Goldstein* · Alexandra Stewart *Mimi* · Hayward Morse *Tony* · Antony Parr *Charlie* ■ *Dir* George Kaczender · *Scr* Noel Hynd, from the novel by Paul Gottlieb

Agent Cody Banks ★★★12
Action comedy adventure
2003 · US · Colour · 97min

Take the traditional plotline and gadgets of a James Bond movie, add an American TV teen heart-throb, throw in some cheeky laughs and you've got a tasty recipe for a boisterous and enjoyable family romp. *Malcolm in the Middle's* Frankie Muniz plays

a high-school student who's also an undercover CIA agent. His first assignment is to befriend class beauty Hilary Duff and spy on her scientist father (Martin Donovan). Though some of the story elements are a little hard to swallow, there's enough humour and excitement to carry the picture. SF Violence. *DVD*

Frankie Muniz *Cody Banks* · Hilary Duff *Natalie Connors* · Angie Harmon *Ronica Miles* · Keith David *CIA Director* · Cynthia Stevenson *Mrs Banks* · Arnold Vosloo *Molay* · Ian McShane *Brinkman* · Martin Donovan (2) *Dr Connors* ■ *Dir* Harald Zwart · *Scr* Ashley Edward Miller, Zack Stentz, Scott Alexander, Larry Karaszewski, from a story by Jeffrey Jurgensen

Agent Cody Banks 2: Destination London ★★PG
Action comedy adventure
2003 · US · Colour · 95min

In this limp, clichéd junior spy caper sequel, director Kevin Allen delivers a hackneyed, picture-postcard vision of Britain. Frankie Muniz returns as the teen CIA operative, this time posing as a gifted pupil at an exclusive music school to track down a mind-control gadget stolen by rogue agent Keith Allen. There are few dramatic visual diversions, and it's littered with low-level humour, but pre-teens may enjoy the chirpy presence of ex-S Club star Hannah Spearritt. SF *DVD*

Frankie Muniz *Cody Banks* · Anthony Anderson *Derek* · Hannah Spearritt *Emily* · Keith Allen *Diaz* · Cynthia Stevenson *Mrs Banks* · Daniel Roebuck *Mr Banks* · Anna Chancellor *Jo Kenworth* · James Faulkner *Lord Kenworth* ■ *Dir* Kevin Allen · *Scr* Don Rhymer, from a story by Rhymer, Dylan Sellers, Harald Zwart, from characters by Jeffrey Jurgensen

Agent of Influence ★★
Spy drama based on a true story
2002 · Can · Colour · 98min

Lies, betrayal and Cold War paranoia combine in this real-life spy tale that dramatises the disturbing events surrounding the 1964 death of diplomat John Watkins (sympathetically portrayed by Christopher Plummer). Formerly Canadian ambassador to Moscow, Watkins was kidnapped by the CIA as a suspected Soviet double agent, subsequently suffering a fatal heart attack that was officially covered up by his interrogators. Plummer performs particularly well, holding the attention in a plodding and stagey film that's more procedural than eventful. SF

Christopher Plummer *John Watkins* · Marina Orsini *Diane Fletcher* · Ted Whittall *Robert Madison* · Shaun Johnston *David Present* · Kurtis Sanheim *Sean Fitzpatrick* · Alain Goulem *Murray Fletcher* ■ *Dir* Michel Poulette · *Scr* Ian and Riley Adams, from the non-fiction book by Ian Adams

Agent Red ★★18
Action thriller 2000 · US/Can · Colour · 91min

In this tatty low-budget effort, Dolph Lundgren plays a special forces ace assigned to escort a lethal chemical bug from the old USSR to the US. However, Russian terrorists take over the nuclear submarine it is being transported on and it is up Lundgren and naval officer Meilani Paul to retake the craft and its deadly load. Routine stuff with ho-hum action scenes and cringe-inducing dialogue. JF

Dolph Lundgren *Matt Hendricks* · Meilani Paul *Linda Christian* · Alexander Kuznetsov *Kretz* · Natalie Radford *Nadia* · Randolph Mantooth *Admiral Edwards* ■ *Dir* Damian Lee · *Scr* Steve Latshaw, Damian Lee, from a story by Latshaw

The Ages of Lulu ★★★18
Erotic thriller 1990 · Sp · Colour · 96min

This was the first film by Bigas Luna to make an international impact. Having already been rejected by numerous actresses, he found Italian star Francesca Neri willing to accept the challenge of playing the innocent who embarks upon a journey of sexual discovery that takes her into the darkest recesses of her psyche. So explicit it was dismissed by many as tasteless porn, this is a surprisingly moral, if

ironic, film. DP Spanish +subtitles.. Sex scenes, swearing, violence. *DVD*

Francesca Neri *Lulu* · Oscar Ladoire *Pablo* · Maria Barranco *Ely* · Fernando Guillen-Cuervo · Rosana Pastor · Javier Bardem ■ *Dir* Bigas Luna · *Scr* Bigas Luna, Almudena Grandes, from the novel by Grandes

Agnes Browne ★★★15
Period drama 1999 · US/Ire · Colour · 88min

Anjelica Huston both directs and stars in this quirky little movie, set in Dublin in 1967. When her husband dies prematurely, Huston and her seven children are catapulted into an emotional maelstrom. Ekeing out an existence selling fruit and veg in the local market, she borrows cash from unpleasant loan shark Ray Winstone and dreams of attending an upcoming Tom Jones concert. Despite being too cute and rather bizarre, this is a watchable slice of whimsy. LH

Anjelica Huston *Agnes Browne* · Marion O'Dwyer *Marion Monks* · Ray Winstone *Mr Billy* · Niall O'Shea *Mark Browne* · Ciaran Owens *Frankie Browne* · Tom Jones ■ *Dir* Anjelica Huston · *Scr* John Goldsmith, Brendan O'Carroll, from the novel *The Mammy* by O'Carroll

Agnes of God ★★★15
Drama 1985 · US · Colour · 94min

Norman Jewison directs this odd adult drama, which promises more than it delivers. Jane Fonda is her usual forthright self as the court psychiatrist investigating the case of a novice nun (the waif-like Meg Tilly) accused of murdering her baby. It is thanks to the three lead performances – Tilly, Fonda and the always dependable Anne Bancroft – that this sustains interest for as long as it does, but even they cannot cover up what is a rather disappointing ending. JB Swearing. *DVD*

Jane Fonda *Dr Martha Livingston* · Anne Bancroft *Mother Miriam Ruth* · Meg Tilly *Sister Agnes* · Anne Pitoniak *Dr Livingston's mother* · Winston Rekert *Detective Langevin* · Gratien Gelinas *Father Martineau* · Guy Hoffman *Justice Joseph Leveau* · Gabriel Arcand *Monsignor* ■ *Dir* Norman Jewison · *Scr* John Pielmeier, from his play

Agnosia ★★★15
Period drama 2010 · Sp · Colour · 105min

A man is coerced into gaining the trust of a woman who may hold the secret to an industrial marvel in this attractively shot tale from Spain. He begins to fall for her, but cannot bring himself to reveal his true identity. It's an intriguing concept, and the various duplicitous goings-on offer a fair few surprises, while the drama unfurls at an elegant, unhurried pace. Although there is a monstrous element to the woman's behaviour, the tragic but strangely touching way in which the relationship is resolved makes for an arresting conclusion. JH Spanish, German +subtitles. *DVD*

Eduardo Noriega (2) *Carles* · Félix Gómez *Vicent* · Bárbara Goenaga *Joana* · Martina Gedeck *Prevert* · Jack Taylor *Meissner* ■ *Dir* Eugenio Mira · *Scr* Eugenio Mira, Antonio Trashorras

Agony ★★★
Historical epic
1975 · USSR · Colour and BW · 148min

Elem Klimov's take on the last days of the Tsar and the baleful influence of Rasputin blends newly shot colour scenes with archive black-and-white footage from 1916-17. The movie manages to be both documentary and speculation, though that didn't stop the Soviet authorities from banning it in 1975. They allowed it to be shown at the 1981 Moscow film festival, however, where it inevitably created a sensation. Klimov went on to run the Russian film studios. AT Russian +subtitles.

Alexei Petrenko *Rasputin* · Velta Linei *Tsarina Alexandra* · Alisa Freindlikh *Anna Vyrubova* · Anatoly Romashin *Tsar Nicholas II* · A Romantsov *Prince Felix* ■ *Dir* Elem Klimov · *Scr* Semion Lungin, Ilya Nusinov

The Agony and the Ecstasy ★★U
Historical drama 1965 · US · Colour · 133min

There's no doubting the sincerity of those involved in the making of this monumental epic, based on Irving Stone's biography about Michelangelo and the painting of the Sistine Chapel ceiling. This is particularly evident in the playing, notably a self-effacing performance from Charlton Heston. Heston was the cinema's man of action at the time and he's ill-suited to the role of the neurotic artist, no matter how hard he tries. Likewise Rex Harrison's Pope Julius II is more Rex than pontiff. TS *DVD*

Charlton Heston *Michelangelo* · Rex Harrison *Pope Julius II* · Diane Cilento *Contessina de Medici* · Harry Andrews *Bramante* · Alberto Lupo *Duke of Urbino* · Adolfo Celi *Giovanni de Medici* · Venantino Venantini *Paris de Grassis* · John Stacy *Sangallo* ■ *Dir* Carol Reed · *Scr* Philip Dunne, from the novel by Irving Stone · *Cinematographer* Leon Shamroy

Agora ★★★12
Historical drama 2009 · Sp · Colour · 121min

Ancient Alexandria is the setting for this epic drama that stars Rachel Weisz as the little-known astronomer Hypatia. When she comes up with the revolutionary idea that the planets revolve around the sun, she is vilified not just because of her gender but because she is considered a pagan in an increasingly Christian world. Director Alejandro Amenábar (*The Sea Inside*) makes a powerful argument for independent thought over religious faith. However, he does also put his heroine on a pedestal and she often seems aloof. Ultimately it's Hypatia's unswerving passion for science, however, that gives the film its pulse. SP

Rachel Weisz *Hypatia* · Max Minghella *Davus* · Oscar Isaac *Orestes* · Ashraf Barhom *Ammonius* · Michael Lonsdale [Michel Lonsdale] *Theon* · Rupert Evans (2) *Synesius* · Homayoun Ershadi *Aspasius* · Sammy Samir [Sami Samir] *Cyril* ■ *Dir* Alejandro Amenábar · *Scr* Alejandro Amenábar, Mateo Gil

The Agronomist ★★PG
Political documentary
2003 · US · Colour · 87min

Jonathan Demme here charts the life and violent death of Jean Dominique, a former farming scientist who became owner of an independent radio station in Haiti, and thorn in the side of various ruling elites. Demme's unimaginative style uses interview and some archival footage to chart Haiti's violent past, but the history he presents is thin and uninformative, and he's hampered by the fact that Dominique ceased co-operating with the project well before his death. Worthy perhaps, but more than a little dull. AS English, French, Creole +subtitles. *DVD*

■ *Dir* Jonathan Demme

Aguirre, Wrath of God ★★★★★PG
Period drama 1972 · W Ger · Colour · 94min

One of the crowning achievements of the New German Cinema, this movie is a typically haunting Werner Herzog picture in which an eccentric character pursues an overpowering obsession in the most inhospitable of environs. Klaus Kinski dominates the action as the 16th-century conquistador who ruinously rebels against his commander in order to continue his fanatical search for the legendary city of El Dorado. As if shooting in the depths of the Peruvian jungle wasn't difficult enough, the cast wasn't permitted to see the script, and it says much for their improvisational powers that there isn't a single weak performance in the film. DP German +subtitles. *DVD*

Klaus Kinski *Don Lope de Aguirre* · Cecilia Rivera *Flores* · Ruy Guerra *Lieutenant Ursua* · Helena Rojo *Inez* · Del Negro *Brother Gaspar* · Peter Berling *Guzman* · Armando Polanah *Armando* · Daniel Ades *Perucho* · Edward Roland *Okello* ■ *Dir/Scr* Werner Herzog

A

Ah, Wilderness! ★★★
Comedy　　　　　　　1935 · US · BW · 97min

Directed by Clarence "Capability" Brown from Eugene O'Neill's play, this is a typical piece of MGM Americana that enshrines small-town values while concentrating on a boy's first love affair and the advice he (Eric Linden) gets from his pop, Lionel Barrymore. Since Mickey Rooney is in the cast as Linden's annoying younger brother, this looks like a dry run for the Andy Hardy series, which started two years later. It was remade in 1948 as the musical *Summer Holiday*, in which Rooney takes over the starring role of the lovestruck Richard Miller. AT

Lionel Barrymore *Nat Miller* • Aline MacMahon *Lily Davis* • Eric Linden *Richard Miller* • Cecilia Parker *Muriel McComber* • Spring Byington *Essie Miller* • Mickey Rooney *Tommy Miller* • Charles Grapewin [Charley Grapewin] *Mr McComber* • Wallace Beery *Uncle Sid* ■ *Dir* Clarence Brown • *Scr* Albert Hackett, Frances Goodrich, from the play by Eugene O'Neill

Ai Weiwei: Never Sorry
★★★ 15
Documentary　　　　2012 · US · Colour · 90min

Shooting over two years and accorded exceptional access, debuting documentary film-maker Alison Klayman has produced a tantalising and at times inspiring, but rarely penetrating, study of controversial Chinese artist Ai Weiwei. Ai is such a master of self-promotion through his various artistic and social networking activities that he consistently sets the agenda, leaving Klayman merely to record rather than question or assess. Fascinating, but frustrating. DP English, Mandarin +subtitles. Swearing. *DVD* BL

■ *Dir/Scr* Alison Klayman

Aileen: Life and Death of a Serial Killer ★★★ 15
Documentary　　　　2003 · UK · Colour · 90min

This follow-up to documentary film-maker Nick Broomfield's *Aileen Wuornos: the Selling of a Serial Killer* is an uncomfortable affair. While the original film was an exposé of the garish media circus that surrounded the trial of America's most prolific female serial killer, this companion piece comes dangerously close to being part of the problem rather than its solution. Broomfield revisits the story as he testifies in an appeal against the death sentence that Wuornos, who murdered seven men, seems doomed to receive. Broomfield is, to his own obvious discomfort, not in control of this depressing final act of a ruined, pitiable life, but this documentary may be more admirable than his more recent fare precisely for that reason. AS *DVD*

Aileen Wuornos ■ *Dir* Nick Broomfield, Joan Churchill • *Cinematographer* Joan Churchill

Aileen Wuornos: the Selling of a Serial Killer ★★★ 18
Documentary　　　　1992 · UK · Colour · 87min

It's ironic that Charlize Theron won her Oscar for playing Aileen Wuornos in *Monster* on the birthday of "America's first female serial killer". All the more so considering the rumpus caused back in 1991 by the revelation that several people involved in the case had attempted to cash in on its notoriety. Exploiting his trademark on-screen disingenuity, Nick Broomfield exposes the cynical greed of Aileen's lawyer, adoptive mother and numerous Florida cops. He also makes shrewd use of courtroom footage to suggest the Angel of Death was herself a victim. But Broomfield was to prove equally culpable of exploitation in the sequel, *Aileen Wuornos: Life and Death of a Serial Killer*. DP Swearing, sexual references. *DVD*

Aileen Wuornos ■ *Dir* Nick Broomfield

Aimée and Jaguar ★★★ 15
Second World War romantic drama
1999 · Ger · Colour · 121min

Based on the true story of the wartime relationship between model mother Lilly Wurst and Jewish lesbian Felice Schragenheim, this study of the indomitability of the lovers and the insidiousness of Nazism might have been more persuasive had debuting director Max Färberböck devoted more time to period authenticity. There may be air raids and Gestapo patrols, but the nitty-gritty of life in 1943 Berlin is missing and this undermines the good efforts of Juliane Köhler and Maria Schrader. Melodramatic, but engrossing. DP German +subtitles. *DVD*

Maria Schrader *Felice Schragenheim, "Jaguar"* • Juliane Köhler *Lilly Wust, "Aimée"* • Johanna Wokalek *Ilse* • Heike Makatsch *Klärchen* • Elisabeth Degen *Lotte* • Detlev Buck *Günther Wust* ■ *Dir* Max Färberböck • *Scr* Max Färberböck, Rona Munro, from the novel by Erica Fischer

L'Aîné des Ferchaux ★★★
Crime drama　　　　1963 · Fr/It · Colour · 102min

Released with the English title *Magnet of Doom*, this is one of Jean-Pierre Melville's lesser known features. Although it opens in Paris, much of the action takes place between New York and New Orleans, as failed boxer Jean-Paul Belmondo seeks to swindle his employer, Charles Vanel, out of the ill-gotten gains that have forced the financier to flee France. Although the pair have their adventures on the road, most notably with hitcher Stefania Sandrelli and stripper Michèle Mercier, the emphasis is firmly on the unexpected bond that develops between these unlikely accomplices. DP French +subtitles.

Jean-Paul Belmondo *Michel Maudet* • Charles Vanel *Dieudonné Ferchaux* • Michèle Mercier *Lou* • Malvina Silberberg *Lina* • Stefania Sandrelli *Angie* • Barbara Sommers *Lou's friend* ■ *Dir* Jean-Pierre Melville • *Scr* Jean-Pierre Melville, from the novel by Georges Simenon

Ain't Misbehavin' ★★ U
Musical comedy　　　1955 · US · Colour · 81min

Rory Calhoun co-stars with Piper Laurie in this somewhat flimsy excuse for a musical with an unmistakeable nod in the direction of *Pygmalion*. He's a millionaire, she's a chorus girl determined to acquire some education and social polish. Edward Buzzell directs the forgettable but agreeable proceedings. Best of the otherwise long-forgotten songs is Fats Waller's famous number, from which the movie takes its title. RK

Rory Calhoun *Kenneth Post* • Piper Laurie *Sarah Hatfield* • Jack Carson *Hal North* • Mamie Van Doren *Jackie* • Reginald Gardiner *Piermont Rogers* • Barbara Britton *Pat* • Dani Crayne *Millie* • Harris Brown *Randall* ■ *Dir* Edward Buzzell • *Scr* Edward Buzzell, Philip Rapp, Devery Freeman, from the story *Third Girl from the Right* by Robert Carson

Ain't Them Bodies Saints
★★★ 15
Drama　　　　　　　2013 · US · Colour · 92min

The aftermath of a failed robbery puts Texas sweethearts Casey Affleck and Rooney Mara on separate sides of prison bars in this atmospheric 1970s-set drama that harks back to the work of director Robert Altman. Writer/director David Lowery eschews many of the obvious confrontations when Affleck escapes, allowing us time to perceive the characters' highly individual blend of skewed morals and grand passion. Affleck and Mara fail to supply that vital electric charge, but the gracefully burnished images and compelling electro-acoustic score suggest that Lowery is a film-maker of rich promise. TJ Violence, some swearing. *DVD*

Rooney Mara *Ruth Guthrie* • Casey Affleck *Bob Muldoon* • Ben Foster *Patrick Wheeler* • Keith Carradine *Skerritt* • Nate Parker *Sweetie* • Rami Malek *Will* ■ *Dir/Scr* David Lowery

Air America ★★★ 15
Action comedy　　　1990 · US · Colour · 107min

This was originally conceived as a blackly satirical comedy by *The Stunt Man* director Richard Rush, but that idea went out the window in favour of a more obviously commercial approach. Roger Spottiswoode took over the directorial reins and the result was an amiable, if somewhat patchy, action comedy. Set in Laos during the Vietnam War, the story follows the adventures of a CIA-organised air freight operation, which was actually smuggling heroin on behalf of local drug barons. JF Violence, swearing. *DVD*

Mel Gibson *Gene Ryack* • Robert Downey Jr *Billy Covington* • Nancy Travis *Corinne Landreaux* • Ken Jenkins *Major Donald Lemond* • David Marshall Grant *Rob Diehl* • Lane Smith *Senator Davenport* • Art La Fleur [Art LaFleur] *Jack Neely* ■ *Dir* Roger Spottiswoode • *Scr* John Eskow, Richard Rush, from the non-fiction book by Christopher Robbins

Air Bud ★★★ U
Sports comedy adventure
1997 · US/Lux/Can · Colour · 93min

Meet Air Bud, the 1990s version of Lassie, in this cute family adventure about a sporty dog who is promoted from team mascot to basketball player. While parents will be more impressed by the animal acrobatics, youngsters will be entertained by the plot, in which a lonely young boy and the dog's abusive owner fight for custody of the talented pooch. With a canine story that's both appealing and amusing, this is particularly suitable for younger viewers. Four sequels followed. JB *DVD*

Michael Jeter *Norm Snively* • Kevin Zegers *Josh Framm* • Wendy Makkena *Jackie Framm* • Bill Cobbs *Arthur Chaney* • Eric Christmas *Judge Cranfield* • Jay Brazeau *Referee No 1* • Nicola Cavendish *Principal Pepper* ■ *Dir* Charles Martin Smith • *Scr* Paul Tamasy, Aaron Mendelsohn, from the character created by Kevin DiCicco

Air Cadet ★★ U
Aviation drama　　　1951 · US · BW · 93min

Directed with brisk efficiency by Joseph Pevney, this movie about pilots training might have been more interesting had the emphasis been on the cadets' backgrounds and not on cocky Richard Long's affair with major Stephen McNally's estranged wife, Gail Russell. The aerial action is better than anything at the Texas air base, but there's not enough of it. DP

Stephen McNally *Major Jack Page* • Gail Russell *Janet Page* • Alex Nicol *Joe Czanoczek* • Richard Long *Russ Coulter* • Charles Drake *Captain Sullivan* • Robert Arthur (1) *Walt Carver* ■ *Dir* Joseph Pevney • *Scr* Joseph Hoffman, Robert L Richards, from a story by Robert W Soderberg, Richards

Un Air de Famille ★★★★ 15
Comedy drama　　　1996 · Fr · Colour · 105min

Adapted by Jean-Pierre Bacri and Agnès Jaoui from their own play, Cédric Klapisch's bourgeois comedy focuses on the spiteful sparring of three siblings unable to shoulder the responsibility for their own disappointments. Cleverly exploiting his claustrophobic set by keeping camera movements to a minimum, Klapisch relies on neat touches rather than grand flourishes, while his use of reflective surfaces recalls the films of Douglas Sirk and Rainer Werner Fassbinder. The performances are uniformly excellent, though the tipsy Catherine Frot steals the show. DP French +subtitles. Swearing, violence.

Jean-Pierre Bacri *Henri Menard* • Agnès Jaoui *Betty Menard* • Jean-Pierre Darroussin *Denis* • Catherine Frot *Yolande, Philippe's wife* • Claire Maurier *Mother* • Wladimir Yordanoff *Philippe Menard* ■ *Dir* Cédric Klapisch • *Scr* Cédric Klapisch, Agnès Jaoui, Jean-Pierre Bacri, from the play by Jaoui, Bacri

Air Force ★★★★ PG
Second World War drama
1943 · US · BW · 119min

This marvellous wartime drama from one of Hollywood's greatest directors, Howard Hawks, is not as famous as his *Scarface*, *The Big Sleep* or *Rio Bravo*, but is still a major achievement. It tells the story of the Mary Ann, a Flying Fortress, and the men who operated her in the war against the Japanese. The action sequences are excitingly filmed, though it is the quieter moments, when the members of the crew express their excitement and their fears, that give the film its strength as a study of comradeship in adversity. AT *DVD*

John Ridgely *Captain Mike Quincannon* • Gig Young *Lt Bill Williams* • Arthur Kennedy *Lt Tommy McMartin* • Charles Drake *Lt Munchauser* • Harry Carey *Sgt Robby White* • George Tobias *Cpl Weinberg* • Ward Wood *Cpl Peterson* • John Garfield *Sgt Joe Winocki* ■ *Dir* Howard Hawks • *Scr* Dudley Nichols

Air Force One ★★★★ 15
Action thriller　　　1997 · US · Colour · 119min

Hollywood loves putting the US president into its movies, and who better to play him as an action hero than Harrison Ford. When the First Family is held hostage on board the Presidential jumbo jet by a ruthless gang of Russian terrorists led by Gary Oldman, Ford decides to fight back and escapes into the plane's hold. Meanwhile Vice President Glenn Close is left to take Oldman's phone calls in Washington. A stunt-filled thriller that's brimming with nasty villains and daring deeds. SuR Swearing, violence. *DVD* BL

Harrison Ford *President James Marshall* • Gary Oldman *Ivan Korshunov* • Glenn Close *Vice President Kathryn Bennett* • Wendy Crewson *Grace Marshall* • Liesel Matthews *Alice Marshall* • Paul Guilfoyle (2) *Chief of Staff Lloyd Shepherd* • Xander Berkeley *Agent Gibbs* • William H Macy *Major Caldwell* • Dean Stockwell *Defense Secretary Walter Dean* • Jürgen Prochnow *General Radek* ■ *Dir* Wolfgang Petersen • *Scr* Andrew W Marlowe

Air Guitar Nation ★★★ 15
Documentary　　　　2006 · US · Colour · 78min

Every year since 1996, the planet's finest air guitarists gather in Oulu, Finland, to pick, pluck and windmill their way to possible world champion status. This wry, entertaining documentary follows the entrance of American hopefuls into the competition in 2003, from the US finals to the grand "air-off" in Finland, where European purists of the phantom plectrum were becoming concerned that their increasing dominance might compromise the form's essential purity. Alexandra Lipsitz directs briskly, letting the array of eccentrics and likeable enthusiasts – all of whom seem to be well aware of the obvious ludicrousness of their passion – speak for themselves. AS Swearing. *DVD*

Peter Cilella *Clayton Sweeney* • Dan Crane *Dan "Bjorn Turoque" Crane* • Gordon Hintz *Krye Tuff* • David S Jung *C-Diddy* • Angela Shelton *Cherry Vanilla* ■ *Dir* Alexandra Lipsitz • *Cinematographer* Anthony Sacco

The Air I Breathe ★★ 15
Romantic crime drama
2007 · US · Colour · 91min

Like *Crash*, *Babel* and *Magnolia*, this convoluted thriller throws interlinked narratives together to illustrate the enigmatic workings of fate. Forest Whitaker (Happiness), Brendan Fraser (Pleasure), Sarah Michelle Gellar (Sorrow) and Kevin Bacon (Love) play the four characters whose disparate lives intersect in a structure based on the four pillars of life according to an Asian proverb, a thematic affectation that weighs proceedings down to an insufferable degree. Music-video director-turned-film-maker Jieho Lee imbues his feature debut with plenty of visual verve, yet can't make his stories individually distinctive. In the end, this tells us little about fate, but quite a lot about pretentious storytelling. JR Violence, swearing, sexual references. *DVD*

Kevin Bacon *Love* • Julie Delpy *Gina* • Brendan Fraser *Pleasure* • Andy Garcia *Fingers* • Sarah Michelle Gellar *Sorrow* • Emile Hirsch *Tony* • Forest Whitaker *Happiness* ■ *Dir* Jieho Lee • *Scr* Jieho Lee, Bob DeRosa

Air Mail ★★
Adventure　　　　　1932 · US · BW · 83min

Director John Ford is more famous for his westerns, but this is his tribute to the pilots who flew the early air mail service across the West. In fact, this remains a typical Ford western in terms of theme and plot, with planes replacing the old Pony Express. Like the best Ford movies, there's lots of hard drinking and bonhomie on the ground and heroics in the air, but it's all pretty routine. AT

Pat O'Brien *Duke Talbot* • Ralph Bellamy *Mike Miller* • Gloria Stuart *Ruth Barnes* • Lillian Bond *Irene Wilkins* • Russell Hopton *Dizzy Wilkins* • Slim Summerville *Slim McCune* • Frank Albertson *Tommy Bogan* ■ *Dir* John Ford • *Scr* Dale Van Every, Frank W Wead [Frank Wead], from a story by Wead

The Air Up There ★★PG
Sports comedy 1993 · US · Colour · 107min

In this so-so basketball movie, Kevin Bacon plays the ambitious coach who heads for Africa to sign up exceptional athlete Charles Gitonga Maina. However, the latter is a local prince and is more interested in protecting his village than shooting hoops. The film is low on belly laughs, despite the plucky playing of Bacon, and the serious bits are just plain mawkish. On the plus side, director Paul Michael Glaser stages the basketball sequences with some style. JF
DVD

Kevin Bacon *Jimmy Dolan* • Charles Gitonga Maina *Jimmy Saleh* • Yolanda Vazquez *Sister Susan* • Winston Ntshona *Urudu* • Mabutho "Kid" Sithole *Nyaga* • Sean McCann *Coach Ray Fox* • Dennis Patrick *Father O'Hara* ■ *Dir* Paul Michael Glaser • *Scr* Max Apple

Airborne ★★★PG
Sports drama 1993 · US · Colour · 86min

Forced to move with his family from California to Cincinnati, laid-back teenager Shane McDermott swaps surfing the waves for rollerblading in the streets to impress his archenemy's sister. This formulaic teen comedy plot is given a welcome makeover by a likeable cast, and the stunt work is thrilling, especially a hair-raising downhill rollerblade chase through heavy traffic. AJ

Shane McDermott *Mitchell Goosen* • Seth Green *Wiley* • Brittney Powell *Nikki* • Chris Conrad *Jack* • Edie McClurg *Aunt Irene* • Patrick O'Brien [Patrick Thomas O'Brien] *Uncle Louie* ■ *Dir* Rob Bowman • *Scr* Bill Apablasa, from a story by Stephen McEveety, Apablasa

Airborne ★18
Action thriller 1997 · Can · Colour · 89min

Steve Guttenberg gets all mean and moody as the head of an elite squad of commando types, who is assigned to track down an international crook threatening to hold the world to ransom with some sort of secret virus. However, can they trust their own employers? Sean Bean manages to stay out of sight for most of the movie. Excruciating tosh. JF Violence, swearing.

Steve Guttenberg *Bill McNeil* • Kim Coates *Bob Murdoch* • Torri Higginson *Sara Gemmel* • Philip Akin *Romeo Cortez* • David Fraser *Mr Samuels* • Sean Bean *Dave Toombs* ■ *Dir* Julian Grant • *Scr* Tony Johnston, Julian Grant

Airheads ★★★15
Comedy 1994 · US · Colour · 88min

A dumb heavy metal band finds fame by hijacking a local radio station in director Michael Lehmann's broad *Wayne's World*-style comedy that lacks the goofy cleverness of that blockbuster hit. Brendan Fraser ably heads the head-banging brigade, with amusing support from dim-witted Adam Sandler and long-haired Steve Buscemi. Never quite as funny as it thinks it is, the amiable anarchy does sometimes hit the screwball spot. AJ Swearing. *DVD*

Brendan Fraser *Cazz* • Steve Buscemi *Rex* • Adam Sandler *Pip* • Chris Farley *Wilson* • Joe Mantegna *Ian* • Michael McKean *Milo* • Judd Nelson *Jimmie Wing* • Ernie Hudson *Sergeant O'Malley* • Amy Locane *Kayla* • Nina Siemaszko *Suzzi* ■ *Dir* Michael Lehmann • *Scr* Rich Wilkes

Airplane! ★★★★★PG
Disaster movie spoof 1980 · US · Colour · 84min

The first, and still the best, of Zucker, Zucker and Abrahams's wonderful movie send-ups. There's hardly a second that passes without an assault by a wickedly accurate spoof, a cringe-inducing pun or inspired sight gag, and the years have not diminished its dumb appeal. Robert Hays

and Julie Hagerty are the nominal stars, but the most fun is had by the distinguished supporting cast. It's the film that made a comedy star out of Leslie ("don't call me Shirley") Nielsen, but a whole troupe of veteran character actors also have a hugely enjoyable time sending up their screen personae. JF Some swearing. *DVD* *Blu* CS

Robert Hays *Ted Striker* • Julie Hagerty *Elaine Dickinson* • Leslie Nielsen *Dr Rumack* • Lloyd Bridges *McCroskey* • Robert Stack *Rex Kramer* • Kareem Abdul-Jabbar *Roger Murdock* • Peter Graves (2) *Captain Oveur* ■ *Dir/Scr* Jim Abrahams, David Zucker, Jerry Zucker

Airplane II: the Sequel ★★15
Comedy 1982 · US · Colour · 80min

Airplane! was always going to be a hard act to follow and this time the scattergun approach to the script carries more misfires and duds than normal. Still, the two leads from the original (Robert Hays and Julie Hagerty) are back on board again and the silliness of it all should win people over. This time the flimsy storyline revolves around the first commercial flight to the Moon. JF Some swearing, brief nudity. *DVD* CS

Robert Hays *Ted Striker* • Julie Hagerty *Elaine* • Lloyd Bridges *McCroskey* • Peter Graves (2) *Captain Oveur* • William Shatner *Murdock* • Chad Everett *Simon* • Sonny Bono *Bomber* • Raymond Burr *Judge* • Chuck Connors *Sarge* • Jack Jones (2) *Singer* ■ *Dir/Scr* Ken Finkleman

Airport ★★★PG
Disaster movie 1970 · US · Colour · 130min

This sprawling disaster movie was brilliantly spoofed in 1980's *Airplane!*, but it's still competent, soapy entertainment. Burt Lancaster, Dean Martin, George Kennedy and the rest of the starry cast (including an Oscar-winning Helen Hayes) are commendably serious throughout, as blizzards and bombs present crises on the ground and in the air. JF *DVD* *Blu*

Burt Lancaster *Mel Bakersfeld* • Dean Martin *Vernon Demerest* • Jean Seberg *Tanya Livingston* • Jacqueline Bisset *Gwen Meighen* • George Kennedy *Joe Patroni* • Helen Hayes *Ada Quonsett* • Van Heflin *DO Guerrero* • Maureen Stapleton *Inez Guerrero* ■ *Dir* George Seaton, Henry Hathaway • *Scr* George Seaton, from the novel by Arthur Hailey

Airport 1975 ★★★PG
Disaster movie 1974 · US · Colour · 101min

When a light aircraft makes an unscheduled landing in the cockpit of a jumbo jet – the 747 being aloft at the time – it causes something of a panic among the surviving crew and passengers. Stewardess Karen Black takes the controls while Gloria Swanson, Myrna Loy and Sid Caesar gibber quietly in the back, and a sick child (played by *The Exorcist*'s Linda Blair) is soothed by a singing nun. Meanwhile, on the ground, George Kennedy talks into a microphone and Charlton Heston prepares to … Well, parting the Red Sea was nothing compared to this stunt. AT Swearing. *DVD*

Charlton Heston *Alan Murdoch* • Karen Black *Nancy* • George Kennedy *Joseph Patroni* • Gloria Swanson • Helen Reddy *Sister Ruth* • Efrem Zimbalist Jr *Captain Stacy* • Sid Caesar *Barney* • Linda Blair *Janice Abbott* • Dana Andrews *Scott Freeman* • Myrna Loy *Mrs Devaney* ■ *Dir* Jack Smight • *Scr* Don Ingalls

Airport '77 ★★★PG
Disaster movie 1977 · US · Colour · 108min

This is the third in the popular midair disaster series and it's one of the best, thanks to a stellar cast led by Jack Lemmon, James Stewart, Joseph Cotten and Olivia de Havilland. The veterans simply sit around and look classy, but Lemmon has to work a tad harder as he tackles a hijack attempt led by co-pilot Robert Foxworth. Not the most nail-biting film you'll ever see, but still entertaining. DP *DVD*

Jack Lemmon *Don Gallagher* • Lee Grant *Karen Wallace* • Brenda Vaccaro *Eve Clayton* • Joseph Cotten *Nicholas Stone III* • Olivia de Havilland *Emily Livingston* • Darren McGavin *Stan Buchek* • Christopher Lee *Martin Wallace* • James Stewart *Philip Stevens* • George Kennedy *Joe Patroni* • Robert Foxworth *Chambers* ■ *Dir* Jerry

Jameson • *Scr* Michael Scheff, David Spector, from a story by HAL Craig, Charles Kuenstle, inspired by the novel *Airport* by Arthur Hailey

Airport '79: the Concorde ★★PG
Disaster movie 1979 · US · Colour · 108min

The fourth *Airport* movie goes supersonic and has more disaster-packed moments than the average genre entry. Pilots George Kennedy and Alain Delon have to deal with a missile chasing the plane, an emergency landing with no brakes, various explosions and a crash-landing into snow. It's very silly, of course, but the starry cast manages to be as over-the-top as the effects, making this fun if mindless. JB Some swearing.
DVD

Alain Delon *Captain Paul Metrand* • Susan Blakely *Maggie Whelan* • Robert Wagner *Dr Kevin Harrison* • Sylvia Kristel *Isabelle* • George Kennedy *Joe Patroni* • Eddie Albert *Eli Sande* • Bibi Andersson *Francine* • Charo *Margarita* • John Davidson *Robert Palmer* • Cicely Tyson *Elaine Gilbert* • David Warner *Peter O'Neill* • Mercedes McCambridge *Nelli* ■ *Dir* David Lowell Rich • *Scr* Eric Roth, Jennings Lang, inspired by the novel *Airport* by Arthur Hailey

Airspeed ★PG
Action adventure 1997 · Can · Colour · 84min

In this low-budget movie, Robert Tinnell takes all the clichés that Jim Abrahams and the Zucker brothers had so mercilessly spoofed in *Airplane!* and plays them dead straight. But you won't be able to keep a straight face for long, as the brattish Elisha Cuthbert takes the controls of daddy Joe Mantegna's private plane after a storm does for the cabin crew. Unmissably awful. DP *DVD*

Elisha Cuthbert *Nicole Stone* • Joe Mantegna *Raymond Stone* • Andrea Prescott *Bronwen Booth* • Lynne Adams (2) *Marilyn Stone* ■ *Dir* Robert Tinnell • *Scr* Richard Goudreau, Roc Lafortune, from a novel by Andrew Sands

Aitraaz ★★★12
Courtroom drama 2004 · Ind · Colour · 159min

This engrossing tale, reminiscent of Barry Levinson's *Disclosure*, is a real change of pace for Akshay Kumar, who stars here as a happily married executive accused of sexual harassment by an old flame, played by former Miss World Priyanka Chopra. The ex-beauty queen is a diabolical delight, slinking and strutting her way through the role of the unscrupulous vamp, while Kumar is both compelling and restrained as the man treated as guilty until proven innocent. OA Hindi +subtitles. *DVD*

Akshay Kumar *Raj Malhotra* • Kareena Kapoor *Priya* • Priyanka Chopra *Sonia Sharma* • Annu Kapoor *Ram Choitrani* • Paresh Rawal *Mr Patel* • Amrish Puri *Ranjit Roy* ■ *Dir* Abbas, Mustan • *Scr* Shyam Goel, Shiraz Ahmed, from their story

Ajami ★★★15
Drama 2009 · Ger/Is/UK · Colour · 120min

Palestinian Scandar Copti and Israeli Yaron Shani impress as co-directors of this Oscar-nominated drama, which provides a sobering insight into the macho culture ruling the mean streets of a multi-ethnic neighbourhood in the Israeli city of Jaffa. Copti and Shani handle their material with great confidence but their determination to be both even-handed and audacious renders this disappointingly conventional in its discussion of the hatred, frustration and violence fuelling the political reality. DP Arabic, Hebrew +subtitles. Violence, swearing, drug abuse.

Shahir Kabaha *Omar* • Youssef Sahwani *Abu Elias* • Fouad Habash *Nasri* • Ibrahim Frege *Malek* • Ranin Karim *Hadir* ■ *Dir/Scr* Scandar Copti, Yaron Shani

Ake and His World ★★★★
Drama 1984 · Swe · Colour · 99min

The terrors that intrude upon the idylls of childhood are explored in this charming tale of village life, set in 1930s Sweden. Martin Lindström is outstanding as the six-year-old boy convinced by the portent of an extinguished candle that he'll be severely punished for accidentally endangering the

life of a neighbour's son. As in *Elvira Madigan*, Jörgen Persson's glossy photography romanticises the action, but this doesn't diminish the film's genuine warmth and humanity. DP Swedish +subtitles.

Martin Lindström *Ake* • Loa Falkman *Father* • Gunnel Fred *Mother* • Katja Blomquist *Sister* • Ulla Sjoblom *Grandma* • Suzanne Ernrup *Anne-Marie* • Bjorn Gustafson *Bergstrom* • Alexander Skarsgård *Kalle* • Stellan Skarsgård *Ebenholtz* ■ *Dir* Allan Edwall • *Scr* Allan Edwall, from the novel by Bertil Malmberg

Akeelah and the Bee ★★★PG
Social drama 2006 · US · Colour · 108min

Spelling is the key to community cohesion in this simplistic but sincere wish-fulfilment drama. Keke Palmer is wonderful as the talented 11-year-old African-American girl who gradually finds the self-belief to ignore her mocking classmates and sceptical mother (Angela Bassett) and enter a televised spelling bee. Crucial to Akeelah's inspirational journey is Laurence Fishburne as her reluctant coach, whose dignified performance helps bolster the film's commendable message. Although the plot is predictable, descending into naïve fantasy as gang members stop their shady activities to root for their local spelling star, it's hard not to get drawn in. SF Some swearing.
DVD

Laurence Fishburne *Dr Larabee* • Angela Bassett *Tanya Anderson* • Keke Palmer *Akeelah Anderson* • Curtis Armstrong *Mr Welch* • Ma Tzi *Mr Chiu* • Lee Thompson Young *Devon* ■ *Dir/Scr* Doug Atchison • *Cinematographer* M David Mullen

Akenfield ★★12
Documentary drama 1974 · UK · Colour · 97min

Sir Peter Hall, one of modern theatre's more innovative directors, clearly felt up to adapting Ronald Blythe's memoir of life in a sleepy Suffolk farming community for a full-length film. But while the largely non-professional cast provides some fascinating insights, the contrasts with their Edwardian ancestors often feel laboured. Moreover, Ivan Strasburg's lyrical widescreen imagery and Michael Tippett's lush score seem unsuited to such a simple tale. It's a bold experiment, but too stylised and sentimental to succeed. DP *DVD* *Blu*

Garrow Shand *Tom Rouse/Old Tom* • Peggy Cole *Dulcie Rouse* • Barbara Tilney *Jean Quantrill* • Lyn Brooks *Charlotte Rouse* • Ida Page *Aunt Ida* • Ted Dedman *Ted* • Charlie Cornish *Charlie* ■ *Dir* Peter Hall • *Scr* Ronald Blythe, from his book • *Cinematographer* Ivan Strasburg • *Music* Michael Tippett

Akira ★★★★15
Animated science-fiction fantasy 1988 · Jpn · Colour · 119min

This is the movie that really broke *manga* in the West and remains one of the gems of the genre. Directed, co-scripted and designed by Katsuhiro Otomo from his own comic strip, it's a pacey, unrelentingly violent post-apocalyptic adventure, in which a gang of Neo-Tokyo slum kids attempts to counter the telekinetic machinations of a rogue buddy. Yet, for all its futuristic elements, this is also a dark and disturbing portrait of contemporary urban life that seeks to expose the lack of empathy between the establishment and modern youth. The cityscapes are awesome, the camerawork is dizzying. If you're new to *manga*, prepare to be converted. DP Japanese +subtitles. Swearing. *DVD* *Blu*

■ *Dir* Katsuhiro Otomo • *Scr* Izo Hashimoto, Katsuhiro Otomo, from Otomo's graphic novel

Akira Kurosawa's Dreams ★★18
Fantasy drama 1990 · Jpn · Colour · 114min

This is one of the Japanese master's weakest films, though still demonstrating the stylistic versatility and genius for composition that characterises his previous works. Here, the 80-year-old Kurosawa reveals a regrettable tendency towards self-indulgence and political naivety. Although

A

his environmentalism is heartfelt, the messages contained in the eight vignettes that make up the film are muddled and often pompously expressed. There is great beauty to be found, however, notably in the vibrant colours of the *Crows* segment, featuring Martin Scorsese as Vincent van Gogh. **DP** Japanese +subtitles.

Akira Terao *"I"* • Mitsuko Baisho *Mother of "I"* • Mieko Harada *Snow fairy* • Yoshitaka Zushi *Private Noguchi* • Martin Scorsese *Vincent van Gogh* • Toshie Negishi *Mother carrying child* • Chosuke Ikariya *Weeping demon* • Chishu Ryu *103-year-old man* ■ *Dir/Scr* Akira Kurosawa

Al Capone ★★★★ 15

Biographical crime drama
1959 · US · BW · 104min

Rod Steiger was a natural to play Al Capone, the gangster finally imprisoned for tax evasion rather than slaughter on the streets of Chicago. Steiger, of course, brings all his Method mannerisms to play and it's fascinating to compare his portrayal with later ones by Jason Robards (*The St Valentine's Day Massacre*) and Robert De Niro (Brian De Palma's *The Untouchables*). Directed by Richard Wilson, a former associate of Orson Welles, the picture revived interest in Capone, and led to the TV series of *The Untouchables*. **AT**

Rod Steiger *Al Capone* • Fay Spain *Maureen Flannery* • Martin Balsam *Keely* • James Gregory *Tom Schaeffer* • Murvyn Vye *Bugs Moran* • Nehemiah Persoff *Johnny Torrio* • Joe De Santis *Big Jim Colosimo* • Lewis Charles *Hymie Weiss* ■ *Dir* Richard Wilson (1) • *Scr* Marvin Wald, Henry Greenberg

Al Jennings of Oklahoma ★★ U

Biographical western 1951 · US · Colour · 77min

The real-life Al Jennings was born in 1863 in Virginia, trained as a lawyer and, after one of his brothers was killed, drifted into crime, serving time in jail. He eventually made his way to Hollywood and became an actor and film-maker. His autobiography is the notional source of this serviceable western, with Ray Nazarro directing in his usual brisk manner. This is myth-making of the most calculating but diverting kind. **DP**

Dan Duryea *Al Jennings* • Gale Storm *Margo St Claire* • Dick Foran *Frank Jennings* • Gloria Henry *Alice Calhoun* • Guinn "Big Boy" Williams *Lon Tuttle* • Raymond Greenleaf *Judge Jennings* • Stanley Andrews *Marshal Slattery* ■ *Dir* Ray Nazarro • *Scr* George Bricker, from the autobiography by Al Jennings, Will Irwin

Aladdin ★★★★★ U

Animated musical adventure
1992 · US · Colour · 95min

For a full-length cartoon featuring some remarkably hip animation, it's amazing how Robin Williams's performance as the Genie steals the show, his ad-lib voicing a perfect match for the beautifully constructed Disney visuals. In this *Arabian Nights* tale, Aladdin (voiced by Scott Weinger) is the street urchin who uses a magical oil lamp and its wish-granting genie to win the love of Princess Jasmine (Linda Larkin, Lea Salonga singing) and defeat the evil Jafar (Jonathan Freeman). Kids will be enchanted by this captivating fable, while adults will appreciate the film's delightful songs and sophisticated references. **TH DVD Blu**

Scott Weinger *Aladdin* • Robin Williams *Genie* • Linda Larkin *Jasmine* • Jonathan Freeman (1) *Jafar* • Frank Welker *Abu/Narrator* • Gilbert Gottfried *Iago* • Douglas Seale *Sultan* • Lea Salonga *Jasmine* ■ *Dir* John Musker, Ron Clements • *Scr* Ron Clements, John Musker, Ted Elliot, Terry Rossio

Aladdin and the King of Thieves ★★★★ U

Animated adventure 1996 · US · Colour · 78min

In this sequel to the 1992 Disney animated adventure *Aladdin*, Robin Williams returns to give the same sharp voice characterisation to the Genie, helping young Aladdin when he discovers that his father is actually the leader of the "40 Thieves". Adults will be just as entertained

as the youngsters, thanks to a well thought-out plot and witty vocals. **JB DVD CS**

Robin Williams *Genie* • Scott Weinger *Aladdin* • Linda Larkin *Jasmine* • John Rhys-Davies *Cassim* • Gilbert Gottfried *Iago* • Jerry Orbach *Sa'luk* • Val Bettin *Sultan* • Frank Welker *Abu* ■ *Dir* Tad Stones • *Scr* Mark McCorkle, Robert Schooley

Alamar ★★★ PG

Drama 2009 · Mex · Colour · 70min

Chronicling five-year-old Natan Machado Palombini's summer sojourn with his father Jorge, Pedro González-Rubio's pseudo-documentary is a touching study of father-son bonding and an insight into the fragile ecosystem of the Banco Chinchorro coral reef off Mexico's Caribbean coast. This compelling record of a unique lifestyle is beautifully captured, but the fact that several incidents have been staged at the director's suggestion leaves the viewer wondering what's real and what's contrived. **DP** Spanish, Italian +subtitles. **DVD**

Jorge Machado *Jorge* • Natan Machado Palombini *Natan* • Néstor Marin *Matraca* • Roberta Palombini *Roberta* ■ *Dir/Scr* Pedro González-Rubio

The Alamo ★★★★ PG

Historical war drama
1960 · US · Colour · 154min

A local priest said a prayer for the production on the first day of shooting, and some said John Wayne's directorial debut needed it. Filmed on a ranch in Brackettville, Texas, where a facsimile was built of the actual mission that saw the most famous battle for Texas independence, this was less a pet project for Wayne and more of an obsession. Taking the role of Davy Crockett only to secure backing, he nonetheless adds heft to an already strong cast. The result, historically sketchy, oozes poignancy and high drama, allowing humour into the mix. Unable to live up to its own publicity, it remains a powerful old-school epic made with passion. **AC DVD**

John Wayne *Colonel David Crockett* • Richard Widmark *Colonel James Bowie* • Laurence Harvey *Colonel William Travis* • Richard Boone *General Sam Houston* • Frankie Avalon *Smitty* • Patrick Wayne *Captain James Butler Bonham* • Linda Cristal *Flaca* • Joan O'Brien *Mrs Dickinson* • Chill Wills *Beekeeper* • Joseph Calleia *Juan Seguin* ■ *Dir* John Wayne • *Scr* James Edward Grant

The Alamo ★★ 12

Historical war drama
2004 · US · Colour · 131min

Many are familiar with the bare facts of the Alamo and how, in 1836, a handful of Texans mounted a suicidal defence of a former mission against the Mexican army. It's a crucial episode in US history and part of the national psyche, but it would be hard to divine exactly why from this lengthy account. Heavy on character and light on exposition, this reduces events to buckskin fringes and big knives, but the starry cast is a draw. **KK** Violence. **DVD**

Dennis Quaid *Sam Houston* • Billy Bob Thornton *Davy Crockett* • Jason Patric *Jim Bowie* • Patrick Wilson *William Travis* • Emilio Echevarría *Antonio López de Santa Anna* • Jordi Mollà *Juan Seguin* • Leon Rippy *Sergeant William Ward* • Tom Davidson *Colonel Green Jameson* ■ *Dir* John Lee Hancock • *Scr* Leslie Bohem, Stephen Gaghan, John Lee Hancock

Alamo Bay ★★★ 15

Drama based on a true story
1985 · US · Colour · 94min

French director Louis Malle made a better study of racism in his acclaimed 1987 film *Au Revoir les Enfants*, but he also tackled the subject to decent effect two years earlier. This examines the conflict between a group of Vietnamese refugees and a Texan shrimp-fishing community, whose members feel threatened by the competition from the hard-working newcomers. Amy Madigan stands out as the on-again, off-again girlfriend (and real-life wife) of chief racist thug Ed Harris. **PF** Some swearing.

Amy Madigan *Glory Scheer* • Ed Harris *Shang Pierce* • Nguyen Ho Dinh • Donald Moffat *Wally Scheer* • Tran Truyen V *Ben* • Rudy Young *Skinner* • Cynthia Carle *Honey* • Martino Lasalle [Martin Lasalle] *Luis* • William Frankfather *Mac* • Lucky Mosley *Ab Crankshaw* • Bill Thurman *Sheriff* ■ *Dir* Louis Malle • *Scr* Alice Arlen

Alan & Naomi ★★★ PG

Period drama 1992 · US · Colour · 91min

This small but touching film has youngsters Lukas Haas and Vanessa Zaoui playing two Jewish children in 1940s New York. Haas is instructed to befriend new neighbour Zaoui, deeply disturbed since she was forced to watch her father's death at the hands of the Nazis. He is initially resistant, but the two children develop a lasting friendship. Debut director Sterling Van Wagenen handles his cast with ease and the result is poignant if a little stagey. **LH**

Lukas Haas *Alan Drucker Silverman* • Vanessa Zaoui *Naomi Kirschenbaum* • Michael Gross *Sol Silverman* • Amy Aquino *Ruth Silverman* • Kevin Connolly *Shaun Kelly* ■ *Dir* Sterling Van Wagenen • *Scr* Jordan Horowitz, from a novel by Myron Levoy

Alan Partridge: Alpha Papa ★★★★ 15

Comedy 2013 · UK · Colour · 86min

No one can accuse Steve Coogan of rushing into a big-screen transfer for his endearingly deluded TV and radio presenter (who debuted in 1991). Here, with his radio station taken over and rebranded by a media conglomerate and fellow DJ Colm Meaney sacked, Alan finds himself acting as mediator in a police siege that inadvertently earns him viral notoriety. Declan Lowney (*Father Ted*) directs the hilarious script with unfussy economy, while Coogan's vanity-free performance is a perpetual turbine. This may not travel further than Cromer, but it's so refreshing to see a British comedy that thinks small and stays local. **AC** Swearing. **DVD Blu**

Steve Coogan *Alan Partridge* • Felicity Montagu *Lynn Benfield* • Simon Greenall *Michael* • Colm Meaney *Pat Farrell* • Tim Key *Simon* • Phil Cornwell *Dave Clifton* ■ *Dir* Declan Lowney • *Scr* Neil & Rob Gibbons

The Alarmist ★★ 15

Comedy crime drama 1997 · US · Colour · 87min

Uncertain pacing and a surfeit of plot padding make Evan Dunsky's indie comedy feel like a neat short that unnecessarily sprawled into mediocrity. David Arquette mugs madly as a home security salesman who becomes convinced that crooked boss Stanley Tucci is responsible for the death of his girlfriend (Kate Capshaw). Tucci revels in his Terry-Thomas villainy, but even he can't enliven the clumsy finale. **DP** Swearing, sex scenes, violence.

David Arquette *Tommy Hudler* • Stanley Tucci *Heinrich Grigoris* • Kate Capshaw *Gale Ancona* • Mary McCormack *Sally* • Ryan Reynolds *Howard Ancona* • Tricia Vessey *April* • Ruth Miller *Mrs Fielding* • Hoke Howell *Mr Fielding* • Lewis Arquette *Bruce Hudler* • Richmond Arquette *Andrew Hudler* ■ *Dir* Evan Dunsky • *Scr* Evan Dunsky, from the play *Life during Wartime* by Keith Reddin

Alaska ★★★ PG

Action adventure 1996 · US · Colour · 104min

Fraser Heston directs his father Charlton in this well-made family adventure about a young brother and sister searching for their missing dad (*The A-Team's* Dirk Benedict) in the Alaskan wilderness. Instead they discover an adorable baby polar bear that's being hunted by a ruthless poacher (Heston). Breathtaking scenery, a deliciously evil portrayal from Chuck and energetic performances from the kids (Thora Birch and Vincent Kartheiser) make this an enjoyable adventure. **JB**

Thora Birch *Jessie Barnes* • Vincent Kartheiser *Sean Barnes* • Dirk Benedict *Jake Barnes* • Charlton Heston *Perry* • Duncan Fraser *Koontz* • Gordon Tootoosis *Ben* • Ben Cardinal *Charlie* • Ryan Kent *Chip* ■ *Dir* Fraser C Heston • *Scr* Andy Burg, Scott Myers

Albatross ★★★ 15

Coming-of-age drama 2011 · UK · Colour · 86min

Screenwriter Tamzin Rafn's fixation with Emily Lloyd in David Leland's *Wish You Were Here* is evident throughout this spirited if unfocused rite-of-passage tale. Jessica Brown Findlay takes on the Lloyd mantle as a wise-before-her-years teenager who counters her boredom by embarking on an affair with a married man (Sebastian Koch) in a seaside town, so jeopardising her friendship with her lover's studious daughter (Felicity Jones). There are few surprises in director Niall MacCormick's debut feature, but a trip to Oxford has its amusing moments. **DP** Swearing, sex scenes, brief nudity. **DVD**

Felicity Jones *Beth* • Sebastian Koch *Jonathan* • Jessica Brown Findlay *Emelia* • Julia Ormond *Joa* • Peter Vaughan *Grandpa* • Harry Treadaway *Jake* ■ *Dir* Niall MacCormick • *Scr* Tamzin Rafn

Albert Nobbs ★★★ 15

Period drama
2011 · UK/Ire/Fr/US · Colour · 109min

This intriguing tale represents a labour of love for Glenn Close, who takes on the title character 30 years after appearing in the off-Broadway play. She stars as a woman who lives as a male servant in 19th-century Dublin, ostensibly to earn a crust in hard times. But as the story unfolds, it's suggested that Nobbs feels protected in men's clothes. She only yearns for liberation after meeting a more bullish transvestite (Janet McTeer, bringing a touch of lightness) and aims to start afresh by courting a housemaid for a wife. The lure of the story is in trying to work out what drives Nobbs to extremes. What frustrates, though, is that even with a captivating performance by the star, the servant remains inscrutable beneath that starched collar. **SP** Some swearing, sex scenes. **DVD**

Glenn Close *Albert Nobbs* • Mia Wasikowska *Helen* • Aaron Johnson *Joe* • Brendan Gleeson *Holloran* • Janet McTeer *Hubert Page* • Jonathan Rhys Meyers *Viscount Yarrell* • Pauline Collins *Mrs Baker* ■ *Dir* Rodrigo García [Rodrigo Garcia] • *Scr* Glenn Close, John Banville, Gabriella Prekop, from a story by István Szabó, from a novella *The Singular Life of Albert Nobbs* by George Moore

Albert, RN ★★★ U

Second World War drama
1953 · UK · BW · 88min

This PoW drama is about a mannequin nicknamed Albert which supposedly stands in for escaped prisoners. A huge hit at the time, it still has bags of charm and a degree of tension, though a starrier cast than the wooden Anthony Steel and American expats such as William Sylvester would have helped considerably. But all is not lost: Anton Diffring plays a Nazi. **AT**

Anthony Steel *Lt Geoffrey Ainsworth* • Jack Warner *Capt Maddox* • Robert Beatty *Lt Jim Reid* • William Sylvester *Lt "Texas" Norton* • Michael Balfour *Lt Henry Adams* • Guy Middleton *Capt Barton* • Anton Diffring *Hauptmann Schultz* ■ *Dir* Lewis Gilbert • *Scr* Vernon Harris, Guy Morgan, from the play by Morgan, Edward Sammis

Albino Alligator ★★ 18

Crime drama 1996 · US/Fr · Colour · 92min

Highly acclaimed actor Kevin Spacey turned director for this far too theatrical and cerebral hostage thriller. An amateur gang, led by Matt Dillon, flees a disastrous heist and holes up in an all-night bar. Tension rises and tempers fray among the lowlifes and drunks being tended to by barmaid Faye Dunaway, as the police surround the place and wait for the criminals to buckle. The over-ripe dialogue and claustrophobic confines of the stagey scenario soon become stifling. **AJ** Swearing, violence. **DVD**

Matt Dillon *Dova* • Faye Dunaway *Janet Boudreaux* • Gary Sinise *Milo* • Viggo Mortensen *Guy Foucard* • Joe Mantegna *GD Browning* • M Emmet Walsh *Dino* • John Spencer *Jack* • William Fichtner *Law* • Skeet Ulrich *Danny Boudreaux* ■ *Dir* Kevin Spacey • *Scr* Christian Forte

The Alchemist ★ 18
Horror   1981 · US · Colour · 83min

The gates of hell are opened when an old woman incants an ancient spell to free her father from the curse of eternal youth. And what's on the other side? Two men running around wearing dodgy demon rubber masks and a couple of awful special effects! Robert Ginty stars in this tedious occult nonsense from straight-to-video horror maestro Charles Band. AJ

Lucinda Dooling *Lenora* • Robert Ginty *Aaron* • Bob Glaudini [Robert Glaudini] *DenGatto* • John Sanderford • Viola Kate Stimpson ■ *Dir* Charles Band • *Scr* Alan J Adler

Aldrich Ames: Traitor Within ★★★ PG
Spy drama based on a true story
1998 · US · Colour · 97min

Made for cable, this is a fascinating account of one of the USA's most notorious double agents, who betrayed the CIA for years for money. Frustrated by lack of promotion and ridden with debt, Aldrich Ames (Timothy Hutton) starts selling agents' names to the enemy. Joan Plowright is the methodical investigator on his tail, while Elizabeth Peña plays his unsuspecting wife. British director John Mackenzie cranks up the suspense, but this is really Hutton's show. JF Some swearing.

Timothy Hutton *Aldrich Ames* • Elizabeth Peña *Rosario Ames* • Joan Plowright *Jeanne Vertefeuille* • Eugene Lipinski *Vlad* • Robert Benedetti *Chief of Operations* • C David Johnson *Brooks* • Patricia Carroll Brown *Connie Dru* ■ *Dir* John Mackenzie (1) • *Scr* Michael Burton

Alex & Emma ★★ 12
Romantic comedy   2003 · US · Colour · 91min

The genesis of Dostoyevsky's novella *The Gambler* is the inspiration for Rob Reiner's feeble romantic comedy. Luke Wilson is devoid of passion, both as the writer trying to pen a bestseller to pay off his gambling debts to some Cuban thugs and as the hero of his 1920s-set story, who is in love with Sophie Marceau's society sophisticate. Kate Hudson overcompensates as the stenographer helping him meet his deadline and as the various maids who bewitch him in the dictation sequences. DP Sex scenes. *DVD*

Kate Hudson *Emma Dinsmore/Ylva/Elsa/Eldora/Anna* • Luke Wilson *Alex Sheldon/Adam Shipley* • Sophie Marceau *Polina Delacroix* • David Paymer *John Shaw* • Rob Reiner *Wirschafter* • Cloris Leachman *Grandmother* • Rip Taylor *Polina's father* ■ *Dir* Rob Reiner • *Scr* Jeremy Leven

Alex and the Gypsy ★★
Romantic drama   1976 · US · Colour · 98min

Jack Lemmon stars as a bailbondsman who falls for one of his clients, gypsy Geneviève Bujold, after she's accused of nearly killing her husband. It's a story of two of society's drop-outs and sits comfortably within the counterculture era. Lemmon seems to be reprising his Oscar-winning performance in *Save the Tiger*, while Bujold is no less of a cliché, that of the European free spirit. It might have worked better had it been played for black comedy instead of schmaltz. AT

Jack Lemmon *Alexander Main* • Geneviève Bujold *Maritza* • James Woods *Crainpool* • Gino Ardito *Golfer* • Robert Emhardt *Judge* • Joseph X Flaherty *Morgan* • Todd Martin *Roy Blake* ■ *Dir* John Korty • *Scr* Lawrence B Marcus, from the novella *The Bailbondsman* by Stanley Elkin

Alex Cross ★★ 15
Mystery thriller   2012 · US · Colour · 97min

Tyler Perry has made a fortune from his *Madea* series of films, in which he plays a mouthy grandmother in a floral-print dress. This makes him an unusual choice to take on the role of homicide detective/forensic psychologist Alex Cross, previously played by Morgan Freeman in *Kiss the Girls* and *Along Came a Spider*. Set in Detroit, the film follows Cross as he hunts a sadistic killer who begins to target the cop's nearest and dearest. Matthew Fox makes a suitably unhinged baddie but this is a thoroughly

ordinary thriller, featuring an incoherent plot and some laughably dumb dialogue. DA Violence, swearing, drug references. *DVD* *Blu-ray*

Tyler Perry *Alex Cross* • Matthew Fox *Picasso* • Edward Burns *Thomas Kane* • Rachel Nichols *Monica Ashe* • Cicely Tyson *Nana Mama* ■ *Dir* Rob Cohen • *Scr* Marc Moss, Kerry Williamson, from the novel *Cross* by James Patterson

Alex in Wonderland ★
Comedy   1970 · US · Colour · 111min

Paul Mazursky directs this horribly self-indulgent and self-conscious bomb about the far-out dilemma of a hippy director searching for a follow-up to his first successful movie. Donald Sutherland plays the navel-gazing auteur who takes LSD for inspiration, pokes fun at 1960s Hollywood and then fantasises about meeting Fellini (who appears as himself, along with Jeanne Moreau). AJ

Donald Sutherland *Alex* • Ellen Burstyn *Beth* • Federico Fellini • Jeanne Moreau • Meg Mazursky *Amy* • Glenna Sergent *Nancy* • Andre Philippe *André* • Michael Lerner *Leo* • Paul Mazursky *Hal Stern* ■ *Dir* Paul Mazursky • *Scr* Larry Tucker, Paul Mazursky

Alexander ★★ 15
Historical biographical drama
2004 · Ger/UK/Neth/US/It/Fr · Colour · 159min

Director Oliver Stone spent 15 years trying to bring the story of military genius Alexander the Great to the big screen. How sad, then, that an obvious labour of love should end up such a pompous and flaccid affair. The film presents key events in the life of the golden-haired Macedonian conqueror (played by Colin Farrell), each lazily linked by the reminiscences of his ageing general, Ptolemy (Anthony Hopkins). The visual detail is meticulous, but this sterling work is undone by preposterous dialogue and leaden performances. SF Violence. *DVD*

Colin Farrell (2) *Alexander* • Angelina Jolie *Olympias* • Val Kilmer *Philip* • Anthony Hopkins *Ptolemy* • Jared Leto *Hephaistion* • Rosario Dawson *Roxane* • Christopher Plummer *Aristotle* ■ *Dir* Oliver Stone • *Scr* Oliver Stone, Christopher Kyle, Laeta Kalogridis

Alexander and the Terrible, Horrible, No Good, Very Bad Day ★★★ PG
Comedy   2014 · US · Colour · 80min

At a lean, mean 80 minutes, Disney's latest live-action family comedy is somewhat shorter than its title. Treading much the same territory as the *Wimpy Kid* films, it stars Steve Carell and Jennifer Garner in the dad and mum roles, and at the core of the chaos is son Ed Oxenbould. He's just had the day from hell. It's now his 12th birthday and, frustrated by a schoolmate's plan to stage a rival mega-party, he wishes that his family could feel what a worst-ever day feels like, too... The movie sometimes spreads its comedy a little thin, but it's big-hearted and, ultimately, upbeat. DA Brief swearing.

Steve Carell *Ben* • Jennifer Garner *Kelly* • Ed Oxenbould *Alexander* • Dylan Minnette *Anthony* • Kerris Dorsey *Emily* • Dick Van Dyke ■ *Dir* Miguel Arteta • *Scr* Rob Lieber, from Judith Viorst's illustrated children's book

Alexander Nevsky ★★★★ PG
Historical epic   1938 · USSR · BW · 104min

The Soviet equivalent to Laurence Olivier's *Henry V*, this historical epic was to serve as propaganda against Hitler's Reich. However, just as Sergei Eisenstein completed the story of the Teutonic invasion of Russia in the 13th century, Stalin and Hitler signed a non-aggression pact, so the film was withdrawn. Then, when Hitler broke the treaty, Stalin ordered the film into release. It is famous for two things – the battle at the frozen lake, filmed in high summer, and Prokofiev's score. Both are worthy of their reputations, but this is offset by some turgid storytelling and excessively theatrical acting. AT Russian +subtitles. *DVD*

Nikolai Cherkassov *Prince Alexander Yaroslavich Nevsky* • Nikolai P Okhlopkov *Vassily Buslai* • Alexandr L Abrikossov *Gavrilo Olexich* ■ *Dir* Sergei Eisenstein • *Scr* Sergei Eisenstein, Pyotr Pavlenko • *Cinematographer* Edouard Tissé

Alexander the Great ★★ U
Epic historical drama
1956 · US/Sp · Colour · 129min

This epic promises more than it delivers, though Richard Burton makes a fair stab at depicting the conqueror of half the known world, even if he remains no match for Fredric March's Philip of Macedonia (Alexander's father). The use of early CinemaScope is superb, as is the deployment of the armies of extras and the key scene of slicing the Gordian knot, but Robert Rossen's long and static movie is wordy and ponderous. TS *DVD*

Richard Burton *Alexander* • Fredric March *Philip of Macedonia* • Claire Bloom *Barsine* • Danielle Darrieux *Olympias* • Barry Jones *Aristotle* • Harry Andrews *Darius* • Stanley Baker *Attalus* • Peter Cushing *Memnon* • Michael Hordern *Demosthenes* ■ *Dir/Scr* Robert Rossen

Alexander's Ragtime Band ★★★ U
Musical   1938 · US · BW · 101min

It doesn't matter that handsome Tyrone Power shows no sense of rhythm, or that the plot is pure hokum, or that the First World War is over in a montage that's quicker than a wink. No... what matters is that this is a glorious Irving Berlin songfest, with Alice Faye and a young Ethel Merman belting out some of Tin Pan Alley's best and brightest. Unfortunately, there is a plot, and it's 20th Century-Fox's old triangular one: guess who gets Alice - Ty or his best friend, Don Ameche? TS

Tyrone Power *Roger Grant* • Alice Faye *Stella Kirby* • Don Ameche *Charlie Dwyer* • Ethel Merman *Jerry Allen* • Jack Haley *Davey Lane* • Jean Hersholt *Professor Heinrich* • Helen Westley *Aunt Sophie* • John Carradine *Taxi driver* ■ *Dir* Henry King • *Scr* Kathryn Scola, Lamar Trotti

Alexandra ★★★★ PG
War drama   2007 · Rus/Fr · Colour · 90min

As the son of a Red Army veteran, director Aleksandr Sokurov spent his youth on military bases across the Soviet Union. He clearly draws on his own experiences in this paean to patriotism set against the backdrop of the Chechen conflict. Opera singer Galina Vishnevskaya excels as the haughty old Russian woman appalled by the conditions that her soldier grandson has to endure at a camp outside Grozny, but also with an empathy for the enemy. DP Russian, Chechen +subtitles. *DVD*

Galina Vishnevskaya *Alexandra Nikolaevna* • Vasily Shevtsov *Denis* • Raisa Gichaeva *Malika* ■ *Dir/Scr* Aleksandr Sokurov

Alexandria Encore ★★★★
Documentary drama
1990 · Fr/Egy · Colour · 100min

Youssef Chahine's cinema-inspired work is a dazzling, if occasionally self-indulgent, treatise on the process of film-making. Chahine stars as a director assessing his achievements during a period of creative block brought on by a row with the star of his proposed production of *Hamlet*. With a Hollywood song-and-dance spectacular recalling the night he triumphed at Berlin, and flashbacks to an unrealised musical homage to Alexander the Great, this is a witty yet wistful exploration of age, authorship, cinematic art and popular taste. An elegant and engaging piece. DP Arabic +subtitles.

Youssef Chahine • Yousra • Hussein Fahmy • Amr Abdel Guelil ■ *Dir/Scr* Youssef Chahine

Alexandria Why? ★★★★
Second World War drama
1979 · Egy/Alg · Colour · 132min

Youssef Chahine, Egypt's most respected film-maker and the man who "discovered" Omar Sharif, directs this stylish wartime tale, which won the Special Jury prize at Berlin. It focuses on a movie-mad schoolboy (Mohsen Mohiedine), obsessed with

Hollywood musicals at a time when everyone else is preoccupied with the advance of Rommel. Packed with cinematic references, the highlights of this study of starstruck ambition include a wonderfully fouled-up school play and Mohiedine's touching friendship with a Jewish girl, Nagla Fathi. DP Arabic +subtitles.

Mohsen Mohiedine *Yehia* • Nagla Fathi *Sarah* • Gerry Sundquist *Tommy* ■ *Dir* Youssef Chahine • *Scr* Youssef Chahine, Mohsen Zayed

Alfie ★★★★ 15
Comedy drama   1966 · UK · Colour · 109min

Receiving five Oscar nominations and rave reviews, this was one of the most talked-about British movies of the 1960s. Today, the frank discussion of pre-marital sex, adultery and illegitimacy may raise fewer eyebrows and the chirpy cockney banter may sound more than a little old hat, but this drama still has much to say about how differently men and women view intimate relationships, and the abortion scene is particularly harrowing. Michael Caine has rarely bettered his performance here, conveying a charm and a naivety that is as troubling as it is accomplished. Of the wronged women, Julia Foster and Vivien Merchant are outstanding. DP Swearing. *DVD*

Michael Caine *Alfie* • Shelley Winters *Ruby* • Millicent Martin *Siddie* • Julia Foster *Gilda* • Jane Asher *Annie* • Shirley Anne Field *Carla* • Vivien Merchant *Lily* • Eleanor Bron *Doctor* • Denholm Elliott *Abortionist* ■ *Dir* Lewis Gilbert • *Scr* Bill Naughton, from his play

Alfie ★★ 15
Comedy drama   2004 · US · Colour · 101min

The 1966 film got by largely on the roguish charm of Michael Caine as the seducer of the title. Here, Jude Law seems to be struggling to believe his character could be such an unconvincing combination of connivance and dimness. With the action transposed to present-day New York, Alfie has his wicked way with a series of ladies before it begins to dawn on him that maybe an endless string of brief sexual encounters isn't what it's all about. A creaky effort. LF Swearing, nudity, sexual references. *DVD*

Jude Law *Alfie Elkins* • Marisa Tomei *Julie* • Omar Epps *Marlon* • Nia Long *Lonette* • Jane Krakowski *Dorie* • Sienna Miller *Nikki* • Susan Sarandon *Liz* ■ *Dir* Charles Shyer • *Scr* Charles Shyer, Elaine Pope, from the film and the play by Bill Naughton • *Cinematographer* Ashley Rowe

Alfie Darling ★★ 18
Comedy drama   1975 · UK · Colour · 97min

This follow-up to the Oscar-nominated *Alfie* (1966) finds pop singer Alan Price replacing Michael Caine as the cockney casanova, with director Ken Hughes taking over from Lewis Gilbert. This time around Alfie is a truck driver involved with the usual bevy of beauties, none of whom makes any impact apart from Jill Townsend. Lacking much of the verve and pathos of the original, this is harmless and charmless. TH

Alan Price *Alfie* • Jill Townsend *Abby* • Joan Collins *Fay* • Rula Lenska *Louise* • Hannah Gordon *Dora* • Vicki Michelle *Bird* • Annie Ross *Claire* • Sheila White *Norma* ■ *Dir* Ken Hughes • *Scr* Ken Hughes, from the character created by Bill Naughton

Alfred the Great ★★★
Historical drama   1969 · UK · Colour · 122min

1960s trendy David Hemmings is a rather implausible Prince of Wessex, later the only British king to be called "great", in director Clive Donner's story of the man who not only burnt the cakes but also built the boats to create the British navy. In Donner's film, Alfred is portrayed as someone whose greatness was thrust upon him, a deep thinker who had once wanted to take holy orders. An interesting theme, but true epic status somehow eludes the movie. TH

David Hemmings *Alfred* • Michael York *Guthrum* • Prunella Ransome *Aelhswith* • Colin Blakely *Asher* • Julian Glover *Athelstan* • Ian McKellen *Roger* • Alan Dobie *Ethelred* • Peter Vaughan *Buhrud* • Julian Chagrin *Ivar* • Barry Jackson

A

Wulfstan • Vivien Merchant *Freda* • Christopher Timothy *Cedric* • Michael Billington *Offa* ■ *Dir* Clive Donner • *Scr* Ken Taylor, James R Webb

Alfredo Alfredo ★★
Comedy   1971 · It · Colour · 97min

Ever the Method actor, Dustin Hoffman took the trouble to learn the Italian dialogue for this laborious comedy, only for the director to shoot in English and then dub all the voices into Italian. A dubbed English version then went on general release in the States. The story veers between cruel slapstick and broad satire as it chronicles Hoffman's doomed relationship with the demanding Stefania Sandrelli. DP Italian dubbed.

Dustin Hoffman *Alfredo* • Stefania Sandrelli *Mariarosa* • Carla Gravina *Carolina* • Clara Colosimo *Carolina's mother* • Daniele Patella *Carolina's father* • Danika La Loggia *Mariarosa's mother* • Saro Urzi *Mariarosa's father* ■ *Dir* Pietro Germi • *Scr* Leo Benvenuti, Piero De Bernardi, Tullio Pinelli, Pietro Germi

Alf's Button Afloat ★★★ U
Fantasy comedy   1938 · UK · BW · 89min

The upstaging talents of "The Crazy Gang" – Bud Flanagan, Chesney Allen, Jimmy Nervo, Teddy Knox, Charles Naughton and Jimmy Gold – have never been in doubt. However, Alastair Sim easily surpasses them as the genie they encounter in this version of WA Darlington's famous farce. As buskers serving in the Marines, the Gang work hard at their music hall routines, but the bumbling Sim steals the show. TH

Bud Flanagan *Alf Higgins* • Chesney Allen *Ches* • Jimmy Nervo *Cecil* • Teddy Knox *Teddy* • Charlie Naughton *Charlie* • Jimmy Gold *Jimmy* • Alastair Sim *Eustace* • Wally Patch *Sergeant Hawkins* • Peter Gawthorne *Captain Driscol* • Glennis Lorimer *Frankie Driscol* ■ *Dir* Marcel Varnel • *Scr* Marriott Edgar, Val Guest, Ralph Smart, from the play *Alf's Button* by WA Darlington

Algiers ★★★ U
Crime drama   1938 · US · BW · 99min

This loose remake of the Jean Gabin movie *Pépé le Moko* has Charles Boyer and Hedy Lamarr clinching in the Casbah, the scene of innumerable shady goings-on from the supporting cast. The hard-boiled dialogue by James M Cain and the lustrous black-and-white photography give this movie irresistible glamour. Producer Hal B Wallis saw how successful it was and immediately ordered a title change to his new production at Warners called *Everybody Comes to Rick's*. The new title? Why, *Casablanca*, of course. AT *DVD*

Charles Boyer *Pépé le Moko* • Sigrid Gurie *Ines* • Hedy Lamarr *Gaby* • Joseph Calleia *Slimane* • Gene Lockhart *Regis* • Alan Hale *Grandpère* ■ *Dir* John Cromwell • *Scr* John Howard Lawson, James M Cain, from the novel *Pépé le Moko* by Detective Roger D'Ashelbe [Henri La Barthe] • *Cinematographer* James Wong Howe

Ali ★★★ 15
Biographical sports drama
2001 · US · Colour · 150min

There's no faulting Will Smith's remarkable impersonation of Muhammad Ali, nor can you underestimate the epic scale and historical authenticity of director Michael Mann's biopic. Where it falls down is in the lack of fresh insight into the enigmatic fighter; familiar events are lavishly re-created (Jon Voight's uncanny transformation into renowned American sportscaster Howard Cosell is one of the highlights) but are not re-examined or explored in any depth. While Mann's bruising approach to the heavyweight contests are riveting, elsewhere the sluggish pace lessens the overall impact. JC Violence, swearing. *DVD*

Will Smith *Muhammad Ali/Cassius Clay* • Jamie Foxx *Drew "Bundini" Brown* • Jon Voight *Howard Cosell* • Mario Van Peebles *Malcolm X* • Ron Silver *Angelo Dundee* • Jeffrey Wright *Howard Bingham* • Mykelti Williamson *Don King* • Jada Pinkett Smith *Sonji Roi* ■ *Dir* Michael Mann • *Scr* Stephen J Rivele, Christopher Wilkinson, Eric Roth, Michael Mann, from a story by Gregory Allen Howard

Ali Baba and the Forty Thieves ★★ U
Adventure   1944 · US · Colour · 87min

Baghdad... and the Mongols have landed, throwing everyone into slavery, except young Master Baba, who escapes into the desert and finds said number of thieves. He grows up to be Jon Hall, and falls for Maria Montez as a princess with attitude. Made by Universal as a follow-up to the money-spinning *Arabian Nights*, this take on an old story has its tongue in its cheek and delivers its cheapo action thrills quite efficiently. AT *DVD* *BL*

Maria Montez *Amara* • Jon Hall *Ali Baba* • Turhan Bey *Jamiel* • Andy Devine *Abdullah* • Kurt Katch *Hulagu Khan* • Frank Puglia *Cassim* • Fortunio Bonanova *Baba* • Moroni Olsen *Caliph* • Ramsay Ames *Nalu* ■ *Dir* Arthur Lubin • *Scr* Edmund L Hartmann

Ali G indahouse ★★★ 15
Comedy   2002 · Ger/US/Fr/UK · Colour · 83min

While by no means an important piece of film-making, this is still so much better than it ought to have been. As forged on TV by Sacha Baron Cohen (who co-writes here), Ali G – the white kid from Staines who behaves like a black rapper from South Central – is essentially a one-joke creation (albeit a good joke). That joke is stretched to breaking point here, but if you laughed the first time, you'll laugh again. This is largely thanks to the ludicrous plot (Ali becomes an MP, exposes sleaze and saves the planet) and a sparkling turn from co-star Martin Freeman as Ali's sidekick. AC Swearing, drug abuse. *DVD* *BL*

Sacha Baron Cohen *Ali G/Borat* • Michael Gambon *Prime Minister* • Charles Dance *David Carlton* • Kellie Bright *Julie* • Martin Freeman *Ricky C* • Rhona Mitra *Kate Hedges* • Barbara New *Nan* ■ *Dir* Mark Mylod • *Scr* Sacha Baron Cohen, Dan Mazer

Ali Zaoua ★★★ 15
Drama   2000 · Fr/Mor/Bel · Colour · 98min

This tale of Casablancan street kids battling poverty and casual brutality in order to give their buddy a decent burial is both touching and perceptive. Contrasting the squalor of the docks and the inner-city wastelands with glossy advertising images and optimistic animated inserts, director Nabil Ayouch celebrates the resilience of the pre-teenage trio, while also suggesting their seemingly inevitable fate. Cinematographer Vincent Mathias gives an unexpected lustre to the neorealist imagery. DP French, Arabic +subtitles.

Mounïm Khab *Kwita* • Mustapha Hansali *Omar* • Hicham Moussoune *Boubker* • Abdelhak Zhayra *Ali Zaoua* • Saïd Taghmaoui *Dib* ■ *Dir* Nabil Ayouch • *Scr* Nathalie Saugeon, Nabil Ayouch

Alias Jesse James ★★★ U
Comedy western   1959 · US · Colour · 92min

Bob Hope stars in yet another western spoof, this time playing an incompetent insurance salesman determined to retrieve the policy he unwittingly sold to outlaw Jesse James (Wendell Corey). Hope provides the jokes, while Rhonda Fleming supplies the pulchritude. The best moments are in the finale, though, when a host of cowboy stars (Roy Rogers, James Garner, Fess Parker) protect Bob from the killers. TH

Bob Hope *Milford Farnsworth* • Rhonda Fleming *Cora Lee Collins* • Wendell Corey *Jesse James* • Jim Davis (1) *Frank James* • Gloria Talbott *Indian maiden* • Will Wright *Titus Queasley* • James Arness *Matt Dillon* • Ward Bond *Major Seth Adams* • Gary Cooper • Bing Crosby • Gail Davis *Annie Oakley* • Hugh O'Brian *Wyatt Earp* • Fess Parker *Davy Crockett* • Roy Rogers • Jay Silverheels *Tonto* • Gene Autry • James Garner *Bret Maverick* ■ *Dir* Norman Z McLeod • *Scr* William Bowers, Daniel D Beauchamp, from a story by Robert St Aubrey, Bert Lawrence

Alias Nick Beal ★★★
Fantasy crime drama   1949 · US · BW · 92min

This political allegory relocates the Faust legend to 20th-century America. Ray Milland is the mysterious Nick Beal, who

materialises to offer honest politician Thomas Mitchell not only wealth but also the charms of Audrey Totter. The former crusader against crime becomes power hungry under the malign influence of "Old Nick". Milland is the personification of evil, while John Farrow does an efficient job directing what was then considered daring material. BB

Ray Milland *Nick Beal* • Audrey Totter *Donna Allen* • Thomas Mitchell *Joseph Foster* • George Macready *Rev Thomas Garfield* • Fred Clark *Frankie Faulkner* ■ *Dir* John Farrow • *Scr* Jonathan Latimer, from the story *Dr Joe Faust* by Mindret Lord

Alibi ★★
Crime drama   1929 · US · BW · 75min

This early gangster movie was made by the maverick independent Roland West who later made *The Bat Whispers*. It has been credited with being the first film to record the sound and show the destruction caused by a tommy-gun simultaneously. Two interrogation scenes are especially shocking, showing the sadistic techniques used by the cops as utterly normal. Chester Morris, in his first starring role, was among those nominated for the second Oscar ceremony. AT

Chester Morris *Chick Williams* • Harry Stubbs *Buck Bachman* • Mae Busch *Daisy Thomas* • Eleanor Griffith *Joan* • Irma Harrison *Toots* • Regis Toomey *Danny McGann* • Al Hill *Brown* • James Bradbury Jr *Blake* ■ *Dir* Roland West • *Scr* Roland West, C Gardner Sullivan, from the play *Nightstick* by John Wray, JC Nugent, Elaine S Carrington

Alice ★★★★ PG
Animated fantasy
1988 · UK/Swi/W Ger · Colour · 82min

This stunning modern-day version of the Lewis Carroll story from Czech director, animator and surrealist Jan Svankmajer uses every live action technique in the special effects manual, and contains dashes of startling eroticism. The absurdist universe he creates plays around liberally with the source material, yet remains true to its spirit. Flesh-and-blood actress Krystyna Kohoutova stars with a host of scary fish, skeleton birds and, most unusually, perambulating raw meat. AJ *DVD* *BL*

Kristyna Kohoutova *Alice* ■ *Dir* Jan Svankmajer • *Scr* Jan Svankmajer, from the novel *Alice's Adventures in Wonderland* by Lewis Carroll

Alice ★★★ 15
Fantasy comedy   1990 · US · Colour · 102min

When this was originally released, several critics attacked Woody Allen for making the same film over and over again. But is there another Allen picture in which a woman is helped to confront her past with the aid of Chinese herbal teas, gets to meet the ghost of an old flame, and spy on her family and friends while invisible? What gives this that familiar feel is the all-too-predictable performance of Mia Farrow, whose bored Manhattan underachiever undoes a lot of the good work by the excellent supporting cast. DP Swearing, drug abuse. *DVD*

Mia Farrow *Alice* • William Hurt *Doug* • Alec Baldwin *Ed* • Joe Mantegna *Joe* • Cybill Shepherd *Nancy Brill* • Blythe Danner *Dorothy* • Bernadette Peters *Muse* • Gwen Verdon *Alice's mother* • Patrick O'Neal (1) *Alice's father* ■ *Dir/Scr* Woody Allen

Alice Adams ★★★★ U
Comedy drama   1935 · US · BW · 95min

Brilliant Hollywood director George Stevens dates this small-town opus as the real start of his career, conveniently neglecting the early comedies that he cut his teeth on. Understandable, really, since his technique, together with a magnificent performance from Katharine Hepburn as Booth Tarkington's titular heroine, make this unforgettable. The dinner table scene, where beau Fred MacMurray comes visiting, is rightly famous, and is a brilliant example of the film-maker's craft, albeit aided by superb casting (in particular Hattie McDaniel's slovenly maid). This is, in fact, a

remake of a 1923 silent version that had Florence Vidor in the lead, but it's Hepburn's version that's remembered. TS

Katharine Hepburn *Alice Adams* • Fred MacMurray *Arthur Russell* • Fred Stone *Mr Adams* • Evelyn Venable *Mildred Palmer* • Frank Albertson *Walter Adams* • Ann Shoemaker *Mrs Adams* • Charles Grapewin *[Charley Grapewin] Mr Lamb* • Grady Sutton *Frank Dowling* • Hedda Hopper *Mrs Palmer* • Hattie McDaniel *Malena* ■ *Dir* George Stevens • *Scr* Dorothy Yost, Mortimer Offner, from the novel by Booth Tarkington

Alice Doesn't Live Here Anymore ★★★★ 15
Drama   1974 · US · Colour · 107min

Ellen Burstyn won an Oscar for her portrayal of bruised widow Alice in this expertly played drama from Martin Scorsese. Hitting the road with her brattish son in order to find herself and dreaming of a new beginning as a singer, Burstyn brilliantly conveys the vulnerability that forces her character first into the arms of the brutal Harvey Keitel and then of taciturn rancher Kris Kristofferson. Scorsese just about keeps the sprawling road movie segment on track, but the film only really comes to life when Burnstyn joins forces with a sassy diner waitress played by Oscar-nominated Diane Ladd. DP Violence, swearing. *DVD*

Ellen Burstyn *Alice Hyatt* • Kris Kristofferson *David Barrie* • Billy Green Bush *Donald Hyatt* • Diane Ladd *Flo* • Lelia Goldoni *Bea* • Lane Bradbury *Rita* • Vic Tayback *Mel* • Jodie Foster *Audrey* • Harvey Keitel *Ben Eberhart* • Alfred Lutter *Tom Hyatt* ■ *Dir* Martin Scorsese • *Scr* Robert Getchell

Alice et Martin ★★★ 15
Drama   1998 · Fr/Sp/US · Colour · 119min

André Téchiné directs this coolly assured but coldly uninvolving film, which is further undermined by improbable characterisation and contrived plotting. At the mercy of her emotions, Juliette Binoche is never less than persuasive as the violinist who sacrifices everything for Alexis Loret, an undeserving narcissist. Aided by crisp photography and a lovely score, Téchiné deftly captures the fragility of the relationship, but doesn't delve too deeply. DP French +subtitles. *DVD*

Juliette Binoche *Alice* • Alexis Loret *Martin Sauvagnac* • Mathieu Amalric *Benjamin Sauvagnac* • Carmen Maura *Jeanine Sauvagnac* • Jean-Pierre Lorit *Frédéric* • Marthe Villalonga *Lucie* • Pierre Maguelon *Victor Sauvagnac* ■ *Dir* André Téchiné • *Scr* André Téchiné, Gilles Taurand, Olivier Assayas • *Cinematographer* Caroline Champetier • *Music* Philippe Sarde

Alice in the Cities ★★★★ U
Road movie   1974 · W Ger · BW · 107min

Wim Wenders's road movie provides an amusing, affectionate and yet quietly critical portrait of 1970s America. Often employing a subjective camera technique, Wenders places the viewer at the heart of the odyssey so that we can experience the sights and sounds of the eastern seaboard exactly as photojournalist Rüdiger Vogler and his nine-year-old companion Yella Rottlander see them. The search for the girl's grandmother is virtually irrelevant, as it's how this odd couple react to each other and their ever-changing environment that is important. DP German +subtitles. *DVD*

Rüdiger Vogler *Philip Winter* • Yella Rottlander *Alice Van Damm* • Elisabeth Kreuzer *Lisa Van Damm* • Edda Köchl *Edda* • Didi Petrikat *Girl* • Ernest Bohm *Policeman* • Sam Presti *Car salesman* • Lois Moran *Airline girl* ■ *Dir* Wim Wenders • *Scr* Wim Wenders, Veith von Fürstenberg • *Cinematographer* Robby Müller

Alice in Wonderland ★★ U
Fantasy   1933 · US · BW · 79min

This laboured attempt to include a vast range of Lewis Carroll's characters from both *Alice's Adventures in Wonderland* and *Through the Looking Glass* is of most interest for the appearance of Paramount's top stars. However, because they're clad in masks and costumes based on the John

Tenniel drawings, the actors are only recognisable by their voices. AE

Charlotte Henry *Alice* • Richard Arlen *Cheshire Cat* • Roscoe Ates *Fish* • William Austin *Gryphon* • Gary Cooper *White Knight* • Jack Duffy (1) *Leg of Mutton* • Leon Errol *Uncle Gilbert* • Louise Fazenda *White Queen* • WC Fields *Humpty Dumpty* • Cary Grant *Mock Turtle* • Edward Everett Horton *Mad Hatter* • Edna May Oliver *Red Queen* • Charlie Ruggles [Charles Ruggles] *March Hare* ■ *Dir* Norman Z McLeod • *Scr* Joseph L Mankiewicz, William Cameron Menzies, from the illustrated children's books *Alice's Adventures in Wonderland/Through the Looking Glass* by Lewis Carroll

Alice in Wonderland ★★★ U
Animated fantasy   1951 · US · Colour · 72min

This brash, colourful and undemanding animated feature contains the best-loved episodes from the Lewis Carroll classic. Where it scores over its live-action rivals is in the depiction of the more fantastic figures, such as the White Rabbit, the Caterpillar, the Cheshire Cat, the March Hare and the Dormouse, who, while always more Disney than Carroll, are all engaging creations. Alice resembles her Tenniel original, but the Mad Hatter, the weedy King and the blustering Queen of Hearts are more imaginative and great fun. DP *DVD*

Kathryn Beaumont *Alice* • Ed Wynn *Mad Hatter* • Richard Haydn *Caterpillar* • Sterling Holloway *Cheshire Cat* • Jerry Colonna *March Hare* • Verna Felton *Queen of Hearts* • J Pat O'Malley *Walrus/Carpenter/Tweedledee/Tweedledum* • Bill Thompson *White Rabbit/Dodo* ■ *Dir* Clyde Geronimi, Hamilton Luske, Wilfred Jackson • *Scr* Bill Peet, Joe Rinaldi and others, from the illustrated children's books *Alice's Adventures in Wonderland/Through the Looking Glass* by Lewis Carroll

Alice in Wonderland ★★ U
Fantasy adventure
1999 · US/UK · Colour · 133min

Stars aplenty surround Tina Majorino in this small-screen adaptation of *Alice's Adventures in Wonderland*, which also benefits from some wondrous Jim Henson puppetry. Yet, somehow, the combination still falls short of the cherished images taken from those first readings of Lewis Carroll's classic tales. There are stand-out performances from the likes of Miranda Richardson as the Queen of Hearts and Gene Wilder as the Mock Turtle, but others are too eager to please, among them Martin Short's Mad Hatter. DP *DVD*

Tina Majorino *Alice* • Martin Short *Mad Hatter* • Miranda Richardson *Queen of Hearts* • Ben Kingsley *Major Caterpillar* • Whoopi Goldberg *Cheshire Cat* • Gene Wilder *Mock Turtle* • George Wendt *Tweedledee* • Robbie Coltrane *Tweedledum* ■ *Dir* Nick Willing • *Scr* Peter Barnes, from the illustrated children's books *Alice's Adventures in Wonderland/Through the Looking Glass* by Lewis Carroll

Alice in Wonderland ★★ PG
Fantasy adventure   2010 · US · Colour · 104min

Tim Burton tackling the nonsense prose of Lewis Carroll would seem something the visionary director could do in his sleep. Which is what this strangely ponderous "re-imagined" mash-up of the two Alice adventures often induces. It's the second journey to "Underland" for the now teenage Alice (Mia Wasikowska), where she again encounters familiar characters such as the Mad Hatter (Johnny Depp), Tweedledum and Tweedledee (Matt Lucas), and the Cheshire Cat (voiced by Stephen Fry). Burton's trademark quirkiness is in full evidence in the trippy, dippy, acid-coloured excursion through Carroll's literary landscapes, particularly in a rather overextended visit to the Red Queen (Helena Bonham Carter), but the wavering tone is as uncertain as Alice's decision-making, while the added-on 3D is as unconvincing as the entire misconceived venture. AJ Violence, *DVD* *BD* *3D*

Mia Wasikowska *Alice Kingsleigh* • Johnny Depp *Mad Hatter* • Michael Sheen *White Rabbit* • Anne Hathaway *White Queen* • Helena Bonham Carter *Red Queen* • Alan Rickman *Absolem, the Blue Caterpillar* • Stephen Fry *Cheshire Cat* • Crispin

Glover *Stayne, Knave of Hearts* • Christopher Lee *Jabberwocky* • Timothy Spall *Bayard, the Bloodhound* • Matt Lucas *Tweedledee/Tweedledum* • Paul Whitehouse *March Hare* ■ *Dir* Tim Burton • *Scr* Linda Woolverton, from the illustrated children's books *Alice's Adventures in Wonderland and Through the Looking Glass, and What Alice Found There* by Lewis Carroll • *Cinematographer* Dariusz Wolski

Alice through the Looking Glass ★★★ PG
Fantasy adventure   2016 · US · Colour · 112min

Although this has little to do with the events in Lewis Carroll's children's book, it retains the amusing absurdity and glorious production design of Tim Burton's 2010 *Alice in Wonderland*. Burton serves as producer, here, with British director James Bobin taking the reins, as Johnny Depp (the Mad Hatter) in another silly wig doing another silly voice looks to Mia Wasikowska's Alice to help him find out what happened to his family years before. While it doesn't all work like a well-oiled machine, kids are likely to take the film as it comes and simply enjoy the ride. SP *BD*

Johnny Depp *Hatter Tarrant Hightopp* • Mia Wasikowska *Alice Kingsleigh* • Anne Hathaway *Mirana, White Queen* • Helena Bonham Carter *Iracebeth, Red Queen* • Sacha Baron Cohen *Time* • Alan Rickman *Absolem* • Stephen Fry *Cheshire Cat* • Matt Lucas *Tweedledee/Tweedledum* • Michael Sheen *McTwisp, White Rabbit* ■ *Dir* James Bobin • *Scr* Linda Woolverton, from the illustrated children's book *Through the Looking Glass and What Alice Found There* by Lewis Carroll • *Music* Danny Elfman

Alice, Sweet Alice ★★★★ 18
Horror thriller   1977 · US · Colour · 108min

This offbeat, multilayered whodunnit first won acclaim for director Alfred Sole's approach (a highly individual blend of pastiche and homage). Sole shot his story of a series of murders in and around a Catholic church in his home town (Paterson, New Jersey) in 1961. The killings (still shockingly realistic) are interspersed with biting portrayals of the dysfunctional family and Catholic ritual. There is also black humour, inspired by Hitchcock, although fans will notice many other influences. DM

Linda Miller *Catherine Spages* • Mildred Clinton *Mrs Tredoni* • Paula Sheppard *Alice Spages* • Niles McMaster *Dominick Spages* • Rudolph Willrich *Father Tom* • Jane Lowry *Aunt Annie* • Alphonso DeNoble *Mr Alphonso* • Brooke Shields *Karen Spages* ■ *Dir* Alfred Sole • *Scr* Rosemary Ritvo, Alfred Sole

Alice's Adventures in Wonderland ★★ U
Fantasy   1972 · UK · Colour · 91min

This all-star version of the Lewis Carroll classic has syrupy music and lyrics by John Barry and Don Black, and casts Fiona Fullerton as Alice. Fullerton had already made a couple of movies and was promoted as a new Julie Andrews, but she has a hard time not being upstaged by her co-stars: Michael Hordern, Ralph Richardson and Spike Milligan. Peter Sellers caused a minor stir by peevishly slagging the film off before it opened. AT *DVD*

Fiona Fullerton *Alice* • Peter Sellers *March Hare* • Michael Crawford *White Rabbit* • Robert Helpmann *Mad Hatter* • Michael Hordern *Mock Turtle* • Michael Jayston *Dodgson* • Roy Kinnear *Cheshire Cat* • Spike Milligan *Gryphon* • Dudley Moore *Dormouse* • Ralph Richardson *Caterpillar* • Flora Robson *Queen of Hearts* ■ *Dir* William Sterling • *Scr* William Sterling, from the illustrated children's books *Alice's Adventures in Wonderland/Through the Looking Glass* by Lewis Carroll

Alice's Restaurant ★★★ 15
Comedy drama   1969 · US · Colour · 106min

Not so much the story of the restaurant in question as an anti-Vietnam hymn celebrating dropouts, this stars folk singer Arlo Guthrie. It is based on his lengthy (more than 18 minutes) hit recording in which he detailed some of his experiences of trying to dodge the draft for a war that he and his comrades didn't believe in. Threaded with visual authority by Arthur

Penn, it has some saving humour, but its narcissistic self-regard detracts from its undoubted sincerity. TH *DVD*

Arlo Guthrie *Arlo* • Pat Quinn [Patricia Quinn] *Alice* • James Broderick *Ray* • Michael McClanathan *Shelly* • Geoff Outlaw *Roger* • Tina Chen *Mari-Chan* • Kathleen Dabney *Karin* • William Obanhein *Officer Obie* • M Emmet Walsh *Group W sergeant* ■ *Dir* Arthur Penn • *Scr* Venable Herndon, Arthur Penn, from the song *The Alice's Restaurant Massacre* by Arlo Guthrie

LANDMARK FILM
Haunted-house horror is transplanted to a claustrophobic spaceship and changes the face of our nightmares

Alien ★★★★★ 18
Science-fiction horror thriller
1979 · US/UK · Colour · 116min

This revolutionary "haunted house in space" thrill-ride is the classic business, stunning you with shock after shock, even when the fascinating creature is exposed in all its hideous glory. The top-notch acting (super-astronaut Sigourney Weaver) and imaginative bio-mechanical production design (with the alien created by Swiss artist HR Giger) succeed in flattering a script culled from many cult sci-fi movies. There's also director Ridley Scott's eye for detail and brilliant way of alternating false scares with genuine jolts, which help to create a seamless blend of gothic horror and harrowing science fiction. The director's cut, released in 2003, boasts a remastered sound mix and sequences cut from the original – until now only available on the *Alien* DVD – including a much-discussed cocoon scene. AJ Violence, swearing. *DVD* *BD*

Tom Skerritt *Captain Dallas* • Sigourney Weaver *Ripley* • Veronica Cartwright *Lambert* • Harry Dean Stanton *Brett* • John Hurt *Kane* • Ian Holm *Ash* • Yaphet Kotto *Parker* • Helen Horton *"Mother"* ■ *Dir* Ridley Scott • *Scr* Dan O'Bannon, from a story by O'Bannon, Ronald Shusett

Aliens ★★★★★ 18
Science-fiction action thriller
1986 · US · Colour · 131min

Surpassing its predecessor in terms of sheer spectacle, this sequel to Ridley Scott's outer-space nightmare from director James Cameron is an outstanding science-fiction thriller. Sigourney Weaver wakes up 57 years after the original events unfolded, only to be told that the planet where she first met the alien predator has been colonised. When all contact with the inhabitants is lost, she's sent in with a crack squad of marines, and hurtles headlong into a hi-tech house of horrors that delivers super shocks and nail-biting suspense. Masterfully controlling the tension and moving the involving plot at a lightning pace, Cameron exploits everyone's worst fears and carries them to the riveting extreme in this consummate Oscar-winning fright-fest. AJ Violence, swearing. *DVD* *BD*

Sigourney Weaver *Ripley* • Carrie Henn *Rebecca Jorden, "Newt"* • Michael Biehn *Corporal Hicks* • Paul Reiser *Carter J Burke* • Lance Henriksen *Bishop* • Bill Paxton *Private Hudson* • William Hope *Lieutenant Gorman* • Jenette Goldstein *Private Vasquez* • Al Matthews *Sergeant Apone* ■ *Dir* James Cameron • *Scr* James Cameron, from a story by Cameron, David Giler, Walter Hill, from characters by Dan O'Bannon, Ronald Shusett

Alien³ ★★★ 18
Science-fiction action thriller
1992 · US · Colour · 109min

Given that the first two films stand up as sci-fi classics in their own right, *Se7en* director David Fincher, in his feature film debut, had a virtually impossible act to follow with this second sequel. He makes a good fist of it, developing the maternal themes of first sequel *Aliens* and providing an exhilarating final showdown. Sigourney Weaver returns as Ripley, who this time crash-lands on a prison colony where another lethal alien is let loose. A fourth instalment, *Alien: Resurrection*, was released in 1997. JF Violence, swearing. *DVD* *BD*

Sigourney Weaver *Warrant Officer Ripley* • Charles S Dutton *Dillon* • Charles Dance *Clemens* • Paul McGann *Golic* • Brian Glover *Superintendent Andrews* • Ralph Brown (2) *Aaron* • Danny Webb *Morse* • Christopher John Fields *Rains* • Holt McCallany *Junior* • Lance Henriksen *Bishop II* ■ *Dir* David Fincher • *Scr* David Giler, Walter Hill, Larry Ferguson, from a story by Vincent Ward, from characters by Dan O'Bannon, Ronald Shusett

Alien: Resurrection ★★★★ 18
Science-fiction action thriller
1997 · US · Colour · 104min

This enticing helter-skelter trip through space opera cliché cleverly conceals the fact there really isn't anything new of note here, just neat tangents off the basic *Alien* concept: nasty ETs relentlessly stalking their human prey through a deserted spaceship. Sigourney Weaver's Ripley is cloned 200 years after the action of *Alien³* because she's carrying an alien queen foetus. French director Jean-Pierre Jeunet's shock thrill-ride showcases some scintillating set pieces and a gallery of grotesque clones-gone-wrong. Tense, mordantly funny, very graphic and bloody, with Weaver on great form as a clone who's gained some interesting alien influences on her personality. AJ Violence, swearing, nudity. *DVD* *BD*

Sigourney Weaver *Ripley* • Winona Ryder *Call* • Dominique Pinon *Vriess* • Ron Perlman *Johner* • Gary Dourdan *Christie* • Michael Wincott *Elgyn* • Kim Flowers *Hillard* • Dan Hedaya *General Perez* ■ *Dir* Jean-Pierre Jeunet • *Scr* Joss Whedon, from characters by Dan O'Bannon, Ronald Shusett

Alien Autopsy ★★ 12
Sci-fi comedy based on a true story
2006 · UK · Colour · 91min

Small-screen favourites Anthony McPartlin and Declan Donnelly (aka Ant and Dec) make their movie-starring debut with this boisterous sci-fi comedy. Trading on their public personas rather than on any great acting skills, they play buddies who stumble on a potential goldmine when they acquire genuine footage from a 1947 alien autopsy at Roswell, New Mexico. Flimsy and long-winded. SF Swearing.

Declan Donnelly *Ray Santilli* • Anthony McPartlin *Gary Shoefield* • Omid Djalili *Melik* • Morwenna Banks *Jasmine* • Jimmy Carr *Gavin* • Madeleine Moffat *Nan* • John Cater *Maurice* • Bill Pullman *Morgan Banner* • Harry Dean Stanton *Harvey* ■ *Dir* Jonny Campbell • *Scr* William Davies

The Alien Dead ★
Science-fiction horror
1980 · US · Colour · 73min

This first movie directed by hack-meister Fred Olen Ray was Buster Crabbe's last. It couldn't be a sadder epitaph for the 1930s *Flash Gordon* star if it tried. Crabbe investigates a crash-landed meteorite in Florida, apparently responsible for turning a houseboat full of teens into raving ghouls. A pretty awful load of old zombie nonsense. AJ

Buster Crabbe [Larry "Buster" Crabbe] *Sheriff Kowalski* • Ray Roberts *Tom Corman* • Linda Lewis *Shawn Michaels* • George Kelsey *Emmett Michaels* • Mike Bonavia *Miller Haze* ■ *Dir* Fred Olen Ray • *Scr* Martin Alan Nicholas, Fred Olen Ray

Alien Hunter ★★ 15
Science-fiction thriller
2003 · US/Bul · Colour · 87min

Contrary to its misleading title, there's not much extraterrestrial hunting going on in this flimsy sci-fi thriller, as cryptologist James Spader helps unfeasibly good-looking polar scientists decode radio signals emitting from a mysterious object discovered in the Antarctic ice. Though an engaging Spader's hardly stretching himself, he and his fellow cast members make the most of the limited material, and the special effects and criminally underused alien are surprisingly decent for a TV movie. SF Violence, swearing. *DVD*

A

James Spader *Julian Rome* • Janine Eser *Dr Kate Brecher* • John Lynch *Dr Michael Straub* • Nikolai Binev *Dr Alexi Gierach* • Leslie Stefanson *Nyla Olson* ■ *Dir* Ron Krauss • *Scr* JS Cardone, from a story by Cardone, Boaz Davidson

Alien Nation ★★★★ 18
Science-fiction thriller
1988 · US · Colour · 86min

This buddy-buddy cop movie has a twist, as this time the mismatched detectives are from different planets. In the near future, an alien race has been uncomfortably integrated into American society, and Earthling cop James Caan and alien cop Mandy Patinkin are reluctantly paired to track down the killers of Caan's old partner. Director Graham Baker expertly combines the sci-fi and thriller elements and is well served by the two leads, particularly Patinkin, who manages to create a moving character while operating under a ton of latex. The movie inspired a rather more humdrum but still popular TV series and five TV movies. **JF** Violence, swearing, drug abuse, sex scenes. *DVD*

James Caan *Matthew Sykes* • Mandy Patinkin *Sam Francisco, "George"* • Terence Stamp *William Harcourt* • Kevyn Major Howard *Rudyard Kipling* • Leslie Bevis *Cassandra* • Peter Jason *Fedorchuk* • George Jenesky *Quint* • Jeff Kober *Josh Strader* ■ *Dir* Graham Baker • *Scr* Rockne S O'Bannon

Alien Terror ★ 18
Science-fiction thriller
1969 · Mex/US · Colour · 73min

The last movie made by veteran horror icon Boris Karloff was also the last of a shoddily assembled quartet of creature features made back-to-back in Los Angeles and Mexico. Barely directed by schlock maestro Jack Hill (the Mexico scenes were the work of Juan Ibanez) and badly edited, the film involves a molecular ray gun that freaks out observing aliens when its inventor (Karloff) accidentally blows a hole in his laboratory roof. **AJ**

Boris Karloff *Professor John Meyer* • Enrique Guzman *Paul* • Christa Linder *Laura* • Yerye Beirute *Convict* • Maura Monti *Isabel* ■ *Dir* Jack Hill • *Scr* Karl Schanzer, Luis Vergara

Aliens in the Attic ★★★ PG
Fantasy adventure
2009 · US · Colour · 82min

Techno-geek Tom (Carter Jenkins) finds cute but ruthless pint-sized space creatures using his family's holiday home as a base for an alien invasion. Having mocked him for being a "mathlete", Tom's siblings and cousins soon realise that his ingenuity may be the only thing standing between them and the destruction of the Earth, while their parents and grandmother remain oblivious to the mayhem surrounding them. This is a thrilling children's yarn that's chock-full of ingenious slapstick set pieces and enough pop-culture references to hold grown-ups' interest. **TeS** *DVD*

Carter Jenkins *Tom Pearson* • Austin Butler *Jake Pearson* • Henri Young *Art Pearson* • Regan Young *Lee Pearson* • Ashley Boettcher *Hannah Pearson* • Ashley Tisdale *Bethany Pearson* • Robert Hoffman *Ricky* • Doris Roberts *Nana Rose* • Josh Peck *Sparks* ■ *Dir* John Schultz • *Scr* Mark Burton, Adam F Goldberg, from a story by Burton

Alive ★★★ 15
Drama based on a true story
1992 · US · Colour · 121min

This harrowing drama is based on the true story of a South American rugby team whose plane crash-landed in the Andes in 1972, leaving the survivors the choice of starving to death or eating their dead to stay alive. Director Frank Marshall stages the mountaintop crash with a terrifying sequence of special effects and makes sure that the subsequent events are tastefully presented. He's also well served by the convincing performances of his cast, but the grim subject matter forces an emotional distance. **TH** Swearing. *DVD*

Ethan Hawke *Nando Parrado* • Vincent Spano *Antonio Balbi* • Josh Hamilton *Roberto Canessa* • Bruce Ramsay *Carlitos Paez* • John Haymes Newton [John Newton (2)] *Tintin* • David Kriegel

Gustavo Zerbino • Kevin Breznahan *Roy Harley* • Sam Behrens *Javier Methol* • Illeana Douglas *Lilliana Methol* ■ *Dir* Frank Marshall • *Scr* John Patrick Shanley, from the non-fiction book by Piers Paul Read

Alive and Kicking ★★★
Comedy
1958 · UK · BW · 91min

Sybil Thorndike, Kathleen Harrison and Estelle Winwood are a joy to behold as three old ladies who escape from a home and set themselves up on an isolated island as the relatives of millionaire Stanley Holloway. Eyes twinkle with mischief as they carve a niche in the local knitwear trade. Director Cyril Frankel's engaging piece of Irish whimsy is slight but diverting, and also notable as the film debut of Richard Harris. DP *DVD*

Sybil Thorndike *Dora* • Kathleen Harrison *Rosie* • Estelle Winwood *Mabel* • Stanley Holloway *MacDonagh* • Liam Redmond *Old man* • Marjorie Rhodes *Old woman* • Richard Harris *Lover* • Olive McFarland *Lover* • John Salew *Solicitor* • Eric Pohlmann *Captain* ■ *Dir* Cyril Frankel • *Scr* Denis Cannan

Alive and Kicking ★★★ 15
Comedy drama
1996 · UK · Colour · 94min

This is a spirited, if not always cinematic, tale by acclaimed dramatist Martin Sherman (*Bent*). Although rooted in the grand old kitchen sink tradition, director Nancy Meckler's grimly comic film is both clichéd and insightful, sad and uplifting. As the ballet dancer coping with the closure of his company and his HIV-positive status, Jason Flemyng gives an unexpectedly poignant performance. But who could compete with Anthony Sher on top form as the paunchy, bald alcoholic who offers him love? DP Swearing.

Jason Flemyng *Tonio* • Antony Sher *Jack* • Dorothy Tutin *Luna* • Anthony Higgins *Ramon* • Bill Nighy *Tristan* • Philip Voss *Duncan* • Diane Parish *Millie* • Aiden Waters *Vincent* • Natalie Roles *Catherine* ■ *Dir* Nancy Meckler • *Scr* Martin Sherman

All about Eve ★★★★★ PG
Classic drama
1950 · US · BW · 132min

"Fasten your seatbelts, it's going to be a bumpy night!", and with the acerbic talents of multi-Oscar-winning writer/director Joseph L Mankiewicz and his magnificent cast – the superb Bette Davis, the acid-tongued George Sanders, Celeste Holm, Thelma Ritter, Marilyn Monroe - it certainly is. On its original release, this tale of the theatre was criticised in some quarters for being over-wordy and arch, though today's audiences revel in its wit and cynicism. The dialogue is especially clever and the performances are first-rate. If the framing flashback structure seems a little contrived, or if Anne Baxter's Eve doesn't quite have the killer instinct required for the role, these are minor blemishes in a classic movie. **TS** *DVD*

Bette Davis *Margo Channing* • Anne Baxter *Eve Harrington* • George Sanders *Addison DeWitt* • Celeste Holm *Karen Richards* • Gary Merrill *Bill Sampson* • Hugh Marlowe *Lloyd Richards* • Gregory Ratoff *Max Fabian* • Barbara Bates *Phoebe* • Marilyn Monroe *Miss Casswell* • Thelma Ritter *Birdie Coonan* ■ *Dir* Joseph L Mankiewicz • *Scr* Joseph L Mankiewicz, from the short story *The Wisdom of Eve* by Mary Orr in *Hearst's International-Cosmopolitan*

All about My Mother ★★★★★ 15
Comedy drama
1999 · Sp/Fr · Colour · 96min

Mature and moving aren't words usually associated with Pedro Almodóvar, but they certainly apply to this inspired comedy drama that's littered with allusions to the Bette Davis classic *All about Eve* and Tennessee Williams's *A Streetcar Named Desire*. Devastated by the death of her son, hospital worker Cecilia Roth leaves Madrid for Barcelona to find her absent father of his existence. Here she finds a whole new purpose in tending to a pregnant HIV-positive nun (Penélope Cruz) and a *grande dame* of the stage nearing the end of his career (Marisa Paredes). This fond, deliciously flamboyant study of

womanhood and friendship is intense without ever being overbearing, and touching but never sentimental. One of the Spanish director's finest achievements, it earned him an Oscar and two Baftas. DP Spanish +subtitles. Drug abuse, swearing, sex scenes. *DVD*

Cecilia Roth *Manuela* • Marisa Paredes *Huma Rojo* • Candela Peña *Nina* • Antonia San Juan *"La Agrado"* • Penélope Cruz *Sister Rosa* • Rosa Maria Sarda *Rosa's mother* • Toni Cantó *Lola, "la Pionera"* • Eloy Azorin *Esteban* ■ *Dir/Scr* Pedro Almodóvar

All about Steve ★★ 12
Romantic comedy
2009 · US · Colour · 94min

Sandra Bullock turns in an excruciatingly kooky performance in this ill-conceived stalker romance. Few scenes escape Bullock's jarring and overbaked wackiness as nerdy crossword-puzzle compiler Mary Horowitz, whose parents arrange for her to go on a blind date with handsome TV cameraman Steve (Bradley Cooper). Ken Jeong (*The Hangover*) makes some impression as a luckless travelling TV producer, but otherwise this too often settles for cheap laughs. **KK** Sexual references. *DVD* *Bl*

Sandra Bullock *Mary Horowitz* • Thomas Haden Church *Hartman Hughes* • Bradley Cooper *Steve* • Ken Jeong *Angus* • DJ Qualls *Howard* • Keith David *Corbitt* • Howard Hesseman *Mr Horowitz* • Beth Grant *Mrs Horowitz* ■ *Dir* Phil Traill • *Scr* Kim Barker

The All American ★★ U
Drama
1953 · US · BW · 82min

Tony Curtis stars as a sports hero whose confidence is shaken when his parents are killed en route to watching him play, causing him to abandon glory for serious study - for a time. An unpretentious little film that effectively combines the ingredients of the rah-rah college football movie with a more intimate drama, it showcases the famous pretty-boy good looks that made Curtis a major star. **RK**

Tony Curtis *Nick Bonelli* • Lori Nelson *Sharon Wallace* • Richard Long *Howard Carter* • Mamie Van Doren *Susie Ward* • Gregg Palmer *Cameron* • Paul Cavanagh *Prof Banning* • Herman Hickman *Jumbo* • Stuart Whitman *Zip Parker* ■ *Dir* Jesse Hibbs • *Scr* DD Beauchamp, Robert Yale Libett, from a story by Leonard Freeman

The All-American Boy ★
Sports drama
1973 · US · Colour · 118min

Jon Voight made this clinker just before his breakthrough in *Midnight Cowboy*, though it sat on the Warner Bros shelf for four years before they re-edited it and released it to an indifferent world. Voight plays a small-town boxer and the movie is artfully structured into six rounds; however, most audiences will have trouble going the distance. **AT**

Jon Voight *Vic Bealer* • EJ Peaker *Janelle Sharkey* • Ned Glass *Arty* • Anne Archer *Drenna Valentine* • Art Metrano *Jay* • Bob Hastings *Ariel* • Carol Androsky *Rodine* • Gene Borkan *Rockoff* ■ *Dir/Scr* Charles Eastman

All Ashore ★★ U
Musical comedy
1953 · US · Colour · 79min

This cut-price imitation of the classic musical *On the Town* doesn't make much impression. Directed by Richard Quine from a screenplay he wrote with Blake Edwards, the movie focuses on the shore-leave escapades of three sailors - Mickey Rooney, Dick Haymes, Ray McDonald - and their romantic involvements with Peggy Ryan, Jody Lawrence and Barbara Bates. It falls almost entirely to the diminutive, multi-talented Rooney, as the patsy of the trio, to provide the fun. **RK**

Mickey Rooney *Francis "Moby" Dickerson* • Dick Haymes *Joe Carter* • Ray McDonald *Skip Edwards* • Peggy Ryan *Gay Night* • Barbara Bates *Jane Stanton* • Jody Lawrence *Jody Lawrence* *Nancy Flynn* • Fay Roope *Commodore Stanton* ■ *Dir* Richard Quine • *Scr* Blake Edwards, Richard Quine, from a story by Robert Wells, Blake Edwards

All Cheerleaders Die ★★★ 15
Comedy horror
2013 · US · Colour · 85min

Cult directors Lucky McKee and Chris Sivertson combine their talents for an engaging rampage through formula high-school horrors, inspired by their 2001 short of the same name. After a well-liked cheerleader dies, an excellent ensemble cast, led by Caitlin Stasey (*Neighbours*), is sent on a supernatural rollercoaster ride of gory death, runestone magic and unusual destruction in a perfect dovetailing of directorial styles. It's remarkably fresh and always blackly amusing. **AJ** Violence, swearing, sex scenes, drug abuse.

Caitlin Stasey *Maddy Killian* • Sianoa Smit-McPhee *Leena Miller* • Brooke Butler *Tracy Bingham* • Amanda Grace Cooper *Hanna Popkin* ■ *Dir/Scr* Lucky McKee, Chris Sivertson

All Creatures Great and Small ★★★ PG
Drama
1974 · UK · Colour · 87min

We all know the animals are incidental in this screen prequel to TV's popular memoirs of vet James Herriot: what really matters is the Yorkshire folk whose emotions are brought out from behind those gruff exteriors by what happens to their creatures' comfort. Episodic, and fairly sentimental, this has warm-hearted performances by Simon Ward as the young Herriot, Lisa Harrow as his future wife Helen and Anthony Hopkins as local vet Siegfried Farnon. **TH** *DVD*

Simon Ward *James Herriot* • Anthony Hopkins *Siegfried Farnon* • Lisa Harrow *Helen Alderson* • Brian Stirner *Tristan Farnon* • Freddie Jones *Cranford* • TP McKenna *Soames* • Brenda Bruce *Miss Harbottle* • John Collin *Mr Alderson* • Christine Buckley *Mrs Hall* ■ *Dir* Claude Whatham • *Scr* Hugh Whitemore, from the novel by James Herriot

All Dogs Go to Heaven ★★★ U
Animated adventure
1989 · Ire · Colour · 81min

Burt Reynolds provides the voice for Charlie B Parkin, a dog in late-1930s Louisiana who is killed by his business partner. Given the choice of remaining in heaven or leaving without being able to return, he decides to go back to Earth to seek revenge. Don Bluth began his career at Disney so, as you would expect, the animation is excellent, but the story is clumsily told and very young children may find some of the darker sequences upsetting. Charlie Sheen took over as the voice of Charlie in the 1996 sequel. DP *DVD*

Burt Reynolds *Charlie* • Dom DeLuise *Itchy* • Vic Tayback *Carface* • Judith Barsi *Anne-Marie* • Loni Anderson *Flo* • Melba Moore *Whippet Angel* • Charles Nelson Reilly *Killer* ■ *Dir* Don Bluth • *Scr* David Weiss

All Fall Down ★★★★
Drama
1962 · US · BW · 110min

The opening shots in Warren Beatty's career created his image as a Hollywood lothario. In this, an intense family saga, he's a loner and a womaniser, idolised by his younger brother Brandon de Wilde. Their father, Karl Malden, hits the bottle; their mother, Angela Lansbury, henpecks. And when lodger Eva Marie Saint falls for Beatty, de Wilde looks on, almost eager for a hard lesson in life. Directed by John Frankenheimer and scripted by playwright William Inge, it is now rather dated, but the cast is matchless. **AT**

Eva Marie Saint *Echo O'Brien* • Warren Beatty *Berry-Berry Willart* • Karl Malden *Ralph Willart* • Angela Lansbury *Annabel Willart* • Brandon de Wilde *Clinton Willart* • Constance Ford *Mrs Mandel* • Barbara Baxley *Schoolteacher* • Evans Evans *Hedy* ■ *Dir* John Frankenheimer • *Scr* William Inge, from the novel by James Leo Herlihy

All for Love ★★ 15
Period drama
1999 · UK · Colour · 84min

This is a botched attempt to combine swashbuckling adventure with costume romance. Jean-Marc Barr cuts a suitable dash as the French officer who is captured and sent to a remote Scottish PoW camp under the command of Richard E Grant. But director Harry Hook seems uncertain where to place the emphasis once the two men begin competing for the affections of Anna Friel and Barr decides to escape with the assistance of long-lost relations. DP Violence, nudity.

Jean-Marc Barr *Captain Jacques St Ives* • Anna Friel *Flora Gilchrist* • Miranda Richardson *Susan Gilchrist* • Richard E Grant *Major Chevening* • Tim Dutton *François* • Jason Isaacs *Alain St Ives* • Michael Gough *Count* • Vernon Dobtcheff *Bonnefoy* ■ *Dir* Harry Hook • *Scr* Joe Gallagher, Allan Cubitt, from the story *St Ives* by Robert Louis Stevenson

All for Mary ★★U
Comedy   1955 · UK · Colour · 75min

In this unfunny comedy, Nigel Patrick and David Tomlinson are rival suitors for the hand of Jill Day, but they contract chickenpox and are forced into quarantine in a Swiss chalet at the mercy of ageing nanny Kathleen Harrison. The invalids become infants as the grown men are brought under control by a dominant female. Sadly, director Wendy Toye takes the joke no further, so all we get is a feeble production that only weakly echoes its successful West End stage origins. TH **DVD**

Nigel Patrick *Clive Morton* • Kathleen Harrison *Nannie Cartwright* • David Tomlinson *Humpy Miller* • Jill Day *Mary* • David Hurst *M Victor* • Leo McKern *Gaston Nikopopoulos* • Nicholas Phipps *General* • Lionel Jeffries *Maître d'hotel* ■ *Dir* Wendy Toye • *Scr* Peter Blackmore, Paul Soskin, from the play by Harold Brooke, Kay Bannerman

All Good Things ★★15
Murder mystery based on a true story
2010 · US · Colour · 96min

After spooking audiences with his 2003 documentary *Capturing the Friedmans*, director Andrew Jarecki comes unstuck here, adapting the real-life 1982 case of Robert Durst who was suspected of causing his wife's disappearance. Slickly shot on impeccable period sets, the story chronicles the twisted tale of a New Yorker who appears to find consolation in a cosy marriage after a tormented childhood. Ryan Gosling gives his all as the damaged anti-hero, but this was a troubled shoot and that's reflected in the movie's muddled structure. DP Violence, swearing, drug abuse. **DVD**

Ryan Gosling *David Marks* • Kirsten Dunst *Katie Marks* • Frank Langella *Sanford Marks* • Kristen Wiig *Lauren Fleck* • Philip Baker Hall *Malvern Bump* ■ *Dir* Andrew Jarecki • *Scr* Marcus Hinchey, Marc Smerling

All Hands on Deck ★★U
Musical comedy   1961 · US · Colour · 98min

Director Norman Taurog – never one to over-tax the grey matter – ensures this lightweight shipboard comedy has a smooth passage. With Lieutenant Pat Boone excused duties to warble a few inoffensive songs, the time passes pleasantly enough. Given that the chief source of hilarity is the romance between Buddy Hackett's turkey and a pelican, though, it's not surprising the film sometimes goes adrift. DP

Pat Boone *Lt Donald* • Buddy Hackett *Screaming Eagle Garfield* • Dennis O'Keefe *Lt Cdr O'Gara* • Barbara Eden *Sally Hobson* • Warren Berlinger *Ensign Rush* • Gale Gordon *Cdr Bintle* • David Brandon *Lt Kutley* • Joe E Ross *Bosun* • Bartlett Robinson *Lt Cdr Anthony* ■ *Dir* Norman Taurog • *Scr* Jay Sommers, from the novel by Donald R Morris

All I Desire ★★U
Period drama   1953 · US · BW · 76min

Barbara Stanwyck finds herself in a town she left long ago, and pays an unfortunate visit to what's left of her family. This slight tosh is under-directed by melodrama favourite Douglas Sirk, who totally fails to rein in Stanwyck's excesses, so losing all sympathy for her character. This never rises above its double-bill status and is really rather tiresome. TS **DVD**

Barbara Stanwyck *Naomi Murdoch* • Richard Carlson *Henry Murdoch* • Lyle Bettger *Dutch Heineman* • Marcia Henderson *Joyce Murdoch* • Lori Nelson *Lily Murdoch* • Maureen O'Sullivan *Sara Harper* • Richard Long *Russ Underwood* • Billy Gray *Ted Murdoch* • Lotte Stein *Lena Engstrom* ■ *Dir* Douglas Sirk • *Scr* James Gunn, Robert Blees, Gina Kaus, from the novel *Stopover* by Carol Brink

All I Want for Christmas ★★U
Seasonal comedy   1991 · US · Colour · 88min

The only thing Ethan Randall and Thora Birch want for Christmas is for their separated parents to be reconciled. Will they never learn? Lauren Bacall is way over the top as their batty but bountiful granny and everything creaks along, coated liberally in sentiment. SH **DVD**

Harley Jane Kozak *Catherine O'Fallon* • Jamey Sheridan *Michael O'Fallon* • Ethan Randall [Ethan Embry] *Ethan O'Fallon* • Kevin Nealon *Tony Boer* • Thora Birch *Hallie O'Fallon* • Lauren Bacall *Lillian Brooks* • Amy Oberer *Stephanie* • Leslie Nielsen *Santa* ■ *Dir* Robert Lieberman • *Scr* Richard Kramer, Thom Eberhardt, Gail Parent, Neal Israel

All I Want for Christmas ★★
Seasonal romantic drama
2007 · US · Colour · 103min

You only need catch the opening few minutes of this seasonal schmaltz-fest to guess the ultimate outcome. An unsophisticated though innocuous advocate for true love, friendship and family, it sees widow Gail O'Grady unwittingly thrown into the media spotlight when her ten-year-old son secretly requests a new husband for her by means of a nationwide Christmas wish competition. But as contrived and simplistic as proceedings are, they possess a crude emotional appeal thanks largely to O'Grady's warm and unaffected performance. SF

Gail O'Grady *Sarah Armstrong* • Robert Mailhouse *Ben Grant* • Jimmy "Jax" Pinchak *Jessie Armstrong* • Greg Germann *Roger Nelson* • Amanda Foreman *Amber* ■ *Dir* Harvey Frost • *Scr* Marc Prey

All in a Night's Work ★★★U
Comedy   1960 · US · Colour · 90min

Some may be enchanted by this glossily produced, one-gag trifle; others may find it simply smutty. Luckily the bright sheen of 1960s Technicolor makes the shenanigans watchable, despite director Joseph Anthony's occasional lapses of pace and humour. Shirley MacLaine is suspected of helping a wealthy publisher to his death, and the man's heir (Dean Martin) tries to seduce her to get at the truth. Both stars are exceedingly adept at this sort of sexy caper, and a fine veteran supporting cast comes along for the ride. TS

Dean Martin *Tony Ryder* • Shirley MacLaine *Katie Robbins* • Charles Ruggles *Dr Warren Kingsley Sr* • Cliff Robertson *Warren Kingsley Jr* • Norma Crane *Marge Coombs* • Gale Gordon *Oliver Dunning* • Jerome Cowan *Sam Weaver* • Jack Weston *Lasker* ■ *Dir* Joseph Anthony • *Scr* Edmund Beloin, Maurice Richlin, Sidney Sheldon, from a play by Owen Elford, from a story by Margit Veszi

All in Good Time ★★★12
Romantic comedy drama
2012 · UK · Colour · 90min

Director Nigel Cole (*Calendar Girls*) and Ayub Khan-Din (the writer of *East Is East*) join forces for this light Anglo-Indian take on the same source material as the 1966 Hywel Bennett/Hayley Mills movie *The Family Way*. Atul (Reece Ritchie) and Vina (Amara Karan) live in Bolton. They're newlyweds, but a cancelled flight forces them to honeymoon at Atul's parents, and consummating the marriage proves problematic. The comedy and cultural jibes are broad and corny, though with a curiously bittersweet undercurrent; the two young leads are attractive, and the all-Indian support is spot-on. DA Some swearing, sexual references. **DVD** **Blu-ray**

Reece Ritchie *Atul* • Amara Karan *Vina* • Meera Syal *Lopa* • Arsher Ali *Etash* • Harish Patel *Eeshwar* ■ *Dir* Nigel Cole • *Scr* Ayub Khan-Din, from the play *Rafta, Rafta...* by Khan-Din, from the play *All in Good Time* by Bill Naughton

All Is Lost ★★★★12
Drama   2013 · US/Can · Colour · 101min

As a follow-up to financial crisis drama *Margin Call*, JC Chandor's next film could not be more different, telling the single-character story of a solo sailor (Robert Redford), far out in the Indian Ocean, whose yacht sustains a hole after a night-time collision. The ensuing drama develops slowly, as the yachtsman patches up the damage, but when a massive storm hits, things become deadly serious. For those tired of superhero movies, this gripping tale is the perfect antidote: a terrifying reminder of the world's natural dangers, and also a soulful homage to man's survival instincts. DW Brief swearing. **DVD**

Robert Redford *Our man* ■ *Dir/Scr* JC Chandor • *Cinematographer* Frank G DeMarco

All Men Are Mortal ★★15
Romantic fantasy
1995 · UK/Neth/Fr · Colour · 86min

A 1960s-style art movie, based on the novel by Simone de Beauvoir, about a temperamental, very actressy actress (Irène Jacob) who abandons her black musician lover for a mysterious stranger, played by Stephen Rea, who reveals himself to be a 700-year-old immortal prince. It's all very metaphysical, existential, philosophical and, for many viewers, downright pretentious. Set in France in the late 1940s, it was actually filmed in Hungary. AT

Stephen Rea *Fosca* • Irène Jacob *Regina* • Colin Salmon *Chas* • Marianne Sägebrecht *Annie* • Maggie O'Neill *Florence* • Steve Nicolson *Laforet* • Chiara Mastroianni *Françoise* ■ *Dir* Ate De Jong • *Scr* Ate de Jong, Olwen Wymark, Steven Gaydos, from the novel by Simone de Beauvoir

All My Good Countrymen ★★★★
Drama   1968 · Cz · Colour · 126min

One of four films "banned for ever" by the Czech authorities in the wake of the Prague Spring, this is an acerbic and acutely observed satire that won Vojtech Jasny the best director prize at Cannes. With its intricate blend of comedy, tragedy, fantasy and bitter reality, it chronicles events in a Moravian village from the end of the Second World War to the spring of 1968, exposing the excesses of communist rule by means of four shocking and suspicious deaths that periodically shatter the rural idyll. Played and directed with consummate skill, this provocative picture is as poetic as it is powerful. DP Czech +subtitles.

Vladimir Mensik *Jozka Pyrk* • Radoslav Brozobohaty *Frantisek* • Vlastimil Brodsky *Ocenas* • Vlaclav Babka *Franta Lampa* • Ilja Prachar *Plecmera* • Pavel Pavlovsky *Postman* ■ *Dir/Scr* Vojtech Jasny

All My Sons ★★
Drama   1948 · US · BW · 93min

The film of Arthur Miller's first play stars Burt Lancaster as the young man who makes the painful discovery that his father, tycoon Edward G Robinson, knowingly sold the US Air Force defective parts for their planes in the Second World War. Seized on by the right-wing as communist propaganda, the movie seems far less contentious today, and its moral debate rather open and shut. Very talkie, too. AT

Edward G Robinson *Joe Keller* • Burt Lancaster *Chris Keller* • Mady Christians *Kate Keller* • Louisa Horton *Ann Deever* • Howard Duff *George Deever* • Frank Conroy *Herbert Deever* • Lloyd Gough *Jim Bayliss* • Arlene Francis *Sue Bayliss* ■ *Dir* Irving Reis • *Scr* Chester Erskine, from the play by Arthur Miller

All Neat in Black Stockings ★12
Drama   1969 · UK · Colour · 95min

There's little to recommend this cheesy mix of peek-a-boo nudity and bawdy humour,

even though it boasts that icon of Swinging Sixties sex appeal, Susan George. The pairing of TV playwright Hugh Whitemore and director Christopher Morahan produces little merit. DP **DVD**

Victor Henry *Ginger* • Susan George *Jill* • Jack Shepherd *Dwyer* • Clare Kelly *Mother* • Anna Cropper *Sis* • Harry Towb *Issur* • Vanessa Forsyth *Carole* ■ *Dir* Christopher Morahan • *Scr* Jane Gaskell, Hugh Whitemore, from the novel by Gaskell

All Night Long ★★15
Drama   1961 · UK · Colour · 87min

The producer/director team of Michael Relph and Basil Dearden (*Sapphire*) tackle Britain's jazz scene with a plot about sexual jealousy that culture vultures may recognise as *Othello*. At the centre of it all is jazz singer Marti Stevens, married to Paul Harris and desired by Patrick McGoohan, jazzmen both. It's shot like a moody *film noir* and its main appeal is the chance to spot hot jazzmen during the frequent musical interludes. AT **DVD** **Blu-ray**

Patrick McGoohan *Johnny Cousin* • Marti Stevens *Delia Lane* • Betsy Blair *Emily* • Keith Michell *Cass Michaels* • Richard Attenborough *Rod Hamilton* • Paul Harris *Aurelius Rex* ■ *Dir* Basil Dearden • *Scr* Nel King, Peter Achilles [Paul Jarrico]

All Night Long ★★★15
Comedy   1981 · US · Colour · 84min

Gene Hackman drops his usual intimidating manner to play the night-manager of a suburban supermarket, who decides to rebel against his staid existence by having an affair with the kooky wife of his cousin, played by Barbra Streisand. Directed by Frenchman Jean-Claude Tramont, the film's strange domestic focus creates an offbeat view of American city life, though some sequences lack continuity and coherence. TH Swearing.

Gene Hackman *George Dupler* • Barbra Streisand *Cheryl Gibbons* • Diane Ladd *Helen Dupler* • Dennis Quaid *Freddie Dupler* • Kevin Dobson *Bobby Gibbons* • William Daniels (2) *Richard H Copleston* • Hamilton Camp *Buggams* • Ann Doran *Grandmother Gibbons* ■ *Dir* Jean-Claude Tramont • *Scr* WD Richter

All of Me ★★★15
Comedy   1984 · US · Colour · 87min

A promising idea and a dynamic performance from Steve Martin aren't enough to distract from this film's shortage of funny moments and an overreliance on half-baked resolutions. As the lawyer whose body is taken over by the soul of deceased millionairess Lily Tomlin, Martin is effective, combining his trademark exasperation with some amazingly energetic slapstick. Tomlin makes the most of appearing almost exclusively in reflection and Richard Libertini is hilarious as a swami, but Victoria Tennant hams shamelessly. DP Violence, swearing. **DVD**

Steve Martin *Roger Cobb* • Lily Tomlin *Edwina Cutwater* • Victoria Tennant *Terry Hoskins* • Madolyn Smith *Peggy Schuyler* • Richard Libertini *Prahka Lasa* • Dana Elcar *Burton Schuyler* • Jason Bernard *Tyrone Wattell* • Selma Diamond *Margo* ■ *Dir* Carl Reiner • *Scr* Phil Alden Robinson

All or Nothing ★★★★18
Social drama   2002 · UK/Fr · Colour · 122min

Dispensing with the caricature that softened the emotional impact of much of his previous work, Mike Leigh delivers a grim and relentless autopsy of working-class life. Beautifully shot and brilliantly acted, the film observes a ragtag group of south London social casualties over a long weekend on a run-down housing estate. The focus is on world-weary minicab driver Timothy Spall (outstanding), his common-law wife Lesley Manville and their two overweight offspring – daughter Alison Garland, who works in an old people's home, and younger son James Corden, an irascible couch potato. It's a poignant and stomach-churning journey into the darkest recesses of human despair, yet, for all its everyday horror, the bittersweet story brims with hope and humanity. SF **DVD**

Timothy Spall *Phil Bassett* • Lesley Manville *Penny Bassett* • Alison Garland *Rachel Bassett* • James Corden *Rory Bassett* • Ruth Sheen *Maureen* • Marion Bailey *Carol* • Paul Jesson *Ron* • Sam Kelly *Sid* ■ *Dir/Scr* Mike Leigh

All over Me ★★★★ 15

Drama 1996 · US · Colour · 89min

A haunting, uncompromising snapshot of urban adolescent life, this exceptional debut never gained the same exposure as the similarly themed *kids*, but packs the same raw power to shock. Written and directed (respectively) by Sylvia and Alex Sichel, the film offers a portrait of two teenage girls: Tara Subkoff is hopelessly in love with drug-taking loser Cole Hauser, while Alison Folland is struggling to come to terms with her own sexuality. A brutal murder in their neighbourhood puts the two friends on a collision course. The cast of unknowns is superb, and the brutally frank script helps create a troubled vision of modern American life. JF Swearing, drug abuse. *DVD*

Alison Folland *Claude* • Tara Subkoff *Ellen* • Cole Hauser *Mark* • Wilson Cruz *Jesse* • Ann Dowd *Anne, Claude's mum* • Leisha Hailey *Lucy* ■ *Dir* Alex Sichel • *Scr* Sylvia Sichel

All over Town ★★ U

Comedy 1937 · US · BW · 71min

There's no denying that the comic team of Ole Olsen and Chic Johnson always were an acquired taste. But they were always very funny, both on stage and screen, and commanded a huge following in their day. This haunted theatre flick has a great deal of typical humour, and should please fans and make converts, even if the Republic studio production values are ropey. TS

Ole Olsen *Olsen* • Chic Johnson *Johnson* • Mary Howard *Joan Eldridge* • Harry Stockwell *Don Fletcher* • Franklin Pangborn *Costumer* • James Finlayson *MacDougal* • Eddie Kane *Bailey* • Stanley Fields *Slug* • Franklin Pangborn *Costumer* ■ *Dir* James Horne [James W Horne] • *Scr* Jack Townley, Jerome Chodorov, from a story by Richard English

All Quiet on the Western Front ★★★★★ PG

Classic First World War drama
1930 · US · BW and Tinted · 125min

This classic Oscar-winning tale has lost none of its ability to shock and involve. As a study of the inhumanity of war, it retains all the impact of the novel by Erich Maria Remarque upon which it is so faithfully based. This epic saga of German schoolboys called up during the First World War marked the coming of age of the war movie, and of Carl Laemmle Jr's Universal Studios, which produced it. It also demonstrated, as an early talkie, the flexibility of the new technique, with staggering trench sequences brilliantly filmed by director Lewis Milestone, who received his second Academy Award for his work. The performances are also exemplary, but it is primarily a film of great moments - the climactic sequence of the young conscript reaching out for a butterfly in the sun - that, once seen, are never forgotten. TS *DVD*

Lew Ayres *Paul Baumer* • Louis Wolheim *Katczinsky* • John Wray *Himmelstoss* • Raymond Griffith *Gérard Duval* • George "Slim" Summerville [Slim Summerville] *Tjærden* • Russell Gleason *Müller* • William Bakewell *Albert* • Scott Kolk *Leer* • Walter Browne Rogers *Behm* • Beryl Mercer *Mrs Baumer* ■ *Dir* Lewis Milestone • *Scr* Del Andrews, Maxwell Anderson, George Abbott, from the novel by Erich Maria Remarque • *Cinematographer* Arthur Edeson

All Quiet on the Western Front ★★★ PG

First World War drama
1979 · US · Colour · 122min

It's a brave man who dares to remake what is still regarded as the most powerful pacifist statement ever committed to celluloid. However, director Delbert Mann does a fine job of adapting Erich Maria Remarque's harrowing study of life in the trenches. In addition to winning Emmys for its editing and special effects, this TV movie

also brought nominations for Mann, Patricia Neal and Ernest Borgnine, here cast as the veteran who puts Richard Thomas and his fellow recruits through their paces. A compelling, affecting insight into the hellishness of war. DP *DVD*

Richard Thomas *Paul Baumer* • Ernest Borgnine *Stanislaus Katczinsky* • Ian Holm *Himmelstoss* • Donald Pleasence *Kantorek* • Patricia Neal *Paul's mother* • Mark Drewry *Tjaden* • Michael Sheard *Paul's father* ■ *Dir* Delbert Mann • *Scr* Paul Monash, from the novel by Erich Maria Remarque

All Stars ★★★ U

Dance comedy 2013 · UK · Colour · 102min

Lively and likeable, *All Stars* is a pre-teen version of all those "Let's put the show on here!" films, such as *Step Up* and *StreetDance*. *Horrid Henry: the Movie's* Theo Stevenson and Akai Osei-Mansfield play the friends who set about staging a dance contest to save their much-loved community centre from being turned into a car park by the local council. Thoroughly corny it may be, but this makes for decent, undemanding entertainment for younger kids. DA *DVD*

Theo Stevenson *Ethan* • Akai [Akai Osei-Mansfield] *Jaden* • Ashley Jensen *Gina* • Ashley Walters *Mark* • Kimberley Walsh *Trish* • John Barrowman *Matthew* ■ *Dir* Ben Gregor • *Scr* Paul Gerstenberger • *Cinematographer* Ben Wheeler

All That Heaven Allows ★★★★ U

Melodrama 1955 · US · Colour · 84min

This is a soapy follow-up to the same team's successful *Magnificent Obsession*, which had made a star out of Rock Hudson the previous year. This is almost as daft, but it's revered in some critical circles as director Douglas Sirk's serious commentary on 1950s American values. While Sirk makes the romance between widow Jane Wyman and her gardener Hudson less than likely, the Technicolor photography by Russell Metty is sumptuous, Hudson is remarkably good, and Agnes Moorehead brings some acerbity to the tale. LB *DVD*

Jane Wyman *Cary Scott* • Rock Hudson *Ron Kirby* • Agnes Moorehead *Sara Warren* • Conrad Nagel *Harvey* • Virginia Grey *Alida Anderson* • Gloria Talbott *Kay Scott* • William Reynolds *Ned Scott* • Jacqueline de Wit *Mona Flash* • Charles Drake *Mick Anderson* ■ *Dir* Douglas Sirk • *Scr* Peggy Fenwick, from a story by Edna and Harry Lee

All That Jazz ★★★★ 15

Musical drama 1979 · US · Colour · 117min

Besides being the only musical featuring a surgical operation, this is unique in being heavily autobiographical about its director and co-writer, Bob Fosse. The talented choreographer closely resembles the lead character, Broadway dance-maestro Joe Gideon, whose philandering with women is only surpassed by his flirtations with the Angel of Death - the symbol of the self-destructiveness that will eventually kill him. Jessica Lange and Ann Reinking are the women in his angst-fuelled life but it's Roy Scheider, as the driven Joe, who dominates in a film that's as brilliantly egotistical as it is flashily self-indulgent. TH *DVD*

Roy Scheider *Joe Gideon* • Jessica Lange *Angelique* • Ann Reinking *Kate Jagger* • Leland Palmer *Audrey Paris* • Cliff Gorman *Davis Newman* • Ben Vereen *O'Connor Flood* • Erzsebet Foldi *Michelle* • Michael Tolan *Dr Ballinger* • Sandahl Bergman *Dancer* ■ *Dir* Bob Fosse • *Scr* Bob Fosse, Robert Alan Aurthur • *Choreography* Bob Fosse • *Cinematographer* Giuseppe Rotunno • *Editor* Alan Heim • *Music Director* Ralph Burns • *Art Directors* Philip Rosenberg, Tony Walton • *Costume Designer* Albert Wolsky

All the Boys Love Mandy Lane ★★★ 18

Horror 2006 · US · Colour · 90min

A crazed stalker is killing anyone who gets close to bedding high-school goddess Mandy Lane (a terrific Amber Heard) in this smart shocker. Director Jonathan Levine inserts a whole raft of subliminal references to little-known teen terrors of old, putting a

playful spin on the visceral horror and making it feel fresh and exhilarating. Certain elements will divide opinion - some will see them as unsettling, some as an annoying cheat. But at least it's another attempt to redefine the genre, and will distinguish this deconstruction of the slasher staple from the moribund rest. AJ Violence, swearing. *DVD*

Amber Heard *Mandy Lane* • Anson Mount *Garth* • Michael Welch *Emmet* • Whitney Able *Chloe* • Edwin Hodge *Bird* • Aaron Himelstein *Red* ■ *Dir* Jonathan Levine • *Scr* Jacob Forman

All the Brothers Were Valiant ★★

Adventure 1953 · US · Colour · 95min

This is a watery yarn about whalers, mutiny, South Seas maidens and exotic pearls. All that's missing is a giant squid and a tidal wave! Robert Taylor and Stewart Granger are on good form as the eponymous siblings, while Lewis Stone - Andy Hardy's dad - puts in an appearance in what was to prove his final film. AT

Robert Taylor (1) *Joel Shore* • Stewart Granger *Mark Shore* • Ann Blyth *Priscilla Holt* • Betta St John *Native girl* • Keenan Wynn *Silva* • James Whitmore *Fetcher* • Kurt Kasznar *Quint* • Lewis Stone *Captain Holt* ■ *Dir* Richard Thorpe • *Scr* Harry Brown, from the novel by Ben Ames Williams

All the Fine Young Cannibals ★★

Drama 1960 · US · Colour · 122min

This bizarre blend of teenage angst movie and Cassavetes-style drama has Robert Wagner as Chet Baker in all but name. Jazz trumpeter and protégé of dipso Pearl Bailey, he's also the father of Natalie Wood's baby - though Wood marries George Hamilton when Wagner jilts her. Having British director Michael Anderson at the helm ensures a blander ride than the subject merits. AT

Robert Wagner *Chad Bixby* • Natalie Wood *Salome Davis* • Susan Kohner *Catherine McDowall* • George Hamilton *Tony McDowall* • Pearl Bailey *Ruby Jones* • Jack Mullaney *Putney Tinker* • Onslow Stevens *Joshua Davis* • Anne Seymour *Mrs Bixby* ■ *Dir* Michael Anderson • *Scr* Robert Thom, from the novel *The Bixby Girls* by Rosamond Marshall

All the King's Men ★★★★ U

Political drama 1949 · US · BW · 105min

This blistering and powerful political drama deservedly won the best picture Oscar, with the best actor award going to gruff Broderick Crawford in the performance of a lifetime as Willie Stark, a thinly disguised portrait of Louisiana demagogue "Kingfish" Huey Long. Mercedes McCambridge is also superb as a political aide, gaining another well-deserved Oscar as best supporting actress. Today this movie may seem a tad hysterical and over-performed, but it's important to view it in the context of when it was made - a time of extreme corruption and bigotry. Editor (and later director) Robert Parrish was responsible for restructuring director Robert Rossen's cut: Parrish added new scenes and dialogue, making the film worthy of its Oscar. TS *DVD*

Broderick Crawford *Willie Stark* • Joanne Dru *Anne Stanton* • John Ireland *Jack Burden* • John Derek *Tom Stark* • Mercedes McCambridge *Sadie Burke* • Shepperd Strudwick *Adam Stanton* • Ralph Dumke *Tiny Duffy* • Anne Seymour *Lucy Stark* • Katharine Warren [Katherine Warren] *Mrs Burden* ■ *Dir* Robert Rossen • *Scr* Robert Rossen, from the novel by Robert Penn Warren

All the King's Men ★★ 12

Political drama 2005 · US · Colour · 122min

In his showy role as wily politician Willie Stark, Sean Penn fails to bring this remake of the 1949 Oscar-winning drama to life. Writer/director Steven Zaillian seems overawed by the task of adapting Robert Penn Warren's Pulitzer Prize-winning novel, which shows Stark (a character inspired by Louisiana governor Huey P Long) gradually being seduced by the lure of power. Jude Law plays Stark's right-hand man, who tries

to avert scandal while battling his own inner demons. Despite the efforts of the A-list cast (Kate Winslet, Anthony Hopkins), significant revelations have little impact among the numerous subplots, and Zaillian is forced to rely on a ponderous voiceover to explain the story. SP Some violence. *DVD* *BL*

Sean Penn *Willie Stark* • Jude Law *Jack Burden* • Kate Winslet *Anne Stanton* • James Gandolfini *Tiny Duffy* • Mark Ruffalo *Adam Stanton* • Patricia Clarkson *Sadie Burke* • Anthony Hopkins *Judge Irwin* • Kathy Baker *Mrs Burden* ■ *Dir* Steven Zaillian • *Scr* Steven Zaillian, from the novel by Robert Penn Warren • *Music* James Horner

All the Little Animals ★★★ 15

Drama 1998 · UK · Colour · 107min

Christian Bale stars as a mentally-impaired young man who runs away from his sinister stepfather (Daniel Benzali) and ends up in Cornwall, helping an eccentric hermit (John Hurt) collect and bury animals that have been hit by cars. While Jeremy Thomas (in his directorial debut) never quite settles on a consistent tone, this is still interesting, thanks to the presence of Benzali and Hurt; Bale, however, seems somewhat overwhelmed in their company. JB Violence.

John Hurt *Mr Summers* • Christian Bale *Bobby* • Daniel Benzali *De Winter* • James Faulkner *Mr Whiteside* • John O'Toole *Lorry driver* • Amanda Royle *Des* • Amy Robbins *Bobby's mother* • John Higgins *Dean* ■ *Dir* Jeremy Thomas • *Scr* Eski Thomas, from the novel by Walker Hamilton

All the President's Men ★★★★★ 15

Political thriller 1976 · US · Colour · 132min

Alan J Pakula's Oscar-winning thriller about the Watergate burglary stars Robert Redford and Dustin Hoffman as the two *Washington Post* reporters (Bob Woodward and Carl Bernstein) whose stubborn digging ultimately brings down President Nixon. William Goldman's script brilliantly clarifies the multilayered labyrinth of corruption, while Pakula's tense direction draws telling parallels between the blazing white, open-plan offices of the *Post* (no secrets here) and the dark, murky world of Washington politics. Great support, too, from Jason Robards as the *Post*'s editor, Ben Bradlee, and Hal Holbrook as the creepy informant "Deep Throat". Along with *The Best Man* and *The Manchurian Candidate*, this is one of the best movies ever made about American politics. AT Swearing. *DVD*

Robert Redford *Bob Woodward* • Dustin Hoffman *Carl Bernstein* • Jack Warden *Harry Rosenfeld* • Martin Balsam *Howard Simons* • Hal Holbrook *Deep Throat* • Jason Robards *Ben Bradlee* • Jane Alexander *Book-keeper* • Meredith Baxter *Debbie Sloan* • Ned Beatty *Dardis* • Stephen Collins *Hugh Sloan Jr* ■ *Dir* Alan J Pakula • *Scr* William Goldman, from the book by Bob Woodward, Carl Bernstein • *Cinematographer* Gordon Willis • *Editor* Robert L Wolfe • *Art Director* George Jenkins

All the Pretty Horses ★★★ 15

Western 2000 · US · Colour · 112min

Fans of Cormac McCarthy's great modern western may not be too enamoured by the overly schematic treatment it has received here under Billy Bob Thornton's measured direction. Despite its many flaws (one being Matt Damon's inability to carry the central emotional load), this retains much of its source novel's power and romantic nostalgia. Finding himself without a home or future when his beloved ranch is sold out from under him by his estranged mother, Damon and his best buddy Henry Thomas head to Mexico to become cowboys. AJ Violence, sex scenes. *DVD*

Matt Damon *John Grady Cole* • Henry Thomas *Lacey Rawlins* • Lucas Black *Jimmy Blevins* • Penélope Cruz *Alejandra* • Rubén Blades *Rocha* • Robert Patrick *Cole* • Bruce Dern *Judge* ■ *Dir* Billy Bob Thornton • *Scr* Ted Tally, from the novel by Cormac McCarthy • *Cinematographer* Barry Markowitz

All the Queen's Men ★★ 12

Second World War comedy
2001 · US/Austria/Ger/Hun · Colour · 97min

Matt LeBlanc stars in this dismal affair, being sent into Germany to infiltrate a factory making Enigma machines after an altercation with twitchy British brass hat Edward Fox. Eddie Izzard's drag queen offers gender-bending tips and LeBlanc indulges in some combat action, but it's infantile stuff from director Stefan Ruzowitzky. DP *DVD*

Matt LeBlanc *Steven O'Rourke* • Eddie Izzard *Tony Parker* • James Cosmo *Archie* • Nicolette Krebitz *Romy* • Udo Kier *Gen Landsdorf* • David Birkin *Johnno* • Edward Fox *Colonel Aiken* ■ *Dir* Stefan Ruzowitzky • *Scr* David Schneider, from a story by Digby Wolfe, Joseph Manduke, June Roberts

All the Real Girls ★★★ 15

Romantic drama   2003 · US · Colour · 103min

This small-town study of love and friendship has the potential either to beguile or to bore audiences. Writer/director David Gordon Green captures the awkwardness of a fledgeling romance, gaining naturalistic honesty from local stud Paul Schneider and his friend's virginal young sister, Zooey Deschanel. The film has mood, courtesy of some lyrical North Carolina landscape photography and an evocative soundtrack, yet the impression lingers of a movie that thinks a little too highly of itself. JC *DVD*

Paul Schneider (2) *Paul* • Zooey Deschanel *Noel* • Patricia Clarkson *Elvira Fine* • Benjamin Mouton *Leland* • Maurice Compte *Bo* • Danny McBride (2) *Bust-Ass* • Shea Whigham *Tip* ■ *Dir* David Gordon Green • *Scr* David Gordon Green, from a story by Paul Schneider, David Gordon Green • *Cinematographer* Tim Orr

All the Right Moves ★★★ 15

Sports drama   1983 · US · Colour · 86min

Respected cinematographer Michael Chapman made his directorial debut with this authentic portrait of small-town life. Indeed, it's such a well-rounded film that it makes his decision to return to cinematography – following criticism handed out to his follow-up, *The Clan of the Cave Bear* – all the more disappointing. The turbulent relationship between a star footballer (Tom Cruise) and his coach (Craig T Nelson) is convincingly established and the gridiron action smacks of the real thing. DP *DVD*

Tom Cruise *Stef Djordjevic* • Craig T Nelson *Vern Nickerson* • Lea Thompson *Lisa Lietske* • Charles Cioffi *Pop* • Paul Carafotes *Salvucci* • Christopher Penn [Chris Penn] *Brian* • Sandy Faison *Suzie* ■ *Dir* Michael Chapman • *Scr* Michael Kane

All the Right Noises ★★★ 12

Drama   1970 · UK · Colour · 87min

This study of age-gap passion in Swinging London sat on a shelf for two years and is a difficult watch in the post-Savile era, given that it follows the developing relationship between 30-something theatre electrician Tom Bell and chorus girl Olivia Hussey. Trouble is, he has forgotten to mention he has a wife and kids, and she's omitted that she's 15 and still at school. Capturing the free love spirit of the time, O'Hara refuses to judge either, but viewed now this is bound to provoke debate. DP Sex scenes.

Tom Bell *Len* • Olivia Hussey *Val* • Judy Carne *Joy* ■ *Dir/Scr* Gerry O'Hara

All the Vermeers in New York ★★★★

Romantic drama   1990 · US · Colour · 87min

Virtually ignored on its original release, this is a subtle and often moving story of unfulfilled love, in which the pace and emptiness of modern life is contrasted with the serenity and beauty of the paintings by Dutch artist Jan Vermeer hanging in New York's art galleries. Proving that the auteur is not yet extinct, versatile Jon Jost not only wrote and directed the film, but also shot, designed and edited it. Jost's imaginative contrasts between art and life and his stylish compositions will linger longest in the memory, and Stephen Lack's passion for Emmanuelle Chaulet will leave you slightly misty-eyed. DP

Emmanuelle Chaulet *Anna* • Katherine Bean *Nicole* • Grace Phillips *Felicity* • Laurel Lee Kiefer *Ariel Ainsworth* • Gracie Mansion • Gordon Joseph Weiss *Gordon* • Stephen Lack *Mark* ■ *Dir/Scr* Jon Jost

All the Way ★★★★

Biographical drama   2016 · US · Colour · 132min

Breaking Bad's Bryan Cranston is flat-out terrific in this political epic as the charming but ferocious Lyndon B Johnson. It's a reworking of an acclaimed play, for which Cranston won a Tony award, and his performance ignites what might otherwise be one of those solid, reverential US history lessons. The plot follows Johnson from the stunned aftermath of JKF's assassination to his own election as president in 1965. In the end this probably glorifies LBJ, but it's how you wish politics worked. DB

Bryan Cranston *Lyndon B Johnson* • Melissa Leo *Lady Bird Johnson* • Anthony Mackie *Martin Luther King Jr* • Bradley Whitford *Hubert Humphrey* • Frank Langella *Richard Russell* ■ *Dir* Jay Roach • *Scr* Robert Schenkkan, from his play

All the Way Home ★★★★

Period drama   1963 · US · BW · 97min

This magnificently acted movie is an adaptation of James Agee's autobiographical *A Death in the Family*. The tale of bereavement and its effect on the young Agee in Tennessee in 1915 is seen through the eyes of a boy, played by Michael Kearney, as his father is suddenly and accidentally killed. Jean Simmons is very moving in the role of the mother, and Robert Preston, as the father, also demonstrates what a fine and subtle actor he could be given the right material. TS

Jean Simmons *Mary* • Robert Preston *Jay* • Pat Hingle *Ralph* • Aline MacMahon *Aunt Hannah* • Thomas Chalmers *Joel* • John Cullum *Andrew* • Ronnie Claire Edwards *Sally* • Michael Kearney *Rufus* ■ *Dir* Alex Segal • *Scr* Philip Reisman Jr, from the play by Tad Mosel, from the novel *A Death in the Family* by James Agee

All the Young Men ★★

War drama   1960 · US · BW · 86min

This is a desperately tedious Korean War tale despite an interesting cast. It's sad to see Alan Ladd, well past his prime, struggling to hold the screen against sturdy Sidney Poitier, who plays a black sergeant trying to gain the respect of a leaderless platoon of marines. TS

Alan Ladd *Kincaid* • Sidney Poitier *Towler* • James Darren *Cotton* • Glenn Corbett *Wade* • Mort Sahl *Crane* • Ana St Clair *Maya* • Joe Gallison *Jackson* • Ingemar Johansson *Torgil* ■ *Dir/Scr* Hall Bartlett

All These Women ★★ PG

Satire   1964 · Swe · Colour · 76min

Ingmar Bergman's first production in colour is one of his few miscalculations. Co-written with actor Erland Josephson, this clumsy costume comedy seeks both to explore the elusive nature of genius and decry the parasitic insolence of critics, whose only acts of creation depend entirely on the destruction of another's work. Although there are flashes of Mack Sennett, Jacques Tati and Federico Fellini in the humour, biographer Jarl Kulle's encounters with a cellist's female entourage are resolutely unfunny. DP Swedish +subtitles. *DVD*

Jarl Kulle *Cornelius* • Bibi Andersson *Humlan* • Harriet Andersson *Isolde* • Eva Dahlbeck *Adelaide* ■ *Dir* Ingmar Bergman • *Scr* Erland Josephson, Ingmar Bergman

All Things Fair ★★★ 15

Second World War romantic drama
1995 · Swe/Den · Colour · 124min

Winner of the Silver Bear at Berlin and recipient of an Oscar nomination for best foreign film, this was something of a return to form for Bo Widerberg. Set in neutral Malmö during the Second World War, it tells of a lonely teenager who begins an affair with one of his teachers. The director's son, Johan, takes the lead, and his amenable performance and the customary beauty of the imagery are the main reasons for watching this often incoherent account of first love. DP Swedish +subtitles. Swearing, sex scenes, mild violence.

Johan Widerberg *Stig* • Marika Lagercrantz *Viola* • Tomas von Brömssen *Kjell* • Karin Huldt *Lisbet* • Björn Kjellman *Sigge* • Frida Lindholm *Olga* ■ *Dir/Scr* Bo Widerberg

All Things to All Men ★★ 15

Crime drama   2012 · UK · Colour · 84min

First-time writer/director George Isaac's capably paced thriller depicts London crime on both sides of the law. Rufus Sewell is flintily amoral as the Scotland Yard detective who busts the drug-dealer son of a gangland bigwig (Gabriel Byrne) and forces him to help set up Toby Stephens's rogue thief. His superiors in the force and the government are as corrupt as he is, but no-one has factored in the conscience of rookie cop Leo Gregory. There's plenty of treachery and violence, but the characterisation is too thin to allow the fine cast to shine. DP Violence, swearing.

Gabriel Byrne *Joseph Corso* • Rufus Sewell *Parker* • Toby Stephens *Riley* • Elsa Pataky *Sophia* • Leo Gregory *Dixon* • Terence Maynard *Sands* ■ *Dir/Scr* George Isaac

All This, and Heaven Too ★★★★ U

Romantic drama   1940 · US · BW · 134min

This sumptuous Warner Bros period melodrama stars Bette Davis as a governess in Paris causing marital problems for her employer Charles Boyer. There's a veritable series of tragedies in scriptwriter Casey Robinson's torrid adaptation of the first half of Rachel Lyman Field's once-popular doorstop *roman à clef*, but Davis is remarkably restrained, and therefore doubly effective, in what must rank as one of her finest screen performances. Despite the length, Anatole Litvak's detailed pacing and Max Steiner's magnificent score render this one unmissable. TS

Bette Davis *Henriette Deluzy Desportes* • Charles Boyer *Duke De Praslin* • Jeffrey Lynn *Reverend Henry Field* • Barbara O'Neil *Duchesse De Praslin* • Virginia Weidler *Louise* • Walter Hampden *Pasquier* • Harry Davenport *Pierre* • Fritz Leiber *Albe* ■ *Dir* Anatole Litvak • *Scr* Casey Robinson, from the novel by Rachel Lyman Field

All through the Night ★★★

Spy drama   1942 · US · BW · 106min

A standard piece of Warner Bros wartime propaganda, this stars Humphrey Bogart as a Broadway gambler who discovers a gang of Nazis plotting to sink a US battleship anchored in New York. The tone of the film is rather jokey, though it was released a year after the bombing of Pearl Harbor and consequently no one thought it was very funny. But Bogart is on decent enough form and the usual suspects including Conrad Veidt and Peter Lorre lurk in the shadows. AT

Humphrey Bogart *Gloves Donahue* • Conrad Veidt *Hall Ebbing* • Kaaren Verne *Leda Hamilton* • Jane Darwell *Ma Donahue* • Frank McHugh *Barney* • Peter Lorre *Pepi* • Judith Anderson *Madame* • William Demarest *Sunshine* • Jackie Gleason *Starchie* • Phil Silvers *Waiter* • Wallace Ford *Spats Hunter* • Barton MacLane *Marty Callahan* ■ *Dir* Vincent Sherman • *Scr* Leonard Spigelgass, Edwin Gilbert, from a story by Spigelgass, Leonard Ross

The All Together ★ 15

Comedy drama   2007 · UK · Colour · 79min

This lower-than-low-budget feature was made with a cast and crew of just 28 in a south London house. Sadly, the corny and contrived end product wasn't worth the effort. Chris (Martin Freeman) is desperate to sell his house, so has ordered his flatmate Bob to let in anyone who calls round. Bob takes this instruction literally, so an American gangster and his British lackey (Danny Dyer) get mistaken for estate agents, and when assorted other callers show up they wind up being held hostage. The two parts of the story seem like separate films and there is nothing funny about either of them. DA Swearing, some violence. *DVD*

Martin Freeman *Chris Ashworth* • Corey Johnson *Mr Gaspardi* • Velibor Topic *Bob Music* • Danny Dyer *Dennis Earle* • Richard Harrington *Jerry Davies* ■ *Dir/Scr* Gavin Claxton

Allan Quatermain and the Lost City of Gold ★★ PG

Adventure   1987 · US · Colour · 95min

This sequel to *King Solomon's Mines* again has Richard Chamberlain and Sharon Stone in search of treasure. If the first film was a remake of a remake that ripped off *Raiders of the Lost Ark*, this one is a remake that rips off *Romancing the Stone*. Lazy direction and hilariously cheap special effects aren't quite awful enough to make it a candidate for the Ed Wood award. AT Some violence and swearing *DVD*

Richard Chamberlain *Allan Quatermain* • Sharon Stone *Jesse Huston* • James Earl Jones *Umslopogaas* • Henry Silva *Agon* • Cassandra Peterson *Sorais* • Robert Donner *Swarma* ■ *Dir* Gary Nelson • *Scr* Gene Quintano, Lee Reynolds, from the novel *Quatermain* by H Rider Haggard

Allegro ★★★ 15

Futuristic romantic drama
2005 · Den · BW and Colour · 87min

Danish director/writer Christoffer Boe follows up his 2003 debut with another intriguing oddity. Concert pianist Ulrich Thomsen loses his emotional memory after his affair with an enigmatic beauty (model Helena Christensen). For ten years, his recollections are surreally trapped in a section of his Copenhagen home town, until an invitation forces the musician to confront his past. Despite its technical elegance, the picture is as cold as its protagonist, rarely demonstrating the passion that it claims to champion. Fortunately, the conclusion has a satisfying poignancy with an unexpected twist to bolster an otherwise basic storyline. SF Danish +subtitles. Swearing. *DVD*

Ulrich Thomsen *Zetterstrom* • Helena Christensen *Andrea* • Henning Moritzen *Tom* • Nicolas Bro *Terence Sander* • Ellen Hillingso *Clara* ■ *Dir* Christoffer Boe • *Scr* Christoffer Boe, Mikael Wulff • *Cinematographer* Manuel Alberto Claro

Allegro non Troppo ★★★ PG

Animated musical comedy
1976 · It · BW and Colour · 74min

Part parody, part homage to Disney's *Fantasia*, Bruno Bozzetto's third feature combines animation and live-action to generally amusing effect. Divided by sections featuring composer Maurizio Nichetti, the best vignettes show the serpent suffering the agony of Eden's apple to the strains of Stravinsky's *Firebird*, a weird menagerie of alien life forms struggling forth from a discarded Coke bottle to Ravel's *Bolero*, and Vivaldi's *Concerto in C Minor* forming the backdrop to a bee's pursuit of pollen in the presence of a courting couple. However, the showpiece is Sibelius's *Valse Triste*, which accompanies a melancholy cat on its nostalgic journey through the ruins of a bombed-out city. DP In Italian.

■ *Dir* Bruno Bozzetto • *Scr* Bruno Bozzetto, Guido Manuli, Maurizio Nichetti • *Animators* Bruno Bozzetto, Guido Manuli

Alleluia ★★★★ 18

Thriller   2014 · Bel/Fr · Colour · 93min

Real-life "Lonely Hearts Killers" Martha Beck and Raymond Fernandez have inspired many films, most notably 1969's *The Honeymoon Killers* and *Deep Crimson* (1996). In the second searing opus in his Ardennes trilogy, which started with *Calvaire*, Belgian director Fabrice du Welz piles on the style in a quirky update full of hypnotic eeriness and stylish voyeurism. Laurent Lucas and Lola Dueñas play an internet dating con artist and a damaged morgue attendant who team up to prey on lonely women, as the film alternates between tension-filled drama and trippy horror, right up to its enigmatic conclusion. AJ French +subtitles. Violence, swearing, sex scenes.

Laurent Lucas *Michel* • Lola Dueñas *Gloria* • Stéphane Bissot *Madeleine* • Edith Le Merdy *Marguerite* • Anne-Marie Loop *Gabriella* • Helena Noguerra *Solange* ■ *Dir* Fabrice du Welz • *Scr* Fabrice du Welz, Vincent Tavier

Alligator ★★★★ 15

Horror   1980 · US · Colour · 87min

The old urban myth about baby alligators thriving in city sewers after being discarded as pets becomes a turbo-driven eco-chiller, thanks to the genuine wit and sardonic wisdom of John Sayles's superb script. Just as he did with *Piranha* and *The Howling* (written with Terence H Winkless), Sayles crafts a monster-on-the-loose scenario that's better than the best of the 1950s movies it resembles. The cast is highly believable and treats the in-jokes with the right amount of tongue-in-cheek deference. Director Lewis Teague (*Cujo*) brings subtle irony to the carnage and infuses the whole radical re-packaging of mutant monster clichés with a likeable sense of insolent fun. AJ *DVD*

Robert Forster *Detective David Madison* • Robin Riker *Marisa Kendall* • Dean Jagger *Slade* • Michael Gazzo [Michael V Gazzo] *Police Chief Clark* • Sidney Lassick [Sydney Lassick] *Lou* • Jack Carter *Mayor Ledoux* • Perry Lang *Kelly* • Henry Silva *Col Brock* ■ *Dir* Lewis Teague • *Scr* John Sayles

Alligator II: the Mutation ★★ 15

Horror   1991 · US · Colour · 90min

The original *Alligator* was a cult delight: John Sayles had a hand in the witty dialogue, while the actors kept theirs tongues firmly in cheek. This sequel reprises the basic plot – mutant reptile wreaks havoc in suburbia – but it's tame stuff, despite a pretty good cast. The creature isn't particularly scary, either. JF *DVD*

Joseph Bologna *David Hodges* • Brock Peters *Chief Speed* • Dee Wallace Stone *Christine Hodges* • Woody Brown *Rich Harmon* • Holly Gagnier *Sheri* • Richard Lynch *Hawkins* • Bill Daily *Anderson* • Steve Railsback *Vincent Brown* ■ *Dir* Jon Hess • *Scr* Curt Allen

An Alligator Named Daisy ★★★ U

Comedy   1955 · UK · Colour · 84min

This bright, if silly, Rank comic romp for sexy Diana Dors and pompous Donald Sinden has one of those compulsively watchable period character casts. J Lee Thompson's hand lies a little too heavy over the proceedings and Pinewood's attempt to match Hollywood in pace and style doesn't happen. But Dors reveals a nice sense of comic timing and Stephen Boyd, who is best known for playing Messala in *Ben-Hur*, makes an early impact. TS *DVD*

Donald Sinden *Peter Weston* • Diana Dors *Vanessa Colebrook* • Jeannie Carson *Moira* • James Robertson-Justice *Sir James* • Stanley Holloway *General* • Margaret Rutherford *Prudence Croquet* • Roland Culver *Colonel Weston* • Stephen Boyd *Albert* • Richard Wattis *Hoskins* • Henry Kendall *Valet* ■ *Dir* J Lee Thompson • *Scr* Jack Davies

The Alligator People ★

Science-fiction horror   1959 · US · BW · 74min

1950s "creature features" don't come any sillier or more insane than this. Down in the Louisiana swamplands, doctor George Macready experiments with an alligator serum intended to help amputee victims grow new limbs. Bruce Bennett is a wounded man who takes the serum and turns into an upright reptile, with the help of an ill-fitting rubber suit. Inept in practically every area. AJ

Beverly Garland *Jane Marvin* • Bruce Bennett *Dr Erik Lorimer* • Lon Chaney Jr *Mannon* • George Macready *Dr Mark Sinclair* • Frieda Inescort *Mrs Henry Hawthorne* • Richard Crane *Paul Webster* ■ *Dir* Roy Del Ruth • *Scr* Orville H Hampton, from a story by Charles O'Neal, Hampton

The Allnighter ★★ PG

Comedy   1987 · US · Colour · 91min

This attempt to turn the Bangles singer Susanna Hoffs into a movie star failed because she's not a very good actress, and the film isn't that great either. Hoffs and co-star Dedee Pfeiffer are out of their depth, but the performances of the more experienced Joan Cusack and Michael Ontkean help make this a passable, slightly saucy comedy. JB

Susanna Hoffs *Molly* • Dedee Pfeiffer *Val* • Joan Cusack *Gina* • John Terlesky *CJ* • James Anthony Shanta *Killer* • Michael Ontkean *Mickey Leroi* • Pam Grier *Sgt MacLeish* • Phil Brock *Brad* ■ *Dir/Scr* Tamar Simon Hoffs

All's Fair ★ 15

Comedy   1989 · US · Colour · 85min

George Segal, once the credible embodiment of harassed middle America, must have been desperate when he agreed to star in this tosh. As chauvinist businessmen take on their wives and female colleagues at a weekend war game, this metaphor for the battle of the sexes is never less than clumsy. A slack, no-laughs comedy. JM Swearing.

George Segal *Colonel* • Sally Kellerman *Florence* • Robert Carradine *Mark* • Jennifer Edwards *Ann* • Jane Kaczmarek *Linda* • John Kapelos *Eddy* • Lou Ferrigno *Klaus* ■ *Dir* Rocky Lang • *Scr* Randee Russell, John Finegan, Tom Rondinella, William Pace, from a story by Watt Tyler, Finegan

Almost ★ PG

Romantic comedy   1990 · Aus · Colour · 81min

Wacky housewife Rosanna Arquette regresses into uninspired fantasy through a combination of sheer boredom and constant arguments with her uncaring husband. Director Michael Pattinson's whimsically challenged, unremarkable comedy is short on wit and long on limp laughs. AJ Some swearing, brief nudity. *DVD*

Rosanna Arquette *Wendy* • Bruce Spence *Ronnie* • Hugo Weaving *Jake* • Kerry Walker *Deidre* • Doreen Warburton *Elsie* • Desirée Smith *Cynthia* • Susan Lyons *Caroline* ■ *Dir* Michael Pattinson • *Scr* Suzanne Hawley

Almost an Angel ★★ PG

Comedy   1990 · US · Colour · 91min

Poor Paul ("Crocodile" Dundee) Hogan plays a crook-turned-angel in what is anything but a divine comedy. He only has himself to blame for the feeble wisecracks and fortune cookie philosophy as he wrote the script, and one suspects that he had as much control over the direction as credited John Cornell. Hogan ambles through the action as if his mind was elsewhere, only perking up when joined by real-life wife Linda Kozlowski, who gives a half-decent performance, as does Elias Koteas as her disabled brother. DP Swearing.

Paul Hogan *Terry Dean* • Linda Kozlowski *Rose Garner* • Elias Koteas *Steve Garner* • Doreen Lang *Mrs Garner* • Robert Sutton *Guido* • Travis Venable *Bubba* • Douglas Seale *Father* • Charlton Heston *God* ■ *Dir* John Cornell • *Scr* Paul Hogan

Almost Famous ★★★★ 15

Comedy drama   2000 · US · Colour · 118min

This funny and touching coming-of-age movie is based on writer/director Cameron Crowe's own experiences as a teenage rock journalist in the early 1970s. Fifteen-year-old William Miller (Patrick Fugit) escapes from the clutches of his delightfully overprotective mother (Frances McDormand) when he's hired to write about rock band Stillwater for *Rolling Stone* magazine. Joining the group on tour, Fugit is sucked into a chaotic world of parties, drugs and clashing egos, falling under the spell of self-styled "band aid" Kate Hudson and lead guitarist Billy Crudup. It loses its way slightly towards the end, but this is still entertaining and affectionate. LH Swearing, brief nudity, drug abuse. *DVD* ⬚

Billy Crudup *Russell Hammond* • Frances McDormand *Elaine Miller* • Kate Hudson *Penny Lane* • Jason Lee *Jeff Bebe* • Patrick Fugit *William Miller* • Anna Paquin *Polexia Aphrodisia* •

Fairuza Balk *Sapphire* • Noah Taylor *Dick Roswell* • Zooey Deschanel *Anita Miller* ■ *Dir/Scr* Cameron Crowe

Almost Heroes ★★ 12

Comedy adventure   1998 · US · Colour · 86min

In his final screen outing Chris Farley is paired with Matthew Perry as 19th-century rivals of the legendary explorers Lewis and Clark. Determined to put their names in the history books, they end up falling foul of Indians, the rugged wilderness and each other. Farley is as energetically crude as ever, but both Perry and director Christopher Guest, who was behind the classic *This Is Spinal Tap*, seem uncomfortable with the material. JF Swearing.

Chris Farley *Bartholomew Hunt* • Matthew Perry *Leslie Edwards* • Bokeem Woodbine *Jonah* • Eugene Levy *Guy Fontenot* • Kevin Dunn *Hidalgo* • Lisa Barbuscia *Shaquinna* • Steven M Porter *Higgins* • David Packer *Bidwell* • Lewis Arquette *Merchant* ■ *Dir* Christopher Guest • *Scr* Boyd Hale, Mark Nutter, Tom Wolfe

Almost Married ★★ 15

Comedy   2014 · UK · Colour · 96min

Dishonesty and hypocrisy quickly sour the mood in this determinedly laddish British farce about the perils of stag-do debauchery. Relentlessly crude, the slimly plotted swear-fest is seldom as funny as it thinks it is, as *Game of Thrones* star Philip McGinley returns home with an STD. After a boisterous opening, first-time writer/director Ben Cookson struggles to mine humour from the serious issues, and the childishly offensive chat about HIV, suicide and paedophilia falls flat, making his characters seem small-minded and unlikeable. SF Swearing, sexual references. *DVD*

Philip McGinley *Kyle* • Emily Atack *Lydia* ■ *Dir/Scr* Ben Cookson

Almost Peaceful ★★★ 15

Period drama   2002 · Fr · Colour · 94min

Michel Deville's film focuses on a group of Jewish tailors toiling in a workshop off the Rue de Soleil in Paris shortly after the Second World War. The ensemble cast evocatively captures the feelings of grief, relief and guilt that pervaded the time, with Zabou Breitman particularly affecting as she realises that she's more attuned to widower Denis Podalydès's melancholy than husband Simon Akbarian's optimism. DP French +subtitles. Nudity.

Simon Abkarian *Monsieur Albert* • Zabou Breitman [Zabou] *Léa* • Lubna Azabal *Jacqueline* • Clotilde Courau *Simone* • Vincent Elbaz *Léon* • Julie Gayet *Madame Andrée* • Stanislas Merhar *Maurice* • Denis Podalydès *Charles* ■ *Dir* Michel Deville • *Scr* Rosaline Deville, from the novel *Quoi de Neuf sur la Guerre?* by Robert Bober

Almost Summer ★★

Romantic drama   1977 · US · Colour · 88min

High-school elections, the teenage dating game and a feel-good soundtrack combine for an initially bright and breezy satire about youth values. It's when the tone gets too serious and preachy that restlessness is likely to set in. Beach Boy Brian Wilson is credited for the title tune and *It's OK*, while fellow group member Mike Love penned and sings *Cruisin* and *Sad, Sad Summer*. While no great addition to the rock cinema genre, this is good natured enough to get by. AJ

Bruno Kirby *Bobby* DeVito • Lee Purcell *Christine Alexander* • John Friedrich *Darryl Fitzgerald* • Didi Conn *Donna* DeVito • Thomas Carter *Dean Hampton* • Tim Matheson *Kevin Hawkins* ■ *Dir* Martin Davidson • *Scr* Judith Berg, Sandra Berg, Martin Davidson, Marc Reid Rubel

Almost You ★★ 15

Romantic drama   1984 · US · Colour · 92min

Griffin Dunne stars as the unhappy husband whose wife Brooke Adams is injured in a car accident. It's not long before he's having an affair with nurse Karen Young, hired to look after her, in a drama that suffers from the fact that few of the characters are sympathetic. This would be a huge problem

were it not for the performance of Dunne, who manages to give his character some credibility and keeps you watching. JB

Brooke Adams *Erica Boyer* • Griffin Dunne *Alex Boyer* • Karen Young *Lisa Willoughby* • Marty Watt *Kevin Danzig* • Christine Estabrook *Maggie* • Josh Mostel *David* • Laura Dean *Jeannie* • Dana Delany *Susan McCall* ■ *Dir* Adam Brooks • *Scr* Mark Horowitz, from a story by Adam Brooks

Aloha ★★ 12A

Comedy   2015 · US · Colour · 104min

Former golden boy Cameron Crowe doesn't half lay the sentimentality on thick, as screwball comedy rubs awkwardly up against spirituality and sappiness. Bill Murray's untrustworthy billionaire is launching a satellite from Hawaii, Bradley Cooper's old stomping ground, and Emma Stone and Rachel McAdams are respectively the mixed-race fighter pilot (bizarre!) Cooper falls for and his ex who has something important to impart. Confusing, unconvincing and frustratingly glib. EAS

Bradley Cooper *Brian Gilcrest* • Emma Stone *Allison Ng* • Rachel McAdams *Tracy Woodside* • Bill Murray *Carson Welch* ■ *Dir/Scr* Cameron Crowe

Aloha, Bobby and Rose ★★★

Crime drama   1975 · US · Colour · 88min

After making an impact with his role in George Lucas's *American Graffiti*, Paul Le Mat starred in this crime melodrama from director Floyd Mutrux. This is just the kind of rock 'n' roll chase movie that influenced Quentin Tarantino and paved the lethal path towards Oliver Stone's *Natural Born Killers*. Note the use of rock standards and an early appearance from Edward James Olmos. TS Violence, swearing.

Paul Le Mat *Bobby* • Dianne Hull *Rose* • Tim McIntire *Buford* • Leigh French *Donna Sue* • Noble Willingham *Uncle Charlie* • Martine Bartlett *Rose's mother* • Robert Carradine *Moxey* • Eddie Olmos [Edward James Olmos] ■ *Dir/Scr* Floyd Mutrux

Aloha Summer ★★★ PG

Drama   1988 · US · Colour · 92min

The secret of surf movies is to ensure there is plenty of sun and sand, and as many shots of muscular, tanned, teen bodies arching through the breakers as decency will allow. Director Tommy Lee Wallace resists the temptation to tamper with what, essentially, is a winning formula, ensuring that this surfing sextet pass through their rites of passage in an orderly fashion to the sound of rock hits of the day. This being Hawaii in 1959, he is able to slip in a few novel touches, such as the Japanese kid who, while thinking his homeland was hard done by in the war, can't accept his father's traditional code. DP

Chris Makepeace *Mike Tognetti* • Yuji Okumoto *Kenzo Konishi* • Don Michael Paul *Chuck Granville* • Tia Carrere *Lani Kepoo* • Sho Kosugi *Yukinaga Konishi* ■ *Dir* Tommy Lee Wallace • *Scr* Mike Greco, Bob Benedetto, from a story by Greco

Alone in the Dark ★★ 18

Horror   1982 · US · Colour · 89min

Donald Pleasence is the head of a New Jersey lunatic asylum keeping its really dangerous criminal inmates – among them Jack Palance and Martin Landau – under electronic surveillance. When a power failure occurs, the violent psychos break out and head to the home of the asylum doctor. Aside from a promising opening dream sequence and an interesting "who's really crazy?" dénouement, this debut horror feature from director Jack Sholder is below par. AJ

Jack Palance *Frank Hawkes* • Erland Van Lidth Ronald "Fatty" Elster • Deborah Hedwall *Nell Potter* • Phillip Clark *Tom Smith/Skagg* • Martin Landau *Bryon "Preacher" Sutcliff* • Dwight Schultz *Dan Potter* ■ *Dir* Jack Sholder • *Scr* Jack Sholder, from a story by Robert Shaye, Michael Harpster, Sholder

Alone on the Pacific ★★★★
Adventure 1963 · Jpn · Colour · 104min

In all his major films, from *The Burmese Harp* to *Tokyo Olympiad*, Kon Ichikawa is concerned with men pushed to extremes. Here, a young yachtsman takes three months to sail from Osaka to San Francisco on a 19-foot craft. Based on the true adventures of Kenichi Horie, it seems an impossible subject for a film. But Ichikawa, using widescreen to magnificent effect and integrating flashbacks to the sailor's life on shore, makes even the dull bits of the voyage interesting. The climactic scene, as the Golden Gate bridge looms out of the mist, is genuinely moving. RB Japanese +subtitles.

Yujiro Ishihara *The youth* • Kinuyo Tanaka *His mother* • Masayuki Mori *His father* • Ruriko Asoka *His sister* • Hajime Hana *His friend* ■ *Dir* Kon Ichikawa • *Scr* Natto Wada, from the logbook of Kenichi Horie

Alone with a Stranger ★★
Thriller 2000 · US · Colour · 90min

Former *Falcon Crest* mainstay William R Moses takes the lead in this decidedly derivative thriller. He simply doesn't have the authority to carry his pivotal double role as twins whose lives have taken very different directions. Director Peter Liapis must take most of the blame for the lack of tension, as he also wrote the screenplay and has a small acting role. JF Swearing.

William R Moses *James/Max Kennington* • Barbara Niven *Sandy Kennington* • Nia Peeples *Beth Jenkins* • Scotty Cox *David Kennington* • Priscilla Barnes *Claire* ■ *Dir* Peter Liapis • *Scr* Peter Liapis, from a story by Liapis, Richard Dana Smith

Along Came a Spider ★★★ 15
Suspense thriller
2001 · US/Ger · Colour · 98min

A prequel to *Kiss the Girls*, this suspense thriller has Morgan Freeman resuming his role as detective and psychologist Alex Cross. A senator's daughter is being held to ransom, and the Secret Service agent (Monica Potter) who should have been protecting her volunteers to assist Cross. Based on the first of James Patterson's bestselling Cross novels, the film boasts a strong cast assuredly led by Freeman. Yet the pace of the film seems forced in order to fit in too many plot contrivances. JF Violence, swearing.

Morgan Freeman *Alex Cross* • Monica Potter *Secret Service Agent Jezzie Flannigan* • Michael Wincott *Gary Soneji/Jonathan Mercuzio* • Penelope Ann Miller *Elizabeth Rose* • Michael Moriarty *Senator Hank Rose* • Dylan Baker *Special Agent Oliver "Ollie" McArthur* ■ *Dir* Lee Tamahori • *Scr* Marc Moss, from the novel by James Patterson

Along Came Jones ★★★ PG
Comedy western 1945 · US · BW · 86min

Fans of the Coasters' immortal 1950s record *Along Came Jones* should check out this undervalued film, in which amiable cowpoke Gary Cooper is mistaken for outlaw Dan Duryea. It's a likeable compendium of western clichés, ably handled by former editor Stuart Heisler. There's much to enjoy here, not least a lovely performance from Loretta Young. The title passed into western movie folklore. TS DVD

Gary Cooper *Melody Jones* • Loretta Young *Cherry de Longpre* • William Demarest *George Fury* • Dan Duryea *Monte Jarrad* • Frank Sully *Cherry's brother* • Russell Simpson *Pop de Longpre* • Arthur Loft *Sheriff* ■ *Dir* Stuart Heisler • *Scr* Nunnally Johnson, from a story by Alan LeMay

Along Came Polly ★★ 12
Romantic comedy 2004 · US · Colour · 86min

Ben Stiller plays a cautious risk assessor who falls for wild former schoolfriend Jennifer Aniston after his new wife cheats on him during their honeymoon. Stiller and Aniston's performances are reassuringly familiar, demonstrating a credible

chemistry. However, director John Hamburg insists on throwing in incongruous gross-out humour that would make even the Farrelly brothers wince. SF DVD BL

Ben Stiller *Reuben Feffer* • Jennifer Aniston *Polly Prince* • Philip Seymour Hoffman *Sandy Lyle* • Debra Messing *Lisa Kramer* • Hank Azaria *Claude* • Bryan Brown *Leland Van Lew* • Alec Baldwin *Stan Indursky* • Jsu Garcia *Javier* ■ *Dir/Scr* John Hamburg

Along the Great Divide ★★
Western 1951 · US · BW · 87min

Kirk Douglas, in his memoirs, remembered this standard revenge western with some distaste. "I hated *Along the Great Divide*," he wrote, "I did it just to get my one picture a year obligation [to Warners] out of the way." He recalled the cruelty to the horses, the risks the stuntmen were forced to take and the sadism of the director, Raoul Walsh: "Critics talk about how Walsh movies have such great pace. They have great pace because he was always in a hurry to finish them." AT

Kirk Douglas *Len Merrick* • Virginia Mayo *Ann Keith* • John Agar *Billy Shear* • Walter Brennan *Tim "Pop" Keith* • Ray Teal *Lou Gray* • Hugh Sanders • Morris Ankrum *Ed Roden* • James Anderson (2) *Dan Roden* • Charles Meredith *The Judge* ■ *Dir* Raoul Walsh • *Scr* Walter Doniger, Lewis Meltzer, from a story by Doniger

Along the Rio Grande ★★ U
Western 1941 · US · BW · 64min

One of cowboy star Tim Holt's RKO series of westerns, featuring a routine plot wherein Tim and two pals join up with an outlaw gang to avenge the murder of their boss. Mind you, it takes some intervention from Sheriff Hal Taliaferro to help our heroes bring the villains to book, but the script is above par for this sort of western. Ray Whitley plays Holt's sidekick Smokey, while leading lady Betty Jane Rhodes is a colourful diversion. TS

Tim Holt *Jeff* • Ray Whitley *Smokey* • Betty Jane Rhodes *Mary Lawry* • Emmett Lynn *Whopper* • Robert Fiske *Doc Randall* • Hal Taliaferro *Sheriff* • Carl Stockdale *Turner* ■ *Dir* Edward Killy • *Scr* Arthur V Jones, Morton Grant, from a story by Stuart Anthony

Alpha and Omega ★ U
Animated adventure 2010 · US · Colour · 87min

She's an alpha female, he's an omega male: they're young wolves and their love is forbidden. This animated adventure never rises above the perfunctory, with tiresome comic-relief geese and bog-standard internecine rivalry in the wolf pack. The visuals deliver some of the grandeur of the Canadian landscapes, but prove less distinctive on facial characterisation, while the voice cast – headed by Justin Long and Hayden Panettiere as the ill-fated central duo – really haven't got much to work with. TJ Some violence. DVD BL 3D

Justin Long *Humphrey* • Hayden Panettiere *Kate* • Dennis Hopper *Tony* • Danny Glover *Winston* • Larry Miller *Marcel* • Christina Ricci *Lilly* ■ *Dir* Anthony Bell, Ben Gluck • *Scr* Christopher Denk, Steve Moore, from a story by Moore

Alpha Beta ★★★
Drama 1973 · UK · Colour · 66min

EA Whitehead's play marked Albert Finney's return to the London stage after a six-year absence. The play is a two-hander, and Finney's co-star was Rachel Roberts, who last acted with him in *Saturday Night and Sunday Morning*. In three lacerating acts, the play defines modern marriage as a battlefield; there is caustic wit, bruising, a lot of metaphorical blood and ample opportunity for great acting. Financed by Finney himself and directed by Anthony Page, who also helmed the original Royal Court production, this is a valuable record of the stage original. AT

Albert Finney *Man* • Rachel Roberts (1) *Woman* ■ *Dir* Anthony Page • *Scr* EA Whitehead, from his play

Alpha Dog ★★★ 15
Crime drama based on a true story
2006 · US · Colour · 112min

A kidnapping goes tragically awry in this rambling crime drama from Nick Cassavetes. Based on the case of Californian drug dealer Jesse James Hollywood, the film explores how a pack mentality and parental disregard can turn even socially respectable teens wild. Emile Hirsch plays a thinly veiled Hollywood – here renamed Johnny Truelove – a wannabe gangster whose privileged life sours when he abducts a junkie debtor's kid brother (Anton Yelchin) and entrusts him to his right-hand man (an impressive Justin Timberlake). The youngster's eventual fate has an unsettling sting, despite Cassavetes's tendency to dilute the impact with showy visuals and faux-documentary inserts. SF Violence, swearing, sex scenes, drug abuse. DVD BL

Emile Hirsch *Johnny Truelove* • Justin Timberlake *Frankie Ballenbacher* • Ben Foster *Jake Mazursky* • Shawn Hatosy *Elvis Schmidt* • Anton Yelchin *Zack Mazursky* • Sharon Stone *Olivia Mazursky* • Bruce Willis *Sonny Truelove* ■ *Dir/Scr* Nick Cassavetes • *Cinematographer* Robert Fraisse

Alpha Male ★★★ 15
Relationship drama
2005 · US/UK · Colour · 95min

There's something strangely compelling about this domestic drama, in which writer/director Dan Wilde cuts between past and present events to explore the impact of a man's death on his family. Businessman and near-perfect father Jim Ferris (Danny Huston) dies suddenly while his children are still young, and his wife (Jennifer Ehle) subsequently takes up with a widower (Patrick Baladi). As the estranged family reunites for son Jack's 21st birthday, Wilde explores new tensions and past indiscretions. The action and the acting are often too meticulous, but the stifling atmosphere of repressed resentments is well sustained. DP Swearing. DVD

Jennifer Ehle *Alice Ferris* • Danny Huston *Jim Ferris* • Trudie Styler *Brede Norton* • Patrick Baladi *Clive Lamis* • Amelia Warner *Elyssa Ferris* • Mark Wells *Jack Ferris* • Christopher Egan *Felix Methuselah* • Arthur Duncan *Young Jack Ferris* ■ *Dir/Scr* Dan Wilde

Alphabet City ★★ 18
Crime drama 1984 · US · Colour · 85min

The most mainstream movie directed by underground film-maker Amos Poe (*Subway Riders*) has style in abundance and a great performance by Vincent Spano but virtually no plot. Tough Spano is a Lower East Side drug dealer with plans to retire until mobsters force him to go on the run. When Spano is centre stage, this violent slice-of-life drama crackles with menacing intensity. Otherwise, it's a rather bland affair that goes over too much familiar ground. AJ

Vincent Spano *Johnny* • Kate Vernon *Angela* • Michael Winslow *Lippy* • Zohra Lampert *Mama* • Jami Gertz *Sophia* • Ray Serra [Raymond Serra] *Gino* ■ *Dir* Amos Poe • *Scr* Amos Poe, Gregory K Heller, Robert Seidman, from a short story by Heller • *Music* Nile Rodgers

The Alphabet Murders ★ U
Comedy mystery 1966 · UK · BW · 95min

Having met with cinematic success with Agatha Christie's Miss Marple as played by Margaret Rutherford, MGM turned to another of Christie's detectives, Hercule Poirot, here incarnated in the unlikely personage of Tony Randall. The film's an unfortunate mess, which is doubly sad since talented satirist director Frank Tashlin should be capable of getting a handle on the whole affair. TS

Tony Randall *Hercule Poirot* • Anita Ekberg *Amanda Beatrice Cross* • Robert Morley *Hastings* • Maurice Denham *Inspector Japp* • Guy Rolfe *Duncan Doncaster* • Sheila Allen *Lady Diane* • Margaret Rutherford *Miss Marple* ■ *Dir* Frank Tashlin • *Scr* David Pursall, Jack Seddon, from the novel by Agatha Christie

Alphaville ★★★★ PG
Futuristic detective drama
1965 · Fr · BW · 94min

This assured blend of sci-fi and *film noir* is perhaps Jean-Luc Godard's most accessible picture: a chilling peek into the future inspired as much by poetry and mythology as pulp fiction. Playing fast and loose with genre conventions, Godard explores themes more readily associated with Michelangelo Antonioni, as world-weary private eye Eddie Constantine searches the far-off metropolis of Alphaville for missing scientist Akim Tamiroff. Anna Karina is genuinely affecting as the robot who discovers emotion, while cinematographer Raoul Coutard miraculously turns Paris into a soulless hell. DP French +subtitles. DVD

Eddie Constantine *Lemmy Caution* • Anna Karina *Natacha Von Braun* • Akim Tamiroff *Henri Dickson* • Howard Vernon *Professor Leonard Nosferatu/Von Braun* • Laszlo Szabo *Chief engineer* • Michel Delahaye *Von Braun's assistant* ■ *Dir/Scr* Jean-Luc Godard

Alpine Fire ★★★ 18
Drama 1985 · Swi · Colour · 118min

Fredi M Murer adapts his own novel with a directorial style as stark as the Alpine landscape, and a power and subtlety usually missing from films about incest. Had the performances not been so innocent and unabashed, however, the realism would have seemed embarrassingly phoney. Johanna Lier impresses as the teenage daughter of a Swiss hill farmer, but it's Thomas Nock who compels as the pubescent deaf-mute who relieves his frustrations by constructing a network of stone monuments. DP Swiss German +subtitles.

Thomas Nock *Boy* • Johanna Lier *Belli* • Dorothea Moritz *Mother* • Rolf Illig *Father* • Tilli Breidenbach *Grandmother* • Joerg Odermatt *Grandfather* ■ *Dir* Fredi M Murer • *Scr* Fredi M Murer, from his novel

Alps ★★★★ 15
Drama 2011 · Gr · Colour · 93min

Bereaved parents, a disgruntled rhythmic gymnast and moonlighting paramedic staff find their paths converging in this Greek drama from director Yorgos Lanthimos, whose previous offering, *Dogtooth*, created quite a stir on the art-house circuit. The film takes its time to reveal its purpose, as a picture emerges of sundry individuals who dedicate themselves to acting as substitutes for lost loved ones, thus salving the pain for surviving relatives. Not everyone will go with Lanthimos's often disarmingly original approach to storytelling, but for those who do, this is a fascinating, slightly mad and ultimately rather affecting portrait of our need for human connections. TJ Greek, English +subtitles. Violence, swearing, sex scenes.

Aggeliki Papoulia *Nurse* • Aris Servetalis *Paramedic* • Ariane Labed *Gymnast* • Johnny Vekris *Coach* ■ *Dir* Yorgos Lanthimos • *Scr* Yorgos Lanthimos, Efthimis Filippou

Alsino and the Condor ★★★
Political drama
1982 · Nic/Cub/Mex/Cos R · Colour · 89min

It's somewhat apt that the first feature produced in Nicaragua under the Sandinistas should have been directed by a Chilean who'd fled the Pinochet regime. Leavening his stylised portrait of the brutal civil war with juvenile escapades and magic realism, Miguel Littín succeeds in fashioning an allegory that, in spite of its anti-American sentiment, received an Oscar nomination for best foreign film. Personifying his nation's need to come of political age, Alan Esquivel is superb as the 12-year-old orphan whose dreams of flying high above the surrounding jungle sustain him through the savagery of the conflict. DP Spanish +subtitles.

Dean Stockwell *Frank* • Alan Esquivel *Alsino* • Carmen Bunster *Alsino's grandmother* • Alejandro Parodi *The Major* ■ *Dir* Miguel Littín • *Scr* Miguel Littín, Isidora Aguirre, Tomas Perez Turrent

A

Altered States ★★★ 18
Horror fantasy   1980 · US · Colour · 98min

Scientist William Hurt tinkers with tribal drug rituals and sensory deprivation tanks until they cause him to regress to a primitive killer-simian state of altered consciousness. The deer-eating Neanderthal man mid-section may seem too over-the-top considering the deliberately excessive whole, but, in general, director Ken Russell power-drives his mad doctor update with trademark visual excess and hits the bullseye. Celebrated screenwriter Paddy Chayefsky, who also wrote the novel on which this is based, removed his name from the film in disgust. AJ Violence, swearing, nudity. DVD

William Hurt *Eddie Jessup* • Blair Brown *Emily Jessup* • Bob Balaban *Arthur Rosenberg* • Charles Haid *Mason Parrish* • Thaao Penghlis *Eccheverria* • Miguel Godreau *Primal man* • Dori Brenner *Sylvia Rosenberg* • Peter Brandon *Hobart* • Drew Barrymore *Margaret Jessup* ■ *Dir* Ken Russell • *Scr* Sidney Aaron [Paddy Chayefsky], from his novel

Altman ★★★ 15
Documentary   2014 · US · Colour and BW · 95min

People often forget that director Robert Altman was 45 when *MASH* (1970) transformed him from a jobbing director to a beloved maverick. Suddenly, critics were talking about an "Altmanesque" mix of roving cameras, large ensembles and overlapping dialogue. Though the peaks and troughs of his career have been ably explored in print, they're largely skirted in Ron Mann's sanitised and rather superficial profile. However, Mann does make fine use of private sources and clips from Altman's lesser works to show how his distinctive style evolved and how trenchant he was in his mistrust of the Hollywood studio system. DP Violence, swearing, drug abuse.

Robert Altman ■ *Dir* Ron Mann • *Scr* Len Blum

Alucarda ★★★ 18
Horror   1975 · Mex · Colour · 74min

In this horror tale from Mexican director Juan Lopez Moctezuma (a former assistant to Alejandro Jodorowsky), the action follows a demonically possessed nun as she exacts hideous revenge on the killers of her bosom buddy. Although the movie typically relies on exploitation, Moctezuma gives this rather more style than the average low-budget horror, which serves to make its bizarre events more convincing. DP Violence, nudity. DVD

Claudio Brook *Dr Oszek/Hunchbacked gypsy* • David Silva *Father Lazaro* • Tina Romero *Alucarda* • Susana Kamini *Justine* • Adriana Roel *Sister Germana* ■ *Dir* Juan Lopez Moctezuma • *Scr* Juan Lopez Moctezuma, Yolanda Lopez Moctezuma, Alexis T Arroyo

Alvarez Kelly ★★★ PG
Western   1966 · US · Colour · 105min

In this oddball American Civil War western, William Holden plays the eponymous rancher who delivers a herd of cattle to the Union army. He's then kidnapped by the Confederates whose colonel, Richard Widmark, wants Holden to steal back the herd in order to feed his own soldiers. At first it's jokey; then Widmark shoots one of Holden's fingers off and things get rather more serious. Waywardly plotted, it's held together by the terrific rivalry and enmity whipped up by Holden and Widmark. AT Violence, some swearing. DVD

William Holden (2) *Alvarez Kelly* • Richard Widmark *Colonel Tom Rossiter* • Janice Rule *Liz Pickering* • Patrick O'Neal (1) *Major Albert Stedman* • Victoria Shaw *Charity Warwick* • Roger C Carmel *Captain Angus Ferguson* ■ *Dir* Edward Dmytryk • *Scr* Franklin Coen, Elliot Arnold, from a story by Coen

Alvin and the Chipmunks ★★ U
Part-animated comedy adventure
2007 · US · Colour · 87min

Alvin, Simon and Theodore are three squeaky-voiced critters who were first radio and recording stars 50 years ago. There seems little point, however, in resurrecting them here as computer-generated cuties. In this mostly live-action tale, Alvin and his chums become global singing sensations when they are given a home by songwriter Jason Lee. But they soon fall foul of an unscrupulous record label boss (David Cross). There is plenty of lowbrow slapstick, most of it targeting the hapless Lee, who definitely needs a better agent, yet the chipmunks themselves are undeniably entertaining in their sweeter moments. This will provide an adequate distraction for the less discerning under-sixes. The sequel is released in December 2009. DA DVD Blu

Jason Lee *Dave Seville* • David Cross (2) *Ian Hawk* • Cameron Richardson *Claire* • Justin Long *Alvin* • Matthew Gray Gubler *Simon* • Jesse McCartney *Theodore* ■ *Dir* Tim Hill • *Scr* Jon Vitti, Will McRobb, Chris Viscardi, from a story by Vitti, from characters by Ross Bagdasarian Sr [Ross Bagdasarian] • *Cinematographer* Peter Lyons Collister

Alvin and the Chipmunks: the Squeakquel ★★★ U
Part-animated comedy adventure
2009 · US · Colour · 84min

Chipmunk pop sensation Alvin and his brothers Simon and Theodore are back in this second big-screen adventure, but this time they have competition. As the boys start school without the support of their mentor Dave (Jason Lee), who's laid up in hospital, they have to face bullying, threats to their friendship and the popularity of upcoming girl band the Chipettes before coming to terms with their new responsibilities. There's possibly too little here for older viewers to enjoy, but youngsters will love the slapstick action and catchy soundtrack. Be warned, though: some of the themes may cause sleepless nights for any children about to start a new school. SuR DVD Blu

Zachary Levi *Toby Seville* • David Cross (2) *Ian Hawke* • Jason Lee *Dave Seville* • Justin Long *Alvin Seville* • Matthew Gray Gubler *Simon Seville* • Jesse McCartney *Theodore Seville* • Amy Poehler *Eleanor* • Anna Faris *Jeanette Miller* • Christina Applegate *Brittany Miller* ■ *Dir* Betty Thomas • *Scr* Jonathan Aibel, Glenn Berger, Jon Vitti, from characters by Ross Bagdasarian, Janice Karman

Alvin and the Chipmunks: Chipwrecked ★★ U
Part-animated comedy adventure
2011 · US · Colour · 83min

Life for Alvin and his chipmunk brothers never runs smoothly, so it's no surprise when a cruise to an awards ceremony goes horribly wrong. The Chipmunks and Chipettes are stranded on an island, and to make matters worse they are separated from dad Dave (Jason Lee). Cue the usual messages about family ties and responsibilities, yet it all seems rather jaded this time around, and even the pop songs (usually a saving grace in these movies) feel tired. Thank goodness for little chipmunk Theodore, who can't help but be adorably cute and cuddly. A third sequel is due in early 2016. SuR DVD Blu

Jason Lee *Dave* • David Cross (2) *Ian* • Jenny Slate *Zoe* • Justin Long *Alvin* • Matthew Gray Gubler *Simon* • Jesse McCartney *Theodore* ■ *Dir* Mike Mitchell • *Scr* Jonathan Aibel, Glenn Berger, from characters by Ross Bagdasarian, Janice Karman

Alvin and the Chipmunks: the Road Chip ★★ U
Part-animated comedy adventure
2015 · US · Colour · 91min

The flagging fourth film in the furry franchise has Alvin and co fearing that hapless human "minder" and resident fall guy Jason Lee is going to dump them for marriage to a single mum with an obnoxious teenage son. So they set out cross-country to scupper his proposal plans. Younger kids just can't seem to get enough of the funny voices, fart jokes and kindergarten comedy. But, despite some cute moments here, it's a formula that's starting to wear thin. DA

Jason Lee *Dave* • Bella Thorne *Ashley Grey* • Justin Long *Alvin* • Matthew Gray Gubler *Simon* • Jesse McCartney *Theodore* ■ *Dir* Walt Becker • *Scr* Randi Mayem Singer, Adam Sztykiel, from characters by Ross Bagdasarian, Janice Karman

Always ★★★ 15
Comedy   1985 · US · Colour · 105min

This distinctive comedy of manners probes the meaning of love and marriage by focusing on three couples, each at different stages of their relationship. Writer/director Henry Jaglom and his former wife Patrice Townsend co-star as a couple about to get divorced; Alan Rachins and Joanna Frank, their best friends in real life, play their best friends on screen; while shooting took place in the house that Jaglom and Townsend shared when they were married. Charming, witty and often perceptive, the film is probably too unconventional to have more than a limited appeal. PF

Henry Jaglom *David* • Patrice Townsend *Judy* • Joanna Frank *Lucy* • Alan Rachins *Eddie* • Melissa Leo *Peggy* • Jonathan Kaufer *Maxwell* • Bud Townsend *Judy's father* • Bob Rafelson *David's neighbour* ■ *Dir/Scr* Henry Jaglom

Always ★★★ PG
Romantic fantasy   1989 · US · Colour · 117min

This was Steven Spielberg's attempt to make a more grown-up fantasy, after he was criticised for pandering to the child in all of us with *ET* and *Raiders of the Lost Ark*. It's effectively an update of the Spencer Tracy film *A Guy Named Joe*, with Richard Dreyfuss as the firefighter pilot who returns from the dead to watch over the love of his life, Holly Hunter. Best pal John Goodman steals the show, and Audrey Hepburn (in her last screen role) gives him a run for his money as an angelic guide. JB DVD Blu

Richard Dreyfuss *Pete Sandich* • Holly Hunter *Dorinda Durston* • Brad Johnson *Ted Baker* • John Goodman *Al Yackey* • Audrey Hepburn *Hap* • Roberts Blossom *Dave* • Keith David *Powerhouse* • Ed Van Nuys *Nails* ■ *Dir* Steven Spielberg • *Scr* Jerry Belson, Diane Thomas, from the film *A Guy Named Joe* by Dalton Trumbo, Frederick Hazlitt Brennan, Chandler Sprague, David Boehm

Always and Forever ★★
Romantic drama   2008 · US · Colour · 86min

Old love is reawakened in this slight yet engaging romantic drama. Rena Sofer plays a divorced interior designer whose life is thrown into turmoil once more following a chance encounter with her high-school sweetheart (Dean McDermott). Though the tale's outcome is obvious from the start, likeable performances and an abundance of warmth keep the familiarity palatable. SF

Rena Sofer *Grace* • Rob Boltin *Phillip Walsh* • Jonathan Chase *James* • Barbara Eden *Mary Anderson* • Max Gail *Bill Anderson* • Dean McDermott *Michael* ■ *Dir* Kevin Connor • *Scr* Riley Weston

Always Goodbye ★★
Melodrama   1938 · US · BW · 75min

This remake of *Gallant Lady* (1934), which starred Ann Harding and Clive Brook, now stars Barbara Stanwyck and Herbert Marshall in the story of an unwed mother who sacrifices her child but then wants him back. Unfortunately, despite the ever-admirable Stanwyck and all the ingredients for a delicious wallow, the movie is directed by Sidney Lanfield with such a heavy overlay of treacle and unsubtle use of close-ups that it ends up an inferior and uninvolving example of the genre. RK

Barbara Stanwyck *Margot Weston* • Herbert Marshall *Jim Howard* • Ian Hunter *Phillip Marshall* • Cesar Romero *Count Giovanni Corini* • Lynn Bari *Jessica Reid* ■ *Dir* Sidney Lanfield • *Scr* Kathryn Scola, Edith Skouras, from a story by Gilbert Emery, Douglas Doty, from the film *Gallant Lady* by Emery, Franc Rhodes, Sam Mintz

Always in My Heart ★★ U
Drama   1942 · US · BW · 93min

This uncomfortable mix of music and drama has the mother of a teenage daughter with singing aspirations about to marry for the second time. Complications ensue when her long-lost husband turns up, having served 13 years in jail for a crime he didn't commit. Kay Francis stars as the mother, with singer Gloria Warren as the daughter, but the honours go to the always splendidly sympathetic Walter Huston. The movie is incredibly silly but perfectly agreeable, and boasts an Oscar-nominated title song. RK

Kay Francis *Marjorie Scott* • Walter Huston *MacKenzie Scott* • Gloria Warren *Victoria Scott* • Patty Hale *Dooley* • Frankie Thomas *Martin Scott* • Una O'Connor *Angie* ■ *Dir* Jo Graham • *Scr* Adele Comandini, from the play *Fly Away Home* by Dorothy Bennett, Irving White

Always Leave Them Laughing ★★★ U
Comedy   1949 · US · BW · 115min

Milton Berle's big feature starring role was not a success in its day, but Miltie went on to greater celebrity in the Golden Era of American television. His face in grimace was not, in truth, well suited to leading roles on the big screen, but he was perfectly cast in this wry saga of a vaudeville comic who becomes a TV star. There was considerable on-screen competition, though, from vaudeville great Bert Lahr, playing the comedian whose shoes Berle aspires to step into, and who immortalises one of his most famous routines in this movie. TS

Milton Berle *Kip Cooper* • Virginia Mayo *Nancy Egan* • Ruth Roman *Fay Washburn* • Bert Lahr *Eddie Egan* • Alan Hale *Mr Washburn* • Grace Hayes *Mrs Washburn* • Jerome Cowan *Elliot Lewis* ■ *Dir* Roy Del Ruth • *Scr* Jack Rose, Melville Shavelson, from a story by Max Shulman, Richard Mealand

Amadeus ★★★★★ PG
Biographical drama   1984 · US · Colour · 153min

The winner of eight Oscars and an unexpected box-office smash, *Amadeus* is simply one of the finest biographical dramas ever made. Reworked rather than simply adapted by Peter Shaffer from his own hit play, the film is as much about the mediocrity and envy of the composer Antonio Salieri as it is about the eccentric genius of his rival Mozart. There is, therefore, a sort of poetic justice in the fact that F Murray Abraham pipped Tom Hulce for the best actor award. Returning to Prague (standing in for Vienna) for the first time since the Soviet invasion in 1968, director Milos Forman and his regular cinematographer Miroslav Ondricek revel in the beauty of the city, but credit must also go to Patrizia von Brandenstein for her superb sets and inspired choice of location interiors. The music is majestic, thanks largely to Neville Marriner's outstanding interpretation of everything from gypsy dances to *Don Giovanni*. DP Some swearing. DVD Blu

F Murray Abraham *Antonio Salieri* • Tom Hulce *Wolfgang Amadeus Mozart* • Elizabeth Berridge *Constanze Mozart* • Simon Callow *Emanuel Schikaneder* • Roy Dotrice *Leopold Mozart* • Christine Ebersole *Katerina Cavalieri* • Jeffrey Jones *Emperor Joseph II* • Charles Kay *Count Orsini-Rosenberg* • Kenny Baker (2) *Parody Commendatore* ■ *Dir* Milos Forman • *Scr* Peter Shaffer, from his play • *Cinematographer* Miroslav Ondricek • *Production Designer* Patrizia von Brandenstein • *Music Director* Neville Marriner

Amandla! A Revolution in Four-Part Harmony ★★★ 12
Documentary   2002 · S Afr/US · Colour · 98min

Nine years in the making, this inspiring documentary reveals the role played by music in sustaining black South Africa's identity during its half-century struggle against apartheid. Director Lee Hirsch uses archive footage and personal reminiscences to chronicle the key events from 1948-98. But this is more specifically a history of the freedom music of Vuyisile Mini and Vusi Mahlasela - as well as such internationally

U SUITABLE FOR ALL   Uc SUITABLE ESPECIALLY FOR YOUNG CHILDREN (DVD ONLY)   PG PARENTAL GUIDANCE   12A UNDER 12s TO BE ACCOMPANIED (CINEMA ONLY)

renowned exiles as Miriam Makeba, Hugh Masekela and Abdullah Ibrahim – that enabled the repressed townships to endure injustice, prejudice and violence even though the outside world seemed to have forgotten them. DP In English, Xhosa. Violence. *DVD*
■ *Dir* Lee Hirsch

Les Amants ★★★★ 15
Drama 1958 · Fr · BW · 86min

A *succès de scandale* on its release, Louis Malle's second feature won him the special jury prize at Venice. Although it may no longer have the power to shock, it's still got plenty to admire, first and foremost Henri Decaë's glossy black-and-white photography that sets the film apart from most other French pictures of the New Wave era. Jeanne Moreau is also superb as the seductive socialite who seeks casual affairs to relieve the boredom of her perfect life. The celebrated 20-minute love scene she shares with Jean-Marc Bory looks a little stylised today, but it remains notable for its bold portrayal of passion and rebellion. DP French +subtitles. A sex scene, nudity. *DVD*
Jeanne Moreau *Jeanne Tournier* • Alain Cuny *Henri Tournier* • Jean-Marc Bory *Bernard Dubois-Lambert* • Judith Magre *Maggy Thiebaut-Leroy* • *Dir* Louis Malle • *Scr* Louis Malle, Louise de Vilmorin, from the novel *Point de Lendemain* by Dominique Vivant • *Cinematographer* Henri Decaë

Les Amants du Pont-Neuf ★★★ 15
Drama 1990 · Fr · Colour · 120min

This is a classic example of the kind of flashy French film whose MTV-inspired visuals and sound-bite dialogue earned them the nickname *cinéma du look* for the emphasis on style over content. Writer/director Leos Carax strains to make a grand statement, but ends up trapped between his attempts to explore the social realities of France during the bicentenary of its Revolution, and his genius for opulent set pieces. The scenes on Paris's oldest bridge between Juliette Binoche, an artist losing her sight, and injured fire-eater Denis Lavant are more often pretentious than touching, but the film is still worth a look. DP French +subtitles. Some violence, nudity. *DVD*
Juliette Binoche *Michèle* • Denis Lavant *Alex* • Klaus-Michael Gruber *Hans* • Daniel Buain *Clochard's friend* • Marion Statens *Marion* • Chrichan Larson *Julien* • Paulette Berthonnier *Sailor* • Roger Berthonnier *Sailor* ■ *Dir/Scr* Leos Carax

Amar Akbar & Tony ★★★ 15
Romantic comedy drama
2014 · UK · Colour · 96min

A multicultural comedy drama, this follows three friends from different backgrounds as they navigate relationships, responsibilities and tragedy in contemporary West London. The film's focus is mainly on the British Asian community, but its exploration of the expectations of traditional families will be familiar to most who see it. Amid the tonal uncertainty and occasionally blunt stereotyping, this is a likeable coming-of-age tale with both brains and heart. JL
Rez Kempton *Amar* • Sam Vincenti *Akbar* • Martin Delaney *Tony* • Karen David *Meera* ■ *Dir/Scr* Atul Malhotra

Amarcord ★★★★★ 15
Comedy drama 1973 · It · Colour · 118min

Deftly tainting childhood memory with adult insight, Federico Fellini's dazzling blend of autobiography, fantasy and wickedly precise satire won an Oscar for best foreign film. Set in a seaside town not dissimilar to the director's native Rimini, *Amarcord* ("I remember") assembles a wonderful cast of characters, as human as they are grotesque, while mocking Mussolini's regime, Roman Catholicism and the prejudices of the parochial bourgeoisie. Touching, coarse and comic, this is a must for fans and, for those yet to be converted,

a superb introduction to the work of a great artist. DP Italian +subtitles. *DVD*
Puppela Maggio *Miranda Biondi* • Magali Noël *Gradisca* • Bruno Zanin *Titta Biondi* • Armando Brancia *Aurelio Biondi* • Ciccio Ingrassia *Uncle Teo* • Nandino Orfei *Pataca* • Luigi Rossi *Lawyer* • Gianfilippo Carcano *Don Baravelli* ■ *Dir* Federico Fellini • *Scr* Federico Fellini, Tonino Guerra • *Cinematographer* Giuseppe Rotunno • *Art Director* Danilo Donati • *Music* Nino Rota

The Amateur ★★ 15
Spy thriller 1981 · Can · Colour · 106min

When terrorists take over the US consulate in Munich and kill a female hostage, the girl's boyfriend – computer boffin John Savage – starts plotting revenge. Despite some well-filmed action scenes, the plotting in this thriller is slow and never plausible, while the performances range from the adequate to the laughable. AT
John Savage *Charles Heller* • Christopher Plummer *Professor Lakos* • Marthe Keller *Elisabeth* • Arthur Hill *Brewer* • Nicholas Campbell *Schraeger* • George Coe *Rutledge* • John Marley *Molton* • Jan Rubes *Kaplan* • Ed Lauter *Anderson* ■ *Dir* Charles Jarrott • *Scr* Robert Littell, Diana Maddox, from the novel by Littell

Amateur ★★★★ 15
Drama 1994 · Fr/UK/US · Colour · 100min

Given that the central characters are an ex-nun turned professional pornographer and a professional pornographer now suffering from amnesia, it doesn't take a genius to recognise that you are in the world of Hal Hartley, a place where humour is so deadpan it makes *Twin Peaks* look like a celebration of slapstick. Isabelle Huppert gives a marvellous performance of wide-eyed innocence, while Martin Donovan retains that unique expression he saves for Hartley films, one that implies he can't quite fathom why everyone else finds his normal behaviour so eccentric. This is in a league (let alone a world) of its own. DP Violence, swearing, sex scenes. *DVD* & Blu-ray
Isabelle Huppert *Isabelle* • Martin Donovan (2) *Thomas* • Elina Lowensohn *Sofia* • Damian Young *Edward* • Chuck Montgomery *Jan* • David Simonds *Kurt* • Pamela Stewart *Officer Melville* ■ *Dir/Scr* Hal Hartley

The Amazing Captain Nemo ★ U
Fantasy adventure 1978 · US · Colour · 98min

Seven writers without a worthwhile idea between them collaborated on the script for this ludicrous movie, edited down from a three-part TV series. José Ferrer brings nothing new to the part of the captain, who is awakened after a century in suspended animation and pitched into battle with a mad professor (Burgess Meredith) bent on world domination. DP
José Ferrer *Captain Nemo* • Burgess Meredith *Professor Waldo Cunningham* • Tom Hallick *Commander Tom Franklin* • Burr DeBenning *Lt Jim Porter* • Lynda Day George *Kate* • Mel Ferrer *Dr Robert Cook* • Horst Buchholz *King Tibor* ■ *Dir* Alex March • *Scr* Norman Katkov, Preston Wood, Robert C Dennis, William Keys, Mann Rubin, Robert Bloch, Larry Alexander

The Amazing Colossal Man ★ PG
Science-fiction drama 1957 · US · BW · 79min

After being exposed to plutonium radiation, Lieutenant Colonel Glen Langan grows ten feet taller per day and rampages through cardboard miniatures on the way to Las Vegas. Truly amazing, because this is considered supremo schlock producer/director Bert I Gordon's best effort. And colossal, because that's exactly what it is – a colossal bore. Amazingly, this spawned a sequel, *War of the Colossal Beast*. AJ
Glen Langan [Glenn Langan] *Lt Col Glenn Manning* • Cathy Downs *Carol Forrest* • William Hudson *Dr Paul Lindstrom* • James Seay *Colonel Hallock* • Larry Thor *Dr Eric Coulter* • Russ Bender *Richard Kingman* • Lyn Osborn *Sergeant Taylor* ■ *Dir* Bert I Gordon • *Scr* Bert I Gordon, Mark Hanna

The Amazing Dobermans ★★
Crime caper 1976 · US · Colour · 96min

Fred Astaire plays a reformed conman who leads five Doberman pinschers plus one undercover treasury agent (James Franciscus) on the trail of racketeers. This was the final film in a series that began in 1972 with *The Doberman Gang* and continued with *The Daring Dobermans* the following year. All offer the sort of family entertainment Disney churned out in the 60s; by the 70s, however, they seemed strangely anachronistic. AT
Fred Astaire *Daniel Hughes* • James Franciscus *Lucky Vincent* • Barbara Eden *Justine Pirot* • Jack Carter *Solly Kramer* ■ *Dir* Byron Ross Chudnow • *Scr* Michael Kraike, William Goldstein, Richard Chapman, from a story by Kraike, Goldstein

The Amazing Dr Clitterhouse ★★★
Crime drama 1938 · US · BW · 87min

Edward G Robinson has a ball in this ingenious gangster picture, co-written by John Huston and directed by Anatole Litvak. Robinson plays a psychiatrist whose study of the criminal mind turns him into a criminal himself, while Humphrey Bogart is the gang leader he studies, emulates and subsequently plans to murder. Morality is very much to the fore, but this is also a first-rate entertainment. AT
Edward G Robinson *Dr Clitterhouse* • Claire Trevor *Jo Keller* • Humphrey Bogart *Rocks Valentine* • Gale Page *Nurse Randolph* • Donald Crisp *Inspector Lane* • Allen Jenkins *Okay* • Thurston Hall *Grant* • Susan Hayward ■ *Dir* Anatole Litvak • *Scr* John Wesley, John Huston, from the play by Barre Lyndon

Amazing Grace ★★★ PG
Biographical political drama
2006 · US/UK · Colour · 112min

The early work of 18th-century abolitionist William Wilberforce is laid bare in this handsome biopic from director Michael Apted. Produced to coincide with the 200th anniversary of Britain's outlawing of the slave trade, it stars an impressive Ioan Gruffudd as the Hull-born reformer. Crackling with energy and wit, this absorbing drama depicts the long battle as an intergenerational struggle, as young Wilberforce and his fellow humanitarians (including Rufus Sewell as Thomas Clarkson) lock horns with the established order. The acting is exemplary, but in visually shying away from slavery's more horrific realities, the film lacks the impact its emotive subject really deserves. SF *DVD*
Ioan Gruffudd *William Wilberforce* • Romola Garai *Barbara Spooner* • Ciaran Hinds *Lord Tarleton* • Rufus Sewell *Thomas Clarkson* • Youssou N'Dour *Olaudah Equiano* • Michael Gambon *Lord Charles Fox* • Albert Finney *John Newton* • Benedict Cumberbatch *William Pitt* ■ *Dir* Michael Apted • *Scr* Steven Knight • *Cinematographer* Remi Adefarasin

Amazing Grace and Chuck ★★ PG
Drama 1987 · US · Colour · 110min

A little league baseball player convinces major athletes on both sides of the Iron Curtain to stop playing sports as a protest over the nuclear arms race in *Four Weddings* director Mike Newell's simple-minded Capra-esque fable. Gregory Peck, as the US President, lends his support to the peacenik effort in a well-intentioned but ultimately squirm-inducing treatise. Jamie Lee Curtis and Boston Celtics player Alex English contribute to the overall embarrassment. AJ
Jamie Lee Curtis *Lynn Taylor* • Alex English *Amazing Grace Smith* • Gregory Peck *President* • William L Petersen *Russell* • Joshua Zuehlke *Chuck Murdock* • Dennis Lipscomb *Johnny B Goode* • Lee Richardson *Jeffries* ■ *Dir* Mike Newell • *Scr* David Field

The Amazing Mr Blunden ★★★ U
Fantasy mystery 1972 · UK · Colour · 94min

In his later years, character actor Lionel Jeffries had a second career as a sympathetic director of films made for and about young people, notably *The Railway Children*. This Antonia Barber period ghost story is also perfectly suitable for adult viewing. There's much to enjoy, especially in the ripe performances from Laurence Naismith in the title role, and from the splendid Diana Dors as Mrs Wickens – gross, warty and every child's nightmare. TS *DVD*
Laurence Naismith *Mr Blunden* • Lynne Frederick *Lucy Allen* • Garry Miller *Jamie Allen* • Dorothy Alison *Mrs Allen* • Diana Dors *Mrs Wickens* • James Villiers *Uncle Bertie* • Madeline Smith *Bella* • Rosalyn Landor *Sarah* ■ *Dir* Lionel Jeffries • *Scr* Lionel Jeffries, from the story *The Ghosts* by Antonia Barber

The Amazing Mr Williams ★★ U
Screwball comedy mystery
1939 · US · BW · 84min

Melvyn Douglas is the over-conscientious detective whose workload gets in the way of his romance with long-suffering fiancée Joan Blondell. To keep one date, Douglas arrives with a murderer in tow, and later he is forced into drag to trap a lady killer, which is the most amazing he gets. Though Blondell and Douglas mesh beautifully on their third pairing, the story has a mechanical feel, which is not helped by Alexander Hall's uninspired direction. AE
Melvyn Douglas *Kenny Williams* • Joan Blondell *Maxine Carroll* • Clarence Kolb *McGovern* • Ruth Donnelly *Effie* • Edward Brophy *Moseby* • Donald MacBride *Bixler* • Don Beddoe *Deever* • Jonathan Hale *Mayor* ■ *Dir* Alexander Hall • *Scr* Dwight Taylor, Sy Bartlett, from a story by Bartlett

The Amazing Mrs Holliday ★★ U
Musical adventure 1943 · US · BW · 93min

The fact that Jean Renoir, the great French director exiled in the US, was considered to be the right man for this sentimental vehicle for the wholesome singing star Deanna Durbin is an example of the mysterious way in which Hollywood works. However, after four weeks work, Renoir decided to withdraw diplomatically on grounds of health. What remains is a superficial film that exploits the theme of war orphans for entertainment. Yet Durbin does well as a missionary in China who smuggles nine Chinese children back to the States. RB *DVD*
Deanna Durbin *Ruth* • Edmond O'Brien *Tom* • Barry Fitzgerald *Timothy* • Arthur Treacher *Henderson* • Harry Davenport *Commodore* ■ *Dir* Bruce Manning • *Scr* Frank Ryan, John Jacoby from a story by Sonya Levien, adapted by Boris Ingster, Leo Townsend

The Amazing Panda Adventure ★★ PG
Adventure 1995 · US · Colour · 80min

The panda is cute and the Chinese countryside is gorgeous, but that's all that can be said for this family film's favour. Ryan Slater (Christian's brother) is incredibly annoying as a spoiled American boy who travels to China to visit his father on a panda reserve. Somewhat better is Yi Ding as the young Chinese girl he teams up with to protect a baby panda from poachers. What's really amazing is that the movie has the gall to reuse the same camera shots and few bars of music repeatedly. KB
Stephen Lang *Dr Michael Tyler* • Ryan Slater *Ryan Tyler* • Yi Ding *Ling* • Wang Fei *Chu* ■ *Dir* Chris Cain [Christopher Cain] • *Scr* Jeff Rothberg, Laurice Elehwany, from a story by John Wilcox, Steven Alldredge

The Amazing Quest of Ernest Bliss ★★ U
Comedy 1936 · UK/US · BW · 61min

An idle millionaire accepts a challenge to earn his living for a year without touching his own means. He takes a serious of humble jobs – greengrocer, chauffeur, salesman and so on – though he decides to lose the bet when his girlfriend's invalid sister needs an operation. A mildly enjoyable, lightweight British film, it's competently directed by Alfred Zeisler, with the main appeal being the presence of imported star Cary Grant. RK *DVD*

Cary Grant *Ernest Bliss* • Mary Brian *Frances* • Peter Gawthorne *Sir James Aldroyd* • Henry Kendall *Lord Honiton* • Leon M Lion *Dorrington* • John Turnbull *Masters* • Arthur Hardy *Crawley* • Iris Ashley *Clare* ■ *Dir* Alfred Zeisler • *Scr* John L Balderston, from the novel by E Phillips Oppenheim

The Amazing Spider-Man ★★★ 12

Fantasy adventure 2012 · US · Colour · 130min

This reboot of the Spider-Man story boasts plenty of action and humour but lacks the charm of Sam Raimi's 2002 film. Andrew Garfield delivers a moodier version of Peter Parker, but his incarnation also borders on the smug when he discovers superpowers bestowed on him by a genetically modified arachnid. Emma Stone provides a steadying influence as girlfriend Gwen Stacy – who also happens to be the protégé of conflicted scientist (and part-time lizard) Dr Connors (a creepy Rhys Ifans). Newcomers may enjoy the novelty, but it's less involving for those who know where it's all headed. SP Some violence. *DVD* Blu *SP*

Andrew Garfield *Peter Parker/Spider-Man* • Emma Stone *Gwen Stacy* • Rhys Ifans *Dr Curt Connors/The Lizard* • Martin Sheen *Uncle Ben* • Sally Field *Aunt May* • C Thomas Howell *Ray Cooper* ■ *Dir* Marc Webb • *Scr* James Vanderbilt, Alvin Sargent, Steve Kloves, from a story by Vanderbilt, from characters by Steve Ditko, Stan Lee

The Amazing Spider-Man 2 ★★★ 12

Fantasy action adventure
2014 · US · Colour · 135min

Thankfully, Andrew Garfield looks a bit less smug in the role of Peter Parker as Marc Webb's sequel turns a shade darker. Problem is, Webb tries to balance comedy, pathos and action in a sprawling plot that brings our hero face-to-face with skeletons in the family closet as well as an eerily blue-lit Jamie Foxx as Electro. And there's push and pull of a different kind with girlfriend Gwen Stacy (Emma Stone) and childhood pal Harry Osborn (a standout Dane DeHaan). Garfield can't match Tobey Maguire's vulnerability in Sam Raimi's franchise, but Webb's saga is getting better, even if it is taking him a while to get into the swing of things. SP Some violence. *DVD* Blu

Andrew Garfield *Peter Parker/Spider-Man* • Emma Stone *Gwen Stacy* • Jamie Foxx *Max Dillon/Electro* • Dane DeHaan *Harry Osborn/Green Goblin* • Chris Cooper *Norman Osborn* • Campbell Scott *Richard Parker* • Embeth Davidtz *Mary Parker* • Paul Giamatti *Aleksei Sytsevich/The Rhino* • Sally Field *Aunt May* ■ *Dir* Marc Webb • *Scr* Alex Kurtzman, Roberto Orci, Jeff Pinkner, from a story by James Vanderbilt, Kurtzman, Orci, Pinkner, from characters by Stan Lee, Steve Ditko • *Music* Hans Zimmer

Amazon Women on the Moon ★★ 15

Comedy 1987 · US · Colour · 80min

This collection of comedy sketches spoofing commercials, sexual mores, tabloid television and old movies misses more targets than it hits. However, it's the fabulous cast of cult icons (director Russ Meyer), camp starlets (Sybil Danning) and Hollywood veterans (Ralph Bellamy) that makes this follow-up to *Kentucky Fried Movie* such a delight for cinema trainspotters. AJ *DVD*

Michelle Pfeiffer *Brenda* • Rosanna Arquette *Karen* • Steve Guttenberg *Jerry* • Steve Forrest *Captain Nelson* • Joey Travolta *Butch* • David Alan Grier *Don Simmons* • Archie Hahn *Harvey Pitnik* • Ed Begley Jr *Griffin* • Matt Adler *George* • Ralph Bellamy *Mr Gower* • Carrie Fisher *Mary Brown* • Sybil Danning • Russ Meyer ■ *Dir* Joe

Dante, Carl Gottlieb, Peter Horton, John Landis, Robert K Weiss • *Scr* Michael Barrie, Jim Mulholland

The Ambassador ★★ 18

Political thriller 1984 · US · Colour · 91min

Elmore Leonard's novel *52 Pick-Up* is oddly transposed to Israel where middle-eastern politics, PLO guerrillas and CIA murkiness are added to the cocktail of adultery and blackmail. It's an overstuffed package, though not without its benefits – most of which come in the shape of Robert Mitchum's cuckolded and blackmailed US ambassador. Rock Hudson plays a security expert in what turned out to be his final film. Two years later, John Frankenheimer adapted this Leonard novel rather more faithfully. AT

Robert Mitchum *Peter Hacker* • Ellen Burstyn *Alex Hacker* • Rock Hudson *Frank Stevenson* • Donald Pleasence *Eretz* • Fabio Testi *Mustapha Hashimi* • Michal Bat-Adam *Tova* ■ *Dir* J Lee Thompson • *Scr* Max Jack, from the novel *52 Pick-Up* by Elmore Leonard

The Ambassador's Daughter ★★★ U

Romantic comedy 1956 · US · Colour · 103min

This old-fashioned comedy, with a plot so featherlight it's in danger of blowing away, is thoroughly enjoyable thanks to glamorous Paris locations, some witty lines and a polished cast that includes Myrna Loy. It deals with the adventures that befall the daughter (Olivia de Havilland) of the ambassador (Edward Arnold) when she sets out to disprove visiting senator Adolphe Menjou's contention that the GIs stationed in the city constitute a moral danger. De Havilland is too old for the role, but carries it off with conviction. RK

Olivia de Havilland *Joan* • John Forsythe *Danny* • Myrna Loy *Mrs Cartwright* • Adolphe Menjou *Senator Cartwright* • Tommy Noonan *Al* • Francis Lederer *Prince Nicholas Obelski* • Edward Arnold *Ambassador Fiske* ■ *Dir/Scr* Norman Krasna

Amber's Story ★★

Biographical crime drama
2006 · US · Colour · 86min

A bereaved mother's relentless campaigning to protect vulnerable children forms the core of this emotional but clumsily constructed true story. *Law & Order's* Elisabeth Rohm is convincing as the anguished Texan who battles for the introduction of an official abduction alert system following her daughter's murder. The film covers Amber's tragic death and its aftermath in procedural drama style, while drip-feeding details of her mum's subsequent mission. The over-sentimental music and a mass of shocking statistics complete the manipulative onslaught. SF Some violence.

Elisabeth Röhm *Donna Whitson* • Teryl Rothery *Sharon Timmons* • Myron Natwick *Glen Park* • Sophie Hough *Amber Hagerman* ■ *Dir* Keoni Waxman • *Scr* Richard Leder

Ambition ★ 15

Psychological drama 1991 · US · Colour · 94min

Some years after his Oscar-winning role in *The Killing Fields* (1984), Haing S Ngor is the best thing in this rambling indulgence written by and starring Lou Diamond Phillips as a ruthless writer who teams up with a mass murderer. It's almost impossible to suspend disbelief in a wild story that looks as though it was initially intended for television. TH

Lou Diamond Phillips *Mitchell* • Clancy Brown *Albert Merrick* • Cecilia Peck *Julie* • Richard Bradford *Jordan* • Willard Pugh *Freddie* • Grace Zabriskie *Mrs Merrick* • Katherine Armstrong *Roseanne* • JD Cullum *[John David Cullum] Jack* • Haing S Ngor *Tatay* ■ *Dir* Scott D Goldstein • *Scr* Lou Diamond Phillips

The Ambulance ★★★★ 15

Black comedy thriller 1990 · US · Colour · 91min

A terrific urban paranoia thriller dosed with engaging black comedy, this marvellous B-movie gem from director Larry Cohen is a fright delight. A vintage ambulance roams Manhattan looking for the stricken and

injured, only to whisk them off to psychotic surgeon Eric Braeden for illegal medical research. Eric Roberts is the comic artist plunged into a medical nightmare when the girl he's trying to date disappears. Witty repartee, unpredictable plot twists and some superb action set pieces make this an instant remedy for boredom. AJ

Eric Roberts *Josh Baker* • James Earl Jones *Lieutenant Spencer* • Red Buttons *Elias* • Megan Gallagher *Sandy Malloy* • Janine Turner *Cheryl* • Richard Bright *Detective* • Eric Braeden *Doctor* • Stan Lee *Stan Lee, Marvel comics editor* ■ *Dir/Scr* Larry Cohen

Ambulance Girl ★★

Comedy drama based on a true story
2005 · US · Colour · 88min

Kathy Bates directs and stars in this offbeat comedy drama based on the memoir of Jane Stern – an American food critic who overcame clinical depression by becoming a Connecticut paramedic. But though Bates delivers a customarily warm and proficient lead performance, she's not quite as adept behind the camera. Too many visual techniques hinder the narrative, while the jarring mix of solemnity and near-slapstick gives the project an unpolished air that betrays its made-for-TV status. Nonetheless, Bates's genial presence ensures the film remains solidly engaging, even if its stylistic indecision dilutes the impact and believability of Stern's life-changing actions. SF

Kathy Bates *Jane Stern* • Robin Thomas *Michael Stern* • Sean McCann *Walter* • Gordon Pinsent *Pete* • Wayne Best *Ed* • Kristina Nicoll *Audrey* ■ *Dir* Kathy Bates • *Scr* Alan Hines, from the autobiography by Jane Stern

Ambush ★★★ U

Western 1949 · US · BW · 88min

Robert Taylor took up making westerns regularly after this cavalry-versus-Indians story showed how steely-eyed and determined he looked in the saddle. Here he's the scout easily persuaded by glamorous Arlene Dahl to help the army look for her young sister who's been abducted by Apaches. The plot proves cumbersome at times, delving into marital strife at the fort, but the film scores in its graphic depiction of the Apaches as cunning and merciless enemies. AE

Robert Taylor (1) *Ward Kinsman* • John Hodiak *Capt Ben Lorrison* • Arlene Dahl *Ann Duverall* • Don Taylor *Lt Linus Delaney* • Jean Hagen *Martha Conovan* ■ *Dir* Sam Wood • *Scr* Marguerite Roberts, from a story by Luke Short

Ambush at Tomahawk Gap ★★

Western adventure 1953 · US · Colour · 72min

This standard adventure featuring John Hodiak and John Derek has a formulaic plot in which four ex-cons seek lost loot in a ghost town. There just aren't enough sharp twists in the story or characterisations to shake it up, but an Apache attack is well done. TH

John Hodiak *McCord* • John Derek *The Kid* • David Brian *Egan* • Ray Teal *Doc* • Maria Elena Marques *Indian girl* • John Qualen *Jonas P Travis* • Otto Hulett *Stranton* ■ *Dir* Fred F Sears • *Scr* David Lang

Ambush Bay ★★ 12

Second World War adventure
1966 · US · Colour · 104min

There's snare too far and too late for this stalled action movie about a group of US marines trying to escape a Japanese-controlled island in the Philippines in 1944. Hugh O'Brian and Mickey Rooney at least look as though they mean it, but James Mitchum, son of Robert, gives a performance as lacklustre as the film. TH Violence *DVD*

Hugh O'Brian *First Sergeant Steve Corey* • Mickey Rooney *Sergeant Ernest Wartell* • James Mitchum *Private First Class James Grenier* • Peter Masterson *Sergeant William Maccone* • Harry Lauter *Cpl Alvin Ross* • Greg Amsterdam *Cpl Stanley Parrish* ■ *Dir* Ron Winston • *Scr* Marve Feinberg, Ib Melchior

Amelia ★★ PG

Biographical drama 2009 · US · Colour · 106min

Hilary Swank (*Boys Don't Cry, Million Dollar Baby*) is in tomboy mode again here, but she lacks a sure stance as 1930s aviatrix Amelia Earhart – the first woman to fly solo across the Atlantic. Earhart talks about living free as a bird, but *Monsoon Wedding* director Mira Nair doesn't show us what really makes her tick. Nair also flits between timelines without logic, or a sense of what's at stake in each daredevil expedition. Sadly, an extraordinary life winds up feeling like a series of random blips on the radar screen. SP *DVD* Blu

Hilary Swank *Amelia Earhart* • Richard Gere *George Putnam* • Ewan McGregor *Gene Vidal* • Christopher Eccleston *Fred Noonan* • Joe Anderson (1) *Bill* • Cherry Jones *Eleanor Roosevelt* • Mia Wasikowska *Elinor Smith* • Aaron Abrams *Slim Gordon* ■ *Dir* Mira Nair • *Scr* Ron Bass, Anna Hamilton Phelan, from the biographies *East to the Dawn* by Susan Butler and *The Sound of Wings* by Mary Lovell

Amelia Earhart: the Final Flight ★★ PG

Biographical drama 1994 · US · Colour · 90min

Diane Keaton was extremely keen to play pioneer American aviator Amelia Earhart, aiming to convey a detailed portrait of a complex woman, but the finished product is less than scintillating. There is something a shade flat about Keaton's portrayal, and Rutger Hauer strides around the place looking mean and moody, but contributing little of solid value. Passable, but it could have been so much more. SH

Diane Keaton *Amelia Earhart* • Bruce Dern *George Putnam* • Rutger Hauer *Fred Noonan* • Paul Guilfoyle (2) *Paul Mantz* • Denis Arndt *Joseph Laughlin* • David Carpenter *Harry Manning* ■ *Dir* Yves Simoneau • *Scr* Anna Sandor, from the book *Amelia Earhart: a Biography* by Doris L Rich

Amélie ★★★★★ 15

Romantic comedy drama
2001 · Fr/Ger · Colour · 116min

Jean-Pierre Jeunet's offering enchants and beguiles with a nostalgic optimism thanks to its glorious visuals and ceaseless invention. Audrey Tautou is guaranteed iconic status as Amélie, the Montmartre waitress whose selfless *joie de vivre* leads her to improve the lives of her friends and neighbours. She only takes a break from her role of good fairy to pursue Mathieu Kassovitz, the handsome loner who collects rejected photo-booth snaps for his album of forgotten smiles. It has to be conceded that complaints of uncosmopolitan conservatism made against this film have some justification. But as a love letter to the City of Light – filmed at locations all around Paris yet retaining the stylised magic of a movie set – this is deliciously romantic and ingeniously mischievous. DP French +subtitles. *DVD* Blu

Audrey Tautou *Amélie Poulain* • Mathieu Kassovitz *Nino Quicampoix* • Rufus *Raphaël Poulain, Amélie's father* • Yolande Moreau *Madeleine Wallace, the concierge* • Artus de Penguern *Hipolito, the writer* • Urbain Cancelier *Collignon, the grocer* • Dominique Pinon *Joseph* ■ *Dir* Jean-Pierre Jeunet • *Scr* Guillaume Laurant, Jean-Pierre Jeunet • *Cinematographer* Bruno Delbonnel

Amen. ★★★ PG

Second World War drama
2002 · Fr/Ger · Colour · 125min

Costa-Gavras's sincere exposé of the shamefully noncommittal Papal-Allied response to the first news of the Holocaust suffers from being a thriller with a foregone outcome. The fact that Kurt Gerstein (Ulrich Tukur), the Christian chemist who unwittingly introduced Zyklon B gas into the concentration camps, is a true-life character, while Mathieu Kassovitz's crusading Jesuit is fictional, lessens the impact. Powerful, but not wholly persuasive. DP English, French, Italian, German +subtitles. *DVD*

Ulrich Tukur *Kurt Gerstein* • Mathieu Kassovitz *Riccardo Fontana* • Ulrich Mühe *Doctor* • Michel Duchaussoy *Cardinal* • Ion Caramitru *Count Fontana* • Marcel Iures *Pope* ■ *Dir* Costa-Gavras • *Scr* Costa-Gavras, Jean-Claude Grumberg, from the play *Der Stellvertreter* by Rolf Hochhuth

America ★★★
Silent historical epic 1924 · US · BW · 135min

Set during the American War of Independence, DW Griffith's failed attempt to repeat the success of *The Birth of a Nation* (1915) is little more than a ponderous patriotic pageant. Claims to historical accuracy are undermined by having George Washington play Cupid to a bland pair of lovers (Neil Hamilton and Carol Dempster, Griffith's then-inamorata). But the battle scenes were filmed magnificently by a team of photographers headed by Billy Bitzer and Hendrik Sartov. RB

Neil Hamilton *Nathan Holden* • Erville Alderson *Justice Montague* • Carol Dempster *Nancy Montague* • Charles Emmett Mack *Charles Philip Edward Montague* • Lee Beggs *Samuel Adams* • John Dunton *John Hancock* • Arthur Donaldson *King George III* • Charles Bennett *William Pitt* • Downing Clarke *Lord Chamberlain* • Lionel Barrymore *Captain Walter Butler* ■ *Dir* DW Griffith • *Scr* John LE Pell, from a story by Robert W Chambers

America ★★★
Drama 2009 · US · Colour · 89min

The "broken" foster-care system is explored through the eyes of a life-scarred adolescent in this thought-provoking and deeply moving drama co-written by and starring Rosie O'Donnell. Teenager Philip Johnson struggles to face his demons after being sent to the residential treatment facility where a low-key O'Donnell is therapist. Subtle storytelling and skilful direction allow this episodic feature to stand head and shoulders above most TV movies, as impactful themes (sexual abuse, self-harm) are sensitively handled. SF

Philip Johnson *America* • Rosie O'Donnell *Dr Maureen Brennan* • Ruby Dee *Mrs Harper* • Jade Yorker *Brooklyn* ■ *Dir* Yves Simoneau • *Scr* Rosie O'Donnell, Joyce Eliason, from ER Frank's novel *America*

America, America ★★★🅿🅶
Drama 1963 · US · Colour · 161min

Elia Kazan based this would-be epic on the experiences of his uncle, who fled a perilous existence within the Ottoman empire to start afresh in New York. Whether Stathis Giallelis has the wherewithal to surmount the problems encountered en route is open to debate. Such is the authenticity of everything around him, however, that the hesitancy of his performance almost becomes an advantage. Gene Callahan's turn-of-the-century designs thoroughly deserved that Oscar, while the supporting turns of Paul Mann, Linda Marsh and the wicked Lou Antonio are exemplary. DP

Stathis Giallelis *Stavros Topouzoglou* • Frank Wolff *Vartan Damadian* • Harry Davis *Isaac* • Elena Karam *Vasso* • Estelle Hemsley *Grandmother* • Gregory Rozakis *Hohanness Gardashian* • Lou Antonio *Abdul* • Salem Ludwig *Odysseus* ■ *Dir* Elia Kazan • *Scr* Elia Kazan, from his book

The American ★★★15
Thriller 2010 · US · Colour · 100min

In this moody Euro-thriller, an assassin heads for a safe house in the Italian countryside after narrowly escaping an attempt on his life. George Clooney brings his taciturn charisma to bear on the central role, which is probably just as well, since this rather self-consciously arty offering strips away the snappy dialogue and action highlights of more traditional espionage fare, concentrating instead on the professional killer questioning his way of life. Director Anton Corbijn's stylishly evocative framing ensures that the proceedings retain a sense of mystery throughout... until a decidedly predictable climactic showdown rather breaks the spell. TJ English, Italian +subtitles. A sex scene, one gory image. **DVD** 🅱

George Clooney *Jack* • Thekla Reuten *Mathilde* • Irina Bjorklund *Ingrid* • Violante Placido *Clara* • Paolo Bonacelli *Father Benedetto* • Johan Leysen *Pavel* • Bruce Altman *Larry* ■ *Dir* Anton Corbijn • *Scr* Rowan Joffe, from the novel *A Very Private Gentleman* by Martin Booth

American Beauty ★★★★★18
Black comedy 1999 · US · Colour · 116min

British theatre director Sam Mendes made an astonishing film debut with this sublime black comedy about midlife crises, starring Kevin Spacey and Annette Bening as a bored couple in suburban America. The sexually frustrated Bening begins an affair with estate agent Peter Gallagher; Spacey, meanwhile, fantasises about Mena Suvari, a teenage friend of his daughter's. Their disparate needs result in a comic tragedy of misunderstanding that combines acute observations with side-splitting scenarios. This truly outstanding film deservedly picked up a clutch of Oscars including best picture, best director and best actor. LH Violence, swearing, sex scenes, drug abuse, nudity. **DVD** 🅱

Kevin Spacey *Lester Burnham* • Annette Bening *Carolyn Burnham* • Thora Birch *Jane Burnham* • Wes Bentley *Ricky Fitts* • Mena Suvari *Angela Hayes* • Peter Gallagher *Buddy Kane* • Allison Janney *Barbara Fitts* • Scott Bakula *Jim Olmeyer* • Sam Robards *Jim Berkley* • Chris Cooper *Colonel Fitts* ■ *Dir* Sam Mendes • *Scr* Alan Ball

American Blue Note ★★★12
Comedy drama 1989 · US · Colour · 96min

Neatly capturing the atmosphere of dingy rehearsal rooms and smoky clubs, director Ralph Toporoff strikes the perfect balance between music and drama, and draws a performance of some sensitivity from Peter MacNicol as the jazz bandleader given a year to make it big or settle for a lifetime of disappointment. Striking all the right notes, this quaint little film is like *The Commitments* in a minor key. DP Some swearing. **DVD**

Peter MacNicol *Jack* • Charlotte D'Amboise *Benita* • Carl Capotorto *Jerry* • Tim Guinee *Bobby* • Bill Christopher-Myers *Lee* • Jonathan Walker *Tommy* • Zohra Lampert *Louise* ■ *Dir* Ralph Toporoff • *Scr* Gilbert Girion, from a story by Toporoff

American Boyfriends ★★★15
Comedy drama 1989 · Can · Colour · 91min

The stars and writer/director of the engagingly quirky *My American Cousin* are reunited for this witty sequel. This time, Canadian Margaret Langrick is grappling with adolescence as she heads back to the US to attend her cousin John Wildman's wedding. The two leads once again deliver pleasing performances and Sandy Wilson demonstrates a keen understanding of teenage rites, although the tone here is more melancholic than in the earlier film. JF

Margaret Langrick *Sandy Wilcox* • John Wildman *Butch Wilcox* • Jason Blicker *Marty Kaplan* • Liisa Repo-Martell *Julie La Belle* • Delia Brett *Lizzie* • Michelle Bardeaux *Thelma* • Troy Mallory *Spider* • Scott Anderson *Daryl* ■ *Dir/Scr* Sandy Wilson

American Buffalo ★★★15
Drama 1995 · US/UK · Colour · 83min

Dustin Hoffman returns to the skid row of *Midnight Cowboy*'s Ratso Rizzo for this talkfest, scripted by David Mamet from his stage play. Hoffman's a petty thief who decides to muscle in on the burglary plans of ghetto junk dealer Dennis Franz, at the expense of Franz's teenage sidekick, Sean Nelson. The plot disappears into the Pinteresque pauses, but the dialogue has such power and the acting such conviction, you hang on every word however obscene it is. TH Violence. **DVD**

Dustin Hoffman *Teach* • Dennis Franz *Donny Dubrow* • Sean Nelson *Bobby* ■ *Dir* Michael Corrente • *Scr* David Mamet, from his play

American Cousins ★★★15
Crime comedy drama 2003 · UK · Colour · 88min

A Glasgow fish and chip shop provides sanctuary for a couple of New Jersey mobsters in this well-performed and charming British crime comedy drama. After a deal goes sour, New Jersey hoods Danny Nucci and Dan Hedaya flee to Scotland to take refuge with their cousin Gerald Lepkowski, fish fryer by day and stamp collector by night. Director Donald Coutts throws in all sorts of Mafia clichés with total disregard for momentum, but there's a cheerful absurdity about it all that is infectious. TH Swearing, violence. **DVD**

Danny Nucci *Gino* • Shirley Henderson *Alice* • Gerald Lepkowski *Roberto* • Vincent Pastore *Tony* • Dan Hedaya *Settimo* • Russell Hunter *Nonno* • Stevan Rimkus *Jo Jo* • Stephen Graham *Henry* • Jake Abraham *Vince* ■ *Dir* Donald Coutts • *Scr* Sergio Casci

American Dragons ★★15
Crime thriller 1997 · US · Colour · 91min

The racial stereotypes are glaring in this mediocre example of a Hollywood attempt to make a successful crime movie in which mismatched Oriental and American detectives tackle mutual adversaries, with both yakuza and Mafiosi being reduced to cyphers engaged in a gun-toting turf war. With Park Joong-Hoon's Korean cop serving as little more than a stooge for his partner's salty insults, Michael Biehn is powerless to rescue the picture. DP Violence, swearing. **DVD**

Michael Biehn *Detective Tony Luca* • Park Joong-Hoon *Kim* • Cary-Hiroyuki Tagawa *Matsuyama* • Don Stark *Rocco* ■ *Dir* Ralph Hemecker • *Scr* Erik Saltzgaber, Keith W Strandberg

An American Dream ★★★
Drama 1966 · US · Colour · 103min

This Warner Bros adaptation of one of Norman Mailer's lesser novels is enjoyable enough to watch, despite the ham-fisted direction from actor Robert Gist. It's all Technicolor gloss when it should be lean and mean, though it did receive an X certificate for its release in Britain as *See You in Hell, Darling*. Stuart Whitman is most unappealing as the talk-show host who murders his wife and tries to pass her death off as a suicide. Janet Leigh, as his nosey ex-girlfriend, is much better. TS

Stuart Whitman *Stephen Rojack* • Eleanor Parker *Deborah Kelly Rojack* • Janet Leigh *Cherry McMahon* • Barry Sullivan *Roberts* • Lloyd Nolan *Barney Kelly* • Murray Hamilton *Arthur Kabot* • JD Cannon *Sergeant Leznicki* • Susan Denberg *Ruta* ■ *Dir* Robert Gist • *Scr* Mann Rubin, from the novel by Norman Mailer

The American Dreamer ★★★
Documentary 1971 · US · Colour · 93min

Long hidden in the vaults of the Walker Art Center in Minneapolis, this is a fascinating if far from revelatory portrait of Dennis Hopper. Made in the wake of *Easy Rider*, it's less an insight into the mind of a counterculture icon than an extended photo opportunity. It allows him to compare himself to Orson Welles and spout a good deal of self-deluded nonsense and, while the insights into his wayward youth are intriguing, Hopper is too canny to allow the camera too close. DP

Dennis Hopper ■ *Dir* Lawrence Schiller, LM Kit Carson • *Scr* Dennis Hopper, LM Kit Carson, Lawrence Schiller

American Dreamer ★★★🅿🅶
Comedy adventure 1984 · US · Colour · 105min

JoBeth Williams throws herself into the part of a bored housewife who bumps her head and regains consciousness convinced that she is the heroine of her own thrill-a-minute tale of romance and intrigue. Tom Conti perhaps overdoes the bemusement as the man she insists is her faithful sidekick, but Giancarlo Giannini looks suitably shifty as her supposed adversary. An enjoyable, sprightly comedy. DP

JoBeth Williams *Cathy Palmer/Rebecca Ryan* • Tom Conti *Alan McMann* • Giancarlo Giannini *Victor Marchand* • Coral Browne *Margaret McMann* • James Staley *Kevin Palmer* • CD Barnes [Christopher Daniel Barnes] *Kevin Palmer Jr* • Huckleberry Fox *Karl Palmer* • Pierre Santini *Klaus* ■ *Dir* Rick Rosenthal • *Scr* Jim Kouf, David Greenwalt, from a story by Ann Biderman

American Dreamz ★★12
Satirical comedy 2006 · US · Colour · 102min

Pop wannabes jostle for stardom in this messy and contrived satire from Paul Weitz starring Hugh Grant, who plays the host of a TV talent show. Dennis Quaid is wasted in this heavy-handed farce as a US president who hardly knows where the Middle East is, let alone how to bring peace to it. Anyway, he's too busy guest judging on America's most popular TV show. There are funny moments, but this satire is as shallow as the celebrity-obsessed culture it lampoons. SP Swearing. **DVD**

Hugh Grant *Martin Tweed* • Dennis Quaid *President Staton* • Mandy Moore *Sally Kendoo* • Marcia Gay Harden *First Lady* • Chris Klein *William Williams* • Jennifer Coolidge *Martha Kendoo* • Willem Dafoe *Chief of Staff* • Sam Golzari *Omer* ■ *Dir/Scr* Paul Weitz

American Flyers ★★🅿🅶
Action drama 1985 · US · Colour · 107min

This tale of rival cycling siblings competing in a Rocky Mountains endurance race is complicated by David Grant's antagonism towards his sports doctor older brother, Kevin Costner. Other distractions in the plot are an anti-Soviet diversion and a terminal illness that Grant may be suffering from. TH Swearing, brief nudity.

Kevin Costner *Marcus Sommers* • David Grant [David Marshall Grant] *David Sommers* • Rae Dawn Chong *Sarah* • Alexandra Paul *Becky* • Luca Bercovici *Muzzin* • Robert Townsend *Jerome* • John Amos *Dr Conrad* • John Garber *Belov* • Janice Rule *Mrs Sommers* • Jennifer Grey *Leslie* ■ *Dir* John Badham • *Scr* Steve Tesich

The American Friend ★★★★15
Crime drama 1977 · W Ger/Fr · Colour · 120min

There are enough *film noir* tricks and dark philosophical insights in this adaptation of Patricia Highsmith's *Ripley's Game* for German director Wim Wenders to turn a bleak road movie into a dazzling psychological thriller. Bruno Ganz is the simple Swiss picture framer who, believing he's dying from a blood disease, is lured into killing Mafia kingpins by shady loner Dennis Hopper. Soon the two men from opposite ends of the human spectrum bond, allowing Wenders to explore his existentialist subtext with exciting wit and enjoyable wisdom. The film features cameos from directors Samuel Fuller and Nicholas Ray, to whom Wenders pays visual homage. AJ **DVD**

Dennis Hopper *Ripley* • Bruno Ganz *Jonathan Zimmermann* • Lisa Kreuzer *Marianne Zimmermann* • Gérard Blain *Raoul Minot* • Nicholas Ray *Derwatt* • Samuel Fuller *American mobster* • Peter Lilienthal *Marcangelo* • Daniel Schmid *Ingraham* ■ *Dir* Wim Wenders • *Scr* Wim Wenders, from the novel *Ripley's Game* by Patricia Highsmith • *Cinematographer* Robby Müller

American Friends ★★★🅿🅶
Romantic drama 1991 · UK · Colour · 91min

In this delightful, understated personal project, Michael Palin stars as a romantically awkward Oxford don, a character allegedly based on his great-grandfather. The stuffy, frock-coated formality of Victorian varsity life is atmospherically conjured up and the insightful script, co-written by director Tristram Powell and Palin, is used to good effect. There are also some lovely performances, particularly from Trini Alvarado as Palin's bouncy teenage love interest and a consummate Connie Booth as her guardian. SH Nudity.

Michael Palin *Rev Francis Ashby* • Connie Booth *Miss Caroline Hartley* • Trini Alvarado *Miss Elinor Hartley* • Alfred Molina *Oliver Syme* • David Calder *Pollitt* • Simon Jones *Anderson* • Robert

Eddison *Rushden* • Alun Armstrong *Dr Weeks* • Sheila Reid *Mrs Weeks* • Edward Rawle-Hicks *John Weeks* • Roger Lloyd Pack *Dr Butler* • Jonathan Firth *Cable* ■ *Dir* Tristram Powell • *Scr* Michael Palin, Tristram Powell

American Gangster

★★★★ **18**

Crime drama based on a true story
2007 · US/UK · Colour · 150min

As this true-life New York crime saga (set between 1968 and 1974) evocatively unfolds, master director Ridley Scott makes "big" look easy. Denzel Washington brings a suave tranquility to his role as Harlem drugs lord Frank Lucas, while, in parallel, Russell Crowe's honest New Jersey cop Richie Roberts juggles divorce, pariah status within a corrupt police department and, eventually, the logistics of bringing Lucas down. Beyond Josh Brolin's poisonously bad cop, a fine supporting cast struggles to make any meaningful impact in the wake of a dominant Washington – not least in the poorly sketched female roles. Nevertheless, this is still a classy crime fable that succeeds despite sidestepping the electric set pieces of such genre maestros as Martin Scorsese or Brian De Palma. Also shown in an extended edition. AC Violence, drug abuse. *DVD* *BL*

Denzel Washington *Frank Lucas* • Russell Crowe *Richie Roberts* • Ruby Dee *Mama Lucas* • Chiwetel Ejiofor *Huey Lucas* • Cuba Gooding Jr *Nicky Barnes* • Josh Brolin *Detective Trupo* • Ted Levine *Lou Toback* • Armand Assante *Dominic Cattano* • John Ortiz (1) *Javier J Rivera* • John Hawkes *Freddie Spearman* • RZA *Moses Jones* • Carla Gugino *Laurie Roberts* ■ *Dir* Ridley Scott • *Scr* Steven Zaillian, from the article *The Return of Superfly* by Mark Jacobson • *Cinematographer* Harris Savides • *Art Directors* Arthur Max, Beth A Rubino • *Editor* Pietro Scalia

American Gigolo

★★★ **18**

Erotic thriller
1980 · US · Colour · 111min

Richard Gere romped his way to stardom in this glossy and controversial (for its time) story of a Los Angeles stud who services the bored wives of Beverly Hills. His detached view of life is threatened, however, when he gets caught up in murder and politics. This hasn't aged well, and is a beautifully designed but transparent walk on the wild side. JF Swearing, sex scenes, nudity. *DVD*

Richard Gere *Julian Kay* • Lauren Hutton *Michelle Stratton* • Hector Elizondo *Detective Sunday* • Nina Van Pallandt *Anne* • Bill Duke *Leon Jaimes* • Brian Davies *Charles Stratton* • Patti Carr *Judy Rheiman* • Tom Stewart *Mr Rheiman* ■ *Dir/Scr* Paul Schrader

American Gothic

★ **18**

Horror 1987 · UK/Can · Colour · 85min

An uneasy mix of old-fashioned off-screen splatter and humour that's supposed to be black (but ends up being merely ludicrous), this vaguely sick shocker stars Rod Steiger and Yvonne De Carlo as backwoods nutcases who live on a remote island with their three mentally handicapped adult children. The suspense refuses to build from the moment six campers arrive on the island and become their victims. AJ *DVD*

Rod Steiger *Pa* • Yvonne De Carlo *Ma* • Sarah Torgov *Cynthia* • Michael J Pollard *Woody* • Fiona Hutchison *Lynn* • William Hootkins *Teddy* ■ *Dir* John Hough • *Scr* John Hough, Terry Lens, Bert Wetanson, Michael Vines

American Graffiti

★★★★★ **PG**

Comedy drama 1973 · US · Colour · 107min

A summer night in the lives of a group of small-town Californian teenagers following their graduation from high school in 1962 is brilliantly captured by director George Lucas in this classic coming-of-age saga that virtually invented juke-box nostalgia. Based on Lucas's own youthful exploits, the golden oldies soundtrack is a perfect counterpoint to the sharp and tender comedy, engagingly played by Richard Dreyfuss and Ronny (Ron) Howard, two of a number of future stars in the cast. Wonderfully evoking the feel and spirit of the era, this is one of those rare movies you live through rather than watch. An inferior sequel, *More American Graffiti*, followed in 1979. AJ Swearing. *DVD* *BL*

Richard Dreyfuss *Curt Henderson* • Ronny Howard [Ron Howard] *Steve Bolander* • Paul Le Mat *John Milner* • Charles Martin Smith *Terry Fields* • Cindy Williams *Laurie* • Candy Clark *Debbie* • Mackenzie Phillips *Carol* • Wolfman Jack *Disc jockey* • Harrison Ford *Bob Falfa* • Bo Hopkins *Joe* • Manuel Padilla Jr *Carlos* ■ *Dir* George Lucas • *Scr* George Lucas, Gloria Katz, Willard Huyck

An American Guerrilla in the Philippines

★★ **U**

Second World War action adventure
1950 · US · Colour · 103min

Retitled *I Shall Return* for the UK market, this ultra-patriotic flag-waver is almost unwatchable today, save for the striking Technicolor and the star presence of Tyrone Power, whose dramatic energy alone goes a long way towards saving the Filipinos, as he shows them how to build radio stations and organise their resistance against the Japanese. Despite its pacey action sequences, this is rather too slow. TS

Tyrone Power *Ensign Chuck Palmer* • Micheline Presle *Jeanne Martinez* • Tom Ewell *Jim Mitchell* • Bob Patten *Lovejoy* • Tommy Cook *Miguel* • Juan Torena *Juan Martinez* • Jack Elam *Speaker* • Robert Barrat *General Douglas Macarthur* • Carleton Young *Colonel Phillips* ■ *Dir* Fritz Lang • *Scr* Lamar Trotti, from the novel by Ira Wolfert

American Gun

★★★ **15**

Murder mystery drama
2002 · US · BW and Colour · 85min

James Coburn gives his final film more than it deserves. It's a steely investigation into the nature of violent crime in the United States, with Coburn as the father who decides to trace the history of the .357 Magnum that killed his daughter (Virginia Madsen) on the streets of his Vermont home. Some of the encounters feel contrived, but the monochrome flashbacks to Coburn's encounters with guns during his childhood and in the Second World War are evocatively staged. DP Swearing, violence, drug abuse. *DVD*

James Coburn *Martin* • Barbara Bain *Anne* • Virginia Madsen *Penny* • Alexandra Holden *Mia* ■ *Dir/Scr* Alan Jacobs

An American Haunting

★★★ **15**

Period horror
2005 · US · Colour and BW · 86min

This supernatural chiller sees a wealthy and respected family in early 19th-century America besieged by an aggressive poltergeist. For four years, the spook terrorised the household, singling out John Bell (Donald Sutherland) and his only daughter Betsy (Rachel Hurd-Wood) in increasingly vicious attacks. While individual elements may seem familiar, they're no less effective and hit all the right scary notes thanks to taut direction and a ruthless exploitation of sound and visuals. SF *DVD*

Donald Sutherland *John Bell* • Sissy Spacek *Lucy Bell* • Rachel Hurd-Wood *Betsy Bell* • James D'Arcy *Richard Powell* • Matthew Marsh *James Johnston* • Thom Fell *John Bell Jr* • Sam Alexander *Joshua Gardner* ■ *Dir* Courtney Solomon • *Scr* Courtney Solomon, from the novel *The Bell Witch: An American Haunting* by Brent Monahan

American Heart

★★ **15**

Drama 1992 · US · Colour · 114min

Top-class performances by Jeff Bridges and Edward Furlong add a glossy sheen to this one-dimensional material. Bridges plays a no-hope drifter who, when released from prison, tries bonding with his alienated teenage son (Furlong), with tragic results. By turns poignant, hard-hitting and annoying, it's only the stars who make director Martin Bell's strained relationship movie work. AJ

Jeff Bridges *Jack Kelson* • Edward Furlong *Nick Kelson* • Lucinda Jenney *Charlotte* • Don Harvey *Rainey* • Tracey Kapisky *Molly* • Shareen Mitchell *Diane* • Christian Frizzell *Rollie* • Maggie Welsh *Freddie* ■ *Dir* Martin Bell • *Scr* Peter Silverman, from a story by Martin Bell, Peter Silverman, Mary Ellen Mark

American History X

★★★★ **18**

Social drama 1998 · US · Colour and BW · 113min

Director Tony Kaye's tough, powerful and uncompromising cautionary tale takes a brutal look at the depths of racial prejudice and the roots of violent hate crimes. Teenager Edward Furlong has been keeping the faith of his older brother Edward Norton, a neo-Nazi who has recently released from jail. However, Norton has undergone a radical transformation through his friendship with a black prison inmate and the moral clarity of solitude. Told in colour with black-and-white flashbacks, Kaye's cutting-edge treatise is a shock to the system filled with unforgettable moments, seriously handled issues and superb acting by Norton, who was deservedly Oscar-nominated. AJ Swearing, nudity, violence. *DVD* *BL*

Edward Norton *Derek Vinyard* • Edward Furlong *Danny Vinyard* • Beverly D'Angelo *Doris Vinyard* • Jennifer Lien *Davina Vinyard* • Ethan Suplee *Seth* • Fairuza Balk *Stacey* • Avery Brooks *Dr Robert Sweeney* • Elliott Gould *Murray* • Stacy Keach *Cameron Alexander* ■ *Dir* Tony Kaye • *Scr* David McKenna

American Honey

★★★★

Comedy drama 2016 · UK/US · Colour

Ditching gritty British drama to shoot an improvised road movie on the freeways of the US, acclaimed director Andrea Arnold follows her dour take on *Wuthering Heights* with an exhilarating celebration of modern youth. Sasha Lane is left in charge of two siblings by her absentee mother, but after a chance meeting she heads off in search of adventure. Despite the arty flourishes, this is an intoxicating experience, mixing the blurry hedonism of youth with jarring, sharply etched vignettes. DW

Sasha Lane *Star* • Shia LaBeouf *Jake* • McCaul Lombardi *Corey* • Arielle Holmes *Pagan* ■ *Dir/Scr* Andrea Arnold

American Hot Wax

★★★

Biographical drama 1977 · US · Colour · 91min

DJ Alan Freed was the man credited with introducing white American teenagers to the sounds that their parents considered the Devil's music. With Tim McIntire solid enough as "the Pied Piper of Rock 'n' Roll", this pleasing pop picture makes a fair fist of re-creating the era. You can forgive director Floyd Mutrux for calling on the services of Chuck Berry and Jerry Lee Lewis, but their obvious age and over-polished performances detract from the aura of amateur authenticity. DP

Tim McIntire *Alan Freed* • Fran Drescher *Sheryl* • Jay Leno *Mookie* • Laraine Newman *Louise* • Jeff Altman *Lennie Richfield* • Moosie Drier *Artie Moress* • John Lehne *District Attorney Coleman* • Stewart Steinberg *Stone* ■ *Dir* Floyd Mutrux • *Scr* John Kaye, from his story with Art Linson

American Hustle

★★★★ **15**

Crime caper based on a true story
2013 · US · Colour · 132min

American Hustle begins as most 1970s-set crime capers do, with a flurry of obvious wigs, polyester suits and iconic chart hits. Unusually, however, it quickly reveals itself to be an intelligent character piece, with a New York conman (Christian Bale) and his lover/partner (Amy Adams) forced into assisting the FBI. David O Russell uses his A-list cast to create a kind of adult pantomime, in which allegiances switch constantly and no one is ever quite who they seem. As is typical, the men drive the story, but it's the women that provide the substance. Adams is terrific, but Jennifer Lawrence steals the show as a likeable ditz whose loose-lipped tendencies might at any minute instigate a bloodbath. DW Swearing. *DVD* *BL*

Christian Bale *Irving Rosenfeld* • Bradley Cooper *Richie DiMaso* • Amy Adams *Sydney Prosser* • Jennifer Lawrence (2) *Rosalyn Rosenfeld* • Jeremy Renner *Mayor Carmine Polito* • Louis CK *Stoddard Thorsen* • Robert De Niro *Victor Tellegio* ■ *Dir* David O Russell • *Scr* David O Russell, Eric Warren Singer [Eric Singer] • *Music* Danny Elfman • *Production Designer* Judy Becker

• *Editors* Jay Cassidy, Crispin Struthers, Alan Baumgarten • *Costume Designer* Michael Wilkinson

An American in Paris

★★★★ **U**

Musical 1951 · US · Colour · 108min

This archetypal glamorous MGM musical was the deserved winner of six Oscars, including best picture, collected by genius producer Arthur Freed, with a special Oscar presented to star Gene Kelly for advancing the art of choreography on screen. It still looks pretty good today, with marvellous Technicolored design, athletic dancing from Kelly and a superb Gershwin score, but some sequences have dated. The climactic 17-minute ballet on the theme of the French Impressionists is a little precious and overstaged by today's standards, but much of the movie remains delightful. TS *DVD* *BL*

Gene Kelly *Jerry Mulligan* • Leslie Caron *Lise* • Oscar Levant *Adam Cook* • Georges Guetary *Henri Baurel* • Nina Foch *Milo Roberts* • Eugene Borden *George Mattieu* • Martha Bamattre *Mathilde Mattieu* ■ *Dir* Vincente Minnelli • *Scr* Alan Jay Lerner • *Cinematographers* John Alton, Alfred Gilks • *Art Directors* Cedric Gibbons, Preston Ames • *Costume Designers* Walter Plunkett, Irene Sharaff, Orry-Kelly

American Madness

★★★ **U**

Period drama 1932 · US · BW · 73min

Frank Capra was a master of the "feel-good factor", long before the phrase was coined. Populist and simplistic it may be, but this dry run for the financial dilemma of *It's a Wonderful Life* is one of his American fantasies, showing how the "little people" can save big institutions. All bank bosses are perhaps not as dynamic as Walter Huston's, and it's unlikely that small depositors would rally round in real life as they do here, but with Capra you take it on trust. TH

Walter Huston *Thomas Dickson* • Pat O'Brien *Matt* • Kay Johnson *Mrs Dickson* • Constance Cummings *Helen* • Gavin Gordon *Cluett* ■ *Dir* Frank Capra • *Scr* Robert Riskin

American Mary

★★★★ **18**

Horror 2012 · Can · Colour · 98min

A debt-ridden medical student takes up a lucrative sideline in extreme body modification in this pulverising horror from the Soska twins (*Dead Hooker in a Trunk*). Katharine Isabelle (*Ginger Snaps*) gives a terrific performance as trainee surgeon Mary Mason, whose dire financial straits force her to take a walk on the dark side after a visit to a sleazy strip club. The sibling directors' second feature is no gratuitous schlock-fest: it's a thoughtful, well-made piece with plenty of gallows humour and a memorable cameo from the Soskas themselves. JA *DVD* *BL*

Katharine Isabelle *Mary Mason* • Antonio Cupo *Billy Barker* • Tristan Risk *Beatress Johnson* • David Lovgren *Dr Grant* • Paula Lindberg *Ruby Realgirl* ■ *Dir/Scr* Jen Soska, Sylvia Soska

American Me

★★★ **18**

Drama 1992 · US · Colour · 120min

This vivid exploration of three generations of a Hispanic-American family growing up in violence-torn Los Angeles marks the directing debut of actor Edward James Olmos. Low self-esteem and abject poverty inspire the criminal behaviour of Santana, a Chicano underworld kingpin whom Olmos plays as an adult. Against the background of the 1943 Pachuco riots, Santana controls the streets from behind bars in this fact-based drama. Olmos gives the action a brutally violent and raw realism. AJ

Edward James Olmos *Santana* • William Forsythe *JD* • Pepe Serna *Mundo* • Danny De La Paz *Puppet* • Evelina Fernandez *Julie* • Cary-Hiroyuki Tagawa *El Japo* • Daniel Villarreal *Little Puppet* ■ *Dir* Edward James Olmos • *Scr* Floyd Mutrux, Desmond Nakano, from a story by Floyd Mutrux, Desmond Nakano

American Ninja ★★ 18

Martial arts action adventure
1985 · US · Colour · 91min

This was the film that made Michael Dudikoff's name, and went on to spawn a fair few sequels, most of which didn't stray too far from the blueprint established here. There are some nice fight scenes, but the acting is about as mindless as the action sequences. Dudikoff returned for the first sequel, but not the three others that followed. JF **DVD** Blu

Michael Dudikoff *Joe* • Guich Koock *Hickock* • Judie Aronson *Patricia* • Steve James (1) *Jackson* • Don Stewart *Ortega* • John LaMotta *Rinaldo* ■ *Dir* Sam Firstenberg • *Scr* Paul de Mielche, from a story by Avi Kleinberger, Gideon Amir

American Outlaws ★★★ 12

Comedy western   2001 · US · Colour · 90min

This cowboy film features young gunslingers who would seem more at home popping pimples than pumping pistols - even when they're up against land-grabbing railroad barons. It's yet another re-telling of the Jesse James story, with Colin Farrell as Jesse and Scott Caan as partner Cole Younger. Director Les Mayfield may portray them as mere run-of-the-mill Robin Hoods, but this is all about attracting the *Dawson's Creek* crowd into the cinema. There's welcome support from Kathy Bates and Timothy Dalton. TH Swearing, violence.
DVD

Colin Farrell (2) *Jesse James* • Scott Caan *Cole Younger* • Ali Larter *Zee Mimms* • Gabriel Macht *Frank James* • Harris Yulin *Thaddeus Rains* • Kathy Bates *Ma James* • Timothy Dalton *Allan Pinkerton* ■ *Dir* Les Mayfield • *Scr* Roderick Taylor, John Rogers, from a story by Taylor

American Pastoral

Drama   2016 · US · Colour

This is a preview - no prints were available to review prior to publication: For his directorial debut, an ambitious Ewan McGregor tackles Philip Roth's lauded novel, often cited as one of the most important books of modern times. He also stars as squeaky-clean "hero" Swede, who has left behind his Jewish roots, married a "shiksa" (Jennifer Connelly) and is raising a daughter (Dakota Fanning). But he threatens everything he has built by joining the 1960s anti-establishment movement. Setting aside his dodgy US accent, McGregor certainly has his work cut out behind the camera. SP

Ewan McGregor *Seymour "Swede" Levov* • Jennifer Connelly *Dawn* • Dakota Fanning *Merry Levov* ■ *Dir* Ewan McGregor • *Scr* John Romano, from Philip Roth's novel

American Perfekt ★★★ 15

Psychological thriller 1997 · US · Colour · 99min

The one-letter misspelling in the title of this weird road movie aims to convey the imperfections of the American Dream. Amanda Plummer has a bizarre accident on her way to the town of Peachblossom. Rescued by Robert Forster, a doctor, she then hitches a lift from David Thewlis. As Plummer's sister Fairuza Balk tries to re-trace her movements the plot corkscrews into mania and murder. Terrific performances add colour and momentum, but Paul Chart's lacklustre direction blunts the point and slackens the tension. TH Violence, a sex scene, swearing, nudity.
DVD

Robert Forster *Dr Jake Gordon Nyman* • Amanda Plummer *Sandra Thomas* • Fairuza Balk *Alice Thomas* • David Thewlis *Ernest Santini* • Paul Sorvino *Sheriff Frank Noonan* • Geoffrey Lewis *Willy* • Chris Sarandon *Deputy Sheriff Sammy Goodall* • Joanna Gleason *Shirley Dutton* • Jay Patterson *Bernie* ■ *Dir/Scr* Paul Chart

American Pie ★★★★ 15

Comedy   1999 · US · Colour · 91min

If you thought *Dumb and Dumber* or *There's Something about Mary* plumbed the depths of grossness, hold on to your lunch - you ain't seen nothing yet. This laughter-packed comedy about four teenage boys who pledge to lose their virginity before prom night has enough crass gags to satisfy the most demanding fierce fans. Yet it also boasts some spot-on performances from a hip young cast that includes Chris Klein, Mena Suvari, Tara Reid and Natasha Lyonne. Must-see fare for those not easily offended. JB Swearing, sex scenes, nudity.
DVD Blu

Jason Biggs *Jim Levenstein* • Chris Klein *Chris "Oz" Ostreicher* • Natasha Lyonne *Jessica* • Thomas Ian Nicholas *Kevin Myers* • Tara Reid *Vicky* • Mena Suvari *Heather* • Eugene Levy *Jim's dad* • Eddie Kaye Thomas *Paul Finch* • Jennifer Coolidge *Stifler's mom* • Seann W Scott [Seann William Scott] *Stifler* • Alyson Hannigan *Michelle Flaherty* • Shannon Elizabeth *Nadia* ■ *Dir* Paul Weitz • *Scr* Adam Herz

American Pie 2 ★★★ 15

Comedy   2001 · US · Colour · 100min

Bawdy comedy *American Pie* was an unexpected success in 1999 and the whole cast returned for this sequel. The humour remains the same - rude, crude and lewd - as the gang gets together for lots of beer and sex at a beach house following their first year in college. The comedy is unsophisticated and often predictable, but you'll be laughing too much to notice. JB
DVD Blu

Jason Biggs *Jim Levenstein* • Shannon Elizabeth *Nadia* • Alyson Hannigan *Michelle Flaherty* • Chris Klein *Chris "Oz" Ostreicher* • Natasha Lyonne *Jessica* • Thomas Ian Nicholas *Kevin Myers* • Tara Reid *Vicky* • Seann William Scott *Stifler* • Mena Suvari *Heather* • Eugene Levy *Jim's dad* ■ *Dir* James B Rogers • *Scr* Adam Herz, from a story by David H Steinberg, Herz, from characters by Herz

American Pie: the Wedding ★★★ 15

Comedy   2003 · US/Ger · Colour · 99min

For some, these adolescent sex comedies are the living proof of how popular cinema has plumbed new depths in taste. For others, they are worthy successors to the classic John Hughes teen-fests of the 1980s. Here, series regulars Jim (Jason Biggs) and Michelle (Alyson Hannigan) attempt to tie the knot. Writer Adam Herz delivers the familiar recipe of unpleasant set pieces, together with a shamelessly upbeat and sentimental ending. AS Sex scenes, swearing, nudity. **DVD** Blu

Jason Biggs *Jim Levenstein* • Alyson Hannigan *Michelle Flaherty* • January Jones *Cadence Flaherty* • Thomas Ian Nicholas *Kevin Myers* • Seann William Scott *Steve Stifler* • Eddie Kaye Thomas *Paul Finch* • Fred Willard *Harold Flaherty* • Eugene Levy *Jim's dad* • Molly Cheek *Jim's mom* ■ *Dir* Jesse Dylan • *Scr* Adam Herz, from his characters

American Pie Presents Band Camp ★ 15

Comedy   2005 · US · Colour · 87min

This straight-to-DVD sequel to the blockbuster teenage franchise sees the saga hit rock bottom. The lead character here is Stifler's equally obnoxious little brother (newcomer Tad Hilgenbrink) who is sentenced to band camp when an end of year school prank goes wrong. There's a tiredness to the gags and even the crudity has a TV tameness about it. JF Swearing, nudity. **DVD**

Eugene Levy *Mr Levenstein* • Tad Hilgenbrink *Matt Stifler* • Arielle Kebbel *Elyse* • Rachel Veltri *Dani* • Angela Little *Sherri* • Omar Benson Miller *Oscar* • Chris Owen *Sherman* ■ *Dir* Steve Rash • *Scr* Brad Riddell, from characters from Adam Herz

American Pie Presents the Naked Mile ★ 15

Comedy   2006 · US · Colour · 97min

The original *American Pie* always felt like a proper feature, but this third straight-to-DVD cash-in is more a badly paced patchwork of vulgar vignettes. The story, for what it's worth, revolves around high-school virgin Erik Stifler (John White) after his girlfriend gives him free rein for a wild weekend. Even fans of teen sex comedies will find the verbal gags repetitive, predictable and often plain unfunny. SF Swearing, sex scenes.

John White (2) *Erik Stifler* • Eugene Levy *Mr Levenstein* • Jessy Schram *Tracy* • Steve Talley *Dwight Stifler* • Candace Kroslak *Brandi* ■ *Dir* Joe Nussbaum • *Scr* Erik Lindsay, from characters by Adam Herz

American Reunion ★★ 15

Comedy   2012 · US · Colour · 108min

Nine years after the third of the *American Pie* movies (disregarding a few forgettable straight-to-DVD efforts), Jim, Oz, Stifler and co are together again. Sadly, it soon becomes apparent that they should all have stayed at home. *Harold and Kumar* writer/directors Jon Hurwitz and Hayden Schlossberg take an age to get things going, and even then there's a palpable air of strained pointlessness to the whole thing. Only a conspicuously buff Seann William Scott manfully tries to inject a little energy and even a subdued note of genuine pathos, and the film loses something when he's not on screen. AS Swearing, sexual references, drug abuse, nudity. **DVD** Blu

Jason Biggs *Jim* • Alyson Hannigan *Michelle* • Tara Reid *Vicky* • Seann William Scott *Stifler* • Chris Klein *Oz* • Jennifer Coolidge *Stifler's mom* • Eugene Levy *Jim's dad* ■ *Dir* Jon Hurwitz, Hayden Schlossberg • *Scr* Jon Hurwitz, Hayden Schlossberg, from characters from Adam Herz

The American President ★★★★ 15

Romantic comedy   1995 · US · Colour · 109min

A gleaming, witty and irresistible romantic comedy, this was one of several White House-based movies made in the wake of Bill Clinton's election. Michael Douglas is the recently widowed president, the father of a young daughter and in need of female company at official functions. Annette Bening, an eco-lobbyist, fits the bill and, after he dances with her in public, the press goes into speculative overdrive. Douglas walks and talks presidentially, while Bening is also terrific. Written by Aaron Sorkin, who went on to create TV's *The West Wing*. AT Swearing. **DVD**

Michael Douglas (1) *Andrew Shepherd* • Annette Bening *Sydney Ellen Wade* • Michael J Fox *Lewis Rothschild* • David Paymer *Leon Kodak* • Martin Sheen *AJ MacInerney* • Anna Deavere Smith *Robin McCall* • Samantha Mathis *Janie Basdin* • Richard Dreyfuss *Senator Rumson* • John Mahoney *Leo Solomon* • Shawna Waldron *Lucy Shepherd* ■ *Dir* Rob Reiner • *Scr* Aaron Sorkin

American Psycho ★★★★ 18

Satirical black comedy drama
2000 · US/Can · Colour · 97min

Director Mary Harron fought for Christian Bale to play Bret Easton Ellis's smooth yuppie killer and her decision is totally vindicated. Bale is brilliant as the wealthy, successful and psychopathic Patrick Bateman. Despite the novel's skin-crawling reputation, most of the violence takes place off-screen. Moreover, the film's satirical swipes at the materialistic 1980s provide laughs amid the carnage, as does Bale's cheesy, game-show host delivery of Bateman's eccentric cultural observations. Aside from a graphic threesome, this is an admirably restrained adaptation, although its cold, aloof tone lessens the impact of Bateman's actions. JC Violence, swearing, sex scenes, drug abuse, nudity. **DVD**

Christian Bale *Patrick Bateman* • Willem Dafoe *Donald Kimball* • Jared Leto *Paul Allen* • Reese Witherspoon *Evelyn Williams* • Samantha Mathis *Courtney Rawlinson* • Chloe Sevigny [Chloë Sevigny] *Jean* • Justin Theroux *Timothy Bryce* ■ *Dir* Mary Harron • *Scr* Guinevere Turner, Mary Harron, from the novel by Bret Easton Ellis • *Music* John Cale

American Psycho II: All American Girl ★★ 18

Black comedy horror thriller
2002 · US/Can · Colour · 84min

This slipshod sequel has very little to do with Mary Harron's adaptation of Bret Easton Ellis's infamous novel. Mila Kunis stars as a girl who, as a child, supposedly slayed the murderous Patrick Bateman, and has become unhealthily fascinated by serial killers. But in chronicling her ruthless bid to become ex-FBI agent William Shatner's teaching assistant, director Morgan J Freeman too often replaces the original's satire with a clumsy brand of gross-out black comedy. DP Violence, swearing.
DVD

Mila Kunis *Rachael Newman* • Geraint Wyn Davies *Dr Eric Daniels* • William Shatner *Robert Starkman* • Robin Dunne *Brian Leads* • Lindy Booth *Cassandra Blaire* • Charles Officer *Keith Lawson* ■ *Dir* Morgan J Freeman • *Scr* Karen Craig, Alex Sanger

An American Rhapsody ★★

Drama   2001 · US · Colour and BW · 106min

Writer/director Eva Gardos charts her amazing life in this careful but controlled autobiography. The opening section focuses on her parents' escape (without her) from Communist Hungary and her itinerant, but contented existence in the tranquil countryside. But after they've summoned her to the United States, the emphasis shifts to her feuds with her over-compensating mother and the lack of chemistry between Nastassja Kinski and Scarlett Johansson reduces the emotional *frisson* to teleplay melodramatics. DP

Nastassja Kinski *Margit* • Scarlett Johansson *Suzanne* • Tony Goldwyn *Peter* • Mae Whitman *Maria* • Agnes Banfalvy *Helen* • Zoltan Seress *George* ■ *Dir/Scr* Eva Gardos

An American Romance ★★ U

Drama   1944 · US · Colour · 150min

This epic film by the great pioneering director of the American cinema, King Vidor, is impressive in both scale and technical expertise. Unfortunately, the tale of a European immigrant's rise to the top of industry is an extraordinarily dull affair, curiously devoid of drama or passion. The lead roles are played by the competent but uncharismatic Brian Donlevy and unknown Australian Ann Richards, neither of whose shoulders are big enough to shoulder the weight. RK

Brian Donlevy *Steve Dangos* • Ann Richards *Anna* • Walter Abel *Howard Clinton* • John Qualen *Anton Dubechek* ■ *Dir* King Vidor • *Scr* Herbert Dalmas, William Ludwig, from a story by King Vidor

American Sniper ★★★★ 15

Action drama based on a true story
2014 · US · Colour · 127min

A confident yet thoughtful performance from Bradley Cooper is the solid centre of director Clint Eastwood's absorbing biopic of the most lethal sniper in US military history. Texas patriot Chris Kyle (Cooper) notched up 160 confirmed kills during two tours of Navy SEAL duty in post 9/11 Iraq, and Eastwood succinctly charts his life through sharpshooting youth, marriage to a long-suffering wife (played by an impressive Sienna Miller) and becoming a reluctant hero. With the final haunting frames bound to surprise those unaware of Kyle's career, this is hard-nosed myth-making at its finest from a director at the top of his game. AJ Violence, swearing. **DVD** Blu

Bradley Cooper *Chris Kyle* • Sienna Miller *Taya Renae Kyle* • Luke Grimes *Marc Lee* • Kyle Gallner *Winston* ■ *Dir* Clint Eastwood • *Scr* Jason Hall, from the non-fiction book by Chris Kyle, Scott McEwen, Jim DeFelice

The American Soldier ★★★★ 18

Crime drama   1970 · W Ger · BW · 76min

A homage to the visual style of American gangster movies, this is often regarded as the prototype Fassbinder film. Bordering on pastiche, it follows Vietnam veteran Karl Scheydt as he assassinates a gypsy rent boy, a pornographer and his own girlfriend. Fassbinder seems more interested in creating a mood and referencing such film-makers as Samuel Fuller than storytelling or social analysis. Yet this brooding non-drama is still highly revelatory of the director's preoccupations: sex and violence are chillingly equated, while emotion and morality are dismissed as fatal flaws. DP German +subtitles. **DVD**

A

Karl Scheydt *Ricky* • Elga Sorbas *Rosa von Praunheim* • Jan George *Jan* • Margarethe von Trotta *Maid* • Hark Bohm *Doc* • Ingrid Caven *Singer* • Rainer Werner Fassbinder *Franz Walsh* • Ulli Lommel *Gypsy* ■ *Dir/Scr* Rainer Werner Fassbinder

American Splendor
★★★★ 15

Biographical drama 2003 · US · Colour · 97min

The mundane life of a working-class everyman is celebrated in all its minor detail in this imaginative biopic of American underground comic book writer Harvey Pekar. It brilliantly captures the humanity and acidic humour of the Cleveland hospital filing clerk who turned his everyday experiences into a cult publication. As well as including authentic archival footage, the directors present the curmudgeonly author in animated form, as his real-life self and, in the picture's main body, as a dramatised character. A total delight. **SF** Swearing. *DVD*

Paul Giamatti *Harvey Pekar* • Hope Davis *Joyce Brabner* • James Urbaniak *Robert Crumb* • Judah Friedlander *Toby Radloff* • Earl Billings *Mr Boats* • James McCaffrey *Fred* ■ *Dir* Shari Springer Berman, Robert Pulcini • *Scr* Shari Springer Berman, from the comic-book series by Harvey Pekar, from the comic book *Our Cancer Year* by Harvey Pekar, Joyce Brabner

American Strays
★★★

Black comedy crime thriller
1996 · US · Colour · 93min

Occupying the same surreal niche as the offbeat work of David Lynch, this is a mordantly funny and intensely bizarre study of the meaning of life and death. It all revolves around Red's Desert Oasis diner, where surly waitress Jennifer Tilly dishes up the very average food and where strangers, travelling salesmen and drifters meet their destinies in anything but average ways. This is a compelling – if perplexing – mystery. Violent and hilarious, it is always intriguing and often likeable. **AJ**

Jennifer Tilly *Patty Mae* • Eric Roberts *Martin* • John Savage *Dwayne* • Luke Perry *Johnny* • Carol Kane *Helen* • Joe Viterelli *Gene* • James Russo *Harv* • Vonte Sweet *Mondo* • Sam Jones *Exterminator* ■ *Dir/Scr* Michael Covert

The American Success Company
★★

Black comedy drama 1979 · US · Colour · 90min

Corporate drone Jeff Bridges gives the "success at any price" business world a taste of its own medicine in this offbeat black comedy about ethics and karma. Director William Richert's follow-up to *Winter Kills* is wildly uneven and caustically toned in a way some may find off-putting. When he does hit his targets, however, Richert really pulls no punches. **AJ**

Jeff Bridges *Harry* • Belinda Bauer *Sarah* • Ned Beatty *Mr Elliot* • Steven Keats *Rick Duprez* • Bianca Jagger *Corinne* • John Glover *Ernst* • Mascha Gonska *Greta* • Michael Durrell *Herman* ■ *Dir* William Richert • *Scr* William Richert, Larry Cohen, from a story by Larry Cohen • *Music* Maurice Jarre

An American Tail ★★★★ U

Animated adventure 1986 · US · Colour · 76min

Directed by ex-Disney animator Don Bluth and with Steven Spielberg as co-executive producer, this handsome feature has the look and feel of a master cartoonist at work. The story of the Mousekewitz family who leave 1880s Russia for the United States because they've heard that the country has no cats and the streets are paved with cheese, ties in nicely with Bluth's stunning animation, and, in true Disney tradition, the Oscar-nominated song *Somewhere Out There* is a major highlight. Three lacklustre sequels followed. **DP** *DVD*

Phillip Glasser *Fievel* • Dom DeLuise *Tiger* • Nehemiah Persoff *Papa Mousekewitz* • Erica Yohn *Mama Mousekewitz* • Madeline Kahn *Gussie Mausheimer* • Christopher Plummer *Henri* • Cathianne Blore *Bridget* ■ *Dir* Don Bluth • *Scr* Judy Freudberg, Tony Geiss, from a story by David Kirschner, Judy Freudberg, Tony Geiss

An American Tail: Fievel Goes West
★★ U

Animated adventure 1991 · US · Colour · 71min

This lacklustre feature following the further adventures of Fievel, the little Russian immigrant mouse. The storyline is practically nonexistent, the songs are unimaginative, and the animation could easily have been done in the 1940s, such is its flat traditionalism. That said, the voiceovers of James Stewart, John Cleese and Dom DeLuise are excellent and they alone earn this poor production its second star. **DP** *DVD*

Phillip Glasser *Fievel* • James Stewart *Wylie Burp* • Erica Yohn *Mama Mousekewitz* • John Cleese *Cat R Waul* • Dom DeLuise *Tiger* • Jon Lovitz *TR Chula* • Amy Irving *Miss Kitty* • Nehemiah Persoff *Papa Mousekewitz* • Cathy Cavadini *Tanya Mousekewitz* ■ *Dir* Phil Nibbelink, Simon Wells • *Scr* Flint Dille, from the story by Charles Swenson, from characters by David Kirschner

American Teen
★★★ 15

Documentary 2008 · US · Colour · 97min

Director Nanette Burstein (*The Kid Stays in the Picture*) details the lives of a bunch of high-school seniors from Warsaw, Indiana, in this enjoyable documentary. Taking five stereotypes – the jock, the princess, the hunk, the geek and the misfit – it explores how young people both create and conform to their own tribes, even when it's against their self-interest, and the unnervingly honest scenes of peer pressure show that, in America at least, the problem is only getting worse. Such revelations, though, are tainted by scenes such as a cruel text message not only being sent but being received. Still, the teenagers do make fascinating case studies. **DW** *DVD*

Hannah Bailey • Colin Clemens • Geoff Haase • Megan Krizmanich • Mitch Reinholt • Jake Tusing ■ *Dir* Nanette Burstein

American: the Bill Hicks Story
★★ 15

Documentary 2010 · UK · Colour · 101min

Scabrous American comedian Bill Hicks died of cancer in 1994 at the age of just 32. This somewhat unenlightening documentary traces his development from a strict southern Baptist upbringing through to his burgeoning international success, though it lacks detail about his personal life and what drove him professionally. Perhaps in the end it was really about the jokes, and those, as the archive footage attests, remain as pungently well-observed today as they were 20 years ago. **AS** Swearing, sexual, drug references. *DVD*

Bill Hicks ■ *Dir* Matt Harlock, Paul Thomas

An American Tragedy ★★★

Romantic melodrama 1931 · US · BW · 96min

This is the first film version of Theodore Dreiser's novel about a social climber who murders his pregnant low-born sweetheart when a society girl makes eyes at him. The story is a classic critique of the American Dream, so Hollywood bravely imported the Soviet Union's greatest director and chief propagandist, Sergei Eisenstein, to write and direct it. But Paramount rejected his script and got Josef von Sternberg to take over, much to Dreiser's fury. Fascinating to compare it to the 1951 remake, *A Place in the Sun*. **AT**

Phillips Holmes *Clyde Griffiths* • Sylvia Sidney *Roberta Alden* • Frances Dee *Sondra Finchley* • Irving Pichel *Orville Mason* • Frederick Burton *Samuel Griffiths* • Claire McDowell *Mrs Samuel Griffiths* ■ *Dir* Josef von Sternberg • *Scr* Samuel Hoffenstein, from the novel by Theodore Dreiser

American Ultra
★★★ 15

Action comedy 2015 · US · Colour · 91min

The stoner comedy gets a new, violent twist as slacker Jesse Eisenberg is unwillingly thrown into a high-octane battle with the government when he discovers he is a highly trained assassin whose memory has been wiped. Eisenberg's bewildered wanderings have an innocence that is hard not to like, and he certainly capitalises on his great chemistry with on-screen girlfriend Kristen Stewart. It may lose its thread towards the blood-spattered finale, but this fast, amiable comedy never outstays its welcome. **JL** Violence, swearing, sexual references, drug abuse. *DVD* *BL*

Jesse Eisenberg *Mike Howell* • Kristen Stewart *Phoebe* • Topher Grace *Adrian Yates* • Tony Hale *Petey Douglas* • John Leguizamo *Rose* ■ *Dir* Nima Nourizadeh • *Scr* Max Landis

An American Werewolf in London
★★★★ 18

Horror comedy 1981 · US · Colour · 93min

Director John Landis (*The Blues Brothers*) pulls off the difficult trick of revitalising the horror genre while parodying it at the same time. David Naughton and Griffin Dunne play the American students who are attacked by werewolves on an English moor. Only Naughton survives, but is visited by his dead friend, who has bad news. Funny, scary and extremely gory – Griffin Dunne's gradual decomposition is an absolute hoot – this lycanthropic lampoon is also a splendid satire on British life, as seen through American eyes. The special effects and Rick Baker's Oscar-winning make-up established new trends in monster metamorphoses. **AJ** Violence, swearing, sex scenes, nudity. *DVD* *BL*

David Naughton *David Kessler* • Jenny Agutter *Alex Price* • Griffin Dunne *Jack Goodman* • John Woodvine *Dr Hirsch* • Brian Glover *Chess player* • Rik Mayall *Second chess player* • David Schofield *Darts player* • Lila Kaye *Barmaid* ■ *Dir/Scr* John Landis

An American Werewolf in Paris
★★ 15

Horror comedy
1997 · US/Lux/Fr/UK · Colour · 94min

Made as a belated sequel to the classic *An American Werewolf in London*, director Anthony Waller's watered-down lycanthrope is frustratingly devoid of the edgy suspense, biting humour and keen visual style of that comedy horror landmark. Three American students go to Paris to bungee jump off the Eiffel Tower and find themselves inducted into a tortured twilight world. **AJ** Violence, swearing, nudity. *DVD*

Tom Everett Scott *Andy* • Julie Delpy *Sérafine* • Vince Vieluf *Brad* • Phil Buckman *Chris* • Julie Bowen *Amy* • Pierre Cosso *Claude* • Thierry Lhermitte *Dr Pigot* • Tom Novembre *Inspector Leduc* ■ *Dir* Anthony Waller • *Scr* Tim Burns, Tom Stern, Anthony Waller, from characters by John Landis

American Yakuza
★★ 18

Action thriller 1994 · US · Colour · 95min

In this hard-edged thriller, Viggo Mortensen is FBI man Nick Davis, dispatched to Los Angeles to infiltrate and dismantle the American arm of the Japanese underworld. Adopted by a powerful crime family, he rises through the ranks. Inevitably, however, he finds his loyalties strained between the forces of law and order, his new-found colleagues in the yakuza and the established Mafia. **JF**

Viggo Mortensen *Nick Davis/David Brandt* • Ryo Ishibashi *Shoji* • Michael Nouri *Campanela* • Robert Forster *Littman* • Franklyn Ajaye *Sam* ■ *Dir* Frank Cappello • *Scr* Max Strom, John Allen Nelson

American Yakuza 2: Back to Back
★★★ 18

Action thriller 1996 · US · Colour · 87min

Outside the presence of the excellent Ryo Ishibashi, this quirky and stylish take on what happens when Japanese gangsters run amok in California bears little resemblance to *American Yakuza* (1994). However, it does feature cult comic and *Police Academy* series regular Bobcat Goldthwait, in a brief but bonkers role as a bank-robbing nutcase. The mood is darkly hip as two yakuza – one with an Elvis fixation, the other (Ishibashi) cool and dangerous – hit town on a revenge mission that is thwarted when Goldthwait takes them and a downbeat cop (Michael Rooker) hostage. Slick, explosive and surprisingly original. **JF** *DVD*

Michael Rooker *Bob Malone* • Ryo Ishibashi *Koji* • Danielle Harris *Chelsea* • John Laughlin *Dussecq* • Bobcat Goldthwait *Psycho* • Koh Takasugi *Hideo* • Tim Thomerson *Thomas* • Stephen Furst *Jimmy* • Vincent Schiavelli *Leonardo* ■ *Dir* Roger Nygard • *Scr* Roger Nygard, Lloyd Keith

Americana
★★★ 15

Drama 1981 · US · Colour · 86min

Shot in 1973, when David Carradine and Barbara Hershey (then known as Seagull) were in the middle of their torrid affair, this allegory on faith, morality and the American Way lay in the vaults for several years before post-production was completed. Although some of its relevance had, by then, been lost, there is still much to admire in this portrait of Mid-West, small-town life. Carradine is laudably restrained as the Vietnam veteran who arouses the ire of the locals when he decides to recondition a neglected merry-go-round. **DP**

David Carradine *Soldier* • Barbara Seagull [Barbara Hershey] *Girl* • Michael Greene *Garage man* • John Blyth Barrymore *Jack* • Greg Walker *Greg* ■ *Dir* David Carradine • *Scr* Richard Carr, David Carradine, from the novel *The Perfect Round* by Henry Morton Robinson

The Americanization of Emily
★★★★

Comedy drama 1964 · US · BW · 115min

This surprisingly acerbic and adult comedy from the usually glossy MGM studio was shot in England and written by the brilliant Paddy Chayefsky. It's magnificently cast, with Julie Andrews in arguably her finest screen role, starring as an English war widow given to comforting US servicemen. James Garner is the cynically treated Yank coward to whom Andrews ministers, and the superb supporting players include a very funny James Coburn, obsessed admiral Melvyn Douglas, plus the venerable Joyce Grenfell. This is director Arthur Hiller's best work, and his own personal favourite. **TS**

James Garner *Lt Cmdr Charles Madison* • Julie Andrews *Emily Barham* • Melvyn Douglas *Admiral William Jessup* • James Coburn *Lt Cmdr "Bus" Cummings* • Joyce Grenfell *Mrs Barham* • Liz Fraser *Sheila* • Edward Binns *Admiral Thomas Healy* • Keenan Wynn *Old sailor* • William Windom *Capt Harry Spaulding* ■ *Dir* Arthur Hiller • *Scr* Paddy Chayefsky, from the novel by William Bradford Huie

The Americano
★★ PG

Western 1955 · US · Colour · 81min

Glenn Ford goes down South America way and meets Frank Lovejoy and Cesar Romero in this amiable western variant, though the Brazilian setting that was a novelty when the film came out may well have lost its appeal by now. Ford's attractive naturalistic style would soon turn him into one of Hollywood's biggest stars. **TS**

Glenn Ford *Sam Dent* • Frank Lovejoy *Bento Hermanny* • Cesar Romero *Manoel* • Ursula Thiess *Marianna Figueirido* • Abbe Lane *Teresa* • Rodolfo Hoyos Jr [Rodolfo Hoyos] *Christino* • Salvador Baguez *Captain Gonzales* ■ *Dir* William Castle • *Scr* Guy Trosper, from a story by Leslie T White

America's Sweethearts
★★★ 12

Romantic comedy 2001 · US · Colour · 98min

Catherine Zeta-Jones and John Cusack play the Hollywood couple who've split up since making their last film together. Billy Crystal is the film publicist who has to get the estranged couple together for a press junket. What he can't account for is Zeta-Jones's current wild-card boyfriend, Hank Azaria, and Cusack transferring his affections from his superstar wife to her sister and personal assistant, Julia Roberts. It's all very funny in a daft, predictable kind of way, but Crystal's script lacks the bite that could have made it so much better. **LH** Swearing. *DVD*

Julia Roberts *Kiki Harrison* • Billy Crystal *Lee Phillips* • Catherine Zeta-Jones *Gwen Harrison* • John Cusack *Eddie Thomas* • Hank Azaria *Hector* • Stanley Tucci *Dave Kingman* • Christopher Walken *Hal Weidmann* • Alan Arkin *Wellness guide* ■ *Dir* Joe Roth • *Scr* Billy Crystal, Peter Tolan

Americathon ★★🅿🄶
Comedy 1979 · US · Colour · 80min

Despite a talented, eclectic cast and an inspired premise – the United States is now so poor it has to stage a telethon to bail itself out – this has to go down as a major disappointment. The film lacks the necessary focus and fails to make the most of its satirical promise. Still, there's fun to be had watching Mel Brooks regular Harvey Korman, future chat-show king Jay Leno and Elvis Costello. JF

Peter Riegert *Eric* • Harvey Korman *Monty Rushmore* • Fred Willard *Vanderhoff* • Zane Buzby *Mouling Jackson* • Nancy Morgan *Lucy Beth* • John Ritter *Chet Roosevelt* • Elvis Costello *Earl Manchester* • Jay Leno *Larry Miller* • Meat Loaf *Oklahoma Roy* ■ *Dir* Neal Israel • *Scr* Neal Israel, Michael Mislove, Monica Johnson, from a play by Peter Bergman, Philip Proctor

Le Amiche ★★★★🅿🄶
Drama 1955 · It · BW · 105min

After enjoying success as a fashion designer in Rome, Eleonora Rossi-Drago returns to her native Turin and becomes involved in the affairs of four of her upper-middle-class girlfriends. The film manages to hold ten characters in almost flawless equilibrium, while simultaneously attending to their individuality and oscillating relationships. Michelangelo Antonioni's gift for positioning actors meaningfully against landscapes is well-demonstrated, notably in an extended afternoon beach sequence. RB
Italian +subtitles. 🄳🅅🄳 🔵

Eleonora Rossi-Drago *Clelia* • Valentina Cortese *Nene* • Yvonne Furneaux *Momina De Stefani* • Gabriele Ferzetti *Lorenzo* • Franco Fabrizi *Cesare Pedoni, the architect* • Ettore Manni *Carlo* ■ *Dir* Michelangelo Antonioni • *Scr* Michelangelo Antonioni, Suso Cecchi D'Amico, Alba De Céspedes, from the story *Tra Donne Sole* by Cesare Pavese

La Amiga ★★★
Drama 1988 · Arg/W Ger · Colour · 110min

Classical myth, Nazi Germany and the Argentinian junta come together in this rather unfocused drama from Jeanine Meerapfel. As children, Liv Ullmann and Cipe Lincovsky wanted to be actresses. But, while the latter gets to play Antigone on stage, the former takes on the role in real life as she becomes a prominent figure in the "Mothers of the Disappeared". The comparison between the two political situations is adequately made, but Meerapfel doesn't always appear to be in control of her material. The performances, however, are strong and assured. DP
Spanish +subtitles.

Liv Ullmann *Maria* • Cipe Lincovsky *Raquel* • Federico Luppi *Pancho* • Victor Laplace *Diego* • Harry Baer *Raquel's friend in Berlin* • Lito Cruz *Chief of Police Tito* ■ *Dir* Jeanine Meerapfel • *Scr* Jeanine Meerapfel, Alcides Chiesa

Amish Grace ★★★
Drama based on a true story
2010 · US · Colour · 88min

Could you forgive your child's murderer? That's the difficult question raised by this poignant true-life drama about a 2006 shooting in an Amish school in Pennsylvania. The movie centres on the crisis of faith suffered by a fictional victim's mother (an affecting Kimberly Williams-Paisley) as she struggles to accept her Amish community's decision to pardon a dead outsider for killing five youngsters. Though the key performances are strong, it's this focus on the tragedy's emotional impact that makes the film and papers over some weaknesses in characterisation and plot. SF

Kimberly Williams-Paisley [Kimberly Williams] *Ida Graber* • Tammy Blanchard *Amy Roberts* • Matt Letscher *Gideon Graber* • Fay Masterson *Jill Green* ■ *Dir* Gregg Champion • *Scr* Sylvie White,

Teena Booth, from the non-fiction book by Donald B Kraybill, Steven M Nolt, David L Weaver-Zercher

Amistad ★★★🄸🄸
Historical courtroom drama
1997 · US · Colour · 148min

Steven Spielberg's lengthy historical courtroom drama has its moments of pure visual poetry, but it fails to ignite the same moral outrage that Schindler's List so poignantly evoked. Anthony Hopkins and Matthew McConaughey lead the all-star cast, and there's an amazing debut by Djimon Hounsou as the leader of a shipload of men from Sierra Leone destined to become slaves, who are charged with murder after a failed attempt to take over the ship. It's a flawed but chilling movie. AJ
Violence. 🄳🅅🄳

Anthony Hopkins *John Quincy Adams* • Matthew McConaughey *Roger Baldwin* • Morgan Freeman *Theodore Joadson* • Djimon Hounsou *Sengbe Pieh, "Cinque"* • Nigel Hawthorne *Martin Van Buren* • David Paymer *Secretary Forsyth* • Pete Postlethwaite *Holabird* • Stellan Skarsgård *Tappan* • Anna Paquin *Queen Isabella* • Jeremy Northam *Judge Coglin* ■ *Dir* Steven Spielberg • *Scr* David Franzoni

The Amityville Horror ★★🄸🄸
Supernatural horror 1979 · US · Colour · 113min

This only marginally watchable schlock horror is based on Jay Anson's allegedly true bestseller about the Lutz family and their Long Island dream house that's possessed by ghostly squatters. Valiant James Brolin and Margot Kidder battle evil spirits, while an overblown religious subplot unfolds starring Rod Steiger. Although a baffling box-office hit, this tepid chiller never matches the flesh-crawling terror contained in Anson's book. Jennifer Jason Leigh will star in a 2015 reboot. AJ 🄳🅅🄳

James Brolin *George Lutz* • Margot Kidder *Kathleen Lutz* • Rod Steiger *Father Delaney* • Don Stroud *Father Bolen* • Natasha Ryan *Amy* • KC Martel *Greg* • Meeno Peluce *Matt* • Michael Sacks *Jeff* • Helen Shaver *Carolyn* ■ *Dir* Stuart Rosenberg • *Scr* Sandor Stern, from the non-fiction book by Jay Anson

Amityville II: the Possession ★★★🄸🄸
Horror 1982 · US · Colour · 99min

Much better overall than the dull first outing, this prequel to *The Amityville Horror* is given a neat European atmosphere by Italian director Damiano Damiani. It tells the full story of the vicious multiple murders that took place a year prior to the Lutz family's infamous tenancy-turned-bestselling book. Standard haunted-house shocks are combined with prowling camerawork for maximum involvement, while unusual imagery and spectacular make-up and special effects make this a handsomely crafted effort. AJ Swearing, violence. 🄳🅅🄳

Burt Young *Anthony Montelli* • Rutanya Alda *Dolores Montelli* • James Olson *Father Adamsky* • Jack Magner *Sonny Montelli* • Diane Franklin *Patricia Montelli* • Andrew Prine *Father Tom* • Leonardo Cimino *Chancellor* • Danny Aiello *First removal man* ■ *Dir* Damiano Damiani • *Scr* Tommy Lee Wallace, from the book *Murder in Amityville* by Hans Holzer

Amityville III: the Demon ★★★🄸🄸
Horror 1983 · US · Colour · 89min

After exposing a pair of phoney spiritualists based in the notorious Long Island town, journalist Tony Roberts laughs at the legend and moves into the famous cursed Amityville house. Almost immediately, strange manifestations occur, resulting in unexplained deaths among his workmates and family. Decent special effects – originally in highly effective 3D – dovetail neatly with director Richard Fleischer's creepy, claustrophobic atmosphere. AJ
Violence, swearing. 🄳🅅🄳 🆂🄳

Tony Roberts *John Baxter* • Tess Harper *Nancy Baxter* • Robert Joy *Elliot West* • Candy Clark *Melanie* • John Beal *Harold Caswell* • Leora Dana

Emma Caswell • John Harkins *Clifford Sanders* • Lori Loughlin *Susan Baxter* • Meg Ryan *Lisa* ■ *Dir* Richard Fleischer • *Scr* William Wales

Amityville: the Evil Escapes ★★🄸🄸
Horror 1989 · US · Colour · 95min

The title conjures up a wonderful image of a detached bungalow loping down the highways to find a new town to terrorise. But, sadly, no, it's only the evil that moves to California, leaving the original house in peace in this third sequel in the series. Director Sandor Stern, who scripted the first film, delivers some neat set pieces, but he is hampered by the constraints of the TV movie format. JF 🄳🅅🄳

Patty Duke *Nancy Evans* • Jane Wyatt *Alice Leacock* • Norman Lloyd *Father Manfred* • Frederic Lehne [Fredric Lehne] *Father Kibbler* • Brandy Gold *Jessica Evans* • Aron Eisenberg *Brian Evans* • Geri Betzler *Amanda Evans* ■ *Dir* Sandor Stern • *Scr* Sandor Stern, from the book by John G Jones

The Amityville Curse ★🄸🄸
Horror 1990 · Can · Colour · 87min

They must have good estate agents in Amityville because this is yet another tale of someone buying a property, only to discover that it has more than just a damp problem. In this pedestrian instalment, a young couple snap up an old house to do it up, only to unwittingly unleash supernatural forces that date back to the murder of a priest. JF 🄳🅅🄳

Kim Coates *Frank* • Dawna Wrightman *Debbie* • Cassandra Gava *Abigail* • Jan Rubes *Priest* • Helen Hughes *Mrs Moriarty* ■ *Dir* Tom Berry • *Scr* Norvell Rose, Michael Krueger, Doug Olson, from a novel by Hans Holzer

Amityville: a New Generation ★★🄸🄸
Horror 1993 · Can · Colour · 91min

This relocates the action to the city with the portal of evil being a mirror rather than a clock this time around. Ross Partridge is the artist who inherits the evil antique from a sinister street bum. Inevitably, it sparks off a series of mysterious slayings in his apartment block. Predictable stuff but genre fans will appreciate the appearances of David Naughton and Terry O Quinn. JF 🄳🅅🄳

Ross Partridge *Keyes* • Julia Nickson-Soul *Suki* • David Naughton *Dick Cutler* • Lala Sloatman *Llanie* • Barbara Howard *Jane Cutler* • Richard Roundtree *Pauli* • Terry O'Quinn *Det Clark* ■ *Dir* John Murlowski • *Scr* Christopher DeFaria, Antonio Toro, from the novel *Amityville: the Evil Escapes* by John G Jones

Amityville Dollhouse ★★🄸🄸
Horror 1996 · US · Colour · 92min

This adds nothing new to the supernatural series, and merely delivers bland and unremarkable horror homages to better efforts in the genre. The Martin family desert the big city rat race for a quiet life in the country. But, when they find a beautifully ornate doll house in their new home, and give it to their daughter, it begins exerting an evil influence over the family. AJ Violence, swearing, sex scenes, brief nudity. 🄳🅅🄳

Robin Thomas *Bill Martin* • Starr Andreeff *Claire* • Allen Cutler *Todd Martin* • Rachel Duncan *Jessica Martin* ■ *Dir* Steve White • *Scr* Joshua Michael Stern

The Amityville Horror ★★🄸🄸
Supernatural horror 2005 · US · Colour · 85min

Although no vast improvement on the popular 1979 original, this slick makeover does return to Jay Anson's bestseller for additional material and emphasises the psychological aspects of the notorious – and now clichéd – haunted-house tale. Here, the harrowing month spent by the Lutz family in their new Long Island home focuses on the mental breakdown suffered by patriarch George (an adequate Ryan Reynolds), who apparently becomes the satanic pawn of an ancient evil.

Aggravatingly ordinary. AJ Swearing, violence. 🄳🅅🄳

Ryan Reynolds *George Lutz* • Melissa George *Kathy Lutz* • Jesse James *Billy Lutz* • Jimmy Bennett *Michael Lutz* • Chloë Grace Moretz *Chelsea Lutz* • Rachel Nichols *Lisa* • Philip Baker Hall *Father Callaway* ■ *Dir* Andrew Douglas • *Scr* Scott Kosar, from the film by Sandor Stern, from the non-fiction book by Jay Anson

Amityville Playhouse ★🄸🄸
Horror 2015 · Can · Colour · 98min

Riding on the coat-tails of a horror legacy is this shabby shock-fest, following young Fawn (Monèle LeStrat) as she and her friends investigate an abandoned cinema left to her by her father. Shooting in a gloomy, amateurish style only underlines the low standards set by British director John R Walker and screenwriter Steve Hardy, whose plot is a half-hearted retread of most of the spin-off films bearing the Amityville name. JL

Monèle LeStrat *Fawn Harriman* • Linden Baker *Kyle Blaker* • Kennie Benoit *Matteus "Matt" Darnell* ■ *Dir* John R Walker • *Scr* Steve Hardy, John R Walker

Amnesia ★★★★
Political thriller 1994 · Chil · Colour · 90min

Set in an unspecified country (that is patently Chile around the time of the 1973 coup), this powerful political thriller flashes back to a desert concentration camp and catalogues the crimes of the brutal regime against the inmates. Switching back to the present, a sadistic sergeant becomes the victim of a revenge plot. Seen only by a few privileged film festival audiences, but a big box-office hit in Chile, Gonzalo Justiniano's uncompromising picture was cited as one of the ten best films ever made in Chile in a poll specially commissioned for the centenary of cinema. DP Spanish +subtitles.

Julio Jung *Zuniga* • Pedro Vicuna *Ramirez* • Nelson Villagra *The Captain* • Jose Secall *Carrasco* ■ *Dir* Gonzalo Justiniano • *Scr* Gonzalo Justiniano, Gustavo Frias

Among Giants ★★★🄸🄸
Romantic drama 1998 · UK · Colour · 94min

It may not have quite the same feel-good comedy spin as his hit *The Full Monty*, but writer Simon Beaufoy's look at unemployed Sheffield friends making do buzzes along thanks to his excellent ear for dialogue and his unerring eye for gritty truthfulness. This time, amateur mountain climber Pete Postlethwaite gets the lads to help him paint pylons in the wilds of northern England against an impossible deadline, for cash in hand. When sexy Australian backpacker Rachel Griffiths joins the team, however, romantic competition starts a rift between Postlethwaite and his best mate James Thornton. An always engaging ensemble piece. AJ Swearing, sex scenes, nudity.

Pete Postlethwaite *Ray* • Rachel Griffiths *Gerry* • James Thornton *Steve* • Lennie James *Shovel* • Andy Serkis *Bob* • Rob Jarvis *Weasel* • Alan Williams (2) *Frank* ■ *Dir* Sam Miller • *Scr* Simon Beaufoy

Among the Living ★★★
Drama 1941 · US · BW · 69min

Albert Dekker had a remarkable talent that only manifested itself on those rare occasions when he was aptly cast. As a demented twin let loose in a sophisticated world, he is both disturbed and disturbing; ultimately, however, he is let down by the poor production values. Today the film's most interesting elements are its two leading ladies: Susan Hayward and the tragedy-strewn Frances Farmer, both of whom are excellent. TS

Albert Dekker *John Raden/Paul Raden* • Susan Hayward *Millie Pickens* • Harry Carey *Dr Ben Saunders* • Frances Farmer *Elaine Raden* • Gordon Jones *Bill Oakley* • Jean Phillips *Peggy Nolan* • Maude Eburne *Mrs Pickens* • Frank M Thomas *Sheriff* ■ *Dir* Stuart Heisler • *Scr* Lester Cole, Garrett Fort, from a story by Brian Marlowe, Lester Cole

A

El Amor Brujo ★★★ PG
Drama 1986 · Sp · Colour · 98min

The concluding part of the "flamenco trilogy" that began with *Blood Wedding* and *Carmen* may be the least successful of the three, but there is still much to admire in Carlos Saura's highly stylised production. The tale of doomed gypsy romance has a woman torn between the spirit of her dead husband and the attentions of his convicted murderer. Teo Escamilla's photography enhances both Gerardo Vera's costume designs and Antonio Gades's choreography, but the non-musical passages are heavy-going. DP Spanish +subtitles. **DVD**

Antonio Gades *Carmelo* • Cristina Hoyos *Candela* • Laura Del Sol *Lucia* • Juan Antonio Jimenez *José* • Emma Penella *Hechicer* • La Polaca *Pastora* • Gomez De Jerez *El Lobo* ■ *Dir* Carlos Saura • *Scr* Antonio Gades, Carlos Saura, from the ballet by Manuel De Falla • *Music* Manuel De Falla

L'Amore ★★★ PG
Drama 1948 · It · BW · 76min

This film from director Roberto Rossellini, comprising two separate tales, is a paean to the breathtaking talents of Anna Magnani, whose presence is the reason for watching it. The first half, an adaptation of Jean Cocteau's famous one-woman stage monologue *The Human Voice*, has the star as an abandoned society lady attempting to reconcile herself with her lover on the telephone; in *The Miracle*, she is a devout peasant woman seduced by Federico Fellini, who claims to be St Joseph. Rossellini's somewhat over-theatrical departure from neorealism was originally banned in New York and in England on grounds of blasphemy. RB Italian +subtitles. **DVD**

Anna Magnani *The woman/Nannina* • Federico Fellini *St Joseph* ■ *Dir* Roberto Rossellini • *Scr* Roberto Rossellini, Tullio Pinelli, from the play *La Voix Humaine* by Jean Cocteau and from a story by Federico Fellini

Amore! ★★
Romantic comedy 1993 · US · Colour · 93min

A starry supporting cast enlivens this otherwise insubstantial slice of movie fluff. Jack Scalia plays a wealthy businessman who rather bizarrely changes his identity and attempts to make it in Hollywood. The plot is ludicrous and Scalia is unconvincing in the lead role, but a string of delightful supporting turns from old troupers almost make it worthwhile. JF

Jack Scalia *Saul Schwartz* • Kathy Ireland *Taylor Christopher* • George Hamilton *Rudolfo Carbonera* • Norm Crosby *Shlomo Schwartz* • Elliott Gould *George Levine* • Katherine Helmond *Mildred Schwartz* ■ *Dir/Scr* Lorenzo Doumani

L'Amore Molesto ★★★ 15
Thriller 1995 · It · Colour · 98min

Italian stage star Anna Bonaiuto is directed by her longtime partner Mario Martone in this atmospheric Neapolitan thriller. Returning to investigate the suspicious death of her elderly mother, Bonaiuto is forced to reacquaint herself with the city of her birth and delve into some long suppressed emotions to make sense of the clues. Although there is much to intrigue in the Freudian flashbacks and the encounters with the dead woman's male friends, the film's main interest lies in Martone's neorealist portrait of Naples. DP Italian +subtitles. Swearing, sex scenes, nudity.

Anna Bonaiuto *Delia* • Angela Luce *Amalia* • Carmela Pecoraro *Delia as a child* • Licia Maglietta *Young Amalia* • Gianni Cajafa *Uncle Filippo* • Anna Calato *Mrs De Riso* • Giovanni Viglietti *Nicola Polledro, "Caserta"* ■ *Dir* Mario Martone • *Scr* Mario Martone, from the novel by Elena Ferrante

Amores Perros ★★★★★ 18
Drama 2000 · Mex · Colour · 147min

With its wealth of hard-bitten characters, intertwining complex plot and nearly three-hour running time, director Alejandro González Iñárritu's internationally acclaimed and multi-award-winning debut feature is a startling original. How a fatal car accident impacts on the disparate lives of a slum teenager (Gael García Bernal) involved in illegal dog fights, a magazine editor (Alvaro Guerrero) who leaves his wife for a perfume campaign model and an ex-con tramp-turned-hired assassin (Emilio Echevarría) is expertly fashioned by Iñárritu into a stunning rumination on the traumas and desperation of love and desire. Shot completely with a hand-held camera, and gaining enormous documentary-style immediacy from this in-your-face device, the film is a truly exhilarating masterpiece. AJ Spanish +subtitles. Violence, swearing, sex scenes. **DVD Blu**

Emilio Echevarría *El Chivo, the "Goat"* • Gael García Bernal *Octavio* • Goya Toledo *Valeria* • Alvaro Guerrero *Daniel* • Vanessa Bauche *Susana* • Jorge Salinas *Luis* • Marco Perez *Ramiro* • Rodrigo Murray *Gustavo* ■ *Dir* Alejandro González Iñárritu • *Scr* Guillermo Arriaga • *Cinematographer* Rodrigo Prieto

The Amorous Adventures of Moll Flanders ★★
Comedy 1965 · UK · Colour · 132min

After *Tom Jones* cleaned up at the box office and the Oscars, this rollicking 18th-century yarn was rushed into production, using the same composer (John Addison) with James Bond's director, Terence Young, at the helm. Adapted from the novel by Daniel Defoe, it's a Hollywood concoction that rarely comes off, while Kim Novak isn't anyone's idea of the English workhouse girl who sleeps her way to the gallows and beyond. AT

Kim Novak *Moll Flanders* • Claire Ufland *Young Moll* • Richard Johnson *Jemmy* • Angela Lansbury *Lady Blystone* • Vittorio De Sica *The Count* • Leo McKern *Squint* • George Sanders *The banker* • Lilli Palmer *Dutchy* • Hugh Griffith *Prison governor* ■ *Dir* Terence Young • *Scr* Denis Cannan, Roland Kibbee, from the novel *Moll Flanders* by Daniel Defoe

The Amorous Milkman ★ 18
Sex comedy 1974 · UK · Colour · 86min

Actor Derren Nesbitt's one and only venture behind the camera is as cheap and cheerful as any soft-core comedy made in the 1970s. Brendan Price does his best, but the most significant thing about this bawdy trash is what it says about the state of the British film industry at the time – it's sad that this was the only work Diana Dors, Roy Kinnear and other talented actors could find. DP Sex scenes, nudity.

Diana Dors *Rita* • Brendan Price *Davy* • Julie Ege *Diana* • Bill Fraser *Gerald* • Roy Kinnear *Sergeant* ■ *Dir* Derren Nesbitt • *Scr* Derren Nesbitt, from his story

The Amorous Prawn ★★ U
Comedy 1962 · UK · BW · 85min

Joan Greenwood plays the general's wife who converts her husband's HQ into a hotel in his absence to fleece visiting Americans and raise some cash. Director Anthony Kimmins also wrote the play on which this is based and he hasn't really opened it out too much for the cinema. As a result, the talents of Ian Carmichael are given little room. TS **DVD**

Joan Greenwood *Lady Fitzadam* • Cecil Parker *General Fitzadam* • Ian Carmichael *Corporal Sidney Green* • Robert Beatty *Larry Hoffman* • Dennis Price *Prawn* • Liz Fraser *Suzie Tidmarsh* • Reg Lye *Uncle Joe* • Bridget Armstrong *Biddy O'Hara* • Derek Nimmo *Willie Maltravers* ■ *Dir* Anthony Kimmins • *Scr* Anthony Kimmins, Nicholas Phipps, from the play by Kimmins

Amos & Andrew ★★ 15
Comedy 1993 · US · Colour · 95min

This silly, offbeat comedy begins as a satire of racial stereotyping before stumbling clumsily into buddy-movie territory. Samuel L Jackson is a successful, politically active author who moves into a wealthy (and very white) neighbourhood. His narrow-minded neighbours assume he's a burglar, cops surround the house, and police chief Dabney Coleman comes up with a hair-brained scheme involving small-time criminal Nicolas Cage that might salvage the situation. Writer/director E Max Frye's interesting anti-racist angle is lost in a comic treatment of the issues that totally misses the mark. JC CS

Nicolas Cage *Amos Odell* • Samuel L Jackson *Andrew Sterling* • Michael Lerner *Phil Gillman* • Margaret Colin *Judy Gillman* • Dabney Coleman *Chief of Police Cecil Tolliver* • Brad Dourif *Officer Donnie Donaldson* • Chelcie Ross *Earl* ■ *Dir/Scr* E Max Frye

Amour ★★★★★ 12
Drama 2012 · Fr/Ger/Austria · Colour · 121min

Part adult romance, part middle-class horror movie, Michael Haneke's Palme d'Or winner is an extraordinary meditation on love and death that succeeds not just on account of its director's intelligence but because of two brilliant performances by its 80-something leads. Jean-Louis Trintignant and Emmanuelle Riva play two self-sufficient Parisians whose close relationship is rocked when Riva suffers a serious stroke. From here, the film becomes a powerful albeit uncomfortably bleak and forensic study of old age, controlled with icy precision by Haneke, but it's the fearless Riva who really makes this such an unforgettable experience. DW French +subtitles. Swearing, brief nudity. **DVD Blu**

Jean-Louis Trintignant *Georges Laurent* • Emmanuelle Riva *Anne Laurent* • Isabelle Huppert *Eva* • Alexandre Tharaud *Alexandre* • William Shimell *Geoff* ■ *Dir/Scr* Michael Haneke

L'Amour Fou ★★★★
Drama 1968 · Fr · BW

Of all the French New Wave directors, Jacques Rivette has remained the most uncompromising. He usually goes in for exceptionally long movies, and this one, shot in both 35mm and 16mm, was originally 256 minutes. (The producers, however, initially distributed it in a two-hour version that the director disowned.) Like many of Rivette's pictures, it is about the art of creation: in this case, a theatre group preparing to stage Racine's *Andromaque* while being filmed by a TV team. There is a fascinating interplay between the characters and the play itself, but Rivette's austere style and cerebral preoccupations require some effort on the part of the viewer. RB In French.

Jean-Pierre Kalfon *Sébastien* • Bulle Ogier *Claire* • André Labarthe *[André S Labarthe] André* • Josée Destoops *Marta* ■ *Dir* Jacques Rivette • *Scr* Jacques Rivette, Marilu Tonilini

Amour Fou ★★★ 12
Period drama 2014 · Austria/Lux/Ger · Colour · 91min

Convinced the world is beyond redemption, German Romantic poet Heinrich von Kleist (Christian Friedel) yearns to end it all in a romantic double suicide. Fate brings him together with a bourgeois housewife and mother, and director Jessica Hausner (*Lourdes*) subtly points up the absurd humour in the poet's pomposity without losing sympathy for those who don't quite fit into the rigid conventions of the world around them. TJ German +subtitles. **DVD**

Christian Friedel *Heinrich von Kleist* • Birte Schnöink *Henriette* • Stephan Grossmann *Vogel* • Sandra Hüller *Marie* ■ *Dir/Scr* Jessica Hausner

L'Amour par Terre ★★ 12
Drama 1984 · Fr · Colour · 169min

A decade after *Celine and Julie Go Boating*, Jacques Rivette returned to similar territory – two women forced to play various roles in a strange house – but with less rewarding results. The director's interest in theatre and literature provides some pleasure (Geraldine Chaplin and Jane Birkin share their names with the Brontë sisters, Charlotte and Emily), as does the chateau setting, but the game-playing becomes tedious after a while. RB French +subtitles. **DVD**

Geraldine Chaplin *Charlotte* • Jane Birkin *Emily* • André Dussollier *Paul* • Jean-Pierre Kalfon *Clément Roquemaure* • Facundo Bo *Silvano* • Laszlo Szabo *Virgil* • Sandra Montaigu *Eléonore* •

The Amsterdam Kill ★★ 15
Thriller 1978 · HK · Colour · 86min

Robert Mitchum sleepwalks through this Hong Kong-financed thriller about a modern opium war fought out in the Far East and Amsterdam. As a former Drug Enforcement Agency man who was fired for corruption, Mitchum is wholly convincing even when the plot is underdeveloped. Co-stars Bradford Dillman and Leslie Nielsen are given little to work with – beyond counting corpses – and the Chinese actors, stars on their home turf, seem frankly amateurish. Boringly predictable, except for Mitchum. AT **DVD**

Robert Mitchum *Quinlan* • Bradford Dillman *Odums* • Richard Egan *Ridgeway* • Leslie Nielsen *Riley Knight* • Keye Luke *Chung Wei* • George Kee Cheung *Jimmy Wong* • Chen Hsing *Assassin* ■ *Dir* Robert Clouse • *Scr* Robert Clouse, Gregory Leifer

Amsterdamned ★★★ 15
Action thriller 1988 · Neth · Colour · 108min

A maniac frogman, horribly scarred after exposure to toxic chemicals during a botched salvage operation, is haunting Amsterdam's canals to take revenge on the uncaring society he's judged responsible for his plight. Dick Maas's thriller is an unusual mix of police procedural and American stalk-and-slash conventions. Maas both scripts and scores the film, but it's his efficient direction and humorously etched character studies that set this nuanced Dutch treat apart. AJ Dutch dubbed. **DVD**

Huub Stapel *Eric Visser* • Monique van de Ven *Laura* • Serge-Henri Valcke *Vermeer* • Tanneke Hartsuiker *Potter* • Wim Zomer *John* • Hidde Maas *Martin* • Lou Landré *Chief* ■ *Dir* Dick Maas • *Music* Dick Maas

Amy ★★ U
Period drama 1981 · US · Colour · 90min

Disney's inability to resist coating the pill undermines this otherwise sincere insight into the educational needs of sight- and hearing-impaired children. Still grieving after the death of her deaf son, Jenny Agutter leaves domineering husband Chris Robinson to work with doctor Barry Newman at a special school, even though such independence was hardly expected of women in the early 1900s. Carefully made, but over-earnest. DP

Jenny Agutter *Amy Medford* • Barry Newman *Dr Ben Corcoran* • Kathleen Nolan *Helen Gibbs* • Chris Robinson *Elliot Medford* • Lou Fant *Lyle Ferguson* • Margaret O'Brien *Hazel Johnson* • Nanette Fabray *Malvina* • Otto Rechenberg *Henry Watkins* ■ *Dir* Vincent McEveety • *Scr* Noreen Stone

Amy ★★★★ 15
Documentary 2015 · UK · Colour · 122min

This captivating, Oscar-winning documentary paints an intimate portrait of Amy Winehouse, the troubled singer/songwriter who died of alcohol poisoning in 2011 at the age of just 27. British film-maker Asif Kapadia (who also made the superb *Senna*) doesn't shy away from the personal problems she faced, but he also celebrates Amy as a highly talented musician with a distinctive voice. There is a wealth of archive footage, which includes several private videos that haven't been seen before, complemented by revealing voiceover interviews. SC Swearing, drug references. **DVD Blu**

Amy Winehouse ■ *Dir* Asif Kapadia

The Amy Fisher Story ★★ 15
Crime drama based on a true story 1993 · US · Colour · 92min

Amy Fisher was a *cause célèbre* in the early 1990s and her case achieved a level of public notoriety that was unusual considering no one was actually killed. Fisher shot the wife of her older lover and became prime front-page fodder. The scandal had repercussions: on three different US TV networks, three different made-for-TV movies of the case premiered within six days of each other. This one is by far the best of the batch, with Drew Barrymore as the sexpot Amy, and Anthony John Denison as her lover, one Joey Buttafuoco. TS

Drew Barrymore *Amy Fisher* • Anthony John Denison *Joey Buttafuoco* • Laurie Paton *Mary Jo Buttafuoco* • Harley Jane Kozak *Amy Pagnozzi* • Linda Darlow *Roseann Fisher* • Ken Pogue *Elliot Fisher* ■ *Dir* Andy Tennant • *Scr* Janet Brownell

Amy Foster ★★15
Romantic melodrama
1997 · UK/US/Fr · Colour · 108min

Also known as *Swept from the Sea*, this is a wildly misjudged adaptation of a haunting Joseph Conrad short story. Director Beeban Kidron goes for the overblown romantic (and very heavy-handed) touch in this melodramatic tale of silent Rachel Weisz who falls in love with Vincent Perez, the sole survivor of a shipwreck. JB Some swearing, violence, a brief sex scene. DVD

Rachel Weisz *Amy Foster* • Vincent Perez *Yanko* • Ian McKellen *Dr James Kennedy* • Kathy Bates *Miss Swaffer* • Joss Ackland *Mr Swaffer* • Tony Haygarth *Mr Smith* • Fiona Victory *Mrs Smith* • Tom Bell *Isaac Foster* • Zoë Wanamaker *Mary Foster* ■ *Dir* Beeban Kidron • *Scr* Tim Willocks, from the story by Joseph Conrad

Anaconda ★★★15
Horror adventure
1997 · US/Bra · Colour · 85min

Director Luis Llosa's cheerful slither-fest shows how a documentary film crew sailing up the Amazon gets used as snake-bait by deranged explorer Jon Voight in his obsessive quest to capture a legendary 40ft anaconda. As the competent cast fights a computer-generated garden hose with fangs, and as Voight's performance goes into camp overdrive, the scaly screams shrink while the screams of laughter increase. Daft fun. AJ Swearing, violence. DVD

Jennifer Lopez *Terri Flores* • Ice Cube *Danny Rich* • Jon Voight *Paul Sarone* • Eric Stoltz *Dr Steven Cale* • Jonathan Hyde *Warren Westridge* • Owen Wilson *Gary Dixon* • Kari Wuhrer *Denise Kalberg* • Vincent Castellanos *Mateo* • Danny Trejo *Poacher* ■ *Dir* Luis Llosa • *Scr* Hans Bauer, Jim Cash, Jack Epps Jr

Anacondas: the Hunt for the Blood Orchid ★★12
Horror adventure
2004 · US · Colour · 92min

It may have been daft fun, but did 1997's *Anaconda* really warrant a sequel (or three... the latest was released in 2009)? Here the giant serpents prey on scientists who are scouring Borneo for a rare orchid with youth-preserving qualities. It takes an age for the predators to slither into action, and the special effects are disappointing. SF Swearing. DVD

Johnny Messner *Bill Johnson* • KaDee Strickland *Samantha "Sam" Rogers* • Matthew Marsden *Dr Jack Byron* • Eugene Byrd *Cole Burris* • Salli Richardson-Whitfield *Gail Stern* • Nicholas Gonzalez *Dr Ben Douglas* • Karl Yune *Tran* • Morris Chestnut *Gordon Mitchell* ■ *Dir* Dwight H Little • *Scr* John Claflin, Daniel Zelman, Michael Miner, Ed Neumeier, from a story by Hans Bauer, Jim Cash, Jack Epps Jr

Analyze This ★★★★15
Crime comedy
1999 · US · Colour · 99min

Robert De Niro gives a great performance in this feel-good Mafia comedy from *Groundhog Day* director Harold Ramis. De Niro stars as a Manhattan Mob boss whose stressful lifestyle causes him to seek undercover therapy from psychiatrist Billy Crystal. De Niro's deadpan responses to the Freudian dissections, together with soon-to-be-married Crystal's increasing entanglement with the "family" business, bring on the laughs. Aided by a clever script packed with fresh repartee, Ramis's skilled timing allows the two dynamic leads to show their full comic potential. AJ Swearing, violence. DVD

Billy Crystal *Ben Sobel* • Robert De Niro *Paul Vitti* • Lisa Kudrow *Laura MacNamara* • Joe Viterelli *Jelly* • Chazz Palminteri *Primo Sindone* • Bill

Macy *Isaac Sobel* • Molly Shannon *Caroline* • Max Casella *Nicky Shivers* ■ *Dir* Harold Ramis • *Scr* Peter Tolan, Harold Ramis, Kenneth Lonergan, from a story by Kenneth Lonergan, Peter Tolan

Analyze That ★★15
Comedy
2002 · US · Colour · 91min

Robert De Niro and Billy Crystal – the double act that struck box-office gold with *Analyze This* – return for this sequel, but fail to conjure up the same magic. After faking a breakdown, De Niro's mobster is released from jail into the custody of psychiatrist Crystal. Soon fed up with his houseguest, Crystal gets De Niro a job as a consultant on a TV show. Crystal's quick-witted neuroses still spark effectively off De Niro's slow charm, but that's just not enough. StH Violence, swearing. DVD

Billy Crystal *Ben Sobel* • Robert De Niro *Paul Vitti* • Lisa Kudrow *Laura Sobel* • Joe Viterelli *Jelly* • Reg Rogers *Raoul Berman* • Cathy Moriarty-Gentile *[Cathy Moriarty] Patti LoPresti* • John Finn *Richard Chapin* • Kyle Sabihy *Michael Sobel* ■ *Dir* Harold Ramis • *Scr* Peter Steinfeld, Harold Ramis, Peter Tolan, from characters by Peter Tolan, Kenneth Lonergan

Anari ★★★U
Drama
1959 · Ind · BW · 156min

Ever the underdog, Raj Kapoor takes the lead in this outspoken attack on capitalism and medical irresponsibility. He plays a worker accused of murdering his landlady, even though a medicine produced by the company that employs him is really to blame. Nutan is charming as the company owner's niece who poses as her own maid to prevent Raj from discovering the extent of her wealth. But the emphasis is clearly as much on the social issues as on escapism, prompting many critics to suggest that Kapoor had as much to do with the direction as Hrishikesh Mukherjee. DP Hindi, Urdu +subtitles. DVD

Raj Kapoor *Raj* • Nutan *Aarti* • Lalita Pawar *Mrs D'Sa* • Motilal *Ramnath* ■ *Dir* Hrishikesh Mukherjee • *Scr* Inder Raj Anand

Anastasia ★★★★U
Period drama
1956 · US · Colour · 100min

Ingrid Bergman gives an exceptional, Oscar-winning performance in this gripping tale of a refugee passed off as the Romanov Grand Duchess by cunning Yul Brynner. A clever, insightful script puts flesh on the bones of an already intriguing mystery, but it is Bergman who makes this one a minor classic. She portrays vulnerability and dignity in equal measure with a rare screen intelligence, and Helen Hayes is also very fine as Anastasia's grandmother. SH DVD

Ingrid Bergman *Anastasia/Ana* • Yul Brynner *Bounine* • Helen Hayes *Empress* • Akim Tamiroff *Chernov* • Martita Hunt *Baroness Von Livenbaum* • Felix Aylmer *Russian Chamberlain* • Sacha Pitoeff *Petrovin* • Ivan Desny *Prince Paul* • Natalie Schafer *Lissenskaia* • Gregoire Gromoff *Stepan* • Karel Stepanek *Vlados* ■ *Dir* Anatole Litvak • *Scr* Arthur Laurents, from the play by Marcelle Maurette, adapted by Guy Bolton

Anastasia ★★★U
Animated musical fantasy
1997 · US · Colour · 90min

History buffs will despair at the liberal use of fiction in this adventure set around the time of the Russian Revolution. Little girls, however, will be enchanted by the tale of Anastasia, the Tsar's young daughter and the only one to survive after the evil Rasputin puts a curse on her family. Ten years later, without any recollection of her past, she meets her grandmother and discovers her heritage. A better-than-average prequel, *Bartok the Magnificent*, followed in 1999. JB DVD

Meg Ryan *Anastasia* • John Cusack *Dimitri* • Kelsey Grammer *Vladimir* • Christopher Lloyd *Rasputin* • Hank Azaria *Bartok* • Bernadette Peters *Sophie* • Kirsten Dunst *Young Anastasia* • Angela Lansbury *Dowager Empress Marie* ■ *Dir* Don Bluth, Gary Goldman • *Scr* Susan Gauthier, Bruce Graham, Bob Tzudiker, Noni White

Anatomy ★★★★18
Horror
2000 · Ger · Colour · 95min

Brilliant but insecure medical student Franka Potente goes to study an anatomy course at the prestigious Heidelberg University and uncovers a sinister secret society infamous for its ruthless research on live bodies. The dissected victims pile up along with the suspenseful shrieks in Austrian director Stefan Ruzowitzky's hugely enjoyable Hammer-style horror that is given a stark hi-tech contemporary makeover with congealed helpings of pharmaceutical fear and surgical shock on the side. AJ German +subtitles. DVD

Franka Potente *Paula Henning* • Benno Fürmann *Hein* • Anna Loos *Gretchen* • Sebastian Blomberg *Casper* • Holger Speckhahn *Phil* • Traugott Buhre *Prof Grombek* ■ *Dir/Scr* Stefan Ruzowitzky

Anatomy of a Murder ★★★★★12
Classic courtroom drama
1959 · US · BW · 153min

Possibly the greatest courtroom drama ever made, this features James Stewart's finest screen performance. Controversial in its day for using words such as "panties" and "spermatogenesis", Otto Preminger's film gives you an "irresistible impulse" to watch for nearly three hours as its story about a rape and murder unfolds. As the country hick lawyer (and jazz fan), Stewart is drawn into the case, suckered by it, and comes up against big-town prosecutor George C Scott. Their courtroom duels and stunts are mesmerising as they show America leaving its traditional old-time moral values behind: this is the America not of apple pie but of *Lolita*. AT Violence, brief nudity. DVD

James Stewart *Paul Biegler* • Lee Remick *Laura Manion* • Ben Gazzara *Lt Frederick Manion* • Arthur O'Connell *Parnell McCarthy* • Eve Arden *Maida* • George C Scott *Claude Dancer* • Kathryn Grant *Mary Pilant* • Joseph N Welch *Judge Weaver* • Duke Ellington *Pie-Eye* ■ *Dir* Otto Preminger • *Scr* Wendell Mayes, from the novel by Robert Traver [John D Voelker]

Anazapta ★★18
Period mystery thriller
2001 · UK · Colour · 110min

Alberto Sciamma's medieval murder mystery achieves a creditable sense of time and place, but the clumsiness of the dialogue and the overacting of the cast undermine its ambitions. The idea of a mysterious French prisoner from the Hundred Years' War bringing pestilence to an isolated, superstitious settlement is splendid. But as the death toll rises, Sciamma can't decide whether he's making a bodice-ripper or a slasher film. DP Violence, swearing. DVD

Lena Headey *Lady Matilda Mellerby* • David La Haye *Jacques de Saint Amant* • Jason Flemyng *Nicholas* • Christopher Fairbank *Steward* • Anthony O'Donnell *Randall* • Jeff Nuttall *Priest* • Hayley Carmichael *Agnes* • Ian McNeice *Bishop* • Jon Finch *Sir Walter Mellerby* ■ *Dir* Alberto Sciamma • *Scr* Alberto Sciamma, Harriet Sand

Anchoress ★★★12
Period drama
1993 · UK/Bel · BW · 104min

Director Chris Newby's film chronicles the gruesome fate of peasant girl Natalie Morse. Seeking solace from her medieval family and tiny hovel, Morse becomes obsessed with the Virgin Mary and seeks to serve her by being walled up for life in her local church. When her mother is tried and convicted of witchcraft, however, she digs her way out of imprisonment and stands to pay for the action with her life. A haunting film shot in striking monochrome that offers an apt period metaphor for contemporary teenage rebellion. LH DVD

Natalie Morse *Christine Carpenter* • Eugene Bervoets *[Gene Bervoets] Reeve* • Toyah Willcox *Pauline Carpenter* • Peter Postlethwaite *[Pete Postlethwaite] William Carpenter* • Christopher Eccleston *Priest* • Brenda Bertin *Meg Carpenter* • Annette Badland *Mary* ■ *Dir* Chris Newby • *Scr* Christine Watkins, Judith Stanley-Smith

Anchorman: the Legend of Ron Burgundy ★★★12
Period comedy
2004 · US · Colour · 90min

This sporadically amusing but thoroughly dumb 1970s-set comedy stars Will Ferrell as a top news anchorman who suddenly finds his job under threat from a woman. When ambitious reporter Christina Applegate joins a top-rated but male chauvinistic San Diego news team, she sets her sights on becoming the first female anchor. However, Ferrell has no intention of sharing the limelight and tries to frustrate the plans of his rival. The jokes are puerile in the extreme, but matters are given a lift by a host of cameo appearances. A sequel is in production. AS DVD BD

Will Ferrell *Ron Burgundy* • Christina Applegate *Veronica Corningstone* • Paul Rudd *Brian Fantana* • Steve Carell *Brick Tamland* • David Koechner *Champ Kind* • Fred Willard *Ed Harken* • Chris Parnell *Garth Holliday* • Kathryn Hahn *Helen* ■ *Dir* Adam McKay • *Scr* Adam McKay, Will Ferrell

Anchorman 2: the Legend Continues ★★★15
Comedy
2013 · US · Colour · 117min

Nearly a decade after Will Ferrell created the character of sexist newsman Ron Burgundy in *Anchorman*, he returns with this rib-tickling tale. Estranged from wife (and news rival) Veronica Corningstone (Christina Applegate), Ron is thrust into the arms of a New York network exec (Meagan Good) and her fledgeling rolling news channel. Ferrell's penchant for silliness is at its best earlier in the movie through the satirical swipes at the dumbing-down of TV news. It's here that, even if Burgundy has lost a bit of his shock value, the craziness still feels scathingly current. An extended version was released in 2014. SP Swearing, sexual references, drug abuse. DVD

Will Ferrell *Ron Burgundy* • Steve Carell *Brick Tamland* • Paul Rudd *Brian Fantana* • David Koechner *Champ Kind* • Christina Applegate *Veronica Corningstone* • Meagan Good *Linda Jackson* • James Marsden *Jack Lime* • Kristen Wiig *Chani Lastname* • Harrison Ford *Mack Harken* ■ *Dir* Adam McKay • *Scr* Will Ferrell, Adam McKay, from characters by Ferrell, McKay

Anchors Aweigh ★★★U
Musical
1945 · US · Colour · 133min

Gene Kelly and Frank Sinatra play two sailors on shore leave in Hollywood, whose plans for their break are changed when they meet young Dean Stockwell and his beautiful aunt Kathryn Grayson. At times it's schmaltzy and overlong, but none of that matters when Kelly and Sinatra are on the screen – they're a joy to watch. The Technicolor is ravishing, George Sidney's direction is technically clever and assured, and that key moment when Kelly shows the second most famous cartoon mouse how to dance is a stroke of genius. TS DVD BD

Gene Kelly *Joseph Brady* • Frank Sinatra *Clarence Doolittle* • Kathryn Grayson *Susan Abbott* • Dean Stockwell *Donald Martin* • Pamela Britton *Girl from Brooklyn* • Rags Ragland *Police sergeant* • Billy Gilbert *Cafe manager* • Henry O'Neill *Admiral Hammond* • José Iturbi ■ *Dir* George Sidney (2) • *Scr* Isobel Lennart, from a story by Natalie Marcin

And Baby Makes Three ★★
Comedy
1949 · US · BW · 83min

Barbara Hale is in the family way and about to marry anew, but really wants to stay with divorced first husband Robert Young. Need you ask more? What you could ask is how such a topic appeased the strict US censor's Breen Office, and then enjoy the amazing number of euphemisms used to describe Hale's condition. This is a trifle, nicely played by Barbara Hale, but its tale of a pregnant wife trying to get out of a second marriage to get her first hubby back leaves a strange taste in the mouth. TS

Robert Young (1) *Vernon Walsh* • Barbara Hale *Jacqueline Walsh* • Robert Hutton *Herbert Fletcher* • Janis Carter *Wanda York* • Billie Burke *Mrs Fletcher* • Nicholas Joy *Mr Fletcher* • Lloyd

A

Corrigan *Dr William Parnell* ■ *Dir* Henry Levin · *Scr* Lou Breslow, Joseph Hoffman from their story

And God Created Woman
★★★ **PG**

Drama 1956 · Fr · Colour · 88min

This was not Brigitte Bardot's first movie, but it was the one that turned her into the world's ultimate sex symbol. Directed by Roger Vadim, her then husband, the film also turned the little fishing village of St Tropez into a glamorous resort – the kind of place where girls leave their bikini tops on the ironing board, pose provocatively in CinemaScope and go with anything in trousers. Curt Jurgens, Jean-Louis Trintignant and Christian Marquand are three of Bardot's conquests in a movie whose funny attitude towards sex made it seem all the more risqué in the 1950s. AT French +subtitles. *DVD*

Brigitte Bardot *Juliette Hardy* · Curt Jurgens *Eric Carradine* · Jean-Louis Trintignant *Michel Tardieu* · Christian Marquand *Antoine Tardieu* · Georges Poujouly *Christian Tardieu* · Jean Tissier *M Vigier-Lefranc* · Jeanne Marken [Jane Marken] *Mme Morin* ■ *Dir* Roger Vadim · *Scr* Roger Vadim, Raoul J Lévy

And God Created Woman
★ **18**

Drama 1988 · US · Colour · 90min

Director Roger Vadim's sad attempt to reclaim his past glory is a tedious retooling of the sensational 1956 original that made Brigitte Bardot an international sex symbol. Rebecca De Mornay is hardly in the same class as an aspiring rock star who sleeps with electrician Vincent Spano and sundry high-powered men to get out of jail and achieve her aim. Vadim's contrived fable collapses into a cliché-ridden heap of melodrama. AJ *DVD*

Rebecca De Mornay *Robin Shay* · Vincent Spano *Billy Moran* · Frank Langella *James Tiernan* · Donovan Leitch *Peter Moran* · Judith Chapman *Alexandra Tiernan* · Jaime McEnnan *Timmy Moran* · Benjamin Mouton *Blue* ■ *Dir* Roger Vadim · *Scr* RJ Stewart

...And God Spoke
★★

Spoof documentary 1993 · US · Colour · 83min

Though there are some laughs to be had in this mock documentary about two skin flick merchants who decide to make a biblical epic on the cheap, *Spinal Tap* it ain't. Clueless duo Michael Riley and Stephen Rappaport have no idea what they're letting themselves in for, and it's fun to see them treat the Bible like a Jackie Collins bestseller and hire such actors as *The Incredible Hulk*'s Lou Ferrigno and Eve Plumb from *The Brady Bunch*. The gags are few and far between, and the film peters out alarmingly. AJ

Michael Riley *Clive Walton* · Stephen Rappaport *Marvin Handleman* · Josh Trossman *Ray/Jesus* · Lou Ferrigno *Cain* · Andy Dick *Abel* · Eve Plumb *Mrs Noah* · Fred Kaz *Noah* · Soupy Sales *Moses* · Michael Medved ■ *Dir* Arthur Borman · *Scr* Gregory S Malins, Michael Curtis, from a story by Arthur and Mark Borman

And Hope to Die
★★★

Crime drama 1972 · Fr/US · Colour · 126min

The penultimate film from veteran French director René Clément is a gangster thriller, filmed mainly in Canada, where fugitive Jean-Louis Trintignant inadvertently finds himself with a million bucks in cash, the price paid by a crime baron (Robert Ryan) to have a state witness assassinated. The plot gets even more complicated when Trintignant is kidnapped by the gang. Clearly intended to rival the crime dramas made by Jean-Pierre Melville, it's undeniably gripping, but not quite in that exalted league. AT In English, French. *DVD*

Robert Ryan *Charley* · Jean-Louis Trintignant *Tony* · Aldo Ray *Mattone* · Lea Massari *Sugar* · Tisa Farrow *Pepper* · Jean Gaven *Rizzio* · Nadine Nabokov *Majorette* · Andre Lawrence *Gypsy* · Daniel Breton *Paul* ■ *Dir* René Clément · *Scr* Sébastien Japrisot

...And Justice for All
★★★ **15**

Courtroom drama 1979 · US · Colour · 116min

Al Pacino stars as an idealistic young lawyer in this courtroom drama that takes a scathing look at the American justice system. First seen in prison where he's serving time for contempt, Pacino's attorney is a crusader, fighting corruption with a zeal that real-life lawyers can only dream of. The script by then husband-and-wife Valerie Curtin and Barry Levinson is, on the whole, solid enough, but the direction by Norman Jewison is rather bloated. AT *DVD*

Al Pacino *Arthur Kirkland* · Jack Warden *Judge Rayford* · John Forsythe *Judge Fleming* · Lee Strasberg *Grandpa Sam* · Jeffrey Tambor *Jay Porter* · Christine Lahti *Gail Packer* · Sam Levene *Arnie* ■ *Dir* Norman Jewison · *Scr* Valerie Curtin, Barry Levinson

And Life Goes On...
★★★

Documentary drama 1991 · Iran · Colour · 100min

In keeping with the rest of Iranian director Abbas Kiarostami's canon, this is a deceptively simple study of the enduring link between cinema and life. Following an earthquake in northern Iran, a director (Farhad Kheradmand representing Kiarostami) travels to see whether the cast of his 1987 film *Where Is the Friend's Home?*, survived the disaster. Taking a precarious mountain route, and in the company of his son, he arrives to discuss with the peoples of Rudbar and Rostamabad their plans for the future and how God could have allowed such suffering. Combining simple narrative with unobtrusive documentary, this is a humane, deeply affecting work. DP Farsi +subtitles.

Farhad Kheradmand *Film director* · Buba Bayour *Film director's son* ■ *Dir/Scr* Abbas Kiarostami

And Millions Will Die!
★★

Science-fiction thriller 1973 · US · Colour · 93min

Leslie Nielsen co-stars with TV regular Richard Baseheart in this story about an unknown force that threatens to unleash poison gas in Hong Kong. It attempts to cash in on the early 1970s demand for disaster movies, but there is little in the way of either star charisma or suspense. JF Some violence, swearing.

Richard Basehart *Dr Pruitt* · Leslie Nielsen *Gallagher* · Joseph First *Franz Kessler* · Susan Strasberg *Heather Kessler* · Alwyn Kurts *Dr Mitchell* · Shariff Medon *Postman* ■ *Dir* Leslie Martinson [Leslie H Martinson] · *Scr* Michael Fisher

And Now for Something Completely Different
★★★★ **PG**

Comedy 1971 · UK · Colour · 84min

Not all that different, though, for British enthusiasts of Monty Python's comic madness, as it's a recycling of some of the team's funniest BBC TV sketches. But this first cinematic celebration was really aimed at American innocents, ignorant of such items as the "Upper Class Twit of the Year Race" and "Hell's Grannies", with Graham Chapman, John Cleese and Terry Gilliam giving vent to a wholly superior form of surrealism. TH Swearing. *DVD*

Graham Chapman · John Cleese · Terry Gilliam · Eric Idle · Terry Jones · Michael Palin · Carol Cleveland · Connie Booth ■ *Dir* Ian MacNaughton · *Scr* Graham Chapman, John Cleese, Terry Gilliam, Eric Idle, Terry Jones, Michael Palin · *Animation* Terry Gilliam

And Now... Ladies and Gentlemen
★★ **PG**

Romantic drama 2002 · Fr/UK · Colour · 123min

Two lost souls are drawn together by fate in veteran French film-maker Claude Lelouch's handsome but clunky melodrama. A curious hotch-potch of travelogue, crime caper and romance, it explores the relationship between an English jewel thief (Jeremy Irons) and a heartbroken French singer (real-life chanteuse Patricia Kaas), who are both suffering mysterious bouts of amnesia. SF French, English +subtitles. *DVD*

Jeremy Irons *Valentin Valentin* · Patricia Kaas *Jane Lester* · Thierry Lhermitte *Thierry* · Alessandra Martines *Françoise* · Jean-Marie Bigard *Dr Lamy/Pharmicist* · Ticky Holgado *Boubou* · Yvan Attal *David* · Amidou *Police inspector* · Claudia Cardinale *Contessa Falconetti* ■ *Dir* Claude Lelouch · *Scr* Claude Lelouch, Pierre Leroux, Pierre Uytterhoeven

And Now My Love
★★

Drama 1974 · Fr/It · Colour · 121min

This flamboyant folly from Claude Lelouch astonishingly earned an Oscar nomination for best original screenplay. Overlong and self-indulgent, it's interminably dull from our first encounter with a pioneering movie cameraman (Charles Denner) at the turn of the century right through to the moment his granddaughter (Marthe Keller) sets her roguish beau (André Dussollier) on the straight and narrow. DP French +subtitles.

Marthe Keller *Sarah/Her mother/Her grandmother* · André Dussollier *Simon Duroc* · Charles Denner *Cameraman/Sarah's father/Sarah's grandfather* · Carla Gravina *Sarah's Italian friend* · Charles Gerard *Charlot, Simon's friend* · Gilbert Bécaud ■ *Dir* Claude Lelouch · *Scr* Claude Lelouch, Pierre Uytterhoeven

And Now the Screaming Starts!
★★ **15**

Horror 1973 · UK · Colour · 90min

Stephanie Beacham marries Ian Ogilvy and is menaced by a dismembered hand, an axe-wielding farmer and other apparitions thanks to an ancient family curse. The presence of horror veterans Peter Cushing and Herbert Lom gives this formula haunted house material a much needed lift, but there's very little action and too few surprises. AJ *DVD*

Peter Cushing *Doctor Pope* · Herbert Lom *Henry Fengriffen* · Patrick Magee *Doctor Whittle* · Ian Ogilvy *Charles Fengriffen* · Stephanie Beacham *Catherine Fengriffen* · Geoffrey Whitehead *Silas Jr/Sr* · Guy Rolfe *Maitland* · Rosalie Crutchley *Mrs Luke* ■ *Dir* Roy Ward Baker · *Scr* Roger Marshall, from the novel *Fengriffen* by David Case

And Now Tomorrow
★★

Drama 1944 · US · BW · 84min

Don't get over-excited by the name Raymond Chandler on the credits of this melodrama. He was only doing it for the money and reserved his best – and least charitable – line until after the movie, describing its star as "a small boy's idea of a tough guy". Actually Ladd deserved better of both writer and film. He plays a doctor with working-class origins who, while working on a cure for deafness caused by meningitis, meets and falls for upper-class Loretta Young. BB

Alan Ladd *Dr Merek Vance* · Loretta Young *Emily Blair* · Susan Hayward *Janice Blair* · Barry Sullivan *Jeff Stoddard* · Beulah Bondi *Aunt Em* · Cecil Kellaway *Dr Weeks* ■ *Dir* Irving Pichel · *Scr* Frank Partos, Raymond Chandler, from the novel by Rachel Field

And Now You're Dead ★★ **18**

Action 1998 · HK · Colour · 90min

Shannon Lee, the daughter of legendary martial artist Bruce Lee, kickboxes and karate chops her way through a threadbare action adventure. She plays a sharpshooter who teams up with her former partner, a professional thief, and two young pickpockets to steal the largest diamond in the Czech Republic. Lee's fine but the double-crossing theatrics and explosive stunts simply aren't in the same league as her fighting proficiency. AJ Cantonese dubbed. *DVD*

Shannon Lee *Mandy* · Michael Wong *Marty* · Anita Yuen *Lucy* · Jordan Chan *Tommy* ■ *Dir* Corey Yuen

And Quiet Flows the Don
★★★★

War drama 1957 · USSR · BW · 108min

Sergei Gerasimov's epic adaptation of Nobel laureate Mikhail Sholokhov's masterpiece has rarely been seen in its sprawling entirety outside the old Soviet bloc. Yet, even in its bowdlerised version, it remains one of the most polished examples of socialist realism. The action initially focuses on Pyotr Glebov's feud with his father, Danilo Ilchenko, who insists he marries Zinaida Kirienko, rather than his lover, Elina Bystritskaya. However, the First World War and the Revolution intervene and change their lives forever. Visually, it's a hugely impressive achievement, although the acting is occasionally bombastic. DP In Russian.

Elina Bystritskaya *Aksinya* · Pyotr Glebov *Grigory* · Zinaida Kirienko *Natalya* · Danilo Ilchenko *Panteleimon Melekhov* ■ *Dir* Sergei Gerasimov · *Scr* Sergei Gerasimov, from the novel *Tikhij Don/And Quiet Flows the Don* by Mikhail Sholokhov

And Quiet Rolls the Dawn
★★★★

Drama 1979 · Ind · Colour · 90min

Less politically strident than his earlier work, this intense treatise on the role of women in Indian society demonstrates Mrinal Sen's total mastery of his art. Moving between the vast courtyard of a Calcuttan tenement and the crowded apartment in which Satya Bannerjee and his family of seven live, Sen uses the overnight absence of a hard-working daughter to expose the family's indolent dependence on her wage. Interspersing dramatic scenes with speeches to camera, he compels and provokes as he probes their middle-class pride and prejudices. DP In Bengali.

Satya Bannerjee *Hrishikesh Sen Gupta* · Gita Sen *Mother* · Mamata Shankar *Chinu* · Sreela Majumdar *Minu* · Tapan Das *Tapu* · Umanath Bhattacharya *Landlord* · Arun Mukherjee *Shyamal, the neighbour* ■ *Dir* Mrinal Sen · *Scr* Mrinal Sen, from the story *Abiroto Chene Mukh* by Amalendu Chakravarty

And She Was
★★

Comedy drama 2007 · US · Colour · 95min

Kirstie Alley plays a veteran scriptwriter taking revenge on the youth-fixated film industry in this simplistic but watchable TV-movie comedy. The initial screwball-style fun gets bogged down by clumsy moralising and two weakly written romances that are both contrived and distracting. Fortunately, lively performances and a slew of entertaining Tinseltown references keep events flowing, while the feature's crucial messages withstand even an overly neat and saccharine finale. SF

Kirstie Alley *Byrdie Langdon* · Eric Christian Olsen *Jason "Krueger" Langdon* ■ *Dir* Graeme Clifford · *Scr* George Beckerman

And So It Goes
★★ **12**

Romantic comedy drama 2014 · US · Colour · 89min

Unsure if it's a crinkly comedy, romantic weepie or a family drama, this is a rather pedestrian offering from the normally reliable Rob Reiner. Michael Douglas plays a misanthropic estate agent who is looking to sell his multimillion home and retire to a life of luxury. Diane Keaton is the amateur lounge singer who lives in a small block of lakeside apartments he also happens to own. The two leads spark off each other nicely, but they're sadly let down by Michael Arbus's predictable script. JF Sexual references. *DVD*

Michael Douglas (1) *Oren Little* · Diane Keaton *Leah* · Paloma Guzman *Selena* · Sterling Jerins *Sarah* ■ *Dir* Rob Reiner · *Scr* Mark Andrus

And So They Were Married
★★★

Romantic comedy 1936 · US · BW · 68min

Widower Melvyn Douglas and his young son Jackie Moran meet widow Mary Astor and her daughter Edith Fellows while vacationing at a winter resort. After a sticky start, the adults fall for each other, but their children set out to sabotage the relationship. A short, neat romantic comedy, directed by the excellent Elliott Nugent, in which the classy expertise of Douglas and Astor is almost buried by the engaging antics of the juveniles. RK

Melvyn Douglas *Hugh "Stephen" Blake* • Mary Astor *Edith Farnham* • Edith Fellows *Brenda Farnham* • Jackie Moran *Tommy Blake* • Donald Meek *Hotel manager* • Dorothy Stickney *Miss Alma Peabody* • Romaine Callender *Mr Ralph P Shirley* • Douglas Scott *Horace* ■ *Dir* Elliott Nugent • *Scr* Doris Anderson, Joseph Anthony, A Laurie Brazee

And Soon the Darkness
★★★ 15

Thriller   1970 · UK · Colour · 94min

This nerve-jangling "missing person" mystery stars Pamela Franklin and Michele Dotrice as English nurses cycling in rural France until one vanishes, forcing the other into a frantic search to find her. Director Robert Fuest eschews the tongue-in-cheek antics of his Dr Phibes films to create a tale of escalating terror, and is well served by a taut script from Brian Clemens (*The Avengers*) and Terry Nation (*Doctor Who*). JA DVD BL

Pamela Franklin *Jane* • Michele Dotrice *Cathy* • Sandor Eles *Paul* • John Nettleton *Gendarme* • Clare Kelly *Schoolmistress* • Hana-Maria Pravda *Madame Lassal* • John Franklyn *Old man* ■ *Dir* Robert Fuest • *Scr* Brian Clemens, Terry Nation

And the Angels Sing ★★★ U

Musical comedy   1944 · US · BW · 95min

Raucous Betty Hutton and glamorous Dorothy Lamour are joined by Diana Lynn and Mimi Chandler to make up a four-girl singing sister act. Their harmonious relationship is fractured by bandleader Fred MacMurray, who helps the quartet to success and finds romance with one of the sisters. This has a good Johnny Burke–Jimmy Van Heusen score that includes the enduring standard, *It Could Happen to You*, plus a couple of stand-out numbers from the irrepressible Hutton. RK

Dorothy Lamour *Nancy Angel* • Fred MacMurray *Happy Marshall* • Betty Hutton *Bobby Angel* • Diana Lynn *Josie Angel* • Mimi Chandler *Patti Angel* • Raymond Walburn *Pop Angel* • Eddie Foy Jr *Fuzzy Johnson* ■ *Dir* George Marshall • *Scr* Melvin Frank, Norman Panama, from a story by Claude Binyon

And the Band Played On
★★★ 12

Documentary drama   1993 · US · Colour · 141min

This made-for-cable adaptation of Randy Shilts's monumental history of Aids is distractingly overloaded with stars, all too willing to prove their political correctness. But, taken as a detective story, this is still a gripping narrative in which French and American scientists search to isolate the virus and seek to find the airline employee who may have brought it from Africa. Matthew Modine's clear-sighted visionary provides the necessary human focus, keeping his integrity while others lose theirs. Director Roger Spottiswoode is hemmed in by too many statistics, yet still produces an absorbing docudrama. TH Some swearing. DVD

Matthew Modine *Dr Don Francis* • Ian McKellen *Bill Kraus* • Lily Tomlin *Dr Selma Dritz* • Richard Gere *Choreographer* • Alan Alda *Dr Robert Gallo* • Glenne Headly *Mary Guinan* • Phil Collins *Eddie Papasano* • Anjelica Huston *Dr Betsy Reisz* • Saul Rubinek *Dr Jim Curran* • Steve Martin *Brother* • Charles Martin Smith *Dr Harold Jaffe* • Elizabeth Taylor ■ *Dir* Roger Spottiswoode • *Scr* Arnold Schulman, from the non-fiction book by Randy Shilts

And the Beat Goes On: the Sonny and Cher Story
★★★ PG

Biographical drama   1999 · US · Colour · 85min

Based on Sonny Bono's controversial autobiography, this TV biopic of the 1960s odd couple is enjoyably camp without veering too far into the cheap and tacky.

Cher is played with respect by lookalike Renee Faia, while Sonny's infectious enthusiasm is ably put across by Jay Underwood. Fans will enjoy the clever soundtrack, which mixes original music with some skilled re-creations. JF

Jay Underwood *Sonny Bono* • Renee Faia *Cher* • Jim Pirri *Buddy Black* • Laura Johnson *Georgia LaPierre* • Christian Leffler *Phil Spector* • Walter Franks *Little Richard* • Bruce Nozick *Art Rupe* • Marie Wilson (2) *Mary Bono* ■ *Dir* David Burton Morris • *Scr* Ellen Weston, from the autobiography by Sonny Bono

And the Same to You ★★ U

Comedy   1960 · UK · BW · 67min

Any film boasting Sid James, Tommy Cooper and Brian Rix in the cast has to be worth a look, but there are few laughs to be had in this screen version of a popular stage farce. Rix stars as a singularly hopeless boxer who has to keep his career hidden from his disapproving archdeacon uncle. John Paddy Carstairs co-wrote the script with John Junkin, but every punch is pulled. DP DVD

Brian Rix *Dickie Dreadnought* • William Hartnell *Wally Burton* • Tommy Cooper *Horace Hawkins* • Dick Bentley *George Nibbs* • Vera Day *Cynthia* • Sidney James *Sammy Gatt* • Leo Franklyn *Vicar* • Renee Houston *Mildred* • Miles Malleson *Bishop* ■ *Dir* George Pollock • *Scr* John Paddy Carstairs, John Junkin, from the play *The Chigwell Chicken* by AP Dearsley

And the Ship Sails On
★★★ 12

Comedy drama   1983 · It/Fr · Colour · 123min

Federico Fellini's idea was to create the last voyage of the old Europe before it was snuffed out by the First World War. So in his mind he builds an ocean liner and lets it sail upon a phoney sea, laden with human cargo – aristocrats, diplomats and a band of opera singers who want to bury a great soprano on an offshore island. The director concocts some simply stunning moments of surreal beauty and impish humour, and the sudden arrival of Balkan refugees has the required impact. But the film is still an awkward mishmash, too long and unevenly acted. AT Italian dubbed. DVD

Freddie Jones *Mister Orlando* • Barbara Jefford *Ildebranda Cuffari* • Victor Poletti *Aureliano Fuciletto* • Peter Cellier *Sir Reginald Dongby* • Elisa Mainardi *Teresa Valegnani* • Norma West *Lady Violet Dongby* • Janet Suzman *Edmea Tetua* ■ *Dir* Federico Fellini, Mike Hodges • *Scr* Federico Fellini, Tonino Guerra, Catherine Breillat

And Then There Were None
★★★★ U

Crime mystery   1945 · US · BW · 97min

Of all the adaptations of Agatha Christie's classic who-, what- and why-dunnit *Ten Little Indians* (or *Ten Little Niggers* as the 1974 film would have it), this is the first and the best. French director René Clair, working in Hollywood, provides a distinctly European creepiness to the story of mysteriously invited guests on a deserted Cornish island being killed off one by one and, even without a Poirot or a Miss Marple, the dénouement is a real shock. Stalwarts such as Barry Fitzgerald, Walter Huston, Louis Hayward and June Duprez form an ensemble as tetchy as they are terrified. AT DVD

Barry Fitzgerald *Judge Francis J Quincannon* • Walter Huston *Dr Edward G Armstrong* • Louis Hayward *Philip Lombard/Charles Morley* • Roland Young *William H Blore* • June Duprez *Vera Claythorne* • Mischa Auer *Prince Nikita Starloff* • C Aubrey Smith *Gen Sir John Mandrake* • Judith Anderson *Emily Brent* ■ *Dir* René Clair • *Scr* Dudley Nichols, from the novel *Ten Little Indians* by Agatha Christie

And Then There Were None
★★★ PG

Crime mystery   1974 · Fr/Sp/W Ger/It · Colour · 102min

This film version of Agatha Christie's whodunnit *Ten Little Niggers* assembles strangers at an isolated Persian palace and bumps them off one by one in retribution. It is lushly filmed by director Peter Collinson

in pre-revolutionary Iran, but stars such as Richard Attenborough, Oliver Reed, Elke Sommer and Herbert Lom are given the task of propping up a dubious proposition, helped by the disembodied voice of narrator Orson Welles, who lends the project more weight than it deserves. TH DVD

Oliver Reed *Hugh Lombard* • Richard Attenborough *Judge Cannon* • Elke Sommer *Vera Clyde* • Gert Froebe [Gert Fröbe] *Wilhelm Blore* • Adolfo Celi *General Soule* • Stéphane Audran *Ilona Bergen* • Herbert Lom *Dr Armstrong* • Charles Aznavour *Michel Raven* • Orson Welles *Voice on tape recorder* ■ *Dir* Peter Collinson • *Scr* Erich Kröhnke, Enrique Llovet, from the novel *Ten Little Niggers* by Agatha Christie

And When Did You Last See Your Father? ★★★★ 12

Biographical drama
2007 · UK/Ire · Colour · 88min

Colin Firth and Jim Broadbent give heart-rending performances in this brilliant adaptation of Blake Morrison's memoirs about his dying father. As the pair grasp for the right words in the older man's final hours, long-held resentments are revealed in flashback. Young actor Matthew Beard holds his own playing the teenage Blake against a formidable Broadbent. The veteran actor dazzles as the charismatic yet sometimes insufferable dad, who is consistently (albeit inadvertently) chipping away at his son's fragile ego. Director Anand Tucker manages to find comedy in these minor indignities, including a camping trip that culminates in the middle of a river. An acutely observed script and moving performances keep things from descending into cliché, and the tragic ending is undeniably powerful. SP Some swearing, sex scenes. DVD

Colin Firth *Blake Morrison* • Jim Broadbent *Arthur Morrison* • Juliet Stevenson *Kim Morrison* • Gina McKee *Kathy Morrison* • Matthew Beard *Teenage Blake Morrison* • Sarah Lancashire *Beaty* • Elaine Cassidy *Sandra* • Claire Skinner *Gillian Morrison* • Bradley Johnson *Young Blake Morrison* • Carey Mulligan *Rachel* ■ *Dir* Anand Tucker • *Scr* David Nicholls, from the memoirs by Blake Morrison • *Cinematographer* Howard Atherton

And Women Shall Weep ★★

Drama   1960 · UK · BW · 65min

This little British B-movie is given great strength by the leading performance of veteran TV character actress Ruth Dunning. She stars as a widow trying to keep her young son Richard O'Sullivan on the straight and narrow. However, her older son Max Butterfield is beyond help. Slight and overplayed. TS

Ruth Dunning *Mrs Lumsden* • Max Butterfield *Terry Lumsden* • Gillian Vaughan *Brenda Wilkes* • Richard O'Sullivan *Godfrey Lumsden* • Claire Gordon *Sadie MacDougall* ■ *Dir* John Lemont • *Scr* John Lemont, Leigh Vance

Andaz ★★★★ PG

Drama   1949 · Ind · BW · 141min

Also known as *A Matter of Style*, this concluded the string of 1940s classics that established Mehboob Khan as one of the key figures in Indian cinema. An allegorical warning to the newly independent state not to lose sight of traditional values, it is a typically knotty melodrama, with ambitious young executive Dilip Kumar coming between his heiress boss Nargis and her feckless husband, Raj Kapoor. The film turned Kumar into a superstar, while also reinforcing the status of his co-stars as the sub-continent's favourite romantic team. DP Hindi +subtitles. DVD

Raj Kapoor *Rajan* • Dilip Kumar *Dilip* • Nargis *Neeta* • Sapru *Badriprasad* ■ *Dir* Mehboob Khan • *Scr* S Ali Raza

The Anderson Tapes ★★★ 15

Crime drama   1971 · US · Colour · 94min

Sean Connery sets out to burgle a luxury apartment block helped by some notable eccentrics, unaware that his every move is

under surveillance from various law enforcement agencies. The implicit ironies – that the agents can't see the larger picture of a major robbery for all their attention to the smaller details – are never quite forged into the intended satire, but director Sidney Lumet does achieve a certain sarcastic humour. TH Swearing. DVD

Sean Connery *Duke Anderson* • Dyan Cannon *Ingrid Everleigh* • Martin Balsam *Tommy Haskins* • Ralph Meeker *Delaney* • Alan King *Pat Angelo* • Christopher Walken *The Kid* • Val Avery *Parelli* • Dick Williams [Dick Anthony Williams] *Spencer* • Margaret Hamilton *Miss Kaler* ■ *Dir* Sidney Lumet • *Scr* Frank R Pierson, from the novel by Lawrence Sanders

Andre ★★★ U

Adventure   1994 · US · Colour · 90min

Set in the early 1960s, this tells the story of the rather cute seal of the title, who is adopted by precocious newcomer Tina Majorino, playing the animal-loving daughter of harbour master Keith Carradine. The local fishing community is worried that Andre will affect their catch, which leads to the inevitable conflict. It's sickly sweet stuff, but Andre (actually played by a sea-lion) is undoubtedly endearing, and youngsters will be enraptured. JF

Keith Carradine *Harry Whitney* • Tina Majorino *Toni Whitney* • Chelsea Field *Thalice Whitney* • Shane Meier *Steve Whitney* • Aidan Pendleton *Paula Whitney* • Shirley Broderick *Mrs McCann* • Andrea Libman *Mary May* • Joshua Jackson *Mark Baker* ■ *Dir* George Miller (1) • *Scr* Dana Baratta, from the non-fiction book *A Seal Called Andre* by Harry Goodridge, Lew Dietz

Andrei Rublev ★★★★★ 15

Biographical drama
1966 · USSR · Colour and BW · 174min

Divided into eight episodes and majestically photographed by Vadim Yusov, this is a remarkable study of the artist Andrei Rublev's struggle to overcome both his own doubts, and the poverty and cruelty of his time, to create works of inspirational power and outstanding beauty. Anatoly Solonitsin plays the 15th-century icon painter as a sort of wandering mystic who takes a vow of silence in protest at conditions in Russia under the Tartars. Andrei Tarkovsky includes too much impenetrable symbolism, but the battle, the balloon flight, the snow crucifixion, the casting of the bell and the colour montage from Rublev's work are stunning. DP Russian +subtitles. DVD BL

Anatoly Solonitsin [Anatoli Solonitsyn] *Andrei Rublev* • Ivan Lapikov *Kirill* • Nikolai Grinko *Daniel Chorny* • Nikolai Sergeyev *Theophanes the Greek* • Irma Rausch *Idiot girl* • Nikolai Burlyaev *Boris* • Yuri Nazarov *The Grand Prince/His brother* ■ *Dir* Andrei Tarkovsky • *Scr* Andrei Tarkovsky, Andrei Mikhalkov-Konchalovsky, *Cinematographer* Vadim Yusov

Andrew & Jeremy Get Married ★★★ 15

Documentary   2004 · UK · Colour · 72min

This low-key documentary from writer/director Don Boyd was produced for the BBC's *Storyville* series, which may explain its rather brief running time and small-screen feel. Filmed over the course of a year, it chronicles the relationship between two very different gay men in the run-up to their "wedding". Jeremy is a patrician 69-year-old English professor with connections to London's upper-crust literati, and Andrew is a 49-year-old former bus driver with a history of promiscuity and drug abuse. They're an engaging if odd couple, as Boyd reveals, and their commitment ceremony at London's City Hall, after five years together, is a moving and uplifting experience. DA DVD

■ *Dir/Scr* Don Boyd

Androcles and the Lion ★★★ U

Satirical comedy   1952 · US · BW · 96min

This RKO movie was a long time in the making, and stars Victor Mature and Jean Simmons found greater success with their next foray into Roman history together, *The*

Robe. The imported British supporting cast, including Robert Newton, behave like fish out of water under Chester Erskine's shambolic direction, but this is still an interesting one-off. **TS**

Jean Simmons *Lavinia* • Alan Young *Androcles* • Victor Mature *Captain* • Robert Newton *Ferrovius* • Maurice Evans *Caesar* • Elsa Lanchester *Megaera* • Reginald Gardiner *Lentulus* • Gene Lockhart *Menagerie keeper* • Alan Mowbray *Editor* ■ *Dir* Chester Erskine • *Scr* Chester Erskine, Ken Englund, from the play by George Bernard Shaw

Android ★★★ 15

Science-fiction fantasy
1982 · US · Colour · 76min

Three space convicts upset the plans of mad scientist Klaus Kinski to replace his companion android, Max 404, with a perfect female version in a low-key slice of cult science-fiction from the Roger Corman factory. Don Opper's portrayal of Max as a nerdy movie buff clone adds extra pop culture playfulness to the enjoyably exciting proceedings. Neat suspense, a few final reel twists and another eccentric Kinski performance make this low-budget gem a winner. **AJ** Swearing, violence. *DVD*

Klaus Kinski *Dr Daniel* • Don Opper *Max 404* • Brie Howard *Maggie* • Norbert Weisser *Keller* • Crofton Hardester *Mendes* • Kendra Kirchner *Cassandra* ■ *Dir* Aaron Lipstadt • *Scr* Don Opper, James Reigle

The Andromeda Strain ★★★★ PG

Science-fiction thriller
1970 · US · Colour · 125min

This super combination of hi-tech thrills and against-the-clock suspense was the first Michael Crichton novel to be adapted for the big screen. Robert Wise's near-documentary direction keeps tension mounting as desperate scientists race to isolate a fatal alien virus from a fallen satellite. More science fact than fiction, and still powerfully relevant, it's a remarkably faithful account of Crichton's biological invasion bestseller, layered with sophisticated special effects by Douglas Trumbull. **AJ** *DVD*

Arthur Hill *Dr Jeremy Stone* • David Wayne *Dr Charles Dutton* • James Olson *Dr Mark Hall* • Kate Reid *Dr Ruth Leavitt* • Paula Kelly *Karen Anson* • George Mitchell *Jackson* • Ramon Bieri *Major Mancheck* • Richard O'Brien *Grimes* ■ *Dir* Robert Wise • *Scr* Nelson Gidding, from the novel by Michael Crichton

Andy Hardy Gets Spring Fever ★★ U

Comedy drama
1939 · US · BW · 85min

The seventh in the series has a new director to marshal the action and those "man to man" talks between Judge Lewis Stone and Mickey Rooney. Here, Rooney falls for a drama teacher and then discovers she's engaged. The teacher is played by Helen Gilbert, a cellist in the MGM studio orchestra until someone gave her a screen test. **DP**

Lewis Stone *Judge James K Hardy* • Mickey Rooney *Andy Hardy* • Cecilia Parker *Marian Hardy* • Ann Rutherford *Polly Benedict* • Fay Holden *Mrs Emily Hardy* • Sara Haden *Aunt Milly* • Helen Gilbert *Rose Meredith* • *Dir* WS Van Dyke II [WS Van Dyke] • *Scr* Kay Van Riper, from characters by Aurania Rouverol

Andy Hardy Meets Debutante ★★ U

Comedy drama
1940 · US · BW · 87min

The ninth film in the series sees Mickey Rooney in the Big Apple trying to secure a meeting with a debutante whose photograph he's seen in a magazine. It isn't all Hollywood pap, however: Andy's dad (Lewis Stone) is also in town, tending to the affairs of an orphanage. This entry is notable only for the appearance of Judy Garland. **AT**

Lewis Stone *Judge James K Hardy* • Mickey Rooney *Andy Hardy* • Fay Holden *Mrs Emily Hardy* • Cecilia Parker *Marian Hardy* • Judy Garland *Betsy Booth* • Sara Haden *Aunt Milly* • Ann Rutherford *Polly Benedict* • Tom Neal

Aldrich Brown ■ *Dir* George B Seitz • *Scr* Annalee Whitmore, Thomas Seller, from characters by Aurania Rouverol

Andy Hardy's Private Secretary ★★ U

Comedy drama
1941 · US · BW · 100min

The gang's all here for this tenth outing, plus 18-year-old Kathryn Grayson making an early screen appearance as the girl Mickey Rooney hires as his secretary as he is about to graduate from high school. She ends up helping him pass his English exam and getting him through high school at the second attempt. Grayson gets to sing and show her star potential, but the formula already shows signs of running out of steam. **AT**

Lewis Stone *Judge James K Hardy* • Mickey Rooney *Andy Hardy* • Fay Holden *Mrs Emily Hardy* • Ian Hunter *Steven Land* • Ann Rutherford *Polly Benedict* • Kathryn Grayson *Kathryn Land* • Todd Karns *Harry Land* • John Dilson *Mr Davis* ■ *Dir* George B Seitz • *Scr* Jane Murfin, Harry Ruskin, from characters by Aurania Rouverol

Andy Hardy's Double Life ★★ U

Comedy drama
1942 · US · BW · 92min

This was one of the last films in this ever-popular series, as MGM couldn't stop Mickey Rooney from growing older. Andy Hardy finally gets to go to college, where he gets embroiled with the opposite sex. Rooney's mugging and the sentimental home-town feel was beginning to wear thin, and there would be only two more films in the series, not including *Andy Hardy Comes Home* in 1958. **TS**

Mickey Rooney *Andy Hardy* • Lewis Stone *Judge James K Hardy* • Esther Williams *Sheila Brooks* • Ann Rutherford *Polly Benedict* • Fay Holden *Mrs Emily Hardy* • Cecilia Parker *Marian Hardy* • Sara Haden *Aunt Milly* • William Lundigan *Jeff Willis* ■ *Dir* George B Seitz • *Scr* Agnes Christine Johnston, from characters by Aurania Rouverol

Andy Hardy's Blonde Trouble ★★ U

Comedy drama
1944 · US · BW · 107min

Mickey Rooney stars in the 14th and penultimate *Andy Hardy* comedy (not counting the straggler made in 1958). As the eternal, archetypal teenager, Rooney enrols in his dad's alma mater but gets into trouble by paying too much attention to girls, mainly Bonita Granville and twin blondes who fancy him and make his life a misery. **AT**

Lewis Stone *Judge James K Hardy* • Mickey Rooney *Andy Hardy* • Fay Holden *Mrs Emily Hardy* • Sara Haden *Aunt Milly* • Herbert Marshall *Dr MJ Standish* • Bonita Granville *Kay Wilson* • Jean Porter *Katy Henderson* • Keye Luke *Dr Lee Wong How* ■ *Dir* George B Seitz • *Scr* Harry Ruskin, William Ludwig, Agnes Christine Johnston, from characters by Aurania Rouverol

Andy Hardy Comes Home ★★ U

Comedy drama
1958 · US · BW · 79min

A dozen years after his last appearance as Andy Hardy, Mickey Rooney returns to the small town of Carvel and finds himself embroiled in a dishonest property deal over an aircraft factory. Trading heavily on the audience's nostalgia for the series – clips from earlier films are featured – this was intended to herald a brand new run of Andy Hardy movies. The series, however, ended here. **AT**

Mickey Rooney *Andy Hardy* • Patricia Breslin *Jane Hardy* • Fay Holden *Mother Hardy* • Cecilia Parker *Marian* • Sara Haden *Aunt Milly* • Jerry Colonna *Doc* • Frank Ferguson *Mayor Benson* • Teddy Rooney *Andy Hardy Jr* ■ *Dir* Howard W Koch • *Scr* Edward Everett Hutshing, Robert Morris Donley, from characters by Aurania Rouverol

Angel ★★

Drama
1937 · US · BW · 90min

Marlene Dietrich was already labelled box-office poison when she made this movie for Ernst Lubitsch, a tale of sexual deception that's halfway between romantic

melodrama and sophisticated comedy. Dietrich is married to Herbert Marshall, but she still fancies former boyfriend Melvyn Douglas. Things get bogged down by plot and, without Josef von Sternberg's camerawork, Dietrich often looks like a plain Jane. **AT**

Marlene Dietrich *Maria Barker* • Herbert Marshall *Sir Frederick Barker* • Melvyn Douglas *Anthony Halton* • Edward Everett Horton *Graham* • Ernest Cossart *Walton* • Laura Hope Crews *Grand Duchess Anna Dmitrievna* • Herbert Mundin *Greenwood* • Ivan Lebedeff *Prince Vladimir Gregorovitch* ■ *Dir* Ernst Lubitsch • *Scr* Samson Raphaelson, Guy Bolton, Russell Medcraft, Melchior Lengyel, from the play by Melchior Lengyel

Angel ★★★★ 15

Crime thriller
1982 · Ire · Colour · 88min

In Neil Jordan's remarkable first feature, Stephen Rea plays a saxophonist who embarks on a bloody trail of revenge after his business manager and a mute girl are gunned down by Irish gangsters. While the Troubles and the sectarian divide are always in the background, Jordan steers a hypnotic and often surreal path through Ulster's underworld, while Rea is perfect as the equivocal hero whose quest becomes almost Arthurian. **AT** *DVD*

Stephen Rea *Danny* • Alan Devlin *Bill* • Veronica Quilligan *Annie* • Peter Caffrey *Ray* • Honor Heffernan *Deirdre* • Ray McAnally *Bloom* ■ *Dir/Scr* Neil Jordan

Angel ★★ 18

Crime comedy drama 1984 · US · Colour · 88min

Writer/director Robert Vincent O'Neil tosses some offbeat comedy and a teenage temptress angle into this tacky follow-up to *Vice Squad*. Dick Shawn serves up the former as a gregarious drag queen, while Donna Wilkes does her best to provide the latter as the class-topping student who becomes a fallen angel by night. **DP**

Cliff Gorman *Lt Andrews* • Susan Tyrrell *Mosler* • Dick Shawn *Mae* • Rory Calhoun *Kit Carson* • John Diehl *Billy Boy* • Donna Wilkes *Angel/Molly* • Robert Acey *Driver/John* ■ *Dir* Robert Vincent O'Neil • *Scr* Robert Vincent O'Neil, Joseph Michael Cala

Angel ★★ 15

Period drama
2006 · Fr/UK/Bel · Colour · 119min

The satirical novel by author Elizabeth Taylor provides ripe material for the first English-language film from French director François Ozon (*Swimming Pool*). It owes a debt to *Gone with the Wind* for both its florid visuals and a heroine you're meant to love to hate. Romola Garai plays Angel, a bratty grocer's daughter who dreams of fame and fortune, and finds it when her trashy romantic novels are snapped up by Edwardian society. But her success doesn't bring her happiness, and her relationships are toxic. **DA** *DVD*

Romola Garai *Angelica "Angel" Deverell* • Sam Neill *Théo Deverell* • Lucy Russell *Nora Howe-Nevinson* • Michael Fassbender *Esmé* • Charlotte Rampling *Hermione Gilbright* • Jacqueline Tong *Mother Deverell* ■ *Dir* François Ozon • *Scr* François Ozon, Martin Crimp, from the novel by Elizabeth Taylor (2)

Angel-A ★★★ 15

Romantic comedy
2005 · Fr · BW · 86min

Luc Besson crafts a love letter to Paris with this whimsical comedy fable, shot in ravishing black and white to capture the city at its most beautiful. In a bittersweet storyline, Jamel Debbouze plays a downtrodden petty crook who decides to jump off a bridge after gangsters call in his loans. However his plans are thwarted by another potential suicide – statuesque blonde Rie Rasmussen – whom he rescues. So begins an unconventional and increasingly surreal relationship, while Besson infuses events with surprising tenderness. **SF** French +subtitles. Swearing. *DVD* *Blu-ray*

Jamel Debbouze *André* • Rie Rasmussen *Angela* • Gilbert Melki *Franck* • Serge Riaboukine *Pedro* ■ *Dir/Scr* Luc Besson

Angel and the Badman ★★★ U

Western
1947 · US · BW · 95min

As Republic's one major star, John Wayne flexed his power to make a producing debut with this absorbingly offbeat western on which he promoted his writer buddy, James Edward Grant, to the director's chair. Wayne stars as the injured gunman, nursed back to health by Quakers, who falls for the daughter of the house, Gail Russell. Can Wayne embrace their peaceful ways and avoid firing his six-gun despite the provocation of bad guy Bruce Cabot? Grant's screenplay delivers some gratifying and ingenious twists en route. **AE** *DVD*

John Wayne *Quirt Evans* • Gail Russell *Penelope* • Harry Carey *Wistful McClintock* • Bruce Cabot *Laredo Stevens* • Irene Rich *Mrs Worth* • Lee Dixon *Randy McCall* • Stephen Grant *Johnny Worth* • Tom Powers *Dr Mangrum* ■ *Dir/Scr* James Edward Grant

Angel and Tony ★★★★ 15

Drama
2010 · Fr · Colour · 83min

Clotilde Hesme (*Mysteries of Lisbon*) emerges as one of French cinema's brightest new stars in this superbly controlled drama by director Alix Delaporte (her feature-length debut). Desperate to find stability after a prison term so she can finally raise her young son, Hesme eventually comes across podgy Normandy fisherman Grégory Gadebois. Claire Mathon's seascapes, the pacey editing and Mathieu Maestracci's score are impeccable, as is Gadebois's performance. But it's the intuitive star/director dynamic that makes this such an authentic and affecting experience. **DP** French +subtitles. Swearing, drug abuse, a sex scene, nudity.

Clotilde Hesme *Angèle* • Grégory Gadebois *Tony* • Evelyne Didi *Myriam* • Jérôme Huguet *Ryan* ■ *Dir/Scr* Alix Delaporte

Angel, Angel Down We Go ★

Crime drama
1969 · US · Colour · 93min

Director Robert Thom's staggering folly stars Hollywood legend Jennifer Jones as a porn-movie actress, Roddy McDowall as a rock group member and future soul singer Lou Rawls. It finds rock star Jordan Christopher moving in on a wealthy Hollywood family only to seduce and kill them. Warped, strange and ridiculous, this is an an infamous cult movie disaster. **AJ**

Jennifer Jones *Astrid Steele* • Jordan Christopher *Bogart* • Roddy McDowall *Santoro* • Holly Near *Tara Nicole Steele* • Lou Rawls *Joe* • Charles Aidman *Willy Steele* • Davey Davison *Anna Livia* ■ *Dir/Scr* Robert Thom

An Angel at My Table ★★★★★ 15

Biographical drama
1990 · NZ/Aus/UK · Colour · 151min

Director Jane Campion went on to win a screenplay Oscar for *The Piano*, but this perceptive film biography of New Zealand author Janet Frame had already served notice of her remarkable talent. Based on Frame's autobiographies and put together from a three-part TV mini-series it charts the writer's difficult life, including the eight years she spent in a mental hospital after being wrongly diagnosed as schizophrenic. What could so easily have become a sensationalist exposé of mental shock treatment comes across as a small masterpiece about one woman's triumph in breaking out of life's straitjacket. *Shallow Grave*'s Kerry Fox and Karen Fergusson give superb performances as the grown-up and teenage Janet. **TH** Swearing, nudity. *DVD*

Kerry Fox *Janet Frame* • Karen Fergusson *Teenage Janet* • Alexia Keogh *Young Janet* • Melina Bernecker *Myrtle Frame* • Glynis Angell *Isabel Frame* • Samantha Townsley *Teenage Isabel* • Katherine Murray-Cowper *Young Isabel* • Sarah Smuts Kennedy *June Frame* ■ *Dir* Jane Campion • *Scr* Laura Jones, from the autobiographical books *To the Is-land*, *An Angel at My Table* and *The Envoy from Mirror City* by Janet Frame

A

Angel Baby ★★★
Drama   1961 · US · BW · 97min

Notable as Burt Reynolds's big-screen debut, this is a steely look at the effects of a no-holds-barred evangelical ministry on the deeply suspicious backwoods population of America's southern states. There's plenty of hootin', hollerin' and speakin' in tongues, but the movie cleverly avoids the obvious targets, choosing instead to concentrate on what happens to people within their own community when a collective subconscious is rattled. SH

George Hamilton *Paul Strand* · Mercedes McCambridge *Sarah Strand* · Salome Jens *Angel Baby* · Joan Blondell *Mollie Hays* · Henry Jones *Ben Hays* · Burt Reynolds *Hoke Adams* · Roger Clark *Sam Wilcox* ■ *Dir* Paul Wendkos · *Scr* Orin Borsten, Paul Mason, Samuel Roeca, from the novel *Jenny Angel* by Elsie Oaks Barber

Angel Baby ★★ 15
Romantic drama   1995 · Aus · Colour · 100min

This tale of doomed love stars John Lynch and Jacqueline McKenzie as two psychiatric patients who decide to live together. The two lovers hit the bottom of mental hell, bouncing off the walls as well as each other and the prognosis does not suggest a happy ending. The film suffers from the fact that the two leads sadly lack the depth to pull it off. LH Swearing, nudity.

John Lynch *Harry* · Jacqueline McKenzie *Kate* · Colin Friels *Morris* · Deborra-Lee Furness *Louise* · Daniel Daperis *Sam* · David Argue *Dave* · Geoff Brooks *Rowan* · Humphrey Bower *Frank* ■ *Dir/Scr* Michael Rymer

Angel Eyes ★★★ 15
Romantic drama   2001 · US · Colour · 99min

Director Luis Mandoki's unconventional romance stars Jennifer Lopez as an embittered Chicago cop who's hopelessly at odds with her father and brother's brutality towards their wives. On the streets, however, she is as aggressive as they are until rescued one day by enigmatic drifter Jim Caviezel. A darker slant makes this intriguing, but it's let down by a finale that reeks of schmaltz. LH DVD

Jennifer Lopez *Sharon Pogue* · Jim Caviezel *Catch* · Terrence Howard *Robby* · Sonia Braga *Josephine Pogue* · Jeremy Sisto *Larry Pogue* · Victor Argo *Carl Pogue* · Shirley Knight *Elanora Davis* ■ *Dir* Luis Mandoki · *Scr* Gerald DiPego

Angel Face ★★★★ PG
Crime drama   1953 · US · BW · 91min

Jean Simmons was never happy under contract to Howard Hughes, who made her chop off her hair and wear a wig. She also felt Otto Preminger brutalised her during the making of *Angel Face*, taking rather too much enjoyment in showing Robert Mitchum how to slap her around. The film, however, is a near classic, in which Simmons's beauty is a mask for psychopathy. In this Freudian melodrama, she bumps off her dad and stepmother before turning her sights on the chauffeur (Mitchum). Passion has rarely been depicted so chillingly. AT DVD

Robert Mitchum *Frank Jessup* · Jean Simmons *Diane Tremayne* · Mona Freeman *Mary* · Herbert Marshall *Mr Tremayne* · Leon Ames *Fred Barrett* · Barbara O'Neil *Mrs Tremayne* · Kenneth Tobey *Bill* · Raymond Greenleaf *Arthur Vance* · Jim Backus *Judson* ■ *Dir* Otto Preminger · *Scr* Frank Nugent, Oscar Millard, from a story by Chester Erskine

Angel Heart ★★★ 18
Mystery thriller   1987 · US · Colour · 108min

In Alan Parker's unpleasant, tense thriller set in 1950s New Orleans, Mickey Rourke plays a private detective who's trying to locate a missing person for sinister client Robert De Niro. The trail leads towards voodoo rites, and Rourke's naked romp with Lisa Bonet, as blood drips from the ceiling, caused considerable controversy and received attention from the censors. The story is utter nonsense, dressed up by Parker with much visual hype. AT Violence, swearing, sex scenes, nudity. DVD

Mickey Rourke *Harry Angel* · Robert De Niro *Louis Cyphre* · Lisa Bonet *Epiphany Proudfoot* · Charlotte Rampling *Margaret Krusemark* · Stocker Fontelieu *Ethan Krusemark* · Brownie McGhee *Toots Sweet* · Michael Higgins *Doctor Fowler* · Elizabeth Whitcraft *Connie* ■ *Dir* Alan Parker, from the novel *Falling Angel* by William Hjortsberg

Angel in Exile ★★★ PG
Western   1948 · US · BW · 86min

Ex-convict John Carroll heads for Mexico to recover a cache of stolen gold hidden in a disused mine. Plans to work a scam go awry when his "discovery" convinces the local peasantry that God has worked a miracle for their prosperity. Co-directed by veteran Allan Dwan and Philip Ford, with a cast that includes Thomas Gomez as the village doctor and Adele Mara as his daughter, this modest western has an unusual, ironic and appealing message to accompany its otherwise stock ingredients. RK

John Carroll *Charlie Dakin* · Adele Mara *Raquel Chavez* · Thomas Gomez *Dr Esteban Chavez* · Barton MacLane *Max Giorgio* · Alfonso Bedoya *Ysidro Alvarez* · Grant Withers *Sheriff* · Paul Fix *Carl Spitz* · Art Smith *Ernie Coons* ■ *Dir* Allan Dwan, Philip Ford · *Scr* Charles Larson

Angel in My Pocket ★★★
Comedy   1968 · US · Colour · 105min

Andy Griffith was at his disturbing best in the box-office failure *A Face in the Crowd*, but he seldom moved beyond the safe character he developed in his TV series. This lightweight trifle is an extension of that soft-hearted soul, though Griffith is acted off the screen by Jerry Van Dyke's performance as the most revolting brother-in-law in movie history. The tale of a new minister trying to win over his resentful new community is very American in theme and outlook. TS

Andy Griffith *Samuel D Whitehead* · Jerry Van Dyke *Bubba* · Kay Medford *Racine* · Edgar Buchanan *Axel Chavez* · Gary Collins *Art Shields* · Lee Meriwether *Mary Elizabeth* · Henry Jones *Will Sinclair* · Parker Fennelly *Calvin* ■ *Dir* Alan Rafkin · *Scr* James Fritzell, Everett Greenbaum

Angel in the Family ★★
Seasonal drama   2004 · US · Colour · 88min

In this manipulative festive tale, warring sisters Tracey Needham and Natasha Gregson Wagner are forced to reunite by their sick father's wish for a traditional Christmas at home. So far so routine... until a miracle delivers an unexpected visitor. The mix of drama and fantasy really doesn't gel, prompting director Georg Stanford Brown to launch a distracting final strike of emotion that will either touch your heart or turn your stomach. SF

Meredith Baxter *Lorraine* · Ronny Cox *Buddy* · Tracey Needham *Sarah* · Natasha Gregson Wagner *Beth* · David Chisum *David* · Tess Harper *Mrs Tomkins* ■ *Dir* Georg Stanford Brown · *Scr* Duane Poole

The Angel Levine ★★
Fantasy drama   1970 · US · Colour · 105min

Jewish tailor Zero Mostel, forever complaining to God about his bad luck, finds that black angel Harry Belafonte has been assigned to his case. But even the heavenly presence gets bored with the grumbles – as do we. There are some admirable performances, but as an affirmation of faith it comes across in a very negative fashion. TH

Zero Mostel *Morris Mishkin* · Harry Belafonte *Alexander Levine* · Ida Kaminska *Fanny Mishkin* · Milo O'Shea *Dr Arnold Berg* · Gloria Foster *Sally* · Barbara Ann Teer *Welfare lady* · Eli Wallach *Store clerk* ■ *Dir* Jan Kadar · *Scr* Bill Gunn, Ronald Ribman, from the story by Bernard Malamud

Angel of Mine ★★★ 12
Psychological thriller   2008 · Fr · Colour · 91min

An innocent child is caught in an obsessive tug-of-love between warring mothers in this highly charged psychological thriller. Catherine Frot (*The Page Turner*) plays a divorced woman going through a child-custody battle who stops in her tracks when collecting her son from a party, clearly feeling an unspoken connection with a little girl in a fairy costume. It's not long before the child's mother (Sandrine Bonnaire) is aware of the other woman's attentions, and from there Safy Nebbou's film is permeated by tension as the confrontation between the two mums acquires a steely edge. Frot delivers a performance that inspires chills and sympathy, and is matched by Bonnaire's assured turn as the privileged housewife with something to hide. TJ French +subtitles. DVD

Catherine Frot *Elsa Valentin* · Sandrine Bonnaire *Claire Vigneaux* · Wladimir Yordanoff *Bernard Vigneaux* · Antoine Chappey *Antoine* · Michel Aumont *Alain Valentin* · Sophie Quinton *Laurence* ■ *Dir* Safy Nebbou · *Scr* Cyril Gomez-Mathieu, Safy Nebbou

Angel on My Shoulder ★★★ PG
Fantasy drama   1946 · US · BW · 101min

One of those whimsical fantasies beloved of Hollywood in the 1940s, this has Paul Muni as a murdered gangster sent back to Earth to seek revenge in a deal with ultra-urbane Devil Claude Rains. Muni enjoys himself in the brash leading role, and Anne Baxter is simply delightful as the confused fiancée of the crusading judge whom Rains is trying to discredit. Veteran director Archie Mayo keeps the action moving along and makes good use of the story by Harry Segall. TS DVD

Paul Muni *Eddie Kagle/Judge Parker* · Anne Baxter *Barbara Foster* · Claude Rains *Nick/the Devil* · Onslow Stevens *Dr Matt Higgins* · George Cleveland *Albert* · Hardie Albright *Smiley Williams* · James Flavin *Bellamy* · Erskine Sanford *Minister* ■ *Dir* Archie Mayo · *Scr* Harry Segall, Roland Kibbee, from a story by Harry Segall · *Music* Dimitri Tiomkin [Dmitri Tiomkin]

Angel on the Right ★★★ 12
Comedy drama   2002 · Fr/It/Swi/Tajikistan · Colour · 88min

Combining the grim realities of post-Soviet Tajikistan with the morality of an old Islamic fable, Djamshed Usmonov's disarmingly offbeat comedy is set in his home village of Asht and bathed in washed-out tones. It's something of a family affair, with the director's brother and mother (Maruf Pulodzoda and Uktamoi Miyasarova) headlining the story of a petty hood who is lured into visiting his ailing parent only to be ensnared by irate creditors, who duly proceed to offer him assistance when he's pursued by a vengeful Moscow mobster. Dark and deadpan. DP Tajik +subtitles. Violence. DVD

Uktamoi Miyasarova *Halima* · Maruf Pulodzoda *Hamro* · Kova Tilavpur *Yatim* · Mardonqul Qulbobo *The Mayor* ■ *Dir/Scr* Djamshed Usmonov

The Angel Who Pawned Her Harp ★★ U
Fantasy comedy   1954 · UK · BW · 76min

In one of her first roles, Australian actress Diane Cilento plays an angel sent on a goodwill mission to Earth. Landing in the Angel, Islington, she pawns her harp, wins some dosh on the greyhounds and sets about sorting out the problems of the ordinary folk she encounters. What this dash of whimsy needs is a modicum of tension or humour. AT

Diane Cilento *The Angel* · Felix Aylmer *Joshua Webman* · Jerry Desmonde *Parker* · Robert Eddison *The Voice* · Sheila Sweet *Jenny Lane* · Alfie Bass *Lennox* · Joe Linnane *Ned Sullivan* · Philip Guard *Len Burrows* ■ *Dir* Alan Bromly · *Scr* Charles Terrot, Sidney Cole, from the novel by Terrot

The Angel Wore Red ★★
Romantic drama   1960 · US · BW · 98min

One of the few features to deal with the Spanish Civil War, this improbable romantic drama suffers from confused ideas and unsuitable casting; no wonder it barely saw the light of day in cinemas, being released a year or so after it was filmed. Dirk Bogarde is the priest who falls for prostitute Ava Gardner, but, despite their off-screen friendship, no real romantic sparks are struck and as a result the movie suffers a crippling blow. TS

Ava Gardner *Soledad* · Dirk Bogarde *Arturo Carrera* · Joseph Cotten *Hawthorne* · Vittorio De Sica *General Clave* · Aldo Fabrizi *Canon Rota* · Arnoldo Foà *Insurgent Major* · Finlay Currie *Bishop* · Rossana Rory *Mercedes* ■ *Dir/Scr* Nunnally Johnson

Angela ★★
Drama   1955 · US/It · BW · 91min

Hollywood actor Dennis O'Keefe found himself increasingly in Europe towards the end of his career, and it was there that he wrote, directed and starred in this low-key combination of *Double Indemnity* and *The Postman Always Rings Twice*. Shot entirely on location in Rome, it was one of the movies that brought Italian heart-throb Rossano Brazzi to the attention of the world. O'Keefe does a workmanlike job, but has a real chemistry with Mara Lane in the title role. TS

Dennis O'Keefe *Steve Catlett* · Mara Lane *Angela Towne* · Rossano Brazzi *Nino* · Arnoldo Foà *Captain Ambrosi* · Galeazzo Benti *Gustavo Venturi* · Enzo Fiermonte *Sergeant Collins* ■ *Dir* Dennis O'Keefe · *Scr* Jonathan Rix [Dennis O'Keefe], Edoardo Anton, from a story by Steven Carruthers

Angela ★★★ 15
Romantic crime drama   2002 · It · Colour · 87min

Roberta Torre radically departs from the musical comedies with which she began her career, in this intense, fact-based tale of forbidden passion among the Sicilian Mafia. Torn between loyalty to husband Mario Pupella and lust for handsome newcomer Andrea Di Stefano, debutante Donatella Finocchiaro shatters the stereotype of the gangland consort, while remaining true to its rigid code of honour. With Daniele Cipri's brooding photography intensifying the sense of danger that envelops the affair, this is also a compelling insight into the Mob's status within Palermo society. DP Italian +subtitles. DVD

Donatella Finocchiaro *Angela* · Andrea Di Stefano *Masino* · Mario Pupella *Saro* · Erasmo Lo Bello *Mimmo* · Tony Gambino *Santino* · Matteo Gulino *Paolino* ■ *Dir/Scr* Roberta Torre

Angela's Ashes ★★★ 15
Biographical drama   1999 · US/Ire · Colour · 139min

Frank McCourt's bestselling, Pulitzer Prize-winning memoir is brought vividly to the screen by Alan Parker with a good cast and top-of-the-line production values. The result is a faithful, sometimes pedestrian movie. Parker's decision to film the terrible poverty of the McCourt family – first in America, then in Ireland – with artistic, anaesthetising cinematography is a touch misguided, and Robert Carlyle as Frank's alcoholic dad has much less to do than Emily Watson. But the three boys playing Frank at various ages are all good, and McCourt's early memories of school and church provide some humorous respite. JC DVD

Emily Watson *Angela* · Robert Carlyle *Dad* · Joe Breen *Young Frank* · Ciaran Owens *Middle Frank* · Michael Legge *Older Frank* · Ronnie Masterson *Grandma Sheehan* · Pauline McLynn *Aunt Aggie* · Liam Carney *Uncle Pa Keating* · Eanna MacLiam *Uncle Pat* ■ *Dir* Alan Parker · *Scr* Laura Jones, Alan Parker, from the book by Frank McCourt · *Music* John Williams · *Cinematographer* Michael Seresin

Angèle ★★★★
Melodrama   1934 · Fr · BW · 164min

As with his famous rural trilogy *Marius, Fanny, César*, director Marcel Pagnol is here concerned with the problems of illegitimate pregnancy. The setting is again the Marseille region where he grew up and began work as a teacher. Peasant girl Orane Demazis (then having an affair with the director) is abandoned by her lover and heads for the city where she has their baby and resorts to prostitution to survive. A complex story develops into a representation of feminism within a realistic docudrama that was well ahead of its time. **BB** French +subtitles.

Orane Demazis *Angèle* • Henri Poupon *Clarius Barbaroux* • Fernandel *Saturnin* • Jean Servais *Albin* • Edouard Delmont *Amédée* ■ *Dir* Marcel Pagnol • *Scr* Marcel Pagnol, from the novel *Un de Baumugnes* by Jean Glono

The Angelic Conversation

★★ 🅿🄶

Experimental drama
1985 · UK · Colour and BW · 77min

Gay icon director Derek Jarman takes Shakespeare's sonnets back to their homoerotic roots in his highbrow rumination on the objectivity of desire. As young male figures wash, decorate and make love to each other on rocky seaside coastlines, a female narrator (Judi Dench) explores the subtext of the playwright's poetry in gay terms. Beautifully shot with painterly textures, Jarman's academic treatise will either bore or delight, depending on one's openness to the subject matter. **AJ** *DVD*

Judi Dench *Narrator* ■ *Dir* Derek Jarman • *Scr* Derek Jarman, from sonnets by William Shakespeare • *Music* Benjamin Britten, Coil

Angels & Demons

★★ 🄻🄸

Mystery thriller 2009 · US · Colour · 132min

Tom Hanks and director Ron Howard return for this disappointing sequel to their hit 2006 adaptation of *The Da Vinci Code*. This time Harvard professor Robert Langdon (Hanks) is called upon after the murder of a top physicist is linked to secret society the Illuminati and its plot to kidnap four cardinals and blow up the Vatican. Dan Brown's original bestseller brimmed over with murder, betrayal and religious conspiracies, yet the transfer to film has only emphasised the farcical aspects. Still, the views around Rome are breathtaking, Hanks rises above the material with an easy charm, and Ewan McGregor as an earnest papal aide does his best to bring plausibility to the proceedings. **SuR** English, Italian, French +subtitles. *DVD* 🄱🄻

Tom Hanks *Robert Langdon* • Ewan McGregor *Camerlengo Patrick McKenna* • Ayelet Zurer *Vittoria Vetra* • Stellan Skarsgård *Commander Richter* • Pierfrancesco Favino *Inspector Ernesto Olivetti* • Nikolaj Lie Kaas *Mr Gray/Assassin* • Armin Mueller-Stahl *Cardinal Strauss* ■ *Dir* Ron Howard • *Scr* Akiva Goldsman, David Koepp, from the novel by Dan Brown • *Cinematographer* Salvatore Totino

Angels and Insects

★★ 🄸🄸

Period drama 1995 · UK/US · Colour · 112min

In this precious adaptation of AS Byatt's novella *Morpho Eugenia*, director Philip Haas and his co-writer Belinda Haas have got some pretty tricky ideas to convey (such as Darwinism and the notion that humans are little more than specimens in a celestial laboratory), but they do so in such a pompous manner that the already stilted performances of Mark Rylance and Patsy Kensit border on the comic. Only Kristin Scott Thomas, as a mousey governess, emerges with any credit. **DP** *DVD*

Mark Rylance *William Adamson* • Patsy Kensit *Eugenia Alabaster* • Saskia Wickham *Rowena Alabaster* • Chris Larkin *Robin Swinnerton* • Douglas Henshall *Edgar Alabaster* • Annette Badland *Lady Alabaster* • Kristin Scott Thomas *Matty Crompton* • Jeremy Kemp *Sir Harald Alabaster* ■ *Dir* Philip Haas • *Scr* Philip and Belinda Haas, from the novella *Morpho Eugenia* by AS Byatt

Angel's Dance

★ 🄸🄸

Black comedy thriller 1999 · US · Colour · 98min

Thrillers don't get much more stupid or obnoxious than this jumbled tale of master hitman James Belushi running rookie Kyle Chandler through his paces. The target is eccentric wallflower Sheryl Lee, who wears an ill-fitting dark wig for the first half, so she can make a dramatic (and ludicrous) transformation to cropped blonde avenger when she decides to strike back. **JC** *DVD*

James Belushi *Stevie Rosellini* • Sheryl Lee *Angelica Chaste* • Kyle Chandler *Tony "The Rock" Greco* • Jon Polito *Uncle Vinnie* • Frank John Hughes *Nick* ■ *Dir/Scr* David L Corley [David Corley]

Angels in the Outfield ★★ 🄐

Sports fantasy 1951 · US · BW · 98min

The rough-tongued and ill-tempered manager of a baseball team in need of success calls on celestial help; Paul Douglas heads a cast that includes Janet Leigh. An odd mix of comedy, whimsy and fantasy, this may appeal to those who like their laughs laced with sentimentality. Distinguished Clarence Brown directs, but his expertise is wasted here. **RK**

Paul Douglas *Guffy McGovern* • Janet Leigh *Jennifer Paige* • Keenan Wynn *Fred Bayles* • Donna Corcoran *Bridget White* • Lewis Stone *Arnold P Hapgood* • Spring Byington *Sister Edwitha* • Bruce Bennett *Saul Hellman* • Marvin Kaplan *Timothy Durney* ■ *Dir* Clarence Brown • *Scr* Dorothy Kingsley, George Wells, from a story by Richard Conlin

Angels in the Outfield ★★ 🄐

Sports fantasy 1994 · US · Colour · 93min

This is a flimsy, overly sentimental baseball comedy that wastes the talents of such respected performers as Danny Glover, Christopher Lloyd and Brenda Fricker. Joseph Gordon-Levitt features as a baseball fan who seeks divine intervention to win back his estranged father (Dermot Mulroney) and help his struggling team end its losing streak. It's sickly sweet, but children may be entertained. A TV sequel of sorts, *Angels in the Endzone*, followed. **JF** *DVD*

Danny Glover *George Knox* • Brenda Fricker *Maggie Nelson* • Tony Danza *Mel Clark* • Christopher Lloyd *Al the Angel* • Ben Johnson (1) *Hank Murphy* • Jay O Sanders *Ranch Wilder* • Joseph Gordon-Levitt *Roger* • Milton Davis Jr *J P* • Matthew McConaughey *Ben Williams* • Dermot Mulroney *Roger's father* ■ *Dir* William Dear • *Scr* Dorothy Kingsley, George Wells, Holly Goldberg Sloan

Angels of Evil ★★★★ 🄸🄸

Biographical crime drama 2010 · It/Fr/US · Colour · 122min

Rising Italian star Kim Rossi Stuart is the standout in this fast-paced biography of Milanese gangster Renato Vallanzasca, who fancied himself something of a Robin Hood figure but was a killer of cops and a frequent fugitive from justice. Flashy and accessible, the film tries to pack too much in, but Stuart's performance is the real draw and his commitment to the role allows us to believe Italy's love/hate relationship with this contradictory man, an outlaw who behaved more like a flamboyant rock 'n' roll star than a criminal. **DW** Italian +subtitles. Violence, swearing, sex scenes, drug abuse. *DVD* 🄱🄻

Kim Rossi Stuart *Renato Vallanzasca* • Filippo Timi *Enzo* • Moritz Bleibtreu *Sergio* • Valeria Solarino *Consuelo* • Paz Vega *Antonella D'Agostino* • Francesco Scianna *Francis Turatello* ■ *Dir* Michele Placido • *Scr* Kim Rossi Stuart, Michele Placido, Antonio Leotti, Toni Trupia, Andrea Leanza, Antonella D'Agostino, from a story by Andrea Purgatori, Angelo Pasquini, from the non-fiction books *Il Fiore del Male (The Flower of Evil)* by Renato Vallanzasca and *Lettera a Renato* by Vallanzasca, D'Agostino

Angels One Five ★★★ 🄐

Second World War drama 1952 · UK · BW · 93min

Jack Hawkins, John Gregson and Michael Denison do well in this low-key, intelligent Second World War drama that attempts to show the reality of service life during the Battle of Britain. Director George More O'Ferrall draws on his first-hand knowledge of the subject gained during his own wartime RAF service to probe the emotions behind the British stiff upper lip. A big hit in its day, and still worth the time now. **PF** *DVD* 🄱🄻

Jack Hawkins *Group Captain "Tiger" Small* • Michael Denison *Squadron Leader Peter Moon* • Dulcie Gray *Nadine Clinton* • John Gregson *Pilot Officer "Septic" Baird* • Cyril Raymond *Squadron Leader Barry Clinton* • Veronica Hurst *Betty*

Carfax • Harold Goodwin (2) *Wailes* ■ *Dir* George More O'Ferrall • *Scr* Derek Twist, from a story by Pelham Groom

Angels over Broadway ★★★ 🄐

Drama 1940 · US · BW · 75min

This is an intriguing, tongue-in-cheek blackly comic drama, in which Douglas Fairbanks Jr tries to embroil a suicidal conman in a poker game with the frantically paced help of Rita Hayworth and Thomas Mitchell, playing a mouthy alcoholic with a big idea. The whole film is not as good as the sum of its many diverse parts, although Mitchell gives a truly terrific performance and takes over the screen whenever he appears. **SH**

Douglas Fairbanks Jr *Bill O'Brien* • Rita Hayworth *Nina Barona* • Thomas Mitchell *Gene Gibbons* • John Qualen *Charles Engle* • George Watts *Hopper* • Ralph Theodore *Dutch Enright* • Eddie Foster *Louie Artino* • Jack Roper *Eddie Burns* ■ *Dir* Ben Hecht, Lee Garmes • *Scr* Ben Hecht

The Angels' Share ★★★ 🄸🄸

Comedy drama 2012 · UK/Fr/It · Colour · 100min

It's been billed as Scotland's answer to *The Full Monty*, but this story of a criminal who develops a taste for fine malt whisky doesn't quite have that film's underdog appeal or Everyman quality. The main character, Robbie (Paul Brannigan), is a volatile troublemaker who viciously assaults an innocent man, a crime that sits uneasily with the gentle, Ealing-style comedy that follows. While doing community service for his crime, Robbie visits a distillery, setting in train a plan to siphon off some extremely rare whisky. Brannigan is an engaging lead, but director Ken Loach struggles to find a balance between the film's comic and serious elements. **DW** Violence, swearing. *DVD* 🄱🄻

Paul Brannigan *Robbie Emerson* • John Henshaw *Harry* • Gary Maitland *Albert* • Jasmine Riggins *Mo* • William Ruane *Rhino* ■ *Dir* Ken Loach • *Scr* Paul Laverty

Angels Wash Their Faces ★★★

Drama 1939 · US · BW · 85min

This is a follow-up, as you might have guessed from the rather arch title, to the previous year's classic *Angels with Dirty Faces*, though sadly bereft of that film's stars James Cagney and Pat O'Brien, not to mention director Michael Curtiz. So here's Ann Sheridan, who appeared in the original but in a different role, trying to keep her brother away from those pesky Dead End Kids in a sentimental social opus. It's expertly made, nattily paced and beautifully acted. **TS**

Ann Sheridan *Joy Ryan* • Ronald Reagan *Pat Remson* • Billy Halop *Billy Shafter* • Bonita Granville *Peggy Finnigan* • Frankie Thomas *Gabe Ryan* • Bobby Jordan *Bernie* • Bernard Punsley *Sleepy Arkelian* • Leo Gorcey *Lee Finegan* • Huntz Hall *Huntz* • Gabriel Dell *Luigi* • Henry O'Neill *Mr Remson Sr* ■ *Dir* Ray Enright • *Scr* Michael Fessier, Niven Busch, Robert Buckner, from an idea by Jonathan Finn

Angels with Dirty Faces ★★★★★ 🅿🄶

Classic crime drama 1938 · US · BW · 93min

This is the definitive Warner Bros gangster movie, starring James Cagney in his image-defining role. It's a knockdown, knockout, fast-paced, gritty melodrama, which, though much copied and even parodied, has never been bettered. The tale of two men – one good, one bad – is given extra weight by the casting of the Dead End Kids, headed by Leo Gorcey and Huntz Hall, as Cagney's would-be disciples, and the moral of the story is still valid today. Michael Curtiz directs with great élan, and the ending, as Cagney walks the famous last "mile" to his execution, is particularly well acted and directed. **TS** *DVD*

James Cagney *"Rocky" Sullivan* • Pat O'Brien *Jerry Connelly* • Humphrey Bogart *James Frazier* • Ann Sheridan *Laury Ferguson* • George Bancroft *Mac Keefer* • Billy Halop *"Soapy"* • Bobby Jordan *"Swing"* • Leo Gorcey *"Bim"* •

Gabriel Dell *"Pasty"* • Huntz Hall *"Crab"* ■ *Dir* Michael Curtiz • *Scr* John Wexley, Warren Duff, from a story by Rowland Brown

Anger Management ★★★ 🄸🄸

Comedy 2003 · US · Colour · 100min

Adam Sandler gives a relatively restrained performance here as a mild-mannered businessman who, after a misunderstanding regarding some in-flight headphones, is ordered into anger management under the counsel of spirited shrink Jack Nicholson. Nicholson's methods are unusual – he moves in with Sandler while making a move on his girlfriend Marisa Tomei – but director Peter Segal never really mines the comedy that this pairing and premise deserve. However, this gets by on star power. **IF** Swearing. *DVD* 🄱🄻

Adam Sandler *Dave Buznik* • Jack Nicholson *Dr Buddy Rydell* • Marisa Tomei *Linda* • Luis Guzman *Lou* • Lynne Thigpen *Judge Daniels* • Woody Harrelson *Galaxia/Security guard* • John Turturro *Chuck* • Kurt Fuller *Frank Head* • Jonathan Loughran *Nate* ■ *Dir* Peter Segal • *Scr* David Dorfman

Les Anges du Péché ★★★★★★

Drama 1943 · Fr · BW · 73min

Robert Bresson's remarkable directorial debut set the tone for his entire career. It's an intense study of spirituality about a young novice (Renée Fauré) who sacrifices herself for the moral redemption of an ex-prisoner (Jany Holt) who murders her lover immediately on release. Set mainly in the confines of a convent, the film details the devotional aspects of the nuns' lives while depicting the relationship between the two women, one damned, the other divine. Bresson's later work became increasingly pared-down and austere, but this first outing is almost melodramatic; and, while nothing specifically sexual occurs, it's suffused with an eerie, unspoken eroticism. **AT** French +subtitles.

Renée Fauré *Anne-Marie* • Jany Holt *Thérèse* • Sylvie *Prioress* • Mila Parely *Madeleine* • Marie-Hélène Dasté *Mother St John* ■ *Dir* Robert Bresson • *Scr* Robert Bresson, Jean Giraudoux, RL Brückberger

Angi Vera ★★★★ 🄸🄸

Political drama 1980 · Hun · Colour · 92min

Set in 1948, as Stalinism tightened its grip on Hungary, this handsome drama provides an unsettling insight into political indoctrination. Veronika Papp is wholly convincing as the spirited teenage nurse who is sentenced to a Party correction centre after complaining about hospital conditions and then slowly succumbs to the allure of belonging and the illusion of status. The ease with which she betrays both her ideals and her lover is chilling, but Pal Gabor's stealthy direction leaves no doubt where the blame lies. **DP** Hungarian +subtitles.

Veronika Papp *Vera Angi* • Erzsi Pasztor *Anna Trajan* • Eva Szabo *Maria Muskat* • Tamas Dunai *Istvan Andre* • Laszlo Halasz *Comrade Sas* ■ *Dir* Pal Gabor • *Scr* Pal Gabor, from the novel by Endre Veszi

Angie ★★ 🄸🄸

Comedy drama 1994 · US · Colour · 103min

This should have been the perfect showcase for the talents of Geena Davis. However, Todd Graff's script is such an unconvincing blend of episode and narrative, comedy and melodrama, that she often seems to be acting in a vacuum. Her search for the mother who abandoned her as a child robs the plot of any momentum gained from the ruckus that occurs when she ditches longtime fiancé James Gandolfini for new beau Stephen Rea. **DP** Swearing, nudity.

Geena Davis *Angie Scaccapensieri* • Stephen Rea *Noel* • James Gandolfini *Vinnie* • Aida Turturro *Tina* • Philip Bosco *Frank* • Jenny O'Hara *Kathy* • Michael Rispoli *Jerry* ■ *Dir* Martha Coolidge • *Scr* Todd Graff, from the novel *Angie, I Says* by Avra Wing

The Angriest Man in Brooklyn ★★ 15

Comedy drama 2014 · US · Colour · 80min

Robin Williams plays a New York curmudgeon whose anger knows no bounds. But when stressed doctor Mila Kunis loses patience, and frustratedly but falsely tells him that he has 90 minutes to live, Williams sets out across the city to reconcile with all the friends and family that he's alienated. Competently directed by Phil Alden Robinson, best known for the far superior *Field of Dreams*, this is contrived and occasionally forced, but watchable for its committed performances and a high calibre cast. DA *DVD*

Robin Williams *Henry Altmann* • Mila Kunis *Dr Sharon Gill* • Peter Dinklage *Aaron Altmann* • Melissa Leo *Bette Altmann* • James Earl Jones *Ruben* ■ *Dir* Phil Alden Robinson • *Scr* Daniel Taplitz, from the film *The 92 Minutes of Mr Baum* by Assi Dayan

The Angry Birds Movie ★★★ U

Animated action comedy 2016 · Fin/US · Colour · 97min

In this animated adventure based on the popular smartphone game, Jason Sudeikis provides the voice of an irritable bird named Red, the only angry bird on an island of happy flightless creatures. But soon Red has to call on all his reserves of rage to save his home. The game wasn't what you'd call complex, so understandably the movie doesn't concern itself with too much plot. Unabashedly silly throughout, it boasts a lack of pretension that's quite charming. JL SP

Jason Sudeikis *Red* • Josh Gad *Chuck* • Danny McBride (2) *Bomb* • Bill Hader *Leonard* • Maya Rudolph *Matilda* • Peter Dinklage *Mighty Eagle* ■ *Dir* Clay Kaytis, Fergal Reilly • *Scr* Jon Vitti

The Angry Hills ★★

Second World War spy drama 1959 · UK · BW · 114min

This adaptation of Leon Uris's novel casts Robert Mitchum as an American war correspondent trapped by a Nazi advance in Greece after agreeing to spy for British intelligence. Most of the time he poses in front of olive groves, tries to avoid Gestapo officer Stanley Baker and dallies with Gia Scala. Apart from Mitchum's unavoidable and irrepressible charisma, this war frolic has little to commend it. AT

Robert Mitchum *Mike Morrison* • Stanley Baker *Konrad Heisler* • Elisabeth Mueller *Lisa Kyriakides* • Gia Scala *Eleftheria* • Theodore Bikel *Tassos* • Sebastian Cabot *Chesney* • Peter Illing *Leonides* • Leslie Phillips *Ray Taylor* ■ *Dir* Robert Aldrich • *Scr* Al Bezzerides, from the novel by Leon Uris

The Angry Red Planet ★★ PG

Science fiction 1959 · US · Colour · 79min

A female astronaut under the influence of drugs recalls an expedition to Mars where her team are greeted by giant man-eating plants, three-eyed Martians, Cyclopean blobs, giant bat-spiders and assorted bad vibes. The expressionistic special effects are red-tinted thanks to the film process "Cinemagic" to approximate the distorted, dream-like quality of Nora Hayden's reminiscences. Renowned science fiction director Ib Melchior gives a diverting spin to the familiar Saturday morning serial antics. AJ

Gerald Mohr *O'Banion* • Nora Hayden *Iris Ryan* • Les Tremayne *Professor Gettell* • Jack Kruschen *Sergeant Jacobs* • Paul Hahn *General Treegar* • J Edward McKinley *Professor Weiner* • Tom Daly *Dr Gordon* • Edward Innes *General Prescott* ■ *Dir* Ib Melchior • *Scr* Ib Melchior, Sid Pink, from a story by Pink

The Angry Silence ★★★ PG

Drama 1960 · UK · BW · 90min

Although this fascinating melodrama was made decades ago, its attitudes to trade unionism and industrial action are curiously contemporary. Screenwriter Bryan Forbes explores a range of political issues, but the practised rhetoric sounds false in the mouths of the rank and file, and the best moments are not the confrontations between strike-breaker Richard Attenborough and his workmates, but those depicting the pressures on his marriage. Attenborough gives a sterling performance, but the acting honours go to Pier Angeli as his distraught wife and Alfred Burke as the devious *agent provocateur*. DP *DVD* *BL*

Richard Attenborough *Tom Curtis* • Pier Angeli *Anna Curtis* • Michael Craig *Joe Wallace* • Bernard Lee *Bert Connolly* • Alfred Burke *Travers* • Geoffrey Keen *Davis* • Lawrence Naismith *Martindale* • Oliver Reed *Mick* ■ *Dir* Guy Green • *Scr* Bryan Forbes, from a story by Michael Craig, Richard Gregson

Anguish ★★★★ 18

Horror 1986 · Sp · Colour · 80min

Catalan director Bigas Luna ventures into experimental horror with this extraordinary study in complicit voyeurism that makes the viewer part of the on-screen mayhem. As a grim Oedipal fable unfolds – a maniac hospital orderly (Michael Lerner) is hypnotised by his loony mother (*Poltergeist*'s Zelda Rubinstein) into gouging out eyeballs – the camera pulls back to reveal the audience watching this movie and then follows a killer apeing Lerner's actions. A blackly comic, metaphorical and metaphysical nightmare. AJ

Zelda Rubinstein *Alice Pressman/Mother* • Michael Lerner *John Pressman* • Paul Talia *Patty* • Angel Jove *Killer* • Clara Pastor *Linda* ■ *Dir/Scr* Bigas Luna

Angus ★★★ 12

Comedy drama 1995 · US · Colour · 86min

There's no way you can watch this charming rites-of-passage picture and not end up smiling. Perfectly pitched without a hint of condescension, this will be an inspiration to all those children who have suffered at school because of their weight. Charlie Talbert gives a truly vibrant performance as the amiable, resilient teenager, who not only overcomes the snide teasing of physique fascist James Van Der Beek, but also steals his girl at the prom. Funny, touching and hugely reassuring. DP

Kathy Bates *Meg* • George C Scott *Ivan* • Charlie Talbert *Angus* • Ariana Richards *Melissa Lefevre* • Chris Owen *Troy Wedberg* • Rita Moreno *Madame Rulenska* • Lawrence Pressman *Principal Metcalf* • Anna Thomson *[Anna Levine]* *April Thomas* ■ *Dir* Patrick Read Johnson • *Scr* Jill Gordon, from a short story by Chris Crutcher

Angus, Thongs and Perfect Snogging ★★★★ 12

Comedy drama 2008 · US · Colour · 95min

Four years after *Bride & Prejudice*, Gurinder Chadha directs this very British coming-of-age yarn. Adapted from the first two books in Louise Rennison's *Confessions of Georgia Nicolson* series, the film stars Georgia Groome as the hormonal heroine who is far too clever for her own good. The material may seem familiar, but Chadha has a light touch and never patronises her audience. Instead of gross-out gags, she exploits the dry humour that comes from Georgia's quiet exasperation with her embarrassing parents (played by Alan Davies and Karen Taylor), uncomfortable undies, and sloppy snogs. And Aaron Johnson is surprisingly soulful as the wannabe rock star heart-throb. SP *DVD*

Georgia Groome *Georgia Nicolson* • Alan Davies *Bob Nicolson* • Karen Taylor *Connie Nicolson* • Aaron Johnson *Robbie* • Eleanor Tomlinson *Jas* • Georgia Henshaw *Rosie* • Manjeeven Grewal *Ellen* • Liam Hess *Peter Dyer* ■ *Dir* Gurinder Chadha • *Scr* Gurinder Chadha, Paul Mayeda Berges, Will McRobb, Chris Viscardi, from the novels *Angus, Thongs and Full-Frontal Snogging*, *It's OK, I'm Wearing Really Big Knickers!* by Louise Rennison

Aniki-Bobó ★★★★

Drama 1942 · Por · BW · 70min

Manoel de Oliveira's first feature is a portrait of Oporto street life that is both poetic and highly political. There's a deep irony in the way the kids play cops and robbers without appreciating how the game presages their futures. But their hopes and fears are also touchingly conveyed by the non-professional cast. Yet, despite much of the action being shot from a juvenile perspective, this is more an exercise in innocence than realism. DP Portuguese +subtitles.

Fernanda Matos *Teresinha* • Horacio Silva *Carlitos* • Antonio Santos Eduardinho • Antonio Morais Soares *Pistarim* ■ *Dir* Manoel de Oliveira • *Scr* Manoel de Oliveira, Antonio Lopes Ribeiro, Nascimento Fernandes, from the story *Meninos Milionarios* by Joao Rodrigues de Freitas

The Animal ★ 12

Comedy 2001 · US · Colour · 79min

This gross-out comedy is so dumbed down it's tongue-tied. Although it doesn't contain as many flatulence jokes as some, it does get a lot of mileage from hints about bestiality. Rob Schneider is an inept cop who's seriously injured when his car goes over a cliff. But mad scientist Michael Caton stitches him together with animal parts and so, before long, Schneider has the olfactory ability of a dog, the sexual urges of a stallion and aquatic skills worthy of Flipper. Beastly. TH *DVD*

Rob Schneider *Marvin Mange* • Colleen Haskell *Rianna* • John C McGinley *Sgt Sisk* • Edward Asner *Chief Wilson* • Michael Caton *Dr Wilder* • Louis Lombardi *Fatty* • Guy Torry *Miles* • Adam Sandler *Townie* ■ *Dir* Luke Greenfield • *Scr* Tom Brady, Rob Schneider, from a story by Tom Brady

Animal Attraction ★★ 12

Romantic comedy 2001 · US · Colour · 93min

Ashley Judd – displaying no real flair for this sort of comedy – plays a TV talent agent who's let down in love and vents her spleen by writing an article in a men's magazine that likens the male of the species to bulls. Support for her hypothesis is provided by her randy roommate played by Hugh Jackman. Rising star Jackman is watchable but he has little to sink his teeth into here. DA *DVD*

Ashley Judd *Jane Goodale* • Greg Kinnear *Ray Brown* • Hugh Jackman *Eddie Alden* • Marisa Tomei *Liz* • Ellen Barkin *Diane Roberts* ■ *Dir* Tony Goldwyn • *Scr* Elizabeth Chandler, from the novel *Animal Husbandry* by Laura Zigman

Animal Behavior ★★ PG

Romantic comedy 1989 · US · Colour · 88min

An excellent cast can do little with this weak romantic comedy set on a college campus. Karen Allen is the psychologist studying animal communication who finds it more difficult to get on with her own species, particularly musician Armand Assante. There appears to be little chemistry between Allen and Assante and they are hardly helped by the indecisive script and direction. JF Swearing.

Karen Allen *Alex Bristow* • Armand Assante *Mark Mathias* • Holly Hunter *Coral Grable* • Josh Mostel *Mel Gorsky* • Richard Libertini *Dr Parrish* • Alexa Kenin *Sheila Sandusky* • Jon Mathews *Tyler Forbes* • Nan Martin *Mrs Norton* ■ *Dir* H Anne Riley [Jenny Bowen], H Anne Riley [Kjehl Rasmussen] • *Scr* Susan Rice

Animal Crackers ★★★★ U

Comedy 1930 · US · BW · 92min

"Hooray for Captain Spaulding, the African explorer!". "Did someone call me schnorrer?" asks Groucho Marx, making one of the great cinematic entrances. A relatively straightforward film version of their Broadway hit of the same name, this has the boys helping to recover a valuable painting stolen from a gala party, and was the last Marx Brothers film to be shot in New York before they moved to Hollywood. The requirements of early sound recording render the action somewhat static, but the clowning is irresistible and Margaret Dumont is a perfect foil as Mrs Rittenhouse. TS *DVD*

Groucho Marx *Captain Jeffrey Spaulding* • Harpo Marx *Professor* • Chico Marx *Signor Emanuel Ravelli* • Zeppo Marx *Horatio Jamison* • Lillian Roth *Arabella Rittenhouse* • Margaret Dumont *Mrs Rittenhouse* ■ *Dir* Victor Heerman • *Scr* Morris Ryskind, from the musical play by Ryskind, George S Kaufman

Animal Factory ★★ 15

Prison drama 2000 · US · Colour · 90min

Steve Buscemi's straightforward version of Edward Bunker's novel gets by on the fine performances of all concerned. Basically it charts the growing father-son relationship between hardened convict Willem Dafoe – the big cheese at a hard-boiled penitentiary – as he teaches new inmate Edward Furlong about the power zones in the prison's perilous infrastructure. Overly subtle and unsentimental in its depiction of life behind bars, it consistently feels dramatically undernourished because of this refined stance. AJ *DVD*

Willem Dafoe *Earl Copen* • Edward Furlong *Ron Decker* • John Heard *James Decker* • Tom Arnold *Buck Rowan* • Mickey Rourke *Jan the Actress* • Seymour Cassel *Lt Seeman* • Edward Bunker *Buzzard* • Danny Trejo *Vito* • Steve Buscemi *AR Hosspack* ■ *Dir* Steve Buscemi • *Scr* Edward Bunker, John Steppling, from the novel by Edward Bunker

Animal Farm ★★★★ U

Animated political satire 1954 · UK · Colour · 69min

Made by the award-winning husband-and-wife team of John Halas and Joy Batchelor, this adaptation of George Orwell's searing political allegory was the first feature-length cartoon produced in Britain. Having decided to target an adult audience, the directors had to create characters that were not only faithful to the novel, but were also capable of arousing emotions without resorting to Disney cuteness. Their success in bringing to life the dictatorial Napoleon, the idealistic Snowball and the noble Boxer is aided by the amazingly individual voices provided by one man, Maurice Denham. This provocative and polished production is an all-too-rare attempt to make an intelligent and entertaining animation for adults. DP *DVD* *BL*

Maurice Denham *Voices* • Gordon Heath *Narrator* ■ *Dir* John Halas, Joy Batchelor • *Scr* John Halas, Joy Batchelor, Lothar Wolff, Borden Mace, Philip Stapp, from the novel by George Orwell

Animal Farm ★★ PG

Political satire 1999 · US · Colour · 87min

In its original literary form, George Orwell's 1946 satire of Stalinist Russia provoked readers' minds with its power and intelligence. Here turned into a TV movie, the political allegory falls flat, losing its impact to show-off animatronics and a "guess the celebrity voice" cast. This story of downtrodden farm animals revolting against their master is relentlessly bleak and often too disturbing and ideologically complex for the youngsters it will attract. SF *DVD*

Pete Postlethwaite *Farmer Jones* • Kelsey Grammer *Snowball* • Ian Holm *Squealer* • Julia Louis-Dreyfus *Mollie* • Julia Ormond *Jessie* • Paul Scofield *Boxer* • Patrick Stewart *Napoleon* • Peter Ustinov *Old Major* ■ *Dir* John Stephenson • *Scr* Martyn Burke, Alan Janes, from the novel by George Orwell

The Animal Kingdom ★★★★ PG

Drama 1932 · US · BW · 84min

This highly sophisticated piece might almost be called a "drawing room drama". A wealthy and unconventional publisher (Leslie Howard), marries an unsuitably conventional and shallow wife (Myrna Loy) to the detriment of his ideals, his lifestyle and his most precious relationship, with an artist (Ann Harding). An unusual approach and the lightest of touches elevates a seemingly well-worn storyline to something special. Credit is due to the impeccable screenplay, the elegance of the accomplished cast, David O Selznick's A-grade production values, and Edward H Griffith's direction. RK *DVD*

Ann Harding *Daisy Sage* • Leslie Howard *Tom Collier* • Myrna Loy *Cecilia Henry* • Neil Hamilton *Owen* • William Garçan *Regan* • Henry Stephenson *Rufus Collier* • Ilka Chase *Grace* •

A

Leni Stengel *Franc* • Donald Dillaway *Joe* ■ *Dir* Edward H Griffith • *Scr* Horace Jackson, from the play by Philip Barry

Animal Kingdom ★★★★★ 18
Crime drama　2009 · Aus · Colour · 108min

Australian writer/director David Michôd's feature debut is an astonishingly assured and powerfully gripping work. When socially inept teenager Joshua (James Frecheville) goes to live with his criminal in-laws, he becomes caught in the centre of a bitter feud between his family and renegade police. The performances are exemplary: Ben Mendelsohn is simmering rage personified as a man whose days of criminal supremacy are now behind him; Oscar-nominated Jacki Weaver is terrifying as the grandmother who'll stop at nothing to protect her boys; and Guy Pearce excels as a straight cop who struggles to get Joshua to do the right thing. With its vivid portrayal of a realistically grimy underworld, this is an exciting and challenging thriller that builds to a stunning conclusion. AJ Violence, swearing, drug abuse. **DVD** **BL**

Ben Mendelsohn *Andrew "Pope" Cody* • Joel Edgerton *Barry "Baz" Brown* • Guy Pearce *Det Senior Sgt Nathan Leckie* • James Frecheville *Joshua "J" Cody* • Jacki Weaver *Janine "Smurf" Cody* • Sullivan Stapleton *Craig Cody* ■ *Dir/Scr* David Michôd

Animals United ★★ U
Animated adventure　2010 · Ger · Colour · 89min

Dubbed by a voice cast to die for, this CGI tale follows a group of animals from around the world who are stranded in Africa by a slew of ecological disasters. A polar bear, two giant Galapagos tortoises, a kangaroo - you get the picture - join forces with a meerkat and a vegetarian lion to battle humans for water. The environmental messages and cod philosophy - humans bad, animals good - are rather simplistic and confused for adults, but the slapstick fun may well keep small children amused. SuR German dubbed. **DVD** **BL** **3D**

James Corden *Billy* • Stephen Fry *Socrates* • Andy Serkis *Charles* • Billie Piper *Bonnie* • Dawn French *Angie* • Joanna Lumley *Giselle* • Vanessa Redgrave *Winifred* • Jim Broadbent *Winston* ■ *Dir* Reinhard Klooss, Holger Tappe • *Scr* Reinhard Klooss, from the novel *Die Konferenz der Tiere* by Erich Kästner

Animalympics ★★ U
Animated comedy　1979 · US · Colour · 75min

A cartoon feature that spoofs the Olympics by having animals as athletes. It's a good idea, but the dull story could have done with more jokes and a little less preaching about taking part being more important than winning. Uninspired animation means that the characters are a pretty resistible bunch and not even the voices of Gilda Radner and Billy Crystal can liven them up. DP

Gilda Radner • Billy Crystal • Harry Shearer • Michael Fremer ■ *Dir* Steven Lisberger • *Scr* Steven Lisberger, Michael Fremer, from a story by Lisberger, Roger Allers, John Norton

Anita & Me ★★★ 12
Comedy drama　2002 · UK · Colour · 88min

Although its light-hearted depiction of a Punjabi family settling in a small Midlands village in the early 1970s is rarely more than one-dimensional, Meera Syal's adaptation of her own novel is consistently amusing. At the heart of the story is Asian teenager Meena (Chandeep Uppal), and her relationship with her white neighbour Anita (Anna Brewster), whose sexual maturity and rebellious behaviour alarm Meena's traditionalist family. The above-average cast adds lustre to this enjoyable, if inconsequential movie. JC **DVD**

Chandeep Uppal *Meena* • Anna Brewster *Anita Rutter* • Sanjeev Bhaskar *Papa* • Ayesha Dharker *Mama* • Lynn Redgrave *Mrs Ormerod* • Mark Williams *Uncle Alan* • Max Beesley *Hairy Neddy* • Alex Freeborn *Sam Lowbridge* • Kathy Burke *Deirdre Rutter* • Meera Syal *Auntie Shaila* ■ *Dir* Metin Hüseyin • *Scr* Meera Syal, from her novel

Ankur ★★★★ 15
Drama　1974 · Ind · Colour · 125min

Shyam Benegal (nephew of Bollywood director Guru Dutt) made his feature debut with this astute drama, a key work in the politically committed alternative to mainstream escapism known as Parallel Cinema. Beautifully capturing the sights and sounds of the countryside, Benegal denounces the caste system and provides a fascinating contrast between urban and rural mores in southern India. Shabana Azmi gives a star-making performance as the married servant girl who is seduced by her employer, Anant Nag. DP Hindi +subtitles.

Shabana Azmi *Laxmi* • Anant Nag *Surya* • Sadhu Meher *Kishtaya* • Priya Tendulkar *Saroj* ■ *Dir* Shyam Benegal • *Scr* Shyam Benegal, Satyadev Dubey

Ann Vickers ★★★
Romantic drama　1933 · US · BW · 74min

Expertly directed by the always reliable John Cromwell as a starring vehicle for Irene Dunne, this manages to combine themes of feminism, social conscience, political comment and romance to absorbing effect. Dunne, dignified as ever, shines as a reforming social worker who surmounts life's knocks to gain fame with her humane approach to prison reform, while Walter Huston manages to win her heart. Gritty entertainment, albeit with an element of soapy melodrama - though that, too, has its appeal. RK

Irene Dunne *Ann Vickers* • Walter Huston *Barney Dolphin* • Conrad Nagel *Lindsay* • Bruce Cabot *Resnick* • Edna May Oliver *Malvina* • Sam Hardy *Russell Spaulding* • Mitchell Lewis *Capt Waldo* • Helen Eby-Rock *Kitty Cignac* • Gertrude Michael *Mona Dolphin* ■ *Dir* John Cromwell • *Scr* Jane Murfin, from the novel by Sinclair Lewis

Anna ★★★ 15
Drama　1987 · US · Colour · 95min

Sally Kirkland landed an Oscar nomination for her performance as a fading Czech actress in this beautifully observed but little seen film. Scripted by the Polish director Agnieszka Holland, it is essentially a reworking of *All about Eve*. Kirkland does a nice line in mournful self-effacement, but she's nowhere near as convincing once she becomes jealous of the adoring hopeful (played by debuting supermodel Paulina Porizkova) she has turned into a star. Director Yurek Bogayevicz handles the cast well, but rather loses his grip on the story. DP Swearing, nudity.

Sally Kirkland *Anna* • Robert Fields *Daniel* • Paulina Porizkova *Krystyna* • Gibby Brand *1st director* • John Robert Tillotson *2nd director* • Julianne Gilliam *Woman author* • Joe Aufiery *Stage manager* • Charles Randall *Agent* • Mimi Weddell *Agent's secretary* • Larry Pine *Baskin* ■ *Dir* Yurek Bogayevicz • *Scr* Agnieszka Holland, from a story by Yurek Bogayevicz, Holland

Anna and the King ★★★ 12
Period drama based on a true story
1999 · US · Colour · 142min

With so many versions of this tale already on film, who doesn't know the story of the Victorian widow who travels with her son to tutor the children of the King of Siam? Here Jodie Foster, boasting an immaculate English accent, stars as the plucky governess who melts the heart of the king, played by a surprisingly sweet-natured Chow Yun-Fat. With a heavy emphasis on complicated political machinations and the odd gruesome scene, it's hardly suitable for young ones. SR **DVD**

Jodie Foster *Anna Leonowens* • Chow Yun-Fat *King Mongkut* • Bai Ling *Tuptim* • Tom Felton *Louis Leonowens* • Alwi Syed *The Kralahome* • Randall Duk Kim *General Alak* • Lim Kay Siu *Prince Chowfa* • Melissa Campbell *Princess Fa-Ying* ■ *Dir* Andy Tennant • *Scr* Peter Krikes, Steve Meerson, from diaries of Anna Leonowens

Anna and the King of Siam ★★★ 12
Period drama based on a true story
1946 · US · BW · 122min

Irene Dunne and Rex Harrison star in a stolid (if expensive) 20th Century-Fox adaptation of Margaret Landon's bestseller about English schoolteacher Anna Leonowens. While Dunne was born to play a governess, Harrison is miscast, with facial features more appropriate to Hampstead than Thailand. John Cromwell's direction suffers in comparison to the liveliness of the musical version and the art direction is relentlessly Hollywood Siam, but the sets won an Oscar, as did Arthur Miller's camerawork. TS **DVD**

Irene Dunne *Anna* • Rex Harrison *The King* • Linda Darnell *Tuptin* • Lee J Cobb *Kralahome* • Gale Sondergaard *Lady Thiang* • Mikhail Rasumny *Alak* • Dennis Hoey *Sir Edward* • Tito Renaldo *Prince, as a man* • Richard Lyon *Louis Owens* • William Edmunds *Monshee* • Mickey Roth *Prince, as a boy* ■ *Dir* John Cromwell • *Scr* Talbot Jennings, Sally Benson, from the non-fiction book by Margaret Landon • *Set Designers* Lyle Wheeler, William Darling, Thomas Little, Frank E Hughes

Anna Boleyn ★★★★
Silent biographical drama
1920 · Ger · Tinted · 100min

Recently restored with the original colour tinting, this sumptuous film has a fine cast headed by Henny Porten, Germany's first superstar, and Emil Jannings as a sensual and cruel Henry VIII. Before German-born Ernst Lubitsch went to Hollywood in 1923, he made his reputation with several ironic historical romances like this one, which led to his first being described as having the "Lubitsch Touch". RB

Henny Porten *Anna Boleyn* • Emil Jannings *King Henry VIII* • Paul Hartmann *Sir Henry Norris* • Ludwig Hartau *Duke of Norfolk* • Aud Egede Nissen *Jane Seymour* • Hedwig Pauly *Queen Catherine* • Hilde Müller *Princess Marie* ■ *Dir* Ernst Lubitsch • *Scr* Norbert Falk [Fred Orbing], Hans Kräly

Anna Christie ★★★ U
Drama　1930 · US · BW · 85min

"Gif me a vhiskey, ginger ale on the side - and don't be stingy, baby." These were the first words spoken on the screen in this, her first talkie, by the great Greta Garbo. She's perfectly cast as Eugene O'Neill's lady with a past in this turgid seafront drama, which plays more than a little creaky today. The Swedish *grande dame* also talked in the simultaneously-shot but shorter German language version of this film, and director Jacques Feyder was much more in sympathy with her angst than was this version's director, Clarence Brown. TS

Greta Garbo *Anna Christie* • Charles Bickford *Matt Burke* • George F Marion *Producer* • Marie Dressler *Marthy Owen* • James T Mack [James Mack] • Lee Phelps *Larry, barman* ■ *Dir* Clarence Brown • *Scr* Frances Marion, from the play by Eugene O'Neill

Anna Karenina ★★★★ U
Period romantic drama　1935 · US · BW · 89min

The great Greta Garbo in one of her best-remembered roles, a fine mating of artist and character. This was her second attempt at *Karenina*, having starred with John Gilbert in a notable silent version of the tale in 1927, retitled *Love*. This is very much a *Reader's Digest* version of the great novel, paring the plot down to the bone; it is also overdependent on a splendid, but sometimes disconcertingly multi-accented cast. Garbo's favourite cameraman William Daniels gives a dynamic sheen to the famous final station scene, but the noted MGM production values look a shade creaky today. TS **DVD**

Greta Garbo *Anna Karenina* • Fredric March *Vronsky* • Freddie Bartholomew *Sergei* • Maureen O'Sullivan *Kitty* • May Robson *Countess Vronsky* • Basil Rathbone *Karenin* • Reginald Owen *Stiva* • Reginald Denny *Yashvin* • Phoebe Foster *Dolly* • Gyles Isham *Levin* ■ *Dir* Clarence Brown • *Scr* Clemence Dane, Salka Viertel, SN

Behrman, from the novel by Leo Tolstoy • *Production Designer* Cedric Gibbons • *Costume Designer* Adrian

Anna Karenina ★★★ PG
Period romantic drama　1947 · UK · BW · 133min

The sumptuous production values of this film, combined with the dazzling beauty of Vivien Leigh as Tolstoy's famously doomed heroine, are not enough to prevent it being ultimately a disappointment. It is too long to support the screenplay and the miscasting of a pretty but dull Kieron Moore as Vronsky robs the drama of weight and conviction. Leigh does her best and there are some affecting moments, but only Ralph Richardson, superbly unbending as Karenin, has the measure of the material. RK **DVD**

Vivien Leigh *Anna Karenina* • Ralph Richardson *Alexei Karenin* • Kieron Moore *Count Vronsky* • Sally Ann Howes *Kitty Scherbatsky* • Niall MacGinnis *Levin* • Martita Hunt *Princess Betty Tversky* • Marie Lohr *Princess Scherbatsky* • Michael Gough *Nicholai* • Hugh Dempster *Stefan Oblonsky* ■ *Dir* Julien Duvivier • *Scr* Jean Anouilh, Guy Morgan, Julien Duvivier, from the novel by Leo Tolstoy • *Cinematographer* Henri Alekan • *Costume Designer* Cecil Beaton

Anna Karenina ★★★ PG
Period romantic drama　1985 · US · Colour · 129min

It can't be easy following in the footsteps of Greta Garbo and Vivien Leigh, but Jacqueline Bisset has a decent stab at it in this lavish made-for-TV version of Tolstoy's classic. Bisset has always been a rather nervy performer, conscious of her beauty, and this helps her portrayal of the neurotic heroine who falls for dashing Count Vronsky (Christopher Reeve) and abandons her boring husband (Paul Scofield), with tragic consequences. James Goldman provides a literate compression of the novel's vast expanses. AT

Jacqueline Bisset *Anna* • Christopher Reeve *Count Vronsky* • Paul Scofield *Karenin* • Ian Ogilvy *Stiva* • Anna Massey *Betsy* • Joanna David *Dolly* • Judi Bowker *Kitty* • Valerie Lush *Annushka* • Judy Campbell *Countess Vronsky* ■ *Dir* Simon Langton • *Scr* James Goldman, from Leo Tolstoy's novel

Anna Karenina ★★ 12
Period romantic drama　1997 · US · Colour · 103min

Despite being the first film adaptation to benefit from authentic locations in St Petersburg and Moscow, this is a fairly negligible version of the classic novel. The problem lies in the leaden script and the Euro-pudding casting. Sophie Marceau is pretty but vacuous in the lead, and only James Fox creates any lasting impression as her cuckolded husband. AT

Sophie Marceau *Anna Karenina* • Sean Bean *Vronsky* • Alfred Molina *Levin* • Mia Kirshner *Kitty* • James Fox *Karenin* • Fiona Shaw *Lydia* • Danny Huston *Stiva* • Phyllida Law *Vronskaya* ■ *Dir* Bernard Rose • *Scr* Bernard Rose, from Leo Tolstoy's novel

Anna Karenina ★★ 12
Period romantic drama　2012 · UK · Colour · 124min

After directing Keira Knightley in *Pride & Prejudice* and *Atonement*, Joe Wright casts her again in this left-field adaptation of Tolstoy's epic novel. Knightley does a commendable job of softening the hard edges of the imprudent Russian ingénue, married to Jude Law's older statesman but risking everything in an affair with Aaron Johnson's moody count. And yet she's upstaged by her director at every turn, as he lays it on thick with incongruous camera moves and flashes of surrealism. Clearly, the artifice is a symbol for the hypocrisy of the upper classes, but it trivialises Karenina's suffering. The end result is a beautiful bore. SP Brief swearing, sex scenes. **DVD** **BL**

Keira Knightley *Anna Karenina* • Jude Law *Karenin* • Aaron Taylor-Johnson [Aaron Johnson] *Vronsky* • Kelly Macdonald *Dolly* •

Matthew Macfadyen *Oblonsky* ▪ *Dir* Joe Wright ▪ *Scr* Tom Stoppard, from Tolstoy's novel ▪ *Costume Designer* Jacqueline Durran

Anna Lucasta ★★★
Melodrama   1949 · US · BW · 85min

The luscious Paulette Goddard stars as Anna, gone to the bad in Brooklyn after being thrown out by her Polish immigrant father (Oscar Homolka). She is lured back to her coarse, poor and feckless family in the Midwest who plot to marry her off for money, but the plans go awry. It's directed with a sure hand by Irving Rapper and there's a stand-out supporting performance from Broderick Crawford as her scheming brother-in-law. Solid entertainment that deftly signals the subtexts of incestuous desire and prostitution. RK

Paulette Goddard *Anna Lucasta* ▪ William Bishop *Rudolf Strobel* ▪ Oscar Homolka *Joe Lucasta* ▪ John Ireland *Danny Johnson* ▪ Broderick Crawford *Frank* ▪ Will Geer *Noah* ▪ Gale Page *Katie* ▪ Mary Wickes *Stella* ▪ Whit Bissell *Stanley* ▪ *Dir* Irving Rapper ▪ *Scr* Philip Yordan, Arthur Laurents, from the play by Yordan

Anna Lucasta ★★
Drama   1958 · US · BW · 96min

Philip Yordan's Broadway play, about a girl whose shady past as a sailors' whore catches up with her and almost destroys her chance of a fresh start, was originally staged with an all-black cast. Columbia filmed it in 1949 as an all-white drama and, here, United Artists had Yordan adapt it again, casting Eartha Kitt as Anna with an all-black cast. Kitt acquits herself reasonably well, but Arnold Laven's direction is stagey and the film is utterly lacking in conviction. RK

Eartha Kitt *Anna Lucasta* ▪ Sammy Davis Jr *Danny Johnson* ▪ Frederick O'Neal *Frank* ▪ Henry Scott *Rudolph Slocum* ▪ Rex Ingram (2) *Joe Lucasta* ▪ Georgia Burke *Theresa* ▪ James Edwards *Eddie* ▪ *Dir* Arnold Laven ▪ *Scr* Philip Yordan, from his play

Anna M. ★★15
Psychological drama   2007 · Fr · Colour · 101min

This painstakingly detailed psychological drama was inspired by a collection of case studies about erotomania – the delusion that someone is in love with you. Isabelle Carré (*Private Fears in Public Places*) plays Anna, a shy woman with a boring job who becomes enthralled by her doctor (Gilbert Melki) after a suicide attempt, an obsession that leads to tragedy. Carré carries the film and Melki is exceptional as the distant object of her affection. But the languid pace and over-meticulous treatment of the topic mean the movie is lacking as either entertainment or education. KK French +subtitles. Sex scenes. *DVD*

Isabelle Carré *Anna M* ▪ Gilbert Melki *Dr Andre Zanevsky* ▪ Anne Consigny *Marie Zanevsky* ▪ Geneviève Mnich *Anna's mother* ▪ Gaëlle Bona *Eleonore* ▪ Francis Renaud *Albert* ▪ *Dir/Scr* Michel Spinosa

Annabel Takes a Tour ★★U
Comedy   1938 · US · BW · 66min

Earlier in 1938, RKO's *The Affairs of Annabel* launched a proposed B-comedy series for Lucille Ball, starring as a giddy movie actress whose press agent (Jack Oakie) dreams up a series of screwball publicity stunts. The movie drew the punters, and this first sequel followed hot on its heels. It was also the last. A laboured and less amusing retread of the first film, it lost money and the studio cancelled the series. However, Ball's high-octane appeal is intact. RK

Lucille Ball *Annabel* ▪ Jack Oakie *Lanny Morgan* ▪ Ruth Donnelly *Josephine* ▪ Bradley Page *Webb* ▪ Ralph Forbes *Viscount* ▪ Frances Mercer *Natalie* ▪ Donald MacBride *Thompson* ▪ *Dir* Lew Landers ▪ *Scr* Bert Granet, Olive Cooper, from a story by Joe Bigelow, from characters by Charles Hoffman

Annabelle ★★15
Horror   2014 · US · Colour · 94min

That creepy grinning doll from *The Conjuring* gets its own origin story in this disappointingly banal supernatural spin-off. John Form (Ward Horton) buys a vintage figure decked out in a wedding dress for his expectant wife (Annabelle Wallis) on the day their neighbours are killed by satanic cult members. Directed by *Conjuring* cinematographer John R Leonetti, *Annabelle* is helped initially by its late-1960s setting, but the fear factor decreases rapidly after the well-staged Manson-esque attack. AJ Violence. *DVD* *Blu*

Annabelle Wallis *Mia* ▪ Ward Horton *John* ▪ Tony Amendola *Father Perez* ▪ Alfre Woodard *Evelyn* ▪ *Dir* John R Leonetti ▪ *Scr* Gary Dauberman

Annapolis ★★12
Sports drama   2005 · US · Colour · 99min

In this amalgam of *Top Gun* and *An Officer and a Gentleman*, James Franco plays a working-class kid whose boxing skills land him a spot at the prestigious Annapolis Naval Academy. Tyrese Gibson plays Franco's sadistic drill sergeant – in other words, the Lou Gossett Jr character – while Jordana Brewster is a sympathetic officer he meets in a bar (that's Kelly McGillis in *Top Gun* covered). As a recruitment film for the US armed forces, this has some dubious merit, but otherwise it's a depressingly predictable affair. JF Swearing *DVD*

James Franco *Jake Huard* ▪ Tyrese Gibson *Cole* ▪ Jordana Brewster *Ali* ▪ Donnie Wahlberg *Lt Burton* ▪ Vicellous Shannon *Twins* ▪ McCaleb Burnett *Whitaker* ▪ *Dir* Justin Lin ▪ *Scr* Dave Collard

An Annapolis Story ★★★
Wartime romance   1955 · US · Colour · 81min

Director Don Siegel makes the most of this tale of two brothers (John Derek and Kevin McCarthy), both cadets at the Annapolis naval academy, who fall out over a girl (Diana Lynn). Their relationship is temporarily poisoned, but the boys eventually settle their differences while on active service in Korea. The personal drama is lent veracity by authentic location filming at Annapolis (complete with flag-waving passing-out parades) and on board a real aircraft carrier. RK

John Derek *Tony Scott* ▪ Diana Lynn *Peggy Lord* ▪ Kevin McCarthy *Jim Scott* ▪ Alvy Moore *Willie* ▪ Pat Conway *Dooley* ▪ LQ Jones *Watson* ▪ John Kirby *Macklin* ▪ Barbara Brown *Mrs Scott* ▪ *Dir* Don Siegel ▪ *Scr* Daniel B Ullman, Geoffrey Homes [Daniel Mainwaring], from a story by Daniel B Ullman

Anne and Muriel ★★★★15
Romantic drama   1971 · Fr · Colour · 124min

Inspired by his fascination with the Brontës, François Truffaut reverses the situation in *Jules et Jim* with this elegiac tale of doomed love. An unbearably sad film, this is as much about the passion of creativity as it is about romance, as Jean-Pierre Léaud's art critic is capable only of appreciating the beauty of English sisters Kika Markham and Stacey Tendeter rather than being captivated by it. Shot in desaturated colour to convey the turn-of-the-century atmosphere, the film also employs written material, voiceovers and a range of cinematic devices to enhance the intimacy of the story. DP French +subtitles. *DVD* *Blu*

Jean-Pierre Léaud *Claude Roc* ▪ Kika Markham *Anne Brown* ▪ Stacey Tendeter *Muriel Brown* ▪ Sylvia Marriott *Mrs Brown* ▪ Marie Mansart *Madame Roc* ▪ Philippe Léotard *Diurka* ▪ François Truffaut *Narration* ▪ *Dir* François Truffaut ▪ *Scr* Jean Gruault, François Truffaut, from the novel by Henri-Pierre Roché

Anne Devlin ★★★PG
Historical drama   1984 · Ire · Colour · 121min

Pat Murphy's film is a fitting tribute to Anne Devlin, the peasant's daughter who, as Robert Emmett's confidante, played a key role in the struggle for Irish independence in the early 19th century. Deftly equating political liberation with female emancipation, Murphy is content to focus on character rather than events, and she's helped by the affecting simplicity of Thaddeus O'Sullivan's photography and

Brid Brennan's committed performance. Her pacing is a touch too deliberate, however. DP

Brid Brennan *Anne Devlin* ▪ Bosco Hogan *Robert Emmett* ▪ Des McAleer ▪ Gillian Hackett ▪ *Dir* Pat Murphy ▪ *Scr* Pat Murphy, from journals by Anne Devlin

Anne Frank Remembered ★★★★
Documentary   1995 · US/UK/Neth · Colour · 122min

The figure of Anne Frank has become so symbolic of the horrors of the Holocaust that the girl behind the Second World War diary has been obscured. But in this powerful, Oscar-winning documentary, writer/director Jon Blair restores the Jewish teenager's humanity, painting a candid and vivid portrait of a vivacious youngster whose promising life was cut short by Nazi oppression. Poignant eyewitness accounts add intimacy to a wealth of extraordinary archival footage and photographs, while Blair's respectful treatment of her tragic fate ensures that the Nazis' other victims – including her own family – are never forgotten. SF

Kenneth Branagh *Narrator* ▪ Glenn Close ▪ *Dir* Jon Blair ▪ *Scr* Jon Blair, from the diary by Anne Frank

Anne of Green Gables ★★★U
Drama   1934 · US · BW · 77min

This is the definitive movie version (it had been filmed before in 1919) of LM Montgomery's popular tale about the teenage orphan. Child actress Dawn O'Day changed her professional name to that of the film's character, and as Anne Shirley delivered an exquisite, utterly charming performance. This is a real one-off: the 1940 sequel *Anne of Windy Poplars* is feeble by comparison, and Shirley was not nearly as beguiling as a grown-up, though she did have a useful screen career. TS

Anne Shirley ▪ Tom Brown *Gilbert Blythe* ▪ OP Heggie *Matthew Cuthbert* ▪ Helen Westley *Marilla Cuthbert* ▪ Sara Haden *Mrs Barry* ▪ Murray Kinnell *Mr Phillips* ▪ Gertrude Messinger *Diana* ▪ June Preston *Mrs Blewett's daughter* ▪ Charley Grapewin *Dr Tatum* ▪ Hilda Vaughn *Mrs Blewett* ▪ *Dir* George Nichols Jr ▪ *Scr* Sam Mintz, from the novel by LM Montgomery

Anne of Windy Poplars ★★U
Drama   1940 · US · BW · 85min

Six years after the charming film version of author LM Montgomery's popular *Anne of Green Gables* came this routine sequel, with the now grown-up Anne teaching in one of those small towns where everyone (except kindly old folks) is hypocritical or corrupt, or both. Anne Shirley is once again played by Anne Shirley, the former Dawn O'Day, who changed her name to that of her character. TS

Anne Shirley ▪ James Ellison *Tony Pringle* ▪ Henry Travers *Matey* ▪ Patric Knowles *Gilbert Blythe* ▪ Slim Summerville *Jabez Monkman* ▪ Elizabeth Patterson *Rebecca* ▪ Louise Campbell *Katherine Pringle* ▪ Joan Carroll *Betty Grayson* ▪ *Dir* Jack Hively ▪ *Scr* Michael Kanin, Jerry Cady, from the novel by LM Montgomery

Anne of the Indies ★★★U
Swashbuckling adventure   1951 · US · Colour · 79min

Jean Peters stars here as the swashbuckling scourge of the Caribbean, shown off in fine Technicolor and surrounded by old reliables James Robertson-Justice as the first mate, Herbert Marshall as the rummy doc and Thomas Gomez as Blackbeard himself. Louis Jourdan is the dashing Frenchman who is forced into luring the pirate queen into a treasure-baited trap, while 1950s icon Debra Paget plays Jourdan's kidnapped wife. Director Jacques Tourneur seems more than comfortable with this splendid seafaring tale. TS

Jean Peters *Anne* ▪ Louis Jourdan *Captain Pierre François La Rochelle* ▪ Debra Paget *Molly* ▪ Herbert Marshall *Dr Jameson* ▪ Thomas Gomez *Blackbeard* ▪ James Robertson-Justice *Red Dougal* ▪ Francis Pierlot *Herkimer* ▪ Sean McClory *Hackett* ▪ Holmes Herbert *English sea captain* ▪ *Dir* Jacques Tourneur ▪ *Scr* Phillip Dunne, Arthur Caesar, from a story by Herbert Ravenel Sass

Anne of the Thousand Days ★★★PG
Historical drama   1969 · US · Colour · 139min

Producer Hal Wallis's inventive and flamboyant slice of English history was a surprising hit, reviving a moribund genre and providing marvellous showcases for Richard Burton, as a roistering but soulful Henry VIII, and Geneviève Bujold, touchingly well cast as Anne Boleyn. The period interiors, largely re-created at Shepperton studios, are beautifully designed and detailed. Margaret Furse's costumes rightly won an Oscar; a shame, then, that the direction is insipid and poorly paced. TS *DVD*

Richard Burton *King Henry VIII* ▪ Geneviève Bujold *Anne Boleyn* ▪ Irene Papas *Catherine of Aragon* ▪ Anthony Quayle *Cardinal Wolsey* ▪ John Colicos *Cromwell* ▪ Michael Hordern *Thomas Boleyn* ▪ Katharine Blake *Elizabeth Boleyn* ▪ Peter Jeffrey *Norfolk* ▪ William Squire *Thomas More* ▪ Valerie Gearon *Mary Boleyn* ▪ Elizabeth Taylor *Courtesan* ▪ *Dir* Charles Jarrott ▪ *Scr* Bridget Boland, John Hale, from the play by Maxwell Anderson, adapted by Richard Sokolove ▪ *Cinematographer* Arthur Ibbetson ▪ *Art Directors* Maurice Carter, Lionel Couch, Patrick McLoughlin

Annie ★★★U
Musical   1982 · US · Colour · 122min

John Huston was the wrong director for this long-winded version of the Broadway musical based on the popular American comic strip. He lacks the necessary light touch that might have made this the equal of the stage production, and he's not helped by the casting of heavyweight Albert Finney as bald Daddy Warbucks and grimacing Tim Curry as a villain. However, Carol Burnett is a zesty Miss Hannigan and Aileen Quinn is appealing as the moppet of the title, while real class is brought to the proceedings by Broadway divas Bernadette Peters and Ann Reinking. TS *DVD* *Blu*

Albert Finney *Daddy Warbucks* ▪ Carol Burnett *Miss Hannigan* ▪ Bernadette Peters *Lily* ▪ Ann Reinking *Grace Farrell* ▪ Tim Curry *Rooster* ▪ Aileen Quinn *Annie* ▪ Geoffrey Holder *Punjab* ▪ Roger Minami *Asp* ▪ *Dir* John Huston ▪ *Scr* Carol Sobieski, from the musical by Thomas Meehan, Charles Strouse, Martin Charnin, from the comic strip *Little Orphan Annie* by Harold Gray

Annie ★★★U
Musical   1999 · US · Colour · 88min

The musical that gives thousands of showbiz mums the chance to push their little darlings on the stage gets the Walt Disney treatment in this occasionally saccharine but enjoyably bumptious TV movie. Newcomer Alicia Morton is little orphan Annie, who gradually thaws the heart of millionaire Daddy Warbucks (Victor Garber). As usual, though, it's the baddie who steals the show, and Kathy Bates is a memorable Miss Hannigan. JF *DVD*

Victor Garber *Daddy Warbucks* ▪ Kathy Bates *Miss Hannigan* ▪ Audra McDonald *Grace Farrell* ▪ Kristin Chenoweth *Lily* ▪ Alan Cumming *Rooster* ▪ Alicia Morton *Annie* ▪ *Dir* Rob Marshall ▪ *Scr* Irene Mecchi, from the musical by Thomas Meehan, Charles Strouse, Martin Charnin, from the comic strip *Little Orphan Annie* by Harold Gray

Annie ★★PG
Musical   2014 · US · Colour · 113min

The 1977 Broadway hit has suffered an overblown 1982 adaptation, a sickly 1999 TV movie and a terrible stage sequel. But the worst hadn't happened to it until this misconceived and sloppy remake. Quvenzhané Wallis from *Beasts of the Southern Wild* is consistently winning as the afro-haired waif under the foster care of benefits grabbing drunk Cameron Diaz (whose performance is way too broad). How Annie and cynical billionaire Will Stacks

A

(a merely adequate Jamie Foxx) help each other find love and family remains the key insight – but only just, under Will Gluck's haphazard direction. AJ **DVD**

Jamie Foxx *Will Stacks* • Quvenzhané Wallis *Annie* • Cameron Diaz *Miss Hannigan* • Rose Byrne *Grace* • Bobby Cannavale *Guy* ■ *Dir* Will Gluck • *Scr* Aline Brosh McKenna, Will Gluck, from the musical by Thomas Meehan, from the comic strip *Little Orphan Annie* by Harold Gray

Annie Get Your Gun
★★★★★ **U**

Musical western   1950 • US • Colour • 103min

MGM's wonderfully zesty film of Irving Berlin's Broadway smash stars a perfectly cast Betty Hutton as Annie Oakley, replacing an ailing (and, to tell the truth, unsuitable) Judy Garland. George Sidney's bravura direction gets the most out of a marvellous score, which includes such classics as *Anything You Can Do (I Can Do Better)* and *There's No Business Like Show Business*. Handsome Howard Keel makes an impressive movie musical debut as sharp-shooting Frank Butler, and the Technicolor and costume design are particularly ravishing. It's hard to see how this could have been any better. TS **DVD**

Betty Hutton *Annie Oakley* • Howard Keel *Frank Butler* • Louis Calhern *Buffalo Bill* • J Carrol Naish *Chief Sitting Bull* • Edward Arnold *Pawnee Bill* • Keenan Wynn *Charlie Davenport* • Benay Venuta *Dolly Tate* • Clinton Sundberg *Foster Wilson* ■ *Dir* George Sidney (2) • *Scr* Sidney Sheldon, from the play by Herbert Fields, Dorothy Fields • *Cinematographer* Charles Rosher • *Music/lyrics* Irving Berlin • *Music* Adolph Deutsch, Roger Edens

LANDMARK FILM
This much-imitated romantic comedy refines the battle-of-the-sexes genre and strengthens the independent sector

Annie Hall
★★★★★ **15**

Romantic comedy   1977 • US • Colour • 89min

Although Woody Allen had still to acquire great technical strength as a film-maker, this was the movie where he found his own singular voice, a voice that echoes across events with a mixture of exuberance and introspection. Peppered with hilarious, snappy insights into the meaning of life, love, psychiatry, ambition, art and New York, this comic delight also gains considerably from the spirited playing of Diane Keaton as the kooky innocent from the Midwest, and Woody himself as the fumbling New York neurotic. The narrative runs parallel to the real-life relationship between the two leads, and the film scooped four Oscars, including best film and screenplay (co-written with Marshall Brickman) for Allen, and best actress for Keaton. JM Swearing. **DVD** **BD**

Woody Allen *Alvy Singer* • Diane Keaton *Annie Hall* • Tony Roberts *Rob* • Carol Kane *Allison* • Paul Simon *Tony Lacey* • Shelley Duvall *Pam* • Janet Margolin *Robin* • Colleen Dewhurst *Mom Hall* • Christopher Walken *Duane Hall* • Donald Symington *Dad Hall* • Helen Ludlam *Grammy Hall* • Mordecai Lawner *Alvy's dad* • Joan Newman *Alvy's mom* • Jonathan Munk *Alvy aged nine* ■ *Dir* Woody Allen • *Scr* Woody Allen, Marshall Brickman

Annie Laurie
★★★ **U**

Silent romantic melodrama
1927 • US • BW and Colour • 96min

Because Lillian Gish's sweet image was out of step with the vogue for flappers and jazz babies, it was said that MGM humiliated her by giving her this, which one critic called "soggy haggis". This tale of clan warfare, in which a governor's daughter has to choose between a Campbell and a MacDonald, is rather tritely handled, yet Gish is as radiant as ever. There is some splendid camerawork, and the recently restored two-tone Technicolor scenes are lovely, but the picture was a box-office failure. RB

Lillian Gish *Annie Laurie* • Norman Kerry *Ian MacDonald* • Creighton Hale *Alastair* • Joseph Striker *Alastair* • Hobart Bosworth *The MacDonald Chieftain* • Patricia Avery *Enid* • Russell Simpson *Sandy* • Brandon Hurst *The Campbell Chieftain* ■ *Dir* John S Robertson • *Scr*

Josephine Lovett, Marian Ainslee (titles), Ruth Cummings (titles), from a story by Josephine Lovett • *Cinematographer* Jack Parker

Annie Oakley
★★★ **U**

Western   1935 • US • BW • 86min

The story of America's most famous female sharpshooter here becomes a vehicle for Barbara Stanwyck. It was her first western, and she copes well enough, though she seems far too contemporary in looks and attitude for the feisty Ms Oakley. However, this is a still a thoroughly enjoyable early work from George Stevens, who went on to direct such classics as *A Place in the Sun* (1951), *Shane* (1953) and *Giant* (1956). Suave Melvyn Douglas and handsome Preston Foster both score highly in a film that studiously ignores history throughout. TS

Barbara Stanwyck *Annie Oakley* • Preston Foster *Toby Walker* • Melvyn Douglas *Jeff Hogarth* • Moroni Olsen *Buffalo Bill* • Pert Kelton *Vera Delmar* • Andy Clyde *Macivor* • Chief Thundercloud *Sitting Bull* • Margaret Armstrong *Mrs Oakley* • Delmar Watson *Wesley Oakley* ■ *Dir* George Stevens • *Scr* Joel Sayre, John Twist, from a story by Joseph A Fields, Ewart Adamson

Annie's Coming Out
★★ **PG**

Drama based on a true story
1984 • Aus • Colour • 88min

A cerebral palsy victim is confined to a state mental institution despite being highly intelligent, and has to fight to prove she is more than a vegetable. An interesting premise – based on a true story – ends up as TV-movie-of-the-week fodder thanks to a cumbersome soundtrack and an annoying tendency to raise questions without actually providing any answers to them. While it never quite rises above a run-of-the-mill weepie, this nonetheless features solid performances from the leads. JB

Angela Punch McGregor *Jessica Hathaway* • Drew Forsythe *David Lewis* • Tina Arhondis *Annie O'Farrell* • Monica Maughan *Vera Peters* • Mark Butler *Dr John Monroe* • Philippa Baker *Sister Waterman* ■ *Dir* Gil Brealey • *Scr* John Patterson, Chris Borthwick, from the non-fiction book by Rosemary Crossley

Annie's Point
★★

Comedy drama   2005 • US • Colour • 84min

The life lessons come thick and fast in this sugary morality tale about following your dreams no matter what. Betty White, star of TV's *The Golden Girls*, sparkles as the titular headstrong pensioner who embarks on an eventful 2,000-mile road trip to scatter her late husband's ashes at his favourite beauty spot. With Annie's aspiring singer granddaughter (Amy Davidson) as a reluctant companion, the two generations find themselves bonding over a series of mischievous escapades. The film is corny, predictable and relentlessly manipulative, but it still leaves you with a warm glow when the end credits roll. SF

Betty White *Annie Eason* • Richard Thomas *Richard Eason* • Amy Davidson *Julia Eason* • Ellen Albertini Dow *Louise Tette* • Robert F Lyons *Jack Backis* • Patrick Weller *John Dybdahl* ■ *Dir* Michael Switzer • *Scr* Mike Leonardo

The Anniversary
★★★ **PG**

Black comedy   1968 • UK • Colour • 90min

Here, Hollywood *grande dame* Bette Davis provides the scares, and some laughs, as an eyepatch-wearing virago ruling an ill-assorted family in England's suburbia. The rest of the cast is no match for Davis, but Sheila Hancock, Jack Hedley and, particularly, James Cossins, hold their own. This Hammer slice of *Grand Guignol* was based on a play and, despite *Brighton Rock* cinematographer Harry Waxman's excellent colour photography, the atmosphere is resolutely theatrical. Still, Davis is always watchable. TS **DVD**

Bette Davis *Mrs Taggart* • Sheila Hancock *Karen Taggart* • Jack Hedley *Terry Taggart* • James Cossins *Henry Taggart* • Christian Roberts *Tom Taggart* • Elaine Taylor *Shirley Blair* • Timothy Bateson *Mr Bird* • Arnold Diamond *Headwaiter* ■ *Dir* Roy Ward Baker • *Scr* Jimmy Sangster, from the play by Bill MacIlwraith

The Anniversary Party
★★★★ **18**

Relationship drama   2001 • US • Colour • 110min

British actor Alan Cumming and American star Jennifer Jason Leigh wrote and directed this tantalising tale about marriage and Hollywood. Set at the sixth anniversary party of an actress (Leigh) and her writer/director husband (Cumming), it gives us a voyeuristic opportunity to imagine the lives of the rich and famous, with inside stories and drug-fuelled revelations. It's made possible by superb performances from a terrific cast, the immediacy of digital video and the straightforward approach of the co-directors. JB Sex scenes, swearing, drug abuse. **DVD**

Alan Cumming *Joe Therrian* • Jennifer Jason Leigh *Sally Nash* • Gwyneth Paltrow *Skye Davidson* • Kevin Kline *Cal Gold* • Phoebe Cates *Sophia Gold* • Jane Adams (2) *Clair Forsyth* • John C Reilly *Mac Forsythe* • John Benjamin Hickey *Jerry Adams* • Parker Posey *Judy Adams* ■ *Dir/Scr* Alan Cumming, Jennifer Jason Leigh

Año Uña
★★★ **15**

Romantic drama
2007 • Mex • Colour and BW • 78min

Jonás Cuarón (son of *Y Tu Mamá También* director Alfonso Cuarón) adopts an innovative approach in this offbeat drama, which is made up entirely of photographs, in the manner of Chris Marker's 1962 sci-fi gem *La Jetée*. Cuarón took the snaps over the course of a year and organised them into a storyline that chronicles the blossoming relationship between Molly (Eireann Harper), an American college student on an exchange programme in Mexico City, and Diego (Diego Cataño), the 14-year-old son of her landlady. At the outset, the technique of using voiceovers to animate the still sequences feels a touch self-conscious. DP English, Spanish +subtitles.

Eireann Harper *Molly* • Diego Cataño *Diego* • Michèle Alban *Grandma Michèle* • Cristina Orozco *Grandma Cristina* • Mariana Elizondo *Mom* • Pia Elizondo *Aunt* ■ *Dir/Scr* Jonás Cuarón

Anomalisa
★★★★★ **15**

Animated comedy drama
2015 • US • Colour • 86min

Charlie Kaufman's achingly humane puppet film isn't quite like anything you've seen before. Pundit Michael (voiced by David Thewlis) arrives at a conference, where everyone around him seems to be from the same mould and speaks with the same voice (that of Tom Noonan). The only exception is Lisa (Jennifer Jason Leigh), a young woman who's ashamed of a facial scar. But to a man bored with the sameness around him, Lisa is a beautiful anomaly. There's no easily extractable message here but somehow the film says something very profound about our need to believe that we and our loved ones are unique and special. LF Swearing, sex scenes, nudity. **DVD** **BD**

David Thewlis *Michael Stone* • Jennifer Jason Leigh *Lisa* • Tom Noonan *Everyone else* ■ *Dir* Charlie Kaufman, Duke Johnson • *Scr* Charlie Kaufman

The Anomaly
★★ **15**

Science-fiction thriller
2014 • UK • Colour • 96min

This admirably ambitious but poorly realised sci-fi thriller from British writer/director/actor Noel Clarke combines elements of *Total Recall*, *The Bourne Identity* and *The Matrix*. The action takes place in the near future, where an ex-soldier (Clarke) keeps waking up in different situations with absolutely no memory of what has happened during the intervening periods. The fight scenes are effectively staged, but a promising premise is let down by ropey acting, inexplicable plot developments and clunky dialogue. SC Violence, swearing, sex scenes, nudity. **DVD** **BD**

Noel Clarke *Ryan* • Ian Somerhalder *Harkin Langham* • Alexis Knapp *Dana* • Luke Hemsworth *Agent Elkin* • Brian Cox (1) *Dr Langham* ■ *Dir* Noel Clarke • *Scr* Simon Lewis

Anonyma: a Woman in Berlin
★★ **15**

Wartime drama
2008 • Ger/Pol • Colour • 126min

This enterprising yet slightly underwhelming fact-based drama details the traumatic experiences of German women left in Berlin when the city fell to the Russians at the end of the Second World War. It's adapted from the memoirs of an anonymous female journalist whose first-hand testimony of the mass rape inflicted by the occupying forces caused shockwaves in Germany when it was published in 1959. (Her identity was revealed as Marta Hillers after her death in 2001.) Max Färberböck's undeniably earnest film rather soft-pedals the horrors of the situation, preferring to trace the unlikely human connection that develops between Nina Hoss's heroine and her high-ranking Soviet protector (a broodingly impressive Yevgeni Sidikhin). TJ In German, Russian. **DVD** **BD**

Nina Hoss *Anonyma* • Yevgeni Sidikhin *Andreij Rybkin* • Irm Herrmann [Irm Hermann] *Witwe* • Rüdiger Vogler *Eckhart* ■ *Dir* Max Färberböck • *Scr* Max Färberböck, from the diary *Eine Frau in Berlin* by Anonyma [Marta Hillers]

Anonymous
★★★★ **12**

Period drama
2011 • US/UK/Ger • Colour • 124min

Director Roland Emmerich, better known for blockbusters such as *Independence Day* and *2012*, abandons over-the-top special effects for this meticulous and seductive period drama. At its heart is the question of who really wrote Shakespeare's works: the Bard (Rafe Spall) is portrayed as an imbecilic actor, while the Earl of Oxford (Rhys Ifans) is shown to be the man truly holding the quill. *Anonymous* is poignant and shocking by turns, while maintaining an entertaining pace. Amid the stellar cast, Ifans, in particular, excels, and the movie also boasts amazing production, lighting and costume design. KK Some violence, sex scenes, swearing. **DVD** **BD**

Rhys Ifans *Earl of Oxford* • Vanessa Redgrave *Queen Elizabeth I* • Joely Richardson *Princess Elizabeth Tudor* • David Thewlis *William Cecil* • Sebastian Armesto *Ben Jonson* • Rafe Spall *William Shakespeare* ■ *Dir* Roland Emmerich • *Scr* John Orloff

Another Country
★★★★ **15**

Drama   1984 • UK • Colour • 86min

This is the film that should have made Rupert Everett a bigger star than he is. His electrifying performance as a homosexual public schoolboy barred from an exclusive prefects' society is at once endearing and arrogant. Directed by Marek Kanievska, from Julian Mitchell's adaptation of his own play about the background to the Burgess/MacLean spy scandal, the tale only clicks into credibility when Everett goes into outsider mode. A wonderfully flamboyant exposure of the making of a traitor, this deserved more acclaim than it got. TH Swearing, a sex scene.

Rupert Everett *Guy Bennett* • Colin Firth *Tommy Judd* • Michael Jenn *Barclay* • Robert Addie *Delahay* • Anna Massey *Imogen Bennett* • Betsy Brantley *Julie Schofield* • Rupert Wainwright *Devenish* • Tristan Oliver *Fowler* • Cary Elwes *Harcourt* ■ *Dir* Marek Kanievska • *Scr* Julian Mitchell, from the play by Julian Mitchell

Another Dawn
★★

Romantic adventure   1937 • US • BW • 74min

Errol Flynn made some classic adventure movies in the 1930s, but this isn't one of them. Everyone involved seems to be treading water: his co-star this time is Kay Francis, who was one of Warner's highest paid female stars until Bette Davis came on the scene. The story is a love triangle, with Francis marrying Ian Hunter yet lusting after Flynn, a British army officer. The Arabs, meanwhile, cause the Empire problems whenever the story gets bogged down. AT

Errol Flynn *Captain Denny Roark* • Kay Francis *Julia Ashton* • Ian Hunter *Colonel John Wister* • Frieda Inescort *Grace Roark* • Herbert Mundin *Wilkins* • Billy Bevan *Hawkins* • Kenneth Hunter *Sir Charles Benton* ■ *Dir* William Dieterle • *Scr* Laird Doyle

Another Day/Another Time ★★★ 12

Music documentary 2013 · US · Colour · 97min

Folk music forms the backbone of the Coen Brothers' exquisitely downbeat *Inside Llewyn Davis*, and this filmed concert, in New York's historic Town Hall in September 2013, features many of the musicians on the soundtrack. Director Chris Wilcha cuts between the stage of this packed, appreciative house and a rehearsal room two days earlier, providing a more intimate, off-duty portrait of players as diverse as Joan Baez, Patti Smith, Jack White and Marcus Mumford of Mumford & Sons. The showstopper is a rendition by Dave Rawlings and house band the Punch Brothers of Woody Guthrie's epochal *This Land Is Your Land*, not heard in the movie. AC Swearing. *DVD* *BL*

T Bone Burnett • Oscar Isaac • Carey Mulligan • Gillian Welch • Joan Baez • Patti Smith • Marcus Mumford • Jack White ■ *Dir* Christopher Wilcha

Another Day in Paradise ★★★★ 18

Drama 1998 · US · Colour · 101min

Director Larry Clark's compelling glimpse into outlaw life in the American Midwest during the 1970s is not as controversial as his first feature, *kids*, but it's just as grim and gritty. In this disturbing look at thug bravado, a charismatic drugs dealer (James Woods) persuades a teenage runaway (Vincent Kartheiser) and his junkie girlfriend (Natasha Gregson Wagner) to help him pull a bank heist. It's when things go horribly wrong and the dysfunctional "family" is torn apart that this devastating road movie really hits home. As Woods's heroin-addicted lover, Melanie Griffith gives the performance of her career in a shocking tale. AJ Violence, swearing, drug abuse. *DVD*

James Woods *Mel* • Melanie Griffith *Sid* • Vincent Kartheiser *Bobbie* • Natasha Gregson Wagner *Rosie* • James Otis *Reverend* • Branden Williams *Danny* • Brent Briscoe *Clem* • Peter Sarsgaard *Ty* • Lou Diamond Phillips *Jules* ■ *Dir* Larry Clark • *Scr* Christopher Landon, Stephen Chin, from the novel by Eddie Little

Another Earth ★★★ 12

Science-fiction drama 2011 · US · Colour · 88min

Destiny and guilt are the twin themes of this low-key sci-fi drama, in which a planet remarkably similar to our own suddenly appears in the sky. Brit Marling stars as a high-school student who is driving under the influence when, distracted by the planet, she slams into another car, putting its driver (William Mapother) into a coma and killing his wife and child. Following her release from prison, Marling poses as a free cleaning service in a desperate bid to make things right. Despite its high-concept premise, this is actually a quiet and often hypnotically beautiful character piece, and its soulful qualities more than make up for some very dubious leaps of logic. DW Some sex scenes. *DVD* *BL*

Brit Marling *Rhoda Williams* • William Mapother *John Burroughs* • Matthew-Lee Erlbach *Alex* • DJ Flava *DJ Flava* • Meggan Lennon *Maya Burroughs* • Jordan Baker *Kim Williams* ■ *Dir* Mike Cahill • *Scr* Mike Cahill, Brit Marling

Another 48 HRS ★★ 18

Comedy thriller 1990 · US · Colour · 91min

Although original stars of *48 HRS*, Eddie Murphy and Nick Nolte, are reunited with director Walter Hill, all three seem to be going through the motions. Nolte is the same rough-and-ready cop who is forced to team up again with con Murphy, this time in a bid to salvage his career. Murphy here verges on self-parody, but the action is

spectacular enough. JF Swearing, violence, nudity. *DVD* *BL*

Eddie Murphy *Reggie Hammond* • Nick Nolte *Jack Cates* • Brion James *Ben Kehoe* • Kevin Tighe *Blake Wilson* • Ed O'Ross *Frank Cruise* • David Anthony Marshall *Willy Hickok* • Andrew Divoff *Cherry Ganz* • Bernie Casey *Kirkland Smith* ■ *Dir* Walter Hill • *Scr* John Fasano, Jeb Stuart, Larry Gross, from a story by Fred Braughton, from characters by Roger Spottiswoode, Walter Hill, Larry Gross, Steven E de Souza

Another Life ★★ 15

Period drama 2000 · UK · Colour · 101min

Back in the early 1920s, the Edith Thompson case was a *cause célèbre*, with thousands signing a petition for leniency after her sailor beau, Freddy Bywaters, murdered her intransigent husband, Percy. However, little of that drama surfaces in Philip Goodhew's unpersuasive period piece. Natasha Little plays Edith with guilt, but neither Ioan Gruffudd nor his victim, Nick Moran, are up to the task. DP

Natasha Little *Edie Thompson* • Nick Moran *Percy Thompson* • Ioan Gruffudd *Freddy Bywaters* • Imelda Staunton *Ethel Graydon* • Rachael Stirling *Avis Graydon* ■ *Dir/Scr* Philip Goodhew

Another Man, Another Chance ★★★

Period romantic drama 1977 · Fr/US · Colour · 127min

This French take on the American western by Claude Lelouch is also a retake, 11 years on, of his most romantic movie of the 1960s, *Un Homme et une Femme*, as the lives of widow Geneviève Bujold, a 19th-century French settler, and widower James Caan, a Yankee vet, intersect. A bit long for what it has to say, but there are some deliciously wry moments (Caan demonstrating he's a worse shot than his young son, for example) and a feeling that people are worth the effort. TH

James Caan *David Williams* • Geneviève Bujold [Geneviève Bujold] *Jeanne* • Francis Huster *Francis Leroy* • Jennifer Warren *Mary* • Susan Tyrrell *Debbie/"Miss Alice"* • Rossie Harris *Simon* • Linda Lee Lyons *Sarah* ■ *Dir/Scr* Claude Lelouch

Another Man's Poison ★

Crime melodrama 1951 · UK · BW · 90min

Bette Davis crossed the Atlantic with her *Now, Voyager* director Irving Rapper and her husband Gary Merrill for this tale of a lady novelist residing on the Yorkshire moors. Engaged in an affair with her secretary's fiancé (Anthony Steel), she is provoked by her husband's return into murdering him. Utter drivel. RK

Bette Davis *Janet Frobisher* • Gary Merrill *George Bates* • Emlyn Williams *"Dr" Henderson* • Anthony Steel *Larry Stevens* • Barbara Murray *Chris Dale* • Reginald Beckwith *Mr Bigley* • Edna Morris *Mrs Bunting* ■ *Dir* Irving Rapper • *Scr* Val Guest, from a play by Leslie Sands

Another 9½ Weeks ★★ 18

Erotic drama 1997 · US · Colour · 100min

Mickey Rourke returns to the role that made him (in)famous but he really shouldn't have bothered – this is an utterly pointless and flaccid affair. Here, moody rich bloke Rourke is still pining for Elizabeth (Kim Basinger in the original) and travels to Paris where he hooks up with a fashion designer (Angie Everhart). Director Anne Goursaud gives it a glossy surface sheen, but Rourke sleepwalks through the film. JF Swearing, violence, sex scenes.

Mickey Rourke *John* • Angie Everhart *Lea* • Agathe de la Fontaine *Claire* • Steven Berkoff *Vittorio* • Dougray Scott *Charlie* ■ *Dir* Anne Goursaud • *Scr* Mick Davis, from a character created by Elizabeth McNeil

Another Part of the Forest ★★

Drama 1948 · US · BW · 106min

Lillian Hellman's prequel to *The Little Foxes* (which was filmed in 1941), shows how the awful Hubbard brood clawed and insinuated their way into Southern high society. The

movie's stage origins are evident in every static scene, while the social criticism points to left-wing views for which director Michael Gordon was later blacklisted. There are some good performances, though, notably from Fredric March and Ann Blyth. AT

Fredric March *Marcus Hubbard* • Ann Blyth *Regina Hubbard* • Edmond O'Brien *Ben Hubbard* • Florence Eldridge *Lavinia Hubbard* • Dan Duryea *Oscar Hubbard* • John Dall *John Bagtry* • Dona Drake *Laurette* ■ *Dir* Michael Gordon • *Scr* Vladimir Pozner, from the play by Lillian Hellman

Another Shore ★★ U

Comedy 1948 · UK · BW · 73min

This is one of the least distinguished films produced by Ealing during its golden age. Part of the problem lies in the unbearable whimsy of the plot, in which customs official Robert Beatty's dreams of living on a South Sea island are brought within touching distance by rich dipsomaniac Stanley Holloway. However, the real problem is the failure of Charles Crichton and his design team to re-create the atmosphere of postwar Dublin. DP *DVD*

Robert Beatty *Gulliver Shiels* • Stanley Holloway *Alastair McNeil* • Moira Lister *Jennifer Stockley* • Michael Medwin *Yellow Bingham* • Maureen Delaney *Mrs Gleason* • Fred O'Donovan *Coghlan* • Sheila Manahan *Nora* • Wilfrid Brambell *Moore* ■ *Dir* Charles Crichton • *Scr* Walter Meade, from the novel by Kenneth Reddin

Another Stakeout ★★ PG

Action comedy 1993 · US · Colour · 104min

Richard Dreyfuss and Emilio Estevez are reteamed for a sequel to the box office smash *Stakeout*, but here the chemistry is missing. Once again, the two bickering cops find themselves on surveillance duty, this time watching a potential witness in a Mob trial, played by Cathy Moriarty, and with feisty Assistant DA Rosie O'Donnell along for the ride. The comic playing between the three leads can't be faulted, but this is just a retread. JF Violence, swearing. *DVD*

Richard Dreyfuss *Chris Lecce* • Emilio Estevez *Bill Reimers* • Rosie O'Donnell *Gina Garrett* • Madeleine Stowe *Maria* • Dennis Farina *Brian O'Hara* • Marcia Strassman *Pam O'Hara* • Cathy Moriarty *Lu Delano* • Miguel Ferrer *Tony Castellano* ■ *Dir* John Badham • *Scr* Jim Kouf, from his characters

Another Thin Man ★★ U

Detective comedy 1939 · US · BW · 98min

The third in the massively popular series appeared after a two-year gap in which star William Powell had been absent from MGM through illness. This reunion with Myrna Loy, Asta the dog and director WS Van Dyke is very much the formula as before - witty and sophisticated Nick and Nora Charles trade wisecracks in between solving a few murders - with the addition of a baby, Nick Jr. Lacking the edge of its predecessors, it signals the decline of the series. *Shadow of the Thin Man* continued the series in 1941. RK *DVD*

William Powell *Nick Charles* • Myrna Loy *Nora Charles* • Virginia Grey *Lois MacFay* • Otto Kruger *Van Slack* • C Aubrey Smith *Colonel MacFay* • Ruth Hussey *Dorothy Waters* • Nat Pendleton *Lt Guild* • Patric Knowles *Dudley Horn* ■ *Dir* WS Van Dyke • *Scr* Frances Goodrich, Albert Hackett, from a story by Dashiell Hammett

Another Time, Another Place ★ U

Second World War melodrama 1958 · UK · BW · 91min

This tale casts the glamorous Lana Turner as an unlikely American news reporter in England during the Second World War, who becomes embroiled in a love affair with married war correspondent Sean Connery (yet to find stardom). Tragedy strikes, and Lana spends the rest of director Lewis Allan's turgid film consoling his widow (Glynis Johns) in the unconvincing setting of a Cornish village. RK *DVD*

Lana Turner *Sara Scott* • Sean Connery *Mark Trevor* • Barry Sullivan *Carter Reynolds* • Glynis Johns *Kay Trevor* ■ *Dir* Lewis Allen • *Scr* Stanley Mann, from the novel by Lenore Coffee

Another Time, Another Place ★★★★ 15

Second World War drama 1983 · UK · Colour · 91min

This was one of the first *Films on Four*, and it set a precedent for the innovative work to come. It also marked the directorial debut of Michael Radford, whose glorious *Il Postino* was nominated for a slew of Oscars in 1996. This thoughtful Second World War drama takes a sharp but sympathetic look at a lonely young woman who becomes fascinated by the Italian prisoners of war incarcerated nearby. Phyllis Logan and Gregor Fisher give sterling performances in a film that subtly avoids the story's obvious pitfalls. SH *DVD*

Phyllis Logan *Janie* • Giovanni Mauriello *Luigi* • Gian Luca Favilla *Umberto* • Claudio Rosini *Paolo* • Paul Young *Dougal* • Gregor Fisher *Beel* • Tom Watson *Finlay* • Jennifer Piercey *Kirsty* • Denise Coffey *Meg* • Yvonne Gilan *Jess* ■ *Dir* Michael Radford • *Scr* Michael Radford, from the novel by Jessie Kesson

Another Woman ★★★★ PG

Drama 1988 · US · Colour · 78min

One of the few Woody Allen movies to have disappeared swiftly on release, this complex, highly structured look at the great questions of life, love and death contains a stunning performance from Gena Rowlands as a rather smug, self-absorbed college professor who is forced to question her assumed truths. This is Allen at his most serious, often verging on pretentiousness, but there is plenty of food for thought and some able support from Ian Holm, Gene Hackman and Mia Farrow before the infamous parting. SH *DVD*

Gena Rowlands *Marion Post* • Mia Farrow *Hope* • Ian Holm *Ken Post* • Blythe Danner *Lydia* • Gene Hackman *Larry* • Betty Buckley *Kathy* • Martha Plimpton *Laura Post* • John Houseman *Marion's father* • Sandy Dennis *Claire* • David Ogden Stiers *Young Marion's father* ■ *Dir/Scr* Woody Allen

Another Woman ★★ 15

Romantic thriller 1994 · Can/US/Ger · Colour · 89min

Unlike her *Family Ties* co-star Michael J Fox, Justine Bateman's film career has failed to shine and she has tended to find herself consigned to formulaic TV fare such as this so-so thriller. She plays a millionaire's wife who, thanks to a convenient bout of amnesia, gets to rebuild her marriage. However, her new-found happiness is soon under threat. Bateman does her best, but the intriguing story never kicks into life. JF Nudity, some violence. *DVD*

Justine Bateman *Lisa Temple* • Peter Outerbridge *Paul Temple* • Kenneth Welsh *Dr Ken Holcross* • Amy Stewart *Bonnie Temple* • James Purcell *Joe Dooley* ■ *Dir* Alan Smythe [Steven Hilliard Stern] • *Scr* Lee Langley, Jim Henshaw, Lyle Slack, from the novel by Margot Dalton

Another Year ★★★★ 12

Comedy drama 2010 · UK · Colour · 124min

A gifted director of women, Mike Leigh follows *Vera Drake* and *Happy-Go-Lucky* with yet another beautifully performed character piece. The focus appears to be happily married couple Jim Broadbent and Ruth Sheen, but into this picture of suburban bliss lurches Lesley Manville, a friend of Sheen's from work whose boozing, flakiness and emotional neediness quickly become a bore for the whole family. Manville's performance, however, gives what could have been an unsympathetic character a fragility and poignancy, providing a profound emotional charge, and Leigh's simple, subtle film is all the richer for it. DW *DVD*

Jim Broadbent *Tom* • Lesley Manville *Mary* • Ruth Sheen *Gerri* • Peter Wight *Ken* • Oliver Maltman *Joe* • David Bradley (2) *Ronnie* • Philip Davis *Jack* • Imelda Staunton *Janet* ■ *Dir/Scr* Mike Leigh

Another You ★ 15
Comedy 1991 · US · Colour · 90min

Richard Pryor looks very ill indeed in this lame comedy. The combined talents of the stars can't paper over a nondescript plot and lacklustre dialogue. There are numerous tasteless jokes about mental illness – Gene Wilder has just been released from the local sanatorium – but nothing can disguise Pryor's deep-seated problems. SH Swearing. *DVD*

Gene Wilder *George/Abe Fielding* • Richard Pryor *Eddie Dash* • Mercedes Ruehl *Elaine/Mimi Kravitz* • Stephen Lang *Dibbs* • Vanessa Williams [Vanessa L Williams] *Gloria* • Jerry Houser *Tim* • Kevin Pollak *Phil* ■ *Dir* Maurice Phillips • *Scr* Ziggy Steinberg

The Ant Bully ★★ U
Animated fantasy adventure
2006 · US · Colour · 85min

The communist ethos of an ant hill is a hefty subject for this animation from the *Jimmy Neutron* team. Moody ten-year-old Lucas finds himself reduced to the size of the ants that he's been pestering. With the help of kindly mentor Hova (voiced by Julia Roberts), Lucas has to learn to work with the ants rather than against them if he's ever to be returned to his natural size. Sadly, in a film that's been so lovingly animated and acutely observed, the message is too overt to be entertaining. And, after the far superior *Antz* and *A Bug's Life*, and the *Honey, I Shrunk the Kids* franchise, little here seems fresh or appealing. SuR *DVD BL*

Julia Roberts *Hova* • Nicolas Cage *Zoc* • Meryl Streep *Queen Ant* • Paul Giamatti *Stan Beals* • Zach Tyler *Lucas Nickle* • Regina King *Kreela* • Bruce Campbell *Fugax* • Lily Tomlin *Mommo* ■ *Dir* John A Davis • *Scr* John A Davis, from a story by John Nickle

Ant-Man ★★★ 12
Action adventure 2015 · US · Colour · 112min

This Marvel superhero is no household name like Spider-Man or the Hulk. Ant-Man made his comic-book debut in 1962, and is the alter ego of scientist Hank Pym, who shrinks to the size of an ant but with super-strength. However, in this light-hearted adventure, Pym (Michael Douglas) recruits ex-con cat burglar Scott Lang (Paul Rudd) to put on the Ant-Man suit to help stop the invention being used for nefarious purposes. Rudd's deadpan quips are on target and the rapid-fire size-changing is effectively handled, too, but it's jesting not jousting that wins out here. JA Some swearing. *DVD BL sp cs*

Paul Rudd *Scott Lang/Ant-Man* • Michael Douglas (1) *Hank Pym* • Evangeline Lilly *Hope Van Dyne* • Corey Stoll *Darren Cross/Yellowjacket* • Michael Peña [Michael Pena] *Luis* • Anthony Mackie *Sam Wilson/Mackie* • Bobby Cannavale *Paxton* • Judy Greer *Maggie* ■ *Dir* Peyton Reed • *Scr* Edgar Wright, Joe Cornish, Paul Rudd, Adam McKay, from a story by Wright, Cornish, from characters by Jack Kirby (artist), Stan Lee, Larry Lieber (writers)

La Antena ★★★★ PG
Fantasy drama 2007 · Arg · BW · 97min

This dazzlingly inventive fantasy from Argentinian director Esteban Sapir is pleasingly intricate and packed with stock heroes and villains. It's set in the "City without a Voice", whose population has been struck dumb by the TV broadcasts of the sinisterly omnipresent Alejandro Urdapilleta. Opposing his nefarious scheme is unassuming inventor Rafael Ferro and it is he alone who can save mystery singer Florencia Raggi and frustrate Urdapilleta's plan to steal the very words of the citizenry. Drawing on the look and mood of such expressionist classics as *Metropolis*, this is a brilliant pastiche of silent screen style with its inspired use of captions, silhouette and studio-bound décor. A gem. DP Spanish +subtitles. *DVD*

Alejandro Urdapilleta *Mr TV* • Valeria Bertuccelli *Mr TV's son* • Julieta Cardinali *Nurse* • Rafael Ferro *The Inventor* • Raúl Hochman *Mouse man* • Jonathan Sandor *Tomas* • Carlos Piñeiro *Doctor Y* • Florencia Raggi *The Voice* ■ *Dir/Scr* Esteban Sapir

Anthony Adverse ★★★★
Period swashbuckling drama
1936 · US · BW · 142min

A mammoth epic based on an even more mammoth popular novel, this splendid Warner Bros period melodrama offers many rewards, most notably the spectacle of a studio in its prime using all its facilities to the utmost. Unsurprisingly, this movie won Oscars for best cinematography, best editing and best score. Apply those elements to a rousing swashbuckler about a hero (an effective Fredric March) whose one true love (Olivia de Havilland at her peak) is swept away from him, and the result is very satisfying. The tale takes its time to unfold, but stick with it, especially for Gale Sondergaard's Oscar-winning debut performance. TS

Fredric March *Anthony Adverse* • Olivia de Havilland *Angela Guessippi* • Edmund Gwenn *John Bonnyfeather* • Claude Rains *Don Luis* • Anita Louise *Maria* • Louis Hayward *Denis Moore* • Gale Sondergaard *Faith Paleologus* • Steffi Duna *Neleta* • Billy Mauch *Anthony as a child* • Donald Woods *Vincent Nolte* • Akim Tamiroff *Carlo Cibo* • Rollo Lloyd *Napoleon Bonaparte* ■ *Dir* Mervyn LeRoy • *Scr* Sheridan Gibney, from the novel by Hervey Allen • *Cinematographer* Tony Gaudio • *Music* Erich Wolfgang Korngold • *Editor* Ralph Dawson

Antibodies ★★★★ 18
Crime thriller 2005 · Ger · Colour · 122min

Gripping from the stylish opening salvo, writer/director Christian Alvart's psycho-thriller is tense, edgy and daring. Did arrested serial killer, the disturbingly deadpan André Hennicke, also kill a girl in a suburban German village? If not, then who did? Upstanding country cop Wotan Wilke Möhring suspects someone local, but the imprisoned lunatic has a malevolent psychodrama in store. The stark twists and fiendishly clever turns taken by this crisply shot frightener are extraordinarily potent. AJ German +subtitles.

Wotan Wilke Möhring *Michael Martens* • Heinz Hoenig *Seiler* • André Hennicke [Andre Hennicke] *Gabriel Engel* • Ulrike Krumbiegel *Rosa Martens* • Hauke Diekamp *Christan* • Nina Proll *Lucy* • Jürgen Schornagel *Sucharzewski* ■ *Dir/Scr* Christian Alvart

Antichrist ★★★ 18
Horror drama
2009 · Den/Ger/Fr/Swe/Pol/It/Bel · Colour and BW · 101min

In Danish auteur Lars von Trier's controversial horror, Willem Dafoe and Charlotte Gainsbourg play nameless characters who make love while their unattended toddler son climbs out of a window and falls to his death. Gainsbourg's grief appears to intensify her sexual appetite as the couple retreat to a rural cabin where Gainsbourg previously worked on an abortive research project on witchcraft. The film is at times revolting (explicit genital mutilation), silly (a talking fox), even tedious. But Von Trier ultimately creates a grey, foreboding world that possesses the oppressive atmosphere of a Grimm fairy tale and then mounts a battle of the sexes that will haunt viewers long after the grisly denouement. BP Sex scenes, violence. *DVD BL*

Willem Dafoe *He* • Charlotte Gainsbourg *She* ■ *Dir/Scr* Lars von Trier • *Cinematographer* Anthony Dod Mantle

Anti-Social ★★ 15
Crime drama 2015 · Hun/UK · Colour · 115min

Taking inspiration from news reports about burka-wearing gangs smashing their way through shopping malls, this caricature of an East End gangster flick is remarkably soft-edged in its brutality. Josh Myers (grandson of the real Michael Myers, the UK distributor John Carpenter named his *Halloween* maniac after) plays the serial robber who drags his sensible street artist brother (Gregg Sulkin) into the shady underworld. Reg Traviss's artless thriller meanders for nearly two long hours as Traviss searches for cockney cool but can't

find it, in the one-note flimsy plot that's worsened by weak acting. AJ

Gregg Sulkin *Dee* • Meghan Markle *Kirsten* • Josh Myers *Marcus* • Christian Berkel *Philip* ■ *Dir/Scr* Reg Traviss

Antitrust ★★ 12
Thriller 2000 · US · Colour · 104min

In this contrived thriller, Ryan Phillippe stars as a computer whizzkid who abandons his idealism to work for giant software corporation Nurv. Once there, he discovers there's a link between the suspicious deaths of computer programmers outside the company and the ground-breaking new codes that Nurv is developing. Tim Robbins's performance as a corporate software executive is worthy of a better film, but Phillipe gets little to do apart from stare at a screen. SuR Brief violence, swearing. *DVD*

Ryan Phillippe *Milo Hoffmann* • Rachael Leigh Cook *Lisa Calighan* • Claire Forlani *Alice Poulson* • Tim Robbins *Gary Winston* • Douglas McFerran *Bob Shrot* • Richard Roundtree *Lyle Barton* • Yee Jee Tso *Teddy Chin* ■ *Dir* Peter Howitt • *Scr* Howard Franklin

Antiviral ★★★★ 15
Science-fiction horror thriller
2012 · Can/Fr · Colour · 103min

Brandon Cronenberg picks up the body-horror baton from father David in this exceptional debut feature that echoes his dad's early sci-fi perversions, *Shivers* and *Videodrome* in particular. In a sterile near future, sick celebrities sell their diseases to obsessed fans. Impeccably cast Caleb Landry Jones (*X-Men: First Class*) smuggles top viruses out of the workplace in his body for illegal pirate use. While the movie is too long for its own good, young Cronenberg never loses his quirky conceptual focus or viscerally unsettling aesthetic in a visually pristine cautionary tale that is not for the faint-hearted. AJ Violence. *DVD*

Caleb Landry Jones *Syd March* • Sarah Gadon *Hannah Geist* • Malcolm McDowell *Dr Abendroth* • Douglas Smith (2) *Edward Porris* • Joe Pingue *Arvid* ■ *Dir/Scr* Brandon Cronenberg

Anton Corbijn: Inside Out ★★★ 15
Documentary
2012 · Ire/Neth/Bel · Colour · 81min

This documentary about rock-star snapper turned film director Anton Corbijn (*Control*, *The American*) shadows him at work and at home, and attempts to paint a fuller picture of the man whose striking and iconic images of the likes of Joy Division, U2 and Depeche Mode have influenced countless other photographers. Director Klaartje Quirijns observes quietly as Corbijn puts George Clooney, Lou Reed and others through their paces. Friends and family offer more intimate assessments of him, but Corbijn ultimately remains, at least partially, a man of mystery. TeS English, Dutch +subtitles. Swearing. *DVD*

Anton Corbijn • *Dir* Klaartje Quirijns

Antonia's Line ★★★ 15
Drama 1995 · Bel/UK/Neth · Colour · 98min

Combining pastoral fantasy and magic realism, feminist polemic and humanist compassion, Marleen Gorris's vibrant drama won the Oscar for best foreign film, albeit in a poor year. Sprawling over five decades, the action boasts a spirited start, as Willeke van Ammelrooy returns to her home village after the war and introduces us to a gallery of eccentric characters. The tale then loses its way, with the opening's life-affirming joy replaced by a stiff sense of moral rectitude. DP Dutch +subtitles. Violence, swearing, sex scenes, nudity. *DVD*

Willeke van Ammelrooy *Antonia* • Els Dottermans *Danielle, Antonia's daughter* • Jan Decleir *Bas* • Marina de Graaf *Deedee* • Mil Seghers *Crooked Finger* • Fran Waller Zeper *Olga* • Jakob Beks *Farmer Daan* • Jan Steen *Loony Lips* ■ *Dir/Scr* Marleen Gorris

Antonio das Mortes ★★★★ 15
Political drama 1969 · Bra · Colour · 99min

Returning to the barren *sertao* plain, Glauber Rocha's sequel to *Black God, White Devil* (1964) was one of the key films in the second phase of the Brazilian *cinema nôvo* revival, known as "cannibal-tropicalist" for its heavy emphasis on allegorical symbolism. Rocha won the best director prize at Cannes for this first colour feature, but the decision to turn Antonio (Maurício do Valle) from an establishment assassin into a revolutionary hero of the peasantry did not impress the junta, and he was hounded into decade-long European exile. Almost politicising the spaghetti western, this is highly stylised yet effective film-making. DP Portuguese +subtitles. *DVD*

Mauricio do Valle *Antonio das Mortes* • Hugo Carvana *Police Chief Mattos* • Odete Lara *Laura* • Othon Bastos *Professor* • Jofre Soares *Colonel Horacio* • Lorival Pariz *Coirana* ■ *Dir/Scr* Glauber Rocha

Antony and Cleopatra ★★★
Historical drama 1972 · UK · Colour · 138min

Charlton Heston played Mark Antony in 1949, then again in 1970, both times in film versions of *Julius Caesar*. Here he begs comparisons with Olivier by directing and starring in an adaptation of the other Shakespeare play in which the character appears. The picture has grandeur, while the English cast members are all excellent, but Chuck's Antony is a bit of a pontificating bore and Hildegard Neil isn't up to the role of Cleopatra. AT

Charlton Heston *Antony* • Hildegard Neil *Cleopatra* • Eric Porter *Enobarbus* • John Castle *Octavius Caesar* • Fernando Rey *Lepidus* • Juan Luis Galiardo *Alexas* • Carmen Sevilla *Octavia* • Freddie Jones *Pompey* • Jane Lapotaire *Charmian* ■ *Dir* Charlton Heston • *Scr* Charlton Heston, from the play by William Shakespeare

Antwone Fisher ★★★ 15
Drama based on a true story
2002 · US · Colour · 115min

Actor Denzel Washington made his directorial debut with this powerful drama, in which he also stars. It's an often harrowing tale of child abuse and its lifelong effects. Derek Luke puts in a compelling performance as the adult Antwone Fisher, a young black sailor whose deep-rooted problems manifest themselves in violent outbursts. When he's forced to seek help from a naval psychiatrist (played by Washington), he learns to face up to his horrific past. Crisply directed and beautifully shot, Washington's tear-jerking drama has the odd mawkish moment, but is still a balanced film. SF *DVD*

Derek Luke *Antwone Fisher* • Joy Bryant *Cheryl Smolley* • Denzel Washington *Jerome Davenport* • Salli Richardson *Berta Davenport* • Earl Billings *James* • Kevin Connolly *Slim* • Viola Davis *Eva* • James Brolin *Fisher's commanding officer* ■ *Dir* Denzel Washington • *Scr* Antwone Fisher, from his autobiography *Finding Fish: a Memoir*

Antz ★★★★ PG
Animated fantasy adventure
1998 · US · Colour · 79min

This charming and witty animated adventure is perhaps even more appealing to adults than it is to children, who are nevertheless sure to be enchanted. Woody Allen is the perfect choice for the voice of Z, an ant who feels insignificant among millions. He sets out to achieve something in his life by winning the heart of Princess Bala (sexily voiced by Sharon Stone). Helping him in his quest for fulfilment is a butch soldier ant (Sylvester Stallone), while Gene Hackman and Christopher Walken give voice to the sinister villains plotting dastardly things for the colony. JB *DVD*

Woody Allen *Z* • Sharon Stone *Bala* • Sylvester Stallone *Weaver* • Gene Hackman *Mandible* • Christopher Walken *Cutter* • Jane Curtin *Muffy* • Jennifer Lopez *Azteca* • John Mahoney *Drunk Scout* • Paul Mazursky *Psychologist* • Anne Bancroft *Queen* • Dan Aykroyd *Chip* • Danny Glover *Barbatus* ■ *Dir* Eric Darnell, Tim Johnson • *Scr* Todd Alcott, Chris Weitz, Paul Weitz

Anvil: the Story of Anvil
★★★★ 15

Music documentary 2008 · US · Colour · 80min

The spirit of Spinal Tap lives on in this documentary about a real Canadian heavy metal band who enjoyed brief success back in the 1980s, touring with the likes of Bon Jovi, Whitesnake and The Scorpions. The director, former roadie and devoted fan Sacha Gervasi, catches up with his idols years later, as the now 50-something rockers go on a tour of Europe and make plans for their 13th studio album. As with Spinal Tap, their story is rich in idiocy and pathos, particularly in a scene where just 174 people show up to see them play at a 10,000-capacity stadium in Transylvania. But the band – singer and guitarist Steve "Lips" Kudlow and drummer Robb Reiner – are lovable characters beneath the hair, studs and leather, giving this short, sharp film a warm glow and good humour that banish any thoughts of a freak show. DW Swearing. *DVD* *SL*

Steve "Lips" Kudlow • Robb Reiner ■ *Dir* Sacha Gervasi

Any Day Now
★★★ 15

Drama 2012 · US · Colour · 98min

Alan Cumming is a tremendous actor, but sometimes the screen struggles to contain him and this touching, fact-based saga suffers as a consequence. Here he's a 1970s LA drag queen who tries to gain custody of his drug-addled neighbour's Down's syndrome-affected son when she's jailed for a variety of offences. During the proceedings, he falls for assistant DA Garret Dillahunt. For all its commitment and compassion, Cumming's performance always feels as embellished as his climactic torch songs. DP Swearing, sexual references, drug abuse.

Alan Cumming *Rudy* • Garret Dillahunt *Paul* • Isaac Leyva *Marco* • Frances Fisher *Judge Meyerson* • Jamie Anne Allman *Marianna* ■ *Dir* Travis Fine • *Scr* Travis Fine, George Arthur Bloom

Any Given Sunday
★★★★ 15

Sports drama 1999 · US · Colour · 150min

Oliver Stone offers his multi-camera perspective on American football in this bruising "us and them" drama. Essentially it's *North Dallas Forty* with a racial subtext, coated in *Jerry Maguire* sentimentality. But this ensemble masterclass is also a hybrid of *Platoon* and *Wall Street*, with Al Pacino even delivering a teamwork variation on Michael Douglas's "Greed is Good" speech. It's no accident that the tin-helmeted players thunder into encounters resembling the beach sequence in *Saving Private Ryan*, for Stone considers them the cannon fodder in a militaristic stratagem. Overlong, but with moments of explosive inspiration. DP Violence, swearing, drug abuse, nudity. *DVD*

Al Pacino *Tony D'Amato* • Cameron Diaz *Christina Pagniacci* • Dennis Quaid *Jack "Cap" Rooney* • James Woods *Dr Harvey Mandrake* • Jamie Foxx *Willie Beamen* • LL Cool J *Julian Washington* • Matthew Modine *Dr Ollie Powers* • Jim Brown *Montezuma Monroe* • Charlton Heston *AFFA football commissioner* • Ann-Margret *Margaret Pagniacci* • Aaron Eckhart *Nick Crozier* ■ *Dir* Oliver Stone • *Scr* John Logan, Oliver Stone, from a story by Daniel Pyne, Logan

Any Number Can Play
★★★

Drama 1949 · US · BW · 102min

Clark Gable runs a casino, much to the embarrassment of his son – until he starts winning, of course. There's a weird moral here: that gambling will make a man of you and cure family problems. But, since it won't do much for your heart condition, quit while you're ahead. The gangster subplot is more conventional, though. AT

Clark Gable *Charley Enley Kyng* • Alexis Smith *Lon Kyng* • Wendell Corey *Robbin Elcott* • Audrey Totter *Alice Elcott* • Frank Morgan *Jim Kurstyn* • Mary Astor *Ada* • Lewis Stone *Ben Gavery Snelerr* • Barry Sullivan *Tycoon* ■ *Dir* Mervyn LeRoy • *Scr* Richard Brooks, from the novel by Edward Harris Heth

Any Number Can Win
★★★

Crime drama 1963 · Fr/It · BW · 118min

Despite the rise of the French New Wave, such competent directors as Henri Verneuil continued to make traditional genre movies like this entertaining albeit familiar heist yarn. This time the Cannes casino is the target of an ageing ex-con and a younger crook. What made it a hit in France was the co-starring of Jean Gabin, a huge box-office star of the 1930s, with Alain Delon, as big a name in the 60s. RB French +subtitles.

Jean Gabin *Charles* • Alain Delon *Francis* • Viviane Romance *Ginette* • Maurice Biraud *Louis* • Carla Marlier *Brigitte* • José-Luis De Villalonga *Grimp* • Germaine Montero *Francis's mother* ■ *Dir* Henri Verneuil • *Scr* Albert Simonin, Michel Audiard, Henri Verneuil, from the novel *The Big Grab* by John Trinian

Any Wednesday
★★★

Comedy 1966 · US · Colour · 109min

From the bimbo Barbarella via political activist to mogul-mate Jane Fonda has been a moll for all seasons. This is an eager-to-please sex farce with Jason Robards as the married executive whose midweekly liaisons with mindless mistress Fonda have become a ritual even his wife (Rosemary Murphy) knows about. Dean Jones, seeking true love, tries to find a way to break the habit so that it all ends happily. Originally cut and called *Bachelor Girl Apartment*, it works better with the risqué bits back in. TH

Jane Fonda *Ellen Gordon* • Jason Robards *John Cleves* • Dean Jones *Cass Henderson* • Rosemary Murphy *Dorothy Cleves* • Ann Prentiss *Miss Linsley* • Jack Fletcher *Felix* • Kelly Jean Peters *Girl in Museum* ■ *Dir* Robert Ellis Miller • *Scr* Julius J Epstein, from the play *Son of Any Wednesday* by Muriel Resnik

Any Which Way You Can
★★★ 15

Action comedy 1980 · US · Colour · 110min

This sequel to *Every Which Way but Loose* typifies the kind of comic vehicles that paid Clint Eastwood's rent in the late 1970s and early 80s. Short on plot, long on slapstick humour and featuring then real-life girlfriend Sondra Locke as his love interest and the likeable Geoffrey Lewis as his best buddy, it has a lightweight charm that makes up for the insignificance of the story. Eastwood plays a car repair mechanic pushed back into bare-knuckle boxing for one last fight by the Mafia. JC Violence, swearing. *DVD*

Clint Eastwood *Philo Beddoe* • Sondra Locke *Lynn Halsey-Taylor* • Geoffrey Lewis *Orville Boggs* • William Smith *Jack Wilson* • Harry Guardino *James Beekman* • Ruth Gordon *Ma Boggs* ■ *Dir* Buddy Van Horn • *Scr* Stanford Sherman, from characters by Jeremy Joe Kronsberg

Anybody's Woman
★★★

Romantic comedy 1930 · US · BW · 80min

A case has been made for this movie's seeming honesty because it was directed by a woman, Dorothy Arzner, who empathised with the plight of a woman who married an alcoholic. The film's strengths are in its depiction of the couple's sleaze-ridden life, and the remarkably strong performances of the fine Clive Brook as the drunken lawyer and the splendid Ruth Chatterton as the cheap stripper he marries. Age has not worn this film well, but it retains its inherent interest. TS

Ruth Chatterton *Pansy Gray* • Clive Brook *Neil Dunlap* • Paul Lukas *Gustav Saxon* • Huntley Gordon *Grant Crosby* • Virginia Hammond *Katherine Malcolm* • Tom Patricola *Eddie Calcio* • Juliette Compton *Ellen* • Cecil Cunningham *Dot* ■ *Dir* Dorothy Arzner • *Scr* Zoe Akins, Doris Anderson, from a story by Gouverneur Morris

Anything Can Happen
★★ U

Comedy 1952 · US · BW · 96min

Two years after his Oscar-winning performance as Cyrano de Bergerac, José Ferrer played a Russian immigrant in this comedy of manners and language, based on the real-life experiences of George and Helen Papashvily. Falling for a court

stenographer (Kim Hunter), Ferrer follows her to California, gets married and starts an orange farm. Director George Seaton's film offers some episodic, fitfully amusing entertainment, though its real aim is to portray America as a haven for the dispossessed of Eastern Europe. AT

José Ferrer *Giorgi* • Kim Hunter *Helen Watson* • Kurt Kasznar *Nuri Bey* • Eugenie Leontovich *Anna Godiedze* • Oscar Karlweis *Uncle Besso* • Oscar Beregi (2) *Uncle John* • Mikhail Rasumny *Tariel Godiedze* • Nick Dennis *Chancho* ■ *Dir* George Seaton • *Scr* George Seaton, George Oppenheimer, from the memoirs of George Papashvily, Helen Papashvily

Anything Else
★★★ 15

Romantic comedy 2003 · US · Colour · 104min

Woody Allen revisits many of the themes explored in *Annie Hall* in this typically acerbic film, but would-be writer Jason Biggs's disintegrating relationship with aspiring actress Christina Ricci departs in several ways from the director's trusted formula. The action filmed in CinemaScope, and it's also darker than usual, with Allen's teacher-cum-gagsmith fixating on firearms and the Holocaust, while the depiction of both Ricci and her wannabe-singer mother (Stockard Channing) is scathing. Fitfully amusing, but disconcerting. DP Drug abuse. *DVD*

Woody Allen *David Dobel* • Jason Biggs *Jerry Falk* • Christina Ricci *Amanda* • Stockard Channing *Paula* • Danny DeVito *Harvey* • Jimmy Fallon *Bob* • KaDee Strickland *Brooke* • Erica Leerhsen *Connie* ■ *Dir/Scr* Woody Allen

Anything for Her
★★★ 15

Thriller 2008 · Fr · Colour · 92min

There's something reassuringly old-fashioned about this visceral thriller, which could easily have been made in the 1970s with Alain Delon or Jean-Paul Belmondo playing the devoted husband who decides to spring his wife from prison after she is falsely accused of murder. The underrated Vincent Lindon exudes macho injustice as the Parisian teacher encountering a variety of lowlifes in plotting Diane Kruger's audacious escape. Debuting director Fred Cavayé hurtles Alain Duplantier's camera through bruising action sequences that contrast with more cerebral moments. The storyline does occasionally require a suspension of disbelief, but overall the movie makes for slick and often gripping entertainment. DP French +subtitles. *DVD*

Vincent Lindon *Julien* • Diane Kruger *Lisa* • Lancelot Roch *Oscar* • Olivier Marchal *Henri Pasquet* • Hammou Graia *Commandant Susini* ■ *Dir* Fred Cavayé • *Scr* Fred Cavayé, Guillaume Lemans, from an idea by Lemans

Anything Goes
★★★ U

Musical 1936 · US · BW · 91min

PG Wodehouse co-wrote the book for the original Cole Porter stage smash on which this is based. This shipboard story of a romantic stowaway who's forced to pose as a criminal is pretty lightweight, but there's still plenty to enjoy, particularly with Ethel Merman repeating her Broadway triumph by belting out such classic tunes as *I Get a Kick Out of You* and the title song. A relaxed Bing Crosby and a radiant Ida Lupino play the lovers, while Charles Ruggles enjoys himself as "Public Enemy #13". DP

Bing Crosby *Billy Crockett* • Ethel Merman *Reno Sweeney* • Charles Ruggles [Charles Ruggles] *Rev Dr Moon* • Ida Lupino *Hope Harcourt* • Grace Bradley *Bonnie Le Tour* • Arthur Treacher *Sir Evelyn Oakleigh* • Robert McWade *Elisha J Whitney* • Richard Carle *Bishop Dobson* ■ *Dir* Lewis Milestone • *Scr* Howard Lindsay, Russel Crouse, from the musical by Guy Bolton (book), PG Wodehouse (book), Cole Porter (music/lyrics) • *Source Writer* Cole Porter

Anything Goes
★★ U

Musical 1956 · US · Colour · 105min

Having already starred in the 1936 film version of Cole Porter's hit musical, Bing Crosby came aboard this Sidney Sheldon-scripted reworking, which is far too loose to be considered a genuine remake. Donald O'Connor co-stars as the vaudevillian who hires showgirl Mitzi Gaynor, unaware that

Crosby has already signed up Zizi Jeanmaire. Crosby revels in the exceptional songbook, while Jeanmaire impresses in a ballet choreographed by her husband, Roland Petit. Yet it all remains stubbornly flat. DP

Bing Crosby *Bill Benson* • Donald O'Connor *Ted Adams* • Zizi Jeanmaire *Gaby Duval* • Mitzi Gaynor *Patsy Blair* • Phil Harris *Steve Blair* • Kurt Kasznar *Victor Lawrence* ■ *Dir* Robert Lewis (1) • *Scr* Sidney Sheldon, from the musical by PG Wodehouse, Guy Bolton • *Music* Cole Porter, Jimmy Van Heusen • *Lyrics* Cole Porter, Sammy Cahn

Anywhere but Here
★★★ 12

Comedy drama 1999 · US · Colour · 109min

Flighty Susan Sarandon and her rebellious daughter Natalie Portman go on a turbulent voyage of self-discovery in an old-fashioned tear-jerker from director Wayne Wang. Familial tension mounts as they drive to Hollywood to fulfil the acting dreams Sarandon has for her embarrassed daughter, though the sudsy script eventually allows its emotional themes to bubble to the surface. Portman breathes fresh life into the overfamiliar, soap-opera plot with grace, charm and wit. AJ Sexual references. *DVD*

Susan Sarandon *Adele August* • Natalie Portman *Ann August* • Eileen Ryan *Lillian* • Ray Baker *Ted* • John Diehl *Jimmy* • Shawn Hatosy *Benny* • Bonnie Bedelia *Carol* • Faran Tahir *Hisham* ■ *Dir* Wayne Wang • *Scr* Alvin Sargent, from the novel by Mona Simpson

Anzio
★★ PG

Second World War drama
1968 · It · Colour · 112min

In this epic Second World War drama, Robert Mitchum stars as an American war correspondent covering the Allied Forces' landing at Anzio Beach in Italy and their costly and bloody march on Rome. This is one of those war movies that poses thunderous moral questions at every turn and gives ordinary Joes statements rather than dialogue. It's a long haul, in every respect. AT *DVD*

Robert Mitchum *Dick Ennis* • Peter Falk *Corporal Rabinoff* • Arthur Kennedy *General Lesly* • Robert Ryan *General Carson* • Earl Holliman *Sergeant Stimler* • Mark Damon *Richardson* • Reni Santoni *Movie* • Joseph Walsh *Doyle* • Thomas Hunter *Andy* • Giancarlo Giannini *Cellini* • Anthony Steel *General Marsh* ■ *Dir* Edward Dmytryk • *Scr* Harry AL Craig, from the novel by Wynford Vaughan-Thomas, adapted by Frank DeFelitta, Duilio Coletti, Giuseppe Mangione, Canestri

Apa
★★★★ 12

Drama 1966 · Hun · BW · 85min

Described by sophomore director István Szabó as "the autobiography of a generation", this is a visually audacious yet highly personal study of the uneasy relationship between postwar Hungary and its past. The fragmentary structure enables Szabó to explore the themes of reputation, heroism and paternalism as student Andras Balint gradually discovers the truth about his deceased partisan father. Committedly played and meticulously constructed, the film gains power and authenticity from the inspired photographic pastiches of *film noir* and State-sponsored newsreel. DP Hungarian +subtitles. *DVD*

Andras Balint *Tako* • Miklos Gabor *Father* • Klari Tolnay *Mother* • Dani Erdelyi *Tako, as a child* • Kati Solyom *Anni* ■ *Dir/Scr* István Szabó • *Cinematographer* Sandor Sara

Apache
★★★★ U

Western 1954 · US · Colour · 87min

This courageous (for its day) film was directed by newcomer Robert Aldrich, who rose to the challenge and turned in a fine and intelligent western with splendid set pieces. He is helped immeasurably by the dynamic athletic presence of Burt Lancaster in the lead as Massai, the last noble Apache, who tried to hold out against the overwhelming forces of the US Army, and so passed into legend. The showing of the so-called growth of western civilisation through Massai's eyes is superbly directed, and the film, though brutal, presents a

A

realistic and wholly sympathetic viewpoint, despite being compromised by the happy ending insisted upon by the distributors. TS *DVD*

Burt Lancaster *Massai* • Jean Peters *Nalinle* • John McIntire *Al Sieber* • Charles Buchinsky [Charles Bronson] *Hondo* • John Dehner *Weddle* • Paul Guilfoyle (1) *Santos* • Ian MacDonald *Clagg* • Walter Sande *Lt Col Beck* • Morris Ankrum *Dawson* • Monte Blue *Geronimo* ■ *Dir* Robert Aldrich • *Scr* James R Webb, from the novel *Bronco Apache* by Paul I Wellman

Apache Drums ★★★ U

Western   1951 · US · Colour · 74min

The fact that this is a darker than usual western is perhaps not too surprising, since it was horror producer Val Lewton's last film. Stephen McNally is excellent as the ne'er-do-well who's run out of town, then returns to help defend the community from an Apache attack. Director Hugo Fregonese isn't daunted by the movie's low budget, and the short running time helps keep the tension taut. TS

Stephen McNally *Sam Leeds* • Coleen Gray *Sally* • Arthur Shields *Rev Griffin* • Willard Parker *Joe Madden* • James Griffith *Lt Glidden* • Armando Silvestre *Pedro-Peter* • Georgia Backus *Mrs Keon* • Clarence Muse *Jehu* ■ *Dir* Hugo Fregonese • *Scr* David Chandler, from the story *Stand at Spanish Boot* by Harry Brown

Apache Rifles ★ 12

Western drama   1964 · US · Colour · 91min

Provoked by gold miners invading their homeland, the Apaches go on the warpath. Audie Murphy's cavalry captain brings about a peace that lasts until the murder of a new Indian agent is blamed on the tribe and the ruthless tactics of officer John Archer make matters worse. Unpolished, with a weak supporting cast. AE *DVD*

Audie Murphy *Jeff Stanton* • Michael Dante *Red Hawk* • Linda Lawson *Dawn Gillis* • LQ Jones *Mike Greer* • Ken Lynch *Hodges* • Joseph Vitale *Victorio* • Robert Brubaker *Sergeant Cobb* • J Pat O'Malley *Captain Thatcher* • John Archer *Colonel Perry* ■ *Dir* William Witney • *Scr* Charles B Smith, from a story by Kenneth Gamet, Richard Schayer, from the 1951 film *Indian Uprising* by Richard Schayer

Apache Territory ★★ PG

Western   1958 · US · Colour · 70min

Rory Calhoun is suitably stoic as the loner hero of this routine B-western, in which he comes to the rescue of a motley group of characters pinned down at a desert water hole by angry Apaches. A callow kid, a traumatised survivor, an old flame and her jealous fiancé are just a few of the stereotypes who need no introduction thanks to the join-the-dots script. Betrayal, greed and fear bubble under the surface but there's very little else, in a noticeably no-budget yarn that could barely afford enough extras to play the hostiles. JA

Rory Calhoun *Logan Cates* • Barbara Bates *Jennifer Fair* • John Dehner *Grant Kimbrough* • Carolyn Craig *Junie Hatchett* • Leo Gordon *Zimmerman* ■ *Dir* Ray Nazarro • *Scr* Charles R Marion, George W George, Frank L Moss, from the novel *Last Stand at Papago Wells* by Louis L'Amour

Apache Trail ★★ U

Western   1942 · US · BW · 65min

This routine but reliable B-western has a pair of estranged brothers (William Lundigan and Lloyd Nolan) thrown together by an Apache uprising. Donna Reed provides the love interest, while Chill Wills supplies the corncob philosophising, but there are very few surprises on this well-rutted cowboy trail. Richard Thorpe's film was later remade as *Apache War Smoke*. TH

Lloyd Nolan *Trigger Bill* • Donna Reed *Rosalia Martinez* • William Lundigan *Tom Folliard* • Ann Ayars *Constance Selden* • Connie Gilchrist *Senora Martinez* • Chill Wills *"Pike" Skelton* • Miles Mander *James V Thorne* ■ *Dir* Richard Thorpe • *Scr* Maurice Geraghty, from a story by Ernest Haycox

Apache Uprising ★★ U

Western   1965 · US · Colour · 91min

Curiosity may have drawn audiences in 1965 to see what had become of stars like Rory Calhoun, Corinne Calvet, Lon Chaney Jr, Richard Arlen and Johnny Mack Brown. Unfortunately it's an utterly routine affair which pits hero Calhoun against Apaches and outlaws. John Russell makes an excellent deep-dyed villain, and DeForest Kelley also scores as a paranoid henchman, but it would be kinder to catch the others when they were in their prime. AE

Rory Calhoun *Jim Walker* • Corinne Calvet *Janice MacKenzie* • John Russell *Vance Buckner* • Lon Chaney [Lon Chaney Jr] *Charlie Russell* • Gene Evans *Jess Cooney* • Richard Arlen *Captain Gannon* • Arthur Hunnicutt *Bill Gibson* • DeForest Kelley *Toby Jack Saunders* • Johnny Mack Brown *Sheriff Ben Hall* • Jean Parker *Mrs Hawkes* • Donald Barry *Henry Belden* ■ *Dir* RG Springsteen • *Scr* Harry Sanford, Max Lamb, from the novel *Way Station* by Max Steeber, Harry Sanford

Apache Woman ★★ U

Western   1955 · US · Colour · 83min

Celebrated B-movie producer/director Roger Corman is perhaps best known for his 1960s adaptations of Edgar Allan Poe stories. He also made notable, if often tacky, contributions to the sci-fi and gangster genres, but westerns like this weren't really his thing, although the story in which Lloyd Bridges is a government agent sent to investigate crimes supposedly committed by a group of renegade Apaches has some surprises. TH

Lloyd Bridges *Rex Moffet* • Joan Taylor *Anne Libeau* • Lance Fuller *Armand* • Morgan Jones (1) *Macey* • Paul Birch *Sheriff* ■ *Dir* Roger Corman • *Scr* Lou Rusoff

Aparajito ★★★★ U

Drama   1956 · Ind · BW · 104min

This central part of Satyajit Ray's celebrated Apu trilogy won the Golden Lion at the Venice film festival. Continuing the story started in *Pather Panchali*, it focuses on Apu's relationship with his mother and the sharp contrasts between his simple country background and the bustle of city life. With his camera scarcely still for a second, Ray paints a fascinating picture of Indian life, considering the clash between western and traditional ideas with the same humanism that characterises all his work. While it lacks some of the poignancy of its predecessor, this is still a remarkable and deeply felt film. DP Bengali +subtitles. *DVD*

Pinaki Sen Gupta *Apu, as a boy* • Smaran Ghoshal *Apu, as an adolescent* • Karuna Bannerjee *Mother* • Kanu Bannerjee *Father* ■ *Dir* Satyajit Ray • *Scr* Satyajit Ray, from the novels *Pather Panchali*, *Aparajito* by Bibhutibhushan Bannerjee

The Apartment ★★★★★ PG

Comedy drama   1960 · US · BW · 122min

This classic from Billy Wilder sees Jack Lemmon's put-upon, snuffling insurance clerk CC Baxter basically offer his apartment to his superiors so that they can indulge in extramarital trysts. That he does it in return for promotions that never come makes "Buddy Boy" Baxter a sad case indeed. But Wilder cleverly veils the plot's darker side and operates the movie as a light romantic comedy. He is helped immensely by Lemmon's skilled performance, which instantly earns our sympathy, and his character's redemption eventually comes through Shirley MacLaine's elevator girl. From such potentially edgy material Wilder and co-writer IAL Diamond sculpt an unforgettable romance that won five Oscars. AC *DVD*

Jack Lemmon *CC "Bud" Baxter* • Shirley MacLaine *Fran Kubelik* • Fred MacMurray *JD Sheldrake* • Ray Walston *Mr Dobisch* • David Lewis (1) *Mr Kirkeby* • Jack Kruschen *Dr Dreyfuss* • Joan Shawlee *Sylvia* • Edie Adams *Miss Olsen* • Hope Holiday *Margie MacDougall* ■ *Dir* Billy Wilder • *Scr* Billy Wilder, IAL Diamond • *Cinematographer* Joseph LaShelle • *Editor* Daniel Mandell • *Art Director* Alexandre Trauner

Apartment for Peggy ★★★

Drama   1948 · US · Colour · 96min

Jeanne Crain and William Holden star as the young married couple trying to find a place to live in the era of postwar housing shortages in this shamelessly sentimental opus. Crain and Holden play off each other nicely, but both leads are given a run for their money by veterans Edmund Gwenn and Gene Lockhart. Professor Gwenn's transformation from suicidal depressive into hopeful optimist does take some swallowing, though the movie's worth perserverimg with for the period Technicolor and the charming performances. TS

Jeanne Crain *Peggy* • William Holden (2) *Jason* • Edmund Gwenn *Professor Henry Barnes* • Gene Lockhart *Professor Edward Bell* • Griff Barnett *Dr Conway* • Randy Stuart *Dorothy* ■ *Dir/Scr* George Seaton

Apartment 143 ★★ 15

Horror thriller   2011 · Sp · Colour · 77min

Originality is jettisoned in favour of atmospherics in this first feature from Carles Torrens. Unevenly scripted by *Buried* director Rodrigo Cortés, the compact chiller plays like *Paranormal Activity* meets *Poltergeist*, as three parapsychologists explore the apparently supernatural disturbances plaguing widower Kai Lennox and his two children in their increasingly oppressive home. A truly traumatised-looking Lennox adds a splash of emotion to the otherwise minimalist story. SF *DVD*

Kai Lennox *Alan White* • Michael O'Keefe *Dr Helzer* • Fiona Glascott *Ellen Keegan* • Rick Gonzalez *Paul Ortega* ■ *Dir* Carles Torrens • *Scr* Rodrigo Cortés

Apartment Zero ★★ 15

Psychological thriller
1988 · UK · Colour · 119min

Colin Firth stars as the manager of a Buenos Aires cinema. Twitchy, timid and totally unconvincing, he falls under the spell of dynamic lodger Hart Bochner. This occasionally intriguing mix of *The Lady from Shanghai* and *The Servant* is often too clever for its own good, and runs out of steam long before the inevitable "housemate from hell" plot kicks in. DP Swearing, nudity.

Colin Firth *Adrian LeDuc* • Hart Bochner *Jack Carney* • Dora Bryan *Margaret McKinney* • Liz Smith *Mary Louise McKinney* • Fabrizio Bentivoglio *Carlos Sanchez-Verne* • James Telfer *"Vanessa"* • Mirella D'Angelo *Laura Werpachowsky* • Juan Vitali *Alberto Werpachowsky* • Francesca D'Aloja *Claudia* ■ *Dir* Martin Donovan (1) • *Scr* Martin Donovan, David Koepp, from a story by Donovan

The Ape ★

Horror   1940 · US · BW · 62min

This has to be the daftest B-movie horror king Boris Karloff ever appeared in. After polio claims the life of his child, Karloff searches for a cure. His discovers his prototype serum will only work if it contains human spinal fluid; so he kills an escaped circus ape, skins it and, disguised in the animal's hide, hunts for more of the precious liquid. A ridiculously dumb potboiler. AJ

Boris Karloff *Dr Bernard Adrian* • Maris Wrixon *Frances Clifford* • Gertrude W Hoffman *Housekeeper* • Henry Hall (1) *Sheriff* ■ *Dir* William Nigh • *Scr* Richard Carroll, Kurt Siodmak [Curt Siodmak], from the play by Adam Hull Shirk

APEX ★★ 15

Science-fiction adventure
1994 · US · Colour · 97min

Richard Keats visits the past, gets trapped there, makes alterations and returns to 2073, with a killer cyborg in hot pursuit, to find an alternate universe thanks to a deadly virus he may have unleashed. Although efficiently directed with some notable moments (the best being the cyborg mating with a heavy metal CD), Phillip J Roth doesn't have the wit, or imagination to pull off such an ambitious concept. JF Violence, swearing. *DVD*

Richard Keats *Nicholas Sinclair* • Mitchell Cox *Shepherd* • Lisa Ann Russell *Natasha Sinclair* • Marcus Aurelius *Taylor* • Adam Lawson *Rasheed* • David Jean Thomas *Dr Elgin* • Brian Richard Peck *Desert Rat* • Anna B Choi *Mishima* ■ *Dir* Phillip J Roth • *Scr* Phillip J Roth, Ronald Schmidt, from a story by Gian Carlo Scandiuzzi, Phillip J Roth

Apocalypse Now ★★★★★ 18

Epic war drama   1979 · US · Colour · 147min

Director Francis Coppola inherited a modest movie about the Vietnam War from writer John Milius and turned it into this phantasmagorical ride, in which Martin Sheen travels up the Mekong river to terminate Marlon Brando's rebel command "with extreme prejudice". Working under difficult conditions in the Philippines and running way over budget, Coppola delivered a harrowing masterwork that bursts with malarial, mystical images. Coppola restored a whopping 50 minutes of extra footage for *Apocalypse Now Redux*, which was released in 2001. Whether the additional scenes greatly enhance an already exhilarating experience is debatable, but they were certainly worth the wait. AT Violence, swearing, drug abuse. *DVD* *BL*

Martin Sheen *Captain Willard* • Marlon Brando *Colonel Kurtz* • Robert Duvall *Lt Col Kilgore* • Frederic Forrest *Chef* • Albert Hall *Chief* • Sam Bottoms *Lance* • Larry Fishburne [Laurence Fishburne] *Clean* • Dennis Hopper *Photo journalist* • GD Spradlin *General* • Harrison Ford *Colonel* • Scott Glenn *Captain Richard Colby* • Bill Graham *Agent* • Francis Ford Coppola *TV director* ■ *Dir* Francis Coppola [Francis Ford Coppola] • *Scr* Francis Coppola, John Milius, from the novella *Heart of Darkness* by Joseph Conrad • *Cinematographer* Vittorio Storaro

Apocalypto ★★★★ 18

Period action adventure
2006 · US · Colour · 132min

At first sight, Mel Gibson's Mayan epic seems intimidating. It's over two hours long, has subtitled Yucatec Maya dialogue and is set in pre-Spanish Mexico. Yet this is no pretentious art house film but a thrilling chase movie in which Mayan warrior Jaguar Paw (Rudy Youngblood) is pursued through the jungle by a rival tribe eager to use him as a blood sacrifice. Gibson matches *The Passion of the Christ*'s bloodsoaked tableaux with a catalogue of gory beheadings and impalements, all set against the forbidding backdrop of Mayan pyramids and lush tropical undergrowth. He directs the set pieces with style, creating an exciting, exhausting adventure that's a strangely compelling mix of Mayan mythology, video nasty and Tarzan. JR Yucatec Maya +subtitles. Violence, gore. *DVD* *BL*

Rudy Youngblood *Jaguar Paw* • Dalia Hernandez *Seven* • Jonathan Brewer *Blunted* • Morris Birdyellowhead *Flint Sky* • Carlos Emilio Baez *Turtles Run* • Amilcar Ramirez *Curl Nose* • Israel Contreras *Smoke Frog* • Israel Rios *Cocoa Leaf* ■ *Dir* Mel Gibson • *Scr* Mel Gibson, Farhad Safinia • *Music* James Horner

Apollo 13 ★★★★ PG

Space drama based on a true story
1995 · US · Colour · 140min

In April 1970, astronaut Jim Lovell contacted mission control with the words: "Houston, we have a problem." It was a classic understatement, signalling a huge, complex problem to be solved. Lovell and his crew, Jack Swigert and Fred Haise, were bound for the Moon when an oxygen tank exploded in their craft, leaving them potentially marooned. Lovell is played by Tom Hanks, whose very ordinariness is the essence of astronaut-man, while Kevin Bacon and Bill Paxton offer welcome contrasts, as does the superb Ed Harris as the chain-smoking mission controller. Filmed in genuine weightless conditions, Ron Howard's movie is a technical tour de force. AT Swearing. *DVD* *BL*

Tom Hanks *Jim Lovell* • Bill Paxton *Fred Haise* • Kevin Bacon *Jack Swigert* • Gary Sinise *Ken Mattingly* • Ed Harris *Gene Kranz* • Kathleen Quinlan *Marilyn Lovell* • Mary Kate Schellhardt *Barbara Lovell* • Emily Ann Lloyd *Susan Lovell* • Joe Spano *Nasa director* • Xander Berkeley

Henry Hurt ■ *Dir* Ron Howard • *Scr* William Broyles Jr, Al Reinert, from the non-fiction book *Lost Moon* by Jim Lovell, Jeffrey Kluger

Apollo 18 ★★ 15

Science-fiction horror thriller
2011 · US · Colour · 82min

A secret 1974 Nasa mission to the moon uncovers a Soviet spacecraft and something much worse in this dull "found footage" thriller. Director Gonzalo López-Gallego takes the now-familiar *Paranormal Activity* route, with long build-ups to shock moments, as astronauts Warren Christie and Lloyd Owen realise they are not alone on the lunar surface. But in this case the jolts hardly seem worth the wait. Some care has been taken to re-create the grainy images of real space missions but this only briefly disguises the fact that nothing much of interest is going on. **AJ** *DVD*

Lloyd Owen *Nate Walker* • Warren Christie *Ben Anderson* • Ryan Robbins *John Grey* • Andrew Airlie *Mission control* ■ *Dir* Gonzalo López-Gallego • *Scr* Brian Miller, Cory Goodman

The Apostle ★★★★ 12

Drama
1997 · US · Colour · 128min

Robert Duvall writes, produces, directs and stars in this beautifully detailed character study of a Pentecostal preacher on a quest for atonement. The journey begins when his wife (Farrah Fawcett) has an affair with a younger minister, forcing him to take a long, hard look at his own life, the rural Texan community he serves and the Word of God itself. Expertly using little-seen Bible Belt locations and a great supporting cast, Duvall then proceeds to act everybody else off the screen. The result is an engrossing labour of love and a literal tour de force. **AJ** Violence.

Robert Duvall *Euliss "Sonny" Dewey, the Apostle EF* • Farrah Fawcett *Jessie Dewey* • Todd Allen *Horace* • John Beasley *Brother Blackwell* • June Carter Cash *Mrs Dewey Sr* • Walton Goggins *Sam* • Billy Joe Shaver *Joe* • Billy Bob Thornton *Troublemaker* • Miranda Richardson *Toosie* ■ *Dir/Scr* Robert Duvall

The Appaloosa ★★★ PG

Western
1966 · US · Colour · 94min

Marlon Brando and his much-prized Appaloosa horse become the target for a Mexican bandit chief in this very 1960s western, flashily directed by Sidney J Furie. Brando is at his mumbliest, moodiest and most masochistic. The highlight is an absurd arm-locking duel fought between Brando and John Saxon over a pair of scorpions – the loser gets stung – and the whole movie has an operatic, parodic quality that recalls the style of Sergio Leone. **AT** *DVD*

Marlon Brando *Fletcher* • Anjanette Comer *Trini* • John Saxon *Chuy Medina* • Emilio Fernandez *Lazaro* • Alex Montoya *Squint Eye* • Miriam Colon *Ana* ■ *Dir* Sidney J Furie • *Scr* James Bridges, Roland Kibbee, from the novel by Robert MacLeod

Appaloosa ★★★★ 15

Western
2008 · US · Colour · 110min

Actor Ed Harris returns to the director's chair – following his critically acclaimed debut with *Pollock* – in what is arguably the best out-and-out western since Kevin Costner's *Open Range*. Harris also co-stars with Viggo Mortensen as the friends and peacekeepers hired by the town council of Appaloosa to bring to justice a crooked ranch boss (Jeremy Irons). Renée Zellweger rounds off a starry cast, playing a widow whose relationship with Harris has consequences for the two men's mission. In terms of plot, *Appaloosa* may sound like pretty standard western fare, but there's a quirky, down-to-earth feel about its dialogue and a marvellously understated interplay between the two leads. **DA** Violence, swearing. *DVD* *Blu*

Ed Harris *Virgil Cole* • Viggo Mortensen *Everett Hitch* • Renée Zellweger *Allison French* • Jeremy Irons *Randall Bragg* • Timothy Spall *Phil Olson* • Lance Henriksen *Ring Shelton* • Ariadna Gil *Abner Raines* ■ *Dir* Ed Harris • *Scr* Ed Harris, Robert Knott, from the novel by Robert B Parker

L'Appartement ★★★★ 15

Romantic mystery drama
1996 · Fr/Sp/It · Colour · 111min

One of the most visually audacious French films of the 1990s, this intricate thriller clearly owes a debt to Hitchcock and Truffaut. Debutant writer/director Gilles Mimouni isn't just a cinematic magpie, however, as these homages are an ingenious means of making us identify with Vincent Cassel's high-flying executive. Suspecting that a long-vanished girlfriend has reappeared, he's duped into a web of deceit and desire, with every icon and flashback drawing him deeper into the mystery. We follow not so much out of a desire to solve the puzzle, but more because we're spellbound by the dazzling imagery. DP French +subtitles. Sex scenes. *DVD*

Romane Bohringer *Alice* • Vincent Cassel *Max* • Jean-Philippe Ecoffey *Lucien* • Monica Bellucci *Lisa* • Sandrine Kiberlain *Muriel* • Olivier Granier *Daniel* • Paul Pavel *Jeweller* ■ *Dir/Scr* Gilles Mimouni

The Appearing ★★ 15

Supernatural horror
2014 · US · Colour · 87min

Heavy-handed biblical references compound the clumsiness of this bitty haunted-house tale. The film begins with mentally fragile Emily Brooks and her detective husband Will Wallace moving to a rural town following a tragedy, only to be caught up in a nightmare involving a missing teen, demonic forces and a spook-filled woodland property. Brooks and an overly frowny Wallace are particularly weak together, though the former at least does a decent solo job when the truth of her situation becomes clear. **SF** Violence. *DVD*

Will Wallace *Michael* • Dean Cain *Dr Shaw* • Emily Brooks *Rachel* • Don Swayze *Sheriff Hendricks* ■ *Dir/Scr* Daric Gates

Applause ★★★★

Musical drama
1929 · US · BW · 80min

This very early talkie should be seen for the heart-rending performance of the legendary stage singer Helen Morgan. Not yet 30, she allowed herself, in her first dramatic film role, to be deglamourised and aged to play the boozy burlesque artiste who sacrifices herself for her teenage daughter. Imaginatively directed by Rouben Mamoulian, *Applause* remains equally notable for being one of the first films to throw off the restrictions on camera movement that the microphone had imposed and to use sound creatively, mixing dialogue with atmospheric background noise. **AE**

Helen Morgan (1) *Kitty Darling* • Joan Peers *April Darling* • Fuller Mellish Jr *Hitch Nelson* • Henry Wadsworth *Tony* • Jack Cameron *Joe King* ■ *Dir* Rouben Mamoulian • *Scr* Garrett Fort, from the novel by Beth Brown

The Apple ★

Science-fiction musical
1980 · US · Colour · 91min

Set in the New York of the future (well, 1994) and borrowing shamelessly from *The Rocky Horror Picture Show*, this follows the foot-tapping efforts of tunesmiths Catherine Mary Stewart and George Gilmour to deliver the world from drug-peddling villain Mr Boogalow and his demonic dance craze, the "Bim". This discordant drivel is best forgotten. DP

Catherine Mary Stewart *Bibi* • George Gilmour *Alphie* • Grace Kennedy *Pandi* • Alan Love *Dandi* • Joss Ackland *Mr Topps* • Ray Shell *Shake/Snake* • Miriam Margolyes *Landlady* ■ *Dir* Menahem Golan • *Scr* Menahem Golan, Coby Recht, Iris Recht, from a story by Coby Recht, Iris Recht

The Apple ★★★★ PG

Biographical drama
1998 · Iran/Fr · Colour · 81min

In her first feature, 17-year-old Samira Makhmalbaf makes a quietly ambitious assault on social injustice and sexual discrimination. Scripted by her director father, Mohsen, it's inspired by a scandal that shocked Iran. The tale of 12-year-old twin sisters who finally experience the world after being imprisoned since birth by their ultra-conservative father is re-enacted by the real-life people involved. Demonstrating an astonishing ease before the camera, Zahra and Massoumeh Naderi stand in wonderfully mischievous contrast to the shame and regret of their father, Ghorban Ali-Naderi. DP Farsi +subtitles. *DVD*

Massoumeh Naderi • Zahra Naderi • Ghorban Ali-Naderi • Zahra Sagharisaz • Amir Hossein Khosrojerdi • Azizeh Mohamadi ■ *Dir* Samira Makhmalbaf • *Scr* Mohsen Makhmalbaf

The Apple Dumpling Gang ★★★ U

Comedy western
1974 · US · Colour · 96min

This charming comedy western from the Disney stable is driven by some fine comic performances. Bill Bixby heads a cast full of amiable and refreshingly believable characters, playing a professional gambler who accompanies three orphans to an abandoned gold mine. An inferior sequel *The Apple Dumpling Gang Rides Again* was made in 1979. **NF** *DVD*

Bill Bixby *Russel Donovan* • Susan Clark *Magnolia Dusty Clydesdale* • Don Knotts *Theodore Ogelvie* • Tim Conway *Amos Tucker* • David Wayne *Colonel TR Clydesdale* • Slim Pickens *Frank Stillwell* • Harry Morgan *Sheriff Homer McCoy* • Brad Savage *Clovis Bradley* ■ *Dir* Norman Tokar • *Scr* Don Tait, from the novel by Jack M Bickham

The Apple Dumpling Gang Rides Again ★ U

Comedy western
1979 · US · Colour · 85min

Don Knotts and Tim Conway, who formed an enduring Disney partnership in the original *Apple Dumpling* adventure, return as the "Hash Knife Outfit" in this substandard sequel. Their buffoonery raises the odd smile, but there's little else to recommend this tiresome tale. DP

Tim Conway *Amos* • Don Knotts *Theodore* • Tim Matheson *Private Jeff Reid* • Kenneth Mars *Marshall* • Elyssa Davalos *Millie* • Jack Elam *Big Mac* • Robert Pine *Lt Ravencroft* • Harry Morgan *Major Gaskill* ■ *Dir* Vincent McEveety • *Scr* Don Tait

The Appointment ★

Romantic melodrama
1968 · US · Colour · 114min

Sidney Lumet went all Euro-arty for this dismal melodrama, quite the worst film he ever made. Omar Sharif plays a lawyer in Rome and Anouk Aimée is his wife who may or may not be a high-class call girl. This leads to a thriller of sorts in which Sharif becomes insanely jealous and worries about the meaning of love and existence as if he's seen one too many Michelangelo Antonioni movies. Gobsmackingly awful. **AT**

Omar Sharif *Federico Fendi* • Anouk Aimée *Carla* • Lotte Lenya *Emma Valadier* • Fausto Tozzi *Renzo* • Ennio Balbo *Ugo Perino* • Didi Perego *Nany* ■ *Dir* Sidney Lumet • *Scr* James Salter, from a story by Antonio Leonviola

Appointment for Love ★★ U

Romantic comedy
1941 · US · BW · 88min

Hollywood's favourite Frenchman of the 1940s, Charles Boyer, and the luminously talented and touching Margaret Sullavan (who would die of an overdose at the age of 49), star in this romantic comedy about a playwright (he) and a doctor (she) who marry, only to be plunged into near-terminal misunderstandings and suspicion. They have separate apartments on honeymoon, and only meet once a day, at 7am. Thin and superficial, the movie gets by thanks to the polished expertise of the stars and the glossy direction. **RK**

Charles Boyer *Andre Casall* • Margaret Sullavan *Jane Alexander* • Rita Johnson *Nancy Benson* • Eugene Pallette *George Hastings* • Ruth Terry *Edith Meredith* • Reginald Denny *Michael Dailey* • Cecil Kellaway *OLeary* • JM Kerrigan *Timothy* ■ *Dir* William A Seiter • *Scr* Bruce Manning, Felix Jackson, from the story by Ladislaus Bus-Fekete

A

Appointment in Honduras ★★★ U

Adventure
1953 · US · Colour · 79min

This furiously fast, all-action jungle drama stars Glenn Ford at his most nobly heroic, bristling with brio and derring-do as an adventurer en route to save the president of Honduras. Director Jacques Tourneur fashions an intelligent, multilayered romp, which on first sight may appear to be little more than "man wrestles baddies and requisite troop of snarling beasts", but opens out to display great performances from all concerned. **SH**

Glenn Ford *Corbett* • Ann Sheridan *Sylvia Sheppard* • Zachary Scott *Harry Sheppard* • Rodolfo Acosta *Reyes* • Jack Elam *Castro* • Ric Roman *Jiminez* ■ *Dir* Jacques Tourneur • *Scr* Karen De Wolfe

Appointment in London ★★ U

Second World War drama
1952 · UK · BW · 92min

This is a routine mission for the reliable Dirk Bogarde, who is slightly off-form as a Second World War pilot grounded on doctor's orders. His determination to continue flying is deflected momentarily by his love for widow Dinah Sheridan and the disappearance of comrade Bryan Forbes. It's all much as you'd expect, but a little more insight into the lives of the air crews would have filled in the gaps left by the absence of flag-waving propaganda. DP *DVD*

Dirk Bogarde *Wing Commander Tim Mason* • Ian Hunter *Captain Logar* • Dinah Sheridan *Eve Canyon* • Bill Kerr *Flight Lieutenant Bill Brown* • Bryan Forbes *Pilot Officer Greeno* • William Sylvester *Mac* ■ *Dir* Philip Leacock • *Scr* John Wooldridge, Robert Westerby

Appointment with Danger ★★★

Film noir
1950 · US · BW · 89min

This nifty little B-thriller finds Alan Ladd working for the Post Office's detective branch, tracking down the murderers of a colleague and foiling a robbery by posing as a corrupt cop. Phyllis Calvert plays a nun on the run who witnessed the murder. Moodily shot by master cameraman John F Seitz, the *film noir* proceedings are smartly handled by Lewis Allen. **AT**

Alan Ladd *Al Goddard* • Phyllis Calvert *Sister Augustine* • Paul Stewart *Earl Boettiger* • Jan Sterling *Dodie* • Jack Webb *Joe Regas* • Stacy Harris *Paul Ferrar* • Henry Morgan [Harry Morgan] *George Soderquist* • David Wolfe *David Goodman* ■ *Dir* Lewis Allen • *Scr* Richard Breen, Warren Duff

Appointment with Death ★★ PG

Crime mystery
1988 · US · Colour · 98min

Peter Ustinov as Hercule Poirot travels to Palestine where a murder awaits a twist of his waxed moustache. The usual assortment of glamorous suspects is on hand, including John Gielgud and Lauren Bacall. Michael Winner was the director, so a good time was probably had by the stars, but with Ustinov making his sixth appearance as Poirot, the formula looks stale to say the least, though some mild amusement can be had from trying to guess whodunnit. **AT** Violence. *DVD*

Peter Ustinov *Hercule Poirot* • Lauren Bacall *Lady Westholme* • Carrie Fisher *Nadine Boynton* • John Gielgud *Colonel Carbury* • Piper Laurie *Mrs Emily Boynton* • Hayley Mills *Miss Quinton* • Jenny Seagrove *Dr Sarah King* • David Soul *Jefferson Cope* • Nicholas Guest *Lennox Boynton* ■ *Dir* Michael Winner • *Scr* Anthony Shaffer, Peter Buckman, Michael Winner, from the novel by Agatha Christie

Appointment with Murder ★★

Detective mystery
1948 · US · BW · 67min

This is far from the best of the Falcon's screen outings, with magician John Calvert paling beside his predecessors George Sanders and Tom Conway. Hamstrung by a

A

minuscule budget, director Jack Bernhard struggles to persuade us that part of the action takes place in Italy. But Jack Reitzen shows well as the mastermind behind a series of art thefts from curator Catherine Craig's gallery. The series ground to a halt with 1949's *Search for Danger*. DP

John Calvert *Michael Waring/"The Falcon"* • Catherine Craig *Lorraine W Brinckley* • Jack Reitzen *Norton Benedict* • Lyle Talbot *Fred Muller* • Peter Brocco *Giuseppe Donatti* ■ *Dir* Jack Bernhard • *Scr* Don Martin, from a story by Joel Malone, Harold Swanton, from the character created by Michael Arlen

Appointment with Venus
★★★ U

Second World War comedy adventure
1951 · UK · BW · 87min

Venus is a pedigree cow that has to be shipped off the German-occupied Channel Island of Armoref by major David Niven, with help from Glynis Johns, during the Second World War. If you can forget the real-life horrors, this light comedy adventure is more than passable. The supporting cast is a *Who's Who* of British cinema, including Kenneth More in an early role, showing real star potential. TS

David Niven *Major Valentine Morland* • Glynis Johns *Nicola Fallaize* • George Coulouris *Captain Weiss* • Kenneth More *Lionel Fallaize* • Noel Purcell *Trawler Langley* • Barry Jones *Provost* • Bernard Lee *Brigadier* • Richard Wattis *Higher executive* ■ *Dir* Ralph Thomas • *Scr* Nicholas Phipps, from the novel *Transit of Venus* by Jerrard Tickell Black

Apprentice to Murder ★★ 15

Mystery thriller 1988 · US/Can · Colour · 88min

Fire and brimstone preacher Donald Sutherland - known locally as the Pow Wow Doctor - is sure a hex has been placed on him by Knut Husebo as an emissary from Satan. With help from the young Chad Lowe, who he's training to detect such evil, the maniac mystic kills Husebo. Both religious fanatics are then given a jail sentence. Loosely based on a true-life murder case, this is initially intriguing, but it's very slow in presenting the offbeat facts of the story. . AJ

Donald Sutherland *John Reese* • Chad Lowe *Billy Kelly* • Mia Sara *Alice Spangler* • Knut Husebo *Lars Hoeglin* • Rutanya Alda *Elma Kelly* • Eddie Jones *Tom Kelly* • Adrian Sparks *Irwin Meyers* ■ *Dir* RL Thomas [Ralph L Thomas] • *Scr* Alan Scott, Wesley Moore

The Apprenticeship of Duddy Kravitz ★★★★ 15

Drama 1974 · Can · Colour · 120min

Richard Dreyfuss confirmed his star quality in this adaptation of Mordecai Richler's novel. As Duddy, a no-holds-barred hustler in 1948 Montreal, he alienates friends and family in his quest to get rich and make his mark. Directed by former TV director Ted Kotcheff, the comic highlights include Denholm Elliott's down-at-heel film director setting up a bar mitzvah as an artsy-fartsy work of art. TH

Richard Dreyfuss *Duddy* • Micheline Lanctôt *Yvette* • Jack Warden *Max* • Randy Quaid *Virgil* • Joseph Wiseman *Uncle Benjy* • Denholm Elliott *Friar* • Henry Ramer *Dingleman* • Joe Silver *Farber* ■ *Dir* Ted Kotcheff • *Scr* Mordecai Richler, Lionel Chetwynd, from the novel by Mordecai Richler

Les Apprentis ★★★ 15

Comedy 1995 · Fr · Colour · 93min

Guillaume Depardieu gave notice that he had finally emerged from the shadow of his famous father Gérard with this César-winning performance. As Fred, the indolent flatmate, he brings some much-needed sanity to the proceedings, as his neurotic buddy François Cluzet comes close to madness wrestling with his literary aspirations. This odd-couple comedy may be short on incident, but it's packed with quirky humour and sly insights into the character of the modern French male. DP French +subtitles. Violence, swearing, nudity.

François Cluzet *Antoine* • Guillaume Depardieu *Fred* • Judith Henry *Sylvie* • Claire Laroche *Agnes* • Philippe Girard *Nicolas* • Bernard Yerles *Patrick* • Jean-Pol Brissard *Magazine editor* • Marie Trintignant *Lorette* ■ *Dir* Pierre Salvadori • *Scr* Pierre Salvadori, Philippe Harel

Appropriate Behaviour
★★★★ 15

Comedy 2014 · UK · Colour · 85min

The female-fronted confessional comedy is given a Middle Eastern twist in Desiree Akhavan's sharply penned feature debut, in which she also stars. She's entertainingly chaotic as a bisexual New Yorker who's unable to come out to her Iranian family. Her misadventures - although recalling both *Obvious Child* and TV's *Girls* - are honest and idiosyncratic enough for this to feel like a fresh take on wobbling your way through your twenties. EAS

Desiree Akhavan *Shirin* • Rebecca Henderson *Maxine* • Scott Adsit *Ken* ■ *Dir/Scr* Desiree Akhavan

Après l'Amour ★★★ 15

Drama 1992 · Fr · Colour · 100min

An air of detached amusement hangs over this assured discourse on the sexual mores of today's sophisticated Parisians, exemplified by novelist Isabelle Huppert and her dalliances with architect Bernard Giraudeau and pop star Hippolyte Girardot. Employing her trademark mix of naturalism and keen social insight, director Diane Kurys suggests that, where love is concerned, liberation is just another form of entanglement. Occasionally struggling for significance, the film is perhaps too insular, but the casting is apposite and Huppert outstanding. DP French +subtitles.

Isabelle Huppert *Lola* • Bernard Giraudeau *David* • Hippolyte Girardot *Tom* • Lio *Marianne* • Yvan Attal *Romain* • Judith Reval *Rachel* • Ingrid Held *Anne* ■ *Dir* Diane Kurys • *Scr* Diane Kurys, Antoine Lacomblez

The April Fools ★★★★

Romantic drama 1969 · US · Colour · 94min

The oddball teaming of Jack Lemmon, the quintessential neurotic American, with Catherine Deneuve, the epitome of cool French charm, might seem like a hoax played on cinema audiences. But it works extraordinarily well, with the two stars playing refugees from tedious New York marriages escaping to Paris and self-discovery. Stuart Rosenberg's direction desperately tries to be 1960s trendy, but there's dramatic poignancy to be experienced all the same. TH

Jack Lemmon *Howard Brubaker* • Catherine Deneuve *Catherine Gunther* • Peter Lawford *Ted Gunther* • Jack Weston *Potter Shrader* • Myrna Loy *Grace Greenlaw* • Charles Boyer *André Greenlaw* • Harvey Korman *Benson* • Sally Kellerman *Phyllis Brubaker* • Melinda Dillon *Leslie Hopkins* • Kenneth Mars *Don Hopkins* • David Doyle *Walters* ■ *Dir* Stuart Rosenberg • *Scr* Hal Dresner

April Fool's Day ★★★ 15

Horror 1986 · US · Colour · 85min

Responsible for the seminal stalk-and-slash movie *When a Stranger Calls*, director Fred Walton made a belated return to the much-maligned genre he helped create with this amusing diversion. Who's the insane maniac gruesomely reducing the ranks of practical joker Deborah Foreman's college pals as they party on her island retreat? There's a surprising twist in the tail of this wittily inventive whodunnit. AJ Swearing, violence, sex scenes. *DVD*

Deborah Foreman *Muffy St John/Buffy* • Deborah Goodrich *Nikki* • Ken Olandt *Rob* • Griffin O'Neal *Skip* • Mike Nomad *Buck* • Leah King Pinsent [Leah Pinsent] *Nan* ■ *Dir* Fred Walton • *Scr* Danilo Bach

April Fool's Day ★★ 15

Horror thriller 2008 · US · Colour · 87min

Another 1980s horror flick gets a 21st-century retread here, but it still feels worn and in severe need of a jump-start. The original 1986 film featured college students meeting a nasty end on an island retreat

and owed as much to Agatha Christie as to *Friday the 13th*. Here it's trustifarian siblings Desiree and Blaine Cartier (Taylor Cole, Josh Henderson) and their bitchy, selfish friends who are stalked a year after a cruel prank at a debutante ball causes a woman's death. But this is vapid stuff, which is odd from directors using the moniker of the Butcher Brothers. JA Violence, swearing. *DVD*

Taylor Cole *Desiree Cartier* • Josh Henderson *Blaine Cartier* • Scout Taylor-Compton *Torrance* • Joe Egender *Ryan* ■ *Dir* The Butcher Brothers [Mitchell Altieri], The Butcher Brothers [Phil Flores] • *Scr* Michael Wigart, from a story by Danilo Bach, from a screenplay (unproduced) by The Butcher Brothers [Mitchell Altieri], [Phil Flores]

April in Paris ★ U

Musical comedy romance
1952 · US · Colour · 95min

This is a leaden would-be romance that never gets off the backlot. The film pairs a hard-working Doris Day with a most unlikely leading man in Ray Bolger and the pair are lumbered with a dud of a plot. The 1950s Technicolor is attractive, but the art direction is garish, the dumb script wastes every opportunity for wit or satire, and the songs are weak. TS *DVD*

Doris Day *Ethel Dynamite Jackson* • Ray Bolger S *Winthrop Putnam* • Claude Dauphin *Philippe Fouquet* • Eve Miller *Marcia* • George Givot *François* • Paul Harvey *Secretary Sherman* • Herbert Farjeon *Joshua Stevens* • Wilson Millar *Sinclair Wilson* ■ *Dir* David Butler • *Scr* Jack Rose, Melville Shavelson

April Love ★★★

Romantic musical 1957 · US · Colour · 99min

A harmless remake of *Home in Indiana*, this musical romance is dressed up as a star vehicle for 1950s teen heart-throb Pat Boone. The controversy at the time was that clean-livin' Boone wouldn't take part in love scenes, and, true to form, the moment when he actually plants a peck on co-star Shirley Jones doesn't raise the temperature. However, Boone and Jones make a very likeable pair and this is mighty pleasant. TS

Pat Boone *Nick Conover* • Shirley Jones *Liz Templeton* • Dolores Michaels *Fran* • Arthur O'Connell *Jed* • Matt Crowley *Dan Templeton* • Jeanette Nolan *Henrietta* • Brad Jackson *Al Turner* ■ *Dir* Henry Levin • *Scr* Winston Miller, from the novel by George Agnew Chamberlain

Aprile ★★★ 15

Comedy drama 1998 · It/Fr · Colour · 74min

Having reinforced his auteur status with *Dear Diary*, Nanni Moretti opted for more of the same in this teasing blend of fact and fiction. Musing on aspects of his own life, as well as the state of Italian politics, this is more calculated and less charming than its predecessor, with the highly personal insights into nationhood, fatherhood and the frustrations of being a film director making for intriguing viewing. The genial honesty of the project keeps you hooked until the bizarre finale, in which Moretti finally succeeds in mounting part of his musical about a politicised pastry cook. DP Italian +subtitles. A scene of drug abuse. *DVD*

Nanni Moretti • Andrea Molaiolo • Silvio Orlando • Silvia Nono • Pietro Moretti • Nuria Schoenberg ■ *Dir/Scr* Nanni Moretti

Apt Pupil ★★★★ 15

Drama 1997 · US/Fr · Colour · 106min

The third work taken from Stephen King's 1982 anthology *Different Seasons* outlines the terrible consequences of a gifted Californian teenager's obsession with the Holocaust and his strange relationship with a Nazi war criminal living in secret in his home town. In a tale that's almost the equal of its predecessors *Stand by Me* and *The Shawshank Redemption*, director Bryan Singer uses smart visual fluency to suggest the appalling and shocking nature of his core story. Ian McKellen gives a stupendous performance as the former SS death-camp officer and the film provides unsettling

viewing that occasionally crosses the bad taste barrier. AJ Swearing, violence. *DVD*

Brad Renfro *Todd Bowden* • Ian McKellen *Kurt Dussander* • Joshua Jackson *Joey* • Mickey Cottrell *Sociology teacher* • Michael Reid MacKay *Nightmare victim* • Ann Dowd *Monica Bowden* • Bruce Davison *Richard Bowden* • James Karen *Victor Bowden* • David Schwimmer *Edward French* ■ *Dir* Bryan Singer • *Scr* Brandon Boyce, from the novella by Stephen King

Aquaman

Action adventure 2018 · US · Colour

This is a preview - no prints were available to review as we went to press: Briefly glimpsed in *Batman v Superman*, the King of the Seven Seas (and Justice League founding member) gets his own solo adventure as DC seeks to rival the success of Marvel. Former Conan and star of *Game of Thrones* Jason Momoa plays the aquatic superhero who hurls a mean trident and can talk to the fishes. Aquaman was a joke in comic-book circles; let's hope this movie won't end up the same way. JA

Jason Momoa *Arthur Curry/Aquaman* ■ *Dir* James Wan • *Scr* Kurt Johnstad, from characters by Paul Norris, Mort Weisinger

Aquamarine ★★ PG

Comedy 2006 · US · Colour · 99min

Florida teenagers Emma Roberts and Joanna "JoJo" Levesque dream of getting a second glance from a hunky lifeguard (the terminally bland Jake McDorman). When mermaid Aquamarine (Sara Paxton) is washed ashore in a tempest, the girls have three days to help her woo their own object of desire and so prove the existence of love - in return for which they'll be granted one wish. This trite fable has about as much depth as a rock pool. SP *DVD*

Emma Roberts *Claire* • Joanna "JoJo" Levesque *Hailey* • Sara Paxton *Aquamarine* • Jake McDorman *Raymond* • Arielle Kebbel *Cecilia* • Claudia Karvan *Ginny* • Bruce Spence *Leonard* • Tammin Sursok *Marjorie* • Roy Billing *Grandpa Bob* ■ *Dir* Elizabeth Allen • *Scr* John Quaintance, Jessica Bendinger, from the novel by Alice Hoffman

The Arab ★★★

Silent adventure 1924 · US · BW · 75min

Having played a key part in the emergence of Rudolph Valentino by directing *The Four Horsemen of the Apocalypse*, Irish firebrand director Rex Ingram drew inspiration from the silent superstar's best-known film, *The Sheik*, for this tempestuous desert romance. However, he had to settle for Hollywood's second-string Latin lover Ramon Novarro, instead of Valentino, to play the disgraced son of a Bedouin chief, now a tour guide, who smoulders missionary Alice Terry into submission. Unusually for the time, this overwrought Metro melodrama was shot on location in North Africa. DP

Ramon Novarro *Jamil Abdullah Azam* • Alice Terry *Mary Hilbert* • Gerald Robertshaw *Dr Hilbert* • Maxudian *Governor* • Count Jean de Limur *Hossein, governor's aide* • Adelqui Millar *Abdulla* ■ *Dir* Rex Ingram (1) • *Scr* Rex Ingram, from the play by Edgar Selwyn

Arabella ★★★

Comedy 1967 · US/It · Colour · 87min

This bizarre and often very funny comedy has Virna Lisi - a minor goddess of the 1960s - trying to raise money so that her eccentric grandmother (Margaret Rutherford) can pay a fortune in back taxes. Naturally, Lisi hasn't the slightest intention of raising the cash legally. It's all done in episodic fashion with quite a flourish, mainly due to the cast. Rutherford is a cigar-chomping joy, and so is Terry-Thomas in each of his four roles. AT

Virna Lisi *Arabella Danesi* • James Fox *Giorgio* • Margaret Rutherford *Princess Ilaria* • Terry-Thomas *Hotel manager/General/Duke/Insurance agent* • Paola Borboni *Duchess Moretti* • Antonio Casagrande *Filberto* ■ *Dir* Mauro Bolognini • *Scr* Adriano Baracco

Arabesque ★★★ 12

Spy drama 1966 · US/UK · Colour · 105min

In the wake of the box-office smash *Charade*, this glamorous trawl through 1960s post-Bond espionage has the same director, Stanley Donen, and stars Gregory Peck and Sophia Loren. The plot is some nonsense about Arab spies , but Alan Badel and Kieron Moore provide fine support. This is lush, mindless and expertly crafted matinée fare, with no small credit going to ace cinematographer Chris Challis's ravishing Panavisioned Technicolor. TS *DVD*

Sophia Loren *Yasmin Azir* • Gregory Peck *David Pollock* • Alan Badel *Beshraavi* • Kieron Moore *Yussef Kassim* • Carl Duering *Hassan Jena* • John Merivale *Sloane* • Duncan Lamont *Webster* • George Coulouris *Ragheeb* ■ *Dir* Stanley Donen • *Scr* Julian Mitchell, Stanley Price, Pierre Marton [Peter Stone], from the novel *The Cipher* by Gordon Cotler

Arabian Adventure ★★ U

Fantasy adventure 1979 · US · Colour · 93min

Former editor-turned-director Kevin Connor here lacks the imagination needed to conjure up the magic of the *Arabian Nights* tales, and he's not helped by a weak turn from Oliver Tobias as the prince battling Christopher Lee's wicked caliph. The eclectic cast keeps it watchable, but the special effects look cheap and let down the whole affair. TS *DVD*

Christopher Lee *Alquazar* • Milo O'Shea *Khasim* • Oliver Tobias *Prince Hasan* • Emma Samms *Princess Zuleira* • John Ratzenberger *Achmed* • Peter Cushing *Wazir Al Wuzara* • Capucine *Vahishta* • Mickey Rooney *Daad El Shur* • Athar Malik [Art Malik] *Mahmoud* ■ *Dir* Kevin Connor • *Scr* Brian Hayles

Arabian Nights ★★★

Adventure 1942 · US · Colour · 86min

This piece of Hollywood exotica, made to cash in on the success of *The Thief of Bagdad*, stars Jon Hall as the Caliph, Sabu as his best buddy and Maria Montez as his suitor. The actors have their tongues firmly in their cheeks and the whole show is on the brink of send-up, which is exactly where it should be. Producer Walter Wanger was one of Tinseltown's more enterprising independents, though he was later brought to his knees by the crippling costs of *Cleopatra*. AT

Jon Hall *Haroun al Raschid* • Sabu *Ali Ben Ali* • Maria Montez *Sherazad* • Leif Erickson *Kamar* • Shemp Howard *Sinbad* • "Wee Willie" Davis [William "Wee Willie" Davis] *Valda* • John Qualen *Aladdin* • Turhan Bey *Captain* • Richard Lane *Corporal* ■ *Dir* John Rawlins • *Scr* Michael Hogan, True Boardman, from the stories by Sir Richard Burton

The Arabian Nights ★★★★ 18

Fantasy adventure
1974 · It/Fr · Colour · 125min

Italian director Pier Paolo Pasolini took almost two years to complete this final, and most polished, offering in his trilogy of great story cycles, the others being *The Decameron* (1970) and *The Canterbury Tales* (1971). *The Arabian Nights* features ten interwoven stories of love, potions and betrayal, connected by the tale of Mur-El-Din (Franco Merli) searching for his kidnapped slave girl. Filmed in Eritrea, Iran, Nepal and Yemen, it reveals the captivating beauty of those countries, while the ribald spirit of the original tales remains thankfully unshackled by Freudian or religious guilt. RB Italian dubbed. *DVD*

Ninetto Davoli *Aziz* • Ines Pellegrini *Zumurrud* • Franco Citti *Demon* • Franco Merli *Mur-El-Din* ■ *Dir* Pier Paolo Pasolini • *Scr* Pier Paolo Pasolini, Danilo Donati

Arachnid ★ 15

Horror 2001 · Sp · Colour · 91min

An air force jet crashes into a UFO and the zoological alien cargo is showered over a South Pacific island. A research team, investigating the outbreak of an unknown virus on the island, find themselves fighting mutant bugs instead. This is saddled with a stupid story, an equally stupid script and duff special effects. AJ

Chris Potter *Valentine* • Alex Reid *Mercer* • José Sancho *Samuel Léon* • Neus Asensi *Susana* • Ravil Isyanov [Ravil Issyanov] *Capri* ■ *Dir* Jack Sholder • *Scr* Mark Sevi

Arachnophobia ★★★★ PG

Comedy horror 1990 · US · Colour · 104min

Steven Spielberg's longtime producer Frank Marshall turned director for this tongue-in-cheek creepy-crawly about deadly tropical spiders invading the small California town where phobic doctor Jeff Daniels has just started up a practice. Marshall shows much of his mentor's touch (Spielberg acted as co-executive producer with Marshall), spinning a tension-laden web full of solid scares and well-timed wit in what is virtually *The Birds* with eight legs. The black humour mixes with the black widows surprisingly well, and John Goodman's exterminator provides some lovely moments. AJ *DVD*

Jeff Daniels *Dr Ross Jennings* • Harley Jane Kozak *Molly Jennings* • John Goodman *Delbert McClintock* • Julian Sands *Dr James Atherton* • Stuart Pankin *Sheriff Parsons* • Brian McNamara *Chris Collins* • Mark L Taylor *Jerry Manley* • Henry Jones *Dr Sam Metcalf* ■ *Dir* Frank Marshall • *Scr* Don Jakoby, Wesley Strick, from a story by Don Jakoby, Al Williams

Arakimentari ★★★ 18

Documentary 2004 · US · Colour · 74min

It's hard to ignore the power of Japanese photographer Nobuyoshi Araki's early street realism, his deeply moving record of his wife's final illness and his stark contribution to events marking the 50th anniversary of the attacks on Hiroshima and Nagasaki. But his iconoclastic voyeurism has earned him the reputation of a pornographer among those offended by his nudes, which frequently depict figures in distressed or objectified situations. Yet, admirers such as Björk and Takeshi Kitano argue in Travis Klose's intriguing portrait that Araki's vision reflects the society in which he lives rather than the misogyny of a perverse mind. DP English, Japanese +subtitles. Nudity. *DVD*

■ *Dir/Scr* Travis Klose

Ararat ★★★ 15

Drama 2002 · Can/Fr · Colour · 110min

How can the crime of genocide be so easily forgotten? That's the question posed by this angry diatribe against the actions of Turkey which, in 1915, slaughtered over a million of its ethnic Armenian population. The world has overlooked the tragedy, which is here brought to our attention by Atom Egoyan (who is of Armenian descent). Beginning with a film-maker's attempts to shoot a movie about the massacre in Turkey, Egoyan fashions a complex story that flashes back and forth in time, revealing the events leading up to the slaughter and its impact on subsequent generations. TH Violence, swearing, a sex scene. *DVD*

David Alpay *Raffi* • Charles Aznavour *Edward Saroyan* • Eric Bogosian *Rouben* • Brent Carver *Philip* • Marie-Josée Croze *Celia* • Bruce Greenwood *Martin/Clarence Ussher* • Arsinée Khanjian *Ani* • Elias Koteas *Ali/Jevdet Bey* • Christopher Plummer *David* ■ *Dir* Atom Egoyan • *Scr* Atom Egoyan, from the non-fiction book *An American Physician in Turkey* by Clarence Ussher

Arbitrage ★★★★ 15

Thriller 2012 · US/Pol · Colour · 102min

Nicholas Jarecki's accomplished directorial debut stars Richard Gere as a hedge fund mogul whose world has begun to fall apart, both professionally and personally. Not only is he caught up in a financial fraud that could scupper his plans to sell his company, but when he leaves the scene of a car accident that results in the death of his mistress (Laetitia Casta), he finds himself facing a potential prison sentence. The old silver fox Gere gives one of his best performances in recent years as the suave corporate shark, and Tim Roth is equally good as the dogged detective who, for once, doesn't want the rich to get away with it. JF Swearing, drug abuse. *DVD* *Blu*

Richard Gere *Robert Miller* • Brit Marling *Brooke Miller* • Tim Roth *Det Michael Bryer* • Nate Parker *Jimmy Grant* • Susan Sarandon *Ellen Miller* • Laetitia Casta *Julie Cote* • Stuart Margolin *Syd Felder* ■ *Dir/Scr* Nicholas Jarecki

The Arbor ★★★ 15

Drama documentary 2010 · UK · Colour · 90min

This ingeniously staged film about the short, tragic life of working-class playwright Andrea Dunbar – author of *Rita, Sue and Bob Too* – re-creates events surrounding her rise to fame from her poverty-stricken roots by using actors lip-synching to recorded interviews with her family and friends. But attention is swiftly switched to Dunbar's daughter Lorraine, whose startling true-life misfortunes dwarf anything in her mother's hard-hitting dramas. The style of the film is always arresting, but when the full horror of Lorraine's situation is revealed, one could argue that a less unorthodox approach might have been more appropriate. DW Swearing, drug abuse. *DVD* *Blu*

Manjinder Virk *Lorraine* • Neil Dudgeon *Steve Saul* • Monica Dolan *Ann Hamilton* • Danny Webb *Max Stafford Clark/father* • Christine Bottomley *Lisa* ■ *Dir/Scr* Clio Barnard

Arch of Triumph ★ U

Romantic drama 1948 · US · BW · 126min

Despite the reteaming of the two stars of *Gaslight* (Ingrid Bergman and Charles Boyer) and the directorial skills of Lewis Milestone, this was a costly failure. Bergman plays a down-on-her-luck courtesan who falls in love with an Austrian doctor (Boyer) escaping from the Nazis. The overall pace is deadly and the re-creation of pre-war Paris is totally without atmosphere. TS *DVD*

Ingrid Bergman *Joan Madou* • Charles Boyer *Dr Ravic* • Charles Laughton *Haake* • Louis Calhern *Morosow* • Ruth Warrick *Kate Hegstroem* • Roman Bohnen *Dr Weber* • Stephen Bekassy *Alex* • Ruth Nelson *Madame Fessier* ■ *Dir* Lewis Milestone • *Scr* Harry Brown, Lewis Milestone, from the novel by Erich Maria Remarque

Archipelago ★★★ 15

Drama 2010 · UK · Colour · 109min

Writer/director Joanna Hogg is fascinated by holidaymakers struggling to leave their cares behind. Here, as in the Tuscan-set *Unrelated*, she relies on phone conversations and off-screen squabbles to show the tensions arising within an affluent family, as Edward (Tom Hiddleston) joins his mother (Kate Fahy) and sister (Lydia Leonard) for a holiday in the Scilly Isles. But the awkward naturalism of the performances becomes increasingly stiff in this pale Ingmar Bergman imitation. Ed Rutherford's photography is superb, however. DP Swearing. *DVD*

Tom Hiddleston *Edward* • Kate Fahy *Patricia* • Lydia Leonard *Cynthia* • Amy Lloyd *Rose* • Christopher Baker *Christopher* ■ *Dir/Scr* Joanna Hogg • *Cinematographer* Ed Rutherford

Arctic Tale ★★★ U

Wildlife documentary
2007 · US · Colour · 82min

National Geographic's gloriously photographed documentary informs and entertains but misses out on the affecting majesty of its clear inspiration, *March of the Penguins*. Experienced naturalists Adam Ravetch and Sarah Robertson shot hundreds of hours of footage in the frozen habitat of polar bear cub Nanu and walrus calf Seela as they battle the effects of global warming in their hunting ground. Breezily narrated by Queen Latifah, the script was co-written by Kristin Gore, daughter of former US vice-president Al Gore (*An Inconvenient Truth*) and brings an authoritative element to the environmental plea finale. But the accent here is on the cute and cuddly. AJ *DVD*

Queen Latifah *Narrator* ■ *Dir* Adam Ravetch, Sarah Robertson • *Scr* Linda Woolverton, Mose Richards, Kristin Gore • *Cinematographer* Adam Ravetch

Are We There Yet? ★★ PG

Road movie comedy 2005 · US · Colour · 90min

A family-friendly mix of sassy dialogue, slapstick and sight gags, this stars Ice Cube as a love-struck singleton who's trying to woo divorcee Nia Long. But when he offers to transport her two monstrous children to see her on a business trip, everything that could go wrong does. The eye-watering clashes and cartoon-style violence that ensue are enjoyable, but the film founders when it becomes overly sentimental, and the youngsters are just too obnoxious. SF *DVD*

Ice Cube *Nick Persons* • Nia Long *Suzanne Kingston* • Jay Mohr *Marty* • MC Gainey *Al* • Aleisha Allen *Lindsey Kingston* • Philip Daniel Bolden *Kevin Kingston* • Tracy Morgan *Satchel Paige* • Nichelle Nichols *Miss Mable* ■ *Dir* Brian Levant • *Scr* Steven Gary Banks, Claudia Grazioso, J David Stern, David N Weiss from a story by Steven Gary Banks, Claudia Grazioso

Are We Done Yet? ★★ PG

Comedy 2007 · US · Colour · 88min

This unnecessary sequel to *Are We There Yet?* features rapper-turned-actor Ice Cube in a (very loose) remake of the 1948 Cary Grant vehicle *Mr Blandings Builds His Dream House*. Downsizing his wife (Nia Long) and her adopted children to a dilapidated house in the countryside, the star gets the opportunity to tackle slapstick favourites like power tools, falling ceiling lights and invasive raccoons. The results are predictably painful and largely unfunny. Ice Cube's perpetually morose persona is hard not to like, though, especially when he's partnered with John C McGinley (from TV's *Scrubs*). JR *DVD* *Blu*

Ice Cube *Nick Persons* • Nia Long *Suzanne Persons* • John C McGinley *Chuck Mitchell Jr* • Aleisha Allen *Lindsey Persons* • Philip Daniel Bolden *Kevin Persons* • Jonathan Katz *Mr Rooney* • Linda Kash *Mrs Rooney* • Magic Johnson ■ *Dir* Steve Carr • *Scr* Hank Nelken, from a story by Nelken, from characters by Steven Gary Banks, Claudia Grazioso, from the film *Mr Blandings Builds His Dream House* by Norman Panama, Melvin Frank

Are You Being Served? ★ PG

Comedy 1977 · UK · Colour · 91min

Grace Brothers opened for business as part of the BBC's *Comedy Playhouse* in the early 1970s, but never in its ten-year history were the shelves as bare as they are in this feeble feature. Abandoning the clothing department for the Costa Plonka, the staff are soon engaging in the usual smutty banter as sun, sand and booze take their toll. DP *DVD*

Mollie Sugden *Mrs Slocombe* • John Inman *Mr Humphries* • Frank Thornton *Captain Peacock* • Trevor Bannister *Mr Lucas* • Wendy Richard *Miss Brahms* • Arthur Brough *Mr Grainger* • Nicholas Smith *Mr Rumbold* • Arthur English *Harman* • Harold Bennett *Young Mr Grace* • Andrew Sachs *Don Bernardo* ■ *Dir* Bob Kellett • *Scr* Jeremy Lloyd, David Croft

Are You with It? ★★ U

Musical comedy 1948 · US · BW · 89min

This hotch-potch of humdrum hokum veers from the sublime (Donald O'Connor's restaurant dance) to the ridiculous (Louis Da Pron's climactic ballet). O'Connor's humourless insurance bod is fired for misplacing a decimal point and seeks solace at the carnival, where he falls for the exotic Olga San Juan, who persuades him to use his mathematical nous to rescue barker Lew Parker's bacon. Musical mediocrity par excellence. DP

Donald O'Connor *Milton Haskins* • Olga San Juan *Vivian Reilly* • Martha Stewart *Bunny LaFleur* • Lew Parker *John Goldie McGoldrick* • Walter Catlett *Jason "Pop" Carter* • Pat Dane *[Patricia Dane] Sally* • Louis Da Pron *Bartender* ■ *Dir* Jack Hively • *Scr* Oscar Brodney, from the musical comedy by Sam Perrin, George Balzer, Harry Revel, from the novel *Slightly Perfect* by George Malcolm-Smith

A

Arena ★★ U
Western drama 1953 · US · Colour · 70min

Sadly no gladiators, for this melodrama concerns itself with rodeo riders and bucking broncos. Gig Young is the seasoned rodeo star thinking of quitting, but thinking mostly about his girlfriend and his wife who wants a divorce. Then his best mate gets killed in the arena and Young gets very gloomy indeed. Filmed in 3D – hence the frequency of shots in which the bulls snort into the camera lens. **AT**

Gig Young *Bob Danvers* · Jean Hagen *Meg Hutchins* · Polly Bergen *Ruth Danvers* · Henry Morgan [Harry Morgan] *Lew Hutchins* · Barbara Lawrence *Sylvia Morgan* · Robert Horton *Jackie Roach* · Lee Van Cleef *Smitty* ■ *Dir* Richard Fleischer · *Scr* Harold Jack Bloom, from a story by Arthur Loew Jr

L'Argent ★★★★★ PG
Crime drama 1983 · Fr/Swi · Colour · 80min

Adhering rigidly to the spirit of a Tolstoy short story, Robert Bresson's final feature is as uncompromising as (but much less admired than) his earlier study of the preordained consequences of crime, *Pickpocket* (1959). Starting with the mischievous exchange of a forged 500 franc note, an inexorable sequence of events culminates in a man murdering his family with an axe. It's a brutal climax to Christian Patey's descent from decency to degradation. Yet, it's hard to accuse Bresson of manipulation, as he views each chillingly logical stage with a dispassion that distressingly echoes that of an even less compassionate society. DP French +subtitles. **DVD**

Christian Patey *Yvon Targe* · Sylvie van den Elsen *Woman* · Michel Briguet *Woman's father* · Caroline Lang *Elise Targe* · Vincent Risterucci *Lucien* ■ *Dir* Robert Bresson · *Scr* Robert Bresson, from the story *The False Note* by Leo Tolstoy

Argentine Nights ★★ U
Comedy musical 1940 · US · BW · 74min

A trio of girl singers, accompanied by their managers (conveniently also numbering three) decamp to Argentina to escape their creditors. This low-budget B-musical is notable for marking the screen debut of immensely popular vocalists the Andrews Sisters, and the Universal debut of former Fox stars, the Ritz Brothers. **RK**

Laverne Andrews *Laverne* · Maxene Andrews *Maxine* · Patty Andrews *Patty* · Al Ritz *Al* · Harry Ritz *Harry* · Jimmy Ritz *Jimmy* · Constance Moore *Bonnie Brooks* · George Reeves *Eduardo* · Peggy Moran *Peggy* · Anne Nagel *Linda* · Kathryn Adams *Carol* ■ *Dir* Albert S Rogell · *Scr* Arthur T Horman, Ray Golden, sid Kuller

Argo ★★★★★ 15
Thriller based on a true story 2012 · US · Colour · 120min

A true story that involves the CIA, Hollywood and the anti-American regime of Iran's Ayatollah Khomeini shouldn't be as seamless as this gripping, beautifully performed and often very funny but dramatic thriller. The year is 1979 and the US embassy in Tehran has been stormed, with many of its workers taken hostage. However, six have fled, and are being secretly sheltered by the Canadian ambassador, but time is running out. The CIA has exhausted every avenue, so when "exfiltration" expert Tony Mendez (Ben Affleck) suggests disguising them as a film crew and scouting locations for a *Star Wars* rip-off, it seems as good an idea as any. Alan Arkin and John Goodman are superb as the operation's jaded Tinseltown connections in a terrific story that deftly offsets tension with comedy. **DW** Swearing.
DVD Blu

Ben Affleck *Tony Mendez* · Alan Arkin *Lester Siegel* · John Goodman *John Chambers* · Bryan Cranston *Jack O'Donnell* · Victor Garber *Ken Taylor* · Tate Donovan *Bob Anders* · Scoot McNairy *Joe Stafford* · Clea DuVall *Cora Lijek* ■ *Dir* Ben Affleck · *Scr* Chris Terrio, from an article by Joshua Bearman

Aria ★★★ 18
Opera anthology 1987 · UK · Colour · 88min

This is the cinematic equivalent of the *Three Tenors* concerts: hummable slices of opera, here interpreted visually by an eclectic selection of film directors. Understandably, it's an uneven affair but, although the true opera buff will be horrified, there are some little gems. The pick of the vignettes is Franc Roddam's take on the *Liebestod* from Wagner's *Tristan and Isolde*, with Bridget Fonda (in her film debut) and James Mathers as a pair of beautiful, tragic lovers. Honourable mention, too, for Robert Altman's segment from *Les Boréades* (with the camera focused entirely on an audience seemingly made up of inmates from an asylum) and Julien Temple's trashy and kitsch version of Verdi's *Rigoletto*. **JF** Sex scenes, nudity.
DVD

John Hurt · Sophie Ward · Theresa Russell · Jackson Kyle · Marianne McLoughlin [Marian McLoughlin] · Buck Henry · Beverly D'Angelo · Anita Morris · Elizabeth Hurley · Peter Birch · Julie Hagerty · Genevieve Page · Bridget Fonda · James Mathers · Linzi Drew · Andreas Wisniewski · Amy Johnson · Tilda Swinton ■ *Dir* Nicolas Roeg, Jean-Luc Godard, Robert Altman, Derek Jarman, Charles Sturridge, Julien Temple, Bruce Beresford, Franc Roddam, Ken Russell, Bill Bryden · *Scr* Nicolas Roeg, Jean-Luc Godard, Robert Altman, Derek Jarman, Charles Sturridge, Julien Temple, Bruce Beresford, Franc Roddam, Ken Russell, Bill Bryden, Don Boyd

Ariane ★★★
Drama 1931 · Ger · BW · 78min

The sixth collaboration between the soon-to-be husband-and-wife team of Hungarian director Paul Czinner and Polish-born actress Elisabeth Bergner was their first venture into talkies. She is positively radiant as the Russian émigrée who is distracted from her studies by sophisticated businessman Rudolf Forster, whose boast that he prefers experienced women prompts her to invent a string of affairs that only alienate his affections. Filmed in both German and English (as *The Loves of Ariane*), the action is as deliciously light as Billy Wilder's 1957 remake *Love in the Afternoon*. DP German +subtitles.

Elisabeth Bergner *Ariane* · Rudolf Forster *Konstantin* · Annemarie Steinsieck *Tante Warwara* · Hertha Guthmar *Olga* · Theodor Loos *The teacher* · Nikolas Wassilieff *The student* · Alfred Gerasch *The doctor* ■ *Dir* Paul Czinner · *Scr* Paul Czinner, Carl Mayer, from a novel by Claude Anet

Ariel ★★★★ 15
Comedy drama 1988 · Fin · Colour · 69min

Aki Kaurismäki puts his habitually offbeat slant on the *film noir* road movie. Quitting Lapland in his Cadillac to seek pastures new, tin miner Turo Pajala makes a typically lugubrious Kaurismäki hero, stumbling into increasingly dangerous situations almost as accidentally as he takes up with single-mom meter maid Susanna Haavisto. The deceptively simple style may seem to subvert traditional social realism, but there's a barbed satirical intent at work here, which blends with the subtle character comedy to pass copious pertinent comments on modern-day Finland. DP Finnish +subtitles. Swearing, violence.

Turo Pajala *Taisto Kasurinen* · Susanna Haavisto *Irmeli* · Matti Pellonpaa *Mikkonen* · Eetu Hilkamo *Riku* · Erkki Pajala *Miner* · Matti Jaaranen *Mugger* ■ *Dir/Scr* Aki Kaurismäki

Arirang ★★★ 12
Drama documentary 2011 · S Kor · Colour · 90min

South Korean auteur Kim Ki-duk quit filmmaking after his lead actress almost suffocated during the shooting of a suicide sequence for *Dream* (2008). This very personal documentary marks Kim's return to the medium and sees him muse about the state of Korean cinema and his status within it. Editing footage to appear as both inquisitor and interviewer, Kim seems genuinely remorseful while berating himself for the *Dream* incident. But the fantasy gun-toting denouement raises doubts about the authenticity of the exercise, which never quite disconcerts as much as it perhaps should. DP Korean +subtitles.

Kim Ki-duk ■ *Dir/Scr* Kim Ki-duk

Arise, My Love ★★★★
Wartime romantic comedy drama 1940 · US · BW · 111min

Claudette Colbert and Ray Milland co-star in this superior comedy-drama-romance from Paramount, which won several Oscar nominations and the award itself for its story, although not, surprisingly for the polished screenplay by the team of Billy Wilder and Charles Brackett. It audaciously combines wit and a love story with headline events of the Spanish Civil War and then the Second World War, both of which Paris-based newswoman Colbert is reporting while becoming involved with Milland. The film is sophisticated and gripping entertainment with a serious theme, and Mitchell Leisen's direction perfectly catches the nuances. **RK**

Claudette Colbert *Augusta Nash* · Ray Milland *Tom Martin* · Dennis O'Keefe *Shep* · Walter Abel *Phillips* · Dick Purcell *Pink* · George Zucco *Prison Governor* · Frank Puglia *Father Jacinto* ■ *Dir* Mitchell Leisen · *Scr* Charles Brackett, Billy Wilder, from the story by Benjamin Glazer, John S Toldy

The Aristocats ★★★★ U
Animated adventure 1970 · US · Colour · 78min

The delight in Wolfgang Reitherman's turn-of-the-century movie, set in a charmingly detailed Paris, is the brilliant matching of voices to visuals. Hermione Baddeley voices the aristo-owner of elegant feline Duchess (Eva Gabor) who, with her three kittens, is befriended by Phil Harris's alley cat after the butler, Edgar (Roddy Maude-Roxby), has tried to do away with them because the old lady has left everything to the cats in her will. The Sherman brothers' songs are out of the top drawer. **TH** **DVD** Blu

Phil Harris *J Thomas O'Malley* · Eva Gabor *Duchess* · Sterling Holloway *Roquefort* · Scatman Crothers *Scat Cat* · Paul Winchell *Chinese Cat* · Lord Tim Hudson *English Cat* · Vito Scotti *Italian Cat* · Thurl Ravenscroft *Russian Cat* · Hermione Baddeley *Madame Bonfamille* · Roddy Maude-Roxby *Butler* ■ *Dir* Wolfgang Reitherman · *Scr* Larry Clemmons, Vance Gerry, Ken Anderson, Frank Thomas, Eric Cleworth, Julius Svendsen, Ralph Wright, Tom Rowe, Tom McGowan · *Animation Director* Frank Thomas

The Aristocrats ★★★ 18
Comedy documentary 2005 · US · Colour · 84min

An infamous filthy joke is told by dozens of comedians and recorded on digital video by film-makers Paul Provenza and Penn Jillette. It always begins with a man telling a talent agent about his family act: "We go on stage and ... " There follows a litany of sexual deviancy, crudity, obscenity and outrageous violence. While the gag's not particularly funny in print, the humour comes from the ways in which each comic riffs its malleably mirthful mid-section. Some of the routines are hilarious, although some of the participants spread the material way too thin and the film does feel a bit long. But this joke is the benchmark of stand-up comedy – used to judge what a comic is truly made of. **AJ** **DVD**

Jason Alexander · Hank Azaria · Billy Connolly · Whoopi Goldberg · Eddie Izzard · Chris Rock · Robin Williams ■ *Dir* Paul Provenza

Arizona ★★★ U
Western 1940 · US · BW · 116min

Jean Arthur plays the first lady settler in Tucson, battling it out with the rogues trying to control her rail freight business. Femininity asserts itself when she falls in love with William Holden, passing through on his travels. Distinguished by Arthur's performance and outstanding photography and action set pieces which reflect the film's then massive production budget, it contains all the ingredients that became standard to the frontier western. **RK**

Jean Arthur *Phoebe Titus* · William Holden (2) *Peter Muncie* · Warren William *Jefferson Carteret* · Porter Hall *Lazarus Ward* · Paul Harvey *Solomon Warner* · George Chandler *Haley* · Byron Foulger *Pete Kitchen* · Regis Toomey *Grant Oury* ■ *Dir* Wesley Ruggles · *Scr* Claude Binyon, from a story by Clarence Budington Kelland · *Cinematographers* Joseph Walker, Harry Hallenberger, Fayte Browne

Arizona Bushwhackers ★
Western 1968 · US · Colour · 87min

Producer AC Lyles's series of plodding westerns stuffed with veteran stars was looking as tired as its principal players when this entry hobbled into release. Lyles coaxed James Cagney out of retirement to speak the narration and the film also introduced Roy Rogers Jr in a small supporting role. Otherwise, there's little pleasure now in the convoluted plot about gunrunning under the anonymous direction of Lesley Selander. **AE**

Howard Keel *Lee Travis* · Yvonne De Carlo *Jill Wyler* · John Ireland *Dan Shelby* · Marilyn Maxwell *Molly* · Scott Brady *Tom Rile* · Brian Donlevy *Major Smith* · Barton MacLane *Sheriff Grover* · James Craig *Ike Clanton* · Roy Rogers Jr *Roy* · James Cagney *Narrator* ■ *Dir* Lesley Selander · *Scr* Steve Fisher, from a story by Steve Fisher, Andrew Craddock

Arizona Dream ★★★ 15
Drama 1991 · Fr · Colour · 134min

Talented European directors often fail to succeed in transferring their specific view of life to English-language cinema, and this sprawling eccentric drama from Bosnian film-maker Emir Kusturica is a case in point. Nevertheless, it remains mesmerisingly watchable, largely owing to the superb performances of an eclectic cast, particularly the marvellous Faye Dunaway in one of her best roles as the emotional wreck that drifter Johnny Depp falls for, and the cleverly cast Jerry Lewis as Depp's uncle. Despite their efforts, it still doesn't really work. **TS** Swearing. **DVD**

Johnny Depp *Axel Backmar* · Jerry Lewis *Leo Sweetie* · Faye Dunaway *Elaine Stalker* · Lili Taylor *Grace Stalker* · Paulina Porizkova *Millie* · Vincent Gallo *Paul Backmar* · Michael J Pollard *Fabian* ■ *Dir* Emir Kusturica · *Scr* David Atkins, Emir Kusturica

The Arizona Kid ★★
Western 1939 · US · BW · 61min

In 1939, Roy Rogers became the third most popular western star in America; Gene Autry came top, while William "Hopalong Cassidy" Boyd was second. With his trademark white hat, twin holsters and geetar, Rogers rode, shot and crooned his way through scores of B-westerns like this one: a Civil War yarn in which our hero, a Confederate captain, must kill his best friend when he realises they are fighting on the wrong side of the moral fence. **AT**

Roy Rogers *Roy* · George "Gabby" Hayes *Gabby Whittaker* · Sally March *Laura Radford* · Stuart Hamblen *McBride* · Dorothy Sebastian *Bess Warren* · Earl Dwire *Dr Radford* ■ *Dir* Joseph Kane · *Scr* Luci Ward, Gerald Geraghty, from a story by Luci Ward

Arizona Raiders ★★
Western 1965 · US · Colour · 89min

This by-the-numbers western is a new version of the 1951 George Montgomery picture *The Texas Rangers*, which helps explain why it seems so old hat. Audie Murphy and Ben Cooper play the convicted members of Quantrill's Raiders, who agree to help Buster Crabbe and the newly formed Arizona Rangers round up the rest of the gang. **AE**

Audie Murphy *Clint* · Michael Dante *Brady* · Ben Cooper *Willie Martin* · Buster Crabbe [Larry "Buster" Crabbe] *Captain Andrews* · Gloria Talbott *Martina* · Ray Stricklyn *Danny Bonner* ■ *Dir* William Witney · *Scr* Alex Gottlieb, Mary and Willard Willingham, from a story by Frank Gruber, Richard Schayer

The Arizonian ★★★ U
Western 1935 · US · BW · 75min

An excellent screenplay by Dudley Nichols (who also wrote *Stagecoach*) enlivens a western which these days rather shows its age. Richard Dix is a marshal working with reformed outlaw Preston Foster to rid Silver City of corrupt Louis Calhern. Nichols won a best screenplay Oscar for his next film, *The Informer*, which also featured Margot Grahame. TS

Richard Dix *Clay Tallant* · Margot Grahame *Kitty Rivers* · Preston Foster *Tex Randolph* · Louis Calhern *Jake Mamien* · James Bush *Orin Tallant* · Ray Mayer *McClosky* ■ *Dir* Charles Vidor · *Scr* Dudley Nichols

Arlington Road ★★★★ 15
Thriller 1998 · US/UK · Colour · 112min

Is college professor Jeff Bridges's new neighbour Tim Robbins an urban terrorist planning to bomb a government target? Or is that theory fuelled by Bridges's paranoia following the death of his FBI agent wife? Director Mark Pellington audaciously chips away at the American psyche to deliver a gripping psychological thriller, powered by a totally sympathetic and believable performance by Bridges. This is seat-edge stuff, with a sobering message. AJ Violence, swearing. *DVD*

Jeff Bridges *Michael Faraday* · Tim Robbins *Oliver Lang* · Joan Cusack *Cheryl Lang* · Hope Davis *Brooke Wolf* · Robert Gossett *FBI Agent Whit Carver* · Mason Gamble *Brady Lang* · Spencer Treat Clark *Grant Faraday* · Stanley Anderson *Dr Archer Scobee* ■ *Dir* Mark Pellington · *Scr* Ehren Kruger

Armaan ★★★ U
Musical romantic drama
2003 · Ind · Colour · 158min

Honey Irani makes her directorial bow with this stellar melodrama scripted with ex-husband and prolific lyricist, Javed Akhtar. Amitabh Bachchan stars as a doctor determined to build a new hospital for his patients, but he dies before his ambition is fulfilled and son Anil Kapoor has to resolve his romantic crisis with Preity Zinta and Gracy Singh before realising his father's dream. With the emphasis more on filial than civic duty, this is a solid, but formulaic drama. DP Hindi +subtitles. *DVD*

Amitabh Bachchan *Dr Siddharth Sinha* · Anil Kapoor *Dr Akash Sinha* · Preity Zinta *Soniya Kapoor* · Gracy Singh *Dr Neha Mathur* · Hrithik Roshan ■ *Dir* Honey Irani · *Scr* Honey Irani, Javed Akhtar, from a story by Honey Irani

Armadillo ★★★★★ 15
War documentary 2010 · Den · Colour · 105min

This eye-opening documentary captures the experiences of a platoon of Danish soldiers at a military base – code-named "Armadillo" – in Afghanistan's Helmand province, where the camera crew risked their own lives facing the same bullets as their subjects. Presented with all the visual intensity of a Stanley Kubrick film, this is not just a vivid dispatch from Afghanistan, it's a classic snapshot of men at war. TJ Danish +subtitles. Swearing. *DVD*

■ *Dir* Janus Metz [Janus Metz Pedersen] · *Scr* Kasper Torsting

Armageddon ★★★ 15
Science-fiction action adventure
1998 · US · Colour · 147min

In this megabucks popcorn-spiller from producer Jerry Bruckheimer and director Michael Bay, there's a meteor "the size of Texas" heading for Earth. It's up to Bruce Willis and his motley oil-drilling gang to blast off and save us all. It's flashy, overwrought and excessive, but there's a knowing irony in the committee-written script and in the performances of Willis, Billy Bob Thornton and Steve Buscemi. AC Violence, swearing. *DVD* *BLU-RAY*

Bruce Willis *Harry S Stamper* · Billy Bob Thornton *Dan Truman* · Ben Affleck *AJ Frost* · Liv Tyler *Grace Stamper* · Will Patton *Charles "Chick" Chapple* · Steve Buscemi *Rockhound* · Keith David *General Kimsey* · Jason Isaacs *Ronald Quincy* · Chris Ellis *Walter Clark* · Charlton Heston *Narrator* ■ *Dir* Michael Bay · *Scr*

Jonathan Hensleigh, Jeffrey Abrams, from a story by Jonathan Hensleigh, Robert Roy Pool, adapted by Tony Gilroy, Shane Salerno

Armed and Dangerous ★ 15
Comedy 1986 · US · Colour · 83min

John Candy often showed very suspect judgement when it came to leading roles and this moronic comedy was a depressing waste of his talents. Teaming up with old chum Eugene Levy, this finds the unlikely duo causing chaos at a private security company and coming up against gangster Robert Loggia. JF *DVD*

John Candy *Frank Dooley* · Eugene Levy *Norman Kane* · Robert Loggia *Michael Carlino* · Kenneth McMillan *Clarence O'Connell* · Meg Ryan *Maggie Cavanaugh* · Brion James *Anthony Lazarus* · Jonathan Banks *Clyde Klepper* · Don Stroud *Sergeant Rizzo* ■ *Dir* Mark L Lester · *Scr* Harold Ramis, Peter Torokvei, from a story by Brian Grazer, Ramis, James Keach

Armored ★★ 12
Action thriller 2009 · US · Colour · 84min

In this workmanlike thriller, security guards plot to rob their own reinforced vans and blame the theft of millions in cash on an outside gang. However, the supposedly perfect crime unsurprisingly goes awry, and the bullets soon start flying. *Stomp the Yard's* Columbus Short provides the film's moral compass, as the new boy on the block who challenges the authority of gruff alpha males Matt Dillon and Laurence Fishburne, neither of whom is called upon to do much more than scowl and get handy with a gun. Director Nimrod Antal's attempts to crank up the tension are telegraphed far too often, meaning this never delivers quite enough bang for your buck. TeS Violence, swearing. *DVD* *BLU-RAY*

Matt Dillon *Mike Cochrane* · Columbus Short *Ty Hackett* · Jean Reno *Quinn* · Laurence Fishburne *Baines* · Amaury Nolasco *Palmer* · Fred Ward *Duncan Ashcroft* · Milo Ventimiglia *Eckehart* · Skeet Ulrich *Dobbs* ■ *Dir* Nimrod Antal · *Scr* James V Simpson

Armored Car Robbery ★★
Crime drama 1950 · US · BW · 67min

This B-movie thriller about a robbery that goes horribly wrong vaguely resembles *The Asphalt Jungle*, which was made the same year, while its ironic climax was copied by Stanley Kubrick for his 1956 movie *The Killing*. Director Richard Fleischer is clearly working on a shoestring, but that doesn't hinder his creation of suspense or atmosphere. The cast, alas, is distinctly third-rate. AT

Charles McGraw *Cordell* · Adele Jergens *Yvonne* · William Talman *Purvus* · Douglas Fowley *Benny* · Steve Brodie *Mapes* · Don McGuire *Ryan* · Don Haggerty *Cuyler* ■ *Dir* Richard Fleischer · *Scr* Earl Fenton, Gerald Drayson Adams, from a story by Robert Angus, Robert Leeds

The Armour of God ★★ 15
Martial arts adventure
1986 · HK · Colour · 84min

Although he has never reached the kung fu heights of Bruce Lee, Jackie Chan's high-vaulting, low-swiping action movies have an endearing humour that almost amounts to wit. This *Raiders of the Lost Ark* rip-off exports him to Europe, where he seeks out a crusader's relic and battles some lethal monks. As director as well as star, his style is not so much cramped as numbed. A sequel, *Operation Condor: the Armour of God II*, followed in 1990. TH Cantonese dubbed. *DVD*

Jackie Chan *Jackie* · Alan Tam *Alan* · Rosamund Kwan *Lorelei* · Lola Forner *May* · Bozidar Smilianic *Bannon* · Ken Boyle *Grand Wizard* · John Ladalski *Chief Lama* · Robert O'Brien (2) *Witch doctor* ■ *Dir* Jackie Chan · *Scr* Edward Tang, Szeto Chuek-Hun, Ken Lowe, John Sheppard, from a story by Barry Wong

The Armstrong Lie ★★★★ 15
Documentary 2013 · US · Colour · 118min

In Alex Gibney's previous film, *We Steal Secrets: the Story of Wikileaks*, Julian Assange was only an archive presence, but

here he has unprecedented access to abrasive fallen cycling idol Lance Armstrong. The original idea was to chart Armstrong's attempt to win the Tour again four years after retiring in 2005, but that film (entitled *The Road Back*) wasn't completed. So Gibney returned to confront Armstrong a mere three hours after his still-startling doping confession to Oprah. The footage is a staggering contrast: on the one hand the aggressive competitor castigating all who accused him of drug taking; on the other, a humbled shadow of a legend forced to accept a spectacular fall from grace. You don't have to be a sports fan to find this an utterly absorbing ride. JA Swearing. *DVD* *BLU-RAY*

Lance Armstrong ■ *Dir/Scr* Alex Gibney

The Army of Crime ★★★★ 15
Second World War drama
2009 · Fr · Colour · 133min

Robert Guédiguian's sobering true-life thriller follows the courageous exploits of Resistance fighters in Paris during the Second World War. The focus is on the members of a cell – a ragtag band scornfully dubbed "the army of crime" by the Vichy authorities - operating under the leadership of an exiled Armenian poet, who finds his non-violent ideals challenged when he realises what's happening to the Jews across the city. The film's authentic tension and palpable anger underline that there are still valuable stories to be told from this testing moment in history, and, moreover, that its moral questions continue to haunt us. TJ French +subtitles. Swearing, nudity. *DVD* *BLU-RAY*

Simon Abkarian *Missak Manouchian* · Virginie Ledoyen *Mélinée Manouchian* · Robinson Stévenin *Marcel Rayman* · Grégoire Leprince-Ringuet *Thomas Elek* · Lola Naymark *Monique Stern* ■ *Dir* Robert Guédiguian · *Scr* Robert Guédiguian, Serge Le Péron, Gilles Taurand, from a story by Le Péron

Army of Darkness ★★ 15
Fantasy horror comedy
1993 · US · Colour · 84min

Director Sam Raimi's juvenile second sequel to his classic *The Evil Dead* is a vapid exercise in watered-down horror kitsch. After a recap of the first two movies, Bruce Campbell battles with pit monsters, sword-wielding skeletons and his evil clone to find the sacred "Book of the Dead" that will help him escape the Dark Ages and return to the present. There's plenty of in-jokes for the discerning horror buff but little actual horror. AJ *DVD* *BLU-RAY*

Bruce Campbell *Ash/Evil Ash* · Embeth Davidtz *Sheila/Evil Sheila* · Marcus Gilbert *Arthur* · Ian Abercrombie *Wiseman* · Richard Grove *Duke Henry* · Michael Earl Reid *Gold Tooth* · Bridget Fonda *Linda* · Ivan Raimi *Fake Shemp* ■ *Dir* Sam Raimi · *Scr* Sam Raimi, Ivan Raimi

Army of Shadows ★★★★★ 12
Second World War drama
1969 · Fr/It · Colour · 138min

Jean-Pierre Melville's reputation rests largely on American-style gangster movies such as *Le Deuxième Souffle* and *Le Samouraï*, but this may be his greatest film. It is a long but utterly mesmerising vengeance thriller, set during the Second World War, with Lino Ventura playing a Resistance fighter searching for the man who betrayed him to the Nazis. With its superb cast, moody photography, marvellous use of Lyons locations and doom-laden flashbacks, this is a war drama par excellence that draws on the director's own experience as a member of the Maquis. AT French, German, English +subtitles. *DVD* *BLU-RAY*

Lino Ventura *Philippe Gerbier* · Paul Meurisse *Luc Jardie* · Simone Signoret *Mathilde* · Jean-Pierre Cassel *Jean-François* · Claude Mann *Le Masque* · Christian Barbier *Le Bison* · Serge Reggiani *Barber* · Alain Libolt *Paul Dounat* · Paul Crauchet *Felix* ■ *Dir* Jean-Pierre Melville · *Scr* Jean-Pierre Melville, from the novel by Joseph Kessel · *Cinematographer* Pierre Lhomme

Around the Bend ★★★ 15
Road movie drama 2004 · US · Colour · 79min

Michael Caine plays the ailing great-grandfather being cared for by his grandson (Josh Lucas) and great-grandson (Jonah Bobo). Then, out of the blue, son Christopher Walken returns home for the first time in 30 years. Following Caine's death, the three men take a road trip to Albequerque. Along the way, family mysteries are slowly solved. Its quirkiness feels rather forced and it lacks tension, but this heartfelt film is well acted and satisfyingly subtle. KK Swearing. *DVD*

Christopher Walken *Turner Lair* · Josh Lucas *Jason Lair* · Michael Caine *Henry Lair* · Glenne Headly *Katrina* · Jonah Bobo *Zach Lair* · Norbert Weisser *Walter* ■ *Dir/Scr* Jordan Roberts

Around the World in 80 Days ★★★★ U
Adventure 1956 · US · Colour · 174min

An epic very much of its time, this vastly entertaining, star-studded travelogue was produced (with some difficulty) by the great showman and charismatic producer Michael Todd, who was awarded the best picture Oscar for his considerable pains. The cast, led by the ultra-urbane David Niven, couldn't be bettered, nor could the use of worldwide locations – 13 countries in all. Todd persuaded 46 guest stars to appear in supporting roles, and spotting them is a delight. TS *DVD*

David Niven *Phileas Fogg* · Cantinflas *Passepartout* · Shirley MacLaine *Princess Aouda* · Robert Newton *Inspector Fix* · Noël Coward *Hesketh-Baggott* · Trevor Howard *Fallentin* · Robert Morley *Ralph* · Hermione Gingold *Sporting lady* · Marlene Dietrich *Dance hall girl, Barbary Coast saloon* · Peter Lorre *Steward* · John Mills *Cabby* · George Raft *Bouncer, Barbary Coast saloon* · Frank Sinatra *Pianist, Barbary Coast saloon* · Buster Keaton *Train conductor* · John Gielgud *Foster* ■ *Dir* Michael Anderson · *Scr* SJ Perelman, James Poe, from the novel by Jules Verne · *Cinematographer* Lionel Lindon · *Music* Victor Young

Around the World in 80 Days ★★ PG
Period comedy adventure
2004 · US/Ger/Ire/UK · Colour · 115min

Inventor Phileas Fogg (Steve Coogan) and his valet Passepartout (Jackie Chan) endeavour to circumnavigate the globe in record time to win a wager set by the villainous Lord Kelvin (Jim Broadbent). Chan delivers his trademark martial arts rough and tumble along the way, but a redundant subplot involving a stolen jade Buddha only serves to slow the action down. The broad comedy is perhaps more suited to Chan's pratfalls than Coogan's wit, but big-name cameos to help pass the time on this laboured journey. GM *DVD*

Jackie Chan *Passepartout/Lao Xing* · Steve Coogan *Phileas Fogg* · Cécile de France *Monique La Roche* · Jim Broadbent *Lord Kelvin* · Kathy Bates *Queen Victoria* · Arnold Schwarzenegger *Prince Hapi* · Jim Cleese *Grizzled sergeant* · Owen Wilson *Wilbur Wright* · Luke Wilson *Orville Wright* · Richard Branson *Balloon man* ■ *Dir* Frank Coraci · *Scr* David Titcher, David Benullo, David Goldstein, from the novel by Jules Verne

The Arrangement ★★ 15
Drama 1969 · US · Colour · 120min

This rather distasteful film from director Elia Kazan is taken from his own novel about a successful New York advertising man, played by Kirk Douglas, who becomes disenchanted with his cosy, privileged world and decides to jettison work, marriage and respectability. A starry cast struggles with a rather old-fashioned premise, while Kazan promotes the abdication of all personal responsibility. SH Some violence, swearing, brief nudity.

Kirk Douglas *Eddie Anderson* · Faye Dunaway *Gwen* · Deborah Kerr *Florence Anderson* · Richard Boone *Sam Anderson* · Hume Cronyn *Arthur* · Michael Higgins *Michael* · John Randolph Jones *Charles* ■ *Dir* Elia Kazan · *Scr* Elia Kazan, from his novel

Arrietty ★★★ U
Animated fantasy adventure
2010 · Jpn · Colour · 90min

Mary Norton's *The Borrowers* gets a beautifully drawn makeover from Japanese animation house Studio Ghibli (*Spirited Away*). It's a coming-of-age story following Arrietty (voiced by Saoirse Ronan), the only child of tiny people surviving on the scraps left by humans, as she forges an unlikely friendship with a frail boy. The storytelling is mild-mannered from first-time director Hiromasa Yonebayashi, and it lacks imaginative verve, but it does tap into the vulnerability of these little folk in a way that's captivating. **TJ** Japanese, dubbed.
DVD Blu

Saoirse Ronan *Arrietty* · Tom Holland (2) *Sho* · Mark Strong *Pod* · Olivia Colman *Homily* · Geraldine McEwan *Haru* · Phyllida Law *Sadako* · Luke Allen-Gale *Spiller* ■ *Dir* Hiromasa Yonebayashi · *Scr* Hayao Miyazaki, Keiko Niwa, from the novel *The Borrowers* by Mary Norton

The Arrival ★★★ 12
Science-fiction thriller
1996 · US · Colour · 110min

Director David Twohy skilfully reworks a number of science-fiction clichés (as well as ideas from his *Waterworld* and *The Fugitive* scripts) to deliver a highly polished entry in the alien-invasion sweepstakes. Charlie Sheen plays an astronomer who goes on the run after he discovers an extraterrestrial conspiracy to change the Earth's climate and prepare it for colonisation. He faces stylish computer-generated effects at every turn, but still emerges as the winner in this pleasing, if low-key, B-movie. **AJ** *DVD*

Charlie Sheen *Zane Ziminski* · Ron Silver *Gordian* · Lindsay Crouse *Ilana Green* · Teri Polo *Char* · Richard Schiff *Calvin* · Tony T Johnson *Kiki* ■ *Dir/Scr* David Twohy

The Arrival of Wang ★★★ 15
Science-fiction horror
2011 · It · Colour · 82min

An interpreter with liberal principles (Francesca Cuttica) is taken to a dank bunker by a shady branch of government and asked to act as interlocutor between a mysterious individual named Wang, who only speaks Mandarin, and his aggressive Italian-speaking interrogator (Ennio Fantastichini). Where does Wang come from, what does he want and is he dangerous? The performances are shaky, the effects even more so and everything takes place pretty much in one room. But the Manetti brothers understand the power of contrasting the mundane with the weird and their plot twists are as humorous as they are dramatic. **SvM** Italian, Mandarin +subtitles. *DVD*

Francesca Cuttica *Gaia* · Ennio Fantastichini *Curti* · Li Yong *Wang* ■ *Dir/Scr* Antonio Manetti, Marco Manetti

Arrow in the Dust ★★ U
Western
1954 · US · Colour · 80min

Prolific director Lesley Selander was one of the unsung heroes of the western, whose feature output embraced such cowboy icons as Buck Jones, Hopalong Cassidy and Tim Holt. This perfectly workmanlike programme filler stars Sterling Hayden as a deserter masquerading as an officer to help out a wagon train. Lee Van Cleef makes an early appearance. **TS**

Sterling Hayden *Bart Laish* · Coleen Gray *Christella* · Keith Larsen *Lt King* · Tom Tully *Crowshaw* · Jimmy Wakely *Carqueville* · Tudor Owen *Tillotson* · Lee Van Cleef *Crew boss* ■ *Dir* Lesley Selander · *Scr* Don Martin, from the novel by LL Foreman

Arrowhead ★★ U
Western
1953 · US · Colour · 105min

This western derives considerable force from its depiction of the intense hatred between Charlton Heston, as the army scout who was raised by the Apaches, and Jack Palance as the college-educated son of the chief. The government wants peace but Heston is sure the Apaches can't be trusted. While Palance is chillingly ruthless

as the native American, Heston remains monotonously grim. The film is distinctly unpleasant in the crude way it deals with a delicate subject. **AE**

Charlton Heston *Ed Bannon* · Jack Palance *Toriano* · Katy Jurado *Nita* · Brian Keith *Capt North* · Mary Sinclair *Lee* · Milburn Stone *Sandy MacKinnon* · Richard Shannon *Lieutenant Kirk* ■ *Dir* Charles Marquis Warren · *Scr* Charles Marquis Warren, from the novel *Adobe Walls* by WR Burnett

Arrowsmith ★★★
Drama
1931 · US · BW · 102min

John Ford wasn't, perhaps, the ideal director for the work of Sinclair Lewis, but this sturdy adaptation of Lewis's novel benefits from a marvellous performance by Ronald Colman as the idealistic doctor of the title who's seeking a cure for bubonic plague. Colman brings a vivid, idealistic freshness to the part and single-handedly justifies this Samuel Goldwyn production. Helen Hayes suffers nobly as his wife and a pre-stardom Myrna Loy excels as the bored society girl with whom Colman has a fling. **TS**

Ronald Colman *Dr Martin Arrowsmith* · Helen Hayes *Leora* · AC Anson *Professor Gottlieb* · Richard Bennett (1) *Sondelius* · Claude King *Dr Tubbs* · Beulah Bondi *Mrs Tozer* · Myrna Loy *Joyce Lanyon* · Russell Hopton *Terry Wickett* ■ *Dir* John Ford · *Scr* Sidney Howard, from the novel by Sinclair Lewis

The Arsenal Stadium Mystery ★★★ PG
Sports murder mystery 1939 · UK · BW · 82min

While not premier league stuff, this far-from-baffling mystery has become something of a cult item in art house circles. There's plenty to enjoy as maverick Scotland Yard inspector Leslie Banks tries to find out who murdered star player Anthony Bushell during a friendly match, not least the chance to see members of the 1937/38 Arsenal championship-winning side in action. Director Thorold Dickinson reveals a talent for authentic detail and there's also a pleasing lightness about the action. **DP** *DVD*

Leslie Banks *Inspector Slade* · Greta Gynt *Gwen Lee* · Ian MacLean *Sergeant Clinton* · Esmond Knight *Raille* · Liane Linden *Inga* · Brian Worth *Philip Morring* · Anthony Bushell *Jack Dyce* ■ *Dir* Thorold Dickinson · *Scr* Thorold Dickinson, Donald Bull, from the novel by Leonard Gribble

Arsene Lupin ★★★
Crime adventure 1932 · US · BW · 84min

The names of John and Lionel Barrymore sharing the marquee guaranteed big audiences for this well-upholstered version of Maurice Leblanc's master criminal. It was the first time the two brothers had starred together on film and that prospect created fireworks in 1932, though today the picture inevitably lacks that resonance and creaks a little. John plays the thief, Lionel the detective on his trail, and director Jack Conway sacrifices plot (the theft of the Mona Lisa from the Louvre) for some elaborate thesping. **AT**

John Barrymore *Duke of Charmerace* · Lionel Barrymore *Guerchard* · Karen Morley *Sonia* · John Miljan *Prefect of Police* · Tully Marshall *Gourney-Martin* ■ *Dir* Jack Conway · *Scr* Carey Wilson, Bayard Veiller, Lenore Coffee, from the play by Maurice Leblanc, Francis de Croisset [François Wiener]

Arsène Lupin ★★★ 15
Period crime adventure
2004 · Fr/UK/Sp/It · Colour · 130min

Maurice Leblanc's notorious *fin-de-siècle* cracksman has already been played on screen by such luminaries as Jules Berry and John Barrymore. But no previous outing can boast the lavish settings and sweeping storyline of Jean-Paul Salomé's rousing adventure. Moving from the daring theft of a necklace that belonged to Marie Antoinette, the story becomes increasingly complex and compelling as master of disguise Romain Duris meets his match in the darkly seductive Kristin Scott Thomas. Duris is well supported by a cracking gallery

of rogues and a director who knows the difference between spectacle and excess. **DP** French +subtitles. Violence.
DVD

Romain Duris *Arsène Lupin* · Kristin Scott Thomas *Joséphine* · Pascal Greggory *Beaumagnan* · Eva Green *Clarisse* · Robin Renucci *Dreux-Soubise* · Patrick Toomey *Léonard* · Mathieu Carrière *Duc d'Orléans* · Philippe Magnan *Bonnetot* · Marie Bunel *Henriette Lupin* · Philippe Lemaire *Cardinal d'Etigues* ■ *Dir* Jean-Paul Salomé · *Scr* Jean-Paul Salomé, Laurent Vachaud, from the novel *La Comtesse de Cagliostro* by Maurice Leblanc

Arsene Lupin Returns ★★★
Crime adventure 1938 · US · BW · 80min

The glamorous criminal was first personified by John Barrymore in 1932, memorably pitted against his brother Lionel, and the ultra-sophisticated thief went down a treat with American audiences. Six years later the same studio, MGM, decided to revive him, this time played by the equally debonair Melvyn Douglas. Trouble is, the French flavour of the original has been Americanised here, with a plot involving Warren William as an overly publicity conscious ex-FBI man. **TS**

Melvyn Douglas *Rene Farrand* · Virginia Bruce *Lorraine Degrissac* · Warren William *Steve Emerson* · John Halliday *Count Degrissac* · Nat Pendleton *Joe Doyle* · Monty Woolley *Georges Bouchet* · EE Clive *Alf* · George Zucco *Prefect of Police* ■ *Dir* George Fitzmaurice · *Scr* James Kevin McGuinness, Howard Emmett Rogers, George Harmon Coxe · *Music* Franz Waxman

Arsenic and Old Lace
★★★★★ PG

Classic black comedy 1944 · US · BW · 113min

From the moment he saw Joseph Kesselring's hit play, Frank Capra was determined to bring it to the screen. Although forced to settle for Raymond Massey after he failed to get Boris Karloff to repeat his stage triumph, Capra was blessed with a sparkling cast. Cary Grant only agreed to take the lead as it gave him the chance to reunite with Jean Adair, but he then proceeded to insist on changes to the script, costumes, sets and the lighting. Grant ended up donating his fee to a range of war charities and rarely spoke of the picture with any fondness. A shame, really, as he hurls himself into the part of the decent nephew who discovers that his respectable aunts (played with hilarious dottiness by Josephine Hull and Adair) are serial killers. Spookily lit and very funny, the film is unmissable, with Grant's wonderful double-takes lightening the pitch-black humour. **DP** *DVD*

Cary Grant *Mortimer Brewster* · Priscilla Lane *Elaine Harper* · Raymond Massey *Jonathan Brewster* · Jack Carson *O'Hara* · Edward Everett Horton *Mr Witherspoon* · Peter Lorre *Dr Einstein* · James Gleason *Lt Rooney* · Josephine Hull *Abby Brewster* · Jean Adair *Martha Brewster* · John Alexander (1) "Teddy Roosevelt" Brewster · Grant Mitchell *Reverend Harper* · Edward McNamara *Brophy* · Garry Owen *Taxi cab driver* ■ *Dir* Frank Capra · *Scr* Julius J & Philip G Epstein, from the play by Joseph Kesselring · *Cinematographer* Sol Polito

The Art of Getting By ★★ 12
Romantic comedy drama
2011 · US · Colour · 83min

Freddie Highmore is the rich, rebellious lad who doesn't get on with his secretly unemployed stepdad and refuses to do his homework. Ever! He finds himself falling in with an even richer crowd headed by Emma Roberts, with whom he begins his first romance. Highmore and Roberts have just enough charm to offset much of the flat, predictable screenplay and this, together with some pretty New York photography from Ben Kutchins ensures that *The Art of Getting By* gets by, but only just. **AS** Some sexual references, brief swearing. *DVD*
Blu

Freddie Highmore *George Zinavoy* · Emma Roberts *Sally Howe* · Sasha Spielberg *Zoe Rubenstein* · Michael Angarano *Dustin* · Marcus Carl Franklin *Will Sharpe* · Rita Wilson *Vivian Sargent* ■ *Dir/Scr* Gavin Wiesen · *Cinematographer* Ben Kutchins

Art of Love ★★★ U
Comedy 1965 · US · Colour · 98min

This is a glossy, very silly but enjoyable example of the Technicolor Universal 1960s style as produced by Ross Hunter. It is bedecked with likeable stars and is a jolly pleasant way to pass the time. The would-be adult plot involves James Garner and Dick Van Dyke as struggling artists in Paris, with Angie Dickinson and Elke Sommer as their chicks and the great Ethel Merman as a singing madame. **TS**

James Garner *Casey* · Dick Van Dyke *Paul* · Elke Sommer *Nikki* · Angie Dickinson *Laurie* · Ethel Merman *Madame Coco* · Carl Reiner *Rodin* · Pierre Olaf *Carnot* ■ *Dir* Norman Jewison · *Scr* Carl Reiner, from a story by Richard Alan Simmons, William Sackheim

The Art of Murder ★★
Suspense thriller 1999 · US · Colour · 100min

Polish-born Joanna Pacula certainly deserves better than this tepid thriller, in which she's blackmailed by slimy Peter Onorati, who threatens to show her wealthy, sozzled husband Michael Moriarty explicit pictures of her cavortings with his supposedly loyal lieutenant, Boyd Kestner. There's a couple of twists that just about pass muster, but you might not consider them worth waiting for. **DP**

Michael Moriarty *Cole* · Joanna Pacula *Elizabeth Sheridan* · Boyd Kestner *Tony Blanchard* · Peter Onorati *Willie* ■ *Dir* Ruben Preuss · *Scr* Sean Smith, Anthony Stark

The Art of the Steal ★★ 15
Heist caper 2013 · Can · Colour · 90min

Art-thief brothers Kurt Russell and Matt Dillon reunite for one last heist after years of bad blood in this old-fashioned caper movie. The cast members have a winning camaraderie, but that can't enliven the self-conscious dialogue, hokey action and telegraphed plot machinations, which all feel like so many Guy Ritchie leftovers. Occasionally charming, yet completely unoriginal, this is dumb fun, no more, no less. **AJ** Swearing, sexual references.

Kurt Russell *Crunch Calhoun* · Jay Baruchel *Francie Tobin* · Matt Dillon *Nicky Calhoun* · Kenneth Welsh *Uncle Paddy* · Chris Diamantopoulos *Guy de Cornet* · Katheryn Winnick *Lola* · Terence Stamp *Samuel Winter* ■ *Dir/Scr* Jonathan Sobol

The Art of War ★★ 18
Action thriller 2000 · Can/US · Colour · 112min

This fails to rise above the ordinary, despite a substantial budget and some star names. The daft and hackneyed plot has Wesley Snipes as a United Nations "dirty tricks" operative who finds himself framed for the assassination of the Chinese ambassador. Snipes only gets really animated in some so-so martial arts sequences, but that's an improvement on Donald Sutherland and Anne Archer, who look bored and listless. **DA** Violence, swearing, drug abuse. *DVD*

Wesley Snipes *Neil Shaw* · Anne Archer *Eleanor Hooks* · Maury Chaykin *Cappella* · Marie Matiko *Julia Fang* · Cary-Hiroyuki Tagawa *David Chan* · Michael Biehn *Bly* · Donald Sutherland *Douglas Thomas* · Liliana Komorowska *Novak* · James Hong *Ambassador Wu* ■ *Dir* Christian Duguay · *Scr* Wayne Beach, Simon Davis Barry, from a story by Wayne Beach

The Art of War II: Betrayal ★ 15
Action thriller 2008 · Can · Colour · 98min

Wesley Snipes adds another clunker to his CV with this lumbering sequel to the 2000 action thriller. Sleepwalking through the generic storyline, he returns as ex-secret agent Neil Shaw, who here finds himself embroiled in a political assassination conspiracy that naturally sees him set up to take the fall. **SF** Violence, swearing. *DVD*

Wesley Snipes *Neil Shaw* · Lochlyn Munro *John Garret* · Athena Karkanis *Heather* · Winston Rekert *Reverend Tim* ■ *Dir* Josef Rusnak · *Scr* Jason Bourque, Keith Shaw

Artemisia ★★★ 18
Biographical drama
1997 · Fr/Ger/It · Colour · 91min

The 17th-century painter Artemisia Gentileschi emerges from this sumptuous biopic as the doomed heroine of a gothic melodrama rather than a courageous artist who challenged the conventions of her day. However, while director Agnès Merlet's approach has appalled purists and feminists alike, she has nevertheless produced a moving portrayal that captures both the flavour of the times and the tragic fate of a passionate artist. Valentina Cervi conveys sensuality rather than creative zest in the title role, but this still succeeds in being a vibrant portrait. DP French, Italian +subtitles. Nudity, sex scenes.
Michel Serrault *Orazio Gentileschi* · Valentina Cervi *Artemisia Gentileschi* · Miki Manojlovic *Agostino Tassi* · Luca Zingaretti *Cosimo* · Brigitte Catillon *Tuzia* ■ *Dir* Agnès Merlet · *Scr* Agnès Merlet, Christine Miller

Arthur ★★★★ 15
Screwball comedy 1981 · US · Colour · 93min

While Dudley Moore's drunken millionaire is outclassed by John Gielgud's disdainful butler, he still shines in this boozy variation on Jeeves and Wooster. As he tries to change his layabout lifestyle for love of working girl Liza Minnelli, Moore displays the charm and timing that helped to make *10* a hit, though his character is sometimes too clichéd. The ever-adaptable Gielgud delivers his lines with such wonderful aplomb that he won an Oscar. A planned remake with Russell Brand can't possibly live up to this marvellous original. TH Swearing. *DVD*
Dudley Moore *Arthur Bach* · Liza Minnelli *Linda Marolla* · John Gielgud *Hobson* · Geraldine Fitzgerald *Martha Bach* · Jill Eikenberry *Susan Johnson* · Stephen Elliot *[Stephen Elliott (1)]* *Burt Johnson* · Ted Ross *Bitterman* ■ *Dir/Scr* Steve Gordon

Arthur 2: On the Rocks ★ PG
Romantic comedy 1988 · US · Colour · 108min

Seven years after the charming if one-joke original, Dudley Moore returned to the role of the drunken millionaire in this disastrous sequel. After a financial takeover by the father of his former girlfriend, Moore is left penniless and has to save his marriage to Liza Minnelli and regain his fortune before the end credits. JB Swearing. *DVD*
Dudley Moore *Arthur Bach* · Liza Minnelli *Linda Marolla Bach* · John Gielgud *Hobson* · Geraldine Fitzgerald *Martha Bach* · Stephen Elliott (1) *Burt Johnson* · Paul Benedict *Fairchild* · Kathy Bates *Mrs Canby* ■ *Dir* Bud Yorkin · *Scr* Andy Breckman, from characters by Steve Gordon

Arthur ★★ 12
Comedy 2011 · US · Colour · 105min

Russell Brand steps into the late Dudley Moore's shoes in this relatively faithful remake, as a playboy drunk under pressure to marry a manipulative executive (Jennifer Garner) so creating a merger between two powerful business families. Trouble is, he's fallen for a free-spirited tour guide (Greta Gerwig). Brand brings plenty of his eloquent stand-up persona to the role, but the much-loved original film looms large over proceedings, while Helen Mirren as Arthur's long-suffering nanny is no match for John Gielgud's pithy butler. The feeling persists that we've seen it all before, and with a great deal more charm. TeS Brief swearing, sexual references. *DVD* *Blu-ray*
Russell Brand *Arthur Bach* · Helen Mirren *Hobson* · Jennifer Garner *Susan Johnson* · Greta Gerwig *Naomi* · Luis Guzman *Bitterman* · Nick Nolte *Burt Johnson* · Geraldine James *Vivienne Bach* ■ *Dir* Jason Winer · *Scr* Peter Baynham, from the 1981 film · *Cinematographer* Uta Briesewitz

Arthur & Mike ★★ 15
Comedy drama 2012 · US · Colour · 93min

British duo Colin Firth and Emily Blunt deliver polished, tender performances in this worthy indie drama. Firth plays an unhappy former golf pro, now slumming it as a penpusher, who fakes his own death and reinvents himself as Arthur Newman (the film's original title). Heading off on a road trip to a new life in Indiana, Arthur meets suicidal thief Mike (Blunt), who also has reasons for travelling under an alias. The leads draw some empathy from the viewer, but the story offers little resolution and its underdeveloped subplots set it on a road to nowhere. JL Swearing, drug abuse, sex scenes, nudity.
Colin Firth *Arthur Newman/Wallace Avery* · Emily Blunt *Mike/Charlotte* · Anne Heche *Mina Crawley* · Sterling Beaumon *Grant* ■ *Dir* Dante Ariola · *Scr* Becky Johnston

Arthur and the Invisibles ★★ U
Part-animated fantasy adventure
2006 · US/Fr · Colour · 89min

This anglicised family fantasy from co-writer/director Luc Besson obviously loses something in translation. Based on his series of French children's books (co-authored with Céline Garcia), the film uses live action and computer-generated effects to tell the story of ten-year-old Arthur (Freddie Highmore), who shrinks himself to enlist the help of a tribe of tiny, elfin beings. Together they set out to find a lost fortune that will save the boy's family home from foreclosure. Despite the presence of such luminaries as Madonna and Robert De Niro, the voice artistry here is decidedly ordinary and the plot may prove too convoluted for younger audiences. DA *DVD*
Freddie Highmore *Arthur* · Mia Farrow *Granny* · Penny Balfour *Arthur's mother* · Douglas Rand *[Doug Rand]* *Arthur's father* · Madonna *Princess Selenia* · Jimmy Fallon *Betameche* · Robert De Niro *The King* · Harvey Keitel *Miro* · Emilio Estevez *Ferryman* · Snoop Dogg *Max* ■ *Dir* Luc Besson · *Scr* Luc Besson, Céline Garcia, from Besson's book *Arthur and the Minimoys*, from an idea by Garcia

Arthur Christmas ★★★ U
Seasonal animated adventure
2011 · UK/US · Colour · 93min

In this seasonal offering from Aardman, James McAvoy voices gangly young Arthur, who is overcome by enthusiasm for the gift-giving season, as his father, the current Santa (Jim Broadbent), slowly creeps towards retirement. But the hi-tech operation to deliver billions of presents in one night comes unstuck, prompting Arthur and the irascible Grandsanta (Bill Nighy) to leap into action and do things the old-fashioned way. Terrific characters and a wonderful mash-up of old and new holiday traditions give this a real sense of occasion, while the animation is inspired and breathtakingly inventive. Sadly, the script does tend to meander in the middle, but our titular hero, with his wonderful holiday jumper, makes a big impression in his colourful film debut. KK *DVD* *Blu-ray* *3D*
James McAvoy *Arthur* · Hugh Laurie *Steve* · Jim Broadbent *Santa* · Bill Nighy *Grandsanta* · Imelda Staunton *Mrs Santa* · Ashley Jensen *Bryony* · Matt Lucas *Santa elf 1* ■ *Dir* Sarah Smith (2) · *Scr* Sarah Smith (2), Peter Baynham

Arthur Miller's The American Clock ★★★
Drama 1993 · US · Colour

An adaptation of Arthur Miller's 1980 play, which Miller described as "a mural of American society in the Depression crisis." This TV version is a three-stranded sprawl, dealing with a powerful family of bankers gone bust, a songwriter faced by eviction and a rich New Yorker whose journey to the rural heartland transforms him into a Marxist. Directed by Bob Clark, it features an impressive cast. AT
Mary McDonnell *Rose Baumler* · Darren McGavin *Older Arthur Huntington* · Kelly Preston *Diana Marley* · David Strathairn *Young Arthur Huntington* · Eddie Bracken *Grandpa* · Tony Roberts *Jesse Livermore* · Jim Dale *Ted Quinn* · Estelle Parsons *Older Doris* ■ *Dir* Bob Clark · *Scr* Frank Galati, from the play by Arthur Miller, from the book *Hard Times* by Studs Terkel

Arthur's Dyke ★★ 15
Comedy drama 2001 · UK · Colour · 103min

This Ealingesque comedy about the eccentricity of the British character doesn't really make the grade. Offa's Dyke provides the magnificent setting for the midlife reunion of college pals Robert Daws, Nicholas Farrell and Richard Graham. Pauline Quirke tops the bill as the woman on a soul-searching mission of her own who travels with the three men. Ribald and occasionally poignant, but without social insight. DP *DVD*
Pauline Quirke *Janet* · Robert Daws *Arthur* · Nicholas Farrell *Geoffrey* · Richard Graham (2) *Andy* · Rebecca Lacey *Phillipa* · Dennis Waterman *Doubleday* · Brian Conley *Dave* · Warren Clarke *Doug* ■ *Dir* Gerry Poulson · *Scr* Jackie Robb, Bernie Stringle

Arthur's Hallowed Ground ★★
Drama 1985 · UK · Colour · 85min

The Arthur of the title (Jimmy Jewel) is an indispensable school groundsman whose main ambition in life is to create the perfect cricket pitch. Cue much fiddling with antiquated machinery, which is as slow-moving as the film itself. This is the directorial debut of the distinguished cinematographer Freddie Young, then 82 years old, but his experience doesn't seem to have helped him succeed as director. LH
Jimmy Jewel *Arthur* · Jean Boht *Betty* · David Swift *Lionel* · Michael Elphick *Len* · Derek Benfield *Eric* · Vas Blackwood *Henry* · John Flanagan *Norman* · Bernard Gallagher *George* ■ *Dir* Freddie Young · *Scr* Peter Gibbs

Article 99 ★ 15
Comedy drama 1992 · US · Colour · 98min

This sets out with two aims, but fails to accomplish either of them. Firstly, it wants to make us angry that Washington neglects the war veterans in its hospitals. Secondly, it seeks to reproduce the gallows humour of *MASH* by having the cast quip endlessly through each crisis. An unrelieved failure. DP Violence, swearing. *DVD*
Ray Liotta *Dr Richard Sturgess* · Kiefer Sutherland *Dr Peter Morgan* · Forest Whitaker *Dr Sid Handleman* · Lea Thompson *Dr Robin Van Dorn* · John C McGinley *Dr Rudy Bobrick* · John Mahoney *Dr Henry Dreyfoos* · Keith David *Luther Jerome* · Kathy Baker *Dr Diane Walton* · Eli Wallach *Sam Abrams* ■ *Dir* Howard Deutch · *Scr* Ron Cutler

The Artist ★★★★★ PG
Silent romantic drama
2011 · Fr/Bel · BW · 96min

Just as they did in their French *OSS 117* spy spoofs, director Michel Hazanavicius and star Jean Dujardin perfectly evoke an authentic period and style in this remarkable re-creation of Hollywood's silent movie era. Dujardin's charm is successfully harnessed as a matinée idol whose career nosedives with the arrival of the talkies, just as that of an extra in one of his movies (Bérénice Bejo) is taking off. Embracing the techniques and look of the times, and paying homage to numerous silent classics and *Citizen Kane*, this loving pastiche is a sheer delight. AJ *DVD* *Blu-ray*
Jean Dujardin *George Valentin* · Bérénice Bejo *Peppy Miller* · James Cromwell *Clifton* · Penelope Ann Miller *Doris* · Malcolm McDowell *The Butler* · Missi Pyle *Constance* ■ *Dir/Scr* Michel Hazanavicius · *Cinematographer* Guillaume Schiffman · *Music* Ludovic Bource

The Artist and the Model ★★★★ 12A
Drama 2012 · Sp/Fr · BW · 105min

Set in the French Pyrenees in 1943 and loosely based on incidents in the lives of Picasso and Matisse, this is a compelling treatise on the ravages of war and time. Claudia Cardinale offers sanctuary to Spanish Civil War fugitive Aida Folch in the hope that her spirit and beauty will inspire her octagenarian sculptor husband, Jean Rochefort. The performances and visuals are superb, while the screenplay (co-written by Trueba and Jean-Claude Carrière) explores notions of heroism, liberty, inspiration and the preciousness of life with rare intelligence and intensity. DP French, Catalan, Spanish +subtitles. Nudity.
Jean Rochefort *Marc Cross* · Claudia Cardinale *Léa* · Chus Lampreave *María* · Götz Otto *[Gotz Otto]* *Werner* · Martin Gamet *Pierre* ■ *Dir* Fernando Trueba · *Scr* Fernando Trueba, Jean-Claude Carrière

Artists and Models ★★★ U
Musical 1937 · US · BW · 97min

Jack Benny's first starring vehicle was made at the height of his radio fame. While the Louis Armstrong and Martha Raye blackface sequences seem tasteless and offensive today, this is a raucous funfest that fairly zips along under Raoul Walsh's canny direction. There's a lovely plot-driving performance from young co-star Ida Lupino that's a joy to watch, and sturdy Richard Arlen also registers strongly. A sequel, *Artists and Models Abroad*, followed in 1938. TS
Jack Benny *Mac Brewster* · Ida Lupino *Paula* · Richard Arlen *Alan Townsend* · Gail Patrick *Cynthia* · Ben Blue *Jupiter Pluvius* · Judy Canova *Toots* · Donald Meek *Dr Zimmer* · Louis Armstrong · Martha Raye ■ *Dir* Raoul Walsh · *Scr* Walter DeLeon, Francis Martin, from a story by Sig Herzig, Gene Thackery · *Choreographers* Vincente Minnelli, LeRoy Prinz · *Music* Victor Young

Artists and Models ★★★★ U
Musical comedy 1955 · US · Colour · 108min

This superior Dean Martin and Jerry Lewis vehicle is gloriously photographed in some brilliant Technicolor. Of course, appreciation really depends on how one feels about Martin and Lewis, here expertly cast as a cartoonist and wacky fantasist, respectively, Dean using Jerry's dreams for inspiration. What gives this lunacy credence is that it's the work of Frank Tashlin, himself a noted cartoon artist, and there's a wonderful stylistic boldness to the design. TS
Dean Martin *Rick Todd* · Jerry Lewis *Eugene Fullstack* · Shirley MacLaine *Bessie Sparrowbush* · Dorothy Malone *Abigail Parker* · Eddie Mayehoff *Mr Murdock* · Eva Gabor *Sonia* · Anita Ekberg *Anita* · George Winslow *Richard Stilton* · Jack Elam *Ivan* ■ *Dir* Frank Tashlin · *Scr* Frank Tashlin, Hal Kanter, Herbert Baker, from a play by Norman Lessing, Michael Davidson · *Cinematographer* Daniel L Fapp

The Aryan Couple ★★ 12
Second World War thriller based on a true story
2004 · US/UK · Colour · 114min

There's a fascinating film to be made about the Europa Plan, which enabled wealthy Jews to buy safe passage from the Third Reich, but this ponderously scripted movie isn't it. Based on a true story, it concerns a Hungarian industrialist (Martin Landau) and his attempt to negotiate his family's freedom. This potentially gripping story is undermined by self-indulgent performances from Danny Webb and Christopher Fulford (as Himmler and his SS henchman), while Landau and Judy Parfitt (as his feisty wife) are also culpable. Veteran film-maker John Daly seems as overawed by key locations such as Auschwitz as he is by the responsibility of doing the tale justice. DP Some violence.
Martin Landau *Joseph Krauzenberg* · Judy Parfitt *Rachel Krauzenberg* · Kenny Doughty *Hans Vassman* · Caroline Carver *Ingrid Vassman* · Christopher Fulford *Edelhein* · Danny Webb *Himmler* · Steven Mackintosh *Eichmann* · Jake Wood *Dressler* ■ *Dir* John Daly · *Scr* John Daly, Kendrew Lascelles, from a story by Lascelles · *Cinematographer* Sergei Kozlov

As Above, So Below ★★★ 15
Horror 2014 · US · Colour · 93min

This by-the-book spook story follows a group of adventurers as they explore the catacombs beneath the streets of Paris in search of ancient artefacts, but find more than they bargained for. Expedition leader Perdita Weeks makes a steely heroine, but her fellow subterranean thrill-seekers are drawn as uninteresting archetypes. It's a perfectly serviceable addition to the "found footage" genre of chillers, but it never quite

A

racks up enough tension for a full-on fright-fest. TeS Violence, swearing. DVD BL

Perdita Weeks *Scarlett Marlowe* • Ben Feldman *George* • Edwin Hodge *Benji* • François Civil *Papillon* • *Dir* John Erick Dowdle • *Scr* John Erick Dowdle, Drew Dowdle

As Good as It Gets
★★★★ 15

Romantic comedy drama
1997 · US · Colour · 138min

Ostensibly, James L Brooks's movie is about Jack Nicholson. He plays Melvin Udall, a homophobic bigot who insults everyone, lives alone, writes trashy novels for a living and has an obsessive-compulsive disorder. However, the movie is really about Helen Hunt, who plays that corniest of Hollywood characters – the lonely waitress with a problem child. Yet Hunt, who was offered the role when Holly Hunter turned it down and, like Nicholson, won an Oscar for her pains, breathes life into the part, trouncing her co-star and his trademark grouchy act. AT Violence, swearing, drug abuse. DVD

Jack Nicholson *Melvin Udall* • Helen Hunt *Carol Connelly* • Greg Kinnear *Simon Bishop* • Cuba Gooding Jr *Frank Sachs* • Skeet Ulrich *Vincent* • Shirley Knight *Beverly* • Yeardley Smith *Jackie* • Lupe Ontiveros *Nora* ■ *Dir* James L Brooks • *Scr* Mark Andrus, James L Brooks, from a story by Mark Andrus

As I Lay Dying
★★★ 15

Drama
2013 · US · Colour · 105min

William Faulkner's experimental novel, a gruelling 1920s-set tale of a family's journey to bury their mother, takes the form of 59 stream-of-consciousness monologues and has long been declared unfilmable. But here James Franco gutsily takes it on, both directing and starring in his own adaptation. He uses split screen, voiceover and some irritating actorly mumbling to reflect the novel's fractured nature, while preserving the sense of isolation and privation that the characters endure. The acting is top notch with Tim Blake Nelson standing out as stubborn patriarch Anse. Ironically, it's only Franco himself who is a little disappointing. AS Violence, a sex scene, brief swearing, nudity.

James Franco *Darl Bundren* • Tim Blake Nelson *Anse* • Danny McBride (2) *Vernon Tull* • Logan Marshall-Green *Jewel Bundren* • Ahna O'Reilly *Dewey Dell* ■ *Dir* James Franco • *Scr* James Franco, from William Faulkner's novel

As Long as They're Happy
★★ U

Comedy
1955 · UK · Colour · 90min

This moderately amusing all-British comedy, with some music, was inspired by the 1950s craze for sob singer Johnny Ray. The plot has an American crying crooner (Jerry Wayne) causing havoc in an English family with whom he stays. Jack Buchanan plays the unamused head of the household and the father of three daughters (Janette Scott, Jean Carson and Susan Stephen) obsessed with the visitor. RK

Jack Buchanan *John Bentley* • Janette Scott *Gwen* • Jean Carson [Jeannie Carson] *Pat* • Susan Stephen *Corinne* • Brenda de Banzie *Stella* • Jerry Wayne *Bobby Denver* • Diana Dors *Pearl* • Joan Sims *Linda* • Dora Bryan *Mavis* ■ *Dir* J Lee Thompson • *Scr* Alan Melville, from the play by Vernon Sylvaine

As Summers Die
★★★ 15

Drama
1986 · US · Colour · 83min

The setting for this drama – based on the novel by Winston Groom, who also wrote *Forrest Gump* – is a small town in America's Deep South during the 1950s. An old-style colonial family is trying to deprive a black woman of her rightful land, and Scott Glenn is the crusading lawyer who attempts to help her. Jean-Claude Tramont's predictable TV movie rises above the norm thanks to the performances of Glenn, Jamie Lee Curtis and the ageing but still wonderful Bette Davis. JB

Jamie Lee Curtis *Whitsey* • Scott Glenn *Willie Croft* • Bette Davis *Aunt Hannah* • CCH Pounder *Priscilla* • Beah Richards *Elvira* • John Randolph

Augustus Tompkins ■ *Dir* Jean-Claude Tramont • *Scr* Jeff Andrus, Ed Namzug, from the novel by Winston Groom

As Tears Go By
★★★ 18

Crime drama
1988 · HK · Colour · 95min

Writer/director Wong Kar-Wai made his transition from scriptwriter to film-maker with this gritty and violent Hong Kong gangster drama. It's a love-versus-loyalty tale in which Andy Lau's low-level Triad "big brother" is torn between his gang allegiance to his hot-tempered "little brother" Jacky Cheung and his blossoming romance with his gentle cousin Maggie Cheung. Encumbered slightly by its synthesiser-heavy soundtrack and poor quality film stock, this debut shows signs of what will become Wong's cinematic signature. Saturated reds and greens add rich, visual texture, while highly stylised set pieces enhance the conventional plot. SF Cantonese +subtitles. Violence, swearing. DVD

Andy Lau *Wah* • Maggie Cheung *Ngor* • Jacky Cheung *Fly* • Alex Man *Tony* ■ *Dir/Scr* Wong Kar-Wai

As the Palaces Burn
★★★ 15

Music documentary
2014 · US/Col/Ind/Is/Ven · Colour · 120min

This watchable fly-on-the-wall documentary initially follows US heavy metal band Lamb of God's preparations for their 2012 tour. However, events take a turn for the unexpected when singer Randy Blythe, now sober after years of alcoholic excess, is arrested in Prague for the death of a teenager two years earlier. Here's where the story becomes genuinely intriguing and more serious issues than rock music take centre stage, as the shell-shocked Blythe battles to prove his innocence. JA Swearing.

■ *Dir* Don Argott

As Time Runs Out
★★

Crime thriller
1999 · Can · Colour · 95min

A promising premise is wasted in this mechanical kidnap drama that spends more time on romance than suspense. Stephen Collins plays the wealthy industrialist whose son is kidnapped and given a booby-trapped teddy bear, but his search is largely devoid of tension, even after we see the kidnapper killed in a bizarre accident. Director Jerry London joins the plot dots without any dramatic or stylistic flourishes, and more time is devoted to Collins's relationship with earnest cop Karen Sillas than his six-year-old's dilemma. Ultimately, time doesn't run out quickly enough. DP

Karen Sillas *Janet Wise* • Stephen Collins *Dan Carlin* • Rick Roberts *Redman* • Emmett Shoemaker *Marcus Carlin* • Fred Henderson *Brad* • Laurie Murdoch *Phil* ■ *Dir* Jerry London • *Scr* Ronald Parker

As You Desire Me
★★★

Melodrama
1932 · US · BW · 69min

It may be slow moving and a shade creaky today, but this Greta Garbo vehicle positively smoulders, and contains some of the most overt sensuality you're likely to see in a Hollywood movie of the period. It's a classy MGM production, with George Fitzmaurice directing and Melvyn Douglas and Erich von Stroheim as Garbo's co-stars. Blonde, fashionably bobbed Garbo plays an Italian countess suffering from amnesia who becomes a nightclub singer. TS

Greta Garbo *Zara* • Melvyn Douglas *Count Bruno Varelli* • Erich von Stroheim *Carl Salter* • Owen Moore *Tony* • Hedda Hopper *Madame Mantari* • Rafaela Ottiano *Lena* ■ *Dir* George Fitzmaurice • *Scr* Gene Markey, from the play by Luigi Pirandello

As You Like It
★★ U

Romantic comedy
1936 · UK · BW · 96min

With her German accent and mispronunciations, Elisabeth Bergner is unintentionally hilarious as Rosalind in this lavish film version of Shakespeare's comedy, directed and produced by her husband Paul Czinner. Laurence Olivier

speaks beautifully but seems awkward as Orlando in his first screen venture into Shakespeare. JM Barrie adds a whimsical edge to the adaptation. AE

Elisabeth Bergner *Rosalind* • Laurence Olivier *Orlando* • Sophie Stewart *Celia* • Leon Quartermaine *Jacques* • Henry Ainley *Exiled Duke* • Mackenzie Ward *Touchstone* • Felix Aylmer *Duke Frederick* • Richard Ainley *Sylvius* • Austin Trevor *Beau* • John Laurie *Oliver* ■ *Dir* Paul Czinner • *Scr* JM Barrie, Robert J Cullen, from the play by William Shakespeare

As You Like It
★ U

Romantic comedy
1992 · UK · Colour · 112min

This ill-fated version of one of the Bard's finest comedies finds the forest of Arden transposed into a contemporary urban environment. Peopled by strays in cardboard boxes, the tale of Orlando's passion for the banished Rosalind misfires conceptually. LH

Emma Croft *Rosalind* • Andrew Tiernan *Orlando/Oliver* • James Fox *Jaques* • Griff Rhys Jones *Touchstone* • Cyril Cusack *Adam* • Miriam Margolyes *Audrey* • Don Henderson *The Dukes* • Celia Bannerman *Celia* • Ewen Bremner *Silvius* ■ *Dir* Christine Edzard • *Scr* from the play by William Shakespeare

As You Like It
★★ 12

Romantic comedy
2006 · US/UK · Colour · 121min

Kenneth Branagh replants the "Forest of Arden" in 19th-century Japan for this, his fifth retelling of a Shakespeare classic. But, aside from providing an excuse for some oriental set dressing, there seems little point to the relocation, as most of the action unfolds in the woods. Bryce Dallas Howard is charming as Rosalind, the daughter of the exiled Duke Senior (Brian Blessed, in one of two roles). She falls for Orlando (David Oyelowo), but after she is also banished from court, Rosalind disguises herself as a man and finds refuge in Arden. Despite sterling support from the likes of Alfred Molina and Kevin Kline, Branagh's blinkered direction means all the magic and intrigue are lost. SP DVD

Brian Blessed *Duke Frederick/Duke Senior* • Bryce Dallas Howard *Rosalind* • Romola Garai *Celia* • Adrian Lester *Oliver de Boys* • Alfred Molina *Touchstone* • Kevin Kline *Jaques* • David Oyelowo *Orlando de Boys* • Richard Briers *Old Adam* ■ *Dir* Kenneth Branagh • *Scr* Kenneth Branagh, from the play by William Shakespeare • *Cinematographer* Roger Lanser

As Young as You Feel
★★★ U

Comedy
1951 · US · BW · 73min

This 20th Century-Fox comedy is still relevant today and provides a marvellous vehicle for Monty Woolley, here playing a 65-year-old print worker who refuses to go quietly when he is asked to retire. The acerbic tale is an early work by writer Paddy Chayefsky, and the supporting cast is particularly fine. Pay attention to that scene-stealing contract blonde – a certain Marilyn Monroe in an early role. TS DVD

Monty Woolley *John Hodges* • Thelma Ritter *Della Hodges* • David Wayne *Joe* • Jean Peters *Alice Hodges* • Constance Bennett *Lucille McKinley* • Marilyn Monroe *Harriet* ■ *Dir* Harmon Jones • *Scr* Lamar Trotti, from a story by Paddy Chayefsky

The Ascent
★★★★ PG

Second World War drama
1976 · USSR · BW · 104min

Filmed in harsh monochrome by Vladimir Chukhnov, this was Larissa Shepitko's fourth feature in a career than spanned 20 years; it was also the last she completed before her fatal car crash. It is clearly the work of an inspired film-maker, though, as she imbues this award-winning tale of desperate survival with a biblical spirit that further ennobles the deeds of the partisans who fought to liberate Belorussia. Refusing to toe the socialist realist line on the Second World War, Shepitko depicts such unpatriotic acts as cowardice and collaboration, as well as suggesting that the

Russian climate was as dangerous an enemy as the Nazis. DP In Russian.

Boris Plotnikov • Vladimir Gostukhin • Sergei Jakovlev • Anatoli Solinitzin ■ *Dir* Larissa Shepitko • *Scr* Yuri Klepikov, Larissa Shepitko, from a novel by Vassil Bykov • *Cinematographer* Vladimir Chukhnov

The Ascent
★★

Second World War adventure
1994 · US · Colour · 96min

This offbeat adventure, set in Africa well away from the front line, centres on a PoW camp where the largely Italian inmates and their British guards get involved in a bizarre challenge to see who can climb a treacherous mountain peak nearby. Ben Cross and John DeVeillers fly the Union flag; Vincent Spano plays the PoW with more than just mountain climbing on his mind. The stunning locations and the oddness of the tale don't really compensate for the uneven script. JF Violence, swearing.

Vincent Spano *Franco* • Ben Cross *Major Farrell* • Rachel Ward *Patricia* • Tony LoBianco *Aldo* • Mark Ingall *Sergeant Thomas* • John DeVeillers *Major Quinn* ■ *Dir* Donald Shebib • *Scr* David Wiltse

Ash Wednesday
★★★ 15

Drama
1973 · US · Colour · 94min

To save her ailing marriage to Henry Fonda, Elizabeth Taylor decides to fly to Italy for a face-lift. Looking beautiful again, she has a fling with Euro-stud Helmut Berger. Sadly this isn't a comedy, but a heavy drama which shows the agonies of plastic surgery in unremitting detail before turning to the emotional pain of a splintering relationship. Playing 55, Taylor was a mere 40-year-old when she made the picture, and she looks utterly ravishing – and that's *before* the surgery. AT

Elizabeth Taylor *Barbara Sawyer* • Henry Fonda *Mark Sawyer* • Helmut Berger *Erich* • Keith Baxter *David* • Maurice Teynac *Dr Lambert* ■ *Dir* Larry Peerce • *Scr* Jean-Claude Tramont

Ash Wednesday
★★ 18

Crime drama
2002 · US · Colour · 94min

Edward Burns produces, directs and stars in this routine, New York-set tale about Irish-American family ties. Elijah Wood plays a young man whose death has to be faked after he thwarts the attempted murder of his hoodlum brother (Burns) by a rival gang. Three years later, Wood "resurrects" himself in order to woo back his wife (Rosario Dawson). Overwrought and underwritten. DA Swearing, violence. DVD

Edward Burns *Francis Sullivan* • Elijah Wood *Sean Sullivan* • Rosario Dawson *Grace Quinonez* • Oliver Platt *Moran* • Pat McNamara *Murph* • James Handy *Father Mahoney* • Michael Mulheren *Detective Pulaski* • Malachy McCourt *Whitey* • Julie Hale *Maggie Shea* ■ *Dir/Scr* Edward Burns

Ashanti
★★ 15

Adventure
1979 · Swi/US · Colour · 112min

This overblown adventure stars Michael Caine and Beverly Johnson as married doctors, who are working for the World Health Organisation in a small West African village when Johnson is kidnapped by slave-trader Peter Ustinov for wealthy prince Omar Sharif. Caine (inanimate and inadequate) sets off to track her down. Heavy-going, thanks to Richard Fleischer's leisurely direction and Ustinov's lack of menace. TH Swearing, violence. DVD

Michael Caine *Dr David Linderby* • Peter Ustinov *Suleiman* • Beverly Johnson *Dr Anansa Linderby* • Kabir Bedi *Malik* • Omar Sharif *Prince Hassan* • Rex Harrison *Brian Walker* • William Holden (2) *Jim Sandell* ■ *Dir* Richard Fleischer • *Scr* Stephen Geller, from the novel *Ebano* by Alberto Vasquez-Figueroa

Ashes
★★★ 15

Drama
2012 · UK · Colour · 96min

Mat Whitecross's contemporary *film noir* is not what you expect. The unsettling story is anchored on Frank (Ray Winstone), a man gripped by Alzheimer's disease, but the plot quickly develops into a tense thriller that keeps its secrets closely guarded right till the end. After months of searching, Frank's estranged son, James (Jim Sturgess), breaks him out of a nursing home and the pair go on the run. A two-hander, filmed almost exclusively on the road, the film lacks the pace and glamour of a Hollywood blockbuster. But it has an intelligent screenplay and fans of Winstone will be interested to see the unexpected delicacy he brings to the role. **ReP** Violence, swearing.

Ray Winstone *Frank* • Jim Sturgess *James* • Lesley Manville *Cathy* • Jodie Whittaker *Ruth* • Luke Evans *JB* ■ *Dir* Mat Whitecross • *Scr* Paul Viragh

Ashes and Diamonds
★★★★★ 12

Drama   1958 · Pol · BW · 102min

This made an overnight star of Zbigniew Cybulski, who was hailed by some as the Polish James Dean. Set on the last day of the Second World War, the film follows an underground guerrilla as he plots to assassinate a communist leader whose views he despises, but whose humanity he admires. Cybulski is quite magnificent as the resistance fighter, whether debating where to draw the line between military and moral duty, romancing barmaid Ewa Krzyzanowska, or paying bitterly for his indecision. Demonstrating a mastery of location shooting, symbolism, characterisation and camera technique, this is Wajda's masterpiece. **DP** Polish +subtitles. **DVD** Bl

Zbigniew Cybulski *Maciek* • Ewa Krzyzanowska *Krystyna* • Adam Pawlikowski *Andrzej* • Waclaw Zastrzezynski *Szczuka* • Bogumil Kobiela *Drewnowski* ■ *Dir* Andrzej Wajda • *Scr* Andrzej Wajda, Jerzy Andrzejewski, from the novel by Andrzejewski • *Cinematographer* Jerzy Wojcik

Ashes of Time
★★★★

Period martial arts drama
1994 · HK/Tai · Colour · 100min

Based on the cult Jin Yong novel *The Eagle-Shooting Heroes* and with A-list stars in its cast, this stylised swashbuckler should have been a huge commercial success. That it wasn't owes much to director Wong Kar-Wai's refusal to tell the story in a linear manner, thus alienating the viewers he hadn't already confused. Yet the exploits of Leslie Cheung's band of assassins are elevated above standard martial arts fare by Wong's fragmentary exploration of time and memory, the mythical atmosphere generated by the desert locations, Christopher Doyle's exquisite lighting and Sammo Hung's kinetic fight sequences. Wong revisited this film in 2008 with *Ashes of Time Redux*, but the re-editing changed surprisingly little. **DP** Cantonese +subtitles.

Leslie Cheung *Feng Ouyang* • Tony Leung Chiu-Wai [Tony Leung (2)] *Blind swordsman* • Tony Leung Kar-Fai [Tony Leung (1)] *Huang Yaoshi* • Brigitte Lin Ching Hsia [Brigitte Lin] *Yin/Murong Yan* • Maggie Cheung *The woman* ■ *Dir* Wong Kar-Wai • *Scr* Wong Kar-Wai, from the novel *The Eagle-Shooting Heroes* by Jin Yong [Louis Cha]

Ashik Kerib
★★★★ PG

Fantasy drama   1988 · USSR · Colour · 73min

This was the last film completed by the extraordinarily talented Georgian film-maker Sergei Paradzhanov. Although actor Dodo Abashidze shares the directorial credit, the astonishing beauty and complexity of the imagery is so reminiscent of such earlier Paradjanov pictures as *The Colour of Pomegranates* that the film's authorship is never in doubt. Loosely based on a story by the Russian writer Mikhail Lermontov, the action follows a poor minstrel on his 1001-day exile from his true love. Cinematic poetry. **DP** Azerbaijani +Georgian voiceover, English subtitles. Some violence. **DVD**

Yuri Mgoyan *Ashik Kerib* • Veronika Metonidze • Levan Natroshvili • Sofiko Chiaureli • R Chkhlkvadze ■ *Dir* Dodo Abashidze, Sergei Paradjanov • *Scr* Giya Badridze, from the story *Ashik Kerib the Lovelorn Minstrel* by Mikhail Lermontov

Ask a Policeman
★★★ U

Comedy   1938 · UK · BW · 74min

Will Hay had a thing about spooky crooks. Just as the villains in *Oh, Mr Porter!* exploited a local legend to keep snoopers at bay, so the smugglers in this corking comedy play on the myth of the headless horseman to go about their business undisturbed. The setting is a sleepy coastal berg where the police station is in danger of being closed down because Sergeant Dudfoot (Hay) claims there is no crime. Co-screenwriter Val Guest directed the shudderingly awful remake, *The Boys in Blue*, 45 years later. **DP** **DVD**

Will Hay *Sgt Dudfoot* • Graham Moffatt *Albert* • Moore Marriott *Harbottle* • Glennis Lorimer *Emily* • Peter Gawthorne *Chief Constable* • Charles Oliver *Squire* • Herbert Lomas *Coastguard* • Pat Aherne *Motorist* ■ *Dir* Marcel Varnel • *Scr* Marriott Edgar, Val Guest, from a story by Sidney Gilliat

Ask Any Girl
★★ U

Comedy   1959 · US · Colour · 97min

This mediocre comedy has a top-notch cast, but George Wells's script is merely good-natured and, while it occasionally bubbles, it's still sparkling wine rather than champagne. Shirley MacLaine is wide-eyed and lovely as a waif with a glut of suitors, who are played with typical aplomb by David Niven, Gig Young and Rod Taylor. **DP**

David Niven *Miles Doughton* • Shirley MacLaine *Meg Wheeler* • Gig Young *Evan Doughton* • Rod Taylor *Ross Taford* • Jim Backus *Mr Maxwell* • Claire Kelly *Lisa* • Elisabeth Fraser *Jeannie Boyden* ■ *Dir* Charles Walters • *Scr* George Wells, from the novel by Winifred Wolfe

Ask the Dust
★★ 15

Period romantic drama
2006 · US · Colour · 112min

Robert Towne revisits 1930s Los Angeles, the setting for his masterful screenplay for *Chinatown*, for this adaptation of John Fante's Depression-era novel. Miscast Colin Farrell is a virginal writer, while Salma Hayek is a Mexican immigrant seeking the American dream. They're stuck with each other for a romance that's intended to be slow-burning, but is actually played out in exasperating fits and starts. **SP** Sex scenes. **DVD**

Colin Farrell (2) *Arturo Bandini* • Salma Hayek *Camilla Lopez* • Donald Sutherland *Hellfrick* • Eileen Atkins *Mrs Hargraves* • Idina Menzel *Vera Rivkin* • Justin Kirk *Sammy* • Jeremy Crutchley *Solomon* ■ *Dir* Robert Towne • *Scr* Robert Towne, from the novel by John Fante

Asoka
★★★ 12

Epic historical drama
2001 · Ind · Colour · 169min

Although its epic sweep contrasts sharply with the intense intimacy of *The Terrorist*, it's clear from the visual lyricism and symbolic preoccupation with water that this rousing historical drama was also directed by Santosh Sivan. His stylised use of close-ups, angles and cross-cutting lends an added personal touch to what is, essentially, a genre film, chronicling the life of the Mauryan emperor, who abandoned tyranny to embrace Buddhism. Shah Rukh Khan is dashing in the title role and Kareena Kapoor impressive as his wife. **DP** Hindi +subtitles. **DVD**

Shah Rukh Khan *Asoka* • Kareena Kapoor *Kaurwaki* • Danny Denzongpa *Virat* • Rahul Dev *Bheema* ■ *Dir* Santosh Sivan • *Scr* Saket Chaudhary, Santosh Sivan

Aspen Extreme
★ 15

Drama   1993 · US · Colour · 113min

It's rather apt that this movie is about skiing, because it really is downhill all the way. Quitting Detroit for a life on the piste, Peter Berg is quickly on the slide, while his buddy Paul Gross slaloms between Teri Polo and Finola Hughes. **DP** **DVD**

Paul Gross *TJ Burke* • Peter Berg *Dexter Rutecki* • Finola Hughes *Bryce Kellogg* • Teri Polo *Robin Hand* • William Russ *Dave Ritchie* • Trevor Eve *Karl Stall* • Martin Kemp *Franc Hauser* ■ *Dir/Scr* Patrick Hasburgh

Asphalt
★★★★ U

Silent drama   1928 · Ger · BW · 93min

Making exceptional use of sequence montage, superimpositions, neon lighting and meticulously re-created interiors, Joe May brings a gritty realism to what is essentially a melodramatic tale of petty crime, seduction and misplaced loyalty. Betty Amann is beguiling as the jewel thief who uses her charms to silence eager policeman Gustav Fröhlich, whose slavish devotion causes him to kill her lover. Combining the visual dynamism of the "city symphony" with the dramatic authenticity of the "street film", this is an astute summation of the styles dominating German cinema at the end of the silent era. **DP** **DVD**

Gustav Fröhlich *Police Constable Albert Holk* • Betty Amann *Else Kramer* • Albert Steinrück *Police Sergeant Holk* • Else Heller *Mrs Holk* • Hans Adalbert von Schlettow *Lagen* ■ *Dir* Joe May • *Scr* Fred Majo, Hans Szekely, Rolf E Vanloo • *Cinematographer* Günther Rittau

The Asphalt Jungle
★★★★★ PG

Crime thriller   1950 · US · BW · 107min

Shot with an almost documentary realism, this exceptional *film noir* from director John Huston continues to influence heist movies today. It has everything you could ask of a thriller. There's a scintillating plot (co-scripted by Ben Maddow and Huston from WR Burnett's novel), in which the perfect plan unravels with compelling inevitability; a seminal performance from Oscar-nominated Sam Jaffe as a criminal mastermind; totally convincing ensemble playing from his bungling gang (including Sterling Hayden and Anthony Caruso); and superb support from Jean Hagen and Marilyn Monroe as molls. Add Miklos Rozsa's atmospheric score and Harold Rosson's gritty photography and you have a masterpiece. **DP** **DVD**

Sterling Hayden *Dix Handley* • Louis Calhern *Alonzo D Emmerich* • Jean Hagen *Doll Conovan* • James Whitmore *Gus Ninissi* • Sam Jaffe *Doc Erwin Riedenschneider* • John McIntire *Police Commissioner Hardy* • Marc Lawrence (1) *Cobby* • Barry Kelley *Lieutenant Ditrich* • Anthony Caruso *Louis Ciavelli* • Marilyn Monroe *Angela Phinlay* ■ *Dir* John Huston • *Scr* Ben Maddow, John Huston, from the novel by WR Burnett

The Asphyx
★★★★ 15

Supernatural horror   1972 · UK · Colour · 82min

This thoughtful horror oddity explores aspects of immortality with a sci-fi spin. The title refers to a soul-snatching being from another dimension that approaches the body at the moment of death. Photographer Robert Stephens captures one such life form in the hope he can claim eternal life. Morbid, intriguing and acted with conviction, director Peter Newbrook's cerebral chiller is a wordy gothic drama masquerading as a supernatural terroriser. **AJ** Violence. **DVD**

Robert Stephens *Hugo Cunningham* • Robert Powell *Giles Cunningham* • Jane Lapotaire *Christina Cunningham* • Alex Scott (1) *President* • Ralph Arliss *Clive Cunningham* • Fiona Walker *Anna Cunningham* • Terry Scully *Pauper* ■ *Dir* Peter Newbrook • *Scr* Brian Comport, from a story by Christina, Laurence Beers

The Assam Garden
★★ U

Drama   1985 · UK · Colour · 90min

Deborah Kerr's first film since 1969 is a mild, inconsequential affair. Returning from Assam to England, Kerr tends her recently deceased husband's eastern garden as a way of cherishing his memory. This, and her friendship with neighbour Madhur Jaffrey, are the means by which she tries to heal her grief. Kerr is as delightful as ever, but the film lacks real substance. **LH**

Deborah Kerr *Helen* • Madhur Jaffrey *Ruxmani Lal* • Alec McCowen *Mr Philpott* • Zia Mohyeddin *Mr Lal* • Anton Lesser *Mr Sutton* • Iain Cuthbertson *Arthur* • Tara Shaw *Sushi* ■ *Dir* Mary McMurray • *Scr* Elisabeth Bond

Assassin
★★

Spy drama   1973 · UK · Colour · 82min

Without the extraneous style and a couple of the more extended scenes, this might have made a decent half-hour TV thriller. Instead, director Peter Crane piles on the flashy visuals in an attempt to turn a humdrum espionage caper into a meaningful tract on the state's dispassionate sanctioning of murder and the isolation of the professional killer. Amid the directorial pyrotechnics, however, Ian Hendry is highly effective. **DP**

Ian Hendry *Assassin* • Edward Judd *MI5 Control* • Frank Windsor *John Stacey* • Ray Brooks *Edward Craig* • John Hart Dyke *Janik* • Verna Harvey *Girl* • Mike Pratt *Matthew* ■ *Dir* Peter Crane • *Scr* Michael Sloan

The Assassin
★★ 18

Thriller   1993 · US · Colour · 103min

Luc Besson's *Nikita*, starring the luminous Anne Parillaud, was a throbbing, stylish look at a convicted murderess who receives secret government training as a hired gun. Remade here with a plodding hand by John Badham and featuring an ill-at-ease Bridget Fonda, what was once witty, if somewhat vacuous, entertainment has been reduced to a series of one-dimensional thrills. **SH** Violence, swearing, sex scenes, nudity. **DVD**

Bridget Fonda *Maggie* • Gabriel Byrne *Bob* • Dermot Mulroney *JP* • Miguel Ferrer *Kaufman* • Anne Bancroft *Amanda* • Olivia D'Abo *Angela* • Richard Romanus *Fahd Bahktiar* • Harvey Keitel *Victor the cleaner* ■ *Dir* John Badham • *Scr* Robert Getchell, Alexandra Seros, from the film *Nikita* by Luc Besson

The Assassin
★★★★ 12

Period drama
2015 · Tai/Chi/HK/Fr · Colour and BW · 101min

The dynamic but treacherous glory days of China's Tang Dynasty are revisited in this beautiful but somewhat enigmatic martial arts drama by veteran Hou Hsiao-Hsien. After a minimalist black and white prologue, the film explodes into gorgeous colour, as a woman with orders to murder a local governor reveals a secret that threatens to compromise the mission. Episodic violence ensues, but martial arts fans should bed in for something more slow and mysterious than the likes of *Crouching Tiger, Hidden Dragon*. **DW** In Mandarin. Some violence. **DVD** Bl

Shu Qi *Nie Yinniang* • Chang Chen *Tian Ji'an, the governor of Weibo* • Yun Zhou *Lady Tian* • Satoshi Tsumabuki *The mirror polisher* ■ *Dir* Hou Hsiao-Hsien • *Scr* Hou Hsiao-Hsien, Chu Tien-Wen, Hai-Meng Hsieh, Zhong Acheng

Assassin of the Tsar
★★★ 15

Psychological drama
1991 · Rus/UK · Colour · 100min

Malcolm McDowell stars as a psychiatric patient who believes he assassinated the Tsar and his family in 1918. From his hospital bed in present-day Moscow, McDowell is taken back to the past by his psychiatrist, Oleg Yankovsky (who also plays the Tsar), in an attempt to free him of his delusion. Shot in both English and Russian versions, its flaws are obvious. However, McDowell's portrait of schizophrenia is often disturbing, and the whole picture is a fascinating and gripping study of madness. **TS** Russian dubbed.

Malcolm McDowell *Timofeev/Yurovsky* • Oleg Yankovsky *Dr Smirnov/Tsar Nicholas Ii* • Armen Dzhigarkhanyan *Alexander Egorovich* • Iurii Sherstnev *Kozlov* • Angela Ptashuk *Marina* • Viktor Seferov *Voikov* ■ *Dir* Karen Shakhnazarov • *Scr* Aleksandr Borodianskii, Karen Shakhnazarov

Assassination
★★ 12

Thriller   1986 · US · Colour · 84min

Charles Bronson is the minder to the American president's wife (here played by Bronson's own wife, Jill Ireland) who goes on the run with her when killers threaten. It has its moments of tension but the relationship never achieves much

A

credibility. Bronson dozes off in scene one and doesn't even begin to stir before the end. JM Swearing, violence. *DVD*

Charles Bronson *Jay Killian* • Jill Ireland *Lara Royce Craig* • Stephen Elliott (1) *Fitzroy* • Jan Gan Boyd *Charlotte Chang* • Randy Brooks *Tyler Loudermilk* • Michael Ansara *Senator Hector Bunsen* • Erik Stern *Reno Bracken* ■ *Dir* Peter Hunt • *Scr* Richard Sale

The Assassination Bureau ★★★★

Period black comedy 1969 · UK · Colour · 111min

This dry period black comedy stars Diana Rigg as a journalist infiltrating a gang of professional killers whose members only accept contracts on those who "deserve" to die. Director Basil Dearden infuses the tale with joyous glee and no little character insight as Rigg persuades the gang's leader, Oliver Reed, to allow himself to become a target as a challenge to his professionalism. It's a clever twist in a madcap yarn by Jack London and Robert Fish. Reed is wonderfully malevolent through his charm, while the quality cast gauges the light tone to perfection. TH

Oliver Reed *Ivan Dragomiloff* • Diana Rigg *Sonya Winter* • Telly Savalas *Lord Bostwick* • Curt Jurgens *General von Pinck* • Philippe Noiret *Lucoville* • Warren Mitchell *Weiss* • Beryl Reid *Madame Otero* • Clive Revill *Cesare Spado* ■ *Dir* Basil Dearden • *Scr* Michael Relph, from the novel *The Assassination Bureau Limited* by Jack London, Robert Fish

The Assassination of Jesse James by the Coward Robert Ford ★★★★ 15

Western drama
2007 · US/Can · Colour · 153min

The overlong title betrays the serious mood of this powerful epic that teases out its fiercely modern theme with unnerving acuity. Brad Pitt delivers a career-topping turn as Jesse James, the notorious outlaw shot by a turncoat member of his own gang, Bob Ford (Casey Affleck), a whining young wannabe who was once his greatest fan. Locking these two protagonists in a deadly embrace, Andrew Dominik turns their story into a timely tragedy about the perils of fame. Unwilling to simply print the legend, Dominik encourages Pitt to play James as a manipulative psychopath. Meanwhile, Affleck's creepily sycophantic assassin is reviled as "The Man Who Shot Jesse James". JR *DVD* *Blu-ray*

Brad Pitt *Jesse James* • Casey Affleck *Robert Ford* • Sam Shepard *Frank James* • Mary-Louise Parker *Zeralda "Zee" James* • Paul Schneider (2) *Dick Liddil* • Jeremy Renner *Wood Hite* • Zooey Deschanel *Dorothy Evans* • Sam Rockwell *Charley Ford* ■ *Dir* Andrew Dominik • *Scr* Andrew Dominik, from Ron Hansen's novel • *Cinematographer* Roger Deakins • *Music* Nick Cave, Warren Ellis (1)

The Assassination of Richard Nixon ★★★ 15

Biographical drama 2004 · US · Colour · 91min

Based on little-known real events of 1974, this stars Sean Penn as Samuel Bicke, an American whose grip on reality fails at the same time as his marriage. As both his personal life and fledgeling business founder, Bicke channels his dissatisfaction into a plan to assassinate the president. The film features a strong performance from Penn, aided by Don Cheadle and Naomi Watts as his friend and his estranged wife. The film misses an opportunity to say something new about what drives disturbed individuals to such acts, but Penn still brings fascinating shades of light and dark to a striking story of American madness. KK Swearing, violence. *DVD*

Sean Penn *Samuel Bicke* • Naomi Watts *Marie Bicke* • Don Cheadle *Bonny Simmons* • Jack Thompson *Jack Jones* • Brad Henke *Martin Jones* • Michael Wincott *Julius Bicke* • Mykelti Williamson *Harold Mann* • April Grace *Mae Simmons* ■ *Dir* Nils Mueller • *Scr* Nils Mueller, Kevin Kennedy

The Assassination of Trotsky ★★ 15

Historical drama 1972 · Fr/It · Colour · 98min

Despite being shot on authentic locations, Joseph Losey's botched film is often dull and fatally lacking in both historical perspective and on-screen drama. Richard Burton acts his socks off as Leon Trotsky, the Russian revolutionary who was gruesomely murdered in Stalin's orders in Mexico City in 1940. However, while Alain Delon has a certain menace as the assassin, he's never a flesh-and-blood character. AT Violence. *DVD*

Richard Burton *Leon Trotsky* • Alain Delon *Frank Jacson* • Romy Schneider *Gita* • Valentina Cortese *Natasha* • Luigi Vannucchi *Ruiz* • Duilio Del Prete *Felipe* • Simone Valère *Mrs Rosmer* ■ *Dir* Joseph Losey • *Scr* Nicholas Mosley, Masolino D'Amico

Assassins ★★★ 15

Action thriller 1995 · US · Colour · 127min

This film should carry a warning: don't look too deeply for rhyme or reason or you'll end up with a nasty headache. Just ignore the holes in the plot and concentrate instead on the rivalry that develops between hitmen Sylvester Stallone and Antonio Banderas, especially when Stallone becomes enamoured of their target, Julianne Moore. Director Richard Donner lets Banderas get away with a lazy performance, but Stallone has rarely been so interesting. DP Swearing, violence. *DVD*

Sylvester Stallone *Robert Rath* • Antonio Banderas *Miguel Bain* • Julianne Moore *Electra* • Anatoly Davydov *Nicolai* • Muse Watson *Ketcham* • Stephen Kahan *[Steve Kahan] Alan Branch* • Kelly Rowan *Jennifer* ■ *Dir* Richard Donner • *Scr* Andy Wachowski, Larry Wachowski, Brian Helgeland, from a story by the Wachowskis

Assassin's Creed

Science-fiction action adventure
2016 · US/UK/Fr · Colour

This is a preview – no prints were available to review prior to publication: Michael Fassbender stars in this sci-fi action adventure as a bartender who is kidnapped by a large corporation – once again the root of all evil, according to the large corporations that run Hollywood. He's then forced to relive the memories of his ancestors, most of whom, judging by the title, weren't employed in the serving of flagons of foaming ale like his good self. TP *DVD*

Michael Fassbender *Callum Lynch/Aguilar* • Marion Cotillard *Dr Sophia Rikkin* • Jeremy Irons *Alan Rikkin* • Brendan Gleeson *Joseph* ■ *Dir* Justin Kurzel • *Scr* Bill Collage, Adam Cooper (1), Michael Lesslie

Assault ★★ 15

Thriller 1970 · UK · Colour · 87min

Suzy Kendall stars as an art teacher whose pupils are being targeted by a killer/rapist. Hoping to trap the murderer before he strikes again, she offers herself to the police as a decoy. Apart from its rather leery approach to the subject matter, this is a resolutely old-fashioned whodunnit, complete with a gallery of not-so-likely suspects, a series of mini-skirted would-be victims and a baffled cop played by Frank Finlay. AT Violence. *DVD*

Suzy Kendall *Julie West* • Frank Finlay *Det Chief Supt John Velyan* • James Laurenson *Dr Gregory Lomax* • Lesley-Anne Down *Tessa Hurst* • Freddie Jones *Denning* • Tony Beckley *Leslie Sanford* • Dilys Hamlett *Mrs Sanford* ■ *Dir* Sidney Hayers • *Scr* John Kruse, from the novel *The Ravine* by Kendal Young

The Assault ★★★ PG

Drama 1986 · Neth · Colour · 120min

Winner of the Oscar for best foreign film, this is a harrowing study of how a victim of the Nazi occupation of Holland is continually reminded of the horrific night when his entire family was arrested and executed in reprisal for the death of a collaborator. Derek De Lint conveys some of the survivor's pain and resilience, but the impact of this shocking incident is rather lost as the film comes up to date, with neither De Lint's encounters with others who were involved in the "assault" nor his moments of crushing guilt and depression having quite the same dramatic intensity. DP Dutch +subtitles.

Derek De Lint *Anton Steenwijk* • Marc Van Uchelen *Anton as a boy* • Monique van de Ven *Truus Coster/Saskia De Graaff* • John Kraaykamp *Cor Takes* • Elly Weller *Mrs Beumer* • Ina Van Der Molen *Karin Korteweg* ■ *Dir* Fons Rademakers • *Scr* Gerard Soeteman, from the novel by Harry Mulisch

Assault at West Point: the Court Martial of John Whittaker ★★★

Historical courtroom drama
1994 · US · Colour · 94min

Based on John F Marszalek's minutely researched book, this is a well-mounted TV re-creation of one of the most shameful episodes in US military history. At the tail end of the 19th century, Johnson Whittaker became the first black cadet at the famed academy, only to be charged with beating himself unconscious (while tied to his bunk) in order to frame his racist persecutors. There are a couple of explosive courtroom sequences featuring Sam Waterston and Samuel L Jackson, but some power is lost thanks to Seth Gilliam's lacklustre performance in the title role. DP

Samuel L Jackson *Richard Greener* • Sam Waterston *Daniel Chamberlain* • Seth Gilliam *Cadet Johnson Whittaker* • Mason Adams *Hyde* • Val Avery *General Sherman* ■ *Dir* Harry Moses • *Scr* Harry Moses, from the non-fiction book *The Court-Martial of Johnson Whittaker* by John F Marszalek

Assault on a Queen ★ U

Crime caper 1966 · US · Colour · 106min

In *Ocean's 11*, Frank Sinatra and his cronies held up five casinos in Las Vegas. In this follow-up, Ol' Blue Eyes and even more cronies raise a U-boat from the ocean shallows to plunder the *Queen Mary* and its well-heeled passengers. It's heavy-handed in all departments, with leaden direction by Jack Donohue. AT

Frank Sinatra *Mark Brittain* • Virna Lisi *Rosa Lucchesi* • Tony Franciosa *[Anthony Franciosa] Vic Rossiter* • Richard Conte *Tony Moreno* • Alf Kjellin *Eric Lauffnauer* • Errol John *Linc Langley* ■ *Dir* Jack Donohue • *Scr* Rod Serling, from the novel by Jack Finney

Assault on Precinct 13 ★★★★★ 15

Thriller 1976 · US · Colour · 90min

Cult director John Carpenter's hybrid of *Rio Bravo* and *Night of the Living Dead* is a model of low-budget film-making and ranks as one of the best B-movies ever made in the urban horror/action genre. In this gripping thriller, a nearly abandoned police station in the worst neighbourhood in Los Angeles is placed under siege for harbouring the killer of a street gang's fearless leader. Paranoia abounds as Austin Stoker and his motley crew of quipping cops are attacked from all sides with no escape route. Carpenter also supplies a taut synthesiser score that adds untold atmosphere to this minor gem. AJ Violence, swearing. *DVD*

Austin Stoker *Ethan Bishop* • Darwin Joston *Napoleon Wilson* • Laurie Zimmer *Leigh* • Martin West *Lawson* • Tony Burton *Wells* • Kim Richards *Kathy* ■ *Dir/Scr* John Carpenter

Assault on Precinct 13 ★★★ 15

Action thriller 2005 · US/Fr · Colour · 104min

John Carpenter's cult classic gets an exciting, contemporary reworking here. This simple urban western is set in an isolated, sparsely manned Detroit police station under siege during its final night before closure. The relentless assailants want laid-back crime lord Laurence Fishburne, which forces the prisoners and cops inside into an uneasy alliance. Director Jean-François Richet cranks up the tension and the acting is enjoyable, too – despite some corny dialogue and clichéd characters – with Ethan Hawke's emotionally scarred police sergeant a particular standout. SF Swearing, violence. *DVD*

Ethan Hawke *Sergeant Jake Roenick* • Laurence Fishburne *Marion Bishop* • John Leguizamo *Beck* • Maria Bello *Alex Sabian* • Jeffrey "Ja Rule" Atkins *[Ja Rule] Smiley* • Drea de Matteo *Iris Ferry* • Matt Craven *Capra* • Brian Dennehy *Jasper O'Shea* • Gabriele Byrne *Marcus Duvall* • Aisha Hinds *Anna* ■ *Dir* Jean-François Richet • *Scr* James DeMonaco, from the film by John Carpenter

Assembly ★★★ 15

War drama based on a true story
2007 · Chi/HK · Colour · 118min

Director Feng Xiaogang's Chinese Civil War epic works best as a blockbuster war movie, the opening hour taking its cue from Spielberg's handheld camera and battlefield carnage in *Saving Private Ryan*. Set in 1948, the story follows communist soldier Captain Guzidi (Zhang Hanyu) as his company holds a fortified position against a superior force of Chinese nationalists, hoping in vain to hear the assembly bugle sound the retreat. Years later, the shell-shocked Guzidi fights to convince the sceptical military authorities that his men died honourably in action, and almost single-handedly tries to retrieve their remains. The peacetime drama can't help but seem an anticlimactic adjunct to the breathless battle sequences, but Zhang's performance as the obsessed, ageing officer remains riveting. JR Mandarin +subtitles. *DVD* *Blu-ray*

Zhang Hanyu *Guzidi* • Deng Chao *Zhao Erdou* • Yuen Wenkang *Wang Jincun* • Tang Yan *Sun Guiqin* • Liao Fan *Jiao Dapeng* ■ *Dir* Feng Xiaogang • *Scr* Liu Heng, from the short story *Lawsuit* by Yang Jingyuan

The Assignment ★★ 18

Thriller 1997 · Can/US · Colour · 114min

Director Christian Duguay dishes up a steady stream of graphic action in this thriller based on the story of real-life terrorist Carlos the Jackal. Aidan Quinn stars in a dual role, as the Jackal himself and an American naval officer with a remarkable resemblance to the wanted man. Donald Sutherland plays a CIA veteran obsessed with getting revenge for past humiliation, with Ben Kingsley as a Mossad agent eager to rid the world of the assassin. Despite the formulaic subject matter, this is well paced and moderately exciting fare. AJ Nudity, swearing, violence. *DVD*

Aidan Quinn *Annibal Ramirez/Carlos* • Donald Sutherland *Jack Shaw/Henry Fields* • Ben Kingsley *Amos* • Claudia Ferri *Maura Ramirez* • Celine Bonnier *Carla* • Vlasta Vrana *KGB Head officer* • Liliana Komorowska *Agnieska* • Von Flores *Koj* ■ *Dir* Christian Duguay • *Scr* Dan Gordon, Sabi H Shabtai

Assignment – Paris ★★ U

Spy drama 1952 · US · BW · 84min

This unremarkable Cold War thriller stars Dana Andrews as a reporter in the Paris office of the *New York Herald Tribune* who uncovers a conspiracy in Budapest. The communists throw him in jail and shoot him full of truth drugs; his editor (George Sanders) tries to forget that Andrews stole his girlfriend (Marta Toren) and fights for his release. Critics at the time thought the whole thing far-fetched; nowadays, however, it's just rather ho-hum. AT

Dana Andrews *Jimmy Race* • Marta Toren *Jeanne Moray* • George Sanders *Nick Strang* • Audrey Totter *Sandy Tate* • Sandro Giglio *Grischa* • Donald Randolph *Anton Borvitch* • Herbert Berghof *Andreas Ordy* ■ *Dir* Robert Parrish • *Scr* William Bowers, Paul Gallico, Jack Palmer White, from the story *Trial by Terror* by Paul Gallico, Pauline Gallico

Assignment Redhead ★ PG

Crime drama 1956 · UK · BW · 76min

Also known as *Million Dollar Manhunt*, this dismal thriller has all the hallmarks of a Butcher's production: shoddy script, cheap settings and a cast of has-beens and no-hopers. Ronald Adam can just about hold his head up as the crook intent on blagging counterfeit Nazi cash, but the rest of the cast is just inept. DP Some violence *DVD*

Richard Denning *Keen* • Carole Mathews *Hedy* • Ronald Adam *Scammel/Dumetrius* • Danny Green *Yottie* • Brian Worth *Ridgeway* • Jan Holden *Sally* ■ *Dir* Maclean Rogers • *Scr* Maclean Rogers, from the novel *Requiem for a Redhead* by Al Bocca

The Assisi Underground
★ **PG**

Second World War drama
1985 · It/US · Colour · 109min

Underground is where this drama should have stayed. Its truth-based story of an Assisi-centred network, smuggling disguised Jewish refugees out of Italy via Franciscan monasteries, needed its own lifeline of credibility but didn't get it from a muddled script and banal direction. TH

Ben Cross *Padre Rufino* • James Mason *Bishop Nicolini* • Irene Papas *Mother Giuseppina* • Maximilian Schell *Colonel Mueller* • Karl-Heinz Hackl [Karlheinz Hackl] *Captain von Velden* ■ *Dir* Alexander Ramati • *Scr* Alexander Ramati, from his novel

The Associate
★★ **PG**

Comedy drama   1996 · US · Colour · 108min

Whoopi Goldberg stars as a Wall Street analyst who can't move up the career ladder because she's a woman. Taking the rather radical action of setting up her own company with a fictitious male partner, matters are further complicated when her excuses for his absences run out and she actually has to produce the mystery man. Despite fun performances from Goldberg, Dianne Wiest and Bebe Neuwirth, there just aren't enough jokes. JB **DVD** **CS**

Whoopi Goldberg *Laurel* • Dianne Wiest *Sally* • Eli Wallach *Fallon* • Tim Daly [Timothy Daly] *Frank* • Bebe Neuwirth *Camille* • Austin Pendleton *Aesop* • Lainie Kazan *Cindy Mason* • George Martin (1) *Manchester* ■ *Dir* Donald Petrie • *Scr* Nick Thiel, from the film *L'Associé* by Jean-Claude Carrière and René Gainville, and the novel *El Socio* by Jenaro Prieto

Assumed Killer
★★

Mystery thriller   2013 · US · Colour · 87min

A journalist wife (Barbie Castro) thinks her husband (Casper Van Dien) is a serial killer in this slow-moving and uneventful mystery thriller. Suffering amnesia after a car accident, Castro becomes convinced that attorney Van Dien is the Florida psycho she was investigating prior to the crash. Some menacing visuals and music, not to mention Van Dien's exaggerated behaviour, suggest she's right, but all this is merely followed by unimpressive twists and a flat climax. SF

Casper Van Dien *Sam Morrow* • Barbie Castro *Daria Valdez Morrow* • Armand Assante *Aaron Banfield* • Christie Lynn Smith *Sara* • Eric Roberts *Taxi driver* ■ *Dir/Scr* Bernard Salzman [Bernard Salzmann]

Asterix the Gaul
★★★ **U**

Animated adventure
1967 · Bel/Fr · Colour · 65min

Almost a decade after the publication of René Goscinny and Albert Uderzo's first comic book, Asterix and his friends found their way on to the big screen. Made in Belgium, this is pretty much an introductory exercise, as the secret of Getafix's magic potion, the story behind Obelix's ludicrous strength and the reasons why Caesar's legions can't conquer a tiny Gaullish village are all explained. But there's also plenty of action as Asterix and his menhir-carrying chum set out to rescue their druid from an ambitious centurion. DP French dubbed.

■ *Dir/Scr* René Goscinny, Albert Uderzo

Asterix and Cleopatra
★★★ **U**

Animated adventure
1968 · Fr/Bel · Colour · 72min

Following on from *Asterix the Gaul*, this is the second animated feature culled from the classic comic books by René Goscinny and Albert Uderzo. Once again, the pair took dual directorial responsibility for this amusing (if racially suspect) odyssey, in which Asterix, Obelix, his pet pooch Dogmatix and the potion-brewing druid Getafix set out to cock a snook at Caesar by

building a palace for the Queen of the Nile. Followed by *The 12 Tasks of Asterix*. DP French dubbed.

■ *Dir* René Goscinny, Albert Uderzo • *Scr* René Goscinny, Albert Uderzo, Pierre Tchernia, from the comic book by Goscinny, Uderzo

Asterix vs Caesar
★★★ **U**

Animated adventure   1985 · Fr · Colour · 73min

Combining plotlines from *Asterix the Legionary* and *Asterix the Gladiator*, this big-screen adaptation of the bestselling adventures of the indomitable Gaul and his doltish sidekick, Obelix, follows on from *The 12 Tasks of Asterix*. The American dubbing grates horribly, but the puns are as deliciously bad as ever. The parodies of *Spartacus* and *Ben-Hur* should amuse. DP French dubbed.

Jack Bearber *Asterix* • Bill Kearns [Billy Kearns] *Obelix* • Allen Wenger *Caius Flavius* • Gordon Heath *Julius Caesar* ■ *Dir* Gaetan Brizzi, Paul Brizzi • *Scr* Pierre Tchernia, from the comic book by René Goscinny, Albert Uderzo

Asterix in Britain
★★★ **U**

Animated adventure   1986 · Fr · Colour · 75min

By Jupiter! How superbus! In another animated movie to be lifted from the text and drawings of Goscinny and Uderzo's books, the pun-struck Gallic heroes come to the aid of a British village thats just been invaded by the Romans. The wily Asterix and the galumphing Obelix are on hand to satirise national stereotypes, and the puns are enough to make "wincemeat" of us all. TH French dubbed.

Jack Beaber *Asterix* • Bill Kearns [Billy Kearns] *Obelix* • Graham Bushnell *Anticlimax/Jolitorax* • Herbert Baskind *Totalapsus* • Jimmy Shuman *Chateaupetrus* • Ed Marcus *Stratocumulus* ■ *Dir* Pino Van Lamsweerde • *Scr* Pierre Tchernia, from the comic book by René Goscinny, Albert Uderzo

Asterix Conquers America
★★ **U**

Animated adventure   1994 · Ger · Colour · 81min

Asterix's adventures are hardly the most politically correct at the best of times, but this adaptation is guilty of some unforgivable racist lapses. The story of Getafix's rescue from the New World is not the strongest in the series, though the anachronistic gags are as sharp as ever, while the familiar drawing style atones for the rather uninspired voiceovers. DP German dubbed.

John Rye *Narrator* • Craig Charles *Asterix* • Howard Lew Lewis *Obelix* • Henry McGee *Caesar* • Christopher Biggins *Lucullus* • Geoffrey Bayldon *Getafix* ■ *Dir* Gerhard Hahn • *Scr* Thomas Platt, Rhett Rooster, from an idea by Pierre Tchernia, Albert Uderzo, from the comic book *Asterix and the Great Crossing* by René Goscinny, Albert Uderzo

Asterix and Obelix Take On Caesar
★★ **PG**

Comedy fantasy adventure
1999 · Fr/Ger/It · Colour · 105min

It may be one of the most expensive French movies ever made, but Claude Zidi's live-action romp has none of the wit or charm of the original comic books. With Christian Clavier and Gérard Depardieu well cast as the indomitable Gauls and Roberto Benigni milking every gag as a scheming centurion, the acting is suitably pantomimic. But the inability of Terry Jones (who penned the English language script and dubbed Depardieu) to duplicate René Goscinny's sublime linguistic games undermines the cast's efforts. DP French dubbed. **DVD**

Christian Clavier *Astérix* • Gérard Depardieu *Obélix* • Roberto Benigni *Detritus* • Marianne Sägebrecht *Bonnemine* • Gottfried John *César* • Laetitia Casta *Falbala* • Michel Galabru *Abaracourcix* • Claude Piéplu *Panoramix* ■ *Dir* Claude Zidi • *Scr* Claude Zidi, Gérard Lauzier, from the comic books by René Goscinny, Albert Uderzo

Asterix & Obelix: Mission Cleopatra
★★★ **PG**

Comedy fantasy adventure
2001 · Fr/Ger · Colour · 103min

More in the spirit of Goscinny and Uderzo than Claude Zidi's Hollywoodised blockbuster *Asterix and Obelix Take on Caesar*, this is still nowhere near as satisfying as reading the original comic book. However, it's a vast improvement, as director Alain Chabat not only trusts his story, but also keeps a much tighter rein on Christian Clavier's exuberance and Gérard Depardieu's buffoonery. Monica Bellucci is perfectly cast as the Egyptian queen who demands that architect Jamel Debbouze build a golden palace within three months to win a bet with Caesar (Chabat). DP French +subtitles. **DVD** **CS**

Gérard Depardieu *Obelix* • Christian Clavier *Asterix* • Jamel Debbouze *Numerobis* • Monica Bellucci *Cleopatra* • Alain Chabat *Julius Caesar* • Claude Rich *Panoramix* ■ *Dir* Alain Chabat • *Scr* Alain Chabat, from the comic book by René Goscinny, Albert Uderzo

Asterix at the Olympic Games
★ **PG**

Comedy fantasy adventure
2008 · Sp/Ger/Fr/It/Bel · Colour · 112min

The worst of the three live-action movies based on the famous Gallic comic books is the most expensive French fantasy ever made. Forced and overplayed, the messy script sidelines Asterix (Clovis Cornillac) and Obelix (Gérard Depardieu) in favour of a plodding romantic triangle. Even superior special effects and surprise cameos (Zinédine Zidane, Michael Schumacher) cannot save this unfunny adventure from being nothing more than a spectacularly epic bore. AJ French +subtitles. **DVD**

Clovis Cornillac *Asterix* • Gérard Depardieu *Obelix* • Alain Delon *Julius Caesar* • Benoît Poelvoorde *Brutus* • Stéphane Rousseau *Alafolix* • Vanessa Hessler *Princess Irina* • Franck Dubosc *Assurancetourix* • Jean-Pierre Cassel *Panoramix* • Michael Schumacher *Schumix* • Zinédine Zidane *Numérodix* ■ *Dir* Frédéric Forestier [Frederic Forestier], Thomas Langmann • *Scr* Alexandre Charlot, Olivier Dazat, Thomas Langmann, Franck Magnier, from the comic book by René Goscinny, Albert Uderzo

Asterix and the Vikings
★★★ **U**

Animated comedy adventure
2006 · Fr/Den · Colour · 74min

Loosely based on the Goscinny and Uderzo comic book *Asterix and the Normans*, the eighth animated outing for Asterix and Obelix sees the hirsute heroes squaring off against an invading band of Viking warriors who've kidnapped the Chief's slacker nephew, Justforkix. Groan-worthy puns and anachronistic gags deliver the biggest laughs, something that will inevitably leave younger children cold. It's a scrappy but likeable entry in the hit-and-miss series that makes up for its lack of action by staying true to the iconic style of the original. JR French dubbed. **DVD**

Paul Giamatti *Asterix* • Sean Astin *Justforkix* • Brad Garrett *Obelix* • John DiMaggio *Timandahaf* • Greg Proops *Cryptograf* • Evan Rachel Wood *Abba* ■ *Dir* Stefan Fjeldmark, Jesper Moller • *Scr* Jean-Luc Goossens, Stefan Fjeldmark, Philip LaZebnik, from the comic book *Asterix and the Normans* by René Goscinny, Albert Uderzo

The Asthenic Syndrome
★★★★

Drama   1989 · USSR · Colour and BW · 153min

Kira Muratova has made only eight features in her 30-year career, and this uncompromising study of the last days of the USSR shows why she had so much trouble with the Soviet censors and why she's ranked among the most important of all women film-makers. The winner of the Special Jury Prize at the Berlin film festival, the film suggests that Communist rule has subjected the entire population to asthenia, a condition that induces dejected passivity in times of stress. The pain of the opening monochrome sequence and the stark

realism of the Moscow scenes make for most uncomfortable yet compelling viewing. DP Russian +subtitles.

Sergei Popov *Nikolai* • Olga Antonova *Natascha* • Natalia Busko *Mascha, the brunette* • Galina Sakurdaeva *Mascha, the blonde* • Aleksandra Ovenskaia *Lehrerin* • Pavel Polischnuk • Natalia Rallewa ■ *Dir* Kira Muratova • *Scr* Kira Muratova, Sergei Popov, Aleksandr Chernitch, Vladimir Pankov

The Astonished Heart
★

Romantic drama   1949 · UK · BW · 87min

Noël Coward stars a psychiatrist whose understanding wife (Celia Johnson) attempts to condone his adultery with her beautiful best friend (Margaret Leighton). A low point in the career of all three principals and co-director Terence Fisher, it sank into almost immediate obscurity. RK

Noël Coward *Christian Faber* • Celia Johnson *Barbara Faber* • Margaret Leighton *Leonora Vail* • Joyce Carey *Susan Birch* • Graham Payn *Tim Verney* • Amy Veness *Alice Smith* • Ralph Michael *Philip Lucas* • Michael Hordern *Ernest* ■ *Dir* Terence Fisher, Anthony Damborough • *Scr* Noël Coward, from his play

The Astounding She-Monster
★★

Science-fiction horror   1958 · US · BW · 59min

A super-tall female alien in skin-tight metallic spacesuit, spangled tights and high heels lands on Earth and uses her glow-in-the-dark touch to kill. A group of loyal citizens band together to fight the intergalactic menace in a prime example of ultra-cheap 1950s trash, which is so bad it's actually quite good fun. Pitiful special effects and deadly dull nocturnal strolls through the forest by the extraordinary-looking She-Monster (Shirley Kilpatrick) add to its camp charm. AJ

Robert Clarke *Dick Cutler* • Kenne Duncan *Nat Burdell* • Marilyn Harvey *Margaret Chaffee* • Jeanne Tatum *Esther Malone* • Shirley Kilpatrick *Monster* • Ewing Brown *Brad Conley* ■ *Dir* Ronnie Ashcroft • *Scr* Frank Hall

The Astral Factor
★ **12**

Horror   1976 · US · Colour · 95min

Shot in 1976, it's not hard to see why this confusing would-be chiller was kept on the shelf until 1984. A boy strangles his mother when she tells him she wishes she had had an abortion. Imprisoned in a mental asylum, he learns an ancient Buddhist technique for becoming invisible and escapes death row to murder all the people responsible for his sentence. A terrible script and amateur-hour direction condemn the viewer to hard labour as well. AJ **DVD**

Robert Foxworth *Lieutenant Charles Barrett* • Stefanie Powers *Candy Barrett* • Elke Sommer *Chris* • Sue Lyon *Miss De Long* • Leslie Parrish *Coleen Hudson* ■ *Dir* John Florea • *Scr* Arthur C Pierce, from the story by Arthur C Pierce, Earle Lyon

Astro Boy
★★★ **PG**

Animated science-fiction adventure
2009 · US/HK · Colour · 89min

The iconic Japanese *anime* character makes his Hollywood debut in this sweet-natured and colourful futuristic adventure. Brilliant scientist Dr Tenma (voiced by Nicolas Cage) is devastated when his equally brilliant son (Freddie Highmore) is accidentally killed during an experiment. Tenma builds a robotic replacement, but abandons him when he doesn't live up to expectations. Left to fend for himself, the robot becomes Astro Boy and discovers the true extent of his powers when an evil force threatens the world. The film presents some fairly adult themes in an understandable way, and it's also less cheesy and sentimental than a lot of animated fare, with some exciting action sequences along the way. LB **DVD** **Blu-ray**

Freddie Highmore *Astro Boy/Toby* • Nicolas Cage *Dr Tenma* • Kristen Bell *Cora* • Samuel L Jackson *Zog* • Bill Nighy *Dr Elefun/Robotsky* • Donald Sutherland *President Stone* • Charlize Theron *"Our Friends" narrator* • Matt Lucas *Sparx* ■ *Dir* David Bowers • *Scr* Timothy Hyde Harris [Timothy Harris], David Bowers, from a story by Bowers, from the comic book by Osamu Tezuka

The Astronaut Farmer
★★ PG

Drama   2006 · US · Colour · 99min

A classic episode of *The Simpsons* had Homer being selected by NASA to undertake a space mission; this excruciating American drama is only slightly less unlikely – and nowhere near as much fun. Billy Bob Thornton plays the rural spaceman, who has given up his flying career to save the family farm, but is still determined to be an astronaut so he builds a rocket ship in his barn. Leaving aside the implausible storyline and saccharine direction, the biggest problem is that it's hard to empathise with this particular underdog. Thornton comes off as a self-obsessed nutter, rather than a lovable eccentric, which makes the loyalty shown by wife Virginia Madsen even more bewildering. Bruce Willis, who has a supporting role as a sympathetic former astronaut, wisely took his name off the credits. JF **DVD**

Billy Bob Thornton *Charles Farmer* · Virginia Madsen *Audrey "Audie" Farmer* · Bruce Dern *Hal* · JK Simmons *Jacobson* · Tim Blake Nelson *Kevin Munchak* · Max Thieriot *Shepard Farmer* · Jon Gries [Jonathan Gries] *FBI Agent Killbourne* · Mark Polish *FBI Agent Mathis* · Jasper Polish *Stanley Farmer* · Logan Polish *Sunshine Farmer* ■ *Dir* Michael Polish · *Scr* Mark and Michael Polish · *Cinematographer* M David Mullen

The Astronaut's Wife ★★ 18
Science-fiction psychological thriller
1999 · US · Colour · 109min

One wonders what an actor with the impeccable taste of Johnny Depp was doing accepting the lead in Rand Ravich's directorial debut. Playing an astronaut who starts behaving oddly after an accident in space, Depp brings an undeserved degree of credibility to what is a derivative and unshocking sci-fi rehash of *Rosemary's Baby*. This is too serious for its own good, and no amount of inventive direction can save it. AC Violence, swearing, sex scenes. **DVD**

Johnny Depp *Spencer Armacost* · Charlize Theron *Jillian Armacost* · Joe Morton *Sherman Reese* · Clea DuVall *Nan* · Samantha Eggar *Doctor* · Donna Murphy *Natalie Streck* · Nick Cassavetes *Alex Streck* · Gary Grubbs *NASA director* ■ *Dir/Scr* Rand Ravich

Asya's Happiness ★★★★★ PG
Drama   1967 · USSR · BW · 97min

Suppressed by the Communist authorities because of the critical political opinions expressed by some of the male characters and not released abroad until the late 1980s, this film exemplifies why director Andrei Mikhalkov-Konchalovsky was one of the USSR's premier directors before decamping to Hollywood and taking on more commercial fare. The magnificent Iya Savvina, supported by a largely non-professional and extraordinarily natural cast, stars in this account of life and hardships in a rural village. This absorbing and moving film is rich in detail, authentic atmosphere and honesty. RK Russian +subtitles.

Iya Savvina *Asya Klyachina* · Lyubov Sokolova · Alexander Surin · Gennady Yegorychev ■ *Dir* Andrei Mikhalkov-Konchalovsky [Andrei Konchalovsky] · *Scr* Ivan Petrov, Yuri Klepikov

Asylum ★★★ 15
Horror   1972 · UK · Colour · 82min

This rippingly good terror anthology of *Psycho* author Robert Bloch's tales showcases re-animated, dismembered limbs, a magic suit, homicidal split personalities and tiny murdering robots. With an ingenious linking device – each story is a mental patient's case history – building to a *Grand Guignol* twist finale, the excellent cast wrings every ounce of horror from a clever script, while the underplayed black humour is a bonus. AJ Violence. **DVD**

Robert Powell *Dr Martin* · Peter Cushing *Smith* · Britt Ekland *Lucy* · Herbert Lom *Byron* · Patrick Magee *Dr Rutherford* · Charlotte Rampling *Barbara* · Richard Todd *Walter* · Barbara Parkins

Bonnie · Barry Morse *Bruno* · Sylvia Syms *Ruth* ■ *Dir* Roy Ward Baker · *Scr* Robert Bloch, from his stories

Asylum ★★★ 15
Psychological romantic drama
2004 · US/Ire · Colour · 95min

Ambitious psychiatrist Hugh Bonneville arrives to take up a post as deputy superintendent at an old Gothic mental institution, along with his wife (Natasha Richardson) and young son. He is boring. She is bored. Richardson soon finds an outlet for her repressed desires in the arms of Marton Csokas, an artist who murdered his unfaithful spouse and is now the star patient of Bonneville's rival Ian McKellen. Powerful performances and the gritty style are just about enough to offset the melodramatic excesses of the plot. BP Sex scenes, violence, swearing. **DVD**

Natasha Richardson *Stella Raphael* · Ian McKellen *Dr Peter Cleave* · Marton Csokas *Edgar Stark* · Hugh Bonneville *Max Raphael* · Judy Parfitt *Brenda Raphael* · Sean Harris *Nick* · Gus Lewis *Charlie Raphael* · Wanda Ventham *Bridie Straffen* ■ *Dir* David Mackenzie · *Scr* Patrick Marber, from the novel by Patrick McGrath

The Asylum ★★★ 18
Horror   2015 · US · Colour and BW · 87min

A surprisingly watchable and entertaining riff on teen slaughter-fest territory, this starts slowly with a loud and lairy group of adolescents mooching about in a dilapidated asylum following a party. But what makes it a cut above the usual fodder is that director Marcus Nispel knows his fear flicks – one droll reference to *The Exorcist* sees the bunch look up a DIY exorcism kit on an app inspired by the 1973 classic. Knowing without being glib, the film is crisply shot and offers plenty of claustrophobic tension. JA **DVD**

Stephen Lang *Father Conway* · Brett Dier *Brad* · Gage Golightly *Amber* ■ *Dir* Marcus Nispel · *Scr* Kirsten Elms, from a story by Marcus Nispel

At Any Price ★★★★ 18
Drama   2012 · US · Colour · 99min

Set in the heartland of Iowa, this engaging, low-key drama has Dennis Quaid as a seed salesman who runs a family farm. He wants this tradition to continue, but one son is travelling the world, while the other (Zac Efron) wants to be a racing driver. Quaid offers one of his best performances, conveying a flawed man who is struggling – and failing – to connect with his son. The story isn't particularly satisfying, but the film is built around a handful of relatable characters, which is enough to set it apart from the average drama. SC Brief sex scene.

Dennis Quaid *Henry Whipple* · Zac Efron *Dean Whipple* · Kim Dickens *Irene Whipple* · Heather Graham *Meredith Crown* ■ *Dir* Ramin Bahrani · *Scr* Ramin Bahrani, Hallie Elizabeth Newton

At Berkeley ★★★★ PG
Documentary   2013 · US · Colour · 244min

Frederick Wiseman's 38th documentary looks at the University of California at Berkeley. It was a hotbed of student radicalism in the 1960s, but is now at a crossroads, as budgetary cutbacks threaten both the teaching programme and the campus's hard-won relationship with the local community. Prioritising ideas and debate over personality and incident, the director's style can feel a little rarefied. But few are better at conveying the ambience of a place and the mindset of the people who uphold its traditions and values. DP

■ *Dir* Frederick Wiseman

At Close Range ★★★★ 15
Biographical drama   1985 · US · Colour · 110min

This powerful drama about crime and misguided family loyalties features a magnificent performance from Sean Penn as the bored son who's lured into the world of gangsters by evil dad Christopher Walken. Downbeat and very tough, the grim tale is even more compelling and chilling for being true. Director James Foley's decision

to shoot with a documentary-style realism is one of the movie's great strengths, as it gives the gripping chain of events a pervasive atmosphere of simmering violence that's tremendously effective. AJ Swearing, violence. **DVD**

Sean Penn *Brad Whitewood Jr* · Christopher Walken *Brad Whitewood Sr* · Mary Stuart Masterson *Terry* · Christopher Penn [Chris Penn] *Tommy Whitewood* · Millie Perkins *Julie Whitewood* · Eileen Ryan *Grandmother* · Kiefer Sutherland *Tim* ■ *Dir* James Foley · *Scr* Nicholas Kazan, from a story by Elliott Lewitt, Kazan · *Cinematographer* Juan Ruiz-Anchia

...At First Sight ★★★
Romantic comedy   1995 · US · Colour · 90min

Jonathan Silverman stars as a lovable schmuck who's dating the lovely Allison Smith. But his pal Dan Cortese bullies him into more adventurous romantic escapades. Like its main characters, however, it doesn't really go anywhere. The film features a hilarious cameo from voice actress Pamela Segall as a wallflower turned vamp. ST

Dan Cortese *Joey Fortone* · Jonathan Silverman *Lenny Kaminski* · Allison Smith *Rhonda Glick* · Monte Markham *Lester Glick* · Kathleen Freeman *Grandma* · Susan Walters *Cindy One* · Pamela Segall *Tracy* ■ *Dir* Steven Pearl · *Scr* Ken Copel

At First Sight ★★★ 12
Drama   1998 · US · Colour · 123min

Like *Awakenings*, this medical melodrama is also drawn from the casebook of Dr Oliver Sacks, but it's not so dramatically satisfying. However, the tale of courage is so remarkable that any filming of it would seem trite and sentimental. Val Kilmer's performance as a blind man who has trouble adjusting when his sight is restored is infuriatingly mannered. But Kelly McGillis as his sister and Mira Sorvino as his lover prevent the material from entering disease-of-the-week TV movie territory. No classic, but thoughtful and solidly crafted. DP Swearing, brief nudity. **DVD**

Val Kilmer *Virgil Adamson* · Mira Sorvino *Amy Benic* · Kelly McGillis *Jennie Adamson* · Steven Weber *Duncan Allanbrook* · Bruce Davison *Dr Charles Aaron* · Nathan Lane *Phil Webster* · Ken Howard *Virgil's father* · Laura Kirk *Betsy Ernst* · Jack Dodick *Dr Goldman* · Oliver Sacks *Reporter* ■ *Dir* Irwin Winkler · *Scr* Steve Levitt, from the article *To See and Not See* from *An Anthropologist on Mars* by Oliver Sacks

At Five in the Afternoon
★★★★ U
Drama   2003 · Iran/Fr · Colour · 101min

Although the focus of this incisive blend of social reality and romantic idealism is on the discrimination still facing women in post-Taliban Afghanistan, Iranian director Samira Makhmalbaf also highlights the extent to which everyone's beliefs and duties are determined by the politico-cultural agendas of the powers that be. The bleak landscape captured by Ebrahim Ghafori's camera reinforces the sense of despair that prompts Abdolgani Yousefrazi to keep his family on the move around a combat-scarred Kabul. But the charmingly expressive Agheleh Rezaie's minor acts of defiance and outspoken self-confidence provide an optimistic challenge to the status quo. DP Farsi +subtitles. **DVD**

Agheleh Rezaie *Nogreh* · Abdolgani Yousefrazi *Father* · Razi Mohebi *Poet* ■ *Dir* Samira Makhmalbaf · *Scr* Samira Makhmalbaf, Mohsen Makhmalbaf

At Gunpoint ★★ U
Western   1955 · US · Colour · 81min

This is a very average Allied Artists western, owing much to *High Noon* in its plotting. It stars a rather glum Fred MacMurray, but the ever-glamorous Dorothy Malone (seemingly born to play frontierswomen) is the main attraction here, doing sterling work as Fred's wife. The whole benefits from being filmed in CinemaScope, but director Alfred Werker's pace is just too slow for comfort. TS

Fred MacMurray *Jack Wright* · Dorothy Malone *Martha Wright* · Walter Brennan *Doc Lacy* · Tommy Rettig *Billy* · John Qualen *Livingstone* ·

Irving Bacon *Ferguson* · Skip Homeier *Bob* · Jack Lambert *Kirk* ■ *Dir* Alfred Werker · *Scr* Daniel B Ullman

At Long Last Love ★★ U
Musical romance   1975 · US · Colour · 114min

Despite predictions that this spoof on 1930s musicals would become a cult classic, it's embarrassing the way aspiration became affectation. Playboy Burt Reynolds, icy-blonde Cybill Shepherd, Broadway star Madeline Kahn and gambler Duilio Del Prete find contrivances to weave in and out of 16 Cole Porter songs, and get lost in the process. TH

Burt Reynolds *Michael Oliver Pritchard III* · Cybill Shepherd *Brooke Carter* · Madeline Kahn *Kitty O'Kelly* · Duilio Del Prete *Johnny Spanish* · Eileen Brennan *Elizabeth* · John Hillerman *Rodney James* · Mildred Natwick *Mabel Pritchard* · Quinn Redeker *Phillip* · M Emmet Walsh *Harold* ■ *Dir/Scr* Peter Bogdanovich · *Music* Cole Porter

At Play in the Fields of the Lord ★★ 15
Adventure drama   1991 · US · Colour · 185min

Unless you're fascinated by the ecological issues raised, Hector Babenco's Amazonian rainforest saga is unlikely to sustain your interest throughout its mammoth running time. This tale of religious, emotional and physical conflict in one of the most beautiful vistas on Earth is sincere, and Aidan Quinn, Kathy Bates and Tom Berenger give committed performances. Alas, the unsympathetic characters, rambling plot and extreme length are hurdles Babenco is ultimately unable to overcome. JC

Tom Berenger *Lewis Moon* · John Lithgow *Leslie Huben* · Daryl Hannah *Andy Huben* · Aidan Quinn *Martin Quarrier* · Tom Waits *Wolf* · Kathy Bates *Hazel Quarrier* · Stenio Garcia *Boronai* ■ *Dir* Hector Babenco · *Scr* Jean-Claude Carrière, Hector Babenco, from the novel by Peter Matthiessen

At the Circus ★★★ U
Comedy   1939 · US · BW · 83min

This picture marked the start of the Marx Brothers' fall from grace, as their humorous anarchy was severely restricted by MGM's big-studio regulations. Here Groucho plays a shyster lawyer who teams up with Harpo and Chico to save a circus from bankruptcy. There are some great moments but the exuberance has been toned down. The trio also seem reluctant to follow the plot, especially if it means being on the same bill as crooner Kenny Baker. TH **DVD**

Groucho Marx *Attorney Loophole* · Chico Marx *Antonio* · Harpo Marx *Punchy* · Kenny Baker (1) *Jeff Wilson* · Eve Arden *Peerless Pauline* · Margaret Dumont *Mrs Dukesbury* · Florence Rice *Julie Randall* · Nat Pendleton *Goliath* ■ *Dir* Edward Buzzell · *Scr* Irving Brecher

At the Earth's Core ★★ PG
Science-fiction adventure
1976 · UK · Colour · 86min

Victorian explorer Doug McClure and fidgety scientist Peter Cushing encounter all manner of unconvincing monsters as they burrow through the Earth with a giant boring device to the subterranean kingdom of Pellucidar. This childish and chintzy adaptation of an Edgar Rice Burroughs novel would be an even bigger patience-tester if not for sultry heroine Caroline Munro and the truly awful man-in-rubber-suit special effects, which will inspire hoots of laughter. AJ **DVD**

Doug McClure *David Innes* · Peter Cushing *Dr Abner Perry* · Caroline Munro *Dia* · Cy Grant *Ra* · Godfrey James *Ghak* · Sean Lynch *Hooja* ■ *Dir* Kevin Connor · *Scr* Milton Subotsky, from the novel by Edgar Rice Burroughs

At the Height of Summer ★★★ PG
Drama   1999 · Fr/Ger/Viet · Colour · 108min

Vietnamese director Tran Anh Hung produces here another film of immense beauty and psychological significance, but it's also a tad convoluted and precious. There is such a focus on aquatic symbolism and the essence of ritual that it's easy to become distracted from the problems facing three Hanoi sisters. Both Le Khanh and Nguyen Nhu Quynh impress as wronged wives, but only Tran Nu Yen Khe's ambiguous relationship with her brother is untainted by soap operatics. DP Vietnamese +subtitles. **DVD**

Tran Nu Yen-Khe *Lien* • Nguyen Nhu Quynh *Suong* • Le Khanh *Khanh* • Ngo Quang Hai *Hai* ■ *Dir/Scr* Tran Anh Hung

At War with the Army
★★★ U

Comedy   1950 · US · BW · 91min

The third film for comedy team Dean Martin and Jerry Lewis was a massive hit. It consolidated their screen images (Martin's the smoothie, Lewis is the nerd) and ensured their success throughout a generation.This is slapdash film-making, but also very funny, and a scene involving a soda machine is priceless. Dean croons three songs as he enjoins Jerry to help him out of female trouble, and Polly Bergen makes an attractive movie debut. TS **DVD**

Dean Martin *Sergeant Puccinelli* • Jerry Lewis *Private Korwin* • Mike Kellin *Sergeant McVey* • Jimmie Dundee *Eddie* • Dick Stabile *Pokey* • Tommy Farrell *Corporal Clark* • Frank Hyers *Corporal Shaughnessy* • Dan Dayton *Sergeant Miller* • Polly Bergen *Helen* ■ *Dir* Hal Walker • *Scr* Fred F Finklehoffe, from the play by James B Allardice

LANDMARK FILM
Jean Vigo's 1930s poetic realist story of barge life in Paris later influences the French New Wave

L'Atalante
★★★★★ PG

Romantic drama   1934 · Fr · BW · 85min

Few films can claim to have inspired two revolutions. Jean Vigo's masterpiece not only established the visual style of 1930s poetic realism, but was also one of the key influences on the New Wave of the late 1950s. It's a simple, almost uneventful picture, chronicling barge captain Jean Dasté's first days of marriage to Dita Parlo. Yet it becomes a mesmerising personal vision thanks to Vigo's sophisticated blend of fairy-tale romance, documentary realism, surrealist fantasy, bawdy humour and song. Michel Simon's scene-stealing improvisation and the exceptional cinematography further enhance the pleasure to be derived from one of the most completely cinematic pictures ever made. DP French +subtitles. **DVD**

Michel Simon *Père Jules* • Jean Dasté *Jean* • Dita Parlo *Juliette* • Gilles Margaritis *Pedlar* • Louis Lefebvre *Cabin boy* • Fanny Clar *Juliette's mother* • Raphael Diligent *Juliette's father* • Charles Goldblatt *Thief* • René Bleck *Best man* ■ *Dir* Jean Vigo • *Scr* Jean Vigo, Albert Riera from a story by Jean Guinée • *Cinematographers* Boris Kaufman, Louis Berger, Jean-Paul Alphen

Atanarjuat: the Fast Runner
★★★★ 15

Drama   2001 · Can · Colour · 161min

Set in the Canadian Arctic and based on ancient Inuit legend, the first film to be written in the Inuktitut language is a sublime cross between an anthropological study and a Jacobean tragedy. Exposing the threat posed to communal security by ambition and desire, Zacharias Kunuk's debut feature has an intimacy that belies its epic scope. After winning the heart of a woman betrothed to the son of an elder, Natar Ungalaaq earns the enmity of the man that erupts into violence. A compelling achievement. DP Inuktitut +subtitles. Violence, sex scenes, nudity. **DVD**

Natar Ungalaaq *Atanarjuat* • Sylvia Ivalu *Atuat* • Peter Henry Arnatsiaq *Oki* • Lucy Tulugarjuk *Puja* ■ *Dir* Zacharias Kunuk • *Scr* Paul Apak

Athena
★★ U

Musical   1954 · US · Colour · 95min

An unusual idea is let down by a paper-thin plot in this musical starring Jane Powell and Debbie Reynolds as two of seven sisters who belong to a family of health and exercise fanatics. Crooner Vic Damone and cardboard cutout Edmund Purdom are their suitors and Mr Universe-turned-movie-star

Steve Reeves is on hand to support the theory about healthy living ensuring the body beautiful. Some pleasant singing livens up the routine proceedings. RK

Jane Powell *Athena* • Debbie Reynolds *Minerva* • Virginia Gibson *Niobe* • Nancy Kilgas *Aphrodite* • Dolores Starr *Calliope* • Jane Fischer *Medea* • Cecile Rogers *Ceres* • Edmund Purdom *Adam Calhorn Shaw* • Vic Damone *Johnny Nyle* • Louis Calhern *Grandpa Mulvain* • Steve Reeves *Ed Perkins* ■ *Dir* Richard Thorpe • *Scr* William Ludwig, Leonard Spigelgass

The Athlete
★★ PG

Sports biography

2009 · US/Ger/Eth · BW and Colour · 92min

This moderate biopic dramatises the rollercoaster life of barefoot marathon runner Abebe Bikila. In the 1960 Rome Olympics, the Ethiopian became the first-ever black African to win Olympic gold, and, four years later in Tokyo, he became the first athlete to win consecutive marathon golds. But a car crash would leave him paralysed from the waist down, and facing challenges of a very different kind, and it's the post-crash period that provides the film's dramatic heart. Script and acting are on the stilted side, but the strength of the story compensates somewhat. DA English, Amharic +subtitles. **DVD**

Rasselas Lakew *Abebe Bikila* • Dag Malmberg *Onni* • Ruta Gedmintas *Charlotte* • Abba Waka Dessalegn *The priest* ■ *Dir* Davey Frankel, Rasselas Lakew • *Scr* Rasselas Lakew, Davey Frankel, Mikael Aemiro Awake

Atlantic City
★★★ U

Musical   1944 · US · BW · 87min

A surprise offering from the poverty row studio Republic, this agreeable little musical chronicles the professional trials, personal tribulations and eventual triumphs of a young impresario (Brad Taylor) as he pursues his ambition to make Atlantic City into a world-class entertainment playground. The plus factors include the presence of Paul Whiteman and Louis Armstrong with their orchestras, some good musical numbers, and Constance Moore lending the turbulent romantic interest. RK

Brad Taylor [Stanley Brown] *Brad Taylor* • Constance Moore *Marilyn Whitaker* • Charley Grapewin *Jake Taylor* • Jerry Colonna *Professor* • Robert B Castaine *Carter Graham* • Adele Mara *Barmaid* • Louis Armstrong • Paul Whiteman • Dorothy Dandridge • Belle Baker ■ *Dir* Ray McCarey • *Scr* Doris Gilbert, Frank Gill Jr, George Carleton Brown, from a story by Arthur Caesar

Atlantic City, USA
★★★★★ 15

Crime drama   1980 · US/Can · Colour · 99min

In this wonderfully beguiling and bizarre study of small-time losers from director Louis Malle, Burt Lancaster stars as a voyeuristic, over-the-hill hood reduced to running a gambling racket and living off fake memories of days with famous gangsters of yesteryear. Paradoxically, this role is one of Lancaster's best, and his performance is matched by that of Susan Sarandon as the woman with whom he becomes involved when a stash of drugs is stolen from the Mafia. Hard to define – it's neither a thriller nor a love story – this gangster movie displays abundant Gallic charm, while Sarandon is the perfect foil for Lancaster. TH Violence, swearing, brief nudity. **DVD**

Burt Lancaster *Lou* • Susan Sarandon *Sally* • Michel Piccoli *Joseph* • Hollis McLaren *Chrissie* • Robert Joy *Dave* • Kate Reid *Grace* • Moses Znaimer *Felix* • Al Waxman *Alfie* • Robert Goulet *Singer* ■ *Dir* Louis Malle • *Scr* John Guare

Atlantis
★★ U

Documentary   1991 · Fr · Colour · 74min

After making *Nikita*, director Luc Besson returned to the ocean depths of *The Big Blue* for a stunningly shot but boring documentary on undersea life that proved he was no Jacques Cousteau. Concentration lapses are numerous for

such a short film, barely released outside his native France. AJ In French. **DVD** **Blu**

■ *Dir/Scr* Luc Besson

Atlantis, the Lost Continent
★★

Fantasy adventure   1960 · US · Colour · 90min

Famed producer/director George Pal came unstuck with this silly fantasy. Anthony Hall is the young Greek sailor facing danger, animal men and atomic death rays in the final days of the fabled city before it slips into the deep, thanks to a volcanic eruption. Even the special effects are below sea level in this uneasy mix of comic book science fiction and tacky sand-and-sandal epic. AJ

Anthony Hall [Sal Ponti] *Demetrios* • Joyce Taylor *Antillia* • John Dall *Zaren* • Bill Smith [William Smith] *Captain of the guard* • Frank De Kova *Sonoy* • Edward Platt *Azor* • Berry Kroeger *Surgeon* ■ *Dir* George Pal • *Scr* Daniel Mainwaring, from the play *Atlanta, a Story of Atlantis* by Gerald Hargreaves

Atlantis: the Lost Empire
★★★★ U

Animated fantasy adventure

2001 · US · Colour · 91min

Taking its cue from Japanese *manga* and the current breed of adult-friendly animation, this visually delightful tale of explorers hunting for a mythical lost continent dispenses with Disney's traditional trademarks of cute animals and foot-tapping songs. Instead, it offers grown-up, multilayered storytelling combined with a relentless pace. Exquisitely animated and voiced, the fantasy presents Atlantis as an earthly paradise, before the consequences of its characters' foibles and ambitions explode into a thrilling climax. A straight-to-video sequel, *Atlantis: Milo's Return*, followed in 2003. SF **DVD**

Michael J Fox *Milo Thatch* • James Garner *Commander Rourke* • Cree Summer *Princess Kida* • Leonard Nimoy *King of Atlantis* • Don Novello *Vinny Santorini* • Claudia Christian *Helga Sinclair* • Jacqueline Obradors *Audrey Ramirez* • John Mahoney *Preston B Whitmore* • Corey Burton *Mole* • David Ogden Stiers *Fenton Q Harcourt* • Jim Varney *Cookie* ■ *Dir* Gary Trousdale, Kirk Wise • *Scr* Tab Murphy, from a story by Kirk Wise, Gary Trousdale, Joss Whedon, Bryce Zabel, Jackie Zabel, Tab Murphy

Atlas
★★ U

Fantasy adventure   1960 · US · Colour · 78min

Muscles and baloney combine in this early outing from exploitation director Roger Corman, here trawling through Greek myths and dredging up risible rubbish about an Olympic champion (Michael Forest) who, despite being bribed by Praximedes (Frank Wolff), opts for democracy and fighting on behalf of the ordinary citizen. The solitary saving grace is that the film was shot in Greece. TH

Michael Forest *Atlas* • Barboura Morris *Candia* • Frank Wolff *Praximedes* • Walter Maslow *Garnis* • Christos Exarchos *Indros* • Andreas Philippides *Talectos* ■ *Dir* Roger Corman • *Scr* Charles Griffith

The Atomic Café
★★★ 12

Satirical political documentary
1982 · US · Colour and BW · 85min

This absorbing documentary, assembled from an amazing array of 1950s government and educational films, reveals how Americans were eased into the atomic era and the threat of possible nuclear annihilation. The film shows soldiers being subjected to A-bomb tests, while schoolchildren are taught how to "duck and cover" under their desks to avoid the harmful effects of fallout. The naive assumption that an atomic war would be survivable is one of the many shocking facts to emerge from this worthwhile nostalgia trip, which is at once scary and hilarious, informative and compelling. AJ

■ *Dir* Jayne Loader, Kevin Rafferty, Pierce Rafferty

The Atomic Kid
★★ U

Science-fiction comedy   1954 · US · BW · 85min

Made at a time when nuclear power could be treated as a joke, this happy-go-lucky tosh has Mickey Rooney as a prospector who survives an atomic test in the desert and finds he's immune to radiation. This comes in handy when he helps the FBI catch a ring of communist spies. TH

Mickey Rooney *Blix Waterberry* • Robert Strauss *Stan Cooper* • Elaine Davis *Audrey Nelson* • Bill Goodwin *Dr Rodell* • Whit Bissell *Dr Edgar Pangborn* ■ *Dir* Leslie H Martinson • *Scr* Benedict Freedman, John Fenton Murray, from a story by Blake Edwards

The Atomic Submarine
★★ PG

Science-fiction drama   1960 · US · BW · 67min

Director Spencer Gordon Bennet sustains a tense atmosphere throughout this endearing piece of hokum about an underwater alien. But the real star of this B-movie is producer Alex Gordon, who assembled a memorable cast for movie buffs. The nominal star is Arthur Franz and in support are a veritable clutch of familiar faces, all past their sell-by dates. TS

Arthur Franz *Reef* • Dick Foran *Wendover* • Brett Halsey *Carl* • Tom Conway *Sir Ian Hunt* • Paul Dubov *Dave* • Bob Steele *Griff* • Victor Varconi *Kent* • Joi Lansing *Julie* ■ *Dir* Spencer G Bennet [Spencer Gordon Bennet] • *Scr* Orville H Hampton

Atomic Twister
★★

Disaster thriller   2002 · US · Colour · 95min

Director Bill Corcoran crosses *Twister* with *The China Syndrome* in this hokey TV movie. The effects are respectable enough, but the script is packed with stock characters, clichéd situations and unintentionally hilarious dialogue. Sharon Lawrence gives it her best shot as the nuclear power-plant supervisor whose workplace is in the way of a tornado. DP

Corbin Bernsen *Sheriff CB Bishop* • Sharon Lawrence *Corinne Maguire* • Mark-Paul Gosselaar *Jake Hannah* • Carl Lewis *Stu* • Daniel Costello *Campbell Maguire* • Charmaine Guest *Ashley* ■ *Dir* Bill Corcoran • *Scr* Ron McGee

Atonement
★★★★★ 15

Period romantic drama
2007 · UK · Colour · 117min

The kind of collaboration that seems designed to produce the perfect British film, this adaptation of Ian McEwan's bestseller from screenwriter Christopher Hampton (*Dangerous Liaisons*) and director Joe Wright (*Pride & Prejudice*) actually pulls it off. Beginning in 1935, the drama pivots on the burgeoning love affair between privileged Keira Knightley and servant's son James McAvoy. An intercepted love letter, sibling jealousy and an assault combine to tear them apart. Their hopes of reunion are further complicated by the outbreak of war, McAvoy's conscription and the 1940 evacuation of Dunkirk - stunningly staged here by Wright. A handsome, heart-thumping, character-based love story, this is impeccably acted - Keira Knightley truly comes of age - and stylishly scored, with a knockout twist that works better on screen than it did on the page. AC English, French +subtitles. **DVD** **Blu**

Keira Knightley *Cecilia Tallis* • James McAvoy *Robbie Turner* • Romola Garai *Briony, aged 18* • Brenda Blethyn *Grace Turner* • Patrick Kennedy *Leon Tallis* • Saoirse Ronan *Briony, aged 13* • Benedict Cumberbatch *Paul Marshall* • Vanessa Redgrave *Older Briony* • Harriet Walter *Emily Tallis* • Gina McKee *Sister Drummond* ■ *Dir* Joe Wright • *Scr* Christopher Hampton, from the novel by Ian McEwan • *Cinematographer* Seamus McGarvey • *Music* Dario Marianelli • *Editor* Paul Tothill • *Production Designers* Sarah Greenwood, Katie Spencer • *Costume Designer* Jacqueline Durran

Attack!
★★★★ PG

Second World War drama
1956 · US · BW · 105min

Director Robert Aldrich didn't have much time for human aspirations, and never less so than in this US Army shocker about a

A

cowardly captain (Eddie Albert) endangering the lives of his men during the Battle of the Bulge. As the heroic platoon leader, Jack Palance has never been better, and neither was Lee Marvin as the colonel presiding over the whole affair. In Aldrich's macho view, war is only hell because men make it so, but his true skill is to make these unattractive characters convincing and understandable. TH *DVD*

Jack Palance *Lieutenant Costa* • Eddie Albert *Captain Cooney* • Lee Marvin *Colonel Bartlett* • Robert Strauss *Private Bernstein* • Richard Jaeckel *Private Snowden* • Buddy Ebsen *Sergeant Tolliver* • William Smithers *Lieutenant Woodruff* ◼ *Dir* Robert Aldrich • *Scr* James Poe, from the play *The Fragile Fox* by Norman Brooks

Attack Force ★ 15
Science-fiction action thriller
2006 · Rom/UK/US · Colour · 90min

This instantly forgettable B-movie is Steven Seagal's first foray into horror. It's also a truly horrible movie. The ponytailed martial arts star is a US military operative whose special ops team is wiped out by a gang of vampire-like villains while working in Paris. The vampires are actually addicts hooked on a top-secret drug called CTX whose side-effects include making users both super-powered and super-cranky. Much of the film's explicit supernatural element was apparently excised in the editing room resulting in an atrocious, semi-coherent mess. JR *DVD*

Steven Seagal *Marshall Lawson* • Lisa Lovbrand *Tia* • David Kennedy *Dwayne Dixon* • Matthew Chambers *Seth* • Danny Webb *Werner* ◼ *Dir* Michael Keusch • *Scr* Steven Seagal, Joe Halpin, from a story by Halpin

Attack Force Z ★★ 15
Second World War drama
1981 · Aus/Tai · Colour · 89min

John Phillip Law is the nominal star of this 1950s-style war yarn, now more notable for featuring an early performance from Mel Gibson, with able support from Sam Neill. A commando group is sent on an impossible mission to rescue the survivors of a plane wreck on a Japanese island. Some decent action scenes (filmed in Taiwan), typically dry humour and Law's trademark teak-forest performance keep the interest going, though the script quickly runs out of ideas. AT

John Phillip Law *Lt JA Veitch* • Mel Gibson *Capt PG Kelly* • Sam Neill *Sgt DJ Costello* • Chris Haywood *Able Seaman AD Bird* • John Waters (3) *Sub Lt EP King* ◼ *Dir* Tim Burstall • *Scr* Roger Marshall, Lee Robinson

Attack of the Crab Monsters ★★★ PG
Science-fiction horror 1957 · US · BW · 60min

Atomic testing on a remote Pacific island causes the crab population to mutate into giant monsters in one of cult director Roger Corman's earliest successes. The crustaceans look shoddy and laughable (you can often glimpse the stuntmen's feet under the costumes), but Charles Griffith's compact script successfully mines the concept for keen menace and gruesome shock. Lunatic but fast-moving fun. AJ *DVD*

Richard Garland *Dale Drewer* • Pamela Duncan *Martha Hunter* • Russell Johnson *Hank Chapman* • Leslie Bradley *Dr Karl Weigand* • Mel Welles *Jules Deveroux* • Richard H Cutting *Dr James Carson* ◼ *Dir* Roger Corman • *Scr* Charles Griffith

Attack of the 50 Foot Woman ★★
Cult science-fiction 1958 · US · BW · 65min

Though it's no more than a barely competent example of low-budget 1950s sci-fi, this poverty row cheapie has come to be regarded as a legendary absurd classic. There's a strangely contemporary feminist slant to the tale, with Allison Hayes teaching her cheating husband a lesson after a bald alien turns her into a giantess, clothed in a bedsheet bikini. However, with the effects at their least special, Hayes's accelerating

voluptuousness also exerts a curious fascination. AJ

Allison Hayes *Nancy Archer* • William Hudson *Harry Archer* • Roy Gordon *Dr Cushing* • Yvette Vickers *Honey Parker* • Ken Terrell *Jessup Stout* • George Douglas *Sheriff Dubbitt* ◼ *Dir* Nathan Hertz [Nathan Juran] • *Scr* Mark Hanna

Attack of the 50 Ft Woman ★ 12
Science fiction 1993 · US · Colour · 85min

This pointless revamp of the beloved 1958 cult classic often looks cheesier than its inspiration. Daryl Hannah narrates and stars as the rich, unhappy wife, abused by both her unfaithful husband and her uncaring father, who takes revenge when she grows to monstrous proportions after being zapped by an alien ray. AJ Some swearing. *DVD*

Daryl Hannah *Nancy Archer* • Daniel Baldwin *Harry Archer* • William Windom *Hamilton Cobb* • Frances Fisher *Dr Cushing* • Cristi Conaway *Honey* • Paul Benedict *Dr Loeb* • O'Neal Compton *Sheriff Denby* • Victoria Haas *Deputy Charlie Spooner* ◼ *Dir* Christopher Guest • *Scr* Joseph Dougherty, from the 1958 film by Mark Hanna

Attack of the Giant Leeches ★ PG
Horror 1960 · US · BW · 62min

A small town in the swampy South is terrorised by bloodthirsty giant leeches (the stuntmen barely covered by their ill-fitting rubber suits) in this thankfully short cheapie produced by cult director Roger Corman. Uninspired trash with a lousy script and inept direction it may be, but starlet Yvette Vickers is good value. AJ *DVD*

Ken Clark *Steve Benton* • Yvette Vickers *Liz Walker* • Jan Shepard *Nan Greyson* • Michael Emmet *Cal Moulton* • Tyler McVey *Doc Greyson* • Bruno VeSota *Dave Walker* • Gene Roth *Sheriff Kovis* ◼ *Dir* Bernard L Kowalski • *Scr* Leo Gordon

Attack of the Killer Tomatoes ★ PG
Horror comedy 1978 · US · Colour · 83min

Behind an irresistible title lurks one of the worst movies ever made. Deliberately planned as a bad movie from the start, the fact that director John DeBello totally achieves his aim is the only good thing to say about this dire spoof, in which giant tomatoes rampage through San Diego to avenge fruit mistreatment. Intentionally awful special effects (the tomatoes are beach balls), ludicrous dialogue and low camp turn this parody of monster movies into a mind-numbing splatter bore. Still, it did spawn three sequels (including *Return of the Killer Tomatoes*, which starred George Clooney) and a television cartoon show. AJ *DVD*

David Miller (2) *Mason Dixon* • George Wilson *Jim Richardson* • Sharon Taylor *Lois Fairchild* • Jack Riley *Agricultural official* • Rock Peace *Wilbur Finletter* • Eric Christmas *Senator Polk* • Al Sklar *Ted Swan* ◼ *Dir* John DeBello • *Scr* Costa Dillon, John DeBello, Steve Peace

Attack on the Iron Coast ★★ PG
Second World War drama
1968 · US/UK · Colour · 89min

As a cinema actor, Lloyd Bridges never really gained major star status, but his TV appearances made his face familiar to millions. He plays a major planning a daring raid on a German naval base in this generally uninvolving action adventure. The film was shot in England, and a supporting cast of British TV names does what is expected of it, but the overall style is curiously flat. TS *DVD*

Lloyd Bridges *Major James Wilson* • Andrew Keir *Capt Owen Franklin* • Sue Lloyd *Sue Wilson* • Mark Eden *Lt Com Donald Kimberley* • Maurice Denham *Sir Frederick Grafton* • Glyn Owen *Lt Forrester* ◼ *Dir* Paul Wendkos • *Scr* Herman Hoffman, from a story by John C Champion

Attack the Block ★★★★ 15
Science-fiction action comedy
2010 · Fr/UK · Colour · 84min

For his feature debut as writer/director, Joe Cornish – of comedy duo Adam and Joe – combines his love of 1980s creature capers like *Gremlins* with a more contemporary concern: fear of teenage hoodies. First seen mugging nurse Jodie Whittaker, the young protagonists are all patois and machismo, but are soon forced to find the hero within when their "block" is targeted by alien invaders. Cornish stages the nonstop siege action like a master – the slang, drugs and council-estate setting may put some audiences off, but they would be missing a socially conscious, energetic horror comedy that's scary and very funny. AC Violence, swearing, drug abuse, gore. *DVD* *BD*

Jodie Whittaker *Sam* • John Boyega *Moses* • Nick Frost *Ron* • Alex Esmail *Pest* • Luke Treadaway *Brewis* • Franz Drameh *Dennis* • Leeon Jones *Jerome* ◼ *Dir/Scr* Joe Cornish

Attacking the Devil: Harold Evans and the Last Nazi War Crime ★★★★ 12A
Documentary
2014 · UK · Colour and BW · 102min

Siblings David and Jacqui Morris build on their impressive debut *McCullin*, with this ambitious profile of Harold Evans and his bid to expose the iniquitous history of controversial morning sickness drug Thalidomide. By combining the 87-year-old Evans's eloquent recollections with interviews with Thalidomide victims, and stark and often shocking monochrome archive footage, the co-directors not only chronicle a landmark scoop but also highlight the importance of investigative journalism. DP Distressing scenes.

Michael Sheen *Narrator* • Harold Evans ◼ *Dir/Scr* David Morris (2), Jacqui Morris

The Attic: the Hiding of Anne Frank ★★★★ PG
Biographical drama
1988 · US/UK · Colour · 95min

This is one of the best of the many film versions of the story of the Frank family, who were forced to hide from the Jew-hunting Gestapo. Told from an unusual perspective – that of Miep Gies – it relates how the courageous Dutch woman (played by the wonderful Mary Steenburgen) gave shelter to her employer Otto Frank (Paul Scofield) and his family, including his daughter Anne. This TV movie successfully conveys a sense of the claustrophobia of the situation and the courage of the family. TH

Mary Steenburgen *Miep Gies* • Paul Scofield *Otto Frank* • Lisa Jacobs *Anne Frank* • Eleanor Bron *Edith Frank* • Frances Cuka *Petronella van Daan* • Victor Spinetti *Herman van Daan* • Ian Sears *Peter van Daan* • Georgia Slowe *Margot Frank* • Jeffrey Robert *Albert Dussel* ◼ *Dir* John Erman • *Scr* William Hanley, from the non-fiction book *Anne Frank Remembered* by Miep Gies, Allison Leslie Gold

Attila Marcel ★★★ 12A
Comedy 2013 · Fr · Colour · 106min

In the first live-action feature from noted French animator Sylvain Chomet (*Belleville Rendez-vous*), meek pianist Guillaume Gouix, rendered mute by losing his parents as a toddler, delves within his childhood memories to seek the truth about the past. He's aided by a splendid Anne Le Ny as Madame Proust, who feeds him magic-mushroom soup and madeleines. The imaginative visuals are still a whimsical treat, thanks to Chomet's eye for witty detail, and there's genuine emotion in the story's life-affirming take on the mental shackles we create for ourselves. TJ In French.

Guillaume Gouix *Paul/Attila Marcel* • Anne Le Ny *Mme Proust* • Bernadette Lafont *Tante Annie* • Hélène Vincent *Tante Anna* ◼ *Dir/Scr* Sylvain Chomet

Attraction ★★ 15
Thriller 2000 · US · Colour · 91min

Matthew Settle stalks ex-girlfriend Gretchen Mol in a slow and baffling drama. It's unconvincing from the off, as Settles's increasingly obsessive behaviour provokes little more than a mild reprimand from Mol and best friend Tom Everett Scott. Samantha Mathis is likeable as an aspiring actress who gets involved with Settle, but her nude performance in an experimental play is little more than an excuse for Russell DeGrazier to provide titillation. JC *DVD*

Samantha Mathis *Corey* • Gretchen Mol *Liz* • Tom Everett Scott *Garrett* • Matthew Settle *Matthew* ◼ *Dir/Scr* Russell DeGrazier

Au Hasard, Balthazar ★★★★★ PG
Drama 1966 · Fr/Swe · BW · 91min

This extraordinary film by director Robert Bresson tells the story of a donkey named Balthazar, who is, at various times, an adored children's playmate, a circus performer and a harsh mill owner's slave. Finally, and fatefully, he carries smugglers' contraband over the mountains. The film is a religious parable, with the donkey – like Jesus – taking the sins of the world upon his back. It is also one of the great masterpieces of cinema: austere, warm, grim, surreal, shocking and heartbreaking. AT French +subtitles. *DVD* *BD*

Anne Wiazemsky *Marie* • François Lafarge *Gérard* • Philippe Asselin *Marie's father* • Nathalie Joyaut *Marie's mother* • Walter Green *Jacques* • JC Guilbert [Jean-Claude Guilbert] *Arnold, the tramp* • Pierre Klossowski *Corn merchant* • Jean Rémignard *Notary* ◼ *Dir/Scr* Robert Bresson

Au Revoir les Enfants ★★★★ PG
Second World War drama
1987 · Fr · Colour · 100min

As a reminiscence of bigotries past, French director Louis Malle's autobiographical memoir has a discreet integrity rare among films dealing with anti-Semitism. A 12-year-old boy at a strict Carmelite convent school in 1944 wonders why a newcomer is treated so differently – bullied by other boys, shielded by teachers. The arrival of the Gestapo shows why: the boy is Jewish. It all works so extremely well because Malle never sentimentalises friendships or cruelty, and the result is a powerful tract in miniature. TH French +subtitles. *DVD*

Gaspard Manesse *Julien Quentin* • Raphael Fejtö *Jean Bonnet* • Francine Racette *Mme Quentin* • Stanislas Carré de Malberg *François Quentin* • Philippe Morier-Genoud *Father Jean* • François Berléand *Father Michel* ◼ *Dir/Scr* Louis Malle

Au Revoir l'Eté ★★★ 12A
Drama 2013 · US/Jpn · Colour · 125min

The spirit of Eric Rohmer pervades this rites-of-passage film, as it shifts focus between Fumi Nikaido who goes to spend the summer house-sitting on the coast with her aunt, and Taiga, a young refugee from the nuclear disaster at Fukushima, who is working at the hotel managed by his uncle. Confused by the way grown-ups behave, Nikaido hopes that a fling with Taiga will help her refocus. In his fourth feature, Koji Fukada shows flashes of wit, but he is a better image-maker than storyteller. DP Japanese +subtitles. Sex scenes, nudity.

Fumi Nikaido *Sakuko* • Mayu Tsuruta *Mikie* • Taiga *Takashi* • Kanji Furutachi *Ukichi* ◼ *Dir/Scr* Koji Fukada

Audition ★★★★ 18
Psychological horror
1999 · Jpn/S Kor · Colour · 110min

Containing scenes of surreal violence and excruciating torture that many will find difficult to watch, this controversial film from cult Japanese director Takashi Miike begins like a typical romantic comedy. A lonely Tokyo widower is persuaded to start looking for a new wife. Together with a producer friend, he holds a fake audition so he can screen a group of beautiful women –

ostensibly for the part of a heroine in a new movie. But, when Ryo Ishibashi picks out ex-ballerina Eihi Shiina and tentatively begins to woo her, events take a shocking turn. With stunning imagery and a mounting sense of puzzled dread, this is a profoundly moving shocker. AJ Japanese +subtitles. DVD BL

Ryo Ishibashi *Shigeharu Aoyama* • Eihi Shiina *Asami Yamazaki* • Tetsu Sawaki *Shigehiko Aoyama* • Jun Kunimara *Yasuhisa Yoshikawa* ■ *Dir* Takashi Miike • *Scr* Daisuke Tengan, from a novel by Ryu Murakami

The Audrey Hepburn Story
★★★ PG

Biographical drama 2000 · US · Colour · 128min

In this TV-movie biopic, buxom teen movie star Jennifer Love Hewitt is neither gamine nor delicately classy enough to embody Hepburn, though she has a fair stab at the emotional points of the actress's life. Told in flashback from the set of *Breakfast at Tiffany's*, the film follows Audrey's experiences in wartime Holland and her early career, but while the tribute is an honourable one, there isn't enough drama to maintain interest until the end. JB DVD

Jennifer Love Hewitt *Audrey Hepburn* • Eric McCormack *Mel Ferrer* • Frances Fisher *Ella* • Keir Dullea *Joseph* • Gabriel Macht *William Holden* ■ *Dir* Steven Robman • *Scr* Marsha Norman

Audrey Rose
★★★ 15

Supernatural thriller 1977 · US · Colour · 108min

Anthony Hopkins hams it up in this cash-in on the 1970s post-*Exorcist* interest in possession and the supernatural, with a tale about a young girl who may in fact be a reincarnation of Hopkins's deceased daughter. The cast is capable, but this is let down by the drawn-out plot and unlikely ending. JB DVD

Anthony Hopkins *Elliot Hoover* • Marsha Mason *Janice Templeton* • John Beck *Bill Templeton* • Susan Swift *Ivy Templeton/Audrey Rose* • Norman Lloyd *Dr Steven Lipscomb* ■ *Dir* Robert Wise • *Scr* Frank De Felitta, from his novel

Auggie Rose
★★★

Crime drama 2000 · US · Colour · 109min

This drama has Jeff Goldblum giving a fun performance as an insurance salesman, bored with his dull life, who takes on the persona of an ex-con who dies in his arms. Goldblum is suitably manic as the man leading a double life, and there's good support from a strong cast. Sadly, towards the end huge plot holes and contrivances begin to emerge, but for the first half this is entertaining stuff. JB DVD

Jeff Goldblum *John C Nolan* • Anne Heche *Lucy Brown* • Timothy Olyphant *Roy Mason* • Nancy Travis *Carol* • Richard T Jones *Officer Decker* • Joe Santos *Emanuel* • Kim Coates *Auggie Rose* ■ *Dir/Scr* Matthew Tabak

August
★★★ PG

Period drama 1995 · UK · Colour · 89min

Chekhov's *Uncle Vanya* is relocated to 19th-century Wales in Anthony Hopkins's handsomely shot directorial debut. Although the new setting and a British cast that includes Leslie Phillips and Kate Burton (Richard's daughter) lend some appeal, the slow pacing and not terribly sympathetic characters will be a turn-off for some. Hopkins gives an energetic performance as the estate manager whose unrequited feelings for Burton and frustration with his lot are fuelled by bouts of drinking. JC Violence.

Anthony Hopkins *Ieuan Davies* • Kate Burton *Helen Blathwaite* • Leslie Phillips *Professor Alexander Blathwaite* • Gawn Grainger *Dr Michael Lloyd* • Rhian Morgan *Sian Blathwaite* • Hugh Lloyd *Thomas "Pocky" Prosser* • Rhoda Lewis *Mair Davies* • Menna Trussler *Gwen* ■ *Dir* Anthony Hopkins • *Scr* Julian Mitchell, from the play *Uncle Vanya* by Anton Chekhov, from the play *August* by Julian Mitchell • *Cinematographer* Robin Vidgeon

August: Osage County
★★★ 15

Comedy drama 2013 · US · Colour · 115min

Queen bitch Meryl Streep abstractedly deals with her poet husband's suicide in Tracy Letts's adaptation of his own Pulitzer Prize-winning stage smash. Meanwhile, Streep's long-suffering family expose festering wounds, rehash bitter feuds and reveal long-buried secrets in attempts to restore stability at the Oklahoma wake. However, the drama is more trailer trash *Dallas* than Tennessee Williams. At least the members of the stellar cast are each given their moment to shine (especially Chris Cooper and Benedict Cumberbatch) and it's eminently watchable, but with every crippling emotional issue from abuse and incest to infidelity covered by rote, it all comes across as risk-averse, over-baked and hollow. AJ Swearing, drug abuse. DVD BL

Meryl Streep *Violet Weston* • Julia Roberts *Barbara Weston* • Ewan McGregor *Bill Fordham* • Chris Cooper *Charles Aiken* • Abigail Breslin *Jean Fordham* • Benedict Cumberbatch *"Little" Charles Aiken* • Juliette Lewis *Karen Weston* ■ *Dir* John Wells • *Scr* Tracy Letts, from his play

August Rush
★★ PG

Fantasy drama 2007 · US · Colour · 108min

Oliver Twist gets a contemporary makeover in this schmaltzy urban fairy tale about a young musical genius. Evan (Freddie Highmore) is the result of a one-night stand between classical cellist Keri Russell and roguish rock musician Jonathan Rhys Meyers. Desperate to find his parents, he flees his orphanage and heads to New York. There his prodigious musical gifts win the attention of Wizard (Robin Williams) who nicknames him August Rush. Kirsten Sheridan's glossily sentimental movie has a woefully contrived storyline that will be too ridiculous for most adults to endure. JR DVD

Freddie Highmore *Evan Taylor/August Rush* • Keri Russell *Lyla Novacek* • Jonathan Rhys Meyers *Louis Connelly* • Terrence Howard *Richard Jeffries* • Robin Williams *Maxwell "Wizard" Wallace* • William Sadler *Thomas* • Leon Thomas III *Arthur* • Jamia Simone Nash *Hope* ■ *Dir* Kirsten Sheridan • *Scr* Nick Castle, James V Hart, from a story by Castle, Paul Castro • *Cinematographer* John Mathieson

Aunt Julia and the Scriptwriter
★★★ 15

Comedy 1990 · US · Colour · 102min

Mario Vargas Llosa's novel is translated to the big screen by director Jon Amiel, while the action is transported from Peru to 1950s New Orleans. Barbara Hershey is the aunt of the title, Keanu Reeves plays her gullible nephew, and Peter Falk steals the show as the gruff, obsessive radio scriptwriter who has more going on than meets the eye. It's enjoyably quirky stuff, beautifully played by the impressive cast. JB DVD

Barbara Hershey *Aunt Julia* • Keanu Reeves *Martin Loader* • Peter Falk *Pedro Carmichael* • Bill McCutcheon *Puddler* • Patricia Clarkson *Aunt Olga* • Richard Portnow *Uncle Luke* • Dan Hedaya *Robert Quince* • Elizabeth McGovern *Elena Quince* • Hope Lange *Margaret Quince* ■ *Dir* Jon Amiel • *Scr* William Boyd, from the novel by Mario Vargas Llosa

Aunt Sally
★★ U

Musical comedy 1933 · UK · BW · 80min

A vehicle for the irrepressible comedian and musical comedy star Cicely Courtneidge, this good-natured and thoroughly silly little British musical has her pretending to be a French nightclub star in order to get a job, only to find herself dealing with gangsters with a grudge against the club's owner (Sam Hardy). This is a romp for addicts of 1930s English nostalgia. RK

Cicely Courtneidge *Mademoiselle Zaza/Sally Bird* • Sam Hardy *Michael "King" Kelly* • Phyllis Clare *Queenie* • Billy Milton *Billy* • Hartley Power *"Gloves" Clark* • Ben Weldon *Casion* • Enrico Naldi *Little Joe* • Ann Hope *Joan* ■ *Dir* Tim Whelan • *Scr* Tim Whelan, Guy Bolton, AR Rawlinson

Auntie Mame
★★★★

Comedy 1958 · US · Colour · 143min

"Life's a banquet and most suckers are starving to death", quips Patrick Dennis's flamboyant aunt in this definitive film version of her fantastical life, following the successful stage show based on Dennis's book. Rosalind Russell is simply fabulous in the outrageous leading role, filling the screen with an ebullience equalled only by Robert Preston in director Morton Da Costa's other Warner Bros hit, *The Music Man*. Forget Beatrice Lillie (who played the role on stage in London) and all of those musical "Mames" – Russell *is* Auntie Mame. TS

Rosalind Russell *Mame Dennis* • Forrest Tucker *Beauregard Burnside* • Coral Browne *Vera Charles* • Roger Smith *Patrick Dennis* • Fred Clark *Mr Babcock* • Peggy Cass *Agnes Gooch* • Patric Knowles *Lindsay Woolsey* ■ *Dir* Morton Da Costa • *Scr* Betty Comden, Adolph Green, from the play by Jerome Lawrence, Robert E Lee, from the novel by Patrick Dennis

El Aura
★★★

Crime thriller 2005 · Arg/Fr/Sp · Colour · 125min

The final feature from Fabien Bielinsky reunited the director with his *Nine Queens* star Ricardo Darín, here playing an epileptic taxidermist who's persuaded to accompany a friend (Alejandro Awada) on a hunting trip after being abandoned by his wife. However, an accident in the woods and the chance discovery of a brutal hotel owner's secret hideaway prompts Darín to assume the role of kingpin in a heist on a nearby casino. Conveniently possessed of a photographic memory, Darín responds to the potential perils of his new guise with an alacrity that belies his taciturn demeanour. But it's Bielinsky's confident control of his material that sustains this ingenious and highly cinematic house of cards. DP Spanish +subtitles.

Ricardo Darín [Ricardo Darin] *Esteban Espinosa (the taxidermist)* • Alejandro Awada *Sontag* • Dolores Fonzi *Diana Dietrich* • Pablo Cedron *Sosa* • Jorge D'Elia *Urien* • Manuel Rodal *Carlos Dietrich* ■ *Dir/Scr* Fabian Bielinsky

Aurora
★★★★ 12A

Crime drama 2010 · Rom/Fr/Swi/Ger · Colour · 183min

The second of Cristi Puiu's proposed "Six Stories from the Outskirts of Bucharest" – the first was *The Death of Mr Lazarescu* in 2005 – is a rigorous study of a man's daily life that also doubles as a gripping thriller, as the director also stars as a motiveless killer waiting to strike. Angry at the world after losing his job, Puiu's middle-aged Viorel endures fractious encounters with his nearest and dearest. But his special ire is reserved for others and Puiu depicts the dispensing of twisted justice with a ruthless efficiency that is all the more chilling for its detachment. DP Romanian +subtitles. Violence, brief nudity. DVD

Cristi Puiu *Viorel Ghenghea* • Clara Voda *Gina Filip* • Valeria Seciu *Pusa* • Catrinel Dumitrescu *Mrs Rodica Livinski* ■ *Dir/Scr* Cristi Puiu

Austenland
★★★ 12

Romantic comedy 2013 · US/UK · Colour · 92min

The enduring appeal of Jane Austen's England is explored in this uneven but often hilarious romp, a comedy – for once – aimed squarely at a female audience. Keri Russell stars as a single girl in her 30s who is obsessed with the BBC's adaptation of *Pride and Prejudice*. She spends her savings on a trip to the UK, to take a holiday in "Austenland", where a cast of actors will re-create the Regency period. Though it often blunders into farce, *Austenland* is nevertheless a warm-hearted and deceptively smart comedy of modern manners, with a scene-stealing turn by Jane Seymour as the theme park's mean-spirited proprietor. DW Some swearing. DVD

Keri Russell *Jane Hayes* • JJ Feild *Mr Henry Nobley* • Jennifer Coolidge *Miss Elizabeth Charming* • Bret McKenzie *Martin* • Jane Seymour (2) *Mrs Wattlesbrook* • Rupert

Vansittart *Mr Wattlesbrook* ■ *Dir* Jerusha Hess • *Scr* Jerusha Hess, Shannon Hale, from Hale's novel

Austin Powers: International Man of Mystery
★★★★ 15

Spy spoof 1997 · US · Colour · 90min

This Swinging Sixties spy spoof is a fast, furious and fabulously funny ride that expertly mocks every groovy fad, psychedelic fashion and musical style of the period. Mike Myers is brilliant as the secret agent-cum-fashion photographer, cryogenically frozen so he can foil the world domination plans of his arch enemy Dr Evil (Myers again) in the 1990s. Witty, sophisticated and hysterically stupid by turns, the movie's side-splitting humour arises from clever culture-clash comedy, knockabout farce, Austin's catchphrases and countless spy-movie references. AJ Swearing, nudity. DVD BL

Mike Myers *Austin Powers/Dr Evil* • Elizabeth Hurley *Vanessa Kensington* • Michael York *Basil Exposition* • Mimi Rogers *Mrs Kensington* • Robert Wagner *Number Two* • Seth Green *Scott Evil* • Fabiana Udenio *Alotta Fagina* • Mindy Sterling *Frau Farbissina* • Burt Bacharach ■ *Dir* Jay Roach • *Scr* Mike Myers

Austin Powers: the Spy Who Shagged Me
★★★★ 12

Spy spoof 1999 · US · Colour · 91min

If you liked the International Man of Mystery's first adventure, then you'll love this shagadelic sequel. Mike Myers goes back to the 1960s to reclaim his "mojo" which has been stolen by his adversary Dr Evil (also played by Myers). While the star and his returning director, Jay Roach, revisit the same free-for-all secret agent spoofing of the original, they do it with just the right degree of retro style, knowing geniality and complete lack of taste and restraint. AJ Swearing. DVD BL CS

Mike Myers *Austin Powers/Dr Evil/Fat Bastard* • Heather Graham *Felicity Shagwell* • Michael York *Basil Exposition* • Robert Wagner *Number Two* • Seth Green *Scott Evil* • Mindy Sterling *Frau Farbissina* • Rob Lowe *Young Number Two* • Gia Carides *Robin Swallows* • Verne Troyer *Mini-Me* • Elizabeth Hurley *Vanessa Kensington* • Kristen Johnson [Kristen Johnston] *Ivana Humpalot* • Burt Bacharach • Elvis Costello • Will Ferrell *Mustafa* ■ *Dir* Jay Roach • *Scr* Mike Myers, Michael McCullers, from characters by Mike Myers

Austin Powers in Goldmember
★★★ 12

Spy spoof 2002 · US · Colour · 90min

Co-writer, producer and star Mike Myers doesn't take many risks with this enjoyable third outing for the groovy secret agent and his nemesis Dr Evil, sticking to his tried and tested formula of cool catchphrases, bad-taste buffoonery and surreal slapstick. He perhaps overstretches himself this time, taking on the additional role of eponymous Dutch villain Goldmember, and there's a distinct feeling of *déjà vu* about his comic schtick. JC Swearing. DVD BL

Mike Myers *Austin Powers/Dr Evil/Fat Bastard/Goldmember* • Michael Caine *Nigel Powers* • Beyoncé Knowles *Foxxy Cleopatra* • Seth Green *Scott Evil* • Michael York *Basil Exposition* • Robert Wagner *Number Two* • Mindy Sterling *Frau Farbissina* • Verne Troyer *Mini-Me* • Fred Savage *Number Three, "The Mole"* ■ *Dir* Jay Roach • *Scr* Mike Myers, Michael McCullers, from characters by Mike Myers

Australia
★★ U

Romantic drama 1989 · Fr/Bel/Swi · Colour · 118min

Set in southern Australia and the Belgian town of Verviers in the 1950s, this plodding drama of sheep farming and adultery instantly pulls the wool over our eyes, and is quite content to let it remain there. Director Jean-Jacques Andrien would have us believe that glossy visuals, authentic period trappings, a stately pace and the presence of such stars as Jeremy Irons and Fanny Ardant are compensation for the fact that virtually nothing happens. DP

A

Jeremy Irons *Edouard Pierson* • Fanny Ardant *Jeanne Gauthier* • Tcheky Karyo *Julien Pierson* • Agnes Soral *Agnès Decker* • Hélène Surgère *Madame Pierson* • Maxime Laloux *François Gauthier* • Patrick Bauchau *André Gauthier* ■ *Dir* Jean-Jacques Andrien • *Scr* Jean-Jacques Andrien, Jean Gruault, Jacques Audiard

Australia ★★ 12
Romantic period drama
2008 · US/Aus · Colour · 158min

There's no faulting Baz Luhrmann's ambition: this old-fashioned, $130 million epic romantic adventure was intended as his *Gone with the Wind*. At the start of the Second World War, Nicole Kidman's English lady arrives in Australia to confront a husband she believes is being unfaithful. The stunning vistas of northern Australia provide built-in splendour, and the spit-and-sawdust world of cattle ranching is personified by Hugh Jackman's cross between Indiana Jones and "Crocodile" Dundee. Unfortunately the action, built around a land feud and a Kidman/Jackman on-off affair, veers from melodramatic to plain silly, with Luhrmann welding screwball comedy to romance, western to war movie (all while not patronising the Aborigines) and aiming for camp excess while demanding that we take the film seriously. One day it may become a cult classic, but for now, *Australia* is really his *Pearl Harbor*. AC *DVD* BD

Nicole Kidman *Lady Sarah Ashley* • Hugh Jackman *The drover* • David Wenham *Neil Fletcher* • Bryan Brown *King Carney* • Jack Thompson *Kipling Flynn* ■ *Dir* Baz Luhrmann • *Scr* Baz Luhrmann, Ronald Harwood, Stuart Beattie, Richard Flanagan • *Cinematographer* Mandy Walker

Author! Author! ★★ PG
Comedy
1982 · US · Colour · 109min

An ill-cast but effective Al Pacino is having a slew of domestic troubles as his new play opens on Broadway, and director Arthur Hiller has a tough time finding the requisite lightness of touch to make all the shenanigans convincing. There is, though, a sort of rough-edged charm to the piece, largely thanks to the blissful performances of clever Dyan Cannon and the sublime Tuesday Weld as the gals in Pacino's life, but the material involving the threesome's respective offspring is tasteless. TS *DVD*

Al Pacino *Ivan Travalian* • Dyan Cannon *Alice Detroit* • Tuesday Weld *Gloria* • Alan King *Kreplich* • Bob Dishy *Finestein* • Bob Elliott *Patrick Dicker* • Eric Curry *Igor* • Elva Leff *Bonnie* • *Dir* Arthur Hiller • *Scr* Israel Horovitz

Auto Focus ★★★★ 18
Biographical drama 2002 · US · Colour · 101min

This is one of Paul Schrader's most sustained and successful treatments of the dark side of sexuality. Based on the life of actor Bob Crane (star of the 1960s US sitcom *Hogan's Heroes*), it charts his descent into a libidinous hell as he becomes addicted to casual sex, videotaping an endless succession of meaningless encounters (aided by Willem Dafoe's noxious video technician). Greg Kinnear is excellent as the vacuous hedonist, and there's also a stand-out performance from Ron Leibman as the tender-hearted agent who watches with horror as his client's life implodes. This is a moral and often funny tour de force. AS Violence, swearing, sex scenes, drug abuse, nudity. *DVD*

Greg Kinnear *Bob Crane* • Willem Dafoe *John Carpenter* • Rita Wilson *Anne Crane* • Maria Bello *Patricia Olsen Crane* • Ron Leibman *Lenny* • Bruce Solomon *Edward H Feldman, producer* • Michael Rodgers *Richard Dawson* • Kurt Fuller *Werner Klemperer/Col Klink* ■ *Dir* Paul Schrader • *Scr* Michael Gerbosi, from the non-fiction book *The Murder of Bob Crane* by Robert Graysmith

Autobiography of a Princess ★★★ PG
Drama 1975 · UK · Colour · 55min

An early (and short) Merchant Ivory offering in their traditional reserved vein, scripted as ever by Ruth Prawer Jhabvala. James Mason and Madhur Jaffrey star as a former secretary to a maharajah and the

maharajah's daughter who meet up in London. Through watching old home movies of India they share caustic reminiscences of their time there and of past relationships. Insubstantial but well-observed. LH *DVD*

James Mason *Cyril Sahib* • Madhur Jaffrey *The princess* • Keith Varnier *Delivery man* • Diane Fletcher *Seductress* • Timothy Bateson *Blackmailer* • Nazruh Rahman *Papa* ■ *Dir* James Ivory • *Scr* Ruth Prawer Jhabvala • *Producer* Ismail Merchant

The Autobiography of Miss Jane Pittman ★★★★★ 12
Drama 1974 · US · Colour · 97min

This ambitious adaptation of Ernest J Gaines's novel won nine Emmys and is one of the finest TV movies ever made. As the 110-year-old African-American woman who experienced both the abolition of slavery at the end of the Civil War and the start of the civil rights movement in the 1960s, Cicely Tyson gives a towering performance. We see her progress from timid innocent to sassy senior citizen, no longer prepared to tolerate the injustices of a supposedly civilised society. Tracy Keenan Wynn's script is occasionally unfocused and overly reliant on journalist Michael Murphy to link the episodes, but, nonetheless, this informative work of fiction makes for compelling viewing. Released on video and DVD as *The White People's Fountain*. DP *DVD*

Cicely Tyson *Jane Pittman* • Michael Murphy (1) *Quentin Lerner* • Richard Dysart *Master Bryant* • Collin Wilcox-Horne [Collin Wilcox Paxton] *Mistress Bryant* • Thalmus Rasulala *Ned* • Dean Smith *Ned, aged 15* • Odetta *Big Laura* • Barbara Chaney *Amma Dean* ■ *Dir* John Korty • *Scr* Tracy Keenan Wynn, from the novel by Ernest J Gaines

Autobus ★★★★ 15
Thriller 1991 · Fr · Colour · 93min

In Eric Rochant's compelling thriller, Yvan Attal is outstanding as the emotionally unstable man who hijacks a school bus in the hope of impressing girlfriend Charlotte Gainsbourg. He veers between menace and confusion as he gets to know teacher Kristin Scott Thomas and the little charmers in her charge. Rochant makes the most of the cramped confines and perfectly judges the shifts in tone. DP French +subtitles.

Yvan Attal *Bruno* • Kristin Scott Thomas *Teacher* • Marc Berman *Driver* • Charlotte Gainsbourg *Juliette* • Renan Mazeas *Bruno's brother* • Francine Olivier *Bruno's mother* • Michèle Foucher *Juliette's mother* • Aline Still *Headmistress* • Daniel Milgram *Brigadier* ■ *Dir/Scr* Eric Rochant

Automatic ★★★ 15
Science-fiction action thriller
1994 · US · Colour · 86min

In this sci-fi thriller, a cutting-edge electronics corporation tries to hush up a homicidal fault that develops within its top-secret prototype, a cyborg bodyguard/servant called J269 (Oliver Gruner), by sending in a SWAT team to eliminate it. Unfortunately, a lowly secretary (Daphne Ashbrook) has witnessed the murderous glitch and will have to be erased, too. There's rarely a dull moment in this effective, well-mounted entertainment. AJ Swearing, violence. *DVD*

Olivier Gruner *J269* • Daphne Ashbrook *Nora Rochester* • John Glover *Goddard Marx* • Jeff Kober *Major West* • Penny Johnson *Julia Rodriguez* • Marjean Holden *Epsilon leader* ■ *Dir* John Murlowski • *Scr* Susan Lambert, Patrick Highsmith

An Autumn Afternoon ★★★★★ PG
Drama 1962 · Jpn · Colour · 110min

Yasujiro Ozu, one of film's great artists, signed off with this typically gentle study of family obligation and the relentless advance of life. Making only his second film in colour, Ozu keeps his camera still and at its customarily low angle, giving us the freedom to explore the meticulously

composed frame. It also allows us to concentrate on Chishu Ryu's touching performance as the widowed bookkeeper who reluctantly convinces his daughter (Shima Iwashita) that it's her duty to wed and leave him to the companionship of his drinking buddies. Suffused with genial humanity, this warm, wise tale is both pure cinema and a sheer delight. DP Japanese +subtitles. *DVD* BD

Chishu Ryu *Shuhei Hirayama* • Shima Iwashita *Michiko Hirayama* • Shinichiro Mikami *Kazuo Hirayama* • Keiji Sada *Koichi Hirayama* • Mariko Okada *Akiko Hirayama* • Nobuo Nakamura *Shuzo Kawai* • Kuniko Miyake *Nobuko Kawai* ■ *Dir* Yasujiro Ozu • *Scr* Yasujiro Ozu, Kogo Noda

Autumn in New York ★ 15
Romantic drama 2000 · US · Colour · 101min

Richard Gere and Winona Ryder are the incredibly unlikely couple in this unbelievable romance. He's the suave restaurateur who can have any babe he wants, she's the quirky hat designer half his age who also happens to be dying. Directed like a Dairy Milk advert by Joan Chen. JB *DVD*

Richard Gere *Will Keane* • Winona Ryder *Charlotte Fielding* • Anthony LaPaglia *John* • Elaine Stritch *Dolly* • Vera Farmiga *Lisa* • Sherry Stringfield *Sarah* ■ *Dir* Joan Chen • *Scr* Allison Burnett

Autumn Leaves ★★★
Melodrama 1956 · US · BW · 108min

In this dark melodrama, Joan Crawford marries her toyboy lover and then discovers that he's a little disturbed, if not totally deranged. This features all the hallmarks of director Robert Aldrich: misogyny, misanthropy and murderous intent. Cliff Robertson puts in a distinguished performance as Crawford's dangerous other half, although his naturalistic acting style clashes somewhat with Crawford's all-stops-out performance. TS

Joan Crawford *Milly Wetherby* • Cliff Robertson *Burt Hanson* • Vera Miles *Virginia* • Lorne Greene *Mr Hanson* • Ruth Donnelly *Liz* • Shepperd Strudwick *Dr Couzzens* • Selmer Jackson *Mr Wetherby* • Maxine Cooper *Nurse Evans* ■ *Dir* Robert Aldrich • *Scr* Jack Jevne [Hugo Butler, Jean Rouverol], Robert Blees, Lewis Metzer

Autumn Moon ★★★★
Drama 1992 · HK/Jpn · Colour · 108min

Set during the days when Hong Kong's post-colonial destiny had been determined but was still some time off, this is an elegant and intelligent exploration of the differences between two of Asia's most vibrant economies. Li Pui Wai is a teenager whose experience of first love eases the worry of her grandmother's illness, while Masatoshi Nagase, as the Japanese visitor she befriends, finds his past flirtations no longer satisfy him. Directed with delicious understatement by Clara Law from a subtle script, this is a thoughtful, intimate drama. DP Cantonese, Japanese, English +subtitles. Sex scenes.

Masatoshi Nagase *Tokio* • Li Pui Wai *Wai* • Choi Siu-wan *Granny* • Maki Kiuchi *Miki* • Suen Ching Hung *Wai's boyfriend* • Sung Lap Yeung *Wai's father* • Tsang Yuet Guen *Wai's mother* • Chu Kit Ming *Wai's brother* ■ *Dir* Clara Law • *Scr* Ling Ching Fong

Autumn Sonata ★★★ 15
Drama 1978 · Swe/W Ger · Colour · 88min

This harrowing film was the result of a difficult shoot, during which Ingmar and Ingrid Bergman frequently fell out and Ms Bergman had to resume treatment for the cancer that eventually killed her. This stifling study of resentment and regret is superbly played, particularly by Liv Ullmann, who can't forgive her musician mother for a childhood of neglect. Yet it was Ingrid who received the Oscar nomination, as, less deservingly, did Ingmar, for a script over-laden with theatrical speeches. DP Swedish +subtitles. *DVD*

Ingrid Bergman *Charlotte* • Liv Ullmann *Eva* • Lena Nyman *Helena* • Halvar Bjork *Viktor* • Arne Bang-Hansen *Uncle Otto* • Gunnar Björnstrand

Paul • Erland Josephson *Josef* • Georg Lokkeberg *Leonardo* • Linn Ullmann *Eva as a Child* ■ *Dir/Scr* Ingmar Bergman • *Producers* Lew Grade, Martin Starger

An Autumn Tale ★★★★ U
Romantic comedy drama
1998 · Fr · Colour · 106min

Eric Rohmer was one of the few contemporary directors still interested in people. This is a typically intimate human drama, in which bookish Marie Rivière becomes overly involved with the lonely heart date (Alain Libolt) she has arranged for her wine-growing friend (Béatrice Romand). This deft, meticulously paced exploration of emotional confusion develops into a delightful comedy of errors, with Rohmer mirroring the plight of his middle-aged leads in the romantic tangles of teenager Alexia Portal. Drawing us inexorably into the lives of characters whose foibles are instantly recognisable, this is a triumph of literate cinema. DP French +subtitles. *DVD*

Marie Rivière *Isabelle* • Béatrice Romand *Magali* • Alain Libolt *Gérard* • Didier Sandre *Etienne* • Alexia Portal *Rosine* • Stéphane Darmon *Léo* • Aurélia Alcaïs *Emilia* • Mathieu Davette *Grégoire* • Yves Alcaïs *Jean-Jacques* ■ *Dir/Scr* Eric Rohmer

Avalanche ★★ 15
Disaster movie 1978 · US · Colour · 86min

Cult director Roger Corman produced this cut-rate disaster movie coasting on the 1970s fascination with the genre. Rich developer Rock Hudson opens a ski resort during avalanche season and watches as the low-rent celebrities fall foul of the "six million tons of icy terror" promised in the ads. Poor effects match the acting in what was supposed to be Corman's ticket to mainstream respectability. Its lacklustre box-office performance sent him back to B-movie territory. AJ

Rock Hudson *David Shelby* • Mia Farrow *Caroline Brace* • Robert Foster *Nick Thorne* • Jeanette Nolan *Florence Shelby* • Rick Moses *Bruce Scott* • Steve Franken *Henry McDade* • Barry Primus *Mark Elliott* ■ *Dir* Corey Allen • *Scr* Corey Allen, Claude Pola

Avalanche Express ★★ PG
Spy drama 1979 · Ire · Colour · 84min

Ruthless CIA agent Lee Marvin uses defector Robert Shaw to entrap Soviet scientist Maximilian Schell in this ill-fated Cold War thriller. Set on a cross-border train impeded by blizzards, the film suffered its own tragedies when both Shaw and director Mark Robson died before production was completed. The repair job on what was left doesn't hide the joins, though the acting has an impressive energy. TH

Robert Shaw *General Marenkov* • Lee Marvin *Colonel Harry Wargrave* • Linda Evans *Elsa Lang* • Maximilian Schell *Nikolai Bunin* • Mike Connors *Haller* • Joe Namath *Leroy* • Horst Buchholz *Scholten* • David Hess *Geiger* ■ *Dir* Mark Robson • *Scr* Abraham Polonsky, from the novel by Colin Forbes

Avalon ★★★ U
Epic drama 1990 · US · Colour · 122min

Director Barry Levinson's lengthy family epic – a sort of *Godfather* without guns – is saved from schmaltz by a wonderfully assured and generous performance by Armin Mueller-Stahl. He plays the head of an immigrant clan who arrives in America on 4 July, 1914. Four generations of family loving and feuding follow, with the bulk of the film taking place just after the Second World War. While Joan Plowright and Elizabeth Perkins are featured, it's primarily a movie about men, though everyone is so talkily eloquent they eventually become tiresome. TH

Aidan Quinn *Jules Krichinsky* • Elizabeth Perkins *Ann Kaye* • Armin Mueller-Stahl *Sam Krichinsky* • Leo Fuchs *Hymie Krichinsky* • Eve Gordon *Dottie Kirk* • Lou Jacobi *Gabriel Krichinsky* • Joan Plowright *Eva Krichinsky* • Kevin Pollak *Izzy Krichinsky* • Elijah Wood *Michael Kaye* ■ *Dir/Scr* Barry Levinson

Avalon ★ 12
Futuristic thriller
2000 · Jpn/Pol/Fr · Colour/Sepia · 102min

Baffling in the extreme, there seems to be no rational explanation for the stylish events that unfold during this convoluted slice of futuristic role-playing. Set in a ruined, nameless metropolis, the story revolves around fearless loner Malgorzata Foremniak, who competes in the deadly and illegal virtual-reality war game Avalon. But once this has been showcased in a magnificent opening sequence, the film loses its way. SF Polish +subtitles. DVD

Malgorzata Foremniak *Ash* • Wladyslaw Kowalski *Game Master* • Jerzy Gudejko *Murphy* • Dariusz Biskupski *Bishop* • Bartek Swiderski *Stunner* • Katarzyna Bargielowska *Receptionist* ■ *Dir* Mamoru Oshii • *Scr* Kazunori Ito

Avalon: beyond the Abyss ★★ PG
Science fiction adventure
1999 · US · Colour · 85min

In this sci-fi adventure, a small island inexplicably explodes, releasing a tide of mutating plankton that starts killing off the marine life. There's an impressive array of diving gadgetry on display, including the world's most sophisticated submersible, and female lead Mehgan Heaney-Grier is suitably qualified as a US record-breaking free-diver (165ft on a single gulp of air, if you're interested). Sadly, the impressive statistics can't disguise the fact that the film isn't that absorbing, and the attempts to spice it up dull any sci-fi edge. DP

Parker Stevenson *John Alden* • Krista Allen *Dr Katherine "K" Harrison* • Mehgan Heaney-Grier *Alyssa Meade* • Billy Rieck *Billy Domino* ■ *Dir* Philip Sgriccia • *Scr* Chris Ruppenthal

Avanti! ★★★★ 12
Romantic comedy   1972 · US · Colour · 140min

Billy Wilder's sublime romantic comedy spins on one of his favourite themes: the confrontation between the brashness of America, where he worked, and the sophistication of Europe, where he was born. Jack Lemmon's harried business executive flies from Baltimore to Italy to collect his father's corpse. Juliet Mills arrives from England to pick up her mother's body, and before you can say "espresso", the odd couple are re-enacting their parents' affair. Though long, the film is impeccably plotted and full of marvellous characters, from Clive Revill's hotel manager to Edward Andrews as a CIA agent whose arrival serves to show the distance Lemmon has travelled. AT Swearing, brief nudity. DVD

Jack Lemmon *Wendell Armbruster* • Juliet Mills *Pamela Piggott* • Clive Revill *Carlo Carlucci* • Edward Andrews *JJ Blodgett* • Gianfranco Barra *Bruno* • Franco Angrisano *Arnold Trotta* • Pippo Franco *Mattarazzo* • Franco Acampora *Armando Trotta* ■ *Dir* Billy Wilder • *Scr* Billy Wilder, IAL Diamond, from the play by Samuel Taylor

LANDMARK FILM
James Cameron's game-changing adventure took so much money at the box-office that 3D became the norm

Avatar ★★★ 12
Epic science-fiction fantasy
2009 · US/UK · Colour · 155min

Think *Dances with Wolves* in space and you'll have the measure of this blockbuster from James Cameron. Sam Worthington stars as a paraplegic US marine drafted to distant planet Pandora to gain the trust of the Na'vi, whose homeland lies above a large deposit of a rare and valuable mineral. There's nothing ground-breaking about the plot. And yet, as a motion-captured Worthington - controlling an alien body (or Avatar) through telepathy - is tutored in the clan's ways by chief's daughter Zoë Saldana, the breathtakingly beautiful CGI landscape pulls audiences into this tale of profit and progress versus nature's power and infinite variety. Three sequels are in production. SuR Violence. DVD BL 3D

Sam Worthington *Jake Sully* • Zoë Saldana *Neytiri* • Sigourney Weaver *Dr Grace Augustine* • Stephen Lang *Colonel Miles Quaritch* • Michelle Rodriguez *Trudy Chacon* • Giovanni Ribisi *Parker Selfridge* • CCH Pounder *Moat* • Wes Studi *Eytukan* ■ *Dir/Scr* James Cameron • *Cinematographer* Mauro Fiore

Avatar 2
Epic science-fiction fantasy
2018 · US · Colour

This is a preview - no prints were available to review prior to publication. Blockbusting film-maker James Cameron returns to the alien world of Pandora for this first of three sequels to *Avatar*, the film that knocked his own *Titanic* off its perch as the biggest grossing film ever. According to producer Jon Landau, the techno wizards have been "working out performance capture for underwater scenes" in a story that will feature more humans among the blue-skinned Na'vi people. Sam Worthington and Zoë Saldana reprise their roles, and Sigourney Weaver makes a comeback. SP

Sam Worthington *Jake Sully* • Zoë Saldana *Neytiri* • Sigourney Weaver *Dr Grace Augustine* • Stephen Lang *Colonel Miles Quaritch* ■ *Dir* James Cameron • *Scr* James Cameron, Josh Friedman, from a story by Rick Jaffa, Amanda Silver, from characters by Cameron

The Avengers ★ 12
Action adventure   1998 · US · Colour · 85min

The cult 1960s TV series gets royally shafted by Hollywood in a stunningly designed blockbuster that's stunningly awful in every other department. Ralph Fiennes and Uma Thurman are miscast as John Steed and Emma Peel, here trying to stop villainous Sir August De Wynter (Sean Connery) holding the world's weather to ransom. Ruthlessly edited before release and packed with arch one-liners, bad puns and vulgar double entendres, this is misguided and misbegotten. AJ Violence, swearing. DVD

Ralph Fiennes *John Steed* • Uma Thurman *Doctor Emma Peel* • Sean Connery *Sir August De Wynter* • Jim Broadbent *Mother* • Fiona Shaw *Father* • Eddie Izzard *Bailey* • Eileen Atkins *Alice* • Shaun Ryder *Donavan* • Patrick Macnee *Invisible Jones* ■ *Dir* Jeremiah Chechik • *Scr* Don MacPherson, from the TV series created by Sydney Newman

Avengers: Age of Ultron ★★★★ 12
Action adventure   2015 · US · Colour · 135min

Marvel's superhero A-team returns with a vengeance in this exhilarating sequel, to take on robot adversary Ultron (chillingly voiced by James Spader), whose aim is to destroy humanity. It doesn't help that he's a Tony Stark experiment gone wrong, as his insider knowledge allows him to take down the Avengers from within. However, director Joss Whedon is just as interested in what makes his characters tick, while the witty repartee leavens the odd lull. And then there's the first appearance of the enigmatic Vision (Paul Bettany)... but whose side is he on? This branch of the Marvel franchise continues with *Avengers: Infinity War Parts 1 & 2* in 2018/19. JA DVD BL 3D CS

Robert Downey Jr *Tony Stark/Iron Man* • Chris Hemsworth *Thor* • Mark Ruffalo *Bruce Banner/Hulk* • Chris Evans *Steve Rogers/Captain America* • Scarlett Johansson *Natasha Romanoff/Black Widow* • Samuel L Jackson *Nick Fury* • Paul Bettany *Jarvis/The Vision* • James Spader *Ultron* ■ *Dir* Joss Whedon • *Scr* Joss Whedon, from characters by Jack Kirby, Stan Lee

Avenging Angel ★ 18
Crime drama   1985 · US · Colour · 93min

Taking on the role played by Donna Wilkes in the original film, *Angel*, Betsy Russell here puts her streetwalking days behind her to search for the killers of the cop who saved her from prostitution. Little more than an excuse for some cheap sex and violence, this is only of interest to western fans curious to see what happened to Rory Calhoun. DP

Betsy Russell *Angel/Molly Stewart* • Rory Calhoun *Kit Carson* • Robert F Lyons *Detective Andrews* • Susan Tyrrell *Solly Mosler* • Ossie Davis *Captain Moradian* • Barry Pearl *Johnny Glitter* • Ross Hagen *Ray Mitchell* ■ *Dir* Robert Vincent O'Neil • *Scr* Robert Vincent O'Neil, Joseph M Cala

Avenging Angel ★★
Western drama   2007 · US · Colour · 81min

This bland and plodding western is a mishmash of genre clichés that borrows liberally from the likes of *Pale Rider* and *Shane*, and is only watchable thanks to the diverting presence of Kevin Sorbo (*Hercules: the Legendary Journeys*). In a hackneyed plotline, he plays a preacher who turns bounty hunter to avenge the murder of his wife and child. Yet despite the premise, there's very little action, leaving it to Sorbo's soulful brooding to just about keep proceedings afloat. SF

Kevin Sorbo *The preacher* • Wings Hauser *Cusack* • Cynthia Watros *Maggie* • Nick Chinlund *Quinn* • Fred Cross *Jacob* • Van Epperson *Mayor* ■ *Dir* David S Cass Sr • *Scr* William Sims Myers

Avenging Angelo ★★ 15
Romantic comedy   2002 · US · Colour · 93min

It's a shame that the late Anthony Quinn's final film was this patchy romantic comedy. Still he handles his fleeting role as a Mob boss with dignity, standing out in a sloppily acted film. Sylvester Stallone stars as a Mafia bodyguard who vows to protect Quinn's secret daughter Madeleine Stowe after the kingpin's murder. Stowe's contribution is little more than hysteria-prone eye candy, though Stallone demonstrating a softer side has its charm. Lame and slack. SF Swearing, violence, sex scenes. DVD

Sylvester Stallone *Frankie Delano* • Madeleine Stowe *Jennifer Barrett Allieghieri* • Raoul Bova *Marcello/Gianni Carboni* • Anthony Quinn *Angelo Allieghieri* • Harry Van Gorkum *Kip Barrett* • Billy Gardell *Bruno* • George Touliatos *Lucio Malestesta* ■ *Dir* Martyn Burke • *Scr* Will Aldis [Will Porter], Steve Mackall

Avenging Force ★★ 18
Martial arts action thriller
1986 · US · Colour · 98min

It's too bad that Steve James exits this movie halfway through. He is not only a much better actor than top-billed Michael Dudikoff, but he shows he had the stuff to be a big action star. Dudikoff plays a retired secret agent who lends his politician buddy (James) a hand when a neo-Nazi group makes him a target. The fight scenes are exciting, but the brutal violence leaves a bad impression. KB DVD

Michael Dudikoff *Matt Hunter* • Steve James (1) *Larry Richards* • James Booth *Admiral Brown* • John P Ryan *Glastenbury* • Bill Wallace *Delaney* • Karl Johnson (3) *Wallace* • Marc Alaimo *Lavall* • Allison Gereighty *Sarah Hunter* ■ *Dir* Sam Firstenberg • *Scr* James Booth

The Avenging Hand ★
Thriller   1936 · UK · BW · 66min

Staying in a gloomy English hotel, Chicago gangster Noah Beery tracks down the killer of an old match-seller with the help of a hotel clerk and then disappears back to America. This somewhat confused thriller is feeble, forgettable and largely forgotten. RK

Noah Beery *Lee Barwell* • Kathleen Kelly *Gwen Taylor* • Louis Borell *Pierre Charrell* • James Harcourt *Sam Hupp* • Charles Oliver *Toni Visetti* • Reginald Long *Charles Mason* • Ben Welden *Slug Clarke* ■ *Dir* Victor Hanbury • *Scr* Akos Talney, Reginald Long

Aventure Malgache ★★★ PG
Second World War adventure
1944 · UK · BW · 29min

The second of the two wartime shorts that Alfred Hitchcock made for the Ministry of Information was prompted by the feuding between the Free French who had worked on the first, *Bon Voyage*. Co-scripting with Angus MacPhail, "Hitch" introduced a note of levity that was unusual for propaganda films of the time to help encourage co-operation between partisans of all regional, personal and political persuasions. Yet the anecdote told by an exiled amateur actor about his Resistance activities against the Vichy regime on Madagascar didn't meet with the approval of Whitehall, and the film was never shown. DP French +subtitles.

■ *Dir* Alfred Hitchcock • *Scr* Angus MacPhail, Alfred Hitchcock

The Aviator ★★ PG
Period drama   1985 · US · Colour · 92min

Christopher Reeve stars as a pilot haunted by the crash that killed his buddy who is ordered to fly rebellious Rosanna Arquette to college to avoid an adultery scandal. It's loathe at first sight, but their bickering ceases when they are forced down in a mountain wilderness. The need to survive brings about the sort of change of heart that only happens in thinly-plotted movies. Reeve and Arquette barely raise a spark. DP DVD

Christopher Reeve *Edgar Anscombe* • Rosanna Arquette *Tillie Hansen* • Jack Warden *Moravia* • Sam Wanamaker *Bruno Hansen* • Scott Wilson *Jerry Stiller* • Tyne Daly *Evelyn Stiller* • Marcia Strassman *Rose Stiller* ■ *Dir* George Miller (1) • *Scr* Marc Norman, from the novel by Ernest K Gann

The Aviator ★★★★ 12
Biographical drama
2004 · US/Ger · Colour · 163min

If *The Aviator* lacks the punch of Martin Scorsese's earlier biopic *Raging Bull*, it's perhaps because Howard Hughes presents him with too much raw material. A millionaire at 18 (he inherited the Hughes Tool Company from his father), Hughes went on to become an aircraft designer and movie mogul. Hughes's childhood is dismissed in a brief prologue that sets up his obsession with cleanliness, then it's straight on to the beginning of his Hollywood career. The film is uneven, seemingly unsure of whether its protagonist is hero or villain, but Leonardo DiCaprio brings an impressive intensity to the role of Hughes. Cate Blanchett is a treat as Katharine Hepburn, but Kate Beckinsale is hopelessly miscast as Ava Gardner. BP DVD BL

Leonardo DiCaprio *Howard Hughes* • Cate Blanchett *Katharine Hepburn* • Kate Beckinsale *Ava Gardner* • John C Reilly *Noah Dietrich* • Alec Baldwin *Juan Trippe* • Alan Alda *Senator Ralph Owen Brewster* • Ian Holm *Professor Fitz* • Danny Huston *Jack Frye* • Gwen Stefani *Jean Harlow* • Jude Law *Errol Flynn* ■ *Dir* Martin Scorsese • *Scr* John Logan

The Aviator's Wife ★★★★ PG
Comedy   1980 · Fr · Colour · 101min

Eric Rohmer launched his *Comedies and Proverbs* series with this shrewd tale of tortured emotions, deceptive appearances and missed opportunities. Racked by the sight of girlfriend Marie Rivière leaving her apartment with pilot Mathieu Carrière, postal worker Philippe Marlaud begins to pursue his rival, enlisting the assistance of amused schoolgirl Anne-Laure Meury. Although Bernard Lutic's photography glories in the parks and backstreets of Paris, this is still a typically garrulous picture. Rohmer's sympathy for these lost souls makes everything most engaging. DP French +subtitles. DVD

Philippe Marlaud *François* • Marie Rivière *Anne* • Anne-Laure Meury *Lucie* • Mathieu Carrière *Christian* • Philippe Caroit *Friend* • Coralie Clément *Colleague* • Lisa Heredia *Girlfriend* ■ *Dir/Scr* Eric Rohmer

L'Avventura ★★★★★ PG
Classic drama   1960 · It/Fr · BW · 142min

Booed at Cannes (where it still won the Special Jury Prize) and branded immoral by the American National League of Decency, Michelangelo Antonioni's masterpiece is a mystery without a solution. This adventure in cinematic technique is a brilliant and troubling study of alienation, privileged indolence and psychological sterility, in which the search for a missing woman gradually becomes irrelevant as her lover and best friend are drawn into an unsatisfying relationship of their own.

A

Antonioni coaxes memorable performances from his cast, while he uses cinematographer Aldo Scavarda's exceptional views to reveal his characters' emotional states. DP Italian +subtitles.
DVD BL

Monica Vitti *Claudia* • Gabriele Ferzetti *Sandro* • Lea Massari *Anna* • Dominique Blanchar *Giulia* • James Addams *Carrado, her husband* • Renzo Ricci *Anna's father* • Esmeralda Ruspoli *Patrizia* • Lelio Luttazzi *Raimondo* ■ *Dir* Michelangelo Antonioni • *Scr* Michelangelo Antonioni, Elio Bartolini, Tonino Guerra, from a story by Antonioni

Awake ★★ 15
Psychological thriller
2007 · US · Colour · 80min

Debut writer/director Joby Harold's medical thriller begins in soap opera territory, as wealthy businessman Clayton Beresford (Hayden Christensen) tries to hide his relationship with Sam (Jessica Alba) from his controlling mother (Lena Olin). But when he's called in for life-saving heart surgery, events in the operating room don't go according to plan. Or do they? Christensen's performance is lethargic, and Terrence Howard provides the only spark of interest as the chief surgeon. Beyond the visceral impact of scalpel breaking skin, there is very little here to get the adrenaline pumping. SP *DVD*

Hayden Christensen *Clayton Beresford Jr* • Jessica Alba *Sam Lockwood* • Lena Olin *Lilith Beresford* • Terrence Howard *Dr Jack Harper* • Christopher McDonald *Dr Larry Lupin* • Fisher Stevens *Dr Puttnam* • Georgina Chapman *Penny Carver* • Sam Robards *Clayton Beresford Sr* • Arliss Howard *Dr Jonathan Neyer* ■ *Dir/Scr* Joby Harold

The Awakening ★ 15
Horror 1980 · UK/US · Colour · 95min

This adaptation of a Bram Stoker novel is a dreadful plod. Surprising, given the cinematography's by the great Jack Cardiff and promising British director Mike Newell is behind the camera. The symbolism is heavy-handed, and Charlton Heston reads the script as if it were the Ten Commandments, forgetting Cecil B DeMille's 11th commandment: Thou Shalt Not Bore. AT Violence, swearing.

Charlton Heston *Matthew Corbeck* • Susannah York *Jane Turner* • Jill Townsend *Anne Corbeck* • Stephanie Zimbalist *Margaret Corbeck* • Patrick Drury *Paul Whittier* • Nadim Sawalha *Dr El Sadek* • Miriam Margolyes *Kadira* ■ *Dir* Mike Newell • *Scr* Allan Scott, Chris Bryant, Clive Exton, from the novel *The Jewel of Seven Stars* by Bram Stoker

The Awakening ★★★ 15
Period supernatural thriller
2011 · Fr/UK · Colour · 102min

Writer/director Nick Murphy and co-writer Stephen Volk (the creative force behind the controversial 1992 TV classic *Ghostwatch*) deliver a mostly effective and unnerving 1920s-set tale here. Rebecca Hall plays a feisty debunker of alleged hauntings, summoned to a remote boys' boarding school by teacher Dominic West, who tells her that her charges are being menaced by a mysterious spectre. Sadly, things go a little haywire in the third act, but if you can forgive the silly conclusion, it's still satisfyingly scary. AS Violence. *DVD BL*

Rebecca Hall *Florence Cathcart* • Dominic West *Robert Mallory* • Imelda Staunton *Maud Hill* • Isaac Hempstead-Wright *Tom* • Joseph Mawle *Edward Judd* • John Shrapnel *Reverend Hugh Purslow* • Cal MacAninch *Freddie Strickland* • Lucy Cohu *Constance Strickland* ■ *Dir* Nick Murphy • *Scr* Nick Murphy, Stephen Volk

Awakening of the Beast ★★★ 18
Horror 1969 · Bra · Colour and BW · 92min

With his top hat, cape and curling talons, Coffin Joe is a Latin horror legend. The alter ego of Brazilian actor/director José Mojica Marins, he's at both his most eccentric and socially conscious in this anti-drugs story, which so outraged the military government of the time that it was banned. Opening with a disturbing injection

sequence, the tone shifts into pseudo-documentary mode as Marins outlines an LSD experiment he has conducted on a quartet of addicts. What makes this film so effective, however, is cinematographer Giorgio Attili's ingenious use of disparate film stocks. DP Portuguese +subtitles. *DVD*

José Mojica Marins *Coffin Joe* • Sergio Hingst *Dr Sergio* • Ozualdo Candeias • Andreia Bryan ■ *Dir/Scr* José Mojica Marins

Awakenings ★★★★ 15
Biographical drama 1990 · US · Colour · 115min

Robert De Niro and Robin Williams star in this powerful dramatisation of neurologist Oliver Sacks's book, based on his real-life success in "awakening" patients who had been trapped in a comatose state for more than 30 years after contracting sleeping sickness in the 1920s. Williams shows his versatility by playing the shy scientist, though it was De Niro who got the Oscar nomination. Too upbeat for some tastes, Penny Marshall's film got mixed reviews on its release, but also earned an Oscar nomination for best picture. PF Some swearing. *DVD*

Robert De Niro *Leonard Lowe* • Robin Williams *Dr Malcolm Sayer* • Julie Kavner *Eleanor Costello* • Ruth Nelson *Mrs Lowe* • John Heard *Dr Kaufman* • Penelope Ann Miller *Paula* • Alice Drummond *Lucy* • Max von Sydow *Dr Peter Ingham* ■ *Dir* Penny Marshall • *Scr* Steven Zaillian, from the non-fiction book by Oliver Sacks

Awara ★★★★ U
Drama 1951 · Ind · BW · 168min

Indian cinema's greatest romantic team, Raj Kapoor and Nargis, light up the screen in this powerful study of class, kinship and criminality. Raised on the street because his judge father believes he was conceived after his mother was raped by a vengeful bandit, Kapoor seeks to rekindle a childhood romance with Nargis. But her guardian is none other than his disapproving father, who stubbornly insists that Kapoor can never escape his heredity. Kapoor invests his character with a Chaplin-like pathos, and there's a palpable sensuality to his scenes with Nargis (particularly after her swim in the sea). DP Hindi +subtitles.

Prithviraj [Prithviraj Kapoor] *Justice Raghunath* • Nargis *Rita* • Raj Kapoor *Raj Raghunath* • KN Singh *Jagga* • Shashiraj [Shashi Kapoor] *Young Raj* ■ *Dir* Raj Kapoor • *Scr* KA Abbas, from a story by Abbas, VP Sathe

Awara Paagal Deewana ★★★ 15
Comedy 2002 · Ind · Colour · 157min

Action sequences inspired by *The Matrix* add a little midair panache to this frenetic crime caper. Gangster Om Puri sets things in motion by bequeathing a diamond stash to his children Rahul Dev and Preeti Jhangiani and her husband, Akshay Kumar, providing they take equal shares. However, the action only starts to hot up when the scene shifts to New York and the eccentric Paresh Rawal and his scheming son-in-law Aftab Shivdasani become embroiled in the dangerous game. DP Hindi +subtitles. *DVD*

Akshay Kumar *Guru Gulab Khatri* • Sunil Shetty *Yeda Anna* • Aftab Shivdasani *Dr Anmol Acharya* • Preeti Jhangiani *Preeti* • Amrita Arora *Mona* • Aarti Chhabria *Tina* • Paresh Rawal *Manilal* • Om Puri • Rahul Dev *Vikrant* ■ *Dir* Vikram Bhatt

Away ★★
Drama 2016 · UK · Colour

In this sombre British drama, two troubled individuals come together to form an unlikely friendship. Timothy Spall plays the older of the two, a boozy, depressed widower who has come to Blackpool to commit suicide. After a failed attempt, he is discovered by a feisty young woman (Juno Temple) who is running away from an abusive relationship. Despite an impressive turn from Temple, the film itself is grim and downbeat to a fault and may be way too bleak for some viewers. SC

Juno Temple *Ria* • Timothy Spall *Joseph* • Matt Ryan *Dex* • Susan Lynch *Angie* ■ *Dir* David Blair (4) • *Scr* Roger Hadfield

Away All Boats ★★★ PG
Second World War drama
1956 · US · Colour · 109min

Today's cynicism would blow this gung-ho Second World War drama out of the water – which is what nearly happens to the wartime attack transport boat *Belinda*. Jeff Chandler is the inevitably unyielding captain who has to encourage a fighting spirit among his dispirited crew. The action scenes pass the time spectacularly enough and there's a very young Clint Eastwood to be spotted. Otherwise, the flag-waving patriotism makes it an interesting curio from a bygone era. TH *DVD*

Jeff Chandler *Captain Jebediah Hawks* • George Nader *Lieutenant MacDougall* • Lex Barker *Commander Quigley* • Julie Adams *Nadine MacDougall* • Keith Andes *Dr Bell* • Richard Boone *Lieutenant Fraser* • William Reynolds *Kruger* • Clint Eastwood ■ *Dir* Joseph Pevney • *Scr* Ted Sherdeman, from the novel by Kenneth Dodson

Away from Her ★★★★ 12
Relationship drama
2006 · Can/UK/US · Colour · 105min

Canadian actress Sarah Polley makes her feature writer/director debut with this mature and deeply poignant meditation on love, loss and memory. In wonderfully understated performances, Gordon Pinsent and Julie Christie play a devoted couple whose 50-year marriage appears unshakeable until the wife develops Alzheimer's disease and moves into a care home. It's a quiet and sensitively handled drama that allows the tragic narrative to speak for itself without sickly sentiment or showy direction. A cliché-free Christie has never been better, but it's Pinsent's affecting restraint in a trickier role that carries the picture. SF Swearing. *DVD*

Julie Christie *Fiona Anderson* • Gordon Pinsent *Grant Anderson* • Olympia Dukakis *Marian* • Michael Murphy (1) *Aubrey* • Kristen Thomson *Kristy* • Wendy Crewson *Madeleine Montpellier* ■ *Dir* Sarah Polley • *Scr* Sarah Polley, from the short story *The Bear Came over the Mountain* by Alice Munro

Away We Go ★★★ 15
Road movie comedy drama
2009 · US/UK · Colour · 93min

After the gloomy *Revolutionary Road*, director Sam Mendes returns to the quirkiness of *American Beauty* for this spin on the road movie, as Colorado residents Burt (John Krasinski) and his partner Verona (Maya Rudolph) hit the road in search of a new home. Along the way they meet various characters from their pasts, ranging from the slightly individualistic to the positively pantomimic. The characterisations are at times overblown, but the first half of the film is great fun. Then they go to Canada, the tone changes, things get serious and the pace slackens. And the dénouement is long in coming and too pat when it does. BP Swearing, sexual references. *DVD*

John Krasinski *Burt Farlander* • Maya Rudolph *Verona De Tessant* • Maggie Gyllenhaal *Ellen, "LN"* • Allison Janney *Lily* • Catherine O'Hara *Gloria Farlander* • Paul Schneider (2) *Courtney Farlander* • Melanie Lynskey *Munch Garnett* ■ *Dir* Sam Mendes • *Scr* Dave Eggers, Vendela Vida

Awaydays ★★ 18
Drama 2009 · UK · Colour · 100min

This would-be bruising story of football hooliganism and social alienation centres on aspiring artist Paul Carty (Nicky Bell) and his friendship with the achingly hip Elvis (Liam Boyle). Director Pat Holden ably recalls the music and fashion trends of late 1970s Merseyside, but the punch-ups are unconvincingly staged and the accents are decidedly dodgy. Ultimately mired in melodrama, this lacks its source novel's laconic humour and owes more to TV soaps *Brookside* and *Hollyoaks* than reality. DP *DVD BL*

Nicky Bell *Paul Carty* • Liam Boyle *Elvis* • Stephen Graham *John Godden* • Holliday Grainger *Molly* • Oliver Lee *Baby* • Sacha Parkinson *Natasha* ■ *Dir* Pat Holden • *Scr* Kevin Sampson, from his novel

Awesome; I F***in' Shot That! ★★★★ 15
Music documentary
2006 · US · Colour and BW · 84min

Grainy hand-held camerawork has been part of the film-maker's armoury for shooting live concerts for years, but the ever-mischievous and street savvy Beastie Boys have gone one step further. For this record of their 2004 gig at Madison Square Garden, they let loose 50 friends and fans with portable digital cameras to film the event as they saw it. Beastie Boy Adam Yauch – using the directorial moniker of Nathanial Hörnblowér – then stitched all the footage together and the result is one of the most innovative concert movies ever made. It's certainly a warts-and-all approach, but one that perfectly captures the band's anarchic punk edge. JF *DVD*

■ *Dir* Nathanial Hörnblowér [Adam Yauch]

The Awful Dr Orlof ★★ 15
Horror 1962 · Sp/Fr · BW · 82min

Trash-meister Jesus Franco's incredible directing career took off with this graphic Spanish shocker (which credits the director as Norbert Moutier, one of many pseudonyms he has taken to avoid France's strict quota laws). Demented Howard Vernon kidnaps starlets to perform skin-graft operations on his disfigured daughter. Franco's early gore landmark is rather talky, but the expressionistic black-and-white photography still impresses. Four sequels followed. AJ Spanish dubbed. Violence, nudity. *DVD*

Howard Vernon *Dr Orlof* • Conrado San Martin *Inspector Tanner* • Diana Lorys *Wanda Bronsky* • Perla Cristal *Arne* • Maria Silva *Dany* • Ricardo Valle *Morpho* • Mara Lasso *Irma Gold* • Venancio Muro *Jean Rousseau* • Felix Dafauce *Inspector* ■ *Dir* Norbert Moutier [Jesus Franco] • *Scr* Jesus Franco, from the novel *Gritos en la Noche* by David Khune [Jesus Franco]

The Awful Truth ★★★★★ U
Classic screwball comedy
1937 · US · BW · 87min

This is a wonderful example of Cary Grant at his screwball comic best, playing one half of a sniping, divorcing couple, who trade insults like gunfire and seek to spoil each other's future plans. Irene Dunne is the superb foil for Grant's laconic asides, and the two leads are assisted by a great supporting cast. Leo McCarey's assured direction was rightly rewarded with an Oscar. Many stars, including Tom Hanks and Hugh Grant, have laid claim to Grant's mantle, but this movie illustrates once again that they are light years away from the man at his best. Remade in 1953 as *Let's Do It Again*. SH

Irene Dunne *Lucy Warriner* • Cary Grant *Jerry Warriner* • Ralph Bellamy *Daniel Leeson* • Alexander D'Arcy [Alex D'Arcy] *Armand Duvalle* • Cecil Cunningham *Aunt Patsy* • Molly Lamont *Barbara Vance* • Esther Dale *Mrs Leeson* • Joyce Compton *Dixie Belle Lee/Toots Binswanger* ■ *Dir* Leo McCarey • *Scr* Viña Delmar [Vina Delmar], from the play by Arthur Richman

An Awfully Big Adventure ★★★ 15
Period black comedy
1994 · UK · Colour · 107min

Underrated on its release, this watchable and entertaining adaptation of Beryl Bainbridge's jet-black comedy novel hits the right cynical notes. Focusing on the romantic intrigues involving the members of a British repertory theatre as they prepare to mount a production of *Peter Pan* in the late 1940s, the film has Hugh Grant cast against type as the egomaniacal director, while Alan Rickman's charismatic portrayal of the ageing matinée idol steals the handsomely mounted show. AJ Swearing, brief nudity.

Alan Rickman *PL O'Hara* • Hugh Grant *Meredith Potter* • Georgina Cates *Stella* • Alun Armstrong *Uncle Vernon* • Peter Firth *Bunny* • Prunella Scales *Rose* • Rita Tushingham *Aunt Lily* • Nicola Pagett *Dotty Blundell* ■ Dir Mike Newell • Scr Charles Wood, from the novel by Beryl Bainbridge

Ay, Carmela! ★★★ 15
War drama 1990 · Sp/It · Colour · 98min

This is a highly enjoyable and eventually moving story of a vaudevillian couple's contact with the opposing sides in the Spanish Civil War. As a political satire, it is less successful, with both the Falangists and the Republicans being drawn as broad caricatures, while the pokes at military bureaucracy, cynical survivalism and the macho nature of Spanish society are as gentle as they are obvious. Nevertheless, director Carlos Saura re-creates the period admirably and coaxes fine performances from Andres Pajares and Carmen Maura. DP Spanish +subtitles. Violence, swearing.

Carmen Maura *Carmela* • Andres Pajares *Paulino* • Gabino Diego *Gustavete* • Maurizzio De Razza *Lieutenant Ripamonte* • Miguel Angel Rellan [Miguel Rellan] *Interrogating lieutenant* • Edward Zentara *Polish officer* • Mario DeCandia *Bruno* • José Sancho *Artillery captain* • Antonio Fuentes *Artillery subaltern* ■ Dir Carlos Saura • Scr Carlos Saura, Rafael Azcona, from the play by José Sanchis Sinistierra

Azur & Asmar: the Princes' Quest ★★★★ U
Animated fantasy adventure
2006 · Sp/It/Bel/Fr · Colour · 98min

French animator Michel Ocelot departs from the stylised West African designs of his Kirikou series in this stunning *Arabian Nights*-inspired tale. It tells the story of childhood friends who are separated when Asmar's nursemaid mother is banished from court by Azur's widowed father and later come together to search for the imprisoned Djinn Fairy. Ocelot's use of colour is particularly dazzling, however, the beauty of the CGI graphics owes as much to medieval and Islamic art as to the cut-out techniques of the great German silhouettist Lotte Reiniger. But this is not just a gorgeous fairy tale, as Ocelot also sprinkles the action with wise words about racial and religious tolerance and the equality of the sexes. DP *DVD*

Steven Kynman *Azur* • Nigel Pilkington *Asmar* • Suzanna Nour *Jenane* • Nigel Lambert *Crapoux* • Leopold Benedict *Azur as a child* • Freddie Benedict *Asmar as a child* ■ Dir/Scr Michel Ocelot, George Roubicek

The BFG ★★★ PG
Fantasy 2016 · US · Colour · 117min

Little orphan Sophie (newcomer Ruby Barnhill) is kidnapped by a benevolent giant (a brilliantly motion-captured Mark Rylance) who blows dreams into the bedrooms of sleeping humans in Steven Spielberg's visually dazzling but emotionally remote adaptation of Roald Dahl's children's classic. It's more a kid-friendly experience than an adult one, and certainly not in the *ET* class, though Melissa Mathison, scripter of both, does happily keep Dahl's gibberish dialogue intact. Twinkly-eyed Rylance's soulfully expert take on the BFG, however, is an asset everyone will love. AJ 3D

Mark Rylance *The BFG* • Ruby Barnhill *Sophie* • Penelope Wilton *The Queen* • Jemaine Clement *Fleshlumpeater* • Rebecca Hall *Mary* • Rafe Spall *Mr Tibbs* ■ Dir Steven Spielberg • Scr Melissa Mathison, from Roald Dahl's illustrated children's book

BF's Daughter ★★
Political romantic drama
1948 · US · BW · 107min

John P Marquand's novel was a serious study in social mores, but the film adaptation became little more than a vehicle for Barbara Stanwyck, who over-emotes as only she can as the rich man's daughter who destroys her weak liberal husband, Van Heflin. Director Robert Z Leonard's pacing is sluggish, yet Stanwyck fans won't want to miss this. TS

Barbara Stanwyck *"Polly" Fulton* • Van Heflin *Thomas W Brett* • Charles Coburn *BF Fulton* • Richard Hart *Robert S Tasmin III* • Keenan Wynn *Martin Delwyn Ainsley* • Margaret Lindsay *"Apples" Sandler* • Spring Byington *Gladys Fulton* ■ Dir Robert Z Leonard • Scr Luther Davis, from the novel by John P Marquand

BMX Bandits ★★ PG
Adventure 1983 · Aus · Colour · 86min

This lively but very ordinary adventure story would probably be gathering dust by now if it weren't for the presence of a pre-stardom Nicole Kidman. She and her chums get mixed up with a gang of crooks who might have got away with it if it weren't for those darned BMX bikes. JF *DVD*

David Argue *Duane Whitey* • John Ley *"Moustache"* • Nicole Kidman *Judy* • James Lugton *Goose* • Bryan Marshall *The Boss* • Angelo D'Angelo *PJ* ■ Dir Brian Trenchard-Smith • Scr Patrick Edgeworth, from a screenplay (unproduced) by Russell Hagg

B Monkey ★★★ 18
Romantic thriller 1996 · UK/US · Colour · 88min

Tired of her life of crime, sexy jewel thief Asia Argento decides to go straight. But as romance with schoolteacher Jared Harris beckons, can she really give up the guns, drugs and glamorous danger of London's underworld? Distinctly old-fashioned, this fast-moving thriller from director Michael Radford features well-drawn characters who help smooth over the bumpier plot jolts. Argento – in her English-language debut – glows with charisma. AJ Sex scenes, swearing, violence, drug abuse.

Asia Argento *Beatrice (B Monkey)* • Jared Harris *Alan* • Rupert Everett *Paul* • Jonathan Rhys Meyers *Bruno* • Tim Woodward *Frank* • Ian Hart *Steve* ■ Dir Michael Radford • Scr Chloe King, Michael Radford, Michael Thomas, from the novel by Andrew Davies

Baadasssss! ★★★★ 15
Drama based on a true story
2003 · US · Colour · 110min

A thoroughly entertaining movie that crackles with raw energy, this offers a dramatised account of the making of Melvin Van Peebles's landmark 1971 blaxploitation picture *Sweet Sweetback's Baad Asssss Song*. Actor/director Mario Van Peebles plays his tenacious dad, who went to extraordinary lengths to get his self-starring tale about a street hustler-turned-revolutionary shot and into theatres. Chronicling the increasingly desperate events with a sharp and blackly comic touch, Mario delivers an enjoyably manic history lesson about the birth of black independent cinema, but what really gives the project its richness is his refusal to glamorise his cigar-chomping father. SF Swearing, sex scenes. *DVD*

Mario Van Peebles *Melvin Van Peebles* • Joy Bryant *Priscilla* • TK Carter *Bill Cosby* • Terry Crews *Big T* • Ossie Davis *Granddad* • David Alan Grier *Clyde Houston* • Nia Long *Sandra* • Paul Rodriguez *Jose Garcia* • Saul Rubinek *Howard "Howie" Kaufman* • Adam West *Bert* ■ Dir Mario Van Peebles • Scr Mario Van Peebles, Dennis Haggerty from the memoir *The Making of Sweet Sweetback's Baadasssss Song* by Melvin Van Peebles

The Baader Meinhof Complex ★★★★ 18
Drama based on a true story
2008 · Ger/Fr/Cz Rep · Colour · 143min

The story of the Baader Meinhof Gang (later the Red Army Faction) is absorbingly told in this controversial German drama. The group, inspired in part by late-1960s student protests, was behind a series of bank raids, bombings, kidnappings and assassinations from the 1960s to the 1990s. Working from Stefan Aust's non-fiction bestseller, director Uli Edel grippingly shows how volatile radical Andreas Baader (a swaggering Moritz Bleibtreu) and disillusioned journalist Ulrike Meinhof (Martina Gedeck) became the driving force behind the increasingly violent terrorists. Intense action-movie flair is blended with news footage and authentic dialogue to accurately portray the group's zeal, and debunk the glamour surrounding their activism. AJ German, English +subtitles. Violence, swearing, nudity *DVD*

Martina Gedeck *Ulrike Meinhof* • Moritz Bleibtreu *Andreas Baader* • Johanna Wokalek *Gudrun Ensslin* • Nadja Uhl *Brigitte Mohnhaupt* • Stipe Erceg *Holger Meins* • Bruno Ganz *Horst Herold* ■ Dir Uli Edel • Scr Bernd Eichinger, Uli Edel, from the non-fiction book by Stefan Aust

Baarìa ★★★★★ 15
Period drama 2009 · It/Fr · Colour · 144min

Director Giuseppe Tornatore's autobiographical epic inspired by his early life in Sicily is one of the most expensive Italian productions ever made – and certainly looks it. From the magical realist opening to the operatic finale, everything in this ravishing scrapbook of sun-kissed memories is sweeping, involving, romantic and disarmingly sentimental. Tornatore's constantly changing landscape is filled with engaging characters and colourful incident, making this another immensely moving and elegant charmer like *Cinema Paradiso* – with yet another wonderful Ennio Morricone score. AJ Italian, English +subtitles. *DVD*

Francesco Scianna *Peppino* • Margareth Madè *Mannina* • Nicole Grimaudo *Sarina (young girl)* • Angela Molina *Sarina (adult)* • Lina Sastri *Tana* • Gaetano Aronica *Cicci (adult)* ■ Dir Giuseppe Tornatore • Scr Giuseppe Tornatore, from his story • Music Ennio Morricone

Baazigar ★★★ 15
Psychological drama 1993 · Ind · Colour · 173min

Not since George Raft has a bad guy been able to trip the light fantastic as well as Shahrukh Khan. One of the most popular villains in recent Bollywood history, he turns in an impeccable performance of malevolent charm in this psychological masala from directing duo Abbas/Mustan. Equally impressive is Kajol, as the beauty who discovers that the supposedly deceased killer of her sister is alive, well and on her trail. DP Hindi +subtitles.

Shahrukh Khan [Shah Rukh Khan] • Kajol • Shilpa Shetty • Dalip Tahil • Siddharth • Johnny Lever • Krish Malik • Anant ■ Dir Abbas, Mustan • Scr Robin Bhatt, Javed Sidique, Akash Khurana

The Babadook ★★★★ 15
Horror 2013 · Aus/Can/Neth · Colour · 89min

Jennifer Kent's striking debut feature is a bold and intensely emotional psychological horror. Struggling to cope with her troubled six-year-old son (Noah Wiseman), who was born on the day her husband violently died, a stressed-out Australian care worker (Essie Davis) reads him a sinister children's book that mysteriously appears on a shelf. From that moment on, the boy can put a name to the "monster in the closet" causing his sleepless nights, while his mother comes to question whether the beast is as fictional as she first thought. Davis gives a monumental performance as the anguished parent who becomes an uncontrollable force of murderous destruction in order to protect her child. AJ Violence, swearing. *DVD* *BL*

Essie Davis *Amelia* • Noah Wiseman *Samuel* • Hayley McElhinney *Claire* • Daniel Henshall *Robbie* • Barbara West *Mrs Roach* ■ Dir/Scr Jennifer Kent

The Babe ★★★ PG
Sports biography 1992 · US · Colour · 109min

This was only released on video in the UK, perhaps because it was felt we would rather count sheep than watch baseball. It is, however, a character study of a flawed talent, baseball legend Babe Ruth, rather than a sports film centred on endless action. John Goodman perfectly captures the hero's enthusiasm, insecurity and weaknesses, and helps distract from the episodic nature of the film. JM *DVD*

John Goodman *George Herman "Babe" Ruth* • Kelly McGillis *Claire Hodgeson-Ruth* • Trini Alvarado *Helen Woodford-Ruth* • Bruce Boxleitner *Jumpin' Joe Dugan* • Peter Donat *Harry Frazee* • James Cromwell *Brother Mathias* ■ Dir Arthur Hiller • Scr John Fusco

Babe ★★★★ U
Fantasy comedy 1995 · Aus · Colour · 88min

This Australian family comedy came out of nowhere to enchant millions around the world. The "babe" of the title is an orphaned piglet, adopted by a family of Border collies, who learns how to handle sheep under the patient training of soft-hearted farmer James Cromwell. The mixture of live action and animatronics brings the animals magically to life (the film won an Oscar for visual effects). A delight from start to finish. JF *DVD* *BL*

James Cromwell *Farmer Arthur Hoggett* • Magda Szubanski *Esme Hoggett* • Christine Cavanaugh *Babe* • Miriam Margolyes *Fly* • Danny Mann *Ferdinand* • Hugo Weaving *Rex* • Miriam Flynn *Maa* • Roscoe Lee Browne *Narrator* ■ Dir Chris Noonan • Scr Chris Noonan, George Miller, from the novel *The Sheep-Pig* by Dick King-Smith

Babe: Pig in the City ★★ U
Fantasy comedy adventure
1998 · US/Aus · Colour · 91min

This rather disappointing sequel isn't anywhere near the equal of the endearing original. Here, Babe finds himself in constant danger when he travels to the city to earn money after Farmer Hoggett is injured. The action is taken at too frantic a pace to let the personalities come through, though the special-effects work with the animals is still quite wonderful and visually impressive. TH *DVD* *BL* *CS*

James Cromwell *Farmer Hoggett* • Magda Szubanski *Esme Hoggett* • Mickey Rooney *Fugly Floom* • Mary Stein *Landlady* • Julie Godfrey *Neighbour* • EG Daily [Elizabeth Daily] *Babe* • Glenne Headly *Zootie* • Steven Wright *Bob* • Miriam Margolyes *Fly* • Hugo Weaving *Rex* ■ Dir George Miller (2) • Scr George Miller, Judy Morris, Mark Lamprell, from characters by Dick King-Smith • Cinematographer Andrew Lesnie

B

The Babe Ruth Story ★★ U
Sports biography   1948 · US · BW · 105min

In the USA George "Babe" Ruth achieved heroic status for helping drag baseball back to respectability after the 1919 White Sox Scandal. Of the several biopics of the famous slugger, this was the first, the most sentimental and least accurate in the omission of his legendary drinking, womanising and gluttony. Bendix does a reasonable impersonation of the burly player, Claire Trevor is good, and there is intercut documentary footage of "Babe" in his heyday. **BB**

William Bendix *George Herman/Babe Ruth* • Claire Trevor *Claire Hodgson Ruth* • Charles Bickford *Brother Matthias* • Sam Levene *Phil Conrad* • William Frawley *Jack Dunn* ■ *Dir* Roy Del Ruth • *Scr* Bob Considine, George Callahan, from the non-fiction book *The Babe Ruth Story* by Babe Ruth as told to Bob Considine

Babel ★★★ 15
Drama   2006 · US/Mex · Colour · 137min

Acclaimed Mexican director Alejandro González Iñárritu once again fashions an ambitious, harrowing narrative from seemingly unconnected stories. As if to top his ideal *Amores Perros* (set in Mexico City) and English-language follow-up *21 Grams* (shot in Memphis), *Babel* crosses three continents. Deftly moving between four strands (involving goatherds in Morocco, a tourist couple played by Brad Pitt and Cate Blanchett, a formidable nanny, and a deaf-mute teenager in Tokyo), the film is grainily handsome and naturalistically acted (the goatherds are non-professionals). But with one of the links predictable and another arbitrarily contrived, the whole isn't quite as profound as it appears. **AC** English, Spanish, Japanese, Arabic +subtitles. Violence, swearing, sexual references, drug abuse. *DVD*

Brad Pitt *Richard* • Cate Blanchett *Susan* • Gael García Bernal *Santiago* • Koji Yakusho *Yasujiro* • Rinko Kikuchi *Chieko* • Adriana Barraza *Amelia* • Boubker Aït El Caid *Yussef* • Said Tarchani *Ahmed* • Elle Fanning *Debbie* ■ *Dir* Alejandro González Iñárritu • *Scr* Guillermo Arriaga, from an idea by Arriaga, Alejandro González Iñárritu

Babeldom ★★★ 15
Part-animated science-fiction documentary   2011 · UK · Colour · 84min

Paul Bush's first feature-length film is a meditation on the modern metropolis, which contains poetic and pretentious moments in equal measure. Constructed around urban explorer Mark Caven's search for archaeologist Youla Boudali, the action opens with a view of Bruegel's 16th-century impression of the Tower of Babel and consists of a series of labyrinthine wanderings through an urban purgatory where it's possible to witness one's own birth and death. This audacious experiment ends up feeling like a scolding upmarket computer game, but there's no denying that Bush's slickly edited and imaginative imagery lingers long in the memory. **DP** Nudity.

Mark Caven *Man* • Youla Boudali *Woman* ■ *Dir/Scr* Paul Bush

Babes in Arms ★★★★ U
Musical   1939 · US · BW · 95min

Not much of Rodgers and Hart's Broadway score was left in this MGM film version, but that didn't matter to audiences who turned out in force to watch Judy Garland and Mickey Rooney. They were brought together in the very first musical produced by genius Arthur Freed, whose later work would include such classics as *On the Town*. Rooney is magnificent, earning an Oscar nomination but losing to Robert Donat. He's a perfect foil for Garland, her wayward vulnerability contrasting with his brashness. Just sit back and enjoy their obvious pleasure in singing *Good Morning*. **TS**

Mickey Rooney *Mickey Moran* • Judy Garland *Patsy Barton* • Charles Winninger *Joe Moran* • Guy Kibbee *Judge Black* • June Preisser *Baby Rosalie Essex* • Grace Hayes *Florrie Moran* ■

Dir Busby Berkeley • *Scr* Jack McGowan, Kay Van Riper, from the musical by Richard Rodgers, Lorenz Hart

Babes in Toyland ★★★★ U
Musical fantasy   1934 · US · BW · 70min

Fairy-tale whimsy with Laurel and Hardy! What could be better for children of all ages? Victor Herbert's light operetta was adapted – to the extent there's nothing left of the original – with Stan and Ollie as incompetent assistants to Santa Claus. They order 100 six-foot wooden soldiers instead of 600 foot-tall toys, but the combatants come in handy when miser Barnaby parts Tom-Tom from his beloved Bo-Peep and tries to take over nurseryland. Released on video and DVD as *March of the Wooden Soldiers*. **TH** *DVD*

Stan Laurel *Stanley Dum* • Oliver Hardy *Oliver Dee* • Charlotte Henry *Little Bo-Peep* • Felix Knight *Tom-Tom* • Henry Kleinbach [Henry Brandon] *Evil Silas Barnaby* • Florence Roberts *Widow Peep* • Ferdinand Munier *Santa Claus* ■ *Dir* Gus Meins, Charles Rogers • *Scr* Nick Grinde, Frank Butler, from the operetta *Babes in Toyland* by Victor Herbert, Glen MacDonough

Babes in Toyland ★★ U
Musical fantasy   1961 · US · Colour · 101min

The second of three film adaptations of Victor Herbert's light opera, this earned a couple of Oscar nominations but it isn't a patch on the classic Laurel and Hardy version. It was personally produced by Walt Disney, but there's a distinct lack of magic. The special effects that allow Tommy Sands to lead an army of toy soldiers to rescue Annette Funicello from the grasp of evil Ray Bolger are clever enough, but Jack Donohue's direction is uninspired. **DP** *DVD*

Ray Bolger *Barnaby* • Tommy Sands *Tom Piper* • Annette Funicello *Mary Contrary* • Ed Wynn *Toymaker* • Tommy Kirk *Grumio* • Kevin Corcoran *Boy Blue* • Henry Calvin *Gonzorgo* ■ *Dir* Jack Donohue • *Scr* Ward Kimball, Joe Rinaldi, Lowell S Hawley, from the operetta by Victor Herbert, Glen MacDonough

Babes in Toyland ★ U
Musical fantasy   1986 · US/W Ger · Colour · 91min

The old Laurel and Hardy picture of 1934 was remade by Disney in 1961, with two TV versions in between. This further TV remake is only of minor interest, even for fans of Drew Barrymore and Keanu Reeves: she was 11, and towards the end of her first flush of success, while he was 21, and yet to find his. The original songs by Victor Herbert and Glen McDonough have been replaced by gooey items by Leslie Bricusse, who wrote *Scrooge* and *Doctor Dolittle*. **AT**

Drew Barrymore *Lisa Piper* • Richard Mulligan *Bernie/Barnaby Barnacle* • Eileen Brennan *Mrs Piper/Widow Hubbard* • Keanu Reeves *Alex/Jack Be Nimble* • Pat Morita *Toymaster* ■ *Dir* Clive Donner • *Scr* Paul Zindel

Babes on Broadway ★★★ U
Musical   1941 · US · BW · 117min

This appallingly contrived, sentimental mishmash was created to suit the talents of its stars, but when those stars are the incomparable Judy Garland and the ineffable Mickey Rooney, frankly they could have dispensed with the plot entirely. As it is, the arch plot structure enables them to go though their paces – Rooney performs an amazing Carmen Miranda impression and Judy pretends to be Sarah Bernhardt. But be warned: the minstrel number seems incredibly tasteless today and there's an air of corny wartime patriotism. **TS**

Mickey Rooney *Tommy Williams* • Judy Garland *Penny Morris* • Fay Bainter *Miss Jones* • Virginia Weidler *Barbara Jo* • Ray McDonald *Ray Lambert* • Richard Quine *Morton "Hammy" Hammond* • Donald Meek *Mr Stone* • Alexander Woollcott ■ *Dir* Busby Berkeley • *Scr* Fred F Finklehoffe, Elaine Ryan, from a story by Fred F Finklehoffe

Babette's Feast ★★★★★ U
Period drama   1987 · Den · Colour · 99min

This Danish film with a French star deservedly won the best foreign film Oscar and transcended the barriers of subtitles to capture the imagination of cinema-goers everywhere. Set in the 1870s, the story unfolds against the background of the grim Jutland peninsula, where two spinster sisters (Bodil Kjer, Birgitte Federspiel), daughters of the former pastor, continue his work in leading the religious sect he founded. Into their lives comes Babette (Stéphane Audran), seeking refuge from war-torn Paris, who becomes their housekeeper. Her presence gradually effects changes in the austere community, culminating in a magnificent feast that she cooks 14 years later. Faithfully and brilliantly adapted by Gabriel Axel, this original and poignant tale is leavened with well-judged humour. **RK** Danish +subtitles. *DVD* *BL*

Stéphane Audran *Babette Hersant* • Jean-Philippe Lafont *Achille Papin* • Gudmar Wivesson *Young Lorenz Lowenhielm* • Jarl Kulle *Old Lorenz Lowenhielm* • Bibi Andersson *Swedish court lady-in-waiting* • Hanne Stensgaard *Young Philippa* ■ *Dir* Gabriel Axel • *Scr* Gabriel Axel, from a story by Isak Dinesen [Karen Blixen]

Babies ★★★ U
Documentary   2010 · Fr · Colour · 75min

The cute quotient couldn't be higher in Thomas Balmès's documentary, but this study of four babies from various parts of the world focuses on the adorable instead of examining differing attitudes to infancy and parenthood. Firstborns Hattie from San Francisco and Mari from Tokyo are endlessly doted over, while Bayar and Ponijao are left to their own devices as they respectively toddle around a Mongolian yurt and a Namibian kraal. Drawing attention to the obvious contrasts between plenty and poverty, Balmès struggles to provide any significant socio-cultural context. **DP** In English, Japanese, Mongolian. *DVD* *BL*

■ *Dir* Thomas Balmès

Babul ★★ U
Romantic drama   1950 · Ind · BW · 124min

A huge hit at the Indian box office, this romance not only takes tragedy to new heights, but also comes pretty close to crossing the boundaries of credibility. It's intrigue all the way as the new village postman becomes the subject of a tug-of-war between his boss's daughter and the spoilt sibling of the local landowner. Dilip Kumar broke all sorts of cinematic conventions by jilting Nargis and opting for the resistible Munawar Sultana, but what they fail to comment on is the ludicrousness of the finale. **DP** Hindi +subtitles.

Dilip Kumar *Ashok* • Nargis *Bela* • Munawar Sultana *Usha* ■ *Dir* SU Sunny • *Scr* Azm Bazidpuri

The Baby ★★★
Horror   1973 · US · Colour · 85min

Kept in nappies by his man-hating mother, taunted by his psycho sister and desired by a well-meaning social worker, life has been anything but easy for teenager David Manzy, and it's going to get worse. Director Ted Post makes a decent fist of this bizarre horror film and is rewarded with good performances from his cast, though his use of actual footage depicting mentally disabled children is in poor taste. **DP**

Ruth Roman *Mrs Wadsworth* • Anjanette Comer *Ann Gentry* • Marianna Hill *Germaine* • Suzanne Zenor *Alba* • Beatrice Manley Blau *Judith* • David Manzy *Baby* ■ *Dir* Ted Post • *Scr* Abe Polsky

The Baby and the Battleship ★★ U
Comedy   1956 · UK · Colour · 91min

It was in Malta, when shooting this picture, that Bryan Forbes coined his nickname for Richard Attenborough. "Bunter" he called him and "Bunter" he remained, owing to Attenborough's addiction to chocolate. Nowadays that little piece of trivia is rather more significant than the movie, which is a juvenile comedy about an Italian baby smuggled aboard HMS *Gillingham* while the ship is docked in Naples. It's all too twee for words and the single joke is stretched beyond endurance. **AT** *DVD*

John Mills *Puncher Roberts* • Richard Attenborough *Knocker White* • Andre Morrell *Marshal* • Bryan Forbes *Professor* • Michael Hordern *Captain* • Harold Siddons *Whiskers* • Clifford Mollison *Sails* • Lionel Jeffries *George* • Gordon Jackson *Harry* • Michael Howard *Joe* • Ernest Clark *Commander Digby* • Lisa Gastoni *Maria* ■ *Dir* Jay Lewis • *Scr* Jay Lewis, Gilbert Hackforth-Jones, from the novel by Anthony Thorne

Baby Boom ★★★ PG
Comedy   1987 · US · Colour · 105min

Diane Keaton stars as a ruthless New York executive whose business ambitions falter when she's forced to foster a dead relative's baby girl. The men in her life – boss Sam Wanamaker and lover Harold Ramis – aren't sympathetic to her new working mother status, so she buys a money-pit mansion in the country and tries to make it on her own, with local veterinarian Sam Shepard popping in. With its mix of cuteness and acuteness, it's one of Keaton's more likeable films. **TH** Some swearing, brief nudity. *DVD*

Diane Keaton *JC Wiatt* • Harold Ramis *Steven Buchner* • Sam Wanamaker *Fritz Curtis* • Sam Shepard *Dr Jeff Cooper* • James Spader *Ken Arrenberg* • Pat Hingle *Hughes Larrabee* • Britt Leach *Vern Boone* • Kristina Kennedy *Elizabeth Wiatt* • Michelle Kennedy *Elizabeth Wiatt* • Kim Sebastian *Robin* ■ *Dir* Charles Shyer • *Scr* Nancy Meyers, Charles Shyer

Baby Boy ★★ 15
Drama   2001 · US · Colour · 124min

Director John Singleton's companion piece to his career-making debut *Boyz N the Hood* falls way short of its predecessor's power, poignancy and perception. Set in South Central Los Angeles, the plot revolves around 20-year-old Tyrese Gibson who still lives at home with his mother and has fathered two children by different women. Little attempt is made to explore Gibson's psychological state, so fringe characters played by Omar Gooding and Ving Rhames prove far more interesting. **DP** *DVD*

Tyrese Gibson *Jody* • Omar Gooding *Sweetpea* • AJ Johnson [Adrienne-Joi Johnson] *Juanita* • Taraji P Henson *Yvette* • Snoop Dogg *Rodney* • Tamara LaSeon Bass *Peanut* • Ving Rhames *Melvin* ■ *Dir/Scr* John Singleton

Baby Doll ★★★ PG
Melodrama   1956 · US · BW · 109min

The film that scandalised America was tamed by the passage of some four decades. It is hard to keep a smile off one's face at the thought of millions of respectable citizens being pinned back in their seats by the emotional G-force emanating from the screen and their own sense of delicious guilt. Yet Tennessee Williams's screenplay is not without its highlights, thanks to the skilled direction of his favourite film-maker, Elia Kazan, notably the scene on a swing in which Eli Wallach, in his film debut, seeks revenge on arsonist Karl Malden by seducing his bride. **DP**

Karl Malden *Archie* • Carroll Baker *Baby Doll* • Eli Wallach *Silva Vacarro* • Mildred Dunnock *Aunt Rose Comfort* • Lonny Chapman *Rock* • Eades Hogue *Town Marshall* • Noah Williamson *Deputy* ■ *Dir* Elia Kazan • *Scr* Tennessee Williams, from his story

Baby Face ★★★
Drama   1933 · US · BW · 68min

A tour-de-force performance from the incomparable Barbara Stanwyck enlivens this tale of a small-town girl who makes it to the mansion by using and abusing every gullible schmuck who crosses her silk-stockinged path. This is essentially a pretty ordinary movie – everything moves along predictably and the clichés have been shared out even-handedly – made extraordinary by its star who is in her sashaying, gimlet-eyed, "don't mess with me" prime. Keep an eye out for a youthful John Wayne, but everyone is acted off the screen by Stanwyck. **SH**

Barbara Stanwyck *Lily "Baby Face" Powers* • George Brent *Trenholm* • Donald Cook *Stevens* • Arthur Hohl *Sipple* • John Wayne *Jimmy McCoy* •

U SUITABLE FOR ALL   Uc SUITABLE ESPECIALLY FOR YOUNG CHILDREN (DVD ONLY)   PG PARENTAL GUIDANCE   12A UNDER 12s TO BE ACCOMPANIED (CINEMA ONLY)

Henry Kolker *Mr Carter* • Margaret Lindsay *Ann Carter* • Theresa Harris *Chico* ■ *Dir* Alfred E Green • *Scr* Gene Markey, Kathryn Scola, from a story by Mark Canfield [Darryl F Zanuck]

Baby Face Morgan ★★
Crime comedy   1942 · US · BW · 60min

In this would-be gangster comedy the camerawork is so inept and the sets so obviously cheap that the very incompetence of the production makes for compulsive viewing. Richard Cromwell plays the title mobster's son who gets embroiled in an insurance scam. This is poor quality stuff, but it's enlivened by sterling work from a cast headed by B-movie girl Mary Carlisle and Robert Armstrong. **TS**

Mary Carlisle *Virginia Clark* • Richard Cromwell *"Baby Face" Morgan* • Robert Armstrong *"Doc" Rogers* • Chick Chandler *Oliver Harrison* • Charles Judels *"Deacon" Davis* • Warren Hymer *Wise Willie* ■ *Dir* Arthur Dreifuss • *Scr* Edward Dein, Jack Rubin, from a story by Oscar Brodney, Jack Rubin

Baby Face Nelson ★★★
Crime drama   1957 · US · BW · 84min

Casting Mickey Rooney, the baby face of all those cutesy MGM movies, was a wonderfully subversive idea, and Rooney turns in an energetic, scary and convincing performance as the notorious gangster of the 1930s. Falling in with Leo Gordon's gang, Rooney goes bonkers and goes on to become America's Public Enemy Number One. Carolyn Jones is the girlfriend who has to put up with his highly charged antics. What distinguishes this movie is its refusal to moralise: it's a slick, stylish celebration of anti-social behaviour. **AT**

Mickey Rooney *Lester "Baby Face Nelson" Gillis* • Carolyn Jones *Sue* • Cedric Hardwicke *Doc Saunders* • Chris Dark [Christopher Dark] *Jerry* • Ted De Corsia *Rocco* • Emile Meyer *Mac* • Tony Caruso [Anthony Caruso] *Hamilton* • Leo Gordon *John Dillinger* • Dan Terranova *Miller* • Elisha Cook *Jr Van Meter* ■ *Dir* Don Siegel • *Scr* Irving Shulman, Geoffrey Homes [Daniel Mainwaring], from a story by Irving Shulman

Baby for Sale ★★
Drama   2004 · US · Colour · 89min

A couple desperate for a baby challenge New York state law in this illuminating TV-movie drama. Dana Delany provides the emotional cement as an affluent woman who draws her husband into a black market bidding war when they try to adopt a Hungarian infant that they've seen on the internet. Naturally, manipulative tear-jerking follows, as director Peter Svatek wrings every last bit of sentiment from the largely routine tale. **SF**

Dana Delany *Nathalie Johnson* • Hart Bochner *Steve Johnson* • Bruce Ramsay *Gabor Szabo* • Romano Orzari *Joey Perrotta* • Elizabeth Marleau *Janka* • Claudia Besso *Laura Jackson* ■ *Dir* Peter Svatek • *Scr* Peter Wierick

Baby Geniuses ★ PG
Comedy fantasy adventure
1999 · US · Colour · 90min

This rotten, infantile comedy marks a career low for Kathleen Turner. She plays a nasty children's magnate who is carrying out tests on a host of brainy litte nippers on the shaky premise that infants can actually converse in a secret language. The slapstick will amuse only toddlers. Jon Voight starred in the equally misguided 2003 sequel. **JF**
DVD

Kathleen Turner *Elena* • Christopher Lloyd *Heep* • Kim Cattrall *Robin* • Peter MacNicol *Dan* • Dom DeLuise *Lenny* • Ruby Dee *Margo* • Kyle Howard *Dickie* • Kaye Ballard *Mayor* ■ *Dir* Bob Clark • *Scr* Bob Clark, Greg Michael, from a story by Steven Paul, Francisca Matos, Robert Grasmere

Baby It's You ★★★ 15
Romantic comedy drama
1983 · US · Colour · 100min

One of the earlier films from independent writer/director John Sayles, this slice-of-life drama, set in 1960s New Jersey, centres on the efforts of an Italian Catholic boy (Vincent Spano) to romance a middle-class Jewish girl (Rosanna Arquette). Sayles's talents weren't yet fully formed and the film rather runs out of steam in the later stages, but the attention to detail, plus some bursts of typically sharp Sayles dialogue are indicative of the movie mastery he would exhibit in later films. **DA** Swearing, drug abuse, sex scenes, nudity.

Rosanna Arquette *Jill Rosen* • Vincent Spano *"Sheik" Capadilupo* • Joanna Merlin *Mrs Rosen* • Jack Davidson *Dr Rosen* • Nick Ferrari *Mr Capadilupo* • Dolores Messina *Mrs Capadilupo* • Robert Downey *Jr Stewart* • Matthew Modine *Steve* ■ *Dir* John Sayles • *Scr* John Sayles, from a story by Amy Robinson

Baby Mama ★★★ 12
Comedy   2008 · US · Colour · 98min

Tina Fey (*30 Rock*) stars in this smart, sassy and often laugh-out-loud comedy about surrogate motherhood. Fey plays Kate, a single and successful 37-year-old company vice-president, who has always put her career before starting a family. But now her biological clock is ticking. After being informed that she has little chance of conceiving naturally, Kate turns to surrogacy – and is paired up with potential mum Angie (Amy Poehler), a walking, talking compendium of "trailer trash" values. Slowly, though, the bickering turns to bonding between the two mums-to-be. With good performances from the leads and spot-on cameos from Sigourney Weaver and Steve Martin, this is saucy, sexy and fun. **DA** *DVD* *Blu*

Tina Fey *Kate Holbrook* • Amy Poehler *Angie Ostrowiski* • Dax Shepard *Carl* • Sigourney Weaver *Chaffee Bicknell* • Greg Kinnear *Rob* • Romany Malco *Oscar* • Maura Tierney *Caroline* • Steve Martin *Barry* ■ *Dir/Scr* Michael McCullers

The Baby of Macon ★★★ 18
Period drama   1993 · UK · Colour · 121min

There's a certain irony in the fact that a film about the deceptiveness of appearance should itself glitter without ever being golden. In a 17th-century theatre, a play is being performed where an elderly mother gives birth to a baby boy. But one of her virginal daughters announces that the child is hers, proclaiming a "miracle birth". Thanks to Sacha Vierny's sumptuous photography, this is a visual if disturbing delight, but director Peter Greenaway allows his twin penchants for thematic controversy and stylistic contrivance to run away with him. **DP** Violence, nudity.

Julia Ormond *Daughter* • Ralph Fiennes *Bishop's son* • Philip Stone *Bishop* • Jonathan Lacey *Cosimo Medici* • Don Henderson *Father Confessor* • Celia Gregory *Mother Superior* • Jeff Nuttall *Major Domo* ■ *Dir/Scr* Peter Greenaway

Baby on Board ★★ PG
Romantic comedy thriller
1993 · Can · Colour · 86min

There are precious few cuddly moments in this thriller, as a posse of Brylcreemed mafiosos follow taxi driver Judge Reinhold and passengers Carol Kane and her young daughter. This is basically one very long and very predictable chase movie, in which squealing brakes and interior car shots dominate so exclusively that the entire cast could have shot this trouserless and we'd be none the wiser. **SH**

Judge Reinhold *Ernie* • Carol Kane *Maria* • Geza Kovacs *Carmine* • Alex Stapley *Angelica* • Conrad Bergschneider *Lorenzo* • Lou Pitoscias *Vincenzo* • Jason Blicker *Frankie* • Holly Stapley *Angelica* ■ *Dir* Francis A Schaeffer • *Scr* Damian Lee, James Shavick, from a story by Doug Moore

Baby: Secret of the Lost Legend ★★★ PG
Comedy adventure   1985 · US · Colour · 88min

Disney's old-fashioned adventure fantasy is a pleasant enough tale about palaeontologist Sean Young and her sports writer husband William Katt discovering a apatosaurus family in Africa. Scientist Patrick McGoohan is the villain of the piece who wants the baby dinosaur brought back to civilisation. Veering from cute to violent, this reworked *Lost World* tale is too bland to properly satisfy. Yet kids will love the huggable Baby, for all its winsome plasticity. **AJ** *DVD*

William Katt *George Loomis* • Sean Young *Susan Matthews-Loomis* • Patrick McGoohan *Dr Erick Kiviat* • Julian Fellowes *Nigel Jenkins* • Kyalo Mativo *Cephu* • Hugh Quarshie *Kenge Obe* • Edward Hardwicke *Dr Pierre Dubois* ■ *Dir* BWL Norton [Bill L Norton] • *Scr* Clifford Green, Ellen Green

The Baby-Sitter's Club ★★★ U
Comedy drama   1995 · US · Colour · 90min

Based on the popular Ann M Martin novels, this agreeable comedy drama directed by former *thirtysomething* star Melanie Mayron concerns a group of young girls dealing with parents and romance while earning extra money looking after children at a day camp. Sissy Spacek's daughter, Schuyler Fisk, appears in her first starring role and, despite a nice performance, has done very little since. **JB**

Schuyler Fisk *Kristy* • Bre Blair *Stacey* • Rachael Leigh Cook *Mary Anne* • Larisa Oleynik *Dawn* • Tricia Joe *Claudia* • Stacey Linn Ramsower *Mallory* • Zelda Harris *Jessi* • Vanessa Zima *Rosie Wilder* • Bruce Davison *Watson* • Ellen Burstyn *Mrs Haberman* ■ *Dir* Melanie Mayron • *Scr* Dalene Young, from the novels by Ann M Martin

Baby, Take a Bow ★★ PG
Crime drama   1934 · US · BW · 72min

This was Shirley Temple's first starring vehicle after Fox signed her to a seven-year contract. She had her sixth birthday while making it and enchanted critics and audiences with her performance as the daughter of an ex-convict (James Dunn) who saves him from false accusations of theft. American women's groups winced at such a young child being seen mixed up with criminals. **AE** *DVD*

Shirley Temple *Shirley Ellison* • James Dunn *Eddie Ellison* • Claire Trevor *Kay Ellison* • Alan Dinehart *Welch* • Ray Walker *Larry Scott* • Dorothy Libaire *Jane* ■ *Dir* Harry Lachman • *Scr* Philip Klein, EE Paramore Jr, from the play *Square Crooks* by James P Judge

Baby the Rain Must Fall ★★★
Drama   1965 · US · BW · 98min

This is one of the great Steve McQueen's more sombre roles. He's fresh out of jail and reunited with his wife, played by Lee Remick, and the daughter he has never seen. He has a nothing job by day but sings with a band at night, though any hopes he has of fame are dashed by his foster mother, a domineering woman who becomes the catalyst for later events. McQueen and Remick are both excellent, while Robert Mulligan's direction not only eschews any easy melodramatics, but also beautifully evokes the flatness and deadness of small-town Texas, all of which acts as a tinderbox for McQueen's pent-up emotions. **AT**

Lee Remick *Georgette Thomas* • Steve McQueen (1) *Henry Thomas* • Don Murray *Slim* • Paul Fix *Judge Ewing* • Josephine Hutchinson *Mrs Ewing* • Ruth White *Miss Clara* • Charles Watts *Mr Tillman* • Carol Veazie *Mrs Tillman* • Estelle Hemsley *Catherine* ■ *Dir* Robert Mulligan • *Scr* Horton Foote

Babycall ★★★ 15
Horror thriller
2011 · Nor/Ger/Swe · Colour · 96min

Writer/director Pal Sletaune's film stars Noomi Rapace (from the original Scandinavian *Dragon Tattoo* trilogy) as a single mother who flees her violent ex-partner and hides out in a secret location with her eight-year-old son. This effective chiller bears more than a passing resemblance to the 2006 Spanish TV horror *The Baby's Room*. But, while the premise is neat, its plausibility is severely tested by plot holes that the creepy atmosphere ultimately stuggles to fill. It's slicky staged, but only superficially tense. **DP** Norwegian, Swedish +subtitles. Violence.

Noomi Rapace *Anna* • Kristoffer Joner *Helge* • Vetle Qvenild Werring *Anders* • Stig Amdam *Ole* • Maria Bock *Grete* ■ *Dir/Scr* Pal Sletaune

Babyfever ★★★
Comedy drama   1994 · US · Colour · 110min

Henry Jaglom's typically talky treatise on babies was clearly inspired by the fact he had just fathered a second child with his wife, the film's star Victoria Foyt. Foyt is so tormented by the ticking of her biological clock that she can barely make a rational choice between dull boyfriend Matt Salinger and her reckless ex, Eric Roberts. The verbosity of the baby-shower scene will alienate many, but some of the insights are disarmingly honest, if not particularly original. **DP** Swearing.

Victoria Foyt *Gena* • Matt Salinger *James* • Dinah Lenney *Roz* • Eric Roberts *Anthony* • Frances Fisher *Rosie* • Elaine Kagan *Milly* • Zack Norman *Mark* ■ *Dir* Henry Jaglom • *Scr* Henry Jaglom, Victoria Foyt

Babylon ★★★ 15
Drama   1980 · UK · Colour · 91min

This ground-breaking British film about contemporary black life in London was not the first of its kind, but it was the first to reflect the significance of such things as sound systems, the Stop-and-Search Law and Rastafarianism to black culture. The action revolves around young garage mechanic Blue, who is trying to take part in a sound-system contest while dealing with domestic, racial and cultural pressures. Natural performances and desolate locations give a vivid impression of south London life prior to the Brixton riots, only a year later. **DM** Violence, swearing *DVD*

Karl Howman *Ronnie* • Trevor Laird *"Beefy"* • Brian Bovell *"Spark"* • Victor Evans Romero *"Lover"* • David N Haynes *Errol* • Archie Pool *"Dreadhead"* • T-Bone Wilson *Wesley* • Mel Smith *Alan* • Bill Moody *Man on balcony* ■ *Dir* Franco Rosso • *Scr* Martin Stellman, Franco Rosso

Babylon AD ★★ 12
Science-fiction action adventure
2008 · US/Fr · Colour · 86min

Despite all its noise and bluster, this big-budget blockbuster is actually a rather slight dystopian sci-fi thriller. And with a running time of just 90 minutes, it's disarmingly brief compared to similarly themed epics like *Blade Runner* or *The Fifth Element*, which it is blatantly trying to emulate. Vin Diesel plays Toorop, a bounty hunter with a heart who accepts "one last job". He must escort a young psychic and her kung fu nun chaperone from a post-nuclear meltdown Russia to the relatively safe haven of a gentrified New York. **AC** *DVD* *Blu*

Vin Diesel *Toorop* • Michelle Yeoh *Sister Rebeka* • Mélanie Thierry *Aurora* • Lambert Wilson *Darquandier* • Mark Strong *Finn* • Gérard Depardieu *Gorsky* • Charlotte Rampling *High priestess* ■ *Dir* Mathieu Kassovitz • *Scr* Mathieu Kassovitz, Eric Besnard, from the novel *Babylon Babies* by Maurice G Dantec

Babymother ★★ 15
Musical comedy drama
1998 · UK · Colour · 78min

Writer/director Julian Henriques's feature debut has in its favour an undeniable energy and a gutsy performance from Anjela Lauren Smith, as the mother of two battling against the odds and the indifference of her partner to become a reggae singer. Yet too often the narrative is hijacked by musical interludes, and there's insufficient dramatic focus. **DP** Swearing, some violence, a sex scene. *DVD*

Anjela Lauren Smith *Anita* • Caroline Chikezie *Sharon* • Jocelyn Esien *Yvette* • Wil Johnson *Byron* • Don Warrington *Luther* • Tameka Empson *Dionne* • Diane Bailey *Bee* • Vas Blackwood *Caesar* • Andrea Francis *Yvette's Sister* ■ *Dir* Julian Henriques • *Scr* Julian Henriques, Vivienne Howard

Baby's Day Out ★★★ PG
Comedy   1994 · US · Colour · 94min

John Hughes (*Home Alone*) here comes up with another successful spin on the small-people-humiliating-adults theme, with a wee baby standing in for Macaulay Culkin. The little tot – the precious child of a wealthy family – is snatched by a bungling trio of

B

kidnappers and proceeds to make their life hell. Wit and subtlety are hardly to the fore, but the action does rip along at a cracking pace, the comic set pieces are executed with precision, and Joe Mantegna, Joe Pantoliano and Brian Haley are good fun as the crooks. JF *DVD*

Joe Mantegna *Eddie Mauser* • Lara Flynn Boyle *Laraine Cotwell* • Joe Pantoliano *Norby LeBlaw* • Brian Haley *Veeko Riley* • Cynthia Nixon *Gilbertine* • Fred Dalton Thompson *FBI agent Grissom* ■ *Dir* Patrick Read Johnson • *Scr* John Hughes

The Baby's Room ★★★★
Supernatural horror 2006 · Sp · Colour · 77min

From *Poltergeist* to *Ring*, there seems to have been a horror film about every conceivable piece of audiovisual gadgetry. But few have made such effective use of a prop as this nerve-jangling chiller. Within hours of moving into a newly renovated home, Javier Gutiérrez becomes convinced that he can hear someone (or something) sinister on the baby monitor. He takes out his increasing paranoia on unnerved wife Leonor Watling. All the more disconcerting for its subtlety, this spine-tingler is a minor gem. DP Spanish +subtitles.

Javier Gutiérrez *Juan* • Leonor Watling *Sonia* • Sancho Gracia *Domingo* • Antonio Dechent *Fernández* • Manuel Tallafé *García* ■ *Dir* Alex de la Iglesia • *Scr* Alex de la Iglesia, Jorge Guerricaechevarría

The Babysitter ★ 18
Erotic thriller 1995 · US · Colour · 85min

This litany of tired sex fantasies went straight to video, and we might never have heard of it at all had not Alicia Silverstone scored such a huge hit in the same year with *Clueless*. She has little to do here but look alluring as her employers and their neighbours contemplate soft-core encounters in a series of daydreams that only rarely rise above the squalid. DP Violence, swearing, substance abuse, sex scenes, nudity.

Alicia Silverstone *Jennifer* • Jeremy London *Jack* • JT Walsh *Harry Tucker* • Lee Garlington *Dolly Tucker* • Nicky Katt *Mark* • Lois Chiles *Bernice Holsten* • George Segal *Bill Holsten* ■ *Dir* Guy Ferland • *Scr* Guy Ferland, from the short story by Robert Coover

Bach and Broccoli ★★★ U
Comedy drama 1986 · Can · Colour · 95min

A box-office sensation in its native Quebec, the *Tales for All* series of children's films won more than 100 international awards. This third entry brought about a reunion between producer Rock Demers and André Melançon, who directed the first film in the series, *The Dog Who Stopped the War*. Mahée Paiement is hugely impressive as the 11-year-old orphan who arrives with her pet skunk to disrupt the ordered life of her uncle, Raymond Legault. Maintaining a light touch, Melançon doesn't labour his life lessons. DP French dubbed.

Mahée Paiement *Fanny* • Raymond Legault *Jonathan* • Harry Marciano *Sean* • Andrée Pelletier *Bernice* ■ *Dir* André Melançon • *Scr* Bernadette Renaud, André Melançon

The Bachelor ★★★
Romantic drama 1990 · It · Colour · 105min

Roberto Faenza directs Keith Carradine, Miranda Richardson and Kristin Scott Thomas in a drama about loss and love, adapted from Arthur Schnitzler's novel. Carradine, a middle-class, middle-aged doctor who has never married, is devastated when his close sibling (Richardson) commits suicide. He subsequently embarks on a string of sexual liaisons with three women, one of whom is played by Richardson in a secondary role. This understated and atmospheric drama about midlife crisis and masculinity is a fine example of good European cinema – an all-too-rare occurrence in the age of the Euro-pudding. LH

Keith Carradine *Dr Emil Grasler* • Miranda Richardson *Frederica/Widow* • Kristin Scott Thomas *Sabine* • Sarah-Jane Fenton *Katerina* • Max von Sydow *Von Schleheim* ■ *Dir* Roberto

Faenza • *Scr* Enrico DeConcini, Roberto Faenza, Hugh Fleetwood (English language version), from the novel *Dr Grasler, Spa Physician* by Arthur Schnitzler • *Music* Ennio Morricone

The Bachelor ★★ 12
Romantic comedy 1999 · US · Colour · 97min

This weak update of Buster Keaton's 1925 classic *Seven Chances* stars Chris O'Donnell as a young man who must get married by his 30th birthday (just 24 hours away) if he is to inherit $100 million from his deceased grandfather. His girlfriend (Renee Zellweger) has already given up on him, so he has to try all his ex-girlfriends. O'Donnell lacks the charisma and comic timing to hold this together. JB *DVD*

Chris O'Donnell *Jimmy Shannon* • Renee Zellweger [Renée Zellweger] *Anne* • Hal Holbrook *O'Dell* • James Cromwell *Priest* • Artie Lange *Marco* • Edward Asner *Gluckman* • Marley Shelton *Natalie* • Sarah Silverman *Carolyn* • Peter Ustinov *Grandad* • Mariah Carey *Ilana* • Brooke Shields *Buckley* ■ *Dir* Gary Sinyor • *Scr* Steve Cohen, from the film *Seven Chances* by Clyde Bruckman, Jean Havez, Joseph A Mitchell, from the play by Roi Cooper Megrue

The Bachelor and the Bobby-Soxer ★★★★ U
Comedy 1947 · US · BW · 90min

Teenager Shirley Temple takes a shine to womaniser Cary Grant (who wouldn't?), so her sister, judge Myrna Loy, orders Grant to wine and dine Temple until she grows sick of him. It's a thin premise for Grant's 50th movie (also known in the UK as *Bachelor Knight*), but sparkling playing and sheer starpower, not to mention Sidney Sheldon's Oscar-winning screenplay, turned this trifle into one of the top box-office hits of its day. Time hasn't dented its appeal. TS *DVD*

Cary Grant *Dick* • Myrna Loy *Margaret* • Shirley Temple *Susan* • Rudy Vallee *Tommy* • Ray Collins *Beemish* • Harry Davenport *Thaddeus* • Johnny Sands *Jerry* • Don Beddoe *Tony* • Lillian Randolph *Bessie* ■ *Dir* Irving Reis • *Scr* Sidney Sheldon

Bachelor Apartment ★★★
Drama 1931 · US · BW · 77min

It's always interesting to see a Hollywood sex comedy from before the puritanical Hays Code pooped the party. Here Lowell Sherman, who made a speciality of playing lecherous lovers, is the confirmed bachelor with three women on the go simultaneously. They are ladylike Irene Dunne (in one of her first films), vampish Mae Murray (in one of her last films) and innocent Claudia Dell. It's a trifle theatrical, but Sherman directs smoothly enough. RB

Lowell Sherman *Wayne Carter* • Irene Dunne *Helene Andrews* • Mae Murray *Agatha Carraway* • Ivan Lebedeff *Henri De Maneau* • Norman Kerry *Lee Graham* • Noel Francis *Janet* • Claudia Dell *Lita Andrews* ■ *Dir* Lowell Sherman • *Scr* John Howard Lawson, J Walter Ruben (adaptation and dialogue)

The Bachelor Father ★★★
Comedy 1931 · US · BW · 91min

This is a rather nice vehicle for the venerable C Aubrey Smith, best known today as a crusty old actor in supporting roles embodying stiff-upper-lippery. Although Marion Davies and Ralph Forbes are billed above Smith, this is his picture all the way. He plays the titular role of a man searching for his three grown-up children. Director Robert Z Leonard stands back and just lets the old ham get on with it. He does achieve some touching moments, but fails to disguise the film's theatrical origins. TS

Marion Davies *Tony Flagg* • Ralph Forbes *John Ashley* • C Aubrey Smith *Sir Basil Winterton* • Ray Milland *Geoffrey Trent* • Guinn "Big Boy" Williams *Dick Berney* • David Torrence *Doctor MacDonald* ■ *Dir* Robert Z Leonard • *Scr* Lawrence E Johnson, from the play by Edward Childs Carpenter

Bachelor Flat ★★★ U
Comedy 1961 · US · Colour · 91min

Director Frank Tashlin scored cinematic bull's-eyes with his colourfully trenchant and hysterical satires, most famously *Son of*

Paleface and *The Girl Can't Help It*. Here he cocks an anti-English snoot at California-style education, as girls run hot and cold through professor Terry-Thomas's beachside apartment. Terry-Thomas has had far better scripts than this to get his gapped teeth into, but he's compulsively watchable. TS

Tuesday Weld *Libby Bushmill* • Richard Beymer *Mike Pulaski* • Terry-Thomas *Professor Bruce Patterson* • Celeste Holm *Helen Bushmill* • Francesca Bellini *Gladys* • Howard McNear *Dr Bowman* • Ann Del Guercio *Liz* ■ *Dir* Frank Tashlin • *Scr* Frank Tashlin, Bud Grossman, from the play by Bud Grossman

Bachelor in Paradise ★★★
Comedy 1961 · US · Colour · 108min

A typical relic of the Eisenhower era, this breezy satire on American lifestyle and morals stars Bob Hope as a famous travel-writer-cum-sociologist who, for tax reasons, adopts a phoney identity and settles down in a model housing development called "Paradise". The film's targets are marriage (Hope causes three divorces) and modern household gadgetry; the result is like a Jacques Tati version of *The Stepford Wives*. Hope quips his way through the jubilantly sexist material and cop-out ending. AT

Bob Hope *Adam J Niles* • Lana Turner *Rosemary Howard* • Janis Paige *Dolores Jynson* • Jim Hutton *Larry Delavane* • Paula Prentiss *Linda Delavane* • Don Porter *Thomas W Jynson* • Virginia Grey *Camille Quinlaw* ■ *Dir* Jack Arnold • *Scr* Valentine Davies, Hal Kanter, from a story by Vera Caspary

Bachelor Mother ★★★ U
Comedy 1939 · US · BW · 82min

Although Ginger Rogers and David Niven are top-billed in this contrived but hugely enjoyable comedy, the real star is that cuddly curmudgeon Charles Coburn. As the department store tycoon who threatens to dismiss Rogers from the toy counter after she finds an abandoned baby, he times every disapproving look to perfection before melting like the big softy he was. Felix Jackson's story earned an Oscar nomination, but it's Norman Krasna's screenplay that merits the praise, along with the slick direction of Garson Kanin. DP *DVD*

Ginger Rogers *Polly Parrish* • David Niven *David Merlin* • Charles Coburn *JB Merlin* • Frank Albertson *Freddie Miller* • EE Clive *Butler* ■ *Dir* Garson Kanin • *Scr* Norman Krasna, from a story by Felix Jackson

Bachelor of Hearts ★★★ U
Romantic comedy 1958 · UK · Colour · 94min

German actor Hardy Kruger stars in this rather charming romantic comedy, directed by the talented Wolf Rilla, and aided by a lovely performance from co-star Sylvia Syms. Today these gauche student antics look a little daft, but they are neatly depicted here by a pair of young screenwriters who have since become much more famous: Leslie Bricusse, distinguished co-writer of *Stop the World I Want to Get Off*, and Frederic Raphael, who collected an Oscar for *Darling*. TS

Hardy Kruger *Wolf* • Sylvia Syms *Ann* • Ronald Lewis *Hugo* • Jeremy Burnham *Adrian* • Peter Myers *Jeremy* • Philip Gilbert *Conrad* • Charles Kay *Tom* ■ *Dir* Wolf Rilla • *Scr* Leslie Bricusse, Frederic Raphael • *Cinematographer* Geoffrey Unsworth

The Bachelor Party ★★★★
Drama 1957 · US · BW · 94min

Screenwriter Paddy Chayefsky's gift for realism-as-fable was never grittier than in this adaptation of his own TV play. A bawdy stag-night becomes an odyssey in which the American male's inherent fear of women is brilliantly explored – from porn movies to strip-show to hooker confrontation - all floated along on a river of alcohol. Nervous groom-to-be Philip Abbott is counterbalanced by Don Murray, the married man wondering if he did the right thing, while office bachelor Jack Warden presents a cheery persona to hide his own loneliness. TH

Don Murray *Charlie Samson* • EG Marshall *Walter* • Jack Warden *Eddie* • Philip Abbott *Arnold* • Larry Blyden *Kenneth* • Patricia Smith *Helen Samson* • Carolyn Jones *Existentialist* • Nancy Marchand *Julie* • Karen Norris *Hostess* ■ *Dir* Delbert Mann • *Scr* Paddy Chayefsky, from his TV play

Bachelor Party ★★ 18
Comedy 1984 · US · Colour · 101min

Chaos ensues as Tom Hanks's bachelor binge degenerates into a bawdy riot, in a plot similar to the formula used in *National Lampoon's Animal House* and *Porky's*. Neal Israel's bid to produce a riotous comedy doesn't really hit the mark and Hanks, already showing early promise, is the film's only redeeming feature. NF Sex scenes, violence, swearing, nudity. *DVD*

Tom Hanks *Rick Gassko* • Tawny Kitaen *Debbie Thompson* • Adrian Zmed *Jay O'Neill* • Robert Prescott *Cole Whittier* • George Grizzard *Mr Thompson* • Barbara Stuart *Mrs Thompson* • William Tepper *Dr Stan Gassko* ■ *Dir* Neal Israel • *Scr* Neal Israel, Pat Proft, from a story by Bob Israel

Bachelorette ★★★ 15
Comedy 2012 · US · Colour · 83min

On paper, *Bachelorette* appears to be a cheap cash-in on the success of *Bridesmaids* with a focus on girls behaving badly on the eve of a wedding. However, it's actually based on Leslye Headland's 2010 play of the same name and is a much more acerbic gal-pal comedy than its big-screen predecessor. Although things do get a little sombre, this is a wonderfully nasty romp, stacked with caustic one liners and boasting terrific turns from the leading trio (Kirsten Dunst, Lizzy Caplan and Isla Fisher) as mean girls reluctantly facing up to adulthood. JF *DVD* *Blu*

Kirsten Dunst *Regan* • Isla Fisher *Katie* • Lizzy Caplan *Gena* • James Marsden *Trevor* • Kyle Bornheimer *Joe* • Rebel Wilson *Becky* ■ *Dir/Scr* Leslye Headland

Back Door to Heaven ★★★
Crime drama 1939 · US · BW · 73min

In its day, this grim 20th Century-Fox melodrama was much-discussed - it's a sort of *Cathy Come Home* about how the underprivileged drift into crime. A teacher awaits the return of former pupils, but one of them has ended up in reform school. Although the nominal star is sturdy Wallace Ford, the most interesting cast member is young Van Heflin as the errant student. Three movies after this one Van Heflin won an Oscar at MGM for *Johnny Eager*. TS

Aline MacMahon *Miss Williams* • Jimmy Lydon [James Lydon] *Frankie as a boy* • Anita Magee *Carol* • William Harrigan *Mr Rogers* • Jane Seymour (1) *Mrs Rogers* • Robert Wildhack *Rudolph Herzing* • Van Heflin *John Shelley as an adult* ■ *Dir* William K Howard • *Scr* William K Howard, John Bright, Robert Tasker

Back Door to Hell ★★
Second World War drama 1964 · US/Phil · BW · 69min

The first of four films Jack Nicholson made with director Monte Hellman is a sparse war drama, shot in the Philippines at the same time as *Flight to Fury* and costing around $80,000. Nicholson plays one of three marines who reconnoitre a Japanese-held island ahead of the American invasion force. As far as Nicholson is concerned, the film allows us to see him learning as he goes along without giving any inkling that a major star was in the process of being born. AT

Jimmie Rodgers *Lieutenant Craig* • Jack Nicholson *Burnett* • John Hackett *Jersey* • Annabelle Huggins *Maria* • Johnny Monteiro *Ramundo* ■ *Dir* Monte Hellman • *Scr* Richard A Guttman, John Hackett, from a story by Richard A Guttman

Back from Eternity ★★★
Adventure drama 1956 · US · BW · 97min

Director John Farrow waited 17 years to remake his movie *Five Came Back* and, if anything, the idea works even better the second time around. Rod Steiger and Robert Ryan star in this story of a plane that crash-lands in cannibal country, using every trick of the acting trade to up-stage each other. It's still an obvious situation, but the budget is better than it was for the 1939 original and the treatment more spectacular. TH

Robert Ryan *Bill* • Anita Ekberg *Rena* • Rod Steiger *Vasquel* • Phyllis Kirk *Louise* • Keith Andes *Joe* • Gene Barry *Ellis* • Fred Clark *Crimp* • Beulah Bondi *Martha* ■ *Dir* John Farrow • *Scr* Jonathan Latimer, from a story by Richard Carroll

Back in Action ★★ 18
Action thriller 1993 · Can · Colour · 79min

When a nasty drug dealer guts his partner, cop Roddy Piper sets his sights on eliminating the gang. At the same time, cabbie Billy Blanks attempts to shelter his uncooperative sister from the same gang, who want her rubbed out because she witnessed the killing. This incredibly brutal film boasts about one shoot-out or bone-breaking fight every ten minutes but, to its credit, it doesn't take itself too seriously. KB *DVD*

"Rowdy" Roddy Piper [Roddy Piper] *Frank Rossi* • Billy Blanks *Billy* • Bobbie Phillips *Helen* • Kai Soremekun *Tara* ■ *Dir* Steve DiMarco • *Scr* Karl Schiffman

Back in the USSR ★ 15
Romantic thriller 1992 · US/Rus · Colour · 83min

This uninspiring thriller propels Frank Whaley from support roles (where he should, quite frankly, have stayed) to lead protagonist as an American getting lost in the Russian underworld. Encountering the feisty Natalya Negoda, the two become romantically entwined. Far from generating excitement, their relationship makes the film about as unappealing as a piece of tripe. LH *DVD*

Frank Whaley *Archer Sloan* • Natalya Negoda *Lena* • Roman Polanski *Kurilov* • Andrew Divoff *Dimitri* • Dey Young *Claudia* • Ravil Issyanov *Georgi* • Harry Ditson *Whittier* • Brian Blessed *Chazov* ■ *Dir* Deran Sarafian • *Scr* Lindsay Smith, from a story by Lindsay Smith, Ilmar Taska

Back of Beyond ★ 15
Romantic crime thriller 1995 · Aus · Colour · 81min

This below-par Australian thriller was actually inspired by the Quentin Tarantino-scripted *True Romance*. Paul Mercurio reveals why we've heard so little of him since *Strictly Ballroom* with his unconvincing portrayal of a garage owner shaken by the motorcycle death of his sister, while a peroxided Colin Friels gives a risible rendition of paranoid villainy. DP

Paul Mercurio *Tom McGregor* • Colin Friels *Connor* • Dee Smart *Charlie* • John Polson *Nick* • Bob Maza *Gilbert* • Rebekah Elmaloglou *Susan McGregor* ■ *Dir* Michael Robertson • *Scr* Richard J Sawyer, Paul Leadon, AM Brooksbank, from a story by Richard J Sawyer, from a treatment by Michael Robertson

Back Roads ★★ 15
Comedy drama 1981 · US · Colour · 94min

A big-hearted hooker in the Deep South falls in love with an unsuccessful boxer who is unable to pay for her services. Together they take to the road to seek better times. Starring Sally Fields and Tommy Lee Jones and directed by Martin Ritt, this cutesy road movie is a journey to nowhere: an unbelievable collection of outmoded clichés and a waste of its talented leads. RK

Sally Field *Amy Post* • Tommy Lee Jones *Elmore Pratt* • David Keith *Mason* • Miriam Colon *Angel* • Michael V Gazzo *Tazio* • Dan Shor *Spivey* • M Emmet Walsh *Arthur* ■ *Dir* Martin Ritt • *Scr* Gary DeVore

Back Room Boy ★★ U
Second World War comedy 1942 · UK · BW · 82min

How many flag-waving British comedies during the Second World War rehashed the old "haunted house full of spies" plot? The year after Will Hay used the premise in *The Ghost of St Michael's*, his regular sidekicks

Graham Moffatt and Moore Marriott cropped up in this inferior version set on an Orkney island lighthouse, tailored for the talents of Arthur Askey. The main problem is that the film hammers home every gag, with Askey particularly at fault. DP

Arthur Askey *Arthur Pilbeam* • Googie Withers *Bobbie* • Moore Marriott *Jerry* • Graham Moffatt *Albert* • Vera Frances *Jane* • Joyce Howard *Betty* ■ *Dir* Herbert Mason • *Scr* Val Guest, Marriott Edgar

Back Street ★★
Romantic melodrama 1932 · US · BW · 84min

This tale of the self-sacrificing mistress of a married man, who comes to grief after over 20 years of "backstreet" fidelity, would be filmed twice more (in 1941 and 1961) to be wept over by successive generations. This first version, directed by John M Stahl, is the least successful, owing to a stilted script and an even more stilted and unattractive performance from John Boles. Ladylike and long-suffering, the accomplished Irene Dunne radiates sweetness. RK

Irene Dunne *Ray Schmidt* • John Boles *Walter Saxel* • June Clyde *Freda Schmidt* • George Meeker *Kurt Schendler* • ZaSu Pitts *Mrs Dole* • Shirley Grey *Francine* • Doris Lloyd *Mrs Saxel* ■ *Dir* John M Stahl • *Scr* Gladys Lehman, Lynn Starling, from the novel by Fannie Hurst

Back Street ★★★★
Romantic melodrama 1941 · US · BW · 88min

This remake of the 1932 film of Fannie Hurst's tear-jerking bestseller about the long-standing mistress of a married man, whose understanding, discretion and fidelity lead only to heartbreak, stars the luminous Margaret Sullavan, who waits in vain for her wealthy banker lover, played by the smoothly sexy Charles Boyer. Both stars pull out all the stops in conveying their torment under the expert direction of Robert Stevenson and with a little help from an excellent supporting cast. An irresistible period romance, requiring a handy box of tissues for an enjoyable wallow. RK

Charles Boyer *Walter Saxel* • Margaret Sullavan *Ray Smith* • Richard Carlson *Curt Stanton* • Frank McHugh *Ed Porter* • Frank Jenks *Harry Niles* • Tim Holt *Richard Saxel* • Peggy Stewart *Freda Smith* • Samuel S Hinds *Felix Darren* ■ *Dir* Robert Stevenson • *Scr* Bruce Manning, Felix Jackson, from the novel by Fannie Hurst

Back Street ★★★★
Romantic melodrama 1961 · US · Colour · 105min

The third and final version of the three-handkerchief weepie about a long-running and painful love affair between a married man and his mistress updates the story and gives it the full Ross Hunter treatment. This time the suffering pair are cast for glamour, with Susan Hayward languishing in luxury and sumptuous clothes by Jean Louis, and the glossily good-looking John Gavin playing the object of her tormented affections. David Miller directs efficiently, while Vera Miles supplies an entertaining turn as Gavin's alcoholic wife. Wildly enjoyable melodrama. RK

Susan Hayward *Rae Smith* • John Gavin *Paul Saxon* • Vera Miles *Liz Saxon* • Charles Drake *Curt Stanton* • Virginia Grey *Janie* • Reginald Gardiner *Dalian* • Tammy Marihugh *Caroline Saxon* • Robert Eyer *Paul Saxon Jr* ■ *Dir* David Miller (1) • *Scr* Eleanore Griffin, William Ludwig, from the novel by Fannie Hurst

Back to Bataan ★★★ PG
Second World War drama 1945 · US · BW · 87min

MGM scored a tremendous success with the then topical war film *Bataan* back in 1943, so it was a Hollywood inevitability that the Philippines would be revisited. However, instead of the searing campaign study that was expected, RKO plumped for a routine action film starring John Wayne. Still exciting for all that, the plot features a surprisingly subdued Duke as a colonel leading his unit of guerrillas in an undercover mission through the rather obvious studio foliage to victory. It's all

expertly directed by former editor Edward Dmytryk. TS *DVD*

John Wayne *Colonel Madden* • Anthony Quinn *Captain Andres Bonifacio* • Beulah Bondi *Miss Bertha Barnes* • Fely Franquelli *Dalisay Delgado* • Richard Loo *Major Hasko* • Philip Ahn *Colonel Kuroki* • "Ducky" Louie *Maximo* ■ *Dir* Edward Dmytryk • *Scr* Ben Barzman, Richard Landau, from a story by Aeneas MacKenzie, William Gordon

Back to God's Country ★★★
Adventure 1953 · US · Colour · 77min

Rock Hudson makes a splendid job of starring in this rugged story set in the far Canadian north. Hudson is a sea captain, married to the rather colourless Marcia Henderson, who has to face up to the tough weather and an even tougher Steve Cochran. Hudson tackles his plight splendidly, or at least well enough to convince his bosses at Universal he was ready for promotion to A-features: next came *Taza, Son of Cochise*, then his star-making performance in *Magnificent Obsession*. TS

Rock Hudson *Peter Keith* • Marcia Henderson *Dolores Keith* • Steve Cochran *Paul Blake* • Hugh O'Brian *Frank Hudson* • Chubby Johnson *Billy Shorter* • Tudor Owen *Fitzsimmons* • John Cliff *Joe* ■ *Dir* Joseph Pevney • *Scr* Tom Reed, from the novel by James Oliver Curwood

Back to School ★★ 15
Comedy 1986 · US · Colour · 92min

This ham-fisted comedy stars Rodney Dangerfield as a wealthy middle-aged man who returns to college to prove there's life in the old dog yet. Dangerfield drives in every gag with the subtlety of a steam hammer. Keith Gordon and Robert Downey Jr try hard as Dangerfield's weedy son and his radical pal, but the standouts are English teacher Sally Kellerman and coach M Emmett Walsh. DP *DVD*

Rodney Dangerfield *Thornton Melon* • Keith Gordon *Jason Melon* • Sally Kellerman *Diane Turner* • Burt Young *Lou* • Robert Downey Jr *Derek* • Paxton Whitehead *Philip Barbay* • Terry Farrell *Valerie Desmond* • M Emmet Walsh *Coach Turnbull* ■ *Dir* Alan Metter • *Scr* Steven Kampmann, Will Porter, Peter Torokvei, Harold Ramis, from a story by Rodney Dangerfield, Greg Fields, Dennis Snee

Back to the Beach ★★★ PG
Satirical comedy 1987 · US · Colour · 88min

Twenty years after hanging up their swimsuits in the highly successful *Beach Party* movies, 1960s teen idols Annette Funicello and Frankie Avalon returned for more fun in the sun in this agreeably nostalgic surf spoon pop culture's trash-filled memory lane. Now married, and living in Ohio, the couple decide to visit their daughter in California. Little do they know she's living with a beach bum, and when Frankie's old flame Connie Stevens also turns up, more rifts occur in the perfect family unit. Cleverly sending up the entire beach genre and crammed with camp cameos, Frankie and Annette parody their own squeaky clean personas with glee. AJ

Frankie Avalon *The Big Kahuna* • Annette Funicello *Annette* • Connie Stevens *Connie* • Lori Loughlin *Sandi* • Tommy Hinkley *Michael* • Demian Slade *Bobby* • Pee-wee Herman [Paul Reubens] *Pee-wee Herman* • Don Adams *Harbor master* ■ *Dir* Lyndall Hobbs • *Scr* Peter Krikes, Steve Meerson, Christopher Thompson, from the story by James Komack, from characters by Lou Rusoff

Back to the Future ★★★★★ PG
Science-fiction comedy adventure 1985 · US · Colour · 111min

This irresistible combination of dazzling effects and sly comedy propelled Michael J Fox to stardom and Robert Zemeckis to the front rank of Hollywood directors. Fox plays the student who travels back in time to the 1950s and acts as matchmaker for his future parents. It's beautifully played by the cast (honourable mentions to Christopher Lloyd, Lea Thompson and Crispin Glover), making the most of an ingenious script, which finds time to poke fun at 50s icons

between the bouts of time travelling. Zemeckis's direction is adroit and he never lets the effects swamp the film. JF Swearing. *DVD* *BL*

Michael J Fox *Marty McFly* • Christopher Lloyd *Dr Emmett Brown* • Lea Thompson *Lorraine Baines* • Crispin Glover *George McFly* • Thomas F Wilson *Biff Tannen* • Claudia Wells *Jennifer Parker* • Marc McClure *Dave McFly* • Wendie Jo Sperber *Linda McFly* ■ *Dir* Robert Zemeckis • *Scr* Robert Zemeckis, Bob Gale • *Special Effects* Kevin Pike

Back to the Future Part II ★★★ PG
Science-fiction comedy adventure 1989 · US · Colour · 107min

After the success of the first time-travelling caper a sequel was inevitable, although this time around director Robert Zemeckis is guilty of over-gilding the lily. Stars Michael J Fox and Christopher Lloyd return, along with Lea Thompson and Thomas F Wilson, but the script is too clever for its own good and the film gets bogged down by cramming in too many ideas and settings (past, future, alternative universes). The effects, however, are even better than in the first film. JF Swearing, violence. *DVD* *BL*

Michael J Fox *Marty McFly/Marty McFly Jr/Marlene McFly* • Christopher Lloyd *Dr Emmett Brown* • Lea Thompson *Lorraine* • Thomas F Wilson *Biff Tannen/Griff Tannen* • Harry Waters Jr *Marvin Berry* • Charles Fleischer *Terry* • Elisabeth Shue *Jennifer* ■ *Dir* Robert Zemeckis • *Scr* Bob Gale, from a story by Bob Gale, Robert Zemeckis

Back to the Future Part III ★★★★ PG
Science-fiction comedy adventure 1990 · US · Colour · 118min

Director Robert Zemeckis's blockbusting trilogy went slightly off the rails with the second segment, but it got right back on track with the concluding instalment. The film is set predominantly in the Old West and, as before, the plot revolves around the need to tinker with time and the problem of how to power the trusty DeLorean car so that Fox can get back to the present. Bob Gale and Zemeckis have come up with an ingenious plot and a clutch of in-jokes, Michael J Fox is on cracking form and Christopher Lloyd's romance with Mary Steenburgen is surprisingly touching. JF Swearing. *DVD* *BL*

Michael J Fox *Marty McFly/Seamus McFly* • Christopher Lloyd *"Doc" Emmett Brown* • Mary Steenburgen *Clara Clayton* • Thomas F Wilson *Buford "Mad Dog" Tannen/Biff Tannen* • Lea Thompson *Maggie McFly/Lorraine McFly* • Elisabeth Shue *Jennifer* • Richard Dysart *Barbed wire salesman* • Pat Buttram *Saloon old timer* • Harry Carey Jr *Saloon old timer* • Dub Taylor *Saloon old timer* ■ *Dir* Robert Zemeckis • *Scr* Bob Gale, from a story by Gale, Robert Zemeckis

Back to the Secret Garden ★ U
Fantasy drama 2000 · Ger/US/UK · Colour · 95min

American film-makers can't resist concocting sequels to beloved children's classics that are invariably a pale shadow of the original. This transatlantic continuation of Frances Hodgson Burnett's charming story couldn't be more winsome or wince-inducing. Misselthwaite Manor has become an orphanage run by Mrs Sowerby (Joan Plowright), who has allowed the garden to run to seed, and its former saviour Mary is now an ambassador's wife (Cherie Lunghi) living in New York. The rejuvenation of the garden is foreshadowed by a string of increasingly improbable incidents. As a result, the characters are ciphers, the message is trite and the magic is utterly dissipated by the cynically populist approach. DP *DVD*

Joan Plowright *Martha Sowerby* • George Baker *Will Weatherstaff* • Cherie Lunghi *Lady Mary Craven* • Leigh Lawson *Sir Colin Craven* • Aled Roberts *Robert* • Florence Hoath *Geraldine* • David Warner *Dr Snodgrass* ■ *Dir* Michael Tuchner • *Scr* Joe Wiesenfeld, from characters by Frances Hodgson Burnett

B

Back to You and Me ★★
Romantic drama 2005 · US · Colour · 92min

A mother and daughter gradually lay to rest the ghosts of the past in this uneven blend of gentle romance and family drama. Lisa Hartman Black is the work-obsessed doctor whose reluctant return home for a high-school reunion reignites her antagonistic relationship with estranged parent Rue McClanahan. Though it's obvious exactly where this film is going, it's a warm and inoffensive enough diversion. Dale Midkiff is particularly charming as the sensitive former flame who gives Hartman Black a second chance of love. SF

Lisa Hartman Black [Lisa Hartman] *Syd Ludwick* • Dale Midkiff *Gus Martin* • Rue McClanahan *Helen Ludwick* • Barbara Niven *Connie Murray* • Larry Manetti *Nelson* ■ *Dir* David S Cass Sr • *Scr* Tom Amundsen

The Back-Up Plan ★★12
Romantic comedy 2010 · US · Colour · 99min

This romantic comedy stars Jennifer Lopez as Zoe, a rather unlikely pet shop owner who uses a sperm donor to get pregnant, only to meet her perfect mate, Stan (Australian actor Alex O'Loughlin), immediately afterwards. The story, by *Will & Grace* writer Kate Angelo, lurches awkwardly from romance to break-up and back again in an attempt to create some tension, but the chemistry between Lopez and O'Loughlin is too stagey to be convincing. Lopez deserves better than this excruciating material. In fact, all actors do. KK Brief swearing, sex scenes. *DVD*

Jennifer Lopez *Zoe* • Alex O'Loughlin *Stan* • Eric Christian Olsen *Clive* • Anthony Anderson *Playground man* • Michaela Watkins *Mona* • Noureen DeWulf *Daphne* • Linda Lavin *Nana* • Tom Bosley *Arthur* ■ *Dir* Alan Poul • *Scr* Kate Angelo

Backbeat ★★★15
Biographical drama 1993 · UK · Colour · 99min

Iain Softley's account of the Fab Four's Hamburg days is rather like their music of the time: loud, raw and full of energy. It also betrays a lack of experience, leaving too much to enthusiasm. Focusing primarily on the relationship between John Lennon and "Fifth Beatle" Stuart Sutcliffe, it descends into tacky melodrama once Sutcliffe falls for photographer Astrid Kirchherr. Ian Hart is solid enough in another of his outings as Lennon (he played the Beatle in *The Hours and Times*), but Stephen Dorff and Sheryl Lee only occasionally convince as the star-crossed lovers. DP Violence, swearing, drug abuse, nudity. *DVD CS*

Sheryl Lee *Astrid Kirchherr* • Stephen Dorff *Stuart Sutcliffe* • Ian Hart *John Lennon* • Gary Bakewell *Paul McCartney* • Chris O'Neill *George Harrison* • Scot Williams *Pete Best* • Kai Wiesinger *Klaus Voormann* • Jennifer Ehle *Cynthia Powell* ■ *Dir* Iain Softley • *Scr* Iain Softley, Michael Thomas, Stephen Ward

Backdraft ★★★★15
Action drama 1991 · US · Colour · 131min

Director Ron Howard has become one of the most accomplished of Hollywood craftsmen, and this sturdy star-studded fare was deservedly a mainstream hit. Kurt Russell and William Baldwin are the two warring, firefighting brothers who have to cope with a rash of fires sparked by a seemingly deranged arsonist, whose lethal "backdrafts" are resulting in death and destruction. The plot is hardly original, but Howard marshals the sprawling elements with great finesse and the fire footage, if harrowing at times, is genuinely exhilarating. JF Swearing, sex scenes, nudity. *DVD*

Kurt Russell *Stephen McCaffrey* • William Baldwin *Brian McCaffrey* • Robert De Niro *Donald Rimgale* • Jennifer Jason Leigh *Jennifer Vaitkus* • Scott Glenn *John Adcox* • Rebecca De Mornay *Helen McCaffrey* • Jason Gedrick *Tim Krizminski* • JT Walsh *Martin Swayzak* • Donald Sutherland *Ronald Bartel* ■ *Dir* Ron Howard • *Scr* Gregory Widen

Backfire ★
Mystery 1950 · US · BW · 91min

With Gordon MacRae and Virginia Mayo in the leads, this ought to be a musical. As an ex-soldier just released from hospital and his obliging nurse, they're clearly unsuited to serious detective work as they investigate the disappearance of Edmond O'Brien, a friend of MacRae's wanted for murder. Too many writers cooked up the convoluted story, with its excess of flashbacks, and Vincent Sherman's direction fails to liven the pace. AE

Virginia Mayo *Julie Benson* • Gordon MacRae *Bob Corey* • Edmond O'Brien *Steve Connolly* • Dane Clark *Ben Arno* • Viveca Lindfors *Lysa Randolph* • Ed Begley *Capt Garcia* ■ *Dir* Vincent Sherman • *Scr* Larry Marcus, Ivan Goff, Ben Roberts

Backfire ★★18
Mystery thriller 1987 · US/Can · Colour · 88min

Occasionally, films get better performances than they deserve. Here it's Karen Allen and Keith Carradine who rise above the predictable plotting. Allen is pretty convincing, although her plan to bump off husband Jeff Fahey and share his loot with lover Dean Paul Martin is gruyère-like in its feasibility. Things perk up a bit when stranger Keith Carradine gives her a taste of her own hallucinogenic medicine, but the direction is too deliberate for any surprises. DP

Karen Allen *Mara* • Keith Carradine *Reed* • Jeff Fahey *Donnie* • Bernie Casey *Clint* • Dean Paul Martin *Jake* ■ *Dir* Gilbert Cates • *Scr* Larry Brand, Rebecca Reynolds

Background ★★PG
Drama 1953 · UK · BW · 79min

This stiff little picture is supposed to be a grown-up drama about the need to adopt a responsible attitude to divorce. However, by overplaying the "for the sake of the children" angle and allowing Valerie Hobson and Philip Friend to bicker in clipped BBC accents, director Daniel Birt succeeds not in discussing a difficult subject in a meaningful way, but only in drawing unintentional laughs. DP Some violence. *DVD*

Valerie Hobson *Barbie Lomax* • Philip Friend *John Lomax* • Norman Wooland *Bill Ogden* • Janette Scott *Jess Lomax* • Mandy Miller (1) *Linda Lomax* • Jeremy Spenser *Adrian Lomax* ■ *Dir* Daniel Birt • *Scr* Warren Chetham Strode, Don Sharp, from the play by Warren Chetham Strode

Background to Danger ★★★
Second World War spy drama 1943 · US · BW · 79min

One of the few starring roles not turned down by Warner Bros contract artist George Raft (he allegedly said no to *The Maltese Falcon* and *Casablanca* among others), this is a rattling good action film, with smoothie Raft battling Nazis in a studio-bound Turkey. Warner stalwarts Sydney Greenstreet and Peter Lorre are on welcome stand-by, but Brenda Marshall (then married to actor William Holden) is unfortunately a rather glamour-less leading lady. TS

George Raft *Joe Barton* • Brenda Marshall *Tamara* • Sydney Greenstreet *Colonel Robinson* • Peter Lorre *Zaleshoff* • Osa Massen *Ana Remzi* • Turhan Bey *Hassan* • Willard Robertson *McNamara* ■ *Dir* Raoul Walsh • *Scr* WR Burnett, from the novel *Uncommon Danger* by Eric Ambler

Backlash ★★★PG
Western 1956 · US · Colour · 80min

This is a bizarre western, with a superbly neurotic Richard Widmark as the gunfighter searching for gold and the sole survivor of a mining party that was massacred by Indians. Made by John Sturges just before his classic *Gunfight at the OK Corral*, this develops into a heavily symbolic Freudian story that has to be seen to be believed. AT *DVD*

Richard Widmark *Jim Slater* • Donna Reed *Karyl Orton* • William Campbell *Johnny Cool* • John McIntire *Jim Bonniwell* • Barton MacLane *George*

Lake • Edward Platt *Sheriff Marson* ■ *Dir* John Sturges • *Scr* Borden Chase, from a novel by Frank Gruber

Backstage ★★15
Music documentary 2000 · US · Colour · 86min

Chris Fiore's boisterous documentary cashes in on the hip-hop phenomenon by offering a purportedly frank and uncensored look at 1999's sell-out US rap extravaganza, the Hard Knock Life Tour. Featuring headlining MCs Jay-Z, DMX, Method Man, Redman and other key artists, the congratulatory film follows the standard formula of concert footage randomly combined with off-stage action and plenty of pointless posturing for the camera. Die-hard fans will doubtless lap up the profanity-riddled shots of stars smoking dope, groping groupies, squabbling and generally stroking their egos, but it's definitely a case of preaching to the converted. Ultimately anyone unfamiliar with the scene will gain little insight, especially since Fiore cuts away when anything really revealing occurs. SF *DVD*

Jay-Z • DM X *DMX* • Method Man • Redman • Beanie Sigel • Memphis Bleek ■ *Dir* Chris Fiore • *Cinematographers* Mark Petersson, Lenny Santiago, Elena Sorre

Backstreet Dreams ★★18
Drama 1990 · US · Colour · 95min

Jason O'Malley has no one to blame but himself as he co-produced, wrote and stars in this self-indulgent, contrived tale. It mixes elements of crime and family dramas to no logical effect, and an interesting cast can do little but flounder. O'Malley plays a small-time crook with an autistic child who finds an unlikely friend in PhD psychology student Brooke Shields when his wife (Sherilyn Fenn) leaves him. JF Violence, swearing, drug abuse.

Brooke Shields *Stephanie Bloom* • Jason O'Malley *Dean Costello* • Sherilyn Fenn *Lucy Costello* • Tony Fields *Manny Santana* • Burt Young *Luca Garibaldi* • Anthony Franciosa *Angelo Carnivale* ■ *Dir* Rupert Hitzig • *Scr* Jason O'Malley

Backtrack ★★★
Western 1969 · US · Colour · 95min

This Wild West reworking of *The Three Musketeers* is an entertaining curiosity. Not only do cast members of hit TV series *The Virginian* and *Laredo* reprise their characters, but background scenes and out-takes from the shows are utilised by director Earl Bellamy. Fernando Lamas revels in his villainy, but he proves no match for Doug McClure as the cowhand who teams up with a trio of Texas Rangers while on a mission to Mexico. But maybe most intriguing is the inclusion of Hollywood sirens Ida Lupino and Rhonda Fleming. DP

Neville Brand *Reese* • James Drury *Ramrod* • Doug McClure *Trampas* • Peter Brown *Chad* • William Smith *Riley* • Philip Carey *Captain Parmalee* • Ida Lupino *Mama Dolores* • Rhonda Fleming *Carmelita Flanagan* • Fernando Lamas *Captain Estrada* • Royal Dano *Faraway* • LQ Jones *Belden* ■ *Dir* Earl Bellamy • *Scr* Borden Chase

Backtrack ★★15
Mystery thriller 2015 · Aus · Colour · 90min

Nothing is what it seems in Michael Petroni's dull and derivative plundering of *The Sixth Sense*, *The Others* and *Don't Look Now*. It's revealed very early on that all the patients on the couch of a bereaved Australian psychologist (Adrien Brody) are actually ghosts from his past, intent on leading him to uncover a dark trauma. If only the reveal was worth the build-up – even the basic supernatural ingredients fail to cohere. AJ Violence, swearing. *DVD*

Adrien Brody *Peter Bower* • Sam Neill *Duncan Steward* • Robin McLeavy *Barbara Henning* • Bruce Spence *Felix* ■ *Dir/Scr* Michael Petroni

Backyard Wedding ★★
Romantic drama 2010 · US · Colour

True love never dies according to this flimsy made-for-TV fluff. Bride-to-be Alicia Witt finds her plans to marry in her parents'

garden disrupted by the reappearance of her childhood sweetheart and ex-husband (Teddy Sears). A thoroughly dislikeable fiancé (Ryan Bittle) adds the last piece to the simplistic jigsaw and ensures viewer support for the cute but far-fetched finale. SF

Frances Fisher *Eleanor* • Markie Post *Aunt Addie* • Alicia Witt *Kim Tyler* • Christie Lynn Smith *Kayla Tyler* ■ *Dir* Bradford May • *Scr* Nina Weinman

Bad ★★★★18
Black comedy 1976 · US · Colour · 58min

Camp icon Carroll Baker (*Baby Doll*) pulls out all the stops as a Queens housewife using her electrolysis business as a front for a freelance assassination operation. Very funny and very sick (the scene where a baby is thrown out of a window is justly infamous), director Jed Johnson's absurdist excursion into John Waters territory is a hugely satisfying satire on rotten 1970s society. Not for those of a nervous disposition. AJ

Carroll Baker *Mrs Aiken* • Perry King *LT* • Susan Tyrrell *Mary Aiken* • Stefania Casini *PG* • Cyrinda Foxe *RC* • Mary Boylan *Grandmother* • Brigid Polk *Estelle* ■ *Dir* Jed Johnson • *Scr* Pat Hackett, George Abagnalo

The Bad and the Beautiful ★★★★PG
Drama 1952 · US · BW · 113min

Riven by political investigation, competition from TV and the realisation that the Golden Age had passed, Hollywood produced a series of withering self-portraits in the early 1950s that revealed, beneath the tinsel, a sordidness worthy of Dorian Gray. Full of insider gags, Vincente Minnelli's fizzing melodrama touches more than a few raw nerves as it charts the decline and fall of a movie mogul (Kirk Douglas) through the eyes of a writer (Dick Powell), a director (Barry Sullivan) and an actress (Lana Turner). Allegedly an amalgam of David O Selznick and Val Lewton, the character of Jonathan Shields is made truly detestable by Douglas. DP *DVD*

Kirk Douglas *Jonathan Shields* • Lana Turner *Georgia Lorrison* • Walter Pidgeon *Harry Pebbel* • Dick Powell *James Lee Bartlow* • Barry Sullivan *Fred Amiel* • Gloria Grahame *Rosemary Bartlow* • Vanessa Brown *Kay Amiel* ■ *Dir* Vincente Minnelli • *Scr* Charles Schnee, from a story by George Bradshaw

Bad Behaviour ★★★15
Comedy drama 1992 · UK · Colour · 99min

This slightly eccentric comedy is in the Mike Leigh school of movie-making; in other words, wry, improvised, rooted in social nuance and dependent on the audience's recognition of character types. Director Les Blair has fashioned an amusing look at the external stresses that can crack a seemingly idyllic partnership, with Stephen Rea and Sinead Cusack as the oddly cast but affecting pair. This bobs along pleasingly, but with a curious lack of soul. SH Drug abuse.

Stephen Rea *Gerry McAllister* • Sinead Cusack *Ellie McAllister* • Philip Jackson *Howard Spink* • Clare Higgins *Jessica Kennedy* • Phil Daniels *The Nunn Brothers* • Mary Jo Randle *Winifred Turner* • Saira Todd *Sophie Bevan* • Amanda Boxer *Linda Marks* ■ *Dir/Scr* Les Blair

Bad Blood ★★★★PG
Biographical crime drama 1982 · UK/NZ · Colour · 110min

This has been rightly hailed as a key release in New Zealand cinema – even if many of those involved are foreign imports. Based on a notorious murder case, it stars Australian Jack Thompson as a reclusive farmer who refuses to surrender his weapons to the authorities during the Second World War, leading to a violent manhunt. British director Mike Newell keeps the tension simmering, while managing to look sympathetically at the farmer's plight. Thompson is superb, but veteran New Zealand character actor Martyn Sanderson steals the show. JF *DVD*

Jack Thompson *Stanley Graham* • Carol Burns *Dorothy Graham* • Denis Lill *Ted Best* • Donna Akersten *Doreen Bond* • Martyn Sanderson *Les North* • Marshall Napier *Trev Bond* ■ *Dir* Mike Newell • *Scr* Andrew Brown, from the book *Manhunt: The Story of Stanley Graham* by Howard Willis

Bad Boy Bubby ★★★ 18

Horror comedy 1993 · Aus/It · Colour · 109min

This experimental attempt at the cinema of the grotesque will not be to everyone's taste. It's the grim and controversial story of an imprisoned, abused, childlike 35-year-old who has never encountered another human being other than his mother, and what happens when the outside world finally crashes in on his squalid existence. Using differing cinematic styles to relate each of Bubby's adventures, director Rolf De Heer lets the viewer feel some of Bubby's disorientation. Hugely effective at best, irritating and shocking at worst. AJ Swearing, sex scenes. SD

Nicholas Hope *Bubby* • Claire Benito *Mom* • Ralph Cotterill *Pop* • Carmel Johnson *Angel* • Syd Brisbane *Yobbo* • Nikki Price *Screaming woman* • Norman Kaye *Scientist* • Paul Philpot *Paul* ■ *Dir/Scr* Rolf De Heer

Bad Boys ★★★ 18

Prison drama 1983 · US · Colour · 104min

Sean Penn stars as a young street thug who tries to steal a pile of drugs from a rival gang, only for it all to go horribly wrong. Penn ends up serving time in the same correctional facility as the rival he tried to cheat. Littered with violence (a revenge rape, shootings, fights) and flashy direction from Rick Rosenthal (*Halloween II*), this can be hard to stomach, but does boast an early strong and neurotic performance from Penn. JB DVD

Sean Penn *Mick O'Brien* • Reni Santoni *Ramon Herrera* • Jim Moody *Gene Daniels* • Eric Gurry *Horowitz* • Esai Morales *Paco Moreno* • Ally Sheedy *JC Walenski* ■ *Dir* Richard L Rosenthal [Rick Rosenthal] • *Scr* Richard DiLello

Bad Boys ★★★★ 18

Action comedy thriller 1995 · US · Colour · 113min

This is a perfect example of debuting director Michael Bay's slick abilities. In fact, this is probably one of the best buddy movies in years, with Bay's eye for cool ultra-violence enhanced by the inspired double-act of Will Smith and Martin Lawrence. The plot revolves around the audacious robbery of a huge cache of heroin. Enter our two heroes: Smith as the womanising bachelor and Lawrence as his married, strait-laced partner, who are forced to swap lifestyles to fool the only witness to the crime (Téa Leoni). JF Violence, swearing. DVD BLU

Martin Lawrence *Marcus Burnett* • Will Smith *Mike Lowrey* • Téa Leoni *Julie Mott* • Tcheky Karyo *Fouchet* • Theresa Randle *Theresa Burnett* • Marg Helgenberger *Alison Sinclair* • Nestor Serrano *Detective Sanchez* ■ *Dir* Michael Bay, *Scr* Michael Barrie, Jim Mulholland, Doug Richardson, from a story by George Gallo

Bad Boys II ★★ 15

Action comedy thriller 2003 · US · Colour · 140min

This overindulgent sequel reteams bickering cops Will Smith and Martin Lawrence and features high-gloss action and brutal bloodshed on a formidable scale. Add a hollow romantic subplot with Gabrielle Union and the banal premise of taking down a Cuban drugs lord, and this extends to a torturous length. By the end, you just want to escape from this smug, sadistic nonsense. JC Violence, swearing. DVD BLU

Martin Lawrence *Det Marcus Burnett* • Will Smith *Det Mike Lowrey* • Jordi Mollà *Hector Juan Carlos "Johnny" Tapia* • Gabrielle Union *Sydney "Syd" Burnett* • Peter Stormare *Alexei* • Theresa Randle *Theresa Burnett* • Joe Pantoliano *Captain Howard* ■ *Dir* Michael Bay • *Scr* Ron Shelton, Jerry Stahl, from a story by Marianne Wibberley, Cormac Wibberley, Ron Shelton, from characters by George Gallo

Bad Company ★★

Crime drama 1931 · US · BW · 73min

Following their success in *Her Man* (1930), director Tay Garnett reunited Ricardo Cortez and Helen Twelvetrees for this hammy Mob melodrama, which survived initial hostility to become one of the genre's real curios. It was one of the first movies to portray organised crime as a family business. Although occasionally prone to excess, Twelvetrees still demonstrates considerable pluck as the bride discovering that both lawyer husband John Garrick and brother Frank Conroy are Cortez's lackeys. DP

Helen Twelvetrees *Helen King* • Ricardo Cortez *Goldie Gorio* • John Garrick *Steven Carlyle* • Paul Hurst *Butler* • Frank Conroy *Markham King* • Frank McHugh *Doc* ■ *Dir* Tay Garnett • *Scr* Tom Buckingham, Tay Garnett, from the novel *Put on the Spot* by Jack Lait

Bad Company ★★★★ 15

Western 1972 · US · Colour · 88min

This oddball take on the American Civil War stars Jeff Bridges as the leader of runaways from conscription. He's joined by Barry Brown, and the crew become outlaws, drifting towards the Mississippi. As an evocation of past times, it's a remarkably successful venture for first-time director Robert Benton, a Robert Altman protégé who co-wrote *Bonnie and Clyde*. Woody Allen's one-time cinematographer, Gordon Willis, provides the autumnal mood that gives the idea an elegiac resonance. TH DVD

Jeff Bridges *Jake Rumsey* • Barry Brown *Drew Dixon* • Jim Davis (1) *Marshal* • David Huddleston *Big Joe* • John Savage *Loney* • Jerry Houser *Arthur Simms* • Damon Cofer *Jim Bob Logan* • Joshua Hill Lewis *Boog Bookin* ■ *Dir* Robert Benton • *Scr* David Newman, Robert Benton

Bad Company ★★★ 18

Thriller 1994 · US · Colour · 86min

Two of video's biggest draws, Lance Henriksen and Eric Roberts, team up for this novel spin on *The Hitcher*. Essentially a two-hander, Henriksen plays a salesman travelling cross-country being stalked by a serial killer. When he hooks up with sinister hitch-hiker Roberts, it becomes apparent that both men have dark secrets to hide. Director Victor Salva edgily plays out the cat-and-mouse games between two dangerous men. JF Violence, sex scenes, swearing, drug abuse.

Lance Henriksen *Jack Powell* • Eric Roberts *Adrian (Dusty)* • Brion James *Sheriff Gordon* • Sasha Jenson *Gerald* • Ana Gabriel *Dahlia* ■ *Dir/Scr* Victor Salva

Bad Company ★★ 15

Thriller 1995 · US · Colour · 103min

On paper this sexy thriller must have looked foolproof, with the two charismatic leads, Laurence Fishburne and Ellen Barkin, capable of generating a fair amount of on-screen steam. However, the plodding direction and an unnecessarily convoluted script put paid to any high expectations. Fishburne plays the newest recruit to a shadowy organisation specialising in industrial espionage, who becomes romantically involved with one of his colleagues (Barkin). JF Swearing, violence, sex scenes.

Ellen Barkin *Margaret Wells* • Laurence Fishburne *Nelson Crowe* • Frank Langella *Vic Grimes* • Spalding Gray *Walter Curl* • Michael Beach *Tod Stapp* • Gia Carides *Julie Ames* ■ *Dir* Damian Harris • *Scr* Ross Thomas

Bad Company ★★ 12

Action comedy thriller 2002 · US · Colour · 111min

This pedestrian take on the traditional buddy movie is a brash, self-satisfied tale, in which Anthony Hopkins's veteran CIA agent must transform unrefined motormouth Chris Rock into a believable replacement for his murdered agent twin brother. While there's no denying everything looks great, strip away the sleek veneer and what remains is a virtual A to Z of action comedy techniques and clichés. Chris Rock is implausible as he repeatedly slips out of character, but the one saving grace is Hopkins, whose dry wit and gentle dignity run rings around Rock's buffoonery. SF Violence, swearing. DVD

Anthony Hopkins *Gaylord Oakes* • Chris Rock *Jake Hayes/Kevin Pope* • Gabriel Macht *Agent Seale* • Peter Stormare *Adrik Vas* • John Slattery *Roland Yates* • Garcelle Beauvais-Nilon *CNN reporter, Nicole* • Kerry Washington *Julie* • Matthew Marsh *Dragan Adjanic* ■ *Dir* Joel Schumacher • *Scr* Jason Richman, Michael Browning, from a story by Gary Goodman, David Himmelstein

Bad Day at Black Rock ★★★★★ PG

Suspense drama 1955 · US · Colour · 78min

An Oscar-nominated Spencer Tracy gives a masterclass in screen acting, playing the one-armed Second World War veteran, who arrives in a small south-western town to visit a Japanese farmer. However, the remote desert community harbours a dark secret that Robert Ryan and his fellow rednecks are prepared to do anything to protect. Director John Sturges and cinematographer William C Mellor achieve an atmosphere of deceptive calm that makes the wait for the surprisingly shocking showdown all the more tense. Ryan is on career-best form, while Ernest Borgnine and Lee Marvin are marvellously malevolent as racist heavies. DP

Spencer Tracy *John J Macreedy* • Robert Ryan *Reno Smith* • Anne Francis *Liz Wirth* • Dean Jagger *Tim Horn* • Walter Brennan *Doc Velie* • John Ericson *Pete Wirth* • Ernest Borgnine *Coley Trimble* • Lee Marvin *Hector David* ■ *Dir* John Sturges • *Scr* Millard Kaufman, Don McGuire (adaptation), from the story *Bad Day at Hondo* by Howard Breslin • *Cinematographer* William C Mellor

Bad Education ★★★ 15

Drama 2004 · Sp · Colour · 101min

Rising film-maker Fele Martínez is approached by an old school pal (Gael García Bernal), who has a story entitled *The Visit*. The friend is revealed to be the director's boyhood love and elements of their story populate *The Visit*, including the abuse Bernal suffered at the hands of a priest. Martínez agrees to film the story with wannabe actor Bernal in the lead, but soon discovers that his leading man is living a shocking lie. Though Pedro Almodóvar skilfully manipulates his labyrinthine storyline, he overcomplicates this tribute to Hollywood melodrama with too many heavy-handed references. AJ Spanish +subtitles. Swearing, sex scenes, drug abuse. DVD

Gael García Bernal *Angel/Zahara/Juan* • Fele Martínez *Enrique Goded* • Daniel Giménez-Cacho [Daniel Gimenez Cacho] *Father Manolo* • Lluís Homar *Señor Berenguer* • Francisco Boira *Ignacio Rodriguez* • Javier Cámara *Paca* • Petra Martínez *Ignacio's mother* • Ignacio Pérez *Young Ignacio* • Raúl García Forneiro *Young Enrique* ■ *Dir/Scr* Pedro Almodóvar

The Bad Education Movie ★★★ 15

Comedy 2015 · UK · Colour · 87min

Jack Whitehall takes the BBC3 comedy he created and brings it to a head in a film version that benefits from his boundless enthusiasm. As haphazard teacher Alfie Wickers, he takes his students on a trip to Cornwall, but it derails quickly after he accidentally becomes aligned with Cornish extremists. Aiming for lowbrow from the outset, the film may befuddle the uninitiated as not every joke hits the mark. However, lovers of lewd humour and fans of the show will find plenty to chuckle at. JL Swearing, sexual references, drug abuse. DVD BLU

Jack Whitehall *Alfie Wickers* • Mathew Horne *Fraser* • Sarah Solemani *Rosie Gulliver* • Harry Enfield *Martin Wickers* • Jeremy Irvine *Atticus Hoye* ■ *Dir* Elliot Hegarty • *Scr* Jack Whitehall, Freddy Syborn

Bad for Each Other ★

Drama 1954 · US · BW · 82min

Doctor Charlton Heston returns from patching up wounded soldiers in Korea and must decide between a practice in the rich area of Pittsburgh or the nearby mining community. He chooses money and Lizabeth Scott until a catastrophe at the mine makes him rethink his priorities. Made before Heston acquired his epic-hero status, this moral medico-melo was panned by critics and was a major flop. AT

Charlton Heston *Dr Tom Owen* • Lizabeth Scott *Helen Curtis* • Dianne Foster *Joan Lasher* • Mildred Dunnock *Mrs Mary Owen* • Arthur Franz *Dr Jim Crowley* • Ray Collins *Dan Reasonover* ■ *Dir* Irving Rapper • *Scr* Irving Wallace, Horace McCoy, from the story *Scalpel* by Horace McCoy

Bad Girl ★★★ U

Melodrama 1931 · US · BW · 90min

A misleading title for the account of a year in the life of a young working-class couple, from their meeting to their marriage and the birth of their first child. James Dunn is a hardworking lad from the tenements intent on bettering himself, Sally Eilers the girl he loves, and Minna Gombell her best friend and his verbal sparring partner. Frank Borzage brings realism and humour to this depiction of life in a more innocent era. RK

Sally Eilers *Dorothy Haley* • James Dunn *Eddie Collins* • Minna Gombell *Edna Driggs* • Frank Darien *Lathrop* • William Pawley *Jim Haley* ■ *Dir* Frank Borzage • *Scr* Edwin Burke, from the novel by Viña Delmar [Vina Delmar], Eugene Delmar, from the play by Viña Delmar [Vina Delmar], Brian Marlowe

Bad Girls ★★ 15

Western 1994 · US · Colour · 96min

You can imagine the pitch: *Young Guns*, but with babes. It succeeds to a degree, despite the weak script. The bad girls of the title are four prostitutes (Andie MacDowell, Madeleine Stowe, Drew Barrymore and Mary Stuart Masterson) who find a price on their heads when Stowe shoots a disagreeable client. Their spirited performances are enjoyable to watch, even if they fail to deliver the toughness promised by the title. JF Violence, swearing, nudity. DVD

Madeleine Stowe *Cody Zamora* • Mary Stuart Masterson *Anita Crown* • Andie MacDowell *Eileen Spenser* • Drew Barrymore *Lilly Laronette* • James Russo *Kid Jarrett* • James LeGros *William Tucker* • Robert Loggia *Frank Jarrett* • Dermot Mulroney *Josh McCoy* ■ *Dir* Jonathan Kaplan • *Scr* Ken Friedman, Yolande Finch, from a story by Albert S Ruddy, Charles Finch, Gary Frederickson

Bad Guy ★★★ 18

Drama 2001 · S Kor · Colour · 102min

Cult Korean director Kim Ki-Duk's stylised view of exploitation and crime on the backstreets of Seoul combines disconcerting realism with moments of grim humour and unexpected tenderness. Duped into prostitution by loan sharks, student Seo Won endures endless humiliation in a gaudy shop-front brothel, while mobster Cho Jae-Hyeon keeps tabs on her through a two-way mirror. It's a sordid neon-lit hell, but the evocative design and doughty performances enable romance and a semblance of redemption to seep through. DP Korean +subtitles. DVD

Cho Jae-Hyeon *Han-gi* • Seo Won *Sun-hwa* • Kim Yoon-Tae *Jung-Tae* • Choi Duk-mun *Hyun-Ja* ■ *Dir/Scr* Kim Ki-Duk

Bad Guys ★ PG

Comedy 1986 · US · Colour · 86min

A dreadful attempt to cash-in on the huge popularity of wrestling, this has Adam Baldwin and Mike Jolly as a pair of bumbling policeman who turn to the ring when they lose their day jobs. However, their bid to become wrestling stars soon arouses enmity among the professional wrestling community. Bottom of the barrel. JF

Adam Baldwin *Skip Jackson* • Mike Jolly *Dave Atkins* • Michelle Nicastro *Janice Edwards* • Ruth Buzzi *Petal McGurk* • James Booth *Lord Percy* • Gene LeBell *Turk McGurk* ■ *Dir* Joel Silberg • *Scr* Brady W Setwater, Joe Gillis

Bad Influence ★★ 18

Mystery thriller 1990 · US · Colour · 94min

In this wildly implausible mystery thriller, a stranger (Rob Lowe) befriends a down-at-heel suit (James Spader) and is soon conducting a cat-and-mouse game of psychological manipulation. This soon disintegrates into pulp that wastes the talents of the gifted Spader. LH Swearing, violence, sex scenes, nudity, drug abuse.

DVD

Rob Lowe *Alex* • James Spader *Michael Boll* • Lisa Zane *Claire* • Christian Clemenson *Pismo Boll* • Kathleen Wilhoite *Leslie* • Tony Maggio *Patterson* • David Duchovny *Clubgoer* ■ *Dir* Curtis Hanson • *Scr* David Koepp

Bad Jim ★★★ PG

Western 1989 · US · Colour · 86min

This affectionate, cosily paced western comes up with a different spin on the story of Billy the Kid. Now it's the late outlaw's horse that is the focus of attention, with the film tracing the stallion's adventures as it falls into the hands of a trio of cowboys. Clyde Ware's direction is perhaps too unhurried, but he is rewarded with some amiable performances from a line-up that is headed by James Brolin and Richard Roundtree and features Clark Gable's son, John Clark Gable, making his film debut. JF

DVD

James Brolin *BD Sweetman* • Richard Roundtree *July* • John Clark Gable *JT Coleman* • Harry Carey Jr *CJ Lee* • Ty Hardin *Tom Jefford* • Rory Calhoun *Sam Harper* • Pepe Serna *Virgilio* • Suzanne Wouk *Elizabeth* ■ *Dir/Scr* Clyde Ware

Bad Karma ★★

Psychological thriller 2001 · US · Colour · 89min

British director John Hough is hamstrung by pedestrian plotting in this adaptation of Douglas Clegg's novel. The premise has mental patient Patsy Kensit go on a Lecter-like spree as she assumes various guises to wreak revenge on Patrick Muldoon, the psychiatrist she believes to be the reincarnation of Jack the Ripper, who murdered her in a previous life. Played with little enthusiasm and directed with even less. DP

Patsy Kensit *Agnes Thatcher* • Patrick Muldoon *Dr Trey Campbell* • Amy Locane *Carly Campbell* • Damian Chapa *Mr Miller* ■ *Dir* John Hough • *Scr* from the novel by Douglas Clegg

Bad Land: Road to Fury ★★ 15

Futuristic action drama
2014 · US · Colour · 95min

In this speculative drama set in the near future, rainfall is virtually unheard of and small farmers face a desperate battle for survival. Michael Shannon's remote holding is now dry as dust, and he clings on by supplying a nearby water-drilling operation with illicit booze, all the while trying to keep daughter Elle Fanning out of the grasp of scheming boyfriend Nicholas Hoult. This ambitious effort from writer director Jake Paltrow (Gwyneth's younger brother) has a lot going for it - except a compelling central storyline, and anticipation dissipates as the narrative wanders hither and thither. It's intermittently arresting but ultimately exasperating. TJ *DVD* *BL*

Michael Shannon *Ernest Holm* • Nicholas Hoult *Flem Lever* • Elle Fanning *Mary Holm* • Kodi Smit-McPhee *Jerome Holm* • Aimee Mullins *Katherine Holm* ■ *Dir/Scr* Jake Paltrow • *Cinematographer* Giles Nuttgens

Bad Lieutenant ★★★★ 18

Crime drama 1992 · US · Colour · 90min

When director Abel Ferrara's films are good, they are exceptionally good, as proved by this highly controversial tale of a corrupt cop (Harvey Keitel) getting one last chance at redemption when he investigates the rape of a nun. The problem is that she has forgiven her attackers and therefore

refuses to name them. This depiction of one man's vice-ridden hell is sexually explicit and brutally violent to an extreme degree, but the intention to shock audiences out of their complacency is Ferrara's point. Keitel gives one of the bravest performances of his career as the lapsed Catholic in serious debt and even worse moral and ethical chaos. AJ Drug abuse, swearing, nudity.

DVD *BL*

Harvey Keitel *Lieutenant* • Victor Argo *Beat cop* • Paul Calderone [Paul Calderon] *Cop* • Leonard Thomas *Cop* • Robin Burrows *Ariane* • Frankie Thorn *Nun* • *Scr* Zoe Tamarlaine Lund, Abel Ferrara • *Dir* Abel Ferrara

The Bad Lieutenant - Port of Call: New Orleans ★★★★ 18

Crime drama 2009 · US · Colour · 116min

Nicolas Cage gives one of the best performances of his career in this borderline insane film. Cage plays a police officer in post-Katrina New Orleans who develops a drug problem after picking up a back injury. But while supposedly investigating a gang murder, the demands of his drug habit, massive gambling debt, alcoholic father and hooker girlfriend (Eva Mendes) begin to take their toll on his increasingly frayed existence. Curiously, director Werner Herzog claims never to have seen or even heard of Abel Ferrara's 1992 cop drama Bad Lieutenant. That's not difficult to believe, as his picture is certainly a livelier, more human and less portentous take on the theme of one man's journey into a kind of personal hell. It's certainly a lot funnier, too. AS Violence, swearing, sex scenes, drug abuse. *DVD* *BL*

Nicolas Cage *Terence McDonagh* • Eva Mendes *Frankie Donnenfield* • Val Kilmer *Stevie Pruit* • Alvin "Xzibit" Joiner [Xzibit] *Big Fate* • Fairuza Balk *Heidi* • Shawn Hatosy *Armand Benoit* • Jennifer Coolidge *Genevieve* ■ *Dir* Werner Herzog • *Scr* William Finkelstein

The Bad Lord Byron ★★

Biographical drama 1949 · UK · BW · 84min

Released at a time when hopes were high that British cinema would be able to compete with Hollywood, this historical fantasy was massacred by the critics. It hasn't really improved with age, although it provided Dennis Price with a useful run-through for the role of Louis Mazzini in the following year's classic Kind Hearts and Coronets. There is precious little biography on display, but the way the script whizzes you round the celebrities of the day is fun. DP

Dennis Price *Lord Byron* • Mai Zetterling *Teresa Guiccioli* • Joan Greenwood *Lady Caroline Lamb* • Linden Travers *Augusta Leigh* • Sonia Holm *Arabella Millbank* • Raymond Lovell *John Hobhouse* • Leslie Dwyer *Fletcher* ■ *Dir* David MacDonald • *Scr* Terence Young, Anthony Thorne, Peter Quennell, Lawrence Kitchen, Paul Holt

Bad Man of Brimstone ★★

Western 1938 · US · BW · 88min

Ugly mug Wallace Beery stars in this western about a gunfighter redeemed when he meets his long-lost son, a boxer turned lawyer played by Dennis O'Keefe. (This was the first time O'Keefe used that name; up to this point, he was billed as Bud Flanagan.) It's the sort of morality tale that only MGM could make, with a message about the evil of violence and the importance of society. AT

Wallace Beery *"Trigger" Bill* • Virginia Bruce *Loretta Douglas* • Dennis O'Keefe *Jeffrey Burton* • Joseph Calleia *Ben* • Lewis Stone *Mr Jack Douglas* • Guy Kibbee *"Eight Ball" Harrison* ■ *Dir* J Walter Reuben • *Scr* Cyril Hume, Richard Maibaum, from a story by J Walter Reuben, Maurice Rapf

Bad Manners ★★★

Psychological drama 1997 · US · Colour · 88min

Jonathan Kaufer was briefly regarded as a promising young talent around Hollywood in the 1980s but his career never seemed to get into gear. This caustic drama shows what we have been missing. A bitter take on

academic and sexual jealousy, it finds David Strathairn and Bonnie Bedelia as married lecturers crossing psychological swords with the latter's former lover (Saul Rubinek) and his young girlfriend (Caroleen Feeney). It's a claustrophobic affair but beautifully played, written and directed. JF

David Strathairn *Wes Westlund* • Bonnie Bedelia *Nancy Westlund* • Saul Rubinek *Matt Carroll* • Caroleen Feeney *Kim Matthews* • Julie Harris (2) *Professor Harper* ■ *Dir* Jonathan Kaufer • *Scr* David Gilman, from his play Ghost in the Machine

Bad Man's River ★★ 12

Comedy western 1971 · Sp/It/Fr · Colour · 88min

There's very little to raise the temperature in this comedy western about an attempt to blow up a Mexican arms arsenal for revolutionary reasons. The bizarre casting of Lee Van Cleef and James Mason as rivals for the affection of Gina Lollobrigida doesn't help this co-production, and neither does the freeze-frame trickery of director Gene Martin. TH *DVD*

Lee Van Cleef *Roy King* • James Mason *Montero* • Gina Lollobrigida *Alicia* • Simon Andreu *Angel Sandos* • Diana Lorys *Dolores* • John Garko *Ed Pace* • Lone Ferk *Conchita* ■ *Dir* Gene Martin [Eugenio Martin] • *Scr* Gene Martin [Eugenio Martin], Philip Yordan

Bad Medicine ★★ 15

Comedy 1985 · US · Colour · 93min

After hitting it big with Police Academy and Cocoon, Steve Guttenberg came a cropper with this dim comedy. He is the lazy student who winds up in a dodgy medical school in Latin America - run by Alan Arkin, complete with preposterous accent - only to discover a conscience. Director Harvey Miller serves up an unappealing menu of old medical jokes and toilet humour, and then gets all sentimental. JF

Steve Guttenberg *Jeff Marx* • Alan Arkin *Dr Ramon Madera* • Julie Hagerty *Liz Parker* • Bill Macy *Dr Gerald Marx* • Curtis Armstrong *Dennis Gladstone* • Candy Milo *Maria Morales* ■ *Dir* Harvey Miller • *Scr* Harvey Miller, from the novel Calling Dr Horowitz by Steven Horowitz, Neil Offen

Bad Moon ★ 18

Horror thriller 1996 · US · Colour · 76min

Michael Paré is mauled by a beast in Nepal and returns home to sister Mariel Hemingway and her son, in the hope their love will stop him having to wear one of the most ill-fitting fur suits in cinematic history. It's up to the family dog to sniff out the truth - and plug the plot holes. AJ Nudity, sex scenes.

Mariel Hemingway *Janet* • Michael Paré *Ted Harrison* • Mason Gamble *Brett* ■ *Dir* Eric Red • *Scr* Eric Red, from the novel Thor by Wayne Smith

Bad Neighbours ★★★ 15

Comedy 2014 · US · Colour · 92min

High School Musical heart-throb Zac Efron continues to dirty up his image by playing the neighbour from hell in this outrageous comedy. His adversary is new dad Seth Rogen, who along with his missus (Rose Byrne), begins a campaign of dirty tricks in an attempt to shut Efron and his frat parties down. But their best-laid plans soon backfire. Director Nicholas Stoller pushes too hard against the boundaries of taste, with the big laughs more often coming when he just lets the actors bounce off each other. SP Swearing, sex scenes, drug abuse, nudity. *DVD* *BL*

Seth Rogen *Mac Radner* • Zac Efron *Teddy Sanders* • Rose Byrne *Kelly Radner* • Christopher Mintz-Plasse *Scoonie* • Dave Franco *Pete* • Lisa Kudrow *Dean Carol Gladstone* ■ *Dir* Nicholas Stoller • *Scr* Andrew Jay Cohen, Brendan O'Brien

Bad Neighbours 2 ★★★★ 15

Comedy 2016 · US · Colour · 92min

Far from appealing only to fans, this sequel subverts the college comedy with a feminist twist - surprising considering it's written by five men (including star Seth Rogen and director Nicholas Stoller). With their house sale delayed, Rogen and Rose Byrne are

once again at the mercy of teenage neighbours, this time in the shape of a rule-breaking sorority led by Chloë Grace Moretz. Moving at a fair old lick, Bad Neighbours 2 feels refreshingly incendiary, while Byrne and old nemesis Zac Efron are terrific. EAS Swearing, sexual references, drug abuse.

Seth Rogen *Mac Radner* • Zac Efron *Teddy Sanders* • Rose Byrne *Kelly Radner* • Chloë Grace Moretz *Shelby* • Selena Gomez *Madison* • Dave Franco *Pete* ■ *Dir* Nicholas Stoller • *Scr* Andrew Jay Cohen, Brendan O'Brien, Evan Goldberg, Seth Rogen, Nicholas Stoller, from characters by O'Brien, Cohen

The Bad News Bears ★★★ PG

Sports comedy 1976 · US · Colour · 97min

Walter Matthau is on fine form in one of the first sports comedies to use the now familiar "underdogs taking on the big boys" scenario. He plays a boozy coach trying to lick a bunch of no-hoper Little League baseball misfits into shape, with a little help from star-pitcher Tatum O'Neal. It's the relationship between coach and team that pulls you in, while the child actors are more than a match for old pro Matthau - especially O'Neal, who has more screen presence than dad Ryan ever had. A small winner. JC

Walter Matthau *Coach Morris Buttermaker* • Tatum O'Neal *Amanda Whurlizer* • Vic Morrow *Roy Turner* • Joyce Van Patten *Cleveland* • Ben Piazza *Councilman Whitewood* • Jackie Earle Haley *Kelly Leak* • Alfred W Lutter [Alfred Lutter] *Ogilvie* ■ *Dir* Michael Ritchie • *Scr* Bill Lancaster

The Bad News Bears in Breaking Training ★★

Sports comedy 1977 · US · Colour · 99min

The plucky Junior League baseball team is preparing for a big game, with the reward being a trip to Japan. Jackie Earle Haley's reunion with her estranged father William Devane affords director Michael Pressman one of several opportunities to explore the problems of growing up, but only wiseacre pitcher Jimmy Baio emerges from the mediocre ensemble in this far-fetched sequel. DP

William Devane *Mike Leak* • Clifton James *Sy Orlansky* • Jackie Earle Haley *Kelly Leak* • Jimmy Baio *Carmen Ronzonni* • Chris Barnes *Tanner Boyle* • Erin Blunt *Ahmad Abdul Rahim* • Jaime Escobedo *Jose Agilar* • George Gonzales *Miguel Agilar* ■ *Dir* Michael Pressman • *Scr* Paul Brickman, from characters by Bill Lancaster

The Bad News Bears Go to Japan ★

Sports comedy 1978 · US · Colour · 91min

Aside from Tony Curtis's star turn as a greedy hustler who takes charge of the titular Little Leaguers, there's little to say about this listless, pointless second sequel. Curtis sees a lucrative dollar opportunity in a tour of Japan, which involves the kids taking on the National Champions. A dud. JC

Tony Curtis *Marvin Lazar* • Jackie Earle Haley *Kelly Leak* • Matthew Douglas Anton *ERW Tillyard III* • Erin Blunt *Ahmad Abdul Rahim* • George Gonzales *Miguel Agilar* • Brett Marx *Jimmy Feldman* • David Pollock *Rudy Stein* ■ *Dir* John Berry • *Scr* Bill Lancaster

Bad News Bears ★★★ 12

Sports comedy 2005 · US · Colour · 108min

Billy Bob Thornton steps up to bat (and into Walter Matthau's shoes) as the grouchy coach in Richard Linklater's remake of the 1976 comedy. This story of an alcoholic ex-baseball pro who's hired to coach a motley team of kids is very formulaic and, as the competitive stakes are raised, the clichés come thick and fast. But it's impossible not to laugh at Thornton's outrageous antics and stinging one-liners. Delightfully disrespectful. SP Swearing. *DVD*

Billy Bob Thornton *Morris Buttermaker* • Greg Kinnear *Roy Bullock* • Marcia Gay Harden *Liz Whitewood* • Sammi Kane Kraft *Amanda Whurlizer* • Jeffrey Davies *Kelly Leak* • Timmy Deters *Tanner Boyle* • Brandon Craggs *Mike Engelberg* • Ridge Canipe *Toby Whitewood* • Troy

Gentile *Matthew Hooper* ■ *Dir* Richard Linklater • *Scr* Bill Lancaster, Glenn Ficara, John Requa, from the 1976 film

Bad Santa ★★★ 15
Seasonal crime black comedy
2003 · US/Ger · Colour · 88min

If Christmas brings out the "bah, humbug" in you, then this pitch-black comedy from *Ghost World* director Terry Zwigoff will be right up your alley. Flouting the sentimental spirit of the season and then some, it stars Billy Bob Thornton as a grouchy, alcoholic safe-cracker who works as a department store Santa so he can rob his employers. But on his last job, the foul-mouthed, determinedly child-unfriendly Stokes becomes involved with a bullied, overweight boy who is apparently immune to the river of bile coming out of Thornton's mouth. Sounds like a recipe for a feel-good ending, but Zwigoff resists that temptation, and with Thornton giving a terrific deadpan performance, this is the perfect antidote to the usual saccharine Christmas confection. A belated sequel is due in late 2016. JA Swearing, violence, sex scenes. DVD BL
Billy Bob Thornton *Willie T Stokes* • Tony Cox *Marcus* • Brett Kelly *The Kid* • Lauren Graham *Sue* • Lauren Tom *Lois* • Bernie Mac *Gin* • John Ritter *Bob Chipeska* ■ *Dir* Terry Zwigoff • *Scr* Glenn Ficarra, John Requa

The Bad Seed ★★★★
Psychological horror 1956 · US · BW · 128min

This is an adaptation of playwright Maxwell Anderson's Broadway and West End success about an irredeemably evil eight-year-old child, played on stage and here on screen by the brilliant Patty McCormack. Also imported from the Broadway production are Nancy Kelly as the girl's mother, Eileen Heckart, as the mother of one of the girl's schoolfriends, and a particularly effective Henry Jones as the venal caretaker. This is *Grand Guignol* stuff, really, but veteran Mervyn LeRoy directs effectively. TS
Nancy Kelly *Christine* • Patty McCormack *Rhoda* • Henry Jones *LeRoy* • Eileen Heckart *Mrs Daigle* • Evelyn Varden *Monica* • William Hopper *Kenneth* • Paul Fix *Bravo* • Jesse White *Emory* ■ *Dir* Mervyn LeRoy • *Scr* John Lee Mahin, from the play by Maxwell Anderson and the novel by William March

Bad Sister ★★ U
Drama 1931 · US · BW · 64min

Extrovert and flirtatious small-town girl Sidney Fox falls for a big-city swindler Humphrey Bogart. The couple elopes, with unhappy consequences, but her actions lead to the happy union of her respectable rejected suitor Conrad Nagel and her demure sister Bette Davis. This flaccid drama is notable only as marking Davis's screen debut – though it gives little intimation of the fact that she wouldn't be playing the subsidiary good girl for long. RK DVD
Conrad Nagel *Dr Dick Lindley* • Sidney Fox *Marianne* • Bette Davis *Laura* • ZaSu Pitts *Minnie* • Slim Summerville *Sam* • Charles Winninger *Mr Madison* • Emma Dunn *Mrs Madison* • Humphrey Bogart *Corliss* ■ *Dir* Hobart Henley • *Scr* Raymond L Schrock, Tom Reed, Edwin H Knopf, from the novel *The Flirt* by Booth Tarkington

The Bad Sleep Well ★★ PG
Crime drama 1960 · Jpn · BW · 127min

In this drama about corporate corruption in postwar Japan, Toshiro Mifune lays down his samurai sword to play a housing company employee who marries the boss's daughter purely to expose his new father-in-law, whom he believes was responsible for his own father's "suicide". Akira Kurosawa turns what should have been a taut thriller into a rather sombre exercise in morality, with Shakespearean themes of revenge and remorse. The film flopped in Japan (critiques of the economic recovery were rare) and led to the collapse of the director's production company. AT Japanese +subtitles. DVD
Toshiro Mifune *Koichi Nishi* • Takeshi Kato *Itakura* • Masayuki Mori *Iwabuchi* • Takashi Shimura *Moriyama* • Akira Nishimura *Shirai* ■

Dir Akira Kurosawa • *Scr* Akira Kurosawa, Shinobu Hashimoto, Hideo Oguni, Ryuzo Kikushima, Eijiro Hisaita

Bad Taste ★★★★ 18
Horror comedy 1987 · NZ · Colour · 87min

Director Peter Jackson began his career began with this cheerfully disgusting Kiwi sickie, made over a four-year period. Directed in chaotic fashion, with epic quantities of gore, flying viscera, macabre humour and wild special effects, Jackson's man-eating alien invasion film remained the bloody benchmark of sci-fi horror, though he topped it five years later with *Braindead*. The title says it all, so those of a sensitive disposition should steer clear. AJ DVD
Peter Jackson *Derek/Robert* • Mike Minett *Frank* • Peter O'Herne *Barry* • Terry Potter *Ozzy* • Craig Smith *Giles* • Doug Wren *Lord Crumb* ■ *Dir/Scr* Peter Jackson

Bad Teacher ★★ 15
Comedy 2011 · US · Colour · 93min

This misfiring comedy stars Cameron Diaz as a hard-drinking, hopeless educator who's desperate to get breast-enhancement surgery. When she hears of a teaching contest with a big-money prize, Diaz vows to turn over a new leaf, believing her new-found conscientiousness and reupholstered cleavage will win the heart of handsome Justin Timberlake. But director Jake Kasdan bundles together a mishmash of high-school movie clichés and off-colour toilet humour, with the flimsy plot and faltering pace providing far too few laughs. TeS Swearing, nudity, drug abuse. DVD BL
Cameron Diaz *Elizabeth Halsey* • Justin Timberlake *Scott Delacorte* • Jason Segel *Russell Gettis* • Lucy Punch *Amy Squirrel* • Phyllis Smith *Lynn* • John Michael Higgins *Principal Wally Snur* ■ *Dir* Jake Kasdan • *Scr* Gene Stupnitsky, Lee Eisenberg

Bad Timing ★★★★ 18
Drama 1980 · UK · Colour · 117min

One to admire or abhor, director Nicolas Roeg's case history of a sexual obsession dazzles with flashbacks and disturbs with "What if?" sidetracks. Art Garfunkel is the psycho-psychiatrist involved with Theresa Russell in a sadistic affair, which starts with the girl's suicide attempt and ends with even nastier revelations about their relationship. Roeg piles on angst-ridden chic to the detriment of human values and sympathy, but it's well worth watching. TH Swearing, sex scenes, nudity. DVD BL
Art Garfunkel *Alex Linden* • Theresa Russell *Milena Flaherty* • Harvey Keitel *Inspector Netusil* • Denholm Elliott *Stefan Vognic* • Dana Gillespie *Amy* • Daniel Massey *Foppish man* ■ *Dir* Nicolas Roeg • *Scr* Yale Udoff

Badge of the Assassin ★★★ 15
Crime drama based on a true story
1985 · US · Colour · 94min

Another tough-guy role for James Woods, though in this hard-edged and controversial film he's on the right side of the law for a change. As assistant district attorney Robert K Tanenbaum, it's his job to find the men responsible for the murder of two police officers. Woods's powerful performance, the strong supporting cast and the tense, fact-based plotline add up to an entertaining TV-movie package. NF
James Woods *Robert K Tanenbaum* • Yaphet Kotto *Cliff Fenton* • Alex Rocco *Bill Butler* • David Harris *Lester May* • Steven Keats *Skelton* • Larry Riley *Herman Bell* • Pam Grier *Alie* • Rae Dawn Chong *Christine* • Richard Bradford *Delsa* ■ *Dir* Mel Damski • *Scr* Lawrence Roman, from the book by Robert K Tanenbaum, Philip Rosenberg

The Badlanders ★★★
Western 1958 · US · Colour · 83min

This decent western, directed by the reliable Delmer Daves, stars Alan Ladd and Ernest Borgnine as ex-convicts who emerge from prison in Yuma with a plan to rob a gold mine. Since this involves blowing up a mountain and escaping with half a ton of rock, it takes some organising. The picture is actually less a western than a suspense thriller, with plenty of surprises, a thrilling chase through a carnival and some excellent performances, notably from Nehemiah Persoff as the gunpowder expert. AT
Alan Ladd *Peter Van Hock* • Ernest Borgnine *John McBain* • Katy Jurado *Anita* • Claire Kelly *Ada Winton* • Kent Smith *Cyril Lounsberry* • Nehemiah Persoff *Vincente* • Robert Emhardt *Sample* • Anthony Caruso *Comanche* • Adam Williams *Leslie* ■ *Dir* Delmer Daves • *Scr* Richard Collins, from the novel *The Asphalt Jungle* by WR Burnett

Badlands ★★★★ 18
Crime drama 1973 · US · Colour · 89min

Reclusive director Terrence Malick's atmospheric crime drama was the *Natural Born Killers* of its day. In a moodily disturbing account of the infamous Charlie Starkweather murders of the 1950s, Martin Sheen plays the alienated killer on a psychopathic rampage through the American Midwest, accompanied by his loyal teenage girlfriend, Sissy Spacek. Both leads are highly effective as the icy duo caught up in a series of horrific events that are dazzlingly and daringly depicted by Malick. Yet, it's this understated approach, defying convention by leaving loose ends, that makes this a truly scary experience. AJ Violence, swearing. DVD
Martin Sheen *Kit Carruthers* • Sissy Spacek *Holly* • Warren Oates *Father* • Ramon Bieri *Cato* • Alan Vint *Deputy* • Gary Littlejohn *Sheriff* • John Carter *Rich man* • Bryan Montgomery *Boy* • Gail Threlkeld *Girl* ■ *Dir/Scr* Terrence Malick

Badman's Territory ★★★ U
Western 1946 · US · BW · 97min

An excellent Randolph Scott western, this features such tried-and-tested supporting players as grizzled George "Gabby" Hayes and the great Chief Thundercloud. Rather like those Universal horror movies that gathered together Dracula, Frankenstein, the monster and the Wolf Man, this RKO special has Jesse and Frank James, Sam Bass, Belle Starr and the Dalton gang as opponents to Scott, as he attempts to turn the Oklahoma territory into a full-grown state. Cleverly directed by Tim Whelan, who doesn't let the clutter of characters spoil the flow. TS
Randolph Scott *Mark Rowley* • Ann Richards *Henryette Alcott* • George "Gabby" Hayes *Coyote* • Steve Brodie *Bob Dalton* • Ray Collins *Colonel Farewell* • Lawrence Tierney *Jesse James* • Tom Tyler *Frank James* • Nestor Paiva *Sam Bass* • Isabel Jewell *Belle Starr* • William Moss *Bill Dalton* ■ *Dir* Tim Whelan • *Scr* Jack Natteford, Luci Ward, Clarence Upson Young, Bess Taffel

Bagdad Café ★★★★ 12
Comedy drama 1987 · W Ger · Colour · 103min

Co-written and co-produced with his wife Eleanore and starring his regular favourite Marianne Sägebrecht, German director Percy Adlon's first American feature is a hypnotic blend of feminist fantasy and Capra-esque feel-good. Set in a run-down diner in the middle of the Arizona desert, the action centres on the impact Sägebrecht has on the claustrophobic local community, in particular on café boss CCH Pounder and an ageing hippy artist, played with an instinctive comic touch by Jack Palance. Although there are some shrewd asides on racial friction, this is still the kind of gentle comedy you can simply sink into your armchair and enjoy. DP Brief swearing, nudity. DVD
Marianne Sägebrecht *Jasmin Münchgstettner* • CCH Pounder *Brenda* • Jack Palance *Rudi Cox* • Christine Kaufmann *Debby* • Monica Calhoun *Phyllis* • Darron Flagg *Sal Junior* • George Aguilar *Cahuenga* • G Smokey Campbell *Sal* • Hans Stadlbauer *Münchgstettner* • Alan S Craig *Eric* ■ *Dir* Percy Adlon • *Scr* Percy Adlon, Eleonore Adlon

Baggage Claim ★★ 12
Romantic comedy 2013 · US · Colour · 92min

If you're happy with the notion that a woman isn't complete without a husband, you won't instantly reject this outdated romantic comedy. Paula Patton plays a flight attendant embarking on an implausible 30-day, 30,000-mile odyssey to man-up in time for her younger sister's wedding. However, you won't be surprised to hear that her search for love ends in a rather more Earth-bound location. It's fun in a dumb kind of way, but it sets feminism back several decades. DA Swearing, sexual references.
Paula Patton *Montana Moore* • Derek Luke *William Wright* • Taye Diggs *Langston Jefferson Battle III* • Boris Kodjce *Graham* • Tremaine Neverson [Trey Songz] *Damon Diesel* • Djimon Hounsou *Quinton Jamison* ■ *Dir* David E Talbert • *Scr* David E Talbert, from his novel

The Bait ★★★★ 15
Crime drama 1995 · Fr · Colour · 111min

Shot in the same uncompromising manner as his *policier*, *L.627*, Bertrand Tavernier's lowlife thriller is darker than the average *film noir* as both the crime and the violence are so chillingly pitiless. Driven by an ambition to open a chain of boutiques in the States, shopgirl-cum-model Marie Gillain agrees to distract her wealthy male contacts while they're burgled by boyfriend Olivier Sitruk and his doltish buddy Bruno Putzulu. The resolution is never in doubt, but the action remains engrossing as Tavernier, aided by a credible cast, strips the daydreams down to their seedy reality. DP French +subtitles.
Marie Gillain *Nathalie* • Olivier Sitruk *Eric* • Bruno Putzulu *Bruno* • Richard Berry *Alain* • Philippe Duclos *Antoine* • Marie Ravel *Karine* • Clotilde Courau *Patricia* • Jean-Louis Richard *Restaurant owner* ■ *Dir* Bertrand Tavernier • *Scr* Colo Tavernier O'Hagan, Bertrand Tavernier, from a book by Morgan Sportes

Bait ★★★★ 18
Horror 2015 · UK · Colour · 83min

In a town in northern Britain, best friends Victoria Smurfit and Joanne Mitchell struggle to expand their market stall, which leaves them at the mercy of a charming but ruthless loan shark (chillingly played by RSC actor Jonathan Slinger). Director Dominic Brunt (*Emmerdale*'s Paddy Kirk) creates an ominous atmosphere punctuated by staccato bursts of shocking violence, while Slinger creates one of British cinema's vilest villains, excruciatingly smug but menacing to boot. JA Violence, swearing, sex scenes. CS
Victoria Smurfit *Bex* • Jonathan Slinger *Jeremy* • Joanne Mitchell *Dawn* • Adam Fogerty *Si* • Rula Lenska *Linda* ■ *Dir* Dominic Brunt • *Scr* Paul Roundell

The Baited Trap ★★★
Crime thriller 1959 · US · Colour · 86min

This tense suspense film from writer/ director Norman Panama – a man more usually known for his comedies – is a better movie than it ought to be thanks to an above-average cast. Lawyer Richard Widmark returns to his small home town of Tula to help villainous Lee J Cobb escape into Mexico. There he must deal with his father (Carl Benton Reid) and his ex-girlfriend (Tina Louise), who's now married to Widmark's brother. TH
Richard Widmark *Ralph Anderson* • Lee J Cobb *Victor Massonetti* • Earl Holliman *Tippy Anderson* • Tina Louise *Linda Anderson* • Carl Benton Reid *Sheriff Anderson* • Lorne Greene *Davis* ■ *Dir* Norman Panama • *Scr* Richard Alan Simmons, Norman Panama

The Baker ★★ 12
Comedy 2007 · UK · Colour · 82min

Despite his inherent charm and sharp comic timing, Damian Lewis cannot sustain this half-baked film written and directed by his younger brother Gareth. Indeed, the first-time director's biggest mistake is to take the focus off Lewis's hitman Milo, who flees to a small Welsh village in search of normality and ends up running a bakery. But he soon discovers that life there is far from normal. The misanthropic local characters overwhelm the story, and even more irritating is the heavy reliance on silly coincidences and misunderstandings to drive the action forward. SP DVD

Damian Lewis *Milo* • Kate Ashfield *Rhiannon* • Nikolaj Coster Waldau [Nikolaj Coster-Waldau] *Bjørn* • Michael Gambon *Leo* • Steven Spiers *Bryn* • Dyfan Dwyfor *Eggs* • William Thomas *Alun* • Annette Badland *Martha* ■ *Dir/Scr* Gareth Lewis

B | Baker's Hawk ★★★

Western   1976 · US · Colour · 96min

Clint Walker only enjoyed brief stardom, but this family western shows what a capable actor he could be. Here he plays the father of Lee H Montgomery, a young boy who helps recluse Burl Ives and his pet hawk escape from hooligans. It could be an episode of the TV series *Cheyenne*, which made Walker's name before that other Clint (Eastwood) moseyed along. However, Lyman D Dayton's direction gives the film a moral dimension that lifts it out of the ordinary. **TH**

Clint Walker *Dan Baker* • Burl Ives *Mr McGraw* • Diane Baker *Jenny Baker* • Lee H Montgomery [Lee Montgomery] *Billy Baker* • Alan Young *Mr Carson* • Taylor Lacher *Sweeney* ■ *Dir* Lyman D Dayton *Lyman Dayton]* • *Scr* Dan Greer, Hal Harrison Jr, from the novel by Jack Bickham

The Baker's Wife ★★★★

Comedy   1938 · Fr · BW · 118min

While Marcel Pagnol's style may be regarded as hopelessly old-fashioned by many post-New Wave critics, there's no escaping the wit and warmth of this tale of simple Provençal folk. Villagers have to band together to disrupt the romance between a shepherd (Charles Moulin) and a faithless wife (Ginette Leclerc) to encourage their cuckolded baker to make bread again. One of the screen's finest comic actors, Raimu is superb as the broken-hearted *boulanger*. But what makes the film so irresistible is Pagnol's attention to detail and mastery at creating the close-knit communal atmosphere. **DP** French +subtitles.

Raimu *Aimable, the baker* • Ginette Leclerc *Aurelie, the baker's wife* • Charles Moulin *Dominique, the shepherd* • Robert Vattier *The priest* • Robert Bassac *The schoolteacher* ■ *Dir* Marcel Pagnol • *Scr* Marcel Pagnol, from the novel *Jean le Bleu* by Jean Giono

Le Bal ★★★

Musical   1983 · Alg/Fr/It · Colour · 107min

In addition to landing a best foreign film Oscar nomination, Ettore Scola won the best director prize at Berlin for this stylised adaptation of Jean-Claude Penchenat's experimental stage play. Original members of the Théâtre du Campagnol cast re-enact routines inspired by events in France from 1936 to the early 1980s. But while their expertise is undeniable and Vladimir Cosma's score cleverly plays on the popular tunes of the different periods, the action says more about Scola's ingenuity than the incidents on which it's supposed to be commenting. **DP** In French.

Etienne Guichard *Provincial student* • Régis Bouquet *Ballroom owner* • Francesco de Rosa *Toni* • Nani Noël *Goodtime girl* • Liliane Delval *Girl with long hair* • Arnault Lecarpentier *Young printer* • Martine Chauvin *Flower girl* ■ *Dir* Ettore Scola • *Scr* Ettore Scola, Ruggero Maccari, Furio Scarpelli, Jean-Claude Penchenat, from the Théâtre du Campagnol stage production, from an original idea by Jean-Claude Penchenat

Bal ★★★★

Drama   2010 · Tur/Ger · Colour · 104min

The winner of the Golden Bear at the 2010 Berlin film festival, writer/director Semih Kaplanoglu's film (the title translates as *Honey*) completes his reverse chronology trilogy, following 2007's *Egg* and 2008's *Milk*. Having already covered his hero Yusuf's adulthood and youth, Kaplanoglu returns to his childhood in the wooded mountains of north-eastern Turkey, where six-year-old Yusuf (Bora Altas) struggles at school and would much rather learn about wildlife with his beekeeping father. It's a poignant study of passing innocence. **DP** Turkish +subtitles.

Bora Altas *Yusuf* • Erdal Besikcioglu *Yakup* • Tulin Ozen *Zehra* • Kamil Yilmaz *Hamdi's father* • Adem Kurkut *Policeman* • Erhan Keskin

---

Policeman ■ *Dir* Semih Kaplanoglu • *Scr* Semih Kaplanoglu, Orcun Koksal • *Cinematographer* Baris Ozbicer

La Balance ★★★★18

Crime thriller   1982 · Fr · Colour · 101min

An American in Paris was responsible for this hard-as-nails thriller, which won several Césars including best picture, best actor and best actress. Stylishly exploiting the seedy streets of Belleville, Bob Swaim brings an unswerving authenticity to this tale of a pimp (Philippe Léotard) who agrees to inform on neighbourhood thug Maurice Ronet to prevent detective Richard Berry from harming the whore he adores. Although Swaim makes the most of the action sequences, the film's real strength lies in the conviction of the performances. Nathalie Baye's hardened hooker is a revelation. **DP** French +subtitles. *DVD*

Nathalie Baye *Nicole* • Philippe Léotard *Dede* • Richard Berry *Inspector Paluzzi* • Christophe Malavoy *Tintin* • Jean-Paul Connart *The Belgian* • Bernard Freyd *The Captain* • Albert Dray *Carlini* • Florent Pagny *Simoni* • Maurice Ronet *Roger Massina* ■ *Dir/Scr* Bob Swaim

The Balcony ★★★15

Drama fantasy   1963 · US · BW · 80min

This is a fascinating film version of Jean Genet's controversial play set in a brothel. While the revolutionaries occupy the streets below, the brothel becomes the headquarters of the government, the state police, religion and the media. The brothel itself is designed like a film studio, with different sets, lighting and even back projection to add "reality" to the clients' sexual fantasies. Deeply allegorical, it captures the off-Broadway ambience of the period. **AT** Swearing, sex scenes. *DVD*

Shelley Winters *Madame Irma* • Peter Falk *Police chief* • Lee Grant *Carmen* • Ruby Dee *Thief* • Peter Brocco *Judge* • Jeff Corey *Bishop* • Joyce Jameson *Penitent* • Arnette Jens *Horse* • Leonard Nimoy *Roger* ■ *Dir* Joseph Strick • *Scr* Ben Maddow, from the play by Jean Genet • *Music* Igor Stravinsky

Ball of Fire ★★★★U

Comedy   1941 · US · BW · 111min

This scintillating and hysterically funny update of *Snow White and the Seven Dwarfs* features Barbara Stanwyck as Sugarpuss O'Shea, a moll on the run who falls in with a group of wacky academics working on a language dictionary. Gawky, lovable Gary Cooper is the professor quizzing fireball Babs (hence the title) about contemporary slang. Director Howard Hawks creates a minor comic masterpiece from the witty screenplay by Billy Wilder and Charles Brackett, and all the performances are spot-on. Hawks remade the film seven years later as *A Song Is Born*. **TS** *DVD*

Gary Cooper *Professor Bertram Potts* • Barbara Stanwyck *Sugarpuss O'Shea* • Oscar Homolka *Professor Gurkakoff* • Henry Travers *Professor Jerome* • SZ "Cuddles" Sakall [SZ Sakall] *Professor Magenbruch* • Tully Marshall *Professor Robinson* • Leonid Kinskey *Professor Quintana* ■ *Dir* Howard Hawks • *Scr* Charles Brackett, Billy Wilder, from the story *From A to Z* by Thomas Monroe, Billy Wilder

Ballad in Blue ★★U

Drama   1964 · UK · BW · 88min

Ray Charles's only major film is a well-intentioned though mawkish tale, in which the singer (playing himself) enriches the lives of a mother and her blind son. Charles is no actor and the rest of the cast seem to have picked up his slow, deliberate pace; but fans will not want to miss him singing a dozen numbers, including *Hit the Road, Jack* and *Busted*. **DM** *DVD* ⊞

Ray Charles • Tom Bell *Steve Collins* • Mary Peach *Peggy Harrison* • Piers Bishop *David Harrison* • Dawn Addams *Gina Graham* • Betty McDowall *Helen Babbidge* • Lucy Appleby *Margaret Babbidge* • Joe Adams *Fred Parker* ■ *Dir* Paul Henreid • *Scr* Burton Wohl, from a story by Paul Henreid, Wohl

---

Ballad of a Soldier ★★★★PG

War drama   1959 · USSR · BW · 84min

The winner of the special jury prize at Cannes, Grigori Chukhrai's picaresque home-front drama is a classic example of the socialist-realist style films that dominated postwar Soviet cinema. As much a statement about the resilience of Stalin's citizenry as a pacifist tract, this is a surprisingly sentimental tale, in which the naive hero (Vladimir Ivashov) encounters a series of people as he travels to spend a four-day leave with his mother. Particularly striking is the contrast between the pitiable infidelity of a comrade's frightened wife and Ivashov's brief romance with peasant girl Shanna Prokhorenko. **DP** Russian +subtitles. *DVD*

Vladimir Ivashov *Alyosha* • Shanna Prokhorenko *Shura* • Antonina Maximova *Alyosha's mother* • Nikolai Kruchkov *General* ■ *Dir* Grigori Chukhrai • *Scr* Grigori Chukhrai, Valentin Yezhov

The Ballad of Cable Hogue ★★★★PG

Comedy western   1970 · US · Colour · 116min

This elegy for the Old West about an itinerant prospector who "found water where there wasn't" is a beautifully crafted and very funny film. Like director Sam Peckinpah's earlier and more explicitly violent *The Wild Bunch*, it leaves an audience with nostalgic pangs for a lifestyle that perhaps only existed in motion pictures. Tender and ironic by turns, it contains marvellous performances from a whimsical Jason Robards (arguably a career best) in the title role as Hogue and sexy Stella Stevens (definitely a career best) as the hooker who becomes his lady. **TS** Swearing. *DVD*

Jason Robards *Cable Hogue* • Stella Stevens *Hildy* • David Warner *Joshua* • Strother Martin *Bowen* • Slim Pickens *Ben* • LQ Jones *Taggart* • Peter Whitney *Cushing* ■ *Dir* Sam Peckinpah • *Scr* John Crawford, Edmund Penney

The Ballad of Gregorio Cortez ★★★15

Western based on a true story
1983 · US · Colour · 105min

This unusual western is based on the true story of a Mexican cowhand, who was mistakenly arrested by Texas Rangers in 1901. He kills a sheriff in the struggle to escape and leads the posse after him on a merry dance. Shot in the locations where the real Cortez was actually imprisoned and tried, this saga of racial bigotry and language barriers gains drama by being told from multiple perspectives. Edward James Olmos makes a sympathetic Cortez, even if the film is a trifle worthy at times. **AJ**

Edward James Olmos *Gregorio Cortez* • James Gammon *Sheriff Frank Fly* • Tom Bower *Boone Choate* • Bruce McGill *Bill Blakely* • Brion James *Captain Rogers* • Alan Vint *Mike Trimmell* • Timothy Scott *Sheriff Morris* ■ *Dir* Robert M Young • *Scr* Victor Villasenor, Robert M Young, from the novel *With His Pistol in His Hands* by Americo Paredes

The Ballad of Jack and Rose ★★15

Drama   2005 · US · Colour · 111min

Daniel Day-Lewis stars in this drama written and directed by his wife, Rebecca Miller, daughter of playwright Arthur Miller. Day-Lewis plays a dying eco-warrior living in the remnants of an idealistic island commune, alone save for his sheltered 16-year-old daughter (Camilla Belle). The acting is spot-on, but the film is dull and dated, with a final, rather obvious "message" that's hammered home. **DA** Swearing. *DVD*

Camilla Belle *Rose Slavin* • Daniel Day-Lewis *Jack Slavin* • Catherine Keener *Kathleen* • Ryan McDonald *Rodney* • Paul Dano *Thaddius* • Jason Lee *Gray* • Jena Malone *Red Berry* • Beau Bridges *Marty Rance* ■ *Dir/Scr* Rebecca Miller

The Ballad of Josie ★★PG

Comedy western   1968 · US · Colour · 97min

Bland is too strong a word for this tepid flick, which never really catches fire despite

---

being directed by western ace Andrew V McLaglen. Doris Day is good, even though by this stage in her career she was becoming hard to cast, but the men are uninteresting - only Andy Devine brings a sense of authenticity to this western where the jeans look newly ironed and the faces are too well scrubbed. **TS**

Doris Day *Josie Minick* • Peter Graves (2) *Jason Meredith* • George Kennedy *Arch Ogden* • Andy Devine *Judge Tatum* • William Talman *Charlie Lord* • David Hartman *Fonse Pruitt* • Guy Raymond *Doc* ■ *Dir* Andrew V McLaglen • *Scr* Harold Swanton

The Ballad of Little Jo ★★★15

Western   1993 · US · Colour · 116min

In director Maggie Greenwald's sobering, beautifully understated western, Suzy Amis gives a superb performance as the socialite driven into exile after a scandal, who is forced to pose as a man to survive in a wild frontier town. Greenwald makes some telling points about chauvinistic attitudes in the Old West and creates a believable picture of the harshness of the life. **JF** Violence, swearing, nudity.

Suzy Amis *Josephine Monaghan* • Bo Hopkins *Frank Badger* • Ian McKellen *Percy Corcoran* • David Chung *Tinman Wong* • Carrie Snodgress *Ruth Badger* • René Auberjonois *Streight Hollander* • Heather Graham *Mary Addie* • Sam Robards *Jasper Hill* • Tom Bower *Lyle* ■ *Dir/Scr* Maggie Greenwald

The Ballad of Lucy Whipple ★★★

Period drama   2001 · US · Colour

Glenn Close is typically effective in this TV movie as the New England widow who transports her young family to Gold Rush California, only for her eldest daughter to rebel and embark on a series of adventures of her own. Thus, it's teenager Jena Malone who carries the bulk of the action, as she learns about life from preacher Robert Pastorelli, cowboy Meat Loaf and sheriff Wilford Brimley. Thanks to the generosity of her co-stars, she handles the responsibility with aplomb. **DP**

Glenn Close *Arvella Whipple* • Jena Malone *Lucy "California" Whipple* • Bruce McGill *Jonas Scatter* • Meat Loaf *Aaron* • Chloe Webb *Sophie* • Dennis Christopher *Joshua "Carrots" Beale* ■ *Dir* Jeremy Paul Kagan • *Scr* Christopher Lofton, from the novel by Karen Cushman

The Ballad of Narayama ★★★U

Drama   1958 · Jpn · Colour · 100min

Kinuyo Tanaka gives a remarkable rendition of stoic resignation in this stylised adaptation of Shichiro Fukazawa's novels. Focusing on the custom of abandoning the elderly to die on a mountain top, Keisuke Kinoshita's heartbreaking drama is consciously played in a Kabuki manner against theatrical settings to remove any vestige of realism and thus increase the folkloric nature of a practice that will seem barbaric to most Western observers. **DP** In Japanese. *DVD*

Kinuyo Tanaka *Orin* • Teiji Takahashi *Tatsuhei* • Yuko Mochizuki *Tama-yan* • Danko Ichikawa *Kesakichi* • Keiko Ogasawara *Mutsu-yan* • Seiji Miyaguchi *Mata-yan* • Yunosuke Ito *Mata-yan's son* • Ken Mitsuda *Teru-yan* ■ *Dir* Keisuke Kinoshita • *Scr* Keisuke Kinoshita, from the novels by Shichiro Fukazawa

The Ballad of Narayama ★★★★15

Drama   1983 · Jpn · Colour · 129min

A far cry from Keisuke Kinoshita's earlier adaptation, Shohei Imamura's Palme d'Or-winning reworking of Shichiro Fukazawa's novels dispassionately places humanity in the context of the natural world, with all its seemingly callous acts of survivalism. Thus, rape, infant mortality and death by burial are presented as nothing more sensational than scrabbling for subsistence in a famine. Stoically accepting the tradition of the elderly being left on a mountain top to ease the communal burden, Sumiko Sakamoto

---

   U SUITABLE FOR ALL   **Uc** SUITABLE ESPECIALLY FOR YOUNG CHILDREN (DVD ONLY)   **PG** PARENTAL GUIDANCE   **12A** UNDER 12s TO BE ACCOMPANIED (CINEMA ONLY)

goes about settling her affairs with a calculation that contrasts with the brutality of the daily grind and the abjection of her final journey. DP Japanese +subtitles.
DVD

Ken Ogata *Tatsuhei* • Sumiko Sakamoto *Orin-yan* • Tonpei Hidari *Risuke, "Smelly"* • Takejo Aki *Tama-yan* • Shoichi Ozawa *Shozo* • Mitsuaki Fukamizu *Tada-yan* • Seiji Kurasaki *Kesakichi* • Junko Takada *Matsu-yan* ■ *Dir* Shohei Imamura • *Scr* Shohei Imamura, from the novels by Shichiro Fukazawa

The Ballad of Tam Lin ★★
Horror　1970 · UK · Colour · 104min

Hollywood star Roddy McDowall's only film as a director may be a product of its Age of Aquarius hippy era, yet it remains a rare curio item. Loosely based on a Robert Burns poem, it stars Ava Gardner as a camp witch trying to control the feckless jet setters she surrounds herself with, so she can stay young. It all ends badly with Ava's object of lust, Ian McShane, being chased through the Scottish woodlands high on LSD. Although interminably slow and hilariously pretentious at times, its aura of faded Swinging Sixties decadence is interesting – as is a cast of future talent that includes Joanna Lumley, Stephanie Beacham and *Withnail & I* director Bruce Robinson. AJ Drug abuse.

Ava Gardner *Michaela Cazaret* • Ian McShane *Tom Lynn* • Richard Wattis *Elroy* • Cyril Cusack *Vicar Julian Ainsley* • Stephanie Beacham *Janet Ainsley* • Sinead Cusack *Rose* • Joanna Lumley *Georgia* • Bruce Robinson *Alan* ■ *Dir* Roddy McDowall • *Scr* William Spier, from a poem by Robert Burns

The Ballad of the Sad Café ★★ 15
Drama　1991 · US/UK · Colour · 100min

A critical success but commercial flop on release, this sometimes brutal directorial debut by actor Simon Callow takes a bizarre but wonderfully written book by Carson McCullers and, by way of Edward Albee's stage version, gives it the enclosed, soundstage-on-a-shoestring-budget treatment. Its toe-curling pretentiousness knows no bounds, crowned by an execrable over-the-top performance by Vanessa Redgrave who attacks her role with full rolling-eyed abandon. SH *DVD*

Vanessa Redgrave *Miss Amelia Evans* • Keith Carradine *Marvin Macy* • Cork Hubbert *Cousin Lymon* • Rod Steiger *Reverend Willin* • Austin Pendleton *Lawyer Taylor* • Beth Dixon *Mary Hale* • Lanny Flaherty *Merlie Ryan* ■ *Dir* Simon Callow • *Scr* Michael Hirst, from the play by Edward Albee, from the novel by Carson McCullers

Ballast ★★★★ 15
Drama　2007 · US · Colour · 96min

Lance Hammer makes his film debut with this intense melodrama set in the Mississippi delta, featuring a cast of largely nonprofessional local actors. Following his twin brother's death from a drug overdose, Lawrence (Micheal J Smith Sr) finds himself responsible for 12-year-old nephew James (JimMyron Ross) when his sister-in-law Marlee (Tarra Riggs) moves back home. Hammer makes exceptional use of evocative imagery and visceral sound design to emphasise the alienation, isolation and frustration of a trio forced to take emotional risks to survive. DP Swearing, drug abuse.

Micheal J Smith Sr *Lawrence* • JimMyron Ross *James* • Tarra Riggs *Marlee* • Johnny McPhail *John* ■ *Dir/Scr* Lance Hammer • *Cinematographer* Lol Crawley • *Sound* Kent Sparling

Ballets Russes ★★★★ PG
Documentary
2005 · US · Colour and BW · 118min

This documentary is a peerless blend of archive footage and personal memoir that not only chronicles the history of a ballet institution between 1909 and the 1960s, but also brings the art form and its finest practitioners to vibrant life. The rivalry between impresarios Colonel Wassily de Basil and René Blum and choreographers

George Balanchine and Leonide Massine is described with clarity and insight. But what makes Dayna Goldfine and Dan Geller's film so glorious are the clips from the various stage triumphs (some of which are in ethereally beautiful colour) and the recollections of many balletic legends. DP *DVD*

Marian Seldes *Narrator* ■ *Dir* Dan Geller, Dayna Goldfine • *Scr* Dan Geller, Dayna Goldfine, Celeste Schaefer Snyder, Gary Weimberg

Ballistic: Ecks vs Sever ★★ 15
Science-fiction action thriller
2002 · US · Colour · 87min

This abysmal tale is too slow and unexciting to deserve its action thriller label. FBI man Antonio Banderas and his agent foe Lucy Liu make insipid leads as they unite to defeat a common enemy who's stolen a deadly, injectable micro-device. With its poorly executed fight scenes, clumsy camerawork and wooden support, this is a painful experience. SF Violence. *DVD*

Antonio Banderas *Jeremiah Ecks* • Lucy Liu *Sever* • Gregg Henry *Robert Gant/Clark* • Ray Park *AJ Ross* • Talisa Soto *Vinn Gant/Rayne* • Miguel Sandoval *Julio Martin* ■ *Dir* Kaos [Wych Kaosayananda] • *Scr* Alan B McElroy

Balls of Fury ★★ 12
Sports comedy　2007 · US · Colour · 86min

Table tennis became an official Olympic event in Seoul in 1988 but it still hasn't shrugged off its family-friendly alter ego, ping pong. This lame comedy stars Dan Fogler (*Good Luck Chuck*) as a former child "ping pong phenom" who lost out at the Seoul Olympics. Nineteen years on, he's hired by the FBI to infiltrate a table tennis tournament run by evil Triad leader Christopher Walken. Stealing its plot from *Enter the Dragon*, this lackadaisical spoof takes a hit-and-miss approach. Walken is amusingly camp in his flamboyant role, but the table tennis tomfoolery generates precious few laughs. JR *DVD*

Dan Fogler *Randy Daytona* • Christopher Walken *Feng* • George Lopez *Agent Ernie Rodriguez* • Maggie Q *Maggie Wong* • James Hong *Master Wong* • Terry Crews *Freddy* • Robert Patrick *Sgt Pete Daytona* • Aisha Tylor *Mahogany* ■ *Dir* Robert Ben Garant • *Scr* Robert Ben Garant, Thomas Lennon (3)

The Baltimore Bullet ★★ 15
Sports comedy　1980 · US · Colour · 98min

The Hustler for wimps, with James Coburn and protégé Bruce Boxleitner touring the pool halls of America and taking on the sharks. A big tournament lies ahead, for which Coburn needs a minimum stake of $20,000 if he is to take on the Deacon (Omar Sharif). Subplots about local gangsters and the drug trade juggle for screen time with the rather repetitive pool games, though the film just about gets by on the charm of its two stars. AT

James Coburn *Nick Casey* • Omar Sharif *Deacon* • Ronee Blakley *Carolina Red* • Bruce Boxleitner *Billie Joe Robbins* • Jack O'Halloran *Max* • Michael Lerner *Paulie* • Calvin Lockhart *Snow White* ■ *Dir* Robert Ellis Miller • *Scr* John Brascia, Robert Vincent O'Neill [O'Neil]

Balto ★★★ U
Animated adventure
1995 · US/UK · Colour · 74min

This well-crafted cartoon tells the story of an outcast sled dog who tries to save the children of the isolated Alaskan town of Nome during a diphtheria epidemic in 1925. Kevin Bacon's voice turns the wolf-dog crossbreed into a no-nonsense hero with a sense of duty that far outweighs the pride of his deadly rival, Steele, while Bob Hoskins's eccentric Russian goose provides the comedy. This is a touch darker than most animated features. A made-for-video sequel followed in 2001. DP *DVD*

Kevin Bacon *Balto* • Bob Hoskins *Boris* • Bridget Fonda *Jenna* • Jim Cummings *Steele* • Phil Collins *Muk/Luk* • Jack Angel *Nikki* ■ *Dir* Simon Wells • *Scr* Cliff Ruby, Elana Lesser, David Steven Cohen [David Cohen], Roger SH Schulman, from a story by Elana Lesser, Cliff Ruby

Balto – Wings of Change ★★ U
Animated adventure　2004 · US · Colour · 78min

Cartoon canine Balto demonstrates his heroism and compassion once again in a second made-for-DVD sequel from director Phil Weinstein. This time, it's son Kodi who needs his dad's assistance to demonstrate that his Alaskan sled dog team can deliver the mail faster than a plane. Subsequent tragedy brings lightly perilous adventure, providing life lessons all round and adding a touch of emotional depth to an otherwise slight affair. SF *DVD*

Maurice LaMarche *Balto* • Sean Astin *Kodi* • Jodi Benson *Jenna* • Keith Carradine *Duke* • Bill Fagerbakke *Ralph* • Jean Smart *Stella* ■ *Dir* Phil Weinstein • *Scr* Elana Lesser, Cliff Ruby

Balzac and the Little Chinese Seamstress ★★★ 12
Period comedy drama
2002 · Fr/Chi · Colour · 106min

Dai Sijie makes his directorial debut with this self-consciously handsome adaptation of his autobiographical novel about life in rural China during the Cultural Revolution. Dai uses Western literature – read to seamstress Zhou Xun by exiled city-dwellers Chen Kun and Liu Ye – to comment on Beijing's current cautious acceptance of external influences. Sentimental and lacking in political rigour, this is still a lyrical study of clashing cultures. DP Mandarin +subtitles. *DVD*

Zhou Xun *Little Chinese seamstress* • Liu Ye *Ma* • Chen Kun *Luo* • Wang Shuangbao *Village chief* • Cong Zhijun *Old tailor* • Wang Hongwei *Four Eyes* ■ *Dir* Dai Sijie • *Scr* Dai Sijie, Nadine Perront, from the novel *Balzac et la Petite Tailleuse Chinoise* by Dai Sijie

Bamako ★★★★ PG
Satirical political drama
2006 · Fr/Mali/US · Colour · 112min

With its hard-hitting content, dense symbolism and seemingly haphazard structure, this treatise on the continuing agonies of Africa is far from an easy watch. In a communal courtyard in the Malian capital of Bamako, an extraordinary "trial" unfolds that involves a counsel for the International Monetary Fund and the World Bank, and witnesses testifying to the continent's systematic exploitation as a result of their financial policies. As the debate continues, the action shifts between moments of everyday drama (a quarrelling couple) and a pastiche western showing on TV (starring Danny Glover and Palestinian director Elia Suleiman). Unconventional and often cuttingly satirical, this is a fascinating and deeply disconcerting experience. DP French +subtitles.

Aïssa Maïga *Melé* • Tiécoura Traoré *Chaka* • Hélène Diarra *Saramba* • Habib Dembélé *Falaï* • Djénéba Koné *Chaka's sister* • Hamadoun Kassogué *Journalist* • William Bourdon *Prosecuting lawyer* • Mamadou Konaté *Defense lawyer* • Danny Glover *Cowboy* • Elia Suleiman *Cowboy* ■ *Dir/Scr* Abderrahmane Sissako

La Bamba ★★★ 15
Biographical drama　1987 · US · Colour · 104min

Most pop biopics are tepid affairs, but the same cannot be said for director Luis Valdez's engrossing re-creation of Ritchie Valens's short life. Los Angeles band Los Lobos perform impassioned versions of the young man's songs, and their playing is mirrored by Lou Diamond Phillips's intense performance, which brings the 1950s rock 'n' roll star to life with a lot of vibrant detail while generally avoiding the usual clichés of the genre. JM Swearing, nudity. *DVD*

Lou Diamond Phillips *Ritchie Valens/Richard Valenzuela* • Esai Morales *Bob Morales* • Rosana De Soto *Connie Valenzuela* • Elizabeth Peña *Rosie Morales* • Danielle Von Zerneck *Donna Ludwig* • Joe Pantoliano *Bob Keene* ■ *Dir/Scr* Luis Valdez

Bambi ★★★★★ U
Classic animated fantasy
1942 · US · Colour · 69min

The classic status of this Disney landmark is merely buffed up by time, as successive generations discover its peerless mix of ecological message and anthropomorphic fun. It traces the formative seasons of a deer – imbued with human characteristics, as are his companions Flower, the shy skunk, and Thumper, the exuberant rabbit – who learns the lessons of life in the forest. The death of his mother at the hands of a hunter ("Man" personified) remains one of cinema's most memorable, though it isn't actually shown. This still has plenty to tell children and strikes a deft artistic balance between naturalism and cartoonery. AC *DVD BLU*

Bobby Stewart *Bambi* • Peter Behn *Thumper* • Stan Alexander *Flower* • Cammie King *Phylline* ■ *Dir* David D Hand [David Hand] • *Scr* Perce Pearce, Larry Morey, from a story by Felix Salten, from his novel

Le Bambole ★★★
Portmanteau comedy
1965 · Fr/It · Colour · 111min

In Dino Risi's *The Telephone Call*, Nino Manfredi takes advantage of Virna Lisi's endless call to flirt with a neighbour, while in Franco Rossi's *The Soup*, Monica Vitti attempts to dispose of her husband. *Treatise on Eugenics* sees Elke Sommer search for the perfect Latin father for her baby, while *Monsignor Cupid* focuses on hotel receptionist Gina Lollobrigida's attempts to seduce the nephew of prelate Akim Tamiroff (Jean Sorel). Portmanteau pictures have always been hit-and-miss affairs, but one expects slightly more from directors of the calibre of Luigi Comencini and Mauro Bolognini, who settle for mischief rather than meaning in their respective episodes. DP In Italian.

Virna Lisi *Luisa, the wife* • Nino Manfredi *Giorgio, the husband* • Elke Sommer *Ulla* • Maurizio Arena *Massimo* • Monica Vitti *Giovanna* • John Karlsen *Alfonso, her husband* • Orazio Orlando *Richetto, her lover* • Gina Lollobrigida *Beatrice* • Akim Tamiroff *Monsignor Arendi* • Jean Sorel *Vincenzo* ■ *Dir* Dino Risi, Luigi Comencini, Franco Rossi, Mauro Bolognini • *Scr* Rodolfo Sonego, Tullio Pinelli (from a story by Luciano Salce, Steno, Luigi Magni), Leo Benvenuti (from a story by Piero De Bernardi, from the story *Il Decamerone* by Giovanni Boccaccio)

The Bamboo Blonde ★★ U
Second World War romance
1946 · US · BW · 67min

Anthony Mann's tenth feature ranks among the least distinguished of his career. Shot quickly and cheaply for RKO, it wavers between being a wartime adventure, a romantic melodrama and a musical. Ultimately, it succeeds only in being a bore, despite Frances Langford's pretty crooning of some catchy ditties. Ralph Edwards is suitably seedy as the Manhattan nightclub boss who exploits Langford, but there's no chemistry among the leading players. DP

Frances Langford *Louise Anderson* • Ralph Edwards *Eddie Clark* • Russell Wade *Patrick Ransom Jr* • Iris Adrian *Montana* • Richard Martin (1) *Jim Wilson* • Jane Greer *Eileen Sawyer* ■ *Dir* Anthony Mann • *Scr* Olive Cooper, Lawrence Kimble, from the story *Chicago Lulu* by Wayne Whittaker

Bamboozled ★★★ 15
Satirical drama　2000 · US · Colour · 130min

Spike Lee's dark, biting satire is both thought provoking and amusing. Damon Wayans plays the only black writer at a network TV station, who's dismayed at his employer's decision to dumb down in a bid to boost ratings. He wants to quit, but station boss Michael Rapaport won't let him. So Wayans decides to get himself fired by creating a programme so controversial that the station won't touch it – an old-style minstrel show, with blacks portrayed as grinning idiots who dwell in watermelon patches. The plan backfires when Rapaport loves the idea. DA Swearing. *DVD*

B

Damon Wayans *Pierre Delacroix* • Savion Glover *Manray/Mantan* • Jada Pinkett Smith *Sloan Hopkins* • Tommy Davidson *Womack/Sleep 'n' Eat* • Michael Rapaport *Dunwitty* • Thomas Jefferson Byrd *Honeycutt* • Paul Mooney *Junebug* ■ *Dir/Scr* Spike Lee

Banacek: Detour to Nowhere ★★★ PG
Crime mystery 1972 · US · Colour · 92min

George Peppard stars as Boston-based insurance investigator Thomas Banacek in this efficiently directed TV crime drama pilot that went on to a two-year run as a series. The Polish-American Banacek is more of a bounty hunter than an authority figure and Peppard plays him with a curt swagger. Aided by Murray Matheson's bookshop owner and rival adjuster Christine Belford, he makes for Texas to track down a missing armoured car packed with gold bullion. DP *Some violence.*

George Peppard *Thomas Banacek* • Christine Belford *Carlie Kirkland* • Don Dubbins *Sheriff Jessup* • Murray Matheson *Felix Mulholland* • Russell C Wiggins [Russell Wiggins] *Earl Lewis* ■ *Dir* Jack Smight • *Scr* Anthony Wilson

Banana Peel ★★★
Comedy 1964 · Fr/It · BW · 97min

Although his father Max was renowned for sparkling sophistication in his films, Marcel Ophüls's debut feature owes more to the brash panache of Hollywood satirist Preston Sturges. Set among the idle rich of the French Riviera and its constant round of double-dealings, this has a couple of sharp swindlers trying to con a miserly millionaire. Revelling in the badinage, Jeanne Moreau and Jean-Paul Belmondo are ideally matched as they cross swords with the far from helpless Gert Fröbe. DP *French +subtitles.*

Jeanne Moreau *Cathy* • Jean-Paul Belmondo *Michel* • Gert Fröbe *Lachard* • Claude Brasseur *Charlie* • Jean-Pierre Marielle *Reynaldo* • Alain Cuny *Bontemps* ■ *Dir* Marcel Ophüls • *Scr* Marcel Ophüls, Claude Sautet, Daniel Boulanger, from the novel *Nothing in Her Way* by Charles Williams

Bananas ★★★ 15
Comedy 1971 · US · Colour · 78min

With a title that refers to both banana republics and the Marx Brothers film *Cocoanuts*, Woody Allen's second picture as director and star is one of his least convincing outings. Packed with nods to cinematic maestros such as Eisenstein, Chaplin, Buñuel and Bergman, it's the work of a comic delighting in his gags rather than a director in control of his material. A touch of political satire might have helped stem the endless flow of throwaway lines and surreal incidents, as well as giving the plot a little more focus. Inconsistent, but when it's funny, it's a riot. DP *DVD* *BL*

Woody Allen *Fielding Mellish* • Louise Lasser *Nancy* • Carlos Montalban *General Emilio M Vargas* • Natividad Abascal *Yolanda* • Jacobo Morales *Esposito* • Miguel Suarez [Miguel Angel Suarez] *Luis* • Sylvester Stallone *Subway thug* ■ *Dir* Woody Allen • *Scr* Woody Allen, Mickey Rose

Band of Angels ★★
Period drama 1957 · US · Colour · 114min

After the death of her father, beautiful Southern belle Yvonne De Carlo discovers that her mother was a slave. As a result she's sold as a slave to millionaire Clark Gable, whose mistress she becomes. Directed by the veteran Raoul Walsh, who must have been forced into it, and with Sidney Poitier as a slave, this utter tosh strains credibility to the limits and has little to recommend it other than De Carlo's glamour. RK

Clark Gable *Hamish Bond* • Yvonne De Carlo *Amantha Starr* • Sidney Poitier *Rau-Ru* • Efrem Zimbalist Jr *Ethan Sears* • Rex Reason *Seth Parton* • Patric Knowles *Charles de Marigny* • Torin Thatcher *Captain Canavan* ■ *Dir* Raoul Walsh • *Scr* John Twist, Ivan Goff, Ben Roberts, from the novel by Robert Penn Warren

Band of Thieves ★★ U
Musical crime drama 1962 · UK · BW · 66min

Nicolas Roeg received his third credit as a cinematographer on this caper comedy. But jazz fans will be more interested in seeing Acker Bilk starring in the second of his three 1960s pictures. Ostensibly, the clarinettist plays himself. But the real Acker presumably didn't use his gigs as a front for stately home robberies! Jimmy Thompson co-stars as the light-fingered socialite who hooks up with Bilk on his release from Gaunstone Jail, while Maudie Edwards and Jennifer Jayne play a dotty duchess and a suspicious hostess, who land the band and their getaway driver Arthur Mullard in big trouble. Slight, but fun. DP

Acker Bilk • Jimmy Thompson *Hon Derek Delaney* • Colin Smith *Flash* • Jonathan Mortimer *Fingers* • Ron McKay *Scouse* • Roy James *Dippy* • Stan Greig *Haggis* • Geoffrey Sumner *Clifford, the prison governor* • Jennifer Jayne *Anne* • Maudie Edwards *Duchess* • Arthur Mullard *Getaway* ■ *Dir* Peter Bezencenet • *Scr* Lyn Fairhurst, from a story by Harold Shampan

Band Waggon ★★★ U
Musical comedy 1939 · UK · BW · 85min

The radio spin-off movie may be unheard of today, but they were all the rage in the 1930s. Although it only ran for some two years, *Band Waggon*, with its quirky characters and rapid-fire humour, was hugely popular. Here, the script restricts the fabled ad-libbing of Arthur Askey and Richard "Stinker" Murdoch, but it's still good fun as the pair stray from their famous flat in the eaves of Broadcasting House only to encounter spies in a haunted castle. DP

Arthur Askey *Big Hearted Arthur* • Richard Murdoch *Stinker* • Jack Hylton • Pat Kirkwood *Pat* • Moore Marriott *Jasper* • Peter Gawthorne *Claude Pilkington* • Wally Patch *Commissionaire* ■ *Dir* Marcel Varnel • *Scr* Marriott Edgar, Val Guest, from the radio series by Harry S Pepper, Gordon Crier, Vernon Harris

The Band Wagon ★★★★★ U
Classic musical 1953 · US · Colour · 107min

This clever and witty backstage musical has Fred Astaire playing a Broadway star who's out of step with the very modern musical he has been hired to headline. It boasts brilliant direction from Vincente Minnelli and fabulous Technicolor production design, and to many marks the peak of Astaire's screen work. The star is stunning as he partners the gorgeous Cyd Charisse in *Dancing in the Dark* and the Mickey Spillane parody, *The Girl Hunt* ballet, superbly choreographed by Michael Kidd and Oliver Smith. This is as good as musicals get. TS *DVD*

Fred Astaire *Tony Hunter* • Cyd Charisse *Gaby Berard* • Jack Buchanan *Jeffrey Cordova* • Oscar Levant *Lester Marton* • Nanette Fabray *Lily Marton* • James Mitchell *Paul Byrd* • Robert Gist *Hal Benton* • Ava Gardner *Movie star* ■ *Dir* Vincente Minnelli • *Scr* Betty Comden, Adolph Green • *Lyrics* Howard Dietz • *Music* Arthur Schwartz

Bande à Part ★★★★ PG
Crime drama 1964 · Fr · Colour · 95min

A playful effort from Jean-Luc Godard has his then wife, the radiant Anna Karina, teaming up with a couple of petty crooks – Sami Frey and Claude Brasseur – in a hair-brained scheme to rob her aunt. In characteristic fashion, Godard drops the plot at every opportunity to indulge in homages to various Hollywood genres and to allow his camera to idolise Karina's beauty. Some may find it irritating beyond endurance, but in its day its freshness was greeted like rain in a drought. Thirty years later, Quentin Tarantino rediscovered the film and liked it so much he named his production company "A Band Apart". AT French +subtitles. *DVD*

Anna Karina *Odile* • Sami Frey *Franz* • Claude Brasseur *Arthur* • Louisa Colpeyn *Madame Victoria* • Danièle Girard *English teacher* • Chantal Darget *Arthur's aunt* • Ernest Menzer *Arthur's uncle* • Jean-Luc Godard *Narration* ■

Dir Jean-Luc Godard • *Scr* Jean-Luc Godard, from the novel *Fool's Gold (Pigeon Vole)* by Dolores Hitchens

Bandido ★★ U
Western 1956 · US · Colour · 91min

This routine 1950s western adventure stars Robert Mitchum as an American soldier of fortune who joins forces with a rebel leader in a bid to intercept a shipment of arms during the Mexican Revolution. Mitchum is better than the script, but the film still offers action, sufficient intrigue and picturesque landscapes. You could do worse. PF

Robert Mitchum *Wilson* • Ursula Thiess *Lisa* • Gilbert Roland *Escobar* • Zachary Scott *Kennedy* • Rodolfo Acosta *Sebastian* • Henry Brandon *Gunther* • Douglas Fowley *McGee* • José I Torvay [José Torvay] *Gonzalez* • Victor Junco *Lorenzo* ■ *Dir* Richard Fleischer • *Scr* Earl Felton

Bandini ★★★★ U
Drama 1963 · Ind · BW · 145min

Bimal Roy's final feature is regarded by many as his crowning achievement. The key lay in persuading Nutan out of her post-nuptial retirement to play the strictly raised, poetry-loving village girl, Kalyani. Her passion for a revolutionary, played by Ashok Kumar, leads first to her imprisonment for murder and then to her redemption through the love of a prison doctor (Dharmendra). The heartbreaking intensity of her performance is considerably enhanced by cinematographer Kamal Bose's authentic re-creation of 1930s Bengal and SD Burman's score, which provided legendary backing singer Gulzar with a memorable debut. DP Hindi +subtitles. *DVD*

Nutan *Kalyani* • Ashok Kumar *Bikash Ghosh* • Dharmendra *Devendra* ■ *Dir* Bimal Roy • *Scr* M Ghosh, Nabendu Ghosh

The Bandit of Sherwood Forest ★★ U
Swashbuckling adventure 1946 · US · Colour · 82min

Cornel Wilde stars as Robin Hood's son, who tries to save the Magna Carta and Britain from the constitutional ravages of Henry Daniell's royal schemer, the wayward Regent. It's really just a western in weird costumes with added peasantry, shot on the Columbia backlot in bright-as-a-button Technicolor. Not a patch on Errol Flynn's classic *The Adventures of Robin Hood*, this is an enjoyable romp just the same. AT *DVD*

Cornel Wilde *Robert of Nottingham* • Anita Louise *Lady Catherine Maitland* • Jill Esmond *Queen Mother* • Edgar Buchanan *Friar Tuck* • Henry Daniell *Regent* • George Macready *Fitz-Herbert* • Russell Hicks *Robin Hood* • John Abbott *Will Scarlet* • Ray Teal *Little John* ■ *Dir* George Sherman, Henry Levin • *Scr* Wilfred H Pettit, Melvyn Levy, from the novel *Son of Robin Hood* by Paul A Castleton

The Bandit of Zhobe ★★ 12
Action adventure 1959 · UK · Colour · 81min

This very silly Northwest Frontier romp stars Victor Mature in dark make-up as a fearsome but noble Indian leader whose family has been massacred by Brits. There ensues much pillage, a lot of smirking by Mature, romantic interest from forgotten starlet Anne Aubrey and some wince-inducing comic mugging from Anthony Newley. Quite a lot of money was thrown at it, but this remains a B-movie. AT

Victor Mature *Kasim Khan* • Anne Aubrey *Zena Crowley* • Anthony Newley *Corporal Stokes* • Norman Wooland *Major Crowley* • Dermot Walsh *Captain Saunders* • Walter Gotell *Azhad* ■ *Dir* John Gilling • *Scr* John Gilling, from a story by Richard Maibaum

Bandit Queen ★★★★ 18
Biographical drama 1994 · Ind/UK · Colour · 114min

Released to a storm of protest throughout the subcontinent and the displeasure of its subject, Phoolan Devi herself, this is a damning condemnation of both the caste system and the subservience of women in modern Indian society. Director Shekhar Kapur deserves great credit for depicting provocative events without the slightest hint of sensationalism, whether it is Devi's gang-rape at the hands of some Uttar Pradeshi bandits or her merciless revenge, which culminated in the Behmai massacre of 1981. Seema Biswas is superb as the folkloric figure who avoided capture for five years before surrendering in 1983. DP Hindi +subtitles. *DVD*

Seema Biswas *Phoolan Devi* • Nirmal Pandey *Vikram Mallah* • Manoj Bajpai *Man Singh* • Rajesh Vivek *Mustaquim* • Raghuvir Yadav *Madho* • Govind Namdeo *Sriram* • Saurabh Shukla *Kailash* • Aditya Srivastava *Puttilal* ■ *Dir* Shekhar Kapur • *Scr* Mala Sen

Bandits ★★★ 12
Crime comedy drama 2001 · US · Colour · 117min

Bruce Willis and Billy Bob Thornton star as charismatic bank robbers in this enjoyable (if utterly nonsensical) film from Barry Levinson. They earn the nickname of "sleepover bandits" because of their habit of casually kidnapping bank managers the night before a job. However, their modus operandi is complicated when they both fall for Cate Blanchett, whom they take along for the ride. The film is at its best when Willis and Thornton exchange witty banter. JB *Swearing, violence.* *DVD*

Bruce Willis *Joe Blake* • Billy Bob Thornton *Terry Collins* • Cate Blanchett *Kate Wheeler* • Troy Garity *Harvey Pollard* • Brian F O'Byrne *Darill Miller* • Stacey Travis *Cloe Miller* ■ *Dir* Barry Levinson • *Scr* Harley Peyton

The Bandits of Corsica ★ U
Adventure 1953 · US · BW · 80min

The 1942 Douglas Fairbanks Jr swashbuckler *The Corsican Brothers* was only loosely based on the characters created by Alexandre Dumas, but this sequel is even further removed. Every expense seems to have been spared in the mounting of this clumping adventure, in which Richard Greene manages to give two poor performances. DP

Richard Greene *Mario/Carlos* • Paula Raymond *Christina* • Raymond Burr *Jonatto* • Dona Drake *Zelda* • Raymond Greenleaf *Paoli* • Lee Van Cleef *Nerva* • Frank Puglia *Riggio* ■ *Dir* Ray Nazarro • *Scr* Richard Schayer, from a story by Frank Burt

Bandolero! ★★ 15
Western 1968 · US · Colour · 101min

This would-be rollicking adventure suffers from chronic miscasting. All-time good guys James Stewart and Dean Martin play outlaw brothers who hold a peculiarly accented Raquel Welch hostage after she loses her husband in a botched bank raid. The actual good guy, surprisingly, is George Kennedy, but he's no match for these particular baddies. This uneven mixture of contemporary violence and traditional western values is a mess, but not unenjoyable. TS *DVD*

James Stewart *Mace Bishop* • Dean Martin *Dee Bishop* • Raquel Welch *Maria* • George Kennedy *Sheriff Johnson* • Andrew Prine *Roscoe Bookbinder* • Will Geer *Pop Chaney* • Clint Ritchie *Babe* • Denver Pyle *Muncie Carter* ■ *Dir* Andrew V McLaglen • *Scr* James Lee Barrett, from the unpublished story *Mace* by Stanley L Hough

Bandslam ★★★ PG
Musical comedy drama 2009 · US · Colour · 106min

The plot of *Bandslam* is a familiar one: a competition for a recording contract attracts a bevy of youngsters, rivalries emerge and friendships are made and broken. What surprises is the believable dialogue and the freshness of the performers, such as *High School Musical*'s Vanessa Hudgens. *Friends* star Lisa Kudrow is credible as the mother of Will (Gaelan Connell), who teams up with popular girls Charlotte and Sa5m (Sam – the five "is silent") to start a band. Though there are a few duff notes, the occasional rough edge is preferable to computer-enhanced perfection. Silly, yet fresh and sparky – with room for a sequel. KK *DVD*

Vanessa Hudgens [Vanessa Anne Hudgens] *Sa5m* • Lisa Kudrow *Karen Burton* • Aly Michalka [Alyson Michalka] *Charlotte* • David Bowie • Gaelan Alexander Connell *Will Burton* • Scott Porter *Ben Wheatley* ■ *Dir* Todd Graff • *Scr* Todd Graff, Josh A Cagan, from a story by Cagan

Bang Gang (A Modern Love Story) ★★★ 18

Romantic drama 2015 · Fr · Colour · 93min

This is a fresh and fluid take on teen sexuality in an age of online exhibitionism. The Bardot-esque Marilyn Lima plays a pretty but insecure schoolgirl who kick-starts a series of orgies, falls out with a pal (Daisy Broom) and ultimately enters into a tender romance with a troubled contemporary (Lorenzo Lefèbvre). Frank and fairly explicit, the events nevertheless unfold through a prism of sensitivity and compassion, credibly capturing the maelstrom of youth. EAS French +subtitles. Swearing, sex scenes, drug abuse, nudity. *DVD*

Finnegan Oldfield *Alex* • Marilyn Lima *George* • Lorenzo Lefèbvre *Gabriel* • Daisy Broom *Laetitia* • Fred Hotier *Nikita* ■ *Dir/Scr* Eva Husson

Bang the Drum Slowly ★★★★

Period sports drama 1973 · US · Colour · 98min

Director John Hancock's moving buddy drama is one of the best baseball movies ever made. Telling the engrossing tale of how New York pitcher Michael Moriarty helps his terminally ill catcher Robert De Niro through one more season, this 1950s-set heartbreaker resonates with emotional truths while evoking nostalgia for an innocent era. It's superlatively performed by De Niro (then unknown) and Moriarty, with excellent support from Vincent Gardenia, as their manager. AJ

Robert De Niro *Bruce Pearson* • Vincent Gardenia *Dutch Schnell* • Phil Foster *Joe Jaros* • Ann Wedgeworth *Katie* • Patrick McVey *Pearson's father* • Heather MacRae *Holly Wiggin* • Selma Diamond *Tootsie* ■ *Dir* John Hancock • *Scr* Mark Harris (2), from his novel

Bang! You're Dead ★★ PG

Crime drama 1954 · UK · BW · 85min

Simply because the plot revolves around a young boy finding a gun and accidentally killing a much detested local man, only for the victim's most outspoken detractor to be arrested for murder, this minor British crime drama has been compared to both 1949's *The Window* and 1952's *The Yellow Balloon*. Yet there's considerably less insight into the boy's guilt-stricken torment than in either of those films, with director Lance Comfort settling for a mildly suspenseful countdown to the predictable climax. DP *DVD*

Jack Warner *Mr Bonsell* • Derek Farr *Detective Grey* • Veronica Hurst *Hilda* • Michael Medwin *Bob Carter* • Gordon Harker *Mr Hare* • Anthony Richmond *Cliff Bonsell* • Sean Barrett (1) *Willy* ■ *Dir* Lance Comfort • *Scr* Guy Elmes, Ernest Borneman

The Banger Sisters ★★★ 15

Comedy drama 2002 · US · Colour · 93min

This is a likeable attempt to see what happens to groupies after the tours and tequila have dried up. Goldie Hawn stars as an over-the-hill rock chick travelling across the country to hook up with former partner-in-crime Susan Sarandon, now a model of suburban respectability. The life lessons are trotted out with predictable regularity and the writing fails to deliver on the promising premise. But Hawn and Sarandon are a winning pairing, and they're ably assisted by Geoffrey Rush. IF Swearing, drug abuse, sex scenes. *DVD*

Goldie Hawn *Suzette* • Susan Sarandon *Lavinia "Vinnie" Kingsley* • Geoffrey Rush *Harry Plumber* • Erika Christensen *Hannah* • Eva Amurri *Ginger* • Robin Rhomas *Raymond* • Matthew Carey *Jules* ■ *Dir/Scr* Bob Dolman

Bangkok Dangerous ★★★ 18

Crime thriller 2000 · Thai · Colour · 105min

Deaf-mute hitman Pavarit Mongkolpisit at first plays it all mean and moody as the archetypal loner, isolated by his profession and his inability to communicate. Then he meets unsuspecting pharmacy assistant Premsinee Ratanasopha and the possibility of a redemptive romance is introduced. However, debuting writers/directors Oxide and Danny Pang are too interested in atmospheric neon nightscapes and pyrotechnics to develop the characters or their relationship, Visually impressive and intermittently involving, but derivative. DP Thai +subtitles. Violence. *DVD*

Pavarit Mongkolpisit *Kong* • Premsinee Ratanasopha *Fon* • Patharawarin Timkul *Aom* ■ *Dir/Scr* Oxide Pang, Danny Pang

Bangkok Dangerous ★★ 18

Action thriller 2007 · US · Colour · 94min

Seven years after the original *Bangkok Dangerous* was released, twin brothers Oxide and Danny Pang have remade it in English. Nicolas Cage plays it mean and moody as Joe, a sniper-assassin who is hired to carry out a number of hits in Bangkok. Joe lives and works by four intractable rules, most of which he manages to break in the film's opening scenes. Small wonder, then, that his Thai employers turn skittish and eventually try to do the dirty on him. Slickly made and with a few decent action scenes, this hitman thriller has a clinically efficient film at its core, but the Pangs overdo things with laughable grandiosity. DA *DVD* *Blu*

Nicolas Cage *Joe* • Shahkrit Yamnarm *Kong* • Charlie Young [Charlie Yeung] *Fon* • Panward Hemmanee *Aom* • Nirattisai Kaliaruck *Surat* • Dom Hetrakul *Aran* ■ *Dir* Oxide Pang, Danny Pang • *Scr* Jason Richman, from the 2000 film

The Banishment ★★★ 12

Drama 2007 · Rus · Colour · 150min

Konstantin Lavronenko won the 2007 best actor prize at Cannes for his performance in this loose adaptation of writer William Saroyan's *The Laughing Matter*. He sustains a disconcerting level of intensity as the taciturn husband who demands that his wife (Maria Bonnevie) have an abortion after he presumes that he's been cuckolded. However, director Andrey Zvyagintsev (*The Return*) allows character motivation to become so submerged beneath religious symbolism and cultural homage that the compelling plot lacks the appropriate emotional resonance. Mikhail Krichman's photography is excellent, though. DP Russian +subtitles. *DVD*

Konstantin Lavronenko *Alex* • Maria Bonnevie *Vera* • Alexander Baluev *Mark* • Maxim Shibaev *Kir* ■ *Dir* Andrey Zvyagintsev • *Scr* Andrey Zvyagintsev, Oleg Negin, from the novel *The Laughing Matter* by William Saroyan • *Cinematographer* Mikhail Krichman

Banjo on My Knee ★★★

Musical drama 1936 · US · BW · 95min

After being abandoned by new husband Joel McCrea, Barbara Stanwyck as riverboat moll Pearl, takes over the whole show: she dances with Buddy Ebsen, sings with Tony Martin and even gets into a fight with Katherine DeMille, adopted daughter of the legendary Cecil B. John Cromwell's direction is perfunctory, but the supporting players are a joy. TS

Barbara Stanwyck *Pearl* • Joel McCrea *Ernie Holley* • Helen Westley *Grandma* • Buddy Ebsen *Puddy* • Walter Brennan *Newt Holley* • Walter Catlett *Warfield Scott* • Anthony Martin [Tony Martin (1)] *Chick Bean* • Minna Gombell *Ruby* • Katherine DeMille *Leota Long* ■ *Dir* John Cromwell • *Scr* Nunnally Johnson, from the novel by Harry Hamilton

The Bank ★★★★

Thriller 2001 · Aus/It · Colour · 106min

Enthralling both as a thriller and as a caustic portrait of corporate greed, writer/director Robert Connolly's superb debut delivers a crowd-pleasing comeuppance to an institution that people love to hate – the bank. David Wenham plays a brilliant Australian mathematician who is close to perfecting a computer programme that will be able to predict major stock market ups and downs. His employer (Anthony LaPaglia), the head of a big Australian bank, has other ideas. Wenham is excellent as a man coping with the conflict between his moral code and a desire to leave his mark on the world of mathematics, while LaPaglia offers up the most monstrous business executive since Michael Douglas's Gordon Gecko. JF

David Wenham *Jim Doyle* • Anthony LaPaglia *Simon O'Reilly* • Sibylla Budd *Michelle Roberts* • Mitchell Butel *Stephen* • Mandy McElhinney *Diane Davis* • Greg Stone *Vincent* ■ *Dir/Scr* Robert Connolly

The Bank Dick ★★★★ U

Comedy 1940 · US · BW · 69min

Scripted by WC Fields under the name of Mahatma Kane Jeeves, this is one of his finest comedies. Fields growls and grumbles his way through some inspired routines as the indolent passer-by who is rewarded with the post of bank detective after inadvertently foiling a raid. Even though several gags are rehashed from his celebrated shorts, they are done to a crisp by Fields and a superb supporting cast, in which Cora Witherspoon, Una Merkel and Jessie Ralph are outstanding as the women who delight in pointing out the shortcomings he considers his assets. DP *DVD*

WC Fields *Egbert Sousé* • Cora Witherspoon *Agatha Sousé* • Una Merkel *Myrtle Sousé* • Evelyn Del Rio *Elsie May Adele Brunch Sousé* • Jessie Ralph *Mrs Hermisillo Brunch* • Franklin Pangborn *J Pinkerton Snoopington* • Shemp Howard *Joe Guelpe* • Richard Purcell [Dick Purcell] *Mackley Q Greene* • Grady Sutton *Og Oggilby* • Russell Hicks *J Frothingham Waterbury* • Pierre Watkin *Mr Skinner* ■ *Dir* Edward Cline • *Scr* Mahatma Kane Jeeves [WC Fields], Richard Carroll

Bank Holiday ★★★

Comedy drama 1938 · UK · BW · 86min

While today it may look slightly laboured, in 1938 this was acclaimed for its naturalism, restraint and shrewd characterisation. Following a group of day-trippers to Brighton, the film is smoothly directed by Carol Reed, who sustains interest in a variety of stock figures by flitting between them in the style of a soap opera instalment. Margaret Lockwood wins sympathy as a nurse who is distracted from a dirty weekend by her concern for a grieving widow, but the stand-out performances come from Kathleen Harrison as a prim cockney wife and Wilfrid Lawson as a world-weary police sergeant. DP

John Lodge *Stephen Howard* • Margaret Lockwood *Catherine* • Hugh Williams *Geoffrey* • René Ray *Doreen* • Merle Tottenham *Milly* • Linden Travers *Ann Howard* • Wally Patch *Arthur* • Kathleen Harrison *May* • Garry Marsh *Manager* ■ *Dir* Carol Reed • *Scr* Rodney Ackland, Roger Burford, from a story by Hans Wilhelm, Rodney Ackland

The Bank Job ★★★ 15

Heist thriller based on a true story 2008 · US/UK/Aus · Colour · 107min

In this good, old-fashioned British heist movie set in the early 1970s, Jason Statham plays the leader of a ragtag bunch of crooks who's persuaded by former flame Saffron Burrows to break into the safety-deposit boxes of a Baker Street bank. But unbeknown to Statham, one of the boxes contains a right royal secret and the shadier elements of Britain's security forces will stop at nothing to ensure that it stays secret. Despite claims that it is founded in fact, *The Bank Job* is fancifully plotted and quite preposterous, but with a fast-moving script from Dick Clement and Ian La Frenais, it still manages to be the sort of Swinging Sixties-style caper film that they don't really make any more. DA Violence, swearing, sex scenes. *DVD* *Blu*

Jason Statham *Terry Leather* • Saffron Burrows *Martine Love* • Stephen Campbell Moore *Kevin Swain* • Daniel Mays *Dave Shilling* • James Faulkner *Guy Singer* • Alki David *Bambas* • David Suchet *Lew Vogel* • Keeley Hawes *Wendy Leather* ■ *Dir* Roger Donaldson • *Scr* Dick Clement, Ian La Frenais

Bank Shot ★★ PG

Crime caper 1974 · US · Colour · 80min

This feeble comedy caper too often stretches credibility as escaped convict George C Scott literally steals a bank by lifting it up and dragging it off. Although there are some neat gags and shrewd ideas, the result is all at sea. TH

George C Scott *Walter Ballantine* • Joanna Cassidy *El* • Sorrell Booke *Al G Karp* • G Wood *FBI Agent Andrew Constable* • Clifton James *Frank "Bulldog" Streiger* • Robert Balaban [Bob Balaban] *Victor Karp* ■ *Dir* Gower Champion • *Scr* Wendell Mayes, from the novel by Donald E Westlake

Banning ★★

Drama 1967 · US · Colour · 101min

This golfing melodrama feels like 101 minutes spent in the deepest bunker with a snooker cue. Robert Wagner takes a job as a country club pro and becomes the focus of attention for a number of women, including the sophisticated Anjanette Cromer. He also finds himself up against old adversary Guy Stockwell for the huge cash prize in a special tournament. DP

Robert Wagner *Mike Banning* • Anjanette Comer *Carol Lindquist* • Jill St John *Angela Barr* • Guy Stockwell *Jonathan Linus* • James Farentino *Chris Patton* • Susan Clark *Cynthia Linus* • Gene Hackman *Tommy Del Gaddo* ■ *Dir* Ron Winston • *Scr* James Lee, from a story by Hamilton Maule

El Baño del Papa ★★★ 15

Comedy drama 2007 · Urug/Bra/Fr/Sp · Colour · 93min

The title of this whimsical South American comedy drama translates as the Pope's toilet, which may sound provocative but is actually a fairly literal description of its subject. When Pope John Paul II announces a visit to the forgotten town of Melo on the Uruguay/Brazil border in 1988, the impoverished inhabitants hope to make a fortune by catering to visiting Brazilian tourists – predicted by an over-excited local media to number up to 200,000. Yet while his neighbours cook up empanadas, local smuggler Beto (César Troncoso) tries to convince his wife and daughter that the family should stretch their finances by opening an outdoor toilet to cater to the needs of the faithful. JR Spanish +subtitles. *DVD*

César Troncoso *Beto* • Virginia Méndez *Carmen* • Mario Silva *Valvulina* • Virginia Ruiz *Silvia* ■ *Dir/Scr* Cesar Charlone, Enrique Fernandez

The Banquet ★★ 15

Period action drama 2006 · Chi · Colour · 125min

Chinese cinema hit paydirt in the early 21st century with a formula of period detail and gravity-defying action, beginning in 2000 with *Crouching Tiger, Hidden Dragon*. Some of that seminal film's talents – notably stunt director Yuen Woo-Ping and star Zhang Ziyi – contribute to this lavish but inferior martial-arts drama, a 10th-century tale of betrayal and revenge. Starting out as a loose take on *Hamlet*, it sees a young prince (Daniel Wu) striking back at the uncle who killed his father and lusts after his stepmother (Zhang). Despite some stirring set pieces, this soon degenerates into a talky bore. Even the climactic feast is a let-down: not so much a banquet as a pretty but insubstantial buffet. DW Mandarin +subtitles. Violence. *DVD* *Blu*

Zhang Ziyi *Empress Wan* • Daniel Wu *Prince Wu Luan* • Zhou Xun *Qing Nu* • Ge You *Emperor Li* • Ma Jingwu *The Minister* • Huang Xiaoming *General Yin* • Zhonghe Zhou *Chamberlain* ■ *Dir* Feng Xiaogang • *Scr* Qiu Gangjian, Sheng Heyu

BAPS ★ 15

Comedy 1997 · US · Colour · 88min

This lame, ludicrous comedy stars Halle Berry and Natalie Desselle as a couple of garishly dressed Georgia homegirls who

B

travel to LA to audition for a music video, but get caught up in a scam involving dying millionaire Martin Landau. The title stands for "Black American Princesses", and the idea seems to be some sort of African-American *Pygmalion*. But the result is insulting and unfunny. **JC**

Halle Berry *Nisi* • Martin Landau *Mr Blakemore* • Ian Richardson *Manley* • Natalie Desselle *Mickey* • Troy Beyer *Tracy* • Luigi Amodeo *Antonio* • Jonathan Fried *Isaac* • Pierre *Ali* • AJ Johnson [Anthony Johnson] *James* ■ *Dir* Robert Townsend • *Scr* Troy Beyer

Barabbas ★★★ PG
Epic biblical drama   1961 · It · Colour · 131min

This is an impressive quasi-biblical epic, produced by Dino De Laurentiis on a grand scale and directed with a fine sense of period by Richard Fleischer. It's best remembered today, however, for the fact that the Crucifixion was photographed against an actual eclipse of the sun. Anthony Quinn does well in the title role as the murderer and thief pardoned in place of Christ, and the climactic arena sequences involving Jack Palance are splendid. However, it's overlong and dull, like the novel on which it is based. **TS** DVD

Anthony Quinn *Barabbas* • Silvana Mangano *Rachel* • Arthur Kennedy *Pontius Pilate* • Katy Jurado *Sara* • Harry Andrews *St Peter* • Vittorio Gassman *Sahak* • Jack Palance *Torvald* • Ernest Borgnine *Lucius* • Valentina Cortese *Julia* ■ *Dir* Richard Fleischer • *Scr* Christopher Fry, Ivo Perilli, Diego Fabbri, Nigel Balchin, from the novel by Par Lagerkvist

Baraka ★★ PG
Documentary   1992 · US · Colour · 92min

Shot on Todd-AO 70mm stock, so that every image positively shimmers, Ron Fricke's heartfelt film is, sadly, a wasted opportunity. The ecological points he makes are blatant and laboured, while his over-reliance on snazzy editing and time-lapse photography draws too much attention to technique at the expense of the visual content. The contrasts between urban jungles and the areas of natural beauty they imperil do, occasionally, strike home, but, while it's easy to look at these often beautiful moving postcards, Fricke presents locations without identifying them, so most viewers will quickly find themselves lost and overwhelmed. **DP** DVD 🅱

■ *Dir* Ron Fricke • *Music* Michael Stearns

Barb Wire ★ 18
Science-fiction adventure
1995 · US · Colour · 94min

"Don't call me babe!" scowls Pamela Anderson, as she roves around Steel Harbor zapping agents of the Congressional Directorate. OK, providing you don't ask us to call this insulting reworking of *Casablanca* a film. Director David Hogan isn't interested in storytelling, which is just as well as he doesn't have much of a tale to tell. **DP** Violence, swearing, nudity. DVD 🅱

Pamela Anderson Lee [Pamela Anderson] *Barb Wire* • Temuera Morrison *Axel Rood* • Victoria Rowell *Cora D* • Jack Noseworthy *Charlie* • Xander Berkeley *Alexander Willis* • Steve Railsback *Colonel Pryzer* • Udo Kier *Curly* ■ *Dir* David Hogan • *Scr* Chuck Pfarrer, Ilene Chaiken, from the story by Ilene Chaiken

Barbara ★★★★ 12
Drama   2012 · Ger · Colour · 100min

Director Christian Petzold's fifth collaboration with muse Nina Hoss often feels like a Douglas Sirk melodrama tinged with a bittersweet "ostalgia" for the repressions and privations of 1980s East Germany. Banished to a remote town for requesting a travel visa, Hoss's Berlin doctor hopes to escape to her boyfriend (Mark Waschke) in the West, but is drawn to her supervisor who is torn between his affection and his official duties. Although tensions mount as the estimable Hoss considers her options, this is not an outright thriller, but also suggests that life under the GDR regime wasn't always intolerable. **DP**

German +subtitles. Some sexual references. DVD

Nina Hoss *Barbara Wolff* • Ronald Zehrfeld *André Reiser* • Jasna Fritzi Bauer *Stella* • Mark Waschke *Jörg* ■ *Dir/Scr* Christian Petzold

Barbara Taylor Bradford's Everything to Gain ★ 12
Romantic crime drama
1996 · US · Colour · 87min

Sean Young stars in this TV movie as a woman who tries to rebuild her life after her husband and two children are murdered. Alone and depressed, she joins forces with gritty detective Jack Scalia to find the thugs responsible for the crime. Unless you're a rabid fan of Barbara Taylor Bradford, you have nothing to gain from this preposterous drivel. **MC** DVD

Sean Young *Mallory Jordan* • Jack Scalia *Detective DeMarco* • Charles Shaughnessy *Andrew Keswick* • Joanna Miles *Jessica Jordan* • Samantha Eggar *Diana Keswick* ■ *Dir* Michael Miller (2) • *Scr* Cathleen Young, from the novel by Barbara Taylor Bradford

Barbarella ★★★ 15
Cult science-fiction fantasy
1967 · Fr/It · Colour · 93min

The famed French comic strip comes to glorious psychedelic life in director Roger Vadim's 41st-century space opera. Once you get past Jane Fonda's infamous antigravity striptease, however, the script turns rather dull. The imaginative sets steal the whole show, as Fonda's nubile intergalactic bimbo experiences close encounters of the sexually bizarre kind. A pleasure machine, cannibalistic dolls and Anita Pallenberg's Black Queen help ease the verbal vacuum. **AJ** Violence, sex scenes. DVD 🅱

Jane Fonda *Barbarella* • John Phillip Law *Pygar* • Anita Pallenberg *Black Queen* • Milo O'Shea *Concierge/Durand-Durand* • David Hemmings *Dildano* • Marcel Marceau *Professor Ping* • Ugo Tognazzi *Mark Hand* • Claude Dauphin *President of Earth* ■ *Dir* Roger Vadim • *Scr* Terry Southern, Brian Degas, Claude Brulé, Jean-Claude Forest, Clement Biddle Wood, Tudor Gates, Vittorio Bonicelli, Roger Vadim, from the comic by Jean-Claude Forest • *Cinematographer* Claude Renoir

The Barbarian ★★★
Romance   1933 · US · BW · 82min

Made when screen idol Ramon Novarro was nearing the end of the peak of his career and Myrna Loy was at the start of hers, this hot-blooded desert romance was of a kind leftover from the silent period, yet its sensibility remains far from old hat. When tourist Loy is cautioned by her uncle that she is hiring as a guide a man she knows nothing about, she replies, "But look at that profile!" Dashing Novarro sings *Love Songs of the Nile*, while sparkling Loy takes an on-screen bath and relishes the risqué pre-code dialogue. This is great fun. **TV**

Ramon Novarro *Jamil* • Myrna Loy *Diana* • Reginald Denny *Gerald* • Louise Closser Hale *Powers* • C Aubrey Smith *Cecil* • Edward Arnold *Achmed* • Blanche Frederici *Mrs Hume* ■ *Dir* Sam Wood • *Scr* Anita Loos, Elmer Harris, from the story by Edgar Selwyn

The Barbarian and the Geisha ★ U
Historical drama   1958 · US · Colour · 100min

Tough-guy director John Huston teamed up with John Wayne for the first and last time to make this historical drama about Townsend Harris, America's first consul to Japan. Wayne and Huston loathed each other from day one, however, and the movie was a disaster. **AT** DVD

John Wayne *Townsend Harris* • Eiko Ando *Okichi* • Sam Jaffe *Henry Heusken* • So Yamamura *Tamura* • Norman Thomson *Ship captain* • James Robbins *Lieutenant Fisher* • Morita *Prime minister* • Kodaya Ichikawa *Daimyo* ■ *Dir* John Huston • *Scr* Charles Grayson, from a story by Ellis St Joseph

The Barbarian Invasions ★★★★ 18
Comedy drama   2003 · Can/Fr · Colour · 95min

In director Denys Arcand's follow-up to his acclaimed 1986 film *The Decline of the American Empire*, a womanising history professor who is dying of cancer reflects on his life. Old lovers and friends congregate to help Rémy Girard celebrate and analyse a life that has earned the disapproval of his son, financial whizzkid Stéphane Rousseau. While this reunites the characters of the earlier film, it does not depend on familiarity with them for its success in painting a picture that is by turns funny and poignant. **BP** French, English +subtitles. DVD

Rémy Girard *Rémy* • Stéphane Rousseau *Sébastien* • Marie-Josée Croze *Nathalie* • Marina Hands *Gaëlle* • Dorothée Berryman *Louise* • Johanne-Marie Tremblay *Sister Constance* • Pierre Curzi *Pierre* • Yves Jacques *Claude* ■ *Dir/Scr* Denys Arcand

Barbarians at the Gate ★★★★ 15
Satirical drama based on a true story
1993 · US · Colour · 102min

Based on Bryan Burrough and John Helyar's bestseller, this superior TV movie recounts one of the most vicious takeover deals in American business history. James Garner is admirable as the head of multinational power player RJR Nabisco, who tries to buy the company when he realises its smokeless cigarette project isn't going to catch light. Stealing the show, however, is Jonathan Pryce as the wheeler-dealer determined to block him. The script is razor-sharp and Glenn Jordan's direction red hot. **DP** Swearing.

James Garner *F Ross Johnson* • Jonathan Pryce *Henry Kravis* • Peter Riegert *Peter Cohen* • Joanna Cassidy *Linda Robinson* • Fred Dalton Thompson *Jim Robinson* • Leilani Ferrer *Laurie Johnson* • Matt Clark *Ed Horrigan* • Jeffrey DeMunn *John Greeniaus* ■ *Dir* Glenn Jordan • *Scr* Larry Gelbart, from the book *Barbarians at the Gate: the Fall of RJR Nabisco* by Bryan Burrough, John Helyar

Barbarosa ★★ PG
Western   1982 · US · Colour · 86min

Country-and-western star Willie Nelson was chosen by director Fred Schepisi to be this film's western legend. But it doesn't work as well as intended, despite Nelson's endearing partnership with goofy farmboy Gary Busey, because the idea of an ageing outlaw forever on the lam is not only predictable but monotonous. **TH** Swearing.

Willie Nelson *Barbarosa* • Gary Busey *Karl* • Gilbert Roland *Don Braulio* • Isela Vega *Josephina* • Danny De La Paz *Eduardo* • Alma Martinez *Juanita* • George Voskovec *Herman Pahmeyer* • Sharon Compton *Hilda* ■ *Dir* Fred Schepisi • *Scr* William D Wittliff

Barbary Coast ★★★ PG
Period action drama   1935 · US · BW · 86min

This rowdy action drama, directed by Howard Hawks, was scripted by Ben Hecht and Charles MacArthur, but Hawks rewrote the script and the pair wanted to have their names taken off the credits. Miriam Hopkins plays a gold-digger who arrives in San Francisco intending to marry a rich man but, when she discovers he's dead, she switches her affections to crime boss Edward G Robinson. Then Joel McCrea shows up and confuses the issue. Sharp performances make this an enjoyable romp. **AT**

Miriam Hopkins *Mary Rutledge* • Edward G Robinson *Louis Charnalis* • Joel McCrea *James Carmichael* • Walter Brennan *Old Atrocity* • Frank Craven *Colonel Marcus* • Brian Donlevy *Knuckles* ■ *Dir* Howard Hawks • *Scr* Ben Hecht, Charles MacArthur

Barbary Coast Gent ★★ U
Western   1944 · US · BW · 86min

The main attraction of this Gold Rush rough-and-tumble is Wallace Beery, starring as a San Francisco conman gloriously named Honest Plush Brannon, who is

forced out of town after a shooting fracas with his enemy John Carradine. Waved goodbye to by his understanding girlfriend Binnie Barnes, he makes for Nevada and strikes gold, but that's not the end of the story. Directed by Roy Del Ruth, it features a cast of familiar character actors, and was produced appropriately by Orville Dull. **RK**

Wallace Beery *Honest Plush Brannon* • Binnie Barnes *Lil Damish* • John Carradine *Duke Cleat* • Bruce Kellogg *Bradford Bellamy III* • Frances Rafferty *Portia Adair* • Chill Wills *Sheriff Hightower* • Noah Beery Sr [Noah Beery] *Pete Hannibal* • Louise Beavers *Bedelia* ■ *Dir* Roy Del Ruth • *Scr* William R Lipman, Grant Garrett, Harry Ruskin

The Barber of Seville ★★★ U
Opera   1946 · It · BW · 96min

Director Mario Costa will go down in film history as the man who discovered Gina Lollobrigida. Yet he also handled several operatic adaptations in the 1940s which, while not particularly inventive in visual terms, do adequate justice to both the music and its performance. American journalist Deems Taylor (who narrated Disney's *Fantasia*) reworked the libretto for the screen to enable Costa to place the emphasis firmly on Rossini's memorable score. As Figaro, the barber who matchmakes lovesick count Ferruccio Tagliavini and miser's ward Nelly Corradi, the flamboyant Tito Gobi is in fine fettle. **DP** Italian +subtitles.

Ferruccio Tagliavini *Count Almaviva* • Tito Gobbi *Figaro* • Nelly Corradi *Rosina* • Vito de Tarranto *Don Bartolo* • Italo Tajo *Don Basilio* • Natalia Nicolini *Berta* • Nino Mazziotti *Fiorello* ■ *Dir* Mario Costa • *Scr* Deems Taylor, from the opera by Giacomo Rossini

The Barber of Siberia ★★ 12
Period drama   1999 · Rus · Colour · 169min

Staged with a grandeur that undermines his trademark intimacy, Nikita Mikhalkov's Tsarist epic suffers from thematic imprecision, uncertainty of tone and excessive length. The lack of spark between American Julia Ormond and soldier Oleg Menshikov further strains the credibility of this long-cherished project, which inexplicably lurches from comedy to melodrama partway through. Thanks to Pavel Lebeshev's glorious photography, the evocation of the 1880s is impeccable. **DP** English, Russian +subtitles. DVD

Julia Ormond *Jane Callahan* • Richard Harris *Douglas McCracken* • Oleg Menshikov *Andre Tolstov* • Alexei Petrenko *General Radlov* • Alexander Yakovlev *Maximich* • Marat Bacharov *Polievsky* • Daniel Olbrychski *Kopnovsky* ■ *Dir* Nikita Mikhalkov • *Scr* Nikita Mikhalkov, Rustam Ibragimbekov, Rospo Pallenberg, from a story by Nikita Mikhalkov

The Barber Shop ★★★★ U
Comedy   1933 · US · BW · 20min

WC Fields engages in surrealist experimentation in his last two-reeler for comic king Mack Sennett. A cello has a romance, a fat man is steamed skeletally thin and a dog develops a taste for severed ears as Fields reworks material that had served him since his vaudeville days. The plotline – about the bungled capture of a fleeing bank robber – is almost an irrelevance; the real interest lies in Fields as Cornelius O'Hare as he absent-mindedly wields a razor and deals with the various eccentrics who enter his shop. Director Arthur Ripley is nominally in charge, but there's only one creative force at work here. **DP** DVD

WC Fields *Cornelius O'Hare* ■ *Dir* Arthur Ripley • *Scr* WC Fields

Barbershop ★★★ 12
Comedy   2002 · US · Colour · 98min

Ice Cube gives a self-assured performance here as the jaded owner of a Chicago hairdressing salon threatened with foreclosure. A warm, but far from tame, slice-of-life comedy, this follows the salon through what could be its last day, as barbers and their customers trade jokes and neighbourhood gossip and the boss struggles to come up with the cash. The message is short on subtlety, and a slapstick subplot about a stolen ATM is a needless distraction. However, the camaraderie and antagonistic banter of the workplace are well observed and brightly performed. JC Violence, swearing. *DVD*

Ice Cube *Calvin Palmer* • Anthony Anderson *JD* • Cedric the Entertainer *Eddie* • Sean Patrick Thomas *Jimmy* • Eve *Terri* • Troy Garity *Isaac Rosenberg* ■ *Dir* Tim Story • *Scr* Mark Brown, Don D Scott, Marshall Todd, from a story by Mark Brown

Barbershop 2: Back in Business ★★★12

Comedy   2004 · US · Colour · 101min

Calvin (Ice Cube) discovers that his shop's future on Chicago's South Side is threatened when super-hairdressing salon Nappy Cutz is set to open across the street. This sequel is more character-driven than the original, with the ever-opinionated Cedric the Entertainer's backstory benefiting from the flashback treatment, while Queen Latifah joins the ranks of eccentrics and oddballs as the proprietress of the beauty shop next door. Director Kevin Rodney Sullivan tries too hard to make it likeable, but that's not at all unwelcome. TH Swearing. *DVD*

Ice Cube *Calvin Palmer* • Cedric the Entertainer *Eddie* • Sean Patrick Thomas *Jimmy* • Eve *Terri* • Troy Garity *Isaac Rosenberg* • Michael Ealy *Ricky Nash* • Leonard Earl Howze *Dinka* • Harry Lennix *Quentin Leroux* • Robert Wisdom *Alderman Brown* • Queen Latifah *Gina* ■ *Dir* Kevin Rodney Sullivan • *Scr* Don D Scott, from characters by Mark Brown

Barbershop: a Fresh Cut ★★★12A

Comedy   2016 · US · Colour · 111min

It may have been a long time coming, but the latest instalment might be the best one yet. We are back at Calvin's Barbershop on the South Side of Chicago, where the neighbourhood has taken a turn for the worse. Calvin (Ice Cube) and his staff are growing tired of gang-related violence, so they decide to do something about it. As with the previous two movies, most of the action takes place inside the shop, where the stylists discuss a variety of timely issues, which are mostly funny and well-observed. SC Swearing, sexual references.

Ice Cube *Calvin* • Cedric the Entertainer *Eddie* • Regina Hall *Angie* • Anthony Anderson *JD* • Eve *Terri* • JB Smoove *One-Stop* ■ *Dir* Malcolm D Lee • *Scr* Kenya Barris, Tracy Oliver, from characters by Mark Brown

Barcelona ★★★★12

Comedy drama   1994 · US · Colour · 96min

Louche observation, tart dialogue and droll wit are director Whit Stillman's hallmarks, and they're all astutely called on in this sophisticated rumination on the sex and social lives of two American cousins living in the cosmopolitan Spanish city during the 1980s. Solemn salesman Taylor Nichols and loudmouth navy officer Christopher Eigeman clash with each other as much as the foreign culture, while roaming the Ramblas and seducing the senoritas in a spot-on view of the Eurotrash disco scene. AJ Some violence, swearing, nudity, substance abuse.

Taylor Nichols *Ted Boynton* • Christopher Eigeman [Chris Eigeman] *Fred Mason* • Tushka Bergen *Montserrat* • Mira Sorvino *Marta Ferrer* • Pep Munne *Ramon* • Hellena Schmied *Greta* • Nuria Badia *Aurora* • Thomas Gibson *Dickie Taylor* ■ *Dir/Scr* Whit Stillman

Barefoot Adventure ★★★

Documentary   1960 · US · Colour · 74min

Filmed at some of the most famous beaches in Hawaii – including North Shore at Oahu and Point Surf at Makaha, where the waves are legendarily huge – Bruce Brown's third feature is the beneficiary of a lucky accident. As the original voice track had been lost, he wrote a completely new commentary that enabled him to reminisce about the US surfing scene in the 1960s, as

well as comment on the action. With an evocative jazz score by Bud Shank and some stunning cinematography (shot from within a Plexiglass case), this is a wry, yet wistful memoir of a gloriously hedonistic lifestyle. DP *DVD*

■ *Dir* Bruce Brown

The Barefoot Contessa ★★★★PG

Drama   1954 · US · Colour · 125min

"The world's most beautiful animal," shrieked the ads for this mordant satire on the movie business, and, unsurprisingly, nobody disputed the fact, for "the animal" was none other than Ava Gardner in her prime, playing a character based on Rita Hayworth. Humphrey Bogart plays her cynical director: "I made her," he snarls, and you believe him. Director/writer Joe Mankiewicz had satirised Broadway in the multi-Oscar winning *All about Eve*, and this is similar, but far less theatrical. Edmond O'Brien collected an Oscar here as the sweaty publicist, and there's a star-making performance from Rossano Brazzi. TS *DVD*

Humphrey Bogart *Harry Dawes* • Ava Gardner *Maria Vargas* • Edmond O'Brien *Oscar Muldoon* • Marius Goring *Alberto Bravano* • Valentina Cortesa [Valentina Cortese] *Eleanora Torlato-Favrini* • Rossano Brazzi *Vincenzo Torlato-Favrini* • Elizabeth Sellars *Jerry* ■ *Dir/Scr* Joseph L Mankiewicz • *Cinematographer* Jack Cardiff

The Barefoot Executive ★★★U

Comedy adventure   1971 · US · Colour · 91min

This Disney comedy may blunt some of its point with whimsy, but it's still an enjoyable spoof of the way TV companies chase ratings. Here, a chimpanzee is discovered to be an ace television programmer, leading to a battle between rival companies to sign up the simian marvel. Human lead Kurt Russell looks bewildered, but the chimp proves what the rest of us have always known about scheduling: it's all just monkey business. TH

Kurt Russell *Steven Post* • Joe Flynn *Francis X Wilbanks* • Harry Morgan *EJ Crampton* • Wally Cox *Mertons* • Heather North *Jennifer Scott* • Alan Hewitt *Farnsworth* • Hayden Rorke *Clifford* • John Ritter *Roger* ■ *Dir* Robert Butler • *Scr* Joseph L McEveety, from a story by Lila Garrett, Bernie Kahn, Stuart C Billett

Barefoot in the Park ★★★★PG

Romantic comedy   1967 · US · Colour · 101min

In this delightful comedy, adapted by Neil Simon from his hit Broadway show, Robert Redford (who appeared in the stage play) and Jane Fonda star as the young married couple attempting to achieve newly wedded bliss. Redford is a joy in a reasonably rare comic role, though Mildred Natwick almost steals the show as Fonda's mother. It's handled well by director Gene Saks, who maintains the humour and a lively pace until half an hour from the end. JB *DVD*

Robert Redford *Paul Bratter* • Jane Fonda *Corie Bratter* • Charles Boyer *Victor Velasco* • Mildred Natwick *Mrs Ethel Banks* • Herb Edelman *Telephone man* • James Stone *Delivery man* • Ted Hartley *Frank* ■ *Dir* Gene Saks • *Scr* Neil Simon, from his play

Barely Legal ★15

Comedy   2003 · US/Ger · Colour · 87min

National Lampoon continues its downward slide with this pitiful teen sex comedy. Hormones run wild as three high-school losers decide to improve their finances and popularity by making a porn flick. Naturally, the "by virgins, for virgins" project brings an array of problems, none of which are funny or titillating. SF Swearing, sexual references, drug abuse. *DVD*

Erik Von Detten *Deacon* • Tony Denman *Fred* • Daniel Farber *Matt* • Sarah-Jane Potts [Sarah Jane Potts] *Ashley* • Amy Smart *Naomi* • Tom Arnold *Mr Lewis* ■ *Dir* David M Evans [David Mickey Evans] • *Scr* David H Steinberg

Barely Lethal ★★12

Spy comedy adventure   2015 · US · Colour · 98min

This teen action comedy follows a 16-year-old girl (Hailee Steinfeld) who is unhappy with her life. The twist is that she happens to be a highly trained assassin. The plot sees her faking her own death and enrolling at a high school in an attempt at a normal life. What follows is elevated by Steinfeld, who is immensely endearing in the lead role, despite the fact that her character is frustratingly inconsistent. The result is a high-school flick that is both knowing and formulaic at the same time. SC Violence, swearing, sexual references.

Hailee Steinfeld *Megan Walsh* • Samuel L Jackson *Maxwell Hardman* • Jessica Alba *Victoria Knox* • Dove Cameron *Liz Larson* ■ *Dir* Kyle Newman • *Scr* John D'Arco

Barfly ★★18

Comedy drama   1987 · US · Colour · 95min

Confirming the notion that there's no one more boring than a drunk, *Barfly* gives Mickey Rourke and Faye Dunaway the chance to slur their words and blur their meaning. Written by Charles Bukowski from his own experiences propping up a bar in a dimly-lit dive in Los Angeles, the story puts the casualties of life who think they are poets or romantics, or both, on display. AT

Mickey Rourke *Henry Chinaski* • Faye Dunaway *Wanda Wilcox* • Alice Krige *Tully Sorenson* • Jack Nance *Detective* • JC Quinn *Jim* • Frank Stallone *Eddie* • Sandy Martin *Janice* • Roberta Bassin *Lilly* • Gloria LeRoy *Grandma Moses* • Joe Unger *Ben* ■ *Dir* Barbet Schroeder • *Scr* Charles Bukowski

The Bargee ★★PG

Comedy   1964 · UK · Colour · 102min

Having failed to make an international movie star out of Tony Hancock with *The Rebel*, Ray Galton and Alan Simpson tried to fashion a film comedy for their *Steptoe and Son* protégé Harry H Corbett. However, in spite of the presence of a number of comic luminaries, the result is disappointing. The poverty of the plot (in which Corbett's "Lothario of the Locks" is duped into matrimony) is nothing next to its intrinsic sexism. DP *DVD*

Harry H Corbett *Hemel Pike* • Hugh Griffith *Joe* • Eric Sykes *The mariner* • Ronnie Barker *Ronnie* • Julia Foster *Christine* • Miriam Karlin *Nellie* • Eric Barker *Foreman* • Derek Nimmo *Dr Scott* • Norman Bird *Waterways supervisor* • Richard Briers *Tomkins* ■ *Dir* Duncan Wood • *Scr* Ray Galton, Alan Simpson

The Barker ★★

Silent drama   1928 · US · BW · 86min

Starring Milton Sills as a fairground barker, this movie captures the colourful milieu of the tent-show world and boasts a cast that includes silent stars Betty Compson and Dorothy Mackaill. With direction by George Fitzmaurice and superior photography from Lee Garmes, it promises good if modest entertainment. Unfortunately, however, it was made as a silent with some sound subsequently added. This is of such poor quality that it becomes a pain to watch the film. RK

Milton Sills *Nifty Miller* • Dorothy Mackaill *Lou* • Betty Compson *Carrie* • Douglas Fairbanks Jr *Chris Miller* • Sylvia Ashton *Ma Benson* • George Cooper (1) *Hap Spissel* ■ *Dir* George Fitzmaurice • *Scr* Benjamin Glazer, Joseph Jackson, Herman J Mankiewicz (titles), from the play by Kenyon Nicholson

The Barkleys of Broadway ★★★U

Musical   1949 · US · Colour · 104min

This movie was originally intended as a vehicle for the successful *Easter Parade* team, but in fact resulted in the reteaming of Ginger Rogers and Fred Astaire after a ten-year break, with Rogers replacing an ailing Judy Garland. Fred is as chirpy and debonair as ever, but time hasn't been kind to Ginger, who has lost her freshness – and she's not helped by some of the hokey

situations. Cherishable, but a bit disappointing. TS *DVD*

Fred Astaire *Josh Barkley* • Ginger Rogers *Dinah Barkley* • Oscar Levant *Ezra Miller* • Billie Burke *Mrs Belney* • *Dir* Charles Walters • *Scr* Betty Comden, Adolph Green • *Choreography* Hermes Pan • *Music* Harry Warren • *Lyrics* Ira Gershwin

Barnacle Bill ★U

Comedy   1957 · UK · BW · 85min

The last of the Ealing comedies, this is a wearisome affair. There are echoes of *Kind Hearts and Coronets* (with Alec Guinness playing his ancestors in several contrived flashbacks), and the action brims over with eccentric characters who could be refugees from any of the film's more illustrious predecessors. An unfunny and slightly embarrassing bore. DP

Alec Guinness *Captain Ambrose/his ancestors* • Irene Browne *Mrs Barrington* • Percy Herbert *Tommy* • Harold Goodwin (2) *Duckworth* • Maurice Denham *Crowley* • Victor Maddern *Figg* • George Rose *Bullen* • Jackie Collins *June* • Warren Mitchell *Artie White* • Donald Pleasence *Teller* ■ *Dir* Charles Frend • *Scr* TEB Clarke

Barney's Great Adventure ★★★U

Fantasy   1998 · US · Colour · 73min

Television's popular purple dinosaur magically appears to teach three vacationing youngsters all about the worlds of the farmyard and the circus as they undertake a quest to find a nearly-hatched alien egg. Devoid of all the usual Hollywood special effects razzmatazz, but not so sugary sweet that it will cause tooth decay, this colourful, energetic and endurable nursery rhyme-style fantasy will have children hitting the rewind button from now until for ever. AJ *DVD*

George Hearn *Grandpa Greenfield* • Shirley Douglas *Grandma Greenfield* • Trevor Morgan *Cody Newton* • Kyla Pratt *Marcella* ■ *Dir* Steve Gomer • *Scr* Stephen White, from a story by Sheryl Leach, Dennis DeShazer, Stephen White, from characters by Kathy Parker, Sheryl Leach, Dennis DeShazer

Barney's Version ★★★15

Drama   2010 · Can/It · Colour · 128min

This drama charts the incident-packed life of Barney (Paul Giamatti), as he stumbles from one bad marriage to another. Helped and hindered in equal measure by his lifelong friends and bon viveur ex-cop father (Dustin Hoffman), Barney seems to have finally found true happiness with Miriam (Rosamund Pike), but another wrong turn is never too far away. Giamatti (*Sideways*) is perfectly cast as the world-weary Barney, while an over-the-top Hoffman and Minnie Driver as Barney's spoilt second wife are the major sources of humour. TeS Swearing, sex scenes. *DVD*

Paul Giamatti *Barney Panofsky* • Dustin Hoffman *Izzy* • Rosamund Pike *Miriam* • Minnie Driver *The 2nd Mrs P* • Rachelle Lefevre *Clara* • Scott Speedman *Boogie* • Bruce Greenwood *Blair* • Mark Addy *Detective O'Hearne* ■ *Dir* Richard J Lewis • *Scr* Michael Konyves, from the novel by Mordecai Richler

Barnyard ★★★PG

Animated comedy   2006 · US · Colour · 85min

This CGI cartoon seems like a cross between *The Lion King* and the skewed world of Gary Larson's *Far Side*, where animals stand up and talk whenever humans aren't looking. Kevin James voices fun-loving male cow Otis, who must face up to his manly responsibility when his father (Sam Elliott) is killed by coyotes. The film brims with often laugh-out-loud sight gags and one-liners but, while younger children may be a little disturbed by the dark undertones, the more literal-minded will feel confused by the muddled biology on view: all the cows, male and female, have udders. LF *DVD*

Kevin James *Otis* • Courteney Cox *Daisy* • Sam Elliott *Ben* • Danny Glover *Miles* • Wanda Sykes *Bessy* • Andie MacDowell *Etta* • Jeff Garcia *Pip* • Maria Bamford *Mrs Beady* ■ *Dir/Scr* Steve Oedekerk

12 15 18 PASSED FOR PEOPLE OF THESE AGES AND OVER   *DVD* RELEASED ON DVD   RELEASED ON BLU-RAY   3D RELEASED IN 3D   CS END CREDIT SEQUENCE

93

B

Baron Blood ★★★ 15
Horror   1972 · It/W Ger · Colour · 93min

One of the most richly visual and atmospheric works in the chill catalogue of Italian horror genius Mario Bava. Joseph Cotten plays the Austrian baron whose ancestral castle is being turned into a luxury hotel and also his moldy-faced reincarnation wanting to put his 16th-century torture chamber to good use again. Elke Sommer screams a lot as she and her lover Antonio Cantafora revive the warlock baron. Commendable for its taut chase scenes, grisly gore and eerie photography. AJ Italian dubbed. DVD BL

Joseph Cotten *Alfred Becker/Otto von Kleist* • Elke Sommer *Eva Arnold* • Massimo Girotti *Uncle Karl Hummel* • Antonio Cantafora *Peter von Kleist* ■ *Dir* Mario Bava • *Scr* William A Bairn, Vincent Fotre, Willibald Eser, Mario Bava, from a story by Vincent Fotre

Baron Münchhausen ★★★ PG
Fantasy   1943 · Ger · Colour · 110min

The eponymous Baron, described as "the greatest liar of all time", was a real-life character who lived in Germany and became an 18th-century folk hero with his outrageous stories. None of them were true; all of them were entertaining. He has formed the basis of three feature films. This first version, directed by the Hungarian Josef von Baky, is an extraordinary technical achievement. The film was commissioned by Joseph Goebbels to celebrate the 25th anniversary of the UFA studios in Berlin. AT German +subtitles. DVD

Hans Albers *Baron Münchhausen* • Brigitte Horney *Catherine the Great* • Wilhelm Bendow *The Man in the Moon* • Michael Bohnen *Prince Karl of Brunswick* • Hans Brausewetter *Frederick von Hartenfeld* • Marina von Ditmar *Sophie von Riedesel* ■ *Dir* Josef von Baky • *Scr* Berthold Bürger [Erich Kästner]

Baron Munchhausen ★★★
Part-animated fantasy adventure
1961 · Cz · Colour · 81min

Czech animator Karel Zeman tackled the fantastic adventures of the notorious mythomaniac by using puppets, cartoons, special effects and live action against painted backdrops. Zeman's inspiration sprang from the 1862 edition of Gottfried Burger's novel, with its drawings by Gustave Doré, and the turn-of-the-century films of conjurer and cinema pioneer Georges Méliès. Visually fascinating, but stilted. RB In Czech.

Milos Kopecky *Baron Munchhausen* • Jana Brejchova *Bianca* • Rudolf Jelinek *Tonik* • Jan Werich *Captain of Dutch ship* • Rudolf Hrusinsky *Sultan* • Eduard Kohout *Commander of the fortress* • Karel Hoger *Cyrano de Bergerac* • Karel Effa *Officer of the guard* ■ *Dir* Karel Zeman • *Scr* Karel Zeman, Jiri Brdecka, Josef Kainar, from the novel *Baron Prásil* by Gottfried Burger and the illustrations by Gustave Doré

The Baron of Arizona ★★
Western   1950 · US · BW · 96min

The second film of maverick writer/director Samuel Fuller, this low-budget, fact-based drama tells the story of a land office clerk in the 19th century who forges documents to prove himself the "Baron of Arizona". The forger is played rather ponderously by Vincent Price and the film becomes bogged down in detail. AE

Vincent Price *James Addison Reavis* • Ellen Drew *Sofia Peralta-Reavis* • Vladimir Sokoloff *Pepito* • Reed Hadley *Griff* • Robert Barrat *Judge Adams* ■ *Dir/Scr* Samuel Fuller

The Baroness and the Butler ★★
Romantic comedy   1938 · US · BW · 79min

French beauty and future wife of Tyrone Power, Annabella, made an uncomfortable Hollywood debut in this whimsy as the wayward baroness daughter of the Hungarian prime minister. William Powell co-stars as the butler to the household who leaves his job to go into politics, becomes Leader of the Opposition, and returns to declare his love for the baroness. The script is silly and Annabella is deficient in both spoken English and light comedy, but this is partly redeemed by the polished Powell and an A-list supporting cast. RK

William Powell *Johann Porok* • Annabella *Baroness Katrina Marissey* • Helen Westley *Countess Sandor* • Henry Stephenson *Count Albert Sandor* • Joseph Schildkraut *Baron Georg Marissey* • J Edward Bromberg *Zorda* ■ *Dir* Walter Lang • *Scr* Sam Hellman, Lamar Trotti, Kathryn Scola, from the play *Jean* by Ladislaus Bus-Fekete

Barquero ★★★ 15
Western   1970 · US · Colour · 104min

A violent American western in the European style, this is one of the few movies to give a decent co-starring role to the estimable Warren Oates. Here, a black-clad Oates is pitted mercilessly against Lee Van Cleef as the tenacious ferryman of the title. There's a moral of sorts amid all the slaughter, and it's interesting to see how veteran western director Gordon Douglas adapts himself to the new, freer style. TS Violence, swearing.

Lee Van Cleef *Travis* • Warren Oates *Jake Remy* • Forrest Tucker *Mountain Phil* • Kerwin Mathews *Marquette* • Mariette Hartley *Anna* • Marie Gomez *Nola* • Brad Weston *Driver* • Craig Littler *Pitney* ■ *Dir* Gordon Douglas • *Scr* George Schenck, William Marks

The Barrens ★★★
Horror   2012 · US/Can · Colour · 94min

True Blood star Stephen Moyer embarks on a family camping trip to the Pine Barrens, ostensibly to scatter his late father's ashes at their favourite holiday spot. However, it soon becomes apparent that Moyer is not a happy camper: he's haunted by a childhood encounter and when fellow campers start turning up disembowelled, he's convinced the demon is back to get him. Director Darren Lynn Bousman has been responsible for some of the more forgettable *Saw* sequels, but in this proficient backwoods chiller, he ratchets up the tension nicely and keeps the viewer guessing right to the end. JF DVD

Stephen Moyer *Richard Vineyard* • Mia Kirshner *Cynthia Vineyard* • Allie MacDonald *Sadie Vineyard* • Peter DaCunha *Danny Vineyard* ■ *Dir/Scr* Darren Lynn Bousman

The Barretts of Wimpole Street ★★★★ U
Biographical drama   1934 · US · BW · 109min

One of the great triumphs of producer Irving G Thalberg's reign at MGM, this managed to be both intelligent in execution and a commercial success. As Elizabeth Barrett, Norma Shearer (Mrs Thalberg) is superb, but the real star is Charles Laughton as Elizabeth's tyrannical father, whose incestuous love for his daughter is hinted at but never addressed. In fact, he was only a year older than his "daughter" Shearer and two years younger than Fredric March, uncomfortably cast as poet Robert Browning. TS

Norma Shearer *Elizabeth Barrett* • Fredric March *Robert Browning* • Charles Laughton *Edward Moulton Barrett* • Maureen O'Sullivan *Henrietta Barrett* • Katharine Alexander [Katherine Alexander] *Arabel Barrett* • Ralph Forbes *Captain Surtees Cook* • Marion Clayton *Bella Hedley* • Una O'Connor *Wilson* ■ *Dir* Sidney Franklin • *Scr* Ernest Vajda, Claudine West, Donald Ogden Stewart, from the play by Rudolf Besier

The Barretts of Wimpole Street ★★ U
Period drama   1956 · UK · Colour · 105min

This recounts the story of the love affair between the invalid poetess Elizabeth Barrett and Robert Browning, with whom she elopes to escape the rigid and frightening control of her father (John Gielgud). Sidney Franklin, who directed the 1934 Hollywood version, also directed this British remake. Although stylish and sober-minded, with a Freudian take on Barrett's relationship with his daughters (Virginia McKenna is featured as the other victim of his wrath), the film emerges as slow, heavy-handed and uninvolving. RK

Jennifer Jones *Elizabeth* • John Gielgud *Barrett* • Bill Travers *Robert Browning* • Virginia McKenna *Henrietta* • Susan Stephen *Bella* ■ *Dir* Sidney Franklin • *Scr* John Dighton, from the play by Rudolf Besier

Barricade ★★
Western   1950 · US · Colour · 75min

This exercise in rough brutality features Raymond Massey as the owner of a mine in the middle of nowhere who slave-drives his labourers with sadistic cruelty, until nemesis arrives in the form of a fugitive from justice (Dane Clark). Both the screenplay and Peter Godfrey's direction are undistinguished, but as a depiction of violence in a different era the movie has its moments. RK

Ruth Roman *Judith Burns* • Dane Clark *Bob Peters* • Raymond Massey *"Boss" Kruger* • Robert Douglas *Aubry Milburn* • Morgan Farley *Judge* • Walter Coy *Benson* • George Stern *Tippy* • Robert Griffin *Kirby* ■ *Dir* Peter Godfrey • *Scr* William Sackheim

Barry Lyndon ★★★★★ PG
Period drama   1975 · UK · Colour · 177min

Stanley Kubrick provides this awesome work with an authentic 18th-century look and a unique atmosphere that totally convinces. It is the slow and utterly hypnotic tale of an Irish youth whose adventures and misfortunes take in the Seven Years' War, the gambling clubs of Europe and marriage into the English aristocracy. In Kubrick's scheme of things, character means less than context, so Ryan O'Neal may appear bloodless and Marisa Berenson wholly vacant, but this turns out to be a strength. There are fine turns by Leonard Rossiter, Hardy Kruger and, best of all, Leon Vitali as O'Neal's stepson. There is also a definitive climactic duel scene, a confiding narration by Michael Hordern and ravishing photography. AT Some violence. DVD BL

Ryan O'Neal *Barry Lyndon* • Marisa Berenson *Lady Lyndon* • Patrick Magee *The Chevalier* • Hardy Kruger *Captain Potzdorf* • Steven Berkoff *Lord Ludd* • Gay Hamilton *Nora* • Leonard Rossiter *Captain Quin* • Godfrey Quigley *Captain Grogan* • Marie Kean *Barry's mother* • Leon Vitali *Lord Bullingdon* ■ *Dir* Stanley Kubrick • *Scr* Stanley Kubrick, from William Makepeace Thackeray's novel • *Cinematographer* John Alcott • *Art Director* Ken Adam

Barry McKenzie Holds His Own ★★ 18
Comedy adventure   1974 · Aus · Colour · 93min

When Dame Edna is mistaken for the Queen, she and her nephew Barry are whisked off to Transylvania by Count Plasma. A lot of this sequel to *The Adventures of Barry McKenzie* is naff, lazily shot and rather boring. But when the actors get fired up and the Aussie slang starts flowing, it's splendidly vulgar and even subversive in its trouncing of racial stereotypes and political hypocrisy. AT

Barry Crocker *Barry McKenzie/Ken McKenzie* • Barry Humphries *Buck-toothed Englishman/Edna Everage/Senator Douglas Manton/Dr Meyer de Lamphrey* • Donald Pleasence *Erich, Count Plasma* • Roy Kinnear *Bishop of Paris* • John Le Mesurier *English emigrant* • Tommy Trinder *Arthur McKenzie* • Dick Bentley *Colonel Lucas* ■ *Dir* Bruce Beresford • *Scr* Barry Humphries, Bruce Beresford, from the comic strip *The Wonderful World of Barry McKenzie* by Barry Humphries

Barsaat ★★★ U
Musical drama   1949 · Ind · BW · 157min

The popular romantic team of Nargis and Raj Kapoor were reunited for this enduring Bollywood classic, which the latter also produced and directed. Defying her father's wishes, country girl Nargis's plans to elope with the wealthy Kapoor are thwarted when she's rescued from near-drowning by a fisherman (KN Singh), who claims her as his bride. The story may be packed with such melodramatic devices as class prejudice, spurned love and incredible coincidence, but there's also a level of social comment in Ramanand Sagar's screenplay, which is reinforced by the moody symbolism of Jal Mistry's photography. DP Hindi +subtitles.

Raj Kapoor *Pran* • Nargis *Reshma* • Premnath *Gopal* • KN Singh *Fisherman* ■ *Dir* Raj Kapoor • *Scr* Ramanand Sagar

Bartleby ★★★
Drama   1971 · UK · Colour · 78min

Herman Melville's short story makes for a unremittingly downbeat yet fascinating movie, mainly due to the riveting interplay between its two stars. John McEnery plays Bartleby, a reclusive, diffident accounts clerk who simply won't accept he has been fired by Paul Scofield. Instead, he carries on accounting until he achieves his ultimate aim, which is total exclusion from society – in other words, death. A mysterious, chilling allegory. AT

Paul Scofield *The accountant* • John McEnery *Bartleby* • Thorley Walters *The colleague* • Colin Jeavons *Tucker* • Raymond Mason *Landlord* • Charles Kinross *Tenant* • Neville Barber *First client* ■ *Dir* Anthony Friedman • *Scr* Anthony Friedman, Rodney Carr-Smith, from the story *Bartleby the Scrivener* by Herman Melville

Bartleby ★★★ PG
Black comedy   2000 · US · Colour · 82min

Written in 1853, Herman Melville's short story provided both a psychological and a satirical insight into urban alienation and the dehumanising effect of monotonous labour. But Jonathan Parker finds the material less cinematically malleable than it first appears. The soul-destroying setting is splendid, as is David Paymer's performance as the record office boss whose inadequacies are exposed by eccentric clerk Crispin Glover's refusal to follow orders or vacate the premises. However, too many minor figures border on caricature, while additions such as the fascistic fantasy sequence prove to be seriously miscalculated. DP

David Paymer *The Boss* • Crispin Glover *Bartleby* • Glenne Headly *Vivian* • Maury Chaykin *Ernie* • Joe Piscopo *Rocky* • Seymour Cassel *Frank Waxman* • Carrie Snodgress *Book publisher* • Dick Martin *The Mayor* ■ *Dir* Jonathan Parker • *Scr* Jonathan Parker, Catherine di Napoli, from the short story *Bartleby the Scrivener* by Herman Melville

Bartok the Magnificent ★★★ U
Animated adventure   1999 · US · Colour · 65min

Reasoning that if Disney can spin off from their cartoon hits so can he, Don Bluth awards the voluble bat from *Anastasia* his chance to shine in this cheap and cheerful prequel. The voice talents are impeccable, enlivening an already noisy story, in which the critters abandon their con trickery to undertake a trio of impossible tasks in order to rescue the Tsarevich from the clutches of his evil tutor. DP

Hank Azaria *Bartok* • Kelsey Grammer *Zozi* • Andrea Martin *Baba Yaga* • Catherine O'Hara *Ludmilla* • Tim Curry *The Skull* • Jennifer Tilly *Piloff* ■ *Dir* Don Bluth, Gary Goldman • *Scr* Jay Lacopo

Barton Fink ★★★★ 15
Period drama   1991 · US · Colour · 112min

This is the most brilliantly observed Hollywood put-down since *Day of the Locust*. Only the Coen brothers would dare to make such a vitriolic attack on the industry supporting them and actually get away with it. Part David Lynch, part Kafka and wholly demanding, this tale features John Turturro as the social realist playwright snapped up by 1940s Hollywood to script a Wallace Beery wrestling picture. But, even as his life collapses around him, and his next-door neighbour (John Goodman) turns serial killer, he just can't sacrifice his ideals on the altar of commercialism. A gorgeously designed paranoid parable packed with sharp detail, great in-jokes and an Oscar-nominated performance by Michael Lerner as the studio mogul from hell. AJ Violence, swearing. DVD BL

The

Bat

B

John Turturro *Barton Fink* • John Goodman *Charlie Meadows* • Judy Davis *Audrey Taylor* • Michael Lerner *Jack Lipnik* • John Mahoney *WP Mayhew* • Tony Shalhoub *Ben Geisler* • Jon Polito *Lou Breeze* • Steve Buscemi *Chet* ■ *Dir* Joel Coen • *Scr* Joel Coen, Ethan Coen

BASEketball ★★★ 15
Sports comedy 1998 · US · Colour · 103min

Unfairly denied a British cinema release after a disastrous US run, this sports spoof from director David Zucker (who made *Airplane!* and the first two *Naked Gun* movies) is wildly offensive fun. It stars *South Park* creators Trey Parker and Matt Stone, playing a pair of infantile slobs who invent a popular new game that combines the hoops of basketball with the runs of baseball – and a few sick twists of their own. JC Swearing. *DVD* CS
Trey Parker *Joseph Cooper* • Matt Stone *Doug Remer* • Robert Vaughn (1) *Baxter Cain* • Ernest Borgnine *Theodore Denslow* • Dian Bachar *Kenny "Squeak" Scolari* • Yasmine Bleeth *Jenna Reed* • Jenny McCarthy *Yvette Denslow* ■ *Dir* David Zucker • *Scr* David Zucker, Robert LoCash, Jeff Wright, Lewis Friedman

Basement ★ 15
Horror thriller 2010 · UK · Colour · 74min

EastEnders star Danny Dyer has been in some clunkers, yet few of his movies are as abysmal as this wafer-thin horror. Weakly written and badly acted, this British snooze-fest sees Dyer's antiwar protester and four student mates (including an embarrassing Jimi Mistry and *Fish Tank* star Kierston Wareing) get trapped in a mysterious bunker in the middle of a forest, only to discover they're being stalked. To say that this pedestrian picture is uneventful is an understatement. SF *DVD*
Danny Dyer *Gary* • Jimi Mistry *Derek* • Kierston Wareing *Sarah* ■ *Dir* Asham Kamboj • *Scr* Ewen Glass

Basic ★★ 15
Thriller 2003 · US/Ger/UK · Colour · 94min

John McTiernan's risible attempt at a military thriller misfires on practically all levels. A platoon of US Army Rangers goes in to the Panamanian jungle on a routine training exercise, and only two come out alive. DEA agent John Travolta is brought in to investigate the killings – alongside inexperienced sidekick Connie Nielsen – and uncovers a nexus of corruption. As the incoherent plotting reveals a layer upon layer of deceit, it is difficult to care about anything. IF *DVD*
John Travolta *Tom Hardy* • Connie Nielsen *Lt Julia Osborne* • Samuel L Jackson *Sgt Nathan West* • Giovanni Ribisi *Levi Kendall* • Brian Van Holt *Raymond Dunbar* • Taye Diggs *Pike* • Tim Daly [Timothy Daly] *Col Bill Styles* ■ *Dir* John McTiernan • *Scr* James Vanderbilt

Basic Instinct ★★★ 18
Erotic thriller 1992 · US · Colour · 122min

Director Paul Verhoeven's reputation is built on his wonderful lack of taste and restraint, and these "qualities" are fully to the fore in this controversial but massively successful thriller. Sharon Stone became a sex symbol of the 1990s thanks to her cool portrayal of the predatory novelist who may or may not be a murderer, but who enjoys tormenting policeman Michael Douglas all the same. Writer Joe Eszterhas shamelessly reworks ideas and themes he had exploited in earlier films, but the sheer overheated nature of Verhoeven's direction makes this extremely watchable. JF Swearing, violence, sex scenes, nudity. *DVD* BD
Michael Douglas (1) *Detective Nick Curran* • Sharon Stone *Catherine Tramell* • George Dzundza *Gus* • Jeanne Tripplehorn *Dr Beth Garner* • Denis Arndt *Lieutenant Walker* • Leilani Sarelle *Roxy* ■ *Dir* Paul Verhoeven • *Scr* Joe Eszterhas

Basic Instinct 2: Risk Addiction ★★ 18
Erotic crime thriller 2006 · Ger/US/Sp/UK · Colour · 109min

Sharon Stone reprises her most famous role in this London-set sequel. Novelist Stone is again under suspicion after her latest lover (played by soccer "bad boy" Stan Collymore) takes a fatal dive into a London dock. David Morrissey plays a psychiatrist who becomes enamoured of his icily erotic new patient. Director Michael Caton-Jones does a workmanlike job of keeping things rattling along, but there's precious little beneath the film's surface glitz. DA Sex scenes. *DVD*
Sharon Stone *Catherine Tramell* • David Morrissey *Dr Michael Glass* • Charlotte Rampling *Dr Milena Gardosh* • David Thewlis *Roy Washburn* • Hugh Dancy *Adam Tower* • Anne Caillon *Laney Ward* • Stan Collymore *Kevin Franks* ■ *Dir* Michael Caton-Jones • *Scr* Leora Barish, Henry Bean, from the character created by Joe Eszterhas

Basil ★★ 15
Period drama 1998 · US · Colour · 98min

Writer/director Radha Bharadwaj here delivers a stiff costume drama, based on the novel by Wilkie Collins. Jared Leto is miscast as rich man's son Basil, who offends his father by marrying the mysterious Claire Forlani and befriending commoner Christian Slater. This being a tale of oppression, love and revenge, you'd expect some twists in the tale. However, Bharadwaj signposts each one so obviously that you know what the characters are up to almost before they do. JB Some violence. *DVD*
Jared Leto *Basil* • Christian Slater *John Mannion* • Jack Wild *Peddler* • Claire Forlani *Julia Sherwin* • Derek Jacobi *Basil's father, Frederick* • David Ross *Mr Sherwin* • Crispin Bonham-Carter *Ralph* ■ *Dir* Radha Bharadwaj • *Scr* Radha Bharadwaj, from the novel *Basil: a Story of Modern Life* by Wilkie Collins

Basil the Great Mouse Detective ★★★ U
Animated adventure 1986 · US · Colour · 73min

An attractive idea, but rather crudely done for Disney animation, this is about a young mouse devotee of Sherlock Holmes who helps to investigate the disappearance of a mouse toymaker and a plot against the Mouse Queen. It's notable for Vincent Price's wonderfully arch voiceover as the master scoundrel Professor Ratigan, proving that villains have all the best lines. TH *DVD*
Vincent Price *Professor Ratigan* • Barrie Ingham *Basil/Bartholomew* • Val Bettin *Dr David Q Dawson/Thug guard* • Diana Chesney *Mrs Judson* • Candy Candido *Fidget* • Susanne Pollatschek *Olivia Flaversham* • Eve Brenner *The Mouse Queen* ■ *Dir* Ron Clements, Dave Michener, John Musker, Burny Mattinson • *Scr* Eve Titus, Paul Galdone

Basket Case ★★★★ 18
Horror comedy 1982 · US · Colour · 87min

This gore-drenched, gutter-trash classic is one of the key horror movies of the 1980s. It tells the bizarre story of the Bradley brothers – normal Duane (Kevin Van Hentenryck) and his hideously deformed Siamese twin Belial, whom he carries around in a wicker basket – and how they wreak revenge on the quack doctor who separated them years before. Graphic blood-letting is juxtaposed with comic relief, but lurking behind its cruel and crude façade is an accomplished shocker laced with great artistry and pathos. AJ *DVD*
Kevin Van Hentenryck *Duane Bradley* • Terri Susan Smith *Sharon* • Beverly Bonner *Casey* • Robert Vogel *Hotel manager* • Diana Browne *Dr Judith Kutter* • Lloyd Pace *Dr Harold Needleman* • Bill Freeman *Dr Julius Lifflander* • Joe Clarke *Brian "Mickey" O'Donovan* ■ *Dir/Scr* Frank Henenlotter

Basket Case 2 ★★ 15
Horror comedy 1990 · US · Colour · 85min

The saga of Duane and Belial, his grotesque Siamese twin, continues as they both escape from hospital and media attention to hide out in a Staten Island shelter for freaks. Suffering from latex monster overkill and with too many references to Tod Browning's *Freaks* for comfort, director Frank Henenlotter's poor follow-up is nothing more than a cash-in. AJ *DVD*
Kevin Van Hentenryck *Duane Bradley* • Annie Ross *Granny Ruth* • Kathryn Meisle *Marcie Elliott* • Heather Rattray *Susan* • Jason Evers *Lou the editor* • Ted Sorel *Phil* • Matt Mitler *Artie* ■ *Dir/Scr* Frank Henenlotter

Basket Case 3: the Progeny ★★★ 18
Horror comedy 1992 · US · Colour · 86min

Director Frank Henenlotter's second sequel to his inspired original is a far less depressing experience than *Basket Case 2*. Dealing more in edgy cartoon craziness than gory splatter, the film follows the Bradley twins, Duane and Belial, as they accompany Granny Ruth to the redneck Deep South. It's when Belial's flesh-hungry offspring are stolen by the police department that Henenlotter's frenzied rubber romp takes off. AJ Violence, swearing. *DVD*
Kevin Van Hentenryck *Duane Bradley* • Annie Ross *Granny Ruth* • Dan Biggers *Uncle Hal* • Gil Roper *Sheriff Griffith* • James O'Doherty *Little Hal* ■ *Dir* Frank Henenlotter • *Scr* Frank Henenlotter, Robert Martin

The Basketball Diaries ★★ 18
Biographical drama 1995 · US · Colour · 102min

This attempts to plumb the depths of adolescent despair but only betrays the pop-video limitations of debut director Scott Kalvert's imagination. Leonardo DiCaprio occasionally comes close to real pathos as the hoop dreamer wallowing in a mire of sex, drugs and squalor, though his misery is founded on cliché. Best buddy Mark Wahlberg and desperate mum Lorraine Bracco are more persuasive. DP Violence, swearing, drug abuse, nudity. *DVD*
Leonardo DiCaprio *Jim Carroll* • Bruno Kirby *Swifty* • Lorraine Bracco *Jim's mother* • Ernie Hudson *Reggie Porter* • Patrick McGaw *Neutron* • James Madio *Pedro* • Mark Wahlberg *Mickey* • Juliette Lewis *Diane Moody* ■ *Dir* Scott Kalvert • *Scr* Brian Goluboff, from the memoirs of Jim Carroll

The Basque Ball: Skin against Stone ★★★ 15
Political documentary 2003 · Sp · Colour · 110min

The refusal of either the Spanish government or the Basque separatist group ETA to participate in this debate about the Basque country conflict clearly diminishes its focus. But such is the scope and balance of Julio Medem's documentary that the political and cultural complexities of the Euskal Herria region of France and Spain become readily apparent. If anything, the film has too many opinions from too many interested parties for non-specialists to follow the arguments, and Medem's clumsy method of introducing speakers in captioned batches hardly helps. But many human tragedies emerge from the confusion of racial intransigence and emotive intellectualising and it's impossible to remain unmoved. DP French, Spanish, Basque +subtitles. Violence. *DVD*
■ *Dir* Julio Medem • *Cinematographers* Javier Aguirre, Jon Elicegui, Ricardo de Gracia

Basquiat ★★★ 15
Biographical drama 1996 · US · Colour · 106min

This is the story of artist Jean-Michel Basquiat (Jeffrey Wright) as told by his friend and contemporary, director Julian Schnabel. Basquiat went from being an angry graffiti artist to one of Andy Warhol's close circle before overdosing on heroin in the late 1980s. Schnabel's aim is to show how the man was uncomfortable being lionised by the bourgeoisie he so despised. But Basquiat comes off more as a tiresome antihero in this well-meaning biopic, which fails to reveal why he's deserving of remembrance. AJ Violence, swearing, drug abuse. *DVD*
Jeffrey Wright *Jean-Michel Basquiat* • Michael Wincott *Andy Warhol* • Benicio Del Toro *Benny Dalmau* • Claire Forlani *Gina Cardinale* • David Bowie *Andy Warhol* • Dennis Hopper *Bruno Bischofberger* • Gary Oldman *Albert Milo* • Christopher Walken *Interviewer* • Willem Dafoe *Electrician* • Parker Posey *Mary Boone* • Paul Bartel (1) *Henry Geldzahler* • Courtney Love *Big Pink* • Tatum O'Neal *Cynthia Kruger* ■ *Dir* Julian Schnabel • *Scr* Julian Schnabel, from a story by Lech J Majewski, John Bowe

Bastards ★★★ 18
Drama 2013 · Fr · Colour · 96min

In this brooding revenge drama from Claire Denis, tanker captain Vincent Lindon returns to Paris to help his sister (Julie Bataille) after her debt-ridden husband commits suicide and their teenage daughter (Lola Créton) is pitilessly assaulted. Shooting in digital for the first time, Denis and regular cinematographer Agnès Godard make fascinating use of intricate long shots and intimate close-ups, which draw viewers into the action only to leave them as far from the truth as ever. While the performances are exceptional, the conceit and execution are self-consciously calculating. DP French +subtitles. Sex scenes, nudity, some violence, swearing. *DVD*
Vincent Lindon *Marco Silvestri* • Chiara Mastroianni *Raphaëlle* • Julie Bataille *Sandra* • Michel Subor *Edouard Laporte* • Lola Créton *Justine* • Alex Descas *Doctor* ■ *Dir* Claire Denis • *Scr* Claire Denis, Jean-Pol Fargeau • *Cinematographer* Agnès Godard

Bastards
Comedy 2016 · US · Colour

This is a preview – no prints were available to review as we went to press: Owen Wilson has had a few partners in comedy – brother Luke, Ben Stiller, Vince Vaughn. This time he's teaming up with Ed Helms of *The Hangover* to play brothers whose mother has lied to them all their lives about their father being dead. Tracking him down is a great excuse for a road trip where comical bickering will surely ensue. JK Simmons, Harry Shearer, Ving Rhames and Glenn Close are all on board, so the pressure is on debuting director Lawrence Sher to make it work. SP
Owen Wilson *Kyle* • Ed Helms *Peter* • JK Simmons • Glenn Close • Ving Rhames *Rod Hamilton* ■ *Dir* Lawrence Sher • *Scr* Justin Malen

Bastille Day ★★★ 15
Action thriller 2016 · US/Fr · Colour · 91min

Director James Watkins (*The Woman in Black*) has shown himself to be a master of suspense, but here he loosens his strangler's grip for an action movie that presses the pedal firmly to the metal. Idris Elba plays part of a CIA surveillance unit in Paris that is pursuing a thief (Richard Madden) who has stolen a bag containing an explosive device. With recent tragedies in France in mind, this may be a tough watch, and having Americans played by Brits gives the film a phoney feel. But it certainly delivers on the thrills front and Elba makes for a charismatic lead. EAS Violence, swearing. *DVD* BD
Idris Elba *Sean Briar* • Richard Madden *Michael Mason* • Charlotte Le Bon *Zoë* • Kelly Reilly *Karen Dacre* ■ *Dir* James Watkins • *Scr* Andrew Baldwin, James Watkins • *Cinematographer* Tim Maurice-Jones

The Bat ★★ PG
Mystery thriller 1959 · US · BW · 80min

Intrepid mystery writer Agnes Moorehead rents a country mansion for the summer, only to be terrorised by a mad hooded killer called "The Bat". Money is stolen, a real bat turns up and Vincent Price becomes the prime suspect in this creaky, improbable thriller. Sluggishly paced and old-fashioned in the extreme, it nevertheless has a comfortably nostalgic appeal. AJ *DVD*

B

Vincent Price *Dr Malcolm Wells* • Agnes Moorehead *Cornelia Van Gorder* • Gavin Gordon *Lieutenant Anderson* • John Sutton *Warner* • Lenita Lane *Lizzie Allen* • Elaine Edwards *Dale Bailey* ■ *Dir* Crane Wilbur • *Scr* Crane Wilbur, from the play by Mary Roberts Rinehart, Avery Hopwood, from their novel *The Circular Staircase*

BAT-21 ★★ 15
War drama   1988 · US · Colour · 100min

Set during the Vietnam War, this drama stars Gene Hackman as an officer (codenamed BAT-21) who crashes behind enemy lines and is brought face to face with the human misery of the conflict. Hackman makes the career soldier a strongly believable character, while Danny Glover is excellent as the pilot trying to track him down. However, the episodic nature of the tale never allows a sense of urgency to surface. TH Violence, swearing. *DVD*

Gene Hackman *Lt Col Iceal Hambleton* • Danny Glover *Captain Bartholomew Clark* • Jerry Reed *Colonel George Walker* • David Marshall Grant *Ross Carver* • Clayton Rohner *Sergeant Harley Rumbaugh* ■ *Dir* Peter Markle • *Scr* William C Anderson, George Gordon, from the novel by William C Anderson

The Bat Whispers ★★★ U
Mystery thriller   1930 · US · BW · 84min

Roland West's talkie remake of his own 1926 silent film *The Bat* is by far the best movie adaptation of the stock spoof horror play set in a creepy mansion. It's also a superior chiller in its own right. Sure, it's a dusty antique, but the impressively surreal imagery is unusual for the period, making it well worth a look. Using remarkable special effects and miniature sets, the fluid camera darts about as much as the titular caped criminal for a fun combination of screams and laughs. AJ

Chester Morris *Detective Anderson* • Grayce Hampton *Cornelia Van Gorder* • Chance Ward *Police lieutenant* • Richard Tucker *Mr Bell* • Wilson Benge *The butler* • Maude Eburne *Lizzie Allen* ■ *Dir* Roland West • *Scr* Roland West, from the play *The Bat* by Mary Roberts Rinehart, Avery Hopwood, from their novel *The Circular Staircase*

Bataan ★★
Second World War drama
1943 · US · BW · 114min

General MacArthur was forced to abandon the Philippines to the Japanese during the Second World War, and this scrappy piece of patriotic action re-creates one of the battles before the pull-out. Robert Taylor and Barry Nelson are among those caught in the jungled MGM backlot, exchanging bullets and sanctimonious dialogue. MacArthur did go back and so did John Wayne, in *Back to Bataan*. AT

Robert Taylor (1) *Sergeant Bill Dane* • George Murphy *Lieutenant Steve Bentley* • Thomas Mitchell *Corporal Jake Feingold* • Lloyd Nolan *Corporal Barney Todd/Danny Burns* • Lee Bowman *Captain Lassiter* ■ *Dir* Tay Garnett • *Scr* Robert D Andrews

La Bataille du Rail ★★★
Second World War drama
1946 · Fr · BW · 87min

Director René Clément's directing debut is about the war waged by the French railway workers against their Nazi oppressors. Using a largely amateur cast of genuine railway personnel (an introduction and narration by Charles Boyer was added for foreign release), Clément depicts in great detail the various acts of sabotage and subtle route changes that were to cause havoc to the German supply lines. AT French +subtitles.

Jean Daurand *Railway worker* • Jacques Desagneaux *Maquis Chief* • Leroy *Station master* • Redon *Mechanic* • Pauléon *Station master at St André* • Charles Boyer *Narrator* ■ *Dir* René Clément • *Scr* Colette Audry, René Clément, Jean Daurand, from stories by Colette Audry

Bathing Beauty ★★★ U
Musical   1944 · US · Colour · 101min

MGM contractee Esther Williams became a star overnight in this, the first of her many swimfests, and who could ever forget her as she steps on to the MGM diving board? Esther had a robust, sexy aura that director George Sidney knew exactly how to exploit, although this movie actually started life as a Red Skelton vehicle, one of those school romps about romance among the co-eds. The film's a little too long, but Esther's worth every single Technicolored frame. TS

Red Skelton *Steve Elliott* • Esther Williams *Caroline Brooks* • Basil Rathbone *George Adams* • Bill Goodwin *Willis Evans* • Ethel Smith *Organist* • Jean Porter *Jean Allenwood* • Carlos Ramírez *Carlos* • Donald Meek *Chester Klazenfrantz* ■ *Dir* George Sidney (2) • *Scr* Dorothy Kingsley, Allen Boretz, Frank Waldman, Joseph Schrank, from a story by Kenneth Earl, MM Musselman

Bathory ★ 15
Drama drama
2008 · Cz Rep/UK/Hun · Colour · 134min

The life and the legend of 16th-century Hungarian noblewoman Elizabeth Bathory, known as the Blood Countess, are explored in this handsome but risible biopic. It attempts to question some of the more dubious stories – her habit of bathing in the blood of virgins – while introducing others (an affair with the famously gay painter Caravaggio). Anna Friel does her best to portray Elizabeth as a wronged woman whose vicious reputation was, in fact, just payback for daring to be strong in a male-dominated world. Around her, though, the late-medieval murk – itself less than historically accurate – plays out more like a Monty Python comedy than a serious drama. DW Violence, nudity, torture. *DVD*

Anna Friel *Erzsebet Bathory* • Hans Matheson *Merisi Caravaggio* • Karel Roden *Count Thurzo* • Franco Nero *King Matthias II* • Bolek Polivka [Boleslav Polivka] *Peter* • Jiri Madl *Monk Cyril* ■ *Dir* Juraj Jakubisko • *Scr* Juraj Jakubisko, John Paul Chapple

Batman ★★★★ U
Action fantasy   1966 · US · Colour · 104min

This is the movie spin-off from the hit TV series of the 1960s, with Adam West as the Caped Crusader and Burt Ward as the Boy Wonder. Lee Meriwether as Catwoman was the least well known of the three actresses who played Catwoman in the 1960s (the others were Julie Newmar and Eartha Kitt). Director Leslie H Martinson lets the pace slacken occasionally, but Lorenzo Semple Jr's script overflows with irresistible throwaway gags. DP *DVD*

Adam West *Batman/Bruce Wayne* • Burt Ward *Robin/Dick Grayson* • Lee Meriwether *Catwoman/Kitka* • Cesar Romero *Joker* • Burgess Meredith *Penguin* • Frank Gorshin *Riddler* • Alan Napier *Alfred* • Neil Hamilton *Commissioner Gordon* • Stafford Repp *Chief O'Hara* • Madge Blake *Aunt Harriet Cooper* ■ *Dir* Leslie H Martinson • *Scr* Lorenzo Semple Jr, from characters by Bob Kane

Batman ★★★★ 15
Action fantasy   1989 · US · Colour · 121min

Only director Tim Burton could take the Caped Crusader into the darkest realms of comic-strip nightmare yet still manage to weave an arresting tale full of doomy Shakespearean irony. From the camera crawling around the Bat symbol under the opening credits to the *Hunchback of Notre Dame*-inspired finale, Burton captures the spirit of artist Bob Kane's creation to produce a sophisticated *film noir*. With Michael Keaton's brooding Batman/Bruce Wayne and Jack Nicholson's garish Joker on the knife-edge of good and evil, Burton cleverly places both tragic characters within the same psychological bracket, making the film one of the most atypical of superhero movies. JF Violence, swearing. *DVD* Blu-ray

Michael Keaton *Batman/Bruce Wayne* • Jack Nicholson *Joker/Jack Napier* • Kim Basinger *Vicki Vale* • Robert Wuhl *Alexander Knox* • Pat Hingle *Commissioner Gordon* • Billy Dee Williams *Harvey Dent* • Michael Gough *Alfred* • Jack Palance *Carl Grissom* • Jerry Hall *Alicia* ■ *Dir* Tim Burton • *Scr* Sam Hamm, Warren Skaaren, from a story by Sam Hamm, from characters by Bob Kane • *Production Designer* Anton Furst

Batman Returns ★★★★ 15
Action fantasy   1992 · US · Colour · 121min

Director Tim Burton refused to lighten up for the second of the Batman movies and the result is another moody, gloomy and occasionally perverse portrait of the Dark Knight. The sets are stunning and, while action may not be Burton's strongest suit, there are still some dazzling set pieces and a range of new gadgets. The only real problem is that all the best lines are bagged by the villains – Danny DeVito's tragic Penguin, Michelle Pfeiffer in *that* suit as Catwoman. It's still impressive stuff. JF Some violence. *DVD* Blu-ray

Michael Keaton *Batman/Bruce Wayne* • Danny DeVito *Oswald Cobblepot/The Penguin* • Michelle Pfeiffer *Catwoman/Selina Kyle* • Christopher Walken *Max Shreck* • Michael Gough *Alfred* • Michael Murphy (1) *Mayor* ■ *Dir* Tim Burton • *Scr* Daniel Waters, from a story by Daniel Waters, Sam Hamm, from characters by Bob Kane

Batman Forever ★★★★ PG
Action fantasy   1995 · US · Colour · 114min

Although it performed well at the box office, the critics were less than convinced by the gloomy turn taken by *Batman Returns*. So, when Tim Burton said no to a third outing, Warners brought in the flamboyant Joel Schumacher. This entry is nowhere near as dark as its predecessors, even though the brooding Val Kilmer took over the Dark Knight's mantle from Michael Keaton. It's easily the funniest in the series, with the action hurtling along at a breakneck pace. Throw in stylish special effects from a team that includes the legendary John Dykstra and Oscar-nominated photography from Stephen Goldblatt, and you have a rousingly undemanding piece of popcorn fodder. DP Violence. *DVD* Blu-ray

Val Kilmer *Batman/Bruce Wayne* • Tommy Lee Jones *Harvey Two-Face/Harvey Dent* • Jim Carrey *The Riddler/Edward Nygma* • Nicole Kidman *Dr Chase Meridian* • Chris O'Donnell *Robin/Dick Grayson* • Michael Gough *Alfred Pennyworth* • Pat Hingle *Commissioner James Gordon* • Debi Mazar *Spice* • Drew Barrymore *Sugar* ■ *Dir* Joel Schumacher • *Scr* Lee Batchler, Janet Scott Batchler, Akiva Goldsman, from a story by Lee Batchler, Janet Scott Batchler, from characters by Bob Kane

Batman and Robin ★★ PG
Action fantasy   1997 · US · Colour · 119min

With the *Batman* franchise looking decidedly tired, Caped Crusader Mark 3 was introduced in the shape of George Clooney in an attempt to pep up the flagging formula. The rugged former TV medic doesn't disgrace himself in this wild special-effects extravaganza that is as close to a cartoon adventure as director Joel Schumacher could get. This is still the least satisfying entry in the series. JF Violence, swearing. *DVD* Blu-ray

George Clooney *Batman/Bruce Wayne* • Arnold Schwarzenegger *Mr Freeze/Dr Victor Fries* • Chris O'Donnell *Robin/Dick Grayson* • Uma Thurman *Poison Ivy/Pamela Isley* • Alicia Silverstone *Batgirl/Barbara Wilson* • Michael Gough *Alfred Pennyworth* ■ *Dir* Joel Schumacher • *Scr* Akiva Goldsman, from characters by Bob Kane

Batman: Mask of the Phantasm ★★★★ PG
Animated action fantasy
1993 · US · Colour · 73min

Released in cinemas after the TV animated series took off, this cartoon feature expertly captures the feel of the comics. The Phantasm is a formidable vigilante who painstakingly executes Gotham's most powerful criminals. After both the police and the underworld mistakenly hold the Dark Knight responsible, Batman must unmask the real culprit. Stylishly drawn and with a strong cast of voices including Stacy Keach and *Star Wars*'s Mark Hamill, this is a spirited riposte to the live-action films. AJ *DVD*

Kevin Conroy *Batman/Bruce Wayne* • Dana Delany *Andrea Beaumont* • Hart Bochner *Councilman Arthur Reeves* • Stacy Keach

Batman Returns ★★★★ 15

Phantasm/Carl Beaumont • Abe Vigoda *Salvatore Valestra* • Dick Miller *Chuckie Sol* ■ *Dir* Eric Radomski, Bruce W Timm • *Scr* Alan Burnett, Paul Dini, Martin Pasko, Michael Reaves, from a story by Alan Burnett, from characters by Bob Kane

Batman of the Future: Return of the Joker ★★★ 12
Animated action adventure
2000 · US · Colour · 70min

The Joker finally gets to be as evil on film as he is in the comics in this darker animation. Although there are still plenty of slapstick pranks, this Clown Prince of Crime is quite prepared to loose a laser on Gotham City and murder anyone in his way. He even starts training a protégé in the mould of the Boy Wonder. Mark Hamill is on excellent vocal form as the Joker, as is Kevin Conroy as the now-retired Bruce Wayne. But Will Friedle doesn't quite cut the mustard as new Caped Crusader Terry McGinnis. DP

Will Friedle *Terry McGinnis/Batman* • Kevin Conroy *Bruce Wayne/Batman* • Mark Hamill *Joker* • Angie Harmon *Commissioner Barbara Gordon* ■ *Dir* Curt Geda • *Scr* Paul Dini, from characters by Bob Kane

Batman: The Killing Joke ★★★ 15
Animated action adventure
2016 · US · Colour · 73min

Writer Alan Moore and artist Brian Bolland distilled the clash between Batman and archvillain the Joker to gob-smacking effect in best-selling graphic novel *The Killing Joke* in 1988. This animated (but not for kids) adaptation sees longtime voice providers Kevin Conroy (Batman) and Mark Hamill (Joker) return for a story that mingles the Clown Prince of Crime's genesis with his latest malevolent scheme. The confrontation between the comic world's ultimate hero and villain is well worth the wait, but the animation is no replacement for Bolland's exquisite artwork. JA *DVD* Blu-ray

Kevin Conroy *Batman/Bruce Wayne* • Mark Hamill *Joker* • Ray Wise *Commissioner Gordon* • Tara Strong *Batgirl/Barbara Gordon* ■ *Dir* Sam Liu • *Scr* Brian Azzarello, from a graphic novel by Alan Moore (2), Brian Bolland, from characters by Bob Kane, Bill Finger, Jerry Robinson

Batman Begins ★★★★ 12
Action fantasy 2005 · US/UK · Colour · 134min

Christopher Nolan directs this gloriously epic comic book yarn starring Christian Bale, who imbues the Caped Crusader with beguiling dignity. Nolan offers a darker, more gripping psychological portrait of Bruce Wayne and his painful evolution into Batman. Bursts of adrenaline-pumping action relieve all the brooding, although the plot sometimes creaks under the strain of so much going on. It also lacks a truly terrifying villain, but a sterling cast stands persuasively for lofty ideals as a climate of fear threatens to bring down Gotham City. This swoops you up and doesn't let go till the end. Nolan's Batman trilogy concluded with *The Dark Knight* (2008) and *The Dark Knight Rises* (2012). SP Violence. *DVD* Blu-ray

Christian Bale *Bruce Wayne/Batman* • Michael Caine *Alfred the butler* • Liam Neeson *Henri Ducard* • Katie Holmes *Rachel Dawes* • Gary Oldman *Detective Sergeant James Gordon* • Cillian Murphy *Dr Jonathan Crane/Scarecrow* • Tom Wilkinson *Carmine Falcone* • Rutger Hauer *Richard Earle* • Morgan Freeman *Lucius Fox* ■ *Dir* Christopher Nolan • *Scr* David S Goyer, Christopher Nolan, from a story by Goyer, from characters by Bob Kane

Batman v Superman: Dawn of Justice ★★★ 12
Action adventure   2016 · US · Colour · 144min

Three years after rebooting the Superman legend, director Zack Snyder earns the dream job of pitting the last son of Krypton against the Dark Knight in the ultimate smackdown. Christian Bale was great, but Ben Affleck proves to be an older, wiser Batman for a post-Christopher Nolan world, leaving Henry Cavill overshadowed as his hero struggles with doubt. Amy Adams is a feisty Lois Lane, but Jesse Eisenberg's Lex Luthor may be too manic for some. The result is a spectacular if overstuffed epic that's a long way from the best of Marvel's blockbusters. JA Some violence, swearing.

DVD Blu-ray 3D

Ben Affleck *Bruce Wayne/Batman* • Henry Cavill *Clark Kent/Superman* • Amy Adams *Lois Lane* • Jesse Eisenberg *Lex Luthor* • Diane Lane *Martha Kent* • Laurence Fishburne *Perry White* • Jeremy Irons *Alfred* • Gal Gadot *Diana Prince/Wonder Woman* ■ *Dir* Zack Snyder • *Scr* Chris Terrio, David S Goyer, from characters by Bob Kane, Joe Shuster, Jerry Siegel, Bill Finger

Bats ★ 15

Horror 1999 · US · Colour · 87min

Genetically enhanced killer bats are released upon an unsuspecting Texas town by a mad scientist. A perky zoologist, her cowardly sidekick and the town's sheriff fight desperately to fend off the flying monsters in this by-the-numbers monster movie, in which the lead characters never say or do anything of any interest. ST Violence, swearing. **DVD**

Lou Diamond Phillips *Emmett Kimsey* • Dina Meyer *Dr Sheila Casper* • Bob Gunton *Dr Alexander McCabe* • Leon *Jimmy Sands* • *Dir* Louis Morneau • *Scr* John Logan

*batteries not included ★★★ PG

Science-fiction fantasy 1987 · US · Colour · 106min

The presence of Hume Cronyn and Jessica Tandy makes this retread of *Cocoon* worth watching. They play residents of a doomed New York block of flats, who find the unlikeliest of allies in the shape of a friendly group of aliens. Director Matthew Robbins lets sentimentality run supreme, but Cronyn and Tandy rise above it all, and children and soft-hearted adults will be enchanted. JF

DVD

Hume Cronyn *Frank Riley* • Jessica Tandy *Faye Riley* • Frank McRae *Harry Noble* • Elizabeth Peña *Marisa* • Michael Carmine *Carlos* • Dennis Boutsikaris *Mason* • Tom Aldredge *Sid* ■ *Dir* Matthew Robbins • *Scr* Brad Bird, Matthew Robbins, Brent Maddock, SS Wilson, from a story by Mick Garris, Steven Spielberg

The Battle at Apache Pass ★★★ U

Western 1952 · US · Colour · 85min

Universal contract star Jeff Chandler created a tremendous impression as the native American chief Cochise in the remarkably liberal (for its time) *Broken Arrow*. Here he reprises the role in another sympathetic western, which deals primarily with Apache warrior Geronimo, played by native American actor Jay Silverheels. Intelligent writing and performances make up for the lack of political depth and there's a splendid staging of the battle. Western fans won't be disappointed. TS

Jeff Chandler *Cochise* • John Lund *Major Jim Colton* • Beverly Tyler *Mary Kearny* • Bruce Cowling *Neil Baylor* • Susan Cabot *Nono* • John Hudson (1) *Lieutenant George Bascom* • Jay Silverheels *Geronimo* ■ *Dir* George Sherman • *Scr* Gerald Drayson Adams

Battle at Bloody Beach ★★

Second World War drama 1961 · US · BW · 83min

Audie Murphy, the most decorated American in the Second World War, is out of uniform in this Pacific adventure as he scours the Philippines for Dolores Michaels, the wife who disappeared when the Japanese interrupted their Manila honeymoon. Convinced he died in the invasion, she's become involved with resistance leader Alejandro Rey, who proceeds to enlist Murphy in his guerrilla rearguard. The jungle sequences are directed with gung-ho efficiency, but the romantic triangle is wearisome. DP

Audie Murphy *Craig Benson* • Gary Crosby *Marty Sackler* • Dolores Michaels *Ruth Benson* • Alejandro Rey *Julio Fontana* • Marjorie Stapp

Caroline Pelham ■ *Dir* Herbert Coleman • *Scr* Richard Maibaum, Willard Willingham [William Willingham], from a story by Richard Maibaum

Battle beneath the Earth ★★ U

Science-fiction action adventure 1968 · UK · Colour · 91min

The Red Chinese have dug a series of tunnels beneath the United States. In go Chinese H-bombs and lasers, and in after them goes Kerwin Matthews, the Harrison Ford of British cinema back in the 1960s, to do a job even 007 might have found taxing. Everyone takes it very seriously and, as a result, it's hugely enjoyable rubbish. AT

Kerwin Mathews *Commander Jonathan Shaw* • Viviane Ventura *Tila Yung* • Robert Ayres *Admiral Felix Hillebrand* • Peter Arne *Arnold Kramer* • Al Mulock *Sergeant Marvin Mulberry* • Martin Benson *General Chan Lu* ■ *Dir* Montgomery Tully • *Scr* Lance Z Hargreaves

Battle beyond the Stars ★★★ PG

Science-fiction adventure 1980 · US · Colour · 98min

This entertaining slice of hokum from Roger Corman production company is great B-movie fodder. Essentially it's *The Magnificent Seven* in space; Corman even manages to rope in one of the original cast, Robert Vaughn, to take his place alongside the likes of John Saxon (as the baddie), George Peppard and Richard Thomas from *The Waltons*. The knowing script is by John Sayles, now better known as the writer/director of such critically acclaimed films as *Passion Fish* and *Lone Star*. JF

Richard Thomas *Shad* • Robert Vaughn (1) *Gelt* • John Saxon *Sador* • George Peppard *Cowboy* • Darlanne Fluegel *Nanelia* • Sybil Danning *St Exmin* • Sam Jaffe *Dr Hephaestus* • Morgan Woodward *Cayman* • Steve Davis *Quopeg* ■ *Dir* Jimmy T Murakami • *Scr* John Sayles, from a story by John Sayles, Ann Dyer

Battle Circus ★★

War drama 1953 · US · BW · 90min

Humphrey Bogart coasts through this movie, playing the commanding officer of a US Army surgical unit during the Korean War, who falls in love with idealistic nurse June Allyson between dodging bullets and indulging in blokeish camaraderie. This was Bogart's second film for writer/director Richard Brooks, who wanted to call this one *MASH 66*, but the studio thought the title was unsuitable. This is clichéd and doesn't have much to say about the conflict. AT

Humphrey Bogart *Major Jeb Webbe* • June Allyson *Lt Ruth McCara* • Keenan Wynn *Sergeant Orvil Statt* • Robert Keith (1) *Lt Col Hillary Whalters* • William Campbell *Captain John Rustford* • Perry Sheehan *Lt Lawrence* • Patricia Tiernan *Lt Rose Ashland* ■ *Dir* Richard Brooks • *Scr* Richard Brooks, from a story by Allen Rivkin, Laura Kerr

Battle Cry ★★★★ PG

Second World War drama 1955 · US · Colour and BW · 142min

It may seem dated today, but this impressive Warner Bros drama based on Leon Uris's semi-fictional account of his own wartime experiences still packs a terrific emotional punch. It is exceptionally well acted, with a key star-making role for Tab Hunter, though top-billed Van Heflin has little to do but act gritty as the leader of "Huxley's Harlots". Watch out, too, for Justus E McQueen as LQ Jones, who took his professional name from the character he portrays here. There's also a rousing Oscar-nominated score by the great Max Steiner. TS In English, Japanese, Navajo.

DVD

Van Heflin *Major Huxley* • Aldo Ray *Andy* • Mona Freeman *Kathy* • Nancy Olson *Pat* • James Whitmore *Sergeant Mac* • Raymond Massey *General Snipes* • Tab Hunter *Danny* • Justus E McQueen [LQ Jones] *LQ Jones* ■ *Dir* Raoul Walsh • *Scr* Leon Uris, from his novel

Battle for Haditha ★★★ 15

War drama based on a true story 2007 · UK · Colour · 92min

Distinguished British documentary-maker Nick Broomfield continues his excursion into narrative drama with this exploration of the war in Iraq. It is based on an actual incident in the city of Haditha in 2005, in which a US marine was killed by a roadside bomb and his buddies allegedly responded by killing pretty much everyone in the vicinity. Broomfield tries hard to represent the motivations and fears of Iraqi insurgents, American soldiers and the locals, without offering judgement on any of them. On the other hand, some characters remain slightly blurred and the action is occasionally muddled. Broomfield is clearly aiming for the tone and style of Gillo Pontecorvo's classic *The Battle of Algiers*. Although he falls short of that masterpiece, his film remains a poignant reflection on the tragedy of modern warfare. BP In English, Arabic. Violence, swearing. **DVD**

Elliot Ruiz *Cpl Ramirez* • Yasmine Hanani *Hiba* • Eric Mehalacopoulos *Sgt Ross* • Andrew McLaren *Capt Sampson* • Matthew Knoll *Cpl Matthews* • Oliver Bytrus *Jafar* ■ *Dir* Nick Broomfield • *Scr* Nick Broomfield, Marc Hoeferlin, Anna Telford

Battle for Terra ★ PG

Animated science-fiction adventure 2007 · US · Colour · 78min

Despite culling ideas from *Planet of the Apes*, *The Day the Earth Stood Still* and *Romeo and Juliet*, this preachy animation parable remains resolutely dull. It focuses on the relationship between an alien (voiced by Evan Rachel Wood) and a human space-station pilot (Luke Wilson), which becomes the key to preventing the intergalactic holocaust proposed by a military madman (Brian Cox). The 3D texturing only throws into sharp relief the lack of depth in the simplistic graphic style and tired alien colonisation metaphors, and the bland overall design soon becomes visually wearing. AJ

Evan Rachel Wood *Mala* • Brian Cox (1) *General Hemmer* • Dennis Quaid *Roven* • Luke Wilson *Jim Stanton* • James Garner *Doron* • Chris Evans *Stewart Stanton* • Danny Glover *President Chen* • Amanda Peet *Maria Montez* • Justin Long *Senn* • Beverly D'Angelo *Interrogator Wright* • Mark Hamill *Elder Orin* ■ *Dir* Aristomenis Tsirbas • *Scr* Evan Spiliotopoulos, from a story by Tsirbas

Battle for the Planet of the Apes ★ PG

Science-fiction fantasy 1973 · US · Colour · 86min

This is the fifth, final and least effective entry in the series. Roddy McDowall heads the cast, as our heroes attempt to restore racial harmony to Earth and make humans social equals. Spotting who's who under the hairy masks will while away the time as this threadbare monkey business wends its time-warp way back to the beginning of the original film. Endless action can't disguise the cheapness of the production or the lack of novelty. AJ **DVD Blu-ray**

Roddy McDowall *Caesar* • Claude Akins *Aldo* • John Huston *Lawgiver* • Natalie Trundy *Lisa* • Severn Darden *Kolp* • Lew Ayres *Mandemus* • Paul Williams *Virgil* • Austin Stoker *MacDonald* • Noah Keen *Teacher* ■ *Dir* J Lee Thompson • *Scr* John William Corrington, Joyce Hooper Corrington, from a story by Paul Dehn, from characters by Pierre Boulle

Battle Hymn ★★★ U

War drama based on a true story 1957 · US · Colour · 108min

From the producer-director team of Ross Hunter and Douglas Sirk, responsible for glossy remakes of classic weepies, comes this earnest biopic about Dean Hess. As a combat flyer he accidentally bombed a German orphanage in the Second World War; how, as a minister in the Korean war, Hess heroically atones for this mistake, forms the stuff of this starring vehicle for Rock Hudson. RK

Rock Hudson *Colonel Dean Hess* • Anna Kashfi *En Soon Yang* • Dan Duryea *Sgt Herman* • Don DeFore *Capt Skidmore* • Martha Hyer *Mary Hess*

• Jock Mahoney *Major Moore* • Alan Hale Jr *Mess Sergeant* • James Edwards *Lt Maples* ■ *Dir* Douglas Sirk • *Scr* Charles Grayson, Vincent B Evans, from the memoirs of Colonel Dean Hess

Battle in Seattle ★★★ 15

Action drama based on a true story 2007 · US/Can/Ger · Colour · 95min

Actor-turned-director Stuart Townsend's intense drama rehashes events in 1999, when demonstrators clashed with police at the World Trade Organisation. It focuses on a handful of characters swept up in the chaos: nonviolent activist Martin Henderson, riot cop Woody Harrelson and his pregnant wife Charlize Theron, and the city's beleaguered mayor, Ray Liotta. The handheld cameras brilliantly capture the anarchy and terror of the protests, but the cardboard characters are less effective, while the "WTO bad" message is about as subtle as being hit over the head with a police baton. JR Violence, swearing. **DVD**

Martin Henderson *Jay* • Michelle Rodriguez *Lou* • Woody Harrelson *Dale* • Charlize Theron *Ella* • Connie Nielsen *Jean* • Ray Liotta *Mayor Jim Tobin* • André Benjamin *Django* ■ *Dir/Scr* Stuart Townsend • *Cinematographer* Barry Ackroyd

Battle Los Angeles ★★★ 12

Science-fiction action drama 2011 · US · Colour · 111min

War of the Worlds meets *The Hurt Locker* in director Jonathan Liebesman's down-and-dirty alien-invasion flick. Aaron Eckhart leads a misfit platoon against intergalactic aggressors in need of Earth's water for fuel. Filming the hectic military operations from the soldiers' point-of-view creates newsreel-type immediacy, but most of the frantic displays of firepower are more tedious than exciting, while the allegorical nods to Afghanistan wear a bit thin, too. Nevertheless, it's a watchable action epic with the odd visual power punch along the way. AJ Violence, swearing. **DVD Blu-ray**

Aaron Eckhart *Staff Sergeant Michael Nantz* • Michelle Rodriguez *Troop Sergeant Elena Santos* • Ramon Rodriguez *Second Lieutenant William Martinez* • Bridget Moynahan *Michele* • Ne-Yo *Corporal Kevin Harris* ■ *Dir* Jonathan Liebesman • *Scr* Christopher Bertolini

The Battle of Algiers ★★★★★ 15

Political war drama 1965 · Alg/It · BW · 116min

The winner of the Golden Lion at Venice and nominated for three Oscars, this stark and compelling drama about the rise of the Front de Libération Nationale in Algeria was banned by a French government still smarting from the recent loss of that country. Yet, one of the strengths of Gillo Pontecorvo's *cinéma-vérité* approach is its refusal to condemn or condone: French and Algerian rhetoric is given an equal airing. Depressingly, this compassionate masterpiece of political analysis still has much contemporary resonance, but it also has a vigour, a commitment and an intelligence that is absent from too much modern cinema. DP French, Arabic +subtitles. Violence. **DVD Blu-ray**

Yacef Saadi *Saari Kader* • Jean Martin *Colonel Mathieu* • Brahim Haggiag *Ali la Pointe* • Tommaso Neri *Captain Dubois* • Michèle Kerbash [Samia Kerbash] *Fathia* ■ *Dir* Gillo Pontecorvo • *Scr* Franco Solinas, from a story by Franco Solinas, Gillo Pontecorvo

The Battle of Austerlitz ★★ U

Historical drama 1960 · Fr/It/Yug · Colour · 122min

Watching international superstars re-enact Napoleon's greatest victory is a pleasant enough way of passing the time. But it's sad to realise that this rather tawdry epic is the penultimate feature of veteran French director Abel Gance. It's barely recognisable as the work of the director of the masterpiece *Napoléon*. TS French, Italian dubbed.

Pierre Mondy *Napoleon Bonaparte* • Jean Mercure *Talleyrand* • Jack Palance *General Weirother* • Orson Welles *Robert Fulton* • Martine Carol *Josephine* • Leslie Caron *Mademoiselle de*

B

Vaudey • Claudia Cardinale *Pauline* • Jean Marais *Carnot* ■ *Dir* Abel Gance • *Scr* Abel Gance, Roger Richebe

Battle of Britain ★★★★ PG

Second World War epic
1969 · UK · Colour · 126min

This worthy tribute to "the few" has spectacular air battles, a memorable re-creation of the Blitz and a terrific cast. It is interesting today to watch so many great names in the twilight of their careers: not just knights Ralph Richardson, Michael Redgrave and Laurence Olivier, but also Trevor Howard, Robert Shaw, Kenneth More and Curt Jurgens. Most of Sir William Walton's original score was dumped and replaced by Ron Goodwin's, but a tantalising fragment remains in the air battles. TS DVD Blu

Laurence Olivier *Air Chief Marshal Sir Hugh Dowding* • Robert Shaw *Squadron Leader Skipper* • Christopher Plummer *Squadron Leader Colin Harvey* • Susannah York *Section Officer Maggie Harvey* • Ian McShane *Sergeant Pilot Andy* • Michael Caine *Squadron Leader Canfield* • Kenneth More *Group Captain Baker* • Trevor Howard *Air Vice-Marshal Keith Park* • Ralph Richardson *British Minister in Switzerland* • Curd Jürgens [Curt Jurgens] *Baron von Richter* • Michael Redgrave *Air Vice-Marshal Evill* ■ *Dir* Guy Hamilton • *Scr* James Kennaway, Wilfred Greatorex, from the book *The Narrow Margin* by Derek Wood, Derek Dempster

The Battle of El Alamein ★★ PG

Second World War drama
1968 · It/Fr · Colour · 101min

This might have been an intriguing, alternative account of the battle that marked a turning point in the war in North Africa. Viewing the conflict from the Axis perspective, it reveals an uneasy alliance, in which the Italian Division Folgore is left high and dry by Rommel's grand design. As the rival field marshals, Robert Hossein and Michael Rennie are adequate, but this is something of a wasted opportunity. DP Italian dubbed.

Michael Rennie *Field Marshal Montgomery* • Robert Hossein *Field Marshal Rommel* • George Hilton *Lieutenant Graham* • Ira Furstenberg [Ira von Fürstenberg] *Marta* • Enrico Maria Salerno *Captain Hubert* • Frederick Stafford *Lt Claudio Borri* ■ *Dir* Calvin Jackson Padget [Giorgio Ferroni] • *Scr* Ernesto Gastaldi

The Battle of Elderbush ★★★

Silent western
1914 · US · BW · 29min

This very early western was the last two-reeler made by DW Griffith before embarking on America's first feature-length films. For this simple tale of Indians attacking a settlement, Griffith constructed a complete three-dimensional town in the San Fernando Valley. Brilliantly shot by Billy Bitzer, the short becomes more and more compelling towards its climax, as a baby whose parents have been killed escapes the shelter of her cabin and must be rescued by a posse. RB

Mae Marsh *The waif* • Alfred Paget *Her uncle* • Charles H Mailes [Charles Hill Mailes] *The ranch owner* • Lillian Gish *Young wife* • Robert Harron *Young husband* • Kate Bruce *Settler* • W Chrystie Miller [Walter Miller] *Settler* • Blanche Sweet *Child* ■ *Dir/Scr* DW Griffith

The Battle of Mary Kay ★★★

Comedy drama based on a true story
2002 · Can/US · Colour · 100min

Hard facts blur into camp kitsch in a madcap re-creation of the rivalry between cosmetics queen Mary Kay Ash and sassy wannabe Jinger Heath. Director Ed Gernon indulges in all manner of visual pyrotechnics, but his attention-seeking style too often distracts from the full-on performances of Shirley MacLaine and Parker Posey. They rip into their roles in this TV biopic with a bitchy glee that's fun to watch. DP

Shirley MacLaine *Mary Kay Ash* • Parker Posey *Jinger Heath* • Shannen Doherty *Lexi Wilcox* • Maggie Butterfield *Doris* • Terri Cherniak *Liz* ■ *Dir* Ed Gernon • *Scr* Patricia Resnick

The Battle of Midway ★★★★

Second World War documentary
1942 · US · Colour · 18min

This is one of a striking series of Second World War documentaries made by the world's greatest film directors – here John Ford, uncredited, for the US Navy. Ford did some of the camerawork himself and captured the searing, tragic sense of destruction in a battle that marked a turning point in the war against Japan. In the cutting rooms, aided by Robert Parrish and some familiar voices Ford wove a structure around his material and made a superb propagandist tract. TS

Henry Fonda • Jane Darwell • Donald Crisp • Irving Pichel ■ *Dir* John Ford • *Cinematographer* John Ford • *Music* Alfred Newman • *Editor* Robert Parrish

Battle of Midway ★★★ PG

Second World War action drama
1976 · US · Colour · 131min

Charlton Heston juts his jaw aggressively and Henry Fonda falters reflectively in this blockbuster drama about the events leading up to the decisive battle fought between the navies of the US and Japan during the Second World War. The techniques of the star-studded cast are blown away somewhat by the big guns of audio technology, though the din of the original ear-blasting Sensurround has been diminished to clarify the narrative. TH DVD

Charlton Heston *Capt Matt Garth* • Henry Fonda *Adm Chester W Nimitz* • James Coburn *Capt Vinton Maddox* • Glenn Ford *Rear Adm Raymond A Spruance* • Hal Holbrook *Cmdr Joseph Rochefort* • Toshiro Mifune *Adm Isoroku Yamamoto* • Robert Mitchum *Adm William F Halsey* • Cliff Robertson *Cmdr Carl Jessop* • Robert Wagner *Lt Cmdr Ernest L Blake* ■ *Dir* Jack Smight • *Scr* Donald S Sanford

The Battle of Russia ★★

Second World War documentary
1943 · US · BW · 80min

Lt Col Frank Capra, Lt Col Anatole Litvak and other ranking Hollywood soldiers made this documentary, one of a series of seven designed to show Americans what the Second World War was all about. This one's about the ally Russia, from the time of Alexander Nevsky to the Nazi invasion. The vast amount of documentary footage is accompanied by Dimitri Tiomkin's copious borrowings from Prokofiev, Tchaikovsky and Shostakovich. AT

Walter Huston *Narrator* • Anthony Veiller *Narrator* ■ *Dir* Frank Capra, Anatole Litvak • *Scr* Anatole Litvak

Battle of the Bulbs ★★

Seasonal comedy drama
2010 · Can/US · Colour · 89min

A Christmas decoration contest renews a 25-year feud between neighbours Daniel Stern and Matt Frewer in this knockabout TV movie. Slapstick and diverting goofiness follow, as the ultra-competitive ex-friends – and eventually their wives, too – go to increasing extremes to outdo and humiliate each other. Of course, moral messages soon start creeping in, ultimately leading everyone to repent with unconvincing haste. Shame they had to over-egg the festive goodwill with a naff, sing-along finale. SF

Daniel Stern *Bob Wallace* • Matt Frewer *Stu Jones* • Allison Hossack *Mindy Wallace* • Teryl Rothery *Mary Jones* ■ *Dir* F Harvey Frost [Harvey Frost] • *Scr* W Paul Thompson

Battle of the Bulge ★★★★ PG

Second World War action drama
1965 · US · Colour · 149min

This truly exciting war epic is based on the last German offensive in 1944, when thousands of tanks smashed their way through the snowy pine forests of the Ardennes. It's a study of resolve on both the American and the German sides; representing Uncle Sam are Robert Ryan and Dana Andrews, with Henry Fonda as the only man who sees the German tactic months before it happens. But the picture is dominated by Robert Shaw as the German colonel, a riveting portrait of military genius infested with paranoia. The climax is *High Noon* with tanks. AT DVD

Henry Fonda *Lt Col Kiley* • Robert Shaw *Colonel Hessler* • Robert Ryan *General Grey* • Dana Andrews *Colonel Pritchard* • George Montgomery *Sergeant Duquesne* • Ty Hardin *Schumacher* • Pier Angeli *Louise* • Barbara Werle *Elena* • Charles Bronson *Wolenski* ■ *Dir* Ken Annakin • *Scr* Philip Yordan, Milton Sperling, John Melson

Battle of the Coral Sea ★★ PG

Second World War drama
1959 · US · BW · 82min

This numbingly predictable war movie has a rather a misleading title, as much of the action takes place in a PoW camp. Cliff Robertson's submarine captain is one of the dullest heroes ever to turn the tables on his captors. There's plenty of square-jawed defiance, but not enough humanity to make us care whether he gets back in time to report on Japanese shipping movements prior to the key 1942 battle. DP

Cliff Robertson *Lieutenant Commander Jeff Conway* • Gia Scala *Karen Philips* • Teru Shimada *Commander Mori* • Patricia Cutts *Lieutenant Peg Whitcomb* • Rian Garrick *Al Schechter* • Gene Blakely *Lieutenant Len Ross* • LQ Jones *Yeoman Halliday* ■ *Dir* Paul Wendkos • *Scr* Stephen Kandel, Dan Ullman [Daniel B Ullman], from a story by Stephen Kandel

Battle of the Damned ★★ 15

Science-fiction horror
2013 · US/Sing · Colour · 84min

Dolph Lundgren never did make it onto the action-star A-list following his breakthrough opposite Sylvester Stallone in 1985's *Rocky IV*. Here the grizzled Lundgren plays a mercenary hired to rescue a VIP's daughter from a virus-hit city infested with slavering ghouls. Up close, the star pulls off the taciturn tough guy act with aplomb, but no amount of judicious editing can disguise the fact he's more geriatric than dynamic in the action scenes. JA Violence, swearing.

Dolph Lundgren *Max Gatling* • Melanie Zanetti *Jude* • Matt Doran *Reese* • David Field *Duke* ■ *Dir/Scr* Christopher Hatton

The Battle of the River Plate ★★★ U

Second World War drama
1956 · UK · Colour · 114min

Though this true-life Second World War drama hardly rates alongside *A Matter of Life and Death* and *The Red Shoes* on the CV of the writing/producing/directing duo Michael Powell and Emeric Pressburger, it is a tale well told and features some impressive location work. Peter Finch pulls off a noble German officer (no mean feat in a British war film, even in the 1950s), captain of pocket battleship the *Graf Spee*, the pursuit of which forms the basis of the action. Despite a surfeit of naval detail, the climax in Montevideo makes it worthwhile. AC DVD

John Gregson *Captain Bell* • Anthony Quayle *Commodore Harwood* • Peter Finch *Captain Langsdorff* • Ian Hunter *Captain Woodhouse* • Jack Gwillim *Captain Barry* • Bernard Lee *Captain Dove* • Lionel Murton *Mike Fowler* • Anthony Bushell *Mr Millington-Drake* • Peter Illing *Dr Guani* • Michael Goodliffe *Captain McCall* • Patrick Macnee *Lt Cmdr Medley* • John Chandos *Dr Langmann* • Douglas Wilmer *M Desmoulins* ■ *Dir/Scr* Michael Powell, Emeric Pressburger

The Battle of the Sexes ★★★

Silent drama
1914 · US · BW · 50min

Long thought lost, this is a five-reeler made by the great film pioneer DW Griffith, one of his amazing total of 495 movies. Like many of Griffith's morality playlets from this period, this drama of a father demanding that his daughter live a moral life to which he himself does not aspire may prove hard to watch today, but there is no denying the sheer creativity at work in the storytelling. Here are close-ups, here, too, a moving camera – tools of the trade we now take for granted. TS

Lillian Gish *Jane Andrews* • Donald Crisp *Frank Andrews* • Mary Alden *Mrs Frank Andrews* • Fay Tincher *Cleo* • Owen Moore *Cleo's lover* • Robert Harron *The son* • WE Lawrence ■ *Dir* DW Griffith • *Scr* From the novel *The Single Standard* by Daniel Carson Goodman

The Battle of the Sexes ★★★ U

Comedy
1960 · UK · BW · 80min

This features one of the most underrated performances by Peter Sellers. He plays a Scottish accountant revenging himself on efficiency expert Constance Cummings, who wants his firm to get rid of old-fashioned impedimenta like him. There's an industrial message that's still relevant today, though director Charles Crichton never seems to be enough in control. TH DVD

Peter Sellers *Mr Martin* • Robert Morley *Robert MacPherson* • Constance Cummings *Angela Barrows* • Ernest Thesiger *Old MacPherson* • Jameson Clark *Andrew Darling* • Moultrie Kelsall *Graham* • Alex Mackenzie *Robertson* ■ *Dir* Charles Crichton • *Scr* Monja Danischewsky, from the short story *The Catbird Seat* by James Thurber

The Battle of the Sexes ★★★ PG

Documentary
2013 · UK/US · Colour · 82min

This illuminating documentary about the notorious 1973 clash between tennis champ Billie Jean King and former Wimbledon winner Bobby Riggs is no mere chronicle of a sporting contest. Women's rights in the 70s was as provocative and emotive an issue in the US as civil rights had been a decade before, so there was a lot riding on a confrontation set to attract a global audience of 100 million. This compendium of revealing archive footage, talking heads and (frankly unnecessary) reconstructions demonstrates the significance of the match and is a vital record of a symbolic event for gender equality in sport and society in general. JA

Billie Jean King • Bobby Riggs ■ *Dir/Scr* James Erskine, Zara Hayes

Battle of the Sexes

Sports comedy drama based on a true story
2017 · US · Colour

This is a preview – no prints were available to review as we went to press: Emma Stone makes an amazing transformation as tennis legend Billie Jean King for her 1973 match with retired pro Bobby Riggs (Steve Carell). The build-up to that day and its aftermath are as much a part of the story, given the sexual politics of the era – and the issue of equal pay still resonates. With a script by our very own Simon Beaufoy (*The Full Monty*), Danny Boyle a producer and Andrea Riseborough the lover who outed King, this could be one of the few times that Brits triumph in tennis. SP

Emma Stone *Billie Jean King* • Steve Carell *Bobby Riggs* • Elisabeth Shue • Sarah Silverman *Gladys Heldman* • Andrea Riseborough *Marilyn Barnett* ■ *Dir* Jonathan Dayton, Valerie Faris • *Scr* Simon Beaufoy

The Battle of the V1 ★★ PG

Second World War drama
1958 · UK · BW · 100min

Weakly cast and excessively long, this fitfully exciting melodrama stars Michael Rennie and David Knight as two Polish patriots who discover the latest Nazi secret weapon – the flying missiles or "doodlebugs" that were eventually unleashed on London. The low-budget production awkwardly mixes documentary footage from old enemy newsreels with standard underground heroics that were filmed in the Sussex countryside. AE DVD

Michael Rennie *Stefan Nowak* • Patricia Medina *Zofia* • Milly Vitale *Anna* • David Knight *Tadek* • Esmond Knight *Stricker* • Christopher Lee *Brunner* ■ *Dir* Vernon Sewell • *Scr* Jack Hanley, Eryk Wlodek, from the novel *They Saved London* by Bernard Newman

The Battle of the Villa Fiorita ★★ U
Romance 1965 · UK/US · Colour · 111min

Hankies out for this slick weepie. Shamelessly emulating the glossy soap-opera style of Douglas Sirk, writer/director Delmer Daves makes the most of the gorgeous Italian scenery, as runaway wife Maureen O'Hara and her composer lover Rossano Brazzi are dogged by the disapproval of her children. Brazzi is suavity personified, but O'Hara's flame-haired ebullience is disappointingly buried beneath an unexpected veneer of suffering. DP

Maureen O'Hara *Moira* • Rossano Brazzi *Lorenzo* • Richard Todd *Darrell* • Phyllis Calvert *Margot* • Martin Stephens *Michael* • Elizabeth Dear *Debby* • Olivia Hussey *Donna* • Maxine Audley *Charmian* • Ursula Jeans *Lady Anthea* ■ *Dir* Delmer Daves • *Scr* Delmer Daves, from the novel by Rumer Godden

Battle of the Year ★★ 12
Dance drama 2013 · US · Colour · 105min

It's yonks since the Yanks last won the annual world dance-crew championships, which now take place in France. B-boy entrepreneur Dante (Laz Alonso) decides that it's time to rectify that situation and persuades a jaded ex-basketball coach (Josh Holloway) to forge a "dream team" from the US's best individual break-dancers. As corny as Kellogg's, this is nevertheless brainlessly watchable. DA Some violence.

DVD 3D

Josh Holloway *Jason Blake* • Laz Alonso *Dante Graham* • Josh Peck *Franklyn* • Caity Lotz *Stacy* • Chris Brown *Rooster* ■ *Dir* Benson Lee • *Scr* Brin Hall, Chris Parker [Christopher Parker]

Battle Royale ★★★★ 18
Futuristic action thriller 2000 · Jpn · Colour · 108min

Much has been made of the violence in Kinji Fukasaku's dark satire of reality TV. The film depicts an annual competition of the future in which, as a lesson to unruly youth, a class of schoolchildren is taken to an island, equipped with various weapons and given just three days to reduce their number to the sole survivor who will then be allowed to rejoin society. This is a film of contrasting moods, with moments of bleak comedy and grotesque horror being interspersed with genuinely touching insights into teen trauma. It's occasionally ragged, and the characterisation is sharp – particularly "Beat" Takeshi as a world-weary former teacher who monitors the teenagers' "progress" – and the murderous set pieces are often inspired. DP Japanese +subtitles. DVD ⬅

"Beat" Takeshi [Takeshi Kitano] *Kitano* • Taro Yamamoto *Shogo Kawada, male student 5* • Masanobu Ando *Kazuo Kiriyama, male student 11* • Sosuke Takaoka *Hiroki Sugimura, male student 11* • Tatsuya Fujiwara *Shuya Nanahara, male student 15* • Hirohito Honda *Niida Yoriyuki, male student 16* • Eri Ishikawa *Yukie Utsumi, female student 2* ■ *Dir* Kinji Fukasaku • *Scr* Kenta Fukasaku, from a novel by Koshun Takami

Battle Royale 2: Requiem ★★ 18
Futuristic action thriller 2003 · Jpn · Colour · 132min

Kinji Fukasaku died shortly after beginning this inferior sequel. His son Kenta took over, and the resulting picture underplays the original's satirical elements in favour of awkward politics and clumsy moralising. Contest survivor-turned-terrorist leader Tatsuya Fujiwara publicly calls for violence against western tyranny. He and his supporters hole up on an island, and the government forcibly dispatches a student class to wipe them out. Far-fetched and tedious. SF Japanese +subtitles. Violence. DVD

Tatsuya Fujiwara *Shuya Nanahara* • Ai Maeda *Shiori Kitano* • Shugo Oshinari *Takuma Aoi* • Ayana Sakai *Nao Asakura* • Haruka Suenaga *Haruka Kuze* • "Beat" Takeshi [Takeshi Kitano] *Kitano* ■ *Dir* Kenta Fukasaku, Kinji Fukasaku • *Scr* Kenta Fukasaku, Norio Kida

Battle Shock ★★
Psychological drama 1956 · US · BW · 88min

Directed by the actor Paul Henreid – better known as the Resistance leader in *Casablanca* – this thriller, released in the States as *A Woman's Devotion*, finds artist Ralph Meeker and wife Janice Rule snarled up in a murder hunt while holidaying in Mexico. TH

Ralph Meeker *Trevor Stevenson* • Janice Rule *Stella Stevenson* • Paul Henreid *Captain Henrique Monteros* • Rosenda Monteros *Maria* • Fanny Schiller *Senora Reidl* • José Torvay *Gomez* • Yerye Beirute *Amigo Herrera* ■ *Dir* Paul Henreid • *Scr* Robert Hill

Battle Taxi ★ U
War drama 1955 · US · BW · 80min

In this Korean War drama, Sterling Hayden plays the commander of a unit of rescue helicopters who's getting trouble from Arthur Franz, a former jet pilot who resents his present assignment and starts launching attacks in his unarmed chopper. Hayden was too good an actor for this dime-budget stuff, which has little time for character development beyond the odd frown. AT

Sterling Hayden *Captain Russ Edwards* • Arthur Franz *Lieutenant Pete Stacy* • Marshall Thompson *2nd Lieutenant Tim Vernon* • Leo Needham *Staff Sergeant Slats Klein* • Jay Barney *Lt Col Stoneham* ■ *Dir* Herbert L Strock • *Scr* Malvin Wald, from a story by Art Arthur, Malvin Wald

Battlefield Earth ★ 12
Science-fiction action adventure 2000 · US · Colour · 112min

This expensive stinker is very much a labour of love for its producer and star, John Travolta. In the year 3000, Earth is controlled by ten-foot-tall aliens from the planet Psychlo; the few remaining humans either hide out in the mountains or live and die as slaves. Barry Pepper dares to rebel against the invaders, bringing him into conflict with the fearsome chief of security, a dreadlocked Travolta. Unfeasibly banal. NS DVD

John Travolta *Terl* • Barry Pepper *Jonnie Goodboy Tyler* • Forest Whitaker *Ker* • Kim Coates *Carlo* • Richard Tyson *Robert the Fox* • Sabine Karsenti *Chrissie* • Michael Byrne *Parson Staffer* ■ *Dir* Roger Christian • *Scr* Corey Mandell, JD Shapiro, from the novel by L Ron Hubbard

Battleground ★★★★ PG
Second World War drama 1949 · US · BW · 113min

This grimy and authentic-looking study of wartime close combat comes from MGM, home of glamour and gloss. The studio supplied an all-star cast, and then proceeded to make the likes of Van Johnson, George Murphy and Ricardo Montalban virtually unrecognisable in combat duds as members of a US Army infantry unit trapped during the siege of Bastogne in 1944. Writer Robert Pirosh actually served at Bastogne, and his screenplay won an Oscar, as did Paul C Vogel's cinematography, though director William A Wellman lost out to Joseph L Mankiewicz. Even those who aren't fans of war movies might find much to appreciate in this one. TS DVD

Van Johnson *Holley* • John Hodiak *Jarvess* • Ricardo Montalban *Rodrigues* • George Murphy *Pop Stazak* • Marshall Thompson *Jim Layton* • Jerome Courtland *Abner Spudler* • Don Taylor *Standiferd* • Bruce Cowling *Wolowicz* • James Whitmore *Kinnie* ■ *Dir* William Wellman [William A Wellman] • *Scr* Robert Pirosh

The Battles of Coronel and Falkland Islands ★★★★ PG
War drama documentary 1927 · UK · BW · 106min

Hailed as one of the best Great War reconstructions, this docu-dramatic account of two key naval encounters completed a trilogy by director Walter Summers, following *Ypres* (1925) and *Mons* (1926). It was filmed with the assistance of the Admiralty and relies less on models and archive footage than many. The maritime action was staged off Malta, while the Isles of Scilly stood in for the Falklands, and the cinematic highlight is the montage sequence showing HMS *Inflexible* and *Invincible* being fitted out at Devonport, suggesting the influence of Abel Gance and Sergei Eisenstein. DP DVD ⬅

Craighall Sherry *Admiral Sturdee* ■ *Dir* Walter Summers • *Scr* John Buchan, Harry Engholm, Frank C Bowen

Battleship ★★★ 12
Science-fiction action adventure 2012 · US · Colour · 125min

The third Hasbro toy-to-film franchise (after Transformers and GI Joe) doesn't mess with a winning format. This is *Transformers* at sea, with rebellious no-hoper Taylor Kitsch turned into a naval hero who must fight off alien invaders – in this case snake-eyed cyborgs who pilot ocean-hopping spacecraft armed with giant yo-yo weaponry. Once the soap opera settles down, director Peter Berg (*Hancock*) delivers grand-scale wanton destruction in an unrelenting special-effects extravaganza: dumb fun personified. Despite her much touted appearance, singer Rihanna barely registers as a gung-ho gunner. AJ Some violence. DVD ⬅

Taylor Kitsch *Lt Alex Hopper* • Alexander Skarsgård *Stone Hopper* • Liam Neeson *Adml Shane* • Rihanna *Cora Raikes* • Tadanobu Asano *Capt Yugi Nagata* • Brooklyn Decker *Sam Shane* ■ *Dir* Peter Berg • *Scr* Erich and Jon Hoeber, from the Hasbro board game

LANDMARK FILM
One of the most influential features ever made, particularly in its much-imitated Odessa Steps sequence

The Battleship Potemkin ★★★★★ PG
Silent historical drama 1925 · USSR · BW · 65min

Originally planned as a brief episode in an epic history of the 1905 Revolution, this silent classic from Sergei Eisenstein – also now available with its original score – remains one of the most influential films ever made. A masterpiece of editorial dexterity, it proved that symbolic imagery could have the same emotional and intellectual impact on an audience as a straightforward narrative. You don't need a working knowledge of Russian history, Marxist dialectic, Japanese pictographs or the techniques of "montage" to appreciate the power of the plate smashing that sparks the mutiny, the fog scene and the legendary massacre on the Odessa Steps. Don't be put off by its highbrow reputation, this is essential cinema. DP DVD

Mikhail Gomarov *Sailor* • Repnikova *Woman on the steps* • Aleksander Antonov *Vakulinchuk the sailor* • Grigori Aleksandrov *Chief Officer Gilyarovsky* • Vladimir Barsky *Captain Golikov* • Alexander Lyovshin *Petty officer* • Beatrice Vitoldi *Mother with baby carriage* • I Bobrov *Humiliated soldier* ■ *Dir* Sergei Eisenstein • *Scr* Sergei Eisenstein, Nina Agadzhanova-Shutko • *Cinematographer* Edouard Tissé

Battlestar Galactica ★★ PG
Science-fiction adventure 1978 · US · Colour · 124min

This feature film spin-off consists of two episodes from the short-lived TV series, cloned from *Star Wars* and unsuccessfully sued for plagiarism by the makers of that blockbuster hit. Lorne Greene stars as the commander of a fleet of starships trying to return to Earth after it has virtually been wiped out by the Cylons, a robot race programmed to destroy mankind. The result is a tacky, juvenile and derivative space opera with a "gee whizz" aesthetic. AJ

Lorne Greene *Commander Adama* • Richard L Hatch [Richard Hatch] *Captain Apollo* • Dirk Benedict *Lieutenant Starbuck* • Maren Jensen *Athena* • Herb Jefferson Jr [Herbert Jefferson Jr] *Lieutenant Boomer* • Terry Carter *Colonel Tigh* • Jane Seymour (2) *Serina* • Noah Hathaway *Boxey* ■ *Dir* Richard A Colla • *Scr* Glen A Larson

Battletruck ★★★ 15
Science-fiction adventure 1982 · US · Colour · 88min

Lone warrior hero Michael Beck takes on bloodthirsty pirates and their super truck after 21st-century oil wars cause a fuel shortage. Further friction occurs when Annie McEnroe, the villain's daughter, is caught between the opposing camps. This may be a rather juvenile *Mad Max* clone, but director Harley Cokliss ensures that the subtle ecological messages don't get in the way of the fast-paced mayhem. AJ

Michael Beck *Hunter* • Annie McEnroe *Corlie* • James Wainwright *Straker* • John Ratzenberger *Rusty* • Randolph Powell *Judd* • Bruno Lawrence *Willie* • Diana Rowan *Charlene* • John Bach *Bone* ■ *Dir* Harley Cokliss • *Scr* Irving Austin, Harley Cokliss, John Beech

Battling Butler ★★★
Silent comedy 1926 · US · BW · 80min

Although this was Buster Keaton's most profitable silent film (and one he once cited as his favourite), it is generally rated among his weaker ventures. The pioneering use of deep-focus photography gives it a certain historical value, but there is too little comic business to relish. Keaton plays a wealthy milksop who is sent into the woods to toughen up, only to be mistaken for a prizefighter by mountain girl Sally O'Neil. The duck shoot is ingeniously staged, and there are a couple of amusing training camp gags, but what lingers longest is the brutality of the final boxing bout. DP

Buster Keaton *Alfred Butler* • Sally O'Neil *Mountain girl* • Snitz Edwards *His valet* • Francis McDonald *Alfred "Battling Butler"* • Mary O'Brien *His wife* • Tom Wilson *The trainer* • Eddie Borden *His manager* • Walter James *The girl's father* ■ *Dir* Buster Keaton • *Scr* Paul Gerard Smith, Albert Boasberg, Charles Smith, Lex Neal, Ballard McDonald, from the play *Battling Butler* by Stanley Brightman, Austin Melford, Walter L Rosemont, Douglas Furber

The Bawdy Adventures of Tom Jones ★★ 15
Period musical romp 1976 · UK · Colour · 88min

The success of Tony Richardson's film *Tom Jones* (1963) led to other Fielding adaptations. Desperation must have set in early, adding hopeful temptation to audiences with promises of Tom's bawdy behaviour. This was inspired by a stage musical, but only three songs intrude on the lacklustre events depicting his life and loves. Nicky Henson, as the rascally hero, heads a memorable cast who all sink without trace. BB

Nicky Henson *Tom Jones* • Trevor Howard *Squire Western* • Terry-Thomas *Mr Square* • Arthur Lowe *Dr Thwackum* • Georgia Brown *Jenny Jones/Mrs Waters* • Joan Collins *Black Bess* • Geraldine McEwan *Lady Bellaston* ■ *Dir* Cliff Owen • *Scr* Jeremy Lloyd, from the musical by Don MacPherson, Paul Holden, from the novel by Henry Fielding

Baxter ★★★
Drama 1973 · UK · Colour · 104min

Actor-turned-director Lionel Jeffries never puts a foot wrong through the quagmire of clichés that can so often swamp stories of ill-adjusted youngsters. The 12-year-old hero (Scott Jacoby) is being treated for his lisp by speech therapist Patricia Neal, which seems to put him at odds with his friends and compounds the problem of his parents splitting up. The acting throughout lives up to the gravitas of the film's theme. TH

Patricia Neal *Dr Clemm* • Jean-Pierre Cassel *Roger Tunnell* • Britt Ekland *Chris Bentley* • Lynn Carlin *Mrs Baxter* • Scott Jacoby *Robert Baxter* • Sally Thomsett *Nemo* • Paul Eddington *Mr Rawling* • Paul Maxwell *Mr Baxter* • Ian Thomson *Dr Walsh* ■ *Dir* Lionel Jeffries • *Scr* Reginald Rose

The Bay ★★★★ 15
Horror thriller 2012 · US · Colour · 81min

Harking back to 1970s eco-horrors like *Doomwatch*, *Piranha* and *Prophecy*, *Rain Man* director Barry Levinson takes an unprecedented plunge into the found-footage genre with this cautionary *Jaws* meets *Paranormal Activity* tale. The film unveils the implosion of Fourth of July celebrations in a small coastal town in Maryland after parasitic isopods terrorise the population. For Levinson, this is not just fantastical genre tosh. Born in Maryland, he has observed the effects of pollution first-hand, and this superbly observed terror tale is an impassioned expression of his own concerns. The combination of fact (isopods do exist) and fiction makes the movie a breathlessly scary experience. JA Violence, swearing. *DVD* *Blu*

Will Rogers (2) *Alex* • Kristen Connolly *Stephanie* • Kether Donohue *Donna Thompson* • Frank Deal *Mayor John Stockman* • Stephen Kunken *Dr Jack Abrams* ■ *Dir* Barry Levinson • *Scr* Michael Wallach, from a story by Levinson, Wallach

Bay Boy ★★★ 15
Period drama 1984 · Can/Fr · Colour · 96min

Kiefer Sutherland's first starring role was in this downbeat but interesting film from Canada. He plays a Nova Scotia lad destined for the priesthood who witnesses the murder of a Jewish couple and keeps quiet about it because he knows the killer, a cop who is the father of the girl he fancies. Set in 1937, Daniel Petrie's tale is semi-autobiographical and rather low-key; even so, Sutherland is appealing and his problems with his mother (Liv Ullmann) are often touching. AT Swearing, nudity.

Liv Ullmann *Mrs Jennie Campbell* • Kiefer Sutherland *Donald Campbell* • Alan Scarfe *Sergeant Tom Coldwell* • Peter Donat *Mr Will Campbell* • Mathieu Carrière *Father Chaisson* • Chris Wiggins *Chief Charles McInnes* • Isabelle Mejias *Mary McNeil* • Leah Pinsent *Saxon Coldwell* • Stéphane Audran *Blanche* ■ *Dir/Scr* Daniel Petrie

Bay of Blood ★★★★ 18
Horror 1971 · It · Colour · 80min

Italian horror maestro Mario Bava's blueprint for the stalk-and-slash flick sees all sorts of folks converge on a remote mansion after the murder of an aged countess. But who's behind the slaughter that erupts? Never mind the inconsistent acting or the 1970s fashions, just sit back and be unnerved by a catalogue of carnage that was to inspire *Friday the 13th* and its imitators. Short, sharp and shocking. JA Italian dubbed. Violence, sex scenes, nudity. *DVD* *Blu*

Claudine Auger *Renata* • Luigi Pistilli *Albert* • Claudio Volonté [Claudio Camaso] *Simon* • Anna Maria Rosati *Laura* ■ *Dir* Mario Bava • *Scr* Mario Bava, Joseph McLee, Filippo Ottoni, from a story by Franco Barberi, Dardano Sacchetti

The Bay of Saint Michel ★★
Adventure 1963 · UK · BW · 73min

That marvellous French monument, Le Mont-Saint-Michel, with its broad sweep of sandy bay, makes a spectacular location for this unassuming little thriller about a commando unit that reforms after the Second World War and sets about finding some buried Nazi loot. American star Keenan Wynn is in charge of the operation, while Mai Zetterling, a Swedish actress who made many movies in Britain, plays a mystery Frenchwoman. AT

Keenan Wynn *Nick Rawlings* • Mai Zetterling *Helene Bretton* • Ronald Howard *Bill Webb* • Rona Anderson *Pru Lawson* • Trader Faulkner *Dave Newton* • Edward Underdown *Col Harvey* • Michael Peake *Capt Starkey* • Rudolph Offenbach *Father Laurent* ■ *Dir* John Ainsworth • *Scr* Christopher Davis

Bay of the Angels ★★★★
Drama 1963 · Fr · BW · 85min

Jacques Demy's second feature is an atmospheric study of seduction and obsession. Yet Jean Rabier's modish monochrome photography and Michel Legrand's cascading score add romance to a tale of ruinous addiction that in less assured hands would have been unbearably melodramatic. As the woman who has abandoned her baby to prowl the tables of the Riviera, Jeanne Moreau vivaciously personifies the thrills and the perils of gambling, as she clings to timorous bank clerk Claude Mann during a typically brief winning streak. Demy's adroit attention to visual detail gives this neglected classic its class. DP French +subtitles.

Jeanne Moreau *Jackie Demaistre* • Claude Mann *Jean Fournier* • Paul Guers *Caron* • Henri Nassiet *Jean's father* ■ *Dir/Scr* Jacques Demy

The Baytown Outlaws ★★★ 15
Action crime comedy 2012 · US · Colour · 94min

Bullets, babes and... bows and arrows are just a few of the ingredients in this ferocious slice of southern-fried mayhem, as three redneck siblings are hired to retrieve sultry Eva Longoria's godson from ex-husband Billy Bob Thornton. There's a definite Tarantino vibe going on in the directorial debut of Barry Battles and he's blessed with eye-catching turns from Thornton, Clayne Crawford (as the lead bad-boy brother) and Andre Braugher as a corrupt sheriff who knows more about the rednecks than he's letting on. And, of course, there's plenty of bullet-laden bloodiness for action fans, although Battles isn't in Tarantino's class quite yet. JA Violence, swearing, drug abuse. *DVD*

Billy Bob Thornton *Carlos* • Eva Longoria *Celeste* • Clayne Crawford *Brick Oodie* • Daniel Cudmore *Lincoln Oodie* • André Braugher *Sheriff Henry Millard* ■ *Dir* Barry Battles • *Scr* Barry Battles, Griffin Hood

Baywatch
Comedy 2017 · US · Colour

This is a preview – no prints were available to review as we went to press: Here comes another spin-off of a beloved TV series – *Baywatch* (1989-2001). Producer/original star David Hasselhoff makes an appearance, but it's Dwayne "The Rock" Johnson who will front the movie as lifeguard Mitch Buchannon. You can expect lots of schoolboy gags about girls with big floatation devices and some slo-mo running from Johnson and fellow lifeguard Zac Efron – let's hope they don't flog the joke to death. SP

Zac Efron *Matt Brody* • Dwayne Johnson *Mitch Buchannon* • Alexandra Daddario *Summer Quinn* • Kelly Rohrbach *CJ Parker* • David Hasselhoff ■ *Dir* Seth Gordon • *Scr* Robert Ben Garant, Justin Malen

The Be All and End All ★★★★ 15
Comedy drama 2009 · UK · Colour · 94min

A teenager is determined to help his terminally ill best mate lose his virginity in this Liverpool-set comedy drama. It's quite a challenge for the film-makers not to let the fatal heart condition that has struck Robbie (Josh Bolt) overshadow everything else. Yet perceptive writing shows how this tragic situation proves the making of his resilient pal (Eugene Byrne). Thankfully, strong performances across the board and a sprinkling of laugh-out-loud moments make amends for a plot that has few surprises up its sleeve. TJ Swearing, sexual references. *DVD*

Josh Bolt *Robbie Wallace* • Eugene Byrne *Ziggy* • Connor McIntyre *Mr Wallace* • Catherine Rice *Mrs Wallace* • Liza Tarbuck *Tina* • Neve McIntosh *Kate* ■ *Dir* Bruce Webb • *Scr* Steve Lewis, Tony Owen

Be Cool ★★ 12
Crime comedy 2005 · US · Colour · 114min

This sequel to *Get Shorty* tries hard to emulate its hip, flip style, but just can't carry it off. This time around, wise guy-turned-movie producer Chili Palmer (John Travolta) has tired of the film business and decides to try his luck with the music industry. Travolta and Uma Thurman exude an easy-going charisma, but this just isn't cool enough. JF Violence, swearing. *DVD* *Blu*

John Travolta *Chili Palmer* • Uma Thurman *Edie Athens* • Vince Vaughn *Raji* • Harvey Keitel *Nick Carr* • The Rock [Dwayne Johnson] *Elliot Wilhelm* • Cedric the Entertainer *Sin LaSalle* • André Benjamin *Dabu* • Danny DeVito *Martin Weir* • Steven Tyler ■ *Dir* F Gary Gray • *Scr* Peter Steinfeld, from the novel by Elmore Leonard

Be Kind Rewind ★★★★ 12
Comedy 2007 · US/Fr/UK · Colour and BW · 97min

Following on from *Eternal Sunshine of the Spotless Mind* and *The Science of Sleep*, director Michel Gondry steams ahead on a surreal train of thought. He also wrote the screenplay for this comedy about video store clerk Mike (Mos Def) whose brash buddy Jerry (Jack Black) becomes magnetised in an industrial accident and inadvertently wipes all the tapes. Instead of switching to DVD, Jerry gets a camcorder and they start remaking popular titles like *Ghost Busters*, *RoboCop* and even *Driving Miss Daisy*. Gondry's film is loosely strung together and ridiculous in the extreme, but with Jack Black in the frame it all makes a strange kind of sense. His puckish enthusiasm is both infectious and funny. SP Brief swearing, sexual references. *DVD* *Blu*

Jack Black *Jerry* • Mos Def *Mike* • Danny Glover *Mr Fletcher* • Mia Farrow *Ms Falewicz* • Melonie Diaz *Alma* • Marcus Carl Franklin *Kid 1* • Chandler Parker *Craig* • Sigourney Weaver *Ms Lawson* ■ *Dir/Scr* Michel Gondry

Be My Baby ★★
Romantic comedy 2006 · US · Colour · 97min

An emotionally wounded woman resorts to extreme methods to get back at cheating men in this predictable and frequently unsavoury romantic comedy. Co-writer and star René Ashton is hard to sympathise with as the duplicitous nursery assistant who "borrows" babies to use as blackmailing tools. But when she targets handsome Brody Hutzler with her scam, events become increasingly complex and implausible. Ultimately, the offbeat narrative is neither cute nor particularly amusing and the film's feel-good finale is obvious from the opening scenes. SF Sexual references, drug abuse.

René Ashton *Rylee* • Brody Hutzler *Jason* • Julia Duffy *Doris* • Cris Judd *Brad* • Lacey Chabert *Tiffany* ■ *Dir* Bryce Olson • *Scr* René Ashton, Chris Kennedy (2)

Be My Guest ★★★ U
Drama 1965 · UK · BW · 78min

The second of two unassuming but spirited little pop musicals (the first was *Live It Up*) released during the British beat boom of the 1960s. David Hemmings is once again the star, this time playing a newspaper office boy, who tries to launch the "Brighton beat", but tangles with unscrupulous music industry bigwigs. The format and mood belong to the earlier rock 'n' roll era (Jerry Lee Lewis is one of the guest stars). But the snappy script is played with verve by all concerned, and the result is a very jolly piece of pop history. DM

David Hemmings *Dave* • Steve Marriott *Ricky* • John Pike *Phil* • Andrea Monet *Erica* • Ivor Salter *Herbert* • Anna King *Margaret* • Avril Angers *Mrs Pucil* ■ *Dir* Lance Comfort • *Scr* Lyn Fairhurst

Be with Me ★★★ 12
Romantic drama 2005 · Sing · Colour · 89min

Eric Khoo has been a key figure in Singaporean cinema since his controversial debut *Mee Pok Man* in 1995. This film is a typically unconventional offering that combines three fictional vignettes with a documentary-style segment, in which the courage demonstrated by deaf-and-blind Theresa Chan acts as the link in a deceptively simple but charming picture. Two of the vignettes (about a teenage lesbian crush and an obese security guard's fixation) have their amusing moments. But they're more formulaic than the best of the three – a poignant plotline involving an ageing shopkeeper and his hospitalised wife. DP English, Mandarin, Hokkien, Cantonese +subtitles. *DVD*

Theresa Chan *Herself* • Seet Keng-yew *Fatty Koh* • Ezann Lee *Jackie* • Samantha Tan *Sam* ■ *Dir* Eric Khoo • *Scr* Eric Khoo, Wong Kim-hoh • *Cinematographer* Adrian Tan

The Beach ★★★★ 15
Adventure thriller 2000 · US/UK · Colour · 114min

This film from the *Trainspotting* team takes a tour round the mind of Leonardo DiCaprio, a young backpacker seeking adventure in Thailand who gets more than he bargained for when drug-crazed madman Robert Carlyle tells him the location of a secret beach. John Hodge's clever, witty script keeps the narrative firmly on track, while leaving director Danny Boyle ample room to luxuriate in the Orient's visual delights. DiCaprio gives a mature, multilayered performance, and Virginie Ledoyen is a great find as the love interest. SR Violence, swearing, drug abuse, nudity. *DVD* *Blu*

Leonardo DiCaprio *Richard* • Tilda Swinton *Sal* • Virginie Ledoyen *Françoise* • Guillaume Canet *Etienne* • Robert Carlyle *Daffy* • Paterson Joseph *Keaty* • Lars Arentz Hansen *Bugs* • Daniel York *Hustler* ■ *Dir* Danny Boyle • *Scr* John Hodge, from the novel by Alex Garland • *Cinematographer* Darius Khondji

Beach Blanket Bingo ★★
Comedy 1965 · US · Colour · 100min

A mindless, pointless title for a mindless, pointless movie, unless you happen to be a fan of AIPs stream of post-*Beach Party* teen films. For those who care, this yet again features those oh-so-nice singing stars Frankie Avalon and Annette Funicello, and it's sad to see the great Buster Keaton paying the rent with a walk-on cameo. The music is utter drivel and the direction nonexistent, but it's an extraordinary time capsule to wonder at. TS

Frankie Avalon *Frankie* • Annette Funicello *Dee Dee* • Deborah Walley *Bonnie Graham* • Harvey Lembeck *Eric Von Zipper* • John Ashley *Steve Gordon* • Jody McCrea *Bonehead* • Linda Evans *Sugar Kane* • Don Rickles *Big Drop* • Paul Lynde *Bullets* • Buster Keaton ■ *Dir* William Asher • *Scr* Sher Townsend, Leo Townsend

Beach Party ★★★ U
Comedy 1963 · US · Colour · 97min

This is the first, and best, of AIP's phenomenally successful surfin' series. These naive frolics proved to a British audience that America, post-Beatles, was positively archaic. Viewed charitably (is there any other way?), this teen-slanted Frankie Avalon/Annette Funicello beach romp is not without charm, though the inclusion of grown-ups Bob Cummings and Dorothy Malone wastes two usually likeable screen performers in a subplot of astounding banality that looks as though it was filmed separately from the rest of the movie. TS

Bob Cummings [Robert Cummings] *Professor Sutwell* • Dorothy Malone *Marianne* • Frankie Avalon *Frankie* • Annette Funicello *Dolores* • Harvey Lembeck *Eric Von Zipper* • Jody McCrea *Deadhead* • John Ashley *Ken* • Morey Amsterdam *Cappy* • Eva Six *Ava* ■ *Dir* William Asher • *Scr* Lou Rusoff

Beach Red ★★★★ 12
Second World War drama 1967 · US · Colour · 99min

Former beefcake star Cornel Wilde became a maverick director to reckon with in later life, producing self-starring vehicles, invariably also featuring his wife, Jean Wallace, as co-star. This ferocious Pacific war opus is one of his better efforts, an uncompromising movie with minimal narrative. The film's editing, by *Bullitt's* Frank P Keller, is stunning, and was rightly Oscar nominated, and the depiction of war's savagery is truly remarkable: no one who has seen this film will ever forget the shot of the soldier leaving his arm behind on the beach. TS Violence, nudity.

U SUITABLE FOR ALL   Uc SUITABLE ESPECIALLY FOR YOUNG CHILDREN (DVD ONLY)   PG PARENTAL GUIDANCE   12A UNDER 12s TO BE ACCOMPANIED (CINEMA ONLY)

Cornel Wilde *Captain MacDonald* • Rip Torn *Sergeant Honeywell* • Dewey Stinger III *Mouse* • Patrick Wolfe *Cliff* • Burr DeBenning *Egan* • Jean Wallace *Julie MacDonald* • Linda Albertano *Girl in Baltimore* • Jan Garrison *Susie* • Gene Blakely *Goldberg* ■ *Dir* Cornel Wilde • *Scr* Clint Johnston, Donald A Peters, Jefferson Pascal, from the novel *Sunday Red Beach* by Peter Bowman

The Beachcomber ★★ U

Drama   1954 · UK · Colour · 78min

W Somerset Maugham's story of the drunken derelict who is reformed by a prissy missionary had been filmed under its original title, *Vessel of Wrath*, in 1938 with Charles Laughton and Elsa Lanchester in the leads. Robert Newton seems so aware of the stature of Laughton's performance that he allows his own to lapse into a slurred variation on Long John Silver. Newton's blustering blows poor Glynis Johns and the rest of a decent cast off the screen. DP

Robert Newton *Ted* • Glynis Johns *Martha* • Donald Sinden *Ewart Gray* • Paul Rogers *Owen* • Donald Pleasence *Tromp* • Walter Crisham *Vederala* • Michael Hordern *Headman* • Auric Lorand *Alfred* ■ *Dir* Muriel Box • *Scr* Sydney Box, from the story *Vessel of Wrath* by W Somerset Maugham

Beaches ★★★ 12

Drama   1988 · US · Colour · 118min

This movie about a lifelong friendship between two women stars powerhouse Bette Midler and Barbara Hershey. They both make the most of their roles as two girls from different backgrounds who meet as 11-year-olds and remain close over the years. Garry Marshall directs slickly and Hershey is very appealing as a poor little rich girl, but the movie belongs to the astonishing Midler, playing a brash, selfish singer. It's at its best when Midler gives free rein to her character rather than when it slips into schmaltz. SH Swearing. *DVD*

Bette Midler *CC Bloom* • Barbara Hershey *Hillary Whitney Essex* • John Heard *John Pierce* • Spalding Gray *Dr Richard Milstein* • Lainie Kazan *Leona Bloom* • James Read *Michael Essex* • Grace Johnston *Victoria Essex* ■ *Dir* Garry Marshall • *Scr* Mary Agnes Donoghue, from the novel by Iris Rainer Dart

The Beaches of Agnès
★★★★ 18

Documentary   2008 · Fr · Colour · 112min

Don't be fooled by footage of the diminutive octogenarian pottering around in this mischievous memoir. Agnès Varda is an exceptional film-maker with a career spanning over 50 years, a woman of fierce intellect, social commitment and artistic tenacity. Having profiled her late husband Jacques Demy in *Jacquot de Nantes* back in 1991, the "godmother of the *nouvelle vague*" here turns her camera on herself. Looking back on the revolutionary politics of the 1960s, messing about on boats or composing shots of beaches on both the Channel coast and on a Parisian street, Varda shows her ability to survive sorrow and disappointment. The result is a work that is as personal as it is compelling and as audacious as it is affectionate. Truly a cineaste's delight. DP French +subtitles. Sex scenes, nudity.

Agnès Varda ■ *Dir/Scr* Agnès Varda

Bean ★★★★ PG

Comedy   1997 · UK · Colour · 85min

This very enjoyable American outing for Rowan Atkinson's celebrated TV character has the bumbling Bean jetting off to the States to oversee the unveiling of the newly acquired *Whistler's Mother*. There are some familiar sketches, but the cohesive, engaging and fast-moving story are perfectly suited to Atkinson's singular style of physical comedy – his close encounter with "America's greatest painting" is an absolute riot. Peter MacNicol's anxiety-ridden American host is the perfect foil to Atkinson and Burt Reynolds is, well, Burt Reynolds in a general's uniform. The film was a massive

international hit and deservedly so. JC
DVD *Blu-ray* *CS*

Rowan Atkinson *Mr Bean* • Peter MacNicol *David Langley* • Pamela Reed *Alison Langley* • Harris Yulin *George Grierson* • Burt Reynolds *General Newton* • Larry Drake *Elmer* • Chris Ellis *Detective Butler* • Johnny Galecki *Stingo Wheelie* ■ *Dir* Mel Smith • *Scr* Richard Curtis, Robin Driscoll, from the character created by Rowan Atkinson, Richard Curtis

The Bear ★★★★ PG

Adventure   1988 · Fr · Colour · 89min

A (tooth-)ripping yarn by director Jean-Jacques Annaud, this tells the adventures of a small bear, befriended by a larger cousin who is a tempting target for a couple of trappers. It's filmed with enormous expertise and the eco-warrior case is put with great sympathy, but its anthropomorphism makes it seem like a glossy and more symbolic version of the Disney real-life stories that used to be all the rage in the 1960s. TH

Jack Wallace *Bill* • Tcheky Karyo *Tom* • André Lacombe *Joseph, the dog handler* ■ *Dir* Jean-Jacques Annaud • *Scr* Gérard Brach, John Brownjohn, Alexander Whitelaw, from the novel *The Grizzly King* by James Oliver Curwood • *Cinematographer* Philippe Rousselot

Bear ★ 15

Thriller   2010 · US · Colour · 78min

A vengeful bear has more screen presence than his human victims in this feeble man-against-nature tale from debut director John Rebel. Brendan Michael Coughlin and Patrick Scott Lewis play the antagonistic brothers who break down with their partners in remote woods, then have to deal with a huge grizzly after shooting dead its mate. It's all very silly, though unfortunately not in an entertaining way, thanks to a disastrous concentration on dialogue over action. What little bear carnage there is comes muted by budget restrictions. SF

Katie Lowes *Christine* • Mary Alexandra Stiefvater *Liz* • Patrick Scott Lewis *Sam* • Brendan Michael Coughlin *Nick* ■ *Dir* Rebel John • *Scr* Roel Reiné, Ethan Wiley

Bear Island ★ PG

Action thriller   1979 · UK/Can · Colour · 102min

Obviously unimpressed by Alistair MacLean's story of fascists bidding for world domination by means of meteorological mastery, director Don Sharp rejects plot in favour of a series action sequences and earnest conversations in ludicrous accents. DP Some swearing, violence. *DVD*

Donald Sutherland *Frank Lansing* • Vanessa Redgrave *Hedi Lindquist* • Richard Widmark *Otto Gerran* • Christopher Lee *Lechinski* • Barbara Parkins *Judith Ruben* • Lloyd Bridges *Smithy* • Lawrence Dane *Paul Hartman* • Patricia Collins *Inge Van Zipper* ■ *Dir* Don Sharp • *Scr* David Butler, Murray Smith, Don Sharp, from the novel by Alistair MacLean

The Bears and I ★★ U

Adventure   1974 · US · Colour · 88min

In attempting to follow in his father John's footsteps, Patrick Wayne set himself a mission impossible. A decade after he appeared in the last in a series of westerns with the Duke himself, Patrick struck out on his own in this passable live-action adventure from Disney. Playing a Vietnam veteran who settles in a national park, he finds himself with the dual problem of preventing native American land from falling into the hands of racist rednecks and of raising a trio of mischievous bear cubs. DP

Patrick Wayne *Bob Leslie* • Chief Dan George *Chief A-Tas-Ka-Nay* • Andrew Duggan *Commissioner Gaines* • Michael Ansara *Oliver Red Fern* • Robert Pine *John McCarten* • Val DeVargas *Sam Eagle Speaker* ■ *Dir* Bernard McEveety • *Scr* John Whedon, from the novel by Robert Franklin Leslie

Beast Cops ★★★ 18

Action thriller   1998 · HK · Colour · 104min

This violent cop thriller cleaned up at the Hong Kong Film Awards in 1999. Anthony Wong is the hard-nosed detective who is prepared to bend all sorts of laws in the constant battle with the Triads; Michael Wong is his more conventional superior, uneasy about his colleague's relationship with the criminal fraternity. It's a familiar enough story but the raw, unflinching direction by Gordon Chan and Dante Lam gives it a gritty ring of truth and the splashes of violence are unsettling. JF Cantonese, English +subtitles. *DVD*

Michael Wong Man-Tak [Michael Wong] *Michael Cheung* • Anthony Wong Chau-Sang [Anthony Wong (1)] *Tung* • Kathy Chow Hoi-Mei *Yoyo* • Roy Cheung Yiu-Yeung [Roy Cheung] *Big Brother* • Sam Lee Chan-Sam [Sam Lee] *Lam* • Patrick Tam Yiu-Man [Patrick Tam] *Ah Wah* ■ *Dir* Gordon Chan Ka-Seung [Gordon Chan], Dante Lam Chiu-yin • *Scr* Gordon Chan, Steve Chan Hing-kai

Beast from Haunted Cave
★★

Horror   1959 · US · BW · 67min

Crooks hiding out in a ski resort get their comeuppance at the paws of a cave-dwelling snow beast. This is a painless, cost-conscious effort typical of producer Roger Corman, made by his company and filmed in Deadwood, South Dakota. Yet it is infused with flair and imagination by director Monte Hellman. Hellman later directed the cult westerns *Ride in the Whirlwind* (1965) and *The Shooting* (1967), and this unusual mobster versus monster melange shows his early promise. AJ

Michael Forest *Gill* • Sheila Carol *Gypsy* • Frank Wolff *Alex* • Richard Sinatra *Marty* • Wally Campo *Byron* • Linne Ahlstrand *Natalie* ■ *Dir* Monte Hellman • *Scr* Charles B Griffith

The Beast from 20,000 Fathoms ★★★★ PG

Science-fiction adventure   1953 · US · BW · 76min

The first prehistoric-monster-on-the-rampage feature and arguably the best. It marked the solo debut of special effects genius Ray Harryhausen, who would refine his stop-motion artistry in the Sinbad fantasies and *Jason and the Argonauts*. Freed from a prehistoric hibernation by an atomic blast at the North Pole, the monster tramples through New York and ends up taking a bite out of the Coney Island roller coaster. This was the *Jurassic Park* of its day and spawned countless imitations. AJ *DVD*

Paul Christian *Tom Nesbitt* • Paula Raymond *Lee Hunter* • Cecil Kellaway *Professor Elson* • Kenneth Tobey *Colonel Evans* • Jack Pennick *Jacob* • Donald Woods *Captain Jackson* • Lee Van Cleef *Corporal Stone* • Steve Brodie *Sergeant Loomis* ■ *Dir* Eugène Lourié • *Scr* Lou Morheim, Fred Freiberger, from the story *The Fog Horn* by Ray Bradbury

The Beast in the Cellar ★ 15

Horror   1970 · UK · Colour · 84min

Two sinister sisters hide a dark secret in their basement in this ponderously talky horror tale. With the title revealing all, James Kelly has nowhere interesting to go and what little atmosphere he conjures up is soon dissipated in a pretty tedious, badly constructed and unsuspenseful affair. AJ Violence. *DVD*

Beryl Reid *Ellie Ballantyne* • Flora Robson *Joyce Ballantyne* • Tessa Wyatt *Joanna Sutherland* • John Hamill *Corporal Alan Marlow* • TP McKenna *Superintendent Paddick* • David Dodimead *Dr Spencer* • Christopher Chittell *Baker* ■ *Dir/Scr* James Kelly

The Beast Must Die ★★ 15

Horror   1974 · UK · Colour · 87min

This is a clumsily contrived variation on the old dark house whodunnit, in which one of the guests invited to Calvin Lockhart's hunting lodge is not merely a murderer but a werewolf to boot. Even with the lame "werewolf break" gimmick (the film

suddenly stops and viewers are asked to guess the lycanthrope's identity), it all boils down to the same horror clichés, with the wolf rather too obviously played by a dressed-up dog. AJ Violence. *DVD*

Calvin Lockhart *Tom Newcliffe* • Peter Cushing *Dr Christopher Lundgren* • Charles Gray *Bennington* • Anton Diffring *Pavel* • Marlene Clark *Caroline Newcliffe* • Ciaran Madden *Davina Gilmore* • Tom Chadbon *Paul Foote* • Michael Gambon *Jan Jarmokowski* ■ *Dir* Paul Annett • *Scr* Michael Winder, from the story *There Shall Be No Darkness* by James Blish

The Beast of Hollow Mountain ★★

Science-fiction western   1956 · US/Mex · Colour · 81min

Based on a story by *King Kong* animator Willis O'Brien, this low-budget production could have done with his stop-motion skills. When the tyrannosaurus finally makes its long-awaited entrance in this cowboys versus prehistoric monster saga, it's a disappointment. This tells the tale of greedy land barons, with Guy Madison giving a plucky performance as a rancher and Patricia Medina making a decent heroine, but their efforts are overshadowed by the hokey effects. AJ

Guy Madison *Jimmy Ryan* • Patricia Medina *Sarita* • Eduardo Noriega (1) *Enrique Rios* • Carlos Rivas *Felipe Sanchez* ■ *Dir* Edward Nassour, Ismael Rodriguez • *Scr* Robert Hill, Jack DeWitt, from the story *Valley of the Mist* by Willis H O'Brien

The Beast of the City ★★★

Crime drama   1932 · US · BW · 86min

In direct response to a request by President Herbert Hoover that the police be glorified on screen rather than gangsters, MGM turned out this crusading drama with Walter Huston well cast as the incorruptible police chief waging war on Jean Hersholt's big shot and his empire of crime. Jean Harlow puts in a torrid appearance as the gangster's moll who proves irresistible to Huston's younger brother, played by Wallace Ford. AE

Walter Huston *Jim Fitzpatrick* • Jean Harlow *Daisy* • Wallace Ford *Edward Fitzpatrick* • Jean Hersholt *Sam Belmonte* • Dorothy Peterson *Mary Fitzpatrick* • Tully Marshall *Michaels* • John Miljan *District attorney* • Emmett Corrigan *Chief of Police* • Sandy Roth *Mac* • Mickey Rooney *Mickey Fitzpatrick* ■ *Dir* Charles Brabin • *Scr* John Lee Mahin, from the story by WR Burnett

The Beast of War ★★★ 18

War drama   1988 · US · Colour · 109min

Yet another movie to prove that war is hell. And yet, with its exotic locations and intense relationships, director Kevin Reynolds's carefully balanced drama brings its message home with a fierce urgency. Set in 1981 during the second year of the Soviet-Afghan war, the beast of the title is a Soviet tank that has helped raze a village to the ground and, becoming separated from its unit, is trapped in a mountainous dead-end by guerrillas bent on reprisals. Emotions within the tank are overheated, with paranoid commander George Dzundza at odds with crew member Jason Patric. TH English, Pashtu +subtitles. Violence, swearing. *DVD*

George Dzundza *Daskal* • Jason Patric *Koverchenko* • Steven Bauer *Taj* • Stephen Baldwin *Golikov* • Don Harvey *Kaminski* • Kabir Bedi *Akbar* • Erick Avari *Samad* ■ *Dir* Kevin Reynolds • *Scr* William Mastrosimone, from his play *Nanawatai*

The Beast with a Million Eyes ★★ PG

Science-fiction thriller   1955 · US · BW · 78min

Made for a paltry $23,000, this Roger Corman executive-produced allegory has been written off because of its peculiar premise and its bargain-basement effects. The prospect of watching birds and barnyard animals turning on humans at the behest of a malevolent alien force may, indeed, seem preposterous. As does the rationale that this evil entity can be tamed by folksy, American love. But the notion

B

that we are being watched over by a potentially malicious presence is actually rather provocative. DP DVD

Paul Birch *Allan Kelley* • Lorna Thayer *Carol Kelley* • Dona Cole *Sandy Kelley* • Dick Sargent *Deputy Larry Brewster* • Leonard Tarver *"Him"* • Chester Conklin *Old Man Webber* ■ *Dir* David Kramarsky • *Scr* Tom Filer

The Beast with Five Fingers ★★★★ 15
Horror 1946 · US · BW · 84min

Peter Lorre acts deliciously deranged, as only he can, when the severed hand of a dead concert pianist returns from the grave to haunt his tortured soul. Or is he just imagining it? Lorre steals the show with a masterfully bravura performance in a superior slice of psychological horror, marshalling the sinister staples of mythic madness and macabre music into a satisfying scare-fest. Give a big hand to Robert Florey for his adept direction, and to the key special effect itself (which Luis Buñuel had a hand in), a marvellously nightmarish image. AJ

Robert Alda *Bruce Conrad* • Andrea King *Julie Holden* • Peter Lorre *Hilary Cummins* • Victor Francen *Francis Ingram* • J Carrol Naish *Ouidio Castanio* • Charles Dingle *Raymond Arlington* • John Alvin *Donald Arlington* • David Hoffman *Duprex* ■ *Dir* Robert Florey • *Scr* Curt Siodmak, from a story by William Fryer Harvey

Beastly ★ 12
Fantasy romance 2010 · US · Colour · 82min

Beauty and the Beast gets a mundane update in a crass adaptation of Alex Flinn's bestseller. It's a flatly embarrassing interpretation, as handsome but obnoxious rich kid Alex Pettyfer upsets emo witch Mary-Kate Olsen and is transformed into a supposedly ugly pierced and tattooed skinhead. Will Vanessa Hudgens say "I love you" within the year to lift the hex? With no magical chemistry between the lacklustre leads, this charmless exercise proves impossible to warm to. The title says it all. AJ Sexual references. DVD

Vanessa Hudgens [Vanessa Anne Hudgens] *Lindy* • Alex Pettyfer *Kyle Kingsbury* • Mary-Kate Olsen *Kendra* • Peter Krause *Rob* • Lisagay Hamilton [Lisa Gay Hamilton] *Zola* • Neil Patrick Harris *Will* ■ *Dir* Daniel Barnz • *Scr* Daniel Barnz, from the novel by Alex Flinn

The Beastmaster ★★★ 15
Fantasy action adventure 1982 · US · Colour · 113min

This is a daft sword-and-sorcery fantasy adventure from director Don Coscarelli of *Phantasm* fame. Muscleman Marc Singer is Dar, a prehistoric Doctor Dolittle, who can telepathically talk to jungle animals and uses them to battle evil magician Maax (an over-the-top Rip Torn), the plunderer of his barbarian village. Lots of glitzy special effects, zombie guards in bondage gear and some amazing animal stunts spice up the proceedings. Two belated sequels also with Singer appeared in the 1990s. AJ Violence, brief nudity. DVD

Marc Singer *Dar* • Tanya Roberts *Kiri* • Rip Torn *Maax* • John Amos *Seth* • Josh Milrad *Tal* • Rod Loomis *Zed* • Ten Hammer *Young Dar's father* • Ralph Strait *Sacco* • Billy Jacoby *Young Dar* ■ *Dir* Don Coscarelli • *Scr* Don Coscarelli, Paul Pepperman, from the novel by Andre Norton

Beasts of No Nation ★★★★ 15
War drama 2015 · US · Colour · 136min

When rebel soldiers invade his village in an unnamed African country, a young boy (Abraham Attah) is recruited by the charismatic yet vicious Commandant (Idris Elba) to his ragtag band of foot soldiers. In an overlong but intense war story, Attah's disintegration from kid to killing machine is not easy to watch, but it's chillingly plausible, while Elba's powerhouse performance depicts a barbarous tyrant who's at heart as lost and lonely as the boys he abuses. DW

Idris Elba *Commandant* • Abraham Attah *Agu* • Kurt Egyiawan *Second in command* • Jude Akuwudike *Supreme Commander Dada*

Goodblood ■ *Dir* Cary Joji Fukunaga [Cary Fukunaga] • *Scr* Cary Joji Fukunaga, from Uzodinma Iweala's novel

Beasts of the Southern Wild ★★★★ 12
Drama 2012 · US · Colour · 89min

This marvellous bayou fable is set at the edge of so-called "civilisation" on the Louisiana levee and revolves around the relationship between a big-hearted six-year-old (Quvenzhané Wallis) and her gruff father (Dwight Henry). They are happy within their shanty-like Delta community, but storm clouds are gathering. Working on a modest budget and using local talent, first-time director Benh Zeitlin impressively juggles elements of magical fantasy with hard-bitten poverty-line realism. As well as being dramatically and visually engaging, the film conjures a living ecosystem that pulses, grips and ultimately enchants. AC DVD

Quvenzhané Wallis *Hushpuppy* • Dwight Henry *Wink* • Levy Easterly *Jean Battiste* • Lowell Landes *Walrus* • Pamela Harper *Little Jo* ■ *Dir* Benh Zeitlin • *Scr* Lucy Alibar, Benh Zeitlin, from Alibar's play *Juicy and Delicious*

The Beat beneath My Feet ★★ 15
Comedy drama 2014 · UK · Colour · 91min

In this escapist low-budget yarn, a shy South London teenager's life is turned around when he realises his new neighbour is a former rock star (Luke Perry) who disappeared years before under mysterious circumstances. The highlights are the imaginative pop-video-style sequences, which make clever use of stop-frame animation to bring the songs to life. If only there was the same vim and vigour elsewhere in this otherwise plodding tale. TJ

Luke Perry *Max Stone, "Steve"* • Nicholas Galitzine *Tom* • Verity Pinter *Felix* • Lisa Dillon *Mary* • Christian O'Connell *Battle of the Band host* ■ *Dir* John Williams (5) • *Scr* Michael Müller [Michael Mueller]

The Beat Generation ★★
Psychological detective drama 1959 · US · BW · 94min

This is one of those mesmerising bad productions with a sordid storyline and a compulsively watchable eclectic period cast. Here we've got tough detective Steve Cochran on the hunt for a sex killer, along the way meeting the likes of blonde sexpot Mamie Van Doren, sex kitten Fay Spain and sexy Maggie Hayes. Talented director Charles Haas makes the grim goings-on compulsive viewing, though without much conviction. TS

Steve Cochran *Dave Culloran* • Mamie Van Doren *Georgia Altera* • Ray Danton *Stan Hess* • Fay Spain *Francee Culloran* • Louis Armstrong • Maggie Hayes [Margaret Hayes] *Joyce Greenfield* • Jackie Coogan *Jake Baron* • Jim Mitchum [James Mitchum] *Art Jester* • Ray Anthony *Harry Altera* • Vampira *Poetess* • Charles Chaplin Jr *Lover Boy* ■ *Dir* Charles Haas • *Scr* Richard Matheson, Lewis Meltzer

Beat Girl ★★ 12
Drama 1960 · UK · BW · 88min

Beatnik parties in backstreet sin cellars, nights in sleazy Soho strip joints, unsupervised drag racing – it's easy to see why this raucous juvenile-delinquency romp raised eyebrows and scared adults back in 1960. But the failed attempt to launch Adam Faith as yet another of Britain's answers to Elvis Presley is now a great pop history lesson in teenage attitudes and rock 'n' roll rebellion, complete with cool jive talk and swinging sounds. AJ Brief swearing, nudity. DVD

David Farrar *Paul Linden* • Noelle Adam *Nichole* • Christopher Lee *Kenny* • Gillian Hills *Jennifer* • Adam Faith *Dave* • Shirley Anne Field *Dodo* • Peter McEnery *Tony* • Claire Gordon *Honey* • Oliver Reed *Plaid shirt* ■ *Dir* Edmond T Gréville • *Scr* Dail Ambler

The Beat That My Heart Skipped ★★★★ 15
Crime drama 2005 · Fr · Colour · 102min

Director Jacques Audiard's simmering remake of James Toback's 1978 crime drama *Fingers* transplants the action from New York to Paris. The earlier film had some implausible moments; here, it's much easier to accept Romain Duris as a man who is torn between following his small-time crook father (Niels Arestrup) into crime and honouring the memory of his mother by becoming a concert pianist. Some may baulk at the lengthy passages in which the gifted but rusty Duris practises piano with patient Chinese tutor Linh-Dan Pham. But such interludes make his inevitable recourse to violence all the more shockingly wasteful. DP French +subtitles. Swearing, violence. DVD

Romain Duris *Tom* • Niels Arestrup *Robert* • Linh-Dan Pham *Miao-Lin* • Emmanuelle Devos *Chris* • Jonathan Zaccaï *Fabrice* • Gilles Cohen *Sami* • Anton Yakovlev *Minskov* ■ *Dir* Jacques Audiard • *Scr* Jacques Audiard, Tonino Benacquista, from the film *Fingers* by James Toback

Beat the Devil ★★★ U
Comedy thriller 1953 · UK/It · BW · 89min

This sophisticated international romp (co-scripted by Truman Capote and John Huston) has a group of eccentric characters setting out to find uranium-rich land in Africa. The splendid cast ensures that the jokes play and the romance works. Peter Lorre and Humphrey Bogart work again here with Huston, with support from Jennifer Jones as the wife of oh-so-English Edward Underdown, and goonish gangsters Robert Morley and Ivor Barnard. Not terribly well appreciated in its day, this quirky one-off has achieved something of a cult status. TS DVD

Humphrey Bogart *Billy Dannreuther* • Jennifer Jones *Gwendolen Chelm* • Gina Lollobrigida *Maria Dannreuther* • Robert Morley *Petersen* • Peter Lorre *O'Hara* • Edward Underdown *Harry Chelm* • Ivor Barnard *Major Ross* • Bernard Lee *CID Inspector* ■ *Dir* John Huston • *Scr* John Huston, Truman Capote, from the novel by James Helvick

Beatrice Cenci ★★★
Historical tragedy 1969 · It · Colour · 99min

Italian director Lucio Fulci regarded this blend of costume melodrama and stylised horror as his finest film. Opening on the morning of the Cenci family's execution, the action is constructed from a series of flashbacks that slowly reveals the fate of the brutal patriarch, George Wilson. But while the torture scenes deter the squeamish, they serve to highlight the unswerving loyalty of Tomas Milian as he seeks to prevent the unworldly Adrienne Larussa from suffering the consequences of her justifiable act of revenge. In stark contrast stands the duplicity of the Catholic Church. DP Italian dubbed.

Tomas Milian *Olimpio* • Adrienne Larussa *Beatrice Cenci* • Georges Wilson *Cenci* • Raymond Pellegrin *Cardinal Lanciani* • Ignazio Spalla *Catalano* ■ *Dir* Lucio Fulci • *Scr* Lucio Fulci, Roberto Gianviti, from the play *The Cenci* by Percy Bysshe Shelley

Beau Brummell ★★★ U
Historical drama 1954 · US · Colour · 111min

Robert Morley had the distinction of playing the late-18th century's two unhappiest monarchs: Louis XVI of France (in *Marie Antoinette*, for which he earned an Oscar nomination) and George III in this over-inflated historical pageant. Stewart Granger cuts a dashing figure as the Regency fop, whose life, loves and dress sense set tongues wagging. Faced with the exuberance of Morley, Granger and Peter Ustinov (deliciously affected as the Prince of Wales), Elizabeth Taylor seems a little daunted. DP

Stewart Granger *Beau Brummell* • Elizabeth Taylor *Lady Patricia* • Peter Ustinov *Prince of Wales* • Robert Morley *King George III* • James Donald *Lord Edwin Mercer* • James Hayter

Mortimer • Rosemary Harris *Mrs Fitzherbert* • Paul Rogers *William Pitt* ■ *Dir* Curtis Bernhardt • *Scr* Karl Tunberg, from the play by Clyde Fitch

Beau Geste ★★★★
Silent adventure 1926 · US · BW · 101min

This is one of the most popular films of the silent era and is still a ripping yarn, thanks to the irresistible appeal of PC Wren's story and the flamboyance of the performances. Ronald Colman, Ralph Forbes and Neil Hamilton are the three English brothers who join the Foreign Legion in search of a family heirloom, the Blue Water diamond. The story unfolds in a series of flashbacks and revelations – quite complex and innovative for the time – and director Herbert Brenon has the knack of combining epic tragedy with lightweight adventure. AT

Ronald Colman *Michael "Beau" Geste* • Neil Hamilton *Digby Geste* • Ralph Forbes *John Geste* • Alice Joyce *Lady Brandon* • Mary Brian *Isobel* • Noah Beery *Sgt Lejeune* • Norman Trevor *Maj de Beaujolais* • William Powell *Boldini* • Victor McLaglen *Hank* ■ *Dir* Herbert Brenon • *Scr* Paul Schofield, John Russell, from the novel by PC Wren

Beau Geste ★★★★★ PG
Classic adventure 1939 · US · BW · 108min

The definitive version of PC Wren's *Boys' Own* classic saga of the Foreign Legion and the events surrounding Fort Zinderneuf. Gary Cooper makes a perfect Beau, while Ray Milland and Robert Preston are well cast as his brothers John and Digby. Also watch out for a very young Donald O'Connor as Beau as a boy. Discerning viewers (and silent movie fans) will spot that this is virtually a shot-for-shot remake of the Ronald Colman version, but a major plus here (apart from sound) is the casting of Brian Donlevy as the evil Sergeant Markoff, who garnered an Oscar nomination. The heroic and romantic attitudes on display may now seem out of date, but that's the fault of the times, not the story. TS

Gary Cooper *Beau Geste* • Ray Milland *John Geste* • Robert Preston *Digby Geste* • Brian Donlevy *Sgt Markoff* • Susan Hayward *Isobel Rivers* • J Carrol Naish *Rasinoff* • Albert Dekker *Schwartz* • Broderick Crawford *Hank Miller* • Charles Barton *Buddy McMonigal* ■ *Dir* William A Wellman • *Scr* Robert Carson, from the novel by PC Wren

Beau Geste ★★
Adventure 1966 · US · Colour · 104min

This is the third – and by far the least impressive – adaptation of PC Wren's foreign legion yarn. Guy Stockwell isn't in the same league as Ronald Colman and Gary Cooper, and only Telly Savalas as the sadistic sergeant major comes close to matching his predecessors. Douglas Heyes takes several liberties with the original story, most notably reducing the three Geste brothers to two and changing their nationality from English to American. Bud Thackery's colour photography of the desert is eye-catching. AT

Telly Savalas *Sergeant Major Dagineau* • Guy Stockwell *Beau* • Doug McClure *John* • Leslie Nielsen *Lieutenant De Ruse* • Robert Wolders *Fouchet* • David Mauro *Boldini* • Leo Gordon *Krauss* ■ *Dir* Douglas Heyes • *Scr* Douglas Heyes, from the novel by PC Wren

Beau Ideal ★★
Adventure 1931 · US · BW · 82min

Beau Geste was such a huge success in 1926 that Paramount knocked out a quickie sequel, *Beau Sabreur*, two years later. This is the second sequel to the original film; Ralph Forbes returns as John Geste, as does original director Herbert Brenon. This time around, John meets up with his childhood buddy in the foreign legion. Loretta Young is the girl back in England who perpetuates their romantic rivalry. AT

Frank McCormack *Carl Neyer* • Ralph Forbes *John Geste* • Lester Vail *Otis Madison* • Otto Matieson *Jacob Levine* • Don Alvarado *Ramon Gonzales* • Bernard Siegel *Ivan Radinoff* • Irene Rich *Lady Brandon* • Myrtle Stedman *Mrs Frank*

Madison • Loretta Young *Isobel Brandon* ■ *Dir* Herbert Brenon • *Scr* Elizabeth Meehan, from the novel by PC Wren

Beau James ★★★★

Biographical drama 1957 · US · Colour · 106min

Bob Hope had been successful in a sentimental semi-comic role in *Seven Little Foys*, and here he is reunited with the underrated writer/director Melville Shavelson for this sparkling biopic of New York's flamboyant former mayor Jimmy Walker. Hope is superb, effortlessly capturing the cynicism and brashness of this son of the Roaring Twenties, and there's a fine support cast. Walter Winchell, the narrator of *The Untouchables* on TV, narrated the American version, with Alistair Cooke, his equivalent in Britain, lending an authenticity belied by the glamorised and inaccurate screen story. TS

Bob Hope *Jimmy Walker* • Vera Miles *Betty Compton* • Paul Douglas *Chris Nolan* • Alexis Smith *Allie Walker* • Darren McGavin *Charley Hand* • Joe Mantell *Bernie Williams* • Horace McMahon *Prosecutor* • Richard Shannon *Dick Jackson* ■ *Dir* Melville Shavelson • *Scr* Jack Rose, Melville Shavelson, from the book by Gene Fowler

Le Beau Mariage ★★★★🅿🅶

Comedy drama 1982 · Fr · Colour · 95min

Having impressed as an adolescent in *Claire's Knee*, Béatrice Romand is reunited with director Eric Rohmer for this bittersweet treatise on the clash between feminist and old-fashioned ideals, winning the Best Actress prize at Venice. The action flits between Paris and Le Mans as Romand's art student decides to quit the romantic rat race and find a husband. However, it soon becomes clear that lawyer André Dussolier is immune to her charms and humiliation is in the offing. Bristling with life, Rohmer's slyly witty film is as chatty and keenly observed as ever. DP French +subtitles. *DVD*

Béatrice Romand *Sabine* • André Dussollier *Edmond* • Arielle Dombasle *Clarisse* • Féodor Atkine *Simon* • Huguette Faget *Antique dealer* • Thamila Mezbah *Mother* • Sophie Renoir *Lise* ■ *Dir/Scr* Eric Rohmer

Beau Sabreur ★★★

Silent adventure 1928 · US · BW · 67min

In this silent movie, Gary Cooper elegantly disports himself in the desert, as a French legionnaire who is sent to the Sahara to negotiate a treaty with an oil-rich sheik and falls in love with Evelyn Brent on the way. It followed *Beau Geste* (1926), and was meant to use up pieces of leftover location film from the first movie. TH

Gary Cooper *Major Henri de Beaujolais* • Evelyn Brent *May Vanbrugh* • Noah Beery Sr [Noah Beery] *Sheikh El Hamel* • William Powell *Becque* • Mitchell Lewis *Suleiman the Strong* • Frank Reicher *Gen de Beaujolais* • Oscar Smith *Djikki* ■ *Dir* John Waters (1) • *Scr* Tom J Geraghty [Tom Geraghty] (story), Julian Johnson (titles), from the story by PC Wren

Le Beau Serge ★★★★🔢

Drama 1958 · Fr · BW · 94min

Traditionally hailed as the first feature of the French New Wave, Claude Chabrol's inconsistent debut was made while he was still working as a film critic, with a small sum inherited by his wife. The picture's American title, *Bitter Reunion*, sums up the story, in which Jean-Claude Brialy returns home to find that his gifted childhood friend Gérard Blain has destroyed his life through drink. Shunning the directorial pyrotechnics associated with contemporaries such as Godard and Truffaut, Chabrol coaxes intelligent performances from his leads. DP French +subtitles. *DVD*

Gérard Blain *Serge* • Jean-Claude Brialy *François Bayon* • Michèle Meritz *Yvonne* • Bernadette Lafont *Marie* • Edmond Beauchamp *Glomaud* • Claude Cerval *The curé* • André Dino *Michel, the doctor* ■ *Dir/Scr* Claude Chabrol

Beau Travail ★★★★🔢

Psychological drama 1999 · Fr · Colour · 89min

Translating Herman Melville's *Billy Budd* from the 18th-century Royal Navy to the modern Foreign Legion, Claire Denis has produced a simmering study of petty tyranny, fatuous duty and homoerotic repression. Spurning the barked histrionics of American boot camp pictures, she uses stylised rhythms to convey the ennui endured by an isolated unit in Djibouti. As the sergeant seized by a pathological hatred of new recruit Grégoire Colin, Denis Lavant gives a remarkable, almost wordless performance that culminates in some astonishing disco gyrations. DP French +subtitles. *DVD*

Denis Lavant *Galoup* • Michel Subor *Commander* • Grégoire Colin *Sentain* • Richard Courcet *Legionnaire* ■ *Dir* Claire Denis • *Scr* Claire Denis, Jean-Pol Fargeau, from the novella *Billy Budd, Sailor* by Herman Melville

Beaufort ★★★🔢

War drama based on a true story 2007 · Is · Colour · 126min

Joseph Cedar's adaptation of Ron Leshem's novel is set during the final months of Israel's occupation of Lebanon. The ancient crusader fortress held by inexperienced commander Oshri Cohen makes a simultaneously spectacular and claustrophobic setting for an isolated unit's desperate rearguard action against Hezbollah guerrillas. Despite the digs at the Israeli high command, the perspective is never wholly impartial. But Cedar (himself a veteran of the campaign) captures the strains of active service in a credible mix of dedication and cynicism in a work that received an Academy Award nomination for best foreign language film. DP Hebrew +subtitles. Swearing. *DVD* 🆂

Oshri Cohen *Liraz* • Itay Tiran *Koris* • Eli Eltonyo *Oshri* • Ohad Knoller *Ziv* • Itay Turgeman *Zitlawy* • Arthur Faradjev *Shpitzer* ■ *Dir* Joseph Cedar • *Scr* Joseph Cedar, Ron Leshem, from the novel *Im Yesh Gan Eden* by Leshem

Beaumarchais l'Insolent ★★★🔢

Historical biographical drama 1996 · Fr · Colour · 96min

Edouard Molinaro directs this breathless biopic of one of France's most dashing heroes, Beaumarchais. In chronicling the playwright's more picaresque activities, from law reform to arms dealing and espionage, fact and fantasy become entangled and there's barely room to mention his love life, let alone celebrate his literary achievement. However, Fabrice Luchini's vibrant performance ensures this isn't merely a series of elegant tableaux, while Molinaro evokes the theatrical milieu to give the action a true sense of pageant and place. DP French +subtitles.

Fabrice Luchini *Pierre-Augustin Caron de Beaumarchais* • Manuel Blanc *Gudin* • Sandrine Kiberlain *Marie-Thérèse* • Michel Serrault *Louis XV* • Jacques Weber *Duc de Chaulnes* • Michel Piccoli *Prince de Conti* • Jean-François Balmer *Sartine* ■ *Dir* Edouard Molinaro • *Scr* Edouard Molinaro, Jean-Claude Brisville, from a play by Sacha Guitry

La Beauté du Diable ★★★

Fantasy drama 1949 · Fr/It · BW · 95min

René Clair is arguably the finest director of comic fantasy in screen history. Though he does not quite hit the heights here, this is still a sparkling version of the Faust legend. The picture uses stylised sets similar to those of pioneer film-maker Georges Méliès and poet-director Jean Cocteau to create a world touched more by magic than evil. Clair's cutest trick, however, is to have Michel Simon and Gérard Philipe swap places after the former sells his soul in return for the latter's devilish good looks. DP French +subtitles.

Michel Simon *Old Mephistopheles/Faust* • Gérard Philipe *Young Faust/Mephistopheles* • Simone Valère *Princess* • Nicole Besnard *Marguerite* • Carlo Ninchi *Prince* • Paolo Stoppa *Prosecutor* ■ *Dir* René Clair • *Scr* René Clair, Armand Salacrou

The Beautician and the Beast ★★🅿🅶

Romantic comedy 1997 · US · Colour · 102min

Fran Drescher made her name as the "hostess with the mostest" in *This Is Spinal Tap*, and this was intended to kickstart her career on the big screen. It's actually not too bad, with Drescher playing the very "Noo Yawk" beautician who mistakenly winds up as governess to the family of the dictator (Timothy Dalton) of an eastern European country and gradually melts his heart. JF *DVD*

Fran Drescher *Joy Miller* • Timothy Dalton *Boris Pochenko* • Ian McNeice *Grushinsky* • Patrick Malahide *Kleist* • Lisa Jakub *Katrina* • Michael Lerner *Jerry Miller* • Phyllis Newman *Judy Miller* • Adam LaVorgna *Karl* ■ *Dir* Ken Kwapis • *Scr* Todd Graff

Beautiful ★★

Comedy drama 2000 · US · Colour · 112min

Actress Sally Field directs her debut feature, which is yet another "tribute" to the beauty pageant. Minnie Driver stars as a girl obsessed with becoming Miss Illinois who is prepared to cheat fourfold to get there. Supported by the bizarrely unconditional love of best friend Joey Lauren Adams, Driver's supremacy is only threatened by exposure from TV news hack Leslie Stefanson. The problem is you care as little for Driver as you do for the principle of the pageant itself. LH

Minnie Driver *Mona* • Hallie Kate Eisenberg *Vanessa* • Joey Lauren Adams *Ruby* • Kathleen Turner *Verna Chickle* • Leslie Stefanson *Joyce Parkins* • Bridgette L Wilson [Bridgette Wilson] *Lorna Larkin, Miss Texas* • Kathleen Robertson *Wanda Love, Miss Tennessee* ■ *Dir* Sally Field • *Scr* Jon Bernstein

The Beautiful Blonde from Bashful Bend ★★★★

Comedy western 1949 · US · Colour · 76min

Though one of Betty Grable's better vehicles, this burlesque western was considered to be one of the major catastrophes of 1949 – a setback for its talented writer/director Preston Sturges, who had acquired a reputation for churning out wacky and risqué comedies. Viewed today, however, this farce can be regarded as a comedy triumph for both star and director, fabulously photographed in gloriously garish Technicolor. TS

Betty Grable *Freddie* • Cesar Romero *Blackie Jobero* • Rudy Vallee *Charles Hingleman* • Olga San Juan *Conchita* • Sterling Holloway *Basserman Boy* • Hugh Herbert *Doctor* • El Brendel *Mr Jorgenson* • Porter Hall *Judge O'Toole* ■ *Dir* Preston Sturges • *Scr* Preston Sturges, from a story by Earl Felton • *Cinematographer* Harry Jackson

Beautiful but Dangerous ★★🆄

Comedy drama 1954 · US · BW · 88min

Having bought RKO in 1948, Howard Hughes took a shine to Jean Simmons and imported her from England, casting her opposite Robert Mitchum in Otto Preminger's torrid *Angel Face*. Since the on-screen chemistry between the two stars was combustible, this second rendezvous was concocted; the mistake was to make it a comedy. Simmons plays an heiress with a guilt complex and Mitchum is the local doctor who rumbles her. Stilted and slackly directed. AT

Robert Mitchum *Doc Sellars* • Jean Simmons *Corby Lane* • Arthur Hunnicutt *Otey* • Edgar Buchanan *Ad Meeker* • Wallace Ford *Joe* • Raymond Walburn *Judge Holbert* ■ *Dir* Lloyd Bacon • *Scr* DD Beauchamp, William Bowers, Richard Flournoy, from the story *Enough for Happiness* by DD Beauchamp

Beautiful but Dangerous ★★

Romantic drama 1955 · It/Fr · Colour · 102min

This pallid period piece, shot in Italy (where it was known as *The World's Most Beautiful Woman*), was one of the last pictures made by Robert Z Leonard. Gina Lollobrigida plays Lina Cavalieri, the 19th-century opera singer who finds love with Prince Sergei Bariatine (Vittorio Gassman), the Russian royal whom she had encountered many years before. A polished but plodding affair. DP Italian dubbed.

Gina Lollobrigida *Lina Cavalieri* • Vittorio Gassman *Prince Sergei Bariatine* • Robert Alda *Doria* • Tamara Lees *Manolita* • Anne Vernon *Carmela* ■ *Dir* Robert Z Leonard • *Scr* Cesare Cavagna, Liana Ferri, Frank Gervasi, Mario Monicelli, Luciano Martino, Piero Pierotti, Franco Solinas, Giovanna Soria, from a story by Maleno Malenotti

The Beautiful City ★★★★

Drama 2004 · Iran · Colour · 101min

The humanism that has informed much Iranian cinema since the late 1980s is readily evident in Asghar Farhadi's affecting and often gently amusing drama. Its insights into Islamic law and the status of women may incense some. But this is much more a study of ordinary people making the best of their situation than a socio-political critique. Taraneh Alidoosti and Babak Ansari impress as the older sister and former cellmate of Hossein Farzi-Zadeh, the teenager who will be executed for murder unless his victim's father agrees to clemency. Their burgeoning romance contrasts with the cruel contradictions of life under a strict theocratic regime. DP Farsi +subtitles.

Babak Ansari *A'la* • Taraneh Alidoosti *Firoozeh* • Hossein Farzi-Zadeh *Akbar* ■ *Dir/Scr* Asghar Farhadi

Beautiful Creatures ★★★🔢

Black comedy thriller 2000 · UK · Colour · 84min

Rachel Weisz and Susan Lynch are two very different women brought together by violence, who then find themselves with a dead body on their hands. This is one of those films where everyone is trying to outwit and double-cross everyone else, but thanks to the stars' winning performances, this is a thoroughly enjoyable film. JB Violence, swearing, drug abuse, sex scenes. *DVD*

Rachel Weisz *Petula* • Susan Lynch *Dorothy* • Iain Glen *Tony* • Maurice Roëves *Ronnie McMinn* • Alex Norton *Detective Inspector George Hepburn* • Tom Mannion *Brian McMinn* ■ *Dir* Bill Eagles • *Scr* Simon Donald

Beautiful Creatures ★★★★🔢

Supernatural drama 2013 · US · Colour · 118min

Based on the first in a series of boy-meets-witch books, this fantasy is the perfect filler for teens left bereft by the end of the *Twilight* films. Alden Ehrenreich plays a bored teenager who falls for the weird new kid (Alice Englert) in his Deep South home town. Turns out Englert's a "Caster" and will come into full possession of her powers on her 16th birthday. But the youngsters' budding romance runs awry when elders Jeremy Irons and Emma Thompson battle to determine whether her powers will be turned towards good or evil. The two young leads are terrific. So, too, are the smartly written early scenes of small-town conservatism and awkward boy/girl smoochy stuff. Though the film's second half doesn't quite cast the spell of the first, this remains decent teen entertainment. DA *DVD*

Alden Ehrenreich *Ethan Wate* • Alice Englert *Lena Duchannes* • Jeremy Irons *Macon Ravenwood* • Viola Davis *Amma* • Emmy Rossum *Ridley Duchaness* • Emma Thompson *Mrs Lincoln/Sarafine* ■ *Dir* Richard LaGravenese • *Scr* Richard LaGravenese, from the novel by Kami Garcia, Margaret Stohl • *Cinematographer* Philippe Rousselot

Beautiful Dreamers ★★🔢

Period drama based on a true story 1990 · Can · Colour · 103min

The underrated Rip Torn gives a tour-de-force performance as legendary American poet Walt Whitman who, while visiting the London Asylum for the Insane in Ontario, encounters psychiatrist Dr Maurice Bucke (Colm Feore). The pair proceed to make waves with their revolutionary ideas on the

B

treatment of mental illness. A little trite and predictable in places, this is more of a Disney-style history lesson than a dissection of Victorian attitudes towards madness. LH

Colm Feore *Dr Maurice Bucke* • Rip Torn *Walt Whitman* • Wendel Meldrum *Jessie Bucke* • Sheila McCarthy *Molly Jessop* • Colin Fox *Rev Randolph Haines* • David Gardner *Dr Lett* ■ *Dir/Scr* John Kent Harrison

Beautiful Girls ★★★ 15
Comedy drama 1996 · US · Colour · 107min

A starry cast illuminates this high-school reunion movie, though the end result is rather disappointingly low-key and lacking in sparkle. Timothy Hutton is the New York pianist at a crossroads in his life who returns to his small-town roots and is depressed to discover that his schoolmates are stuck in dead-end jobs. If director Ted Demme's situations are stereotypical, the film is made memorable by writer Scott Rosenberg's cutting dialogue and sharp-edged script. The bigger stars are upstaged by Natalie Portman as Hutton's intelligent and surprisingly mature teenage neighbour. LH Violence, swearing, sexual references, drug abuse. *DVD* *BL*

Matt Dillon *Tommy "Birdman" Rowland* • Timothy Hutton *Willie Conway* • Noah Emmerich *Michael "Mo" Morris* • Annabeth Gish *Tracy Stover* • Lauren Holly *Darian Smalls* • Rosie O'Donnell *Gina Barrisano* • Martha Plimpton *Jan* • Natalie Portman *Marty* • Michael Rapaport *Paul Kirkwood* • Mira Sorvino *Sharon Cassidy* • Uma Thurman *Andera* • David Arquette *Bobby Conway* ■ *Dir* Ted Demme • *Scr* Scott Rosenberg

Beautiful Joe ★★ 15
Romantic drama 2000 · UK/US · Colour · 93min

Sharon Stone plays a trailer-trash mom who is pursued by gangsters after she steals a small fortune from Billy Connolly, an Irish florist who has been mistaken for a syndicate bigwig by crime boss Ian Holm. Shifting from Kentucky to Vegas, this caper comedy is short on laughs and originality, while the direction is energetic, but uninspired. DP Swearing, some violence, sex scenes. *DVD*

Sharon Stone *Hush* • Billy Connolly *Joe* • Ian Holm *The geek* • Gil Bellows *Elton* • Jurnee Smollett *Vivien* ■ *Dir/Scr* Stephen Metcalfe

Beautiful Kate ★★★ 15
Drama 2009 · Aus · Colour · 101min

Actress-turned-director Rachel Ward transfers Newton Thornberg's novel from Chicago to a remote farm in South Australia, and creates a skilfully modulated drama. She also brings the best out of husband Bryan Brown, as the dying patriarch visited by his estranged middle-aged son, writer Ned (Ben Mendelsohn). This reunion forces them both to recall a long-ago summer, when the lives of a teenage Ned and his vivacious twin sister Kate were touched by tragedy. A whiff of Southern Gothic occasionally threatens to overpower the film's flashbacks, but the impassioned performances ensure this is compelling rather than contrived. DP Swearing, sex scenes. *DVD*

Ben Mendelsohn *Ned Kendall* • Rachel Griffiths *Sally Kendall* • Bryan Brown *Bruce Kendall* • Maeve Dermody *Toni* • Sophie Lowe *Kate Kendall* • Scott O'Donnell *Young Ned* ■ *Dir* Rachel Ward • *Scr* Rachel Ward, from a novel by Newton Thornburg • *Cinematographer* Andrew Commis

Beautiful Lies ★★ 12
Romantic comedy 2010 · Fr · Colour · 100min

Audrey Tautou has never quite repeated the success she had with *Amélie*, but she consistently turns out light and likeable films. Here, she plays the co-owner of a hair salon who is secretly adored by the shop's handyman, and decides to send his anonymous love notes to her lovelorn mum (Nathalie Baye) who needs a boost for her confidence. Cue much confusion. The French perhaps like this sort of comedy of chaos more than we do, but *Beautiful Lies* is enjoyable enough. DA French +subtitles. Some swearing. *DVD* *BL*

Audrey Tautou *Emilie Dandrieux* • Nathalie Baye *Maddy Dandrieux* • Sami Bouajila *Jean* • Stéphane Lagarde *Sylvia* ■ *Dir* Pierre Salvadori • *Scr* Benoît Graffin, Pierre Salvadori • *Cinematographer* Gilles Henry

A Beautiful Mind ★★★ 12
Biographical drama 2001 · US · Colour · 129min

The true story of maths genius John Forbes Nash Jr, who battled paranoid schizophrenia at the height of his academic success and won the Nobel Prize for economics, is tailor-made Oscar fare (it won four). It has the triumph-over-tragedy theme going for it, plus a powerhouse performance from Russell Crowe. Nash is presented as a difficult man with a complex psychological condition – reduced to a series of delusional episodes to furnish a thriller subplot – who has devoted his life to an almost insurmountably dry subject, namely advanced mathematics theory. Sadly, the film's desire to be taken seriously gets in the way of the story. AC *DVD* *BL*

Russell Crowe *John Forbes Nash Jr* • Ed Harris *William Parcher* • Jennifer Connelly *Alicia Larde Nash* • Paul Bettany *Charles Herman* • Adam Goldberg *Sol* • Judd Hirsch *Helinger* • Josh Lucas Hansen • Anthony Rapp *Bender* • Christopher Plummer *Dr Rosen* ■ *Dir* Ron Howard • *Scr* Akiva Goldsman, from the book *A Beautiful Mind: a Biography of John Forbes Nash Jr* by Sylvia Nasar

Beautiful People ★★★ 15
Comedy drama 1999 · UK · Colour · 103min

Jasmin Dizdar's debut feature is a creditable achievement, especially bearing in mind it cost a mere £1.1 million. It includes snippets from an affair between a Tory MP's doctor daughter and an exiled war criminal, and follows a TV reporter filming a football hooligan's accidental transformation into a hero. These diverse plot strands ambitiously attempt to meld romance, black comedy and political critique. The ensemble cast brings commitment and wit to the proceedings, which, while rarely credible, are never dull. DP

Charlotte Coleman *Portia Thornton* • Rosalind Ayres *Nora Thornton* • Siobhan Redmond *Kate Higgins* • Nicholas Farrell *Doctor Mouldy* • Edin Dzandzanovic *Pero Guzina* ■ *Dir/Scr* Jasmin Dizdar

Beautiful Stranger ★
Crime drama 1954 · UK · BW · 89min

Ginger Rogers, moving inexorably towards her sell-by date, stars in this thriller set on the French Riviera. She plays a woman who, let down by her wealthy and married racketeer lover Stanley Baker, contemplates killing herself but, instead, hooks up with Frenchman Jacques Bergerac and finds herself implicated in murder. Labyrinthine and unconvincing. RK

Ginger Rogers *Johnny Victor* • Herbert Lom *Emil Landosh* • Stanley Baker *Louis Galt* • Jacques Bergerac *Pierre Clement* • Margaret Rawlings *Marie Galt* • Eddie Byrne *Luigi* • Ferdy Mayne *Chief of Police* • Coral Browne *Helen* ■ *Dir* David Miller (I) • *Scr* Robert Westerby, Carl Nystrom, from a story by Rip Van Ronkel, David Miller

The Beautiful Swindlers ★★
Portmanteau crime comedy
1964 · Fr/It/Jpn/Neth · BW · 90min

Despite a promising premise, this is a pretty lame portmanteau picture. Things might have been better had Jean-Luc Godard decided not to withdraw his contribution and release it as the short, *Le Grand Escroc*. Yet, Claude Chabrol's *Paris*, in which a gullible hick buys the Eiffel Tower, has its amusing moments, while Hiromichi Horikawa's *Tokyo*, about a barmaid charged with murder after she attempts to pawn an old man's false teeth, smacks of life's grim desperation. Unlike the necklace at its core, Roman Polanski's *Amsterdam* is a gaudy bauble, while Ugo Gregoretti's *Naples* is a trivial anecdote about a double-dealing pimp. DP

Nicole Karen • Jan Tuelings • Gabriella Giorgelli • Jean-Pierre Cassel • Catherine Deneuve • Mie Hama ■ *Dir* Roman Polanski, Ugo Gregoretti, Claude Chabrol, Hiromichi Horikawa • *Scr* Roman Polanski, Gérard Brach

Beautiful Thing ★★★ 15
Drama 1995 · UK · Colour · 87min

Two teenage neighbours on a London council estate discover they are gay in director Hettie MacDonald's urban fairy tale. How the boys deal with their sexual awakening is endearingly explored via a rough kitchen sink backdrop, camp one-liners and a soundtrack leaning heavily on hits from Mama Cass. Newcomers Glen Berry and Scott Neal give purposely raw-edged performances to match their on-screen naivety, but it's Linda Henry who shines as the indomitable single mother. AJ Violence, swearing, nudity. *DVD*

Glen Berry *Jamie Gangel* • Linda Henry *Sandra Gangel* • Scott Neal *Ste Pearce* • Ben Daniels *Tony* • Tameka Empson *Leah* • Meera Syal *Miss Chauhan* ■ *Dir* Hettie MacDonald • *Scr* Jonathan Harvey, from his play

Beauty ★★★ 18
Drama 2011 · S Afr/Fr · Colour · 100min

South African director Oliver Hermanus follows up the excellent *Shirley Adams* (2009) with this unflinching, if not always entirely convincing, treatise on the post-apartheid emasculation of the Afrikaaner male. In less sensitive hands, the contradictions in sawmill owner Deon Lotz's lifestyle would seem ludicrously contrived. But such is the seething sense of injustice and self-loathing that underpins his boorish behaviour that it seems almost plausible that this macho, churchgoing, racist homophobe would harbour a crush on a family friend's student son. While the performances are admirable, Hermanus ultimately sacrifices authenticity in trying to address too many contentious sociopolitical taboos. DP Afrikaans, English +subtitles. Violence, sex scenes. *DVD*

Deon Lotz *Francois van Heerden* • Charlie Keegan *Christian Roodt* • Michelle Scott *Elena van Heerden* • Albert Maritz *Willem Roodt* ■ *Dir* Oliver Hermanus • *Scr* Oliver Hermanus, Didier Costet

Beauty and the Beast ★ U
Period fantasy 1962 · US · Colour · 79min

Duke Mark Damon, condemned by a curse to roam his castle by night as a growling beast, is set free by the love of Joyce Taylor and regains his handsome, human identity. This Technicolor travesty of the fairy tale is substandard in every department. RK

Joyce Taylor *Lady Althea* • Mark Damon *Duke Eduardo* • Eduard Franz *Baron Orsini* • Michael Pate *Prince Bruno* • Merry Anders *Princess Sybil* • Dayton Lummis *Count Roderick* ■ *Dir* Edward L Cahn • *Scr* George Bruce, Orville H Hampton, from the fairy tale *La Belle et la Bête* by Jeanne-Marie Leprince de Beaumont

Beauty and the Beast ★★ U
Fantasy 1987 · US · Colour · 89min

In another reworking of the classic tale of the young woman taken hostage by a half-man, half-beast whom she eventually falls in love with, Rebecca De Mornay (*The Hand that Rocks the Cradle*) is bland as Beauty, while John Savage (*The Deer Hunter*) is gruffly enjoyable as the Beast. But they both flounder during the duff song and dance numbers in the middle. JB

Rebecca De Mornay *Beauty* • John Savage *Beast/Prince* • Yossi Graber *Father* • Michael Schneider *Kuppel* • Carmela Marner *Bettina* • Ruth Harlap *Isabella* • Joseph Bee *Oliver* ■ *Dir* Eugene Marner • *Scr* Carole Lucia Satrina, from the fairy tale *La Belle et la Bête* by Jeanne-Marie Leprince de Beaumont

Beauty and the Beast
Animated musical fantasy ★★★★★ U
1991 · US · Colour · 91min

The first feature-length cartoon to be nominated for the best picture Oscar, this is one of the most ambitious films ever produced by Disney. Three and a half years

in the making, the movie was one of the first animations to include computer-generated imagery, seen to best advantage during the ballroom and *Be Our Guest* sequences. With visuals based on such French artists as Fragonard and a storyline inspired by the famous fairy tale, the film also boasts the voices of Angela Lansbury (who sings the Oscar-winning title song), Paige O'Hara and Robby Benson. DP *DVD* *BL*

Paige O'Hara *Belle* • Robby Benson *Beast* • Rex Everhart *Maurice* • Richard White *Gaston* • Jesse Corti *Le Fou* • Angela Lansbury *Mrs Potts* • Jerry Orbach *Lumiere* • David Ogden Stiers *Cogsworth/Narrator* • Bradley Michael Pierce [Bradley Pierce] *Chip* ■ *Dir* Gary Trousdale, Kirk Wise • *Scr* Linda Woolverton, from a story by Brenda Chapman, Burny Mattinson, Brian Pimental, Joe Ranft, Kelly Asbury, Christopher [Chris] Sanders, Kevin Harkey, Bruce Woodside, Tom Ellery, Robert Lence, from the fairy tale *La Belle et la Bête* by Jeanne-Marie Leprince de Beaumont

Beauty and the Beast
Fantasy adventure 2017 · US · Colour

This is a preview – no prints were available to review prior to publication: Kenneth Branagh proved there's still plenty of mileage in traditional fairy tales with his enjoyable *Cinderella*, and now director Bill Condon throws a hefty budget and a starry cast at this old favourite. Condon should know what pushes the buttons of teenage girls after two movies in the *Twilight* saga, and the casting of Emma Watson as Belle and *Downton Abbey's* Dan Stevens as the Beast should ensure a cross-generational audience. The combined weight of Ian McKellen, Emma Thompson, Stanley Tucci and Gugu Mbatha-Raw proves this is to be no small-scale take on the classic tale. TP *BL*

Emma Watson *Belle* • Dan Stevens *Beast* • Luke Evans *Gaston* • Josh Gad *LeFou* • Emma Thompson *Mrs Potts* • Kevin Kline *Maurice* • Ewan McGregor *Lumiere* • Ian McKellen *Cogsworth* ■ *Dir* Bill Condon • *Scr* Stephen Chbosky, Evan Spiliotopoulos, from the 1991 film, from the fairy tale *La Belle et la Bête* by Jeanne-Marie Leprince de Beaumont

Beauty and the Beast: the Enchanted Christmas ★★★ U
Animated fantasy 1997 · US · Colour · 67min

This made-for-video sequel to the wonderful 1991 Disney animated musical fantasy finds Belle still a prisoner in the castle and attempting to convince the Beast to celebrate Christmas. While many of the cast return to lend their voices, this doesn't quite have the production values or charm of the original, but it should enchant young children if not their more fussy parents. Haley Joel Osment replaced Bradley Pierce as the voice of Chip. JB *DVD*

Paige O'Hara *Belle* • Robby Benson *Beast* • Jerry Orbach *Lumiere* • David Ogden Stiers *Cogsworth* • Bernadette Peters *Angelique* • Tim Curry *Forte* • Haley Joel Osment *Chip* • Paul Reubens *Fife* • Angela Lansbury *Mrs Potts* ■ *Dir* Andy Knight • *Scr* Flip Kobler, Cindy Marcus, Bill Motz, Bob Roth

Beauty for the Asking ★★
Drama 1939 · US · BW · 68min

Leaving Lucille Ball's outstanding comic gifts on the back burner, RKO cast her to play straight in this plodding and uncertain tale of a beautician who, after being jilted by smooth Patric Knowles, comes up with a new face cream that makes millions. It's directed without distinction by Glenn Tryon, but there's some fun to be had from the backroom bitching in the cosmetics industry. RK

Lucille Ball *Jean Russell* • Patric Knowles *Denny Williams* • Donald Woods *Jeffrey Martin* • Frieda Inescort *Flora Barton* • Inez Courtney *Gwen Morrison* • Leona Maricle *Eva Harrington* • Frances Mercer *Patricia Wharton* • Whitney Bourne *Peggy Ponsby* ■ *Dir* Glenn Tryon • *Scr* Doris Anderson, Paul Jerrico

The Beauty Jungle ★★
Drama 1964 · UK · Colour · 114min

Portraying the seedier side of beauty contests in the early 1960s, this is a bustling but predictable rise-and-fall story, in which Janette Scott discovers that fame sometimes doesn't even last 15 minutes. Charting her progress to the Miss Globe title, Val Guest's film unerringly descends upon the tawdry and the fake, whether exposing the cattiness behind the catwalk or the emptiness behind celebrity. Scott is suitably naive, while Ian Hendry and Edmund Purdom reek of insincerity as the men promising her stardom. **DP**

Ian Hendry *Don Mackenzie* • Janette Scott *Shirley* • Ronald Fraser *Walter* • Edmund Purdom *Carrick* • Jean Claudio *Armand* • Kay Walsh *Mrs Freeman* • Norman Bird *Freeman* • Janina Faye *Elaine* • Tommy Trinder *Charlie Dorton* • David Weston *Harry* ■ *Dir* Val Guest • *Scr* Robert Muller, Val Guest

Beauty Shop ★★⏳
Comedy 2005 · US · Colour · 100min

Barbershop 2's sassy hairdresser-next-door, Gina (Queen Latifah), gets her own movie in this companion piece to the male-focused comedy franchise. It's a sprightly, raucous affair in which Gina, now relocated to Atlanta, tells her flamboyant, condescending boss Kevin Bacon to stick his job and sets about establishing her own beauty shop. There are a fair few laugh-out-loud moments, but the film is too clichéd and sprawling. **SF** Swearing, sexual references. 📀

Queen Latifah *Gina Norris* • Alicia Silverstone *Lynn* • Andie MacDowell *Terri Green* • Alfre Woodard *Ms. Josephine* • Mena Suvari *Joanne Marcus* • Kevin Bacon *Jorge Christophe* • Djimon Hounsou *Joe* ■ *Dir* Bille Woodruff • *Scr* Kate Lanier, Norman Vance Jr, from a story by Elizabeth Hunter

The Beaver ★★★⏳
Comedy drama 2010 · US · Colour · 87min

Mel Gibson's off-screen exploits have lumbered him with some heavy baggage, so it's surprising to see him embrace that vulnerability in Jodie Foster's oddball comedy. Gibson plays a depressed toy executive who begins to build a bridge back to his former wellbeing by using a furry puppet – the Beaver – to speak through, adopting a voice that sounds unnervingly like Ray Winstone. Foster co-stars as his long-suffering wife and also directs, skilfully balancing comedy and tragedy. Thanks to her light-handed touch, the film remains surprisingly moving and upbeat, even when the line between Gibson's recovery and insanity begins to blur. **SP** Brief swearing. 📀

Mel Gibson *Walter Black* • Jodie Foster *Meredith Black* • Anton Yelchin *Porter Black* • Jennifer Lawrence (2) *Norah* • Cherry Jones *Vice president* • Riley Thomas Stewart *Henry Black* ■ *Dir* Jodie Foster • *Scr* Kyle Killen

Beavis and Butt-head Do America ★★★⏳
Animated comedy 1996 · US · Colour · 77min

Moronic animated twosome Beavis and Butt-head (voiced by creator and director Mike Judge) star in this entertaining full-length feature that sees them uprooted from their couch in front of the TV. The exotic plot has the sniggering pair chased across the country after they become unwitting carriers of a lethal chemical weapon. Bruce Willis and Demi Moore score as the villains, while Robert Stack is spot-on as the head of the FBI. **JF** A sex scene, brief nudity, some swearing. 📀

Mike Judge *Beavis/Butt-head* • Cloris Leachman *Old woman on plane and bus* • Robert Stack *Agent Flemming* • Eric Bogosian *Ranger* • Richard Linklater *Tour bus driver* • Bruce Willis *Muddy Grimes* • Demi Moore *Dallas Grimes* ■ *Dir* Mike Judge • *Scr* Mike Judge, Joe Stillman

Bebe's Kids ★★★⏳
Animated musical comedy 1992 · US · Colour · 69min

Based on the characters invented by comedian Robin Harris and scripted by Reginald Hudlin, this was the only animated feature released during the black cinema boom of the early 1990s. Some of the snipes at African-American and white

culture are predictable, others are way off beam. Yet when they do hit the target, they are both sassy and funny. The gruff voice of baby Pee-Wee is provided by rap singer Tone Loc. **DP**

Faizon Love *Robin Harris* • Vanessa Bell Calloway *Jamika* • Wayne Collins Jr *Leon* • Jonell Greene *LaShawn* • Marques Huston *Kahlil* • Tone Loc *Pee-Wee* • Myra J *Dorothea* • Nell Carter *Vivian* • Reynaldo Rey *Lush* ■ *Dir* Bruce Smith • *Scr* Reginald Hudlin, from characters by Robin Harris

Because I Said So ★★⏳
Romantic comedy drama 2007 · US · Colour · 97min

Diane Keaton stars as a meddlesome mother who is determined that her unwed youngest daughter (Mandy Moore) should not make the same marital mistake she did. Accordingly, she vets potential suitors via an ad on the internet. But her bid to play Cupid turns awry. Relative newcomer Moore tries to play even her weakest lines with conviction, but this cheesy chick flick is really old hand Keaton's film and she milks it for the little it's worth. **DA** Sexual references. 📀

Diane Keaton *Daphne Wilder* • Mandy Moore *Milly* • Piper Perabo *Mae* • Lauren Graham *Maggie* • Gabriel Macht *Johnny* • Tom Everett Scott *Jason* ■ *Dir* Michael Lehmann • *Scr* Karen Leigh Hopkins, Jessie Nelson

Because of Him ★★★⏳
Musical romance 1946 · US · BW · 83min

Ten years after she arrived as a teenage singing star to save Universal studios from bankruptcy and two years before her retirement from the screen at the age of 27, Deanna Durbin starred in this "grown-up" version of her previous adolescent-dream-come-true movies. The plot has waitress Durbin determinedly seeking the help of famous actor Charles Laughton to establish her stage career. Franchot Tone is the playwright who is initially immune to her charms. **RK**

Deanna Durbin *Kim Walker* • Franchot Tone *Paul Taylor* • Charles Laughton *Sheridan* • Helen Broderick *Nora* • Stanley Ridges *Charlie Gilbert* • Donald Meek *Martin* • Charles Halton *Mr Dunlap* ■ *Dir* Richard Wallace • *Scr* Edmund Beloin, from the story by Edmund Beloin, Sig Herzig

Because of Winn-Dixie ★★★⏳
Comedy drama 2004 · US · Colour · 101min

Wayne Wang directs this homespun fairy tale, brimming with old-fashioned values and charm. AnnaSophia Robb is delightful as a kind-hearted ten-year-old, who moves to a small Florida town with her single parent father and preacher, Jeff Daniels. Lonely and struggling to fit in, she adopts a stray dog that she names after the local supermarket. The leisurely adventures that follow have a whimsical feel as girl and pooch bring together the eclectic community. **SF** 📀

AnnaSophia Robb *Opal* • Jeff Daniels *Preacher* • Cicely Tyson *Gloria Dump* • Eva Marie Saint *Miss Franny* • Dave Matthews *Otis* • Courtney Jines *Amanda Wilkinson* • Nick Price *Dunlap Dewberry* • Elle Fanning *Sweetie Pie Thomas* • Luke Benward *Stevie Dewberry* • BJ Hopper *Mr Alfred* ■ *Dir* Wayne Wang • *Scr* Joan Singleton, from the novel by Kate DiCamillo

Because They're Young ★★★
Drama 1960 · US · Colour · 98min

This little Columbia teenage angst flick was given street credibility by the starring presence of *American Bandstand* host Dick Clark, who unfortunately proved to be no thespian. The student cast is a teen dream: Tuesday Weld and James Darren (who also recorded the theme song), plus *Cat Ballou*'s Michael Callan and *Blue Denim*'s Warren Berlinger. **TS**

Dick Clark *Neil* • Michael Callan *Griff* • Tuesday Weld *Anne* • Victoria Shaw *Joan* • Roberta Shore *Ricky* • Warren Berlinger *Buddy* • Doug McClure *Jim* • Linda Watkins *Frances McCalla* • James

Darren • Duane Eddy • The Rebels ■ *Dir* Paul Wendkos • *Scr* James Gunn, from the novel *Harrison High* by John Farris

Because You're Mine ★★⏳
Musical comedy 1952 · US · Colour · 103min

Amazingly selected as the 1953 Royal Command Film, this Mario Lanza vehicle is memorable today as the feeble follow-up to his biggest success, *The Great Caruso*. This is a thankless affair, with Lanza as an opera star conscripted into the army who falls for his sergeant's sister, less than winningly played by Broadway *Kismet* star Doretta Morrow. However, apart from the rich period Technicolor, there's little to sing about in this lacklustre MGM musical. **TS**

Mario Lanza *Renaldo Rossano* • Doretta Morrow *Bridget Batterson* • James Whitmore *Sgt Batterson* • Dean Miller *Ben Jones* • Paula Corday [Rita Corday] *Francesca Landers* • Jeff Donnell *Patty Ware* • Spring Byington *Mrs Montville* ■ *Dir* Alexander Hall • *Scr* Karl Tunberg, Leonard Spigelgass, from a story by Ruth Brooks Flippen, Sy Gomberg • *Music* Sammy Cahn

Becket ★★★★⏳
Historical drama 1964 · UK/US · Colour · 142min

This drama is distinguished by a couple of charismatic performances from Richard Burton and Peter O'Toole. Edward Anhalt's Oscar-winning script from Jean Anouilh's stage play tells of the friendship, at the 12th-century court, between Henry II (O'Toole) and Archbishop Becket (Burton) – here seen as friends from childhood. The insights into their power struggle are more modern than medieval, but they make for an engrossing portrayal of the past. **TH** 📀

Richard Burton *Thomas Becket* • Peter O'Toole *King Henry II* • John Gielgud *King Louis VII of France* • Donald Wolfit *Bishop Folliot* • Martita Hunt *Queen Matilda* • Pamela Brown *Queen Eleanor* • Paolo Stoppa *Pope Alexander III* • Gino Cervi *Cardinal Zambelli* • Sian Phillips *Gwendolen* ■ *Dir* Peter Glenville • *Scr* Edward Anhalt, from the play *Becket, ou l'Honneur de Dieu* by Jean Anouilh • *Producer* Hal B Wallis • *Cinematographer* Geoffrey Unsworth • *Costume Designer* Margaret Furse

LANDMARK FILM
This first three-strip Technicolor feature takes colour to a new level of intensity

Becky Sharp ★★★★
Period drama 1935 · US · Colour · 84min

Rouben Mamoulian's picture is notable as the first full-length feature in three-strip Technicolor. And what exquisite colour it is! The costumes are dazzling and are seen at their best in the ball scenes on the eve of Waterloo. Francis Edward Faragoh's script focuses on the famous central character from Thackeray's *Vanity Fair*, romping through her rise and fall in a breathtakingly audacious bowdlerisation and distortion of the original. An Oscar-nominated Miriam Hopkins makes a spirited if unsubtle and hoydenish Becky, while most of the supporting characters are reduced to fleeting cardboard cutouts or caricatures. Never dull. **RK**

Miriam Hopkins *Becky Sharp* • Frances Dee *Amelia Sedley* • Cedric Hardwicke *Marquis of Steyne* • Billie Burke *Lady Bareacres* • Alison Skipworth *Miss Crawley* • Nigel Bruce *Joseph Sedley* ■ *Dir* Rouben Mamoulian • *Scr* Francis Edward Faragoh, from a play by Langdon Mitchell, from the novel *Vanity Fair* by William Makepeace Thackeray • *Cinematographer* Ray Rennahan

Becoming Colette ★★⏳
Biographical drama 1991 · Ger/UK/Fr · Colour · 96min

A stilted account of the life and early career of the French author who wrote as Colette (played by Mathilda May), this details her transformation from a naive country girl to a Paris socialite, her disastrous marriage to Henri Gauthier-Villars (Klaus Maria Brandauer) and her sexual awakening. A rather superficial and empty period piece with indifferent performances from the lead actors, this proves director Danny Huston is no match for his father John. **AJ**

Klaus Maria Brandauer *Henri Gauthier-Villars* • Mathilda May *Sidonie Gabrielle Colette* • Virginia Madsen *Polaire Sorel* • Paul Rhys *Chapo* • John Van Dreelen *Albert* • Jean-Pierre Aumont *Captain* • Lucienne Hamon *Sido* • Georg Tryphon *Creditor* ■ *Dir* Danny Huston • *Scr* Ruth Graham, Burt Weinshanker

Becoming Jane ★★★⏳
Biographical romantic drama 2006 · US/UK · Colour · 115min

Jane Austen became one of England's most famous authors by writing about the social conventions of the 19th century, and especially affairs of the heart. And yet she never married, which is the starting point for this fictionalised romantic drama. After 20-year-old Jane (Anne Hathaway) meets a young Irishman (James McAvoy), their initial dislike evolves into a mutual attraction. But the path of true love never runs smooth. American actress Hathaway is convincing as the rural clergyman's daughter with literary ambitions, while McAvoy is similarly impressive as the wild Irish lawyer who ruffles genteel country feathers. And Maggie Smith, Julie Walters and Ian Richardson (in his final screen role) get ample opportunity to strut their acting stuff. **BP** Brief sexual references. 📀 💿

Anne Hathaway *Jane Austen* • James McAvoy *Tom Lefroy* • Julie Walters *Mrs Austen* • James Cromwell *Rev Austen* • Maggie Smith *Lady Gresham* • Joe Anderson (1) *Henry Austen* • Ian Richardson *Judge Langlois* • Anna Maxwell Martin *Cassandra Austen* ■ *Dir* Julian Jarrold • *Scr* Kevin Hood, Sarah Williams • *Cinematographer* Eigil Bryld

Bed and Board ★★★⏳
Comedy drama 1970 · Fr · Colour · 93min

Antoine Doinel, the hero of *The 400 Blows*, is now married to Claude Jade but still can't settle down. He has an affair with a Japanese girl and enters a ludicrous Zen period; after a variety of pointless jobs, he appears to mature by writing a novel and becoming a father. While *Bed and Board* is not in the same class as its gorgeous predecessor, *Stolen Kisses*, the gentle comedy and romance make for an utterly charming film, shot through with Truffaut's trademark optimism about human nature. **AT** French +subtitles. 📀 💿

Jean-Pierre Léaud *Antoine Doinel* • Claude Jade *Christine Doinel* • Hiroko Berghauer *Kyoko* • Daniel Ceccaldi *Lucien Darbon* • Claire Duhamel *Madame Darbon* • Daniel Boulanger *Tenor* • Barbara Laage *Monique* ■ *Dir* François Truffaut • *Scr* François Truffaut, Claude de Givray, Bernard Revon

Bed & Breakfast ★★★⏳
Romantic comedy 1992 · US · Colour · 92min

A modest yet entertaining comedy from *Reuben, Reuben* director Robert Ellis Miller, this contains a surprisingly good performance by Roger Moore. He stars as a conman whose arrival in a small New England community brings a sparkle to the lives of widow Colleen Dewhurst, her daughter Talia Shire and granddaughter Nina Siemaszko. Barely released in the cinema, this pleasantly unusual and self-effacing movie was the swan song of Dewhurst, who died of cancer in 1991. **TH** 📀

Roger Moore *Adam* • Talia Shire *Claire* • Colleen Dewhurst *Ruth* • Nina Siemaszko *Cassie* • Ford Rainey *Amos* • Stephen Root *Randolph* • Jamie Walters *Mitch* ■ *Dir* Robert Ellis Miller • *Scr* Cindy Myers

Bed of Roses ★★⏳
Romantic comedy drama 1995 · US · Colour · 84min

Life isn't always rosy in this uncertain attempt to combine realism and romance. Christian Slater is a florist whose wife died giving birth. Grieving, he gradually falls for "suit" Mary Stuart Masterson. As their relationship develops, both attempt to heal past wounds. Well meaning, this wilts rather than blooms. **LH**

B

Christian Slater *Lewis* • Mary Stuart Masterson *Lisa* • Pamela Segall *Kim* • Josh Brolin *Danny* • Gina Torres *Francine* • Ally Walker *Wendy* ▪ *Dir/Scr* Michael Goldenberg

The Bed Sitting Room ★★★ PG

Comedy	1969 · UK · Colour · 87min

One of comic genius Spike Milligan's two great West End hits, this anti-war play by Milligan and John Antrobus seemed ideal screen material. It's set three years after the great nuclear holocaust and the cast gradually transmutes into various altered physical states (Arthur Lowe becomes a parrot). Ralph Richardson stars, joined by a cast full of priceless British eccentrics. Richard Lester is quite at home in this surreal world, but despite its undoubted originality, this fails to transfer successfully from stage to screen. Watch carefully for Marty Feldman in his movie debut. TS
DVD BD

Ralph Richardson *Lord Fortnum* • Rita Tushingham *Penelope* • Peter Cook *Inspector* • Dudley Moore *Sergeant* • Arthur Lowe *Father* • Roy Kinnear *Plastic Mac Man* • Mona Washbourne *Mother* • Michael Hordern *Captain Bules Martin* • Spike Milligan *Mate* • Harry Secombe *The Shelter Man* • Jimmy Edwards *Nigel* • Marty Feldman *Nurse Arthur* ▪ *Dir* Richard Lester • *Scr* John Antrobus, from the play by Spike Milligan, John Antrobus

Bedazzled ★★★ PG

Comedy	1967 · UK · Colour · 99min

From the days when London was swinging and Peter Cook and Dudley Moore were a partnership made in comedy heaven, this Faustian fantasy has Dud as a cook lusting after waitress Eleanor Bron and being granted seven wishes by Pete, as a drawlingly engaging Devil hungry for Dud's soul. A briefly clad, briefly glimpsed Raquel Welch is one of the Deadly Sins, while Barry Humphries turns in a hilarious performance as Envy. Director Stanley Donen settles for quirky comedy instead of razor-sharp satire. TH DVD

Peter Cook *George Spiggot* • Dudley Moore *Stanley Moon* • Raquel Welch *Lillian Lust* • Eleanor Bron *Margaret* • Alba *Vanity* • Robert Russell *Anger* • Barry Humphries *Envy* • Parnell McGarry *Gluttony* • Daniele Noel *Avarice* • Howard Goorney *Sloth* ▪ *Dir* Stanley Donen • *Scr* Peter Cook, from a story by Peter Cook, Dudley Moore • *Music* Dudley Moore

Bedazzled ★★★ 12

Comedy	2000 · US/Ger · Colour · 89min

Liz Hurley is the Devil in disguise in this remake of the 1967 Dudley Moore/Peter Cook comedy. In a contemporary riff on the Faustian premise, Satan Hurley grants geeky Brendan Fraser seven wishes in exchange for his soul. Fraser uses these to try to attain the object of his affections, Frances O'Connor, while Hurley uses them to subvert his desires. Extremely funny in places, this is director Harold Ramis at his superficial best. LH Swearing, drug abuse. DVD

Brendan Fraser *Elliott Richards* • Elizabeth Hurley *The Devil* • Frances O'Connor *Alison Gardner/Nicole* • Miriam Shor *Carol/Penthouse hostess* • Orlando Jones *Dan/Esteban/Beach jock/Sportscaster/African party guest* • Paul Adelstein *Bob/Roberto/Beach jock/Sportscaster/Lincoln aide* • Toby Huss *Jerry/Alejandro/Beach jock/sportscaster/Lance* ▪ *Dir* Harold Ramis • *Scr* Harold Ramis, Peter Tolan, Larry Gelbart, from the 1967 film

Bedelia ★★

Crime drama	1946 · UK · BW · 89min

Made when Britain's glamorous and highly popular "wicked lady" Margaret Lockwood was at the peak of her stardom, the postwar public flocked to this tale of a classy married woman who, having poisoned three husbands, is planning to dispose of the present one (Ian Hunter). Lance Comfort directs this utter drivel, which offers a nice twist ending, photography by Frederick A Young and a giggly *frisson* for Lockwood fans. RK

Margaret Lockwood *Bedelia Carrington* • Ian Hunter *Charlie Carrington* • Barry K Barnes *Ben Chaney* • Anne Crawford *Ellen Walker* • Jill Esmond *Nurse Harris* • Barbara Blair *Sylvia Johnstone* ▪ *Dir* Lance Comfort • *Scr* Vera Caspary, Herbert Victor, from the novel by Vera Caspary

Bedevilled ★

Crime drama	1955 · US · Colour · 85min

Anne Baxter is wasted as a nightclub singer on the run who finds refuge in a church and the sensitive arms of priest-to-be Steve Forrest, who gives a terribly wooden performance. The production itself was bedevilled with so many problems that MGM chief Dore Schary fired director Mitchell Leisen towards the end of shooting and had John Sturges take over. AT

Anne Baxter *Monica Johnson* • Steve Forrest *Gregory Fitzgerald* • Victor Francen *Father Du Rocher* • Simone Renant *Francesca* • Maurice Teynac *Trevelle* • Robert Christopher *Tony Lugacetti* • Ina De La Hye *Mama Lugacetti* • Joseph Tomelty *Father Cunningham* ▪ *Dir* Mitchell Leisen • *Scr* Jo Eisinger

The Bedford Incident ★★★★ PG

Adventure	1965 · UK · BW · 101min

This superior Cold War sea drama-cum-chase movie, directed by Stanley Kubrick's one-time producer James B Harris, explores similar nuclear fears to Kubrick's *Dr Strangelove*, but in more sober fashion. Richard Widmark gives a notable performance as the captain of a nuclear-armed American naval destroyer, who has become overly zealous in his hunt for Russian subs. Sidney Poitier plays a journalist along for the ride. PF DVD

Richard Widmark *Captain Eric Finlander* • Sidney Poitier *Ben Munceford* • James MacArthur *Ensign Ralston* • Martin Balsam *Lieutenant Commander Chester Potter* • Wally Cox *Sonar operator* • Eric Portman *Commander Wolfgang Schrepke* • Michael Kane *Commander Allison* • Donald Sutherland *Pharmacist's mate* ▪ *Dir* James B Harris • *Scr* James Poe, from the novel by Mark Rascovich

Bedknobs and Broomsticks ★★★ U

Part-animated musical fantasy
1971 · US · Colour · 112min

This was a conscious effort on the part of Disney to repeat the success of *Mary Poppins*. Angela Lansbury is splendidly dotty as amateur witch Eglantine Price, but neither David Tomlinson nor the trio of cockney evacuees offer her much support. But then neither does the story, cobbled together from a couple of Mary Norton novels, in which the Nazi invasion of Britain is repelled by magic. The animated sequences are easily the highlights of the film, which is now available in full (for many years we had to make do with a 98-minute version). DP English, German +subtitles.
DVD

Angela Lansbury *Eglantine Price* • David Tomlinson *Emelius Browne* • Roddy McDowall *Mr Jelk* • Sam Jaffe *Bookman* • John Ericson *Colonel Heller* • Bruce Forsyth *Swinburne* • Reginald Owen *General Teagler* • Tessie O'Shea *Mrs Hobday* ▪ *Dir* Robert Stevenson • *Scr* Bill Walsh, Don DaGradi, from the book *The Magic Bed-Knob* and *Bonfires and Broomsticks* by Mary Norton

Bedlam ★★★ PG

Horror	1946 · US · BW · 79min

Was there ever a star who played sadistic men with as much relish as Boris Karloff? He's given ample room to snarl here as an asylum boss in 18th-century London who interns an innocent woman to stop her from exposing his harsh rule. Intelligently written and acted, with its production design modelled on Hogarth's engravings, this atmospheric chiller is let down by Mark Robson's rather pedestrian direction. RS

Boris Karloff *Master Sims* • Anna Lee *Nell Bowen* • Billy House *Lord Mortimer* • Jason Robards [Jason Robards Sr] *Oliver Todd* • Richard Fraser *Hannay* • Glenn Vernon *The gilded boy* • Ian Wolfe *Sidney Long* • Leyand Hodgson [Leyland Hodgson] *John Wilkes* ▪ *Dir* Mark Robson • *Scr*

Carlos Keith [Val Lewton], Mark Robson, from the engraving by William Hogarth • *Cinematographer* Nicholas Musuraca

The Bedroom Window ★★★ 15

Thriller	1987 · US · Colour · 108min

Steve Guttenberg must have seen this thriller as a means of escaping being typecast in the zany *Police Academy* series. Unfortunately, for all his efforts, he comes off second best to his female co-stars, Elizabeth McGovern and Isabelle Huppert. Writer/director Curtis Hanson keeps this bright and entertaining, but he eventually runs into trouble when he tries to resolve the many intrigues and plot twists. TH Swearing, sex scenes, brief nudity. DVD

Steve Guttenberg *Terry Lambert* • Elizabeth McGovern *Denise Connelly* • Isabelle Huppert *Sylvia Wentworth* • Paul Shenar *Collin Wentworth* • Carl Lumbly *Detective Quirke* • Wallace Shawn *Henderson's attorney* ▪ *Dir* Curtis Hanson • *Scr* Curtis Hanson, from the novel *The Witnesses* by Anne Holden

Bedrooms and Hallways ★★★ 15

Romantic comedy	1998 · UK · Colour · 91min

Rose Troche's second feature is an intelligent and funny examination of 1990s sexuality. Homosexual Kevin McKidd starts exploring his masculinity in an overly serious men's group, where he meets James Purefoy. Embarking on a relationship with him, McKidd is distraught to discover Purefoy is the boyfriend of his first love and good friend Jennifer Ehle. Impressive in its open attitude, where the characters' sexual bent is not as important as their essential humanity, this is funny and perceptive. LH Swearing, sex scenes.

Kevin McKidd *Leo* • Jennifer Ehle *Sally* • Simon Callow *Keith* • Hugo Weaving *Jeremy* • Christopher Fulford *Adam* • Julie Graham *Angie* • Tom Hollander *Darren* • Harriet Walter *Sybil* • James Purefoy *Brendan* ▪ *Dir* Rose Troche • *Scr* Robert Farrar

Bedtime for Bonzo ★★ U

Comedy	1951 · US · BW · 83min

Apart from the fact that this wretched farce starred an actor destined to be President of the United States, this nature-versus-nurture joke has little going for it. The story, which looks at how environment shapes personality, is about a chimpanzee being brought up as a human baby and the monkey business which ensues. It's an amiable idea, perhaps, but director Frederick De Cordova's cramped style of approach affords it little room for comic manoeuvre. TH

Ronald Reagan *Professor Peter Boyd* • Diana Lynn *Jane* • Walter Slezak *Professor Hans Neumann* • Lucille Barkley *Valerie Tillinghast* • Jesse White *Babcock* • Herbert Heyes *Dean Tillinghast* • Herb Vigran *Lt Daggett* ▪ *Dir* Frederick De Cordova • *Scr* Val Burton, Lou Breslow, from a story by Raphael David Blau [Raphael Blau], Ted Berkman

Bedtime Stories ★★★ PG

Fantasy comedy	2008 · US · Colour · 95min

Adam Sandler plays the plucky underdog yet again in this inventive, family-friendly Disney fantasy comedy about a put-upon hotel handyman whose tall tales not only entertain his niece and nephew, but have a funny way of coming true. It's not hard to see where this feel-good frolic is going, but there are plenty of amusing diversions on the way. The stories themselves whisk us amiably to medieval England, the Wild West and outer space, and if the movie's never quite laugh-out-loud funny, it's jaunty enough and skips along at a decent clip. Sandlerphobes can rest assured that he's less irritating than usual, and there are the additional curiosities of Guy Pearce's alarmingly camp hotel manager, and Russell Brand on best behaviour as our hero's wisecracking pal. TJ DVD BD

Adam Sandler *Skeeter Bronson* • Keri Russell *Jill* • Guy Pearce *Kendall* • Courteney Cox *Wendy* • Russell Brand *Mickey* • Teresa Palmer *Violet* • Lucy Lawless *Aspen* • Richard Griffiths *Barry*

Nottingham • Jonathan Pryce *Marty Bronson* ▪ *Dir* Adam Shankman • *Scr* Matt Lopez, Tim Herlihy

Bedtime Story ★★★

Screwball comedy	1942 · US · BW · 84min

Sparks fly when the starry actress wife (Loretta Young) of a theatre-obsessed playwright (Fredric March) insists on retiring from the stage. A rather over-extended one-joke situation is enlivened by sporadically successful attempts at screwball comedy, but eventually it wears a bit thin and the formidable March is somewhat unsympathetic. The ravishing Young holds it together, however, with the aid of an excellent supporting cast. RK

Fredric March *Lucius Drake* • Loretta Young *Jane Drake* • Robert Benchley *Eddie Turner* • Allyn Joslyn *William Dudley* • Eve Arden *Virginia Cole* • Helen Westley *Emma Harper* • Joyce Compton *Beulah* • Tim Ryan *Mac* ▪ *Dir* Alexander Hall • *Scr* Richard Flournoy, from a story by Horace Jackson, Grant Garrett

Bedtime Story ★★★★ PG

Comedy	1964 · US · Colour · 98min

Marlon Brando - the ultimate method actor - and David Niven - the ultimate exponent of relaxed, intuitive style - make for an unlikely double act, but the results are absolutely hilarious. They play two rival conmen on the French Riviera who try to trick TV soap star Shirley Jones out of her riches. Besides Niven's irresistible debonair charm, we have Brando's extraordinary catalogue of accents and disguises, notably his Ruritanian prince Ruprecht. It's marred by some phoney sets and back projection, but it deserves to be known in its own right rather than just as the basis for the Michael Caine/Steve Martin remake, *Dirty Rotten Scoundrels*. AT DVD

Marlon Brando *Freddy Benson* • David Niven *Lawrence Jameson* • Shirley Jones *Janet Walker* • Dody Goodman *Fanny Eubank* • Aram Stephan *Andre* • Parley Baer *Colonel Williams* • Marie Windsor *Mrs Sutton* • Rebecca Sand *Miss Trumble* ▪ *Dir* Ralph Levy • *Scr* Stanley Shapiro, Paul Henning

The Bee Keeper ★★★ 18

Drama	1986 · Gr/Fr · Colour · 121min

Marcello Mastroianni is an elderly schoolteacher, at the end of his life and his tether, who sets out to visit his beloved beehives, family and old friends before his intended suicide. Along the road he picks up a teenage hitch-hiker (Nadia Mourouzi) who may or may not revive him spiritually and sexually. This is a beautifully shot, but over-extended allegory, though Mastroianni delivers a detailed and very moving performance. AT Greek +subtitles.

Marcello Mastroianni *Spyros* • Nadia Mourouzi *Girl* • Serge Reggiani *Sick man* • Jenny Roussea *Spyros's wife* • Dinos Iliopoulos *Spyros's friend* ▪ *Dir* Theodoros Angelopoulos [Theo Angelopoulos] • *Scr* Thodoru Angelopoulos, Dimitris Nollas, Tonino Guerra • *Cinematographer* Yorgos Arvanitis

Bee Movie ★★★★ U

Animated comedy	2007 · US · Colour · 86min

This appealing animated adventure marks the first high-profile big-screen venture for comedian Jerry Seinfeld, who co-wrote the screenplay and provides the voice for the story's hero, Barry B Benson. Young Barry is a honey bee from New Hive City who rebels against the prospect of a life spent toiling away for the Honex corporation. On a foray into Manhattan, he meets a florist called Vanessa (voiced by Renée Zellweger), and the pair strike up an inter-species friendship that is strictly forbidden in his world. From there the plot takes off in several directions, but the screenplay deftly treads the tightrope between keeping the kids amused and entertaining adults with some more topical gags. The supporting voice cast includes John Goodman as a lawyer and Chris Rock as a mosquito, while Ray Liotta and Sting (naturally) contribute fun cameos. DA DVD BD

Jerry Seinfeld *Barry B Benson* • Renée Zellweger *Vanessa Bloome* • Matthew Broderick *Adam Flayman* • John Goodman *Layton T Montgomery*

U SUITABLE FOR ALL • **Uc** SUITABLE ESPECIALLY FOR YOUNG CHILDREN (DVD ONLY) • **PG** PARENTAL GUIDANCE • **12A** UNDER 12s TO BE ACCOMPANIED (CINEMA ONLY)

• Chris Rock *Mooseblood* • Patrick Warburton *Ken* • Megan Mullally *Trudy* • Kathy Bates *Janet Benson* • Rip Torn *Lou Lo Duca* • Ray Liotta • Sting ■ *Dir* Steve Hickner, Simon J Smith • *Scr* Jerry Seinfeld, Barry Marder, Spike Feresten, Andy Robin

Bee Season ★★ 12
Drama   2005 · US · Colour · 100min

Richard Gere and Juliette Binoche star as a high-achieving dysfunctional Jewish couple whose alienated children are left to discover their own ways into the worlds of spirituality and intellect. While their sensitive daughter (Flora Cross) hones her penchant for spelling, their son (portrayed by Max Minghella, son of director Anthony) secretly joins the Hare Krishnas with his new-age girlfriend (Kate Bosworth). Playing obsessively with words and hidden meanings, the film often leaves the audience bewildered. KK In English, Hebrew. Swearing. *DVD*

Richard Gere *Saul Naumann* • Juliette Binoche *Miriam Naumann* • Flora Cross *Eliza Naumann* • Max Minghella *Aaron Naumann* • Kate Bosworth *Chali* ■ *Dir* Scott McGehee, David Siegel • *Scr* Naomi Foner Gyllenhaal [Naomi Foner], from a novel by Myla Goldberg

Beefcake ★★★ 18
Erotic drama documentary
1998 · Can/UK/Fr/It · Colour · 91min

This is a worthy attempt at a documentary about American "male physique" photographer Bob Mizer. A surprising amount of Mizer's pictures and films have survived but, with the notable exception of Warhol superstar Joe Dallesandro, a Mizer model in 1967, those who worked in the semi-illicit world of nude photography tend not to have done. Much of Mizer's life is therefore reconstructed by actors. Thom Fitzgerald initially pretends, as did Mizer, that the blatantly homoerotic material is artistic and non-sexual. The truth emerges in a climactic court case (transcripts are used as dialogue). DM *DVD*

Daniel MacIvor *Bob Mizer* • Josh Peace [Joshua Peace] *Neil O'Hara* • Carroll Godsman *Delia Mizer* • Jack Griffin Mazeika *Red* • Jonathan Torrens *David* • Joe Dallesandro • Jack LaLanne ■ *Dir* Thom Fitzgerald • *Scr* Thom Fitzgerald, from a non-fiction book by F Valentine Hooven III

Beer ★ 15
Comedy   1985 · US · Colour · 79min

An old-fashioned and rather naive satire on the Madison Avenue advertising industry, this strains to be funny and credible but ends up being bland and unsubtle. Aggressive executive Loretta Swit comes up with an outrageous advertising campaign which upsets various minority groups due to the sleazy, sexist and camp approach taken by its alcoholic director, Rip Torn. AJ

Loretta Swit *BD Tucker* • Rip Torn *Buzz Beckerman* • Kenneth Mars *AJ Norbecker* • David Alan Grier *Elliot Morrison* • William Russ *Merle Draggett* • Saul Stein *Frankie Falcone* • Peter Michael Goetz *Harley Feemer* • Dick Shawn *Talk show host* ■ *Dir* Patrick Kelly • *Scr* Allan Weisbecker

Beerfest ★★ 18
Comedy adventure   2006 · US · Colour · 111min

Broken Lizard, the zany American troupe behind *Broken Lizard's Club Dread*, unleashes another daft but likeable comedy. A fratboy-style drinking film that's best watched half-soaked, it follows two American siblings (Erik Stolhanske, Paul Soter) on a trip to Munich's legendary Oktoberfest to spread the ashes of their ale-loving grandfather. At its most absurd, the tale is hilarious, reminiscent of John Landis's early work. However, despite some priceless "frog-milking" and sausage gags, the boisterous frivolity runs out of steam – only redeeming itself in an endearingly stupid finale. The 15 certificate cinema version was re-edited to an 18 certificate on DVD. SF Swearing, sex scenes, drug abuse. *DVD*

Erik Stolhanske *Todd Wolfhouse* • Paul Soter *Jan Wolfhouse* • Jay Chandrasekhar *Barry* • Kevin Heffernan *Landfill* • Steve Lemme *Fink* • Will Forte *Otto* • Cloris Leachman *Great Gam Gam* ■ *Dir* Jay Chandrasekhar • *Scr* Broken Lizard [Jay Chandrasekhar, Kevin Heffernan, Steve Lemme, Paul Soter, Erik Stolhanske]

Bees in Paradise ★★
Musical comedy   1943 · UK · BW · 75min

Co-scripted by director Val Guest and gagsmith Marriott Edgar, this is one of Arthur Askey's lesser-known vehicles. This may be because there's a sauciness to the dialogue and lyrics that makes it rather risqué for its time. As one of four pilots stranded on a South Sea island, Askey revels in the attentions of the local maidens, only to discover that it's traditional for husbands to commit suicide once the honeymoon is over. DP

Arthur Askey *Arthur Tucker* • Anne Shelton *Rouana* • Peter Graves (1) *Peter Lovell* • Max Bacon *Max Holer* • Jean Kent *Jani* • Ronald Shiner *Ronald Wild* • Antoinette Cellier *Queen* • Joy Shelton *Almira* ■ *Dir* Val Guest • *Scr* Val Guest, Marriott Edgar

Beethoven ★★★
Biographical romance   1936 · Fr · BW · 115min

Abel Gance, the great Romantic of French cinema, idolised Ludwig van Beethoven, the great Romantic of German music. Unfortunately, the loss of sound for Beethoven and the coming of sound for Gance were almost equally agonising. Gance was not at his best with dialogue, as this rather leaden biopic demonstrates. But it does have the expected visual flourishes, such as the poignant sequence when the hero loses his hearing, revealed by the silent shots of violins, bells and birds singing. RB French +subtitles.

Harry Baur *Ludwig van Beethoven* • Annie Ducaux *Thérèse de Brunswick* • Jany Holt *Giulietta Glucciardi* • Jean-Louis Barrault *Karl* • Jane Marken *Esther* • Jean Debucourt *Le Comte Gallenberg* • André Nox *Humpholz* ■ *Dir* Abel Gance • *Scr* Stève Passeur, Abel Gance

Beethoven ★★★★ U
Comedy   1992 · US · Colour · 83min

This is a cute comedy about an adorable St Bernard dog named Beethoven and the effect he has on an American family. Charles Grodin is the father who ends up with a puppy he doesn't want, which turns into a huge eating and slobbering machine. *The Flintstones* director Brian Levant keeps the comedy coming fast and furious so this never lapses into soppy territory, while Beethoven is gorgeous enough to soften even the hardest dog-hater's heart. JB *DVD*

Charles Grodin *George Newton* • Bonnie Hunt *Alice Newton* • Dean Jones *Dr Varnick* • Nicholle Tom *Ryce* • Christopher Castile *Ted* • Sarah Rose Karr *Emily* • Oliver Platt *Harvey* • Stanley Tucci *Vernon* • David Duchovny *Brad* • Patricia Heaton *Brie* ■ *Dir* Brian Levant • *Scr* Edmond Dantes [John Hughes], Amy Holden Jones

Beethoven's 2nd ★★★ U
Comedy   1993 · US · Colour · 84min

This cosy sequel sees the Newton children trying to hide a litter of ultra-cute St Bernard puppies from their still dog-shy father, Charles Grodin. While all eyes will be on the four pups, let's not forget the amiable performances of Grodin and Bonnie Hunt, and the Cruella-like villainy of scheming Debi Mazar, who dognaps Missy (Beethoven's beloved) to use as a pawn in her divorce. DP *DVD*

Charles Grodin *George Newton* • Bonnie Hunt *Alice Newton* • Nicholle Tom *Ryce* • Christopher Castile *Ted* • Sarah Rose Karr *Emily* • Debi Mazar *Regina* • Chris Penn *Floyd* • Ashley Hamilton *Taylor* • Danny Masterson *Seth* ■ *Dir* Rod Daniel • *Scr* Len Blum, from characters by Edmond Dantes [John Hughes], Amy Holden Jones

Beethoven's 3rd ★★ U
Comedy   2000 · US · Colour · 94min

Charles Grodin hands the leash over to Judge Reinhold for the huggable St Bernard's next adventure. Realising that the disaster-laden trip to California is short on

laughs, Reinhold (who returned for a further sequel the following year) overcompensates by playing each scene as if it were an amateur-dramatics pantomime. 2003 and 2008 saw two more sequels. DP *DVD*

Judge Reinhold *Richard Newton* • Julia Sweeney *Beth Newton* • Joe Pichler *Brennan Newton* • Michaela Gallo *Sara Newton* • Mike Ciccolini *Tommy* • Jamie Marsh *Bill* • Frank Gorshin *Uncle Morrie* ■ *Dir* David M Evans [David Mickey Evans] • *Scr* Jeff Schechter, from characters by Edmond Dantes [John Hughes], Amy Holden Jones

Beetle Juice ★★★★ 15
Horror comedy   1988 · US · Colour · 88min

This refreshingly flaky fantasy from director Tim Burton is a landmark supernatural comedy that ingeniously showcases monstrously zany special effects, demonic one-liners and offbeat performances. Michael Keaton is amazing as the unstable freelance exorcist called in to help recently deceased Geena Davis and Alec Baldwin rid their new home of human pests. Burton's marvellously imaginative view of the afterlife as a ghoulish extension of mundane earthbound problems is a visionary masterstroke crammed with wit and invention. AJ Violence, swearing. *DVD* *BL*

Michael Keaton *Betelgeuse* • Geena Davis *Barbara Maitland* • Alec Baldwin *Adam Maitland* • Catherine O'Hara *Delia Deetz* • Winona Ryder *Lydia Deetz* • Jeffrey Jones *Charles Deetz* • Robert Goulet *Maxie Dean* • Sylvia Sidney *Juno* ■ *Dir* Tim Burton • *Scr* Michael McDowell, Warren Skaaren, from a story by Michael McDowell, Larry Wilson • *Special Effects Supervisor* Chuck Gaspar • *Special Effects* Robert Short • *Visual Effects* Peter Kuran

Before and After ★★ 12
Drama   1996 · US · Colour · 103min

Meryl Streep and Liam Neeson's lives are irrevocably changed when their son is accused of murdering his girlfriend in director Barbet Schroeder's unfocused pseudo-thriller. A turgid pace coupled with poor plotting stretches credibility to breaking point in a bland morality melodrama, notable only for Streep's fine performance. AJ Violence, swearing.

Meryl Streep *Carolyn Ryan* • Liam Neeson *Ben Ryan* • Edward Furlong *Jacob Ryan* • Julia Weldon *Judith Ryan* • Alfred Molina *Panos Demeris* • Daniel Von Bargen *Fran Conklin* • John Heard *Wendell Bye* • Ann Magnuson *Terry Taverner* ■ *Dir* Barbet Schroeder • *Scr* Ted Tally, from the book by Rosellen Brown

Before Dawn ★★★★ 18
Horror   2012 · UK · Colour · 82min

The countryside becomes a terrifying place for *Emmerdale*'s Dominic Brunt in this surprisingly effective blend of zombie horror and relationship drama (think George A Romero meets Mike Leigh). Brunt is way out of his soap opera comfort zone here, as a husband eager to patch up his failing marriage by taking wife Joanne Mitchell to a remote rural retreat. Trouble is, their weekend idyll is interrupted by the small matter of a zombie apocalypse. But, before you say "low-budget gorefest", be assured that Brunt's accomplished directorial debut is no full-on horror – it's primarily an intimate portrait of a couple trying to rekindle their love. And when feral zombies do crash the peace and quiet of the Yorkshire Dales it makes for an unnerving and ultimately poignant experience. JA Violence, swearing. *DVD*

Dominic Brunt *Alex* • Joanne Mitchell *Meg* • Nicky Evans *Stephen* • Alan French *Peter* ■ *Dir* Dominic Brunt • *Scr* Mark Illis, from a story by Joanne Mitchell

Before I Go to Sleep
★★★★ 15
Mystery thriller   2014 · UK · Colour · 88min

Based on the bestselling thriller by SJ Watson, this is a memorable example of fine British film-making. Nicole Kidman plays a vulnerable amnesiac who must record her memories every day lest she lose further

track of her forgotten life. Husband Colin Firth is fiercely protective, unaware that doctor Mark Strong has other ideas about her affliction. But should Kidman trust her spouse or her doctor? A sexy, chilling, stylish trick of the light, this psychological thriller knows exactly what it's doing. KK Violence, swearing, some sexual references. *DVD* *BL*

Nicole Kidman *Christine Lucas* • Colin Firth *Ben Lucas* • Mark Strong *Dr Nash* • Anne-Marie Duff *Claire* • Dean-Charles Chapman *Adam* • Jing Lusi *Nurse Kate* ■ *Dir* Rowan Joffe • *Scr* Rowan Joffe, from SJ Watson's novel

Before I Hang ★★★
Horror   1940 · US · BW · 62min

This short and sweet programme filler allows Boris Karloff to veer superbly between brilliant scientist and rabid madman. This time he's dabbling in serums to combat old age and uses a criminal's blood for some behind bars experimentation after he's imprisoned for a "mercy killing". There's loads of fun psychobabble about medicine being for the good of mankind, but what it eventually turns into is another twist on the *Frankenstein* theme. AJ

Boris Karloff *Dr John Garth* • Evelyn Keyes *Martha Garth* • Bruce Bennett *Dr Paul Ames* • Edward Van Sloan *Dr Ralph Howard* • Ben Taggart *Warden Thompson* ■ *Dir* Nick Grinde • *Scr* Robert D Andrews

Before I Wake ★★★★
Supernatural horror   2015 · US · Colour

Occupying the same horror fantasy niche as *Pan's Labyrinth*, Mike Flanagan's elegant chiller is a stunningly beautiful, emotionally intense and often quite alarming treat. Kate Bosworth and Thomas Jane can't wait to foster after their own son tragically dies. However, they soon discover that their new ward has a unique gift: his vivid and imaginative dreams come to life while sleeping. A gorgeous blend of *The Orphanage* and *The Babadook*, with a wonderfully shaded performance from Bosworth. AJ

Kate Bosworth *Jessie* • Thomas Jane *Mark* • Annabeth Gish *Natalie* • Jacob Tremblay *Cody* ■ *Dir* Mike Flanagan • *Scr* Mike Flanagan, Jeff Howard • *Music* Danny Elfman

Before Night Falls ★★★★ 15
Biographical drama   2000 · US · Colour · 127min

Director Julian Schnabel's follow-up to *Basquiat* is another compelling portrait of a troubled artist, this time gay Cuban poet Reinaldo Arenas, brought to moving life by Spanish superstar Javier Bardem, who won an Oscar nomination for his searing portrayal. From Arenas's birth in rural Cuba, 1943, to his Aids-related death in New York, 1990, Schnabel's polished, visually distinctive and confident biography covers the key episodes in the poet's traumatic life. An intelligent and affecting masterpiece that succinctly captures the spirit of Arenas himself. AJ English, Spanish +subtitles. *DVD*

Javier Bardem *Reina\do Arenas* • Olivier Martinez *Lázaro Gómez Carilles* • Andrea Di Stefano *Pepe Malas* • Johnny Depp *Bon Bon/Lieutenant Victor* • Sean Penn *Cuco Sánchez* • Michael Wincott *Herberto Zorilla Ochoa* ■ *Dir* Julian Schnabel • *Scr* Julian Schnabel, Cunningham O'Keefe, Lázaro Gómez Carilles, from the memoir *Antes que Anochezca* by Reinaldo Arenas • *Cinematographers* Xavier Pérez Grobet, Guillermo Rosas

Before Sunrise ★★★★ 15
Romantic drama   1995 · US · Colour · 96min

When American slacker Ethan Hawke meets French student Julie Delpy on a train to Vienna, the romantic sparks fly and they spend one eventful night together in this exhilarating drama. Announcing his presence as a major talent after grabbing attention with *Dazed and Confused*, director Richard Linklater's understated use of gorgeous Viennese backgrounds, coupled with a smart, funny and touching script, make this ultra-modern romance hip yet timeless. AJ Swearing. *DVD* *BL*

B

Ethan Hawke *Jesse* • Julie Delpy *Céline* • Andrea Eckert *Wife on train* • Hanno Poschl *Husband on train* • Karl Bruckschwaiger *Guy on bridge* • Tex Rubinowitz *Guy on bridge* • Erni Mangold *Palm reader* • Dominik Castell *Street poet* ■ *Dir* Richard Linklater • *Scr* Richard Linklater, Kim Krizan

Before Sunset ★★★ 15
Romantic drama   2004 · US · Colour · 76min

Nine years after their brief encounter in Vienna in *Before Sunrise*, director Richard Linklater reunites his two lovers for a second tryst, this time in Paris. Meeting "by chance" in a city bookshop, the pair converse during a 70-minute stroll that plays out in real time. Ethan Hawke and Julie Delpy reprise their roles, and Linklater directs his often perceptive script with quiet style, but the characters are a bit pretentious. **DA** Swearing. **DVD** **BL**

Ethan Hawke *Jesse Wallace* • Julie Delpy *Céline* • Vernon Dobtcheff *Bookstore manager* • Louise Lemoine Torres *Journalist number one* • Rodolphe Pauly *Journalist number two* • Mariane Plasteig *Waitress* • Diabolo *Philippe* • Albert Delpy *Man at grill* • Marie Pillet *Woman in courtyard* ■ *Dir* Richard Linklater • *Scr* Richard Linklater, Julie Delpy, Ethan Hawke, from a story by Richard Linklater, Kim Krizan

Before Midnight ★★★★ 15
Romantic drama
2013 · US/Gre · Colour · 108min

The magic is still alive in director Richard Linklater's third astute probe into the developing relationship between Ethan Hawke and Julie Delpy (previously chronicled in *Before Sunrise* and *Before Sunset*). Nine more years have passed and the two lovers live in Paris with their twin daughters. At the end of an idyllic Greek holiday, they talk honestly about their life together in relaxed, long takes, and the intelligent banter, sharp humour and emotional truths show the duo clearly comfortable in their characters' skin, but the core concerns remain mortality, regret, romantic maintenance and an optimistic outlook, in what has turned out to be an outstanding indie trilogy. **AJ** Swearing, sex scenes. **DVD** **BL** **⊃**

Ethan Hawke *Jesse Wallace* • Julie Delpy *Celine* • Seamus Davey-Fitzpatrick *Hank* • Jennifer Prior *Ella* • Charlotte Prior *Nina* ■ *Dir* Richard Linklater • *Scr* Richard Linklater, Julie Delpy, Ethan Hawke, from characters by Linklater, Kim Krizan

Before the Devil Knows You're Dead ★★★★ 15
Crime thriller   2007 · US · Colour · 111min

Veteran director Sidney Lumet is once again on familiar territory with this New York-set thriller that takes its title from an old Irish toast – "May you be in heaven half an hour before The Devil knows you're dead". It's an effective blend of crime flick and family melodrama that features a pair of finely judged performances from Philip Seymour Hoffman and Ethan Hawke as the brothers afflicted by financial, relationship and substance abuse problems. Increasingly desperate, they come up with a scheme to rob the family jewellery store. But their enterprise is a disaster that ends in violence and soon the net of retribution closes in. Hoffman is predictably excellent as a son full of fury at his father (a wildly overacting Albert Finney), but equally impressive is Hawke as his messed-up younger sibling. **AS** Swearing, a sex scene, drug abuse. **DVD** **BL**

Philip Seymour Hoffman *Andy Hanson* • Ethan Hawke *Hank Hanson* • Marisa Tomei *Gina Hanson* • Albert Finney *Charles Hanson* • Rosemary Harris *Nanette Hanson* • Brian F O'Byrne *Bobby* • Amy Ryan *Martha* • Aleksa Palladino *Chris* ■ *Dir* Sidney Lumet • *Scr* Kelly Masterson • *Cinematographer* Ron Fortunato

Before the Night ★★ 18
Erotic thriller   1995 · US · Colour · 93min

Talia Shire makes her directorial debut with this instantly forgettable erotic thriller, with ex-husband David Shire composing the score, while older brother Francis Ford Coppola and his mentor Roger Corman

helped out behind the scenes. Coppola regular Frederic Forrest even crops up as the father whose daughter may or may not have been murdered by A Martinez, the very man with whom lonely Ally Sheedy has a one-night stand. **DP** Swearing, sex scenes, nudity.

Ally Sheedy *Michelle "Mickey" Sanderson* • A Martinez *Jack Gillman* • Frederic Forrest *Michael Joslyn* • Don Novello *Warren Miller* • Diane Salinger *Barbara Joslyn* ■ *Dir* Talia Shire • *Scr* Marty Casella

Before the Rain ★★★ 15
Portmanteau drama
1994 · Mac/UK/Fr · Colour · 108min

Winner of the Golden Lion at Venice and nominated for the best foreign film Oscar, this was the first film produced in the newly formed Republic of Macedonia. Director Milcho Manchevski brings an imposing portentousness to this portmanteau picture, but too often he mistakes ponderousness for gravity. **DP** Macedonian, Albanian, English +subtitles.

Josif Josifovski *Father Marko* • Rade Serbedzija *Aleksandar* • Grégoire Colin *Kiril* • Labina Mitevska *Zamira* • Boris Delcevski *Petre* • Dejan Velkov *Mate* • Kiril Ristoski *Father Damjan* • Mladen Krstevski *Trifun* • Dzemail Maksut *Kuzman* • Katrin Cartlidge *Anne* • Phyllida Law *Anne's mother* • Jay Villiers *Nick* ■ *Dir/Scr* Milcho Manchevski

Before the Rains ★★★ 12
Period romantic drama
2007 · Ind/UK/US · Colour · 93min

Santosh Sivan delivers both exoticism and eroticism in this tale of illicit passion in 1930s India. Against a backdrop of burgeoning Indian nationalism, British spice planter Henry Moores (Linus Roache) plans the construction of a new road with his Indian assistant TK (Rahul Bose). Their friendship is tested by Henry's ill-advised affair with Sajani, his married Indian housemaid. When Henry's wife and child return from England, he sends his lover away – with disastrous consequences. It's a steamy tale of colonial hanky-panky, but Sivan, writer/director of *The Terrorist* and *Asoka*, draws decent performances from Roache, Jennifer Ehle as his wife and Nandita Das as the tormented housemaid. **DA** English, Malayalam +subtitles. Violence. **DVD**

Linus Roache *Henry Moores* • Nandita Das *Sajani* • Jennifer Ehle *Laura Moores* • Rahul Bose *TK Neelan* • Leopold Benedict *Peter* • John Standing *Charles Humphries* ■ *Dir* Santosh Sivan • *Scr* Cathy Rabin, from the film *Yellow Asphalt* by Dan Verete

Before the Revolution ★★★★ 12
Political drama
1964 · It · BW · 107min

The second feature from Bernardo Bertolucci tells of a young man whose involvement with radical politics and affair with an aunt is countered by his need to conform and settle down with a pretty girl. Bertolucci refined these themes over and over again, notably in his masterpiece *The Conformist* (1969). This is a fascinating apprentice effort, even if it is full of dated, gimmicky effects apparently borrowed from Jean-Luc Godard. **AT** Italian +subtitles. Some swearing, sex scenes. **DVD** **BL**

Adriana Asti *Gina* • Francesco Barilli *Fabrizio* • Morando Morandini *Cesare* • Allen Midgette *Agostino* • Cristina Pariset *Clelia* • Domenico Alpi *Fabrizio's father* ■ *Dir/Scr* Bernardo Bertolucci

Before the Winter Chill ★★★ 15
Relationship drama
2013 · Fr/Lux · Colour · 102min

Another middle-class, midlife crisis unfolds here in the way French cinema does so well. Daniel Auteuil is as watchable as ever as a surgeon whose neatly regulated existence begins to dismantle after a chance encounter with fascinating barmaid Leila Bekhti. Between them, Auteuil and writer/director Philippe Claudel ensure that the story avoids older-man lechery, focusing instead on the regrets of a life lived for

others. Kristin Scott Thomas's role as the bored, increasingly suspicious wife is slightly ill-defined, but overall the assured performances and a patina of Gallic elegance make this a well-heeled time-passer. **TJ** French +subtitles. Swearing, some violence, brief nudity.

Daniel Auteuil *Paul* • Kristin Scott Thomas *Lucie* • Leila Bekhti *Lou* • Richard Berry *Gérard* • Vicky Krieps *Caroline* ■ *Dir/Scr* Philippe Claudel

Before Winter Comes ★★★
Drama   1968 · UK · Colour · 107min

Instead of merrily fiddling on the roof, here's Topol cheerfully trifling with the truth. He plays a Russian deserter, masquerading as a Slav interpreter who speaks 13 languages, helping major David Niven run a displaced persons camp in Austria at the end of the Second World War. Both are in conflict over local girl Anna Karina, but J Lee Thompson's relaxed direction fails to generate sufficient tension. Niven's punctilious dignity is as memorable as ever, however. **TH**

David Niven *Major Giles Burnside* • Topol *Janovic* • Anna Karina *Maria Holz* • John Hurt *Lieutenant Francis Pilkington* • Anthony Quayle *Brigadier-General Bewley* • Ori Levy *Captain Kamenev* • John Collin *Sergeant Woody* • Karel Stepanek *Count Kerassy* ■ *Dir* J Lee Thompson • *Scr* Andrew Sinclair, from the story *The Interpreter* by Frederick L Keefe in *New Yorker*

Before Women Had Wings ★★★ 15
Drama   1997 · US · Colour · 88min

Once you get past the naff title, there's actually some decent drama to be found in this TV movie "presented by" Oprah Winfrey. The film stars Oprah (of course) as the kindly woman who takes in the children of downtrodden mother Ellen Barkin. While Winfrey goes for melodrama, Barkin adds much needed class and grit and is backed up by nice performances from hot young actress Julia Stiles. **DP** **DVD**

Oprah Winfrey *Miss Zora* • Ellen Barkin *Glory Marie Jackson* • Tina Majorino *"Bird"* • Julia Stiles *Phoebe Jackson* • John Savage *Billy Jackson* • Burt Young *Mr Ippolito* • William Lee Scott *Hank* • Louis Crugnali *LJ Ippolito* • David Hart *Sheriff* ■ *Dir* Lloyd Kramer • *Scr* Connie May Fowler, from her novel

Before You Go ★★★ 15
Comedy drama   2002 · UK · Colour · 91min

Bravura turns by Julie Walters, Joanne Whalley and Victoria Hamilton inject vivacity into this old-fashioned, fantasy-tinged tragicomedy. The trio play three sisters returning home for their formidable mother's funeral who each find their own way of coping with the loss. Troubled Whalley is haunted by visions of their mother's ghost, while health fanatic Walters sparkles in yet another eccentric role and Hamilton mops up the left over laughter as the stoned nymphomaniac. Tom Wilkinson and John Hannah support the sardonic edge of this low-key melodrama. **AJ** **DVD**

Julie Walters *Teresa* • John Hannah *Mike* • Joanne Whalley *Mary* • Victoria Hamilton *Catherine* • Patricia Hodge *Violet Heaney* • Tom Wilkinson *Frank* • Hugh Ross *Mr Berry* ■ *Dir* Lewis Gilbert • *Scr* Shelagh Stephenson, from her play *The Memory of Water*

Before You Say "I Do" ★★ PG
Fantasy romantic comedy
2009 · US · Colour · 86min

Romance outstrips realism in this increasingly preposterous fantasy comedy. Filled with not so much plot holes as craters, it sees an advertising executive (David Sutcliffe) trying to prevent his divorced fiancée (Jennifer Westfeldt) from marrying her first husband after inadvertently travelling back in time. Despite the encouragement of Westfeldt's eccentric pal (a wasted Lauren Holly), Sutcliffe's over-enthusiastic behaviour is more scary than heart-warming – and unlikely to have led to the tale's predictable

but happy ending. **SF** Some swearing. **DVD**

David Sutcliffe *George Murray* • Jennifer Westfeldt *Jane Gardner* • Lauren Holly *Mary* ■ *Dir* Paul Fox • *Scr* Elena Krupp

Beggars of Life ★★★
Drama   1928 · US · BW · 80min

After killing her brutal stepfather, farm girl Louise Brooks, disguised as a boy, flees into hiding in company with youthful hobo Richard Arlen. Much of the action famously has them hopping freight trains and dossing down in a community of tramps, where Wallace Beery is top dog. Director William A Wellman, filming on location on railways and in the Californian desert, creates strong atmosphere and Brooks is beguiling, but the film is slow and sketchy. It was filmed as a silent movie, but some snatches of dialogue and a music track were added to qualify it, a little dubiously, as Paramount's first talkie feature. **RK**

Wallace Beery *Oklahoma Red* • Louise Brooks *Nancy* • Richard Arlen *Jim* • Edgar Blue Washington *Mose* • HA Morgan [Horace Morgan] *Skinny* • Andy Clark *Skelly* • Mike Donlin *Bill* ■ *Dir* William A Wellman • *Scr* Benjamin Glazer, Jim Tully, from the story by Jim Tully

The Beggar's Opera ★★★ U
Operetta   1953 · US · Colour · 94min

What with Laurence Olivier launching into lilting vocals as highwayman MacHeath, and Dorothy Tutin in exasperated voice as Polly Peachum, this debut movie of radical stage producer Peter Brook had some distinguished credentials. But John Gay's satirical operetta comes across as stagey and stilted, despite music arranged by Sir Arthur Bliss and a script by playwrights Dennis Cannan and Christopher Fry. But it does have some visual delights that make it an intriguing spectacle. **TH** **DVD**

Laurence Olivier *Capt MacHeath* • Stanley Holloway *Lockit* • George Devine *Peachum* • Mary Clare *Mrs Peachum* • Athene Seyler *Mrs Trapes* • Dorothy Tutin *Polly Peachum* • Daphne Anderson *Lucy Lockit* • Hugh Griffith *The Beggar* • Margot Grahame *The actress* ■ *Dir* Peter Brook • *Scr* Dennis Cannan, Christopher Fry, from the comic opera by John Gay • *Cinematographer* Guy Green

Begin Again ★★★★ 15
Romantic comedy drama
2013 · US · Colour · 99min

Two damaged souls attempt to heal themselves through music in this uplifting crowd-pleaser. The first is a washed-up record producer (Mark Ruffalo), whose glory days are a distant memory. The second is a British singer/songwriter (Keira Knightley), heartbroken after splitting up with her boyfriend-cum-recording partner. Both their lives are changed for the better when he persuades her to record an album on the streets of New York. The original songs are lovely and the always excellent Ruffalo delivers plenty of rumpled charm. **SC** Swearing, sexual references. **DVD** **BL**

Keira Knightley *Gretta* • Mark Ruffalo *Dan* • Hailee Steinfeld *Violet* • Adam Levine *Dave* • James Corden *Steve* • Yasiin Bey [Mos Def] *Saul* ■ *Dir/Scr* John Carney • *Cinematographer* Yaron Orbach

Beginners ★★★ 15
Drama   2010 · US · Colour · 99min

In this quirky fable, Ewan McGregor plays Oliver, a tortured artist who's given guidance by his father, Hal (Christopher Plummer) – who finally comes out as gay at the age of 75. Writer/director Mike Mills (*Thumbsucker*) creates a colourful scrapbook of Oliver's life, flitting between observations of his father's new-found joy with a younger partner (*ER's* Goran Visnjic) and his own attempts to achieve intimacy. Plummer gives a textured portrayal, but it's the sensitive playing of McGregor that rings truest, even when he takes advice from a subtitled dog. **SP** Swearing, sexual references. **DVD** **BL**

Ewan McGregor *Oliver* • Christopher Plummer *Hal* • Mélanie Laurent *Anna* • Goran Visnjic *Andy* • Kai Lennox *Elliot* • Mary Page Keller *Georgia* ■ *Dir/Scr* Mike Mills

Beginning of the End ★

Science-fiction horror   1957 · US · BW · 72min

An atomic radiation leak kills off scores of farmers in the Midwest and produces giant grasshoppers that march in formation on hapless Chicago, slaughtering everyone who stands in their way. Featuring performances from Peter Graves is a baffled boffin and Peggy Castle as a boggled journalist, this rubbishy horror is cheesy and hammy. AT

Peggie Castle *Audrey* • Peter Graves (2) *Ed Wainwright* • Morris Ankrum *General Hanson* • Richard Benedict *Corporal Mathias* • James Seay *Captain Barton* ■ *Dir* Bert I Gordon • *Scr* Fred Freiberger, Lester Gorn

The Beginning or the End
★★★ **U**

Historical drama   1947 · US · BW · 111min

MGM's dramatisation of America's development of the atom bomb is a portentous and turgid, yet absolutely fascinating, relic of the Cold War era. Hume Cronyn plays the scientist, J Robert Oppenheimer, while a cast of dozens play other real-life personages, including Einstein, Roosevelt and Harry Truman. The movie celebrates Yankee know-how, but also wonders if the invention might herald an apocalyptic dawn and wipe out humanity for good. There's a framing device about a time capsule to be opened in the year 2446 that's simply mind-boggling. AT

Brian Donlevy *Maj-Gen Leslie R Groves* • Robert Walker *Col Jeff Nixon* • Tom Drake *Matt Cochran* • Beverly Tyler *Ann Cochran* • Audrey Totter *Jean O'Leary* • Hume Cronyn *Dr J Robert Oppenheimer* • Hurd Hatfield *Dr John Wyatt* • Godfrey Tearle *President Roosevelt* • Ludwig Stossel *Dr Albert Einstein* • Art Baker *President Truman* ■ *Dir* Norman Taurog • *Scr* Frank Wead

The Beguiled ★★★ **15**

Western drama   1970 · US · Colour · 100min

An eccentric change of pace for Clint Eastwood and action director Don Siegel who successfully collaborated on *Dirty Harry*, this could be entitled "Sex and the Single Girls". For it is the frustrated sexuality of the young ladies in the Southern school run by Geraldine Page that leads to the downfall of Eastwood's wounded Unionist soldier, whom they nurse and protect. It might have played better as a languid black comedy – Siegel's camera is too energetic for its own good – but it's still effective. TH Some nudity. **DVD**

Clint Eastwood *John McBurney* • Geraldine Page *Martha Farnsworth* • Elizabeth Hartman *Edwina Dabney* • Jo Ann Harris *Carol* • Darleen Carr *Doris* • Mae Mercer *Hallie* • Pamelyn Ferdin *Amy* • Melody Thomas *Abigail* • Peggy Drier *Lizzie* • Pattye Mattick [Patricia Mattick] *Janie* ■ *Dir* Don Siegel • *Scr* John B Sherry, Grimes Grice, from the novel by Thomas Cullinan

Behind Enemy Lines ★★ **12**

Wartime action drama
2001 · US · Colour · 101min

Owen Wilson plays a naval reconnaissance pilot who's shot down over Bosnia after inadvertently filming evidence of war crimes. Gene Hackman is the maverick admiral who battles Nato caution to find his flyboy before the pursuing Serbs do. Former commercials director John Moore proves a dab hand at the action stuff but, pyrotechnics aside, the rest of film is less enthralling. DA **DVD** **Blu-ray**

Owen Wilson *Lieutenant Chris Burnett* • Gene Hackman *Reigart* • Gabriel Macht *Stackhouse* • Charles Malik Whitfield *Rodway* • Joaquim de Almeida *Piquet* • David Keith *O'Malley* • Olek Krupa *Lokar* ■ *Dir* John Moore (3) • *Scr* David Veloz, Zak Penn, from a story by James Thomas, John Thomas

Behind Enemy Lines II: Axis of Evil ★ **15**

Action thriller   2006 · US · Colour · 91min

Original star Owen Wilson wisely bailed at the end of the previous outing leaving Nicholas Gonzalez to head up the cast of this shoddy sequel, as the leader of a team of Navy SEALs sent into North Korea to dismantle a nuclear missile. Laden with a stolid screenplay more interested in the minutiae of the chain of command than nonstop action, the story stutters like a jammed machine gun. The boredom is only briefly enlivened by the inestimable Keith David, playing a ferocious drill sergeant. JR Violence, swearing. **DVD**

Nicholas Gonzalez *Lieutenant Robert James* • Matt Bushell *Master Chief Neil "Spaz" Calahan* • Peter Coyote *US President* • Keith David *Scott Boytano* • Ben Cross *Commander Tom Mackey* ■ *Dir/Scr* James Dodson

Behind the Candelabra
★★★★ **15**

Biographical drama   2013 · US · Colour · 113min

Steven Soderbergh's bittersweet, often hilarious biopic sketches out the last seven years in the life of flamboyant Vegas entertainer Wladziu Valentino "Lee" Liberace, as seen through the eyes of his assistant and lover Scott (Matt Damon). Dripping with gold, silver, diamante and mink, Soderbergh's often dark yet somehow good-hearted portrait could so easily have fallen into camp caricature, but Douglas's powerhouse central performance exquisitely captures Liberace's peculiarly self-aware charm. Rather than being a study in sleaze and excess, it prefers to tell a misguided father/son story, and although the sexual content would be considered strong even without the A-list names involved, what lasts longest in the mind is not the film's bold gay love scenes but its affectionate tip of the hat to a great, unapologetic American eccentric. DW Swearing, sex scenes, drug abuse. **DVD** **Blu-ray**

Michael Douglas (1) *Liberace* • Matt Damon *Scott Thorson* • Dan Aykroyd *Seymour Heller* • Scott Bakula *Bob Black* • Rob Lowe *Dr Jack Startz* • Tom Papa *Ray Arnett* • Debbie Reynolds *Frances Liberace* ■ *Dir* Steven Soderbergh • *Scr* Richard LaGravenese, from the memoir by Scott Thorson, Alex Thorleifson • *Cinematographer* Peter Andrews [Steven Soderbergh] • *Editor* Mary Ann Bernard [Steven Soderbergh]

Behind the Forbidden City
★★★★ **15**

Drama   1996 · Chi/Fr/Neth · Colour · 90min

Announced as the first Chinese film to tackle homosexuality, this intense interrogation drama is also an allegory on the complex relationship between the people and the forces of law and order. Si Han uses flashbacked episodes from his life to force a sexually ambivalent cop, Hu Jun, to confront his own preferences. Set around the public toilets on the edge of Tiananmen Square, which gives the film its slang title, this controversial drama led to the confiscation of Zhang Yuan's passport and the formation of the Film Bureau to outlaw production of unapproved independent pictures. Released on DVD in the UK as *East Palace, West Palace*. DP Mandarin +subtitles. **DVD**

Si Han *A-Lan* • Hu Jun *Shi Xiaohua* ■ *Dir* Zhang Yuan • *Scr* Zhang Yuan, Xiaobo Wang

Behind the Headlines ★★★

Drama   1937 · US · BW · 58min

Having played Hildy Johnson on Broadway in the jewel of newsroom dramas, *The Front Page*, Lee Tracy was frequently cast as fast-talking, sharp-witted reporters on screen. This superior B-melodrama finds him playing just such a character. Good at getting scoops, Tracy finds his relationship with his reporter girlfriend (Diana Gibson) threatened by their rivalry, though circumstances eventually require him to rescue her from danger. Well directed by

Richard Rosson, with good performances from the leads and supporting cast. RK

Lee Tracy *Eddie Haines* • Diana Gibson *Mary Bradley* • Donald Meek *Potter* • Paul Guilfoyle (1) *Art Martin* • Philip Huston *Bennett* • Frank M Thomas *Naylor* ■ *Dir* Richard Rosson • *Scr* J Robert Bren, Edmund L Hartmann, from a story by Thomas Ahearn

Behind the Headlines ★★ **U**

Thriller   1956 · UK · BW · 67min

This is elevated above the morass of British crime B-movies by a sure sense of newsroom atmosphere that owes more to Hollywood than Pinewood. This tale of showgirls, blackmail and murder presents an unromanticised view of journalism and there's a convincing seediness about the backstage milieu thanks to Geoffrey Faithfull's unfussy photography, but it lacks suspense and newsman Paul Carpenter is short on charisma. DP

Paul Carpenter *Paul Banner* • Adrienne Corri *Pam Barnes* • Hazel Court *Maxine* • Ewen Solon *Supt Faro* • Alfie Bass *Sammy* • Harry Fowler *Alfie* • Tom Gill *Creloch* ■ *Dir* Charles Saunders • *Scr* Allan MacKinnon, from the novel by Robert Chapman

Behind the Mask ★★

Medical drama   1958 · UK · Colour · 108min

Much of this potboiling drama about feuding surgeons, put-upon housemen and devoted nurses is taken up with a dispute between Michael Redgrave and Niall MacGinnis over the management of their hospital. Director Brian Desmond Hurst seems unable to choose between realism and melodrama, leaving his actors unsure how to pitch their performances. DP

Michael Redgrave *Sir Arthur Benson Gray* • Tony Britton *Philip Selwood* • Carl Mohner *Dr Carl Romek* • Niall MacGinnis *Neil Isherwood* • Vanessa Redgrave *Pamela Gray* • Ian Bannen *Alan Crabtree* • Brenda Bruce *Elizabeth Fallon* • Lionel Jeffries *Walter Froy* • Ann Firbank *Mrs Judson* ■ *Dir* Brian Desmond Hurst • *Scr* John Hunter, from the novel *The Pack* by John Rowan Wilson

Behind the Mask ★★ **PG**

Drama based on a true story
1999 · US · Colour · 90min

Donald Sutherland plays a doctor who suffers a heart attack while running a facility for the disabled in this TV movie. When a mentally challenged janitor (Matthew Fox) saves his life, he becomes the doctor's surrogate son – much to the chagrin of Sutherland's own son, who has long felt neglected by his father. Fox and Sutherland deliver honest, powerful performances under Tom McLoughlin's steady direction. MC **DVD**

Donald Sutherland *Dr Bob Shushan* • Matthew Fox *James Jones* • Bradley Whitford *Brian Shushan* • Sheila Larken *Dana* • Lorena Gale *Mrs Flowers* • Currie Graham *Geller* • Mary McDonnell *Mary Shushan* ■ *Dir* Tom McLoughlin • *Scr* Gregory Goodell

Behind the Screen ★★★ **U**

Silent satire   1916 · US · BW · 20min

At a time when movies had scarcely moved out of the freak-show stage, the novelty of Charlie Chaplin's sophisticated slapstick made a star of him. In this Biograph silent, he satisfied the public's curiosity about the new medium by taking us behind the scenes at a movie studio. Also known as *The Pride of Hollywood*, its story is simple – Charlie, in Little Tramp guise, sneaks into a studio where a film is being made. Several film personalities can be seen in passing and, although dated, it's a fascinating glimpse of a bygone age. TH **DVD**

Charles Chaplin *David, a stagehand* • Eric Campbell *Goliath, his boss* • Edna Purviance *Girl seeking film job* • Frank J Coleman *Assistant director* • Albert Austin *A stagehand* • Henry Bergman *Dramatic director* • Lloyd Bacon *Comedy director* ■ *Dir* Charles Chaplin • *Scr* Charles Chaplin

Behind the Sun ★★★ **12**

Period drama
2001 · Bra/Swi/Fr · Colour · 88min

This handsome tale of feuding families in the Brazilian badlands of the early 20th century brandishes its art house credentials like a badge of honour. Every composition devised by director Walter Salles and his *Central Station* cinematographer Walter Carvalho is painstakingly exquisite, as Rodrigo Santoro hits the road with circus performer Flavia Marco Antonio and tries to experience life before his destiny overtakes him. However, for all gushing pathos, there's no real thematic or emotional depth to the proceedings. DP Portuguese +subtitles. **DVD**

José Dumont *Father* • Rodrigo Santoro *Tonho* • Rita Assemany *Mother* • Luiz Carlos Vasconcelos *Salustiano* • Ravi Ramos Lacerda *Pacu* ■ *Dir* Walter Salles • *Scr* Walter Salles, Sergio Machado, Karim Aïnouz, from the novel *Abril Despedaçado* by Ismail Kadaré

Behold a Pale Horse ★★★

Drama   1964 · US · BW · 119min

As an exiled former Spanish Civil War guerrilla, Gregory Peck is drawn into a confrontation years later with brutal police chief Anthony Quinn, in a story based on a novel by Emeric Pressburger. Director Fred Zinnemann continues his *High Noon* tradition of combining moral dilemmas with violent action, and the film contains one of Peck's finest – and least heroic – performances. Omar Sharif is miscast as a young priest, however, spouting the message of virtue versus vengeance a little too blatantly. TH

Gregory Peck *Manuel Artiguez* • Anthony Quinn *Captain Vinolas* • Omar Sharif *Father Francisco* • Mildred Dunnock *Pilar* • Raymond Pellegrin *Carlos* • Paolo Stoppa *Pedro* • Daniela Rocca *Rosanna* • Christian Marquand *Lieutenant Zaganar* ■ *Dir* Fred Zinnemann • *Scr* JP Miller, from the novel *Killing a Mouse on Sunday* by Emeric Pressburger

Beijing Bastards ★★★

Musical drama   1993 · HK/Chi · Colour · 88min

Director Zhang Yuan fell foul of the Chinese authorities with this film, which resulted in his blacklisting. This semi-documentary study of teenage delinquency focuses on the disillusion of post-Tiananmen Square youth with the party hierarchy and the social system it maintains, and features subversive pop icon Cui Jian. Zhang's aggressive direction adds to the pace and punch of the picture, but style too often counts for more than content, and his preoccupation with provocative images makes it hard to identify with the characters. DP Mandarin +subtitles.

Wei Li *Karzi* • Cui Jian *Rock singer* ■ *Dir* Zhang Yuan • *Scr* Cui Jian, Tang Danian, Zhang Yuan

Beijing Bicycle ★★★★ **PG**

Drama   2001 · Chi/Tai/Fr · Colour · 113min

Wang Xiaoshuai explores the socio-psychological pressure of making one's mark in the world in this homage to the neorealist classic *Bicycle Thieves*. Cui Lin's progress as a pedal-bike courier is cut short when his only means of support is swiped. But Wang's portrayal of this event is less an attempt to elicit sympathy for him than the conscious establishment of a contrast to the need demonstrated by teenager Li Bin. He refuses to part with the bike he acquired at a flea market, as his status at school depends upon it. DP Mandarin +subtitles. **DVD**

Cui Lin *Guei* • Li Bin (2) *Jian* • Zhou Xun *Qin* • Gao Yuanyuan *Xiao* ■ *Dir* Wang Xiaoshuai • *Scr* Wang Xiaoshuai, Tang Danian, Peggy Chiao Hsiung-Ping, Hsu Hsiao-Ming

Being at Home with Claude
★★★ **18**

Crime drama
1992 · Can · Colour and BW · 85min

This stylised blend of romantic drama and mystery thriller makes the most of its claustrophobic setting to focus our attention on the motive for the crime committed in the arresting opening sequence. Cutting between a series of graphic black and white flashbacks and the intense interview between gay hustler Roy Dupuis and police inspector Jacques Godin, director Jean Beaudin reveals why Dupuis loved his partner to death – literally. Occasionally self-indulgent, this is still well staged and impeccably acted. DP French +subtitles.

Roy Dupuis *Yves* • Jacques Godin *Inspector* • Jean-François Pichette *Claude* • Gaston Lepage *Stenographer* • Hugo Dube *Policeman* • Johanne-Marie Tremblay *Inspector's wife* ■ *Dir* Jean Beaudin • *Scr* Jean Baudin, from the play by René-Daniel Dubois

Being Cyrus ★★★12
Mystery drama   2005 · Ind · Colour · 81min

An apparently innocuous family saga erupts into a hotbed of murder, betrayal and revenge in this engaging yet convoluted drama. Mixing Indian and western sensibilities to unusual effect, it stars Bollywood heart-throb Saif Ali Khan as a young drifter who sets off a dark chain of events when he takes employment with a reclusive sculptor (Naseeruddin Shah) and his scheming wife (Dimple Kapadia). Despite some overacting with minor characters, the cast copes perfectly with the English-language script, while debuting director Homi Adajania demonstrates confidence and visual flair. SF *DVD*

Saif Ali Khan *Cyrus Mistry* • Naseeruddin Shah *Dinshaw Sethna* • Dimple Kapadia *Katy Sethna* • Boman Irani *Farokh Sethna* • Simone Singh *Tina Sethna* • Honey Chhaya *Fardounjee Sethna* • Manjoi Pahwa *Inspector Lovely* ■ *Dir* Homi Adajania • *Scr* Homi Adajania, Kersi Khambatta

Being Elmo: a Puppeteer's Journey ★★★
Documentary   2011 · US · Colour · 76min

This documentary narrated by Whoopi Goldberg offers a happy glance at Baltimore native Kevin Clash, who went from being teased in high school for "playing with dolls" to being part of Jim Henson's Muppet clan and becoming the man who "is" Elmo from *Sesame Street*. The film moves snazzily along, using interviews, visits to Clash's childhood home and snippets of archive footage to illustrate his rise to success – with only brief mentions of the price he may have had to pay for his devotion to work. KK *DVD*

Kevin Clash • Whoopi Goldberg *Narrator* ■ *Dir* Constance Marks, Philip Shane • *Scr* Philip Shane, Justin Weinstein

Being Flynn ★★★15
Drama based on a true story
2012 · US · Colour · 97min

Nick Flynn (Paul Dano) is astonished one day to stumble across his long-absent dad (Robert De Niro) at a homeless shelter. As his father's downward spiral continues, he is forced to come to grips with his own demons. De Niro is terrific as the delusional bigot and he is well supported by Dano and Julianne Moore as the latter's mother. Writer/director Paul Weitz is occasionally guilty of over-egging the melodrama, but impresses with a sobering, unsentimental portrait of the plight of New York's underclasses. JF Swearing, drug abuse, brief nudity.

Robert De Niro *Jonathan* • Paul Dano *Nick Flynn* • Julianne Moore *Jody Flynn* • Olivia Thirlby *Denise* • Lili Taylor *Joy* ■ *Dir* Paul Weitz • *Scr* Paul Weitz, from Nick Flynn's memoirs

Being Human ★★★15
Comedy drama   1994 · UK/US · Colour · 116min

This unclassifiable picture very nearly spelt the end for director Bill Forsyth. Shelved after its disastrous US opening, the film re-emerged with an added narration by Theresa Russell that was supposed to tie together the five tales spanning 6,000 years. For all the ingenious interplay of recurrent themes and motifs, none of these understated stories is particularly memorable in itself, yet this is a thoughtful, if obscure, experiment, with Robin Williams endlessly inventive as a caveman, a Roman

slave, a medieval wanderer, a 17th-century nobleman and a modern-day New Yorker. DP

Robin Williams *Hector* • John Turturro *Lucinnius* • Kelly Hunter *Deirdre* • Anna Galiena *Beatrice* • Vincent D'Onofrio *Priest* • Jonathan Hyde *Francisco* • Lizzy McInnerny *Ursula* • Hector Elizondo *Dom Paulo* • Ewan McGregor *Alvarez* • Helen Miller *Betsy* • Lindsay Crouse *Janet* • Lorraine Bracco *Anna* • William H Macy *Boris* • Theresa Russell *The Storyteller* ■ *Dir/Scr* Bill Forsyth • *Producers* David Puttnam, Robert F Colesberry

Being John Malkovich
★★★★★15
Fantasy comedy   1999 · US · Colour · 108min

Spike Jonze's crazy, surreal comedy consistently dazzles while never losing its grip on unreality. The daringly original, metaphysical fantasy still finds time to ponder the human status quo, sexual gender and identity, as down-on-his-luck street puppeteer John Cusack takes a job at a strange Manhattan firm where a small door hidden behind a filing cabinet reveals a dark tunnel that leads into the head of movie star John Malkovich. When he tells co-worker Catherine Keener about his new-found celebrity joy ride, they form a business partnership that offers jaded New Yorkers the chance to be the actor for 15 minutes at $200 a time. Jonze's Kafka-esque mind trip is super-smart, hip and darkly subversive. AJ Swearing, sex scenes. *DVD* ⬚

John Cusack *Craig Schwartz* • Catherine Keener *Maxine* • Cameron Diaz *Lotte Schwartz* • John Malkovich *John Horatio Malkovich* • Orson Bean *Dr Lester* • Mary Kay Place *Floris* • Carlos Jacott *Larry the agent* • Charlie Sheen *Charlie* • Brad Pitt • Sean Penn ■ *Dir* Spike Jonze • *Scr* Charlie Kaufman

Being Julia ★★★12
Period comedy drama
2004 · Can/UK/Hun/US · Colour · 99min

The glamour and superficiality surrounding the London theatre scene of the 1930s is stylishly brought to life by István Szabó. Annette Bening is the 40-something stage actress and society queen, who begins a turbulent affair with a gold-digging young American (Shaun Evans). Initially energised by their illicit meetings, the married diva is increasingly pained by Evans's playboy ways, particularly his relationship with a beautiful acting hopeful (Lucy Punch). This benefits from solid performances and a sharply amusing script, although Bening occasionally overplays her role. SF Swearing. *DVD*

Annette Bening *Julia Lambert* • Jeremy Irons *Michael Gosselyn* • Bruce Greenwood *Lord Charles* • Miriam Margolyes *Dolly de Vries* • Juliet Stevenson *Evie* • Shaun Evans *Tom Fennel* • Lucy Punch *Avice Crichton* • Maury Chaykin *Walter Gibbs* • Sheila McCarthy *Grace Dexter* • Michael Gambon *Jimmie Langton* • Rita Tushingham *Aunt Carrie* ■ *Dir* István Szabó • *Scr* Ronald Harwood, from the novella *Theatre* by W Somerset Maugham

Being There ★★★★12
Satirical comedy   1979 · US · Colour · 124min

Hal Ashby's satirical parable on the way the USA surrenders itself to homespun evangelicals gives Peter Sellers the role of a lifetime as the naive, illiterate gardener thrust into an outside world that takes his ignorance for philosophical depth. TV-nurtured, he comments to a seductive Shirley MacLaine that he likes watching and gives her entirely the wrong idea. Veteran Melvyn Douglas refuses to be upstaged by Sellers and thoroughly deserved his Oscar for best supporting actor. TH *DVD* ⬚

Peter Sellers *Chance* • Shirley MacLaine *Eve Rand* • Melvyn Douglas *Benjamin Rand* • Jack Warden *President, "Bobby"* • Richard Dysart *Dr Robert Allenby* • Richard Basehart *Vladimir Skrapinov* • Ruth Attaway *Louise* • Dave Clennon [David Clennon] *Thomas Franklin* ■ *Dir* Hal Ashby • *Scr* Jerzy Kosinski, from his novel

Bel Ami ★★15
Period drama   2010 · UK/Fr/It · Colour · 98min

This decorous but fake-looking dramatisation of Guy de Maupassant's oft-filmed French novel sees *Twilight* heart-throb Robert Pattinson as an ex-soldier on the make in *Belle Epoque* Paris. As his lovers, Uma Thurman, Kristin Scott Thomas and Christina Ricci do their best with an English-sounding script, but director Declan Donnellan struggles to convert the material into a convincing cinematic whole. No doubt, Twihards will simply be satisfied with the glimpse of Pattinson's bare bottom. AC Swearing, sex scenes, nudity. *DVD* ⬚

Robert Pattinson *Georges Duroy* • Uma Thurman *Madeleine Forestier* • Kristin Scott Thomas *Madame Rousset* • Christina Ricci *Clotilde de Marelle* • Colm Meaney *Rousset* • Philip Glenister *Charles Forestier* • Holliday Grainger *Suzanne Rousset* ■ *Dir* Declan Donnellan, Nick Ormerod • *Scr* Rachel Bennette, from Guy de Maupassant's novel

Bela Lugosi Meets a Brooklyn Gorilla ★
Comedy horror   1952 · US · BW · 74min

The last film Bela Lugosi made before he fell into the clutches of Ed Wood, this cheapie was produced (in just two weeks) to cash in the "success" of the Lon Chaney Jr vehicle, *Bride of the Gorilla*. Although Lugosi was the nominal star, producer Jack Broder was much more interested in showcasing the negligible talents of his Martin and Lewis lookalikes, Duke Mitchell and Sammy Petrillo. DP

Bela Lugosi *Dr Zabor* • Duke Mitchell • Sammy Petrillo • Charlita *Nona* • Muriel Landers *Salome* • Al Kikume *Chief Rakos* ■ *Dir* William Beaudine • *Scr* Tim Ryan

A Belfast Story ★15
Drama   2013 · Ire · Colour · 94min

The Northern Ireland peace process still has some way to go in this Ulster-set thriller, in which a spate of murders targeting former IRA terrorists seems destined to stir up old enmities. On the case is Colm Meaney's world-weary, Loyalist-leaning cop, who feels despite the past he still has a job to do serving justice in the present. It's a dilemma with dramatic possibilities, but convoluted plotting, unspeakable dialogue and scenery-chewing performances soon put paid to them. TJ Violence. *DVD* ⬚

Colm Meaney *Detective* • Malcolm Sinclair *Chief Constable* • Tommy O'Neill *First Minister* • Patrick Rocks *Eammon* • Damien Hasson *Damien* ■ *Dir/Scr* Nathan Todd

Believe ★★★PG
Sports drama   2012 · UK/US · Colour · 95min

Legendary Manchester United manager Matt Busby decides to encourage a team of gifted youngsters in director David Scheinmann's fictional drama. The retired Sir Matt (Brian Cox) takes it upon himself to coach the side whose star player has stolen his wallet. Whether wondering why he survived the 1958 Munich air disaster or bantering with lads, who have no idea who he is, Cox is a delight, and is ably supported by Philip Jackson and Anne Reid. But a bit more grit would have helped. DP

Brian Cox (1) *Sir Matt Busby* • Natascha McElhone *Erica Gallagher* • Anne Reid *Jean Busby* • Philip Jackson *Bob* • Toby Stephens *Dr Farquar* ■ *Dir* David Scheinmann • *Scr* David Scheinmann, Massimiliano Durante, Carmelo Pennisi

The Believer ★★★★15
Biographical drama   2001 · US · Colour · 98min

Though controversial, screenwriter-turned-director Henry Bean's feature debut is no cheap-trick shocker. Instead, the story of Danny Balint, a young Jewish New Yorker who rejects his faith in favour of rabid fascism and a role as a neo-Nazi mouthpiece, makes its mark with rawness, intelligence and maturity. Devoid of sensationalism yet truly unnerving, the stomach-churning drama reinforces its grit with choppy camerawork and grainy visuals. Ryan Gosling's enigmatic and blisteringly feral lead performance is

perfectly judged. SF Violence, swearing, sex scenes. *DVD*

Ryan Gosling *Danny Balint* • Summer Phoenix *Carla Moebius* • Glenn Fitzgerald *Drake* • Theresa Russell *Lina Moebius* • Billy Zane *Curtis Zampf* • Elizabeth Reaser *Miriam* ■ *Dir* Henry Bean • *Scr* Henry Bean, from a story by Henry Bean, Mark Jacobson

The Believers ★★★18
Horror   1987 · US · Colour · 109min

John Schlesinger directs this tale of a voodoo cult holding Manhattan in a grip of terror, but clearly feels the material is beneath him and tries upgrading it to a *Rosemary's Baby*-style exercise in paranoia. Wrong choice. Despite the presence of the ever-dependable Martin Sheen, as a police psychiatrist trying to save his son from Satan, and a very polished style, this uninspired suspense tale is more depressing than chilling. AJ Swearing, violence. *DVD*

Martin Sheen *Cal Jamison* • Helen Shaver *Jessica Halliday* • Harley Cross *Chris Jamison* • Robert Loggia *Lieutenant Sean McTaggert* • Elizabeth Wilson *Kate Maslow* • Harris Yulin *Donald Calder* • Lee Richardson *Dennis Maslow* • Richard Masur *Marty Wertheimer* ■ *Dir* John Schlesinger • *Scr* Mark Frost, from the novel *The Religion* by Nicholas Conde

Belizaire the Cajun ★★★
Historical drama   1985 · US · Colour · 101min

This indie effort dramatises the persecution of French-speaking Cajuns by landowners and their henchmen in the 1850s. The main characters are Armand Assante as a Cajun herbalist, Gail Youngs as his former girlfriend and Will Patton as her common-law husband. All are happy to farm the land and keep themselves to themselves, but are inexorably caught up in the violence and necktie parties. The film was developed at Robert Redford's Sundance Institute with the active support of Robert Duvall, who makes a cameo appearance. AT Violence, swearing.

Armand Assante *Belizaire Breaux* • Gail Youngs *Alida Thibodaux* • Michael Schoeffling *Hypolite Leger* • Stephen McHattie *James Willoughby* • Will Patton *Matthew Perry* • Nancy Barrett *Rebecca* • Robert Duvall *Preacher* ■ *Dir/Scr* Glen Pitre

Bell, Book and Candle ★★★U
Supernatural romantic comedy
1958 · US · Colour · 98min

James Stewart and Kim Novak are pleasant enough in this screen version of the theatre hit about a publisher who falls in love with a witch. But they are left struggling in a lush but charmless adaptation, sadly lacking the right magical brew. Still, the Oscar-nominated art direction/set decoration is effective, there's a fine performance from Pyewacket the cat, and rival witches Hermione Gingold and Elsa Lanchester are good fun. TS *DVD*

James Stewart *Shepherd Henderson* • Kim Novak *Gillian Holroyd* • Jack Lemmon *Nicky Holroyd* • Ernie Kovacs *Sidney Redlitch* • Hermione Gingold *Mrs De Pass* • Elsa Lanchester *Queenie* ■ *Dir* Richard Quine • *Scr* Daniel Taradash, from the play by John Van Druten • *Art Director* Cary Odell • *Set Designer* Louis Diage

Bell-Bottom George ★★U
Second World War comedy
1943 · UK · BW · 93min

This wartime comedy is so full of tired plot that it could easily have been assembled after a recce of the cutting room floor. George Formby is rejected by the armed forces only to find himself in the thick of the action after he puts on a handy uniform. Like so many British flag-wavers, the storyline concerns a nest of Nazi spies. DP *DVD*

George Formby *George* • Anne Firth *Pat* • Reginald Purdell *Birdie Edwards* • Peter Murray Hill *Shapley* • Charles Farrell (2) *Jim Benson* • Eliot Makeham *Johnson* • Manning Whiley *Church* ■ *Dir* Marcel Varnel • *Scr* Peter Fraser, Edward Dryhurst, from a story by Richard Fisher, Peter Cresswell

A Bell for Adano ★★★
Second World War drama
1945 · US · BW · 103min

The prolific director Henry King was always a safe pair of hands but rarely an inspired artist in a film career that spanned half a century, and this is a typical example of his work. No masterpiece, in other words, but still a gentle and engaging Second World War tale about a US Army unit that occupies an Italian town and wins over the locals by, among other things, providing them with a new bell after the old one had been melted down for the war effort. PF

Gene Tierney *Tina* • John Hodiak *Major Victor Joppolo* • William Bendix *Sgt Borth* • Glenn Langan *Lt Livingstone* • Richard Conte *Nicolo* • Stanley Prager *Sgt Trampani* • Henry Morgan [Harry Morgan] *Capt Purvis* ■ *Dir* Henry King • *Scr* Lamar Trotti, Norman Reilly Raine, from the novel by John Hersey

Bella ★★☒
Romantic drama
2006 · US/Mex · Colour · 88min

There's something quaintly old-fashioned about Alejandro Gomez Monteverde's romantic melodrama, which follows chef Jose (Eduardo Verástegui) and pregnant waitress Nina (Tammy Blanchard) on an eventful day around New York. Such sentimental storytelling might have passed muster if it wasn't for Monteverde's habit of continually switching visual style, as the awkwardly structured script simply doesn't warrant such overly busy camerawork and fussy editing. DP English, Spanish +subtitles. Some swearing. **DVD**

Eduardo Verástegui *Jose* • Tammy Blanchard *Nina* • Manny Perez *Manny* • Ali Landry *Celia* • Angelica Aragon [Angélica Aragón] *Mother* • Jaime Tirelli *Father* ■ *Dir* Alejandro G Monteverde [Alejandro Gomez Monteverde] • *Scr* Alejandro G Monteverde, Patrick Million, Leo Severino

The Bellboy ★★★☒
Comedy
1960 · US · BW · 71min

After 17 films with partner Dean Martin, and a further seven solo, Jerry Lewis persuaded Paramount to let him take on the directorial duties for the first time in one of his own films. Little more than a series of sketches set in the famous Fontainebleau Hotel in Miami, this very funny movie (which Lewis also produced and wrote) confirmed a clear directorial style, and proved Lewis well capable of continuing the tradition of American comedy auteurs. Unfortunately, his talent has only really been recognised in France; most British critics still loathe Lewis's humour. TS **DVD**

Jerry Lewis *Stanley* • Alex Gerry *Manager* • Bob Clayton *Bell Captain* • Herkie Styles *Bellboy* • Sonny Sands *Bellboy* • Eddie Shaeffer *Bellboy* • David Landfield *Bellboy* ■ *Dir/Scr* Jerry Lewis

Belle ★★★★☒
Period drama based on a true story
2013 · US/UK · Colour · 99min

It's hard to imagine the story of Britain's first mixed-race aristocrat being told more elegantly than in this warm and funny period piece, which brings a subtle gravitas to its central fairy-tale romance. Dido Belle (Gugu Mbatha-Raw) is the illegitimate child of a slave and a nobleman, who is taken to live with her great uncle (Tom Wilkinson) in a life of luxury. The horror of slavery is addressed, but the film does so from a place of hope and love, expanding the Regency world of Jane Austen while delivering all the wit and spectacle of top-flight costume drama. DW **DVD**

Gugu Mbatha-Raw *Dido Elizabeth Belle* • Tom Wilkinson *Lord Mansfield* • Sam Reid *John Davinier* • Sarah Gadon *Lady Elizabeth Murray* • Penelope Wilton *Lady Mary Murray* • Miranda Richardson *Lady Ashford* • Tom Felton *James Ashford* ■ *Dir* Amma Asante • *Scr* Misan Sagay • *Music* Rachel Portman

Belle and Sebastian – the Adventure Continues ★★★☒
Adventure
2015 · Fr · Colour · 92min

Viewers of a certain vintage will have nothing but fond memories of *Belle and Sebastian*, which was a fixture on the BBC's school holiday schedules in the late 1960s and early 70s. Clearly, the French recall the adventures of a boy and his Pyrenean Mountain dog with similar affection, as this is the second film in the revival, with Félix Bossuet returning as the 1940s youngster living with surrogate grandfather Tcheky Karyo and his niece. Christian Duguay makes the most of the handsome photography, but the action dawdles in places. DP French, Italian +subtitles.

Félix Bossuet *Sébastien* • Tcheky Karyo *César* • Margaux Chatelier *Angelina* • Thierry Neuvic *Pierre* ■ *Dir* Christian Duguay • *Scr* Juliette Sales, Fabien Suarez, from characters by Cécile Aubry

Belle de Jour ★★★★★☒
Psychological drama
1967 · Fr/It · Colour · 96min

Luis Buñuel embarked on this picture convinced it would be his last. However, the receipt of the Golden Lion at Venice and universal critical acclaim persuaded him to undertake five further features, each one a masterpiece. Stunningly photographed by Sacha Vierny, this complex parable on social, sexual and emotional repression flits between dream and reality with such deft sleights of hand that we are never sure whether we are watching episodes from Catherine Deneuve's life or sharing her fantasies. Deneuve is utterly beguiling as the housewife who seeks escape in prostitution, but the director is the film's true star. DP French +subtitles. Sex scenes, swearing, violence. **DVD**

Catherine Deneuve *Séverine Sérizy* • Jean Sorel *Pierre Sérizy* • Geneviève Page [Genevieve Page] *Mme Anaïs* • Michel Piccoli *Henri Husson* • Pierre Clémenti *Marcel* • Macha Méril *Renée Févret* • Francisco Rabal *Hyppolite* ■ *Dir* Luis Buñuel • *Scr* Luis Buñuel, Jean-Claude Carrière, from the novel by Joseph Kessel

Belle Epoque ★★★★☒
Comedy drama
1992 · Sp/Por/Fr · Colour · 109min

Winner of the best foreign language film Oscar, this charming picture recalls not only a key moment in Spanish history, at the dawning of the short-lived Republic, but also a golden age in film-making when romantic comedies were about innocence, discovery and love. Director Fernando Trueba claims his only mentor is Billy Wilder, but there is more than a touch of Buñuel about the opening sequences and the down-to-earth-with-a-bump finale. Although the romantic entanglements involving army deserter Jorge Sanz and the four bewitching sisters hold centre stage, the film is stolen by Fernando Fernán Gómez as their anarchist artist father. DP Spanish +subtitles. Some swearing, sex scenes. **DVD**

Fernando Fernán Gómez *Manolo* • Jorge Sanz *Fernando* • Maribel Verdú *Rocio* • Ariadna Gil *Violeta* • Miriam Diaz-Aroca *Clara* • Penélope Cruz *Luz* • Mary Carmen Ramirez *Amalia, Manola's wife* • Gabino Diego *Juanito* ■ *Dir* Fernando Trueba • *Scr* Rafael Azcona, from a story by Rafael Azcona, José Luis García Sanchez , Fernando Trueba

La Belle Equipe ★★★★
Drama
1936 · Fr · BW · 101min

Jean Renoir was originally to make this classic example of the poetic realist style that dominated French cinema under the Popular Front. However, Julien Duvivier makes a fine job of juggling the quirks and concerns of the five nobodies who decide to invest their lottery winnings in a run-down inn. Jean Gabin is outstanding, as camaraderie turns to contempt and the pals fall out over the renovation and the beguiling Viviane Romance. A revised ending is now generally shown, although the pessimistic version is perhaps more revealing about the fragility of happiness. DP French +subtitles.

Jean Gabin *Jean, "Jeannot"* • Charles Vanel *Charles, "Charlot"* • Raymond Aimos *Raymond, "Tintin"* • Charles Dorat *Jacques* • Raphael Medina *Mario* • Micheline Cheirel *Huguette* • Viviane Romance *Gina* • Marcelle Géniat *The grandmother* • Raymond Cordy *Drunk* ■ *Dir* Julien Duvivier • *Scr* Charles Spaak, Julien Duvivier

La Belle et la Bête ★★★★★☒
Fantasy
1946 · Fr · BW · 89min

Although René Clément got a co-directing credit for his technical assistance, this adaptation of the timeless fairy tale is clearly the work of the poet-director Jean Cocteau. With interiors that owe much to the paintings of Doré and Vermeer, this visual feast is enhanced by the magical realism of Henri Alekan's photography, exquisite costumes and Georges Auric's audacious score. Josette Day is a delight as Beauty, while Jean Marais, in his dual role as the Beast and the Prince, manages to be truly touching beneath the superb make-up. DP French +subtitles.

Jean Marais *Avenant/The Beast/The Prince* • Josette Day *Beauty* • Marcel André *The Merchant* • Mila Parely *Adelaide* • Nane Germon *Felice* • Michel Auclair *Ludovic* ■ *Dir* Jean Cocteau, René Clément • *Scr* Jean Cocteau • *Costume Designers* Christian Bérard, Antonio Castillo, Marcel Escoffier

Une Belle Fille comme Moi ★★☒
Black comedy
1973 · Fr · Colour · 93min

François Truffaut so misjudges the tone of this black comedy that brusque becomes strident and risqué becomes tasteless. He has Bernadette Lafont recall in flashback to sociologist André Dussolier the experiences that landed her in jail. Stuffing the action with in-jokes, autobiographical snippets and cinematic allusions, Truffaut succeeds in making his characters seem as one-dimensional as the satire. DP In French. **DVD**

Bernadette Lafont *Camille Bliss* • Claude Brasseur *Monsieur Murène* • Charles Denner *Arthur* • Guy Marchand *Sam Golden* • André Dussollier *Stanislas Previne* • Philippe Léotard *Clovis Bliss* • Michel Delahaye *Marchal* ■ *Dir* François Truffaut • *Scr* François Truffaut, Jean-Loup Dabadie, from the novel *Such a Gorgeous Kid* by Henry Farrell

La Belle Noiseuse ★★★★★☒
Drama
1991 · Fr · Colour · 228min

In its full form (as opposed to the 125-minute *Divertimento*), this is a majestic study of art and the agonies of creation from one of the masters of the French New Wave, Jacques Rivette. The sophisticated seduction games played by artist Michel Piccoli as he sketches his new model Emmanuelle Béart make for fascinating viewing, but nothing is as compelling as the artist's hand at work. The sight of the drawing taking shape and the sound of the charcoal or nib scratching paper are hypnotic. A courageous, rewarding masterpiece. DP French +subtitles. Nudity. **DVD**

Michel Piccoli *Frenhofer* • Jane Birkin *Liz* • Emmanuelle Béart *Marianne* • David Bursztein *Nicolas* • Marianne Denicourt *Julienne* • Gilles Arbona *Porbus* • Bernard Dufour *The painter* ■ *Dir* Jacques Rivette • *Scr* Pascal Bonitzer, Christine Laurent, from Honoré de Balzac's story *Le Chef d'Oeuvre Inconnu*

The Belle of New York ★★★★☒
Musical
1952 · US · Colour · 80min

Utterly charming, this MGM Technicolor musical stars the inimitable Fred Astaire as an idle playboy (a role perfectly suited to his screen persona) and the often underrated Vera-Ellen as the social worker he falls for. The film offers many delights along the way, notably Astaire's superb *I Wanna Be a Dancin' Man* number. Vera-Ellen dazzles in partnership (with vocals dubbed by an uncredited Anita Ellis), and unfairly neglected director Charles Walters turns this elderly Broadway show into a tiptop Metro musical. TS

Fred Astaire *Charlie Hill* • Vera-Ellen *Angela Bonfils* • Marjorie Main *Mrs Phineas Hill* • Keenan Wynn *Max Ferris* • Alice Pearce *Elsie Wilkins* • Clinton Sundberg *Gilfred Spivak* • Gale Robbins *Dixie McCoy* • Lisa Ferraday *Frenchie* ■ *Dir* Charles Walters • *Scr* Robert O'Brien, Irving Elinson, Chester Erskine (adaptation), from a play by Hugh Morton

Belle of the Nineties ★★★☒
Comedy
1934 · US · BW · 70min

Following her smash-hits *She Done Him Wrong* and *I'm No Angel*, queen of the double entendre Mae West returned with more of the same in a lavish production under Leo McCarey's expert direction. The screenplay – originally entitled *It Ain't No Sin* until the Hays Office said no – was penned by the buxom star herself. It's no great shakes (St Louis saloon singer engages in two romances while fending off a third), but the innuendos flow, and Mae's musical numbers are backed up by Duke Ellington and his Orchestra. RK **DVD**

Mae West *Ruby Carter* • Roger Pryor *Tiger Kid* • John Mack Brown [Johnny Mack Brown] *Brooks Claybourne* • John Miljan *Ace Lamont* • Katherine DeMille *Molly Brant* • James Donlan *Kirby* • Stuart Holmes *Dirk* ■ *Dir* Leo McCarey • *Scr* Mae West

Belle of the Yukon ★★
Musical western
1944 · US · Colour · 84min

Set in the gold rush days, this stars Randolph Scott as a conman, so convincing that he is dubbed "Honest John" by the Klondike miners who entrust their gold dust to his safekeeping. Scott's plans are hindered by his romance with the Belle of the title, played by famous stripper Gypsy Rose Lee. Some nice comedy and lively performances contribute to the sporadic pleasures of an over complicated screenplay. RK

Randolph Scott *Honest John Calhoun* • Gypsy Rose Lee *Belle Devalle* • Dinah Shore *Lettie Candless* • Charles Winninger *Pop Candless* • Bob Burns (2) *Sam Slade* • Florence Bates *Viola Guinn "Big Boy"* • Williams *Marshall Maitland* ■ *Dir* William A Seiter • *Scr* James Edward Grant, from a story by Houston Branch

Belle Starr ★★
Western
1941 · US · Colour · 87min

The inexperience of the beautiful Gene Tierney, relatively early in her career, shows through in her unconvincing performance as a Missouri slave-owner determined to see off the Yankees. This shameless rewriting of history converts America's famous 19th-century female bandit into a Southern plantation owner, complete with loyal "mammy" (Louise Beavers) and a husband (Randolph Scott) who leads guerrilla actions against the North. Short on action and characterisation, with a weak script. RK

Randolph Scott *Sam Starr* • Gene Tierney *Belle Starr* • Dana Andrews *Major Thomas Crall* • John Shepperd [Shepperd Strudwick] *Ed Shirley* • Elizabeth Patterson *Sarah* • Chill Wills *Blue Duck* • Louise Beavers *Mammy Lou* • Olin Howlin *Jasper Tench* ■ *Dir* Irving Cummings • *Scr* Lamar Trotti, from a story by Niven Busch, Cameron Rogers

Belle Starr's Daughter ★★☒
Western
1948 · US · BW · 85min

Seven years after the 1941 original, 20th Century-Fox made this lacklustre sequel. Ruth Roman, playing Belle's daughter, chases marshal George Montgomery who she thinks (wrongly, of course) shot and killed her mother. Not much more than an average co-feature, it's of interest today as one of the higher-budgeted westerns directed by Lesley Selander, who made almost 200 such films for the big screen. TS

George Montgomery *Tom Jackson* • Rod Cameron *Bob "Bittercreek" Yauntis* • Ruth Roman *Rose of Cimarron* • Wallace Ford *Bailey* • Charles Kemper *Gaffer* • William Phipps *Yuma*

Edith King *Mrs Allen* • Jack Lambert *Brone* • Isabel Jewell *Belle Starr* ■ *Dir* Lesley Selander • *Scr* WR Burnett

Belle Toujours ★★15

Drama   2006 · Por/Fr · Colour · 65min

This sequel of sorts to Luis Buñuel's daring 1967 masterpiece *Belle de Jour* proves little more than an intriguing oddity in the hands of veteran Portuguese writer/director Manoel de Oliveira. Michel Piccoli reprises his role as spurned admirer Henri Husson, who, 38 years after the events in the original movie, plots to avenge his wounded ego after he spots Séverine (now played by Bulle Ogier, who lacks the icy sophistication of Catherine Deneuve) at a concert. Playful winks to surrealism provide a visual link back to Buñuel, but they feel incongruous in an otherwise staid and literal affair. SF French +subtitles. *DVD*

Michel Piccoli *Henri Husson* • Bulle Ogier *Séverine Sérizy* • Ricardo Trepa *Benedito, barman* • Leonor Baldaque *Young prostitute* • Julia Buisel *Old prostitute* • Lawrence Foster ■ *Dir/Scr* Manoel de Oliveira

Les Belles de Nuit ★★★★

Fantasy drama   1952 · Fr · BW · 89min

From René Clair, one of the great stylists of European cinema, comes this wistful, ironic and sexy fantasy about a shy young man who escapes his bleak life by dreaming of adventure and romantic encounters in different places at different historical periods. The star is the devastatingly handsome Gérard Philipe, one of France's great actors as well as the premier matinée idol of his generation. The main purveyors of feminine pulchritude in this dream-like film are Gina Lollobrigida and Martine Carol. RK French +subtitles.

Gérard Philipe *Claude* • Gina Lollobrigida *Leila* • Magali Vendeuil *Suzanne* • Marilyn Buferd *Bonny* • Raymond Cordy *Gaston* • Martine Carol *Edmée* ■ *Dir/Scr* René Clair

Belle's Magical World ★★U

Animated adventure   1997 · US · Colour · 67min

A quartet of simple, stand-alone stories continues the cartoon adventures of Belle and her enchanted friends in this second made-for-video spin-off from Disney's *Beauty and the Beast*. But while the Oscar-winning original was both charming and visually ambitious, the dull and poorly animated material presented here just smacks of cheap cash-in. SF

Paige O'Hara *Belle* • Robby Benson *Beast* • Jerry Orbach *Lumiere* • David Ogden Stiers *Cogsworth* • Anne Rogers *Mrs Potts* ■ *Dir* Cullen Blaine, Daniel de la Vega

The Belles of St Trinian's ★★★U

Comedy   1954 · UK · BW · 86min

Most people's memory of the *St Trinian's* films dates from their own youth, when the wonderful indiscipline of the tearaways and the debauched indifference of the staff had them longing for their own school to be run along similar lines. In 1954 nothing had ever been seen to compare with this anarchic adaptation of Ronald Searle's cartoons, which turned traditional ideas of female gentility on their heads. Alastair Sim's Miss Fritton and George Cole's Flash Harry became icons of British comic lore, but the real star of the film is Joyce Grenfell. Followed by *Blue Murder at St Trinian's*. DP *DVD* BL

Alastair Sim *Millicent Fritton/Clarence Fritton* • Joyce Grenfell *Sergeant Ruby Gates* • George Cole *Flash Harry* • Vivienne Martin *Arabella* • Eric Pohlmann *Sultan of Makyad* • Lorna Henderson *Princess Fatima* • Hermione Baddeley *Miss Drownder* • Betty Ann Davies *Miss Waters* ■ *Dir* Frank Launder • *Scr* Frank Launder, Sidney Gilliat, Val Valentine, from the drawings by Ronald Searle

Belles on Their Toes ★★★U

Comedy   1952 · US · Colour · 85min

A delightful and equally popular sequel to *Cheaper by the Dozen*, this has Edward Arnold romancing newly widowed Myrna Loy but not wanting to take her extraordinarily large family with him to the altar. Jeanne Crain heads up the brood and Clifton Webb appears briefly, so don't blink in the finale. Loy battles hard on her own in this early feminist tract, backed by a typical 1950s cast. TS *DVD*

Jeanne Crain *Ann Gilbreth* • Myrna Loy *Mrs Lillian Gilbreth* • Debra Paget *Martha* • Jeffrey Hunter *Dr Bob Grayson* • Edward Arnold *Sam Harper* • Hoagy Carmichael *Tom Bracken* • Barbara Bates *Ernestine* • Robert Arthur (1) *Frank Gilbreth* ■ *Dir* Henry Levin • *Scr* Phoebe Ephron, Henry Ephron, from a novel by Frank B Gilbreth Jr, Ernestine Gilbreth Carey

Belleville Rendez-vous ★★★★12

Animated adventure   2003 · Fr/Can/Bel/UK · Colour/BW · 77min

This animated adventure a graphic delight and a triumph of invention. Effortlessly combining slapstick, character quirk and nostalgia, it follows a club-footed grandmother and her pudgy mutt across the Atlantic as they attempt to rescue the cyclist grandson who has been kidnapped from the Tour de France by two sinister gangsters. Splendid set pieces abound and, while there's the occasional longueur, the throwaway gags and passing homages give this ambitious entertainment a unique charm. DP In French. *DVD* CS

■ *Dir/Scr* Sylvain Chomet

Bellissima ★★★PG

Drama   1951 · It · BW · 109min

Italian aristocrat Luchino Visconti is best known for his sumptuous, operatic approach in films such as *Senso* and *The Leopard*. His early career, however, saw him as a pioneer of neorealism, focusing on the harsh reality of working-class life. In this, his third feature film, the powerful, uninhibited Anna Magnani plays a mother from the slums attempting to get her small daughter into a film at Rome's Cinecittà studios. The portrayal of life in the contrasting worlds of the tenements and the film studio is fascinating. RK Italian +subtitles. *DVD*

Anna Magnani *Maddalena Cecconi* • Walter Chiari *Alberto Annovazzi* • Tina Apicella *Maria Cecconi* • Gastone Renzelli *Spartaco Cecconi* ■ *Dir* Luchino Visconti • *Scr* Suso Cecchi D'Amico, Francesco Rosi, Luchino Visconti, from the story by Cesare Zavattini

Bellman & True ★★★15

Crime thriller   1987 · UK · Colour · 121min

This low-budget British crime thriller proves that there's sentiment, if not honour, among thieves. Bernard Hill is the alcoholic computer ace, forever telling bedtime stories to his small stepson (Kieran O'Brien), who's leaned on by villains (Derek Newark, Richard Hope) to hack into a bank prior to a heist. Despite stereotypes – the sinisterly silken chief crook calls victims "Dear Heart" – this includes some great moments of tension, especially the tragicomic break-in. TH Swearing, violence. *DVD*

Bernard Hill *Hiller* • Derek Newark *Guv'nor* • Richard Hope *Salto* • Ken Bones *Gort* • Frances Tomelty *Anna* • Kieran O'Brien *Boy* • John Kavanagh *The Donkey* • Arthur Whybrow *The Peterman* ■ *Dir* Richard Loncraine • *Scr* Desmond Lowden, Richard Loncraine, Michael Wearing, from the novel by Desmond Lowden

Bells Are Ringing ★★★U

Musical comedy   1960 · US · Colour · 125min

Judy Holliday's Broadway performance as a telephone operator who becomes wrapped up in the lives of her callers was enshrined for ever when she repeated it in this sophisticated but lacklustre Vincente Minnelli musical. By the time this was made, MGM had lost its magic touch and it was a case of *The Party's Over* for its stylish brand of musical tonic. But there's still much pleasure to be had in watching the radiant Holliday in her last screen appearance before her tragically early death from cancer in 1965. TS

Judy Holliday *Ella Peterson* • Dean Martin *Jeffrey Moss* • Fred Clark *Larry Hastings* • Eddie Foy Jr Jr *Otto Prantz* • Jean Stapleton *Sue* • Ruth Storey *Gwynne* • Dort Clark *Inspector Barnes* • Frank

Gorshin *Blake Barton* ■ *Dir* Vincente Minnelli • *Scr* Betty Comden, Adolph Green, from the musical play by Betty Comden, Adolph Green, Jule Styne

The Bells Go Down ★★U

Comedy drama   1943 · UK · BW · 85min

From wartime days, when British film-makers thought the lower orders all spoke cockney and made cups of tea in times of crisis, comes this uneasy Ealing chronicle of the work of a London firefighting unit, which still fascinates for its social documentation and class conflict. As a tribute to the Auxiliary Fire Service, it has an embarrassingly contrived plot, but comedian Tommy Trinder and James Mason still manage to convince by sheer force of personality. TH

Tommy Trinder *Tommy Turk* • James Mason *Ted Robbins* • Philip Friend *Bob* • Mervyn Johns *Sam* • Billy Hartnell [William Hartnell] *Bookes* • Finlay Currie *Dist Officer MacFarlane* • Philippa Hiatt *Nan* • Meriel Forbes *Susie* ■ *Dir* Basil Dearden • *Scr* Roger MacDougall, from the novel by Stephen Black

Bells of Coronado ★★★

Musical western   1950 · US · Colour · 67min

It's business as usual for crooning cowboy Roy Rogers in this routine B-movie western. Here Rogers goes undercover for an insurance company to investigate the suspicious death of a mine owner. Despite lacking the power the plot deserves, it's an entertaining, easy-going yarn, with Rogers his usual energetic self and an array of cheerful songs and quirky characters. MF

Roy Rogers • Dale Evans *Pam Reynolds* • Pat Brady *Sparrow Biffle* • Grant Withers *Craig Bennett* ■ *Dir* William Witney • *Scr* Sloan Nibley

Bells of Rosarita ★★★

Western   1945 · US · BW · 68min

According to this offbeat Roy Rogers picture, cowboy stars are just as resourceful in real life as they are on screen. Rogers is making a western on location at a circus when he finds out the pretty owner (Dale Evans) is in danger of being cheated out of her property. Roy summons five of his fellow Republic stars to stage a benefit on her behalf and they end up corralling the bad guys. AE

Roy Rogers • George "Gabby" Hayes *Baggy Whittaker* • Dale Evans *Sue Farnum* • Adele Mara *Patty Phillips* • Wild Bill Elliott [Bill Elliott] • Allan "Rocky" Lane [Allan Lane] • Donald Barry • Robert Livingston • Sunset Carson ■ *Dir* Frank McDonald • *Scr* Jack Townley

The Bells of St Mary's ★★★U

Musical drama   1945 · US · BW · 125min

A massively popular success in its day, this pairs Bing Crosby with Ingrid Bergman. Crosby reprises the role that won him an Oscar, that of wise and lovable Father O'Malley from *Going My Way*. Today, Crosby's priest seems rather insufferable as he helps Sister Ingrid fix up her run-down mission with a bit of song and a lot of charm. Crosby fans will brook no arguments, of course, but others may feel director Leo McCarey has his tongue well and truly in his cheek and only made this for the money. TS *DVD*

Bing Crosby *Father O'Malley* • Ingrid Bergman *Sister Benedict* • Henry Travers *Mr Bogardus* • Joan Carroll *Patsy* • Martha Sleeper *Patsy's mother* • William Gargan *Joe Gallagher* • Ruth Donnelly *Sister Michael* • Dickie Tyler *Eddie* ■ *Dir* Leo McCarey • *Scr* Dudley Nichols, from a story by Leo McCarey

Bells of San Angelo ★★U

Western   1947 · US · Colour · 77min

This was the Republic studio movie intended to toughen up the image of Roy Rogers, whose hand-tailored outfits had never previously shown any signs of dirt, and whose morals outweighed his screen presence. Here, villain John McGuire actually beats up our hero, and, at last, in the fight sequences there's a realistic feeling of characters being hurt. Rogers

moves as comfortably in the action sequences as he does wielding a guitar. TS

Roy Rogers • Dale Evans *Lee Madison* • Andy Devine *Cookie* • John McGuire *Rex Gridley* • Olaf Hytten *Lionel Bates* ■ *Dir* William Witney • *Scr* Sloan Nibley

Belly ★★18

Crime thriller   1998 · US · Colour · 95min

This frenetic thriller, as directed by rap video film-maker Hype Williams, is all stuttering edits and flash visuals, as it tells of the decline and fall of two violent young black men (played by rap musicians Nas and DMX) in the last weeks of 1999. TH Swearing, violence.

Nas [Nasir Jones] *Sincere* • DMX [Earl Simmons] *Tommy Brown* • Taral Hicks *Kisha* • Tionne "T-Boz" Watkins *Tionne* • Method Man *Shameek* • Tyrin Turner *Big* ■ *Dir* Hype Williams • *Scr* Hype Williams, from a story by Anthony Bodden, Nas [Nasir Jones]

The Belly of an Architect ★★★15

Psychological drama   1987 · It/UK · Colour · 113min

This features Peter Greenaway's trademark strongly visual approach and multiple referencing to birth, death and the insubstantial human condition. Brian Dennehy stars as a self-obsessed American architect travelling to Italy to supervise an exhibition about an 18th-century French architect. His work is subverted by his preoccupation with his own stomach pains and with his wife Chloe Webb's attempts to conceive. This won't disappoint Greenaway fans, but others may prefer to avoid. LH

Brian Dennehy *Stourley Kracklite* • Chloe Webb *Louisa Kracklite* • Lambert Wilson *Caspasian Speckler* • Sergio Fantoni *Io Speckler* • Stefania Casini *Flavia Speckler* • Vanni Corbellini *Frederico* • Alfredo Varelli *Julio Ficcone* • Geoffrey Copleston *Caspetti* • Francesco Carnelutti *Pastarri* ■ *Dir/Scr* Peter Greenaway

Belly of the Beast ★★15

Action drama   2003 · Can/HK/UK · Colour · 87min

There's nothing particularly original or coherent about the plotline of this kidnap-rescue thriller starring Steven Seagal. However, the action, which sees ex-CIA agent Seagal out to rescue his daughter, receives a welcome infusion of panache from ace Hong Kong fight choreographer Tony Ching Siu-tung, who directs with a control and conviction that gives even the cheesiest wire-fu and bullet-time effects a touch of class. DP In English, Thai. Swearing, violence, sex scenes, nudity. *DVD*

Steven Seagal *Jake Hopper* • Byron Mann *Sunti* • Monica Lo *Lulu* • Tom Wu *General Jantapan* • Sarah Malukul Lane *Jessica Hopper* • Patrick Robinson *Leon Washington* • Vincent Riotta *Fitch McQuaid* ■ *Dir* Tony Ching Siu-tung [Ching Siu-Tung] • *Scr* James Townsend, from a story by Steven Seagal

Beloved ★★15

Period drama   1998 · US · Colour · 164min

Despite a strong lead performance from Oprah Winfrey, this gets bogged down in a laborious attempt to make something worthy. Winfrey is the ex-slave who killed her own daughter to prevent her being taken into slavery, only to have a young, childlike woman (Thandie Newton) turn up on her doorstep years later who seems to have all the characteristics of the child she killed. JB Violence, nudity.

Oprah Winfrey *Sethe* • Danny Glover *Paul D* • Thandie Newton *Beloved* • Kimberly Elise *Denver* • Beah Richards *Baby Suggs* • Lisa Gay Hamilton *Younger Sethe* • Albert Hall *Stamp Paid* ■ *Dir* Jonathan Demme • *Scr* Akosua Busia, Richard LaGravenese, Adam Brooks, from the novel by Toni Morrison

Beloved ★★15

Romantic musical drama   2011 · Fr/UK/Cz Rep · Colour · 138min

Catherine Deneuve and Chiara Mastroianni, mother and daughter in real life, find romantic conflict crossing generational lines in this melodrama with music from French writer/director Christophe Honoré. Spanning the decades, the action begins in late 1960s Paris with a younger Deneuve – played by Ludivine Sagnier – marrying a handsome yet feckless Czech doctor. Their daughter (a convincingly disturbed Mastroianni) grows up to have man trouble, too, falling for Paul Schneider's American musician. It's hard to fault the actors and it's moderately watchable, yet the heartstrings remain untouched. TJ In French, Czech, English. Swearing, sex scenes, nudity.

Chiara Mastroianni *Véra* • Catherine Deneuve *Madeleine* • Ludivine Sagnier *Young Madeleine* • Louis Garrel *Clément* • Milos Forman *Jaromil* • Paul Schneider (2) *Henderson* ■ *Dir/Scr* Christophe Honoré

Beloved Enemy ★★★U

Romantic drama　　1936 · US · BW · 82min

One of the few mainstream Hollywood movies to deal with the political upheaval in Ireland in the early part of the 20th century, this features top-billed Merle Oberon falling for Irish rebel leader Brian Aherne. Though the title's of literary derivation, the plot clearly isn't. Nevertheless, it's intelligent and well-made, and marked the movie debut of director HC ("Hank") Potter. TS

Merle Oberon *Helen Drummond* • Brian Aherne *Dennis Riordan* • Karen Morley *Cathleen* • Theodore von Eltz *O'Brian* • Jerome Cowan *O'Rourke* • David Niven *Gerald Preston* • John Burton *Hall* ■ *Dir* HC Potter • *Scr* John Balderston, Rose Franken, William Brown Meloney, David Hart, from a story by John Balderston

Beloved/Friend ★★★

Drama　　1998 · Sp · Colour · 91min

Catalan director Ventura Pons is renowned for ensemble pieces in which emotions are revealed through earnest conversation. Such is the case here, as a group of friends fall out over the contents of a dying academic's will. Adapted from his own play by Josep M Benet I Jornet, the action retains a staginess that enhances the airless atmosphere of this enclosed world. However, it's the intensity of the performances that really gives the intricate drama its fascination. DP Catalan +subtitles.

Josep Maria Pou [José Maria Pou] *Jaume Clara* • Rosa Maria Sarda *Fanny* • Mario Gas *Pere Roure* • David Selvas *David Vila* • Irene Montalà *Alba* ■ *Dir* Ventura Pons • *Scr* Josep M Benet I Jornet from his play *Testament*

Beloved Infidel ★★★

Romantic drama　　1959 · US · Colour · 122min

This screen version of Sheilah Graham's bestselling memoir is sunk by the staggering miscasting of Gregory Peck as F Scott Fitzgerald, though Deborah Kerr makes a brave stab at Graham. Director Henry King concentrates on the period feel, and the CinemaScope photography is stunning, but to no avail. Legend has it that Peck was annoyed that the first edit of the film favoured Kerr, and summoned brilliant film editor William Reynolds to see him. "Why do you think they pay me a fortune to do this?" demanded Peck. "I really can't imagine," replied Reynolds. TS

Gregory Peck *F Scott Fitzgerald* • Deborah Kerr *Sheilah Graham* • Eddie Albert *Carter* • Philip Ober *John Wheeler* • Herbert Rudley *Stan Harris* • John Sutton *Lord Donegal* • Karin Booth *Janet Pierce* • Ken Scott (1) *Robinson* ■ *Dir* Henry King • *Scr* Sy Bartlett, from the book by Sheilah Graham, Gerold Frank • *Cinematographer* Leon Shamroy

The Beloved Vagabond ★★U

Musical drama　　1936 · UK · BW · 73min

Made simultaneously in English and French, this take on a twice-filmed William J Locke novel was one of several Euro musicals that Maurice Chevalier made in the mid-30s after his Hollywood star began to fade. He scarcely convinces as an architect in London who resigns under a cloud after trying to help boss Charles Carson pay his debts, but he comes into his own on hitting

the open road in France with buddy Desmond Tester. While the songs aren't particularly memorable, Chevalier sells them with trademark insouciance. DP 📀

Maurice Chevalier *Gaston de Nera "Paragot"* • Betty Stockfeld *Joanna Rushworth* • Margaret Lockwood *Blanquette* • Desmond Tester *Asticot* • Charles Carson *Charles Rushworth* ■ *Dir* Kurt Bernhardt • *Scr* Kurt Bernhardt, Greta Heller, Wells Root, Arthur Wimperis, Walter Creighton, Hugh Mills, from the novel *Der Geliebte Vagabund* by William J Locke

Below ★★★15

Supernatural horror thriller　　2002 · US · Colour · 101min

A supernatural presence haunts an American submarine during the Second World War in director David Twohy's ghost tale. Or does it? After the USS *Tiger Shark* rescues three survivors from a torpedoed hospital ship, the low-key tension and claustrophobia mounts as the crew members attempt to conceal their dark, mutinous secrets against a battle-weary and psychologically intense backdrop. Twohy doesn't quite mine the creepy premise for all its macabre potential, but this will tingle undemanding spines. AJ Violence, swearing. 📀

Matt Davis [Matthew Davis] *Ensign Douglas O'Dell* • Bruce Greenwood *Lt Brice* • Olivia Williams *Claire Paige* • Holt McCallany *Loomis* • Scott Foley *Coors* • Zach Galifianakis *Weird Wally* • Jason Flemyng *Stumbo* • Dexter Fletcher *Kingsley* ■ *Dir* David Twohy • *Scr* Lucas Sussman, Darren Aronofsky, David Twohy

The Belstone Fox ★★PG

Drama　　1973 · UK · Colour · 98min

In this workmanlike adaptation of David Rook's novel, Eric Porter is the huntsman who adopts an abandoned fox cub and rears it with a litter of puppy hounds. When the hunting season starts, the fox reverts to its role as quarry and Porter lives to regret his moment of weakness. The film impresses more for its wildlife photography than for its dramatic interest. PF 📀

Eric Porter *Asher* • Rachel Roberts (1) *Cathie* • Jeremy Kemp *Kendrick* • Bill Travers *Tod* • Dennis Waterman *Stephen* ■ *Dir* James Hill • *Scr* James Hill, from the novel *Ballad of the Belstone Fox* by David Rook • *Cinematographers* John Wilcox, James Allen

Ben ★★

Horror　　1972 · US · Colour · 94min

This sequel to *Willard* is probably best known for its theme song (which was a hit for Michael Jackson), as few horror aficionados have much time for its unconvincing blend of gore and gushing sentimentality. Yet it's a polished piece of work, with Lee Harcourt Montgomery fine as the kid sheltering the rodent hordes, and Joseph Campanella business-like as the pursuing cop who discovers who is leading a pack of killer rats. DP

Lee Harcourt Montgomery [Lee Montgomery] *Danny Garrison* • Joseph Campanella *Cliff Kirtland* • Arthur O'Connell *Bill Hatfield* • Rosemary Murphy *Beth Garrison* • Meredith Baxter *Eve Garrison* • Kaz Garas *Joe Greer* • Paul Carr *Kelly* • Richard Van Fleet *Reade* ■ *Dir* Phil Karlson • *Scr* Gilbert A Ralston, from characters by Stephen Gilbert [Gilbert A Ralston]

Ben-Hur ★★★★★PG

Period epic　　1959 · US · Colour · 213min

Back in 1959, this epic was the most costly movie ever made. Many believe that it is not a match for the 1925 silent version, while it certainly lasts almost as long as the Roman Empire itself. Nor will it ever win any prizes for experimental film-making. But, never mind, enjoy Charlton Heston's chariot-driving, galley-rowing and toga-wearing, and, above all, feel the vital statistics. A thousand-strong force toiled for a year to construct the 18-acre chariot arena, which was eventually filled with 8,000 extras for the 20-minute race that forms the famous climax. The film, in all, used over 300 sets, 40,000 tons of sand (for the chariot track) and swept up a record 11 Oscars, a total that was equalled in 1998 by James Cameron's

Titanic and in 2004 by Peter Jackson's *The Return of the King*. PF 📀 ⬜

Charlton Heston *Ben-Hur* • Stephen Boyd *Messala* • Haya Harareet *Esther* • Jack Hawkins *Quintus Arrius* • Hugh Griffith *Sheik Ilderim* • Martha Scott *Miriam* • Cathy O'Donnell *Tirzah* • Frank Thring *Pontius Pilate* • Sam Jaffe *Simonides* • Finlay Currie *Balthasar* ■ *Dir* William Wyler • *Scr* Karl Tunberg, from the novel by Lew Wallace • *Music* Miklos Rozsa • *Cinematographer* Robert L Surtees [Robert Surtees] • *Special Effects* A Arnold Gillespie, Robert MacDonald, Milo Lory • *Art Directors* Edward Carfagno, William A Horning • *Costume Designer* Elizabeth Haffenden • *Editors* Ralph E Winters, John Dunning

Ben-Hur

Period epic　　2016 · US · Colour

This is a preview – no prints were available to review prior to publication: A retelling of the story of Judah Ben-Hur, the Jewish nobleman sold into slavery who fights his way back to take his revenge. With both the 1925 film, starring Ramon Novarro, and the 1959 Charlton Heston version seen as classics, this looks like an act of mad bravado by all concerned. But with action ace Timur Bekmambetov (*Night Watch*) at the helm and rising star Jack Huston in the lead role, it's going to be interesting at the very least. And what will Bekmambetov do with the iconic chariot race? SvM 🇪🇸

Jack Huston *Judah Ben-Hur* • Toby Kebbell *Messala* • Morgan Freeman *Ildarim* • Nazanin Boniadi *Esther* ■ *Dir* Timur Bekmambetov • *Scr* Keith R Clarke, John Ridley, from the novel *Ben-Hur, a Tale of the Christ* by Lew Wallace

Ben-Hur: a Tale of the Christ ★★★★★PG

Silent period epic　　1925 · US · BW and Colour · 142min

A landmark movie in every respect, this story of the friendship and hatred between a Jew and a Roman allowed for plenty of moralising as well as rousing action scenes. Lew Wallace's novel – a Victorian potboiler – had been a Broadway hit and MGM almost broke the bank buying the rights. Filming was due to begin in Italy with George Walsh as Ben-Hur, under the direction of Charles Brabin. But the footage was so terrible MGM junked everything and fired Walsh. He was replaced by Ramon Novarro, and Fred Niblo took over as director. The result flabbergasted critics and audiences alike, but its final cost of $4 million was too much to see any profit. AT

Ramon Novarro *Ben-Hur* • Francis X Bushman *Messala* • May McAvoy *Esther* • Betty Bronson *Mary* • Claire McDowell *Princess of Hur* • Kathleen Key *Tirzah* ■ *Dir* Fred Niblo • *Scr* Bess Meredyth, Carey Wilson, June Mathis, from the novel by Lew Wallace

Ben X ★★★15

Drama　　2007 · Bel/Neth/Rom · Colour · 89min

Ben (Greg Timmermans) is a bullied teenager with Asperger's syndrome. But Ben X, his digital alter ego, is a troll-slaying warrior in an online fantasy world, where a lack of social skills isn't an impediment. Belgian writer/director Nic Balthazar offers a moving portrait of autism, placing us in his character's head through some jittery and disorientating camerawork. Loosely based on a true story, the film builds steadily as young Ben begins to lose touch with reality, imagining his playground tormentors as evil trolls. A series of talking-head interviews with his family and teachers prepare us for the inevitably bloody conclusion, until Balthazar hoodwinks us with an unexpected – and ambiguous – finale. JR Dutch +subtitles. 📀

Greg Timmermans *Ben* • Laura Verlinden *Scarlite* • Marijke Pinoy *Mother* • Pol Goossen *Father* • Titus De Voogdt *Bogaert* • Maarten Claeyssens *Desmet* ■ *Dir* Nic Balthazar • *Scr* Nic Balthazar, from his novel *Niets Is Alles Wat Hij Zei*

The Benchwarmers ★★12

Sports comedy　　2006 · US · Colour · 85min

This gross-out comedy stars Rob Schneider, David Spade and Jon Heder as childhood victims of bullies who must defeat the

current offenders in the neighbourhood – at baseball. To succeed, they enlist the help of billionaire super-nerd Jon Lovitz, who puts up the money for a tournament. There is some snappy dialogue, but the direction is uneven and the pacing saggy. KK 📀

Rob Schneider *Gus Matthews* • David Spade *Richie Goodman* • Jon Heder *Clark* • Jon Lovitz *Mel* • Craig Kilborn *Coach Jerry* • Molly Sims *Liz Matthews* • Tim Meadows *Coach Wayne* • Nick Swardson *Howie* ■ *Dir* Dennis Dugan • *Scr* Allen Covert, Nick Swardson

Bend It like Beckham ★★★12

Sports comedy drama　　2001 · Ger/UK · Colour · 107min

This feel-good teen-orientated comedy drama has two things going for it, besides its opportunistic title: it's set in the world of female football and against a background of intransigent first-generation Indian tradition in suburban Britain. Newcomer Parminder Nagra is skilled in both acting and ball-control as the teenager who "worships" at her shrine to England captain David Beckham, and culture clashes are played with knowing humour. But the predictability of the storyline and wooden co-star Keira Knightley let this down. AC Swearing. 📀 ⬜

Parminder Nagra *Jess Bhamra* • Keira Knightley *Jules* • Jonathan Rhys Meyers *Joe* • Anupam Kher *Mr Bhamra* • Archie Panjabi *Pinky Bhamra* • Juliet Stevenson *Paula* ■ *Dir* Gurinder Chadha • *Scr* Guljit Bindra, Gurinder Chadha, Paul Mayeda Berges

Bend of the River ★★★★PG

Western　　1952 · US · Colour · 87min

This is a magnificent western, one of a superb postwar series of films starring James Stewart and directed by Anthony Mann. Here, Stewart is a wagon train scout trying to hide his past, pitted against former partner Arthur Kennedy in a story that takes on the dimensions of Greek tragedy. Watch, too, for an early star-making performance from Rock Hudson, who forms a bond with reformed outlaw Stewart. A satisfying work, with action sequences and performances that repay several viewings. TS 📀

James Stewart *Glyn McLyntock* • Arthur Kennedy *Cole Garett* • Rock Hudson *Trey Wilson* • Julia Adams [Julie Adams] *Laura Baile* • Lori Nelson *Marjie* • Stepin' Fetchit [Stepin Fetchit] *Adam* ■ *Dir* Anthony Mann • *Scr* Borden Chase, from the novel *Bend of the Snake* by Bill Gulick

Benda Bilili! ★★★★12

Music documentary　　2010 · Congo/Fr · Colour · 82min

Few rags-to-riches documentaries can match this profile of the Congolese busking band Staff Benda Bilili, as it charts the group's rise from the depths of poverty in Kinshasa to wow audiences on its first European tour. The combo (most of whom are paraplegic) perfected a catchy blend of samba and rhythm 'n' blues that became even more distinctive after recruiting 13-year-old street kid Roger Landu, who plays a stringed instrument fashioned from a curved piece of wood and an empty tin can. Four years of interminable struggle pass before the band finally gets its shot at the big time. The concerts are exhilarating, but it's the footage of Benda Bilili's humble origins that has a lasting impact. DP Lingala, French +subtitles. 📀 ⬜

■ *Dir/Scr* Renaud Barret, Florent de la Tullaye

Beneath ★★15

Horror thriller　　2007 · US · Colour · 78min

The MTV production team behind this slow-paced and cheap-looking psychological horror are desperate for it to be creepy. But it's so heavy-handed in every respect that any hint of atmosphere is quickly lost, as supposedly traumatised 20-something Nora Zehetner returns to her home town six years after her sister's death, convinced that the young woman was buried alive. A game-changing climax perks up the final act, though anyone who's watched a few chillers will know what's coming. **SF**

Nora Zehetner *Christy* • Carly Pope *Vanessa* • Matthew Settle *John* • Jessica Amlee *Amy* ■ *Dir* Dagen Merrill • *Scr* Kevin Burke, Dagen Merrill

B

Beneath the Planet of the Apes ★★★15

Science-fiction adventure
1969 · US · Colour · 90min

The first sequel to the enormously successful *Planet of the Apes* is also the best. Less subtle and profound than its predecessor, it's still an exciting and colourful action adventure. This time out, astronaut James Franciscus and chimpanzee scientist Kim Hunter search for Charlton Heston (star of the first film) in the nuclear-devastated future, evading militaristic apes only to stumble upon an underground community of mutant, telepathic humans. Three more progressively silly sequels followed, with *Escape from the Planet of the Apes* (1971) the next in the series. **AJ** Violence. **DVD**

James Franciscus *Brent* • Charlton Heston *Taylor* • Kim Hunter *Dr Zira* • Maurice Evans *Dr Zaius* • Linda Harrison *Nova* • Paul Richards (1) *Mendez* • Victor Buono *Fat man* • James Gregory *Ursus* • Roddy McDowall *Narrator* ■ *Dir* Ted Post • *Scr* Paul Dehn, from a story by Mort Abrahams, Paul Dehn, from characters by Pierre Boulle

Beneath the 12-Mile Reef ★★U

Adventure 1953 · US · Colour · 100min

Having already shot the Crucifixion (*The Robe*) and Marilyn Monroe (*How to Marry a Millionaire*) in CinemaScope, 20th Century-Fox took its new wonder process underwater for this scuba-frolic. Robert Wagner cuts a dash as a sponge diver, Gilbert Roland is his dad, Terry Moore is the love interest, Richard Boone the heavy and an octopus shows up when the plot begins to leak. **AT DVD**

Robert Wagner *Tony Petrakis* • Gilbert Roland *Mike Petrakis* • J Carrol Naish *Soak* • Richard Boone *Thomas Rhys* • Harry Carey Jr *Griff Rhys* • Terry Moore *Gwyneth Rhys* • Peter Graves (2) *Arnold* • Angela Clarke *Mama* ■ *Dir* Robert D Webb • *Scr* Al Bezzerides

Beneath the Valley of the Ultra Vixens ★★★18

Cult sex comedy 1979 · US · Colour · 92min

This quintessential sex comedy is Russ Meyer's last movie to date as director, and it's all here: comic violence, insatiable busty women, religion, necrophilia, impotent bumbling men, chainsaws and Martin Bormann. The plot revolves around stripper Kitten Natividad's attempts to steer her husband away from perversion, with Anne Marie and Uschi Digard along for the rollercoaster ride through Meyer's lusty small-town landscape. The director plays himself in this satirical semi-autobiography, which has a strong moral code at its soft-core centre. **AJ DVD**

Francesca "Kitten" Natividad [Kitten Natividad] *Lavonia/Lola Langusta* • Anne Marie *Eufaula Roop* • Ken Kerr *Lamar Shedd* • June Mack *"Junk-yard" Sal* • Uschi Digard *Supersoul* ■ *Dir* Russ Meyer • *Scr* Roger Ebert, Russ Meyer

The Benefactor ★★15

Drama 2015 · US · Colour · 88min

Richard Gere is still a leading man of some stature and it's his show, in this good-looking but unfocused drama, playing a wealthy but guilt-wracked philanthropist who returns to public life after withdrawing for five years following the death of his married best friends. When their orphaned daughter (Dakota Fanning) re-enters his life, he is unable to resist using his money to improve her lot, but altruism swiftly turns to suffocating omnipresence. The only problem is, Fanning has so little meat to her role, she ends up a cipher to Gere. **JA** Swearing, drug abuse. **DVD**

Richard Gere *Franny* • Theo James *Luke* • Dakota Fanning *Olivia* • Cheryl Hines *Mia* • Dylan Baker *Bobby* ■ *Dir/Scr* Andrew Renzi

Benefit of the Doubt ★★★18

Thriller 1993 · US/Ger · Colour · 87min

This modest, occasionally gripping little thriller manages some neat variations on a familiar theme. An almost unrecognisable Amy Irving is the struggling single mum who is less than enamoured when she learns that her father (Donald Sutherland) is about to be released from prison, particularly because it was her testimony as a child that convicted him of the murder of her mother. The two leads, particularly the ambivalent Sutherland, are good, but the film is let down by a half-hearted climax. **JF** Violence, swearing, nudity.

Donald Sutherland *Frank Braswell* • Amy Irving *Karen Braswell* • Rider Strong *Pete Braswell* • Christopher McDonald *Dan* • Graham Greene (2) *Sheriff Calhoun* • Theodore Bikel *Gideon Lee* • Gisele Kovach *Susanna* • Ferdinand Mayne [Ferdy Mayne] *Mueller* • Julie Hasel *Young Karen* ■ *Dir* Jonathan Heap • *Scr* Christopher Keyser, Jeffrey Polman, Michael Lieber

Bengazi ★★

Adventure 1955 · US · BW · 79min

Richard Conte here makes the most of a script that seems content to rehash a job-lot of clichés and assorted dead ends. Recalling his peak of fame as a hard-nut gangster, Conte is energetically gritty playing an unsavoury character trying to unearth hidden gold in North Africa. Sadly, director John Brahm's laudable attempts at style are punctured by moments of unplanned hilarity. **JM**

Richard Conte *Gilmore* • Victor McLaglen *Donovan* • Richard Carlson *Levering* • Mala Powers *Aileen Donovan* • Richard Erdman *Selby* • Hillary Brooke *Nora* • Maury Hill *Peters* • Jay Novello *Basim* • Albert Carrier *MacMillan* ■ *Dir* John Brahm • *Scr* Endre Bohem, Louis Vittes, from a story by Jeff Bailey

Benjamin Britten: Peace and Conflict ★★★PG

Drama documentary
2013 · UK/Aus/Fin/Nor · Colour · 108min

Released to mark the centenary of Benjamin Britten's birth, this is a sincere and informed, if frequently random, profile of one of this country's greatest composers. Already a prodigious talent by the time he enrolled at Gresham's School in Norfolk in 1928, Britten acquired the abhorrence of violence that made him a committed opponent of blood sports and an avowed pacifist. Director Tony Britten (no relation) mixes expert analysis, archive material and reverential performance with dramatic reconstruction, but falls prey to meandering anecdotes and mawkish symbolism. **DP**

John Hurt *Narrator* • Alex Lawther *Benjamin Britten* • Christopher Theobold *Donald Maclean* ■ *Dir/Scr* Tony Britten

Benji ★★★Uc

Adventure 1974 · US · Colour · 85min

So what if the production values are shoddy, the kids can't act and the plot was old hat when Rin Tin Tin was a pup. This is a cheer-to-the-rafters adventure, thanks to the exuberant ingenuity and adorably expressive face of a mongrel called Higgins. A veteran of TV's *Petticoat Junction*, the 18-year-old dog was brought out of retirement for this role of a lifetime, as the family pet who foils a kidnapping attempt. Benji pulls off a series of truly amazing tricks that won him the Georgie for the animal act of the year. A first sequel, *For the Love of Benji*, followed in 1977. **DP**

Patsy Garrett *Mary* • Allen Fiuzat *Paul* • Cynthia Smith *Cindy* • Peter Breck *Dr Chapman* • Edgar Buchanan *Bill* ■ *Dir* Joe Camp

Benji the Hunted ★★U

Adventure 1987 · US · Colour · 85min

A litter of cuddly cougar cubs comes close to upstaging our cute hero in the fourth film in the Benji series. It was made seven years after *Oh, Heavenly Dog!*, but the passage of time did little to refresh director Joe Camp's imagination, as the plot is nothing more than a cross-breed between a Lassie movie and Disney adventures.

However, with a shipwreck, a trek through the wilderness and a series of murderous attacks, it's packed with enough incident to retain the interest of children. Camp directed a further sequel, *Benji: Off the Leash*, 17 years later. **DP DVD**

Red Steagall *Hunter* • Nancy Francis *Newscaster* • Frank Inn • Mike Francis *TV cameraman* ■ *Dir/Scr* Joe Camp

Benny & Jolene ★★15

Comedy 2014 · UK · Colour · 87min

This slight comedy follows the fortunes of a winsome teenage indie folk duo (Craig Roberts and Charlotte Ritchie), catapulted into the spotlight when their debut single becomes a surprise chart-topper. The improvised "mockumentary" style makes comparisons to *This Is Spinal Tap* inevitable, but here the parodying of the superficial music industry rarely convinces, as one lazy stereotype after another is wheeled out. The best lines are delivered by Dolly Wells as Ritchie's mother. **TeS** Swearing, sexual references.

Charlotte Ritchie *Jolene* • Craig Roberts *Benny* • Rosamund Hanson *Nadia* • Dolly Wells *Rosamund* ■ *Dir/Scr* Jamie Adams

Benny & Joon ★★★12

Comedy drama 1993 · US · Colour · 94min

You'll either find this so-so romantic fable a whimsical joy or annoyingly eccentric, as beguiling man-child Johnny Depp woos unstable Mary Stuart Masterson, much to her brother's concern. It's one of those "lunatics are saner than the rest of us" polemics: heartfelt, but too underwritten to put its message across properly. However, the performances do wonders in papering over the credibility gaps, and Depp's silent movie skills are truly remarkable. **AJ DVD**

Johnny Depp *Sam* • Mary Stuart Masterson *Joon Pearl* • Aidan Quinn *Benny Pearl* • Julianne Moore *Ruthie* • Oliver Platt *Eric* • CCH Pounder *Doctor Garvey* • Dan Hedaya *Thomas* • Joe Grifasi *Mike* • William H Macy *Randy Burch* ■ *Dir* Jeremiah Chechik • *Scr* Barry Berman, from a story by Barry Berman, Leslie McNeil

The Benny Goodman Story ★★U

Musical biography 1955 · US · Colour · 116min

Universal had a surprise smash hit with *The Glenn Miller Story* and this forlorn follow-up proved that lightning doesn't strike twice, despite the great Benny himself playing clarinet to Steve Allen's miming. TV chat show host Allen lacks both the screen charisma and acting experience to make this involving, even though he's surrounded by real-life musicians and has Donna Reed as co-star. **TS**

Steve Allen *Benny Goodman* • Donna Reed *Alice Hammond* • Berta Gersten *Mom Goodman* • Herbert Anderson *John Hammond* • Robert F Simon *Pop Goodman* • Sammy Davis Sr *Fletcher Henderson* • Dick Winslow *Gil Rodin* ■ *Dir/Scr* Valentine Davies

Benny's Video ★★★★15

Drama 1992 · Austria/Swi · Colour · 105min

The desensitising nature of popular culture is a theme that recurs throughout most of Michael Haneke's films, but rarely has it been more chillingly debated than in this almost nonchalant study of dysfunction and death. Technically, the tactic of viewing the world through a camcorder lens may not be original. But the dispassionate way in which Arno Frisch – a spoiled but neglected teenager who subsists on violent movies – murders the stranger he has lured to the family home is as stupefyingly horrific as the callous passivity with which his parents learn of the crime. A subtly disturbing experience. **DP** German +subtitles. **DVD**

Arno Frisch *Benny* • Angela Winkler *Mother* • Ulrich Mühe *Father* • Ingrid Stassner *Young girl* ■ *Dir/Scr* Michael Haneke

Bent ★★18

Drama 1996 · UK/US/Jpn · Colour · 100min

Lothaire Bluteau and Clive Owen star as fellow prisoners and lovers against the background of the appallingly cruel

conditions of the Nazi concentration camps. Martin Sherman adapted his own West End play about Nazi homophobia and persecution, while theatre stalwart Sean Mathias directs. Mathias fails to give the film any emotional urgency, so it's the actors, including Ian McKellen, who have to carry the main burden. They stagger a bit, but provide the impetus the direction lacks. **TH** Violence, swearing, sex scenes. **DVD BL**

Lothaire Bluteau *Horst* • Clive Owen *Max* • Ian McKellen *Uncle Freddie* • Mick Jagger *Greta/George* • Brian Webber *Rudy* • Nikolaj Waldau [Nikolaj Coster-Waldau] *Wolf* • Jude Law *Stormtrooper* ■ *Dir* Sean Mathias • *Scr* Martin Sherman

Bent Keltoum ★★★

Drama 2001 · Tun/Fr/Bel · Colour · 116min

Despite its surface superficiality, the story of a Swiss-based model who returns to her Saharan homeland to discover why she was abandoned for adoption has much to say about the social mores and grinding poverty that exist in northern Africa. Director Mehdi Charef takes a chance in allowing Cylia Malki to adopt such a superior attitude towards her compatriots, as her disregard for their basic amenities and traditional customs frequently appears supercilious. But the relentless depiction of deprivation and the humanity of the Maghreb locals root this in a reality beyond the travelogue visuals. **DP** French, Arabic +subtitles.

Cylia Malki *Rallia* • Baya Belal *Nedjma* • Jean-Roger Milo *Djibril* • Deborah Lamy *Kaltoum* ■ *Dir/Scr* Mehdi Charef

Benzina ★★★15

Crime thriller 2001 · It · Colour · 85min

Monica Stambrini's adaptation is more concerned with exposing intolerance within Italian society than with exploring the seemingly disparate personalities of mousy Regina Orioli and her mechanic lover Maya Sansa. The action opens with the accidental death of Orioli's disapproving mother and alternates between the couple's desire to dump the body and embark on a new life and their encounters on the road with a thuggish twosome, whose voyeuristic girlfriend films their increasingly hostile antics. It's packed with incident and ideas, but it's also decidedly inconsistent. **DP** Italian +subtitles. Swearing, sex scenes. **DVD**

Maya Sansa *Stella* • Regina Orioli *Lenni* • Mariella Valentini *Lenni's mother* • Chiara Conti *Pippi* • Marco Quaglia *Sandro* • Pietro Ragusa *Filippo* • Luigi Maria Burruano *Padre Gabriele* ■ *Dir* Monica Lisa Stambrini • *Scr* Monica Stambrini, Elena Stancanelli, AnneRitte Ciccone, from the novel by Elena Stancanelli

Beowulf ★★★★12

Animated fantasy adventure
2007 · US · Colour · 109min

Myth and technology combine in this spectacular animated fantasy that reworks the English language's oldest surviving poem using 21st-century computer power. As in *The Polar Express*, director Robert Zemeckis employs "performance capture" techniques to turn his cast – including Ray Winstone and Anthony Hopkins – into digital avatars. The entertaining script by Neil Gaiman (*Stardust*) and *Pulp Fiction* co-writer Roger Avary adds a bold new dimension to the story of Beowulf's battle against the monstrous Grendel in 6th-century Denmark. Zemeckis creates a dark fantasy full of haunting images, not least Angelina Jolie's sultry turn as Grendel's demonic mother. **JR DVD BL**

Ray Winstone *Beowulf* • Angelina Jolie *Grendel's mother* • Crispin Hellion Glover [Crispin Glover] *Grendel* • Anthony Hopkins *King Hrothgar* • John Malkovich *Unferth* • Robin Wright Penn [Robin Wright] *Queen Wealthow* • Chris Coppola *Olaf* • Brendan Gleeson *Wiglaf* • Alison Lohman *Ursula* ■ *Dir* Robert Zemeckis • *Scr* Neil Gaiman, Roger Avary, from the epic poem by Anonymous • *Cinematographer* Robert Presley

Bequest to the Nation ★★

Historical drama   1972 · UK · Colour · 116min

Though lofty in tone, playwright Terence Rattigan's account of the relationship between Lord Nelson and Lady Hamilton reduces it to the Trafalgar hero's "little bit on the side". Fine performances by Peter Finch as Nelson and Glenda Jackson as Hamilton do little to animate the walking-waxworks style of what amounts to video history. **TH**

Glenda Jackson *Lady Emma Hamilton* • Peter Finch *Lord Horatio Nelson* • Michael Jayston *Captain Hardy* • Anthony Quayle *Lord Minto* • Margaret Leighton *Lady Frances Nelson* • Dominic Guard *Master George Matcham Jr* • Nigel Stock *George Matcham Sr* • Barbara Leigh-Hunt *Catherine "Catty" Matcham* ■ *Dir* James Cellan Jones • *Scr* Terence Rattigan, from his play

Berberian Sound Studio ★★★★ 15

Horror   2012 · UK · Colour · 88min

A shy sound engineer (a masterfully restrained Toby Jones) leaves Dorking and nature documentaries to work for the Italian exploitation industry in this evocative celebration and sly deconstruction of 1970s Eurotrash horror. Soon life begins to imitate art for Jones, as sonic realities shift and professional bewilderment gives way to witchcraft mayhem. Director Peter Strickland cleverly forces the viewer to question what they are hearing and how it links into Jones's spiralling nightmare, while every sound effect reverberates with multiple meanings. **AJ** *DVD* *BL*

Toby Jones *Gilderoy* • Tonia Sotiropoulou *Elena* • Cosimo Fusco *Francesco Coraggio* • Antonio Mancino *Santini* • Fatma Mohamed *Silvia* • Susanna Cappellaro *Veronica* ■ *Dir/Scr* Peter Strickland

Berkeley Square ★★★★ U

Period romantic fantasy   1933 · US · BW · 89min

Leslie Howard is so entranced by the early 18th-century diaries of his namesake ancestor that he takes on his identity and finds himself transported back to a periwigged past, where he consorts with the likes of Sir Joshua Reynolds. This quaint and delightful fantasy, ornamented with immaculate and sumptuous period detail, has Howard repeating the role he created on Broadway with all the polished elegance and poetic presence that made him a star of stage and screen. The accomplished direction is by Scottish-born Frank Lloyd. **RK**

Leslie Howard *Peter Standish* • Heather Angel *Helen Pettigrew* • Valerie Taylor *Kate Pettigrew* • Irene Browne *Lady Ann Pettigrew* • Beryl Mercer *Mrs Barwick* • Colin Keith-Johnston *Tom Pettigrew* • Alan Mowbray *Maj Clinton* • Lionel Belmore *Innkeeper* ■ *Dir* Frank Lloyd • *Scr* Sonya Levien, John L Balderston, from the play by John L Balderston

Berlin ★★★★ 12

Concert documentary
2007 · US/Ger · Colour · 80min

Lou Reed's concept album *Berlin* flopped spectacularly on its original release in 1973. More than three decades later, Reed showed his confidence in the material by performing it live for the first time at a series of gigs in Brooklyn, New York. Julian Schnabel's film showcases the proficiency of Reed's band and the strikingly contemporary feel of both the music and the lyrics, although it's slightly less successful at capturing the visceral power of the concerts. In addition to such album highlights as *How Do You Think It Feels* and *The Bed*, Reed also throws in renditions of *Rock Minuet* and *Candy Says*. **DP** *DVD*

Lou Reed • Emmanuelle Seigner *Caroline* ■ *Dir* Julian Schnabel • *Cinematographer* Ellen Kuras

Berlin Alexanderplatz ★★★

Drama   1931 · Ger · BW · 90min

With sound still in its infancy, it was the visual aspect of this adaptation of Alfred Döblin's sprawling novel that made the greatest impression, even though the author co-wrote the screenplay. Clearly influenced by the "city symphony" style so popular in the late silent era, director Phil Jutzi captures the sights and rhythms of Berlin with a vibrancy that stands in stark contrast to the grim Depression existence of reformed criminal Heinrich George, whose obsession with Margarete Schlegel prompts him to return to his wicked ways. **DP** German +subtitles.

Heinrich George *Franz Bieberkopf* • Bernhard Minetti *Reinhold* • Margarete Schlegel *Mieze* • Albert Florath *Pums* • Paul Westermeier *Henschke* ■ *Dir* Phil Jutzi • *Scr* Alfred Döblin, Hans Wilhelm, from the novel by Alfred Döblin

Berlin Alexanderplatz ★★★★★ 15

Drama   1980 · W Ger/It · Colour · 902min

Originally screened as a 13-part TV series, this epic study of sexual obsession is far superior to Phil Jutzi's 1931 version, even though Alfred Döblin, who wrote the source novel, was among that film's scriptwriters. The book was Rainer Werner Fassbinder's lifelong inspiration and his fascination with its themes and central character, Franz Biberkopf, is evident from the deeply personal epilogue. As played by Günther Lamprecht, Biberkopf is the plaything of a callous society that would rather destroy him than allow him to thrive as an individual. A remarkable undertaking that has to be seen. **DP** German +subtitles. *DVD*

Hanna Schygulla *Eva* • Günther Lamprecht [Günter Lamprecht] *Franz Biberkopf* • Franz Buchrieser *Meck* • Gottfried John *Reinhold* • Barbara Sukowa *Mieze* • Peter Kolleck *Nachum* • Elisabeth Trissenaar *Lina* • Brigitte Mira *Frau Bast* • Hans Zander *Eliser* • Mechthild Grossmann *Paula* • Karin Baal *Minna* ■ *Dir* Rainer Werner Fassbinder • *Scr* Rainer Werner Fassbinder, from the novel by Alfred Döblin

Berlin Correspondent ★★ U

Second World War spy drama
1942 · US · BW · 69min

This routine, low-budget wartime espionage drama is set in the days before Pearl Harbor, with Dana Andrews as an American radio journalist in Berlin whose broadcasts contain coded information about Nazi plans. He is rumbled by beautiful Virginia Gilmore who, naturally, is about to forsake her Nazi beliefs. **AT**

Virginia Gilmore *Karen Hauen* • Dana Andrews *Bill Roberts* • Mona Maris *Carla* • Martin Kosleck *Captain von Rau* • Sig Rumann [Sig Ruman] *Dr Dietrich* • Kurt Katch *Weiner* • Erwin Kalser *Mr Hauen* • Hans Schumm *Gunther* ■ *Dir* Eugene Forde • *Scr* Steve Fisher, Jack Andrews

Berlin Express ★★★

Spy thriller   1948 · US · BW · 86min

The nondescript title hides a really tense suspense tale from talented cult director Jacques Tourneur, in his *film noir* period before he hit his swashbuckling stride with *The Flame and the Arrow* and *Anne of the Indies*. Paul Lukas plays the suave German democrat kidnapped by an underground group of Nazis opposed to the unification of their country. Merle Oberon and the impressive Robert Ryan star as the fellow travellers who become involved in the plot. The Nazis are strictly clichéd, but the view of postwar Germany rings very true and Tourneur keeps up the tension throughout. **TS** In English, German, French, Russian.

Merle Oberon *Lucienne Mirbeau* • Robert Ryan *Robert Lindley* • Charles Korvin *Henri Perrot* • Paul Lukas *Dr Heinrich Bernhardt* • Robert Coote *James Sterling* ■ *Dir* Jacques Tourneur • *Scr* Harold Medford, from a story by Curt Siodmak

Berlin Jerusalem ★★★

Drama   1989 · Fr/Is/Neth/UK · Colour · 89min

Israeli director Amos Gitai's film may be an uphill struggle for many viewers, but it's still a fascinating attempt to depict the lives and friendship of two little-known, real-life women in the 1920s and 1930s: the German poet Else Lasker-Schüler and the Russian revolutionary Tania Shochat. The ambition often outpaces the technique, but Gitai is helped by the sheer artistry of cinematographer Henri Alekan. **TS** German, Hebrew +subtitles.

Lisa Kreuzer *Else* • Rivka Neuman *Tania* • Markus Stockhausen *Ludwig* • Vernon Dobtcheff *Editor* • Veronica Lazare [Veronica Lazar] *Secretary* • Bernard Eisenschitz *Man in Berlin café* ■ *Dir* Amos Gitai • *Scr* Amos Gitai, Gudie Lawaeyz

Berlin: Symphony of a Great City ★★★★★

Experimental silent documentary
1927 · Ger · BW · 77min

As with so much in German silent cinema, this artistic masterpiece was conceived by the screenwriter Carl Mayer, who was to disassociate himself from the project when director Walter Ruttman opted for an abstract, rather than a sociological, approach. Applying still novel theories of montage to Karl Freund's vibrant imagery, Ruttman created a rhythmical portrait of the city, which seems to last a day, but was, in fact, the product of 18 months of candid photography. Dropping in on various workplaces and night spots, the film pulses with life and remains as inventive and viscerally thrilling as it must have seemed in 1927. **DP**

■ *Dir* Walter Ruttmann • *Scr* Walter Ruttmann, Karl Freund, from an idea by Carl Mayer

The Bermuda Mystery ★★

Crime mystery   1944 · US · BW · 65min

This watchable little 1940s B-movie is the usual mixture of murder and money, featuring the rather too stolid Preston Foster in the lead and an interesting support cast. Ann Rutherford, perhaps best known as Polly Benedict in the Andy Hardy films, makes a charming leading lady, while the rather camp Charles Butterworth gives added value. **TS**

Preston Foster *Steve Carromond* • Ann Rutherford *Constance Martin* • Charles Butterworth *Dr Tilford* • Helene Reynolds *Angela* • Jean Howard *Mrs Tilford* • Richard Lane *Detective Donovan* • Roland Drew *Mr Best* ■ *Dir* Benjamin Stoloff [Ben Stoloff] • *Scr* W Scott Darling, from a story by John Larkin

Bermuda Triangle ★★

Mystery adventure   1996 · US · Colour · 96min

British TV exile Ian Toynton (*Minder, Bergerac, The Sweeney*) makes a decent fist of this sci-fi variation on *Swiss Family Robinson*, but he simply didn't have the budget to make it credible. Stephen McPherson and Elizabeth Bradley's storyline is reasonably ingenious, as it shifts a New York family from their Bermudian cruise on to an uncharted island in the 27th Dimension. There they encounter strangers from various times and places who have similarly fallen victim to the mysterious Triangle. Watch out for a young Naomi Watts, appearing here a decade before *King Kong*. **DP**

Sam Behrens *Dr John Everman* • Susanna Thompson *Dr Grace Everman* • David Gallagher *Sam Everman* • Lisa Jakub *Annie Everman* • Michael Reilly Burke *Michael* • Jerry Hardin *Slick* • Naomi Watts *Amanda* • Dennis Neal *Calvin* ■ *Dir* Ian Toynton • *Scr* Stephen McPherson, Elizabeth Bradley

Bernard and Doris ★★★ 15

Biographical drama
2006 · US/UK · Colour · 102min

In 1993, the story of billionaire tobacco heiress Doris Duke and her gay, Irish butler Bernard Lafferty created a flood of tabloid headlines after her will made him into a millionaire. But was it an act of love, or could she have been manipulated, or worse? This semi-fictionalised account of the pair's relationship turns their unlikely friendship into an impressive, if sluggish, showcase for an Emmy-nominated Susan Sarandon and Ralph Fiennes. But, as we're never quite sure of Lafferty's intentions towards his employer, the movie ends up feeling half-complete. Did the butler do it or not? **JR** Swearing, sex scenes, drug abuse. *DVD*

Susan Sarandon *Doris Duke* • Ralph Fiennes *Bernard Lafferty* • James Rebhorn *Waldo Taft* • Nick Rolfe *Ben* ■ *Dir* Bob Balaban • *Scr* Hugh Costello

Bernie ★★★ 12

Black comedy based on a true story
2011 · US · Colour · 95min

This curio from indie stalwart Richard Linklater is the blackly comedic true story of the 39-year-old mortician's assistant who in 1996 shot his 81-year-old companion. Jack Black gives a touching, low-key performance as Bernie Tiede, a generous, God-fearing man who regards chaste friendships with elderly widows as part of the service. Shirley MacLaine has less chance to shine as the wealthy heiress whose nagging finally drives him to murder. Dangerously blurring fact and fiction, Linklater interviews countless local people, whose down-home testimony - often unintentionally amusing - drives the story, but also slows it down. **AC** Swearing. *DVD*

Jack Black *Bernie Tiede* • Shirley MacLaine *Marjorie Nugent* • Matthew McConaughey *Danny Buck Davidson* • Brady Coleman *Scrappy Holmes* • Richard Robichaux *Lloyd Hornbuckle* ■ *Dir* Richard Linklater • *Scr* Richard Linklater, Skip Hollandsworth, from an article in *Texas Monthly* by Hollandsworth

Berserk ★★ 12

Mystery thriller   1967 · UK · Colour · 92min

Here, in the twilight of her career, Joan Crawford stars in a tale about murderous goings-on in a circus, which is at least marginally better than her caveman fiasco *Trog*. It's a shame to watch an actress of Crawford's stature gawking at such explicit sadism, for many that is this tawdry flick's main appeal. Cheap and nasty. **TS**

Joan Crawford *Monica Rivers* • Ty Hardin *Frank Hawkins* • Diana Dors *Matilda* • Michael Gough *Dorando* • Judy Geeson *Angela Rivers* • Robert Hardy *Det Supt Brooks* • Geoffrey Keen *Commissioner Dalby* ■ *Dir* Jim O'Connor • *Scr* Aben Kandel, Herman Cohen, from their story

Bert Rigby, You're a Fool ★★ 15

Musical comedy   1989 · US · Colour · 90min

American director Carl Reiner was so impressed by Robert Lindsay in a West End show that he wrote this wish-fulfilling fable for him. He's a striking miner, whose impersonations of Gene Kelly and Fred Astaire take him to Hollywood stardom, and collisions with clichéd characters such as Anne Bancroft, portraying the frustrated wife of a film producer. **TH**

Robert Lindsay *Bert Rigby* • Anne Bancroft *Meredith Perlestein* • Corbin Bernsen *Jim Shirley* • Robbie Coltrane *Sid Trample* • Cathryn Bradshaw *Laurel Pennington* • Jackie Gayle II *Perlestein* • Bruno Kirby *Kyle DeForest* • Liz Smith *Mrs Rigby* ■ *Dir/Scr* Carl Reiner

Besieged ★★ PG

Romantic drama   1998 · It · Colour · 89min

Originally intended as a 60-minute TV drama, the tale of a timid pianist's obsession with his housekeeper is intriguing without ever being wholly engaging. Thandie Newton is solid enough as the medical student forced into service to make ends meet after fleeing a tyrannical African regime, but David Thewlis is wildly erratic as her besotted benefactor. A very minor work. **DP** Brief nudity.

Thandie Newton *Shandurai* • David Thewlis *Jason Kinsky* • Claudio Santamaria *Agostino* • John C Ojwang *Singer* • Cyril Nri *Priest* • Massimo De Rossi *Patient* • Andrea Quercia *Child pianist* • Mario Mazzetti Di Pietralata *Piano buyer* ■ *Dir* Bernardo Bertolucci • *Scr* Clare Peploe, Bernardo Bertolucci, from a story by James Lasdun

The Bespoke Overcoat ★★★

Supernatural drama   1955 · UK · BW · 33min

Director Jack Clayton was a teenager when he got his first job in a British film studio, graduating to editor, associate producer and eventually director with this atmospheric version of a ghost story by Gogol. His debut won many awards,

B

including a 1956 Oscar for best short film. In this two-reeler, a poor clerk working in a clothing factory is refused a coat by his bosses. A tailor friend agrees to make him one, but the clerk's death from freezing before it's finished leaves his ghost to seek retribution. Wolfgang Suschitzky's superb chiaroscuro camerawork helps belie the modest budget. BB

Alfie Bass *Fender* • David Kossoff *Morry* • Alan Tilvern *Ranting* • Alf Dean *Gravedigger* • *Dir* Jack Clayton • *Scr* Wolf Mankowitz, from the short story by Nikolai Gogol

Best ★★ 15
Sports biographical drama
1999 · UK · Colour · 102min

This is a shoddy biography of soccer genius George Best. Normally, it's the match scenes that let football films down: you either have actors who can't play, or players who can't act. Ironically, though, the match scenes here, a blend of grainy original footage and cleverly integrated re-creations, are one of its few plus points. The bulk of the film, however, focuses on Best's downward spiral into alcoholism and unfulfilled potential. It's muddled in structure, melodramatic in direction and boringly repetitive. DA Swearing. *DVD*

John Lynch *George Best* • Ian Bannen *Sir Matt Busby* • Jerome Flynn *Bobby Charlton* • Ian Hart *Nobby Stiles* • Patsy Kensit *Anna* • Cal MacAninch *Paddy Crerand* • Linus Roache *Denis Law* • Roger Daltrey *Rodney Marsh* • *Dir* Mary McGuckian • *Scr* Mary McGuckian, John Lynch, George Best (script consultant)

Best Boy ★★★★ U
Documentary
1979 · US · Colour · 104min

Disregarding the documentarist's supposed duty to remain impartial, Ira Wohl directly influences the action in this life-affirming Oscar winner, as he prises his 52-year-old cousin, Philly, away from the parents who have devotedly cossetted him on account of his mental incapacity. Realising that they are ageing (indeed, the father is dying), Wohl attempts to prepare Philly for life on his own. Nonetheless, he remains sensitive to the fact that each small accomplishment is as much a source of regret as of pride for the selfless people witnessing their son's dependence on them diminishing. Movingly inspirational. A sequel, *Best Man*, followed. DP

■ *Dir/Scr* Ira Wohl

Best Defense ★★ 18
Comedy
1984 · US · Colour · 90min

This anti-establishment comedy was filmed as a Dudley Moore vehicle, but the result pleased nobody. After previews, the movie was recalled, rewritten and partially reshot, incorporating an expensive Eddie Murphy, billed as "Strategic guest star". The anti-Russian material is tasteless and the comedy unfunny, but Kate Capshaw and Helen Shaver make it watchable. TS Swearing, sex scenes, brief nudity. *DVD*

Dudley Moore *Wylie Cooper* • Eddie Murphy *Landry* • Kate Capshaw *Laura* • George Dzundza *Loparino* • Helen Shaver *Claire Lewis* • Mark Arnott *Brank* • Peter Michael Goetz *Frank Joyner* ■ *Dir* Willard Huyck • *Scr* Gloria Katz, Willard Huyck, from the novel *Easy and Hard Ways Out* by Robert Grossbach

The Best Exotic Marigold Hotel ★★★★ 12
Comedy drama
2011 · US · Colour · 118min

Masterfully directed by John Madden (*Shakespeare in Love*), this audaciously manipulative charmer is a deft adaptation of Deborah Moggach's novel *These Foolish Things*, in which a group of British pensioners outsource their retirement to India, lured by the promise of cheap luxury. Though the establishment of the title, managed by ever-optimistic Dev Patel (a sweetly subtle performance), turns out to be a dump, the pensioners' shared experiences transform their lives. The film does become slightly predictable – Maggie Smith's xenophobia mellows, henpecked Bill Nighy finds himself and Judi Dench is faced with a romantic conundrum – yet the

treasure trove of British stars offers a tale that never once strays from satisfying, feel-good magic. AJ Some swearing, sexual references. *DVD* ■ 🅱

Judi Dench *Evelyn* • Bill Nighy *Douglas* • Maggie Smith *Muriel* • Tom Wilkinson *Graham* • Dev Patel *Sonny* • Penelope Wilton *Jean* • Ronald Pickup *Norman* • Celia Imrie *Madge* ■ *Dir* John Madden • *Scr* Ol Parker, from the novel *These Foolish Things* by Deborah Moggach

Best Foot Forward ★★★ U
Musical
1943 · US · Colour · 95min

This early MGM Technicolor musical is a movie adaptation of a famous George Abbott Broadway show, and is notable for importing many of the Broadway cast to MGM. Although the feeble leading men didn't stay the course, Hollywood fell for peppy June Allyson and zesty Nancy Walker. The plot revolves around movie star Lucille Ball visiting a military academy. The glamorous Gloria DeHaven steals every scene in which she appears. Period nonsense, but watchable. TS

Lucille Ball • William Gaxton *Jack O'Riley* • Virginia Weidler *Helen Schlessenger* • Tommy Dix *Elwood* • Nancy Walker *Nancy* • Gloria DeHaven *Minerva* • Kenny Bowers *Dutch* • June Allyson *Ethel* ■ *Dir* Edward Buzzell • *Scr* Irving Brecher, Fred F Finklehoffe

Best Friends ★★★ PG
Comedy
1982 · US · Colour · 104min

Before he became the director of such hits as *Rain Man* and *Disclosure*, Barry Levinson worked as a scriptwriter, often in collaboration with his first wife, Valerie Curtin. Proving that the couple who write together also fight together, this overexcitable comedy is a dramatic exaggeration of their real-life relationship. Burt Reynolds and Goldie Hawn are well-matched as the Hollywood scriptwriters and, once the bickering begins, they hurl their lines at each other with some enthusiasm, but this only partly atones for the fact that they are never very funny. DP

Burt Reynolds *Richard Babson* • Goldie Hawn *Paula McCullen* • Jessica Tandy *Eleanor McCullen* • Barnard Hughes *Tim McCullen* • Audra Lindley *Ann Babson* • Keenan Wynn *Tom Babson* • Ron Silver *Larry Weisman* • Carol Locatell *Nellie Ballou* ■ *Dir* Norman Jewison • *Scr* Valerie Curtin, Barry Levinson

The Best House in London ★★★
Period comedy
1968 · UK · Colour · 98min

Scripted Denis Norden and directed with bawdy good humour by Philip Saville, this tale of the Home Secretary agreeing to open a licensed brothel in Victorian London ranks among the most lavish soft-core comedies ever produced in Britain. David Hemmings enjoys a dual role as a mild-mannered PR man smitten with anti-smut campaigner Joanna Pettet and as the opportunistic manager of the brothel in question. There's much fun to be had in the celebrity cameos, but the choices moment involves George Saunders and John Cleese attempting to take tiffin under fire. DP

David Hemmings *Walter Leybourne/Benjamin Oakes* • Joanna Pettet *Josephine Pacefoot* • George Sanders *Sir Francis Leybourne* • Dany Robin *Babette* • Warren Mitchell *Count Pandolfo* • John Bird *Home secretary* • William Rushton *Sylvester Wall* • Bill Fraser *Inspector Macpherson* • Maurice Denham *Editor of "The Times"* • Martita Hunt *Headmistress* • Clement Freud *Mr Mason* ■ *Dir* Philip Saville • *Scr* Denis Norden

Best in Show ★★★★ 12
Satire
2000 · US · Colour · 86min

After lampooning a heavy metal band in *This Is Spinal Tap* and amateur dramatics in *Waiting for Guffman*, "mockumentary" maestro Christopher Guest scores again with this howlingly funny look at dog owners. Guest co-writes, directs and acts in this sharp, but never malicious satire that follows a cross section of contestants preparing for a (fictional) Philadelphia dog show. The impeccable ensemble improvises its way through an inspired series of keenly observed set pieces. This is laugh-out-loud

comedy with pedigree and bite. DP Some swearing. *DVD*

Christopher Guest *Harlan Pepper* • Eugene Levy *Gerry Fleck* • Catherine O'Hara *Cookie Fleck* • Michael McKean *Stefan Vanderhoof* • John Michael Higgins *Scott Donlan* • Fred Willard *Buck Laughlin* • Jennifer Coolidge *Sherri Ann Ward Cabot* • Jane Lynch *Christy Cummings* • Parker Posey *Meg Swan* • Michael Hitchcock *Hamilton Swan* • Bob Balaban *Dr Theodore W Millbank III* ■ *Dir* Christopher Guest • *Scr* Christopher Guest, Eugene Levy

Best Intentions ★★★★ PG
Drama
1992 · Swe · Colour · 173min

Although a six-hour version was made for Swedish TV, director Bille August here settled on half that time to explore the tempestuous early relationship of Ingmar Bergman's parents. The great film-maker's script returns to the theme of troubled young love that informed so many of his early features, but there's also plenty of the spiritual and emotional angst that characterised much of his later work. The difficulties facing Samuel Froler and Pernilla August (Bille's wife) provide plenty of dramatic interest, especially when they come in the form of the disapproving father, magisterially played by Max von Sydow. This is the first of an autobiographical trilogy, that continues with *Sunday Children* and *Private Confessions*. DP Swedish +subtitles. *DVD*

Samuel Froler *Henrik Bergman* • Pernilla August *Anna Akerblom* • Max von Sydow *Johan Akerblom* • Ghita Norby *Karin Akerblom* • Mona Malm *Alma Bergman* • Lena Endre *Frida Strandberg* • Keve Hjelm *Fredrik Bergman* • Björn Kjellman *Ernst Akerblom* • Börje Ahlstedt *Carl Akerblom* ■ *Dir* Bille August • *Scr* Ingmar Bergman

Best Laid Plans ★★★ 15
Crime thriller
1999 · US · Colour · 89min

Alessandro Nivola is called to Josh Brolin's house in the middle of the night where his friend confesses that he has been accused of raping a girl (Reese Witherspoon). To make matters worse, it turns out she is only 16 and Brolin has her tied up downstairs. All is not what it seems, however. Director Mike Barker creates a complex tale of robbery and deception, and displays a sympathetic eye for the small-town, blue-collar backdrop to the film. JF Sex scenes, violence, swearing. *DVD*

Alessandro Nivola *Nick* • Reese Witherspoon *Lissa* • Josh Brolin *Bryce* • Rocky Carroll *Bad ass dude* • Michael G Hagerty *Charlie* • Terrence Howard *Jimmy* • Jamie Marsh *Barry* ■ *Dir* Michael Barker [Mike Barker] • *Scr* Ted Griffin

Best Laid Plans ★★ 15
Drama
2011 · UK · Colour · 103min

This Nottingham-set attempt to update John Steinbeck's Depression masterpiece *Of Mice and Men* is essentially sound, but contrived plotting and characterisation undermine it at every turn. Adewale Akinnuoye-Agbaje plays the gentle giant who does everything wheeler-dealing protector Stephen Graham asks of him, but he unwittingly jeopardises their safety when he becomes besotted with equally simple soul Maxine Peake. Director David Blair makes gutsy use of his run-down locations, but struggles to staunch the sentiment and cliché. DP Violence, swearing, drug abuse, sex scenes, nudity. *DVD* ■ 🅱

Stephen Graham *Danny* • Adewale Akinnuoye-Agbaje *Joseph* • Emma Stansfield *Lisa* • David O'Hara *Curtis* • Maxine Peake *Isabel* ■ *Dir* David Blair (4) • *Scr* Chris Green

The Best Little Whorehouse in Texas ★★★ 15
Musical comedy
1982 · US · Colour · 109min

This lightweight version of the much grittier long-running Broadway musical stars Dolly Parton and Burt Reynolds, two performers noted for their sex appeal, but who fail to ignite the proper sparks here. Parton plays the madam of the Chicken Ranch brothel, who comes to blows with her sheriff lover (Reynolds) when TV evangelist Dom

DeLuise tries to close the place down. Some great routines and new songs keep it all on a lively and likeable keel. AJ

Burt Reynolds *Sheriff Dodd* • Dolly Parton *Miss Mona* • Dom DeLuise *Melvin* • Charles Durning *Governor* • Jim Nabors *Deputy Fred* • Robert Mandan *Senator Wingwood* • Lois Nettleton *Dulci Mae* ■ *Dir* Colin Higgins • *Scr* Larry L King, Peter Masterson, Colin Higgins, from the musical by Peter Masterson

The Best Man ★★★★ PG
Political drama
1964 · US · BW · 97min

Political satire is a tough subject to convey successfully in a movie, but director Franklin J Schaffner succeeded brilliantly with Gore Vidal's scabrous look at the underbelly of Washington. Not surprisingly a commercial failure, this brilliantly cast, superbly acted drama got lost on its release. Daring in its day – two political rivals have deep and dark secrets in their past – this is a mature and satisfying work, and contains an almost career-best performance from the great Henry Fonda. TS *DVD*

Henry Fonda *William Russell* • Cliff Robertson *Joe Cantwell* • Edie Adams *Mabel Cantwell* • Margaret Leighton *Alice Russell* • Shelley Berman *Sheldon Bascomb* • Lee Tracy *Art Hockstader* • Ann Sothern *Mrs Gamadge* • Gene Raymond *Don Cantwell* • Kevin McCarthy *Dick Jensen* ■ *Dir* Franklin Schaffner [Franklin J Schaffner] • *Scr* Gore Vidal, from his play

The Best Man ★★★ PG
Period romantic drama
1998 · It · Colour · 100min

Pupi Avati's melodrama is set on the last day of the 19th century and its resulting symbolism is heavy-handed. There's no faulting Pasquale Rachini's sumptuous photography or the lavish attention to period detail. But there's something damningly novelettish about Inès Sastre's attempt to circumvent her marriage to doddering tycoon Dario Cantarelli by addressing her vows to Diego Abatantuono, his dashingly mysterious best man. DP Italian +subtitles.

Diego Abatantuono *Angelo Beliossi* • Inès Sastre *Francesca Babini* • Dario Cantarelli *Edgardo Osti* • Cinia Mascoli *Peppina Campeggi* • Valeria D'Obici *Olimpia Campeggi Babini* ■ *Dir/Scr* Pupi Avati

The Best Man ★★ 15
Comedy drama
1999 · US · Colour · 115min

In this first feature from writer/director Malcolm D Lee (cousin of Spike), Taye Diggs discovers that his debut novel, as yet unpublished, has been leaked to his friends as they prepare to reunite for a wedding. Since the book is drawn from his own experiences, they're none too pleased with his representation of them. The dud script undermines the talents of the stars. LH *DVD*

Nia Long *Jordan* • Taye Diggs *Harper* • Morris Chestnut *Lance* • Terrence Howard *Quentin* • Harold Perrineau Jr [Harold Perrineau] *Murch* • Sanaa Lathan *Robin* • Monica Calhoun *Mia* • Melissa De Sousa *Shelby* • Victoria Dillard *Anita* ■ *Dir/Scr* Malcolm D Lee

The Best Man ★★ 15
Romantic comedy
2005 · UK/US/Ger/Hun · Colour · 91min

It never quite reaches the bawdy, cynical, clever or enchanting heights to which it aspires, but this gentle pastiche of the *Four Weddings* subgenre is still watchable. Asked to be best man for estranged college pal Steve John Shepherd, struggling writer Stuart Townsend finds himself falling for James's bride-to-be, Amy Smart, unaware that a porn-loving estate agent (a scene-stealing Seth Green) is covertly seeking to sabotage the engagement. If you're in the mood for undemanding entertainment this might fit the bill. DP Swearing, sexual references. *DVD*

Stuart Townsend *Olly Pickering* • Amy Smart *Sarah Marie Barker* • Seth Green *Murray* • Kate Ashfield *Becka* • Steve John Shepherd *James* • Simon Callow *Publisher* • Jodhi May *Tania* • Anna Chancellor *Dana* ■ *Dir* Stefan Schwartz • *Scr* Ed Roe, Stefan Schwartz

B

The Best Man Holiday
★★★ 15

Comedy drama · 2013 · US · Colour · 123min

This belated sequel to 1999's The Best Man has author Taye Diggs persuaded to write a biography about his ex-best friend, NFL star Morris Chestnut, who he's barely spoken to in years. The drama is generally effective, although each narrative turn is predictable, while the attempts at farcical humour feeling jarring and unnecessary. But the heart-warming moments and the winning performances from Diggs and Chestnut do compensate. SC Swearing, sexual references.

Taye Diggs *Harper* · Morris Chestnut *Lance* · Terrence Howard *Quentin* · Regina Hall *Candace* ▪ *Dir* Malcolm D Lee · *Scr* Malcolm D Lee, from characters by Lee

Best Men
★ 15

Crime comedy drama
1997 · US/UK · Colour · 86min

Just released from prison, and on the way to his wedding with Drew Barrymore, Luke Wilson finds himself in trouble when one of the friends driving him to church makes an unscheduled stop to rob a bank. In predictable fashion, the bungled heist quickly escalates into a full-scale hostage situation. It's a ridiculous story, made worse by the clueless direction. AJ *DVD*

Drew Barrymore *Hope* · Dean Cain *Sergeant Buzz Thomas* · Andy Dick *Teddy Pollack* · Sean Patrick Flanery *Billy Phillips* · Mitchell Whitfield *Sol Jacobs* · Luke Wilson *Jesse Chandler* · Fred Ward *Sheriff Bud Phillips* ▪ *Dir* Tamra Davis · *Scr* Art Edler Brown, Tracy Fraim

The Best of Benny Hill
★★★ PG

Comedy compilation · 1974 · UK · Colour · 83min

No matter where you stand on the content of Benny Hill's bawdy comedy, there's no escaping the fact that he was one of British television's biggest ever stars. Featuring such familiar characters as Fred Scuttle, this compilation comes from sketches that originally appeared in his Thames series between 1969 and 1972. Regulars such as Bob Todd, Jenny Lee Wright and Henry McGee do their usual selfless stooging, and there's the inevitable "Hill's Angels" chase to Boots Randolph's immortal *Yakety Sax* theme. DP *DVD*

Benny Hill *Benny Hill/Fred Scuttle/Mervyn Cruddy* · Bob Todd · Anne Irving · Bettine Le Beau · David Prowse [Dave Prowse] · Henry McGee · Nicholas Parsons · Patricia Hayes · Jenny Lee Wright ▪ *Dir* John Robins · *Scr* Benny Hill

The Best of Enemies
★★★ PG

Second World War comedy drama
1961 · UK/It · BW · 99min

As the rival commanders, David Niven and Alberto Sordi are given admirable support by such stalwarts as Michael Wilding, Harry Andrews and Bernard Cribbins. The great Nino Rota composed the score, while Fellini's regular cameraman Giuseppe Rotunno provides some stunning visuals. Yet, in spite of Guy Hamilton's steady direction and the odd amusing moment, this account of the misadventures of a British army unit in Abyssinia in the early 1940s never really gathers momentum. DP

David Niven *Major Richardson* · Alberto Sordi *Capt Blasi* · Michael Wilding *Lt Burke* · Amedeo Nazzari *Major Fornari* · Harry Andrews *Capt Rootes* · Noel Harrison *Lt Hilary* · David Opatoshu *Captain Bernasconi* · Aldo Giuffre *Sgt Todini* · Duncan Macrae *Sgt Trevethan* · Bernard Cribbins *Pvt Tanner* · Ronald Fraser *Cpl Prefect* ▪ *Dir* Guy Hamilton · *Scr* Jack Pulman, Age Scarpelli [Agenore Incrocci and Furio Scarpelli] (adaptation), Suso Cecchi D'Amico (adaptation), from a story by Luciano Vincenzoni

Best of Enemies
★★★★ 15

Documentary
2015 · US · Colour and BW · 88min

If the level of political debate on TV leaves you cold, then this stunning, blast-from-the-past documentary should stave off the torpor. The televised face-off between political pundits and literary big beasts Gore Vidal and William Buckley Jr during the campaign for the US Presidency in 1968 was a game-changer. In the red corner Vidal, fiery *enfant terrible* of the liberal left who wields intellect like a stiletto; in the blue corner Buckley, conservative commentator and rigorous critic of all things progressive. Utterly absorbing, their blistering verbal jousts make Jeremy Paxman's *Newsnight* look like a playground. JA Swearing. *DVD*

Gore Vidal · William Buckley Jr · Christopher Hitchens · John Lithgow · Kelsey Grammer · Dick Cavett ▪ *Dir/Scr* Robert Gordon, Morgan Neville

The Best of Everything ★★

Romantic drama · 1959 · US · Colour · 120min

"We've proven romance is still the best of everything," croons Johnny Mathis over the titles, but this preposterous 20th Century-Fox tosh is not really a romance: it's a steamy melodrama about power and glamour in the New York publishing jungle. An ageing and predatory Joan Crawford chews the scenery with aplomb, making mincemeat of Fox's young contract players Hope Lange and Suzy Parker. TS

Joan Crawford *Amanda Farrow* · Hope Lange *Caroline Bender* · Stephen Boyd *Mike* · Louis Jourdan *David Savage* · Suzy Parker *Gregg* · Martha Hyer *Barbara* · Diane Baker *April* · Brian Aherne *Mr Shalimar* · Robert Evans *Dexter Key* · Brett Halsey *Eddie* ▪ *Dir* Jean Negulesco · *Scr* Edith Sommer, Mann Rubin, from the novel by Rona Jaffe

The Best of Me
★ 12

Romantic drama · 2014 · US · Colour · 112min

This adaptation of the Nicholas Sparks novel follows the reunion of two childhood sweethearts (James Marsden and Michelle Monaghan) at a friend's funeral. Through flashbacks we see the events of the past that tore them apart. The film follows the Sparks-adaptation formula (forbidden love, small town drama, dying father figure) as it heads off in ludicrous directions. As the plot takes its third or fourth twist, it's clear that the script's only intention is to make as sad a film as possible, plausibility be damned. Cynical and lazy. JL *DVD* BL

James Marsden *Dawson Cole* · Michelle Monaghan *Amanda Collier* · Liana Liberato *Young Amanda* · Luke Bracey *Young Dawson* · Gerald McRaney *Tuck* ▪ *Dir* Michael Hoffman · *Scr* J Mills Goodloe, Will Fetters, Michael Hoffman, from Nicholas Sparks's novel

Best of the Badmen ★★ U

Western · 1951 · US · Colour · 83min

A collection of noted western outlaws ride together in this innocuous RKO film. Robert Ryan is top billed as a former Confederate colonel pitted against a rather bland Robert Preston. Walter Brennan makes the most of his role as an ex-Quantrill's raider who wonders why there's now a price on his head for doing something which brought him glory in the Civil War. Too talky. TS

Robert Ryan *Jeff Clanton* · Claire Trevor *Lily* · Jack Buetel *Bob Younger* · Robert Preston *Matthew Fowler* · Walter Brennan *Doc Butcher* · Bruce Cabot *Cole Younger* · John Archer *Curley Ringo* · Lawrence Tierney *Jesse James* · Barton MacLane *Joad* ▪ *Dir* William D Russell · *Scr* Robert Hardy Andrews, John Twist, from a story by Robert Hardy Andrews

Best of the Best ★★ 15

Martial arts sports drama
1989 · US · Colour · 93min

The US karate team take on the Koreans in a slick "against the odds" martial arts drama that alternates between body blows and tugs on the heartstrings. Formulaic in the extreme, with nice fighter Eric Roberts given every possible reason to triumph (his son's in a coma after a traffic accident and he has a nasty shoulder injury), this compendium of clichés is undone by sentimentality and paper-thin characterisation. JC *DVD*

Eric Roberts *Alex Grady* · James Earl Jones *Coach Couzo* · Sally Kirkland *Catherine Wade* · Phillip Rhee *Tommy Lee* · Chris Penn *Travis Brickley* ▪ *Dir* Robert Radler · *Scr* Paul Levine, from a story by Phillip Rhee, Paul Levine

Best of the Best II ★★ 18

Action thriller · 1992 · US · Colour · 95min

The original was a glossy, straight-to-video action tale that benefited from a surprisingly good cast. There's no James Earl Jones this time around, but Eric Roberts, Chris Penn and martial arts expert Phillip Rhee are reunited for another bout of mindless but entertaining biffing. Two more sequels followed. JF *DVD*

Eric Roberts *Alex Grady* · Phillip Rhee *Tommy Lee* · Edan Gross *Walter Grady* · Ralph Moeller *Brakus* · Chris Penn *Travis Brickley* · Sonny Landham *James* · Wayne Newton *Weldon* · Meg Foster *Sue* ▪ *Dir* Robert Radler · *Scr* Max Strom, John Allen Nelson, from characters by Paul Levine

The Best of Times ★★ 15

Comedy drama · 1986 · US · Colour · 99min

All-American whimsy, set in small-town California, where Robin Williams and Kurt Russell are two of life's failures. Williams is a banker, living in the shadow of a missed pass at a high school football game; Russell was the school's star quarterback, now also on the skids. The characters are one dimensional, there aren't any jokes, and the tone is glutinous. AT Swearing.

Robin Williams *Jack Dundee* · Kurt Russell *Reno Hightower* · Pamela Reed *Gigi Hightower* · Holly Palance *Elly Dundee* · Donald Moffat *The Colonel* · Margaret Whitton *Darla* · M Emmet Walsh *Charlie* · Donovan Scott *Eddie* ▪ *Dir* Roger Spottiswoode · *Scr* Ron Shelton

The Best Pair of Legs in the Business ★

Comedy drama · 1972 · UK · Colour · 87min

Taking a break from the buses, Reg Varney finds himself at a holiday camp in this old-fashioned seaside comedy. Although he's the world's worst entertainer, our Reg is convinced that the big time is just a soft-shoe shuffle away. A trouper through and through, Varney always tries to make the most of even the lowest grade material, yet even he struggles to pep up this maudlin mess. DP Swearing.

Reg Varney *"Sherry" Sheridan* · Diana Coupland *Mary Sheridan* · Jean Harvey (2) *Emma* · Lee Montague *Charlie* · David Lincoln *Ron* · George Sweeney *Dai* ▪ *Dir* Christopher Hodson · *Scr* Kevin Laffan

Best Revenge ★★ 18

Thriller · 1983 · Can · Colour · 91min

John Heard can be electric in a part with some depth, but here he is saddled with a film that has none. Instead, he is required to wrestle with the obviously episodic story of a small-potatoes drugs runner who is arm-twisted into undertaking a larger errand when a friend is taken hostage. As he tries to bring unseemly quantities of cannabis from Morocco to America, all the regulation nastiness is given full rein. JM

John Heard *Charlie Grainger* · Levon Helm *Bo* · Alberta Watson *Dinah* · Stephen McHattie *Brett Munro* · Moses Znaimer *Leo Ellis* · John Rhys-Davies *Mustapha* · Benjamin Gordon *Willy* ▪ *Dir* John Trent · *Scr* David Rothberg, Rick Rosenthal, Logan N Danforth, from a story by David Rothberg

Best Seller ★★★★ 18

Thriller · 1987 · US · Colour · 91min

In between making his own quirky horror films, Larry Cohen turned his writing skills to the crime genre and the result was this ingenious, electric thriller. Brian Dennehy is the policeman-turned-writer who forms an uneasy alliance with hitman James Woods, who has promised to put him back on the bestseller lists. Cohen delivers a typically witty script and director John Flynn is a dab hand at the action set pieces. Dennehy is as dependable as ever, while Woods mesmerises as the strangely likeable professional killer. JF Swearing, violence. *DVD*

Brian Dennehy *Dennis Meechum* · James Woods *Cleve* · Victoria Tennant *Roberta Gillian* · Allison Balson *Holly Meechum* · Paul Shenar *David Madlock* · George Coe *Graham* · Ann Pitoniak [Anne Pitoniak] *Mrs Foster* · Mary Carver *Cleve's mother* · Sully Boyar *Monks* ▪ *Dir* John Flynn · *Scr* Larry Cohen

The Best Things in Life Are Free ★★★★ U

Musical biographical drama
1956 · US · Colour · 104min

Director Michael Curtiz's stirring musical biopic is about the songwriting team of BG De Sylva, Ray Henderson and Lew Brown. It matters not a jot if you've never heard of them, since they're played with tremendous verve by Gordon MacRae, Dan Dailey and Ernest Borgnine. Sheree North simply sizzles in two superb dance routines, a vibrant (and definitive) Birth of the Blues with the great Jacques d'Amboise and a very snazzy Black Bottom. TS

Gordon MacRae *BG "Buddy" De Sylva* · Dan Dailey *Ray Henderson* · Ernest Borgnine *Lew Brown* · Sheree North *Kitty* · Tommy Noonan *Carl* · Murvyn Vye *Manny* · Phyllis Avery *Maggie Henderson* · Jacques d'Amboise *Speciality dancer* ▪ *Dir* Michael Curtiz · *Scr* William Bowers, Phoebe Ephron, from a story by John O'Hara

The Best Years of Our Lives ★★★★★ U

Drama · 1946 · US · BW · 170min

Undoubtedly one of the finest and most satisfying achievements in American cinema. Despite its length, it still retains its capacity to move an audience. The tale of three returning GIs adjusting to civilian life after the Second World War may have lost some relevance post-Vietnam, but there's no denying the magnificent craftsmanship as director William Wyler and photographer Gregg Toland (Citizen Kane) bring Robert E Sherwood's vivid screenplay to life. Stars Fredric March, Myrna Loy and Dana Andrews are at their postwar peaks here, but it is the performance of real-life wartime amputee Harold Russell that is most touching, and he rightly won two Academy Awards for his role (a special award for bringing hope to other veterans along with that of best supporting actor). Awarded six other Oscars, this movie is hard to overpraise. TS *DVD*

Myrna Loy *Milly Stephenson* · Fredric March *Al Stephenson* · Dana Andrews *Fred Derry* · Harold Russell *Homer Parrish* · Teresa Wright *Peggy Stephenson* · Virginia Mayo *Marie Derry* · Cathy O'Donnell *Wilma Cameron* · Hoagy Carmichael *Butch Engle* ▪ *Dir* William Wyler · *Scr* Robert E Sherwood, from the blank verse novella *Glory for Me* by MacKinlay Kantor · *Cinematographer* Gregg Toland · *Editor* Daniel Mandell · *Music* Hugo Friedhofer

La Bête ★★★ 18

Erotic fantasy drama 1975 · Fr · Colour · 94min

The perverse sexual content of this erotic fairy tale earned it a notoriety that detracted from its value as a savage social satire and a film of painterly beauty. Polish-born former animator Walerian Borowczyk errs on the wrong side of political correctness in contrasting the experiences of an 18th-century bride and an American heiress, both about to marry into the same aristocratic family. The bestial nature of some of the dream-diary sequences might cause offence, but there is a playfulness about the eccentric couplings. DP French +subtitles. *DVD* BL

Sirpa Lane *Romilda de l'Espérance* · Lisbeth Hummel *Lucy Broadhurst* · Elizabeth Kaza [Elisabeth Kaza] *Virginia Broadhurst* · Pierre Benedetti *Mathurin de l'Espérance* · Guy Tréjan *Pierre, Marquis Pierre de l'Espérance* · Dalio [Marcel Dalio] *Duc Rommondelo de Balo* · Pascale Rivault *Clarisse de l'Espérance* ▪ *Dir/Scr* Walerian Borowczyk

La Bête Humaine ★★★★★ PG

Crime drama 1938 · Fr · BW · 98min

Zola's dark, fatalistic novel of the railway tracks was turned by Jean Renoir into one of the classics of pre-war French cinema. The incomparable Jean Gabin stars as the train driver who acquires a young mistress, and together they plot to murder her husband. Hollywood would use Zola's yarn as a template for many *films noirs* but Renoir's film is every inch their equal. It's a wonderful, painterly evocation of the railway and a poetic drama that just gets grimmer. Fritz Lang remade it in Hollywood as *Human Desire* with Glenn Ford and Gloria Grahame, a dead ringer for this film's pathetic heroine, Simone Simon. AT French +subtitles. *DVD*

Jean Gabin *Jacques Lantier* • Simone Simon *Séverine* • Fernand Ledoux *Roubaud, Séverine's husband* • Julien Carette *Pecqueux* • Blanchette Brunoy *Flore* • Jean Renoir *Cabuche, the poacher* • Gérard Landry *Dauvergne's son* • Jenny Hélia *Philomène* ■ *Dir* Jean Renoir • *Scr* Jean Renoir, from the novel by Emile Zola

Bethune: the Making of a Hero ★★★ 15
Biographical drama
1990 · Can/Fr/Chi · Colour · 111min

Having already played controversial Canadian doctor Norman Bethune in Eric Till's 1977 biopic, Donald Sutherland returned to the role for this troubled co-production. He gives a warts-and-all portrayal of the surgeon whose detestation of fascism led him first to participate in the Spanish Civil War, and then to assist Mao Tse-tung on his famous Long March. Strikingly filmed by Mike Molloy and Raoul Coutard, the scenery makes an imposing impression. DP

Donald Sutherland *Dr Norman Bethune* • Helen Mirren *Frances Penny Bethune* • Helen Shaver *Ms Dowd* • Colm Feore *Chester Rice* • James Pax *Mr Tung* • Ronald Pickup *Alan Coleman* • Da Guo *Dr Chian* • Harrison Liu *Dr Fong* • Anouk Aimée *Marie-France Coudaire* ■ *Dir* Phillip Borsos • *Scr* Ted Allan

Betrayal ★★★★ 15
Romantic drama   1982 · UK · Colour · 91min

This film version of Harold Pinter's 1978 play has Patricia Hodge married to Ben Kingsley but having an affair with Jeremy Irons. The story - a sort of sexual charade - starts at the end and works backwards, dealing with a sequence of betrayals between the three friends. Razor sharp in its depiction of a rather pretentious literary London, it includes an unforgettable scene in a restaurant when Kingsley goes ballistic. This was distinguished producer Sam Spiegel's final film. AT Swearing.

Jeremy Irons *Jerry* • Ben Kingsley *Robert* • Patricia Hodge *Emma* • Avril Elgar *Mrs Banks* • Ray Marioni *Waiter* • Caspar Norman *Sam* ■ *Dir* David Jones (3) • *Scr* Harold Pinter, from his play

Betrayal from the East ★★
Second World War drama
1945 · US · BW · 82min

Lee Tracy is enlisted by the Japanese in 1941 to spy for them. In particular they want the defence plans for the Panama Canal, which they apparently hope to destroy. But Tracy, though broke, isn't morally bankrupt, and intends to trick the Japanese with the help of double agent Nancy Kelly. This cheapo war drama isn't the expected flag-waver. AT

Lee Tracy *Eddie* • Nancy Kelly *Peggy* • Richard Loo *Tanni* • Abner Biberman *Yamato* • Regis Toomey *Scott* • Philip Ahn *Kato* • Addison Richards *Capt Bates* • Bruce Edwards *Purdy* ■ *Dir* William Berke • *Scr* Kenneth Gamet, Aubrey Wisberg, from the book by Alan Hynd

Betrayed ★★★
Thriller   1944 · US · BW · 67min

This effective, moody B-thriller was originally titled *When Strangers Marry* but was quickly changed to *Betrayed* when people expected a marital comedy. It stars Kim Hunter as the latest wife of Dean Jagger, whom she suspects may be a murderer. Hunter's fears are calmed by her former boyfriend Robert Mitchum, whose hulking, laconic presence dominates the picture. AT

Robert Mitchum *Fred* • Kim Hunter *Millie* • Dean Jagger *Paul* • Neil Hamilton *Blake* • Lou Lubin *Houser* • Milton Kibbee *Charlie* • Dewey Robinson *News stand man* • Claire Whitney *Middle-aged woman* ■ *Dir* William Castle • *Scr* Philip Yordan, Dennis J Cooper, from a story by George V Moscov

Betrayed ★★ U
Second World War spy drama
1954 · US · Colour · 108min

Directed by Gottfried Reinhardt at MGM's British studios, this old-fashioned, plodding film about spies, Resistance workers and traitors is chiefly notable for marking the end of Clark Gable's 22-year tenure with the studio, before he went lucratively freelance for his remaining years. Co-starring with Victor Mature and Lana Turner, the ageing "King" of Hollywood was hardly challenged by this outmoded melodrama. RK

Clark Gable *Colonel Pieter Deventer* • Lana Turner *Carla Van Oven* • Victor Mature *"The Scarf"* • Louis Calhern *General Ten Eyck* • OE Hasse *Colonel Helmuth Dietrich* • Wilfrid Hyde White *General Charles Larraby* • Ian Carmichael *Captain Jackie Lawson* • Niall McGinnis *"Blackie"* • Nora Swinburne *"The Scarf's" mother* • Roland Culver *General Warsleigh* ■ *Dir* Gottfried Reinhardt • *Scr* Ronald Millar, George Froeschel

Betrayed ★★★★ 18
Political thriller   1988 · US · Colour · 121min

This intelligent and intriguing political thriller from director Costa-Gavras follows an undercover FBI agent (played by the excellent Debra Winger) sent to investigate a Midwest farmer who's suspected of having links with a white supremacist organisation. Tom Berenger is suitably charming and chilling as Winger's prey, but Costa-Gavras gives the convoluted plot such a plethora of twists and turns that cohesive tension is ultimately lost. The performances and set pieces raise it up, but this film is simply too long. SH Violence, swearing. *DVD*

Debra Winger *Cathy Weaver/Katie Phillips* • Tom Berenger *Gary Simmons* • John Heard *Michael Carnes* • Betsy Blair *Gladys Simmons* • John Mahoney *Shorty* • Ted Levine *Wes* • Jeffrey DeMunn *Flynn* • Albert Hall *Al Sanders* • David Clennon *Jack Carpenter* ■ *Dir* Costa-Gavras • *Scr* Joe Eszterhas

The Betsy ★★ 18
Drama   1978 · US · Colour · 120min

It was said when this film was first released that it was too up-market to be a successful adaptation of a Harold Robbins novel. Well, if your idea of sophistication is the sight of Laurence Olivier bouncing around on a bed, then director Daniel Petrie's full-throttle tale of cars, lust and greed will be right up your street. Ageing 50 years over a series of flashbacks, Olivier acts up a storm, and is joined at the ham counter by Tommy Lee Jones and Lesley-Anne Down. DP Swearing, nudity.

Laurence Olivier *Loren Hardeman Sr* • Robert Duvall *Loren Hardeman III* • Katharine Ross *Sally Hardeman* • Tommy Lee Jones *Angelo Perino* • Jane Alexander *Alicia Hardeman* • Lesley-Anne Down *Lady Bobby Ayres* • Joseph Wiseman *Jake Weinstein* • Kathleen Beller *Betsy Hardeman* ■ *Dir* Daniel Petrie • *Scr* Walter Bernstein, William Bast, from the novel by Harold Robbins

Betsy's Wedding ★★★ 15
Comedy   1990 · US · Colour · 90min

A movie directed by Alan Alda means a touch of Woody Allen meets vaudeville and that's the case with this tale of a group of eccentric New Yorkers all trying to get Betsy married off. Molly Ringwald is neatly understated as the title gal who wishes to make an honest man of a nice boy who is neither Jewish like Ringwald's mom (an excellent Madeline Kahn) nor makes breakfast seem like a scene from *Tosca*, as does her Italian dad (Alda, at his best). SH Violence, swearing. *DVD*

Alan Alda *Eddie Hopper* • Madeline Kahn *Lola Hopper* • Molly Ringwald *Betsy Hopper* • Ally Sheedy *Connie Hopper* • Anthony LaPaglia *Stevie Dee* • Joe Pesci *Oscar Henner* • Catherine O'Hara

Gloria Henner • Joey Bishop *Eddie's father* • Samuel L Jackson *Mickey, taxi dispatcher* ■ *Dir/Scr* Alan Alda

Better Late than Never ★★ PG
Comedy   1983 · UK · Colour · 91min

Great talent, shame about the script. David Niven and Art Carney are a couple of conmen competing for the affections of a ten-year-old heiress (Kimberley Partridge). Her grandmother (Maggie Smith) is a dithering amnesiac, so it's up to the girl to decide which one is her true grandfather. Writer/director Bryan Forbes is as flat-footed here as he was with *International Velvet*. TH

David Niven *Nick Cartland* • Art Carney *Charley Dunbar* • Maggie Smith *Anderson* • Kimberley Partridge *Bridget* • Catherine Hicks *Sable* • Lionel Jeffries *Hargreaves* • Melissa Prophet *Marlene* ■ *Dir/Scr* Bryan Forbes

A Better Life ★★★★ 12
Social drama   2011 · US · Colour · 93min

After working for years to turn the American Dream into reality, Carlos Galindo (Demian Bichir) must choose whether to buy his own business, or tout for work each day on construction sites. The choice seems simple, except that Galindo is an illegal immigrant in LA. It is a touching story of a father struggling to give his son a future, and a son (José Julián) torn between home and the ways of the street. With beautiful performances and direction (from Chris Weitz, *About a Boy*), this is insightful as well as entertaining. AIS Violence, brief swearing, drug abuse. *DVD*

Demián Bichir [Demian Bichir] *Carlos Galindo* • José Julián *Luis Galindo* • Dolores Heredia *Anita* • Chelsea Rendon *Ruthie* ■ *Dir* Chris Weitz • *Scr* Eric Eason, from a story by Roger L Simon

Better Living through Chemistry ★★ 15
Comedy drama   2014 · US/UK · Colour · 87min

A peculiar take on suburban rebellion, this stars Sam Rockwell as a frustrated pharmacist who enters a dangerous world of sex, drugs and murder when he meets bored housewife Olivia Wilde. The script is funny in places, but the central pair's sloppy homicide plot lacks edge. With a protracted ending that wraps everything up in a neat, disappointing bow, it's a dark comedy that, much like its lead character, could do with taking a few more risks. JL Swearing, sex scenes, drug abuse. *DVD*

Sam Rockwell *Doug Varney* • Olivia Wilde *Elizabeth Roberts* • Michelle Monaghan *Kara Varney* • Ray Liotta *Jack Roberts* • Jane Fonda *Jane Fonda/narrator* ■ *Dir/Scr* Geoff Moore, David Posamentier

Better Luck Tomorrow ★★★ 15
Crime drama   2001 · US · Colour · 95min

High-school clichés are explored and often exploded in this slick first solo feature from *Fast & Furious* director Justin Lin. A low-budget, coming-of-age drama, it follows overachieving yet disillusioned Asian-American teens as they start committing minor crimes for kicks, shielded by their perfect grades. Heavily stylised and hyper-kinetic visuals mirror the group's inevitable downward-spiralling experiences, but while these invigorating aesthetics demonstrate Lin's ability to work serious magic with limited funds, they also expose the episodic film's lack of narrative and emotional substance. SF

Parry Shen *Ben Manibag* • Jason J Tobin *Virgil Hu* • Sung Kang *Han* • Roger Fan *Daric Loo* • John Cho *Steve Choe* ■ *Dir* Justin Lin • *Scr* Ernesto M Foronda [Ernesto Foronda], Justin Lin, Fabian Marquez

Better Mus' Come ★★★
Crime drama   2010 · Jam · Colour · 104min

The gang wars of late 1970s Jamaica are shown through the eyes of a morally conflicted single father in native writer/director Storm Saulter's ambitious and visually vibrant debut. Shot on location, this

fact-based tale impressively captures the look and feel of 1978 Kingston, as charismatic newcomer Sheldon Shepherd's impoverished community leader and gangster finds the violence he's embroiled in escalating out of control. Despite some technical prowess, there's a lack of narrative focus, and the crucial emotional aspects of Shepherd's ultimately tragic story are underplayed. SF Violence, swearing, sex scenes.

Sheldon Shepherd *Ricky* • Nicole "Sky" Grey *Kemala* • Ricardo Orgil *Flames* • Everaldo Creary *Shortman* ■ *Dir* Storm [Storm Saulter] • *Scr* Storm [Storm Saulter], from a story by Paul Bucknor, Joshua Bratter, from Saulter's idea

Better Off Dead ★★ 15
Comedy   1985 · US · Colour · 92min

John Cusack is suicidal after being dumped by his beautiful but shallow girlfriend (Amanda Wyss) - and that's just the start of his problems. Writer/director Savage Steve Holland surrounds the always engaging star with a variety of quirky neighbourhood characters and slapstick sight gags. This is pretty lightweight compared to such classier Cusack comedies as *The Sure Thing*. JC *DVD*

John Cusack *Lane Myer* • David Ogden Stiers *Al Myer* • Kim Darby *Jenny Myer* • Demian Slade *Johnny Gasparini* • Scooter Stevens *Badger Myer* • Diane Franklin *Monique Junet* ■ *Dir/Scr* Savage Steve Holland

Better Things ★★★★ 15
Social drama   2007 · UK/Ger · Colour · 89min

Writer/director Duane Hopkins's first feature is a compelling and highly credible insight into the deterioration of life in rural Britain. Making evocative use of his Cotswold locations, he creates a multi-stranded narrative that powerfully captures the genuine sense of isolation and torpor felt by the community, from young heroin addicts to a dying grandmother. But for all the desolation of the landscape and the oppressiveness of the silences, there are moments of optimism here. Hopkins uses a predominantly non-professional cast and their performances match the sullen naturalism of Lol Crawley's cinematography and Douglas MacDougall's disconcerting sound design, making this an impressive debut. DP *DVD*

Liam McIlfatrick *Rob* • Che Corr *David* • Tara Ballard *Sarah* • Megan Palmer *Rachel* • Rachel McIntyre *Gail Wilson* • Frank Bench *Mr Gladwin* ■ *Dir/Scr* Duane Hopkins • *Cinematographer* Lol Crawley • *Sound* Douglas MacDougall

A Better Tomorrow ★★★★ 18
Action thriller   1986 · HK · Colour · 90min

One of the defining films in Hong Kong action cinema, this not only made names out of director John Woo and star Chow Yun-Fat, but also exerted a considerable influence over one Quentin Tarantino. Chow takes his now familiar role as the lethal but honorable crook - in this case a counterfeiter - who, with his weary partner in crime (Ti Lung), attempts to go straight but is led back into a battle to the death with a ruthless gangster. The artfully choreographed scenes of slow-motion destruction more than compensate for the occasional lapses into clumsy sentimentality. This is available on video in both dubbed and subtitled versions, although the latter is unintentionally funny because of dubious translation. JF In Cantonese. *DVD*

Chow Yun-Fat *Mark* • Ti Lung *Ho* • Leslie Cheung *Kit Sung* • Lee Waise *Shing* ■ *Dir/Scr* John Woo

A Better Tomorrow II ★★★ 18
Action thriller   1987 · HK · Colour · 99min

Less a sequel than a remake, this nevertheless consolidated John Woo's reputation as the hippest of Hong Kong's action directors. Most of the stars of the original are back on board: Chow Yun-Fat this time plays the brother of the master counterfeiter of the first film, while Ti Lung

B

and Leslie Cheung return as the two brothers from different sides of the law. The childish attempts at humour will leave some embarrassed, but once again the set pieces are stunning. JF Cantonese +subtitles.

Chow Yun-Fat *Ken* • Ti Lung *Ho* • Leslie Cheung *Kit* • Dean Shek *Lung* ■ *Dir* John Woo • *Scr* John Woo, Tsui Hark • *Producer* Tsui Hark

A Better Tomorrow III ★★**18**

Action thriller   1989 · HK · Colour · 116min

John Woo jumped ship after the first two *Better Tomorrow* films, so producer Tsui Hark took over the directorial reins. This one is a prequel, although it bares only a passing resemblance to the first two. Chow Yun-Fat is back on board, although his co-star Tony Leung takes centre stage, as he attempts to bring his relatives out of South Vietnam as the communists move in. Not in the same league as the first two. JF Cantonese +subtitles.

Chow Yun-Fat *Cheung Chi-Keung (Mark)* • Anita Mui *Chow Ying-Kit (Kitty Chow)* • Tony Kar-Fai Leung [Tony Leung (1)] *Cheung Chi Mun (Mun)* • Saburo Tokito *Ho Cheung-Ching* • Cheng Wai Lan *Pat* • Shek Kin *Uncle* • Maggie Cheung *Ling* ■ *Dir* Tsui Hark • *Scr* Tai Fu-Ho, Leung Yiu-Ming

A Better Way to Die ★★**18**

Action thriller   2000 · US · Colour · 97min

Scott Wiper is a minor-leaguer, but he still had sufficient clout to write, direct and co-star in this boorish road movie. He's certainly an imposing presence and stages some sequences with blustering bravura. But his talents do not lie in screenwriting. The dialogue consists solely of threats, curses and platitudes, while the story of a disillusioned cop who is mistaken for the quarry of a private eye, the FBI and the Chicago underworld is one long cliché. DP *DVD*

André Braugher *Cleveland* • Scott Wiper *Boomer* • Lou Diamond Phillips *Special Agent William Dexter* • Natasha Henstridge *Kelly* • Matt Gallani *Laslov* • Wayne Duvall *Rifkin* • Joe Pantoliano *Flash* ■ *Dir/Scr* Scott Wiper

Betty Blue ★★★★★**18**

Drama   1986 · Fr · Colour · 116min

Blessed with a beautiful score by Gabriel Yared, this is the finest example of the type of French film known, rather snipingly, as *cinéma du look*. The usual accusation of all style and no content simply can't be aimed at Jean-Jacques Beineix's Oscar-nominated return to form after *Moon in the Gutter*. The tragic relationship of Betty and Zorg is as compelling as it is chic. Béatrice Dalle is unbelievably vibrant as the waitress living on the edge of her passions, but Jean-Hugues Anglade does manage to keep up as the would-be novelist coping with her exhilarating highs and destructive lows. DP French +subtitles. Violence, swearing, sex scenes, nudity. *DVD*

Béatrice Dalle *Betty* • Jean-Hugues Anglade *Zorg* • Consuelo de Haviland *Lisa* • Gérard Darmon *Eddy* • Clémentine Célarié *Annie* • Jacques Mathou *Bob* • Claude Confortes *Zorg's boss* ■ *Dir* Jean-Jacques Beineix • *Scr* Jean-Jacques Beineix, from the novel by Philippe Djian

Betty Fisher and Other Stories ★★★**15**

Psychological crime thriller
2001 · Fr/Can · Colour · 98min

Director Claude Miller's adaptation of a Ruth Rendell novel is an intriguing combination of psychological chic, lowlife graft and bourgeois irony. Unless you can accept a world in which bestselling authors accept kidnap victims as substitutes for deceased sons, abusive mothers twist reality for their own devices and conmen are left mansions by erstwhile lovers, then you will spend the entire film looking for holes in its tortuous logic. But if you surrender to the spirited performances, the kooky atmosphere will keep you interested. DP French +subtitles. Violence, swearing. *DVD*

Sandrine Kiberlain *Betty Fisher* • Nicole Garcia *Margot Fisher* • Mathilde Seigner *Carole Novacki* • Edouard Baer *Alex Basato* • Stéphane Freiss *Edouard* ■ *Dir* Claude Miller • *Scr* Claude Miller, from the novel *The Tree of Hands* by Ruth Rendell

The Betty Ford Story ★★★★

Biographical drama   1987 · US · Colour · 96min

Gena Rowlands gives a stunning performance as the president's wife who battled an addiction to prescription drugs and alcohol in this powerful TV movie, based on Mrs Ford's autobiography. The story is told with candour and the film offers an intimate view of the emotional pain Ford and her family suffered because of her destructive behaviour. The drama is bolstered by strong acting from the supporting cast, especially Josef Sommer as Gerald Ford. MC

Gena Rowlands *Betty Ford* • Josef Sommer *President Gerald Ford* • Nan Woods *Susan Ford* • Concetta Tomei *Jan* • Jack Radar *First doctor* • Joan McMurtrey *Diane* • Kenneth Tigar *Dr Lukash* • Laura Leigh Hughes *Gayle Ford* ■ *Dir* David Greene • *Scr* Karen Hall, from the autobiography *The Times of My Life* by Betty Ford, Chris Chase

Between ★

Mystery thriller
2005 · US/Mex · Colour and BW · 91min

David Ocanas makes a less than prepossessing directorial debut with this metaphysical thriller that is not only a wildly convoluted tale but also clumsily staged. Poppy Montgomery (*Without a Trace*) stars as a high-flying American lawyer who heads to Tijuana (against the advice of husband Adam Kaufman) to find her missing sister, and encounters some mind-bending dead-ends. Ocanas directs with such thudding deliberation that the action frequently risks descending into farce and Montgomery's earnest performance doesn't help much, either. With its moments of mystery, symbolism and shock all being unintentionally hilarious, this is impossible to take seriously. DP

Poppy Montgomery *Nadine Roberts* • Adam Kaufman *James Roberts* ■ *Dir* David Ocanas • *Scr* Robert Nelms, from a story by David Ocanas

Between Friends ★★★**15**

Drama   1983 · US · Colour · 95min

Forget the old hat story and enjoy watching two great stars strut their stuff as middle-aged divorcees from different backgrounds who meet by accident and help each other through their midlife crises. In a neat twist, Carol Burnett plays the object of all men's desire, while Elizabeth Taylor can't even get close to a boyfriend. The two leads give incandescent performances in this cable television movie. AJ

Elizabeth Taylor *Deborah Shapiro* • Carol Burnett *Mary Catherine Castelli* • Barbara Bush [Barbara Tyson] *Francie Castelli* • Henry Ramer *Sam Tucker* • Bruce Gray *Malcolm Hollan* • Charles Shamata [Chuck Shamata] *Dr Seth Simpson* • Lally Cadeau *Lolly James* ■ *Dir* Lou Antonio • *Scr* Shelley List, Jonathan Estrin, from the novel *Nobody Makes Me Cry* by Shelley List

Between Heaven and Hell ★★**PG**

Second World War drama
1956 · US · Colour · 89min

Skilled Richard Fleischer (*The Vikings, Compulsion*) directs this routine 20th Century-Fox feature. The plot favours the 1950s psychological approach, as rich southern recruit Robert Wagner suffers in combat under psychotic bully Broderick Crawford, but the structure is messy and confused, and Wagner's brilliantined hairstyle is anachronistic. TS

Robert Wagner *Sam Gifford* • Terry Moore *Jenny* • Broderick Crawford *Waco* • Buddy Ebsen *Willie* • Robert Keith (1) *Colonel Gozzens* • Brad Dexter *Joe Johnson* • Mark Damon *Terry* • Ken Clark *Morgan* ■ *Dir* Richard Fleischer • *Scr* Harry Brown, from the novel *The Day the Century Ended* by Francis Gwaltney

Between the Lines ★★★★**15**

Comedy   1977 · US · Colour · 101min

This is a warm-hearted comedy revolving around staff members of a Boston underground newspaper just before it's sold to a profit-minded publisher. The perceptive humour comes from the last bastion of 1960s political radicalism taking on corporate thinking, coupled with a brilliant ensemble cast milking every moment for wit and poignancy. Rock critic Jeff Goldblum's ad-libbed music lecture is a hoot, while photographer Lindsay Crouse's feminist rapport with stripper Marilu Henner is another highlight. Engrossing and believable. AJ

John Heard *Harry* • Bruno Kirby *David* • Lindsay Crouse *Abbie* • Gwen Welles *Laura* • Jeff Goldblum *Max* • Stephen Collins *Michael* • Jill Eikenberry *Lynn* • Michael J Pollard *Hawker* • Marilu Henner *Danielle* ■ *Dir* Joan Micklin Silver • *Scr* Fred Barron, from a story by Fred Barron, David Helpern

Between Two Worlds ★★★

Fantasy drama   1944 · US · BW · 111min

This is a revamped and updated version of Sutton Vane's allegorical play *Outward Bound*, which was filmed in 1930. It has a shipload of "dead" Warner Bros contract players en route to the next world, some going on to Heaven and others to Hell. Rather turgid stuff, it has good performances from Isobel Elsom, as a dreadful snob, Edmund Gwenn, as the steward, and Sydney Greenstreet as God's great divider, which make it worth watching, while John Garfield overacts. RB

John Garfield *Tom Prior* • Paul Henreid *Henry* • Sydney Greenstreet *Thompson* • Eleanor Parker *Ann* • Edmund Gwenn *Scrubby* • George Tobias *Pete Musick* • George Coulouris *Lingley* • Faye Emerson *Maxine* ■ *Dir* Edward A Blatt • *Scr* Daniel Fuchs, from the play *Outward Bound* by Sutton Vane

The Beverly Hillbillies ★★**PG**

Comedy   1993 · US · Colour · 89min

Hollywood loves rehashing old TV shows into movies and this transfer of the 1960s show to the big screen seems just as pointless as the others of its ilk, despite Penelope Spheeris's direction, which tries hard to put a modern edge on nostalgia. The cast, including Dabney Coleman and Cloris Leachman, mainly mimics their predecessors. AT *DVD*

Jim Varney *Jed Clampett* • Diedrich Bader *Jethro/Jethrine* • Erika Eleniak *Elly May* • Cloris Leachman *Granny* • Lily Tomlin *Miss Hathaway* • Dabney Coleman *Mr Drysdale* • Lea Thompson *Laura* • Rob Schneider *Tyler* • Dolly Parton • Buddy Ebsen *Barnaby Jones* • Zsa Zsa Gabor ■ *Dir* Penelope Spheeris • *Scr* Lawrence Konner, Mark Rosenthal, Jim Fisher, Jim Staahl, Rob Schneider, Alex Herschlag, from a story by Lawrence Konner, Mark Rosenthal, from the TV series by Paul Henning

Beverly Hills Chihuahua ★**U**

Fantasy comedy   2008 · US · Colour · 87min

Lapdogs get their cinematic day in this tiresome Disney comedy, with Drew Barrymore as the voice of Chloe, a pampered LA pooch who's dognapped while away in Baja, California. As her human dog-sitter (Piper Perabo) combs Mexico for her, Chloe befriends a grumpy German shepherd (voiced by Andy García). Director Raja Gosnell was responsible for both *Scooby-Doo* live-action movies, and here he attempts to appeal to tots as tiny as his starring pooch. Adults may feel it redefines the term animal cruelty. Two sequels went straight to DVD in 2011 and 2012. JR *DVD*

Piper Perabo *Rachel* • Manolo Cardona *Sam Cortez* • Jamie Lee Curtis *Aunt Viv* • José María Yazpik *Vasquez* • Drew Barrymore *Chloe* • Andy García *Delgado* • George Lopez *Papi* • Cheech Marin [Richard "Cheech" Marin] *Manuel* ■ *Dir* Raja Gosnell • *Scr* Analisa LaBianco, Jeff [Jeffrey] Bushell, from a story by Bushell

Beverly Hills Cop ★★★★**15**

Action comedy   1984 · US · Colour · 100min

This was the blockbuster that propelled Eddie Murphy to superstardom at a time when his brash, confident swagger still appeared fresh and he hadn't descended into caricature. In the first and best of the trilogy, he stars as the Detroit street cop who causes a major upset in posh Beverly Hills when he turns up to investigate the murder of an old friend. Director Martin Brest orchestrates the senseless set pieces with slick precision and British actor Steven Berkoff pops up as the villain of the piece. JF Violence, swearing. *DVD* *BD*

Eddie Murphy *Axel Foley* • Judge Reinhold *Detective Billy Rosewood* • Lisa Eilbacher *Jenny Summers* • Steven Berkoff *Victor Maitland* • John Ashton *Sergeant Taggart* • Ronny Cox *Lieutenant Bogomil* • James Russo *Mikey Tandino* • Jonathan Banks *Zack* • Bronson Pinchot *Serge* ■ *Dir* Martin Brest • *Scr* Daniel Petrie Jr, from a story by Daniel Petrie Jr, Danilo Bach

Beverly Hills Cop II ★★**15**

Action comedy   1987 · US · Colour · 98min

Eddie Murphy is back and the set pieces are even more spectacular – shame they forgot about the script. This blockbusting sequel replays the plot of the original, but any wit goes largely by the wayside and Murphy's mugging becomes increasingly irritating. Jürgen Prochnow and Brigitte Nielsen ham it up as the obligatory foreign-accented baddies, but fail to make much impact. JF Swearing, violence. *DVD* *BD*

Eddie Murphy *Axel Foley* • Judge Reinhold *Billy Rosewood* • Jürgen Prochnow *Maxwell Dent* • Ronny Cox *Andrew Bogomil* • John Ashton *John Taggart* • Brigitte Nielsen *Karla Fry* • Allen Garfield *Harold Lutz* • Dean Stockwell *Charles "Chip" Cain* ■ *Dir* Tony Scott • *Scr* Larry Ferguson, Warren Skaaren, from a story by Eddie Murphy, Robert D Wachs, from characters by Danilo Bach, Daniel Petrie Jr

Beverly Hills Cop III ★★**15**

Action comedy   1994 · US · Colour · 99min

Eddie Murphy and Judge Reinhold go through their paces for a third time, beginning once again on Murphy's home turf in Detroit and moving to Beverly Hills and a theme park called Wonder World. John Landis does pull off the occasional visual joke. If Murphy looks bored by the whole thing, that fine character actor Hector Elizondo adds some genuine quirkiness. AT *DVD* *BD*

Eddie Murphy *Axel Foley* • Judge Reinhold *Billy Rosewood* • Hector Elizondo *Jon Flint* • Timothy Carhart *Ellis DeWald* • Stephen McHattie *Steve Fulbright* • Theresa Randle *Janice* • John Saxon *Orrin Sanderson* • Bronson Pinchot *Serge* ■ *Dir* John Landis • *Scr* Steven E de Souza, from characters by Danilo Bach, Daniel Petrie Jr

Beverly Hills Ninja ★★★**12**

Martial arts comedy   1997 · US · Colour · 84min

A box-office number one in the States, this features one of the last performances of comic Chris Farley. An American baby washes up on the shores of Japan and is brought up by a clan of martial arts masters. Now Haru (Farley), a willing but clumsy pupil, must journey to the "Hills of Beverly" to rescue a beautiful American girl from yakuza counterfeiters. Slapstick fun for the undemanding. JF Swearing, violence. *DVD*

Chris Farley *Haru* • Nicollette Sheridan *Alison* • Robin Shou *Gobei* • Nathaniel Parker *Tanley* • Soon-Tek Oh [Soon-Teck Oh] *Sensei* • Keith Cooke Hirabayashi *Nobu* • Chris Rock *Joey* • François Chau *Izumo* • John Farley *Policeman* • Kevin Farley *Policeman* ■ *Dir* Dennis Dugan • *Scr* Mark Feldberg, Mitch Klebanoff

Beware, My Lovely ★★★

Drama   1952 · US · BW · 76min

In this tense drama, vulnerable widow Ida Lupino hires craggy handyman Robert Ryan to help her prepare for Christmas, only to discover that he's a psychopath. Director Harry Horner creates such a claustrophobic atmosphere of pervasive nastiness that this film was rightly given an

B

X certificate for its cinema release in Britain. Much disliked by the critics of the day, this is tough stuff, indeed. It was produced by Lupino's second husband, Collier Young. TS

Ida Lupino *Helen Gordon* • Robert Ryan *Howard Wilton* • Taylor Holmes *Mr Armstrong* • Barbara Whiting *Ruth Williams* • James Willmas *Mr Stevens* • OZ Whitehead *Mr Franks* ■ *Dir* Harry Horner • *Scr* Mel Dinelli, from his story and play *The Man*

Beware of a Holy Whore
★★★ 15

Comedy　　　　1970 · W Ger/It · Colour · 99min

Inspired by Rainer Werner Fassbinder's own unhappy experience of shooting *Whity* in Spain, this is a real eye-opener for those who doggedly believe in cinema as a glamorous business. A brutally honest – if self-indulgent – auto-critique, this is as much about the frustration of failing to find a means of expression as the dangerous vanity of artists. Yet there is still much satirical fun to be had at the expense of director Lou Castel, his bolshy film crew and the preening star, played with conscious irony by Eddie Constantine. DP German +subtitles. *DVD*

Lou Castel *Jeff, the director* • Eddie Constantine *Eddie Constantine, lead actor* • Marquard Bohm *Ricky, lead actor* • Hanna Schygulla *Hanna, lead actress* • Rainer Werner Fassbinder *Sascha Berling, production manager* • Margarethe von Trotta *Babs, production secretary* ■ *Dir* Rainer Werner Fassbinder • *Scr* Rainer Werner Fassbinder

Beware of Mr Baker
★★★★ 15

Documentary　　　2012 · US · Colour · 88min

Legendary drummer Ginger Baker is, arguably, as well known today for his short temper and erratic behaviour as he is for the music he made with the likes of Cream, Blind Faith and Public Image Ltd. Baker's inner demons are unflinchingly addressed in this documentary that opens with the 73-year-old breaking the nose of director Jay Bulger. It's an engrossing portrait of a supremely talented but troubled man who, seemingly, lashes out at everything around him, both drum kit and contemporaries. Bulger mixes interviews with Baker at his South African home with reams of archive footage showing him in action on stage; a whirling dervish of drumsticks and cymbals. TeS Violence, swearing, drug abuse. *DVD* ◈

Ginger Baker ■ *Dir/Scr* Jay Bulger

Beware of Pity
★★

Romantic drama　　1946 · UK · BW · 102min

Lilli Palmer is touchingly vulnerable as the disabled baroness whose happiness with army officer Albert Lieven is jeopardised when she discovers the real motive for his attentions. Having learnt his trade in the silent era, director Maurice Elvey can't resist overplaying the melodrama, but the cast keeps things on track. DP

Lilli Palmer *Baroness Edith* • Albert Lieven *Lt Anton Marek* • Cedric Hardwicke *Dr Albert Condor* • Gladys Cooper *Klara Condor* • Linden Travers *Ilona Domansky* • Ernest Thesiger *Baron Emil de Kekesfalva* • Peter Cotes *Cusma* • Freda Jackson *Gypsy* ■ *Dir* Maurice Elvey • *Scr* WP Lipscomb, from the novel by Stefan Zweig

Beware! The Blob
★ 15

Science-fiction horror 1971 · US · Colour · 86min

Noteworthy only for being directed by Larry (*Dallas*) Hagman – it was re-released in the 1980s with the tagline "The film that JR shot!" – this pointless sequel to the 1958 classic rehashes virtually the same plot, but dumbs it down with amateurish special effects and strained acting. Godfrey Cambridge brings a globule of alien jelly back from the Arctic, which thaws out to become a homicidal protoplasm that increases its size by attacking partygoers and bowling alleys. AJ

Robert Walker Jr *Bobby Hartford* • Gwynne Gilford *Lisa Clark* • Godfrey Cambridge *Chester* • Richard Stahl *Edward Fazio* • Richard Webb *Sheriff Jones* • Carol Lynley *Leslie* • Shelley

Berman *Hairdresser* • Larry Hagman *Cop* ■ *Dir* Larry Hagman • *Scr* Anthony Harris, Jack Woods, from a story by Richard Clair, Anthony Harris

Bewitched
★★

Suspense drama　　1945 · US · BW · 65min

Arch Oboler, a radio producer who turned to movies, is nowadays best known, if at all, for his ground-breaking 3D feature *Bwana Devil*. This adaptation of his story *Alter Ego* was the first of a series of films that invariably featured bizarre or supernatural themes. Phyllis Thaxter plays a woman suffering from a dual personality disorder, an unusual subject for this period, but the sheer talkiness betrays the writer/director's background in radio. TS

Phyllis Thaxter *Joan Alris Ellis* • Edmund Gwenn *Dr Bergson* • Henry H Daniels Jr *Bob Arnold* • Addison Richards *John Ellis* • Kathleen Lockhart *Mrs Ellis* • Francis Pierlot *Dr George Wilton* ■ *Dir* Arch Oboler • *Scr* Arch Oboler, from his story *Alter Ego*

Bewitched
★★ PG

Romantic comedy fantasy
2005 · US · Colour · 97min

Toil and trouble sums up this tepid rehash of the 1960s sitcom. Director Nora Ephron betrays a profound misunderstanding of the show's appeal by taking a sexy and sassy character and replacing her with a simpering idiot. Nicole Kidman plays the real-life witch who is offered the part of Samantha in a remake of the show. Will Ferrell conjures up some laughs as Kidman's mortal love interest, but it isn't enough to save the asinine plot. SP *DVD*

Nicole Kidman *Isabel Bigelow* • Will Ferrell *Jack Wyatt* • Shirley MacLaine *Iris Smythson* • Michael Caine *Nigel Bigelow* • Jason Schwartzman *Richie* • Kristin Chenoweth *Maria Kelly* • Heather Burns *Nina* • Jim Turner *Larry* ■ *Dir* Nora Ephron • *Scr* Nora Ephron, Delia Ephron, from the TV series created by Sol Saks

Beyond a Reasonable Doubt
★★★★ PG

Film noir　　　　1956 · US · BW · 76min

While perhaps overdependent on coincidence and contrivance, this deft thriller guards its secret right to the end and proved a fitting swan song to Fritz Lang's Hollywood career. Dana Andrews brings a chilling calculation to the role of a journalist whose crusade against circumstantial evidence results in a murder rap, while Joan Fontaine is the loyal fiancée who campaigns to prove his innocence. But it is Lang's teasing direction that keeps the viewer guessing as his camera alights on seemingly inconsequential details that are just as likely to be red herrings as vital clues. A Michael Douglas remake is due out in late 2009. DP *DVD*

Dana Andrews *Tom Garrett* • Joan Fontaine *Susan Spencer* • Sidney Blackmer *Austin Spencer* • Philip Bourneuf *Roy Thompson* • Shepperd Strudwick *Wilson* • Arthur Franz *Bob Hale* • Edward Binns *Lt Kennedy* ■ *Dir* Fritz Lang • *Scr* Douglas Morrow

Beyond a Reasonable Doubt
★★ 12

Mystery drama　　2009 · US · Colour · 101min

Not for the first time, *Narrow Margin* director Peter Hyams revisits a classic 1950s thriller. Trouble is, *Desperate Housewives's* Jesse Metcalfe is a long way from being Gene Hackman. Metcalfe merely goes through the motions as a TV reporter who's convinced that DA Michael Douglas has been planting evidence to secure a string of questionable convictions. So Metcalfe plants evidence of his own to suggest he is a murderer, in a desperate attempt to expose the prosecutor. Fritz Lang's original 1956 film was tense and atmospheric, but any atmosphere here is lost in a wordy script, which Douglas hams it up to little effect. Only Amber Tamblyn is a breath of fresh air as the DA's assistant in love with Metcalfe. The final twist just isn't worth the wait. SuR Violence, brief swearing, a sex scene. *DVD* ◈

Michael Douglas (1) *Mark Hunter* • Jesse Metcalfe *CJ Nicholas* • Amber Tamblyn *Ella* • Joel David Moore *Corey Finley* • Orlando Jones *Ben Nickerson* • Sewell Whitney *Weldon* ■ *Dir* Peter Hyams • *Scr* Peter Hyams, from the 1956 film

Beyond Bedlam
★ 18

Psychological thriller 1993 · UK · Colour · 85min

Director Vadim Jean displays little talent in this convoluted, violent and ineffectual thriller. The cat-and-mouse tale involves a detective (Craig Fairbrass) who stumbles upon a scientist (Elizabeth Hurley) conducting gross experiments on serial killer Keith Allen. The B-list British cast doesn't bode well. LH *DVD*

Craig Fairbrass *Terry Hamilton* • Elizabeth Hurley *Stephanie Lyell* • Keith Allen *Marc Gilmour* • Anita Dobson *Judith Hamilton* • Craig Kelly (2) *Matthew Hamilton* • Georgina Hale *Sister Romulus* • Jesse Birdsall *Scott* ■ *Dir* Vadim Jean • *Scr* Rob Walker, Vadim Jean, from the novel *Bedlam* by Harry Adam Knight

Beyond Borders
★★ 15

Wartime romantic drama
2003 · US/Ger · Colour · 121min

Thanks to Phil Meheux's glossy photography, poverty and repression have rarely looked so picturesque as in this well-meaning but naive melodrama. Clive Owen's militant maverick throws himself into aiding the destitute of Ethiopia, Cambodia and Chechnya, but succeeds only in alienating an audience whose credibility has already been strained by do-gooding socialite Angelina Jolie, who periodically abandons husband Linus Roache to lend Owen some moral and romantic support. DP English, Khmer +subtitles. Swearing, violence. *DVD*

Angelina Jolie *Sarah Jordan* • Clive Owen *Nick Callahan* • Teri Polo *Charlotte Jordan* • Linus Roache *Henry Bauford* • Noah Emmerich *Elliott Hauser* • Yorick van Wageningen *Steiger* • Timothy West *Lawrence Bauford* ■ *Dir* Martin Campbell • *Scr* Caspian Tredwell-Owen

Beyond Clueless
★★★ 15

Documentary　　　2014 · UK · Colour · 88min

Teen movies from the 1990s onwards are the subject of this debut documentary from British film blogger Charlie Lyne. But instead of the usual interviews and anecdotes, Lyne takes a more critical tack, delivering a kind of taxonomy of the genre supported by clips from over 200 films. Lyne clearly has great affection for his subject, and snappy editing and a great original score by the band Summer Camp do much to alleviate what often becomes a bit of a slog. AS

Fairuza Balk *Narrator* ■ *Dir/Scr* Charlie Lyne

Beyond Rangoon
★★★★ 15

Drama　　　　　1995 · US · Colour · 99min

John Boorman's powerful indictment of Burma's oppressive military regime stars Patricia Arquette as a naive American doctor who becomes embroiled in the country's problems. She finds herself drawn to the campaign of Aung San Suu Kyi, the democratic leader under house arrest. Filmed in neighbouring Malaysia, it follows *The Year of Living Dangerously* and *The Killing Fields* by using a westerner as its protagonist: "Some people have found that her grief is in some sense trivial against the horrors of a nation's bloodshed," said Boorman, "but my feeling was that this woman shares the audience's ignorance... she's drawn into it and learns about it as we do." AT

Patricia Arquette *Laura Bowman* • U Aung Ko • Frances McDormand *Andy* • Spalding Gray *Jeremy Watt* • Tiara Jacquelina *Desk clerk* • Kuswadinath Bujang *Colonel* • Victor Slezak *Mr Scott* • Jit Murad *Sein Htoo* • Ye Myint *Zaw Win* • Adelle Lutz *Aung San Suu Kyi* ■ *Dir* John Boorman • *Scr* Alex Lasker, Bill Rubenstein

Beyond Reasonable Doubt
★★★ PG

Drama based on a true story
1980 · NZ · Colour · 103min

David Hemmings gives his best performance since he became a Swinging

Sixties sensation, playing a malicious New Zealand cop planting evidence to put a noose around the neck of a feeble-minded farmer (John Hargreaves) accused of a husband-and-wife murder. The farmer went for two trials, was found guilty and then pardoned. John Laing directs without any sense of urgency, but the fact that it's a true story makes it memorable. TH Some violence.

David Hemmings *Inspector Hutton* • John Hargreaves *Arthur Allen Thomas* • Martyn Sanderson *Lem Demler* • Tony Barry *Detective John Hughes* • Grant Tilly *David Morris* • Diana Rowan *Vivien Thomas* ■ *Dir* John Laing • *Scr* David Yallop, from his non-fiction book

Beyond the Blackboard
★★★

Drama based on a true story
2011 · US · Colour · 95min

Adapted from the memoir of real-life American educator Stacey Bess, this inspirational teaching drama centres on a likeable turn by Emily VanCamp (star of TV's *Revenge*) as a 24-year-old, middle-class idealist forced to overcome her fears and prejudices when she's hired to school homeless children living in a shelter in 1980s Salt Lake City. The story is predictable and simplistic, but the events are enthusiastically performed, with the well-chosen young actors proving particularly endearing. SF

Emily VanCamp *Stacey Bess* • Steve Talley *Greg Bess* • Timothy Busfield *School HR representative* • Treat Williams *Dr Warren* ■ *Dir* Jeff Bleckner • *Scr* Camille Thomasson, from the non-fiction book *Nobody Don't Love Nobody: Lessons on Love from the School with No Name* by Stacey Bess

Beyond the Blue Horizon
★★★

Musical comedy　　1942 · US · Colour · 76min

Sporting her trademark sarong in yet another of her popular South Seas movies, Dorothy Lamour stars as an orphan who has grown up living native on a tropical isle with a tiger and a chimp for company. Richard Denning supplies the romance, while Lamour's discovery that she's a millionairess peps up the plot. Treated as the fantastical nonsense it is by director Alfred Santell, this is gloriously tongue-in-cheek, escapist fare. RK

Dorothy Lamour *Tama* • Richard Denning *Jakra* • Jack Haley *Squidge* • Walter Abel *Thornton* • Helen Gilbert *Carol* • Patricia Morison *Sylvia* • Frances Gifford *Charlotte* • Elizabeth Patterson *Mrs Daly* ■ *Dir* Alfred Santell • *Scr* Frank Butler, from a story by E Lloyd Sheldon, Jack DeWitt

Beyond the Call
★★★ 15

Drama　　　　　1996 · US · Colour · 96min

In this moving TV movie, Sissy Spacek plays a housewife who becomes involved in a battle to save the life of David Strathairn, a former boyfriend and Vietnam veteran who is on death row after murdering a policeman. She learns that the tragedy was the result of post-traumatic stress syndrome, but her campaign puts her own marriage to Arliss Howard in jeopardy. The performances are first rate and the direction from Tony Bill is sympathetically understated. JF Violence, swearing. *DVD*

Sissy Spacek *Pam O'Brien* • David Strathairn *Russell Gates* • Arliss Howard *Keith O'Brien* • Janet Wright *Fran* • Lindsay Murrell *Rebecca O'Brien* • Andrew Sardella *Mark O'Brien* ■ *Dir* Tony Bill • *Scr* Doug Magee

Beyond the Clouds
★★ 18

Portmanteau drama
1995 · It/Ger/Fr · Colour · 104min

At the age of 82 and in poor health, Michelangelo Antonioni filmed this quartet of short stories, linked by John Malkovich as a film director looking for his next idea. At times the visuals betray the presence of a master film-maker, but otherwise this is a flimsy enterprise. AT English, French, Italian +subtitles. Swearing, nudity. *DVD*

John Malkovich *The Director* • Sophie Marceau *Young woman* • Inés Sastre *Carmen* • Kim Rossi Stuart *Silvano* • Chiara Caselli *Olga* • Peter Weller

Husband • Jean Reno *Carlo* • Fanny Ardant *Patricia* • Irène Jacob *Girl* • Vincent Perez *Boy* • Marcello Mastroianni *Maestro* • Jeanne Moreau *Woman* ■ *Dir* Michelangelo Antonioni • *Scr* Michelangelo Antonioni, Wim Wenders, Tonino Guerra, from the short story collection *That Bowling Alley on the River Tiber* by Michelangelo Antonioni

Beyond the Curtain ★☆
Thriller   1960 · UK · BW · 84min

This shoddy propaganda piece is bargain-basement nonsense. It stars Richard Greene as a pilot who drops behind the Iron Curtain to prise air hostess Eva Bartok out of the clutches of the communists. Faced with a dismal script and locations that would shame poverty row, the unfortunate cast doesn't even try to convince. DP *DVD*

Richard Greene *Captain Jim Kyle* • Eva Bartok *Karin von Seefeldt* • Marius Goring *Hans Koertner* • Lucie Mannheim *Frau von Seefeldt* • Andrée Melly *Linda* • George Mikell *Pieter* • John Welsh *Turner* • Dennis Shaw [Denis Shaw] *Krumm* ■ *Dir* Compton Bennett • *Scr* John Cresswell, Compton Bennett, from the novel *Thunder Above* by Charles F Blair

Beyond the Edge ★★★ PG
Drama documentary 2013 · NZ · Colour · 86min

Kiwi director Leanne Pooley has worked wonders in bringing Sir Edmund Hillary and Tenzing Norgay's historic conquest of Mount Everest vividly to life by pacing it like a thriller. There are no talking heads: instead Pooley uses audio interviews to provide a soundtrack to the visuals – a nimbly assembled blend of still photos, old 16mm film and, best of all, some stunningly shot re-enactments. The wealth of detail provided about what now seems very primitive equipment, further reinforces the ground-breaking nature of the 1953 expedition. JF *DVD*

Chad Moffitt *Edmund Hillary* • Sonam Sherpa *Tenzing Norgay* • John Wraight *John Hunt* • Joshua Rutter *George Lowe* ■ *Dir* Leanne Pooley • *Scr* Leanne Pooley, from a story by Matthew Metcalfe, Pooley • *Cinematographer* Richard Bluck

Beyond the Fire ★★ 15
Drama   2008 · UK/Ire · Colour · 76min

It isn't usually a good sign when a film boasts more producers than cast principals – and this has 16 of them. As a result, writer/director Maeve Murphy seems to have been striving to please too many people while balancing a number of thorny issues in this sincere but overwrought drama. At its core is a tentative romance between rape victim Cara Seymour and Irish ex-priest Scot Williams, who has come to London after being released from prison to find the mentor who abused him as a young curate. Murphy is not afraid to tackle taboos, but this unflinching indictment of Catholic hypocrisy lacks nuance. DP *DVD*

Scot Williams *Sheamy* • Cara Seymour *Katie* • Chris O'Neill *Rory* • Hugh Sachs *Father Brendan* ■ *Dir/Scr* Maeve Murphy

Beyond the Forest ★★
Melodrama   1949 · US · BW · 76min

The great Bette Davis occasionally teetered on the edge of farce, only saved from producing a parody of herself by a strong directorial hand on the tiller. Sadly, King Vidor does not provide it here. Davis is the disenchanted wife of a hick doctor – a competent Joseph Cotten – stuck in a small town and soon embroiled in a murder puzzle. Vidor tries too hard and fails miserably to engender an atmosphere of tension and menace, while Davis at her most arch and uncontained is not a pretty sight. SH

Bette Davis *Rosa Moline* • Joseph Cotten *Dr Lewis Moline* • David Brian *Neil Latimer* • Ruth Roman *Carol* • Minor Watson *Moose* • Dona Drake *Jenny* • Regis Toomey *Sorren* • Sara Selby [Sarah Selby] *Mildred* ■ *Dir* King Vidor • *Scr* Lenore Coffee, from the novel by Stuart Engstrand

Beyond the Hills ★★★★ 12
Drama   2012 · Rom/Fr/Bel · Colour · 145min

A monastery in rural Romania is the location for a fierce conflict between implacable faith and liberated secular desires in this fact-based drama. At its core is a love story between two young women brought up in a state orphanage, who meet again when Cristina Flutur returns from working in Germany to visit her beloved Cosmina Stratan, now a nun at a religious community. Director Cristian Mungiu rewards the patient viewer with a powerful portrayal of the carnage inflicted by good intentions, closed minds and sheer incomprehension. It's a demanding yet worthwhile film, whose courageous female leads went on to share the best actress award at Cannes in 2012. TJ Romanian +subtitles. Swearing, brief nudity.

Cosmina Stratan *Voichita* • Cristina Flutur *Alina* • Valeriu Andriuta *Papa, priest* • Dana Tapalaga *Mother Superior* ■ *Dir* Cristian Mungiu • *Scr* Cristian Mungiu, from the non-fiction novels by Tatiana Niculescu Bran

Beyond the Law ★★★ U
Detective drama   1968 · US · BW · 85min

This abrasive second film from novelist-turned-director Norman Mailer shows the off-duty hours of three Manhattan cops. Mailer himself plays the senior detective, while his colleagues are all racist bigots who bend the rules in their quest for a collar. The style is *cinéma vérité* – the cameraman is noted documentarist DA Pennebaker – and the script consists of improvised dialogue made up on the spot. It's a grubby, shambolic movie with some terrible scenes, but there's also some powerful stuff here, most of it involving Rip Torn as a hippy accused of murder. AT

Rip Torn *Popcorn* • George Plimpton *Mayor* • Norman Mailer *Lieutenant Francis Xavier Pope* • Mickey Knox *Mickey Berk* • Buzz Farbar *Rocco Gibraltar* • Beverly Bentley *Mary Pope* • Mara Lynn *Ilse Fuchs* • Marcia Mason *Marcia Stillwell* ■ *Dir/Scr* Norman Mailer

Beyond the Lights ★★★ 12
Music drama   2014 · US · Colour · 116min

Essentially a riff on *The Bodyguard*, this cheesy but entertaining "fame is pain" tearjerker offers rising British actress Gugu Mbatha-Raw a very different lead role from the one she played in period drama *Belle*. She plays a hip-hop superstar who's been groomed for success since childhood by pushy mum Minnie Driver. But she now feels lost inside her artificial showbiz persona, and attempts suicide only to be saved by hunky cop-cum-minder Nate Parker. Unashamedly corny, this leaves no music-biz cliché unmined, but Mbatha-Raw is undoubtedly a star in the making. DA *DVD*

Gugu Mbatha-Raw *Noni* • Nate Parker *Kaz* • Minnie Driver *Macy Jean* • Danny Glover *Captain Nicol* • Darryl Stephens *Quentin* ■ *Dir/Scr* Gina Prince-Bythewood

Beyond the Mat ★★★★ 15
Sports documentary 1999 · US · Colour · 98min

Barry W Blaustein, an ex-*Saturday Night Live* writer, makes his directorial debut with this behind-the-scenes look at the World Wrestling Federation. Highlighting the sport's meticulously choreographed showmanship, Blaustein focuses specifically on the way hard-nosed commercialism drives the stars to push themselves to the limits of physical endurance. However, while Terry Funk is seemingly content to wrestle on at the age of 53, the sport has clearly ruined the life of Jake "the Snake" Roberts, whose relationship with his daughter provides painful moments matched only by Mick Foley seeing the impact his fearless style has on his kids. Glib in places, but sympathetic. DP *DVD*

■ *Dir/Scr* Barry W Blaustein • *Cinematographer* Michael Grady

Beyond the Pole ★★★ 15
Satirical comedy   2009 · UK · Colour · 86min

Starting out as a BBC Radio Four series, this entertaining mockumentary succeeds in setting a green agenda while also cracking some decent gags. Determined to do their bit for the planet, ordinary joes Stephen Mangan and Rhys Thomas set out to become the first carbon neutral, vegetarian and organic expedition to reach the North Pole and end up in a race against two Norwegians. Splendidly filmed by Stuart Biddlecombe, this largely improvised romp works best when focusing on the intrepid duo and makes its potent ecological points with unexpectedly affecting poignancy. DP In English, Norwegian. Swearing. *DVD* *BL*

Stephen Mangan *Mark Bark Jones* • Rhys Thomas *Brian Tongue* • Helen Baxendale *Becky* • Alexander Skarsgård *Terje* • Mark Benton *Graham* • Rosie Cavaliero *Sandra* ■ *Dir* David L Williams • *Scr* David L Williams, Neil Warhurst, from the BBC Radio 4 series by Warhurst, Paul Barnhill

Beyond the Poseidon Adventure ★★ 12
Disaster movie   1979 · US · Colour · 109min

It's ironic that this sequel to the blockbuster that initiated the disaster movie cycle should effectively finish off the genre and the career of its king, Irwin Allen. Michael Caine, Sally Field and Karl Malden play the members of a salvage team who come to the rescue of the overturned *Poseidon* passenger liner and find themselves fighting off villainous Telly Savalas, who is after the ship's valuable secret cargo. Even the effects aren't up to much. JF

Michael Caine *Captain Mike Turner* • Sally Field *Celeste Whitman* • Telly Savalas *Stefan Svevo* • Peter Boyle *Frank Mazzetti* • Jack Warden *Harold Meredith* • Shirley Knight *Hannah Meredith* • Shirley Jones *Gina Rowe* • Karl Malden *Wilbur Hubbard* • Veronica Hamel *Suzanne Constantine* • Slim Pickens *Tex* • Mark Harmon *Larry Simpson* ■ *Dir* Irwin Allen • *Scr* Nelson Gidding, from the novel by Paul Gallico

Beyond the Reach ★★★ 12
Thriller   2014 · US · Colour · 87min

The vast majority of this lean, sun-bleached thriller takes place in the Mojave Desert, where Jeremy Irvine's wilderness guide is on a hunting expedition with wealthy Michael Douglas. Realising that a gun mishap could jeopardise an ongoing business deal, Douglas turns nasty, attempting to lose Irvine in the desert. The transformation isn't exactly convincing, but it plays to Douglas's strengths, and he remains highly watchable throughout, despite being lumbered with some ropey dialogue. As for the film, it starts to feel somewhat repetitive, yet is still passable entertainment. SC *DVD* *BL*

Michael Douglas [1] *Madec* • Jeremy Irvine *Ben* • Hanna Mangan Lawrence *Laina* • Ronny Cox *The Sheriff* • Patricia Bethune *Secretary* ■ *Dir* Jean-Baptiste Léonetti • *Scr* Stephen Susco, from Robb White's novel *Deathwatch*

Beyond the Reef ★★ PG
Adventure   1981 · US · Colour · 87min

This picturesque South Seas adventure about the bond shared by a Polynesian youth and a tiger shark plays like a melodrama and a nature documentary spliced together. It follows the relationship between Tikoyo (Dayton Ka'ne), his sweetheart Diana (Maren Jensen) and the man-eating creature that he befriended as a boy. Slight and simply directed, events are accompanied by poor dialogue and unconvincing acting that practically bury the film's poignant messages about the erosion of traditional cultures. SF *DVD*

Dayton Ka'ne *Tikoyo* • Maren Jensen *Diana* • Kathleen Swan *Milly* • Keahi Farden *Jeff* • Oliverio Maciel Diaz *Manidu* ■ *Dir* Frank C Clark • *Scr* Louis La Russo II, Jim Carabatsos, from the novel *Tikoyo and His Shark* by Clement Richer • *Music* Francis Lai

Beyond the River ★★
Drama   1956 · US · Colour · 88min

The original American title, *The Bottom of the Bottle*, should alert you to the content of this maudlin adaptation of a Georges Simenon novel. The physically similar Van Johnson and Joseph Cotten are well cast as psychologically mismatched brothers, one an alcoholic fugitive, the other a respected attorney. Despite veteran director Henry Hathaway's expert handling, the story barely fills the CinemaScope screen; it would have worked better as a tight, black-and-white production. TS

Van Johnson *Donald Martin* • Joseph Cotten *PM* • Ruth Roman *Nora Martin* • Jack Carson *Hal Breckinridge* • Margaret Hayes *Lil Breckinridge* • Bruce Bennett *Brand* • Brad Dexter *Stanley Miller* • Peggy Knudsen *Ellen Miller* ■ *Dir* Henry Hathaway • *Scr* Sydney Boehm, from a novel by Georges Simenon

Beyond the Sea ★★★ 12
Musical biographical drama
2004 · UK/Ger · Colour · 113min

This is very much a labour of love for Kevin Spacey, who, as well as taking the all-singing, all-dancing lead, co-wrote and directed this biopic of crooner Bobby Darin. Charting the singer's astonishing life from an illness-ridden childhood to his death at the tragically young age of 37, it takes in Darin's recording triumphs, marriage to Sandra Dee (Kate Bosworth) and success in Vegas and Hollywood. Spacey is outstanding as Darin, but the film's structure – a strange blend of flashbacks and fantasy – will prove too odd for some viewers. AS Swearing. *DVD*

Kevin Spacey *Bobby Darin* • Kate Bosworth *Sandra Dee* • John Goodman *Steve Blauner* • Bob Hoskins *Charlie Cassotto Maffia* • Brenda Blethyn *Polly Cassotto* • Greta Scacchi *Mary Duvan* • Caroline Aaron *Nina Cassotto Maffia* • Peter Cincotti *Dick Behrke* ■ *Dir* Kevin Spacey • *Scr* Lewis Colick, Kevin Spacey

Beyond the Stars ★★★ PG
Drama   1988 · Can/US · Colour · 87min

A very young looking Christian Slater is the teenager who dreams of becoming an astronaut in this charming drama. His life changes for ever when he discovers that a reclusive neighbour (Martin Sheen) actually took part in a Moon landing, and the two form an uneasy friendship. Both Slater and Sheen are delightful in this enjoyable tale, and they are joined by an impressive cast, which includes F Murray Abraham, Robert Foxworth and a pre-*Basic Instinct* Sharon Stone. JB Swearing. *DVD*

Martin Sheen *Paul Andrews* • Christian Slater *Eric Mason* • Robert Foxworth *Richard Michaels* • Sharon Stone *Laurie McCall* • Olivia D'Abo *Mara Simons* • F Murray Abraham *Harry* ■ *Dir/Scr* David Saperstein

Beyond the Time Barrier ★★ U
Science-fiction adventure
1960 · US · BW · 75min

Pilot Robert Clarke breaks the time barrier in an experimental hypersonic aircraft, crosses the fifth dimension, and finds himself on post-World War III Earth where the underground civilisation is menaced by mutants caused by "the cosmic nuclear plague of 1971". This flimsy fantasy from cult director Edgar G Ulmer is saddled with a dreadful script, amateur acting and a crudely expressed "ban the bomb" political message. AJ

Robert Clarke *Maj William Allison* • Darlene Tompkins *Trirene* • Arianne Arden *Markova* • Vladimir Sokoloff *The Supreme* ■ *Dir* Edgar G Ulmer • *Scr* Arthur C Pierce

Beyond the Valley of the Dolls ★★★★ 18
Cult satirical melodrama
1970 · US · Colour · 104min

Dubbed "BVD" by die-hard trash lovers, soft-core porn king Russ Meyer's hilarious exposé of Hollywood sex, drugs and rock 'n' roll is platinum-plated cult camp. Telling the fabulous rags-to-bitches story of all-girl

B

band the Carrie Nations as they scale the dizzy heights of rock-star fame and then crash-land into decadent sleaze, Meyer's pneumatic parody flashes between soap-opera morality, caricature deviance, flower-power lunacy and shock horror with such breathless audacity that you'll watch it in open-mouthed disbelief. AJ Swearing, nudity. *DVD* *Blu*

Dolly Read *Kelly MacNamara* • Cynthia Myers *Casey Anderson* • Marcia McBroom *Petronella Danforth* • John La Zar [John LaZar] *Z-Man* • Michael Blodgett *Lance Rocke* • David Gurian *Harris Allworth* • Edy Williams *Ashley St Ives* • Erica Gavin *Roxanne* • Charles Napier *Baxter Wolfe* ■ *Dir* Russ Meyer • *Scr* Roger Ebert

Beyond the Walls ★★ 18

Prison drama 1984 · Is · Colour · 98min

An Israeli contender for the best foreign film Oscar, this is an overloud and hysterical prison drama. The plot is naive: in a maximum security jail an Israeli criminal and an Arab terrorist team up to start a prison strike and stop the escalation of violence between inmates and guards. Director Uri Barbash's simplistic premise is that these Israeli-Arab prison relationships serve as a metaphor for the Middle East conflict. TS Hebrew +subtitles.

Arnon Zadok *Uri* • Muhamad Bakri *Issam* • Assi Dayan *Assaf* • Hilel Ne'eman *Hershko, the security officer* • Rami Danon *Fittusi* • Boaz Sharaabi *"The Nightingale"* • Adib Jahashan *Malid* • Roberto Polak *Yechiel* • Naffi Salach *Sanji* ■ *Dir* Uri Barbash, Arnon Zadok, Muhamad Bakri, Rudy Cohen • *Scr* Benny Barbash, Eran Preis, Uri Barbash

Beyond Therapy ★★★ 15

Comedy 1987 · US · Colour · 89min

With his scattergun style, director Robert Altman tends to miss as many targets as he hits. So it proves in this weirdly wacky love story, in which bisexual Jeff Goldblum's relationship with neurotic Julie Hagerty is helped and hindered by their respective psychiatric agony aunts. Glenda Jackson intimidates everyone and there are some great one-liners, but this might have worked better with a more coherent approach. TH *DVD*

Julie Hagerty *Prudence* • Jeff Goldblum *Bruce* • Glenda Jackson *Charlotte* • Tom Conti *Dr Stuart Framingham* • Christopher Guest *Bob* • Genevieve Page *Zizi* • Cris Campion *Andrew* • Sandrine Dumas *Cindy* ■ *Dir* Robert Altman • *Scr* Christopher Durang, Robert Altman, from the play by Christopher Durang

Beyond This Place ★★

Drama 1959 · UK · BW · 90min

Cameraman-turned-director Jack Cardiff was still finding his feet with this, his second film. It's a rather turgid tale about a grown-up wartime evacuee who returns to England to clear his dad of murder. Anglophile Van Johnson is not an ideal lead, though he furrows his brow nicely, but there's a fine British supporting cast. The budget limitations are obvious, despite the presence of US import Vera Miles and a brief location shoot in Liverpool. TS

Van Johnson *Paul Mathry* • Vera Miles *Lena Anderson* • Emlyn Williams *Enoch Oswald* • Bernard Lee *Patrick Mathry* • Jean Kent *Louise Birt* • Leo McKern *McEvoy* • Rosalie Crutchley *Ella Mathry* • Vincent Winter *Paul, as a child* ■ *Dir* Jack Cardiff • *Scr* Kenneth Taylor, from a novel by AJ Cronin

Bhaji on the Beach ★★★ 15

Comedy drama 1993 · UK · Colour · 96min

Gurinder Chadha's debut feature is an astute look at what it means to be Asian, female and British. Following a group of Brummies on a day trip to Blackpool, the film's great strength is the way it interweaves the different plot strands so that each one develops into a fascinating little story in its own right before being neatly brought together at the end. Chadha and scriptwriter Meera Syal were a touch overambitious in trying to tackle so many themes, but their insights are often provocative. DP Violence, swearing. *DVD*

Kim Vithana *Ginder* • Jimmi Harkishin *Ranjit* • Sarita Khajuria *Hashida* • Mo Sesay *Oliver* • Lalita Ahmed *Asha* • Shaheen Khan *Simi* • Zohra Segal *Pushpa* • Amer Chadha-Patel *Amrik* • Nisha Nayar [Nisha K Nayar] *Ladhu* ■ *Dir* Gurinder Chadha • *Scr* Meera Syal, from a story by Meera Syal, Gurinder Chadha

Bhoot ★★★ 15

Horror thriller 2003 · Ind · Colour · 110min

Director Ram Gopal Varma scored a major box-office success by dispensing with any song 'n' dance routines and concentrating on the supernatural in this haunted house chiller. The central plot strand owes much to *The Exorcist*, but the emphasis is on atmosphere and the use of camera and soundtrack to generate suspense and shock. Urmila Matondkar impresses as the wife terrorised in a Mumbai apartment, with Nana Patekar's cop, Seema Biswas's maid and Rekha's medium offering scene-stealing support. The dénouement is a disappointment, however. DP Hindi +subtitles. *DVD*

Ajay Devgan *Vishal* • Urmila Matondkar *Swati* • Rekha *Witch doctor* • Victor Banerjee *Dr Rajan* • Nana Patekar *Inspector Liyacat* • Tanuja *Mrs Khosla* • Seema Biswas *Maid* ■ *Dir* Ram Gopal Varma • *Scr* Lalit Marathe, Sameer Sharma

Bhowani Junction ★★

Period drama 1956 · US · Colour · 109min

Director George Cukor's record with action was far from enviable when he set off for Pakistan to shoot this adaptation about inflamed political and romantic passions in the last days of the Raj. Yet the crowd scenes and the acts of Communist terror are the best parts of this rather turgid melodrama, in which Cukor fails to coax any kind of performance out of Ava Gardner. Stewart Granger and Bill Travers are scarcely more animated. DP

Ava Gardner *Victoria Jones* • Stewart Granger *Colonel Rodney Savage* • Bill Travers *Patrick Taylor* • Abraham Sofaer *Surabhai* • Francis Matthews *Ranjit Kasel* • Marne Maitland *Govindaswami* • Peter Illing *Ghanshyam* • Edward Chapman *Thomas Jones* ■ *Dir* George Cukor • *Scr* Sonya Levien, Ivan Moffat, from the novel by John Masters

The Bible... in the Beginning ★★ U

Religious epic 1966 · US/It · Colour · 163min

This is a reverential but onerous adaptation of the first 22 chapters of Genesis. Director John Huston makes a lovely job of the Creation, but the stellar casting too often works against the drama. George C Scott is imposing as Abraham, however, while Huston himself makes a suitably humble Noah. Giuseppe Rotunno's photography is striking, but Toshiro Mayuzumi's Oscar-nominated score is somewhat overbearing. DP *DVD* *Blu*

Michael Parks *Adam* • Ulla Bergryd *Eve* • Richard Harris *Cain* • John Huston *Noah* • Stephen Boyd *Nimrod* • George C Scott *Abraham* • Ava Gardner *Sarah* • Peter O'Toole *Three Angels* • Franco Nero *Abel* ■ *Dir* John Huston • *Scr* Christopher Fry, Jonathan Griffin, Ivo Perilli, Vittorio Bonicelli

Bicentennial Man ★★ PG

Science-fiction comedy drama 1999 · US · Colour · 125min

Based on the work of two of science fiction's literary giants, Isaac Asimov and Robert Silverberg, this could have become a poignant tale about what it means to be human. Unfortunately, Robin Williams plays for tears as the android butler assembled to serve one family over four generations. The marvellous effects and ideas are scuppered by sentimentality. TH Swearing. *DVD*

Robin Williams *Andrew* • Embeth Davidtz *Little Miss/Portia* • Sam Neill *Sir* • Oliver Platt *Rupert Burns* • Wendy Crowson *Ma'am* • Stephen Root *Dennis Mansky* ■ *Dir* Chris Columbus • *Scr* Nicholas Kazan, from a short story by Isaac Asimov and from the novel *The Positronic Man* by Isaac Asimov, Robert Silverberg

Les Biches ★★★★ 15

Erotic drama 1968 · Fr/It · Colour · 94min

New Wave director Claude Chabrol entered a new phase – which would ultimately lead to such masterpieces as *Le Boucher* – with this cool study of a *ménage à trois* between rich lesbian Stéphane Audran, her penniless young plaything Jacqueline Sassard, and handsome architect Jean-Louis Trintignant. Set on the Riviera, the movie has a marvellously fluid style that matches the seesawing sexuality of the characters and builds towards a startling climax. AT French +subtitles. *DVD*

Stéphane Audran *Frederique* • Jean-Louis Trintignant *Paul* • Jacqueline Sassard *Why* • Nane Germon *Violetta* • Henri Attal *Robeque* • Dominique Zardi *Riais* • Claude Chabrol *Film-maker* ■ *Dir* Claude Chabrol • *Scr* Claude Chabrol, Paul Gégauff

LANDMARK FILM
A masterpiece of Italian neorealism influences directors worldwide

Bicycle Thieves ★★★★★ U

Social drama 1948 · It · BW · 86min

Co-scripted by Cesare Zavattini and directed by Vittorio De Sica, this urban parable is the masterwork of the neorealist movement. Exploring the response of ordinary people to the sociopolitical changes sweeping postwar Italy, the film adopts a "flow of life" structure, comprising vignettes of differing emotional intensity as it follows Lamberto Maggiorani and his son, Enzo Staiola, around Rome in search of the stolen bicycle on which the family depends for its livelihood. Alternating travelling shots of poetic symbolism with stark close-ups of his non-professional leads, De Sica achieves an ironic humanism that can't fail to touch the heart. DP Italian +subtitles. *DVD* *Blu*

Lamberto Maggiorani *Antonio Ricci* • Lianella Carell *Maria Ricci* • Enzo Staiola *Bruno Ricci* • Elena Altieri *The Lady* • Vittorio Antonucci *The Thief* ■ *Dir* Vittorio De Sica • *Scr* Cesare Zavattini, Suso Cecchi D'Amico, Vittorio De Sica, Oreste Biancoli, Adolfo Franci, Gherardo Gherardi, Guerrier Gerardo, from a novel by Luigi Bartolini • Cinematographer Carlo Montuori

Bienvenido Mr Marshall ★★★★ U

Satirical comedy 1953 · Sp · BW · 83min

A prime example of Spanish neorealism, this gentle satire was accused of being anti-American on its release. Cannes juror Edward G Robinson was particularly annoyed by the dream sequences that depict a spoof western, a Ku Klux Klan lynching and a House Un-American Activities Committee hearing. Yet, while Luis Garcia Berlanga is swift to poke fun at US philanthropic pomposity, he saves most of his barbs for the residents of a small Castilian village, whose greed at the prospect of receiving aid from the Marshall Plan only worsens their plight. DP Spanish +subtitles.

Lolita Sevilla *Carmen Vargas* • Manolo Moran *Manolo* • Jose Isbert *Don Pablo, el alcalde* • Alberto Romea *Don Luis, el caballero* ■ *Dir* Luis Garcia Berlanga • *Scr* Juan Antonio Bardem, Luis Garcia Berlanga, Miguel Mihura, from a story by Juan Antonio Bardem, Luis Garcia Berlanga

Big ★★★★ 12

Comedy 1988 · US · Colour · 99min

Oscar winner Tom Hanks only received a nomination for this performance as a 12-year-old boy transplanted by a carnival wishing contraption into a man's body. Elizabeth Perkins also makes an impact as a co-worker who finds herself strangely attracted to Hanks's little big man. This may well be a formula fantasy movie, but Penny Marshall's polished direction combined with Hanks's gauche charm make it the best of the spate of body-swap movies that were turned out by Hollywood in the late 1980s. PF Swearing. *DVD* *Blu*

Tom Hanks *Josh Baskin* • Elizabeth Perkins *Susan Lawrence* • Robert Loggia *"Mac" MacMillan* • John Heard *Paul Davenport* • Jared Rushton *Billy Kopeche* • David Moscow *Young Josh* • Jon Lovitz *Scotty Brennen* • Mercedes

Ruehl *Mrs Baskin* • Josh Clark *Mr Baskin* ■ *Dir* Penny Marshall • *Scr* Gary Ross, Anne Spielberg

Big Ass Spider ★★★ 15

Science-fiction comedy horror 2013 · US · Colour · 77min

After a typical creature feature opening – science interferes with nature; spider grows to larger-than-normal size - this turns into a fun ride of mammoth proportions. The performances, especially from the likeable Greg Grunberg (the burly cop in *Heroes*), are far better than the concept deserves, as a spider (the twist is it's alien) grows larger with every victim it bites. Troma films producer Lloyd Kaufman appears in cameo as a jogger, lending the film some schlock kudos. SuR *DVD*

Ray Wise *Major Braxton Tanner* • Greg Grunberg *Alex Mathis* • Lin Shaye *Mrs Jefferson* • Clare Kramer *Lieutenant Karly Brant* • Lloyd Kaufman *Jogger* ■ *Dir* Mike Mendez • *Scr* Gregory Gieras

Big Bad Mama ★★★ 18

Crime drama 1974 · US · Colour · 80min

Angie Dickinson comes on strong in a typical early 1970s B-movie from the Roger Corman production line, clearly based on *Bonnie and Clyde* and *Bloody Mama*. Dickinson plays a high-spirited widow in 1930s Texas who goes on a bank-robbing spree with her two nubile daughters when the Depression bites. Full of sex, violence, machine guns and banjo music, it's a rambunctious quickie effortlessly touching each exploitation base. *Star Trek*'s William Shatner turns up to romance Dickinson, and her eye-popping nude scenes have made this one a cult favourite. AJ *DVD*

Angie Dickinson *Wilma McClatchie* • William Shatner *William J Baxter* • Tom Skerritt *Fred Diller* • Susan Sennett *Billy Jean McClatchie* • Robbie Lee *Polly McClatchie* • Noble Willingham *Barney* • Joan Prather *Jane Kingston* • Royal Dano *Reverend Johnson* • William O'Connell *Preacher* ■ *Dir* Steve Carver • *Scr* William Norton, Frances Doel

Big Bad Mama II ★★★ 18

Crime drama 1987 · US · Colour · 80min

A cheap and cheerful follow-up – albeit 13 years later - to Roger Corman's cult gangster hit, with Angie Dickinson reviving her role as the gun-toting matriarch. In this adventure, she takes time off from her bank-robbing activities to do battle with slimy politician Bruce Glover, with journalist Robert Culp also on her trail. Although this lacks the knockabout charm and the eclectic casting of the original, director Jim Wynorski delivers a lightweight, knowing slice of exploitation. JF Violence, swearing, nudity.

Angie Dickinson *Wilma McClatchie* • Robert Culp *Daryl Pearson* • Danielle Brisebois *Billie Jean McClatchie* • Julie McCullough *Polly McClatchie* • Bruce Glover *Crawford* • Jeff Yagher *Jordan Crawford* ■ *Dir* Jim Wynorski • *Scr* RJ Robertson, Jim Wynorski

Big Bad Wolves ★★★ 18

Crime thriller 2013 · Is · Colour · 105min

Following on from Israel's first horror movie (*Rabies*), directors Aharon Keshales and Navot Papuhado prove themselves equally adept at dark comic thrillers. This is a grisly tale of murder, abduction and revenge, in which the lives of a loose-cannon cop, a vengeful father and a suspect released by the police collide. Keshales and Papushado push their luck with some of the more risqué humour, but even so, with a score that evokes Bernard Herrmann's best work, it's a film that successfully reels you in. DP In Hebrew. Violence, torture. *DVD*

Lior Ashkenazi *Miki* • Rotem Keinan *Dror* • Tzahi Grad *Gidi* • Doval'e Glickman *Yoram* ■ *Dir/Scr* Aharon Keshales, Navot Papushado

The Big Bird Cage ★★ 18

Blaxploitation 1972 · US · Colour · 86min

The sequel to *The Big Doll House* is more of the same - a blaxploitation mix of broad humour, random violence and dodgy politics. Anitra Ford is jailed in a bamboo sugar mill for knowing too much about a banana republic's revolutionary government and gets imprisoned in the titular torture device. Sid Haig, meanwhile, swoops in to rescue his girlfriend (Pam Grier) and incite a bloody insurrection. This is predictable escapist mayhem with the accent on laughs. AJ *DVD*

Pam Grier *Blossom* • Anitra Ford *Terry* • Candice Roman *Carla* • Teda Bracci *Bull Jones* • Carol Speed *Mickie* • Karen McKevic *Karen* • Sid Haig *Django* ■ *Dir/Scr* Jack Hill

The Big Blockade ★★★ U
Second World War drama
1942 · UK · BW · 71min

Initially conceived as a propaganda short for the Ministry of Information, this Ealing flag-waver sought to emphasise the importance of winning the economic war while Europe remained occupied. Adopting the docudramatic style that would be the prime legacy of British wartime cinema, Charles Frend expounds his message efficiently enough. However, Robert Morley and his fellow Nazis are embarrassing caricatures to set alongside the committed gravitas of Michael Redgrave's Russian and the dignified heroism of Michael Rennie and John Mills. DP *DVD*

Will Hay *Skipper, Royal Navy* • Bernard Miles *Mate, Royal Navy* • John Stuart *Naval officer, Royal Navy* • David Evans *David, Royal Air Force* • John Mills *Tom, Royal Air Force* • Michael Rennie *George, Royal Air Force* • Robert Morley *von Geiselbrecht* • Michael Wilding *Captain* • Thora Hird *Waitress* • Michael Redgrave *Russian* ■ *Dir* Charles Frend • *Scr* Angus MacPhail, Charles Frend

The Big Blue ★★★★ 15
Romantic adventure
1988 · US · BW and Colour · 114min

Action director Luc Besson (*The Fifth Element*) pays homage to the ocean-exploring documentaries of Jacques Cousteau with this stunning, if long and slightly pretentious, underwater cult epic. The story – about two rival deep-sea divers (Besson regular Jean Reno and Jean-Marc Barr) who are crazy about dolphins – is a little shallow, and Rosanna Arquette's role, as a New York insurance investigator who meets Barr in Peru, does seem rather like an afterthought. But Reno mines great humour from his macho mother's boy role, Barr looks impossibly handsome, and the sensational ocean photography is absolutely magnificent. AJ *DVD* *BL*

Rosanna Arquette *Joanna Cross* • Jean-Marc Barr *Jacques Mayol* • Jean Reno *Enzo Molinari* • Paul Shenar *Dr Laurence* • Sergio Castellitto *Novelli* • Jean Bouise *Uncle Louis* • Marc Duret *Roberto* • Griffin Dunne *Duffy* ■ *Dir* Luc Besson • *Scr* Luc Besson, Robert Garland, Marilyn Golding, Jacques Mayol, Marc Perrier, from a story by Luc Besson • *Cinematographer* Carlo Varini

The Big Boss ★★★ 18
Martial arts drama
1971 · HK · Colour · 94min

Bruce Lee's breakthrough Hong Kong film may be a bit rough around the edges, but it remains an electrifying example of the martial arts master at work. The plot is fairly perfunctory: Lee is a young man who travels to Thailand, promising to keep out of trouble only to find himself caught up with a drugs ring. However, his graceful charisma shines throughout and director Lo Wei and fight co-ordinator Han Ying-Chieh (who also plays the villain of the piece) orchestrate some stunning set pieces. JF Cantonese dubbed. Violence. *DVD* *BL*

Bruce Lee *Cheng Chao-An* • Maria Yi *Lin Hau-Mei* • James Tien *Hsu Chien* • Nora Miao *Prostitute* • Hang Ying-Chieh ■ *Dir/Scr* Lo Wei

The Big Bounce ★
Crime drama
1969 · US · Colour · 102min

Ryan O'Neal makes his big screen debut as a cucumber picker who jumps in and out of bed with various women and ends up accused of murder. One of his dalliances (then wife Leigh Taylor-Young) likes having sex in graveyards; another (Lee Grant) commits suicide. Made in 1969, this is one of those "youth movies" that's full of hippy characters, free sex, "daring" nudity and a general air of social rebellion. AT

Ryan O'Neal *Jack Ryan* • Leigh Taylor-Young *Nancy Barker* • Van Heflin *Sam Mirakian* • Lee Grant *Motel resident* • James Daly *Ray Richie* • Robert Webber *Bob Rogers* • Cindy Eilbacher *Cheryl* ■ *Dir* Alex March • *Scr* Robert Dozier, from the novel by Elmore Leonard

The Big Bounce ★★ 12
Crime comedy thriller
2004 · US · Colour · 84min

Owen Wilson plays a laid-back petty thief whose roving eye gets him into serious trouble when he falls for the criminally-minded thrill-seeker Sara Foster. Despite being perfectly cast, Wilson's easy charm is never completely convincing, and he struggles to carry the feature. It's partly due to the weak script and unnecessarily convoluted plot, which twists and turns without any real explanation or character development to support it. Even the entertaining smart-talk rapidly degenerates into farce. SF *DVD*

Owen Wilson *Jack Ryan* • Morgan Freeman *Walter Crewes* • Gary Sinise *Ray Ritchie* • Sara Foster *Nancy Hayes* • Vinnie Jones *Lou Harris* • Charlie Sheen *Bob Rogers Jr* • Bebe Neuwirth *Alison Ritchie* • Harry Dean Stanton *Bob Rogers Sr* • Willie Nelson *Joe Lurie* • Andrew Wilson (1) *Ned Coleman* ■ *Dir* George Armitage • *Scr* Sebastian Gutierrez, from the novel by Elmore Leonard

The Big Brawl ★★ 15
Martial arts comedy
1980 · US · Colour · 91min

This was an early tilt at the American market from Jackie Chan – although he would have to wait for more than a decade before breaking through. Chan plays a martial arts star in 1930s America who decides to take part in a no-holds barred fighting competition, bringing him into conflict with local gangsters. Robert Clouse expertly stages the many fight sequences, although even then Chan was putting equal emphasis on comedy. The period trappings add a fresh flavour to the otherwise predictable plotting. JF

Jackie Chan *Jerry* • José Ferrer *Dominici* • Kristine DeBell *Nancy* • Mako *Herbert* • Ron Max *Leggetti* • David Sheiner *Morgan* • Rosalind Chao *Mae* • Lenny Montana *John* ■ *Dir* Robert Clouse • *Scr* Robert Clouse, from a story by Fred Weintraub, Robert Clouse

The Big Broadcast ★★★★
Musical comedy
1932 · US · BW · 83min

Radio was huge in the 1930s and families listening in at home was starting to pose a threat to cinema, so Paramount cleverly exploited the trend by making this vehicle for radio stars on the big screen. The paper-thin plot has Stuart Erwin taking over a failing radio station run by George Burns and – guess what? – putting on an all-star show. So successful was this flick that three sort-of sequels followed, all successful. Somehow they lack the quaint and specific charm of the original, which even manages to bring some fresh cleverness to its familiar triangle subplot. TS

Bing Crosby *Bing Hornsby* • Stuart Erwin *Leslie McWhinney* • Leila Hyams *Anita Rogers* • Sharon Lynne *Mona* • George Burns *George* • Gracie Allen *Gracie* • George Barbier *Clapsaddle* • Ralph Robertson *Announcer* ■ *Dir* Frank Tuttle • *Scr* George Marion Jr, from the play *Wild Waves* by William Ford Manley

The Big Broadcast of 1936 ★★★★ U
Musical comedy
1935 · US · BW · 94min

In this second of Paramount's all-star collections of radio stars on the silver screen the linking plot seems strangely prophetic, as Gracie Allen's alleged uncle invents a device called television that can send pictures of artistes performing to anywhere in the world. Jack Oakie is the nominal star, as a radio station owner. But more importantly this is your opportunity to catch such major period names as Amos 'n' Andy (Freeman Gosden and Charles Correll, blackfaced), Ethel Merman, the great Bill Robinson and the Vienna Boys' Choir. TS

Jack Oakie *Spud* • George Burns *George* • Gracie Allen *Gracie* • Fayard Nicholas *Dash* • Harold Nicholas *Dot* • Akim Tamiroff *Boris* • Bing Crosby • Ethel Merman • Amos n' Andy • Bill Robinson ■ *Dir* Norman Taurog • *Scr* Walter DeLeon, Francis Martin, Ralph Spence

The Big Broadcast of 1937 ★★★ U
Musical comedy
1936 · US · BW · 104min

The third of Paramount's showcases for big radio names ostensibly stars the great George Burns and Gracie Allen, but actually teams Gracie with the incorrigible Jack Benny, to great and hilarious effect. There is a plot of sorts involving Ray Milland and Shirley Ross going on the town. But, as ever, this is really just an excuse for some of the biggest stars of the day to strut their stuff. TS

Jack Benny *Jack Carson* • George Burns *Mr Platt* • Gracie Allen *Mrs Platt* • Bob Burns (2) *Bob Black* • Frank Forest *Frank Rossman* • Ray Milland *Bob Miller* • Shirley Ross *Gwen Holmes* • Martha Raye *Patsy* • Benny Goodman • Leopold Stokowski ■ *Dir* Mitchell Leisen • *Scr* Walter DeLeon, Francis Martin, from a story by Barry Trivers, Arthur Kober, Erwin Gelsey

The Big Broadcast of 1938 ★★ U
Musical comedy
1937 · US · BW · 90min

The last and frankly weakest of Paramount's all-star series is missing George Burns and Gracie Allen, but benefits from starring the great WC Fields. Though nearly crippled by a dumb plot about racing ocean liners, the film does include a moment that bequeaths immortality upon it – a radio comic called Bob Hope, making his film debut, joins star Shirley Ross in a specially written bittersweet duet entitled *Thanks for the Memory*. The song rightfully won an Oscar and became Bob Hope's theme song. TS

WC Fields *T Frothingill Bellows/SB Bellows* • Martha Raye *Martha Bellows* • Dorothy Lamour *Dorothy Wyndham* • Shirley Ross *Cleo Fielding* • Russell Hicks *Capt Stafford* • Dorothy Howe *Joan Fielding* • Lionel Pape *Lord Droopy* • Bob Hope *Buzz Fielding* • Kirsten Flagstad ■ *Dir* Mitchell Leisen • *Scr* Walter DeLeon, Francis Martin, Ken Englund, Howard Lindsay, Russel Crouse, from a story by Frederick Hazlitt Brennan

Big Brown Eyes ★★★
Crime drama
1936 · US · BW · 76min

This crime drama sought to emulate the success of *The Thin Man* in its teaming of Cary Grant and Joan Bennett, but it has rather more violence and action, including the accidental shooting of a baby. Grant is a little awkward as the two-fisted detective who finds his vaudeville past as a ventriloquist useful in a tight spot, but Bennett is on top form as the wisecracking hotel manicurist turned reporter, who helps him collar Walter Pidgeon's suave racketeer. AE

Cary Grant *Danny Barr* • Joan Bennett *Eve Fallon* • Walter Pidgeon *Richard Morey* • Lloyd Nolan *Russ Cortig* • Alan Baxter *Cary Butler* • Marjorie Gateson *Mrs Cole* • Isabel Jewell *Bessie Blair* • Douglas Fowley *Benny Battle* ■ *Dir* Raoul Walsh • *Scr* Raoul Walsh, Bert Hanlon, from the short stories *Hahsit Babe* and *Big Brown Eyes* by James Edward Grant

Big Bully ★ PG
Comedy
1996 · US · Colour · 86min

Chances are you've never heard of this awful comedy from horror specialist Steve Miner, and for good reason. The plot is unappealing (boy bullied at school grows up to be Rick Moranis and continues to be tormented by Tom Arnold), the black humour falls flat and the notion that Arnold can find renewed meaning in his life through thuggery is vaguely offensive. JC

Rick Moranis *David Leary* • Tom Arnold *Rosco Bigger (Fang)* • Julianne Phillips *Victoria* • Carol Kane *Faith* • Jeffrey Tambor *Art* • Curtis Armstrong *Clark* • Faith Prince *Betty* ■ *Dir* Steve Miner • *Scr* Mark Steven Johnson

The Big Bus ★★ PG
Disaster movie spoof 1976 · US · Colour · 84min

In this intended parody of the 1970s disaster movie genre, the usual bunch of misfits climbs aboard the world's first nuclear-powered coach, travelling from New York to Denver. More like *The Big Blunderbuss* in its scattergun attack on its targets, the likes of Joseph Bologna, Stockard Channing, Lynn Redgrave and Ned Beatty make a lot of noise to occasionally comic effect. SR *DVD*

Joseph Bologna *Dan Torrance* • Stockard Channing *Kitty Baxter* • John Beck *Shoulders* • René Auberjonois *Father Kudos* • Ned Beatty *Shorty Scotty* • Bob Dishy *Dr Kurtz* • José Ferrer *Ironman* • Ruth Gordon *Old lady* • Harold Gould *Professor Baxter* • Larry Hagman *Parking lot doctor* • Sally Kellerman *Sybil Crane* ■ *Dir* James Frawley • *Scr* Fred Freeman, Lawrence J Cohen

Big Business ★★★★★ U
Silent comedy
1929 · US · BW · 18min

Hailed by some critics as the greatest Laurel and Hardy comedy ever filmed, this has the dynamic duo fighting back in an orgy of reciprocal destruction. They're door-to-door salesmen selling Christmas trees in sunny California, up against their ever-wrathful stooge, James Finlayson – he of the pop-eyes and belligerent moustache – as a householder driven to take apart, bit by bit, their car, while they tear up his house and garden. Stan's crocodile tears win over the on-guard policeman, but Ollie's giveaway grin ruins any chance of a happy-ever-after finale. Outstanding. TH *DVD*

Stan Laurel *Stan* • Oliver Hardy *Ollie* • James Finlayson *Homeowner* • Tiny Sandford *Policeman* • Lyle Tayo *Husbandless woman* • Retta Palmer *Neighbor* ■ *Dir* James W Horne • *Scr* Leo McCarey, HM Walker (titles)

Big Business ★★ PG
Comedy
1988 · US · Colour · 93min

This strains the talents and energy levels of Bette Midler and Lily Tomlin to breaking point, along with the audience, who are asked to not so much suspend disbelief as leave their brains on the sideboard during viewing. This could have been enormous fun – a brace of old comedy pros playing two sets of identical twins juggled at birth and meeting years later in a posh New York hotel. But director Jim Abrahams jettisons coherent narrative in favour of giving his leads enough rope to hang themselves. SH *DVD*

Bette Midler *Sadie Shelton/Sadie Ratliff* • Lily Tomlin *Rose Shelton/Rose Ratliff* • Fred Ward *Roone Dimmick* • Edward Herrmann *Graham Sherbourne* • Michele Placido *Fabio Alberici* • Daniel Gerroll *Chuck* • Barry Primus *Michael* • Michael Gross *Dr Jay Marshall* • Deborah Rush *Binky Shelton* • Seth Green *Jason* ■ *Dir* Jim Abrahams • *Scr* Dori Pierson, Marc Rubel

The Big Caper ★★★
Crime thriller
1957 · US · BW · 84min

Rory Calhoun is part of a motley gang of fruitcakes and no-hopers who plan to be a million dollars richer by robbing a bank. Things don't quite go to plan, however. This dime-budget thriller is directed by Robert Stevens, who maintains the tension and evokes the small-town atmosphere well. AT

Rory Calhoun *Frank Harber* • Mary Costa *Kay* • James Gregory *Flood* • Robert Harris *Zimmer* • Corey Allen *Roy* • Roxanne Arlen *Doll* • Paul Picerni *Harry* • Pat McVey *[Patrick McVey] Sam Loxley* ■ *Dir* Robert Stevens • *Scr* Martin Berkeley, from a novel by Lionel White

The Big Chance ★★ PG
Crime drama
1957 · UK · BW · 58min

This is an efficient but hackneyed variation on the well-worn movie notion that crime must never pay. From the moment travel agent William Russell claps eyes on foxy socialite Adrienne Corri and decides to abandon his humdrum married existence for a life of South American excess, we know it will end in tears. Events move at such a pace that there's scarcely time to notice the poverty of the plot and the stiffness of the acting. DP *DVD*

B

Adrienne Corri *Diana Maxwell* • William Russell *Bill Anderson* • Ian Colin *Adam Maxwell* • Penelope Bartley *Betty* • Ferdy Mayne *Alpherghis* • John Rae *Jarvis* • Douglas Ives *Stan Willett* ■ *Dir* Peter Graham Scott • *Scr* Peter Graham Scott, from the novel by Pamela Barrington

The Big Chill ★★★★ 15
Drama 1983 · US · Colour · 100min

At one time a cult movie among 20-somethings, this chic comedy is now also known as the picture from which Kevin Costner had all his scenes cut. Smartly written by director Lawrence Kasdan and Barbara Benedek, the Oscar-nominated script clearly owes a debt to John Sayles's overlooked and superior reunion drama *The Return of the Secaucus Seven*. However, there are still plenty of original insights into both 1960s counterculture and the pretensions of the chattering classes. There's a dream cast, while the soundtrack is packed with the anthems of an age. Over clever, but very slick. DP Swearing, drug abuse, brief nudity. *DVD*

Kevin Kline *Harold Cooper* • Glenn Close *Sarah Cooper* • William Hurt *Nick* • Jeff Goldblum *Michael* • Tom Berenger *Sam* • Meg Tilly *Chloe* • JoBeth Williams *Karen* • Mary Kay Place *Meg* • Don Galloway *Richard* ■ *Dir* Lawrence Kasdan • *Scr* Lawrence Kasdan, Barbara Benedek

The Big Circus ★★★ U
Adventure 1959 · US · Colour · 103min

Cult favourite Joseph M Newman directs a fine, though slightly second-rung, cast, headed by world-weary Victor Mature and featuring such stars as Peter Lorre (as a neurotic clown) and Gilbert Roland (as the tightrope walker). Although clearly hindered by budget limitations, this is a worthy attempt to break new ground. Though not a box-office hit, this remains a treat. TS

Victor Mature *Hank Whirling* • Red Buttons *Randy Sherman* • Rhonda Fleming *Helen Harrison* • Kathryn Grant *Jeannie Whirling* • Vincent Price *Hans Hagenfeld* • David Nelson (1) *Tommy Gordon* • Gilbert Roland *Zach Colino* • Peter Lorre *Skeeter* ■ *Dir* Joseph M Newman • *Scr* Irwin Allen, Charles Bennett, Irving Wallace, from a story by Irwin Allen

Big City ★★
Drama 1937 · US · BW · 79min

Rival New York cab companies are at loggerheads but you'd think the Third World War had broken out, so overwrought is this movie. Cabs get smashed, faces get smashed, the unions march in and then bombs go off and the city teeters on anarchy. Spencer Tracy, as one of the cabbies, tries to stay calm, while his pregnant Russian immigrant wife, Luise Rainer, is accused of causing explosions. Just awful, but compulsive viewing. AT

Spencer Tracy *Joe Benton* • Luise Rainer *Anna Benton* • Charley Grapewin *Mayor* • Janet Beecher *Sophie Sloane* • Eddie Quillan *Mike Edwards* • Victor Varconi *Paul Roya* • Oscar O'Shea *John C Andrews* ■ *Dir* Frank Borzage • *Scr* Dore Schary, Hugo Butler, from a story by Norman Krasna

The Big City ★★★★ PG
Drama 1963 · Ind · BW · 136min

Satyajit Ray won the best director prize at Berlin for this, the first of his films with a contemporary setting. Although thematically related to the "salaryman" comedies of Yasujiro Ozu, the stylistic references to Jean Renoir and neorealism remain consistent with Ray's earliest work. Touching on the mores of Anglo-Indians, the film deals primarily with the social role of women, as it traces Madhabi Mukherjee's progress from traditional housewife to middle-class heroine. Minutely observed and flawlessly acted, this is a gently satirical study of the changing face of Calcutta. DP Bengali +subtitles. *DVD*

Madhabi Mukherjee *Arati* • Anil Chatterjee *Subrata Mazumdar* • Haradhan Bannerjee *Mukherjee* • Haren Chatterjee *Father* • Vicky Redwood *Edith Simmons* • Jaya Bhaduri [Jaya Bachchan] *Sister* ■ *Dir* Satyajit Ray • *Scr* Satyajit Ray, from Narendranath Mitra's novel *Abataranika*

The Big Clock ★★★
Film noir 1948 · US · BW · 95min

Charles Laughton plays a publisher who murders his mistress and then gets one of his employees, crime editor Ray Milland, to investigate. What Laughton doesn't know is that Milland shared the same girlfriend, so lots of juicy complications ensue, especially as Milland hates Laughton for his oppressive business practices. With the huge office clock ticking away like a countdown to doom, this is highly effective. AT

Ray Milland *George Stroud* • Charles Laughton *Earl Janoth* • Maureen O'Sullivan *Georgette Stroud* • George Macready *Steven Hagen* • Rita Johnson *Pauline York* • Elsa Lanchester *Louise Patterson* • Harold Vermilyea *Don Klausmeyer* • Dan Tobin *Ray Cordette* ■ *Dir* John Farrow • *Scr* Jonathan Latimer, from the novel by Kenneth Fearing

The Big Combo ★★★★ PG
Film noir 1955 · US · BW · 87min

This is as tough and nasty as they come, and that's a recommendation! Cult director Joseph H Lewis trawls the mean streets as cop Cornel Wilde turns over the local rocks to see what slime crawls out from underneath. A co-feature on its original release, and barely noticed, this movie was accorded a reissue in repertory cinemas in the 1980s. A whole new audience responded to the amorality and the raw violence, delighting in the twisted viciousness of evil Richard Conte. TS

Cornel Wilde *Diamond* • Richard Conte *Brown* • Brian Donlevy *McClure* • Jean Wallace *Susan* • Robert Middleton *Peterson* • Lee Van Cleef *Fante* • Ted De Corsia *Bettini* • Helen Walker *Alicia* ■ *Dir* Joseph H Lewis • *Scr* Philip Yordan

The Big Country ★★★★★ PG
Western 1958 · US · Colour · 159min

Unfairly neglected today, this major western is a film of truly epic dimensions. It tells the tale of a greenhorn sent to the wide-open spaces, a role to which co-producer and star Gregory Peck is particularly suited – he is one of the few actors whose innate pacificism rings true. Thanks to the combination of top director William Wyler and a superb cast that includes Jean Simmons, Charlton Heston and the Oscar-winning Burl Ives the film never palls, despite its length. It also features a great theme tune, a triumph for composer Jerome Moross. Though misused by a score of commercials, when heard in context, the music rightfully lifts this distinguished movie to the realm of screen classic. TS *DVD*

Gregory Peck *James McKay* • Jean Simmons *Julie Maragon* • Carroll Baker *Patricia Terrill* • Charlton Heston *Steve Leech* • Burl Ives *Rufus Hannassey* • Charles Bickford *Major Henry Terrill* • Alfonso Bedoya *Ramon* • Chuck Connors *Buck Hannassey* ■ *Dir* William Wyler • *Scr* James R Webb, Robert Wilder, Sy Bartlett, Robert Wyler, from the novel by Donald Hamilton, adapted by Jessamyn West, Robert Wyler • *Cinematographer* Franz F Planer [Franz Planer]

The Big Cube ★
Drama 1969 · US/Mex · Colour · 98min

This sad coda to the great Lana Turner's career came three years after her last glamorous Ross Hunter/Universal production, *Madame X*. Co-stars George Chakiris, Richard Egan and Dan O'Herlihy – all well past their prime – lend this demented melodrama a camp attraction. But its sheer ineptitude, combined with Turner's ravaged looks and (to be kind) uncertain performance, make it hard to watch, let alone take seriously. TS

Lana Turner *Adriana Roman* • George Chakiris *Johnny Allen* • Richard Egan *Frederick Lansdale* • Dan O'Herlihy *Charles Winthrop* • Karin Mossberg *Lisa Winthrop* • Pamela Rodgers *Bibi* ■ *Dir* Tito Davison • *Scr* William Douglas Lansford, from a story by Tito Davison, Edmundo Baez

Big Daddy ★★★★ 12
Comedy 1999 · US · Colour · 89min

This "adoption-by-proxy" comedy is a perfect example of how a sparkling central performance can make even the most crudely sentimental fluff hilariously palatable. Thanks to slacker superstar Adam Sandler and his infectious goofball sweetness, this film works like a charm, even though the story springs few surprises (lazy loafer takes his flatmate's love-child under his wing; they bond; and the parental challenges change him sufficiently to win the hand of Miss Right, Joey Lauren Adams). Yes, it's contrived, mawkish and manipulative, but director Dennis Dugan's effortless handling of the tale and Sandler's confident puppy-dog demeanour ensure that it delivers huge laughs. AJ Swearing. *DVD*

Adam Sandler *Sonny Koufax* • Joey Lauren Adams *Layla* • Jon Stewart *Kevin* • Cole Sprouse *Julian* • Dylan Sprouse *Julian* • Josh Mostel *Mr Brooks* • Leslie Mann *Corinne* • Allen Covert *Phil* • Rob Schneider *Delivery guy* • Kristy Swanson *Vanessa* • Joseph Bologna *Mr Koufax* • Steve Buscemi *Homeless guy* ■ *Dir* Dennis Dugan • *Scr* Steve Franks, Tim Herlihy, Adam Sandler, from a story by Steve Franks

Big Deal on Madonna Street ★★★★
Heist comedy 1958 · It · BW · 91min

This is a smashing comedy, mainly a send-up of *Rififi*, about a band of incompetent layabouts and petty crooks who plan a major heist by breaking into an empty flat and drilling through to the bank vault next door. The plan goes slightly awry and leads to a hilarious twist in the tale. Made quickly and cheaply, it stars Marcello Mastroianni and Vittorio Gassman, the latter made up to hide his Latin lover image completely. Louis Malle remade it in 1984 as *Crackers*; it was remade again in 2002 as *Welcome to Collinwood*. AT In Italian.

Vittorio Gassman *Peppe* • Marcello Mastroianni *Tiberio* • Toto *Dante* • Renato Salvatori *Mario* • Carla Gravina *Nicoletta* • Claudia Cardinale *Carmelina* • Memmo Carotenuto *Cosimo* • Tiberio Murgia *Ferribotte* ■ *Dir* Mario Monicelli • *Scr* Mario Monicelli, Suso Cecchi D'Amico, Age Scarpelli [Agenore Incrocci and Furio Scarpelli]

The Big Easy ★★★★ 15
Crime thriller 1986 · US · Colour · 96min

After watching this sizzling crime thriller, you'll wonder why director Jim McBride and stars Dennis Quaid and Ellen Barkin failed to go on to take Hollywood by storm. Rather than the start of something big, this was the career peak of all three, but what heights they attained! Sparks fly from the moment cop Quaid and assistant district attorney Barkin come together to investigate a New Orleans Mob killing, but their conflicting moral codes threaten to take the heat out of their steamy affair. Ned Beatty and John Goodman provide gritty support, while McBride brings the city to throbbing life. DP Violence, swearing, sex scenes. *DVD*

Dennis Quaid *Remy McSwain* • Ellen Barkin *Anne Osborne* • Ned Beatty *Jack Kellom* • Ebbe Roe Smith *Detective Dodge* • John Goodman *Detective DeSoto* • Lisa Jane Persky *Detective McCabe* • Charles Ludlam *Lamar* • Thomas O'Brien *Bobby* ■ *Dir* Jim McBride • *Scr* Daniel Petrie Jr, Jack Baran

Big Eden ★★ PG
Romantic drama 2000 · US · Colour · 115min

In the mythical Montana town of Big Eden, where all the local yokels are pro-gay, non-racist and open to suggestion, closeted New York artist Arye Gross arrives to look after his grandfather. But the accepting townsfolk guess his secret and force him to choose between a relationship with his hunky ex-schoolfriend Tim DeKay and the American Indian general store owner Eric Schweig. Although saccharine and awkwardly scripted, this exerts a certain charm. AJ *DVD*

Arye Gross *Henry Hart* • Eric Schweig *Pike Dexter* • Tim DeKay *Dean Stewart* • Louise Fletcher *Grace Cornwell* • George Coe *Sam Hart* • Nan Martin *Widow Thayer* ■ *Dir/Scr* Thomas Bezucha

Big Eyes ★★★ 12
Biographical drama 2014 · US · Colour · 101min

Director Tim Burton turns his sorcerer's sights on this real-life story, adding a smattering of the fantastic to a tale of fraud and female subjugation in the 1950s and 60s. Amy Adams stars as artist Margaret Keane, whose paintings of doe-eyed children were phenomenally successful, and Christoph Waltz plays her conman husband, manipulating her in order to take credit for her work. Burton's directorial style is a good visual match for the subject matter, and an over-the-top Waltz is balanced by Adams, who acts with bewitching delicacy to anchor the film. EAS *DVD BLU*

Amy Adams *Margaret Keane* • Christoph Waltz *Walter Keane* • Danny Huston *Dick Nolan* • Jason Schwartzman *Ruben* • Terence Stamp *John Canaday* ■ *Dir* Tim Burton • *Scr* Scott Alexander, Larry Karaszewski

Big Fat Liar ★★ PG
Comedy 2002 · US/Ger · Colour · 84min

Frankie Muniz plays a 14-year-old habitual liar who's understandably disbelieved by his mum and dad when he tells the far-fetched truth for once: that an unscrupulous Hollywood film producer (Paul Giamatti) has filched his latest tall tale, and is turning it into the summer's movie blockbuster. Muniz heads for Beverly Hills – cue lights, camera and mean-spirited slapstick as the pilfering producer gets his comeuppance. DA *DVD*

Frankie Muniz *Jason Shepherd* • Paul Giamatti *Marty Wolf* • Amanda Bynes *Kaylee* • Amanda Detmer *Monty Kirkham* • Lee Majors *Vince* • Donald Faison *Frank Jackson/Kenny Trooper* ■ *Dir* Shawn Levy • *Scr* Dan Schneider, from a story by Dan Schneider, Brian Robbins

Big Fella ★★ U
Musical drama 1937 · UK · BW · 73min

Paul Robeson stars as an idle vagabond on the Marseille waterfront, known to all for his great singing voice. Hired to find a missing boy, he succeeds in his mission, but the child is a runaway who threatens him with accusations of kidnapping if he is returned to his family. This is unworthy of its star, but it does offer a few twists and turns and the pleasure of seeing the splendid Elisabeth Welch in her prime. RK

Paul Robeson *Joe* • Elizabeth Welch [Elisabeth Welch] *Manda* • Roy Emerton *Spike* • James Hayter *Chuck* • Lawrence Brown *Corney* • Eldon Grant *Gerald Oliphant* ■ *Dir* J Elder Wills • *Scr* Ingram D'Abbes, Fenn Sherie, from the novel *Banjo* by Claude McKay

Big Fish ★★ PG
Fantasy drama 2003 · US · Colour · 119min

Director Tim Burton returns to familiar territory here – a strange place somewhere between reality and fantasy, dream and nightmare. Albert Finney plays Edward Bloom, a travelling salesman whose apparent selfishness and ridiculous stories of his exploits have driven a wedge between him and son Billy Crudup. Called to his father's deathbed, Crudup is infuriated when his wife is regaled with tall tales featuring young Edward (Ewan McGregor). Intent on exposing his father, the disgruntled son sets out to learn the truth. This drifts colourfully along, but lacks edge. BP *DVD BLU*

Ewan McGregor *Young Edward Bloom* • Albert Finney *Edward Bloom* • Billy Crudup *Will Bloom* • Jessica Lange *Sandra Bloom* • Helena Bonham Carter *Jenny/The Witch* • Alison Lohman *Young Sandra* • Robert Guillaume *Dr Bennett* • Marion Cotillard *Josephine* ■ *Dir* Tim Burton • *Scr* John August, from the novel *Big Fish, a Story of Mythic Proportions* by Daniel Wallace

The Big Fisherman ★★ U
Biblical drama 1959 · US · Colour · 166min

Howard Keel is competent enough as Simon Peter in this biblical saga, directed by Frank Borzage, an Oscar-winning veteran of the 1920s and 1930s. The film is handsomely mounted and photographed, as befits the epic genre, but it's still a plodding bore, the main excitement in which comes from a princess (Susan Kohner) out to kill

U SUITABLE FOR ALL   Uc SUITABLE ESPECIALLY FOR YOUNG CHILDREN (DVD ONLY)   PG PARENTAL GUIDANCE   12A UNDER 12s TO BE ACCOMPANIED (CINEMA ONLY)

Herod (Herbert Lom) and a prince (John Saxon) who is hopelessly in love with her. AJ

Howard Keel *Simon Peter* • Susan Kohner *Fara* • John Saxon *Voldi* • Martha Hyer *Herodias* • Herbert Lom *Herod Antipas* • Ray Stricklyn *Deran* ■ *Dir* Frank Borzage • *Scr* Howard Estabrook, Rowland V Lee, from a novel by Lloyd C Douglas

The Big Fix ★★★ 15
Comedy detective drama
1978 · US · Colour · 103min

Richard Dreyfuss turned actor/producer for this off-the-wall private eye thriller that takes in the demise of 1960s radicalism, Latino tensions and what might be summed up as post-Watergate disenchantment. Dreyfuss plays the Jewish gumshoe Moses Wine, a former campus activist with an ex-wife, two kids and a heap of debt. Then the plot kicks in – something about dirty tricks during a political campaign – and quickly gets very complicated. Principally a character study, superbly portrayed by Dreyfuss, it flopped. AT

Richard Dreyfuss *Moses Wine* • Susan Anspach *Lila* • Bonnie Bedelia *Suzanne* • John Lithgow *Sam Sebastian* • Ofelia Medina *Alora* • Nicolas Coster *Spitzler* • F Murray Abraham *Eppis* • Fritz Weaver *Oscar Procari Sr* • Mandy Patinkin *Pool man* ■ *Dir* Jeremy Paul Kagan • *Scr* Roger L Simon, from his novel

Big Game ★★★ 15
Action adventure
2014 · Fin/UK/Ger/Fr · Colour · 86min

The tone veers all over the place in this light-hearted, if far-fetched, thriller. But if you like your Boy's Own adventure with jokey snatches of edgy terrorist violence, Jalmari Helander's follow-up to the cult Christmas thriller *Rare Exports* is a pleasing enough escapist diversion. During a rite-of-passage solo hunt in the scenic Finnish mountains, young Onni Tommila (the kid from *Exports*) saves the crash-landed US President (Samuel L Jackson) from assassination after Air Force One is shot down in a coup attempt. The cliffhanger action is outlandish but the direction is lively and things move at a brisk clip. AJ

DVD *Blu*

Samuel L Jackson *The President* • Onni Tommila *Oskari* • Ray Stevenson *Morris* • Victor Garber *Vice President* • Mehmet Kurtulus *Hazar* • Ted Levine *General Underwood* • Felicity Huffman *CIA Director* • Jim Broadbent *Herbert* ■ *Dir/Scr* Jalmari Helander

The Big Green ★★ U
Sports comedy
1995 · US · Colour · 95min

After the success of ice-hockey movie *The Mighty Ducks* (which, with the help of likeable Emilio Estevez, spawned two sequels), it probably seemed a good idea to use the same ingredients (little team does good and the players learn more about themselves and each other in the process) for other sports. However, here the plot is rehashed for a movie about soccer, and Estevez is replaced by a man whose career is even further in the dumpster, Steve Guttenberg. JB *DVD*

Steve Guttenberg *Sheriff Tom Palmer* • Olivia D'Abo *Anna Montgomery* • Jay O Sanders *Jay Huffer* • John Terry *Edwin V Douglas* • Chauncey Leopardi *Evan Schiff* • Patrick Renna *Larry Musgrove* • Billy L Sullivan *Jeffrey Luttrell* • Yareli Arizmendi *Marbelly Morales* ■ *Dir/Scr* Holly Goldberg Sloan

A Big Hand for a Little Lady ★★★ U
Comedy western
1966 · US · Colour · 91min

This amiable comedy western was originally devised as a 50-minute TV programme. Although there are a few visible stretch marks, screenwriter Sidney Carroll and director Fielder Cook have done a creditable job in filling it out to feature length. It is slickly acted by Henry Fonda and Joanne Woodward, playing two homesteaders heading for Texas who check in to a hotel where the year's biggest poker game is in progress. DP

Henry Fonda *Meredith* • Joanne Woodward *Mary* • Jason Robards *Henry Drummond* • Charles Bickford *Benson Tropp* • Burgess Meredith *Doc Scully* • Kevin McCarthy *Otto Habershaw* • Robert Middleton *Dennis Wilcox* • Paul Ford *Ballinger* ■ *Dir* Fielder Cook • *Scr* Sidney Carroll, from his teleplay *Big Deal at Laredo*

The Big Hangover ★★★ U
Comedy drama
1950 · US · BW · 82min

This engaging comedy has Van Johnson working for a law firm and trying to conceal an allergy to alcohol brought on during the war when the cellar he was hiding in flooded with brandy. This is where Elizabeth Taylor comes in. She's the boss's daughter and an amateur shrink, who sets out to cure our hero of his allergy. Taylor, in her first adult role, could probably persuade any man to overcome any phobia. AT

Van Johnson *David* • Elizabeth Taylor *Mary Belney* • Percy Waram *John Belney* • Fay Holden *Martha Belney* • Leon Ames *Carl Bellcap* • Edgar Buchanan *Uncle Fred Mahoney* • Selena Royle *Kate Mahoney* ■ *Dir/Scr* Norman Krasna

The Big Heat ★★★★ 15
Film noir
1953 · US · BW · 85min

Glenn Ford crusades against Mob-led civic corruption and hunts for vengeance in this classic *film noir* from director Fritz Lang. Its most famous scene, when moll Gloria Grahame is scalded by hot coffee hurled by crook Lee Marvin, was trimmed by the censors before the movie could be released in Britain with an X certificate. Now fully restored, it's tame by today's standards, but still packs a punch. Ford is excellent as the cop with a mission – his character was based on the investigators during the televised 1950s Estes Kefauver Senate investigations – and Lang gives the vicious exposé a sleek and glossy surface. TS *DVD*

Glenn Ford *Dave Bannion* • Gloria Grahame *Debby Marsh* • Jocelyn Brando *Katie Bannion* • Alexander Scourby *Mike Lagana* • Lee Marvin *Vince Stone* • Jeanette Nolan *Bertha Duncan* • Peter Whitney *Tierney* • Willis Bouchey *Lt Wilkes* ■ *Dir* Fritz Lang • *Scr* Sydney Boehm, from the serial in *The Saturday Evening Post* by William P McGivern • *Cinematographer* Charles B Lang [Charles Lang]

The Big Heist ★★
Crime drama based on a true story
2001 · US/Can · Colour · 92min

It might be based on a true crime story, but this dramatisation of the 1978 Lufthansa heist doesn't feel very authentic. Part of that's down to lead Donald Sutherland, whose accent fluctuates absurdly as a small-time, Irish-American crook who incurs brutal Mafia "justice" after carrying out the then biggest cash theft in US history (a pivotal incident in *GoodFellas*). Veteran director Robert Markowitz's show-off visuals and generally erratic editing obstruct the narrative, while excessive artistic licence makes events seem clichéd and ultimately contrived. SF Violence, swearing, drug abuse.

Donald Sutherland *Jimmy Burke* • John Heard *Richard Woods* • Jamie Harris *Frankie Burke* • Janet Kidder *Maria* • Nick Sandow *Henry Hill* • Michael P Moran *Louis the whale* ■ *Dir* Robert Markowitz • *Scr* Jere Cunningham, Gary Hoffman, from the book *The Heist* by Ernest Volkman, John Cummings

Big Hero 6 ★★★★ PG
Animated action adventure
2014 · US · Colour · 97min

Disney's Oscar-winning animation combines an East-meets-West story of brotherly love and loss, heroism and villainy, with a plethora of action sequences that are carefully structured for maximum intensity. In seaside city San Fransokyo (geddit?), young robotics genius Hiro Hamada is forced into a battle with an evil megalomaniac. For Marvel comic fans, this has little to do with the original series, with central character Baymax transformed from a shape-shifting powerhouse on page into the cutest and cuddliest of balloon buddies on screen. Kids will love the whooshing and swooping of the characters

in what is a multicoloured sugar-rush of a movie. SuR *DVD* *Blu* *CS*

Scott Adsit *Baymax* • Ryan Potter *Hiro Hamada* • Daniel Henney *Tadashi Hamada* • TJ Miller *Fred* • Jamie Chung *GoGo Tomago* • Damon Wayans Jr *Wasabi* • Genesis Rodriguez *Honey Lemon* • James Cromwell *Robert Robert Callaghan* ■ *Dir* Don Hall (2), Chris Williams • *Scr* Daniel Gerson, Robert L Baird, Jordan Roberts, from the comic books by Duncan Rouleau, Steven T Seagle

The Big Hit ★★ 18
Action thriller
1998 · US · Colour · 87min

This tries very hard to be offbeat and quirky, but ends up as merely dumb and annoying. Mark Wahlberg does well as the girl-juggling assassin, though Lou Diamond Phillips overdoes his performance as Wahlberg's accomplice. This isn't clever, funny or engaging enough to be the exercise in killer cool it craves to be. JC Violence, swearing, brief nudity. *DVD* *Blu*

Mark Wahlberg *Melvin Smiley* • Lou Diamond Phillips *Cisco* • Christina Applegate *Pam Shulman* • Avery Brooks *Paris* • Bokeem Woodbine *Crunch* • Antonio Sabato Jr *Vince* • China Chow *Keiko Nishi* • Lainie Kazan *Jeanne Shulman* • Elliott Gould *Morton Shulman* • Sab Shimono *Jiro Nishi* ■ *Dir* Che-Kirk Wong [Kirk Wong] • *Scr* Ben Ramsey

The Big House ★★★★
Prison drama
1930 · US · BW · 84min

This powerful exposé of conditions in a men's prison, prompted by newspaper headlines of rioting convicts, was such as a smash hit that it served as a template for dozens of pictures. Robert Montgomery is the new inmate, a well-bred weakling sentenced for manslaughter, who has to share a cell with Wallace Beery's tough gangster and Chester Morris's repentant forger. Co-written by a leading female screenwriter, Frances Marion, and directed by her husband, George Hill, the film vividly evokes the grimness of prison life, from overcrowded cells to a spell in solitary. The long take down the empty corridor of the solitary wing as the inmates call out to each other for company is unforgettable. AE

Chester Morris *John Morgan* • Wallace Beery *Butch Schmidt* • Lewis Stone *Warden James Adams* • Robert Montgomery *Kent Marlowe* • Leila Hyams *Ann Marlowe* • George F Marion *Pop Riker* • JC Nugent *Mr Marlowe* • Karl Dane *Olsen* ■ *Dir* George Hill • *Scr* Frances Marion, Joe Farnham, Martin Flavin • *Cinematographer* Harold Wenstrom

Big House, USA ★★★
Action crime drama
1955 · US · BW · 82min

This is a tight, compressed thriller about a kidnapped boy, buried ransom money and the heavies and psychos who break out of jail intending to dig it up. All the while, FBI man Reed Hadley lies in wait. A strong cast of B-movie regulars – Broderick Crawford, Charles Bronson and Ralph Meeker, as the kidnapper – contribute some agreeably cheesy characterisations. AT

Broderick Crawford *Rollo Lamar* • Ralph Meeker *Jerry Barker* • Reed Hadley *James Madden* • Randy Farr *Nurse Emily Evans* • William Talman *Machinegun Mason* • Lon Chaney Jr *Alamo Smith* • Charles Bronson *Benny Kelly* • Peter Votrian *Danny Lambert* ■ *Dir* Howard W Koch • *Scr* John C Higgins

Big Jake ★★ 15
Western
1971 · US · Colour · 105min

It might just as well have been titled *Big John*, because that's all it is, really: close-ups of the grizzled John Wayne, in the twilight of his career, nostalgically paired (for the fifth and last time) with an elegantly ageing Maureen O'Hara. There's precious little plot, though, and George Sherman's direction is lazy and untidy. Still, William Clothier's outdoor photography is worth a look and Richard Boone makes a fine larger-than-life baddie. But the whole sad enterprise is altogether too routine, and the leads just look too old. TS *DVD* *Blu*

John Wayne *Jacob McCandles* • Richard Boone *John Fain* • Maureen O'Hara *Martha McCandles* • Patrick Wayne *James McCandles* • Chris Mitchum [Christopher Mitchum] *Michael McCandles* •

Bobby Vinton *Jeff McCandles* • Bruce Cabot *Sam Sharpnose* ■ *Dir* George Sherman • *Scr* Harry Julian Fink, Rita M Fink

Big Jim McLain ★ U
Spy drama
1952 · US · BW · 86min

John Wayne produced and starred in this nasty piece of propaganda in which he and James Arness, as House Un-American Activities Committee investigators, rout out communist spies in Hawaii. The astonishingly crude script portrays communists as inadequate human beings who behave like gangsters and make stupid mistakes. AE *DVD*

John Wayne *Big Jim McLain* • Nancy Olson *Nancy Vallon* • James Arness *Mal Baxter* • Alan Napier *Sturak* • Veda Ann Borg *Madge* • Gayne Whitman *Dr Gelster* • Hal Baylor *Poke* ■ *Dir* Edward Ludwig • *Scr* James Edward Grant, Richard English, Eric Taylor

The Big Job ★★★ U
Comedy
1965 · UK · BW · 84min

Sidney James is the leader of a gang of incompetent crooks who discover a police station has been built on the site where they stashed the loot from their last robbery. Partners-in-crime Sylvia Syms, Dick Emery and Lance Percival bungle his recovery plans with practised buffoonery, but they are often reduced to slapstick props. In contrast, Joan Sims's landlady, Jim Dale's goofy plod and Deryck Guyler's idle desk sergeant are much more fully developed comic creations. DP

Sidney James *George Brain* • Sylvia Syms *Myrtle Robbins* • Dick Emery *Fred "Booky" Binns* • Lance Percival *Tim "Dipper" Day* • Joan Sims *Mildred Gamely* • Jim Dale *Harold* • Edina Ronay *Sally Gamely* • Deryck Guyler *Police sergeant* ■ *Dir* Gerald Thomas • *Scr* Talbot Rothwell

The Big Kahuna ★★★ 15
Drama
1999 · US · Colour · 87min

Kevin Spacey plays one of a trio of salesmen who have gathered at a hotel for a convention. Spacey, all hyperactive bluster, is determined to secure a major client – the Big Kahuna of the title. However, it's new boy Peter Facinelli who may hold the key to capturing the elusive prize. This claustrophobic drama struggles to shake off its stage origins, but Spacey delivers a bravura turn and is more than matched by Danny DeVito as his world-weary partner. JF Swearing. *DVD*

Kevin Spacey *Larry Mann* • Danny DeVito *Phil Cooper* • Peter Facinelli *Bob Walker* ■ *Dir* John Swanbeck • *Scr* Roger Rueff, from his play *Hospitality Suite*

The Big Knife ★★★★ PG
Drama
1955 · US · BW · 107min

This intelligent, haunting film is full of wonderful performances, particularly from Jack Palance (never better) and Rod Steiger as, respectively, the movie star coming apart at the seams and the studio boss who wants to cover up the paranoia at any price. This is one of the more successful films that Hollywood has made about itself, blessed with a marvellously literate script from the play by Clifford Odets and able direction from Robert Aldrich. A great movie suffused with realistic tension and lacerating satire. SH *DVD*

Jack Palance *Charles Castle* • Ida Lupino *Marion Castle* • Shelley Winters *Dixie Evans* • Wendell Corey *Smiley Coy* • Jean Hagen *Connie Bliss* • Rod Steiger *Stanley Hoff* ■ *Dir* Robert Aldrich • *Scr* James Poe, from the play by Clifford Odets

The Big Land ★★★ U
Western
1957 · US · Colour · 92min

Called *Stampede* in the UK, this was one of star Alan Ladd's production ventures, made by his own company Jaguar. Ladd's wife and agent, former actress Sue Carol, often chose these projects, and cocooned her husband with quality factors. In this case he is reunited with Virginia Mayo and Gordon Douglas, his co-star and director respectively from *The Iron Mistress* (1952). Ladd is now sadly unfashionable and almost forgotten, but there was much more to him than *Shane*. Watch how effortlessly he

B

turns this ordinary western into an impressive star vehicle. **TS**

Alan Ladd *Chad Morgan* • Virginia Mayo *Helen* • Edmond O'Brien *Jagger* • Anthony Caruso *Brog* • Julie Bishop *Kate Johnson* • John Qualen *Sven Johnson* • Don Castle *Draper* • David Ladd *David Johnson* ■ *Dir* Gordon Douglas • *Scr* David Dortort, Martin Rackin, from an adaptation by David Dortort of the novel *Buffalo Grass* by Frank Gruber

Big Leaguer ★★ U
Sports drama   1953 · US · BW · 53min

Robert Aldrich made his directing debut with this baseball drama, shot in 16 days in the area of Florida that was to become Cape Canaveral. Edward G Robinson stars as real-life John B Lobert, who ran a training camp for the New York Giants' potential recruits. Vera-Ellen plays Robinson's niece, while Richard Jaeckel is among the young hopefuls. Most of the story is concerned with the kids' social background - rich and poor, cocky and shy, Cuban and American - and paints Robinson's character as one of the world's kindest people. **AT**

Edward G Robinson *John B "Hans" Lobert* • Vera-Ellen *Christy* • Jeff Richards *Adam Polachuk* • Richard Jaeckel *Bobby Bronson* • William Campbell *Julie Davis* • Carl Hubbell • Paul Langton *Brian McLennan* ■ *Dir* Robert Aldrich • *Scr* Herbert Baker, from a story by John McNulty, Louis Morheim

The Big Lebowski ★★★★ 18
Comedy   1997 · US/UK · Colour · 112min

While not in the same class as the Coen brothers' previous film, *Fargo*, this goofy tribute to Raymond Chandler and *film noir* still comes gift-wrapped with enough good lines, ingenious plot twists and eccentric characters to satisfy the siblings' dedicated army of fans. There are in fact two Lebowskis: one is Jeff Bridges, who calls himself "the Dude", an ageing hippy who becomes embroiled in the kidnapping of the other Lebowski's wife, aided and abetted by tenpin bowling chum John Goodman. What follows is an insane labyrinth of plot that encompasses the drug and porn underworlds, Busby Berkeley fantasies and bathtime with a savage marmot, sharply edited by the Coens (under the pseudonym of Roderick Jaynes). **AT** Drug abuse, violence, swearing. *DVD* Blu

Jeff Bridges *Jeff "The Dude" Lebowski* • John Goodman *Walter Sobchak* • Julianne Moore *Maude Lebowski* • Steve Buscemi *Donny* • David Huddleston *The Big Lebowski* • Philip Seymour Hoffman *Brandt* • John Turturro *Jesus Quintana* • Tara Reid *Bunny Lebowski* ■ *Dir* Joel Coen • *Scr* Ethan Coen, Joel Coen • *Producer* Ethan Coen

The Big Lift ★★★ PG
Drama   1950 · US · BW · 119min

The talented and tragic Montgomery Clift only completed 17 features, but each movie is of supreme interest. That's because Clift was the forerunner of today's naturalistic school of screen acting, predating Brando's film debut by a good couple of years. This is one of five films Clift made with a German or militarist theme - a propaganda piece celebrating the airlift into postwar Berlin. Paul Douglas plays the blustering mouthpiece for American policy, and Cornell Borchers smooches with Clift. **TS** *DVD*

Montgomery Clift *Danny MacCullough* • Paul Douglas *Hank* • Cornell Borchers *Frederica* • Bruni Lobel *Gerda* • OE Hasse *Stieber* ■ *Dir/Scr* George Seaton

The Big Man ★ 15
Sports drama   1990 · UK · Colour · 111min

What a shame that Liam Neeson got his first starring role in this ham-fisted drama. He plays an unemployed Scottish miner who becomes a bare-knuckle fighter, a Spartacus for corrupt businessman Ian Bannen. The picture is irredeemably dull, and was a resounding flop that hastened the demise of the ailing Palace Pictures. **AT** Violence, swearing. *DVD*

Liam Neeson *Danny Scoular* • Joanne Whalley-Kilmer [Joanne Whalley] *Beth Scoular* • Billy Connolly *Frankie* • Ian Bannen *Matt Mason* • Maurice Roëves *Cam Colvin* • Hugh Grant *Gordon* • Kenny Ireland *Tony* ■ *Dir* David Leland • *Scr* Don MacPherson, from the novel by William McIlvanney

Big Miracle ★★★ PG
Wildlife adventure based on a true story
2012 · US · Colour · 102min

It's *Free Willy* times three in this wildlife adventure, which focuses on a family of grey whales that become trapped by ice in the far north of Alaska. Their plight becomes a global *cause célèbre*, prompting a race-against-time rescue that involves not only the US and Russian militaries, but also conservationist Drew Barrymore, oil tycoon Ted Danson and the Alaskan locals. Inspired by a true story from the Glasnost-era late 1980s, *Big Miracle* is unashamedly corny and manipulative. But the whales are so appealing, and the fight to free them so feel-good, that all cynicism is put aside. **DA** *DVD* Blu

Kristen Bell *Jill Jerard* • Vinessa Shaw *Kelly Meyers* • Drew Barrymore *Rachel Kramer* • John Krasinski *Adam Carlson* • Dermot Mulroney *Colonel Scott Boyer* • Ted Danson *JW McGraw* ■ *Dir* Ken Kwapis • *Scr* Jack Amiel, Michael Begler, from the non-fiction book *Freeing the Whales* by Thomas Rose

Big Momma's House ★★★ 12
Comedy   2000 · US/Ger · Colour · 94min

Martin Lawrence plays an "underblubber" agent, trying to catch escaped bank robber Terrence Howard by posing as the 300lb southern momma of the villain's ex-girlfriend Nia Long. The comedy derives both from Lawrence's roly-poly impersonation and from his falling for the girl he's guarding. The humour is pretty obvious, but Lawrence works hard to give this one-joke film enough crowd-pleasing moments to justify the ticket price. **DA** Violence, swearing. *DVD* Blu

Martin Lawrence *Malcolm Turner* • Nia Long *Sherry* • Paul Giamatti *John* • Jascha Washington *Trent* • Terrence Howard *Lester* ■ *Dir* Raja Gosnell • *Scr* Darryl Quarles, Don Rhymer, from a story by Darryl Quarles

Big Momma's House 2 ★★ PG
Action comedy   2006 · US · Colour · 94min

Martin Lawrence embraces his feminine side once again in this uninspired sequel. When a deadly computer "worm" threatens national security, FBI agent Lawrence disguises himself as a chubby grandma and poses as a nanny to infiltrate the home of suspect Mark Moses. Despite occasional moments of crude hilarity, this is a lazy cash-in. **SF** *DVD* Blu

Martin Lawrence *Malcolm Turner* • Nia Long *Sherry Pierce* • Emily Procter *Leah Fuller* • Zachary Levi *Kevin Keneally* • Mark Moses *Tom Fuller* • Kat Dennings *Molly* • Chloë Grace Moretz *Carrie* ■ *Dir* John Whitesell • *Scr* Don Rhymer, from characters by Darryl Quarles

Big Mommas: Like Father, like Son ★★ PG
Comedy   2011 · US · Colour · 102min

Martin Lawrence's FBI man plays second fiddle to his wannabe rapper stepson (Brandon T Jackson) in this third instalment of the crass but popular cross-dressing comedy series. Here, both undercover agent and teenager don fatsuits and frillies to hunt missing evidence inside a girls' performing arts school. The well-established *Big Momma* combination of cheap and cheesy chuckles, sex-obsessed banter and slapstick provides humour so broad that even the biggest of mommas could easily hide behind it. **DA** Some violence, sexual references. *DVD* Blu

Martin Lawrence *Malcolm/Big Momma* • Brandon T Jackson *Trent/Charmaine* • Jessica Lucas *Haley* • Michelle Ang *Mia* • Portia Doubleday *Jasmine* ■ *Dir* John Whitesell • *Scr* Matthew Fogel, from a story by Fogel, Don Rhymer and characters by Darryl Quarles

The Big Money ★★ U
Comedy   1956 · UK · Colour · 86min

There are too many British comedies in which the talents of a superb cast are wasted by an inferior script. This offering is a case in point, though it does boast a decent story about a family of crack crooks whose eldest son couldn't pass a counterfeit note in a game of Monopoly. Ian Carmichael is perfectly cast in the lead, but director John Paddy Carstairs hammers every gag into place, and staying the course seems like a life sentence. **DP**

Ian Carmichael *Willie Frith* • Belinda Lee *Gloria* • Kathleen Harrison *Mrs Frith* • Robert Helpmann *The Reverend* • James Hayter *Mr Frith* • George Coulouris *The Colonel* • Jill Ireland *Doreen Frith* • Renee Houston *Bobby* • Leslie Phillips *Receptionist* ■ *Dir* John Paddy Carstairs • *Scr* John Baines

The Big Mouth ★ U
Comedy   1967 · US · Colour · 102min

Comedian Jerry Lewis opens his mouth to the usual embarrassingly idiotic effect as a less-than-aggressive little guy who is the double of a gangster and becomes involved in a search for stolen diamonds. Directed, produced and co-written by Lewis, the film focuses almost continually on the star, which is a pity. **TH**

Jerry Lewis *Gerald Clamson* • Harold J Stone *Thor* • Susan Bay *Suzie Cartwright* • Buddy Lester *Studs* • Del Moore *Mr Hodges* • Paul Lambert *Moxie* • Leonard Stone *Fong* • Jeannine Riley *Bambi Berman* ■ *Dir* Jerry Lewis • *Scr* Jerry Lewis, Bill Richmond, from a story by Bill Richmond

Big News ★★★
Crime drama   1929 · US · BW · 75min

This early talkie entry in the popular reporter-turned-detective cycle is directed with a good feel for authenticity by Gregory La Cava and is marked by some witty exchanges and a breezy leading performance from Robert Armstrong. He plays a reckless newspaper reporter with a taste for drinking in speakeasies, who courts trouble in his determination to nail a narcotics gang. Carole Lombard - not yet a star - demonstrates why she became one. **RK**

Robert Armstrong *Steve Banks* • Carole Lombard *Margaret Banks* • Tom Kennedy *Sgt Ryan* • Warner Richmond *Phelps* • Wade Boteler *O'Neil* • Sam Hardy *Joe Reno* • Louis Payne *Hensel* • James Donlan *Deke* • Cupid Ainsworth *Vera Wilson* • Lew Ayres *Copy Boy* ■ *Dir* Gregory La Cava • *Scr* Walter DeLeon, Jack Jungmeyer, from the play *For Two Cents* by George S Brooks

The Big Night ★★ 12
Drama   1951 · US · BW · 72min

When sports columnist Howard St John beats up widowed ex-boxer Preston Foster for no apparent reason, the victim's young son, John Barrymore Jr, goes on a night-long quest for the attacker through murky nightclubs, bars and hotels. Barrymore Jr lacks the weight of his famous father, and this is flashily directed (and co-written) by Joseph Losey, who offers a compendium of nightlife underbelly clichés. **RK** *DVD*

John Barrymore Jr [John Drew Barrymore] *George La Main* • Preston Foster *Andy La Main* • Joan Lorring *Marion Rostina* • Howard St John *Al Judge* • Dorothy Comingore *Julie Rostina* • Philip Bourneuf *Dr Lloyd Cooper* • Howland Chamberlin *Flanagan* • Emil Meyer [Emile Meyer] *Packingpaugh* ■ *Dir* Joseph Losey • *Scr* Stanley Ellin, Joseph Losey, from the novel *Dreadful Summit* by Stanley Ellin

Big Night ★★★★ 15
Period comedy drama
1996 · US · Colour · 104min

Actors Campbell Scott and Stanley Tucci impress as promising directors in this small-scale 1950s tale, a gastronomic dream for all lovers of fine Italian food that offers a crisp chianti of comedy as accompaniment. Brothers Tony Shalhoub and Tucci run a not particularly successful restaurant in New Jersey. Their constant bickering reaches a crescendo with the prospect that entertainer Louis Prima will come to dinner

and help resurrect their failing business. Superb in support, Isabella Rossellini and Minnie Driver supply the love interest. **LH** Swearing, sex scenes.

Stanley Tucci *Secondo* • Tony Shalhoub *Primo* • Isabella Rossellini *Gabriella* • Ian Holm *Pascal* • Minnie Driver *Phyllis* • Marc Anthony *Cristiano* • Campbell Scott *Bob* ■ *Dir* Stanley Tucci, Campbell Scott • *Scr* Joseph Tropiano, Stanley Tucci

The Big Noise ★★★
Silent comedy   1928 · US · BW · 80min

Former vaudevillian, circus clown and Keystone Kop, Chester Conklin, a great comedy favourite of the silent era, stars in this efficiently made romp combining farce and satire. Sporting his trademark moustache, Conklin plays an ineffectual New York subway guard who accidentally falls on the track in front of an oncoming express. When a daily tabloid turns the incident into a heroic deed, he temporarily becomes a "big noise". It's a bit creaky now, but it has its moments for fans of the early comic style. **RK**

Chester Conklin *John Sloval* • Alice White *Sophie Sloval* • Bodil Rosing *Ma Sloval* • Sam Hardy *Philip Hurd* • Jack Egan *Bill Hedges* • Ned Sparks *William Howard* • David Torrence *Managing editor* ■ *Dir* Allan Dwan • *Scr* Thomas J Geraghty [Tom Geraghty], George Marion (titles), from a story by Ben Hecht

The Big Noise ★★ U
Comedy   1944 · US · BW · 73min

Laurel and Hardy are on the skids in this incompetently staged story of two dumb-luck detectives, hired to guard an inventor's new bomb - the titular "Big Noise". Biggest laughs are in the performance of Jack Norton, whose "drunk" routine has its moments. The rest, though, has scarcely any. **TH**

Stan Laurel *Stan* • Oliver Hardy *Ollie* • Doris Merrick *Evelyn* • Arthur Space *Hartley* • Louis Arco *German officer* • Beal Wong *Japanese officer* • Veda Ann Borg *Mayme* • Bobby Blake [Robert Blake] *Egbert* • Jack Norton *Drunk* ■ *Dir* Mal St Clair [Malcolm St Clair] • *Scr* Scott Darling

Big Nothing ★★★ 15
Black comedy thriller
2006 · UK/Can · Colour · 82min

Jean-Baptiste Andrea's blackly comic second feature is a marked improvement on 2003's *Dead End*, quirkily blending *film noir* aesthetics with the darkest of slapstick. *Shaun of the Dead* star Simon Pegg shines as sneaky conman Gus, who entices unemployed teacher Charlie (David Schwimmer) into a supposedly foolproof blackmailing scheme. Inevitably, they find their simple plan spiralling outrageously out of control. Snuff movies, missing bodies and even a local serial killer get thrown into the visually surreal mix, delivering a traditional "crime never pays" message with sledgehammer subtlety and a splash of seat-edge tension. **SF** Violence, swearing, sex scenes. *DVD*

Simon Pegg *Gus Dickinson* • David Schwimmer *Charlie Wood* • Alice Eve *Josie McDunn* • Natascha McElhone *Penelope* • Jon Polito *Agent Hymes* • Mimi Rogers *Mrs Smalls* • Billy Asher *Deputy Garman* • Julian Glover *80-year-old blind man* ■ *Dir* Jean-Baptiste Andrea • *Scr* Jean-Baptiste Andrea, Bill [Billy] Asher • *Cinematographer* Richard Greatrex

The Big One ★★★★ PG
Satirical documentary
1997 · US/UK · Colour · 86min

Documentary film-maker Michael Moore is something of a thorn in the side of politicians and big business in the United States. He's tackled General Motors, George W Bush and the gun industry, but here he turns the camera on his very own book tour for his bestseller *Downsize This!* with a mix of comedy, political commentary, observation, and his singular distrust of corporate America. It's a superbly realised, often funny and sometimes depressing documentary, but it's never boring. Indeed, it's worth it just to see Moore's suggestion that Nike should move their factory to Flint, or even his attempts to get past security guards to interview millionaire company chairmen. JB *DVD*

Michael Moore (2) *Narrator* • Phil Knight • Garrison Keillor • Bill Clinton ■ *Dir/Scr* Michael Moore (2) • *Cinematographers* Brian Danitz, Chris Smith

The Big Operator ★★★

Crime drama   1959 · US · BW · 90min

It's small beer today, but in 1959 this was a real toughie, beginning with a man being chucked into a cement mixer. It stars Mickey Rooney as a sadistic racketeer who takes the fifth while under investigation by the Senate. Rooney had already essayed Baby Face Nelson, and here he creates another memorable and plausible psycho. Co-star Mamie Van Doren adds allure as the wife of Steve Cochran, whom Rooney has tortured, while Mel Tormé cruises along nicely until Mickey has him torched. AT

Mickey Rooney *Little Joe Braun* • Steve Cochran *Bill Gibson* • Mamie Van Doren *Mary Gibson* • Mel Tormé *Fred McAfee* • Ray Danton *Oscar Wetzel* • Jim Backus *Cliff Heldon* • Ray Anthony *Slim Clayburn* • Jackie Coogan *Ed Brannell* • Charles Chaplin Jr *Bill Tragg* ■ *Dir* Charles Haas • *Scr* Robert Smith, Allen Rivkin, from a story by Paul Gallico

The Big Parade ★★★★★★

Silent war drama   1925 · US · BW and Colour

Rich industrialist's idle son John Gilbert enlists in the army when America enters the First World War and is sent to France. Billeted in a village, he meets and falls in love with French farm girl Renée Adorée before going to the front. A simple synopsis doesn't begin to convey the beauty of the love story, the poignancy of comradeship among men almost certainly facing death, or the authentic power and horror of the battle. Director King Vidor's approach to his subject, and his great artistry in executing it, has given us one of the great anti-war films – an unqualified masterpiece, enacted by a uniformly first-class cast. RK

John Gilbert (1) *James Apperson* • Renée Adorée *Mélisande* • Hobart Bosworth *Mr Apperson* • Claire McDowell *Mrs Apperson* • Claire Adams *Justyn Reed* • Robert Ober *Harry* • Tom O'Brien *Bull* • Karl Dane *Slim* • Rosita Marstini *French mother* ■ *Dir* King Vidor • *Scr* Henry Behn, Joseph Farnham (titles), from a story by Laurence Stallings • *Cinematographers* John Arnold, Henrik Sartov

The Big Parade ★★★★

Drama   1986 · Chi · Colour · 137min

Thanks to the imposing finale, filmed with suitable pomp and scale by Zhang Yimou, this study of soldiers preparing for China's National Day parade was embraced by the authorities as a fitting tribute to the People's Liberation Army. Yet Chen Kaige was ordered to add this triumphant ending to lessen the impact of the gruelling training sequences, which were criticised for glorifying the achievements of the individual. Chen's main aim is a critique of the communist system, but this is also a powerful paean to the indomitability of the human spirit. DP Mandarin +subtitles.

Wang Xueqi *Li Weicheng* • Sun Chun *Sun Fang* • Lu Lei *Jiang Junbiao* • Wu Ruofu *Lu Chun* • Guan Qiang *Liu Guoqiang* • Kang Hua *Hao Xiaoyuan* ■ *Dir* Chen Kaige • *Scr* Lili Gao

The Big Picture ★★★★

Satire   1989 · US · Colour · 96min

Three years before *The Player*, this criminally neglected satire hit the same Hollywood targets first. But what else would you expect from director Christopher Guest and his *This Is Spinal Tap* co-writer Michael McKean? Hilariously detailing just how much film student Kevin Bacon is willing to compromise his integrity to get his first feature made, Guest smartly dissects the movie industry with malicious glee, film buff in-jokes and gentle humour, while also providing a fascinating insight into its power plays and studio politics. The cast is uniformly excellent. AJ Some swearing, nudity.

Kevin Bacon *Nick Chapman* • Emily Longstreth *Susan Rawlings* • JT Walsh *Allen Habel* • Jennifer Jason Leigh *Lydia Johnson* • Martin Short *Neil Sussman* • Michael McKean *Emmett Sumner* • Kim Miyori *Jenny Sumner* • Teri Hatcher *Gretchen* • John Cleese *Bartender* • Elliott Gould *Attorney* ■ *Dir* Christopher Guest • *Scr* Michael Varhol, Christopher Guest, Michael McKean, from a story by Michael Varhol, Christopher Guest

The Big Picture ★★ 15

Drama   2010 · Fr · Colour · 111min

This slick but implausible French drama stars Gallic heart-throb Romain Duris (*The Beat That My Heart Skipped* as a disgruntled lawyer and amateur photographer who seizes the chance to change his circumstances after he accidentally kills his wife's lover. Eric Lartigau's film is glossily watchable, but it's hampered by a central conceit that never really convinces and not even a cameo from screen legend Catherine Deneuve can lift proceedings. DA French +subtitles. Violence, swearing, sex scenes. *DVD*

Romain Duris *Paul Exben* • Marina Foïs *Sarah Exben* • Niels Arestrup *Bartholomé* • Branka Katic *Ivana* • Catherine Deneuve *Anne* ■ *Dir* Eric Lartigau • *Scr* Eric Lartigau, Laurent de Bartillat, from the novel by Douglas Kennedy

The Big Pond ★★★

Romantic musical   1930 · US · BW · 78min

This vehicle for Maurice Chevalier is not in the same class as the previous year's hit *The Love Parade*, though he received a joint Oscar nomination for both films in 1929/1930. (This was the era of split-year Academy Awards.) The featherbrained screenplay, with additional dialogue from future master of satire Preston Sturges, has the star as a French tour guide in Venice falling for wealthy American tourist Claudette Colbert. Hobart Henley directs competently enough, and Chevalier, oozing his usual Gallic charm, sings a clutch of excellent songs. RK

Maurice Chevalier *Pierre Mirande* • Claudette Colbert *Barbara Billings* • George Barbier *Mr Billings* • Marion Ballou *Mrs Billings* • Elaine Koch *Jennie* • Nat Pendleton *Pat O'Day* • Frank Lyon *Ronnie* • Andrée Corday *Toinette* ■ *Dir* Hobart Henley • *Scr* Robert Presnell, Garrett Fort, Preston Sturges, from the play by George Middleton, AE Thomas

Big Red ★ U

Adventure   1962 · US · Colour · 85min

This Disney wildlife adventure is about an Irish setter called Big Red and the young orphan boy who trains him. Their friendship is put to the test when old curmudgeon Walter Pidgeon decides to split them up. Set in Quebec, this is a movie of unspeakable treacliness. AT

Walter Pidgeon *James Haggin* • Gilles Payant *René Dumont* • Em le Genest *Emile Fornet* • Janette Bertrand *Terese Fornet* • George Bouvier *Baggageman* • Doris Lussier *Farmer Mariot* • Roland Bedard *Conductor* ■ *Dir* Norman Tokar • *Scr* Louis Pelletier, from the novel by Jim Kjelgaard

The Big Red One ★★★★ 15

Second World War drama   1980 · US · Colour · 108min

Samuel Fuller's skills had been blunted by working in American TV in the 1960s, but the director returned to form on the big screen with this graphic war movie, arguably one of his most accomplished features. An infantryman in the Second World War, Fuller drew on the brutalities that he had witnessed and recorded to produce a powerful and, at times, poetic tale of five soldiers who experience the shocking realities of combat. The squad is lead by Lee Marvin, a perfect choice as the tight-jawed, bullish, growling sergeant. The 2005 reconstructed version of the film contains 47 minutes of restored footage cut by the studio on its initial release and is as close to the late director's original vision. JM Violence, swearing. *DVD*

Lee Marvin *Sergeant* • Mark Hamill *Griff* • Robert Carradine *Zab* • Bobby DiCicco *Vinci* • Kelly Ward *Johnson* • Siegfried Rauch *Schroeder* • Stéphane

Audran *Walloon* • Serge Marquand *Rensonnet* • Charles Macaulay *General/Captain* ■ *Dir/Scr* Samuel Fuller ■

The Big Short ★★★★ 15

Drama   2015 · US · Colour · 130min

Swinging masterfully between irreverence and incredulity, this courageously tells the story of the men who saw the 2008 financial crash coming and decided to bet it all on global economic catastrophe. Based on Michael Lewis's non-fiction bestseller, it apes the restless swagger of the world of high finance with energetic editing, fidgety camerawork and cocksure humour. The charismatic cast (Christian Bale, Steve Carell, Brad Pitt) is uniformly superb, and the film manages to be entertaining and accessible as well as frighteningly credible. EAS Swearing, nudity. *DVD* *Blu*

Christian Bale *Michael Burry* • Steve Carell *Mark Baum* • Ryan Gosling *Jared Vennett* • Brad Pitt *Ben Rickert* • Melissa Leo *Georgia Hale* • Rafe Spall *Danny Moses* • Marisa Tomei *Cynthia Baum* • Karen Gillan *Evie* ■ *Dir* Adam McKay • *Scr* Adam McKay, Charles Randolph, from Michael Lewis's non-fiction book

The Big Shot ★★★

Crime drama   1942 · US · BW · 81min

This was one of the movies Humphrey Bogart made just before *Casablanca* that consolidated the cynical, hard-boiled, louche image he had established in 1941's *The Maltese Falcon*. It comes as no surprise, then, to discover that this flick is little more than a standard Warner Bros potboiler, albeit with a slightly more clever exposition than most, with Bogie as a self-styled three-time loser framed after a heist. He virtually carries the movie single-handedly. TS

Humphrey Bogart *Duke Berne* • Irene Manning *Lorna Fleming* • Richard Travis *George Anderson* • Susan Peters *Ruth Carter* • Stanley Ridges *Martin Fleming* • Minor Watson *Warden Booth* • Chick Chandler *Dancer* ■ *Dir* Lewis Seiler • *Scr* Bertram Millhauser, Abem Finkel, Daniel Fuchs

Big Shot's Funeral ★★★ PG

Satirical comedy   2001 · Chi/HK · Colour · 96min

In this over-striving satire, Ge You stars as a frustrated cinematographer, who is hired by Rosamund Kwan to make a documentary record of Hollywood honcho Donald Sutherland's bid to shoot a costume drama in the Forbidden City. There's a relaxed buddiness about the dispirited Sutherland's relationship with the chipper cameraman, but the humour becomes strained after Sutherland is fired and Ge misunderstands his joking invitation to arrange a "comedy funeral" for him. Fun, but hardly subtle. DP Mandarin, English +subtitles. *DVD*

Ge You *YoYo* • Rosamund Kwan *Lucy* • Donald Sutherland *Don Tyler* • Paul Mazursky *Tony* • Ying Da *Louis Wang* ■ *Dir* Feng Xiaogang • *Scr* Feng Xiaogang, Li Xiaoming, Shi Kang

The Big Show ★★★ U

Drama   1961 · US · Colour · 112min

This lavish circus epic stars the fabulous Esther Williams, her MGM swimming pool days behind her and her Amazonian physique now deployed on the high wire. Esther is super to watch, as is the young star she has the hots for, Cliff Robertson. While it doesn't quite come off, the European circus background is enthralling. TS

Esther Williams *Hillary Allen* • Cliff Robertson *Josef Everard* • Nehemiah Persoff *Bruno Everard* • Robert Vaughn (1) *Klaus Everard* • Margia Dean *Carlotta Martinez* • David Nelson (1) *Eric Solden* • Carol Christensen *Garda Everard* ■ *Dir* James B Clark • *Scr* Ted Sherdeman

The Big Sky ★★★★ U

Western adventure   1952 · US · BW · 122min

An eventful epic western, directed with great flair by maestro Howard Hawks, this could have been a great one with better casting. Kirk Douglas in the lead, good though he is, looks too urbane, not to mention intense, for this particular role, while his co-stars are not up to the splendour of Dudley Nichols's fine screenplay. There's a problem of taste too

– the finger amputation scene is played for laughs – but the film overall is so satisfying you'll forgive its faults. TS *DVD*

Kirk Douglas *Jim Deakins* • Dewey Martin *Boone Caudill* • Arthur Hunnicutt *Zeb* • Elizabeth Threatt *Teal Eye* • Steven Geray *Jourdonnais* • Buddy Baer *Romaine* • Hank Worden *Poordevil* • Jim Davis (1) *Streak* ■ *Dir* Howard Hawks • *Scr* Dudley Nichols, from the novel by AB Guthrie

The Big Sleep ★★★★★★ PG

Classic detective drama   1946 · US · BW · 109min

This ultra-witty romantic thriller from director Howard Hawks – the second screen pairing of real-life lovers Humphrey Bogart and Lauren Bacall – is one of the great pleasures of the silver screen. Its original release was delayed to give Hawks time to exploit and build up the Bogie-Bacall scenes, and as a result the movie sizzles with sexual chemistry as each exchange hides a censor-baiting double or triple entendre. The Raymond Chandler plot is notoriously confusing, and ultimately irrelevant, but the delights are many: Martha Vickers's sexy Carmen ("She tried to sit in my lap when I was standing up"), Dorothy Malone's bookshop flirt and Elisha Cook Jr's sad fall guy. The pace never lets up, and the result is a classic. TS *DVD*

Humphrey Bogart *Philip Marlowe* • Lauren Bacall *Vivian Rutledge* • John Ridgely *Eddie Mars* • Martha Vickers *Carmen Sternwood* • Dorothy Malone *Girl in bookshop* • Peggy Knudsen *Mona Mars* • Regis Toomey *Bernie Ohls* • Charles Waldron *General Sternwood* • Charles D Brown *Norris, the butler* • Bob Steele *Canino* • Elisha Cook Jr *Harry Jones* • Louis Jean Heydt *Joe Brody* • Sonia Darren *Agnes* ■ *Dir* Howard Hawks • *Scr* William Faulkner, Jules Furthman, Leigh Brackett, from the novel by Raymond Chandler • *Cinematographer* Sid Hickox • *Music* Max Steiner

The Big Sleep ★★ 15

Detective drama   1978 · UK · Colour · 95min

Having given an excellent account of himself in *Farewell, My Lovely*, Robert Mitchum returned to the role of Philip Marlowe for this curious reworking of Raymond Chandler's hard-boiled novel. Shifted to 1970s London, the action loses nearly all of its shadowy atmosphere and, although Michael Winner sticks closer to the book than the writers responsible for Howard Hawks's seminal 1946 version, he's not in the same class. DP *DVD*

Robert Mitchum *Philip Marlowe* • Sarah Miles *Charlotte Regan* • Richard Boone *Lash Canino* • Candy Clark *Camilla Sternwood* • Joan Collins *Agnes Lozelle* • Edward Fox *Joe Brody* • John Mills *Inspector Carson* • James Stewart *General Sternwood* • Oliver Reed *Eddie Mars* • Harry Andrews *Norris* ■ *Dir* Michael Winner • *Scr* Michael Winner, from the novel by Raymond Chandler

The Big Stampede ★★ U

Western   1932 · US · BW · 51min

The second of six B-westerns John Wayne dashed off for Warner Bros early in his career, its big studio pedigree puts this a cut above Wayne's subsequent poverty row efforts. It has character actor Berton Churchill as New Mexico Governor Lew Wallace dispatching John Wayne's deputy sheriff to deal with cattle rustlers. AE

John Wayne *John Steele* • Noah Beery *Sam Crew* • Mae Madison *Ginger Malloy* • Luis Alberni *Sonora Joe* • Berton Churchill *Gov Lew Wallace* ■ *Dir* Tenny Wright • *Scr* Kurt Kempler, from a story by Marion Jackson

The Big Steal ★★★ PG

Film noir   1949 · US · BW · 72min

Don Siegel's third feature is a thriller with more mirth than menace, and the sexual banter between Robert Mitchum and Jane Greer sometimes rivals that of Bogart and Bacall. The plot is simple – $300,000 of army payroll money has gone missing – and the extended chase throws up a great deal of subplots and shifty characters, notably Ramon Novarro as a lazy police chief. Real locations, rather than studio backdrops, are an asset, and Siegel never lets the pace sag or the shoestring budget show. AT *DVD*

B

Robert Mitchum *Lieutenant Duke Halliday* • Jane Greer *Joan Graham* • William Bendix *Captain Vincent Blake* • Patric Knowles *Jim Fiske* • Ramon Novarro *Colonel Ortega* • Don Alvarado *Lieutenant Ruiz* • John Qualen *Julius Seton* • Pasqual Garcia Peña *Manuel* ■ *Dir* Don Siegel • *Scr* Geoffrey Homes [Daniel Mainwaring], Gerald Drayson Adams, from the story *The Road to Carmichael's* by Richard Wormser

The Big Steal ★★★ 15
Comedy   1990 · Aus · Colour · 96min

Fans of the 1986 Australian comedy *Malcolm* will enjoy this equally quirky offering from the husband-and-wife team of director Nadia Tass and writer/cameraman David Parker. This comedy of cars and romance stars Ben Mendelsohn (*The Year My Voice Broke*) as a shy teenager who craves a Jaguar so that he can woo a local beauty. When his dad gives him a battered old Nissan, our hero gets involved with shady car dealers and a 1973 Jag of dubious provenance. It's a slight but charming movie. AT

Ben Mendelsohn *Danny Clark* • Claudia Karvan *Joanna Johnson* • Steve Bisley *Gordon Farkas* • Marshall Napier *Desmond Clark* • Damon Herriman *Mark Jorgensen* • Angelo D'Angelo *Vangeli Petrakis* • Tim Robertson *Desmond Johnson* • Maggie King *Edith Clark* • Sheryl Munks *Pam Schaeffer* ■ *Dir* Nadia Tass • *Scr* David Parker, Max Dunn

The Big Store ★★★★ U
Comedy   1941 · US · BW · 79min

The last of five MGM comedies by the Marx Brothers, this has more plot than is usual for them. They play ramshackle detectives hired to guard a vast emporium in which customers take second place to the various under-the-counter shenanigans, in which the Brothers participate. As usual, Groucho woos massive Margaret Dumont, with insult amounting to injury but, more unusually, the romantic subplot is let loose, and allows Tony Martin to sing *Tenement Symphony*. TH *DVD*

Groucho Marx *Wolf J Flywheel* • Chico Marx *Ravelli* • Harpo Marx *Wacky* • Tony Martin (1) *Tommy Rogers* • Virginia Grey *Joan Sutton* • Margaret Dumont *Martha Phelps* • William Tannen (1) *Fred Sutton* ■ *Dir* Charles Reisner • *Scr* Sid Kuller, Hal Fimberg, Ray Golden, from a story by Nat Perrin

The Big Street ★★★
Comedy melodrama   1942 · US · BW · 88min

Writer Damon Runyon produced this movie version of his own short story, *Little Pinks*, which has an oddly cast Henry Fonda playing the busboy with a crush on moll Lucille Ball. When Ball is injured by her sadistic boss, Fonda leaps at the chance to care for her and prove his devotion. It's sentimental stuff, but Runyon's unique streetwise dialogue and brilliantly sketched gallery of eccentric supporting characters make this a pleasure. TS

Henry Fonda *Little Pinks* • Lucille Ball *Gloria* • Barton MacLane *Case Ables* • Eugene Pallette *Nicely Nicely Johnson* • Agnes Moorehead *Violette* • Sam Levene *Horsethief* • Ray Collins *Professor B* • Marion Martin *Mrs Venus* ■ *Dir* Irving Reis • *Scr* Leonard Spigelglass, from the short story *Little Pinks* by Damon Runyon

The Big TNT Show ★★★★
Music concert documentary
1966 · US · BW · 93min

Shot in Electronovision on 29 November 1965 at the Moulin Rouge nightclub in Hollywood, this fabulous concert film delivers one legendary performance after another and captures the precise moment old school rock 'n' roll turned hippy. The happy-go-lucky atmosphere is infectious as The Byrds, Petula Clark, Bo Diddley, The Ronettes, The Lovin' Spoonful, Roger Miller and other contemporary acts sock out their hits and drive the crowd wild, with the orchestra swelling under Phil Spector's giant production. A superb pop time capsule and an ideal companion piece to the earlier (and very similar) *The TAMI Show*. AJ

■ *Dir* Larry Peerce • *Producer* Phil Spector

The Big Tease ★★ 15
Comedy   1999 · US/UK · Colour · 82min

Gay Scottish crimper Craig Ferguson believes that, thanks to his talent with the curling tongs, he's been invited to Los Angeles to take part in an international hairdressing competition. His hopes are dashed, however, when he realises he's only been summoned to appear in the celebrity audience. Refusing to curl up and dye, he charms his way into the contest via hard-nosed Hollywood agent Frances Fisher, millionaire sponsor Charles Napier and the usual bunch of eccentrics. The result is intermittently amusing. AJ Swearing. *DVD*

Craig Ferguson *Crawford Mackenzie* • Frances Fisher *Candace "Candy" Harper* • Mary McCormack *Monique Geingold* • Donal Logue *Eamonn McGarvey* • Larry Miller *Dunston Cactus, hotel manager* • Charles Napier *Senator Warren Crockett* • Michael Paul Chan *Clarence* • David Hasselhoff ■ *Dir* Kevin Allen • *Scr* Sacha Gervasi, Craig Ferguson

Big Time ★ PG
Music documentary   1988 · US · Colour · 92min

Put together by singer/songwriter Tom Waits, his wife Kathleen Brennan and Levis 501 commercials director Chris Blum, this indulgent concert documentary was shot during the raspy lounge lizard's 1987 tour and contains all, or snatches of, 22 songs in his haphazard repertoire. Anyone other than the ardent fan will find *Big Time* a hard time. AJ

■ *Dir* Chris Blum • *Scr* Tom Waits, Kathleen Brennen, Chris Blum

The Big Tip Off ★
Crime drama   1955 · US · BW · 78min

In one of Hollywood's first efforts to discredit its burgeoning rival, television, journalist Richard Conte is duped by gangster Bruce Bennett who diverts funds from a charity telethon into his own pocket. The telethon scam is only one of several strands in a baffling plot. The treatment is decidedly lacklustre, and the minor stars are generally a wan bunch. AT

Richard Conte *Johnny Denton* • Constance Smith *Penny Conroy* • Bruce Bennett *Bob Gilmore* • Cathy Downs *Sister Joan* • James Millican *Lt East* • Dick Benedict *First hood* • Sam Flint *Father Kearney* • Mary Carroll *Sister Superior* • George Sanders ■ *Dir* Frank McDonald • *Scr* Steve Fisher

Big Top Pee-wee ★★★ U
Comedy   1988 · US · Colour · 81min

As a bizarre star, he blazed only briefly in this and *Pee-wee's Big Adventure* before his career was abruptly halted by ignominy. But Pee-wee Herman, alias Paul Reubens, and his childish eccentricity of manner and dress contrived an odd originality, at least in this account of his funny farm - a hot-dog tree is the least of it - into which Kris Kristofferson's circus is blown during a storm. The talking pig is amusingly oinkish, but for most of the time the film has all the eerie fascination of a freak show - with Pee-wee as the main exhibit. TH

Pee-wee Herman [Paul Reubens] *Pee-wee Herman* • Penelope Ann Miller *Winnie* • Kris Kristofferson *Mace Montana* • Valeria Golino *Gina* • Wayne White *Vance the Pig* • Susan Tyrrell *Midge Montana* • Albert Henderson *Mr Ryan* • Jack Murdock *Otis* • Terrence V Mann [Terrence Mann] *Snowball the Clown* • Benicio Del Toro *Duke, the Dog-Faced Boy* ■ *Dir* Randal Kleiser • *Scr* Paul Reubens, George McGrath, from character created by Paul Reubens

The Big Town ★★ 15
Drama   1987 · US · Colour · 105min

Matt Dillon plays an extremely sulky would-be high-roller in this formulaic, sepia-toned, crap-shooting movie. Director Ben Bolt ladles on the fug and finger snappin' with a heavy-handed trowel, but this remains a fruitless, sterile exercise with deep pretentions to style but little discernible substance. That said, there are solid performances from the always interesting Tommy Lee Jones and the pouting Diane Lane, as a deeply unsavoury couple who

inveigle Dillon into further dodgy doings. SH Some swearing.

Matt Dillon *JC Cullen* • Diane Lane *Lorry Dane* • Tommy Lee Jones *George Cole* • Bruce Dern *Mr Edwards* • Lee Grant *Ferguson Edwards* • Tom Skerritt *Phil Carpenter* • Suzy Amis *Aggie Donaldson* • David Marshall Grant *Sonny Binkley* ■ *Dir* Ben Bolt • *Scr* Robert Roy Pool, from the novel *The Arm* by Clark Howard

The Big Trail ★★★★ U
Western   1930 · US · BW · 116min

Fox made this truly epic western to celebrate the centenary of a famous pioneers' trek from Independence, Missouri. Under director Raoul Walsh, the cast and crew arduously re-created the highlights of that journey, lowering wagons and horses down cliff-faces, fighting heat, blizzards, raging rivers and Indians, giving the film an amazing documentary look. It was shot for both 70mm widescreen (the shortlived Fox Grandeur process) and for standard 35mm. A then-unknown John Wayne took the lead: some of his lines are awkwardly spoken but he makes an authoritative figure of the wagon train scout. Unfairly, he took most of the flack for the film's failure, and was relegated to minor parts for a while. AE *DVD*

John Wayne *Breck Coleman* • Marguerite Churchill *Ruth Cameron* • El Brendel *Gussie* • Tully Marshall *Zeke* • Tyrone Power [Tyrone Power Sr] *Red Flack* • David Rollins *Dave Cameron* • Ian Keith *Bill Thorpe* • Frederick Burton *Pa Bascom* • Russ Powell *Windy Bill* ■ *Dir* Raoul Walsh • *Scr* Jack Peabody, Marie Boyle, Florence Postal, Fred Sersen, from a story by Hal G Evarts, Raoul Walsh

The Big Trees ★★★ PG
Drama   1952 · US · Colour · 89min

This saga is about a forest of giant redwood trees that lumberjack Kirk Douglas wants to cut down, much to the horror of the local Quaker community. Cue drama and romance with a demure Quaker girl, played by Eve Miller. For Douglas, still chasing after real stardom, this low-budget movie was a way out of a stifling contract with Warner Bros: he did the picture for nothing and earned his independence. Filmed in Oregon, the picture is routinely exciting and delivers a powerful environmental message for the time. AT *DVD*

Kirk Douglas *John Fallon* • Eve Miller *Alicia Chadwick* • Patrice Wymore *Daisy Fisher* • Edgar Buchanan *Yukon Burns* • John Archer *Frenchy Lecroix* • Alan Hale Jr *Tiny* ■ *Dir* Felix Feist • *Scr* John Twist, James R Webb, from a story by Kenneth Earl

Big Trouble ★★★ 15
Comedy   1985 · US · Colour · 89min

This is an odd switch of tactics for the great improvisational director, John Cassavetes - a blandly contrived take-off of *Double Indemnity*, with insurance man Alan Arkin conniving with Beverly D'Angelo to take out a lethal kind of insurance policy on her husband Peter Falk. So far, so conventional. But there are enough off-the-wall surprises to raise it just above the average spoof thriller - one of which is that Arkin needs the money to send his trio of musical children to Yale. TH Some violence, swearing. *DVD*

Peter Falk *Steve Rickey* • Alan Arkin *Leonard Hoffman* • Beverly D'Angelo *Blanche Rickey* • Charles Durning *O'Mara* • Paul Dooley *Noozel* • Robert Stack *Winslow* • Valerie Curtin *Arlene Hoffman* • Richard Libertini *Dr Lopez* ■ *Dir* John Cassavetes • *Scr* Warren Bogle

Big Trouble ★★ 12
Crime comedy   2002 · US · Colour · 81min

Barry Sonnenfeld's manic, Miami-based ensemble comedy faced post-September 11 release problems in the US because of its climactic satirising of poor airport security, which allows a nuclear bomb onto a plane. There's barely enough plot to cover the short running time of this crime farce, as chance, coincidence and an explosive suitcase bring together a dozen characters. Tim Allen and Rene Russo are the nominal stars, but this appealing partnership is

hampered by puerile plotting and overacting supporting players. JC *DVD*

Tim Allen *Eliot Arnold* • Rene Russo *Anna Herk* • Stanley Tucci *Arthur Herk* • Tom Sizemore *Snake* • Johnny Knoxville *Eddie* • Dennis Farina *Henry* • Jack Kehler *Leonard* • Janeane Garofalo *Monica Romero* • Barry Sonnenfeld *Confused sports radio caller* ■ *Dir* Barry Sonnenfeld • *Scr* Robert Ramsey, Matthew Stone, from the novel by Dave Barry

Big Trouble in Little China ★★ 15
Action adventure   1986 · US · Colour · 95min

Horror maestro John Carpenter is clearly in awe of Hong Kong movies, but this brave attempt to fuse martial arts action with a westernised adventure story sadly doesn't gel. Kurt Russell makes an amiably inept hero as the lorry driver who gets mixed up with ancient Chinese magic when he ventures beneath the streets of San Francisco. The fight scenes are surprisingly stodgy, however, and the special effects take over. JF *DVD* *BLU*

Kurt Russell *Jack Burton* • Kim Cattrall *Gracie Law* • Dennis Dun *Wang Chi* • James Hong *Lo Pan* • Victor Wong (2) *Egg Shen* • Kate Burton *Margo* • Donald Li *Eddie Lee* • Carter Wong *Thunder* ■ *Dir* John Carpenter • *Scr* Garry Goldman, David Z Weinstein, WD Richter

The Big Wedding ★★ 15
Comedy   2013 · US · Colour · 85min

Robert De Niro and Diane Keaton head a starry cast in this comedy remake of a 2006 French film that goes down like an old vol-au-vent - puffed up, stale and unsatisfying. Years after their divorce, ex-partners De Niro and Keaton are forced to play house to mollify the strictly religious mother of their adopted son (Ben Barnes) as the family gathers to see him marry a vapid Amanda Seyfried. Writer/director Justin Zackham tries desperately to inject some colour into the proceedings, but his gags clang as loudly as church bells. SP Swearing, sexual references, brief nudity. *DVD* *BLU*

Robert De Niro *Don Griffin* • Katherine Heigl *Lyla Griffin* • Diane Keaton *Ellie Griffin* • Amanda Seyfried *Missy* • Ben Barnes *Alejandro* ■ *Dir* Justin Zackham • *Scr* Justin Zackham, from the film *Mon frère se marie* by Jean-Stéphane Bron, Karine Sudan

Big Wednesday ★★★★ PG
Sports drama   1978 · US · Colour · 114min

It's easy to dismiss this Malibu surfing saga as pretentious nonsense, with beach bums Jan-Michael Vincent, William Katt and Gary Busey forever seeking the great Californian wave that will give meaning to their lives. However, director John Milius - who went on to script *Apocalypse Now* - shows a personal commitment to all the mystical bonding. The result rises above the pseudo-intellectual twaddle to make a poignant statement about the lack of purpose in the 1960s, and the way Vietnam forced even infantile hunks such as these to take on responsibility. TH *DVD*

Jan-Michael Vincent *Matt Johnson* • William Katt *Jack Barlow* • Gary Busey *Leroy Smith* • Patti D'Arbanville *Sally Johnson* • Lee Purcell *Peggy Gordon* • Darrell Fetty *Jim "Waxer" King* • Sam Melville *"The Bear"* • Barbara Hale *Mrs Barlow* ■ *Dir* John Milius • *Scr* John Milius, Dennis Aaberg

The Big Wheel ★★ U
Motor racing drama   1949 · US · BW · 88min

Tough guy Mickey Rooney gets back into the driving seat again, this time to prove he's as good as his old man, who, of course, died on the track. Clichéd stuff, but done with confidence and bravura, though alas without much style. Rooney continues to amaze, giving real credence to the duffest dialogue and situations, but don't expect too much. TS *DVD*

Mickey Rooney *Billy Coy* • Thomas Mitchell *Red Stanley* • Michael O'Shea (1) *Vic Sullivan* • Mary Hatcher *Louise Riley* • Spring Byington *Mary Coy* • Lina Romay (1) *Dolores Raymond* • Steve Brodie *Happy* • Allen Jenkins *George* ■ *Dir* Edward Ludwig • *Scr* Robert Smith

The Big White ★★ 15
Crime black comedy
2005 · Ger/US/UK/Can/NZ · Colour · 100min

Alaskan-based travel agent Robin Williams has been worn to a frazzle by debts and caring for his troubled wife Holly Hunter, who thinks she has Tourette syndrome. When he finds a dead body in a dumpster, he tries scamming his insurance company into thinking that it's the corpse of his long-lost brother in order to collect on a million-dollar policy. Director Mark Mylod tries hard to manage the script's snowstorm of Coen brothers-style whimsical detail and abrupt tonal shifts, but the result is a slushy mess. LF Swearing, violence. *DVD*

Robin Williams *Paul Barnell* • Holly Hunter *Margaret Barnell* • Giovanni Ribisi *Ted Watters* • Woody Harrelson *Raymond Barnell* • Tim Blake Nelson *Gary* • Alison Lohman *Tiffany* • W Earl Brown *Jimbo* ■ *Dir* Mark Mylod • *Scr* Colin Friesen

The Big Year ★★ PG
Comedy drama   2011 · US · Colour · 95min

Steve Martin, Jack Black and Owen Wilson play rival birdwatchers taking part in "The Big Year" competition. On paper, the trio looks like a comedy dream team. On film, however, they're amiably ordinary. Director David Frankel (who directed Wilson in *Marley & Me*) doesn't fully exploit the line-up of talent. Martin's silky comic skills, Black's broader schtick and Wilson's likeable patter are lost in a story that's neither funny nor dramatic, and there's a distinct lack of tension between the characters. Britain's own birders might be lured by the subject matter alone, but even they would fail to be transfixed by a feather-light tale that never really takes off. DA *DVD* *BL*

Steve Martin *Stu Preissler* • Jack Black *Brad Harris* • Owen Wilson *Kenny Bostick* • Brian Dennehy *Raymond* • Anjelica Huston *Annie Auklet* • Rashida Jones *Ellie* • Rosamund Pike *Jessica* • Dianne Wiest *Brenda* ■ *Dir* David Frankel • *Scr* Howard Franklin, from the non-fiction book by Mark Obmascik

The Bigamist ★★★ PG
Drama   1953 · US · BW · 79min

This is a gritty but far-fetched tale, directed by and co-starring Ida Lupino, in which feckless travelling salesman Edmond O'Brien ends up with two wives – Lupino and the suffering Joan Fontaine. This is adult material and director Lupino really makes you believe in O'Brien's dilemma. It's an unusual and serious subject that is given a dramatic outing for a change. The only weakness is in the framing story, with lovable Edmund Gwenn as an investigator. TS *DVD*

Edmond O'Brien *Harry Graham* • Joan Fontaine *Eve Graham* • Ida Lupino *Phyllis Martin* • Edmund Gwenn *Mr Jordan* • Jane Darwell *Mrs Connelley* • Kenneth Tobey *Tom Morgan* • John Maxwell *Judge* ■ *Dir* Ida Lupino • *Scr* Collier Young, from a story by Larry Marcus, Lou Schor

Bigfoot and the Hendersons ★★ PG
Comedy   1987 · US · Colour · 106min

This resembles a watered-down, terrestrial remake of *ET*, and is produced by Steven Spielberg's company Amblin Entertainment. A Seattle family adopts America's answer to the abominable snowman and suffers the ludicrous consequences, while trying to keep it a secret from the neighbours. It's cosier, cutesier and even more sentimental than the Spielberg norm and became a short-lived TV sitcom. AJ *DVD*

John Lithgow *George Henderson* • Melinda Dillon *Nancy Henderson* • Margaret Langrick *Sarah Henderson* • Joshua Rudoy *Ernie Henderson* • Kevin Peter Hall *Harry* • David Suchet *Jacques Lafleur* • Lainie Kazan *Irene Moffitt* • Don Ameche *Dr Wallace Wrightwood* • M Emmet Walsh *George Henderson Sr* ■ *Dir* William Dear • *Scr* William Dear, William E Martin, Ezra D Rappaport

Bigga than Ben: a Guide to Ripping Off London ★★★ 15
Biographical black comedy
2007 · UK · Colour · 81min

Barbed laughs in the *Borat* mould make for brisk and boisterously un-PC entertainment in writer/director Suzie Halewood's low-budget satire. Based on the controversial diaries of Russian immigrants Pavel Tetersky and Sergei Sakin, it's a loosely plotted travelogue in which two self-confessed "pieces of Moscow scum" (played by Russian heart-throb Andrei Chadov and Ben Barnes from *The Chronicles of Narnia: Prince Caspian*) dodge conscription and flee to London, intent on scamming their way to a fortune. SF Swearing, drug abuse. *DVD*

Ben Barnes *Cobakka* • Andrei Chadov *Spiker* • Ovidiu Matesan *Artash* • Hero Fiennes-Tiffin *Spartak* • Andrew Byron *Sergei* • Jeff Mirza *Dennis* ■ *Dir* Suzie Halewood • *Scr* Suzie Halewood, from the diaries *Bol'she Ben* by Pavel Tetersky, Sergei Sakin

A Bigger Splash ★★★ 15
Biographical documentary
1974 · UK · Colour · 98min

Jack Hazan's documentary portrait of artist David Hockney admirably captures the visual style of the artist, without ever quite breaking through his defences. Touching on the closeness of his friendships and his penchant for revisiting favourite haunts, the action mostly concerns his relationship with his latest sitter, Peter Schlesinger. The film is less concerned with Hockney's methods than with the way in which he relates to his model and how he copes with the completion of his work. DP

David Hockney • Peter Schlesinger ■ *Dir* Jack Hazan • *Scr* Jack Hazan, David Mingay

A Bigger Splash ★★★★ 15
Drama   2015 · It/Fr · Colour · 119min

This sexy, sun-baked drama is the sort of film that engrosses and amuses in equal measure. Set on a small island in Sicily, it revolves around Tilda Swinton's Bowie-like rock star who is enjoying a relaxing holiday with her younger partner (Matthias Schoenaerts). However, the peace is shattered by the arrival of talkative, hedonistic record producer Ralph Fiennes. What follows is cool, funny and sexually charged, as tensions start to rise. The leads are superb, but Fiennes steals the show, dominating a scene whenever he appears. SC Swearing, sex scenes, nudity, drug abuse. *DVD* *BL*

Tilda Swinton *Marianne Lane* • Ralph Fiennes *Harry Hawkes* • Matthias Schoenaerts *Paul de Smedt* • Dakota Johnson *Penelope* • Aurore Clément *Mireille* ■ *Dir* Luca Guadagnino • *Scr* David Kajganich, from the film *The Swimming Pool* by Jean-Emmanuel Conil, Jacques Deray, Jean-Claude Carrière, from a story by Alain Paige [Jean-Emmanuel Conil]

Bigger than Life ★★★★ 12
Psychological drama   1956 · US · Colour · 91min

One of those legendary 1950s melodramas, this was treated as a routine release in America and Britain, but hailed as a major work of art by the French (notably Jean-Luc Godard and François Truffaut) because it is a film by Nicholas Ray, the director of *Rebel without a Cause* and *They Live by Night*. James Mason, in one of his best roles, is a mild-mannered teacher whose life is wrecked by his addiction to cortisone, which turns him into a monster. Made in CinemaScope and famous for its dramatic colour scheme (New York cabs are at their yellowest), it is a real humdinger. AT *DVD*

James Mason *Ed Avery* • Barbara Rush *Lou* • Walter Matthau *Wally* • Robert Simon *[Robert F Simon] Dr Norton* • Christopher Olsen *Richie Avery* • Roland Winters *Dr Rurich* • Rusty Lane *La Porte* ■ *Dir* Nicholas Ray • *Scr* Cyril Hume, Richard Maibaum, from the article *Ten Feet Tall* by Berton Roueche • *Cinematographer* Joseph MacDonald [Joe MacDonald]

The Biggest Bundle of Them All ★★
Crime comedy   1968 · US/It · Colour · 107min

Robert Wagner kidnaps rival mobster Vittorio De Sica. When no one offers to pay the ransom, De Sica takes over the gang and proposes stealing $5 million of valuable platinum. The resulting caper is a little too frantic for its own good. However, Edward G Robinson is on excellent form as the mastermind who plans the heist, while Raquel Welch adds a lot of fizz. AT

Vittorio De Sica *Cesare Celli* • Raquel Welch *Juliana* • Robert Wagner *Harry* • Godfrey Cambridge *Benny* • Edward G Robinson *Professor Samuels* ■ *Dir* Ken Annakin • *Scr* Sy Salkowitz, Josef Shaftel, Riccardo Aragno, from a story by Josef Shaftel

Biggie & Tupac ★★ 15
Documentary   2001 · US · Colour · 107min

British documentary maker Nick Broomfield investigates the unsolved murders of US rap stars Tupac Shakur and Christopher Wallace (aka Biggie Smalls, The Notorious BIG), throwing up allegations of conspiracy, corruption and police complicity in the killings. With a sound unit strapped satchel-style across his chest, Broomfield comes across as a diligent scholar. Doggedly chasing his interview subjects, he's both relentless and meticulous in his approach, and for this he's rewarded with some fascinating, though sometimes questionable, testimonies. Broomfield's gaffes and preambles are included, as in his previous projects, but the assumed air of bumbling incompetence gives the film an inappropriate humorous touch, and weakens the power of his case. SF *DVD*

■ *Dir* Nick Broomfield • *Cinematographer* Joan Churchill

Biggles ★ PG
Science-fiction adventure
1986 · UK · Colour · 88min

A hero to a generation of young readers, Captain WE Johns's immortal flying ace is made to look very foolish in this ghastly spoof, directed with a leaden touch by John Hough. Neil Dickson does his best to give Biggles his customary gung-ho cheeriness, but his efforts are shot to pieces by a shambles of a story in which burger-bar boss Alex Hyde-White is whisked from modern America back to the First World War to join his time-twin, the flying ace on a secret mission. However, the saddest aspect of this sorry episode is that it was Peter Cushing's final film. DP *DVD* *BL*

Neil Dickson *James "Biggles" Bigglesworth* • Alex Hyde-White *Jim Ferguson* • Fiona Hutchison *Debbie Stevens* • Peter Cushing *Colonel Raymond* • Marcus Gilbert *Eric von Stalhein* • William Hootkins *Chuck* • Michael Siberry *Algy* ■ *Dir* John Hough • *Scr* John Groves, Ken Walwin, from characters by Captain WE Johns

Les Bijoutiers du Clair de Lune ★★ PG
Crime thriller   1957 · Fr/It · Colour · 87min

The respective contours of the Spanish landscape and Brigitte Bardot are all that interest director Roger Vadim in this sordid little thriller. Beset by shooting difficulties, the tension between Bardot and Stephen Boyd is tangible, although it doesn't make them any more credible as a protective convent girl and the man who killed her uncle and seduced her aunt. The sex scenes that were considered frisky in their day have now lost their oomph. DP French +subtitles. *DVD*

Brigitte Bardot *Ursula* • Alida Valli *Aunt Florentine* • Stephen Boyd *Lambert* • Pepe Nieto [José Nieto] *Count Ribera* • Maruchi Fresno *Conchita* • Adriano Dominguez *Fernando* ■ *Dir* Roger Vadim • *Scr* Roger Vadim, Jacques Rémy, Peter Viertel, from the novel *The Midnight Jewellers* by Albert Vidalie

Bike Boy ★★★★
Experimental satire   1967 · US · Colour · 96min

An endlessly amusing Warhol specimen, this Factory model appeared shortly after the artist's big-screen triumph, *The Chelsea Girls*, and took its cue from that film's languid obsession with flagrantly uninhibited (and unhinged) characters who aren't the least bit camera-shy. It features none-hit-wonder Joe Spencer as an intrinsically uninteresting biker hunk who wanders in for a series of static episodes in which he is subjected to some of the more entertainingly impossible members of the Warhol set. The conspicuous editing, the playful tensions between artifice and naturalism and the camp appeal of people doing "being" make for a fluid, modern experience. DO

Joe Spencer *Motorcyclist* • Viva *Girl on couch* • Brigid Polk *Woman with husband* • Ingrid Superstar *Girl in kitchen* • Vera Cruz *Other motorcyclist* • George Ann *Salesman* • Bruce Ann *Salesman* • Ed Hood *Florist* • Valerie Solanas [Valerie Solanas] *Valerie Solanas* ■ *Dir/Scr* Andy Warhol

Biker Boyz ★★ 12
Action drama   2003 · US · Colour · 106min

This tepid drama is centred around underground motorcycle gangs burning rubber in the streets of California. After a full-throttle opening, in which a spectacular crash leaves brash teen Derek Luke fatherless, the film decelerates into a standard tale of a talented racer desperate to prove himself the best of the best. Laurence Fishburne, as the undefeated veteran, is a picture of coolness, though he and the rest of the cast are held back by their formulaic characters. JC Violence, swearing. *DVD*

Laurence Fishburne *Smoke* • Derek Luke *Kid* • Orlando Jones *Soul Train* • Djimon Hounsou *Motherland* • Lisa Bonet *Queenie* • Brendan Fehr *Stuntman* • Larenz Tate *Wood* ■ *Dir* Reggie Rock Bythewood • *Scr* Craig Fernandez, Reggie Rock Bythewood, from the article in the *New Times* by Michael Gougis

Bikini Beach ★★★ U
Comedy   1964 · US · Colour · 99min

The third in the fun-in-the-sun teen series features Frankie Avalon in two roles – his usual lovesick surfer lusting after Annette Funicello and a British pop idol named the Potato Bug with the same idea. There's the usual quota of beach frolics, disapproving adults, camp Hell's Angels and drag races, while fluffy pop ditties from the leads are complemented by appearances from Little Stevie Wonder, The Exciters and The Pyramids. This go-go delight is one of the best in the series, even though Avalon's English accent, Beatle wig and "yeah yeahs" strain the wafer-thin credibility. AJ

Frankie Avalon *Frankie/Potato Bug* • Annette Funicello *Dee Dee* • Martha Hyer *Vivien Clements* • Harvey Lembeck *Eric Von Zipper* • Don Rickles *Big Drag* • John Ashley *Johnny* • Little Stevie Wonder [Stevie Wonder] *Little Stevie Wonder* • Keenan Wynn *Harvey Huntington Honeywagon* • Boris Karloff *Art dealer* ■ *Dir* William Asher • *Scr* William Asher, Leo Townsend, Robert Dillon

Bill ★★★★ PG
Biographical drama   1981 · US · Colour · 91min

Almost 60 years after making his showbiz debut, mini-dynamo Mickey Rooney turns in what many rate a career-best performance, playing a mentally retarded man who has to learn to survive on his own in New York City after spending almost half a century in institutions. The film teeters on the edge of over-sentimentality. But, thanks to the sheer class of Rooney's performance, it never quite topples over. Made for TV, *Bill* earned Rooney an Emmy. Had it been made for the cinema, it might well have earned him an Oscar. Dennis Quaid co-stars in this true story, which spawned a sequel, *Bill: On His Own*. DA

Mickey Rooney *Bill Sackter* • Dennis Quaid *Barry Morrow* • Largo Woodruff *Bev Morrow* • Harry Goz *Thomas Walz* • Anna Maria Horsford *Marge Keating* • Kathleen Maguire *Florence Archer* • Jenny Rebecca Dweir *Amy Hill* • Tony Turco *Dr Peters* ■ *Dir* Anthony Page • *Scr* Corey Blechman, from a story by Barry Morrow

Bill ★★★ PG

Comedy   2014 · UK · Colour · 90min

The original cast of *Horrible Histories* make a promising feature debut with this ribald period romp, as a restless Bill Shakespeare (Matthew Baynton) leaves his family in Stratford to make his fortune penning plays in London. Unknown to him, however, our Bard-in-waiting becomes the patsy in a plot by Philip II of Spain to kill Good Queen Bess. The production works wonders with its modest budget, while the Pythonesque tomfoolery is hard to resist, and Helen McCrory's grotesque Elizabeth I is hilarious. JH *Some violence, sexual references, brief swearing.* DVD

Mathew Baynton *William Shakespeare/Lord Burghley/English messenger/customs official* • Simon Farnaby *Earl of Croydon/Juan Domingo/ sausage/Dimitri Alexandrovitch/fur seller* • Martha Howe-Douglas *Anne Hathaway/Molly/ Spanish courtier/body collector* • Ben Willbond *King Phillip II of Spain/Earl of Southampton/ grubby thief/Alexander Dimitrievitch/head of guards/* • Helen McCrory *Queen Elizabeth I* ■ *Dir* Richard Bracewell • *Scr* Laurence Rickard, Ben Willbond

Bill & Ted's Excellent Adventure ★★★★ PG

Comedy   1988 · US · Colour · 86min

A nonstop giggle from start to finish, this beguiling grab-bag of time-travel clichés, hard-rock music and Valley-speaking cool dudes is a flawless, purpose-built junk movie. Director Stephen Herek's scattershot style perfectly complements the wayward cosmic capers, and Keanu Reeves (in his pre-sex symbol days) bravely takes on comedian Alex Winter in competing for the "Most Witlessly Appealing Airhead" crown. Reeves resembles a moronic puppet with loose strings ambling amiably through this happy-go-lucky voyage into the short circuits of history. Engaging to the max. AJ *Swearing.* DVD BD

Keanu Reeves *Ted "Theodore" Logan* • Alex Winter *Bill S Preston* • George Carlin *Rufus* • Terry Camilleri *Napoleon* • Dan Shor *Billy the Kid* • Tony Steedman *Socrates* • Rod Loomis *Sigmund Freud* • Al Leong *Genghis Khan* • Jane Wiedlin *Joan of Arc* ■ *Dir* Stephen Herek • *Scr* Chris Matheson, Ed Solomon

Bill & Ted's Bogus Journey ★★★★ PG

Comedy   1991 · US · Colour · 89min

Wayne's World heroes Wayne and Garth may have won at the box office, but Bill and Ted remain the original and best dudes. This time around the two airheads (played with enormous energy by Alex Winter and Keanu Reeves) are still trying to get their band together when they are murdered by their robotic doppelgangers, sent from the future by the evil Joss Ackland. This sequel lacks the inspired stupidity of the first, but it is still a hoot, especially the knowing nods to Ingmar Bergman's classic *The Seventh Seal* as the duo play battleships with the Reaper. Reeves and Winter are once again cheerfully inept, and director Peter Hewitt stages the spectacular set pieces with panache. JF *Swearing.* DVD CS

Keanu Reeves *Ted/Evil Ted* • Alex Winter *Bill/Evil Bill* • George Carlin *Rufus* • Joss Ackland *De Nomolos* • Sarah Trigger *Joanna* • Annette Azcuy *Elizabeth* • Hal Landon Jr *Captain Logan* • William Sadler *Grim Reaper* ■ *Dir* Peter Hewitt • *Scr* Ed Solomon, Chris Matheson

Bill Cunningham New York ★★★★ 12A

Documentary   2010 · US · Colour · 84min

In his role as photographer for the society and street-style pages of the *New York Times*, Bill Cunningham has been the city's leading fashion chronicler for more than 30 years. Richard Press's documentary turns the lens back on the man who, even at the age of 80, hasn't lost his ability to capture the trends being sported along Manhattan's bustling avenues all the way up to the catwalks of Paris. Cunningham comes across as a man out of time, but his eager grin and old-world charm mask an

uncompromising perfectionist who has given his entire life to fashion and who, in one scene, offers an unexpected glimpse of a secret sadness in his life. Echoing the respect the lensman famously accords his own subjects, Press doesn't pry like an overbearing paparazzo. As such, this isn't the confessional exposé some would hope, but it is a reverent profile of a fascinating, funny and inspirational gentleman. JH *English, French +subtitles.*

Bill Cunningham ■ *Dir* Richard Press • *Cinematographers* Tony Cenicola, Richard Press

A Bill of Divorcement ★★★ U

Drama   1932 · US · BW · 68min

More of interest for its place in cinema history than its dramatic content, this film features Katharine Hepburn's screen debut and introduced Hepburn to her favourite director, George Cukor. Star John Barrymore, though prone to ham, is moving as the former mental asylum inmate reunited with his family, including daughter Hepburn. Billie Burke is also effective as Barrymore's wife, but many of today's viewers may find both the acting style and proscenium-based direction very creaky. TS

John Barrymore *Hilary Fairfield* • Katharine Hepburn *Sydney Fairfield* • Billie Burke *Margaret Fairfield* • David Manners *Kit Humphrey* • Elizabeth Patterson *Aunt Hester* • Paul Cavanagh *Gray Meredith* • Henry Stephenson *Dr Alliot* ■ *Dir* George Cukor • *Scr* Howard Estabrook, Harry Wagstaff Gribble, from the play by Clemence Dane

A Bill of Divorcement ★★★ PG

Drama   1940 · US · BW · 74min

Confined to an asylum for 20 years and unaware that his wife has divorced him and is to remarry, Adolphe Menjou suddenly regains sanity and unexpectedly returns to the family home, precipitating emotional havoc. The 1932 version marked the screen debut of Katharine Hepburn and was a box-office hit. This straight remake was unfavourably compared to the original but, sacrilegious as it might be to say this, stands up better for a modern audience. It creaks in the same places, but offers a stunning performance from Maureen O'Hara, while John Farrow directs with depth and sensitivity. RK

Maureen O'Hara *Sydney Fairfield* • Adolphe Menjou *Hilary Fairfield* • Fay Bainter *Margaret Fairfield* • Herbert Marshall *Gray Meredith* • Dame May Whitty *Hester Fairfield* • Patric Knowles *John Storm* • C Aubrey Smith *Dr Alliot* • Ernest Cossart *Dr Pumphrey* ■ *Dir* John Farrow • *Scr* Dalton Trumbo, from the play by Clemence Dane

Billabong Odyssey ★★ PG

Sports documentary
2003 · US/Bra · Colour · 87min

The pitch for this occasionally spectacular but ultimately disappointing documentary is certainly enticing. Some of the world's most advanced big-wave surfers embark on an 18-month project to find the biggest waves on the planet and to surf them. It brings to mind Bruce Brown's seminal surfing film *Endless Summer*, which perfectly captured both the questing character of the athletes and the sheer physical poetry of the sport at its best. Sadly, this mostly delivers the usual competition footage and none of the personal, meditative flavour or camaraderie of its superior predecessor. AS DVD

■ *Dir* Philip Boston

Billie ★★★ U

Musical comedy   1965 · US · Colour · 86min

An Oscar winner at 16 for her startling performance as the young Helen Keller in *The Miracle Worker* (1962), Patty Duke returned to the screen three years later to play a tomboy whose astonishing prowess at athletics humiliates her male team-mates, bruises her beau's ego and embarrasses her mayoral candidate father. Directed with a pleasingly light touch by

Don Weis, this high-school comedy is both innocuous and entertaining. RK

Patty Duke *Billie Carol* • Jim Backus *Howard G Carol* • Jane Greer *Agnes Carol* • Warren Berlinger *Mike Benson* • Billy De Wolfe *Mayor Davis* • Charles Lane (2) *Coach Jones* • Dick Sargent *Matt Bullitt* • Susan Seaforth *Jean Matthews* • Ted Bessell *Bob Matthews* ■ *Dir* Don Weis • *Scr* Ronald Alexander, from the play *Time Out for Ginger* by Ronald Alexander

Billion Dollar Brain ★★ PG

Spy thriller   1967 · UK · Colour · 103min

The third of the Harry Palmer pictures (after *The Ipcress File* and *Funeral in Berlin*) has a story that smacks of substandard Bond, as Michael Caine travels to Finland to infiltrate power-crazed Ed Begley's secret organisation and prevent him from taking over the world. Ken Russell was perhaps an unlikely choice as director, but his exuberance prevents the plot from lapsing into predictability. In 1995, Harry Palmer was brought out of retirement for *Bullet to Beijing* and *Midnight in St Petersburg*. DP DVD

Michael Caine *Harry Palmer* • Karl Malden *Leo Newbigin* • Françoise Dorléac *Anya* • Oscar Homolka *Colonel Stok* • Ed Begley *General Midwinter* • Guy Doleman *Colonel Ross* • Vladek Sheybal *Dr Eiwort* • Milo Sperber *Basil* ■ *Dir* Ken Russell • *Scr* John McGrath, from the novel by Len Deighton

Billy Bathgate ★★★ 15

Crime drama   1991 · US · Colour · 102min

Dustin Hoffman as infamous mobster Dutch Schultz gives one of his more over-egged performances, but Nicole Kidman is sterling in support as a society moll. The credentials of this mahogany-toned movie are pretty impressive - original novel by EL Doctorow, script by Tom Stoppard - and there is an obvious intelligence that shines through the many nasty killings on offer. SH *Violence, swearing, nudity.* DVD

Dustin Hoffman *Dutch Schultz* • Nicole Kidman *Drew Preston* • Loren Dean *Billy Bathgate* • Bruce Willis *Bo Weinberg* • Steven Hill *Otto Berman* • Steve Buscemi *Irving* • Billy Jaye *Mickey* ■ *Dir* Robert Benton • *Scr* Tom Stoppard, from the novel by EL Doctorow • *Cinematographer* Nestor Almendros

Billy Budd ★★★ U

Adventure drama   1962 · UK · BW · 124min

Although this allegory about good versus evil is more suited to declamatory opera than cinema, writer/director Peter Ustinov's adaptation of Herman Melville's novel about life aboard an 18th-century British warship has a cannonade of powerful performances, notably from Ustinov as the indecisive captain, Robert Ryan as the sadistic Master-at-Arms, and an Oscar-nominated Terence Stamp as the innocent Billy. The film backs off from the fable that Melville intended, but it's a rather plodding treatment. TH

Terence Stamp *Billy Budd* • Peter Ustinov *Captain Edward Fairfax Vere* • Robert Ryan *Master-at-Arms John Claggart* • Melvyn Douglas *The Dansker* • Ronald Lewis *Jenkins* • David McCallum (1) *Lt Wyatt* • John Neville *Lt John Ratcliffe* • Ray McAnally *O'Daniel* ■ *Dir* Peter Ustinov • *Scr* Peter Ustinov, DeWitt Bodeen, Robert Rossen, from the play by Louis O Coxe and Robert H Chapman, from the novel *Billy Budd, Foretopman* by Herman Melville

Billy Elliot ★★★★ 15

Drama   2000 · UK · Colour · 107min

Stage director Stephen Daldry made his feature debut with this amiable study of daring to be different in the face of intractable tradition. The decision to set the story of an 11-year-old north-easterner's bid to become a ballet dancer against the backdrop of the 1984 miners' strike has more emotional resonance than social relevance. It's the heart, not the conscience, that Daldry is keenest to tweak, and he succeeds triumphantly, thanks largely to Jamie Bell's eager performance in the title role, and the marvellous supporting turns from Gary Lewis as the lad's reactionary dad and Julie Walters as his chain-smoking dance instructor. DP *Swearing.* DVD BD

Julie Walters *Mrs Wilkinson* • Gary Lewis *Dad* • Jamie Draven *Tony* • Jean Heywood *Grandmother* • Jamie Bell *Billy* • Stuart Wells *Michael* • Mike Elliot *George Watson* ■ *Dir* Stephen Daldry • *Scr* Lee Hall

Billy Galvin ★★★ PG

Drama   1986 · US · Colour · 90min

This pleasingly gritty blue-collar drama is held together by a powerful performance from screen veteran Karl Malden. In a neat twist on a familiar story, he plays a stubborn construction worker who doesn't want his rebellious son Lenny Von Dohlen to join him on the scaffolding. John E Gray's direction is admirably low key. JF *Swearing.*

Karl Malden *Jack Galvin* • Lenny Von Dohlen *Billy Galvin* • Joyce Van Patten *Mae* • Toni Kalem *Nora* • Keith Szarabajka *Donny* • Alan North *Georgie* • Paul Guilfoyle (2) *Nolan* • Barton Heyman *Kennedy* ■ *Dir/Scr* John E Gray [John Gray]

Billy Liar ★★★★★ PG

Comedy drama   1963 · UK · BW · 94min

A hit on page and stage, Keith Waterhouse and Willis Hall's *Billy Liar* was brought to the screen by John Schlesinger as a faultless blend of social realism and satirical fantasy. Tom Courtenay is at his career best - so far - as the undertaker's assistant who escapes from his mundane existence into the neverland of Ambrosia, where he is supreme dictator. The performances are all first rate, notably Julie Christie and Helen Fraser as two of the three women in his life, Wilfred Pickles and Mona Washbourne as his long-suffering parents, and Leonard Rossiter as his humourless boss. DP DVD BD

Tom Courtenay *Billy Fisher* • Julie Christie *Liz* • Wilfred Pickles *Geoffrey Fisher* • Mona Washbourne *Alice Fisher* • Ethel Griffies *Florence, grandmother* • Finlay Currie *Duxbury* • Rodney Bewes *Arthur Crabtree* • Helen Fraser *Barbara* • Leonard Rossiter *Shadrack* ■ *Dir* John Schlesinger • *Scr* Keith Waterhouse, Willis Hall, from their play and the novel by Keith Waterhouse

Billy Madison ★★★ PG

Comedy   1995 · US · Colour · 85min

Your enjoyment of this gimmicky comedy will depend on your feelings about the lowbrow comedy of Adam Sandler. He plays an infantile loser who won't be given control of his father's business empire unless he agrees to repeat his school education in just 24 weeks. Exploiting the star's talent for slapstick stupidity, this has some entertaining moments as he clashes with junior classmates and falls for his pretty teacher (Bridgette Wilson). JC DVD BD

Adam Sandler *Billy Madison* • Darren McGavin *Brian Madison* • Bridgette Wilson *Veronica* • Bradley Whitford *Eric Gordon* • Josh Mostel *Max Anderson* • Norm MacDonald *Frank* • Mark Beltzman *Jack* • Larry Hankin *Carl Alphonse* ■ *Dir* Tamra Davis • *Scr* Tim Herlihy, Adam Sandler

Billy Rose's Diamond Horseshoe ★★★ U

Musical   1945 · US · Colour · 100min

This is probably the best of the Betty Grable vehicles, and here she plays a beautiful showgirl, with Dick Haymes as the medical student who falls for her. For once, she had a decent director in George Seaton, who ensured that the garish 20th Century-Fox production was well appointed and that the songs were well above the usual recycled standard of the period. This is the film that introduced the endearing hit *The More I See You*. TS

Betty Grable *Bonnie Collins* • Dick Haymes *Joe Davis Jr* • Phil Silvers *Blinky Walker* • William Gaxton *Joe Davis Sr* • Beatrice Kay *Claire Williams* • Margaret Dumont *Mrs Standish* • Roy Benson *Harper* • George Melford *Pop* • Hal K Dawson *Carter* ■ *Dir* George Seaton • *Scr* George Seaton, from a play by John Kenyon Nicholson • *Music* Alfred Newman, Charles Henderson • *Costume Designers* Kay Nelson, Rene Hubert, Sascha Brastoff, Bonnie Cashin

Billy the Kid ★★★★

Western   1930 · US · BW · 95min

The first sound film about Billy the Kid tells a now familiar story of his friendship with a kindly British rancher and his relentless pursuit of the man's killers who have the law in their pocket. It shows its age at times, but director King Vidor presents the story in an austere, anti-romantic fashion, with a realistic regard for the effects of hunger and thirst on men under siege – and for the pain and finality of violent death. Johnny Mack Brown makes an excellent Kid, while Wallace Beery is restrained as the fair-minded sheriff Pat Garrett. The film was shot with alternative endings, tragic and upbeat; it is the latter which is now usually shown. AE

John Mack Brown [Johnny Mack Brown] *Billy* • Wallace Beery *Barrett* • Kay Johnson *Claire* • Karl Dane *Swenson* • Wyndham Standing *Tunston* • Russell Simpson *McSween* • Blanche Frederici *Mrs McSween* ■ *Dir* King Vidor • *Scr* Wanda Tuchock, Laurence Stallings, Charles MacArthur, from the novel *The Saga of Billy the Kid* by Walter Noble Burns

Billy the Kid ★★★

Western   1941 · US · Colour · 94min

The superb use of three-strip Technicolor doesn't altogether compensate for a certain dullness in this portrayal of the west's most famous outlaw, played by Robert Taylor dressed entirely in black. First-time feature director and former editor David Miller has the benefit of the MGM production process, but, despite Gene Fowler's literate and inventive screenplay, which makes Billy and his nemesis Pat Garrett (here renamed Jim Sherwood) childhood friends, fans of this oft-told tale may be disappointed. TS

Robert Taylor (1) *Billy Bonney* • Brian Donlevy *Jim Sherwood* • Ian Hunter *Eric Keating* • Mary Howard *Edith Keating* • Gene Lockhart *Dan Hickey* • Lon Chaney Jr *Spike Hudson* • Henry O'Neill *Tim Ward* • Guinn Williams [Guinn "Big Boy" Williams] *Ed Bronson* ■ *Dir* David Miller (1) • *Scr* Gene Fowler, from a story by Howard Emmett Rogers, Bradbury Foote, suggested by the book *The Saga of Billy the Kid* by Walter Noble Burns

Billy the Kid vs Dracula ★★ PG

Horror western   1966 · US · Colour · 71min

This example of high-camp fun bordered on exploitation and came at the end of William Beaudine's career. John Carradine stars as Dracula (a role he had last played 20 years before) who's way out west and lusting after the blood of a pretty ranch owner. Unluckily for the Count, her fiancé is the reformed outlaw Billy the Kid. Let battle commence in a cheap but not nasty B-picture. BB

Chuck Courtney *Billy the Kid* • John Carradine *Count Dracula* • Melinda Plowman *Betty Bentley* • Virginia Christine *Eva Oster* • Walter Janovitz *Franz Oster* ■ *Dir* William Beaudine • *Scr* Carl K Hittleman, from a story by Carl K Hittleman

Billy Two Hats ★★★ 15

Western   1973 · UK/US · Colour · 95min

An example of how Hollywood's elder statesmen (here Gregory Peck) tried to connect with the new "youth" audience of the 1970s by co-starring with fresh talent, in this case Desi Arnaz Jr, best known for being the son of Desi Arnaz and Lucille Ball. It's a western about a bungled robbery, filmed in Israel, which looks like Spain pretending to be New Mexico. It offers some decent action sequences and the novelty of the usually presidential Peck ostensibly playing a baddie. AT Swearing. *DVD*

Gregory Peck *Deans* • Desi Arnaz Jr *Billy* • Jack Warden *Gifford* • Sian Barbara Allen *Esther* • David Huddleston *Copeland* • John Pearce *Spencer* • Dawn Littlesky *Squaw* ■ *Dir* Ted Kotcheff • *Scr* Alan Sharp

Billy's Hollywood Screen Kiss ★★★ 15

Romantic comedy drama
1998 · US · Colour · 88min

Director Tommy O'Haver's gay comedy drama serves up some disarmingly honest truths about confused passion in a camp cascade of glossy style, glamorous drag queens and glorous vamping. Wannabe LA photographer Sean P Hayes shoots homoerotic portraits based on famous Hollywood kisses and falls in lust with one of his models, the sexually confused Brad Rowe. Although never quite scalpel-sharp, O'Haver's classy confection is an engaging enough diversion held together by Hayes's central turn. AJ Swearing.

Sean P Hayes [Sean Hayes] *Billy* • Brad Rowe *Gabriel* • Meredith Scott Lynn *Georgiana* • Richard Ganoung *Perry* • Armando Valdes-Kennedy *Fernando* • Paul Bartel (1) *Rex Webster* • Matthew Ashford *Whitey* • Carmine Giovinazzo *Gundy* ■ *Dir/Scr* Tommy O'Haver

Biloxi Blues ★★★★ 15

Second World War comedy
1988 · US · Colour · 102min

Playwright Neil Simon's semi-autobiographical trilogy began with *Brighton Beach Memoirs* (1986) and ended with *Broadway Bound* (1991), but this second instalment is the most entertaining of the three. Matthew Broderick plays Simon's altered ego Eugene Jerome, whose army boot-camp training involves him in the lives of the various soldiers around him – from Christopher Walken's surprisingly desolate sergeant to Matt Mulhern's dumb-ox bully boy. Director Mike Nichols makes up for the lack of momentum with character-revealing conversation and the result is comic and poignant. TH *DVD*

Matthew Broderick *Eugene* • Christopher Walken *Sgt Toomey* • Matt Mulhern *Wykowski* • Corey Parker *Epstein* • Markus Flanagan *Selridge* • Casey Siemaszko *Carney* • Michael Dolan *Hennessey* • Penelope Ann Miller *Daisy* • Park Overall *Rowena* ■ *Dir* Mike Nichols • *Scr* Neil Simon, from his play

Bingo ★★ PG

Adventure   1991 · US · Colour · 86min

This tale of a boy's tearful split from his faithful canine companion has enough sentiment to make you cringe. Every cliché in the "youngsters and pets" genre is played out from the moment Robert J Steinmiller Jr adopts a circus dog. Despite the earnest nature of the performances, this will stretch the patience of even the most soft-hearted viewer. SH Swearing, violence. *DVD*

Cindy Williams *Natalie Devlin* • David Rasche *Hal Devlin* • Robert J Steinmiller Jr *Chuckie Devlin* • Kurt Fuller *Lennie* • Joe Guzaldo *Eli* • David French *Chickie Devlin* • Glenn Shadix *Duke* • Suzie Plakson *Ginger* ■ *Dir* Matthew Robbins • *Scr* Jim Strain, from the film *The Littlest Hobo* by Dorrell McGowan

The Bingo Long Travelling All-Stars and Motor Kings ★★★★ 15

Period sports comedy
1976 · US · Colour · 106min

This sports comedy set in 1939 takes a less than serious look at the issue of racial prejudice. Billy Dee Williams and James Earl Jones are the stars of a black baseball team, who decide to set up their own club in defiance of Negro League boss Ted Ross. Needless to say the bosses don't like it and try to put the All-Stars out of business. In this crowd-pleasing mix of skill and farce, Richard Pryor almost steals the show with his attempts to crash the race barrier. TH

Billy Dee Williams *Bingo Long* • James Earl Jones *Leon* • Richard Pryor *Charlie Snow* • Rico Dawson *Willie Lee* • Sam "Birmingham" Briston *Louis* • Jophery Brown *Champ Chambers* • Leon Wagner *Fat Sam* • Tony Burton *Isaac* ■ *Dir* John Badham • *Scr* Hal Barwood, Matthew Robbins, from a novel by William Brashler

Bio-Dome ★ 12

Comedy   1996 · US · Colour · 93min

This excruciatingly awful comedy is about a couple of crude, lewd and generally nauseating brothers (Pauly Shore and Stephen Baldwin) who accidentally gatecrash a year-long science bio-dome experiment. Naturally, they trash the place. The braindead brothers' juvenile antics grate and the plotting is an insult. JC *DVD*

Pauly Shore *Bud Macintosh* • Stephen Baldwin *Doyle Johnson* • William Atherton *Dr Noah Faulkner* • Denise Dowse *Olivia Biggs* • Dara Tomanovich *Mimi Simkins* • Kevin West *TC Romulus* • Kylie Minogue *Petra Von Kant* • Joey Adams [Joey Lauren Adams] *Monique* • Patricia Hearst *Doyle's mother* • Roger Clinton *Professor Bloom* ■ *Dir* Jason Bloom • *Scr* Kip Koenig, Scott Marcano, from a story by Adam Leff, Mitchell Peck, Jason Blumenthal

Birch Interval ★★★★

Drama   1976 · US · Colour · 103min

Not shown in British cinemas, this marvellous film is touching and sensitive in its telling of the story of a young American girl growing up in the midst of an Amish community. Finely directed by Delbert Mann, this features an exceptionally strong cast headed by veterans Eddie Albert and Rip Torn, and marks a last return to film by blacklisted Oscar winner Anne Revere. Little seen, this is a minor classic in search of recognition. TS

Eddie Albert *Pa Strawacher* • Rip Torn *Thomas* • Ann Wedgeworth *Marie* • Susan McClung *Jesse* • Brian Part *Samuel* • Jann Stanley *Esther* • Bill Lucking [William Lucking] *Charlie* • Anne Revere *Mrs Tanner* • Joanna Crawford *Lady on Bus* ■ *Dir* Delbert Mann • *Scr* Joanna Crawford, from her novel

Bird ★★★★ 15

Biographical drama   1988 · US · Colour · 154min

Charlie Parker, the black American alto saxophonist who was the driving force behind the bebop jazz revolution, sacrificed his wellbeing, and that of his lover, to the tempting whirlwind of his music. As Parker, Forest Whitaker gives a pumping performance, with Diane Venora no second best as his lady, who goes from strutting dancer to empty soul. Director Clint Eastwood is perfectly in tune with his subject, giving the film a claustrophobic atmosphere as it portrays the anarchy of bebop. The innovative soundtrack, enhancing Parker's recordings using present-day musicians, is a perfect accompaniment. JM Swearing. *DVD*

Forest Whitaker *Charlie "Yardbird" Parker* • Diane Venora *Chan Richardson* • Michael Zelniker *Red Rodney* • Samuel E Wright *Dizzy Gillespie* • Keith David *Buster Franklin* • Michael McGuire *Brewster* • James Handy *Esteves* • Damon Whitaker *Young Bird* ■ *Dir* Clint Eastwood • *Scr* Joel Oliansky

Bird of Paradise ★★★

Romantic adventure   1932 · US · BW · 81min

Producer David O Selznick wheeled in the big guns at RKO for this romance about love across the racial divide on a Polynesian island, sending Joel McCrea, the luscious Dolores Del Rio and distinguished director King Vidor off to locations in Hawaii. Appalling weather plagued the shoot, but can't be blamed for the turgid and messy screenplay, which deadens the drama. The production values are first-rate, though, while the doom-laden tale is played with conviction. RK

Dolores Del Rio *Luana* • Joel McCrea *Johnny Baker* • John Halliday *Mac* • Richard "Skeets" Gallagher *Chester* • Creighton Chaney [Lon Chaney Jr] *Thornton* • Bert Roach *Hector* • Napoleon Pukui *The King* • Sofia Ortega *Mahumahu* ■ *Dir* King Vidor • *Scr* Wells Root, Leonard Praskins, Wanda Tuchok, from a play by Richard Walton Tully

Bird of Paradise ★

Romantic adventure   1951 · US · Colour · 100min

Bird of Paradise was originally filmed in black and white by RKO in 1932, with stellar leads, a top-class director and loads of authentic atmosphere. This pointless

Technicolor remake from Fox has no merit, despite being written and directed by the usually reliable Delmer Daves. The over-lush visuals engulf the human drama. RK

Louis Jourdan *Andre Laurence* • Debra Paget *Kalua* • Jeff Chandler *Tenga* • Everett Sloane *The beachcomber* • Maurice Schwartz *The Kahuna* • Jack Elam *The Painter* • Prince Leilani *Chief* • Otto Waldis *Skipper* ■ *Dir* Delmer Daves • *Scr* Delmer Daves, from a play by Richard Walton Tully

Bird on a Wire ★★★ 15

Comedy action thriller
1990 · US · Colour · 105min

Mel Gibson plays a former small-time drugs runner who has been in hiding since turning state's evidence, but who ends up on the run with an old flame (Goldie Hawn) when his cover is broken. It's frothy nonsense for the most part, but expertly packaged by director John Badham. Hawn is an able if sometimes irritating foil, while David Carradine, Bill Duke and Stephen Tobolowsky are an entertaining trio of villains. JF Swearing, violence. *DVD*

Mel Gibson *Rick Jarmin* • Goldie Hawn *Marianne Graves* • David Carradine *Eugene Sorenson* • Bill Duke *Albert Diggs* • Stephen Tobolowsky *Joe Weyburn* • Joan Severance *Rachel Varney* • Harry Caesar *Marvin* • Jeff Corey *Lou Baird* ■ *Dir* John Badham • *Scr* David Seltzer, Louis Venosta, Eric Lerner, from a story by Louis Venosta, Eric Lerner

The Bird with the Crystal Plumage ★★★★ 15

Suspense thriller
1969 · It/W Ger · Colour · 91min

Who is the new Jack the Ripper holding Rome in a grip of terror? American author Tony Musante knows he's witnessed a vital clue to the chilling conundrum – but what is it exactly? Dario Argento's *giallo* trendsetter (*giallo*, or "yellow", being a term for all Italian thrillers more concerned with the modus operandi of the bloody murders than their whodunnit aspect) is a glossy, cosmopolitan and jagged mystery firmly entrenched in Hitchcockian paranoia. A seminal work, it shows Argento's visual flair for horrific set pieces. AJ Italian +subtitles. *DVD*

Tony Musante *Sam Dalmas* • Suzy Kendall *Julia* • Eva Renzi *Monica* • Enrico Maria Salerno *Morosini* • Mario Adorf *Berto* • Renato Romano *Dover* • Umberto Rano *Ranieri* ■ *Dir/Scr* Dario Argento • *Music* Ennio Morricone • *Cinematographer* Vittorio Storaro

The Birdcage ★★★ 15

Comedy   1996 · US · Colour · 114min

The knives were out for this camp comedy from the start. Film snobs were convinced it would besmirch the memory of *La Cage aux Folles*, and the gay lobby denounced the making of such a cosy film in the Aids era. Yet, in the end, nearly everyone was pleasantly surprised by a picture that trivialised neither its source nor its sensitive issues. Robin Williams underplays sensibly, Nathan Lane almost matches the peerless Michel Serrault, and Gene Hackman shows again what a deft comic he can be. Less assured, however, is director Mike Nichols and writer Elaine May's clumsy political satire. DP Swearing. *DVD*

Robin Williams *Armand Goldman* • Gene Hackman *Senator Keeley* • Nathan Lane *Albert* • Dianne Wiest *Louise Keeley* • Dan Futterman *Val Goldman* • Calista Flockhart *Barbara Keeley* • Hank Azaria *Agador* • Christine Baranski *Katherine* ■ *Dir* Mike Nichols • *Scr* Elaine May, from the film *La Cage aux Folles* by Jean Poiret, Francis Veber, Edouard Molinaro, Marcello Danon, from the play *La Cage aux Folles* by Jean Poiret

Birdman of Alcatraz ★★★★ PG

Biographical drama   1962 · US · BW · 145min

Real-life killer Robert Stroud was apparently quite unlike the tough, taciturn inmate portrayed by Burt Lancaster in director John Frankenheimer's thought-provoking study of one man's attempt to survive an unforgiving prison system. Stroud used his years in solitary confinement to become a world authority on ornithology, despite the cruel injustices meted out by the prison warden (convincingly played by Karl Malden). Lancaster was Oscar-nominated for a performance that is ranked by many to be one of the finest of his career, while Burnett Guffey's claustrophobic black-and-white photography is masterly. DP **DVD**

Burt Lancaster *Robert Stroud* • Karl Malden *Harvey Shoemaker* • Thelma Ritter *Elizabeth Stroud* • Betty Field *Stella Johnson* • Neville Brand *Bull Ransom* • Edmond O'Brien *Tom Gaddis* • Hugh Marlowe *Roy Comstock* • Telly Savalas *Feto Gomez* • Crahan Denton *Kramer* ■ *Dir* John Frankenheimer • *Scr* Guy Trosper, from the non-fiction book *Birdman of Alcatraz; the Story of Robert Stroud* by Thomas E Gaddis

Birdman or (The Unexpected Virtue of Ignorance) ★★★★★ 15

Comedy drama 2014 · US · Colour · 114min

The midlife crisis of a fading star is the basis of this surprisingly profound and kinetic satire about success in the age of social media. Michael Keaton stars as an actor who found fame in the 1990s with a trilogy of superhero films, and is now suffering from the woes of debuting his first play as writer and director. As the stress mounts, Keaton begins to hear the persuasive voice of his one-time alter ego. The Birdman conceit is a good excuse for some great effects but really this is an excellent drama about a man on the edge, with Keaton outstanding and Edward Norton superb as his nemesis, the Method actor from hell. DW **DVD** ⬙

Michael Keaton *Riggan Thomson/Birdman* • Edward Norton *Mike Shiner* • Zach Galifianakis *Brandon Vander Hay* • Andrea Riseborough *Laura* • Emma Stone *Sam Thomson* • Naomi Watts *Lesley* • Amy Ryan *Sylvia* • Lindsay Duncan *Tabitha* ■ *Dir* Alejandro González Iñárritu • *Scr* Alejandro González Iñárritu, Nicolás Giacobone, Alexander Dinelaris, Armando Bo

The Birds ★★★★★ 15

Classic horror 1963 · US · Colour · 113min

This Hitchcock classic strayed from favour for a while, yet it is now rivalled only by *Vertigo* and *Psycho*. Set in the coastal town of Bodega Bay, the story concerns a small group of dissatisfied creatures. Two women and a young girl are all fixed on one man (Rod Taylor), and when a fourth (Tippi Hedren) arrives from San Francisco to vie for his attention, a menacing populace of birds descends on the town, wreaking terror and havoc, right up until the film's inscrutable ending. As ever, despite the horror pervading the action, Hitchcock's sense of humour shines through. AJ Violence. **DVD** ⬙

Rod Taylor *Mitch Brenner* • "Tippi" Hedren [Tippi Hedren] *Melanie Daniels* • Jessica Tandy *Lydia Brenner* • Suzanne Pleshette *Annie Hayworth* • Veronica Cartwright *Cathy Brenner* • Ethel Griffies *Mrs Bundy* • Charles McGraw *Sebastian Sholes* • Ruth McDevitt *Mrs MacGruder* ■ *Dir* Alfred Hitchcock • *Scr* Evan Hunter, from the short story by Daphne du Maurier

The Birds and the Bees ★★ U

Comedy 1956 · US · Colour · 94min

Directed by Norman Taurog with Mitzi Gaynor, David Niven and George Gobel, this is a direct copy of Preston Sturges's *The Lady Eve*, the story of a father-daughter duo of cardsharps who fleece a gullible millionaire, which is a magic amalgam of satire, farce, slapstick and romance. While the original is now regarded as an enduring gem of screwball comedy, this Technicolor remake is only mildly amusing and short on charm. RK

George Gobel *George Hamilton* • Mitzi Gaynor *Jean Harris* • David Niven *Colonel Harris* • Reginald Gardiner *Gerald* • Fred Clark *Mr Hamilton* • Harry Bellaver *Marty Kennedy* • Hans Conried *Duc Jacques de Montaigne* • Margery Maude *Mrs Hamilton* ■ *Dir* Norman Taurog • *Scr* Sidney Sheldon, Preston Sturges, from a story by Monckton Hoffe

Birds Anonymous ★★★★ U

Animated comedy 1957 · US · Colour · 6min

Fritz Freleng's distinguished career spanned the fledgeling Disney studios in the 1920s and his own DePatie-Freleng organisation of the 1960s and beyond, with a lengthy period at Warner Bros in between (he was their longest serving director). At Warners, he developed into a master of timing, rivalling Avery in sharpness if not in wackiness. In this imaginative Tweety and Sylvester vehicle, Sylvester the cat is within inches of eating the sadistic canary when another feline interrupts him with an invitation to an AA-style meeting for canary addicts. This film received an Academy Award for best short cartoon of its year (one of five awarded to Freleng). CLP

Mel Blanc *Sylvester/Tweety* ■ *Dir* Friz Freleng • *Scr* Warren Foster • *Music* Milt Franklyn

Birds of Prey ★★ PG

Mystery 1930 · UK · BW · 91min

Adapted from AA Milne's play *The Fourth Wall*, this is an intriguing variation on the country-house whodunnit. It shouldn't prove too difficult to deduce who killed host C Aubrey Smith because of his past deeds as a policeman in South Africa. However, nephew Frank Lawton struggles to spot the clues as he engages in a spot of amateur sleuthing. Unfortunately, the film suffers from the fact it was made in the early days of the talkie, with concealed mics restricting the action. DP **DVD**

Robert Loraine *Carter* • Warwick Ward *Laverick* • Frank Lawton *Jimmy Hilton* • C Aubrey Smith *Arthur Hilton* ■ *Dir* Basil Dean • *Scr* Basil Dean, AA Milne, from Milne's play *The Fourth Wall*

The Birds, the Bees, and the Italians ★★

Comedy 1965 · Fr/It · BW · 115min

Bursting with Italianate gusto, director Pietro Germi's film is one of the many compendium works from Italy with sex as the subject of their intentionally humorous tales. This contribution, in which Virna Lisi is the best-known name, offers three episodes dealing variously with a deceived husband, a henpecked husband and an underage girl who is the favoured bed-mate of most of the male population of her village. Efficient enough, it now seems rather dated, though British audiences found it hilarious in its day. RK In Italian.

Virna Lisi *Milena Zulian* • Gastone Moschin *Osvaldo Bisigato* • Nora Ricci *Gilda Bisigato* • Alberto Lionello *Toni Gasparini* • Olga Villi *Ippolita Gasparini* • Franco Fabrizi *Lino Benedetti* • Beba Loncar *Noemi Castellan* ■ *Dir* Pietro Germi • *Scr* Age Scarpelli [Agenore Incrocci and Furio Scarpelli], Luciano Vincenzoni, Pietro Germi, from a story by Scarpelli [Agenore Incrocci and Furio Scarpelli], Germi

BirdWatchers ★★★ 15

Drama 2008 · It/Bra · Colour · 103min

In the Brazilian rainforest, a group of tribespeople come into conflict with a wealthy white farmer as they try to reclaim some of their ancestral land. Featuring real-life members of the Guarani-Kaiowá tribe in leading roles, director Marco Bechis's film feels like a *National Geographic* photo spread sprung into vivid life. Beautiful cinematography captures the slow erosion of the Amazon as modern agriculture encroaches on an ancient way of living. Sketching the drama in broad strokes, the film hammers its point home as the tribe's trainee shaman (Abrísio da Silva Pedro) falls for the farmer's teenage daughter. Bechis elucidates it all with a keen eye for anthropological detail and uses the religious mysticism of the tribe to offer a powerfully creepy sense of how unseen forces (from evil spirits to capitalist greed) can overturn lives. JR Portuguese, Guarani +subtitles. Sex scenes, violence. **DVD**

Claudio Santamaria *Roberto* • Alicélia Batista Cabreira *Lia* • Chiara Caselli *Beatrice* • Abrísio da Silva Pedro *Osvaldo* • Ademilson Concianza Verga *Irineu* • Ambrósio Vilhava *Nádio* ■ *Dir* Marco Bechis • *Scr* Marco Bechis, Luiz Bolognesi

Birdy ★★★★ 15

Drama 1984 · US · Colour · 115min

This engrossing psychological drama features powerful performances from Matthew Modine and Nicolas Cage as lifelong friends who are both scarred by the trauma of fighting in Vietnam. Director Alan Parker shows his versatility by adapting William Wharton's complex novel with sensitivity and skill, while Modine is exceptional as the boy who believes he's a bird. PF Violence, swearing, sex scenes. **DVD**

Matthew Modine *Birdy* • Nicolas Cage *Al Columbato* • John Harkins *Dr Weiss* • Sandy Baron *Mr Columbato* • Karen Young *Hannah Rourke* • Bruno Kirby *Renaldi* • Nancy Fish *Mrs Prevost* • George Buck *Birdy's father* • Dolores Sage *Birdy's mother* ■ *Dir* Alan Parker • *Scr* Sandy Kroopf, Jack Behr, from the novel by William Wharton

Birth ★★★★ 15

Mystery drama 2004 · US/Ger · Colour · 100min

A ten-year-old boy claims to be the reincarnation of a woman's dead husband in director Jonathan Glazer's utterly captivating New York-set fairy tale. This gripping film considers the overriding power of love and how the strength of belief can lead individuals into moral minefields. Nicole Kidman gives a performance of haunting intensity as the about-to-be-remarried widow whose life is turned upside down by Cameron Bright's intrusive pre-pubescent. This is elegantly shot and intriguingly ambiguous. AJ Nudity, a sex scene. **DVD**

Nicole Kidman *Anna* • Cameron Bright *Sean* • Danny Huston *Joseph* • Lauren Bacall *Eleanor* • Alison Elliott (2) *Laura* • Arliss Howard *Bob* • Anne Heche *Clara* • Peter Stormare *Clifford* ■ *Dir* Jonathan Glazer • *Scr* Jean-Claude Carrière, Milo Addica, Jonathan Glazer

LANDMARK FILM
A staggeringly racist Civil War epic that pioneers such concepts as the close-up and cross-cutting between scenes

The Birth of a Nation ★★★★ 15

Silent historical epic 1915 · US · BW · 192min

This colossal, majestic Civil War epic from pioneer director DW Griffith is one of the most successful films of all time. In terms of film history, the film was ground-breaking: a long and epic narrative telling a complex tale interweaving two families' fortunes, with dramatic reconstructions of key events including the assassination of Abraham Lincoln, not to mention accurate (and costly) re-creations of Civil War battlefields. But – and it's a very big "but" – the source material is fervently racist, and Griffith remains true to his source. It's hard to applaud a film where the Ku Klux Klan rides triumphantly to the rescue, and this, alas, undoes all the sterling work put in earlier and the wonderful performances. TS **DVD** ⬙

Lillian Gish *Elsie Stoneman* • Mae Marsh *Flora Cameron* • Henry B Walthall *Ben Cameron* • Miriam Cooper *Margaret Cameron* • Mary Alden *Lydia Brown* • Ralph Lewis *Hon Austin Stoneman* • George Siegmann *Silas Lynch* • Walter Long *Gus* • Jack Ford [John Ford] *Klansman* ■ *Dir* DW Griffith • *Scr* DW Griffith, Frank E Woods, from the novel and the play *The Clansman* and the novel *The Leopard's Spots* by Thomas Dixon Jr • *Cinematographer* Billy Bitzer

The Birth of the Blues ★★★ U

Musical 1941 · US · BW · 82min

Bing Crosby, Brian Donlevy, Mary Martin and real-life trombonist Jack Teagarden head the line-up in this rather flimsy fiction about a pioneering group of musicians who progress from being street entertainers to taking New Orleans by storm as the original Dixieland jazz band. Plot and characterisation, however, are secondary to such great numbers as *St Louis Blues*, *Melancholy Baby* and the title number. It's a good-natured, well-directed film that will delight fans of the music. RK **DVD**

Bing Crosby *Jeff Lambert* • Mary Martin *Betty Lou Cobb* • Brian Donlevy *Memphis* • Carolyn Lee *Aunt Phoebe* • Eddie "Rochester" Anderson *Louie* • Jack Teagarden *Pepper* • J Carrol Naish *Blackie* • Warren Hymer *Limpy* ■ *Dir* Victor Schertzinger • *Scr* Harry Tugend, Walter DeLeon, from a story by Harry Tugend

Birthday Girl ★★★ 15

Romantic comedy drama 2001 · UK/US · Colour · 89min

Worth seeing for Nicole Kidman's downbeat and brave performance as a Russian mail-order bride, this blackly comic film suffers from a genre identity crisis. Ben Chaplin is the suburban bank clerk who summons Kidman to England via the internet. But once she's ensconced in his semi, Chaplin is disappointed with her lack of English and grunge style, but forgives her when she compensates with action in the bedroom. Then two men claiming to be Kidman's relatives arrive and soon all he holds dear is in danger. Noot quite funny or hard enough. LH Swearing, sex scenes, violence. **DVD**

Nicole Kidman *Sophia/"Nadia"* • Ben Chaplin *John Buckingham* • Vincent Cassel *Alexei* • Mathieu Kassovitz *Yuri* • Kate Evans *Clare* • Alexander Armstrong *Robert Moseley* • Sally Phillips *Karen* ■ *Dir* Jez Butterworth • *Scr* Jez Butterworth, Tom Butterworth

The Birthday Party ★★★ 15

Drama 1968 · UK · Colour and BW · 118min

Directing his second film, William Friedkin opted for a safe and rather uncinematic approach to Harold Pinter's first full-length play. This is all about text and performance, and, compelling though the action is, it's clearly diminished by the loss of the immediacy you get in the theatre. Robert Shaw is too sturdy an actor to convince as the frightened mystery man hiding away in a seaside B&B. Veterans Sydney Tafler and Dandy Nichols are left to steal the show with performances that suggest both had been rather wasted during their earlier movie careers. DP **DVD**

Robert Shaw *Stanley Weber* • Patrick Magee *Shamus McCann* • Dandy Nichols *Meg Bowles* • Sydney Tafler *Nat Goldberg* • Moultrie Kelsall *Petey Bowles* ■ *Dir* William Friedkin • *Scr* Harold Pinter, from his play

The Birthday Present ★★ U

Drama 1957 · UK · BW · 96min

Pat Jackson directs this doleful, overlong slice of surburban life, in which Tony Britton shows why he never made it as even a minor movie star, playing a toy salesman whose world falls apart when he is arrested for smuggling a wrist watch. Sylvia Syms, as the long-suffering wife who can take no more, deserves better than this. DP **DVD**

Tony Britton *Simon Scott* • Sylvia Syms *Jean Scott* • Jack Watling *Bill Thompson* • Walter Fitzgerald *Sir John Dell* • Geoffrey Keen *Colonel Wilson* • Howard Marion-Crawford *George Bates* • John Welsh *Chief customs officer* • Lockwood West *Mr Barraclough* ■ *Dir* Pat Jackson • *Scr* Jack Whittingham

The Biscuit Eater ★★★ U

Adventure drama 1940 · US · BW · 80min

Stuart Heisler, a former editor then assistant to John Ford, made his solo debut with this simple and deeply affecting story of two boys – one black, one white – who are given the runt of a litter of dogs and turn their aptly named Promise into a champion. Superbly shot on Georgia locations, this was the first of several socially committed films from a neglected director. BB

Billy Lee *Lonnie McNeil* • Cordell Hickman *Text* • Richard Lane *Harvey McNeil* • Lester Matthews *Mr Ames* • Helene Millard *Mrs McNeil* ■ *Dir* Stuart Heisler • *Scr* Stuart Anthony, Lillie Hayward, from the short story *The Biscuit Eater* by James Street in *The Saturday Evening Post*

The Biscuit Eater ★★ U

Adventure drama 1972 · US · Colour · 86min

As the pals who overcome the racial prejudices of the adults around them to transform a wild hunting dog into a champion, Johnny Whitaker and George

Spell avoid the winsome boyishness usually portrayed in Hollywood outdoor adventures. But director Vincent McEveety tub-thumps the liberal American values and allows sentiment to turn to mush in this sugar-coated Disney offering. DP

Earl Holliman *Harve McNeil* • Lew Ayres *Mr Ames* • Godfrey Cambridge *Willie Dorsey* • Patricia Crowley [Pat Crowley] *Mrs McNeil* • Beah Richards *Charity Tomlin* • Johnny Whitaker *Lonnie McNeil* • George Spell *Text Tomlin* • Clifton James *Mr Eben* ■ *Dir* Vincent McEveety • *Scr* Lawrence Edward Watkin, from the short story by James Street in *The Saturday Evening Post*

The Bishop's Wife ★★★ U
Fantasy comedy   1947 · US · BW · 104min

Cary Grant stars as an angel who descends from heaven to put the marriage of irritable, materialistic bishop David Niven and Loretta Young in order, and to raise money for a new church. There were tensions on the set as Grant clashed with Young and director Henry Koster over the script, which Grant thought substandard. However, the playing from all three stars is enjoyable and the festive setting allows Grant to trim a Christmas tree with the flick of a finger. Remade in 1996 as *The Preacher's Wife*. DP DVD

Cary Grant *Dudley* • David Niven *Henry Brougham* • Loretta Young *Julia Brougham* • Monty Woolley *Professor Wutheridge* • James Gleason *Sylvester* • Gladys Cooper *Mrs Hamilton* • Elsa Lanchester *Matilda* ■ *Dir* Henry Koster • *Scr* Robert E Sherwood, Leonardo Bercovici, from the novel *In Barleyfields* by Robert Nathan

A Bit of Scarlet ★★★ 12
Documentary
1996 · UK · Colour and BW · 74min

While not as good as its American counterpart *The Celluloid Closet*, this miscellany of gay and lesbian clips culled from British movies of the past 60 years has a fun time contrasting its stereotypical images with the supposed rules of the genre: "All relationships must end with broken hearts", "You will not be the main character", "Go to public school". The usual suspects are all here – *The Killing of Sister George*, *Victim*, Charles Hawtrey, *Carry On Spying* – and though it's messily assembled, it's narrated with ironic aplomb by Ian McKellen. AJ

Ian McKellen *Narrator* ■ *Dir* Andrea Weiss • *Scr* Andrea Weiss, Stuart Marshall

The Bit Player ★★★
Comedy   1973 · Fr · Colour · 96min

Marcello Mastroianni stars as a bit-part actor, separated from his wife (Carla Gravina) and children, and living with his jealous mistress (Françoise Fabian). When she leaves him, he tries to go back to his wife, who is now carrying another man's child. Directed by Yves Robert, who undermines the sardonic comedy with a dollop of sentimentality, the film depends for its appeal on Mastroianni's entertaining, melancholy performance,and that of Jean Rochefort as his friend. RB French dubbed.

Marcello Mastroianni *Nicolas* • Françoise Fabian *Peggy* • Jean Rochefort *Clement* • Carla Gravina *Elizabeth* ■ *Dir* Yves Robert • *Scr* Jean-Loup Dabadie, Yves Robert

The Bitch ★★★ 18
Erotic drama   1979 · UK · Colour · 88min

This kitsch classic – a sequel to *The Stud* – follows the further adventures of promiscuous club owner Fontaine Khaled (Joan Collins) as she goes through a messy divorce and tries to get her London disco back in the celebrity limelight. Add a jewel robbery, handsome conmen, horse racing and glamorous parties, and you have the usual Jackie Collins cocktail of sexy sleaze and camp hysteria. AJ DVD

Joan Collins *Fontaine Khaled* • Michael Coby *Nico Cantafora* • Kenneth Haigh *Arnold Rinstead* • Ian Hendry *Thrush Feather* • Carolyn Seymour *Polly* • Sue Lloyd *Vanessa* • Mark Burns *Leonard* • John Ratzenberger *Hal* ■ *Dir* Gerry O'Hara • *Scr* Gerry O'Hara, from the novel by Jackie Collins

Bite the Bullet ★★★ PG
Western adventure   1975 · US · Colour · 125min

This gripping al egorical drama about a 700-mile horse race from writer/director Richard Brooks pits old-school values against the sha lowness of capitalism. Filmed amid the stunning scenery of Nevada, Colorado and New Mexico, the picture is perhaps too long, with too many trough-stops for discourses about machismo and the motives of the competitors. But on the hoof it's an excellent adventure with a splendid cast and some spectacular turn-of-the-century settings. AT DVD

Gene Hackman *Sam Clayton* • Candice Bergen *Miss Jones* • James Coburn *Luke Matthews* • Ben Johnson (1) *Mister* • Jan-Michael Vincent *Carbo* • Ian Bannen *Norfolk* • Mario Arteaga *Mexican* ■ *Dir/Scr* Richard Brooks

Bitter Harvest ★★ 12
Drama   1963 · UK · Colour · 91min

As the young Welsh innocent who is abused by various London ne'er-do-wells, Janet Munro exhibits not only a touching vulnerability but also a credible inner reserve, which sustains her after she herself exploits a kindly barman (John Stride). Scripted by Ted Willis, this lacks the bite of contemporary examples of social realism, but it's solidly made. DP DVD

Janet Munro *Jeannie Jones* • John Stride *Bob Williams* • Anne Cunningham *Ella* • Alan Badel *Karl Denny* • Vanda Godsell *Mrs Pitt* • Norman Bird *Mr Pitt* • Terence Alexander *Andy* • Richard Thorp *Rex* ■ *Dir* Peter Graham Scott • *Scr* Ted Willis, from the novel *The Street Has a Thousand Skies* by Pamela Hamilton

Bitter Harvest ★★ 18
Erotic crime thriller   1993 · US · Colour · 93min

If you've ever wanted to watch beautiful women throwing themselves at Stephen Baldwin for no apparent reason, then this is for you. Baldwin plays Travis, a young man who has just inherited his father's house. And it's not a coincidence that, at the same time as he takes possession of the house, two attractive blondes start hanging around and trying to seduce him at every opportunity. ST

Patsy Kensit *Jolene* • Stephen Baldwin *Travis Graham* • Jennifer Rubin *Kelly Ann* • M Emmet Walsh *Sheriff Bob* • Adam Baldwin *Bobby* ■ *Dir* Duane Clark • *Scr* Randall Fontana

Bitter Moon ★★★ 18
Drama   1992 · Fr/UK · Colour · 133min

Roman Polanski s slickly told dramaset on board a liner tries to make sexual sadism into a metaphor for human relationships. Innocents Hugh Grant and Kristin Scott Thomas become entangled in the fantasies of paralysed writer Peter Coyote and Emmanuelle Seigner (Polanski's wife). It should have been played as a Buñuel-esque comedy, but it's no laughing matter, and ponderous solemnity finally makes it seem like a psychiatric casebook. TH Sex scenes, violence, swearing, nudity. DVD

Peter Coyote *Oscar* • Emmanuelle Seigner *Mimi* • Hugh Grant *Nigel Dobson* • Kristin Scott Thomas *Fiona Dobson* • Victor Bannerjee [Victor Banerjee] *Mr Singh* • Sophie Patel *Amrita* • Patrick Albenque *Steward* • Stockard Channing *Beverly* ■ *Dir* Roman Polanski • *Scr* Roman Polanski, Gérard Brach, John Brownjohn, from the novel *Lunes de Fiel* by Pascal Bruckner

Bitter Rice ★★★
Drama   1949 · It · BW · 107min

This Italian film about a woman (Silvana Mangano) who comes from the city each year to labour in the rice fields of the Po valley and falls in love with a macho petty villain (Vittorio Gassman), who is planning to steal the crop, caused a sensation in its day. The reason was not, however, the Academy Award-nominated original story, but the presence of the then 19-year-old, voluptuous beauty Mangano, clad in skimpy shorts and emanating sexuality from every pore. The story is no longer original, but the steamy eroticism is intact. RK Italian +subtitles.

Silvana Mangano *Silvana* • Doris Dowling *Francesca* • Vittorio Gassman *Walter* • Raf Vallone *Marco* • Checco Rissone *Aristide* • Nico Pepe *Beppe* • Adriana Sivieri *Celeste* • Lia Croelli *Amelia* ■ *Dir* Giuseppe De Santis • *Scr* Giuseppe De Santis, Carlo Lizzani, Gianni Puccini, from a story by Giuseppe De Santis, Carlo Lizzani

Bitter Springs ★★★ U
Period adventure   1950 · Aus/UK · BW · 88min

Dismissed by many critics as a mere outback western, this is a typical Ealing attempt to humanise a pressing social problem. In this case, it's the relationship between Australia's white and Aboriginal populations. There is an adventure element to the clash over water rights between pioneer Chips Rafferty and tribesman Henry Murdoch. However, while the action is set in the early 20th century, it has an obvious contemporary resonance -- right down to the uncomfortable truce. Tommy Trinder is the unlikely star. DP

Tommy Trinder *Tommy* • Chips Rafferty *Wally King* • Gordon Jackson *Mac* • Jean Blue *Ma King* • Charles "Bud" Tingwell [Charles Tingwell] *John King* • Nonnie Piper *Emma King* • Nicky Yardley *Charlie* • Michael Pate *Trooper* ■ *Dir* Ralph Smart • *Scr* WP Lipscomb, Monja Danischewsky, from a story by Ralph Smart • *Producer* Michael Balcon

Bitter Suite ★★
Romantic comedy
2000 · US/Ger · Colour · 91min

Nastassja Kinski and Timothy Dalton don't have great track records when it comes to comedy, and this uninspired TV holiday romance won't improve the situation. It's loathe at first sight when Kinski's humourless scientist and Dalton's pernickety cook discover they've double booked a beach house. The direction is determinedly sunny, but there's a real desperation about some of the slapstick set pieces. DP Swearing.

Nastassja Kinski *Julia* • Timothy Dalton *Matt* • Kevin Zegers *Thomas* • Cameron Finley *Max* • Billy Kay *Lewis* ■ *Dir* Sharon von Wietersheim • *Scr* Eric Tuchman

Bitter Sweet ★★
Operetta   1933 · UK · BW · 94min

Produced, directed and partly written by Herbert Wilcox from Noël Coward's operetta, and starring his future wife Anna Neagle, this wistful period piece recounts the tale of a girl who elopes with her music teacher to 1870s Vienna. They live in happy poverty until tragedy strikes – but the movie's message is optimistically romantic. MGM remade it as a ludicrously sumptuous vehicle for Jeanette MacDonald and Nelson Eddy in 1940. RK

Anna Neagle *Sari Linden* • Fernand Graavey [Fernand Gravet] *Carl Linden* • Esme Percy *Hugh Devon* • Clifford Heatherley *Herr Schlick* • Ivy St Helier *Manon La Crevette* • Miles Mander *Captain August Lutte* • Pat Paterson *Dolly* ■ *Dir* Herbert Wilcox • *Scr* Herbert Wilcox, Lydia Hayward, Monckton Hoffe, from the operetta by Noël Coward

Bitter Sweet ★★★ U
Operetta   1940 · US · Colour · 93min

Jeanette MacDonald shocks her family when she runs off to Vienna with her music teacher Nelson Eddy on the eve of her marriage. Deciding to photograph in sumptuous and expensive three-strip Technicolor was a clear indication of how highly studio boss Louis B Mayer prized his team of songbirds, and although Eddy is now almost unwatchable, the songs are fabulous; this is one of the greatest of Noël Coward's scores, lavishly redone by MGM in the heart of their golden era. TS

Jeanette MacDonald *Sarah Millick* • Nelson Eddy *Carl Linden* • George Sanders *Baron Von Tranisch* • Ian Hunter *Lord Shayne* • Felix Bressart *Max* • Edward Ashley *Harry Daventry* • Lynne Carver *Dolly* • Diana Lewis *Jane* ■ *Dir* WS Van Dyke II [WS Van Dyke] • *Scr* Lesser Samuels, from the operetta by Noël Coward

The Bitter Tea of General Yen ★★★★ PG
Drama   1932 · US · BW · 90min

This genuinely exotic oddity is superbly performed by stars Barbara Stanwyck and the Swedish actor Nils Asther, and magnificently directed by a young Frank Capra. The first film ever to play the famous Radio City Music Hall, New York, this deeply sensuous movie was banned throughout the UK and the Commonwealth for dealing so blatantly with the then taboo subject of miscegenation. Stanwyck is magnificent, and the final close-up of her face deserves to be as well known in cinema annals as the similar shot of Garbo at the end of *Queen Christina*. Sensual and disturbing. TS

Barbara Stanwyck *Megan Davis* • Nils Asther *General Yen* • Gavin Gordon *Dr Robert Strike* • Lucien Littlefield *Mr Jackson* • Toshia Mori *Mah-Li* • Richard Loo *Captain Li* • Clara Blandick *Mrs Jackson* • Walter Connolly *Jones* ■ *Dir* Frank Capra • *Scr* Edward Paramore, from the novel by Grace Zaring Stone • *Editor* Edward Curtiss

The Bitter Tears of Petra von Kant ★★★★ 18
Melodrama   1972 · W Ger · Colour · 118min

Inspired by both his own experiences as a gay man and Joseph L Mankiewicz's *All about Eve*, this is Rainer Werner Fassbinder's tribute to the Hollywood "woman's picture". Petra von Kant (Margit Carstensen) is the fashion designer who embarks on a stormy lesbian affair with her model Hanna Schygulla. Fassbinder shows the classic relationship issues of dominance, submission and jealousy are just as prevalent in homosexual affairs as straight ones. The production is heavily stylised but such is the elegance of the gliding camerawork and the symbolic kitsch of the furnishings that the action never feels stagey. DP German +subtitles. DVD Blu

Margit Carstensen *Petra von Kant* • Hanna Schygulla *Karin Thimm* • Irm Hermann *Marlene* • Katrin Schaake *Sidonie von Grasenabb* • Eva Mattes *Gabriele von Kant* • Gisela Fackeldey *Valerie von Kant* ■ *Dir/Scr* Rainer Werner Fassbinder • *Cinematographer* Michael Ballhaus

Bitter Victory ★★★ PG
Second World War drama
1957 · Fr/US · BW · 101min

In this fraught tale, Richard Burton and Curt Jurgens lead an assault on Rommel's HQ. But as the mission proceeds, Jurgens cracks after learning that Burton has been having an affair with his wife. As the picture veers from realism to surrealism and then to overblown melodrama, Jurgens is an impressive fraudulent hero, while Burton comes across strongly as a TE Lawrence figure, the neurotic scholar-soldier. Filmed in Libya, it was heavily cut for US release. AT

Richard Burton *Captain Leith* • Curt Jurgens *Major Brand* • Ruth Roman *Mrs Brand* • Raymond Pellegrin *Makron* • Anthony Bushell *General Paterson* • Alfred Burke *Lt Col Callander* • Christopher Lee *Sergeant Barney* ■ *Dir* Nicholas Ray • *Scr* Rene Hardy, Nicholas Ray, Gavin Lambert, from the novel by Rene Hardy

A Bittersweet Life ★★★ 18
Thriller   2005 · S Kor · Colour · 113min

South Korean Kim Ji-woon writes and directs this ultra-violent, visually stunning gangster thriller. It's a sumptuous and nihilistic urban *noir*, skilfully infused with jet-black humour. Lee Byung-hun is terrific as the unfortunate henchman who pays a horrendous price for disobeying orders to kill his Mob boss's unfaithful girlfriend. As the grisly action sequences nudge towards *manga*-type unreality, the film loses some of its heart, relying on style and energy to reach its powerfully ambiguous climax. SF Korean +subtitles. Violence.

Lee Byung-hun *Kim Sun-woo* • Kim Young-chul *Kang* • Shin Min-a *Hee-soo* • Kim Roi-ha *Moon suk* • Lee Ki-young *Oh Mu-sung* • Oh Dai-soo *Myung Ku* ■ *Dir/Scr* Kim Ji-woon

B

Bittersweet Love ★★

Drama · 1976 · US · Colour · 90min

Meredith Baxter and Scott Hylands fall in love. She becomes pregnant. Then they discover they're half-siblings as a result of the one-night stand of her mother (Lana Turner) and his father (Robert Lansing) who are married, respectively, to Robert Alda and Celeste Holm. Starting from a not uninteresting idea, this degenerates into an endless debate about whether Baxter should have an abortion. RK

Lana Turner *Claire* • Robert Lansing *Howard* • Celeste Holm *Marian* • Robert Alda *Ben* • Meredith Baxter Birney [Meredith Baxter] *Patricia* • Scott Hylands *Michael* • Gail Strickland *Roz* ■ *Dir* David Miller (1) • *Scr* Adrian Morrall, DA Kellogg

Biutiful ★★★ 15

Drama · 2009 · Sp/Mex/UK · Colour · 141min

Writer/director Alejandro González Iñárritu abandons the multi-stranded narratives of his previous work (*21 Grams, Babel*) for this relatively simple but still heart-rending drama. It's set in Barcelona, where hustler Uxbal (Javier Bardem) manages illegal street traders and reluctantly runs a sideline as a psychic, comforting relatives of the dead. However, he also has an angry, bipolar ex-wife (Maricel Alvarez) to deal with, while trying to save his father's burial plot from developers. Then a tragedy throws his life of petty crime into turmoil. *Biutiful* deals with some heavy themes, but thanks to the subtle gravity Bardem brings to the role they are never overwhelming. DW Spanish, English +subtitles. Swearing, drug abuse, nudity. *DVD* *BL*

Javier Bardem *Uxbal* • Maricel Alvarez *Marambra* • Hanaa Bouchaib *Ana* • Guillermo Estrella *Mateo* • Eduard Fernández *Tito* • Cheikh Ndiaye *Ekweme* ■ *Dir* Alejandro González Iñárritu • *Scr* Alejandro González Iñárritu, Armando Bo, Nicolás Giacobone, from a story by Iñárritu

Black ★★★★ 12

Drama · 2004 · Ind · Colour · 124min

Amitabh Bachchan plays the dedicated mentor who attempts to teach the blind and deaf Rani Mukherji. By encouraging, coaxing and even bullying the intelligent, determined girl, he succeeds, but Bachchan's own life begins to change when he is diagnosed with Alzheimer's disease. As he comes to rely on his former student, the pair form a deep bond. The camaraderie between the two central characters is convincing, and Sanjay Leela Bhansali's meticulously crafted film captures the determination of the human spirit with understated elegance. OA Hindi +subtitles. *DVD*

Amitabh Bachchan *Debraj Sahai* • Rani Mukherjee [Rani Mukherji] *Michelle McNally* • Ayesha Kapoor *Young Michelle McNally* • Shernaz Patel *Catherine McNally* • Dhritiman Chaterji [Dhritiman Chatterjee] *Paul McNally* • Nandana Sen *Sara McNally* ■ *Dir* Sanjay Leela Bhansali • *Scr* Bhavani Iyer, Prakash Kapadia

Black and White ★★ 15

Police thriller · 1998 · US · Colour · 93min

Gina Gershon's compelling performance as a hard-nosed detective is the main reason for watching this otherwise routine thriller. Bristling with attitude and allure, she's the prime suspect for a string of lowlife murders, but her rookie partner and new lover, Rory Cochrane, is convinced that a tyre track at the scene of the latest slaying will lead elsewhere. DP Violence, swearing, sex scenes, nudity. *DVD*

Gina Gershon *Nora Hugosian* • Rory Cochrane *Chris O'Brien* • Ron Silver *Simon Herzel* • Alison Eastwood *Lynn Dombrowsky* • Ross Partridge *Michael Clemence* ■ *Dir* Yuri Zeltser • *Scr* Yuri Zeltser, Leon Zeltser

Black and White ★★★ 18

Drama · 1999 · US · Colour · 95min

A group of affluent white teens obsessed with hip-hop culture are at the heart of James Toback's provocative look at race relations in contemporary America. A web of tenuously connected storylines covers everything from blackmail to documentary film-making and there's an eclectic cast that includes Robert Downey Jr, Claudia Schiffer, boxer Mike Tyson, and Oliver "Power" Grant (from Wu-Tang Clan), as a thug trying to go legit as a rap music producer. The largely improvised script gives the film a raw energy at the expense of a cohesive narrative. Tyson, portraying himself, gives a performance that's surprisingly wise. ST *DVD*

Robert Downey Jr *Terry* • Brooke Shields *Sam* • Stacy Edwards *Sheila King* • Allan Houston *Dean* • Scott Caan *Scotty* • Gaby Hoffman [Gaby Hoffmann] *Raven* • Kidada Jones *Jesse* • Jared Leto *Casey* • Marla Maples *Muffy* • Power [Oliver "Power" Grant] *Rich Bower* • Claudia Schiffer *Greta* • Mike Tyson ■ *Dir/Scr* James Toback

Black and White ★★ 15

Historical drama · 2002 · Aus/UK/Swe · Colour · 97min

The trial of Max Stuart, the Aborigine accused of murdering a nine-year-old girl in the South Australian resort of Ceduna in December 1958, proved a turning point in the career of newspaperman Rupert Murdoch. But, despite its care and muted sense of outrage, Craig Lahiff's re-creation never captures the significance of the case. Robert Carlyle lacks conviction as the lawyer duelling with crown prosecutor Charles Dance, while Kerry Fox is wasted as his assistant. DP Swearing, violence. *DVD*

Robert Carlyle *David O'Sullivan* • Charles Dance *Roderic Chamberlain* • Kerry Fox *Helen Devaney* • Colin Friels *Father Tom Dixon* • Ben Mendelsohn *Rupert Murdoch* • David Ngoombujarra *Max Stuart* ■ *Dir* Craig Lahiff • *Scr* Louis Nowra

Black and White in Color ★★★

First World War satire · 1976 · Fr/Iv C/Swi · Colour · 91min

Set in a remote trading post in a French colony in West Africa on the outbreak of the First World War, this co-production deals with a group of French colonists, who mobilise the natives to attack a German fort. A rather specious satire on colonialism, it certainly has many amusing moments, but most of the humour is largely dependent on racist and sexist stereotypes. The debut feature of former TV-commercials director Jean-Jacques Annaud, it won the Oscar for the best foreign film in a bad year. RB French +subtitles.

Jean Carmet *Sergeant Bosselet* • Jacques Dufilho *Paul Rechampot* • Catherine Rouvel *Marinette* • Jacques Spiesser *Hubert Fresnoy* • Dora Doll *Maryvonne* • Maurice Barrier *Caprice* • Claude Legros *Jacques Rechampot* • Jacques Monnet *Père Simon* ■ *Dir* Jean-Jacques Annaud • *Scr* Georges Conchon, Jean-Jacques Annaud

Black Angel ★★

Film noir · 1946 · US · BW · 80min

Dan Duryea stars in this darkish thriller as a songwriter whose wife is strangled, presenting him with any number of suspects. It turns out she had been blackmailing someone, and then... well, it gets a little too complicated for its own good. Duryea's profession as a tunesmith is merely an excuse to cram in some musical sequences with June Vincent, set mainly in Peter Lorre's nightclub. The film is anonymously directed by Roy William Neill, and Duryea doesn't really have leading man appeal. AT

Dan Duryea *Martin Blair* • June Vincent *Catherine* • Peter Lorre *Marko* • Broderick Crawford *Captain Flood* • Wallace Ford *Joe* • Hobart Cavanaugh *Jake* • Constance Dowling *Marvis Marlowe* • Freddie Steele *Lucky* ■ *Dir* Roy William Neill • *Scr* Roy Chanslor, from a novel by Cornell Woolrich

The Black Arrow ★★ U

Historical adventure · 1948 · US · BW · 75min

There's trouble brewing in Ye Olde House of York, as Louis Hayward discovers when he returns from the War of the Roses. Uncle George Macready has seized power, hacking off many heads in the process, including that of Hayward's father. Loosely based (they used the title) on Robert Louis Stevenson's novel, it's moderately entertaining, with Hayward looking fetching in shining armour and cooing over demure Janet Blair. AT

Louis Hayward *Richard Shelton* • Janet Blair *Joanna Sedley* • George Macready *Sir Daniel Brackley* • Edgar Buchanan *Lawless* • Lowell Gilmore *Duke of Gloucester* • Russell Hicks *Sir Harry Shelton* ■ *Dir* Gordon Douglas • *Scr* Richard Schayer, David P Sheppard, Thomas Seller, from the novel by Robert Louis Stevenson

Black Beauty ★★ U

Drama · 1933 · US · BW · 47min

This version of Anna Sewell's famous horsey tale is a very average low-budgeted, competently directed by studio hack Phil Rosen, with former silent star Esther Ralston topping a largely forgettable cast. The horse sequences may look vaguely familiar, since they went into the studio stock library and used material featured in many other films of that time. TS

Esther Ralston *Leila Lambert* • Alexander Kirkland *Henry Cameron* • Hale Hamilton *Bledsoe* • Gavin Gordon *Captain Jordan* • Don Alvarado *Renaldo* • George Walsh *Junk man* ■ *Dir* Phil Rosen • *Scr* Charles Logue, from Anna Sewell's novel

Black Beauty ★★ U

Drama · 1946 · US · BW · 73min

An early score from ace composer Dimitri Tiomkin distinguishes this pallid version of Anna Sewell's equine classic. Although this is set in England, none of the cast seriously modify their Yank accents. Ingénue Mona Freeman would appear in many horse operas later on. A moderate low-budget film, drably directed by Polish expatriate Max Nosseck. A belated sequel, *Courage of Black Beauty*, was released in 1957. TS

Mona Freeman *Anne Wendon* • Richard Denning *Bill Dixon* • Evelyn Ankers *Evelyn Carrington* • Charles Evans *Squire Wendon* • JM Kerrigan *John* • Moyna MacGill *Mrs Blake* • Terry Kilburn *Joe* • Tom Dillon [Thomas P Dillon] *Skinner* ■ *Dir* Max Nosseck • *Scr* Lillie Hayward, Agnes Christine Johnston, from the novel by Anna Sewell

Black Beauty ★★ PG

Drama · 1971 · UK/W Ger/Sp · Colour · 101min

This version of Anna Sewell's classic children's story doesn't really hit the mark, despite starring the winsome Mark Lester. Director James Hill obviously knows how to work with animals, having made both *Born Free* and *The Belstone Fox*, but his talent couldn't save this muddled and undistinguished Euro-pudding, produced at German and Spanish studios with a pan-European cast, but made in English. SG *DVD*

Mark Lester (2) *Joe* • Walter Slezak *Hackenschmidt* • Peter Lee Lawrence *Gervaise* • Ursula Glas *Marie* • Patrick Mower *Sam Greene* • John Nettleton *Sir William* • Maria Rohm *Anne* • Eddie Golden *Evans* ■ *Dir* James Hill • *Scr* Wolf Mankowitz, from the novel by Anna Sewell

Black Beauty ★★★ U

Drama · 1994 · UK/US · Colour · 84min

This glossy reworking of Anna Sewell's much-filmed classic marked the directorial debut of Caroline Thompson, a writer whose successes include *Edward Scissorhands* and *The Addams Family*. The horses look superb and Beauty even sounds convincing, thanks to Alan Cumming's clever voiceover. The largely British cast does its bit, too, with Sean Bean and David Thewlis revealing previously unsuspected soft centres, but the acting honours go to Peter Cook and Eleanor Bron, as Lord and Lady Wexmire. DP *DVD* *BL*

Sean Bean *Farmer Grey* • David Thewlis *Jerry Barker* • Jim Carter *John Manly* • Peter Davison *Squire Gordon* • Alun Armstrong *Reuben Smith* • John McEnery *Mr York* • Eleanor Bron *Lady Wexmire* • Peter Cook *Lord Wexmire* • Andrew Knott *Joe Green* • Alan Cumming *Black Beauty* ■ *Dir* Caroline Thompson • *Scr* Caroline Thompson, from the novel by Anna Sewell

Black Belt Jones ★★ 18

Martial arts crime thriller · 1974 · US · Colour · 80min

Having pulled off a major box office coup with *Enter the Dragon*, producers Fred Weintraub and Paul Heller were denied the services of their recently deceased star, Bruce Lee. So they turned to karate champion Jim Kelly for this rollicking (albeit overplotted) mixture of blaxploitation and kung fu. Kelly teams up with Scatman Crothers and his daughter (Gloria Hendry) to prevent property developer Malik Carter and mobster André Phillipe from taking over their run-down martial arts school. Robert Wall's fight sequences are slickly choreographed. A sequel followed in 1978. DP

Jim Kelly *Black Belt Jones* • Gloria Hendry *Sydney* • Scatman Crothers *Pop* • Alan Weeks *Tippy* • Eric Laneuville *Quincy* • Andre Philippe *Don Steffano* • Vincent Barbi *Big Tuna* • Nate Esfornes *Roberts* ■ *Dir* Robert Clouse • *Scr* Oscar Williams, from a story by Alex Rose, Fred Weintraub • *Choreographer* Robert Wall

The Black Bird ★★★★

Silent crime drama · 1926 · US · BW · 75min

In seedy Limehouse, a master criminal known as the Black Bird covers his crimes by assuming the identity of his disabled "twin" and uses a charity mission house as an elaborate front. Thanks to a brilliant performance by Lon Chaney, kept in a deliberate and darkly fantastic key by director Tod Browning, a preposterous premise is transformed into convincing entertainment. There's a nasty sting in the tall tale and the plot's essential irrationalities are masked by Browning's masterful direction, as he distracts viewer attention by remaining on the dangerous side of farce. An exaggerated vision of the shadowy underworld from two seminal masters of silent shock. AJ

Lon Chaney *The Blackbird/The Bishop of Limehouse* • Owen Moore *West End Bertie* • Renée Adorée *Fifi* • Doris Lloyd *Limehouse Polly* • Andy MacLennan *The Shadow* • William Weston Red • Eric Mayne *Sightseer* • Sidney Bracey *Bertie's No 1 Man* • Ernie S Adams *Bertie's No 2 Man* ■ *Dir* Tod Browning • *Scr* Waldemar Young, from the story *The Mockingbird* by Tod Browning

The Black Bird ★★

Detective spoof · 1975 · US · Colour · 97min

This send-up of *The Maltese Falcon* has Sam Spade Jr (George Segal) discovering the priceless statuette among his dad's old files. It's a nice idea, thoroughly botched - it simply isn't funny, tense or even nostalgic. There is, however, one clever in-joke. Anxious to raise some money for the falcon, Segal takes it to a pawnbroker named Kerkorian, who offers him a paltry $15. This is a reference to Kirk Kerkorian, who owned MGM at the time and sold off its most famous props. AT

George Segal *Sam Spade Jr* • Stéphane Audran *Anna Kemidov* • Lionel Stander *Gordon Andre* Jackson *Immerman* • Lee Patrick *Effie* • Elisha Cook Jr *Wilmer* • Felix Silla *Litvak* • Signe Hasso *Dr Crippen* • John Abbot *DuQuai* • Howard Jeffrey *Kerkorian* ■ *Dir* David Giler • *Scr* David Giler, from a story by Don M Mankiewicz, Gordon Cotler, from characters by Dashiell Hammett

Black Book ★★★ 15

Second World War thriller · 2006 · UK/Neth/Bel/Ger · Colour · 139min

Paul Verhoeven's first film in Holland since 1983's *The Fourth Man* (he left for Hollywood and the likes of *RoboCop* and *Basic Instinct*) returns to the subject of the Dutch Resistance, which he first tackled in 1977's *Soldier of Orange*. Based loosely on a real character, Rachel (Carice van Houten) is a Jewish singer who infiltrates the local Nazi HQ. Verhoeven delivers a rollicking yarn that's surprisingly traditional if convoluted. The performances are good and the bloody action is typically well handled but, while *Black Book* certainly entertains, it lacks the cultural tensions and mischievous satire of his best American films. AS Dutch, English, German, Hebrew

U SUITABLE FOR ALL   Uc SUITABLE ESPECIALLY FOR YOUNG CHILDREN (DVD ONLY)   PG PARENTAL GUIDANCE   12A UNDER 12s TO BE ACCOMPANIED (CINEMA ONLY)

+subtitles. Violence, swearing, nudity. **DVD**

Carice van Houten *Rachel Steinn/Ellis de Vries* • Sebastian Koch *Ludwig Müntze* • Thom Hoffman *Hans Akkermans* • Halina Reijn *Ronnie* • Waldemar Kobus *Günther Franken* • Derek de Lint [Derek De Lint] *Gerben Kuipers* ■ *Dir* Paul Verhoeven • *Scr* Gerard Soeteman, Paul Verhoeven, from a story by Soeteman

Black Butler ★★★★ 15
Crime drama   2014 · Jpn · Colour · 119min

An adaptation of the immensely popular manga, starring Ayame Goriki as Shiori Genpo, a noblewoman determined to avenge the murder of her parents, alongside her "butler" Sebastian (Hiro Mizushima), a demon who has agreed to aid her in her quest in exchange for her soul. Energetic and stylish, the film is part action, part detective story, with acrobatic set pieces punctuating a plot that is intricate without being complicated. JL Japanese, English +subtitles.

Hiro Mizushima *Sebastian* • Ayame Goriki *Shiori Genpo/Kiyoharu* • Yuka Hanae *Wakatsuki* • Mizuki Yamamoto *Rin* ■ *Dir* Kentaro Otani, Kei'ichi Sato • *Scr* Tsutomu Kuroiwa, from the manga TV series by Yana Toboso

Black Caesar ★★★ 18
Blaxploitation crime drama
1973 · US · Colour · 89min

Tried and tested gangster themes are updated using elements of the blaxploitation genre of the early 1970s in B-movie maestro Larry Cohen's funky inner-city thriller. Former American football star Fred Williamson gives one of his best performances as the shoeshine boy who rises through the mobster ranks to become Harlem's crime lord. Violent heroics clash with relative morality, but in its quieter moments this spirited action pic offers tender moments brimming with emotional truth. Williamson and Cohen returned for the sequel *Hell Up in Harlem*. AJ Swearing, violence, nudity. **DVD**

Fred Williamson *Tommy Gibbs* • Phillip Roye *Joe Washington* • Gloria Hendry *Helen* • Julius W Harris [Julius Harris] *Mr Gibbs* • Val Avery *Cardoza* • Minnie Gentry *Mama Gibbs* • Art Lund *John McKinney* • D'Urville Martin *Reverend Rufus* ■ *Dir/Scr* Larry Cohen

The Black Castle ★★ PG
Gothic horror   1952 · US · BW · 78min

Swashbuckling adventurer Richard Greene believes that sinister Austrian count Stephen MacNally has captured and killed two of his friends in this half-hearted *Most Dangerous Game* rerun. So it's off to the count's sinister castle where he braves secret passageways, torture chambers, prowling leopards and a moat filled with alligators before falling in love with the count's unhappy wife (Rita Corday). Boris Karloff does little but stand around looking ominous as the imprisoned doctor in this tame, dull gothic horror. AJ **DVD**

Richard Greene *Sir Ronald Burton/Richard Beckett* • Boris Karloff *Dr Meissen* • Stephen McNally *Count Karl von Bruno* • Rita Corday *Countess Elga von Bruno* • Lon Chaney Jr *Gargon* • Michael Pate *Count Ernst von Melcher* ■ *Dir* Nathan Juran • *Scr* Jerry Sackheim

The Black Cat ★★★★★★ 15
Horror   1934 · US · BW · 62min

One of the landmark horror films of the 1930s, this was the first feature to double bill Boris Karloff and Bela Lugosi, both of whom were given reverential sole surname billing on the credits. Karloff is the Satanist playing chess with doctor Lugosi for innocent lives. More Aleister Crowley than the Edgar Allan Poe story it's actually based on, it's a triumph of bizarre Art Deco sets, innovative style, classical music and eerie tension. This timeless classic is superbly directed by Edgar G Ulmer before his career lurched into the quickie arena. Lugosi has never been so sympathetic or Karloff so evil and the heady finale is incredibly potent stuff for the era. AJ **DVD**

Karloff [Boris Karloff] *Hjalmar Poelzig* • Bela Lugosi *Dr Vitus Verdegast* • David Manners *Peter Allison* • Jacqueline Wells [Julie Bishop] *Joan Allison* • Lucille Lund *Karen* • Egon Brecher *Majordomo* • Henry Armetta *Sergeant* • Albert Conti *Lieutenant* ■ *Dir* Edgar G Ulmer • *Scr* Edgar G Ulmer, Peter Ruric, from the story by Edgar Allan Poe • *Cinematographer* John J Mescall • *Art Director* Charles D Hall

The Black Cat ★★
Horror   1941 · US · BW · 70min

It's sad to see such great horror icons as Bela Lugosi, Basil Rathbone and Gale Sondergaard in this unremarkable creepie which is based on a story by Edgar Allan Poe. Real-estate promoter Broderick Crawford and dizzy antiques collector Hugh Herbert gate-crash the reading of a will. To make up for the film's simple-mindedness, the old dark house atmosphere is elegantly photographed by Stanley Cortez. Alan Ladd makes a brief appearance. TH

Basil Rathbone *Hartley* • Hugh Herbert *Mr Penny* • Broderick Crawford *Hubert Smith* • Bela Lugosi *Eduardo* • Gale Sondergaard *Abigail Doone* • Anne Gwynne *Elaine Winslow* • Gladys Cooper *Myrna Hartley* • Alan Ladd *Richard Hartley* ■ *Dir* Albert S Rogel • *Scr* Robert Lees, Fred Rinaldo, Eric Taylor, Robert Neville, from the story by Edgar Allan Poe

The Black Cat ★★ 18
Horror   1981 · It/UK · Colour · 88min

This is a lopsided version of the classic Edgar Allan Poe tale, shot through with Italian director Lucio Fulci's trademark gore theatrics. Medium Patrick Magee tries to contact dead people via electrical equipment, American photographer Mimsy Farmer snaps murder victims, and Scotland Yard detective David Warbeck investigates local disappearances, all while supernatural forces are unleashed by a cat's death. The best thing about this oddly atmospheric chiller is the terrific score by Pino Donaggio. AJ **DVD**

Patrick Magee *Robert Miles* • Mimsy Farmer *Jill Travers* • David Warbeck *Inspector Gorley* • Dagmar Lassander *Mrs Grayson* • Daniela Dorio *Maureen* ■ *Dir* Lucio Fulci • *Scr* Lucio Fulci, Biagio Proietti, from a story by Biagio Proietti, from a short story by Edgar Allan Poe

Black Cat, White Cat ★★★★ 15
Comedy drama
1998 · Fr/Ger/Ser · Colour · 123min

Vowing to quit after the savage press reception for his Cannes Palme d'Or winner *Underground*, director Emir Kusturica returned with this riotous blend of crime, comedy and romance. Originally planned as a documentary about gypsy musicians, this is a scattershot affair, with offbeat hilarity competing with coarse slapstick. The network of fictional relationships between the various Romany families takes time to establish but, once all are assembled for a wedding, this gleeful romp goes into overdrive. Far from subtle, but thanks to exuberant storytelling, it is irresistible. DP Serbo-Croat, German, Romany +subtitles. Swearing, drug abuse.

Bajram Severdzan *Matko Destanov* • Srdjan Todorovic *Dadan Karambolo* • Florijan Ajdini *Zare Destanov* • Salija Ibraimova *Afrodita Karambolo, "Ladybird"* • Jasar Destani *Grga Veliki* • Sabri Sulejmani *Grga Pitic* ■ *Dir* Emir Kusturica • *Scr* Gordan Mihic, Emir Kusturica

The Black Cauldron ★★★ U
Animated adventure   1985 · US · Colour · 76min

The most distinguished element of this medium-rated Disney animation, from a Tolkien-like series by Lloyd Alexander, is the solemn intonation of narrator John Huston. Otherwise, it's standard stuff about likeable teenagers (of course) trying to stop the Horned King from using a magic cauldron to raise an Army of the Dead. As swords and sorcery goes, it's potboiling stuff. TH **DVD**

John Huston *Narrator* • Grant Bardsley *Taran* • Susan Sheridan *Princess Eilonwy* • Freddie Jones *Dallben* • Nigel Hawthorne *Fflewddur* • Arthur Malet *King Eidilleg* • John Byner *Gurgi/Doli* • John Hurt *Horned King* ■ *Dir* Ted Berman,

Richard Rich • *Scr* David Jonas, Vance Gerry, Ted Berman, Richard Rich, Al Wilson, Roy Morita, Peter Young, Art Stevens, Joe Hale, from the book series *The Chronicles of Prydain* by Lloyd Alexander

Black Christmas ★★★★ 18
Horror thriller   1974 · Can · Colour · 97min

This underrated horror pre-dated the *Halloween* cycle and practically established the genre's hard-and-fast rules. A maniac is on the loose in a closed-for-Christmas girls' boarding school. Director Bob Clark's neat little chiller scores scares thanks to stylish visuals, fiendishly inventive slaughter and unexpected twists. Promoted at the time with the wicked tagline "If this picture doesn't make your skin crawl, it's on too tight!", the film also features above-average performances from Olivia Hussey and Margot Kidder. AJ Violence, swearing. **DVD**

Olivia Hussey *Jess* • Keir Dullea *Peter* • Margot Kidder *Barb* • Andrea Martin *Phyl* • John Saxon *Lieutenant Fuller* • Marian Waldman *Mrs Mac* • Art Hindle *Chris* • Lynne Griffin *Clare Harrison* • James Edmond *Mr Harrison* ■ *Dir* Bob Clark • *Scr* Roy Moore

Black Christmas ★★★ 15
Horror thriller   2006 · Can/US · Colour · 80min

Bob Clark's 1974 movie paved the way for the likes of *Halloween* and *Friday the 13th*. This cheeky but no less brutal remake pays its dues to Clark's cult classic, borrowing wholesale from its gruesome tableaux as a killer stalks a sorority house in the run-up to Christmas. Producer James Wong cut his teeth on the *Final Destination* franchise and employs the same mix of gore and black comedy here, as the incongruities of murder in a Christmas setting are lent a grotesque spin, giving an otherwise forgettable horror some likeable chutzpah. JR Violence, swearing, some sex scenes. **DVD**

Katie Cassidy *Kelli Presley* • Mary Elizabeth Winstead *Heather Lee* • Lacey Chabert *Dana Mathis* • Michelle Trachtenberg *Melissa Kitt* • Oliver Hudson *Kyle* • Andrea Martin *Barbara MacHenry* ■ *Dir* Glen Morgan • *Scr* Glen Morgan, from the film by Roy Moore

Black Coal, Thin Ice ★★★★ 15
Crime thriller   2014 · Chi/HK · Colour · 109min

Diao Yinan makes a positive impression with this atmospheric *noir*, which delights in flouting generic convention at every twisting turn. Five years after bungling a 1999 murder case, security guard Liao Fan drinks to cope with his guilt and the break-up of his marriage. However, when a former cop colleague informs him about a spate of copycat killings, Liao can't resist a little private investigation. Nothing is quite as it seems in this teasingly digressive story, and Diao's wintry sense of place is impeccable, as are his allusions to classic Hollywood thrillers and the price China has had to pay for its economic transformation. DP Mandarin +subtitles.

Liao Fan *Zhang Zili* • Gwei Lun Mei *Wu Zhizhen* • Wang Xuebing *Liang Zhijun* ■ *Dir/Scr* Diao Yinan

The Black Dahlia ★★★ 15
Crime drama
2006 · Ger/US · Colour and BW · 115min

This adaptation of James Ellroy's crime novel from Brian De Palma showcases all his strengths, as well as some of his faults. Loosely inspired by an unsolved murder case from the 1940s, this stylish movie sees tough cops Bleichert (Josh Hartnett) and Blanchard (Aaron Eckhart) investigating the grisly demise of a would-be actress. Meanwhile, Bleichert becomes involved with Blanchard's glamorous wife (Scarlett Johansson). The cast is strong, with Hartnett surprisingly good as the basically decent gumshoe. Dante Ferretti's sumptuous design is atmospherically shot by veteran Vilmos Zsigmond and, although De Palma's enthusiastic style doesn't always extend to the humanity of his characters, this is still a watchable piece. AS Violence, sex scenes, swearing. **DVD**

Josh Hartnett *Officer Dwight "Bucky" Bleichert* • Aaron Eckhart *Sergeant Leland "Lee" Blanchard* • Scarlett Johansson *Kay Lake* • Hilary Swank *Madeleine Linscott* • Mia Kirshner *Elizabeth Short* • Mike Starr *Russ Millard* • Fiona Shaw *Ramona Linscott* ■ *Dir* Brian De Palma • *Scr* Josh Friedman, from the novel by James Ellroy • *Cinematographer* Vilmos Zsigmond • *Production Designer* Dante Ferretti

Black Death ★★★★ 15
Horror mystery   2010 · UK/Ger · Colour · 97min

Director Christopher Smith (*Severance, Triangle*) delivers a superior interpretation of medieval history and superstition in this thought-provoking horror. In 1348, knight Sean Bean and his mercenary band of torturers are sent by the church to investigate rumours that necromancy is holding the plague at bay in a remote rural community. Their guide is a conflicted monk (Eddie Redmayne, giving a hugely affecting performance) who's put to the ultimate test by a playful sorceress (Carice van Houten). Smith's film is a frightening journey into the social fabric of evil, religious persecution, pathological cruelty and supernatural possibility, which builds to a transfixing finale. AJ Violence. **DVD** **BD**

Sean Bean *Ulric* • Eddie Redmayne *Osmund* • David Warner *Abbot* • Carice van Houten *Langiva* • John Lynch *Wolfstan* • Tim McInnerny *Hob* • Andy Nyman *Dalywag* • Kimberley Nixon *Averill* ■ *Dir* Christopher Smith • *Scr* Dario Poloni

Black Dog ★★★ 12
Action road movie   1998 · US · Colour · 84min

This Patrick Swayze action drama was waved into the straight-to-video lane in Britain, but it's a shame, because it's entertaining enough in a rough-hewn kind of way. Swayze is the ex-convict trucker caught up in a feud with a religious zealot (Meat Loaf) after he is duped into delivering a cargo of stolen weapons. It's not subtle, but the vehicular destruction will bring a nostalgic tear to the eyes of *Smokey and the Bandit* fans. JF Swearing, violence.

Patrick Swayze *Jack Crews* • Randy Travis *Earl* • Meat Loaf *Red* • Gabriel Casseus *Sonny* • Brian Vincent *Wes* • Brenda Strong *Melanie* • Graham Beckel *Cutler* • Charles Dutton [Charles S Dutton] *Agent Ford* ■ *Dir* Kevin Hooks • *Scr* William Mickelberry, Dan Vining

Black Dynamite ★★★ 15
Action comedy   2009 · US · Colour · 80min

Blaxploitation gets a hilarious grindhouse makeover in this send-up. Michael Jai White's martial arts chops have always been more impressive than his acting ability and he's in his element here, channelling old 1970s stars like Jim Brown into his role as a former CIA agent on a mission to find out who murdered his brother. From the jive-talking dialogue to the shaky camerawork, director Scott Sanders affectionately re-creates both the look and feel of the classic blaxploitation flicks, and although it's played mainly for laughs, White still has plenty of opportunities to kick ass. JF Some violence, swearing, sex scenes, nudity. **DVD**

Michael Jai White *Black Dynamite* • Obba Babatundé *Osiris* • Kevin Chapman *O'Leary* • Tommy Davidson *Cream Corn* • Richard Edson *Dino* • Arsenio Hall *Tasty Freeze* ■ *Dir* Scott Sanders • *Scr* Michael Jai White, Byron Minns, Scott Sanders, from a story by White, Minns

Black Eagle ★★★ 15
Martial arts thriller   1988 · US · Colour · 99min

Malta is the location for this Jean-Claude Van Damme martial arts film. Remember the Cold War? CIA and KGB agents hurtling around the globe in pursuit of top secret weapons? Well, there is nothing hush-hush about this action fest, in which the "Muscles from Brussels" plays a Soviet killing machine intent on seizing a laser device lost in a plane crash, before high-kicking hero Sho Kosugi can lay his mitts on it. Directed with maximum noise by Eric Karson. DP Swearing, violence.

Sho Kosugi *Ken Tani* • Jean-Claude Van Damme *Andrei* • Doran Clark *Patricia Parker* • Vladimir Skomarovsky *Vladimir Klimenko* • Bruce French *Father Joseph Bedelia* • Dorota Puzio *Natasha* •

William Bassett *Dean Rickert* ■ Dir Eric Karson • Scr AE Peters, Michael Gonzales, from a story by Shimon Arama

The Black Fox ★★★
Documentary 1962 · US · BW · 89min

The winner of the Oscar for best documentary feature, this is a fascinating exploration of the historical factors that led to the rise (and fall) of Adolf Hitler. Narrated by Marlene Dietrich (who refused Nazi overtures to make a triumphant return to the Fatherland), Louis Clyde Stoumen's film resorts to some overly familiar newsreel footage. But it also offers some perceptive insights into the general European situation and the nature of the German people, who so readily accepted a fascist dictatorship. Less successful are the references to Goethe's retelling of the medieval fable of *Reynard the Fox*. DP

Marlene Dietrich *Narrator* ■ Dir Louis Clyde Stoumen • Scr Louis Clyde Stouman

Black Fury ★★
Drama based on a true story
1935 · US · BW · 93min

A committed social melodrama torn, as Warner Bros was wont to say, from the headlines, this is about a mine worker who falls victim to corrupt employers and racketeers. Paul Muni's presence guarantees some "serious" acting and serious make-up, but there are compensations, notably Michael Curtiz's pacey direction and an extraordinary full-scale underground mine built on the Warner Bros ranch. A box-office flop, it was banned in Pennsylvania where the main industry is coal mining. AT

Paul Muni *Joe Radek* • Karen Morley *Anna Novak* • William Gargan *Slim* • Barton MacLane *McGee* • John Qualen *Mike Shemanski* • J Carrol Naish *Steve Croner* • Vince Barnett *Kubanda* • Henry O'Neill *JW Hendricks* ■ Dir Michael Curtiz • Scr Abem Finkel, Carl Erickson, from the play *Bohunk* by Henry R Irving and the story *Jan Volkanik* by Judge MA Musmanno

Black Girl ★★★
Drama 1972 · US · Colour · 96min

Lurking behind the catchpenny, blaxploitation title is a rather perceptive and thought-provoking study of foster parenting and the integration of children within a caring family unit. Louise Stubbs is the put-upon mother trying to cope with her two daughters and their new half-sister, who aspires to be a dancer and makes life intolerable in the process. Astutely directed by actor Ossie Davis, it has a ring of truth. AJ

Brock Peters *Earl* • Leslie Uggams *Netta* • Claudia McNeil *Mu' Dear* • Louise Stubbs *Mama Rosie* • Gloria Edwards *Norma* • Loretta Greene *Ruth Ann* • Kent Martin *Herbert* • Peggy Pettit *Billie Jean* ■ Dir Ossie Davis • Scr JE Franklin, from his play

Black God, White Devil ★★★★ 12
Western drama 1964 · Bra · BW · 118min

Glauber Rocha was one of the driving forces behind Brazilian *cinema nôvo*. Set in the 1940s and exhibiting both indigenous cultural and international filmic influences, this *sertao* western epitomises the movement's initial preoccupation with the politicisation of the peasantry. Alternately presented in long takes and montage sequences, the action follows Geraldo d'el Rey as he veers between bandit Othon Bastos and his sworn enemy Maurício de Valle. In so doing, Rocha illustrates how difficult it was for uneducated farmhands to know where to place allegiance in the struggle against the oppression of the pitiless landowners. De Valle would return in the sequel, *Antonio das Mortes* (1969). DP Portuguese +subtitles. *DVD*

Geraldo Del Rey *Manuel* • Yona Magalhaes *Rosa* • Othon Bastos *Sebastian* • Maurício de Valle *Antonio Das Mortes* • Lidio Silva *Corisco* • Sonia dos Humildes *Dada* ■ Dir/Scr Glauber Rocha

Black Gold ★★ U
Melodrama 1947 · US · Colour · 89min

Named after the winner of the 1924 Kentucky Derby, this minor drama gave Anthony Quinn his first starring role as an illiterate Indian who becomes an oil tycoon and horse-racing enthusiast. Quinn's then-wife Katherine DeMille co-stars as the native American's well-educated spouse with "Ducky" Louie playing the Chinese boy they adopt. Harsh Cinecolor and a dreary plot emphasising tears and tolerance leaves Quinn's dynamic performance as the stand-out feature of the production. AE

Anthony Quinn *Charley Eagle* • Katherine DeMille *Sarah Eagle* • Elyse Knox *Ruth Frazer* • Kane Richmond *Stanley Lowell* • "Ducky" Louie *Davey* • Raymond Hatton *Bucky* • Thurston Hall *Colonel Caldwell* ■ Dir Phil Karlson • Scr Agnes Christine Johnston, from a story by Caryl Coleman

Black Gold ★★ U
Adventure 1962 · US · BW · 98min

This Warner Bros drama is one of those curious pictures that was made in the interim between the decline of the B-movie and the advent of the teleplay. Philip Carey and James Best feature as buddies who go searching for oil in 1920s Oklahoma and fall out over Diane McBain. Claude Akins steals the show as a tycoon who lets the wildcatters take all the risks before staking his claim to their strike. Leslie H Martinson directs with efficiency, but little style. DP

Philip Carey *Frank McCandless* • Diane McBain *Ann Evans* • James Best *Jericho Larkin* • Fay Spain *Julie* • Claude Akins *Chick Carrington* • William Phipps *Albert Mailer* • Dub Taylor *Doc* ■ Dir Leslie H Martinson • Scr Bob Duncan, Wanda Duncan, from a story by Henry Whittington

Black Gold ★★★ U
Documentary 2006 · UK/US · Colour · 77min

While it may prompt some to think again next time they're ordering a latte, this well-meaning insight into the coffee business is better at lauding the good guys than taking the multinationals to task. Director brothers Marc and Nick Francis refuse to mince their words and trenchantly expose the flaws in a system that has existed since the deregulation of the market in 1989. But, while they state the obvious solutions with tenacious clarity, they fail to confront those at fault with their misgivings. They're more persuasive, however, in profiling the manager of the Oromo Coffee Farmers Co-op, whose 70,000 members in Ethiopia depend on him striking fair trade deals with conglomerates. DP English, Amharic, Italian +subtitles. *DVD*

Tadesse Meskela • Joe O'Neill • Dr Ernesto Illy • Burte Arba • Simon Wakefield • Dr Ahmed Mahamadi ■ Dir Marc Francis, Nick Francis

Black Gold ★★ 12
Epic period drama 2011 · Fr · Colour · 124min

Jean Jacques-Annaud's misty-eyed morality tale stars Mark Strong and Antonio Banderas as rival leaders who spill blood and oil in the Arabian desert in the 1930s. But it's Tahar Rahim who has the meatiest role here, playing Strong's scholarly son who's given up as a child to Banderas's wily emir to guarantee peace between the tribes – an agreement that is broken when the Americans detect oil between their lands. Strong oozes charisma as the noble warrior, while Banderas relishes his turn as the villain of the piece. However, Rahim (so effective in *A Prophet*) is miscast as a supposed leader of men, upstaged at every turn by Riz Ahmed (*Four Lions*) as his quick-witted half-brother. SP Some violence, a brief sex scene. *DVD*

Tahar Rahim *Prince Auda* • Antonio Banderas *Nesib* • Mark Strong *Sultan Amar* • Freida Pinto *Princess Leyla* • Riz Ahmed [Rizwan Ahmed] *Ali* • Akin Gazi *Prince Saleeh* ■ Dir Jean-Jacques Annaud • Scr Menno Meyjes, from the novel *Arab* by Hans Ruesch • Music James Horner

The Black Hand ★★
Crime drama 1950 · US · BW · 90min

A potentially fascinating study of the roots of the Mafia in turn-of-the-century New

York is not helped by its odd casting and by the MGM studio gloss that makes this feature look artificial. Precisely why casting directors thought Gene Kelly should play the young Italian seeking to avenge his father's death is beyond comprehension. The Pittsburgh-Irish Kelly is wrong, and his earnest manner grates. Richard Thorpe's not the director for this kind of material, either, and the whole seems a rare miscalculation. TS

Gene Kelly *Johnny Columbo* • J Carrol Naish *Louis Lorelli* • Teresa Celli *Isabella Gomboli* • Marc Lawrence (1) *Caesar Xavier Serpi* • Frank Puglia *Carlo Sabballera* • Barry Kelley *Captain Thompson* • Mario Siletti *Benny Danetta* ■ Dir Richard Thorpe • Scr Luther Davis, from a story by Leo Townsend

Black Hawk Down ★★★ 15
War drama 2001 · US · Colour · 138min

The fact that this noisy, gung-ho modern war movie is based on the disastrous 1993 "Battle of Mogadishu" in Somalia does not temper its flag-waving, pro-American militarism.The film's poster tagline "Leave no man behind" disguises what was a strategic American mess – in reality, 18 Americans were killed, as were hundreds of Somalis during a 15-hour firefight. It's sensitive, cool-headed and intelligent, but its call for "heroes" makes it little more than a recruitment film. AC Violence, swearing. *DVD* *Blu-ray*

Josh Hartnett *Ranger Staff Sgt Matt Eversmann* • Ewan McGregor *Ranger Spec Grimes* • Tom Sizemore *Ranger Lt Col Danny McKnight* • Eric Bana *Delta Sgt First Class "Hoot" Gibson* • William Fichtner *Delta Sgt First Class Jeff Sanderson* • Ewen Bremner *Specialist Shawn Nelson* • Sam Shepard *Maj Gen William F Garrison* • Gabriel Casseus *Ranger Spec Mike Kurth* • Kim Coates *Delta Master Sgt Chris "Wex" Wexler* • Hugh Dancy *Ranger Sgt First Class Kurt Schmid* • Ron Eldard *Chief Warrant Officer Mike Durant* • Ioan Gruffudd *Ranger Beales* • Jeremy Piven *Chief Warrant Officer Cliff Wolcott* • Jason Isaacs *Captain Mike Steele* • Orlando Bloom *Private First Class Todd Blackburn* ■ Dir Ridley Scott • Scr Ken Nolan, Steve Zaillian, from a non-fiction book and articles by Mark Bowden

The Black Hole ★★★ PG
Science-fiction adventure
1979 · US · Colour · 97min

It seems strange now, but there was a time in the 1970s when Disney seemed to have lost its magic touch, and this unwieldy sci-fi epic didn't really succeed in halting the decline of the period. It's actually not too bad, boasting some stunning special effects and an intriguing story about a disturbed scientist (Maximilian Schell) who is about to boldly go where no man has been before into a black hole in space. The cast is dependable, but it's a bit staid. JF *DVD*

Maximilian Schell *Dr Hans Reinhardt* • Anthony Perkins *Dr Alex Durant* • Robert Forster *Captain Dan Holland* • Joseph Bottoms *Lieutenant Charles Pizer* • Yvette Mimieux *Dr Kate McCrae* • Ernest Borgnine *Harry Booth* • Tommy McLoughlin *Captain STAR* ■ Dir Gary Nelson • Scr Jeb Rosebrook, Gerry Day, from a story by Bob Barbash, Richard Landau, Jeb Rosebrook • Special Effects Peter Ellenshaw, Art Cruickshank, Eustace Lycett, Danny Lee, Harrison Ellenshaw, Joe Hale

Black Horse Canyon ★★ U
Western 1954 · US · Colour · 81min

Joel McCrea may be top billed in this fitfully entertaining Universal western, but his limelight is stolen by a superb wild stallion called Outlaw who won the 1955 Patsy Award of Excellence for animal actors. Here, Outlaw plays the horse that McCrea's co-stars Mari Blanchard and Murvyn Vye want to capture for breeding purposes – and that's about it as far as the plot is concerned. It's directed by Jesse Hibbs from a warm-hearted screenplay by the prolific Daniel Mainwaring. TS

Joel McCrea *Del Rockwell* • Mari Blanchard *Aldia Spain* • Race Gentry *Ti* • Murvyn Vye *Jennings* • Irving Bacon *Doc* • Ewing Mitchell *Sheriff* • John Pickard *Duke* • Pilar Del Rey *Juanita* ■ Dir Jesse Hibbs • Scr Daniel Mainwaring, from the novel *The Wild Horse* by Les Savage Jr, adapted by David Lang

Black Jack ★★
Drama 1952 · US/Fr · BW · 101min

Julien Duvivier was one of the finest exponents of the poetic realist style, which laid bare the soul of France in the 1930s. However, he never recovered his assured sense of atmosphere and place after a wartime sojourn in Hollywood. Co-scripted by Duvivier and his longtime collaborator Charles Spaak, this wearying tale of duplicity among the idle rich of the Riviera is never as frothy or intricate as the makers intend it to be. DP

George Sanders *Mike Alexander* • Patricia Roc *Ingrid* • Herbert Marshall *James* • Agnes Moorehead *Emily* • Marcel Dalio *Captain* ■ Dir Julien Duvivier • Scr Julien Duvivier, Charles Spaak

Black Jack ★★
Satirical comedy 1972 · US · Colour · 87min

Produced by exploitation hive American International Pictures, this demented Cold War satire is a sort of poor man's *Dr Strangelove*. Georg Stanford Brown and Brandon de Wilde star as a couple of escaped peaceniks who hijack a B-52 so they can drop an atom bomb on Fort Knox. William T Naud wrote, directed, produced and edited this scattershot portrait of a nation torn apart by Vietnam fallout. However, its main significance is that it marked the last appearance of 30-year-old de Wilde. DP

Georg Stanford Brown *Lynch* • Brandon de Wilde *Josh* • Keenan Wynn *General Harry Gobohare* • Tim O'Connor *Senator Bob Recker* • Dick Gautier *Diver* • Robert Lansing *Major Reason* • Larry Hovis *Captain Breen* • Bernie Kopell *Penrat* ■ Dir William T Naud • Scr Dick Gautier, William T Naud, from a story by Peter Marshall, Dick Gautier, William T Naud

Black Jack ★★★ PG
Period adventure 1979 · UK · Colour · 97min

This family film evokes the atmosphere of its setting brilliantly, but a real star might have made it more coherent. Burt Lancaster wanted to play the hero, but director Ken Loach's aversion to stars meant that French actor Jean Franval took the role of the 18th-century rogue. His escape from hanging – by lodging a bullet in his throat – leads to adventures with young Stephen Hirst and Louise Cooper. TH *DVD*

Jean Franval *Black Jack* • Stephen Hirst *Tolly* • Andrew Bennet *Hatch* • Louise Cooper *Belle* • Packie Byrne *Dr Carmody* • John Young *Dr Hunter* • Russell Waters *Dr Jones* • Pat Wallis *Mrs Gorgandy* • William Moore *Mr Carter* ■ Dir Kenneth Loach [Ken Loach] • Scr Kenneth Loach, from the novel by Leon Garfield

Black Joy ★★ 15
Comedy 1977 · UK · Colour · 94min

Although writer Anthony Simmons's film tries to say something significant about the experience of being black in Brixton in the mid-1970s, he and co-writer Jamal Ali fail to achieve a consistent tone, as they veer between back-street realism and frontline comedy. There are a few rough-hewn gems hidden in the dialogue, but the acting is as variable as the writing, with only Norman Beaton (as a wily waster) and Trevor Thomas (as the young Guyanan he dupes) convincing throughout. DP Swearing, sex scenes. *DVD*

Norman Beaton *Dave King* • Trevor Thomas *Benjamin Jones* • Floella Benjamin *Miriam* • Dawn Hope *Saffra* • Oscar James *Jomo* • Paul Medford *Devon* • Shango Baku *Raastaman* ■ Dir Anthony Simmons • Scr Anthony Simmons, Jamal Ali, from the play *Dark Days and Light Nights* by Jamal Ali

The Black Knight ★★★ U
Period romantic adventure
1954 · UK/US · Colour · 86min

This underrated Alan Ladd vehicle was released a year after his leading role in the classic western *Shane*. Skilled director Tay Garnett brings a fair amount of boisterous charm to this not-to-be-taken-seriously studio-bound Arthurian romp. The 1950s Technicolor is absolutely splendid and the supporting cast of British stalwarts is a joy to behold. A better script wouldn't really have helped – and doesn't really matter. **TS**

Alan Ladd *John* • Patricia Medina *Linet* • Andre Morell [André Morell] *Sir Ontzlake* • Harry Andrews *Earl of Yeonil* • Peter Cushing *Sir Palamides* • Anthony Bushell *King Arthur* • Laurence Naismith *Major Domo* • Patrick Troughton *King Mark* ■ *Dir* Tay Garnett • *Scr* Alec Coppel

Black Knight ★★ PG
Comedy 2001 · US · Colour · 91min

This struggles to turn a loose version of Mark Twain's *A Connecticut Yankee in King Arthur's Court* into a suitable vehicle for comic Martin Lawrence, whose inconsistent performance doesn't help the cause. Lawrence plays an underachieving employee at on-the-skids theme park Medieval World. After falling into a moat, he is magically zapped back to a 14th-century England, that he initially fails to comprehend because "they're all such good actors". Director Gil Junger seems unable to control Lawrence's tedious cheeky-chappy persona and leaves little room for laughs, action or other characters. **TH**
DVD

Martin Lawrence *Jamal Walker* • Marsha Thomason *Victoria* • Tom Wilkinson *Sir Knolte* • Vincent Regan *Sir Percival* • Kevin Conway *King Leo* • Jeannette Weegar *Princess Regina* ■ *Dir* Gil Junger • *Scr* Darryl J Quarles, Peter Gaulke, Gerry Swallow

The Black Legion ★★★
Crime drama 1937 · US · BW · 83min

A young Humphrey Bogart stars as a devoted family man and factory worker who becomes hopelessly and tragically embroiled with a Ku Klux Klan-style secret society, which is dedicated to "cleansing" America of so-called foreigners. Straight from the heart of Warner Bros social conscience cycle, the drama is grim and the moral message against intolerance strong. Basically a B-picture, it's elevated by its subject and some supporting performances. **RK**

Humphrey Bogart *Frank Taylor* • Dick Foran *Ed Jackson* • Erin O'Brien-Moore *Ruth Taylor* • Ann Sheridan *Betty Grogan* • Robert Barrat *Brown* • Helen Flint *Pearl Davis* • Joseph Sawyer [Joe Sawyer] *Cliff Moore* • Addison Richards *Prosecuting Attorney* ■ *Dir* Archie Mayo • *Scr* Abem Finkel, William Wister Haines, from a story by Robert Lord

Black like Me ★★
Biographical drama 1964 · US · BW · 107min

This relates the real-life experiences of white writer John Howard Griffin, who decided to pose as a black man in the South. The consequences of this and the racial discrimination that he suffers are wholly predictable. James Whitmore and the supporting cast, most notably Clifton James and Roscoe Lee Browne, try to make a slack script taut but, despite good intentions, this never convinces other than as a piece of 1960s anti-racist propaganda. **TH**

James Whitmore *John Finley Horton* • Clifton James *Eli Carr* • Lenka Peterson *Lucy Horton* • Roscoe Lee Browne *Christopher* • Sorrell Booke *Doctor Jackson* ■ *Dir* Carl Lerner • *Scr* Gerda Lerner, Carl Lerner, from the book by John Howard Griffin

Black Magic ★★
Swashbuckling drama 1949 · US · BW · 105min

Orson Welles's hobby was conjuring, but no sleight of hand can disguise the ramshackle nature of this swashbuckler, one of those low-grade acting jobs he took to raise funds to make his Shakespearean films, *Macbeth* and *Othello*. He plays a notorious court magician around the time of the French Revolution, who becomes part of a plot to switch Marie Antoinette for a servant girl (both played by Nancy Guild). Ponderous rubbish. **TH**

Orson Welles *Cagliostro* • Nancy Guild *Marie Antoinette/Lorenza* • Akim Tamiroff *Gitano* • Frank Latimore *Gilbert* • Valentina Cortesa [Valentina Cortese] *Zoraida* • Margot Grahame *Madame Dubarry* • Stephen Bekassy *DeMontagne* • Berry Kroeger *Alexandre Dumas*

Sr • Gregory Gaye *Chambord* • Raymond Burr *Alexandre Dumas Jr* • *Dir* Gregory Ratoff • *Scr* Charles Bennett, from the novel *Joseph Balsamo* by Alexandre Dumas

Black Mama, White Mama ★★ 18
Blaxploitation action adventure 1972 · US · Colour · 81min

The Defiant Ones changes sex and gets the blaxploitation treatment in hack Filipino director Eddie Romero's trashy action filler. Hooker Pam Grier and guerrilla fighter Margaret Markov are the chicks in chains who escape from a prison and flee disguised as nuns. This was the movie (amazingly from a story co-written by future director Jonathan Demme) that apparently convinced future black superstar Grier to become a full-time actress – so it wasn't a complete waste of everyone's time. **AJ** Violence, swearing, nudity. *DVD*

Pam Grier *Lee Daniels* • Margaret Markov *Karen Brent* • Sid Haig *Ruben* • Lynn Borden *Densmore* • Zaldy Zshornack *Ernesto* • Laurie Burton *Logan* ■ *Dir* Eddie Romero • *Scr* HR Christian, from a story by Joseph Viola, Jonathan Demme

The Black Marble ★★★ 15
Romantic comedy 1980 · US · Colour · 105min

Dognapping would hardly seem to be the stuff of riveting drama. Yet this cop thriller, taken from Joseph Wambaugh's bestseller, is a thoughtful look at the human side of police work. Transferred from the homicide department after a gruelling child murder case, burnt-out Robert Foxworth teams up with Paula Prentiss to investigate animal burglary. Strong acting takes up the slack. **AJ**

Robert Foxworth *Sgt Valnikov* • Paula Prentiss *Sgt Natalie Zimmerman* • James Woods *Fiddler* • Harry Dean Stanton *Philo* • Barbara Babcock *Madeline Whitfield* • John Hancock *Clarence Cromwell* • Raleigh Bond *Capt Hooker* • Judy Landers *Pattie Mae* • Pat Corley *Itchy Mitch* ■ *Dir* Harold Becker • *Scr* Joseph Wambaugh, from his novel

Black Mask ★★★★ 18
Martial arts action thriller 1996 · HK · Colour · 83min

This was the film that introduced UK audiences to Hong Kong action star Jet Li. The deliriously bonkers plot has Li as a former member of an elite group of assassins who, after radical nerve surgery, feel neither pain nor emotion. He escapes to take up a new life – as a librarian! – but is forced back into action. Director Daniel Lee takes the action sequences to mind-boggling new extremes with some jaw-dropping ultra-violence, while Li gets to showcase his dazzling physical talents. The star didn't return for the dismal 2001 sequel directed by Tsui Hark. **JF** Cantonese dubbed. Violence, swearing, sex scenes. *DVD*

Jet Li *Tsui* • Lau Ching Wan *Shi* • Karen Mok *Tracy* • Françoise Yip *Yu Lan* • Patrick Lung-Kang *Commander Hung* ■ *Dir* Daniel Lee • *Scr* Hark Tsui, Hui Kuan, Teddy Chen, Joe Ma

Black Mass ★★★ 15
Crime drama based on a true story 2015 · US · Colour · 118min

Johnny Depp gives his best performance in years, despite being caked in latex, as real-life Boston crime lord Whitey Bulger, who's made untouchable by the FBI – specifically by childhood pal Agent John Connolly (Joel Edgerton) - when he forges an alliance to topple the Italian mafia in the city. There's a terrifying glint of mania visible in Depp's eyes in his carefully measured portrayal, but there's surprisingly little screen-time for Benedict Cumberbatch as Whitey's brother, and director Scott Cooper misses too many opportunities to add depth to a fascinating story. **SP** Violence, swearing, sexual references, drug abuse. *Blu-ray*

Johnny Depp *James "Whitey" Bulger* • Joel Edgerton *John Connolly* • Benedict Cumberbatch *Billy Bulger* • Rory Cochrane *Steve Flemmi* • Jesse Plemons *Kevin Weeks* ■ *Dir* Scott Cooper • *Scr* Scott Cooper, from a screenplay by Mark

Mallouk, from the non-fiction book *Black Mass: Whitey Bulger, the FBI, and a Devil's Deal* by Dick Lehr, Gerard O'Neill

Black Moon ★★★ 12
Fantasy drama 1974 · Fr · Colour · 96min

Beautifully photographed by Sven Nykvist, Louis Malle's first film in English is a weird, futuristic fantasy set in a countryside where symbols abound. Not all of this enigmatic movie comes off, but Malle's Wonderland is full of surprising things, including talking rats, unicorns and ex-Andy Warhol hunk Joe Dalessandro. Cathryn Harrison, Rex's granddaughter, is adequate as the Alice figure; the title refers to the time of chaos that precedes some cataclysmic change. **RB**
DVD

Cathryn Harrison *Lily* • Thérèse Giehse *The old lady* • Alexandra Stewart *Sister* • Joe Dalessandro *Brother* ■ *Dir* Louis Malle • *Scr* Louis Malle, Ghislain Uhry, Joyce Buñuel

Black Moon Rising ★★ 18
Action thriller 1985 · US · Colour · 97min

Director Harley Cokliss plays too safe, here sticking to a standard action-thriller format. Similarly, there are solid but not outstanding performances from the cast, with the exception of the ever-excellent Tommy Lee Jones as a burglar on the trail of a stolen computer tape. Linda Hamilton and Robert Vaughn provide able support, but even they are not at their best. Co-written by John Carpenter from his own story, it could have been so much better with him as director. **NF** Violence, swearing, nudity. *DVD*

Tommy Lee Jones *Quint* • Linda Hamilton *Nina* • Robert Vaughn (1) *Ryland* • Richard Jaeckel *Earl Windom* • Lee Ving *Marvin Ringer* • Bubba Smith *Johnson* • Dan Shor *Billy Lyons* • William Sanderson *Tyke Thayden* • Keenan Wynn *Iron John* • Nick Cassavetes *Luis* ■ *Dir* Harley Cokliss • *Scr* John Carpenter, Desmond Nakano, William Gray, from a story by John Carpenter

Black Mountain Poets ★★★ 15
Comedy 2015 · UK · Colour · 85min

Two scatterbrained thieves (Alice Lowe, Dolly Wells) pose as poets in this slight but entertaining offering. The duo in question steal a JCB and head to a poetry retreat in the Black Mountains of Wales, where they have their sights set on a big cash prize. Although it lacks context and never really rises above sitcom-style farce, the film is lifted by its leads - a neurotic, subtly sorrowful Wells and an amusingly demented Lowe. But the absence of depth and structure means it flails in tandem with its heroines. **EAS** Swearing. *DVD*

Alice Lowe *Lisa Walker* • Dolly Wells *Claire Walker* • Tom Cullen *Richard* • Rosa Robson *Louise Cabaye* ■ *Dir/Scr* Jamie Adams

Black Narcissus ★★★★★ U
Classic drama 1947 · UK · Colour · 100min

Winner of Oscars for art design and cinematography, Michael Powell and Emeric Pressburger's adaptation of Rumer Godden's simmering novel is one of the most striking examples of studio-controlled artifice in film history. Jack Cardiff's lush colour images not only enhance the beauty of the stylised Himalayan scenery, but also bring a certain grandeur to the melodramatic events at a remote mountain mission, where the visit of English agent David Farrar is causing passions to run dangerously out of control among the nuns. Kathleen Byron's eye-rolling jealousy awakens the occasionally sleepy plot and her scene with Deborah Kerr on the bell-tower is a true classic. **DP** *DVD* *Blu-ray*

Deborah Kerr *Sister Clodagh* • Sabu *Dilip Rai, the Young General* • David Farrar *Mr Dean* • Flora Robson *Sister Philippa* • Esmond Knight *The old General* • Jean Simmons *Kanchi* • Kathleen Byron *Sister Ruth* • Jenny Laird *Blanche, Sister Honey* ■ *Dir* Michael Powell, Emeric Pressburger • *Scr* Michael Powell, Emeric Pressburger, from Rumer Godden's novel • *Cinematographer* Jack Cardiff • *Art Director* Alfred Junge

The Black Orchid ★★ U
Drama 1959 · US · BW · 98min

Hollywood, on the whole, gave the luscious Sophia Loren a raw deal, leaving her native Italy to provide worthy vehicles for her talent. Without her, and Anthony Quinn's excellent co-starring performance, this New York-based saga about a widower (Quinn) fighting his children's opposition to his marrying a gangster's widow (Loren) would hardly be worth staying in for. Nonetheless, the Italian star won the acting award at the Venice film festival for her sterling efforts. **RK**

Sophia Loren *Rose Bianco* • Anthony Quinn *Frank Valente* • Ina Balin *Mary Valente* • Mark Richman [Peter Mark Richman] *Noble* • Jimmy Baird *Ralphie Bianco* • Virginia Vincent *Alma Gallo* • Naomi Stevens *Guilia Gallo* • Frank Puglia *Henry Gallo* ■ *Dir* Martin Ritt • *Scr* Joseph Stefano

Black Orpheus ★★★ PG
Romance 1958 · Fr/Bra/It · Colour · 103min

Winner of the Oscar for best foreign film and the Palme d'Or at Cannes, this transposition of the myth of Orpheus and the Underworld to Rio de Janeiro at Carnival time is a riot of exotic colour and dynamic movement. Yet there's also an overweening sentimentality about trolleybus conductor Breno Mello's doomed affair with Marpessa Dawn, and director Marcel Camus is guilty of a certain naivety in his political symbolism and of failing to compensate for the limitations of his inexperienced cast. Yet, this remains a visually exhilarating and, thanks to a superb score, vibrant experience. **DP** Portuguese +subtitles. *DVD*

Breno Mello *Orpheus* • Marpessa Dawn *Eurydice* • Lourdes de Oliveria *Mira* • Lea Garcia *Serafina* • Ademar da Silva *Death* • Alexandro Constantino *Hermes* • Waldetar de Souza *Chico* ■ *Dir* Marcel Camus • *Scr* Jacques Viot, Marcel Camus, from the play *Orfeu da Conceicao* by Vinicius De Moraes • *Cinematographer* Jean Bourgoin • *Music* Antonio Carlos Jobim, Luiz Bonfa

Black Panther
Action adventure 2018 · US · Colour ·

This is a preview - no prints were available to review prior to publication: Following breakout roles as baseball icon Jackie Robinson (*42*) and soul legend James Brown (*Get on Up*), Chadwick Boseman is primed for superstar status with his casting as Marvel's premier black superhero. The character of T'Challa, a prince of the African state of Wakanda who takes up the mantle of the Black Panther after his father is murdered, is due to appear here in his first solo adventure. Membership of the Avengers then beckons. **JA**

Chadwick Boseman *T'Challa/Black Panther* • Andy Serkis *Ulysses Klaue/Klaw* ■ *Dir* Ryan Coogler • *Scr* Joe Robert Cole

The Black Panthers: Vanguard of the Revolution ★★★ 15
Documentary 2015 · US · Colour and BW · 114min

The problems that created the Black Panthers still haunt America, so this compelling piece of film history couldn't be more timely. Formed to bring better education and nutrition into the African-American community, the Panthers are famous for taking on persistent police and racial abuse via rallies and protests. In a film that's both educational and entertaining, the rise and fall of the most alluring and controversial black organisation of late 60s America comes to life via facts, vivid images and unique statements. **KK** Swearing, disturbing scenes. *DVD*

■ *Dir* Stanley Nelson • *Cinematographers* Antonio Rossi, Rick Butler

The Black Pirate ★★★★ PG
Silent swashbuckling adventure 1926 · US · Colour · 97min

Hailed as the first full-length feature to be made in two-tone Technicolor, this was one of the most spectacular swashbucklers

B

undertaken by Douglas Fairbanks (who also took a story credit as Elton Thomas). It was a stormy production, with co-star Donald Crisp being ousted from the director's chair in favour of the more malleable Albert Parker. This ripsnorting adventure has the aristocratic Fairbanks joining a pirate band to avenge the death of his father. The knife-blade descent down a billowing sail thrilled audiences of the day. DP *DVD*

Douglas Fairbanks *The Black Pirate* • Billie Dove *The Princess* • Anders Randolf *Pirate leader* • Donald Crisp *McTavish* • Tempe Pigott *Duenna* • Sam De Grasse *Pirate* • Charlie Stevens [Charles Stevens] *Powder man* • Charles Belcher *Chief passenger* ■ *Dir* Albert Parker • *Scr* Lotta Woods, Jack Cunningham, from a story by Elton Thomas [Douglas Fairbanks]

Black Point ★★15
Crime drama   2001 · Can · Colour · 102min

As an ex-soldier trying to restart his life in the Pacific Northwest, David Caruso is taken for a ride by *femme fatale* Susan Haskell. Thomas Ian Griffith (who also co-scripted) plays the abusive husband whose stolen Mob money is in Haskell's sights. This is *film noir* by numbers. DP Violence, swearing. *DVD*

David Caruso *John Hawkins* • Susan Haskell *Natalie Travis* • Thomas Ian Griffith *Gus Travis* • Miguel Sandoval *Malcolm* • Gordon Tootoosis *Standing Bear* ■ *Dir* David Mackay • *Scr* Greg Mellot, Thomas Ian Griffith

Black Pond ★★★★15
Black comedy drama   2011 · UK · Colour · 82min

This original black comedy from two first-time writer/directors does not waste a penny of its £25,000 budget. The tale of an average, middle-class Surrey family that becomes infamous after being accused of murder rustles up suburban satire, horror-movie dread and some memorable flashes of visual imagination in the form of animations and dream sequences. A terrific, low-key cast includes Chris Langham as the well-meaning but muddled father, who invites a stranger for tea while walking his dog, and former stand-up Simon Amstell (in his film debut) as a comic shrink. While the dialogue recalls the poetic mundanity of Mike Leigh, the story also packs a sense of palpable unease. AC Swearing. *DVD*

Chris Langham *Tom Thompson* • Simon Amstell *Eric Sacks* • Amanda Hadingue *Sophie Thompson* • Colin Hurley *Blake* • Will Sharpe *Tim Tanaka* • Helen Cripps *Jess Thompson* ■ *Dir* Tom Kingsley, Will Sharpe • *Scr* Will Sharpe, from a story by Kingsley, Sharpe

The Black Power Mixtape 1967-1975 ★★★★12A
Documentary
2011 · Swe/US/Nor/Ger/Swi/Fin/Gre · Colour and BW · 95min

The most astonishing thing about this documentary charting the most militant years of African-American politics in the United States is not the intimate, up-close footage of such firebrands as Stokely Carmichael, Eldridge Cleaver and Huey P Newton, but that it was found sitting quietly in the basement of a Swedish TV station. While the US media were trying to demonise these figures, who were questioning the non-violent stance of Martin Luther King and the civil rights movement, the Swedes adopted a neutral approach that proves surprisingly effective. The film does require some prior knowledge, but as a primer it's fascinating, and the smooth soundtrack by hip-hop/soul outfit the Roots counterbalances the unsettling rage of its subjects. DW Drug references. *DVD*

■ *Dir/Scr* Goran Olsson [Goran Hugo Olsson]

Black Rain ★★★★PG
Drama   1988 · Jpn · BW · 122min

From its devastating re-creation of the atomic bombing of Hiroshima, this intense and affecting drama exercises the fiercest of grips. Set mainly five years on from the blast, the story focuses on a woman whose marriage prospects have been dashed

because the male population of her country village fear she contracted radiation sickness. Yoshiko Tanaka gives an exceptional performance, as does Keisuke Ishida as the tormented stonemason with whom she strikes up an uneasy relationship. However, the powerful insights into the social and psychological aftermath of the bomb make this very much director Shohei Imamura's film. DP Japanese +subtitles.

Yoshiko Tanaka *Yasuko* • Kazuo Kitamura *Shigematsu Shizuma* • Etsuko Ichihara *Shigeko Shizuma* • Shoichi Ozawa *Shokichi* ■ *Dir* Shohei Imamura • *Scr* Shohei Imamura,Toshiro Ishido, from the novel by Masuji Ibuse

Black Rain ★★★15
Thriller   1989 · US · Colour · 125min

This tense, glossy and violent film stars Michael Douglas and Andy Garcia as New York cops on assignment in Japan where yakuza gangsters wield swords and where Kate Capshaw hangs out in a nightclub à la Marlene Dietrich. This being a Ridley Scott film, the atmosphere is so hyped up that the picture threatens to burst an artery. Jan De Bont's photography delights in the neon-lit locations and makes the city of Osaka look like a vision of hell, but beneath all this is a very conventional cop thriller. AT Violence, swearing. *DVD*

Michael Douglas (1) *Nick Conklin* • Andy Garcia *Charlie Vincent* • Ken Takakura *Masahiro Matsumoto* • Kate Capshaw *Joyce Kingsley* • Yusaku Matsuda *Sato* • Tomisaburo Wakayama *Sugai* • Shigeru Koyama *Ohashi* • John Spencer *Oliver* ■ *Dir* Ridley Scott • *Scr* Craig Bolotin, Warren Lewis

Black Rainbow ★★★★15
Supernatural thriller   1989 · UK · Colour · 98min

Achieving a ring of truth very few fantasies aspire to, Mike Hodges's most personal movie is an intriguing psychic thriller containing numerous eerie surprises. One of the main shocks is Rosanna Arquette, in her finest role to date, as the Doris Stokes-type medium who can plug into the link between this world and the spiritual one – the "black rainbow" of the title. And when she successfully predicts a murder, the unusual scene is set for a clairvoyant cat-and-mouse chase through previously uncharted suspense territory. AJ Swearing, brief nudity. *DVD*

Rosanna Arquette *Martha Travis* • Jason Robards *Walter Travis* • Tom Hulce *Gary Wallace* • Mark Joy *Lloyd Harley* • Ron Rosenthal *Detective Irving Weinberg* • John Bennes *Ted Silas* • Linda Pierce *Mary Kuron* • Olek Krupa *Tom Kuron* ■ *Dir/Scr* Mike Hodges

The Black Rider ★★U
Crime caper   1954 · UK · BW · 65min

This amiable low-budget crime caper takes the idea of using spooks to cover a smuggling operation and adds a dash of *Famous Five* exuberance to create a formula familiar to fans of the cartoon series *Scooby Doo*. The plot zips along like one of the motorbikes owned by the club members who expose the villains with the help of a crusading journalist. A pleasing enough time-passer. DP *DVD*

Jimmy Hanley *Jerry Marsh* • Rona Anderson *Mary* • Leslie Dwyer *Robert* • Beatrice Varley *Mrs Marsh* • Lionel Jeffries *Brennan* • Valerie Hanson *Karen* • Vincent Ball *Ted Lintott* ■ *Dir* Wolf Rilla • *Scr* AR Rawlinson

Black Robe ★★★15
Historical drama
1991 · Can/Aus · Colour · 96min

This saga about the clash between native Americans and Jesuits in the 17th century was adapted by Brian Moore from his own novel. Directed by Bruce Beresford amid stunning forest scenery in Quebec, it's an austere, small-scale epic that turns on the sexuality of the Indians and the morality of organised, colonialist religion. It's a dark, intense piece, powerfully acted by Lothaire Bluteau (*Jesus of Montreal*) as the head priest, and Sandrine Holt as the chief's daughter who falls in love with a Frenchman. AT English, French +subtitles.

Lothaire Bluteau *Father Laforgue* • Aden Young *Daniel* • Sandrine Holt *Annuka* • August Schellenberg *Chomina* • Tantoo Cardinal *Chomina's wife* • Billy Two Rivers *Ougebmat* • Lawrence Bayne *Neehatin* • Harrison Liu *Awondoie* • Wesley Cote *Oujita* ■ *Dir* Bruce Beresford • *Scr* Brian Moore, from his novel

Black Rock ★★15
Horror thriller   2012 · US · Colour · 76min

Black Rock is essentially a female twist on *Deliverance*, but it fails to deliver on the promise of that premise. Kate Bosworth, Lake Bell and Katie Aselton (who also directs) play childhood friends who reunite for a girlie weekend on a remote island off the coast of Maine. But a cosy campfire get-together with three local hunters leads to attempted rape and murder, forcing the girls to turn feral to survive. Aselton demonstrates an assured touch in the early character-based scenes, but she lacks the same control when it comes to handling the action. DA Violence, swearing, sexual references, nudity. *DVD*

Katie Aselton [Kathryn Aselton] *Abby* • Kate Bosworth *Sarah* • Lake Bell *Lou* • Will Bouvier *Henry* • Jay Paulson *Derek* ■ *Dir* Katie Aselton [Kathryn Aselton] • *Scr* Mark Duplass, from a story by Aselton

The Black Room ★★★
Horror   1935 · US · BW · 66min

Boris Karloff plays 19th-century twins in a standard gothic melodrama in which an evil brother murders the good one and impersonates him until an ancient family curse comes true. Generally effective, with the "black room" debauchery, sadism and torture implied rather than shown, it's primarily a showcase for Karloff to display his acting range between "hateful" and "sympathetic". He does it brilliantly. AJ

Boris Karloff *Baron Gregor de Berghman/Anton de Berghman* • Marian Marsh *Thea Hassel* • Robert Allen *Lt Albert Lussan* • Thurston Hall *Col Hassel* • Katherine DeMille *Mashka* • John Buckler *Beran* • Henry Kolker *Baron de Berghman* ■ *Dir* Roy William Neill • *Scr* Arthur Strawn, Henry Myers, from a story by Arthur Strawn

The Black Rose ★★U
Romantic adventure   1950 · UK · Colour · 120min

This sweeping yarn set in the 13th century stars Tyrone Power as the bastard son of a Saxon nobleman who travels from England to the Far East. On the way to Cathay, he rescues a blonde slave girl (the diminutive French actress Cécile Aubry) and confronts a Mongolian warlord (Orson Welles, hamming it up behind heavy Oriental make-up). The film looks good, but most of the dialogue is so bad it's painful to listen to. RB

Tyrone Power *Walter of Gurnie* • Orson Welles *Bayan* • Cécile Aubry *Maryam* • Jack Hawkins *Tristram* • Michael Rennie *King Edward* • Finlay Currie *Alfgar* • Herbert Lom *Anthemus* • Mary Clare *Countess of Lessford* • Bobby Blake [Robert Blake] *Mahmoud* ■ *Dir* Henry Hathaway • *Scr* Talbot Jennings, from the novel by Thomas B Costain

Black Sabbath ★★★★15
Portmanteau horror
1963 · US/Fr/It · BW · 92min

This chillingly effective portmanteau piece is from the Italian master of horror and suspense, Mario Bava. Veteran Boris Karloff, acting as master of ceremonies, introduces three classic tales. In the first a woman steals a ring from a corpse only to be haunted by her spirit. In the second a prostitute is terrified by a phantom telephone caller and lastly Karloff himself turns in one of his creepiest performances as a vampire cursed to chew only upon his own family. Pictorially stunning, this also has a script of above average intelligence for a horror movie. Two versions of the film exist – in Italian and English – with slight variations. RS Some dialogue dubbed. *DVD*

Jacqueline Pierreux [Jacqueline Soussard] *Helen Corey* • Milli Monti *Maid* • Michèle Mercier *Rosy* • Lidia Alfonsi *Mary* • Gustavo de Nardo *Frank* • Boris Karloff *Gorka* • Mark Damon *Vladimir*

D'Urfe • Susy Anderson *Sdenka* ■ *Dir* Mario Bava • *Scr* Marcello Fondato, Alberto Bevilacqua, Mario Bava • *Cinematographer* Ubaldo Terzano

The Black Scorpion ★★★
Science-fiction drama   1957 · US · BW · 87min

The slumber of giant scorpions is disturbed by volcanic activity in director Edward Ludwig's low-budget sci-fi drama. The leader of the angry arachnids takes one look at the desert and heads straight for Mexico City and a showdown with a cast headed by B-movie regulars Richard Denning and Mara Corday. Special effects come courtesy of Willis O'Brien, who helped give life to King Kong. The film's climax, in the Mexico City stadium, is wonderfully schlocky. AT

Richard Denning *Henry Scott* • Mara Corday *Teresa* • Carlos Rivas *Arturo Ramos* • Mario Navarro *Juanito* • Carlos Muzquiz *Doctor Velasco* • Pasqual Garcia Peña *Jose de la Cruz* ■ *Dir* Edward Ludwig • *Scr* David Duncan, Robert Blees, from a story by Paul Yawitz

Black Sea ★★★★15
Adventure thriller
2014 · US/UK · Colour · 109min

Although it pits westerners against Russians in a decrepit submarine, there's nothing of the Cold War in this tense undersea thriller. Instead, there's an undertow of recession-era desperation, with Jude Law as a recently laid-off submarine pilot who recruits a motley bunch of sailors to search for a missing trove of Nazi gold in Russian waters. The way enmities quickly escalate is a little bit of a stretch, but otherwise this is a smartly handled, old-school adventure, and British director Kevin Macdonald proves himself adept with tension as well as character. DW Violence, swearing. *DVD*

Jude Law *Captain Robinson* • Scoot McNairy *Daniels* • Ben Mendelsohn *Fraser* • David Threlfall *Peters* • Jodie Whittaker *Chrissy* • Konstantin Khabenskiy [Konstantin Khabensky] *Blackie* ■ *Dir* Kevin Macdonald • *Scr* Dennis Kelly (2)

Black Sheep ★★
Crime drama   1935 · US · BW · 70min

Returning to Hollywood after a brief sojourn in Britain, veteran director Allan Dwan resumed his career with this shipboard melodrama. Edmund Lowe stars as the transatlantic gambler who prevents Tom Brown from the taking the rap for a jewel robbery – without letting the boy know he's really his father. While never riveting, Lowe and Trevor are admirable, and Adrienne Ames is hissable as a scheming vamp. DP

Edmund Lowe *John Francis Dugan* • Claire Trevor *Janette Foster* • Tom Brown *Fred Curtis* • Eugene Pallette *Col Upton Calhoun Belcher* • Adrienne Ames *Mrs Millicent Caldwell Bath* ■ *Dir* Allan Dwan • *Scr* Allen Rivkin, from the story *Baa Baa Black Sheep* by Allan Dwan

Black Sheep ★★12
Comedy   1996 · US · Colour · 82min

Wayne's World director Penelope Spheeris continues her erratic career with this mindless vehicle for double act Chris Farley and David Spade. Farley is the overweight, accident-prone brother of would-be State Governor Tim Matheson. To get Farley out of the way, the caustic Spade is enlisted to "babysit". There's chemistry between the leads, but the jokes are uninspired. JC *DVD*

Chris Farley *Mike Donnelly* • David Spade *Steve Dodds* • Tim Matheson *Al Donnelly* • Christine Ebersole *Governor Tracy* • Gary Busey *Drake Sabitch* • Grant Heslov *Robbie Mieghem* • Timothy Carhart *Roger Kovary* • Bruce McGill *Neuschwender* • "Gypsy" Spheeris *Pocket pool lady* • Kevin P Farley [Kevin Farley] *Bouncer* • John Farley *Bouncer* ■ *Dir* Penelope Spheeris • *Scr* Fred Wolf

Black Sheep ★★★★15
Horror comedy   2006 · NZ · Colour · 82min

It's appropriate that Peter Jackson's Weta Workshop provided the effects for this Kiwi horror comedy, as it's powered by the same gleeful tastelessness that the director brought to his early cult hits like *Braindead*. Here, Nathan Meister plays the sheep-phobic farmer's son who reluctantly returns to the family holdings to formally sign everything over to his bullying brother Peter Feeney. However, Meister soon discovers that his sibling has been playing around with nature, and that the usually docile flock now has a taste for human flesh. Naturally, evil scientists are the villains of the piece, and director Jonathan King has just as much fun sending up the politically correct antics of the greenies. The film's finest moment comes when the blood-crazed flock come thundering down the hill to lay waste to a group of investors. JF **DVD** **BL**

Nathan Meister *Henry Oldfield* • Danielle Mason *Experience* • Peter Feeney *Angus Oldfield* • Tammy Davis *Tucker* • Oliver Driver *Grant* • Glenis Levestam *Mrs Mac* • Tandi Wright *Dr Rush* • Matthew Chamberlain *Oliver Oldfield* • Kevin McTurk *Wereshed* • Mick Rose *Mike* • Nick Blake *Taxi driver* ■ *Dir/Scr* Jonathan King

The Black Sheep of Whitehall ★★★★ U
Comedy   1941 · UK · BW · 73min

Co-directing, as well as starring, Will Hay is at his blithering best as the incompetent principal of a correspondence college. He stumbles across a dastardly plot involving Nazi Felix Aylmer masquerading as a famous economist so that he and treacherous journalist Basil Sydney can disrupt a vital trade pact between Britain and South America. Adopting a series of hilariously transparent disguises, Hay and sole pupil John Mills finally capture the villains in a corking chase sequence, with Hay (dressed as a nurse) being dragged along in a Bath chair. This wonderful wartime comedy is the neglected classic in the Hay canon. DP **DVD**

Will Hay *Professor Davis* • John Mills *Bobby* • Basil Sydney *Costello* • Henry Hewitt *Professor Davys* • Felix Aylmer *Crabtree* • Frank Cellier *Innsbach* • Joss Ambler *Sir John* • Frank Allenby *Onslow* ■ *Dir* Will Hay, Basil Dearden • *Scr* Angus MacPhail, John Dighton

The Black Shield of Falworth ★★ U
Swashbuckling adventure
1954 · US · Colour · 95min

Janet Leigh and Tony Curtis made six films together during their marriage, and here the glamorous couple cavort across Ye Merrie Olde Englande (or the Universal backlot) to save Henry IV from a fate worse than a Kenneth Branagh remake. This swashbuckler features suave Herbert Marshall, decent swordfights, early CinemaScope photography and some wonderful Brooklyn accents. AT **DVD**

Tony Curtis *Myles Falworth* • Janet Leigh *Lady Anne* • David Farrar *Earl of Alban* • Barbara Rush *Meg Falworth* • Herbert Marshall *Earl of Mackworth* • Torin Thatcher *Sir James* • Dan O'Herlihy *Prince Hal* • Rhys Williams *Diccon Bowman* • Ian Keith *King Henry IV* ■ *Dir* Rudolph Maté • *Scr* Oscar Brodney, from the novel *Men of Iron* by Howard Pyle

The Black Sleep ★
Horror thriller   1956 · US · BW · 82min

In order to cure his wife's catalepsy, mad doctor Basil Rathbone performs surgery on innocent victims to unlock the secrets of the brain. His failed lobotomy experiments eventually escape their cellar prison and rebel against him. Aside from the unique spectacle of seeing such horror heavies as Rathbone, Bela Lugosi, Lon Chaney Jr, John Carradine, Tor Johnson and Akim Tamiroff, this is barely watchable. AJ

Basil Rathbone *Sir Joel Cadman* • Akim Tamiroff *Odo* • Lon Chaney Jr *Mungo* • John Carradine *Borg* • Bela Lugosi *Casimir* • Herbert Rudley *Dr Gordon Ramsay* • Patricia Blake *Laurie* • Tor Johnson *Curry* ■ *Dir* Reginald Le Borg • *Scr* John C Higgins

Black Snake Moan ★★★ 15
Melodrama   2006 · US · Colour · 110min

Christina Ricci oozes raw sexuality in this outrageous Deep South melodrama as

small-town nymphomaniac Rae, who's left for dead by the roadside following a wild night. A God-fearing former blues musician (Samuel L Jackson) decides to cure the scantily clad girl of her lasciviousness – by chaining her to his radiator. Evoking the ambience of 1970s exploitation films, writer/director Craig Brewer delivers a questionable yet surprisingly entertaining morality tale about sex, race and the redemptive power of the blues. Juicy dialogue and a sizzling soundtrack add to the guilty pleasure, and there's strong support from Justin Timberlake as Rae's soldier boyfriend. SF Swearing, sexual references. **DVD**

Samuel L Jackson *Lazarus* • Christina Ricci *Rae* • Justin Timberlake *Ronnie* • S Epatha Merkerson *Angela* • John Cothran Jr *Reverend RL* • David Banner *Tehronne* • Michael Raymond-James *Gill* • Adriane Lenox *Rose Woods* ■ *Dir/Scr* Craig Brewer

Black Souls ★★★★ 15
Crime drama   2014 · It/Fr · Colour · 108min

Francesco Munzi's layered, believable look at the reach and consequences of criminality hones in on three siblings: mid-level drug trafficker Marco Leonardi; corrupt money man Peppino Mazzotta; and their elder brother, seemingly pious goat-herd Fabrizio Ferracane. It recalls *Animal Kingdom* in its realistic depiction of a criminal clan in freefall and the restrained, never-less-than-riveting approach allows Munzi to deliver an ending of formidable impact. EAS Italian +subtitles. Violence, swearing, drug abuse, brief nudity.

Marco Leonardi *Luigi* • Peppino Mazzotta *Rocco* • Fabrizio Ferracane *Luciano* • Barbora Bobulova *Valeria* ■ *Dir* Francesco Munzi • *Scr* Francesco Munzi, Maurizio Braucci, Fabrizio Ruggirello, from the novel *Anime Nere* by Gioacchino Criaco

The Black Stallion ★★★★★ U
Adventure   1979 · US · Colour · 112min

This is among the most magical children's films ever made. Making his debut as director, Carroll Ballard blends stunning visuals with a heart-warming story in which a small boy trains the horse he rescued from a shipwreck. The storm and the desert island scenes are breathtaking, and, if the training and racing sequences have all been done before, they have an energy and an eye-catching splendour that more than compensate. Mickey Rooney earned an Oscar nomination as a has-been trainer, but the true stars are 11-year-old Kelly Reno and the horse Cass-ole. DP **DVD**

Mickey Rooney *Henry Dailey* • Kelly Reno *Alec Ramsey* • Teri Garr *Alec's mother* • Clarence Muse *Snoe* • Hoyt Axton *Alec's father* • Michael Higgins *Jim Neville* • Ed Wolff *Arab* • Doghmi Larbi *Arab* ■ *Dir* Carroll Ballard • *Scr* Melissa Mathison, Jeanne Rosenberg, William Witliff, from the novel by Walter Farley • *Executive Producer* Francis Ford Coppola • *Cinematographer* Caleb Deschanel • *Editor* Robert Dalva

The Black Stallion Returns ★★ U
Adventure   1983 · US · Colour · 98min

Having edited Carroll Ballard's original film, Robert Dalva made his directorial debut with this substandard sequel, which is short on both fantasy and charm. Although the action is handsomely photographed by Carlo Di Palma and Caleb Deschanel, too few risks are taken with the storyline, which again sees Kelly Reno and his horse overcome all manner of trials to reunite for a big race. DP **DVD**

Hoyt Axton *Narrator* • Kelly Reno *Alec Ramsay* • Vincent Spano *Raj* • Allen Goorwitz [Allen Garfield] *Kurr* • Woody Strode *Meslar* • Ferdy Mayne *Abu Ben Ishak* • Jodi Thelen *Tabari* • Teri Garr *Alec's mother* ■ *Dir* Robert Dalva • *Scr* Richard Kletter, Jerome Kass, from the novel by Walter Farley • *Executive Producer* Francis Ford Coppola

Black Sunday ★★★★ 15
Crime thriller   1976 · US · Colour · 137min

John Frankenheimer is on top form with this thriller based on the novel by Thomas

Harris, author of *The Silence of the Lambs*, about terrorists planning to cause mayhem at a Super Bowl football game. Maniacs on both sides of the law (Robert Shaw and Bruce Dern) explain their motives, but it's the violent action that makes the film so fraught and yet so exciting. The clash between police helicopters and a hijacked blimp is the highlight of the outstanding set pieces. TH Swearing, violence.

Robert Shaw *Major Kabakov* • Bruce Dern *Michael Lander* • Marthe Keller *Dahlia Iyad* • Fritz Weaver *Corley* • Steven Keats *Robert Moshevsky* • Bekim Fehmiu *Fasil* • Michael V Gazzo *Muzi* • William Daniels (2) *Pugh* • Tom McFadden *Farley* ■ *Dir* John Frankenheimer • *Scr* Ernest Lehman, Kenneth Ross, Ivan Moffat, from the novel by Thomas Harris

The Black Swan ★★★★ PG
Swashbuckling adventure
1942 · US · Colour · 81min

The kind of movie they used to make before they stopped making them like that any more, this is a rip-roaring tale of swashbuckling, buccaneering and damsel-wooing, starring Tyrone Power. Power plays a reformed sea wolf, whose former partner in piracy (Laird Cregar) is made governor of Jamaica. They join forces to rid the neighbourhood of assorted rogues and one-eyed knaves. Much swordplay – plus intermittent courtship of Maureen O'Hara by Power – ensues, all captured by Oscar-winning colour cinematography. Vintage stuff. PF **DVD**

Tyrone Power *James Waring* • Maureen O'Hara *Margaret Denby* • Laird Cregar *Captain Henry Morgan* • Thomas Mitchell *Tommy Blue* • George Sanders *Captain Billy Leech* • Anthony Quinn *Wogan* • George Zucco *Lord Denby* • Edward Ashley *Roger Ingram* ■ *Dir* Henry King • *Scr* Ben Hecht, Seton I Miller, from the novel by Rafael Sabatini • *Cinematographer* Leon Shamroy

Black Swan ★★★★ 15
Psychological thriller
2010 · US · Colour · 103min

Darren Aronofsky's dark, hypnotic study of obsession is set in the punishing world of ballet, where serious hard graft doesn't always guarantee results and stardom is perhaps at its most fleeting. Natalie Portman plays Nina, an aspiring lead with a New York dance company, who's determined to win the coveted role of the Swan Queen in an upcoming production of *Swan Lake*. However, the ballet's director (Vincent Cassel) is sceptical. The arrival of the talented and rebellious Lily (Mila Kunis) raises the stakes, and as Nina wrestles with her demons, the film hurtles towards an exhilarating and disturbing climax. Logic and originality are sometimes lacking, but Aronofsky's bravura direction and Portman's sincere, mesmerising performance paper over those particular cracks. BW Violence, swearing, sex scenes. **DVD**

Natalie Portman *Nina Sayers/The Swan Queen* • Vincent Cassel *Thomas Leroy/The Gentleman* • Mila Kunis *Lily/The Black Swan* • Barbara Hershey *Erica Sayers/The Queen* • Winona Ryder *Beth MacIntyre/The Dying Swan* • Benjamin Millepied *David/The Prince* ■ *Dir* Darren Aronofsky • *Scr* Mark Heyman, John McLaughlin [John J McLaughlin], Andrés Heinz [Andres Heinz], from a story by Heinz

The Black Tent ★★ PG
Second World War drama
1956 · UK · Colour · 88min

Brian Desmond Hurst directs this contrived drama in which wounded officer Anthony Steel joins Bedouin sheikh André Morell to confound the Nazis. The romance with Anna-Maria Sandri sits awkwardly alongside the action, while Donald Sinden's clipped bravado as Steel's brother occasionally borders on the comic. The script by Robin Maugham and Bryan Forbes is undistinguished. DP **DVD**

Anthony Steel *David Holland* • Donald Sinden *Charles Holland* • Anna-Maria Sandri *Mabrouka* • André Morell *Sheikh Salem* • Ralph Truman *Croft* • Donald Pleasence *Ali* • Anthony Bushell *Baring* • Michael Craig *Faris* • Anton Diffring *German*

officer • Frederick Jaeger *German officer* ■ *Dir* Brian Desmond Hurst • *Scr* Robin Maugham, Bryan Forbes

The Black Torment ★★ 12
Gothic horror   1964 · UK · Colour · 82min

This barnstorming period horror is no longer the marrow-chiller it once was. Nevertheless, it has a literate script and still delivers some mild shocks as it wheels out a time-honoured tale of suicide, gloomy castles, ghosts and mad relatives locked in the attic. It's directed by Robert Hartford-Davis, an unsung hero of British horror, and actors John Turner and Heather Sears work miracles in making this gothic melodrama believable. AJ **DVD** **BL**

John Turner *Sir Richard Fordyke* • Heather Sears *Lady Elizabeth* • Ann Lynn *Diane* • Peter Arne *Seymour* • Raymond Huntley *Colonel Wentworth* • Annette Whiteley *Mary* • Norman Bird *Harris* • Roger Croucher *Apprentice* • Joseph Tomelty *Sir Giles* • Patrick Troughton *Ostler* • Edina Ronay *Lucy Judd* ■ *Dir* Robert Hartford-Davis • *Scr* Donald Ford, Derek Ford

The Black Tulip ★★
Historical adventure   1963 · Fr · Colour · 110min

French superstar Alain Delon stars in this Alexandre Dumas tale about the exploits of *La Tulipe Noire*, a sort of Robin Hood figure of 18th-century France. He also has a twin brother, so it's as much a dual role as a duelling one. Virna Lisi makes a glamorous heroine, and Akim Tamiroff hams away as the local big *fromage*. It's slackly directed by Christian-Jaque, who shows none of the style that won him the best director award at Cannes for the swashbuckler *Fanfan la Tulipe*. AT French dubbed.

Alain Delon *Guillaume de Saint-Preux/Julien de Saint-Preux* • Virna Lisi *Caroline* • Dawn Addams *Marquise de Vigogne* • Francis Blanche *Plantin* • Akim Tamiroff *Marquis de Vigogne* • Robert Manuel *Prince Alexander de Grassilach* ■ *Dir* Christian-Jaque • *Scr* Henri Jeanson, from the novel *La Tulipe Noire* by Alexandre Dumas

A Black Veil for Lisa ★
Crime thriller   1969 · It/W Ger · Colour · 87min

One of John Mills's lowest career points, this is a Euro-pudding cop thriller that dredges up every cliché of the British B-movie, relocates them to Hamburg and adds some nudity and violence. Mills is a detective more concerned with the infidelities of his wife (Luciana Paluzzi) than solving the various high-profile drug trafficking cases on his desk. AT Some dialogue dubbed.

John Mills *Bulon* • Luciana Paluzzi *Lisa* • Robert Hoffmann *Max* • Renata Kasche *Marianne* • Tullio Altamura *Ostermeyer* • Carlo Hintermann *Mansfeld* • Enzo Fiermonte *Siegert* • Loris Bazzocchi *Kruger* ■ *Dir* Massimo Dallamano • *Scr* Giuseppe Belli, Vittoriano Petrilli, Massimo Dallamano, Audrey Nohra, from a story by Belli

Black Water ★★★ 15
Horror thriller   2007 · Aus/UK · Colour · 85min

Mining the same territory as *Open Water* and *Adrift*, co-directors Andrew Traucki and David Nerlich's nature-takes-revenge saga is an economical nail-biter. Set in Australia's Northern Territory and inspired by a true story, this has three tourists coming under attack from a saltwater crocodile when their boat capsizes in a mangrove swamp. The would-be victims find temporary safety up a tree, but as the hours slip by with no sign of a rescue, they must take decisive action to escape the predator relentlessly stalking them. It's small scale, but the tension generated by the film's simple premise pays dividends, while stylish visuals make the sudden jolts all the more startling and effective. AJ **DVD**

Maeve Dermody *Lee* • Diana Glenn *Grace* • Andy Rodoreda *Adam* • Ben Oxenbould *Jim* • Fiona Press *Pat* ■ *Dir/Scr* David Nerlich, Andrew Traucki

Black Widow ★★
Murder mystery   1954 · US · Colour · 94min

A starry cast, a decent build-up of tension and a surprise dénouement overcome a slow start and a superficial screenplay in this moderately enjoyable murder mystery. Van Heflin is the producer suspected of killing a young Broadway hopeful, and Ginger Rogers his poisonous leading lady; the glamorous Gene Tierney plays another stage star, while George Raft is the purposeful investigating detective. RK

Ginger Rogers *Lottie* • Van Heflin *Peter* • Gene Tierney *Iris* • George Raft *Detective Bruce* • Peggy Ann Garner *Nancy Ordway* • Reginald Gardiner *Brian* • Virginia Leith *Claire Amberly* • Otto Kruger *Ling* ■ *Dir* Nunnally Johnson • *Scr* Nunnally Johnson, from the novel by Patrick Quentin [Hugh Wheeler]

Black Widow ★★★ 15
Thriller 1987 · US · Colour · 97min

It's not quite in the same league as his dense psychological dramas from the early 1970s, but this intriguing thriller marked a return to form for Bob Rafelson. Theresa Russell is the black widow of the title, who specialises in bumping off wealthy millionaires, among them Dennis Hopper and Nicol Williamson. Debra Winger is the uptight FBI agent who sets out to bring her to justice. The cat-and-mouse games played by Winger and Russell crackle with tension and there is a lovely twist. JF Violence, swearing, nudity. *DVD* *BL*

Debra Winger *Alexandra Barnes* • Theresa Russell *Catharine* • Sami Frey *Paul Nuytten* • Dennis Hopper *Ben Dumers* • Nicol Williamson *William Macauley* • Terry O'Quinn *Bruce* • James Hong *Shin* • Diane Ladd *Etta* ■ *Dir* Bob Rafelson • *Scr* Ronald Bass

Black Widow ★★
Mystery thriller 2007 · US · Colour · 89min

The bland and unconvincing scripting of this thriller does a hackneyed storyline no favours, as an LA photojournalist (Alicia Coppola) immediately suspects her best pal's beautiful new girlfriend (Elizabeth Berkley) of nefarious deeds. Gut instinct provides the lame explanation for this obsessive distrust, prompting a repetitive, secret investigation that allows all the genre's stylistic and narrative clichés to be trotted out. Director Armand Mastroianni injects a modicum of tension, but generally falls down by relying on score for atmosphere. SF

Elizabeth Berkley *Olivia* • Alicia Coppola *Mel* • Brady Smith *Lucas* • Jeremy Howard *Henry* ■ *Dir* Armand Mastroianni • *Scr* Riley Weston, from a story by Jeremy Bernstein, Weston

Black Widow Murders ★★★
Crime drama based on a true story
1993 · US · Colour · 92min

Elizabeth Montgomery gives a convincing performance in this TV crime drama as a North Carolina widow respected in the community, who hides the secrets of childhood abuse and her resultant anger against all men, until two of her suitors die in similar ways. Tautly directed, this is a gripping story made all the more so by Montgomery's portrayal and the truth of the tale. JB

Elizabeth Montgomery *Blanche Taylor Moore* • David Clennon *Reverend Dwight Moore* • John M Jackson *Raymond Reid* • Grace Zabriskie *Ethel* • Bruce McGill *Morgan* • Mark Rolston *O'Keefe* • Guy Boyd *Kevin Denton* ■ *Dir* Alan Metzger • *Scr* Judith Paige Mitchell, from the book *Preacher's Girl* by Jim Schutze

The Black Windmill ★★ 12
Spy thriller 1974 · UK · Colour · 101min

A disappointing thriller from *Dirty Harry* director Don Siegel, this stars Michael Caine as an agent whose son is kidnapped by a mysterious military organisation, which demands diamonds in return for his release. The plot is over-thickened with cat-and-mouse sequences and Siegel's acclaimed naturalistic style is intrusive here, but the performances are fine. DP Swearing. *DVD*

Michael Caine *Major John Tarrant* • Donald Pleasence *Cedric Harper* • John Vernon *McKee* • Janet Suzman *Alex Tarrant* • Delphine Seyrig *Ceil Burrows* • Joss Ackland *Chief Superintendent Wray* • Joseph O'Conor *Sir Edward Julyan* • Clive Revill *Alf Chesterman* ■ *Dir* Don Siegel • *Scr* Leigh Vance, from the novel *Seven Days to a Killing* by Clive Egleton

Black Zoo ★★★
Horror 1963 · US · Colour · 88min

Michael Gough stars in this gleefully eccentric, but decidedly macabre chiller. Throwing restraint to the winds, Gough indulges himself as the owner of a private zoo whose obsession with big cats has brought nothing but misery to his wife, Jeanne Cooper, and his mute son, Rod Lauren. The sequence in which Gough plays the organ for his brood encapsulates the picture's camp tone, but there are moments of genuine unease as the furtive animal-worshipping cultist disposes of those opposed to his twisted schemes. DP

Michael Gough *Michael Conrad* • Jeanne Cooper *Edna Conrad* • Rod Lauren *Carl* • Virginia Grey *Jenny* • Jerome Cowan *Jeffrey Stengle* • Elisha Cook Jr *Joe* ■ *Dir* Robert Gordon • *Scr* Herman Cohen, Aben Kandel

Blackball ★ 15
Comedy 2003 · UK · Colour · 92min

This charmless comedy is rooted in the same kind of so-called humour that one hoped had died out in the 1970s with the likes of *On the Buses*. Paul Kaye plays an obnoxious bad boy of bowls who's blackballed by his stuffy club, then reluctantly re-instated to take on the visiting Aussie champions. Despite a likeable cast, the laughs are way off-target. DA *DVD*

Paul Kaye *Cliff Starkey* • James Cromwell *Ray Speight* • Alice Evans *Kerry Speight* • Bernard Cribbins *Mutley* • Johnny Vegas *Trevor* • Vince Vaughn *Rick Schwartz* • Imelda Staunton *Bridget* • James Fleet *Alan the Pipe* • David Ryall *Giles Wilton* • Ian McNeice *Hugh the Sideburns* • Kenneth Cranham *Chairman Collins* ■ *Dir* Mel Smith • *Scr* Tim Firth

Blackbeard the Pirate ★★ PG
Swashbuckling adventure
1952 · US · Colour · 98min

RKO producer Val Lewton had, at one time, planned this swashbuckler as a vehicle for Boris Karloff, and, in view of the outlandish performance by Robert Newton, one can only lament the fact that he didn't take the starring role. Newton throws in every cliché ever used by a pantomime pirate and occasionally comes close to making this almost unwatchable. Fortunately, director Raoul Walsh's sure handling of the action sequences and a good supporting cast keep the thing afloat. DP *DVD*

Robert Newton *Blackbeard* • Linda Darnell *Edwina* • William Bendix *Worley* • Keith Andes *Maynard* • Torin Thatcher *Sir Henry Morgan* • Irene Ryan *Alvina* • Alan Mowbray *Noll* ■ *Dir* Raoul Walsh • *Scr* Alan LeMay, from a story by DeVallon Scott

Blackbeard's Ghost ★★★ U
Comedy 1967 · US · Colour · 102min

This Disney caper is overlong and short on inspiration, but it does have a lively lead in the incomparable Peter Ustinov as the buccaneer condemned to wander in limbo until he performs a good deed. Poaching the picture from him, however, is Elsa Lanchester, as one of the old dears he must save from gambling gangsters. It's corny and over the top, but entertaining nonetheless. DP *DVD*

Peter Ustinov *Captain Blackbeard* • Dean Jones *Steve Walker* • Suzanne Pleshette *Jo Anne Baker* • Elsa Lanchester *Emily Stowecroft* • Joby Baker *Silky Seymour* • Elliott Reid *TV commentator* • Richard Deacon *Dean Wheaton* • Norman Grabowski *Virgil* ■ *Dir* Robert Stevenson • *Scr* Bill Walsh, Don DaGradi, from the novel by Ben Stahl

The Blackboard Jungle ★★★ 12
Drama 1955 · US · BW · 96min

This teenage angst picture, following hot on the heels of James Dean's *Rebel without a Cause*, has Glenn Ford as the gauche schoolteacher who wonders why his class beat him up and "don't wanna loin nuthin'". Anne Francis offers him a shoulder to cry on, while American parents everywhere sobbed in sympathy. Director Richard Brooks's film rams home his message

without much subtlety. It has a footnote in history for introducing rock music to mainstream cinema, courtesy of Bill Haley's *Rock around the Clock*, which is played over the credit titles. AT

Glenn Ford *Richard Dadier* • Anne Francis *Anne Dadier* • Louis Calhern *Jim Murdock* • Margaret Hayes *Lois Judby Hammond* • John Hoyt *Mr Warneke* • Richard Kiley *Joshua Y Edwards* • Emile Meyer *Mr Halloran* • Warner Anderson *Dr Bradley* ■ *Dir* Richard Brooks • *Scr* Richard Brooks, from the novel by Evan Hunter • *Cinematographer* Russell Harlan

Blackboards ★★★★ PG
Political drama
2000 · Iran/It/Jpn · Colour · 81min

In stark contrast to the easy urban charm of *The Apple*, Samira Makhmalbaf's second feature is a bleakly neorealistic account of life in Iran's hostile borderlands. Examining the value of education to the dispossessed Kurds whose sole concern is survival, it boldly blends hard-hitting drama with comic diversion and towering vistas with moments of acute intimacy. Said Mohamadi and Bahman Ghobadi admirably convey a sense of dignity and desperation as the peripatetic teachers touting for work. This is both courageous and compelling. DP Kurdish +subtitles. *DVD*

Said Mohamadi *Said, teacher* • Behnaz Jafari *Halaleh, young woman* • Bahman Ghobadi *Reeboir, teacher* • Mohamad Karim Rahmati *Father* • Rafat Moradi *Ribvar* ■ *Dir* Samira Makhmalbaf • *Scr* Samira Makhmalbaf, Mohsen Makhmalbaf

Blackfish ★★★★ 15
Documentary 2013 · US · Colour · 82min

Director Gabriela Cowperthwaite's second feature goes into marine parks to look at the effect of life there on its inhabitants. The main focus is on Tilikum, the orca that has killed three people since 1991. Cowperthwaite presents cogent evidence from behavioural experts and ex-trainers to reveal the psychological damage that captivity can cause these clever, sociable creatures who never attack humans in the wild. Some of the archive footage is harrowing, and few will be able to watch this without a growing sense of outrage. DP *DVD* *BL*

■ *Dir* Gabriela Cowperthwaite • *Scr* Gabriela Cowperthwaite, Eli B Despres

Blackhat ★★ 15
Action crime drama 2015 · US · Colour · 127min

This tale of international cyber-espionage from magisterial action director Michael Mann sees the US and China forced to co-operate when they experience related cyber-attacks. The original architect of the offending malware - a hacker played by Chris Hemsworth - is sprung from jail to assist the investigation, but early attempts to render the subject matter cinematic bode ill, as sparking circuit boards and glowing cables prove less than thrilling. Punchy, enlivening action is dotted throughout, lest the audience forget who's at the helm when faced with reams of spirit-sapping computer code, but *Blackhat* is an inconsistent, ill-conceived affair that rarely, if ever, rings true. EAS In English, Spanish. *DVD* *BL*

Chris Hemsworth *Nicholas Hathaway* • Tang Wei *Chen Lien* • Viola Davis *Carol Barrett* ■ *Dir* Michael Mann • *Scr* Morgan Davis Foehl, Michael Mann

Blackmail ★★★ PG
Thriller 1929 · UK · BW · 81min

Alfred Hitchcock's first talking picture was also the earliest in which he used a famous landmark to stage the finale. The visuals are eerily expressionistic, the trick photography in the British Museum sequence is first class and the recurrence of the word "knife" on the soundtrack is amusingly ghoulish. But the restrictions placed on film-makers by primitive sound recording techniques render the action and the acting fatally stilted. There is a predominantly silent version of this film, which is infinitely better. DP

Anny Ondra *Alice White* • John Longden *Frank Webber* • Donald Calthrop *Tracy* • Sara Allgood *Mrs White* • Charles Paton *Mr White* • Cyril Ritchard *Artist* • Harvey Braban *Inspector* • Phyllis Monkman *Gossip* • Hannah Jones *Landlady* ■ *Dir* Alfred Hitchcock • *Scr* Alfred Hitchcock, Benn W Levy, Charles Bennett, Michael Powell (uncredited), from the play *Blackmail* by Charles Bennett • *Cinematographer* Jack Cox

Blackmail ★★★
Prison drama 1939 · US · BW · 80min

Edward G Robinson fights fires on Oklahoma's oil fields but serves time on a chain-gang for a crime he did not commit, and is then blackmailed by Gene Lockhart. MGM was trying to splice two genres here - the social drama, such as *I Am a Fugitive from a Chain Gang*, and the sexy melodrama. It works, sort of, mainly due to the powerful performances of Robinson and Lockhart, as well as some well-handled scenes of burned-out oil-rigs and burned-out convicts. AT

Edward G Robinson *John R Ingram* • Ruth Hussey *Helen Ingram* • Gene Lockhart *William Ramey* • Bobs Watson *Hank Ingram* • Guinn Williams [Guinn "Big Boy" Williams] *Moose McCarthy* • John Wray *Diggs* • Arthur Hohl *Rawlins* • Esther Dale *Sarah* • Charles Middleton *First deputy* ■ *Dir* HC Potter • *Scr* David Hertz, William Ludwig, Brown Holmes, Nathalie Buchnall, from a story by Endre Bohem, Dorothy Yost

Blackout ★★
Thriller 1950 · UK · BW · 73min

Directed by Robert S Baker, this is a fanciful project, about a blind man (Maxwell Reed) who recovers his sight in time to tackle a counterfeiting ring led by supposed air-crash victim Kynaston Reeves. Written by future horror director John Gilling, this is a by-the-numbers thriller, although the photography is atmospheric. DP

Maxwell Reed *Chris Pelley* • Dinah Sheridan *Patricia Dale* • Eric Pohlmann *Otto* • Patric Doonan *Chalky* • Michael Brennan *Mickey* • Michael Evans (1) *Sinclair* • Annette Simmonds *Lila Drew* • Campbell Singer *Inspector* ■ *Dir* Robert S Baker • *Scr* Robert S Baker, John Gilling • *Cinematographer* Monty Berman

The Blackout ★★ 18
Thriller 1997 · US/Fr · Colour · 94min

Abel Ferrara uses a rather blunt scalpel to expose the living hell of Hollywood stardom in another of his typically unrestrained rants. Matty (played with autobiographical candour by Matthew Modine) is a high-living movie celebrity who can't curtail his booze and drug lifestyle despite increasing blackouts. Did he commit murder during one such bout of unconsciousness? AJ Swearing, violence, drug abuse, sex scenes. *DVD*

Matthew Modine *Matty* • Claudia Schiffer *Susan* • Béatrice Dalle *Annie 1* • Sarah Lassez *Annie 2* • Dennis Hopper *Mickey Wayne* • Steven Bauer *Mickey's studio actor* ■ *Dir* Abel Ferrara • *Scr* Abel Ferrara, Marla Hanson, Christ Zois

Blackrock ★★★
Drama 1997 · Aus · Colour · 100min

Based on a true event, this compulsive Aussie drama deals with various personal and social issues, although there's an element of exploitation alongside the high-mindedness. Young Laurence Breuls throws a party for his surfing pal Simon Lyndon. Matters get desperately out of hand when several of the boys drunkenly rape a teenage girl, who is found dead the following day. Stargazers should watch out for Heath Ledger in a small part. BB

Laurence Breuls *Jared Kirby* • Linda Cropper *Diane Kirby* • Simon Lyndon *Ricko* • Chris Haywood *Det Sgt Wilansky* • Rebecca Smart *Cherie* • Essie Davis *Det Gilhooley* • Heath Ledger *Toby* ■ *Dir* Steven Vidler • *Scr* Nick Enright

Blackthorn ★★★ 15
Western 2011 · Sp/US/Bol/Ind · Colour · 97min

Blackthorn is a thoroughly decent western that takes up where *Butch Cassidy and the Sundance Kid* left off. Actor/playwright Sam Shepard is a grizzled, bewhiskered Butch, who somehow escaped the Bolivian shoot-out in which he was reportedly killed. Twenty years later, he goes by the name of James Blackthorn and is living quietly on a remote Bolivian ranch. But he has to take up his guns again when he crosses paths with a Sundance-style kid (Eduardo Noriega). With westerns rarer than hen's teeth, and decent westerns even rarer, this is certainly one that genre fans should seek out. DA English, Spanish +subtitles. Violence, swearing. *DVD* *BL*

Sam Shepard *James Blackthorn* • Eduardo Noriega *Eduardo Apodaca* • Stephen Rea *Mackinley* • Magaly Solier *Yana* • Nikolaj Coster-Waldau *Young James* • Padraic Delaney *Sundance* ■ *Dir* Mateo Gil • *Scr* Miguel Barros

Blackwood ★★★ 15
Thriller 2013 · UK · Colour · 86min

This haunted house story blends the spectral and the psychological with some success. Ed Stoppard stars as a mentally fragile college professor who relocates with wife Sophia Myles and their son to the isolated country house of the title. Soon, traditionally spooky stuff starts happening. But are these events real, or merely the products of Stoppard's increasingly unsettled mind? Director Adam Wimpenny never quite digs the film out of the hole that some early complexity drops it into, but there are decent performances, a suitably creepy atmosphere and genuinely scary moments. DA Violence. *DVD*

Ed Stoppard *Ben Marshall* • Sophia Myles *Rachel Marshall* • Russell Tovey *Jack Otterley* • Paul Kaye *Father Patrick* • Joanna Vanderham *Jessica* • Greg Wise *Dominic* ■ *Dir* Adam Wimpenny • *Scr* JS Hill

Blacula ★★★ 15
Blaxploitation horror 1972 · US · Colour · 89min

This is one of the better novelty blaxploitation horror romps, despite its eventual turn toward predictable genre conventions in the last half. Noted Shakespearean actor William Marshall stars as an African prince turned into a vampire by Count Dracula, who arrives in contemporary Los Angeles and starts cleaning up the ghetto by putting the bite on drug dealers, pimps and homosexuals. The tongue-in-cheek humour makes this undemanding fun. AJ Swearing. *DVD* *BL*

William Marshall *Blacula* • Vonetta McGee *Tina* • Denise Nicholas *Michelle* • Thalmus Rasulala *Gordon Thomas* • Gordon Pinsent *Lieutenant Peters* • Charles McCauley *Dracula* • Emily Yancy *Nancy* ■ *Dir* William Crain • *Scr* Joan Torres, Raymond Koenig

Blade ★★★ 18
Fantasy action adventure 1998 · US · Colour · 115min

Wesley Snipes plays the half-mortal, half-vampire who hunts down creatures of the night in this flashy action adventure based on the popular comic. Aided by gruff-and-tough Kris Kristofferson, he sets out to thwart the evil schemes of fellow vampire Stephen Dorff, whose plans include running a nightclub that will supply humans for his fiendish pals to feed on. This is far-fetched stuff indeed, but Snipes looks great in leather, it's snappily paced and the performances are perfectly tongue in cheek. JB Swearing, violence. *DVD*

Wesley Snipes *Blade* • Stephen Dorff *Deacon Frost* • Kris Kristofferson *Whistler* • Kevin Patrick Walls *Krieger* • N'Bushe Wright *Karen* • Donal Logue *Quinn* • Arly Jover *Mercury* • Udo Kier *Dragonetti* • Traci Lords *Raquel* ■ *Dir* Stephen Norrington • *Scr* David S Goyer, from characters created for Marvel Comics by Marv Wolfman, Gene Colan

Blade II ★★★ 18
Fantasy action adventure 2002 · US/Ger · Colour · 112min

Mexican genre maestro Guillermo del Toro directs this episode in the Daywalker chronicles, based on the character from cult Marvel comic *Tomb of Dracula*. Pitching the moody half-vampire/half-human Blade (Wesley Snipes) as a sort of nocturnal James Bond with gadgets and gimmicks galore, the film's unrelenting action never

flags. This time Blade reluctantly joins forces with vampire overlord Damaskinos (Thomas Kretschmann) to wipe out a new breed of super-vampires. It looks fabulous, but has zero character substance and isn't remotely scary. AJ *DVD* *BL*

Wesley Snipes *Blade* • Kris Kristofferson *Whistler* • Ron Perlman *Reinhardt* • Leonor Varela *Nyssa* • Norman Reedus *Scud* • Thomas Kretschmann *Damaskinos* • Luke Goss *Nomak* ■ *Dir* Guillermo del Toro • *Scr* David S Goyer, from the character created by Marv Wolfman, Gene Colan

Blade: Trinity ★ 15
Fantasy action adventure 2004 · US · Colour · 108min

Franchise fatigue shows in all areas of this third Blade outing, directed by series writer David S Goyer. The plot is an incoherent mess, with Wesley Snipes's half-vampire vigilante teaming up with Ryan Reynolds and Jessica Biel to take on a vampire leader Parker Posey. Compared to the previous instalments, the horror is negligible and the action scenes tepid and repetitive. AJ Violence, swearing. *DVD* *BL*

Wesley Snipes *Blade* • Kris Kristofferson *Abraham Whistler* • Jessica Biel *Abigail Whistler* • Ryan Reynolds *Hannibal King* • Parker Posey *Danica Talos* • Dominic Purcell *Dracula/"Drake"* • Triple H [Paul Michael Levesque] *Jarko Grimwood* • Natasha Lyonne *Sommerfield* ■ *Dir* David S Goyer • *Scr* David S Goyer, from characters by Marv Wolfman, Gene Colan

LANDMARK FILM
A major departure from prevailing futuristic visions of squeaky-clean, hermetic societies and post-apocalyptic wastelands

Blade Runner ★★★★★ 15
Futuristic science-fiction thriller 1982 · US · Colour · 111min

A super Philip K Dick story, about superdick Harrison Ford battling rebellious replicants, translates here into a violent eye-popper, based in a futuristic American Chinatown, which set the acid rain/neon-drenched metropolis design standard for 1980s sci-fi. As influential as *2001: a Space Odyssey* and *Star Wars*, and as thought provoking as the Kubrick classic, Ridley Scott's atmospheric downer is a compelling *noir* thriller pleading for harmony between man and machine. Rutger Hauer is exceptional as the blond humanoid who, like the others, has been implanted with memories of a nonexistent youth. The Director's Cut, which drops Ford's voiceover, adds depth, allowing the full masterpiece to shine through. Scott also produced a Final Cut in 2007, over which he had complete artistic control. AJ Violence, swearing, brief nudity. *DVD* *BL*

Harrison Ford *Rick Deckard* • Rutger Hauer *Roy Batty* • Sean Young *Rachael* • Edward James Olmos *Gaff* • M Emmet Walsh *Bryant* • Daryl Hannah *Pris* • William Sanderson *Sebastian* • Brion James *Leon* ■ *Dir* Ridley Scott • *Scr* Hampton Fancher, David Peoples, from the novel *Do Androids Dream of Electric Sheep?* by Philip K Dick • *Cinematographer* Jordan Cronenweth • *Music* Vangelis • *Production Design* Lawrence G Paull • *Special Effects* Douglas Trumbull

Blade Runner 2
Futuristic science-fiction thriller 2017 · US · Colour ·

This is a preview - no prints were available to review prior to publication: Thirty years or so after the original, it looks like we're finally going to get a sequel to the groundbreaking sci-fi drama. Harrison Ford looks certain to return as replicant (or was he?) Deckard, with Ryan Gosling also in the cast. But no Ridley Scott on directing duties. That job has gone to Denis Villeneuve. Plot details are well under wraps, of course, with Scott saying it "relates well to the first one". And with so many versions of the first one, that leaves a lot of scope. TP

Harrison Ford *Rick Deckard* • Ryan Gosling • Robin Wright ■ *Dir* Denis Villeneuve • *Scr* Hampton Fancher, Michael Green, from a story by Fancher, Ridley Scott, inspired by Philip K Dick's novel *Do Androids Dream of Electric Sheep?* • *Cinematographer* Roger Deakins

Blades of Glory ★★★ 12
Sports comedy 2007 · US · Colour · 89min

After *Elf*, *Anchorman* and *Talladega Nights*, ungainly *Saturday Night Live* alumnus Will Ferrell further proves his versatility in this enjoyable if trite sports movie spoof. Ferrell plays a sex-addicted, skating bad boy who, along with his effeminate nemesis (*Napoleon Dynamite*'s goofy Jon Heder) is banned from the sport after an unseemly brawl. It's a technical triumph, as real-life skating action is mixed with some spectacular effects-based moves, but Ferrell and Heder provide funky physical comedy in close-up, too. There's also fine support from Amy Poehler and *Arrested Development*'s Will Arnett as their camp opponents. AC Some violence, sexual references. *DVD* *BL* *CS*

Will Ferrell *Chazz Michael Michaels* • Jon Heder *Jimmy MacElroy* • Will Arnett *Stranz Van Waldenberg* • Amy Poehler *Fairchild Van Waldenberg* • Craig T Nelson *Coach* • Jenna Fischer *Katie Van Waldenberg* • William Fichtner *Darren MacElroy* • Romany Malco *Jesse* ■ *Dir* Will Speck, Josh Gordon • *Scr* John Altschuler, Craig and Jeff Cox, Dave Krinsky, from a story by Craig and Jeff Cox, Busy Philipps

LANDMARK FILM
A landmark film for the quality of its marketing, rather than of its making

The Blair Witch Project ★★★★ 15
Supernatural horror 1998 · US · Colour and BW · 77min

Made on a shoestring ($35,000), this no-frills, no-stars, no-effects horror yarn was released amid expectations that might have been hard to live up to had the film not been so different and so simple. Through arch use of the internet and word-of-mouth, it became a box-office sensation. A campfire ghost story in which three students go into the Maryland woods to film their own search for a mythical monster, the film's rough, video-diary edge and shaky point-of-view camerawork - while demanding on the eye - take the viewer right into the unfolding story. Scary without being explicit, it is a 1990s cinematic landmark, and best judged away from the hype. A disgraceful sequel, *Book of Shadows: Blair Witch 2*, followed in 2000. AC Swearing. *DVD* *BL*

Heather Donahue *Michael* • Michael Williams • Joshua Leonard • Bob Griffith *Interviewee* • Jim King *Interviewee* • Sandra Sanchez *Interviewee* • Ed Swanson *Interviewee* ■ *Dir* Daniel Myrick, Eduardo Sanchez • *Scr* Eduardo Sanchez, Daniel Myrick

Blame ★★
Horror 2006 · Sp · Colour · 72min

In this ineffectual Spanish chiller, financially strapped nurse Gloria (Montse Mostaza) and her daughter move into the house of a gynaecologist (Nieve de Medina) in return for Gloria becoming her assistant. But events turn sinister when it transpires that the private practice is actually an abortion clinic. Although made for the *Films to Keep You Awake* TV series, the feature fails to live up to its initial promise. The narrative is underdeveloped and overstretched, while the ending is truly preposterous. SF Spanish +subtitles.

Nieve de Medina *Ana* • Montse Mostaza *Gloria* • Alejandra Lorenzo *Vicky* • Mariana Cordero *Teresa* • Asunción Díaz *Consuelo* ■ *Dir* Narciso Ibáñez Serrador • *Scr* Luis Peñafiel [Narciso Ibáñez Serrador], from a story by Luis Murillo • *Cinematographer* José Luis Alcaine

Blame It on Fidel ★★★ 12
Period drama 2006 · It/Fr · Colour · 94min

Early 1970s radicalism is seen through the eyes of a nine-year-old Parisian girl in this charming and perceptive coming-of-age tale from documentary director Julie Gavras (daughter of political film-maker Costa-Gavras). Her assured feature debut is carried by newcomer Nina Kervel-Bey's delightful performance as the pouting youngster whose bourgeois life is snatched away when her parents abruptly become left-wing activists. Gavras applies a skilfully

light touch to increasingly serious issues and the child-level camera provides some of the most impactful moments. SF French +subtitles. *DVD*

Nina Kervel [Nina Kervel-Bey] *Anna de la Mesa* • Julie Depardieu *Marie de la Mesa* • Stefano Accorsi *Fernando de la Mesa* • Benjamin Feuillet *François de la Mesa* ■ *Dir* Julie Gavras, from the novel *Tutta Colpa di Fidel* by Domitilla Calamai

Blame It on Rio ★★ 15
Comedy 1984 · US · Colour · 95min

Michael Caine and Joseph Bologna may give decent enough performances as best friends on a spree in Rio, but the romance that develops between Caine and Bologna's teenage daughter (Michelle Johnson) is just too leery for comfort. The holiday atmosphere is well evoked, but the bad taste from director Stanley Donen is an unpleasant surprise. TH Swearing, nudity. *DVD* *BL*

Michael Caine *Matthew Hollis* • Joseph Bologna *Victor Lyons* • Valerie Harper *Karen Hollis* • Michelle Johnson *Jennifer Lyons* • Demi Moore *Nicole Hollis* • José Lewgoy *Eduardo Marques* • Lupe Gigliotti *Signora Botega* • Michael Menaugh *Peter* ■ *Dir* Stanley Donen • *Scr* Charlie Peters, Larry Gelbart, from the film *Un Moment d'Egarement* by Claude Berri

Blame It on the Bellboy ★★★ 12
Comedy 1992 · UK · Colour · 75min

A bellboy (Bronson Pinchot in a wonderfully farcical turn) is responsible for a series of mistaken identity mix-ups at a Venice hotel in this daft but fun slapstick-style comedy. Dudley Moore, Bryan Brown and Patsy Kensit are among the people getting confused in an intermittently hilarious tale that which owes much of its charm to the supporting performances from Richard Griffiths, Penelope Wilton and the always reliable Alison Steadman. JB Swearing. *DVD*

Dudley Moore *Melvyn Orton* • Bryan Brown *Charlton Black/Mike Lawton* • Richard Griffiths *Maurice Horton* • Patsy Kensit *Caroline Wright* • Andreas Katsulas *Scarpa* • Alison Steadman *Rosemary Horton* • Penelope Wilton *Patricia Fulford* • Bronson Pinchot *Bellboy* • Jim Carter *Rossi* ■ *Dir/Scr* Mark Herman

Blame It on the Night ★★ PG
Drama 1984 · US · Colour · 84min

Of most note since the screenplay is based on an original story by director Gene Taft and rock legend Mick Jagger, this shoddy, misbegotten family drama also showcases rock stars Billy Preston and Merry Clayton. Nick Mancuso plays an ageing rock star trying to buy the affections of his illegitimate son and one can only suppose that the plot has resonance for Mr Jagger, because there's little here for any audience. Tatty and ludicrous. TS

Nick Mancuso *Chris Dalton* • Byron Thames *Job Dalton* • Leslie Ackerman *Shelly* • Dick Bakalyan [Richard Bakalyan] *Manzini* • Leeyan Granger *Melanie* • Rex Ludwick *Animal* • Michael Wilding Jr *Terry* • Merry Clayton • Billy Preston ■ *Dir* Gene Taft • *Scr* Len Jenkin, from a story by Gene Taft, Mick Jagger

Blancanieves ★★★★ 12A
Silent fantasy drama 2011 · Sp/Fr/Bel · BW · 100min

Writer/director Pablo Berger's slick transposition of the Snow White story to 1920s Spain is every bit as sincere in its homage to silent cinema as Michel Hazanavicius's *The Artist*. Maribel Verdú plays the ambitious nurse who marries disabled bullfighter Daniel Giménez Cacho and tries to have his young daughter, Carmencita (played by Sofía Oria), murdered. Carmencita survives, is taken in by a troupe of bullfighting dwarves and becomes a famous matador. Berger's mastery of image and tone makes for an entrancing movie, and there's an exceptional score from Alfonso de Villalonga. DP

Maribel Verdú *Encarna* • Daniel Giménez Cacho [Daniel Gimenez Cacho] *Antonio Villalta* • Macarena Garcia *Carmen* • Sofia Oria *Carmencita* • Pere Ponce *Genaro* ■ *Dir* Pablo Berger • *Scr* Pablo Berger, from a fairy tale by Jacob & Wilhelm Grimm • *Music* Alfonso de Villalonga

Blanche ★★★★🅿🅶
Period drama   1971 · Fr · Colour · 89min

Fairy tale, morality play and wry political allegory, Walerian Borowczyk's remarkable period drama is as visually alluring as it's tantalisingly ambiguous. Set in the castle of Michel Simon's 13th-century French baron, it considers such diverse themes as allegiance and honour, passion and possession, pride and folly, as his son, Lawrence Trimble, attempts to protect his stepmother's purity from the lustful advances of king Georges Wilson and his page, Jacques Perrin. Simon is gloriously grotesque as the slavering vassal, while Ligia Branice's porcelain stillness demurely conveys Borowczyk's vision of sacrificial perfection. DP French +subtitles. 📀 💿

Ligia Branice *Blanche* • Michel Simon *The Baron* • Lawrence Trimble *Nicolas* • Jacques Perrin *Bartolomeo* • Georges Wilson *The King* • Denise Péronne *Lady Harcourt* ■ *Dir* Walerian Borowczyk • *Scr* Walerian Borowczyk, from the novel *Mazepa* by Juliusz Slowacki

Blanche Fury ★★★★🅿🅶
Melodrama   1948 · UK · Colour · 90min

This dark, brooding tale about inheritance and forbidden passion is set in a rambling English country home and stars an impressive Stewart Granger as a maverick estate manager. Granger is pitted against the best that British melodrama had to offer at the time, including Valerie Hobson in the title role, Maurice Denham and Michael Gough. This also benefits from an excellent screenplay and some taut direction from Marc Allégret, but it's the distinctive atmosphere that lingers in the memory. SH

Valerie Hobson *Blanche Fury* • Stewart Granger *Philip Thorn* • Walter Fitzgerald *Simon Fury* • Michael Gough *Lawrence Fury* • Maurice Denham *Major Frazer* • Sybilla Binder *Louisa* • Edward Lexy *Colonel Jenkins* • Allan Jeayes *Wetherby* ■ *Dir* Marc Allégret • *Scr* Audrey Erskine Lindop, Hugh Mills, Cecil McGivern, from the novel by Joseph Shearing • *Cinematographers* Guy Green, Geoffrey Unsworth

Blank Check ★★🅿🅶
Comedy   1994 · US · Colour · 93min

Clearly hoping to cash in on the success of *Home Alone*, Disney seemingly produced this kiddie comedy with nothing but the urgency of the release date in mind. The story of how pre-teen Brian Bonsall forges a cheque, sets himself up in the lap of luxury and then defends his patch is patently ludicrous – but with a little more imagination it might have made an entertaining romp. DP 📀

Brian Bonsall *Preston Waters* • Karen Duffy *Shay Stanley* • James Rebhorn *Fred Waters* • Jayne Atkinson *Sandra Waters* • Michael Faustino *Ralph Waters* • Chris Demetral *Damian Waters* • Miguel Ferrer *Quigley* • Michael Lerner *Biderman* ■ *Dir* Rupert Wainwright • *Scr* Blake Snyder, Colby Carr

Blank City ★★★
Documentary
2010 · US · Colour and BW · 94min

Director Céline Danhier's documentary focuses on the shoestring-budget work of New York's independent film-makers in the 1970s, such as Richard Kern, Vivienne Dick and James Nares, who often collaborated with musicians like Debbie Harry and Richard Hell. What emerges is an affectionate portrait of an artistic community based in the derelict tenements and lofts of a run-down city. Big names, including director Jim Jarmusch and actor Steve Buscemi, talk about their early struggles, offering a fascinating insight into the DIY ethic at the heart of films that both shocked the mainstream and inspired those who followed. TeS 📀

Deborah Harry • Fab Five Freddy • Jim Jarmusch • John Waters • Lydia Lunch • Steve Buscemi ■ *Dir* Céline Danhier

Blankman ★★★12
Comedy   1994 · US · Colour · 91min

Nerdy inventor Damon Wayans creates a bulletproof fabric, fashions a ridiculous superhero costume from it and becomes an inept crime-fighter battling ghetto gangsters in this above-average comedy. Despite having no superpowers and with only his daft inventions and luck on his side, Wayans sets out to beat underworld kingpin Jon Polito and get the girl – TV news reporter Robin Givens. AJ

Damon Wayans *Darryl Walker/Young Kevin Walker* • David Alan Grier *Kevin Walker* • Robin Givens *Kimberly Jonz* • Christopher Lawford *Mayor Marvin Harris* • Lynne Thigpen *Grandma Walker* • Jon Polito *Michael "The Suit" Minelli* • Nicky Corello *Sammy the Blade* • Jason Alexander *Mr Stone* • Michael Wayans *Young Darryl* • Greg Kinnear *Talk show host* • Arsenio Hall ■ *Dir* Mike Binder • *Scr* JF Lawton, Damon Wayans, from a story by Damon Wayans

Blast from the Past ★★★12
Comedy   1998 · US · Colour · 98min

Convinced that an atomic bomb is about to drop on 1960s America, married couple Sissy Spacek and Christopher Walken seal themselves in a fallout shelter for 35 years. What will their naive son Brendan Fraser make of the cynical 1990s when he's sent out into the world for the first time, enlisting the aid of streetwise Alicia Silverstone in his quest for supplies? Though the tone is sweet, the gags fail to bite in this somewhat laboured "culture clash" romantic comedy, but Fraser's goofy charm is winning. AJ Swearing. 📀

Brendan Fraser *Adam* • Christopher Walken *Calvin* • Sissy Spacek *Helen* • Alicia Silverstone *Eve* • Dave Foley *Troy* • Joey Slotnick *Soda jerk* • Rex Linn *Dave* ■ *Dir* Hugh Wilson • *Scr* Bill Kelly, Hugh Wilson, from a story by Bill Kelly

Blaze ★★★15
Biographical drama   1989 · US · Colour · 112min

The story of the passionate love affair between feisty Louisiana governor Earl Long and infamous New Orleans stripper Blaze Starr in the strait-laced 1950s is sanitised in director Ron Shelton's sometimes insightful look into the dangerous and volatile mix of sex and politics. Paul Newman has fun moments as the uninhibited maverick who advocated black voting rights and Lolita Davidovich gives a memorable performance as the well-endowed hillbilly burlesque queen. While the combination of truth and comedy doesn't quite work, the two stars deliver a fair account of the tabloid scandal, and the real Blaze appears as backstage stripper Lily in a tiny cameo. AJ Swearing, nudity. 📀

Paul Newman *Earl Kemp Long* • Lolita Davidovich *Fannie Belle Fleming/Blaze Starr* • Jerry Hardin *Thibodeaux* • Gailard Sartain *LaGrange* • Jeffrey DeMunn *Tuck* • Garland Bunting *Doc Ferriday* • Richard Jenkins *Times-Picayune Reporter* • Brandon Smith *Arvin Deeter* ■ *Dir* Ron Shelton • *Scr* Ron Shelton, from the autobiography *Blaze Starr: My Life as Told to Huey Perry* by Blaze Starr, Huey Perry

Blaze of Noon ★★
Adventure drama   1947 · US · BW · 90min

William Holden, returning to civvy street and Paramount studios after four years of active service, stars in this tale of stunt-circus flying brothers who switch to the commercial world of airmail delivery. Set in the 1920s and adapted from a novel by Ernest K Gann for maximum excitement in the air – it collapses on the ground thanks to the turgidly scripted relationship between Holden and Anne Baxter. RK

Anne Baxter *Lucille Stewart* • William Holden (2) *Colin McDonald* • William Bendix *Porkie* • Sonny Tufts *Roland McDonald* • Sterling Hayden *Tad McDonald* • Howard Da Silva *Gafferty* • Johnny Sands *Keith McDonald* • Jean Wallace *Poppy* •

Edith King *Mrs Murphy* ■ *Dir* John Farrow • *Scr* Frank Wead, Arthur Sheekman, from the novel by Ernest K Gann

Blazing Saddles ★★★★15
Spoof western   1974 · US · Colour · 88min

Mel Brooks's all-singing, all-belching western spoof remains one of his finest creations. Cleavon Little is the railway worker who is appointed the first black sheriff to a hell-raising western town; Gene Wilder is the drunken gunman who helps him out. The two stars are great, but there are even better performances from Madeline Kahn (sending up Marlene Dietrich) and the crazed Harvey Korman. There's not a lot of subtlety, but loads of slapstick, and even more jokes about bodily functions. JF Swearing. 📀 💿

Cleavon Little *Bart* • Gene Wilder *Jim, the Waco Kid* • Slim Pickens *Taggart* • Harvey Korman *Hedley Lamarr* • Madeline Kahn *Lili Von Shtupp* • Mel Brooks *Governor Le Petomane/Indian chief* • David Huddleston *Olson Johnson* • Liam Dunn *Rev Johnson* • Alex Karras *Mongo* ■ *Dir* Mel Brooks • *Scr* Mel Brooks, Norman Steinberg, Andrew Bergman, Richard Pryor, Alan Uger, from a story by Bergman

Bleak Moments ★★★★🅿🅶
Drama   1971 · UK · Colour · 106min

Written and directed by Mike Leigh and produced and edited by Leslie Blair, this may be the work of two dedicated realists, but it isn't quite the depressing prospect suggested by the title. However, it is an unflinching look at the everyday difficulties facing people leading quietly extraordinary lives. Among them is Anne Raitt, who struggles to communicate with those she knows, from her mentally disabled sister and her daydreaming office-mate to the hippy in her garage and her kindly teacher boyfriend. Everyone remembers the Chinese meal, but it's the aggregate of little episodes that makes this so moving. DP 📀

Anne Raitt *Sylvia* • Sarah Stephenson *Hilda* • Eric Allan *Peter* • Joolia Cappleman *Pat* • Mike Bradwell *Norman* • Liz Smith *Pat's mother* ■ *Dir/Scr* Mike Leigh

Bleeder ★★★18
Drama   1999 · Den · Colour · 93min

Questioning the truism that movies are responsible for violence in society, and containing one of the most sadistic modes of execution ever witnessed on screen, this has much in common with Nicolas Winding Refn's debut feature, *Pusher*. However, while Kim Bodnia's abusive relationship with pregnant girlfriend Rikke Louise Andersson is sickening in the extreme, there's a hint of optimism in video geek Mads Mikkelsen's timid regard for waitress Liv Corfixen. Flawed but provocative. DP Danish +subtitles. Violence. 📀

Kim Bodnia *Leo* • Mads Mikkelsen *Lenny* • Rikke Louise Andersson *Louise* • Liv Corfixen *Lea* • Levino Jensen *Louis* • Zlatko Buric *Kitjo* • Claus Fluggare *Joe* ■ *Dir/Scr* Nicolas Winding Refn

Blended ★★12
Comedy   2014 · US · Colour · 112min

Adam Sandler and Drew Barrymore have chemistry and history. Sadly, this bloated romantic comedy isn't in the same class as *The Wedding Singer* or *50 First Dates*. Here the stars play single parents who, after a disastrous blind date, unexpectedly find themselves and their five kids on the same African safari. The combination of kids and critters ensures much lowbrow slapstick, as well as the occasional subtler moment. But ultimately, this comedy is long and laboured, and is at its best when it's not trying too hard to be funny. DA Some sexual references, swearing. 📀 💿

Adam Sandler *Jim Friedman* • Drew Barrymore *Lauren Reynolds* • Kevin Nealon *Eddy* • Terry Crews *Nickens* • Wendi McLendon-Covey *Jen* ■ *Dir* Frank Coraci

Bless the Child ★★15
Supernatural thriller
2000 · US/Ger · Colour · 103min

Kim Basinger plays a nurse who rears her drug-addicted sister's baby as her own, until the sister turns up with a creepy new husband (Rufus Sewell) and demands the return of the youngster, who's started to manifest all sorts of magical powers. Basinger teams up with an FBI officer (Jimmy Smits) to track the child down. Utter nonsense, but entertaining in a daft sort of way. JB Swearing, violence. 📀

Kim Basinger *Maggie O'Connor* • Jimmy Smits *John Travis* • Rufus Sewell *Eric Stark* • Ian Holm *Reverend Grissom* • Angela Bettis *Jenna* • Holliston Coleman *Cody* • Christina Ricci *Cheri* ■ *Dir* Chuck Russell • *Scr* Tom Rickman, Clifford Green, Ellen Green, from a novel by Cathy Cash Spellman

Bless This House ★★🆄
Comedy   1972 · UK · Colour · 85min

In the 1970s, there was a misguided belief among British film-makers that successful sitcoms could be transferred to the big screen. The majority proved to be huge disappointments, and this was no exception, although it does have the incomparable Sidney James. He is the grouchy father, married to Diana Coupland, who is trying to come to grips with his teenage children and his neighbours (Terry Scott and June Whitfield). There are more laughs in the naff 1970s fashions than in the script. JF 📀

Sidney James *Sid Abbot* • Diana Coupland *Jean Abbot* • Sally Geeson *Sally Abbot* • Terry Scott *Ronald Baines* • June Whitfield *Vera Baines* • Peter Butterworth *Trevor Lewis* • Robin Askwith *Mike Abbot* • Bill Maynard *Oldham* • Wendy Richard *Carol* ■ *Dir* Gerald Thomas • *Scr* Dave Freeman

Blessed ★★🆄
Drama   2007 · UK · Colour · 119min

City trader James Nesbitt becomes a lighthouse keeper on a remote Scottish island following the deaths of his wife and children. But after using isolation to bury his emotions, he's forced to finally confront them when a little girl (Lillian Woods) is washed ashore. Quirkiness then takes precedence over melancholy, as the youngster tries to befriend her saviour by employing the tricks of her still-missing-at-sea magician dad, while Nesbitt maintains a vow of silence. But soon self-conscious whimsy turns into silly unrealism that robs the climax of its dramatic punch. SF 📀

James Nesbitt *Peter* • Natascha McElhone *Lou* • Gary Lewis *Howie* • Lillian Woods *Charlotte* • Phillip Bird *Freddie* • Peggy Nesbitt *Rachel* ■ *Dir/Scr* Mark Aldridge

Blessed Event ★★★
Comedy drama   1932 · US · BW · 82min

Band singer Dick Powell, who would go on to have a successful career in both musicals and tough-guy roles, made his screen debut in this version of a hit Broadway play set in the worlds of newspapers and showbiz. However, the movie belongs to its star, Lee Tracy, in the role of a newspaperman. Aided by dialogue that snaps, crackles and pops, he gives the performance of his career as a ruthless gossip columnist tangling with colleagues, crooners and chorus girls – though Ned Sparks, as a misogynistic journalist, gives him a run for his money. Amusing, authentic and entertaining. RK

Lee Tracy *Alvin Roberts* • Mary Brian *Gladys Price* • Allen Jenkins *Frankie Wells* • Ruth Donnelly *Miss Stevens* • Ned Sparks *George Moxley* • Dick Powell *Bunny Harmon* ■ *Dir* Roy Del Ruth • *Scr* Howard J Green, from the play by Manuel Seff, Forrest Wilson

Blind ★★★★18
Drama   2014 · Nor · Colour · 92min

Memory and imagination collide in Norwegian Eskil Vogt's debut feature, which forever leaves the viewer uncertain whether the action is taking place in reality or in the mind of 30something Ellen Dorrit Petersen. She seeks to come to terms with her recent blindness by concocting fictitious

🆄 SUITABLE FOR ALL   🆄ᶜ SUITABLE ESPECIALLY FOR YOUNG CHILDREN (DVD ONLY)   🅿🅶 PARENTAL GUIDANCE   12A UNDER 12s TO BE ACCOMPANIED (CINEMA ONLY)

narratives to reinforce her recollection of the world she can no longer see. Every twist adds to the complexity, ingenuity and artistic bravura of this mesmerising treatise on the refusal to be beaten by disability. **DP** In Norwegian. **DVD BL**

Ellen Dorrit Petersen *Ingrid* • Henrik Rafaelsen *Morten* • Vera Vitali *Elin* • Marius Kolbenstvedt *Einar* ■ *Dir/Scr* Eskil Vogt

Blind Adventure ★★U
Spy comedy drama   1933 · US · BW · 62min

Robert Armstrong is the American in London who gets mixed up with a bunch of criminal rogues that includes charming burglar Roland Young. Helen Mack is the heroine of this routine film, which is defeated by a tediously muddled plot. **RK**

Robert Armstrong *Richard Bruce* • Helen Mack *Rose Thorne* • Roland Young *Holmes, the burglar* • Ralph Bellamy *Jim Steele* • John Miljan *Regan* • Laura Hope Crews *Lady Rockingham* ■ *Dir* Ernest B Schoedsack • *Scr* Ruth Rose, Robert Benchley (additional dialogue)

Blind Alley ★★★
Crime thriller   1939 · US · BW · 69min

Remade in 1948 with William Holden as *The Dark Past*, this adaptation of James Warwick's play keeps the original Broadway title. Chester Morris is interestingly cast as a thug who holds a psychologist prisoner, getting himself analysed in the process. (This was one of the first films to offer a Freudian explanation for a character's behaviour.) Likeable Ralph Bellamy is sympathetic as the shrink hostage. **TS**

Chester Morris *Hal Wilson* • Ralph Bellamy *Dr Shelby* • Ann Dvorak *Mary* • Joan Perry *Linda Curtis* • Melville Cooper *George Curtis* • Rose Stradner *Doris Shelby* • John Eldredge *Dick Holbrook* • Ann Doran *Agnes* • Marc Lawrence (1) *Buck* ■ *Dir* Charles Vidor • *Scr* Phillip MacDonald, Michael Blankfort, Albert Duffy, from the play by James Warwick

A Blind Bargain ★★★
Silent science-fiction mystery   1922 · US · BW

In this Dr Moreau-style melodrama, Lon Chaney's misguided surgeon plans to perform a glandular operation on penniless soldier Raymond McKee, only to be confounded by one of his hideously deformed cast-offs, a piteous simian hunchback. Typically, the Man of a Thousand Faces plays both creator and creation, and it's worth noting the similarity between his apeman make-up and that of Fredric March's alter ego in the 1931 version of *Dr Jekyll and Mr Hyde*. **DP**

Lon Chaney *Dr Arthur Lamb/Hunchback* • Raymond McKee *Robert Sandell* • Virginia True Boardman *Mrs Sandell* • Fontaine La Rue *Mrs Lamb* • Jacqueline Logan *Angela Marshall* ■ *Dir* Wallace Worsley • *Scr* JG Hawks, from Barry Pain's novel *The Octave of Claudius*

Blind Chance ★★★18
Drama   1987 · Pol · Colour · 113min

The basic premise of this politically loaded drama is essentially sound. Boguslaw Linda runs for a train and three potential fates ensue: the first sees him become a Communist aparatchik; the next reveals him dabbling in underground protest and religion; while the third shows him pursuing an apolitical medical career. However, the rigidity of the structure prevents director Krzysztof Kieslowski from exploring his themes in any depth. Indeed, he recognised the flaws while editing and always deemed the film a failure. Yet its historical context and its anticipation of the ideas considered in *The Double Life of Véronique* and *Three Colours Red* enhance its significance. **DP** Polish +subtitles. Swearing, sex scenes, nudity. **DVD**

Boguslaw Linda *Witek* • Tadeusz Lomnicki *Werner* • Zbigniew Zapasiewicz *Adam* • Marzena Trybala *Werka* • Jacek Borkowski *Marek* • Monika Gozdzik *Olga* • Zygmunt Hübner *Dzirkan* ■ *Dir/Scr* Krzysztof Kieslowski

Blind Date ★★★PG
Crime drama   1959 · UK · BW · 91min

This usually overlooked entry in the Joseph Losey canon is actually quite a daring and

---

sophisticated investigation into British attitudes towards sex, class and the establishment in the late 1950s. The story is pretty unremarkable, but Losey's assured handling of character and location forces you to share the plight of Dutch painter Hardy Kruger, as he becomes embroiled in a political scandal after the mistress he shares with the French ambassador in London is murdered. Stanley Baker investigates. **DP DVD**

Hardy Kruger *Jan van Rooyen* • Stanley Baker *Inspector Morgan* • Micheline Presle *Jacqueline Cousteau* • Robert Flemyng *Sir Brian Lewis* • Gordon Jackson *Police sergeant* • John Van Eyssen *Westover* ■ *Dir* Joseph Losey • *Scr* Ben Barzman, Millard Lampell, from the novel by Leigh Howard

Blind Date ★18
Crime thriller   1984 · US · Colour · 99min

Blind Joseph Bottoms is able to see again after doctor Keir Dullea fits him up with a computer implant. But what's the link between him and a mad serial killer? You won't care in this Greece-set slasher that's so high on tortuous logic and so low on conviction that only the scriptwriters could swallow. Writer/director Nico Mastorakis gets it wrong in every area, especially the inane dialogue. **AJ**

Joseph Bottoms *Jonathon Ratcliffe* • Kirstie Alley *Claire Simpson* • James Daughton *Dave* • Lana Clarkson *Rachel* • Keir Dullea *Dr Steiger* • Charles Nicklin *Robert* • Marina Sirtis *Hooker* ■ *Dir* Nico Mastorakis • *Scr* Nico Mastorakis, Fred C Perry

Blind Date ★★15
Comedy   1987 · US · Colour · 91min

When Bruce Willis's feature debut was released, it was mauled by the critics and some predicted he would join the many TV stars who had attempted to cross over into Hollywood and failed. The film's box-office success and the subsequent career of the former *Moonlighting* actor have proved the critics wrong, but this would-be comedy hasn't improved with age. Willis is fixed up with the blind date from hell in the shape of Kim Basinger. The two leads are likeable enough, but Blake Edwards's direction is crass and chaotic. **JF** Violence, swearing, drug abuse. **DVD**

Bruce Willis *Walter Davis* • Kim Basinger *Nadia Gates* • John Larroquette *David Bedford* • William Daniels (2) *Judge Harold Bedford* • George Coe *Harry Gruen* • Mark Blum *Denny Gordon* • Phil Hartman *Ted Davis* ■ *Dir* Blake Edwards • *Scr* Dale Launer

Blind Dating ★★15
Romantic comedy   2005 · British Virgin Islands/US/UK · Colour · 95min

This unremarkable romantic comedy would surely have slipped into obscurity if it wasn't for the fact that leading man Chris Pine is now better known as Captain Kirk in the rebooted *Star Trek* franchise. He plays a young blind man who leads a fulfilling life apart from the fact that he longs to have a normal relationship with a woman. Things start looking up when he meets his doctor's new Indian receptionist, Anjali Jay. The pair fall for each other but, unbeknown to Pine, she is already engaged and set to have an arranged marriage. Pine gives an appealing performance, but the film runs out of steam well before the end. **JF** Swearing, sexual references. **DVD**

Chris Pine *Danny* • Eddie Kaye Thomas *Larry* • Anjali Jay *Leeza* • Stephen Tobolowsky *Dr Perkins* • Jane Seymour *Dr Evans* • Steven Wellington *Young Danny* • Austin Rogers *Young Larry* ■ *Dir* James Keach • *Scr* Christopher Theo

Blind Flight ★★★★15
Biographical drama   2003 · UK/Ger/Ire · Colour · 92min

This powerful drama recounts the true story of hostages Brian Keenan and John McCarthy and their years of captivity in Lebanon. Following their release, both men published books on their ordeal as well as helping to shape the screenplay for writer/director John Furse's feature debut. Ian Hart (as Keenan) and Linus Roache (as McCarthy) bring the experiences of these

---

two very different men vividly to life, as their resolve is tested by the indignities, hardships and horrors of a life of incarceration. But what is surprising is the understanding extended to the kidnappers ("We all have our reasons," says McCarthy), that serves only to enhance the unfolding human drama. **TH** Violence, swearing. **DVD**

Ian Hart *Brian Keenan* • Linus Roache *John McCarthy* • Bassem Breish *Joker* • Ziad Lahoud *Said* • Mohamad Chamas *Abed* ■ *Dir* John Furse • *Scr* Brian Keenan, John McCarthy, John Furse

Blind Fury ★★★18
Action thriller   1990 · US · Colour · 82min

Two years after he hit the big time with the fabulous *Dead Calm*, Australian director Phillip Noyce made this nifty martial arts saga, in which blind Vietnam veteran Rutger Hauer rescues his buddy's son from evil gangsters and then hits the road, bonding with the boy while fending off the bad guys. It's a gimmicky, but above-average, action adventure (based on the hugely popular Japanese *Zatoichi* film series). **AJ** Violence, swearing.

Rutger Hauer *Nick Parker* • Terrance O'Quinn [Terry O'Quinn] *Frank Devereaux* • Brandon Call *Billy Devereaux* • Lisa Blount *Annie Winchester* • Randall "Tex" Cobb *Slag* • Noble Willingham *MacCready* • Meg Foster *Lynn Devereaux* • Sho Kosugi *Assassin* ■ *Dir* Phillip Noyce • *Scr* Charles Robert Carner

The Blind Goddess ★★
Drama   1948 · UK · BW · 87min

Nobody can do decent coves caught in a dilemma quite like Michael Denison and he's perfectly cast again in this screen version of Patrick Hastings's hit stage play as a secretary who shops his embezzling boss. But, unfortunately, this reunion with director Harold French (after the same year's *My Brother Jonathan*) suffers from some uncertain handling, with the courtroom scenes in particular sapped of the suspense that made them so compelling in the theatre. **DP**

Eric Portman *Sir John Dearing* • Anne Crawford *Lady Brasted* • Hugh Williams *Lord Brasted* • Michael Denison *Derek Waterhouse* • Nora Swinburne *Lady Dearing* • Raymond Lovell *Mr Mainwaring* • Frank Cellier *Judge* • Maurice Denham *Butler* ■ *Dir* Harold French • *Scr* Muriel Box, Sydney Box, from the play by Patrick Hastings

Blind Horizon ★★15
Thriller   2003 · US · Colour · 95min

This employs all manner of bewildering visual flourishes and plot devices in an attempt to make a drab tale seem vaguely intriguing. Yet the stylish touches merely render it pretentious, and even more disappointing is the sight of a calibre cast thrashing around in the muddled storyline. Chief casualty is Val Kilmer, who appears in the New Mexican desert suffering from amnesia with a vague notion that the life of the US president is under threat. **DP** A sex scene, violence, swearing. **DVD**

Val Kilmer *Frank Kavanaugh* • Neve Campbell *Chloe Richards* • Sam Shepard *Sheriff Jack Kolb* • Noble Willingham *Deputy Shirl Cash* • Amy Smart *Liz Culpepper* • Gil Bellows *Dr Theodore Conway* • Giancarlo Esposito *JC Reynolds* • Faye Dunaway *Ms K* ■ *Dir* Michael Haussman • *Scr* F Paul Benz, Steve Tomlin

Blind Husbands ★★★★
Silent melodrama   1919 · US · BW · 129min

After the First World War, when Erich von Stroheim's "Horrible Hun" roles were no longer in demand, he persuaded Universal to let him direct this cynical, witty and erotic drama set in the Alps. Von Stroheim also wrote the script, designed the sets and played the lead role of the dashing Lieutenant von Steuben, who seduces a bored American wife on holiday. With its careful attention to detail in the decor and costumes, and the acute psychological observation of the characters, von Stroheim's debut movie prefigured his later, more mature work. The picture was a

---

commercial as well as critical success. **RB DVD**

Sam De Grasse *Dr Robert Armstrong* • Francelia Billington *Margaret Armstrong* • Erich von Stroheim *Lieutenant von Steuben* • TH Gibson-Gowland [Gibson Gowland] *Sepp* • Fay Holderness *Vamp waitress* • Ruby Kendrick *"A Village Blossom"* ■ *Dir* Erich von Stroheim • *Scr* Erich von Stroheim, Lillian Ducey (titles), from the story *The Pinnacle* by Erich von Stroheim • *Cinematographer* Ben Reynolds

Blind Man ★★★
Spaghetti western   1971 · US/It · Colour · 95min

This spaghetti curio is not only produced by controversial Beatles lawyer Allen Klein, but also co-stars his former client Ringo Starr. The actual star of the piece is Tony Anthony, who plays the titular, sightless antihero, sympathy for whom is rather lacking as he's a human trafficker. Still, he's a whole lot friendlier than the gang who've appropriated his female cargo before wiping out his men in cold blood. With its twisted morality, outright misogyny and unlikely chief protagonist, this is wayward yet compulsively watchable fare. **JH**

Tony Anthony *Blind man* • Ringo Starr *Candy* • Lloyd Battista *Domingo* • Magda Konopka *Sweet Mama* ■ *Dir* Ferdinando Baldi • *Scr* Piero Anchisi, Tony Anthony, Vincenzo Cerami

Blind Shaft ★★★★15
Drama   2003 · Ger/HK · Colour · 88min

Li Yang's debut feature relates a tale that's as bleak as its northern Chinese setting. By merely implying the desperation of the men drawn to the region's poorly regulated coal mines, Li condemns the society that allows such poverty to exist. Yet neither does he condone the iniquitous racket run by Wang Shuangbao and Li Yixiang, who persuade strangers to pose as their relatives to secure employment and then kill them in faked accidents in order to blackmail the pit owners into paying illicit compensation. **DP** Mandarin +subtitles. Swearing, sex scenes. **DVD**

Li Yixiang *Song Jinming* • Wang Shuangbao *Tang Zhaoyang* • Wang Baoqiang *Yuan Fengming* ■ *Dir* Li Yang • *Scr* Li Yang, from the novel *Shenmu [Sacred Wood]* by Liu Qingbang

The Blind Side ★★★★12
Sports drama based on a true story   2009 · US · Colour · 128min

This refreshingly heartfelt drama is based on the life of Michael Oher (Quinton Aaron), who grew up neglected and impoverished but went on to become an American football star. Sandra Bullock won an Oscar for playing Leigh Anne Tuohy, the gun-toting, wealthy, white southern Christian who bucks convention to shelter, educate and love the homeless black teenager. Once viewers grow accustomed to the enormous physical differences between Bullock and Aaron – who nevertheless convince as eventual mother and son – this inspiring film will burrow in and work its magic. Oher's miserable start in life shouldn't have happened, but it did – and *The Blind Side* is a film that shouldn't work, but does. **KK** Some violence, swearing, sexual references. **DVD BL**

Sandra Bullock *Leigh Anne Tuohy* • Tim McGraw *Sean Tuohy* • Quinton Aaron *Michael Oher* • Jae Head *SJ Tuohy* • Lily Collins *Collins Tuohy* • Ray McKinnon *Coach Cotton* • Kathy Bates *Miss Sue* ■ *Dir* John Lee Hancock • *Scr* John Lee Hancock, from the non-fiction book *The Blind Side: Evolution of a Game* by Michael Lewis

Blind Spot: Hitler's Secretary ★★★PG
Documentary   2002 · Austria · Colour · 87min

Shortly before her death in 2002, and after 50 years of silence, Traudl Junge, who worked as one of Adolf Hitler's secretaries, finally told her story to André Heller and Othmar Schmiderer. Sadly the resulting film doesn't do justice to the often fascinating intimate detail of daily life with one of history's most monstrous men. The film-makers' decision to include no archive material at all and to simply present a "talking head" leaves the frustrating

---

B

impression that there is still plenty of raw material for an excellent documentary. **AS** German +subtitles. *DVD*

■ *Dir/Scr* André Heller, Othmar Schmiderer

Blind Terror ★★ 15
Thriller 1971 · UK · Colour · 83min

Blind Mia Farrow splashes mud on a young drifter's cowboy boots while travelling to her uncle's isolated mansion. In revenge, he slaughters her entire family and relentlessly pursues her around the old dark house. Written by Brian Clemens on what must clearly have been an off-day, this cumbersome chiller has minimal suspense. **AJ**

Mia Farrow *Sarah* · Robin Bailey *George Rexton* · Dorothy Alison *Betty Rexton* · Norman Eshley *Steve Reding* · Diane Grayson *Sandy Rexton* · Paul Nicholas *Jacko* · Christopher Matthews *Frost* · Brian Rawlinson *Barker* · Michael Elphick *Gypsy Tom* ■ *Dir* Richard Fleischer · *Scr* Brian Clemens

Blind Trust ★★
Crime drama 2007 · Can · Colour · 90min

An entertaining, yet ludicrous twist proves the saving grace of this otherwise snooze-worthy TV movie, in which actuary Jessica Capshaw (daughter of actress Kate) is wrongly accused of murdering her boyfriend and her best mate. But despite having Art Hindle's eminent defence lawyer fighting her case – and over-acting with aplomb – she decides to go AWOL and do her own investigation. This contrived sleuthing is as unexciting as the courtroom and legal office scenes that precede it, leaving the pumping soundtrack to drive the dull events forward. **SF**

Jessica Capshaw *Cassie Stewart* · Art Hindle *LG Mennick* · Chad Willett *Detective Rudy Shatz* · Robin Wilcock *Jerry* · Carlo Mestroni *Detective Getty* ■ *Dir* Louis Bolduc · *Scr* Tom Gates

Blinded ★★★ 15
Psychological thriller 2004 · UK · Colour · 88min

In this admirable feature debut, writer/director Eleanor Yule draws upon the haunting style of Danish painter Hammershoi to capture the bleakness of the Scottish setting. She also references the Scandinavian artist in the character of Mike Hammershoi (Anders W Berthelsen), a Danish backpacker who goes in search of work at a farm owned by Peter Mullan. There, Berthelsen witnesses the tyranny the blind man imposes on his young wife (Jodhi May) and his meek mother (Phyllida Law). **DP** Sex scenes, swearing, violence. *DVD*

Peter Mullan *Francis Black* · Jodhi May *Rachel Black* · Anders W Berthelsen *Mike Hammershoi* · Phyllida Law *Bella Black* · Samantha Bond (2) *Caroline Lamar* · Kenny Ireland *Lachie McNeill* · Kate Donnolly *PC King* ■ *Dir/Scr* Eleanor Yule

Blindfold ★★★ U
Comedy mystery 1966 · US · Colour · 101min

Had Philip Dunne resisted the temptation to parody Hitchcock, this might have been a first-rate thriller. The levity undercuts the tension that develops as society psychiatrist Rock Hudson begins to realise that Alejandro Rey (the patient he's been seeing in such secrecy that he's blindfolded to and from their consultations) is actually in grave danger. The romance with Rey's sister Claudia Cardinale and some uncomfortable slapstick prevent the action from being nail-biting. **DP**

Rock Hudson *Dr Bartholomew Snow* · Claudia Cardinale *Victoria Vail/Vicky Vincenti* · Jack Warden *General Pratt* · Guy Stockwell *Fitzpatrick* · Brad Dexter *Harrigan* · Anne Seymour *Smitty* · Alejandro Rey *Arthur Vincenti* · Hari Rhodes *Captain Davis* ■ *Dir* Philip Dunne · *Scr* Philip Dunne, WH Menger, from the novel by Lucille Fletcher

Blindness ★★ 18
Drama
2008 · Jpn/Bra/Can/UK/It · Colour · 116min

After his kinetic Oscar-friendly thriller *The Constant Gardener*, Fernando Meirelles's follow-up is a much bleaker affair. A man

who's stuck in traffic realises he has gone blind. Within hours, all those who've come into contact with him are blind, too, and the first wave of infected are put into isolation. As the outside world follows suit, it seems that the only person who can see is timid Julianne Moore, who follows her doctor husband (Mark Ruffalo) into confinement. It's a promising premise, and there are some truly arresting visuals (notably the blurred, milky-white world of the sightless). But the film strangely declines to pursue the obvious drama in its apocalyptic scenario in favour of something more abstract and frustrating. Brave but unsatisfying. **DW** English, Japanese +subtitles. Violence. *DVD*

Julianne Moore *Doctor's wife* · Mark Ruffalo *Doctor* · Danny Glover *Old man with black eye patch/Narrator* · Gael García Bernal *Bartender/King of Ward 3* · Alice Braga *Woman with dark glasses* · Yusuke Iseya *First blind man* · Sandra Oh *Minister of Health* ■ *Dir* Fernando Meirelles · *Scr* Don McKellar, from the novel by José Saramago

The Bling Ring ★★★★ 15
Crime drama based on a true story
2013 · US/UK/Ger/Jpn · Colour · 86min

The fifth film by *Lost in Translation* director Sofia Coppola is a dryly funny but really rather perceptive take on a very modern kind of crime. Set in the late noughties, it concerns a group of high-school kids (among them former Hermione Granger, Emma Watson), who become so obsessed with tabloid stars' private lives that they decide to burgle their houses. Though nominally not a comedy, there are plenty of laughs to be had, mostly from the outlaw band's incursions into the gaudy real-life home of Paris Hilton. More seriously, the movie addresses our obsession with celebrity, investigating a post-reality-TV world where anybody can be not just famous for 15 minutes, but rich, too. **DW** Swearing, drug abuse. *BL*

Katie Chang *Rebecca* · Israel Broussard *Marc* · Emma Watson *Nicki* · Claire Julien *Chloe* · Taissa Farmiga *Sam* · Leslie Mann *Laurie* ■ *Dir/Scr* Sofia Coppola

Blink ★★★ 18
Thriller 1994 · US · Colour · 101min

The concept is not new – blind woman in peril fights back – but, thanks to a winning, sassy performance from Madeleine Stowe, this rises above the routine. Stowe is a folk fiddle player recovering from an operation that will eventually allow her to see again. For the time being, she gets fleeting moments of vision and during one of these periods she catches sight of a murderer, thereby putting her own life in danger. Aidan Quinn is the sceptical policeman assigned to watch over her. Director Michael Apted competently cranks up the tension, and Stowe's faltering flashes of sight are brilliantly realised. **JF** Violence, swearing, nudity. *DVD*

Madeleine Stowe *Emma Brody* · Aidan Quinn *Detective John Hallstrom* · James Remar *Thomas Ridgely* · Peter Friedman *Doctor Ryan Pierce* · Bruce A Young *Lieutenant Mitchell* · Laurie Metcalf *Candice* · Matt Roth *Crowe* · Paul Dillon *Neal Booker* ■ *Dir* Michael Apted · *Scr* Dana Stevens

Bliss ★★★★ 18
Black comedy 1985 · Aus · Colour · 107min

A movie of great charm and style, this concentrates on the hoary old "cheating death and rediscovering life" chestnut, but gives it some fresh and funny topspin. The performances, particularly from frenzied Barry Otto as a hapless advertising executive, are universally excellent, but it is Ray Lawrence's adroit and deft direction that turns a simple and oft-told tale – about a man who dramatically changes his life after a heart attack – into a miniature comic tour de force. **SH** Swearing.

Barry Otto *Harry Joy* · Lynette Curran *Bettina Joy* · Helen Jones *Honey Barbara* · Miles Buchanan *David Joy* · Gia Carides *Lucy Joy* · Tim Robertson *Alex Duval* · Jeff Truman *Joel* · Bryan

Marshall *Adrian* · Jon Ewing *Aldo* ■ *Dir* Ray Lawrence · *Scr* Ray Lawrence, Peter Carey, from Carey's novel

Bliss ★★ 18
Erotic drama 1997 · US · Colour · 99min

Despite the high production values, a quality cast and a wordy script, this is not that different from many formulaic erotic thrillers. Craig Sheffer and Sheryl Lee star as a newly married couple whose sex life is proving to be a damp squib. In desperation they turn to therapist Terence Stamp, who introduces them to a new world of sexual experience. Stamp steals the show from the unconvincing leads, while the soft-focus photography undermines the film's worthy intentions. **JF** Swearing.

Terence Stamp *Baltazar Vincenza* · Craig Sheffer *Joseph* · Sheryl Lee *Maria* · Spalding Gray *Alfred* · Casey Siemaszko *Tanner* · Ken Camroux *Hank* · Pamela Perry *Dottie* · Blu Mankuma *Nick* ■ *Dir/Scr* Lance Young

The Bliss of Mrs Blossom ★★
Comedy 1968 · UK · Colour · 93min

Shirley MacLaine stars in this otherwise all-British comedy, written by Alec Coppel and Denis Norden and directed by Joseph McGrath. She plays the wife of a brassière manufacturer (Richard Attenborough), who manages to conceal her lover (James Booth), one of her husband's employees, in the attic for three years before her husband tumbles to the situation. A kind of screwball farce, it is played with evident gusto by MacLaine. **RK**

Shirley MacLaine *Harriet Blossom* · Richard Attenborough *Robert Blossom* · James Booth *Ambrose Tuttle* · Freddie Jones *Detective Sergeant Dylan* · William Rushton *Dylan's assistant* · Bob Monkhouse *Dr Taylor* · Patricia Routledge *Miss Reece* · John Bluthal *Judge* · Barry Humphries *Mr Wainwright, art dealer* · Clive Dunn *Man* · John Cleese *Clerk* ■ *Dir* Joseph McGrath · *Scr* Alec Coppel, Denis Norden, from the story by Josef Shaftel, from Coppel's play *A Bird in the Nest*

Blithe Spirit ★★★★ U
Comedy fantasy 1945 · UK · Colour · 91min

In this polished adaptation of Noël Coward's comedy, widower Rex Harrison is happily remarried to Constance Cummings and visited by the ghost of his first wife, Kay Hammond. The architect of this event is a dotty old medium, played by the unforgettable Margaret Rutherford. David Lean directed – Coward was away in America and the great British director was worried he was the wrong man for the job. According to Kevin Brownlow's monumental biography of Lean, Coward attended the first preview and was distinctly unimpressed. The critics lapped it up, though, and the dainty special effects won an Oscar. **AT** *DVD*

Rex Harrison *Charles Condomine* · Constance Cummings *Ruth Condomine* · Kay Hammond *Elvira* · Margaret Rutherford *Madame Arcati* · Hugh Wakefield *Dr Bradman* · Joyce Carey *Mrs Bradman* · Jacqueline Clark *Edith* ■ *Dir* David Lean · *Scr* Anthony Havelock-Allan, David Lean, Ronald Neame, from the play by Noël Coward · *Cinematographer* Ronald Neame · *Special Effects* Thomas Howard

Blitz ★★ 18
Crime thriller 2010 · UK · Colour · 93min

An unconventional London detective with an anger-management problem finds himself on the trail of a serial killer targeting cops in Elliott Lester's violent crime thriller. Action star Jason Statham is handy with his fists and ready with a wry one-liner, but an unoriginal plot and a general lack of excitement don't do justice to either him or the high-calibre supporting cast.To his credit, Lester comes up with a fresh vision of London but should have worked harder to make his film live up to its evident franchise potential. **TJ** Violence, swearing. *DVD* *BL*

Jason Statham *Det Brant* · Paddy Considine *Sgt Porter Nash* · Aidan Gillen *Barry Weiss/Blitz* · David Morrissey *Harold Dunlop* · Luke Evans

Stokes · Nicky Henson *The Super* ■ *Dir* Elliott Lester (2) · *Scr* Nathan Parker, from the novel by Ken Bruen

The Blob ★★★ 12
Science-fiction drama 1958 · US · Colour · 82min

Steve McQueen got his first starring role in this musty delight about a giant red alien jelly terrorising small-town America and absorbing the population. A quintessential 1950s classic (which spawned a successful 1988 remake), the gaudy colours, self-mocking tone and the neat title creature add up to loads of unsettling fun. The scene where the outer space ooze invades a local cinema has become one of science-fiction cinema's key images. **AJ** Some violence. *DVD* *BL*

Steven McQueen [Steve McQueen (1)] *Steve* · Aneta Corseaut *Judy* · Earl Rowe *Police lieutenant* · Olin Howlin *Old man* · Steven Chase [Stephen Chase (1)] *Doctor* · John Benson *Sergeant Jim Bert* · Vince Barbi *George* · Tom Ogen · Julie Cousins · Ralph Roseman ■ *Dir* Irvin S Yeaworth Jr · *Scr* Irvin S Yeaworth Jr, Theodore Simonson, Ruth Phillips, from an idea by Irvine H Millgate

The Blob ★★★★ 18
Science-fiction horror 1988 · US · Colour · 90min

The Space Sponge returns in a super remake of the cult monster movie from sci-fi's golden era. Director Chuck Russell gets his revamp exactly right. By re-interpreting all the potent moments from the Steve McQueen original in today's sophisticated special-effects terms, and updating the plot to include contemporary mores and political issues, Russell creates a breakneck crowd-pleaser with a fun nostalgic pulse. **AJ**

Shawnee Smith *Meg Penny* · Donovan Leitch *Paul Taylor* · Kevin Dillon *Brian Flagg* · Ricky Paull Goldin *Scott Jeskey* · Billy Beck *Can man* · Jeffrey DeMunn *Sheriff Herb Geller* · Candy Clark *Fran Hewitt* · Beau Billingslea *Moss Woolsey* ■ *Dir* Chuck Russell · *Scr* Chuck Russell, Frank Darabont

Block Busters ★★ U
Comedy 1944 · US · BW · 60min

Before the East Side Kids became the Bowery Boys, there was a pleasing rough edge to their comedy, and here a new French kid on the block proves to be the very model of international camaraderie as he helps the boys win their local baseball game. Symbolic, you betcha! Back in the dark days of the Second World War, this was a lesson in how to be good neighbours for all audiences. **TH**

Leo Gorcey *Muggs* · Huntz Hall *Glimpy* · Gabriel Dell *Skinny* · Billy Benedict *Butch* · Jimmy Strand *Danny* · Bill Chaney *Tobey* · Minerva Urecal *Amelia* · Roberta Smith *Jinx* · Noah Beery Sr [Noah Beery] *Judge* · Harry Langdon *Higgins* ■ *Dir* Wallace Fox · *Scr* Houston Branch

Blockade ★★ PG
War drama 1938 · US · BW · 83min

The Spanish Civil War was a crusade for many Hollywood liberals and one might have expected a screenwriter such as John Howard Lawson, later one of the original Hollywood Ten, to have produced something less lily-livered than this. The picture tells us that war is wrong and nothing else. Henry Fonda and Madeleine Carroll are mixed up in it – he's a peasant, she's one of dozens of spies – but the story is hopelessly muddled. **AT** *DVD*

Henry Fonda *Marco* · Madeleine Carroll *Norma* · Leo Carrillo *Luis* · John Halliday *Andre* · Vladimir Sokoloff *Basil* · Robert Warwick *General Vallejo* ■ *Dir* William Dieterle · *Scr* John Howard Lawson

Blockheads ★★★★ U
Classic comedy 1938 · US · BW · 54min

Stan Laurel, left to guard a trench in 1917, is discovered two decades later with a pile of empty bean cans, still on guard. Ollie takes the trench hero home, where they become involved in a farcical situation with jealous big-game hunter Billy Gilbert. One to relish for its innuendos and sight gags, John G Blystone's remake of the short

Unaccustomed As We Are is one of Laurel and Hardy's more appealing comedies. TH **DVD**

Stan Laurel *Stan* • Oliver Hardy *Ollie* • Billy Gilbert *Mr Gilbert* • Patricia Ellis *Mrs Gilbert* • Minna Gombell *Mrs Hardy* • James Finlayson *Mr Finn* ■ *Dir* John G Blystone • *Scr* Felix Adler, Arnold Belgard, Harry Langdon, James Parrott, Charles Rogers

The Blockhouse ★★★ 12
Second World War drama based on a true story
1973 · UK · Colour · 91min

An almost unseen Peter Sellers movie, this features the star in a rare straight role. In wartime Germany, slave workers from all over Europe are used to build German coastal fortifications while the Allies bombard the sites. Several workers take refuge in a network of underground tunnels and are subsequently sealed in. Although the bunkers contain ample supplies, the workers undergo a tortuous time in their subterranean prison. This grim movie based on real-life events (two men were discovered in 1951, having been trapped for six years in a similar situation). This difficult film sat on the shelf for several years, before surfacing briefly in 1978. DF Violence, swearing. **DVD**

Peter Sellers *Rouquet* • Charles Aznavour *Visconti* • Per Oscarsson *Lund* • Peter Vaughan *Aufret* • Jeremy Kemp *Grabinski* • Leon Lissek *Kozhek* • Nicholas Jones *Kramer* • Alfred Lynch *Larshen* ■ *Dir* Clive Rees • *Scr* John Gould, Clive Rees, from the novel *Le Blockhaus* by Jean Paul Clebert

Blond Cheat ★ U
Comedy 1938 · US · BW · 62min

Intended as a farce with an English slant, this miserable offering from RKO and director Joseph Santley needed five writers to dream up the tale of a British millionaire (Cecil Kellaway) who offers to finance a new show for an actress (Joan Fontaine, before her career took off with *Rebecca*) on condition she breaks up the romance between his daughter (Lilian Bond) and a smooth socialite (Derrick DeMarney). There is little to recommend it. RK

Joan Fontaine *Julie Evans* • Derrick DeMarney *Michael Ashburn* • Cecil Cunningham *Genevieve Trent* • Lillian Bond *Roberta Trent* • Robert Coote *Gilbert Potts* • Olaf Hytten *Paul Douglas* • Gerald Hamer *Waiter* • Cecil Kellaway *Rufus Trent* ■ *Dir* Joseph Santley • *Scr* Charles Kaufman, Paul Yawitz, Viola Brothers Shore, Harry Segall, from a story by Aladar Lazlo

Blonde Ambition ★★ 12
Romantic comedy 2007 · US · Colour · 88min

No amount of surface gloss can hide the fact that Jessica Simpson's first starring vehicle is pretty much a shallow retread of *Legally Blonde*, even down to Luke Wilson in support. A sweet-natured country girl takes up residence in the city after a surprise visit to her fiancé ends badly. A couple of scheming corporate execs (Penelope Ann Miller and Andy Dick) engineer her appointment as their boss's PA, but this blonde proves to be smarter than she looks. The supporting players give it their best but the toothsome star lacks the comic chops to pull this sort of frothy confection off. JF Some swearing, sexual references. **DVD**

Jessica Simpson *Katie* • Luke Wilson *Ben* • Rachael Leigh Cook *Haley* • Penelope Ann Miller *Debra* • Andy Dick *Freddy* ■ *Dir* Scott Marshall • *Scr* David McHugh, John Cohen, Matthew Flanagan

Blonde Bombshell ★★★★
Comedy 1933 · US · BW · 90min

Jean Harlow stars in this perceptive yet affectionate satire on Hollywood itself, with the peroxide sex symbol playing movie sexpot Lola Burns, desperate for a life away from the cameras. It's quite a wacky farce with some biting observations, and Harlow really proves her worth, keeping sentimentality at bay while revealing a warm yet snappy comedic style. This movie is directed by one of Hollywood's most underrated craftsmen, Victor Fleming, who

squeezes every inch of mileage out of a plot one suspects he understood very well. TS

Jean Harlow *Lola* • Lee Tracy *Space* • Frank Morgan *Pops* • Franchot Tone *Gifford Middleton* • Pat O'Brien *Brogan* • Una Merkel *Mae* • Ted Healy *Junior* • Ivan Lebedeff *Marquis* • Mary Forbes *Mrs Middleton* • C Aubrey Smith *Mr Middleton* ■ *Dir* Victor Fleming • *Scr* Jules Furthman, John Lee Mahin, from the play by Caroline Francke, Mack Crane

Blonde Crazy ★★★
Crime comedy drama 1931 · US · BW · 78min

Fast-talking James Cagney's follow-up to his smash hits *Public Enemy* and *Smart Money* was this nifty little melodrama, shown in the UK as *Larceny Lane*. Here, he's a conman and she's his business partner/girlfriend who marries a relative newcomer to Hollywood, a startlingly young looking Ray Milland. The pace never lets up, and the success of this movie forced boss Jack Warner to up Cagney's salary to a richly deserved $1,000 per week after the star threatened to go elsewhere. TS

James Cagney *Bert Harris* • Joan Blondell *Ann Roberts* • Louis Calhern *Dapper Dan Barker* • Noel Francis *Helen Wilson* • Raymond Milland [Ray Milland] *Joe Reynolds* • Guy Kibbee *Rupert Johnson* • Polly Walters *Peggy* • Charles Lane (2) *Four-eyes, desk clerk* ■ *Dir* Roy Del Ruth • *Scr* Kubec Glasmon, John Bright

Blonde Fever ★★
Comedy drama 1944 · US · BW · 68min

Based on Ferenc Molnar's play *Delila*, this familiar tale of a married man falling for the charms of a gold-digger needed a Lubitsch but instead got the uninspired direction of Richard Whorf. It remains watchable due to the MGM production gloss, Gloria Grahame, in her screen debut as the scheming waitress, and a beautiful performance by veteran Mary Astor, as the wife. TV

Philip Dorn *Peter Donay* • Mary Astor *Delilah Donay* • Felix Bressart *Johnny* • Gloria Grahame *Sally Murfin* ■ *Dir* Richard Whorf • *Scr* Patricia Coleman, from the play *Delila* by Ferenc Molnar

Blonde Fist ★ 15
Comedy drama 1991 · UK · Colour · 98min

Real-life brother and sister Frank and Margi Clarke fail to live up to early promise as, respectively, writer/director and star of this lumbering film about a working-class woman with a mess of a life but a socking right hook, inherited from her bare-knuckle boxing dad. One to duck. PF Violence, swearing.

Margi Clarke *Ronnie O'Dowd* • Carroll Baker *Lovelle Summers* • Ken Hutchison *John O'Dowd* • Sharon Power *Mary* • Angela Clarke *Brenda Doyle* • Lewis Bester *Young Tony* • Gary Mavers *Tony Bone* • Jeff Weatherford *Dan* ■ *Dir/Scr* Frank Clarke

A Blonde in Love ★★★★ 15
Romantic comedy 1965 · Cz · BW · 88min

Combining sly situation comedy with charming observation, Milos Forman's second feature thoroughly merited its Oscar nomination – all the more so considering the inexperienced cast improvised much of its dialogue. Hana Brejchova is superb as the small-town factory girl whose earnest (and one-sided) pursuit of pianist Vladimir Pucholt comes to a head when she follows him to his parents' house in Prague. Full of the affectionate irony that characterises Forman's early studies of naive youth, this is also a subtly acerbic social satire. DP Czech +subtitles. **DVD**

Hana Brejchova *Andula* • Vladimir Pucholt *Milda* • Vladimir Mensik *Vacovsky* • Milada Jezkova *Milda's mother* • Josef Sebanek *Milda's father* • Ivan Kheil *Manas* • Jiri Hruby *Burda* • Marie Salacova *Marie* ■ *Dir* Milos Forman • *Scr* Milos Forman, Jaroslav Papousek, Ivan Passer

Blonde Venus ★★★★★ PG
Drama 1932 · US · BW · 93min

The fifth of director Josef von Sternberg's collaborations with Marlene Dietrich is unfortunately only ever wheeled out for teasing snatches of its dazzling club scene involving Dietrich and a gorilla suit, when in

fact the film offers many more riches. The story, with Dietrich's medically dependant husband Herbert Marshall unsettled by his wife's friendly, financial connection to tycoon Cary Grant is, as ever with von Sternberg, merely a departure point for more important matters. You'll not see many films superior to this in their use of visual detail, tempo, humour and double-edged significance. Art as entertainment, from the original "all is not what it seems" director. DO

Marlene Dietrich *Helen Faraday/Helen Jones* • Herbert Marshall *Edward Faraday* • Cary Grant *Nick Townsend* • Dickie Moore *Johnny Faraday* • Gene Morgan *Ben Smith* • Rita La Roy *"Taxi Belle" Hooper* • Robert Emmett O'Connor *Dan O'Connor* • Sidney Toler *Detective Wilson* • Morgan Wallace *Doctor Pierce* • Hattie McDaniel *Cora, Helen's maid* • Francis Sayles *Charlie Blaine* ■ *Dir* Josef von Sternberg • *Scr* SK Lauren, Jules Furthman, from a story by Jules Furthman, Josef von Sternberg • *Cinematographer* Bert Glennon • *Costume Designer* Travis Banton

Blondes Have More Guns ★★ 18
Comedy 1995 · US · Colour · 89min

Trash specialist Troma attempts a *Naked Gun*-style parody in this scattershot collection of crass puns and crude sight gags. *Basic Instinct* is the prime target, although *Indecent Proposal* and *The Crying Game* don't escape, as cop Michael McGahan strives to track down a *femme fatale* with a serial addiction to chainsaw slaughter. Subtlety is not the name of the game here. DP

Michael McGahan *Harry Bates* • Elizabeth Key *Montana Beaver-Shotz* • Richard Neil *Dick Smoker* • Gloria Lusiak *Dakota Beaver* • André Brazeau *Captain Hook* • Brian A York *The Doctor* ■ *Dir* George Merriweather • *Scr* George Merriweather, Dan Goodman, Mary Guthrie

Blondie! ★★★ U
Comedy 1938 · US · BW · 69min

This was the first in the long-running series of films – 28 episodes over 12 years – about the chaotic household of Blondie and Dagwood Bumstead, based on the strip cartoon by Chic Young. In this introduction to the family, Dagwood loses his job; his attempts to keep this a secret cause Blondie to suspect him of infidelity. Penny Singleton's delightfully dippy housewife makes an amusing mate for the bumbling Arthur Lake, while the audience of the time could readily identify with the family's dilemmas. TH

Penny Singleton *Blondie Bumstead* • Arthur Lake *Dagwood Bumstead* • Larry Simms *Baby Dumpling* • Gene Lockhart *CP Hazlip* • Jonathan Hale *JC Dithers* • Gordon Oliver *Chester Franey* • Danny Mummert *Alvin* • Kathleen Lockhart *Blondie's mother, Mrs Miller* • Ann Doran *Elsie Hazlip* • Dorothy Moore *Dorothy* • Fay Helm *Mrs Fuddle* • Irving Bacon *Mailman* ■ *Dir* Frank R Strayer • *Scr* Richard Floumoy, from the comic strip by Chic Young

Blondie of the Follies ★★★
Musical comedy 1932 · US · BW · 91min

The plotline of this musical comedy must have titillated those in the know at the time. Scorned by nice young Robert Montgomery, Marion Davies becomes the kept plaything of older man Douglass Dumbrille. Davies was the mistress of newspaper magnate William Randolph Hearst, whose Cosmopolitan film company funded this opus. Parallels aside, this is a likeable romp, which really centres on Davies and Billie Dove vying for Montgomery's affections. TS

Marion Davies *Blondie McClune* • Robert Montgomery *Larry Belmont* • Billie Dove *Lottie Callahan* • Jimmy Durante *Jimmy* • James Gleason *Pa McClune* • ZaSu Pitts *Gertie* • Sidney Toler *Pete* • Douglass Dumbrille *Murchenson* ■ *Dir* Edmund Goulding • *Scr* Frances Mario, Anita Loos

Blood ★★ 15
Crime thriller 2012 · UK · Colour · 88min

Nick Murphy's intense British cop movie has a cracking cast and is atmospherically set

on a washed-out Wirral coast, but it's somewhat less than the sum of its parts, leaving few genre clichés unmined. Paul Bettany and Stephen Graham play brothers, both detectives, who live in the shadow of their police chief dad (Brian Cox) who was notorious for his strong-arm tactics. Bill Gallagher's adaptation of his own BBC series *Conviction* is an intriguing tale of machismo and mixed-up morality, but it's perhaps better suited to the small screen. DA Violence, swearing, sexual references. **DVD** **Blu-ray**

Paul Bettany *Joe Fairburn* • Stephen Graham *Chrissie Fairburn* • Brian Cox (1) *Lenny Fairburn* • Mark Strong *Robert Seymoore* • Adrian Edmondson *Tom Tiernan* ■ *Dir* Nick Murphy • *Scr* Bill Gallagher, from his TV series *Conviction*

Blood Alley ★★ U
Adventure 1955 · US · Colour · 110min

The first film to be made by John Wayne's production company, Batjac, this began shooting with Robert Mitchum playing the American seafarer who leads 180 villagers in an escape from Communist China to Hong Kong. Mitchum and director William A Wellman clashed and Wayne was obliged to fire Mitchum. When Gregory Peck and Humphrey Bogart's demands for high fees were turned down, Wayne himself stepped in as Mitchum's replacement. The result is a typical piece of Yellow Peril propaganda, sluggish and predictable. AT

John Wayne *Wilder* • Lauren Bacall *Cathy* • Paul Fix *Mr Tso* • Joy Kim *Susu* • Berry Kroeger *Old Feng* • Mike Mazurki *Big Han* • Anita Ekberg *Wei Long* • Henry Nakamura *Tak* • WT Chang *Mr Han* ■ *Dir* William Wellman [William A Wellman] • *Scr* AS Fleischmann, from his novel

Blood and Black Lace ★★★★★ 18
Horror thriller
1964 · Fr/It/W Ger · Colour · 84min

Director Mario Bava's grisly fever dream is an elegantly mounted, visually stunning and erotically charged catalogue of homicidal cruelty. The models at Eva Bartok's fashion house are violently murdered by a sadistic masked assailant, for a diary containing incriminating scandal in an ahead-of-its time psycho-chiller that has influenced everyone from Martin Scorsese to Dario Argento. A spectacular study in voyeuristic delirium and shadowy atmospheric terror, Bava's seminal blueprint for all the spaghetti thrillers of the 1970s is a *Grand Guignol* masterpiece. AJ Italian dubbed. **DVD** **Blu-ray**

Eva Bartok *Cristina* • Cameron Mitchell *Max Martan* • Thomas Reiner *Inspector Silvester* • Arianna Gorini *Nicole* • Mary Arden *Peggy* • Franco Ressel *Marquis Richard Morell* ■ *Dir* Mario Bava • *Scr* Marcel Fondat [Marcel Fondat], Joe Barilla, Mario Bava

Blood and Bone ★★★ 18
Action crime drama 2009 · US · Colour · 89min

Michael Jai White is the holder of all sorts of martial arts black belts and this terrific action yarn makes full use of both his mighty fighting skills and his imposing physique. He plays an ex-con who infiltrates the underground fight circuit to avenge the death of his friend. As with most martial arts stars, White struggles with the actual acting side of things, but when you can fight as well as him, that's largely irrelevant. The gob-smacking opening scene alone makes this essential viewing for any action buff. JF Violence. **DVD** **Blu-ray**

Michael Jai White *Isaiah Bone* • Julian Sands *Franklin McVeigh* • Eamonn Walker *James* • Dante Basco *Pinball* • Nona Gaye *Tamara* ■ *Dir* Ben Ramsey • *Scr* Michael Andrews

Blood and Chocolate ★★ 12
Romantic fantasy horror
2006 · Ger/UK/Rom/US · Colour · 94min

Like a watered-down version of the same producers' *Underworld*, director Katja von Garnier's fantasy horror is a clumsily and radically altered adaptation of Annette Curtis Klause's immensely popular novel for young adults. Werewolf Agnes Bruckner must mate with Olivier Martinez, the leader of her Romanian pack, but instead she falls

B

for human comic-book artist Hugh Dancy, who's researching her lycanthropic kind for his latest graphic novel. And so the stage is set for silly romantic montages scored with schmaltzy music, a deliberately styled rock-video atmosphere, derivative action and slapdash special effects. AJ Violence, drug references. *DVD*

Agnes Bruckner *Vivian* • Hugh Dancy *Aiden* • Olivier Martinez *Gabriel* • Katja Riemann *Astrid* • Bryan Dick *Rafe* • Chris Geere *Ulf* ■ *Dir* Katja von Garnier • *Scr* Ehren Kruger, Christopher Landon, from the novel by Annette Curtis Klause

Blood and Roses ★★★
Horror   1960 • Fr/It • Colour • 84min

Brigitte Bardot's Svengali, Roger Vadim, updated Sheridan Le Fanu's gothic horror story, *Carmilla*, setting it among Rome's idle rich. His then wife Annette plays Carmilla, who believes she is possessed by the spirit of a vampire and attacks her cousin Mel Ferrer's fiancée Elsa Martinelli. Although the film was a commercial failure, cameraman Claude Renoir creates elegant images of women gliding around house and garden. The highlight in a pared-down, uneventful storyline is the striking dream sequence, which utilised new optical technology. DM

Mel Ferrer *Leopoldo De Karnstein* • Elsa Martinelli *Georgia Monteverdi* • Annette Vadim *Carmilla von Karnstein* • Jacques-René Chauffard *Dr Verari* • Marc Allégret *Judge Monteverdi* ■ *Dir* Roger Vadim • *Scr* Roger Vadim, Roger Vailland, Claude Brulé, Claude Martin, Peter Viertel, from the story *Carmilla* by J Sheridan Le Fanu

Blood and Sand ★★★ U
Silent epic   1922 • US • Tinted • 79min

Hot on the heels of the previous year's *Four Horsemen of the Apocalypse* and *The Sheik* came this third smash hit for superstar Rudolph Valentino. This time, the first of the screen's Latin lovers plays a matador led into temptation by a decadent vamp (Nita Naldi). Almost gored to death in the bull ring, he recovers through the tender loving care of his wife (Lila Lee). Fred Niblo's film defies modern criticism, so far are we from its exaggerated histrionics and early techniques. However, it's clear why Valentino's potent presence captured the female hearts of a generation. RK *DVD*

Rudolph Valentino *Juan Gallardo* • Lila Lee *Carmen* • Rosa Rosanova *Senora Augustias* • George Periolat *Marquise de Guevara* • Nita Naldi *Doña Sol* • Walter Long *Plumitas* • Rosita Marstini *El Carnacione* ■ *Dir* Fred Niblo • *Scr* June Mathis, from the play *Blood and Sand* by Tom Cushing, from the novel *Sangre y Arena* by Vicente Blasco Ibanez

Blood and Sand ★★★★ PG
Romantic drama   1941 • US • Colour • 119min

This expensively mounted 20th Century-Fox treatment of the famous novel about a young matador is as sexy as 1940s censorship would allow. Rita Hayworth, in a star-making performance, taunts unlikely bullfighter Tyrone Power, who is handsome but miscast. The pace is slow and the attitudes astoundingly naive, but there is a fine lushness and a wonderful symbolic use of Technicolor that gives the film a rare distinction, and the sheer soppiness of the whole enterprise is breathtakingly endearing. TS

Tyrone Power *Juan Gallardo* • Linda Darnell *Carmen Espinosa* • Rita Hayworth *Dona Sol des Muire* • Anthony Quinn *Manolo de Palma* • Alla Nazimova *Senora Augustias* • J Carrol Naish *Garabato* • John Carradine *Nacional* • Laird Cregar *Natalio Curro* • Lynn Bari *Encarnacion* ■ *Dir* Rouben Mamoulian • *Scr* Jo Swerling , from the novel *Sangre y Arena* by Vicente Blasco Ibanez • *Choreographer* Budd Boetticher

Blood and Sand ★★ 18
Drama   1989 • Sp/US • Colour • 96min

Sharon Stone stars in the third – and weakest – screen version of Vicente Blasco Ibanez's novel. Christopher Rydell is happily married to Ana Torrent and nurses a burning ambition to become a famous toreador. A rehearsal with a dangerous bull the night before a big fight backfires, and it

is left to Stone to show him the ropes. Lacking the gusto of a real bullfight, this is a piece of Euro-pudding nonsense. LH

Christopher Rydell *Juan Gallardo* • Sharon Stone *Doña Sol* • Ana Torrent *Carmen* • Antonio Flores *Chiripa* • Simon Andreu *Juan's uncle* • Albert Vidal ■ *Dir* Javier Elorrieta • *Scr* Rafael Azcona, Ricardo Franco, Thomas Fucci, from the novel *Sangre y Arena* by Vicente Blasco Ibanez

Blood and Wine ★★★ 15
Crime thriller 1996 • US/UK/Fr • Colour • 96min

Paired for the first time, Jack Nicholson and Michael Caine are supremely sleazy as a couple of businessmen/thieves who steal a costly necklace from one of wine dealer Nicholson's affluent Florida clients. It's a delicious double act: Nicholson is, well, Nicholson, and Caine, with dyed black hair and an alarming cough, creates his vilest villain since *Mona Lisa*. Stephen Dorff and Jennifer Lopez offer sexy support, while director Bob Rafelson stylishly juggles the complexities. JC Swearing, violence.

Jack Nicholson *Alex Gates* • Stephen Dorff *Jason* • Jennifer Lopez *Gabriela* • Judy Davis *Suzanne Gates* • Michael Caine *Victor Spansky* • Harold Perrineau Jr [Harold Perrineau] *Henry* • Robyn Peterson *Dina* • Mike Starr *Mike* • John Seitz *Frank* ■ *Dir* Bob Rafelson • *Scr* Nick Villiers, Alison Cross, from a story by Bob Rafelson, Nick Villiers

Blood Beach ★★
Horror   1981 • US • Colour • 89min

What's sucking sun-worshippers and concerned locals under the sand on a south California beach? Nothing more than a stock papier-mâché monster in this workmanlike update of a formula 1950s B-movie. A little atmosphere is created when heroine Mariana Hill finds the creature's lair by accident, but elsewhere director Jeffrey Bloom's first foray into the horror genre is familiar territory. AJ

David Huffman *Harry Caulder* • Mariana Hill [Marianna Hill] *Catherine* • John Saxon *Captain Pearson* • Otis Young *Lieutenant Piantadosi* • Stefan Gierasch *Dr Dimitrios* • Burt Young *Sergeant Royko* • Darrell Fetty *Hoagy* ■ *Dir* Jeffrey Bloom • *Scr* Jeffrey Bloom, from a story by Steven Nalevansky, Jeffrey Bloom

The Blood Beast Terror ★★ 12
Horror   1967 • UK • Colour • 77min

Peter Cushing considered this clumsy chiller the worst picture he ever made. In many respects he was right. He's the policeman investigating vampiristic murders carried out by a giant death's-head moth masquerading as the "daughter" of a renowned Victorian entomologist. It must have seemed a good idea at the time. AJ *DVD*

Peter Cushing *Inspector Quennell* • Robert Flemyng *Professor Mallinger* • Wanda Ventham *Clare Mallinger* • Vanessa Howard *Meg Quennell* • Roy Hudd *Morgue attendant* • David Griffin *William* • Kevin Stoney *Grainger* • Glynn Edwards *Sergeant Allan* ■ *Dir* Vernon Sewell • *Scr* Peter Bryan

Blood Car ★★★ 18
Comedy horror   2007 • US • Colour • 75min

This gleefully gory horror romp atones for some strained satire and the odd technical glitch with a glut of genuinely funny dialogue and slaughter scenes of determinedly dubious taste. Mike Brune gives a bravura performance as the vegan kindergarten teacher who's determined to solve the world fuel crisis with an engine using wheatgrass juice. But he discovers that his formula works better with a dash of human blood. Director Alex Orr revels in the gruesome comedy, but a more incisive lampooning of American capitalism could have elevated this above its B-movie origins. DP Violence, swearing, sex scenes, nudity. *DVD*

Mike Brune *Archie Andrews* • Anna Chlumsky *Lorraine* • Katie Rowlett *Denise* • Matt Hutchinson *Donald Watkins* • Marla Malcolm *Hitchhiker* ■ *Dir* Alex Orr • *Scr* Alex Orr, Adam Pinney, from a story by Orr, Pinney, Hugh Braselton

Blood Creek ★★★ 18
Horror thriller   2009 • US • Colour • 86min

Stylish chills and riotous suspense are well conveyed in director Joel Schumacher's welcome return to harrowing horror form. Evil Nazi Michael Fassbender arrives in the 1936 Midwest in search of immortality for Hitler's war effort. Fast forward to today and marine Dominic Purcell, thought AWOL from Iraq, and his older brother take on the hideous blood-drinking monster Fassbender has become. With its distinctive atmosphere and nonstop splatter action, this quickly captures the imagination and furnishes some highly unusual shocks – a reminder of just how good a terror technician Schumacher can be. AJ Violence, swearing. *DVD* *BL*

Dominic Purcell *Victor Marshall* • Henry Cavill *Evan Marshall* • Michael Fassbender *Richard Wirth* • Emma Booth *Liese Wollner* • Rainer Winkelvoss *Otto Wollner* ■ *Dir* Joel Schumacher • *Scr* Dave Kajganich

Blood Diamond ★★★ 15
Action thriller
2006 • US/S Afr • Colour • 143min

A mercenary diamond smuggler might seem a stretch for Leonardo DiCaprio, but this thought-provoking action thriller offers a superb showcase for his growing talents. For a time it seems the film will be as good, starting with the surprisingly savage attack on a tiny fishing community by guerrillas in war-torn 1990s Sierra Leone. DiCaprio agrees to help survivor Djimon Hounsou (a wonderfully low-key performance) find the family from which he was taken in return for recovering a priceless diamond, so, along with crusading journalist Jennifer Connelly, they set off on the perilous quest. Sadly, it's here that the provocative, uncomfortable tale turns predictable and disappointing. DW Violence, swearing. *DVD* *BL*

Leonardo DiCaprio *Danny Archer* • Djimon Hounsou *Solomon Vandy* • Jennifer Connelly *Maddy Bowen* • Michael Sheen *Simmons* • Arnold Vosloo *Colonel Coetzee* • Kagiso Kuypers *Dia Vandy* • David Harewood *Captain Poison* • Stephen Collins *Ambassador Walker* ■ *Dir* Edward Zwick • *Scr* Charles Leavitt, from a story by Leavitt, C Gaby Mitchell • *Music* James Newton Howard • *Editor* Steven Rosenblum

Blood Father ★★★ 15
Action thriller   2016 • Fr • Colour • 88min

Mel Gibson reclaims his action hero mojo in this slick pulp thriller, even if it does feel like a trashier carbon copy of *Taken*. The grizzled Gibson is clearly having a ball playing an alcoholic outlaw Hell's Angel, whose estranged teenage daughter (Erin Moriarty) is on the run. Gibson's determination to do the right thing leads to bracing road movie thrills and spills. Not to be taken seriously at any point, this is just a crowd-pleasingly nasty revenge saga that builds to a surprising and unexpectedly downbeat desert showdown. AJ

Mel Gibson *John Link* • William H Macy *Kirby Curtis* • Diego Luna *Jonah* • Michael Parks *Preacher* ■ *Dir* Jean-François Richet • *Scr* Peter Craig, Andrea Berloff, from Craig's novel

Blood Feast ★ 18
Horror   1963 • US • Colour • 66min

Although it virtually invented the splatter genre, the first in director Herschell Gordon Lewis's infamous gore trilogy (*Two Thousand Maniacs!* and *Color Me Blood Red* being the other two) is also one of the sickest, stupidest and most inept exploitation movies ever made. Mal Arnold kills young women in brutal fashion so body parts can be used in an ancient Egyptian ritual. The fake, hokey, yet powerfully gruesome mutilations are relieved by Lewis's hopelessly amateur directing and the consummate bad acting. He directed a belated sequel in 2002. AJ *DVD*

Thomas Wood [William Kerwin] *Pete Thornton* • Mal Arnold *Fuad Ramses* • Connie Mason *Suzette* • Scott H Hall *Police captain* • Lyn Bolton *Mrs Fremont* • Toni Calvert *Trudy* ■ *Dir* Herschell G Lewis [Herschell Gordon Lewis] • *Scr* Allison Louise Downe

Blood Feud ★
Drama   1979 • It • Colour • 112min

In the mid-1970s, Italian director Lina Wertmuller became a sensation in America, mainly because *Seven Beauties* (1976) made her the first woman ever to be nominated for a best director Oscar. After that, Wertmuller cashed in on her fame by making her work increasingly pretentious. Set in Sicily at the birth of fascism, this has Marcello Mastroianni and Sophia Loren making their umpteenth film together and probably regretting every second of it. AT Italian dubbed.

Sophia Loren *Titina Paterno* • Marcello Mastroianni *Spallone* • Giancarlo Giannini *Nick* • Turi Ferro *Baron* ■ *Dir/Scr* Lina Wertmuller

Blood for Dracula ★★★ 18
Horror   1974 • It • Colour • 103min

In contrast to this film's Andy Warhol-produced companion piece, *Flesh for Frankenstein* in 3D, The Factory's in-house director Paul Morrissey here accents wit over gore in a clever twist on the vampire myth. Udo Kier is tragicomic as the anaemic Transylvanian Count looking for "wirgin" blood in an Italian household of females. Trouble is, sexy handyman Joe Dallesandro keeps deflowering his prospective prey. Heavy bloodshed is lightened by the consistently humorous tone of the tale. Directors Vittorio De Sica and Roman Polanski put in telling cameos in this funny fang farce. AJ *DVD*

Joe Dallesandro *Mario* • Udo Kier *Dracula* • Vittorio De Sica *Marquis* • Maxime McKendry *Marquisa* • Arno Juerging *Anton* • Milena Vukotic *Esmeralda* • Dominique Darel *Saphiria* • Stefania Casini *Rubinia* • Roman Polanski • Vittorio De Sica ■ *Dir/Scr* Paul Morrissey

Blood from the Mummy's Tomb ★★★ 15
Horror   1971 • UK • Colour • 89min

Statuesque Valerie Leon is possessed by the spirit of an ancient Egyptian queen in this cult Hammer horror based on Bram Stoker's *The Jewel of Seven Stars*. With hardly a bandage in sight, director Seth Holt tried to radically rethink the mummy genre, and largely succeeded in creating a fascinating fantasy with a menacing atmosphere dripping in delicious irony. Sadly, Holt died during shooting; Hammer boss Michael Carreras took over and the film is not as interesting as it should have been. AJ *DVD*

Andrew Keir *Professor Fuchs* • Valerie Leon *Margaret/Tera* • James Villiers *Corbeck* • Hugh Burden *Dandridge* • George Coulouris *Berigan* • Mark Edwards *Tod Browning* • Rosalie Crutchley *Helen Dickerson* • Aubrey Morris *Dr Putnum* • David Markham *Dr Burgess* ■ *Dir* Seth Holt, Michael Carreras • *Scr* Christopher Wicking, from the novel *The Jewel of Seven Stars* by Bram Stoker

Blood Glacier ★★★ 15
Horror   2013 • Austria • Colour • 93min

Adding a whole new meaning to the phrase "cold fusion", this fascinating continental twist on *The Thing* sees infected glacial liquid cause nature to run amok as a trio of scientists and a brooding tech guy at a remote Alpine station become the prey of hungry hybrid beasties. The slow-burn pace works nicely here and careful reveals of the mutated monstrosities only increase anticipation about what weird thingamajig will go on the rampage next. Yes, the effects are ropey, but this is still a monster movie to remember. JA German +subtitles. Violence. *DVD*

Gerhard Liebmann *Janek* • Edita Malovcic *Tanja* • Brigitte Kren *Ministerin Bodicek* • Hille Beseler *Birte* ■ *Dir* Marvin Kren • *Scr* Benjamin Hessler, Marvin Kren

Blood In Blood Out ★★ 18
Drama   1992 • US • Colour • 172min

Co-written by poet Jimmy Santiago Baca, this is based on his real-life experiences. Director Taylor Hackford blunts his treatise on the cultural ties that bind through excessive length and off-putting violence.

Three Chicano cousins take the viewer on a gruelling journey through the Latino experience, as they go from the gang-run streets of East LA to the brutal confines of San Quentin prison. The unknown leads turn in strong performances and Hackford intermittently packs the sermonising saga with a powerfully emotional punch. **AJ**

Damian Chapa *Miklo* • Jesse Borrego *Cruz* • Benjamin Bratt *Paco* • Enrique J Castillo [Enrique Castillo] *Montana* • Victor Rivers *Magic Mike* • Delroy Lindo *Bonafide* • Tom Towles *Red Ryder* • Carlos Carrasco *Popeye* ■ *Dir* Taylor Hackford • *Scr* Jimmy Santiago Baca, Jeremy Iacone, Floyd Mutrux, from a story by Ross Thomas

Blood in the Mobile ★★12A
Documentary
2010 · Den/Ger/Congo/Uganda/Fr/Fin/Nor/Gre/Ire/Hun/Neth/Is · Colour · 85min

Examining the financial link between a 15-year war in the Congo, in which over five million people have lost their lives, and the mining of rare minerals used in mobile phone production, this documentary condemns those western companies – most specifically Nokia – who seem reluctant to take their corporate responsibility seriously. But director Frank Piasecki Poulen's worthy rhetoric doesn't bring any new insight to the African experience of western business. As a plea for urgent action, this is a poorly conceived and unconvincing calling card, full of sound and fury but signifying very little. **SuR** English, French +subtitles.

■ *Dir* Frank Piasecki Poulsen

Blood Money ★★18
Martial arts western
1974 · It/HK/Sp · Colour · 95min

This is an unappetising mix of spaghetti western and chop-socky action movie. Lee Van Cleef snarls in the accustomed manner as a bounty hunter seeking four women who have the clues to buried treasure tattooed on their bodies. Italian director Antonio Margheriti (struggles to sustain the blistering pace expected of a martial arts movie. The brutality of the fight sequences are definitely not for the faint-hearted. **DP**

Lee Van Cleef *Dakota* • Lo Lieh *Wang Ho Kiang* • Karen Yeh *Yeh Ling Chih/Lia Hua* • Julian Ugarte *Deacon Yancy Hobbitt* • Goyo Peralta *Indio* • Al Tung *Wang* ■ *Dir* Anthony M Dawson [Antonio Margheriti] • *Scr* Barth Jules Sussman

Blood Money ★★15
Political thriller
1988 · US · Colour · 90min

This sweaty, muddled political thriller is notable mainly for the presence of two actors on the cusp of stardom: Andy Garcia and Ellen Barkin. Garcia is a petty crook who gets way out of his depth when he starts sniffing around a scheme to smuggle guns to the Contra rebels in Nicaragua. The star is a touch over-the-top, but Barkin is sympathetic as a prostitute who also gets caught up in the plot. **JF** *DVD*

Andy Garcia *Clinton Dillard* • Ellen Barkin *Nadine Powers* • Morgan Freeman *Dorsey Pratt* • Michael Lombard *James Conrad* • John C McGinley *Turner* • Brad Sullivan *General John Anson* • Alan North *Detective Rayburn* ■ *Dir* Jerry Schatzberg • *Scr* Robert Foster

Blood Moon ★★15
Western horror
2014 · UK · Colour · 82min

It's cowboys v werewolves in this rare British western, in which a stagecoach full of passengers and a pair of brutal bank robbers fall prey to a "skinwalker" in a Colorado ghost town. A blend of *Stagecoach* and lycanthrope horror sounds intriguing but, apart from Shaun Dooley's mysterious gunslinger (by way of Clint Eastwood), this anaemic tale has little going for it. Even an unpretentious, low-budget flick shot in the backwoods of Kent should have more chills, thrills and gore than this. **JA** Violence, swearing. *DVD*

Shaun Dooley *Calhoun* • George Blagden *Jake Norman* • Anna Skellern *Marie* • Corey Johnson *Hank Norton* ■ *Dir* Jeremy Wooding • *Scr* Alan Wightman

Blood Oath ★★★★15
Courtroom drama
1990 · Aus · Colour · 103min

Bryan Brown has been a considerable lean and leathery presence in Australian movies, notably in this courtroom drama in which he's the Aussie officer prosecuting an Oxford-educated Japanese commander (George Takei) for war crimes. His task is complicated by Americans wanting a "not guilty" verdict for reasons of political expediency. Brown's role is based on the experiences of the father of co-scriptwriter Brian A Williams, and Brown brings a sardonic edge to the search for motives. **TH** Violence, swearing.

Bryan Brown *Captain Robert Cooper* • George Takei *Vice-Admiral Baron Takahashi* • Terry O'Quinn *Major Tom Beckett* • John Bach *Major Frank Roberts* • Toshi Shioya *Lieutenant Hideo Tanaka* • John Clarke (2) *Mike Sheedy* • Deborah Unger [Deborah Kara Unger] *Sister Carol Littell* • Jason Donovan *Private Talbot* • Russell Crowe *Lieutenant Jack Corbett* ■ *Dir* Stephen Wallace • *Scr* Denis Whitburn, Brian A Williams

The Blood of a Poet ★★★PG
Experimental drama
1930 · Fr · BW · 50min

Jean Cocteau's first film – made when he was 41, his fame already established as a writer, poet and artist – follows the dream-like encounters and observations of a young poet as he views the world on the other side of a mirror. Highly experimental and devoid of any conventional narrative, the film offers a series of arresting images (executions, hermaphrodites, opium smokers), and exerted a strong influence on the American avant-garde. The surreal symbolism is inaccessible to the majority of viewers, however, who are more likely to appreciate Cocteau's ravishing *La Belle et la Bête*. **RK** French +subtitles. *DVD*

Lee Miller *The statue* • Pauline Carton *Child's tutor* • Odette Talazac • Enrico Rivero *The poet* • Jean Desbordes *The friend in Louis XV costume* • Fernand Dichamps • Lucien Jager • Féral Benga *The black angel* • Barbette *Spectator in lodge* • Jean Cocteau *Narrator* ■ *Dir/Scr* Jean Cocteau • *Cinematographer* Georges Périnal

Blood of Dracula ★★PG
Horror
1957 · US · BW · 69min

A routine 1950s "schlock 'n' roller", this is great drive-in movie trash. As is so often the case in these morality-tinged horrors, carnal thoughts equal out-of-control monsterhood, as staid college girl Sandra Harrison turns tramp vamp when hypnotised by a magic amulet owned by her evil chemistry teacher. The solemn intensity Harrison brings to her ludicrous tight-sweater role is a joy to behold. A scream, but not quite in the way anyone intended. **AJ** *DVD*

Sandra Harrison *Nancy Perkins* • Louise Lewis (1) *Miss Branding* • Gail Ganley *Myra* • Jerry Blaine *Tab* • Heather Ames *Nola* • Malcolm Atterbury *Lieutenant Dunlap* • Mary Adams *Mrs Thorndyke* • Thomas B Henry [Thomas Browne Henry] *Mr Perkins* • Don Devlin *Eddie* ■ *Dir* Herbert L Strock • *Scr* Ralph Thornton

Blood of Dracula's Castle ★
Horror
1967 · US · Colour · 84min

This dreadful attempt by exploitation maverick Al Adamson to update the Dracula myth finds high-class vampires Alex D'Arcy and Paula Raymond living in a castle in modern California. A half-wit hunchback keeps the cellar stocked with nubile victims, who are drained of blood for gruesome cocktail hours. An S&M-tinged tacky terror. **AJ**

John Carradine *George* • Paula Raymond *Countess Townsend* • Alex D'Arcy *Count Townsend* • Robert Dix *Johnny* • Gene O'Shane *Glen Cannon* • Barbara Bishop *Liz* ■ *Dir* Al Adamson • *Scr* Rex Carlton

The Blood of Fu Manchu ★★15
Horror
1968 · US/UK/Sp/W Ger · Colour · 89min

Actually more like a western, thanks to its Brazilian setting and bandit subplot, the fourth outing for Christopher Lee as Sax Rohmer's insidious Oriental is cheaply-made horror exotica. Lee's stiff performance doesn't help the daft story, as Fu Manchu endows ten gorgeous girls with the "kiss of death" via an Inca poison deadly only to the male and programmes them to kill any influential power-broker who touches their passionate lips. **AJ** Violence, swearing. *DVD*

Christopher Lee *Fu Manchu* • Götz George *Carl Janson* • Richard Greene *Nayland Smith* • Howard Marion-Crawford *Dr Petrie* • Tsai Chin *Lin Tang* • Maria Rohm *Ursula* • Shirley Eaton *Black Widow* ■ *Dir* Jess Franco [Jesus Franco] • *Scr* Harry Alan Towers

The Blood of Others ★★15
Second World War drama
1984 · Can/Fr · Colour · 263min

Adapted from the novel by Simone De Beauvoir, and with additional dialogue by the Irish-Canadian author Brian Moore, this wartime drama efficiently captures the claustrophobic paranoia of Occupied Paris, without ever involving us in the fate of its protagonists. Torn between her loyalty to imprisoned Resistance fighter Michael Ontkean and a love of luxury that draws her towards pro-Nazi businessman Sam Neill, Jodie Foster gives one of her least credible performances. **DP**

Jodie Foster *Hélène* • Michael Ontkean *Jean Blomart* • Sam Neill *Bergman* • Lambert Wilson *Paul* • Stéphane Audran *Gigi* • Jean-Pierre Aumont *André Blomart* • Micheline Presle *Denise* ■ *Dir* Claude Chabrol • *Scr* Brian Moore, from the novel *Le Sang des Autres* by Simone de Beauvoir

Blood of the Vampire ★★
Horror
1958 · UK · Colour · 85min

Universal nabbed Hammer's gore theatrics along with their resident scriptwriter, Jimmy Sangster, in the effort to beat the House of Horror at its own game. The result is enjoyable hokum with, for the era, some edgily gruesome torture chamber scenes. Thespian legend Donald Wolfit goes predictably over the top as Doctor Callistratus, who needs blood to stay alive and uses victims from his insane asylum for the grisly transfusion purpose. Hammer heroine Barbara Shelley adds the glamour, while Victor Maddern wears the daftest make-up imaginable as the scarred servant of the mad doctor. **AJ**

Donald Wolfit *Dr Callistratus* • Vincent Ball *Dr John Pierre* • Barbara Shelley *Madeleine* • Victor Maddern *Carl* • William Devlin *Kurt Urah* • Andrew Faulds *Wetzler* • Hal Osmond *Sneak thief* • Bernard Bresslaw *Sneak thief* • John Le Mesurier *Chief Justice* ■ *Dir* Henry Cass • *Scr* Jimmy Sangster

Blood on My Hands ★★
Crime drama
1948 · US · BW · 77min

Set in a Hollywood studio re-creation of postwar London, this stars Burt Lancaster as the violent war veteran who accidentally kills a man in a pub and goes on the run. He's blackmailed by a witness (played with exaggerated relish by Robert Newton) and befriended by a nurse (Joan Fontaine in her most sensitive mode). Despite some visual flair from Norman Foster's direction and Russell Metty's photography, plus one of Miklos Rozsa's best scores, this is mostly tedious and unbelievable. **AE**

Joan Fontaine *Jane Wharton* • Burt Lancaster *Bill Saunders* • Robert Newton *Harry Carter* • Lewis L Russell *Tom Widgery* • Aminta Dyne *Landlady* • Grizelda Hervey *Mrs Paton* • Jay Novello *Sea captain* • Colin Keith-Johnston *Judge* ■ *Dir* Norman Foster • *Scr* Leonardo Bercovici, Walter Bernstein, Hugh Gray, Ben Maddow, from the novel *Kiss the Blood off My Hands* by Gerald Butler

Blood on Satan's Claw ★★★18
Horror
1970 · UK · Colour · 92min

Devil-worshipping children in 17th-century England cause havoc for their village in this super-stylish supernatural shocker with a strong period flavour. While this is more sensational, violent and crude than its obvious model *Witchfinder General*, Piers Haggard's tense direction keeps the cauldron of fiendish orgies, demonic tortures and Linda Hayden's sultry turn as the devil's advocate bubbling at an even terror temperature until the satanic slow-motion climax. Vintage British horror at its lip-smacking best. **AJ** Violence, nudity *DVD*

Patrick Wymark *Judge* • Linda Hayden *Angel* • Barry Andrews *Ralph* • Michele Dotrice *Margaret* • Wendy Padbury *Cathy* • Anthony Ainley *Reverend Fallowfield* • Charlotte Mitchell *Ellen* • Tamara Ustinov *Rosalind* ■ *Dir* Piers Haggard • *Scr* Robert Wynne, Piers Haggard

Blood on the Moon ★★★PG
Western
1948 · US · BW · 87min

If there's such a thing as "western noir", then this is it, as director Robert Wise and distinguished photographer Nicholas Musuraca team up for this psychological take on the genre. Robert Mitchum brings some weighty experience to his role as a drifter forced to turn against his one-time mentor (an oily Robert Preston). The mood is satisfyingly dark and the actual confrontation scene, set in a saloon where light only leaks through sporadically, is masterly, while the violence is surprising for the time. **TS** *DVD*

Robert Mitchum *Jim Garry* • Barbara Bel Geddes *Amy Lufton* • Robert Preston *Tate Riling* • Walter Brennan *Kris Barden* • Phyllis Thaxter *Carol Lufton* • Frank Faylen *Jake Pindalest* • Tom Tully *John Lufton* ■ *Dir* Robert Wise • *Scr* Willie Hayward, from the novel *Gunman's Chance* by Luke Short, adapted by Harold Shumate

Blood on the Sun ★★★PG
Period drama
1945 · US · BW · 93min

The Cagney brothers chose a formidable subject for their second independent production, with Bill producing and Jimmy starring as an aggressive editor of an American newspaper in Tokyo, who daringly publishes the Japanese Master Plan for world domination. This doesn't go down too well with Colonel Tojo, nor did the film with the public when it was released. As scripted by blacklisted left-wing Hollywood Ten veteran Lester Cole, the movie packs a powerhouse message, appropriate in its day and still worth heeding. But the propaganda content overwhelms the drama. **TS** *DVD*

James Cagney *Nick Condon* • Sylvia Sidney *Iris Hilliard* • Wallace Ford *Ollie Miller* • Rosemary DeCamp *Edith Miller* • Robert Armstrong *Colonel Tojo* • John Emery *Premier Tanaka* • Leonard Strong *Hijikata* • Frank Puglia *Prince Tatsugi* • John Halloran *Captain Oshima* ■ *Dir* Frank Lloyd • *Scr* Lester Cole, from a story by Garrett Fort

Blood Orange ★★
Crime drama
1953 · UK · BW · 80min

Made for Hammer's B-movie outlet, Exclusive, this is an unremarkable offering from director Terence Fisher, who went on to make some of the studio's best horrors. Jan Read's tepid story about a retired FBI agent who gets involved with jewel thieves following the murder of model Delphi Lawrence gives him little to work with. The real problem, however, is Tom Conway's lacklustre performance. **DP**

Tom Conway *Conway* • Mila Parely *Helen Pascall* • Naomi Chance *Gina* • Eric Pohlmann *Mercedes* • Andrew Osborn *Captain Simpson* • Richard Wattis *Macleod* • Margaret Halstan *Lady Marchant* • Eileen Way *Fernande* • Delphi Lawrence *Chelsea* ■ *Dir* Terence Fisher • *Scr* Jan Read

Blood Orange ★★★15
Thriller
2016 · UK/Sp · Colour · 83min

Intrigued by the mix of passion and pragmatism that keeps age-gap couples together, veteran promo director Toby Tobias puts the relationship between reclusive rocker Bill (Iggy Pop) and trophy wife Isabelle (Kacey Barnfield) at the centre of his debut feature. Simmeringly shot under a scorching sun by Mark Patten, this slow-burning thriller suffers when the "Godfather of Punk" is off screen and the twist isn't entirely concealed, but it is surprisingly atmospheric and artful. **DP** Violence, swearing, nudity.

Iggy Pop *Bill* • Kacey Barnfield *Isabelle* • Ben Lamb *Lucas* • Antonio Magro *David* ■ *Dir/Scr* Toby Tobias

Blood Red ★ 15
Period action drama 1988 · US · Colour · 87min

Immigrant Sicilian grape farmers try to stop tycoon Dennis Hopper from building a railroad through the Napa Valley wine country of the late 19th century in this weak action adventure. It's interesting for two reasons: future superstar Julia Roberts makes her screen debut; and it's the only film she's made with her brother Eric (she plays his sister). The over-ripe script quickly withers on the vine. AJ

Eric Roberts *Marco Collogero* • Giancarlo Giannini *Sebastian Collogero* • Dennis Hopper *William Bradford Berrigan* • Burt Young *Andrews* • Carlin Glynn *Miss Jeffreys* • Lara Harris *Angelica* • Francesca De Sapio *Rosa Collogero* • Julia Roberts *Maria Collogero* • Michael Madsen *Enzio* • Elias Koteas *Silvio* ■ *Dir* Peter Masterson • *Scr* Ron Cutler

Blood Relatives ★★★ 18
Crime drama 1977 · Can/Fr · Colour · 90min

Adapted from an Ed McBain novel, this is directed by the French master Claude Chabrol with a sharp eye for the middle-class hypocrisies of a Canadian community. Donald Sutherland is the detective investigating the assault and murder of a young Montreal girl, with accusations and confessions flying thick and fast, though it's only in the film's final section that there's any real tension. The rest of the drama is – astonishing for Chabrol – actually a little wooden and flat. TH Violence, swearing.
DVD

Donald Sutherland *Steve Carella* • Aude Landry *Patricia Lowery* • Lisa Langlois *Muriel* • Laurent Malet *Andy Lowery* • Stéphane Audran *Mrs Lowery* • Donald Pleasence *Doniac* • David Hemmings *Jack Armstrong* • Walter Massey *Mr Lowery* ■ *Dir* Claude Chabrol • *Scr* Claude Chabrol, Sydney Banks, from the novel by Evan Hunter [Ed McBain]

Blood Simple ★★★★ 18
Thriller 1983 · US · Colour · 98min

A jealous Texas husband hires a sleazy private eye to murder his adulterous wife and her lover in the Coen brothers' feature debut. Blending elements of James M Cain, *film noir*, Hitchcock thrillers and contemporary horror movies, this dark morality tale deviates imaginatively from the 1940s murder mysteries it evokes. The acting is first rate and the atmosphere appropriately brooding. The Coens' use of light and space is impressive, and the innovative camerawork to increase the suspense is breathtaking. A modern classic. AJ Sex scenes, violence, swearing.
DVD

John Getz *Ray* • Frances McDormand *Abby* • Dan Hedaya *Julian Marty* • M Emmet Walsh *Visser* • Samm-Art Williams *Maurice* • Deborah Neumann *Debra* • Raquel Gavia *Landlady* • Van Brooks *Man from Lubbock* ■ *Dir* Joel Coen • *Scr* Ethan Coen, Joel Coen • *Cinematographer* Barry Sonnenfeld

Blood Surf ★ 18
Science-fiction horror 2000 · US/S Afr · Colour · 84min

A TV film crew travelling to a tropical island to document surfers ends up battling a giant crocodile. A subplot about crusty sea captain Duncan Regehr who sees the croc as his own personal nemesis fills out the threadbare story. This comes complete with variable special effects, rubber reptiles, elongated sex scenes and a barely-there script. AJ DVD

Dax Miller *Bog* • Matt Borlenghi *Zach Jardine* • Joel West *Jeremy* • Kate Fischer *Cecily* • Duncan Regehr *John Dirks* • Taryn Reif *Arly* ■ *Dir* James DR Hickox [James Hickox] • *Scr* Sam Bernard, Robert L Levy

Blood: the Last Vampire ★★ 18
Horror thriller 2008 · HK/Jpn/Fr · Colour · 84min

This live-action remake of a Japanese *anime* has half-human, half-vampire Gianna hunting for vampires in postwar Japan by enrolling in a US airbase high school. Despite lifting his opening sequence shot-for-shot, director Chris Nahon then debases

it by saddling Gianna with a dull American sidekick and even duller backstory. It requires a peculiar talent to take the excitement out of samurai sword duels between vampires and a woman dressed in a schoolgirl sailor uniform, but Nahon's quick-fire editing blurs everything into vagueness. The only highlight is a battle in an autumnal forest where vampire warriors emerge from the ground, their blades poking through the forest floor like shark fins. JR Violence. DVD BL

Gianna [Gianna Jun] *Saya* • Allison Miller *Alice Mckee* • JJ Feild *Luke* • Koyuki *Onigen* ■ *Dir* Chris Nahon • *Scr* Kenji Kamiyama, Ronny Yu, Chris Chow, from characters by Kamiyama, Katsuya Terada

Blood Ties ★★★ 15
Crime drama 2013 · US/Fr · Colour · 122min

This 1970s-set crime thriller is a tale of two brothers on opposite sides of the law. Set in Brooklyn, it hinges on the fateful return of Chris (Clive Owen), a career criminal who attempts to go straight. He moves in with his younger brother Frank (Billy Crudup), a law-abiding cop, but before long he returns to his old ways. As much a family drama as a crime thriller, *Blood Ties* is sparing in terms of action, although the regular eruptions of violence pack a genuine punch. A few of the players are under-served, but the ensemble cast is generally excellent. SC Violence, swearing, drug abuse, a sex scene, brief nudity. DVD BL

Clive Owen *Chris* • Billy Crudup *Frank* • Marion Cotillard *Monica* • Mila Kunis *Natalie* • Zoë Saldana *Vanessa* ■ *Scr* Guillaume Canet, James Gray, from the screenplay *Les Liens de Sang* by Jacques Maillot, Pierre Chosson, Eric Veniard, from the novel *Deux Frères, Flic et Truand* by Michel & Bruno Papet

Blood Wedding ★★★★ U
Dance drama 1981 · Sp · Colour · 67min

Setting the minimalist tone that persisted through *Carmen* and *El Amor Brujo*, the first of Carlos Saura's "flamenco trilogy" is an exhilarating blend of passionate choreography and rhythmic camerawork. By setting the action on a bare stage with the minimum of props, Saura focuses our attention on the intricacy and symbolism of the dance. As well as designing the flamboyant routines, Antonio Gades stars as one of the troupe rehearsing a musical version of the celebrated play by Federico Garcia Lorca, in which a jilted husband pursues the wife who abandoned him at the altar. DP Spanish +subtitles. DVD

Antonio Gades *Leonardo* • Cristina Hoyos *Bride* • Juan Antonio Jimenez *Groom* • Pilar Cardenas *Mother* • Carmen Villena *Wife* • Pepe Blanco *Wedding guest* • Lario Diaz *Wedding guest* • Enrique Esteve *Wedding guest* ■ *Dir* Carlos Saura • *Scr* Carlos Saura, from a play by Federico Garcia Lorca • *Choreographer* Antonio Gades • *Cinematographer* Teo Escamilla

Blood Work ★★ 15
Murder mystery thriller 2002 · US · Colour · 105min

This is one of director Clint Eastwood's depressingly average efforts. Eastwood also stars as an FBI agent who leaves the agency after a heart attack. While recovering from a transplant, he is brought out of retirement for one last case – the twist is that the victim was his organ donor. Apart from that, it's a routine police thriller with an unconvincing romance thrown in. StH DVD

Clint Eastwood *Terry McCaleb* • Jeff Daniels *Buddy Noone* • Anjelica Huston *Dr Bonnie Fox* • Wanda De Jesús *Graciela Rivers* • Tina Lifford *Jaye Winston* • Paul Rodriguez *Det Ronaldo Arrango* • Dylan Walsh *Det John Waller* • Mason Lucero *Raymond* ■ *Dir* Clint Eastwood • *Scr* Brian Helgeland, from the novel by Michael Connelly

Bloodbath at the House of Death ★ 18
Horror comedy 1983 · UK · Colour · 91min

Lampoons everything from *Carrie* and *ET* to *Star Wars* and *Friday the 13th* are dragged screaming through this painfully

thin comedy starring Kenny Everett and Pamela Stephenson as paranormal researchers investigating Vincent Price's devil-worshipping cult at Headstone Manor. Nothing more than an excuse for Everett and his chums to indulge in low-grade lavatorial humour. AJ

Kenny Everett *Dr Lucas Mandeville* • Pamela Stephenson *Dr Barbara Coyle* • Vincent Price *Sinister man* • Gareth Hunt *Elliot Broome* • Don Warrington *Stephen Wilson* • John Fortune *John Harrison* • Sheila Steafel *Sheila Finch* • John Stephen Hill *Henry Noland* • Cleo Rocos *Deborah Kedding* • Barry Cryer *Police inspector* • Ray Cameron *Policeman* ■ *Dir* Ray Cameron • *Scr* Ray Cameron, Barry Cryer

Bloodbrothers ★★
Drama 1978 · US · Colour · 116min

Richard Gere is surprisingly good in the unlikely role of an aspiring social worker in this familiar tale of conflict in an Italian-American family. Gere wants to work with children but Dad (Tony LoBianco) wants him to stay in the macho world of construction. Any insights are diverted by way of narrative short cuts. TH

Paul Sorvino *Chubby DeCoco* • Tony LoBianco *Tommy DeCoco* • Richard Gere *Stony DeCoco* • Lelia Goldoni *Marie* • Yvonne Wilder *Phyllis* • Kenneth McMillan *Banion* • Floyd Levine *Doctor Harris* • Marilu Henner *Annette* ■ *Dir* Robert Mulligan • *Scr* Walter Newman, from the novel by Richard Price

Bloodfist ★ 18
Martial arts action drama 1989 · US · Colour · 82min

Three times world kickboxing champion Don "The Dragon" Wilson plays it safe in his first major role cast as – yes, you've guessed it – a kickboxer who travels from Los Angeles to Manila to avenge the death of his brother by competing in a fight tournament. Director Terence H Winkless offers nothing new to the martial arts genre, serving up uninspired fight sequences with the stunt guys missing each other's jaws by miles. Although Wilson demonstrates little screen presence, he went on to star in all seven of the *Bloodfist* sequels. RS DVD

Don "The Dragon" Wilson *Jake Raye* • Joe Mari Avellana *Kwong* • Michael Shaner *Baby Davies* • Riley Bowman *Nancy* • Rob Kaman *Raton* • Billy Blanks *Black Rose* • Kris Aguilar *Chin Woo* • Vic Diaz *Detective* ■ *Dir* Terence H Winkless • *Scr* Robert King

Bloodhounds of Broadway ★★★ U
Musical 1952 · US · Colour · 89min

This enjoyable 20th Century-Fox musical gives the marvellous Mitzi Gaynor the chance to sing such super numbers as *I Wish I Knew*, in a whirl of Damon Runyon-inspired nonsense. Gaynor's co-star is Scott Brady, and watch out for a typecast Charles Buchinski (later Charles Bronson). This was remade in 1989 with an all-star cast, but that film only received a limited release. This version is both breezier and bawdier, and much closer to Runyon in spirit. TS

Mitzi Gaynor *Emily Ann Stackerlee* • Scott Brady *Numbers Foster* • Mitzi Green *Tessie Sammis* • Marguerite Chapman *Yvonne* • Michael O'Shea (1) *Inspector McNamara* • Wally Vernon *Poorly Sammis* • Henry Slate *Dave the Dude* • George E Stone *Ropes McGonigle* ■ *Dir* Harmon Jones • *Scr* Sy Gomberg, from the short stories by Damon Runyon

Bloodhounds of Broadway ★★ PG
Comedy drama 1989 · US · Colour · 83min

Not to be confused with the (better) 1952 musical of the same name, this is an adaptation of a collection of short stories by Damon Runyon. Set in New York on New Year's Eve, 1928, it traces the ins and outs of a group of Mafia gangsters and their molls. Madonna, Jennifer Grey, Matt Dillon, Randy Quaid and Rutger Hauer star, but even their combined efforts fail to make Howard Brookner's film anything more than a lacklustre amalgam of tales and cabaret. LH DVD

Madonna *Hortense Hathaway* • Randy Quaid *Feet Samuels* • Matt Dillon *Regret* • Josef Sommer *Waldo Winchester* • Jennifer Grey *Lovey Lou* • Tony Longo *Crunch Sweeney* • Rutger Hauer *The Brain* • Stephen McHattie *Red Henry* • Steve Buscemi *Whining Willie* • Tony Azito *Waiter* ■ *Dir* Howard Brookner • *Scr* Howard Brookner, Colman deKay, from the short stories by Damon Runyon

Bloodline ★★ 18
Mystery melodrama 1979 · US/W Ger · Colour · 111min

An anaemic script pumps little in the way of drama into this tedious thriller, adapted from Sidney Sheldon's novel. Audrey Hepburn is the heiress to a pharmaceutical conglomerate, who takes control of the company only to find that she's in fear for her life. James Mason, Ben Gazzara and Omar Sharif try for some smoothly silken menace, but it comes across as hair-shirt denim. Ennio Morricone's music is probably best appreciated without the accompanying dialogue. TH

Audrey Hepburn *Elizabeth Roffe* • Ben Gazzara *Rhys Williams* • James Mason *Sir Alec Nichols* • Claudia Mori *Donatella* • Irene Papas *Simonetta Palazzi* • Michelle Phillips *Vivian Nichols* • Maurice Ronet *Charles Martin* • Romy Schneider *Helene Martin* • Omar Sharif *Ivo Palazzi* • Beatrice Straight *Kate Erling* ■ *Dir* Terence Young • *Scr* Laird Koenig, from the novel by Sidney Sheldon

Bloodsport ★★ 18
Martial arts action drama 1987 · US · Colour · 88min

This is the movie that consolidated Jean-Claude Van Damme's standing in the martial arts film world. Loosely based on a true story, it stars Van Damme as the first western fighter to enter a lethal martial arts tournament in Hong Kong. The always frightening Bolo Yeung is the man standing in his way. The Belgian star merits few acting plaudits, but director Newt Arnold concentrates on the violent bouts. Two belated sequels appeared a decade later starring Daniel Bernhardt rather than Van Damme. JF Violence, swearing, nudity.
DVD

Jean-Claude Van Damme *Frank Dux* • Donald Gibb *Ray Jackson* • Leah Ayres *Janice* • Norman Burton *Helmer* • Forest Whitaker *Rawlins* • Roy Chiao *Senzo "Tiger" Tanaka* • Philip Chan *Captain Chen* ■ *Dir* Newt Arnold • *Scr* Sheldon Lettich, Christopher Cosby, Mel Friedman, from a story by Sheldon Lettich

Bloodsport II: The Next Kumite ★★ 18
Martial arts action 1996 · US · Colour · 82min

The original *Bloodsport* catapulted Jean-Claude Van Damme to stardom, but the sequel didn't do the same for fellow biffer Daniel Bernhardt. He plays a gentleman thief who ends up in a Thai jail and discovers that his only passport out is to fight in the legendary *kumite*, a last-man-standing martial arts championship. There's plenty of bone-crunching action, but the plotting and acting is strictly average. A further sequel followed in 1997. JF DVD

Daniel Bernhardt *Alex* • Pat Morita *Leung* • Donald Gibb *Tiny* • Lori Lynn Dickerson *Janine* • Philip Tan *John* • James Hong *Sun* • Nick Hill *Sergio* • Ron Hall *Cliff* ■ *Dir* Alan Mehrez • *Scr* Jeff Schechter

Bloodsucking Bosses ★★★ 15
Comedy horror 2015 · US · Colour · 87min

Nothing should be taken too seriously in this wonderfully lewd tale. Meek and mild office drone Fran Kranz is desperate to get on but when an old college foe (a gleefully sleazy Pedro Pascal) is promoted above him, it's too much to bear. He's then too distracted to notice his colleagues are falling prey to a vampire, but thankfully his best friend, gung-ho security guard Joey Kern, is there to help him save the day. Not especially original, this still has enough snappy patter and laugh-out-loud moments to be bloody good fun. JA Violence, swearing. DVD

Fran Kranz *Evan Sanders* • Emma Fitzpatrick *Amanda* • Pedro Pascal *Max* • Joey Kern *Tim* • Joel Murray *Ted* ■ *Dir* Brian James O'Connell • *Scr* Dr God [Brian James O'Connell, Sean Cowhig, Neil Garguilo, David Park, Justin Ware], Ryan Mitts

The Bloody Judge ★★ 18
Horror 1969 · It/UK/Sp/W Ger · Colour · 89min

Christopher Lee says his portrayal of the depraved 17th-century Lord Chief Justice Judge Jeffreys, who cruelly condemned women as witches to further his political and sexual needs, is one of his best performances. Shame it's wasted in this cheap *Witchfinder General* imitation from Spanish hack Jess Franco. The plot revolves around Maria Rohm romancing the son of the Earl of Wessex, and submitting to the judge's perversions in order to save her rebel lover from the death sentence. Badly structured, often boring. AJ *DVD*

Christopher Lee *Lord George Jeffreys* • Leo Genn *Earl of Wessex* • Maria Schell *Mother Rosa* • Maria Rohm *Mary Gray* • Margaret Lee *Alicia Gray* ■ *Dir* Jess Franco [Jesus Franco] • *Scr* Enrico Colombo, Jess Franco [Jesus Franco]

Bloody Kids ★★★ 15
Drama 1979 · UK · Colour · 87min

Originally made for TV, Stephen Frears's bleak study of early Thatcherite Britain is a fascinating blend of *Play for Today* sensationalism and Film4 kitchen sink. Scripted by Stephen Poliakoff with Caroline Embling, and set in a place that's more dead end than Southend, the film places delinquency at the door of an uncaring society. Yet there's a wilfulness about the antics of Richard Thomas (not of *The Waltons*) and Peter Clark, the 11-year-olds whose knife-fight prank backfires, that lands one in hospital and the other in the clutches of a gang. Two decades later, little has changed apart from the fashions. DP Swearing. *DVD*

Derrick O'Connor *Richie* • Gary Holton *Ken* • Richard Thomas (2) *Leo* • Peter Clark *Mike* • Gwyneth Strong *Jan* • Caroline Embling *Susan* ■ *Dir* Stephen Frears • *Scr* Stephen Poliakoff, Caroline Embling • *Cinematographer* Chris Menges

Bloody Mama ★★★ 18
Period crime drama 1970 · US · Colour · 86min

Shelley Winters is the quintessential Ma Barker in cult director Roger Corman's gangster movie about her infamous bank-robbing brood who terrorised the Depression-hit Midwest during the 1930s. Corman's supposedly true crime saga is a riotous stew of sentimental blood-bonding and perverse bloody violence. In one of his earliest appearances, Robert De Niro is electrifying as the drug-addicted son. Satisfyingly sleazy. AJ *DVD*

Shelley Winters *Kat "Ma" Barker* • Pat Hingle *Sam Pendlebury* • Don Stroud *Herman Barker* • Diane Varsi *Mona Gibson* • Bruce Dern *Kevin Kirkman* • Clint Kimbrough *Arthur Barker* • Robert Walden *Fred Barker* • Robert De Niro *Lloyd Barker* • Alex Nicol *George Barker* ■ *Dir* Roger Corman • *Scr* Robert Thom, from a story by Robert Thom, Don Peters

Bloody Sunday ★★★★ 15
Historical drama
2001 · Ire/UK · Colour · 105min

Based on Don Mullan's acclaimed book, this is an unblinking account of the events of 30 January 1972 that resulted in 13 civilians being killed by members of the Parachute Regiment while on an unruly and violent protest march through the city of Londonderry. Employing a gritty, *vérité* filming style that is complemented by superb editing, writer/director Paul Greengrass not only captures the tension between the sectarian communities and the British forces, but also conveys the shattered hopes of the civil rights movement and the march organisers. Powerful and provocative. DP *DVD*

James Nesbitt *Ivan Cooper* • Tim Pigott-Smith *Maj Gen Ford* • Nicholas Farrell *Brigadier Patrick MacLellan* • Gerard McSorley *Chief Supt Lagan* • Kathy Keira Clarke *Frances* • Allan Gildea *Kevin McCorry* • Gerard Crossan *Eamonn McCann* •

Mary Moulds *Bernadette Devlin* ■ *Dir* Paul Greengrass • *Scr* Paul Greengrass, from the non-fiction book *Eyewitness Bloody Sunday* by Don Mullan

bl,.m ★★ 18
Period drama 2003 · Ire · Colour · 113min

This brave attempt to film James Joyce's masterpiece fails to find the audiovisual equivalent of the dexterous stream of consciousness that dazzled and scandalised readers in the 1920s. Moreover, neither Stephen Rea nor Hugh O'Conor comes close to capturing the personalities of wittily bitter cuckold Leopold Bloom and self-absorbed poet Stephen Dedalus. Most disappointing, however, is director Sean Walsh's handling of the novel's most important character, Dublin on 16 June 1904. DP Sex scenes.

Stephen Rea *Leopold Bloom* • Angeline Ball *Molly Bloom* • Hugh O'Conor *Stephen Dedalus* • Patrick Bergin *The Citizen* • Alan Devlin *Simon Dedalus* • Phelim Drew *Martin Cunningham* ■ *Dir* Sean Walsh • *Scr* Sean Walsh, from the novel *Ulysses* by James Joyce

Bloomfield ★ PG
Sports drama 1969 · UK/Is · Colour · 91min

Richard Harris made a disastrous directorial debut with this blend of soccer and sentiment. He also stars as the Israeli footballer who, though well past his sell-by date, goes a game too far because he's been offered a car to fix the result. The soccer sequences are poorly staged, while the vistas that accompany ten-year-old Yossi Yadin on his trek to Jaffa to see his hero are achingly dull. DP

Richard Harris *Eitan* • Romy Schneider *Nira* • Kim Burfield *Nimrod* • Maurice Kaufmann *Yasha* • Yossi Yadin *Weiner* • Shraga Friedman *Chairman* • Aviva Marks *Teddy* ■ *Dir* Richard Harris • *Scr* Wolf Mankowitz, from a story by Joseph Gross

Blossom Time ★★ U
Musical romance 1934 · UK · BW · 91min

Fans of Richard Tauber, once the world's most popular Viennese tenor, will enjoy this period romance with music set in the Hapsburg capital of the 1820s. Tauber plays a composer who not only gracefully concedes defeat when the girl he loves falls for a titled Royal dragoon of the Archduchess's regiment, but also persuades the Archduchess to give his rival permission to marry a commoner. Old-fashioned, formulaic and slow, but undeniably charming. RK

Richard Tauber *Schubert* • Jane Baxter *Vicki* • Carl Esmond *Rudi* • Athene Seyler *Archduchess* • Paul Graetz *Wimpassinger* • Charles Carson *Lafont* • Marguerite Allan *Baroness* • Edward Chapman *Meyerhoffer* ■ *Dir* Paul L Stein • *Scr* Roger Burford, GH Clutsam, John Drinkwater

The Blossoming of Maximo Oliveros ★★★ 15
Comedy drama 2005 · Phil · Colour · 100min

Filipino director Auraeus Solito's debut feature is dominated by Nathan Lopez's bold performance as the camp 12-year-old of the title, who lives in a rundown district of Manila with his father and two older brothers. But when one brother accidentally kills a student, the boy's friendship with – and crush on – an incorruptible cop becomes a cause for concern among his criminal relatives. Tackling the subject of pre-teen sexuality with wit and sensitivity, Solito paints an unsentimental portrait of the poverty and survival instincts of his marginalised characters, but he can't prevent the action from becoming increasingly melodramatic. DP Tagalog +subtitles. Swearing. *DVD*

Nathan Lopez *Maximo "Maxi" Oliveros* • Soliman Cruz *Mang Paco Oliveros* • JR Valentin *Victor Perez* • Neil Ryan Sese *Boy Oliveros* • Ping Medina *Bogs Oliveros* • Bodjie Pascua *Police chief* ■ *Dir* Auraeus Solito • *Scr* Michiko Yamamoto

Blossoms in the Dust ★★★
Biographical drama 1941 · US · Colour · 100min

All the MGM gloss in the world can't hide the fact that this is a tear-jerker of the first

order, but director Mervyn LeRoy and stars Greer Garson and Walter Pidgeon embrace the subject head on, and knowingly create a fine biopic, enhanced by Oscar-winning interior decoration and some first-rate Technicolor. This is the tale of Edna Gladney, who started the Texas Children's Home and Aid Society of Fort Worth, caring for orphans and strays. Despite the film's undoubted worthiness, Garson's refusal to age alongside the narrative reduces the drama to bathos. TS

Greer Garson *Edna Gladney* • Walter Pidgeon *Sam Gladney* • Felix Bressart *Dr Max Breslar* • Marsha Hunt *Charlotte* • Fay Holden *Mrs Kahly* • Samuel S Hinds *Mr Kahly* • Kathleen Howard *Mrs Keats* • George Lessey *Mr Keats* ■ *Dir* Mervyn LeRoy • *Scr* Anita Loos, from a story by Ralph Wheelwright • *Cinematographers* Karl Freund, W Howard Greene • *Set Designers* Cedric Gibbons, Urie McCleary, Edwin B Willis

Blow ★★★ 18
Biographical drama 2001 · US · Colour · 118min

The rise and fall of the 1970s biggest cocaine importer, George Jung, is charted in Ted Demme's vivid biopic. Johnny Depp lends an affable charm to his portrayal of the naive entrepreneur who gets in way over his head. There's also a clutch of fine characterisations from the likes of Paul Reubens as a camp hairdresser cum dealer, and Ray Liotta and Rachel Griffiths as Jung's parents. Aside from a certain predictability in Jung's slippery slope, the film's weakness lies in the unbalanced pacing and direction. The period details are outstanding though, with particular praise reserved for Depp's spectacular range of bad-hair days. JC *DVD* *BL*

Johnny Depp *George Jung* • Penélope Cruz *Mirtha* • Franka Potente *Barbara* • Rachel Griffiths *Ermine Jung* • Paul Reubens *Derek Foreal* • Jordi Mollà *Diego Delgado* • Ray Liotta *Fred Jung* ■ *Dir* Ted Demme • *Scr* David McKenna, Nick Cassavetes

Blow Dry ★★ 15
Comedy drama
2000 · UK/Ger/US · Colour · 86min

The glitz and glamour of the British hairdressing championships form the backdrop to this bittersweet comedy drama. It's set in a sleepy Yorkshire town, where ex-champion barber Alan Rickman faces stiff competition from favourite Bill Nighy. Sadly, it's a bit of a mess – a subplot involving Natasha Richardson as Rickman's cancer-afflicted estranged wife – jars with some farcical stylist skulduggery. There are some affecting moments, but the laughs are few. JC Swearing, nudity. *DVD*

Alan Rickman *Phil Allen* • Natasha Richardson *Shelley* • Rachel Griffiths *Sandra* • Rachael Leigh Cook *Christina* • Josh Hartnett *Brian* • Bill Nighy *Ray Robertson* • Warren Clarke *Tony* • Rosemary Harris *Daisy* • Hugh Bonneville *Louis* ■ *Dir* Paddy Breathnach • *Scr* Simon Beaufoy

Blow Out ★★★★ 18
Thriller 1981 · US · Colour · 103min

Long before *Pulp Fiction*, John Travolta's best role was in Brian De Palma's audio version of Michelangelo Antonioni's *Blowup*, laced with the director's usual quota of Hitchcockian black humour and startling suspense. Travolta is marvellous as the cheesy horror flick sound-effects man who accidentally tapes events leading to the drowning of a presidential candidate. Nothing is what it seems in a paranoid mystery deliciously overflowing with De Palma's trademark high style right up until the knockout ending. AJ Violence, swearing, nudity. *DVD* *BL*

John Travolta *Jack Terry* • Nancy Allen *Sally Badina* • John Lithgow *Burke* • Dennis Franz *Manny Karp* • John Aquino *Detective Mackey* • Peter Boyden *Sam* • Curt May *Donahue* • John McMartin *Lawrence Henry* • Deborah Everton *Hooker* ■ *Dir/Scr* Brian De Palma

Blowback ★★ 18
Science-fiction crime thriller
1999 · US · Colour · 87min

In this preposterous thriller, James Remar's serial killer is secretly saved from execution by a shady government group that wants

him as an assassin. Mario Van Peebles does his usual humourless work as the cop who becomes certain that his apparently dead adversary is disposing of the jury who sent him to the gas chamber. It all makes little sense, but Remar makes a decent villain and director Mark L Lester manages some serviceable suspense. JC Sex scenes, swearing, violence, nudity. *DVD*

James Remar *John Matthew Whitman/Schmidt* • Mario Van Peebles *Don Morrell* • Gladys Jimenez *Charlotte Hart-Morrell* • Sharisse Baker *Monica Ricci* • David Groh *Captain Barnett* ■ *Dir* Mark L Lester • *Scr* Randall Frakes, Jeffrey Goldenberg, Bob Held

Blowing Wild ★★★
Adventure 1953 · US · BW · 89min

"Marina mine..." belted out Frankie Laine over the opening titles of this 1930s-set oil-rig melodrama, securing himself a substantial hit. Marina is played by Barbara Stanwyck. She's married to tycoon Anthony Quinn, but has the hots for former lover Gary Cooper, a wildcatter from her past who turns up in her life just when she shouldn't. Director Hugo Fregonese makes the most of the Mexican locations, even though he seems incapable of reining in the full-throttle performances of his stars. TS

Barbara Stanwyck *Marina Conway* • Gary Cooper *Jeff Dawson* • Ruth Roman *Sal* • Anthony Quinn *Paco Conway* • Ward Bond *Dutch Peterson* • Juan Garcia *El Gavilan* • Ian MacDonald *Jackson* ■ *Dir* Hugo Fregonese • *Scr* Phillip Yordan

Blown Away ★★ 15
Thriller 1994 · US · Colour and BW · 115min

Jeff Bridges stars as a bomb disposal expert and Tommy Lee Jones is his former colleague who wants Bridges blown away in this bungled hi-tech thriller. The film aims to deliver a tense sequence every 15 minutes or so, while Bridges and Jones, two of the best around, can make nothing of the thinly written, often tasteless, material. AT Brief nudity, violence, swearing. *DVD*

Jeff Bridges *Jimmy Dove* • Tommy Lee Jones *Ryan Gaerity* • Suzy Amis *Kate* • Lloyd Bridges *Max O'Bannon* • Forest Whitaker *Anthony Franklin* • Stephi Lineburg *Lizzy* • John Finn *Captain Roarke* • Caitlin Clarke *Rita* • Chris De Oni *Cortez* ■ *Dir* Stephen Hopkins • *Scr* Joe Batteer, John Rice, from a story by John Rice, Joe Batteer, M Jay Roach [Jay Roach]

Blowup ★★★ 15
Mystery drama 1966 · UK/It · Colour · 106min

One of the true tests of a great work of art is its ability to transcend time. Film can have the shortest shelf life of any art form, and Michelangelo Antonioni's first English language feature is a case in point. Hailed in its day as a work of genius, an intriguing, if self-indulgent, challenge to the idea that the camera never lies, this might-be murder mystery is now often dismissed as ostentatious and exploitative. Sarah Miles walked out during production, leaving Vanessa Redgrave to strip off, look gawky and fidget while David Hemmings puts on a jazz record. If you can ignore the pretensions, this does contain fleeting moments of brilliance. DP Swearing, nudity. *DVD*

David Hemmings *Thomas* • Vanessa Redgrave *Jane* • Sarah Miles *Patricia* • John Castle *Patricia's artist husband* • Jane Birkin *Teenager* • Gillian Hills *Teenager* • Peter Bowles *Ron* • Verushka [Veruschka Von Lehndorff] *Model* ■ *Dir* Michelangelo Antonioni • *Scr* Michelangelo Antonioni, Tonino Guerra, Edward Bond, from the short story *Final del Juego* by Julio Cortázar • *Cinematographer* Carlo di Palma [Carlo Di Palma]

Blue ★★
Western 1968 · US · Colour · 112min

Strikingly photographed by Stanley Cortez, this is an otherwise undistinguished western from Silvio Narizzano. As the adopted son of Mexican bandit Ricardo Montalban, Terence Stamp rescues respectable Karl

B

Malden and his daughter Joanna Pettet only to learn the hard facts of life in the Old West. Archly acted and heavy-handed in its symbolism, this is a long haul. DP

Terence Stamp *Blue/Azul* • Joanna Pettet *Joanne Morton* • Karl Malden *Doc Morton* • Ricardo Montalban *Ortega* • Anthony Costello *Jess Parker* • Joe De Santis *Carlos* • James Westerfield *Abe Parker* • Stathis Giallelis *Manuel* • Sally Kirkland *Sara Lambert* • Peggy Lipton *Laurie Kramer* ■ *Dir* Silvio Narizzano • *Scr* Meade Roberts, Ronald M Cohen, from the story by Ronald M Cohen

Blue ★★★★ 15
Experimental 1993 · UK · Colour · 75min

Derek Jarman's work has been overpraised by critics desperate for an original voice in British cinema, but there is no doubting the courage and sincerity of this deeply moving swan song. The screen remains a shimmering shade of blue for the entire film, while Nigel Terry, John Quentin, Tilda Swinton and the director himself read extracts from Jarman's diary and other writings to the accompaniment of Simon Fisher Turner's imaginative score. The meditations might meander now and then, but there is no self-pity or bitterness in his comments on Aids, the loss of his friends, his own blindness and the inevitability of death. DP Swearing. *DVD*

Derek Jarman • John Quentin • Nigel Terry • Tilda Swinton ■ *Dir/Scr* Derek Jarman • *Music* Simon Fisher Turner

The Blue Angel ★★★★ PG
Drama 1930 · Ger · BW · 106min

Contrary to popular myth, 28-year-old Marlene Dietrich had already appeared in almost 20 (admittedly minor) films in her native Germany when Josef von Sternberg cast her as Lola, the sensual cabaret singer who enslaves, humiliates and finally destroys middle-aged professor Emil Jannings. The film did, however, bring about the famous von Sternberg/Dietrich Hollywood collaboration. Jannings, making his first talking picture, has some wonderful moments in an uneven performance. But it was the cruel and seductive Dietrich, in top hat and black stockings, perched on a bar stool and huskily singing *Falling in Love Again*, that became one of the cinema's great iconic images. RK German +subtitles. *DVD*

Emil Jannings *Professor Immanuel Rath* • Marlene Dietrich *Lola Frohlich* • Kurt Gerron *Kiepert, a magician* • Rosa Valette *Guste Kiepert, his wife* • Hans Albers *Mazeppa* • Eduard Von Winterstein *School principal* • Reinhold Bernt *The clown* • Hans Roth *Beadle* ■ *Dir* Josef von Sternberg • *Scr* Carl Zuckmayer, Karl Vollmöller, Robert Liebmann, from the novel *Professor Unrat* by Heinrich Mann • *Music* Friedrich Holländer

The Blue Angel ★
Drama 1959 · US · Colour · 107min

This is a seriously misguided attempt by 20th Century-Fox to remake Josef von Sternberg's 1930 German classic, about a cabaret singer who destroys the middle-aged professor obsessionally in love with her. Placed in a modern setting and filmed in CinemaScope, this is truly awful, losing the atmosphere, resonance and credibility of the original. RK

Curt Jurgens *Professor Immanuel Rath* • May Britt *Lola-Lola* • Theodore Bikel *Klepert* • John Banner *Principal Harter* • Fabrizio Mioni *Rolf* • Ludwig Stossel *Professor Braun* • Wolfe Barzell *Clown* • Ina Anders *Gussie* ■ *Dir* Edward Dmytryk • *Scr* Nigel Balchin, from the film by Carl Zuckmeyer, Karl Vollmöller, Robert Liebmann, from the novel *Professor Unrat* by Heinrich Mann

The Blue Bird ★★★ U
Fantasy 1940 · US · Colour · 82min

Twentieth Century-Fox's answer to MGM's *The Wizard of Oz* was this lavish version of the Maurice Maeterlinck play about a woodcutter's daughter, played by Shirley Temple, seeking the blue bird of happiness. Enjoy the fantastic settings and the fine Technicolor, for the characters here come to life and the handling is too literal. This was Temple's first box-office flop and her

career never really recovered. Gale Sondergaard, though, is splendid, playing the treacherous family cat. AE

Shirley Temple *Mytyl* • Spring Byington *Mummy Tyl* • Nigel Bruce *Mr Luxury* • Gale Sondergaard *Tylette* • Eddie Collins *Tylo, the dog* • Edwin Maxwell *Oak* • Thurston Hall *Father Time* ■ *Dir* Walter Lang • *Scr* Ernest Pascal, Walter Bullock, from the play *L'Oiseau Bleu* by Maurice Maeterlinck

The Blue Bird ★★ U
Fantasy 1976 · US/USSR · Colour · 97min

Patsy Kensit is in the glittering company of Liz Taylor, Ava Gardner and Jane Fonda in this retelling of the Maeterlinck theatrical fairy tale. Two children, Kensit and her brother Todd Lookinland, set out on a journey to find the blue bird of happiness accompanied by the human manifestations of, among others, a dog, a cat, a loaf of bread and fire. Despite the stellar cast, this first US/Soviet co-production is a turgid affair and is doubtful entertainment, even for the children it's aimed at. LH

Elizabeth Taylor *Mother/Light/Maternal Love/ Witch* • Jane Fonda *Night* • Cicely Tyson *Cat* • Ava Gardner *Luxury* • Patsy Kensit *Mytyl* • Todd Lookinland *Tyltyl* • Mona Washbourne *Grandmother* • George Cole *Dog* • Robert Morley *Father Time* • Harry Andrews *Oak* ■ *Dir* George Cukor • *Scr* Hugh Whitemore, Alfred Hayes, Alexei Kapler, from the play *L'Oiseau Bleu* by Maurice Maeterlinck

Blue Black Permanent ★★★★ PG
Drama 1992 · UK · Colour · 85min

We watch, moved, as Scottish photographer Celia Imrie tells her boyfriend Jack Shepherd the heart-rending story of her mother's death when she was a child, coming to realise as she does just how much the event has shaped her life. Superbly performed, this is an unusual and thought-provoking drama about coping with loss and the guilt that comes with it, filled with unusual imagery that punctuates each emotion. While it doesn't always work, this is nonetheless an stunning debut full of emotion and meaning. JB

Celia Imrie *Barbara Thorburn* • Jack Shepherd *Philip Lomax* • Gerda Stevenson *Greta Thorburn* • James Fleet *Jim Thorburn* • Sean Scanlan *Andrew Cunningham* • Hilary Maclean *Wendy* • Walter Leask *Sam Kelday* • Sheana Marr *Mrs Kemp* • Eoin MacDonald *Dan of Fea* ■ *Dir/Scr* Margaret Tait

Blue Blood ★ 18
Psychological thriller 1973 · UK · Colour · 78min

It's hard to describe just how abysmal this reworking of *The Servant* really is. It is directed with revolting enthusiasm by Andrew Sinclair, who has not been entrusted with many features since. As the vicious butler intent on destabilising his weak-kneed aristocratic employer (Derek Jacobi), Oliver Reed gesticulates and rolls his eyes. DP

Oliver Reed *Tom* • Derek Jacobi *Gregory* • Fiona Lewis *Lily* • Anna Gael *Carlotta* • Meg Wynn Owen *Beate Krug* • John Rainer *Clurman* • Richard Davies (2) *Jones* • Gwyneth Owen *Agnes* ■ *Dir* Andrew Sinclair • *Scr* Andrew Sinclair, from the novel *The Carry-Cot* by Alexander Thynne

Blue Blood ★★★ 15
Sports documentary 2006 · UK · Colour · 96min

Offering some trenchant insights into the class system in Tony Blair's Britain, Stevan Riley's fond if rather formulaic documentary follows a group of wannabes who join the Oxford University Amateur Boxing Club in the hope of being selected for the annual varsity bout against Cambridge. Under the tutelage of a no-nonsense builder named Des, the novices get a few painful lessons in boxing and life. They are a mixed bunch, but their various trials and tribulations make for sturdy docusoap-style viewing, with the "town versus gown" match and a sobering night at Sandhurst military academy standing out before the varsity showdown finale. DP Swearing. *DVD*

Des Brackett • Chris Kavanagh • Fred Brown • Charlie Ogilvie • Justin Bronder • James Boyle ■ *Dir/Scr* Stevan Riley • *Music* Itamar Ziegler

Blue Canadian Rockies ★★ U
Western 1952 · US · Sepia · 57min

This Saturday morning fare is only for die-hard fans of the immensely popular singing cowboy Gene Autry. This programmer is a typical vehicle, with Autry's regular sidekick Pat Buttram also along for the ride. The real co-star, though, is Champion, who went on to become the only cowboy horse to have his own TV series. TS

Gene Autry • Pat Buttram *"Rawhide" Buttram* • Gail Davis *Sandra Higbee* • Carolina Cotton • Ross Ford *Todd Markley* ■ *Dir* George Archainbaud • *Scr* Gerald Geraghty

Blue Car ★★★ 15
Drama 2001 · US · Colour · 87min

Familiar themes such as adolescent angst, domestic dysfunction and betrayed trust are given a new lease in Karen Moncrieff's affecting debut. Desperate to find a father figure to compensate for the neglect of her overworked mother and the stress of coping with a disturbed sister, teenager Agnes Bruckner's growing dependence on teacher David Strathairn reaches a predictable climax when he persuades her to enter a poetry contest in Florida. DP

David Strathairn *Auster* • Agnes Bruckner *Meg* • Margaret Colin *Diane* • Regan Arnold *Lily* • Frances Fisher *Delia* • AJ Buckley *Pat* ■ *Dir/Scr* Karen Moncrieff

Blue Chips ★★★ 15
Sports drama 1994 · US · Colour · 103min

Ron Shelton is probably the finest writer of sports movies Hollywood has produced. Although not up there with *Bull Durham*, this is still a perceptive take on the machinations of the American sporting industry. This time the target is basketball, with an excellent Nick Nolte as the honourable college coach under pressure to succumb to the dodgy practices of his peers by secretly paying for young stars to join his team. Director William Friedkin films the set pieces with aplomb. DP Swearing.

Nick Nolte *Pete Bell* • Mary McDonnell *Jenny* • JT Walsh *Happy* • Ed O'Neill *Ed* • Alfre Woodard *Lavada McRae* • Bob Cousy *Vic* • Shaquille O'Neal *Neon* • Louis Gossett Jr *Father Dawkins* ■ *Dir* William Friedkin • *Scr* Ron Shelton

Blue City ★★ 18
Thriller 1986 · US · Colour · 79min

Though the sublime Ry Cooder supplies part of the soundtrack, this is an overwrought, largely forgettable, crime drama, in which Judd Nelson attempts to discover the truth behind the death of his father. Nelson and Ally Sheedy look out of their depth. Only the reliable Paul Winfield emerges from this mess with reputation intact. JF Swearing, violence.

Judd Nelson *Billy Turner* • Ally Sheedy *Annie Rayford* • David Caruso *Joey Rayford* • Paul Winfield *Luther Reynolds* • Scott Wilson *Perry Kerch* • Anita Morris *Malvina Kerch* • Luis Contreras *Lieutenant Ortiz* • Julie Carmen *Debbie Torez* ■ *Dir* Michelle Manning • *Scr* Lukas Heller, Walter Hill, from the novel by Ross MacDonald

Blue Collar ★★★★ 18
Drama 1978 · US · Colour · 108min

After writing the scripts for *Taxi Driver* and an early version of *Close Encounters of the Third Kind*, Paul Schrader made his directorial debut with *Blue Collar*, a rare Hollywood feature in that it deals with America's industrial relations in a factory, more the province of British realist pictures of the 1960s. It's the grinding boredom of the production line that interests Schrader and how his three workers – Richard Pryor, Harvey Keitel, Yaphet Kotto – plan to break free of it by robbing their union. It's tough, convincing and littered with ripe language. AT Swearing, drug abuse, brief nudity. *DVD*

Richard Pryor *Zeke Brown* • Harvey Keitel *Jerry Bartowski* • Yaphet Kotto *Smokey* • Ed Begley Jr *Bobby Joe* • Harry Bellaver *Eddie Johnson* • George Memmoli *Jenkins* • Lucy Saroyan *Arlene Bartowski* ■ *Dir* Paul Schrader • *Scr* Paul Schrader, Leonard Schrader, from source material by Sydney A Glass

Blue Crush ★★★ 12
Romantic sports drama 2002 · US · Colour · 99min

Unlike the usual babes-in-bikinis epics, this looks at the reality behind an adrenaline-fuelled life on the ocean wave. The film centres on three girls (Kate Bosworth, Michelle Rodriguez and Sanoe Lake) who work at a luxury Hawaiian resort in order to support their surf addiction. Bosworth is the favourite to win the upcoming tournament and turn pro, but she has distractions: a kid sister to look after and a budding romance with a visiting American football player. Director John Stockwell provides the exciting wave action, and brilliantly shot it is, too. TH Swearing. *DVD*

Kate Bosworth *Anne Marie* • Matthew Davis *Matt* • Michelle Rodriguez *Eden* • Sanoe Lake *Lena* • Mika Boorem *Penny* • Chris Taloa *Drew* • Kala Alexander *Kala* • Ruben Tejada *JJ* ■ *Dir* John Stockwell • *Scr* Lizzy Weiss, from her story, from the article *Surf Girls of Maui* by Susan Orlean

The Blue Dahlia ★★★★ PG
Film noir 1946 · US · BW · 95min

This terrifically taut thriller was written for the screen from his own original story by the great Raymond Chandler, with lines and whole scenes as hard-boiled and witty as in the better known *films noirs*. Steely-eyed, supercool Alan Ladd returns from the war to cheating wife Doris Dowling who winds up dead, and he becomes the chief murder suspect. He meets sultry Veronica Lake, and their scenes together simply sizzle. TS *DVD* BL

Alan Ladd *Johnny Morrison* • Veronica Lake *Joyce Harwood* • William Bendix *Buzz Wanchek* • Howard Da Silva *Eddie Harwood* • Doris Dowling *Helen Morrison* • Tom Powers *Captain Hendrickson* • Hugh Beaumont *George Copeland* • Howard Freeman *Corelli* ■ *Dir* George Marshall • *Scr* Raymond Chandler, from his story • *Music* Victor Young • *Cinematographer* Lionel Lindon

Blue Denim ★★★
Drama 1959 · US · BW · 89min

Considered shocking in its day, Philip Dunne's drama stands in stark contrast to the more frivolous teen pictures produced in the late 1950s. There's an undeniable sweetness about the way alienated high school kids Brandon de Wilde and Carol Lynley fall in love, which makes their need to visit an abortionist all the more distressing. However, this being Hollywood under the Production Code, what would have been the inevitable conclusion in life is hijacked by moral rectitude. DP

Carol Lynley *Janet Willard* • Brandon de Wilde *Arthur Bartley* • Macdonald Carey *Maj Malcolm Bartley, Ret* • Marsha Hunt *Jessie Bartley* • Warren Berlinger *Ernie* • Buck Class *Axel Sorenson* • Nina Shipman *Lillian Bartley* ■ *Dir* Philip Dunne • *Scr* Edith Sommer, Philip Dunne, from the play by James Leo Herlihy, William Noble

Blue Eyelids ★★★ 15
Romantic comedy drama 2007 · Mex/US · Colour · 99min

This droll Spanish look at chance and coincidence proves that romantic comedies don't always have to be about beautiful people lurching from one quirky escapade to another. Having won a beach holiday for two, timid factory clerk Marina (Cecilia Suárez) is without the companion she needs to qualify for the prize, until she befriends the equally lonesome Victor (Enrique Arreola). But their practice dates prove to be anything but idyllic. This slow-burning charmer is played without any mawkish whimsy by the perfectly matched leads. And while romance eventually finds a way, director Ernesto Contreras wisely leaves you wondering whether this discreet comedy of manners will actually end happily ever after. **DP** Spanish +subtitles. Sex scenes, nudity.

Cecilia Suárez *Marina Farfán* • Enrique Arreola *Victor Mina* • Tiaré Scanda *Lucía Farfán* • Ana Ofelia Murguía *Lulita* • Luisa Huertas *Mercedes* • Laura De Ita *Lola* ■ *Dir* Ernesto Contreras • *Scr* Carlos Contreras

The Blue Gardenia ★★★
Film noir   1953 · US · BW · 90min

Director Fritz Lang, one of the great expressionists and innovators of cinema (*Metropolis, M*) fled the Nazis in 1936 and made a second career in Hollywood. Reined in by studio executives who tampered with his vision, he nonetheless established himself as a master of *film noir*. This modest offering stars Anne Baxter who, duped into drunkenness by baddie Raymond Burr, comes to in his apartment, finds him dead and flees the scene. Co-star Richard Conte is a powerful newspaper columnist who invites the unknown killer to surrender. The plot and the dénouement are incredible, but it's made with Langian flair. Entertaining. **RK**

Anne Baxter *Norah Larkin* • Richard Conte *Casey Mayo* • Ann Sothern *Crystal Carpenter* • Raymond Burr *Harry Prebble* • Jeff Donnell *Sally Ellis* • Richard Erdman *Al* • George Reeves *Police Captain Haynes* • Ruth Storey *Rose Miller* • Nat King Cole ■ *Dir* Fritz Lang • *Scr* Charles Hoffman, from the story *Gardenia* by Vera Caspary

Blue Hawaii ★★★ PG
Musical comedy drama
1961 · US · Colour · 96min

Though one of Elvis Presley's biggest successes, this movie was directly responsible for turning him from the new James Dean into the king of pap. Confronted with the huge box office grosses, Elvis's controllers – venal manager Colonel Tom Parker and film producer Hal Wallis – decided that every movie their boy made from then on would be the same mix of girls, songs and exotic locations. Thirty films later, they'd sacrificed both their audience and Presley's screen credibility. For all that, this is colourful, amiable fluff. **TS** DVD

Elvis Presley *Chad Gates* • Joan Blackman *Maile Duval* • Nancy Walters *Abigail Prentace* • Roland Winters *Fred Gates* • Angela Lansbury *Sarah Lee Gates* • John Archer *Jack Kelman* • Howard McNear *Mr Chapman* • Flora Hayes *Mrs Manaka* ■ *Dir* Norman Taurog • *Scr* Hal Kanter, from a story by Allan Weiss • *Cinematographer* Charles Lang Jr [Charles Lang]

Blue Heat ★★★ 15
Police action drama   1990 · US · Colour · 101min

Brian Dennehy looks fearsome enough to go off like a one-man firework display, and he co-stars here with Joe Pantoliano, Jeff Fahey and Bill Paxton, playing members of an elite unit working for the Los Angeles police. Striving to be a political allegory, the story works better as a tale of Dennehy and his unit against the drugs barons, even when the action sequences fall flat. **JM** Drug abuse, swearing, violence.

Brian Dennehy *Frank Daly* • Joe Pantoliano *Wayne Gross* • Jeff Fahey *Ricky Rodriguez* • Bill Paxton *Howard "Hojo" Jones* • Michael C Gwynne *Anthony Reece* • Henry Stolow *Stant* • Guy Boyd *RJ Norringer* • Henry Darrow *Captain Joe Torres* • Deborra-Lee Furness *Linda Daly* ■ *Dir* John Mackenzie (1) • *Scr* Jere Cunningham, Thomas Lee Wright, George Armitage, from a story by Jere Cunningham

Blue Ice ★★ 15
Thriller   1992 · US/UK · Colour · 100min

Michael Caine stars in this thriller featuring a central character who resembles a warmed-up version of *The Ipcress File's* Harry Palmer, and a performance from Sean Young that is all mannerism and no depth. Russell Mulcahy's direction is all gloss and no suspense. Still, at least a London of dark encounters and ne'er-do-wells looks properly seedy. **JM** Swearing, violence, nudity.

Michael Caine *Harry Anders* • Sean Young *Stacy Mansdorf* • Ian Holm *Sir Hector* • Bobby Short *Buddy* • Alun Armstrong *Det Sgt Osgood* • Sam

Kelly *George* • Jack Shepherd *Stevens* • Philip Davis *Westy* ■ *Dir* Russell Mulcahy • *Scr* Ron Hutchinson, from the character created by Ted Allbeury

The Blue Iguana ★ 15
Crime comedy   1988 · US · Colour · 86min

An off-target attempt to satirise gumshoe pictures, B-movies and *film noir*, this is directed by John Lafia, who displays no grasp of basic comic timing. The story concerns a hopeless bounty hunter who heads south of the border to retrieve $20 million in drug money. **JM** Violence, swearing, drug abuse.

Dylan McDermott *Vince Holloway* • Jessica Harper *Cora* • James Russo *Reno* • Pamela Gidley *Dakota* • Yano Anaya *Yano* • Flea *Floyd* ■ *Dir/Scr* John Laf a

Blue in the Face ★★★ 15
Comedy drama   1995 · US · Colour · 79min

A funny thing happened after director Wayne Wang and novelist Paul Auster completed *Smoke*, their excellent look at Brooklyn life as distilled through Harvey Keitel's cigar shop. The actors had had such a good time making it, they didn't want to go home, and Wang and Auster had the set for another week. Hence this bookend featuring mainly improvised scenes on the power of the weed, mixed in with video documentary footage. Self-indulgent at times, but in its own small way entertaining. **AJ** Swearing, nudity. DVD

Harvey Keitel *Auggie Wren* • Michael J Fox *Peter* • Roseanne Barr *Dot* • Mel Gorham *Violet* • Lily Tomlin *Derelict* • Madonna *Singing telegram girl* • Jim Jarmusch • Lou Reed • Jared Harris *Jimmy Rose* ■ *Dir/Scr* Wayne Wang, Paul Auster

Blue Is the Warmest Colour ★★★ 18
Romantic drama
2013 · Fr/Bel/Sp · Colour · 172min

The talk of the 2013 Cannes film festival with its simulated but nevertheless convincingly explicit lesbian sex scenes, this tastefully told coming-of-age tale is perhaps too slight and too long to create much of a stir with multiplex audiences. The film dwells mostly on teenage heroine Adèle Exarchopoulos, who makes a botched attempt at a relationship with a male schoolfriend before falling for the blue-haired and openly gay Léa Seydoux, and the pair begins a full-on but ill-fated affair. The two leads, not to mention the direction, are excellent, justifying the film's first-ever joint Palme d'Or win for all three. As for the story, though, many will wonder what the fuss was about. **DW** French +subtitles. Swearing, sex scenes, nudity. DVD BL

Léa Seydoux *Emma* • Adèle Exarchopoulos *Adèle* • Salim Kechiouche *Samir* • Aurélien Recoing *Adèle's father* • Catherine Salée *Adèle's mother* • Benjamin Siksou *Antoine* ■ *Dir* Abdellatif Kechiche [Abdel Kechiche] • *Scr* Abdellatif Kechiche [Abdel Kechiche], Ghalia Lacroix, from a graphic novel by Julie Maroh

Blue Jasmine ★★★★ 12
Drama   2013 · US · Colour · 94min

Woody Allen's strongest drama in years is an updated homage to *A Streetcar Named Desire*, with Cate Blanchett as a Blanche Dubois to Sally Hawkins's Stella. Blanchett plays Jasmine, a New York socialite forced to live with estranged sister Ginger (Hawkins) in a low-rent area of San Francisco. Jasmine's vodka-fuelled reveries flash back to her life of privilege with financial expert Hal (Alec Baldwin). With laughs derived from death, depression and denial, this is Allen at his tartest and most observant. Sensational. **KK** Swearing. DVD BL

Cate Blanchett *Jasmine* • Alec Baldwin *Hal* • Louis CK *Al* • Bobby Cannavale *Chili* • Andrew Dice Clay *Augie* • Sally Hawkins *Ginger* • Peter Sarsgaard *Dwight* ■ *Dir/Scr* Woody Allen

Blue Jean Cop ★★★ 18
Action crime thriller 1988 · US · Colour · 92min

Forget the implausibilities in the dumb plot of this *Lethal Weapon* copy and marvel at

how director James Glickenhaus choreographs the truly spectacular stuntwork. With highlights such as undercover cop Sam Elliott swinging off 42nd Street cinema balconies like an urban Tarzan and the frenetic Coney Island rollercoaster chase, this kinetic sleaze-fest delivers the action goods. **AJ** Violence, swearing.

Peter Weller *Roland Dalton* • Sam Elliott *Richie Marks* • Richard Brooks (2) *Michael Jones* • Jude Ciccolella *Patrick O'Leary* • Tom Waites [Thomas G Waites] *Officer Kelly* • George Loros *Officer Varelli* • Daryl Edwards *Dr Watson* • Antonio Fargas *Nicky Carr* ■ *Dir/Scr* James Glickenhaus

Blue Juice ★★ 15
Comedy drama   1995 · UK · Colour · 94min

What's this? A British movie about surfing! Since it's set on the rocky, chilly beaches of Cornwall, it's no wonder you see little of the sport itself. Instead, director Carl Prechezer focuses on the less interesting dilemma facing surfer Sean Pertwee. Terrified of turning 30, he must choose between his woman (Catherine Zeta-Jones) and the waves. One look at the weather throughout this contrived melodrama and there's no contest. Watch for Ewan McGregor's drug-popping psycho. **AJ** DVD

Sean Pertwee *JC* • Catherine Zeta-Jones *Chloe* • Ewan McGregor *Dean Raymond* • Steven Mackintosh *Josh Tambini* • Peter Gunn *Terry Colcott* • Heathcote Williams *Shaper* • Colette Brown *Junior* • Michelle Chadwick *Sarah* • Keith Allen *Mike* ■ *Dir* Carl Prechezer • *Scr* Peter Salmi, Carl Prechezer, from an idea by Peter Salmi, Carl Prechezer, Tim Veglio

The Blue Kite ★★★★ 12
Drama   1992 · HK/Chi · Colour · 134min

Banned by the Chinese authorities, this is a rich and courageous study of the impact that the policies pursued by the Communist Party between 1949 and 1967 had on ordinary people. Based on director Tian Zhuangzhuang's memories and the stories told to him by family and friends, this tough film combines strident criticisms of Mao's regime with moments of great personal drama as careers, romances, friendships and rivalries are affected by momentous political and historical events. **DP** Mandarin +subtitles.

Yi Tian *Tietou as an infant* • Zhang Wenyao *Tietou as a child* • Chen Xiaoman *Tietou as a teenager* • Lu Liping *Mum (Chen Shujuan)* • Pu Quanxin *Dad (Lin Shaolong)* • Guo Baochang *Stepfather (Lao Wu)* ■ *Dir* Tian Zhuangzhuang • *Scr* Xiao Mao

The Blue Knight ★★★
Police drama   1973 · US · Colour · 102min

This police drama was originally made for American television, ran at nearly four hours and was shown on four consecutive nights. After it won several awards, it was cut by two-thirds and released in cinemas in Britain. Based on the bestselling book by former cop Joseph Wambaugh, it's set among the drug dealers and lowlifes of Los Angeles, but concentrates on the character of weary, craggy patrolman William Holden, who is obsessed with finding the killer of a prostitute. **AT**

William Holden (2) *"Bumper" Morgan* • Lee Remick *Cassie* • Joe Santos *Sergeant Cruze* • Eileen Brennan *Glenda* • Emile Meyer *Bartender* • Sam Elliott *Homicide detective* • Ernest Esparza III *Rudy Garcia* • Anne Archer *Call-girl* • Vic Tayback *Retired cop* ■ *Dir* Robert Butler • *Scr* E Jack Neuman, from the novel by Joseph Wambaugh

The Blue Lagoon ★★★
Romantic adventure 1949 · UK · Colour · 103min

This is an immensely popular and very likeable British version of the sexy little tale by Henry Devere Stacpoole about two children marooned on a desert island paradise, growing up to discover sex and their attraction to each other. The book had to be slightly modified to meet the needs of the censor (a problem not encountered by the ludicrous 1980 remake with Brooke Shields). Here the castaways are played

with great charm by Donald Houston and lovely Jean Simmons. **TS**

Jean Simmons *Emmeline Foster* • Susan Stranks *Emmeline as child* • Donald Houston *Michael Reynolds* • Peter Jones *Michael as child* • Noel Purcell *Paddy Button* • James Hayter *Dr Murdoch* • Cyril Cusack *James Carter* • Nora Nicholson *Mrs Stannard* ■ *Dir* Frank Launder • *Scr* Frank Launder, John Baines, Michael Hogan, from the novel by Henry de Vere Stacpoole • *Cinematographer* Geoffrey Unsworth

The Blue Lagoon ★★ 15
Romantic adventure 1980 · US · Colour · 100min

This is a remake of the 1949 British film, in which two children were shipwrecked on a deserted island. In this update, teenage self-discovery and love ensue as Brooke Shields and co-star Christopher Atkins grow up isolated from the world. It's beautifully shot and there's much nudity and suggested sex, but it's all very, very silly, as the lovebirds conform to traditional marriage-and-baby values. Don't waste your time with the 1991 sequel, *Return to the Blue Lagoon*. **LH** Sex scenes, nudity. DVD

Brooke Shields *Emmeline* • Christopher Atkins *Richard* • Leo McKern *Paddy Button* • William Daniels (2) *Arthur Lestrange* • Elva Josephson *Young Emmeline* • Glenn Kohan *Young Richard* • Alan Hopgood *Captain* • Gus Mercurio *Officer* ■ *Dir* Randal Kleiser • *Scr* Douglas Day Stewart, from the novel by Henry de Vere Stacpoole

The Blue Lamp ★★★★ PG
Crime drama   1949 · UK · BW · 81min

Jack Warner rose from the dead to star in TV's *Dixon of Dock Green* after his character was bumped off by petty crook Dirk Bogarde in this crime classic. Produced by Michael Balcon and scripted by TEB Clarke (a former policeman who penned many an Ealing comedy), the film yet again revealed the influence of the documentary on postwar British cinema, with its realistic depiction of the austere times that pushed some people to crime. Jimmy Hanley is a touch lightweight, but the rest of director Basil Dearden's cast is outstanding. **DP** DVD

Jack Warner *PC George Dixon* • Jimmy Hanley *PC Andy Mitchell* • Dirk Bogarde *Tom Riley* • Robert Flemyng *Sergeant Roberts* • Gladys Henson *Mrs Dixon* • Bernard Lee *Inspector Cherry* • Peggy Evans *Diana Lewis* • Patric Doonan *Spud* • Bruce Seton *Constable Campbell* • Dora Bryan *Maisie* ■ *Dir* Basil Dearden • *Scr* TEB Clarke

The Blue Light ★★★★
Drama   1932 · Ger · BW · 77min

The mountain film was hugely popular with German audiences in the 1930s. Having starred in four features for the master of the genre, Dr Arnold Fanck, Leni Riefenstahl made her directorial debut with this tale of a Dolomite villager who is denounced as a witch for her ability to climb the unscaleable Mount Cristallo. As the maiden who plunges to her death after her lover removes the peak's magic crystals, Riefenstahl does a steady job. However, it's the stylised beauty of her direction that takes this simple moral fable on to a higher plane and landed her the post of Hitler's film-maker. **DP** In Italian, German.

Leni Riefenstahl *Junta* • Mattias Weimann *Vigo* • Max Holzboer *Innkeeper* • Beni Führer *Tonio* • Franz Maldacea *Guzzi* • Martha Mair *Lucia* ■ *Dir* Leni Riefenstahl • *Scr* Leni Riefenstahl, Béla Balázs • *Cinematographer* Hans Schneeberger

The Blue Max ★★★★ PG
First World War drama
1966 · UK/US · Colour · 137min

A film about the short lives and lengthy lusts of German First World War fighter aces – it sounds luridly sensational, but action director John Guillermin makes it a rare treat of aerial excitement. George Peppard is the reckless high-flier who endangers his comrades and beds Ursula Andress, wife of commander James Mason. The love story is unconvincingly staged and compares badly with the camaraderie of men under stress. But the superb in-flight photography reveals the grit as well as the glamour of their escapades. **TH** DVD

B

George Peppard *Bruno Stachel* • James Mason *Count von Klugermann* • Ursula Andress *Countess Kaeti* • Jeremy Kemp *Willi von Klugermann* • Karl Michael Vogler *Heidemann* • Anton Diffring *Holbach* • Harry Towb *Kettering* • Peter Woodthorpe *Rupp* • Derek Newark *Ziegel* ■ *Dir* John Guillermin • *Scr* David Pursall, Jack Seddon, Gerald Hanley, Ben Barzman, Basilio Franchina, from the novel *The Blue Max* by Jack D Hunter • *Cinematographer* Douglas Slocombe

Blue Murder at St Trinian's ★★★ U
Comedy   1957 · UK · BW · 82min

While hugely enjoyable, the second of Frank Launder and Sidney Gilliat's adaptations of Ronald Searle's popular cartoons is something of a disappointment after the riotous success of *The Belles of St Trinian's*. The main problem is that there's only a fleeting glimpse of Alastair Sim as Miss Fritton, but the plot – about a tour of Europe and some stolen gems – is also somewhat under par. However, the flirting between coach company owner Terry-Thomas and undercover cop Joyce Grenfell is a comic delight. Followed by *The Pure Hell of St Trinian's*. DP

Joyce Grenfell *Sergeant Gates* • Terry-Thomas *Romney Carlton-Ricketts* • George Cole *Flash Harry* • Alastair Sim *Miss Amelia Fritton* • Sabrina (1) *Virginia* • Lionel Jeffries *Joe Mangan* • Lloyd Lamble *Superintendent* • Raymond Rollett *Chief Constable* ■ *Dir* Frank Launder • *Scr* Sidney Gilliat, Frank Launder, Val Valentine, from the drawings by Ronald Searle

The Blue Parrot ★★
Crime drama   1953 · UK · BW · 71min

This features an unoriginal plot and a title that recalls the Graham Greene-inspired thriller *The Green Cockatoo*. The budget was tight and the story, about an American cop who solves a case and falls for a pretty English girl while on secondment to Scotland Yard, is hardly riveting stuff. Dermot Walsh does his best with lacklustre material, and John Le Mesurier turns up in a supporting slot, but there's little else to recommend it. DP

Dermot Walsh *Bob Herrick* • Jacqueline Hill *Maureen* • Ballard Berkeley *Supt Chester* • Ferdy Mayne *Stevens* • Valerie White *Eva West* • John Le Mesurier *Henry Carson* • Richard Pearson (1) *Quinney* • June Ashley *Gloria* ■ *Dir* John Harlow • *Scr* Allan MacKinnon, from the story *Gunman* by Percy Hoskins

The Blue Peter ★★★ U
Comedy drama   1955 · UK · Colour · 94min

Group 3 was a government-backed British film production company set up to make low-budget projects utilising new talent. This adventure romp was co-written by talented director Don Sharp and directed by equally talented writer Wolf Rilla. It brought Irish hunk Kieron Moore back from Hollywood to play a Korean War veteran teaching Aberdovey students at an outdoor camp. The youngsters include Anthony Newley and Harry Fowler. TS

Kieron Moore *Mike Merriworth* • Greta Gynt *Mary Griffith* • Sarah Lawson *Gwyneth Thomas* • Mervyn Johns *Captain Snow* • John Charlesworth *Andrew Griffin* • Harry Fowler *Charlie Barton* • Mary Kerridge *Mrs Snow* • Ram Gopal *Dr Tigara* • Russell Napier *Raymond Curtiss* • Anthony Newley *Sparrow* • Vincent Ball *Digger* ■ *Dir* Wolf Rilla • *Scr* Don Sharp, John Pudney

Blue Ruin ★★★★ 15
Revenge thriller   2013 · US · Colour · 86min

Director Jeremy Saulnier's first film, the comedy horror *Murder Party*, may have been an inauspicious debut but his sophomore effort, an unusually minimalist revenge thriller, is pure gold. Bearded vagrant Macon Blair is shaken from his torpor by the release of the man responsible for killing his parents, and sets off to take action. Understated, atmospheric and compelling, *Blue Ruin* has an art house indie aesthetic reminiscent of the Coen brothers' debut *Blood Simple*, and that's high praise, indeed. JA Violence, swearing. *DVD* ⦿

Macon Blair *Dwight* • Devin Ratray *Ben Gaffney* • Amy Hargreaves *Sam* • Kevin Kolack *Teddy Cleland* • Brent Werzner *Carl Cleland* ■ *Dir/Scr* Jeremy Saulnier

Blue Scar ★★★ U
Drama   1947 · UK · BW · 102min

A year after her outstanding documentary study of postwar Plymouth, *The Way We Live*, Jill Craigie made her fiction debut with this openly political drama. Craigie and producer William MacQuitty raised the budget themselves and shot much of the action in a converted cinema in South Wales. The director later dismissed the tale of mining engineer Emrys Jones's visit to London as "amateurish". The acting of the largely nonprofessional cast is certainly stilted, but this is still a bold attempt to present a truthful portrait. DP

Emrys Jones *Tom Thomas* • Gwyneth Vaughan *Olwen Williams* • Rachel Thomas *Gwyneth Williams* • Anthony Pendrell [Tony Pendrell] *Alfred Collins* • Prysor Williams *Ted Williams* • Madoline Thomas *Granny* • Jack James *Dai Morgan* • Kenneth Griffith *Thomas Williams* ■ *Dir/Scr* Jill Craigie

Blue Skies ★★★ U
Musical   1946 · US · Colour · 99min

When dancer Paul Draper turned out to be unsuitable, Paramount called up the great Fred Astaire to replace him opposite crooner Bing Crosby in this garishly Technicolored Irving Berlin songfest. Thank goodness. Beside the divine Astaire, Crosby looks clumsy as they declare that they're *A Couple of Song and Dance Men*. The undoubted highlight is Astaire's classic solo dance routine during *Puttin' On the Ritz*. The girls are weak, the comedy's patchy, the plot's paper-thin, but who cares when Astaire's on screen? TS *DVD*

Fred Astaire *Jed Potter* • Bing Crosby *Johnny Adams* • Joan Caulfield *Mary O'Hara* • Billy De Wolfe *Tony* • Olga San Juan *Nita Nova* • Mikhail Rasmuny *François* • Carol Andrews *Dolly* • Dorothy Barrett *Showgirl* • Robert Benchley *Businessman* ■ *Dir* Stuart Heisler • *Scr* Arthur Sheekman, from an idea by Irving Berlin

Blue Sky ★★★★ 12
Drama   1991 · US · Colour · 96min

This fragmented yet compelling drama is distinguished by Jessica Lange's merciless, Oscar-winning performance as a wife who's a walking nervous breakdown. Tommy Lee Jones matches her every spasm as her US Army husband, an atomic scientist facing the risk of meltdown in both his work and his marriage when Lange sets his sights on commanding officer Powers Boothe. Set in the early 1960s, veteran director Tony Richardson's final film uses the couple's personal crises to echo the nation's nuclear dilemma. TH Violence, swearing, nudity. *DVD*

Jessica Lange *Carly Marshall* • Tommy Lee Jones *Hank Marshall* • Powers Boothe *Vince Johnson* • Carrie Snodgress *Vera Johnson* • Amy Locane *Alex Marshall* • Chris O'Donnell *Glenn Johnson* • Mitchell Ryan *Ray Stevens* ■ *Dir* Tony Richardson • *Scr* Rama Laurie Stagner, Arlene Sarner, Jerry Leichtling, from a story by Arlene Stagner

Blue Steel ★★ U
Western   1934 · US · BW · 54min

A programme filler made for Monogram Studios, this stars John Wayne before he had managed to break free from such routine fare. There's not a lot to commend here: George "Gabby" Hayes makes a watchable tobacco-chewing sheriff and Yakima Canutt, a mainstay of this series, appears as the quaintly monikered Polka Dot Bandit. The plot's that old chestnut about the marshal disguising himself to nail the baddies, and there's little artistry in Robert N Bradbury's direction. TS *DVD*

John Wayne *John Beaumont* • Eleanor Hunt *Betty Mason* • George "Gabby" Hayes *Sheriff Jake* • Ed Peil Sr [Edward Peil Sr] *Melgrove* • Yakima Canutt *Danti, The Polka Dot Bandit* • George Cleveland *Hank* • George Nash *Bridegroom* ■ *Dir/Scr* Robert N Bradbury

Blue Steel ★★★★ 18
Thriller   1990 · US · Colour · 97min

Made a year before the male-dominated *Point Break*, this intelligent, provocative thriller from director Kathryn Bigelow stars Jamie Lee Curtis as the rookie police officer who tries to prevent an armed robbery in a supermarket. Ron Silver is the businessman and firearms nut who picks up the robber's gun and embarks on a chilling game of cat and mouse with her. Curtis is outstanding as the harassed officer and Silver is genuinely creepy. Bigelow skilfully defines the almost fetishistic attraction of guns, and stages some exhilarating action set pieces. JF Sex scenes, violence, swearing. *DVD*

Jamie Lee Curtis *Megan Turner* • Ron Silver *Eugene Hunt* • Clancy Brown *Nick Mann* • Elizabeth Peña *Tracy Perez* • Louise Fletcher *Shirley Turner* • Philip Bosco *Frank Turner* • Kevin Dunn *Assistant Chief Stanley Hoyt* • Tom Sizemore *Wool cap* ■ *Dir* Kathryn Bigelow • *Scr* Kathryn Bigelow, Eric Red

Blue Streak ★★★ 12
Crime comedy   1999 · US · Colour · 90min

Emerging from prison, thief Martin Lawrence is horrified to find that the construction site where he hid a stolen jewel is now a police station. Joining the boys in blue, his "wrong side of the law" approach to crime-solving yields some extraordinary results. Unlike so many action comedies, Les Mayfield's film boasts an intricate and cleverly structured plot, though the tension is undermined by Lawrence's wild overacting. SR Swearing, violence. *DVD* ⦿

Martin Lawrence *Miles Logan* • Luke Wilson *Carlson* • Peter Greene *Deacon* • Dave Chappelle *Tulley* • Nicole Ari Parker *Melissa Green* • Graham Beckel *Rizzo* • Robert Miranda *Glenfiddish* • Olek Krupa *LaFleur* ■ *Dir* Les Mayfield • *Scr* Michael Berry, John Blumenthal, Steve Carpenter [Stephen Carpenter]

Blue Suede Shoes ★★
Music documentary   1980 · UK · Colour · 95min

Some critics will tell you that the truest form of documentary is one in which the director resists the temptation either to participate or impose an editorial slant. However, the simple recording of events without any spin invariably makes for very dull viewing. This is a film brimming with personalities as director Curtis Clark poses the question, "Why do these people dress in long outmoded threads and hurl themselves around to music the devil no longer seems to have a use for?" Shot with all the vibrance of a Pat Boone B-side. DP

■ *Dir* Curtis Clark

Blue Sunshine ★★★★ 18
Horror thriller   1977 · US · Colour · 94min

One of the best shockers produced in the 1970s, director Jeff Lieberman's cult classic is a psychedelic chiller of the highest order. Intriguing pulp fiction invades subversive David Cronenberg territory as the ten-year-delayed after-effects of an LSD derivative result in a group of former Stanford University students losing their hair, then their cool, before turning into crazed, vicious killers. Directed with economic flair and sly black humour, this drug-culture allegory sizzles with invention and frenetical horror. AJ Violence, swearing *DVD*

Zalman King *Jerry Zipkin* • Deborah Winters *Alicia Sweeney* • Mark Goddard *Edward Flemming* • Robert Walden *David Blume* • Charles Siebert *Detective Clay* • Ann Cooper *Wendy Flemming* • Ray Young *Wayne Mulligan* • Brion James *Tony* ■ *Dir/Scr* Jeff Lieberman

Blue Thunder ★★★ 15
Action thriller   1983 · US · Colour · 104min

Directed by John Badham, this is a *Boys' Own*-style action drama involving a super-helicopter, complete with hi-tech surveillance gadgets and mega-weapons. It's flown by LA cop Roy Scheider, who learns that his bitter enemy Malcolm McDowell plans to sabotage the machine. This slick if somewhat predictable

adventure was spun off into a TV series starring James Farentino and *Wayne's World*'s Dana Carvey. JB Violence, swearing, nudity. *DVD* ⦿

Roy Scheider *Frank Murphy* • Malcolm McDowell *Colonel Cochrane* • Candy Clark *Kate* • Warren Oates *Captain Braddock* • Daniel Stern *Lymangood* • Paul Roebling *Icelan* • David Sheiner *Fletcher* ■ *Dir* John Badham • *Scr* Dan O'Bannon, Don Jakoby

Blue Tiger ★★★ 18
Action crime thriller 1994 · US · Colour · 84min

Japanese gangsters were briefly in vogue in the mid-1990s, mainly on the back of *Rising Sun*. This, along with *American Yakuza*, is the pick of the straight-to-video bunch, thanks to a charismatic turn from Virginia Madsen in the lead role. She plays a mother who, after her son is killed during a gun battle, goes gunning for the yakuza. Director Norbeto Barba keeps the foot firmly on the accelerator and serves up some slick scenes of ultra-violence. JF *DVD*

Virginia Madsen *Gina Hayes* • Toru Nakamura *Seiji* • Dean Hallo *Henry Soames* • Ryo Ishibashi *Gan* • Sal Lopez *Luis* • Yuji Okumoto *Sakagami* • Harry Dean Stanton *Smith* • Brenda Varda *Emily* ■ *Dir* Norberto Barba • *Scr* Joel Soisson, from a story by Taka Ichise

The Blue Tower ★★
Romantic thriller   2008 · UK · Colour · 85min

Trapped in an arranged marriage and facing the prospect of a dead-end job with his shady father-in-law, Abhin Galeya embarks on an affair with ailing aunt Indira Joshi's nurse, Alice O'Connell, which culminates in an attempt to rob the old woman. But Galeya's guilt begins to manifest itself in visions of a mysterious blue tower. A combination of multicultural treatise and dark domestic thriller, this marks a new departure for British-Asian cinema. Yet Smita Bhide's clichéd screenplay ultimately defeats the willing but not always convincing cast. DP

Abhin Galeya *Mohan* • Alice O'Connell *Judy* • Manjinder Virk *Asha* • Indira Joshi *Kamla* ■ *Dir/Scr* Smita Bhide

Blue Valentine ★★★★ 15
Relationship drama   2010 · US · Colour · 107min

From the first stirrings of romance to the fractious acrimony of its death throes, this intimate drama offers an in-depth portrait of a marriage hitting the skids. Thanks to strong performances from Michelle Williams and Ryan Gosling, there's a genuine emotional credibility to Derek Cianfrance's film, though it's by no means comfortable viewing. The relationship is well observed throughout, and Williams's turn as the hard-working nurse frustrated by Gosling's apparent lack of ambition is heart-rending indeed. TJ Swearing, sex scenes. *DVD* ⦿

Ryan Gosling *Dean* • Michelle Williams *Cindy* • Faith Wladyka *Frankie* • John Doman *Jerry* • Mike Vogel *Bobby* • Jen Jones *Gramma* ■ *Dir* Derek Cianfrance • *Scr* Derek Cianfrance, Joey Curtis, Cami Delavigne

Blue Valley Songbird ★★ PG
Musical drama   1999 · US · Colour · 91min

Dolly Parton's spirited performance here is undermined by the formulaic melodramatics of this mediocre TV movie. Director Richard A Colla overplays the comparisons between the abuse inflicted on the teenage country singer by her father and the control freakery of her boyfriend-cum-manager, John Terry, whose fear that he will be dumped if Dolly finds fame is preventing her shot at the big time. Parton handles the songs with expected aplomb, but all else fails to convince. DP *DVD*

Dolly Parton *Leanna Taylor* • John Terry *Hank* • Billy Dean *Bobby* • Kimberley Kates *Thelma Russell* ■ *Dir* Richard A Colla • *Scr* Ken Carter, Annette Haywood-Carter

B

The Blue Veil ★★★★
Romantic drama 1951 · US · BW · 108min

Already an Oscar winner for *Johnny Belinda* and a best actress nominee for *The Yearling*, Jane Wyman arrived at RKO on loan from Warner Bros. She picked up another nomination and delivered a massive profit for the small and often troubled studio. Wyman plays a a woman who devotes her life to caring for the children of others and winning their devotion, only to descend into lonely poverty. The star's convincing and dignified portrayal, together with an exceptional set of supporting performances from Joan Blondell (also Oscar-nominated), Charles Laughton, Agnes Moorehead and 13-year-old Natalie Wood, makes for a satisfying, classy tear-jerker. RK

Jane Wyman *Louise Mason* · Charles Laughton *Fred K Begley* · Joan Blondell *Annie Rawlins* · Richard Carlson *Gerald Kean* · Agnes Moorehead *Mrs Palfrey* · Don Taylor *Dr Robert Palfrey* · Audrey Totter *Helen Williams* · Cyril Cusack *Frank Hutchins* · Natalie Wood *Stephanie Rawlins* ■ *Dir* Curtis Bernhardt · *Scr* Norman Corwin, from a story by François Campaux

LANDMARK FILM
A massively influential film that takes weirdness into the mainstream

Blue Velvet ★★★★★ 18
Cult mystery thriller 1986 · US · Colour · 115min

This is the most complete of David Lynch's films, made before his disturbing black vision of small-town American life veered into self-parody. The dark tone is set from the opening sequence, which starts with white picket fences and cheery firemen but ends with a man suffering a stroke in his garden while insect life seethes beneath the lawn. Lynch regular Kyle MacLachlan is the young innocent who gets sucked into the bizarre sadomasochistic relationship between nightclub singer Isabella Rossellini and monstrous local crime boss Dennis Hopper, who resurrected his career with his crazed portrait of evil. Listening to Roy Orbison's *In Dreams* will never be the same again. JF Violence, swearing, drug abuse, sex scenes, nudity. *DVD* *BD*

Kyle MacLachlan *Jeffrey Beaumont* · Isabella Rossellini *Dorothy Vallens* · Dennis Hopper *Frank Booth* · Laura Dern *Sandy Williams* · Hope Lange *Mrs Williams* · Dean Stockwell *Ben* · George Dickerson *Detective Williams* · Brad Dourif *Raymond* · Jack Nance *Paul* ■ *Dir/Scr* David Lynch · *Cinematographer* Frederick Elmes · *Music* Angelo Badalamenti

The Blue Villa ★★★
Drama 1994 · Bel/Fr/Swi · Colour · 100min

More than 30 years after electrifying world cinema with his screenplay for *Last Year at Marienbad*, Alain Robbe-Grillet was still playing intellectual games with structure and perception. Shuffling dreams, memory and reality, Robbe-Grillet and co-director Dimitri de Clercq ally us with a Greek policeman, as he tries to decide whether a sailor (who could be a ghost) was responsible for the murder of the daughter of a screenwriter – or whether she is still alive and a resident of the local brothel. The control is as admirable as it's arch. DP French +subtitles.

Fred Ward *Frank* · Arielle Dombasle *Sarah-la-Blonde* · Charles Tordjman *Edouard Nordmann* · Sandrine Le Berre *Santa* · Dimitri Poulikakos *Thieu* · Christian Maillet *The Father* · Muriel Jacobs *Kim* ■ *Dir/Scr* Alain Robbe-Grillet, Dimitri de Clercq

Blue Water, White Death ★★★ U
Documentary 1971 · US · Colour · 98min

Four years before *Jaws* made seaside swimming seem a hazardous occupation for tourists, director Peter Gimbel mined the same deep-water fears in this outstanding documentary. Using the device of divers searching for the hunting grounds of the great white shark, Gimbel's cameras get unflinchingly up close and dangerously personal with the ocean's eating machines. Yet the film manages to avoid the clichés that have become the norm since the success of Steven Spielberg's shocker. Fans of wildlife programmes will love it. AJ

■ *Dir* Peter Gimbel, James Lipscomb · *Scr* Peter Gimbel

Bluebeard ★★★
Horror 1944 · US · BW · 71min

It wasn't often that poverty row studio PRC (Producers Releasing Corporation) came up with a film worth watching, but it did give the highly talented director Edgar G Ulmer some artistic freedom. Here he coaxes a beautifully restrained performance from the flamboyant character actor John Carradine, in one of his few starring roles, as the artist and puppeteer in 19th-century Paris who has an irresistible urge to murder his models. With production values that transcend the low budget, this is a small miracle of polished film-making. AE

John Carradine *Gaston* · Jean Parker *Lucille* · Nils Asther *Insp Lefevre* · Ludwig Stossel *Lamarte* · George Pembroke *Insp Renard* · Teala Loring *Francine* · Sonia Sorel *Renee* · Iris Adrian *Mimi* ■ *Dir* Edgar G Ulmer · *Scr* Pierre Gendron, from a screenplay (unproduced) by Arnold Phillips, Werner H Furst

Bluebeard ★★★
Crime drama 1962 · Fr/It · Colour · 115min

Claude Chabrol gave Charles Denner his first leading film role in this true story of Landru, a man who charmed a number of unsuspecting women and then murdered them. The magnetic Denner, with bald dome, bushy eyebrows and black beard, was an ideal interpreter of Chabrol's characteristic acid wit. But the screenplay by novelist Françoise Sagan lacks the sympathy or death that Charlie Chaplin brought to the same subject in *Monsieur Verdoux* (1947). However, the photography, the sets, and the bevy of beautiful actresses are pleasing to the eye. RB French dubbed.

Michèle Morgan *Celestine Buisson* · Danielle Darrieux *Berthe Heon* · Charles Denner *Henri-Désire Landru* · Hildegarde Knef [Hildegarde Neff] *Madame Ixe* · Juliette Mayniel *Anna Colomb* · Stéphane Audran *Fernande Segret* · Mary Marquet *Madame Guillin* ■ *Dir* Claude Chabrol · *Scr* Françoise Sagan, Claude Chabrol · *Cinematographer* Jean Rabier · *Costume Designer* Maurice Albray

Bluebeard ★
Crime thriller 1972 · It/Fr/W Ger · Colour · 123min

This take on the infamous serial killer is likely to offend almost everyone. The execution is so ham-fisted, and the murders so exploitative, that the film is oddly repugnant. Richard Burton apparently took the role because he fancied a trip to Budapest, while his female victims are encouraged to strip and camp it up before they meet their untimely ends. AT

Richard Burton *Baron Von Sepper* · Raquel Welch *Magdalena* · Joey Heatherton *Anne* · Virna Lisi *Elga* · Nathalie Delon *Erika* · Marilu Tolo *Brigitte* · Karin Schubert *Greta* · Agostina Belli *Caroline* ■ *Dir* Edward Dmytryk · *Scr* Ennio Di Concini, Edward Dmytryk, Maria Pia Fusco, from a story by Ennio Di Concini, Edward Dmytryk, Maria Pia Fusco

Bluebeard ★★★★ 15
Fantasy drama 2009 · Fr · Colour · 78min

Director Catherine Breillat (*A Ma Soeur!*) returns to the theme of squabbling siblings to impart a feminist twist on Charles Perrault's gruesome fairy tale. When 17th-century teenagers Daphné Baïwir and Lola Créton are forced to leave their convent school, they have little option but to compete for the affections of nobleman Bluebeard (Dominique Thomas), despite his reputation as a serial wife killer. There are echoes here of Angela Carter's short story *The Bloody Chamber*, and the disconcerting saga springs two particularly nasty surprises. DP French +subtitles. *DVD*

Dominique Thomas *Bluebeard* · Lola Créton *Marie-Catherine* · Daphné Baïwir *Anne* · Marilou Lopes-Benites *Catherine* · Lola Giovannetti *Marie-Anne* · Farida Khelfa *Mother Superior* · Isabelle Lapouge *Mother* ■ *Dir* Catherine Breillat · *Scr* Catherine Breillat, from a story by Charles Perrault

Bluebeard's Eighth Wife ★★
Screwball comedy 1938 · US · BW · 84min

An impoverished daughter of the French nobility becomes the eighth wife of a millionaire who finds he has finally met his match. Marking the first screenplay collaboration of Charles Brackett and Billy Wilder, and directed by Ernst Lubitsch, this romantic comedy promises much but, alas, delivers little. After the delightful opening sequence, in which the stars "meet cute" in a store's pyjama department, the famous "Lubitsch touch" disappears and gives way to increasing tedium. RK

Claudette Colbert *Nicole de Loiselle* · Gary Cooper *Michael Brandon* · Edward Everett Horton *de Loiselle* · David Niven *Albert De Regnier* · Elizabeth Patterson *Aunt Hedwige* · Herman Bing *Monsieur Pepinard* · Charles Halton *Monsieur de la Coste* · Barlowe Borland *Uncle Fernandel* · Warren Hymer *Kid Mulligan* · Franklin Pangborn *Assistant hotel manager* ■ *Dir* Ernst Lubitsch · *Scr* Charles Brackett, Billy Wilder, from the translation by Charlton Andrews of the play *La Huitième Femme de Barbe-Bleu* by Alfred Savoir

Blueberry ★★★ 15
Western adventure 2004 · Fr/UK/Mex · Colour · 124min

Jan Kounen allows his technology to get the better of him in this inconsistent adaptation of Jean "Moebius" Giraud's cult comic books. Too much time is spent in the morphed mind of Cajun sheriff Vincent Cassel, as he strives to settle an old score with Michael Madsen, the hissable adventurer who caused the death of Cassel's first love and now seeks the secret of some sacred mountains. The supporting cast ably captures the spirit of the Old West, but the visuals swamp the slender storyline. DP French, English, German, Spanish +subtitles. Nudity.

Vincent Cassel *Mike S Blueberry* · Juliette Lewis *Maria Sullivan* · Michael Madsen *Wally Blount* · Temuera Morrison *Runi* · Djimon Hounsou *Woodhead* · Colm Meaney *Jimmy McClure* · Tcheky Karyo *The Uncle* · Ernest Borgnine *Rolling Star* · Nichole Hiltz *Lola* · Eddie Izzard *Prosit* ■ *Dir* Jan Kounen · *Scr* Gérard Brach, Matt Alexander, Jan Kounen, from the comic book series by Jean "Moebius" Giraud, Jean-Michel Charlier

The Blueblack Hussar ★★★
Documentary 2013 · UK · Colour · 99min

One of the biggest pop stars of the 1980s, Adam Ant suffered a nervous breakdown and, he reckons, lost 15 years of creativity. Filmed over the course of a year, Jack Bond's film follows Ant as he tries to rebuild his career. Resembling Johnny Depp doing a Russell Brand impression, Ant fizzes with ideas, opinions and wisecracks, and encounters with famous friends, though staged, still confirm the esteem in which he is held. While old fans may feel a bit short-changed on the nostalgia front, Ant's new persona, the Blueblack Hussar, makes for splendidly eclectic viewing. DP

Adam Ant ■ *Dir* Jack Bond

The Blues, a Musical Journey: Feel like Going Home ★★★★★ U
Music documentary 2003 · US · Colour and BW · 81min

This is the first in the seven-film documentary series, and the only instalment to be directed by the driving force behind it, Martin Scorsese. Tracing the progress and evolution of the music, Scorsese never loses sight of the historical legacy of slavery, poverty and repression that underpins its pain and pathos. But he also succeeds in recapturing the mood, method and message of such Delta legends as Robert Johnson and Charley Patton. Guitarist Corey Harris proves an amiable travelling companion - his conversations with the likes of Ali Farka Toure, Taj Mahal and Keb' Mo' are as captivating as the music, which retains all its affecting power. DP *DVD*

■ *Dir* Martin Scorsese · *Scr* Peter Guralnick

The Blues, a Musical Journey: Godfathers and Sons ★★★★ 15
Documentary 2003 · US · Colour and BW · 95min

In 1968, Muddy Waters released *Electric Mud* on the Chess label and was slammed by the critics for betraying the spirit of the Blues. Director Marc Levin attempts to reassess the reputation of this much-maligned album in this stylish but always gutsy entry in the documentary series. Levin follows Chicago producer Marshall Chess (whose father, Leonard, co-founded the label) and rapper Chuck D as they bid to reunite Waters's band and rethink the music for a new generation. In so doing, he succeeds in establishing the links between Muddy and Howlin' Wolf and the hip-hop stars of today. DP *DVD*

■ *Dir* Marc Levin · *Cinematographer* Mark Benjamin

The Blues, a Musical Journey: Piano Blues ★★★ 15
Documentary 2003 · US · Colour and BW · 88min

Clint Eastwood's penchant for jazz blurs the lines in this highly personal contribution to the series. Starting off with 1930s ragtime and boogie-woogie, Eastwood detours around Art Tatum and Oscar Peterson, trades tales with Dave Brubeck before meandering back – via some Kansas City big band and pseudo-classical interludes – to West Coast Blues in the company of Ray Charles. Purists are going to protest at every turn, but newcomers will be intrigued by the intermingling of styles. DP *DVD*

■ *Dir* Clint Eastwood

The Blues, a Musical Journey: Red, White & Blues ★★★ 15
Documentary 2003 · US · Colour and BW · 92min

British director Mike Figgis has always lavished care on his film soundtracks and this passion for music comes across in his contribution to the series. Taking 1940s British jazz as his starting point, Figgis shows how this evolved into 1950s skiffle and the 1960s electric Blues perfected by the likes of the Rolling Stones, the Animals and the Spencer Davis Group. The musical highlights are provided by Van Morrison and the unlikely duo of Jeff Beck and Lulu. More reliant on talking heads than other entries, but this is still fascinating. DP *DVD*

■ *Dir* Mike Figgis

The Blues, a Musical Journey: The Road to Memphis ★★★★ PG
Documentary 2003 · US · Colour · 88min

The sense of a parade passing along Beale Street and into history drives director Richard Pearce's melancholic entry in the series. A veteran film-maker who got his start on DA Pennebaker's Bob Dylan documentary *Don't Look Back*, Pearce is torn between celebrating Memphis's almost forgotten black musical roots and emphasising the struggle experienced by the city's remaining blues practitioners. Consequently, the reminiscences are more telling and the sound produced by the quartet of BB King, Rosco Gordon, Ike Turner and Bobby Rush is all the more poignant. As much about the artists as their music, this is a nostalgic and authentic portrait. DP *DVD*

■ *Dir* Richard Pearce · *Scr* Robert Gordon

The Blues, a Musical Journey: The Soul of a Man ★★★★ 12
Documentary 2003 · US/Ger · Colour and BW · 99min

One of the highlights of the series, this technically audacious and musically sincere tribute to Blind Willie Johnson, Skip James and JB Lenoir from director Wim Wenders reveals the enduring legacy of three bluesmen whose songs have previously been the preserve of aficionados. The performances of Lou Reed, Bonnie Raitt and John Mayall and the Bluesbreakers are memorable in themselves. What makes this documentary so enticing, however, are the archive pastiches by cinematographer Lisa Rinzler, which not only bring these elusive figures back to life, but also re-create the Depression-era realities in which they lived and worked. DP *DVD*

■ *Dir/Scr* Wim Wenders • *Narrator* Laurence Fishburne

The Blues, a Musical Journey: Warming by the Devil's Fire ★★ 12

Drama documentary
2003 · US · Colour and BW · 88min

We don't learn as much as we should about such 78rpm recording stars as Ma Rainey, Rosetta Tharpe, Charley Patton and T-Bone Walker in this lacklustre episode of the series. Director Charles Burnett rather capriciously elects to explore their careers through the encyclopedic anecdotes told by a streetwise 1950s New Orleans uncle to his barely enthralled 11-year-old nephew. The fact that so much superb music is short-changed makes the selection of this contrived road movie format all the more disappointing. DP *DVD*

■ *Dir/Scr* Charles Burnett

The Blues Brothers ★★★★ 15

Musical comedy
1980 · US · Colour · 127min

This wonderful sprawling mess of a movie remains one of the best musical comedies of modern times. John Belushi and Dan Aykroyd are the criminally minded brothers on a mission from God, who resurrect their rhythm-and-blues band to raise money for their old orphanage. The skimpiest of plots provides the excuse for a string of rousing musical numbers and cameo appearances from music legends such as Ray Charles, Aretha Franklin and Cab Calloway. When the music runs out, director John Landis stages a spectacular car chase involving the massed forces of law and order, a country-and-western band and neo-Nazis. JF Swearing. *DVD* ☐

John Belushi *"Joliet" Jake Blues* • Dan Aykroyd *Elwood Blues* • Kathleen Freeman *Sister Mary Stigmata* • James Brown (2) *Reverend Cleophus James* • Cab Calloway *Curtis* • Carrie Fisher *Mystery woman* • Ray Charles *Ray* • Aretha Franklin *Soul Food Cafe owner* • John Candy *Burton Mercer* • Henry Gibson *Nazi leader* • Steven Spielberg *Cook county clerk* • Twiggy *Chic lady* • Paul Reubens *Waiter* ■ *Dir* John Landis • *Scr* John Landis, Dan Aykroyd

Blues Brothers 2000 ★★★ PG

Musical comedy
1998 · US · Colour · 118min

It took 18 years for actor Dan Aykroyd and director John Landis to "get the band back together". Although viewers will miss the marvellous slapstick slobbishness of the late John Belushi, this sequel is still a lot of fun. The wafer-thin plot has Elwood Blues (Aykroyd) hooking up with the band's former musicians. But the movie's *raison d'être* is the irresistible R 'n' B numbers performed by Aykroyd, his co-star John Goodman and dynamic vocalists such as Aretha Franklin, BB King and James Brown. Self-indulgent but worth catching. JC Swearing, violence. *DVD* ☐

Dan Aykroyd *Elwood Blues* • John Goodman *Mighty Mack McTeer* • Joe Morton *Cabel Chamberlain* • J Evan Bonifant *Buster* • Aretha Franklin *Mrs Murphy* • James Brown (2) *Reverend Cleophus James* • BB King *Malvern Gasperon* • Steve Cropper *"The Colonel" Cropper* • Donald Dunn *Donald "Duck" Dunn* ■ *Dir* John Landis • *Scr* John Landis, Dan Aykroyd, from their film *The Blues Brothers*

Blues in the Night ★★

Musical drama
1941 · US · BW · 87min

This tough, interesting Warner Bros drama purports to deal honestly with the life of itinerant jazz musicians, with murky direction by Anatole Litvak. The film almost works, but the pivotal role of a musician bent on self-destruction is played by the bland Richard Whorf. The support, though, is excellent, and includes a young, acting Elia Kazan playing (or miming) the clarinet. But, despite the gritty look, the film never quite hangs together. TS

Priscilla Lane *Ginger* • Betty Field *Kay Grant* • Richard Whorf *Jigger Pine* • Lloyd Nolan *Del Davis* • Jack Carson *Leo Powell* • Wally Ford [Wallace Ford] *Brad Ames* • Elia Kazan *Nickie Haroyan* ■ *Dir* Anatole Litvak • *Scr* Robert Rossen, from the play by Edwin Gilbert

Blume in Love ★★★★ 15

Comedy drama
1973 · US · Colour · 110min

One of the best sex comedies from the fast-and-loose 1970s, this has a wonderfully warm performance from George Segal as a lawyer whose harassed humour endears us to his infidelities. His wife (Susan Anspach), alas, feels differently, throwing him out on his ear to repent at leisure and ponder passions past. Writer/director Paul Mazursky – who made *Bob & Carol & Ted & Alice* four years earlier – indulges his usual predilection for lengthy exposition, while the Italian locations add more travelogue gloss than emotional point. Segal's characterisation makes it all worthwhile, however. TH

George Segal *Blume* • Susan Anspach *Nina Blume* • Kris Kristofferson *Elmo* • Marsha Mason *Arlene* • Shelley Winters *Mrs Cramer* • Donald F Muhich *Analyst* • Paul Mazursky *Blume's partner* ■ *Dir/Scr* Paul Mazursky

Boardwalk ★★

Drama
1979 · US · Colour · 100min

American theatre luminaries Lee Strasberg and Ruth Gordon star as a happily married Jewish couple approaching their golden wedding anniversary whose lives – and those of their friends – are blighted by the disintegration of their Brooklyn neighbourhood. Steven Verona's depressing and ineptly-made film offers no insight into the problems it exaggeratedly depicts. RK

Ruth Gordon *Becky Rosen* • Lee Strasberg *David Rosen* • Janet Leigh *Florence* • Joe Silver *Leo Rosen* • Eli Mintz *Mr Friedman* • Eddie Barth *Eli Rosen* ■ *Dir* Stephen Verona • *Scr* Stephen Verona, Leigh Chapman

The Boat That Rocked ★★ 15

Period comedy
2009 · US/Ger/UK/Fr · Colour · 129min

Writer/director Richard Curtis finds himself all at sea with this tribute to the offshore 1960s pirate radio stations that changed the way Britain listened to music. The golden-oldie hits come thick and fast, much like the vignettes passed off as plot in this tale of the good ship *Radio Rock*. The main thrust follows a teenager (Tom Sturridge) who is sent aboard to find direction, and along the way learns which of the resident superstar DJs is his father. There's a decent cast, including a louche Bill Nighy as the station boss and Kenneth Branagh as the uptight MP trying to ban the broadcasts. It's just a shame that nominal star Philip Seymour Hoffman has so little to do. AJ Swearing, some sexual references, brief nudity. *DVD* ☐

Philip Seymour Hoffman *The Count* • Bill Nighy *Quentin* • Rhys Ifans *Gavin Kavanagh* • Nick Frost *Dave* • Kenneth Branagh *Sir Alistair Dormandy* • Tom Sturridge *Carl* • Chris O'Dowd *Simon* • Rhys Darby *Angus* • January Jones *Elenore* • Gemma Arterton *Desiree* ■ *Dir/Scr* Richard Curtis

Boat Trip ★ 15

Comedy
2002 · US/Ger · Colour and BW · 90min

Cuba Gooding Jr stars in this limp comedy about two straight men who wind up on an all-gay ocean cruise. The film-makers also

contrive to get the bikini-clad lovelies of a Swedish tanning team on board. The humour is as subtle as dynamite and about as funny, though Roger Moore's cameo as an ageing queen produces one or two amusing lines. DA Swearing. *DVD*

Cuba Gooding Jr *Jerry* • Horatio Sanz *Nick* • Roger Moore *Lloyd* • Roselyn Sanchez *Gabriella* • Vivica A Fox *Felicia* • Lin Shaye *Sonya* • Victoria Silvstedt *Inga* • Bob Gunton *Captain* • Richard Roundtree *Malcolm* ■ *Dir* Mort Nathan • *Scr* Mort Nathan, William Bigelow, Brian Pollack, Mert Rich

The Boatniks ★★ U

Comedy adventure
1970 · US · Colour · 99min

Rocking the boat with his outrageous mugging, Phil Silvers eventually capsizes this unremarkable Disney comedy. As a smart-talking, but decidedly minor league jewel thief, he fails to outwit the equally gormless Robert Morse, who, up to that point, had been carving his little niche as the worst-ever coastguard in the history of California. A much firmer hand was needed on the tiller than that applied by director Norman Tokar, but there are a couple of neat set pieces. DP

Robert Morse *Ensign Thomas Garland* • Stefanie Powers *Kate Fairchild* • Phil Silvers *Harry Simmons* • Norman Fell *Max* • Mickey Shaughnessy *Charlie* • Don Ameche *Commander Taylor* • Wally Cox *Jason Bennett* ■ *Dir* Norman Tokar • *Scr* Arthur Julian, from a story by Marty Roth

Bob & Carol & Ted & Alice ★★★ 15

Comedy
1969 · US · Colour · 101min

This slice of flower-power permissiveness alarmed some at the time because of promised revelations, but disappointed others because romance got in the way. Natalie Wood, Robert Culp, Elliott Gould and Dyan Cannon make up the two Californian couples who go in for group therapy and confessing to extramarital sin. The result is too many words and too little action courtesy of director Paul Mazursky. There's an intimidating sentimentality, too, but this was a landmark in its day. TH Swearing, drug abuse, nudity. *DVD*

Natalie Wood *Carol* • Robert Culp *Bob* • Elliott Gould *Ted* • Dyan Cannon *Alice* • Horst Ebersberg *Horst* • Lee Bergere *Emelio* • Donald F Muhich *Psychiatrist* • Noble Lee Holderread Jr *Sean* • KT Stevens *Phyllis* ■ *Dir* Paul Mazursky • *Scr* Paul Mazursky, Larry Tucker • *Cinematographer* Charles Lang

Bob Le Flambeur ★★★★ PG

Crime comedy drama
1955 · Fr · BW · 97min

This little-known classic counts as one of Jean-Pierre Melville's very best. It's a bizarre heist movie that spins on a delicious irony: Bob plans to rob the casino at Deauville but wins the money at the tables. There are tragic overtones, but this is still an absurdist comedy with bags of atmosphere, romance, jazz music, pretentious dialogue, great locations and a wonderfully brooding performance from Roger Duchesne. AT French +subtitles. *DVD*

Isabelle Corey *Anne* • Roger Duchesne *Robert "Bob" Montagné* • Daniel Cauchy *Paolo* • Guy Decomble *Inspector Ledru* • André Garret *Roger* • Claude Cerval *Jean* • Gérard Buhr *Marc* • Howard Vernon *McKimmie* ■ *Dir* Jean-Pierre Melville • *Scr* Jean-Pierre Melville, Auguste Le Breton

Bob Roberts ★★★★ 15

Spoof political documentary
1992 · US · Colour · 99min

1992 was the year of Tim Robbins. Not only did he star in Robert Altman's savage Hollywood satire *The Player* but he also starred in, wrote and directed this hilarious pseudo-documentary about a folk-singing right-wing politician running for the US Senate. Taking its style from *This Is Spinal Tap* with a deliberate on-screen homage to the Bob Dylan tour movie *Don't Look Back*, this is both witty and wickedly pointed, if a shade smug at times. Immaculately cast, with telling performances from Alan Rickman, Gore Vidal and John Cusack, the

film was a substantial achievement. TS Swearing. *DVD*

Tim Robbins *Bob Roberts* • Giancarlo Esposito *Bugs Raplin* • Ray Wise *Chet MacGregor* • Rebecca Jenkins *Delores Perrigrew* • Harry Lennix *Franklin Dockett* • John Ottavino *Clark Anderson* • Robert Stanton *Bart Macklerooney* • Alan Rickman *Lukas Hart III* • Gore Vidal *Senator Brickley Paiste* • James Spader *Chuck Marlin* • Helen Hunt *Rose Pondell* • Susan Sarandon *Tawna Titan* • John Cusack *TV host* ■ *Dir/Scr* Tim Robbins

Bob, Son of Battle ★★ U

Drama
1947 · US · Colour · 103min

Clean-cut Lon McCallister is in love with his dog in a movie directed by Louis King. Peggy Ann Garner is sweet, Edmund Gwenn as watchable as ever and the scenery attractive, but this is only for those who particularly enjoy boy-and-dog movies. TS

Edmund Gwenn *Adam McAdam* • Lon McCallister *David McAdam* • Peggy Ann Garner *Maggie Moore* • Reginald Owen *James Moore* • Charles Irwin *Long Kirby* • Dave Thursby *Samuel Thornton* ■ *Dir* Louis King • *Scr* Jerome Cady, from the novel by Alfred Ollivant

Bobbikins ★ U

Fantasy comedy
1959 · UK · BW · 89min

Even die-hard Max Bygraves fans will be hard pressed to squeeze much enjoyment out of this cinematic lemon. Impoverished entertainer Bygraves becomes rich after his 14-month-old baby begins picking up financial titbits from his park bench conversations with Chancellor Charles Carson. Preposterous. DP

Max Bygraves *Benjamin Barnaby* • Shirley Jones *Betty Barnaby* • Steven Stacker *Bobbikins* • Billie Whitelaw *Lydia* • Barbara Shelley *Valerie* • Colin Gordon *Dr Phillips* • Charles Tingwell *Luke* • Lionel Jeffries *Gregory Mason* • Charles Carson *Sir Jason Crandall* ■ *Dir* Robert Day • *Scr* Oscar Brodney

Bobby ★★★ PG

Musical romance
1973 · Ind · Colour · 160min

Movie references abound in this colourful masala, which is not only packed with memorable songs, but also manages to tack a happy ending on to the *Romeo and Juliet* story. Director Raj Kapoor is in playful mood throughout, making many of the love scenes between his son Rishi and Dimple Kapadia mirror classic moments from his own on-screen teaming with 1950s superstar Nargis. DP Hindi +subtitles.

Rishi Kapoor *Raj Nath* • Dimple Kapadia *Bobby* • Pran *Rishi's father* • Premnath *Bobby's father* • Prem Chopra ■ *Dir* Raj Kapoor • *Scr* KA Abbas, VP Sathe

Bobby ★★★★ 15

Period drama
2006 · US · Colour · 112min

Despite the title, this is not a biopic of US presidential hopeful Robert Kennedy but a snapshot of a time and place in history. The drama unfolds on a single momentous day in 1968 at the hotel that acted as Kennedy's campaign headquarters. Writer/director Emilio Estevez personalises the story with glimpses into the lives of staff, guests and members of the senator's team, played by a starry ensemble cast that includes Estevez himself and his father Martin Sheen. But it's Sharon Stone who impresses the most, barely recognisable as the hotel stylist whose manager husband (William H Macy) is having an affair with a switchboard operator (Heather Graham). What the movie lacks in narrative drive, it makes up for by brilliantly re-creating the mood of the time. While the real Bobby Kennedy seems reduced to a supporting player, the promise he represented infuses everything. BP Violence, swearing, drug abuse. *DVD*

William H Macy *Paul Ebbers* • Christian Slater *Timmons* • Anthony Hopkins *John Casey* • Sharon Stone *Miriam Ebbers* • Harry Belafonte *Nelson* • Emilio Estevez *Tim Fallon* • Laurence Fishburne *Edward Robinson* • Heather Graham *Angela* • Helen Hunt *Samantha Stevens* • Ashton Kutcher *Fisher* • Lindsay Lohan *Diane* • Demi Moore *Virginia Fallon* • Martin Sheen *Jack Stevens* • Elijah Wood *William* ■ *Dir/Scr* Emilio Estevez • *Cinematographer* Michael Barrett (3) • *Editor* Richard Chew

Bo66y ★★★★ PG

Documentary
2016 · UK · Colour and BW · 93min

The stars of the football world come out for this documentary charting the life and career of Bobby Moore, from his zenith as England's only World Cup winning captain to struggles later in life and untimely death aged just 51. Fascinating and vibrant footage of the 1966 World Cup Final hammers home just what Moore and his team-mates achieved, while a host of football figures from the past share stories that are funny, inspiring, and heartbreaking. A fitting tribute to an icon. JL *DVD* *BL*

Bobby Moore · Pelé *Pele* · Frank Lampard · Wayne Rooney · Ray Winstone · Russell Brand ■ *Dir* Ron Scalpello

Bobby Deerfield ★★★ PG

Romantic drama 1977 · US · Colour · 118min

This self-consciously arty (and often just plain dumb) yet strangely compelling melodrama stars Al Pacino as a Formula One racing driver who falls in love with a terminally ill Italian beauty, played by Marthe Keller. Thanks to Pacino's addiction to speed, there's a death sentence hanging over both of them, making this a peculiarly morbid experience. It's worth watching for the quality of Pacino's performance and director Sydney Pollack's assured coverage of the races and use of Florence locations. AT

Al Pacino *Bobby Deerfield* · Marthe Keller *Lillian Morelli* · Anny Duperey *Lydia* · Walter McGinn *Leonard* · Romolo Valli *Uncle Luigi* · Stephan Meldegg *Karl Holtzmann* · Jaime Sanchez *Delvecchio* ■ *Dir* Sydney Pollack · *Scr* Alvin Sargent, from the novel *Heaven Has No Favorites* by Erich Maria Remarque

Bobby Fischer against the World ★★★ 12A

Documentary
2011 · US/UK/Ire · Colour and BW · 93min

In the early 1970s, the mercurial American Bobby Fischer generated front-page headlines for chess all over the world. This riveting documentary from director Liz Garbus pivots on Fischer's great 1972 duel – at the height of the Cold War – against Soviet grandmaster Boris Spassky. The prize: the title of chess world champion. However, the movie's title says it all, for despite being a genius whose skill put him at the centre of a superpower confrontation, he was unable to conquer his own demons and ended up an obsessive fugitive figure no longer welcome in his own country. KK Swearing.

■ *Dir* Liz Garbus

Bobby Jones: Stroke of Genius ★★ PG

Sports biography 2004 · US · Colour · 123min

Rowdy Herrington stages some credible golfing sequences in this hagiographic memoir, but he fails to distinguish between the events that made up perpetual amateur Bobby Jones's unrivalled Grand Slam success. Consequently, aficionados will be left frustrated, while casual viewers will be dissuaded by the sanctimonious dismissal of professionalism. Jim Caviezel mistakes sincerity for charisma in the title role and is gloriously upstaged by Jeremy Northam. DP *DVD*

Jim Caviezel *Bobby Jones* · Claire Forlani *Mary Jones* · Jeremy Northam *Walter Hagen* · Connie Ray *Clara Jones* · Brett Rice *Big Bob* · Malcolm McDowell *OB Keeler* ■ *Dir* Rowdy Herrington · *Scr* Rowdy Herrington, Tony DePaul, Bill Pryor, from a story by Rowdy Herrington, Kim Dawson

The Bobo ★★ PG

Comedy 1967 · UK · Colour · 98min

This bizarre Peter Sellers vehicle was one of a string of ill-chosen projects that tarnished Sellers's reputation before he returned to the Clouseau role in the mid-1970s. Here he plays an unsuccessful matador who has to seduce Barcelona's most desirable lady in order to get a booking as a singer. It's not very funny, but the locations are gorgeous,

and the sublime Hattie Jacques is a treat. TS *DVD*

Peter Sellers *Juan Bautista* · Britt Ekland *Olimpia Segura* · Rossano Brazzi *Carlos Matabosch* · Adolfo Celi *Francisco Carbonell* · Hattie Jacques *Trinity Martinez* · Alfredo Lettieri [Al Lettieri] *Eugenio* · Kenneth Griffith *Gamazo* · Marne Maitland *Castillo* ■ *Dir* Robert Parrish · *Scr* David R Schwartz, from his play

Bob's Weekend ★★ 15

Comedy 1996 · UK · Colour · 89min

In first-time director Jevon O'Neill's amiable but underwritten odd-couple comedy, Bruce Jones plays a Manchester security guard who's fired from his job and cuckolded by his wife Anna Jaskolka. He heads for Blackpool determined to throw himself off the pier, but a chance encounter with perky psychology student Charlotte Jones affords him a new lease on life. Their unlikely friendship is engagingly played. DP Violence, swearing. *DVD*

Bruce Jones *Bob* · Charlotte Jones (2) *Angela* · Anna Jaskolka *Brenda* · Brian Glover *The Boss* · Ricky Tomlinson *Jack* ■ *Dir* Jevon O'Neill · *Scr* Jevon O'Neill, Jayson Rothwell

Bodies, Rest & Motion ★★★ 15

Drama 1993 · US · Colour · 90min

In an average "20-something" tale, Phoebe Cates, Bridget Fonda, Tim Roth and Eric Stoltz bum around Arizona musing about life, love and shallow relationships that no one will particularly care about except them. A disappointment from director Michael Steinberg, who previously made the moving and meaningful drama *The Waterdance*. JB Swearing.

Phoebe Cates *Carol* · Bridget Fonda *Beth* · Tim Roth *Nick* · Eric Stoltz *Sid* · Alicia Witt *Elizabeth* · Sandra Lafferty *Yard-sale lady* · Sidney Dawson *TV customer* · Jon Proudstar *Station attendant* ■ *Dir* Michael Steinberg · *Scr* Roger Hedden, from his play

The Body ★★ 12

Religious thriller
2000 · US/Ger/Is · Colour · 104min

A sliver of originality is rapidly buried beneath the rubble in this torpid thriller from first-time director Jonas McCord. When archaeologist Olivia Williams discovers what appears to be the body of Jesus Christ in the back streets of Jerusalem, Vatican troubleshooter Antonio Banderas is sent to refute the claim that the Resurrection is a myth. This lacks both depth and pace, and compounds matters by trivialising the region's political complexities and opting for a tacky romance and a crude action finale. DP *DVD*

Antonio Banderas *Father Matt Gutierrez* · Olivia Williams *Sharon Golban* · Derek Jacobi *Dr Pierre Lavelle* · John Wood (2) *Cardinal Pesci* · Jason Flemyng *Father Walter Winstead* · John Shrapnel *Moshe Cohen* ■ *Dir* Jonas McCord · *Scr* Jonas McCord, from the novel by Richard Ben Sapir

Body and Soul ★★

First World War spy drama
1931 · US · BW · 81min

The principal interest today of this apparently lost First World War flying-and-spying drama is the brief appearance of Humphrey Bogart. He plays an American flyer in France who dies trying to shoot down a German observation balloon. After Bogie's demise, Charles Farrell falls for his dead pal's widow Elissa Landi, who comes under suspicion of being a spy. The arrival of Myrna Loy, also claiming to have been Bogart's dame, complicates matters. AE

Charles Farrell (1) *Maj Andrews* · Elissa Landi *Carla* · Humphrey Bogart *Jim Watson* · Myrna Loy *Alice Lester* · Donald Dillaway *Tap Johnson* · Crawford Kent [Crauford Kent] *Major Burke* · Pat Somerset *Major Knowles* · Ian MacLaren *Gen Trofford Jones* ■ *Dir* Alfred Santell · *Scr* Jules Furthman, from the play *Squadrons* by AE Thomas and the story *Big Eyes and Little Mouth* by Elliot White Springs

Body and Soul ★★★★★ PG

Sports drama 1947 · US · BW · 100min

One of the greatest boxing movies of all time, this looks like a cross between 1940s melodrama and *film noir*. James Wong Howe's in-the-ring photography set landmark standards, as he dispensed with tripods and roller skated with a hand-held camera. Robert Parrish's Oscar-winning editing (with Francis D Lyon) prefigured his directing career, as did Robert Aldrich's assistant direction. John Garfield is superb as the champ with an uncertain sense of ethics, and Lilli Palmer simply mouthwatering as his doll. There's a tautness in Robert Rossen's direction that he would recapture 14 years later in his equally masterly *The Hustler*. TS *DVD*

John Garfield *Charley Davis* · Lilli Palmer *Peg Born* · Hazel Brooks *Alice* · Anne Revere *Anna Davis* · William Conrad *Quinn* · Joseph Pevney *Shorty Polaski* · Canada Lee *Ben Chaplin* · Lloyd Goff *Roberts* ■ *Dir* Robert Rossen · *Scr* Abraham Polonsky

Body and Soul ★★ 18

Sports drama 1981 · US · Colour · 93min

This pallid remake of the powerful 1947 John Garfield boxing classic is remarkable for all the wrong reasons. Hidden away near the bottom of the cast list are two of the most charismatic figures in popular culture: Muhammad Ali, playing himself in a brief cameo, and Rat Packer Peter Lawford, here cast, oddly enough, as a gangster. FL

Leon Isaac Kennedy *Leon Johnson* · Jayne Kennedy *Julie Winters* · Michael V Gazzo *Frankie* · Peter Lawford *Big Man* · Perry Lang *Charles Golphin* · Kim Hamilton *Mrs Johnson* · Muhammad Ali ■ *Dir* George Bowers · *Scr* Leon Isaac Kennedy

Body Count ★★ 18

Crime drama 1997 · US/UK · Colour · 80min

After the massive success of the first series of *NYPD Blue*, its star David Caruso seemed destined for bigger things. So far his big screen career hasn't gone quite to plan, though this is one of his better efforts. He's part of a bickering gang of robbers who, having just pulled off a multimillion- dollar art heist, must now get to Miami to cash in their haul. Lower-league Tarantino. JF Drug abuse, swearing, violence. *DVD*

David Caruso *Hobbs* · Linda Fiorentino *Natalie* · John Leguizamo *Chino* · Ving Rhames *Pike* · Donnie Wahlberg *Booker* · Forest Whitaker *Crane* · Michael Corrigan *Security officer no 1* · Michael Hunter *Security officer no 2* ■ *Dir* Robert Patton-Spruill · *Scr* Theodore Witcher

Body Double ★★★★ 18

Erotic thriller 1984 · US · Colour · 109min

No one is better at apeing Alfred Hitchcock than director Brian De Palma. In this engrossingly sly shocker, he combines the master's predilection for kinky storytelling with his own engaging high style and taste for designer violence. Little does B-movie horror actor Craig Wasson know when he spies on Deborah Shelton undressing in her Hollywood home that it will lead him to witnessing murder. Tense, deliciously sleazy and blackly comic – and sporting a gorgeous Pino Donaggio score – De Palma's *Rear Window* update is his most outrageous and voyeuristic film to date. AJ Violence, swearing, sex scenes, nudity. *DVD*

Craig Wasson *Jake Scully* · Melanie Griffith *Holly Body* · Gregg Henry *Sam Bouchard* · Deborah Shelton *Gloria Revelle* · Guy Boyd *Jim McClean* · Dennis Franz *Rubin* · David Haskell *Drama teacher* · Rebecca Stanley *Kimberly* ■ *Dir* Brian De Palma · *Scr* Brian De Palma, Robert Avrech, from a story by Brian De Palma

Body Heat ★★★★ 18

Thriller 1981 · US · Colour · 108min

Lawrence Kasdan's dazzling directorial debut packs a steamy punch. William Hurt plays the small-town lawyer who falls for *femme fatale* Kathleen Turner only to find himself ensnared in a tortuous plot to murder her wealthy husband (Richard Crenna). Kasdan respectfully tips his hat to classics such as *Double Indemnity*, but the intricate plotting and sly humour ensure

that his film stands in its own right. The performances are first rate, too: Turner positively sizzles, while Hurt is excellent as the ordinary Joe getting increasingly out of his depth. There's also a creepy cameo from Mickey Rourke and a jolly supporting role for the then unknown Ted Danson. JF Violence, swearing, sex scenes, nudity. *DVD*

William Hurt *Ned Racine* · Kathleen Turner *Matty Walker* · Richard Crenna *Edmund Walker* · Ted Danson *Peter Lowenstein* · JA Preston *Oscar Grace* · Mickey Rourke *Teddy Lewis* · Kim Zimmer *Mary Ann* · Jane Hallaren *Stella* · Lanna Sanders *Roz Kraft* ■ *Dir/Scr* Lawrence Kasdan

Body Melt ★★ 18

Horror comedy 1993 · Aus · Colour · 79min

Inhabitants of a suburban Melbourne cul-de-sac become unwitting guinea pigs for a new body enhancement drug in this splatter satire from Australian director Philip Brophy. Exploding genitalia, kangaroo cannibalism and placentas taking on lives of their own are a few of the gross-outs in this stomach-churner. Hysterical acting and pointless horror homages lessen the confrontational nature of Brophy's *Knots Landing in Hell*. AJ *DVD*

Gerard Kennedy *Det Sam Phillips* · Andrew Daddo *Johnno* · Ian Smith *Dr Carrera* · Vincent Gil *Pud* · Regina Gaigalas *Shaan* ■ *Dir* Philip Brophy · *Scr* Philip Brophy, Rod Bishop

Body of Evidence ★★★ 18

Erotic thriller 1992 · US · Colour · 96min

With this erotic thriller, director Uli Edel attempted to out-steam the same year's *Basic Instinct*, but, although it makes for rather hokey fun, it lacks the outrageous flair of Paul Verhoeven's notorious hit. Madonna is the *femme fatale* accused of killing her elderly millionaire boyfriend; Willem Dafoe is the lawyer who gets seduced into a dangerous affair with his client. The story is absolute rot, and it's more interesting to guess how much of the erotic footage survived the snip. JF Swearing, violence, sex scenes, nudity. *DVD*

Madonna *Rebecca Carlson* · Willem Dafoe *Frank Dulaney* · Joe Mantegna *Robert Garrett* · Anne Archer *Joanne Braslow* · Julianne Moore *Sharon Dulaney* · Stan Shaw *Charles Biggs* · Jürgen Prochnow *Dr Alan Paley* ■ *Dir* Uli Edel · *Scr* Brad Mirman

Body of Lies ★★★ 15

Political thriller 2008 · US · Colour · 122min

Two of Hollywood's biggest stars, Leonardo DiCaprio and Russell Crowe, join Crowe's regular collaborator, director Ridley Scott, in this Middle East-set political thriller. But the whole is decidedly less than the sum of its parts. DiCaprio plays CIA agent Roger Ferris, who is sent to Jordan by his boss Ed Hoffman (Crowe) to track down a terrorist mastermind. However, he soon finds himself caught between Hoffman's Machiavellian games and local intelligence chief Hani Salaam (Mark Strong), who doesn't trust his US allies. Scott orchestrates the action with his usual flair and there are some telling points about America's war on terror. However, the movie lacks the depth and sweep of a film like *Syriana* and the muted playing of DiCaprio and Crowe provides few fireworks. JF In English, Arabic. Violence, swearing. *DVD* *BL*

Leonardo DiCaprio *Roger Ferris* · Russell Crowe *Ed Hoffman* · Mark Strong *Hani Salaam* · Golshifteh Farahani *Aisha* · Oscar Isaac *Bassam* · Alon Aboutboul *Al-Saleem* · Simon McBurney *Garland* · Vince Colosimo *Skip* ■ *Dir* Ridley Scott · *Scr* William Monahan, from the novel by David Ignatius

Body Parts ★★★ 18

Horror thriller 1991 · US · Colour · 84min

From the writers of novels that inspired the film classics *Les Diaboliques* and *Vertigo* comes this not-so-classic sci-fi horror, blending hi-tech surgery with low-grade shocks. After a car accident, prison psychiatrist Jeff Fahey has the arm of an executed killer grafted on to his shoulder,

B

which develops a murderous life of its own. Then he meets other recipients of the psycho's body parts suffering similar symptoms. Eric Red directs all this sinister lunacy with a sure hand. **AJ** Swearing, violence.

Jeff Fahey *Bill Chrushank* • Lindsay Duncan *Dr Webb* • Kim Delaney *Karen Chrushank* • Brad Dourif *Remo Lacey* • Zakes Mokae *Detective Sawchuk* • Peter Murnik *Mark Draper* • Paul Ben-Victor *Ray Kolberg* • John Walsh *Charlie Fletcher* ■ *Dir* Eric Red • *Scr* Eric Red, Norman Snider, from a story by Patrica Herskovic, Joyce Taylor, from the novel *Choice Cuts* by Thomas Narcejac, Pierre Boileau

Body Shot ★★ 18
Erotic crime thriller 1994 · US · Colour · 93min

Not many people would root for a member of the paparazzi, but at least the unlikely hero lends a novel twist to an otherwise by-the-numbers thriller. A blond Robert Patrick plays a sleazy snapper who is obsessed with reclusive rock superstar Michelle Johnson. Things go pear-shaped when he ends up framed for her murder. The plot stretches credibility to the limit, but the dependable cast makes it just about bearable. **JF** *DVD*

Robert Patrick *Mickey Dane* • Michelle Johnson *Danielle Wilde/Chelsea* • Ray Wise *Dwight Frye* • Jonathan Banks *Simon Deverau/Blake Donner* • Kim Miyori *Christine Wyler* • Peter Koch *Elmer Hatch* • William Steis *Curt Lomann* ■ *Dir* Dimitri Logothetis • *Scr* Robert Ian Strauss

Body Shots ★★★ 18
Drama 1999 · US · Colour · 99min

Michael Cristofer directs this debate-sparking study of 20-something morality. It looks like we've a long night ahead of us as eight near-identical Los Angelenos go through their pre-club rituals. However, when wannabe actress Tara Reid accuses pro-footballer Jerry O'Connell of date rape, the fun stops and sides are taken. Snappily shot in hip image bites by Rodrigo Garcia and astutely structured by writer David McKenna (*American History X*), this breaks no new ground but still manages to tease, amuse and provoke. **DP**

Sean Patrick Flanery *Rick Hamilton* • Jerry O'Connell *Michael Penorisi* • Amanda Peet *Jane Bannister* • Tara Reid *Sara Olswang* • Ron Livingston *Trent Barber* • Emily Procter *Whitney Bryant* • Brad Rowe *Shawn Denigan* • Sybil Temchen *Emma Cooper* ■ *Dir* Michael Cristofer • *Scr* David McKenna

The Body Snatcher
Horror ★★★★★ PG
1945 · US · BW · 78min

Producer Val Lewton's magnificent version of Robert Louis Stevenson's Burke and Hare-like corpse-stealing short story is a horror masterpiece. Striking attention to historical authenticity and a magnificently evil performance from Boris Karloff as the vile cab driver supplying cadavers to desperate anatomist Henry Daniell make for a grippingly literate and macabre shocker. Sinister support from Bela Lugosi and imaginative direction from Robert Wise give the tale a restrained ominousness and unseen terror until the justifiably famous hallucination climax. **AJ**

Boris Karloff *John Gray* • Bela Lugosi *Joseph* • Henry Daniell *Dr MacFarlane* • Edith Atwater *Meg Camden* • Russell Wade *Donald Fettes* • Rita Corday *Mrs Marsh* • Sharyn Moffett *Georgina Marsh* • Donna Lee *Street singer* ■ *Dir* Robert Wise • *Scr* Carlos Keith [Val Lewton], Philip MacDonald, from a short story by Robert Louis Stevenson

Body Snatchers ★★★★ 15
Science-fiction horror
1993 · US · Colour · 83min

Those interstellar pods capable of duplicating humans return for a third sinister attempt on mankind's individual identities in director Abel Ferrara's masterly reinterpretation of the classic Jack Finney terror tale. On an empathic par with the 1956 original chiller *Invasion of the Body Snatchers*, Ferrara's keen contemporary eye, controlled vision and heartless shock tactics make the underlying message seem as pertinent and vital as ever. Meg Tilly and

Gabrielle Anwar make indelible impressions as they take on the horrifying enemy infiltrating their military home base. **AJ** Violence, swearing, nudity. *DVD*

Terry Kinney *Steve Malone* • Meg Tilly *Carole Malone* • Gabrielle Anwar *Marty Malone* • Forest Whitaker *Doctor Collins* • Reilly Murphy *Andy Malone* • Billy Wirth *Tim Young* • Christine Elise *Jenn Platt* • R Lee Ermey *General Platt* ■ *Dir* Abel Ferrara • *Scr* Stuart Gordon, Dennis Paoli, Nicholas St John, from a story by Larry Cohen, Raymond Cistheri, from the novel *The Body Snatchers* by Jack Finney

The Body Stealers ★ PG
Science-fiction adventure
1969 · US/UK · Colour · 86min

Parachutists pass through a red mist and disappear into thin air. And before long you will, too! There is little point in sticking around to find out it's alien Maurice Evans putting sky divers in suspended animation and substituting duplicates. Talky, laughably low-budget and hopelessly inept. **AJ** *DVD*

George Sanders *General Armstrong* • Maurice Evans *Dr Matthews* • Patrick Allen *Bob Megan* • Neil Connery *Jim Radford* • Hilary Dwyer *Julie Slade* • Robert Flemyng *WC Baldwin* • Lorna Wilde *Lorna* • Allan Cuthbertson *Hindesmith* ■ *Dir* Gerry Levy • *Scr* Mike St Clair, Peter Marcus

Bodyguard ★★★
Crime thriller 1948 · US · BW · 62min

Lawrence Tierney plays a cop in this efficient thriller from director Richard Fleischer. However, soon after quitting the police force to watch over wealthy widow Elisabeth Risdon, Tierney becomes the prime suspect in a murder case. With Philip Reed and Steve Brodie providing hissable support, and Priscilla Lane giving a nicely weighted performance as Tierney's fiancée, this admirably demonstrates why so many lament the passing of the B-movie. **DP**

Lawrence Tierney *Mike Carter* • Priscilla Lane *Doris Brewster* • Philip Reed *Freddie Dysen* • June Clayworth *Connie* • Elisabeth Risdon *Gene Dysen* • Steve Brodie *Fenton* ■ *Dir* Richard Fleischer • *Scr* Harry Essex, Fred Niblo Jr, from a story by George W George, from a story by Robert B Altman [Robert Altman]

The Bodyguard ★★★ 15
Romantic thriller 1992 · US · Colour · 123min

Kevin Costner and Whitney Houston fall in love, she trilling all the while, amid a highly charged atmosphere of jealousy and death threats in this entertaining load of old baloney. Director Mick Jackson created a wildly successful film, much to several critics' snooty chagrin, by teaming two megastars and adding a daft but jaunty script, loud rock soundtrack and a few well-staged exciting moments. Costner is a trifle stern, but Houston makes a very creditable acting debut. **SH** Violence, swearing, a sex scene. *DVD* *BL*

Kevin Costner *Frank Farmer* • Whitney Houston *Rachel Marron* • Gary Kemp *Sy Spector* • Bill Cobbs *Devaney* • Ralph Waite *Herb Farmer* • Tomas Arana *Portman* • Michele Lamar Richards *Nicki* • Mike Starr *Tony* ■ *Dir* Mick Jackson • *Scr* Lawrence Kasdan, from his story

Bodysong ★★★★★ 18
Experimental documentary
2002 · UK · Colour and BW · 78min

American poet Walt Whitman encouraged us to *Sing the Body Electric*, and director Simon Pummell has done just that with this bold and experimental documentary. Laying out his themes of birth, growth, sex, violence, death and dreams as a laudatory hymn to human existence, the film occasionally backs off from the truly shocking - such as the casual slaughter of the Vietnam War - but does capture the sudden appalled awareness of a newborn child. Radiohead's Jonny Greenwood has boosted some remarkable archive images with his music and, while there seem to be some strange blanks in the film's understanding of the human condition, this is put together with a wit and craft that defy expectations. **TH** *DVD*

■ *Dir/Scr* Simon Pummell • *Music* Jonny Greenwood • *Editor* Daniel Goddard

Boeing Boeing ★★★
Romantic comedy 1965 · US · Colour · 102min

Marc Camoletti's hit play achieved astoundingly long theatrical runs throughout the world, so a screen version of this latter-day Feydeauesque farce was an inevitability. With a genuinely funny plot about a casanova of the airlines skewed by modern technology, this is beautifully cast by skilled producer Hal Wallis and features two great comedians - the incorrigibly brash Tony Curtis and a disciplined and subdued Jerry Lewis - who work together impeccably. **TS**

Jerry Lewis *Robert Reed* • Tony Curtis *Bernard Lawrence* • Dany Saval *Jacqueline Grieux* • Christiane Schmidtmer *Lise Bruner* • Suzanna Leigh *Vicky Hawkins* • Thelma Ritter *Bertha* • Lomax Study *Pierre* • Françoise Ruggieri *Taxi driver* ■ *Dir* John Rich • *Scr* Edward Anholt, from the play by Marc Camoletti • *Cinematographer* Lucien Ballard

Boesman & Lena ★★ 15
Period drama
2000 · Fr/S Afr · Colour and BW · 84min

Danny Glover stars as the alcoholic outsider forced to reappraise his relationship with both his wife and the unjust world, after his shanty-town home is demolished. Despite some probing camerawork and the inclusion of a couple of flashbacks to show Glover and Angela Bassett in happier times, veteran director John Berry singularly fails to prise this adaptation away from its proscenium confines. **DP** Swearing. *DVD*

Danny Glover *Boesman* • Angela Bassett *Lena* • Willie Jonah *Old African* ■ *Dir* John Berry • *Scr* John Berry, from a play by Athol Fugard

The Bofors Gun ★ 15
Drama 1968 · UK · Colour · 102min

The setting for this drama of violent personal conflict is a British army camp in Germany; the year is 1954. David Warner plays an indecisive corporal in charge of a guard detail, while Nicol Williamson is the abrasive, self-despising Irish gunner under his command. Too talkative and claustrophobic by half, this unremittingly downbeat study of futility, weakness and hatred takes an inordinate time to reach its very predictable conclusion. **AE** *DVD*

Nicol Williamson *O'Rourke* • Ian Holm *Flynn* • David Warner *Evans* • Richard O'Callaghan *Rowe* • Barry Jackson *Shone* • Donald Gee *Crawley* • John Thaw *Featherstone* • Peter Vaughan *Sergeant Walker* ■ *Dir* Jack Gold • *Scr* John McGrath, from his play *Events While Guarding the Bofors Gun*

Bogus ★★ PG
Fantasy comedy 1996 · US · Colour · 106min

Moonstruck director Norman Jewison has Whoopi Goldberg and Gérard Depardieu at his disposal for this fantasy comedy, as well as *Sixth Sense* star Haley Joel Osment, and all he produces is sentimental codswallop. Admittedly, the clichéd story doesn't give him much to aim at. The recently orphaned Osment is sent to live with his child-loathing aunt (Goldberg) and develops a relationship with an imaginary friend called Bogus (Depardieu) in order to survive the ordeal. Trite stuff. **LH**

Whoopi Goldberg *Harriet Franklin* • Gerard Depardieu [Gérard Depardieu] *Bogus* • Haley Joel Osment *Albert* • Andrea Martin *Penny* • Nancy Travis *Lorraine* • Denis Mercier *M Antoine* • Ute Lemper *Babette* • Sheryl Lee Ralph *Ruth Clark* ■ *Dir* Norman Jewison • *Scr* Alvin Sargent, from a story by Jeff Rothberg, Francis X McCarthy

Bogus Bandits ★★ U
Comedy opera 1933 · US · BW · 88min

A very dubious outing for Laurel and Hardy, this has the glorious boobies playing second fiddle to a *Desert Song*-style operetta. Dennis King is a dashing brigand in 18th-century Italy, wooing Thelma Todd, the neglected wife of lord James Finlayson. Stan and Ollie are vagrants trying to earn a living as bandits. There are some wonderful music-hall moments, but they can't shine

through the clichéd, ridiculous plot. **TH** *DVD*

Stan Laurel *Stanlio* • Oliver Hardy *Olio* • Dennis King *Fra Diavolo/Marquis de San Marco* • Thelma Todd *Lady Pamela* • James Finlayson *Lord Rocberg* ■ *Dir* Charles Rogers, Hal Roach • *Scr* Jeanie Macpherson, from the opera *Fra Diavolo* by Daniel F Auber

Bogwoman ★★★ 15
Drama 1997 · Ire · Colour · 77min

This is a provocative study of how 1960s Northern Irish politics impacted on people's everyday lives. Rachel Dowling gives a mettlesome performance as the single mother who crosses the border to settle in Derry's Bogside and, having married, comes to realise she's capable of more than just slaving for her chauvinistic husband (Peter Mullan). Tom Collins's film is given added resonance by the fact that it ends on the eve of the Troubles. **DP** Swearing.

Rachel Dowling [Rachael Dowling] *Maureen* • Sean McGinley *Mr D* • Peter Mullan *Barry* • Noelle Brown *Mrs D* ■ *Dir/Scr* Tom Collins

La Bohème ★★ U
Silent romantic drama 1926 · US · BW · 106min

A characteristically soulful and touching Lillian Gish and an athletically exuberant and sincere John Gilbert are the lovers doomed to be parted by death in this silent enactment of the story familiar to those who know Puccini's popular opera. Director King Vidor expertly steers the changes of mood from the boisterous to the tragic in the Latin quarter of Paris. Despite its virtues, however, its style is too outmoded to hold much appeal for audiences now. **RK**

Lillian Gish *Mimi* • John Gilbert (1) *Rodolphe* • Renée Adorée *Musette* • George Hassell *Schaunard* • Roy D'Arcy *Vicomte Paul* • Edward Everett Horton *Colline* • Karl Dane *Benoit* • Mathilde Comont *Madame Benoit* ■ *Dir* King Vidor • *Scr* Ray Doyle, Harry Behn, Fred De Gresac, William Conselman (titles), Ruth Cummings (titles), from the novel *Scènes de La Vie de Bohème (The Latin Quarter)* by Henri Murger

La Bohème ★★★ PG
Opera 2008 · Aus/Ger · Colour · 114min

This film version of Puccini's much-loved opera plays its absolutely straight and does a decent job of it. Re-creating 19th-century Paris in the studio, it preserves the tragic story of a starving artist's ill-fated love for an ailing seamstress without unnecessarily jazzing it up - but without adding very much either. The soaring melodies are present and correct as the camera lingers on two of the opera world's hot properties, Mexican tenor Rolando Villazón, who plays the poet Rodolfo, and Russian soprano Anna Netrebko as his consumptive love interest. Neither of them lacks charisma, though his hang-dog features seem rather more suited to comedy. **TJ** Italian +subtitles.

Anna Netrebko *Mimi* • Rolando Villazón *Rodolfo* • Nicole Cabell *Musetta* • Ioan Holender *Alcindoro* ■ *Dir* Robert Dornhelm • *Scr* from the opera by Giuseppe Giacosa, Luigi Illica, Giacomo Puccini, from the novel *Scènes de la Vie de Bohème* by Henri Murger

The Bohemian Girl ★★ U
Comedy 1936 · US · BW · 67min

Not even the great Laurel and Hardy can lift the spirits of this damp adaptation of the operetta by Michael Balfe, about gypsies who, in revenge, kidnap a nobleman's daughter and bring her up as one of their own. Stan and Ollie are snatch-purses, not that it matters much. Their gags disappear in the banal and confused plot and they look as embarrassed as audiences feel. This was the last film of their regular co-star Thelma Todd, who died of carbon monoxide poisoning just after this film was completed. **TH**

Stan Laurel *Stan* • Oliver Hardy *Ollie* • Thelma Todd *Gypsy Queen's daughter* • Antonio Moreno *Devilshoof* • Jacqueline Wells [Julie Bishop] *Arline* • Mae Busch *Mrs Hardy* • James Finlayson *Captain Finn* ■ *Dir* James W Horne, Charles Rogers • *Scr* Alfred Bunn, from the opera by Michael Balfe

B

Boiler Room ★★★★ 15
Drama 2000 · US · Colour · 114min

This amorality tale of financial swizz-kids focuses on young chancer Giovanni Ribisi who joins an "off-Broadway" brokerage firm that offers sky-high pay cheques to successful agents. Fuelled by equal measures of drink, drugs, adrenaline and testosterone, the young fiends of the firm's high-pressure "boiler room" are an obnoxious bunch. Writer/director Ben Younger worked in a real-life "boiler room" to research the film, and the result is a dynamite debut. There's great acting, too. DA Drug abuse, violence, swearing. *DVD*

Giovanni Ribisi *Seth Davis* · Nia Long *Abby Halperin* · Vin Diesel *Chris* · Ben Affleck *Jim Young* · Tom Everett Scott *Michael* · Ron Rifkin *Marty Davis* · Nicky Katt *Greg* · Bill Sage *Agent Drew* ■ *Dir/Scr* Ben Younger

Boiling Point ★★★★ 15
Thriller 1990 · Jpn · Colour · 96min

Takeshi "Beat" Kitano followed up his excellent directorial debut, *Violent Cop*, with this equally assured mix of abrasive action and earthy humour. Set again in the sinister world of the yakuza, the film focuses on the efforts of daydreaming greenhorn Masahiko Ono to protect his boss after he lands him in a gangster's bad books. As the manic former hood Ono hires to save the day, Takahito Iguchi gives a performance as hilarious as it is disturbing. This is essentially a samurai tale given an urban twist, and Kitano makes the city of Okinawa look a particularly forbidding place. Brutal, perhaps, but great fun, too. DP Japanese +subtitles. Violence, nudity. *DVD*

Masahiko Ono *Masaki* · Yuriko Ishida *Sayaka* · Takahito Iguchi *Takashi* · Minoru Iizuka *Kazuo* · Makoto Ashikawa *Akira* · Hitoshi Ozawa *Kanai* · Hisashi Igawa *Otomo, gang boss* ■ *Dir/Scr* Takeshi Kitano

Boiling Point ★★★★ 15
Thriller 1993 · US · Colour · 88min

On its cinema release, this was promoted as a straightforward action thriller, but it's far more intelligent than that. Wesley Snipes plays a treasury agent who hits the vengeance trail when his partner is killed during an undercover operation that goes wrong. Dennis Hopper and Viggo Mortensen are his targets, who are also trying to keep one step ahead of the Mob. While there are some excellent action set pieces, director James B Harris is more interested in exploring the relationships between the hunters and the hunted, and delivers a melancholy tale of crime and punishment. JF Swearing, violence. *DVD*

Wesley Snipes *Jimmy Mercer* · Dennis Hopper *Red* · Lolita Davidovich *Vikki* · Viggo Mortensen *Ronnie* · Valerie Perrine *Mona* · Seymour Cassel *Leach* · Jonathan Banks *Max* · Christine Elise *Carol* · Tony LoBianco *Dio* · James Tolkan *Levitt* ■ *Dir* James B Harris · *Scr* James B Harris, from the novel *Money Men* by Gerald Petievich

El Bola ★★★ 15
Drama 2000 · Sp · Colour · 83min

Made with the assistance of Unicef, this is an important film that focuses on a still largely taboo topic. Juan José Ballesta excels as the timorously rebellious 12-year-old who lives in dread of his short-fused father, Mañuel Marón, and envies the normality of buddy Pablo Galan's home life. Playing on the deceptiveness of social appearances (Marón is a respected shopkeeper, while Galan's dad, played by Alberto Gimenez, is a tattoo artist), first-time director Achero Mañas explores the contentious issue of domestic violence with great sensitivity, while also highlighting the difficulties in bringing such abuse to the attention of the authorities. DP Spanish +subtitles. *DVD*

Juan José Ballesta *Pablo* · Pablo Galán *Alfredo* · Alberto Jimenez *José* · Mañuel Morón *Mariano* ■ *Dir/Scr* Achero Mañas

The Bold and the Brave ★★ PG
Second World War drama 1956 · US · BW · 84min

If you can stand Mickey Rooney at full throttle, you may warm to this Second World War drama set on the front line in Italy. Rooney, as the soldier who wins a fortune in a marathon crap game, is contrasted with sensitive infantryman Wendell Corey, who fears he may have turned yellow, and Don Taylor, as the puritanical sergeant involved with Nicole Maurey, a local girl who hasn't been as good as she should have been. The film plays down the heroics and doesn't run to major battle scenes. AE

Wendell Corey *Fairchild* · Mickey Rooney *Dooley* · Don Taylor *Preacher* · Nicole Maurey *Fiamma* · John Smith *Smith* · Race Gentry *Hendricks* · Ralph Votrian *Wilbur* ■ *Dir* Lewis R Foster · *Scr* Robert Lewin

Bolero ★★★
Romantic drama 1934 · US · BW · 82min

A romantic drama with a good script, expertly directed by Wesley Ruggles, has stars George Raft and Carole Lombard as a dancing duo competing for attention with the hypnotic spell of Ravel's *Bolero*. He opens a smart nightclub in Paris, she goes off to marry a wealthy man, but they're reunited unexpectedly after the First World War, dancing to the aforementioned number as a lead-up to a dramatic climax. RK

George Raft *Raoul DeBaere* · Carole Lombard *Helen Hathaway* · Sally Rand *Annette* · Frances Drake *Leona* · William Frawley *Mike DeBaere* · Ray Milland *Lord Robert Coray* · Gloria Shea *Lucy* · Gertrude Michael *Lady D'Argon* ■ *Dir* Wesley Ruggles · *Scr* Carey Wilson Kubec Glasmon, Horace Jackson (adaptation), from an idea by Ruth Ridenour · *Music* Ralph Rainger, Maurice Ravel

Bolero ★ 18
Period erotic drama 1984 · US · Colour · 100min

One of the funniest bad movies ever made. Virginal heiress Bo Derek goes to the Sahara desert and Spain in search of pure sexual ecstasy, and ends up making love with a sheik and a bullfighter. Set in the 1920s for no apparent reason, director John Derek's anti-erotic valentine to his wife is packed with hilariously awful encounters that are further undermined by insipid dialogue. AJ

Bo Derek *Ayre McGillvary* · George Kennedy *Cotton* · Andrea Occhipinti *Angel Contreras* · Ana Obregon *Catalina* · Greg Bensen *Sheik* · Olivia D'Abo *Paloma* · Ian Cochrane *Robert Stewart* ■ *Dir/Scr* John Derek

Bollywood Calling ★★★ 15
Satirical comedy 2000 · Ind · Colour · 101min

Following the acute social criticism of his pioneering Indian independent film *Hyderabad Blues*, director Nagesh Kukunoor disappointingly settles for easy targets in this patchy satire on the chaos that is the subcontinent's movie capital. The incomparable Om Puri stars as gregarious producer Subra. His brainchild is to import washed-up Hollywood action man Pat Cusick to play the long-lost American brother of ageing superstar Navin Nischol in a corny melodrama called *Maut*. Puri is excellent, Cusick a revelation, but this fast and furious farce lacks finesse. DP English, Hindi +subtitles. *DVD*

Om Puri *Subramaniam, "Subra"* · Pat Cusick *Pat Stormare* · Navin Nischol *Manu Kapoor* ■ *Dir/Scr* Nagesh Kukunoor

Bollywood/Hollywood ★★★ 12
Musical comedy romance 2002 · Can · Colour · 105min

This culture-clash satire is a breezy parody of Bollywood conventions from Deepa Mehta. The movie spoofs are shrewd and the byplay between wealthy Indian-Canadian Rahul Khanna and Lisa Ray - the escort he hires to pose as his fiancée in order to assuage his fussing family - has an old-fashioned screwball energy. The supporting turns are equally worthy, but the musical numbers are disappointingly average. DP English, Hindi +subtitles. *DVD*

Rahul Khanna *Rahul Seth* · Lisa Ray *Sue "Sunita" Singh* · Moushumi Chatterjee *Mummy Ji/Ruby Seth* · Dina Pathak *Grandma Ji* · Kalbhushan Kharbanda *Mr Singh* · Ranjit Chowdhry *Rocky* · Jessica Paré *Kimberly* ■ *Dir/Scr* Deepa Mehta · *Music* Sandeep Chowta

Bollywood Queen ★★ PG
Musical romantic drama 2002 · UK · Colour · 85min

Jeremy Wooding makes a shaky feature debut with this unpersuasive mix of Bollywood masala and backstreet realism. Essentially a Romeo-and-Juliet story with a dash of culture-clash controversy tossed in, the romance between East End Indian Preeya Kalidas and country boy James McAvoy feels as contrived as the song-and-dance routines, which are staged without the stylised exuberance that makes Bollywood musicals so unique. DP English, Hindi +subtitles. *DVD*

Preeya Kalidas *Geena* · James McAvoy *Jay* · Ciaran McMenamin *Dean* · Ray Panthaki *Anil* · Ian McShane *Frank* · Kat Bhathena *Anjali* ■ *Dir* Jeremy Wooding · *Scr* Neil Spencer, Jeremy Wooding

Bolshoi Babylon ★★★ PG
Documentary 2015 · UK · Colour · 86min

As he examines the January 2013 acid attack that left Bolshoi Ballet artistic director Sergei Filin with third-degree burns and blind in one eye, British documentary maker Nick Read reveals how one of Russia's most revered institutions is rotten to the core. Tellingly, little actual dancing is shown as Read snoops backstage, but he really only scratches the surface of the scandal, though with plenty of simmering intrigue and splendid archive material on show. DP Some swearing, sexual references.

■ *Dir* Nick Read, Mark Franchetti

Bolt ★★★★ PG
Animated comedy adventure 2008 · US · Colour · 92min

There's an element of *The Truman Show* to this animated charmer about cute white shepherd dog Bolt (eloquently voiced by John Travolta). He's the star of a hit TV show and thinks his superhero exploits and powers are genuine. That is until a packing accident has the pooch shipped to Manhattan, where reality bites during an eventful cross-country journey back to LA and his caring TV co-star Penny (Miley Cyrus). This first digital Disney cartoon produced under the guidance of *Toy Story* director John Lasseter blends imaginative action, visual wit, cultural savvy and gentle character comedy. AJ *DVD* *Blu* *3D*

John Travolta *Bolt* · Miley Cyrus [Miley Ray Cyrus] *Penny* · Susie Essman *Mittens* · Mark Walton *Rhino* · Malcolm McDowell *Dr Calico* ■ *Dir* Byron Howard, Chris Williams · *Scr* Chris Williams, Dan Fogelman

Bolwieser ★★★
Drama 1977 · W Ger · Colour · 201min

This bitter study of marital discord, social rigidity and incipient fascism was edited down from a two-part television film. Kurt Raab cuts a pathetically dignified figure as the genial stationmaster who is twice cuckolded by wife Elisabeth Trissenaar, whose desire for freedom ultimately results in her husband's imprisonment. In exploring the dispiriting notion that love has no place in the law, director Rainer Werner Fassbinder was also keen to show that, even in a supposedly patriarchal society, the female is the deadlier of the species. The result is subtlety symbolic, yet uncompromisingly bleak. DP German +subtitles.

Kurt Raab *Bolwieser* · Elisabeth Trissenaar *Frau Hanni* · Gustl Bayrhammer *Hanni's father* · Bernhard Helfrich *Merkl* · Udo Kier *Schaffthaler* · Volker Spengler *Mangst* ■ *Dir* Rainer Werner Fassbinder · *Scr* Rainer Werner Fassbinder, from the novel by Oskar Maria Graf

Bombardier ★★
Second World War adventure 1943 · US · BW · 99min

An airborne propaganda picture, this follows a bomber crew on a mission to Japan. At times the picture has all the excitement of a technical manual - no switch, no scanner, no nut and bolt is ignored by the script. Released after Japan's attack on Pearl Harbor - though production started before - the story is filled with vengeance and the Japanese are, of course, depicted as perpetrators of hideous cruelty, and lacking in military know-how. Routine, but lifted by a decent cast. AT

Pat O'Brien *Major Chick Davis* · Randolph Scott *Captain Buck Oliver* · Anne Shirley *Burt Hughes* · Eddie Albert *Tom Hughes* · Robert Ryan *Joe Connors* · Walter Reed *Jim Carter* · Barton MacLane *Sergeant Dixon* ■ *Dir* Richard Wallace · *Scr* John Twist, from a story by John Twist, Martin Rackin

Bombay ★★★ 12
Drama 1995 · Ind · Colour · 135min

Shot in southern India and recalling the civil unrest that occurred in Bombay in the early 1990s, this film achieved several things. It confirmed the reputation of Mani Rathnam as one of the most uncompromising contemporary Indian directors, while also sealing the celebrity of now red-hot composer AR Rahman. But, more importantly, this story of a couple's search for their missing children proved that masala musicals could be suitable vehicles for social comment. Indeed, the film was so effective that it was banned, yet it still became a box-office smash. DP Tamil, Hindi +subtitles.

Tinnu Anand · Manisha Koirala · Nazar · Arvind Swamy ■ *Dir/Scr* Mani Rathnam

Bombay Beach ★★
Documentary 2011 · US · Colour · 80min

A ragtag community on the shores of California's inland Salton Sea is the subject of Alma Har'el's documentary. Once a rich man's paradise, Bombay Beach is now home to a motley collection of social misfits, including an ornery old-timer selling bootlegged cigarettes, and a slightly bemused fugitive from South Central LA's deadly gang culture. Although this peek into other people's daily travails is moderately engrossing, former music video director Har'el often seems more interested in them as aesthetic objects than real individuals. TJ

■ *Dir* Alma Har'el · *Music* Zach Condon

Bombay Boys ★★★
Drama 1998 · Ind · Colour · 105min

This modern Indian drama takes an uncompromising look at the seedier side of Bombay and the influence returning prodigals have upon it. New Yorker Naveen Andrews arrives with ambitions of Bollywood stardom; gay musician Alexander Gifford leaves London looking for love, while Aussie Rahul Bose is in search of his brother. Director Kaizad Gustad sets out to shock and succeeds triumphantly. DP Sex scenes, nudity.

Naveen Andrews *Krishna Sahni* · Rahul Bose *Ricardo Fernandez* · Alexander Gifford *Xerxes Mistry* · Naseeruddin Shah *Don Mastana* · Roshan Seth *Pesi* ■ *Dir/Scr* Kaizad Gustad

Bombay Talkie ★★ PG
Romantic drama 1970 · Ind · Colour · 105min

There's a hollow ring to this Merchant Ivory tale of the doomed romance between a self-centred western novelist and an image-conscious Bollywood star. The opening parody of masala musicals creates something of a false impression; this is a melodrama of the old school, in which Jennifer Kendal toys in a callously destructive manner with the affections of Shashi Kapoor. Mediocre outing. DP *DVD*

Shashi Kapoor *Vikram* · Jennifer Kendal *Lucia Lane* · Zia Mohyeddin *Hari* · Aparna Sen *Mala* · Utpal Dutt *Bose* · Nadira *Anjana Devi* · Pincho Kapoor *Swamiji* ■ *Dir* James Ivory · *Scr* Ruth

Prawer Jhabvala, James Ivory, from a story by Ruth Prawer Jhabvala • Producer Ismail Merchant

The Bomber Boys ★★
Crime adventure 1995 • US • Colour • 90min

This slight but amusing children's film is of interest to grown-ups thanks to the quality of its cast. Martin Sheen, Rod Steiger, Joe Mantegna and star Kate Mulgrew lend their talents to this tale of a group of young boys who discover an old atomic bomb and use it to get the President to cancel school. All the adults spend their time bumbling around and this results in a few laughs. JB

Martin Sheen *Jeff Snyder* • Joe Mantegna *Joey Franelli* • Joanna Pacula *Brenda Franelli* • Joe Piscopo *Mr Wareman* • Rod Steiger *The President* • Ryan Thomas Johnson *The Slug* • Joshua Schaefer *Mickey Boyle* • Michael Bower *Frank Pescoe* • Kate Mulgrew *Mrs Pesco* ■ *Dir/Scr* Charles Gale

Bombers B-52 ★★ U
Drama 1957 • US • Colour • 106min

Released in the UK under the title *No Sleep till Dawn*, this is a clumsy melodrama directed with little sense of either drama or irony by Gordon Douglas. Karl Malden might not have had the greatest range in Hollywood, but he could fret like few others. Here he gets the chance to work himself into a right old lather as he considers a move into civvy street, as well as daughter Natalie Wood's romance with flashy flyboy Efrem Zimbalist Jr. DP

Natalie Wood *Lois Brennan* • Karl Malden *Sergeant Chuck Brennan* • Marsha Hunt *Edith Brennan* • Efrem Zimbalist Jr *Colonel Jim Herlihy* • Don Kelly *[Don O'Kelly] Sergeant Darren McKind* ■ *Dir* Gordon Douglas • *Scr* Irving Wallace, from a story by Sam Rolfe • *Cinematographer* William Clothier

Bombón - El Perro ★★★★ 15
Drama 2004 • Arg/Sp • Colour • 93min

Argentinian director Carlos Sorín's award-winning film is an understated, intensely human depiction of life's little miracles. Sorín unfolds a quiet fable about an unemployed garage mechanic's depressed existence changing for the better when he is given a dog in return for a favour. But this dog is not any old pet - it's a game-hound of noble pedigree and a potential dog-show winner. Newcomer Juan Villegas (a car-park attendant in real life) gives a remarkable and totally unaffected performance as an individual making the best of the harsh realities he's been dealt. How his canine-career dream transforms into an attainable goal is utterly believable and yet still quite magical. AJ Spanish +subtitles. Swearing. *DVD*

Juan Villegas *Juan "Coco" Villegas* • Walter Donado • Pascual Condito *Pascual* • Mariela Diaz *Coco's daughter* • Rosa Valsecchi *Susana* ■ *Dir* Carlos Sorín • *Scr* Carlos Sorín, Santiago Calori, Salvador Roselli, from an idea by Carlos Sorín

Bon Voyage ★★★ U
Spy drama 1944 • UK • BW • 25min

Returning from Hollywood at the behest of the Ministry of Information, Alfred Hitchcock commanded a weekly rate of just £10 for this propaganda boost for the French Resistance. It also served to advocate general vigilance, as a superbly controlled flashback sequence reveals to doltish RAF pilot John Blythe the tell-tale signs he missed as he was escorted back from a PoW camp by a Gestapo agent masquerading as a Pole. With its shocking dénouement, this provocative short was atmospherically shot by the exiled Günther Krampf, who'd also filmed such key expressionist silents as *Pandora's Box*. DP French +subtitles. *DVD*

John Blythe *John Dougall* ■ *Dir* Alfred Hitchcock • *Scr* JOC Orton, Angus MacPhail, from an idea by Arthur Calder-Marshall

Bon Voyage! ★★★ U
Comedy 1962 • US • Colour • 126min

There have been plenty of movies about Americans in Paris, and this Disney offering is an inoffensive family-friendly comedy. The family in question, headed by Fred MacMurray and Jane Wyman, have a series of comic misadventures you can see coming a mile off, while the open-mouthed awe with which they greet all things European is that of the simple-minded for the sophisticated. That said, the various twists and turns have a rather endearing innocence, and the costumes were nominated for an Academy Award. TH

Fred MacMurray *Harry Willard* • Jane Wyman *Katie Willard* • Michael Callan *Nick O'Mara* • Deborah Walley *Amy Willard* • Jessie Royce Landis *La Countessa* • Tommy Kirk *Elliott Willard* • Georgette Anys *Madame Clebert* ■ *Dir* James Neilson • *Scr* Bill Walsh, from the novel by Marrijane Hayes, Joseph Hayes • *Costume Designer* Bill Thomas

Bon Voyage ★★★★ 12
Second World War black comedy 2003 • Fr • Colour • 110min

Impeccably mounted and played with relish by a stellar cast, this is an unashamedly old-fashioned entertainment that oozes class. Director Jean-Paul Rappeneau ably combines romance, suspense and dark comedy as Isabelle Adjani's scheming screen star exploits both lustful government minister Gérard Depardieu and aspiring author Grégori Derangère to cover up a killing. Beneath all the surface sophistication, Rappeneau explores the deeper issues concerning the move to Vichy control. DP French +subtitles. Violence. *DVD*

Isabelle Adjani *Viviane Denvert* • Gérard Depardieu *Minister Jean-Etienne Beaufort* • Virginie Ledoyen *Camille* • Yvan Attal *Raoul* • Grégori Derangère *Frédéric Auger* • Peter Coyote *Alex Winkler* • Jean-Marc Stehlé *Professor Kopolski* • Aurore Clément *Jacqueline de Lusse* ■ *Dir* Jean-Paul Rappeneau • *Scr* Jean-Paul Rappeneau, Patrick Modiano, Gilles Marchand, Jérôme Tonnerre, Julian Rappeneau

Bon Voyage, Charlie Brown ★★★ U
Animation 1980 • US • Colour • 72min

Inspired by Charles Schulz's long-running *Peanuts* comic strip, this animated feature proves the gently sardonic tone that hooked millions is present and correct by appending the bracketed rider (*And Don't Come Back*) to the title. Heading to Europe for an exchange visit, the worldly-wise toddlers find themselves living it up in a French château at the expense of a mysterious patron. There are some nice cultural asides, but what makes this so enjoyable is the trademark philosophising - plus, of course, Snoopy who, after years of practice against the garage door, finally gets to play at Wimbledon. DP

■ *Dir* Bill Melendez • *Scr* Charles M Schulz, from his comic strip *Peanuts*

El Bonaerense ★★★ 15
Police drama 2002 • Arg/Neth/Fr/Chil • Colour • 94min

Exposés of police corruption are nothing new, but this cynical, realist insight into the prejudice and ineptitude of the Buenos Aires force also considers the extent to which these problems are exacerbated by under-funding. Locksmith-turned-rookie Jorge Román is forced to begin again after events conspire against him. But he wrecks a potentially redemptive relationship with police academy lecturer Mimí Ardú before using the pernicious skills he's learned on the job to extricate himself from his plight. DP Spanish +subtitles. Swearing, violence, sex scenes. *DVD*

Jorge Román *Zapa/Enrique* • Orlando Mendoza • Darío Levy *Deputy Inspector Gallo* • Mimí Ardú *Mabel* • Hugo Anganuzzi *Polaco* • Víctor Hugo Carrizo *Inspector Molinari* • Graciana Chironi *Graciana, Zapa's mother* ■ *Dir/Scr* Pablo Trapero

Bond Street ★★ 12
Portmanteau drama 1948 • UK • BW • 105min

Clearly inspired by *Tales of Manhattan*, in which dozens of guest stars helped director Julien Duvivier tell the life story of a tail coat, this portmanteau drama, set around the preparations for a wedding, works best when it's funny and drags when it's not. The stars of the show are undoubtedly Kathleen Harrison as a chirpy seamstress and Roland Young as the befuddled father of the bride. Kenneth Griffith is suitably hissable as disabled Patricia Plunkett's ne'er-do-well spouse, but Derek Farr is embarrassingly unconvincing as a twitchy killer. DP *DVD*

Jean Kent *Ricki Merritt* • Roland Young *George Chester-Barrett* • Kathleen Harrison *Mrs Brawn* • Derek Farr *Joe Marsh* • Hazel Court *Julia Chester-Barrett* • Ronald Howard *Steve Winter* • Paula Valenska *Elsa* • Patricia Plunkett *Mary* ■ *Dir* Gordon Parry • *Scr* Anatole de Grunwald, Terence Rattigan, Rodney Ackland, from an idea by JG Brown

Bonded by Blood ★★ 18
Crime drama based on a true story 2010 • UK • Colour • 92min

In 1995, three career criminals were brutally gunned down in a remote country lane in Essex. Their lives and violent deaths were the subject of both 1999's *Essex Boys* and 2006's *Rise of the Footsoldier*. The same events have been filmed for a third time here, with Tamer Hassan, Vincent Regan and Adam Deacon heading an all-British, all-hardman cast. There's nothing especially wrong with the film, though the acting is a touch strident at times. But one must question whether it needs to exist at all, ploughing as it does an already well-worn crime-film furrow. DA Violence, swearing, drug abuse. *DVD* *SL*

Terry Stone *Tony Tucker* • Tamer Hassan *Pat Tate* • Neil Maskell *Craig Rolfe* • Dave Legeno *Jack Whomes* • Vincent Regan *Mickey Steele* • Adam Deacon *Darren Nicholls* • Kierston Wareing *Kate Smith* ■ *Dir* Sacha Bennett • *Scr* Sacha Bennett, Graeme Muir

Bone ★ 18
Black comedy 1972 • US • Colour • 94min

Also known as *Housewife* and *Beverly Hills Nightmare*, this piece of schlock was released in Britain in 1979 as *Dial Rat for Terror*. Yaphet Kotto stars, along with a lot of cockroaches, a dead rat in a swimming pool and a Beverly Hills couple going bananas. There's an allegory about wealth and white privilege lurking among the wooden performances and silly shock effects. AT Violence, swearing, sex scenes, nudity. *DVD*

Yaphet Kotto *Bone* • Andrew Duggan *Bill* • Joyce Van Patten *Bernadette* • Jeannie Berlin *Girl* ■ *Dir/Scr* Larry Cohen

The Bone Collector ★★★ 15
Crime thriller 1999 • US • Colour • 113min

A run-of-the-mill story is turned into an above-average thriller, thanks to impressive central performances from Denzel Washington and Angelina Jolie as two very different cops who team up to track down a serial killer. Washington plays a decorated police officer now confined to his bed, virtually paralysed following an accident on the job. Jolie's the young rookie who's brought in to explore the deepest, darkest areas of Manhattan under his instruction as they follow the trail of a sadistic murderer. This benefits from Phillip Noyce's fast-paced direction. JB Violence, swearing. *DVD* *SL*

Denzel Washington *Lincoln Rhyme* • Angelina Jolie *Amelia Donaghy* • Queen Latifah *Thelma* • Michael Rooker *Captain Howard Cheney* • Mike McGlone *Detective Kenny Solomon* • Luis Guzman *Eddie Ortiz* • Leland Orser *Richard Thompson* • John Benjamin Hickey *Dr Barry Lehman* • Ed O'Neill *Detective Paulie Sellitto* ■ *Dir* Phillip Noyce • *Scr* Jeremy Iacone, from the novel by Jeffery Deaver

Bone Daddy ★★★ 18
Horror thriller 1998 • US • Colour • 87min

Ex-medical examiner Rutger Hauer writes a fictional bestseller about a serial killer, who then gets up to his old tricks again in this above-average horror thriller. Hauer is put back on the case when bones - removed from the still-living body of his literary agent - begin arriving at police headquarters. The suspects mount up with little sense of suspense or hope of a satisfying resolution, but Hauer acquits himself well in a role tailor-made for his talents. AJ Violence, some swearing. *DVD*

Rutger Hauer *William Palmer* • Barbara Williams (2) *Sharon Hewlett* • RH Thomson *Marshall Stone* • Joseph Kell *Peter Palmer* • Robin Gammell *Cobb* • Blu Mankuma *Trent* ■ *Dir* Mario Azzopardi • *Scr* Thomas Szollosi

Bone Tomahawk ★★★★ 18
Western horror 2015 • US • Colour • 126min

A hunt for a kidnapped wife takes four men into the heart of darkness in this grim but gripping prairie tale from director S Craig Zahler. Zahler's debut stars Kurt Russell as the tough-as-teak sheriff who heads into the wilderness with hobbled husband Patrick Wilson, dandy gunslinger Matthew Fox and befuddled deputy Richard Jenkins when Wilson's wife is abducted by a terrifying tribe of troglodytes. This may move at a slow pace, but it's quirky and entertaining, and the final confrontation is not for the faint-hearted. JA Violence, a sex scene, nudity. *DVD* *SL*

Kurt Russell *Sheriff Hunt* • Patrick Wilson *Arthur* • Matthew Fox *Brooder* • Richard Jenkins *Chicory* ■ *Dir/Scr* S Craig Zahler

Bones ★★ 18
Black comedy horror 2001 • US • Colour • 92min

US rapper Snoop Dogg struts his stuff as a reanimated avenger in this blaxploitation-style supernatural horror. The star cuts a classy figure as a murdered neighbourhood kingpin who comes back from the dead to get even with his killers. However, aside from the schlock elements, there's little to hold the attention, since the tale lacks atmosphere, the visual effects are substandard and the performances cartoonish. SF *DVD*

Snoop Dogg *Jimmy Bones* • Pam Grier *Pearl* • Michael T Weiss *Lupovich* • Clifton Powell *Jeremiah Peet* • Ricky Harris *Eddie Mack* • Bianca Lawson *Cynthia* • Khalil Kain *Patrick* ■ *Dir* Ernest Dickerson [Ernest R Dickerson] • *Scr* Adam Simon, Tim Metcalfe

The Bonfire of the Vanities ★★★ 15
Drama 1990 • US • Colour • 120min

Brian De Palma's adaptation of Tom Wolfe's scathing attack on the yuppie lifestyles of the Wall Street rich and Park Avenue famous is, admittedly, a flawed satire (the casting of Tom Hanks and Melanie Griffith didn't help). Nonetheless, it's hardly the irredeemably awful disaster most critics led you to believe. Even a lesser De Palma picture is a whole lot more interesting than many A-list directors' good ones. Purely from a technical standpoint, it's brilliant - the opening four-minute continuous shot, for example - and, with hindsight, its subtle entertainment values now shine through. AJ Violence, sex scenes, swearing, nudity. *DVD*

Tom Hanks *Sherman McCoy* • Bruce Willis *Peter Fallow* • Melanie Griffith *Maria Ruskin* • Kim Cattrall *Judy McCoy* • Saul Rubinek *Jed Kramer* • Morgan Freeman *Judge White* • F Murray Abraham *Abe Weiss* • John Hancock *Reverend Bacon* • Kevin Dunn *Tom Killian* ■ *Dir* Brian De Palma • *Scr* Michael Cristofer, from the novel by Tom Wolfe • *Cinematographer* Vilmos Zsigmond

Le Bonheur ★★★★
Romantic drama 1965 • Fr • Colour • 79min

The underrated Agnès Varda here produced one of new French cinema's most controversial films. Few could find fault with her elliptical narrative, elegant compositions and psychological use of colour. But debates raged over her motive for having an adulterous carpenter settle down happily with his mistress and children after his wife drowns herself, rather than accept a suggested *ménage à trois*. Irrespective of the film's mischievous morality, the romantic imagery and Mozart score provide an ironic contrast to the contentious sexual politics, which were given an added *je ne sais quoi* by the fact that Jean-Claude Drouot's screen kin were played by his own family. DP French +subtitles.

Jean-Claude Drouot *François* • Claire Drouot *Thérèse* • Sandrine Drouot *Gisou* • Olivier Drouot *Pierrot* • Marie-France Boyer *Emilie* ■ *Dir/Scr* Agnès Varda

Le Bonheur Est dans le Pré ★★★ 15

Comedy 1995 · Fr · Colour · 101min

Etienne Chatiliez is no stranger to the themes of belonging and dislocation. But here he seems less interested in astute social observations than in relating the simple story of toilet king Michel Serrault, who seizes the opportunity presented by a case of mistaken identity to abandon his work-shy employees and grasping wife, Sabine Azéma, to enjoy a rural idyll with Carmen Maura. Although an amiable picture, this lacks a satirical edge. DP French +subtitles. Some swearing. *DVD*

Michel Serrault *Francis Bergeaud* • Eddy Mitchell *Gérard* • Sabine Azéma *Nicole Bergeaud* • Carmen Maura *Dolores Thivart* • François Morel *Pouillaud* • Eric Cantona *Lionel* ■ *Dir* Etienne Chatiliez • *Scr* Florence Quentin

Bonjour Tristesse ★★★ PG

Drama 1958 · US · Colour and BW · 89min

Otto Preminger's Riviera-set romantic drama stars David Niven as the widower whose affair with Deborah Kerr is subverted by his daughter, Jean Seberg. Loosely based on the novel by Françoise Sagan, it's fluffy stuff, enjoyable for Niven's deft playing and for Seberg, whose radiant performance caused a stir not unlike the one caused by Audrey Hepburn in *Roman Holiday*. The film was a huge hit in France, and Seberg became an overnight cult sensation. TH *DVD*

Deborah Kerr *Anne Larsen* • David Niven *Raymond* • Jean Seberg *Cecile* • Mylène Demongeot *Elsa Mackenbourg* • Geoffrey Horne *Philippe* • Juliette Greco *Nightclub singer* • Walter Chiari *Pablo* ■ *Dir* Otto Preminger • *Scr* Arthur Laurents, from the novel by Françoise Sagan

Bonne Chance ★★★★

Comedy 1935 · Fr · Colour · 78min

Establishing the mischievous style that was to become his trademark, this sprightly comedy was once believed lost. As the struggling artist and ingénue who split the cost of a lottery ticket and risk the ire of her soldier boyfriend by spending their winnings on a luxury holiday, they make a splendid team and are much better suited than Ginger Rogers and Ronald Colman in the 1940 remake, *Lucky Partners*. DP French +subtitles.

Sacha Guitry *Claude* • Jacqueline Delubac *Marie* • André Numès *Prosper* • Robert Darthez *Gastion Lepeltier* • Pauline Carton *Mother* ■ *Dir/Scr* Sacha Guitry

Les Bonnes Femmes ★★★★

Drama 1960 · Fr/It · BW · 98min

Meeting no great critical acclaim on its first release, this is now rated one of Claude Chabrol's early masterpieces and a major film of the French New Wave. The "good girls" of the title are four young Parisian women, who make up for the ennui of their working life in an electrical goods shop by regularly hitting the town in search of glamour and romance. Chabrol's mixture of documentary-style realism, slice-of-life drama and black humour combines with stunning photography and fine performances to impressive effect. PF French +subtitles.

Bernadette Lafont *Jane* • Lucile Saint-Simon *Rita* • Clothilde Joano *Jacqueline* • Stéphane Audran *Ginette* • Mario Davia *André Lapierre* • Claude Berri *André* • Claude Chabrol ■ *Dir* Claude Chabrol • *Scr* Paul Gégauff, Claude Chabrol • *Cinematographer* Henri Decaë

Bonneville ★★★ PG

Road movie 2006 · US · Colour · 88min

Jessica Lange plays a recently widowed woman in this well-crafted if rather bland chick flick, a sort of middle-aged *Thelma & Louise* minus the rebellion. Kathy Bates and Joan Allen join her on a cross-country trip in an old Bonneville convertible to deliver her husband's ashes to California at the insistence of her resentful step-daughter (Christine Baranski). En route, Lange reminisces, Bates gets to romance laidback trucker Tom Skerritt and the uptight Allen frets about their behaviour. Not a lot happens, but it doesn't get too treacly and the A-list leads are effortless in familiar roles. JF *DVD*

Jessica Lange *Arvilla Holden* • Kathy Bates *Margene Cunningham* • Joan Allen *Carol Brimm* • Christine Baranski *Francine Holden Packard* • Victor Rasuk *Bo* • Tom Amandes *Bill Packard* • Tom Skerritt *Emmett L Johnson* ■ *Dir* Christopher N Rowley • *Scr* Daniel D Davis, from a story by Davis, Christopher N Rowley

LANDMARK FILM
Sets a milestone for stylish and graphic violence on screen

Bonnie and Clyde ★★★★★ 18

Crime drama 1967 · US · Colour · 106min

"They're young! They're in love! And they kill people!" When this stylish and uncompromising gangster picture was released, graphic screen violence was very rare, and this influential film was misread by some American critics, who dismissed it as a gimmicky, gory crime thriller. However, it proved to be the box-office hit of the year, and scooped ten Oscar nominations. Faye Dunaway and Warren Beatty excel as the gun-toting criminals who roamed the American Midwest during the Depression, while David Newman and Robert Benton's sizzling script (originally offered to both François Truffaut and Jean-Luc Godard) and Arthur Penn's bravura direction are as fresh as ever. DP *DVD* *Blu-ray*

Warren Beatty *Clyde Barrow* • Faye Dunaway *Bonnie Parker* • Michael J Pollard *CW Moss* • Gene Hackman *Buck Barrow* • Estelle Parsons *Blanche* • Denver Pyle *Frank Hamer* • Dub Taylor *Ivan Moss* • Evans Evans *Velma Davis* • Gene Wilder *Eugene Grizzard* ■ *Dir* Arthur Penn • *Scr* David Newman, Robert Benton, Robert Towne (uncredited) • *Cinematographer* Burnett Guffey • *Costume Designer* Theadora Van Runkle

Bonnie Prince Charlie ★ U

Historical drama 1948 · UK · Colour · 113min

This shoddy costume drama must rank as one of the worst films ever made in the UK. It contains some quite dreadful dialogue delivered in atrocious accents by an all-star cast led by a hopelessly miscast David Niven. The studio sets look home-made, but they are nowhere near as embarrassing as the twee score. DP

David Niven *Bonnie Prince Charlie* • Margaret Leighton *Flora MacDonald* • Judy Campbell *Clementine Walkinshaw* • Jack Hawkins *Lord George Murray* • Morland Graham *Donald* • Finlay Currie *Marquis of Tullibardine* • Elwyn Brook-Jones *Duke of Cumberland* • John Laurie *Blind Jamie* ■ *Dir* Anthony Kimmins • *Scr* Clemence Dane

Bonnie Scotland ★★★★ U

Comedy 1935 · US · BW · 76min

An overcomplicated plot – and some comedy routines from previous movies – can't prevent this from being one of the most delightful comedies from the "golden period" of the Laurel and Hardy series of laughter-makers. It includes a litter-picking exercise by the twosome that becomes a soft-shoe shuffle – a classic of fanciful timing. Stan and Ollie go to Scotland to claim Stan's inheritance, which turns out to be bagpipes and a snuff box, and from there they are unwittingly recruited to the British Army in India. There's the added bonus of James Finlayson as a dastardly sergeant major, making up for the wan love interest provided by June Lang. TH *DVD*

Stan Laurel *Stanley McLaurel* • Oliver Hardy *Ollie* • Anne Grey *Lady Violet Ormsby* • David Torrence *Mr Miggs* • June Lang *Lorna McLaurel* •

William Janney *Alan Douglas* • James Mack Butler • James Finlayson *Sergeant Major* ■ *Dir* James W Horne • *Scr* Frank Butler, Jefferson Moffitt

Bonobo ★★★ 15

Comedy drama 2013 · UK · Colour · 82min

In this eccentric but unexpectedly touching drama, prim widow Judith (Tessa Peake-Jones) vows to bring her 20-something daughter home from a commune inspired by the behaviour patterns of bonobo monkeys. However, on meeting stubborn resistance, she agrees to see how founder Josie Lawrence puts this philosophy into action. Far too few films address the concerns of middle-aged women and, although some of the film's New Age sequences feel a touch twee, this offers some shrewd insights. DP

Tessa Peake-Jones *Judith* • Josie Lawrence *Anita* • James Norton *Ralph* • Eleanor Wyld *Lily* • Carolyn Pickles *Celia* • Patricia Potter *Eva* ■ *Dir* Matthew Hammett Knott • *Scr* Matthew Hammett Knott, Joanna Benecke

Boo, Zino and the Snurks ★★ U

Animated fantasy 2004 · Ger/Sp/UK · Colour · 87min

The first computer-generated movie produced in Germany features Boo and Zino, a pair of furry creatures who present their own TV series on Gaya. They hurtle into action - in the company of their co-stars, Princess Alanta and a trio of reprehensible Snurks - when a scheming professor, who's jealous of their success, steals the precious stone that gives their world its energy. Director Lenard Fritz Krawinkel relentlessly sustains the adventure's breakneck pace, but the principal characters could have been more appealing. DP *DVD*

Alan Mariot *Boo* • Glenn Wrage *Zino* • Patrick Stewart *Albert Drollinger* • Emily Watson *Alanta* • John Schwab *Zeck* • John Guerrasio *Galger* • Red Pepper *Bramph* • Lorelei King *Susi/Female Gayan* ■ *Dir* Lenard Fritz Krawinkel • *Scr* Bob Shaw, Donald McEnery, Jan Berger

Booby Trap ★

Crime thriller 1957 · UK · BW · 72min

This dire British B-feature was barely seen when it first came out. Absent-minded boffin Tony Quinn invents an explosive fountain pen, timed to go off on the first stroke of Big Ben. The pen falls into the hands of drug peddler Sydney Tafler who, as it happens, hides his wares in fountain pens. The build-up is feeble and none of the characters engage one's interest. AE

Sydney Tafler *Hunter* • Patti Morgan *Jackie* • Tony Quinn *Professor Hasdane* • John Watson *Major Cunliffe* • Jacques Cey *Bentley* • Richard Shaw *Richards* • Harry Fowler *Sammy* ■ *Dir* Henry Cass • *Scr* Peter Bryan, Bill Luckwell, from a novel by Peter Bryan

Boogeyman ★★ 15

Horror thriller 2005 · US · Colour · 85min

This may be sloppily written, nonsensical and unconvincing, but it still manages a few shivers and jolts, thanks to director Stephen T Kay's well-oiled if clichéd style. Barry Watson returns to his childhood home to confront his greatest fear, the monster that he believes dwells in his bedroom closet and that snatched his father when he was eight years old. There are gaping plot holes, but also some cheap thrills. AJ *DVD* *Blu-ray*

Barry Watson *Tim* • Emily Deschanel *Kate* • Skye McCole Bartusiak *Franny* • Tory Mussett *Jessica* • Andrew Glover *Boogeyman* • Lucy Lawless *Tim's mother* • Charles Mesure *Tim's father* ■ *Dir* Stephen T Kay [Stephen Kay] • *Scr* Eric Kripke, Juliet Snowdon, Stiles White, from a story by Eric Kripke

Boogie ★★★ 15

Comedy drama 2007 · Rom · Colour · 98min

Having captured the chaos that followed the collapse of the Ceausescu regime in *The Paper Will Be Blue* in 2006, Romanian director Radu Muntean moves on to more universal themes - with political undercurrents - in this sombre seaside drama. Married couple Bogdan (Dragos Bucur) and Smaranda (Anamaria Marinca) refuse to let a chill wind spoil their May Day break with their toddler son. But it also blows Bogdan's footloose school buddies (Mimi Branescu, Adrian Vancica) back into his life after several years. Making adroit use of enclosed spaces and mundane dialogue, Muntean conveys the mix of nostalgia, disappointment and doubt that lures Bucur away from his pregnant wife and into the company of a hooker. DP Romanian +subtitles. Swearing, sexual references, nudity. *DVD*

Dragos Bucur *Bogdan "Boogie" Ciocazanu* • Anamaria Marinca *Smaranda Ciocazanu* • Mimi Branescu *Penescu* • Adrian Vancica *Iordache* • Vlad Muntean *Adrian "Adi" Ciocazanu* ■ *Dir* Radu Muntean • *Scr* Alexandra Baciu, Radu Muntean, Razvan Radulescu

The Boogie Man Will Get You ★★★

Comedy horror 1942 · US · BW · 66min

The fun cast in this lively programme filler cheered up many a wartime audience. Boris Karloff plays a demented scientist who attempts to turn salesmen into supermen in a crazy plot, which also involves the Peter Lorre and juvenile lead Larry Parks. Lew Landers successfully juggles the lunatic elements of plot and action. TS

Boris Karloff *Professor Nathaniel Billings* • Peter Lorre *Dr Lorentz* • Maxie Rosenbloom *Maxie* • Larry Parks *Bill Leyden* • Jeff Donnell *Winnie Leyden* • Maude Eburne *Amelia Jones* • Don Beddoe *J Gilbert Brampton* ■ *Dir* Lew Landers • *Scr* Edwin Blum, Paul Gangelin (adaptation), from a story by Hal Fimberg, Robert E Hunt

Boogie Nights ★★★★★ 18

Drama 1997 · US · Colour · 149min

Pornography, drugs and disco are the driving forces of Paul Thomas Anderson's potent parable of the partying 1970s. Spanning the height of the disco era, this is a visually stunning and poignant exploration of the adult entertainment world. Charting the rise, fall and rise again of bus boy-turned-porn star Mark Wahlberg, Anderson's surreal take on the American Dream is as startling as it is highly entertaining. Burt Reynolds and Julianne Moore were Oscar-nominated and there's scintillating support from Heather Graham, while the opening Steadicam shot is breathtaking. AJ Violence, swearing, sex scenes, drug abuse, nudity. *DVD* *Blu-ray*

Mark Wahlberg *Eddie Adams/Dirk Diggler* • Burt Reynolds *Jack Horner* • Julianne Moore *Amber Waves* • John C Reilly *Reed Rothchild* • Don Cheadle *Buck Swope* • Heather Graham *Rollergirl* • William H Macy *Little Bill* ■ *Dir/Scr* Paul Thomas Anderson

Boogie Woogie ★★ 15

Comedy 2009 · UK/US/British Virgin Islands · Colour · 90min

Money makes the London art scene go round in director Duncan Ward's debut feature, a satire of venal dealers, grasping collectors and ambitious artists. When cash-strapped spouse Joanna Lumley contemplates selling elderly hubby Christopher Lee's prize Mondrian canvas (from the artist's *Boogie Woogie* series, hence the title), suave London art dealer Danny Huston eyes a hefty commission, unaware his own gallery director Heather Graham is secretly conniving with wealthy collector Stellan Skarsgård to snaffle the painting. Ward's tiresomely smug offering is desperately obvious - thankfully, the cast makes the clunky dialogue and paper-thin characterisation seem a whole lot better than they are. TJ Swearing, sex scenes, nudity, drug abuse. *DVD*

Gillian Anderson *Jean Maclestone* • Alan Cumming *Dewey Dalamanatousis* • Heather Graham *Beth Freemantle* • Danny Huston *Art Spindle* • Jack Huston *Jo Richards* • Christopher Lee *Alfred Rhinegold* • Joanna Lumley *Alfreda Rhinegold* • Charlotte Rampling *Emille* • Amanda Seyfried *Paige Prideaux* • Stellan Skarsgård *Bob Maclestone* ■ *Dir* Duncan Ward • *Scr* Danny Moynihan, from his novel

B

The Book of Eli ★★★ 15
Futuristic action drama
2009 · US · Colour · 112min

The Hughes Brothers (*Dead Presidents*, *From Hell*) apply their own distinctive stamp to this curious blend of futuristic western and sombre meditation on the uses and abuses of faith. Denzel Washington cuts an iconic figure, playing a lone adventurer in a scorched post-apocalypse America, who fights to keep possession of a book he believes carries sacred powers. As the deliberately paced story sets Washington and ruthless Gary Oldman in bloody conflict over the eponymous tome, it's not too hard to guess the identity of the good book in question. In a world of anonymous production-line action flicks, a nod of respect is due to the Hughes boys for sticking to their own idiosyncratic path, even if it's undoubtedly a wayward one. TJ Violence, swearing. *DVD* *BL*

Denzel Washington *Eli* • Gary Oldman *Carnegie* • Mila Kunis *Solara* • Ray Stevenson *Redridge* • Jennifer Beals *Claudia* • Frances de la Tour *Martha* • Michael Gambon *George* • Tom Waits *Engineer* ■ *Dir* The Hughes Brothers [Albert Hughes], The Hughes Brothers [Allen Hughes] • *Scr* Gary Whitta

The Book of Life ★★★★ 12
Satirical black comedy
1998 · Fr/US · Colour · 63min

Director Hal Hartley is never dull but he remains an acquired taste. Playing on millennial fears of a potential apocalypse, Hartley presents a discussion between the Devil (Thomas Jay Ryan), Jesus (Martin Donovan) and Magdalena (PJ Harvey) on New Year's Eve, 1999, about the survival of the human race. This is a fascinating black comedy, in which we have Christ and his assistant wandering round JFK airport lamenting mortals and Satan getting drunk in a hotel bar. Bizarre, and yet at times brilliant. LH Swearing.

Martin Donovan (2) *Jesus Christ* • PJ Harvey *Magdalena* • Thomas Jay Ryan *Satan* • David Simonds *Dave* • Miho Nikaido *Edie* • DJ Mendel *Lawyer* ■ *Dir/Scr* Hal Hartley

Book of Life ★★★★ U
Animated comedy 2014 · US · Colour · 91min

This bold, bright animated comedy is inspired by the Mexican Day of the Dead holiday (and includes *Hellboy* director Guillermo del Toro as one of its producers). It follows Mexican troubadour and reluctant bullfighter Manolo (Diego Luna) through the Lands of the Living, the Dead and the Forgotten driven by his love for local beauty Maria (a sassy Zoë Saldana). Channing Tatum voices Manolo's bumptious pal Joaquin, who also aims to make Maria his wife, and he ups the laugh count by striving to prove his macho credentials. Writer/director Jorge R Gutierrez tackles the subject of death with glorious gusto, the characters are vividly drawn and the psychedelic landscapes have incredible depth and detail. SP *DVD* *BL* *3D*

Diego Luna *Manolo* • Zoë Saldana *Maria* • Channing Tatum *Joaquin* • Ron Perlman *Xibalba* • Christina Applegate *Mary Beth* • Ice Cube *Candle Maker* • Kate del Castillo *La Muerte* ■ *Dir* Jorge R Gutierrez • *Scr* Douglas Langdale, Jorge R Gutierrez

Book of Numbers ★★★ 15
Blaxploitation period drama
1972 · US · Colour · 81min

Directed by its star, Raymond St Jacques, this is a rare blaxploitation venture into period drama. St Jacques joins with fellow city slacker Philip Thomas in an attempt to beat the Depression by setting up a numbers racket in a small Arkansas town. But can our roguish duo overcome the threat posed by racist gangster Gilbert Greene? Although budgetary constraints leave it looking a little ragged around the edges, this is a mostly entertaining caper movie. DP Swearing, violence.

Raymond St Jacques *Blueboy Harris* • Freda Payne *Kelly Simms* • Philip Thomas [Philip Michael Thomas] *Dave Greene* • Hope Clarke *Pigmeat Goins* • Willie Washington Jr *Makepeace*

Johnson • Doug Finell *Eggy* • Sterling St Jacques *Kid Flick* ■ *Dir* Raymond St Jacques • *Scr* Larry Spiegel, from the novel by Robert Deane Pharr

The Book of Revelation ★★★ 18
Erotic mystery thriller
2006 · Aus · Colour · 117min

On paper, the plot of this Melbourne-set mystery thriller adapted from Rupert Thomson's novel, reads like a porn film. A male dancer (Tom Long) is abducted by three masked women and forced to become their sex slave, before reappearing 12 days later in a deeply traumatised state, much to the consternation of Isabel (Greta Scacchi), his choreographer. Long, who is better known for his comic roles in *The Dish* and *Two Hands*, then reveals the full extent of his ordeal in uncomfortably graphic flashblacks. However, this is no slice of cheap exploitation, rather a provocative, if somewhat pretentious, study of sexual power. JF Violence, sex scenes.

Tom Long *Daniel* • Greta Scacchi *Isabel* • Colin Friels *Olsen* • Anna Torv *Bridget* • Deborah Mailman *Julie* • Zoe Coyle *Renate* • Zoe Naylor *Astrid* • Odette Joannidis *Maude* ■ *Dir* Ana Kokkinos • *Scr* Ana Kokkinos, Andrew Bovell, from the novel by Rupert Thomson

Book of Shadows: Blair Witch 2 ★ 15
Supernatural horror 2000 · US · Colour · 86min

First of all, there is no mention of a book of any sort in this sequel to the phenomenally successful *The Blair Witch Project*. Second, there are hardly any scares, either. The story begins as some misfits sign up for a tour of Burkittsville, where the first movie was set. Whether you love or hate the original, there's no denying that it was an innovative idea, brilliantly marketed. This is just a dud. JB Violence, swearing. *DVD*

Kim Director *Kim* • Jeffrey Donovan *Jeff* • Erica Leerhsen *Erica* • Tristen Skyler *Tristen* • Stephen Barker Turner *Stephen* ■ *Dir* Joe Berlinger • *Scr* Dick Beebe, Joe Berlinger

The Book Thief ★★★ 12
Wartime drama 2014 · US · Colour · 125min

On the eve of the Second World War in Germany, young orphan Liesel (Sophie Nélisse) is taken in by foster parents (played by Geoffrey Rush and Emily Watson) who help her discover the joy of reading just as the locals are burning books in the town square. While so many stories from the era have rightly explored anti-Semitism, this adaptation of the acclaimed novel instead puts the emphasis on the plight of ordinary Germans who didn't buy into Nazi propaganda. The couple do their best for Liesel, but their decision to hide a Jew in the basement puts them all at risk. Director Brian Percival might have milked greater tension from this scenario, but his well-acted, thoughtful drama carefully builds a convincing picture of the rising tide of prejudice. TJ *DVD* *BL*

Geoffrey Rush *Hans Hubermann* • Emily Watson *Rosa Hubermann* • Sophie Nélisse *Liesel Meminger* • Ben Schnetzer *Max* • Roger Allam *Narrator/Death* ■ *Dir* Brian Percival • *Scr* Michael Petroni, from Markus Zusak's novel

The Bookfair Murders ★★
Mystery thriller
2000 · Can/Ger · Colour · 93min

Eli Wallach, Geneviève Bujold and Saul Rubinek are among the decent cast assembled for this adaptation of Anna Porter's whodunnit. But it's Samantha Bond and Linda Kash who take centre stage, playing an editor and a journalist seeking the killer of an author at the Frankfurt book fair. The action drifts somewhat after novelist Bujold goes into hiding and Kash keeps prompting Bond to arrange an interview with her client. However, director Wolfgang Panzer ably captures the preening glamour of the literary world, while also passing incisive comment on big business and the enduring legacy of the Holocaust. DP

Samantha Bond (2) *Marsha Hillier* • Linda Kash *Judith Cass* • Saul Rubinek *Martin P Barrett* • Bernd Michael Lade [Michael Lade] *Ernst Murnau* • Geneviève Bujold *Margaret Dourie Cantor* • Eli Wallach *Erich Schmidt* ■ *Dir* Wolfgang Panzer • *Scr* Herman FG Stuck, from the novel by Anna Porter

Boom ★★ 12
Drama 1968 · UK/US · Colour · 107min

This piece of preening self-indulgence by Richard Burton and Elizabeth Taylor comes from a time when the two stars thought they could be forgiven anything. An adaptation by Tennessee Williams of his play, it clashes symbols with its study of life among the idle rich. Taylor is a six-times married virago, while Burton is a freeloading poet. Noël Coward gives it all some semblance of life as Taylor's confidant – but can't make up for the film's deficiencies. TH *DVD*

Elizabeth Taylor *Flora Goforth* • Richard Burton *Chris Flanders* • Noël Coward *Witch of Capri* • Joanna Shimkus *Blackie* • Michael Dunn *Rudy* • Romolo Valli *Doctor Luilo* • Howard Taylor *Journalist* ■ *Dir* Joseph Losey • *Scr* Tennessee Williams, from his play *The Milk Train Doesn't Stop Here Anymore*

Boom Town ★★★★
Adventure drama 1940 · US · BW · 118min

After the huge success of *San Francisco* and *Test Pilot*, Clark Gable and Spencer Tracy were reunited for another sprawling adventure, this time about two pioneers in the oil business. Although there were reports of behind-the-scenes tensions, the two stars give memorably larger-than-life performances and the female leads, Claudette Colbert and Hedy Lamarr, are on equally good form. Director Jack Conway stages some stunning set pieces (notably a burning oil field) and keeps the action roaring along. JF

Clark Gable *Big John McMasters* • Spencer Tracy *Square John Sand* • Claudette Colbert *Betsy Bartlett* • Hedy Lamarr *Karen Vanmeer* • Frank Morgan *Luther Aldrich* • Lionel Atwill *Harry Compton* • Chill Wills *Harmony Jones* ■ *Dir* Jack Conway • *Scr* John Lee Mahin, from a story by James Edward Grant

Boomerang! ★★★★ PG
Crime drama based on a true story
1947 · US · BW · 87min

Dana Andrews stars as a politically ambitious attorney, assigned to prosecute a vagrant who has confessed to the cold-blooded murder of a priest in this riveting crime drama. Quintessential 1940s icon Andrews heads a fine cast that flourishes under Elia Kazan's direction. If the dénouement seems contrived, remember this is based on a true story. TS *DVD* *BL*

Dana Andrews *Henry L Harvey* • Jane Wyatt *Mrs Harvey* • Lee J Cobb *Chief Robinson* • Cara Williams *Irene Nelson* • Arthur Kennedy *John Waldron* • Sam Levene *Woods* • Taylor Holmes *Wade* • Robert Keith (1) *McCreery* ■ *Dir* Elia Kazan • *Scr* Richard Murphy, from the *Reader's Digest* article *The Perfect Case* by Anthony Abbott

Boomerang ★★★ 15
Comedy 1992 · US · Colour · 111min

After a few years in the wilderness following flops such as *The Golden Child* and *Harlem Nights*, Eddie Murphy returned with this amiable if slightly overlong comedy from director Reginald Hudlin. Murphy is on form as the womaniser who gets his comeuppance when he tries his smooth-talking ways on canny Robin Givens. However, it is the supporting performances from Grace Jones and Eartha Kitt that really give the film a buzz. JB Sex scenes, nudity, swearing. *DVD*

Eddie Murphy *Marcus Graham* • Robin Givens *Jacqueline* • Halle Berry *Angela* • David Alan Grier *Gerard* • Martin Lawrence *Tyler* • Grace Jones *Strangé* • Geoffrey Holder *Nelson* • Eartha Kitt *Lady Eloise* • Chris Rock *Bony T* • Lela Rochon *Christie* ■ *Dir* Reginald Hudlin • *Scr* Barry W Blaustein, David Sheffield, from a story by Eddie Murphy

---

The Boondock Saints ★★ 18
Crime thriller
1999 · Can/US · Colour and BW · 103min

This dated, annoyingly stylised crime thriller presents one of Willem Dafoe's most embarrassing screen performances. Sean Patrick Flanery and Norman Reedus are the "saints" of the title, a couple of working class lads from Boston's Irish community who embark on a bloody vigilante rampage against Mafia types. Dafoe is the gay FBI agent who begins to develop a grudging admiration for the young killers. JF *DVD*

Willem Dafoe *Paul Smecker* • Sean Patrick Flanery *Connor MacManus* • Norman Reedus *Murphy MacManus* • David Della Rocco *Rocco* • Billy Connolly *Il Duce* ■ *Dir/Scr* Troy Duffy

The Boost ★★★ 18
Drama 1988 · US · Colour · 90min

Better known for the rumours behind the scenes than for the action in front of the camera (during the filming stars Sean Young and James Woods allegedly had an affair that ended rather bitterly in lawsuits), this overlooked drama from director Harold Becker has moments of insight in between the screaming matches. The film catalogues a couple's descent into drug addiction. Although more time is spent banging home the anti-drug message than on developing character, both Woods and Young give gutsy performances. JB Violence, swearing, sex scenes, drug abuse, nudity. *DVD*

James Woods *Lenny Brown* • Sean Young *Linda Brown* • John Kapelos *Joel* • Steven Hill *Max Sherman* • Kelle Kerr *Rochelle* • John Rothman *Ned Leavis* • Amanda Blake *Barbara* • Grace Zabriskie *Sheryl* • Marc Poppel *Mark* ■ *Dir* Harold Becker • *Scr* Darryl Ponicsan, from the novel *Ludes* by Benjamin Stein

Boot Hill ★★ PG
Spaghetti western 1969 · It · Colour · 91min

As the vogue for spaghetti westerns began to wane, Italian actors Mario Girotti and Carlo Pedersoli created a subgenre based on the new-found traditions, effectively imitating the imitators. They gave themselves the American-sounding names of Terence Hill and Bud Spencer respectively, and became immensely popular (and rich) primarily for a series of films featuring "Trinity" or "Nobody" in the titles. This movie pre-dates those, and non-fans will find the inept dubbing and poor story structure irritating. TS Italian dubbed. Violence.

Bud Spencer *Hutch Bessy* • Woody Strode *Thomas* • Edward Ciannelli [Eduardo Ciannelli] *Boone* • Terence Hill *Cat Stevens* ■ *Dir/Scr* Giuseppe Colizzi

Das Boot: the Director's Cut ★★★★ 12
Second World War action drama
1981/1997 · W Ger · Colour · 199min

With its spruced up visuals, overhauled sound and an hour's worth of restored footage, this version of Wolfgang Petersen's sprawling U-boat epic certainly improves on the original cinema release (no longer available on TV or DVD), particularly in respect of fleshing out the characters. Petersen depicts steely captain Jürgen Prochnow and his crew as courageous conscripts serving a cause to which they are not wholeheartedly committed. The action, based on actual incidents during the 1941 battle for the North Atlantic, inevitably alternates between tense periods of silent stalking and frantic moments of engagement. This claustrophobic existence is brilliantly captured by cinematographer Jost Vacano, who received one of the film's six Oscar nominations – high praise indeed for a foreign-language film. DP German +subtitles. *DVD* *BL*

Jürgen Prochnow *Captain* • Herbert Grönemeyer *Lieutenant Werner/Correspondent* • Klaus Wennemann *Chief Engineer* • Hubertus Bengsch *First Lieutenant/Number One* • Martin Semmelrogge *Second Lieutenant* • Bernd Tauber *Chief Quartermaster* ■ *Dir* Wolfgang Petersen • *Scr* Wolfgang Petersen, from the novel by Lothar-Guenther Buchheim • *Cinematographer* Jost Vacano

---

U SUITABLE FOR ALL U₅ SUITABLE ESPECIALLY FOR YOUNG CHILDREN (DVD ONLY) PG PARENTAL GUIDANCE 12A UNDER 12s TO BE ACCOMPANIED (CINEMA ONLY)

Bootmen ★★★ 15
Dance drama   2000 · Aus/US · Colour · 88min

Set in the run-down Australian town of Newcastle, this working-class fantasy traces the origins of the Tap Dogs and Steel City dance troupes. Defying his homophobic father, Adam Garcia attempts to stage a benefit for his jobless buddies. But with most of the blokes obsessed with sporting muscle and amber nectar, getting a crew together proves an uphill battle. With too much time spent on sub-plots, Dein Perry skimps on the industrial dance sequences, which is frustrating, as they have a real kinetic kick. DP Swearing, violence. DVD

Adam Garcia *Sean* • Sophie Lee *Linda* • Sam Worthington *Mitchell* • William Zappa *Walter* • Richard Carter *Gary* • Susie Porter *Sara* • Anthony Hayes *Huey* ■ *Dir* Dein Perry • *Scr* Steve Worland, from a story by Hilary Linstead, Dein Perry, Steve Worland

Boots! Boots! ★★ U
Musical   1934 · UK · BW · 71min

Now here's a collector's item. If you ignore a 1915 film called *By the Shortest of Heads*, in which he appeared when he was only 11, George Formby made his proper screen debut in this cheap hotel comedy. It's not hard to spot that much of the action was filmed in a single room above a Manchester garage, but what is of more interest is the fact that George's co-star is Beryl, the domineering wife who exerted such a firm grip on his career that she tried to prevent him from kissing any of his later heroines. Dated, but a must for fans. DP

George Formby *John Willie* • Beryl Formby *Beryl* • Arthur Kingsley *Manager* • Tonie Forde *Chambermaid* • Lilian Keyes *Lady Royston* • Donald Reid *Sir Alfred Royston* • Betty Driver *Betty* ■ *Dir* Bert Tracy • *Scr* George Formby, Arthur Mertz

Boots Malone ★★ U
Sports drama   1951 · US · BW · 103min

Although William Holden had already made *Sunset Blvd* and *Born Yesterday*, Paramount still loaned him out for rubbish such as this family movie. It's an awfully sentimental tale, set at a racing stables where Johnny Stewart is a rich kid who loves horses. Holden is a jockey's agent who hasn't won a race in years but who thinks "The Kid" might change his luck. Veteran director William Dieterle had the chore of calling the shots, and he relies heavily on Holden's innate charm. AT

William Holden (2) *Boots Malone* • Johnny Stewart *"The Kid"* • Stanley Clements *Stash Clements* • Basil Ruysdael *Preacher Cole* • Carl Benton Reid *John Williams* • Ed Begley *Howard Whitehead* ■ *Dir* William Dieterle • *Scr* Milton Holmes, Harold Buchman (uncredited)

Booty Call ★★ 18
Comedy   1997 · US · Colour · 75min

Jamie Foxx and Tommy Davidson are absolutely determined to score with their girls before the night's out. But as they search for contraceptives, Vivica A Fox and Tamala Jones refuse to give in that easily in this lame battle-of-the-sexes comedy. If you find testicular surgery, baby urine and butt-sniffing remotely funny, then this deliberately raw gross-out will be just your *National Lampoon*-style cup of tea. AJ Swearing.

Jamie Foxx *Bunz* • Tommy Davidson *Rushon* • Tamala Jones *Nikki* • Vivica A Fox *Lysterine* • Scott LaRose *Chiub* • Ric Young *Mr Chiu* • Art Malik *Akmed* ■ *Dir* Jeff Pollack • *Scr* Takashi Bufford, Bootsie

Bopha! ★★★ 15
Political drama   1993 · US · Colour · 113min

Morgan Freeman made his directorial debut with this powerful study of apartheid, which presented South Africa from the viewpoint of the black population rather than white liberals. As the police sergeant torn between the comforts his career provides and the inescapable consequences of prejudice, Danny Glover gives one of his finest performances. Alfre Woodard is also impressive as his wife, while Maynard

Eziashi shows great promise as the son whose support for active protest turns the family's world upside down. Malcolm McDowell keeps on just the right side of caricature as a sadistic Special Branch officer. DP Violence, swearing. DVD

Danny Glover *Micah Mangena* • Malcolm McDowell *De Villiers* • Alfre Woodard *Rosie Mangena* • Marius Weyers *Van Tonder* • Maynard Eziashi *Zweli Mangena* • Malick Bowens *Pule Rampa* ■ *Dir* Morgan Freeman • *Scr* Brian Bird, John T Wierick, from Percy Mtwa's play

Borat: Cultural Learnings of America for Make Benefit Glorious Nation of Kazakhstan ★★★★ 15
Satirical comedy   2006 · US/UK · Colour · 80min

For those unfamiliar with Borat, he is a leading Kazakhstani journalist who, for this project, travels America learning about its culture. He is also a complete fabrication, the work of Ali G creator Sacha Baron Cohen. Thus Borat's scatologically uproarious investigation includes a scene in which he attends a posh dinner party and returns from the bathroom with his excrement in a plastic bag. He also destroys a Civil War memorabilia shop and lets loose a chicken on the New York subway. In cinematic terms, it's absolutely nothing special: there's no real reason for it to be a movie at all. But as an example of a comedian willing to take absurd risks for his art, this film - one of the funniest of 2006 - is unsurpassed. AS Swearing, sexual references. DVD BD

Sacha Baron Cohen *Borat Sagdiyev* • Ken Davitian *Azamat Bagatov* • Luenell • Pamela Anderson • *Dir* Larry Charles • *Scr* Sacha Baron Cohen, Anthony Hines, Peter Baynham, Dan Mazer, from a story by Baron Cohen, Hines, Baynham, Todd Phillips, from the character created by Baron Cohen

The Border ★★ 18
Drama   1981 · US · Colour · 103min

It's good cop Jack Nicholson versus bad cop Harvey Keitel on the Tex-Mex border of El Paso, trying to stop "wetbacks" illegally entering America. Well-meaning Nicholson pities the poor immigrants and takes on the corrupt Keitel's smuggling operations in this bland and simplistic human rights drama. However, it's a limp look at what still remains a hot issue. The ending was changed to make Nicholson's character more heroic. AJ

Jack Nicholson *Charlie Smith* • Harvey Keitel *Cat* • Valerie Perrine *Marcy Smith* • Warren Oates *Red* • Elpidia Carrillo *Maria* • Shannon Wilcox *Savannah* • Manuel Viescas *Juan* • Jeff Morris *JJ* ■ *Dir* Tony Richardson • *Scr* Deric Washburn, Walon Green, David Freeman

Border Incident ★★★
Film noir   1949 · US · BW · 95min

This is one of Hollywood's early attempts to tackle the thorny topic of illegal immigration across the Mexican-American border, though the so-called "wetbacks" play second fiddle to a routine plot about racketeering. It was one of several film noir-style thrillers from director Anthony Mann, and is an intelligent picture that belies its low budget. Top-billed Ricardo Montalban gives a fine performance. AT

Ricardo Montalban *Pablo Rodriguez* • George Murphy *Jack Bearnes* • Howard Da Silva *Owen Parkson* • James Mitchell *Juan Garcia* • Arnold Moss *Zopilote* • Alfonso Bedoya *Cuchillo* • Teresa Celli *Maria* ■ *Dir* Anthony Mann • *Scr* John C Higgins, from a story by John C Higgins, George Zuckerman

Border Shootout ★★
Western   1990 · US · Colour · 110min

You don't expect a western from big-city writer Elmore Leonard (*Get Shorty*), but the plot, adapted from his novel, is the best thing in this morality tale. Townsfolk elect an unworldly farmer (Cody Glenn) as deputy sheriff to ageing lawman Glenn Ford so that they can go vigilante lynching. There's an intriguing set-up, but the

production is as simple-minded as the deputy and even Ford is subdued. TH

Glenn Ford *Sheriff Danahar* • Cody Glenn *Kirby Frye* • Charlene Tilton *Edith Hanasain* • Jeff Kaake *Phil Sundeen* • Danny Nelson *Harold Mendez* • Michael Ansara *Chuluka* • Sergio Calderone [Sergio Calderon] *Juaquin* ■ *Dir* Chris McIntyre • *Scr* Chris McIntyre, from the novel *The Law at Randado* by Elmore Leonard

The Borderlands ★★★ 15
Horror   2013 · UK · Colour · 88min

Although a standard "found footage" horror in many respects, writer/director Elliot Goldner's well-crafted feature wins extra points for having at its core the appealing double act of Gordon Kennedy and Robin Hill (*Down Terrace*) as a Vatican-sanctioned paranormal investigator and a tech-head sent to an isolated West Country church to gather evidence of an insidious presence. The pair's easy-going chemistry firmly anchors this slow-burning shocker, which remains witty even as things turn unnerving. AJ Swearing. DVD

Gordon Kennedy *Deacon* • Aidan McArdle *Mark* • Robin Hill *Gray* • Luke Neal *Father Crellick* ■ *Dir/Scr* Elliot Goldner

Borderline ★★★ PG
Romantic crime caper   1950 · US · BW · 88min

A rare example of comic noir, this intriguing road movie has a disconcerting relevance as drugs continue to pour into the States across the Mexican border. Determined to nail supplier Raymond Burr, LAPD narcotics cop Claire Trevor poses as a cheap showgirl. However, when she is snatched, along with a consignment of drugs, by Fred MacMurray, Trevor has no idea he is a federal agent rather than the hired hand of a rival gang boss. The race to sanctuary is slickly staged with plenty of flirtatious banter. DP DVD

Fred MacMurray *Johnny McEvoy aka Johnny Macklin* • Claire Trevor *Madeleine Haley aka Gladys La Rue* • Raymond Burr *Pete Ritchie* • Jose Torvay [José Torvay] *Miguel* ■ *Dir* William A Seiter • *Scr* Devery Freeman, from his story

Borderline ★★ 15
Crime drama   1980 · US · Colour · 99min

In this lacklustre thriller, Charles Bronson stars as a patrolman on the US-Mexican border out to thwart those who make a profit out of illegal immigrants. Ed Harris, in his first major role, is outstanding as the chief baddie, but Bronson can't smuggle any expression of any kind onto that Mount Rushmore face of his. Director Jerrold Freedman tries valiantly to squeeze fresh blood from the script's collection of clichés. TH DVD

Charles Bronson *Jeb Maynard* • Bruno Kirby *Jimmy Fante* • Bert Remsen *Carl Richards* • Michael Lerner *Henry Lydell* • Kenneth McMillan *Malcolm Wallace* • Ed Harris *Hotchkiss* • Karmin Murcelo *Elena Morales* • Enrique Castillo *Arturo* ■ *Dir* Jerrold Freedman • *Scr* Steve Kline, Jerrold Freedman

Bordertown ★★★
Crime drama   1935 · US · BW · 90min

This super-pacey melodrama from Warner Bros stars Paul Muni as a disbarred lawyer who heads south to the US-Mexico border in search of work. There he finds sex in the form of playgirl Margaret Lindsay and hotblood Bette Davis. Davis's role, which culminates in a tremendous trial sequence, is quite sympathetic, since her lust for Muni is presented as entirely understandable because she's married to the gross Eugene Pallette. Daring then, and still stirring now. TS

Paul Muni *Johnny Ramirez* • Bette Davis *Marie Roark* • Margaret Lindsay *Dale Elwell* • Eugene Pallette *Charlie Roark* • Soledad Jiminez *Mrs Ramirez* • Robert Barrat *Padre* • Gavin Gordon *Brook Mandillo* ■ *Dir* Archie Mayo • *Scr* Laird Doyle, Wallace Smith, from the novel by Carroll Graham

Bordertown Cafe ★★★
Comedy drama   1991 · Can · Colour · 101min

This wry, warm-hearted Canadian comedy drama takes an affectionate look at the

relationship between a divorced woman and her troubled adolescent son. Susan Hogan is a larger-than-life owner of a café, something of an embarrassment to her teenage offspring who longs for a normal existence. There are shades of *Bagdad Café* in the rich mix of eccentric characters, but director Norma Bailey also succeeds in making some telling points about the generation gap. JF Swearing.

Susan Hogan *Marlene* • Janet Wright *Maxime* • Lora Schroeder *Linda* • Gordon Michael Woolvett • Sean McCann • Nicholas Campbell ■ *Dir* Norma Bailey • *Scr* Kelly Rebar

Born Again ★ PG
Biographical drama   1978 · US · Colour · 104min

A weird, inferior appendage to the Watergate scandal, this chronicles the rise of White House employee Charles Colson, who served time in prison for his involvement in the affair and became a born-again Christian. Former blues singer (and born-again) Christian Dean Jones plays Colson. The cringe factor is high. AT

Dean Jones *Charles Colson* • Anne Francis *Patty Colson* • Jay Robinson *David Shapiro* • Dana Andrews *Tom Phillips* • Raymond St Jacques *Jimmy Newsom* • George Brent *Judge Gerhard Gesell* • Harry Spillman *President Richard M Nixon* • Peter Jurasik *Henry Kissinger* • Richard Caine *HR Haldeman* ■ *Dir* Irving Rapper • *Scr* Walter Bloch

Born and Bred ★★★★ 15
Drama   2006 · Arg/UK/It · Colour · 95min

Argentinian film-maker Pablo Trapero here gives a masterly demonstration of how environment can be used to explore a character's psychological state. Life seemingly couldn't be better for interior designer Guillermo Pfening, as his family luxuriates in a Buenos Aires dream house. But an inevitable tragedy pitches the grieving Pfening into a Patagonian exile, where his sense of hopelessness is reinforced by the vast, snowy expanses surrounding the tiny airport where he works with everymen Federico Esquerro and Tomás Lipán. The pair's cheerful resignation to their lot - respectively, impending fatherhood and an ailing wife - contrasts with Pfening's emotional fragility. The ending is a touch too sentimental, but it's always implied that redemption is waiting beyond cinematographer Guillermo Nieto's forbidding vistas. DP Spanish +subtitles. DVD

Guillermo Pfening *Santiago* • Federico Esquerro *Robert* • Martina Gusman *Milli* • Tomás Lipán *Cacique* • Victoria Vescio *Josefina* • Nilda Raggi *Victoria* ■ *Dir* Pablo Trapero • *Scr* Pablo Trapero, Mario Rulloni • *Cinematographer* Guillermo Nieto

Born Free ★★★★ U
Biographical wildlife adventure   1966 · US/UK · Colour · 91min

Beautifully shot and sensitively staged by director James Hill, this charming adaptation of Joy Adamson's bestseller is one of the great animal films. It goes without saying that all eyes will be on Elsa the lioness whenever she is on the screen, with her reluctance to take the first steps back into the wild bringing a lump to every throat. But the human performances are also first rate, with Virginia McKenna and Bill Travers bringing real warmth to their roles, while Geoffrey Keen excels as the kindly commissioner who persuades them to part with their pet. *Living Free* continued the story. DP DVD

Virginia McKenna *Joy Adamson* • Bill Travers *George Adamson* • Geoffrey Keen *Kendall* • Peter Luckoye *Nuru* • Omar Chambati *Makkede* • Bill Godden *Sam* • Bryan Epsom *Baker* • Robert Cheetham *Ken* ■ *Dir* James Hill • *Scr* Gerald LC Copley [Lester Cole], from the books by Joy Adamson • *Cinematographer* Ken Talbot

Born in East LA ★★ 15
Comedy drama   1987 · US · Colour · 80min

Based on Cheech Marin's parody of Bruce Springsteen's rock anthem *Born in the USA*, this weak-kneed effort lacks the wit of the Marin recording and cannot even muster a fraction of the Boss's own power. This tale

B

of a third-generation Hispanic American who is wrongly deported to Tijuana starts by taking a handful of amiable pot shots, but eventually allows itself to be smothered by blandness. JM Swearing.

Cheech Marin [Richard "Cheech" Marin] *Rudy Robles* • Daniel Stern *Jimmy* • Paul Rodriguez *Javier* • Kamala Lopez [Kamala Dawson] *Dolores* • Jan-Michael Vincent *McCalister* • Lupe Ontiveros *Rudy's mother* • Urbanie Lucero *Rudy's sister* • Chastity Ayala *Rudy's niece* ■ *Dir/Scr* Richard Marin [Richard "Cheech" Marin]

Born in Flames ★★★ 15
Drama   1983 · US · Colour · 79min

In a futuristic New York, ten years after a peaceful revolution has made all men equal, three feminists from different backgrounds (the army, radio and performance arts) join together to fight for the rights of women irrespective of their race or sexual preference. A classic women's rights movie that utilises an in-your-face, *cinéma vérité* style, poignant arguments and razor-sharp humour to put across the hopeful fantasy of liberation against oppression. Among the cast is future Oscar-winning director Kathryn Bigelow (*The Hurt Locker*). AJ

Honey • Adele Bertei *Isabel* • Jeanne Satterfield *Adelaide* • Flo Kennedy *Zella* • Pat Murphy *Newspaper editor* • Kathryn Bigelow *Newspaper editor* ■ *Dir* Lizzie Borden • *Scr* Hisa Tayo, from a story by Lizzie Borden

Born in 68: We'll Love Each Other until Death Do Us Part ★★★ 15
Drama   2008 · Fr · Colour · 173min

Set over a period of four decades, Olivier Ducastel and Jacques Martineau's film is a meticulously made survey of recent French history. It begins in 1968 and focuses on Catherine (Laetitia Casta), a Parisian student who joins the cause of the radical activists and leaves the city to set up a commune in an abandoned Dordogne farm with lovers Yves (Yannick Renier) and Hervé (Yann Trégouët). Given the scope of the feature, it's not surprising that the directors occasionally lapse into art house soap. And while it may lack the political trenchancy of the equally sweeping Italian film *The Best of Youth* (2003) and the narrative genius of the German *Heimat* cycle, this remains a laudably ambitious project. DP French +subtitles. Violence, swearing, sex scenes, nudity, drug abuse.

Laetitia Casta *Catherine* • Yannick Renier *Yves* • Yann Trégouët [Yann Tregouet] *Hervé* • Christine Citti *Maryse* • Marc Citti *Serge* • Sabrina Seyvecou *Ludmilla* • Théo Frilet *Boris* ■ *Dir* Olivier Ducastel, Jacques Martineau • *Scr* Olivier Ducastel, Jacques Martineau, from a screenplay (unproduced) by Guillaume Le Touze

Born Losers ★★★ 18
Crime drama   1967 · US · Colour · 106min

Don't be fooled by the credits for director TC Frank, screenwriter E James Lloyd and producer Donald Henderson – they are all pseudonyms for Tom Laughlin, the rough-and-ready auteur who also starred in this bruising encounter between a mixed-race ex-Green Beret and a sadistic biker gang. Nowadays it's hard to fathom why this crude exploitation flick was one of the 1960s highest grossers. But the rescue of Elizabeth James was attended by such sickening violence that audiences were shocked to the edge of their seats. Laughlin would revive the character for three disappointing sequels, beginning with *Billy Jack* in 1971. DP

Tom Laughlin *Billy Jack* • Elizabeth James *Vicky Barrington* • Jane Russell *Mrs Shorn* • Jeremy Slate *Danny Carmody* • William Wellman Jr *Child* • Robert Tessier *Cue Ball* • Jeff Cooper *Gangrene* • Edwin Cook *Crabs* ■ *Dir* TC Frank [Tom Laughlin] • *Scr* E James Lloyd [Tom Laughlin]

Born on the Fourth of July ★★★★★ 18
Biographical drama   1989 · US · Colour · 138min

The second film in director Oliver Stone's Vietnam trilogy is a masterpiece, on a much broader canvas than its predecessor

Platoon. It stars Tom Cruise as Ron Kovic, who enlists in the marines because he loves his country. Then he is hideously wounded, endures the rat-infested hell of a veterans' hospital and comes home to find the Stars and Stripes being burned in the streets. He drops out in Mexico, then returns to America to conduct an anti-war campaign from his wheelchair. Stone had won the director's Oscar for *Platoon* and he won it again for his work here. Sadly, Cruise had to settle for a nomination, but his transformation from golden boy to embittered paraplegic is utterly convincing. AT Violence, sex scenes, swearing, nudity. DVD BL

Tom Cruise *Ron Kovic* • Kyra Sedgwick *Donna* • Raymond J Barry *Mr Kovic* • Caroline Kava *Mrs Kovic* • Willem Dafoe *Charlie* • Josh Evans *Tommy Kovic* • Jamie Talisman *Jimmy Kovic* • Tom Berenger *Recruiting sergeant* • Oliver Stone *News reporter* ■ *Dir* Oliver Stone • *Scr* Oliver Stone, Ron Kovic, from Ron Kovic's autobiography

Born Reckless ★★
Crime drama   1930 · US · BW · 73min

A Little Italy gangster, arrested for robbery, is given the opportunity to serve his country rather than serve a prison sentence. He accepts and becomes a hero on the battlefield but, home again, he's drawn back into the underworld and gets involved in bootlegging. This suffers from a miscast Edmund Lowe and an inept screenplay. However, it's also an early example of John Ford's work before he became the premier director of westerns, and, as such, is of some cinematic interest. RK

Edmund Lowe *Louis Beretti* • Catherine Dale Owen *Joan Sheldon* • Lee Tracy *Bill O'Brien* • Marguerite Churchill *Rosa Beretti* • Warren Hymer *Big Shot* • William Harrigan *Good News Brophy* ■ *Dir* John Ford • *Scr* Dudley Nichols, from the novel *Louis Beretti* by Donald Henderson Clarke

Born Reckless ★
Crime drama   1937 · US · BW · 60min

Racing driver Brian Donlevy becomes a cabbie, but finds the cab company under threat from ruthless racketeer Barton MacLane who wants to own it. Donlevy joins forces with MacLane's moll (Rochelle Hudson) to collect evidence that will put the heavy behind bars. Directed by Malcolm St Clair, this crime drama is so pointless and feeble that it caused the *New York Times* critic to dismiss it as "a little cinematic starveling". RK

Rochelle Hudson *Sybil Roberts* • Brian Donlevy *Bob "Hurry" Kane* • Barton MacLane *Jim Barnes* • Robert Kent *Les Martin* • Harry Carey *Dad Martin* ■ *Dir* Malcolm St Clair • *Scr* John Patrick, Robert Ellis, Helen Logan, from a story by Jack Andrews

Born Reckless ★
Musical drama   1959 · US · BW · 79min

The same title was used for an early John Ford failure about bootlegging, and again in 1937 for a programme filler about taxi wars. This time around, it's used for a feeble musical with a western theme. The almost non-existent plot has luckless rodeo cowboy Jeff Richards taking to the road with his old-timer pal Arthur Hunnicutt and sexy blonde trick rider Mamie Van Doren. RK

Mamie Van Doren *Jackie Adams* • Jeff Richards *Kelly Cobb* • Arthur Hunnicutt *Cool Man* • Carol Ohmart *Liz* • Tom Duggan *Wilson* • Tex Williams • Don "Red" Barry [Donald Barry] *Oakie* • Nacho Galindo *Papa Gomez* ■ *Dir* Howard W Koch • *Scr* Richard Landau, from a story by Aubrey Schenck, Richard Landau

Born Romantic ★★★ 15
Romantic comedy   2000 · UK · Colour · 92min

Writer/director David Kane returns to the territory of his debut feature *This Year's Love* with this enjoyable London-based romantic comedy. The setting is a salsa club, where 3-somethings Jane Horrocks, Olivia Williams and Catherine McCormack interact with Craig Ferguson, Jimi Mistry and David Morrissey. Cabbie Adrian Lester provides transport and some much-needed

advice to these romantic no-hopers. There's whimsical humour rather than belly laughs, and good performances, but it's all a little over familiar. JB DVD

Craig Ferguson *Frankie* • Ian Hart *Second cab driver* • Jane Horrocks *Mo* • Adrian Lester *Jimmy* • Catherine McCormack *Jocelyn* • Jimi Mistry *Eddie* • David Morrissey *Fergus* • Olivia Williams *Eleanor* ■ *Dir/Scr* David Kane

Born to Be Bad ★★ U
Romantic drama   1934 · US · BW · 59min

Loretta Young rarely played schemers and she looks decidedly uneasy in this clumsy melodrama warning against the dangers of allowing Depression despair to crush American decency. As the unmarried mother of potential urchin Jackie Kelk, she abandons protective bookseller Henry Travers and tries to scam milk millionaire Cary Grant, first by faking Kelk's injury in a road accident and then, after Grant has adopted the boy, by breaking up his marriage to the angelic Marion Burns. The potboiling storyline has dated badly and Lowell Sherman's direction is mawkish and manipulative. Yet this remains a fascinating example of 1930s Hollywood's attempts to shape national morality. DP DVD

Loretta Young *Letty Strong* • Cary Grant *Malcolm Trevor* • Jackie Kelk *Mickey Strong* • Marion Burns *Mrs Alyce Trevor* • Henry Travers *Fuzzy* • Paul Harvey *Attorney Brian* ■ *Dir* Lowell Sherman • *Scr* Ralph Graves, from his story

Born to Be Bad ★★ PG
Drama   1950 · US · BW · 89min

Unfortunately for RKO, Joan Fontaine was put on this earth to be timid and twee and nice did not come easily. She fails to convince in this flat drama, playing an ambitious, callous woman who arrives in San Francisco determined to have it all her own way. Robert Ryan and Zachary Scott look unconvinced as the men caught up in her wiles. DP DVD

Joan Fontaine *Christabel Caine* • Robert Ryan *Nick Bradley* • Zachary Scott *Curtis Carey* • Joan Leslie *Donna Foster* • Mel Ferrer *Gobby* • Harold Vermilyea *John Caine* • Virginia Farmer *Aunt Clara* ■ *Dir* Nicholas Ray • *Scr* Edith Sommer, Robert Soderberg, George Oppenheimer, Charles Schnee (adaptation), from the novel *All Kneeling* by Anne Parrish

Born to Be Blue ★★★★ 15
Music biography   2015 · UK/Can/US · Colour and BW · 97min

Jazz trumpeters are traditionally troubled souls. This time it's Chet Baker, the "James Dean of jazz", battling personal demons after a drug dealer's brutal beating leaves his mouth wrecked and his playing ability severely impaired. Filmed in a mix of coloured "present" and black-and-white flashbacks, *Born to Be Blue* is a brilliant, often brutal biopic that's cool for cats of any persuasion, whether jazz fans or otherwise. DA DVD BL

Ethan Hawke *Chet Baker* • Carmen Ejogo *Jane/Elaine* • Callum Keith Rennie *Dick* • Stephen McHattie *Dad* ■ *Dir/Scr* Robert Budreau

Born to Be Wild ★★ U
Adventure   1995 · US · Colour · 94min

Only the youngest viewers will fail to spot that animal star Katie is nothing more than a fur-covered collection of gears and wires in this simian reworking of *Free Willy*. It's a shame, as the story of a lonely kid who befriends a three-year-old gorilla in a behavioural study lab is actually quite entertaining, at least until it reaches the ponderous courtroom sequences. Wil Horneff interacts well with the animatronic ape, while Peter Boyle comes up with some deliciously hammed-up villainy. DP

Wil Horneff *Rick Heller* • Helen Shaver *Margaret Heller* • John C McGinley *Max Carr* • Peter Boyle *Gus Charnley* • Jean Marie Barnwell *Lacey Carr* • Marvin J McIntyre *Bob the paramedic* • Gregory Itzin *Walter Mallinson* ■ *Dir* John Gray • *Scr* Paul Young, John Bunzel, from a story by Paul Young

Born to Boogie ★★★
Music documentary   1972 · UK · Colour · 63min

Glam rock fans won't be able to resist this invaluable record of Marc Bolan and T Rex's concert at the Empire Pool, Wembley, on 18 March 1972. All the classic tracks are trotted out with pouting proficiency, and there are also a couple of studio treats, as Elton John and director Ringo Starr jam along on versions of *Tutti-Frutti* and *Children of the Revolution*. Some may find the surreal interludes self-indulgent, but they're hugely revealing of Bolan's view of himself and his art. A memorable snapshot of the glam rock era in all its gaudy glory. DP DVD

Marc Bolan • Ringo Starr • Elton John ■ *Dir* Ringo Starr

Born to Dance ★★★ U
Musical   1936 · US · BW · 105min

This vintage MGM musical has a young and lovable James Stewart crooning (in his own inimitable voice) to Eleanor Powell – she is the mesmerising tap shoes. Stewart is especially amiable, but there's also talented support from loose-limbed Buddy Ebsen and lovely Virginia Bruce, and the fine Cole Porter score includes the classic *I've Got You under My Skin*. Those glossy MGM production values give a rare sheen to the proceedings and the black and white is positively luminous, making you care less about the extremely silly plot. TS

Eleanor Powell *Nora Paige* • James Stewart *Ted Barker* • Virginia Bruce *Lucy James* • Una Merkel *Jenny Saks* • Sid Silvers *Gunny Saks* • Frances Langford *Peppy Turner* • Raymond Walburn *Captain Dingby* • Alan Dinehart *McKay* ■ *Dir* Roy Del Ruth • *Scr* Jack McGowan, Sid Silvers, from a story by Jack McGowan, Sid Silvers, BG DeSylva, Cinematographer Ray June

Born to Fight ★★ 18
Martial arts action   2004 · Thai · Colour · 91min

Set in a remote rural Thai village, this B-movie bone-crusher has a burnt-out young policeman (Dan Chupong) and a team of top athletes among the hostages taken by an invading guerrilla army. The vigilante violence that follows as athletes and villagers hit back at their brutal captors is often stagey and repetitive. SF Thai +subtitles. DVD

Dan Chupong [Chupong Changprung] *Deaw* • Noppol Gomarachun [Nappon Gomarachun] *General Yang* • Santhisook Promsiri *Lor Fai* • Peeyapong Piew-orn *Tuk* • Somrak Kumsing *Tub* • Amorthep Waesang *Moo* • Suebsak Pansueb *Jo* ■ *Dir* Panna Rittikrai • *Scr* Morakat Kaewthanek, Thanapat Taweesuk, from a story by Panna Rittikrai

Born to Raise Hell ★★ 18
Action thriller   2010 · US · Colour · 92min

A mumbling Steven Seagal is out for vengeance once again in this self-penned ego trip that feels more like an episode of a TV show than a fully formed feature. Sleepwalking his way through the clichés, Seagal stars as an Interpol agent in Romania who's driven into an unorthodox alliance to catch the psychotic gangster responsible for murdering his new partner. Pointlessly gimmicky visuals compound the overall tedium – only supporting actor Dan Badarau demonstrates any skill, bringing surprising weight to his unimaginatively written role as a Russian crime lord. SF Violence. DVD BL

Steven Seagal *Bobby* • Darren Shahlavi *Costel* • Zoltan Butuc *Dada* • D Neil Mark *Steve* • Dan Badarau *Dimitri* ■ *Dir* Lauro Chartrand • *Scr* Steven Seagal

Born to Win ★★ 15
Black comedy   1971 · US · Colour · 85min

Robert De Niro appeared in more than ten movies before his real breakthrough parts in *Mean Streets* and *The Godfather Part II*. One of his early films, directed by Czech émigré Ivan Passer, this deals lightly with the New York drug scene. George Segal is the shaggy-haired ex-crimper who needs $100 a day to pay for his heroin habit, but can't even seem to rob a diner successfully. De Niro shows little star potential. AT DVD

U SUITABLE FOR ALL   Ue SUITABLE ESPECIALLY FOR YOUNG CHILDREN (DVD ONLY)   PG PARENTAL GUIDANCE   12A UNDER 12s TO BE ACCOMPANIED (CINEMA ONLY)

George Segal *Jay Jay* • Karen Black *Parm* • Jay Fletcher *Billy Dynamite* • Hector Elizondo *The Geek* • Marcia Jean Kurtz *Marlene* • Robert De Niro *Danny* • Paula Prentiss *Veronica* • Sylvia Syms *Cashier* ■ *Dir* Ivan Passer • *Scr* David Scott Milton, Ivan Passer

Born Yesterday ★★★★★★ U
Romantic comedy   1950 · US · BW · 98min

This is a wonderfully funny look at Washington corruption and the age-old battle between the sexes. As Billie Dawn, mistress to Broderick Crawford's junk trader-made-good, Judy Holliday affects a voice that could curdle cream and a persona that will melt your heart. It's a measure of her performance that she beat both Bette Davis (for *All About Eve*) and Gloria Swanson (for *Sunset Blvd*) to the best actress Oscar. Garson Kanin's dialogue is acid on toast, and director George Cukor cleverly knows when to let the action play in splendid long takes: the gin rummy scene is cinematic perfection. As the nice guy, William Holden demonstrates the subtle charm that would make him a movie legend. TS *DVD*

Judy Holliday *Billie Dawn* • Broderick Crawford *Harry Brock* • William Holden (2) *Paul Verrall* • Howard St John *Jim Devery* • Frank Otto *Eddie* • Larry Oliver *Norval Hedges* • Barbara Brown *Mrs Hedges* • Grandon Rhodes *Sanborn* ■ *Dir* George Cukor • *Scr* Albert Mannheimer, from the play by Garson Kanin • *Cinematographer* Joseph Walker

Born Yesterday ★★★ PG
Romantic comedy   1993 · US · Colour · 96min

If you can put George Cukor's original Oscar-winning charmer to the back of your mind, this makes for an amiable, easy-going journey. Melanie Griffith takes the Judy Holliday role of the sassy, deceptively smart girlfriend of rich businessman John Goodman. He wants her smartened up for Washington, so he hires jaded journalist Don Johnson. Johnson looks uncomfortable with light comedy, while Griffith lacks Holliday's razor-sharp comic timing. However, John Goodman is, as always, a delight. JF Violence, swearing. *DVD*

Melanie Griffith *Billie Dawn* • John Goodman *Harry Brock* • Don Johnson *Paul Verrall* • Edward Herrmann *Ed Devery* • Max Perlich *JJ* • Michael Ensign *Philippe* • Benjamin C Bradlee *Secretary Duffee* ■ *Dir* Luis Mandoki • *Scr* Douglas McGrath, from the play by Garson Kanin

Borrowed Time ★★★ 15
Comedy drama   2012 · UK · Colour · 87min

The ever-dependable Phil Davis brings a touch of class to this quirky, middling British comedy. He plays a curmudgeonly, Steptoe-style pensioner, who strikes up an unlikely relationship with gormless youth Theo Barklem-Biggs when the latter tries to burgle his home to settle a debt with a local crime kingpin. Together, the old man and the young offender turn the tables on the tyrant. First-time writer/director Jules Bishop rather overdoes things, but Barklem-Biggs is impressive, and the movie does have its heart in the right place. DA Swearing. *DVD*

Philip Davis *Philip* • Theo Barklem-Biggs *Kevin* • Perry Benson *Ted* • Juliet Oldfield *Becky* • Warren Brown *Nigel* ■ *Dir/Scr* Jules Bishop

The Borrower ★★★ 18
Science-fiction horror thriller
1989 · US · Colour · 87min

John McNaughton's follow-up to the hugely controversial *Henry: Portrait of a Serial Killer* finds him in more straightforward sci-fi horror territory. The story tracks an alien creature with a penchant for ripping the heads off unsuspecting humans and plonking them on his own neck. Rae Dawn Chong and Don Gordon are the puzzled detectives on its trail. McNaughton has some fun playing around with genre conventions and it offers enough scares to keep horror fans happy. JF Swearing.

Rae Dawn Chong *Diana Pierce* • Don Gordon *Charles Krieger* • Antonio Fargas *Julius Caesar Roosevelt* • Tom Towles *Bob Laney* • Neil Giuntoli *Scully* • Pam Gordon *Connie* • Mädchen Amick *Megan* • Larry Pennell *Captain Scarcelli* ■

Dir John McNaughton • *Scr* Sam Egan [Mason Nage], Richard Fire, from a story by Sam Egan [Mason Nage]

The Borrowers ★★★ U
Fantasy adventure   1997 · UK · Colour · 83min

Mary Norton's charming children's stories about a diminutive family (the "Borrowers" of the title) are here turned into a delightful family film. Jim Broadbent is the head of the tiny brood while John Goodman is the unscrupulous full-sized lawyer who intends to demolish their home. Peter Hewitt directs this fun children's adventure, which features a host of British comedy talent, but it's the clever special effects that steal the show. JB *DVD*

John Goodman *Ocious P Potter* • Jim Broadbent *Pod Clock* • Mark Williams *Exterminator Jeff* • Celia Imrie *Homily Clock* • Hugh Laurie *Officer Steady* • Ruby Wax *Town hall clerk* • Bradley Pierce *Pete Lender* • Flora Newbigin *Arietty Clock* ■ *Dir* Peter Hewitt • *Scr* Gavin Scott, John Kamps, from the novels by Mary Norton • *Special Effects* Digby Milner, Lyn Nicholson, Peter Chiang, Tim Field

Borsalino ★★★★ 15
Crime thriller   1970 · Fr/It · Colour · 119min

Jean-Paul Belmondo and Alain Delon are in top serio-comic form as two small-time hoodlums breaking into the Marseille criminal underworld of the 1930s. The superb period detailing and Claude Bolling's hum-along score are additional delights in Jacques Deray's bloody gangster pastiche, which liberally borrows ideas from the work of Howard Hawks and Jean-Pierre Melville, among others. It's *The Public Enemy*, Gallic-style, with engaging tongue-in-cheek wit and a cheeky comic-strip atmosphere. AJ French +subtitles.

Jean-Paul Belmondo *Capella* • Alain Delon *Siffredi* • Michel Bouquet *Rinaldi* • Catherine Rouvel *Lola* • Françoise Christophe *Mme Escarguel* • Corinne Marchand *Mme Rinaldi* ■ *Dir* Jacques Deray • *Scr* Jean-Claude Carrière, Claude Sautet, Jacques Deray, Jean Cau, from the novel *Bandits à Marseille* by Eugène Soccomare

Borsalino and Co ★★
Thriller   1974 · Fr/It/W Ger · Colour · 110min

Gangster Alain Delon fights heroin addiction and his Mob enemies for control of the criminal underworld in 1930s Marseille in a hackneyed rehash of the far superior *Borsalino*. While clearly taking pointers from *French Connection II*, it fails to do anything interesting with them. Despite the sleazy dockside glamour setting, director Jacques Deray's lazy sequel is for Delon completists only. AJ French dubbed.

Alain Delon *Roch Siffredi* • Riccardo Cucciolla *Volpone* • Reinhardt Kolldehoff [Reinhard Kolldehoff] *Sam* • Lionel Vitrant *Lionel* • Catherine Rouvel *Lola* • Daniel Ivernel *Fanti* ■ *Dir* Jacques Deray • *Scr* Jacques Deray, Pascal Jardin

The Boss ★★ 15
Comedy   2015 · US/Jpn · Colour · 98min

Melissa McCarthy and her husband, director Ben Falcone, re-team following their 2014 comedy *Tammy* for another round of cheap, lazy gags that involve McCarthy working very hard for little or no pay-off. This time she plays multimillionaire businesswoman Michelle Darnell, whose assets are frozen after accusations of insider trading. No doubt McCarthy is hugely talented as a comic actress, but getting in people's faces at full volume with nothing else to balance the account is just bad business. SP Swearing, sexual references, drug abuse.

Melissa McCarthy *Michelle Darnell* • Kristen Bell *Claire* • Kathy Bates *Ida Dell Marquette* • Tyler Labine *Mike Beals* • Peter Dinklage *Renault* ■ *Dir* Ben Falcone • *Scr* Melissa McCarthy, Ben Falcone, Steve Mallory

The Boss, Anatomy of a Crime ★★★
Crime drama   2014 · Arg/Ven · Colour · 98min

A morally taxing courtroom drama from Argentina, exploring the case of a shop

worker who is driven to murdering his manipulative and abusive boss, a corrupt butcher. Questions of right and wrong are littered throughout this story, which asks if the act of murder is always inexcusable. Despite an unsatisfying resolution, this is a worthy drama that raises some important social issues. JL Spanish +subtitles.

Joaquín Furriel *Hermógenes* • Luis Ziembrowski *Don Latuada* • Mónica Lairana *Gladys* ■ *Dir* Sebastián Schindel • *Scr* Sebastián Schindel, Javier Olivera, Nicolás Batlle, from the novel *El Patrón: Radiografía de un Crimen* by Elías Neuman

The Boss of It All ★★★ 15
Satirical comedy
2006 · Den/Swe/Fr/It/Ger · Colour · 118min

After the sombre *Dogville* and *Manderlay*, writer/director Lars von Trier lightens up with this quirky, fish-out-of-water comedy. Jobbing actor Jens Albinus is hired to play a fictional company owner to help the real boss sell his IT firm. The inadequately briefed thespian then struggles to perform his "role" when faced with the business's employees. With the humour centred on the absurdities of white-collar working and the oddball characters' idiosyncrasies, the simple satire plays like a twisted version of TV's *The Office*. Unfortunately, for all its laugh-out-loud irreverence, the film's appeal is reduced by its experimental visual style – the constant jump cuts quickly grate. SF Danish, Icelandic, Russian, English +subtitles. *DVD*

Jens Albinus *Kristoffer* • Peter Gantzler *Ravn* • Fridrik Thór Fridriksson *Finnur* • Benedikt Erlingsson *Interpreter* • Iben Hjejle *Lise* • Henrik Prip *Nalle* ■ *Dir/Scr* Lars von Trier

Boss'n Up ★ 18
Musical crime drama   2005 · US · Colour · 88min

Rap star Snoop Dogg turns "honey into money" in this ludicrous urban drama, inspired by his multi-platinum-selling 2004 album *R & G Rhythm & Gangsta: the Masterpiece*. Playing like an extended music promo spliced with a flimsy storyline, it's a glossy but vacuous account of a supermarket assistant (Snoop) who decides to capitalise on his success with the ladies by becoming a pimp. This is a badly acted string of incidents, based on warped male fantasies. SF Swearing, drug abuse. *DVD*

Snoop Dogg *Cordé Christopher* • Hawthorne James *OJ* • Larry McCoy *Mint Condition* • Shillae Anderson *Chardonnay* • Lil' Jon *Sheriff* • Scruncho *Hucky G* • Caryn Ward *Dominique* • Sundy Carter *Tricel* ■ *Dir/Scr* Pook Brown

Le Bossu ★★ PG
Swashbuckling adventure
1959 · Fr/It · Colour · 101min

This French swashbuckler stars Jean Marais as an adventurer who cares for a small girl when her nobleman father is murdered. As the dashing hero, Marais avenges his friend's death by infiltrating the enemy camp disguised as a hunchback. It's all a bit *Three Musketeers* – not surprising, since director André Hunebelle had already adapted the Dumas classic in 1953, while Marais played D'Artagnan in *Le Masque de Fer* (1962). AT French dubbed. *DVD*

Jean Marais *Chevalier de Legardère* • André Bourvil [Bourvil] *Passepoil* • Sabina Selman [Sabina Sesselman] *Aurore de Nevers, Isabelle de Caylus* • Hubert Noël *Duc de Nevers* • François Chaumette *Gonzague* • Jean Le Poulain *Monsieur de Peyrolles* • Paulette Dubost *Dame Marthe* ■ *Dir* André Hunebelle • *Scr* Jean Halain, Pierre Foucaud, from the novel by Paul Féval

Le Bossu ★★★ 15
Swashbuckling adventure
1997 · Fr/It/Ger · Colour · 123min

This most recent version of Paul Féval's classic adventure feels more like a serial than a seamless narrative. That said, this pacey and polished picture is never anything less than sabre-rattling entertainment. Although not known for action heroics, Daniel Auteuil emerges from this rousing romp with flying colours, as he hones his fencing skills and assumes the disguise of a hunchback to avenge the murder of Vincent Perez by scheming

financier Fabrice Luchini. Director Philippe de Broca is a master swashbuckler, but his handling of Auteuil's romance with Marie Gillain is less assured. DP French +subtitles. Some violence, swearing. *DVD*

Daniel Auteuil *Lagardère/The Hunchback (Le Bossu)* • Fabrice Luchini *Gonzague* • Vincent Perez *Duc de Nevers* • Marie Gillain *Aurore* • Yann Colette *Peyrolles* • Jean-François Stévenin *Cocardasse* • Didier Pain *Passepoil* • Charles Nelson [Charlie Nelson] *Aesop* • Philippe Noiret *Philippe d'Orléans* ■ *Dir* Philippe de Broca • *Scr* Philippe de Broca, Jean Cosmos, Jérôme Tonnerre, from the novel by Paul Féval

Boston Kickout ★★★ 18
Black comedy   1995 · UK · Colour · 100min

Youthful exuberance and an affectionate eye for suburban life help paper over the technical deficiencies of this oddball black comedy. John Simm plays a confused teen desperate to get out of his dead-end life, as his friends drift improbably into crime. It's a bit erratic but there are some nice lines, plus a memorably off-kilter turn from Marc Warren (*The Vice*, *Game On*). JF Swearing, violence, sex scenes. *DVD*

John Simm *Phil* • Emer McCourt *Shona* • Andrew Lincoln *Ted* • Nathan Valente *Matt* • Richard Hanson *Steve* • Marc Warren (1) *Robert* • Derek Martin *Ray* ■ *Dir* Paul Hills • *Scr* Paul Hills, Diane Whitley, Roberto Troni, from a story by Paul Hills

The Boston Strangler ★★★★ 18
Biographical crime drama
1968 · US · Colour · 111min

This is a suspenseful and often disturbing re-creation of the crimes, capture and psychoanalysis of Albert DeSalvo (played here by Tony Curtis), who confessed to being the notorious Boston Strangler, the killer of 13 women in the early 1960s. Director Richard Fleischer deftly captures the pensive atmosphere of a frightened city with a stark, documentary-style approach that makes good use of split-screen sequences. As an all-star line-up of lawmen tightens the net around the elusive maniac, Curtis proves beyond doubt he could act with a nuanced performance of considerable depth and power. AJ Violence, nudity. *DVD*

Tony Curtis *Albert DeSalvo* • Henry Fonda *John S Bottomly* • George Kennedy *Phil Di Natale* • Mike Kellin *Julian Soshnick* • Hurd Hatfield *Terence Huntley* • Murray Hamilton *Frank McAfee* • Jeff Corey *John Asgeirsson* • Sally Kellerman *Dianne Cluny* ■ *Dir* Richard Fleischer • *Scr* Edward Anhalt, from the book by Gerold Frank • *Cinematographer* Richard H Kline

The Bostonians ★★ PG
Period drama   1984 · UK · Colour · 116min

This Merchant Ivory production is adapted by Ruth Prawer Jhabvala from the Henry James novel. Vanessa Redgrave stars as the Bostonian suffragette who gets involved with a faith healer's daughter, while Christopher Reeve appears out of his depth as the cousin who falls for the girl. James is notoriously difficult to convey on film and this moves at a snail's pace. As a result, it's a tad dull, despite the loving attention paid to period detail. LH *DVD*

Christopher Reeve *Basil Ransome* • Vanessa Redgrave *Olive Chancellor* • Madeleine Potter *Verena Tarrant* • Jessica Tandy *Miss Birdseye* • Nancy Marchand *Mrs Burrage* • Wesley Addy *Dr Tarrant* • Barbara Bryne *Mrs Tarrant* • Linda Hunt *Dr Prance* ■ *Dir* James Ivory • *Scr* Ruth Prawer Jhabvala, from the novel by Henry James

Botany Bay ★★★
Adventure   1952 · US · Colour · 93min

Alan Ladd is a medical student unjustly transported to Australia, and James Mason is the sadistic captain of the prison ship that takes him there. While Ladd and Mason square up to each other, Patricia Medina sets both their hearts fluttering. In the end, after some flogging, snogging and an outbreak of plague, they all arrive Down Under, where Aborigines sort out the unresolved plotlines. AT

B

Alan Ladd *Hugh Tallant* • James Mason *Capt Paul Gilbert* • Patricia Medina *Sally Munroe* • Cedric Hardwicke *Governor Phillips* • Murray Matheson *Rev Thynne* • Malcolm Lee Beggs *Nick Sabb* • Jonathan Harris *Tom Oakley* • Dorothy Patten *Mrs Nellie Garth* ■ *Dir* John Farrow • *Scr* Jonathan Latimer, from the novel by Charles Nordhoff, James Norman Hall

Botched ★★★ 15

Crime black comedy horror
2007 · Ger/Ire/UK/US · Colour · 90min

Black comedy horror is a difficult genre to get right. But director Kit Ryan hits more often than he misses with this bizarre hybrid of crime caper and serial-killer thriller that has lashings of slapstick gore. Stephen Dorff stars as the professional thief who's in debt to the Russian Mafia and so agrees to steal a priceless crucifix from a Moscow penthouse. The robbery ends in murder, hostage-taking and getting trapped on the unused 13th floor, where someone is on a beheading spree. A warped sense of humour is needed to fully enjoy this live-action cartoon and its sparkling assortment of weird characters, psycho mobsters, campy villains and full-on splatter. AJ English, Russian +subtitles. Violence, swearing. *DVD*

Stephen Dorff *Ritchie* • Jamie Foreman *Peter* • Jaime Murray *Anna* • Sean Pertwee *Mr Groznyi* • Russell Smith *Yuri* • Bronagh Gallagher *Sonya* • Geoff Bell *Boris* • Hugh O'Conor *Dmitry* ■ *Dir* Kit Ryan • *Scr* Derek Boyle, Eamon Friel, Raymond Friel

The Bothersome Man ★★★ 15

Black comedy drama
2006 · Nor/Ice · Colour · 91min

This dystopian satire from Norwegian director Jens Lien has shades of Buster Keaton, Samuel Beckett and Jacques Tati in its deadpan absurdism. Arriving in a new town, amnesiac Andreas (Trond Fausa Aurvag) quickly acquires an untaxing job, an attractive wife (Petronella Barker) and a compliant mistress (Birgitte Larsen). But despite this seemingly pleasant set-up, he soon realises that his environment is mind-numbingly bland. Leavening the bleakness of his nightmarish world with bursts of cartoonish violence, Lien succeeds in slyly exposing the soullessness of modern life. Yet, for all the enjoyably disconcerting moments, the dénouement is something of a disappointment. DP Norwegian +subtitles. Violence. *DVD*

Trond Fausa Aurvag *Andreas* • Petronella Barker *Anne Britt* • Per Schaaning *Hugo* • Birgitte Larsen *Ingeborg* • Johannes Joner *Havard* ■ *Dir* Jens Lien • *Scr* Per Schreiner

Bottle Rocket ★★★ 15

Comedy crime drama 1996 · US · Colour · 87min

This agreeably eccentric comedy crime tells the story of a dopey trio (Luke and Owen Wilson, Robert Musgrave) who bewilderingly think they are cut out for a life in crime. Debuting Wes Anderson observes their bungling antics and personality disorders with obvious affection, while continually taking the episodic tale in unexpected directions. The leads deliver expertly judged performances and there's a nice cameo from James Caan. JF Violence, swearing, a sex scene, brief nudity. *DVD*

Luke Wilson *Anthony Adams* • Robert Musgrave *Bob Mapplethorpe* • Owen C Wilson [Owen Wilson] *Dignan* • Lumi Cavazos *Inez* • James Caan *Mr Henry* • Andrew Wilson (1) *Future Man* • Ned Dowd *Dr Nichols* • Shea Fowler *Grace* ■ *Dir* Wes Anderson • *Scr* Owen C Wilson, Wes Anderson

Bottle Shock ★★ 12

Comedy drama based on a true story
2008 · US · Colour · 104min

This "triumph of the underdog" comedy drama is set in the snooty world of international wine-tasting. Alan Rickman proves uncharacteristically low-key as Steven Spurrier, an English wine merchant who sets up a contest between the unfashionable cabernets and chardonnays of California and the best of the French

wines. However, while the film is inspired by an actual competition, dubbed the "Judgment of Paris", which took place in 1976, it rather struggles to keep its story on track all the way to the big finale. There's a welcome demystification of the wine-making process, but the movie's clunky knockabout comedy and predictable ending rather limit its appeal. TJ Brief swearing, sexual references, drug references. *DVD*

Alan Rickman *Steven Spurrier* • Chris Pine *Bo Barrett* • Bill Pullman *Jim Barrett* • Rachael Taylor *Sam* • Freddy Rodriguez *Gustavo Brambila* • Dennis Farina *Maurice Cantavale* • Bradley Whitford *Professor Saunders* • Eliza Dushku *Joe* ■ *Dir* Randall Miller • *Scr* Jody Savin, Randall Miller, Ross Schwartz, from a story by Schwartz, Lannette Pabon, Savin, Miller

Bottoms Up ★★ U

Comedy 1959 · UK · BW · 88min

Frank Muir, Denis Norden and Michael Pertwee collaborated on the script for this school-based comedy, which sought to cash in on the successful Jimmy Edwards *Whack-O!* TV series. Leslie Howard's brother Arthur again plays stooge to Jimmy's cane-wielding headmaster, as he tries to raise the profile of his academy by passing off his bookie's son as eastern royalty. The strong supporting cast makes a solid contribution to an otherwise hit-and-miss comedy. DP

Jimmy Edwards *Professor Jim Edwards* • Arthur Howard (2) *Oliver Pettigrew* • Martita Hunt *Lady Gore-Willoughby* • Sydney Tafler *Sid Biggs* • Raymond Huntley *Garrick Jones* • Reginald Beckwith *Bishop Wendover* • Vanda Hudson *Matron* • Richard Briers *Colbourne* • Melvyn Hayes *Cecil Biggs* ■ *Dir* Mario Zampi • *Scr* Michael Pertwee, with additional dialogue by Frank Muir, Denis Norden

Le Boucher ★★★★ 15

Psychological drama
1969 · Fr/It · Colour · 88min

One of Claude Chabrol's most accomplished and celebrated films has the director returning to the provincial world of his first film *Le Beau Serge* a decade later. Chabrol's then wife, Stéphane Audran plays a village schoolteacher who gradually comes to realise that her new friend, a shy butcher (Jean Yanne), is the sex murderer the police are searching for. With certain nods to Chabrol's idol Alfred Hitchcock, the film is much more than a thriller – it's a sympathetic psychological study of sexual frustration. The two leads are superb, and the film is brilliantly shot by Jean Rabier, Chabrol's usual cinematographer. RB French +subtitles. *DVD*

Stéphane Audran *Hélène* • Jean Yanne *Popaul* • Antonio Passalia *Angelo* • Mario Beccaria *Léon Hamel* • Pasquale Ferone *Père Cahrpy* • Roger Rudel *Police Inspector Grumbach* ■ *Dir/Scr* Claude Chabrol

Boudu, Saved from Drowning ★★★★ PG

Comedy 1932 · Fr · BW · 80min

Jean Renoir's classic farce-cum-satire of bourgeois ways will seem familiar to anyone who has seen *Down and Out in Beverly Hills*, Hollywood's 1986 remake. Boudu, a particularly smelly and ill-natured tramp, is saved from suicide in the Seine by a nice, middle-class chap, who invites Boudu into his home. Once installed, the tramp shows his gratitude by wreaking havoc on the household. It's a neat idea, executed to fine comic effect by a master film-maker. PF French +subtitles. *DVD*

Michel Simon *Boudu* • Charles Granval *Monsieur Lestingois* • Marcelle Hainia *Madame Lestingois* • Sévérine Lerczynska *Anne-Marie* • Jean Dasté *Student* • Max Dalban *Godin* • Jean Gehret *Vigour* • Jacques Becker *Poet on bench* ■ *Dir* Jean Renoir • *Scr* Jean Renoir, from the play by René Fauchois

The Boulangère de Monceau ★★★

Romantic drama 1962 · Fr · BW · 26min

Rohmer worked as an influential critic and director for 12 years before announcing his "Six Moral Tales" - a series of similarly

themed works of which this elegant short was the first. He promised that each story would deal "less with what people do, than with what is going on in their mind while they are doing it". The sextet view relationships from the male perspective - in this case a vague young man (Barbet Schroeder) who approaches one girl, then a second arranging a meeting with both on the same day. The series, with its intellectual intimacy, unifying structure and cool detachment, established his international reputation. BB French +subtitles.

Barbet Schroeder • Claudine Soubrier • Michèle Girardon • Bertrand Tavernier • Fred Junck • Michel Mardore ■ *Dir/Scr* Eric Rohmer

Boulevard ★★★ 15

Drama 2014 · US · Colour · 84min

This bittersweet drama tells the story of a man who is living a lie. A kind, mild-mannered loan manager (played by Robin Williams), he works at a small bank, lives with his wife (Kathy Baker), and is on the verge of a big promotion. But none of this makes him happy. It soon becomes clear that Nolan is gay, and that he has been hiding this secret for a very long time. In his final dramatic role, Williams - who committed suicide not long after - delivers a performance that is filled with sadness and regret. As a result, the film is quietly heartbreaking. SC Swearing. *DVD*

Robin Williams *Nolan Mack* • Kathy Baker *Joy* • Roberto Aguire *Leo* • Giles Matthey *Eddie* ■ *Dir* Dito Montiel

Bounce ★★ 12

Romantic drama 2000 · US · Colour · 102min

Ben Affleck is the brash advertising guy who gives up his seat on a plane to a man who wants to get home to his wife - only to hear the next morning that the plane crashed, killing all on board. Racked with guilt, Affleck takes refuge in the bottle and later seeks out the man's widow (Gwyneth Paltrow). Paltrow is moving as the bereaved young wife, while Affleck is well cast as the arrogant young lothario whose life almost falls apart, but this is slow in places and overly sentimental in others. JB Swearing. *DVD*

Ben Affleck *Buddy Amaral* • Gwyneth Paltrow *Abby Janello* • Joe Morton *Jim Weller* • Natasha Henstridge *Mimi* • Tony Goldwyn *Greg Janello* • Johnny Galecki *Seth* • Alex D Linz *Scott Janello* ■ *Dir/Scr* Don Roos

Bound ★★★★ 18

Crime thriller 1996 · US · Colour · 104min

This original and intensely black comedy thriller from Larry and Andy Wachowski stars Jennifer Tilly and Gina Gershon as lesbian lovers who, following a series of steamy liaisons, hatch a plan to steal a fortune from the Mob. Tilly and Gershon form a convincing *Thelma & Louise*-style team, who take their punches like men, while Joe Pantoliano, as Tilly's crooked boyfriend, is an able foil to their conniving. Visually dynamic and strong on gallows humour, this is further proof that the Wachowski brothers' subsequent success with *The Matrix* wasn't merely a flash in the pan. LH Swearing, sex scenes, nudity. *DVD* 🅑

Jennifer Tilly *Violet* • Gina Gershon *Corky* • Joe Pantoliano *Caesar* • John P Ryan *Mickey Malnato* • Christopher Meloni *Johnny Marconi* • Richard C Sarafian *Gino Marzzone* • Barry Kivel *Shelly* • Mary Mara *Bartender* ■ *Dir/Scr* Larry Wachowski [Lana Wachowski], Andy Wachowski [Lilly Wachowski]

Bound & Gagged: a Love Story ★★★ 18

Black comedy 1992 · US · Colour · 89min

More a road movie than the love story the title suggests, this focuses on Ginger Lynn Allen, who escapes her thuggish husband by beginning an affair with another woman. However, this romance takes on a bizarre turn when her lover kidnaps her after Allen refuses to divorce her husband, and takes her on a journey through the badlands of Minnesota. Strange and often funny

stuff, this is capably handled and features two strong lead performances. JB

Ginger Lynn Allen *Leslie* • Karen Black *Carla* • Chris Denton *Cliff* • Elizabeth Saltarrelli *Elizabeth* • Mary Ella Ross *Lida* • Chris Mulkey *Steve* ■ *Dir/Scr* Daniel B Appleby

Bound by a Secret ★★

Drama 2008 · US · Colour · 97min

In this reflective melodrama, two lifelong pals face a moral dilemma when one of them is diagnosed with terminal cancer. Lesley Ann Warren gives an affecting performance as the ailing former actress who's anxious to share a potentially devastating secret, while Meredith Baxter provides solid support in her more low-key best-friend role. The film is bitty and emotionally uneven, but at least Warren and Baxter keep events anchored, infusing their characters' intimacies with an absorbing honesty and depth. SF

Lesley Ann Warren *Jane* • Meredith Baxter *Ida Mae* • Bridget Ann White [Bridget White] *Kate* • Holt McCallany *Jimmy* • Timothy Bottoms *Will* ■ *Dir* David S Cass Sr • *Scr* Darrell V Orme Mann

Bound for Glory ★★★★ PG

Biographical drama 1976 · US · Colour · 142min

This is a moving account of the folk singer Woody Guthrie, a real-life rebel who travelled through the Dust Bowl during the Depression years, singing and whingeing as he went along. David Carradine, who provides his own vocals, makes a credible Guthrie, while director Hal Ashby creates many a vivid composition lit by flashes of real insight. Guthrie influenced many of today's balladeers; watching this, it's not hard to see why. TH *DVD*

David Carradine *Woody Guthrie* • Ronny Cox *Ozark Bule* • Melinda Dillon *Mary Guthrie* • Gail Strickland *Pauline* • John Lehne *Locke* • Ji-Tu Cumbuka *Slim Snedeger* • Randy Quaid *Luther Johnson* • Elizabeth Macey *Liz Johnson* ■ *Dir* Hal Ashby • *Scr* Robert Getchell, from Woody Guthrie's autobiography

The Bounty ★★★★ 15

Historical drama 1984 · UK · Colour · 130min

Unlike the Charles Laughton/Clark Gable and Trevor Howard/Marlon Brando versions of *The Mutiny on the Bounty*, this sticks closely to historical fact. Consequently, Lieutenant - as he was at the time of the mutiny - William Bligh emerges as a gentleman bound by duty and loyalty who expected nothing less of his crew, while Fletcher Christian comes across as a man driven by heartfelt but half-digested notions of liberty and romance. Mel Gibson is acted off the screen by the magnificent Anthony Hopkins, who holds together this intelligent film. DP Violence, nudity *DVD*

Mel Gibson *Fletcher Christian* • Anthony Hopkins *Lieutenant William Bligh* • Laurence Olivier *Admiral Hood* • Edward Fox *Captain Greetham* • Daniel Day-Lewis *John Fryer* • Bernard Hill *Cole* • John Sessions *Smith* • Philip Davis *Young* • Liam Neeson *Churchill* ■ *Dir* Roger Donaldson • *Scr* Robert Bolt, from the non-fiction book *Captain Bligh and Mr Christian* by Richard Hough

The Bounty Hunter ★★★ PG

Western 1954 · US · Colour · 75min

A straightforward yet satisfying Randolph Scott western has the stone-faced one setting out after three marauding bank robbers, all of whom are in disguise as respectable townsfolk. These Andre De Toth directed horse operas were screened as co-features, often with a minor musical or thick-ear thriller (this one partnered the original *Dragnet* on its release), and provided satisfactory, value-for-money programming. TS

Randolph Scott *Jim Kipp* • Dolores Donlon *Julie Spencer* • Marie Windsor *Alice* • Howard Petrie *Sheriff Brand* • Harry Antrim *Dr Spencer* • Robert Keys *George Williams* • Ernest Borgnine *Rachin* • Dub Taylor *Danvers* ■ *Dir* Andre De Toth • *Scr* Winston Miller, from a story by Miller, Finlay McDermid

The Bounty Hunter ★★ 12
Romantic action comedy
2010 · US · Colour · 106min

This knockabout comedy from *Hitch* director Andy Tennant tries to tick too many boxes – thriller, romance, farce – and tends to rely on the radiant star power of Jennifer Aniston to distract viewers from its shortcomings. Cop-turned-bounty hunter Milo Boyd (Gerard Butler) is assigned to track down his bail-jumping reporter ex-wife Nicole (Aniston), but gets sucked into a story she's working on about the police cover-up of a murder. Aniston is charmingly spiky throughout, as is Christine Baranski as her mother, but the laughs are few and far between. TeS Some violence, swearing, sexual references. *DVD* Blu

Gerard Butler *Milo Boyd* · Jennifer Aniston *Nicole Hurley* · Christine Baranski *Kitty Hurley* · Jason Sudeikis *Stewart* · Jeff Garlin *Sid* ■ *Dir* Andy Tennant · *Scr* Sarah Thorp

Bounty Killer ★★★ 18
Futuristic action thriller
2013 · US · Colour · 88min

In a post-apocalypse wasteland, smart-suited city slickers are now the prey of rival bounty hunters. Director Henry Saine's second feature is lively comic-book stuff (no surprise it's based on a graphic novel) that packs in a frenetic mix of tongue-in-cheek humour, kick-ass action (including an outrageous nod to John Ford's *Stagecoach*) and juicy grindhouse-style splatter. It's hokum, of course, but it's the sort of stylish hokum with appealing leads that B-movie maestro Roger Corman would have loved to make. JA Violence, swearing, sex scenes, nudity. *DVD*

Matthew Marsden *Drifter* · Christian Pitre *Mary Death* · Kristanna Loken *Catherine* · Gary Busey *Van Sterling* · Beverly D'Angelo *Lucille* ■ *Dir* Henry Saine · *Scr* Jason Dodson, Colin Ebeling, Henry Saine, from a story by Dodson

The Bourne Identity ★★★★ 12
Spy action thriller
2002 · US/Cz Rep · Colour · 117min

In this hip and energetic tale from former indie director Doug Liman, Matt Damon stars as an amnesiac who's found floating half-dead in the Mediterranean with no identification, except for a device embedded in his hip containing a Swiss bank account number. Unaware that he's actually a top CIA assassin, he sets off to Zurich to investigate, facing cops and government killers as his employers try to wipe out their now renegade operative. The film is fast-paced and slickly executed, with an edgy sophistication. SF Violence, swearing. *DVD* Blu

Matt Damon *Jason Bourne* · Franka Potente *Marie Kreutz* · Chris Cooper *Ted Conklin* · Clive Owen *The Professor* · Brian Cox (1) *Ward Abbott* · Adewale Akinnuoye-Agbaje *Nykwana Wombosi* ■ *Dir* Doug Liman · *Scr* Tony Gilroy, William Blake Herron, from the novel by Robert Ludlum

The Bourne Supremacy ★★★★ 12
Spy action thriller
2004 · US/Ger · Colour · 104min

British film-maker Paul Greengrass takes over the directing duties from Doug Liman for this sequel to *The Bourne Identity*. Two years after ex-CIA operative Matt Damon apparently escaped the attentions of his spymasters, a corrupt Russian businessman frames him for a double assassination, which drags Damon back into the murky world of international espionage. Greengrass uses his drama documentary background to good effect, delivering consistently exciting action without ever pushing the bounds of credibility. Damon impresses in a role that goes against his wholesome image. AS Violence, swearing. *DVD* Blu

Matt Damon *Jason Bourne* · Franka Potente *Marie Kreutz* · Brian Cox (1) *Ward Abbott* · Julia Stiles *Nicolette "Nicky" Parsons* · Karl Urban *Kirill* · Gabriel Mann *Zorn* · Joan Allen *Pamela Landy* ·

Marton Csokas *Jarda* · Tom Gallop *Tom Cronin* ■ *Dir* Paul Greengrass · *Scr* Tony Gilroy, from the novel by Robert Ludlum

The Bourne Ultimatum ★★★★★ 12
Spy action thriller
2007 · US · Colour · 110min

In this third film based on Robert Ludlum's bestsellers, Matt Damon never lets the pulse-pounding pace slacken. The intelligence of the subtly economic script is dazzling as Damon, in his definitive trained assassin role, zips through stunning global locations to take revenge on the rogue CIA element responsible for his brainwashed plight. Using the same hand-held camera technique that he did with *Supremacy*, director Paul Greengrass increases the urgent immediacy, cynical edge and up-close-and-personal thrills. With stars Joan Allen and Julia Stiles returning to marvellous effect, this instalment is essentially one long chase that never loses its grip. Nothing is over-played, from the scary surveillance methods to high-level corruption, in this superbly crafted masterclass in action film-making. *The Bourne Legacy* (2012) starred Jeremy Renner but then a fifth film, *Jason Bourne*, brought Matt Damon back to the franchise. AJ English, French, Arabic, Russian, Spanish +subtitles. *DVD* Blu

Matt Damon *Jason Bourne* · Julia Stiles *Nicolette "Nicky" Parsons* · David Strathairn *Noah Vosen* · Joan Allen *Pamela Landy* · Paddy Considine *Simon Ross* · Edgar Ramirez *Paz* · Scott Glenn *Ezra Kramer* · Albert Finney *Dr Albert Hirsch* ■ *Dir* Paul Greengrass · *Scr* Tony Gilroy, Scott Z Burns, George Nolfi, from a story by Gilroy, from the novel by Robert Ludlum · *Cinematographer* Oliver Wood

The Bourne Legacy ★★★ 12
Action thriller
2012 · US · Colour · 129min

Trained killer Aaron Cross (a steely Jeremy Renner) goes on the run with a genetic scientist (Rachel Weisz) who holds the secret to his enhanced biology. They're both targeted for assassination following the public fallout of the Jason Bourne saga. After a convoluted beginning, in which the film confusingly connects with the other three *Bourne* movies, director Tony Gilroy begins to pick up the pace. The stunts don't have as big an impact as in previous films, but this is still a nimble and well-crafted chase thriller. A fifth film, *Jason Bourne*, brought Matt Damon back to the franchise. AJ Violence. *DVD* Blu

Jeremy Renner *Aaron Cross* · Rachel Weisz *Dr Marta Shearing* · Edward Norton *Retired Col Eric Byer* · Stacy Keach *Retired Adm Mark Turso* · Joan Allen *Pam Landy* · Albert Finney *Dr Albert Hirsch* · Scott Glenn *Ezra Kramer* ■ *Dir* Tony Gilroy · *Scr* Tony and Dan Gilroy, from characters by Robert Ludlum

The Bowery ★★★
Drama
1933 · US · BW · 94min

Lovable Wallace Beery and child star Jackie Cooper had a huge public and critical success in *The Champ* (1931), and here they're reunited in a film based on some romantic legends of old New York. Tough guy George Raft is Steve Brodie, who (in)famously jumped off the Brooklyn Bridge in 1886 (an incident shown to dramatic effect here), while Beery plays his sparring partner in this fast-paced Raoul Walsh production, complete with colourful Bowery language and even more colourful Bowery characters. TS

Wallace Beery *Chuck Connors* · George Raft *Steve Brodie* · Jackie Cooper *Swipes McGurk* · Fay Wray *Lucy Calhoun* · Pert Kelton *Trixie Odbray* · George Walsh *John L Sullivan* · Oscar Apfel *Mr Herman* ■ *Dir* Raoul Walsh · *Scr* Howard Estabrook, James Gleason, from the novel *Chuck Connors* by Michael L Simmons, Bessie Ruth Solomon

The Bowery Boys Meet the Monsters ★★★
Comedy horror
1954 · US · BW · 65min

In 1946 surviving members of the Dead End Kids, who'd come to prominence in films such as in *Angels with Dirty Faces*, became

the Bowery Boys to feed the nation's adolescents with juvenile slapstick comedies of which this was the most commercially successful. A monster spoof, this has the Boys running foul of a family that makes the Addams clan look like something out of Enid Blyton. Although not particularly funny, it's directed by Edward Bernds at such a pace that boredom doesn't get a look in. RS

Leo Gorcey *Slip* · Huntz Hall *Sach* · Bernard Gorcey *Louie* · Lloyd Corrigan *Anton* · Ellen Corby *Amelia* · John Dehner *Derek* · Laura Mason *Francine* ■ *Dir* Edward Bernds · *Scr* Elwood Ullman, Edward Bernds

Bowery Champs ★★★
Comedy
1944 · US · BW · 61min

This is one of the more amusing entries in the *East Side Kids* series, thanks to a super in-joke that has former *Dead End Kid* Bobby Jordan playing himself. The running gag is threaded throughout this daft tale of Muggs (Leo Gorcey) getting himself involved – yet again – in a murder hunt. Journeyman director William Beaudine keeps the pace up. TS

Leo Gorcey *Muggs* · Huntz Hall *Glimpy* · Billy Benedict *Skinny* · Jimmy Strand *Danny* · Bobby Jordan *Kid* · Bud Gorman *Shorty* · Anne Sterling *Jane* · Gabriel Dell *Jim* ■ *Dir* William Beaudine · *Scr* Earle Snell

Bowfinger ★★★★ 12
Comedy
1999 · US · Colour · 92min

A bang-on-target satire of low-budget Hollywood film-making features Steve Martin's best comic performance since *Dirty Rotten Scoundrels*. He's an ambitious but financially challenged director who can't get A-list action star Eddie Murphy for his new sci-fi project. So he follows the actor around, setting up various silly scenarios and filming Murphy's shocked reactions. Martin – who also wrote the hilarious screenplay – is immensely engaging, and there's sparkling support from Murphy (in dual roles) and Heather Graham, as a talentless actress who's quite happy to sleep her way to a larger role. JC Some swearing. *DVD*

Steve Martin *Bowfinger* · Eddie Murphy *Kit Ramsey/Jeff Ramsey* · Heather Graham *Daisy* · Christine Baranski *Carol* · Jamie Kennedy *Dave* · Barry Newman *Kit's agent* · Adam Alexi-Malle *Afrim* · Terence Stamp *Terry Stricter* · Robert Downey Jr *Jerry Renfro* ■ *Dir* Frank Oz · *Scr* Steve Martin

Bowling for Columbine ★★★★★ 15
Documentary
2002 · US/Can/Ger · Colour · 114min

In his 1989 debut *Roger & Me*, "people's film-maker" Michael Moore went after the CEO of General Motors. Here, his quest is much broader: what actually causes America's alarming gun-related annual death toll? Whether opening a bank account that comes with a free rifle or harassing retail giant K-Mart to persuade them to stop selling the type of bullets used at the 1999 Columbine school massacre, Moore leaves no stone unturned, addressing issues such as foreign policy, race, welfare and the post-11 September climate of fear. Shifting with surprising ease between humour and pathos, this is an important, outspoken film, if not an easy one to watch. Moore's confrontation with National Rifle Association president Charlton Heston proves especially uncomfortable, but, at a time when Moore could be branded "unpatriotic" for his views, here is a rousing film that urges you think about what patriotism really means. AC *DVD*

Michael Moore (2) *Michael Moore* · Charlton Heston · Marilyn Manson · Dick Clark · James Nichols · Matt Stone ■ *Dir/Scr* Michael Moore (2)

The Box ★★ 12
Science-fiction thriller
2008 · US · Colour · 110min

In *Donnie Darko* director Richard Kelly's convoluted chiller, a mysterious stranger

(Frank Langella) offers a strange proposition to married couple Cameron Diaz and James Marsden. The film's simple premise – if you could get rich by pushing a button causing a total stranger's death, would you? – is suitably eerie, but Kelly confuses matters with oddball tangents and plot twists, while Diaz and Marsden are horribly stilted. The film may be stylish looking, but it soon collapses under the weight of its lofty pretensions. AJ *DVD* Blu

Cameron Diaz *Norma Lewis* · James Marsden *Arthur Lewis* · Frank Langella *Arlington Steward* · James Rebhorn *Norm Cahill* · Holmes Osborne *Dick Burns* · Sam Oz Stone *Walter Lewis* ■ *Dir* Richard Kelly · *Scr* Richard Kelly, from the short story *Button, Button* by Richard Matheson

Box of Moonlight ★★★★ 15
Comedy
1996 · US · Colour · 106min

Electrical engineer John Turturro lives by the clock, plays by the book and is as boring as hell, until the day he hears what his co-workers truly think of him and decides to go back to the lake where he spent his childhood. There he meets Sam Rockwell, a free spirit who lives in a dilapidated trailer and steals garden gnomes for a living. How his new companion's chaotic existence changes Turturro's attitudes is highly engaging, very affecting and always amusing. Beautifully shot and scripted, this allegorical fairy tale is a box of sheer delights. AJ Swearing, violence.

John Turturro *Al Fountain* · Sam Rockwell *Bucky, "Kid"* · Catherine Keener *Floatie Dupre* · Lisa Blount *Purlene Dupre* · Annie Corley *Deb Fountain* · Rica Martens *Doris* · Ray Aranha *Soapy* · Alexander Goodwin *Bobby Fountain* ■ *Dir/Scr* Tom DiCillo

Boxcar Bertha ★★★ 18
Biographical crime drama
1972 · US · Colour · 88min

Director Martin Scorsese broke into the big time with this Roger Corman-produced bloodfest that clearly signalled he was a major film-maker in waiting. This is a good girl-gone-bad picture, with Barbara Hershey as the farmer's daughter driven to crime by misfortune and an uncaring system. There's the occasional bravura shot and some coal-black humour, but Scorsese is bound too tightly by Corman's usual exploitation formula to have space for such luxuries as character development. DP Swearing, violence, nudity. *DVD*

Barbara Hershey *Boxcar Bertha* · David Carradine *Big Bill Shelley* · Barry Primus *Rake Brown* · Bernie Casey *Von Morton* · John Carradine *H Buckram Sartoris* · Victor Argo *One of the McIvers* · David R Osterhout *One of the McIvers* · Michael Powell *Chicken Holleman* · Emeric Pressburger *Graham Pratt* ■ *Dir* Martin Scorsese · *Scr* Joyce H Corrington, John William Corrington, from characters in *Sister of the Road, the Autobiography of Boxcar Bertha Thompson* by Bertha Thompson, Dr Ben L Reitman

The Boxer ★★★ 15
Political drama
1997 · Ire/UK/US · Colour · 108min

A knockout performance by Daniel Day-Lewis embellishes this otherwise under-nourished tale that seems at times to be a polemic for the Irish Republican cause. He plays an IRA prisoner who returns to his former profession of boxing and establishes a gym, giving delinquents the chance to pummel their way to a better life. Directed and co-written by Jim Sheridan, it feels as sweatily authentic as the inside of a boxing glove, but the flatness of the narrative makes it seem rather dull. TH Swearing, some violence. *DVD*

Daniel Day-Lewis *Danny Flynn* · Emily Watson *Maggie* · Brian Cox (1) *Joe Hamill* · Ken Stott *Ike Weir* · Gerard McSorley *Harry* · Eleanor Methven *Patsy* · Ciaran Fitzgerald *Liam* · David McBlain *Sean* ■ *Dir* Jim Sheridan · *Scr* Jim Sheridan, Terry George

Boxing Day ★★ 15
Drama
2012 · UK/US · Colour · 94min

British director Bernard Rose's adaptation of Tolstoy's story *Master and Man* stars Danny Huston as a ruthless California property developer who abandons his family on Boxing Day to hunt for foreclosures in Colorado. Huston's taken on his quest by local taxi driver Matthew Jacobs, whose world is slowly falling apart. The wintry journey through ice and snow, intertwined with snatched insights into the men's unhappy lives, suggests that little good can come of this, but any such portentous tension soon fades. Huston, as ever, does the devil's work to perfection, but this soon becomes a very long and tiresome slog. DW Swearing. _DVD_

Danny Huston *Basil* • Matthew Jacobs *Nick* • Edie Dakota *Nathalie* • Lisa Enos *Marianne* • Jo Farkas *Rosemary* ■ *Dir* Bernard Rose • *Scr* Bernard Rose, from the short story *Master and Man* by Leo Tolstoy

Boxing Helena ★★18
Erotic thriller   1993 · US · Colour · 100min

Infamous for provoking a feminist controversy and a lawsuit (Kim Basinger was sued for backing out of the lead role), the directorial debut of Jennifer Lynch is a fudged allegorical fantasy about aberrant human behaviour and sexual complexes. Sick surgeon Julian Sands falls in love with Sherilyn Fenn and, after she has a car accident, removes her legs and arms to keep her captive on a pedestal. By turns macabre and silly. AJ

Julian Sands *Dr Nick Cavanaugh* • Sherilyn Fenn *Helena* • Bill Paxton *Ray O'Malley* • Kurtwood Smith *Dr Alan Harrison* • Art Garfunkel *Dr Lawrence Augustine* • Betsy Clark *Anne Garrett* • Nicolette Scorsese *Fantasy lover/Nurse* • Meg Register *Marion Cavanaugh* ■ *Dir* Jennifer Lynch [Jennifer Chambers Lynch] • *Scr* Jennifer Chambers Lynch, from the story by Philippe Caland

The Boxtrolls ★★★PG
Animated adventure 2014 · US · Colour · 92min

Those with a soft spot for chaotic critters will delight in this fun adaptation of the illustrated novel *Here Be Monsters!* from Laika, the stop-motion animation studio behind *ParaNorman* and *Coraline*. The blue-skinned, miscellaneously misshapen boxtrolls are a triumph of design and painstaking execution, but the film suffers from a simplistic, sometimes hastened-through plot, as a boy raised by these misunderstood creatures befriends a lonely girl (voiced by Elle Fanning). EAS _DVD_

Blu _DVD_

Elle Fanning *Winnie* • Isaac Hempstead-Wright *Eggs* • Ben Kingsley *Archibald Snatcher* • Simon Pegg *Herbert Trubshaw* • Toni Collette *Lady Portley-Rind* ■ *Dir* Graham Annable, Anthony Stacchi • *Scr* Irena Brignull, Adam Pava, from the novel *Here Be Monsters!* by Alan Snow

The Boy ★★15
Horror thriller
2016 · US/Chi/Can · Colour · 93min

The Walking Dead's Lauren Cohan is a nanny hired to take care of a young boy, but she's shocked to discover he's actually a life-sized doll. However, when she disobeys the rules for taking care of the "boy", terrifying things begin to happen. Dolls in horror movies are a guaranteed way to create an unnerving atmosphere, but the obviousness of the plot here makes it all a little disappointing. JL Violence. _DVD_ _Blu_

Lauren Cohan *Greta* • Rupert Evans (2) *Malcolm* • Ben Robson *Cole* • Diana Hardcastle *Mrs Heelshire* • Jim Norton *Mr Heelshire* ■ *Dir* William Brent Bell • *Scr* Stacey Menear

A Boy, a Girl and a Bike
★★U
Comedy drama   1949 · UK · BW · 87min

A minor, good-natured British comedy romance, this follows the adventures and love affairs of the youthful members of a Yorkshire cycling club. Future Avenger Honor Blackman is the girl whose affections are vied for by humble Patrick Holt and rich boy John McCallum, while Anthony Newley and Diana Dors play other members of the group. The cosy enterprise demonstrates why, with certain notable exceptions, the public preferred American films. RK _DVD_

John McCallum *David Howarth* • Honor Blackman *Susie Bates* • Patrick Holt *Sam Walters* • Diana Dors *Ada Foster* • Maurice Denham *Bill Martin* • Leslie Dwyer *Steve Hall* • Anthony Newley *Charlie Ritchie* • Megs Jenkins *Nan Ritchie* • Thora Hird *Mrs Bates* ■ *Dir* Ralph Smart • *Scr* Ted Willis, from a story by Ralph Keene, John Sommerfield

A Boy and His Dog ★★★★15

Science-fiction black comedy
1975 · US · Colour · 86min

Featuring a very early screen appearance by Don Johnson, this film remains one of his best. He's actually not particularly brilliant in it as he is upstaged by his canine co-star, but this offbeat sci-fi black comedy has deservedly become a cult favourite. Set in a post-apocalyptic world, the story follows the adventures of Johnson and his super intelligent dog when they get mixed up with a strange subterranean community, unable to reproduce sexually. Director LQ Jones works wonders with a tiny budget and maintains a pleasingly black tone throughout. JF _DVD_

Don Johnson *Vic* • Susanne Benton *Quilla June* • Jason Robards Jr [Jason Robards] *Mr Craddock* • Alvy Moore *Dr Moore* • Helene Winston *Mez* • Charles McGraw *Preacher* • Hal Baylor *Michael* • Ron Feinberg *Fellini* • Mike Rupert *Gary* ■ *Dir* LQ Jones • *Scr* LQ Jones, from the novella by Harlan Ellison

A Boy Called Dad ★★15
Coming-of-age drama
2009 · UK · Colour · 76min

Echoes of the past return to haunt a 14-year-old boy in this bittersweet coming-of-age tale. Kyle Ward makes a notable film debut as Robbie, whose unexpected fathering of a child brings back memories of his own father, Joe (Ian Hart), who abandoned him and his mother. Robbie's resentment is reignited when he encounters Joe again, and these feelings and a violent confrontation soon see the boy on the run. Though the influence of Ken Loach looms large, there's just not enough substance to this tale of two fathers. A pity, as the leads both give fine performances. JA Violence, swearing.

Ian Hart *Joe* • Kyle Ward *Robbie* • Charlene McKenna *Nia* • Sacha Parkinson *Leanne* • Steve Evets *Mr Whippy* • Crissy Rock *Chip shop woman* ■ *Dir* Brian Percival • *Scr* Julie Rutterford

A Boy Called Hate ★★★15
Road movie   1995 · US · Colour · 93min

Scott Caan makes his film debut alongside his more famous dad, James, in this intriguing road movie. Caan Jr plays a delinquent teenager who comes to the aid of would-be rape victim Missy Crider and ends up on the run from both the law and the girl's guardian. First-time director Mitch Marcus coaxes intense performances out of his two young leads, while Caan Sr and Elliott Gould add class to the proceedings. JF Swearing, violence, sex scenes.

Scott Caan *Steve "Hate" Bason* • Missy Crider *Cindy* • James Caan *Jim* • Elliott Gould *Richard* • Adam Beach *Billy Little Plume* ■ *Dir/Scr* Mitch Marcus

The Boy David Story ★★PG
Documentary   2002 · UK · Colour · 99min

This condensed update of journalist Desmond Wilcox's award-winning TV series about Scottish surgeon Ian Jackson's bid to reconstruct the disease-disfigured face of abandoned Peruvian baby David Lopez is a remarkable account of courage, compassion and medical ingenuity, as well as a scathing exposé of the bureaucratic iniquities inherent in the US immigration system. Having endured around 100 operations, David's determination to make his mark as an artist is truly inspirational, but Dougray Scott's narration is needlessly florid, and the score is riddled with pan pipe clichés. DP

Dougray Scott *Narrator* ■ *Dir* Alex McCall • *Scr* Desmond Wilcox, Alex McCall • *Music* Christopher Gunning

Boy, Did I Get a Wrong Number ★U
Comedy   1966 · US · Colour · 98min

Not even an ageing Bob Hope can save this cheapskate, dumbed-down comedy, in which he plays an estate agent who becomes involved with sexy starlet Elke Sommer after she runs away from the set of her latest film. It's hard to believe that director George Marshall is the same man who directed such classics as *The Blue Dahlia* and *Destry Rides Again*. TH

Bob Hope *Tom Meade* • Elke Sommer *Didi* • Phyllis Diller *Lily* • Cesare Danova *Pepe* • Marjorie Lord *Martha Meade* • Kelly Thordsen *Schwartz* • Benny Baker *Regan* • Terry Burnham *Doris Meade* ■ *Dir* George Marshall • *Scr* Burt Syler, Albert E Lewin, George Kennett, from a story by George Beck

Boy Eats Girl ★★★18
Horror comedy   2005 · Ire · Colour · 76min

Director Stephen Bradley's witty Irish zombie comedy has lovelorn David Leon accidentally hanging himself after spying Samantha Mumba supposedly making out with another schoolmate. He is brought back to life by his mother using an ancient voodoo ritual and infects the class bully, unleashing a horde of ravenous undead. But will he ever have the guts (or anybody else's) to tell Mumba his true feelings? Drawing good-natured strength from deliberate tongue-in-cheek cheesiness and B-movie cheapness, Bradley artfully builds to moments of pure horror hilarity. AJ _DVD_

Samantha Mumba *Jessica* • David Leon *Nathan* • Deirdre O'Kane *Grace* • Mark Huberman *Samson* • Tadhg Murphy *Diggs* • Denis Conway *Craig* • Bryan Murray *Mr Frears* ■ *Dir* Stephen Bradley • *Scr* Derek Landy

The Boy Friend ★★★U
Musical comedy   1971 · UK · Colour · 104min

Indebted to the Warner Bros classic *42nd Street*, this is an energetic and invigorating adaptation of Sandy Wilson's stage success, in which the members of a provincial rep company discover their true selves in the process of putting on a show. A warm-hearted tribute to master choreographer Busby Berkeley, the film unsurprisingly lacks his inspiration. Yet Ken Russell makes a fair fist of the song and dance numbers, while Twiggy is ideally cast as the willing gofer who gets the chance to become a star when the lead (an uncredited Glenda Jackson) injures an ankle. DP

Twiggy *Polly Browne* • Christopher Gable *Tony Brockhurst* • Barbara Windsor *Hortense* • Moyra Fraser *Mme Dubonnet* • Bryan Pringle *Percy Parkhill* • Max Adrian *Max* • Catherine Willmer *Lady Brockhurst* • Vladek Sheybal *De Thrill* • Tommy Tune *Tommy* ■ *Dir* Ken Russell • *Scr* Ken Russell, from a play by Sandy Wilson

The Boy from Mercury
★★★★PG
Drama   1996 · UK/Fr/Ire · Colour · 83min

Martin Duffy made his debut as a writer/director with this semi-autobiographical tale set at the dawn of the space age. Paying homage to both 1950s sci-fi and 1960s kitchen sink drama, Duffy not only gets the fashions and furnishings right, but also re-creates the cinematic look of the period thanks to Seamus Deasy's ingeniously faded photography. James Hickey is magnificent as the eight-year-old who compensates for the loss of his dad by adopting Flash Gordon as his hero and claiming interstellar ancestry. A gem. DP

James Hickey *Harry* • Tom Courtenay *Uncle Tony* • Rita Tushingham *Harry's mother* • Hugh O'Conor *Paul* • Joanne Gerrard *Sarah, Paul's girlfriend* • Sean O'Flanagan *Sean McCarthy* ■ *Dir/Scr* Martin Duffy

The Boy from Oklahoma
★★★U
Western   1954 · US · Colour · 88min

This pleasant film stars Roy Rogers Jr as a law student who becomes the peace-loving sheriff of Bluerock. Rogers Jr didn't have

what it took to become a star, but a minor cowboy player in this movie did become one of America's most famous chat-show hosts: watch out for Merv Griffin in his early incarnation as an actor. TS

Will Rogers Jr *Tom Brewster* • Nancy Olson *Katie Brannigan* • Lon Chaney Jr *Crazy Charlie* • Anthony Caruso *Barney Turlock* • Wallace Ford *Wally Higgins* • Clem Bevans *Pop Pruty* • Merv Griffin *Steve* • Louis Jean Heydt *Paul Evans* ■ *Dir* Michael Curtiz • *Scr* Frank Davis, Winston Miller, from a story by Michael Fessier in *The Saturday Evening Post*

The Boy in Blue ★★15
Biographical sports drama
1986 · Can · Colour · 93min

This Canadian curio is not the most compelling picture Nicolas Cage has ever been in. But a screen biography of Ned Hanlan, the Ontario-based ne'er-do-well who held the world speed sculling title towards the end of the last century, was never likely to be. Cage deserves some credit for involving us in Hanlan's struggles, but it's mostly dispiriting stuff and the rowing scenes are largely devoid of energy and tension. DP Swearing, nudity.

Nicolas Cage *Ned* • Christopher Plummer *Knox* • Cynthia Dale *Margaret* • David Naughton *Bill* • Sean Sullivan *Walter* • Melody Anderson *Dulcie* • Walter Massey *Mayor* ■ *Dir* Charles Jarrott • *Scr* Douglas Bowie, from an original idea by John Trent

The Boy in the Plastic Bubble ★★★12
Drama based on a true story
1976 · US · Colour · 93min

This teleplay became part of another true-life tragedy when John Travolta's lover, Diana Hyland, who won an Emmy for her portrayal of his mother, died of cancer within a year of its release. The role of a teenager born with an acute immunity deficiency was a risk for Travolta, who was then cutting a dash in the sitcom *Welcome Back, Kotter*. But his combination of courage and vulnerability does him credit, while Randal Kleiser avoids undue schmaltz in depicting his relationship with neighbour Glynnis O'Connor. Spoofed in 2001's *Bubble Boy*. DP _DVD_

John Travolta *Tod Lubitch* • Glynnis O'Connor *Gina Biggs* • Robert Reed *Johnny Lubitch* • Diana Hyland *Mickey Lubitch* • Karen Morrow *Martha Biggs* • Ralph Bellamy *Dr Ernest Gunther* ■ *Dir* Randal Kleiser • *Scr* Douglas Day Stewart, from a story by Douglas Day Stewart, Joe Morgenstern

The Boy in the Striped Pyjamas ★★★12
Second World War drama
2008 · UK/US · Colour · 90min

Childish innocence provides stark contrast to the darkest depravities of Nazism in *Brassed Off* director Mark Herman's affecting adaptation of John Boyne's bestselling novel. The film follows Bruno (Asa Butterfield), an eight-year-old boy living in Berlin, who is uprooted with his family to the countryside when his Nazi officer father (David Thewlis) is promoted. Bruno mistakes the nearby concentration camp for a farm and, through the barbed wire, befriends another little boy (Jack Scanlon) wearing striped pyjamas. For both grown-ups and children, it's a morality tale that prompts more questions than answers. That's fine, as long as audiences are open to having this conversation. SP _DVD_ _Blu_

Asa Butterfield *Bruno* • Jack Scanlon *Shmuel* • Amber Beattie *Gretel* • David Thewlis *Bruno's father* • Vera Farmiga *Elsa, Bruno's mother* • Richard Johnson *Grandpa* • Sheila Hancock *Grandma* • Rupert Friend *Lt Kotler* ■ *Dir* Mark Herman • *Scr* Mark Herman, from the novel by John Boyne

Boy Meets Girl ★★★
Screwball comedy   1938 · US · BW · 87min

When you see the picture, you'll discover that the title isn't as corny at as it sounds, but ironic. For this is a frenetic screwball comedy with James Cagney and Pat O'Brien as screenwriters who take the strut out of an arrogant star (Dick Foran) by casting him opposite a scene-stealing infant. As always, Cagney's presence is highly combustible, and the direction by Lloyd Bacon (of *42nd Street* fame) is suitably breezy. Real-life radio announcer Ronald Reagan is played by... Ronald Reagan. AT

James Cagney *Robert Law* • Pat O'Brien *J Carlyle Benson* • Marie Wilson *Susie* • Ralph Bellamy *E Elliott Friday* • Dick Foran *Larry Toms* • Frank McHugh *Rosetti* • Bruce Lester *Rodney Bevan* • Ronald Reagan *Announcer* ∎ *Dir* Lloyd Bacon • *Scr* Samuel Spewack, Bella Spewack, from their Broadway play

Boy Meets Girl ★★★ 15
Romantic drama 1984 · Fr · BW · 99min

A debuting Leos Carax was only 23 when he made this meandering but poetic tale of love, loss and alienation. Shot in gorgeous black and white, it stars his muse Denis Lavant as the semi-autobiographical Alex (Carax's real name), a darkly philosophical youth mourning a romance while wandering night-time Paris. Former movie critic Carax shows his passion for cinema in every considered frame, but the gloomy dialogue keeps the characters distant, making this Cannes winner a decidedly polarising affair. SF French, English +subtitles. DVD

Denis Lavant *Alex* • Mireille Perrier *Mireille* • Carroll Brooks *Helen* • Christian Cloarec *Thomas* ∎ *Dir/Scr* Leos Carax

The Boy Mir: Ten Years in Afghanistan ★★★★ PG
Documentary 2011 · UK · Colour · 94min

Phil Grabsky's fascinating follow-up to his 2004 documentary *The Boy Who Plays on the Buddhas of Bamiyan* is a return to the unforgiving mountain terrain of central Afghanistan, primarily to observe the coming of age of young Mir, who acted as the human focus of that original film. Grabsky charts Mir's journey from impish eight-year-old, living in a cave with his refugee family, to virtual manhood ten years later, back in his home village and wondering whether to pursue an education or settle into a life of manual labour. The beauty of the country contrasts markedly with the hardship endured by the family as they attempt to survive in a post-Taliban world. JA Dari, English +subtitles. DVD

∎ *Dir/Scr* Phil Grabsky

A Boy Named Charlie Brown ★★★ U
Animated musical comedy
1969 · US · Colour · 77min

The first of four feature-length films starring Charles M Schulz's much loved *Peanuts* gang finds the eternal no-hoper Charlie Brown filled with anxiety as he prepares for a national spelling competition and the opening day of baseball season. Director Bill Melendez, a veteran of the Disney and Warner Bros animation studios and countless animated commercials, puts his expertise to charming and imaginative effect, though the gentle antics and excruciatingly twee songs - Oscar-nominated at the time - have dated badly. AME

Peter Robbins *Charlie Brown* • Pamelyn Ferdin *Lucy Van Pelt* • Glenn Gilger *Linus Van Pelt* • Andy Pforsich *Schroeder* • Sally Dryer *Patty* • Anne Altieri *Violet* • Erin Sullivan *Sally* • Linda Mendelson *Frieda* ∎ *Dir* Bill Melendez • *Scr* Charles M Shulz, from his comic strip *Peanuts*

The Boy Next Door ★★
Crime thriller 2008 · Can · Colour · 90min

A small-town murder provides both aggravation and literary inspiration for mystery writer Dina Meyer when she becomes the prime suspect in this obvious and uneventful whodunnit. Naturally, it's up to Meyer to play Nancy Drew and prove she didn't kill her hunky neighbour (Christopher Russell) - a way-too-easy endeavour that's not only increasingly unrealistic but also deadly dull. With clues conveniently just dropping into her lap and no proper action

until the predictable climax, there's little for Meyer to do except look attractive. A surfeit of pointless shots of her jogging or getting in and out of her car accentuate the feature's flimsiness, while the underused and forgettable supporting cast, including late *Glee* star Cory Monteith, seem to exist more for padding than plot development. SF

Dina Meyer *Sara Wilde* • Woody Jeffreys *Sayers* • Marc Menard *Walsh* • Barclay Hope *Edward* ∎ *Dir* Neill Fearnley • *Scr* Peter Layton

The Boy Next Door ★★★ 15
Thriller 2015 · US · Colour · 90min

After a night of ill-judged passion with much younger neighbour Ryan Guzman, newly divorced Jennifer Lopez becomes increasingly frightened of his erratic behaviour. As obsession turns dangerous, the screenplay reveals itself to be a collection of trite plot points, though some entertainment can be had in watching Rob Cohen's direction pushing things even further from reality. This may be of some interest to those looking for late night schlock, but for most it will mark a low point in Lopez's career. JL Violence, swearing.

Jennifer Lopez *Claire Peterson* • Ryan Guzman *Noah Sandborn* • John Corbett *Garrett Peterson* • Ian Nelson *Kevin Peterson* • Kristin Chenoweth *Vicky Lansing* • Lexi Atkins *Allie Callahan* ∎ *Dir* Rob Cohen • *Scr* Barbara Curry

Boy on a Dolphin ★ U
Adventure 1957 · US · Colour · 106min

This is a dreary mismatch of the voluptuous Sophia Loren, in her first film for a Hollywood studio, with the ageing Alan Ladd, a last-minute replacement for Robert Mitchum. She's a Greek sponge diver, he's an American archaeologist, and the slight but protracted story is about the raising of a priceless statue from the bed of the Aegean. Loren towered over Ladd, so the island where filming took place was riddled with trenches to even up their heights. AE

Alan Ladd *Dr James Calder* • Sophia Loren *Phaedra* • Clifton Webb *Victor Parmalee* • Jorge Mistral *Rhif* • Laurence Naismith *Dr Hawkins* • Alexis Minotis *Government Man* • Piero Giagnoni *Niko* ∎ *Dir* Jean Negulesco • *Scr* Ivan Moffat, Dwight Taylor, from the novel by David Divine

The Boy She Met Online ★★
Crime thriller 2010 · Can · Colour · 90min

In this unconvincing tale about the dangers of social networking, 17-year-old Tracy Spiridakos falls for a college undergraduate (Jon Cor) she meets online. But the sweet-talking hunk is not who he claims to be and it's not long before he embroils the A-grade student in his downward spiralling life. What little action there is proves poorly staged and emotionally limited, making even the climax lack tension and oomph. One-time *Baywatch* babe Alexandra Paul is particularly underwhelming as Spiridakos's over-protective mum. SF

Alexandra Paul *Tori Winters* • Tracy Spiridakos *Cami Winters* • Jon Cor *Jake Myers* • Thea Gill *Kendra Oliver* • Eddie Guillaume *Dewayne Jackson* ∎ *Dir* Curtis Crawford • *Scr* Christine Conradt

Boy Slaves ★★★
Drama 1938 · US · BW · 66min

This drama about forced labour on the turpentine farms of the American South during the Depression has the excellent Anne Shirley as a victim trapped by the system. In a largely unknown cast, teen-gang leader James McCallion and runaway Roger Daniel are standouts. This is harrowing stuff, melodramatic and preachy by turns, but credit should go to producer/director PJ Wolfson for getting it made at all. TS

Anne Shirley *Annie* • Roger Daniel *Jesse* • James McCallion *Tim* • Alan Baxter *Graff* • Johnny Fitzgerald *Knuckles* • Walter Ward *Miser* • Charles Powers *Lollie* • Walter Tetley *Pee Wee* ∎ *Dir* PJ Wolfson • *Scr* Albert Bein, Ben Orkow, from a story by Albert Bein

The Boy Who Could Fly ★★★ PG
Fantasy drama 1986 · US · Colour · 103min

With a touch more imagination and a little less saccharin, this could have been one of the best family films of the 1980s, but writer/director Nick Castle couldn't resist the flights of fancy that hijack the action. It's a touching tale about an autistic boy, whose attempts to fly from the roof of his house attract the attention of a girl who has moved to the neighbourhood after her father's suicide. Jay Underwood and Lucy Deakins are splendid as the teenage friends, while Bonnie Bedelia and Colleen Dewhurst provide sympathetic support. DP

Lucy Deakins *Milly Michaelson* • Jay Underwood *Eric Gibb* • Bonnie Bedelia *Charlene Michaelson* • Fred Savage *Louis Michaelson* • Colleen Dewhurst *Mrs Sherman* • Fred Gwynne *Uncle Hugo* • Mindy Cohen *Geneva* • Janet MacLachlan *Mrs D'Gregario* ∎ *Dir/Scr* Nick Castle

The Boy Who Cried Bitch ★★★
Psychological drama 1991 · US · Colour · 101min

Disturbed adolescent Harley Cross is expelled from prep school, and ends up in a psychiatric hospital where he threatens his roommate, torches the hallway and has convulsions in the classroom. Eventually his mother brings him home, where he leads his brothers astray and threatens her with a gun. Argentinian director Juan José Campanella builds up an all-too believable scenario in his desire to show what Charles Manson, and other similar mass murderers, were probably like as children. AJ

Harley Cross *Dan Love* • Karen Young *Candice Love* • Jesse Bradford *Mike Love* • JD Daniels *Nick Love* • Gene Canfield *Jim Cutler* • Moira Kelly *Jessica* • Adrien Brody *Eddy* • Dennis Boutsikaris *Orin Fell* ∎ *Dir* Juan José Campanella • *Scr* Catherine May Levin

The Boy Who Had Everything ★ 18
Drama 1984 · Aus · Colour · 90min

Chariots of Fire meets *Oedipus Rex* in this inconsequential tale of overachieving college student Jason Connery. He's caught between his mother (Diane Cilento, his real mother) and a blonde girlfriend and loyalty to a private school where sadistic humiliation rites are the norm, despite his athletic ability. Awkwardly acted and preciously directed, Stephen Wallace's old-fashioned melodrama has little to say about growing up. AJ

Jason Connery *John* • Diane Cilento *Mother* • Laura Williams *Robin* • Lewis Fitz-Gerald *Vandervelt* • Ian Gilmour *Pollock* • Nique Needles *Cummerford* • Michael Gow *Kaplin* ∎ *Dir/Scr* Stephen Wallace

The Boy Who Stole a Million ★ PG
Comedy 1960 · UK · BW · 77min

Co-written by director Charles Crichton and one-time documentarist John Eldridge, the story of a Spanish boy who steals from a bank to help his impoverished family is supposed to be gnawingly realistic. However, not even the drab photography or the run-down locations can increase the authenticity of the protracted pursuit by some sniffy bank officials and a gang of sneaky criminals. A cloying and unconvincing disappointment. DP DVD

Virgilio Texera [Virgilio Teixeira] *Miguel* • Maurice Reyna *Paco* • Marianne Benet *Maria* • Harold Kasket *Luis* • George Coulouris *Bank manager* • Bill Nagy *Police chief* • Warren Mitchell *Pedro* • Tutte Lemkow *Mateo* ∎ *Dir* Charles Crichton • *Scr* Charles Crichton, John Eldridge, from a story by Neils West Larsen, Antonio de Leon

The Boy Who Turned Yellow ★★ U
Science-fiction fantasy
1972 · UK · Colour · 51min

It is a film-making tragedy that, after 1960's *Peeping Tom*, director Michael Powell's reputation took a nose dive. This peculiar little film, which was the final teaming of

Powell with longtime collaborator Emeric Pressburger, sadly did nothing to resurrect his career. Here, schoolboy Mark Dightman takes a trip to the Tower of London and loses his pet mouse. Sent home from school later for falling asleep in a class on electricity, he dreams (or does he?) that the people on the tube and in the street have turned yellow. LH DVD

Mark Dightman *John* • Robert Eddison *Nick* • Helen Weir *Mrs Saunders* • Brian Worth *Mr Saunders* • Esmond Knight *Doctor* • Laurence Carter *Schoolteacher* • Patrick McAlinney *Supreme Beefeater* ∎ *Dir* Michael Powell • *Scr* Emeric Pressburger

The Boy with Green Hair ★★★ U
Fantasy drama 1948 · US · Colour · 82min

One of the last pictures studio chief Dore Schary made at RKO, this somewhat clumsy mix of whimsy and allegory marked the Hollywood feature debut of director Joseph Losey. Howard Hughes ordered wholesale changes to the film when he bought the studio, but the tolerance theme that he detested so much remained largely intact. Dean Stockwell does well as the orphan whose hair changes colour. Most notable, however, are the splendid performances of Robert Ryan and Pat O'Brien. DP

Robert Ryan *Dr Evans* • Dean Stockwell *Peter* • Pat O'Brien *Gramp* • Barbara Hale *Miss Brand* • Richard Lyon *Michael* • Walter Catlett *"The King"* • Samuel S Hinds *Dr Knudson* • Regis Toomey *Mr Davis* ∎ *Dir* Joseph Losey • *Scr* Ben Barzman, Alfred Lewis Levitt, from a story by Betsy Beaton

Boycott ★★★★ PG
Historical drama
2001 · US · Colour and BW · 108min

Biopics by American cable network HBO are generally of a high standard and this is no exception, re-creating with intelligence and clarity the 1955 boycott of Alabama buses by its segregated black population. An excellent Jeffrey Wright is perfectly cast as Martin Luther King, whose fearless and committed involvement - in the face of death threats and police corruption - was crucial in the development of the modern civil rights movement. Time and place are wonderfully evoked and the variety of film stocks and cinematic techniques used, including direct addresses to camera by Alabama citizens, heightens, rather than deflects, the drama. JC DVD

Jeffrey Wright *Martin Luther King Jr* • Terrence Howard *Ralph Abernathy* • CCH Pounder *Jo Ann Robinson* • Carmen Ejogo *Coretta King* • Reg E Cathey *ED Nixon* ∎ *Dir* Clark Johnson • *Scr* Herman Daniel Farrell III, Timothy J Sexton, from the non-fiction book *Daybreak of Freedom* by Stewart Burns

The Boyfriend School ★★ 15
Romantic comedy 1990 · US · Colour · 97min

Steve Guttenberg is a cartoonist with Hodgkin's disease whose recent dose of chemotherapy has left him bald, bloated and with little hope of finding a girlfriend. So his sister (Shelley Long) decides to help by transforming him into a grizzled Kiwi biker. Soon Guttenberg is being pursued by Jami Gertz, a girl attracted to the wrong sort of guy. Clumsy. Released on video in the UK under the title *Don't Tell Her It's Me*. DF

Shelley Long *Lizzie Potts* • Steve Guttenberg *Gus Kubicek* • Jami Gertz *Emily Pear* • Kyle MacLachlan *Trout* • Kevin Scannell *Mitchell Potts* • Mädchen Amick *Mandy* ∎ *Dir* Malcolm Mowbray • *Scr* Sarah Bird, from her novel

Boyfriends ★★★ 18
Drama 1996 · UK · Colour · 81min

Co-directors Neil Hunter and Tom Hunsinger's promising feature debut shows consummate skill in getting under the skin of homosexual neuroses, as it follows the exploits of three troubled gay couples on a country weekend. A shining example of British low-budget film-making, this accurately scrutinises gay sex and love in the 1990s. AJ Swearing, sex scenes, nudity. DVD

James Dreyfus *Paul* • Mark Sands *Ben* • Andrew Ableson *Owen* • Michael Urwin *Matt* • David Coffey *Will* • Darren Petrucci *Adam* • Michael McGrath *James* • Russell Higgs *Mark* ■ *Dir/Scr* Neil Hunter, Tom Hunsinger

Boyhood ★★★★★ 15

Drama   2014 · US · Colour · 158min

Richard Linklater is a film-maker obsessed with time – both its passing and the difficulty of ever truly capturing it on film. With this extraordinary story about a young American boy (Ellar Coltrane), shot at intervals over 12 years with the same cast, the director comes closer than ever to achieving the impossible. Tracking Coltrane up to the age of 18, the film is told not through births, marriages and deaths but the moments in between – midnight Harry Potter book launches, the 2003 invasion of Iraq and the wave of optimism that swept Obama to power. Elevated by fantastic performances and told with Linklater's trademark generosity and lightness of touch, *Boyhood* is an epic of the everyday, as uplifting as it is universal. SI Swearing, sexual references, drug abuse. DVD Blu

Patricia Arquette *Olivia* • Ethan Hawke *Mason Sr* • Ellar Coltrane [Ellar Salmon] *Mason* • Lorelei Linklater *Samantha* • Zoe Graham *Sheena* ■ *Dir/Scr* Richard Linklater

The Boys ★★

Courtroom drama   1961 · UK · BW · 123min

This badly dated courtroom drama from Sidney J Furie proves that some things never change – Jess Conrad, Dudley Sutton and their pals are suspected of murder simply because they're young and rebellious. The film becomes both patronising and predictable as canny lawyer Richard Todd champions the lads' cause, but the strong cast redeems the movie. DP

Richard Todd *Victor Webster* • Robert Morley *Lewis Montgomery* • Felix Aylmer *Judge* • Dudley Sutton *Stan Coulter* • Ronald Lacey *Billy Herne* • Tony Garnett *Ginger Thompson* • Jess Conrad *Barney Lee* • Wilfred Bramble [Wilfrid Brambell] *Robert Brewer* • Wensley Pithey *Mr Coulter* ■ *Dir* Sidney J Furie • *Scr* Stuart Douglas

The Boys ★★★ PG

Black comedy   1991 · US · Colour · 90min

Based on the careers of William Link and Richard Levinson, this is a film *à clef*, in other words a biopic with the names changed to allow a little dramatic latitude. Link and Levinson were the writing duo behind such TV hits as *Columbo* and *Murder, She Wrote*, until the latter died from cancer contracted from inhaling the former's cigarette smoke. Written by Link, the film is directed without mawkishness by Glenn Jordan. The inspired teaming of James Woods and John Lithgow lifts this TV movie a notch above the pack. DP

James Woods *Walter Farmer* • John Lithgow *Artie Margulies* • Joanna Gleason *Marie Margulies* • Eve Gordon *Amanda Freeman* • Alan Rosenberg *Psychiatrist* • Rosemary Dunsmore *Helene Farmer* ■ *Dir* Glenn Jordan • *Scr* William Link

Boys ★★ 15

Romantic drama   1995 · US · Colour · 82min

In a flimsy but watchable teen drama, Lukas Haas is the boarding school boy whose friends discover sexy and mysterious Winona Ryder unconscious in a field. He decides to smuggle her back to his dormitory. Unfortunately, the unravelling secrets of her past aren't quite as thrilling as one would hope for. But both Haas and Ryder give good turns, and there are some nice supporting performances. JB Swearing, drug abuse, violence. DVD

Winona Ryder *Patty Vare* • Lukas Haas *John Baker Jr* • Skeet Ulrich *Bud Valentine* • John C Reilly *Officer Kellogg Curry* • Bill Sage *Officer Bill Martone* • Matt Malloy *Bartender* • Wiley Wiggins *John Phillips* • Russell Young *John Van Slieder* • Marty McDonough *Teacher* • Charlie Hofheimer *John Cooke* • James LeGros *Fenton Ray* • Chris Cooper *Mr John Baker* ■ *Dir* Stacy Cochran • *Scr* Stacy Cochran, from the short story *Twenty Minutes* by James Salter

The Boys ★★★★ 18

Drama   1998 · Aus/UK · Colour · 81min

This Australian-set drama is the bleak, disorienting flipside to *Neighbours*. David Wenham, just released from prison, returns to his suburban home, where he immediately begins to torment girlfriend Toni Collette, his sleazy weak-willed brothers, their girlfriends and even his long-suffering mother. Although confined largely to one set, director Rowan Woods sustains an almost suffocating air of menace, which is further heightened by dislocating flash-forwards to an unknown future crime. Collette demonstrates once again her range, but the real star here is Wenham, who delivers frighteningly believable portrait of a sociopath. JF Violence, swearing. DVD

David Wenham *Brett Sprague* • Toni Collette *Michelle* • Lynette Curran *Sandra Sprague* • John Polson *Glenn Sprague* • Jeanette Cronin *Jackie* • Anthony Hayes *Stevie Sprague* • Anna Lise *Nola* • Pete Smith *George "Abo"* ■ *Dir* Rowan Woods • *Scr* Stephen Sewell, from the play by Gordon Graham

The Boys & Girl from County Clare ★★★ 15

Comedy drama   2003 · UK/Ger · Colour · 87min

Levity and geniality are key to John Irvin's tale of 1960s sibling rivalry, which sees Colm Meaney head home for the first time since he stole Charlotte Bradley from brother Bernard Hill and left her to raise their daughter alone. Returning to face the music simply to compete in an annual band contest is a whopping contrivance. Yet the evocative photography and a willing cast (that includes Andrea Corr of Irish band The Corrs) make it easy to forgive the narrative flaws. DP Swearing, sex scenes, nudity. DVD

Andrea Corr *Anne* • Colm Meaney *Jimmy* • Bernard Hill *John Joe* • Charlotte Bradley *Maisie* • Shaun Evans *Teddy* ■ *Dir* John Irvin • *Scr* Nicholas Adams

Boys and Girls ★ 12

Romantic comedy   2000 · US · Colour · 89min

A miscast Claire Forlani forms a close friendship with Freddie Prinze Jr, taking the entire movie to reach the obvious amorous conclusion. This patchwork quilt of clichés is not aided by the clumsy episodic structure and grating, one-dimensional characters. JC DVD

Freddie Prinze Jr *Ryan* • Claire Forlani *Jennifer* • Jason Biggs *Hunter* • Heather Donahue *Megan* • Amanda Detmer *Amy* • Alyson Hannigan *Betty* ■ *Dir* Robert Iscove • *Scr* The Drews [Andrew Lowery, Andrew Miller]

The Boys Are Back ★★★ 12

Drama based on a true story
2009 · UK/Aus/NZ · Colour · 99min

Based on the memoir by Simon Carr, this drama from *Shine* director Scott Hicks stars Clive Owen as Joe Warr, a British sports writer living in Australia, and follows the expat's unconventional attempts to raise his eight-year-old son following the untimely death of his wife. But when his estranged teenage son from a previous marriage comes to visit, a rudderless Joe has to concentrate on re-establishing his relationship with him, too. Though decently directed, the film covers little unexplored territory. However, Clive Owen's multi-faceted performance at least gives some substance to a rather flimsy plot. DA Sexual references. DVD

Clive Owen *Joe Warr* • Emma Booth *Laura* • Laura Fraser *Katy* • George MacKay *Harry* • Nicholas McAnulty *Artie* • Julia Blake *Barbara* • Chris Haywood *Tom* • Erik Thomson *Digby* ■ *Dir* Scott Hicks • *Scr* Allan Cubitt, from the memoirs by Simon Carr

Boys Don't Cry ★★★ 18

Drama based on a true story
1999 · US · Colour · 113min

The tragic true-life case history of Teena Brandon, a young girl from Nebraska who disguised herself as a man and was brutally raped and murdered in 1993, is compassionately brought to the screen by writer/director Kimberly Peirce. While Oscar winner Hilary Swank gives a remarkable performance as the hero(ine), there's an exploitative sordidness to the enterprise that limits our sympathy. NS DVD

Hilary Swank *Teena Brandon/Brandon Teena* • Peter Sarsgaard *John* • Chloë Sevigny *Lana* • Brendan Sexton III *Tom* • Alison Folland *Kate* • Alicia Goranson *Candace* • Matt McGrath *Lonny* • Rob Campbell *Brian* ■ *Dir* Kimberly Peirce • *Scr* Kimberly Peirce, Andy Bienen

The Boys from Brazil ★★★ 18

Thriller   1978 · US · Colour · 119min

Ira Levin's ingenious novel about the cloning of Hitler's body tissue, producing identical little boys who would revive the Third Reich, is given the epic treatment by director Franklin J Schaffner. Masterminding the genetic engineering is the infamous Dr Mengele, played by Gregory Peck in a convincing departure from his usual good-guy roles. James Mason is his accomplice and Laurence Olivier is the Nazi-hunter modelled on Simon Wiesenthal who tracks them down. More plausible now than it was in the late 1970s and still an accomplished, globe-trotting thriller. AT Violence. DVD Blu

Gregory Peck *Dr Josef Mengele* • Laurence Olivier *Ezra Lieberman* • James Mason *Eduard Seibert* • Lilli Palmer *Esther Lieberman* • Uta Hagen *Frieda Maloney* • Rosemary Harris *Herta Doring* • Jeremy Black *Bobby/Jack/Erich/Simon* • Steve Guttenberg *Barry Kohler* • John Rubinstein *David Bennett* • Michael Gough *Mr Harrington* • Bruno Ganz *Professor Bruckner* • Denholm Elliott *Sidney Beynon* • Prunella Scales *Mrs Harrington* ■ *Dir* Franklin J Schaffner • *Scr* Heywood Gould, from the novel by Ira Levin

The Boys from Syracuse ★★★ U

Musical comedy   1940 · US · BW · 73min

Undercast (and in desperate need of colour), this jolly romp is the film of Rodgers and Hart's Broadway hit, itself based on Shakespeare's *Comedy of Errors*. Only Martha Raye and Joe Penner seem to capture the requisite Broadway brashness, and a wan Allan Jones in the lead looks uncomfortable and strained. Period comedians Charles Butterworth and Eric Blore have a camp old time. TS

Allan Jones *Antipholus of Ephesus/Antipholus of Syracuse* • Martha Raye *Luce* • Joe Penner *Dromio of Ephesus/Dromio of Syracuse* • Rosemary Lane *Phyllis* • Charles Butterworth *Duke of Ephesus* • Irene Hervey *Adriana* • Alan Mowbray *Angelo* • Eric Blore *Pinch* • Samuel S Hinds *Aegon* ■ *Dir* Edward Sutherland [A Edward Sutherland] • *Scr* Leonard Spigelgass, Charles Grayson, from the play by George Abbott, with music and lyrics by Richard Rodgers, Lorenz Hart, from the play *Comedy of Errors* by William Shakespeare

The Boys in Blue ★ PG

Comedy   1983 · UK · Colour · 87min

This is a serious contender for the unwanted title of worst British film ever made. Over 40 years after he helped adapt Sidney Gilliat's story for the Will Hay vehicle *Ask a Policeman*, director Val Guest returned for this shudderingly awful remake, with TV comedy duo Tommy Cannon and Bobby Ball as the bumpkin bobbies whose station is reprieved when a gang of villains moves into their manor. DP DVD

Bobby Ball *Police Constable Bobby Ball* • Tommy Cannon *Sergeant Tommy Cannon* • Suzanne Danielle *Kim* • Roy Kinnear *Hector Lloyd* • Eric Sykes *Chief Constable* • Jack Douglas *Chief Superintendent* • Edward Judd *Hilling* • Jon Pertwee *Coastguard* • Arthur English *Farmer* ■ *Dir* Val Guest • *Scr* Val Guest, from Sidney Gilliat's story for the film *Ask a Policeman*

Boys in Brown ★★★

Crime drama   1949 · UK · BW · 85min

Former variety comedian Jack Warner brings quiet conviction to one of the avuncular roles that brought him film fame in the 1940s. This time he's the governor of a boys' reformatory who does his best to convert his charges to the straight and narrow. Based on a play by Reginald Beckwith, this is a taut tale with a gallery of fine player; the most unregenerate of the delinquents is played by Dirk Bogarde, who was to menace Warner in the classic thriller *The Blue Lamp*. TV

Jack Warner *Governor* • Richard Attenborough *Jackie Knowles* • Dirk Bogarde *Alfie Rawlins* • Jimmy Hanley *Bill Foster* • Barbara Murray *Kitty Hurst* • Patrick Holt *Tigson* • Andrew Crawford *Casey* • Thora Hird *Mrs Knowles* ■ *Dir* Montgomery Tully • *Scr* Montgomery Tully, from a play by Reginald Beckwith

The Boys in Company C ★★★

War drama   1978 · US/HK · Colour · 125min

This Vietnam War drama was designed as a quickie to cash in on the then-imminent release of *Apocalypse Now*. Following a bunch of raw recruits played by a largely unknown cast, the movie explores the ideas and moral terrain later refined by *Platoon*. But this tour of duty ends surprisingly with a soccer match between GIs and a Vietnamese team, effectively reducing the war to an absurdist symbol. AT

Stan Shaw *Tyrone Washington* • Andrew Stevens *Billy Ray Pike* • James Canning *Alvin Foster* • Michael Lembeck *Vinnie Fazio* • Craig Wasson *Dave Bisbee* • Scott Hylands *Captain Collins* • James Whitmore Jr *Lieutenant Archer* • Noble Willingham *Sergeant Curry* • Lee Ermey [R Lee Ermey] *Sergeant Loyce* ■ *Dir* Sidney J Furie • *Scr* Rick Natkin, Sidney J Furie

The Boys in the Band ★★★ 15

Comedy drama   1970 · US · Colour · 114min

The first Hollywood film on the subject of male homosexuality, director William Friedkin's stagey version of the off-Broadway hit captures early glimmers of gay liberation while dealing with the self-hating, straight-acting and overly camp stereotypes of the era. Eight gay men gather for a Manhattan birthday party and a heterosexual visitor from the host's past turns up, adding vicious bitchiness to the proceedings. It's all very dated, but some of the lines are still hilarious. AJ

Kenneth Nelson *Michael* • Leonard Frey *Harold* • Frederick Combs *Donald* • Cliff Gorman *Emory* • Reuben Greene *Bernard* • Robert La Tourneaux *Cowboy* • Laurence Luckinbill *Hank* • Keith Prentice *Larry* • Peter White *Alan* ■ *Dir* William Friedkin • *Scr* Mart Crowley, from his play

The Boys Next Door ★★ 18

Crime drama   1985 · US · Colour · 86min

Penelope Spheeris, best known for *Wayne's World*, directs this tough, grim drama about two 18-year-olds (played by Maxwell Caulfield and Charlie Sheen) who embark on a series of brutal murders for no apparent reason. Although a sometimes shocking look at teen violence, the film eventually seems too slick for its own good, and any message Spheeris may have been trying to get across is lost in a cacophony of flashiness and moody glares from the two leads. JB

Maxwell Caulfield *Roy Alston* • Charlie Sheen *Bo Richards* • Christopher McDonald *Woods* • Hank Garrett *Detective Ed Hanley* • Patti D'Arbanville *Angie* ■ *Dir* Penelope Spheeris • *Scr* Glen Morgan, James Wong

The Boys Next Door ★★★

Comedy drama   1996 · US · Colour · 99min

This high-class made-for-TV drama grabbed a bag of award nominations in the US. The feel-good tale focuses on four men – Nathan Lane, Robert Sean Leonard, Courtney B Vance and Michael Jeter – with mental health disorders watched over by sympathetic social worker Tony Goldwyn, who is helping them learn to fend for themselves. Sensitively acted by the top-notch cast, it occasionally gets too syrupy, but only the most cynical will fail to be moved. JF

Nathan Lane *Norman Bulansky* • Robert Sean Leonard *Barry Klemper* • Tony Goldwyn *Jack Palmer* • Michael Jeter *Arnold Wiggins* •

Courtney B Vance *Lucien P Singer* • Mare Winningham *Sheila* ■ *Dir* John Erman • *Scr* William Blinn, from the play by Tom Griffin

Boys' Night Out ★★
Comedy 1962 · US · Colour · 113min

A bachelor and his three married friends decide to rent an apartment with a dishy blonde inside and use it, and her, for a week each. What they don't know is that the lady of the night is actually a sociology student doing her thesis on the American male, and she is singularly inimpressed with the men's ability to sustain a playboy lifestyle. This may be revealing of early 1960s sexual mores but falls absolutely flat as a comedy. **AT**

Kim Novak *Cathy* • James Garner *Fred Williams* • Tony Randall *George Drayton* • Howard Duff *Doug Jackson* • Janet Blair *Marge Drayton* • Patti Page *Joanne McIlenny* • Jessie Royce Landis *Ethel Williams* • Oscar Homolka *D Prokosch* ■ *Dir* Michael Gordon • *Scr* Ira Wallach, Marion Hargrove (adaptation), from a story by Marvin Worth, Arne Sultan

The Boys of Paul Street ★★★ U
Comedy drama 1968 · US/Hun · Colour · 104min

Previously filmed in Hollywood by Frank Borzage as *No Greater Glory* in 1934, this Oscar-nominated adaptation by Zoltan Fabri of Ferenc Molnar's autobiographical novel returned to its original Budapest locations. Although intended as an allegory on the futility of war, the feud between two rival gangs over an unclaimed patch of land also has a Party angle, as it's the benevolent forces of authority that eventually claim the lot for building work. The film still has the freshness that typified most Eastern European cinema in the mid-1960s. **DP** In Hungarian, English.

Anthony Kemp *Nemecsek* • William Burleigh *Boka* • Julien Holdaway *Feriats* • Peter Delmar *Older Pasztor* • Andras Avar *Szabo* • Mari Torocsik *Nemecsek's mother* • Sandor Pecsi *Professor Racz* ■ *Dir* Zoltan Fabri • *Scr* Zoltan Fabri, Endre Bohém, from the novel *A Pal Utcai Fiuk* by Ferenc Molnar

Boys of the City ★★
Crime comedy 1940 · US · BW · 68min

The first in the series featuring the East Side Kids, after they were the Dead End Kids and before they were the Bowery Boys, was typical of the films of the streetwise gang – whatever they were called. The crude farce (also known as *The Ghost Creeps*) has the lads, headed by Leo Gorcey and Bobby Jordan, sent to the country where they get involved with murder in a haunted house. **RB**

Bobby Jordan *Danny* • Leo Gorcey *Muggs* • Dave O'Brien *Knuckles Dolan* • George Humbert *Tony* • Hally Chester [Hal E Chester] *Boy* • Sunshine Morrison ["Sunshine Sammy" Morrison] *Morrison* *Scruno* ■ *Dir* Joseph H Lewis • *Scr* William Lively, from his story

Boys on the Side ★★★★ 15
Drama 1995 · US/Fr · Colour · 112min

Director Herbert Ross's emotional rollercoaster ride has three crackerjack central performances oiling this unconventional fugitive tale. Lesbian Whoopi Goldberg, HIV-positive Mary-Louise Parker and pregnant Drew Barrymore head for California, but find themselves grounded in Arizona when Parker falls ill. It's a tender drama that's smart, sassy and really quite special, and when Roy Orbison's *You Got It* strikes up there won't be a dry eye in the house. **AJ** Brief nudity, violence, swearing.

Whoopi Goldberg *Jane DeLuca* • Mary-Louise Parker *Robin Nickerson* • Drew Barrymore *Holly* • Matthew McConaughey *Abe Lincoln* • James Remar *Alex* • Billy Wirth *Nick* • Anita Gillette *Elaine* • Dennis Boutsikaris *Massarelli* • Estelle Parsons *Louise* • Amy Aquino *Anna* ■ *Dir* Herbert Ross • *Scr* Don Roos

Boys Town ★★★
Biographical drama 1938 · US · Sepia · 92min

In this corny and manipulative tear-jerker, Spencer Tracy plays Father Flanagan, a Nebraskan priest who wants to set up a sanctuary for society's lost causes, while Mickey Rooney is one of the juvenile delinquents he tries to save. When the picture opened, the real Father Flanagan complained about the studio gloss and how that had affected donations since people assumed his refuge was rolling in money. Mayer went on the radio saying, "Boys Town does need your money, so keep it coming, Americans!" Tracy won his second consecutive Oscar for this film and dedicated it to Flanagan. **AT**

Spencer Tracy *Father Edward Flanagan* • Mickey Rooney *Whitey Marsh* • Henry Hull *Dave Morris* • Leslie Fenton *Dan Farrow* • Addison Richards *Judge* • Edward Norris *Joe Marsh* • Gene Reynolds *Tony Ponessa* • Minor Watson *Bishop* ■ *Dir* Norman Taurog • *Scr* John Meehan, Dore Schary, from a story by Dore Schary, Eleanore Griffin

Boys Will Be Boys ★★★ U
Comedy 1935 · UK · BW · 72min

Although Will Hay had included the "Fourth Form at St Michael's" sketch in his music-hall act since the early 1920s, this was the first time he donned the familiar mortar board, gown and pince-nez on the screen. He plays Dr Alec Smart, whose rogue's progress takes him from a prison classroom to the headmaster's study of that school for crooks, Narkover. The script is based on characters invented by JB Morton for the legendary "Beachcomber" newspaper column, and Hay retains the blend of bluster and dishonesty that makes his films irresistible. **DP** DVD

Will Hay *Dr Alec Smart* • Gordon Harker *Faker Brown* • Claude Dampier *Theo P Finch* • Jimmy Hanley *Cyril Brown* • Davy Burnaby *Colonel Crableigh* • Norma Varden *Lady Korking* • Charles Farrell (2) *Louis Brown* • Percy Walsh *Governor* ■ *Dir* Will Beaudine • *Scr* Will Hay, Robert Edmunds, from characters by JB Morton

Boyz N the Hood ★★★★★ 15
Drama 1991 · US · Colour · 112min

Alongside Quentin Tarantino's *Reservoir Dogs*, this was the most astonishing and hard-hitting directorial debut of the 1990s. John Singleton was a mere 23 when he wrote and directed this powerhouse picture about growing up black in inner-city America. Rougher and readier than Spike Lee on the same subject, Singleton largely avoids sermonising to present a brutally candid view of the realities of LA street life. Cuba Gooding Jr and co-stars Morris Chestnut and Ice Cube impress as the friends for whom the future looks uncertain (if not downright unlikely), while Laurence Fishburne is outstanding as Gooding's disciplinarian father. **DP** Violence, swearing, drug abuse, nudity.

Larry Fishburne [Laurence Fishburne] *Furious Styles* • Ice Cube *Doughboy Baker* • Cuba Gooding Jr *Tre Styles* • Nia Long *Brandi* • Morris Chestnut *Ricky Baker* • Tyra Ferrell *Mrs Baker* • Angela Bassett *Reva Styles* • Redge Green *Chris* ■ *Dir/Scr* John Singleton

Braddock: Missing in Action III ★ 18
Action thriller 1988 · US · Colour · 98min

Dispatching Colonel James Braddock to 1980s Vietnam to find both the wife he believed dead and the son he never knew he had, this is a sequel too far for Chuck Norris and his director brother Aaron. Not only is this gung-ho action tosh morally dubious, but it's also exceedingly dull. **DP**

Chuck Norris *Colonel James Braddock* • Roland Harrah III *Van Tan Cang* • Aki Aleong *General Quoc* • Miki Kim *Lin Tang Cang* • Yehuda Efroni *Reverend Polanski* • Ron Barker *Mik* ■ *Dir* Aaron Norris • *Scr* James Bruner, Chuck Norris, from the character created by Arthur Silver, Larry Levinson, Steve Bing

The Brady Bunch Movie ★★★ 12
Comedy 1995 · US · Colour · 84min

In the 1990s, Hollywood studios desperately ransacked their old TV archives for cinema remakes, with very mixed results. This one is probably the most innovative of the lot, even if it doesn't always work. If anyone can't remember, the Brady bunch were a cute-as-pie American family suffering the mildest of 1970s domestic discord every week. And in this remake, the same applies, except that everyone else is now living in the 1990s. A cue, then, for loads of postmodernist laughs, expertly served up by a cast headed by Shelley Long and Gary Cole. **JF** Some swearing. DVD

Shelley Long *Carol Brady* • Gary Cole *Mike Brady* • Michael McKean *Mr Dittmeyer* • Christine Taylor *Marcia Brady* • Christopher Daniel Barnes *Greg Brady* • Jennifer Elise Cox *Jan Brady* • Paul Sutera *Peter Brady* • Olivia Hack *Cindy Brady* • Jesse Lee *Bobby Brady* • Henriette Mantel *Alice* ■ *Dir* Betty Thomas • *Scr* Laurice Elehwany, Rick Copp, Bonnie Turner, Terry Turner, from characters by Sherwood Schwartz

The Brain ★★★ 12
Science fiction 1962 · W Ger/UK · BW · 83min

Hammer Horror veteran Freddie Francis does a decent job directing this version of Curt Siodmak's *Donovan's Brain*. Peter Van Eyck is the scientist controlled by the power-crazed organ of a sadistic tycoon kept alive after a plane crash. More of a mystery than an all-stops-out horror, the moody tale has some eerie moments and is efficiently involving. A competent cast injects new life into a familiar story. **AJ**

Anne Heywood *Anna* • Peter Van Eyck *Doctor* • Peter Corrie • Cecil Parker *Stevenson* • Bernard Lee *Frank Shears* • Ellen Schwiers *Ella* • Maxine Audley *Marion* • Jeremy Spenser *Martin* • Ann Sears *Secretary* ■ *Dir* Freddie Francis • *Scr* Robert Stewart, Phil Macki, from the novel *Donovan's Brain* by Curt Siodmak

The Brain ★ PG
Comedy caper 1969 · Fr/US/It · Colour · 95min

David Niven plays a master criminal in this frenetic French comedy that needs a brain transplant in the script department. Put in charge of security for the transportation of Nato's military funds – which he intends to snatch – Niven finds himself competing for the loot with two French rogues (Jean-Paul Belmondo and Bourvil) as well as with the Mafia. A mess. **TH** French dubbed.

David Niven *The Brain* • Jean-Paul Belmondo *Arthur* • Bourvil *Anatole* • Eli Wallach *Scannapieco* • Silvia Monti *Sofia* • Fernand Valois *Bruno* ■ *Dir* Gérard Oury • *Scr* Gérard Oury, Marcel Julian, Daniele Thompson

Brain Damage ★★★★ 18
Horror comedy 1988 · US · Colour · 85min

This outrageously gory and excessively violent fable is infused with the junk culture and trash aesthetic of cult director Frank Henenlotter's demented imagination. Elmer, the all-singing, all-dancing alien parasite, injects a euphoric hallucinogenic fluid into his host, Rick Herbst, in return for donors it can suck brains from. Quirky, inventive and completely offensive – some death scenes deliberately use pornographic imagery – this is a wickedly humorous slice of warped genius. **AJ**

Rick Herbst *Brian* • Gordon MacDonald *Mike* • Jennifer Lowry *Barbara* • Theo Barnes *Morris Ackerman* • Lucille Saint-Peter *Martha Ackerman* • Vicki Darnell *Blonde in Hell Club* • Joe Gonzales *Guy in shower* • Bradlee Rhodes *Night watchman* • Don Henenlotter *Policeman* ■ *Dir/Scr* Frank Henenlotter

Brain Dead ★★★ 15
Psychological horror 1990 · US · Colour · 80min

Neurologist Bill Pullman is blackmailed by business friend Bill Paxton into studying the case history of paranoid accountant-turned-serial killer Bud Cort in order to unlock the secrets in his mind. After brain surgery and shock therapy, however, Cort switches personalities with Pullman, turning director Adam Simon's enjoyably quirky *Twilight Zone* update into a crazed splatter romp. Lively and interesting, even if it is hard to follow exactly what's going on. **AJ**

Bill Pullman *Rex Martin* • Bill Paxton *Jim Reston* • Bud Cort *Jack Halsey* • Patricia Charbonneau *Dana Martin* • Nicholas Pryor *Conklin/Ramsen* • George Kennedy *Vance* • Brian Brophy *Ellis* ■ *Dir* Adam Simon • *Scr* Charles Beaumont, Adam Simon, from a story by Charles Beaumont

Brain Donors ★ PG
Comedy 1992 · US · Colour · 76min

Director Dennis Dugan's flat farce has the occasional flash of high-energy outrageousness, but little else to commend it. Shyster lawyer John Turturro and his two wacky assistants, Bob Nelson and Mel Smith, take over rich widow Nancy Marchand's ballet company, with suitably dire consequences. Dugan's laboured burlesque throws every tired gag into the frantic action hoping it hits the fan – sorry, screen. **AJ**

John Turturro *Roland T Flakfizer* • Bob Nelson *Jacques* • Mel Smith *Rocco Melonchek* • Nancy Marchand *Lillian Oglethorpe* • John Savident *Lazlo* • George De La Pena *"The Great" Volare* • Spike Alexander *Alan* • Juli Donald *Lisa* • Teri Copley *Blonde* ■ *Dir* Dennis Dugan • *Scr* Pat Proft

The Brain Eaters ★★ PG
Science-fiction adventure 1958 · US · BW · 60min

An uncredited adaptation of Robert Heinlein's landmark alien invasion novel *The Puppet Masters*, this routine B-movie exemplifies the atomic-era paranoia genre. Despite the laughable, hairy, neck-burrowing parasites and the stock scientist-versus-the-military scenario, director Bruno VeSota creates an imaginatively bleak atmosphere through tilted camera angles and crisp photography. Though no great shakes, this sci-fi adventure is only an hour long and *Star Trek* fanatics can see Leonard Nimoy in an early role. **AJ** DVD

Edwin Nelson [Ed Nelson] *Dr Kettering* • Joanna Lee *Alice* • Jody Fair *Elaine* • Alan Frost *Glenn* • Jack Hill *Senator Powers* • David Hughes (2) *Dr Wyler* • Robert Ball *Dan Walker* • Greigh Phillips *Sheriff* • Orville Sherman *Cameron* • Leonard Nimoy *Protector* ■ *Dir* Bruno VeSota • *Scr* Gordon Urquhart

The Brain from Planet Arous ★★ PG
Science-fiction thriller 1958 · US · BW · 70min

This all-time camp schlock classic stars bad-movie icon John Agar, an absolute hoot as the nuclear physicist possessed by a floating alien brain called Gor, in its first step towards Earth domination. Soon Agar is sporting silver contact lenses and setting model planes on fire with a glance, while his pet dog is taken over by Gor's rival for the final axe battle. Unsurprisingly, director Nathan Hertz changed his name to Nathan Juran later the same year. **AJ** DVD

John Agar *Steve* • Joyce Meadows *Sally Fallon* • Robert Fuller *Dan* • Thomas Browne Henry *John Fallon* • Henry Travis *Colonel Grogley* • Tim Graham *Sheriff Paine* ■ *Dir* Nathan Hertz [Nathan Juran] • *Scr* Ray Buffum

The Brain Machine ★★ U
Crime thriller 1954 · UK · BW · 79min

This British B-movie begins, promisingly, in sci-fi mode but soon lapses into routine thrillerdom. The machine of the title, known as an "electroencephalograph", is attached to an accident victim who may also be a psychopath. Despite its cheap production values and leaden acting, the picture has a trashy energy that can be enjoyed if you disengage your own brain. **AT**

Patrick Barr *Dr Geoffrey Allen* • Elizabeth Allan *Dr Philippa Roberts* • Maxwell Reed *Frank Smith* • Russell Napier *Inspector Durham* • Gibb McLaughlin *Spencer Simon* • Edwin Richfield *Ryan* • Neil Hallett *Sergeant John Harris* • Vanda Godsell *Mae* • Bill Nagy *Charlie* ■ *Dir/Scr* Ken Hughes

Brain Smasher... a Love Story ★★ PG
Comedy action adventure 1993 · US · Colour · 84min

In straight-to-video director Albert Pyun's mildly amusing action comedy, bouncer Andrew Dice Clay joins supermodel Teri Hatcher and her botanist sister to stop a sacred mystical lotus flower, which holds the key to unlimited power over matter, from falling into the hands of a suave band of Chinese ninja monks. **AJ** DVD

B

Andrew Dice Clay *Ed Malloy* • Teri Hatcher *Samantha Crain* • Deborah Van Valkenburgh *Cammy Crain* • Yuji Okamoto *Wu* • Brion James *Brown* • Tim Thomerson *Black* • Charles Rocket *Jones* ▪ *Dir/Scr* Albert Pyun

The Brain That Wouldn't Die ★

Horror thriller · 1959 · US · BW · 81min

After decapitating his fiancée Virginia Leith in a car crash, demented surgeon Jason Evers decides to transplant her still living head onto the body of a facially scarred stripper. But Leith wants to die and telepathically manipulates the giant pinhead mutant locked up in Evers's cupboard to go on the rampage. This rock-bottom fantasy exploitation pic reaches high levels of engaging absurdity through poverty-row production values and ludicrous, blood-soaked action. This appalling cheapie has nonetheless become a brainless cult classic. AJ

Jason Evers *Dr Bill Cortner* • Leslie Daniel *Kurt* • Paula Maurice *B-Girl* • Virginia Leith *Jan Compton* • Adele Lamont *Doris* • Bruce Brighton *Doctor* • Lola Mason *Donna Williams* • Audrey Devereau *Jeannie* ▪ *Dir* Joseph Green • *Scr* Joseph Green, from a story by Rex Carlton, Joseph Green

Braindead ★★★★★ 18

Comedy horror · 1992 · NZ · Colour · 99min

New Zealand director Peter Jackson's horrendously funny gross-out shocker is a brilliant black comedy and the ultimate gore movie. Timothy Balme's mother gets bitten by a Sumatran "rat monkey" carrying a living-dead virus and turns into a rabid zombie with terrible table manners. Cue zombie sex, kung fu priests, re-animated spinal columns and half-eaten craniums, all building towards a final, gore-drenched massacre. Jackson's outrageously sick ground-breaker is a virtuoso *Grand Guignol* masterpiece. AJ Sex scenes, violence, swearing. **DVD**

Timothy Balme *Lionel* • Diana Peñalver *Paquita* • Liz Moody *Mum* • Ian Watkin *Uncle Les* • Brenda Kendall *Nurse McTavish* • Stuart Devenie *Father McGruder* • Jed Brophy *Void* • Elizabeth Brimilcombe *Zombie mum* • Peter Jackson *Undertaker's assistant* ▪ *Dir* Peter Jackson • *Scr* Peter Jackson, Stephen Sinclair, Frances Walsh [Fran Walsh]

Brainscan ★★★ 15

Science-fiction horror
1994 · Can/US/UK · Colour · 90min

Misfit loner Edward Furlong sends off for the virtual reality game *Brainscan*, advertised as the ultimate in terror, only to wake up with memory loss and a severed foot in the refrigerator. Frank Langella is the cop on his trail. But will he believe the murder is really the work of the Trickster, a vile demon who represents the dark side of anybody playing the game? Despite some inferior special effects, this bleak and intense chiller uses the virtual reality hook effectively. AJ **DVD**

Edward Furlong *Michael Brower* • Frank Langella *Detective Hayden* • T Rider-Smith *Trickster* • Amy Hargreaves *Kimberly* • Jamie Marsh *Kyle* • Victor Ertmanis *Martin* • David Hemblen *Dr Fromberg* • Vlasta Vrana *Frank* ▪ *Dir* John Flynn • *Scr* Andrew Kevin Walker, from a story by Brian Owens

Brainstorm ★★

Crime thriller · 1965 · US · BW · 114min

Portly actor William Conrad, best remembered for his television cop Frank Cannon, directs here. Jeffrey Hunter plots to kill Dana Andrews, not because Andrews's acting is extremely dull and boring, but because Hunter's in love with the latter's wife, the beautiful Anne Francis. Meanwhile, wise Viveca Lindfors counsels from the wings. Hunter acquits himself well, but the film would have worked better with some judicious editing. TS

Jeff Hunter [Jeffrey Hunter] *James Grayam* • Anne Francis *Lorrie Benson* • Dana Andrews *Cort Benson* • Viveca Lindfors *Dr Elizabeth Larstadt* ▪ *Dir* William Conrad • *Scr* Mann Rubin, from a story by Larry Marcus

Brainstorm ★★★★ 15

Science-fiction thriller
1983 · US · Colour · 101min

In later films, such as *The Lawnmower Man* and *Strange Days*, it's called virtual reality. But when *2001: a Space Odyssey* special effects genius Douglas Trumbull directed this film (which turned out to be Natalie Wood's last), he termed it "telepathic engineering". Louise Fletcher (giving a stand-out performance) and Christopher Walken invent a headset enabling the wearer to experience the sensory recordings of others. Although flawed and naive, Trumbull's metaphysical odyssey is a technically dazzling triumph. AJ

Christopher Walken *Michael Brace* • Natalie Wood *Karen Brace* • Cliff Robertson *Alex Terson* • Louise Fletcher *Lillian Reynolds* • Donald Hotton *Landon Marks* • Joe Dorsey *Hal Abramson* • Darrell Larson *Security technician* ▪ *Dir* Douglas Trumbull • *Scr* Robert Statzel, Phillip Frank Messina, from a story by Bruce Joel Rubin

Brainwaves ★★ 18

Science-fiction thriller
1982 · US · Colour · 76min

This suffers from a low budget and some clumsy writing and direction. Suzanna Love plays a woman who regains consciousness after a coma only to discover that, thanks to some ground-breaking surgery, she has inherited the brainwaves of a murdered woman. There are some nifty moments but the main point of interest is the eclectic casting: as well as Vera Miles and Keir Dullea there is Tony Curtis in a ripe cameo as an improbable brain surgeon. JF

Keir Dullea *Julian Bedford* • Suzanna Love *Kaylie Bedford* • Vera Miles *Marian* • Percy Rodrigues *Dr Robinson* • Tony Curtis *Dr Clavius* • Paul Wilson [Paul Willson] *Dr Schroder* • Ryan Seitz *Danny Bedford* • Nicholas Love *Willy Meiser* ▪ *Dir* Ulli Lommel • *Scr* Ulli Lommel, Suzanna Love

Bram Stoker's Dracula ★★★★ 18

Horror · 1992 · US · Colour · 121min

Eerie, romantic and operatic, this exquisitely mounted revamp of the undead legend is a supreme artistic achievement. Francis Ford Coppola's film is grandiose in visual approach and uses every cinematic trick – from the basic atmospheric lighting of the silent era to today's more sophisticated techniques – to accentuate the poetic sensuality of Bram Stoker's novel rather than the more exploitative bloodsucking elements. Keanu Reeves's acting may not be to everyone's taste, but, as the tired count who has overdosed on immortality, Gary Oldman's towering performance holds centre stage and burns itself into the memory. AJ Violence, nudity. **DVD** **BL**

Gary Oldman *Dracula* • Winona Ryder *Mina Murray/Elisabeta* • Anthony Hopkins *Professor Abraham Van Helsing* • Keanu Reeves *Jonathan Harker* • Richard E Grant *Doctor Jack Seward* • Cary Elwes *Lord Arthur Holmwood* • Bill Campbell *Quincey P Morris* • Sadie Frost *Lucy Westenra* • Tom Waits *RM Renfield* ▪ *Dir* Francis Ford Coppola • *Scr* James V Hart, from the novel by Bram Stoker • *Cinematographer* Michael Ballhaus

Bram Stoker's Legend of the Mummy ★★ 15

Horror · 1998 · US · Colour · 95min

This is a familiar cocktail of ancient curses and dusty bandages from B-movie veteran Jeffrey Obrow. When her father incurs the wrath of the re-animated Queen Tera, Amy Locane enlists the aid of retired tomb raider Louis Gossett Jr to return the Egyptian ruler to eternal rest. This blunt-edged chiller features the least believable mummy make-up in horror history. AJ Swearing, nudity. **DVD**

Louis Gossett Jr *Corbeck* • Amy Locane *Margaret Trelawny* • Eric Lutes *Robert Wyatt* • Mark Lindsay Chapman *Daw* • Lloyd Bochner *Abel Trelawny* • Mary Jo Catlett *Mrs Grant* • Aubrey Morris *Dr Winchester* • Laura Otis *Lily* ▪ *Dir* Jeffrey Obrow • *Scr* Jeffrey Obrow, Lars Hauglie, John Penney, from the novel *The Jewel of the Seven Stars* by Bram Stoker

Bram Stoker's Shadowbuilder ★ 18

Horror · 1997 · US/Can · Colour · 96min

A demon tries to open the gates of hell by sacrificing an innocent child during a solar eclipse. A renegade, chain-smoking priest must stop the ancient prophecy coming true in a silly, sexed-up shocker that has more to do with Jackie Collins than Bram Stoker. This is a death, darkness and blasphemy-fuelled wash-out. AJ Some swearing, violence, nudity. **DVD**

Kevin Zegers *Chris Hatcher* • Tony Todd *Evert Covey* • Michael Rooker *Father Vassey* ▪ *Dir* Jamie Dixon • *Scr* Michael Stokes, from the short story by Bram Stoker

The Bramble Bush ★★

Drama · 1960 · US · Colour · 93min

Richard Burton is ill at ease here as a New England doctor who returns to his Cape Cod home town and falls in love with his dying friend's wife. Adapted from a bestseller by Charles Mergendahl, it's a soap opera lacking in strong characters and situations, though corruption and adultery figure as prominently as ever. Barbara Rush and the great Jack Carson are suitably angst-ridden for the material, but Burton looks all at sea. TH

Richard Burton *Guy Montford* • Barbara Rush *Mar McFie* • Jack Carson *Bert Mosley* • Angie Dickinson *Fran* • James Dunn *Stew Schaeffer* • Henry Jones *Parker Welk* • Tom Drake *Larry McFie* • Frank Conroy *Dr Kelsey* ▪ *Dir* Daniel Petrie • *Scr* Milton Sperling, Philip Yordan, from the novel by Charles Mergendahl

Branches of the Tree ★★

Drama · 1990 · Fr/Ind · Colour · 120min

Satyajit Ray's penultimate film as a director is anything but the work of a master. Mostly set in a single room, the film explores the relationship between a wealthy man who has a heart attack and his four sons, one of whom is mentally disturbed. As the declamatory speeches become longer and more turgid, each brother rejects his upbringing and the values of a bygone era. The overwrought acting is certainly off-putting, but it's Ray's theatrical staging that is so dismaying. DP Hindi +subtitles.

Ajit Bannerjee *Ananda Majumdar* • Haradhan Bannerjee *Probodh* • Soumitra Chatterjee *Prashanto* • Dipankar Dey ▪ *Dir/Scr* Satyajit Ray • *Co-producer* Gérard Depardieu

Brand: a Second Coming ★★★★ 15

Documentary · 2015 · UK/US · Colour · 100min

Regardless of one's views on Russell Brand as a comedian, celebrity, actor and political theorist, it's impossible to deny his energy and eloquence. But, as director Ondi Timoner quickly discovers, Brand is equally driven by egotism. Having inherited the project from five previous directors, she sometimes struggles to manage the material, while the interviews with celebrities like Mike Tyson and David Lynch sit particularly uncomfortably. However, Brand's fans and foes alike will find much to delight and disquiet them here. DP Swearing, sexual references, drug abuse. **DVD** **BL**

Russell Brand • Simon Amstell • Stephen Merchant • David Lynch • Katy Perry ▪ *Dir/Scr* Ondi Timoner

The Brand New Testament ★★★ 15

Comedy drama
2015 · Bel/Fr/Lux · Colour · 109min

Belgian director Jaco Van Dormael struggles to build upon an inspired premise in this scattershot satire on faith and fanaticism in an increasingly secular world. The ten-year-old daughter of God is so fed up with her dad tormenting humanity that she escapes into modern-day Brussels. So the Almighty ventures forth from his Belgian apartment to find her, only to discover how cruel the world really is. Van Dormael can't be faulted for his ambition here, but his corking idea never quite pays off. DP French, German +subtitles. Swearing, sex scenes, nudity.

Pili Groyne *Ea, God's daughter* • Benoît Poelvoorde *God* • Catherine Deneuve *Martine* • François Damiens *François* • Yolande Moreau *God's wife* ▪ *Dir* Jaco Van Dormael • *Scr* Thomas Gunzig, Jaco Van Dormael

Branded ★★★

Western · 1950 · US · Colour · 94min

More psychological than most westerns – and the better for it – this lavish Paramount picture stars Alan Ladd as the gunman who is persuaded to impersonate the long-lost son of wealthy rancher Charles Bickford. Predictably, Ladd becomes sick of the deception when he comes under the warm and loving embrace of a family that includes Mona Freeman as the beautiful daughter. Putting director Rudolph Maté, previously an outstanding cinematographer, with one of Hollywood's finest practising cameramen, Charles Lang, results in a visually arresting western in glorious Technicolor, and Ladd shows what an underrated actor he was. AE

Alan Ladd *Choya* • Mona Freeman *Ruth Lavery* • Charles Bickford *Mr Lavery* • Robert Keith (1) *Leffingwell* • Joseph Calleia *Rubriz* • Peter Hansen [Peter Hanson] *Tonio* • Selena Royle *Mrs Lavery* • Milburn Stone *Dawson* • Tom Tully *Ransome* ▪ *Dir* Rudolph Maté • *Scr* Sydney Boehm, Cyril Hume, from the novel by Evan Evans

Branded to Kill ★★★★ 18

Thriller · 1967 · Jpn · Colour · 90min

Filmed the year after the surreal crime comedy *Tokyo Drifter* and the uncompromising political drama *Elegy to Violence*, director Seijun Suzuki outdid himself with this astonishing blend of yakuza movie, *film noir* and *nouvelle vague*. The picture starts off in classic crime mode, with a ruthless hitman goaded by a *femme fatale* into a confrontation with his deadliest rival. As our hero begins to lose his grip, however, the tone changes completely and we are bombarded with a dizzying array of cinematic tricks. DP Japanese +subtitles. Violence, nudity. **DVD** **BL**

Jo Shishido *Goro Hanada* • Mariko Ogawa *Mami Hanada* • Koji Nanbara *Number One Killer* • Mari Annu *Nakajo Misako* ▪ *Dir* Seijun Suzuki • *Scr* Hachiro Guryu

Brandy for the Parson ★★ U

Comedy · 1951 · UK · BW · 78min

Director John Eldridge makes leisurely use of the coastal locations as holidaymakers James Donald and Jean Lodge become entangled with genial smuggler Kenneth More. A few more comic set pieces wouldn't have gone amiss, but this is still an amiable entertainment. DP

Kenneth More *Tony Rackman* • James Donald *Bill Harper* • Jean Lodge *Petronella Brand* • Frederick Piper *Customs Inspector* • Charles Hawtrey *George Crumb* • Michael Trubshawe *Redworth* • Alfie Bass *Dallyn* • Wilfred Caithness *Mr Minch* ▪ *Dir* John Eldridge • *Scr* John Dighton, Walter Meade, from the novel by Geoffrey Household

Brannigan ★★★ 15

Crime drama · 1975 · UK · Colour · 106min

Richard Attenborough plays the Scotland Yard police officer whose job it is to make sure visiting American cop John Wayne plays things by the book. It's essentially a western transported to London, with red double-deckers instead of stagecoaches and hangovers from swinging London. AT Violence, swearing. **DVD**

John Wayne *Jim Brannigan* • Richard Attenborough *Commander Swann* • Judy Geeson *Jennifer Thatcher* • Mel Ferrer *Mel Fields* • John Vernon *Larkin* • Daniel Pilon *Gorman* • Del Henney *Drexel* • John Stride *Traven* • Lesley-Anne Down *Luana* • Barry Dennen *Julian* ▪ *Dir* Douglas Hickox • *Scr* Christopher Trumbo, Michael Butler, William P McGivern, William Norton, from a story by Christopher Trumbo, Michael Butler

The Brass Bottle ★★
Comedy　　1964 · US · Colour · 89min

Tony Randall never seems to get a chance to show off his comedic talents, though this witless farce – adapted from F Anstey's perennial bestseller – tries to do so. Randall is a naive architect who opens an antique brass bottle and releases a genie that makes threats and offers to grant wishes. There's good back-up from Burl Ives and Barbara Eden, but the material is too thin to stretch very far and it soon splits disastrously. TH

Tony Randall *Harold Ventimore* • Burl Ives *Fakrash* • Barbara Eden *Sylvia* • Edward Andrews *Professor Kenton* • Ann Doran *Martha Kenton* ■ *Dir* Harry Keller • *Scr* Oscar Brodney, from the novel by F Anstey

The Brass Legend ★★★
Western　　1956 · US · BW · 79min

This impressive B-western has Raymond Burr as the psychotic killer captured by Arizona lawman Hugh O'Brian, who then has to deal with various factions within the town and keep Burr from escaping. Critics at the time admired the showdown between the two antagonists, which was filmed like a medieval joust with the two men facing each other down on charging horses. However, the whole movie has an admirable tension and a neatly dovetailed gallery of characters. AT

Hugh O'Brian *Sheriff Wade Adams* • Nancy Gates *Linda* • Raymond Burr *Tris Hatten* • Reba Tassell *Millie* • Donald MacDonald *Clay* • Robert Burton *Gipson* • Eddie Firestone *Shorty* • Willard Sage *Tatum* ■ *Dir* Gerd Oswald • *Scr* Don Martin, from a story by George Zuckerman, Jess Arnold

The Brass Monkey ★★ U
Comedy thriller　　1948 · UK · BW · 81min

This is a bizarre combination of a Saki-esque parable and a vehicle for radio talent scout Carroll Levis. Here he's pitted against an evil connoisseur bent on obtaining the titular Buddhist artefact. This was the penultimate film (not released until 1951) of tragic Hollywood actress Carole Landis, who committed suicide after breaking up with the married Rex Harrison. TS *DVD*

Carole Landis *Kay Sheldon* • Carroll Levis • Herbert Lom *Peter Hobart* • Avril Angers • Ernest Thesiger *Ryder-Harris* • Henry Edwards *Inspector Miller* • Edward Underdown *Max Taylor* ■ *Dir* Thornton Freeland • *Scr* Alec Coppel, Thornton Freeland, C Denis Freeman, from the story by Alec Coppel

Brass Target ★★ 15
Thriller　　1978 · US · Colour · 106min

Thick layers of plot make for a very thin enterprise in a film that lacks any central focus point. It's the kind of picture that is so mesmerised by the detail of its basic idea – what if General Patton was killed just after the war in the course of his investigation into a gold bullion heist? – that it allows class performers to wander in and out of the story, spouting slabs of dialogue rather than developing their roles. JM Violence, swearing.

Sophia Loren *Mara* • John Cassavetes *Major Joe De Lucca* • George Kennedy *Gen George S Patton Jr* • Robert Vaughn (1) *Colonel Donald Rogers* • Patrick McGoohan *Colonel Mike McCauley* • Bruce Davison *Colonel Robert Dawson* • Edward Herrmann *Colonel Walter Gilchrist* • Max von Sydow *Shelley/Webber* • Ed Bishop *Colonel Stewart* ■ *Dir* John Hough • *Scr* Alvin Boretz, from the novel *The Algonquin Project* by Frederick Nolan

Brassed Off ★★★★ 15
Drama　　1996 · UK/US · Colour · 103min

There's a certain Ealing-like quality in the way the mining town of Grimley rallies around the colliery's brass band as it progresses to the national finals amid talk of pit closures and redundancies. But there's no coy comedy here – the humour is acerbic and near the knuckle. Also missing is the Capra-esque last act in which the everyday folk triumph over adversity. Instead, there's only the promise of more struggle and the grim realisation that a way of life has gone for ever. But the edgy pace

---

Mark Herman brings to the drama and his presentation of the musical sequences can't be faulted, and he draws remarkable performances from a strong cast. DP Swearing. *DVD* ▸

Pete Postlethwaite *Danny* • Tara FitzGerald *Gloria* • Ewan McGregor *Andy* • Stephen Tompkinson *Phil* • Jim Carter *Harry* • Ken Colley [Kenneth Colley] *Greasley* • Peter Gunn *Simmo* • Mary Healey *Ida* • Melanie Hill *Sandra* • Philip Jackson *Jim* • Sue Johnston *Vera* ■ *Dir/Scr* Mark Herman

bratz ★★ PG
Musical comedy adventure
2007 · US · Colour · 97min

Determined to remain "BFF" (Best Friends Forever), four teenage girls start high school. But they find their pact difficult to stick to, as divisive cliques pull them in different directions. Two years later with their friendship renewed, they decide to challenge the system. With a paper-thin plot and strained central performances, this adventure (inspired by the Bratz range of fashion dolls) has little to recommend it, other than to its own captive market of five-to seven-year-old girls. However, parents may wonder about exposing even them to a film whose message is not "It's what's on the inside that counts", but rather "If you don't have the money to buy new clothes, get it from a friend." Jon Voight as the high school principal is barely recognisable, hiding behind a false nose. And who can blame him? SuR *DVD*

Nathalia Ramos *Yasmin* • Janel Parrish *Jade* • Logan Browning *Sasha* • Skyler Shaye *Cloe* • Chelsea Staub *Meredith* • Anneliese van der Pol *Avery* • Malese Jow *Quinn* • Jon Voight *Principal Dimly* ■ *Dir* Sean McNamara • *Scr* Susan Estelle Jansen, from a story by Adam De La Peña, David Eilenberg, from the toy range by MGA Entertainment

The Bravados ★★ PG
Western　　1958 · US · Colour · 93min

Gregory Peck tracks down a gang he thinks raped and murdered his wife. What is intended here is a parable about revenge that shows Peck descending into madness and seeking religious salvation at the end. It's a good story, but the treatment needs far more emotional conviction than either Peck or director Henry King give it. Joan Collins co-stars in an under-written role. AT *DVD*

Gregory Peck *Jim Douglas* • Joan Collins *Josefa Velarde* • Stephen Boyd *Bill Zachary* • Albert Salmi *Ed Taylor* • Henry Silva *Lujan* • Kathleen Gallant *Emma* • Barry Coe *Tom* • Lee Van Cleef *Alfonso Parral* ■ *Dir* Henry King • *Scr* Philip Yordan, from the novel by Frank O'Rourke

Brave ★★★★ PG
Animated fairy tale　　2012 · US · Colour · 89min

Pixar's 13th full-length film is the studio's first to feature a female as its central character. And a memorable creation she is, too. Merida (voiced by Kelly Macdonald) is a Scottish princess whose head of unruly red hair (a technical marvel) conveys her fiery spirit: this is a young woman who prefers riding and shooting to the restrictive life of the court. When Merida learns that her mother (Emma Thompson) plans for her to marry to preserve peace in the kingdom, the princess begs a witch for a spell that will change her mother's mind. Bad idea. *Brave* looks stunning and is very entertaining, but it serves up some lazy clichès in its depiction of the kingdom's menfolk and lacks the audacious spirit of the studio's earlier offerings. BP *DVD* ▸ CS

Kelly Macdonald *Merida* • Billy Connolly *King Fergus* • Emma Thompson *Queen Elinor* • Julie Walters *The Witch* • Kevin McKidd *Lord MacGuffin/Young MacGuffin* • Robbie Coltrane *Lord Dingwall* • Craig Ferguson *Lord Macintosh* ■ *Dir* Mark Andrews, Brenda Chapman • *Scr* Brenda Chapman, Irene Mecchi

The Brave Bulls ★★
Drama　　1951 · US · BW · 112min

This is a fraught exploration of the psychology of a bullfighter (Mel Ferrer), whose fear before a fight intensifies after his girlfriend (Czech actress Miroslava) dies

---

in a car crash. Co-star Anthony Quinn, who plays Ferrer's personal manager, claims the film as one of his personal favourites but blamed its lack of commercial success on the studio, which dumped it when director Robert Rossen was named a communist in the McCarthy hearings. As a result of being made by a "Red", the film never found a large following, but it's pretty average. AT

Mel Ferrer *Luis Bello* • Miroslava *Linda de Calderon* • Anthony Quinn *Raul Fuentes* • Eugene Iglesias *Pepe Bello* • José Torvay *Eladio Gomez* • Charlita *Raquelita* • Jose Luis Vasquez *Yank Delgado* • Alfonso Alvirez *Loco Ruiz* ■ *Dir* Robert Rossen • *Scr* John Bright, from a novel by Tom Lea

The Brave Don't Cry ★★ U
Disaster drama　　1952 · UK · BW · 91min

In this downbeat reconstruction of a true-life Scottish mining disaster, Philip Leacock admirably captures the stoicism of the hundred or so men trapped in a suffocating chamber following a landslide. However, he is less successful in eliciting credible performances from the non-professionals who make up the villagers. DP

John Gregson *John Cameron* • Meg Buchanan *Margaret Wishart* • John Rae *Donald Sloan* • Fulton Mackay *Dan Wishart* • Andrew Keir *Charlie Ross* • Wendy Noel *Jean Knox* • Russell Walters *Hughie Aitken* • Jameson Clark *Dr Andrew Keir* ■ *Dir* Philip Leacock • *Scr* Montagu Slater

The Brave Little Toaster ★★★★ U
Animated adventure　　1987 · US · Colour · 90min

A good number of ex-Disney personnel were involved in crafting this imaginative, unofficial remake of Disney favourite *The Incredible Journey*, substituting household appliances for the animals in the classic Disney house style. And, knowing a good thing when it sees it, Disney snapped the film up for release on its video label in America. The songs are a bit of a letdown, but the sharp humour and heart-warming sentiments make it marvellous fun for all the family. AJ *DVD*

Jon Lovitz *Radio* • Tim Stack [Timothy Stack] *Lampy* • Timothy E Day *Blanky* • Thurl Ravenscroft *Kirby* • Deanna Oliver *Toaster* • Phil Hartman *Air conditioner/hanging lamp* • Joe Ranft *Elmo St Peters* ■ *Dir* Jerry Rees • *Scr* Jerry Rees, Joe Ranft, Brian McEntee, from the novella by Thomas M Disch

Brave New Girl ★★
Coming-of-age drama
2004 · US · Colour · 120min

Britney and Lynne Spears's book *A Mother's Gift* is the inspiration for this coming-of-age drama about a Texas teen's determination to make the most of her talents in the face of competition and prejudice. Lindsey Haun takes the title role of the wannabe from the school choir whose chances at a prestigious performing arts academy are jeopardised by the cattiness of her fiercest rival, Barbara Mamabolo. Luckily, she has golden-hearted roommate Jackie Rosenbaum and self-sacrificing single mom Virginia Madsen to fall back on. It's pretty tacky stuff, but those hooked on TV talent shows should find enough to amuse them. DP

Lindsey Haun *Holly Lovell* • Virginia Madsen *Wanda Lovell* • Jackie Rosenbaum *Ditz* • Barbara Mamabolo *Angela* • Aaron Ashmore *Tyler* • Joanne Boland *Zoe Moscatel* ■ *Dir* Bobby Roth • *Scr* Amy Talkington, from a story by Talkington, from the novel *A Mother's Gift* by Britney & Lynne Spears

The Brave One ★★★ U
Drama　　1956 · US · Colour · 94min

Owing to the anti-communist blacklist that operated in Hollywood throughout the 1950s, Dalton Trumbo had to wait until 1975 to collect the best story Oscar he won (under the pseudonym of Robert Rich) for this charming tale of childlike innocence and loyalty. Transposing events that occurred in Barcelona in the mid-1930s to Mexico allows the screenplay to concentrate on the peasant sensibility of

---

Michel Ray, the farm boy who doggedly follows his pet bull all the way to the Plaza de Mexico. DP

Michel Ray *Leonardo* • Rodolfo Hoyos *Rafael Rosillo* • Elsa Cardenas *Maria* • Carlos Navarro *Don Alejandro* • Joi Lansing *Marion Randall* • George Trevino [Jorge Treviño] *Salvador* • Carlos Fernandez *Manuel* ■ *Dir* Irving Rapper • *Scr* Harry Franklin, Merrill G White, from a story by Robert Rich [Dalton Trumbo]

The Brave One ★★ 18
Revenge thriller
2007 · US/Aus · Colour · 117min

After a brutal attack lands her in hospital and leaves her fiancé dead, radio talk-show host Erica Bain (Jodie Foster) is driven to take the law into her own hands. Foster brings real emotional depth to the role, particularly in the first half hour when Erica struggles to step outside her New York apartment. Quite rightly, director Neil Jordan doesn't take short cuts to the point where she finally picks up a gun, but as Erica descends into a spiral of violence, it becomes increasingly difficult to stick with her. Her empathy with an unwitting cop (Terrence Howard) is one of many grating contrivances that serves to justify her actions. It's a gutsy turn by Foster, but a shame the film-makers lacked the courage to follow through. SP Violence, swearing. *DVD* ▸

Jodie Foster *Erica Bain* • Terrence Howard *Detective Mercer* • Naveen Andrews *David* • Nicky Katt *Detective Vitali* • Mary Steenburgen *Carol* • Carmen Ejogo *Jackie* • Lenny Venito *Mortell* ■ *Dir* Neil Jordan • *Scr* Cynthia Mort, Bruce A Taylor, Roderick Taylor, from a story by Bruce A Taylor, Roderick Taylor

Braveheart ★★★★ 15
Historical drama　　1995 · US · Colour · 179min

Mel Gibson directs this 13th-century saga of Scottish revolt against English tyranny with a claymore-like flourish, defying the criticism that there are moments as bogus as plastic haggis. Gibson's rebel leader and rabble-rouser William Wallace is an intrepid champion from the mould of Hollywood heroes, made believable by the grace of the star. However, Patrick McGoohan as the villainous King Edward "Longshanks" is a jeering, sneering cliché too far. As director, Gibson's control over thousands of extras in the swift succession of gruesome hand-to-hand battles is effective, but when the action moves in for the emotional kill, the film loses credibility. TH Violence, swearing, some nudity. *DVD* ▸

Mel Gibson *William Wallace* • Sophie Marceau *Princess Isabelle* • Patrick McGoohan "Longshanks", *King Edward I* • Catherine McCormack *Murron* • Brendan Gleeson *Hamish* • James Cosmo *Campbell* • David O'Hara *Stephen* • Angus MacFadyen *Robert the Bruce* • Ian Bannen *Leper* ■ *Dir* Mel Gibson • *Scr* Randall Wallace

Brazil ★★★ U
Musical comedy　　1944 · US · BW · 91min

A Brazilian composer (Tito Guizar) takes exception to an uncomplimentary book called *Why Marry a Latin?* and sets out to put the record straight with its attractive American author (Virginia Bruce). A big-budget musical from a little studio (Republic), Joseph Santley's film doesn't set the world on fire, but it is pleasing and lively. RK

Virginia Bruce *Nicky Henderson* • Tito Guizar *Miguel "Mike" Soares* • Edward Everett Horton *Everett St John Everett* • Robert Livingston *Rod Walker* • Richard Lane *Edward Graham* • Roy Rogers • Aurora Miranda *Speciality dancer* ■ *Dir* Joseph Santley • *Scr* Frank Gill Jr, Laura Kerr, from a story by Richard English

Brazil ★★★★★ 15
Science-fiction fantasy
1985 · US/UK · Colour · 137min

In this extraordinary vision of a futuristic bureaucratic hell from director Terry Gilliam, Jonathan Pryce stars as the Orwellian hero, a permanently harassed clerk at the all-seeing Department of Information Retrieval. Pryce is only kept sane by his vivid daydreams, which see him

---

B

as a heroic flying warrior coming to the aid of a beautiful woman (Kim Greist). As unpredictable as Gilliam's Monty Python animations, this daring and dazzling take on *1984* creates a weird world inhabited by an assortment of crazy characters, including Robert De Niro as an SAS-style repairman. The movie's sledgehammer conclusion gave studio executives sleepless nights. Expect the same. JC *DVD* Blu

Jonathan Pryce *Sam Lowry* • Robert De Niro *Archibald "Harry" Tuttle* • Katherine Helmond *Mrs Ida Lowry* • Ian Holm *Mr Kurtzmann* • Bob Hoskins *Spoor* • Michael Palin *Jack Lint* • Ian Richardson *Mr Warrenn* • Peter Vaughan *Mr Eugene Helpmann* • Kim Greist *Jill Layton* • Jim Broadbent *Dr Jaffe* ■ *Dir* Terry Gilliam • *Scr* Terry Gilliam, Tom Stoppard, Charles McKeown

Breach ★★★★ 12

Spy drama based on a true story
2006 · US · Colour · 105min

The plot of this bracingly grown-up thriller is taken from recent history. In 2001, the FBI unmasked Robert Hanssen, one of the Bureau's own counter-intelligence specialists, as a KGB mole. The man who toppled this spymaster's 22-year deception was fresh-faced Eric O'Neill (played with suitable rigidity by Ryan Phillippe), a lowly agent-in-training who was used as bait in a complicated sting operation. Sticking close to the facts of the case, co-writer/director Billy Ray's take on "the worst breach in American history" plays out as a suspenseful and cerebral game of human chess. Veteran actor Chris Cooper excels as the enigmatic Hanssen in this riveting human drama about the lies men tell and the personal cost of straying so far from the truth. JR Sexual references, brief swearing. *DVD*

Chris Cooper *Robert Hanssen* • Ryan Phillippe *Eric O'Neill* • Laura Linney *Kate Burroughs* • Dennis Haysbert *Dean Plesac* • Caroline Dhavernas *Juliana O'Neill* • Gary Cole *Rich Garces* • Bruce Davison *John O'Neill* • Kathleen Quinlan *Bonnie Hanssen* ■ *Dir* Billy Ray • *Scr* Adam Mazer, William Rotko, Billy Ray, from a story by Mazer, Rotko • *Cinematographer* Tak Fujimoto

Breach of Trust ★★ PG

Drama   1999 · US · Colour · 85min

Derry-born Roma Downey must have needed the patience of a saint to cope with the melodramatic demands made on her in this tear-jerking TV movie. Also known as *A Secret Life*, it's the kind of film they'd once have made with, say, Jane Wyman as the wife who discovers her husband has a mistress after he's been left comatose in a plane crash and Margaret O'Brien as the love child from that illicit union. Downey and Kristina Malota do well enough in the roles, but this is pretty heavy going. DP *DVD*

Roma Downey *Cassie Whitman* • William Russ *Mark Whitman* • Kristina Malota *Erica* ■ *Dir* Larry Peerce

Bread and Roses ★★★ 15

Political drama
2000 · UK/Ger/Sp/Fr/It · Colour · 105min

Ken Loach seems to be British cinema's sole surviving social conscience. It's disappointing, therefore, that he should decamp to Los Angeles for this naively over-simplified account of a janitorial workforce's struggle for representation. The mainly non-professional cast seems uncomfortable with his improvisational style, but Pilar Padilla embodies Loachian zeal as she unites with Adrien Brody's rabble-rouser to expose indifference and corruption. DP Spanish, English +subtitles. Swearing, brief nudity. *DVD*

Pilar Padilla *Maya* • Adrien Brody *Sam* • Elpidia Carrillo *Rosa* • Jack McGee *Bert* • Frankie Davila *Luis* ■ *Dir* Ken Loach • *Scr* Paul Laverty

Bread and Tulips ★★★ 12A

Romantic comedy
2000 · It/Swi · Colour · 116min

Directed with humour and humanity by Silvio Soldini, this is a delightful midlife rebellion comedy, set against the glorious vistas of Venice. Accidentally abandoned by

her lowbrow family on a cut-price coach tour, Licia Maglietta decides to treat herself to an adventure and finds professional fulfilment in an elderly anarchist's flower shop and unexpected romance with Icelandic waiter Bruno Ganz. The all-round geniality is reinforced by the amiably bungling performance of Giuseppe Battiston, as the inept plumber/private eye hired to track her down. DP Italian +subtitles. Swearing.

Licia Maglietta *Rosalba Barletta* • Bruno Ganz *Fernando Girasoli* • Marina Massironi *Grazia* • Giuseppe Battiston *Costantino* • Felice Andreasi *Fermo* • Antonio Catania *Mimmo Barletta* ■ *Dir* Silvio Soldini • *Scr* Doriana Leondeff, Silvio Soldini, from their story

Bread, Love & Dreams ★★★

Comedy   1953 · It · BW · 97min

Dated now, this is a typically frothy Italian comedy of the postwar years, set in a mountain village and dominated by Gina Lollobrigida. "La Lollo" plays the wild beauty lusting in love with a young policeman. She also catches the eye of Vittorio De Sica, playing the newly arrived police chief, who locks her up in his jail. Village elders and the priest frown at the sexual intrigue. A huge hit in Italy and released widely abroad, it led to a quickie sequel, *Bread, Love and Jealousy*, which reunited the cast and director. AT In Italian.

Vittorio De Sica *The marshal* • Gina Lollobrigida *The girl/"Frisky"* • Marisa Merlini *The midwife/ "Annarella"* • Roberto Risso *The carabiniere/ "Stelluti"* • Virgilio Riento *Priest "/Dom Emidio"* • Maria Pia Casilio *Priest's niece/"Paoletta"* • Memmo Carotenuto *Another carabiniere* • Tina Pica *Housekeeper/"Caramel"* ■ *Dir* Luigi Comencini • *Scr* Ettore Margadonna [Ettore Maria Margadonna], Luigi Comencini, from a story by Ettore Margadonna [Ettore Maria Margadonna]

The Break ★★ 12

Mystery thriller   1962 · UK · BW · 100min

Lance Comfort directs this plodding whodunnit, in which a detective, a novelist, a fleeing crook and his sister stumble upon dark deeds on a Devon farm. Tony Britton does his best in the lead, but the mystery isn't likely to put too much strain on your little grey cells. DP

Tony Britton *Greg Parker* • William Lucas *Jacko Thomas* • Eddie Byrne *Judd Tredegar* • Robert Urquhart *Pearson* • Sonia Dresdel *Sarah* • Edwin Richfield *Moses* • Gene Anderson *Jean Tredegar* ■ *Dir* Lance Comfort • *Scr* Pip Baker, Jane Baker

Break in the Circle ★★ U

Adventure drama   1955 · UK · BW · 90min

Adventurer Forrest Tucker is hired by wealthy foreign baron Marius Goring to smuggle a Polish scientist out of East Germany. However, he is nabbed in Hamburg by the gang who are holding the boffin captive. The glamorous Eva Bartok comes to his rescue, but things are not what they seem. Written and directed by Val Guest, this is an efficient and energetic British thriller, not without the odd moment of humour. RK

Forrest Tucker *Skip Morgan* • Eva Bartok *Lisa* • Marius Goring *Baron Keller* • Eric Pohlmann *Emile* • Guy Middleton *Hobart* • Arnold Marlé *Kudnic* • Fred Johnson *Farquarson* • Reginald Beckwith *Dusty* ■ *Dir* Val Guest • *Scr* Val Guest, from the novel by Philip Lorraine

Break of Hearts ★★★ U

Romantic drama   1935 · US · BW · 77min

This is one of a string of RKO features that lead to cinema exhibitors listing Katharine Hepburn as box-office poison. She plays a struggling young composer in Greenwich Village who falls for a famous international conductor, played by French heart-throb Charles Boyer. They both suffer unmercifully and he becomes a lush. Of course, she nurses him. Taken in the right spirit, on a wet matinée afternoon, this tosh has pleasure to offer, but the story is so familiar that there are no real surprises in store. TS

Katharine Hepburn *Constance Roberti* • Charles Boyer *Fritz Roberti* • John Beal *Johnny* • Jean Hersholt *Talma* • Sam Hardy *Marx* • Inez Courtney *Miss Wilson* • Helene Millard *Sylvia* ■ *Dir* Philip Moeller • *Scr* Sarah Y Mason, Anthony Veiller, Victor Heerman, from a story by Lester Cohen

Break Up ★ 18

Crime thriller   1998 · US · Colour · 96min

Bridget Fonda is the battered wife - deaf thanks to one of her husband's beatings - who is suspected of his murder when a charred body is found in his burnt-out car. Kiefer Sutherland and Steven Weber are the cops who only discover clues when the plot has slowed to the point of stagnation, while Penelope Ann Miller and Tippi Hedren are among the cast wondering what they did to deserve a daft film like this. JB

Bridget Fonda *Jimmy Dade* • Kiefer Sutherland *John Box* • Hart Bochner *Frankie Dade* • Steven Weber *Ramsey* • Penelope Ann Miller *Grace* • Tippi Hedren *Mom* ■ *Dir* Paul Marcus • *Scr* Anne Amanda Opotowsky

The Break-Up ★★ 12

Relationship comedy drama
2006 · US · Colour · 101min

The title of *The Break-Up* refers to Vince Vaughn and Jennifer Aniston's crumbling relationship (they play estranged lovers living under the same roof). But it could equally be applied to the film's disjointed script, which veers awkwardly between comedy and drama. Starting with a funny chat-up scene between tour guide Vaughn and gallery worker Aniston, this quickly descends into a soapy lather punctuated by their bickering. There are some nice moments between Vaughn and his old *Swingers* buddy Jon Favreau and with Vincent D'Onofrio (as his brother), but they can't hold this yarn together. SP Some sexual references, brief swearing. *DVD* Blu

Vince Vaughn *Gary Grobowski* • Jennifer Aniston *Brooke Meyers* • Joey Lauren Adams *Maddie* • Jason Bateman *Riggleman* • Vincent D'Onofrio *Dennis Grobowski* • Jon Favreau *Johnny O* • Cole Hauser *Lupus Grobowski* ■ *Dir* Peyton Reed • *Scr* Jeremy Garelick, Jay Lavender, from a story by Garelick, Lavender, Vince Vaughn

Breakdance ★★ PG

Musical drama   1984 · US · Colour · 82min

Adolfo "Shabba-Doo" Quinones and Michael "Boogaloo Shrimp" Chambers teach white waitress Lucinda Dickey their moves so that she can win a dance contest in a film that was rush-released to cash in on the short-lived breakdance craze. Great street choreography comes a poor second to the yawn-inducing, youth-versus-establishment plot with *Flashdance* trappings. Still, this dance culture is where hip-hop and rap found their acceptable public face. AJ *DVD*

Lucinda Dickey *Kelly* • Adolfo "Shabba-Doo" Quinones *Ozone* • Michael "Boogaloo Shrimp" Chambers [Michael Chambers (1)] *Turbo* • Phineas Newborn III *Adam* • Christopher McDonald *James* ■ *Dir* Joel Silberg • *Scr* Allen DeBevoise, from a story by Allen DeBevoise, Charles Parker

Breakdance 2 – Electric Boogaloo ★★ PG

Musical drama   1984 · US · Colour · 89min

This super-quick sequel finds the same lead characters using their dance talents once more to save their run-down community centre. Adolfo "Shabba-Doo" Quinones and Michael "Boogaloo Shrimp" Chambers put on a show to raise cash and halt the urban developers who want to turn the centre into a shopping mall. Stereotypical humour undercuts its breeziness. AJ *DVD*

Lucinda Dickey *Kelly* • Adolfo "Shabba-Doo" Quinones *Ozone* • Susie Bono *Rhonda* • Harry Caesar *Byron Smith* • Jo De Winter *Mrs Bennett* • John Christy Ewing *Mr Bennett* • Michael "Boogaloo Shrimp" Chambers [Michael Chambers (1)] *Turbo* ■ *Dir* Sam Firstenberg • *Scr* Jan Ventura, Julie Reichert, from characters by Charles Parker, Allen DeBevoise

Breakdown ★★★★ 15

Thriller   1997 · US · Colour · 89min

Director Jonathan Mostow twists the knife with a certain taut flair in this gripping thriller, in which Kurt Russell and Kathleen Quinlan play a city couple moving west, whose car breaks down in the middle of nowhere. Trucker JT Walsh gives Quinlan a lift to the nearest phone, but when she subsequently vanishes he denies ever seeing her. This is enjoyably old-fashioned, with Russell giving an engaging performance. The resolution isn't as clever as you might think, but you'll be too busy chewing your cuticles to really care. JC Swearing, violence. *DVD*

Kurt Russell *Jeff Taylor* • JT Walsh *Red Barr* • Kathleen Quinlan *Amy Taylor* • MC Gainey *Earl* • Jack Noseworthy *Billy* • Rex Linn *Sheriff Boyd* • Ritch Brinkley *Al* • Moira Harris *Arleen* ■ *Dir* Jonathan Mostow • *Scr* Sam Montgomery, Jonathan Mostow, from a story by Jonathan Mostow

Breakdown ★★★ 15

Crime thriller   2015 · UK · Colour · 110min

Since leaving *EastEnders* in 2001, Craig Fairbrass has carved out a career in a wave of tough, home-grown crime flicks. Here, he flexes his muscles as an ageing hitman haunted by his murderous past and heading for a meltdown. It's the last thing you need when you work for a brutal boss (a menacing James Cosmo). A solid if lengthy thriller, this certainly has some tense moments, as the increasingly frazzled Fairbrass heads towards a bloody reckoning. JA Violence, swearing, drug abuse. *DVD*

Craig Fairbrass *Alfie Jennings* • James Cosmo *Albert Chapman* • Emmett J Scanlan *Connor Moran* • Mem Ferda *Hakan Abaci* • Olivia Grant *Catherine Jennings* • Tamer Hassan *Iraz Kartal* ■ *Dir/Scr* Jonnie Malachi

Breaker Morant ★★★★ PG

War drama based on a true story
1979 · Aus · Colour · 102min

Bruce Beresford directs this true story of three soldiers (led by Edward Woodward) fighting the Boers, who are court-martialled by the British in need of scapegoats for war crimes. What Beresford sometimes lacks in subtlety, he makes up for in an impassioned sense of injustice and he draws powerful performances from Woodward, reluctant counsel Jack Thompson and Bryan Brown. JF *DVD*

Edward Woodward *Lt Harry Harbord "Breaker" Morant* • Jack Thompson *Major JF Thomas* • John Waters (3) *Captain Alfred Taylor* • Bryan Brown *Lt Peter Handcock* • Charles Tingwell *Lt Col Denny* • Terence Donovan *Captain Simon Hunt* • Vincent Ball *Colonel Ian "Johnny" Hamilton* • Chris Haywood *Corporal Sharp* ■ *Dir* Bruce Beresford • *Scr* Jonathan Hardy, David Stevens, Bruce Beresford, from the play by Kenneth Ross and the book *The Breaker* by Kit Denton

Breakfast at Tiffany's ★★★★★ PG

Romantic drama   1961 · US · Colour · 110min

Audrey Hepburn's Holly Golightly has passed, happily, into cinematic folklore. Director Blake Edwards's hymn to New York high style and high living, with its charming heroine and those wonderful Johnny Mercer *Moon River* lyrics, has hardly dated since its release. Originally a creation of writer Truman Capote, Holly, as written for the screen by George Axelrod and portrayed by Hepburn, is quite enchanting, even though period censorship makes it rather unclear what she actually does for a living. Despite the presence of handsome George Peppard and Patricia Neal, this is Hepburn's movie, her black dress and long cigarette holder ready to start a fashion revolution. Only Mickey Rooney's phoney caricature of a Japanese gent seems out of kilter in what is otherwise a thoroughly entertaining movie. TS *DVD* Blu

Audrey Hepburn *Holly Golightly* • George Peppard *Paul Varjak* • Patricia Neal *"2-E"* • Buddy Ebsen *Doc Golightly* • Martin Balsam *OJ Berman* • Mickey Rooney *Mr Yunioshi* • Vilallonga [José-

Luis De Villalonga] Jose • Dorothy Whitney *Mag Wildwood* • John McGiver *Tiffany's clerk* • *Dir* Blake Edwards • *Scr* George Axelrod, from the novella by Truman Capote • *Cinematographer* Franz F Planer [Franz Planer] • *Music* Henry Mancini

The Breakfast Club ★★★★ 15

Drama   1985 · US · Colour · 92min

One of the high-water marks of the 1980s teen pic, John Hughes's Saturday detention drama has lost some of its freshness in the face of time and endless inferior imitations. Yet this still rings true often enough to be relevant to both overgrown teenagers and the disgruntled kids of today. Brat Packers Emilio Estevez, Judd Nelson and Ally Sheedy are joined by teen favourite of the time Molly Ringwald and the underestimated Anthony Michael Hall for this mix of justified grievances, self-pitying whinges and hard-hitting home truths. The cast breathes life into their essentially clichéd characters. **DP** Swearing, drug abuse. 𝐃𝐕𝐃 Blu

Emilio Estevez *Andrew Clark* • Molly Ringwald *Claire Standish* • Judd Nelson *John Bender* • Ally Sheedy *Allison Reynolds* • Anthony Michael Hall *Brian Johnson* • Paul Gleason *Richard Vernon* • John Kapelos *Carl* • Perry Crawford *Allison's father* • John Hughes *Brian's father* ■ *Dir/Scr* John Hughes

Breakfast for Two ★★★ U

Screwball comedy   1937 · US · BW · 67min

This little known screwball comedy gives Barbara Stanwyck and Herbert Marshall plenty of opportunities to strike sparks off each other. She's a Texan heiress and he's a playboy who prefers the bottle to facing up to his responsibilities as heir to a shipping line. Stanwyck buys the company as part of her plan to reform and marry him. Running at barely over an hour, the picture has bags of energy and a strong supporting cast. **AT**

Barbara Stanwyck *Valentine Ransome* • Herbert Marshall *Jonathan Blair* • Glenda Farrell *Carol Wallace* • Eric Blore *Butch* • Etienne Girardot *Meggs* • Donald Meek *Justice of the peace* ■ *Dir* Alfred Santell • *Scr* Charles Kaufman, Paul Yawitz, Viola Brothers Shore

Breakfast of Champions ★ 15

Black comedy   1999 · US · Colour · 105min

As the richest man in a small town, Bruce Willis is having an existential crisis in this tedious adaptation of the Kurt Vonnegut Jr novel. He spends most of the movie contemplating ending it all and, after enduring two hours of this mess, you might too. An able cast is hindered by an incoherent script and uncertain direction. **ST**

Bruce Willis *Dwayne Hoover* • Albert Finney *Kilgore Trout* • Barbara Hershey *Celia Hoover* • Nick Nolte *Harry Le Sabre* • Glenne Headly *Francine Pefko* • Lukas Haas *Bunny Hoover* • Omar Epps *Wayne Hoobler* • Buck Henry *Fred T Barry* ■ *Dir* Alan Rudolph • *Scr* Alan Rudolph, from the novel by Kurt Vonnegut Jr

Breakfast on Pluto ★★★ 15

Black comedy drama   2005 · Ire/UK · Colour · 123min

Set in the glam-rock-soaked 1970s, Neil Jordan's whimsical movie is the flamboyant yet poignant story of cross-dressing teen Patrick "Kitten" Braden (Cillian Murphy), whose determination to find his real mother leads to an outrageous series of misadventures. While crackling with political tension and sinister unease, events are largely played for laughs - albeit of the darkest variety. Occasionally the film is too self-consciously left-field, but it's hard not to be won over by the sheer optimism of Jordan's colourful fantasy. **SF** Swearing, violence. 𝐃𝐕𝐃

Cillian Murphy *Patrick "Kitten" Braden* • Stephen Rea *Bertie* • Brendan Gleeson *John Joe Kenny* • Liam Neeson *Father Liam* • Eva Birthistle *Eily Bergin* • Liam Cunningham *Mosher, 1st biker* • Bryan Ferry *Mr Silky String* • Ruth Negga *Charlie* ■ *Dir* Neil Jordan • *Scr* Neil Jordan, Patrick McCabe, from the novel by Patrick McCabe

Breakfast with Jonny Wilkinson ★★ 15

Comedy   2013 · UK · Colour · 95min

This mildly amusing comedy is set around England's historic appearance in the final of the 2003 rugby World Cup. The focus is on Jake (George Mackay), the star player at a small-time rugby club, who believes he's psychically linked to superstar Jonny Wilkinson. Additional plot strands include plans to sell off the club for development, a power struggle over its chairmanship, and the presence in the suspiciously empty club bar of a cynical local reporter. It's stagily overplayed, corny and contrived. **DA** Swearing, a sex scene, brief nudity.

George MacKay *Jake Whittam* • Norman Pace *Dave Dowson* • Nigel Lindsay *Nigel Maitland* • Michael Beckley *Matt Holden* • Gina Varela *Lena* ■ *Dir* Simon Sprackling • *Scr* Chris England, from his play

Breakheart Pass ★★ PG

Western murder mystery   1976 · US · Colour · 93min

This Alistair MacLean caper has Charles Bronson on the trail of gunrunners and running into a murder mystery. And, if that wasn't enough, the plot is thickened by an outbreak of diphtheria. There are more red herrings than a chef could wave a skillet at, for this is really Agatha Christie in western garb, complete with a wonderful old steam train that steals every scene. **AT** 𝐃𝐕𝐃

Charles Bronson *John Deakin* • Ben Johnson (1) *Nathan Pearce* • Richard Crenna *Richard Fairchild* • Jill Ireland *Marcia Scoville* • Charles Durning *Frank O'Brien* • Ed Lauter *Major Claremont* • David Huddleston *Dr Molyneux* • Roy Jenson *Banlon* ■ *Dir* Tom Gries • *Scr* Alistair MacLean, from his novel

Breakin' All the Rules ★★★ 12

Romantic comedy   2004 · US · Colour · 81min

Oscar winner Jamie Foxx stars in this boisterous exploration of modern romance. Sharply scripted by director Daniel Taplitz, it sees Foxx go from heartbroken to sizzling when he writes a bestselling break-up guide for men after being dumped by his fiancée. Though the screwball events that follow as he tries to help others practice what he preaches verge on TV sitcom territory, they're no less enjoyable, benefiting from perky performances and spot-on delivery. **SF** Swearing. 𝐃𝐕𝐃

Jamie Foxx *Quincy Watson* • Gabrielle Union *Nicky Callas* • Morris Chestnut *Evan Fields* • Peter MacNicol *Phillip Gascon* • Jennifer Esposito *Rita Monroe* • Bianca Lawson *Helen Sharp* • Jill Ritchie *Amy* ■ *Dir/Scr* Daniel Taplitz

Breaking and Entering ★★★ 15

Social drama   2006 · US/UK · Colour · 113min

Writer/director Anthony Minghella (*The English Patient*) captures the cultural and social maelstrom of the King's Cross area of London in this tale of a young architect working on its regeneration. After opening an office in the heart of the district, Will (Jude Law) is infuriated by two break-ins. He follows one of the young thieves home, but instead of reporting him to the police, Will begins a tentative relationship with the boy's mother (Juliette Binoche), a Bosnian refugee. Minghella has assembled an impressive cast for this thoughtful and articulate drama, but it's weighed down by an excess of metaphors and ultimately seems cold and contrived. **BP** Swearing, sex scenes. 𝐃𝐕𝐃 Blu

Jude Law *Will Francis* • Juliette Binoche *Amira* • Robin Wright Penn [Robin Wright] *Liv* • Martin Freeman *Sandy* • Ray Winstone *Bruno Fella* • Vera Farmiga *Oana* • Rafi Gavron *Miro* • Juliet Stevenson *Rosemary* • Mark Benton *Legge* • Anna Chancellor *Kate* ■ *Dir/Scr* Anthony Minghella • *Cinematographer* Benoît Delhomme

Breaking Away ★★★★ 12

Comedy sports drama   1979 · US · Colour · 96min

Director Peter Yates's delightfully unpredictable comedy uses a local bicycle race to uncover the sexual, class and economic tensions within an all-American community. The Oscar-winning script by Steve Tesich has a wry wit and great sensitivity. The performances are marvellous, especially from Dennis Quaid and, more particularly, Dennis Christopher, who plays a character so enamoured of the Italian cycling team that he speaks with an Italian accent, bursts into Verdi arias and re-names his cat Fellini. Costing a mere $2.4 million to make, it was destined to be dumped by the studio, but became a huge box-office success. **AT** Swearing. 𝐃𝐕𝐃

Dennis Christopher *Dave Stohler* • Dennis Quaid *Mike* • Daniel Stern *Cyril* • Jackie Earle Haley *Moocher* • Barbara Barrie *Mrs Stohler* • Paul Dooley *Mr Stohler* • Robyn Douglass *Katherine* • Hart Bochner *Rod* • Amy Wright *Nancy* ■ *Dir* Peter Yates • *Scr* Steve Tesich

Breaking Dawn Part One ★★ 12

Romantic horror fantasy   2011 · US · Colour · 112min

The fourth and final book in Stephenie Meyer's *Twilight* saga is split in two for clear commercial reasons, but is really just ponderous melodrama. As it deals with Bella's lavish marriage to undead lover Edward, their Rio honeymoon and her pregnancy, all the lead actors have got their roles down pat by now; a certain ennui has set in, however, that's not helped by the banal dialogue and thin plotting. Twihards will no doubt love the movie irrespective of its flaws, insipid pop soundtrack and focus on glamour over acting talent. But this absurdly self-serious vampire love story sadly comes off as nothing more than a parody of the fine first film. **AJ** Some violence, brief sex scenes. 𝐃𝐕𝐃 Blu

Kristen Stewart *Bella Swan* • Robert Pattinson *Edward Cullen* • Taylor Lautner *Jacob Black* • Billy Burke *Charlie Swan* • Michael Sheen *Aro Volturi* • Anna Kendrick *Jessica Stanley* ■ *Dir* Bill Condon • *Scr* Melissa Rosenberg, from the novel by Stephenie Meyer

Breaking Dawn Part Two ★★★ 12

Romantic horror fantasy   2012 · US · Colour · 110min

For the final film of the series, Bill Condon pulls off an amazing visual coup that will satisfy the many millions of Twihards and possibly convert a few others. Bella and Edward are now Mr and Mrs Cullen, who have a half human/half vampire daughter - the oddly named Renesmee. When the Volturi - ancient warlike vampires who act as judges of the vampire world - come to believe that Renesmee is an immortal child (which is forbidden by their laws), they set out to kill the entire Cullen family. Despite stupid CGI wolves, dodgy red contact lenses and blotchy facepaint, this glossy finale remains true to the world of *Twilight* and the eternal love story at its heart. **KK** Some violence, a sex scene. 𝐃𝐕𝐃 Blu

Kristen Stewart *Bella Cullen* • Robert Pattinson *Edward Cullen* • Taylor Lautner *Jacob Black* • Michael Sheen *Aro Volturi* • Dakota Fanning *Jane* • Billy Burke *Charlie Swan* • Mackenzie Foy *Renesmee Cullen* ■ *Dir* Bill Condon • *Scr* Melissa Rosenberg, from Stephenie Meyer's novel

Breaking Glass ★★ 15

Musical drama   1980 · UK · Colour · 99min

Singer Hazel O'Connor claws her way into the charts, with help from spiv promoter Phil Daniels, only to find the glitter of fame tarnished. Efficiently directed by Brian Gibson, this hopelessly dated musical is completely formulaic yet intriguing from a New Wave nostalgia perspective. O'Connor, who wrote all the songs, hit the Top Ten with *Eighth Day* before fading into obscurity. The "life imitating art" subtext adds another level of interest to what is basically a chronicle of music-biz clichés. **AJ**

Phil Daniels *Danny Price* • Hazel O'Connor *Kate Crawley* • Jon Finch *Bob Woods* • Jonathan Pryce *Ken* • Peter-Hugo Daly *Mick Leaf* • Mark Wingett *Tony* • Paul McCartney • Rod Stewart ■ *Dir/Scr* Brian Gibson

Breaking In ★★★ 15

Comedy   1989 · US · Colour · 90min

This proved to be an over-optimistic title for Scottish director Bill Forsyth, who was making his second attempt at a Hollywood breakthrough after the British success of *Gregory's Girl* and *Local Hero*. Burt Reynolds, as an ageing burglar teaching his skills to a younger man (Casey Siemaszko), suits the humorous style, but John Sayles's script stresses mildness at the expense of momentum. The resulting story possesses a measure of charm, but more bite would have helped. **TH** Swearing. 𝐃𝐕𝐃

Burt Reynolds *Ernie Mullins* • Casey Siemaszko *Mike Lefebb* • Sheila Kelley (1) *Carrie* • Lorraine Toussaint *Delphine* • Albert Salmi *Johnny Scat* • Harry Carey [Harry Carey Jr] *Shoes* • Maury Chaykin *Tucci* • Stephen Tobolowsky *District attorney* ■ *Dir* Bill Forsyth • *Scr* John Sayles

The Breaking Point ★★★

Drama   1950 · US · BW · 97min

Ernest Hemingway's short novel, *To Have and Have Not*, became a classic movie in 1944, starring Humphrey Bogart and Lauren Bacall. This version, directed by Michael Curtiz, co-stars John Garfield and Patricia Neal. Hawks's version at least used Hemingway's title. This movie doesn't even bother to do that, replacing the tale of wartime gunrunning with one of peacetime smuggling, but retaining its core relationship about an unlucky guy, a bunch of hoodlums and a girl in the middle. Efficient. **AT**

John Garfield *Harry Morgan* • Patricia Neal *Leona Charles* • Phyllis Thaxter *Lucy Morgan* • Juano Hernandez *Wesley Park* • Wallace Ford *Duncan* • Edmond Ryan [Edmon Ryan] *Rogers* • Ralph Dumke *Hannagan* • Guy Thomajan *Danny* • William Campbell *Concho* ■ *Dir* Michael Curtiz • *Scr* Ranald MacDougall, from the novel *To Have and Have Not* by Ernest Hemingway

The Breaking Point ★ U

Crime thriller   1961 · UK · BW · 58min

If stars were awarded for plot contrivance, this low-budget thriller would be well into double figures. There's a banknote printer with a gambling debt, revolutionaries with a counterfeiting plan, an armed robbery, a bomb, a touch of adultery and a speeding plane finale. Not one character rings true nor is one fragment of the storyline credible. **DP**

Peter Reynolds *Eric Winlatter* • Dermot Walsh *Robert Wade* • Joanna Dunham *Cherry Winlatter* • Lisa Gastoni *Eva* • Brian Cobby *Peter de Savory* • Jack Allen *Ernest Winlatter* ■ *Dir* Lance Comfort • *Scr* Peter Lambert, from a novel by Laurence Meynell

Breaking Point ★

Crime drama   1976 · Can · Colour · 91min

Bo Svenson, a sort of expressionless forerunner of fellow Swede Dolph Lundgren, takes the stand against the Mafia and is set up with another identity by decent cop Robert Culp. But the Mafia soon sniff Svenson out and threaten his family and then we're into *Death Wish* vigilante land. **AT**

Bo Svenson *Michael McBain* • Robert Culp *Frank Sirrianni* • John Colicos *Vincent Karbone* • Belinda Montgomery [Belinda J Montgomery] *Diana McBain* • Stephen Young *Peter Stratis* • Linda Sorenson *Helen McBain* ■ *Dir* Bob Clark • *Scr* Roger Swaybill, Stanley Mann, from a story by Roger Swaybill

Breaking the Bank ★★ 12A

Comedy   2014 · UK · Colour · 105min

In this combination of romantic farce and economic chicanery, Kelsey Grammer (a long way from the brilliance of *Frasier*) dons a plummy English accent to play the bumbling aristocratic head of a long-established London bank, whose self-inflicted travails wreck his life and his marriage to Tamsin Greig. There are lots of lovely helicopter shots of the City of London, yet it's nowhere near enough fun. **TJ** Sexual references.

Kelsey Grammer *Sir Charles Banbury* • Tamsin Greig *Penelope Banbury* • Mathew Horne *Nick Freeman* • Pearce Quigley *Oscar* • Andrew Sachs

B

Jenkins ■ *Dir* Vadim Jean • *Scr* Roger Devlin, Stephen Keyworth, Vadim Jean, James McIllwraith, Tom Swanston

Breaking the Waves
★★★★★ **18**

Drama   1996 · Den/Swe/Fr · Colour · 152min

A staggeringly honest performance from newcomer Emily Watson and a wrenching central theme – the meaning of true love – illuminate this moving testament to the human spirit, which marked the English-language debut of Danish director Lars von Trier. Set in a remote Scottish village, and shot in pseudo home-video style to keep the profound events real and exposed, it tells the heartbreaking story of a devoutly religious and simple-minded woman who sacrifices everything for the man she adores. An often uncompromising and uncomfortable saga of faith, hope and charity. AJ Violence, swearing, sex scenes, nudity. *DVD* Blu

Emily Watson *Bess* • Stellan Skarsgård *Jan* • Katrin Cartlidge *Dodo* • Jean-Marc Barr *Terry* • Udo Kier *Man on the trawler* • Adrian Rawlins *Doctor Richardson* • Jonathan Hackett *The minister* • Sandra Voe *Bess's mother* ■ *Dir* Lars von Trier • *Scr* Lars Von Trier, Peter Asmussen

Breaking Up
★ **15**

Romantic drama   1996 · US · Colour · 85min

The talented Russell Crowe and Salma Hayek are both completely wasted in this low-budget, endlessly drawn-out explanation of a marriage. Scriptwriter Michael Cristofer clearly had a great deal of emotional baggage to sort through; perhaps he should've kept it to himself. LH Swearing, sex scenes, nudity.

Russell Crowe *Steve* • Salma Hayek *Monica* • Abraham Alvarez *Minister* ■ *Dir* Robert Greenwald • *Scr* Michael Cristofer

Breakout
★★★ **15**

Action adventure   1975 · US · Colour · 92min

In this off-target thriller, adventurer Charles Bronson rescues Robert Duvall from the Mexican prison he's been languishing in since being framed by father-in-law John Huston. The film starts rather slowly, but the tension builds as Duvall seeks revenge. Huston is nearly as villainous as he was in *Chinatown*, though the best work in the movie comes from Randy Quaid, Sheree North and Alejandro Rey in supporting roles. TH *DVD*

Charles Bronson *Nick Colton* • Robert Duvall *Ray Wagner* • Jill Ireland *Ann Wagner* • John Huston *Harris Wagner* • Randy Quaid *Hawk Hawkins* • Sheree North *Myrna* • Alejandro Rey *Sanchez* • Paul Mantee *Cable* ■ *Dir* Tom Gries • *Scr* Howard B Kreitsek, Marc Norman, Elliott Baker, from a novel by Warren Hinckle, William Turner, Eliot Asinof

Breakthrough
★★

Second World War drama
1950 · US · BW · 90min

This tale of an infantry platoon's progress through Europe following the Normandy landings has been wholly sanitised by the screenwriters. From David Brian's blokish captain down, each man is a caricature, but none more so than John Agar's green lieutenant, who turns out to be a natural born warrior. Director Lewis Seiler might have been advised to keep inserting archival footage, as in the boot-camp segment, but he lets his cast banter inanely. DP

David Brian *Captain Hale* • John Agar *Lieutenant Joe Mallory* • Frank Lovejoy *Sergeant Bell* • William Campbell *Dominick* • Paul Picerni *Private Ed Rojeck* • Greg McClure *Private Frank Finlay* ■ *Dir* Lewis Seiler • *Scr* Bernard Girard, Ted Sherdeman, from a story by Joseph I Breen Jr [Joseph Breen]

Breakthrough
★ **15**

Second World War drama
1978 · W Ger · Colour · 92min

A sorry sequel to Sam Peckinpah's classic war drama *Cross of Iron*, this tawdry affair has Richard Burton as Sergeant Steiner, the role so magnificently created by James Coburn, and features a totally wasted all-

star support cast. Burton doesn't seem interested in making his character believable, and it's hard to disguise the lack of both production values and a decent script. TS

Richard Burton *Sergeant Steiner* • Rod Steiger *General Webster* • Robert Mitchum *Colonel Rogers* • Curt Jurgens *General Hoffmann* • Helmut Griem *Major Stransky* • Michael Parks *Sergeant Anderson* • Klaus Loewitsch [Klaus Löwitsch] *Corporal Krueger* • Veronique Vendell *Yvette* ■ *Dir* Andrew V McLaglen • *Scr* Tony Williamson

Breast Men
★★★ **18**

Black comedy   1997 · US · Colour · 91min

Lawrence O'Neil's witheringly cynical direction offers up a mordant picture of beauty-obsessed America in this racy and frequently hilarious history of the fake boob industry. David Schwimmer and Chris Cooper star as the pioneering surgeons who make a fortune through their silicone implants in the drug-fuelled 1970s, only to fall out. Schwimmer relishes his first major chance to drop his lovable *Friends* persona, and he receives first-class support from a talented cast. JF Nudity, swearing. *DVD*

David Schwimmer *Dr Christopher Saunders/Kevin Saunders* • Chris Cooper *Dr William Larson* • Emily Procter *Laura Larson* • Matt Frewer *Gerald* • Terry O'Quinn *Hersch Lawyer* • Kathleen Wilhoite *Tammi-Jean Lingley* • John Stockwell *Robert Renaud* • Louise Fletcher *Mrs Saunders* • Lyle Lovett *Research scientist* ■ *Dir* Lawrence O'Neil • *Scr* John Stockwell

A Breath of Scandal
★★

Romance   1960 · US · Colour · 97min

The costumes are nice, the colour's lovely and Sophia Loren looks gorgeous. But there's little ace director Michael Curtiz can do to make this somewhat misguided version of Ferenc Molnar's hoary old play sparkle, especially when wooden John Gavin is cast as the light in Loren's eye. Still, Maurice Chevalier and Isabel Jeans delight both eye and ear and Angela Lansbury plays Loren's lying arch rival, so there's some pleasure to be had among the tedium. TS

Sophia Loren *Princess Olympia* • John Gavin *Charlie Foster* • Maurice Chevalier *Prince Philip* • Isabel Jeans *Princess Eugenie* • Angela Lansbury *Countess Lina* • Tullio Carminati *Albert* • Roberto Risso *Aide* • Carlo Hintermann *Prince Ruprecht* • Milli Vitale *Can-can girl* ■ *Dir* Michael Curtiz • *Scr* Walter Bernstein, Ring Lardner Jr, Sidney Howard, from the play *Olympia* by Ferenc Molnar

Breathe In
★★★★ **15**

Relationship drama   2013 · US · Colour · 93min

In this powerful relationship movie from Drake Doremus (*Like Crazy*), Guy Pearce plays a music teacher in upstate New York who is in the early throes of a midlife crisis. Into his life comes British foreign-exchange student Felicity Jones, who is a precocious talent in more ways than one. Though he is impressed enough by her musical skills, Pearce soon starts to see this beautiful, intelligent young woman as a soul mate and an exit route from his stale marriage. The two leads are wonderful, especially Jones as the seemingly guileless heartbreaker. DW Swearing. *DVD* Blu

Guy Pearce *Keith Reynolds* • Amy Ryan *Megan Reynolds* • Felicity Jones *Sophie* • Mackenzie Davis *Lauren Reynolds* • Matthew Daddario *Aaron* • Ben Shenkman *Sheldon* • Kyle MacLachlan *Peter Sebeck* ■ *Dir* Drake Doremus • *Scr* Drake Doremus, Ben York Jones

Breathing
★★★★ **15**

Drama   2011 · Austria · Colour · 89min

Austrian cinema has acquired a reputation for bleakness, but Karl Markovics restores some of its compassion in this, his directorial debut. Orphaned 19-year-old Roman Kogler (Thomas Schubert) dreams of becoming a diving instructor, but has to be content with a job transporting cadavers to the Vienna morgue. When he collects a victim who shares his surname, Kogler is prompted to search for the mother who abandoned him and, in the process, makes a much more important discovery. Evocatively photographed by Martin

Gschlacht, this is a compelling and impressively played and paced study of a lost soul coming to terms with himself and his situation. DP German, English +subtitles. *DVD* Blu

Thomas Schubert *Roman Kogler* • Karin Lischka *Margit Kogler* • Gerhard Liebmann *Walter Fakler* • Stefan Matousch *Gerhard Schorn* • Georg Friedrich *Rudolf Kienast* ■ *Dir/Scr* Karl Markovics • *Cinematographer* Martin Gschlacht

Breathing Lessons
★★★

Drama   1994 · US · Colour · 93min

Joanne Woodward and James Garner star in this made-for-TV adaptation of Anne Tyler's novel about a bickering married couple who drive down from Baltimore to a funeral in Pennsylvania. As far as road movies go, this one only lasts a day and doesn't take in the great sweep of America, but as the couple married for 29 years, Woodward and Garner make several breaks in their journey and learn a lot about each other. Their performances are as good as one could wish for. AT

James Garner *Ira Moran* • Joanne Woodward *Maggie Moran* • Kathryn Erbe *Fiona* • Joyce Van Patten *Serena* • Eileen Heckart *Mabel* • Paul Winfield *Mr Otis* • Henry Jones *Sam, Ira's father* ■ *Dir* John Erman • *Scr* Robert W Lenski, from the novel by Anne Tyler

Breathless
★★★ **15**

Crime drama   1983 · US · Colour · 95min

This remake of Jean-Luc Godard's 1959 classic *A Bout de Souffle* suffers greatly in comparison, but judged on its own merits it's a fair attempt at an on-the-run-style drama. Driving a stolen car, Richard Gere kills a cop and then heads into the arms of Valérie Kaprisky, a French student with whom he's had a brief affair. As the police close in, director Jim McBride seems most interested in getting both his actors to display as much flesh as possible. It's stylish but shallow, and Gere fits his superficial role like a glove. JB Violence, swearing, nudity. *DVD*

Richard Gere *Jesse Lujack* • Valérie Kaprisky *Monica* • Art Metrano *Birnbaum* • John P Ryan *Lieutenant Parmental* • William Tepper *Paul* • Robert Dunn (1) *Sergeant Enright* • Garry Goodrew *Berutti* • Lisa Persky [Lisa Jane Persky] *Salesgirl* ■ *Dir* Jim McBride • *Scr* Jim McBride, LM "Kit" Carson [LM Kit Carson], from the film *A Bout de Souffle* by Jean-Luc Godard, from a story by François Truffaut

Breathless
★★★ **18**

Crime drama   2009 · S Kor · Colour · 130min

Violence breeds violence in this intense and well-shot South Korean tale, as a vicious young debt collector (the film's talented, first-time writer/director Yang Ik-Joon) forms an unlikely friendship with a wilful high-school girl (Kim Kot-Bi). The resulting torrent of aggression and strong language is not for the faint-hearted, but there's an emotional complexity to events that keeps them gripping. Yang and Kim are superb and the unsentimental scripting gives extra weight to a predictably dramatic climax. SF Violence, swearing. *DVD*

Yang Ik-Joon *Sang-Hoon* • Kim Kot-bi *Yeon-Hue* • Jeong Man-shik *Man-sik* • Lee Hwan *Yeong-Jae* ■ *Dir/Scr* Yang Ik-Joon

The Breed
★★★ **18**

Futuristic action horror
2001 · US · Colour · 87min

Adrian Paul has a nice line in deadpan humour as a Polish bloodsucker teaming-up with vampire-hating cop Bokeem Woodbine in this slickly enjoyable futuristic thriller. Director Michael Oblowitz adds an impressive surface sheen to a fast-paced effort, shot in moody Budapest locations. Beneath the novelty window-dressing, it's merely a standard, formulaic buddy movie, but there are some noteworthy narrative touches. JC *DVD*

Adrian Paul *Aaron Gray* • Bokeem Woodbine *Steve Grant* • Bai Ling *Lucy Westenra* • Peter Halasz *Cross* ■ *Dir* Michael Oblowitz • *Scr* Ruth C Fletcher, Christos N Gage

The Breed
★ **15**

Horror thriller
2006 · S Afr/US/Ger · Colour · 87min

Some horror movies are terrible but great fun, others are simply terrible. This lazy B-movie is certainly the latter, with a story about genetically modified killer dogs pursuing students across a deserted island. Michelle Rodriguez (TV's *Lost*) phones in her performance as the film's heroine, and director Nick Mastandrea makes every mistake possible, with "canine cam" point-of-view shots proving laughably silly, a screenplay that leaves several plot points unresolved and a cast out-acted by their furry co-stars. JR Violence. *DVD*

Michelle Rodriguez *Nikki* • Oliver Hudson *John* • Taryn Manning *Sara* • Eric Lively *Matt* • Hill Harper *Noah* ■ *Dir* Nick Mastandrea • *Scr* Robert Conte, Peter Martin Wortmann

A Breed Apart
★★ **15**

Drama   1984 · US · Colour · 91min

Rutger Hauer plays a damaged and eccentric Vietnam veteran who's chosen to live as a recluse on a remote island. There he turns into a bird fancier and is pitted against Powers Booth, who has been hired by a rich egg collector to steal from Rutger's nest of eagles. Add to this unlikely scenario Kathleen Turner, who initiates an improbable love triangle, and you have a picture as risible as the moment when Hauer rides his white steed across the island, dressed as a pirate and carrying a crossbow. LH Violence, swearing.

Rutger Hauer *Jim Malden* • Kathleen Turner *Stella Clayton* • Powers Boothe *Michael Walker* • Donald Pleasence *Whittier* • Jayne Bentzen *Amy Rollings* • Adam Fenwick *Adam Clayton* • John Dennis Johnston *Peyton* • Brion James *Miller* ■ *Dir* Philippe Mora • *Scr* Paul Wheeler • *Music* Maurice Gibb

Breezy
★★★

Drama   1973 · US · Colour · 107min

In 1973, this gentle, middle-age romance marked a real departure for Clint Eastwood as director, though he stopped short of taking the main role himself. Instead the craggy and irresistibly charming William Holden plays the cynical divorcee who becomes infatuated with a young girl named Breezy, the sort of hippy who says, "I love being horizontal." There are vague echoes of the heyday of Ernst Lubitsch, Leo McCarey and Billy Wilder, along with some echoes of Eastwood's private life (he tested Sondra Locke for the part but gave it to the younger Kay Lenz). AT

William Holden (2) *Frank Harmon* • Kay Lenz *Breezy* • Roger C Carmel *Bob Henderson* • Marj Dusay *Betty Tobin* • Joan Hotchkis *Paula Harmon* • Jamie Smith-Jackson *Marcy* ■ *Dir* Clint Eastwood • *Scr* Jo Heims

Brenda Starr
★★ **PG**

Fantasy adventure   1989 · US · Colour · 93min

This cheap and cheerful comic-strip adaptation is let down by a plastic performance from Brooke Shields in the title role. She is the annoyingly intrepid ace reporter on the trail of a mad inventor and pursued by a posse of rival journalists and baddies. The latter are the most fun, while Timothy Dalton is the romantic interest. There are some camp moments, but it's not trashy enough to be truly enjoyable. JF Violence, some swearing. *DVD*

Brooke Shields *Brenda Starr* • Timothy Dalton *Basil St John* • Tony Peck *Mike Randall* • Diana Scarwid *Libby "Lips" Lipscomb* • Nestor Serrano *José, seaplane pilot* • Jeffrey Tambor *Vladimir* • June Gable *Luba* • Charles Durning *Francis I Livright, editor* ■ *Dir* Robert Ellis Miller • *Scr* Noreen Stone, James David Buchanan, Delia Ephron, from a story by Noreen Stone, James David Buchanan, from the comic strip by Dale Messick

Brewster McCloud
★★ **15**

Comedy   1970 · US · Colour · 105min

Robert Altman had just made *MASH* and was deluged by offers from the major studios. He chose to make this eccentric movie, starring Bud Cort as a modern-day Icarus who kits himself out with wings and

B

wants to fly in the Houston Astrodome. Altman probably felt he had a giant symbol on his hands – an allegory for freedom – when he simply had a Disney-ish story without the layers of syrup. Making things even wackier is Shelley Duvall in her first film role. AT Swearing, nudity.

Bud Cort *Brewster McCloud* • Sally Kellerman *Louise* • Michael Murphy (1) *Frank Shaft* • William Windom *Sheriff Weeks* • Shelley Duvall *Suzanne* • René Auberjonois *Lecturer* • Stacy Keach *Abraham Wright* • John Schuck *Policeman Johnson* ■ *Dir* Robert Altman • *Scr* Doran William Cannon

Brewster's Millions ★★ U
Comedy 1945 · US · BW · 79min

The idea of a young man who must spend a million to inherit many times that amount is one of the most popular comedy plots, with film versions dating back almost to the dawn of cinema. This time Dennis O'Keefe is the guy who finds it harder to spend his loot than he expects. Although only sporadically amusing, this fast-paced farce is still probably the funniest take on the tale. SR

Dennis O'Keefe *Monty Brewster* • Helen Walker *Peggy Gray* • Eddie "Rochester" Anderson *Jackson* • June Havoc *Trixie Summers* • Gail Patrick *Barbara Drew* • Mischa Auer *Michael Michaelovich* ■ *Scr* Sig Herzig, Charles Rogers, Wilkie Mahoney, from the novel by George Barr McCutcheon, from the play by Winchell Smith, Byron Ongley

Brewster's Millions ★★ PG
Comedy 1985 · US · Colour · 97min

Director Walter Hill and comedy are always an uneasy combination, and this hackneyed, overlong tale glaringly proves the point. Add the manic, rolling-eyed Richard Pryor, and you have a major disappointment that fell flat even when it was made. This was the seventh time the story had been filmed – man left millions in will but first has to spend large amount in 30 days – which should have sounded a note of caution all round, but didn't. As usual, Pryor overacts wildly. SH Some swearing. *DVD*

Richard Pryor *Montgomery Brewster* • John Candy *Spike Nolan* • Lonette McKee *Angela Drake* • Stephen Collins *Warren Cox* • Jerry Orbach *Charley Pegler* • Pat Hingle *Edward Roundfield* • Tovah Feldshuh *Marilyn* • Hume Cronyn *Rupert Horn* • Rick Moranis *Morty King* • Reni Santoni *Vin Rapelito* ■ *Dir* Walter Hill • *Scr* Herschel Weingrod, Timothy Harris, from the novel by George Barr McCutcheon

Brian's Song ★★★★ PG
Biographical sports drama
1971 · US · Colour · 74min

This tragic true story brought a new respectability to that despised genre, the TV movie, proving that real quality was possible. James Caan finally achieved stardom (his next role would be Sonny in *The Godfather*) as Brian Piccolo, a Chicago Bears football star dying of cancer. This moving story was based on the real-life account entitled *I Am Third* written by Piccolo's friend Gale Sayers, here played by Billy Dee Williams. Underrated director Buzz Kulik (*Warning Shot*) displays a remarkable sensitivity, and Michel Legrand's score is wonderful. Remade in 2001, also as a TV movie. TS

James Caan *Brian Piccolo* • Billy Dee Williams *Gale Sayers* • Jack Warden *Coach George Halas* • Shelley Fabares *Joy Piccolo* • Judy Pace *Linda Sayers* • Bernie Casey *JC Caroline* • David Huddleston *Ed McCaskey* • Ron Feinberg *Doug Atkins* ■ *Dir* Buzz Kulik • *Scr* William E Blinn, from the book *I Am Third* by Gale Sayers with Al Silverman • *Music* Michel Legrand

The Bribe ★★★
Crime drama 1949 · US · BW · 97min

This was as close as that home of gloss, MGM, got to making a genuine *film noir*. Federal agent Robert Taylor heads south of the border to encounter a cleverly cast assortment of genre clichés, including ailing crook John Hodiak and sultry singer Ava Gardner. Villains Charles Laughton and Vincent Price are both seemingly well out of directorial control, which is perhaps not surprising as the movie was started by arch stylist Vincente Minnelli and finished by the credited director Robert Z Leonard. TS

Robert Taylor (1) *Rigby* • Ava Gardner *Elizabeth Hintten* • Charles Laughton *JJ Bealler* • Vincent Price *Carwood* • John Hodiak *Tug Hintten* • Samuel S Hinds *Dr Warren* • John Hoyt *Gibbs* ■ *Dir* Robert Z Leonard • *Scr* Marguerite Roberts, from the short story by Frederick Nebel

Brick ★★★ 15
Mystery drama 2005 · US · Colour · 105min

This promising debut movie has a bizarre conceit - a bunch of high-school students talk and behave as if they're straight out of a Dashiell Hammett novel. The plot is similarly hard-boiled: Joseph Gordon-Levitt is a tough-natured teen who investigates the mysterious disappearance of his ex-girlfriend, Emilie de Ravin, only to be pulled into the grimy underbelly of school culture. Rian Johnson's film is deliberately overly complex though stylishly done. AS Violence, swearing. *DVD* *BLU*

Joseph Gordon-Levitt *Brendan* • Nora Zehetner *Laura* • Lukas Haas *The Pin* • Noah Fleiss *Tugger* • Matt O'Leary *The Brain* • Emilie de Ravin *Emily* • Noah Segan *Dode* • Richard Roundtree *Assistant VP Trueman* ■ *Dir/Scr* Rian Johnson

Brick Lane ★★★★ 15
Drama 2007 · UK · Colour · 97min

Sarah Gavron's accomplished feature debut does justice to the spirit of Monica Ali's expansive novel. Teenager Nazneen (Tannishtha Chatterjee) leaves her village in Bangladesh for an arranged marriage to the older Chanu (Satish Kaushik) and life in a drab East London council block. Sixteen years and two children later, we see how thwarted dreams have taken their toll on Chanu, while his wife remains largely an observer until she meets cocky young Karim (Christopher Simpson). Fans of the book may be disappointed by the film's emphasis on London, but the real strength of the film lies in the accumulation of small-scale domestic details, and in the subtle, humorous and compassionate performances of the lead actors as they negotiate the confines of their characters' relationship. SS Swearing. *DVD*

Tannishtha Chatterjee *Nazneen Ahmed* • Satish Kaushik *Chanu Ahmed* • Christopher Simpson *Karim* • Harvey Virdi *Razia* • Lalita Ahmed *Mrs Islam* • Naeema Begum *Shahana Ahmed* • Lana Rahman *Bibi Ahmed* • Zafreen *Hasina* ■ *Dir* Sarah Gavron • *Scr* Laura Jones, Abi Morgan, from Monica Ali's novel

Brick Mansions ★ 15
Action crime drama
2014 · Fr/Can · Colour · 90min

Filmed before the death of star Paul Walker in 2013, this is a ghastly remake of *District 13*, a far better French action thriller from 2004. Proceedings are relocated from a near-future Paris to a near-future Detroit, but the plot remains the same: an undercover cop (Walker) has to team up with a vigilante free runner (David Belle, from the original) to take down a drugs kingpin. But any similarities between this and the original end there. The film is poorly directed, edited, scripted, acted and everything else, and does scant justice to Walker's presence and Belle's prodigious free-running skills. DA Violence. *DVD* *BLU*

Paul Walker *Damien Collier* • David Belle *Lino* • RZA *Tremaine* • Catalina Denis *Lola* • Ayisha Issa *Rayzah* ■ *Dir* Camille Delamarre • *Scr* Luc Besson, from the film *District 13* by Besson, Bibi Naceri

The Bridal Path ★★ U
Comedy 1959 · UK · Colour · 95min

Frank Launder and Sidney Gilliat's powers were clearly on the wane when they made this slipshod romantic comedy. Bill Travers presents only a slight variation on his performance in the same team's earlier film, *Geordie*, as a tetchy Scottish giant whose doltish unwillingness to come to terms with modern life precipitates what is intended to be rib-tickling confusion. Hamming gleefully, George Cole and Gordon Jackson only emphasise Travers's one-dimensional acting. DP

Bill Travers *Ewan McEwan* • Alex Mackenzie *Finlay* • Eric Woodburn *Archie* • Jack Lambert *Hector* • John Rae *Angus* • Roddy McMillan *Murdo* • Jefferson Clifford *Wallace* • Nell Ballantyne *Jessie* • George Cole *Sergeant Bruce* • Fiona Clyne *Katie* • Gordon Jackson *Constable Alec* ■ *Dir* Frank Launder • *Scr* Frank Launder, Geoffrey Willans, Nigel Tranter, from the novel by Nigel Tranter

The Bride ★★ 15
Gothic horror drama 1985 · US · Colour · 114min

This is one of the more unnecessary versions of Mary Shelley's man-makes-monster story. A bizarre cast has Sting as Baron Frankenstein, bringing Jennifer Beals to life under the gaze of monster number one Clancy Brown, whose touching scenes with the late David Rappaport effortlessly steal the movie. Michael Seymour's production design is lush and impressive, as is Maurice Jarre's score, but this one is a non-starter. TS *DVD*

Sting *Baron Frankenstein* • Jennifer Beals *Eva* • Anthony Higgins *Clerval* • Clancy Brown *Viktor* • David Rappaport *Rinaldo* • Geraldine Page *Mrs Baumann* • Alexei Sayle *Magar* • Phil Daniels *Bela* • Veruschka [Veruschka Von Lehndorff] *Countess* • Quentin Crisp *Dr Zalhus* ■ *Dir* Franc Roddam • *Scr* Lloyd Fonvielle, from characters by Mary Shelley • *Music* Maurice Jarre • *Editor* Michael Ellis • *Production Designer* Michael Seymour

Bride & Prejudice ★★★ 12
Romantic comedy
2004 · UK/Ger · Colour · 106min

Jane Austen's classic story is transposed to India and given a Bollywood makeover here by director Gurinder Chadha. Aishwarya Rai takes the Elizabeth Bennet role as Lalita, one of four eligible daughters from a good family. She meets handsome but haughty American Will Darcy (Martin Henderson) at a wedding, and soon the sparks are flying and saris whirling for cast-of-hundreds musical numbers. The script nimbly pulls off the location and time shift of Austen's tale, but there's a lack of chemistry between the two leads and the stretches between the singing occasionally fall flat. LF *DVD*

Aishwarya Rai *Lalita Bakshi* • Martin Henderson *Will Darcy* • Naveen Andrews *Balraj Bingley* • Indira Varma *Kiran Bingley* • Namrata Shirodkar *Jaya Bakshi* • Peeya Rai Chodhuri *Lucky Bakshi* • Meghnaa *Maya Bakshi* • Nadira Babbar *Mrs Bakshi* • Anupam Kher *Mr Bakshi* • Daniel Gillies *Johnny Wickham* • Nitin Ganatra [Nitin Chandra Ganatra] *Mr Kholi* ■ *Dir* Gurinder Chadha • *Scr* Gurinder Chadha, Paul Mayeda Berges, from the novel *Pride and Prejudice* by Jane Austen

The Bride and the Beast ★ PG
Psychological horror 1958 · US · BW · 73min

What else could this painfully cheap *King Kong* variant be but junk, when its author is Ed Wood Jr, the world's worst director? On their wedding night, Charlotte Austin is curiously attracted to hubby Lance Fuller's pet ape. Under hypnosis, she learns that in a previous incarnation she was queen of the gorillas. So it's off on an African safari (cue endless stock footage) to meet her hairy destiny. Laughably inept. AJ

Charlotte Austin *Laura* • Lance Fuller *Dan* • Johnny Roth *Taro* • Steve Calvert *Beast* • William Justine *Dr Reiner* • Jeanne Gerson *Marka* • Gil Frye *Captain Cameron* ■ *Dir* Adrian Weiss • *Scr* Edward D Wood Jr, from a story by Adrian Weiss

Bride by Mistake ★★
Comedy 1944 · US · BW · 81min

Lovely Laraine Day nearly achieved stardom in the mid-1940s, having built up a following as Mary Lamont in MGM's popular *Dr Kildare* series. This minor feature, in which she plays a rich heiress who swaps roles with her secretary to discover the worth of a prospective suitor, showcased her charms and let to a number of co-starring roles. TS

Alan Marshal *Tony Travis* • Laraine Day *Norah Hunter* • Marsha Hunt *Sylvia* • Allyn Joslyn *Phil Vernon* • Edgar Buchanan *Connors* • Michael St Angel *Corey* ■ *Dir* Richard Wallace • *Scr* Phoebe Ephron, Henry Ephron, from a story by Norman Krasna

The Bride Came COD ★★★ U
Romantic comedy 1941 · US · BW · 87min

The unlikely comic pairing of movie greats James Cagney and Bette Davis may seem a mite arch, but they seem to enjoy each other's company. The plot is a heavily diluted comic caper about mistaken identities and runaway brides - he's a flier, she's an heiress and, for some obscure reason, they spend a lot of time together marooned in a desert ghost town. Cagney gives Davis a pretty good run for her money and is better at the farcical moments, especially as most of the jokes involve Davis losing her dignity. Still, Davis was a born trouper, and rises above this nonsense with style. TS *DVD*

James Cagney *Steve Collins* • Bette Davis *Joan Winfield* • Stuart Erwin *Tommy Keenan* • Jack Carson *Allen Brice* • George Tobias *Peewee* • Eugene Pallette *Lucius K Winfield* • Harry Davenport *Pop Tolliver* • William Frawley *Sheriff McGee* ■ *Dir* William Keighley • *Scr* Julius J Epstein, Philip G Epstein, from a story by Kenneth Earl, MM Musselman

The Bride Comes Home ★★★ U
Comedy 1935 · US · BW · 82min

Having chalked up a success by pairing Claudette Colbert and newcomer Fred MacMurray in the romantic comedy *The Gilded Lily* (1935), Paramount recycled the formula - same stars, same director (Wesley Ruggles) and the same screenwriter (Claude Binyon). Once again the delightful Colbert is in a tug of war between two suitors. She's now an impoverished but feisty heiress involved in a magazine-publishing venture with mega-rich and sweet-natured Robert Young. MacMurray is Young's poor sidekick. No prizes for guessing which man she chooses in the end. RK

Claudette Colbert *Jeanette Desmereau* • Fred MacMurray *Cyrus Anderson* • Robert Young (1) *Jack Bristow* • William Collier Sr *Alfred Desmereau* • Donald Meek *The judge* • Richard Carle *Frank* • Johnny Arthur *Otto* ■ *Dir* Wesley Ruggles • *Scr* Claude Binyon, from a story by Elizabeth Sanxay Holding

Bride for Sale ★★★
Romantic comedy 1949 · US · BW · 87min

Although her career would extend another two decades, this was the last comedy made by the sparkling Claudette Colbert. It's slight stuff - she's torn between sturdy George Brent and cheerful Robert Young - made watchable by its attractive stars. Colbert's next role was to have been Margo Channing in *All about Eve*, but she injured her back. TS

Claudette Colbert *Nora Shelly* • Robert Young (1) *Steve Adams* • George Brent *Paul Martin* • Max Baer *Litka* • Gus Schilling *Timothy* • Charles Arnt *Dobbs* • Mary Bear *Miss Stone* • Ann Tyrrell *Miss Swanson* ■ *Dir* William D Russell • *Scr* Bruce Manning, Islin Auster, from a story by Joseph Fields

The Bride Is Too Beautiful ★★ PG
Romantic comedy 1956 · Fr · BW · 93min

This Brigitte Bardot vehicle was made when the "sex kitten" could break your heart with a look. Also featuring Louis Jourdan, the film has Bardot as a girl from the sticks who becomes a top model after she is spotted by the publishers of a Paris magazine. Micheline Presle brings class to the silly proceedings in a lightweight offering. Released on video/DVD as *Her Bridal Night*. TS French dubbed. *DVD*

Brigitte Bardot *Chouchou* • Micheline Presle *Judith* • Louis Jourdan *Michel* • Marcel Amont *Tom* • Jean-François Calvé *Patrice* • Roger Dumas *Marc* • Madeleine Lambert *Aunt Agnès* • Marcelle Arnold *Madame Victoire* ■ *Dir* Pierre Gaspard-Huit • *Scr* Philippe Agostini, Odette Joyeux, Juliette Saint-Giniez, from a story by Odette Joyeux

Bride of Chucky ★★★ 18

Horror spoof   1998 · US · Colour · 85min

This fourth encounter with devilish doll Chucky is the most entertaining of the *Child's Play* series, thanks to Ronny Yu's colourful direction, a wickedly humorous tone and the irresistible presence of Jennifer Tilly. There's more laughter than slaughter as Chucky and new dolly girl Tiffany plot to escape their diminutive frames. Although the story is lightweight, the witty references to horror classics and the hilarious interplay between the rubber lovers resurrect this series. Chucky and Tiffany returned in 2004's *Seed of Chucky*. JC Swearing, violence. **DVD**

Jennifer Tilly *Tiffany* • Brad Dourif *Chucky* • Katherine Heigl *Jade* • Nick Stabile *Jesse* • Alexis Arquette *Damien Baylock* • Gordon Michael Woollett *David* • John Ritter *Chief Warren Kincaid* • Lawrence Dane *Lieutenant Preston* ■ *Dir* Ronny Yu • *Scr* Don Mancini

Bride of Frankenstein ★★★★★ PG

Classic horror   1935 · US · BW · 71min

James Whale's extravagantly produced sequel to his own *Frankenstein* still ranks as one of horrordom's greatest achievements. From his wittily eccentric direction and Elsa Lanchester's electric hairdo, to Ernest Thesiger's ingenious portrayal of the perverse Dr Pretorius and Boris Karloff's alternately poignant and pushy monster, it's a class act from amazing start to religious-slanted finish. They don't get any better than this and some scenes – the unveiling of the bride to the sound of wedding bells, the miniature people in bell jars – are classics. *Son of Frankenstein* followed in 1939. AJ **DVD BL**

Boris Karloff *Monster* • Colin Clive *Henry Frankenstein* • Valerie Hobson *Elizabeth* • Ernest Thesiger *Doctor Pretorius* • Elsa Lanchester *Mary Wollstonecraft Shelley/Monster's mate* • Gavin Gordon *Lord Byron* • Douglas Walton *Percy Bysshe Shelley* • Una O'Connor *Minnie* ■ *Dir* James Whale • *Scr* William Hurlbut, John Balderston [John L Balderston], Tom Reed (uncredited), from the novel *Frankenstein; or, the Modern Prometheus* by Mary Wollstonecraft Shelley • *Cinematographer* John J Mescall • *Art Director* Charles D Hall • *Special Effects* John P Fulton • *Make-up* Jack Pierce

Bride of Re-Animator ★★ 18

Horror comedy   1991 · US · Colour · 92min

Nowhere near as impactful, witty or fresh as the original HP Lovecraft-based cult movie *Re-Animator*, director Brian Yuzna's gloriously gory sequel sadly ventures more into standard Frankenstein territory. Jeffrey Combs is good value as the mad doctor with the luminous green serum that revives dead tissue to create a living woman out of assorted body parts. Gruesomely over-the-top; followed by a second sequel, *Beyond Re-Animator* (2003). AJ Violence, swearing. **DVD**

Jeffrey Combs *Herbert West* • Bruce Abbott *Dan Cain* • Claude Earl Jones *Lieutenant Leslie Chapham* • Fabiana Udenio *Francesca Danelli* • David Gale *Doctor Carl Hill* • Kathleen Kinmont *Gloria – The Bride* ■ *Dir* Brian Yuzna • *Scr* Woody Keith, Rick Fry, from a story by Brian Yuzna, Woody Keith, Rick Fry, from the character *Herbert West – the Re-Animator* by HP Lovecraft

Bride of the Monster ★ PG

Horror   1955 · US · BW · 68min

Many will know about this movie purely because Tim Burton expertly re-created key scenes in his superb *Ed Wood* biopic. The movie itself is pure torture to watch. Bela Lugosi, in his only true starring role in an Ed Wood exploiter, is a fugitive Russian scientist trying to create a race of super-beings in his swamp-based hideout. The whole sorry affair comes complete with light-bulb special effects and the infamous pit fight between Lugosi and a lifeless rubber octopus stolen from a John Wayne movie. AJ **DVD**

Bela Lugosi *Dr Eric Vornoff* • Tor Johnson *Lobo* • Tony McCoy *Lieutenant Dick Craig* • Loretta King *Janet Lawton* • Harvey B Dunn *Captain Robbins* •

George Becwar *Professor Strowski* • Paul Marco *Kelton* • Don Nagel *Martin* ■ *Dir* Edward D Wood Jr • *Scr* Edward D Wood Jr, Alex Gordon

Bride of the Wind ★

Biographical drama   2001 · US/UK/Ger · Colour · 99min

Bruce Beresford's bio pic of Alma Mahler, wife of Gustav Mahler is a sorry affair. Alma (Sarah Wynter) bed-hops through the Viennese rich and famous. First she meets and seduces Mahler (Jonathan Pryce). Then the hussy is repeatedly unfaithful to him – blaming his passion for music as her just cause. Dire performances and a dry script don't improve matters much either. To be avoided. LH

Sarah Wynter *Alma Mahler* • Jonathan Pryce *Gustav Mahler* • Vincent Perez *Oskar Kokoschka* • Simon Verhoeven *Walter Gropius* • Gregor Seberg *Franz Werfel* • Dagmar Schwarz *Anna Moll* • Wolfgang Hubsch *Karl Moll* • August Schmolzer *Gustav Klimt* ■ *Dir* Bruce Beresford • *Scr* Marilyn Levy

Bride of Vengeance ★

Drama   1949 · US · BW · 92min

The Borgias get up to all sorts of shady dealings in Renaissance Italy, especially Lucretia, who is sent out to kill a man, but falls in love with him. This was a disaster for all concerned – director Michael Keisen loathed the script, and Ray Milland refused to appear in it and was suspended by the studio. So bad were the reviews, and so thin was the box office, that Paramount sacked its contract star, Paulette Goddard. AT

Paulette Goddard *Lucretia Borgia* • John Lund *Alfonso D'Este* • Macdonald Carey *Cesare Borgia* • Albert Dekker *Vanetti* • John Sutton *Bisceglie* • Raymond Burr *Michelotto* • Charles Dayton *Bastino* • Donald Randolph *Tiziano* • Billy Gilbert *Beppo* ■ *Dir* Mitchell Leisen • *Scr* Cyril Hume, Michael Hogan, Clemence Dane, from a story by Michael Hogan

The Bride Walks Out ★★

Comedy   1936 · US · BW · 80min

This Barbara Stanwyck vehicle demonstratesd that, without a strong director and clever script, comedy was not her forte. She tries hard as a model who becomes a housewife, but the material defeats her. Yet, there's still pleasure to be had in watching a cast that includes such super character players as Ned Sparks and Hattie McDaniel. TS

Barbara Stanwyck *Carolyn Martin* • Gene Raymond *Michael Martin* • Robert Young (1) *Hugh McKenzie* • Ned Sparks *Paul Dodson* • Helen Broderick *Mattie Dodson* • Willie Best *Smokie* • Robert Warwick *Mr McKenzie* • Billy Gilbert *Donovan* • Hattie McDaniels [Hattie McDaniel] *Maime* ■ *Dir* Leigh Jason • *Scr* PJ Wolfson, Philip G Epstein, Edmund Joseph (uncredited), from a story by Howard Emmett Rogers

Bride Wars ★★ 12

Comedy   2008 · US · Colour · 85min

Anne Hathaway and Kate Hudson head the cast of director Gary Winick's comedy about brides behaving badly. Teacher Emma (Hathaway) and lawyer Liv (Hudson) are best pals who share everything, until a mix-up causes their respective weddings to be booked for the same date at their dream venue – New York's Plaza Hotel. With neither woman willing to budge, the claws come out and anyone and anything is fair game. Hathaway and Hudson make convincing friends, but despite their natural charms there's a lack of credibility to their bitchy antics. SP Brief swearing, sexual references. **DVD BL**

Anne Hathaway *Emma* • Kate Hudson *Liv* • Kristen Johnston *Deb* • Candice Bergen *Marion St Claire* • Bryan Greenberg *Nate* • Steve Howey *Daniel* ■ *Dir* Gary Winick • *Scr* Greg DePaul, Casey Wilson, June Diane Raphael, from a story by DePaul

The Bride with White Hair ★★★★ 18

Martial arts fantasy romance   1993 · HK · Colour · 88min

The extraordinary Hong Kong movie that created a massive fan base for Ronny Yu

(later to make *Bride of Chucky* and *The 51st State*), this is an intoxicating fantasy. Brigitte Lin's wolf-raised killing machine and Leslie Cheung's warrior fall in love and face the wrath of Lin's evil, dual-sexed Siamese twin fiancée. No, really. Much of the huge budget went on the amazing sets, which complement Yu's phenomenal eye for composition, dazzling fight choreography, stunning photography and artistic blood-letting. It was followed by a sequel produced by Yu. JC Cantonese +subtitles. **DVD**

Leslie Cheung *Zhou Yihang* • Brigitte Lin *Lian Nichang* • Ng Chun-yu [Francis Ng] *Ji Wu Shang, Siamese male twin* • Elaine Lui *Ji Wu Shang, Siamese female twin* ■ *Dir* Ronny Yu • *Scr* Lam Kei Tou, Tseng Pik Yin, David Wu, Ronny Yu

The Bride Wore Black ★★★★

Mystery   1967 · Fr/It · Colour · 107min

In adapting Cornell Woolrich's novel and hiring Bernard Herrmann for the score, François Truffaut paid his most conscious tribute to Alfred Hitchcock. Jeanne Moreau gives a chameleon-like performance as the widow seeking retribution from the quintet who accidentally killed her husband on their wedding day. Each of them is an archetype of male boorishness, yet their deaths invoke a mixture of emotions and flashbacks to reveal the extent of Moreau's loss temper the callousness of her crimes. DP French +subtitles.

Jeanne Moreau *Julie Kohler* • Jean-Claude Brialy *Corey* • Michel Bouquet *Coral* • Charles Denner *Fergus* • Claude Rich *Bliss* • Daniel Boulanger *Holmes/Delvaux* • Michel Lonsdale *Rene Morane* • Serge Rousseau *David* ■ *Dir* François Truffaut • *Scr* François Truffaut, Jean-Louis Richard, from the novel by William Irish [Cornell Woolrich] • *Cinematographer* Raoul Coutard

The Bride Wore Boots ★★

Comedy   1946 · US · BW · 86min

This comedy of marital disharmony has Barbara Stanwyck detesting her husband Robert Cummings's interest in the Civil War and Cummings detesting her love of horses. There's a divorce, a horse that's in love with Cummings and a championship steeplechase. And that's about it, really, with both stars making the most of their modest material. AT

Barbara Stanwyck *Sally Warren* • Robert Cummings *Jeff Warren* • Diana Lynn *Mary Lou Medford* • Patric Knowles *Lance Gale* • Peggy Wood *Grace Apley* • Robert Benchley *Tod Warren* • Willie Best *Joe* • Natalie Wood *Carol Warren* ■ *Dir* Irving Pichel • *Scr* Dwight Michael Wiley, from a story by Dwight Michael Wiley, from a play by Harry Segall

The Bride Wore Red ★★★ U

Drama   1937 · US · BW · 103min

In this fairly typical, though slightly eccentric Joan Crawford vehicle, the star plays a cabaret singer who gets to travel to the obviously studio-bound and back-projected Austrian Tyrol and can't choose between handsome and dashing playboy Robert Young or handsome and dashing postman Franchot Tone. Not, of course, that it matters one jot in this entertaining tosh, directed by the only woman director in mainstream Hollywood at the time, Dorothy Arzner. TS

Joan Crawford *Anni* • Franchot Tone *Giulio* • Robert Young (1) *Rudi Pal* • Billie Burke *Contessa di Milano* • Reginald Owen *Admiral Monti* • Lynne Carver *Magdalena Monti* • George Zucco *Count Armalia* • Mary Phillips [Mary Philips] *Maria* ■ *Dir* Dorothy Arzner • *Scr* Tess Slesinger, Bradbury Foote, from the play *The Girl from Trieste* by Ferenc Molnar

The Brides of Dracula ★★★★ 12

Horror   1960 · UK · Colour · 82min

While Christopher Lee worried about typecasting, Hammer went ahead anyway with this sequel (in name only) to its huge 1958 hit *Dracula*. Anaemic David Peel as Baron Meinster is a poor substitute for Lee's more full-blooded undead Count, but that's the only point of contention in a

classic Terence Fisher-directed shocker. The marvellous atmosphere drips with a lingering gothic ghoulishness, the sexuality is remarkably upfront for its time, and the climax set in the shadow of a moonlit windmill is the stuff of fairy-tale nightmare. AJ **DVD**

Peter Cushing *Dr Van Helsing* • Martita Hunt *Baroness Meinster* • Yvonne Monlaur *Marianne* • Freda Jackson *Greta* • David Peel *Baron Meinster* • Miles Malleson *Dr Tobler* • Henry Oscar *Herr Lang* • Mona Washbourne *Frau Lang* ■ *Dir* Terence Fisher • *Scr* Jimmy Sangster, Peter Bryan, Edward Percy, from characters by Bram Stoker

The Brides of Fu Manchu ★★ U

Crime drama   1966 · UK · Colour · 89min

The second outing for Christopher Lee as Sax Rohmer's mastermind (after *The Face of Fu Manchu*) was the first step down the slippery slope of inadequate stories and deteriorating quality for the series. In this bid for world domination, Fu Manchu kidnaps the daughters of 12 international diplomats to cause political chaos. Don Sharp's direction rarely lives up to his surname, although Lee's performance is as entertaining as always. *The Vengeance of Fu Manchu* followed in 1967. AJ **DVD**

Christopher Lee *Fu Manchu* • Douglas Wilmer *Nayland Smith* • Marie Versini *Marie Lentz* • Heinz Drache *Franz Baumer* • Howard Marion-Crawford *Dr Petrie* • Kenneth Fortescue *Sergeant Spier* • Joseph Furst *Otto Lentz* • Carole Gray *Michele* ■ *Dir* Don Sharp • *Scr* Peter Welbeck [Harry Alan Towers], from characters by Sax Rohmer

Brideshead Revisited ★★★ 12

Period drama   2008 · UK/US · Colour · 127min

Like the 2005 adaptation of *Pride & Prejudice*, this take on a literary classic is destined to be compared to the landmark TV serialisation that came before it. ITV's 1981 production of Evelyn Waugh's between-the-wars tale was memorably brought to life by Anthony Andrews and Jeremy Irons as the leads. Here Matthew Goode takes the role of Charles Ryder, a middle-class scholar who is drawn into the upper-class world of fellow Oxford undergraduate Lord Sebastian Flyte (Ben Whishaw). *Becoming Jane* director Julian Jarrold's film has much to commend it, particularly the performances of Whishaw (charming, camp, dangerous) and co-stars Emma Thompson and Patrick Malahide. And although the bookend sequences do feel rather like awkward appendages, the loss of lesser characters and changes to the book's structure shouldn't offend purists too much. BP A sex scene. **DVD BL**

Matthew Goode *Charles Ryder* • Ben Whishaw *Sebastian Flyte* • Hayley Atwell *Julia Flyte* • Emma Thompson *Lady Marchmain* • Michael Gambon *Lord Marchmain* • Greta Scacchi *Cara* • Patrick Malahide *Edward Ryder* • Felicity Jones *Cordelia Flyte* ■ *Dir* Julian Jarrold • *Scr* Jeremy Brock, Andrew Davies, from the novel by Evelyn Waugh

The Bridesmaid ★★★ 15

Psychological thriller   2004 · Fr/Ger/It · Colour · 110min

Director Claude Chabrol returns to the work of crime novelist Ruth Rendell for this sinister thriller. Sales rep Benoît Magimel loses his grip on reality after falling for Laura Smet (sadly lacking sufficient *femme fatale* quality) after being struck by her similarity to a garden statue that his mother Aurore Clément had given to her lover Bernard Le Coq. While Chabrol generates a typically unnerving atmosphere here, the storyline is short on surprises. DP French +subtitles. Sex scenes.

Benoît Magimel *Philippe Tardieu* • Laura Smet *Stéphanie "Senta" Bellange* • Aurore Clément *Christine Tardieu* • Bernard Le Coq *Gérard Courtois* • Solène Bouton *Sophie Tardieu* • Anna Mihalcea *Patricia Tardieu* • Michel Duchaussoy *The tramp* • Suzanne Flon *Mrs Crespin* ■ *Dir* Claude Chabrol • *Scr* Claude Chabrol, Pierre Leccia, from the novel by Ruth Rendell

Bridesmaids ★★★

Drama   1989 · US · Colour · 120min

Five friends reunite at a wedding and attempt to resolve past problems while new ones crop up during the countdown to the nuptials. Nothing tremendously exciting or revealing happens, but the cast of US TV regulars including Sela Ward, Shelley Hack, Brooke Adams and Jack Coleman is amiable enough to make this pleasant entertainment. **JB** Swearing.

Shelley Hack *Kimberly Bradstreet* · Sela Ward *Caryl Fox* · Stephanie Faracy *Beth Babyak* · Brooke Adams *Pat McClinton* · Jack Coleman *Matt* · Audra Lindley *Lulu* ■ *Dir* Lila Garrett · *Scr* Bett Eyre

Bridesmaids ★★★★★ 15

Comedy   2011 · US · Colour · 119min

Can women be funny? Can they disgust us and appal us but still have us in stitches and loving them? The answer is yes – and *Bridesmaids* is the proof. Loser singleton Kristen Wiig is asked by lifelong pal Maya Rudolph to be maid of honour at her upcoming wedding. But their friendship is torn asunder by Rudolph's new friend, icky perfectionist Rose Byrne. So Wiig musters a motley crew of bridesmaids and attempts to get her best friend back. The script and direction are brilliant, and the whole thing is spiked with outrageous humour. Wiig is fantastic among the assembled gem-like cluster of comedic actresses, but credit should also go to *The IT Crowd*'s Chris O'Dowd as her love interest and Melissa McCarthy as the awkward but lovable weirdo in the bridal party. **KK** Swearing, sexual references. *DVD* BD

Kristen Wiig *Annie* · Rose Byrne *Helen* · Maya Rudolph *Lillian* · Melissa McCarthy *Megan* · Chris O'Dowd *Officer Rhodes* · Ellie Kemper *Becca* · Matt Lucas *Gil* · Jon Hamm *Ted* ■ *Dir* Paul Feig · *Scr* Annie Mumolo, Kristen Wiig

The Bridge ★★★★ PG

Second World War drama
1959 · W Ger · BW · 98min

Although many German features in the 1950s tackled the aftermath of the Second World War (the so-called "rubble films") few dealt with the conflict itself. Actor Bernhard Wicki made his debut as writer/director with this docudramatic reconstruction of an actual incident involving seven teenage recruits who were ordered to defend a strategically irrelevant bridge in the last days of the American advance. Rarely has the rigidity of Nazi discipline or the futility of war been as powerfully exposed as in this Oscar-nominated drama. **DP** German +subtitles. *DVD*

Volker Bohnet *Hans Scholten* · Fritz Wepper *Albert Mutz* · Michael Hinz *Walter Forst* · Frank Glaubrecht *Jurgen Borchert* · Karl Michael Balzer *Karl Horber* · Volker Lechtenbrink *Klaus Hager* · Gunther Hoffmann *Sigi Bernhard* ■ *Dir* Bernhard Wicki · *Scr* Michael Mansfeld, Karl-Wilhelm Vivier, from the novel *Die Brucke* by Manfred Gregor

The Bridge ★★ 15

Period drama   1990 · UK · Colour · 97min

This genteel British period piece lacks both subtlety and dynamism. The brilliant Saskia Reeves is underused as a bored wife who falls head over heels for a young artist (David O'Hara) while on holiday with her children. Even with the acting clout of Joss Ackland, Geraldine James and Rosemary Harris behind him, director Sydney Macartney simply doesn't have the artistry of a James Ivory. **LH**

Saskia Reeves *Isobel Hetherington* · David O'Hara *Philip Wilson Steer* · Joss Ackland *Smithson* · Rosemary Harris *Aunt Jude* · Anthony Higgins *Reginald Hetherington* · Geraldine James *Mrs Todd* · Tabitha Allen *Emma Hetherington* · Dominique Rossi *Mary* ■ *Dir* Sydney Macartney · *Scr* Adrian Hodges, from the novel by Maggie Hemingway

The Bridge ★★★

Drama   1999 · Fr · Colour · 88min

Gérard Depardieu explores the randomness of attraction in this measured drama, which he co-directed with Frédéric Auburtin. In a bid to reinforce his themes, Depardieu archly cast his off-screen lover, Carole Bouquet, as the perfect wife who has an affair with Charles Berling, an engineer working on the same bridge as her husband. The film is truthful but slightly lacking in dramatic impetus. **DP** French +subtitles.

Gérard Depardieu *Georges* · Carole Bouquet *Mina* · Charles Berling *Matthias* · Stanislas Crevillen *Tommy* · Dominique Reymond *Claire Daboval* · Mélanie Laurent *Lisbeth* ■ *Dir* Gérard Depardieu, Frédéric Auburtin · *Scr* François Dupeyron, from a novel by Alain LeBlanc

The Bridge ★ 18

Documentary   2006 · UK/US · Colour · 93min

Director Eric Steel's cynical documentary combines footage culled from a year-long vigil at San Francisco's Golden Gate Bridge and interviews with the grieving friends and family of suicide victims whose deaths were captured on camera. Steel protested that the film was intended to highlight the taboo topics of mental illness and self-harm, and he insisted (tellingly off-camera) that every effort was made to alert the authorities to potential jumpers. But this remains an exploitative exercise that callously builds up voyeuristic suspense while prying into the raw emotions of those who blame themselves for not averting disaster. **DP** *DVD*

■ *Dir* Eric Steel · *Scr* Inspired by the *New Yorker* article *Jumpers* by Tad Friend · *Cinematographer* Peter McCandless

The Bridge at Remagen ★★★ PG

Second World War drama
1969 · US · Colour · 112min

George Segal lifts this "war is hell" saga out of the ordinary with a world-weary performance as a die-hard platoon leader who's trying to reach the bridge of the title before the Germans can destroy it. Filming in Czechoslovakia and interrupted by the actual Russian invasion, big-budget director John Guillermin was clearly trying something different here by adding sober measures of cynical disenchantment to the conventional melodramatic mix. **AJ** *DVD*

George Segal *Lieutenant Phil Hartman* · Robert Vaughn (1) *Major Paul Kreuger* · Ben Gazzara *Sergeant Angelo* · Bradford Dillman *Major Barnes* · EG Marshall *Brig Gen Shinner* · Peter Van Eyck *General von Brock* · Matt Clark *Colonel Jellicoe* · Fritz Ford *Colonel Dent* ■ *Dir* John Guillermin · *Scr* Richard Yates, William Roberts, Ray Rigby, from a story by Roger Hirson [Roger O Hirson], from the novel by Kenneth William Hechler

Bridge of Dragons ★★ 18

Action thriller   1999 · US · Colour · 87min

Dolph Lundgren remains a popular draw in videoland and this won't disappoint his fans. Set in a post-apocalyptic future, it stars Lundgren as a programmed killing machine – an always helpful plot device since it explains the wooden acting. When he comes to the rescue of a princess, he incurs the wrath of evil warlord Cary-Hiroyuki Tagawa. **JF** *DVD*

Dolph Lundgren *Warchyld* · Cary-Hiroyuki Tagawa *Ruecheng* · Rachel Shane [Valerie Chow] *Halo* ■ *Dir* Isaac Florentine · *Scr* Carlton Holder

Bridge of Spies ★★★★ 12

Spy thriller based on a true story
2015 · US · Colour and BW · 135min

Steven Spielberg's gloriously glossy espionage drama spins a complex story of political intrigue into timeless entertainment. Inspired by real events and set during the height of the Cold War, it follows Tom Hanks's principled insurance lawyer as he agrees to represent unassuming artist and Soviet spy Mark Rylance. Spielberg finds humour in the escalating subterfuge and includes plenty of eye-catching period detail. It all seems slowed to match the pace of Rylance's riveting performance, while its compassionate message is written all over his face. **EAS** Violence, swearing. *DVD* BD

Tom Hanks *James B Donovan* · Mark Rylance *Rudolf Abel* · Amy Ryan *Mary Donovan* · Scott Shepherd *Hoffman* · Sebastian Koch *Vogel* · Alan Alda *Thomas Watters Jr* ■ *Dir* Steven Spielberg · *Scr* Matt Charman, Ethan Coen, Joel Coen

The Bridge on the River Kwai ★★★★★ PG

Second World War epic
1957 · UK · Colour · 155min

Few Second World War films are as enduring as director David Lean's multi-Oscar-winning examination of the stiff upper lip. Alec Guinness plays Colonel Nicholson, the epitome of British dignity and resolve who, after brutal treatment at the hands of his Japanese captors in Burma, leads his men in the building of a strategically vital railway bridge for the enemy, as an exercise in keeping up their – and his – morale. This is interesting enough, but the ironies of war are further pointed up by the subplot in which wily American escapee William Holden is dispatched back into the jungle to blow up said bridge. The central performances are first rate, including Sessue Hayakawa as the Japanese commander, but it's Guinness who stands out, imbuing Nicholson with a brand of pride, patriotism and courage that speaks of another age. **AC** *DVD* BD

William Holden (2) *Shears* · Alec Guinness *Colonel Nicholson* · Jack Hawkins *Major Warden* · Sessue Hayakawa *Colonel Saito* · James Donald *Major Clipton* · Geoffrey Horne *Lieutenant Joyce* · André Morell *Colonel Green* · Peter Williams *Captain Reeves* · John Boxer *Major Hughes* ■ *Dir* David Lean · *Scr* Pierre Boulle (front for Carl Foreman, Michael Wilson), from the novel by Pierre Boulle · *Music* Malcolm Arnold · *Editor* Peter Taylor

Bridge to Terabithia ★★★★ PG

Fantasy adventure   2006 · US · Colour · 91min

Based on Katherine Paterson's children's novel, this charming fantasy is an emotionally rich testament to the life-changing power of friendship. Josh Hutcherson and AnnaSophia Robb are wonderful as ten-year-old misfits who are drawn together by their mutual alienation and delightful creativity. After an awkward introduction, they become inseparable, inventing an imaginary kingdom known as Terabithia (a homage to CS Lewis) in their local woods. Yet it's the duo's mundane experiences and the way their secret empowers them at school that are the story's greatest strengths. Former *Rugrats* animator Gabor Csupo tackles pre-teen issues with wit and sensitivity, while an unexpectedly tragic turn makes the final segment particularly affecting. **SF** Scary scenes. *DVD* BD

Josh Hutcherson *Jess Aarons* · AnnaSophia Robb *Leslie Burke* · Zooey Deschanel *Ms Edmonds* · Robert Patrick *Jack Aarons* · Kate Butler *Nancy Aarons* · Bailee Madison *May Belle Aarons* · Devon Wood *Brenda Aarons* ■ *Dir* Gabor Csupo · *Scr* Jeff Stockwell, David Paterson, from the novel by Katherine Paterson · *Cinematographer* Michael Chapman

Bridge to the Sun ★★ U

Second World War biographical drama
1961 · US/Fr · BW · 112min

Carroll Baker stars as an American girl who marries Japanese diplomat James Shigeta and accompanies him to Japan in time for Pearl Harbor. Needless to say, the couple endure social, cultural and emotional difficulties as well as wartime hardships, and suffer a tragedy at the war's end. Based on an autobiography by Gwen Terasaki, the subject itself is fascinating, but, although proficient, the film remains dull and uninvolving. **RK**

Carroll Baker *Gwen Terasaki* · James Shigeta *Hidenari Terasaki* · James Yagi *Hara* · Tetsuro Tamba *Jiro* · Sean Garrison *Fred Tyson* · Ruth Masters *Aunt Peggy* ■ *Dir* Etienne Périer · *Scr* Charles Kaufman, from the autobiography by Gwen Terasaki

A Bridge Too Far ★★★ 15

Second World War drama
1977 · UK · Colour · 168min

Richard Attenborough's epic retelling of one of the Second World War's biggest debacles is impressive enough, with its eye-catching list of stars, fabulous parachute-drop sequences and superb Panavision photography from Geoffrey Unsworth. But the depressing nature of this story of human suffering and sacrifice makes for grim, unedifying viewing, no matter how cleverly writer William Goldman has created drama from the event. Only Sean Connery and Edward Fox really shine in an all-star cast. **TS** Violence, swearing. *DVD* BD

Dirk Bogarde *Lt Gen Frederick Browning* · James Caan *Staff Sergeant Eddie Dohun* · Michael Caine *Lt Col Joe Vandeleur* · Sean Connery *Maj Gen Robert Urquhart* · Edward Fox *Lt Gen Brian Horrocks* · Elliott Gould *Colonel Bobby Stout* · Gene Hackman *Maj Gen Stanislaw Sosabowski* · Anthony Hopkins *Lt Col John Frost* · Hardy Kruger *Maj Gen Ludwig* · Laurence Olivier *Dr Spaander* · Ryan O'Neal *Brig Gen James M Gavin* · Robert Redford *Major Julian Cook* · Maximilian Schell *Lt Gen Bittrich* ■ *Dir* Richard Attenborough · *Scr* William Goldman, from the book by Cornelius Ryan

The Bridges at Toko-Ri ★★★★ U

War drama   1954 · US · Colour · 98min

This glossy, star-laden Korean War movie manages to be both superbly entertaining and extremely moving, thanks to solid direction from the underrated Mark Robson. The source material is from the prolific writer James A Michener, and his view of the futility of the war in Korea is given expert emphasis by the fine performances of William Holden as a reserve officer recalled to service and Fredric March as a gruff admiral. Grace Kelly is simply luminous as Holden's navy wife. **TS** *DVD*

William Holden (2) *Lieutenant Harry Brubaker* · Fredric March *Rear Admiral George Tarrant* · Grace Kelly *Nancy Brubaker* · Mickey Rooney *Mike Forney* · Robert Strauss *Beer Barrel* · Charles McGraw *Commander Wayne Lee* · Keiko Awaji *Kimiko* · Earl Holliman *Nestor Gamidge* · Richard Shannon *Lieutenant Olds* ■ *Dir* Mark Robson · *Scr* Valentine Davies, from a novel by James A Michener

The Bridges of Madison County ★★★★ 12

Romantic drama   1995 · US · Colour · 129min

Clint Eastwood directs and stars in this romantic drama based on Robert James Waller's bestseller. He plays a photographer drawn into an intense love affair with rancher's wife Meryl Streep when he arrives in Iowa to take pictures of Madison County's covered bridges. Told in flashback after Streep's death, when her grown-up children discover a diary and realise how deeply affected their mother was by the experience. Eastwood's moving film avoids easy sentimentality, and this is beautifully photographed and directed with an intimate maturity. **TH** Swearing. *DVD*

Clint Eastwood *Robert Kincaid* · Meryl Streep *Francesca Johnson* · Annie Corley *Carolyn Johnson* · Victor Slezak *Michael Johnson* · Jim Haynie *Richard* · Sarah Kathryn Schmitt *Young Carolyn* · Christopher Kroon *Young Michael* · Phyllis Lyons *Betty* ■ *Dir* Clint Eastwood · *Scr* Richard LaGravenese, from the novel by Robert James Waller

Bridget Jones's Diary ★★★★ 15

Romantic comedy
2001 · UK/US · Colour · 93min

So well adapted by Richard Curtis that it appeals to both sexes, the film is actually far better than the book. Star Renée Zellweger, as the 1990s heroine, is far more endearing than the book's Bridget. Then one cannot imagine Helen Fielding ever having the luxury of suitor super duo Hugh Grant and Colin Firth, who both surpass expectations. What we have here is the best in British romantic comedy, well directed by newcomer Sharon Maguire, well acted by

B

an ensemble of stellar cast and very, very funny indeed. Daft, delicious, decidedly dippy and quite brilliant. LH Sex scenes, swearing, nudity. DVD SL

Renée Zellweger *Bridget Jones* • Colin Firth *Mark Darcy* • Hugh Grant *Daniel Cleaver* • Jim Broadbent *Bridget's dad* • Gemma Jones *Bridget's mum* • Sally Phillips *Sharon* • Shirley Henderson *Jude* • James Callis *Tom* • Embeth Davidtz *Natasha* • Celia Imrie *Una Alconbury* • Honor Blackman *Penny Husbands-Bosworth* ■ *Dir* Sharon Maguire • *Scr* Helen Fielding, Andrew Davies, Richard Curtis, from the novel by Helen Fielding

Bridget Jones: the Edge of Reason ★★★ 15
Romantic comedy
2004 · UK/US/Fr/Ire · Colour · 103min

This occasionally tiresome sequel has the gormless but lovable Bridget (Renée Zellweger) no longer single, having hooked dishy but taciturn Mark Darcy (Colin Firth). It's not long, however, before they're squabbling, so Bridget heads off to Thailand with handsome cad Hugh Grant. The characterisations are once more excellent, but the script lets it down. BP Swearing, sex scenes. DVD SL

Renée Zellweger *Bridget Jones* • Hugh Grant *Daniel Cleaver* • Colin Firth *Mark Darcy* • Jim Broadbent *Bridget's dad* • Gemma Jones *Bridget's mum* • Sally Phillips *Shazzer* • Shirley Henderson *Jude* • Neil Pearson *Richard Finch* ■ *Dir* Beeban Kidron • *Scr* Helen Fielding, Andrew Davies, Richard Curtis, Adam Brooks, from the novel by Helen Fielding

Bridget Jones's Baby ★★★★
Romantic comedy
2016 · UK · Colour

Over a decade after Bridget said "yes" to her Mr Darcy, she is alone, again, in a total hoot of a sequel, outdoing the second film by far (and almost matching the first). Renée Zellweger reprises the role with gusto, celebrating her 43rd birthday with a cupcake and plenty of wine, older but no wiser despite putting her newsroom career first for once. Helen Fielding's third novel had fans up in arms, so director Sharon Maguire (making her feature debut) works instead from a script based on Fielding's columns for *The Independent* in 2005. Even if the machinations of the plot are unlikely and a tad predictable, it is in the end, a bundle of joy. SP

Renée Zellweger *Bridget Jones* • Colin Firth *Mark Darcy* • Patrick Dempsey *Jack Qwant* • Jim Broadbent *Bridget's dad* • Celia Imrie *Una Alconbury* • Sally Phillips *Shazzer* • Gemma Jones *Bridget's mum* • Ed Sheeran ■ *Dir* Sharon Maguire • *Scr* Emma Thompson, Helen Fielding, David Nicholls, from characters by Fielding

Brief Ecstasy ★★★ U
Romantic drama
1937 · UK · BW · 66min

Linden Travers is so heartbroken when handsome aviator Hugh Williams leaves for India to tend his dying father that she throws herself at ageing scientist Paul Lukas. However, just as Travers is becoming accustomed to her loveless domestic regime, Williams makes an unexpected reappearance as Lukas's ward. Director Edmond T Gréville conspires with cinematographer Ronald Neame to expertly capture the mood of simmering lust and emphasise Travers's growing emotional turmoil. DP DVD

Paul Lukas *Prof Paul Bernardy* • Hugh Williams *Jim Wyndham* • Linden Travers *Helen Norwood Bernardy* • Marie Ney *Martha Russell* • Renee Gadd *Marjorie* ■ *Dir* Edmond T Gréville • *Scr* Basil Mason • *Cinematographer* Ronald Neame

Brief Encounter ★★★★★ PG
Classic romantic drama 1945 · UK · BW · 83min

Co-adapted by Noël Coward from his own one-act play *Still Life*, this is one of the finest films ever made in Britain. What makes the illicit love between doctor Trevor Howard and housewife Celia Johnson so memorable is their sheer ordinariness – they really could be anybody sitting in the dark or in the comfort of their armchair. Romancing to the strains of Rachmaninov's

Second Piano Concerto, the leads are outstanding, but credit should also go to Cyril Raymond, whose decent dullness as Johnson's husband makes those stolen Thursdays seem so special. DP DVD SL

Celia Johnson *Laura Jesson* • Trevor Howard *Dr Alec Harvey* • Cyril Raymond *Fred Jesson* • Stanley Holloway *Albert Godby* • Joyce Carey *Myrtle Bagot* • Everley Gregg *Dolly Messiter* • Margaret Barton *Beryl Waters* • Dennis Harkin *Stanley* • Irene Handl *Organist* ■ *Dir* David Lean • *Scr* Noël Coward, David Lean, Ronald Neame, from the play *Still Life* by Noël Coward • *Cinematographer* Robert Krasker

Brief Encounter ★★ PG
Romantic drama 1974 · UK/US · Colour · 99min

Richard Burton and Sophia Loren step uncomfortably into Trevor Howard and Celia Johnson's shoes as the married strangers drifting into a poignant affair. There's no denying the bittersweet source material still packs an emotional punch even in this lavish treatment. But the ever-gorgeous Loren, as an Italian housewife who married into the English middle class, barely convinces. AJ DVD

Richard Burton *Alec Harvey* • Sophia Loren *Anna Jesson* • Jack Hedley *Graham Jesson* • Rosemary Leach *Mrs Gaines* • John Le Mesurier *Stephen* • Gwen Cherrell *Dolly* ■ *Dir* Alan Bridges • *Scr* John Bowne, from the play *Still Life* by Noël Coward

A Brief History of Time ★★★
Documentary 1992 · US/UK · Colour · 80min

Using computers and synthesizers to circumvent the devastating effects of amyotrophic lateral sclerosis, Stephen Hawking succeeded in transforming our notions about the formation of the universe and, through his bestseller *A Brief History of Time*, became the world's most famous theoretical physicist. Steering scrupulously clear of Hawking's then-complex love life, innovative documentarist Errol Morris delves into his past to discover a rebellious student whose mental faculties sharpened as his physical condition deteriorated. With stylised graphics illuminating the theories, and Philip Glass's score imbuing them with a suitable sense of awesomeness, this is a fascinating study. DP

■ *Dir* Errol Morris • *Scr* Stephen Hawking, from his book

Brigadoon ★★★★ U
Musical romantic fantasy
1954 · US · Colour · 103min

This beguiling MGM version of Alan J Lerner and Frederick Loewe's magical stage musical about a Scottish village that comes to life every hundred years is an overlooked and often derided movie: time has proved there's no reason for such harsh judgement. It boasts a wonderful score and magnificent arrangements, plus an imaginative studio set, while the use of early CinemaScope enhances the brilliant lateral stage choreography. Yet the real heart of the film lies in the casting. The great Gene Kelly could not be bettered as the American in love in a faraway time and a foreign clime. His duet with Cyd Charisse - *The Heather on the Hill* – is enchanting and, as Kelly's buddy-in-booze, Van Johnson shines. TS DVD

Gene Kelly *Tommy Albright* • Van Johnson *Jeff Douglas* • Cyd Charisse *Fiona Campbell* • Elaine Stewart *Jane Ashton* • Barry Jones *Mr Lundie* • Hugh Laing *Harry Beaton* • Albert Sharpe *Andrew Campbell* • Virginia Bosler *Jean Campbell* ■ *Dir* Vincente Minnelli • *Scr* Alan Jay Lerner, from the musical by Alan Jay Lerner, Frederick Loewe • *Choreographer* Gene Kelly • *Art Directors* Cedric Gibbon, Preston Ames • *Set Designers* Edwin B Willis, Keogh Gleason • *Costume Designer* Irene

Brigham Young ★★
Historical drama 1940 · US · BW · 112min

It was jolly difficult to tell the true story of the Mormon trek westward when the censor forbade polygamy on the screen. Director Henry Hathaway gets around this by ignoring the facts and concentrating

instead on such eye-catching events as an impressive locust attack on the Mormons' first spring crop. The title role is played by Dean Jagger with a sense of rugged integrity and conviction. TS

Tyrone Power *Jonathan Kent* • Linda Darnell *Zina Webb* • Dean Jagger *Brigham Young* • Brian Donlevy *Angus Duncan* • Jane Darwell *Eliza Kent* • John Carradine *Porter Rockwell* • Mary Astor *Mary Ann Young* • Vincent Price *Joseph Smith* • Jean Rogers *Clara Young* ■ *Dir* Henry Hathaway • *Scr* Lamar Trotti, from the story by Louis Bromfield

Bright ★★ PG
Fantasy crime drama 2017 · US · Colour

This is a preview - no prints were available to review as we went to press. *Suicide Squad*, writer/director David Ayer re-teams with that film's star Will Smith, this time pairing him with Joel Edgerton for a cop drama with a kooky twist. Straying from his usual LA beat, Ayer has set this movie in a fantastical world where orcs and fairies live among humans. The *Men in Black* series has a similar premise, but given Ayer's track record in gritty policiers, the mood will more likely be pitch black. SP

Will Smith • Joel Edgerton ■ *Dir* David Ayer • *Scr* Max Landis, David Ayer

Bright Angel ★★ 15
Road movie 1990 · US · Colour · 89min

A heavenly cast are rather lost at sea in this over-stylised thriller. Dermot Mulroney plays a Montana boy inveigled by runaway hippy Lili Taylor to go to Wyoming and find a man who will spring her brother from jail. A pair of innocents, their road trip places them up to their necks in unpleasant but interesting characters. A depressing examination of Midwest life and "Generation X". LH

Dermot Mulroney *George Russell* • Lili Taylor *Lucy* • Sam Shepard *Jack Russell* • Valerie Perrine *Aileen Russell* • Burt Young *Art Falcone* • Bill Pullman *Bob* • Benjamin Bratt *Claude* • Mary Kay Place *Judy* • Delroy Lindo *Harley* ■ *Dir* Michael Fields • *Scr* Richard Ford

Bright Days Ahead ★★★ 15
Romantic drama 2013 · Fr · Colour · 94min

Marion Vernoux's study of late-life passion is slickly staged and luminously photographed, but short on drama and depth. Fanny Ardant plays the 60-something woman who's retired from the dental practice she ran with husband Patrick Chesnais on the Nord-Pas-de-Calais coast, who embarks upon a reckless fling with 30-something computer tutor Laurent Lafitte. Ardant effortlessly combines glamour and vulnerability, but the plotline comes perilously close to soap opera. DP French, English +subtitles. Swearing, sex scenes, nudity.

Fanny Ardant *Caroline ("Caro")* • Laurent Laffite *Julien* • Patrick Chesnais *Philippe* • Jean-François Stévenin *Roger* • Fanny Cottençon *Chantal* ■ *Dir* Marion Vernoux • *Scr* Marion Vernoux, Fanny Chesnel, Marc Syrigas, from Chesnel's novel *Une Jeune Fille aux Cheveux Blancs*

Bright Eyes ★★ U
Comedy 1934 · US · BW · 81min

A must for Shirley Temple fans (but others beware) as here, at six years' old, she performs her most famous song, *On the Good Ship Lollipop*. In the last of some ten 1934 screen appearances, the hard-working moppet is the daughter of a maid killed in a road accident. Her mother's employers grudgingly look after Temple to keep in with a rich relative (Charles Sellon) who dotes on her. In memorable contrast to Hollywood's favourite moppet is Jane Withers in her first substantial role as a spoiled and sadistic brat. Two years older than Temple, she went on to become a child star in her own right. AE DVD

Shirley Temple *Shirley Blake* • James Dunn *Loop Merritt* • Jane Darwell *Mrs Higgins* • Judith Allen *Adele Martin* • Lois Wilson *Mary Blake* • Charles Sellon *Uncle Ned Smith* • Walter Johnson *Thomas, the chauffeur* • Jane Withers *Joy Smythe* ■ *Dir* David Butler • *Scr* William Conselman, Edwin Burke, David Butler

Bright Leaf ★★
Drama 1950 · US · BW · 110min

After appearing together in *The Fountainhead*, Gary Cooper and Patricia Neal were reunited for this turgid melodrama about rival tobacco barons. Cooper gives a lazy performance that stands in stark contrast to Donald Crisp and Neal, who both overact wildly as the father and daughter who seek to ruin him. DP

Gary Cooper *Brant Royle* • Lauren Bacall *Sonia Kovac* • Patricia Neal *Margaret Jane Singleton* • Jack Carson *Chris Malley* • Donald Crisp *Major James Singleton* • Gladys George *Rose* • Elizabeth Patterson *Tabitha Jackson* ■ *Dir* Michael Curtiz • *Scr* Ranald MacDougall, from the novel by Foster Fitz-Simons

Bright Leaves ★★★★ PG
Documentary 2003 · US/UK · Colour · 107min

Ross McElwee's reputation for personal documentaries with a deceptively wider perspective is reinforced with this investigation into his North Carolina family's role in the corporatisation of the tobacco business. Seeking to establish whether the character played by Gary Cooper in Michael Curtiz's 1950 melodrama *Bright Leaf* was based on his great-grandfather, McElwee winds up considering everything from cinematic license to the capricious nature of history and public health. He approaches his subject with wry, self-deprecating sagacity and the result is disarmingly charming. DP

■ *Dir/Scr* Ross McElwee

Bright Lights, Big City ★★ 18
Drama 1988 · US · Colour · 102min

The archetypal 1980s movie, this has oodles of RayBans, credit cards, minimalist furniture, naked ambition and enough South American nose candy to make antihero Michael J Fox's coffee table look like Mount Kilimanjaro. At the time, though, it all creaked and groaned, largely due to Fox's inability to portray the complexities of a young New York novelist on the skids. SH Swearing, drug abuse. DVD

Michael J Fox *Jamie Conway* • Kiefer Sutherland *Tad Allagash* • Phoebe Cates *Amanda* • Swoosie Kurtz *Megan* • Frances Sternhagen *Clara Tillinghast* • Tracy Pollan *Vicky* • John Houseman *Mr Vogel* • Charlie Schlatter *Michael* • Jason Robards *Alex Hardy* • Dianne Wiest *Mother* ■ *Dir* James Bridges • *Scr* Jay McInerney, from his novel

Bright Road ★★★ U
Drama 1953 · US · BW · 68min

A modest second feature, this is about a pupil (Philip Hepburn) in an all-black school, emotionally troubled as a result of racism and a depressed home life, who overcomes his difficulties with the dedicated help of teacher Dorothy Dandridge. It's a worthy, well-acted effort with some touching moments, but it's hampered by a screenplay that pulls its punches. RK

Dorothy Dandridge *Jane Richards* • Philip Hepburn *CT Young* • Harry Belafonte *School principal* • Barbara Ann Sanders *Tanya* • Robert Horton *Dr Mitchell* • Maidie Norman *Tanya's mother* • Renee Beard *Booker T Jones* ■ *Dir* Gerald Mayer • *Scr* Emmett Lavery, from the short story *See How They Run* by Mary Elizabeth Vroman

Bright Star ★★★ PG
Romantic drama based on a true story
2009 · UK/Aus · Colour · 114min

This bittersweet love story from *The Piano* director Jane Campion reveals the inspiration behind some of the finest work of English Romantic John Keats. Ben Whishaw (*Perfume: the Story of a Murderer*) plays the tubercular 23-year-old poet, who is living in Hampstead and finds his creative juices reanimated by teenager Fanny Brawne (a stern Abbie Cornish), who lives next door. The headstrong Brawne soon becomes Keats's muse and an intense relationship is initiated, but the poet's ill-health casts a gloom over the picture-perfect romance. There's a spellbinding, painterly quality to the way Campion depicts the changing seasons and it sets a mood that complements the poet's vivid and sensuous style. SP *DVD*

Abbie Cornish *Fanny Brawne* • Ben Whishaw *John Keats* • Paul Schneider (2) *Charles Brown* • Kerry Fox *Mrs Brawne* • Edie Martin *Toots* • Thomas Brodie-Sangster *Samuel* ■ *Dir/Scr* Jane Campion • *Cinematographer* Greig Fraser

Bright Victory ★★★

Drama   1951 · US · BW · 97min

Blinded in the war, soldier Arthur Kennedy faces another kind of battle as he attempts to adjust to his disability, first in hospital, then back home, where his girlfriend Julia Adams is waiting for him. A moving, if sentimental drama, this is lent added interest by its insight into the rehabilitation methods for the blind. Kennedy gives a superbly convincing performance that earned him a deserved Oscar nomination. RK

Arthur Kennedy *Larry Nevins* • Peggy Dow *Judy Greene* • Julia Adams [*Julie Adams*] *Chris Paterson* • James Edwards *Joe Morgan* • Will Geer *Mr Nevins* • Minor Watson *Mr Paterson* • Jim Backus *Bill Grayson* • Joan Banks *Janet Grayson* • Rock Hudson *Cpl John Flagg* ■ *Dir* Mark Robson • *Scr* Robert Buckner, from the novel *Lights Out* by Bayard Kendrick

Bright Young Things ★★★ 15

Period comedy drama
2003 · UK · Colour · 101min

Stephen Fry's adaptation of Evelyn Waugh's classic novel *Vile Bodies* is a solid enough directorial debut. The tale of inter-war youthful plutocrats engaging in endless partying and occasional spasms of self-loathing has been semi-faithfully transferred to the screen. Stephen Campbell Moore stars as a frustrated writer who sets out to marry his girlfriend Emily Mortimer, but it's Fenella Woolgar who really shines as a ditzy socialite. Some of Waugh's finely wrought style evaporates in the transfer and the film drags occasionally as a result. AS Drug abuse. *DVD*

Stephen Campbell Moore *Adam Fenwick-Symes* • Emily Mortimer *Nina Blount* • Fenella Woolgar *Agatha Runcible* • James McAvoy *Lord Simon Balcairn* • Michael Sheen *Miles* • David Tennant *Ginger* • Guy Henry *Archie* • Dan Aykroyd *Lord Monomark* • Jim Broadbent *Drunken Major* • Simon Callow *King of Anatolia* • Stockard Channing *Mrs Melrose Ape* • Julia McKenzie *Lottie Crump* • Sir John Mills [*John Mills*] *Gentleman at party* • Peter O'Toole *Colonel Blount* • Harriet Walter *Lady Metroland* • Bill Paterson *Sir James Brown* • Margaret Tyzack *Lady Throbbing* • Stephen Fry *Chauffeur* ■ *Dir* Stephen Fry • *Scr* Stephen Fry, from the novel *Vile Bodies* by Evelyn Waugh

Brighton Beach Memoirs ★★★ 15

Comedy drama   1986 · US · Colour · 104min

Neil Simon is an expert at angst-ridden autobiography and loves to mine the seam of Jewish family life. Nobody does this particular brand of head-banging better, and this slice of strudel boasts a lovely, acerbic portrayal from Jonathan Silverman as Simon's adolescent doppelgänger, Eugene Jerome. However, Simon has fails to open out his stage play enough for the film to breathe. SH *DVD*

Jonathan Silverman *Eugene* • Blythe Danner *Kate* • Bob Dishy *Jack* • Brian Drillinger *Stanley* • Stacey Glick *Laurie* • Judith Ivey *Blanche* • Lisa Waltz *Nora* ■ *Dir* Gene Saks • *Scr* Neil Simon, from his play

Brighton Rock ★★★★ PG

Crime drama   1947 · UK · BW · 88min

This is one of the most sinister crime films ever made in Britain and, but for several cuts by the censor, it would also have been one of the most shocking. However, Graham Greene, scripting from his own novel (not in collaboration with Terence Rattigan, as many sources state), also drew some of the film's teeth by allowing gullible waitress Carol Marsh the faint hope that her malicious husband might love her after all.

Richard Attenborough turns in the best performance of his career. DP *DVD* *Blu-ray*

Richard Attenborough *Pinkie Brown* • Hermione Baddeley *Ida Arnold* • William Hartnell *Dallow* • Carol Marsh *Rose* • Nigel Stock *Cubitt* • Wylie Watson *Spicer* • Harcourt Williams *Prewitt* • Alan Wheatley *Fred Hale/Kolley Kibber* ■ *Dir* John Boulting • *Scr* Graham Greene, from his novel

Brighton Rock ★★★ 15

Period crime thriller
2010 · Fr/UK · Colour · 106min

Rowan Joffe insists his directorial debut adapts Graham Greene's pre-war novel rather than remakes the 1947 film, though comparisons to the latter are inevitable. The action still centres on hoodlum Pinkie (Sam Riley) and his attempts to cover his tracks after a murder, but it's been arbitrarily relocated from the 1930s to the 1960s. This apart, the new *Brighton Rock* is not so radically different, beyond the melodramatic cranking up of the book's Catholicism. Riley is suitably morose, and the older cast – Helen Mirren, John Hurt, Phil Davis – dependable, but the real star is Andrea Riseborough as corrupted waitress Rose. AC Violence, swearing. *DVD* *Blu-ray*

Sam Riley *Pinkie* • Andrea Riseborough *Rose* • Helen Mirren *Ida* • John Hurt *Phil Corkery* • Phil Davis [*Philip Davis*] *Spicer* • Nonso Anozie *Dallow* • Craig Parkinson *Cubitt* • Andy Serkis *Colleoni* • Steve Evets *Mr Wilson* ■ *Dir* Rowan Joffe • *Scr* Rowan Joffe, from the novel by Graham Greene • *Music* Martin Phipps

The Brighton Strangler ★★★

Thriller   1945 · US · BW · 67min

Set in Britain during the Second World War, but filmed (extremely quickly and cheaply) in Hollywood, this intriguing little programme filler was directed by Max Nosseck. This stars a rather wooden John Loder, who appears on stage as "the Brighton Strangler", and, after a blow to the head, begins to live out his stage role in real life. Cleverly done, and really quite eerie. TS

John Loder *Reginald/Edward* • June Duprez *April* • Michael St Angel *Bob* • Miles Mander *Allison* • Rose Hobart *Dorothy* • Gilbert Emery *Dr Manby* • Rex Evans *Shelton* • Matthew Boulton *Inspector Graham* ■ *Dir* Max Nosseck • *Scr* Arnold Phillips, Max Nosseck

brilliantlove ★ 18

Erotic drama   2010 · UK · Colour · 96min

Manchester (Liam Browne) and Noon (Nancy Trotter Landry) live in a lock-up garage and spend much of their time having sex, and taking pictures to prove it. When pornographer Michael Hodgson happens upon these images, Manchester is offered an art show to exhibit them. Noon, though, is unsurprisingly less pleased at being exposed to the world, prompting a falling out between the pair. *brilliantlove* is competently made and adequately acted, but unless you're a fan of films featuring bouts of explicit love-making, it's likely to come across as nothing more than a self-indulgent bore. DA Sex scenes. *DVD*

Liam Browne *Manchester* • Nancy Trotter Landry *Noon* • Michael Hodgson *Franny* • Arabella Arnott *Leah* ■ *Dir* Ashley Horner • *Scr* Sean Conway

Brimstone and Treacle ★★★ 18

Black comedy thriller 1982 · UK · Colour · 83min

The movie version of Dennis Potter's controversial television play (taped by the BBC, but then promptly banned) emerges as an uneven and theatrical thriller with dark religious underpinnings. Demonic Sting is the cunning stranger who worms his way into the household of an atheist hymn composer (Denholm Elliot) his devout wife (Joan Plowright) and their comatose daughter (Suzanna Hamilton) for nefarious reasons. It's persuasively performed and typical Potter – by turns unpleasant and thought-provoking – but director Richard Loncraine goes for mood and atmosphere above any sense of logic or reality. AT *DVD*

Sting *Martin Taylor* • Denholm Elliott *Thomas Bates* • Joan Plowright *Norma Bates* • Suzanna Hamilton *Patricia Bates* • Mary McLeod *Valerie Holdsworth* • Benjamin Whitrow *Businessman* ■ *Dir* Richard Loncraine • *Scr* Dennis Potter

Bring It On ★★ 12

Comedy   2000 · US · Colour · 94min

Kirsten Dunst swaps the cut-throat world of beauty pageants (*Drop Dead Gorgeous*) for the equally competitive arena of high-school cheerleading. Dunst takes over as leader of a crack San Diego high-school squad whose prowess is in stark contrast to the shambolic football team they support. Things don't go smoothly. Peyton Reed's rah!-rah!-rah! chronicle lacks a satirical edge. The 2004 sequel went straight to video. TH *DVD*

Kirsten Dunst *Torrance Shipman* • Eliza Dushku *Missy Pantone* • Jesse Bradford *Cliff Pantone* • Gabrielle Union *Isis* • Sherry Hursey *Christine Shipman* • Holmes Osborne *Bruce Shipman* ■ *Dir* Peyton Reed • *Scr* Jessica Bendinger

Bring Me the Head of Alfredo Garcia ★★★★ 18

Crime drama   1974 · US · Colour · 107min

Sam Peckinpah's enormous talent was on the wane when he made this gruesome Mexican crime drama. But if you can bear to look beneath its gory exterior as piano player Warren Oates becomes caught up with bounty hunters pursuing *that* head for a wealthy landowner, there are still enough moments when Peckinpah's greatness shines through. Excitingly told, this is like *The Wild Bunch*, but even wilder. TH English, Spanish +subtitles. Swearing, violence, nudity. *DVD*

Warren Oates *Bennie* • Isela Vega *Elita* • Gig Young *Quill* • Robert Webber *Sappensly* • Helmut Dantine *Max* • Emilio Fernandez *El Jefe* • Kris Kristofferson *Paco* • Chano Urueta *One-armed bartender* ■ *Dir* Sam Peckinpah • *Scr* Sam Peckinpah, Gordon Dawson, from a story by Frank Kowalski

Bring Me the Head of Mavis Davis ★ 15

Comedy   1997 · UK · Colour · 95min

Rik Mayall plays a record producer who realises that his pride and joy, singer Jane Horrocks, is worth more to him dead than alive. So he hires a hitman to do the dirty deed. Mayall's shouting and Horrocks's shrieking are almost unbearable, and there are some pretty unpleasant gags to boot. LH Swearing, violence. *DVD*

Rik Mayall *Marty Starr* • Jane Horrocks *Marla Dorland* • Danny Aiello *Rathbone* • Ronald Pickup *Percy Stone* • Philip Martin Brown *Inspector Furse* • Ross Boatman *Rock star* • Paul Shearer *Presenter 1980* • Stuart Bunce *Aspirant* ■ *Dir* John Henderson • *Scr* Craig Strachan, from an idea by Joanne Reay

Bring Me the Head of the Machine Gun Woman ★★★ 18

Crime action drama 2013 · Chil · Colour · 73min

Slacker Santiago (Matías Oviedo) spends his time playing violent shoot-'em-ups and DJs at a club run by a gangster. Overhearing mobsters discussing a planned hit, the only way to escape is by volunteering to do what they've failed to do: stop vengeful killer the Machine Gun Woman. From there, the timid Santiago must perform all the criminal activities he can do so well virtually, only for real. With its tongue firmly in its cheek, this is grimy, gimmicky and over all too quickly, but Fernanda Urrejola's title killer – an impossibly sexy, semi-clad, bullet-spraying fury – is assured cult-icon status. JH Spanish +subtitles. Violence, swearing, a sex scene. *DVD* *Blu-ray*

Fernanda Urrejola *Machine Gun Woman* • Matías Oviedo *Santiago Fernández* • Jorge Alis *Che Longana* • Sofía García *Shadeline Soto* • Alex Rivera *Flavio* • Felipe Avello *Jonny Medina* ■ *Dir/Scr* Ernesto Díaz Espinoza

Bring On the Girls ★★

Romantic musical comedy
1945 · US · Colour · 91min

Millionaire Eddie Bracken joins the navy hoping that, as a humble sailor, he'll find a girl who'll love him for himself. Around such thin stuff is woven a feeble assembly-line musical comedy which, under Sidney Lanfield's dull direction, wastes the considerable talents of Bracken, star of such gems as *Hail the Conquering Hero*. RK

Veronica Lake *Teddy Collins* • Sonny Tufts *Phil North* • Eddie Bracken *J Newport Bates* • Marjorie Reynolds *Sue Thomas* • Grant Mitchell *Uncle Ralph* • Johnny Coy *Benny Lowe* • Peter Whitney *Swede* ■ *Dir* Sidney Lanfield • *Scr* Karl Tunberg, Darrell Ware, from a story by Pierre Wolff

Bring On the Night ★★ 15

Music documentary   1985 · UK · Colour · 96min

As the brains behind TV's seminal *7 Up* series, Michael Apted is no stranger to documentary. But he fails to prevent this behind-the-scenes account of Sting's *Dream of the Blue Turtles* tour from becoming a pretentious, self-glorifying vehicle for the one-time Police frontman. While it's fascinating to watch him rehearsing his new band in a palatial French mansion, the talking-head pieces (whether discussions of music or more serious issues) are less than inspiring. The songs, however, are superb. DP *DVD*

Sting • Kenny Kirkland • Branford Marsalis • Trudie Styler • Miles Copeland ■ *Dir* Michael Apted

Bring Your Smile Along ★★★ U

Musical comedy   1955 · US · Colour · 82min

The dynamic singer Frankie Laine made five musicals for producer Jonie Taps in the 1950s and this is the best, brightened by the assured comic touch of writer/director Blake Edwards, making his directorial debut. The plot, which has a timid schoolmarm venturing to the big city and writing the lyrics for a string of hit songs recorded by Laine, is an amusing trifle, filling the spaces between Frankie's electrifying musical renditions. TV

Frankie Laine *Jerry Dennis* • Keefe Brasselle *Martin Adams* • Constance Towers *Nancy Willows* • Lucy Marlow *Marge Stevenson* • William Leslie *David Parker* • Mario Siletti *Ricardo* • Ruth Warren *Landlady* • Jack Albertson *Jenson* ■ *Dir* Blake Edwards • *Scr* Blake Edwards, from a story by Blake Edwards, from a story by Richard Quine

Bringing Down the House ★ 12

Comedy   2003 · US · Colour · 100min

Steve Martin stars in this unfunny, sentimental mush as an uptight lawyer whose perfectly ordered life is turned upside down by an escaped black female convict (Queen Latifah) who's determined to have him prove her innocence. Martin and Latifah's chemistry feels forced, and many will detect racism and homophobia in the film's crass manipulation of stereotypes. AS *DVD*

Steve Martin *Peter Sanderson* • Queen Latifah *Charlene Morton* • Eugene Levy *Howie Rottman* • Joan Plowright *Mrs Arness* • Jean Smart *Kate* • Kimberly J Brown *Sarah Sanderson* • Angus T Jones *Georgey Sanderson* • Betty White *Mrs Kline* ■ *Dir* Adam Shankman • *Scr* Jason Filardi

Bringing Out the Dead ★★★ 18

Drama   1999 · US · Colour · 115min

Martin Scorsese lends his customary intensity and visual razzle-dazzle to this 72-hour insight into the exhausting lives of New York paramedics. The director reunites with his *Taxi Driver* collaborator Paul Schrader to conjure up a powerful, blackly comic and often hallucinatory portrait, with Nicolas Cage perfectly cast as crumbling protagonist Frank Pierce. However, the other performances are so unhinged and the episodic encounters so overwrought,

B

that the drama never really grabs as it should. JC *DVD*

Nicolas Cage *Frank Pierce* • Patricia Arquette *Mary Burke* • John Goodman *Larry* • Ving Rhames *Marcus* • Tom Sizemore *Tom Wolls* • Marc Anthony *Noel* • Mary Beth Hurt *Nurse Constance* • Martin Scorsese *Dispatcher* ■ *Dir* Martin Scorsese • *Scr* Paul Schrader, from the novel by Joe Connelly

LANDMARK FILM

The quintessential screwball comedy, this perfectly encapsulates Katharine Hepburn's comic screen persona

Bringing Up Baby ★★★★★ U
Classic screwball comedy
1938 · US · BW · 102min

How sublime can movies get? This is perfectly cast (Katharine Hepburn in a celebrated screwball role), brilliantly written by Hagar Wilde and Dudley Nichols and fabulously directed by Howard Hawks. It's a genuinely funny original that repays repeated viewings, especially to marvel at the variety of subtle expressions on the face of Cary Grant, who gives one of the most wonderful comic performances ever to grace the silver screen. Regarded as too wacky by half when it was released, this shimmering dissection of the male-female relationship is now regarded as a classic. By the way, "Baby" is a pet leopard. TS *DVD*

Katharine Hepburn *Susan Vance* • Cary Grant *Dr David Huxley* • Charlie Ruggles *[Charles Ruggles] Major Horace Applegate* • Walter Catlett *Constable Slocum* • Barry Fitzgerald *Mr Gogarty* • May Robson *Mrs Carleton Random, Aunt Elizabeth* • Fritz Feld *Dr Fritz Lehmann* • Leona Roberts *Mrs Hannah Gogarty* • George Irving *Mr Alexander Peabody* • Tala Birell *Mrs Lehmann* • Virginia Walker *Alice Swallow* ■ *Dir* Howard Hawks • *Scr* Dudley Nichols, Hagar Wilde, from a short story by Wilde in *Collier's* • *Cinematographer* Russell Metty • *Art Director* Van Nest Polglase

The Brink's Job ★★★ PG
Crime comedy
1978 · US · Colour · 98min

William Friedkin directs this wild, but often hugely entertaining heist comedy. Re-creating what was then dubbed "the crime of the century", it stars Peter Falk as the leader of a gang of amateur crooks who knock over a Boston security firm to the tune of nearly $3 million. The art direction team notched up an Oscar nomination for their stylish period designs, but it's the cast that catches the eye, with Warren Oates a standout as Falk's doltish sidekick. DP

Peter Falk *Tony Pino* • Peter Boyle *Joe McGinnis* • [Allen Garfield] *Vinnie Costa* • Warren Oates *Specs O'Keefe* • Gena Rowlands *Mary Pino* • Paul Sorvino *Jazz Maffie* • Sheldon Leonard *J Edgar Hoover* • Gerard Murphy *Sandy Richardson* ■ *Dir* William Friedkin • *Scr* Walon Green, from the book *Big Stick Up at Brink's* by Noel Behn • *Art Directors* Dean Tavoularis, Angelo Graham • *Set Designers* George R Nelson, Bruce Kay

Britannia Hospital ★★★ 15
Black comedy
1982 · UK · Colour · 111min

Director Lindsay Anderson's top-heavy symbolism all but crushes the satirical life out of this attempt to lampoon the state of the nation, with a run-down hospital expecting a royal visit to celebrate its 500th anniversary used as a metaphor for Britain's moral decay. Media hacks, strike-bent workers, bureaucratic chaos and sinister laboratory experiments are the targets, although the burlesque humour makes it seem closer to "Carry On Casualty". TH Violence, swearing, nudity. *DVD*

Leonard Rossiter *Potter* • Graham Crowden *Millar* • Malcolm McDowell *Mick Travis* • Joan Plowright *Phyllis Grimshaw* • Marsha Hunt [Marsha A Hunt] *Nurse Amanda Persil* • Frank Grimes *Sammy* • Jill Bennett *MacMillan* • Robin Askwith *Ben Keating* • Peter Jeffrey *Sir Geoffrey* • Fulton Mackay *Chief Superintendant Johns* • Dandy Nichols *Florrie* • Alan Bates *Macready* • Mark Hamill *Red* ■ *Dir* Lindsay Anderson • *Scr* David Sherwin

Britannia Mews ★★★
Drama
1949 · UK · BW · 91min

Twentieth Century-Fox made this interesting version of part of Margery

Sharp's excellent but dour novel about Victorian class relationships to use up part of their frozen UK assets. It's a striking and original film, though undermined by the bizarre casting of the usually dependable Dana Andrews in a dual role as Maureen O'Hara's two husbands, in one of which he is rather weirdly revoiced. Nevertheless, O'Hara is striking as ever and the British contingent makes this sordid opus compulsively watchable. TS

Maureen O'Hara *Adelaide Culver* • Dana Andrews *Gilbert Lauderdale/Henry Lambert* • Sybil Thorndike *Mrs Mounsey* • June Allen *Adelaide as a child* • Anthony Tancred *Treff Culver* • Anthony Lamb *Treff as a child* • Wilfrid Hyde White *Mr Culver* • Fay Compton *Mrs Culver* ■ *Dir* Jean Negulesco • *Scr* Ring Lardner Jr, from the novel by Margery Sharp

Britannic ★★★ 15
First World War drama
2000 · US · Colour · 93min

The appeal of this TV movie is its cheeky attempt to rip off James Cameron's 1997 blockbuster – but on a fraction of its budget. True, the *Titanic*'s sister ship, the *Britannic*, was also sunk (in November 1916), but whether the hospital ship was torpedoed because of espionage activities is one of the weaker points of the movie. Actually the special effects aren't bad, but the inevitable romance unnecessarily pads out the final voyage. DM *DVD*

Edward Atterton *Reynolds* • Amanda Ryan *Vera Campbell* • Jacqueline Bisset *Lady Lewis* • Ben Daniels *First Officer Townsend* • John Rhys-Davies *Captain Barrett* • Bruce Payne *Dr Baker* ■ *Dir* Brian Trenchard-Smith • *Scr* Kim Smith, Brett Thompson, Dennis A Pratt, Brian Trenchard-Smith

British Agent ★★★ U
Historical spy adventure 1934 · US · BW · 79min

This historical drama dares to show ungentlemanly conduct on the part of the British Government, which is here shown trying to stop the Bolsheviks making peace with Germany in 1917. Leslie Howard stars as Britain's unofficial representative, who is readily betrayed when he becomes a political embarrassment to his country. Luckily, he has more on his mind than politics after meeting the delectable Kay Francis, who is – as she puts it – a woman first and a Russian agent second. Laird Doyle's screenplay is often tiresome, but director Michael Curtiz brings his usual pace and visual flair to the proceedings. AE

Leslie Howard *Stephen Locke* • Kay Francis *Elena Moura* • William Gargan *Bob Medill* • Phillip Reed [Philip Reed] *Gaston LeFarge* • Irving Pichel *Sergei Pavlov* • Ivan Simpson *Evans Poohbah* • Halliwell Hobbes *Sir Walter Carrister* • J Carroll Naish [J Carrol Naish] *Commissioner for War Trotsky* • Walter Byron *Stanley* • Cesar Romero *Tito Del Val* ■ *Dir* Michael Curtiz • *Scr* Laird Doyle, Roland Pertwee, from the novel by RH Bruce Lockhart

The British Guide to Showing Off ★★★★
Documentary 2011 · UK · Colour · 97min

Artist Andrew Logan has been running his convention-defying pageant, the Alternative Miss World, on and off since the 1970s. Director Jes Benstock follows the delightfully dotty Logan through preparations for the 2009 event, while also compiling highlights from previous years. Competitors and audience members included Divine, Leigh Bowery, Brian Eno and Derek Jarman, and the film traces an eye-popping history of non-mainstream styles, sexuality and identity. This assemblage of mind-boggling costumery and hilarious interviews offers a surprisingly life-affirming paean to British eccentricity at its finest. TJ Swearing, nudity. *DVD* *Blu-ray*

Brian Eno • Andrew Logan • Richard O'Brien • Grayson Perry • Zandra Rhodes • Derek Jarman ■ *Dir* Jes Benstock

British Intelligence ★★★ PG
Spy drama 1940 · US · BW · 60min

This is an intriguing thriller, which used the Great War and its terrifying zeppelin raids

as a means of boosting British morale during the Second World War Blitz. As the butler to a cabinet minister, Boris Karloff appears to change sides as often as the enigmatic Margaret Lindsay. But the wilful obscurity of the storyline is part of its appeal, along with Karloff's sinister geniality. DP *DVD*

Boris Karloff *Valdar* • Margaret Lindsay *Helene von Lorbeer* • Bruce Lester *Frank Bennett* • Leonard Mudie *James Yeats* • Holmes Herbert *Arthur Bennett* • Austin Fairman *George Bennett* ■ *Dir* Terry Morse • *Scr* John Kangan, Lee Katz, from the play *Three Faces East* by Anthony Paul Kelly

Broadcast News ★★★★ 15
Comedy drama 1987 · US · Colour · 126min

In an environment where superegos pursue serious news, a romantic triangle develops between three self-serving Washington-based TV journalists. Vying for the affections of hard-nosed producer Holly Hunter are undervalued William Hurt, as a newscaster who can bring phoney tears to his eyes, and the underused Albert Brooks, as a seasoned investigator. But it's Hunter who really provokes the sorrow and the pity of lives at the mercy of their careers. TH Swearing, brief nudity. *DVD*

William Hurt *Tom Grunick* • Albert Brooks *Aaron Altman* • Holly Hunter *Jane Craig* • Jack Nicholson *Bill Rorich, news anchor* • Lois Chiles *Jennifer Mack* • Joan Cusack *Blair Litton* • Peter Hackes *Paul Moore* • Christian Clemenson *Bobby* ■ *Dir/Scr* James L Brooks

Broadway ★★★
Musical crime drama
1929 · US · BW and Colour · 105min

One of the most eye-catching of the early sound musicals, this boasts elaborate settings for its production numbers. It also has an entertainingly suspenseful plot, in which a dancer Glenn Tryon becomes unwittingly caught up in a murder. Robert Ellis is an effective villain, while Evelyn Brent scores as a chorus girl. Director Paul Fejos devised a versatile and high-speed crane specially for the film, and the climactic nightclub sequence is photographed in "natural" colour. RK

Glenn Tryon *Roy Lane* • Evelyn Brent *Pearl* • Merna Kennedy *Billie Moore* • Thomas E Jackson *Dan McCorn* • Robert Ellis *Steve Crandall* • Otis Harlan *"Porky" Thompson* • Paul Porcasi *Nick Verdis* • Marion Lord *Lil Rice* ■ *Dir* Paul Fejos • *Scr* Edward T Lowe Jr, Charles Furthman, from the play by Philip Dunning, George Abbott • *Cinematographer* Hal Mohr • *Choreographer* Maurice L Kusell

Broadway ★★★
Musical crime drama 1942 · US · BW · 91min

George Raft stars in this remake of the 1929 musical, which was taken, in turn, from a 1927 Broadway hit. This version is a crime melodrama with a decent helping of snappy songs, some dance and the neat twist of having Raft play himself. As he reminisces about the Roaring Twenties, when bootleggers and mobsters were part of the New York showbiz scene, his memories fold into flashback to tell a tale of backstage murder in which he once found himself involved. Broderick Crawford is excellent as the villain of the piece. RK

George Raft • Pat O'Brien *Dan McCorn* • Janet Blair *Billie* • Broderick Crawford *Steve Crandall* • Marjorie Rambeau *Lili* • Anne Gwynne *Pearl* • SZ Sakall *Nick* • Edward S Brophy [Edward Brophy] *Porky* ■ *Dir* William A Seiter • *Scr* Felix Jackson, John Bright, from the play by Philip Dunning, George Abbott

Broadway Bill ★★★ U
Drama 1934 · US · BW · 102min

The title is the name of the racehorse bought by businessman Warner Baxter, who gives up everything to run the horse. Baxter's sister-in-law Myrna Loy believes in him, so therefore we all should. A Frank Capra movie, this is simply brimming over with nice people and good intentions - you may find a little of it goes a long way, but then you'd be being churlish. Capra remade it in 1950 as *Riding High* with Bing Crosby

(who, unlike Warner Baxter, actually liked horses). TS *DVD*

Warner Baxter *Dan Brooks* • Myrna Loy *Alice Higgins* • Walter Connolly *JL Higgins* • Raymond Walburn *Colonel Pettigrew* • Clarence Muse *Whitey* • Helen Vinson *Margaret Brooks* • Douglas Dumbrille [Douglass Dumbrille] *Eddie Morgan* • Lynne Overman *Happy McGuire* • Lucille Ball ■ *Dir* Frank Capra • *Scr* Robert Riskin, from a story by Mark Hellinger

Broadway Bound ★★★ PG
Comedy drama 1991 · US · Colour · 89min

Has any modern playwright made as many dramatic mountains out of his life's domestic molehills as Neil Simon? Made as a TV movie but shown in cinemas in Britain, this is the final segment – its predecessors were *Brighton Beach Memoirs* and *Biloxi Blues* – of an autobiographical trilogy. Here, Simon's alter ego Eugene (Corey Parker) makes it to the big time with his brother Stan (Jonathan Silverman). The strong cast skilfully puts acting flesh on skeletal memory. TH

Anne Bancroft *Kate Jerome* • Hume Cronyn *Ben* • Corey Parker *Eugene Morris Jerome* • Jonathan Silverman *Stan Jerome* • Jerry Orbach *Jack Jerome* • Michele Lee *Blanche* • Marilyn Cooper *Mrs Pitkin* • Pat McCormick *Announcer* ■ *Dir* Paul Bogart • *Scr* Neil Simon, from his play

Broadway Danny Rose ★★★★ PG
Comedy 1984 · US · BW · 80min

Romping gleefully rather than analysing deeply, Woody Allen as director, writer and star brings his own light touch to every frame of this film. Putting egotistical, arty Manhattan on hold, and cutting down on his verbal wit to boot, Allen rings the changes not only by taking us to the swamps of New Jersey but also by squeezing humour primarily from situation and character rather than dialogue. Allen the director keeps the caper aspect on a beautifully tight leash at all times and, as the star, he fairly sparkles with eccentricity as a small-fry showbiz agent, while Mia Farrow is amusingly, nasally blunt as a gangster's moll with daft hair. JM *DVD*

Woody Allen *Danny Rose* • Mia Farrow *Tina Vitale* • Nick Apollo Forte *Lou Canova* • Craig Vandenburgh *Ray Webb* • Herb Reynolds *Barney Dunn* • Paul Greco *Vito Rispoli* • Frank Renzulli *Joe Rispoli* • Edwin Bordo *Johnny Rispoli* ■ *Dir/Scr* Woody Allen

The Broadway Melody ★★★
Musical comedy 1929 · US · BW · 102min

The first Hollywood musical, and the prototype for the backstage musical romance that grew, flourished and evolved to become a unique cinematic art form for some three decades. Bessie Love and Anita Page star as a vaudeville sister act, vying for the attentions of dancer Charles King. The drama is woven around a marvellous musical score that includes the enduring title number, as well as the even more ageless *Give My Regards to Broadway*. The movie was voted best picture at the 1928/1929 Oscar ceremony with nominations for director Harry Beaumont and Love. Stylistically dated, but there is still much to enjoy. RK

Anita Page *Queenie* • Bessie Love *Hank* • Charles King (1) *Eddie* • Jed Prouty *Uncle Jed* • Kenneth Thomson *Jock Warriner* • Edward Dillon *Stage manager* ■ *Dir* Harry Beaumont • *Scr* James Gleason, Norman Houston, Sarah Y Mason, from a story by Edmund Goulding • *Art Director* Cedric Gibbons

Broadway Melody of 1936 ★★★★ U
Musical comedy 1935 · US · BW · 100min

A terrific MGM follow-up to its smash hit *The Broadway Melody*, this has a fabulous Arthur Freed and Nacio Herb Brown score, which includes most of those songs that you probably heard for the first time in *Singin' in the Rain*. Eleanor Powell taps up a storm, and she is well backed by Jack Benny as a theatre columnist and handsome hero Robert Taylor. TS

B

Jack Benny *Bert Keeler* • Eleanor Powell *Irene Foster* • Robert Taylor (1) *Bob Gordon* • Una Merkel *Kitty Corbett* • Sid Silvers *Snoop* • Buddy Ebsen *Ted* • June Knight *Lillian Brent* • Vilma Ebsen *Sally* ■ *Dir* Roy Del Ruth • *Scr* Jack McGowan, Sid Silvers, Harry Cohn, from a story by Moss Hart • *Choreographer* Dave Gould • *Music Director* Alfred Newman

Broadway Melody of 1938 ★★★ U

Musical comedy   1937 · US · BW · 105min

For connoisseurs, this contains some knockout routines from that fabulous tap dancer Eleanor Powell. For fans of Judy Garland, it has something unforgettable – the song *Dear Mr Gable*. It was originally written to be performed at a birthday party on the MGM lot, sung by the young Garland to the tune of the standard *You Made Me Love You*, with additional lyrics by Roger Edens. TS

Robert Taylor (1) *Steve Raleigh* • Eleanor Powell *Sally Lee* • George Murphy *Sonny Ledford* • Binnie Barnes *Caroline Whipple* • Buddy Ebsen *Peter Trot* • Sophie Tucker *Alice Clayton* • Judy Garland *Betty Clayton* ■ *Dir* Roy Del Ruth • *Scr* Jack McGowan, from a story by Jack McGowan, Sid Silvers • *Music Director* George Stoll

Broadway Melody of 1940 ★★★★★ U

Musical   1940 · US · BW · 97min

The fourth and last of MGM's great *Broadway Melody* series is perfection in rhythm. Fred Astaire and George Murphy play sparring dance partners, though together they perform terrifically; the seemingly effortless sophistication of *Please Don't Monkey with Broadway* is utterly beguiling. The movie's undoubted highlight is Astaire sublimely performing a tap with toothy Eleanor Powell to Cole's *Begin the Beguine* on a glossy, highly polished black-and-white set. As Frank Sinatra said in *That's Entertainment!*: "You can wait around and hope, but you'll never see its like again." TS DVD

Fred Astaire *Johnny Brett* • Eleanor Powell *Clara Bennett* • George Murphy *King Shaw* • Frank Morgan *Bob Casey* • Ian Hunter *Bert C Matthews* • Florence Rice *Amy Blake* • Lynne Carver *Emmy Lou Lee* • Ann Morriss *Pearl* ■ *Dir* Norman Taurog • *Scr* Leon Gordon, George Oppenheimer, from a story by Jack McGowan, Dore Schary • *Music Director* Alfred Newman

Broadway Rhythm ★★ U

Musical   1944 · US · Colour · 114min

George Murphy stars as a Broadway producer beset by various problems in mounting his extravagant new revue-style show. And that's about the size of it. This is excessively lengthy, devoid of any appreciable narrative and directed without flair by Roy del Ruth. What it does offer is an excuse to parade a string of talented performers. RK

George Murphy *Johnnie Demming* • Ginny Simms *Helen Hoyt* • Charles Winninger *Sam Demming* • Gloria DeHaven *Patsy Demming* • Nancy Walker *Trixie Simpson* • Ben Blue *Felix Gross* • Lena Horne *Fernway De La Fer* • Eddie "Rochester" Anderson *Eddie* ■ *Dir* Roy Del Ruth • *Scr* Dorothy Kingsley, Harry Clark, from a story by Jack McGowan, from the musical *Very Warm for May* by Jerome Kern, Oscar Hammerstein II

Broadway Serenade ★★

Musical   1939 · US · BW · 113min

Marital problems inevitably arise between a songwriter husband (Lew Ayres) and his singer wife (Jeanette MacDonald) when she soars to stardom and he doesn't. MacDonald, minus Nelson Eddy, doesn't fare too well in this opulent but otherwise leaden offering. A lumbering production in which even a grand finale choreographed by Busby Berkeley goes horribly wrong. RK

Jeanette MacDonald *Mary Hale* • Lew Ayres *James Geoffrey Seymour* • Ian Hunter *Larry Bryant* • Frank Morgan *Cornelius Collier Jr* • Wally Vernon *Joey, the Jinx* • Rita Johnson *Judy Tyrrell* • Virginia Grey *Pearl* ■ *Dir* Robert Z Leonard • *Scr* Charles Lederer, from a story by Lew Lipton, from John Taintor Foote, Hans Kräly

Broadway through a Keyhole ★★★★

Musical   1933 · US · BW · 92min

Famous New York gossip columnist Walter Winchell wrote the story, using himself and his broadcasts on the Broadway and gangland scenes as a framework for the plot. The story is simple: mobster Paul Kelly falls for decent Constance Cummings and gets her a job in Texas Guinan's nightclub, where the shows are directed by volatile Gregory Ratoff. Grateful Cummings tries to stay loyal, but falls in love with crooner Russ Columbo. Directed with style and pace by Lowell Sherman, this is sophisticated, unusual and vastly entertaining. RK

Constance Cummings *Joan Whelan* • Russ Columbo *Clark Brian* • Paul Kelly (1) *Hank Rocci* • Blossom Seeley *Sybil Smith* • Gregory Ratoff *Max Mefooski* • Texas Guinan *Tex Kaley* • Hugh O'Connell *Chuck Haskins* ■ *Dir* Lowell Sherman • *Scr* Gene Towne, C Graham Baker, from a story by Walter Winchell • *Music Director* Alfred Newman

Broadway to Hollywood ★★★

Musical   1933 · US · BW and Colour · 87min

This chronicles the struggles of a showbusiness family across three generations, with Eddie Quillan ending up as a Hollywood star almost half a century after his grandparents (Frank Morgan and the gutsy Alice Brady) started out on the hard road of vaudeville. This is a sentimental but lively look at a vanished era. Featuring a 13-year-old Mickey Rooney, it marks the screen debut of Nelson Eddy. RK

Alice Brady *Lulu Hackett* • Frank Morgan *Ted Hackett* • Madge Evans *Anne Ainslee* • Russell Hardie *Ted Hackett Jr* • Jackie Cooper *Ted Hackett Jr as a child* • Eddie Quillan *Ted the Third* • Mickey Rooney *Ted the Third as a child* • Tad Alexander *David* • Jimmy Durante *Hollywood character* • Nelson Eddy *John Sylvester* ■ *Dir* Willard Mack • *Scr* Willard Mack, Edgar Allan Woolf

LANDMARK FILM
For the first time, a gay-specific narrative transcends its subject matter without short-changing the issues

Brokeback Mountain ★★★★★ 15

Romantic western drama
2005 · US/Can · Colour · 128min

Ang Lee's epic love story about two cowboys is so much more than just a "gay" western; it's an exquisitely made and moving account of the corrosive nature of suppressed love. Jake Gyllenhaal and Heath Ledger are superb as the two men who, in the 1960s, find employment minding sheep on the slopes of the titular mountain. They fall for each other, at first just physically (their sex scenes are far from explicit and would be deemed coy if the couplings were heterosexual), but then much more deeply. Later, after both marry to satisfy convention, they resume their impossible affair via "fishing trips" during which few fish are actually caught. Lee avoids any proselytising or preaching, leaving the agony of the situation to speak for itself. And with its final, wrenching sequence, the film delivers what might be the nearest thing to an anguished sob yet committed to celluloid. AS Swearing, violence, sex scenes. DVD

Heath Ledger *Ennis Del Mar* • Jake Gyllenhaal *Jack Twist* • Linda Cardellini *Cassie* • Anna Faris *Lashawn Malone* • Anne Hathaway *Lureen Newsome* • Michelle Williams *Alma* • Randy Quaid *Joe Aguirre* • Kate Mara *Alma Jr, age 19* ■ *Dir* Ang Lee • *Scr* Larry McMurtry, Diana Ossana, from the short story by E Annie Proulx

Brokedown Palace ★★ 12

Prison drama   1999 · US · Colour · 96min

If it weren't for sterling performances from Claire Danes and Kate Beckinsale, this would be yet another turgid rehash of the plot in which nice American kids get burnt by Bangkok drug laws. Slammed in a *Tenko*-style women's prison (whose most bizarre inmate is a cockney-accented Amanda de Cadenet), they pin their hopes on renegade lawyer Bill Pullman. The film, subsequently cold-shouldered by both stars, is formulaic, predictable and dull. LH Swearing. DVD

Claire Danes *Alice Marano* • Bill Pullman *Henry "Yank Hank" Greene* • Kate Beckinsale *Darlene Davis* • Lou Diamond Phillips *Roy Knox* • Jacqueline Kim *Yon Greene* • Daniel Lapaine *Skip Kahn, "Nick Parks"* • Tom Amandes *Doug Davis* ■ *Dir* Jonathan Kaplan • *Scr* David Arata, from a story by Adam Fields, David Arata

The Broken ★★★ 15

Horror thriller   2008 · Fr/UK · Colour · 88min

Delivering atmosphere rather than innovation, this brooding tale stars an icy Lena Headey as a London radiologist who becomes convinced she's being stalked by her doppelganger. Having glimpsed her mysterious double driving down the street and then confronted her in an off-screen encounter, the traumatised 30-something crashes her car and winds up in an amnesiac state. Slow-drip dread replaces genuine scares, as writer/director Sean Ellis interweaves his own highly stylised vision with a reverential plundering of the work of genre masters from Hitchcock to early Polanski. The languid pacing enhances the precision-crafted tension, while the fractured narrative skilfully mirrors the protagonist's mental disintegration – though ultimately the project's technical prowess far outweighs its content. SF

Lena Headey *Gina McVey* • Melvil Poupaud *Steve* • Richard Jenkins *John McVey* • Asier Newman *Daniel* • Michelle Duncan *Kate* • Ulrich Thomsen *Dr Robert Zachman* ■ *Dir/Scr* Sean Ellis

Broken ★★★ 15

Drama   2012 · UK · Colour · 87min

This modest but often very moving British film marks the feature debut of theatre director Rufus Norris. Newcomer Eloise Laurence plays Skunk, an 11-year-old girl living in a suburban cul-de-sac with her single father (Tim Roth), older brother (Bill Milner) and their au pair (Zana Marjanovic). Skunk's life is normal until her upstart teenage neighbours declare war on a young, emotionally damaged man (Robert Emms) who lives opposite. Though this has elements of lurid melodrama, it is the quiet moments that define Norris's atmospheric and elegant film, making for an unusual coming-of-age story set against the disconnect of today's "broken" Britain. DW Violence, swearing, a sex scene, nudity, drug abuse.

Tim Roth *Archie* • Cillian Murphy *Mike Kiernan* • Rory Kinnear *Bob Oswald* • Eloise Laurence *Skunk* • Robert Emms *Rick Buckley* ■ *Dir* Rufus Norris • *Scr* Mark O'Rowe, from Daniel Clay's novel (inspired by Harper Lee's *To Kill a Mockingbird*)

Broken Arrow ★★★★ PG

Western   1950 · US · Colour · 88min

Director Delmer Daves's massively influential western was among the first to tell the native American side of the story. James Stewart heads the cast as a war-weary scout who falls, controversially, for Apache maiden Debra Paget during his mission to negotiate a truce. Jeff Chandler became an international star following his performance here as Cochise, a role he was to reprise twice. The screenplay credited to Michael Blankfort was nominated for an Oscar, but was actually written by blacklisted author Albert Maltz. TS DVD

James Stewart *Tom Jeffords* • Jeff Chandler *Cochise* • Debra Paget *Sonseeahray* • Basil Ruysdael *General Howard* • Will Geer *Ben Slade* • Joyce MacKenzie *Terry* • Arthur Hunnicutt *Duffield* • Raymond Bramley *Colonel Bernall* • Jay Silverheels *Goklia* ■ *Dir* Delmer Daves • *Scr* Michael Blankfort (front for Albert Maltz), from the novel *Blood Brother* by Elliott Arnold

Broken Arrow ★★★ 15

Action thriller   1996 · US · Colour · 103min

Director John Woo teams up with reinvented hard man John Travolta for this techno-thriller. Despite rattling along at a breakneck pace, this is a cliché-ridden tale, but Travolta charismatically milks his new-found icon status as an amoral stealth-bomber pilot. Christian Slater is an able good guy, pursuing his manic adversary across the desert into ever more ludicrous action set pieces, while Samantha Mathis is refreshingly capable as Slater's sidekick. AJ Violence, swearing. DVD Blu-ray

John Travolta *Vic Deakins* • Christian Slater *Riley Hale* • Samantha Mathis *Terry Carmichael* • Delroy Lindo *Colonel Max Wilkins* • Bob Gunton *Pritchett* • Frank Whaley *Giles Prentice* • Howie Long *Kelly* • Vondie Curtis-Hall *Lt Col Sam Rhodes* • Jack Thompson *Chairman, Joint Chiefs of Staff* ■ *Dir* John Woo • *Scr* Graham Yost

Broken Blossoms ★★★★ PG

Silent drama   1919 · US · BW and Tinted · 94min

Set in London's Limehouse, this melodrama is the last of director DW Griffith's undisputed masterpieces. Shot in just 18 days, the story of brutalised waif Lillian Gish's chaste relationship with noble Chinese merchant Richard Barthelmess was Griffith's most expensive film to date. It marked both his earliest experiment with tinted film stock and his first exclusive use of studio sets. The atmosphere of misty dilapidation was achieved by cinematographer Billy Bitzer and effects expert Hendrik Sartov, but it's the way in which Griffith exploits his seedy setting to enhance the ethereality of the romance between the girl and the merchant that makes the film so memorable. DP DVD

Lillian Gish *Lucy* • Donald Crisp *"Battling" Burrows* • Arthur Howard (1) *Burrows's manager* • Richard Barthelmess *Cheng Huan* • Edward Peil [Edward Peil Sr] *Evil Eye* • Norman Selby *A prizefighter* • George Beranger *The Spying One* ■ *Dir* DW Griffith • *Scr* DW Griffith, from the short story *The Chink and the Child* by Thomas Burke from the collection *Limehouse Nights*

Broken Blossoms ★★

Drama   1936 · UK · BW · 88min

Five years after directing his last feature, DW Griffith – the father of narrative film – was invited by Twickenham Studios to remake his 1919 classic about doomed love in London's Limehouse. When he dropped out, Emlyn Williams hurriedly produced a script based on the Griffith original, and German exile John Brahm was hired to direct. The result is better than might be expected, with Brahm emulating the visual delicacy of the silent version. However, the dialogue is excruciating in places, and the cast is no match for the original. DP

Dolly Haas *Lucy Burrows* • Emlyn Williams *Chen* • Arthur Margetson *Battling Burrows* • Gibb McLaughlin *Evil Eye* • Donald Calthrop *Old Chinaman* • Ernest Sefton *Manager* • Jerry Verno *Bert* • Bertha Belmore *Daisy* • Ernest Jay *Alf* ■ *Dir* John Brahm • *Scr* Emlyn Williams, from the story *The Chink and the Child* by Thomas Burke, from the 1919 film • *Cinematographer* Curt Courant

Broken Bridges ★★ PG

Music drama   2006 · US · Colour · 100min

You'd have trouble squeezing any more clichés into this vehicle for country music star Toby Keith (in his film debut). Resembling a poor TV movie, the bitty and unimpactful drama does none of its bored-looking cast any favours, as a military tragedy brings both Keith's washed-up musician and his ex-love Kelly Preston back to their home town after years away. Clueless direction makes the film feel like a convenient series of happenings rather than a cohesive emotional journey, but Willie Nelson does make an appearance. SF DVD

Toby Keith *Bo Price* • Kelly Preston *Angela Delton* • Lindsey Haun *Dixie Leigh Delton* • Burt Reynolds *Jake Delton* ■ *Dir* Steven Goldmann • *Scr* Cherie Bennett, Jeff Gottesfeld

The Broken Circle Breakdown ★★★ 15

Drama   2012 · Bel/Neth · Colour · 107min

It's not often that the editing is the standout aspect of a film, but the controlled cutting across time frames and between moods is crucial to this drama's emotional impact. Johan Heldenbergh excels as the Belgian bluegrass singer who falls for tattoo artist Veerle Baetens but finds his world rocked by events to come. There's deft use of some inspired musical choices to reinforce the depth of feeling and the moments of exhilaration and agony experienced by the couple, but the dénouement seems melodramatic rather than authentic. **DP** Flemish, English +subtitles. *DVD*

Johan Heldenbergh *Didier Bontinck, "Monroe"* • Veerle Baetens *Elise Vandevelde, "Alabama"* • Nell Cattrysse *Maybelle* • Geert Van Rampelberg *William* ■ *Dir* Felix van Groeningen • *Scr* Felix van Groeningen, Carl Joos, from the play *The Broken Circle Breakdown featuring the Cover-ups of Alabama* by Johan Heldenbergh, Mieke Dobbels

Broken City ★★ 15
Crime thriller 2013 · US · Colour · 104min

Mark Wahlberg looks nonplussed from the start in this old-fashioned *film noir* that feels at odds with its contemporary New York setting. He plays private detective Billy Taggart, struggling to make ends meet seven years after a shooting incident got him dismissed from the NYPD. Russell Crowe mostly just sneers as the mayor who hires him to find out who his wife (Catherine Zeta-Jones) has been seeing. Taggart slowly realises he's mixed up in more than a case of infidelity. Director Allen Hughes (*The Book of Eli*) might have got away with the pedestrian story if the characters had been more complex, but the pieces of the puzzle just slot together too easily. **SP** Violence, swearing, sexual references. *DVD* *BL*

Mark Wahlberg *Billy Taggart* • Russell Crowe *Mayor Nicholas Hostetler* • Catherine Zeta-Jones *Cathleen Hostetler* • Barry Pepper *Jack Valliant* • Kyle Chandler *Paul Andrews* • Jeffrey Wright *Carl Fairbanks* ■ *Dir* Allen Hughes • *Scr* Brian Tucker

Broken Embraces ★★★ 15
Thriller 2009 · Sp · Colour · 121min

Fans of the flamboyant Spanish iconoclast will find plenty to mull over in Pedro Almodóvar's pensive, *noir*-tinged melodrama. A blind former film-maker (Lluís Homar) – who chooses to be known only by his pen name "Harry Caine" – recounts a torrid affair with a beautiful starlet (Penélope Cruz) that ruined his movie career and ended in tragedy. It sounds like the perfect starting point for one of the director's usual lurid romps, but Almodóvar goes easy on the passion, focusing instead on the heartbreak and pain. Cruz is mesmerising throughout, but this reteaming of the director and his *Volver* star might be too low-key for many. **DW** Spanish, English +subtitles. Swearing, sexual references. *DVD* *BL*

Penélope Cruz *Magdalena Rivero, "Lena"* • Lluís Homar *Mateo Blanco, "Harry Caine"* • Blanca Portillo *Judit García* • José Luis Gómez *Ernesto Martel* • Rubén Ochandiano *Ray X* • Tamar Novas *Diego* • Angela Molina *Lena's mother* • Rossy de Palma *Julieta* ■ *Dir/Scr* Pedro Almodóvar

Broken Flowers ★★★★ 15
Comedy drama 2005 · US/Fr · Colour · 101min

Bill Murray stars as a middle-aged, committed bachelor whose sedentary life is interrupted by a letter informing him that he may have a son who is searching for him. Jim Jarmusch's charmingly laid-back film engages mainly due to Murray's typically laconic performance as a man who seems to want to avoid life but who finds himself unexpectedly sucked into it. Here, it's when his amateur detective neighbour (a superb Jeffrey Wright) encourages him to go on a road trip to visit former girlfriends Sharon Stone, Frances Conroy, Jessica Lange and Tilda Swinton. **AS** Swearing, nudity. *DVD*

Bill Murray *Don Johnston* • Jeffrey Wright *Winston* • Sharon Stone *Laura* • Frances Conroy *Dora* • Jessica Lange *Carmen* • Tilda Swinton *Penny* • Julie Delpy *Sherry* • Mark Webber *The kid* • Chloë Sevigny *Carmen's assistant* ■ *Dir* Jim Jarmusch • *Scr* Jim Jarmusch, from an idea by Bill Raden, Sara Driver

Broken Harvest ★★
Historical epic
1994 · Ire · Colour and BW · 101min

The period immediately following the Irish civil war has been relatively neglected by film-makers. However, Maurice O'Callaghan's study of the tensions that remained after independence admirably captures the atmosphere of retrenchment and remembrance that characterised the early De Valera years. Yet there's a predictability about the storyline, in which two men refuse to call a ceasefire in the feud that began decades before over a woman. **DP**

Colin Lane *Arthur O'Leary* • Niall O'Brien *Josie McCarthy* • Marian Quinn *Catherine O'Leary* • Darren McHugh *Jimmy O'Leary* • Joy Florish *Mary Finnegan* • Joe Jeffers *Willie Hogan* ■ *Dir* Maurice O'Callaghan • *Scr* Maurice O'Callaghan, Kate O'Callaghan, from the story *The Shilling* by Maurice O'Callaghan

The Broken Hearts Club: a Romantic Comedy ★★★ 15
Comedy drama 2000 · US · Colour · 91min

Simmering with bitchy insults, lustful laments and slyly understated truths, this gay ensemble comedy is unoriginal but amusing. Every one of Timothy Olyphant's team-mates on John Mahoney's softball team flirts with stereotype. Yet they all emerge as credible characters, whether they're flightily gay, podgily insecure or posturingly macho. Writer/director Greg Berlanti judges the mix of camp quippery, Hollywood affectation and romantic pathos to a nicety. **DP** Swearing, drug abuse, sex scenes. *DVD*

Timothy Olyphant *Dennis* • Andrew Keegan *Kevin* • John Mahoney *Jack* • Dean Cain *Cole* • Matt McGrath *Howie* • Zach Braff *Benji* • Ben Weber *Patrick* • Billy Porter *Taylor* • Justin Theroux *Marshall* • Mary McCormack *Anne* ■ *Dir/Scr* Greg Berlanti

Broken Horses ★★ 15
Crime drama 2015 · US · Colour · 100min

A frustratingly old-fashioned morality tale, this never quite matches its beautiful prairie visuals. Beginning with a flashback that sees a young, mentally challenged boy witnessing the murder of his father, the film fast-forwards to the present, with his older brother returning before his impending marriage – but the two boys (Anton Yelchin, Chris Marquette) are now worlds apart. The drama plays out with a simplicity that may be too slow for some, but this thoughtful fare has a slowburn quality that makes it endearing. **DW** Swearing, violence.

Anton Yelchin *Jacob Heckum* • Chris Marquette [Christopher Marquette] *Buddy Heckum* • Sean Patrick Flanery *Ignacio* • Vincent D'Onofrio *Julius Hench* • Thomas Jane *Gabriel Heckum* ■ *Dir* Vidhu Vinod Chopra • *Scr* Vidhu Vinod Chopra, Abhijat Joshi

Broken Journey ★★ U
Melodrama 1948 · UK · BW · 85min

A plane full of mismatched characters comes down in the Alps. Guess what happens next? Watching painfully earnest tales like this makes you wonder why anyone bothers with disaster movies, and why it took so long for *Airplane!* to come along and mock them. Director Ken Annakin, on his third picture, has little idea how to freshen up the stock situations, while there are few hidden depths in the overfamiliar characters. **DP**

Phyllis Calvert *Mary Johnstone* • Margot Grahame *Joanna Dane* • James Donald *Bill Haverton* • Francis L Sullivan *Anton Perami* • Raymond Huntley *Edward Marshall* • Derek Bond *Richard Faber* • Guy Rolfe *Captain Fox* • Sonia Holm *Anne Stevens* ■ *Dir* Ken Annakin • *Scr* Robert Westerby

Broken Lance ★★★★ U
Western 1954 · US · Colour · 92min

This splendid western stars a magnificently grizzled Spencer Tracy in the role he was born to play – King Lear. Even though the daughters have become sons, this is the (uncredited) westernisation of

Shakespeare's tragedy about the royal patriarch and his disparate family. Still, despite the claims for Akira Kurosawa's *Ran*, this is the definitive screen version of the Bard's celebrated work, and the western setting provides a dimension of grandeur: it's no accident, surely, that this was one of the first subjects used to show off the then new CinemaScope process. **TS** *DVD*

Spencer Tracy *Matt Devereaux* • Robert Wagner *Joe Devereaux* • Jean Peters *Barbara* • Richard Widmark *Ben* • Katy Jurado *Senora Devereaux* • Hugh O'Brian *Mike Devereaux* • Eduard Franz *Two Moons* • Earl Holliman *Denny Devereaux* • EG Marshall *Governor* ■ *Dir* Edward Dmytryk • *Scr* Richard Murphy, from a story by Philip Yordan

Broken Lines ★★ 15
Drama 2008 · UK · Colour · 97min

TV director Sallie Aprahamian makes a disappointing big-screen debut with this soapy North London melodrama. Co-scripted by its leads, it chronicles the illicit relationship between B (Doraly Rosa), a waitress nursing an ex-boxer who's had a stroke, and Jake (Dan Fredenburgh) a successful property executive planning his wedding. There's a tangible spark between the leads, but Olivia Williams and Harriet Walter are wasted as Jake's prim fiancée and his estranged mother, while Paul Bettany is allowed to overact as the resentful former boxer. **DP** Swearing. *DVD*

Dan Fredenburgh *Jake Levy* • Doraly Rosa *B* • Paul Bettany *Chester* • Olivia Williams *Zoe* • Harriet Walter *Leah* • Nathan Constance *Yoss* ■ *Dir* Sallie Aprahamian • *Scr* Dan Fredenburgh, Doraly Rosa

Broken Lizard's Club Dread ★★ 15
Comedy horror 2004 · US · Colour · 113min

Unlike comedy group Broken Lizard's own *Super Troopers*, this feature has an obvious plot (albeit derivative) and a relatively coherent structure, even if it's not sure what genre it wants to be. It's a schlocky horror comedy, in which a machete-wielding psycho picks off the incompetent staff at the booze-soaked party resort of Coconut Pete's Pleasure Island. The group blends juvenile, goofball laughs with extreme gore, and it won't have much appeal beyond its target teen audience. **SF** Swearing, violence. *DVD*

Bill Paxton *Coconut Pete* • Jay Chandrasekhar *Putnam Livingston* • Kevin Heffernan *Lars* • Steve Lemme *Juan Castillo* • Paul Soter *Dave* • Erik Stolhanske *Sam* • Brittany Daniel *Jenny* • MC Gainey *Hank* • Jordan Ladd *Penelope* ■ *Dir* Jay Chandrasekhar • *Scr* Broken Lizard [Jay Chandrasekhar, Kevin Heffernan, Steve Lemme, Paul Soter, Erik Stolhanske]

Broken Sun ★ 15
Second World War drama
2007 · Aus · Colour · 91min

This well-intentioned but uninvolving character-based drama seeks to explore universal truths about the nature of conflict. It's set during 1944 in New South Wales, where Japanese soldiers break out of a local PoW camp and shake things up for a local farmer. But what sounds moderately interesting on paper proves a real drag on screen, since the film-makers keep interrupting the story to fill us in on the details of both men's previous combat traumas, a generation and a world apart. The film's noble purpose is obvious, but the drama just never gets going. **TJ** In English, Japanese. Violence. *DVD*

Jai Koutrae *Jack* • Shingo Usami *Masaru* ■ *Dir* Brad Haynes • *Scr* Dacre Timbs

Broken Trust ★★★ 12
Thriller 1995 · US · Colour · 92min

A thoughtful, made-for-TV legal drama, this takes a hard-eyed look at corruption at the very top of the justice system. Tom Selleck plays a dedicated judge who is persuaded by FBI agent Elizabeth McGovern to go undercover, in order to expose senior legal figures on the take. However, he faces a tricky dilemma when he discovers that

some of his closest friends may be implicated in the scandal. It's not in the same league as Sidney Lumet's classic films about legal corruption, but it's still an absorbing piece. **JF**

Tom Selleck *Tim Nash* • Elizabeth McGovern *Janice Diller* • William Atherton *Neil Roemer* • Marsha Mason *Ruth Fraser* • Charles Haid *Harold Ashley* • Stanley DeSantis *Vince Escobar* ■ *Dir* Geoffrey Sax • *Scr* Joan Didion, John Gregory Dunne, from the novel *Court of Honor* by William P Wood

Broken Wings ★★★ 15
Drama 2002 · Is · Colour · 80min

A fascinating portrait of getting by in a patriarchal society emerges in Nir Bergman's debut feature, as middle-class Israeli 40-something Orli Zilberschatz-Banay struggles to raise four children following the demise of her husband. Yet the burden of the daily routine largely falls on her teenage daughter, Maya Maron, who jeopardises her chances of a singing career to atone for the guilt she feels over her father's death. The insights into grieving and coping are sensitive and sensible. **DP** Hebrew +subtitles. *DVD*

Orli Banay-Zilverschatz *Dafna Ulman* • Maya Maron *Maya Ulman* • Nitai Gvirtz *Yair Ulman* • Vladimir Freedman [Vladimir Friedman] *Dr Valentin Goldman* • Mooki Niv [Danny Niv] *Yoram* ■ *Dir/Scr* Nir Bergman

Bronco Billy ★★★ PG
Comedy western 1980 · US · Colour · 111min

Director Clint Eastwood also takes the starring role as a shoe sales clerk who dreams of becoming a cowboy in this small-scale charmer. Eastwood assembles a bunch of other no-hopers and oddballs, among them Sondra Locke, who launch a Wild West show. Eastwood deftly plays with his image as a solitary man of action, and there's sufficient edge and wit to keep bathos at bay. **AT**

Clint Eastwood *"Bronco Billy" McCoy* • Sondra Locke *Antoinette Lily* • Geoffrey Lewis *John Arlington* • Scatman Crothers *"Doc" Lynch* • Bill McKinney *"Lefty" LeBow* • Sam Bottoms *Leonard James* • Dan Vadis *Chief Big Eagle* • Sierra Pecheur *Lorraine Running Water* ■ *Dir* Clint Eastwood • *Scr* Dennis Hackin

Bronco Bullfrog ★★★ 15
Social drama 1970 · UK · BW · 83min

This product of the British social realist school was much admired in its day with director Barney Platts-Mills being favourably compared to Ken Loach. Made on a shoestring in London's East End with a cast of non-professionals, the film shows how Del, a 17-year-old in a dead-end job, is lured into crime by a borstal boy nicknamed Bronco Bullfrog. Although rough around the edges and containing some weak supporting performances, the depiction of the restless, day-to-day existence of ordinary youngsters is authentic. **DM** *DVD* *BL*

Del Walker *Del Quant* • Anne Gooding *Irene Richardson* • Sam Shepherd *Jo Saville/Bronco Bullfrog* • Roy Haywood *Roy* • Freda Shepherd *Mrs Richardson* • Dick Philpott *Del's father* • Chris Shepherd *Chris* ■ *Dir/Scr* Barney Platts-Mills

Bronson ★★★ 18
Biographical prison drama
2008 · UK/Cay · Colour · 88min

This eccentric and often unsavoury biopic charts the rise to infamy of a small-time Luton crook who changed his name and bulked his frame in the mid-1980s to become Britain's most violent and feared prisoner. Tom Hardy gives a stunning performance as moustached reprobate Charles Bronson, who has spent two-thirds of his life in jail, and most of that in solitary confinement. As there's little in the way of biographical fact to contend with, director Nicolas Winding Refn attempts instead to poke around in his subject's psyche. The violence may be too extreme and message too non-judgemental for mainstream viewers, but Hardy does an admirable job of making this monster human. **DW** Violence, swearing. *DVD* *BL*

U SUITABLE FOR ALL   **Uc** SUITABLE ESPECIALLY FOR YOUNG CHILDREN (DVD ONLY)   **PG** PARENTAL GUIDANCE   **12A** UNDER 12s TO BE ACCOMPANIED (CINEMA ONLY)

Tom Hardy *Charles Bronson/Michael Peterson* • Matt King *Paul Daniels* • Terry Stone *Nurse* • Amanda Burton *Charlie's mum* • Hugh Ross *Uncle Jack* • Kelly Adams *Irene* • Edward Bennett-Coles *Brian* • Joe Tucker *John White* ■ *Dir* Nicolas Winding Refn • *Scr* Brock Norman Brock, Nicolas Winding Refn

The Brontë Sisters ★★
Biographical drama 1979 · Fr · Colour · 115min

The major interest in this alternative take on the literary sisters is provided by the casting of three of France's most talented actresses: the Isabelles Adjani and Huppert, and Marie-France Pisier. Director André Téchiné seems to have a misplaced vision of the claustrophobic life lived by the famous family in their remote Yorkshire parsonage and, in concentrating on the tortured life of the sisters' doomed brother Branwell (Pascal Greggory) detracts from the carefully constructed period atmosphere. RB French +subtitles.

Isabelle Adjani *Emily* • Marie-France Pisier *Charlotte* • Isabelle Huppert *Anne* • Pascal Greggory *Branwell* • Patrick Magee *Father* • Hélène Surgère *Mrs Robinson* • Roland Bertin *Nicholls* ■ *Dir* André Téchiné • *Scr* Pascal Bonitzer, André Téchiné, Jean Gruault

A Bronx Tale ★★★★ 15
Crime drama 1993 · US · Colour · 116min

Robert De Niro directs this intelligent portrait of a time (the 1960s) and place (New York's Little Italy). Goodness is a hard quality to depict without sentimentality, yet De Niro manages to convey it well, as a bus driver whose impressionable young son (Lillo Brancato) is attracted to a sharp-dressing local gangster (played by Chazz Palminteri). The debuting director's sense of place and pace and screenwriter Palminteri's autobiographical insights make this a compelling picture. DP Swearing, violence. *DVD*

Robert De Niro *Lorenzo Anello* • Chazz Palminteri *Sonny* • Lillo Brancato *Calogero Anello, aged 17* • Francis Capra *Calogero Anello, aged nine* • Taral Hicks *Jane* • Katherine Narducci *Rosina Anello* • Clem Caserta *Jimmy Whispers* • Alfred Sauchelli Jr *Bobby Bars* • Joe Pesci *Carmine* ■ *Dir* Robert De Niro • *Scr* Chazz Palminteri, from his play

The Brood ★★★★ 18
Horror 1979 · Can · Colour · 88min

Oliver Reed, a doctor experimenting with the new science of psychoplasmics, persuades Samantha Eggar to "shape her rage" and give birth to deformed children with killer instincts in another of director David Cronenberg's disturbing shockers. An intriguing metaphor for both unexplained bodily changes and the mental abuse some parents heap on their offspring, this genuinely creepy and upsetting stomach-churner is a modern horror classic. Eggar's performance gives a poignant emotional depth to Cronenberg's complex chiller. AJ *DVD*

Oliver Reed *Dr Hal Raglan* • Samantha Eggar *Nola Carveth* • Art Hindle *Frank Carveth* • Cindy Hinds *Candice Carveth* • Nuala Fitzgerald *Julianna Kelly* • Henry Beckman *Barton Kelly* • Susan Hogan *Ruth Mayer* • Michael McGhee *Inspector Mrazek* ■ *Dir/Scr* David Cronenberg

The Brooke Ellison Story ★★
Biographical drama 2004 · US · Colour · 90min

The title of Christopher Reeve's last directorial outing is something of a misnomer. Rather than focusing on the 11-year-old who was rendered quadriplegic by a road accident, this well-meaning if sentimentally intense TV movie concentrates essentially on the sacrifices made by her parents to help her come to terms with her injuries and then fulfil her dream of going to Harvard. Consequently, Mary Elizabeth Mastrantonio and John Slattery carry the dramatic burden, although Vanessa Marano and Lacey Chabert do well enough as the adolescent and 20-something Brooke. However, Reeve leaves a few ends untied, especially those

involving the younger, neglected siblings. DP

Mary Elizabeth Mastrantonio *Jean Ellison* • John Slattery *Ed Ellison* • Lacey Chabert *Brooke Ellison* • Vanessa Marano *Young Brooke Ellison* • Jenson Goins *Young Kysten Ellison* • Devon Gearhart *Young Reed Ellison* • Lauren Barrett *Older Kysten Ellison* • Ryan Hudson *Reed Ellison* ■ *Dir* Christopher Reeve • *Scr* Camille Thomasson, from the autobiography *Miracles Happen: One Mother, One Daughter, One Journey* by Brooke & Jean Ellison

Brooklyn ★★★★ 12
Romantic comedy drama 2015 · UK/Ire · Colour · 107min

Adapted by Nick Hornby from the novel by Colm Toibin, this is the crowd-pleasing tale of a young woman (Saiorse Ronan) torn between two worlds and two loves during the austere 1950s. She's a small-town Irish girl despatched to a church-funded job in Brooklyn, New York. Surviving both acute homesickness and the jibes of others, Ronan eventually finds romance. Then there's a tragedy back home, and she's torn not only between Ireland and New York, but also between new and old loves, the latter in the shape of Domhnall Gleeson. This breaks no new territory, but it's still a hugely likeable piece of old-fashioned entertainment. DA Swearing, sex scenes. *DVD*

Saoirse Ronan *Eilis Lacey* • Domhnall Gleeson *Jim Farrell* • Julie Walters *Mrs Kehoe* • Jim Broadbent *Father Flood* • Emily Bett Rickards *Patty* ■ *Dir* John Crowley • *Scr* Nick Hornby, from Colm Toibin's novel

Brooklyn Rules ★★ 15
Coming-of-age drama 2007 · US · Colour · 95min

The mean streets of 1980s New York are paved with clichés in this dull and flimsy drama. Scripted by *Sopranos* screenwriter Terence Winter, it sees a miscast Freddie Prinze Jr and his two 20-something buddies trying to make their way in a Mob-controlled neighbourhood. One-note performances and stale dialogue do little to convince of this trio's lifelong bonds, while the *GoodFellas*-style voiceover and an intrusive period soundtrack are overused. Only Alec Baldwin as a charismatic local mafioso has any oomph. SF Violence, swearing, sex scenes. *DVD*

Freddie Prinze Jr *Michael Turner* • Scott Caan *Carmine Mancuso* • Jerry Ferrara *Bobby Canzoneri* • Alec Baldwin *Caesar Manganaro* • Mena Suvari *Ellen* ■ *Dir* Michael Corrente • *Scr* Terence Winter

Brooklyn's Finest ★★★ 18
Crime drama 2009 · US · Colour · 127min

In this gritty police drama, three disparate New York cops (veteran patrolman Richard Gere, troubled family man Ethan Hawke and undercover agent Don Cheadle) hurtle towards their dates with destiny, their paths only briefly crossing as they face personal and professional hardships on the city's mean streets. The violent outbursts are often shocking but rarely gratuitous, as director Antoine Fuqua returns to the familiar territory of his Oscar-winning *Training Day*, weaving together three storylines with confidence and a steady hand. Of the three leads, Cheadle is the most impressive, giving a textured performance that keeps the narrative rooted in realism. TeS Violence, sex scenes, nudity. *DVD*

Richard Gere *Eddie* • Don Cheadle *Tango* • Ethan Hawke *Sal* • Wesley Snipes *Caz* • Will Patton *Lieutenant Bill Hobarts* • Ellen Barkin *Agent Smith* • Brian F O'Byrne *Ronny Rosario* • Vincent D'Onofrio *Carlo* ■ *Dir* Antoine Fuqua • *Scr* Michael C Martin

Brother ★★★★ 18
Crime drama 1997 · Rus · Colour · 95min

A controversial hit in Russia, Alexei Balabanov's unflinchingly naturalistic *noir* equates democratic St Petersburg with the Chicago of the 1920s. Crime is as unavoidable as American consumerism, rabid nationalism, urban decay and dehumanising poverty, so ex-soldier Sergei

Bodrov Jr has little option but to emulate his assassin brother, Viktor Sukhorukov, to survive. It's a perilous existence, though the wages of sin afford him the chance to rescue tram driver Svetlana Pismichenko from her abusive marriage. Grimly impressive. A sequel followed in 2000. DP Russian +subtitles. *DVD*

Sergei Bodrov Jr *Danila Bragov* • Viktor Sukhorukov *Viktor Bragov* • Svetlana Pismichenko *Sveta* ■ *Dir/Scr* Alexei Balabanov

Brother ★★★ 18
Crime drama 2000 · Jpn/UK/US/Fr · Colour · 108min

Takeshi Kitano attempts to reach a wider audience with this typically deadpan tale of a yakuza, set – for the first time – in the US. It's essentially a greatest hits movie, enticing the uninitiated while providing knowing winks to aficionados, as Kitano's gangster flees a Tokyo turf war only to precipitate an equally bloody showdown in Los Angeles. Exploring cultural contrasts, the criminal code and notions of brotherhood, this is over-customised but still polished and perceptive. DP English, Japanese +subtitles. Violence, swearing, brief nudity. *DVD*

"Beat" Takeshi [Takeshi Kitano] *Yamamoto* • Omar Epps *Denny* • Claude Maki *Ken* • Masaya Kato *Shirase* • Susumu Terajima *Kato* ■ *Dir/Scr* Takeshi Kitano

Brother Bear ★★★ U
Animated fantasy adventure 2003 · US · Colour · 81min

This Disney film is an old-fashioned morality tale with bold messages of love, trust and loyalty. A flighty young native American man, Kenai, learns his life lessons the hard way after the Great Spirits turn him into a bear. It's a movie with considerable charm, beautifully animated, and the characters are well developed, helped by excellent voice talent. Phil Collins's uncharacteristically restrained songs further emphasise the comedy and emotion. SF *DVD* *CS*

Joaquin Phoenix *Kenai* • Jeremy Suarez *Koda* • Rick Moranis *Rutt* • Dave Thomas *Tuke* • DB Sweeney *Sitka* • Jason Raize *Denahi* • Joan Copeland *Tanana* ■ *Dir* Aaron Blaise, Robert Walker (2) • *Scr* Steve Bencich, Lorne Cameron, Ron J Friedman, David Hoselton, Tab Murphy

The Brother from Another Planet ★★★ 15
Science-fiction satire 1984 · US · Colour · 109min

This is a beguiling and thoughtful example of science fiction as social satire from independent writer/director John Sayles. Joe Morton gives a tour-de-force performance as the mute ET wandering Harlem streets in a daze, whose "magical touch" enables him to mend any household object. The provocative device provides opportunities for a fine roster of supporting characters to be spiritually "fixed". AJ Drug abuse, violence, swearing. *DVD*

Joe Morton *The Brother* • Daryl Edwards *Fly* • Steve James (1) *Odell* • Leonard Jackson *Smokey* • Bill Cobbs *Walter* • Maggie Renzi *Noreen* • Tom Wright *Sam* • Ren Woods *Bernice* ■ *Dir/Scr* John Sayles

Brother John ★★
Fantasy drama 1970 · US · Colour · 95min

The title role is so admirably suited to the saintly-looking Sidney Poitier, it's almost a cliché in itself. A black man returns to his Alabama home town to see if racial tensions have eased over the years. It turns out he's an angel who's recording it all for the heavenly host. As a fantasy it's pleasant enough, but James Goldstone's film could have been been much more searching in its implications. TH

Sidney Poitier *John Kane* • Will Geer *Doc Thomas* • Bradford Dillman *Lloyd Thomas* • Beverly Todd *Louisa MacGill* • Ramon Bieri *Orly Ball* • Warren J Kemmerling [Warren Kemmerling] *George* ■ *Dir* James Goldstone • *Scr* Ernest Kinoy

Brother Orchid ★★★
Crime comedy 1940 · US · BW · 87min

There is always a down side to Warner Bros gangster pictures – a rather out-of-place moral dimension, meant to counterbalance the fast-living world of guys and molls. The down side here, after the pleasure of watching Edward G Robinson and Humphrey Bogart as partners who fall out, is having to watch Robinson transform himself into a pious friar. The two stars are on good form as they run rival protection rackets and rub out the lesser names on the cast list. Lloyd Bacon directs with machine-gun speed. AT

Edward G Robinson *Little John Sarto* • Humphrey Bogart *Jack Buck* • Ann Sothern *Flo Addams* • Donald Crisp *Brother Superior* • Ralph Bellamy *Clarence Fletcher* • Allen Jenkins *Willie the Knife* • Charles D Brown *Brother Wren* • Cecil Kellaway *Brother Goodwin* • Morgan Conway *Philadelphia Powell* ■ *Dir* Lloyd Bacon • *Scr* Earl Baldwin, from the *Collier's Magazine* article by Richard Connell

Brother Sun, Sister Moon ★ PG
Biographical religious drama 1972 · It/UK · Colour · 115min

Avoid this insipid rendering of the early life of St Francis of Assisi. As seen by Franco Zeffirelli, Francesco di Bernadone was a prototype hippy with flowers in his hair who approved of free love (the only sort he could afford) and social equality. To play him, Zeffirelli first fancied the young Al Pacino, but the studio said "Who?". So Graham Faulkner, another unknown, was hired. AT *DVD*

Graham Faulkner *Francesco* • Judi Bowker *Clare* • Leigh Lawson *Bernardo* • Kenneth Cranham *Paolo* • Lee Montague *Pietro di Bernardone* • Valentina Cortese *Pica di Bernardone* • Alec Guinness *Pope Innocent III* ■ *Dir* Franco Zeffirelli • *Scr* Suso Cecchi D'Amico, Kenneth Ross, Lina Wertmuller, Franco Zeffirelli

The Brotherhood ★★
Crime drama 1968 · US · Colour · 96min

Made before *The Godfather* revealed how fascinating and complex a subject the Mafia could be, this is a straightforward tale of generational conflict within the criminal "family". Kirk Douglas (who also produced) stars as the traditionalist at odds with his younger brother (Alex Cord), although the real drama arises when each has to carry out the role of executioner. There are strong performances, but it suffers as a result of failing to synthesise the good and bad aspects of Douglas's character. AE

Kirk Douglas *Frank Ginetta* • Alex Cord *Vince Ginetta* • Irene Papas *Ida Ginetta* • Luther Adler *Dominick Bertolo* • Susan Strasberg *Emma Ginetta* • Murray Hamilton *Jim Egan* ■ *Dir* Martin Ritt • *Scr* Lewis John Carlino

Brotherhood ★★★ 15
Epic war drama 2004 · S Kor · Colour · 142min

A phenomenal success in its native South Korea, this reworks Steven Spielberg's *Saving Private Ryan* for the Korean War. When brothers Jin-tae (Jang Dong-gun) and Jin-seok (Won Bin) are drafted into the army to fight the Communist invaders, Jin-tae transforms himself into a one-man killing machine after learning that winning the medal of honour will spare his brother from frontline duty. While throwing gore and severed limbs around the screen with terrifying abandon, there is also plenty of scope for maudlin melodrama. JR Korean +subtitles. Violence, swearing. *DVD*

Jang Dong-gun *Jin-tae* • Won Bin *Jin-seok* • Lee Eun-joo *Young-shin* • Gong Hyung-jin *Young-man* • Lee Young-ran *Mother* ■ *Dir* Kang Je-gyu • *Scr* Kang Je-gyu, Kim Sang-don, Han Ji-hoon

Brotherhood ★★★ 15
Thriller 2010 · US/Ger · Colour · 75min

Will Canon's slickly scripted tale pitches the viewer straight into the action, maintains a cracking pace and also allows a few moments of bleak humour, as college frat-house president Frank (Jon Foster) and new pledge Adam (Trevor Morgan) become

B

caught up in an escalating series of crises after an initiation ritual at a convenience store culminates in a shooting. The clash of codes between the die-hard brother and the scruple-racked rookie is key to the conceit, and Canon adds suspense by returning to the bleeding wound of gunshot victim Kevin (Lou Taylor Pucci). Punchily played and cannily directed, this may be a touch contrived, but it's still highly entertaining. DP Violence, swearing, sex scenes. *DVD*

Jon Foster (1) *Frank* • Trevor Morgan *Adam* • Arlen Escarpeta *Mike* • Lou Taylor Pucci *Kevin* ■ *Dir* Will Canon • *Scr* Will Canon, Doug Simon

Brotherhood ★★★★ 15

Drama   2016 · UK · Colour · 104min

Noel Clarke writes, directs and stars in this conclusion to his "Sam and Curtis" trilogy, which kicked off in 2005 with *Kidulthood*, then continued in 2008 with *Adulthood*. An accomplished piece of film-making, *Brotherhood* is less edgy, less "street" than its predecessors, with principal character Sam (Clarke) striving to stay settled now he has kids and responsibilities. But his violent past comes brutally back to haunt him. DA

Noel Clarke *Sam Peel* • Tonia Sotiropoulou *Janette* • Steven Cree *Brick* • Olivia Chenery *Sariya* ■ *Dir/Scr* Noel Clarke

Brotherhood of Justice ★★ 15

Action drama   1986 · US · Colour · 93min

Proving that everyone has to start somewhere, this high-school version of *Death Wish* finds a young Keanu Reeves, in one of his early roles, deciding to fight back against rising crime at school and in the city. However, it's not long before the junior vigilantes get out of control. This made-for-TV crime drama is not without curiosity value, but it has little else to offer. JF *DVD*

Keanu Reeves *Derek* • Lori Loughlin *Christie* • Kiefer Sutherland *Victor* • Joe Spano *Bob Grootemat* • Darren Dalton *Scottie* • Evan Mirand *Mule* • Billy Zane *Les* ■ *Dir* Charles Braverman • *Scr* Noah Jubelirer, Jeffrey Bloom, from a story by Jubelirer

Brotherhood of Satan ★★★ 18

Horror   1970 · US · Colour · 88min

Strother Martin heads a Californian devil cult kidnapping local children for soul transference purposes. This eerie witchcraft extravaganza packs an unsettling punch because of its ordinary setting and the imaginative and versatile use of its low-budget trappings. It's a great example of what can be achieved with very little, enhanced by good acting, classy direction by Bernard McEveety and clever small-scale special effects. An unpretentious winner. AJ

Strother Martin *Don Duncan* • LQ Jones *Sheriff* • Charles Bateman *Ben* • Anna Capri *[Ahna Capri] Nicky* • Charles Robson Knox *[Charles Knox Robinson] Priest* • Alvy Moore *Tobey* ■ *Dir* Bernard McEveety • *Scr* William Welch, from an idea by Sean MacGregor

Brotherhood of the Wolf ★★★ 15

Period action fantasy 2001 · Fr · Colour · 139min

Blending historical fact with hysterical fiction, this flamboyant fantasy attempts to give substance to France's own Loch Ness Monster legend - the fabled Beast of Gévaudan that killed more than a hundred women and children between 1764 and 1767. Taking this still unexplained visceral mystery as his inspiration, Christophe Gans details how forward-thinking naturalist Samuel Le Bihan and his Iroquois blood brother Mark Dacascos are sent by King Louis XV to destroy the mythical creature. A visual tour de force, but hollow. AJ French +subtitles. *DVD Blu*

Samuel Le Bihan *Grégoire de Fronsac* • Vincent Cassel *Jean-François de Morangias* • Emilie Dequenne *Marianne de Morangias* • Monica Bellucci *Sylvia* • Jérémie Rénier *Thomas d'Apcher* • Mark Dacascos *Mani* • Jean Yanne

Count de Morangias ■ *Dir* Christophe Gans • *Scr* Stéphane Cabel, Christophe Gans, from a treatment by Stéphane Cabel

The Brothers ★★ PG

Period drama   1947 · UK · BW · 87min

Cecil B DeMille's one-time assistant David MacDonald returned to his native Scotland for this tempestuous melodrama. While Stephen Dade's images of Skye are highly evocative, there's little passion in the romance between Patricia Roc and Andrew Crawford, even though she's the housekeeper of his deadliest rival (Finlay Currie). Part of the problem is the strait-laced nature of postwar British cinema, which kept emotions firmly in check. DP

Patricia Roc *Mary* • Will Fyffe *Aeneas McGrath* • Maxwell Reed *Fergus Macrae* • Finlay Currie *Hector Macrae* • Duncan Macrae *John Macrae* • John Laurie *Dugald* • Andrew Crawford *Willie McFarish* • James Woodburn *Priest* ■ *Dir* David MacDonald • *Scr* Muriel Box, Sydney Box, Paul Vincent Carroll, David MacDonald, from a novel by LAG Strong

Brothers ★ 18

Comedy drama   1999 · UK · Colour · 94min

Debut director Martin Dunkerton proves that sheer enthusiasm does not a good movie make. This tale of lads abroad puking, farting and drinking would offend even the most loyal reader of *Loaded*. Badly acted, poorly realised, terribly written. JB *DVD*

Justin Brett *Matt "Mystic Matey" Davidson* • Daren Jacobs *Chris "Beercan" Sullivan* • Daniel Fredenburgh *Julian "The King" Davidson* • Rebecca Cardinale *Anna Stefanos* ■ *Dir* Martin Dunkerton • *Scr* Martin Dunkerton, Nick Valentine

The Brothers ★★★ 15

Comedy drama   2001 · US · Colour · 98min

This sharply written film spurns the usual African-American stereotypes and focuses on the universal themes of romantic commitment and the bonds of friendship. Four well-to-do young black men have to reassess their lives, loves and loyalties when one of their friends suddenly announces that he's getting married, despite having once sworn to remain single for ever. In the characters' familiar fears of commitment, there are sharp echoes of real life. DA *DVD*

Morris Chestnut *Jackson Smith* • DL Hughley *Derrick West* • Bill Bellamy *Brian Palmer* • Shemar Moore *Terry White* • Tamala Jones *Sheila West* ■ *Dir/Scr* Gary Hardwick

Brothers ★★★ 15

Drama   2004 · Den/UK/Swe/Nor · Colour · 112min

When the helicopter carrying army major Ulrich Thomsen is shot down in Afghanistan, his family back home in Copenhagen is told he is missing, presumed dead. The tragedy forges a bond between his wife Connie Nielsen and wayward brother Nikolaj Lie Kaas that develops into sexual attraction. But then it transpires Thomsen is alive and recovering from his brutal treatment at the hands of the Taliban. The film's hand-held cinematography lends immediacy while some finely observed touches freshen up the potentially overwrought plot. LF Danish +subtitles. Swearing, violence. *DVD*

Connie Nielsen *Sarah* • Ulrich Thomsen *Michael* • Nikolaj Lie Kaas *Jannik* • Bent Mejding *Henning* • Solbjorg Hojfeldt *Else* • Paw Henriksen *Niels Peter, "NP"* • Laura Bro *Ditte* ■ *Dir* Susanne Bier • *Scr* Thomas Anders Jensen from a story by Thomas Anders Jensen, Susanne Bier

Brothers ★★★ 12

Wartime melodrama   2009 · US · Colour · 100min

When US marine captain Tobey Maguire is presumed killed in action in Afghanistan, the process of healing brings spouse Natalie Portman and black-sheep brother Jake Gyllenhaal closer together. A fairly faithful remake of a fine 2004 Scandinavian film, this contemporary melodrama shows that the story is arguably even more relevant in

this US setting, where the siblings' ex-soldier father (Sam Shepard) is as proud of one brother's service record as he is withering towards the other's shiftless ways. If the other key performances were as persuasive as Gyllenhaal's, this might be something really special, yet a slightly bland Portman and an overwrought Maguire rather highlight the contrived turns in the plotting of what is a respectable effort but not all it could have been. TJ Violence, swearing. *DVD Blu*

Tobey Maguire *Sam Cahill* • Jake Gyllenhaal *Tommy Cahill* • Natalie Portman *Grace Cahill* • Sam Shepard *Hank Cahill* • Bailee Madison *Isabelle Cahill* • Taylor Geare *Maggie Cahill* • Patrick Flueger *Private Joe Willis* • Carey Mulligan *Cassie Willis* ■ *Dir* Jim Sheridan • *Scr* David Benioff, from the 2004 film

The Brothers Bloom ★★★★ 12

Comedy drama   2008 · US · Colour · 108min

In writer/director Rian Johnson's cunning and witty yarn, Adrien Brody is wonderfully engaging as a conman who's fed up with living a lie. He wants a real and meaningful existence and assures his big brother, Mark Ruffalo, that their next job will be their last. Unfortunately, the target is wealthy bookworm Rachel Weisz, who captures Brody's heart with her eagerness to experience the world beyond New Jersey. That's the cue for a globetrotting adventure that moves at a screwball pace through atmospheric eastern European locations. It lags a touch towards the end and it's ultra quirky, but it delivers unexpected rewards. SP In English, French. Some violence, swearing, sexual references. *DVD Blu*

Rachel Weisz *Penelope* • Adrien Brody *Bloom* • Mark Ruffalo *Stephen* • Rinko Kikuchi *Bang Bang* • Robbie Coltrane *The Curator* • Nora Zehetner *Rose* • Maximilian Schell *Diamond Dog* ■ *Dir/Scr* Rian Johnson

The Brothers Grimm ★★★ 12

Period fantasy adventure
2005 · Cz Rep/US · Colour · 113min

Set in Germany in the late 18th century, this is a grotesque, freewheeling period fantasy from director Terry Gilliam. Here, the future purveyors of scary fairy tales, Jacob (Heath Ledger) and Wilhelm Grimm (Matt Damon), are travelling conmen who become embroiled in the mystery of a haunted forest from which youngsters continue to disappear. Ledger and Damon - sporting fine English accents - carry the film with their bickering schtick. The sketchy script and occasional CGI effects may leave a little to be desired but, after a plodding start, the momentum picks up for a barnstorming third act. AC Violence. *DVD Blu*

Matt Damon *Wilhelm Grimm* • Heath Ledger *Jacob Grimm* • Peter Stormare *Cavaldi* • Lena Headey *Angelika* • Jonathan Pryce *Delatombe* • Monica Bellucci *Mirror Queen* • Jeremy Robson *Young Jacob* ■ *Dir* Terry Gilliam • *Scr* Ehren Kruger

Brothers in Law ★★★★ U

Comedy   1956 · UK · BW · 90min

The Boulting brothers' delightfully witty follow-up to their smash hit *Private's Progress* features many of the same cast. Its source novel is by Henry Cecil, himself a distinguished QC, and hopefully quite unlike the absent-minded QC played by Miles Malleson to whom our hero Ian Carmichael is apprenticed. Carmichael is surrounded here by a cast of accomplished character actors, including the splendid Terry-Thomas and the redoubtable Richard Attenborough as a smarmy fellow barrister. This is still very funny and relevant today. TS *DVD*

Richard Attenborough *Henry Marshall* • Ian Carmichael *Roger Thursby* • Terry-Thomas *Alfred Green* • Jill Adams *Sally Smith* • Miles Malleson *Kendall Grimes* • Eric Barker *Alec Blair* • Irene Handl *Mrs Potter* • John Le Mesurier *Judge Ryman* • Raymond Huntley *Tatlock* • Nicholas Parsons *Charles Poole* ■ *Dir* Roy Boulting • *Scr* Roy Boulting, Frank Harvey, Jeffrey Dell, from the novel by Henry Cecil

Brothers in Trouble ★★★ 15

Drama   1995 · UK · Colour · 97min

Director Udayan Prasad betrays his inexperience with narrative in this well-meaning but rather contrived drama about illegal immigrants living in 1960s Britain. While making atmospheric use of the cramped house in which the 18 illegals live, Prasad also draws fine performances from his cast, but the story begins to disintegrate when the script abandons telling observation in favour of sensationalist melodrama. DP Swearing, a sex scene, nudity.

Om Puri *Hussein Shah* • Angeline Ball *Mary* • Pavan Malhotra *Amir* • Ahsen Bhatti *Irshad* • Bhasker *Gholam* • Pravesh Kumar *Sakib* • Lesley Clare O'Neill *Prostitute* • Kulvinder Ghir *Agent* • Badi Uzzaman *Old Ram* ■ *Dir* Udayan Prasad • *Scr* Robert Buckler, from the novel *Return Journey* by Abdullah Hussein

The Brothers Karamazov ★★★

Drama   1958 · US · Colour · 145min

Most famous in its day for the fact that Marilyn Monroe wanted to play Grushenka - or so she breathily gasped to an assembled press - this rather stodgy but undeniably well-made MGM epic could well have benefited from such courageous casting, for, excellent though Maria Schell is, she just isn't Monroe. The brothers themselves are superb, with Yul Brynner a dashing Dmitri, Richard Basehart as Ivan, and William Shatner as the young Alexey. Although long, this is accessible, capturing the essence of Dostoyevsky without losing substance or tone. TS

Yul Brynner *Dmitri Karamazov* • Maria Schell *Grushenka* • Claire Bloom *Katya* • Lee J Cobb *Fyodor Karamazov* • Richard Basehart *Ivan Karamazov* • Albert Salmi *Smerdyakov* • William Shatner *Alexey Karamazov* • Judith Evelyn *Madame Anna Hohlakov* • Edgar Stehli *Grigory* ■ *Dir* Richard Brooks • *Scr* Richard Brooks, from the novel by Fyodor Dostoyevsky, adapted by Julius J Epstein, Philip G Epstein

The Brothers McMullen ★★★ 15

Comedy drama   1995 · US · Colour · 94min

Edward Burns made his directorial debut with this endearing look at the mixed up romantic lives of three Irish Catholic brothers who share the family home in New York following their widowed mother's return to Ireland. Dealing with unusually heavyweight topics for a comedy drama, such as religious ethics and sexual morality, the literate and amusing script keeps things bubbling along nicely. AJ Swearing. *DVD*

Edward Burns *Barry* • Mike McGlone *Patrick* • Jack Mulcahy *Jack* • Shari Albert *Susan* • Maxine Bahns *Audry* • Catharine Bolz *Mrs McMullen* ■ *Dir/Scr* Edward Burns

Brothers of the Head ★★★ 18

Drama   2005 · UK · Colour and BW · 89min

Brian Aldiss's cult novel is the inspiration for this messy but oddly compelling 1970s-set tale of a pair of Siamese twins spotted by a music promoter who determines to turn them into a freakish rock act. Directors Keith Fulton and Louis Pepe (whose first fiction film this is, having previously made the excellent documentary *Lost in La Mancha*), deliver a patchwork mockumentary about the brother's rise and tragic fall. It's all a bit too tightly packed in the end, but the film's real strength is a beguiling pair of performances from Harry and Luke Treadaway. AS Swearing, drug abuse. *DVD*

Harry Treadaway *Tom Howe* • Luke Treadaway *Barry Howe* • Bryan Dick *Paul Day (1970s)* • Sean Harris *Nick Sidney* • Tania Emery *Laura Ashworth (1970s)* ■ *Dir* Keith Fulton, Louis Pepe • *Scr* Tony Grisoni, from the novel by Brian Aldiss

The Brothers Rico ★★★

Crime drama   1957 · US · BW · 91min

As *film noir* disappeared in the late 1950s, this crude example of the genre emerged. Richard Conte is the gangster turned successful businessman whose younger brothers have been earmarked for assassination by the Mob. The *noir* element is provided by Conte's meaningless quest and the disorderly world around him, but director Phil Karlson piles on enough violence to flatten the subtleties of French writer Georges Simenon's original story. TH

Richard Conte *Eddie Rico* • Dianne Foster *Alice Rico* • Kathryn Grant *Norah* • Larry Gates *Sid Kubik* • James Darren *Johnny Rico* • Argentina Brunetti *Mrs Rico* • Lamont Johnson *Peter Malaks* • Harry Bellaver *Mike Lamotta* ▪ *Dir* Phil Karlson • *Scr* Lewis Meltzer, Ben Perry, from the novella *Les Frères Rico* by Georges Simenon

The Brothers Solomon ★ 15

Comedy 2007 · US · Colour · 89min

This terrible comedy stars Will Arnett and Will Forte as John and Dean Solomon, a pair of sexually clueless but permanently cheerful brothers. After their dad (Lee Majors) slips into a coma, the siblings try to fulfil his wish for a grandchild, in the hope that it will aid his recovery. Veering between the moronic and the crass, this is a pitiful collection of gags about sperm banks, pregnancy and fatherhood. Neither Arnett nor Forte - veterans of TV's *Arrested Development* and *Saturday Night Live*, respectively - has the charisma to pull off the edgier moments. JR Swearing, sexual references. *DVD*

Will Arnett *John Solomon* • Will Forte *Dean Solomon* • Chi McBride *James* • Kristen Wiig *Janine* • Malin Akerman *Tara* • Lee Majors *Ed Solomon* ▪ *Dir* Bob Odenkirk • *Scr* Will Forte

The Brown Bunny ★★★ 18

Erotic road movie drama
2003 · US/Jpn/Fr · Colour · 89min

Famously reviled by many critics when it premiered at the Cannes film festival, but also championed by a passionate few, this is both a tone poem about lost love and a singularly uneventful road movie where nothing much happens until the notorious, supposedly for-real oral-sex scene at the end. For most of the running time, writer/editor/director/star Vincent Gallo drives across the US, starring moodily into a lens and meeting a variety of women who instantly fall in love with him. Enjoyment is aided by a high tolerance for Gordon Lightfoot songs and slow, unbroken and quite beautiful shots of scenery. LF *DVD*

Vincent Gallo *Bud Clay* • Chloë Sevigny *Daisy* • Cheryl Tiegs *Lilly* • Elizabeth Blake *Rose* • Anna Vareschi *Violet* ▪ *Dir/Scr* Vincent Gallo

Brown Sugar ★★ 12

Romantic comedy drama
2002 · US · Colour · 104min

A simple "follow your heart" romantic comedy is dressed up in hip-hop clothing here, as New York record company exec Taye Diggs and urban music magazine editor Sanaa Lathan take their time to recognise the obvious - that they're crazy about each other. But although their formulaic journey from childhood friends to lovers is appropriately messy and melodramatic, it rarely makes you root for the pair's happiness. SF Brief swearing. *DVD*

Taye Diggs *Dre* • Sanaa Lathan *Sidney* • Mos Def *Chris* • Nicole Ari Parker *Reese* • Boris Kodjoe *Kelby* • Queen Latifah *Francine* ▪ *Dir* Rick Famuyiwa • *Scr* Michael Elliot, Rick Famuyiwa, from a story by Elliot

The Browning Version ★★★★ U

Drama 1951 · UK · BW · 86min

This is another expert collaboration between writer Terence Rattigan and director Anthony Asquith. What makes this version of Rattigan's hit play so memorable is the mesmerising performance of Michael Redgrave as the classics teacher whose life is as redundant as his subject. The supporting cast is also first rate, with Jean Kent chillingly heartless as Redgrave's adulterous wife and Nigel Patrick suitably cocky as the man who cuckolds him. The shabby gentility of the school is neatly captured and the merciless revelation of

each new woe is, thanks to Redgrave's dignified self-pity, agonising to watch. DP *DVD*

Michael Redgrave *Andrew Crocker-Harris* • Jean Kent *Millie Crocker-Harris* • Nigel Patrick *Frank Hunter* • Wilfrid Hyde White *Frobisher* • Brian Smith (1) *Taplow* • Bill Travers *Fletcher* • Ronald Howard *Gilbert* • Paul Medland *Wilson* ▪ *Dir* Anthony Asquith • *Scr* Terence Rattigan, from his play • *Art Director* Carmen Dillon

The Browning Version ★★★ 15

Drama 1994 · UK · Colour · 93min

Mike Figgis's version of Terence Rattigan's play is a polished, if slightly old-fashioned piece of work. However, it doesn't bear comparison with Anthony Asquith's 1951 adaptation, with Albert Finney giving a less finely shaded performance than Michael Redgrave in the role of the timid, under-appreciated schoolmaster. A curious choice for its director, perhaps, but still an affecting tale. DP Violence, swearing, brief nudity.

Albert Finney *Andrew Crocker-Harris* • Greta Scacchi *Laura Crocker-Harris* • Matthew Modine *Frank Hunter* • Julian Sands *Tom Gilbert* • Michael Gambon *Dr Frobisher* • Ben Silverstone *Taplow* • Maryam D'Abo *Diana Rafferty* • James Sturgess [Jim Sturgess] *Bryant* ▪ *Dir* Mike Figgis • *Scr* Ronald Harwood, from the play by Terence Rattigan

Brown's Requiem ★★ 18

Crime drama 1998 · US · Colour · 100min

This competent adaptation of James Ellroy's first novel suffers from comparisons with the superb film version of the author's *LA Confidential*. Michael Rooker has the appropriately intimidating frame and throaty voice for Fritz Brown, a low-rent, ex-alcoholic private investigator assigned to keeping an eye on a young girl who's involved with a local heavy. Although Jason Freeland creates a convincing shady milieu, the flawed characters and cynical voiceover are pretty run of the mill. JC *DVD*

Michael Rooker *Fritz Brown* • Selma Blair *Jane Baker* • Jack Conley *Richard Ralston* • Harold Gould *Solly K* • Tobin Bell *Stan the Man* • Brad Dourif *Edwards* • Brion James *Cathcart* ▪ *Dir* Jason Freeland • *Scr* Jason Freeland, from the novel by James Ellroy

Brubaker ★★★★ 15

Prison drama 1980 · US · Colour · 124min

Robert Redford stars as the new warden of a state prison farm, who is determined to introduce more humane conditions after he masquerades as an inmate and is appalled by the brutality and corruption. Director Stuart Rosenberg piles on the agony with sequences of bleak action, while the acting is formidable enough to take on all that social responsibility. A touch downbeat, and at times ponderous and sanctimonious, this prison drama still sends out an ominous message to those who care about what society does with its misfits. TH Violence, swearing. *DVD*

Robert Redford *Henry Brubaker* • Yaphet Kotto *Richard "Dickie" Coombes* • Jane Alexander *Lillian Gray* • Murray Hamilton *Deach* • David Keith *Larry Lee Bullen* • Morgan Freeman *Walter* • Matt Clark *Purcell* • Tim McIntire *Huey Rauch* • Richard Ward *Abraham* ▪ *Dir* Stuart Rosenberg • *Scr* WD Richter, from the story by WD Richter, Arthur Ross, from a book by Thomas O Murton, Joe Hyams

The Bruce ★ 15

Historical adventure 1996 · UK · Colour · 106min

This is a ramshackle historical drama about Robert the Bruce, the Scots hero who, according to legend, was inspired by the persistence of a stranded spider to renew his bid to expel the English from Scotland. Less low-budget than no-budget, the film was largely funded by public subscriptions. DA

Sandy Welch *Robert the Bruce* • Brian Blessed *King Edward* • Michael van Wijk *De Bohun* • Oliver Reed *Bishop Wisharton* ▪ *Dir* Bob Carruthers • *Scr* Bob Carruthers, Michael Leighton

Bruce Almighty ★★★ 12

Comedy fantasy 2003 · US · Colour · 97min

When professionally wacky TV news reporter Jim Carrey is passed over for promotion, he vents his anger live on air, is sacked and curses God for doing a lousy job. Rising to the bait, the Almighty - a coolly majestic Morgan Freeman - gives the sceptical Carrey the chance to see if he can do any better. He does what you might expect: enlarges girlfriend Jennifer Aniston's boobs, performs a Red Sea-style parting of his tomato soup and pulls the Moon out of its usual orbit to create a romantic moment. A neat premise and plenty of laughs, but hardly memorable. BP Swearing. *DVD* *BL*

Jim Carrey *Bruce Nolan* • Morgan Freeman *God* • Jennifer Aniston *Grace Connelly* • Philip Baker Hall *Jack Keller* • Catherine Bell *Susan Ortega* • Lisa Ann Walter *Debbie* ▪ *Dir* Tom Shadyac • *Scr* Steve Koren, Mark O'Keefe, Steve Oedekerk, from a story by Steve Koren, Mark O'Keefe

Brüno ★★★ 18

Spoof comedy 2009 · US · Colour · 77min

British comedian Sacha Baron Cohen struck gold with *Borat* and employs similar tactics here as a gay Austrian fashion journalist on a mission to become world famous. Once again Baron Cohen goes undercover in the US (albeit in a most conspicuous way) to bait bigots and get belly laughs. He also ventures to the Middle East and ends up being chased, Benny Hill-style, by angry clerics. This makes for moments that are both funny and toe-curling, and it is a no-holds-barred approach that will offend some people. Overall it's a hit-and-miss affair that works best when Baron Cohen doesn't just make a spectacle of himself through cheap gags but shines a spotlight on the real-life oddballs along his way. Also shown in a slightly edited 15 certificate version as *Brüno (Snipped)*. SP Sex scenes, sexual references. *DVD* *BL*

Sacha Baron Cohen *Brüno* • Gustaf Hammarsten *Lutz* • Paula Abdul • Harrison Ford • Ron Paul ▪ *Dir* Larry Charles • *Scr* Dan Mazer, Sacha Baron Cohen, Anthony Hines, Jeff Schaffer, from a story by Mazer, Baron Cohen, Hines, Peter Baynham, from characters by Baron Cohen

Brute Force ★★★★ 12

Prison drama 1947 · US · BW · 93min

This is one of the great prison dramas, tough even by today's standards, and a film whose parallels to the Nazi concentration camps would have been obvious to the audience of the time. Hume Cronyn is a sadistic prison warden whose staff systematically brutalise their captives. Burt Lancaster, in his second picture, leads the prisoners in a *Spartacus*-style revolt. Apart from the flashbacks showing prisoners with their wives and girlfriends, this is a masterpiece of escalating violence. It's a disturbing, powerful picture, handled in an urgent, documentary style by Jules Dassin. AT *DVD* *BL*

Burt Lancaster *Joe Collins* • Hume Cronyn *Capt Munsey* • Charles Bickford *Gallagher* • Whit Bissell *Tom Lister* • Sam Levene *Louie* • John Hoyt *Spencer* • Yvonne De Carlo *Gina* • Ann Blyth *Ruth* • Ella Raines *Cora* • Anita Colby *Flossie* ▪ *Dir* Jules Dassin • *Scr* Richard Brooks, from a story by Robert Patterson • *Cinematographer* William Daniels (1)

El Bruto ★★★ 12

Drama 1952 · Mex · BW · 77min

This simmering drama is among director Luis Buñuel's more interesting failures. Although he has little sympathy with the worker who becomes a boss's lackey, Buñuel clearly demonstrates the desperate domestic situation that would compel a man to betray his class. Shot in a mere 18 days, the film looks rough, but this only reinforces the atmosphere of life around Mexico City's abattoirs. Katy Jurado is superb, but Pedro Armendáriz seems more interested in preserving his macho image than giving a germane performance. DP Spanish +subtitles.

Pedro Armendáriz *Pedro, El Bruto* • Katy Jurado *Paloma* • Rosita Arenas *Meche* • Andres Soler *Andres Cabrera* • Beatriz Ramos *Doña Marta* • Paco Martinez *Don Pepe* ▪ *Dir* Luis Buñuel • *Scr* Luis Buñuel, Luis Alcoriza

The Brylcreem Boys ★★★ 15

Second World War comedy drama
1996 · UK · Colour · 101min

Loosely based on actual events, this PoW film is set in the Republic of Ireland, which, as a neutral country during the Second World War, was committed to interning both German and Allied personnel - in the same camp. Canadian flier Bill Campbell and German air ace Angus MacFadyen are the two newest internees who come to blows over the conflict and a local farm girl. There are some pleasing supporting turns while director/co-writer Terence Ryan affably melds together the comic, romantic and dramatic elements. JF Swearing, violence. *DVD*

Bill Campbell *Myles Keogh* • William McNamara *Sam Gunn* • Angus MacFadyen *Rudolph Von Stegenbek* • John Gordon-Sinclair *Richard Lewis* • Oliver Tobias *Hans Jorg Wolff* • Jean Butler *Mattie Guerin* • Joe McGann *Captain Deegan* • Hal Fowler *Bunty Winthrop* • Gabriel Byrne *Commandant O'Brien* ▪ *Dir* Terence Ryan • *Scr* Terence Ryan, Jamie Brown, Susan Morrall

Bubba Ho-tep ★★★ 15

Black comedy horror
2002 · US · Colour · 88min

This irreverent, B-movie-style horror comedy offers an alternative version of what became of Elvis Presley. In an astonishingly spot-on performance, Bruce Campbell plays the king of rock 'n' roll, now an elderly unknown living in an East Texas rest home. When fellow pensioners start inexplicably dying, Campbell teams up with a black resident (Ossie Davis), who believes he's President Kennedy, to solve the mystery. Crudely hilarious, this frolic combines below-the-belt geriatric wit with Three Stooges-type slapstick. The climax, however, is disappointing. SF Swearing, sexual references. *DVD* *BL*

Bruce Campbell *Elvis* • Ossie Davis *Jack* • Ella Joyce *The nurse* • Heidi Marnhout *Callie* • Bob Ivy *Bubba Ho-tep* • Edith Jefferson *Elderly woman* ▪ *Dir* Don Coscarelli • *Scr* Don Coscarelli, from the short story by Joe R Lansdale

The Bubble ★★

Science-fiction drama
1966 · US · Colour · 93min

Arch Oboler is the man who brought us the first ever 3-D movie, *Bwana Devil* in 1952. While Hollywood lost interest in the costly process, Oboler persisted and finally perfected Space-Vision (his own 3D system) and released *The Bubble*. Ironically this overly talky movie about three people trapped in a town populated by mindless zombies and surrounded by an energy shield hardly merited or benefited from 3D exposure. RS

Michael Cole *Mark* • Deborah Walley *Catherine* • Johnny Desmond *Tony* • Kassid McMahon ▪ *Dir/Scr* Arch Oboler

Bubble Boy ★★ 12

Comedy 2001 · US · Colour · 80min

In this wildly uneven comedy, Jake Gyllenhaal plays a young man with immune deficiencies who is forced by his worried mum (Swoosie Kurtz) to live his life in a bubble. However, when he falls for the girl next door (Marley Shelton), who is about to marry a sleazy musician, the boy and his bubble set off cross-country to reclaim his true love. It's deeply politically incorrect - in the US, the Immune Deficiency Foundation called for a boycott - but it has its moments and is enthusiastically played. JF *DVD*

Jake Gyllenhaal *Jimmy Livingston* • Swoosie Kurtz *Mrs Livingston* • Marley Shelton *Chloe* • Danny Trejo *Slim* • John Carroll Lynch *Mr Livingston* ▪ *Dir* Blair Hayes • *Scr* Cinco Paul, Ken Daurio

12 **15** **18** PASSED FOR PEOPLE OF THESE AGES AND OVER · *DVD* RELEASED ON DVD · *BL* RELEASED ON BLU-RAY · *3D* RELEASED IN 3D · *CS* END CREDIT SEQUENCE

185

B

The Buccaneer ★★ U
Swashbuckling adventure
1938 · US · BW · 125min

Cecil B DeMille's lavish juggernaut of a swashbuckler is set during the British-American war of 1812-15, but rather lacks the lightness and humour the genre needs. Fredric March plays the pirate Jean Lafitte, who sides with President Andrew Jackson and runs the British out of New Orleans. The leading lady is Franciska Gaal, a Hungarian discovery of DeMille's who subsequently went home and vanished without a trace. Anthony Quinn, DeMille's son-in-law at the time, plays one of March's henchmen. In 1958 Quinn remade the film, as his sole directorial effort. AT

Fredric March *Jean Lafitte* · Franciska Gaal *Gretchen* · Akim Tamiroff *Dominique You* · Margot Grahame *Annette* · Walter Brennan *Ezra Peavey* · Ian Keith *Crawford* · Spring Byington *Dolly Madison* · Douglass Dumbrille *Governor Claiborne* · Hugh Sothern *Andrew Jackson* · Anthony Quinn *Beluche* ■ *Dir* Cecil B DeMille · *Scr* Edwin Justus Mayer, Harold Lamb, C Gardner Sullivan, Jeanie Macpherson, from the book *Lafitte the Pirate* by Lyle Saxon

The Buccaneer ★★★ U
Swashbuckling adventure
1958 · US · Colour · 118min

This is actor Anthony Quinn's only film as director and while it's a little long and drawn out, the Technicolor is splendid and it boasts quite a cast. A bewigged Yul Brynner stars as the dashing pirate Lafitte, who gets caught up in the War of 1812. His women are Claire Bloom and Inger Stevens, while Charlton Heston appears as General Andrew Jackson. The most impressive sequence is a well-mounted but studio-bound Battle of New Orleans. The anti-British sentiments might put off some, but this is still worth a look. TS

Yul Brynner *Jean Lafitte* · Charlton Heston *General Andrew Jackson* · Claire Bloom *Bonnie Brown* · Charles Boyer *Dominique You* · Inger Stevens *Annette Claiborne* · Henry Hull *Ezra Peavey* · EG Marshall *Governor Claiborne* · Lorne Greene *Mercier* ■ *Dir* Anthony Quinn · *Scr* Jesse L Lasky Jr, Bernice Mosk, from the 1938 film, from the book *Lafitte the Pirate* by Lyle Saxon

Buchanan Rides Alone ★★★ U
Western
1958 · US · Colour · 79min

This colourful B-western was co-produced by star Randolph Scott and Harry Joe Brown for their Ranown independent production company, and directed by the talented Budd Boetticher. It's based on a novel in a cowboy series (the "Buchanan" books by Jonas Ward) and features a rather more cheerful, humorous hero than usually portrayed by the craggy, taciturn Scott. The myriad plot convolutions are mightily effective, too, but there are no standouts in the rather feeble supporting cast. TS

Randolph Scott *Buchanan* · Craig Stevens *Abe Carbo* · Barry Kelley *Lou Agry* · Tol Avery *Simon Agry* · Peter Whitney *Amos Agry* · Manuel Rojas *Juan* · LQ Jones *Pecos Bill* · Robert Anderson (2) *Waldo Peek* ■ *Dir* Budd Boetticher · *Scr* Charles Lang, from the novel *The Name's Buchanan* by Jonas Ward

La Bûche ★★★ 15
Comedy drama
1999 · Fr · Colour · 107min

Screenwriter Danièle Thompson's directorial debut is the kind of women's picture Hollywood can't do any more without submerging it in life-affirming sentiment. There will be clichéd characters in any ensemble piece, but rarely will they be as well played as they are here. Everyone impresses, from Charlotte Gainsbourg's lonely career girl and Emmanuelle Béart's jilted model housewife to their pregnant singer sister Sabine Azéma and her indecisive married lover, Jean-Pierre Darroussin. Though the episodes seem mundane, they vibrate with wit and warmth. DP French +subtitles. Swearing, sex scenes.

Sabine Azéma *Louba* · Emmanuelle Béart *Sonia* · Charlotte Gainsbourg *Milla* · Claude Rich *Stanislas* · Françoise Fabian *Yvette* · Christopher Thompson *Joseph* · Jean-Pierre Darroussin *Gilbert* · Isabelle Carré *Annabelle* ■ *Dir* Danièle Thompson · *Scr* Danièle Thompson, Christopher Thompson

Buck and the Preacher ★★★ PG
Western
1972 · US · Colour · 98min

Sidney Poitier's first film as director is a lively reworking of the *Wagon Train* idea, with Poitier as leader of a group of slaves, newly freed after the American Civil War, making their way through the wilderness despite harassment by white nightriders trying to take them back to the plantations. A mainly black cast notably avoids "hush-mah-mouth" clichés, while Harry Belafonte gives real edge to his conman preacher whose slickness turns eventually to integrity. TH Swearing. DVD

Sidney Poitier *Buck* · Harry Belafonte *Preacher* · Ruby Dee *Ruth* · Cameron Mitchell *Deshay* · Denny Miller *Floyd* · Nita Talbot *Madame Esther* · John Kelly (3) *Sheriff* · Tony Brubaker *Headman* · James McEachin *Kingston* ■ *Dir* Sidney Poitier · *Scr* Ernest Kinoy, from a story by Ernest Kinoy, Drake Walker

Buck Benny Rides Again ★★★ U
Comedy
1940 · US · BW · 84min

A knockabout throwback to the golden age of American radio, this spin-off from Jack Benny's beloved programme is a gleeful mishmash of in-jokes, inspired lunacy and silly situations. Determined to impress aspiring singer Ellen Drew, Benny convinces her he's a rodeo-rouser and then has to live up to his boasts when they meet up on a dude ranch. Sprightly entertainment, even during the occasionally intrusive musical numbers. DP

Jack Benny · Ellen Drew *Joan Cameron* · Eddie "Rochester" Anderson *Rochester* · Phil Harris *Phil* · Dennis Day *Dennis* · Virginia Dale *Virginia* · Ward Bond *Outlaw* · Morris Ankrum *Outlaw* ■ *Dir* Mark Sandrich · *Scr* William Morrow, Edmund Beloin, from the short story *Woman Handled* by Arthur Stringer, adapted by Zion Myers

Buck Privates ★★★ U
Comedy
1941 · US · BW · 80min

A decade after they first joined forces as a vaudeville act, Abbott and Costello went stellar with this, their second film. It's hard to see why the picture grossed over $10 million at the US box office – a phenomenal sum for the times – though it's amusing enough. Here Bud and Lou find themselves having to adjudicate in a military *ménage à trois* between Alan Curtis, Lee Bowman and Jane Frazee. The Andrews Sisters sing some top-notch tunes, including the Oscar-nominated *Boogie Woogie Bugle Boy from Company B.* DP DVD

Bud Abbott *Slicker Smith* · Lou Costello *Herbie Brown* · Lee Bowman *Randolph Parker III* · Alan Curtis *Bob Martin* · Jane Frazee *Judy Gray* · Laverne Andrews · Maxene Andrews · Patty Andrews ■ *Dir* Arthur Lubin · *Scr* Arthur T Horman, John Grant

Buck Privates Come Home ★ U
Comedy
1947 · US · BW · 77min

After the huge success of Abbott and Costello's second feature, a sequel was inevitable. But Bud and Lou had packed 18 movies into the six years that separated the two films, and it's all too obvious to see how thinly the material has been spread. The story sees the boys having to babysit a French orphan who has been smuggled home by their army buddy. Time weighs heavily. DP

Bud Abbott *Cpl Slicker Smith* · Lou Costello *Herbie Brown* · Tom Brown *Bill Gregory* · Joan Fulton *Sylvia Hunter* · Nat Pendleton *Sgt Collins* · Don Beddoe *Mr Roberts* · Don Porter *Captain* ■ *Dir* Charles Barton · *Scr* John Grant, Frederic I Rinaldo, Robert Lees, from a story by Richard Macauley, Bradford Ropes

Buck Rogers in the 25th Century ★★ 15
Science-fiction adventure
1979 · US · Colour · 84min

Only American television could luridly update a 1930s film serial and make it more trivial and corny than the original. Even funnier, in the post-*Star Wars* glow of space warriors, cute cyborgs and colourful spectacle, is the fact that people actually paid money to see this TV pilot in the cinema. Hunky Gil Gerard jockeys his way through the pastiche, with added comedy relief, and the whole thing remains strictly kids' stuff. AJ

Gil Gerard *"Buck" Rogers* · Pamela Hensley *Princess Ardala* · Erin Gray *Colonel Wilma Deering* · Henry Silva *Kane* · Tim O'Connor *Dr Huer* · Felix Silla *Twiki* · Mel Blanc *Twiki* · Joseph Wiseman *Draco* ■ *Dir* Daniel Haller · *Scr* Glen A Larson, Leslie Stevens, from characters by Robert C Dille

The Bucket List ★★★ 12
Road movie comedy drama
2008 · US · Colour · 93min

In this mild comedy about confronting the inevitable, two cancer patients escape their hospital room and set out to cross every entry off a "bucket list" (things they want to do before they kick the bucket). That the two men are Jack Nicholson and Morgan Freeman is the only good reason to see this well-intentioned yet overly sentimental tale. It's charming, if predictable, and certainly doesn't hang about trying to make its point – the boys are in hospital, then they're driving race cars, then they're in Tibet, and then... Well, let's retain what surprises there are. Freeman and Nicholson are not a natural double act, yet they handle even a soppy little number like this with aplomb. KK Brief swearing. DVD Blu

Jack Nicholson *Edward Cole* · Morgan Freeman *Carter Chambers* · Sean Hayes *Thomas* · Beverly Todd *Virginia Chambers* · Alfonso Freeman *Roger Carter* · Rowena King *Angelica* · Rob Morrow *Dr Hollins* ■ *Dir* Rob Reiner · *Scr* Justin Zackham

A Bucket of Blood ★★★ 15
Horror comedy
1959 · US · BW · 64min

Hopeless as a horror film, but priceless as a hip black comedy, this essential Roger Corman beatnik variation on *House of Wax* has coffee-bar worker Walter Paisley (wonderfully played by Corman regular Dick Miller) hailed as a cool "art" genius when he turns dead bodies into sculpture. Filmed in five days, Corman's cult sickie-quickie is a brilliant satire on the whole Beat Generation scene. Corman remade it in 1995 as *Dark Secrets*. AJ DVD

Dick Miller *Walter Paisley* · Barboura Morris *Carla* · Antony Carbone *Leonard* · Julian Burton *Brock* · Ed Nelson *Art Lacroix* · John Brinkley *Will* · John Shaner *Oscar* ■ *Dir* Roger Corman · *Scr* Charles B Griffith

Buckskin ★★ U
Western
1968 · US · Colour · 97min

The only thing worse in Hollywood westerns than a tyrannical cattle baron was a grasping tycoon trying to make a quick buck out of the railroad. Wendell Corey combines both villainous aspects in this routine saddle opera. Sheriff Lon Chaney Jr summons no-nonsense marshal Barry Sullivan to restore the backwater to such decent citizens as Barbara Hale's grieving mother and Joan Caulfield's teacher-turned-saloon floozy. DP

Barry Sullivan *Chaddock* · Wendell Corey *Rep Marlowe* · Joan Caulfield *Nora Johnson* · Lon Chaney Jr *Sheriff Tangley* · John Russell *Patch* · Barbara Hale *Sarah Cody* · Bill Williams *Frank Cody* ■ *Dir* Michael D Moore [Michael Moore (1)] · *Scr* Michael Fisher

Buddha Collapsed out of Shame ★★★ PG
Drama
2007 · Iran/Fr · Colour · 76min

Director Hana Makhmalbaf follows up her 2003 documentary *Joy of Madness* with this simple but affecting tale set among the demolished Buddhas of Bamiyan,

Afghanistan. Nikbakht Noruz is disarming as the six-year-old girl who simply doesn't understand why she's not allowed to join her mischievous male neighbour at the local school. Her quest to raise the funds for a notebook and pencil meets with indifference and hostility. Some have criticised the lack of sophistication in Makhmalbaf's film, but it's a sobering reminder of the extent to which the harshness of life has enabled the Taliban influence to persist – even after the liberation – and of how children can be persuaded to accept anything as truth. DP Farsi +subtitles.

Nikbakht Noruz *Bakhtay* · Abbas Alijome *Abbas* ■ *Dir* Hana Makhmalbaf · *Scr* Marziyeh Meshkini

Buddy ★★★ U
Biographical drama
1997 · US · Colour · 83min

This sweet but unassuming film stars Rene Russo as Trudy Lintz, a woman in the 1920s who became known for the collection of animals she looked after at her Long Island home. Director Caroline Thompson focuses on Lintz's attempts to raise Buddy, a baby gorilla whom she treats as her own child. Robbie Coltrane plays Lintz's husband and fellow Scot Alan Cumming also appears. JB DVD

Rene Russo *Trudy Lintz* · Robbie Coltrane *Dr Lintz* · Alan Cumming *Dick* · Irma P Hall *Emma* · Paul Reubens *Professor Spatz* · John Aylward *Mr Bowman* · Mimi Kennedy *Mrs Bowman* ■ *Dir* Caroline Thompson · *Scr* Caroline Thompson, from a story by William Joyce, Caroline Thompson, from the book *Animals Are My Hobby* by Gertrude Davies Lintz

Buddy Boy ★★ 18
Psychological thriller
1999 · US · Colour · 105min

The repressed mummy's boy meets the guilt-ridden voyeur in this self-consciously cultish thriller. Director Mark D Hanlon shovels in an excess of religious iconography and laboured macabre comedy to set the tone. Aidan Gillen plays the loner who finds release from the demands of his bedridden stepmother in the arms of Emmanuelle Seigner, but it's Susan Tyrrell who dominates the unlikely proceedings with her grotesque display of alcoholic tyranny. DP Violence, swearing, drug abuse.

Aidan Gillen *Francis* · Emmanuelle Seigner *Gloria* · Susan Tyrrell *Sal* · Mark Boone Junior *Vic* · Harry Groener *Father Gillespie* · Hector Elias *Mr Salcedo* · Richard Assad *Haroonian* ■ *Dir/Scr* Mark D Hanlon

Buddy Buddy ★★ 15
Comedy
1981 · US · Colour · 91min

Ever since their first film together Jack Lemmon and Walter Matthau have been the odd couple of the movies, as inseparable as Laurel and Hardy. But this farce marks the low point in their chalk-and-cheese collaboration, with slapstick usurping the biting wit of previous productions. Matthau is a hitman who's hampered in his job by a suicide-bent Lemmon. Adapted from the funnier French comedy, *A Pain in the A...!*, its jokes are ill-timed and tedious. TH

Jack Lemmon *Victor Clooney* · Walter Matthau *Trabucco* · Paula Prentiss *Celia Clooney* · Klaus Kinski *Dr Zuckerbrot* · Dana Elcar *Captain Hubris* · Miles Chapin *Eddie the bellhop* · Michael Ensign *Assistant manager* · Joan Shawlee *Receptionist* ■ *Dir* Billy Wilder · *Scr* Billy Wilder, IAL Diamond, from the story and play *A Pain in the A ...* by Francis Veber

The Buddy Holly Story ★★★★ PG
Biographical drama
1978 · US · Colour · 108min

This is a stunningly well-made biopic of the legendary rock 'n' roller, who met his tragically premature end in a plane crash in 1959. Gary Busey has never matched the marvellous Oscar-nominated performance he gives here, contenting himself instead with a rogues' gallery of roles as cops and psychos ever since. Director Steve Rash has likewise never managed to recapture the verve he conjures up here. The movie is made doubly enjoyable by the knowledge that Busey and the movie's Crickets actually do their own singing and playing, generating their own very palpable raw energy in the process. TS *DVD* *BL*

Gary Busey *Buddy Holly* • Don Stroud *Jesse Clarence* • Charles Martin Smith *Ray Bob Simmons* • William Jordan *Riley Randolph* • Maria Richwine *Maria Elena Santiago* • Conrad Janis *Ross Turner* • Albert Popwell *Eddie Foster* • Amy Johnston *Cindy Lou* ■ *Dir* Steve Rash • *Scr* Robert Gittler, from a story by Alan Swyer, from the biography *Buddy Holly His Life and Music* by John Coldrosen

The Buddy System ★★🅟🅖

Romantic comedy drama
1984 · US · Colour · 105min

From the doldrums of Richard Dreyfuss's movie career comes this pale imitation of *The Goodbye Girl*. This time round he is a frustrated writer, forced to take a security job at the local school where he pals up with single mom Susan Sarandon's precocious 11-year-old son. You'd think that such a cast would be box-office gold, but the pair fail to sizzle. FL

Richard Dreyfuss *Joe* • Susan Sarandon *Emily* • Nancy Allen *Carrie* • Jean Stapleton *Mrs Price* • Wil Wheaton *Tim* • Edward Winter *Jim Parks* • Keene Curtis *Dr Knitz* ■ *Dir* Glenn Jordan • *Scr* Mary Agnes Donoghue

Buddy's Song ★★🅟🅖

Drama
1990 · UK · Colour · 102min

Nigel Hinton has done his popular teen novel a major disservice with his clumsy adaptation that fails to convince. Roger Daltrey gives a knowing and willing performance as Chesney Hawkes's teddy boy dad, but Sharon Duce and Michael Elphick settle for caricatures. DP Swearing, brief nudity.

Roger Daltrey *Terry Clark* • Chesney Hawkes *Buddy* • Sharon Duce *Carol* • Michael Elphick *Des King* • Douglas Hodge *Bobby Rosen* • Paul McKenzie *Julius* • Lee Ross *Jason* • Nick Moran *Mike* ■ *Dir* Claude Whatham • *Scr* Nigel Hinton, from his novel

Buena Vista Social Club ★★★★

Music documentary 1998 · Ger · Colour · 100min

This charming documentary from director Wim Wenders follows in the footsteps of the album by legendary guitarist Ry Cooder, capturing the rhythm and blues of a group of elderly Cuban musicians – the oldest over 90. Their music had largely been forgotten (some of the musicians featured had long been in retirement), but now it can be heard by a world that had consigned them to a bygone age. The visual style sometimes detracts from the lyrical substance – the camera circles the soloists to an irritating degree – but, despite that, this is still one of the best music documentaries ever made and a compelling testament to the strength of the human spirit. TH English, Spanish +subtitles. *DVD*

■ *Dir* Wim Wenders

Buffalo Bill ★★★

Western 1944 · US · Colour · 86min

You won't learn much about the real William Frederick Cody from this conventional western, with a stalwart, though rather dull, Joel McCrea in the lead. Still, redhead Maureen O'Hara and the striking locations were made for Fox Technicolor – though these days you have to take Anthony Quinn and Linda Darnell made-up as Cheyenne Indians with a pinch of salt. Director William A Wellman keeps the film moving. TS *DVD*

Joel McCrea *Buffalo Bill* • Maureen O'Hara *Louisa Cody* • Linda Darnell *Dawn Starlight* • Thomas Mitchell *Ned Buntline* • Edgar Buchanan *Sergeant Chips* • Anthony Quinn *Yellow Hand* • Moroni Olsen *Senator Frederici* • Frank Fenton *Murdo Carvell* ■ *Dir* William A Wellman • *Scr* Aeneas MacKenzie, Clements Ripley, Cecile Kramer, from a story by Frank Winch • *Cinematographer* Leon Shamroy

Buffalo Bill and the Indians, or Sitting Bull's History Lesson ★★🅟🅖

Western 1976 · US · Colour · 118min

Like so many of Robert Altman's pictures, this is a glorious, infuriating mess, a whirl of half-baked ideas, missed opportunities and startling moments. Paul Newman plays Buffalo Bill with golden locks and a twinkle in his eye, a phoney and a showman, who hires Sitting Bull for his travelling Wild West show. Co-stars drift in and out of a picture driven solely by Altman's unfocused vision of a people on the edge of extinction and a country in turmoil. AT *DVD*

Paul Newman *Buffalo Bill* • Joel Grey *Nate Salsbury* • Burt Lancaster *Ned Buntline* • Kevin McCarthy *Major John Burke* • Harvey Keitel *Ed Goodman* • Allan Nicholls *Prentiss Ingraham* • Geraldine Chaplin *Annie Oakley* • John Considine *Frank Butler* • Frank Kaquitts *Sitting Bull* ■ *Dir* Robert Altman • *Scr* Alan Rudolph, Robert Altman, from the play *Indians* by Arthur Kopit

Buffalo '66 ★★★★ 15

Drama 1998 · Can/US · Colour · 109min

Touted by actor/director Vincent Gallo as a self-styled masterpiece, this searing view of disillusionment is indeed as arrogantly conceited as the man himself. But his grimy, ironic look at uncaring family life, and the emotional pain it causes, is also an amazing slice of neo-existentialism that takes some breathtaking risks. Gallo plays the born loser desperate for a lucky break, who unknowingly finds one when he kidnaps Christina Ricci to play his wife during an overdue family visit. Sharp dialogue and unusual flashbacks lead to an uplifting payoff that is well worth the wait. This is a minor gem. AJ Swearing, violence, nudity. *DVD*

Vincent Gallo *Billy Brown* • Christina Ricci *Layla* • Ben Gazzara *Jimmy Brown* • Mickey Rourke *The Bookie* • Rosanna Arquette *Wendy Balsam* • Jan-Michael Vincent *Sonny* • Anjelica Huston *Janet "Jan" Brown* ■ *Dir* Vincent Gallo • *Scr* Vincent Gallo, Alison Bagnall, from a story by Vincent Gallo • *Music* Vincent Gallo

Buffalo Soldiers ★★★ 15

Western drama 1997 · US · Colour · 90min

Based on actual events, this quality TV movie is well worth a look. In post-Civil War New Mexico, an all-black cavalry troop under the leadership of a fearless ex-slave (Danny Glover) pursues an Apache marauder through the territory. The tight-knit group must also suffer the endless degradation heaped upon them by white officers in the segregated army. Glover gives an excellent performance, and the action is handled efficiently by ex-*Hill Street Blues* veteran Charles Haid. MC Violence.

Danny Glover *Sergeant Wyatt* • Bob Gunton *Colonel Grierson* • Carl Lumbly *Horse* • Glynn Turman *Sergeant Joshua "Joju" Judges Ruth* • Mykelti Williamson *Corporal William Christy* • Lamont Bentley *Corporal Sea* • Tom Bower *General Pike* • Timothy Busfield *Major Robert Carr* ■ *Dir* Charles Haid • *Scr* Frank Military, Susan Rhinehart, from a story by Jonathan Klein, Frank Military

Buffalo Soldiers ★★★★ 15

Black comedy drama 2001 · UK/Ger/US · Colour · 94min

You know you're in satirical territory when a stoned US soldier stationed in Germany watches live news footage of the Berlin Wall coming down and asks: "Where's Berlin?". Gregor Jordan's self-consciously hip adaptation of Robert O'Connor's novel presents the US military – as embodied by Joaquin Phoenix's charismatic wheeler-dealer – as bored and morally bankrupt. But the film makes the serious point that warriors in peacetime will go looking for conflict. Given the post "9/11", post-Iraq War climate, this entertaining and nihilistic black comedy now carries a greater political significance than ever could have been intended. AC Swearing, violence, drug abuse. *DVD*

Joaquin Phoenix *Ray Elwood* • Ed Harris *Col Wallace Berman* • Scott Glenn *Sgt Robert Lee* • Anna Paquin *Robyn Lee* • Elizabeth McGovern

Mrs Berman • Dean Stockwell *Gen Lancaster* • Leon Robinson *[Leon] Stoney* ■ *Dir* Gregor Jordan • *Scr* Gregor Jordan, Eric Axel Weiss, Nora Maccoby, from the novel by Robert O'Connor

Buffet Froid ★★★ 12

Black comedy 1979 · Fr · Colour · 89min

Not since *The Treasure of the Sierra Madre* has a son directed his father with such a mischievous sense of respect as in this savage black comedy. As the inspector drawn into a series of bizarre murders, Bernard Blier is given full rein by his son, Bertrand, who also coaxes a full-throttled display of blue collar boorishness from Gérard Depardieu as the killer caught up in the crimes of maniac Jean Carmet. DP French +subtitles. *DVD*

Gérard Depardieu *Alphonse Tram* • Bernard Blier *Inspector Morvandieu* • Jean Carmet *Murderer* • Genevieve Page *Widow* • Denise Gence *Hostess* • Carole Bouquet *Young girl* • Michel Serrault *Man in subway* ■ *Dir/Scr* Bertrand Blier

Buffy the Vampire Slayer ★★★ 15

Comedy horror 1992 · US · Colour · 81min

This engagingly silly yet knowing horror comedy deserves cult status. Kristy Swanson is cheerfully dim-witted as LA teenager Buffy, who's surprised to discover that she is actually the only person who can save the city from suave Rutger Hauer and his fellow vampires. Director Fran Rubel Kuzui rightly plays it like a comic strip and draws perfectly judged performances from an eclectic cast that also includes teen heart-throb Luke Perry, Donald Sutherland, an unrecognisable Paul Reubens (Pee-wee Herman) and an uncredited appearance from Ben Affleck. Fun, but fans of the TV series will be disappointed. JF *DVD*

Kristy Swanson *Buffy* • Donald Sutherland *Merrick* • Paul Reubens *Amilyn* • Rutger Hauer *Lothos* • Luke Perry *Pike* • Michele Abrams *Jennifer* • Hilary Swank *Kimberly* • Paris Vaughn *Nicole* • David Arquette *Benny* ■ *Dir* Fran Rubel Kuzui • *Scr* Joss Whedon

Bug ★★ 15

Horror 1975 · US · Colour · 95min

The last film produced by William Castle, the king of gimmick cinema (*The Tingler*, *Macabre*), is one of his better efforts. An earthquake unleashes a swarm of fire-making insects and scientist Bradford Dillman mates them with the common cockroach in order to communicate with them. The initial nature-revenge plot tends to get lost once the routine mad-doctor thread takes over, but zestful direction and tongue-in-cheek acting eke out some decent thrills and chills from the implausible tale. AJ

Bradford Dillman *James Parmiter* • Joanna Miles *Carrie Parmiter* • Richard Gilliland *Metbaum* • Jamie Smith-Jackson *Norma Tacker* • Alan Fudge *Mark Ross* • Jesse Vint *Tom Tacker* • Brenden Dillon *Charlie* ■ *Dir* Jeannot Szwarc • *Scr* Thomas Page, William Castle, from the novel *The Hephaestus Plague* by Thomas Page

Bug ★ 18

Psychological thriller 2006 · US · Colour · 97min

Despite misleading genre trappings, nasty gore and director William Friedkin's *Exorcist* fame, this alienating, exhausting rant is not a horror film but a psychological drama. Trailer-trash waitress Ashley Judd (giving a fearless yet wasted performance) and traumatised soldier Michael Shannon shack up in a tacky motel room and feed off each other's paranoid delusions. Each becomes more hysterical as manic fantasy takes over from fact, with Friedkin pushing the final ludicrous third act into dead-end grotesque camp. AJ Violence. *DVD*

Ashley Judd *Agnes White* • Michael Shannon *Peter Evans* • Harry Connick Jr *Jerry Goss* • Lynn Collins *RC* • Brian F O'Byrne *Dr Sweet* ■ *Dir* William Friedkin • *Scr* Tracy Letts, from his play

Bugles in the Afternoon ★★ U

Western 1952 · US · Colour · 84min

This disappointing, would-be stirring Warner Bros western is seriously hampered by poor casting. The urbane Ray Milland looks uncomfortable out west and fails to convince as a disgraced cavalry officer who re-enlists as a private at a remote outpost in Sioux territory. He's not helped by a sub-par supporting cast and a totally inadequate leading lady in Helena Carter. Nevertheless, the exterior Technicolor location photography is impressive. TS

Ray Milland *Kern Shafter* • Helena Carter *Josephine Russell* • Hugh Marlowe *Captain Edward Garnett* • Forrest Tucker *Private Donovan* • Barton MacLane *Captain Myles Moylan* • George Reeves *Lieutenant Smith* • James Millican *Sergeant Hines* ■ *Dir* Roy Rowland • *Scr* Geoffrey Homes [Daniel Mainwaring], Harry Brown, from a novel by Ernest Haycox • *Music* Dmitri Tiomkin • *Cinematographer* Wilfred M Cline [Wilfred M Cline]

Bugs Bunny 1001 Rabbit Tales ★★★ U

Animation compilation
1982 · US · Colour · 70min

This slickly assembled compilation film was produced by Friz Freleng, the genius behind many of the most popular Warner Bros cartoon characters and a pioneer of the crash-bang style of animation known as "socko". Voiced, as ever, by the legendary Mel Blanc, Bugs Bunny and Daffy Duck here find themselves reliving some classic capers as they try to sell books to some highly resistant customers. As you would expect, the quality is inconsistent, but there are some cracking slapstick gags and lots of cringe-worthy puns. DP

Mel Blanc ■ *Dir* David Detiege, Art Davis, Bill Perez, Friz Freleng • *Scr* John Dunn, David Detiege, Friz Freleng

The Bugs Bunny/Road Runner Movie ★★★★ U

Animation compilation
1979 · US · Colour · 93min

Not really a film in the true sense of the word, this is essentially the best of Bugs tenuously linked by the presence of the much loved rabbit. But as it brings together some of the most memorable shorts devised by animation legend Chuck Jones, who's complaining? Along with Bugs, his long-suffering adversaries Daffy Duck and Porky Pig get plenty of screen time, while Wile E Coyote gets to suffer endless humiliation at the hands of his nemesis, Road Runner. JF

Mel Blanc ■ *Dir* Chuck Jones, Phil Monroe • *Scr* Chuck Jones, Michael Maltese

A Bug's Life ★★★★ U

Animated adventure 1998 · US · Colour · 93min

Director John Lasseter's follow-up to the ground-breaking *Toy Story* may have less beguiling characters than Woody and Buzz Lightyear, but the computer-animated effects are if anything even more wondrous. In an ant colony, clumsy worker Flik (voiced by Dave Foley) accidentally destroys the grain that's regularly offered to appease a band of hostile grasshoppers led by the bullying Hopper (a superb characterisation by Kevin Spacey). As the ants struggle to find twice as much grain, Flik employs a flea circus of colourful eccentrics to do battle with the grasshoppers. The result is a witty variation on *The Seven Samurai*. TH *DVD* *BL* *CS*

Dave Foley *Flik* • Kevin Spacey *Hopper* • Julia Louis-Dreyfus *Princess Atta* • Hayden Panettiere *Princess Dot* • Phyllis Diller *Queen* • Richard Kind *Molt* • David Hyde Pierce *Slim* • Denis Leary *Francis* • Jonathan Harris *Manny* • Madeline Kahn *Gypsy* • Bonnie Hunt *Rosie* • Mike McShane [Micheal McShane] *Tuck/Roll* • Roddy McDowall *Mr Soil* ■ *Dir* John Lasseter • *Scr* Andrew Stanton, Donald McEnery, Bob Shaw, from the story *The Ant and the Grasshopper* by Aesop

B

Bugsy ★★★★ 🔞

Crime drama 1991 · US · Colour · 130min

While avoiding the usual gangster film clichés, director Barry Levinson also insists that Warren Beatty does more than coast through the movie on matinée idol looks and easy charm. Beatty is charismatically dangerous as gangster Benjamin "Bugsy" Siegel, switching unnervingly from flirtation to rage, even if his on-screen romance with Annette Bening never really catches fire (unlike their off-screen relationship, which led to marriage and parenthood). This double Oscar winner (for costume and art direction) is strong on pumping narrative and strewn with memorable scenes and distinctive criminals. JM Violence, swearing. *DVD*

Warren Beatty *Benjamin "Bugsy" Siegel* · Annette Bening *Virginia Hill* · Harvey Keitel *Mickey Cohen* · Ben Kingsley *Meyer Lansky* · Elliott Gould *Harry Greenberg* · Joe Mantegna *George Raft* · Richard Sarafian [Richard C Sarafian] *Jack Dragna* · Bebe Neuwirth *Countess Di Frasso* ■ *Dir* Barry Levinson · *Scr* James Toback, from the book *We Only Kill Each Other: the Life and Bad Times of Bugsy Siegel* by Dean Jennings · *Art Director* Dennis Gassner · *Set Designer* Nancy Haigh · *Costume Designer* Albert Wolsky

Bugsy Malone ★★★★ Ⓤ

Spoof crime musical 1976 · UK · Colour · 89min

Alan Parker's debut feature, following a number of social-realist scripts for the BBC, was a deliberate attempt to get attention. And, by casting children as American gangsters whose Tommy guns fire gunk, Parker achieved his ambition: the movie was the toast of the Cannes film festival and a flamboyant career was under way. Using techniques borrowed from old Hollywood movies, as well as the polish that he learned from his many TV commercials, Parker creates a vibrant pastiche that hovers just on the brink of cuteness. The children - most notably Jodie Foster - have an edge to their performances that cuts through sentiment . AT *DVD* *BL*

Scott Baio *Bugsy Malone* · Jodie Foster *Tallulah* · Florrie Dugger *Blousey* · John Cassisi *Fat Sam* · Martin Lev *Dandy Dan* · Paul Murphy *Leroy* · "Humpty" Albin Jenkins *Fizzy* · Davidson Knight *Cagey Joe* ■ *Dir/Scr* Alan Parker · *Music/lyrics* Paul Williams

Build My Gallows High
★★★★★ 🅿🅶

Classic film noir 1947 · US · BW · 96min

This classic 1940s *film noir* - better known in America as *Out of the Past* - contains a memorably languid performance by Robert Mitchum as the hard-boiled former private eye who falls for the woman (Jane Greer) he's been hired to track by gangster Kirk Douglas. Unfairly underrated for many years, this is in fact a stylish, atmospheric, highly watchable and strongly recommended masterpiece from genre expert Jacques Tourneur. Remade in 1984 as the inferior *Against All Odds* (with Jeff Bridges and Rachel Ward). PF

Robert Mitchum *Jeff Bailey/Jeff Markham* · Jane Greer *Kathie Moffat* · Kirk Douglas *Whit Sterling* · Rhonda Fleming *Meta Carson* · Richard Webb *Jim* · Steve Brodie *Jack Fisher* · Virginia Huston *Ann Miller* · Paul Valentine *Joe Stefanos* ■ *Dir* Jacques Tourneur · *Scr* Geoffrey Homes [Daniel Mainwaring], from his novel · *Cinematographer* Nicholas Musuraca

Bula Quo! ★★ 🅿🅶

Comedy action adventure 2013 · UK/British Virgin Islands/Fiji · Colour · 90min

You don't see that old chestnut, the pop group movie, often these days. Now veteran rockers Status Quo unexpectedly revive the tradition, with band frontmen Francis Rossi and Rick Parfitt flying to Fiji for a series of gigs, stumbling upon an illicit Russian Roulette ring and finding themselves on the run from criminals. Fiji looks fabulous, and Rossi and Parfitt acquit themselves creditably in a cast that also includes Craig Fairbrass as their minder/manager. Of course, the whole concept is slight and silly, but it's not quite the car crash it could have been. DA

Francis Rossi *Francis* · Rick Parfitt *Rick* · Craig Fairbrass *Simon* · Laura Aikman *Caroline* · Jon Lovitz *Wilson* ■ *Dir* Stuart St Paul · *Scr* Stuart St Paul, Jean Heard

Bull Durham ★★★★ 🔞

Comedy sports drama 1988 · US · Colour · 106min

Director Ron Shelton has proved something of a specialist with baseball movies, and in this winning comedy drama his detailed love of the sport shines through. The result is a smart, witty character piece that eschews the stale sports flick formula, concentrating instead on the electric attraction between baseball groupie Susan Sarandon and hot young pitcher Tim Robbins, as old pro Kevin Costner broods convincingly in the wings. All three actors make the picture sizzle. JM Swearing, nudity. *DVD*

Kevin Costner *Crash Davis* · Susan Sarandon *Annie Savoy* · Tim Robbins *Ebby Calvin "Nuke" LaLoosh* · Trey Wilson *Joe "Skip" Riggins* · Robert Wuhl *Larry Hockett* · William O'Leary *Jimmy* · David Neidorf *Bobby* · Danny Gans *Deke* ■ *Dir/Scr* Ron Shelton

Bulla... Big Fat Gypsy Gangster ★★ 🔞

Crime comedy 2011 · UK · Colour and BW · 91min

This dodgy offering from writer/director/star Ricky Grover features his alter ego Bulla (the hardman star from C4's *11 o'Clock Show*), who is released from a 16-year prison sentence into the hands of a documentary film crew. The film starts promisingly enough, but degenerates into a chaotic and tasteless mess. There are some notable cameos (Peter Capaldi, Steven Berkoff, Omid Djalili) but nevertheless this is a painful example of what happens when you stretch a fun 90-second skit to a 90-minute feature. TP Swearing. *DVD*

Ricky Grover *Bulla* · Omid Djalili *Jik Jickels* · Laila Morse *Aunt Queenie* · Peter Capaldi *Peter Van Gellis* · Steven Berkoff *Guru Shah* ■ *Dir* Bulla [Ricky Grover] · *Scr* Ricky Grover, Maria Grover

The Bulldog Breed ★★ 🅿🅶

Comedy 1960 · UK · BW · 93min

There is no doubt where the fun lies in this merely adequate comedy - it's in the brief sight of Michael Caine and Oliver Reed playing second fiddle to Norman Wisdom. Norman is not at his best as the fumbling shop assistant whose career in the navy culminates in an ill-fated moonshot. The script does him few favours. DP *DVD*

Norman Wisdom *Norman Puckle* · Ian Hunter *Admiral Sir Bryanston Blyth* · David Lodge *CPO Knowles* · Robert Urquhart *Commander Clayton* · Edward Chapman *Mr Philpots* · John Le Mesurier *Prosecuting counsel* · Michael Caine *Sailor* · Oliver Reed ■ *Dir* Robert Asher · *Scr* Jack Davies, Henry Blyth, Norman Wisdom

Bulldog Drummond ★★★

Detective mystery adventure 1929 · US · BW · 90min

Suave Ronald Colman's first talkie revealed to movie-goers the dulcet tones and perfect enunciation that would become a model for all future screen matinée idols. As the ex-army adventure hero of HC "Sapper" McNeile's popular novels, Colman is splendidly cast. He provides a Drummond that others found impossible to better, while Claud Allister is the definitive Algy, Drummond's constant companion. Creaky, but with value. TS

Ronald Colman *Bulldog Drummond* · Joan Bennett *Phyllis Benton* · Lilyan Tashman *Erma Peterson* · Montagu Love *Carl Peterson* · Lawrence Grant *Doctor Lakington* · Wilson Benge *Danny* · Claud Allister *Algy Longworth* ■ *Dir* F Richard Jones · *Scr* Wallace Smith, Sidney Howard, from the play by HC "Sapper" McNeile

Bulldog Drummond Strikes Back ★★★

Detective mystery adventure 1934 · US · BW · 83min

This is Ronald Colman's rarely seen second outing as supersleuth and 007 precursor Bulldog Drummond. Colman is suave, fearless and witty, while co-star Loretta Young is there to look pretty and to be kidnapped more than once. Nunnally Johnson's screenplay has a few sharp lines and Roy Del Ruth, best known for his breezy musicals, directs with dollar efficiency to disguise the dime budget. AT

Ronald Colman *Captain Hugh Drummond* · Loretta Young *Lola Field* · C Aubrey Smith *Inspector Nielsen* · Charles Butterworth *Algy Longworth* · Una Merkel *Gwen* · Warner Oland *Prince Achmed* · George Regas *Singh* · Mischa Auer *Hassan* ■ *Dir* Roy Del Ruth · *Scr* Nunnally Johnson, Henry Lehrman, from the novel by HC "Sapper" McNeile

Bulldog Drummond Escapes ★★ Ⓤ

Detective mystery adventure 1937 · US · BW · 64min

Ray Milland is somewhat miscast in the first of Paramount's low-budget adaptations from the casebook of Bulldog Drummond. Drummond's bid to deliver helpless heiress Heather Angel from the clutches of an avaricious admirer never gathers any momentum as too much time is spent introducing his devoted sidekicks, Reginald Denny, EE Clive and Scotland Yard supremo Guy Standing. DP *DVD*

Ray Milland *Captain Hugh "Bulldog" Drummond* · Sir Guy Standing [Guy Standing] *Inspector Nielson* · Heather Angel *Phyllis Clavering* · Reginald Denny *Algy Longworth* · Porter Hall *Norman Merridew* · Fay Holden *Natalie* · EE Clive *Tenny* ■ *Dir* James Hogan · *Scr* Edward T Lowe, from the play *Bulldog Drummond Again* by HC "Sapper" McNeile, Gerard Fairlie

Bulldog Drummond Comes Back ★★ Ⓤ

Detective mystery adventure 1937 · US · BW · 58min

It may seem an ignominious end for one of the greatest American actors of his day to guest in a B-movie series, but John Barrymore seems to enjoy himself in this film, one of his three outings as Scotland Yard hotshot Colonel Nielson. He certainly upstages John Howard, whose Drummond seems a very dull dog by comparison. The story turns around the kidnapping of Louise Campbell by J Carrol Naish, who leaves clues to lure the detecting duo into a trap. DP *DVD*

John Barrymore *Colonel Nielson* · John Howard (1) *Capt Hugh "Bulldog" Drummond* · Louise Campbell *Phyllis Clavering* · Reginald Denny *Algy Longworth* · EE Clive *Tenny* · J Carrol Naish *Mikhail Valdin* ■ *Dir* Louis King · *Scr* Edward T Lowe, from the novel *The Female of the Species* by HC "Sapper" McNeile

Bulldog Drummond's Revenge ★★ Ⓤ

Detective mystery adventure 1937 · US · BW · 55min

Director Louis King was more of a western specialist than a master of suspense. Consequently, there's a fatal slackness about this adaptation of HC "Sapper" McNeile's novel, which is itself a pretty routine espionage yarn. John Howard this time locks horns with master thief Frank Puglia, who absconds with a consignment of explosive material. But Howard's lack of charisma means that he's easily overshadowed by John Barrymore as Nielson. DP

John Barrymore *Colonel Nielson* · John Howard (1) *Captain Hugh "Bulldog" Drummond* · Louise Campbell *Phyllis Clavering* · Reginald Denny *Algy Longworth* · EE Clive *Tenny* · Frank Puglia *Draven Nogais* ■ *Dir* Louis King · *Scr* Edward T Lowe, from the novel *The Return of Bulldog Drummond* by HC "Sapper" McNeile

Bulldog Drummond's Peril ★★ Ⓤ

Detective mystery adventure 1938 · US · BW · 66min

In the last of John Barrymore's guest appearances as Colonel Nielson, he effortlessly outshines the nominal star, John Howard, despite being marginalised for much of the picture. This has Drummond forced once more to postpone his wedding to Phyllis Clavering (again played by Louise Campbell) as he pursues a gang that has purloined some synthetic diamonds. Porter Hall chews the scenery as the villain. DP

John Barrymore *Colonel Nielson* · John Howard (1) *Captain Hugh "Bulldog" Drummond* · Louise Campbell *Phyllis Clavering* · Reginald Denny *Algy Longworth* · EE Clive *Tenny* · Porter Hall *Dr Max Botulian* · Elizabeth Patterson *Aunt Blanche* ■ *Dir* James Hogan · *Scr* Stuart Palmer, from the novel *The Third Round* by HC "Sapper" McNeile

Bulldog Drummond in Africa ★★ Ⓤ

Detective mystery adventure 1938 · US · BW · 58min

John Howard returns as the dapper troubleshooter in a pretty shoddy affair, with stock footage and unconvincing sets standing in for master criminal J Carrol Naish's jungle lair. Typically, Naish revels in his villainy as he readies Scotland Yard inspector HB Warner for some long-overdue revenge. However, he counted without Howard's rescue party, in which fiancée Heather Angel seems to be along for the ride only so that she can be imperilled. DP

John Howard (1) *Captain Hugh "Bulldog" Drummond* · Heather Angel *Phyllis Clavering* · HB Warner *Colonel Nielson* · J Carrol Naish *Richard Lane/Charles Mega* · Reginald Denny *Algy Longworth* · EE Clive *Tenny* · Anthony Quinn *Deane Fordine* ■ *Dir* Louis King · *Scr* Garnett Weston, from the novel *Challenge* by HC "Sapper" McNeile

Bulldog Drummond's Bride ★★ 🅿🅶

Detective mystery adventure 1939 · US · BW · 56min

Paramount wound down its undistinguished crime series with this routine adaptation. Yet again, the sole reason for watching is the malevolent ingenuity of the villain - in this case the lugubrious Eduardo Ciannelli's master of disguise. Director James Hogan packs plenty into the budget running time, but much of it feels like padding, particularly where John Howard's wedding to Heather Angel is concerned. DP *DVD*

John Howard (1) *Captain Hugh C Drummond* · Heather Angel *Phyllis Clavering* · HB Warner *Colonel Nielson* · Reginald Denny *Algy Longworth* · EE Clive *Tenny* · Elizabeth Patterson *Aunt Blanche* · Eduardo Ciannelli *Henri Armides* ■ *Dir* James Hogan · *Scr* Stuart Palmer, Garnett Weston, from the short story *Bulldog Drummond and the Oriental Mind* by HC "Sapper" McNeile

Bulldog Drummond Strikes Back ★

Detective mystery adventure 1947 · US · BW · 64min

One of the 20-odd movies to feature the James Bond forerunner Bulldog Drummond, created by HC "Sapper" McNeile as a post-First World War clubland hero whose daring exploits sold in their millions. Kicked off in 1929 with Ronald Colman, the series quickly went down-market as various British and American studios bought and sold the franchise. This dismal entry stars Ron Randell, an Australian actor who played Drummond twice. AT

Ron Randell *Bulldog Drummond* · Gloria Henry *Ellen Curtiss* · Pat O'Moore [Patrick O'Moore] *Algy Longworth* · Anabel Shaw *Ellen Curtiss #2* · Holmes Herbert *Inspector McIver* · Wilton Graff *Cedric Mason* · Matthew Boulton *William Cosgrove* · Terry Kilburn *Seymour* ■ *Dir* Frank McDonald · *Scr* Edward Anhalt, Edna Anhalt, from the novel by HC "Sapper" McNeile

Bulldog Jack ★★★ Ⓤ

Detective comedy adventure 1934 · UK · BW · 69min

British comedies have rarely travelled well across the Atlantic, but none has been so mistreated as this Gaumont spoof on the Bulldog Drummond myth, which was shown in the States as a straight thriller with all the gags removed! In his only screen teaming with his brother Claude, Jack Hulbert is all jutting chin and silly expressions as he pursues villainous Ralph Richardson and rescues 1930s scream queen Fay Wray. DP

Fay Wray *Ann Manders* • Jack Hulbert *Jack Pennington* • Claude Hulbert *Algy Longworth* • Ralph Richardson *Morelle* • Paul Graetz *Salvini* • Gibb McLaughlin *Denny* • Atholl Fleming *Bulldog Drummond* ■ *Dir* Walter Forde • *Scr* HC "Sapper" McNeile, Gerard Fairlie, JOC Orton, Sidney Gilliat, from an idea by Jack Hulbert, from a character created by HC "Sapper" McNeile

Bullet ★ 18

Crime drama   1995 · US · Colour · 90min

The first few moments of Mickey Rourke (in his late 30s) acting and dressing like a gang-banger must be some of the most unintentionally hilarious footage ever shot for a motion picture. Unfortunately, the laughs soon evaporate when he starts to mutter in his infamous style and his performance is enough to bury any other good impressions that this snail-paced movie could have generated. KB Swearing, sex scenes, violence. *DVD*

Mickey Rourke *Butch "Bullet" Stein* • Tupac Shakur *Tank* • Ted Levine *Louis* • Donnie Wahlberg *Big Balls* • John Enos III *(John Enos) Lester* • Adrien Brody *Ruby* • Jerry Grayson *Sol Stein* ■ *Dir* Julien Temple • *Scr* Bruce Rubinstein, Sir Eddie Cook

Bullet Boy ★★★ 15

Crime drama   2004 · UK · Colour · 85min

The rise of inner-city gun crime is at the heart of this low-budget British film, set and filmed around Hackney, east London, near the area nicknamed "Murder Mile". A minor street fracas spirals into tragedy and caught up in the ensuing tit-for-tat carnage are teenager Ricky (Ashley Walters), freshly released from youth custody, and, most shockingly, his 12-year-old brother. Walters – better known as So Solid Crew member Asher D – is joined by many first-time actors in this rough-and-ready film that is still convincing enough in its depiction of corrupted innocence. DA Swearing, violence, sex scenes. *DVD*

Ashley Walters *Ricky* • Luke Fraser *Curtis* • Leon Black *Wisdom* • Clare Perkins *Beverley* • Sharea-Mounira Samuels *Shea* • Curtis Walker *Leon* • Rio Tison *Rio* • Clark Lawson *Godfrey* ■ *Dir* Saul Dibb • *Scr* Saul Dibb, Catherine R Johnson

Bullet for a Badman ★★★ PG

Western   1964 · US · Colour · 76min

This is a rare decent role for Audie Murphy, and the baby-faced war hero rises to the occasion, making one regret that he had so few opportunities to fulfil his potential. This RG Springsteen western has Murphy vying with baddie Darren McGavin for Ruta Lee, as he heads a posse escorting McGavin back to town for justice. Photographed by the great Joe Biroc and featuring a marvellous supporting cast of familiar faces, this is a pleasure to watch. TS *DVD*

Audie Murphy *Logan Keliher* • Darren McGavin *Sam Ward* • Ruta Lee *Lottie* • Beverley Owen *Susan* • Skip Homeier *Pink* • George Tobias *Diggs* • Alan Hale Jr *Leach* • Berkeley Harris *Jeff* ■ *Dir* RG Springsteen • *Scr* Mary Willingham, Willard Willingham, from the novel by Marvin H Albert

A Bullet for Joey ★★

Spy crime drama   1955 · US · BW · 86min

A disappointing reunion of Edward G Robinson and George Raft, this economically made crime melodrama revolves about a communist spy's use of an exiled gangster to kidnap an atomic scientist. Raft plays the gangster, while Robinson is the police inspector who uncovers the scheme. The two stars' climactic encounter on a boat takes far too long to materialise. AE

Edward G Robinson *Inspector Raoul Leduc* • George Raft *Joe Victor* • Audrey Totter *Joyce Geary* • George Dolenz *Carl Macklin* • Peter Hanson *Fred* • Peter Van Eyck *Eric Hartman* ■ *Dir* Lewis Allen • *Scr* Geoffrey Homes [Daniel Mainwaring], Al Bezzerides, from a story by James Benson Nablo

A Bullet for Sandoval ★★

Spaghetti western   1970 · It/Sp · Colour · 91min

Well, the climax is good: a battle between four desperate gringos and hundreds of Mexican soldiers, all crowded into a bullring where they blast each other to pieces. It's the sort of deadly, crimson-coloured ballet that Sergio Leone made famous, and one which Julio Buchs stages with just as much arty brio. Until then, though, it's the usual overcooked spaghetti, with Ernest Borgnine wading through a botched revenge plot. AT Italian dubbed.

Ernest Borgnine *Don Pedro Sandoval* • George Hilton *Warner* • Alberto de Mendoza *Lucky boy* • Leo Anchoriz *Padre* • Antonio Pica *Sam* • José Manuel Martin *Cross-eyed man* • Manuel de Blas *Jose* • Manuel Miranda *Francisco* ■ *Dir* Julio Buchs • *Scr* Ugo Guerra, Jose Luis Martinez Molla, Federico De Urrutia, Julio Buchs, from a story by Jose Luis Martinez Molla, Federico De Urrutia

A Bullet for the General ★★★ 15

Spaghetti western   1966 · It · Colour · 112min

Think spaghetti western and Sergio Leone will always spring to mind. Other directors who toyed with the form are generally overlooked, including Italian Damiano Damiani, whose film is a very decent stab at the genre. Capably instilling the violence with intelligent, probing moral concern, Damiani, and there is a creative tension throughout. JM Italian dubbed. *DVD*

Gian Maria Volonté *El Chuncho* • Klaus Kinski *Santo* • Lou Castel *Bill Tate* • Jaime Fernandez *General Elias* • Andrea Checchi *Don Felipe* • Spartaco Conversi *Cirillo* • Joaquin Parra *Picaro* • José Manuel Martin *Raimundo* ■ *Dir* Damiano Damiani • *Scr* Salvatore Laurani, Franco Solinas

Bullet in the Head ★★★ 18

Crime drama   1990 · HK · Colour · 125min

One of the more personal films in John Woo's canon and one which combines the highly stylised themes and motifs of his gangster films with a grittier than usual edge. Tony Leung, Jacky Cheung and Lee Waise play a trio of Hong Kong chums who see the chance to make a fortune in 1960s Vietnam, but find their friendship pushed to the limit by the war. It's not without its flaws, but bravura direction from Woo carries the day and it provides a fascinating view of a conflict usually seen from a western perspective. JF Cantonese +subtitles. Violence, swearing. *DVD*

Tony Chiu-Wai Leung [Tony Leung (2)] *Ben* • Jacky Cheung *Frank* • Lee Waise *Paul* • Simon Yam *Luke* • Fennie Yeun *Jane* ■ *Dir* John Woo • *Scr* John Woo, Patrick Leung, Janet Chung

A Bullet Is Waiting ★ U

Crime drama   1954 · US · Colour · 81min

The audience is waiting, too – for something, *anything* to happen. The film starts with a plane crash that strands Stephen McNally's sheriff at a sheep ranch with his captive (Rory Calhoun), an alleged murderer. It becomes bogged down in endless talk as lonely shepherdess Jean Simmons takes a shine to Calhoun. AE

Jean Simmons *Cally Canham* • Rory Calhoun *Ed Stone* • Stephen McNally *Sheriff Munson* • Brian Aherne *David Canham* ■ *Dir* John Farrow • *Scr* Thames Williamson, Casey Robinson, from a story by Thames Williamson

Bullet to Beijing ★★ 15

Spy thriller
1995 · UK/Can/Rus · Colour · 100min

Thirty years after the film of Len Deighton's novel *The Ipcress File*, Michael Caine resurrects his British spy Harry Palmer. In this very average affort, Palmer is in Russia, working with former KGB agents to prevent North Korea from using biological weapons. Michael Gambon plays a Russian magnate and there's the casting in-joke of Sean Connery as a Russian agent. Caine and Connery made a second Palmer movie, *Midnight in St Petersburg*, back to back with this one. AT Violence, swearing, brief nudity. *DVD*

Michael Caine *Harry Palmer* • Jason Connery *Nikolai* • Mia Sara *Natasha* • Michael Sarrazin *Craig* • Michael Gambon *Alexei* • John Dunn-Hill *Louis* • Burt Kwouk *Kim Soo* • Sue Lloyd *Jean* ■ *Dir* George Mihalka • *Scr* Peter Welbeck [Harry Alan Towers], from Len Deighton's novel

Bullet to the Head ★★★ 15

Action crime thriller   2012 · US · Colour · 87min

Sylvester Stallone and director Walter Hill team up for an endearingly retro action film that harks back to the veteran director's 1980s heyday of hit buddy-cop movies like *48 HRS* and *Red Heat*. It sees Stallone's tattooed hitman reluctantly teaming up with a straight-arrow cop (Sung Kang) to face a mutual foe in Jason Momoa's scene-stealing killer. Of course, the plot is familiar and derivative, but some pithy one-liners and bone-crunching fights more than compensate in a film that's surely bound for guilty pleasure status. DA Violence, swearing, drug abuse. *DVD* *BLU*

Sylvester Stallone *James Bonomo, "Jimmy Bobo"* • Sung Kang *Taylor Kwon* • Jason Momoa *Keegan* • Christian Slater *Marcus Baptiste* • Sarah Shahi *Lisa Bonomo* ■ *Dir* Walter Hill • *Scr* Alessandro Camon, from the graphic novel *Du Plomb dans la Tête* by Matz [Alexis Nolent] and Colin Wilson

Bulletproof ★ 15

Action adventure   1987 · US · Colour · 90min

Gary Busey stars in this preposterous action film that gives new meaning to the word derivative. He plays the indestructible Frank "Bulletproof" McBain, lured out of retirement to retrieve a secret weapon. Steve Carver fills the screen with enough comic book characters to keep Marvel in business for years. RS *DVD*

Gary Busey *Frank McBain* • Darlanne Fluegel *Lieutenant Devon Shepard* • Henry Silva *Colonel Kartiff* • Thalmus Rasulala *Billy Dunbar* • LQ Jones *Sergeant O'Rourke* • Rene Enriquez *General Brogado* ■ *Dir* Steve Carver • *Scr* TL Lankford, Steve Carver, from a story by Fred Olen Ray, TL Lankford

Bulletproof ★ 18

Action comedy   1996 · US · Colour · 80min

Director Ernest Dickerson (a brilliant cinematographer on Spike Lee's earlier movies) delivers some slick shoot-outs in this buddy movie, but everything else here is all wrong. Undercover cop Damon Wayans and drug dealer Adam Sandler are utterly unappealing as ex-friends forced to team up against crime lord James Caan. The performances are annoying, the tasteless jokes are lame and the violence is plain nasty. JC Swearing, violence, nudity. *DVD* *BLU*

Adam Sandler *Moses* • Damon Wayans *Keats* • James Caan *Frank Colton* • Jeep Swenson *Bledsoe* • James Farentino *Captain Jensen* • Kristen Wilson *Traci* • Larry McCoy *Detective Sulliman* • Allen Covert *Detective Jones* ■ *Dir* Ernest R Dickerson • *Scr* Lewis Colick, Joe Gayton, from a story by Joe Gayton

Bulletproof Monk ★ 12

Fantasy action adventure
2002 · US · Colour · 99min

This fantasy produced by John Woo is based on a late 1990s cult comic book. The plot concerns an ancient life-prolonging Tibetan scroll that's protected by nameless monk Chow Yun-Fat and his pickpocket disciple Seann William Scott, who are pursued by former Nazi officer Karl Roden. Combining daft fortune-cookie philosophy and overdone stunts, this cheesy misadventure soon collapses. AJ English, Tibetan +subtitles. *DVD* *BLU*

Chow Yun-Fat *Monk with No Name* • Seann William Scott *Kar* • Jaime King *Jade/Bad Girl* • Karel Roden *Struker* • Victoria Smurfit *Nina* • Marcus Jean Pirae *Mr Funktastic* • Mako *Mr Kojima* ■ *Dir* Paul Hunter • *Scr* Ethan Reiff, Cyrus Voris, from the Flypaper Press comic book

Bullets or Ballots ★★★ PG

Crime drama   1936 · US · BW · 78min

This taut and tough crime drama stars Edward G Robinson as a New York City cop who infiltrates the rackets run by Barton MacLane. Warner Bros churned this type of

film out by the yard in the 1930s, claiming they were good for the nation's morals, but the casts and the straightforward style makes them seem rather special nowadays. This one co-stars feisty Joan Blondell and Humphrey Bogart, who has a great showdown with Robinson and the director is William Keighley, a second-string contract director who usually got the job done well. AT *DVD*

Edward G Robinson *Johnny Blake* • Joan Blondell *Lee Morgan* • Barton MacLane *Al Kruger* • Humphrey Bogart *Nick "Bugs" Fenner* • Frank McHugh *Herman* • Joseph King (1) *Captain Dan McLaren* • Richard Purcell [Dick Purcell] *Ed Driscoll* ■ *Dir* William Keighley • *Scr* Seton I Miller, from a story by Martin Mooney

Bullets over Broadway ★★★★ 15

Period crime comedy   1994 · US · Colour · 95min

Woody Allen celebrates the heyday of New York's theatreland, but remains behind the camera, allowing his typically excellent ensemble cast to shine. As the earnest playwright making his Broadway debut, John Cusack rather fumbles some classic Woodyisms. Dianne Wiest thoroughly deserved her best supporting actress Oscar, but Chazz Palminteri is, perhaps, even more remarkable. Providing teasing insights into how Allen views his own body of work, this is essentially a debate about whether the artist's duty is to retain his own integrity or pander to popular taste. It's also darn good entertainment. DP Swearing. *DVD*

John Cusack *David Shayne* • Chazz Palminteri *Cheech* • Dianne Wiest *Helen Sinclair* • Jennifer Tilly *Olive Neal* • Jim Broadbent *Warner Purcell* • Jack Warden *Julian Marx* • Joe Viterelli *Nick Valenti* • Rob Reiner *Sheldon Flender* • Mary-Louise Parker *Ellen* • Harvey Fierstein *Sid Loomis* ■ *Dir* Woody Allen • *Scr* Woody Allen, Douglas McGrath

The Bullfighter and the Lady ★★★

Drama   1951 · US · BW · 87min

Director Budd Boetticher and his co-writer Ray Nazarro were Oscar-nominated for the story, but the story's the least of it. For the love of pretty senorita Joy Page, clean-cut, all-American guy Robert Stack goes to Mexico to become a bullfighter, ending up a hero in the final fade. On this flimsy and unconvincing premise, Boetticher builds a colourful and absorbing account of the training and art of the matador. Filming on location, he captures all the excitement of this bloody sport. RK

Robert Stack *Chuck Regan* • Joy Page *Anita de la Vega* • Gilbert Roland *Manolo Estrada* • Virginia Grey *Lisbeth Flood* • John Hubbard *Barney Flood* • Katy Jurado *Chelo Estrada* • Antonio Gomez ■ *Dir* Budd Boetticher • *Scr* James Edward Grant, from a story by Budd Boetticher, Ray Nazarro

The Bullfighters ★ PG

Comedy   1945 · US · BW · 60min

Laurel and Hardy's final Hollywood film was, as Stan said later, "a vast disappointment". Not only were their usual hairstyles changed and slicked down, but the studio (20th Century-Fox) only allowed a brief snatch of their "cuckoo theme" in the music. This time around they're private detectives in Mexico, where Stan finds he's the spitting image of a famous matador. The studio really had it in for them. TH

Stanley Laurel [Stan Laurel] *Stan* • Oliver Hardy *Ollie* • Margo Woods *Tangerine* • Richard Lane *Hot Shot Coleman* • Carol Andrews *Hattie Blake* ■ *Dir* Malcolm St Clair • *Scr* W Scott Darling

Bullhead ★★★ 15

Crime thriller   2011 · Bel/Neth · Colour · 128min

Belgian film-maker Michael R Roskam landed an Oscar nomination for best foreign film with this intense rural thriller, inspired by the murder of a vet investigating the use of illegal growth hormones in cattle. Aware that the heat is on following the slaying of a local cop and unsure who to trust, hulking farmer Matthias Schoenaerts is reluctant to cut a deal with a gangland beef trafficker.

Roskam is uncertain whether to focus on the crime drama or the flashbacks, overcomplicating two straightforward storylines, but the director at least generates a palpable sense of unease. DP Dutch, French +subtitles. Violence, swearing, sexual references. *DVD* *Blu*

Matthias Schoenaerts *Jacky Vanmarsenille* • Jeroen Perceval *Diederik Maes* • Barbara Sarafian *Eva Forrestier* • Jeanne Dandoy *Lucia Schepers* • Sam Louwyck *Marc de Kuyper* ■ *Dir/Scr* Michael R Roskam

Bullitt ★★★★ 15

Crime thriller 1968 · US · Colour · 108min

Steve McQueen did better work in his tragically shortened career, but this is one of the films that helped make him a screen icon. He's at his deadpan best as the maverick cop who's assigned to protect a key government witness against a crime syndicate. Director Peter Yates gives it more, in terms of urban reality, than the predictable script deserves, while Frank P Keller won an Oscar for editing the famous San Francisco hill-bouncing car chase. But it's always McQueen's movie, and he's snappy, laconic and cynical in equal doses. TH Some violence, swearing. *DVD* *Blu*

Steve McQueen (1) *Bullitt* • Robert Vaughn (1) *Chalmers* • Jacqueline Bisset *Cathy* • Don Gordon *Delgetti* • Robert Duvall *Weissberg* • Simon Oakland *Captain Bennett* • Norman Fell *Baker* • Georg Stanford Brown *Dr Willard* ■ *Dir* Peter Yates • *Scr* Alan R Trustman, Harry Kleiner, from the novel *Mute Witness* by Robert L Pike

Bullseye! ★ 15

Comedy thriller 1990 · US · Colour · 88min

This hideously unfunny comedy of errors from Michael Winner must rank as a career low for nearly all involved. Poor old Michael Caine and Roger Moore play conmen who set out to steal gems from under the noses of their lookalikes. Neither seems comfortable for a second, while the glamorous locations and the glut of cameos can't plug the gaps in an awful script. DP

Michael Caine *Sidney Lipton/Dr Daniel Hicklar* • Roger Moore *Gerald Bradley-Smith/Sir John Bavistock* • Sally Kirkland *Willie Metcalfe* • Deborah Barrymore [Deborah Moore (1)] *Flo Fleming* • Lee Patterson *Darrell Hyde* • Mark Burns *Nigel Holden* • Derren Nesbitt *Inspector Grosse* ■ *Dir* Michael Winner • *Scr* Leslie Bricusse, Laurence Marks, Maurice Gran, from a story by Leslie Bricusse, Michael Winner, Nick Mead

Bullshot ★ PG

Spoof adventure 1983 · UK · Colour · 82min

This risible spoof of the Bulldog Drummond stories stars Alan Shearman, Ron House and Diz White, who wrote the screenplay and the stage play on which it is based. Shearman plays the fearless "Bullshot" Crummond with all the subtlety of a salesman on commission. Every pun and sight gag in this atrocious tale of German cads pursuing a top-secret formula demands to be rammed home with steam-hammer finesse. DP *DVD*

Alan Shearman *"Bullshot" Crummond* • Diz White *Rosemary Fenton* • Ron House *Count Otto von Bruno* • Frances Tomelty *Fraulein Lenya Von Bruno* • Ron Pember *Dobbs* • Mel Smith *Crouch* • Michael Aldridge *Rupert Fenton* • Billy Connolly *Hawkeye McGillicuddy* • Nicholas Lyndhurst *Nobby Clark* ■ *Dir* Dick Clement • *Scr* Ron House, Alan Shearman, Diz White, from their play

Bullwhip ★★★ U

Western 1958 · US · Colour · 80min

Rhonda Fleming plays a part-Cheyenne Indian with money-making ambitions in the fur trade who wields a bullwhip to get her way. When she requires a spouse in order to inherit property, she makes a deal with condemned cowboy Guy Madison. Loosely based on Shakespeare's *The Taming of the Shrew*, this unusual B-western was written by genre veteran Adele Buffington, and while the over-the-top comedy elements are a little hard to take, it's decently acted and photographed in attractive Technicolor. RK

Guy Madison *Steve* • Rhonda Fleming *Cheyenne* • James Griffith *Karp* • Don Beddoe *Judge* • Peter Adams (1) *Parnell* • Dan Sheridan *Podo* ■ *Dir* Harmon Jones • *Scr* Adele Buffington

Bully ★★★★ 18

Biographical revenge drama 2001 · US/Fr · Colour · 107min

Stylistically echoing his brutal yet dazzling debut feature *kids*, director Larry Clark here unleashes a superbly shot drama that's not so much entertainment as a stomach-churning life-lesson. Based on the true story of a sadistic Florida teenager who was hideously murdered by the friends he victimised, the film presents a terrifying snapshot of alienated young America. An ultra-realistic portrayal of morally corrupt youth, illuminated by startling performances from the largely unknown cast, it turns from powerful social commentary into an authentic horror movie as the nerve-shredding events unfold. SF *DVD*

Brad Renfro *Mario "Marty" Puccio* • Rachel Miner *Lisa Connelly* • Nick Stahl *Bobby Kent* • Bijou Phillips *Alice "Ali" Willis* • Michael Pitt *Donny Semenec* • Kelli Garner *Heather Swallers* ■ *Dir* Larry Clark • *Scr* Zachary Long, Roger Pullis, from the book *Bully: a True Story of High School Revenge* by Jim Schutze

Bulworth ★★★★ 18

Political comedy drama 1998 · US · Colour · 103min

Warren Beatty's astonishingly fearless political satire is one of the boldest studio films to come out of Hollywood in years. Beatty, who writes and directs, also stars as a disillusioned liberal senator who takes out a contract on his own life, giving him three days to start saying what he really believes. Just when you think Beatty won't dare to be more radical than his acidic (and very funny) swipes at just about everybody, he re-invents himself as a streetwise urban rapper. Sharp and risky, the film succeeds as both a startlingly original comedy and a fang-baring assault on the American political system. JC Drug abuse, swearing, sex scenes. *DVD*

Warren Beatty *Jay Bulworth* • Halle Berry *Nina* • Paul Sorvino *Graham Crockett* • Christine Baranski *Constance Bulworth* • Kimberly Deauna Adams *Denisha* • Vinny Argiro *Debate director* • Sean Astin *Gary* • Kirk Baltz *Debate producer* ■ *Dir* Warren Beatty • *Scr* Warren Beatty, Jeremy Pikser, from a story by Warren Beatty

A Bunch of Amateurs ★★ 15

Comedy 2008 · UK · Colour · 92min

In this impossibly twee British comedy, Burt Reynolds takes centre stage as an over-the-hill Hollywood action hero, Jefferson Steel. Lacking any other options, he accepts an offer to tread the boards in an amateur production of Shakespeare's *King Lear* in the English village of Stratford (but crucially, not upon-Avon). Reynolds is supposed to be portraying a bad actor but he takes this character trait off stage as well, sleepwalking through the entire film. He can hardly be blamed for this as the writers struggle to find any jokes beyond the central premise. SP Swearing. *DVD* *Blu*

Burt Reynolds *Jefferson Steel* • Samantha Bond (2) *Dorothy Nettle* • Derek Jacobi *Nigel Dewberry* • Imelda Staunton *Mary* • Charles Durning *Charlie Rosenberg* • Peter Gunn *Frank Dobbins* ■ *Dir* Andy Cadiff • *Scr* Nick Newman, John Ross, Ian Hislop, Jonathan Gershfield

Bundle of Joy ★★ U

Musical comedy 1956 · US · Colour · 98min

This perfectly preserved slice of pop culture from a bygone era is a starring vehicle for "America's Sweethearts", Eddie Fisher, king of the pre-rock 'n' roll pop charts, and his new bride Debbie Reynolds. It's a remake of the popular Ginger Rogers movie *Bachelor Mother* with music added, but Fisher is no film star and the movie remains a silly, laboured farce. TS

Debbie Reynolds *Polly Parrish* • Eddie Fisher *Dan Merlin* • Adolphe Menjou *JB Merlin* • Tommy Noonan *Freddie Miller* • Nita Talbot *Mary* • Una Merkel *Mrs Dugan* • Melville Cooper *Adams* • Bill

Goodwin *Mr Creely* ■ *Dir* Norman Taurog • *Scr* Norman Krasna, Robert Carson, Arthur Sheekman, from a story by Felix Jackson

Bundy ★★ 18

Biographical crime drama 2002 · UK/US · Colour · 95min

This biopic of notorious serial killer Ted Bundy (he was the first multiple murderer to whom the term was applied, having bludgeoned, raped and mutilated a large number of women in the 1970s) never really attempts to find a motive for his actions. Instead, director Matthew Bright concentrates on re-creating his sadistic attacks in as much unpleasant detail as possible. Michael Reilly Burke is plausible as the suave psychopath, but the screenplay engages in unwarranted speculation about what Bundy did with his victims as well as delivering a leering, gratuitous final scene. AS *DVD*

Michael Reilly Burke *Ted Bundy* • Boti Ann Bliss *Lee* • Steffani Brass *Julie* • Marina Black *Kate* • Wayne Morse *Bob* • Renee Madison Cole *Cutler* ■ *Dir* Matthew Bright • *Scr* Stephen Johnston, Matthew Bright

The Bunker ★★★ 15

Second World War horror 2001 · UK · Colour · 87min

German soldiers face their darkest demons while sheltering in a haunted bunker in director Rob Green's feature debut. Their supposedly safe haven is built over the site of a medieval massacre and soon the soldiers start experiencing mysterious occurrences. Expertly making the most of one prime location and relying heavily on the shadowy and unseen to crank up the suspense, Green delivers a modest miniature that's an effective haunted house of shell-shocked horror. AJ Violence. *DVD*

Jason Flemyng *Cpl Baumann* • Charley Boorman *Pte First Class Franke* • Jack Davenport *Lance Cpl Ebert* • Andrew Lee Potts *Pte Neumann* • Christopher Fairbank *Sgt Heydrich* • Nicholas Hamnett *Pte Engels* ■ *Dir* Rob Green • *Scr* Clive Dawson

Bunny & the Bull ★★★ 15

Comedy 2009 · UK/Fr · Colour · 97min

Empty takeaway cartons, heaving bookshelves and clutter-filled boxes provide the raw material for this whimsical road movie, undertaken by a lonely obsessive-compulsive agoraphobic from the confines of his London flat. Grieving for his lost pal Bunny (Simon Farnaby), Stephen Turnbull (Edward Hogg) retraces their experiences on a European holiday, recalling how they liberated both a stuffed grizzly bear and a frustrated Spanish waitress (Verónica Echegui). In his feature debut, *The Mighty Boosh* director Paul King's use of rough-edged animation techniques give this potentially morbid, bittersweet tale a much-needed lightness. Slight, silly and somewhat familiar it may be, but this off-the-wall comedy has enough freewheeling charm and likeable personality to cover its cracks. DW Swearing, sexual references, nudity. *DVD* *Blu*

Edward Hogg *Stephen Turnbull* • Simon Farnaby *Bunny* • Verónica Echegui *Eloisa* • Noel Fielding *Javier* • Julian Barratt *Attila* • Richard Ayoade *Museum curator* ■ *Dir/Scr* Paul King (2)

Bunny Chow: Know Thyself ★★★ 15

Comedy 2006 · S Afr/Swe · BW · 168min

Bunny Chow is a South African dish made by hollowing out half a loaf of bread and filling it with a spicy mixture of vegetables. It's a fine metaphor for this comic melting pot about three young stand-up comedians from Johannesburg on a trip to the Oppi Koppi rock festival. Dave (David Kibuuka) is a wannabe comic battling terminal stage fright. His friend Kags (Kagiso Lediga) is more experienced but an incorrigible womaniser, while lax Muslim Joey (Joey Rasdien) suffers pangs of conscience about his unorthodox profession. Shot in black and white and bursting with life, the film paints a refreshingly upbeat picture of South African youth. A great soundtrack of

Johannesburg dub and rap rounds off a movie that – much like the fast food it's named after – is a messy but satisfying light bite. JR *DVD*

David Kibuuka *Dave* • Kim Engelbrecht *Kim* • Kagiso Lediga *Kagiso "Kags"* • Joey Rasdien *Joey* • Jason Cope *Cope* • Keren Neumann *Carla* ■ *Dir* John Barker • *Scr* John Barker, David Kibuuka, from a story by Joey Rasdien, Salah Sabiti, Barker, Kibuuka

Bunny Lake Is Missing ★★★ 12

Mystery drama 1965 · US · BW · 102min

Laurence Olivier (as a leaden-paced, raincoated British copper) and Noël Coward may have regarded this as a bit of slumming, judging by the way they camp it up. However, director Otto Preminger uses their archness to consolidate the nightmarish quality of this story about Carol Lynley's illegitimate little girl being absent without mum's leave. Keir Dullea demonstrates that, even prior to *2001: a Space Odyssey*, he was an unconventional actor, and his performance reflects the illusory atmosphere of the movie. TH *DVD*

Laurence Olivier *Newhouse* • Carol Lynley *Ann* • Keir Dullea *Steven* • Noël Coward *Wilson* • Martita Hunt *Ada Ford* • Anna Massey *Elvira* • Clive Revill *Andrews* • Finlay Currie *Doll maker* • Richard Wattis *Shipping Clerk* ■ *Dir* Otto Preminger • *Scr* John Mortimer, Penelope Mortimer, from the novel by Evelyn Piper

Bunny O'Hare ★

Crime comedy 1971 · US · Colour · 92min

In her golden years, veteran diva Bette Davis took on practically any role to prove she was still alive and a viable actress. But nothing can really explain why she sank as low as this dreadful gimmick flick, where she's a bored grandmother in hippy gear and a long blonde wig, who decides to rob banks with ageing partner-in-crime Ernest Borgnine. Appalling. AJ

Bette Davis *Bunny O'Hare* • Ernest Borgnine *Bill Green* • Jack Cassidy *Detective Greeley* • Joan Delaney *RJ Hart* • Jay Robinson *Banker* • Reva Rose *Lulu* ■ *Dir* Gerd Oswald • *Scr* Stanley Z Cherry, Coslough Johnson, from a story by Stanley Z Cherry

Bunraku ★★ 15

Fantasy action drama 2010 · US · Colour · 119min

A cowboy without a gun and a samurai with no sword pitch up in a town lorded over by a gang of killers in this superficially dazzling action yarn. Writer/director Guy Moshe's genre mish-mash of martial arts, pulp crime and western takes the vibrant visuals of *Dick Tracy* and adds a post-*Sin City* CGI sheen. There are plenty of neat touches, but an increasingly unnecessary narration simply adds to the suspicion that most of the film was put together after the actors went home. All nominal star Josh Hartnett is required to do is to look good in a moustache and a Stetson, in what turns out to be a colourful but flimsy confection. JH English, Japanese +subtitles. Violence, swearing. *DVD* *Blu*

Josh Hartnett *The drifter* • Woody Harrelson *The bartender* • Gackt Camui [Gackt] *Yoshi* • Kevin McKidd *Killer no 2* • Ron Perlman *Nicola* • Demi Moore *Alexandra* ■ *Dir* Guy Moshe • *Scr* Guy Moshe, from a story by Boaz Davidson

Buona Sera, Mrs Campbell ★★★

Comedy drama 1968 · It · Colour · 112min

Gina Lollobrigida looks a treat in director Melvin Frank's rather tasteless comedy drama about an Italian single mother whose promiscuous wartime past comes back to haunt her. There's earnest support from Phil Silvers, Telly Savalas and suave Peter Lawford as the three American airmen who each believe they fathered Lollobrigida's child 20 years ago, and who have been paying child support ever since. This farce is a glossy romp. TS

Gina Lollobrigida *Carla* • Telly Savalas *Walter Braddock* • Shelley Winters *Shirley Newman* • Phil Silvers *Phil Newman* • Peter Lawford *Justin Young* • Lee Grant *Fritzie Braddock* • Janet

Margolin *Gia* • Marian Moses *Lauren Young* ■ *Dir* Melvin Frank • *Scr* Melvin Frank, Sheldon Keller, Denis Norden

The 'Burbs ★★★★ 12
Comedy   1989 · US · Colour · 97min

When the Klopeks move into a run-down house in an otherwise spick-and-span suburb, Tom Hanks – playing a one-man neighbourhood watch scheme – starts to fret. Just what are the Klopeks up to, digging in the garden and making all those clanking noises at night? This light-hearted and very funny comedy is an askew parable about small-town America, with Hanks as the ultimate conformist surrounded by weirdos. Bruce Dern and Carrie Fisher offer fine support to the affable Hanks. Director Joe Dante excels at this sort of thing and this is a constantly intriguing picture. AT Swearing, violence. *DVD* *BL*

Tom Hanks *Ray Peterson* • Bruce Dern *Mark Rumsfield* • Carrie Fisher *Carol Peterson* • Rick Ducommun *Art Weingartner* • Corey Feldman *Ricky Butler* • Henry Gibson *Dr Werner Klopek* • Brother Theodore *Uncle Reuben Klopek* • Courtney Gains *Hans Klopek* ■ *Dir* Joe Dante • *Scr* Dana Olsen

Burden of Dreams ★★★★ 12
Documentary   1982 · US · Colour · 94min

This remarkable documentary by Les Blank is about the appalling slog involved in making Werner Herzog's *Fitzcarraldo*. In telling the story of an opera lover (Klaus Kinski) who hauls a ship through the South American jungle to bring music to the natives, the visionary German director embarked upon an overtaxing labour of love that frayed tempers and stirred skirmishes with the locals. Rarely have the rigours of location filming been so dramatically chronicled. TH *DVD*

■ *Dir* Les Blank • *Scr* Michael Goodwin

Bureau of Missing Persons ★★★
Comedy thriller   1933 · US · BW · 73min

This pacey action movie from Warner Bros is, in effect, a selection of different overlapping stories, tightly held together by the direction of Roy Del Ruth. The central tale features Bette Davis, who may or may not have killed her husband, and tough-talking cop Pat O'Brien, who has to sort out the mystery. There's much pleasure to be had from watching Warners' hard-boiled rep company goes through their paces. TS

Bette Davis *Norma Phillips* • Lewis Stone *Captain Webb* • Pat O'Brien *Butch Saunders* • Glenda Farrell *Belle* • Allen Jenkins *Joe Musik* • Ruth Donnelly *Pete* • Hugh Herbert *Slade* • Alan Dinehart *Therme Roberts* ■ *Dir* Roy Del Ruth • *Scr* Robert Presnell, from the book *Missing Men* by John H Ayres, Carol Bird

The Burglar ★★★
Film noir   1956 · US · BW · 90min

This little gem is the real thing, a sordid little *film noir* flick with great style, directed with panache by cult favourite Paul Wendkos, who went on to make hard edged TV movies. Here, a thief plots to steal a valuable necklace with the help of his gang and his half-sister, but a corrupt policeman is also after the loot. The cast is well worth tuning in for: Dan Duryea is the disturbed titular crook, while Jayne Mansfield, and Martha Vickers provide terrific female support. Bleak and bizarre. TS

Dan Duryea *Nat Harbin* • Jayne Mansfield *Gladden* • Martha Vickers *Della* • Peter Capell *Baylock* • Mickey Shaughnessy *Dohmer* • Wendell Phillips *Police captain* • Phoebe Mackay *Sister Sara* ■ *Dir* Paul Wendkos • *Scr* David Goodis, from his novel

Burglar ★★ 15
Comedy thriller   1987 · US · Colour · 97min

Whoopi Goldberg stars in this disappointing mix of humour and action, and even the added talents of Bob "Bobcat" Goldthwait and John Goodman have little impact on the comedy. Goldberg is the burglar of the title who witnesses a murder and then finds herself suspected of the crime, but even the actress's comic timing and acting talents can't keep you from guessing what will happen way before her character does. JB Violence, swearing.

Whoopi Goldberg *Bernice Rhodenbarr* • Bob Goldthwait [Bobcat Goldthwait] *Carl Hefler* • GW Bailey *Ray Kirschman* • Lesley Ann Warren *Dr Cynthia Sheldrake* • James Handy *Carson Verrill* • Anne De Salvo *Detective Todras* • John Goodman *Detective Nyswander* ■ *Dir* Hugh Wilson • *Scr* Joseph Loeb III, Matthew Weisman, Hugh Wilson, from the books by Lawrence Block

The Burglars ★★ 18
Crime drama   1971 · Fr/It · Colour · 109min

The worldwide success of *The Sicilian Clan* meant that French director Henri Verneuil could call on an international cast and a high-powered location shoot for his next movie. Jean-Paul Belmondo and Omar Sharif co-star in this colourful remake of the 1956 *noir* thriller, *The Burglar*, this time shot in Greece and containing some of the most irritating dubbing you're ever likely to hear. TS French dubbed.

Jean-Paul Belmondo *Azad* • Omar Sharif *Abel Zacharia* • Dyan Cannon *Lena* • Robert Hossein *Ralph* • Nicole Calfan *Hélène* • Renato Salvatori *Renzi* ■ *Dir* Henri Verneuil • *Scr* Henri Verneuil, Vahe Katcha, from the film and novel *The Burglar* by David Goodis

Buried ★★★★ 15
Thriller   2009 · Sp/US · Colour · 91min

The spirit of Alfred Hitchcock's single-set 1940s movies (*Rope* and *Lifeboat*) is deliberately evoked in this fascinating thriller, which stars Ryan Reynolds as a US contractor working in Iraq who's been kidnapped by insurgents. When he awakes – which is right where the movie starts – he finds himself buried six feet underground in a coffin, with just a mobile phone, a lighter and a glow-stick at his disposal. The film occasionally sags in its effort to stretch to a respectable running time, but it's still an intense experience, inventively filmed and powerfully performed by Reynolds as the story's flawed but unnecessarily hard-done-by everyman. DW Swearing. *DVD* *BL*

Ryan Reynolds *Paul Conroy* • Robert Paterson *Dan Brenner* • José Luis García Pérez *Jabir* • Stephen Tobolowsky *Alan Davenport* • Samantha Mathis *Linda Conroy* • Warner Loughlin *Donna Mitchell* ■ *Dir* Rodrigo Cortés • *Scr* Chris Sparling

Buried Alive ★ 18
Horror   1990 · US · Colour · 86min

This is a shoddy rehash of Edgar Allan Poe (misspelt Allen in the credits!) plonked down in South Africa and directed by one-time porn film-maker Gérard Kikoine. Robert Vaughn runs the Ravenscroft Institute, populated by shady students and eccentric teachers (including grey-wigged Donald Pleasence), where Poe's psychological horrors are made stupidly literal. John Carradine's appearance as a walled-up victim was his last and saddest. AJ Swearing, violence. *DVD*

Robert Vaughn (1) *Dr Gary* • Donald Pleasence *Dr Schaeffer* • Karen Witter *Janet* • John Carradine *Jacob* • Nia Long *Fingers* • Ginger Lynn Allen *Debbie* • Bill Butler [William Butler] *Tim* • Janine Denison *Shiro* ■ *Dir* Gérard Kikoine • *Scr* Jake Clesi, Stuart Lee, from stories by Peter Welbeck [Harry Alan Towers], Edgar Allan Poe

Buried Alive ★★★ 12
Thriller   1990 · US · Colour · 89min

This superior TV-movie thriller stars Tim Matheson as a businessman who survives not only poisoning but also burial by his adulterous wife. Matheson does well as the unsuspecting husband and Jennifer Jason Leigh is equally as good as his scheming spouse. This was well enough received to spawn a sequel called, rather unoriginally, *Buried Alive II*. PF Violence, swearing. *DVD*

Tim Matheson *Clint Goodman* • Jennifer Jason Leigh *Joanna Goodman* • William Atherton *Cortland Van Owen* • Hoyt Axton *Sheriff Sam Eberly* ■ *Dir* Frank Darabont • *Scr* Mark Patrick Carducci

Buried Loot ★★
Crime drama   1934 · US · BW · 18min

This two-reeler initiated MGM's *Crime Does Not Pay* series, which ran to 48 titles over 12 years, giving movie houses quality shorts and enabling the studio to try out new talent. Here the recently signed 23-year-old Robert Taylor was given the principal role of the thief who hides his loot, aiming to recover it after serving time in prison. What with a jailbreak, plastic surgery and a twist ending, it packed a full B-feature plot into 18 minutes. Taylor soon became a star, while later *Crime Does Not Pay* entries became informative exposés of rackets that were fooling the public. AE

Robert Taylor (1) *Al Douglas* • Robert Livingston ■ *Dir* George B Seitz • *Scr* George B Seitz, from a story by Marty Brooks

Burke & Hare ★ 15
Horror   1971 · UK · Colour · 90min

This dire effort is more *Carry On Bodysnatching* than anything even loosely based on the facts about the two Irish immigrants who sold dubiously procured cadavers for dissection classes at Edinburgh Medical College. Burke and Hare (Derren Nesbitt and Glynn Edwards) come across as period Likely Lads instead of purveyors of corpses, and with lots of time-wasting brothel scenes featuring copious female nudity, the accent is on sleazy sexploitation and bawdy comedy rather than anything truly macabre or frightening. AJ Violence, nudity. *DVD*

Derren Nesbitt *Burke* • Harry Andrews *Dr Knox* • Glynn Edwards *Hare* • Yootha Joyce *Mrs Hare* • Françoise Pascal *Marie* • Robin Hawdon *Lord Angus McPhee* ■ *Dir* Vernon Sewell • *Scr* Ernie Bradford • *Cinematographer* Desmond Dickinson

Burke & Hare ★★★ 15
Black comedy thriller based on a true story   2010 · UK · Colour · 87min

Director John Landis's take on the grisly tale of the Edinburgh corpse-sellers is a sinister black comedy that's very much in the old Ealing tradition. Simon Pegg (Burke) and Andy Serkis (Hare) make a well-matched double act – pitched as a sort of entrepreneurial Morecambe and Wise – and the gags run the hit-and-miss gamut from the subtly understated (pot shots at Wordsworth, Lister and Gretfriars Bobby) to crass slapstick. Mildly amusing more than laugh-out-loud funny, the film benefits from a cast of well-known British comics (Ronnie Corbett, Bill Bailey, Paul Whitehouse) and a beautifully evoked Georgian period setting. AJ Sex scenes, gore. *DVD* *BL*

Simon Pegg *William Burke* • Andy Serkis *William Hare* • Isla Fisher *Ginny Hawkins* • Jessica Hynes [Jessica Stevenson] *Lucky* • Tom Wilkinson *Dr Robert Knox* • Ronnie Corbett *Captain Tam McLintoch* • Tim Curry *Dr Alexander Monro* • Stephen Merchant *Hollyrood footman* • Christopher Lee *Old Joseph* • Paul Whitehouse *Gentleman drunk* • Bill Bailey *Hangman* ■ *Dir* John Landis • *Scr* Piers Ashworth, Nick Moorcroft

Burke and Wills ★★★
Historical drama   1985 · Aus · Colour · 140min

Robert Burke and William Wills, who with two others were the first explorers to cross Australia from south to north, are here played with lantern-jawed determination by Jack Thompson and Nigel Havers. There are certain grandiose moments that border on parody and so nudge the film towards unintended hilarity. Otherwise the extended scenes of bravery and endurance have an authentic period atmosphere and psychological resonance. JM Some violence, swearing.

Jack Thompson *Robert O'Hara Burke* • Nigel Havers *William John Wills* • Greta Scacchi *Julia Matthews* • Matthew Fargher *John King* • Ralph Cotterill *Charley Gray* • Drew Forsythe *William Brahe* ■ *Dir* Graeme Clifford • *Scr* Michael Thomas

Burlesque ★★★ 12
Musical drama   2010 · US · Colour · 114min

There's an innocent sweetness about this showcase for Christina Aguilera's vocal and dance skills that just about excuses its utter hokiness. The superstar songstress plays an Iowa waitress following her showbiz dreams, who finds her way to Cher's ailing burlesque theatre on LA's Sunset Strip. With Bob Fosse-inspired choreography and Alan Cumming channelling Joel Grey's MC in *Cabaret*, writer/director Steven Antin's movie springs few surprises as the super-nice Aguilera moves from lip-synching chorus girl to diva belter. AJ Swearing. *DVD* *BL*

Cher *Tess* • Christina Aguilera *Ali Rose* • Stanley Tucci *Sean* • Cam Gigandet *Jack* • Kristen Bell *Nikki* • Alan Cumming *Alexis* ■ *Dir/Scr* Steve Antin

Burlesque Undressed ★★ 15
Documentary   2009 · UK · Colour · 88min

Striptease sensation Immodesty Blaize lifts the veil on the noughties burlesque revival in writer/director Alison Grist's flimsy but playful documentary. Essentially a glossy promotional vehicle for Blaize's ultra-glamour-meets-high-camp art form, the canny cash-in combines a gossipy overview of the scene with extensive performance footage. When retro-style saucepot Blaize isn't strutting her stuff on stage or sharing personal recollections, hip-shaking stars like veteran vixen Satan's Angel offer their own spirited reminiscences. Yet for all its titillating titbits and glitzy visuals, the film simply can't capture burlesque's electrifying atmosphere and appeal. Instead, Grist's attempts to dissect the subject actually take away its sparkle, scarcely doing justice to the talents featured. SF Nudity.

Immodesty Blaize • Marc Almond • Satan's Angel ■ *Dir/Scr* Alison Grist

Burma VJ: Reporting from a Closed Country ★★★ 12A
Documentary   2008 · Den/Swe/It/UK/Ger/Neth/Nor/Is/Sp/Bel · Colour · 89min

In September 2007, journalists from underground activist group the Democratic Voice of Burma risked their lives to transmit to the outside world digital video footage of the peaceful protests being led by Buddhist monks against Burma's military regime. Their efforts were co-ordinated by a colleague known as Joshua, and director Anders Ostergaard and editors Thomas Papapetros and Janus Billeskov Jansen have done a fine job in piecing the often shocking material into a coherent narrative. But, even though Ostergaard ably places the grainy guerrilla footage in context, his studio re-creations of Joshua's phone conversations with his cameramen are less persuasive. Nevertheless, this movie is a fitting tribute to those who filmed the protesters' selfless courage. DP Burmese, English +subtitles.

■ *Dir* Anders Ostergaard • *Scr* Anders Ostergaard, Jan Krogsgaard • *Editors* Thomas Papapetros, Janus Billeskov Jansen

The Burmese Harp ★★★★ 12
War drama   1956 · Jpn · BW · 116min

Adapted from Michio Takeyama's novel by director Kon Ichikawa's wife, Natto Wada, this lyrical epic is among the most moving acts of atonement made by the postwar Japanese film industry. Yet the decision of a young musician (Shoji Yasui) to renounce his homeland and remain in Burma as a Buddhist monk is less an indictment of militarism and more a cry of anguish on behalf of all those who suffered during the Second World War. Ichikawa occasionally allows sincerity to lapse into sentimentality, but he clearly felt deeply about the story, which he remade (less memorably) in 1985. DP Japanese +subtitles. *DVD* *BL*

Rentaro Mikuni *Captain Inouye* • Shoji Yasui *Private Yasuhiko* • Tatsuya Mihashi *Defence Commander* • Tanie Kitabayashi *Old woman* • Yunosuke Ito *Village head* ■ *Dir* Kon Ichikawa • *Scr* Natto Wada, from the novel by Michio Takeyama

B

The Burmese Harp ★★★ 12
War drama 1985 · Jpn · Colour · 116min

Strikingly filmed in colour by Setsuo Kobayashi, Kon Ichikawa's remake of his 1956 classic lacks the original's contemporary resonance. This time, in seeking to expose the fanaticism and brutality of the militarist tendency, Ichikawa overdoes the humanist earnestness that inspires a soldier musician to remain in Burma after the Imperial Army's retreat and join the Buddhist monks in burying the dead. This moving film would, perhaps, have been more effective had it not been quite so deliberate. DP In Japanese. *DVD*

Koji Ishizaka *Captain Inoue* • Kiichi Nakai *Private Mizushima* • Takuzo Kawatani *Sgt Ito* • Atsushi Watanabe *PteKobayashi* • Fujio Tokita *Old man* • Tanie Kitabayashi *Old woman* • Bunta Sugawara *Commander of Sankaku Mountain Platoon* ■ *Dir* Kon Ichikawa • *Scr* Natto Wada, from the novel by Michio Takeyama

Burn! ★★★★ 12
Period drama 1970 · It/Fr · Colour · 107min

Even at the height of his stardom, Marlon Brando was prepared to take chances by accepting challenging roles. In this attack on colonial manipulation – a period swashbuckler with attitude – he plays a cynical British secret agent who ignites a Caribbean island revolution against the ruling Portuguese using slave labour on a sugar-cane plantation. It's clumsily handled at times by director Gillo Pontecorvo, but it still has scenes of enormous visual power. Brando is magnificent. TH *DVD*

Marlon Brando *Sir William Walker* • Evaristo Marquez *Jose Dolores* • Renato Salvatori *Teddy Sanchez* • Norman Hill *Shelton* • Tom Lyons *General Prada* • Wanani *Guarina* • Joseph Persuad *Juanito* • Giampiero Albertini *Henry* ■ *Dir* Gillo Pontecorvo • *Scr* Franco Solinas, from a story by Gillo Pontecorvo, Franco Solinas, Giorgio Arlorio • *Cinematographer* Marcello Gatti

Burn after Reading ★★★★ 15
Black comedy crime drama 2008 · US/UK/Fr · Colour · 91min

This crime caper from the Coen brothers highlights their talent for blending sophistication and silliness. John Malkovich goes totally over the top as Osborne Cox, an indignant, heavy-drinking CIA veteran who begins writing an unauthorised memoir after he's fired. When the computer disc containing his book is mislaid at a gym, fitness instructor Brad Pitt and his frumpy colleague Frances McDormand try to blackmail him. This is the springboard for many madcap cloak-and-dagger antics, which also involve Cox's wife (a hard-nosed Tilda Swinton) and her lover, a federal marshal brilliantly played by George Clooney. The plot is overly complicated and rather ridiculous, but therein lies the fun. SP Swearing, sexual references, brief violence. *DVD* *BD*

George Clooney *Harry Pfarrer* • Frances McDormand *Linda Litzke* • Brad Pitt *Chad Feldheimer* • John Malkovich *Osborne Cox* • Tilda Swinton *Katie Cox* ■ *Dir/Scr* Ethan Coen, Joel Coen • *Cinematographer* Emmanuel Lubezki • *Editors* Roderick Jaynes [Ethan Coen], Roderick Jaynes [Joel Coen]

Burn Hollywood Burn ★ 15
Satirical comedy 1997 · US · Colour · 81min

In this monumentally awful celebrity-packed Hollywood "mockumentary", Eric Idle plays Allan Smithee, the joke being that this is the pseudonym used by directors who don't want to have their real name credited on a movie. Sylvester Stallone, Jackie Chan and Whoopi Goldberg look embarrassed playing themselves, which is unsurprising given that the Joe Eszterhas script makes his *Showgirls* work read like Shakespeare. Unsubtle, unfunny and an unbelievable waste of time. JC Swearing.

Ryan O'Neal *James Edmunds* • Coolio *Dion Brothers* • Chuck D *Leon Brothers* • Eric Idle *Alan Smithee* • Leslie Stefanson *Michelle Rafferty* • Sandra Bernhard *Ann Glover* • Cherie Lunghi *Myrna Smithee* • Harvey Weinstein *Sam Rizzo* •

Naomi Campbell *Attendant no 2* • Sylvester Stallone • Whoopi Goldberg • Jackie Chan • Robert Evans • Joe Eszterhas ■ *Dir* Alan Smithee [Arthur Hiller] • *Scr* Joe Eszterhas

The Burning ★ 18
Horror 1981 · US · Colour · 91min

This highly derivative *Friday the 13th* clone found itself on the infamous "video nasty" list that caused a furore in the early 1980s. A horribly-burned summer camp caretaker returns with scissors and shears to take bloody vengeance on the promiscuous teens responsible for the joke-gone-wrong that caused his fiery scars. Inept direction by Tony Maylam and a predictable script cause boredom to set in very early on. AJ *DVD*

Brian Matthews *Todd* • Leah Ayres *Michelle* • Brian Backer *Alfred* • Larry Joshua *Glazer* • Jason Alexander *Dave* • Ned Eisenberg *Eddy* • Fisher Stevens *Woodstock* • Holly Hunter *Sophie* ■ *Dir* Tony Maylam • *Scr* Peter Lawrence, Bob Weinstein, from a story by Harvey Weinstein, Tony Maylam, Brad Grey

The Burning ★★★ 15
Drama 2014 · Arg/Mex/Bra/Fr/US · Colour · 96min

In the wilds of Argentina, unscrupulous business interests use brutal mercenaries to clear the land of farmers. But salvation could be at hand, in this eco-warrior drama with a mythic twist. Gael García Bernal plays the mysterious avenger who emerges half-naked from the forest to track down the villains who've parted a powerless peasant from his isolated patch. He makes the most of a slightly woolly conceit, while Argentinian director Pablo Fendrik conjures startling images from the local flora and fauna. TJ In Spanish, English.

Gael García Bernal *Kai* • Alice Braga *Vania* • Chico Diaz *Joao* • Claudio Tolcachir *Tarquinho* ■ *Dir/Scr* Pablo Fendrik

The Burning Bed ★★★★ 15
Biographical drama 1984 · US · Colour · 91min

Farrah Fawcett left her blonde bimbo *Charlie's Angels* image behind with this superb performance as a battered wife who takes revenge on her husband by setting him on fire while he is sleeping. Based on a true story, this Emmy-nominated drama from Robert Greenwald is carefully and sensitively handled, and never lapses into melodrama. Thought-provoking, moving and exceptionally well played. JB

Farrah Fawcett *Francine Hughes* • Paul Le Mat *Mickey Hughes* • Richard Masur *Aryon Greydanus* • Grace Zabriskie *Flossie Hughes* • Penelope Milford *Gaby* • Christa Denton *Christy, aged 12* • James Callahan *Berlin Hughes* • Gary Grubbs *District Attorney* ■ *Dir* Robert Greenwald • *Scr* Rose Leiman Goldemberg, from a book by Faith McNulty

The Burning Hills ★★ PG
Western 1956 · US · Colour · 88min

This minor western has Tab Hunter setting out on a vengeance trail and finding Mexican-American Natalie Wood who nurses him when he's shot. Casting these two young and pretty things to star in a western was unusual in those days, a studio ploy to lure teenagers away from their dance halls and TV sets. Hunter proves himself a rather anaemic hero, though his popularity later gained him his own TV show. AT

Tab Hunter *Trace Jordan* • Natalie Wood *Maria Colton* • Skip Homeier *Jack Sutton* • Eduard Franz *Jacob Lantz* • Earl Holliman *Mort Bayliss* • Claude Akins *Ben Hindeman* • Ray Teal *Joe Sutton* ■ *Dir* Stuart Heisler • *Scr* Irving Wallace, from the novel by Louis L'Amour

The Burning Plain ★★★★ 15
Drama 2008 · US/Arg · Colour · 102min

Writer Guillermo Arriaga (*21 Grams*, *Babel*) makes an impressive directorial debut with this brooding drama about the corrosive effects of guilt. In windswept Portland, Oregon, emotionally distant restaurateur Sylvia (Charlize Theron) is confronted by a stranger who brings news from her past. Her story is intercut with flashbacks to a

New Mexico border town, revealing how teenager Mariana (Jennifer Lawrence) reacts to the affair between her mother Gina (Kim Basinger) and Nick (Joaquin de Almeida) and its tragic aftermath. Arriaga's enthusiasm for complex, non-linear narratives can sometimes make for frustrating viewing, but here the gradual unravelling of the three women's stories proves intriguing as it builds towards a devastating climax. SS English, Spanish +subtitles. Swearing, sex scenes, nudity. *DVD* *BD*

Charlize Theron *Sylvia* • Kim Basinger *Gina* • Jennifer Lawrence (2) *Mariana* • John Corbett *John* • Joaquin de Almeida *Nick Martinez* • Robin Tunney *Laura* • Brett Cullen *Robert* ■ *Dir/Scr* Guillermo Arriaga

The Burning Season ★★★★ 15
Biographical drama 1994 · US · Colour · 117min

In one of his last roles before his tragically early death, Raul Julia is both committed and convincing as Chico Mendes, the Brazilian union leader who was assassinated in 1990. Superbly scripted, and directed with power by John Frankenheimer, this superior TV movie never allows its passionate support for Mendes and his cause (the preservation of the Amazon rainforests) to deteriorate into either hagiography or melodrama. Green film-making at its best. DP Swearing, violence.

Raul Julia *Chico Mendes* • Kamala Dawson *Ilzamar* • Edward James Olmos *Wilson Pinhairo* • Sonia Braga *Regina De Carvaiho* • Esai Morales *Jair* • Carmen Argenziano *Allredo Sezero* • Enrique Novi *Nilo Sergio* • Jorge Zepeda *Thomas Sanjos* • Nigel Havers *Steven Kaye* ■ *Dir* John Frankenheimer • *Scr* Michael Tolkin, Ron Hutchinson, William Mastrosimone, from the novel by Andrew Revkin

Burning Secret ★★★ PG
Period drama 1988 · US/UK/W Ger · Colour · 103min

Director Andrew Birkin shows a sure grasp of child psychology in this thoughtful child's-eye view of the charged relationship that develops between an asthmatic boy's mother (Faye Dunaway) and a rakish Austrian baron (Klaus Maria Brandauer) during the youth's treatment at a mountain spa town after the First World War. The pace occasionally slackens, but there is the consolation of the beauties of Prague (standing in for Vienna). DP

Faye Dunaway *Sonya Tuchman* • Klaus Maria Brandauer *Baron Alexander Maria von Hauenschild* • David Eberts *Edmund Tuchman* • Ian Richardson *Father* • Martin Obernigg *Concierge* • John Nettleton *Dr Weiss* • Vaclav Stekl *Asst concierge* ■ *Dir* Andrew Birkin • *Scr* Andrew Birkin, from the short story *Brennendes Geheimnis* by Stefan Zweig

Burnt ★★ 15
Comedy drama 2015 · US · Colour · 96min

Bradley Cooper is a sparky presence at the head of this comedy drama about a head chef who, after going off the rails on booze and drugs, is given a second chance by his former boss (Daniel Brühl) at a prestigious London restaurant. Director John Wells aims to dissect the chef's obsessive-compulsive mind, but he doesn't get in deep enough. Naturally, with dishes designed by celebrity chef Marcus Wareing, there's lots of food porn, but the overall sensation is one of emptiness. SP Swearing, sexual references. *DVD* *BD*

Bradley Cooper *Adam Jones* • Sienna Miller *Helene* • Omar Sy *Michel* • Daniel Brühl *Tony* • Riccardo Scamarcio *Max* • Emma Thompson *Dr Rosshilde* ■ *Dir* John Wells • *Scr* Steven Knight

Burnt Barns ★★
Murder mystery 1973 · Fr · Colour · 95min

A dead woman is discovered on a farm, and suspicion falls on the son of Simone Signoret, a widowed matriarch who rules her family with a rod of iron. Alain Delon plays the local magistrate, who uncovers the sort of familial resentment that can only be put down to peasant tradition and in-

breeding. The presence of Signoret and Delon made Jean Chapot's sombre film a sure-fire hit in France, although it's really rather ordinary. AT French dubbed.

Alain Delon *Larcher* • Simone Signoret *Rose* • Paul Crauchet *Pierre* • Catherine Allégret *Françoise* • Bernard Le Coq *Paul* • Miou-Miou *Monique* ■ *Dir* Jean Chapot • *Scr* Sebastian Roulet, Frantz-Andre Burget

Burnt by the Sun ★★★★★ 15
Period drama 1995 · Rus/Fr · Colour · 146min

This period drama from director Nikita Mikhalkov plunges into the heart of darkness that was Stalin's Russia in the mid-1930s. Mikhalkov also stars as a complacent military hero of the Soviet Revolution, whose country house is visited unexpectedly by his young wife's former childhood sweetheart. Against the backdrop of a lazy summer's day, the truth behind Stalin's rule and the reason for the visit become apparent. Winner of the Oscar for best foreign film, this masterpiece of visual audacity – the vast balloon displaying an image of Stalin is a highlight – depicts, with vivid candour, a nation's paranoia grievously turned in upon itself. TH Russian +subtitles. Violence, swearing, sex scenes, nudity. *DVD*

Nikita Mikhalkov *Sergei Petrovich Kotov* • Oleg Menshikov *Dmitrii* • Ingeborga Dapkunaite *Marusia Kotov* • Nadia Mikhalkova *Nadia* • André Umansky *Philippe* • Vyacheslav Tikhonov *Vsevolod Konstantinovich* • Svetlana Kriuchkova *Mokhova* ■ *Dir* Nikita Mikhalkov • *Scr* Nikita Mikhalkov, Rustam Ibragimbekov, from a story by Nikita Mikhalkov • *Cinematographer* Vilen Kaliuta

Burnt Offerings ★ 15
Horror 1976 · US · Colour · 110min

In this chiller, Karen Black, Oliver Reed and family take a house for the summer. The fact that the house is owned by that old fruitcake Burgess Meredith should have told them at the start that things will soon get very bumpy in the night. Too long and not at all scary. AT *DVD*

Karen Black *Marian* • Oliver Reed *Ben* • Burgess Meredith *Brother* • Eileen Heckart *Roz* • Lee Montgomery *David* • Dub Taylor *Walker* • Bette Davis *Aunt Elizabeth* ■ *Dir* Dan Curtis • *Scr* William F Nolan, Dan Curtis, from the novel by Robert Marasco

Bury My Heart at Wounded Knee ★★★ 15
Historical western drama 2007 · US · Colour · 177min

Published in 1970, Dee Brown's landmark history of the American Indian struggle altered perceptions about the taking of the West. Despite including plenty of visceral conflict, this feature-length HBO dramatisation hasn't quite shed the scholarliness of the source material. Nevertheless, Aidan Quinn and Adam Beach are strong as politician Henry Dawes (during whose land negotiations the native tribes suffered great losses) and Ohiyesa, a Sioux boy whose father took him from the tribe to the schoolroom. Renamed Charles Eastman, the latter became a doctor and lobbied for native American rights, but was working within a system hopelessly skewed against his people's way of life. ES Violence, swearing. *DVD*

Aidan Quinn *Henry Dawes* • Adam Beach *Charles Eastman* • August Schellenberg *Sitting Bull* • Anna Paquin *Elaine Goodale* • Colm Feore *General Sherman* • Fred Thompson [Fred Dalton Thompson] *President Ulysses S Grant* • JK Simmons *McLaughlin* • Wes Studi *Wovoka* ■ *Dir* Yves Simoneau • *Scr* Daniel Giat, from the non-fiction book by Dee Brown

Bus 174 ★★★★ 15
Crime documentary 2002 · Bra · Colour and BW · 131min

An outstanding example of the crusading documentary, this account of the tragic life and times of Rio street kid Sandro do Nascimento lays bare the inhumanity, incompetence and indifference that allow so many born into poverty to sink into depravity. On 12 June 2000, Sandro hijacked a bus and held the occupants hostage for more than four hours. The stand-off was broadcast live to the nation and José Padilha and co-director Felipe Lacerda make compelling use of the contemporary TV footage. They also reveal his traumatic childhood and interview friends, SWAT officers and surviving hostages. The violent dénouement is perhaps over-dramatised but, by then, the film-makers' points about Sandro, urban decay and the class divide in Brazilian society have been more than well made. DP Portuguese +subtitles. Swearing, violence. *DVD*

■ Dir José Padilha, Felipe Lacerda

Bus Riley's Back in Town ★★★
Drama 1965 · US · Colour · 93min

Michael Parks shuffles and mumbles his way through this small-town melodrama. He plays a former sailor twice jilted by the voluptuous Ann-Margret, who has married a sugar daddy but still fancies Parks. He is something of a weakness but this is a quiet, understated study of frustrated ambition. The original author, noted playwright William Inge, demanded his real name be removed from the credits and the movie bombed. AT

Ann-Margret *Laurel* • Michael Parks *Bus Riley* • Janet Margolin *Judy* • Brad Dexter *Slocum* • Jocelyn Brando *Mrs Riley* • Larry Storch *Howie* • Crahan Denton *Spencer* ■ Dir Harvey Hart • Scr Walter Gage [William Inge]

Bus Stop ★★★★ U
Romantic comedy 1956 · US · Colour · 90min

This was the film that proved Marilyn Monroe was a considerable screen actress, and capable of much, much more than her sexpot image indicated. Whether Monroe's performance is a result of director Joshua Logan's patience or Lee and Paula Strasberg's legendary coaching is irrelevant: she is superb as the down-at-heel saloon chanteuse whom young cowboy Don Murray (impressive in his film debut) decides to marry. Based on William Inge's stage play, this is a movie that rewards – especially memorable is Monroe's delivery of an off-kilter *That Old Black Magic*. TS *DVD*

Marilyn Monroe *Cherie* • Don Murray *Bo* • Arthur O'Connell *Virgil* • Betty Field *Grace* • Eileen Heckart *Vera* • Robert Bray *Carl* • Hope Lange *Elma* • Hans Conried *Life photographer* • Casey Adams [Max Showalter] *Life reporter* ■ Dir Joshua Logan • Scr George Axelrod, from the play by William Inge

Bush Christmas ★★★ U
Adventure 1947 · Aus/UK · BW · 61min

The first film made for J Arthur Rank's Children's Cinema Club, this adventure was beautifully photographed in the sultry Blue Mountains of New South Wales with an all-Australian cast and crew. Chips Rafferty, at the time the only world-famous Australian actor, heads the cast in the tale of a group of children who trek through the bush in order to catch the rustlers who have stolen their father's horses. The film doesn't talk down to its youthful audience and is fine family fare. TV

Chips Rafferty *Long Bill* • John Fernside *Jim* • Stan Tolhurst *Blue* • Pat Penny *Father* • Thelma Grigg *Mother* • Clyde Combo *Old Jack* • John McCallum *Narrator* • Helen Grieve *Helen* ■ Dir/Scr Ralph Smart • Cinematographer George Heath

Bush Christmas ★★★
Adventure 1983 · Aus · Colour · 91min

A remake of the 1947 original, this amiable outdoor adventure is of primary interest for marking the screen debut of Nicole Kidman. Along with brother Mark Spain, English cousin James Wingrove and Aboriginal stablehand Manalpuy, she spends much of the film pursuing roguish horse thieves John Ewart and John Howard. Directed with a kid-friendly mix of humour and action by Henri Safran and splendidly shot by Malcolm Richards and Ross Berryman, this is family fare of a high order. DP

Nicole Kidman *Helen* • Mark Spain *John* • James Wingrove *Michael* • Manalpuy • John Ewart *Bill* • John Howard (2) *Sly* ■ Dir Henri Safran • Scr Ted Roberts, from the film by Ralph Smart

Bushwhacked ★ PG
Comedy 1995 · US · Colour · 86min

This calamitous comedy might appeal to those youngsters who thought that Daniel Stern being pummelled in *Home Alone* was hilariously funny. Here, Stern is a doltish delivery man who poses as a scout leader while trying to beat a murder rap. Unsubtle slapstick. DP Swearing. *DVD*

Daniel Stern *Max Grabelski* • Jon Polito *Agent Palmer* • Brad Sullivan *Jack Erickson* • Ann Dowd *Mrs Patterson* • Anthony Heald *Bragdon* • Tom Wood *Agent McMurrey* ■ Dir Greg Beeman • Scr John Jordan, Danny Byers, Tommy Swerdlow, Michael Goldberg, from a story by John Jordan, Danny Byers

The Business ★★★ 18
Crime drama 2005 · UK/Sp · Colour · 91min

In this boisterous 1980s-set crime drama, Danny Dyer stars as the young Londoner who goes on the run to Malaga, only to be initiated into a violent world of drugs and organised crime by flamboyant ex-con Tamer Hassan. The film perfectly captures the era's social and sartorial excesses, providing a hilarious sense of nostalgia that complements the tale's overall black humour. Despite a predictable storyline, the actors acquit themselves well, delivering a torrent of bad language and witticisms with skill and relish. SF Violence. *DVD* *Blu*

Danny Dyer *Frankie* • Tamer Hassan *Charlie* • Geoff Bell *Sammy* • Georgina Chapman *Carly* • Eddie Webber *Ronnie* • Adam Bolton *Danny* • Linda Henry *Shirley* • Roland Manookian *Sonny* ■ Dir/Scr Nick Love

A Business Affair ★★ 15
Romantic comedy 1993 · Fr/UK/Ger/Sp · Colour · 97min

It's hard to believe the combined talents of Christopher Walken and Jonathan Pryce could make such a lacklustre film. Pryce plays a novelist whose writer's block is seriously aggravated when his wife Carole Bouquet achieves sudden success as a novelist. To make matters worse, she elopes with her husband's literary agent (Walken). Charlotte Brandstrom's film is simply too fluffy for its heavyweight cast. LH

Christopher Walken *Vanni Corso* • Carole Bouquet *Kate Swallow* • Jonathan Pryce *Alec Bolton* • Sheila Hancock *Judith* • Anna Manahan *Bianca* • Fernando Guillen-Cuervo *Angel* • Tom Wilkinson *Bob* ■ Dir Charlotte Brandstrom • Scr William Stadiem, from a story by Charlotte Brandstrom, William Stadiem, from the books *Tears Before Bedtime* and *Weep No More* by Barbara Skelton

Business as Usual ★★ 15
Drama 1987 · UK · Colour · 85min

Lezli-An Barrett's debut feature has a tendency towards the didactic. Glenda Jackson plays a Liverpool boutique manager who becomes a supporter of workers' rights when she's sacked by her boss for complaining about the sexual harassment of an employee. Very 1980s and anti-Thatcher in its approach, the film is watchable thanks to the conviction of the cast, but not helped by the heavy-handed treatment. LH

Glenda Jackson *Babs Flynn* • John Thaw *Kieran Flynn* • Cathy Tyson *Josie Patterson* • Mark McGann *Stevie Flynn* • Eamon Boland *Mr Barry* • James Hazeldine *Mark* • Buki Armstrong *Paula Douglas* • Stephen McGann *Terry Flynn* ■ Dir/Scr Lezli-An Barrett

Business Is Business ★★★ 18
Comedy drama 1971 · Neth · Colour · 88min

The huge success of this spicy comedy drama in Holland allowed first-time feature director Paul Verhoeven to helm his international breakthrough hit *Turkish Delight*. Based on a booklet of anecdotes about prostitutes working in Amsterdam's red light district, it follows the risqué adventures of Ronnie Bierman and Sylvia

de Leur as they ply their trade, specialising in deviant sex for mainly upper-class clients, avoiding trouble with pimps in the process. Engrossing and highly entertaining. AJ Dutch dubbed. *DVD*

Ronnie Bierman *Blonde Greet* • Sylvia de Leur *Nel* • Piet Romer *Piet* • Bernhard Droog ■ Dir Paul Verhoeven • Scr Gerard Soeteman, from a book by Albert Mol

The Business of Strangers ★★★ 15
Drama 2001 · US · Colour · 80min

Patrick Stettner's debut feature begins with a confidence that makes its descent into melodrama all the more disappointing. Sassy assistant Julia Stiles incessantly scrutinises the vulnerability beneath Stockard Channing's crisp professional demeanour, but her irresponsible duplicity, and the brutal treatment of smarmy headhunter Frederick Weller, upsets the delicate dramatic balance of this dark satire. Channing's multilayered performance proves that she's still one of the most underrated actresses around. DP Swearing, sex scenes. *DVD*

Stockard Channing *Julie Styron* • Julia Stiles *Paula Murphy* • Frederick Weller *Nick Harris* • Mary Testa *Receptionist* • Jack Hallett *Mr Fostwick* ■ Dir/Scr Patrick Stettner

Busman's Honeymoon ★★
Crime thriller 1940 · UK · BW · 98min

Lord Peter Wimsey gets married and vows to drop all his detective work until a corpse appears in his honeymoon hideaway in Devon. It's based on the novel by Dorothy L Sayers and you can almost hear the stage boards creaking. However, Robert Montgomery and Constance Cummings, while the clear camerawork is by Freddie Young, who later won Oscars for *Lawrence of Arabia* and *Doctor Zhivago*. AT

Robert Montgomery *Lord Peter Wimsey* • Constance Cummings *Harriet Vane* • Leslie Banks *Inspector Kirk* • Seymour Hicks *Bunter* • Robert Newton *Frank Crutchley* • Googie Withers *Polly* • Frank Pettingell *Puffett* • Joan Kemp-Welch *Aggie Twitterton* ■ Dir Arthur B Woods • Scr Monckton Hoffe, Angus MacPhail, Harold Goldman, from the novel by Dorothy L Sayers

Buster ★★★ 15
Biographical crime drama 1988 · UK · Colour · 92min

Phil Collins takes on his first lead movie role, playing Buster Edwards, one of the gang involved in the Great Train Robbery. Julie Walters plays his wife and they make the most of their roles as lovably cheeky Cockney sparrers chirruping away in Acapulco after fleeing London. *EastEnders*-style clichés fall as thick and fast as the pair's "aitches", and, while Collins does his best, it's Walters who scores as a woman missing the comforts of home. Too squeaky clean to be believable, this is a fairy-tale view of law-breaking. TH Swearing, violence, nudity. *DVD*

Phil Collins *Buster Edwards* • Julie Walters *June Edwards* • Larry Lamb *Bruce Reynolds* • Stephanie Lawrence *Franny Reynolds* • Ellen Beaven *Nicky Edwards* • Michael Attwell *Harry* • Ralph Brown (2) *Ronnie* • Christopher Ellison *George* • Sheila Hancock *Mrs Rothery* ■ Dir David Green • Scr Colin Shindler

Buster and Billie ★★★ 18
Period drama 1974 · US · Colour · 95min

Rural Georgia in 1948: local boys loaf about eying the girls and wonder how far they will go in a sexual relationship. The exception is Joan Goodfellow who lives in squalor on the other side of the tracks and entertains the boys at the drop of a hat. When Jan-Michael Vincent abandons his childhood sweetheart for her, things come to a head. The movie should have been a potboiler but it's a bit too well behaved, too self-consciously "literate" and too preoccupied with period trappings to be more than just absorbing. AT

Jan-Michael Vincent *Buster Lane* • Joan Goodfellow *Billie* • Pamela Sue Martin *Margie Hooks* • Clifton James *Jake* • Robert Englund *Whitey* • Jessie Lee Fulton *Mrs Lane* • JB Joiner

Mr Lane • Dell C Payne *Warren* ■ Dir Daniel Petrie • Scr Ron Turbeville, from a story by Ron Baron, Ron Turbeville

The Buster Keaton Story ★ U
Biographical comedy drama 1957 · US · BW · 91min

Blockbuster novelist Sidney Sheldon was responsible (as co-writer, co-producer and director) for this insult to the comic genius of the Great Stone Face. Even though Keaton himself supervised the re-created moments of peerless slapstick, he was so furious at the flagrant fictions littering the script that he almost walked out of the Hollywood premiere in disgust. Tacky and inaccurate. DP

Donald O'Connor *Buster Keaton* • Ann Blyth *Gloria* • Rhonda Fleming *Peggy Courtney* • Peter Lorre *Kurt Bergner* • Larry Keating *Larry Winters* • Richard Anderson *Tom McAffee* • Dave Willock *Joe Keaton* • Claire Carleton *Myrna Keaton* • Jackie Coogan *Elmer Case* • Cecil B DeMille ■ Dir Sidney Sheldon • Scr Sidney Sheldon, Robert Smith

Buster's World ★★★
Comedy drama 1984 · Den · Colour · 77min

This charming rite-of-passage picture is considerably more personal than Bille August's more internationally acclaimed study of childhood, *Pelle the Conqueror*. Mads Bugge Andersen gives a wonderfully eccentric performance as the daydreaming pre-teen who uses his grandfather's magic kit not only to ward off the bullies who threaten his crippled sister, but also to further his chances with the poor little rich girl he meets at the fair. This is an astute blend of pathos and comedy. DP Danish +subtitles.

Mads Bugge Andersen *Buster* • Katerina Stenbeck *Buster's sister* • Peter Schrøder *Father* • Kirsten Rolffes *Joanna's mother* • Berthe Qvistgaard *Mrs Larsen* • Buster Larsen *Shopkeeper* • Signe Dahl Madsen *Joanna* • Katja Miehe-Renard *Mother* ■ Dir Bille August • Scr Bjarne Reuther, from his novel

Bustin' Down the Door ★★★ 15
Documentary 2008 · US · Colour · 95min

Fans of both surfing and all things retro will enjoy this solid documentary. Edward Norton narrates the story of how a small group of Australian and South African surfers changed the face of the sport when they came to Oahu's North Shore in the mid-1970s, stoking tensions with the Hawaiian locals. Jeremy Gosch's film is composed mainly of middle-aged men telling their war stories, interspersed with scratchy yet evocative Super-8 film footage. Pleasing nostalgia for some; but for others, this group's achievement is bittersweet, as the amateur pastime has evolved into today's corporate-sponsored sport. AS Swearing, drug abuse.

Edward Norton *Narrator* ■ Dir Jeremy Gosch • Scr Jeremy Gosch, Monika Gosch, Phil Jarratt, Robert Traill, Shaun Tomson

Bustin' Loose ★★★ 15
Comedy 1981 · US · Colour · 88min

Richard Pryor wrote and co-produced this story of an ex-convict who shepherds teacher Cicely Tyson and her class of maladjusted children to a rural retreat, revealing that sentiment is as much his line as deadpan wisecracks. The film took two years to complete, because it was interrupted by Pryor's near-fatal drug-related accident, and, as a result, theatre director Oz Scott, in his film debut, was left with discrepancies in continuity. Despite a queasy mix of pratfalls and pathos, Pryor still comes across as hugely likeable. TH Swearing, violence.

Richard Pryor *Joe Braxton* • Cicely Tyson *Vivian Perry* • Alphonso Alexander *Martin* • Kia Cooper *Samantha* • Edwin Deleon *Ernesto* • Jimmy Hughes *Harold* • Edwin Kinter *Anthony* ■ Dir Oz Scott • Scr Roger L Simon, Lonne Elder III, from a story by Richard Pryor

Busting ★★ 18
Crime drama 1974 · US · Colour · 87min

This is an early attempt to show the Los Angeles police as corrupt, bureaucratic and just like any other government department. While Elliott Gould and Robert Blake are the vice detectives forced to crack down on minor drug dealers, top managers are taking payoffs from high ranking mobsters. Peter Hyams's direction bustles farcically to make its case that the LAPD is lapdog to the Syndicate, but it's too raucous to make the point at all coherently. TH

Elliott Gould *Michael Keneely* · Robert Blake *Patrick Farrell* · Allen Garfield *Carl Rizzo* · William Sylvester *Mr Weldman* · Logan Ramsey *Dr Berman* · Richard X Slattery *Desk sergeant* · John Lawrence *Sergeant Kenfick* ■ *Dir/Scr* Peter Hyams

The Busy Body ★★★
Black comedy 1967 · US · Colour · 101min

This is a black comedy about Mafia folk and is based on the novel by Donald E Westlake, author of *Point Blank*. Sid Caesar is the Mafia employee suspected of stealing a bundle, Robert Ryan, always a joy to watch, is the *numero uno* mobster and there's rich support from Anne Baxter and Richard Pryor in his screen debut. Sloppy in places, this is nonetheless a delightful tongue-in-cheek piece for connoisseurs of the crime movie. AT

Sid Caesar *George Norton* · Robert Ryan *Charley Barker* · Anne Baxter *Margo Foster* · Kay Medford *Ma Norton* · Jan Murray *Murray Foster* · Richard Pryor *Whittaker* · Arlene Golonka *Bobbi Brody* · Dom DeLuise *Kurt Brock* ■ *Dir* William Castle · *Scr* Ben Starr, from the novel by Donald E Westlake

But I'm a Cheerleader ★★ 15
Satire 1999 · US · Colour · 88min

This sugar-coated satire sacrifices the important points it makes regarding homophobia and prejudice for the sake of an easy gag. Teenager Natasha Lyonne is suspected of being a lesbian by her friends and family, so she's shipped off to a rehabilitation camp that promises to "cure" her sexual preference. But there she meets the sexy Clea DuVall. Lyonne is good value and drag artist RuPaul is fun as the butch camp counsellor whose job it is to straighten the kids out. However, the initial spoofing of gay culture soon loses its edge. AJ *DVD*

Natasha Lyonne *Megan Bloomfield* · Clea DuVall *Graham Eaton* · RuPaul Charles [RuPaul] *Mike* · Eddie Cibrian *Rock* · Bud Cort *Peter* · Melanie Lynskey *Hilary* · Mink Stole *Nancy Bloomfield* · Cathy Moriarty *Mary Brown* · Julie Delpy *Lipstick lesbian* ■ *Dir* Jamie Babbit · *Scr* Brian Wayne Peterson, from a story by Jamie Babbit

But Not for Me ★★★ U
Romantic comedy 1959 · US · BW · 104min

Here Clark Gable stars as a fading theatre producer who almost succumbs to the charms and devotion of his new secretary (Carroll Baker). A pleasingly suitable vehicle for its ageing star, the film lacks effervescence, but Walter Lang directs with polish, while Lilli Palmer is ideal as the woman who boxes more to Gable's weight. RK

Clark Gable *Russell Ward* · Carroll Baker *Eleanor Brown* · Lilli Palmer *Kathryn Ward* · Lee J Cobb *Jeremiah MacDonald* · Barry Coe *Gordon Reynolds* · Thomas Gomez *Demetrios Bacos* · Charles Lane (2) *Atwood* · Wendell Holmes *Montgomery* ■ *Dir* Walter Lang · *Scr* John Michael Hayes, from the play *Accent on Youth* by Samson Raphaelson

Butch and Sundance: the Early Days ★★★ PG
Comedy western 1979 · US · Colour · 106min

Completely inconsequential when measured against its phenomenally successful progenitor, this fictional version of the early outlaw careers of Butch Cassidy and the Sundance Kid is still an enjoyable romp. William Katt and Tom Berenger emit oodles of charm as the cowboy heroes' younger selves, and director Richard Lester laces the ambitious material with the same wit and irony he brought to *The Three Musketeers*. AJ *DVD*

William Katt *Sundance Kid* · Tom Berenger *Butch Cassidy* · Jeff Corey *Sheriff Ray Bledsoe* · John Schuck *Harvey Logan* · Michael C Gwynne *Mike Cassidy* · Peter Weller *Joe LeFors* · Brian Dennehy *OC Hanks* · Chris Lloyd [Christopher Lloyd] *Bill Carver* ■ *Dir* Richard Lester · *Scr* Allan Burns

Butch Cassidy and the Sundance Kid ★★★★★ PG
Western comedy drama 1969 · US · Colour · 105min

Director George Roy Hill's freewheeling, Oscar-winning comic western was one of the biggest box-office hits in the genre's history. It features the unforgettable pairing of Paul Newman and Robert Redford, whose exhilarating performances turn the ruthless real-life desperados of fact into loveable rogues and, ultimately, tragic heroes. Some of the credit must go to the Oscar-winning trio of William Goldman, Conrad Hall and Burt Bacharach for the witty script, luminous photography and jaunty score respectively, but all of the charm of this ever-popular picture lies with the charismatic outlaws. DP Violence, swearing. *DVD* ⓑ

Paul Newman *Butch Cassidy* · Robert Redford *Sundance Kid* · Katharine Ross *Etta Place* · Strother Martin *Percy Garris* · Henry Jones *Bike salesman* · Jeff Corey *Sheriff Bledsoe* · George Furth *Woodcock* · Cloris Leachman *Agnes* · Ted Cassidy *Harvey Logan* ■ *Dir* George Roy Hill · *Scr* William Goldman

The Butcher Boy ★★★★
Silent comedy 1917 · US · BW · 30min

Although the career of silent film comedian Roscoe "Fatty" Arbuckle was to end in scandal, this shows just how deft and delicate he could be in fast-moving farce. It's a simple-minded tale of love among the meat-hooks, the first of the Comique films he signed up for with Paramount's Joseph Schenck. The occasional vulgarity of his Keystone movies was left behind and, generously, he gave a first chance to one of his vaudeville friends whose routine with a coin and molasses in the film almost upstaged "Fatty" himself. The friend? Buster Keaton, who supported Arbuckle after scandal had ruined his career. TH

Roscoe "Fatty" Arbuckle *Butcher boy* · Buster Keaton *Customer* · Al St John *Rival* · Josephine Stevens *Proprietor's daughter/Pupil at girls' boarding school* ■ *Dir* Roscoe "Fatty" Arbuckle · *Scr* Roscoe "Fatty" Arbuckle, from a story by Joe Roach [Joseph Anthony Roach]

The Butcher Boy ★★★★ 15
Black comedy drama 1997 · Ire/US · Colour · 105min

Novelist Patrick McCabe's portrait of small-town Irish life in the 1960s is viewed through dark-tinted glasses in this shocking, often surreal adaptation by Neil Jordan. Armed only with comics, movies and visions of the Virgin Mary (Sinead O'Connor), Eamonn Owens excels as the breezy teenager whose grip on reality begins to loosen as he returns from a pitiless Catholic remand home to witness the descent of father Stephen Rea into alcoholism and mother Aisling O'Sullivan into madness. DP Swearing, violence.

Stephen Rea *Da Brady* · Fiona Shaw *Mrs Nugent* · Eamonn Owens *Francie Brady* · Ian Hart *Uncle Alo* · Sinead O'Connor *Our Lady/Colleen* · Ardal O'Hanlon *Mr Purcell* · Milo O'Shea *Father Sullivan* ■ *Dir* Neil Jordan · *Scr* Neil Jordan, Patrick McCabe, from the novel by Patrick McCabe

The Butcher's Wife ★★★ 15
Romantic comedy 1991 · US · Colour · 100min

In this quirky but quiet romantic comedy, Demi Moore plays a blonde psychic who cheerfully tries to sort out the lives of her lonely neighbours in New York, who include besotted Jeff Daniels, Mary Steenburgen and Frances McDormand. Director Terry Hughes succeeds in conjuring up a bittersweet, magical atmosphere which is rarely cloying, and he is well served by a talented cast. JF Some swearing. *DVD*

Demi Moore *Marina* · Jeff Daniels *Alex* · George Dzundza *Leo* · Mary Steenburgen *Stella* · Frances McDormand *Grace* · Margaret Colin *Robyn* · Max Perlich *Eugene* · Miriam Margolyes *Gina* ■ *Dir* Terry Hughes · *Scr* Ezra Litwak, Marjorie Schwartz

The Butler ★★ 12A
Historical drama based on a true story 2013 · US · Colour · 132min

Lee Daniels (*Precious*) directs this drama about a black White House butler (inspired by real-life butler Eugene Allen) who served seven US presidents from the 1950s to the 1980s. It's a sprawling, soapy affair with the butler (Forest Whitaker) portrayed as something of a Forrest Gump figure, stolidly standing stock-still while significant moments of 20th-century history swirl past. There's a certain pleasure to be derived from the star casting – Robin Williams as Dwight D Eisenhower, Alan Rickman as Ronald Reagan – but there's also an underlying TV-movie ambience to the tale. DA Some violence, brief swearing. *DVD* ⓑ

Forest Whitaker *Cecil Gaines* · Oprah Winfrey *Gloria Gaines* · David Oyelowo *Louis Gaines* · John Cusack *Richard Nixon* · Robin Williams *Dwight Eisenhower* · Jane Fonda *Nancy Reagan* · Alan Rickman *Ronald Reagan* ■ *Dir* Lee Daniels · *Scr* Danny Strong, from the article *A Butler Well Served by This Election* by Wil Haygood

Butley ★★★ 15
Drama 1973 · UK · Colour · 123min

Alan Bates gives a tour de force performance in this filmed play – made for the American Film Theatre – of Simon Gray's drama about an academic whose wit and know-all attitude lacerates those around him. In the end, though, his self-destructiveness hurts no one but himself. Playwright Harold Pinter directs with a laconic style that has little to do with cinema. TH *DVD*

Alan Bates *Ben Butley* · Jessica Tandy *Edna Shaft* · Richard O'Callaghan *Joey Keyston* · Susan Engel *Anne Butley* · Michael Byrne *Reg Nuttall* · Georgina Hale *Miss Heasman* ■ *Dir* Harold Pinter · *Scr* Simon Gray, from his play

Buttercup Bill ★★★ 18
Romantic drama 2014 · UK/US · Colour · 95min

This intriguing, if ultimately self-indulgent movie is the debut feature from singer Tony Bennett's granddaughter, Remy, and co-writer/director Emilie Richard-Froozan. It's a dark psychological study of estranged friends forever connected by a dreadful secret, starring Bennett and Evan Louison as once inseparable lovers who resume their sexual power games in a Louisiana backwater. Yet they find it impossible to take their relationship to the next level. The leads have a potent chemistry, but this drama doesn't entirely engage. DP Swearing, sex scenes, drug abuse, nudity. *DVD*

Remy Bennett *Pernilla* · Evan Louison *Patrick* · Pauly Lingerfelt *Joey* · Mallory June *Mena* ■ *Dir/Scr* Remy Bennett, Emilie Richard-Froozan

The Buttercup Chain ★
Drama 1970 · UK · Colour · 94min

Filled with the psychosexual babble of the Swinging Sixties, this awful movie has Hywel Bennett as the founder member of a group of four inseparable friends who swap partners, generally relate to each other and are clearly destined for an unhappy ending. Bennett is sullen throughout while Jane Asher and Leigh Taylor-Young model some short skirts as the story flits around Europe. AT

Hywel Bennett *France* · Leigh Taylor-Young *Manny* · Jane Asher *Margaret* · Sven-Bertil Taube *Fred* · Clive Revill *George* · Roy Dotrice *Martin* · Carr-Gibbons · Michael Elphick *Chauffeur* ■ *Dir* Robert Ellis Miller · *Scr* Peter Draper, from a novel by Janice Elliott

Butterfield 8 ★★ 15
Drama 1960 · US · Colour · 108min

Elizabeth Taylor's Oscar-winning performance as an up-market whore with a heart is the chief interest of this otherwise dated drama. The film's attitude to sex was controversial on its release, but is tepid stuff today. Eddie Fisher, Taylor's husband at the time, fails to convince as the call girl's long-time friend, while Laurence Harvey looks uncomfortable as the married man with whom she has an affair. PF

Elizabeth Taylor *Gloria Wandrous* · Laurence Harvey *Weston Liggett* · Eddie Fisher *Steve Carpenter* · Dina Merrill *Emily Liggett* · Mildred Dunnock *Mrs Wandrous* · Betty Field *Mrs Fanny Thurber* · Jeffrey Lynn *Bingham Smith* ■ *Dir* Daniel Mann · *Scr* Charles Schnee, John Michael Hayes, from the novel by John O'Hara

Butterflies Are Free ★★ PG
Drama 1972 · US · Colour · 104min

Eileen Heckart won a best supporting actress Oscar for her role as blind Edward Albert's possessive mother, trying to protect her son from the advances of free spirit Goldie Hawn. Unfortunately, this often laughably corny product of the flower power era hasn't dated well, but it may offer some nostalgic pleasure for those old enough to remember. AT Some swearing.

Goldie Hawn *Jill* · Edward Albert *Don Baker* · Eileen Heckart *Mrs Baker* · Michael Glaser [Paul Michael Glaser] *Ralph* · Mike Warren [Mike Warren] *Roy* ■ *Dir* Milton Katselas · *Scr* Leonard Gershe, from his play

Butterfly ★★ 18
Drama 1982 · US · Colour · 103min

James M Cain's tough and complex crime novel about silver mines, incest and murder becomes a patience-testing sexploitation thriller thanks to Matt Cimber's soft-focus direction and a mind-numbing, Lolita-style performance from low-rent starlet Pia Zadora. Stacy Keach plays Zadora's long-lost father who succumbs to her feminine wiles and ore-stripping scam. Orson Welles cameos as a lecherous judge, while Ennio Morricone supplies the music. Too camp to miss. AJ

Stacy Keach *Jeff Tyler* · Pia Zadora *Kady* · Orson Welles *Judge Rauch* · Lois Nettleton *Belle Morgan* · Edward Albert *Wash Gillespie* · James Franciscus *Moke Blue* · Stuart Whitman *Rev Rivers* · Ed McMahon *Mr Gillespie* ■ *Dir* Matt Cimber · *Scr* Matt Cimber, John Goff, from the novel by James M Cain

The Butterfly Effect ★★★ 15
Supernatural thriller 2003 · US/Can · Colour · 108min

Ashton Kutcher stars in this ambitious film based on the idea of chaos theory, which speculates that the smallest of events can have the hugest of consequences. Kutcher plays a troubled college student who discovers he has the ability to go back in time and re-write the past. Touching on provocative themes such as child abuse, disability and terminal illness, J Mackye Gruber and Eric Bress have created a powerful and disturbing tale. It's spoilt by a rushed conclusion, but the performances are strong. SF Swearing, violence. *DVD* ⓑ

Ashton Kutcher *Evan Treborn* · Amy Smart *Kayleigh Miller* · Eric Stoltz *George Miller* · William Lee Scott *Tommy Miller* · Elden Henson *Lenny Kagan* · Ethan Suplee *Thumper* · Melora Walters *Andrea Treborn* · Callum Keith Rennie *Jason Treborn* ■ *Dir/Scr* Eric Bress, J Mackye Gruber

Butterfly Kiss ★★ 18
Crime drama 1994 · UK · Colour and BW · 84min

This weird British road movie stars Amanda Plummer as a lesbian serial killer and Saskia Reeves as her willing associate. Reeves plays the extremely dense shop assistant picked up by punkette Plummer at a service station. Instead of being shockingly original, it's merely drab and depressing. AT Violence, swearing, sex scenes, nudity. *DVD*

Amanda Plummer *Eunice* • Saskia Reeves *Miriam* • Ricky Tomlinson *Robert* • Des McAleer *Eric* • Paul Bown *Gary* • Freda Dowie *Elsie* • Fine Time Fontayne *Tony* ■ *Dir* Michael Winterbottom • *Scr* Frank Cottrell Boyce, from an idea by Frank Cottrell Boyce, Michael Winterbottom

The Butterfly Murders★★★
Martial arts mystery horror
1979 · HK · Colour · 88min

Tsui Hark made his directorial debut with this eerie hybrid of the horror and swordplay genres. Edgar Allan Poe's *The Masque of the Red Death* is the clear inspiration for this elaborate tale of killer butterflies, hidden identities and fantastical contraptions. By reinforcing the claustrophobic atmosphere of the labyrinthine castle setting, Fan Jinyu's photography makes the explosive action all the more dynamic and ethereal as warrior/scholar Liu Zhaoming seeks to eradicate the lepidopteran peril. DP Cantonese +subtitles.

Liu Zhaoming *Fang Hongye* • Michelle Mee *Green Shadow* • Huang Shutang *Tian Feng* • Zhang Guozhu *Shen Qing* • Chen Qiqi *Lady Shen* • Wang Jiang Li *"The Thousand Hands"* • Gao Ziong *Guo "The Magic Fire"* ■ *Dir* Tsui Hark • *Scr* Lin Fan

Butterfly on a Wheel ★★🔲
Crime thriller 2007 · Can/US · Colour · 91min

After losing out to Daniel Craig as Bond, Pierce Brosnan revelled in a string of bad-boy roles: *The Matador, Married Life* – and this. Brosnan plays a gun-toting thug who takes hostage a successful and seemingly happily married couple (Gerard Butler, Maria Bello), tells them he is holding their child, then blackmails them into dismantling their perfectly ordered lives. There is, of course, a hidden agenda for it all. Brosnan overacts a bit, as he has a habit of doing. And the twist ending strains credulity somewhat. But decent performances and glossy production values mean this just about sustains the interest. DA Swearing, sexual references. *DVD*

Pierce Brosnan *Tom Ryan* • Maria Bello *Abby Randall* • Gerard Butler *Neil Randall* • Emma Karwandy *Sophie Randall* • Claudette Mink *Judy* • Desiree Zurowski *Helen Schriver* ■ *Dir* Mike Barker • *Scr* William Morrissey

Butterfly's Tongue ★★★🔲
Period drama 1999 · Sp · Colour · 95min

Lushly photographed and indulgently nostalgic, José Luis Cuerda's pre-Spanish Civil War drama has an anecdotal structure and a surface charm that barely suggest the political torrent raging beneath. However, such a disarmingly genial approach suits Cuerda's intention of exploring the cruel irrationality and agonising consequences of dogmatic strife. As the maverick schoolteacher, Fernando Fernán Gómez exudes the wisdom and humanity that charms young Manuel Lozano, an adorable yet potentially dangerous bundle of curiosity. DP Spanish +subtitles. A sex scene.

Fernando Fernán Gómez *Don Gregorio* • Manuel Lozano *Moncho* • Uxía Blanco *Rosa* ■ *Dir* José Luis Cuerda • *Scr* Rafael Azcona, from a stories by Manuel Riva

Buy & Cell ★★🔲
Comedy 1988 · US · Colour · 92min

Filmed at the height of Wall Street's insider trading crisis, this slight comedy stars Robert Carradine as the naive stockbroker taking the rap for his crooked boss with Malcolm McDowell as the disreputable prison warden. Although the latter has his moments, a good idea has been frittered away by a lacklustre script. Consequently, the satire is slapdash and the inmates are stereotypes. DP Swearing.

Malcolm McDowell *Warden Tennant* • Robert Carradine *Herbie Altman* • Michael Winslow *Sly* • Randall "Tex" Cobb *Wolf* • Ben Vereen *Shaka* • Lise Cutter *Dr Ellen Scott* ■ *Dir* Robert Boris • *Scr* Neal Israel, Larry Siegel

Buy It Now ★★🔲
Documentary drama 2005 · US · Colour · 60min

Starting life as an award-winning short, this docudrama about a girl who sells her virginity on eBay was later expanded. Unfortunately, the mishmash of styles only confuses the issues that the film wants to address. Investigating what might drive someone to turn themselves into a commodity, writer/director Antonio Campos's snapshot of teen angst actually adds up to less than one might expect, especially since the split-format structure saps its impact. No doubt there's an incisive story waiting to be told about teens, the internet and sexual exploitation, but this hour-long film only hints at it. JR Swearing, sexual references, drug abuse. *DVD*

■ *Dir* Antonio Campos

Buying the Cow ★🔲
Romantic comedy 2000 · US · Colour · 84min

A decent 30-something cast is laid low in this head-on collision between a romantic comedy and a gross-out farce. Given two months by longtime girlfriend Bridgette Wilson to rid himself of his "why buy the cow when you can get the milk for free" mentality, slacker Jerry O'Connell goes on a bender with buddies Ryan Reynolds and Bill Bellamy. Puerile, offensive and unfunny. DP *DVD*

Jerry O'Connell *David Collins* • Bridgette L Wilson [Bridgette Wilson] *Sarah* • Ryan Reynolds *Mike* • Bill Bellamy *Jonesy* • Alyssa Milano *Amy* • Jon Tenney *Andrew Hahn* • Annabeth Gish *Nicole* ■ *Dir* Walt Becker • *Scr* Walt Becker, Peter Nelson

Bwana Devil ★
Action adventure 1952 · US · Colour · 79min

The film that launched the 3D craze of the 1950s with its slogan "A lion in your lap! A lover in your arms!" did record business as a novelty attraction. However, writer/producer/director Arch Oboler's film was so flat dramatically that it saddled the stereoscopic process with the reputation of being all gimmick. The substandard colour certainly didn't help, either. AE 🔲

Robert Stack *Bob Hayward* • Barbara Britton *Alice Hayward* • Nigel Bruce *Dr Angus Ross* • Ramsay Hill *Maj Parkhurst* • Paul McVey *Commissioner* • Hope Miller *Portuguese girl* ■ *Dir/Scr* Arch Oboler

By Appointment Only ★★
Thriller 2007 · US · Colour · 93min

Precise direction and taut pacing make a contrived and simple TV movie surprisingly watchable, as recently widowed estate agent Ally Walker (from TV's *Sons of Anarchy*) is embroiled in a dangerous plot when the owner of a multimillion-dollar home she's selling disappears. Good use of music heightens the tension, even though Walker's self-penned and frequently unrealistic script is packed with too many visual and verbal tip-offs. SF

Ally Walker *Val Spencer* • Currie Graham *Jake Brenner* • Marnette Patterson *Angie* • Jordan Garrett *Nick Spencer* ■ *Dir* John Terlesky • *Scr* Ally Walker, Richard O Lowry

By Candlelight ★★★
Romantic comedy 1934 · US · BW · 70min

During a European train journey, a nobleman's manservant (Paul Lukas) is mistaken for his employer (Nils Asther) by a lovely woman (Elissa Landi) and he does nothing to disillusion her. In due course, the nobleman turns up and is taken for his servant. Universal Studios' James Whale, the star director of its famous horror cycle, trespasses here on territory more generally associated with Paramount and Ernst Lubitsch. While not quite up to the rival studio's standard of sophisticated romantic comedies peopled by aristocrats, this is a more than respectably assembled film, well directed and well acted. RK

Elissa Landi *Marie* • Paul Lukas *Josef* • Nils Asther *Count von Bommer* • Dorothy Revier *Countess von Rischenheim* • Lawrence Grant *Count von Rischenheim* • Esther Ralston *Baroness von Ballin* • Warburton Gamble *Baron von Ballin* • Lois January *Ann* ■ *Dir* James Whale

• *Scr* Hans Kräly, F Hugh Herbert, Karen De Wolf, Ruth Cummings, from the play *Candlelight* by Siegfried Geyer

By Dawn's Early Light ★★★🔲
Thriller 1990 · US · Colour · 96min

Powers Boothe gives another powerful performance in this effective TV dramatisation of what might happen to bring about the Third World War. Like *Crimson Tide*, this successfully poses the nuclear threat question, and, even though you could only really have one of two outcomes, director Jack Sholder manages to keep the tension building, helped by a solid cast which includes James Earl Jones, Martin Landau and Rip Torn. JB Swearing.

Powers Boothe *Cassidy* • Rebecca De Mornay *Moreau* • Martin Landau *US President* • James Earl Jones *Alice* • Rip Torn *Colonel Fargo* • Darren McGavin *Condor* • Peter MacNicol *Sedgewick* • Jeffrey DeMunn *Harpoon* • Nicolas Coster *Icarus* ■ *Dir* Jack Sholder • *Scr* Bruce Gilbert, from the novel *Trinity's Child* by William Prochnau

By Love Possessed ★★★★
Romantic drama 1961 · US · Colour · 115min

Meriting four stars for excess rather than consistent quality, this heavenly example of the sleazy, lurid and luxurious finds the gorgeous Lana Turner saddled with an impotent husband (Jason Robards) and an opulent wardrobe of designer gowns. So she drowns her sorrows in drink, riding and the willing arms of Efrem Zimbalist Jr. Her lover's father-in-law (Thomas Mitchell) is an embezzler, while his son (George Hamilton) is up on a rape charge. And that's just for starters! The only normal person in director John Sturges's cast of characters is Barbara Bel Geddes as Zimbalist's estranged wife. RK

Lana Turner *Marjorie Penrose* • Efrem Zimbalist Jr *Arthur Winner* • Jason Robards Jr [Jason Robards] *Julius Penrose* • George Hamilton *Warren Winner* • Susan Kohner *Helen Detweiler* • Barbara Bel Geddes *Clarissa Winner* • Thomas Mitchell *Noah Tuttle* • Everett Sloane *Reggie* • Yvonne Craig *Veronica Kovacs* • Carroll O'Connor *Bernie Breck* ■ *Dir* John Sturges • *Scr* John Dennis [Charles Schnee], Isobel Lennart, William Roberts, Ketti Frings, from the novel *By Love Possessed* by James Gould Cozzens • *Costume Designer* Bill Thomas

By Our Selves ★★★★🔲
Drama 2015 · UK · BW and Colour · 83min

Andrew Kötting re-teams with writer and "psychogeographer" Iain Sinclair for this engagingly loopy meditation on the work of 19th-century poet John Clare. In 1841, a penniless Clare absconded from the asylum in which he had been confined and walked 80 miles from Epping Forest to Northamptonshire. In a mesmerising and surprisingly moving film, Kötting and Sinclair re-create the walk, while Toby Jones plays the poet wandering through modern and forest landscapes as past and present collide. AS Some swearing. *DVD* 🔵

Toby Jones *Younger John Clare* • Freddie Jones *Older John Clare* • Alan Moore (2) *Alan Moore* • Iain Sinclair *Goat impersonator/Ermine Street irregular* ■ *Dir* Andrew Kötting

By the Light of the Silvery Moon ★★★🔲
Musical comedy 1953 · US · Colour · 101min

Following the success of *On Moonlight Bay*, Warners Bros brought back its top songbird, the fabulous Doris Day (her hair a slightly blonder shade), and her sweetheart Gordon MacRae for this sequel in which they cope with life in the 1920s. The Technicolor styling is superb, the treatment of the old songs enchanting and veterans Leon Ames and, particularly, Mary Wickes as the maid are fun to watch. But it's the combination of Day and MacRae that is irresistible, a couple who manage to convey the pleasure of their work to an audience. TS

Doris Day *Marjorie Winfield* • Gordon MacRae *William Sherman* • Leon Ames *George Winfield* • Rosemary DeCamp *Mrs Winfield* • Billy Gray

Wesley • Mary Wickes *Stella* • Russell Arms *Chester Finley* • Maria Palmer *Miss LaRue* ■ *Dir* David Butler • *Scr* Robert O'Brien, Irving Elinson, from the *Penrod* stories by Booth Tarkington

By the Sea ★★★🔲
Romantic drama 2015 · US/Jpn · Colour · 117min

Angelina Jolie Pitt's third film as director (and the first under her married name) is a fusion of the existential angst of Michelangelo Antonioni with the marital acrimony of *Who's Afraid of Virginia Woolf?* (plus a soupçon of Hitchcock for good measure). The cinematography groans under the weight of its gorgeousness and Pitt turns in a natural performance, making fine use of his easy charm. Sadly, Jolie Pitt spends most of the film lounging despondently, and under the scrutiny of her own directorial gaze appears self-conscious. EAS In English, French. Swearing, sex scenes, nudity. *DVD* 🔵

Brad Pitt *Roland* • Angelina Jolie Pitt [Angelina Jolie] *Vanessa* • Mélanie Laurent *Lea* • Melvil Poupaud *François* • Niels Arestrup *Michel* ■ *Dir/Scr* Angelina Jolie Pitt [Angelina Jolie]

By the Sword ★★🔲
Sports drama 1992 · US · Colour and BW · 87min

This made-for-TV fencing movie has two teachers clashing on the honourable way of fighting: F Murray Abraham is the mysterious elderly pupil who turns up at the school run by undefeated Olympic champion Eric Roberts and the two are soon locked in a personal battle. The plotting is confused and Roberts is over the top. JF Swearing. *DVD*

F Murray Abraham *Max Suba* • Eric Roberts *Alexander Villard* • Mia Sara *Erin Clavelli* • Christopher Rydell *Jimmy Trebor* • Elaine Kagan *Rachel* • Brett Cullen *Danny Gallagher* • Doug Wert *Hobbs* • Stoney Jackson *Johnson* • Caroline Barclay *Tatiana* ■ *Dir* Jeremy Kagan [Jeremy Paul Kagan] • *Scr* John McDonald, James Donadio

Bye Bye Birdie ★★★★🔲
Musical comedy 1963 · US · Colour · 110min

This is a wonderfully energetic and colourful adaptation of the smash Broadway hit that satirised the traumatic induction of one Elvis Presley into the US Army. Named Conrad Birdie here (a reference to contemporary country and western star Conway Twitty), this focuses on the legendary rocker bestowing "one last kiss" on a small-town girl – a gimmick started by the star's promoter, played by Dick Van Dyke re-creating his Broadway role. It's splendid stuff and, although the satire has dated, the sheer exuberance of veteran director George Sidney's guiding hand endures, as does the talent of Ann-Margret. Remade (badly) for television in 1995. TS

Janet Leigh *Rosie DeLeon* • Dick Van Dyke *Albert Peterson* • Ann-Margret *Kim McAfee* • Maureen Stapleton *Mama* • Bobby Rydell *Hugo Peabody* • Jesse Pearson *Conrad Birdie* • Ed Sullivan • Paul Lynde *Mr McAfee* ■ *Dir* George Sidney (2) • *Scr* Irving Brecher, from the musical comedy by Michael Stewart, with music and lyrics by Charles Strouse, Lee Adams

Bye Bye Blues ★★★🔲
Romantic drama 1989 · Can · Colour · 116min

Post-Second World War cinema was so intent on telling tales of male heroism or sympathising with the problems of returning veterans that it completely ignored the dilemmas facing women who had spread their wings while their men were away fighting. Based on the experiences of director Anne Wheeler's own mother, this tear-jerker shows just how much of an upheaval the war was for women. Helped by a nostalgic dance band soundtrack, this is warm, wise and beautifully acted. DP Brief nudity.

Rebecca Jenkins *Daisy Cooper* • Luke Reilly *Max Gramley* • Michael Ontkean *Teddy Cooper* • Stuart Margolin *Slim Godfrey* • Wayne Robson

Pete • Robyn Stevan *Frances Cooper* • Leon Pownall *Bernie Blitzer* • Sheila Moore *Doreen Cooper* ■ *Dir/Scr* Anne Wheeler

Bye Bye Braverman ★★★★
Comedy drama   1968 · US · Colour · 94min

This wickedly acerbic midlife crisis comedy anticipates *The Big Chill* in plot and theme, as a group of New York intellectuals mourn a deceased childhood friend and reflect on the state of their own lives on the way to his funeral. Brilliantly acted by a cast headed by George Segal and *Dr No*'s Joseph Wiseman, with comedian Alan King superb as a rabbi, this deserves to be better known, though its mordant theme almost certainly restricted its initial theatrical release. Director Sidney Lumet is not usually recognised for lightness of touch, but acquits himself extremely well here. **TS**

George Segal *Morroe Rieff* • Jack Warden *Barnet Weiner* • Joseph Wiseman *Felix Ottensteen* • Sorrell Booke *Holly Levine* • Jessica Walter *Inez Braverman* • Phyllis Newman *Myra Mandelbaum* • Zohra Lampert *Etta Rieff* • Godfrey Cambridge *Taxicab driver* • Alan King *Rabbi* ■ *Dir* Sidney Lumet • *Scr* Herbert Sargent, from the novel *To an Early Grave* by Wallace Markfield

Bye Bye Love ★★🄬
Comedy   1995 · US · Colour · 101min

Some ghastly slapstick and several clumsy social situations ruin any chance this smarmy comedy has of success. The premise of showing how three divorced fathers cope with life after marriage is essentially a sound one, but not only is the screenplay littered with lines begging to be cut, but director Sam Weisman also has a knack for playing each scene at precisely the wrong pace. **DP** Swearing. **DVD**

Matthew Modine *Dave* • Randy Quaid *Vic* • Paul Reiser *Donny* • Janeane Garofalo *Lucille* • Amy Brenneman *Susan* • Eliza Dushku *Emma* • Ed Flanders *Walter* • Maria Pitillo *Kim* • Lindsay Crouse *Grace* • Rob Reiner *Dr Townsend* ■ *Dir* Sam Weisman • *Scr* Gary David Goldberg, Brad Hall

Bye Bye Monkey ★★★🄳
Black comedy drama
1978 · It/Fr · Colour · 89min

Euro director Marco Ferreri, who had an international hit with *La Grande Bouffe*, made this fable in New York with rising star Gérard Depardieu and old master Marcello Mastroianni. Depardieu keeps a pet chimpanzee and is an electrician in a radical theatre where he's raped; Mastroianni is an asthmatic eccentric who lives in a rat-infested hovel and is on the verge of suicide. Praised at Cannes but barely released, this follows the descent of man from ape to human, from tenderness into barbarism among the rotting skyscrapers of Manhattan. Mastroianni rated his performance among his best. **AT** Violence, nudity, sexual situations, swearing.

Gérard Depardieu *Gérard Lafayette* • Marcello Mastroianni *Luigi Nocello* • James Coco *Andreas Flaxman* • Gail Lawrence *Angelica* • Geraldine Fitzgerald *Toland* • Avon Long *Miko* ■ *Dir* Marco Ferreri • *Scr* Marco Ferreri, Gérard Brach, Rafael Azcona

Bypass ★★🄵
Thriller   2014 · UK · Colour · 104min

Writer/director Duane Hopkins veers into lamentable self-indulgence with this formulaic study of domestic boredom. The arty "Brit-crime" trappings are every bit as miscalculated as the melodramatic use of lens flare and slow motion. Yet, despite the fussily fidgety visuals, this still manages to pack an emotional punch, as twentysomething Tim (George MacKay) turns to crime to care for his rebellious younger sister (Lara Peake) and pregnant girlfriend (Charlotte Spencer). For all the naturalism of the performances, the photography, editing and sound design, the film feels detached from the reality it's supposed to be conveying. **DP**

George MacKay *Tim* • Charlotte Spencer *Lilly* • Benjamin Dilloway *Greg* • Donald Sumpter *Grandfather* ■ *Dir/Scr* Duane Hopkins

Byzantium ★★★★🄵
Horror thriller   2012 · Ire/UK · Colour · 113min

Interview with the Vampire director Neil Jordan returns triumphantly to the bloodsucking genre with this unique horror thriller, light years away from the juvenilia of *Twilight* and its ilk. Gemma Arterton and Saoirse Ronan are radiant as the damaged mother and daughter running a seedy seaside bordello to escape the secret society that has been hunting them through the centuries. The film offers a whole new magical perspective on traditional vampire imagery, while the time-shifting flashbacks and upfront depiction of sexuality simply add to what is a haunting, touching and visually sublime reinvention of undead mythology. **AJ** Violence, swearing, sex scenes, nudity. **DVD** **Blu**

Gemma Arterton *Clara* • Saoirse Ronan *Eleanor* • Sam Riley *Darvell* • Jonny Lee Miller *Ruthven* • Daniel Mays *Noel* ■ *Dir* Neil Jordan • *Scr* Moira Buffini, from her play *A Vampire Story*

CB4 ★★★🄳
Satirical comedy   1993 · US · Colour · 84min

Although this comedy lacks cohesion and feels like a series of loosely linked sketches, it takes several well-aimed pot shots at both gangsta rap and the culture that engendered it. Surprisingly, considering it was directed by a woman, it somewhat ducks the issue of sexism, but *Saturday Night Live* alumnus Chris Rock and his rappers clearly have a ball. **DP** Swearing, sex scenes, drug abuse, nudity.

Chris Rock *Albert* • Allen Payne *Euripides* • Deezer D *Otis* • Chris Elliott *A White* • Phil Hartman *Virgil Robinson* • Charles Q Murphy [Charlie Murphy (1)] *Gusto* • Ice-T • Ice Cube • Flavor Flav • Shaquille O'Neal ■ *Dir* Tamra Davis • *Scr* Chris Rock, Nelson George, Robert LoCash, from a story by Chris Rock, Nelson George

CJ7 ★★★🄿🄶
Science-fiction comedy
2008 · HK/Chi · Colour · 84min

CJ7 is a canine-like extraterrestrial who's adopted by bullied schoolboy Dicky (played by female actress Xu Jiao) and is being accidentally left on Earth by his mother ship. Possessing rubbery shape-shifting abilities and heart-melting eyes, CJ7 looks like a radioactive chihuahua with an Afro, but quickly proves a hit with the kids, especially after Dicky realises it has magic powers. Reining in the martial arts – but little of the chaotic energy – of his earlier outings like *Kung Fu Hustle*, Stephen Chow's offbeat family comedy delivers all the slapstick havoc of a Looney Tunes cartoon. Cute little CJ7 is a delight, but the endless platitudes surrounding Dicky's relationship with his cash-strapped dad (a raggedly comic Chow) may well sap the enjoyment. **JR** Cantonese +subtitles. **DVD**

Stephen Chow *Ti* • Xu Jiao *Dicky* • Kitty Zhang *Miss Yuen* • Lee Sheung-ching *Mr Cao* • Fun Min-hun *PE teacher* • Huang Lei *Johnny* ■ *Dir* Stephen Chow • *Scr* Stephen Chow, Vincent Kok, Tsang Kan-Cheong [Kan-Cheung], Lam Fung, Sandy Shaw, Fung Chih-chiang

CSA: the Confederate States of America ★★★🄸🄰
Spoof documentary
2004 · US · Colour and BW · 89min

Produced on a modest budget by onetime academic Kevin Willmott, this Ken Burns-style cod-documentary (produced by the "British Broadcasting Services") ponders what America would be like today if the Confederacy had won the Civil War. The idea is suitably ingenious and some of the faux material that Willmott generates to illustrate his thesis is credible and slick. But the chronicle becomes increasingly far-fetched as it enters the 20th century. However, it's the lack of satirical bite and some truly subversive revisionism that renders this something of a missed opportunity. **DP**

Evamarii Johnson *Barbara Johnson* • Rupert Pate *Sherman Hoyle* • Larry J Peterson *Ambroise Fauntroy* • Charles Frank *Narrator* ■ *Dir/Scr* Kevin Willmott

CSNY/Déjà Vu ★★★★🄵
Music documentary   2008 · US · Colour · 96min

In this heartfelt documentary, Iraq war correspondent Mike Cerre follows the re-formed Crosby Stills Nash & Young as they embark on the 2006 "Freedom of Speech" tour built largely around Neil Young's *Living with War* album. While the other three members are certainly not just along for the ride, this is very much Young's project.

He directs (under the pseudonym Bernard Shakey) and takes a reasonably balanced view of events surrounding the tour, with both dissenting and supportive voices given room to be heard. The music is first rate, but it's the powerful anti-war message that shines through. **TP**

Stephen Stills • Neil Young (1) *Neil Young* • David Crosby • Graham Nash • Mike Cerre ■ *Dir* Bernard Shakey [Neil Young (1)] • *Scr* Neil Young (1), Mike Cerre

Ca Commence Aujourd'hui ★★★★🄬
Drama   1999 · Fr · Colour · 113min

The winner of the international critics prize at Berlin, this film recalls the fluid starkness of Bertrand Tavernier's police thriller *L.627*, as the camera restlessly prowls headmaster Philippe Torreton's school to witness how his staff make light of financial constraints to fascinate and protect their pupils. Whether challenging an abusive "uncle", encouraging youngsters or lambasting the mayor, Torreton is outstanding in his energy and insight. Apart from the disappointingly cosy conclusion, this is social drama at its best. **DP** French +subtitles. **DVD**

Philippe Torreton *Daniel Lefebvre* • Maria Pitarresi *Valéria* • Nadia Kaci *Samia Damouni* • Véronique Ataly *Madame Liénard* ■ *Dir* Bertrand Tavernier • *Scr* Dominique Sampiero, Tiffany Tavernier, Bertrand Tavernier

Cabaret ★★★★★ 🄵
Musical drama   1972 · US · Colour · 118min

This is a tremendously effective and affecting adult musical version of writer Christopher Isherwood's Berlin memoirs. The tale is transformed here through the Oscar-winning magic of director Bob Fosse (replacing first choice Gene Kelly) and star Liza Minnelli into a lasting screen classic, pulling no punches as it depicts the rise of Hitler and the spread of anti-Semitism through the twilight world of the Berlin cabaret. As the emcee of the Kit-Kat club, Joel Grey positively exudes decadence, and also collected one of the movie's eight Oscars. Fosse achieves several compelling cinematic moments, notably a chilling crescendo of emotion as a young Nazi sings Kander and Ebb's hymn-like *Tomorrow Belongs to Me*. If brash Minnelli seems a mite too talented for the Sally Bowles character, it really doesn't matter: she is, quite simply, magnificent. **TS** Some violence, swearing and drug abuse. **DVD** **Blu**

Liza Minnelli *Sally Bowles* • Joel Grey *Master of Ceremonies* • Michael York *Brian Roberts* • Helmut Griem *Maximilian von Heune* • Fritz Wepper *Fritz Wendel* • Marisa Berenson *Natalia Landauer* ■ *Dir* Bob Fosse • *Scr* Jay Presson Allen, from the musical by Joe Masteroff, from the play *I Am a Camera* by John Van Druten, from the short story collection *Goodbye to Berlin* by Christopher Isherwood • *Choreography* Bob Fosse • *Cinematographer* Geoffrey Unsworth • *Conductor/Music arranger* Ralph Burns • *Editor* David Bretherton • *Art Directors* Rolf Zehetbauer, Jurgen Kiebach

Cabin Boy ★★🄬
Comedy   1994 · US · Colour · 76min

This "fish out of water" comedy gets low marks for originality but succeeds in raising the odd laugh. Chris Elliott plays a spoilt brat who mistakes a fishing boat for a luxury cruise liner and gets a lesson in life from the salty crew. Elliott is fine in the lead role, and watch for some interesting cameos. **JF** Swearing.

Chris Elliott *Nathanial Mayweather* • Ritch Brinkley *Captain Greybar* • James Gammon *Paps* • Brian Doyle-Murray *Skunk* • Brion James *Big Teddy* ■ *Dir* Adam Resnick • *Scr* Adam Resnick, from a story by Adam Resnick, Chris Elliott

Cabin Fever ★★🄵
Horror thriller   2002 · US · Colour · 88min

Five college friends are struck down at their forest cabin retreat by a deadly flesh-eating virus in Eli Roth's cultish, gory exploitation flick. Designed as an all-out gratuitous splatter-fest in the "video nasty" tradition, this delights in delivering toe-curling shocks. Roth's direction is assured, but it's hard to know if this is a parody or a straight horror, or a mixture of both. AJ Violence, swearing. **DVD** **Blu** **CS**

Rider Strong *Paul* • Cerina Vincent *Marcy* • James DeBello *Bert* • Jordan Ladd *Karen* • Joey Kern *Jeff* • Arie Verveen *Hermit* • Eli Roth *Justin* ■ *Dir* Eli Roth • Randy Pearlstein, from a story by Eli Roth

Cabin Fever ★ 15
Horror 2016 · US · Colour · 94min

Coming just 14 years after Eli Roth's 2002 original, this new version of his gratuitous splatter flick once again finds several college students spending the weekend in (you guessed it) a remote cabin, and coming under attack from a horrific flesh-eating virus. This new bout of fever stands out as a spectacular misfire, however, even in the less-than-glorious history of horror remakes. JL Violence, swearing, drug abuse, sex scenes, nudity. **DVD** **Blu**

Gage Golightly *Karen* • Matthew Daddario *Jeff* • Samuel Davis *Paul* • Nadine Crocker *Marcy* ■ *Dir* Travis Z [Travis Zariwny] • *Scr* Randy Pearlstein, Eli Roth, from the 2002 film

Cabin in the Cotton ★★ U
Drama 1932 · US · BW · 79min

Caught between loyalty to his own people – poor tenant farmers – and the friendship of his plantation-owner boss, sharecropper Richard Barthelmess faces problems when he betrays his sweetheart (Dorothy Jordan) by succumbing to the shameless advances of the boss's predatory daughter (Bette Davis). The dramatic tension is dissipated by a poor script and run-of-the-mill direction by Michael Curtiz. RK

Richard Barthelmess *Marvin* • Dorothy Jordan *Betty* • Bette Davis *Madge* • Berton Churchill *Lane Norwood* • Walter Percival *Cleve Clinton* • William LeMaire *Jake Fisher* ■ *Dir* Michael Curtiz • *Scr* Paul Green, from the novel by Harry Harrison Kroll

Cabin in the Sky ★★★★ U
Musical 1943 · US · BW · 94min

This is an all-black fable about heaven and hell fighting for one man's soul. Sounds patronising, doesn't it? Well, this little gem is one of the cinema's great surprises: a stunning directorial debut from Vincente Minnelli, featuring a sublime score performed by Lena Horne, Ethel Waters, Louis Armstrong and the Duke Ellington Orchestra. The film's theatrical origins are subsumed in Minnelli's clever and stylish direction, and Eddie "Rochester" Anderson's performance in the pivotal role of Joe is a revelation. Viewed today, the black stereotypes on display here may be deemed offensive. TS

Ethel Waters *Petunia Jackson* • Eddie "Rochester" Anderson *Little Joe Jackson* • Lena Horne *Georgia Brown* • Louis Armstrong *Trumpeter* • Rex Ingram (2) *Lucius/Lucifer Jr* • Kenneth Spencer *Rev Green/The General* • John "Bubbles" Sublett *Domino Johnson* ■ *Dir* Vincente Minnelli • *Scr* Joseph Schrank, from the musical play by Lynn Root • *Music Director* George Stoll

The Cabin in the Woods ★★★★ 15
Horror thriller 2010 · US · Colour · 91min

Five friends on a forest retreat uncover an ancient conspiracy in this enterprising directorial debut from Drew Goddard (writer of *Lost* and *Cloverfield*) and producer Joss Whedon (*Buffy the Vampire Slayer*). It's a witty deconstruction of fantasy genres in the post-modern *Scream* vein and a weirdly wonderful twist on the whole *Evil Dead* scenario that ensures continual surprises. No shocker stone is left unturned, as creatures from our collective worst nightmares are invoked for unparalleled monster mayhem, leading to a daringly nihilistic Lovecraftian finale. A genuinely captivating original, with some sly performances and a bravura last-minute unbilled cameo. AJ Violence, swearing, drug abuse, a sex scene, brief nudity. **DVD** **Blu**

Kristen Connolly *Dana* • Chris Hemsworth *Curt* • Anna Hutchison *Jules* • Fran Kranz *Marty* • Jesse Williams *Holden* • Richard Jenkins *Sitterson* • Sigourney Weaver *The Director* ■ *Dir* Drew Goddard • *Scr* Drew Goddard, Joss Whedon

The Cabinet of Caligari ★★
Horror 1962 · US · BW · 102min

Horror clichés abound in this pseudo-Freudian nonsense, as a young woman's car breaks down near a mansion and she is held prisoner by its sinister owner, played with exuberant vigour by Dan O'Herlihy. There are moments of delirium and suspense featuring scenes of murder and voyeurism, but mostly it's a bore. RS

Glynis Johns *Jane Lindstrom* • Dan O'Herlihy *Paul/Caligari* • Richard Davalos *Mark* • Lawrence Dobkin *David* • Constance Ford *Christine* ■ *Dir* Roger Kay • *Scr* Robert Bloch

LANDMARK FILM
Highly stylised, distinctive German horror that refines the idea of a psychological, as opposed to physical, terror

The Cabinet of Dr Caligari
★★★★★ U
Silent horror 1919 · Ger · BW · 51min

Like *The Battleship Potemkin*, this silent classic changed the way movies were made and appreciated. Adapting techniques from the German theatrical expressionist style, it introduces us to psychopathic fairground showman Dr Caligari, whose exhibit, Cesare, is said to have been asleep since birth. What follows is a twisted tale of murder, kidnap, madness and an ancient book, all told in flashback by a young man from a park bench. The lopsided sets, odd camera angles and general weirdness caused a sensation at the time, and still look amazing. But modern audiences may find the exaggerated acting and stilted movements dated and rather laughable. AT **DVD** **Blu**

Werner Krauss *Dr Caligari* • Conrad Veidt *Cesare* • Friedrich Feher *Francis* • Lil Dagover *Jane* • Hans von Twardowski *Alan* • Rudolf Lettinger *Dr Olson* • Rudolph Klein-Rogge *A criminal* ■ *Dir* Robert Wiene • *Scr* Carl Mayer, Hans Janowitz, from the film *Das Kabinett des Dr Caligari* by Robert Wiene • *Cinematographer* John L Russell

Cabiria ★★★★
Silent epic 1914 · It · BW · 210min

The international success of this Italian spectacle, the longest and most expensive motion picture made up to that date, allowed DW Griffith to gain support for his large-scale projects. The film, which took an unprecedented six months to shoot in studios and locations in Sicily, the Alps and Tunisia, follows the adventures of Cabiria, a kidnapped girl, and Maciste, her giant slave companion, during the Second Punic War. Giovanni Pastrone directed, but the lion's share of the credit went to Gabriele D'Annunzio, although the latter's contribution was limited to the intertitles. RB

Italia Almirante Manzini *Sophonisba* • Vitale de Stefano *Massinissa* • Bartolomeo Pagano *Maciste* • Lidia Quaranta *Cabiria* • Umberto Mozzato *Fulvio Axilla* • Enrico Gemelli *Archimedes* • Ignazio Lupi *Arbace* ■ *Dir* Piero Fosco [Giovanni Pastrone] • *Scr* Giovanni Pastrone

The Cable Guy ★★★ 12
Satirical comedy 1996 · US · Colour · 91min

Jim Carrey was afforded the opportunity to do something different in this jet-black satire on the power of television, and he responded with a performance that brings a dark edge to his wacky persona. Carrey is on top form as a manic cable television engineer who takes a special interest in customer Matthew Broderick. Psycho stalker Carrey starts invading every aspect of Broderick's life, with both hilarious and sobering results. Ben Stiller's film may suffer from dull patches, but it's much better than you may have heard. AJ Violence, swearing. **DVD**

Jim Carrey *Chip Douglas* • Matthew Broderick *Steven Kovacs* • Leslie Mann *Robin* • Jack Black *Rick* • George Segal *Steven's father* • Diane Baker

Steven's mother • Ben Stiller *Sam Sweet* • Eric Roberts • Janeane Garofalo *Waitress* ■ *Dir* Ben Stiller • *Scr* Lou Holtz Jr

Cactus ★★★ PG
Drama 1986 · Aus · Colour · 91min

Isabelle Huppert, on holiday Down Under, has a car crash and loses sight in one eye. Doctors recommend she has the eye removed to prevent sympathetic blindness in the other. Her choice is complicated when she falls in love with a blind man and contemplates total blindness. A painful topic is handled with naturalism and insight in a drama that weaves in and out of Huppert's life and the lives of her family and friends. LH

Isabelle Huppert *Colo* • Robert Menzies *Robert* • Norman Kaye *Tom* • Monica Maughan *Bea* • Banduk Marika *Banduk* • Sheila Florance *Martha* ■ *Dir/Scr* Paul Cox

Cactus Flower ★★★ PG
Comedy 1969 · US · Colour · 99min

Goldie Hawn won a best supporting actress Oscar for converting her lovable *Laugh-In* bimbo into a believable screen persona as dentist Walter Matthau's young girlfriend. Matthau deflects Hawn's talk of marriage by presenting his receptionist Ingrid Bergman (in one of several screen comebacks) as his wife. Hawn is enchanting and Matthau is always watchable, but the material is wafer thin, and Bergman seems ill at ease in this glossy adaptation. TS **DVD**

Walter Matthau *Julian Winston* • Ingrid Bergman *Stephanie Dickinson* • Goldie Hawn *Toni Simmons* • Jack Weston *Harvey Greenfield* • Rick Lenz *Igor Sullivan* • Vito Scotti *Senor Sanchez* • Irene Hervey *Mrs Durant* ■ *Dir* Gene Saks • *Scr* IAL Diamond, from the play by Abe Burrows, from the French play by Barillet & Gredy

Cactus Jack ★ PG
Comedy western 1979 · US · Colour · 85min

This attempt to spoof old westerns stars Arnold Schwarzenegger and Kirk Douglas in what sounds like a comic meeting of the two chins. The former is the handsome hero, the latter a bumbling gunslinger attempting to kidnap Ann-Margret (as striking as ever). This is, sadly, an example of crass comic mistiming in the extreme, lacking imagination. JM **DVD**

Kirk Douglas *Cactus Jack* • Ann-Margret *Charming Jones* • Arnold Schwarzenegger *Handsome Stranger* • Paul Lynde *Nervous Elk* • Foster Brooks *Bank clerk* • Ruth Buzzi *Damsel in distress* • Jack Elam *Avery Simpson* • Strother Martin *Parody Jones* ■ *Dir* Hal Needham • *Scr* Robert G Kane

Caddie ★★
Period drama 1976 · Aus · Colour · 106min

This worthy drama from Down Under is about a woman who is forced to make radical changes to her lifestyle when she leaves her cheating husband. Helen Morse gives a dignified performance as the woman trying to make her own way in the very macho world of Australia between the wars, and Jack Thompson is as reliable as ever. Donald Crombie's direction, however, is uninspired. JF

Helen Morse *Caddie* • Takis Emmanuel *Peter* • Jack Thompson *Ted* • Jacki Weaver *Josie* • Melissa Jaffer *Leslie* • Ron Blanchard *Bill* • Deborah Kounnas *Ann Marsh aged 2* ■ *Dir* Donald Crombie • *Scr* Joan Long, from the autobiography by "Carrie"

The Caddy ★★ U
Comedy 1953 · US · BW · 95min

Relying on the popularity and appeal of Dean Martin and Jerry Lewis, this hotchpotch of a comedy is chiefly memorable for spawning the Oscar-nominated smash hit, *That's Amore*. The unfocused screenplay has Lewis caddying for Martin, with predictably chaotic consequences. Donna Reed and Barbara Bates are the boys' girls, and golfers Sam Snead and Ben Hogan put in appearances. RK

Jerry Lewis *Harvey Miller* • Dean Martin *Joe Anthony* • Donna Reed *Kathy Taylor* • Barbara Bates *Lisa* • Joseph Calleia *Papa Anthony* •

Clinton Sundberg *Charles* • Howard Smith *Golf official* • Marshall Thompson *Bruce Reeber* ■ *Dir* Norman Taurog • *Scr* Danny Arnold

Caddyshack ★★★ 15
Comedy 1980 · US · Colour · 93min

This wonderfully crass comedy from director Harold Ramis breezes along in a cheerfully tasteless manner. Loud-mouth millionaire Rodney Dangerfield gets up snobbish Ted Knight's nose when he attempts to take over the golf club, setting the scene for a climactic contest on the links. Bill Murray nearly steals the show as a psychopathic groundsman continuing a running battle with the club's resident gophers. JF Violence, sex scenes, swearing, nudity. **DVD** **Blu**

Chevy Chase *Ty Webb* • Rodney Dangerfield *Al Czervik* • Ted Knight *Judge Smails* • Michael O'Keefe *Danny Noonan* • Bill Murray *Carl Spackler* • Sarah Holcomb *Maggie O'Hooligan* • Scott Colomby *Tony D'Annunzio* • Cindy Morgan *Lacey Underall* ■ *Dir* Harold Ramis • *Scr* Brian Doyle-Murray, Harold Ramis, Douglas Kenney

Caddyshack II ★ 15
Comedy 1988 · US · Colour · 93min

Take away some of the talent from the original – Bill Murray, Rodney Dangerfield, director Harold Ramis – and you're left with this mess. Here you have Jackie Mason as a self-made millionaire who decides to take revenge when he's refused membership to a country club. JB Swearing. **DVD**

Jackie Mason *Jack Hartounian* • Robert Stack *Chandler Young* • Dina Merrill *Cynthia Young* • Dyan Cannon *Elizabeth Pearce* • Jonathan Silverman *Harry* • Randy Quaid *Peter Blunt* • Chevy Chase *Ty Webb* • Dan Aykroyd *Captain Tom Everett* ■ *Dir* Allan Arkush • *Scr* Harold Ramis, Peter Torokvei

Cadillac Man ★★★ 15
Comedy drama 1990 · US · Colour · 93min

After his success with *Good Morning, Vietnam*, Robin Williams was still having difficulty finding another star vehicle equal to his talents when he accepted the lead in this comedy from Roger Donaldson. The role of the sleazy car salesman having a very bad day was not Williams's best career choice, but luckily his comedic skills give the film the life it needs. Also on hand to keep things going is Tim Robbins, playing a gun-toting husband who holds up the car lot. JB Swearing, violence, nudity. **DVD**

Robin Williams *Joey O'Brien* • Tim Robbins *Larry* • Pamela Reed *Tina O'Brien* • Fran Drescher *Joy Munchack* • Zack Norman *Harry Munchack* • Annabella Sciorra *Donna* • Lori Petty *Lila* • Paul Guilfoyle (2) *Little Jack Turgeon* • Bill Nelson *Big Jack Turgeon* ■ *Dir* Roger Donaldson • *Scr* Ken Friedman

Cadillac Ranch ★★ 15
Comedy 1996 · US · Colour · 98min

Three sisters hit the road with some stolen loot in a muddled journey made palatable by likeable performances from Suzy Amis, Renee Humphrey and Caroleen Feeney. Lisa Gottlieb's movie has plenty going on – and that's the problem. Female bonding, a hint of idealised romance, reminiscences about their criminal dad and a killer on their trail make this a recipe with too many ingredients. JC Swearing, violence, nudity.

Christopher Lloyd *Wood Grimes* • Suzy Amis *CJ Crowley* • Caroleen Feeney *Frances Crowley* • Renee Humphrey *Mary Katherine Crowley* • Jim Metzler *Travis Crowley* ■ *Dir* Lisa Gottlieb • *Scr* Jennifer Cecil

Cadillac Records ★★★ 15
Musical biographical drama
2008 · US · Colour · 104min

This glossy musical drama charts the fortunes of the pioneering Chicago-based blues and rock 'n' roll record label Chess Records, during the 1950s and 60s. With a roster of stars that includes Muddy Waters, Chuck Berry and Etta James, the studio earned its nickname from owner Leonard Chess (Adrien Brody) giving his artists sleek new cars in lieu of royalty payments. But writer/director Darnell Martin rarely scratches below the surface of the

C

company's dubious accounting, and addresses the racial tensions of the period in a similarly piecemeal fashion. Though Beyoncé Knowles sizzles across the screen as the feisty but fragile James, it's Jeffrey Wright's beefy portrayal of Waters that gives the story its true heart. TeS **DVD**

Adrien Brody *Leonard Chess* • Jeffrey Wright *Muddy Waters* • Gabrielle Union *Geneva Wade* • Columbus Short *Little Walter* • Cedric the Entertainer *Willie Dixon* • Emmanuelle Chriqui *Revetta Chess* • Eamonn Walker *Howlin' Wolf* • Mos Def *Chuck Berry* • Beyoncé Knowles *Etta James* ■ *Dir/Scr* Darnell Martin

Caesar and Cleopatra ★★ U
Historical drama 1945 · UK · Colour · 122min

Legend has it that Hungarian producer Gabriel Pascal managed to convince George Bernard Shaw he was the only person who could do justice to the great man's plays. Unfortunately, Pascal wasn't content to be merely producer here: he also directed, with astounding ineptitude.There's no denying the Technicolor is splendid, but, despite the spirited efforts of Claude Rains and Vivien Leigh as the titular couple, there's no sexual chemistry at all. TS **DVD**

Vivien Leigh *Cleopatra* • Claude Rains *Caesar* • Stewart Granger *Apollodorus* • Flora Robson *Ftatateeta* • Francis L Sullivan *Pothinus* • Basil Sydney *Rufio* • Cecil Parker *Britannus* • Raymond Lovell *Lucius Septimius* • Antony Eustrel [Anthony Eustrel] *Achillas* • Ernest Thesiger *Theodotus* • Anthony Harvey *Ptolemy* ■ *Dir* Gabriel Pascal • *Scr* Majorie Deans, from the play by George Bernard Shaw

Caesar Must Die ★★★ 12A
Prison documentary drama 2012 · It · BW and Colour · 76min

In Rome's notorious Rebibbia prison, theatre director Fabio Cavalli prepares to stage a production of *Julius Caesar* with inmates. Film directors Paolo and Vittorio Taviani capture the action in colour scenes to bookend their otherwise monochrome Golden Bear-winning documentary, which explores themes of honour, brotherhood and guilt. These have a dual resonance with his cast, most of whom are incarcerated for Mafia-related crimes. Some of the confidences spoken to camera sound scripted, while scenes shot in cavernous rooms and the open air diminish the claustrophobic mood, but the Tavianis do capture the tragedy's redemptive effect with rare acuity and compassion. DP Italian +subtitles. Swearing.

Cosimo Rega *Cassio* • Salvatore Striano *Bruto* • Giovanni Arcuri *Cesare* • Antonio Frasca *Marcantonio* • Juan Dario Bonetti *Decio* ■ *Dir* Paolo Taviani, Vittorio Taviani • *Scr* Paolo & Vittorio Taviani, from the play *Julius Caesar* by William Shakespeare

Café de Flore ★★★★★ 15
Romantic drama 2011 · Can/Fr · Colour · 120min

Haunting and heartbreaking, director Jean-Marc Vallée's romantic drama is an electrifying multilayered experience. The struggle faced by a mother of a boy with Down's syndrome in 1969 Paris (a remarkable performance from Vanessa Paradis) is interwoven with the globetrotting life of a present-day Montreal DJ (singer/songwriter Kevin Parent) whose ex-wife just can't let go of her soulmate. Both intriguing stories eventually connect with a shattering genre-bending assurance that asks big questions about the power of love, parenting skills and the paranormal. Just like in Vallée's breakthrough hit *CRAZY*, music is a vital element to the mix, with Matthew Herbert's title track and selections from Sigur Rós, the Cure and Pink Floyd fitting perfectly with Vallée's images. AJ In French. Swearing, sex scenes, drug abuse, nudity. **DVD**

Vanessa Paradis *Jacqueline* • Kevin Parent *Antoine Godin* • Hélène Florent *Carole* • Evelyne Brochu *Rose* • Marin Gerrier *Laurent* ■ *Dir/Scr* Jean-Marc Vallée

Café Flesh ★★ 18
Cult erotic drama 1982 · US · Colour · 69min

Although only a classy porn movie with artistic pretensions, Stephen Sayadian's cult classic (directed under his pseudonym Rinse Dream) is extraordinarily prophetic when viewed in an Aids-related context. Well-made and acted for a picture that features only one heavy-duty porn queen (Michelle Bauer, aka Pia Snow), initial intrigue in the plot soon wears off as genre clichés take over. AJ

Andrew Nichols [Andy Nichols] *Max Melodramatic* • Paul McGibboney *Nick* • Pia Snow [Michelle Bauer] *Lana* • Marie Sharp *Angel* • Dondi Bastone *Spike* ■ *Dir* Rinse Dream [Stephen Sayadian] • *Scr* Rinse Dream [Stephen Sayadian], Herbert W Day [Jerry Stahl], FX Pope [Stephen Sayadian] • *Cinematographer* FX Pope [Stephen Sayadian]

Café Lumière ★★★★ U
Drama 2003 · Jpn/Tai · Colour · 103min

This exquisite drama was made to commemorate the centenary of the birth of director Yasujiro Ozu. Hou Hsiao-Hsien not only replicates the style of the Japanese auteur, he also captures the essence of Ozu's deceptive simplicity. At the heart of the story is the delightful relationship between writer Yo Hitoto and train buff Tadanobu Asano. So it comes as a surprise to learn that she is pregnant by the Taiwanese boyfriend she has no desire to marry. Hou recalls Ozu's preoccupation with the urban landscape, but he also explores his key themes, including the tension between parents and children and the absence of effective communication in the modern world. DP Japanese +subtitles. **DVD**

Yo Hitoto *Yoko Inoue* • Tadanobu Asano *Hajime Takeuchi* • Masato Hagiwara *Seiji* • Kimiko Yo *Yoko's stepmother* • Nenji Kobayashi *Yoko's father* ■ *Dir* Hou Hsiao-Hsien • *Scr* Hou Hsiao-Hsien, Chu Tien-wen

Café Metropole ★★★
Romantic comedy 1937 · US · BW · 83min

A complicated plot involving the suave, less than honest, proprietor of a Paris restaurant, a penniless Ivy Leaguer who gets into trouble over a hefty gambling debt to the aforesaid gentleman, an American heiress whom the handsome gambler courts in the guise of Russian royalty, and a refugee waiter who is the real prince, makes for a jolly romp. Tyrone Power and Loretta Young are gorgeous a romantic duo as one could wish for, and are surrounded by a first-class supporting cast, all of whom bring the requisite light touch to a pleasingly amiable and sophisticated script. RK

Loretta Young *Laura Ridgeway* • Tyrone Power *Alexis Paneiev/Alexander Brown* • Adolphe Menjou *Monsieur Victor Lobard* • Gregory Ratoff *Paul* • Charles Winninger *Joseph Ridgeway* • Helen Westley *Margaret Ridgeway* ■ *Dir* Edward H Griffith • *Scr* Jacques Deval, from a story by Gregory Ratoff

Café Society ★★★ 12A
Romantic comedy 2016 · US · Colour · 96min

Woody Allen uses his latest film to indulge his affection for 1930s LA. Jesse Eisenberg stars as a young New Yorker who heads west to Hollywood to work for his uncle (Steve Carell), a major talent agent. But Eisenberg falls for his PA, unaware of the consequences of pursuing her. The set-up is light and fun, LA made luminous by Vittorio Storaro's magnificent camerawork. As unusually for Allen, things simply trundle to a close, ending on a morose note of arty ambiguity that smacks more of indecision than intent. DW

Steve Carell *Phil Stern* • Jesse Eisenberg *Bobby* • Kristen Stewart *Vonnie* • Blake Lively *Veronica* ■ *Dir/Scr* Woody Allen • *Cinematographer* Vittorio Storaro

Cage ★★★ 18
Action drama 1989 · US · Colour · 96min

Incredible Hulk star Lou Ferrigno gives his best performance in this violent movie. He and Reb Brown play Vietnam veterans who run a Los Angeles bar in an area where

fixed, no-holds-barred fights are the latest illegal money-spinner. Ferrigno is conned into entering the bare-knuckle "cage" and putting his life on the line for Chinatown mobsters. Sleazy, obnoxiously racist and nasty it may be, but Lang Elliott's carnage caper delivers the goods in bloody excitement. A less successful sequel followed in 1994. AJ

Lou Ferrigno *Billy Thomas* • Reb Brown *Scott Monroe* • Michael Dante *Tony Baccola* • Al Leong *Tiger Joe* • Mike Moroff *Mario* • James Shigeta *Tim Lum Yin* • Marilyn Tokuda *Morgan Garrett* • Branscombe Richmond *Diablo* ■ *Dir* Lang Elliott • *Scr* Hugh Kelley

La Cage aux Folles ★★★★ 15
Comedy 1978 · Fr/It · Colour · 92min

One of the most successful foreign films ever released, this frilly farce led to two sequels, a Broadway hit musical and a Hollywood remake starring Robin Williams (1996's *The Birdcage*). It's the remarkably inoffensive and non-threatening tale of what happens when the gay owners of a St Tropez transvestite club meet the straight parents of the daughter their heterosexual son (don't ask!) wants to marry. Cue much mistaken identity humour, mainly revolving around the exaggerated effeminacy of brilliant Michel Serrault as the highly strung diva. AJ French +subtitles. **DVD**

Michel Serrault *Albin, "Zaza"* • Ugo Tognazzi *Renato* • Michel Galabru *Charrier* • Claire Maurier *Simone* • Remi Laurent *Laurent* • Benny Luke *Jacob* • Carmen Scarpitta *Madame Charrier* • Luisa Maneri *Andrea* ■ *Dir* Edouard Molinaro • *Scr* Marcello Danon, Edouard Molinaro, Francis Veber, Jean Poiret, from the play by Jean Poiret

La Cage aux Folles II ★★ 12
Comedy 1980 · Fr/It · Colour · 95min

Michel Serrault and Ugo Tognazzi return as the bickering lovers in this so-so sequel to the 1978 camp classic. Complete with spies, corpses and secret microfilms, the espionage elements of the plot get in the way of the much more amusing character farce. However, director Edouard Molinaro makes the most of the unlikely situations, especially when Serrault has to pretend to be Tognazzi's bride to fool the latter's ultra-conservative mother. DP French +subtitles. **DVD**

Michel Serrault *Albin, "Zaza"* • Ugo Tognazzi *Renato* • Marcel Bozzuffi *Broca* • Paola Borboni *Signora Baldi* • Giovanni Vettorazzo *Milan* • Glauco Onorato *Luigi* • Roberto Bisacco *Ralph* • Benny Luke *Jacob* • Michel Galabru *Charrier* ■ *Dir* Edouard Molinaro • *Scr* Jean Poiret, Francis Veber, Marcello Danon, from characters by Jean Poiret

La Cage aux Folles III: "Elles" Se Marient ★ 15
Comedy 1985 · Fr/It · Colour · 87min

The second sequel to the popular French farce *La Cage aux Folles* finds drag queen nightclub owner Michel Serrault forced to sire a child so he can inherit a fortune. His partner Ugo Tognazzi can only stand back and watch the shrieking and high camp tantrums that this outrageous ultimatum precipitates. It's all too strident, loud and silly. AJ French +subtitles.

Michel Serrault *Albin, "Zaza"* • Ugo Tognazzi *Renato* • Michel Galabru *Charrier* • Benny Luke *Jacob* • Stéphane Audran *Matrimonia* • Antonella Interlenghi *Cindy* ■ *Dir* Georges Lautner • *Scr* Philippe Nicaud, Christine Carère, Marcello Danon, Jacques Audiard, Michel Audiard, Georges Lautner, Gérard Lamballe, from a story by Philippe Nicaud, Christine Carère, Marcello Danon, from characters by Jean Poiret

Cage of Gold ★★
Crime drama 1950 · UK · BW · 83min

Basil Dearden directs this overwrought melodrama, with David Farrar cast somewhat against type as an RAF rogue who, having cheated on Jean Simmons with French singer Madeleine Lebeau during the war, deserts the pregnant Simmons shortly after their marriage in order to smuggle jewels for Paris club owner Herbert Lom. Too many underdrawn characters flit in and

out of the increasingly preposterous plot. DP

Jean Simmons *Judith Moray* • David Farrar *Bill Brennan* • James Donald *Alan Keane* • Herbert Lom *Rahman* • Madeleine Lebeau *Marie* • Maria Mauban *Antoinette* • Bernard Lee *Inspector Grey* ■ *Dir* Basil Dearden • *Scr* Jack Whittingham, Paul Stein, from a story by Jack Whittingham

A Cage of Nightingales ★★★ U
Musical drama 1945 · Fr · BW · 88min

A young working man (Noël-Noël) writes a novel about his life, which includes a spell in a reformatory. His past is revealed to his girlfriend (Micheline Francey) when she reads the book; we see the tale unfold in flashback as she does so. A neat blend of past and present, this modest film from Jean Dréville is a truthful, sober and understanding picture of juvenile delinquency, offering excellent performances and a positive message. RK French +subtitles.

Noël-Noël *Clément* • Micheline Francey *Martine* • George Biscot *Raymond* • René Génin *Maxence* • René Blancard *Rachin* • Marquerite Ducouret *Mme Martine* ■ *Dir* Jean Dréville • *Scr* Noël-Noël, René Wheeler, Georges Chaperot

Caged ★★★
Melodrama 1950 · US · BW · 91min

An unglamorous (and rightly Oscar-nominated) Eleanor Parker stars as the innocent victim who grows tougher after exposure to the brutality of life on the inside in this typical Warner Bros prison melodrama. There's an interesting censor-circumventing prison matron who clearly displays lesbian tendencies, played convincingly by Hope Emerson. It's a slow, absorbing work, and its very drabness renders it rather tedious. TS

Eleanor Parker *Marie Allen* • Agnes Moorehead *Ruth Benton* • Ellen Corby *Emma* • Hope Emerson *Evelyn Harper* • Betty Garde *Kitty Stark* • Jan Sterling *Smoochie* • Lee Patrick *Elvira Powell* • Jane Darwell *Isolation Matron* • Sheila Stevens *Helen* ■ *Dir* John Cromwell • *Scr* Virginia Kellogg, Bernard C Schoenfeld

Caged Heat ★★★ 18
Prison drama 1974 · US · Colour · 73min

Jonathan Demme's debut as writer/director bears all the hallmarks of his mentor, exploitation maestro Roger Corman, who was making this kind of "babes-behind-bars" flick back in the late 1950s. Horror icon Barbara Steele returns to the screen after a five-year absence to play the sadistic wheelchair-using governor, a role that had been written specially for her. There's plenty of humour to leaven the story of naive Juanita Brown's struggle against the system, but the biggest laughs come from the 1970s outfits. DP Violence, swearing, nudity.

Juanita Brown *Maggie* • Roberta Collins *Belle Tyson* • Erica Gavin *Jacqueline Wilson* • Barbara Steele *Mcqueen* • Ella Reid *Pandora Williams* ■ *Dir/Scr* Jonathan Demme

Cagney & Lacey ★★★★ 15
Police drama 1981 · US · Colour · 91min

This is the pilot of the hugely popular TV series about two lady cops, here played by Tyne Daly (who continued her role in the series) and Loretta Swit (who was replaced by Meg Foster and, subsequently, Sharon Gless). As many fans will remember, the series got a bit ropey in later years, but this pilot is a reminder of how great *Cagney & Lacey* was in the beginning. Daly looks youthful (well, it was 1981) and Swit is suitably tough-as-nails as her partner. One can only assume Gless was brought in to be a younger, more glamorous version of Chris Cagney when the producers realised the series would run for almost a decade. JB

Loretta Swit *Christine Cagney* • Tyne Daly *Mary Beth Lacey* • Al Waxman *Detective Samuels* • Joan Copeland *Mrs Friedlander* • Ronald Hunter *Harvey* ■ *Dir* Ted Post • *Scr* Barbara Avedon

Cahill, United States Marshal ★★★ 15

Western 1973 · US · Colour · 97min

Director Andrew V McLaglen could always be depended upon to hammer out gruff, good-looking westerns from the most unpromising material. Here he saddles up John Wayne for a parable on the extent to which modern youth had been corrupted while America was away solving the problems of the world. As a political statement, it's reactionary and naive, and the Duke looks every day of his 66 years as the absentee father out to teach George Kennedy a lesson for enticing his sons into crime. DP Violence. *DVD*

John Wayne *JD Cahill* • George Kennedy *Abe Fraser* • Gary Grimes *Danny Cahill* • Neville Brand *Lightfoot* • Clay O'Brien *Billy Joe Cahill* • Marie Windsor *Mrs Green* • Morgan Paull *Struther* • Dan Vadis *Brownie* • Royal Dano *MacDonald* • Scott Walker (1) *Ben Tildy* ■ *Dir* Andrew V McLaglen • *Scr* Harry Julian Fink, Rita M Fink, from a story by Barney Slater

The Caiman ★★★ 12A

Comedy drama 2006 · It · Colour · 112min

Italian film-maker Nanni Moretti (*The Son's Room*) wrestles with a mix of political satire, family friction and showbiz shenanigans in this unwieldy comedy drama. Fortunately, veteran actor Silvio Orlando has the charisma needed as Bruno, a washed-up producer attempting to stage a comeback with a scathing film about Silvio Berlusconi (then prime minister of Italy), believing the project could save both his company and his failing marriage. The strands just don't weave together satisfactorily, instead creating a tangle of half-finished political musings. Yet despite these flaws, The Caiman remains a colourful, warmly drawn portrait of a man in the jaws of a midlife crisis. SP Italian +subtitles. Some violence, sexual references.

Silvio Orlando *Bruno* • Margherita Buy *Paola* • Daniele Rampello *Andrea* • Giacomo Passarelli *Giacomo* • Jasmine Trinca *Teresa* • Cecilia Dazzi *Luisa* • Michele Placido *Marco Pulici* ■ *Dir* Nanni Moretti • *Scr* Nanni Moretti, Francesco Piccolo, Federica Pontremoli, from a story by Moretti, Heidrun Schleef • *Cinematographer* Arnaldo Catinari

Cain and Mabel ★★ U

Musical comedy 1936 · US · BW · 90min

This is the penultimate movie of talented star Marion Davies, best known today for being the mistress and protégée of newspaper magnate William Randolph Hearst. It's an unfortunate way to remember the delightful actress, here woefully miscast as a Broadway star pretending to romance a boxer for publicity. Since the heavyweight is played by Clark Gable, Davies has trouble holding the screen. There's a clever cast, some witty dialogue and a production number of such vulgarity that it takes the breath away. TS

Marion Davies *Mabel O'Dare* • Clark Gable *Larry Cain* • Allen Jenkins *Dodo* • Roscoe Karns *Aloysius K Reilly* • Walter Catlett *Jake Sherman* • David Carlyle [Robert Paige] *Ronny Cauldwell* • Hobart Cavanaugh *Milo* ■ *Dir* Lloyd Bacon • *Scr* Laird Doyle, Earl Baldwin (uncredited), from a story by HC Witwer

The Caine Mutiny ★★★★ U

Drama 1954 · US · Colour · 119min

This first-rate wartime drama has an Oscar-nominated Humphrey Bogart playing against type as Queeg, the martinet captain of a US minesweeper during the Second World War. His arrival causes a stir among its war-weary crew (including Fred MacMurray and Lee Marvin) but mockery soon turns to outright mutiny when Van Johnson's second officer relieves a panicking Queeg of his command. Bogart gives a mighty performance as the snivelling Queeg, and yet he still arouses our sympathy. JA *DVD* *Blu-ray*

Humphrey Bogart *Captain Queeg* • José Ferrer *Lt Barney Greenwald* • Van Johnson *Lt Steve Maryk* • Fred MacMurray *Lt Tom Keefer* • Robert Francis *Ensign Willie Keith* • Tom Tully *Captain DeVriess* • EG Marshall *Lt Cmdr Challee* • Lee

Marvin *Meatball* ■ *Dir* Edward Dmytryk • *Scr* Stanley Roberts, from Herman Wouk's novel/play • *Music* Max Steiner

The Caine Mutiny Court-Martial ★★★ U

Courtroom drama 1988 · US · Colour · 99min

This 1988 TV-movie adaptation of The Caine Mutiny is one of Robert Altman's better efforts from the 1980s, as he strips away the on-board melodrama of the Hollywood version and focuses purely on the court martial at the heart of the tale. Jeff Daniels is suitably upright as the officer accused of mutiny. Most of the "action" is confined to the courtroom and although it's no 12 Angry Men, Altman expertly builds the tension and creates an engrossing drama replete with his signature use of naturalistic, overlapping dialogue. JA

Eric Bogosian *Lt Barney Greenwald* • Jeff Daniels *Lt Steve Maryk* • Brad Davis *Lt Commander Philip Francis Queeg* • Peter Gallagher *Lt Commander John Challee* ■ *Dir* Robert Altman • *Scr* Herman Wouk, from his play

Cairo ★

Crime drama 1962 · US/UK · BW · 90min

This is a sand-blown remake of just about every caper movie ever made. George Sanders plays a master thief who decides to steal Tutankhamen's jewels from the Cairo museum, so he forms a gang of rogues to execute his plan. Directed by Wolf Rilla, this is a real letdown with some very listless patches of narrative. TH

George Sanders *Major Pickering* • Richard Johnson *Ali* • Faten Hamama *Amina* • John Meillon *Willy* • Ahmed Mazhar *Kerim* • Eric Pohlmann *Nicodemos* • Walter Rilla *Kuchuk* • Salah Nazmi *Commandant* ■ *Dir* Wolf Rilla • *Scr* Joan Scott, from the novel The Asphalt Jungle by WR Burnett

Cairo Road ★★ U

Crime drama 1950 · UK · BW · 86min

Eric Portman stars as an Egyptian detective and Laurence Harvey is his ambitious assistant in this British B-movie about drug smuggling. While Portman rather overplays his part, Harvey is fascinating to watch as a scene-stealing star on the rise. Despite some location sequences (a rarity for a low budget production), the action is fairly slow and routine. AT

Eric Portman *Colonel Youssef Bey* • Laurence Harvey *Lieutenant Mourad* • Maria Mauban *Marie* • Anna Michelis *Camelia* • Harold Lang *Humble* • Coco Aslan *Lombardi* ■ *Dir* David MacDonald • *Scr* Robert Westerby

Cairo Station ★★★★

Drama 1958 · Egy · BW · 86min

Brimming with life and adroitly balancing harsh reality with glimmers of optimism, this drama established Egyptian director Youssef Chahine on the international stage. He also plays the key role of the disabled news vendor whose obsession with soft drinks seller Hind Rustum (herself besotted with porter Farid Shawqi) precipitates a tragic accident. Exploring the impact of western ideas on cultural and religious tradition, as well as the dire poverty in which many of the station workers exist, Chahine exploits his location to suggest a country in flux. DP Arabic +subtitles.

Youssef Chahine *Kenaoui* • Hind Rostum *Hanouma* • Farid Shawqi *Abou Serib* ■ *Dir* Youssef Chahine • *Scr* Abdel Hay Adib

Cake ★★ 15

Drama 2015 · US · Colour · 97min

Jennifer Aniston (all greasy hair and grey cardigans) plays against type here as a woman suffering a bad back and addicted to painkillers following a car accident. Aniston proves she doesn't have to be cute and ingratiating to be engaging, but her deadpan retorts in therapy are a thin veil for what is essentially a saccharine confection of clichés that are hard to swallow. SP In English, Spanish. *DVD* *Blu-ray*

Jennifer Aniston *Claire Bennett* • Adriana Barraza *Silvana* • Felicity Huffman *Annette* • William H Macy *Leonard* • Anna Kendrick *Nina* • Sam Worthington *Roy* ■ *Dir* Daniel Barnz • *Scr* Patrick Tobin

Cal ★★★★ 15

Romantic thriller 1984 · UK · Colour · 98min

Pat O'Connor made his feature debut with this adaptation by Bernard MacLaverty of his own novel. At times treading a mite too carefully along the sectarian divide, this is nevertheless a credible and often compelling look at how the Troubles intrude upon what should be the events of everyday life. There's a genuine warmth in the relationship between widow Helen Mirren (who won best actress at Cannes) and John Lynch, the getaway driver on the IRA mission that resulted in the death of her RUC husband. But the tension amid which their romance blossoms is also well conveyed by O'Connor and his impressive supporting cast. DP

Helen Mirren *Marcella* • John Lynch *Cal* • Donal McCann *Shamie* • John Kavanagh *Skeffington* • Ray McAnally *Cyril Dunlop* • Stevan Rimkus *Crilly* ■ *Dir* Pat O'Connor • *Scr* Bernard MacLaverty, from his novel

Calamity Jane ★★★★★ U

Musical comedy western 1953 · US · Colour · 96min

The opening of this wonderful musical is pure pleasure, as Doris Day rides the Deadwood stage across the screen and into our hearts. This isn't the real Wild West, of course, but Warner Bros Technicolor riposte to MGM's Annie Get Your Gun: the studio even poached the same leading man, Howard Keel, who is excellent here as Wild Bill Hickok. The score is a treat, but the strength of the movie is Day giving a marvellous musical comedy performance in her finest role, creating a warm, robust yet tender character; just marvel at her timing in Just Blew In from the Windy City, while Secret Love, recorded by Day in just one take, won the best song Oscar and is beautifully staged by choreographer Jack Donohue. TS *DVD*

Doris Day *Calamity Jane* • Howard Keel *Wild Bill Hickok* • Allyn McLerie [Allyn Ann McLerie] *Katie Brown* • Philip Carey *Lt Gilmartin* • Dick Wesson *Francis Fryer* • Paul Harvey *Henry Miller* • Chubby Johnson *Rattlesnake* • Gale Robbins *Adelaide Adams* ■ *Dir* David Butler • *Scr* James O'Hanlon • *Music* Sammy Fain • *Lyrics* Paul Francis Webster

Calamity Jane and Sam Bass ★★ U

Western 1949 · US · Colour · 85min

Martha Jane Burke, Calamity Jane of western lore, was played by Jean Arthur for Cecil B DeMille in The Plainsman (1936), and would soon be immortalised by a ripsnortin' Doris Day in the Warner Bros musical. But here she's incarnated by exotic Yvonne De Carlo in a routine western that plays fast and loose with the facts. Former radio star Howard Duff is cast as the romantic interest, outlaw Sam Bass, whose character is whitewashed beyond recognition. TS

Yvonne De Carlo *Calamity Jane* • Howard Duff *Sam Bass* • Dorothy Hart *Katharine Egan* • Willard Parker *Sheriff Will Egan* • Norman Lloyd *Jim Murphy* • Lloyd Bridges *Joel Collins* • Marc Lawrence (1) *Dean* ■ *Dir* George Sherman • *Scr* Maurice Geraghty, Melvin Levy, from a story by George Sherman

The Calcium Kid ★ 15

Sports comedy 2003 · UK/Fr/US · Colour · 84min

Orlando Bloom plays a milkman-turned-boxer in this dire comedy. The daft premise has Bloom so fond of the white stuff he delivers that his bones have become rock hard as a result. When Bloom accidentally knocks out Britain's top challenger in a sparring match, he becomes the next in line for a shot at the world title. DA Swearing. *DVD*

Orlando Bloom *Jimmy Connelly* • Omid Djalili *Herbie Bush* • Rafe Spall *Stan* • Tamer Hassan *Pete Wright* • Michael Peña [Michael Pena] *Jose*

Mendez • Michael Lerner *Artie Cohen* • Billie Piper *Angel* ■ *Dir* Alex De Rakoff • *Scr* Alex De Rakoff, Raymond Friel, Derek Boyle

Calculated Risk ★

Crime drama 1963 · UK · BW · 71min

The only thing of interest about this tatty little drama is a cameo from Warren Mitchell as a dodgy market trader who sells William Lucas the explosives he needs for his bank job. The story isn't a bad one – about a gang that comes across an unexploded Second World War bomb while tunnelling into a vault – but Norman Harrison directs with no sense of suspense. DP Swearing.

John Rutland *Kip* • William Lucas *Steve* • Dilys Watling *Julie* • Warren Mitchell *Simmie* • Shay Gorman *Dodo* • Terence Cooper *Nodge* ■ *Dir* Norman Harrison • *Scr* Edwin Richfield

Calcutta ★★★

Thriller 1947 · US · BW · 83min

Clean-cut, good-looking Alan Ladd and pug-faced William Bendix, his frequent on-screen partner, trawl the threatening back alleys, colourful bazaars and sleazy hotels of India's teeming city (built on the Paramount backlot). There Ladd's search for whoever killed his friend gets them entangled with the underworld and its questionable inhabitants. The result is an old-fashioned, low-budget formula thriller, but still entertaining viewing. RK

Alan Ladd *Neale Gordon* • William Bendix *Pedro Blake* • Gail Russell *Virginia Moore* • June Duprez *Marina* • Lowell Gilmore *Eric Lasser* • Edith King *Mrs Smith* • Paul Singh *Malik* • Gavin Muir *Kendricks* ■ *Dir* John Farrow • *Scr* Seton I Miller

The Calendar ★★

Thriller 1948 · UK · BW · 79min

British cinema was heavily dependent on the mysteries of Edgar Wallace in the early talkie era. Few of these creaky thrillers were ever remade, until someone at Gainsborough Productions felt the need to bring this veritable stage warhorse under starter's orders for a second time. It's all clipped accents and impossibly earnest hamming from the off, as trainer Greta Gynt tries to prove that owner John McCallum didn't throw a race to improve the odds of his horse at a later Ascot meeting. DP

Greta Gynt *Wenda* • John McCallum *Garry* • Raymond Lovell *Willie* • Sonia Holm *Mollie* • Leslie Dwyer *Hillcott* • Charles Victor *John Dory* • Felix Aylmer *Lord Forlingham* • Diana Dors *Hawkins* ■ *Dir* Arthur Crabtree • *Scr* Geoffrey Kerr, from the play by Edgar Wallace

Calendar ★★★

Drama 1993 · Can/Arm/Ger · BW and Colour · 75min

This fascinating treatise on communication, appreciation and the limits of the static image co-stars Armenian-Canadian director Atom Egoyan and real-life partner Arsinée Khanjian as a couple who drift apart during a visit to Armenia to photograph churches for a calendar. As one would expect of this most inventive of film-makers, Egoyan isn't content simply to tell his story through flashbacks, but uses video footage to recall the breakdown of his relationship and lush colour film to show how his life since then has been dominated by disappointing dinner dates and painful memories. Compelling viewing. DP

Arsinée Khanjian *Translator* • Ashot Adamian *Driver* • Atom Egoyan *Photographer* ■ *Dir/Scr* Atom Egoyan

Calendar Girl ★★ 15

Period comedy drama 1993 · US · Colour · 87min

TV heart-throb Jason Priestley gives a surprisingly understated performance here. Set in the early 1960s, the story follows the adventures of a trio of teenagers who leave their small town to go to Hollywood to meet their idol Marilyn Monroe. Although it's marred by some Animal House-style slapstick, it remains an affectionate coming-of-age comedy. JF Swearing, drug abuse, nudity.

Jason Priestley *Roy Darpinian* • Gabriel Olds *Ned Bleuer* • Jerry O'Connell *Scott "The Dood" Foreman* • Joe Pantoliano *Uncle Harvey Darpinian* • Kurt Fuller *Arturo Gallo* • Stephen Tobolowsky *Antonio Gallo* ■ *Dir* John Whitesell • *Scr* Paul W Shapiro

Calendar Girl Murders ★★★ 15

Crime thriller   1984 · US · Colour · 91min

A chance to see Sharon Stone on the early road to stardom in this steamy tale of a serial killer with a penchant for bumping off centrefolds. Detective Tom Skerritt struggles successfully to keep a straight face in the eye of a storm of hoary clichés, as the meticulous killer works his way through the months like an over-zealous accountant. It's saved by a racy, stops-out dénouement. SH

Tom Skerritt *Dan Stoner* • Sharon Stone *Cassie Bascomb* • Barbara Bosson *Nancy Stoner* • Robert Beltran *Mooney* • Pat Corley *Tony* • Robert Morse *Nat Couray* • Robert Culp *Richard Trainor* ■ *Dir* William A Graham • *Scr* Scott Swanton, Gregory S Dinallo, from a story by Gregory S Dinallo

Calendar Girls ★★★★ 12

Biographical comedy drama
2003 · UK/US · Colour · 103min

Often compared to *The Full Monty*, Nigel Cole's film is actually less broad in its comedy and much gentler in tone. It is the very genteel nature of the North Yorkshire Women's Institute milieu that provides the film with its "high concept" (middle-aged women strip for charity). While the pivotal shooting of the calendar itself provides comic gold (during which the spare-part husbands gather in the pub like expectant fathers – a lovely touch), there is a moving, fallible humanity to the performances that keeps the whole thing this side of farce. Julie Walters, Helen Mirren and Linda Bassett shine from a spotless cast of "ladies of a certain age". AC *DVD*

Helen Mirren *Chris* • Julie Walters *Annie* • Penelope Wilton *Ruth* • Annette Crosbie *Jessie* • Celia Imrie *Celia* • Linda Bassett *Cora* • Georgie Glen *Kathy* • Angela Curran *May* • Rosalind March *Trudy* • Ciaran Hinds *Rod* • John Alderton *John* • Philip Glenister *Lawrence* • John-Paul MacLeod *Jem* • Geraldine James *Marie* • John Fortune *Frank* ■ *Dir* Nigel Cole • *Scr* Juliette Towhidi, Tim Firth • *Cinematographer* Ashley Rowe

California ★★

Western   1946 · US · Colour · 98min

This routine Gold Rush western has Ray Milland drinking too much and Barbara Stanwyck shuffling stacked decks as the woman with a history. Directed by John Farrow in his customary no-nonsense manner, it breezes along nicely. Paramount lavished bright-as-a-button Technicolor on it, as well as a couple of songs mimed by Stanwyck and a good supporting cast. AT

Ray Milland *Jonathan Trumbo* • Barbara Stanwyck *Lily Bishop* • Barry Fitzgerald *Michael Fabian* • George Coulouris *Pharoah Coffin* • Albert Dekker *Mr Pike* • Anthony Quinn *Don Luis* ■ *Dir* John Farrow • *Scr* Frank Butler, Theodore Strauss, from the story by Boris Ingster

The California Dolls ★★ 18

Comedy drama   1981 · US · Colour · 108min

Although this dismal final effort from Robert Aldrich purports to be about women's wrestling, it's actually a shameless plug for MGM's Grand Hotel in Reno, Nevada, the glitzy casino where much of the action takes place. What the picture needed was a light satirical touch, not Aldrich's heavy-handed approach which tends to leer when it should laugh. Even so, Peter Falk as the girls' manager and Burt Young as the shady promoter provide the few seedy element and provide the few moments of interest. AT

Peter Falk *Harry* • Vicki Frederick *Iris* • Laurene Landon *Molly* • Burt Young *Eddie Cisco* • Tracy Reed *Diane* • Ursaline Bryant-King *June* • Richard Jaeckel *Reno Referee* ■ *Dir* Robert Aldrich • *Scr* Mel Frohman

California Dreamin' ★★★★ 15

Comedy drama   2007 · Rom · Colour · 148min

This tense, astute and often amusing fact-based satire stands as testament to the late director Cristian Nemescu. A genuine talent, Nemescu here explores the concept of freedom from the perspective of US soldiers en route to Kosovo in 1999, a corrupt Romanian stationmaster and factory workers who are protesting their exploitation by new capitalist bosses. The ensemble acting is uniformly impressive, but it's Nemescu himself who is the driving force, using restless, realist imagery to capture both eastern Europe's post-Communist confusion and America's arrogant assumption that it has the right to police global democracy. DP Romanian, English, Spanish, Italian +subtitles. *DVD*

Armand Assante *Captain Jones* • Jamie Elman *Sergeant David McLaren* • Razvan Vasilescu *Doiaru* • Maria Dinulescu *Monica* • Alex Margineanu [Alexandru Margineanu] *Andrei* ■ *Dir* Cristian Nemescu • *Scr* Catherine Linstrum, Cristian Nemescu, Tudor Voican

California Man ★★ PG

Comedy fantasy   1992 · US · Colour · 84min

This was an attempt to cash in on *Bill & Ted*-style comic capers, but by now Californian teen speak was becoming more irritating than funny. Sean Astin and Pauly Shore dig up a deep-frozen caveman (Brendan Fraser) and educate him in the ways of adolescent etiquette. Fraser makes for a pleasingly gormless hunk and there are a few amusing moments. Released in the USA as *Encino Man*. JF Drug abuse. *DVD*

Sean Astin *Dave Morgan* • Brendan Fraser *Link* • Pauly Shore *Stoney Brown* • Megan Ward *Robyn Sweeney* • Robin Tunney *Ella* • Michael DeLuise *Matt* • Patrick Van Horn *Phil* • Dalton James *Will* • Richard Masur *Mr Morgan* • Rose McGowan *Nora* ■ *Dir* Les Mayfield • *Scr* Shawn Schepps, from a story by Shawn Schepps, George Zaloom

California Split ★★★

Comedy drama   1974 · US · Colour · 108min

Robert Altman's off-the-wall insight into macho men is too wordy, but still has enough gambling action to hold the attention while leads Elliott Gould and George Segal drink themselves through casino-surfing romps. As the girls sidelined by the men's fixation with the tables, Ann Prentiss and Gwen Welles give as bad as they get but it's really the disintegration of the buddies' friendship that forms the core of a rewarding movie. TH

George Segal *Bill Denny* • Elliott Gould *Charlie Walters* • Ann Prentiss *Barbara Miller* • Gwen Welles *Susan Peters* • Edward Walsh *Lew* • Joseph Walsh *Sparkie* • Jay Fletcher *Robber* ■ *Dir* Robert Altman • *Scr* Joseph Walsh

California Straight Ahead ★★★ U

Action adventure   1937 · US · BW · 68min

This vintage chase movie – a kind of Depression-era precursor to *The Cannonball Run* – is made extremely watchable by the casting of John Wayne, trapped in a career no man's land in the years between *The Big Trail* and *Stagecoach*. Ignore the shaky back projection and enjoy the sight of Big John playing one of a pair of truckers engaged in dangerous rivalry. Director Arthur Lubin keeps it all going at a rate of knots. TS

John Wayne *Biff Smith* • Louise Latimer *Mary Porter* • Robert McWade *Corrigan* • Theodore von Eltz *James Gifford* • Tully Marshall *Harrison* • Emerson Treacy *Charlie Porter* ■ *Dir* Arthur Lubin • *Scr* Scott Darling, from a story by Herman Boxer

California Suite ★★★★ 15

Comedy   1978 · US · Colour · 98min

Neil Simon is at his most rapier-witted with this adaptation of his hit Broadway comedy, a classy confection of oddball sequences set in the up-market Beverly Hills Hotel. The cast is a blend of seasoned performers and acting heavyweights, all having a ball with Simon's quick-fire one-liners. The stand-out turns are from Walter Matthau and Elaine May, whose antics almost take the movie into the surreal, and Maggie Smith, who won the best supporting actress Oscar for her performance as, coincidentally, an actress preparing for the Academy Awards. SH Swearing. *DVD*

Alan Alda *Bill Warren* • Michael Caine *Sidney Cochran* • Bill Cosby *Dr Willis Panama* • Jane Fonda *Hannah Warren* • Walter Matthau *Marvin Michaels* • Elaine May *Millie Michaels* • Richard Pryor *Dr Chauncey Gump* • Maggie Smith *Diana Barrie* ■ *Dir* Herbert Ross • *Scr* Neil Simon, from his play

Caligula ★ 18

Historical drama   1979 · US/It · Colour · 156min

This purports to be a biographical drama about the infamous Roman emperor, but it's nothing more than toga-dropping soft porn. Malcolm McDowell glares balefully as the lustful, unhinged emperor, embarking on a sadistic road to destruction. Italian director Tinto Brass couldn't quite plumb the depths demanded, so extra scenes of titillation were allegedly added. TH Violence, sex scenes, nudity. *DVD* *BL*

Malcolm McDowell *Caligula* • Theresa Ann Savoy [Teresa Ann Savoy] *Drusilla* • Peter O'Toole *Tiberius* • John Gielgud *Nerva* • Helen Mirren *Caesonia* ■ *Dir* Tinto Brass • *Scr* Gore Vidal

The Call ★★ 15

Thriller   2013 · US · Colour · 93min

There is nothing wrong with the premise here: an emergency services operator (Halle Berry) finds herself in a race against time to locate a kidnapped teenage girl (Abigail Breslin) who has managed to dial 911 from the boot of a car. However, there is really nowhere for that idea to develop further without all credibility disappearing out the window. And while director Brad Anderson (*The Machinist*) generates some suspense in the early scenes, his heart doesn't seem to be in this tired generic exercise. JF Violence, swearing. *DVD* *BL*

Halle Berry *Jordan Turner* • Abigail Breslin *Casey Welson* • Morris Chestnut *Officer Paul Phillips* • Michael Eklund *Michael Foster* • David Otunga *Officer Jake Devans* • Ella Rae Peck *Autumn* ■ *Dir* Brad Anderson • *Scr* Richard D'Ovidio, from a story by Richard & Nicole D'Ovidio, Jon Bokenkamp

Call Girl ★★★★ 18

Drama
2012 · Swe/Nor/Fin/Ire · Colour · 139min

Set in Sweden during the 1970s, *Call Girl* begins as a sort of social exposé drama that peels away the country's seemingly affluent, egalitarian veneer to reveal a rather more sordid reality underneath. The story focuses on two youngsters from a juvenile home who fall into the clutches of a manipulative madam. At this point, the film switches to political thriller, with a police detective picking up on the case and possible links to people in high places. The shift is a little jarring yet it does provide fresh momentum, thanks to director Mikael Marcimain's assured handling of the material. BP Swedish +subtitles.

Sofia Karemyr *Iris Dahl* • Simon J Berger *John Sandberg* • Pernilla August *Dagmar Glans* • David Dencik *Aspen Thorin* ■ *Dir* Mikael Marcimain • *Scr* Marietta von Hausswolff von Baumgarten

Call Him Savage ★★★

Romantic comedy   1975 · Fr · Colour · 107min

There's much to enjoy in this screwball comedy that trades heavily on the appeal of its French megastars, Catherine Deneuve and Yves Montand. The story kicks off in South America where Deneuve walks out on her fiancé and into the arms of next door neighbour Montand, who is himself on the run from his wife. Together they sail to the South Seas. AT French +subtitles.

Catherine Deneuve *Nelly* • Yves Montand *Martin* • Luigi Vannucchi *Vittorio* • Tony Roberts *Alex* • Dana Wynter *Wife* ■ *Dir* Jean-Paul Rappeneau • *Scr* Jean-Paul Rappeneau, Elizabeth Rappeneau, Jean-Loup Dabadie

Call Me ★★ 18

Thriller   1988 · US · Colour · 90min

Patricia Charbonneau is the New York journalist who gets all excited when she gets an obscene phone call, thinking it's from her boyfriend. Things change, however, when she learns that the guy at the other end is a cold-blooded killer. There are more holes than in a piece of Swiss cheese, and Charbonneau is stuck with a character who is so naive you can't believe she has survived this long. JB

Patricia Charbonneau *Anna* • Patti D'Arbanville *Cori* • Boyd Gaines *Bill* • Stephen McHattie *Jellybean* • John Seitz *Pressure* • David Strathairn *Sam* • Ernest Abuba *Boss* • Steve Buscemi *Switchblade* ■ *Dir* Sollace Mitchell • *Scr* Karyn Kay, from a story by Sollace Mitchell, Kay

Call Me Bwana ★★★ U

Comedy adventure
1963 · US/UK · Colour · 93min

Viewed as outrageously patronising nowadays, this comedy stars Bob Hope as a bogus, bumbling explorer who helps CIA agent Edie Adams find an American space capsule lost in deepest, darkest Africa. Anita Ekberg and Lionel Jeffries play the enemy spies trying to thwart the mission. Despite its political incorrectness, this isn't bad considering the rubbish Hope was churning out at the time. TH

Bob Hope *Matt Merriwether* • Anita Ekberg *Luba* • Edie Adams *Frederica Larsen* • Lionel Jeffries *Dr Ezra Mungo* • Arnold Palmer ■ *Dir* Gordon Douglas • *Scr* Nate Monaster, Johanna Harwood • *Producer* Harry Saltzman

Call Me Claus ★★★ PG

Seasonal comedy   2001 · US · Colour · 86min

Nigel Hawthorne tries to convince Whoopi Goldberg that she should take over the reindeer reins as Santa Claus for the next 200 years. This TV vehicle for Goldberg's grouchy, sharp-tongued schtick has her playing a home shopping channel producer who discovers a money magnet in Hawthorne, whose jolly, sincere demeanour charms the viewers. The stars acquit themselves well enough and despite some manipulative moments, there's an amusing sideline in Christmas cynicism. JC *DVD*

Whoopi Goldberg *Lucy Cullins* • Nigel Hawthorne *Nick* • Brian Stokes Mitchell *Cameron* • Victor Garber *Taylor* • Taylor Negron *Ralph* ■ *Dir* Peter Werner • *Scr* Sara Bernstein, Gregory Bernstein, Brian Bird, from a story by Paul Mooney • *Music* Garth Brooks

Call Me Madam ★★★★ U

Musical comedy   1953 · US · Colour · 114min

After 644 performances as "the hostess with the mostest" in Irving Berlin's hit Broadway show, Ethel Merman repeated her tour de force for the rest of the world's benefit. Acting and singing up a storm with her foghorn voice, whirlwind energy and larger-than-life personality, Merman dominates this lively, lavish movie. Yet she doesn't quite outdo the scintillating dancing of Donald O'Connor and Vera-Ellen; nor does she upstage the suave George Sanders, who steals Merman's heart and has his own musical number. RK

Ethel Merman *Mrs Sally Adams* • Donald O'Connor *Kenneth* • Vera-Ellen *Princess Maria* • George Sanders *Cosmo Constantine* • Billy De Wolfe *Pemberton Maxwell* • Walter Slezak *Tantinnin* ■ *Dir* Walter Lang • *Scr* Arthur Sheekman, from the musical by Howard Lindsay, Russel Crouse • *Music* Irving Berlin • *Choreographer* Robert Alton

Call Me Mister ★★★ U

Musical   1951 · US · Colour · 95min

This long-running Broadway revue made it to the screen on a Betty Grable/Dan Dailey vehicle. It's pleasant enough and the dance routines are choreographed by the great Busby Berkeley, though he's well past his prime. The supporting cast is a veritable roster of rising stars, Grable is attractive and Dailey is, as ever, outstanding. The plot deteriorates into a "putting on a show in an army camp" piece of nothingness. **TS**

Betty Grable *Kay Hudson* • Dan Dailey *Shep Dooley* • Danny Thomas *Stanley* • Dale Robertson *Captain Johnny Comstock* • Benay Venuta *Billie Barton* • Richard Boone *Mess Sergeant* ■ *Dir* Lloyd Bacon • *Scr* Albert E Lewin, Burt Styler, from the musical by Harold J Rome, Arnold M Auerbach

Call Me Mrs Miracle ★★
Seasonal fantasy 2010 · Can · Colour · 88min

Everybody Loves Raymond matriarch Doris Roberts returns as uncanny problem-fixer Mrs "Miracle" in this ultra-simplistic TV-movie sequel. Working in a struggling New York department store in the run-up to Christmas, she combines magic, meddling, and traditional values to hurriedly bring festive cheer to the emotionally needy souls who cross her path. A playful Roberts charms whenever she's on screen, but unfortunately not all the cast share her gentle appeal, with Lauren Holly, in particular, a pantomimic embarrassment as a bitchy boss. **SF**

Doris Roberts *Emily Merkle/Mrs Miracle* • Lauren Holly *Lindy Lowe* • Eric Johnson (3) *Jake Finley* • Jewel Staite *Holly Wilson* ■ *Dir* Michael Scott • *Scr* Nancey Silvers, from the novel by Debbie Macomber

Call Northside 777 ★★★★ U
Crime drama based on a true story
1948 · US · BW · 106min

James Stewart doesn't always convince as the investigating reporter trying to clear Richard Conte of a murder he didn't commit, but the growing sense of injustice carries you along in director Henry Hathaway's crime drama based on a real-life story. With producer Louis de Rochemont, Hathaway had forged a new style of gritty movie-making that reconstructed true stories with a realism and attention to the details of police procedure that made them seem more like documentaries than thrillers. The technique soon became clichéd, but this still works as a crusading piece of film-making. **DP** DVD

James Stewart *McNeal* • Richard Conte *Frank Wiecek* • Lee J Cobb *Brian Kelly* • Helen Walker *Laura McNeal* • Betty Garde *Wanda Skutnik* • Kasia Orzazewski *Tillie Wiecek* ■ *Dir* Henry Hathaway • *Scr* Jerome Cady, Jay Dratler, from articles by James P McGuire in the *Chicago Times*, adapted by Leonard Hoffman, Quentin Reynolds • *Music* Alfred Newman

The Call of the Wild ★★★
Adventure 1935 · US · BW · 93min

While not exactly true to Jack London's source novel, this is still an enjoyable romantic adventure. It was during the making of this movie that Clark Gable had a brief affair with his co-star, the lovely Loretta Young, resulting in an illegitimate daughter who for years didn't know who her father was. The movie is tremendous fun, with a great sense of pace. **TS**

Clark Gable *Jack Thornton* • Loretta Young *Claire Blake* • Jack Oakie *Shorty Hoolihan* • Frank Conroy *John Blake* • Reginald Owen *Smith* • Sidney Toler *Groggin* ■ *Dir* William Wellman [William A Wellman] • *Scr* Gene Fowler, Leonard Praskins, from the novel by Jack London

Call of the Wild ★ PG
Adventure 1972 · UK · Colour · 100min

This version of the yarn about the Yukon gold rush stars a husky dog and Charlton Heston, who, in his memoirs, considers it "the worst movie I ever made." Heston blames the mess on a British producer and the fact that finance came from Germany, France, Italy and Spain. "It was a United Nations of a movie," he wrote, "using actors according to nationality rather than ability." **AT** DVD

Charlton Heston *John Thornton* • Michèle Mercier *Calliope Laurent* • Raimund Harmstorf *Pete* ■ *Dir* Ken Annakin • *Scr* Peter Wellbeck [Harry Alan Towers], Wyn Wells, Peter Yeldman, from the novel by Jack London

The Call of the Wild ★★★ 12
Adventure 1996 · Can · Colour · 86min

Yet another version of this story about the dog with the heart of an ox. Richard Dreyfuss is the narrator upon whom director Peter Svatek relies to bring London's richly evocative words to the screen and get into the mind of its canine legend, Buck. The actors, headed by Rutger Hauer as John Thornton, are not so well-served, though the famous sled-race scene is as heartstopping as ever. **FL** DVD

Rutger Hauer *John Thornton* • Luc Morissette *Perrault* • Richard Dreyfuss *Buck/Narrator* • Charles Powell *Hal* • Robert Pierre Cote *François* • Burke Lawrence *Charles* ■ *Dir* Peter Svatek • *Scr* Graham Ludlow, from the novel by Jack London

Call Out the Marines ★★ U
Musical spy comedy 1941 · US · BW · 67min

Victor McLaglen and Edmund Lowe were one of the screen's great comic partnerships, co-starring as the roistering Captain Flagg and Sergeant Quirt in the 1926 silent war classic *What Price Glory?* and continuing in a popular series of boisterous follow-ups. By the time they made this semi-musical spy story, however, they were both well past their sell-by date. Here the duo vie for the love of nightclub hostess Binnie Barnes. **TS**

Victor McLaglen *Jimmy McGinnis* • Edmund Lowe *Harry Curtis* • Binnie Barnes *Vi Hall* • Paul Kelly (1) *Jim Blake* • Robert Smith *Billy Harrison* • Dorothy Lovett *Mitzi* • Franklin Pangborn *Wilbur* • Corinna Mura *Rita* ■ *Dir/Scr* Frank Ryan, William Hamilton

Callan ★★★ 15
Spy drama 1974 · UK · Colour · 101min

In 1967, James Mitchell turned his novel *A Red File for Callan* into an *Armchair Theatre* production called *A Magnum for Schneider*. This movie expands that play to feature-length status to cash in on the success of the popular TV series. The film is disappointingly slow off the mark, but thanks to Don Sharp's slick direction, the pace eventually begins to pick up, with Edward Woodward excelling as the ex-agent whose ruthless professionalism belies a highly developed conscience. **DP**

Edward Woodward *Callan* • Eric Porter *Hunter* • Carl Mohner *Schneider* • Catherine Schell *Jenny* • Peter Egan *Meres* • Russell Hunter *Lonely* • Kenneth Griffith *Waterman* • Dave Prowse *Arthur* • Don Henderson *George* ■ *Dir* Don Sharp • *Scr* James Mitchell, from his TVplay *A Magnum for Schneider*, from his novel *A Red File for Callan*

Callas Forever ★★ 15
Fantasy music drama
2002 · It/UK/Fr/Rom/Sp · Colour · 108min

In the 1970s, Franco Zeffirelli tried to persuade the Greek diva Maria Callas to lip-sync her way through movie versions of her operatic triumphs. Ultimately, she declined. But the veteran director was clearly so tantalised by the concept that he used it as the premise of this unpersuasive fantasy. Jeremy Irons plays a gay, ponytailed impresario who attempts to rescue the ailing career of Callas (Fanny Ardant) by staging a glossy rendition of Bizet's *Carmen*. The arias have passion and panache, while Ardant captures something of the insecurity that beset Callas. However, the remainder is rather precious and old-fashioned. **DP** Swearing.

Fanny Ardant *Maria Callas* • Jeremy Irons *Larry Kelly* • Joan Plowright *Sarah Keller* • Jay Rodan *Michael* • Gabriel Garko *Marco* • Manuel de Blas *Esteban Gomez* ■ *Dir* Franco Zeffirelli • *Scr* Martin Sherman, Franco Zeffirelli

Callaway Went Thataway ★★★ U
Comedy western 1951 · US · BW · 81min

When the old movies of forgotten western star "Smoky" Callaway enjoy a resurgence of popularity on TV, publicists Fred MacMurray and Dorothy McGuire hire a dim-witted lookalike to impersonate him in personal appearances. In due course, the genuine article - now a washed-up drunk -

materialises. Howard Keel plays both roles. This is an agreeable, if slightly dated satire that offers a reasonable quota of laughs. **RK**

Fred MacMurray *Mike Frye* • Dorothy McGuire *Deborah Patterson* • Howard Keel *"Stretch" Barnes/"Smoky" Callaway* • Jesse White *George Markham* • Fay Roope *Tom Lorrison* • Natalie Schafer *Martha Lorrison* • Clark Gable • Elizabeth Taylor • Esther Williams ■ *Dir/Scr* Norman Panama, Melvin Frank

Calle Mayor ★★★
Comedy drama 1956 · Sp/Fr · BW · 94min

Things do not go according to plan when virile young José Suarez accepts a bet from his friends to court plain spinster Betsy Blair. Also known as *Main Street* and *The Love Maker*, this is one of the films that put the dissident Spanish film-maker Juan Antonio Bardem on the international map. Skilfully capturing the stifling atmosphere of Franco's Spain (indeed, Bardem was arrested and jailed while filming it), it is not uninteresting. **RK** Spanish dubbed.

Betsy Blair *Isabelle* • José Suarez *Juan* • Yves Massard *Jean* • Dora Doll *Antonia* • Lila Kedrova *Mme Pepita* • René Blancard ■ *Dir/Scr* Juan Antonio Bardem

The Caller ★ 18
Suspense drama 1987 · US · Colour · 92min

This is a curious two-hander - which premiered at Cannes and was hardly seen again - in which Malcolm McDowell mysteriously shows up at Madolyn Smith's remote log cabin. As a TV play, this might have worked; as a movie, though, it never stood a chance. **AT**

Malcolm McDowell *The caller* • Madolyn Smith *The girl* ■ *Dir* Arthur Allan Seidelman • *Scr* Michael Sloan

The Calling ★★★ 15
Comedy drama 2009 · UK · Colour · 109min

Gypo writer/director Jan Dunn here works wonders with a limited budget. Ignoring the misgivings of her mother and best friend, Joanna (Emily Beacham) goes on retreat to St Bertha's priory. There, she promptly falls foul of some of the more dubious nuns, but a progressive Sister (Brenda Blethyn) sees potential in the new postulant - especially when Joanna is faced with some trying personal matters. It may veer a touch too brusquely from gentle comedy to soap operatics, but this is still an entertaining insight into the effect that human frailty can have on even the strongest faith. **DP** Swearing, some sex scenes.

Brenda Blethyn *Sister Ignatious* • Emily Beecham *Joanna* • Susannah York *The Prioress* • Rita Tushingham *Sister Gertrude* • Pauline McLynn *Sister Hilda* • Joanna Scanlan *Sister Kevin* • Susannah Harker *Sister Ambrose* • Amanda Donohoe *Trish* • Corin Redgrave *The Bishop* • Chloe Sirene *Vivie* ■ *Dir/Scr* Jan Dunn

The Calling ★★ 15
Thriller 2014 · US · Colour · 107min

A series of religiously motivated murders drive the plot in this chilly crime thriller. The setting is a small, wintry town in Ontario, where world-weary detective Hazel Micallef (Susan Sarandon) discovers that a local woman has been gruesomely murdered. After more victims are found, Hazel and a newly arrived officer (Topher Grace) notice a pattern. *The Calling* isn't so much an awful film as a flat and unremarkable one, and, although Sarandon is always worth watching, the impressive supporting cast is largely wasted. **SC** Violence, swearing.

Susan Sarandon *Hazel Micallef* • Topher Grace *Ben Wingate* • Gil Bellows *Detective Ray Green* • Ellen Burstyn *Emily Micallef* • Donald Sutherland *Father Price* ■ *Dir* Jason Stone • *Scr* Scott Abramovitch, from Inger Ash Wolfe's novel

Calling Bulldog Drummond ★★ U
Detective mystery adventure
1951 · UK · BW · 79min

Bulldog Drummond had last been seen doing B-feature duties in a Hollywood series at Fox when MGM claimed him for this more

substantial one-off picture, filmed at its British studios. Walter Pidgeon plays the sleuth who helps Scotland Yard nail a gang of thieves by going undercover, while the strong supporting cast includes Margaret Leighton as his police assistant. Freddie Young's photography lends some class. **AE**

Walter Pidgeon *Hugh Drummond* • Margaret Leighton *Sergeant Helen Smith* • Robert Beatty *"Guns"* • David Tomlinson *Algy Longworth* • Peggy Evans *Molly* • Charles Victor *Inspector McIver* ■ *Dir* Victor Saville • *Scr* Gerard Fairlie, Howard Emmett Rogers, Arthur Wimperis, from the story by Gerard Fairlie, from characters by HC "Sapper" McNeile

Calling Dr Death ★★
Mystery 1943 · US · BW · 62min

Universal launched its short-lived B series based on the cult radio show *Inner Sanctum* (which was itself derived from a collection of pulp thrillers) with this taut but ultimately unsurprising mystery. It's narrated (somewhat intrusively) by Lon Chaney Jr, who also stars as a neurologist who is haunted by the impression he may have murdered unfaithful wife, Ramsay Ames, during one of his increasingly recurrent blackouts. It's a fascinating clash of acting styles. **DP**

Lon Chaney [Lon Chaney Jr] *Doctor Mark Steele* • Patricia Morison *Stella Madden* • J Carrol Naish *Inspector Gregg* • David Bruce *Robert Duval* • Ramsay Ames *Maria Steele* • Fay Helm *Mrs Duval* • Holmes Herbert *Bryant, butler* ■ *Dir* Reginald LeBorg [Reginald Le Borg] • *Scr* Edward Dein, from the radio series Inner Sanctum Mysteries

Calling Dr Gillespie ★★★
Medical drama 1942 · US · BW · 83min

With the departure of Dr Kildare from Blair General, the focus of attention in MGM's popular medical series shifted on to the crotchety Dr Gillespie. Disguising his soft centre beneath a thick crust as usual, Lionel Barrymore rose to the challenge and carried the franchise for a further six cases. Here he puts his new Dutch assistant Philip Dorn through his paces, although the central plot strand involves the demented attempts of Phil Brown to dispatch the senior surgeon. Efficiently combining mystery with melodrama, director Harold S Bucquet also finds time to squeeze in a walk-on for a young Ava Gardner. **DP**

Lionel Barrymore *Dr Leonard Gillespie* • Philip Dorn *Dr John Hunter Gerniede* • Donna Reed *Marcia Bradburn* • Phil Brown *Roy Todwell* • Nat Pendleton *Joe Wayman* • Alma Kruger *Molly Byrd* • Ava Gardner *Student at Miss Hope's* ■ *Dir* Harold S Bucquet • *Scr* Willis Goldbeck, Harry Ruskin, Lawrence P Bachmann, from a story by Kubec Glasmon, from characters by Max Brand

Calling Dr Kildare ★★
Medical drama 1939 · US · BW · 86min

The second in MGM's hospital series (after 1938's *Young Dr Kildare*) finds the Blair General intern (Lew Ayres) packed off by crusty but kind-hearted Dr Gillespie (Lionel Barrymore) to a humble neighbourhood clinic for a lesson in life. This is well-made, pleasant and sanitised stuff, despite the intrusion of the criminal underworld and Lana Turner as a wounded gunman's glamorous sister. The movie cemented the popularity of the series. *The Secret of Dr Kildare* followed later the same year. **RK**

Lew Ayres *Dr James Kildare* • Lionel Barrymore *Dr Leonard Gillespie* • Laraine Day *Mary Lamont* • Nat Pendleton *Joe Wayman* • Lana Turner *Rosalie* • Samuel S Hinds *Dr Stephen Kildare* • Walter Kingsford *Dr Walter Carew* • Alma Kruger *Molly Byrd* ■ *Dir* Harold S Bucquet • *Scr* Harry Ruskin, Willis Goldbeck, from a story by Max Brand

Calling Paul Temple ★★ U
Crime mystery 1948 · UK · BW · 88min

John Bentley and Dinah Sheridan assume the roles of Paul and Steve Temple for the second time in the sleuthing series produced for low-budget specialists Butcher's Film Service. Adapted from Francis Durbridge's radio serial *Paul Temple and the Canterbury Case*, it's a surprisingly sinister mystery that follows the duo into Kent on the trail of a murderer who signs

C

off as "Rex" at every crime scene. Director Maclean Rogers makes adept use of locations around the cathedral and the climax in the crypt of a ruined monastery is suitably tense, but the early scenes seem padded and the treatment of a Burmese servant is regrettably patronising. DP **DVD**

John Bentley *Paul Temple* • Dinah Sheridan *Steve Temple* • Margaretta Scott *Mrs Trevellyan* • Abraham Sofaer *Dr Kohima* • Celia Lipton *Norma Rice* ■ *Dir* Maclean Rogers • *Scr* Kathleen Butler, AR Rawlinson, from a radio series by Francis Durbridge

Calling the Tune ★★ PG
Musical   1936 · UK · BW · 74min

This variety showcase afforded former editor Thorold Dickinson an opportunity to try his hand at directing alongside the experienced but pedestrian Reginald Denham. The plot feels like an Ealing comedy: Clifford Evans adores Sally Grey, whose father, Sam Livesey, has made his fortune in the gramophone business by pilfering ideas from Evans's inventor dad, Lewis Casson. But the real purpose is the party pieces, including Charles Penrose (*The Laughing Policeman*) and conductor Sir Henry Wood, the brains behind the Proms. DP **DVD**

Adele Dixon *Julia Harbord* • Clifford Evans *Peter Mallory* • Sam Livesey *Bob Gordon* • Sally Gray *Margaret Gordon* • Donald Wolfit *Dick Finlay* • Lewis Casson *John Mallory* ■ *Dir* Reginald Denham, Thorold Dickinson • *Scr* Reginald Denham

Calm Chaos ★★★★ 15
Drama   2008 · It/UK · Colour · 107min

This subtly modulated adaptation of Sandro Veronesi's novel stars Nanni Moretti as a workaholic father whose life takes a bizarre turn after his wife dies on the same day that he rescues two women from drowning on a beach. He then becomes obsessed with supporting his ten-year-old daughter (Blu Yoshimi) through the trauma of his bereavement, conducting his life from a park bench near her school. Moretti's vigil could have lapsed into cheap sentiment, but he sustains such a high level of brittle desperation that his sojourn never seems contrived. A climactic sexual encounter seems a little jarring, but this remains a charming, mature and perceptive insight into the need to keep living in the wake of loss. DP Italian +subtitles. **DVD**

Nanni Moretti *Pietro Paladini* • Valeria Golino *Marta* • Isabella Ferrari *Eleonora Simoncini* • Alessandro Gassman *Carlo* • Blu Yoshimi *Claudia* • Hippolyte Girardot *Jean Claude* ■ *Dir* Antonello Grimaldi • *Scr* Nanni Moretti, Laura Paolucci, Francesco Piccolo, from the novel *Caos Calmo* by Sandro Veronesi

Calvaire ★★★ 18
Black comedy horror
2004 · Bel/Fr/Lux · Colour · 87min

Director Fabrice du Welz's spaced-out spooky feature debut has amateur cabaret singer Laurent Lucas taking a wrong turn to a Christmas gig and ending up in a remote inn run by demented Jackie Berroyer. Berroyer wants a perfect wife as a substitute for the one he never forgave for adultery, and soon Lucas is being debased in drag and facing mental torture and crucifixion in a woodland community of dangerous village idiots. This is disgusting, shocking and delightful in equal proportion. AJ French +subtitles. **DVD**

Laurent Lucas *Marc Stevens* • Jackie Berroyer *Paul Bartel* • Philippe Nahon *Robert Orton* • Jean-Luc Couchard *Boris* • Brigitte Lahaie *Mademoiselle Vicky* • Gigi Coursigni *Madame Langhoff* • Philippe Grand'Henry *Thomas Orton* • Jo Prestia *Mylène* ■ *Dir* Fabrice du Welz • *Scr* Fabrice du Welz, Romain Protat • *Cinematographer* Benoît Debie

Calvary ★★★★ 15
Drama   2013 · Ire/UK · Colour · 98min

The Guard writer/director John Michael McDonagh reteams with Brendan Gleeson for this unique drama. Gleeson plays a "good priest" in an Irish village who is given a week to live by a vengeful mystery man in the confessional. McDonagh's strange brew

---

of comedy, tragedy and melodrama shouldn't work but it does, and although the plot contains an element of spot-the-killer, it's more concerned with the oddball village characters. Gleeson is superb, as usual, but the supporting cast is uniformly excellent, with Kelly Reilly, Chris O'Dowd and Dylan Moran outstanding in a soulful, thought-provoking and warmly human fable. LB Violence, swearing, sexual references, drug abuse. **DVD** **Blu**

Brendan Gleeson *Father James* • Kelly Reilly *Fiona* • Chris O'Dowd *Jack Brennan* • Dylan Moran *Fitzgerald* • Isaach De Bankolé [Isaach de Bankole] *Simon Asamoah* • Aidan Gillen *Dr Frank Harte* ■ *Dir/Scr* John Michael McDonagh

Camelot ★★★★ U
Period musical romance
1967 · US · Colour · 172min

Despite Joshua Logan's stodgy staging, this sumptuous screen version of the Arthurian musical by Lerner and Loewe still pierces the heart in Excalibur fashion. Vanessa Redgrave as Guenevere convincingly enthrals King Arthur (Richard Harris), Lancelot (Franco Nero) and us. The stars may not be exactly tuneful, but they compensate for that with their dramatic and moving interpretation of the glorious songs. TH **DVD**

Richard Harris *King Arthur* • Vanessa Redgrave *Queen Guenevere* • Franco Nero *Lancelot Du Lac* • David Hemmings *Mordred* • Lionel Jeffries *King Pellinore* • Laurence Naismith *Merlyn* • Pierre Olaf *Dap* • Estelle Winwood *Lady Clarinda* ■ *Dir* Joshua Logan • *Scr* Alan J Lerner, from the musical by Alan J Lerner, Frederick Loewe, from the novel *The Once and Future King* by TH White

The Camels Are Coming ★★ U
Comedy   1934 · UK · BW · 71min

Directed by American Tim Whelan, this was hardly a feather in producer Michael Balcon's cap. But comedies of this kind went down a treat with audiences in the 1930s and it was their success that later enabled Balcon to make the Gainsborough costume dramas and Ealing comedies. Star Jack Hulbert teamed with Guy Bolton and WP Lipscomb on the script, and he and Anna Lee make a pleasing partnership as they unmask desert drug smugglers. DP

Jack Hulbert *Jack Campbell* • Anna Lee *Anita Rodgers* • Hartley Power *Nicholas* • Harold Huth *Dr Zhiga* • Allan Jeayes *Sheikh* • Peter Gawthorne *Colonel Fairley* ■ *Dir* Tim Whelan • *Scr* Guy Bolton, Jack Hulbert, WP Lipscomb, from a story by Tim Whelan, Russell Medcraft

Camera Buff ★★★★ 12
Drama   1979 · Pol · Colour · 107min

Despite being one of the key titles in the Cinema of Moral Anxiety that helped shape Poland's fate in the Solidarity era, this scathing satire is Krzysztof Kieslowski's most accessible and amusing feature. Exploring both the addictive nature of film-making and the way in which visual imagery can be corrupted by its context, the story of Jerzy Stuhr's journey from home-movie novice to factory PR lackey and prize-winning auteur is related in a deceptively light tone that belies the intensity of Kieslowski's detestation of censorship and state control. Stuhr is typically excellent, although Malgorzata Zabkowska and Stefan Czyzewski also impress as his alienated wife and hectoring boss. DP Polish +subtitles. **DVD**

Jerzy Stuhr *Filip Mosz* • Malgorzata Zabkowska *Irka Mosz* • Ewa Pokas *Anna Wlodarczyk* • Stefan Czyzewski *Director* • Jerzy Nowak *Osuch* • Tadeusz Bradecki *Witek* ■ *Dir/Scr* Krzysztof Kieslowski

The Cameraman ★★★★★
Silent comedy   1928 · US · BW · 67min

This is a superb example of Buster Keaton's comic genius. He's a street photographer who wants to become a newsreel cameraman to get close to Marceline Day with whom he's fallen in love. The film was remade for comedian Red Skelton as *Watch the Birdie* in 1950, but that went nowhere compared with the original. In one bit of

---

knockabout Keaton hitches a ride on a fire engine to get a scoop, only to find it's returning from the fire. TH

Buster Keaton *Luke Shannon/Buster* • Marceline Day *Sally Richards* • Harold Goodwin (1) *Harold Stagg* • Sidney Bracy [Sidney Bracey] *Edward J Blake, boss of film office* • Harry Gribbon *Hennessey the cop* • Edward Brophy *Fat man in bathhouse* ■ *Dir* Edward Sedgwick • *Scr* Clyde Bruckman, Lew Lipton, Richard Schayer, Joe W Farnham [Joseph Farnham]

Cameraman: the Life & Work of Jack Cardiff ★★★★ PG
Documentary   2010 · UK · Colour · 85min

Craig McCall's documentary is an absorbing history of the first cinematographer awarded an honorary Oscar. It traces Cardiff's career from humble beginnings as a silent movie child actor to becoming Michael Powell and Emeric Pressburger's go-to lighting genius (*Black Narcissus*, *The Red Shoes*), to his own directorial career (starting with *Sons and Lovers* in 1960). Offering insights into his working methods – he was influenced by classic painters such as Vermeer – this illuminating profile finds Cardiff (who died aged 94 in 2009) on engaging and endearing form. The film is packed with movie clips, significant on-set photos and well-chosen archive material, while Lauren Bacall, Charlton Heston and Kirk Douglas are among the stars offering their memories of Cardiff's vintage era. AJ

Jack Cardiff • Thelma Schoonmaker • Martin Scorsese • Kirk Douglas • Lauren Bacall • Richard Attenborough • Marilyn Monroe ■ *Dir* Craig McCall

Cameron's Closet ★ 18
Supernatural horror   1988 · UK · Colour · 83min

This indigestible slice of 1980s horror pulp centres on a boy whose telekinetic powers conjure up a red-eyed monster that resides in his closet. The result is an odd mix of mawkish family drama and graphic gore; 1950s star Tab Hunter has the right idea when he exits this dull affair early on. When it arrives, the Carlo Rambaldi-designed creature wouldn't terrify a Muppets fan. RS

Cotter Smith *Sam Talliaferro* • Mel Harris *Nora Haley* • Scott Curtis *Cameron Lansing* • Chuck McCann *Ben Majors* • Leigh McCloskey *Det Pete Groom* • Tab Hunter *Owen Lansing* ■ *Dir* Armand Mastroianni • *Scr* Gary Brandner

Camila ★★★ 15
Period drama   1984 · Arg · Colour · 107min

Such was the contemporary resonance of this true-life period drama that director Maria Luisa Bemberg was denied permission to film it for many years. Those pillars of Argentinian society – the church, the state and the family – come in for pitiless barrage as Buenos Aires socialite Susu Pecoraro and Jesuit priest Imanol Arias briefly defy the conventions extant under the brutal de Rosas dictatorship to set up housekeeping in a country village. DP Spanish +subtitles.

Susu Pecoraro *Camila O'Gorman* • Imanol Arias *Father Ladislao Gutierrez* • Héctor Alterio *Adolfo O'Gorman* • Elena Tasisto *Dona Joaquina O'Gorman* • Carlos Munoz *Monsignor Elortondo* ■ *Dir* Maria Luisa Bemberg • *Scr* Maria Luisa Bemberg, Beda Docampo Feijo, Juan Batista Stagnaro

Camilla ★★★ 12
Road movie drama
1993 · Can/UK · Colour · 94min

It's impossible to watch this variation on the road movie theme without getting a lump in your throat. In her final role, Jessica Tandy gives a performance of regal impudence as an eccentric violinist that helps elevate a rather undistinguished film to something worth cherishing. The scenes she shares with husband of 51 years Hume Cronyn are exquisitely poignant, but they're over far too soon as Tandy and Bridget Fonda leave in pursuit of the latter's musical dream. DP Swearing. **DVD**

Bridget Fonda *Freda Lopez* • Jessica Tandy *Camilla Cara* • Elias Koteas *Vincent Lopez* • Maury Chaykin *Harold Cara* • Graham Greene (2)

Hunt Weller • Hume Cronyn *Ewald* • Ranjit Chowdhry *Kapur* • George Harris (2) *Jerry* ■ *Dir* Deepa Mehta • *Scr* Paul Quarrington

Camille ★★
Silent romantic drama   1921 · US · BW · 72min

The great Russian actress Alla Nazimova stars as Marguerite in an updated version of Alexandre Dumas's frequently filmed novel which, unaccountably and unacceptably, removes Armand from the famous deathbed finale, leaving the consumptive heroine to expire in the company of her servants. The bob-haired star displays her considerable range of emotions to the full, and is well-partnered by an elegant, handsome and suitably restrained Rudolph Valentino. RK

Alla Nazimova *Camille/Marguerite Gautier* • Rudolph Valentino *Armand Duval* • Arthur Hoyt *Count de Varville* • Zeffie Tillbury *Prudence* • Rex Cherryman *Gaston* • Edward Connelly *Duke* ■ *Dir* Ray C Smallwood • *Scr* June Mathis, from the novel *La Dame aux Camélias* by Alexandre Dumas fils

Camille
Silent romantic drama   1927 · US · BW · 95min

Yet another in the string of silent adaptations of Dumas's famous novel, starring one of America's queens of the silent screen, Norma Talmadge, as the ill-fated Marguerite and a bland Gilbert Roland as her lover, Armand. This is, sadly, a lost film and is on the American Film Institute's "most wanted" list. However, along with previous attempts, it has been overshadowed by MGM's deathless sound version, made ten years later with Greta Garbo. RK

Norma Talmadge *Camille/Marguerite* • Gilbert Roland *Armand* • Lilyan Tashman *Olympe* • Maurice Costello *Monsieur Duval* • Harvey Clark *The Baron* • Alec B Francis *The Duke* ■ *Dir* Fred Niblo • *Scr* Olga Printzlau, Chandler Sprague, Fred De Gresac, from the novel *La Dame aux Camélias* by Alexandre Dumas fils

Camille ★★★★ PG
Romantic drama   1937 · US · BW · 104min

Greta Garbo never won an Oscar for a specific role (she received a special one in 1954), but the New York film critics did give her their best actress gong for what is now one of her most famous performances, as the doomed heroine in George Cukor's sumptuous film of the younger Alexandre Dumas's classic play and novel. She certainly pulls out all the stops, whether expressing her love for young Armand (Robert Taylor), modelling a glamorous wardrobe, or finally breathing her last in one of cinema's most celebrated death scenes. Cukor handles the whole thing with confidence, but it is Garbo's movie all the way. PF

Greta Garbo *Marguerite* • Robert Taylor (1) *Armand* • Lionel Barrymore *Monsieur Duval* • Elizabeth Allan *Nichette* • Jessie Ralph *Nanine* • Henry Daniell *Baron De Varville* • Lenore Ulric *Olympe* • Laura Hope Crews *Prudence* • Rex O'Malley *Gaston* • Russell Hardie *Gustave* ■ *Dir* George Cukor • *Scr* Zoe Akins, Frances Marion, James Hilton, from the novel *La Dame aux Camélias* by Alexandre Dumas fils • *Costume Designer* Adrian

Camille Claudel ★★★ PG
Biographical drama   1988 · Fr · Colour · 165min

It is fascinating to discover that Rodin's mistress Camille Claudel was a talented sculptress, and agonising to watch her sublimation beneath Rodin. Isabelle Adjani and Gérard Depardieu are well cast in this re-creation of the relationship, which makes the journey through the emotional maelstrom akin to walking barefoot over broken glass. Adjani was nominated for an Oscar, and her descent into self-destruction is moving. LH French +subtitles. **DVD**

Isabelle Adjani *Camille Claudel* • Gérard Depardieu *Auguste Rodin* • Laurent Crevill *Paul Claudel* • Alain Cuny *Mr Claudel* • Madeleine Robinson *Madame Claudel* • Katrine Boorman *Jessie* ■ *Dir* Bruno Nuytten • *Scr* Marilyn Goldin, from a biography by Reine-Marie Paris, Bruno Nuytten

---

Camille Claudel 1915
★★★★ **PG**

Biographical drama 2013 · Fr · Colour · 95min

Austere director Bruno Dumont's challenging film about French sculptor Camille Claudel is set nearly two decades after the end of her notorious affair with fellow artist Rodin. It finds Claudel (Juliette Binoche) locked up in a remote mental institution, convinced that someone is trying to poison her. Claudel's daily life is a tough watch, but things pick up with the arrival of her poet brother Paul (Jean-Luc Vincent). Binoche is excellent in a part that trades not on her beauty but her mind, portraying a woman whose talent made her dangerous in less enlightened times. DW French +subtitles. Brief nudity. *DVD*

Juliette Binoche *Camille Claudel* · Jean-Luc Vincent *Paul Claudel* · Robert Leroy *Doctor* · Emmanuel Kauffman *Priest* · Marion Keller *Mlle Blanc* ■ *Dir* Bruno Dumont · *Scr* Bruno Dumont, from Camille & Paul Claudel's letters

Camorra
★★ **18**

Crime thriller 1985 · It · Colour · 89min

Lina Wertmuller's muddle of Mob thriller and moral melodrama is further evidence of the controversial director's fall from critical grace. Here, she adopts a neo-tabloid manner that has little to do with the harsh realism to which the action aspires. There's no doubting the sincerity of the maternal indignation that prompts Angela Molina – a former prostitute who runs a hostel with loyal friend Daniel Ezralow – to take on the drug pushers polluting her Neopolitan neighbourhood. But Wertmuller fails to keep the lid on proceedings after Molina is assaulted and a serial killer begins bumping off the dealers. DP

Angela Molina *Annunziata* · Francisco Rabal *Guaglione* · Harvey Keitel *Frankie Acquasanta* · Daniel Ezralow *Antonio* · Paolo Bonacelli *Tango* · Isa Danieli *Carmela* ■ *Dir* Lina Wertmuller · *Scr* Elvio Porta, Lina Wertmuller

Camouflage
★★★ **15**

Comedy satire 1977 · Pol · Colour · 97min

Made by Krzysztof Zanussi and considered by many to be a landmark of Polish cinema, this intelligent and subtly understated film explores the themes of bureaucratic pettiness and the crushing of idealism. Using a summer seminar for linguistic students, held at a palatial country estate as his fulcrum, Zanussi addresses the concerns of the generation gap through youthful liberal professor Piotr Garlicki, who confronts the cynicism of the status quo and older colleague Zbigniew Zapasiewicz. RB In Polish. *DVD*

Piotr Garlicki *Jaroslaw Kruszynski* · Zbigniew Zapasiewicz *Jakub Szelestowski* · Christine Paul-Podlasky *Mary* · Mariusz Dmochowski *Vice-rector* ■ *Dir/Scr* Krzysztof Zanussi

Camp
★★★ **12**

Musical comedy drama 2003 · US · Colour · 105min

Think *Fame* in a summer camp for teenage Broadway hopefuls and that's actor/writer Todd Graff's sweet, feel-good directorial debut in a nutshell. Despite a variable tone, this sparkling celebration of musical theatre lives up to its title. Fame-hungry types gather at Camp Ovation to rehearse four shows every two weeks for the locals. Talented (and straight) new student Daniel Letterle becomes everyone's lust object as he engineers a benefit finale written by Broadway-has-been-turned-counselor Don Dixon. Graff handles complex issues of teen sexuality in totally un-clichéd ways, and this is a treat for all theatre geeks. AJ *DVD*

Daniel Letterle *Vlad* · Joanna Chilcoat *Ellen* · Robin de Jesus *Michael* · Don Dixon *Bert Hanley* · Steven Cutts *Shaun* · Vince Rimoldi *Spitzer* · Tiffany Taylor *Jenna* · Sasha Allen *Dee* · Alana Allen *Jill* · Anna Kendrick *Fritzi* · Stephen Sondheim ■ *Dir/Scr* Todd Graff

Camp Hell
★★ **15**

Horror 2010 · US · Colour · 95min

Horror is in short supply in this curious tale of an unseen evil stalking a remote summer camp for Christian youths. Hormonally charged Tommy (Will Denton) is already questioning his parents' fervent beliefs when sinister goings-on begin to escalate, and a charismatic but unhinged priest (Bruce Davison) suspects the troubled teen may have brought the devil with him from the outside world. With little in the way of shocks or surprises, writer/director George VanBuskirk fashions a lightweight drama that ponders religious fanaticism but never seems sure of its message. TeS

Will Denton *Tommy Leary* · Bruce Davison *Father Phineas McAllister* · Jesse Eisenberg *Daniel* · Dana Delany *Patricia Leary* · Andrew McCarthy *Michael Leary* · Valentina de Angelis *Melissa* ■ *Dir/Scr* George VanBuskirk

The Camp on Blood Island
★★★

Second World War drama 1958 · UK · BW · 82min

The Hammer House of Horror took a rest from gothic gore to take a grim look at the real-life horrors of the Second World War. A sensation in its day, Hammer faced condemnation on all fronts for daring to tell the moving tale of British PoWs fearing a massacre if their cruel captors learn that the war has ended. Based on a true story, Hammer still didn't flinch from the subject's pathos or its sadistic shock value. A sequel, *The Secret of Blood Island*, followed in 1965. AJ *DVD*

Carl Mohner *Piet Van Elst* · André Morell *Colonel Lambert* · Edward Underdown *Dawes* · Walter Fitzgerald *Beattie* · Barbara Shelley *Kate* ■ *Dir* Val Guest · *Scr* Jon Manchip White, Val Guest, from a story by Jon Manchip White

Camp Rock
★★ **U**

Musical romantic comedy 2008 · US · Colour · 94min

Less successful than Disney's *High School Musical* but just as wholesome, this child-friendly tale is set in a summer camp for wannabe rock stars. Disney regular Demi Lovato is the shy new kid who lies about her mother's job in an attempt to ingratiate herself. Meanwhile, the egotistical lead singer of chart-topping group Connect 3 (played by real-life boy band star Joe Jonas) has been sent to teach at camp to atone for a series of scandals. It's breezily forgettable, but Lovato's smiley heroine is at least endearing. A sequel was released on DVD in 2010. JR

Demi Lovato *Mitchie Torres* · Joe Jonas *Shane Gray* · Kevin Jonas *Jason* · Nick Jonas *Nate* · Alyson Stoner *Caitlyn Geller* ■ *Dir* Matthew Diamond · *Scr* Karin Gist, Regina Hicks [Regina Y Hicks], Julie Brown, Paul Brown

The Campaign
★★★★ **15**

Comedy 2012 · US · Colour · 81min

There's plenty of muck-raking in this outrageous comedy from director Jay Roach (*Austin Powers*, *Meet the Parents*), which pits Will Ferrell against Zach Galifianakis in a battle for political power. Ferrell's incumbent senator and ladies' man recalls *Anchorman*, with a touch of his George W Bush impression thrown in, and Galifianakis is unusually endearing as the dithering tourist guide that billionaire bigwigs John Lithgow and Dan Aykroyd would rather see installed as senator so they can secure a shady trade deal. Don't look for wry satire – the gags are big and brash – but with the duelling stars on top form, *The Campaign* scores high in the approval ratings. SP Swearing, sex scenes, some violence. *DVD* *BL*

Will Ferrell *Cam Brady* · Zach Galifianakis *Marty Huggins* · Jason Sudeikis *Mitch* · Dylan McDermott *Tim Wattley* · John Lithgow *Glen Motch* · Dan Aykroyd *Wade Motch* · Brian Cox (1) *Raymond Huggins* ■ *Dir* Jay Roach · *Scr* Shawn Harwell, Chris Henchy

Campbell's Kingdom
★★ **U**

Adventure 1957 · UK · Colour · 97min

Dirk Bogarde dons some checked shirts and sets out to prove that he can stand up to mean Stanley Baker, who is out to swipe his land, in this unconvincing adventure set in Canada. There is some stunning location photography and a reliable British supporting cast, but director Ralph Thomas looks a little out of his depth in this genre. JF *DVD*

Dirk Bogarde *Bruce Campbell* · Stanley Baker *Owen Morgan* · Michael Craig *Boy Bladen* · Barbara Murray *Jean Lucas* · James Robertson-Justice *James Macdonald* · Athene Seyler *Miss Abigail* · John Laurie *Mac* · Sidney James *Driver* ■ *Dir* Ralph Thomas · *Scr* Robin Estridge, from the novel by Hammond Innes

Can-Can
★★ **U**

Period romantic musical 1960 · US · Colour · 124min

Although based on Cole Porter's Broadway hit, set in turn-of-the-century Paris, this loses some of Porter's best material, notably the brilliant lyric to *Can-Can* itself, and is resolutely anachronistic. Shirley MacLaine is the nightclub owner staging the daring illegal dance, while lawyer Frank Sinatra defends her right to do so. TS

Frank Sinatra *François Durnais* · Shirley MacLaine *Simone Pistache* · Maurice Chevalier *Paul Barrière* · Louis Jourdan *Philippe Forrestier* · Juliet Prowse *Claudine* · Marcel Dalio *Head waiter* ■ *Dir* Walter Lang · *Scr* Dorothy Kingsley, Charles Lederer, from the musical by Abe Burrows, Cole Porter

Can Heironymus Merkin Ever Forget Mercy Humppe and Find True Happiness?
★★

Musical comedy 1969 · UK · Colour · 117min

Anthony Newley's sprawling musical fantasy, a Fellini-esque hotch-potch of dream-like sequences and irreverent whimsy, is a film that could only have been made in the 1960s. Heironymus Merkin sits on a beach surrounded by the flotsam and jetsam of his life, including a film biography which he projects to his family. We learn his story from the vignettes contained in the film-within-the-film. Meanwhile, back in the present, the film company expresses its concern that his movie still has no ending. Joan Collins, Newley's wife at the time, shows off her assets. DF

Anthony Newley *Heironymus Merkin* · Joan Collins *Polyester Poontang* · Milton Berle *Good Time Eddie Filth* · George Jessel *The Presence* · Stubby Kaye *Fat Writer* · Bruce Forsyth *Uncle Limelight* · Patricia Hayes *Grandma* · Victor Spinetti *Sharpnose* ■ *Dir* Anthony Newley · *Scr* Herman Raucher, Anthony Newley

Can She Bake a Cherry Pie?
★★★★ **15**

Comedy 1983 · US · Colour · 90min

Maverick director Henry Jaglom continues on his own sweet way with this entrancing tale of opposites attracting. Mostly improvising their lines, the leads are simply superb. When she's not belting out blues numbers, kooky Karen Black frets over her divorce and the impossibility of finding romance the second time around. Meanwhile, fussy, balding Michael Emil declaims at great length about anything and everything. Teetering on the brink of self-indulgence, this meticulously-paced picture allows us to get to know the characters, whose eccentricities and opinions inexorably reel us in. DP

Karen Black *Zee* · Michael Emil *Eli* · Michael Margotta *Larry* · Frances Fisher *Louise* · Martin Harvey Friedberg *Mort* ■ *Dir/Scr* Henry Jaglom

Can You Keep It Up for a Week?
★★ **18**

Sex comedy 1974 · UK · Colour · 93min

This is one of the better-known British sex comedies of the 1970s. The flesh count is high, but there are also some giggles along the way as Jeremy Bulloch tries to resist temptation and hang on to a job for a week so that his girlfriend will marry him. DP Sex scenes, nudity. *DVD*

Jeremy Bulloch *Gil* · Neil Hallett *Gerry Grimwood* · Jill Damas *Annette* · Joy Harrington *Mrs Grimwood* ■ *Dir* Jim Atkinson · *Scr* Robin Gough

Canadian Bacon
★★ **PG**

Satirical comedy 1995 · US · Colour · 90min

Director Michael Moore has impressed with his satirical documentaries, but he came a cropper with his feature debut. The story has US President Alan Alda declaring war on Canada to boost his popularity rating. There should have been some incisive cross-border comedy, but Moore too often goes for easy laughs and settles for national stereotypes instead of fully rounded characters. DP *DVD*

Alan Alda *President* · John Candy *Bud B Boomer* · Rhea Perlman *Deputy Honey* · Kevin Pollak *Stuart Smiley* · Rip Torn *General Dick Panzer* · Kevin J O'Connor *Roy Boy* · Bill Nunn *Kabral* · Steven Wright *Niagara Mountie* · James Belushi *Charles Jackal* ■ *Dir/Scr* Michael Moore (2)

The Canal
★★★ **15**

Horror mystery 2014 · Ire/Neth/UK · Colour · 93min

Making the most of a wrenching central performance by *Hellboy* veteran Rupert Evans, this Irish chiller lurches from unspoken eeriness to outright horror as it plots a familiar paranormal trajectory. Evans plays a film archivist who moves into a beautiful period house only to find it was the scene of a ghastly murder. Ivan Kavanagh directs the unsettling tale with a no-frills professionalism heavy on ambiguity, dark atmosphere and creeping unease, while Steve Oram (*Sightseers*) adds welcome light touches as a deadpan policeman. AJ

Rupert Evans (2) *David* · Antonia Campbell Hughes [Antonia Campbell-Hughes] *Claire* · Hannah Hoekstra *Alice* · Kelly Byrne *Sophie* · Steve Oram *McNamara* ■ *Dir/Scr* Ivan Kavanagh

The Canary Murder Case
★★★

Detective mystery 1929 · US · BW · 80min

This first of 15 films from SS Van Dine's novels featuring sophisticated sleuth Philo Vance has William Powell in the role (which he would play four times). It made a welcome change from the gallery of rogues for which the actor was becoming known and paved the way for his famously urbane detective, Nick Charles, in the *Thin Man* series. The "canary" of this case is Louise Brooks, an alluring beauty not above a bit of blackmail. Shot as a silent by Malcom St Clair, it was reworked by Frank Tuttle as a talkie before its release. RK

William Powell *Philo Vance* · Louise Brooks *Margaret O'Dell* · James Hall *Jimmy Spotswoode* · Jean Arthur *Alice LaFosse* · Gustav von Seyffertitz *Dr Ambrose Linquist* · Charles Lane (1) *Charles Sportswoode* ■ *Dir* Malcolm St Clair, Frank Tuttle · *Scr* Florence Ryerson, Albert S LeVino, Herman J Mankiewicz, from a novel by SS Van Dine

Cancel My Reservation
★ **U**

Comedy western 1972 · US · Colour · 86min

This incompetent farce from Bob Hope – one of the last he made – reprises so many themes from his earlier movies it feels like a remake. Hope does his cowardly lion routine as a TV talk-show host who becomes entangled with murder and Eva Marie Saint while vacationing in Arizona. TH

Bob Hope *Dan Bartlett* · Eva Marie Saint *Sheila Bartlett* · Ralph Bellamy *John Ed* · Forrest Tucker *Reese* · Anne Archer *Crazy* · Keenan Wynn *Sheriff Riley* ■ *Dir* Paul Bogart · *Scr* Arthur Marx, Robert Fisher, from the novel *The Broken Gun* by Louis L'Amour

The Candidate
★★★★ **PG**

Political drama 1972 · US · Colour · 105min

Robert Redford's engaging performance breathes fresh life into the all-power-corrupts theme, and the sharply observed situations won an Oscar for scriptwriter Jeremy Larner. Redford stars as an idealistic lawyer who succumbs to mass-merchandising politics when he sets out to be a senator. With a campaign engineered by party managers Peter Boyle and Allen Garfield, he ends up alienating his wife Karen Carlson and compromising his principles. Director Michael Ritchie gives a

documentary-like credibility to the piece. TH
DVD

Robert Redford *Bill McKay* • Peter Boyle *Marvin Lucas* • Don Porter *Senator "Crocker" Jarmon* • Allen Garfield *Howard Klein* • Karen Carlson *Nancy McKay* • Quinn Redeker *Rich Jenkin* • Michael Lerner *Paul Corliss* • Melvyn Douglas *John J McKay* ■ *Dir* Michael Ritchie • *Scr* Jeremy Larner

Candlelight in Algeria ★★ U
Second World War spy drama
1943 · UK · BW · 81min

Throughout the Second World War, Allied intelligence chiefs were worried that the image of the doltish Nazi depicted in films might make people underestimate the Germans as an enemy. Certainly, the officers on parade in this tepid potboiler pose few problems for James Mason as he attempts to steal the film that will betray the location of a top-secret meeting. Director George King misses out on suspense and authenticity. DP *DVD*

James Mason *Alan Thurston* • Carla Lehmann *Susan Foster* • Walter Rilla *Dr Muller* • Raymond Lovell *Von Alven* • Enid Stamp-Taylor *Maritza* • Pamela Stirling *Yvette* ■ *Dir* George King • *Scr* Brock Williams, Katherine Strueby, from a story by Dorothy Hope

Candleshoe ★★★ U
Comedy   1977 · UK/US · Colour · 96min

In her fifth outing for Disney, Jodie Foster is in fine fettle as a tomboy turning the tables on bungling crook Leo McKern. The star of the show is David Niven, who is clearly having a ball beneath his various disguises, but there's also solid support from Helen Hayes as the owner of a stately children's hostel that will be closed down unless some buried treasure is unearthed. Solid entertainment, with a good story and fine acting. DP

Jodie Foster *Casey Brown* • Helen Hayes *Lady St Edmund* • David Niven *Priory* • Leo McKern *Harry Bundage* • Veronica Quilligan *Cluny* ■ *Dir* Norman Tokar • *Scr* David Swift, Rosemary Anne Sisson, from the novel *Christmas at Candleshoe* by Michael Innes

Candy ★
Comedy   1968 · US/It/Fr · Colour · 124min

This is a sex farce of mind-boggling ineptitude. The impressive roster of co-stars were each paid $50,000 for a week's work, though it's such a shambolic, episodic mess that the movie seems a monument to the arrogance and indifference of stars tanked up on drugs, booze and undiluted ego. Marlon Brando, a close friend of director Christian Marquand and the film's prime mover, plays an Indian guru addicted to sex. AT

Ewa Aulin *Candy* • Charles Aznavour *The hunchback* • Marlon Brando *Grindl* • Richard Burton *McPhisto* • James Coburn *Dr Krankeit* • John Huston *Dr Dunlap* • Walter Matthau *General Smight* • Ringo Starr *Emmanuel* • John Astin *Daddy/Uncle Jack* • Anita Pallenberg *Nurse Bullock* ■ *Dir* Christian Marquand • *Scr* Buck Henry, from the novel by Terry Southern

Candy ★★★★ 15
Relationship drama
2005 · Aus · Colour · 103min

Heath Ledger returned to his Australian homeland to star in this uncompromising but moving tale of drug addiction. Ledger plays a would-be poet who falls head over heels for a young artist (*Somersault's* Abbie Cornish). The couple's increasingly desperate, drug-addled lifestyle eventually puts an impossible strain on their relationship. Like the very best films about addiction (*Trainspotting, Requiem for a Dream*), this doesn't moralise about heroin, which makes the couple's disintegration even more painful. Neil Armfield's direction is sympathetically low-key with the cold turkey scenes truly harrowing, while Geoffrey Rush almost steals the show as a fellow substance abuser. JF Drug abuse, swearing, nudity. *DVD* BL

Heath Ledger *Dan* • Abbie Cornish *Candy* • Geoffrey Rush *Casper* • Tony Martin (2) *Mr Wyatt* • Noni Hazlehurst *Mrs Wyatt* • Tom Budge *Schumann* ■ *Dir* Neil Armfield • *Scr* Neil Armfield, Luke Davies, from Davies's novel

The Candy Man ★
Crime thriller   1969 · US · Colour · 97min

This deservedly obscure kidnapping drama shot on location in Mexico City stars George Sanders as a British drug pusher who decides to branch out by abducting the daughter of an American film star. Sanders's tired performance is typical of the boredom that drove him to suicide three years later; in contrast, Leslie Parrish over-emotes as the frantic mother. AE

George Sanders *Sidney Carter* • Leslie Parrish *Julia Evans* • Manolo Fabregas *Lieutenant Garcia* • Gina Ronan *Greta Hansen* • Carlos Cortez *Rick Pierce* • Pedro Galvan *Roger West* ■ *Dir* Herbert J Leder • *Scr* Herbert J Leder, from a story by Francis Swann

Candy Mountain ★★★ 15
Road movie   1987 · US · Colour · 91min

Ambitious musician Kevin J O'Connor pretends to know a legendary guitar-maker named Elmore Silk (Harris Yulin) in order to get a job with rocker David Johansen's band. When his bluff is finally called, he attempts to track Silk down via encounters with friends, lovers and relatives. The result is a quirky, if downbeat road movie that's more a celebration of the marginal than a straight story with a cohesive narrative. In a difficult, O'Connor sustains the interest right up to the uplifting payoff. AJ

Kevin J O'Connor *Julius Book* • Harris Yulin *Elmore Silk* • Tom Waits *Al Silk* • Bulle Ogier *Cornelia* • Roberts Blossom *Archie* • Leon Redbone *Huey* • Dr John *Henry* • Rita MacNeil *Winnie* • Joe Strummer *Mario* • Laurie Metcalf *Alice* • David Johansen *Keith* ■ *Dir* Robert Frank, Rudy Wurlitzer • *Scr* Rudy Wurlitzer

Candyman ★★★★ 18
Horror   1992 · US · Colour · 95min

Horror maestro Clive Barker's short story *The Forbidden* is the inspiration for director Bernard Rose's electrifying shocker in which student Virginia Madsen, researching urban legends in Chicago, uncovers a hook-handed mythical killer who then catapults her into the chilling realms of dread and destiny. Intelligent, gripping and refreshingly gimmick-free, this adult-orientated study in psychological fear is a breath of fresh scare. Madsen is terrific, giving a well-shaded performance as the emotionally abandoned heroine, and Rose's bold direction milks every terrifying moment of this compelling and atmospheric movie. AJ Violence, swearing, nudity. *DVD* BL

Virginia Madsen *Helen Lyle* • Tony Todd *Candyman* • Xander Berkeley *Trevor Lyle* • Kasi Lemmons *Bernadette Walsh* • Vanessa Williams *Anne-Marie McCoy* • DeJuan Guy *Jake* • Marianna Eliott *Clara* • Ted Raimi *Billy* • Ria Pavia *Monica* • Mark Daniels *Student* ■ *Dir* Bernard Rose • *Scr* Bernard Rose, from the short story *The Forbidden* by Clive Barker

Candyman: Farewell to the Flesh ★★ 18
Horror   1995 · US · Colour · 90min

Director Bill Condon shows little of the flair or fluency he would bring to his Oscar-winning *Gods and Monsters* in this long-winded and utterly conventional sequel to a marvellous original. Tony Todd returns as the hook-handed slave spirit, this time terrorising New Orleans during Mardi Gras. Not even the colourful carnival backdrop makes up for the predictable plot. AJ Violence, swearing, brief nudity. *DVD*

Tony Todd *Candyman/Daniel Robitaille* • Kelly Rowan *Annie Tarrant* • Timothy Carhart *Paul McKeever* • Veronica Cartwright *Octavia Tarrant* • William O'Leary *Ethan Tarrant* • Fay Hauser *Pam Carver* • Bill Nunn *Reverend Ellis* ■ *Dir* Bill Condon • *Scr* Rand Ravich, Mark Kruger, from a story by Clive Barker

Candyman: Day of the Dead ★ 18
Horror   1999 · US · Colour · 89min

In this dreadful made-for-video sequel, Tony Todd returns to little effect as the hook-handed bogeyman who tries to frame his artist descendant (Donna D'Errico) for the nasty murders of her best friends so she'll join him as a spectral legend and ease his netherworld loneliness. Overdoing the gore to a laughable degree, this remains yawningly predictable and unrelentingly stupid. AJ *DVD*

Tony Todd *Candyman/Daniel Robitaille* • Donna D'Errico *Caroline McKeever* • Wade Andrew Williams *Detective Samuel Kraft* • Nick Corri *David de la Paz* • Alexia Robinson *Tamara* ■ *Dir* Turi Meyer • *Scr* Al Septien, Turi Meyer, from the character created by Clive Barker

Cane Toads – an Unnatural History ★★★ PG
Cult documentary   1987 · Aus · Colour · 46min

Those who believe nature is rendered safe by the urbane explanations of David Attenborough might well be checking behind the sofa or under the bed after this rude shock. It's a wonderfully dotty history lesson about the wholesale import of cane toads into Australia in 1935 to annihilate the cane beetle, showing how the utter uselessness of the attempt bordered on the surreal. Not only were they unfit for the job, but the grubby beasts devoured everything in sight except for their targets. JM

■ *Dir/Scr* Mark T Lewis

Cane Toads: the Conquest ★★★ PG
Documentary   2010 · US/Aus · Colour · 83min

Imagine a small football with legs, a mouth and goggle eyes. That's pretty much the size and shape of the cane toad, a toxic import from the Americas via Hawaii that's laying siege to wildlife across an ever-increasing swathe of northern Australia. Film-maker Mark Lewis's second documentary about them ropes in an array of the equally obsessed as interviewees. The often humorously told mix of real footage and occasional dramatic re-enactment is a fascinating watch for anyone interested in oversized amphibians and eco-disasters. DA *DVD* BL SD

■ *Dir/Scr* Mark Lewis [Mark T Lewis]

Cannery Row ★★★ 15
Drama   1982 · US · Colour · 115min

Raquel Welch was originally cast in David S Ward's overly reverential production of two John Steinbeck novels, but was fired midway through filming. It's a pity, as her buxom sexuality might have roused this story of waterfront bums from its languor. Ward wrote *The Sting*, but his screenplay here lacks that movie's zip and suffers from an episodic narrative. Debra Winger takes on the Welch role of a hooker who yearns for Nick Nolte, excellent as a baseball star-turned-marine biologist. TH

Nick Nolte *Doc* • Debra Winger *Suzy* • Audra Lindley *Fauna* • Frank McRae *Hazel* • M Emmet Walsh *Mack* • Tom Mahoney *Hughie* • John Malloy *Jones* • James Keane *Eddie* • John Huston *Narrator* ■ *Dir* David S Ward • *Scr* David S Ward, from the novels *Cannery Row* and *Sweet Thursday* by John Steinbeck

Cannibal Girls ★
Comedy horror   1973 · Can · Colour · 83min

Before making the grade in Hollywood, Ivan Reitman churned out this dismal horror spoof featuring improvised patter by Second City TV alumni Eugene Levy and Andrea Martin. The couple play a musician and his girlfriend who breakdown in the Canadian backwoods where they encounter a trio of *femme fatales* with a penchant for flesh. This fails to deliver either laughs or shivers. AJ

Eugene Levy *Clifford Sturges* • Andrea Martin *Gloria Wellaby* • Ronald Ulrich *Reverend Alex St John* • Randall Carpenter *Anthea* • Bonnie Neilson *Clarissa* • Mira Pawluk *Leona* ■ *Dir* Ivan Reitman • *Scr* Robert Sandler

Cannibal Holocaust ★★★ 18
Horror   1979 · It · Colour · 97min

One of the titles most often quoted during the British "video nasties" scandal of the early 1980s, this gruesome offering is probably the finest of that bad bunch, and certainly the best of the cannibal genre. A New York professor (Robert Kerman alias porn actor Richard Bolla) goes to the Amazon jungle in search of a missing documentary film crew and finds horrifying evidence of their fate. Although the script is banal, director Ruggero Deodato makes the hunt for the film-makers exciting. Newspapers perpetuated the myth that the murders enacted were genuine well into the 1990s. The film was not legally available in Britain until 2001 when it was passed (with 5 minutes 44 seconds of cuts). DM Italian dubbed. *DVD* BL

Robert Kerman *Professor Harold Monroe* • Francesca Ciardi *Faye Daniels* • Perry Pirkanen *Jack Anders* • Luca Barbareschi *Mark Tommaso* ■ *Dir* Ruggero Deodato • *Scr* Gianfranco Clerici, from his story

Cannibal! the Musical ★★★ 18
Musical comedy horror
1993 · US · Colour · 97min

Only the creators of *South Park*, Trey Parker and Matt Stone, could have come up with this "all singing, all dancing, all flesh-eating" gore flick that's a weird, wonderfully awful mix of western spoof, *Scream*-style horror and cod Hollywood musical. The satire features the sole survivor of an ill-fated mining expedition who tells how his taste for gold was replaced by one for human flesh while singing of gay love, horses and snowmen. AJ Violence. *DVD*

Juan Schwartz [Trey Parker] *Alferd Packer* • Ian Hardin *Shannon Bell* • Matthew Stone [Matt Stone] *James Humphrey* • Jon Hegel *Israel Swan* • Jason McHugh *Frank Miller* • Dian Buchar *George Noon* ■ *Dir/Scr* Trey Parker

Cannibal Women in the Avocado Jungle of Death ★ 12
Comedy adventure   1989 · US · Colour · 85min

Can any film with a title this great be any good? "No" is the short answer, as far as this deadpan feminist send-up is concerned. Tough anthropologist Shannon Tweed is sent by the CIA on an expedition into the Californian wilderness to locate a legendary tribe of man-eating cannibal babes. The safari is a mix of stupid sex farce and talky rhetoric on women's issues. AJ Some nudity, swearing, violence.

Shannon Tweed *Dr Margo Hunt* • Adrienne Barbeau *Dr Kurtz* • Bill Maher *Jim* • Karen Mistal *Bunny* • Brett Stimely *Jean-Pierre* ■ *Dir/Scr* JF Lawton

Cannon for Cordoba ★★★ 12
Western   1970 · US · Colour · 99min

The Wild Bunch it ain't, but this western adventure is still an entertaining affair. George Peppard is a suitably heroic lead, playing an American soldier battling Mexican bandits in the early 20th century, and there's enough action to satisfy fans. The director is Paul Wendkos, an experienced Hollywood hand who since the 1970s has concentrated mainly on made-for-TV movies. JF Swearing, violence.

George Peppard *Captain Rod Douglas* • Giovanna Ralli *Leonora Cristobal* • Raf Vallone *Cordoba* • Pete Duel *Andy Rice* • Don Gordon *Sergeant Jackson Harkness* ■ *Dir* Paul Wendkos • *Scr* Stephen Kandel

Cannonball ★★ 12
Adventure thriller
1976 · HK/US · Colour · 90min

This is nothing more than a poor retread of director Paul Bartel's wilder and wittier *Death Race 2000*, with all the expensive futuristic trappings removed and loads more epic car crashes added. David Carradine is "Cannonball" Buckman, who signs up for the illegal Trans-American Grand Prix cross-country car race between

Los Angeles and New York, where no rules apply and underhand sabotage is *de rigueur*. Great stunts, shame about the formula-one plot. AJ **DVD**

David Carradine *Coy "Cannonball" Buckman* • Bill McKinney *Cade Redman* • Veronica Hamel *Linda* • Gerrit Graham *Perman Waters* • Robert Carradine *Jim Crandell* • Belinda Balaski *Maryann* • Martin Scorsese *Mafioso* • Roger Corman • Sylvester Stallone • Joe Dante ■ *Dir* Paul Bartel (1) | *Scr* Paul Bartel, Donald C Simpson

Cannonball Fever ★ PG
Comedy 1989 · US · Colour · 91min

Depressingly, this is one of the most expensive movies ever filmed in Canada. It's impossible to see where all the money went, for this third instalment in the *Cannonball Run* series is so bad it's embarrassing. This time a bunch of minor celebrities find themselves behind the wheels after the original racers are jailed by sheriff Peter Boyle. DP

John Candy *Charlie Cronyn* • Donna Dixon *Tiffany* • Matt Frewer *Alec* • Joe Flaherty *Vic* • Tim Matheson *Jack* • Mimi Kuzyk *Heather* • Melody Anderson *Lee* • Shari Belafonte *Margaret* • Peter Boyle *Chief Spiro T Edsel* • Lee Van Cleef *Grandfather* ■ *Dir* Jim Drake • *Scr* Michael Short

The Cannonball Run ★★ PG
Action comedy 1981 · US · Colour · 91min

This big-budget take on the illegal coast-to-coast car race movie was made at the height of Burt Reynolds's stardom and Roger Moore's tenure as James Bond. Not surprisingly it was a global smash, but as entertainment it leaves a lot to be desired. There are not nearly enough pile-ups and too many duff jokes from a cameo-studded cast, who act as if they're starring in each other's home movies. RS **DVD** **BL**

Burt Reynolds *JJ McClure* • Roger Moore *Seymour* • Farrah Fawcett *Pamela* • Dom DeLuise *Victor* • Dean Martin *Jamie Blake* • Sammy Davis Jr *Fenderbaum* • Jack Elam *Doctor* • Adrienne Barbeau *Marcie* • Terry Bradshaw *Terry* • Jackie Chan *First Subaru driver* • Jamie Farr *Sheik* • Peter Fonda *Chief biker* • Bianca Jagger *Sheik's sister* ■ *Dir* Hal Needham • *Scr* Brock Yates

Cannonball Run II ★ PG
Action comedy 1983 · US · Colour · 103min

One of the worst films ever made, this stars a plethora of old has-beens who try in vain to recapture the whimsical success of the original. It purports to be an all-action comedy, but should be approached with extreme caution. SH Swearing. **DVD** **BL**

Burt Reynolds *JJ McClure* • Dom DeLuise *Victor* • Dean Martin *Jamie Blake* • Sammy Davis Jr *Fenderbaum* • Jamie Farr *Sheik* • Telly Savalas *Hymie* • Shirley MacLaine *Veronica* • Jackie Chan *Jackie* • Frank Sinatra ■ *Dir* Hal Needham • *Scr* Hal Needham, Albert S Ruddy, Harvey Miller, from characters by Brock Yates

Can't Buy Me Love ★★ 15
Comedy 1987 · US · Colour · 92min

Fed up with his nerdy reputation at high school, Patrick Dempsey pays sexpot senior Amanda Peterson a hard-earned $1,000 to pose as his girlfriend for a month. The image-building works fine until she blows the gaff. A very predictable boy meets, hires and loses girl saga, this is given far too sentimental a spin to work well as romantic comedy. AJ Swearing. **DVD**

Patrick Dempsey *Ronald Miller* • Amanda Peterson *Cindy Mancini* • Courtney Gains *Kenneth Wurman* • Tina Caspary *Barbara* • Seth Green *Chuckie Miller* • Dennis Dugan *David Miller* ■ *Dir* Steve Rash • *Scr* Michael Swerdlick

Can't Hardly Wait ★ 12
Romantic comedy 1998 · US · Colour · 96min

Flat characters are stuck in underdeveloped situations in first-time directors Deborah Kaplan and Harry Elfont's attempt to recapture the mood of a John Hughes 1980s teen comedy. Set around a post-graduation party where couples meet, get drunk, indulge in bonding and gross slapstick, every stereotypical situation is exploited to little effect. AJ Swearing. **DVD**

Jennifer Love Hewitt *Amanda Beckett* • Ethan Embry *Preston Meyers* • Charlie Korsmo *William Lichter* • Lauren Ambrose *Denise Fleming* • Peter Facinelli *Mike Dexter* • Melissa Joan Hart *Yearbook girl* ■ *Dir/Scr* Harry Elfont, Deborah Kaplan

Can't Help Singing ★★ U
Musical western 1944 · US · Colour · 86min

This is an apt title for this Deanna Durbin vehicle, and her cevotees will doubtless embrace this western, vaguely influenced by the Broadway success of *Oklahoma!* Non-Durbin fans, however, will struggle with the dumb plot (Deanna heads west to marry, then changes her mind), uncharismatic leading man Robert Paige and director Frank Ryan's non-existent grasp of film narrative. TS **DVD**

Deanna Durbin *Caroline* • Robert Paige *Lawlor* • Akim Tamiroff *Gregory* • David Bruce *Latham* • Leonid Kinskey *Koppa* • Ray Collins *Senator Frost* • June Vincent *Miss MacLean* • Andrew Tombes *Sad Sam* ■ *Dir* Frank Ryan • *Scr* Lewis R Foster, Frank Ryan, from the novel *Girl of the Overland Trail* by Curtis B Warshawsky, Samuel J Warshawsky

Can't Stop the Music ★★★ PG
Musical 1980 · US · Colour · 117min

Aspiring songwriter Steve Guttenberg and girlfriend Valerie Perrine scour Greenwich Village looking for singers to do justice to his music in this heavily fictionalised account of how disco sensation the Village People rose to fame. All references to the group's gay genesis were placed on the periphery for commercial safety, although much fun can be had spotting the deliberate clues planted by director Nancy Walker. Reviled at the time for being dishonest, from a distance this camp catastrophe is fun and sums up the era. AJ

Valerie Perrine *Samantha Simpson* • Bruce Jenner *Ron White* • Steve Guttenberg *Jack Morell* • Paul Sand *Steve Waits* • Tammy Grimes *Sydney Channing* • June Havoc *Helen Morell* • Barbara Rush *Norma White* • Ray Simpson *Ray, policeman* • David Hodo *David, construction worker* • Felipe Rose *Felipe, Indian* • Randy Jones *Randy, cowboy* • Glenn Hughes *Glenn, leatherman* • Alexander Briley *Alexander, GI* ■ *Dir* Nancy Walker • *Scr* Bronte Woodard, Allan Carr

El Cantante ★ 15
Musical biographical drama 2006 · US · Colour · 109min

Caricatures and contrivances abound in this overwrought biopic of Hector Lavoe, the Puerto Rican singer who helped launch the salsa boom in the mid-1960s. A curiously inanimate Marc Anthony plays the charismatic Lavoe and Jennifer Lopez (the real-life Mrs Anthony) co-stars as the performer's strong-willed New York-born wife, Puchi. A surfeit of clichéd montage sequences chron cles the salsa pioneer's career, while Lopez struts, pouts and sulks her way through 30 years of celebrity, domestic discord and substance abuse without even having the grace to age in the interim. DP English, Spanish +subtitles. **DVD**

Marc Anthony *Héctor Lavoe* • Jennifer Lopez *Puchi* • John Ortiz (1) *Willie Colón* • Manny Perez *Eddie* ■ *Dir* Leon Ichaso • *Scr* Leon Ichaso, David Darmstaedter, Todd Anthony Bello, from a story by Darmstaedter, Eello

A Canterbury Tale ★★★★ U
Second World War drama 1944 · UK · BW · 119min

Michael Powell and Emeric Pressburger's re-think of Chaucer is a peculiar piece of wartime propaganda. Two army sergeants (one British, one American) and a girl arrive at a Kentish village which is within praying distance of Canterbury. There, girls who fraternise with servicemen are having glue poured into their hair as punishment. While it's hard to convey the film's eerie shifts of mood, it impresses as a study of a community resistant to change. This far-sighted film was dismissed at the time but is a lyrical celebration of a disappearing England. AT **DVD**

Eric Portman *Thomas Colpeper* • Sheila Sim *Alison Smith* • John Sweet *Bob Johnson* • Dennis Price *Peter Gibbs* • Charles Hawtrey *Thomas Duckett* • Hay Petrie *Woodcock* ■ *Dir/Scr* Michael Powell, Emeric Pressburger

The Canterbury Tales ★★★
Historical comedy drama 1971 · It/Fr · Colour · 104min

Coming between *The Decameron* and *Arabian Nights* in Pier Paolo Pasolini's classic tales trilogy, this adaptation of Chaucer's masterpiece outraged the purists with its bawdy bowdlerisation. Reinforcing his status as auteur, Pasolini also guests as the poet accompanying the party of pilgrims, who relieve the tedium of their journey to Beckett's shrine with a variety of tales. Glorying in the filth and vulgarity of medieval life and the grotesqueness of the characters, this is a film teeming with life and insight. DP In English, Italian.

Pier Paolo Pasolini *Geoffrey Chaucer* • Tom Baker *Jenkin* • Laura Betti *Wife of Bath* • JP Van Dyne *Cook* • Derek Deadman *Pardoner* • George Bethell Datch *Host of the Tabard* ■ *Dir* Pier Paolo Pasolini • *Scr* Pier Paolo Pasolini, from the stories by Geoffrey Chaucer

The Canterville Ghost ★★★
Supernatural comedy 1944 · US · BW · 95min

This enjoyable MGM version of Oscar Wilde's story has the wonderfully irascible Charles Laughton in the title role as the spirit who can only free himself from eternally roaming by performing one good deed. Made in the heat of wartime, this dated owing to its emphasis on harmonising Anglo-American relationships. However, a super cast handles the stilted sentiments with aplomb. TS

Charles Laughton *Sir Simon De Canterville/The Ghost* • Robert Young (1) *Cuffy Williams* • Margaret O'Brien *Lady Jessica De Canterville* • William Gargan *Sergeant Benson* • Reginald Owen *Lord Canterville* • Peter Lawford *Anthony De Canterville* ■ *Dir* Jules Dassin • *Scr* Edwin Harvey Blum, from the story by Oscar Wilde

The Canterville Ghost ★★★ U
Supernatural comedy 1996 · US · Colour · 87min

A fine TV adaptation of Oscar Wilde's fun fantasy about a cursed ghost and the young girl he befriends. This features *Star Trek: the Next Generation*'s Patrick Stewart (who also produced) and *Scream*'s Neve Campbell, who both deliver superb performances. The comedy side of the story is deliberately played down and the pathos brought centre stage. AJ **DVD**

Patrick Stewart *Sir Simon de Canterville* • Neve Campbell *Virginia Otis* • Edward Wiley *Hiram Otis* • Cherie Lunghi *Lucille Otis* • Ciaran Fitzgerald *Adam Otis* • Raymond Pickard *Washington Otis* • Donald Sinden *Mr Umney* • Joan Sims *Mrs Umney* • Leslie Phillips *Lord Henry* ■ *Dir* Sydney Macartney • *Scr* Robert Benedetti, from the story by Oscar Wilde

Canticle of the Stones ★★★
Documentary drama 1990 · Bel/UK/Ger · Colour · 110min

Following the acclaimed *Wedding in Galilee*, Michel Khleifi attempted to meld drama with archive footage in this study of life in Gaza between the riots of the 1960s and the Intifada. The documentary material is particularly provocative, as various Palestinians recall the fighting that reduced their settlements to rubble and decimated a generation of their youth. The fictional segments, however, involving reunited lovers Bushra Karaman and Makram Khouri, are awash with pompous pronouncements which trivialise the tragedy of this troubled region. DP Arabic +subtitles.

Bushra Karaman • Makram Khouri ■ *Dir* Michel Khleifi

Canyon Passage ★★★★ U
Western 1946 · US · Colour · 91min

This routine story of harsh frontier life was one of the first mature postwar westerns. Director Jacques Tourneur makes wonderful use of the Oregon locations and

lifts the material by his thoughtful staging of everything from a cabin-raising ceremony for a newly married couple to the saloon fight between hero Dana Andrews and heavy Ward Bond. Alas, Britain's Patricia Roc – making her bid for Hollywood fame – is no match for the fiery Susan Hayward. AE

Dana Andrews *Logan Stuart* • Brian Donlevy *George Camrose* • Susan Hayward *Lucy Overmire* • Patricia Roc *Caroline Marsh* • Ward Bond *Honey Bragg* • Andy Devine *Ben Dance* ■ *Dir* Jacques Tourneur • *Scr* Ernest Pascal, from the novel by Ernest Haycox

The Canyons ★★★ 18
Thriller 2013 · US · Colour · 96min

Director Paul Schrader and writer Bret Easton Ellis join forces for this micro-budget morality piece. Lindsay Lohan is pretty terrific in an otherwise flawed movie, as a shallow but ultimately sympathetic Los Angeles woman who has hooked up with a trust-fund brat (played by porn actor James Deen, whose bad acting somehow suits). But the plot is beside the point: Schrader and Ellis are more interested in capturing the moral lassitude of modern LA, where everyone is distracted, and sex and love are meaninglessly interchangeable. LF Swearing, sex scenes, nudity.

Lindsay Lohan *Tara* • James Deen *Christian* • Nolan Funk [Nolan Gerard Funk] *Ryan* • Amanda Brooks *Gina* • Gus Van Sant *Dr Campbell* ■ *Dir* Paul Schrader • *Scr* Bret Easton Ellis

Cape Fear ★★★★ 15
Classic thriller 1962 · US · BW · 101min

This is a gripping and tension-laden thriller about embittered ex-con Robert Mitchum terrorising the frightened family of the meek lawyer (Gregory Peck) who put him in prison. Great shocks increase the climactic suspense, with Mitchum giving a portrayal of villainy that's unforgettably vicious and sadistic. Director J Lee Thompson's skilful use of light and shadow enhances the mood, while Bernard Herrmann's score counterpoints the growing dread with precision. AJ **DVD** **BL**

Gregory Peck *Sam Bowden* • Robert Mitchum *Max Cady* • Polly Bergen *Peggy Bowden* • Lori Martin *Nancy Bowden* • Martin Balsam *Mark Dutton* • Jack Kruschen *Dave Grafton* • Telly Savalas *Charles Sievers* ■ *Dir* J Lee Thompson • *Scr* James R Webb, from the novel *The Executioners* by John D MacDonald • *Cinematographer* Sam Leavitt

Cape Fear ★★★★ 18
Thriller 1991 · US · Colour · 122min

Martin Scorsese has flirted with Hollywood in the past, but did this remake of the 1962 classic was an unashamed bid for the mainstream. Robert De Niro takes the Robert Mitchum role, playing a vicious ex-convict who torments his former attorney Nick Nolte. De Niro is way over the top as the Bible-babbling psychopath, but where Scorsese scores is in his portrayal of Nolte and his family (Jessica Lange, Juliette Lewis). In the original they were the embodiment of apple-pie American values, but here they are falling apart at the seams. Scorsese brings a dazzling array of cinematic techniques to the party and only loses his way in a ludicrous finale. JF Swearing, violence. **DVD** **BL**

Robert De Niro *Max Cady* • Nick Nolte *Sam Bowden* • Jessica Lange *Leigh Bowden* • Juliette Lewis *Danielle Bowden* • Joe Don Baker *Claude Kersek* • Robert Mitchum *Lieutenant Elgart* • Gregory Peck *Lee Heller* • Martin Balsam *Judge* • Illeana Douglas *Lori Davis* ■ *Dir* Martin Scorsese • *Scr* Wesley Strick, from the 1962 film, from the novel *The Executioners* by John D MacDonald • *Cinematographer* Freddie Francis

Capitalism: a Love Story ★★★ 12
Documentary 2009 · Can/US · Colour · 122min

Having tackled George W Bush's foreign policy (*Fahrenheit 9/11*) and America's healthcare system (*Sicko*), Michael Moore here turns his attention to corporate greed. His line of argument is that benevolent capitalism has given way to the ruthless

C

machinations of Wall Street, and many ordinary Americans are victims as a result. These include underpaid airline pilots who have to take a second job and a widow whose so-called "Dead Peasants" insurance policy has generated a handsome profit for her late husband's employers. Moore comes up with enough of these startling moments to keep us watching, though he's certainly stronger on huff and puff than concrete solutions. TJ Swearing. **DVD**

Michael Moore (2) *Michael Moore* • Wallace Shawn ■ *Dir/Scr* Michael Moore (2)

Capone ★★★ 18

Biographical crime drama
1975 · US · Colour · 97min

Ben Gazzara gained 20 pounds by eating spaghetti for the title role in this slick exploitation biography of Al Capone. Showing the rise of the iron-hearted, death-dealing kingpin of Chicago's machine-gun mobs in the Roaring Twenties, his fall at the hands of the tax men and descent into syphilitic madness, director Steve Carver emphasises fast-paced action, copious blood-letting and speakeasy atmospheres above the true facts. Sylvester Stallone plays Frank "The Enforcer" Nitti, Capone's treacherous lieutenant. AJ **DVD**

Ben Gazzara *Al Capone* • Susan Blakely *Iris Crawford* • Harry Guardino *Johnny Torrio* • John Cassavetes *Frankie Yale* • Sylvester Stallone *Frank Nitti* ■ *Dir* Steve Carver • *Scr* Howard Browne

Capote ★★★★ 15

Biographical drama
2005 · US/Can · Colour · 109min

Truman Capote caused a literary sensation with his 1966 "non-fiction novel" *In Cold Blood*, about the real-life slayings of a Kansas family in 1959. The book was filmed a year later, but here director Bennett Miller tackles the equally fascinating story of how the writing of Capote's masterwork consumed the author's life over a period of six years. Travelling to Kansas, Capote (Philip Seymour Hoffman) gains the trust of the townsfolk and chief investigator Alvin Dewey (Chris Cooper), but the heart of the film lies in Capote's strange ambivalence towards the murderers, especially Perry Smith (played by Clifton Collins Jr). Hoffman brilliantly captures the mercurial, effeminate mannerisms and distinctive tones of the Manhattan literary star. AS Violence. **DVD BL**

Philip Seymour Hoffman *Truman Capote* • Catherine Keener *Nelle Harper Lee* • Clifton Collins Jr *Perry Smith* • Chris Cooper *Alvin Dewey* • Bruce Greenwood *Jack Dunphy* • Bob Balaban *William Shawn* • Amy Ryan *Marie Dewey* • Mark Pellegrino *Dick Hickock* ■ *Dir* Bennett Miller • *Scr* Dan Futterman, from the non-fiction book *Capote: a Biography* by Gerald Clarke

Caprice ★★★ U

Comedy thriller
1967 · US · Colour · 93min

The later movies of Doris Day now look like period artefacts; in this confection, co-produced by her then-husband Martin Melcher, she plays an agent working for an international cosmetics company. Director Frank Tashlin shows his usual deft hand with a daft plot and is skilled in getting the most out of Leon Shamroy's cinematography, despite Day's apparent insistence that her close-ups were filmed through multilayered gauze. Day's co-star is a quaintly cast Richard Harris, whose own insistence on wearing blue eye shadow effectively sabotages his right to be taken seriously. TS **DVD BL**

Doris Day *Patricia Foster* • Richard Harris *Christopher White* • Ray Walston *Stuart Clancy* • Jack Kruschen *Matthew Cutter* • Edward Mulhare *Sir Jason Fox* • Lilia Skala *Madame Piasco* • Michael J Pollard *Barney* ■ *Dir* Frank Tashlin • *Scr* Jay Jayson, Frank Tashlin, from a story by Martin Hale

Capricious Summer ★★★★★

Period comedy drama 1968 · Cz · Colour · 78min

It's not often that you come across a method director, but Jiří Menzel learned to walk the tightrope for his role as an

itinerant showman in this enchanting period comedy drama. He also manages to slip a little subversive allegory into the story of a trio of friends whose tranquil existence is shaken by the appearance of Menzel's stunning wife, Jana Drchalova. Perfectly capturing the ambience of provincial life, the film's real strength is the impeccable performances of swimming pool boss Rudolf Hrusinsky and priest Frantisek Rehak. DP Czech +subtitles.

Rudolf Hrusinsky *Dura* • Vlastimil Brodsky *Major Hugo* • Mila Myslikova *Durova* • Frantisek Rehak *Abbé Roch* • Jana Drchalova *Anna* • Jiří Menzel *Arnostek* ■ *Dir* Jiří Menzel • *Scr* Jiří Menzel, from a novel by Vladislav Vancura, Vaclau Nyult

Capricorn One ★★★★ PG

Thriller 1978 · US · Colour · 118min

Did the Americans really land on the Moon, or did they fake it in a TV studio? That's the premise of this ingenious thriller, in which three men are bound for Mars until there's a technical hitch on the launch pad. The astronauts end up faking the mission to save face but their space capsule (which went without them) burns up on re-entry. Problem one: three embarrassingly alive astronauts. Problem two: their distraught families. Problem three: Elliott Gould as a nosey reporter. Directed by Peter Hyams with real flair, this is hugely enjoyable with a gripping finale. AT **DVD BL**

Elliott Gould *Robert Caulfield* • James Brolin *Charles Brubaker* • Sam Waterston *Peter Willis* • Brenda Vaccaro *Kay Brubaker* • OJ Simpson *John Walker* • Hal Holbrook *Dr James Kelloway* • Karen Black *Judy Drinkwater* • Telly Savalas *Albain* ■ *Dir/Scr* Peter Hyams

The Captain ★★★

Period drama 1960 · Fr/It · Colour · 115min

While it is hard to fault the period trappings and sense of time and place created by director André Hunebelle, this is a pale imitation of the kind of rousing swashbuckler that came from the pen of Alexandre Dumas. Set in 17th-century France, it concerns the plot of Marie de Medicis to murder her son, Louis XIII. Jean Marais is more statuesque than ever as a loyal courtier, and not even the attentions of Elsa Martinelli can rouse him from his lethargy. DP French dubbed.

Jean Marais *François de Capestang* • Elsa Martinelli *Gisele d'Angoulême* • Bourvil *Cogolin* • Arnoldo Foà *Concini* • Pierrette Bruno *Giuseppa* • Christian Fourçade *Louis XIII* ■ *Dir* André Hunebelle • *Scr* Jean Halain, André Hunebelle, Pierre Foucaud, from the novel by Michel Zevaco

Captain America ★★ U

Fantasy adventure 1979 · US · Colour · 93min

It's odd that the most patriotic superhero of all, in the United States at least, is the one who had failed to take off until the recent reboot. In this TV movie, Reb Brown has the necessary physique but little else as he dons the stars-and-stripes costume to save Phoenix from being blown up by a neutron bomb. An even sillier sequel followed, and there was a movie version in 1990, but in both cases the concept failed to grab the public's imagination. JF

Reb Brown *Steve Rogers/Captain America* • Len Birman *Dr Simon Mills* • Heather Menzies *Dr Wendy Day* • Steve Forrest *Lou Brackett* • Robin Mattson *Tina Hayden* ■ *Dir* Rod Holcomb • *Scr* Don Ingalls, from a story by Chester Krumholz, Ingalls

Captain America ★★ PG

Action adventure 1990 · US · Colour · 93min

This is another botched attempt to revive the popular American cartoon character, with Matt Salinger battling the evil Red Skull. Albert Pyun is a competent director of sci-fi and martial arts action movies, but this tough, brooding comic book fantasy suffers in comparison to other big-budget superhero adventures, and Salinger lacks charisma as the hero. JF Violence.

Matt Salinger *Steve Rogers/Captain America* • Ned Beatty *Sam Kolawetz* • Scott Paulin *Red Skull* • Ronny Cox *President Tom Kimball* •

Darren McGavin *General Fleming* • Melinda Dillon *Mrs Rogers* ■ *Dir* Albert Pyun • *Scr* Stephen Tolkin

Captain America: the First Avenger ★★★ 12

Wartime action adventure
2011 · US · Colour · 119min

In this sturdy Marvel Comics tale, an asthmatic is enhanced to the peak of human perfection to help the US war effort. Director Joe Johnston cheerfully emulates the cheesy charms of old Hollywood, while Chris Evans's performance in the title role is engagingly straightforward. Whether a CGI head on a 90lb weakling body or muscled up in patriotic uniform with indestructible shield, he is perfectly matched by gruff Tommy Lee Jones, sassy Hayley Atwell and power-crazed Hugo Weaving. Despite the retro environment, there's enough sci-fi paraphernalia to stop this becoming old-fashioned. A sequel, *Captain America: the Winter Soldier*, is due in 2014. AJ Some violence. **DVD BL CS**

Chris Evans *Steve Rogers/Captain America* • Hugo Weaving *Johann Schmidt/Red Skull* • Tommy Lee Jones *Colonel Chester Phillips* • Hayley Atwell *Peggy Carter* • Sebastian Stan *James Buchanan "Bucky" Barnes* • Toby Jones *Arnim Zola* ■ *Dir* Joe Johnston • *Scr* Christopher Markus, Stephen McFeely, Joss Whedon, from characters by Jack Kirby, Joe Simon • *Production designer* Rick Heinrichs

Captain America: the Winter Soldier ★★★★ 12

Action adventure 2014 · US · Colour · 130min

Chris Evans returns as the star-spangled super-soldier who here joins forces with Scarlett Johansson's Black Widow and newcomer to the franchise Anthony Mackie, playing airborne wingman Falcon. The colourful cast of heroes, undercover villains and ghosts from the past bring nimble nuance to a deviously well-constructed story that plays like an old-school political thriller as much as a classy comic-book adventure. The resulting action covers the full gamut of spectacular destruction, from highway car chases to heli-carrier sky battles. Yet it's the character interplay, astute direction and emotionally strong themes that add weight to no less than two end credit sequences. Part 3 is due in 2016. AJ **DVD BL CS**

Chris Evans *Steve Rogers/Captain America* • Samuel L Jackson *Nick Fury* • Scarlett Johansson *Natasha Romanoff/Black Widow* • Anthony Mackie *Sam Wilson/The Falcon* • Sebastian Stan *James Buchanan "Bucky" Barnes/The Winter Soldier* • Robert Redford *Alexander Pierce* • Toby Jones *Arnim Zola* • Jenny Agutter *World Security Council member* ■ *Dir* Anthony Russo, Joe Russo • *Scr* Christopher Markus, Stephen McFeely, from characters by Jack Kirby, Joe Simon

Captain America: Civil War ★★★★ 12A

Action adventure 2016 · US · Colour · 147min

More *Avengers 2.5* than a solo adventure, this exhilarating threequel sees Chris Evans's shield-flinging super-soldier battling over friendship and principle as much as the nefarious plans of the bad guys. Superhero registration is demanded and a world-weary Tony Stark (Robert Downey Jr) agrees, which puts him at loggerheads with a sceptical Cap. Loyalties are shattered, the team disassembles and the mother of all smackdowns looms, with old hands (Hawkeye, War Machine) and fresh recruits (Ant-Man, the debuting Black Panther) signing up to Team Cap or Team Iron Man. Pace, thumping action and sharp fight scenes combine with crisp character interplay. Stupendous stuff. JA Violence, some swearing. **3D CS**

Chris Evans *Steve Rogers/Captain America* • Robert Downey Jr *Tony Stark/Iron Man* • Scarlett Johansson *Natasha Romanoff/Black Widow* • Sebastian Stan *Bucky Barnes/Winter Soldier* ■ *Dir* Anthony Russo, Joe Russo • *Scr* Christopher Markus, Stephen McFeely, from characters by Joe Simon, Jack Kirby

Captain Apache ★★★ 12

Western 1971 · US/Sp · Colour · 90min

This is one of a series of ferociously violent westerns produced by a group of left-leaning American expatriates in Spain in the late 1960s and early 1970s. Director Alexander Singer once made the now forgotten mini-masterpiece, *A Cold Wind in August*, but he seems less happy here. Nevertheless, there's some real tension generated amid the excellent use of the landscape, while English character actor Percy Herbert holds his own against such western stalwarts as Stuart Whitman and Lee Van Cleef. TS Swearing. **DVD**

Lee Van Cleef *Captain Apache* • Carroll Baker *Maude* • Stuart Whitman *Griffin* • Percy Herbert *Moon* • Elisa Montés *Rosita* • Tony Vogel *Snake* • Charles Stalnaker *O'Rourke* • Charlie Bravo *Sanchez* ■ *Dir* Alexander Singer • *Scr* Milton Sperling, Philip Yordan, from the novel by SE Whitman

Captain Blood ★★★★ PG

Swashbuckling adventure
1935 · US · BW · 94min

"Come, feel the wind that fills the sails that carry us all to freedom!" Errol Flynn, a last-minute substitute for asthma sufferer Robert Donat, stars as Peter Blood, doctor-turned-pirate, in Michael Curtiz's marvellous adventure. Today, it's a little long and creaks in places, but the camera loved Flynn's devil-may-care arrogance, and *Captain Blood* remains important as the first leading role of a movie legend. TS **DVD**

Errol Flynn *Captain Blood* • Olivia de Havilland *Arabella Bishop* • Lionel Atwill *Colonel Bishop* • Basil Rathbone *Captain Levasseur* • Ross Alexander (1) *Jeremy Pitt* • Guy Kibbee *Hagthorpe* ■ *Dir* Michael Curtiz • *Scr* Casey Robinson, from the novel by Rafael Sabatini

Captain Boycott ★★★

Historical drama 1947 · UK · BW · 92min

This "serious comedy" from the team of Frank Launder and Sidney Gilliat is about absentee British landowners in Ireland and their rebellious Irish workers. Set in the 1880s, it stars Stewart Granger and Kathleen Ryan, with Cecil Parker as the unpleasant Boycott, whose name entered the language after a failed attempt to collect the rent by force. Lavishly made, it falls uneasily between adventure and political lampoon. AT

Stewart Granger *Hugh Davin* • Kathleen Ryan *Anne Killain* • Cecil Parker *Captain Boycott* • Robert Donat *Charles Stewart Parnell* • Mervyn Johns *Watty Connell* • Alastair Sim *Father McKeogh* • Niall MacGinnis *Mark Killain* • Maurice Denham *Lt Col Strickland* ■ *Dir* Frank Launder • *Scr* Frank Launder, Wolfgang Wilhelm, from the novel by Philip Rooney

Captain Carey, USA ★★

Spy drama 1950 · US · BW · 82min

Alan Ladd is the US army captain sent to an Italian town to root out Nazi collaborators who betrayed his compatriots during the Second World War. A promising premise, but the plot is a mass of confusion that defeats director Mitchell Leisen and leaves the viewer feeling as numb as Ladd looks. The only real success is the Oscar-winning song *Mona Lisa*, which sold a million copies for Nat King Cole. RK

Alan Ladd *Webster Carey* • Wanda Hendrix *Giula* • Celia Lovsky *Contessa Francesca De Cresci* • Angela Clarke *Serafina* • Richard Avonde *Count Carlo De Cresci* • Joseph Calleia *Dr Lunati* ■ *Dir* Mitchell Leisen • *Scr* Robert Thoeren, from the novel *After Midnight* by Martha Albrand

Captain Corelli's Mandolin ★★ 15

Second World War romantic drama
2001 · US/Fr/UK · Colour · 126min

Louis de Bernière's surprise bestseller about an Italian then Nazi-occupied Greek island during the Second World War was so much more than the picture-postcard love story depicted here. Director John Madden and cinematographer John Toll certainly fashion a sumptuous holiday brochure out of Cephalonia, while a sanitised version of the multilayered book plays out like a carnival of dodgy accents. Nicolas Cage's mandolin-plucking Italian is a cartoon, and the miscast Penélope Cruz plays the doctor's daughter Pelagia as a Spanish Greek. **AC** Violence, swearing. *DVD*

Nicolas Cage *Captain Antonio Corelli* • Penélope Cruz *Pelagia* • John Hurt *Dr Iannis* • Christian Bale *Mandras* • David Morrissey *Captain Gunther Weber* • Irene Papas *Drosoula* ■ *Dir* John Madden • *Scr* Shawn Slovo, from the novel by Louis de Bernières • *Cinematographer* John Toll

Capt Eddie ★★★ U

Biographical drama   1945 · US · BW · 107min

The life and times of Eddie Rickenbacker, the First World War flying ace and racing driver, are re-created in this lavish biopic. The focal point is the time when he crashed his plane and nearly drowned in the middle of the Pacific, an event which makes his whole life pass in front of him - and us. Fred MacMurray handles the part with his customary charm; you really believe he's a hero who can handle everything with a shrug and a grin. The film is episodic and not without its dull stretches, but it's still a genuine slice of Americana. **AT**

Fred MacMurray *Eddie Rickenbacker* • Lloyd Nolan *Lieutenant Whittaker* • Charles Bickford *William Rickenbacker* • Thomas Mitchell *Ike Howard* • Lynn Bari *Adelaide Frost* • Mary Phillips [Mary Philips] *Elsie Rickenbacker* • Richard Conte *Bartek* ■ *Dir* Lloyd Bacon • *Scr* John Tucker Battle

Captain Fantastic ★★★ 15

Drama   2015 · US · Colour · 118min

A road movie about a family of social justice warriors who risk being taken into care to attend their late mother's funeral, this bittersweet feelgood comedy ticks plenty of boxes. Viggo Mortensen is the radically left-wing father of six who keeps his brood out in the wild, teaching them about art and literature but mostly about survival. But the film's commercial ambitions undermine the political points it scores; indeed, it's hard to see what viewers will make of a film that has its heroes shun Christmas to celebrate Noam Chomsky Day. **DW** Swearing.

Viggo Mortensen *Ben* • George MacKay *Bodevan* • Missi Pyle *Ellen* • Steve Zahn *Dave* • Frank Langella *Jack* ■ *Dir/Scr* Matt Ross

Captain from Castile ★★★ PG

Period adventure   1947 · US · Colour · 135min

This expansive and sumptuous 20th Century-Fox epic is set around the 16th-century conquest of Mexico by Cortez (one of Cesar Romero's best performances) and distinguished by one of the finest musical scores in Hollywood history. Today's audiences may be less tolerant of its length, and a miscast Tyrone Power grows ever more wooden as the tortuous tale of revenge and greed unfurls. Despite its shortcomings, though, this is diverting and colourful entertainment. **TS** *DVD*

Tyrone Power *Pedro De Vargas* • Jean Peters *Catana Perez* • Cesar Romero *Hernando Cortez* • Lee J Cobb *Juan Garcia* • John Sutton *Diego De Silva* • Antonio Moreno *Don Francisco* ■ *Dir* Henry King • *Scr* Lamar Trotti, from the novel by Samuel Shellabarger

The Captain Hates the Sea ★★★

Comedy   1934 · US · BW · 84min

Comedy tends to date more than any other genre, but there's still enjoyment to be had from this slightly wacky film based around the captain of an ocean liner, played by Walter Connolly. An episodic plot about some of the passengers includes an appearance by John Gilbert - ex-silent star, close companion of Garbo and notorious alcoholic - as a man trying to give up the bottle. Unusually for the time, the film was shot on location, and director Lewis Milestone keeps a tight rein on the various plot strands. **SG**

Victor McLaglen *Schulte* • Helen Vinson *Janet Grayson* • John Gilbert (1) *Steve Bramley* • Alison Skipworth *Mrs Magruder* • Wynne Gibson *Mrs Jeddock* • Walter Connolly *Captain Helquist* ■ *Dir* Lewis Milestone • *Scr* Wallace Smith

Captain Horatio Hornblower RN ★★ U

Swashbuckling adventure   1951 · UK · Colour · 116min

Based on three CS Forester stories about the scourge of Napoleon's navy, this sprawling, handsome but flat feature suffers from too many shifts of emphasis between action adventure and psychological study. Gregory Peck (in a role originally meant for Errol Flynn) plays Hornblower as a high-principled stuffed shirt and thus confounds director Raoul Walsh's efforts to inject some pace. What should have been stirring stuff spends too much time becalmed. **DP**

Gregory Peck *Captain Horatio Hornblower* • Virginia Mayo *Lady Barbara Wellesley* • Robert Beatty *Lieutenant William Bush* • James Robertson-Justice *Quist* • Terence Morgan *Lieutenant Gerard* • Stanley Baker *Mr Harrison* • Christopher Lee *Captain* ■ *Dir* Raoul Walsh • *Scr* Ivan Goff, Ben Roberts, Aeneas MacKenzie, from the novels by CS Forester

Captain Jack ★★★ PG

Comedy adventure   1998 · UK · Colour · 96min

This slight but genial seafaring adventure has Bob Hoskins playing the good captain of the title. Tiring of endless pleasure cruises, Jack decides to re-create the journey of an 18th-century whaler, Captain Scoresby, who sailed from Whitby to the Arctic. He assembles a disparate crew of loners and losers and together they set off on the adventure of a lifetime. Jack Rosenthal's script lacks the sharpness of his best TV work, but the scenery is nice, the performances adept and the direction from Robert Young uncynical. **JF** *DVD*

Bob Hoskins *Captain Jack* • Anna Massey *Phoebe* • Gemma Jones *Eunice* • David Troughton *Emmett* • Peter McDonald *Andy* • Sadie Frost *Tessa* • Maureen Lipman *Miss Barbara Bostock* • Patrick Malahide *Mr Lancing* ■ *Dir* Robert Young (2) • *Scr* Jack Rosenthal, from articles by Nick Davies

Captain January ★★★ U

Musical drama   1936 · US · BW · 72min

This perky Shirley Temple vehicle casts her as a little girl rescued from a shipwreck that claims the life of her parents. Adopted by Guy Kibbee's kindly lighthouse keeper, she runs into trouble when the local truant officer (Sara Haden) decides to dispatch her to boarding school. The highlight is the Temple and Buddy Ebsen singing and dancing *At the Codfish Ball* to Jack Donahue's choreography. This was one of four 1936 releases that maintained Temple as the biggest box-office draw in America for the second year running. **AE** *DVD*

Shirley Temple *Star* • Guy Kibbee *Captain January* • Slim Summerville *Captain Nazro* • June Lang *Mary Marshall* • Buddy Ebsen *Paul Roberts* • Sara Haden *Agatha Morgan* • Jane Darwell *Eliza Croft* ■ *Dir* David Butler • *Scr* Sam Hellman, Gladys Lehman, Harry Tugend, from a story by Laura E Richards

Captain Kidd ★★★ U

Swashbuckling adventure   1945 · US · BW · 88min

Charles Laughton, his triumph as Captain Bligh in *Mutiny on the Bounty* behind him, takes to the high seas again in this swashbuckler. The star is in barnstorming form as the devious and bloodthirsty pirate, while his larger-than-life posturings are both fearful and funny. Gilbert Roland and John Carradine make fine henchmen, Randolph Scott is the hero, while Barbara Britton is the film's fleeting gesture towards romance. **RK** *DVD*

Charles Laughton *Captain William Kidd* • Randolph Scott *Adam Mercy* • Barbara Britton *Lady Anne* • Reginald Owen *Cary Shadwell* • John Carradine *Orange Povey* • Gilbert Roland *Jose Lorenzo* • John Qualen *Bert Blivens* ■ *Dir* Rowland V Lee • *Scr* Norman Reilly Raine, from a story by Robert H Lee

Captain Kidd and the Slave Girl ★★ U

Period adventure   1954 · US · Colour · 84min

This is a second-league but reasonably entertaining swashbuckler-cum-romance in about a wicked earl using a beautiful young woman as bait to discover the whereabouts of Captain Kidd's treasure. Trouble is the pirate and the lady fall in love. No big star names here, but Anthony Dexter, who looks more like a nerdy executive than a famous pirate, and the younger, less famous Gabor sister, Eva, are fine. **RK**

Anthony Dexter *Captain Kidd* • Eva Gabor *Slave girl* • Alan Hale Jr ■ *Dir* Lew Landers • *Scr* Jack Pollexfen, Aubrey Wisberg

Captain Kronos: Vampire Hunter ★★★ 15

Horror   1972 · UK · Colour · 87min

In a bid to revitalise the genre during the 1970s, Hammer gave writer/director Brian Clemens, the brains behind *The Avengers*, carte blanche to bring new blood to the vampire myth. The result is a bright and breezy blend of horror, comedy, swashbuckler and Italian western that follows Horst Janson as he tracks down aristocratic bloodsuckers, with a little help from hunchback professor John Cater and exotic gypsy dancer Caroline Munro. A fun fear-frolic that became an instant Hammer cult. **AJ** Violence *DVD*

Horst Janson *Captain Kronos* • John Carson *Dr Marcus* • John Cater *Professor Grost* • Shane Briant *Paul Durward* • Caroline Munro *Carla* • Ian Hendry *Kerro* • Wanda Ventham *Lady Durward* ■ *Dir/Scr* Brian Clemens

Captain Lightfoot ★★ U

Period adventure   1955 · US · Colour · 94min

Rock Hudson stars as a 19th-century Irish rebel who joins an outfit led by Jeff Morrow to fight against the English. Morrow is wounded and leaves the heroics to Hudson, who, between battles, romances the boss's daughter (Barbara Rush). Authentic locations do little to rescue this dreary and basically uneventful adventure story, produced by Ross Hunter and directed by Douglas Sirk. **RK**

Rock Hudson *Michael Martin* • Barbara Rush *Aga Doherty* • Jeff Morrow *John Doherty (Captain Thunderbolt)* • Kathleen Ryan *Lady Anne More* • Finlay Currie *Callahan* ■ *Dir* Douglas Sirk • *Scr* WR Burnett, Oscar Brodney, from a story by WR Burnett

Captain Nemo and the Underwater City ★ U

Fantasy adventure   1969 · UK · Colour · 105min

Did anyone have faith in this project? Robert Ryan as Nemo looks as if experiencing the "bends" would be preferable to participating in the picture, which has barely adequate effects and a shoddy script of borrowed ideas. **DP**

Robert Ryan *Captain Nemo* • Chuck Connors *Senator Robert Fraser* • Nanette Newman *Helena* • John Turner *Joab* • Luciana Paluzzi *Mala* • Bill Fraser *Barnaby* • Kenneth Connor *Swallow* • Allan Cuthbertson *Lomax* • Christopher Hartstone *Philip* ■ *Dir* James Hill • *Scr* Jane Baker, R Wright Campbell, from characters by Jules Verne

Captain Newman, MD ★★★ 12

Comedy drama   1963 · US · Colour · 120min

Gregory Peck is the military hospital psychiatrist dealing with three cases involving guilt. Corporal Bobby Darin believes himself to be a coward; colonel Eddie Albert feels responsible for the deaths of his men in combat; while Robert Duvall hates himself for hiding out in Nazi territory. The actors are good, and it's entertaining up to a point, but suffers from its uncomfortable mix of drama, sentimentality and comedy. **RK**

Gregory Peck *Capt Josiah J Newman* • Tony Curtis *Corp Jackson Laibowitz* • Angie Dickinson *Lieut Francie Corum* • Bobby Darin *Corporal Jim Tompkins* • Eddie Albert *Col Norval Algate Bliss* • Bethel Leslie *Mrs Paul Cabot Winston* • Larry

Storch *Corporal Gavoni* • Jane Withers *Lieut Grace Blodgett* • Robert Duvall *Capt Paul Cabot Winston* ■ *Dir* David Miller (1) • *Scr* Richard L Breen, Phoebe Ephron, Henry Ephron, from a novel by Leo Rosten

Captain Phillips ★★★★★ 12

Drama based on a true story   2013 · US · Colour · 128min

Director Paul Greengrass pulls no punches with this true-life tale, which sees Tom Hanks as Richard Phillips, the captain of a US cargo ship hijacked by Somali pirates in 2009. As with his 9/11 drama *United 93*, Greengrass re-creates the shocking events with a heart-pounding urgency. But the director's greatest skill is conveying the growing desperation of both Phillips and lead pirate Muse (Barkhad Abdi) after the initial, breathtakingly staged raid goes awry. Even when the US Navy turns up, the tension continues to escalate, as the political ramifications of the kidnapping call for a decisive solution. It all builds to a dizzying emotional crescendo in the final scenes, with Hanks at the very peak of his powers. **SP** English, Somali +subtitles. Violence, swearing. *DVD* +Blu-ray

Tom Hanks *Captain Richard Phillips* • Catherine Keener *Andrea Phillips* • Barkhad Abdi *Muse* • Michael Chernus *Shane Murphy* ■ *Dir* Paul Greengrass • *Scr* Billy Ray, from the autobiography *A Captain's Duty: Somali Pirates, Navy SEALs, and Dangerous Days at Sea* by Richard Phillips with Stephan Talty

Captain Ron ★★ 12

Comedy   1992 · US · Colour · 95min

There's not much worth noting in this Disney attempt at maritime comedy, in which Kurt Russell dons an eye-patch and something that looks like a bikini. When businessman Martin Short and his wife Mary Kay Place set sail with their sassy kids, they hire Russell for his supposed sailing expertise. Although the film contains some hilarious moments, they are too few and far between. **TH** Swearing, brief nudity *DVD*

Kurt Russell *Captain Ron* • Martin Short *Martin Harvey* • Mary Kay Place *Katherine Harvey* • Benjamin Salisbury *Benjamin Harvey* • Meadow Sisto *Caroline Harvey* • Emmanuel Logrono *General Armando* • Jorge Luis Ramos *General's translator* • JA Preston *Magistrate* ■ *Dir* Thom Eberhardt • *Scr* Thom Eberhardt, John Dwyer, from a story by John Dwyer

Captain Scarlett ★★ U

Period action adventure   1953 · US · Colour · 74min

The Mexican locations and supporting cast are a major stumbling block for this would-be swashbuckler that is actually set in post-Napoleonic France. Director Thomas Carr seems as indifferent to the location as he is to the pacing and content. Mercifully, Richard Greene is on noble form, as he returns from war to find his estates misappropriated by scheming duke Manolo Fabregas and princess Leonora Amar in the clutches of count Eduardo Noriega. **DP** *DVD*

Richard Greene *Captain Scarlett* • Leonora Amar *Princess Maria* • Nedrick Young *Pierre DuCloux* • Manolo Fabregas *Duke of Corlaine* • Eduardo Noriega (1) *Count Villiers* • Isobel del Puerto *Josephine* • Carlos Muzquiz *Etienne Dumas* • George Trevino [Jorge Treviño] *Friar* ■ *Dir* Thomas Carr • *Scr* Howard Dimsdale

Captain Sindbad ★★★ PG

Fantasy adventure   1963 · US/W Ger · Colour · 81min

With ingenious effects and vigorously directed by Byron Haskin, this is an enjoyable adventure, despite its dark undertones. Gnarled Mexican veteran Pedro Armendáriz steals the show as the villainous sultan whose indefatigability depends on his heart remaining outside his body! But American lug Guy Williams makes a serviceable hero as he delivers the inanimate Heidi Brühl from Armendáriz's castle. **DP**

Guy Williams *Capt Sindbad* • Heidi Brühl *Princess Jana* • Pedro Armendáriz *El Kerim* • Abraham Sofaer *Galgo* • Bernie Hamilton *Quinius* • Helmut

C

Schneider *Bendar* ■ *Dir* Byron Haskin • *Scr* Samuel B West [Ian McLellan Hunter], Harry Relis [Guy Endore], from a story by West [Hunter]

Captain Webb ★★★ 12

Period drama based on a true story
2014 · UK · Colour · 87min

"Who was the first man to swim the English Channel?" used to be a regular quiz question in years gone by. In giving an answer, director Justin Hardy (son of Robin Hardy) puts some much-needed flesh on the answer. Hardy's homage to his doughty Victorian hero (played by Warren Brown) chronicles Webb's trials and tribulations but also reflects on a time when such derring-do was as much showbiz as personal triumph. An unshowy sense of period and plenty of wry humour help to sustain this delightful dip into the past. JA Sex references, violence, mild swearing.

Warren Brown *Captain Matthew Webb* • Steve Oram *Professor Beckwith* • Georgia Maguire *Agnes Beckwith* • Terry Mynott *Captain Paul Boyton* ■ *Dir* Justin Hardy • *Scr* Jemma Kennedy, from the non-fiction book *The Crossing* by Kathy Watson

Captains Courageous ★★★★ U

Adventure
1937 · US · BW · 111min

Spencer Tracy landed an Oscar for the unlikely role of a Portuguese fisherman with a penchant for sea shanties in MGM's big-budget rendering of Rudyard Kipling's adventure tale. A pampered young toff (Freddie Bartholomew) falls off a liner and is scooped from the briny by a fishing crew, who teach him the basics of life. A box-office hit at the time, it now shows its age, while Tracy's Portuguese lilt takes a while to get used to. But the sum of the parts remains wholesome family entertainment. PF *DVD*

Spencer Tracy *Manuel* • Freddie Bartholomew *Harvey* • Lionel Barrymore *Disko* • Melvyn Douglas *Mr Cheyne* • Mickey Rooney *Dan* • Charley Grapewin *Uncle Salters* • John Carradine *"Long Jack"* • Oscar O'Shea *Cushman* ■ *Dir* Victor Fleming • *Scr* John Lee Mahin, Marc Connelly, Dale Van Every, from the novel by Rudyard Kipling

Captains of April ★★★

Historical drama
2000 · Fr/Por/It · Colour · 124min

Maria de Medeiros directs this accomplished and ambitious drama set against the overthrow of the fascist dictatorship in 1975. Naively exuberant in its revolutionary zeal and occasionally cumbersome in its structure, the story of the army captains who bungled their way towards democracy is, nevertheless, imbued with a genuine longing for the period's misplaced innocence and political passion. De Medeiros draws a bemusedly determined performance from Stefano Accorsi as the rookie rebel and handles the crowd scenes with considerable aplomb. DP Portuguese +subtitles.

Stefano Accorsi *Maia* • Maria de Medeiros *Antonia* • Joaquim de Almeida *Gervasio* • Frédéric Pierrot *Manuel* • Fele Martínez *Lobao* ■ *Dir* Maria de Medeiros • *Scr* Eve Deboise, Maria de Medeiros

Captains of the Clouds ★★★ U

Second World War drama
1942 · US · Colour · 113min

Happy to support the war effort, Warner Bros recruited some of their finest, led by James Cagney, to join the Royal Canadian Air Force and fight the Germans. Despite Cagney's initial cockiness (irritating to Canadians who knew there was more at stake than American machismo), the result was this patriotic propaganda piece, directed with his usual efficiency by Michael Curtiz. TH

James Cagney *Brian MacLean* • Dennis Morgan *Johnny Dutton* • Brenda Marshall *Emily Foster* • Alan Hale *Tiny Murphy* • George Tobias *Blimp Lebec* • Reginald Gardiner *Scrounger Harris* • Reginald Denny *Commanding officer* ■

Dir Michael Curtiz • *Scr* Arthur T Horman, Richard Macaulay, Norman Reilly Raine, from a story by Arthur T Horman, Roland Gillette

The Captain's Paradise ★★★ U

Comedy
1953 · UK · BW · 85min

Alec Coppel received an Oscar nomination for the original story of this self-satisfied comedy, in which bigamy is laughed off as the ideal solution to the sociosexual vacillation of an outwardly charming sea captain. Called upon to do little more than vegetate in Gibraltar and tango around Tangier, Alec Guinness cruises through this lightweight picture, which charts an even more predictable course than the ferry he commands. Yvonne De Carlo confuses noise with exoticism, but Celia Johnson is splendid as the mouse wife. DP *DVD*

Alec Guinness *Captain Henry St James* • Yvonne De Carlo *Nita* • Celia Johnson *Maud* • Charles Goldner *Chief Officer Ricco* • Miles Malleson *Lawrence St James* • Bill Fraser *Absalom* • Tutte Lemkow *Principal dancer* ■ *Dir* Anthony Kimmins • *Scr* Alec Coppel, Nicholas Phipps, from a story by Alec Coppel

The Captain's Table ★★ U

Comedy
1958 · UK · Colour · 86min

Richard Gordon's *Doctor* series had been the mainstay of the Rank Organisation in the 1950s. In this adaptation of another Gordon novel as almost every scene seems like an out-take from *Doctor at Sea*. At the helm is John Gregson as a bluff sea cove whose colourful cargo-ship banter is hardly suitable for the passengers of the luxury liner he now commands. The class clash throws up the usual cosy gags. DP

John Gregson *Captain Ebbs* • Peggy Cummins *Mrs Judd* • Donald Sinden *Shawe-Wilson* • Nadia Gray *Mrs Porteous* • Maurice Denham *Major Broster* • Reginald Beckwith *Burtweed* • Bill Kerr *Bill Coke* • Joan Sims *Maude Pritchett* ■ *Dir* Jack Lee (2) • *Scr* John Whiting, Bryan Forbes, Nicholas Phipps, from the novel by Richard Gordon

Captive ★★★ 18

Thriller
1986 · UK/Fr · Colour · 94min

Wealthy heiress Irina Brook is kidnapped, brainwashed and eventually re-educated by terrorists to recognise the hollowness of her existence in a vague approximation of the Patty Hearst story. Multilayered in thematic structure (as one would expect from writer/director Paul Mayersberg, who wrote the screenplay for Nicolas Roeg's *The Man Who Fell to Earth*), this is a constantly intriguing, if overly intellectual polemic on privilege and self-discovery. AJ

Irina Brook *Rowena Le Vay* • Oliver Reed *Gregory Le Vay* • Xavier Deluc *D* • Corinne Dacla *Bryony* • Hiro Arai *Hiro* • Nick Reding *Leo* • Annie Leon *Pine* ■ *Dir/Scr* Paul Mayersberg

The Captive ★★★ 15

Drama
2000 · Fr/Bel · Colour · 112min

All film-maker Chantal Akerman's trademarks are contained in this rigidly controlled adaptation of Marcel Proust's short story *La Prisonnière*. However, these trademarks - the long takes and impeccable compositions, the fascination with corridors and journeys, and the justifiable anger at cinema's continuing fixation with objectifying women - all serve to distance us from the disturbing storyline. This is often intriguing, but the solemnity of the staging makes it's difficult to engage with either the impassive Sylvie Testud or Stanislas Merhar, the jealous suitor who hires her best friend, Olivia Bonamy, to spy on her. DP French +subtitles. *DVD*

Stanislas Merhar *Simon* • Sylvie Testud *Ariane* • Olivia Bonamy *Andrée* • Liliane Rovère *Françoise* • Françoise Bertin *The grandmother* • Aurore Clément *Léa* ■ *Dir* Chantal Akerman • *Scr* Chantal Akerman, Eric de Kuyper, from the novel *La Prisonnière* by Marcel Proust

The Captive ★★ 15

Thriller
2014 · Can · Colour · 106min

When evidence emerges that a young girl kidnapped eight years ago by a paedophile may still be alive, a curious chain of events

is set in motion. As Rosario Dawson and Scott Speedman investigate, the girl's parents (Ryan Reynolds and Mireille Enos) suffer the trauma anew in very different ways. As cult Canadian director Atom Egoyan customises the thriller chassis with preoccupations of his own - voyeurism, grief and dysfunctional family life - it ought to work but somehow it doesn't, with none of the lyricism that makes Egoyan's work so distinctive. LF Swearing

Ryan Reynolds *Matthew* • Scott Speedman *Jeffrey* • Rosario Dawson *Nicole* • Mireille Enos *Tina* • Kevin Durand *Mika* ■ *Dir* Atom Egoyan • *Scr* Atom Egoyan, David Fraser (2), from Egoyan's story

Captive ★★ 12

Crime thriller based on a true story
2015 · US · Colour · 96min

A drama starring David Oyelowo as Brian Nichols, an escaped prisoner who takes a troubled young mother (Kate Mara) hostage in her own apartment. As the pressure mounts, faith and family drives both captor and hostage toward redemption. Based on true events, the film is let down by a slow-moving plot, stilted dialogue and a religious message that feels quite forced, with the interesting story lost in heavy-handed preaching. JL Violence, drug abuse. *DVD*

David Oyelowo *Brian Nichols* • Kate Mara *Ashley Smith* • Michael K Williams [Michael Kenneth Williams] *Detective John Chestnut* • Mimi Rogers *Aunt Kim* • Jessica Oyelowo *Meredith Mackenzie* ■ *Dir* Jerry Jameson • *Scr* Brian Bird, from the non-fiction book *Captive: The Untold Story of the Atlanta Hostage Hero* by Ashley Smith

The Captive City ★★★

Crime drama
1952 · US · BW · 91min

This exposé of organised crime is seen through the eyes of small-town newspaper editor John Forsythe. Using the documentary approach, director Robert Wise creates an authentic atmosphere of corruption. The story is framed in flashback during Forsythe's journey to Washington where he testifies to the Senate Crime Investigating Committee headed by Senator Kefauver (who makes a cameo appearance). Estes Kefauver was a feared figure in Hollywood, having criticised the studios' glamorising of crime. AT

John Forsythe *Jim Austin* • Joan Camden *Marge Austin* • Harold J Kennedy *Don Carey* • Ray Teal *Chief Gillette* • Marjorie Crossland *Mrs Sirak* • Victor Sutherland *Murray Sirak* ■ *Dir* Robert Wise • *Scr* Karl Kamb, Alvin M Josephy Jr, from a story by Alvin M Josephy Jr

Captive City ★★

Second World War drama
1962 · It · BW · 91min

The city? Athens. The period? The dog days of the Second World War. The exact location? A hotel where a disparate group of actors are in search of work and offshore payments. This Euro-pudding of a movie was cobbled together by three writers and put into the hands of former actor and dancer-turned-director, Joseph Anthony. A formulaic piece about British forces defending an arms cache, it depicts the characters behaving well, interestingly or badly. BB

David Niven *Major Peter Whitfield* • Lea Massari *Lelia* • Ben Gazzara *Capt George Stubbs* • Daniela Rocca *Doushka* • Martin Balsam *Feinberg* • Michael Craig *Captain Elliot* ■ *Dir* Joseph Anthony • *Scr* Guy Elmes, Marc Brandel, Eric Bercovici, from the novel *Captive City* by John Appleby,

The Captive Heart ★★★★ PG

Second World War drama
1946 · UK · BW · 94min

British cinema produced many fine prisoner-of-war movies, but this, made within a year of the liberation of the camps, is one of the best. Perhaps the most notable thing about this evocative production is the almost documentary-like re-creation of the boredom, frustration and claustrophobia of stalag life. Basil Dearden's meticulous direction keeps melodrama at bay, but the real power of the piece comes from the

performance of Michael Redgrave, who is superb as the frightened Czech whose deceptions arouse suspicions. DP *DVD* *Blu*

Michael Redgrave *Captain Karel Hasek* • Rachel Kempson *Celia Mitchell* • Frederick Leister *Mr Mowbray* • Mervyn Johns *Private Evans* • Rachel Thomas *Mrs Evans* • Jack Warner *Corporal Horsfall* • Gladys Henson *Mrs Horsfall* • Gordon Jackson *Lieutenant Lennox* ■ *Dir* Basil Dearden • *Scr* Angus MacPhail, Guy Morgan, from a story by Patrick Kirwan

Captive Heart ★★

Period drama
1996 · US · Colour · 91min

A delightfully convoluted tale that is so bizarre it must be true. Louis Gossett Jr plays a wealthy black Canadian, married to Kate Nelligan, whose mixed-race daughter (Rachael Crawford) is sold into slavery by her evil husband Peter Outerbridge. The couple must then make a perilous journey posing as mistress and slave to rescue her from the Deep South. The stranger-than-fiction TV movie is given credibility by the committed performances. JF Violence.

Louis Gossett Jr *James Mink* • Kate Nelligan *Elizabeth Mink* • Rachael Crawford *Mary Mink* • Peter Outerbridge *William Johnson* • Winston Rekert *Sherman Clay* • Ruby Dee *Indigo* ■ *Dir* Bruce Pittman • *Scr* Brian Bird, John Wierick, from a story by Bryon White

Captive of the Desert ★★★★ PG

Biographical drama
1990 · Fr · Colour · 101min

In this remarkable true-life tale a try, Sandrine Bonnaire gives a powerful performance portraying the story of Françoise Claustre, the Frenchwoman who was kidnapped as a political protest by a tribe of nomadic rebels in Chad in 1975. Director Raymond Depardon captures Bonnaire's shift from desperation to acclimatisation with great subtlety, while he records the daily rituals of the desert people with a respectful curiosity that makes the mundane seem fascinating. DP French +subtitles.

Sandrine Bonnaire *Frenchwoman* • Dobi Kor • Fadi Taha • Dobi Wachink • Badei Barka • Atchi Wahi-li ■ *Dir/Scr* Raymond Depardon

Captives ★★★ 15

Drama
1994 · UK · Colour · 95min

In this drama made by the BBC and given a limited cinema release, Julia Ormond stars as a dentist with marital problems who takes work in a high security prison where she falls for a dangerous criminal, played by Tim Roth. From this decidedly offbeat premise emerges a strange love story and suspense thriller, tightly directed by Angela Pope and sharply written by Frank Deasy. AT Violence, swearing, sex scenes.

Tim Roth *Philip Chaney* • Julia Ormond *Rachel Clifford* • Keith Allen *Lenny* • Siobhan Redmond *Sue* • Peter Capaldi *Simon* • Colin Salmon *Towler* • Richard Hawley *Sexton* • Annette Badland *Maggie* • Jeff Nuttall *Harold* • Kenneth Cope *Dr Hockley* • Mark Strong *Kenny* ■ *Dir* Angela Pope • *Scr* Frank Deasy

Captivity ★★★ 18

Horror thriller
2006 · US/Rus · Colour · 81min

Director Roland Joffé (*The Mission*) and cult writer Larry Cohen (*Phone Booth*) have both done far better work than this psycho-thriller copycat of *Saw*, but still drum up a fair number of shocks. Supermodel Elisha Cuthbert wakes up in a cellar after being kidnapped by a serial killer. She's not alone. In another cell, separated by a glass wall, is equally dazed Daniel Gillies. As the unseen maniac plays sadistic cat-and-mouse games with the duo, the full horror of the situation hits home. Despite a well-telegraphed twist and the gory action turning more conventional, the pace never flags and Cohen's precision script keeps the film on track. AJ *DVD* *Blu*

Elisha Cuthbert *Jennifer Tree* • Daniel Gillies *Gary* • Pruitt Taylor Vince *Ben* • Michael Harney *Det Bettiger* • Laz Alonso *Det Disantos* ■ *Dir* Roland Joffé • *Scr* Larry Cohen, Joseph Tura, from a story by Cohen • *Cinematographer* Daniel Pearl

The Capture ★★★
Drama　1950 · US · BW · 90min

This is a nifty little flashback movie from the pen of Niven Busch, who's then-wife, Teresa Wright, gives a typically adroit performance as the widow involved with oil executive Lew Ayres, blissfully unaware that he killed her husband during an investigation of a payroll robbery. The script is occasionally overcooked, but the leads and the ever-sinister Victor Jory are eminently watchable. DP

Lew Ayres *Vanner* • Teresa Wright *Ellen* • Victor Jory *Father Gomez* • Jacqueline White *Luanda* • Jimmy Hunt *Mike* • Barry Kelley *Mahoney* • Duncan Renaldo *Carlos* • William Bakewell *Tobin* • Edwin Rand *Tevlin* ■ *Dir* John Sturges • *Scr* Niven Busch

Capture the Flag ★★★PG
Animated comedy adventure
2015 · Sp · Colour · 94min

Made in Spain but voiced in "American", this space-race cartoon is fast-paced, fun and shamelessly rooted in the notion of the importance of family. It may lack the finesse of animation from Pixar, Disney or DreamWorks, but it's a decent yarn for younger kids who want something to watch on a rainy day. The plot has a power-mad energy mogul bidding to claim the Moon and its minerals by destroying all trace of the original 1969 lunar landing. Some nice in-jokes will keep the adults happy, but entranced youngsters will need no such sweeteners. DA Spanish, Catalan dubbed. Some swearing.

Sam Fink *Richard Carson* • Paul Kelleher *Frank Goldwing* • Andrew Hamblin *Bill Gags* • Derek Siow *Steve Gigs* ■ *Dir* Enrique Gato • *Scr* Patxi Amezcua

Captured ★★★18
Psychological thriller　1998 · US · Colour · 91min

Car thief Andrew Divoff makes a second stab at stealing the flashy motor of stressed-out developer Nick Mancuso, falling foul of a sneaky new security system. Essentially, this is a dogless variation on Stephen King's *Cujo*, with the car-caged Divoff taunted and tortured by his unbalanced captor in a number of sadistic ways. Although hampered by limited locations (mainly a small garage), bland direction and crazed overacting from Mancuso, this does maintain interest and provokes some interesting ideas, albeit in a deranged fashion. JC DVD

Nick Mancuso *Holden Downs* • Andrew Divoff *Robert Breed* • Michael Mahonen *Joey Breed* • Linda Hoffman *Faye Downs* • Seth Peterson *Buddy* ■ *Dir/Scr* Peter Liapis

Capturing the Friedmans ★★★★15
Documentary　2003 · US · Colour · 103min

Director Andrew Jarecki refuses to adjudicate whether the story of a retired Long Island teacher's arrest for paedophilia is a suburban scandal or a hysterical conspiracy. Accused of assaulting boys attending lessons in the family basement, Arnold Friedman's fall from grace represented a domestic tragedy for his unforgiving wife, Elaine, and his largely supportive sons, David, Seth and Jesse (who was also jailed on child abuse charges). Comprising the Friedmans' own revealing home movies, interviews and news footage, this compelling film raises disturbing questions about the law's attitude to those accused of sex crimes. DP DVD

■ *Dir* Andrew Jarecki • *Editor* Richard Hankin • *Music* Andrea Morricone

The Car ★★★12
Horror　1977 · US · Colour · 92min

This schlock horror about a demonic killer car is not particularly original, but is nonetheless surprisingly effective. What success it does achieve is largely owing to its excellent use of night shooting and a superb dramatic use of sound from dubbing editor John Stacy. The cast is interesting, but the star is really the car. TS DVD

James Brolin *Deputy Sheriff Wade Parent* • Kathleen Lloyd *Lauren* • John Marley *Sheriff Everett Peck* • RG Armstrong *Amos* • John Rubinstein *John Morris* • Elizabeth Thompson *Margie* ■ *Dir* Elliot Silverstein • *Scr* Dennis Shryack, Michael Butler, Lane Slate, from a story by Dennis Shryack

Car of Dreams ★★U
Musical comedy　1935 · UK · BW · 68min

The British film industry has never been renowned for its musicals, but this romantic frippery is made more palatable by the sight of John Mills doing a spot of crooning and hoofing. Mills plays the son of a musical instrument tycoon, who poses as a chauffeur to win the heart of factory girl Grete Mosheim. The songs are pretty dire, but the presence of J Robertson Hare more than compensates. DP DVD

John Mills *Robert Miller* • Mark Lester (1) *Miller Sr* • Norah Howard *Anne Fisher* • J Robertson Hare [Robertson Hare] *Henry Butterworth* • Grete Mosheim *Vera Hart* • Margaret Withers *Mrs Hart* ■ *Dir* Graham Cutts, Austin Melford • *Scr* C Stafford Dickens, R Benson, from a story by Austin Melford

Car Trouble ★15
Comedy　1985 · UK · Colour · 89min

This tale of an adulterous wife who steals her husband's beloved Jaguar and proceeds to get stuck, literally, in flagrante with an obsequious car dealer would barely have provided enough sniggers for a sitcom. But director David Green strings it out to an excruciating length that taxes even Julie Walters's ingenuity. DP DVD

Julie Walters *Jacqueline Spong* • Ian Charleson *Gerald Spong* • Stratford Johns *Reg Sampson* • Vincenzo Ricotta *Kevin* • Hazel O'Connor *Maureen* ■ *Dir* David Green • *Scr* James Whaley, AJ Tipping

Car Wash ★★★★PG
Comedy　1976 · US · Colour · 92min

This great little movie was made for small change but deservedly became a major hit. The simple premise is bursting with energy and high octane joy: a bevy of finger snappin', jive talkin' car-wash attendants josh and joke their way through 24 hours in their downmarket establishment's precarious life. A largely unknown cast, a barely known director and one run-down location add up to a minor movie classic. SH DVD

Franklyn Ajaye *TC* • Sully Boyar *Mr B* • Richard Brestoff *Irwin* • George Carlin *Taxi driver* • Professor Irwin Corey *Mad Number* • Bill Duke *Duane* • Antonio Fargas *Lindy* • Richard Pryor *Daddy Rich* ■ *Dir* Michael Schultz • *Scr* Joel Schumacher

Les Carabiniers ★★★
War drama　1963 · Fr/It · BW · 79min

Jean-Luc Godard's bleak semi-documentary follows two uncouth peasant boys who sign up for war, commit terrible crimes and are stunned when they are not regarded as heroes. The movie adopts a casual approach to violence that is reflected in the attitudes of its main characters. Critical reaction was so hostile that the film was initially withdrawn, while modern audiences may be confused by Godard's cultural teasing. That said, it remains a provocative study of war. AT French +subtitles.

Marino Mase *Ulysses* • Albert Juross *Michel-Ange* • Genevieve Galéa *Vénus* • Catherine Ribeiro *Cléopâtre* • Gérard Poirot *1st Carabinier* • Jean Brassat *2nd Carabinier* • Alvaro Gheri *3rd Carabinier* • Barbet Schroeder *Car salesman* ■ *Dir* Jean-Luc Godard • *Scr* Jean-Luc Godard, Jean Gruault, Roberto Rossellini, from the play *I Carabinieri* by Benjamino Joppolo, adapted by Jacques Audiberti

Caramel ★★★★PG
Romantic comedy drama
2007 · Fr/Leb · Colour · 91min

A women's hairdressing salon might seem an obvious location for a female-bonding drama, but this assured debut from director/star Nadine Labaki is much richer than it seems. Labaki plays the proprietor of a Beirut beauty parlour where the stylists and clients meet to share their problems and have a good gossip. Their universally recognisable woes take priority over the gloomy spectre of potentially alienating Middle Eastern politics. The pacing is staccato at times as the camera weaves the various vignettes together – Labaki mooning over her married lover; the selfless seamstress saddled with a demanding, crazy sister – but the movie has a warm-hearted sense of togetherness that makes an affecting patchwork of some beautifully observed moments. DW Arabic, French +subtitles. DVD

Nadine Labaki *Layale* • Yasmine Al Masri *Nisrine* • Joanna Moukarzel *Rima* • Gisele Aouad *Jamale* • Adel Karam *Youssef* • Siham Haddad *Rose* ■ *Dir* Nadine Labaki • *Scr* Nadine Labaki, Rodney Al Haddad [Rodney El Haddad], Jihad Hojeily

Carancho ★★★15
Romantic crime drama
2010 · Arg/Chil/Fr/SK · Colour · 107min

Argentinian director Pablo Trapero is a master of mood, environment and character, but strays into genre territory with this tale of the relationship between a conscience-stricken insurance agent and an overworked doctor. *The Secret in Their Eyes* star Ricardo Darín gives another impressive performance as Sosa, a disbarred lawyer who tries to help his impoverished clients while cashing in on Buenos Aires's traffic accident epidemic. Neither the exposé nor the thriller it could have been, *Carancho* certainly has its flaws, yet it remains a slick and intriguing proposition. DP Spanish +subtitles.

Ricardo Darin [Ricardo Darín] *Sosa* • Martina Gusman *Luján* • Carlos Weber *Perro* • José Luis Arias *Casal* • Fabio Ronzano *Pico* ■ *Dir* Pablo Trapero • *Scr* Pablo Trapero, Alejandro Fadel, Martín Mauregui, Santiago Mitre

Carandiru ★★★★15
Prison drama based on a true story
2003 · Bra/US · Colour · 139min

Hector Babenco's harrowing true story of conditions inside Carandiru, the biggest prison in South America, leaves you scorched and exhausted. The jail's brutality and squalor is introduced through the eyes of a new doctor (Luiz Carlos Vasconcelos), brought in to help control an escalating Aids epidemic. Despite the depravity, he finds solidarity and a lust for life among the inmates, who divulge their stories to him. This sprawling film uses at least a thousand extras in its second-half riot scenes and, while Babenco's control over everything might not be altogether firm, his device of letting inhabitants explain themselves to camera is highly effective. TH Portuguese +subtitles. Swearing, violence, drug abuse. DVD

Luiz Carlos Vasconcelos *Doctor* • Milton Goncalves *Chico* • Ivan de Almeida *Ebony* • Ailton Graca *Highness* • Maria Luisa Mendonca *Dalva* • Aida Leiner *Rosirene* ■ *Dir* Hector Babenco • *Scr* Victor Navas, Hector Babenco, Fernando Bonassi, from the novel *Estação Carandiru* by Drauzio Varella

Caravaggio ★★★★18
Biographical drama　1986 · UK · Colour · 88min

With Nigel Terry excelling in the lead, this portrait of the artist as a gay man is Derek Jarman's most accessible, revealing and beautiful work. Jarman frees himself from the constraints of the traditional biopic by slotting anachronistic details into a *mise en scène* that is almost mannerist in its solemn grandeur. He investigates not only the painter's relationships with male model Sean Bean and his mistress, Tilda Swinton, but also the source of his inspiration. And, since this is a study of a visual medium, he forces us to seek significance in gestures, silences and exquisitely reproduced tableaux. DP Violence, swearing, nudity. DVD

Nigel Terry *Caravaggio* • Sean Bean *Ranuccio Thomasoni* • Tilda Swinton *Lena* • Garry Cooper *Davide* • Spencer Leigh *Jerusaleme* • Nigel Davenport *Giustiniani* • Robbie Coltrane *Scipione Borghese* • Michael Gough *Cardinal Del Monte* ■ *Dir/Scr* Derek Jarman • *Cinematographer* Gabriel Beristain

Caravan ★★
Musical drama　1934 · US/Fr · BW · 98min

This was filmed in both French and American versions, both starring Charles Boyer and directed by Erik Charell. A young Hungarian countess (Loretta Young/Annabella) inherits a large estate, conditional on getting married. Ignoring the suggestion of the local baron (C Aubrey Smith/Jules Racourt) that his son, whom she has never met, would make a suitable husband, she marries gypsy musician Boyer. Then the baron's son (Phillips Holmes/Pierre Brasseur) appears on the scene. Although eye-catchingly filmed, with leading ladies to match, this whimsical, operetta-style movie is long and largely tedious, not helped by Boyer hamming it up. RK

Charles Boyer *Lazi* • Annabella *Princess Wilma (French version)* • Loretta Young *Countess Wilma (US version)* • Pierre Brasseur *Lieutenant of Tokay (French version)* • Phillips Holmes *Lieutenant von Tokay (US version)* • Conchita Montenegro *Tinka (French version)* • Jean Parker *Tinka (US version)* • Marcel Vallée *Innkeeper (French version)* • Noah Beery *Innkeeper (US version)* • Jules Racourt *Baron de Tokay (French version)* • C Aubrey Smith *Baron von Tokay (US version)* ■ *Dir* Erik Charell • *Scr* (French version) Samson Raphaelson, Robert Liebmann, Arthur Ripley; (US verison) Hans Kraly, Raymond Van Sickel, Erik Charell; from the short story *Gypsy Melody* by Melchior Lengyel

Caravan ★★★
Period romantic drama　1946 · UK · BW · 122min

Set in 19th century Spain, this period melodrama from Gainsborough Studios was a huge hit in 1946, with Stewart Granger's derring-do just the thing to take cinema audiences' minds off postwar rationing. Granger plays an impoverished writer who dallies with Jean Kent's gypsy dancer, but his heart is really set on Anne Crawford's lady of the manor. Meanwhile Dennis Price oozes caddishness from every pore as his deadly rival. Overdressed, overheated and deliriously silly. AT

Stewart Granger *Richard* • Anne Crawford *Oriana* • Jean Kent *Rosal* • Dennis Price *Francis* • Robert Helpmann *Wycroft* • Gerard Heinz *Don Carlos* • Arthur Goullet *Suiza* • John Salew *Diego* ■ *Dir* Arthur Crabtree • *Scr* Roland Pertwee, from the novel by Lady Eleanor Smith

Caravan to Vaccares ★★15
Action adventure　1974 · UK/Fr · Colour · 93min

Caravan to vacuity, more like, in this implausible adaptation of a far-fetched Alistair MacLean novel in which boorish American David Birney and seductress Charlotte Rampling team up to try to smuggle Hungarian scientist Michel Bryant from Provence to New York. The lush Camargue locations and co-star Michel Lonsdale's ironic asides are two meagre reasons to watch. TH

Charlotte Rampling *Lila* • David Birney *Neil Bowman* • Michael Lonsdale [Michel Lonsdale] *Duc de Croytor* • Marcel Bozzuffi *Henri Czerda* • Michael Bryant *Stefan Zuger* ■ *Dir* Geoffrey Reeve • *Scr* Paul Wheeler, from the novel by Alistair MacLean

Carbine Williams ★★
Biographical drama　1952 · US · BW · 91min

James Stewart stars as Marsh Williams, the inventor of the M-1 carbine, a weapon that revolutionised modern warfare. One interesting feature of this rather dour story, directed by Richard Thorpe in a pedestrian manner, was that Williams did his work on the rifle while in prison for bootlegging. RB

James Stewart *Marsh Williams* • Jean Hagen *Maggie Williams* • Wendell Corey *Capt HT Peoples* • Carl Benton Reid *Claude Williams* • Paul Stewart *"Dutch" Kruger* • Otto Hulett *Mobley* • Rhys Williams *Redwick Karson* • Herbert Heyes *Lionel Daniels* ■ *Dir* Richard Thorpe • *Scr* Art Cohn

C

C

Carbon Copy ★ 15
Comedy drama   1981 · US · Colour · 87min

This tepid race satire drives its point home with sledgehammer subtlety. The usually dependable George Segal is wasted here as a successful business executive whose life falls apart following the sudden arrival of the son he never knew he had. Shock, horror – the boy (Denzel Washington) is black! Heavy-going for all concerned. **DF**

George Segal *Walter Whitney* • Susan Saint James *Vivian Whitney* • Jack Warden *Nelson Longhurst* • Denzel Washington *Roger Porter* • Dick Martin *Victor Bard* • Paul Winfield *Bob Garvey* • Vicky Dawson *Mary Ann* ■ *Dir* Michael Schultz • *Scr* Stanley Shapiro

The Card ★★★ U
Comedy drama   1952 · UK · BW · 87min

Adapted from Arnold Bennett's 1911 novel, this is a stylish, if rather empty, rags to riches story set in the author's beloved Five Towns. Eric Ambler's script is full of smart situations and witty lines, but Alec Guinness is hardly stretched as the laundress's son who achieves wealth and respectability through his machiavellian schemes. There is admirable support from Glynis Johns and Valerie Hobson as the women in his life, but the film suffers from the attempt to cast it in the Ealing comedy mould. **DP** *DVD*

Alec Guinness *Edward Henry "Denry" Machin* • Glynis Johns *Ruth Earp* • Valerie Hobson *Countess of Chell* • Petula Clark *Nellie Cotterill* • Edward Chapman *Mr Duncalf* • Joan Hickson *Mrs Codleyn* • Michael Hordern *Bank manager* ■ *Dir* Ronald Neame • *Scr* Eric Ambler, from the novel by Arnold Bennett

The Card Player ★★ 15
Crime thriller   2004 · It · Colour · 99min

In this lethargic whodunnit, a psychopath challenges Roman policewoman Stefania Rocca to games of Internet poker for the lives of abducted women. If she loses, the screaming victims are murdered live on webcam. Can Rocca and Irish cop Liam Cunningham uncover the weird clues to the cyber assassin's identity? Sporting little of director Dario Argento's signature flair or flamboyant style, this is a dreary-looking and bloodless bust. **AJ** English, Italian +subtitles. Swearing, violence. *DVD*

Stefania Rocca *Anna Mari* • Liam Cunningham *John Brennan* • Silvio Muccino *Remo* • Adalberto Maria Merli *Chief of Police* • Claudio Santamaria *Carlo Sturni* • Fiore Argento *Lucia* ■ *Dir* Dario Argento • *Scr* Dario Argento, Franco Ferrini

Cardboard Cavalier ★★ U
Period comedy   1949 · UK · BW · 99min

Popular music hall duo Sid Field and Jerry Desmonde team up for this eager period comedy that, in spite of some spirited playing, soon outstays its welcome. Set during the Cromwellian Commonwealth, the story, in which Field's barrow boy carries secret messages for Desmonde's Royalist spy, has all the appearances of being a flag-waver left over from the war, with puritanism being equated with fascism. Field's high-camp style is an acquired taste. **DP**

Sid Field *Sidcup Buttermeadow* • Margaret Lockwood *Nell Gwynne* • Jerry Desmonde *Lovelace* • Jack McNaughton *Uriah Croup* • Alfie Dean *Murdercasket* • Brian Worth *Tom Pride* • Irene Handl *Lady Agnes* ■ *Dir* Walter Forde • *Scr* Noel Langley

The Cardinal ★★★
Epic drama   1963 · US · Colour · 175min

This is an earnest though rather long adaptation of one of those American doorstop novels about faith, produced on a vast transworld scale by director Otto Preminger. Despite its sweep, scale and obvious intelligence, this failed to make a dent at the box office. The blame lies in the serious miscasting of Tom Tryon in the pivotal title role, as he lacks both range and sympathy. But Preminger surrounds him with a strong supporting cast, while the Technicolor photography is impressive. **TS**

Tom Tryon *Stephen Fermoyle* • John Huston *Cardinal Glennon* • Raf Vallone *Cardinal Quarenghi* • Romy Schneider *Annemarie* • Carol Lynley *Mona/Regina Fermoyle* • Dorothy Gish *Celia Fermoyle* • Burgess Meredith *Father Ned Halley* • Ossie Davis *Father Gillis* • Cecil Kellaway *Monsignor Monaghan* ■ *Dir* Otto Preminger • *Scr* Robert Dozier, from the novel by Henry Morton Robinson • *Cinematographer* Leon Shamroy

Cardinal Richelieu ★★★ U
Biographical drama   1935 · US · BW · 82min

This diverting biopic stars George Arliss as Louis XIII's first minister, whose plans to unify France earned him the enmity of the disaffected nobility and the king's womenfolk. Director Rowland V Lee has a tenuous grasp of the period atmosphere, but this scarcely matters as the historical facts are little more than an excuse for a series of melodramatic intrigues from which Arliss emerges triumphant like some scarlet-caped crusader. **DP**

George Arliss *Cardinal Richelieu* • Maureen O'Sullivan *Lenore* • Edward Arnold *Louis XIII* • Cesar Romero *Andre de Pons* • Douglass Dumbrille *Baradas* • Francis Lister *Gaston* • Halliwell Hobbes *Father Joseph* ■ *Dir* Rowland V Lee • *Scr* Maude Howell, Cameron Rogers, WP Lipscomb, from the play *Richelieu* by Sir Edward Bulwer-Lytton [Edward George Bulwer-Lytton]

The Care Bears Movie ★★ U
Animated adventure 1985 · Can · Colour · 75min

Only teen bands have shorter life cycles than children's television characters, so it will be interesting to see how a generation reared on the Teletubbies reacts to their 1980s equivalents. Although 1960s luminaries Carole King and John Sebastian supply some tunes, there's not much in this for adults, and the animation is tame. The film spawned two sequels and a TV series. **JF** *DVD*

Mickey Rooney *Mr Cherrywood* • Jackie Burroughs *The Spirit* • Harry Dean Stanton *Lion* • Sunny Besen Thrasher *Jason* • Georgia Engel *Love-a-Lot* ■ *Dir* Arna Selzick • *Scr* Peter Sauder

Career ★★★
Drama   1959 · US · BW · 106min

Anthony Franciosa is excellent in this screen version of James Lee's Broadway play about an aspiring actor waiting for his big break in New York. Directed by Joseph Anthony with an A-list cast – Shirley MacLaine as Franciosa's alcoholic wife, Dean Martin as a stage director, Carolyn Jones as a talent scout – the movie is too long and a little plodding. However, it is gritty and authentic, and earned cinematographer Joseph LaShelle an Oscar nomination. **RK**

Anthony Franciosa *Sam Lawson* • Dean Martin *Maury Novak* • Shirley MacLaine *Sharon Kensington* • Carolyn Jones *Shirley Drake* • Joan Blackman *Barbara* • Robert Middleton *Robert Kensington* • Donna Douglas *Marjorie Burke* • Frank McHugh *Charlie* ■ *Dir* Joseph Anthony • *Scr* James Lee, from his play

Career Girls ★★★★ 15
Comedy drama   1997 · UK · Colour · 83min

Mike Leigh isn't cinema's foremost realist, but he's definitely its most perceptive people-watcher. The deceptively simple characters he favours reveal hidden depths that make them utterly fascinating. Here, arrogantly affected Katrin Cartlidge and twitchily timid Lynda Steadman are pretty resistible during the flashbacks to their college days. But they capture our sympathies during a series of low-key misadventures with three old friends and a detestable newcomer. With its tentatively optimistic ending, this may be a small, rather safe film, yet it's also funny, touching and plausible. **DP** Swearing, also a sex scene. *DVD*

Katrin Cartlidge *Hannah Mills* • Lynda Steadman *Annie* • Kate Byers *Claire* • Mark Benton *Richard "Ricky" Burton* • Andy Serkis *Mr Evans* • Joe Tucker *Adrian Spinks* • Margo Stanley *Ricky's Nan* • Michael Healy *Lecturer* ■ *Dir/Scr* Mike Leigh

Career Opportunities ★★ 15
Comedy   1991 · US · Colour · 79min

Written by teen chronicler John Hughes, this unexciting story has Frank Whaley as a young, incompetent conman hired as night watchman at a department store. On his first night on the job, he finds town beauty Jennifer Connelly asleep in a changing room and thwarts some would-be thieves. It might have worked with a touch of fantasy, but the straightforward treatment means this is never more than routine. **TH**

Frank Whaley *Jim Dodge* • Jennifer Connelly *Josie McClellan* • Dermot Mulroney *Nestor Pyle* • Kieran Mulroney *Gil Kinney* • John M Jackson *Bud Dodge* • Jenny O'Hara *Dotty Dodge* • Barry Corbin *Officer Don* • John Candy *Store manager* ■ *Dir* Bryan Gordon • *Scr* John Hughes

Carefree ★★ U
Musical comedy   1938 · US · BW · 79min

It may be one of the weakest of the Astaire/Rogers features, but there's still plenty to enjoy in this rather silly comedy. Astaire looks uneasy as a psychiatrist trying to find a cure for best pal Ralph Bellamy's dippy, wedding-shy fiancée (Rogers), and she looks mortified at having to endure hypnotic mischief sequences. The highlight is Astaire's exquisite golfing routine to the title song. **SH** *DVD*

Fred Astaire *Tony Flagg* • Ginger Rogers *Amanda Cooper* • Ralph Bellamy *Stephen Arden* • Luella Gear *Aunt Cora* • Jack Carson *Connors* • Walter Kingsford *Dr Powers* • Kay Sutton *Miss Adams* ■ *Dir* Mark Sandrich • *Scr* Ernest Pagano, Allan Scott, from a story by Dudley Nichols, Hagar Wilde, Marian Ainslee, Guy Endore • *Music* Irving Berlin

Careful ★★★★
Period black comedy drama 1992 · Can · Colour · 100min

Director Guy Maddin is something of a cult figure in Canadian cinema and this costume curio is one of his most ambitious and enjoyable projects. Shot to look like a 1920s melodrama – complete with stylised silent acting, dialogue captions and whole scenes tinted in atmospheric colours – it tells of the secret passions that lurk behind the respectable façade of the Bavarian town of Tolzbad, which is in such peril from avalanches that everyone talks in whispers or in specially soundproofed rooms to prevent disaster. **DP** Sex scenes, nudity.

Kyle McCulloch *Grigorss* • Gosia Dobrowolska *Zenaida* • Sarah Neville *Klara* • Brent Neale Johann • Paul Cox *Count Knotgers* • Victor Cowie *Herr Trotta* ■ *Dir* Guy Maddin • *Scr* Guy Maddin, George Toles

Careful, He Might Hear You ★★★★ PG
Drama   1983 · Aus · Colour · 112min

In adapting Sumner Locke Elliott's novel for the screen, Carl Schultz has been careful to ensure that much of the action is seen from orphan Nicholas Gledhill's perspective as his aunts struggle for custody. Yet he also emphasises several adult themes, among them Australia's relationship with the "mother country", the impact of the Depression on all strata of society, and the role of women in a repressive patriarchy. John Stoddart's sets and John Seale's photography give the film a nostalgic glow. **DP**

Wendy Hughes *Vanessa* • Robyn Nevin *Lila* • Nicholas Gledhill *PS* • John Hargreaves *Logan* • Geraldine Turner *Vere* • Isabelle Anderson *Agnes* • Peter Whitford *George* • Colleen Clifford *Ettie* • Julie Nihill *Diana* ■ *Dir* Carl Schultz • *Scr* Michael Jenkins, from the novel by Sumner Locke Elliott

Careful, Soft Shoulder ★★★★ U
Second World War comedy drama 1942 · US · BW · 69min

This is an engaging and intelligently subversive movie from director Oliver HP Garrett, who co-scripted *Duel in the Sun* with David O Selznick. Virginia Bruce stars as a world-weary social butterfly who casually mentions at a cocktail party that she fancies spying for the Nazis. Aubrey

Mather takes her up on it. Told primarily in flashback by Bruce, whom Garrett interestingly makes sympathetic, this is a classy film with a witty central performance. It's all the more remarkable when one considers the majority of gung-ho dross on offer at the time. **SH**

Virginia Bruce *Connie Mathers* • James Ellison *Thomas Aldrich* • Aubrey Mather *Mr Fortune* • Sheila Ryan *Agatha Mathers* • Ralph Byrd *Elliot Salmon* • Sigurd Tor *Milo* • Charles Tannen *Joe* ■ *Dir/Scr* Oliver HP Garrett

The Careless Years ★★
Drama   1957 · US · BW · 72min

Arthur Hiller waited five years to follow up this uneasy feature debut, but he later hit the box-office and Oscar jackpot with *Love Story*. Here the romance is less sugary and tells of high school girl Natalie Trundy who falls in love with handsome fellow student Dean Stockwell. The trouble is, her parents are rich and his are poor, and both sides disapprove. **BB**

Dean Stockwell *Jerry Vernon* • Natalie Trundy *Emily Meredith* • John Larch *Sam Vernon* • Barbara Billingsley *Helen Meredith* • John Stephenson *Charles Meredith* • Maureen Cassidy *Harriet* ■ *Dir* Arthur Hiller • *Scr* Edward Lewis, front for John Howard Lawson, Mitch Lindemann

The Carer ★★★★ 15
Comedy drama   2015 · UK · Colour · 88min

Brian Cox gives a wonderful performance in a surprisingly enjoyable tale about two people who form an unlikely friendship. A retired Shakespearean thespian suffering from Parkinson's finally comes to accept his young Hungarian carer, who tolerates his cantankerous, foul-mouthed behaviour. All of this is entirely predictable, but it is funnier than you might expect, with Cox grabbing numerous laughs along the way. He seems to relish the spiky dialogue that he's given, and his performance ensures that the film is a pleasant surprise. **SC**

Brian Cox (1) *Sir Michael* • Anna Chancellor *Milly* • Emilia Fox *Sophia* • Coco König *Dorottya* • Selina Cadell *Mrs Trudeau* • Roger Moore ■ *Dir* Janos Edelenyi • *Scr* Gilbert Adair, Janos Edelenyi, Tom Kinninmont

The Caretaker ★★★ PG
Drama   1963 · UK · BW · 100min

One of Harold Pinter's most famous plays – a study in sinister pauses and comic shifts of emphasis – is wonderfully given over to its fine cast of actors. Alan Bates and Robert Shaw play two brothers who give shelter to Donald Pleasence, a scruffy tramp forever on his way to Sidcup. Either a doomy allegory or a realistic drama with menaces, it's directed without fuss by Clive Donner. A memorable piece of theatre, if not particularly effective as cinema. **TH** *DVD*

Donald Pleasence *Davies* • Alan Bates *Mick* • Robert Shaw *Aston* ■ *Dir* Clive Donner • *Scr* Harold Pinter, from his play

The Caretakers ★
Melodrama   1963 · US · BW · 97min

Considering its subject matter and setting (a mental hospital), producer/director Hall Bartlett's incident-packed melodrama is almost insulting in its lack of seriousness, accuracy or insight. However, it's the kind of awful film which, viewed decades later, entertains for all the wrong reasons – notably Joan Crawford as a senior psychiatric nurse, locked in disagreement with medic Robert Stack's compassionate approach to the disturbed inmates. Hysterical, in every sense of the word. **RK**

Robert Stack *Dr Donovan MacLeod* • Polly Bergen *Lorna Melford* • Joan Crawford *Lucretia Terry* • Janis Paige *Marion* • Herbert Marshall *Dr Jubal Harrington* • Robert Vaughn (1) *Jim Melford* ■ *Dir* Hall Bartlett • *Scr* Henry F Greenberg, from a story by Hall Bartlett, Jerry Paris and a novel by Dariel Telfer

The Carey Treatment ★★ 15
Murder mystery   1972 · US · Colour · 96min

This bizarre murder mystery involves a *Coma*-style hospital racket in body parts, with James Coburn failing to convince as the Californian pathologist trying to disentangle a colleague from a murder frame-up. It's directed by Blake Edwards, who is better known for *The Pink Panther* comedies, and he is clearly not at home with this sort of drama. As the body count rises, this veers towards self parody. **TH** Some swearing.

James Coburn *Peter Carey* • Jennifer O'Neill *Georgia Hightower* • Pat Hingle *Captain Pearson* • Skye Aubrey *Angela Holder* • Elizabeth Allen *Evelyn Randall* • John Fink *Murphy* • Dan O'Herlihy *JD Randall* ■ *Dir* Blake Edwards • *Scr* James P Bonner, from the novel *A Case of Need* by Jeffrey Hudson

The Cariboo Trail ★★ U
Western adventure 1950 · US · Colour · 79min
This moderately interesting Randolph Scott vehicle was produced by western veteran Nat Holt. Victor Jory is Scott's usual snarling foe, but the real interest lies in the use of primitive two-strip Cinecolor. The implacable Scott is eminently watchable, but the plot and direction are routine. **TS**
Randolph Scott *Jim Redfern* • George "Gabby" Hayes *Grizzly* • Bill Williams *Mike Evans* • Karin Booth *Frances* • Victor Jory *Frank Walsh* • Douglas Kennedy *Murphy* • Jim Davis (1) *Miller* • Dale Robertson *Will Gray* ■ *Dir* Edwin L Marin • *Scr* Frank Gruber, from a story by John Rhodes Sturdy

Carla's Song ★★★ 15
Drama 1996 · UK/Ger/Sp · Colour · 106min
Robert Carlyle stars in this sombre story of love among the revolutionaries from director Ken Loach. Carlyle is the Glasgow bus driver who falls in love with exotic Oyanka Cabezas, a refugee from war-torn Nicaragua. He insists they go there so that she can confront her demons, only for him to learn just what she's had to suffer. The story runs out of steam once the action moves from Scotland, but Loach is a persuasive propagandist and Carlyle has enormous charm. **TH** English, Spanish +subtitles. Violence, swearing. **DVD**
Robert Carlyle *George* • Oyanka Cabezas *Carla* • Scott Glenn *Bradley* • Salvador Espinoza *Rafael* • Louise Goodall *Maureen* • Richard Loza *Antonio* • Gary Lewis *Sammy* • Subash Singh Pall *Victor* • Stewart Preston *McGurk* ■ *Dir* Ken Loach • *Scr* Paul Laverty

Carlito's Way ★★★★ 18
Crime drama 1993 · US · Colour · 138min
Ten years after *Scarface*, Al Pacino and director Brian De Palma reunited for another crime-doesn't-pay drama. Pacino plays Puerto Rican hoodlum Carlito Brigante, sprung from jail by his lawyer Sean Penn and determined to go straight. But Penn, who fancies himself as a gangster, scoffs at the idea, and when Pacino meets up with his old acquaintances, he's soon back in trouble. Bolstered by regular scriptwriter David Koepp's smart and funny script, De Palma's visual flair comes into its own in the seedy milieu of New York's clubs and backstreet dives. The set pieces are among the most thrilling De Palma has ever filmed, while Pacino gives a restrained performance. **AT** Violence, sex scenes, swearing, drug abuse, nudity. **DVD**
Al Pacino *Carlito Brigante* • Sean Penn *Dave Kleinfeld* • Penelope Ann Miller *Gail* • John Leguizamo *Benny Blanco* • Ingrid Rogers *Steffie* • Luis Guzman *Pachanga* • James Rebhorn *Norwalk* • Viggo Mortensen *Lalin* ■ *Dir* Brian De Palma • *Scr* David Koepp, from the novels *Carlito's Way* and *After Hours* by Edwin Torres

Carlos ★★★ 15
Biographical crime drama 2010 · Fr/Ger · Colour · 158min
Ilich Ramirez Sanchez aka "Carlos" aka "The Jackal" gained notoriety in 1975 after taking hostages at a meeting of the international oil cartel Opec, to draw attention to the plight of displaced Palestinians. This grand-scale character study by French writer/director Olivier Assayas suggests that Carlos (played with unnerving intensity by Venezuelan actor Edgar Ramirez) was actually a terrorist without a cause, most interested in building

his own myth. Assayas is deft with action, moving at a fast pace across continents, but this version of the film (edited down from a three-part TV miniseries) may be a little too hasty. The fictionalised account of Carlos's personal life is intriguing, but the deeper root of his anger remains unclear. **SP** English, French, German, Spanish, Arabic +subtitles. Violence, sex scenes. **DVD**
Edgar Ramirez *Ilich Ramirez Sanchez, "Carlos"* • Alexander Scheer *Johannes Weinrich* • Nora von Waldstätten *Magdalena Kopp* • Christoph Bach *Hans-Joachim Klein, "Angie"* • Ahmad Kaabour *Wadie Haddad* • Fadi Abi Samra *Michel Moukharbal, "André"* ■ *Dir* Olivier Assayas • *Scr* Olivier Assayas, Dan Franck, from an idea by Daniel Leconte

Carlton-Browne of the FO ★★ U
Satire 1958 · UK · B/W · 86min
A talented cast is put to disappointing use in this slightly silly Boulting brothers farce. Struggling with a rather bizarre script, Terry-Thomas plays a bungling diplomat who's dispatched to a faraway but suddenly mineral-rich British colony. His mission is to save the day for Blighty, but he blusters and blunders instead. The antics only manage to raise an occasional titter. **PF** **DVD**
Terry-Thomas *Cadogen de Vere Carlton-Browne* • Peter Sellers *Prime Minister Amphibulos* • Ian Bannen *Young king* • Thorley Walters *Colonel Bellingham* • Raymond Huntley *Foreign Office minister* • John Le Mesurier *Grand Duke* • Luciana Paluzzi *Princess Ilyena* ■ *Dir/Scr* Roy Boulting, Jeffrey Dell

Carmen ★★★★ U
Silent drama 1915 · US · B/W · 62min
One of the great Cecil B DeMille's biggest early hits, this was one of the movies actually responsible for popularising cinema itself. Unfairly vilified later for his naive and expansive film spectacles, DeMille was one of the film industry's pioneers, and the first to exploit the climate of the Californian orange grove known as Hollywood. As producer, he also pioneered the multiple picture contract; starring here, in the first movie of a three-picture deal, is Metropolitan Opera soprano Geraldine Farrar. She is superb, but Wallace Reid's career ended tragically, his life eroded by drug abuse. **TS**
Geraldine Ferrar *Carmen* • Wallace Reid *Don José* ■ *Dir* Cecil B DeMille • *Scr* William C DeMille, from the novel by Prosper Mérimée and the opera by Georges Bizet

Carmen ★★★★ PG
Dance drama 1983 · Sp · Colour · 97min
Coming between *Blood Wedding* and *El Amor Brujo*, this is the best-known segment of Carlos Saura's "flamenco trilogy". Bringing a new zest to the old cliché that life imitates art, Saura cross-cuts between rehearsals and performance as Antonio Gades becomes fatally bewitched with tempestuous co-star Laura Del Sol. As Teo Escamilla's camera is choreographed as meticulously as the dancers, the action is at once joyous and tragic; while the blend of folk music and opera manages to both send up and celebrate Bizet's famous score. With its exemplary editing, this passionate picture is both kinetic and cinematic. **DP** Spanish +subtitles. **DVD**
Antonio Gades *Antonio* • Laura Del Sol *Carmen* • Paco de Lucia *Paco* • Cristina Hoyos *Cristina* • Juan Antonio Jimenez *Juan* • Sebastian Moreno *Escamillo* • Jose Yepes *Pepe Giron* • Pepa Flores ■ *Dir* Carlos Saura • *Scr* Carlos Saura, Antonio Gades, from the novel by Prosper Mérimée and the opera by Georges Bizet • *Cinematographer* Teo Escamila • *Editor* Pedro del Rey

Carmen ★★★★ PG
Opera 1984 · Fr/It · Colour · 148min
Georges Bizet's adaptation of Prosper Mérimée's novel is here cloaked in realism by Italian director Francesco Rosi. There's nothing stylised about the Andalusian settings in which the fiercely independent Julia Migenes-Johnson exploits her relationship with besotted soldier Placido Domingo. Poverty gnaws at the bones of

everyone who works in the hellish cigarette factory, yet cinematographer Pasqualino De Santis's control of colour is so inspired that he makes the run-down buildings seem the perfect place for passion. A treat for both eye and ear. **DP** French +subtitles. **DVD**
Julia Migenes-Johnson *Carmen* • Placido Domingo *Don José* • Ruggero Raimondi *Escamillo* • Faith Esham *Micaëla* • Jean-Philippe Lafont *Dancaïre* • Gérard Garino *Remendado* • Lilian Watson *Frasquita* ■ *Dir* Francesco Rosi • *Scr* Francesco Rosi, Tonino Guerra, from the novel by Prosper Mérimée and the opera by Georges Bizet

Carmen ★★★ 15
Romantic drama 2003 · Sp/UK/It · Colour · 119min
Vincente Aranda returns to Mérimée's original story for this account of the doomed romance between a tempestuous beauty and a lovesick soldier. Paz Vega suitably in the title role, but Leonardo Sbaraglia struggles to convey reckless obsession. Similarly, Aranda's storytelling is not always as crisp as cinematographer Paco Femenía's evocation of 1830s Andalucia. Handsomely staged, but short on real passion. **DP** Spanish +subtitles.
Paz Vega *Carmen* • Leonardo Sbaraglia *José Lizarrabengoa* • Jay Benedict *Prospero* • Antonio Dechent *Tuerto* • Joan Crosas *Dancaire* • Joe Mackay *Teniente* • Josep Linuesa [José Linuesa] *Lucas* ■ *Dir* Vicente Aranda • *Scr* Joaquín Jordá, Vicente Aranda, from the novel by Prosper Mérimée

Carmen Jones ★★★★ U
Musical melodrama 1954 · US · Colour · 103min
This is 20th Century-Fox's all-black version of Bizet's opera *Carmen*, based on the Oscar Hammerstein II Broadway triumph. As the ultimate *femme fatale* Carmen Jones, Dorothy Dandridge sizzles on screen, although her singing voice was dubbed by the then unknown Marilyn Horne. LeVern Hutcherson sings for handsome Harry Belafonte, but the rest of the cast largely sings for itself. The music has an enjoyable Hollywood zest and *Carmen* fans will warm to the wit of this interpretation. **TS** **DVD**
Dorothy Dandridge *Carmen* • Harry Belafonte *Joe* • Olga James *Cindy Lou* • Pearl Bailey *Frankie* • Diahann Carroll *Myrt* • Roy Glenn *Rum* • Nick Stewart *Dink* • Joe Adams *Husky* • Brock Peters *Sergeant Brown* • Sandy Lewis *T-Bone* ■ *Dir* Otto Preminger • *Scr* Harry Kleiner, from the musical by Oscar Hammerstein II, from the opera by Georges Bizet

Carmen Miranda: Bananas Is My Business ★★★★
Documentary 1994 · US/Bra · Colour · 92min
Born Maria do Carmo Miranda da Cunha near Lisbon in Portugal, Carmen Miranda became an international symbol of Brazilian pizzazz, and her sudden death at 46 was the cause of national mourning. A star of Brazilian films and Broadway before she conquered Hollywood, Miranda was unquestionably wasted by producers who thought that all she had to offer was a genius for mangling the English language and an exoticism that could brighten up an ordinary musical with a few colourful routines. As this revealing documentary tribute proves, she was capable of much more. **DP** Portuguese, English +subtitles.
Cynthia Adler *Luella Hopper* • Erick Barreto *Carmen Miranda (fantasy sequences)* • Leticia Monte *Carmen Miranda (as a teenager)* • Helena Solberg *Narrator* ■ *Dir* Helena Solberg

Carnage ★★★★ 15
Comedy drama 2011 · Fr/Ger/Pol/Sp · Colour · 76min
Roman Polanski's adaptation of Yasmina Reza's hit play is a tightly wound, enjoyably cynical little chamber piece that features four indecently entertaining performances courtesy of Kate Winslet, Jodie Foster, Christoph Waltz and John C Reilly. Taking place in a cramped Brooklyn apartment, it has a quartet of New Yorkers discussing a fight in the park during which one of their sons has sustained a couple of damaged

teeth. But slowly their superficial civility melts away in an escalating cacophony of drowned mobile phones and projectile vomiting, and shows Polanski at the peak of his powers. **AS** Swearing. **DVD** **BL**
Kate Winslet *Nancy Cowan* • Jodie Foster *Penelope Longstreet* • Christoph Waltz *Alan Cowan* • John C Reilly *Michael Longstreet* ■ *Dir* Roman Polanski • *Scr* Roman Polanski, Yasmina Reza, from Reza's play *God of Carnage*

Carnal Knowledge ★★★★ 18
Drama 1971 · US · Colour · 93min
This 1970s drama featured one of the roles which brought Jack Nicholson to international attention and was a precursor to the emerging debate into the price the sexual revolution had on personal relationships. Mike Nichols directs a tale of two old college chums traversing life with some incisive flair, and Ann-Margret is especially fine as a vulnerable partner eager to salvage honesty from the emotional debris. If Nicholson is a touch too vulpine, the film admirably retains its edge and pace. **SH** Swearing. **DVD**
Jack Nicholson *Jonathan* • Arthur Garfunkel [Art Garfunkel] *Sandy* • Ann-Margret *Bobbie* • Candice Bergen *Susan* • Rita Moreno *Louise* • Cynthia O'Neal *Cindy* • Carol Kane *Jennifer* ■ *Dir* Mike Nichols • *Scr* Jules Feiffer

Carnegie Hall ★★★ U
Musical 1947 · US · B/W · 144min
That venerable New York institution is presented here in an over-stuffed, overlong pudding of a picture that has the sublime merit of featuring many of the greatest classical performers of its day, including Leopold Stokowski, Jascha Heifetz, Artur Rubinstein, Lily Pons and Rise Stevens. Big bandsters Harry James and Vaughn Monroe provide some populist appeal, but the music is somewhat dissipated by the thin plot, which sees Marsha Hunt trying to get her offspring onto the concert stage. **TS**
Marsha Hunt *Nora Ryan* • William Prince *Tony Salerno Jr* • Frank McHugh *John Donovan* • Martha O'Driscoll *Ruth Haines* • Hans Jaray *Tony Salerno Sr* • Joseph Buloff *Anton Tribik* • Olin Downes • Emile Boreo *Henry* • Alfonso D'Artega *Tchaikovsky* ■ *Dir* Edgar G Ulmer • *Scr* Karl Kamb, from a story by Seena Owen

Un Carnet de Bal ★★★★
Portmanteau drama 1937 · Fr · B/W · 129min
Boasting an exceptional cast and Maurice Jaubert's haunting melody, *Valse Grise*, this episodic drama won the Coupe Mussolini at Venice and earned its director, Julien Duvivier, an invitation to Hollywood. Marie Bell holds centre stage as a widow who decides to trace the men with whom she danced at her first ball. Naturally, the majority have strayed from the straight and narrow, giving each encounter its socio-symbolic tone. There's also plenty of humour and an affecting finale in this old-fashioned showcase to treasure. **DP** French +subtitles.
Harry Baur *Alain Regnault* • Marie Bell *Christine Surgère* • Pierre Blanchar *Thierry* • Fernandel *Fabien Coutissol* • Jeanne Fusier-Gir *Newspaper vendor* • Louis Jouvet *Pierre Verdier/Jo* • Milly Mathis *Cécile* • Raimu *François Patusset* • Françoise Rosay *Mme Audié* • Pierre Richard-Willm *Eric Irvin* • Sylvie *Thierry's mistress* ■ *Dir* Julien Duvivier • *Scr* Julien Duvivier, Jean Sarment, Pierre Wolff, Yves Mirande, Bernard Zimmer, Henri Jeanson

Carnival ★★
Romantic melodrama 1946 · UK · B/W · 93min
Ballet dancer Sally Gray falls in love with sculptor Michael Wilding, but refuses to compromise her honour by living with him. When he leaves her, she makes the unhappy mistake of marrying Cornish farmer Bernard Miles. This drama is a relentlessly morose and uninteresting film with a melodramatically tragic ending. **RK**
Michael Wilding *Maurice Avery* • Stanley Holloway *Charlie Raeburn* • Bernard Miles *Trewhella* • Jean Kent *Irene Dale* • Catherine Lacey *Florrie Raeburn* • Hazel Court *May*

Raeburn ■ Dir Stanley Haynes • Scr Eric Maschwitz, Stanley Haynes, Peter Ustinov, Guy Green, from a story by Compton Mackenzie

Carnival in Flanders ★★★ 12
Period comedy   1935 • Fr/Ger • BW • 109min

Directed and co-written by Jacques Feyder, this witty and sophisticated farce is set in 17th-century Flanders, wonderfully conjured up by Lazare Meerson's terrific sets and costumes. The accomplished Françoise Rosay stars as the wife of a mayor whose small town is invaded by Spanish troops. The men take fright and go into hiding; the women enjoy the attentions of the occupiers. Although not nearly as daring as it seemed in the 1930s, the film remains a charming romp. RK French +subtitles. DVD

Françoise Rosay Madame Burgomaster • Jean Murat The Duke • André Alerme Burgomaster • Louis Jouvet The Priest • Lynne Clévers Fishmonger's wife • Micheline Cheirel Siska ■ Dir Jacques Feyder • Scr Bernard Zimmer, Charles Spaak, Jacques Feyder, from a story by Charles Spaak

Carnival of Souls ★★★★ 12
Cult horror   1962 • US • BW • 79min

A young church organist finds herself in a strange limbo, haunted by spectral ghouls, in the creepy cult classic that director George A Romero credits as being his major inspiration for Night of the Living Dead. Representing the ultimate triumph of talent over budget, Herk Harvey's sole film as director is a crude but compelling chiller evoking a genuinely eerie atmosphere. Harvey also plays the lead phantom pursuing the heroine (the excellent Candace Hilligoss). AJ DVD

Candace Hilligoss Mary Henry • Herk Harvey The Man • Frances Feist Landlady • Sidney Berger John Linden • Art Ellison Minister ■ Dir Herk Harvey • Scr John Clifford, from a story by John Clifford, Herk Harvey

Carnival of Souls ★★★ 18
Horror   1999 • US • Colour • 83min

The black-and-white 1962 original remains a genuinely creepy tale of possession – fertile material for modern horror maestro Wes Craven. Sadly, though, he only served as executive producer on this slick update. Bobbie Phillips plays a young woman who is haunted by visions of her hated stepfather (comic actor Larry Miller in a surprisingly creepy performance), who she insists is trying to kill her. Problem is, the police insist he is already dead! Director Adam Grossman piles on some jolting shocks, but never manages to re-create the haunting melancholy of Herk Harvey's cult classic. JF DVD

Bobbie Phillips Alex • Larry Miller Louis • Shawnee Smith Sandra ■ Dir/Scr Adam Grossman

Carnival Story ★★ PG
Drama   1954 • US • Colour • 94min

Anne Baxter stars as a German girl seeking refuge from unhappiness by joining a carnival. She falls prey to a lustful cad (Steve Cochran), marries the troupe's high-diver (Lyle Bettger) and... well, see for yourself. This is tacky, but the erotic and suspenseful big-top atmosphere exerts its usual fascination. RK DVD

Anne Baxter Willie • Steve Cochran Joe Hammond • Lyle Bettger Frank Colloni • George Nader Vines • Jay C Flippen Charley • Helene Stanley Peggy • Adi Berber Groppo ■ Dir Kurt Neumann • Scr Hans Jacoby, Kurt Neumann, from the story by Marcel Klauber, CB Williams

Carny ★★★★ 18
Drama   1980 • US • Colour • 102min

Set behind the scenes of a travelling carnival, this very dark tale stars Robbie Robertson (formerly of rock group The Band) as a conman and fixer, Gary Busey as an insane dimwit, and Jodie Foster as the teenage runaway who comes between them. The setting, complete with authentic sideshows and genuine freaks, gives an added creepiness to the proceedings, and, although director Robert Kaylor tries to

concentrate on buddy bonding and life on the road, it's the strangeness of it all that leaves the biggest impression. Unusual, but also unmissable. JB Swearing.

Jodie Foster Donna • Gary Busey Frankie Chipman • Robbie Robertson Patch Beaudry • Meg Foster Gerta • Kenneth McMillan Heavy St John • Elisha Cook [Elisha Cook Jr] "On Your Mark" • Tim Thomerson Doubles • Theodore Wilson [Teddy Wilson (2)] Nails • John Lehne Skeet ■ Dir Robert Kaylor • Scr Thomas Baum, from a story by Phoebe Taylor, Robert Kaylor, Robbie Robertson

Carol ★★★★★ 15
Romantic drama   2015 • UK/US • Colour • 113min

Patricia Highsmith's lesbian novel The Price of Salt is brought to the screen by Todd Haynes in resplendent Far from Heaven fashion. Trapped in a marriage of convenience, uptown Cate Blanchett begins an affair with naive shop girl Rooney Mara. But this is early 1950s Manhattan and scandal beckons. With two high-calibre leads exercising coiffed poise and era-sensitive intelligence in every fabulous-looking frame, this is a stunning masterpiece full of atmosphere and poignant tenderness. AJ Swearing, sex scenes. DVD

Cate Blanchett Carol Aird • Rooney Mara Therese Belivet • Sarah Paulson Abby Gerhard • Jake Lacy Richard • John Magaro Dannie • Cory Michael Smith Tommy • Kyle Chandler Harge Aird ■ Dir Todd Haynes • Scr Phyllis Nagy, from Patricia Highsmith's novel The Price of Salt

A Carol Christmas ★★ 12
Seasonal comedy fantasy   2003 • US • Colour • 85min

Tori Spelling turns in a bravura performance in this TV movie as a self-centred chat show host, who makes life a nightmare for producer Michael Landes and PA Nina Siemaszko, as they prepare for her Christmas special. The showbiz satire is occasionally amusing, but this is more pantomime than morality tale. DP DVD

Tori Spelling Carol Cummings • William Shatner Doctor Bill/Ghost of Christmas Present • Nina Siemaszko Roberta Timmons • Dinah Manoff Marla • Michael Landes Jimmy Fields • Gary Coleman Ghost of Christmas Past ■ Dir Matthew Irmas • Scr Tom Amundsen

Caroline? ★★★★
Mystery drama   1990 • US • Colour • 100min

Here's a made-for-TV movie that's way above average, transferring an old Hollywood standby plot to the glossy world of "movie of the week". Stephanie Zimbalist returns to claim her inheritance after her family thought she was dead. Of course, Anastasia-like, they don't think she's who she says she is. This won Emmys for outstanding drama and the direction of Joseph Sargent. TS

Stephanie Zimbalist Caroline • Pamela Reed Grace Carmichael • George Grizzard Paul Carmichael • Shawn Phelan Winston Carmichael • Jenny Jacobs Heidi Carmichael • Patricia Neal Mrs Trollope • Dorothy McGuire Mrs Adkin ■ Dir Joseph Sargent • Scr Michael de Guzman, from the novel Father's Arcane Daughter by EL Konigsburg

Carousel ★★★★ U
Musical   1956 • US • Colour • 123min

This is a marvellous screen version of what is arguably Rodgers and Hammerstein's finest Broadway show, immaculately cast and filmed in part on glorious Maine locations. Some may find this tale of a reprobate's return to Earth to look out for his daughter arch in the extreme, but it is a tribute to the superb score and sensitive handling of the material that the film is moving. Gordon MacRae and Shirley Jones have the roles of their lives, though they're done no favours by the static direction. TS DVD

Gordon MacRae Billy Bigelow • Shirley Jones Julie • Cameron Mitchell Jigger • Barbara Ruick Carrie • Claramae Turner Cousin Nettie • Robert Rounseville Mr Snow • Gene Lockhart Starkeeper • Audrey Christie Mrs Mullin ■ Dir Henry King •

Scr Phoebe Ephron, Henry Ephron, from the musical by Richard Rodgers, Oscar Hammerstein II, Benjamin F Glazer, Ferenc Molnar

The Carpetbaggers ★★★★
Drama   1964 • US • Colour • 143min

With the lustre of age, nostalgia for its stars and that vanished art of storytelling know-how, this trashy tale has now acquired a certain fascination. Based on the Harold Robbins potboiler, it sprawls across three decades, focusing on the life and loves of tycoon George Peppard. Alan Ladd, as a cowboy star, makes his final screen appearance and Hollywood sexpot Carroll Baker drapes herself over both of them. It's lumpen, lavish and lascivious, a gripping cocktail of melodrama and moralising. AT

George Peppard Jonas Cord Jr • Alan Ladd Nevada Smith • Carroll Baker Rina • Bob Cummings [Robert Cummings] Dan Pierce • Martha Hyer Jennie Denton • Elizabeth Ashley Monica Winthrop • Martin Balsam Bernard B Norman • Lew Ayres McAllister • Tom Tully Amos Winthrop ■ Dir Edward Dmytryk • Scr John Michael Hayes, from the novel by Harold Robbins

Carpool ★★ PG
Comedy   1996 • US • Colour • 85min

The ex-Mr Roseanne Barr, Tom Arnold, won the "Razzie" award for worst actor for his performance in this annoying chase movie. Ironically, though, he's the only reason for watching it. His affably juvenile persona can be grating at times, but it suits his role here as a bumbling crook holding a carload of kids hostage. This runs out of gas before the end. RS Swearing.

Tom Arnold Franklin Laszlo • David Paymer Daniel Miller • Rhea Perlman Martha • Rod Steiger Mr Hammerman • Kim Coates Detective Erdman • Rachael Leigh Cook Kayla ■ Dir Arthur Hiller • Scr Don Rhymer

Carrie ★★★ U
Period romantic melodrama   1952 • US • BW • 116min

Not be confused with Brian De Palma's horror classic, this William Wyler-directed romantic drama is set in Chicago at the beginning of the 20th century. It stars Jennifer Jones as the girl from the Midwest whose youthful optimism is gradually denuded by her time in the Windy City. Jones is fine in the lead role but it's Laurence Olivier who takes the honours here as the middle-aged, married restaurateur who gives up everything for the love of Carrie. JA DVD

Jennifer Jones Carrie Meeber • Laurence Olivier George Hurstwood • Miriam Hopkins Julia Hurstwood • Eddie Albert Charlie Drouet • Basil Ruysdael Mr Fitzgerald • Ray Teal Allan • Barry Kelley Slawson ■ Dir William Wyler • Scr Ruth Goetz, Augustus Goetz, from the novel Sister Carrie by Theodore Dreiser

Carrie ★★★★★ 18
Horror   1976 • US • Colour • 93min

Brian De Palma's modern gothic fairy tale, based on Stephen King's bestseller, offers a tense and lyrical web of emotions. Sissy Spacek is heartbreaking as the telekinetic Cinderella turning her school prom into a bloody massacre after a macabre joke is played on her by vicious teens (including John Travolta). Piper Laurie as Spacek's religious fanatic mother is equally striking and her symbolic "crucifixion" is a thrilling highlight in an unforgettable package of pop psychology and psychic phenomena. Despite a much-copied plot and even more copied shock climax, De Palma's best movie remains a transfixing experience. A belated, very inferior sequel of sorts, The Rage: Carrie 2, followed in 1999 and a remake is due in 2013 featuring Chloë Grace Moretz and Julianne Moore. AJ Violence, swearing, nudity. DVD

Sissy Spacek Carrie White • Piper Laurie Margaret White • Amy Irving Sue Snell • William Katt Tommy Ross • John Travolta Billy Nolan • Nancy Allen Chris Hargensen • Betty Buckley Miss Collins • Priscilla Pointer Mrs Snell ■ Dir Brian De Palma • Scr Lawrence D Cohen, from the novel by Stephen King

Carrie ★★★ 15
Horror   2013 • US • Colour • 99min

Boys Don't Cry director Kimberly Peirce's film is more of a homage to Brian De Palma's 1976 horror classic than a back-to-basics adaptation of Stephen King's novel. The core scary fairy tale remains – teenage Carrie White (Chloë Grace Moretz) is picked on by her classmates until she unleashes full telekinetic revenge at the school prom – but the movie has some updated social media frills and extraneous gore, and completely lacks the captivating poignancy at the heart of the original. The performances are fine, just not in the same class as iconic Sissy Spacek or Piper Laurie, and showing Carrie to be in control of her powers makes it much less emotionally engaging. AJ DVD BD

Chloë Grace Moretz Carrie White • Julianne Moore Margaret White • Judy Greer Miss Desjardin • Portia Doubleday Chris Hargensen • Gabriella Wilde Sue Snell ■ Dir Kimberly Peirce • Scr Roberto Aguirre-Sacasa, Lawrence D Cohen, from Stephen King's novel

La Carrière de Suzanne ★★★★ PG
Drama   1963 • Fr • BW • 52min

The second of Eric Rohmer's "Six Moral Tales" is a witty, wise and wonderfully told story about the gulf in emotional maturity that exists between young men and women. The men behaving badly here are a medical student whose worthless friendship with his lothario buddy costs him not only his meagre supply of cash, but also his chance of romance with Suzanne, the interpreter who at first tolerates and then repudiates their childish games. No one films Paris better than Rohmer, and he coaxes naturalistic performances from his young cast. DP French +subtitles. DVD

Catherine Sée Suzanne • Philippe Beuzen Bertrand • Christian Charrière Guillaume • Diane Wilkinson Sophie ■ Dir/Scr Eric Rohmer

Carriers ★★★ 15
Horror thriller   2008 • US • Colour • 81min

The premise of this horror thriller may not be the most original – a deadly virus has wiped out much of humanity and a band of survivors tries to fight its way to safety – but sibling writer/directors Alex and David Pastor use their tiny budget wisely. They concentrate not on cheap effects or extreme gore but on a mounting sense of doom. Chris Pine (Kirk in Star Trek) and Lou Taylor Pucci are believable as brothers who, along with female companions Piper Perabo and Emily VanCamp, are desperate to find refuge. The movie's convincing bleakness and its absence of shocks are impressive. AS Violence, swearing. DVD BD

Lou Taylor Pucci Danny • Chris Pine Brian • Piper Perabo Bobby • Emily VanCamp Kate • Chris Meloni [Christopher Meloni] Frank • Kiernan Shipka Jodie ■ Dir/Scr Alex Pastor, David Pastor

Carrington ★★★★ 18
Biographical drama   1995 • UK • Colour • 117min

The extraordinary romance between androgynous painter Dora Carrington and homosexual writer Lytton Strachey is captivatingly portrayed by Emma Thompson and Jonathan Pryce in the directing debut of Christopher Hampton. Few love stories have been so intense or unusual as this account of the non-sexual relationship between the Bloomsbury group twosome, who shared their nonconformist alliance with Carrington's husband and Strachey's occasional boyfriends. Hampton's fascinating account is beautifully crafted, wittily scripted and intelligently realised, with Pryce giving the performance of a lifetime. Costume drama is rarely this compelling or moving. AJ DVD

Emma Thompson Carrington • Jonathan Pryce Lytton Strachey • Steven Waddington Ralph Partridge • Samuel West Gerald Brenan • Rufus Sewell Mark Gertler • Penelope Wilton Lady Ottoline Morrell • Janet McTeer Vanessa Bell • Peter Blythe Phillip Morrell • Jeremy Northam Beacus Penrose • Alex Kingston Frances

Partridge ■ *Dir* Christopher Hampton • *Scr* Christopher Hampton, from the book *Lytton Strachey* by Michael Holroyd

Carrington VC ★★★ PG

Courtroom drama 1954 · UK · BW · 101min

David Niven had no formal acting training, but he was capable of giving performances of both subtlety and power. Unfortunately, producers typecast him in debonair roles and only rarely gave him the chance to tackle more demanding characters. Here he shows the depth of his instinctive talent as a war hero driven to theft by delays in repayments of his expenses. Niven's shifts between despair, dignity and determination are masterly, and he is well supported by Margaret Leighton. DP **DVD**

David Niven *Major Carrington VC* • Margaret Leighton *Valerie Carrington* • Noelle Middleton *Captain Alison Graham* • Allan Cuthbertson *Lt Col Henniker* • Victor Maddern *Owen* • Raymond Francis *Maj Jim Mitchell* • Geoffrey Keen *President of the Court* • Laurence Naismith *Major Panton* • Clive Morton *Lt Col Huxford* • Maurice Denham *Lt Col Reeve* ■ *Dir* Anthony Asquith • *Scr* John Hunter, from a play by Dorothy Christie, Campbell Christie

Carry On Abroad ★★ PG

Comedy 1972 · UK · Colour · 85min

This disappointing outing is every bit as jerry-built as the Elsbels Palace Hotel itself. With a stingy quota of jokes, the team's holiday to Spain rapidly descends into innuendo and second-rate slapstick. There are one or two neat observations on the British abroad, but there's too little for the regulars to do, and it's a sad series swan song for the inimitable Charles Hawtrey. DP **DVD**

Sidney James *Vic Flange* • Kenneth Williams *Stuart Farquhar* • Charles Hawtrey *Tuttle* • Peter Butterworth *Pepe* • Joan Sims *Cora Flange* • Kenneth Connor *Stanley Blunt* • Jimmy Logan *Bert Conway* • Barbara Windsor *Sadie* • June Whitfield *Evelyn Blunt* • Hattie Jacques *Floella* • Bernard Bresslaw *Brother Bernard* • Jack Douglas *Harry* • Patsy Rowlands *Miss Dobbs* ■ *Dir* Gerald Thomas • *Scr* Talbot Rothwell

Carry On Admiral ★★ U

Comedy 1957 · UK · BW · 78min

This is not one of the *Carry Ons*, but an unremarkable screen adaptation of an almost forgotten stage farce. Also known as *The Ship Was Loaded*, this comedy of errors has more in common with radio hit *The Navy Lark* than its saucier namesakes. David Tomlinson and Brian Reece goof gamely as the civil servant and the sailor whose identities get muddled, but it's AE Matthews (at the ripe old age of 87) who steals the show. DP **DVD**

David Tomlinson *Tom Baker* • Peggy Cummins *Susan Lashwood* • Brian Reece *Peter Fraser* • Eunice Gayson *Jane Godfrey* • AE Matthews *Admiral Godfrey* • Joan Sims *Mary* ■ *Dir* Val Guest • *Scr* Val Guest, from the play *Off the Record* by Ian Hay, Stephen King-Hall

Carry On Again Doctor ★★★★ PG

Comedy 1969 · UK · Colour · 85min

The 18th *Carry On* is easily the funniest of the medical capers. Rejoicing under the glorious name of Dr Nookey, Jim Dale holds centre stage with some aplomb, most notably matching Sid James gag for gag during the wonderfully sleazy Beatific Island scenes. Charles Hawtrey also has one of his better outings, hissing bitterly as the covetous Dr Stoppidge who is forced to resort to drag in order to discover the secret of Dale's revolutionary slimming tonic. As usual, Talbot Rothwell litters his script with witty one-liners. DP **DVD**

Kenneth Williams *Frederick Carver* • Jim Dale *Dr James Nookey* • Sidney James *Gladstone Screwer* • Charles Hawtrey *Dr Ernest Stoppidge* • Joan Sims *Ellen Moore* • Hattie Jacques *Matron* • Barbara Windsor *Goldie Locks* • Patsy Rowlands *Miss Fosdick* ■ *Dir* Gerald Thomas • *Scr* Talbot Rothwell

Carry On at Your Convenience ★★ PG

Comedy 1971 · UK · Colour · 86min

Among the weakest of the *Carry Ons*, this is toilet humour in every sense of the phrase. Plumbing the depths of his imagination, screenwriter Talbot Rothwell throws up a spoof on "everybody out" trade unionism that is hardly flush with originality. To relieve the comic drought, he packs bosses and workers alike into a charabanc for a works outing that has all the appearance of a desperate time-filler. DP **DVD**

Sidney James *Sid Plummer* • Kenneth Williams *WC Boggs* • Charles Hawtrey *Charles Coote* • Joan Sims *Chloe Moore* • Hattie Jacques *Beattie Plummer* • Bernard Bresslaw *Bernie Hulke* • Patsy Rowlands *Miss Withering* • Bill Maynard *Fred Moore* ■ *Dir* Gerald Thomas • *Scr* Talbot Rothwell

Carry On Behind ★★ PG

Comedy 1975 · UK · Colour · 86min

This caravan version of *Carry On Camping* marked the beginning of the end for the classic comedy series, with neither Sid James nor scriptwriter Talbot Rothwell on board. This woeful effort from writer Dave Freeman, a series newcomer, attempts to combine caravan-holiday capers and archaeological high jinks. The only fragments of fun come from Kenneth Williams and Elke Sommer as relic hunters on a dig. DP **DVD**

Elke Sommer *Professor Anna Vrooshka* • Kenneth Williams *Professor Roland Crump* • Joan Sims *Daphne Barnes* • Bernard Bresslaw *Arthur Upmore* • Jack Douglas *Ernie Bragg* • Windsor Davies *Fred Ramsden* • Kenneth Connor *Major Leep* • Liz Fraser *Sylvia Ramsden* • Peter Butterworth *Barnes* ■ *Dir* Gerald Thomas • *Scr* Dave Freeman

Carry On Cabby ★★★ PG

Comedy 1963 · UK · BW · 88min

The best of the black-and-white *Carry Ons* began life as a script by the then little known Talbot Rothwell entitled *Call Me a Cab*. Having just parted company with regular scriptwriter Norman Hudis, producer Peter Rogers brought Rothwell into the fold and he went on to pen the next 19 films in the series. Pitting Sid James against the long-suffering Hattie Jacques, the battle between Speedee Taxis and Glamcabs is packed with hilarious incidents and cracking performances, not least from Kenneth Connor and Esma Cannon as the respective loyal lieutenants and Charles Hawtrey as the hapless Pint-Pot. DP **DVD**

Sidney James *Charlie* • Hattie Jacques *Peggy* • Kenneth Connor *Ted* • Charles Hawtrey *Pintpot* • Esma Cannon *Flo* • Liz Fraser *Sally* • Bill Owen *Smiley* • Milo O'Shea *Len* • Jim Dale *Expectant father* • Amanda Barrie *Anthea* ■ *Dir* Gerald Thomas • *Scr* Talbot Rothwell, from a story by Sidney Green [SC Green], Richard Hills [RM Hills]

Carry On Camping ★★★ PG

Comedy 1969 · UK · Colour · 85min

The 17th outing is one of the liveliest *Carry Ons*, with the cast making light of the fact that they were shooting in freezing temperatures in fields that were so muddy they were sprayed green to give the impression of high summer. Yet again, the big slapstick finale is a disappointment after all the wonderful double entendre incidents, but there is the compensation of Sid James as a hippy, while Peter Butterworth has his finest hour as the miserly site owner. DP **DVD**

Sidney James *Sid Boggle* • Kenneth Williams *Dr Soaper* • Joan Sims *Joan Fussey* • Charles Hawtrey *Charlie Muggins* • Bernard Bresslaw *Bernie Lugg* • Terry Scott *Peter Potter* • Barbara Windsor *Babs* • Hattie Jacques *Miss Haggerd* • Peter Butterworth *Joshua Fiddler* ■ *Dir* Gerald Thomas • *Scr* Talbot Rothwell

Carry On Cleo ★★★★ PG

Comedy 1964 · UK · Colour · 87min

Mercilessly mocking Elizabeth Taylor's disastrous *Cleopatra*, this corking ancient history lesson sees the *Carry On* team at the peak of its powers. The puns have never been better ("Infamy, infamy, they've all got

it in for me!") and the sets are positively luxuriant (and very familiar!). Amanda Barrie is exquisitely dippy in the title role, and Kenneth Connor and Jim Dale do well as the Britons in the imperial guard. But topping them all are Sid James's lecherous Mark Antony and Kenneth Williams's snivelling Caesar. DP **DVD** ⓢ

Sidney James *Mark Antony* • Kenneth Williams *Julius Caesar* • Kenneth Connor *Hengist Pod* • Charles Hawtrey *Seneca* • Joan Sims *Calpurnia* • Jim Dale *Horsa* • Amanda Barrie *Cleo* • Julie Stevens *Gloria* • Sheila Hancock *Senna Pod* • Warren Mitchell *Spencius* ■ *Dir* Gerald Thomas • *Scr* Talbot Rothwell

Carry On Columbus ★ PG

Comedy 1992 · UK · Colour · 87min

Oh dear. With many of the original *Carry On* regulars no longer with us or (sensibly) otherwise engaged, it was left to more contemporary comedians to put the final nail in the *Carry On* coffin with a cacophony of puerile jokes and general atrociousness. This mainly fails because the *Carry On* films are, like many other historic things, probably best remembered rather than re-created. JB **DVD**

Jim Dale *Christopher Columbus* • Peter Richardson *Bart* • Alexei Sayle *Achmed* • Sara Crowe *Fatima* • Julian Clary *Diego* • Bernard Cribbins *Mordecai Mendoza* • Richard Wilson (3) *Don Felipe* • Keith Allen *Pepi* • Nigel Planer *Wazir* • Rik Mayall *Sultan* • Tony Slattery *Baba* • Maureen Lipman *Countess Esme* • Jon Pertwee *Duke of Costa Brava* • Leslie Phillips *King Ferdinand* • June Whitfield *Queen Isabella* • Martin Clunes *Martin* ■ *Dir* Gerald Thomas • *Scr* Dave Freeman

Carry On Constable ★★★ U

Comedy 1960 · UK · BW · 83min

The fourth in the *Carry On* series is the first to feature the excellent Sid James, who stars as the sergeant detailed to wet nurse rookies Kenneth Williams, Leslie Phillips, Charles Hawtrey and Kenneth Connor. Having studied the policeman's lot at Slough, screenwriter Norman Hudis confessed he could find nothing funny about pounding the beat, but he still turned in a chucklesome script. The bungling bobbies have their moments, but their thunder is stolen by seasoned supports Joan Hickson, Irene Handl and Esma Cannon, inevitably playing their usual eccentrics. DP **DVD**

Sidney James *Sergeant Frank Wilkins* • Kenneth Williams *Constable Benson* • Hattie Jacques *Sergeant Laura Moon* • Eric Barker *Inspector Mills* • Kenneth Connor *Constable Charlie Constable* • Charles Hawtrey *Special Constable Gorse* • Leslie Phillips *Constable Potter* • Joan Sims *Policewoman Gloria Passworthy* ■ *Dir* Gerald Thomas • *Scr* Norman Hudis, from an idea by Brock Williams

Carry On Cowboy ★★★ PG

Comedy 1965 · UK · Colour · 90min

When Marshall P Knutt (Jim Dale) rides into Stodge City, Judge Burke (Kenneth Williams) is convinced that he is the lawman who will rid him of the Rumpo Kid (Sid James) and his band of desperados. But to a sanitary engineer like Knutt, cleaning up the town has a totally different meaning. Shot in the untamed wilds of Pinewood Studios, the 11th *Carry On* finds the team in mid-season form. All the regulars impress, but Charles Hawtrey steals the picture as the firewater-swilling Chief Big Heap. DP **DVD** ⓢ

Sidney James *Rumpo Kid* • Kenneth Williams *Judge Burke* • Jim Dale *Marshall P Knutt* • Charles Hawtrey *Chief Big Heap* • Joan Sims *Belle* • Angela Douglas *Annie Oakley* • Bernard Bresslaw *Little Heap* • Peter Butterworth *Doc* • Jon Pertwee *Sheriff Earp* ■ *Dir* Gerald Thomas • *Scr* Talbot Rothwell

Carry On Cruising ★★★ U

Comedy 1962 · UK · Colour · 89min

The first in colour and the last *Carry On* written by Norman Hudis, this is the most charming film in the series. Set aboard the SS *Happy Wanderer*, it charts the course of captain Sid James's tenth anniversary cruise, during which the members of his

new crew seek to find their sea legs. Kenneth Connor enjoys one of his best outings as the nervous ship's doctor and Lance Percival has fun as the cook-it-and-see chef. DP **DVD**

Sidney James *Captain Crowther* • Kenneth Williams *Leonard Marjoribanks* • Kenneth Connor *Arthur Binn* • Liz Fraser *Gladys Trimble* • Dilys Laye *Flo Castle* • Lance Percival *Wilfred Haines* • Esma Cannon *Bridget Madderley* ■ *Dir* Gerald Thomas • *Scr* Norman Hudis, from a story by Eric Barker

Carry On Dick ★★★ PG

Comedy 1974 · UK · Colour · 86min

Packed with more than the usual amount of smutty innuendo, this spoof on period adventures does not live up to the team's previous best. It is chiefly memorable for being Sid James's 19th and last *Carry On*. He plays feared highwayman Dick Turpin, who masquerades as country vicar the Reverend Flasher. Also leading a double life, Barbara Windsor gives one of her best performances of the series as Turpin's sidekick. DP **DVD**

Sidney James *Dick Turpin/Reverend Flasher* • Barbara Windsor *Harriet/Harry* • Kenneth Williams *Captain Desmond Fancey* • Hattie Jacques *Martha Hoggett* • Bernard Bresslaw *Sir Roger Daley* • Joan Sims *Madame Desiree* • Kenneth Connor *Constable* • Peter Butterworth *Tom "Doc" Scholl* • Jack Douglas *Sergeant Jock Strapp* ■ *Dir* Gerald Thomas • *Scr* Talbot Rothwell, from a treatment by Lawrie Wyman, George Evans

Carry On Doctor ★★★ PG

Comedy 1968 · UK · Colour · 90min

After seven consecutive spoofs of other movies, the *Carry On* crew returned to the world of work for this lively comedy that virtually takes up from where *Carry On Nurse* left off. The timing of another hospital picture couldn't have been better for Sid James, who was genuinely bedridden for much of the production. Consequently, most of the workload falls upon Kenneth Williams as a sneering consultant, Jim Dale as the clumsy Dr Kilmore, and Frankie Howerd, making an impressive series debut as a faith healer. DP **DVD**

Frankie Howerd *Francis Bigger* • Sidney James *Charlie Roper* • Kenneth Williams *Dr Tinkle* • Charles Hawtrey *Mr Barron* • Jim Dale *Dr Kilmore* • Barbara Windsor *Sandra May* • Joan Sims *Chloe Gibson* • Hattie Jacques *Matron* • Bernard Bresslaw *Ken Biddle* • Peter Butterworth *Mr Smith* ■ *Dir* Gerald Thomas • *Scr* Talbot Rothwell

Carry On – Don't Lose Your Head ★★★★ PG

Comedy 1966 · UK · Colour · 86min

Originally not intended to be a *Carry On*, this turns out to be one of the jewels in the series. Hilariously spoofing *The Scarlet Pimpernel*, Talbot Rothwell's script is stuffed with comic incidents and names ranging from Sir Rodney Ffing to the Duc de Pommfrit. Sid James is superb, whether camping it up as a society fop or cutting a dash as the Black Fingernail, while Kenneth Williams's Citizen Camembert is great as "the big cheese" of the French Revolution. Joan Sims also excels as Desirée Dubarry, who poses as the Duchess de la Plume de ma Tante to lure Sid to Paris. DP **DVD**

Sidney James *Sir Rodney Ffing/The Black Fingernail* • Kenneth Williams *Citizen Camembert* • Jim Dale *Lord Darcy* • Charles Hawtrey *Duc de Pommfrit* • Joan Sims *Desirée Dubarry* • Peter Butterworth *Citizen Bidet* ■ *Dir* Gerald Thomas • *Scr* Talbot Rothwell

Carry On Emmannuelle ★ 15

Comedy 1978 · UK · Colour · 84min

Spoofing the series of erotic movies starring Sylvia Kristel, this was the last *Carry On* made during the series' golden age. Sadly, it's the weakest of the lot. Lance Peters's script is a gag-free zone that is utterly dependent on smutty innuendo and severely taxes the talents of the few regulars on duty. DP Some swearing, sex scenes, brief nudity. **DVD**

C

Suzanne Danielle *Emmanuelle Prevert* • Kenneth Williams *Emile Prevert* • Kenneth Connor *Leyland* • Jack Douglas *Lyons* • Joan Sims *Mrs Dangle* • Peter Butterworth *Richmond* • Beryl Reid *Mrs Valentine* ■ *Dir* Gerald Thomas • *Scr* Lance Peters

Carry On England ★ PG
Comedy 1976 · UK · Colour · 85min

The real secret of the *Carry Ons* success was in the scriptwriting, which provided the actors with an endless supply of stinging ammunition. This woeful effort about a Battle of Britain anti-aircraft battery leaves what is essentially a B-team with nothing to fire but blanks. It's a strong contender for worst entry in the comedy series. DP *DVD*
Kenneth Connor *Captain S Melly* • Windsor Davies *Sergeant Major "Tiger" Bloomer* • Patrick Mower *Sergeant Len Able* • Judy Geeson *Sergeant Tilly Willing* • Jack Douglas *Bombardier Ready* • Melvyn Hayes *Gunner Shorthouse* • Joan Sims *Private Sharpe* • Peter Jones *Brigadier* • Peter Butterworth *Major Carstairs* ■ *Dir* Gerald Thomas • *Scr* David Pursall, Jack Seddon

Carry On Follow That Camel ★★ PG
Comedy 1967 · UK · Colour · 90min

Originally released under the title *Follow That Camel*, this disappointing spoof on *Beau Geste* was only later added to the *Carry On* series and it sits uncomfortably alongside the rest. Although many of the regular team are on duty, the presence of Phil Silvers overbalances the story. There are comic oases along the way, however, with the Mustapha Leek joke being the most memorable. DP *DVD*
Phil Silvers *Sergeant Nocker* • Jim Dale *Bertram Oliphant West* • Peter Butterworth *Simpson* • Charles Hawtrey *Captain Le Pice* • Kenneth Williams *Commandant Burger* • Anita Harris *Corktip* • Joan Sims *Zigzig* • Bernard Bresslaw *Abdul* • Angela Douglas *Lady Jane Ponsonby* • John Bluthal *Corporal Clotski* ■ *Dir* Gerald Thomas • *Scr* Talbot Rothwell

Carry On Girls ★★ PG
Comedy 1973 · UK · Colour · 84min

When councillor Sidney Fiddler (Sid James) decides that a beauty contest is the only way to put the sleepy seaside resort of Fircombe on the map, the local feminists are soon up in arms. The least focused of the *Carry On* series, this combines the gentle social satire of an Ealing comedy with the sniggering sauciness of a Donald McGill postcard. It's not one of Talbot Rothwell's best scripts, but there are some splendid supporting performances. DP *DVD*
Sidney James *Sidney Fiddler* • Joan Sims *Connie Philpotts* • Kenneth Connor *Frederick Bumble* • Barbara Windsor *Hope Springs* • Bernard Bresslaw *Peter Potter* • June Whitfield *Augusta Prodworthy* • Peter Butterworth *Admiral* • Jack Douglas *William* • Patsy Rowlands *Mildred Bumble* • Joan Hickson *Mrs Dukes* • Wendy Richard *Ida Downs* ■ *Dir* Gerald Thomas • *Scr* Talbot Rothwell

Carry On Henry ★★★ PG
Comedy 1971 · UK · Colour · 86min

This raucous history lesson is something of an on-off affair. For once, Talbot Rothwell's script isn't as sharp as an executioner's axe, but there are still plenty of wicked one-liners and savage parodies. Sid James makes a suitably merry monarch, while Joan Sims gives her best performance of the series as his garlic-gobbling queen. Exceptional support is provided by Kenneth Williams and Charles Hawtrey as the wonderfully named Sir Roger de Lodgerley. DP *DVD*
Sidney James *Henry VIII* • Kenneth Williams *Thomas Cromwell* • Charles Hawtrey *Sir Roger de Lodgerley* • Joan Sims *Queen Marie* • Terry Scott *Cardinal Wolsey* • Barbara Windsor *Bettina* • Kenneth Connor *Lord Hampton of Wick* • Bill Maynard *Fawkes* ■ *Dir* Gerald Thomas • *Scr* Talbot Rothwell

Carry On Jack ★★ PG
Comedy 1963 · UK · Colour · 87min

The innuendos continue as the *Carry On* crew takes to the seas in the first of the

historical costume parodies tackled by the team. Alas, some of the regulars are missing, making it one of the less memorable productions in the series. Bernard Cribbins in the lead role doesn't carry the same clout as Sid James, but director Gerald Thomas keeps the fun shipshape and Bristol fashion. NF *DVD* *Blu-ray*
Bernard Cribbins *Albert Poop-Decker* • Kenneth Williams *Captain Fearless* • Juliet Mills *Sally* • Charles Hawtrey *Walter* • Donald Houston *Howett* • Percy Herbert *Angel* ■ *Dir* Gerald Thomas • *Scr* Talbot Rothwell

Carry On Loving ★★ PG
Comedy 1970 · UK · Colour · 86min

Containing more double entendres than an exhibition of smutty postcards, Talbot Rothwell's script for this patchy effort spends too much time in the company of Terry Scott and the other clients of the Wedded Bliss Marriage Bureau. Consequently, we get not enough of the bureau's proprietors: Hattie Jacques and Sid James, amorous spinster Joan Sims and marriage guidance counsellor Kenneth Williams. The sound you can hear during the slapstick wedding finale is barrels being scraped. DP *DVD*
Sidney James *Sidney Bliss* • Kenneth Williams *Percival Snooper* • Charles Hawtrey *James Bedsop* • Joan Sims *Esme Crowfoot* • Hattie Jacques *Sophie* • Terry Scott *Terence Philpot* • Bernard Bresslaw *Gripper Burke* • Patsy Rowlands *Miss Dempsey* • Joan Hickson *Mrs Grubb* • Bill Maynard *Mr Dreery* ■ *Dir* Gerald Thomas • *Scr* Talbot Rothwell

Carry On Matron ★★★ PG
Comedy 1972 · UK · Colour · 85min

Subtitled *From Here to Maternity*, the fourth *Carry On* to be set in a hospital is the last in the series that manages to be consistently funny throughout. The regulars are all present, with Hattie Jacques in the title role as the object of consultant Kenneth Williams's confused affections, while crooked Sid James leads a raid on the clinic where they work to steal contraceptive pills. Amid the innuendo, cross-dressing and crude slapstick, there are lovely cameos from Kenneth Connor and Joan Sims. DP *DVD*
Sidney James *Sid Carter* • Kenneth Williams *Sir Bernard Cutting* • Charles Hawtrey *Dr Francis Goode* • Joan Sims *Mrs Tidey* • Hattie Jacques *Matron* • Bernard Bresslaw *Ernie* • Kenneth Cope *Cyril Carter* • Terry Scott *Dr Prodd* • Barbara Windsor *Nurse Susan Ball* • Kenneth Connor *Mr Tidey* • Bill Maynard *Freddy* • Patsy Rowlands *Evelyn Banks* ■ *Dir* Gerald Thomas • *Scr* Talbot Rothwell

Carry On Nurse ★★★ PG
Comedy 1959 · UK · BW · 85min

The second film in the *Carry On* series overdoses on bedpan, large needle and inedible food gags, but, as most of them are funny, no one will mind in the slightest. Hattie Jacques is superb as the bullying matron whose clipped supervision of nurses Shirley Eaton and Joan Sims prompts Kenneth Connor, Leslie Phillips and Kenneth Williams to give her a taste of her own medicine, while Wilfrid Hyde White has fun as a lecherous colonel in a private ward. DP *DVD*
Kenneth Connor *Bernie Bishop* • Charles Hawtrey *Mr Hinton* • Hattie Jacques *Matron* • Shirley Eaton *Dorothy Denton* • Wilfrid Hyde White *Colonel* • Bill Owen *Percy Hickson* • Leslie Phillips *Jack Bell* • Joan Sims *Stella Dawson* • Kenneth Williams *Oliver Reckitt* • Terence Longdon *Ted York* ■ *Dir* Gerald Thomas • *Scr* Norman Hudis, from the play *Ring for Catty* by Patrick Cargill, Jack Searle

Carry On Regardless ★★★ PG
Comedy 1960 · UK · BW · 86min

The fifth *Carry On* is unique in that it does not have a single storyline, but consists of a loose collection of sketches linked by the "Helping Hands" employment agency, run by Sid James to tackle the oddest of jobs. The assignments vary in comic value, but the ones in which Joan Sims gets

hammered at a snooty wine tasting and Kenneth Williams babysits a chimpanzee stand out. The inimitable Esma Cannon simpers and sniggers superbly as Sid's assistant, but Charles Hawtrey and Kenneth Connor have little to do. DP *DVD*
Sidney James *Bert Handy* • Kenneth Connor *Sam Twist* • Kenneth Williams *Francis Courtenay* • Charles Hawtrey *Gabriel Dimple* • Joan Sims *Lily Duveen* • Liz Fraser *Delia King* • Bill Owen *Mike Weston* • Hattie Jacques *Frosty-faced Sister* • Terence Longdon *Montgomery Infield-Hopping* • Joan Hickson *Matron* • Esma Cannon *Miss Cooling* ■ *Dir* Gerald Thomas • *Scr* Norman Hudis

Carry On Screaming ★★★★ PG
Comedy 1966 · UK · Colour · 92min

This is one of the finest entries in Britain's most popular comedy series. Mocking that other bastion of British cinema in the 1960s, the Hammer horror film, Talbot Rothwell's script positively bristles with classic one-liners, the most memorable being Kenneth Williams's gleeful "Frying tonight!" as he sinks into a bubbling cauldron. In his only *Carry On*, Harry H Corbett is superb as the Holmesian detective and Fenella Fielding revels in her role as a vampish vampire, but the picture belongs to Williams as the undead Dr Watt, an amalgam of every mad scientist who ever set foot in a lab. DP *DVD* *Blu-ray*
Kenneth Williams *Dr Watt* • Harry H Corbett *Detective Sergeant Bung* • Fenella Fielding *Valeria* • Jim Dale *Albert Potter* • Charles Hawtrey *Dan Dann* • Joan Sims *Emily Bung* • Bernard Bresslaw *Sockett* • Peter Butterworth *Detective Constable Slobotham* • Jon Pertwee *Dr Fettle* ■ *Dir* Gerald Thomas • *Scr* Talbot Rothwell

Carry On Sergeant ★★★ U
Comedy 1958 · UK · BW · 80min

This is the first of a phenomenon. Like many of the early outings, it centres on an occupation at the heart of British life and is, therefore, closer to Ealing whimsy than the raucous fun of the later *Carry Ons*. William Hartnell (who became a household name as the first Doctor Who) stars as the sergeant determined to make soldiers out of his final batch of national service conscripts. Alongside Bob Monkhouse, a handful of regulars are on duty, with Kenneth Connor splendid as a weedy hypochondriac, Kenneth Williams as a smarmy know-all, and Charles Hawtrey as the wonderfully named Private Golightly. DP *DVD*
William Hartnell *Sergeant Grimshawe* • Bob Monkhouse *Charlie Sage* • Shirley Eaton *Mary* • Eric Barker *Captain Potts* • Dora Bryan *Nora* • Bill Owen *Corporal Copping* • Charles Hawtrey *Peter Golightly* • Kenneth Connor *Horace Strong* • Kenneth Williams *James Bailey* • Hattie Jacques *Captain Clark* ■ *Dir* Gerald Thomas • *Scr* Norman Hudis, from the novel *The Bull Boys* by RF Delderfield

Carry On Spying ★★★ U
Spy spoof 1964 · UK · BW · 83min

Mercilessly ribbing the Bond movies and Graham Greene's espionage entertainments, the ninth *Carry On* saw Barbara Windsor make her series debut as the most resourceful of a hamstrung quartet of agents sent to Vienna to recover a secret formula. The Casbah scenes rather slow things down, but the action picks up pace in STENCH's underground HQ (a wonderfully observed 007 send-up). Bernard Cribbins, Charles Hawtrey and Kenneth Williams are on form as Babs's weak-kneed accomplices and there are splendid turns from Jim Dale and Eric Barker. DP *DVD*
Kenneth Williams *Desmond Simpkins* • Barbara Windsor *Daphne Honeybutt* • Bernard Cribbins *Harold Crump* • Charles Hawtrey *Charlie Bind* • Eric Barker *Chief* • Dilys Laye *Lila* • Jim Dale *Carstairs* ■ *Dir* Gerald Thomas • *Scr* Talbot Rothwell, Sid Colin

Carry On Teacher ★★★ U
Comedy 1959 · UK · BW · 82min

The third in the *Carry On* series is a gentle comedy about the concerted efforts of both the pupils and staff of Maudlin Street

School to dissuade headmaster Ted Ray from accepting a post elsewhere. The pranks are Bash Street Kids' calibre and raise few laughs, but the staff-room infighting is good value, with drama teacher Kenneth Williams and educational psychologist Leslie Phillips squabbling with maths teacher Kenneth Connor over corporal punishment, and gym mistress Joan Sims feuding with school assessor Rosalind Knight over weedy Kenneth Connor. DP *DVD*
Ted Ray *William Wakefield* • Kenneth Connor *Gregory Adams* • Charles Hawtrey *Michael Bean* • Leslie Phillips *Alistair Grigg* • Joan Sims *Sarah Allcock* • Kenneth Williams *Edwin Milton* • Hattie Jacques *Grace Short* • Rosalind Knight *Felicity Wheeler* ■ *Dir* Gerald Thomas • *Scr* Norman Hudis

Carry On Up the Jungle ★★★ PG
Comedy 1970 · UK · Colour · 86min

This is one of the weaker of the genre spoofs, but there's still much to raise a titter as Frankie Howerd and Kenneth Connor lead an expedition to Africa (Pinewood sets at their most gloriously economical) in order to find the Oozalum bird. Along for the ride are Joan Sims in search of her long-lost son and Sid James seeking a rumble in the jungle. The reception committee includes Terry Scott as an infantile Tarzan and Charles Hawtrey as the Great Tonka, a tribal chief with a guilty secret. DP *DVD*
Frankie Howerd *Professor Inigo Tinkle* • Sidney James *Bill Boosey* • Charles Hawtrey *Tonka/Walter* • Joan Sims *Lady Evelyn Bagley* • Terry Scott *Jungle Boy* • Kenneth Connor *Claude Chumley* • Bernard Bresslaw *Upsidasi* ■ *Dir* Gerald Thomas • *Scr* Talbot Rothwell

Carry On Up the Khyber ★★★★ PG
Comedy 1968 · UK · Colour · 85min

Only the *Carry Ons* could get away with using a wooden gate in Snowdonia as the farthest flung outpost of the British Empire! Originally to be called *Carry On the Regiment*, this is rightly regarded as one of the best in the series. Affectionately mocking Hollywood's Raj adventures, Talbot Rothwell's script is stuffed with ludicrous names, classic one-liners and memorable moments, none better than the dinner under fire. Kenneth Williams is superb as the Khasi of Kalabar, but it's Sid James and Joan Sims who steal the show. DP *DVD*
Sidney James *Sir Sidney Ruff-Diamond* • Kenneth Williams *Khasi of Kalabar* • Charles Hawtrey *Private James Widdle* • Roy Castle *Captain Keene* • Joan Sims *Lady Ruff-Diamond* • Bernard Bresslaw *Bungdit Din* • Terry Scott *Sergeant Major MacNutt* ■ *Dir* Gerald Thomas • *Scr* Talbot Rothwell

Cars ★★★ PG
Animated comedy fantasy 2006 · US · Colour · 111min

This fantasy set in a world where all the characters are motor vehicles is a slightly disappointing outing from animation studio Pixar. Red racer Lightning McQueen (voiced by Owen Wilson) is a hot-shot track star who gets stranded on his way to a big match in the small town of Radiator Springs, just off old Route 66. There, the residents, including a cute Porsche (Bonnie Hunt) and a wise old-timer (Paul Newman), teach McQueen a few lessons about life. The jokes are a touch below par, but the racing sequences are mini-masterpieces of editing and the animation is state of the art. LF *DVD* *Blu-ray* *CS*
Owen Wilson *Lightning McQueen* • Paul Newman *Doc Hudson* • Bonnie Hunt *Sally Carrera* • Larry the Cable Guy *Mater* • Richard "Cheech" Marin *Ramone* • George Carlin *Filmore* • Richard Petty *The King* • Michael Keaton *Chick Hicks* • Tony Shalhoub *Luigi* • John Ratzenberger *Mack* ■ *Dir* John Lasseter, Joe Ranft • *Scr* Dan Fogelman, John Lasseter, Dan Gerson, from a story by Jorgen Klubien, Philip Loren, Kiel Murray, Joe Ranft

Cars 2 ★★★ U
Animated comedy   2011 · US · Colour · 101min

Star racer Lightning McQueen (voiced by Owen Wilson) and his trusty tow-truck sidekick Mater (Larry the Cable Guy) return in Pixar's sequel, leaving Radiator Springs behind to take part in the first ever World Grand Prix. Michael Caine joins the voice cast as slick super spy Finn McMissile, in a convoluted story with perhaps too much plot getting in the way of the fun. Director John Lasseter delivers some exciting race sequences, but the stop-start nature of the yarn results in a rare instance of Pixar failing to fire on all cylinders. TeS DVD Ⓑ

Owen Wilson *Lightning McQueen* • Michael Caine *Finn McMissile* • Emily Mortimer *Holley Shiftwell* • Jason Isaacs *Siddeley* • John Ratzenberger *Mack* • Bonnie Hunt *Sally* • Tony Shalhoub *Luigi* • Michael Keaton *Chick Hicks* ■ *Dir* John Lasseter, Brad Lewis • *Scr* Ben Queen, from a story by John Lasseter, Brad Lewis, Dan Fogelman

The Cars That Ate Paris ★★★★ 15
Black comedy   1974 · Aus · Colour · 83min

Peter Weir's directorial debut could not be more different from his later films such as *Picnic at Hanging Rock*, *Witness* and the Oscar-nominated *The Truman Show*. It's a darkly comic tale of a small Australian town that feeds on passing travellers for their car parts; Terry Camilleri is the newcomer who decides to fight back. Rough edges notwithstanding, it's a sharp, vaguely unsettling affair and fortunately free of some of the portentous imagery that occasionally mars Weir's other films. JF Swearing. DVD

Terry Camilleri *Arthur* • John Meillon *Mayor* • Melissa Jaffa *Beth* • Kevin Miles *Dr Midland* • Max Gillies *Metcalfe* • Peter Armstrong *Gorman* ■ *Dir* Peter Weir • *Scr* Peter Weir, Keith Gow, Piers Davies

Carson City ★★★ U
Western   1952 · US · Colour · 86min

Randolph Scott stars as a railway foreman in director Andre De Toth's roistering western, leading the fight against villain Raymond Massey and his gang of bandits. De Toth had a good rapport with Scott, and this is one of the best of their several westerns together. It's also notable for being one of the first movies filmed in Warnercolor, Warner Bros' short-lived rival to Technicolor. TS

Randolph Scott *Jeff Kincaid* • Lucille Norman *Susan Mitchell* • Raymond Massey *Big Jack Davis* • Richard Webb *Alan Kincaid* • James Millican *Jim Squires* • Larry Keating *William Sharon* • Don Beddoe *Zeke Mitchell* ■ *Dir* Andre De Toth • *Scr* Sloan Nibley, Winston Miller, from a story by Sloan Nibley

Cartel Land ★★★ 15
War documentary
2015 · Mex/US · Colour · 100min

Matthew Heineman went above and beyond in making this documentary about the efforts of vigilante groups to combat the drug cartels operating on either side of the Rio Grande. Yet for all the risks he and his crew took recording firefights, gunpoint interrogations and torture sessions, the result is frustrating. The handheld footage is often terrifyingly full-on, but Heineman is too content to allow his subjects to strike heroic and ethical poses, with the result that his film lacks objectivity. DP In English, Spanish. Swearing, disturbing scenes. DVD

■ *Dir* Matthew Heineman • *Cinematographer* Matthew Heineman

The Cartier Affair ★★ PG
Comedy thriller   1984 · US · Colour · 91min

Fans of kitsch will be in seventh heaven: not only does this boast Joan Collins at her most flamboyant, but her male lead is *Baywatch* star David Hasselhoff. He plays a charming rogue out to fleece his rich employer Collins, only to end up falling in love with her. Director Rod Holcomb tries to whip it all up into witty froth, but he is hampered by the ever-wooden Hasselhoff

and a clumsy script. Collins, however, has a ball sending up her soap-queen image, while Telly Savalas makes a splendid villain. JF DVD

Joan Collins *Cartier Rand* • David Hasselhoff *Curt Taylor* • Telly Savalas *Phil Drexler* • Randi Brooks *Shirl* • Jordan Charney *Ben Foley* ■ *Dir* Rod Holcomb • *Scr* Eugenie Ross-Leming, Brad Buckner, from a story by Ross-Leming, Buckner, Michael Devereaux

Cartouche ★★★ 15
Swashbuckling comedy adventure
1961 · Fr/It · Colour · 110min

Cartouche was a Gallic cousin of Robin Hood and he makes an irresistible hero, especially when played by Jean-Paul Belmondo with dashing charm. No true swashbuckler would be complete without an utterly unscrupulous enemy and a beautiful heroine. Philippe Lemaire is the slimy Chief of Police, while Claudia Cardinale is the new addition to Belmondo's band of robbers. DP French dubbed.

Jean-Paul Belmondo *Cartouche* • Claudia Cardinale *Vénus* • Odile Versois *Isabelle de Ferrussac* • Philippe Lemaire *Le Ferrussac* • Marcel Dalio *Malichot* • Noël Roquevert *Recruiting sergeant* • Jess Hahn *La Douceur* ■ *Dir* Philippe de Broca • *Scr* Philippe De Broca, Charles Spaak, Daniel Boulanger

Carve Her Name with Pride ★★★★ PG
Second World War biographical drama
1958 · UK · BW · 114min

Made by the same team of director Lewis Gilbert and co-writer Vernon Harris that had previously brought us the Douglas Bader biopic *Reach for the Sky*, this is another well-crafted biographical film inspired by real-life heroism beyond the call of duty in the Second World War. Virginia McKenna gives an understated performance as Violette Szabo, a glamorous young woman who, after her French officer husband was killed in action, became a British spy on the continent. PF DVD

Virginia McKenna *Violette Szabo* • Paul Scofield *Tony Fraser* • Jack Warner *Mr Bushell* • Denise Grey *Mrs Bushell* • Alain Saury *Etienne Szabo* • Maurice Ronet *Jacques* • Bill Owen *NCO Instructor* • Billie Whitelaw *Winnie* • Michael Caine ■ *Dir* Lewis Gilbert • *Scr* Vernon Harris, Lewis Gilbert, from the novel by RJ Minney

Casa de los Babys ★★
Drama   2003 · US · Colour · 95min

Although he's capable of profound socio-political insight, writer/director John Sayles is also occasionally prone to unsubtle soap-boxing and this self-conscious – not to say cliché-ridden – study of six women awaiting to adopt in an unnamed South American country is one of his least persuasive efforts. Only Susan Lynch's Irish exile avoids broad-brush caricature and, thus, manages to express some genuine emotion. Other characters are merely cyphers for Sayles's opinions on religion, US imperialism and the state of modern womanhood. DP English, Spanish +subtitles.

Maggie Gyllenhaal *Jennifer* • Marcia Gay Harden *Nan* • Daryl Hannah *Skipper* • Susan Lynch *Eileen* • Mary Steenburgen *Gayle* • Lili Taylor *Leslie* • Rita Moreno *Señora Muñoz* • Vanessa Martinez *Asuncion* ■ *Dir/Scr* John Sayles

Casa de Mi Padre ★★★ 15
Comedy   2011 · US · Colour · 80min

Will Ferrell mocks the conventions of spaghetti westerns and daytime Mexican soap operas in this intermittently funny saga about a family of south-of-the-border ranchers under threat from a vicious criminal. While the film has the feel of an extended comedy sketch (both director Matt Piedmont and writer Andrew Steele are *Saturday Night Live* alumni), Ferrell's straight-faced portrayal and impeccable comic timing keep things lively. Performing the entire film in Spanish is a bold move that some may find frustrating, but there are plenty of winks to the audience about clichéd low-budget melodramas to keep us in on the joke. TeS English, Spanish

+subtitles. Violence, swearing, a sex scene, drug abuse, some nudity. DVD Ⓑ

Will Ferrell *Armando Alvarez* • Gael García Bernal *Onza* • Diego Luna *Raul* • Genesis Rodriguez *Sonia* • Pedro Armendáriz Jr *Miguel Ernesto Alvarez* • Nick Offerman *Agent Parker* ■ *Dir* Matt Piedmont • *Scr* Andrew Steele

Casablanca ★★★★★ U
Classic romantic drama   1942 · US · BW · 98min

Like *Citizen Kane* and *Gone with the Wind*, this classic has been dissected to within an inch of its life by scholars. It's a timeless love story wrapped inside a gripping wartime thriller, written with such wit and meaning it's still quoted (and misquoted) decades later. Humphrey Bogart gives a career best performance as Rick, the cynical, seemingly apolitical expat nightclub owner, who becomes embroiled with Paul Henreid's Resistance leader. Henreid fetches up with Bogart's old flame, the luminous Ingrid Bergman, and two exit visas wind up in the piano. Memorable support comes from Peter Lorre, Conrad Veidt and Claude Rains, and Max Steiner's score is superb, but the final credit must go to director Michael Curtiz, who pieces it all together with verve, symbolism and torrid emotion. AC DVD ⒷⒹ

Humphrey Bogart *Rick Blaine* • Ingrid Bergman *Ilsa Lund* • Paul Henreid *Victor Laszlo* • Claude Rains *Louis Renault* • Conrad Veidt *Major Strasser* • Sydney Greenstreet *Ferrari* • Peter Lorre *Ugarte* • SZ Sakall *Carl* • Madeleine Lebeau *Yvonne* • Dooley Wilson *Sam* ■ *Dir* Michael Curtiz • *Scr* Julius J Epstein, Philip G Epstein, Howard Koch, from the unproduced play *Everybody Comes to Rick's* by Murray Burnett, Joan Alison • *Producer* Hal B Wallis • *Cinematographer* Arthur Edeson • *Music* Max Steiner

Casanova ★★★★
Silent drama   1927 · Fr · BW and Tinted · 132min

This jewel of the French silent cinema arrived to some controversy in Paris when it premiered in a censored version in 1931. Finished in 1927, the same year as Abel Gance's mighty *Napoléon*, it stars the great Russian émigré Ivan Mosjoukine, who makes a droll, if temperamental Casanova. The hand-tinted colour sequences of the carnival of Venice were meticulously restored in 1988 and a new score was commissioned from Georges Delerue. A treasure from the glory days of silent cinema. TS

Ivan Mosjoukine *Casanova* • Diana Karenne *Maria Mari* • Suzanne Bianchetti *Catherine II* • Jenny Jugo *Therese* • Rina De Liguro *Corticelli* • Nina Kochitz *Countess Vorontzoff* • Olga Day *Baroness Stanhope* ■ *Dir* Alexandre Volkoff • *Scr* Norbert Falk, Ivan Mosjoukine, Alexandre Volkoff

Casanova ★★★ 15
Biographical historical drama
1976 · It · Colour · 147min

Federico Fellini variously considered this sprawling period fantasy, filmed in both English and Italian versions, to be the worst film he ever made and his "most complete, expressive and courageous" vision. The answer lies somewhere in between. Private distractions, labour disputes and a tense shoot, in which the director's relationship with Donald Sutherland deteriorated daily, hardly facilitated creative endeavour. Yet it was Fellini's determination to undermine accepted notions of romantic love and depict the legendary lothario as a pompous, decadent sex machine that rendered the action so cold and detached. DP DVD

Donald Sutherland *Giacomo Casanova* • Tina Aumont *Henriette* • Cicely Browne *Madame D'Urfe* • Carmen Scarpitta *Madame Charpillon* • Clara Algranti *Marcolina* • Daniela Gatti *Giselda* • Margareth Clementi *Sister Maddalena* • Olimpia Carlisi *Isabella* ■ *Dir* Federico Fellini • *Scr* Federico Fellini, Bernardino Zapponi, Anthony Burgess (English language version), from the autobiography *Histoire de Ma Vie* by Giacomo Casanova de Seingalt • *Music* Nino Rota • *Costume Designer* Danilo Donati

Casanova ★★ 12
Period comedy   2005 · US · Colour · 106min

History's legendary lover finally meets his romantic match in this attractive period

comedy from director Lasse Hallström. Set in 18th-century Venice, it gives a contemporary sheen to the myth of the serial bed-hopper who, as portrayed by Heath Ledger, uses sex as a diversion while hunting for the woman of his dreams. Predictably, she turns out to be the only female ever to refuse his advances: proto-feminist Sienna Miller. What follows is a patchy mix of slapstick, swashbuckling and *Carry On*-style antics. SF Sexual references. DVD

Heath Ledger *Giacomo Casanova* • Jeremy Irons *Bishop Pucci* • Sienna Miller *Francesca Bruni* • Oliver Platt *Papprizzio* • Lena Olin *Andrea Bruni* • Omid Djalili *Lupo* • Stephen Greif *Donato* • Ken Stott *Dalfonso* • Charlie Cox *Giovanni Bruni* ■ *Dir* Lasse Hallström • *Scr* Jeffrey Hatcher, Kimberly Simi, from a story by Simi, Michael Cristofer

Casanova & Co ★
Comedy
1976 · Austria/It/Fr/W Ger · Colour · 101min

Tony Curtis's Casanova conceals his impotence by hiring a man of prodigious sexual appetite who also happens to be his exact double. Released soon after Fellini's sumptuous take on the notorious womaniser, this is really just a soft-core skin flick featuring an army of semi-naked women. AT

Tony Curtis *Giacomo Casanova/Giacomino* • Marisa Berenson *Calipha of Shiraz* • Hugh Griffith *Caliph of Shiraz* • Marisa Mell *Duchess Francesca* • Britt Ekland *Countess Trivulzi* ■ *Dir* François Legrand [Franz Antel] • *Scr* Joshua Sinclair, Tom Priman

Casanova Brown ★★
Comedy   1944 · US · BW · 91min

About to marry for the second time, Gary Cooper learns that his ex-wife Teresa Wright has given birth to his child and is about to have it adopted. Horrified, he spirits the baby away and hides out in a downmarket hotel. Sam Wood's film is not a fraught drama, but a rather undernourished comedy that only raises an occasional smile. RK

Gary Cooper *Casanova "Cas" Q Brown* • Teresa Wright *Isabel Drury* • Frank Morgan *JJ Ferris* • Anita Louise *Madge Ferris* • Edmund Breon *Mr Drury* • Patricia Collinge *Mrs Drury* • Jill Esmond *Dr Martha Zernerke* ■ *Dir* Sam Wood • *Scr* Nunnally Johnson, Joe St Armand, from the play *The Little Accident* by Floyd Dell, Thomas Mitchell, and the novel *An Unmarried Father* by Floyd Dell

Casanova '70 ★★★ 15
Comedy   1965 · Fr/It · Colour · 110min

Six writers contributed to the Oscar-nominated screenplay for this smug sex comedy from Mario Monicelli, which aimed to satirise the effect of female emancipation on the modern male. Marcello Mastroianni, on the other hand, signed up to play the Nato official who discovers he can only rise to the occasion in moments of peril in a bid to debunk the tired image of the Latin lover. Neither director nor star totally succeeded in their intentions, but Marcello exhibits all his Fellini-esque foibles, while Virni Lisi is quite enchanting. DP Italian +subtitles. DVD

Marcello Mastroianni *Major Andrea Rossi-Colombetti* • Virna Lisi *Gigliola* • Michèle Mercier *Noelle* • Marisa Mell *Thelma* • Marco Ferreri *Count Ferreri* • Bernard Blier *Commissioner* ■ *Dir* Mario Monicelli • *Scr* Furio Scarpelli, Agenore Incrocci, Suso Cecchi D'Amico, Mario Monicelli, from a story by Tonino Guerra, Giorgio Salvioni

Casanova's Big Night ★★★ U
Musical comedy   1954 · US · Colour · 82min

Bob Hope's self-created screen image always cast him as a *faux-naïf* - leching yet never leched after. It's interesting, then, to find him playing a Casanova substitute, perpetually mistaken for Vincent Price's genuine womaniser. The film is beautifully designed, and Paramount's Technicolor Venice capably stands in for the real thing. With Basil Rathbone as a suave arch villain, this is one of Hope's better comic vehicles. TS

Bob Hope *Pippo Popolino* • Joan Fontaine *Francesca Bruni* • Basil Rathbone *Lucio* • Raymund Burr *Bragadin* • Audrey Dalton *Elena* • Vincent Price *Casanova* • John Carradine *Minister Foressi* • Lon Chaney Jr *Emo* ■ *Dir* Norman Z McLeod • *Scr* Hal Kanter, Edmund Hartmann [Edmund L Hartmann], from a story by Aubrey Wisberg

Casbah ★★★★ PG
Musical drama 1948 · US · BW · 81min

Crooner Tony Martin steps into the shoes of Charles Boyer in this thoroughly entertaining remake of *Algiers*, which was itself a reworking of the classic *Pépé le Moko*. This is enthrallingly romantic or excruciatingly corny, depending on your point of view, but there's no denying the pleasure afforded by Harold Arlen and Leo Robin's musical numbers. Peter Lorre gives arguably his best Hollywood performance, there's the sultry allure of Yvonne De Carlo, and watch very closely for the briefest glimpse of a young Eartha Kitt. TS

Yvonne De Carlo *Inez* • Tony Martin (1) *Pépé le Moko* • Peter Lorre *Slimane* • Marta Toren *Gaby* • Hugo Haas *Omar* • Thomas Gomez *Louvain* • Douglas Dick *Carlo* • Eartha Kitt ■ *Dir* John Berry • *Scr* L Bus-Fekete, Arnold Manoff, from a story by Erik Charell, from the novel *Pépé le Moko* by Detective Roger D'Ashelbe [Henri La Barthe]

A Case for PC 49 ★
Crime drama 1950 · UK · BW · 78min

Unfortunately, every expense was spared in relating this tale of models, millionaires and murder. Hardly fitting treatment for Brian Reece, British crime fiction's first uniformed hero, who solved over a hundred cases on the airwaves between 1947 and 1953. Such was his popularity that he starred in the *Eagle* comic and in his own board game, *Burglars*. DP

Brian Reece *Archibald Berkeley-Willoughby* • Joy Shelton *Joan Carr* • Christine Norden *Della Dainton* • Leslie Bradley *Victor Palantine* • Gordon McLeod *Inspector Wilson* ■ *Dir* Francis Searle • *Scr* Alan Stranks, Vernon Harris, from their radio series

The Case of Dr Laurent ★★★
Drama 1957 · Fr · Colour · 111min

An intense yet sensitive performance from Jean Gabin holds together this medical melodrama from writer/director Jean-Paul Le Chanois. Quitting his Parisian practice for a rural village, Gabin tries to win the locals round to his ideas on natural childbirth. With opposition to the doctor's theories duly provided, the action could easily have lapsed into a typical "tradition v progress" tirade. Thanks to Henri Alekan's evocative photography and Joseph Kosma's delicate soundtrack, however, the story has stealthily captured the imagination by the time Nicole Courcel has her baby. The birth was actually shown on screen and became a source of some controversy. DP French +subtitles.

Jean Gabin *Dr Laurent* • Nicole Courcel *Francine* • Sylvia Monfort *Catherine Loubet* • Arius *Dr Bastide* • Daxely *Simonet the baker* • Michel Barbey *André Loubet* • Yvonne Gamy *Midwife* ■ *Dir* Jean-Paul Le Chanois • *Scr* Jean-Paul Le Chanois, Rene Barjavel

A Case of Honor ★★ 15
Action adventure 1988 · Phil · Colour · 88min

Timothy Bottoms stars in this unsubtle Vietnam War action adventure. Bottoms booms out his dialogue with more competence than conviction as he joins his fellow PoWs in an audacious escape bid after a decade's illegal detention. Veteran Filipino director Eddie Romero rams the pieces into place as the group liberates some hookers before attempting to fix an abandoned US helicopter, while Russian and Vietnamese patrols close in. Strictly routine. DP

Timothy Bottoms *Sergeant Joseph "Hard" Case* • John Phillip Law *Captain Roger LBarnes* • Candy Raymond *Charlene "Charlie" Delibes* • Nick Nicholson *Pops* ■ *Dir* Eddie Romero • *Scr* John Trayne

The Case of Lena Smith ★★★
Silent romantic drama 1929 · US · BW · 68min

While on holiday in Vienna, naive and pretty peasant girl Esther Ralston falls in love with army officer James Hall and marries him. Back at his family manse, Ralston is tyrannised by her father-in-law Gustave von Seyffertitz and pilloried by society because of her lowly origins. A silent melodrama of quality but unrelieved gloom, this is a searing attack on the evils of pre-1914 class prejudice in Europe. Director Josef von Sternberg's feeling for Vienna permeates the film and gives it an authentic feel. RK

Esther Ralston *Lena Smith* • James Hall *Franz Hofrat* • Gustav von Seyffertitz *Herr Hofrat* • Emily Fitzroy *Frau Hofrat* • Fred Kohler *Stefan* ■ *Dir* Josef von Sternberg • *Scr* Jules Furthman, Julian Johnson (titles), from a story by Samuel Ornitz

The Case of the Black Cat ★★★
Mystery 1936 · US · BW · 66min

The debonair, wise-cracking Warren William was replaced by Ricardo Cortez for this entry in the Perry Mason series, in which the puzzling death of a bedridden millionaire sets off a chain of killings. This is one of the better Mason movies, even though Cortez is a poor actor and Della Street (June Travis) is reduced to a bit part. AJ

Ricardo Cortez *Perry Mason* • June Travis *Della Street* • Jane Bryan *Wilma Laxter* • Craig Reynolds *Frank Oafley* • Carlyle Moore Jr *Douglas Keene* • Gordon Elliott [Bill Elliott] *Sam Laxter* ■ *Dir* William McGann • *Scr* F Hugh Herbert, from the story *The Case of the Caretaker's Cat* by Erle Stanley Gardner

The Case of the Howling Dog ★★
Mystery 1934 · US · BW · 75min

A year after Erle Stanley Gardner created him, Perry Mason made his screen debut in this teasing murder mystery. Although Warren William had just finished playing another detective, Philo Vance, his portrayal of the ingenious attorney owed more to William Powell's soused sleuth, Nick Charles, in cult hit *The Thin Man*. Alan Crosland keeps the clues close to his chest and shifts suspicion between Mary Astor and her fellow suspects with some skill. DP

Warren William *Perry Mason* • Mary Astor *Bessie Foley* • Helen Trenholme *Della Street* • Allen Jenkins *Sgt Holcomb* • Grant Mitchell *Claude Drumm* ■ *Dir* Alan Crosland • *Scr* Ben Markson, from a novel by Erle Stanley Gardner

The Case of the Lucky Legs ★★
Mystery 1935 · US · BW · 78min

The law and Perry Mason are on the trail of a crooked sponsor of "best legs" contests. When he is found murdered, however, the hunt becomes one for his killer. Warren William, the best of the actors to play Erle Stanley Gardner's lawyer/sleuth, stars in this entry, with Genevieve Tobin providing a vivacious Della Street. Alas, the script is so jokey as to bury any possibility of interest in the complicated mystery. RK

Warren William *Perry Mason* • Genevieve Tobin *Della Street* • Patricia Ellis *Margie Clune* • Lyle Talbot *Dr Doray* • Allen Jenkins *Spudsy* • Barton MacLane *Bissonette* • Peggy Shannon *Thelma Bell* ■ *Dir* Archie Mayo • *Scr* Brown Holmes, Ben Markson, Jerome Chodorov, from a novel by Erle Stanley Gardner

The Case of the Mukkinese Battle Horn ★★★ U
Spoof mystery 1955 · UK · BW · 28min

Dick Emery stands in for Harry Secombe in this pseudo-Goons picture. The theft of the eponymous instrument is of virtually no significance other than to give Peter Sellers

the opportunity to play three characters. Spike Milligan also gets to reprise his beloved character, Eccles. The opening "Crime Does Not Pay" pastiche and the door-knocking sequence are the highlights. DP

Peter Sellers *Narrator/Superintendent Quilt/Assistant Commissioner Sir Jervis Fruit/Henry Crun* • Spike Milligan *Sgt Brown/J Smith/Minnie Bannister/Catchpole Burkington* • Dick Emery *Mr Nodule/Mr Crimp/Maurice Ponke/Maxie/Wormscrew* ■ *Dir* Joseph Sterling • *Scr* Harry Booth, Spike Milligan, Peter Sellers, Larry Stephens, from a story by Larry Stephens

The Case of the Stuttering Bishop ★★ U
Mystery 1937 · US · BW · 71min

Lacking the enlivening presence of Warren William, the first and best of the Perry Masons, this run-of-the-mill episode stars Donald Woods as the investigative lawyer and Ann Dvorak as Della Street. The plot finds Mason having to determine whether the granddaughter of a millionaire is the genuine article or an impostor. The uninspiring action culminates in the courtroom. RK

Donald Woods *Perry Mason* • Ann Dvorak *Della Street* • Anne Nagel *Janice Alma Brownley* • Linda Perry *Janice Seaton* • Craig Reynolds *Gordon Bixter* ■ *Dir* William Clemens • *Scr* Don Ryan, Kenneth Gamet, from the novel by Erle Stanley Gardner

The Case of the Velvet Claws ★★★
Mystery 1936 · US · BW · 64min

One of the better entries in the Perry Mason series, featuring the urbane Warren William as the investigating lawyer, which finds him actually married to his loyal secretary Della Street, played this time around by Claire Dodd. The honeymoon, however, is delayed when Mason is forced at gunpoint to take on a blackmail case. Moderately sinister and quite amusing. RK

Warren William *Perry Mason* • Claire Dodd *Della Street* • Winifred Shaw *Eva Belter* • Gordon Elliott [Bill Elliott] *Carl Griffin* • Joseph King (1) *George C Belter* • Eddie Acuff *Spudsy* ■ *Dir* William Clemens • *Scr* Tom Reed, from a story by Erle Stanley Gardner

Case 39 ★★★ 15
Horror thriller 2008 · US · Colour · 104min

Social worker Emily Jenkins (Renée Zellweger) fosters a ten-year-old girl she seemingly saves from atrocious child abuse. But when Lilith Sullivan (Jodelle Ferland) begins showing her true demonic colours and causes Jenkins's friends to die in horrific ways, the social worker realises the parents were acting in self-defence. While the viewer will remain one step ahead of the story at all times, director Christian Alvart (*Antibodies*) manages to keep the emotionally charged events moving at a fair clip to gloss over the mounting credibility problems. Zellweger does the stunned bewilderment bit well, but it's *Tideland* star Ferland who truly shines as the manipulative fiend hiding behind wide-eyed innocence. AJ Violence. DVD

Renée Zellweger *Emily Jenkins* • Jodelle Ferland *Lilith Sullivan* • Ian McShane *Detective Mike Barron* • Bradley Cooper *Doug* • Callum Keith Rennie *Edward Sullivan* • Adrian Lester *Wayne* ■ *Dir* Christian Alvart • *Scr* Ray Wright

Casey's Shadow ★★★ PG
Drama 1978 · US · Colour · 92min

A charming portrayal by Walter Matthau carries this fairly insubstantial family drama. Overlong (though trimmed considerably for its UK release) and relentlessly soft-hearted, it nevertheless offers the welcome sparring of horse-trainer Matthau with horse-breeder Alexis Smith. The action is in the firm but sensitive hands of *Hud* director Martin Ritt. TS Swearing.

Walter Matthau *Lloyd Bourdelle* • Alexis Smith *Sarah Blue* • Robert Webber *Mike Marsh* • Murray Hamilton *Tom Patterson* • Andrew A Rubin [Andrew Rubin] *Buddy Bourdelle* ■ *Dir* Martin Ritt • *Scr* Carol Sobieski, from the short story *Ruidoso* by John McPhee

Ca$h ★★ 12
Crime caper 2008 · Fr · Colour · 98min

It's somehow apt that a film about heists should pilfer so liberally from pictures like Norman Jewison's *The Thomas Crown Affair* (1968), George Roy Hill's *The Sting* (1973) and Steven Soderbergh's *Ocean's Eleven* (2001). But there are only so many plot cracks that can be papered over with freeze frames, split screens and jump cuts and writer/director Eric Besnard settles for contrived ways out of the narrative cul-de-sacs into which he pitches resourceful crook Jean Dujardin, as he falls foul of a ruthless foe in seeking revenge for the death of his con man brother (Clovis Cornillac). Dujardin always exudes dapper charm, but he has to work hard at holding the scenario together. DP English, French +subtitles.

Jean Dujardin *Cash* • Jean Reno *Maxime* • Valeria Golino *Julia* • Alice Taglioni *Garance* ■ *Dir/Scr* Eric Besnard

Ca$h! ★★ 15
Crime thriller 2010 · US · Colour · 103min

Chris Hemsworth's debut feature is increasingly far-fetched and struggles to combine dark humour with bursts of gritty violence. Skint Chicago marrieds Hemsworth and Victoria Profeta spend wildly after stumbling upon some stolen cash, only for quirky bad guy Sean Bean to turn up and demand back every last cent. Bean's entertainingly composed hardman forces them into behaviour that they seem to accept ridiculously quickly. Yet even then events have no bite, with a lack of meat and tension resulting in a particularly flat climax. SF

Sean Bean *Pyke Kubic/Reese Kubic* • Chris Hemsworth *Sam Phelan* • Victoria Profeta *Leslie Phelan* • Mike Starr *Melvin Goldberg* ■ *Dir/Scr* Stephen Milburn Anderson [Steve Anderson (1)]

Cash McCall ★★ U
Romantic comedy 1960 · US · Colour · 101min

Warner Bros was enjoying commercial success at the time with glossy adaptations of popular novels, but this film version of the bestseller by *Executive Suite* writer Cameron Hawley suffered from poor development on its way to the screen. Despite a good cast headed by James Garner – terrific as the title tycoon – and a radiant Natalie Wood in her first adult role, it's too superficial. TS

James Garner *Cash McCall* • Natalie Wood *Lory Austen* • Nina Foch *Maude Kennard* • Dean Jagger *Grant Austen* • EG Marshall *Winston Conway* • Henry Jones *Gil Clark* • Otto Kruger *Will Atherson* ■ *Dir* Joseph Pevney • *Scr* Lenore Coffee, Marion Hargrove, from the novel by Cameron Hawley

Cash on Demand ★★★★ U
Crime thriller 1961 · UK · BW · 88min

One of the best British second features ever made, this is a tense thriller, which hooks the viewer from the beginning, then springs surprises right until the end. The life of truculent bank manager Peter Cushing (in one of his least-known but most complex roles) is changed when he is visited by "insurance investigator" André Morell. Director Quentin Lawrence, whose TV credits include *Coronation Street* and *The Avengers*, controls the suspense with such skill that it's a surprise his movie career didn't take off. DM

Peter Cushing *Fordyce* • André Morell *Hepburn* • Richard Vernon *Pearson* • Norman Bird *Sanderson* • Kevin Stoney *Detective Inspector Mason* • Barry Lowe *Peter Harvill* ■ *Dir* Quentin Lawrence • *Scr* David T Chantler, Lewis Greifer, from the teleplay *The Gold Inside* by Jacques Gillies

Cashback ★★ 15
Comedy drama 2005 · UK · Colour · 97min

Teenage angst comes with a surreal twist in this British comedy drama from writer/director Sean Ellis. A droopy-eyed Sean Biggerstaff takes centre stage as Ben, an insomniac art student working the night shift at Sainsbury's. Ellis adapted it from his 2004 Oscar-nominated short and the concept does feel stretched beyond its limits. The budding romance (with weary checkout girl Emilia Fox) at the heart of the story never really takes flight and, although visually there's plenty to admire, it's all rather let down by the sketchy script. SP *DVD*

Sean Biggerstaff *Ben* • Emilia Fox *Sharon* • Shaun Evans *Sean* • Michelle Ryan *Suzy* • Stuart Goodwin *Jenkins* • Michael Dixon *Barry* • Michael Lambourne *Matt* ■ *Dir* Sean Ellis • *Scr* Sean Ellis, adapted from the short film by Ellis

Casino ★★★★ 18
Crime drama 1995 · US · Colour · 178min

GoodFellas goes to Las Vegas in Martin Scorsese's underrated tale of power, money and depravity. Robert De Niro plays a master bookie turned big-shot casino manager whose head for business deserts him when he marries ex-hooker Sharon Stone. But it's when Joe Pesci, De Niro's boyhood acquaintance, arrives in town with an ambitious agenda of his own that things take a further downward spiral. Written by Nicholas Pileggi, an Oscar nominee for *GoodFellas*, *Casino* goes for absorbing realism, intriguing subplots and expertly drawn characters, while Stone is a revelation in her demanding role. AJ Violence, swearing, sex scenes, drug abuse, nudity. *DVD*

Robert De Niro *Sam "Ace" Rothstein* • Sharon Stone *Ginger McKenna* • Joe Pesci *Nicky Santoro* • James Woods *Lester Diamond* • Don Rickles *Billy Sherbert* • Alan King *Andy Stone* • Kevin Pollak *Phillip Green* ■ *Dir* Martin Scorsese • *Scr* Nicholas Pileggi, Martin Scorsese, from the novel by Nicholas Pileggi

The Casino Murder Case ★★
Detective mystery 1935 · US · BW · 82min

Several actors played SS Van Dine's popular sleuth Philo Vance. The first, and best, was William Powell, who made four films in the series; by 1935, Warren William and Basil Rathbone had each had an outing. This information is more interesting than the seventh film, which stars a miscast Paul Lukas on the trail of a mad poisoner who succeeds in killing three members of a bizarre family. RK

Paul Lukas *Philo Vance* • Rosalind Russell *Doris* • Alison Skipworth *Mrs Llewellyn* • Donald Cook *Lynn* • Arthur Byron *Kincaid* • Ted Healy *Sgt Heath* ■ *Dir* Edwin L Marin • *Scr* Florence Ryerson, Edgar Allan Woolf, from a novel by SS Van Dine

Casino Royale ★★★ PG
Spy spoof 1967 · UK · Colour · 125min

It is perhaps wise not to think of this unwieldy spy caper as a James Bond movie at all. Though nominally based on Ian Fleming's first 007 novel (originally dramatised in a 1954 TV show starring Barry Nelson and remade in 2006 with Daniel Craig), it is in actual fact a spoof, in which David Niven's retired Bond rounds up assorted 007 agents to avenge the death of "M" (John Huston). A surfeit of screenwriters and directors lends the whole a chaotic air, but there is still much fun to be had. AC *DVD*

David Niven *Sir James Bond* • Peter Sellers *Evelyn Tremble* • Ursula Andress *Vesper Lynd* • Orson Welles *Le Chiffre* • Joanna Pettet *Mata Bond* • Woody Allen *Jimmy Bond/Dr Noah* • Deborah Kerr *Agent Mimi/Lady Fiona McTarry* • William Holden (2) *Ransome* • Charles Boyer *Le Grand* • John Huston *McTarry/M* • Jean-Paul Belmondo *French legionnaire* • George Raft • Barbara Bouchet *Moneypenny* • Peter O'Toole *Scotch piper* • Geoffrey Bayldon *"Q"* • Ronnie Corbett *Polo* • Bernard Cribbins *Taxi driver* • Jacky Bisset [Jacqueline Bisset] *Miss Goodthighs* • Derek Nimmo *Hadley* ■ *Dir* John Huston, Ken Hughes, Val Guest, Robert Parrish, Joe McGrath [Joseph McGrath] • *Scr* Wolf Mankowitz, John Law, Michael Sayers (with uncredited contributions from Billy Wilder, Val Guest, Joseph Heller, Ben Hecht, Terry Southern), from the novel by Ian Fleming

Casino Royale ★★★★ 12
Spy adventure 2006 · UK/Cz Rep/Ger/US · Colour/BW · 138min

Daniel Craig effortlessly makes James Bond his own in this resoundingly entertaining spy adventure. *GoldenEye* director Martin Campbell, influenced by the Bourne franchise, gives Bond a gritty new image, upping the violence (the opening sequence is particularly brutal) and stripping back the camp humour. The plot is essentially an origins story, as the rough-around-the-edges agent gains his two zeros (the two kills he needs for his infamous licence) before tackling villain Le Chiffre (a splendid Mads Mikkelsen) at poker. Craig's humanised interpretation of the role balances Campbell's physical direction, while Eva Green provides an alluring love interest. Apart from an overlong last act, this 21st in the series is a triumphant new beginning. AS *DVD* Blu

Daniel Craig *James Bond* • Eva Green *Vesper Lynd* • Mads Mikkelsen *Le Chiffre* • Jeffrey Wright *Felix Leiter* • Judi Dench *M* • Giancarlo Giannini *Rene Mathis* • Richard Branson *Man at airport* ■ *Dir* Martin Campbell • *Scr* Neal Purvis, Robert Wade, Paul Haggis, from the novel by Ian Fleming • *Cinematographer* Phil Méheux [Phil Meheux] • *Music* David Arnold • *Editor* Stuart Baird

Casper ★★★★ PG
Supernatural comedy fantasy 1995 · US · Colour · 95min

With comic books and cartoon series full of muscle-bound superheroes vying for big-screen superstardom, it's nice to see a gentler character making such an impact in his first film outing. Here, Casper the Friendly Ghost is doing his bit to make Whipstaff Manor a homelier place for lonely Christina Ricci to live in, but it's his ghoulish uncles Stretch, Stinkie and Fatso who scare up all the fun in this enchanting family comedy. Cathy Moriarty's hissable villainy nearly steals the show. DP *DVD*

Christina Ricci *Kat Harvey* • Bill Pullman *Dr James Harvey* • Cathy Moriarty *Carrigan Crittenden* • Eric Idle *Dibs* • Malachi Pearson *Casper* • Joe Nipote *Stretch* • Joe Alaskey *Stinkie* • Brad Garrett *Fatso* • Clint Eastwood • Mel Gibson ■ *Dir* Brad Silberling • *Scr* Sherri Stoner, Deanna Oliver, from a story by Joseph Oriolo, Seymour Reit, from characters by Joseph Oriolo • *Special Effects* Michael Lantieri

Casper: a Spirited Beginning ★★ U
Supernatural comedy 1997 · US · Colour · 91min

The friendly ghost does a runner from the ghost training centre and makes friends with a bullied young boy (Brendon Ryan Barrett) in this charmless straight-to-video sequel. Steve Guttenberg stars as the boy's workaholic building contractor dad, and Lori Loughlin is Barrett's teacher who's trying to stop Guttenberg demolishing a local mansion. Cheesy and clumsy. JC *DVD*

Brendon Ryan Barrett *Chris Carson* • Steve Guttenberg *Tim Carson* • James Earl Jones *Kibosh* • Pauly Shore *Snivel* • Michael McKean *Bill Case* • Rodney Dangerfield *Mayor Johnny Hunt* • James Ward *Stretch* • Bill Farmer *Stinkie* • Jeff Harnell *Fatso* • Jeremy Foley *Casper* ■ *Dir* Sean McNamara • *Scr* Jymn Magon, Thomas Hart, from the comic book *Harvey Comics' Casper the Friendly Ghost* by Joseph Oriolo,

Casper Meets Wendy ★ U
Supernatural comedy 1998 · US · Colour · 90min

Teri Garr, Cathy Moriarty and Shelley Duvall reach career low points as a trio of witches hiding away at a summer resort in a straight-to-video release that makes *Home Alone* look like an exercise in subtlety. Their niece Wendy (the helium-voiced Hilary Duff) is being sought by warlock George Hamilton. Unbearable. JC *DVD*

Hilary Duff *Wendy* • Jeremy Foley *Casper* • Shelley Duvall *Gabby* • Teri Garr *Fanny* • Cathy Moriarty *Geri* • George Hamilton *Desmond Spellman* ■ *Dir* Sean McNamara • *Scr* Jymn Magon, Rob Kerchner, from characters by Joseph Oriolo

Casque d'Or ★★★★ PG
Drama 1952 · Fr · BW · 94min

Based on an actual *crime passionnel*, this is one of the jewels of that much-maligned strain of literate French film-making, cynically dubbed, by François Truffaut, the "tradition of quality". In re-creating the underworld Paris of the Impressionists, director Jacques Becker creates a vibrant world of amiable rogues and sensual delight. Radiant at its centre is Simone Signoret, whose golden beauty prompts the tragic rivalry between naive carpenter Serge Reggiani and calculating gangster Claude Dauphin. DP In French. *DVD* Blu

Simone Signoret *Marie* • Serge Reggiani *Manda* • Claude Dauphin *Félix Leca* • Raymond Bussières *Raymond* • William Sabatier *Roland* • Gaston Modot *Danard* • Loleh Bellon *Billy* • Claude Castaing *Fredo* ■ *Dir* Jacques Becker • *Scr* Jacques Companeez

Cass ★★ 18
Biographical crime drama 2008 · UK · Colour · 108min

The true story of reformed football thug Cass Pennant, based on his autobiography, offers a new layer of intrigue to the "hooligan porn" genre typified by books like *The Football Factory* and *Green Street*. Unfortunately, the novelty of the race issue – Pennant was a black orphan raised by white parents – is not enough to remove the film from the very familiar turf of pub, underpass, pub. Played as an adult by the imposing Nonso Anozie, Cass escapes a childhood of racist bullying and finds acceptance among West Ham FC's notorious Inter City Firm. Despite flashes of warmth and insight, *Cass* falls too easily into episodic chunks and is overly reliant on narration, with the facile use of newsreel to create a sense of time passing. AC Violence, swearing, drug abuse. *DVD*

Nonso Anozie *Cass* • Natalie Press *Elaine* • Leo Gregory *Freeman* • Gavin Brocker *Prentice* • Tamer Hassan *Ray* • Ralph Ineson *Sergeant Mullins* • Paul Kaye *CP* ■ *Dir* Jon S Baird • *Scr* Jon S Baird, from the non-fiction book by Cass Pennant, Mike Ridley

Cass Timberlane ★★★★
Romantic drama 1947 · US · BW · 118min

Cass Timberlane (Spencer Tracy) is a highly respected judge in a small Minneapolis town, beloved of the country club set but living alone since the death of his wife. When he falls passionately in love with a beautiful girl from the "wrong" side of town (Lana Turner), a series of shock waves, professional and personal, are unleashed. A good, old-fashioned drama that reveals Turner's often overlooked and mismanaged talent and offers Tracy at his magnificently nuanced best. Zachary Scott's womanising lawyer and Mary Astor's society bitch add extra bite. RK

Spencer Tracy *Cass Timberlane* • Lana Turner *Virginia Marshland* • Zachary Scott *Brad Criley* • Tom Drake *Jamie Wargate* • Mary Astor *Queenie Havock* • Albert Dekker *Boone Havock* ■ *Dir* George Sidney (2) • *Scr* Donald Ogden Stewart, Sonya Levien, from the novel by Sinclair Lewis

Cassadaga ★★ 18
Horror thriller 2011 · US · Colour · 112min

A violently persistent spirit forces grieving deaf woman Kelen Coleman into a hunt for a serial killer in *Dread* director Anthony DiBlasi's unsatisfying genre mash-up. Slow-paced and lacking in bite, the cluttered and forgettably performed murder mystery tries to combine too many ideas. Consequently, it seems incoherent and overlong while even the film's stereotypical psycho has insufficient impact and depth. SF Violence. *DVD* CS

Kelen Coleman *Lily* • Louise Fletcher *Claire* • Rus Blackwell *Christian Burton* • Kevin Alejandro *Mike* ■ *Dir* Anthony DiBlasi • *Scr* Bruce Wood, Scott Poiley, from Wood's story/characters

Cassandra ★★★ 18
Supernatural thriller 1987 · Aus · Colour · 89min

This interesting little movie from Australia belts along effectively enough, featuring Tessa Humphries as a young woman who discovers that her brother has been jailed for causing their mother's death. As if this isn't enough of a shock, her brother has escaped from prison. The jolts are expertly placed, the cast is nicely twitchy and, despite the fact that Humphries shows an uncommon stoicism, this film is intriguing stuff. SH Violence, nudity. *DVD*

Tessa Humphries *Cassandra* • Shane Briant *Steven Roberts* • Briony Behets *Helen Roberts* • Susan Barling *Libby* ■ *Dir* Colin Eggleston • *Scr* Colin Eggleston, John Ruane, Chris Fichett

The Cassandra Crossing ★ PG
Disaster thriller 1976 · UK/It/W Ger · Colour · 123min

A terrorist has passed on a deadly plague to the passengers of a luxury express train, which has to be rerouted across a rickety bridge to a deserted concentration camp in order to prevent an epidemic. Burt Lancaster has the right idea when he suggests blowing up the train – ideally with the film inside. DP *DVD*

Richard Harris *Dr Jonathan Chamberlain* • Sophia Loren *Jennifer Rispoli Chamberlain* • Burt Lancaster *Col Stephen Mackenzie* • Ava Gardner *Nicole Dressler* • Martin Sheen *Robby Navarro* • Ingrid Thulin *Dr Elena Stradner* • Lee Strasberg *Herman Kaplan* • John Phillip Law *Major Stack* • Ann Turkel *Susan* • OJ Simpson *Father Haley* ■ *Dir* George Pan Cosmatos • *Scr* Tom Mankiewicz, Robert Katz, George Pan Cosmatos, from a story by Robert Katz, George Pan Cosmatos

Cassandra's Dream ★★ 12
Crime drama 2007 · US/Fr · Colour · 103min

Like *Match Point* and the little-seen *Scoop*, this darkly comic tale from the prolific Woody Allen is also set in London. Ewan McGregor and Colin Farrell play cockney brothers whose attempts to enjoy the good life leave them debt-ridden. Their saviour is Uncle Howard (Tom Wilkinson), a shadowy international businessman who offers them a loan – if they will get rid of a troublesome colleague for him. With its leads' dodgy cockney accents, the script's working-class clichés and some self-conscious asides on fate and inevitability, this is far from vintage Allen. JR *DVD*

Ewan McGregor *Ian* • Colin Farrell (2) *Terry* • Hayley Atwell *Angela* • Sally Hawkins *Kate* • Tom Wilkinson *Howard* • Phil Davis [Philip Davis] *Martin Burns* • Jim Carter *Garage boss* ■ *Dir/Scr* Woody Allen • *Music* Philip Glass

Casshern ★★★ 15
Science-fiction action fantasy 2004 · Jpn · Colour · 141min

This Japanese action fantasy is set in a not-too-distant future where a race of super robots is trying to take over the world. Into this mayhem comes the heroic but troubled Casshern, who has been made similarly invincible by his dear old scientist dad's plundered technology. Though hampered by a fiendishly complicated plot, *Casshern* is ravishing to look at and sets a new standard for the melding of live action, digital effects and animation. LF Japanese +subtitles. Violence. *DVD*

Yusuke Iseya *Casshern/Tetsuya Azuma* • Kumiko Aso *Luna Kozuki* • Toshiaki Karasawa *Burai* • Akira Terao *Professor Kotaro Azuma* • Kanako Higuchi *Midori Azuma* • Fumiyo Kohinata *Dr Kozuki* • Hiroyuki Miyasako *Akbone* • Mayumi Sada *Sagray* ■ *Dir* Kazuaki Kiriya • *Scr* Kazuaki Kiriya, Shotaro Suga, Dai Sato, from the animated TV series *Shinzo ningen Casshern* by Tatsuo Yoshida

Cast a Dark Shadow ★★★
Drama thriller 1957 · UK · BW · 82min

After murdering his wife Mona Washbourne for her money, Dirk Bogarde marries canny Margaret Lockwood who proves less easy to dispose of. When he meets Kay Walsh, however, murder is back on the agenda. A modest but entertaining melodrama, directed by Lewis Gilbert with a stylish and proficient cast. Lockwood, who would return to the screen only once more two decades later, is particularly effective. RK

Dirk Bogarde *Edward Bare* • Mona Washbourne *Monica Bare* • Margaret Lockwood *Freda Jeffries* • Kay Walsh *Charlotte Young* • Kathleen Harrison *Emmie* ■ *Dir* Lewis Gilbert • *Scr* John Cresswell, from the play *Murder Mistaken* by Janet Green

Cast a Giant Shadow ★★★ PG

War drama 1966 · US · Colour · 132min

This expensive epic tells one of the great stories of the early days in Israel's struggle for independence. The role of American-born colonel David "Mickey" Marcus is ruggedly incarnated by Kirk Douglas, apt casting for the orthodox Jew, born Issur Danielovitch. Marcus's story is impressive enough without the array of guest stars writer/director Melville Shavelson assembled in a distracting attempt to ensure box office respectability. For an absolutely hilarious account of the filming, read Shavelson's own book, *How to Make a Jewish Movie*. TS *DVD*

Kirk Douglas *Colonel David "Mickey" Marcus* • Senta Berger *Magda Simon* • Angie Dickinson *Emma Marcus* • Gary Merrill *Pentagon Chief of Staff* • Haym Topol [Topol] *Abou Ibn Kader* • Frank Sinatra *Vince* • Yul Brynner *Asher Gonen* • John Wayne *General Mike Randolph* ■ *Dir* Melville Shavelson • *Scr* Melville Shavelson, from a biography by Ted Berkman

Cast a Long Shadow ★★ U

Western drama 1959 · US · BW · 82min

It's illegitimacy that casts the long shadow here, turning Audie Murphy's cowpoke into an embittered, hard-drinking, gambling drifter. Then he inherits the estate of a wealthy rancher who may have been his father, whereupon he becomes an intolerant trail boss during an arduous cattle drive. The script sorts him out in due course, but leaves some irritating loose ends. AE

Audie Murphy *Matt Brown* • Terry Moore *Janet Calvert* • John Dehner *Chip Donohue* • James Best *Sam Mullen* • Rita Lynn *Hortensia* • Denver Pyle *Harrison* ■ *Dir* Thomas Carr • *Scr* Martin G Goldsmith, John McGreevey, from a novel by Wayne D Overholser, from a story by Martin G Goldsmith

Cast Away ★★★ 12

Adventure drama 2000 · US · Colour · 137min

Proving, to an extent, that the old ideas are often the best, Tom Hanks plays a Robinson Crusoe for the 21st century in this near one-man show from his *Forrest Gump* director, Robert Zemeckis. Hanks is alone on screen for most of the film's duration, and his plight makes for riveting viewing as he struggles to keep body and soul together. It's only when he arrives home to a woolly, unsatisfying conclusion that the film unravels. AC Swearing. *DVD* *Blu*

Tom Hanks *Chuck Noland* • Helen Hunt *Kelly Frears* • Nick Searcy *Stan* • Lari White *Bettina Peterson* ■ *Dir* Robert Zemeckis • *Scr* William Broyles Jr • *Cinematographer* Don Burgess

Castaway ★★ 15

Drama based on a true story 1986 · UK · Colour · 112min

This is Nicolas Roeg's version of the real-life experiences of Lucy Irvine, who replied to a newspaper advert from Gerald Kingsland for a woman to join him for a year on a desert island. Both Amanda Donohoe and Oliver Reed cope well with their roles as the castaway and the sex-mad, middle-aged man who is her companion, but in the end you can't help feeling the nudity is only there to spice up a tale of two selfish people who probably deserved each other. JB Swearing, sex scenes, nudity. *DVD*

Oliver Reed *Gerald Kingsland* • Amanda Donohoe *Lucy Irvine* • Georgina Hale *Sister St Margaret* • Frances Barber *Sister St Winifred* ■ *Dir* Nicolas Roeg • *Scr* Allan Scott, from the books *Castaway* by Lucy Irvine and *The Islander* by Gerald Kingsland

The Castaway Cowboy ★★★ U

Western 1974 · US · Colour · 87min

The ever-amiable James Garner is the best thing in this Disney family movie about the first big cattle ranch to be set up in the Hawaiian islands. Garner plays a Texan cowboy who helps pretty widow Vera Miles convert her land from potatoes to beef. Robert Culp is a shady operator and Garner's romantic rival, and natives are on hand to cause trouble. AT *DVD*

James Garner *Lincoln Costain* • Vera Miles *Henrietta MacAvoy* • Robert Culp *Bryson* • Eric Shea *Booton MacAvoy* • Elizabeth Smith *Liliha* • Manu Tupou *Kimo* ■ *Dir* Vincent McEveety • *Scr* Don Tait, from a story by Don Tait, Richard Bluel, Hugh Benson

The Castilian ★★ U

Historical adventure 1963 · US/Sp · Colour · 129min

This uninvolving costume epic concerns the 10th-century legend of Fernan Gonzales, who tried to free Spain from the Moors. First, though, he has to unite Spain, despite fierce opposition from Broderick Crawford. This is one of a clutch of second-rate pictures Crawford made between *Highway Patrol* and *The Private Files of J Edgar Hoover*. JG

Cesar Romero *Jeronimo* • Frankie Avalon *Jerifan* • Broderick Crawford *Don Sancho* • Alida Valli *Queen Teresa* • Espartaco Santoni *Fernan Gonzales* • Teresa Velazquez *Sancha* • Fernando Rey *Ramiro II, King of Leon* • George Rigaud [Georges Rigaud] *Saint Milan* ■ *Dir* Javier Seto • *Scr* Paulino Rodrigo Diaz, Javier Seto, Luis de los Arcos, Sidney Pink, from the epic poem by Fernan Gonzales

The Castle ★★★★ 15

Comedy 1997 · Aus · Colour · 81min

This utterly splendid Aussie comedy didn't make a big impact in the UK, but don't let that deter you – although it flags a little at the end it remains one of the funniest films of the decade. Michael Caton and Anne Tenney are the engagingly dim heads of the Kerrigan family who are delighted with their dream home, which borders the runway of Melbourne's airport. When the airport authority decides to purchase their property to make way for expansion, the bumbling Kerrigans go into battle against the authorities. JF Swearing. *DVD*

Michael Caton *Darryl Kerrigan* • Anne Tenney *Sal Kerrigan* • Stephen Curry *Dale Kerrigan* • Anthony Simcoe *Steve Kerrigan* • Sophie Lee *Tracey Kerrigan* • Wayne Hope *Wayne Kerrigan* ■ *Dir* Rob Sitch • *Scr* Rob Sitch, Santo Cilauro, Tom Gleisner, Jane Kennedy

Castle Keep ★★★ 15

Second World War drama 1969 · US · Colour · 102min

Sydney Pollack's fourth film as director is strange indeed: a heavily allegorical Second World War drama about a squad of American soldiers who defend a Belgian castle, its impotent count and art treasures from the approaching Germans. Often pretentious, often startling and rooted in symbol and unreality, it's as if maverick director Sam Fuller had remade *Last Year at Marienbad*. AT Swearing. *DVD*

Burt Lancaster *Major Abraham Falconer* • Peter Falk *Sergeant Orlando Rossi* • Patrick O'Neal (1) *Captain Lionel Beckman* • Jean-Pierre Aumont *Henri Tixier, Comte De Maldorais* • Bruce Dern *Lieutenant Billy Byron Bix* ■ *Dir* Sydney Pollack • *Scr* Daniel Taradash, David Rayfiel, from the novel by William Eastlake

The Castle of Cagliostro ★★★★ PG

Animated mystery adventure 1979 · Jpn · Colour · 100min

Master thief Lupin infiltrates an impenetrable stronghold that contains more hidden tricks, traps and secrets than a Magic Circle convention in this outstanding action *anime*. Directed with cinematic style and pace by Japanese pioneer Hayao Miyakazi, it combines the neat gadgetry and death-defying confrontations of James Bond with the comic irreverence of silent slapstick. The simplistic character animation doesn't detract from an elaborate, entertaining story and even those normally disconcerted by the genre's philosophising will enjoy Lupin's clear-cut mission to get the girl, beat the bad guy and take the treasure. Available in both dubbed and subtitled versions. JC Japanese +subtitles. *DVD*

■ *Dir* Hayao Miyazaki • *Scr* Hayao Miyazaki, Haruya Yamazaki, from a story by Monkey Punch • *Animator* Yasuo Otsuka

Castle of Evil ★

Horror 1966 · US · Colour · 80min

Relatives of a dead, mad scientist gather in his creepy castle for the reading of the will, only to be systematically murdered by a robot fashioned in the image of the deceased. The result is a ridiculously bad mixture of Agatha Christie and schlock horror, featuring 1940s sex goddess Virginia Mayo as the madman's ex-mistress. AJ

Scott Brady *Matt Granger* • Virginia Mayo *Sable* • Lisa Gaye *Carol Harris* • David Brian *Robert Hawley* • Hugh Marlowe *Dr Corozal* • William Thourlby *The robot* • Shelley Morrison *Lupe Tekal d'Esperanza* ■ *Dir* Francis D Lyon • *Scr* Charles A Wallace

The Castle of Fu Manchu ★ PG

Horror 1968 · W Ger/Sp/It/UK · Colour · 88min

The appalling final entry in the series featuring Sax Rohmer's Oriental arch-villain has Christopher Lee once more plotting world domination on a shoestring budget. Richard Greene is Scotland Yard's Nayland Smith, trying to halt the evil Asian's plan to turn oceans into ice from his base in Istanbul. Atrocious. AJ *DVD*

Christopher Lee *Fu Manchu* • Richard Greene *Nayland Smith* • Howard Marion-Crawford *Dr Petrie* • Tsai Chin *Lin Tang* • Günther Stoll *Curt* ■ *Dir* Jess Franco [Jesus Franco] • *Scr* Harry Alan Towers

Castle on the Hudson ★★★

Prison drama 1940 · US · BW · 74min

The castle in question is Sing Sing penitentiary, where John Garfield is serving a long stretch for robbery. Girlfriend Ann Sheridan campaigns for his release; when she's injured in a car crash, the prison warden (Pat O'Brien, who else?) goes soft and lets Garfield out. Despite this B-movie's relatively short running time, it still manages to veer off into a typical Warner Bros exposé of prison brutality. It's breathless and dated, though Garfield's strengths still shine through. AT

John Garfield *Tommy Gordon* • Ann Sheridan *Kay* • Pat O'Brien *Warden Long* • Burgess Meredith *Steven Rockford* • Henry O'Neill *District Attorney* • Jerome Cowan *Ed Crowley* • Guinn "Big Boy" Williams *Mike Cagle* ■ *Dir* Anatole Litvak • *Scr* Seton I Miller, Brown Holmes, Courtenay Terrett [Courtney Terrett], from the book *20,000 Years in Sing Sing* by Lewis E Lawes

Castles in the Sky ★★

Drama based on a true story 2014 · UK · Colour · 89min

This modest BBC drama details the story of Robert Watson-Watt (Eddie Izzard), the visionary Scottish engineer who pioneered the radar technology that helped defend Britain during the Second World War. The fact that the system must be ready in time for war provides the narrative with a ticking clock, but in spite of this the film rarely generates much in terms of tension. It is engaging in places, and Izzard is appealing as the unlikely hero, but the story is painted in broad strokes, and as a result the end product is fairly unremarkable. SC

Eddie Izzard *Robert Watson-Watt* • Alex Jennings *Henry Tizard* • David Hayman *Frederick Lindemann* • Laura Fraser *Margaret Watson-Watt* • Karl Davies *Skip Wilkins* ■ *Dir* Gillies MacKinnon • *Scr* Ian Kershaw

Casual Sex? ★★★ 18

Comedy 1988 · US · Colour · 83min

This talky but likeable post-Aids comedy might equally have been called *Sex and the Single Girl*. The setting is an up-market health centre, where Lea Thompson and Victoria Jackson hope to bump into a hunky, healthy guy. While they're at it, they reflect on the new sexual realities of the late 1980s. Comedian Andrew Dice Clay shows that he can be more than just an offensive stand-up with an amusing cameo as a New Jersey male with an attitude problem. PF

Lea Thompson *Stacy* • Victoria Jackson *Melissa* • Stephen Shellen *Nick* • Jerry Levine *Jamie* • Andrew Dice Clay *Vinny* • Mary Gross *Ilene* ■ *Dir* Genevieve Robert • *Scr* Wendy Goldman, Judy Toll, from their play

Casualties ★★★ 18

Psychological thriller 1997 · US · Colour · 82min

After supporting roles in Hollywood movies such as *Disclosure* and *White Squall*, UK actress Caroline Goodall gets top billing in her own right in this creepy American indie chiller. She plays the abused wife of cop Jon Gries who strikes up a friendship with seemingly nice Mark Harmon, a fellow student in her cookery class. However, it quickly becomes apparent that her idealised "new man" is more than a couple of eggs short of an omelette. Alex Graves's direction is appreciably claustrophobic. JF

Mark Harmon *Tommy Nance* • Caroline Goodall *Annie Summers* • Jon Gries [Jonathan Gries] *Bill Summers* • Michael Beach *Clark* • John Diehl *Polito* ■ *Dir* Alex Graves • *Scr* Gary Preisler, Alex Graves

Casualties of War ★★★★ 18

War drama 1989 · US · Colour · 108min

This disturbing and provocative Vietnam War tale has at its centre the fact-based story of a Vietnamese woman who is kidnapped and brutally raped by four GIs. While battle-scarred Sean Penn leads the assault, new recruit Michael J Fox stands back but doesn't help her. The film's compassion for the woman hits us directly, as does the way director Brian De Palma sets up the episode by showing the brutalisation of Penn and his colleagues in the preceding scenes. Filmed with all of the director's technical bravura, it heads towards an epilogue that reaches an emotional precipice and then leaps confidently over it. AT Violence, sex scenes, swearing, nudity. *DVD*

Michael J Fox *Eriksson* • Sean Penn *Sergeant Tony Meserve* • Don Harvey *Corporal Thomas E Clark* • John C Reilly *Herbert Hatcher* • John Leguizamo *Diaz* • Thuy Thu Le *Oanh* • Erik King *Sergeant Frank Brown* • Jack Gwaltney *Rowan* • Ving Rhames *Lieutenant Reilly* ■ *Dir* Brian De Palma • *Scr* David Rabe, from the book by Daniel Lang

Cat and Mouse ★★★

Drama 1958 · UK · BW · 85min

This claustrophobic thriller denies documentary director Paul Rotha the chance to demonstrate his facility with realism. Yet he still generates a fair amount of suspense as Ann Sears finds herself caught between an American army deserter and the villains searching for the diamonds stolen by her recently executed father. With Hilton Edwards and Lee Paterson imposing as her pursuers, this is superior to the majority of British B-movies made at the time. DP

Lee Patterson *Rod Fenner* • Ann Sears *Ann Coltby* • Hilton Edwards *Mr Scruby* • Victor Maddern *Superintendent Harding* • George Rose *Dealer* ■ *Dir* Paul Rotha • *Scr* Paul Rotha, from the novel *Cat and Mouse* by Michael Halliday

The Cat and the Canary ★★★★

Silent mystery 1927 · US · BW · 82min

Paul Leni was the first of the great expressionist German directors to go to Hollywood, and he made his US debut with this silent mystery that was a strong influence on subsequent horror movies.

Moodily shot, this classic "old dark house" picture is played mostly for laughs. The canary is a wealthy old man and the cat, or rather cats, are those who gather at midnight 20 years after his death to hear a reading of the will. It was remade with Bob Hope in 1939, and again in 1979. Leni died of blood poisoning in 1929, aged 44. RB

Laura La Plante *Annabelle West* • Creighton Hale *Paul Jones* • Forrest Stanley *Charles Wilder* • Tully Marshall *Roger Crosby* • Gertrude Astor *Cecily Young* • Arthur Edmund Carewe *Harry Blythe* • Flora Finch *Susan Sillsby* ◼ *Dir* Paul Leni • *Scr* Robert F Hill, Alfred A Cohn, from the play by John Willard

The Cat and the Canary ★★★★ PG

Mystery comedy   1939 · US · BW · 73min

Unfairly neglected today, this also suffered on release from the fact that 1939 was the *annus mirabilis* of Hollywood's Golden Era. This is the definitive haunted-house movie, much copied, never bettered, in which Bob Hope cements his screen image: at once cowardly, lecherous, vulnerable and attractive. Lovely Paulette Goddard makes a fine foil for Hope; so successful were they together that they were immediately re-teamed in *The Ghost Breakers*. This is a remake of an equally good silent version, and was itself remade by porn king Radley Metzger in 1979. TS *DVD*

Bob Hope *Wally Campbell* • Paulette Goddard *Joyce Norman* • John Beal *Fred Blythe* • Douglass Montgomery *Charlie Wilder* • Gale Sondergaard *Miss Lu* • George Zucco *Lawyer Crosby* • Elizabeth Patterson *Aunt Susan* ◼ *Dir* Elliott Nugent • *Scr* Walter DeLeon, Lynn Starling, from the play by John Willard

The Cat and the Canary ★★ 15

Murder mystery   1979 · UK · Colour · 102min

This remake is not a patch on either Paul Leni's silent original or Bob Hope's cornball reworking. An all-star British cast works hard to raise both laughs and the hairs on the back of your neck, but only succeeds in being annoying. Radley Metzger's tepid direction almost completely misses the eerie atmosphere and grisly graveyard humour that made John Willard's play such a natural for the screen. DP *DVD*

Honor Blackman *Susan Sillsby* • Edward Fox *Hendricks* • Michael Callan *Paul Jones* • Wendy Hiller *Allison Crosby* • Olivia Hussey *Cicily Young* • Beatrix Lehmann *Mrs Pleasant* • Carol Lynley *Annabelle West* • Daniel Massey *Harry Blythe* • Peter McEnery *Charlie Wilder* • Wilfrid Hyde White *Cyrus West* ◼ *Dir* Radley Metzger • *Scr* Radley Metzger, from the play by John Willard

The Cat and the Fiddle ★★★ U

Romantic musical
1934 · US · BW and Colour · 88min

This witty film stars the actress who was undoubtedly queen of movie operetta, "iron butterfly" Jeanette MacDonald. She's paired here with silent screen idol Ramon Novarro, whose matinée good looks and singing voice endured in talkies until his notorious private life led to a severe fall-off in screen popularity. This is good fun, with a sparkling script and the bonus of a last reel in early three-strip Technicolor. TS

Ramon Novarro *Victor* • Jeanette MacDonald *Shirley* • Frank Morgan *Daudet* • Charles Butterworth *Charles* • Jean Hersholt *Professor* ◼ *Dir* William K Howard • *Scr* Bella Spewack, Sam Spewack, from the musical by Jerome Kern, Otto Harbach

Cat Ballou ★★★★ PG

Comedy western   1965 · US · Colour · 92min

In this very entertaining comedy western, Jane Fonda's schoolteacher hires a gunman to avenge her murdered father. The man she hires is Kid Shelleen, a long-haired, buckskinned gunfighter played by Lee Marvin, who wakes up sozzled and gets worse by the minute. Even his horse is a drunkard, leaning against a barn for support. This showpiece role won an Oscar for Marvin, who also plays straight man to himself as Shelleen's psychopathic

adversary, a killer with a silver nose. Nat King Cole and Stubby Kaye string along for a singalong in what is a very amiable affair. AT *DVD*

Jane Fonda *Cat Ballou* • Lee Marvin *Kid Shelleen/Tim Strawn* • Michael Callan *Clay Boone* • Dwayne Hickman *Jed* • Tom Nardini *Jackson Two-Bears* • John Marley *Frankie Ballou* • Reginald Denny *Sir Harry Percival* • Arthur Hunnicutt *Butch Cassidy* ◼ *Dir* Elliot Silverstein • *Scr* Frank R Pierson [Frank Pierson], Walter Newman, from the novel by Roy Chanslor

Cat Chaser ★★ 18

Thriller   1989 · US · Colour · 86min

This tough political thriller, adapted from the Elmore Leonard novel, is a disappointment. Peter Weller is the ex-soldier who gets lured into an affair and dangerous intrigue with former flame Kelly McGillis, now the wife of a particularly nasty Latin American policeman. Weller is fine as the tormented hero, but McGillis is an unconvincing *femme fatale*. JF Violence, swearing, sex scenes, nudity. *DVD*

Peter Weller *George Moran* • Kelly McGillis *Mary de Boya* • Charles Durning *Jiggs Scully* • Frederic Forrest *Nolan Tyner* • Tomas Milian *Andres de Boya* ◼ *Dir* Abel Ferrara • *Scr* Elmore Leonard, James Borrelli, Alan Sharp, from the novel by Elmore Leonard

The Cat Concerto ★★★★★

Animated musical comedy
1947 · US · Colour · 8min

This classic Tom and Jerry cartoon makes wonderful slapstick comedy around Liszt's *Second Hungarian Rhapsody* as Tom the cat's initially pompous, concert-hall rendition of the piece is reduced to rubble by Jerry the mouse, who is disturbed while sleeping in Tom's piano. During production, a mix-up at the Technicolor labs caused a similar Warner Bros cartoon, *Rhapsody Rabbit* (1946), to be delivered to MGM by mistake. MGM then rushed production of their film in order to submit it for that spring's Oscar nominations, later winning the award. A deserved gain for William Hanna and Joseph Barbera, as this is arguably their finest cartoon. CLP

◼ *Dir* William Hanna, Joseph Barbera • *Animators* Kenneth Muse, Ed Barge, Irv Spence, Bob Gentle • *Music* Scott Bradley

The Cat from Outer Space ★★ U

Comedy   1978 · US · Colour · 94min

This is harmless Disney matinée fodder, with an alien feline grounded on Earth and in need of human dexterity to repair its disabled spacecraft. Startling similarities to *ET* add an unforeseen layer of entertainment value to a bland package that could have done with a bit of Spielberg magic. A pretty uninspired juvenile romp. AJ *DVD*

Ken Berry *Dr Frank Wilson* • Sandy Duncan *Dr Liz Bartlett* • Harry Morgan *General Stilton* • Roddy McDowall *Stallwood* • McLean Stevenson *Dr Carl Link* • Jesse White *Earnest Ernie* • Alan Young *Dr Wenger* ◼ *Dir* Norman Tokar • *Scr* Ted Key

The Cat Gang ★★ U

Crime drama   1959 · UK · BW · 50min

Based on a story by George Ewart Evans, this featurette might have kept kids amused in the late 1950s. However, the demands of young audiences have changed dramatically since those more innocent times, and a tale of smuggling devoid of special effects will now have few takers. That said, their parents will no doubt be fascinated to see a youthful Francesca Annis among the gang assisting a grumpy customs officer in the recovery of valuable contraband. DP

Francesca Annis *Sylvia* • John Pike *John* • Jeremy Bullock [Jeremy Bulloch] *Bill* • John Gabriel *Mason* • John Stacy *Dodds* • Paddy Joyce *Banks* ◼ *Dir* Darrell Catling • *Scr* John Eldridge, from a story by G Ewart Evans [George Ewart Evans]

A Cat in Paris ★★ PG

Animated crime mystery
2010 · Fr/Neth/Swi/Bel · Colour · 64min

This modest French children's thriller about a mute, fatherless girl whose cat leads a double life as the accomplice of a conveniently benign human jewel thief was surprisingly nominated for best animated feature at the 2012 Oscars. Its promising echoes of Disney's *The Aristocats* are limited to the Parisian setting, as the unfortunate dub into American English – the voice cast includes luminaries such as Matthew Modine and Anjelica Huston – sucks away any remaining Gallic subtlety. No matter how slight the film, it didn't deserve to lose so much in translation. AC *DVD*

Matthew Modine *Lucas* • Anjelica Huston *Claudine* • Steve Blum [Steven Jay Blum] *Nico* • JB Blanc *Victor Costa* • Marcia Gay Harden *Jeanne* ◼ *Dir* Jean-Loup Felicioli, Alain Gagnol • *Scr* Alain Gagnol, Jacques-Rémy Girerd

Cat on a Hot Tin Roof ★★★★ 15

Drama   1958 · US · Colour · 103min

This is Tennessee Williams at his most overheated, with familial strife in the Deep South coming atmospherically alive in all its steamy, fly-blown and shutters slammin' glory. Elizabeth Taylor overdoes the Southern accent, though Paul Newman is splendid as the sullen but only upright member of a thoroughly dislikeable clan. The surprise plus is Burl Ives as the dying patriarch Big Daddy. One of the sounder screen adaptations of the playwright's work, even if the play's references to the homosexuality of Newman's character were watered down for the film. SH *DVD*

Elizabeth Taylor *Maggie Pollitt* • Paul Newman *Brick Pollitt* • Burl Ives *Big Daddy Pollitt* • Jack Carson *Gooper Pollitt* • Judith Anderson *Big Mama Pollitt* • Madeleine Sherwood *Mae Pollitt* • Larry Gates *Dr Baugh* • Vaughn Taylor *Deacon Davis* ◼ *Dir* Richard Brooks • *Scr* Richard Brooks, James Poe, from the play by Tennessee Williams

Cat o'Nine Tails ★★★ 18

Thriller   1971 · Fr/It/W Ger · Colour · 107min

Blind Karl Malden and journalist James Franciscus unravel a tortuous mystery combining industrial espionage, homosexuality and genetic dementia in director Dario Argento's visually creative study in terror. Thrilling subjective camerawork masks the maniac's identity in a triumph of style over content. The train platform murder and the skylight finale are textbook examples of what Argento calls "violence as art." AJ Some dubbed. *DVD*

Karl Malden *Franco Arno* • James Franciscus *Carlo Giordani* • Catherine Spaak *Anna Terzi* • Cinzia De Carolis *Lori* • Carlo Alighiero *Dr Calabresi* • Vittorio Congia *Righetto* • Aldo Reggiani *Dr Casoni* ◼ *Dir* Dario Argento • *Scr* Dario Argento, from a story by Luigi Collo, Dardano Sacchetti, Dario Argento • *Cinematographer* Erico Menczer

LANDMARK FILM
Horror producer Val Lewton leaves an indelible mark by manipulating fear through shadow and suggestion

Cat People ★★★★ PG

Psychological horror   1942 · US · BW · 72min

Produced by Val Lewton and directed by the great Jacques Tourneur, this was one of the first Hollywood horrors to play on the audience's fears rather than expose it to ghouls and monsters. Simone Simon makes one of cinema's most sensual menaces as the sketch artist who turns into a panther as a result of an ancient Serbian curse. Apart from Simon, the acting's pretty ropey, but the film is packed with eerie moments – the famous walk through the park gave rise to the term "bus", meaning a false shock (you'll have to watch to see what we mean). DP *DVD*

Simone Simon *Irena Dubrovna* • Tom Conway *Dr Judd* • Jane Randolph *Alice Moore* • Jack Holt *Commodore* • Kent Smith *Oliver Reed* • Alan Napier *Carver* • Elizabeth Dunne *Miss Plunkett* •

Elizabeth Russell *The cat woman* • Mary Halsey *Blondie* ◼ *Dir* Jacques Tourneur • *Scr* DeWitt Bodeen • *Cinematographer* Nicholas Musuraca

Cat People ★★★ 18

Horror   1982 · US · Colour · 112min

Paul Schrader's stylish remake of producer Val Lewton's horror classic features a well-cast Nastassja Kinski as one of the last survivors of a race of beings who transform into felines in the heat of passion. Malcolm McDowell is her kinky brother and John Heard the zookeeper unaware that not all of the animals are behind bars. Driven by nudity, gore and sensuality, Schrader's emotionally cold fantasy begins well, but degenerates into a surrealistic mess. AJ Violence, swearing, sex scenes, nudity. *DVD* *Blu*

Nastassia Kinski [Nastassja Kinski] *Irena Gallier* • Malcolm McDowell *Paul Gallier* • John Heard *Oliver Yates* • Annette O'Toole *Alice Perrin* • Ruby Dee *Female* • Ed Begley Jr *Joe Creigh* ◼ *Dir* Paul Schrader • *Scr* Alan Ormsby, from the film by DeWitt Bodeen • *Music* Giorgio Moroder

The Cat Returns ★★ U

Animated fantasy
2002 · Jpn/US · Colour · 75min

Made by the same studio that gave us *Spirited Away*, Hiroyuki Morita's film just isn't on a par with its enchanting, Oscar-winning stablemate. This tells the tale of teenager Haru, who's invited to visit the Kingdom of Cats after saving the life of a moggie prince. But then the king decides that Haru should marry his son and never return to the human world. The storyline is disappointingly simple, while the visuals rarely impress. SF Japanese dubbed. *Blu*

Anne Hathaway *Haru Yoshioka* • Cary Elwes *Baron* • Peter Boyle *Muta* • Elliott Gould *Toto* • Andrew Bevis *Prince Lune* • Tim Curry *Cat King* • Judy Greer *Yuki* • Kristen Bell *Hiromi* • René Auberjonois *Natori* ◼ *Dir* Hiroyuki Morita • *Scr* Reiko Yoshida, Cindy Davis Hewitt (English version), Donald H Hewitt (English version), from the comic book *Baron the Cat Baron* by Aoi Hiiragi

The Catamount Killing ★★★

Crime drama   1974 · W Ger/US · Colour · 97min

Coming between those landmarks in Polish cinema, *Illumination* and *Camouflage*, this English-language crime drama may seem something of an aberration on the part of Krzysztof Zanussi. Yet, as banker Horst Buchholz and his lover Ann Wedgeworth flee with the proceeds of their heist, it becomes clear the director's recurrent themes of moral decline and the disintegration of meaningful relationships are both present and correct. DP

Horst Buchholz *Mark Kalvin* • Ann Wedgeworth *Kit Loring* • Chip Taylor *Ken Travers* • Louise Clark *Iris Loring* • Patricia Joyce *Alice Craig* ◼ *Dir* Krzysztof Zanussi • *Scr* Julien More, Sheila More, from the novel *I'd Rather Stay Poor* by James Hadley Chase

Catch a Fire ★★ 12

Political drama based on a true story
2006 · UK/S Afr/US/Fr · Colour · 97min

Rabbit-Proof Fence director Phillip Noyce once again tackles explosive issues of racial persecution with this true story set in South Africa in 1980. Black oil-refinery foreman Patrick Chamusso (Derek Luke) is called in for questioning when the plant is sabotaged. The brutality of his treatment in detention, under the supervision of the creepy Colonel Vos (a rather too avuncular Tim Robbins), helps to radicalise the previously apolitical Patrick into becoming an active participant in the battle against apartheid. Noyce's movie is decently made and acted, but it is also oddly uninvolving and offers no new insights into this explosive era in South Africa's recent history. DA English, Afrikaans, Zulu +subtitles. Violence, brief swearing. *DVD*

Tim Robbins *Nic Vos* • Derek Luke *Patrick Chamusso* • Bonnie Henna *Precious Chamusso* • Mncedisi Shabangu *Zuko September* • Tumisho K Masha *Obadi* • Sithembiso Khumalo *Sixpence* • Terry Pheto *Miriam* ◼ *Dir* Phillip Noyce • *Scr* Shawn Slovo

Catch and Release ★★ 12

Romantic comedy drama
2007 · US · Colour · 106min

After a pre-wedding boating accident leaves her single, Gray Wheeler (Jennifer Garner) makes an unwelcome discovery about the man she almost married. A secret bank account reveals a fortune from which monthly payments are made to a massage therapist (Juliette Lewis) and her young son. *Erin Brockovich* writer Susannah Grant – making her big-screen directorial debut – tries hard to blend grief and light-hearted moments into a weepie comedy drama. However, it rarely works as the contrived storyline stretches both credibility and goodwill. JR Sexual references. *DVD* Blu

Jennifer Garner *Gray Wheeler* · Timothy Olyphant *Fritz* · Sam Jaeger *Dennis* · Kevin Smith (2) *Sam* · Juliette Lewis *Maureen* · Joshua Friesen *Mattie* · Fiona Shaw *Mrs Douglas* ■ *Dir/Scr* Susannah Grant

Catch Me a Spy ★★

Spy thriller
1971 · UK · Colour · 94min

This lame spy thriller about missing secret files has a sometimes clever and witty script by the ace TV team of Dick Clement and Ian La Frenais. However, it's rather let down by Clement's uncertain direction, while Kirk Douglas's peculiar intensity isn't best suited to a comedy. Trevor Howard and Tom Courtenay seem more at home with the spy spoof material, though. AT

Kirk Douglas *Andrej* · Marlène Jobert *Fabienne* · Trevor Howard *Sir Trevor Dawson* · Tom Courtenay *Baxter Clarke* · Patrick Mower *John Fenton* · Bernadette Lafont *Simone* · Bernard Blier *Webb* ■ *Dir* Dick Clement · *Scr* Dick Clement, Ian La Frenais, from the novel by George Marton, Tibor Meray

Catch Me Daddy ★★★ 15

Thriller
2014 · UK · Colour · 107min

An Asian family hunts for a runaway daughter in rural Yorkshire in this dark thriller. Laila (promising newcomer Sabeena Jameen Ahmed) is a free spirit, while her partner Aaron (*Neds* star Conor McCarron) is more circumspect, understandable given that Laila's domineering father has hired men to track them down. This works best as a nightmarish visual experience, the darkness of the moors at night suggesting the depths of inhumanity as the pursuit unfolds. However, the hot-button issue of "honour killing" is rather more complex than the film's bare-bones storytelling allows. TJ In English, Punjabi. Violence, swearing, drug abuse. *DVD* Blu

Sameena Jabeen Ahmed *Laila* · Conor McCarron *Aaron* · Gary Lewis *Tony* · Wasim Zakir *Tariq* · Anwar Hussain *Junaid* · Barry Nunney *Barry* ■ *Dir/Scr* Daniel Wolfe, Matthew Wolfe · *Cinematographer* Robbie Ryan

Catch Me If You Can ★★★★ 12

Biographical comedy drama
2002 · US · Colour · 134min

Director Steven Spielberg backtracks to the 1960s for this stylish slice of entertainment. Leonardo DiCaprio exudes movie-star charisma as Frank Abagnale Jr who, while still a teenager, charmed and cheated his way across America, posing as an airline pilot, doctor and lawyer in order to cash forged cheques. Tom Hanks turns in an unshowy supporting performance as Carl Hanratty, the dogged FBI agent who obsessively pursued the larcenous young man. Sentimentality is allowed to intrude with the depiction of Abagnale's family life, but not into Christopher Walken's superb turn as the conman's father. Despite these momentary dips, the deft blend of comedy and suspense, great period detail and sheer directorial class ensures that this is one of Spielberg's most purely enjoyable movies. IF Some swearing. *DVD*

Leonardo DiCaprio *Frank William Abagnale Jr/ Frank Taylor/Frank Conners/Barry Allen* · Tom Hanks *Carl Hanratty* · Christopher Walken *Frank William Abagnale Sr* · Martin Sheen *Roger Strong* · Nathalie Baye *Paula Abagnale* · Amy Adams *Brenda Strong* · James Brolin *Jack Barnes* · Brian Howe *Tom Fox* · Jennifer Garner *Cheryl*

Ann • Frank W Abagnale *French policeman* ■ *Dir* Steven Spielberg • *Scr* Jeff Nathanson, from the autobiography *Catch Me If You Can: the Amazing True Story of the Most Extraordinary Liar in the History of Fun and Profit* by Frank Abagnale Jr, Stan Redding

Catch My Soul ★

Musical
1973 · US · Colour · 95min

Lance LeGault, the demonic leader of a desert-based religious commune, manipulates black preacher Richie Havens into murdering his white hippy wife Season Hubley in a fit of jealous rage. This updated musical version of Shakespeare's *Othello* is to be avoided by all but the most dedicated fans of 1970s rock operas. Boring when it doesn't infuriate. RK

Richie Havens *Othello* · Lance LeGault *Iago* · Season Hubley *Desdemona* · Tony Joe White *Cassio* · Susan Tyrrell *Emilia* ■ *Dir* Patrick McGoohan · *Scr* Jack Good, from the play *Othello* by William Shakespeare · *Music* Tony Joe White

Catch That Kid ★★★ PG

Action adventure
2004 · US · Colour · 87min

Its "crime pays" message may be dubious for a family film, but this fast-paced *Mission: Impossible*-style adventure is still imaginative, exciting and entertaining. Kristen Stewart plays a young girl who teams up with two male friends to carry out a hi-tech bank heist to get the cash to pay for a costly operation for her paralysed father. Though the plot's far-fetched, it's well-executed, balancing intelligence, suspense and humour. The acting, too, is engaging. SF Swearing. *DVD*

Kristen Stewart *Maddy* · Corbin Bleu *Austin* · Max Thieriot *Gus* · Jennifer Beals *Molly* · Sam Robards *Tom* · John Carroll Lynch *Mr Hartman* · James Le Gros [James LeGros] *Ferrell* · Michael Des Barres *Brisbane* · Stark Sands *Brad* ■ *Dir* Bart Freundlich · *Scr* Michael Brandt, Derek Haas, from the film *Klatretøsen* by Nikolaj Arcel, Hans Fabian Wullenweber, Erlend Loe

Catch-22 ★★★ 15

War satire
1970 · US · Colour · 116min

Alan Arkin is splendid as Captain Yossarian, the innocent abroad at a US Air Force base in the Mediterranean, in this war satire based on Joseph Heller's bestseller. It's more violent burlesque than tragi-farce, but it certainly draws attention to its hero's "no win situation" as he struggles to cope with sham, hypocrisy and the deaths of too many comrades. Mike Nichols's direction of Buck Henry's script is an organisational tour de force, though the episodic structure requires concentration and the black comedy seems, at times, a bit laboured. TH Violence, swearing, brief nudity. *DVD*

Alan Arkin *Capt Yossarian* · Martin Balsam *Col Cathcart* · Richard Benjamin *Major Danby* · Art Garfunkel *Capt Nately* · Jack Gilford *Doc Daneeka* · Buck Henry *Lt Col Korn* · Bob Newhart *Major Major* · Anthony Perkins *Chaplain Tappman* · Paula Prentiss *Nurse Duckett* · Martin Sheen *Lt Dobbs* · Jon Voight *Milo Minderbinder* · Orson Welles *Gen Dreedle* · Bob Balaban *Capt Orr* · Charles Grodin *Aarfy Aardvark* · Austin Pendleton *Col Moodus* ■ *Dir* Mike Nichols · *Scr* Buck Henry, from the novel by Joseph Heller

Catch Us If You Can ★★ PG

Musical
1965 · UK · BW · 87min

Despite a run of jolly, sunny-sounding pop hits, the Dave Clark Five chose former documentarist John Boorman to direct this starkly black-and-white and unexpectedly bleak first feature. It's no *A Hard Day's Night*, but it paved the way for Boorman to make the massively influential *Point Blank*. Clark and the lads are singularly charmless and unskilled at thesping, but Barbara Ferris does a nice turn as a model on the lam. TS *DVD*

Dave Clark *Steve* · Lenny Davidson *Lenny* · Rick Huxley *Rick* · Mike Smith *Mike* · Denis Payton *Denis* · Barbara Ferris *Dinah* · David Lodge *Louis* · Robin Bailey *Guy* ■ *Dir* John Boorman · *Scr* Peter Nichols

Catchfire ★★★ 15

Thriller
1989 · US · Colour · 98min

Disowned by director Dennis Hopper (hence the Alan Smithee directorial credit), this remains an oddly watchable mess. Hopper also stars as the Mafia hitman who is ordered to assassinate a witness to a gangland killing (Jodie Foster), only to fall in love with his victim. It's an offbeat combination of black comedy and gangster thriller, but the tone is uneven. However, Hopper and Foster spark off each other nicely, while a starry supporting cast keeps you hooked. JF Violence, sex scenes, swearing, nudity. *DVD*

Jodie Foster *Anne Benton* · Dennis Hopper *Milo* · Dean Stockwell *John Luponi* · Vincent Price *Lino Avoca* · John Turturro *Pinella* · Joe Pesci *Leo Carelli* · Fred Ward *Pauling* · Charlie Sheen *Bob* ■ *Dir* Alan Smithee [Dennis Hopper] · *Scr* Rachel Kronstadt-Mann, Ann Louise Bardach, Stephen L Cotler, Lanny Cotler, from a story by Rachel Kronstadt-Mann

The Catered Affair ★★★ U

Comedy
1956 · US · BW · 93min

Bette Davis is miscast as a downtrodden Bronx taxi driver's wife, but she used to glory in shedding the glamour now and then. A passably fine script from Gore Vidal and a good supporting cast (including Ernest Borgnine and Debbie Reynolds) made this a major hit in its day, but when compared to the rest of Davis's cinematic work it's just a good B-league effort. SH

Bette Davis *Mrs Tom Hurley* · Ernest Borgnine *Tom Hurley* · Debbie Reynolds *Jane Hurley* · Barry Fitzgerald *Uncle Jack Conlon* · Rod Taylor *Ralph Halloran* · Robert Simon [Robert F Simon] *Mr Halloran* · Madge Kennedy *Mrs Halloran* ■ *Dir* Richard Brooks · *Scr* Gore Vidal, from the TV play by Paddy Chayefsky

Catfish ★★★★ 12

Documentary
2010 · US · Colour · 83min

Billed as a "reality thriller", this tantalising documentary follows the misadventures of New York photographer Nev Schulman. He begins an online correspondence with a Michigan family, whose eight-year-old daughter has been sending him her paintings based on his pictures of dancers. Surprises are in store, however, when Nev and the film-makers (his brother Ariel, plus co-director Henry Joost) decide to drop by for a visit. The unfolding events prove unsettling, creepy and, ultimately, quite poignant, as all concerned discover that real-world human interaction and Facebook friendship are rather different things. TJ Sexual references. *DVD* Blu

Nev Schulman · Ariel Schulman ■ *Dir* Henry Joost, Ariel Schulman

Catholic Boys ★★★ 15

Comedy
1985 · US · Colour · 99min

Angst, guilt and raging hormones combine to provide a fresh, affecting glimpse of life behind the steel doors of a Catholic boys' school – its regime is so strict that it makes the institutions envisioned by Dickens look positively luxurious. There are a clutch of strong performances, most notably from Andrew McCarthy and Kevin Dillon, while Donald Sutherland is at his brooding best as chief monk and administrator of major whackings. In his feature film debut, director Michael Dinner deals intelligently with a well-worn theme and injects some subtle nuances. SH Swearing.

Andrew McCarthy *Michael Dunn* · Kevin Dillon *Rooney* · Donald Sutherland *Brother Thadeus* · John Heard *Brother Timothy* · Mary Stuart Masterson *Danni* · Kate Reid *Grandma* · Wallace Shawn *Father Abruzzi* · Philip Bosco *Brother Paul* · Patrick Dempsey *Corbet* ■ *Dir* Michael Dinner · *Scr* Charles Purpura

Catlow ★★ PG

Western
1971 · Sp · Colour · 92min

Yul Brynner takes the title role, a cattle rustler caught between marshal Richard Crenna, who wants to lock him up, and bounty hunter Leonard Nimoy, who wants him dead. It's an unpretentious effort that veers more towards knockabout comedy than spaghetti-style ketchup. Silent movie aficionados will relish the brief appearance by Bessie Love. AT

Yul Brynner *Catlow* · Richard Crenna *Cowan* · Leonard Nimoy *Miller* · Daliah Lavi *Rosita* · Jo Ann Pflug *Christina* · Jeff Corey *Merridew* · Michael Delano *Rio* · Julian Mateos *Recalde* · Bessie Love *Mrs Frost* ■ *Dir* Sam Wanamaker · *Scr* Scot Finch [Scott Finch], JJ Griffith, from the novel by Louis L'Amour

Cats & Dogs ★★ PG

Part-animated fantasy comedy
2001 · US/Aus · Colour · 94min

This mixes live action, animatronics and computer-generated animation to create a covert struggle for world domination between cats and dogs. It's a nice concept but messy execution and a weak script serve to undermine any potential charm. The problem lies in the uneasy switch from real animal actors – the cute central beagle Lou (voiced by Tobey Maguire), various innocent looking kitties – to all-too-obvious puppets. AC *DVD* Blu

Jeff Goldblum *Professor Brody* · Elizabeth Perkins *Mrs Brody* · Miriam Margolyes *Sophie* · Alexander Pollack [Alexander Pollock] *Scott Brody* · Tobey Maguire *Lou* · Alec Baldwin *Butch* · Sean Hayes *Mr Tinkles* · Susan Sarandon *Ivy* · Joe Pantoliano *Peek* · Charlton Heston *The Mastiff* ■ *Dir* Lawrence Guterman · *Scr* John Requa, Glenn Ficarra

Cats & Dogs: the Revenge of Kitty Galore ★★★ U

Part-animated comedy fantasy
2010 · US/Aus · Colour · 82min

The claws are out in this belated sequel, as deranged and hairless moggy Kitty Galore seeks revenge on humans by turning the world's dogs against mankind. But disgraced police canine Diggs is soon on Kitty's trail. The film owes much of its look and ideas to the James Bond franchise, including a villainous sidekick akin to Jaws and Roger Moore voicing the feline equivalent of M. However, too much time is spent on the wordy script and sly tributes to other more adult films including *The Silence of the Lambs* to keep youngsters entertained throughout. But, thanks to improvements in CGI and a sympathetic canine lead, this is a slight improvement on the original, with the prize for the best voice acting going to Bette Midler, who lends Kitty a devilish rasp that's one of the joys of the film. SuR *DVD* Blu CG

James Marsden *Diggs* · Bette Midler *Kitty Galore* · Nick Nolte *Butch* · Christina Applegate *Agent Catherine* · Katt Williams *Seamus* · Chris O'Donnell *Shane Larson* · Neil Patrick Harris *Lou* · Sean Hayes *Mr Tinkles* · Michael Clarke Duncan *Sam* · Joe Pantoliano *Peek* · Roger Moore *Tab Lazenby* ■ *Dir* Brad Peyton · *Scr* Ron J Friedman, Steve Bencich, from characters by John Requa, Glenn Ficarra

Cats Don't Dance ★★ U

Animated musical comedy
1998 · US · Colour · 71min

This overly ambitious animated musical is set in late-1930s Hollywood. Danny (voiced by Scott Bakula) is a Gene Kelly-type small-town feline who discovers that animals are relegated to the background, while the humans hog the movie limelight. Interestingly, Kelly himself acted as consultant for the film's sprightly dance choreography, which deserves praise for its energy and originality. Unfortunately, the characters are rather dull and Randy Newman's tunes disappointing. JC

Scott Bakula *Danny* · Jasmine Guy *Sawyer* · Natalie Cole *Sawyer* · Ashley Peldon *Darla Dimple* · Lindsay Rideway *Darla Dimple* · Kathy Najimy *Tillie* · John Rhys-Davies *Woolie* · George Kennedy *LB Mammoth* · René Auberjonois *Flanigan* · Hal Holbrook *Cranston* ■ *Dir* Mark Dindal · *Scr* Roberts Gannaway [Robert Gannaway], Cliff Ruby, Elana Lesser, Theresa Pettengill, from a story by Rick Schneider, Robert Lence, Mark Dindal, Brian McEntee, David Womersley, Kelvin Yasuda

Cat's Eye ★★★ 15
Horror　　　　1984 · US · Colour · 90min

This is a generally entertaining trilogy of terror tales from the ubiquitous Stephen King, the Big Mac of horror literature. James Woods tries an unorthodox method of quitting smoking, *Airplane!*'s Robert Hays is forced into a deadly bet and Drew Barrymore comes under attack from a rather unappetising gnome-like monster in a swift-paced anthology that works more often than not because of strong casting and a refreshingly throwaway tone. AJ Violence, swearing. *DVD*

Drew Barrymore *Girl* • James Woods *Morrison* • Alan King *Dr Donatti* • Kenneth McMillan *Cressner* • Robert Hays *Norris* • Candy Clark *Sally Ann* • James Naughton *Hugh* • Tony Munafo *Junk* ■ *Dir* Lewis Teague • *Scr* Stephen King, from his short stories *Quitters Inc, The Ledge* and *The General*

The Cat's Meow ★★★ 12
Period comedy drama
2001 · Ger/UK/US · Colour · 109min

Peter Bogdanovich investigates the mysterious demise of Thomas Ince, the Hollywood pioneer whose trip aboard tycoon William Randolph Hearst's yacht dominated the front pages of November 1924. Unfortunately, the approach is more Agatha Christie than *Citizen Kane*, with teleplay plastic visuals depicting an all-star cast bandying bon mots in stitch-perfect costumes. Yet, for all its shallowness, this is still entertaining with careful performances. DP *DVD*

Kirsten Dunst *Marion Davies* • Edward Herrmann *William Randolph Hearst* • Eddie Izzard *Charlie Chaplin* • Cary Elwes *Thomas Ince* • Joanna Lumley *Elinor Glyn* • Jennifer Tilly *Louella Parsons* ■ *Dir* Peter Bogdanovich • *Scr* Steven Peros, from the play by Steven Peros

The Cat's Paw ★★★ U
Comedy　　　　1934 · US · BW · 101min

Harold Lloyd, the silent comedian archivists usually overlook, stars in a comedy that shows off little of his acutely timed talents. He plays Ezekiel Cobb, a missionary's son raised in China who arrives in America to find himself up to his spectacles in corrupt politicians. From the man who used cliffhanger comedy so brilliantly in *Safety Last*, this film comes as something of a disappointment. TH

Harold Lloyd *Ezekiel Cobb* • Una Merkel *Petunia Pratt* • George Barbier *Jake Mayo* • Nat Pendleton *Strozzi* • Grace Bradley *Dolores Dace* ■ *Dir* Sam Taylor • *Scr* Sam Taylor, from a story by Clarence Budington Kelland

Cattle Annie and Little Britches ★★★
Western　　　　1980 · US · Colour · 97min

In this cheerful family western, never released in Britain, Diane Lane and Amanda Plummer play a pair of teenage girls intent on joining Burt Lancaster's gang of bank robbers, while Rod Steiger is the lawman determined to bring them all to justice. The scenes where he discusses changing times with Lancaster are the most memorable moments in Lamont Johnson's film, which manages to be quite enjoyable despite an irritating banjo-strumming soundtrack. TH

Burt Lancaster *Bill Doolin* • John Savage *Bittercreek Newcomb* • Rod Steiger *Tilghman* • Diane Lane *Jenny/Little Britches* • Amanda Plummer *Annie/Cattle Annie* • Scott Glenn *Bill Dalton* ■ *Dir* Lamont Johnson • *Scr* David Eyre, Robert Ward, from a story and novel by Robert Ward

Cattle Drive ★★★ U
Western　　　　1951 · US · Colour · 77min

Dean Stockwell, better known to today's audiences for TV's *Quantum Leap*, had a major career as a child star. In this Universal western, he plays a spoiled rich brat growing up out west alongside grizzled trail boss Joel McCrea, learning the cowboy ropes from the likes of veterans Chill Wills and Bob Steele. Kurt Neumann directs with warmth and understanding, and the

Technicolor photography of the Death Valley locations is superb. TS

Joel McCrea *Dan Mathews* • Dean Stockwell *Chester Graham Jr* • Chill Wills *Dallas* • Leon Ames *Mr Graham* • Henry Brandon *Jim Currie* • Howard Petrie *Cap* • Bob Steele *Careless* • Griff Barnett *Conductor O'Hara* ■ *Dir* Kurt Neumann • *Scr* Jack Natteford, Lillie Hayward • *Cinematographer* Maury Gertsman

Cattle Empire ★★ U
Western　　　　1958 · US · Colour · 82min

Little more than a B-feature, this routine western dates from the twilight of veteran Joel McCrea's career, a period when his name could only guarantee co-feature status. McCrea lends real authority to the tale, but classic western fans will shy away from this Charles Marquis Warren confection, as he brings all the TV production values that enabled him to produce such long-running series as *Gunsmoke* and *Rawhide* quickly and economically. TS

Joel McCrea *John Cord* • Gloria Talbott *Sandy* • Don Haggerty *Ralph Hamilton* • Phyllis Coates *Janice Hamilton* • Bing Russell *Douglas Hamilton* • Paul Brinegar *Tom Jeffrey* • Hal K Dawson *George Jeffrey* • Duane Grey *Aruzza* ■ *Dir* Charles Marquis Warren • *Scr* Eric Norden, Endre Bohem, from a story by Daniel B Ullman

Cattle King ★★ U
Western　　　　1963 · US · Colour · 89min

Robert Taylor drifts through this B-western, which tells an all-too-familiar story of Wyoming settlers who want to fence in their land and evil ranchers who think their cows should roam free. Guns come out, cattle stampede, and the dispute goes all the way to the president. AT

Robert Taylor (1) *Sam Brassfield* • Joan Caulfield *Sharleen Travers* • Robert Loggia *Johnny Quatro* • Robert Middleton *Clay Mathews* ■ *Dir* Tay Garnett • *Scr* Thomas Thompson

Cattle Queen of Montana ★★★ PG
Western　　　　1954 · US · Colour · 84min

Barbara Stanwyck stars as a gun-toting pioneer, determined to make a success of her Montana ranch after her father is killed by native Americans. Aided by thoughtful direction from the prolific and talented Allan Dwan, this low-budget western now has great curiosity value, in that the leading man is former US president Ronald Reagan, a bland performer when pitted against screen villains Gene Evans and Jack Elam. The location scenery is very attractive, the action sequences well-staged, and Stanwyck as tough as ever. TS

Barbara Stanwyck *Sierra Nevada Jones* • Ronald Reagan *Farrell* • Gene Evans *Tom McCord* • Lance Fuller *Colorados* • Anthony Caruso *Natchakoa* • Jack Elam *Yost* • Yvette Dugay *Starfire* • Morris Ankrum *JI "Pop" Jones* • Chubby Johnson *Nat* ■ *Dir* Allan Dwan • *Scr* Robert Blees, Howard Estabrook, from a story by Thomas Blackburn

Catwoman ★★ 12
Fantasy action adventure
2004 · US/Aus · Colour · 99min

Director Pitof's lame fantasy action adventure is a spin-off from the *Batman* franchise in name only. Halle Berry gives an uneven performance as scatty artist Patience Phillips, who's revived by a mystical cat after being murdered to become the eponymous superheroine. Using her new-found skills, Berry sets about uncovering a plot to flood the world with a toxic face cream, a scheme fronted by the excellent Sharon Stone. A romantic subplot involving sexy policeman Benjamin Bratt serves only to muddy the main story, while the special effects are poor. KK Violence, sexual references. *DVD*

Halle Berry *Patience Phillips/Catwoman* • Benjamin Bratt *Tom Lone* • Lambert Wilson *George Hedare* • Frances Conroy *Ophelia Powers* • Sharon Stone *Laurel Hedare* • Alex Borstein *Sally* • John Cassini *Graphologist* ■ *Dir* Pitof • *Scr* John Brancato, Michael Ferris, John Rogers, from a story by Theresa Rebeck, Michael Ferris, John Brancato, from the character created by Bob Kane

Caught ★★ U
Romantic melodrama　1949 · US · BW · 84min

In this trite soap opera, the attractive wife (Barbara Bel Geddes) of a neurotic and unpleasant millionaire (Robert Ryan) falls in love with an idealistic doctor (James Mason). The only surprise in this romantic melodrama is that it is directed by the distinguished Max Ophüls, whose expertise and commitment bring some texture and gloss to the dour proceedings. The film marked Mason's Hollywood debut. RK *DVD*

James Mason *Larry Quinada* • Barbara Bel Geddes *Leonora Eames* • Robert Ryan *Smith Ohlrig* • Ruth Brady *Maxine* • Curt Bois *Franzi* • Frank Ferguson *Dr Hoffman* • Natalie Schafer *Dorothy Dale* • Art Smith *Psychiatrist* • Sonia Darrin *Miss Chambers* ■ *Dir* Max Ophüls • *Scr* Arthur Laurents, from the novel *Wild Calendar* by Libbie Bloch

Caught ★★★ 18
Drama　　　　1996 · US · Colour · 105min

This menacing adult drama is bolstered by fine performances. Edward James Olmos plays a New Jersey fish merchant who takes drifter Arie Verveen under his wing, only for the kid to strike up a steamy affair with his wife (Maria Conchita Alonso). Trouble brews when the couple's shifty son (Steven Schub) returns home and smells something fishy. It all ends in tears. DA

Edward James Olmos *Joe* • Maria Conchita Alonso *Betty* • Arie Verveen *Nick* • Steven Schub *Danny* • Bitty Schram *Amy* ■ *Dir* Robert M Young • *Scr* Edward Pomerantz

Cauldron of Blood ★ 15
Horror　　　　1967 · US/Sp · Colour · 94min

Boris Karloff plays a blind sculptor using real human bones in his statues, courtesy of his psychopathic spouse, who kills people and dumps them in an acid bath in the basement. Filmed in 1967 but not released until 1971, two years after the star's death, this co-production offers grisly tedium and few chills. RS Spanish dubbed.

Jean-Pierre Aumont *Claude Marchand* • Boris Karloff *Franz Badulescu* • Viveca Lindfors *Tania Badulescu* • Jacqui Speed *Pilar* • Rosenda Monteros *Valerie* • Ruben Rojo *Lover* ■ *Dir* Edward Mann [Santos Alcocer] • *Scr* John Melson, Jose Luis Bayonas, Edward Mann, from a story by Edward Mann

Cause for Alarm ★★★
Film noir　　　　1951 · US · BW · 73min

This *film noir* has a blacker shade than usual, as finger-fluttering, saucer-eyed Loretta Young tries to retrieve a letter sent by her bedridden husband before his death that blames her for his demise. Director Tay Garnett may have been an MGM hack, but, despite some risibly optimistic touches, his craftsmanship is very evident. TH

Loretta Young *Ellen Jones* • Barry Sullivan *George Z Jones* • Bruce Cowling *Dr Grahame* • Margalo Gillmore *Mrs Edwards* • Bradley Mora *Billy* • Irving Bacon *Carston* • Georgia Backus *Mrs Warren* • Don Haggerty *Russell* ■ *Dir* Tay Garnett • *Scr* Tom Lewis, Mel Dinelli, from a story by Larry Marcus

Cavalcade ★★★ U
Historical drama　　1933 · US · BW · 111min

Noël Coward uses a well-to-do family as a microcosm in this look at British life down the years, from the Boer War to the Great Depression. Critics at the time loved this rather sanctimonious jaunt through history. Seen from the vantage point of post-Second World War egalitarianism, however, it all appears quaint and riddled with accepted class differences. While Coward, via director Frank Lloyd, pulls out all the stops, a modern audience will remain resolutely dry-eyed. SH

Diana Wynyard *Jane Marryot* • Clive Brook *Robert Marryot* • Herbert Mundin *Alfred Bridges* • Una O'Connor *Ellen Bridges* • Ursula Jeans *Fanny Bridges* • Beryl Mercer *Cook* ■ *Dir* Frank Lloyd • *Scr* Reginald Berkeley, from the play by Noël Coward

Cavalry Scout ★★ U
Western　　　　1951 · US · Colour · 77min

This minor western, photographed in the elementary Cinecolor process, centres around the efforts of an army scout (granite-faced Rod Cameron) to prevent stolen Gatling guns from falling into the hands of hostile Indians. Audrey Long is the trader whose wagons are being surreptitiously used to transport weapons by villain James Millican. AE

Rod Cameron *Kirby Frye* • Audrey Long *Claire* • Jim Davis (1) *Lt Spaulding* • James Millican *Martin Gavin* • James Arness *Barth* • John Doucette *Varney* • William Phillips [William "Bill"] *Phillips* • *Sgt Wilkins* • Stephen Chase (1) *Col Drumm* • Rory Mallinson *Corporal* ■ *Dir* Lesley Selander • *Scr* Dan Ullman [Daniel B Ullman], Thomas Blackburn

The Cave ★★ 12
Horror action thriller
2005 · US · Colour · 93min

When a group of cave divers explore an uncharted area in the Carpathian mountains, they are trapped by an underwater cave-in and soon become the prey of a pack of bloodthirsty creatures. There's little originality in director Bruce Hunt's visual arsenal, although the underwater photography is decent enough, but this is formulaic and chill-free. AJ *DVD*

Cole Hauser *Jack* • Eddie Cibrian *Tyler* • Morris Chestnut *Top Buchanan* • Lena Headey *Kathryn* • Piper Perabo *Charlie* • Rick Ravanello *Philip Briggs* • Marcel Iures *Dr Nicolai* • Daniel Dae Kim *Alex Kim* • Kieran Darcy-Smith *Vince Strode* ■ *Dir* Bruce Hunt • *Scr* Michael Steinberg, Tegan West

Cave of Forgotten Dreams ★★★★ U
Documentary
2010 · Fr/Can/US/UK/Ger · Colour · 90min

After travelling to the Arctic for 2007's *Encounters at the End of the World*, Werner Herzog continues to document the world of wonder with this fascinating look at the Chauvet-Pont-d'Arc caves. In 1994, a trio of cavers inched their way through a small opening high on a rock face in the French Ardèche and discovered vast caverns filled with stunning Paleolithic art. Herzog is the first film-maker to be allowed inside and reveals this ancient equivalent to the Sistine Chapel in all its incredible, vivid glory. The undoubted highlight is an extended sequence in which, using the bare minimum of equipment, he brings the paintings to life using shadows, camera movement and Ernst Reijseger's haunting score. AS English, German +subtitles. *DVD* Blu-ray 3D

Werner Herzog ■ *Dir* Werner Herzog • *Cinematographer* Peter Zeitlinger • *Music* Ernst Reijseger

Cave of Outlaws ★★ U
Western　　　　1951 · US · Colour · 75min

Long before William Castle hit his stride as the maker of gimmick horror films and producer of the classic *Rosemary's Baby*, he cut his teeth directing B-features, invariably minor swashbucklers or routine westerns. Here, a bland MacDonald Carey stars as the robber released from prison who decides to go back for the hidden loot. The only distinction is the location filming at New Mexico's Carlsbad Caverns where the climactic shoot-out takes place. TS

Macdonald Carey *Pete Carver* • Alexis Smith *Liz Trent* • Edgar Buchanan *Dobbs* • Victor Jory *Ben Cross* • Hugh O'Brian *Garth* ■ *Dir* William Castle • *Scr* Elizabeth Wilson

Cave of the Yellow Dog ★★★★ U
Drama　　　　2005 · Ger · Colour · 93min

Byambasuren Davaa's follow-up to the Oscar-nominated *The Story of the Weeping Camel* chronicles a Mongolian girl's determination to keep her adopted pet, even though her nomadic shepherd father is convinced it will pester his livestock. Told with touching simplicity against the stunning steppe backdrops, this is not only an enchanting fable, but also provides an enthralling insight into the everyday existence of the Batchuluun family, who play their parts with an earnest naturalism that only adds to the fascination. Six year-old Nansal is particularly impressive, whether she's riding a horse at the head of the flock or defying her parents with a michievous spirit. This may be anthropology "lite", but it more than atones in genial humanity. DP Mongolian +subtitles. *DVD*

■ *Dir* Byambasuren Davaa • *Scr* Byambasuren Davaa, inspired by a story by Gantuya Lhagva

Caveman ★★★ PG
Comedy adventure 1981 · US · Colour · 87min

Ringo Starr is perfectly cast as a hapless cave-dweller in an endearingly stupid prehistoric romp that introduced a couple of future stars to the world. The former Beatle is a caveman drummed out of his tribe for making eyes at the chief's woman (played by his real-life wife Barbara Bach). So he teams up with fellow misfits Shelley Long and Dennis Quaid to advance man's evolution. The result is dumb slapstick fun. JF *DVD*

Ringo Starr *Atouk* • Dennis Quaid *Lar* • Shelley Long *Tala* • Barbara Bach *Lana* • John Matuszak *Tonda* • Avery Schreiber *Ock* • Jack Gilford *Gog* • Cork Hubbert *Ta* ■ *Dir* Carl Gottlieb • *Scr* Carl Gottlieb, Rudy DeLuca

Cecil B Demented ★★★ 18
Satirical comedy 2000 · US · Colour · 84min

This is a maliciously witty, if disjointed, Hollywood satire from John Waters. Stephen Dorff plays the lunatic film-maker of the title, who kidnaps pampered, petulant star Melanie Griffith and forces her into headlining his underground art film, which uses the "ultimate reality" of real people and real terror. Waters's Tinseltown put-down sends up everything from industry protocol and recent hits to porno movies and celebrity gossip. The problem is that the movie revels in its plethora of in-jokes at the expense of entertaining its audience. AJ *DVD*

Stephen Dorff *Cecil B Demented* • Melanie Griffith *Honey Whitlock* • Alicia Witt *Cherish* • Adrian Grenier *Lyle* • Larry Gilliard Jr *Lewis* • Maggie Gyllenhaal *Raven* • Jack Noseworthy *Rodney* • Mike Shannon [Michael Shannon] *Petie* ■ *Dir/Scr* John Waters (2)

Cedar Rapids ★★★★ 15
Comedy 2011 · US · Colour · 83min

This superb comedy stars Ed Helms as a naive and homely insurance agent despatched to a cut-throat sales convention in the Iowa city that gives the film its name. Away from his comfort zone for the first time, he falls in with a wild crowd that includes boorish John C Reilly and flighty good-time gal Anne Heche, and their escalating stunts and japes threaten to derail his company's goal of picking up a prestigious award for a fourth straight year. *The Hangover* star Helms never strays too far from the nerdy but good-hearted salesman he plays in the US version of *The Office*, but Reilly as the fouled-mouthed veteran steals all his scenes with a master class in vulgarity. TeS Swearing, sexual references, drug abuse. *DVD* *BL*

Ed Helms *Tim Lippe* • John C Reilly *Dean Ziegler* • Anne Heche *Joan Ostrowski-Fox* • Isiah Whitlock Jr *Ronald Wilkes* • Stephen Root *Bill Krogstad* • Kurtwood Smith *Orin Helgesson* • Alia Shawkat *Bree* • Sigourney Weaver *Macy Vanderhei* ■ *Dir* Miguel Arteta • *Scr* Phil Johnston

Ceiling Zero ★★★
Adventure 1935 · US · BW · 95min

Director and erstwhile pilot Howard Hawks proved the ideal guiding hand for this version of flying expert and author Frank "Spig" Wead's Broadway play. Though most of the activity takes place on the ground in the office of a commercial airline, the incidents and tensions never let up. However, despite a terrific performance from James Cagney as the daredevil pilot and knockout verbal sparring with Pat O'Brien, the movie creaks a bit today, with phoney back projection sky sequences and poor model shots. TS

James Cagney *Dizzy Davis* • Pat O'Brien *Jack Lee* • June Travis *Tommy Thomas* • Stuart Erwin *Texas Clark* • Henry Wadsworth *Tay Lawson* • Isabel Jewell *Lou Clark* • Barton MacLane *Al Stone* ■ *Dir* Howard Hawks • *Scr* Frank Wead, from his play

Celà S'Appelle l'Aurore ★★
Drama 1956 · Fr/It · BW · 102min

Luis Buñuel adapted an Emmanuel Roblès novel for his first film in Europe after 23 years of exile, setting it in Corsica and casting the implacable and uncharismatic Georges Marchal as a doctor who falls in love with widow Lucia Bosé in his wife's absence. Essentially a melodrama whose level is raised by the director's unmistakeable social consciousness, the film is solidly assembled, but minor. RB In French.

Georges Marchal *Doctor Valerio* • Lucia Bosé *Clara* • Gianni Esposito *Sandro* • Julien Bertheau *Fasaro* • Nelly Borgeaud *Angela* • Jean-Jacques Delbo *Gorzone* ■ *Dir* Luis Buñuel • *Scr* Jean Ferry, Luis Buñuel, from a novel by Emmanuel Roblès

Celebrity ★★★ 15
Comedy drama 1998 · US · BW · 113min

After having his private life splashed all over the tabloids, writer/director Woody Allen uses his own cameras to probe the nature of celebrity. Kenneth Branagh steps up to play the Allen-esque "Ordinary Joe" who finds himself mixing with supermodels (Charlize Theron), spoiled stars (Leonardo DiCaprio) and oversexed actresses (Melanie Griffith), while his ex-wife (Judy Davis) tries to find her own identity as a TV presenter. While not vintage Allen, this amusement has some choice moments. JB Drug abuse, swearing. *DVD*

Hank Azaria *David* • Kenneth Branagh *Lee Simon* • Joe Mantegna *Tony Gardella* • Judy Davis *Robin Simon* • Winona Ryder *Nola* • Leonardo DiCaprio *Brandon Darrow* • Famke Janssen *Bonnie* • Melanie Griffith *Nicole Oliver* • Charlize Theron *Supermodel* • Bebe Neuwirth *Hooker* ■ *Dir/Scr* Woody Allen

Celeste & Jesse Forever ★★★ 15
Comedy drama 2012 · US · Colour · 92min

There are countless films about falling in love, but this smart and bittersweet movie is one of the few about falling out of it. Rashida Jones and Andy Samberg play driven trend-spotter Celeste and surfing slacker Jesse. These former high-school sweethearts are now 30-ish and married, but heading for divorce. It seems like the perfect break-up, though: they're still best buddies and they hang out together. Then Jesse gets involved with another woman, and everything changes. Celeste and Jesse aren't the most likeable of characters and the pacing is a little sluggish at times, but a healthy dose of wit and insight compensate for the film's flaws. DA Swearing, sexual references, drug abuse.

Rashida Jones *Celeste* • Andy Samberg *Jesse* • Chris Messina *Paul* • Ari Graynor *Beth* • Emma Roberts *Riley* • Elijah Wood *Scott* ■ *Dir* Lee Toland Krieger • *Scr* Rashida Jones, Will McCormack

Celia ★★★★ 15
Period drama 1988 · Aus · Colour · 98min

The innocence and dark horrors of childhood have rarely been better portrayed than in this bewitching, often disturbing Australian drama. Set in the dull suburban Melbourne of the 1950s, Ann Turner's striking directorial debut focuses on a nine-year-old girl (a startlingly good performance by Rebecca Smart), whose confusion and resentment over adult behaviour sees her slip into a fantasy world, with tragic consequences. Turner beautifully captures the stuffy conservatism of the period, as well as the sheer wonder of growing up in what is, to a young child, a very strange world. JF *DVD*

Rebecca Smart *Celia Carmichael* • Nicholas Eadie *Ray Carmichael* • Mary-Anne Fahey *Pat Carmichael* • Margaret Ricketts *Granny* • Victoria Longley *Alice Tanner* • Alexander Hutchinson *Steve Tanner* ■ *Dir/Scr* Ann Turner

Celine and Julie Go Boating ★★★★★ 15
Experimental supernatural drama 1974 · Fr · Colour · 185min

Inspired by two Henry James stories and intended as a homage to Lewis Carroll and Jean Cocteau, this astonishing film alludes to so many writers, artists and film-makers that it's impossible to begin listing them. Constantly blurring the line between fantasy and reality, Jacques Rivette dazzles us with his control and inventiion, as magician Juliet Berto takes librarian Dominique Labourier on a series of adventures around a mysterious town house inhabited by the equally fantastic Bulle Ogier and Marie-France Pisier. DP French +subtitles. *DVD*

Juliet Berto *Celine* • Dominique Labourier *Julie* • Bulle Ogier *Camille* • Marie-France Pisier *Sophie* • Barbet Schroeder *Olivier* • Philippe Clevenot *Guilou* • Nathalie Asnar *Madlyn* • Marie-Therese Saussure *Poupie* ■ *Dir* Jacques Rivette • *Scr* Eduardo de Gregorio, Juliet Berto, Dominique Labourier, Bulle Ogier, Marie-France Pisier, Jacques Rivette, from stories by Henry James

The Cell ★★★ 18
Psychological horror thriller 2000 · US/Ger · Colour · 104min

Music-video maestro Tarsem Singh makes a visually audacious debut with this sci-fi hybrid. Psychotherapist Jennifer Lopez employs cutting-edge brain-jaunting technology to enter the subconscious of comatose serial killer Vincent D'Onofrio and help rescue his latest victim. Singh reinforces his credentials as a magpie imagist, employing a barrage of digital trickery to conjure up the nightmarish mindscape of a psychopath. His grasp of plotting and pacing is less assured. DP Sex scenes, violence, swearing, nudity. *DVD*

Jennifer Lopez *Catherine Deane* • Vince Vaughn *Agent Peter Novak* • Vincent D'Onofrio *Carl Stargher* • Marianne Jean-Baptiste *Dr Miriam Kent* ■ *Dir* Tarsem Singh • *Scr* Mark Protosevich

Cell ★★★ 15
Science-fiction horror thriller 2016 · US · Colour · 97min

Based on the Stephen King book, *Cell* starts out like yet another zombie movie, though with its mindless mayhem triggered not by the usual global pandemic, but by a mysterious cellphone signal. There's nothing wrong with a film that makes your brain hurt a bit. But this, to which John Cusack and Samuel L Jackson bring their middling star power, is a touch too enigmatic for its own good. DA

Samuel L Jackson *Tom McCourt* • John Cusack *Clay Riddell* • Isabelle Fuhrman *Alice Naxwell* • Stacy Keach *Charles Ardai* ■ *Dir* Tod Williams • *Scr* Adam Alleca, Stephen King, from King's novel

Cell 211 ★★★ 18
Action drama 2009 · Sp/Fr · Colour · 107min

A rookie guard is forced to impersonate an inmate when a prison riot breaks out during his introductory tour, in director Daniel Monzón's award-winning Spanish thriller. The film is shot in a documentary-style that's enhanced by using actual convicts as extras. But the solid opening soon loses focus as personal back-stories, political machinations and double-crosses are introduced. These twists do add some surprises to the slick proceedings, but they also lessen the gripping tension that was so well established at the outset. AJ Spanish, Basque, English +subtitles. Violence. *DVD* *BL*

Luis Tosar *Malamadre* • Alberto Ammann *Juan Oliver* • Antonio Resines *José Utrilla* • Mañuel Morón *Ernesto Almansa* • Carlos Bardem *Apache* ■ *Dir* Daniel Monzón • *Scr* Jorge Guerricaechevarría, Daniel Monzón, from the novel *Celda 211* by Francisco Pérez Gandul

Cellular ★★ 15
Action thriller 2004 · US/Ger · Colour · 90min

This blackly comic action thriller is never quite as tense as it should be. The opening scenes are gripping, with science teacher

and mother Kim Basinger the victim of a brutal kidnapping. Young slacker Chris Evans races to save her after she randomly calls his mobile using the remains of a shattered phone. However, Basinger's chief abductor, Jason Statham, is too weak a villain for us to ever believe she's in real jeopardy. SF Violence, swearing. *DVD*

Kim Basinger *Jessica Martin* • Chris Evans *Ryan* • William H Macy *Mooney* • Eric Christian Olsen *Chad* • Jessica Biel *Chloe* • Jason Statham *Ethan* • Brendan Kelly *Mad Dog* • Richard Burgi *Craig Martin* ■ *Dir* David R Ellis • *Scr* Chris Morgan, from a story by Larry Cohen

The Celluloid Closet ★★★★★ 15
Documentary 1995 · US · Colour and BW · 101min

How gays and lesbians have fared on the big screen is the subject of this hilarious and poignant documentary. Narrated by Lily Tomlin and featuring candid interviews with Gore Vidal, Susan Sarandon and Shirley MacLaine, to name just a few, this is both a history of homosexual images and a damning indictment of the cavalier way Hollywood has shaped views on sexuality. But mostly it's a feast for cinephiles with more than a hundred clips from early Thomas Edison shorts to *Philadelphia*, assembled with wit, care and precision to illustrate a spicy and thought-provoking study. AJ

Lily Tomlin *Narrator* • Quentin Crisp • Tony Curtis • Harvey Fierstein • Whoopi Goldberg • Shirley MacLaine • Susan Sarandon • John Schlesinger ■ *Dir* Rob Epstein, Jeffrey Friedman • *Scr* Armistead Maupin, from a story by Rob Epstein, Jeffrey Friedman, Sharon Wood, Vito Russo

Celtic Pride ★★★ 12
Sports comedy 1996 · US · Colour · 86min

This sports comedy stars Daniel Stern and Dan Aykroyd as die-hard fans of the Boston Celtics basketball team. Starting out with some fairly astute knocks at the superstitions that fans have about their teams, director Tom DeCerchio becomes a bit heavy-handed once Stern and Aykroyd have kidnapped the arrogant star (played by Daman Wayans) of their arch-rivals. The three leads make it a watchable, if not rib-tickling, experience. JF Swearing. *DVD*

Damon Wayans *Lewis Scott* • Daniel Stern *Mike O'Hara* • Dan Aykroyd *Jimmy Flaherty* • Gail O'Grady *Carol* • Adam Hendershott *Tommy* • Paul Guilfoyle (2) *Kevin O'Grady* ■ *Dir* Tom DeCerchio • *Scr* Judd Apatow, from a story by Colin Quinn, Judd Apatow

Celui Qui Doit Mourir ★★
Political religious drama 1957 · Fr/It · BW · 126min

The radical Jules Dassin directs this sturdy version of the Nikos Kazantzakis novel, filmed on the island of Crete in visually arresting black-and-white CinemaScope. It tells of Greek villagers, under Turkish rule in 1921, who are rehearsing a Passion Play. Nearby compatriots plead for help when attacked by Turks but are refused, until the player Christ intervenes. Though well meaning, this is probably too wordy and pretentious for modern audiences. BB French +subtitles.

Jean Servais *Fotis, the Pope* • Carl Mohner *Lukas* • Grégoire Aslan *Agha* • Gert Froebe [Gert Fröbe] *Patriarchéas, lord of the village* • Teddy Bilis *Hadji Nikolis, the schoolteacher* ■ *Dir* Jules Dassin • *Scr* Ben Barzman, Jules Dassin, André Obey, from the novel *Le Christ Recrucifié* by Nikos Kazantzakis • *Cinematographer* Jacques Natteau

The Cement Garden ★★★★ 18
Drama 1992 · Ger/Fr/UK · Colour · 100min

This is one of the few films based on Ian McEwan's psychologically complex novels that actually works, thanks to some outstanding acting and a script from director Andrew Birkin that sticks closely to its source material. This disturbing story is about children and their reactions to death and loss, and it refuses to conform to any cosy notion of grief. As such, with its central theme about sexual desire and incest, it

makes for uncomfortable, intellectually challenging viewing. **SH** Swearing, a sex scene, nudity. *DVD*
Andrew Robertson *Jack* • Charlotte Gainsbourg *Julie* • Sinead Cusack *Mother* • Alice Coulthard *Sue* • Ned Birkin *Tom* • Hanns Zischler *Father* • Jochen Horst *Derek* ■ *Dir* Andrew Birkin • *Scr* Andrew Birkin, from the novel by Ian McEwan

The Cemetery Club ★★★ 15
Comedy drama   1993 · US · Colour · 106min
Bill Duke directs this gentle comedy drama, which scores highly by having three fine actresses top the bill. Ellen Burstyn, Diane Ladd and Olympia Dukakis play Pittsburgh widows who meet up, chat and help each other cope with their problems. At times, however, Duke's film looks like the pilot for a TV series, while some viewers may feel it betrays its stage origins. **AT** Swearing. *DVD*
Ellen Burstyn *Esther Moskowitz* • Olympia Dukakis *Doris Silverman* • Diane Ladd *Lucille Rubin* • Danny Aiello *Ben Katz* • Christina Ricci *Jessica* • Bernie Casey *John* • Wallace Shawn *Larry* ■ *Dir* Bill Duke • *Scr* Ivan Menchell, from the play by Ivan Menchell

Cemetery Junction ★★★ 15
Comedy drama   2010 · UK · Colour · 90min
The Invention of Lying – the first directorial effort from Ricky Gervais – was a critical and commercial flop. For his second effort, Gervais has wisely taken on both screenwriting and directing duties alongside his long-time collaborator (and co-creator of *The Office*) Stephen Merchant. Set in a nicely re-created Reading of the 1970s, it features a trio of young friends (played by relative unknowns Christian Cooke, Tom Hughes and Jack Doolan) all on the brink of their first jobs, first loves and, at some point, preferably getting the hell out of town. The result is a charming and sweet-natured English take on American coming-of-age movies like *American Graffiti* that's deftly written, unobtrusively directed and nicely acted. **AS** Swearing, sexual references. *DVD* *BL*
Christian Cooke *Freddie Taylor* • Felicity Jones *Julie Kendrick* • Tom Hughes *Bruce Pearson* • Jack Doolan *Snork* • Emily Watson *Mrs Kendrick* • Matthew Goode *Mike Ramsay* • Ralph Fiennes *Mr Kendrick* • Ricky Gervais *Mr Taylor* • Julia Davis *Mrs Taylor* ■ *Dir/Scr* Ricky Gervais, Stephen Merchant

Cemetery Man ★★★★ 18
Horror   1994 · It/Fr · Colour · 98min
This highly acclaimed Italian horror masterpiece dwells on the more metaphysical elements of the genre. Graveyard undertaker Rupert Everett is seduced by zombie Anna Falchi and embarks on a crusade against the living. Beautifully directed by Michele Soavi with wit, style and emotional substance, Everett gives a bravura central performance in a unique original bursting with both gore and brains. Soavi's sophisticated shocker is a mordant delight. **AJ** Italian dubbed. *DVD*
Rupert Everett *Francesco Dellamorte* • François Hadji-Lazaro *Gnaghi* • Anna Falchi *She* • Stefano Masciarelli *Mayor* • Mickey Knox *Marshall Straniero* ■ *Dir* Michele Soavi • *Scr* Gianni Romoli, from the novel *Dellamorte Dellamore* by Tiziano Sclavi

Cemetery of Splendour ★★★★ 12A
Fantasy
2015 · Thai/UK/Fr/Ger/Mal/S Kor/Mex/US/Nor/Neth/HK · Colour · 120min
Echoes of Apichatpong Weerasethakul's previous films (*Uncle Boonmee Who Can Recall His Past Lives* won the Palme D'Or at Cannes) reverberate around this languid meditation on spirits, deities, memory, patriotism and mortality. At the core is the relationship between Banlop Lomnoi, a soldier suffering from a mysterious sleeping sickness, and disabled volunteer Jenjira Pongpas Widner, who communicates with her patient through a medium. The measured action is dotted with moments of quirky humour, making this distinctive blend of lyricism and mysticism quite an

experience. **DP** Thai +subtitles. Some violence.
Jenjira Pongpas Widner [Jenjira Pongpass] *Jenjira* • Banlop Lomnoi *Itt* • Jarinpattra Rueangram *Keng* • Petcharat Chaiburi *Nurse Tet* ■ *Dir/Scr* Apichatpong Weerasethakul

Les Cent et Une Nuits ★★★
Documentary   1995 · Fr/UK · Colour · 125min
Produced to celebrate the centenary of cinema, Agnès Varda's quirky history of the medium demonstrates that her approach to the moving image is just as lively as it was when she launched the *nouvelle vague* with the short *La Pointe Courte* in 1954. The veritable who's who of international stars proves the esteem in which she's held. She even ropes in Michel Piccoli to play Simon Cinéma, the archivist who guides student Julie Gayet through his collection of clips and memorabilia. Highly personal, entirely accessible and most enjoyable. **DP** French +subtitles.
Michel Piccoli *Simon Cinéma* • Marcello Mastroianni *The Italian friend* • Henri Garcin *Firmin, the butler* • Julie Gayet *Camille* • Mathieu Demy *Mica* • Emmanuel Salinger *Vincent* ■ *Dir/Scr* Agnès Varda

Centennial Summer ★★★ U
Period musical   1946 · US · Colour · 102min
This nostalgic musical is set in Philadelphia in 1876, where the Great Exposition is a cause for excitement. Jeanne Crain and Linda Darnell star as sisters whose relationship suffers when they both take a fancy to dashing Frenchman Cornel Wilde. Veterans Dorothy Gish and Walter Brennan play the girls' parents, but the real star of Otto Preminger's undemanding trifle is the music, composed by Jerome Kern shortly before his death. **RK**
Jeanne Crain *Julia* • Cornel Wilde *Philippe Lascalles* • Linda Darnell *Edith Rogers* • William Eythe *Benjamin Franklin Phelps* • Walter Brennan *Jesse Rogers* • Constance Bennett *Zenia Lascalles* • Dorothy Gish *Harriet Rogers* ■ *Dir* Otto Preminger • *Scr* Michael Kanin, from the novel by Albert E Idell

The Center of the World ★★ 18
Erotic drama   2001 · US · Colour · 84min
It's a sad fact that the naturalism and intimacy of the digital video format encourages directors to focus on "breaking down the barriers" at the expense of actual storytelling. Wayne Wang's disappointing character study is a case in point: it's an inert, lifeless exploration of the Las Vegas weekend shared by rich but lonely computer mogul Peter Sarsgaard and the uninhibited stripper Molly Parker he pays to "entertain" him. Despite the film's candour, the attempt at psychological depth feels as fake and contrived as Vegas itself. **JC** *DVD*
Peter Sarsgaard *Richard Longman* • Molly Parker *Florence* • Mel Gorham *Roxanne* • Jason McCabe *Calacanis* • Carla Gugino *Jerri* • Balthazar Getty *Brian Pivano* • Pat Morita *Taxi driver* ■ *Dir* Wayne Wang • *Scr* Ellen Benjamin Wong [Wayne Wang, Paul Auster, Siri Hustvedt], from a story by Wayne Wang, Miranda July, Paul Auster, Siri Hustvedt

Center Stage ★ 12
Drama   2000 · US · Colour · 110min
Idealistic Amanda Schull gets accepted into a top New York ballet school, finds it tougher than expected, and becomes romantic focus for resident hunk Ethan Stiefel and boring but true Sascha Radetsky. The tedious sub-*Fame* proceedings aren't helped by a teeth-grindingly bad script, wooden performances and hilarious dance numbers. **JB** *DVD*
Amanda Schull *Jody* • Zoe Saldana [Zoë Saldana] *Eva* • Susan May Pratt *Maureen* • Peter Gallagher *Jonathan* • Donna Murphy *Juliette* • Debra Monk *Nancy* • Ethan Stiefel *Cooper* • Sascha Radetsky *Charlie* ■ *Dir* Nicholas Hytner • *Scr* Carol Heikkinen • *Cinematographer* Geoffrey Simpson

Central Airport ★ U
Adventure   1933 · US · BW · 74min
This tedious airborne romance finds pilot Richard Barthelmess jilted by parachutist Sally Eilers when she marries his brother Tom Brown instead. This never gets off the ground. Blame the script, not to mention the papier-mâché planes. **AT**
Richard Barthelmess *Jim* • Tom Brown *Neil* • Sally Eilers *Jill* • Grant Mitchell *Mr Blaine* • James Murray (1) *Eddie* ■ *Dir* William A Wellman • *Scr* Rian James, from a story by Jack Moffitt, James Seymour

Central Intelligence ★★★ 12A
Comedy adventure   2016 · US · Colour · 107min
Kevin Hart plays an accountant who's lured into an international spy mission by a former classmate and then social outcast (Dwayne Johnson) now working for the CIA. The film will be wholly familiar to fans of Hart's work, as he once again plays the fast-talking comedy whirlwind who's in over his head. But of Hart's many action comedies, this is one of the more enjoyable thanks to the entertaining star collaboration and a heartfelt anti-bullying message. **JL** Violence, some swearing.
Dwayne Johnson *Bob Stone/Robbie Weirdicht* • Kevin Hart *Calvin Joyner* • Amy Ryan *Agent Pamela Harris* • Danielle Nicolet *Maggie* • Jason Bateman *Trevor* ■ *Dir* Rawson Marshall Thurber • *Scr* Ike Barinholtz, David Stassen, Rawson Marshall Thurber, from a story by Barinholtz, Stassen

Central Station ★★★★ 15
Drama   1998 · Bra/Fr/Sp/Jpn · Colour · 105min
This captivating Brazilian road movie picked up awards all around the world, as well as a deserved Oscar nomination for 69-year-old actress Fernanda Montenegro. Initially shown as selfish and uncaring, her character's gradual softening as she accompanies young Vinicius de Oliveira on a quest to find his dad makes for compelling viewing. Director Walter Salles's filming of their journey of discovery stunningly captures an unglamorous land, seen from the perspective of two travellers whose final destination is far from certain. **JC** Portuguese +subtitles. Some swearing. *DVD*
Fernanda Montenegro *Dora* • Marilia Pêra *Irene* • Vinicius de Oliveira *Josue* • Sôia Lira *Ana* • Othon Bastos *César* ■ *Dir* Walter Salles • *Scr* João Emanuel Carneiro, Marcos Bernstein, from an idea by Walter Salles

Centurion ★★ 15
Period action drama
2009 · UK/US/Fr · Colour · 93min
Writer/director Neil Marshall examines the fate of Rome's legendary Ninth Legion in this dull take on the myth. In Britain in AD 117, they are sent to vanquish the Picts, only to face a sustained onslaught under the command of the mute Etain (Bond girl Olga Kurylenko). Hero Quintus (a weak Michael Fassbender) and his fast-diminishing platoon must then evade capture as they race for the Roman frontier. Marshall takes the survival template from his previous films, but fails to invest his core characters with any personality, so who lives or dies becomes immaterial. It's technically impressive and has an epic sweep, but the lack of emotional involvement makes this little more than a chase movie in ancient garb. **AJ** English, Scottish Gaelic +subtitles. Violence, swearing, sexual references. *DVD* *BL*
Michael Fassbender *Centurion Quintus Dias* • Dominic West *General Titus Flavius Virilus* • Olga Kurylenko *Etain* • Noel Clarke *Macros* • Liam Cunningham *Brick* • David Morrissey *Bothos* • Riz Ahmed [Rizwan Ahmed] *Tarak* • JJ Feild *Thax* ■ *Dir/Scr* Neil Marshall

Century ★★★ 15
Period drama   1993 · UK · Colour · 107min
Stephen Poliakoff takes an absorbing look at a frantic culture in the midst of technological advancement and uncertainty about the future. Clive Owen is the hot-

headed medical researcher on the loose in late-Victorian London who exposes the dubious practices of eminent professor Charles Dance. Robert Stephens steals the sumptuously mounted show as Owen's eccentric Romanian father and brings a welcome touch of humour to what many will find a rather arch conceit. **AJ** Some nudity.
Charles Dance *Professor Mandry* • Clive Owen *Paul Reisner* • Miranda Richardson *Clara* • Robert Stephens *Mr Reisner* • Joan Hickson *Mrs Whiteweather* • Lena Headey *Miriam* ■ *Dir/Scr* Stephen Poliakoff

La Cérémonie ★★★★ 15
Thriller   1995 · Fr · Colour · 107min
Two of France's greatest current female stars, Sandrine Bonnaire and Isabelle Huppert, help make director Claude Chabrol's adaptation of British thriller writer Ruth Rendell's novel *A Judgement in Stone* an authentically chilling account of the way the French middle class brings ruin upon itself. Bonnaire is the new housekeeper, hired by a sweet-natured but condescending Breton family, whose relationship with envious postmistress Huppert results in a shocking finale. **TH** French +subtitles. Violence, swearing. *DVD*
Sandrine Bonnaire *Sophie* • Isabelle Huppert *Jeanne* • Jacqueline Bisset *Catherine* • Jean-Pierre Cassel *Georges* • Virginie Ledoyen *Melinda* ■ *Dir* Claude Chabrol • *Scr* Claude Chabrol, Caroline Eliacheff, from the novel *A Judgement in Stone* by Ruth Rendell

The Ceremony ★★
Crime drama   1963 · US/Sp · BW · 107min
Few actors were as chilling as Laurence Harvey, who also directed and produced this oddity in Spain. Harvey plays a bank robber, sentenced to death, whose 11th-hour escape is arranged by his brother disguised as a priest. Sarah Miles is the girl in the middle. This is a half-baked religious allegory, with every scene screaming "I am an Art Movie". The result barely works as an oddball thriller. **AT**
Laurence Harvey *Sean McKenna* • Sarah Miles *Catherine* • Robert Walker Jr *Dominic* • John Ireland *Prison Warden* ■ *Dir* Laurence Harvey • *Scr* Ben Barzman, Alun Falconer, Laurence Harvey

Certain Fury ★★ 18
Action crime drama   1985 · US · Colour · 82min
It's not often you get to watch two Oscar winners making total prats of themselves, so sit back and enjoy this risible rubbish from director Stephen Gyllenhaal. Tatum O'Neal and Irene Cara play two fugitives, handcuffed together and on the run after a violent court break-out. Any chance of exploring racial tensions between the women is sacrificed on the altar of a fast-moving plot. **RS**
Tatum O'Neal *Scarlet* • Irene Cara *Tracy* • Nicholas Campbell *Sniffer* • George Murdock *Lieutenant Speier* • Moses Gunn *Doctor Freeman* • Peter Fonda *Rodney* • Rodney Gage *Superman* ■ *Dir* Stephen Gyllenhaal • *Scr* Michael Jacobs

A Certain Smile ★★
Romantic drama   1958 · US · Colour · 104min
Directed by Jean Negulesco with an eye for the visual possibilities of Paris and the French Riviera, this adaptation of Françoise Sagan's precocious bestseller is an otherwise limp and lacklustre affair. Christine Carere plays a student who gets involved with the middle-aged Rossano Brazzi before returning to the more suitable Bradford Dillman; Joan Fontaine co-stars as Brazzi's betrayed wife. Johnny Mathis's performance of the title song is all that's noteworthy. **RK**
Rossano Brazzi *Luc* • Joan Fontaine *Françoise Ferrand* • Christine Carere *Dominique Vallon* • Bradford Dillman *Bertrand* • Eduard Franz *M Vallon* ■ *Dir* Jean Negulesco • *Scr* Frances Goodrich, Albert Hackett, from the novel by Françoise Sagan

Certified Copy ★★★ 12

Drama 2009 · Fr/It/Bel · Colour · 102min

Abbas Kiarostami's first film produced outside his native Iran is an unconventional love story, whose unfolding intellectual discourse seems at odds with the sun-dappled Tuscan setting. Juliette Binoche's French gallery owner orchestrates a meeting with a visiting English academic and a chance conversation with a café owner leads them into their own "copy" of intimacy. Kiarostami's film touches on love, marriage and art, feeling at times like a dry seminar. But thanks to its more profound notes, usually arising from the warmth and vulnerability of Binoche's performance, it takes on an ethereal quality. AC French, English +subtitles. DVD BL

Juliette Binoche *She* • William Shimell *James Miller* • Gianna Giachetti *café owner* • Adrian Moore *son* ■ *Dir/Scr* Abbas Kiarostami

Cervantes ★★

Historical drama
1968 · Fr/It/Sp · Colour · 111min

Horst Buchholz takes the title role in this dismal European co-production, which doesn't seem to bear much relation to the life of the famous Spanish writer. While on a secret mission from the Pope, Buchholz gets waylaid at real times in a series of adventures involving the likes of Gina Lollobrigida, José Ferrer and Louis Jourdan. JF

Horst Buchholz *Miguel de Cervantes* • Gina Lollobrigida *Giulia* • José Ferrer *Hassan Bey* • Louis Jourdan *Cardinal Acquaviva* • Fernando Rey *King Philip II of Spain* ■ *Dir* Vincent Sherman • *Scr* David Karp, Enrique Llovet, Enrico Bomba, from the book by Bruno Frank

César ★★★★

Drama 1936 · Fr · BW · 125min

The third and final film in writer Marcel Pagnol's sublime trilogy, which began with *Marius* in 1931 and continued with *Fanny* in 1932, is the only one of the three directed by Pagnol himself. It is 20 years later, and Marius (Pierre Fresnay) is working in a garage in Toulon. Fanny (Orane Demazis) tells her son Césariot (André Fouché) that Marius is his real father; with help from his grandfather, César (Raimu), the lovers are reunited. If Pagnol's direction is less expert than that of his predecessors, it's still a satisfying end to his humorous, sympathetic and acute portrait of Marseille life. RK French +subtitles.

Raimu *César* • Orane Demazis *Fanny* • Pierre Fresnay *Marius* • Fernand Charpin *Panisse* • Milly Mathis *Aunt Claudine* • André Fouché *Césariot* • Maupi *Chauffeur* ■ *Dir/Scr* Marcel Pagnol

César and Rosalie ★★★ 12

Comedy 1972 · Fr · Colour · 106min

Claude Sautet is a keen observer of the mores and susceptibilities of middle-aged, middle-class France, and this deft study of personal freedom and the pain involved in securing it proves. There's nothing particularly new about the romantic triangle formed by single mother Romy Schneider, wealthy lover Yves Montand and her old flame, Sami Frey. But thanks to a thoughtful script and plausible performances, this is a civilised, witty and ultimately moving drama. DP In French. Nudity. DVD BL

Yves Montand *César* • Romy Schneider *Rosalie* • Sami Frey *David* • Umberto Orsini *Antoine* • Isabelle Huppert *Marite* ■ *Dir* Claude Sautet • *Scr* Claude Sautet, Jean-Loup Dabadie

C'est la Vie ★★★★ 12

Period drama
1990 · Fr · Colour · 96min

Set in the seaside resort of La Baule in 1958, this charming evocation of childhood summers concludes Diane Kurys's autobiographical trilogy, which began with *Diabolo Menthe* and continued with *Entre Nous*. Each little moment of mischief, amusement and affection is as fresh and colourful as a holiday snap, thus making the sudden intrusion of real life seem all the more shocking and sad. Julie Bataille and Candice Lefranc are splendid as the sisters by the sea, whether fooling with their cousins, teasing their nanny or responding with dismay to the news that their parents, Nathalie Baye and Richard Berry, are splitting up. DP French +subtitles.

Nathalie Baye *Lena* • Richard Berry *Michel* • Zabou *Bella Mandel* • Jean-Pierre Bacri *Léon Mandel* • Julie Bataille *Frédérique* • Candice Lefranc *Sophie* ■ *Dir* Diane Kurys • *Scr* Diane Kurys, Alain Le Henry

Chachi 420 ★★★ PG

Comedy drama 1997 · Ind · Colour · 158min

Mrs Doubtfire gets the Bollywood treatment in this highly entertaining comedy drama from actor/director Kamal Haasan. Forced to pose as a nanny to secure access to his daughter, divorced choreographer Haasan attempts to win back the affection of his ex-wife, Tabu, only to find himself fighting off the attentions of her tycoon father, Amrish Puri. Although the excellent Om Puri provides a little villainy, this is much more innocent than Robin Williams's blockbuster Hollywood version. DP Hindi +subtitles. DVD

Kamal Haasan *Jayaprakash* • Amrish Puri *Seth Durga* • Tabu *Jhanki* • Om Puri *Bhanwari* ■ *Dir* Kamal Haasan

Chad Hanna ★★★ U

Period romantic drama
1940 · US · Colour · 88min

Director Henry King displays a strong eye for Americana, and his film is full of offbeat episodes and oddball characters. The trouble is that nothing substantial ever really happens. Henry Fonda is well-cast as the country boy who becomes so infatuated with Dorothy Lamour's bareback rider that he joins the travelling circus where she performs. Wonderful Technicolor and a marvellous feeling for life on the road in upstate 1840s New York are the main assets here. AE

Henry Fonda *Chad Hanna* • Dorothy Lamour *Albany Yates* • Linda Darnell *Caroline* • Guy Kibbee *Huguenine* • Jane Darwell *Mrs Huguenine* • John Carradine *Bisbee* • Ted North *Fred Shepley* ■ *Dir* Henry King • *Scr* Nunnally Johnson, from the story *Red Wheels Rolling* by Walter D Edmonds

The Chain ★★ PG

Comedy 1984 · UK · Colour · 92min

Two giants of British television, writer Jack Rosenthal and director Jack Gold, use the *La Ronde* style of storytelling to depict that most British of institutions: the housing chain. However, despite the presence of Denis Lawson, Nigel Hawthorne, Billie Whitelaw, Warren Mitchell and Leo McKern, the jokes fall flat. SR

Denis Lawson *Keith* • Maurice Denham *Grandpa* • Nigel Hawthorne *Mr Thorn* • Billie Whitelaw *Mrs Andreos* • Judy Parfitt *Deidre* • Leo McKern *Thomas* • Bernard Hill *Nick* • Warren Mitchell *Bamber* • Anna Massey *Betty* • David Troughton *Dudley* • Phyllis Logan *Alison* ■ *Dir* Jack Gold • *Scr* Jack Rosenthal

Chain Lightning ★★ U

Second World War drama
1950 · US · BW · 94min

This B-movie casts Humphrey Bogart as a fighter pilot, morbidly droning on about causing the death of his buddy (Richard Whorf) while testing an experimental safety device in a new-fangled jet. The clichés are thick on the ground, but Bogart has a face you have to look at. AT

Humphrey Bogart *Matt Brennan* • Eleanor Parker *Jo Holloway* • Raymond Massey *Leland Willis* • Richard Whorf *Carl Troxall* • James Brown (1) *Major Hinkle* ■ *Dir* Stuart Heisler • *Scr* Liam O'Brien, Vincent Evans, from a story by J Redmond Prior [Lester Cole]

The Chain Reaction ★★★ 15

Thriller 1980 · Aus · Colour · 88min

Boasting chase sequences by *Mad Max*'s George Miller, this chunk of Australian exploitation knocks spots off similar big-budget Hollywood offerings. Director Ian Barry's smart use of both camera and sound effects transforms many of the action set pieces. Unfortunately, the characterisations are comic book level, and Steve Bisley and Arna Maria Winchester's bid to expose a leak at a nuclear plant is predictable. DP

Steve Bisley *Larry Stillson* • Arna-Maria Winchester *Carmel Stillson* • Ross Thompson *Heinrich Schmidt* • Ralph Cotterill *Grey* • Hugh Keays-Byrne *Eagle* ■ *Dir/Scr* Ian Barry

Chain Reaction ★★★ 12

Action thriller 1996 · US · Colour · 106min

Keanu Reeves as a scientist seeking to make cheap power out of water is a little hard to take. But after he and fellow researcher Rachel Weisz go on the run from mysterious saboteurs after cracking the formula, director Andrew Davis's muddled suspense tale finally takes flight. With an unfocused script that's hazy on explanations, the film survives thanks to the pell-mell action that papers over the weak links in the convoluted plot. AJ Some violence, swearing. DVD BL

Keanu Reeves *Eddie Kasalivich* • Morgan Freeman *Paul Shannon* • Rachel Weisz *Lily Sinclair* • Fred Ward *FBI Agent Ford* • Kevin Dunn *FBI Agent Doyle* • Brian Cox (1) *Lyman Earl Collier* • Joanna Cassidy *Maggie McDermott* • Chelcie Ross *Ed Rafferty* ■ *Dir* Andrew Davis • *Scr* JF Lawton, Michael Bortman, from a story by Josh Friedman, Arne L Schmidt, Rick Seaman

Chaindance ★★ 15

Prison drama 1991 · US · Colour · 104min

Michael Ironside plays a convict roped into a radical rehabilitation programme in which prisoners are used to help at a hospital for the physically handicapped. With Brad Dourif as his reluctant patient and Rae Dawn Chong as a sympathetic social worker, the casting can't be faulted, but the over-earnest script makes the plot difficult to swallow. JF Swearing, violence, brief nudity.

Michael Ironside *JT Blake* • Rae Dawn Chong *Ilene* • Brad Dourif *Johnny Reynolds* • Bruce Glover *Casey* ■ *Dir* Allan A Goldstein • *Scr* Michael Ironside, Alan Aylward

Chained ★★★

Romantic drama 1934 · US · BW · 75min

In this handsome romantic drama, Joan Crawford has to choose between shipping magnate Otto Kruger and playboy Clark Gable. The problem is, Crawford is already married Kruger and has several ocean liners in her name. What does Gable have that the older man doesn't? This sort of thing was a breeze for Gable and Crawford, in their fifth film together. Smartly written and stylishly directed, Clarence Brown's film motors along on star power and Crawford's show-stopping costumes. AT

Joan Crawford *Diane Lovering* • Clark Gable *Mike Bradley* • Otto Kruger *Richard Field* • Stuart Erwin *Johnny* • Una O'Connor *Amy* ■ *Dir* Clarence Brown • *Scr* John Lee Mahin, from a story by Edgar Selwyn

Chained ★★★ 18

Horror thriller 2012 · US · Colour · 90min

Jennifer Lynch's debut feature was the critical bomb *Boxing Helena* in 1993. Her fifth film is a vast improvement, though it isn't for everyone, being a violent study of a serial killer. It opens with a young boy taking a taxi with his mother (Julia Ormond), who's brutally murdered in front of him. Flash-forward several years and the boy is now a terrified teenager who lives with his captor (Vincent D'Onofrio) in rural isolation. The scenes of torture and killing that follow are strong but not gratuitous, and the heavy air of malice is leavened by D'Onofrio's strangely human performance. It may lack the style and wicked humour of Lynch's father David's best work, but *Chained* is just as intelligent. DW Violence. DVD BL

Vincent D'Onofrio *Bob* • Eamon Farren *Older Rabbit* • Julia Ormond *Sarah Fittler* • Evan Bird *Younger Rabbit* ■ *Dir* Jennifer Lynch [Jennifer Chambers Lynch] • *Scr* Jennifer Lynch [Jennifer Chambers Lynch], from a screenplay (unproduced) by Damian O'Donnell

Chained Heat ★★★ 18

Drama 1983 · US/W Ger · Colour · 92min

This lip-smackingly good women-in-prison saga finds *Exorcist* star Linda Blair learning the cell block ropes the hard way via degenerate guards, domineering inmates and the usual lesbian quota. Bolstered by a great B-movie cast, this sequel to The *Concrete Jungle* (1982) might arguably be the ultimate jail-and-jiggle trash-fest. John Vernon is an absolute hoot as the sleazy warden who videotapes desperate lags in his office hot-tub while feeding them cocaine. *Chained Heat II* followed in 1993 starring Brigitte Nielsen. AJ Swearing, sex scenes, violence. DVD

Linda Blair *Carol* • John Vernon *Warden Backman* • Sybil Danning *Ericka* • Tamara Dobson *Duchess* • Stella Stevens *Captain Taylor* • Sharon Hughes *Val* • Henry Silva *Lester* • Edy Williams ■ *Dir* Paul Nicholas • *Scr* Vincent Mongol, Paul Nicholas

Chains of Gold ★★ 15

Crime drama 1989 · US · Colour · 91min

One of the low points of John Travolta's wilderness years, this weak crime drama was sold to cable TV after failing to secure a theatrical release. Travolta actually turns in a reasonable performance as a social worker who goes undercover to find a kid who's been abducted by a vicious drug gang. But the script (which Travolta had a go at polishing) veers wildly between the nasty and the sentimental. DP Swearing, violence, drug abuse. DVD

John Travolta *Scott Barnes* • Marilu Henner *Jackie* • Joey Lawrence *Tommy Burke* • Bernie Casey *Sergeant Palco* • Ramon Franco *James* • Hector Elizondo *Lieutenant Ortega* • Benjamin Bratt *Carlos* • Conchata Ferrell *Martha* ■ *Dir* Rod Holcomb • *Scr* John Petz, Linda Favila, Anson Downes, John Travolta

The Chairman ★★★ PG

Spy thriller 1969 · UK · Colour · 93min

J Lee Thompson's effective countdown thriller uses the old comic-strip chestnut of a microchip implanted in an agent's skull that's either a transmitter or a bomb detonator, depending upon the success of their mission. Here, Gregory Peck is the imperilled spy on an assignment in Red China to track down a miraculous crop-growing formula. Laboured dashes of political sermonising aside, the story is laced with enough outrageous twists and suspense to grab full attention. AJ DVD

Gregory Peck *John Hathaway* • Anne Heywood *Kay Hanna* • Arthur Hill *Shelby* • Alan Dobie *Benson* • Conrad Yama *Chairman* • Zienia Merton *Ting Ling* • Ori Levy *Shertov* ■ *Dir* J Lee Thompson • *Scr* Ben Maddow, from the novel by Jay Richard Kennedy

Chalet Girl ★★★ 12

Romantic comedy
2010 · UK/Ger/Austria · Colour · 92min

Now a household name thanks to her eye-catching turn in The *Theory of Everything*, Felicity Jones makes a winning heroine as a working-class Cinderella at a jet-set winter resort. Her aim is to bag a cash prize in an upcoming snowboarding competition and save widowed dad Bill Bailey from total despair. It's a formulaic comedy, with the central romance suffering because rich boy Ed Westwick seems more in love with himself than anyone else, but best friend Tamsin Egerton is fun to watch, not least because she can be snotty, hilarious and endearing simultaneously. SP DVD BL

Felicity Jones *Kim* • Ed Westwick *Jonny* • Tamsin Egerton *Georgie* • Ken Duken *Mikki* • Bill Nighy *Richard* • Bill Bailey *Bill* • Brooke Shields *Caroline* ■ *Dir* Phil Traill • *Scr* Tom Williams

The Chalk Garden ★★★ U

Melodrama 1964 · UK · Colour · 106min

Director Ronald Neame has made little effort to hide the stage origins of Enid Bagnold's play in this adaptation. It's not merely a case of filmed theatre, however, as John Michael Hayes's screenplay shifts the emphasis away from Edith Evans's dotty grandmother and Deborah Kerr's mysterious governess, placing it instead on the precocious teenager played with typical bravado by Hayley Mills. With father John offering neat support as the family butler, this is a rather talkative acting showcase, while the Oscar-nominated Evans steals the limelight from the hesitant Kerr. DP

Deborah Kerr *Madrigal* • Hayley Mills *Laurel* • John Mills *Maitland* • Edith Evans *Mrs St Maugham* • Felix Aylmer *Judge McWhirrey* • Elizabeth Sellars *Olivia* • Lally Bowers *Anna* ■ *Dir* Ronald Neame • *Scr* John Michael Hayes, from the play by Enid Bagnold

The Challenge ★★★ PG
Adventure 1938 · UK · BW · 73min

This remarkable mountaineering film is about the scaling of the Matterhorn by Edward Whymper, here played by Robert Douglas. The film was co-directed by the great climber and film-maker Luis Trenker, who also made a simultaneous German version called *Der Berg Ruft*. It may seem a little creaky today, but there's genuine tension in the Alpine sequences and a sense of joy and achievement that is quite rare in cinema. TS

Robert Douglas *Edward Whymper* • Luis Trenker *Jean-Antoine Carrel* • Mary Clare *Carrel's mother* • Fred Groves *Favre* • Frank Birch *Rev Charles Hudson* • Joan Gardner *Felicitas* • Geoffrey Wardwell *Lord Francis Douglas* ■ *Dir* Milton Rosmer, Luis Trenker • *Scr* Patrick Kirwan, Milton Rosmer, from a story by Emeric Pressburger

The Challenge ★★ 12
Crime drama 1960 · UK · BW · 90min

Sometimes films are so mesmerisingly bad that they offer a diverse selection of delights to the viewer, though not all are intentional. This is one such movie, amazingly pairing Hollywood sexpot Jayne Mansfield and British classical actor Anthony Quayle in a crime thriller of murky intent and ludicrous result. Mansfield makes the least convincing criminal mastermind you'll ever clap eyes on, but Quayle is smitten with her all the same, and goes to jail to ensure the police don't capture the loot from a heist. TS

Jayne Mansfield *Billy Lacrosse* • Anthony Quayle *Jim Maxton* • Carl Mohner *Kristy* • Peter Reynolds *Buddy* ■ *Dir* John Gilling • *Scr* John Gilling, from his story

The Challenge ★★ 18
Thriller 1982 · US · Colour · 109min

American boxer Scott Glenn helps Japanese descendants of revered samurai warriors reclaim their ancient heirlooms in this strange martial arts drama, co-written by John Sayles and directed by John Frankenheimer with little of his renowned flair. The basic thrust of the piece sets honourable traditions against venal westernised capitalism. The film is full of great kung fu fighting and Sayles's trademark ironies, but it's far too slow for a thriller. AJ

Scott Glenn *Rick* • Toshiro Mifune *Yoshida* • Donna Kei Benz *Akiko* • Atsuo Nakamura *Hideo* • Miiko Taka *Keiko* ■ *Dir* John Frankenheimer • *Scr* John Sayles, Richard Maxwell, Ivan Moffatt

A Challenge for Robin Hood ★★ PG
Adventure 1967 · UK · Colour · 95min

Although it will always be best known for its horrors, Hammer had something of a reputation for swashbuckling in the 1960s. Sadly, this adventure isn't half as much fun as Hammer's earlier Robin Hood outings. Barrie Ingham dons the Lincoln green to take on John Arnatt, here promoted to Sheriff of Nottingham after several seasons playing his scheming deputy in the 1950s TV series. The action is staged with little imagination, but compensation comes in the ample form of James Hayter's Friar Tuck. DP DVD

Barrie Ingham *Robin* • James Hayter *Friar Tuck* • Leon Greene *Little John* • Peter Blythe *Roger de Courtenay* • Gay Hamilton *Maid Marian* • Jenny Till *Lady Marian* • John Arnatt *Sheriff of Nottingham* ■ *Dir* CM Pennington-Richards • *Scr* Peter Bryan

Challenge to Be Free ★★ U
Adventure 1972 · US · Colour · 83min

Released four years after it was completed, and also shown as *Mad Trapper of the Yukon*, this was the last of the nearly 50 features directed by Tay Garnett (although he did get a little assistance from experienced action specialist Ford Beebe). The Hollywood veteran also takes a cameo role as the lawman in hot pursuit of fur trapper Mike Mazurki across Alaska. This is family entertainment of the tepid, worthy kind. DP

Mike Mazurki *Trapper* • Jimmy Kane *Old Tracks* • Fritz Ford *Sergeant* • Tay Garnett *Marshall McGee* • John McIntire *Narrator* ■ *Dir* Tay Garnett, Ford Beebe • *Scr* Chuck D Keen, Anne Bosworth, Tay Garnett

Challenge to Lassie ★★★ U
Period drama 1949 · US · Colour · 75min

This is a major character role for this best-loved pooch, as the famed collie retreats to 19th-century Edinburgh from the great American outdoors to play a faithful dog who keeps returning to a churchyard where her master is buried. Sound familiar? It's Disney's 1960 film *Greyfriars Bobby*, which was an uncredited remake of this MGM film. Lassie is utterly splendid in the lead, and the late 1940s Technicolor is ravishing. TS

Edmund Gwenn *John Traill* • Donald Crisp *"Jock" Gray* • Geraldine Brooks *Susan Brown* • Reginald Owen *Sergeant Davie* • Alan Webb *James Brown* • Ross Ford *William Traill* ■ *Dir* Richard Thorpe • *Scr* William Ludwig, from the novel *Greyfriars Bobby* by Eleanor Atkinson

La Chamade ★★
Romantic drama 1968 · Fr/It · Colour · 95min

Apart from the mesmerising *Thérèse* (1986), director Alain Cavalier's sparse output lacks real distinction. He was fortunate in attracting Catherine Deneuve, fresh from her triumph in *Belle de Jour*, for this version of a novel by Françoise Sagan. It has the elegant star as the lover of a wealthy man who leaves her for a summer romance, only to discover that she was happier before. BB French +subtitles.

Catherine Deneuve *Lucile* • Michel Piccoli *Charles* • Roger Van Hool *Antoine* • Irène Tunc *Diane* • Jacques Sereys *Johnny* • Philippine Pascal *Claire* ■ *Dir* Alain Cavalier • *Scr* Françoise Sagan, Alain Cavalier, from a novel by Françoise Sagan

The Chamber ★★ 15
Mystery thriller 1996 · US · Colour · 107min

Gene Hackman gives a sensational performance in a bleak, static potboiler, based on the John Grisham bestseller. Hackman is the Ku Klux Klansman held responsible for racial murders in 1967, with 28 days left before his execution. Grandson Chris O'Donnell grudgingly defends the white supremacist he hates. Director James Foley tries hard to make us care about the colourless characters, but interest remains low throughout the very draggy proceedings. AJ Swearing, violence. DVD

Chris O'Donnell *Adam Hall* • Gene Hackman *Sam Cayhall* • Faye Dunaway *Lee Bowen* • Robert Prosky *E Garner Goodman* • Raymond J Barry *Rollie Wedge* • Bo Jackson *Sergeant Packer* • Lela Rochon *Nora Stark* • Josef Sommer *Phelps Bowen* ■ *Dir* James Foley • *Scr* William Goldman, Chris Reese, from the novel by John Grisham

Chamber of Horrors ★★★★
Period horror 1966 · US · Colour · 97min

Demented killer Patrick O'Neal chops off his own manacled hand to escape the hangman and terrorise 19th-century Baltimore in a great neglected shocker. Originally made as a TV series pilot, featuring Cesare Danova and Wilfrid Hyde White as crime-solving wax museum owners but considered too lurid to air, director Hy Averback's nifty nightmare had gimmicks added for its cinema audience, with "Horror Horn" and "Fear Flasher" warnings of when to close your eyes to the terror. A textbook example of classic 1960s American horror. AJ

Patrick O'Neal (1) *Jason Cravette* • Cesare Danova *Anthony Draco* • Wilfrid Hyde White *Harold Blount* • Laura Devon *Marie Champlain* • Patrice Wymore *Vivian* • Suzy Parker *Barbara Dixon* • Tun Tun *Señor Pepe de Reyes* • Tony Curtis *Mr Julian* ■ *Dir* Hy Averback • *Scr* Stephen Kandel, from a story by Stephen Kandel, Ray Russell

Chameleon Street ★★★★
Biographical comedy drama 1989 · US · Colour · 98min

This is a riveting, true-life account of the life of William Douglas Street, a black man from Detroit who imitated a *Time* reporter, an exchange student, a lawyer and a surgeon – without any qualifications whatsoever! Written, directed and starring Wendell B Harris Jr, this biographical comedy drama won raves on the festival circuit, but received only a nominal release in the US. TH

Wendell B Harris Jr *William Douglas Street* • Angela Leslie *Gabrielle* • Amina Fakir *Tatiana* • Paula McGee • Mano Breckenridge *Neelish Ratnayaka* • Richard David Kiley Jr *Dr Hand* ■ *Dir/Scr* Wendell B Harris Jr

The Champ ★★★★
Sports melodrama 1931 · US · BW · 86min

In this classic weepie, a divorced, washed-up boxer (Wallace Beery) turns his back on drinking and gambling and goes into training for a return to the ring, accompanied by his adoring son (Jackie Cooper). MGM was a dab hand at tear-jerkers such as this, though the film's success owes much to Beery's performance and even more to young Cooper, who is disarmingly natural and precociously gifted. A massive hit in its day, it won Oscars for Beery and the story, and nominations for best picture and for its distinguished director, King Vidor. RK

Wallace Beery *Champ* • Jackie Cooper *Dink* • Irene Rich *Linda* • Roscoe Ates *Sponge* • Edward Brophy *Tim* • Hale Hamilton *Tony* • Jesse Scott *Jonah* ■ *Dir* King Vidor • *Scr* Leonard Praskins, from a story by Frances Marion

The Champ ★★★ PG
Sports drama 1979 · US · Colour · 117min

Director Franco Zeffirelli made his Hollywood debut with this rather routine remake. Jon Voight takes on the washed-up prizefighter role made famous by Wallace Beery, while Ricky Schroder, as the son is determined to make a splashy comeback for, wrings the emotions so effectively he must have shares in Kleenex. Ex-wife Faye Dunaway returns to undermine Voight and son's growing understanding, yet even her unconvincing performance can't sabotage the weepie finale. AJ

Jon Voight *Billy Flynn* • Faye Dunaway *Annie* • Ricky Schroder [Rick Schroder] *TJ Flynn* • Jack Warden *Jackie* • Arthur Hill *Mike* • Strother Martin *Riley* • Joan Blondell *Dolly Kenyon* ■ *Dir* Franco Zeffirelli • *Scr* Walter Newman, from a story by Frances Marion

Champagne ★★★
Silent comedy 1928 · UK · BW · 86min

Alfred Hitchcock abhorred his final silent, which stars Betty Balfour. Her descent into poverty is all part of a ruse by her millionaire father, Gordon Harker, to ensure that fiancé Jean Bradin isn't a gold-digger. The looming presence of Ferdinand von Alten provides a wisp of mystery, but the emphasis is firmly on frivolity. Minor fare maybe, but the use of subjective camera and expressionist fantasy is fascinating. DP

Betty Balfour *Betty* • Jean Bradin *The boy* • Gordon Harker *The father* • Ferdinand von Alten *The cosmopolitan* • Theo von Alten *The man* • Clifford Heatherley *The manager* • Jack Trevor *The officer* ■ *Dir* Alfred Hitchcock • *Scr* Alfred Hitchcock, Eliot Stannard, from an original story by Walter C Mycroft

Champagne Charlie ★★★ PG
Period comedy drama 1944 · UK · BW · 100min

This period romp from Ealing Studios gave the great Tommy Trinder one of his best screen roles. As music-hall star George Leybourne, he is engaged in a contest with

bellicose Stanley Holloway to secure "the most popular drinking song of the era" – the era in question being the 1860s, beautifully re-created and superbly photographed by Wilkie Cooper. Director Alberto Cavalcanti obviously loves the Victorian music hall and has a fine eye for period detail. The film is well cast, with Betty Warren and Jean Kent as the leading ladies. TS DVD

Tommy Trinder *George Leybourne* • Stanley Holloway *The Great Vance* • Betty Warren *Bessie Bellwood* • Jean Kent *Dolly Bellwood* • Austin Trevor *The Duke* • Peter De Greeff *Lord Petersfield* • Leslie Clarke *Fred Saunders* • Eddie Phillips *Tom Sayers* ■ *Dir* Alberto Cavalcanti • *Scr* Austin Melford, Angus MacPhail, John Dighton

Champagne for Caesar ★★★ U
Satire 1950 · US · BW · 99min

One of the very earliest satires on the media, this little-known film is still topical in these days of million-pound quiz shows. Ronald Colman, in one of his last roles, is the unemployed mastermind who applies for a job at a soap company only to be snubbed by boss Vincent Price. In revenge, he enters a radio quiz show and proceeds to win a fortune, much to the chagrin of venal sponsor Price. Celeste Holm then poses as a nurse to try to sabotage Colman's winning run. Not quite as sharp or as funny as it might have been a decade later but nevertheless remarkably watchable. TS

Ronald Colman *Beauregard Bottomley* • Celeste Holm *Flame O'Neil* • Vincent Price *Burnbridge Waters* • Barbara Britton *Gwenn Bottomley* • Art Linkletter *Happy Hogan* ■ *Dir* Richard Whorf • *Scr* Hans Jacoby, Fred Brady Black

The Champagne Murders ★
Crime mystery 1966 · Fr · Colour · 98min

A husband and wife (Anthony Perkins, Yvonne Furneaux), helped by Stéphane Audran, embark on an elaborate plan to convince playboy Maurice Ronet that he is a murderer. This is a deeply mediocre and offensive film from Claude Chabrol, going through career doldrums before rescuing his reputation with the stifling mastery of *The Butcher* three years later. A corked grotesquerie. RB French dubbed.

Anthony Perkins *Christopher Balling* • Maurice Ronet *Paul Wagner* • Stéphane Audran *Jacqueline* • Yvonne Furneaux *Christine Balling* • Suzanne Lloyd *Evelyn Wharton* • Catherine Sola *Denise* ■ *Dir* Claude Chabrol • *Scr* Claude Brule, Derek Prouse, from a story by William Benjamin, Paul Gegauff

Champion ★★★★ PG
Sports drama 1949 · US · BW · 98min

Kirk Douglas here gives one of the definitive performances of his career as ruthless boxer Midge Kelly, who will stop at almost nothing to become a success. Douglas betrays his disabled brother (Arthur Kennedy), his watchful manager (Paul Stewart) and the women in his life (Marilyn Maxwell and Ruth Roman among them) right up until his fist-breaking comeuppance. It's a punishment producer Stanley Kramer must have wished he could have inflicted upon Douglas in real life after the star had a nose job halfway through production, meaning nobody could lay a glove on him. TH DVD

Kirk Douglas *Midge Kelly* • Marilyn Maxwell *Grace Diamond* • Arthur Kennedy *Connie Kelly* • Paul Stewart *Tommy Haley* • Ruth Roman *Emma Bryce* • Lola Albright *Mrs Harris* ■ *Dir* Mark Robson • *Scr* Carl Foreman, from a story by Ring Lardner

Champions ★★★ PG
Biographical drama 1983 · UK · Colour · 109min

Having always looked a bit on the wasted side, John Hurt was the perfect choice to play Bob Champion in this true story of a jockey who overcame cancer, an injured horse and the rest of the field to make a heroic comeback and win the Grand National. The film lacks psychological depth and risks going too far in avoiding hagiography, but this tear-jerking tale holds the attention. PF Swearing. **DVD**

John Hurt *Bob Champion* • Edward Woodward *Josh Gifford* • Ben Johnson (1) *Burly Cocks* • Jan Francis *Jo Beswick* • Peter Barkworth *Nick Embiricos* • Ann Bell *Valda Embiricos* • Judy Parfitt *Dr Merrow* • Alison Steadman *Mary Hussey* • Kirstie Alley *Barbara* • Michael Byrne *Richard Hussey* ■ *Dir* John Irvin • *Scr* Evan Jones, from the book *Champion's Story* by Bob Champion, Jonathan Powell

Chan Is Missing ★★★ 15
Comedy   1982 · US · BW · 72min

Debunking Charlie Chan stereotypes and faintly echoing *The Third Man*, this gently pulsating study of life in San Francisco's Chinatown was filmed for a mere $22,000. The search for "Chan", who owes cabbies Wood Moy and Marc Hayashi a small fortune, almost becomes an irrelevance as director Wayne Wang guides us through a community that is not only isolated from the rest of the country, but is also divided within itself by homeland political rivalries and cross-generational attitudes. Comic and intriguing, this was one of the first films to show what the American indie sector was capable of. DP **DVD**

Wood Moy *Jo* • Marc Hayashi *Steve* • Laureen Chew *Amy* • Jud Y Nihei *Lawyer* • Peter Wang *Henry the cook* • Presco Tabios *Presco* • Frankie Alarcon *Frankie* ■ *Dir* Wayne Wang • *Scr* Wayne Wang, Isaac Cronin, Terrel Seltzer

Chance of a Lifetime ★★ U
Comedy drama   1950 · UK · BW · 92min

Played with conviction by a solid ensemble cast, this is a nostalgic look back to the days when people still believed in the co-operation of capital and labour. Regarded by some as a flight of fancy even on its original release, the story of a striking workforce that takes control of its factory seems more naive than ever. But there's more than a hint of truth behind many of the political platitudes and the finale has a pleasingly Capra-esque ring to it. DP

Basil Radford *Dickinson* • Niall MacGinnis *Baxter* • Bernard Miles *Stevens* • Julien Mitchell *Morris* • Kenneth More *Adam* • Geoffrey Keen *Bolger* • Josephine Wilson *Miss Cooper* • Patrick Troughton *Kettle* • Hattie Jacques *Alice* ■ *Dir* Bernard Miles, Alan Osbiston • *Scr* Bernard Miles, Walter Greenwood

Chance or Coincidence ★★★★★ PG
Romantic drama   1999 · Fr/Can · Colour · 116min

A young widow on a global odyssey to all the sights her dead son would have loved to visit – polar bears in the Arctic, the divers of Acapulco, a Montreal hockey game – is the thrust of director Claude Lelouch's touching rumination on the vital role that chance and coincidence play in life. Yet it's only when her camcorder is stolen and the sentimental images it contains strike a chord with its buyer, that Lelouch's unique romance begins to take flight. Superbly acted by Alessandra Martines, this is one of those movies where it's impossible to guess what's going to happen next. AJ French +subtitles. Brief swearing.

Alessandra Martines *Myriam Lini* • Pierre Arditi *Pierre Turi* • Marc Hollogne *Marc Deschamps* • Laurent Hilaire *Laurent* • Véronique Moreau *Catherine Desvilles* • Patrick Labbé *Michel Bonhomme* • Geoffrey Holder *Gerry* • Luigi Bonino *Mauro Lini* ■ *Dir/Scr* Claude Lelouch

Chances Are ★★★ PG
Romantic fantasy comedy
1989 · US · Colour · 103min

The principle of reincarnation has provided fascinating material for film-makers over the years. While this slightly sexy romantic comedy visits the same territory as 1941's *Here Comes Mr Jordan*, it doesn't reach that film's high plateau. Here, a dead husband returns to Earth in a new body, but with a partial memory of his previous life, and falls for the daughter he never knew he had. Cybill Shepherd, Robert Downey Jr and Ryan O'Neal give the idea their best shot, but Emile Ardolino's direction misses the target. TH Some swearing. **DVD**

Cybill Shepherd *Corinne Jeffries* • Robert Downey Jr *Alex Finch* • Ryan O'Neal *Philip Train* • Mary Stuart Masterson *Miranda Jeffries* • Christopher McDonald *Louie Jeffries* • Josef Sommer *Judge Fenwick* ■ *Dir* Emile Ardolino • *Scr* Perry Howze, Randy Howze

Chandu the Magician ★★★ U
Thriller   1932 · US · BW · 72min

As played by Gayne Whitman in the 1931 children's radio serial, Chandu was a figure of mystery and magic. The casting of the urbane Edmund Lowe, therefore, somewhat hamstrung this serial-like adventure, especially as his unassuming presence was utterly swamped by the scene-stealing excesses of Bela Lugosi as his Egyptian nemesis. A breakneck tale of stolen death-rays and cliffhanging perils with stunning sets and effects, the film suffers from an uncertainty of tone. DP

Edmund Lowe *Chandu* • Irene Ware *Princess Nadji* • Bela Lugosi *Roxor* • Herbert Mundin *Albert Miggles* • Henry B Walthall *Robert Regent* ■ *Dir* Marcel Varnel, William C Menzies [William Cameron Menzies] • *Scr* Barry Connors, Philip Klein, from the radio series by Harry A Earnshaw, Vera M Oldham, RR Morgan

Chanel Solitaire ★★ 15
Biographical drama
1981 · UK/Fr · Colour · 106min

Rutger Hauer made his English language debut in this disappointing fantasy on the early life of Coco Chanel. Crediting her with little inspiration, Julian More's screenplay suggests she rose from rags to riches simply by recognising the moment and exploiting everyone she knew. However, Marie-France Pisier suggests something of the sorrowful isolation of an icon whose affairs were all doomed to failure. DP

Marie-France Pisier *Gabrielle "Coco" Chanel* • Timothy Dalton *Boy Capel* • Rutger Hauer *Etienne de Balsan* • Karen Black *Emilienne D'Alençon* • Catherine Allégret ■ *Dir* George Kaczender • *Scr* Julian More, from a novel by Claude Delay

Chang ★★★★
Silent documentary drama
1927 · US · BW · 69min

Jungle fever had infected film-makers Merian C Cooper and Ernest B Schoedsack, even before they made *King Kong* in 1933, as this plot-driven silent docudrama shows. Set in the jungles of Siam (now Thailand), it's the story of the farmer Kru and his family, fighting for survival amid the indifferent forces of nature and rampaging wild animals, including a herd of elephants ("Chang" is the Thai word for elephant). A blend of dramatic re-creations, invented narrative (bizarrely, the title cards even give Bimbo the monkey a couple of lines of dialogue) and astonishing documentary footage, this is a marvellous record of a vanishing way of life and an incredible piece of cinema history. TH

■ *Dir/Scr* Merian C Cooper, Ernest B Schoedsack

Change of Habit ★ PG
Musical comedy drama
1969 · US · Colour · 88min

A change of pace and style for Elvis Presley, here playing a doctor working in an ghetto whose three new helpers, unbeknown to him, are novice nuns. The talented Mary Tyler Moore co-stars, though she looks distinctly uncomfortable. Presley's film career was in free fall by this time, and the scripts and situations were becoming increasingly desperate. DF **DVD**

Elvis Presley *Dr John Carpenter* • Mary Tyler Moore *Sister Michelle* • Barbara McNair *Sister Irene* • Jane Elliot *Sister Barbara* • Leora Dana *Mother Joseph* • Edward Asner *Lieutenant Moretti* • Robert Emhardt *The banker* ■ *Dir* William Graham [William A Graham] • *Scr* James Lee, SS Schweitzer, Eric Bercovici, from a story Richard Morris, John Joseph

Change of Heart ★★ U
Romantic drama   1934 · US · BW · 77min

The once magical and sure-fire box-office pairing of Janet Gaynor and Charles Farrell had lost its sheen by 1934 and this innocuous little offering couldn't arrest the decline. Here, the duo are joined by Ginger Rogers and James Dunn to make up a quartet of West Coast college graduates who head off to seek their fortunes in New York City. Gaynor wants to write, Farrell plans to become a lawyer and Dunn a radio crooner, while Rogers pursues stage stardom. Their ups and downs and various romances make for a mildly entertaining movie. RK

Janet Gaynor *Catherine Furness* • Charles Farrell (1) *Chris Thring* • James Dunn *Mack McGowan* • Ginger Rogers *Madge Rountree* • Nick Foran *Nick* • Beryl Mercer *Harriet Hawkins* • Gustav von Seyffertitz *Dr Nathan Kurtzman* • Shirley Temple *Shirley* • Jane Darwell *Mrs McGowan* ■ *Dir* John G Blystone • *Scr* Sonya Levien, James Gleason, from the novel *Manhattan Love Story* by Kathleen Norris

Change of Heart ★★★ U
Musical   1943 · US · BW · 88min

Songwriter John Carroll, burnt out and devoid of inspiration, teams up with Midwest girl Susan Hayward who obligingly ghosts his songs for him. A slender hook on which to hang a host of musical numbers and speciality acts, but this production, directed by Albert S Rogell for Poverty Row studio Republic, does just that. Wisecracking Eve Arden is on hand in a supporting role, Dorothy Dandridge performs, while Count Basie appears with his orchestra. A modest, cheerfully amusing musical romance. RK

John Carroll *Rick Farrell* • Susan Hayward *Jill Wright* • Gail Patrick *Toni Jarrett* • Eve Arden *Belinda Wright* • Melville Cooper *Bradley Cole* • Walter Catlett *J MacClellan Davis* • Tom Kennedy *Westinghouse* • Dorothy Dandridge ■ *Dir* Albert S Rogell • *Scr* Frank Gill Jr

A Change of Seasons ★★ 15
Romantic drama   1980 · US · Colour · 97min

When college professor Anthony Hopkins has an affair with student Bo Derek, his wife Shirley MacLaine retaliates by taking Michael Brandon to bed. In *Bob & Carol & Ted & Alice* fashion, they all take a holiday at a Vermont skiing resort just to show how broad-minded they are. Unfortunately, the leads are let down by a lacklustre script, co-written by *Love Story's* Erich Segal, and the film rapidly runs out of steam. TH Swearing, nudity.

Shirley MacLaine *Karen Evans* • Anthony Hopkins *Adam Evans* • Bo Derek *Lindsey Rutledge* • Michael Brandon *Pete Lachapelle* • Mary Beth Hurt *Kasey Evans* • Ed Winter [Edward Winter] *Steven Rutledge* • Paul Regina *Paul DiLisi* ■ *Dir* Richard Lang • *Scr* Erich Segal, Fred Segal, Ronni Kern, from a story by Martin Ransohoff, Erich Segal

The Change-Up ★★★★ 15
Comedy   2011 · US · Colour · 113min

The body-swap comedy gets a mighty shake-up, cheerfully breaking all boundaries of taste, when single, foul-mouthed bed-hopping Ryan Reynolds changes places with high-flying, strait-laced married lawyer Jason Bateman. The beauty of the genre is that they actually become more likeable when lost in each other's bodies after a drunken pee in an enchanted fountain. Director David Dobkin (*The Wedding Crashers*) has a knack for such silliness, so it's the laughs, not the sentimentality, that'll make your eyes water. SP Swearing, sex scenes, nudity. **DVD**

Jason Bateman *Dave Lockwood* • Ryan Reynolds *Mitch Planko* • Leslie Mann *Jamie Lockwood* • Olivia Wilde *Sabrina McArdle* • Alan Arkin *Mitch's dad* ■ *Dir* David Dobkin • *Scr* Jon Lucas, Scott Moore

The Changeling ★★★ 15
Supernatural thriller
1980 · Can · Colour · 102min

In this satisfying twist on the haunted house movie, George C Scott plays a recently

widowed composer who moves into an old house in Seattle (really Vancouver) run by the local historic society. Before long, the house starts croaking, juddering and generally behaving badly. With the help of local historian Trish Van Devere (Scott's then-wife), a century-old murder is discovered; the shocks are neatly handled by director Peter Medak. AT **DVD**

George C Scott *John Russell* • Trish Van Devere *Claire Norman* • Melvyn Douglas *Senator Joseph Carmichael* • Jean Marsh *Mrs Joanna Russell* • Barry Morse *Dr Pemberton* • Bernard Behrens *Robert Lingstrom* ■ *Dir* Peter Medak • *Scr* William Gray, Diana Maddox, from a story by Russell Hunter

Changeling ★★★★★ 15
Mystery thriller based on a true story
2008 · US · Colour · 141min

Clint Eastwood's directorial career shows no sign of losing momentum as he tackles this compelling story of cops, killers, incompetence and corruption in 1920s Los Angeles.Angelina Jolie stars as a telephone exchange manageress whose son disappears. But when he's supposedly found six months later, Jolie's protestations that the boy is not her own – he's even several inches shorter – don't go down well with the city's crisis-hit police department. Based on a true story, Eastwood's film is a beautifully stylised mix of mystery and classic Hollywood human interest drama. In an Oscar-worthy performance, Jolie is terrific as the crusading mother whose only ally, a seemingly paranoiac preacher (John Malkovich), is all that's between her and insanity. Eastwood handles the movie with sincerity and ease, weaving it all together in tense courtroom scenes that cement his reputation as a modern American master. DW Violence, swearing. **DVD** **Blu**

Angelina Jolie *Christine Collins* • John Malkovich *Reverend Gustav Briegleb* • Jeffrey Donovan *Captain JJ Jones* • Colm Feore *Chief James E Davis* • Jason Butler Harner *Gordon Northcott* • Amy Ryan *Carol Dexter* • Michael Kelly (2) *Detective Lester Ybarra* • Devon Conti *Arthur Hutchins* • Eddie Alderson *Sanford Clark* ■ *Dir* Clint Eastwood • *Scr* J Michael Straczynski • *Music* Clint Eastwood

Changing Habits ★★
Romantic comedy drama
1997 · US · Colour · 95min

Moira Kelly stars as a troubled young woman unable to have relationships with men thanks to her difficult upbringing with alcoholic father Christopher Lloyd. Retreating to a convent, Kelly begins a mural in the basement with materials shoplifted from her local art supplier (Dylan Walsh). At least the performances from the leads compensate for the psychological baggage. LH

Moira Kelly *Soosh Teagarden* • Christopher Lloyd *Theo Teagarden* • Dylan Walsh *Felix Shepherd* • Shelley Duvall *Sister Agatha* • Bob Gunton *Bishop Creighton* • Eileen Brennan *Mother Superior* • Teri Garr *Connie* ■ *Dir* Lynn Roth • *Scr* Scott Davis Jones

Changing Lanes ★★★★ 15
Drama   2002 · US · Colour · 94min

This offbeat drama charts the escalating urban warfare between self-absorbed attorney Ben Affleck and recovering alcoholic Samuel L Jackson following a minor road accident that causes both to miss important appointments. As they struggle to right their desperate situations, they are drawn into an increasingly vindictive battle of wills. Their duelling remains gripping throughout, with the deftly structured script and emotionally rich performances lending the slim premise unexpected weight. Director Roger Michell also encourages exceptional work from Toni Collette and Sydney Pollack. JC Violence, swearing. **DVD**

Ben Affleck *Gavin Banek* • Samuel L Jackson *Doyle Gipson* • Toni Collette *Michelle* • Sydney Pollack *Delano* • William Hurt *Doyle's sponsor* • Amanda Peet *Cynthia Banek* • Kim Staunton *Valerie Gipson* • Richard Jenkins *Walter Arnell* ■ *Dir* Roger Michell • *Scr* Chap Taylor, Michael Tolkin, from a story by Chap Taylor

C

Changing Times ★★★
Romantic drama 2004 · Fr · Colour · 98min

Catherine Deneuve's seventh collaboration with Gérard Depardieu (and her fourth with director André Téchiné) is a convoluted study of thwarted desire that could easily have lapsed into melodrama in less skilled hands. Arriving in Tangier for work, construction engineer Depardieu is also hoping to hook up with radio host Deneuve, who is still the only woman he has ever loved three decades after their break-up. While this is polished and impeccably played, it's a touch too deliberate to be wholly involving. DP French +subtitles.

Gérard Depardieu *Antoine Lavau* • Catherine Deneuve *Cécile* • Gilbert Melki *Natan* • Malik Zidi *Sami* ■ *Dir* André Téchiné • *Scr* André Téchiné, Laurent Guyot, Pascal Bonitzer

Un Chant d'Amour ★★★ 18
Silent erotic drama 1950 · Fr · BW · 25min

Jean Genet's only film is a silent ciné-poem containing many of the French novelist and playwright's themes and obsessions. Ex-thief Genet started writing in prison, and the setting of men alone in cells is a milieu he knew at first hand. Although the graphic scenes of masturbation and homosexual sex make this an intensely physical film, its lyrical evocation of passion and love raises it above the category of gay porn. RB DVD

■ *Dir/Scr* Jean Genet

The Chant of Jimmie Blacksmith ★★★★ 18
Period drama 1978 · Aus · Colour · 112min

This is not so much a chant by the half-Aborigine, played with conviction by Tommy Lewis, as a war cry of ferocious rebellion. In one of director Fred Schepisi's most powerful movies, Jimmie really believes he's a stakeholder in the new federation of Australian States announced at the turn of the century. The tragedy is that, discovering he's still of Aborigine, and therefore inferior, status in white eyes, he goes on a murderous rampage. TH Violence, swearing.

Tommy Lewis *Jimmie* • Freddy Reynolds *Mort* • Ray Barrett *Farrell* • Jack Thompson *Reverend Neville* • Angela Punch [Angela Punch McGregor] *Gilda Marshall* • Steve Dodds *Uncle Tabidgi* • Julie Dawson *Mrs Neville* ■ *Dir* Fred Schepisi • *Scr* Fred Schepisi, from Thomas Keneally's novel

Chaos ★★★★ 15
Crime thriller 1999 · Jpn · Colour · 103min

Dazzlingly deceitful and ingeniously intricate, Hideo Nakata's kidnap thriller consistently defies expectations as it shifts perspectives and time frames to compelling effect. Miki Nakatani's disappearance after a lunch date with wealthy husband Ken Mitsuishi comes out of the blue, but it's nothing compared to the twists and double-crosses that follow the ransom demand delivered by Masato Hagiwara. The labyrinthine plot wilfully confuses, but set pieces keep the nerves on edge until the audacious climax. DP Japanese +subtitles. Swearing. DVD

Masato Hagiwara *Goro Kuroda* • Miki Nakatani *Satomi Tsushima* • Ken Mitsuishi *Takayuki Komiyama* • Jun Kunimura *Detective Hamaguchi* ■ *Dir* Hideo Nakata • *Scr* Hisashi Saito, from a novel by Shogo Utano

Chaos ★★ 15
Action crime thriller 2006 · US/UK/Can · Colour · 101min

Jason Statham's frenzied athleticism takes a back seat for this pedestrian crime thriller. Instead it's a weak American accent that dominates his nonchalant performance as a Seattle detective sent to negotiate following a botched bank raid. With hammy head criminal Wesley Snipes deliberately engineering chaos to hide his true aims, events become increasingly convoluted. Ultimately, writer/director Tony Giglio strives for "clever and edgy" but achieves neither, sealing the film's banality with a disappointing climax and contrived final twist. SF DVD

Jason Statham *Quentin Connors* • Ryan Phillippe *Shane Dekker* • Wesley Snipes *Lorenz/Jason York* • Henry Czerny *Capt Martin Jenkins* • Justine Waddell *Det Teddy Galloway* • Nicholas Lea *Det Vincent Durano* • Jessica Steen *Karen Cross* ■ *Dir/Scr* Tony Giglio

Chaplin ★★★ 15
Biographical drama 1992 · UK/US · Colour and BW · 138min

This epic about the early part of Charlie Chaplin's life from co-producer/director Richard Attenborough is, for the most part, entertaining and intelligent, with Oscar-nominated Robert Downey Jr superb in the title role. The opening sequences are genuinely affecting, with Geraldine Chaplin playing Chaplin's mother (and her own grandmother), a music-hall singer who ended her days in an asylum. Yet, overall, the depiction of early Hollywood is too rose-tinted and the true tragic tale of a misunderstood comic genius is reduced to a series of star-studded vignettes. TS Swearing, brief nudity. DVD BD

Robert Downey Jr *Charlie Chaplin* • Geraldine Chaplin *Hannah Chaplin* • Paul Rhys *Sydney Chaplin* • John Thaw *Fred Karno* • Moira Kelly *Hetty Kelly/Oona O'Neill* • Anthony Hopkins *George Hayden* • Dan Aykroyd *Mack Sennett* • Marisa Tomei *Mabel Normand* • Penelope Ann Miller *Edna Purviance* • Kevin Kline *Douglas Fairbanks* • Milla Jovovich *Mildred Harris* • Kevin Dunn *J Edgar Hoover* • Diane Lane *Paulette Goddard* • James Woods *Lawyer Scott* • David Duchovny *Rollie Totheroh* ■ *Dir* Richard Attenborough • *Scr* William Boyd, Bryan Forbes, William Goldman, from a story by Diana Hawkins, the biography *Chaplin: His Life And Art* by David Robinson and the autobiography by Charles Chaplin

The Chapman Report ★★
Drama 1962 · US · Colour · 149min

For "Chapman", read "Kinsey" in this glossy examination of four Los Angeles women with psychosexual difficulties: a bored housewife (the normally ebullient Shelley Winters); a nymphomaniac (the usually ice-cold Claire Bloom); a frigid widow (sexy Jane Fonda); and a romantic adulteress (coy Glynis Johns). Not even distinguished veteran George Cukor can dispel the impression that this is no more than a sleazy exploitation of early 1960s permissiveness. RK

Efrem Zimbalist Jr *Paul Radford* • Shelley Winters *Sarah Garnell* • Jane Fonda *Kathleen Barclay* • Claire Bloom *Naomi Shields* • Glynis Johns *Teresa Harnish* • Andrew Duggan *Dr George Chapman* ■ *Dir* George Cukor • *Scr* Wyatt Cooper, Don M Mankiewicz, from the novel by Irving Wallace

Chappie ★★★ 15
Science-fiction thriller 2015 · Mex/US · Colour · 115min

If RoboCop and WALL-E had a baby it would be Chappie, a decommissioned law enforcement android secretly hardwired with consciousness. Forbidden by his corporate boss (Sigourney Weaver) to experiment with the damaged droid, IT designer Dev Patel gives Chappie artificial intelligence so that he learns like a human child. But then he's kidnapped. This is a return to director Neill Blomkamp's old stomping grounds - the dusty South African oppression of *District 9*. While Hugh Jackman's appearance as a mullet-wearing bad guy is largely forgettable, this futuristic thriller is pacey and perky, and the punkish production design looks very *Mad Max*. KK Violence, swearing. DVD BD

Sharlto Copley *Chappie* • Hugh Jackman *Vincent* • Dev Patel *Deon* • Sigourney Weaver *Michelle* • Yo-Landi Visser *Yolandi Visser* • Brandon Auret *Hippo* ■ *Dir* Neill Blomkamp • *Scr* Neill Blomkamp, Terri Tatchell

Chapter Two ★★ PG
Comedy drama 1979 · US · Colour · 121min

Novelist James Caan suffers guilt over remarrying after the death of his first wife; his anxieties cause problems in his second marriage. Adapted by Neil Simon from his semi-autobiographical Broadway play, the movie is heavy on wisecracks which defuse the potentially serious subject matter. Unfortunately, it's also heavy on talky and rather tedious argument. Caan is good, though, and Oscar-nominated Marsha Mason (the second Mrs Simon) is terrific. RK

James Caan *George Schneider* • Marsha Mason *Jennie MacLaine* • Joseph Bologna *Leo Schneider* • Valerie Harper *Faye Medwick* • Alan Fudge *Lee Michaels* • Judy Farrell *Gwen Michaels* ■ *Dir* Robert Moore • *Scr* Neil Simon, from his play

Character ★★★★ 15
Period drama 1997 · Neth · Colour · 119min

Adapted from Ferdinand Bordewijk's novel, a recognised classic of modern Dutch literature, Mike van Diem's Oscar-winning debut is demanding but hugely rewarding. Set in 1920s Rotterdam, it tells the story of a merciless bailiff (the ferociously austere Jan Decleir) and his twisted relationship with his illegitimate son (Fedja Van Huet). Victor Löw contributes a wonderfully eccentric performance, while the handsomely dour photography complements the stylised art direction. DP Dutch +subtitles. Brief nudity, violence, swearing.

Jan Decleir *Dreverhaven* • Fedja Van Huet *Jacob Katadreuffe* • Betty Schuurman *Joba Katadreuffe* • Tamar van den Dop *Lorna Te George* • Victor Löw *De Gankelaar* ■ *Dir* Mike van Diem • *Scr* Mike van Diem, Laurens Geels, Ruud van Megen, from the novel *Karakter* by Ferdinand Bordewijk • *Cinematographer* Rogier Stoffers • *Art Director* Jelier & Schief

Charade ★★★★★ PG
Romantic comedy thriller 1963 · US · Colour · 108min

This absolutely wonderful comedy thriller from director Stanley Donen nearly out-Hitchcocks Hitchcock. With a twist you'll never guess, and a dream cast of Cary Grant and Audrey Hepburn on ravishing Parisian locations, what more could you possibly want in the way of movie entertainment? There's a clever plot that never lets up, a wondrously romantic score (by Henry Mancini), star-making turns from Walter Matthau and James Coburn, and set pieces that deserve classic status: Grant taking a shower fully-clothed; Audrey and Cary falling in love on a Paris river boat; and a one-handed villain in a roof-top cliffhanger. TS DVD BD

Cary Grant *Peter Joshua* • Audrey Hepburn *Regina "Reggie" Lampert* • Walter Matthau *Hamilton Bartholomew* • James Coburn *Tex Panthollow* • George Kennedy *Herman Scobie* • Ned Glass *Leopold Gideon* • Jacques Marin *Inspector Edouard Grandpierre* ■ *Dir* Stanley Donen • *Scr* Peter Stone, from the story *The Unsuspecting Wife* by Peter Stone, Marc Behm • *Costume Designer* Givenchy

The Charge at Feather River ★★★ U
Western 1953 · US · Colour · 95min

A group of reprobates are rounded up and sent into Cheyenne territory to rescue two white women in this marvellous western that anticipates the plot of *The Searchers*. Unfortunately, it is marred by the miscasting of Guy Madison in the lead. It was originally shown in 3-D, which explains why objects keep crashing towards the camera. Even without its gimmick, this is well-written and well-directed. TS 3D

Guy Madison *Miles Archer* • Frank Lovejoy *Sergeant Baker* • Helen Westcott *Ann McKeever* • Vera Miles *Jennie McKeever* • Dick Wesson *Cullen* ■ *Dir* Gordon Douglas • *Scr* James R Webb

The Charge of the Light Brigade ★★★★ PG
Historical war drama 1936 · US · BW · 110min

This splendid early Errol Flynn vehicle bears little relation to historical fact, but who cares? It's a wonderful swashbuckler set largely in India, but which fetches up in the Crimea in time for a stunningly spectacular charge, punctuated by on-screen quotes from Tennyson. The great Michael Curtiz directs, with Olivia de Havilland returning as Flynn's love interest a year after their screen partnership began with *Captain Blood*. The magnificent score was Max Steiner's first for Warner Bros, and it provides the perfect accompaniment to this thunderingly good movie. TS

Errol Flynn *Maj Geoffrey Vickers* • Olivia de Havilland *Elsa Campbell* • Patric Knowles *Capt Perry Vickers* • Henry Stephenson *Sir Charles Macefield* • Nigel Bruce *Sir Benjamin Warrenton* • Donald Crisp *Col Campbell* • David Niven *Capt James Randall* • C Henry Gordon *Surat Khan* • Spring Byington *Lady Octavia Warrenton* ■ *Dir* Michael Curtiz • *Scr* Michel Jacoby, Rowland Leigh, from a story by Michel Jacoby, inspired by the poem by Alfred Lord Tennyson

The Charge of the Light Brigade ★★★★★ PG
Historical war drama 1968 · UK · Colour · 130min

The charge of 1854, immortalised by Tennyson, is etched deep in our national psyche as a blunder of heroic proportions. Tony Richardson's film of the event was a failure on release, but it's a great, unsung masterpiece, filled with extraordinary set pieces and chillingly funny performances. Richardson and his writer Charles Wood are less concerned with the "reason why" than with social context, a theme mirrored by Richard Williams's witty cartoon sequences. And the charge itself, brilliantly edited by Kevin Brownlow and Hugh Raggett, evokes the carnage as pure chaos. AT DVD

Trevor Howard *Lord Cardigan* • Vanessa Redgrave *Clarissa Codrington* • David Hemmings *Captain Nolan* • John Gielgud *Lord Raglan* • Harry Andrews *Lord Lucan* • Jill Bennett *Mrs Duberly* • Peter Bowles *Paymaster Duberly* • Corin Redgrave *Featherstonhaugh* • Rachel Kempson *Mrs Codrington* ■ *Dir* Tony Richardson • *Scr* Charles Wood • *Editors* Kevin Brownlow, Hugh Raggett

Chariots of Fire ★★★★★ PG
Sports drama based on a true story 1981 · UK · Colour · 118min

Unfairly dismissed by some as an empty exercise in cheap schmaltz, this has an old-fashioned innocence that celebrates the human spirit with a lot of careful detail. It's the powerful tale of two British athletes - one a contemplative Scottish missionary, the other an anxious Jewish student - aiming for glory in the 1924 Olympics, and it contains a compelling study of their characters and those of their competitors. Their experiences are drawn in thoughtfully by Hugh Hudson's direction and Colin Welland's Oscar-winning script. JM DVD BD

Ben Cross *Harold Abrahams* • Ian Charleson *Eric Liddell* • Nigel Havers *Lord Andrew Lindsay* • Nicholas Farrell *Aubrey Montague* • Ian Holm *Sam Mussabini* • John Gielgud *Master of Trinity* • Lindsay Anderson *Master of Caius* • Nigel Davenport *Lord Birkenhead* • Cheryl Campbell *Jennie Liddell* • Alice Krige *Sybil Gordon* • Dennis Christopher *Charles Paddock* • Brad Davis *Jackson Scholz* • Patrick Magee *Lord Cadogan* • Richard Griffiths *Head Porter, Caius College* • Ruby Wax *Bunty* ■ *Dir* Hugh Hudson • *Scr* Colin Welland • *Cinematographer* David Watkin • *Editor* Terry Rawlings • *Music* Vangelis • *Costume Designer* Milena Canonero

Charles Dickens's England ★★★ U
Documentary 2009 · UK · Colour · 123min

Few authors drew on their environs and experiences to more evocative effect than Charles Dickens, and this dense but always engaging documentary takes in the highways and byways that inspired his timeless writings. Director Julian Richards sets a cracking pace and the uninitiated may feel a little lost. But Derek Jacobi does an expert job in relating how Dickens's stories exposed the iniquities and injustices of Victorian England as he tours various museums, inns and residences across the country. The locations visited include County Durham's Dotheboys Hall (from *Nicholas Nickleby*), the graveyard at Cooling Church in Kent (where Pip encounters Magwitch in *Great Expectations*) and the

Isle of Wight retreat where Dickens wrote *David Copperfield*. DP

Derek Jacobi *Presenter* • Roy Hattersley • Lee Ault • Adrian Wootton ■ *Dir* Julian Richards • *Scr* David Nicholas Wilkinson, Emlyn Price

Charley and the Angel ★★ U
Fantasy comedy   1973 · US · Colour · 90min

This tolerable piece of family fare mismatches plot devices from *It's a Wonderful Life* and Dickens's *A Christmas Carol*. Although Fred MacMurray does a nice line in hangdog expressions, he lacks the look of tousled desperation that made James Stewart's performance in Capra's original so heart-rending, while Harry Morgan comes a long way behind Henry Travers in the role of the angel coaxing his charge into reassessing his contribution to life. DP

Fred MacMurray *Charley Appleby* • Cloris Leachman *Nettie Appleby* • Harry Morgan *Angel* • Kurt Russell *Ray Ferris* • Kathleen Cody *Leonora Appleby* ■ *Dir* Vincent McEveety • *Scr* Roswell Rogers, from the novel *The Golden Evenings of Summer* by Will Stanton

Charley Moon ★★★ U
Musical drama   1956 · UK · Colour · 90min

This distinctly downbeat showbiz melodrama was co-written (with John Cresswell) by Leslie Bricusse, who went on to notch up ten Oscar nominations as a composer and songwriter. Here he paints a particularly lurid picture of life in the music halls, as Max Bygraves takes no prisoners on his way to the top before conscience finally triumphs over ambition. Offering fewer insights into the loneliness of the long-distance performer than, say, John Osborne's *The Entertainer*, the film nevertheless has a ring of authenticity. DP

Max Bygraves *Charley Moon* • Dennis Price *Harold Armytage* • Michael Medwin *Alf Higgins* • Florence Desmond *Mary Minton* • Shirley Eaton *Angel Dream* • Patricia Driscoll *Rose* ■ *Dir* Guy Hamilton • *Scr* Leslie Bricusse, John Cresswell, from the novel by Reginald Arkell

Charley Varrick ★★★★ 15
Crime drama   1973 · US · Colour · 105min

Walter Matthau stars as a small-time crook who lands himself in hot water when he mistakenly steals a small fortune belonging to the Mafia. Hitman Joe Don Baker is soon on his trail, but the cunning Matthau has a few tricks up his sleeve. Don Siegel directs the clever, exciting script with verve, and also contributes a brief cameo as a table-tennis player. Unlike other crime thrillers of the period, this still seems fresh and invigorating. SR *DVD*

Walter Matthau *Charley Varrick* • Joe Don Baker *Molly* • Felicia Farr *Sybil Fort* • Andy Robinson [Andrew Robinson] *Harman Sullivan* • Sheree North *Jewell Everett* • John Vernon *Maynard Boyle* • Jacqueline Scott *Nadine Varrick* ■ *Dir* Don Siegel • *Scr* Howard Rodman, Dean Riesner, from the novel *The Looters* by John Reese

Charley's Aunt ★★★ U
Comedy   1930 · US · BW · 90min

Having previously been filmed silently in 1925, this was the first sound adaptation of Brandon Thomas's theatrical warhorse. Updating the action from 1895, Canadian veteran Al Christie uses all the experience gained from churning out countless slapstick shorts to input as much physical business as possible into Charlie Ruggles's impersonation of the spinster from Brazil, when he's pressed into posing as a chaperon to Oxford undergraduates Hugh Williams and Rodney McLennon and their visiting belles. However, the play's cheeky wit survives intact, as the action descends into broad farce. DP

Charlie Ruggles [Charles Ruggles] *Lord Babberly* • June Collyer *Amy Spettigue* • Hugh Williams *Charlie Wykeham* • Doris Lloyd *Donna D'Alvadores* • Halliwell Hobbes *Stephen Spettigue* • Flora Le Breton *Ela Delahay* • Rodney McLennon *Jack Chesney* • Flora Sheffield *Kitty Verdun* • Phillips Smalley *Sir Francis Chesney* • Wilson Benge *Brassett* ■ *Dir* Al Christie • *Scr* F McGrew Willis, from the story and play by Brandon Thomas

Charley's Aunt ★★★ U
Comedy   1941 · US · BW · 81min

Brandon Thomas's memorable creation is this time immortalised by the great Jack Benny, who always seemed strangely at home in drag. True, he's a little long in the tooth as an Oxford student, and, if it all seems a mite familiar, that's probably because this is one of several film versions. There's a super pace to this one, though, and a fabulous supporting cast, headed by the oh-so-elegant Kay Francis and a very young and lovely Anne Baxter. TS

Jack Benny *Babbs* • Kay Francis *Donna Lucia* • James Ellison *Jack Chesney* • Anne Baxter *Amy Spettigue* • Edmund Gwenn *Stephen Spettigue* • Reginald Owen *Redcliff* • Laird Cregar *Sir Francis Chesney* ■ *Dir* Archie Mayo • *Scr* George Seaton, from the play by Brandon Thomas

Charley's (Big Hearted) Aunt ★★ U
Comedy   1940 · UK · BW · 75min

Brandon Thomas's classic farce first saw the light of day on stage in 1892, an era when well-behaved young ladies required a chaperone while on a date. Hence the plot, in which an Oxford University student masquerades as the aunt of one of his friends in order to fulfil the function – providing the most famous and enduring of drag roles. This is lacklustre, with English comedian Arthur Askey taking an only adequate stab at the role. RK

Arthur Askey *Arthur Linden-Jones* • Richard Murdoch *Stinker Burton* • Graham Moffatt *Albert Brown* • Moore Marriott *Jerry* • JH Roberts *Dean Bowgate* • Felix Aylmer *Henry Crawley, the proctor* ■ *Dir* Walter Forde • *Scr* Marriott Edgar, Ralph Smart, JOC Orton

Charlie ★★ 18
Biographical crime drama   2003 · UK · Colour · 90min

One-time Bros sensation Luke Goss takes on the role of Charlie Richardson, the gang boss who terrorised London south of the river during the 1960s. This brutal biopic has a banged-up Richardson reminiscing about the days when pliers, planks and electrodes were the tools of his trade. Malcolm Needs's film is a mishmash of styles and morally questionable, but it's slickly made. DA *DVD*

Luke Goss *Charlie Richardson* • Steven Berkoff *Charlie Richardson Sr* • Leslie Grantham *Richard Waldeck* • Anita Dobson *Mrs Richardson Sr* • Nicole Sherwin *Jean Le Grange* • Marius Weyers *General Van den Bergh* • Douglas McFerran *Richard Aubury* • Antony Carrick *Judge Lawton* • Langley Kirkwood *Eddy Richardson* ■ *Dir/Scr* Malcolm Needs

Charlie & Boots ★★ 12
Road movie comedy drama   2009 · Aus · Colour · 97min

An ageing Paul Hogan plays crotchety father to Shane Jacobson's estranged son in this bitty and predictable Aussie road-trip comedy. More flat than funny, the routine male-bonding tale wastes its strong leads, as Jacobson tries to help his devastated dad get over his wife's sudden death by chauffeuring him 3,000 miles to fish off the country's northernmost tip. Ironically with joker Hogan on board, the most successful moments are the melancholy ones. SF *DVD* *CS*

Paul Hogan *Charlie* • Shane Jacobson *Boots* • Morgan Griffin *Jess* • Roy Billing *Roly* ■ *Dir* Dean Murphy • *Scr* Stewart Faichney, Dean Murphy

Charlie and the Chocolate Factory ★★★ PG
Fantasy adventure   2005 · US/UK · Colour · 110min

A fashionable but superfluous backstory aside, Tim Burton sticks faithfully to the text of Roald Dahl's much loved book: poverty-stricken Charlie Bucket (Freddie Highmore) is one of five competition winners on a guided tour of Willy Wonka's sweet factory. Johnny Depp's camp, childlike Wonka is fun but ultimately too distant to recapture the love generated by Gene Wilder in the 1971 musical version, *Willie Wonka and the Chocolate Factory*. But the production design looks good enough to eat, employing computer animation to dazzling effect. AC *DVD* Blu

Johnny Depp *Willy Wonka* • Helena Bonham Carter *Mrs Bucket* • James Fox *Mr Salt* • Christopher Lee *Dr Wilbur Wonka* • Freddie Highmore *Charlie Bucket* • David Kelly *Grandpa Joe* • Missi Pyle *Mrs Beauregarde* • AnnaSophia Robb *Violet Beauregarde* • Philip Wiegratz *Augustus Gloop* • Julia Winter *Veruca Salt* ■ *Dir* Tim Burton • *Scr* John August, from Roald Dahl's illustrated children's book

Charlie Bartlett ★★★ 15
Comedy   2007 · US · Colour · 92min

In this irreverent and energetic teen comedy, Anton Yelchin (*Alpha Dog*) stars as the rich kid whose illegal enterprises see him ousted from private education and sent to regular high school. Friendless and bullied, Charlie courts popularity by setting up a toilet-stall confessional from where he dispenses both advice and prescription drugs to his peers. Though all the genre clichés are included, they're camouflaged by sharply amusing dialogue and an agreeably darker and more realistic exploration of adolescent angst. Strong turns from Hope Davis as his eccentric mother and Robert Downey Jr as his troubled principal help smooth the film's rough edges. SF *DVD*

Anton Yelchin *Charlie Bartlett* • Hope Davis *Marilyn Bartlett* • Robert Downey Jr *Principal Gardner* • Kat Dennings *Susan Gardner* • Tyler Hilton *Murphy Bivens* • Mark Rendall *Kip Crombwell* ■ *Dir* Jon Poll • *Scr* Gustin Nash

Charlie Bubbles ★★★
Drama   1967 · UK · Colour · 89min

Albert Finney, an archetypally 1960s British screen icon, directed this contemporary romantic drama, as well as playing the title role. Charlie is a northern working-class lad made good – a popular theme of the time. A successful novelist, he's fed up with glitzy metropolitan values and decides to go in search of his roots. Rich in resonances of the era. RK

Albert Finney *Charlie Bubbles* • Colin Blakely *Smokey Pickles* • Billie Whitelaw *Lottie Bubbles* • Liza Minnelli *Eliza* • Timothy Garland *Jack Bubbles* • Richard Pearson (1) *Accountant* ■ *Dir* Albert Finney • *Scr* Shelagh Delaney

Charlie Casanova ★★ 18
Crime thriller   2012 · Ire · Colour · 93min

Supposedly the first feature conceived entirely on Facebook, Terry McMahon's directorial debut is very much a film for the times, as it uses the taming of the Celtic Tiger as the backdrop for a chilling but ultimately ill-disciplined study of bourgeois amorality and arrogance. Owing much to *American Psycho*, the film follows Dublin businessman Emmett J Scanlan as he becomes convinced he's untouchable after seeming to get away with the hit-and-run death of a girl on a run-down housing estate. Scanlon is terrifyingly terrific. But the pretentious verbiage and garish visual style fatally sap this courageously unpleasant picture's dramatic power. DP
Violence, swearing, sexual references, drug abuse, sex scenes, nudity.

Emmett J Scanlan *Charlie Casanova* • Leigh Arnold *Una* • Damien Hannaway *Kevin* • Ruth McIntyre *Soairse* • Anthony Murphy *Donald* • Valeria Bandino *Linda* ■ *Dir/Scr* Terry McMahon

Charlie Chan and the Curse of the Dragon Queen ★★ PG
Detective comedy   1981 · US · Colour · 91min

This comedy is best viewed today as the film that introduced Michelle Pfeiffer to international audiences. It's an ill-advised attempt to resuscitate author Earl Derr Bigger's wily, politically incorrect Oriental detective, listlessly played by Peter Ustinov. Brian Keith, Lee Grant and Rachel Roberts throw away their dignity for the cash, but Richard Hatch, as Chan's half-Jewish, half-Chinese grandson, has some amusing moments. TS

Peter Ustinov *Charlie Chan* • Angie Dickinson *Dragon Queen* • Lee Grant *Mrs Lupowitz* • Richard Hatch *Lee Chan Jr* • Brian Keith *Police Chief* • Roddy McDowall *Gillespie* • Rachel Roberts (1) *Mrs Dangers* • Michelle Pfeiffer *Cordelia* • Paul Ryan *Masten* ■ *Dir* Clive Donner • *Scr* Stan Burns, David Axelrod, from a story by Jerry Sherlock, from characters by Earl Derr Biggers

Charlie Chan at Monte Carlo ★★
Mystery   1937 · US · BW · 71min

This proved to be the Swedish-born Warner Oland's final outing as Earl Derr Biggers's Chinese detective. The storyline offers plenty of twists and turns, but Eugene Forde takes the action at such a clip that it's never easy to remember who's deceiving whom and which of the various characters assembled at a Monte Carlo hotel has been in contact with Sidney Blackmer's stolenbonds. DP

Warner Oland *Charlie Chan* • Keye Luke *Lee Chan* • Virginia Field *Evelyn Grey* • Sidney Blackmer *Karnoff* • Harold Huber *French police inspector* • Kay Linaker *Joan Karnoff* ■ *Dir* Eugene Forde • *Scr* Charles Belden, Jerry Cady, from a story by Robert Ellis, Helen Logan, from characters by Earl Derr Biggers

Charlie Chan at the Circus ★★★
Mystery   1936 · US · BW · 71min

Warner Oland's 11th outing as Earl Derr Biggers's Oriental detective was directed by Harry Lachman. Set to investigate the murder of circus owner Paul Stanton, Oland uncovers a conspiracy involving blackmail, forged documents and a gorilla suit. However, there's also time for Number One Son Keye Luke to provide some comic relief, as his agrizoophobia ruins a hot date. Midget siblings George and Olive Brasno come close to stealing the show, but there's stiff competition from fellow suspects Francis Ford (brother of director John Ford) and J Carrol Naish, who played Chan on TV in the 1950s. DP

Warner Oland *Charlie Chan* • Keye Luke *Lee Chan* • George Brasno *Tim* • Olive Brasno *Tiny* • Francis Ford *John Gaines* • Maxine Reiner *Marie Norman* ■ *Dir* Harry Lachman • *Scr* Robert Ellis, Helen Logan, from characters by Earl Derr Biggers

Charlie Chan at the Olympics ★★ U
Mystery   1937 · US · BW · 71min

As if the presence of Hitler wasn't enough to blight the 1936 Berlin Games, the activities of a nest of spies nearly prevent Keye Luke from taking his place on the US swimming team. He's kidnapped when Warner Oland gets too close to discovering who is after the plans for a top-secret autopilot mechanism. But the villains had not taken into consideration the debut appearance of Number Two Son (Layne Tom Jr), or Chan's unlikely alliance with the Nazi police. DP

Warner Oland *Charlie Chan* • Katherine DeMille *Yvonne Roland* • Pauline Moore *Betty Adams* • Allan Lane *Richard Masters* • Keye Luke *Lee Chan* • C Henry Gordon *Arthur Hughes* • John Eldredge *Cartwright* • Layne Tom Jr *Charlie Chan Jr* • Jonathan Hale *Hopkins* ■ *Dir* H Bruce Humberstone • *Scr* Robert Ellis, Helen Logan, from a story by Paul Burger, Earl Derr Biggers

Charlie Chan at the Opera ★★★
Mystery   1936 · US · BW · 64min

The famously inscrutable Chinese shamus, exquisitely played by Warner Oland, tackles an elaborate mystery in a prime puzzler from the solidly entertaining series. Boris Karloff plays the amnesiac baritone who escapes from a mental asylum and is blamed for the murder of his wife and her lover during a performance of *Carnival* (a fake opera composed especially for the film by Oscar Levant). Karloff's singing voice may be dubbed, but his presence adds a formidable *frisson* to the usual suspenseful scenario. AJ

U SUITABLE FOR ALL   **Uc** SUITABLE ESPECIALLY FOR YOUNG CHILDREN (DVD ONLY)   **PG** PARENTAL GUIDANCE   **12A** UNDER 12s TO BE ACCOMPANIED (CINEMA ONLY)

Warner Oland *Charlie Chan* • Boris Karloff *Gravelle* • Keye Luke *Lee Chan* • Charlotte Henry *Mlle Kitty* • Margaret Irving *Mme Lilli Rochelle* • Thomas Beck *Phil Childers* • Gregory Gaye *Enrico Barelli* ■ *Dir* H Bruce Humberstone • *Scr* Scott Darling, Charles Belden, from a story by Bess Meredyth, from characters by Earl Derr Biggers

Charlie Chan at Treasure Island ★★

Mystery   1939 · US · BW · 73min

Treasure Island was the name of a popular fairground attraction in San Francisco, which is the only reason for the title of this entry in the long-running series. Sidney Toler is Chan, upset by a friend's suicide and looking into the activities of racketeering astrologers as a result. Director Norman Foster keeps the story moving along pre-ordained lines. **AT**

Sidney Toler *Charlie Chan* • Cesar Romero *Fred Rhadini* • Pauline Moore *Eve Cairo* • Victor Sen Yung *James Chan* • Douglas Fowley *Peter Lewis* • June Gale *Myra Rhadini* • Douglass Dumbrille *Thomas Gregory* ■ *Dir* Norman Foster • *Scr* John Larkin, from characters by Earl Derr Biggers

Charlie Chan in Egypt ★★★

Mystery   1935 · US · BW · 73min

This was the first of nine cases penned by Robert Ellis and Helen Logan, and it's easily one of the most exciting. At his inscrutable best, Warner Oland is called in by the managers of a French museum to investigate the rash of murders that follows the opening of a high priest's tomb. Young Rita Hayworth makes in her fourth credited appearance, still being billed as Rita Cansino. **DP**

Warner Oland *Charlie Chan* • Pat Paterson *Carol Arnold* • Thomas Beck *Tom Evans* • Rita Cansino [Rita Hayworth] *Nayda* • Jameson Thomas *Dr Anton Racine* • Frank Conroy *Professor John Thurston* ■ *Dir* Louis King • *Scr* Robert Ellis, Helen Logan, from characters by Earl Derr Biggers

Charlie Chan in London ★★★ U

Mystery   1934 · US · BW · 78min

Even though this was Swedish-born Warner Oland's sixth outing as Earl Derr Biggers's Oriental detective, this is only our second chance to see him in action as, sadly, *Charlie Chan Carries On*, *Charlie Chan's Chance*, *Charlie Chan's Courage* and *Charlie Chan's Greatest Case* have all perished. A teasing mystery and a superb supporting cast make this one of the most enjoyable entries in the series, as Chan investigates a murder among the hunting, shooting and fishing set. DP *DVD*

Warner Oland *Charlie Chan* • Drue Leyton *Pamela Gray* • Douglas Walton *Paul Gray* • Alan Mowbray *Geoffrey Richmond* • Mary Brian *Becky Fothergill* ■ *Dir* Eugene Forde • *Scr* Philip MacDonald, from characters by Earl Derr Biggers

Charlie Chan in Paris ★★ U

Mystery   1935 · US · BW · 71min

Produced by Sol M Wurtzel, who later supervised 20th Century-Fox's other Oriental sleuth series, Mr Moto, the seventh case featuring Warner Oland is notable primarily for the introduction of Keye Luke as Lee Chan ("Number One Son"). Together they make short work of a gang of counterfeiters plaguing the City of Light with a batch of forged bonds. Toss in a little blackmail and murder and you have a briskly directed, sturdy thriller. DP

Warner Oland *Charlie Chan* • Mary Brian *Yvette Lamartine* • Thomas Beck *Victor Descartes* • Erik Rhodes *Max Corday* • Keye Luke *Lee Chan* • Perry Ivins *Bedell* ■ *Dir* Lewis Seiler • *Scr* Edward T Lowe, Stuart Anthony, from a story by Philip MacDonald, from characters by Earl Derr Biggers

Charlie Chan in Reno ★★★

Mystery   1939 · US · BW · 70min

Having handled several entries in Peter Lorre's Mr Moto series, director Norman Foster switched Oriental detectives for this brisk Fox programme filler. It was back

projection all the way, as Sidney Toler (making only his second appearance as Earl Derr Biggers's sleuth) leaves Honolulu, in the company of "Number Two Son" Victor Sen Yung, to investigate why Hawaiian neighbour Pauline Moore is being framed for murder. DP

Sidney Toler *Charlie Chan* • Ricardo Cortez *Dr Ainsley* • Phyllis Brooks *Vivian Wells* • Slim Summerville *Sheriff Fletcher* • Kane Richmond *Curtis Whitman* • Victor Sen Yung *James Chan* • Pauline Moore *Mary Whitman* ■ *Dir* Norman Foster • *Scr* Frances Hyland, Albert Ray, Robert E Kent, from the story *Death Makes a Decree* by Philip Wylie and characters by Earl Derr Biggers

Charlie Chan in Rio ★★

Mystery   1941 · US · BW · 61min

Charlie Chan goes to Brazil for Sidney Toler's tenth outing in this long-running B-movie franchise. Director Harry Lachman exploits his exotic location to provide a lively musical background to this tale of double murder. Yet, in spite of featuring some of the series' most ingenious clues and, most unusually, a brief burst of Mandarin (complete with subtitles), this is one of the least satisfying Chan mysteries. DP

Sidney Toler *Charlie Chan* • Mary Beth Hughes *Joan Reynolds* • Cobina Wright Jr *Grace Ellis* • Ted North *Carlos Dantas* • Victor Jory *Alfredo Marina* • Harold Huber *Chief Souto* • Victor Sen Yung *Jimmy Chan* ■ *Dir* Harry Lachman • *Scr* Samuel G Engel, Lester Ziffren, from characters by Earl Derr Biggers

Charlie Chan in Shanghai ★★ U

Mystery   1935 · US · BW · 70min

Swedish actor Warner Oland makes his ninth screen appearance as fabled Oriental sleuth Charlie Chan in this vintage tale of intrigue and murder. The suave Chinese detective is back on his home turf here, investigating an international opium ring. However, this is more of a children's picture than a smoky, sinister excursion, with "Number One Son" (Keye Luke) taking up a lot of screen time. **AT**

Warner Oland *Charlie Chan* • Irene Hervey *Diana Woodland* • Charles Locher [Jon Hall] *Philip Nash* • Russell Hicks *James Andrews* • Keye Luke *Lee Chan* • Halliwell Hobbes *Chief of Police* ■ *Dir* James Stone • *Scr* Edward T Lowe, Gerald Fairlie, from characters by Earl Derr Biggers

Charlie Chan in The Chinese Cat ★★ PG

Mystery   1944 · US · BW · 62min

The second and best of director Phil Rosen's six Charlie Chan pictures has more than a whiff of *The Maltese Falcon* about it, as the key to the case lies in a prized statue. Aided again by "Number Three Son", Benson Fong, Sidney Toler uncovers the dealings of a diamond smuggling racket, whose ringleader should be readily apparent, despite the deliberately obfuscating pace. However, the involvement of a gloved criminologist and a pair of identical twins residing in a fun-house at the end of a pier gives the story a twist. DP *DVD*

Sidney Toler *Charlie Chan* • Joan Woodbury *Leah Manning* • Mantan Moreland *Birmingham Brown* • Benson Fong *Tommy Chan* • Ian Keith *Dr Paul Recknik* • Cy Kendall *Webster Deacon* • Weldon Heyburn *Harvey Dennis* ■ *Dir* Phil Rosen • *Scr* George Callahan, from characters by Earl Derr Biggers

Charlie Chan in the Secret Service ★★ U

Mystery   1944 · US · BW · 61min

Two years after 20th Century-Fox dropped its option on Earl Derr Bigger's crime series, Sidney Toler acquired the rights and continued his stint in the title role at B-movie outfit Monogram Pictures. Having quit Honolulu, Chan enlists as a government agent to track down torpedo plans stolen from a murdered inventor. Much of the action takes place within the victim's Washington home, but the gallery of sinister suspects enables Russian-born

director Phil Rosen to sustain pace and interest. DP *DVD*

Sidney Toler *Charlie Chan* • Gwen Kenyon *Inez Arranto* • Mantan Moreland *Birmingham Brown* • Arthur Loft *Jones* • Marianne Quon *Iris Chan* • Lelah Tyler *Mrs Winters* • Benson Fong *Tommy Chan* ■ *Dir* Phil Rosen • *Scr* George Callahan, from characters by Earl Derr Biggers

Charlie Chan on Broadway ★★★

Mystery   1937 · US · BW · 68min

An impressive cast was assembled for this above-average entry in the series. But was it newspaper tycoon J Edward Bromberg, ace reporter Donald Woods, nightclub boss Douglas Fowley or mobster Leon Ames who was responsible for the murder of the showgirl whose missing diary contains incriminating gangland details? One thing's for sure: "Number One Son" Keye Luke isn't the guilty party, but it still takes all of Warner Oland's ingenuity to convince the cops. DP

Warner Oland *Charlie Chan* • Keye Luke *Lee Chan* • Joan Marsh *Joan Wendall* • J Edward Bromberg *Murdock* • Douglas Fowley *John Burke* • Harold Huber *Insp Nelson* • Donald Woods *Speed Patten* ■ *Dir* Eugene Forde • *Scr* Charles Belden, Jerry Cady [Jerome Cady], from a story by Art Arthur, Robert Ellis, Helen Logan, from characters by Earl Derr Biggers

Charlie Countryman ★★★ 15

Romantic crime comedy
2013 · US/Rom · Colour · 103min

The culture clash between America and the rest of the world is used to entertaining effect here. Shia LaBeouf stars as a Chicago boy grieving for his dead mother (Melissa Leo in a brief cameo). Inspired by her ghost, LaBeouf takes off for Bucharest, befriending an old man who is returning to see his daughter (Evan Rachel Wood). Part romance and part thriller, with some daft flourishes that don't quite gel, this works best in its action scenes, featuring impressive stunts and some truly heart-pounding music by Moby. DW In English, Romanian. *DVD*

Shia LaBeouf *Charlie Countryman* • Evan Rachel Wood *Gabi Ibanescu* • Mads Mikkelsen *Nigel* • Rupert Grint *Karl* • James Buckley *Luke* ■ *Dir* Fredrik Bond • *Scr* Matt Drake • *Music* Moby

Charlie: the Life and Art of Charles Chaplin ★★★★ PG

Documentary
2003 · US · BW and Colour · 126min

This is, without question, the most comprehensive documentary study of cinema's first superstar. Directed and scripted by critic Richard Schickel and narrated with enthusiasm by Sydney Pollack, it makes impeccable use of stills, newsreels, home movies and Chaplin's canon from *Kid Auto Races at Venice* (1914), for which he devised his famous Tramp character. But it's the quality of the talking-head contributions that makes this so compelling, with the memories of such co-stars as Norman Lloyd and Claire Bloom complementing the assessments of Richard Attenborough, Marcel Marceau, Milos Forman, Martin Scorsese and Woody Allen (who isn't always complimentary). DP

Sydney Pollack *Narrator* • Charles Chaplin ■ *Dir/Scr* Richard Schickel

Charlie Wilson's War ★★★★ 15

Biographical comedy drama
2007 · US · Colour · 97min

Tom Hanks leads the charge as a larger-than-life US congressman in this quick-fire comedy drama from director Mike Nichols. Adapted from George Crile's book, it's the true story of how Texas politician Charlie Wilson raised millions of dollars to fund the Mujahidin's secret war against the Soviets in 1980s Afghanistan. He's aided and abetted by a sharp-tongued Julia Roberts as war-mongering socialite Joanne Herring, and by Philip Seymour Hoffman, who's simply brilliant as gruff CIA agent Gust Avrakotos. Hanks muddies his normally

clean-cut image as Wilson – a booze hound and womaniser – but never enough to compromise his trademark likeability. This is a clever, compelling and (given the subject matter) surprisingly funny film that also boasts an impressive supporting cast. SP Swearing. *DVD* *Blu*

Tom Hanks *Charlie Wilson* • Julia Roberts *Joanne Herring* • Philip Seymour Hoffman *Gust Avrakotos* • Amy Adams *Bonnie Bach* • Emily Blunt *Jane Liddle* • Ken Stott *Zvi* • Om Puri *President Zia* • Ned Beatty *Doc Long* ■ *Dir* Mike Nichols • *Scr* Aaron Sorkin, from the non-fiction book by George Crile • *Cinematographer* Stephen Goldblatt

Charlie's Angels ★★ 15

Action comedy adventure
2000 · US/Ger · Colour · 94min

This take on one of the most popular TV shows of the 1970s is a gossamer-thin, pop culture patchwork. With its reheated plot, trashy single-entendre humour and ho-hum thrills, this rickety adventure charmlessly sashays its bland way from one kitsch set piece to the next. Star and co-producer Drew Barrymore is part of the vampy super agent trio, alongside Cameron Diaz and Lucy Liu, hired to find a kidnapped software genius. Thank heavens for Bill Murray, whose presence rescues the whole thing from total doom. AJ Swearing, violence. *DVD* *Blu*

Cameron Diaz *Natalie* • Drew Barrymore *Dylan* • Lucy Liu *Alex* • Bill Murray *Bosley* • Sam Rockwell *Eric Knox* • Tim Curry *Roger Corwin* • Kelly Lynch *Vivian Wood* • Crispin Glover *Thin Man* • John Forsythe *Charlie Townsend* • Matt LeBlanc *Jason* ■ *Dir* McG [Joseph McGinty Nichol] • *Scr* Ryan Rowe, Ed Solomon, John August, from the TV series created by Ben Roberts, Ivan Goff

Charlie's Angels: Full Throttle ★ 12

Action comedy adventure
2003 · US · Colour · 101min

No amount of special effects, irritating cameos and tedious skits can disguise the fact that this sequel is celluloid trash. Cameron Diaz, Drew Barrymore and Lucy Liu are all very cute as they reprise their special agent roles – this time hunting two stolen rings encrypted with the true identities of incognito federal witnesses – but their endless costume changes and innuendo-riddled dialogue need a plot to support them. SF *DVD*

Cameron Diaz *Natalie Cook* • Drew Barrymore *Dylan Sanders* • Lucy Liu *Alex Munday* • Bernie Mac *Jimmy Bosley* • Crispin Glover *The Thin Man* • Justin Theroux *Seamus O'Grady* • Robert Patrick *Ray Carter* • Demi Moore *Madison Lee* • John Forsythe *Charlie Townsend* • Shia LaBeouf *Max* • Matt LeBlanc *Jason Gibbons* • John Cleese *Mr Munday* ■ *Dir* McG [Joseph McGinty Nichol] • *Scr* John August, Cormac Wibberley, Marianne Wibberley, from a story by John August, from the TV series created by Ben Roberts, Ivan Goff

Charlie's Country ★★★★ 15

Drama   2013 · Aus · Colour · 103min

This extraordinary study of Aboriginal life in the Northern Territory of Australia not only captures some of the sad realities of today but also tells a poignant and universal story of a man struggling to come to terms with his place in a changing society. David Gulpilil (*Walkabout*) stars as the put-upon Charlie, who, when we first meet him, is struggling with a welfare system that refuses him even the most basic housing rights. So Charlie heads out into the wild, only to find that the past is now barely more than a dream. It could be depressing, but instead it's a haunting and beautiful lament for times long gone that ends with a much-needed glimmer of hope. DW English, Yolngu +subtitles. *DVD*

David Gulpilil *Charlie* • Peter Djigirr *Black Pete* • Luke Ford *Luke* • Bobby Bununngurr *Bobby* ■ *Dir* Rolf de Heer [Rolf De Heer] • *Scr* Rolf de Heer, David Gulpilil

Charlie's Ghost Story ★★ PG

Supernatural comedy drama
1994 · US · Colour · 85min

Trenton Knight is the misunderstood son of Anthony Edwards, an archaeologist more comfortable with ancient artefacts than parenting. When Edwards discovers the remains of the Spanish explorer Coronado, his ghost (Cheech Marin) starts doling out fatherly advice to Knight while ensuring his bones get properly buried. Occasionally funny. AJ

Anthony Edwards *Dave* • Cheech Marin [Richard "Cheech" Marin] *Coronado* • Linda Fiorentino *Marta* • Trenton Knight *Charlie* • Charles Rocket *Van Leer* • JT Walsh *Darryl* • Daphne Zuniga *Penni* ■ *Dir* Anthony Edwards • *Scr* Lance W Dreesen, Clint Hutchison, from a short story by Mark Twain

Charlotte Gray ★★ 15
Second World War romantic drama
2001 · UK/Aus/Ger · Colour · 116min

Cate Blanchett stars as the eponymous wartime agent, a Scots woman who parachutes into occupied France in pursuit of her missing lover, pilot Rupert Penry-Jones. On the ground she meets up with Resistance contact Billy Crudup and joins his unit on sabotage missions. The problem with this rather unconvincing portrait of wartime derring-do is that Blanchett appears to be merely along for the ride, and her performance is let down by the unlikely story. TH Sex scenes, violence, swearing. DVD

Cate Blanchett *Charlotte Gray* • Billy Crudup *Julien Levade* • Michael Gambon *Levade* • Rupert Penry-Jones *Peter Gregory* • Anton Lesser *Renech* • James Fleet *Richard Cannerley* ■ *Dir* Gillian Armstrong • *Scr* Jeremy Brock, from the novel by Sebastian Faulks

Charlotte's Web ★★★ U
Animated musical 1973 · US · Colour · 90min

This charming animated adaptation of EB White's children's classic is one of the few features produced by celebrated cartoon team Hanna-Barbera. The critters are brought to life by some superb voiceovers as Charlotte the spider (Debbie Reynolds) joins with Templeton the rat (Paul Lynde) to save petrified porker Wilbur (Henry Gibson). The animation isn't up to Disney standard, and the Sherman brothers' songs are rather hit and miss, but it's still pleasing. DP DVD

Debbie Reynolds *Charlotte* • Paul Lynde *Templeton* • Henry Gibson *Wilbur* • Rex Allen *Narrator* • Martha Scott *Mrs Arable* • Dave Madden *Old sheep* • Danny Bonaduce *Avery* • Don Messick *Geoffrey* • Herb Vigran *Lurvy* • Agnes Moorehead *The goose* ■ *Dir* Charles A Nichols, Iwao Takamoto • *Scr* Earl Hamner Jr, from the novel by EB White

Charlotte's Web ★★★ U
Part-animated fantasy comedy drama
2006 · US · Colour · 92min

Author EB White's classic fable gets the full *Babe* treatment in this warm live-action fantasy. Gently introducing younger viewers to the cycle of life, it explores how a clever spider called Charlotte (tenderly voiced by Julia Roberts) uses her web-spinning talents to save a small pig from the chop. Combining live animals and CGI effects with delightful results, piglet Wilbur is so endearing (as is Charlotte) that you can understand farmer's daughter Fern (a likeable Dakota Fanning) begging for his life. Sadly, the barnyard creatures that surround him don't share this charm. Voiced by the likes of Robert Redford and Steve Buscemi, their tone-lowering flatulence and constant jokes make the finale less poignant than it should be. SF DVD

Julia Roberts *Charlotte* • Dakota Fanning *Fern* • Steve Buscemi *Templeton* • John Cleese *Samuel* • Oprah Winfrey *Gussy* • Dominic Scott Kay *Wilbur* • Cedric the Entertainer *Golly* • Kathy Bates *Bitsy* • Reba McEntire *Betsy* • Robert Redford *Ike* • Sam Shepard *Narrator* ■ *Dir* Gary Winick • *Scr* Susannah Grant, Karey Kirkpatrick, from the novel by EB White • *Music* Danny Elfman

Charly ★★★★ PG
Drama 1968 · US · Colour · 99min

Cliff Robertson found himself cast as heroic types after he played the young John F Kennedy in *PT 109*, but the most rewarding role of his career came with this Oscar-winning portrayal of a mentally disabled

man whose life is transformed by a brain operation. The scenes between Robertson and Claire Bloom are touching, and Algernon the mouse is unforgettable, so director Ralph Nelson can be forgiven for playing down some of the fascinating possibilities raised by Stirling Silliphant's script. An unassuming charmer. DP DVD

Cliff Robertson *Charly Gordon* • Claire Bloom *Alice Kinian* • Leon Janney *Dr Richard Nemur* • Lilia Skala *Dr Anna Straus* • Dick Van Patten *Bert* • William Dwyer *Joey* ■ *Dir* Ralph Nelson • *Scr* Stirling Silliphant, from the short story and novel *Flowers for Algernon* by Daniel Keyes

Charms for the Easy Life ★★
Period drama 2001 · Can/US · Colour · 111min

Female empowerment is celebrated in this bitty but beautifully performed period drama. It follows three generations of North Carolina women in the early 1900s as they defy the era's traditional gender roles. Gena Rowlands is particularly fine as the headstrong matriarch constantly encouraging her daughter Mimi Rogers and granddaughter Susan May Pratt to feed their intellects and pursue their dreams. While the film covers too much ground, it has a subtle poignancy that keeps events engaging. SF Violence.

Gena Rowlands *Charlie Kate Birch* • Mimi Rogers *Sophia* • Susan May Pratt *Margaret* • Geordie Johnson *Richard Baines* • Ken Mitchell *Tom Hawkings* ■ *Dir* Joan Micklin Silver • *Scr* Angela Shelton, from the novel by Kaye Gibbons

Charro! ★ PG
Western 1969 · US · Colour · 94min

By this stage in his career, Elvis Presley must have been desperate to get away from the fluffy nonsense of his musicals, but he should have chosen a far more convincing alternative than this bungled, "serious" western. The King struggles with his role as a supposedly hard-bitten gunfighter who fights to clear his name when he is set up by his old partners in crime, and the rest of the cast is not convincing either. JF

Elvis Presley *Jess Wade* • Ina Balin *Tracy* • Barbara Werle *Sara Ramsey* • Lynn Kellogg *Marcie* • Victor French *Vince* • Solomon Sturges *Billy Roy* • James Sikking [James B Sikking] *Gunner* ■ *Dir* Charles Marquis Warren • *Scr* Charles Marquis Warren, from a story by Frederic Louis Fox

Charulata ★★★★ U
Period drama 1964 · Ind · BW · 120min

This beautifully observed study of 19th-century domestic habits, also known as *The Lonely Wife*, won Satyajit Ray the best director prize at the Berlin film festival. Never has his debt to the great French film-maker Jean Renoir been more apparent than in this gently ironic tale. Mocking both male authority and the gentility of Victorian society, it also boasts a superb performance by Madhabi Mukherjee as the neglected wife who sees an affair with her husband's cousin as a way of boosting her self-esteem and her writing ambitions. DP Bengali +subtitles. DVD

Madhabi Mukherjee *Charulata* • Soumitra Chatterjee *Amal* • Sailen Mukherjee *Bhupati* • Shyamal Ghosal *Umapada* • Gitali Roy *Mandakini* ■ *Dir* Satyajit Ray • *Scr* Satyajit Ray, from the story *Nastaneer* by Rabindranath Tagore

The Chase ★★★★ PG
Film noir 1946 · US · BW · 83min

Pretentious, bizarre and fascinating, this rarely shown psychological thriller stars Robert Cummings as the shell-shocked ex-soldier who becomes chauffeur to Steve Cochran's wealthy and sadistic gangster – a man whose favourite hobby is outrunning trains at level crossings. Michèle Morgan plays his dissatisfied wife, while Peter Lorre is his bodyguard. Cleverly written by Philip Yordan from a novel by the outstanding crime writer Cornell Woolrich, with moody photography by Franz Planer, the result is a most dream-like *film noir*. AE DVD

Robert Cummings *Chuck* • Michèle Morgan *Lorna* • Peter Lorre *Gino* • Steve Cochran *Roman* • Lloyd Corrigan *Johnson* • Jack Holt *Davidson* ■ *Dir* Arthur Ripley • *Scr* Philip Yordan, from the novel *The Black Path of Fear* by Cornell Woolrich

The Chase ★★★★ 15
Drama 1966 · US · Colour · 127min

Before he directed *Bonnie and Clyde*, Arthur Penn made this impressively cast and wondrously overcooked drama about a Texan sheriff who protects an escaped convict against a town that has run out of control. Marlon Brando has immense stature as the sheriff, while Robert Redford is perfect as the angelic convict he protects. In one sense, Lillian Hellman's script is like an updated western; in another, it evokes the madness and violence that gripped America in the aftermath of the Kennedy assassination. Although Penn virtually disowned the picture after producer Sam Spiegel had it re-edited, it remains a disturbing evocation of that traumatic era. AT DVD

Marlon Brando *Sheriff Calder* • Jane Fonda *Anna Reeves* • Robert Redford *Bubber Reeves* • EG Marshall *Val Rogers* • Angie Dickinson *Ruby Calder* • Janice Rule *Emily Stewart* • Miriam Hopkins *Mrs Reeves* • Robert Duvall *Edwin Stewart* • James Fox *Jake Rogers* ■ *Dir* Arthur Penn • *Scr* Lillian Hellman, from the novel and play by Horton Foote

The Chase ★★★ 15
Action adventure 1994 · US · Colour · 84min

Charlie Sheen stars as the lovable con who kidnaps millionaire's daughter Kristy Swanson, prompting a massive manhunt and a media frenzy. The two leads are seriously lightweight, but still spark off each other nicely, although the best performances come from supporting players Ray Wise and punk idol Henry Rollins, cast against type as a psychopathic policeman. JF Violence, swearing. CS

Charlie Sheen *Jack Hammond* • Kristy Swanson *Natalie Voss* • Henry Rollins *Officer Dobbs* • Josh Mostel *Officer Figus* • Wayne Grace *Chief Boyle* • Rocky Carroll *Byron Wilder* ■ *Dir/Scr* Adam Rifkin

Chase a Crooked Shadow ★★★ U
Mystery thriller 1957 · UK · BW · 84min

Coming off the back of *The Dam Busters*, *1984* and *Around the World in 80 Days*, director Michael Anderson was destined for a disappointment, but it is to his credit that this ludicrously contrived thriller not only holds the attention, but also actually manages to induce a short intake of breath at the totally unexpected dénouement. Anne Baxter gives her one of her best performances as a recuperating neurotic who is convinced long-lost brother Richard Todd is after her diamonds. DP DVD

Richard Todd *Ward* • Anne Baxter *Kimberley* • Herbert Lom *Vargas* • Alexander Knox *Chandler Brisson* • Faith Brook *Mrs Whitman* • Alan Tilvern *Carlos* ■ *Dir* Michael Anderson • *Scr* David D Osborn, Charles Sinclair

The Chaser ★★★ 18
Crime thriller 2008 · S Kor · Colour · 119min

Debut director Na Hong-jin's breathless true-crime drama is yet another Asian hit seemingly destined for a US remake. Set in Seoul, the film stars Kim Yoon-suk as a disgraced cop-turned-pimp whose girls keep disappearing. As he searches for one of them, he runs into the man he senses is responsible for the torture and murder of these women. But though he brings in the suspected serial killer, the police can't find enough evidence to arrest him - even though he confesses. The unlikely hero must then redeem himself by tracking down the last, barely alive, victim and nailing the murderer. AJ Korean +subtitles. Violence. DVD

Kim Yoon-suk *Jung-ho* • Ha Jung-woo *Young-min* • Seo Young-hee *Mi-jin* • Jeong In-gi *Detective Lee* • Park Hyo-ju *Detective Oh* ■ *Dir* Na Hong-jin • *Scr* Hong Won-chan, Lee Shin-ho, Na Hong-jin

Chasers ★★ 15
Comedy 1994 · US · Colour · 101min

Dennis Hopper, once the notorious film maverick, must have been keen to show that he could direct a movie with mainstream appeal. Here he certainly succeeds, but the result is a bland comedy, indistinguishable from all the other high concept projects that roll off the Hollywood production line. Tom Berenger and William McNamara are the bickering navy military policemen who are called in to transport a troublesome sailor to jail. It's amiable enough, but lacks a quirky edge. JF Swearing, nudity.

Tom Berenger *Rock Reilly* • William McNamara *Eddie Devane* • Erika Eleniak *Toni Johnson* • Crispin Glover *Howard Finster* • Dean Stockwell *Salesman Stig* • Gary Busey *Sergeant Vince Banger* • Seymour Cassel *Master Chief Bogg* ■ *Dir* Dennis Hopper • *Scr* Joe Batteer, John Rice, Dan Gilroy, from a story by Joe Batteer, John Rice

Chasing a Dream ★★
Drama 2009 · US · Colour · 89min

In this over-sentimental drama, high-school football star Andrew Lawrence clashes with his football coach dad (Treat Williams) when he switches to athletics to honour his dead best friend. Lawrence acts more petulant than distraught, making his emotional and physical challenges as he strives to run a four-minute mile far less affecting than obviously intended. But although the sporting part of the film feels too flat for the inspirational storyline, the fractured father/son relationship keeps things watchable. SF

Andrew Lawrence *Cameron "Cam" Stiles* • Jake McLaughlin *John Van Horn* • Treat Williams *Gary Stiles* • Joanna Going *Diane Stiles* ■ *Dir* David Burton Morris • *Scr* Bryce Zabel, Jackie Zabel

Chasing Amy ★★★★ 18
Romantic comedy 1996 · US · Colour · 108min

Writer/director Kevin Smith comes up trumps with this cool, hilarious and sexy romantic comedy. New Jersey comic book writer Ben Affleck falls for pal Joey Lauren Adams, despite the fact she's a lesbian. In addition to the chemistry between the two leads, it has an insightful and even heartbreaking script from Smith, hilarious support from Jason Lee as Affleck's sceptical pal, plus Jason Mewes and the director himself returning as regular characters Jay and Silent Bob. One of the hippest love stories of the 1990s. JB Swearing, nudity. DVD Blu

Ben Affleck *Holden* • Joey Lauren Adams *Alyssa* • Jason Lee *Banky* • Dwight Ewell *Hooper* • Jason Mewes *Jay* • Ethan Suplee *Fan* • Scott Mosier *Collector* • Casey Affleck *Little kid* • Guinevere Turner *Singer* • Matt Damon *Executive* • Kevin Smith (2) *Silent Bob* ■ *Dir/Scr* Kevin Smith (2)

Chasing Dreams ★★
Sports melodrama 1982 · Can · Colour · 94min

Yet another dull story about a young lad's dream of playing college baseball is notable only for an early appearance from Kevin Costner. The actor would return to the subject nine years later in *Field of Dreams* - thankfully, to much greater effect. NF

David G Brown *Gavin Thompson* • John Fife *Parks* • Jim Shane *Mr Thompson* • Matthew Clark *Ben* • Kevin Costner *Ed* ■ *Dir* Sean Roche, Therese Conte • *Scr* David G Brown

Chasing Ice ★★★
Documentary 2012 · US · Colour · 80min

In 2007, photographer James Balog began venturing into the frozen wilds to set up cameras that would show how fast the glaciers were retreating. First-time director Jeff Orlowski treats Balog with perhaps too much reverence here, and his glorying in the time-lapse sequences capturing glaciers receding in Greenland, Iceland, Alaska and Montana means it would be easy to dismiss this documentary as being too much in love with the stunning visuals. But the evidence gathered by Balog for his Extreme Ice Survey seems so disconcertingly conclusive that this becomes much more than a breathtaking record of nature in all its terrifying beauty: the film is, instead, intended as a warning. DP *DVD* *BL*

James Balog ■ *Dir* Jeff Orlowski • *Scr* Mark Monroe

Chasing Legends ★★★ 15

Sports documentary 2010 · US · Colour · 95min

This efficient if unimaginative sports documentary follows the travails of Team HTC-Columbia and their superstar rider Mark Cavendish in 2009's Tour de France. There's plenty of spectacular race footage and neophytes might be surprised at the extent to which the race is a team sport as well as one of gruelling feats of individual stamina. But the history lesson aspect, covering the founding of the Tour in 1903, is more perfunctory and the allegations of drug-enhanced performances that have dogged the sport are hardly mentioned. AS Swearing.

Phil Liggett • Mark Cavendish ■ *Dir* Jason Berry

Chasing Liberty ★★ 12

Romantic comedy
2004 · US/UK · Colour · 106min

Mandy Moore stars as the daughter of the US president, who's fed up with being hemmed in for security reasons. During a trip to Europe, she makes a dash for it with handsome stranger Matthew Goode. Director Andy Cadiff seeks out all the postcard touristy bits, while you keep hoping for a bit of action to liven up the travelogue. TH Swearing. *DVD*

Mandy Moore *Anna Foster* • Matthew Goode *Ben Calder* • Jeremy Piven *Agent Alan Weiss* • Annabella Sciorra *Agent Cynthia Morales* • Caroline Goodall *First Lady Michelle Foster* • Mark Harmon *President James Foster* ■ *Dir* Andy Cadiff • *Scr* Derek Guiley, David Schneiderman

Chasing Mavericks ★★ PG

Sports drama based on a true story
2012 · US · Colour · 116min

Acting can be a perilous business: Gerard Butler almost drowned while filming this true-life Californian surf story, in which he plays veteran surfer Frosty Hesson, who befriends troubled teen Jay Moriarity (Jonny Weston). Jay's dream is to ride the Mavericks – some of the biggest breakers in the world – and he wants Frosty to help him do it. That's the cue for some *Karate Kid*-style mentoring in matters physical, mental, emotional and spiritual. It's a little long, and a little laboured, but the surf scenes, which are spectacular, just about compensate for its shortcomings. DA

Gerard Butler *Frosty Hesson* • Jonny Weston *Jay Moriarity* • Elisabeth Shue *Kristy Moriarity* • Abigail Spencer *Brenda Hesson* • Leven Rambin *Kim Moriarity* • Taylor Handley *Sonny* ■ *Dir* Curtis Hanson, Michael Apted • *Scr* Kario Salem, from a story by Brandon Hooper, Jim Meenaghan

Chasing Secrets ★★★

Period drama 1999 · US · Colour · 120min

An elderly African-American couple provide refuge for a maltreated young white girl in this heart-rending Old South drama based on the book *Childhood's Thief* by Rose Mary Evans. Della Reese and Ossie Davis radiate warmth as the compassionate rural duo, and director Bruce Pittman handles his material confidently, poignantly exploring the difficult topics of abuse and racism without resorting to sickly melodrama. SF Swearing, violence.

Della Reese *Honey* • Crystal Bernard *Marie Foley* • Ossie Davis *Too Tall* • Madeline Zima *Jo-Ann Foley age 14* • Yvonne Zima *Jo-Ann Foley age 7* • Ron White *Hank Foley* ■ *Dir* Bruce Pittman • *Scr* Bill C Davis, Quinton Peeples, from the non-fiction book *Childhood's Thief* by Rose Mary Evans

Chasing the Deer ★★★ PG

Historical drama 1994 · UK · Colour · 90min

Director Graham Holloway works wonders with a tiny budget for this Scottish labour of love, a gritty period piece about the events leading up to the ill-fated Battle of Culloden. The story focuses on a proud Highland family who unwittingly get drawn into – and

are divided by – the Jacobite rebellion against the hated English. Money considerations means it doesn't have the epic sweep that is needed, but the talented cast make up for any budget deficiencies. JF In English, Scottish Gaelic.

Brian Blessed *Major Elliot* • Iain Cuthbertson *Tullibardine* • Matthew Zajac *Alistair Campbell* • Fish *Angus Cameron* • Brian Donald *Old Campbell* • Sandy Welch *Old Cameron* • Peter Gordon *McKinnon* • Carolyn Konrad *Morag* ■ *Dir* Graham Holloway • *Scr* Jerome Vincent, Bob Carruthers, Steve Gillham, from an idea by Michele Ayson

Chastity ★★

Drama 1969 · US · Colour · 83min

In an effort to change their hippy image and be more credible to the Woodstock generation, pop sensations Sonny and Cher produced this banal road movie. Written and scored by Sonny Bono, the film casts Cher as a teenage hitch-hiker who gets involved in a robbery on the way to Mexico and discusses world problems while encountering prostitution and lesbianism. The fiasco may have ruined them financially, but the couple still named their daughter after it. AJ

Cher *Chastity* • Barbara London *Diana Midnight* • Stephen Whittaker (1) *Eddie* • Tom Nolan *Tommy* • Danny Zapien *Cab driver* • Elmer Valentine *1st truck driver* • Burke Rhind *Salesman* • Richard Armstrong *Husband* ■ *Dir* Alessio DePaola • *Scr* Sonny Bono

Le Château de Ma Mère ★★★★ U

Drama 1990 · Fr · Colour · 94min

Surpassing *La Gloire de Mon Père*, this is as delightful a film as you could wish to see. The characters are old friends by now and in comparison with the boorish game hunting of the original, the encounter with a family of fraudulent Bohemians and the duel with a grouchy watchman and his dog make for much more compelling viewing. Jean Rochefort is superb as the sham pseud and Robert Alazraki's photography of Provence is sublime. Yves Robert directs with a leisure that suggests long, hot summer days, while the ending is sure to bring a lump to your throat. DP French +subtitles. Some swearing. *DVD*

Philippe Caubère *Joseph Pagnol* • Nathalie Roussel *Augustine Pagnol* • Didier Pain *Uncle Jules* • Thérèse Liotard *Aunt Rose* • Julien Ciamaca *Marcel* • Victorien Delamere *Paul* ■ *Dir* Yves Robert • *Scr* Jérôme Tonnerre, Yves Robert, from the story by Marcel Pagnol

Chato's Land ★★ 18

Western 1971 · UK · Colour · 95min

This trashily enjoyable western is flashily directed on a tiny budget by Michael Winner, with Charles Bronson as the eponymous mixed-race Apache, slowly picking off the posse that is chasing him. Bronson is his usual craggy, monosyllabic self, while Jack Palance and James Whitmore complete a formidable trio. AT *DVD*

Charles Bronson *Pardon Chato* • Jack Palance *Quincey Whitmore* • Richard Basehart *Nye Buell* • James Whitmore *Joshua Everette* • Simon Oakland *Jubal Hooker* • Ralph Waite *Elias Hooker* • Victor French *Martin Hall* ■ *Dir* Michael Winner • *Scr* Gerald Wilson

Chatroom ★★ 15

Thriller 2010 · UK · Colour · 93min

This macabre cyber-thriller stars Aaron Johnson as William, a charismatic outsider who creates an intimate internet chatroom where guests are hand-picked for membership. But what his new online friends don't realise is that he is also a dangerous individual who has chosen them for their flaws and is manipulating them all, culminating in an effort to force one of them into suicide. Johnson shines as this amoral Pied Piper, and his sinister mission gives rise to some truly disturbing moments. Sadly, these plausible chills are offset by the film's clumsy youth-movie trimmings. DW Sexual references. *DVD* *BL*

Aaron Johnson *William* • Imogen Poots *Eva* • Matthew Beard *Jim* • Hannah Murray *Emily* • Daniel Kaluuya *Mo* ■ *Dir* Hideo Nakata • *Scr* Enda Walsh, from his play

Chattahoochee ★★ 15

Biographical drama 1989 · US · Colour · 92min

Korean War veteran Emmett Foley (Gary Oldman) returns to his Southern home as a hero, goes on a shooting spree and ends up in a brutal insane asylum. The portrayal of his attempts to expose the nightmarish conditions in the 1950s psychiatric facility owe as much to Hammer horror as documentary-style realism in director Mick Jackson's grim drama, which is straight-jacketed by mental illness clichés. AJ

Gary Oldman *Emmett Foley* • Dennis Hopper *Walker Benson* • Frances McDormand *Mae Foley* • Pamela Reed *Earlene* • Ned Beatty *Doctor Harwood* • M Emmet Walsh *Morris* • William De Acutis *Missy* • Lee Wilkof *Vernon* ■ *Dir* Mick Jackson • *Scr* James Hicks

Che! ★★ 15

Biographical drama 1969 · US · Colour · 91min

Hollywood's take on the Cuban revolution stars Omar Sharif as Che Guevara and Jack Palance as Fidel Castro. Sharif looks oddly convincing – just like the poster every middle-class Marxist had over his bed – and the movie certainly celebrates Che's status as a revolutionary martyr and Robin Hood figure. As Castro, though, Palance is a rascal and a drunkard, a caricature of the man every patriotic American loves to hate. Richard Fleischer directs efficiently, but this is not remotely believable. AT Violence. *DVD*

Omar Sharif *Che Guevara* • Jack Palance *Fidel Castro* • Cesare Danova *Ramon Valdez* • Robert Loggia *Faustino Morales* • Woody Strode *Guillermo* • Barbara Luna *Anita Marquez* ■ *Dir* Richard Fleischer • *Scr* Michael Wilson, Sy Bartlett, from a story by David Karp, Sy Bartlett

Che Part One ★★★★ 15

Biographical drama
2008 · US/Sp/Fr · Colour and BW · 128min

A complex figure gets a complex treatment in Steven Soderbergh's sprawling yet selective two-part biopic, which effectively tells the same story twice. In this opening instalment, the young Guevara (Benicio Del Toro) is recruited by Fidel Castro to take part in the Cuban revolution of the late 1950s. Then the action jumps to the closing months of the war, with re-enactments in between of Che's passionate 1964 address to the United Nations. Though tough to follow at times, it's a refreshing alternative to the usual spoon-feeding of history. Key to the film's success is a charismatic performance by Del Toro, who brings a sense of a real life being lived out in the sweat and dirt of the jungle. DW Spanish, English +subtitles. *DVD* *BL*

Benicio Del Toro *Ernesto "Che" Guevara de la Serna* • Julia Ormond *Lisa Howard* • Demián Bichir [Demian Bichir] *Fidel Castro* • Rodrigo Santoro *Raul Castro* • María Isabel Díaz *María Antonia* • Ramón Fernández *Héctor* • Yul Vázquez *Alejandro Ramírez* • José Caro *Esteban* ■ *Dir* Steven Soderbergh • *Scr* Peter Buchman, from the memoirs *Reminiscences of the Cuban Revolutionary War* by Ernesto "Che" Guevara • *Cinematographer* Peter Andrews [Steven Soderbergh]

Che Part Two ★★★ 15

Biographical drama
2008 · US/Sp/Fr · Colour · 127min

Though it stands alone as a self-contained movie, the second part of Steven Soderbergh's epic biopic works best when seen in conjunction with *Part One*. Where the earlier film was a sweeping, triumphant account of the rebel leader's part in the Cuban revolution, this feels like a darker, more jittery study of his attempts to liberate Bolivia in the 1960s. But here none of Che's tricks work. Just how much of that failure is down to arrogance or simple human folly is left for the viewer to decide. As Che, Benicio Del Toro gives another impressive but inscrutable performance that reveals much of Guevara's inner

turmoil. DW Spanish, English +subtitles. Some violence, swearing. *DVD* *BL*

Benicio Del Toro *Ernesto "Che" Guevara de la Serna* • Carlos Bardem *Moisés Guevara* • Demián Bichir [Demian Bichir] *Fidel Castro* • Joaquim de Almeida *Barrientos* • Eduard Fernández *Ciro Algarañaz* • Marc-André Grondin *Régis Debray* • Matt Damon *Father Schwartz* • Franka Potente *Tania* ■ *Dir* Steven Soderbergh • *Scr* Peter Buchman, Benjamin A Van der Veen, from the memoirs *The Bolivian Diary* by Ernesto "Che" Guevara

The Cheap Detective ★★★★ PG

Detective parody 1978 · US · Colour · 92min

An innuendo-laden and shamelessly silly spoof of classic Humphrey Bogart vehicles, this overlooked Neil Simon-scripted gem is a kind of chaser to his *Murder by Death* from two years earlier, with Robert Moore once again directing and Peter Falk in similar mode as a frustrated trench-coat-wearing detective. As spot-on as Falk is as the endearingly shady sleuth investigating the murder of Floyd Merkle, he's graciously upstaged by a sextet of actresses in their prime, including Eileen Brennan, Stockard Channing, Marsha Mason and, in particular, Madeline Kahn. The film is unusually well-photographed for a comedy and zips along with a stream of one-liners. DO

Peter Falk *Lou Peckinpaugh* • Ann-Margret *Jezebel Dezire* • Eileen Brennan *Betty DeBoop* • Sid Caesar *Ezra Dezire* • Stockard Channing *Bess* • James Coco *Marcel* • Dom DeLuise *Pepe Damascus* • Louise Fletcher *Marlene DuChard* • John Houseman *Jasper Blubber* • Madeline Kahn *Mrs Montenegro* • Fernando Lamas *Paul DuChard* • Marsha Mason *Georgia Merkle* • Phil Silvers *Hoppy* • Nicol Williamson *Colonel Schlussel* • Scatman Crothers *Tinker* ■ *Dir* Robert Moore • *Scr* Neil Simon

Cheap Thrills ★★★ 15

Black comedy thriller 2013 · US · Colour · 83min

What would you do if a stranger offered you piles of cash to do anything on a dare? That's the premise of this razor-sharp morality tale, in which Pat Healy's debt-ridden family man and an old buddy from high school (Ethan Embry) are tempted to take up seemingly frivolous bets offered by a thrill-seeking couple they meet in a bar. Any laughs here are of the darkest hue, as the thought-provoking ride brings desperation and temptation, a combination that can make anyone consider the unthinkable. JA Violence, swearing, a sex scene, drug abuse. *DVD* *BL*

Pat Healy *Craig* • Ethan Embry *Vince* • Sara Paxton *Violet* • Amanda Fuller *Audrey* • David Koechner *Colin* • Laura Covelli *Caryn* ■ *Dir* EL Katz • *Scr* Trent Haaga, David Chirchirillo

Cheaper by the Dozen ★★★ U

Period comedy 1950 · US · Colour · 82min

The success of *Meet Me in St Louis* and *Life with Father* led to a postwar hunger for early 20th-century nostalgia, and no studio managed to so regularly recapture those halcyon days as 20th Century-Fox, whose backlot was turned permanently into a standing period set. Here the Gilbreth family of 12 children, headed by the ineffable Clifton Webb and the incandescent Myrna Loy, raise a ruckus and proved so popular that a follow-up (*Belles on Their Toes*) was immediately ordered. TS

Clifton Webb *Frank Bunker Gilbreth* • Jeanne Crain *Ann Gilbreth* • Myrna Loy *Mrs Lillian Gilbreth* • Betty Lynn *Libby Lancaster* • Edgar Buchanan *Dr Burton* • Barbara Bates *Ernestine* • Mildred Natwick *Mrs Mebane* • Sara Allgood *Mrs Monahan* ■ *Dir* Walter Lang • *Scr* Lamar Trotti, from the book by Frank B Gilbreth Jr, Ernestine Gilbreth Carey

Cheaper by the Dozen ★★ PG

Comedy 2003 · US · Colour · 94min

This is basically an over-extended sitcom that owes little allegiance to the original book or the delightful 1950 comedy starring Clifton Webb and Myrna Loy. Here the weight of the humour is on Steve Martin, who plays the father of 12 children. When

C

his author wife Bonnie Hunt is called away for a book launch, he has to cope with his unruly offspring. TH *DVD*

Steve Martin *Tom Baker* • Bonnie Hunt *Kate Baker* • Piper Perabo *Nora Baker* • Tom Welling *Charlie Baker* • Hilary Duff *Lorraine Baker* • Kevin G Schmidt *Henry Baker* • Alyson Stoner *Sarah Baker* • Jacob Smith *Jake Baker* • Liliana Mumy *Jessica Baker* • Morgan York *Kim Baker* • Forrest Landis *Mark Baker* ■ *Dir* Shawn Levy • *Scr* Sam Harper, Joel Cohen, Alec Sokolow, from a story by Craig Titley, from the novel by Frank Bunker Gilbreth Jr [Frank B Gilbreth Jr], Ernestine Gilbreth Carey

Cheaper by the Dozen 2 ★★ PG
Comedy 2005 · US · Colour · 89min

This limp sequel sees Steve Martin reprising his role as the daddy of the 12-strong Baker brood, who revives an old rivalry with ultra-competitive neighbour Eugene Levy – also the father of a sizeable horde of kids – during a summer camping vacation. Though the children get on, that doesn't stop the two posturing dads from a spot of macho one-upmanship. Tired and obvious. DA *DVD*

Steve Martin *Tom Baker* • Bonnie Hunt *Kate Baker* • Eugene Levy *Jimmy Murtaugh* • Piper Perabo *Nora Baker* • Tom Welling *Charlie Baker* • Hilary Duff *Lorraine Baker* • Carmen Electra *Sarina Murtaugh* • Jaime King *Anne Murtaugh* • Kevin G Schmidt *Henry Baker* • Alyson Stoner *Sarah Baker* • Jacob Smith *Jake Baker* • Forrest Landis *Mark Baker* • Liliana Mumy *Jessica Baker* ■ *Dir* Adam Shankman • *Scr* Sam Harper, from characters by Craig Titley, from the novel by Frank Bunker Gilbreth Jr [Frank B Gilbreth Jr], Ernestine Gilbreth Carey

The Cheat ★★★
Silent melodrama 1915 · US · BW · 55min

Directed by Cecil B DeMille, this melodrama caused a huge scandal in its day. Though its great age has blurred its quality and dramatic impact, it is interesting as an early example of lurid trash presented as high art. The plot concerns a society woman (Fannie Ward) who loses money that isn't hers on the stock market and borrows from a wealthy Oriental (Sessue Hayakawa) to pay her debts. When she refuses him her favours, he exacts a sadistic punishment. RK

Fannie Ward *Edith Hardy* • James Neill *Jones* • Utaka Abe *Tori's valet* • Dana Ong *District attorney* • Hazel Childers *Mrs Reynolds* • Judge Arthur H William *Courtroom judge* • Sessue Hayakawa *Haka Arakau* • Jack Dean *Dick Hardy* ■ *Dir* Cecil B DeMille • *Scr* Hector Turnbull, Jeanie MacPherson

The Cheaters ★★★ U
Comedy 1945 · US · BW · 90min

Billie Burke is the dizzy, spendthrift wife of a put-upon financier Eugene Pallette and soon their family of wealthy, upper-class eccentrics faces ruin. A solution presents itself when a rich uncle leaves his fortune to an actress (Ona Munson) he never met. After a plethora of plot complications, the situation is sorted out with the help of an attractive, down-on-his-luck actor (Joseph Schildkraut giving an outstanding performance). Directed at an appropriate pace by Joseph Kane, the result is an enjoyable melange of comedy and sentimentality. RK

Joseph Schildkraut *Mr M* • Billie Burke *Mrs Pidgeon* • Eugene Pallette *Mr Pidgeon* • Ona Munson *Florrie* • Raymond Walburn *Willie* • Anne Gillis [Ann Gillis] *Angela* • Ruth Terry *Therese* • Robert Livingston *Stephen Bates* ■ *Dir* Joseph Kane • *Scr* Frances Hyland, from a story by Frances Hyland, Albert Ray

Cheating Fate ★★
Mystery drama 2007 · US · Colour · 110min

In this meandering time-travelling adventure, bizarre things start happening after bereaved workaholic Brooke Burns unearths a mysterious music box while renovating her late aunt's home. Whenever she opens it, she is propelled into a different parallel universe, confusing her – and the viewers – as the plot holes mount. Poorly fleshed characters compound the weak

execution, meaning it's only the twisted concept that keeps you interested. Sadly, even that's undermined by the predictable feel-good resolution. SF Violence.

Brooke Burns *Anna Malone* • Paul Anthony *Billy Moss* • Beau Starr *Mac Walkin* • Christina Jastrzembska *Mrs Walkin* • Ben Cotton *Charlie* ■ *Dir* Penelope Buitenhuis • *Scr* David Golden (2)

Check and Double Check ★★
Comedy 1930 · US · BW · 77min

Hollywood's stereotyping of Mantan Moreland and Stepin Fetchit as scaredy cats was iniquitous enough, but Amos and Andy were white men Freeman Gosden and Charles Correll in blackface make-up. Consequently, it's almost impossible to watch this haunted house comedy without shuddering for all the wrong reasons. Back in the early 1930s, the proprietors of the Harlem Fresh Air Taxicab Company were among US radio's biggest stars. But the physical reality of their racial deception is embarrassing to behold. DP

Freeman F Gosden *Amos* • Charles J Correll *Andy* • Sue Carol *Jean Blair* • Charles Norton *Richard Williams* • Ralf Harolde *Ralph Crawford* • Edward Martindel *John Blair* ■ *Dir* Melville Brown [Melville W Brown] • *Scr* J Walter Ruben, from a story by Bert Kalmar, Harry Ruby

Checkers ★★ U
Sports comedy 1937 · US · BW · 78min

This is a modest, cutesy, but enjoyably event-filled rural comedy-cum-domestic drama involving the conventional devices of the genre: money problems down on the farm, a flint-hearted bank manager, and so on. The plot concerns a horse who breaks his leg, but is saved by surgery and goes on to run the movie's climactic big race to the relief of his desperate owner Stuart Erwin and the delight of Jane Withers. RK

Jane Withers *Checkers/Judy* • Stuart Erwin *Edgar Connell* • Una Merkel *Mamie Appleby* • Marvin Stephens *Jimmy Somers* • Andrew Tombes *Tobias Williams* ■ *Dir* H Bruce Humberstone • *Scr* Lynn Root, Frank Fenton, Robert Chapin, Karen De Wolf

Checking Out ★ 15
Black comedy 1988 · UK · Colour · 90min

Barely released in cinemas, this was another nail in the coffin of George Harrison's already troubled HandMade Films. Jeff Daniels stars as an advertising executive who becomes deeply neurotic after his colleague dies of a heart attack. His odyssey isn't worth the journey. AT Swearing, nudity.

Jeff Daniels *Ray Macklin* • Melanie Mayron *Jenny Macklin* • Michael Tucker *Harry Lardner* • Kathleen York *Diana* • Ann Magnuson *Connie Hagen* • Allan Havey *Pat Hagen* • Jo Harvey Allen *Barbara* • Ian Wolfe *Mr D'Amato* ■ *Dir* David Leland • *Scr* Joe Eszterhas

Checkpoint ★★ PG
Action adventure 1956 · UK · Colour · 80min

Although they promise fast-paced action, fiction films about motor racing rarely get out of first gear. At least here there is the compensation of some nifty auto action to pep up an otherwise pedestrian tale of industrial espionage, in which Stanley Baker tries to poach top-secret car designs. DP *DVD*

Anthony Steel *Bill Fraser* • Odile Versois *Francesca* • Stanley Baker *O'Donovan* • James Robertson-Justice *Warren Ingram* • Maurice Denham *Ted Thornhill* • Michael Medwin *Ginger* • Paul Muller *Petersen* ■ *Dir* Ralph Thomas • *Scr* Robin Estridge

Cheech & Chong's Up in Smoke ★★★ 18
Cult comedy 1978 · US · Colour · 81min

A good decade before the phrase was even coined, Richard "Cheech" Marin and Tommy Chong came up with what for some remains the ultimate "slacker" movie. Cheech and Chong had started off on albums only, but they made a surprisingly successful transition to the big screen; the duo made six movies together, all essential

viewing for students around the world. The first (and best) of all their films finds the genially stoned pair looking to find the best grass in town. Stacy Keach is the deranged cop on their trail, while the car made of cannabis is a hoot. JF *DVD*

Richard "Cheech" Marin *Pedro* • Thomas Chong [Tommy Chong] *Man* • Stacy Keach *Sergeant Stedenko* • Tom Skerritt *Strawberry* • Strother Martin *Arnold Stoner* ■ *Dir* Lou Adler • *Scr* Thomas Chong [Tommy Chong], Richard "Cheech" Marin

Cheech and Chong's Next Movie ★★ 18
Comedy 1980 · US · Colour · 90min

Tommy Chong made his directorial debut (he would go on to direct three more of the Cheech and Chong series) in this hit-and-miss follow-up to *Up in Smoke*, a massive cult hit around the world. The plotting this time around is even more episodic than before, but the subject matter and humour still seemed fresh and anarchic at the time. The result drifts along in an amiable, if hazy fashion. JF *DVD*

Richard "Cheech" Marin *Cheech* • Thomas Chong [Tommy Chong] *Chong* • Evelyn Guerrero *Donna* • Betty Kennedy *Candy* • Sy Kramer *Mr Neatnik* • Rikki Marin *Gloria* • Michael Winslow *Welfare comedian* • Paul Reubens *Pee-wee Herman/Desk clerk* ■ *Dir* Thomas Chong [Tommy Chong] • *Scr* Thomas Chong, Richard "Cheech" Marin

Cheech and Chong's Nice Dreams ★★ 18
Comedy 1981 · US · Colour · 83min

Number three in the series, and if you didn't appreciate the joke by now, you were never going to be won over. Stacy Keach returns from the original, Paul "Pee-wee Herman" Reuben pops up, while the sharp-eyed will spot an early film appearance by Sandra Bernhard. There's even room for a cameo from 1960s drug icon Timothy Leary, playing himself. Otherwise it's the usual sloppy mix of dope chat and slapstick from the two stars, "Cheech" Marin and Tommy Chong. JF

Tommy Chong *Chong* • Richard "Cheech" Marin *Cheech* • Stacy Keach *The Sarge* • Evelyn Guerrero *Donna* • Paul Reubens *Howie Hamburger* • Michael Masters *Willard "Animal" Bad* • Sandra Bernhard *Angie* ■ *Dir* Thomas Chong [Tommy Chong] • *Scr* Thomas Chong, Richard "Cheech" Marin

Cheech & Chong's Still Smokin' ★ 18
Comedy 1983 · US · Colour · 86min

As the medical authorities continue to tell us, smoking too much marijuana can be bad for your health. Sadly, the same applies to Cheech and Chong movies. While the duo can't be blamed for wanting to visit a cannabis mecca like Amsterdam, the resulting film is the weakest in the series: a lazy mixture of rambling sketches and concert footage. JF *DVD*

Richard "Cheech" Marin *Cheech* • Thomas Chong [Tommy Chong] *Chong* • Carol Van Herwijnen *Hotel Manager* • Shireen Strooker *Assistant manager* ■ *Dir* Thomas Chong [Tommy Chong] • *Scr* Thomas Chong, Richard "Cheech" Marin

Cheech & Chong's The Corsican Brothers ★ 15
Comedy 1984 · US · Colour · 86min

The stoner duo obviously enjoyed romping around in period dress in *Yellowbeard*, judging by this unwise departure from their successful dopehead formula. Loosely based on the classic novel by Alexandre Dumas, with the duo mugging their way through a variety of unfunny roles, this is a dreadful comic caper. JF Violence, swearing. *DVD*

Richard "Cheech" Marin *Luis (Corsican brother)* • Thomas Chong [Tommy Chong] *Lucien (Corsican brother)* • Roy Dotrice *The Evil Fuckaire/Ye Olde Jailer* • Shelby Fiddis *1st Princess* • Rikki Marin *2nd Princess* ■ *Dir* Thomas Chong [Tommy Chong] • *Scr* Richard "Cheech" Marin, Thomas Chong

Cheeni Kum ★★ PG
Romantic comedy 2007 · Ind · Colour · 134min

Set in London and Delhi, this lightweight comedy stars Bollywood stalwart Amitabh Bachchan as Buddhadev, an irascible 64-year-old chef who falls in love with 34-year-old Nina (Tabu). He travels to Delhi to ask for Nina's hand in marriage, only to find that his potential father-in-law is six years younger than him, and not happy about his proposal. It's a bit slow in exposition and hindered by repetitive dialogue and heavy-handed sentiment. But London landmarks, a memorable theme tune and a great comic performance from Zohra Sehgal as Buddhadev's elderly but perky mother lend some quality to this tale. KK Hindi +subtitles. Brief swearing, sexual references. *DVD* BL

Amitabh Bachchan *Buddhadev Gupta* • Tabu *Nina Verma* • Paresh Rawal *Omprakash Verma* • Zohra Sehgal [Zohra Segal] *Buddhadev's mother* • Swini Khara *Sexy* • Annie Vanders *Nosey London neighbour* ■ *Dir/Scr* R Balki

Cheer Boys Cheer ★★★ U
Comedy 1939 · UK · BW · 83min

A pleasing British comedy about two warring breweries: one mechanised, the other traditional. CV France runs the good ale plant and makes the better brew; bullying Edmund Gwenn manages the other. In a subplot not a million miles from *Romeo and Juliet*, their offspring – lovely Nova Pilbeam (France's daughter) and dapper Peter Coke (Gwenn's son) – fall in love. TS *DVD*

Nova Pilbeam *Margaret Greenleaf* • Edmund Gwenn *Edward Ironside* • Jimmy O'Dea *Matt Boyle* • Moore Marriott *George* • Graham Moffatt *Albert* • CV France *Tom Greenleaf* • Peter Coke *John Ironside* • Alexander Knox *Saunders* ■ *Dir* Walter Forde • *Scr* Roger MacDougall, Allan MacKinnon, from a story by Ian Dalrymple, Donald Bull

Cheers for Miss Bishop ★★★ U
Drama 1941 · US · BW · 94min

After 50 years as a dedicated schoolteacher, Miss Bishop (Martha Scott) relives her life in flashback at a banquet in her honour. As the tale of her life unfolds, we learn why this attractive woman never married. Directed by Tay Garnett, this poignant weepie co-stars William Gargan as the grocer who carries a hopeless torch for the teacher, while Donald Douglas and Sidney Blackmer play the two men she loved and lost. RK

Martha Scott *Ella Bishop* • William Gargan *Sam Peters* • Edmund Gwenn *Corcoran* • Sterling Holloway *Chris Jensen* • Sidney Blackmer *John Stevens* • Mary Anderson *Amy Saunders* ■ *Dir* Tay Garnett • *Scr* Stephen Vincent Benet, Adelaide Heilbron, Sheridan Gibney, from the novel *Miss Bishop* by Bess Streeter Aldrich

Cheetah ★★★ U
Adventure 1989 · US · Colour · 80min

Disney decamped to Kenya for what amounts to a children's version of *Born Free*. It's an amiable adventure about two Californian youngsters teaming up with a Masai boy to raise an orphaned cheetah cub, but there are few surprises in the storyline. Where the film does pick up points, however, is in the splendid photography of the Kenyan bush, the fascinating glimpses of the Masai lifestyle and the unsentimental way in which the harsh realities of nature are explained. DP *DVD*

Keith Coogan *Ted Johnson* • Lucy Deakins *Susan Johnson* • Collin Mothupi *Morogo* • Timothy Landfield *Earl Johnson* • Breon Gorman *Jean Johnson* • Ka Vundla *Kipoin* ■ *Dir* Jeff Blyth • *Scr* Erik Tarloff, John Cotter, Griff Du Rhone, from the book *The Cheetahs* by Alan Caillou • *Cinematographer* Thomas Burstyn

Chef ★★★★ 15
Comedy 2014 · US/UK/Rus · Colour · 110min

Director/star Jon Favreau's feel-good foodie film will have you salivating within minutes. He plays the stellar chef who quits his upmarket job so he can rediscover his culinary mojo. So he, ex-wife Sofia Vergara and son Emjay Anthony wind up in Miami with a food truck for an uplifting road trip back to LA that produces delicious morsels of family bonding. There is some delicious support playing (Scarlett Johansson, Robert Downey Jr), while Favreau skilfully cooks up a film that's sweet and spicy. KK Swearing, sexual references. **DVD** **BL**

Jon Favreau *Carl Casper* • Sofia Vergara *Inez* • Robert Downey Jr *Marvin* • Scarlett Johansson *Molly* • John Leguizamo *Martin* • Dustin Hoffman *Riva* ▪ *Dir/Scr* Jon Favreau

LANDMARK FILM
Andy Warhol's underground film is the 1960s precursor of reality TV

The Chelsea Girls ★★★★
Classic experimental movie
1966 · US · BW and Colour · 210min

This was the first Andy Warhol film to emerge from the underground and play at art houses. The original version comprised two films projected side by side, with a combined running time of three-and-a-half hours. The version premiered in London in 1968, which still runs so occasionally, is one film lasting two hours. It consists of 12 virtually unedited takes in which such Warhol regulars as Nico, Ingrid Superstar and International Velvet improvise dialogue in rooms at New York's Chelsea Hotel. Many are boring or inaudible, but some of them are real shockers – like the "confession" scene in which "Pope" Ondine becomes genuinely violent. DM

Ondine *"Pope"* • Angelica *"Pepper" Davis* • Ingrid Superstar • Albert René Ricard • Mary Might [Mary Woronov] *Hanoi Hanna* • International Velvet [Susan Bottomly] • Brigid Polk • Ed Hood *Ed* • Patrick Flemming • Edie Sedgwick *Edie* • Arthur Loeb • Nico ▪ *Dir* Andy Warhol • *Scr* Andy Warhol, Ronald Tavel • *Music* The Velvet Underground

Chemical Wedding ★★ 18
Supernatural thriller
2008 · UK · Colour · 106min

The life and works of notorious British occultist Aleister Crowley are the inspiration for this cheesy supernatural thriller. Co-written by Iron Maiden frontman Bruce Dickinson, the film sees Simon Callow's stuttering Cambridge professor possessed by Crowley after a botched experiment. Pompous dialogue and gleeful scenery-chewing follow, as the so-called "wickedest man in the world" transforms the don into a depraved murderer, intent on performing the eponymous occult rite. More campy than creepy, the feature exudes self-importance, yet plays like a poor Hammer horror parody with only Callow's hammy exuberance in its favour. SF Violence, sex scenes, nudity, drug abuse.

Simon Callow *Oliver Haddo* • Kal Weber *Mathers* • Lucy Cudden *Lia* • Jud Charlton *Victor* • Paul McDowell *Symonds* • John Shrapnel *Crowley* ▪ *Dir* Julian Doyle • *Scr* Bruce Dickinson, Julian Doyle

Chéri ★★★ 15
Period romantic drama
2009 · UK/Fr/Ger/Cay · Colour · 88min

More than 20 years after *Dangerous Liaisons*, Michelle Pfeiffer, director Stephen Frears and writer Christopher Hampton return to a world of frisky French money-grubbers and their romantic intrigues, this time with a dramatisation of two celebrated novels by Colette. Pfeiffer plays an ageing courtesan living in pre-First World War Paris who is given the job of educating decadent 19-year-old Chéri (Rupert Friend) for marriage. But passion overwhelms them, and they settle into a loving, long-term but ultimately doomed relationship. Up to this point the film is an idle fancy, but Pfeiffer steps up a gear and provides much-needed depth when forced to accept her innermost feelings and her fading beauty. SP **DVD**

Michelle Pfeiffer *Léa de Lonval* • Kathy Bates *Madame Peloux* • Rupert Friend *Chéri* • Felicity Jones *Edmée* • Frances Tomelty *Rose* • Anita Pallenberg *La Copine* • Harriet Walter *La Loupiote* • Iben Hjejle *Marie-Laure* • Stephen

Frears *Narrator* ▪ *Dir* Stephen Frears • *Scr* Christopher Hampton, from the novels *Chéri* and *The Last of Chéri* by Colette

Chernobyl Diaries ★★★ 15
Horror thriller
2012 · US · Colour · 87min

Debut director Brad Parker's horror tale is all about the location, as six backpackers on an eastern European "extreme tour" explore Pripyat, the abandoned town next to the infamous Chernobyl nuclear reactor, and fight for their lives against mysterious marauders. The novelty value of the desolate setting keeps things interesting, and the eeriness increases as the survivors descend towards the location of the core meltdown, even though the predictable climax is well telegraphed by this point. AJ In English, Russian. Violence, swearing. **DVD** **BL**

Devin Kelley *Amanda* • Jonathan Sadowski *Paul* • Ingrid Bolso Berdal *Zoe* • Olivia Taylor Dudley [Olivia Dudley] *Natalie* • Jesse McCartney *Chris* • Nathan Phillips *Michael* • Dimitri Diatchenko *Uri* ▪ *Dir* Brad Parker • *Scr* Oren Peli, Carey Van Dyke, Shane Van Dyke, from a story by Peli

Cherokee Strip ★★
Western
1940 · US · BW · 84min

Richard Dix was no stranger to the Wild West, having earned an Oscar nomination for his role in the 1931 version of *Cimarron*, but he's rather looking his age in this unremarkable story about a square-jawed marshal taking on a gang of desperados. Lesley Selander, best known for his collaborations with Tim Holt and William "Hopalong Cassidy" Boyd, directs with undue fuss. DP

Richard Dix *Dave Morrell* • Florence Rice *Kate Cross* • Victor Jory *Clay Barrett* • Andy Clyde *Tex Crawford* • George E Stone *Abe Gabbert* • Morris Ankrum *Hawk* ▪ *Dir* Lesley Selander • *Scr* Norman Houston, Bernard McConville, from a story by Bernard McConville

Cherry ★★ 18
Drama
2012 · US · Colour · 97min

Tales of youngsters drawn into the murky world of adult entertainment are nothing new and this strangely sterile film has little to add. Ashley Hinshaw stars as the wide-eyed teenager who leaves her troubled home behind to make something of herself in San Francisco. Heather Graham plays a film-maker, echoing her involvement in *Boogie Nights* – arguably the best movie about the porn industry and the lost souls within it. But here subplots remain undeveloped and there's just not enough edge or indeed any point to it at all. JA **DVD** **BL**

Ashley Hinshaw *Angelina* • James Franco *Frances* • Heather Graham *Margaret* • Lili Taylor *Phyllis* • Dev Patel *Andrew* ▪ *Dir* Stephen Elliott (2) • *Scr* Stephen Elliott (2), Lorelei Lee

Cherry Falls ★★★ 18
Horror thriller
1999 · US · Colour · 87min

A masked maniac is killing only the virgins among the local high-school teens in *Romper Stomper* director Geoffrey Wright's sprightly shocker. Cleverly toying with genre conventions, Wright's unpretentious psycho chiller reverses the "have sex and die" theme of the late 1970s, as the rush to get deflowered at a student organised orgy has the parents' blessing. The brisk script sparkles with quirky characters, off-kilter situations and crisp campus dialogue. AJ Violence, swearing, brief nudity. **DVD**

Brittany Murphy *Jody Marken* • Michael Biehn *Sheriff Brent Marken* • Gabriel Mann *Kenny Ascott* • Jesse Bradford *Rod Harper* • Jay Mohr *Leonard Marliston* • Douglas Spain *Mark* • Keram Malicki-Sanchez *Timmy* • Natalie Ramsey *Sandy* • Candy Clark *Marge Marken* ▪ *Dir* Geoffrey Wright • *Scr* Ken Selden

Cherry, Harry & Raquel ★★★ 18
Sex drama
1969 · US · Colour · 72min

This is a seminal trip down mammary lane for Russ Meyer, the "King Leer" of the American soft-core sexploitation industry. The plot has something to do with corrupt sheriff Harry (Charles Napier, a Meyer

favourite) trying to keep the lid on his marijuana-smuggling scam when threatened with exposure. Punctuating the flimsy story are sharply-edited bedroom scenes showing Harry, nurse Cherry and mob mistress Raquel in all manner of sexual situations. Witty and compact, this was co-scripted by famed author Tom Wolfe under the pseudonym Thomas J McGowan. AJ Swearing, violence. **DVD**

Larissa Ely *Raquel* • Linda Ashton *Cherry* • Charles Napier *Harry* • Bert Santos *Enrique* • Franklin H Bolger [Franklin Bolger] *Mr Franklin* • Astrid Lillimor [Uschi Digard] *Soul* • Michele Grand *Millie* • John Milo *Apache* • Robert Aiken *Tom* • Russ Meyer ▪ *Dir* Russ Meyer • *Scr* Russ Meyer, Thomas J McGowan [Tom Wolfe], from a story by Russ Meyer • *Producer* Russ Meyer

The Cherry Orchard ★★★ PG
Drama
1998 · Gr/Cyp/Fr · Colour · 141min

Anton Chekhov called his play a comedy, but there's nothing comic about this version from Greek director Michael Cacoyannis, which places the emphasis squarely on melancholy. Charlotte Rampling leaves an unhappy affair in Paris for a family estate inhabited by dissolute relatives. There, the only way to stave off bankruptcy is to have the orchard chopped down to make way for money-making new houses. Alan Bates plays Rampling's indecisive brother, Frances de la Tour is a deliciously mad governess, and it all looks stunning. The satire is missing, however, and the film is dour to the point of being lugubrious. TH

Charlotte Rampling *Lyubov Andreyevna (Ranevskaya)* • Alan Bates *Gaev (Leonid Andreyevich)* • Katrin Cartlidge *Varya (Varvara Mihailovna)* • Owen Teale *Lopahin (Yermolai Alexeyevich)* • Frances de la Tour *Charlotta* ▪ *Dir* Michael Cacoyannis • *Scr* Michael Cacoyannis, from the play by Anton Chekhov

Cherry Tree Lane ★★ 18
Horror thriller
2010 · UK · Colour · 74min

British film-maker Paul Andrew Williams followed his stunning debut, crime drama *London to Brighton*, with bizarre horror *The Cottage*, and this, his third film, plays like a difficult marriage of both genres. A middle-class couple (Rachael Blake and Tom Butcher) are terrorised in their home by a gang of youths and though the violence happens off-screen, it still feels exploitative. Both Blake and Ashley Chin, as one of the youths, give impressive performances but generally the characters lack depth and the story is as aimless as the gang. SP Violence, swearing. **DVD**

Rachael Blake *Christine* • Tom Butcher *Mike* • Ashley Chin *Asad* • Sonny Muslim *Teddy* • Jumayn Hunter *Rian* • Jennie Jacques *Beth* ▪ *Dir/Scr* Paul Andrew Williams

Cherry 2000 ★★ 15
Science-fiction thriller
1988 · US · Colour · 94min

Set in the year 2017 when sexual partners have been replaced by robot playmates, it follows the travails of David Andrews, who heads off into the desert for spare parts with expert scavenger Melanie Griffith when his mechanical dream girl breaks down. Some nice effects can't hide the B-movie performances. JB Violence, swearing, sex scenes.

Melanie Griffith *E Johnson* • David Andrews (2) *Sam Treadwell* • Ben Johnson (1) *Six Finger Jake* • Tim Thomerson *Lester* • Brion James *Stacy* • Pamela Gidley *Cherry 2000* • Harry Carey Jr *Snappy Tom* • Cameron Milzer *Ginger* ▪ *Dir* Steve De Jarnatt • *Scr* Michael Almereyda, from a story by Lloyd Fonvielle

Cherrybomb ★★ 15
Drama
2008 · UK/Ire · Colour · 82min

In this tale of rebellious Belfast teenagers, high-flying student Malachy (Rupert Grint) and his wayward pal Luke (Robert Sheehan) are looking forward to an idyllic post-exams summer. But when the flirtatious Michelle (Kimberley Nixon) appears, the boys embark on a series of drug-fuelled dares to impress her. Directors Lisa Barros D'Sa and Glenn Leyburn aim for sexually charged edginess, but fall back on glib outrage and

spend little time examining what makes their characters tick. TeS **DVD**

Rupert Grint *Malachy* • Robert Sheehan *Luke* • Kimberley Nixon *Michelle* • James Nesbitt *Crilly* • Lalor Roddy *Smiley* ▪ *Dir* Lisa Barros D'Sa, Glenn Leyburn • *Scr* Daragh Carville

The Chess Player ★★★★ U
Silent period drama
1927 · Fr · BW and Tinted · 135min

Although it boasts sumptuous production values, what most impresses about this period drama is the way in which director Raymond Bernard subtly uses silent imagery to convey exactly what all the characters are feeling. Hiding in a chess-playing automaton to avoid capture, Pierre Blanchar is surprisingly expressive as the Polish rebel who is delivered into the court of Catherine II (Marcelle Charles-Dullin). Banned by the Nazis in 1940, this exquisite film was restored 50 years later by archivist Kevin Brownlow from prints found in four different countries. DP

Edith Jehanne *Sophie Novinska* • Pierre Blanchar *Boleslas Vorowski* • Pierre Batcheff *Prince Serge Oblomoff* • Charles Dullin *Baron von Kempelen* • Marcelle Charles-Dullin *Catherine II* ▪ *Dir* Raymond Bernard • *Scr* Raymond Bernard, Jean-José Frappa, from the novel *Le Joueur d'Échecs* by Henri Dupuy-Mazuel

The Chess Players ★★★★ PG
Historical drama
1977 · Ind · Colour · 115min

Largely dismissed for its precise symbolism and deliberate pacing, this is one of Satyajit Ray's most undervalued features. Exquisitely re-creating the opulence of Lucknow on the eve of the Indian Mutiny, this historical satire exposes both the ruthless ambition of the imperialists and the indolence of the local rulers. As the chess-playing noblemen who are as uninterested in their families as they are in affairs of state, Sanjeev Kumar and Saeed Jaffrey are deftly comic in their inability to equate their game with the power struggle going on around them. DP Hindi, English +subtitles. **DVD**

Sanjeev Kumar *Mirza* • Saeed Jaffrey *Mir* • Amjad Khan *Wajid Ali Shah* • Richard Attenborough *General Outram* • Shabana Azmi *Mirza's wife* • Farida Jalal *Mir's wife* ▪ *Dir* Satyajit Ray • *Scr* Satyajit Ray, from a story by Munshi Premchand

Le Cheval d'Orgueil ★★★
Period drama
1980 · Fr · Colour · 118min

Claude Chabrol, no stranger to the provinces, adopts an almost anthropological stance in chronicling the lives of a Breton family in the years preceding the Great War. Yet while he faithfully records the costumes and customs of the indomitable people celebrated in Pierre-Jakez Helias's book, he dilutes their socio-political problems by romanticising their poverty. DP French +subtitles.

Jacques Dufilho *Alain Le Goff* • Bernadette Le Saché *Anne-Marie Le Goff* • François Cluzet *Pierre-Alain Le Goff* • Ronan Hubert *Pierre-Jacques aged 7* • Arnel Hubert *Pierre-Jacques aged 17* ▪ *Dir* Claude Chabrol • *Scr* Claude Chabrol, Daniel Boulanger, from the novel by Pierre-Jakez Helias

Chevalier ★★ 18
Comedy
2015 · Gr · Colour · 105min

Set on a luxury yacht in the Aegean, this cryptic comedy finds six middle-aged men deciding to ratchet up their holiday banter by turning it into a competition. Starting with a series of mundane tasks, the aim of the game is to single out the man who is "the best in general". That the rules are never explained is part of the film's perverse charm – but after a bawdily amusing erection contest, this really doesn't have much more to say on the subject of male one-upmanship. DW Greek +subtitles. Nudity, sexual references.

Yiorgis Kendros *The Doctor* • Panos Koronis *Yorgos* • Vangelis Mourikis *Joseph* • Efthymis Papadimitriou *Dimitris* ▪ *Dir* Athina Rachel Tsangari • *Scr* Athina Rachel Tsangari, Efthimis Filippou

C

Cheyenne Autumn ★★★★ U

Epic western 1964 · US · Colour · 124min

The last western made by the great John Ford is effectively an apology for the many wrongs done by Hollywood to the American Indian. It maintains tremendous dignity in those sections actually dealing with the tragic resettlement of the Cheyenne by the US government, but it is undermined by a tasteless would-be comic central section set in Dodge City. Still, here's Ford's beloved Monument Valley and a distinguished cast headed by the underrated Richard Widmark in a story of genuine epic scale. TS

Richard Widmark *Captain Thomas Archer* · Carroll Baker *Deborah Wright* · Karl Malden *Captain Oscar Wessels* · James Stewart *Wyatt Earp* · Edward G Robinson *Secretary of the Interior* · Sal Mineo *Red Shirt* · Dolores Del Rio *Spanish Woman* · Ricardo Montalban *Little Wolf* · Gilbert Roland *Dull Knife* · Arthur Kennedy *Doc Holliday* · John Carradine *Major Jeff Blair* ■ *Dir* John Ford · *Scr* James R Webb, from the novel by Mari Sandoz

The Cheyenne Social Club ★★★

Comedy western 1970 · US · Colour · 101min

Gene Kelly was seriously underrated as a director in his post-MGM period, but his dry wit is given full rein in this rather tame western, about a couple of cowboys (James Stewart and Henry Fonda) who inherit a brothel. The photography (by western veteran William Clothier) looks good, but some may be deterred by Kelly's rather smutty treatment of the subject matter. TS Swearing, nudity.

James Stewart *John O'Hanlan* · Henry Fonda *Harley Sullivan* · Shirley Jones *Jenny* · Sue Ane Langdon *Opal Ann* · Elaine Devry *Pauline* · Robert Middleton *Barman* · Arch Johnson *Marshal Anderson* · Dabbs Greer *Willowby* ■ *Dir* Gene Kelly · *Scr* James Lee Barrett

Chicago ★★★★ 12

Musical comedy drama
2002 · US/Ger · Colour · 108min

Renée Zellweger plays Roxie Hart, the ambitious newcomer who dreams of singing and dancing in one of the city's jazz clubs, and Catherine Zeta-Jones is Velma, the established performer. After the shootings of a lover and a faithless husband, they end up in prison, where they find that the publicity surrounding a capital murder case can be a boon to a career in showbusiness. Director Rob Marshall licks the problem of how to film a musical that was presented as vaudeville on stage by re-creating the musical numbers as fantasies in Roxie's head. He loses none of the energy of the stage version nor its dark subtext on the corrupting nature of stardom. BP Violence, sexual references. DVD Blu

Catherine Zeta-Jones *Velma Kelly* · Renée Zellweger *Roxie Hart* · Richard Gere *Billy Flynn* · Queen Latifah *Matron "Mama" Morton* · Christine Baranski *Mary Sunshine* · John C Reilly *Amos Hart* · Taye Diggs *The Band Leader* · Dominic West *Fred Casely* · Lucy Liu *Go-to-Hell Kitty* · Colm Feore *Martin Harrison* ■ *Dir* Rob Marshall · *Scr* Bill Condon, from the musical by Fred Ebb, John Kander, Bob Fosse, from the play by Maurine Dallas Watkins [Maurine Watkins] · *Cinematographer* Dion Beebe · *Production Designer* John Myhre · *Costume Designer* Colleen Attwood · *Editor* Martin Walsh

Chicago Cab ★★★

Drama 1998 · US · Colour · 89min

Cameos from Gillian Anderson, Julianne Moore and John Cusack are what will draw most viewers to this overlooked day-in-the-life drama. But it'll be Paul Dillon's performance you'll remember: he adroitly captures the range of emotions that a taxi driver experiences on the streets, as he picks up such diverse passengers as zealous church-goers, a rape victim, smug businessmen, wasted party animals and a pregnant couple in a hurry. He's abetted by an assured sense of location from married directors Mary Cybulski and John Tintori. DP Swearing, drug abuse, a sex scene.

Paul Dillon *Cab driver* · Gillian Anderson *Southside girl* · John Cusack *Scary man* · Moira Harris *Religious mother* · Michael Ironside *Al* · Laurie Metcalf *Ad executive* · Julianne Moore *Distraught woman* · Kevin J O'Connor *Southside guy* · John C Reilly *Steve* ■ *Dir* Mary Cybulski, John Tintori · *Scr* Will Kern, from his play *Hellcab*

Chicago Confidential ★★★

Crime drama 1957 · US · BW · 73min

In one of those gangster exposés that flourished in the late 1950s, the sincere and honest leader of a trade union is framed for murder by a gambling syndicate that wants to take over his organisation. Brian Keith, Beverly Garland and Elisha Cook Jr manage to hold the interest, while cowboy actor Dick Foran gets down from his horse to play the victimised union leader. It all feels rather predictable now, though. TH

Brian Keith *Jim Fremont* · Beverly Garland *Laura* · Dick Foran *Blane* · Beverly Tyler *Sylvia* · Elisha Cook Jr *Candymouth* · Paul Langton *Jake Parker* · Tony George *Duncan* ■ *Dir* Sidney Salkow · *Scr* Raymond T Marcus [Bernard Gordon], from the story by Hugh King (uncredited) and the book by Jack Lait, Lee Mortimer

Chicago Joe and the Showgirl ★★ 18

War drama based on a true story
1989 · UK · Colour · 98min

English showgirl (Emily Lloyd, annoying) and an American GI (Kiefer Sutherland, over the top) become lovers in England during the Second World War and go on a crime and murder spree. However, because no one knows to this day why the pair actually committed the crimes, director Bernard Rose and his scriptwriter David Yallop resort to clichés. JB Swearing. DVD

Kiefer Sutherland *Karl Hulten/"Ricky Allen"* · Emily Lloyd *Elizabeth Maud Jones/"Georgina Grayson"* · Patsy Kensit *Joyce Cook* · Keith Allen *Lenny Bexley* · Liz Fraser *Mrs Evans* ■ *Dir* Bernard Rose · *Scr* David Yallop

Chick Lit ★★ 15

Comedy 2016 · UK · Colour · 95min

Needing £300,000 to save the local pub, journalist Christian McKay persuades his mates to co-write a BDSM shocker. But when agents Eileen Atkins and John Hurt find a publisher, McKay has to talk her sister-in-law, Dakota Blue Richards, into posing as the author. Smoothly played and eminently watchable (for all its contrivances), this rattles through its predictable twists. But a resistible chauvinism colours the jokes about female reading habits and, even though the gents have the tables turned on them, this feels a touch parochial and smug. DP

Christian McKay *David Rose* · Dakota Blue Richards *Zoe* · Caroline Catz *Jen* · David Troughton *Justin* · Miles Jupp *Marcus* · John Hurt *Francis Bonar* · Eileen Atkins *Peggy Law* ■ *Dir* Tony Britten · *Scr* Tony Britten, Oliver Britten

Chicken ★★★ 15

Coming-of-age drama
2015 · UK · Colour · 85min

Scott Chambers reprises the role he originated on stage in debuting director Joe Stephenson's careful, if not always convincing, adaptation of Freddie Machin's 2011 play. As a 15-year-old with learning difficulties who shares a rickety caravan in Norfolk with his temperamental older brother and his pet chicken, Chambers exudes naive optimism, trusting implicitly in his brother's protection. The eventual twist exposes Stephenson's tonal uncertainty, but Chambers's performance is compelling. DP Violence, swearing.

Scott Chambers *Richard* · Yasmin Paige *Annabel* · Morgan Watkins *Polly* · Gina Bramhill *Tara* · Michael Culkin *McClint* ■ *Dir* Joe Stephenson · *Scr* Chris New, from Freddie Machin's play

The Chicken Chronicles ★★ 18

Comedy 1977 · US · Colour · 90min

Not a particular highpoint for Phil Silvers in the twilight of his career, though he still comes off best from this cheap teen comedy. Silvers aside, this is notable only

for providing a very early film role for Steve Guttenberg, who plays a randy adolescent trying to make sense of his life. It's amusing, but tame. JF

Phil Silvers *Max Ober* · Ed Lauter *Mr Nastase* · Steve Guttenberg *David Kessler* · Lisa Reeves *Margaret Shaffer* · Meredith Baer *Tracy* · Branscombe Richmond *Mark* · Will Seltzer *Weinstein* ■ *Dir* Francis Simon · *Scr* Paul Diamond, from his novel

Chicken Every Sunday ★★

Period comedy 1948 · US · BW · 94min

Dan Dailey stars as the husband who thinks he can reject honest hard work in favour of ill-judged scheming. As he is taught his life's lesson very slowly, we are left to wonder what a nice all-American "gal" like Celeste Holm is doing with him in the first place. This is a very dated slice of mom's apple pie served over the white picket fence with a side order of regulation family values. SH

Dan Dailey *Jim Hefferen* · Celeste Holm *Emily Hefferen* · Colleen Townsend *Rosemary Hefferen* · Alan Young *Geoffrey Lawson* · Natalie Wood *Ruth* ■ *Dir* George Seaton · *Scr* George Seaton, Valentine Davies, from the play by Julius J Epstein, Philip G Epstein, from a novel by Rosemary Taylor

Chicken Little ★★ U

Animated comedy adventure
2005 · US · Colour · 77min

Diminutive Chicken Little (voiced by Zach Braff) is mocked by the other animal residents of Oakey Oaks after his mistaken claim that the sky is falling. However, the bird's paranoia eventually proves to be well founded when an alien invasion begins. Disney's first fully computer-generated animated feature is technically accomplished, but not innovative, while the manic yet flimsy characters draw attention to the unfocused plotline and uneven tone. SF DVD Blu CG

Zach Braff *Chicken Little* · Garry Marshall *Buck Cluck* · Joan Cusack *Abby Mallard* · Steve Zahn *Runt of the litter* · Amy Sedaris *Foxy Loxy* · Don Knotts *Mayor Turkey Lurkey* · Harry Shearer *Dog announcer* · Patrick Stewart *Mr Woolensworth* · Wallace Shawn *Principal Fetchit* ■ *Dir* Mark Dindal · *Scr* Steve Bencich, Ron J Friedman, Ron Anderson, from a story by Mark Dindal, Mark Kennedy

Chicken Run ★★★★ U

Animated comedy adventure
2000 · US/UK · Colour · 80min

This feathered pastiche of such PoW classics as *The Great Escape* and *Stalag 17* is an awesome achievement by consummate film-makers Aardman Animation. Rocky (voiced by Mel Gibson), a "lone free-ranger" rooster, promises to help the hens in Mr and Mrs Tweedy's high-security egg farm find a way to freedom. The nods to classic film moments are funny and plentiful, the largely British voice cast lends moments of humour and pathos, and the set pieces are exhilarating in their ingenuity and élan. DP DVD

Mel Gibson *Rocky* · Julia Sawalha *Ginger* · Imelda Staunton *Bunty* · Jane Horrocks *Babs* · Miranda Richardson *Mrs Tweedy* · Phil Daniels *Fetcher* · Timothy Spall *Nick* ■ *Dir* Nick Park, Peter Lord · *Scr* Karey Kirkpatrick, from a story by Nick Park, Peter Lord

Chicken Tikka Masala ★★ 15

Romantic comedy 2005 · UK · Colour · 95min

Sally Bankes's brassy turn isn't enough to save this mediocre comedy, made on a shoestring by first-time director Harmage Singh Kalirai. Chris Bisson plays a young Indian groom-to-be who can't bring himself to tell his parents he's gay and very much in love with Peter Ash. To make matters even more unlikely, misunderstandings lead his family to believe that Bisson is in a relationship with his landlady (Bankes). Contrived and sluggishly paced. DP Swearing.

Chris Bisson *Jimi* · Peter Ash *Jack* · Saeed Jaffrey *Mr CP Chopra* · Sally Bankes *Vanessa* · Zohra Segal *Grandmother* · Jamila Massey *Mrs Asha Chopra* · Jinder Mahal *Simran* · Sushil

Chudasama *Ravi Chopra* ■ *Dir* Harmage Singh Kalirai · *Scr* Roopesh Parekh, from an idea by Sanjay Tandon, Rony Ghosh

Chico & Rita ★★★ 15

Animated musical romance
2010 · Sp/UK · Colour · 89min

This animated musical for grown-ups charts the turbulent relationship of a gifted jazz pianist and his sultry chanteuse from 1940s Cuba right up to the modern day. There's much to admire in the film's vividly imagined backgrounds, taking in pre-Castro Havana, the Big Apple's thriving nightclub scene and bohemian Paris. With so many positives, it's a shame that the film-makers never really bring the central characters to life, meaning that Chico and Rita's stormy relationship is not that involving. Overall, this is captivating as a riot of rhythm and colour, but somewhat disappointing in the story department. TJ Spanish, English +subtitles. Swearing, a brief sex scene, nudity. DVD Blu

Eman Xor Oña *Chico* · Bebo Valdés *Chico* · Limara Meneses *Rita* · Idania Valdés *Rita* ■ *Dir* Javier Mariscal, Fernando Trueba, Tono Errando · *Scr* Ignacio Martínez de Pisón, Fernando Trueba

Chief Crazy Horse ★★

Biographical western 1955 · US · Colour · 86min

Victor Mature is improbably cast as the great leader of the Sioux nation, but newcomers Ray Danton and Keith Larsen are on hand to add dignity, and veteran John Lund looks good in a cavalry outfit. There's no real thought or style on show here, and the target audience seems to have been a very young one. TS

Victor Mature *Crazy Horse* · Suzan Ball *Black Shawl* · John Lund *Major Twist* · Ray Danton *Little Big Man* · Keith Larsen *Flying Hawk* · Paul Guilfoyle (1) *Worm* · David Janssen *Lieutenant Cartwright* · Robert Warwick *Spotted Tail* ■ *Dir* George Sherman · *Scr* Franklin Coen, Gerald Drayson Adams, from a story by Gerald Drayson Adams

LANDMARK FILM

Luis Buñuel's surrealist collaboration with Salvador Dali sets the pace with its juxtaposition of ideas and images

Un Chien Andalou ★★★★★ 15

Silent experimental classic
1928 · Fr · BW · 15min

How best to recommend a film that runs for less than 20 minutes, with no discernible plot, and that opens with one of cinema's most abidingly shocking sequences? The term "surreal" is nowadays used as a critical cover-all, but in this case director Luis Buñuel and co-writer Salvador Dali were setting the pace, and this is still regarded, rightly, as a cinematic landmark. Search for deeper meaning with due care and attention, or simply sit back and enjoy the abandon with which this juxtaposes ideas and images, sometimes jarringly, occasionally as visual rhymes, such as the cloud slicing across the moon that becomes a razor blade swiped across a woman's eyeball (still the film's greatest coup). AC DVD

Pierre Batcheff *Young man* · Simone Mareuil *Girl* · Luis Buñuel *Man with razor* · Salvador Dalí *Marist priest* · Jaime Miravilles *Seminarist* ■ *Dir* Luis Buñuel · *Scr* Luis Buñuel, Salvador Dali

La Chienne ★★★★

Romantic drama 1931 · Fr · BW · 100min

Unhappily married cashier and part-time artist Michel Simon becomes infatuated with prostitute Janie Marèze, and is callously exploited by her and her violent pimp Georges Flament. This moral fable, in which Simon inexorably slips down the criminal scale towards murder, was filmed by Jean Renoir on the streets of Montmartre – an influential break from the usual studio sets – and still makes for compelling viewing. Simon gives a superbly expressive performance. Remade in Hollywood by Fritz Lang as *Scarlet Street*. AT French +subtitles.

Michel Simon *Maurice* • Janie Marèze *Lulu* • Georges Flament *André* ■ *Dir* Jean Renoir • *Scr* Jean Renoir, André Girard, from a novel by Georges de la Fouchardière

Les Chiens ★★★ 15
Psychological thriller 1978 · Fr · Colour · 99min

Alain Jessua directs this brave and intriguing movie, a severe portrait of life in an impersonal environment depicted as a microcosm of a fascist state. In a town surrounded by mountains, a young doctor sets up practice and finds that he is treating a number of severe wounds. When the town's mayor is murdered, he and his girlfriend try to escape the inhabitants, who have trained vicious dogs to subdue guest workers. While at times confusing and not an easy watch, this is still original and thought provoking. **BB** French +subtitles.

Gérard Depardieu *Morel* • Victor Lanoux *Dr Henri Féret* • Nicole Calfan *Elisabeth Barrault* • Pierre Vernier *Gauthier* • Fanny Ardant *Nurse* ■ *Dir* Alain Jessua • *Scr* André Ruellan, Alain Jessua

Le Chignon d'Olga ★★★★ 15
Comedy drama 2002 · Fr/Bel · Colour · 92min

Jérôme Bonnell's debut feature combines the idealism of youth with mundane reality without romanticising or demeaning either. Set in Louveciennes in late summer, the story charts teenager Hubert Benhamdine's growing obsession with glamorous bookshop assistant Delphine Rollin, which serves as an emotional buffer to the harsher reality of the recent death of his mother that has also had a traumatic effect on his father (Serge Riaboukine) and sister (Florence Loiret Caille). It's a literate, compassionate study of survival. **DP** French +subtitles. *DVD*

Hubert Benhamdine *Julien* • Nathalie Boutefeu *Alice* • Serge Riaboukine *Gilles* • Florence Loiret Caille *Emma* • Antoine Goldet *Basile* • Delphine Rollin *Olga* • Valérie Stroh *Nicole* ■ *Dir/Scr* Jérôme Bonnell

Chihwaseon (Drunk on Women and Poetry)
★★★★ 15
Biographical drama
2002 · S Kor · Colour · 116min

Im Kwon-taek shared the director's prize at Cannes for this stately study of Jang Seung-up, the self-taught peasant who became Oh-won, the most important Korean artist of the late-19th century. Choi Min-sik gives a burly performance as the bibulous, womanising non-conformist who embraced external influences, loved a persecuted Catholic and defied dignitaries and monarchs alike. Handsomely mounted and packed with incident and transient characters, this is complex and compelling. But the real fascination lies in watching Oh-won's breathtaking imagery take shape on the fragile roll paper, particularly when the black outlines are emblazoned with dramatic colour. **DP** Korean +subtitles. *DVD*

Choi Min-sik *Jang Seung-up, Oh-won* • You Ho-jeong *Mae-hyang* • Ahn Sung-kee *Kim Byung-moon* • Kim Yeo-jin *Jin-hong* • Son Ye-jin *So-woon* ■ *Dir* Im Kwon-taek • *Scr* Kim Young-oak, Im Kwon-taek

Chiko ★★★ 18
Crime drama 2007 · Ger/It · Colour · 92min

Ozgur Yildirim's unflinching debut feature focuses on the limited options open to young Turks in Hamburg's tough Dulsberg district. Best buddies through adversity, Chiko (Denis Moschitto) and Tibet (Volkan Ozcan) are so close that Chiko is like a second son to his friend's ailing mother (Lilay Huser). But when they begin drug dealing for music producer Brownie (Moritz Bleibtreu), their relationship is severely tested. "Pusher" pictures trade in clichés and caricatures and Yildirim allows himself to be seduced by them here, much as Chiko is by the trappings of his success. The film is maybe more effective as a social study – the role that Islam plays in the daily lives of the antiheroes is fascinating. **DP** German,

Turkish +subtitles. Violence, swearing, sex scenes, nudity, drug abuse.

Denis Moschitto *Chiko* • Moritz Bleibtreu *Brownie* • Volkan Ozcan *Tibet* • Fahri Ogun Yardim *Curly* • Reyhan Sahin *Meryem* ■ *Dir/Scr* Ozgur Yildirim

Child 44 ★★★ 15
Thriller 2014 · US · Colour · 131min

This adaptation of Tom Rob Smith's bestseller shakes up the serial killer flick, transposing the customary grisly crimes to the Stalin-era Soviet Union. It follows tarnished MGB agent Tom Hardy and his clandestine pursuit of a child killer, accompanied by his plucky wife, Noomi Rapace. Swedish director Daniel Espinosa's efforts to balance the political context, murder hunt and romance are muddled, but his moody, interrogative approach suits the subject and Hardy is believably tortured as an apparently monstrous man who we come to admire. **EAS** *DVD* *BL*

Tom Hardy *Leo Demidov* • Gary Oldman *General Mikhail Nesterov* • Noomi Rapace *Raisa Demidov* • Joel Kinnaman *Vasili* • Jason Clarke (2) *Anatoly Tarasovich Brodsky* • Philip Seymour Hoffman ■ *Dir* Daniel Espinosa • *Scr* Richard Price, from Tom Rob Smith's novel

Child in the House ★★★ U
Drama 1956 · UK · BW · 87min

With her mother in hospital and her father (Stanley Baker) on the run, 11-year-old Mandy Miller is sent to live with her sniffy aunt Phyllis Calvert and rigid uncle Eric Portman. Her presence has an unexpected effect on all concerned. A modest British-made drama, co-directed by Cy Endfield (*Zulu*) and jam-packed with such stalwarts of the acting profession as Dora Bryan, Joan Hickson and Alfie Bass. Good for a tear or two. **RK**

Phyllis Calvert *Evelyn Acheson* • Eric Portman *Henry Acheson* • Stanley Baker *Stephen Lorimer* • Mandy Miller (1) *Elizabeth Lorimer* • Dora Bryan *Cassie* • Joan Hickson *Cook* • Victor Maddern *Bert* • Alfie Bass *Ticket collector* ■ *Dir* C Raker Endfield [Cy Endfield], Charles de Lautour • *Scr* C Raker Endfield [Cy Endfield], from the novel by Janet McNeill

A Child Is Waiting ★★★ PG
Drama 1962 · US · BW · 100min

After John Cassavetes had shot this drama, producer Stanley Kramer fired him and edited it himself, turning what was reputedly a rather tough movie into a sentimental one that tub-thumps its message about the care of an autistic child, played by Bruce Ritchey. Burt Lancaster and Judy Garland star as the child's psychologists, and Gena Rowlands (Cassavetes's wife) and Steven Hill play its parents. Often powerful and always well acted. **AT** *DVD*

Burt Lancaster *Dr Matthew Clark* • Judy Garland *Jean Hansen* • Gena Rowlands *Sophie Widdicombe* • Steven Hill *Ted Widdicombe* • Bruce Ritchey *Reuben Widdicombe* • Gloria McGehee *Mattie* • Paul Stewart *Goodman* ■ *Dir* John Cassavetes • *Scr* Abby Mann, from his story

Child of Divorce ★★★
Drama 1946 · US · BW · 62min

This poignant B-movie is given strength and focus by Sharyn Moffet's performance as a little girl whose parents separate. It is the feature debut of Richard Fleischer, who went on to direct such fine films as *Compulsion* and *10 Rillington Place*. Only an hour long, this is a good deal more touching than many a bigger film on the subject. **TS**

Sharyn Moffett *Bobby* • Regis Toomey *Ray* • Madge Meredith *Joan* • Walter Reed *Michael* • Una O'Connor *Nora* • Doris Merrick *Louise* ■ *Dir* Richard D Fleischer [Richard Fleischer] • *Scr* Lillie Hayward, from the play *Wednesday's Child* by Leopold Atlas

The Childhood of a Leader
★★★ 12A
Period psychological thriller
2015 · US/Can/Fr/Swe/Bel/UK · Colour · 115min

This challenging psychodrama chronicles the childhood experiences of a future

dictator. The father (Liam Cunningham) is always busy with work, leaving his wife (Berenice Bejo) to discipline their seven-year-old son (Tom Sweet) but, as time passes, the boy is increasingly wilful and defiant. This is where the film is most effective, with Sweet providing a disquieting performance as the little sociopath at the centre of the story. The pace may be too deliberate for some, but this is still a bold film that draws you in. **SC**

Bérénice Bejo *Mother* • Liam Cunningham *Father* • Robert Pattinson *Charles* • Stacy Martin *Teacher* • Yolande Moreau *Maid* ■ *Dir/Scr* Brady Corbet

The Children ★★
Drama 1990 · UK/W Ger · Colour · 91min

Previously filmed in 1929 as *The Marriage Playground*, Edith Wharton's novel is here respectfully adapted by playwright Timberlake Wertenbaker. Ben Kingsley gives a typically sensitive performance as the Europe-based engineer whose plans to marry widow Kim Novak are waylaid by his growing obsession with Siri Neal. Though pictorially resplendent and played with precision, the film is technically naive and dramatically unsatisfying. **DP**

Ben Kingsley *Martin Boyne* • Kim Novak *Rose Sellars* • Geraldine Chaplin *Joyce Wheater* • Joe Don Baker *Cliff Wheater* • Siri Neal *Judith* • Britt Ekland *Lady Wrench* • Donald Sinden *Lord Wrench* • Karen Black *Sybil Lullmer* • Rupert Graves *Gerald Omerod* • Rosemary Leach *Miss Scope* • Terence Rigby *Duke of Mendip* • Robert Stephens *Dobree* ■ *Dir* Tony Palmer • *Scr* Timberlake Wertenbaker, from the novel by Edith Wharton

The Children ★★★ 15
Horror 2008 · UK/Cay · Colour · 80min

Two families celebrating the Christmas holidays in a remote cottage face an unexplained nightmare when their young children suddenly turn into vicious killers. The prospect of having to kill your own offspring is the distressing theme of this highly suspenseful horror, which cleverly stages its shocks in broad daylight for maximum psychological dread. It borrows from *Village of the Damned* and *Don't Look Now*, and wrings epic tension from close-up moments and small details. Terrific performances give weight to the life-or-death dilemmas, with Hannah Tointon superb as the moody teen blamed for leading the younger kids astray. **AJ** Violence, swearing, drug abuse

Eva Birthistle *Elaine* • Stephen Campbell Moore *Jonah* • Jeremy Sheffield *Robbie* • Rachel Shelley *Chloe* • Hannah Tointon *Casey* • Rafiella Brooks *Leah* ■ *Dir* Tom Shankland • *Scr* Tom Shankland, from a story by Paul Andrew Williams

The Children Are Watching Us
★★★★
Drama 1943 · It · BW · 85min

Somewhat overshadowed by the masterpieces that followed, this marked director Vittorio De Sica and screenwriter Cesare Zavattini's first excursion into the territory that would be called neorealism. Although it never consistently avoids sentiment, the authentic approach to the disintegrating family's domestic plight is handled with surprising sensitivity. His unpatronising direction of young Luciano De Ambrosis, as the toddler embroiled in bourgeois businessman Emilio Cigoli and adulterous Isa Pola's marital strife, is particularly impressive. **DP** Italian +subtitles.

Luciano De Ambrosis *Pricò* • Isa Pola *Ines, his mother* • Emilio Cigoli *Andrea, his father* • Adriano Rimoldi *Roberto* • Giovanna Cigoli *Agnese* ■ *Dir* Vittorio De Sica • *Scr* Vittorio De Sica, Adolfo Franci, Gherarado Gherhardi, Margherita Maglione, Cesare Giulio Viola, Cesare Zavattini, from the novel *Pricò* by Cesare Giulio Viola

Children Galore ★★ U
Comedy 1954 · UK · BW · 60min

In launching the famous Hammer horror cycle, Terence Fisher secured his place in history. However, this early comedy did nothing for his reputation even though, with

its quaint country setting, it has a vaguely Ealing feel. By deciding to build a cottage for the family with the most grandchildren, squire Peter Evan Thomas sends the village of Tussock into turmoil, with neighbours jeopardising decades of friendship as the search for cute kids intensifies. **DP**

Eddie Byrne *Zacky Jones* • Marjorie Rhodes *Ada Jones* • June Thorburn *Milly Ark* • Peter Evan Thomas *Lord Redscarfe* • Marjorie Hume *Lady Redscarfe* • Lucy Griffiths *Miss Prescott* ■ *Dir* Terence Fisher • *Scr* John Bonnet, Emery Bonnet, Peter Plaskett

Children of a Lesser God
★★★★ 15
Romantic drama 1986 · US · Colour · 114min

This adaptation of Mark Medoff's poignant play, about a woman for whom life's challenge is the fact that she cannot hear, picks up even more resonance in its understanding of the casual slights we inflict upon the hearing-impaired. William Hurt is subtly complex as the speech therapist attracted to his pupil, but it's the first-time performance by deaf actress Marlee Matlin that brilliantly articulates both a character and a condition. She deservedly won an Oscar for her powerful portrayal. **TH** Swearing, nudity. *DVD*

William Hurt *James Leeds* • Marlee Matlin *Sarah Norman* • Piper Laurie *Mrs Norman* • Philip Bosco *Dr Curtis Franklin* • Allison Gompf *Lydia* • John F Cleary *Johnny* • Philip Holmes *Glen* • Georgia Ann Cline *Cheryl* • William D Byrd *Danny* • Frank Carter Jr *Tony* • John Limnidis *William* • Bob Hiltermann *Orin* ■ *Dir* Randa Haines • *Scr* Hesper Anderson, Mark Medoff, from the play by Mark Medoff

The Children of Heaven
★★★★
Comedy drama 1997 · Iran · Colour · 88min

This delightful comedy from Majid Majidi, a key member of the younger generation of Iranian film-makers, proved something of a favourite on the festival circuit. Like *The White Balloon* and *The Apple*, it confirms the Iranian industry's genius for movies about children, with Mohammad Amir Naji and Mir Farrokh Hashemian wondrously natural as the impoverished siblings who try to disguise the loss of the latter's shoes by sharing a pair for school. This enchants as much as it entertains. **DP** Farsi +subtitles.

Mohammad Amir Naji *Ali* • Mir Farrokh Hashemian *Zahra* • Bahareh Seddiqi *Nasifeh* • Jafar Mohammadi *Roya* • Fereshte Sarabandi *Ali's mother* • Kamal Mirkarimi *Principal* • Bezhad Rafi'im *Coach* ■ *Dir/Scr* Majid Majidi

Children of Men ★★★★ 15
Futuristic thriller
2006 · US/UK · Colour · 104min

England, 2027: this green and pleasant land is now a crumbling society in which humanity has become infertile and terrorists fight the fascist powers that be. Submerged in this chaos is alcoholic bureaucrat Theo Faron (Clive Owen), until a surprise visit from an ex-lover (Julianne Moore) offers an unlikely glimmer of hope. Mexican director Alfonso Cuarón delivers a truly startling take on PD James's downbeat novel, reworking its apocalyptic theme through the cracked prism of the post-9/11 era. Owen is excellent and there's a glorious turn from Michael Caine as an ageing, pot-smoking cartoonist. True, the proceedings are occasionally marred by a surfeit of plot exposition, but ultimately the film is a stark triumph for Cuarón. **JR** Violence, swearing. *DVD* *BL*

Clive Owen *Theodore Faron* • Julianne Moore *Julian* • Michael Caine *Jasper* • Chiwetel Ejiofor *Luke* • Charlie Hunnam *Patric* • Claire-Hope Ashitey *Kee* • Pam Ferris *Miriam* • Danny Huston *Nigel* • Peter Mullan *Syd* ■ *Dir* Alfonso Cuarón • *Scr* Alfonso Cuarón, Timothy J Sexton, David Arata, Mark Fergus, Hawk Ostby, from the novel by PD James • *Cinematographer* Emmanuel Lubezki

Children of My Heart ★★

Biographical drama
2000 · Can · Colour · 105min

Whether it's Robin Williams in *Dead Poets Society* or Hilary Swank in *Freedom Writers*, screen teachers – and especially those based on real people – have a habit of ruffling the feathers of both the students in their charge and the superiors who hire them. Geneviève Désilets as Gabrielle Roy proves no exception to the rule in this run-of-the-mill TV movie. The innocent young woman arrives in a small prairie town in the middle of the Depression determined to make a difference. However, it's not just her innovative classroom methods that make an impression on one 15-year-old boy. The ensuing events are melodramatic, but never sensationalist. DP

Geneviève Désilets *Gabrielle Roy* • Geneviève Bujold *Older Gabrielle Roy* • Michael Moriarty *Rodrigue Emyard* • Yani Gellman *Mederic Emyard* • Isabella Fink *Claire* • Mark Ellis *Charlie Roebuck* ■ *Dir* Keith Ross Leckie • *Scr* Keith Ross Leckie, from the autobiography by Gabrielle Roy

The Children of Sanchez ★★

Drama
1978 · US/Mex · Colour · 126min

This is a slow drama about a poor Mexican trying to keep his small army of offspring from starving. Anthony Quinn is as professional as ever, but the real interest lies in the role of Grandma, played by Dolores Del Rio. Trivia gatherers may like to know that she was silent movie star Ramon Navarro's second cousin, and that she retired shortly afterwards. FL

Anthony Quinn *Jesus Sanchez* • Lupita Ferrer *Consuelo* • Dolores Del Rio *Grandma* • Stathis Giallelis *Roberto* • Lucia Mendez *Marta* • Duncan Quinn *Manuel* • Katy Jurado *Chata* • Carmen Montejo *Aunt Guadalupe* ■ *Dir* Hall Bartlett • *Scr* Cesare Zavattini, Hall Bartlett, from the novel by Oscar Lewis

Children of the Corn ★ 18

Horror
1984 · US · Colour · 93min

Adapted from a short story in Stephen King's *Night Shift* anthology, this is a lame horror yarn padded to feature length with tepid special effects and ludicrous dialogue. Travellers Peter Horton and Linda Hamilton narrowly avoid being sacrificed to the "Corn God" in a rural Nebraska community, held in a grip of pagan terror by a 12-year-old preacher. Once past the atmospheric opening sequence – kids slaughtering their parents in a café – it's downhill all the way for this tacky nightmare. AJ *DVD*

Peter Horton *Dr Burt Stanton* • Linda Hamilton *Vicky Baxter* • John Franklin *Isaac* • Courtney Gains *Malachai* • RG Armstrong *Diehl* • Robby Kiger *Job* • Annemarie McEvoy *Sarah* • John Philbin *Amos* • Julie Maddalena *Rachel* ■ *Dir* Fritz Kiersch • *Scr* George Goldsmith, from the short story by Stephen King

Children of the Corn II: the Final Sacrifice ★★ 18

Horror
1993 · US · Colour · 89min

Tabloid journalists gather in Gatlin, Nebraska, to unravel the cause of the original massacre just as "He who walks behind the Rows" returns to manipulate the community's children into murdering again. Director David F Price's modestly mounted but efficient slice of horror is a quantum leap over the first film in terms of acting quality, homicidal set pieces and effective shock tactics. The endless nosebleed is a highlight. AJ *DVD*

Terence Knox *John Garrett* • Paul Scherrer *Danny Garrett* • Ryan Bollman *Micah Balding* • Christie Clark *Lacey Hellerstar* • Rosalind Allen *Angela Casual* ■ *Dir* David F Price • *Scr* AL Katz, Gilbert Adler, from the short story *Children of the Corn* by Stephen King

Children of the Corn III: Urban Harvest ★★★ 18

Horror
1995 · US · Colour · 88min

A refugee from the original corn cult of killer kids devises a plan to take their doctrine of dread to Chicago before going global. The enterprising second sequel to

the Stephen King-based tale of terror is easily the best of the series, because director James Hickox (brother of horror veteran Anthony) knows how to use his low budget without sacrificing credibility or top-notch scares. Three more sequels followed. AJ *DVD*

Ron Melendez *Joshua* • Jim Metzler *William Porter* • Daniel Cerny *Eli* • Nancy Grahn *Alice* • Michael Ensign *Father Frank* ■ *Dir* James DR Hickox [James Hickox] • *Scr* Dode B Levenson, from the short story *Children of the Corn* by Stephen King

Children of the Damned ★★ 12

Science-fiction thriller
1964 · UK · BW · 85min

In this less-than-thrilling sequel to *Village of the Damned*, six children of assorted nationalities with deadly extra-sensory powers escape from their respective London embassies. The alien kids demonstrate their lethal gifts against the armed forces who are trying to destroy them in the name of world security. However, despite a literate script and thoughtful direction by Anton M Leader, the film quickly runs out of steam. AJ *DVD*

Ian Hendry *Colonel Tom Lewellin* • Alan Badel *Dr David Neville* • Barbara Ferris *Susan Eliot* • Alfred Burke *Colin Webster* • Sheila Allen *Diana Looran* • Clive Powell *Paul* ■ *Dir* Anton M Leader • *Scr* John Briley, from the novel *The Midwich Cuckoos* by John Wyndham

The Children of the Marshland ★★★★ PG

Period comedy drama
1998 · Fr · Colour · 110min

Fans of such art house classics as *Jean de Florette* will warm to this gentle portrait of rural France in the early 1930s. A sort of Gallic *Last of the Summer Wine*, Jean Becker's comedy disappointingly skirts around its darker themes. However, there's plenty of nostalgic pleasure to be had from the adventures of shell-shocked soldier Jacques Gamblin, disgruntled peasant Jacques Villeret, world-weary millionaire Michel Serrault and timid bachelor André Dussollier. Complete with a cameo from Eric Cantona, this may be lightweight and sentimental, but it's also undeniably cinematic. DP French +subtitles.

Jacques Villeret *Riton* • Jacques Gamblin *Garris* • André Dussollier *Amedée* • Michel Serrault *Pépé* • Isabelle Carré *Marie* • Eric Cantona *Jo Sardi* • Suzanne Flon *Old Cri Cri* ■ *Dir* Jean Becker • *Scr* Sébastien Japrisot, from the novel *Les Enfants du Marais* by Georges Montforez

Children of the Revolution ★★★★

Political comedy drama
1996 · Aus · Colour · 101min

This classy black comedy from Australia boasts the combined talents of Judy Davis, Sam Neill, Rachel Griffiths and Geoffrey Rush. Joan (Davis) is a die-hard Stalinist living in 1940s Oz. After writing weekly letters to the great man, she ends up at the 1952 Party Congress and subsequently beds him. Their son (Richard Roxburgh) grows up to become a political agitator who brings the Australian government into a state of crisis. Director Peter Duncan deftly mixes newsreel footage, montage sequences and musical comedy, with hysterical results. LH

Judy Davis *Joan Fraser* • Sam Neill *Nine* • Richard Roxburgh *Joe* • Rachel Griffiths *Anna* • F Murray Abraham *Stalin* • Russell Kiefel *Barry* • John Gaden *Dr Wilf Wilke* • Geoffrey Rush *Zachary Welch* ■ *Dir/Scr* Peter Duncan

Children of the Revolution ★★★

Documentary
2010 · Ire/UK/Ger · Colour and BW · 92min

In the 1970s, Ulrike Meinhof and Fusako Shigenobu were among the most wanted women in the world, as they resorted to violence to achieve their revolutionary aims in Europe and the Middle East. Director Shane O'Sullivan makes innovative use of exclusive interviews and archive footage to reveal a fascinating examination of the domestic lives of these two notorious

terrorists and the impact their crimes had on their daughters. The emphasis here falls more on the mothers than their offspring, with powerful first-hand insights into subversive activity in an era of corrupted idealism. DP English, German, Japanese +subtitles. *DVD*

■ *Dir* Shane O'Sullivan

The Children of Theatre Street ★★★ U

Documentary
1977 · US/USSR · Colour · 92min

It needed to be a special assignment to lure the former Grace Kelly out of cinematic retirement, and Robert Dornhelm and Earle Mack's fly-on-the-wall study of the Kirov Ballet School is exactly that. While recalling such great names of the past as Nijinsky, Pavlova, Nureyev and Baryshnikov, this Oscar-nominated documentary is also keen to concentrate on the stars of tomorrow as it follows three aspiring students through their stringent training. The reverential enthusiasm of Princess Grace's narration should fire the imagination of younger viewers, especially those already hooked on ballet's romantic elegance. DP English, Russian +subtitles.

Princess Grace of Monaco [Grace Kelly] *Narrator* ■ *Dir* Robert Dornhelm, Earle Mack • *Scr* Beth Gutcheon (uncredited)

The Children's Hour ★★★ 12

Drama
1961 · US · BW · 103min

Retitled *The Loudest Whisper* in the UK, this screen remake of the notorious Lillian Hellman play about a pupil who falsely accuses two teachers of being lesbians is emphatically not for youngsters. Director William Wyler had filmed it before as *These Three* back in 1936 and, despite being shorn of its overt lesbian theme, the earlier version has considerably more power than this rather quiet and bloodless drama. Perhaps a few years on from 1961 the lesbian elements could have been properly dealt with, but here their muting harms the movie and both Audrey Hepburn and Shirley MacLaine fail to convince. James Garner, though, is very impressive, particularly in his weeping scene: many actors could not have done as well. TS *DVD*

Audrey Hepburn *Karen Wright* • Shirley MacLaine *Martha Dobie* • James Garner *Dr Joe Cardin* • Miriam Hopkins *Lily Mortar* • Fay Bainter *Amelia Tilford* • Karen Balkin *Mary Tilford* • Veronica Cartwright *Rosalie* ■ *Dir* William Wyler • *Scr* John Michael Hayes, from the play by Lillian Hellman

The Children's Midsummer Night's Dream ★★★ U

Comedy drama fantasy
2001 · UK · Colour · 113min

Opening in a charming puppet theatre and performed among quaintly contrived woodland nooks, Christine Edzard's ambitious take on Shakespeare is the best school production you're ever likely to see. But, as a feature film, it lacks the immediacy that might have made it magical. The main problem is that the youngsters rarely seem comfortable with the poetry, their "recital by rote" style exposed by luminaries such as Derek Jacobi, who provide the voices of the marionettes. Yet its honesty and homely ingenuity render this an impossible film to dislike. DP

Derek Jacobi • Frances Barber ■ *Dir* Christine Edzard • *Scr* from the play *A Midsummer Night's Dream* by William Shakespeare

Child's Play ★★★ U

Satirical comedy
1954 · UK · BW · 68min

In this energetic film, which plays upon the 1950s anxiety regarding nuclear science, the son of a scientist working at an atomic research plant invents radioactive popcorn. Margaret Thompson directs this quaintly backward look at the nuclear age, while Mona Washbourne heads a cast of otherwise unfamiliar names. RK

Mona Washbourne *Miss Goslett* • Peter Martyn *PC Parker* • Dorothy Alison *Margery Chappell* • Ingeborg Wells *Lea Blotz* • Carl Jaffe *Carl Blotz* •

Ballard Berkeley *Dr Nightingale* • Joan Young *Mrs Chizzler* ■ *Dir* Margaret Thompson • *Scr* Peter Blackmore, from a story by Don Sharp

Child's Play ★★

Drama
1972 · US · Colour · 99min

This melodramatic nonsense from Sidney Lumet is set in a Roman Catholic boarding school for boys, where hateful teacher James Mason is being victimised and discredited by fellow master Robert Preston. Despite having a mother dying of cancer and a stockpile of pornographic pin-ups, Mason becomes an almost heroic figure when set against the bluff and blustering Preston. TH

James Mason *Jerome Malley* • Robert Preston *Joseph Dobbs* • Beau Bridges *Paul Reis* • Ronald Weyand *Father Mozian* • Charles White *Father Griffin* • David Rounds *Father Penny* • Kate Harrington *Mrs Carter* • Jamie Alexander *Sheppard* ■ *Dir* Sidney Lumet • *Scr* Leon Prochnik, from the play by Robert Marasco

Child's Play ★★★ 15

Horror
1988 · US · Colour · 83min

Six-year-old Alex Vincent's must-have "Good Guy" doll, Chucky, is possessed by the soul of dead serial killer Brad Dourif and goes on a wisecracking murder spree to get revenge on the cop (Chris Sarandon) who put him away. A steady stream of standard scares is dragged from a thinly stretched, formula slasher plot, thanks to panache beyond the call of duty from director Tom Holland. Novelty value and great special effects made this dummy run a big hit. AJ *DVD* ☐

Catherine Hicks *Karen Barclay* • Chris Sarandon *Mike Norris* • Alex Vincent *Andy Barclay* • Brad Dourif *Charles Lee Ray* • Dinah Manoff *Maggie Peterson* • Tommy Swerdlow *Jack Santos* • Jack Colvin *Dr Ardmore* • Neil Giuntoli *Eddie Caputo* ■ *Dir* Tom Holland (1) • *Scr* Don Mancini, Tom Holland, John Lafia, from a story by Don Mancini

Child's Play 2 ★★ 15

Horror
1990 · US · Colour · 80min

Chucky, the living "Good Guy" doll, returns to continue stalking his former owner (Alex Vincent) and terrorise his new foster parents (Jenny Agutter and Gerrit Graham). Still nobody believes the kid's possessed Action Man story – until two seconds before they're brutally murdered, of course – resulting in a predictable rehash of the original. A few neat touches lighten the load. AJ

Alex Vincent *Andy Barclay* • Jenny Agutter *Joanne Simpson* • Gerrit Graham *Phil Simpson* • Christine Elise *Kyle* • Brad Dourif *Chucky* • Grace Zabriskie *Grace Poole* ■ *Dir* John Lafia • *Scr* Don Mancini

Child's Play 3 ★ 18

Horror
1991 · US · Colour · 85min

Brought back to life when the "Good Guy" doll assembly line is reactivated, Chucky – the plastic Terminator – traces his former owner (Justin Whalin, taking over from moppet Alex Vincent) to military school and starts decimating the student body. Bottom-of-the-barrel, slice-and-dice nonsense, this entry in the series is now infamous for being cited in the tabloid frenzy surrounding the Jamie Bulger murder case in Britain. Three further films followed: *Bride of Chucky* in 1998; *Seed of Chucky* in 2004 and *Curse of Chucky* in 2013. AJ

Justin Whalin *Andy Barclay* • Perrey Reeves *DeSilva* • Jeremy Sylvers *Tyler* • Travis Fine *Shelton* • Dean Jacobson *Whitehurst* • Brad Dourif *Chucky* • Peter Haskell *Sullivan* ■ *Dir* Jack Bender • *Scr* Don Mancini

Child's Pose ★★★ 15

Drama
2013 · Rom · Colour · 109min

Luminita Gheorghiu makes the most of her first starring role in this acerbic assault on the Romanian nouveau riche. Determined to ensure her wastrel son gets off when a boy dies as a result of his careless driving, Gheorghiu's fearsome architect seeks to use her status to get her own way. For all her machinations, however, this is still very much a man's world, where inequality, iniquity and injustice exist in equal measure. Despite the power of the performances, this drama lacks the darkly satirical edge of the best Romanian New Wave cinema. DP In Romanian. Swearing.

Luminita Gheorghiu *Cornelia Kerenes, mother* • Bogdan Dumitrache *Barbu, son* • Ilinca Goia *Carmen* • Natasa Raab *Olga Cerchez* ■ *Dir* Calin Peter Netzer • *Scr* Calin Peter Netzer, Razvan Radulescu

Chill Factor ★★ 15

Comedy action thriller
1999 · US · Colour · 97min

Just three years after winning an Oscar for *Jerry Maguire*, Cuba Gooding Jr turned up in this bad rip-off of *Speed*. Diner employee Skeet Ulrich hijacks the truck of ice cream delivery driver Gooding Jr in order to transport a secret chemical weapon that will annihilate everything for miles around if its temperature rises above 50 degrees. Both stars are totally wasted in this routine thriller. ST DVD

Cuba Gooding Jr *Arlo* • Skeet Ulrich *Tim Mason* • Peter Firth *Captain Andrew Brynner* • David Paymer *Doctor Richard Long* • Hudson Leick *Vaughn* ■ *Dir* Hugh Johnson • *Scr* Drew Gitlin, Mike Cheda

Chiller ★★★ 15

Horror   1985 · US · Colour · 87min

In this better-than-average TV movie from *Scream* director Wes Craven, Michael Beck is thawed out after being cryogenically frozen for ten years. Alas, a machine malfunction during his hibernation causes him to lose his soul and start acting in strange ways as he climbs the corporate ladder. A slim idea is elaborately carried off by Craven, who keeps the suspense mounting and makes great use of first-class make-up effects. AJ

Michael Beck *Miles Creighton* • Beatrice Straight *Marion Creighton* • Paul Sorvino *Rev Penny* • Jill Schoelen *Stacey* • Dick O'Neill *Clarence Beeson* • Laura Johnson *Leigh* ■ *Dir* Wes Craven • *Scr* JD Feigelson

Chilly Scenes of Winter ★★★

Drama   1979 · US · Colour · 98min

Originally released as *Head over Heels*, this was something of a disappointment after Joan Micklin Silver's earlier directorial efforts. As a take on modern American love, it has a ring of authenticity. In its keenness to avoid any kind of romantic cliché, however, the story ends up having too little heart, and we're left with John Heard's memories of an idyllic past and his increasingly irritating entreaties to Mary Beth Hurt to give it another try. DP

John Heard *Charles* • Mary Beth Hurt *Laura* • Peter Riegert *Sam* • Kenneth McMillan *Pete* • Gloria Grahame *Clara* • Nora Heflin *Betty* • Jerry Hardin *Patterson* • Tarah Nutter *Susan* • Griffin Dunne *Dr Mark* ■ *Dir* Joan Micklin Silver • *Scr* Joan Micklin Silver, from the novel *Head over Heels* by Ann Beattie

The Chiltern Hundreds ★★★ U

Comedy   1949 · UK · BW · 84min

Although John Paddy Carstairs directed several Norman Wisdom vehicles, this wry political satire is his most accomplished picture. Adapted by William Douglas Home from his own play, the film takes its title from the nominal office MPs take when they wish to resign. Recalling the gentle class comedies produced by Ealing, the election battle between an earl's socialist son (David Tomlinson) and his true blue butler (Cecil Parker) is full of sly observations. DP

Cecil Parker *Benjamin Beecham* • AE Matthews *Lord Lister* • David Tomlinson *Tony, Viscount Pym* • Lana Morris *Bessie Sykes* • Marjorie Fielding *Lady Lister* • Joyce Carey *Lady Caroline* • Tom Macauley *Jack Cleghorn* ■ *Dir* John Paddy Carstairs • *Scr* William Douglas Home, Patrick Kirwan, from the play by William Douglas Home

Chimes at Midnight ★★★★ PG

Historical comedy drama
1966 · Swi/Sp · BW · 115min

This magnificent adaptation of five of the Bard's plays by director Orson Welles is a funny, poignant tribute that charts the relationship between bloated boozer Falstaff and impressionable Prince Hal (Keith Baxter), as the royal heir evolves from debauched wastrel to warrior king Henry V. Welles gives a masterful performance as Falstaff, a cherubic rogue (although admittedly a cherub who has let himself go) whose love of wine, women and more wine is eventually rejected by his protégé. Shakespeare has rarely been rendered so cleverly. JA Some violence, brief nudity. DVD ◐

Orson Welles *Falstaff* • Keith Baxter *Prince Hal, later King Henry V* • John Gielgud *Henry IV* • Margaret Rutherford *Mistress Quickly* • Jeanne Moreau *Doll Tearsheet* • Norman Rodway *Henry Percy, "Hotspur"* • Fernando Rey *Worcester* • Ralph Richardson *Narrator* ■ *Dir* Orson Welles • *Scr* Orson Welles, from *The Chronicles of England* by Raphael Holinshed, from the plays by William Shakespeare

Chimpanzee ★★★ U

Documentary   2012 · US/UK/Fr · Colour · 78min

This family friendly docudrama from Disney's nature division depicts the trials and tribulations of a young chimp called Oscar. He's orphaned when his mother dies in a jungle rumble between rival groups and is subsequently adopted by Freddy, the tribe's alpha male. It's well filmed, the baby chimps are unquestionably cute, and there's a light-hearted narration by actor Tim Allen (*Toy Story*, *Galaxy Quest*). Although there are some moments of mild peril, it's nothing too scary - younger kids will lap up all the monkey business. DA

Tim Allen *Narrator* ■ *Dir* Alastair Fothergill, Mark Linfield • *Scr* Alastair Fothergill, Mark Linfield, Don Hahn

China ★★

Second World War drama
1943 · US · BW · 78min

An American trader, in China to make money, changes his priorities after the bombing of Pearl Harbor and joins a band of Chinese guerrillas. Directed by John Farrow, an expert manipulator of emotions, and starring Alan Ladd as the grimly determined hero who manages to blow up the Japanese forces almost singlehandedly, this patriotic wartime flag-waver feels laughably dated now. RK

Loretta Young *Carolyn Grant* • Alan Ladd *Mr Jones* • William Bendix *Johnny Sparrow* • Philip Ahn *Lin Cho* • Iris Wong *Kwan Su* • Victor Sen Yung *Lin Wei* • Marianne Quon *Tan Ying* • Jessie Tai Sing *Student* ■ *Dir* John Farrow • *Scr* Frank Butler, from the play *Fourth Brother* by Archibald Forbes

China Clipper ★★ U

Drama   1936 · US · BW · 89min

Former pilot Pat O'Brien sacrifices friends and marriage to an obsession to start a trans-Pacific airline, flying from America to China. The now defunct Pan Am gets a big screen credit for assistance, with the picture clearly intended as an advert for them, and the script is by Frank "Spig" Wead, an aviation hero later played by John Wayne in *The Wings of Eagles*. The wonky flying scenes and dime-novel melodramas on the ground don't help, though. AT

Pat O'Brien *Dave Logan* • Beverly Roberts *Jean Logan* • Ross Alexander (1) *Tom Collins* • Humphrey Bogart *Hap Stuart* • Marie Wilson *Sunny Avery* • Henry B Walthall *Dad Brunn* ■ *Dir* Raymond Enright [Ray Enright] • *Scr* Frank Wead

China Cry ★★★ 15

Drama based on a true story
1990 · Tai/US · Colour · 101min

China's cultural upheaval in the 1950s meant no culture and a great deal of repression. This devotedly earnest retelling of a true story shows how a privileged girl witnessed some of Chairman Mao's

atrocities before she escaped to Hong Kong, moving from there to the United States, where she has now settled. Julia Nickson-Soul portrays the girl as more than just a passive spectator, but the film remains too aloof from a nation's anguish for it to be anything more than just a harrowing tale that's moderately well told. TH Violence. DVD

Julia Nickson-Soul *Sung Neng Yee* • Russell Wong *Lam Cheng Shen* • James Shigeta *Dr Sung* • France Nuyen *Mrs Sung* • Philip Tan *Colonel Cheng* • Elizabeth Sung *Interrogator* • Bennett Ohta *Labour camp doctor* • Daphne Cheung *Chung Shing* ■ *Dir* James F Collier • *Scr* James F Collier, from the book by Nora Lam [Sung Neng Yee], Irene Burke

China Doll ★★

Second World War romantic drama
1958 · US · BW · 99min

This out-and-out tear-jerker marked the return of director Frank Borzage, Hollywood's most dedicated sentimentalist, after ten years in the McCarthyite wilderness. Alas, this tale of an American air force officer in China who marries his housekeeper is so overlaid with sugary sentimentality that it felt dated even in the 1950s. Worth a look, though, for fans of its male star, Victor Mature. RK

Victor Mature *Cliff Brandon* • Li Li Hua *Shu-Jen* • Ward Bond *Father Cairns* • Bob Mathias *Phil Gates* • Johnny Desmond *Steve Hill* • Elaine Curtis *Alice Nichols* ■ *Dir* Frank Borzage • *Scr* Kitty Buhler, from the story *China Doll* by James Benson Nablo, Thomas F Kelly and the story *Time Is a Memory* by Kitty Buhler

China Gate ★★★

War drama   1957 · US · BW · 90min

American soldier Gene Barry hooks up with his estranged Eurasian wife Angie Dickinson, a political activist, to lead a guerrilla assault on a Chinese ammunition dump in French-controlled Vietnam. The marital war between the couple, caught in a love/hate relationship, parallels the battle against the Reds in this tough-minded movie, produced, written and directed by Samuel Fuller. Lee Van Cleef plays the communist leader, and Nat King Cole does a good job as a veteran GI. RK Violence

Gene Barry *Brock* • Angie Dickinson *Lucky Legs* • Nat King Cole *Goldie* • Paul Dubov *Captain Caumont* • Lee Van Cleef *Major Cham* • George Givot *Corporal Pigalle* • Gerald Milton *Private Andreades* ■ *Dir/Scr* Samuel Fuller

China Girl ★★

Second World War drama
1942 · US · BW · 95min

American news cameraman George Montgomery, in Mandalay just before the attack on Pearl Harbor and carrying secret military information, is pursued by two traitorous army personnel (Victor McLaglen, Lynn Bari) in the pay of the Japanese. Then he falls in love with a beautiful, American-educated Chinese girl (Gene Tierney). Director Henry Hathaway injects as much tension as possible into this melodrama, helped by some good action sequences. RK

Gene Tierney *Miss Young* • George Montgomery *Johnny Williams* • Lynn Bari *Captain Fifi* • Victor McLaglen *Major Bull Weed* • Alan Baxter *Chinese boy* • Sig Ruman *Jarubi* • Myron McCormick *Shorty* • Bobby Blake [Robert Blake] *Chinese boy* ■ *Dir* Henry Hathaway • *Scr* Ben Hecht, from a story by Melville Crossman [Darryl F Zanuck]

China Girl ★★★ 18

Romantic drama   1987 · US · Colour · 86min

This is Abel Ferrara's stylised reworking of *Romeo and Juliet*. Even when he's misfiring, Ferrara can never be accused of being dull, and he makes superb use here of both Little Italy and Chinatown as Richard Penebianco and Sari Chang find love across the criminal codes. The cast buckles under Ferrara's demands. DP

Richard Panebianco *Tony* • Sari Chang *Tye* • James Russo *Alby* • David Caruso *Mercury* ■ *Dir* Abel Ferrara • *Scr* Nicholas St John

China Moon ★★★ 18

Romantic thriller   1994 · US · Colour · 95min

Fine acting and a surprising climactic revelation are the main virtues of this *film noir* from John Bailey, whose brilliant work as cinematographer includes *Cat People*, *Silverado*, *Mishima* and *As Good As It Gets*. The typical genre storyline sees detective Ed Harris and abused wife Madeleine Stowe succumb to passion in Florida, but although the main plot adds nothing new, there are enough original touches and tasty performances to sustain interest. JC DVD

Ed Harris *Kyle Bodine* • Madeleine Stowe *Rachel Munro* • Charles Dance *Rupert Munro* • Patricia Healy *Adele* • Benicio Del Toro *Lamar Dickey* • Tim Powell *Fraker* ■ *Dir* John Bailey (2) • *Scr* Roy Carlson

China 9, Liberty 37 ★★★

Spaghetti western   1978 · It · Colour · 98min

Director Monte Hellman's unusual mix of Sergio Leone and Sam Peckinpah (who has a bit part) is very interesting indeed. Gunslinger Fabio Testi is released from jail on condition he shoots rancher Warren Oates, enabling corrupt railroad barons to seize his land, However, once he meets Oates and falls for his sexually frustrated wife (Jenny Agutter), he finds the task difficult to accomplish. This is gritty, violent and erotic, with a great score composed by Pino Donaggio. AJ Some dialogue dubbed.

Warren Oates *Matthew* • Fabio Testi *Clayton* • Jenny Agutter *Catherine* • Sam Peckinpah *Wilbur Olsen* • Isabel Mestres *Barbara* ■ *Dir* Monte Hellman • *Scr* Gerald F Harvey, Douglas Venturelli

China O'Brien ★★ 18

Martial arts action thriller
1988 · US · Colour · 85min

The breakthrough role - well, for the video market at least - for martial arts star Cynthia Rothrock, who provides a welcome antidote to the macho heroics of Chuck Norris et al. Here she plays a police officer who turns in her badge when she uses her martial arts skills to kill a villain in self-defence. A sequel followed. JF Violence, swearing.

Cynthia Rothrock *China O'Brien* • Richard Norton *Matt* • Keith Cooke *Dakota* • Patrick Adamson *Lickner* • David Blackwell *Sheriff O'Brien* ■ *Dir* Robert Clouse • *Scr* Robert Clouse, from the story by Sandra Weintraub

China Seas ★★★★ PG

Romantic adventure   1935 · US · BW · 83min

The plot's tosh, the setting preposterous and the crew rip-roaring in this expensive MGM action melodrama. But who cares when the cast is solid gold? Clark Gable's the captain, sailing south to Singapore; Wallace Beery's a mutinous pirate; Rosalind Russell's the captain's aristocratic former mistress; and, best of all, Jean Harlow is the blonde floozy and another of Gable's ex-lovers. Splendidly directed by the underrated Tay Garnett, this is a major treat. TS DVD

Clark Gable *Captain Alan Gaskell* • Jean Harlow *China Doll "Dolly Portland"* • Wallace Beery *Jamesy MacArdle* • Lewis Stone *Tom Davids* • Rosalind Russell *Sybil Barclay* • Dudley Digges *Dawson* • C Aubrey Smith *Sir Guy Wilmerding* • Robert Benchley *Charlie McCaleb* ■ *Dir* Tay Garnett • *Scr* Jules Furthman, James Kevin McGuinness, from the novel by Crosbie Garstin

China Sky ★★

Second World War drama
1945 · US · BW · 78min

RKO planned this adaptation of a novel by the once popular Pearl S Buck as a major starring vehicle for Claudette Colbert. But she took one look at the script and turned it down, leaving Ruth Warrick, Randolph Scott and Ellen Drew to co-star in what is a rather mundane romantic melodrama. Scott and Warrick play American doctors in a remote Chinese village threatened by Japanese forces; Drew is Scott's jealous viper of a wife, while Anthony Quinn is the local guerrilla leader. RK

Randolph Scott *Thompson* • Ruth Warrick *Sara* • Ellen Drew *Louise* • Anthony Quinn *Chen Ta* • Carol Thurston *Siu Mei* • Richard Loo *Col Yasuda* • "Ducky" Louie *"Little Goat"* • Philip Ahn *Dr Kim* ◼ *Dir* Ray Enright • *Scr* Brenda Weisberg, Joseph Hoffman, from Pearl S Buck's noel

The China Syndrome ★★★★ PG
Political drama 1979 · US · Colour · 116min

In this genuinely chilling "what if..." thriller, savvy foreman Jack Lemmon just prevents an atomic meltdown at a nuclear power station. The government tries to hush it up, but TV newswoman Jane Fonda (in one of her best performances) and radical cameraman Michael Douglas (who also produced) probe for the truth in a solidly exciting movie still packed with political relevance. The cautionary conclusions were given a great deal of credence by life imitating art when the Three Mile Island near-tragedy occurred a few weeks after the movie opened. Note the complete lack of background music – Douglas felt it would trivialise the events. AJ *DVD*

Jane Fonda *Kimberly Wells* • Jack Lemmon *Jack Godell* • Michael Douglas (1) *Richard Adams* • Scott Brady *Herman De Young* • James Hampton *Bill Gibson* • Peter Donat *Don Jacovich* • Wilford Brimley *Ted Spindler* ◼ *Dir* James Bridges • *Scr* Mike Gray, TS Cook, James Bridges

Chinatown ★★★★★ 15
Period thriller 1974 · US · Colour · 125min

Jack Nicholson here gives his best ever performance, playing a private eye called Jake Gittes, who pokes his nose rather too deeply into the lives of Faye Dunaway and her father, John Huston, a corrupt Los Angeles tycoon. Writer Robert Towne planned a trilogy about LA, and this first part, set in the 1930s, deals with the city's water supply and how that source of life leads to death and profit. The script is brilliantly organised, though the ending was changed when Roman Polanski arrived as director: Towne's story never got to Chinatown; Polanski insisted the climax was set there. The result was acrimony behind the scenes and genius on the screen in a masterpiece that repays any number of viewings. Nicholson reprised his role in the distinctly less successful *The Two Jakes*. AT Violence, swearing. *DVD* BD

Jack Nicholson *JJ Gittes* • Faye Dunaway *Evelyn Mulwray* • John Huston *Noah Cross* • Perry Lopez *Escobar* • John Hillerman *Yelburton* • Darrell Zwerling *Hollis Mulwray* • Diane Ladd *Ida Sessions* • Roy Jenson *Mulvihill* • Roman Polanski *Man with knife* ◼ *Dir* Roman Polanski • *Scr* Robert Towne • *Cinematographer* John A Alonzo • *Music* Jerry Goldsmith • *Art Directors* Richard Sylbert, W Stewart Campbell • *Editor* Sam O'Steen • *Costume Designer* Anthea Sylbert

Chinese Box ★★★★
Romantic drama 1997 · Jpn/Fr/US · Colour · 109min

The brilliant Wayne Wang directs Jeremy Irons and Gong Li in a drama based around Hong Kong's return to China in 1997. Irons is a disgruntled journalist who discovers he has six months to live. Does he return to Britain or remain in Hong Kong, where he's fallen for bar girl Li (in her first English-speaking role)? As New Year's Eve approaches, there's a strange ambiguity about what the future holds. The allegory is clear: Irons represents the dying colonial past, while Li's boss (Michael Hui) is the future. Fascinating, and full of minute nuances. LH English, Mandarin +subtitles.

Gong Li *Vivian* • Jeremy Irons *John* • Rubén Blades *Jim* • Maggie Cheung *Jean* • Michael Hui *Chang* • Jared Harris ◼ *Dir* Wayne Wang • *Scr* Jean-Claude Carrière, Larry Gross, from a story by Paul Theroux, Wayne Wang, Jean-Claude Carrière

A Chinese Ghost Story ★★★★ 15
Martial arts horror 1987 · HK · Colour · 91min

This marvellous example of the ghost genre popular in Hong Kong and most Asian areas is a real treat that combines excellent martial art sequences with lavish fantasy scenes and slapstick. A tax collector falls in love with a ghost and is drawn into a battle for her soul, but the plot is secondary to the haunting visuals and set pieces that make it a classic of its type. DF Cantonese +subtitles. *DVD*

Leslie Cheung *Ning Tsai-Shen* • Wang Zuxian *Nieh Hsiao-Tsing* • Wu Ma *Yen Che-Hsia* ◼ *Dir* Ching Siu-Tung • *Scr* Ruan Jizhi

Chinese Odyssey 2002 ★★★ U
Period romantic comedy 2002 · HK/Jpn/Chi · Colour · 86min

Lampooning everything from Peking Opera and Communist propaganda to chop socky and blaxploitation, Jeff Lau's scattershot period comedy is a breathless assault on social, sexual and cinematic stereotypes. The focus falls on hectoring Tony Leung and his restaurateur sister Vicky Zhao Wei and their encounters with cross-dressing princess Faye Wong and her fashion-conscious emperor brother, Chang Chen. The plot, however, is rarely as important as the plethora of in-jokes and when the gags run dry, Lau struggles to sustain the momentum. But there's still much to enjoy in the buoyant performances and glorious photography. DP Mandarin +subtitles. *DVD*

Tony Leung (2) *Li Yilong* • Faye Wong *Princess Wushuang* • Vicky Zhao Wei [Zhao Wei] *Phoenix* • Chang Chen *Emperor Zheng De* ◼ *Dir* Jeff Lau • *Scr* Ji An [Jeff Lau] • *Cinematographer* Ngor Chi Kwan

Chinese Puzzle ★★★ 15
Romantic comedy drama 2013 · Fr/Bel · Colour · 117min

Following *Pot Luck* (2002) and *Russian Dolls* (2005), the third part of the trilogy reveals what happens when Romain Duris leaves his European comfort zone and moves to New York. Although familiarity with the earlier films will enhance your enjoyment, it's not essential for this fish-out-of-water tale that finds our hero struggling to get to grips with the New World while juggling commitment to his children, friends and lovers past and present. Marbled with writer/director Cédric Klapisch's trademark whimsical touches, philosophical musings and flights of fantasy, this is a warm, lovable film. LF English, French, Spanish, Mandarin, Yiddish +subtitles.

Romain Duris *Xavier* • Audrey Tautou *Martine* • Cécile de France *Isabelle* • Kelly Reilly *Wendy* • Sandrine Holt *Ju* ◼ *Dir/Scr* Cédric Klapisch

Chinese Roulette ★★★ 15
Drama 1976 · W Ger · Colour · 82min

Alexander Allerson and Margit Carstensen are tricked by their disabled daughter, Andrea Schober, into spending a weekend in the country with their respective lovers. Inevitably, this world of cheap deceptions and stylised poses is shattered as psychic shots give way to lethal lead during the eponymous truth game. Rainer Werner Fassbinder uses a roaming camera and reflective surfaces to expose their coldheartedness; alas, his cynical detachment leaves us appalled but unmoved. DP German +subtitles. Some swearing, sex scenes. *DVD* BD

Margit Carstensen *Ariane* • Ulli Lommel *Kolbe* • Anna Karina *Irene* • Alexander Allerson *Gerhard* • Andrea Schober *Angela* • Macha Méril *Traunitz* • Brigitte Mira *Kast* ◼ *Dir/Scr* Rainer Werner Fassbinder • *Cinematographer* Michael Ballhaus

Chinese Zodiac ★★ 12
Martial arts adventure 2012 · Chi · Colour · 118min

Jackie Chan is back on the treasure-hunting trail after a 20-year lay-off. If you've seen the previous *Armour of God* instalments, this is very much business as usual, blending the likes of *Mission: Impossible*, *National Treasure* and the Indiana Jones films to cartoonish, family-friendly effect. The story sees Chan's genial mercenary hired by shady Oliver Platt to retrieve a series of priceless bronze animal heads. The plotting is largely incomprehensible, the multilingual dialogue exchanges are confusing and the CGI embellishments are slapdash, but the action whizzes along at a breakneck pace and the slapstick fight in a photo studio is vintage Jackie. JH English, French, Mandarin, Spanish, Russian +subtitles. *DVD* BD

Jackie Chan *JC* • Kwone Sang Woo *Simon* • Liao Fan *David* • Yao Xingtong *Coco* ◼ *Dir* Jackie Chan • *Scr* Jackie Chan, Stanley Tong, Edward Tang, Frankie Chan

La Chinoise ★★★★ PG
Experimental political drama 1967 · Fr · Colour · 92min

Marking Jean-Luc Godard's passage from mainstream maverick to militant outsider, this diatribe on Maoism and the possibility of western revolution was also his first collaboration with Jean-Pierre Gorin, with whom he would work until 1972 within the Dziga Vertov co-operative. With the ever-engaging Jean-Pierre Léaud leading a discussion as naive as it's impassioned, the film was accused of trivialising socialism, particularly through Godard's use of agitprop slogans, calligraphic gimmicks and poster imagery. Beneath the surface superficiality and glib wit, however, this was a radical and prescient political statement that represented a determined break from the tyranny of screen narrative. DP French +subtitles. *DVD*

Anne Wiazemsky *Véronique* • Jean-Pierre Léaud *Guillaume* • Michel Semeniako *Henri* • Lex de Bruijn *Kirilov* • Juliet Berto *Yvonne* ◼ *Dir/Scr* Jean-Luc Godard

Chisum ★★ PG
Western 1970 · US · Colour · 106min

This John Wayne movie, handsomely photographed by western veteran William H Clothier, uses a fictional variation on the Lincoln County cattle war to tell the tale of the man who first hired Billy the Kid. The Duke is well served by director Andrew V McLaglen, Forrest Tucker makes an imposing villain, and the Dominic Frontiere score is above average, but the plot rambles. TS *DVD*

John Wayne *John Chisum* • Forrest Tucker *Lawrence Murphy* • Christopher George *Dan Nodeen* • Ben Johnson (1) *James Pepper* • Glenn Corbett *Pat Garrett* • Bruce Cabot *Sheriff Brady* • Richard Jaeckel *Jess Evans* ◼ *Dir* Andrew V McLaglen • *Scr* Andrew J Fenady

Chitty Chitty Bang Bang ★★★★ U
Musical fantasy 1968 · UK · Colour · 139min

When this splendid musical was released in 1968, it was unfairly compared with Disney's *Mary Poppins*. No surprise as it shared *Poppins* star Dick Van Dyke, a super sing-a-long score by the Sherman brothers and a picture-book Edwardian setting. However, this fabulous family film about an eccentric inventor and his onomatopoeically named flying car has toe-tapping songs, glorious sets and a top-notch, as well as a nightmare-inducing baddie in the Child catcher. It's long but it still looks fantastic and is pure evergreen entertainment. JA *DVD* BD

Dick Van Dyke *Caractacus Potts* • Sally Ann Howes *Truly Scrumptious* • Lionel Jeffries *Grandpa Potts* • Gert Frobe [Gert Fröbe] *Baron Bomburst* • Anna Quayle *Baroness Bomburst* • Benny Hill *Toymaker* • James Robertson-Justice *Lord Scrumptious* ◼ *Dir* Ken Hughes • *Scr* Roald Dahl, Richard Maibaum, Ken Hughes, from Ian Fleming's illustrated children's book

Chloe ★★★ 15
Erotic thriller 2009 · Can/Fr · Colour · 92min

Atom Egoyan's involving remake of 2003 French film *Nathalie...* has a starry cast and a twisty, Hitchcock-inspired plot. Julianne Moore plays a middle-aged doctor who suspects that her lecturer husband Liam Neeson is having an affair. She hires high-class prostitute Amanda Seyfried to pose as a student and test his fidelity. Seyfried reports back that Neeson took the bait and provides Moore with a blow-by-blow account. It seems no one can keep their passions or emotions in check and the whole thing becomes more than a little overwrought as it moves towards the climax, but this is always fun to watch, even if it does ultimately stretch credibility beyond breaking point. BP *DVD* BD

Julianne Moore *Catherine Stewart* • Liam Neeson *David Stewart* • Amanda Seyfried *Chloe* • Max Thieriot *Michael Stewart* • RH Thomson *Frank* • Nina Dobrev *Anna* ◼ *Dir* Atom Egoyan • *Scr* Erin Cressida Wilson, from the 2003 film Nathalie...

Le Choc ★★★
Thriller 1982 · Fr · Colour · 100min

The hardships of a professional killer when he decides to retire are well known, but none more so than those suffered by Alain Delon when he decides to rest his trigger finger. His boss wants him to keep working, while Catherine Deneuve offers sympathetic compensation. Directed with some style by Robin Davis from a bestselling novel, it's a romantic thriller of dubious ethics but great pace. TH French dubbed.

Alain Delon *Martin Terrier* • Catherine Deneuve *Claire* • Philippe Léotard *Felix* • Etienne Chicot *Michel* • Stéphane Audran *Mme Faulques* • François Perrot *Cox* ◼ *Dir* Robin Davis • *Scr* Alain Delon, Robin Davis, Claude Veillot, Dominique Robelet, from the novel *La Position du Tireur Couché* by Jean-Patrick Manchette

Chocolat ★★★★ PG
Drama 1988 · Fr · Colour · 99min

Set in the Cameroons, *Chocolat* is both a highly intelligent political allegory and a sensitive study of adult interaction and emotion, seen through the eyes of a child. In her directorial debut, Claire Denis makes exceptional use of the parched landscape and the isolation of district governor François Cluzet's quarters to intensify the relationship between his young daughter and a black servant. In this environment, the arrival of a party of plane crash survivors seems an even more portentous intrusion. Isaach de Bankolé is supremely dignified as the misused houseboy, while Cécile Ducasse is impish and vulnerable as his devoted little friend. DP French +subtitles. *DVD*

Isaach de Bankole *Protée* • Giulia Boschi *Aimée* • François Cluzet *Marc* • Jean-Claude Adelin *Luc* • Laurent Arnal *Machinard* • Kenneth Cranham *Boothby* • Jacques Denis *Delpich* • Cécile Ducasse *France as a child* • Mireille Perrier *France* ◼ *Dir* Claire Denis • *Scr* Claire Denis, Jean-Pol Fargeau

Chocolat ★★★★ 12
Romantic comedy drama 2000 · UK/US · Colour · 116min

Director Lasse Hallström follows up *The Cider House Rules* with this delightful fable, adapted from the novel by Joanne Harris. Set in the late 1950s, the film stars Juliette Binoche as a rootless mother who appears overnight in a small French village and brazenly opens a chocolate shop during Lent. Staunch Catholic mayor Alfred Molina disapproves of her lifestyle and fears the challenge to his authority, but Binoche's confections are soon raising spirits (and more) particularly among the local wives. The arrival of handsome river gypsy Johnny Depp further inflames passions. A truly delicious experience. LH Swearing. *DVD* BD

Juliette Binoche *Vianne Rocher* • Lena Olin *Josephine Muscat* • Johnny Depp *Roux* • Judi Dench *Armande Voizin* • Alfred Molina *Comte de Reynaud* • Peter Stormare *Serge Muscat* • Carrie-Anne Moss *Caroline Clairmont* • Leslie Caron *Madame Audel* ◼ *Dir* Lasse Hallström • *Scr* Robert Nelson Jacobs, from the novel by Joanne Harris • *Cinematographer* Roger Pratt • *Production Designer* David Gropman • *Costume Designer* Renee Ehrlich Kalfus

Chocolate ★★★★ 18
Martial arts drama 2008 · Thai · Colour · 88min

The breakthrough success of 2003's *Ong-Bak* gave the martial arts genre a serious kick up the pants, thanks to the fighting styles of Thailand and the film's breathtakingly athletic star Tony Jaa. *Chocolate* is an equally bone-pounding proposition, showcasing the talents of another exciting performer – JeeJa Yanin.

She's sensational as the autistic girl whose lightning-fast reactions and sponge-like ability to absorb moves allow her to wreak revenge on her sick mother's former gang. This twisted tale is overwrought and ridiculous in equal measure, but it's never less than riveting. JH Thai, Japanese +subtitles. Violence. *DVD* Blu

Yanin Vismitananda [JeeJa Yanin] *Zen* • Hiroshi Abe *Masashi* • Pongpat Wachirabunjong *No 8* • Ammara Siriphong *Zin* ■ *Dir* Prachya Pinkaew • *Scr* Nepalee, Matthew Sakveerakul

The Chocolate Soldier ★★★U

Musical comedy 1941 · US · BW · 101min

Not the Oscar Straus operetta from which it takes its title (and retains some of its songs), but Ferenc Molnar's famous play *The Guardsman* (filmed in 1931) rejigged as a musical. Nelson Eddy is the husband whose insane jealousy leads him to disguise himself and court his wife to test her fidelity; then up-and-coming opera soprano Risë Stevens co-stars. The story now creaks with age, but Eddy's masquerade as an over-the-top Cossack officer is wonderful. RK

Nelson Eddy *Karl Lang/Vassily Vassilievitch* • Risë Stevens *Maria Lanyi* • Florence Bates *Mme Helene Pugsy* • Nydia Westman *Liesel "Maid"* ■ *Dir* Roy Del Ruth • *Scr* Leonard Lee, Keith Winter, Ernest Vajda, Claudine West, from the play *Testör/The Guardsman* by Ferenc Molnar

The Chocolate War ★★★15

Drama 1988 · US · Colour · 99min

Actor Keith Gordon made a creditable debut as writer/director with this brooding study of peer pressure gone mad. As the new boy who refuses the tradition of selling chocolates to boost school funds, Ilan Mitchell-Smith gives a stubborn rather than stoic performance, better at standing up to tyrannical headmaster John Glover than he is at resisting the ruthlessly persuasive methods of the Vigils, a senior elite charged with upholding Catholic principles. Making its points without undue insistence, this is as polished as it's provocative. DP

John Glover *Brother Leon* • Ilan Mitchell-Smith *Jerry* • Wallace Langham [Wally Ward] *Archie* • Doug Hutchison *Obie* • Adam Baldwin *Carter* • Brent Fraser *Emille* • Bud Cort *Brother Jacques* ■ *Dir* Keith Gordon • *Scr* Keith Gordon, from the novel by Robert Cormier

The Choice ★★12A

Romantic drama 2016 · US · Colour · 110min

Yet another Nicholas Sparks sudser brings us love on the North Carolina coast before roguish local vet Benjamin Walker and his new neighbour, medic Teresa Palmer, decide that they don't hate each other after all. The fateful final reel takes tear-jerking to cynical extremes as the ramifications of that title are played out, but along the way there are sunlit beaches, moonlight trysts, puppies in baskets and a rippling piano score offering a full payload of sappy romantic clichés. Meagre fare, even by Sparks standards. TJ Sexual references.

Benjamin Walker *Travis Parker* • Teresa Palmer *Gabby Holland* • Tom Welling *Ryan* • Alexandra Daddario *Monica* • Maggie Grace *Stephanie Parker* ■ *Dir* Ross Katz • *Scr* Bryan Sipe, from Nicholas Sparks's novel

Choice of Arms ★★★★

Crime drama 1981 · Fr · Colour · 135min

Having moved on from the thuggish persona that helped establish his credentials, Gérard Depardieu was reluctant to commit to Alain Corneau's *policier*. However, he gives an imposing performance as an escapee on the run who, along with Michel Galabru, seeks sanctuary on the stud farm of retired gangster Yves Montand. Although the action is often ferocious, Corneau deglamorises the violence by emphasising its finality. Though uncompromisingly staged and bleak in both tone and theme, this is superbly acted and touchingly concluded. DP French +subtitles.

Yves Montand *Noel* • Gérard Depardieu *Mickey* • Catherine Deneuve *Nicole* • Michel Galabru *Bonnafot* • Gérard Lanvin *Sarlat* • Marc Chapiteau *Savin* • Pierre Forget *Serge* • Christian Marquand *Jean* ■ *Dir* Alain Corneau • *Scr* Alain Corneau, Michel Grisolia

The Choir ★★★PG

Drama 2014 · US · Colour · 102min

A petulant young boy is given a life-changing opportunity in this passable music drama. Newcomer Garrett Wareing plays an 11-year-old troublemaker gifted with an angelic singing voice, who winds up at America's National Boychoir Academy after his mother dies. There he comes into conflict with both the pupils and hard-to-please conductor Dustin Hoffman. The singing is beautiful and the performances are solid, and the movie, overall, a harmless crowd-pleaser. SC Some violence, swearing.

Dustin Hoffman *Carvelle* • Kathy Bates *Headmistress* • Debra Winger *Ms Steel* • Josh Lucas *Gerard* • Eddie Izzard *Drake* ■ *Dir* François Girard • *Scr* Ben Ripley

The Choirboys ★18

Black comedy drama 1977 · US · Colour · 119min

This confused cop movie shows an LAPD squad's on- and off-duty behaviour. Supposedly a raunchy comedy, it's directed by Robert Aldrich with all the subtlety of a rampaging rhino, and the result is a catalogue of bigoted attitudes that dismally fails to amuse. Joseph Wambaugh, who wrote the book on which this is based, successfully took legal action to have his name removed from the credits. AT Violence, swearing, sex scenes, drug abuse, nudity.

Charles Durning *"Spermwhale" Whalen* • Louis Gossett Jr *Calvin Motts* • Perry King *Baxter Slate* • Clyde Kusatsu *Francis Tanaguchi* • Stephen Macht *Spencer Van Moot* • Tim McIntire *Roscoe Rules* • Randy Quaid *Dean Proust* • Don Stroud *Sam Lyles* • James Woods *Harold Bloomguard* • Burt Young *Sergeant Dominic Scuzzi* • Robert Webber *Deputy Chief Riggs* ■ *Dir* Robert Aldrich • *Scr* Christopher Knopf

Choke ★★★18

Comedy drama 2008 · US/Cay · Colour · 88min

The second film adaptation of a novel by cult author Chuck Palahniuk (the first was *Fight Club*), this is a typically dark slice of modish strangeness. Victor (an appealingly weird Sam Rockwell) is a theme-park worker, sex-addict and conman, who fakes choking fits in expensive restaurants to extract money from those who "save" him. Most of this cash is spent on the care bills for his demented mother Ida (Anjelica Huston), who rarely recognises him. Things get more complicated for Victor when he becomes involved with Paige (Kelly Macdonald), a nurse who works in Ida's hospital. Loosely shot and for the most part nicely played, this still doesn't amount to much more than a series of ribald sketches. AS *DVD*

Sam Rockwell *Victor Mancini* • Anjelica Huston *Ida Mancini* • Kelly Macdonald *Paige Marshall* • Brad William Henke *Denny* • Jonah Bobo *Young Victor* • Paz de la Huerta *Nico* • Clark Gregg *Lord High Charlie* • Joel Grey *Phil* ■ *Dir* Clark Gregg • *Scr* Clark Gregg, from the novel by Chuck Palahniuk

Chokher Bali ★★★PG

Period drama 2003 · Ind · Colour · 123min

This is an intense and meticulously made melodrama about a liberated widow (played by Aishwarya Rai), who becomes a companion to the mother of the man who once spurned her, and then proceeds to drive a wedge between him and his wife (Raima Sen). The atmosphere of Bengal prior to the 1905 partition is ably conveyed, but Ghosh's realist approach does not gel with the superstar aura of Bollywood icon Rai, who comes across a touch too modern. DP Bengali +subtitles. *DVD*

Lily Chakraborty [Lily Chakravarty] *Rajlakshmi* • Prosenjit Chatterjee *Mahendra* • Tota Raychowdhury *Behari* • Aishwarya Rai *Binodini* • Raima Sen *Ashalata* ■ *Dir* Rituparno Ghosh • *Scr* Rituparno Ghosh, from the novel by Rabindranath Tagore

Choking Man ★★15

Drama 2006 · US/UK · Colour · 82min

Ecuadorian immigrant Jorge (Octavio Gómez Berríos) is a painfully shy dishwasher in a New York diner in Jamaica, Queens, in this modest feature from Steve Barron. In his imagination he conjures animated visions of Chinese dragons and bunny rabbits; in reality he barely has the courage to remove his hoodie. Former MTV favourite Barron (he directed the video for a-ha's *Take On Me*) delivers what feels like an overstretched short here. He compensates for the thinness by laying on the quirky cuteness with a trowel, but neither that nor the occasional dashes of urban magical realism can save the plot from its own inertia. JR English, Spanish +subtitles. *DVD*

Octavio Gómez Berríos *Jorge* • Eugenia Yuan *Amy* • Aaron Paul *Jerry* • Mandy Patinkin *Rick* ■ *Dir/Scr* Steve Barron

CHOMPS ★★PG

Comedy 1979 · US · Colour · 86min

Based on a story by Joseph Barbera (of Hanna-Barbera cartoon fame), this film falls between two stools. It's a bit gritty for younger children and too simplistic for the pre-teens, so its mix of crime and comedy won't find many takers. The title refers to the Canine Home Protection System designed in the shape of a robotic dog by inventor Wesley Eure in a bid to save Conrad Bain's security company. The slapstick has the feel you'd expect of the man who'd helped create Tom and Jerry. DP Some swearing.

Wesley Eure *Brian Foster* • Valerie Bertinelli *Casey Norton* • Conrad Bain *Ralph Norton* • Chuck McCann *Brooks* • Red Buttons *Bracken* • Larry Bishop *Ken Sharp* • Hermione Baddeley *Mrs Flower* ■ *Dir* Don Chaffey • *Scr* Dick Robbins, Duane Poole, Joseph Barbera, from a story by Joseph Barbera

Choose Me ★★★★15

Romantic comedy drama 1984 · US · Colour · 102min

A languid psychological mosaic from writer/director Alan Rudolph, this film resembles a slowed-down version of his mentor Robert Altman's output. In the neon-lit bar that is the focal point of this romantic comedy drama, the main characters are the bar's owner (Lesley Ann Warren) and a radio agony aunt (Geneviève Bujold). Both offer sex, but are frustrated until newcomer Mickey (Keith Carradine) becomes the man in their lives. Rudolph's work is an acquired taste; once acquired, though, it's addictive. TH *DVD*

Geneviève Bujold *Dr Nancy Love* • Keith Carradine *Mickey* • Lesley Ann Warren *Eve* • Patrick Bauchau *Zack Antoine* • Rae Dawn Chong *Pearl Antoine* • John Larroquette *Billy Ace* ■ *Dir/Scr* Alan Rudolph

Chop Suey ★★15

Documentary 2000 · US · Colour and BW · 94min

Having garnered an Oscar nomination for *Let's Get Lost*, photographer Bruce Weber ended a decade's sabbatical from cinema with this unfocused, if fittingly compulsive, treatise on obsession. It's a dazzling scrapbook of changing visual styles, but in allowing his fascination with dullard hunk Peter Johnson to seep into the foreground, Weber disappointingly marginalises such intriguing characters as Robert Mitchum, lesbian jazz legend Frances Faye and *Vogue* editor Diana Vreeland. Very much a vanity project. DP *DVD*

■ *Dir* Bruce Weber

Chopper ★★★★★18

Biographical crime drama 2000 · Aus · Colour · 90min

An extraordinary movie about an extraordinary man, this is the boldest Australian film in decades. Downbeat, gritty and ultra-violent, the sensational feature debut of rock-video director Andrew Dominik is a long, sharp shock to the system and has a show-stopping central performance from Eric Bana. This totally unclassifiable biography of notorious criminal Mark "Chopper" Read mixes startling facts from his numerous bestsellers (one was titled *How to Shoot Friends and Influence People*) with large doses of pulp fiction regarding the supposed 19 murders he committed. Using a wild array of stylistic tricks, Dominik's fascinating, funny and frightening look at Read's playful sadism is a masterpiece of innovation. AJ Violence, swearing, drug abuse. *DVD*

Eric Bana *Mark Brandon "Chopper" Read* • Simon Lyndon *Jimmy Loughnan* • David Field *Keithy George* • Dan Wyllie *Bluey* • Bill Young *Detective Downey* • Vince Colosimo *Neville Bartos* • Kenny Graham *Keith Read* ■ *Dir* Andrew Dominik • *Scr* Andrew Dominik, from the books (including *Chopper: From the Inside*) by Mark Brandon Read

Chopper Chicks in Zombietown ★15

Comedy horror 1990 · US · Colour · 85min

At no-budget film empire Troma, a film's title is usually more important than the content. This is no exception. On paper it sounds suitably wacky: an all-girl biker gang ride into a small town and face their toughest test when they confront a population of zombies. However, the direction is inept, the script and performances are awful, and it scores low in the bad-taste stakes as well. JF *DVD*

Jamie Rose *Dede* • Catherine Carlen *Rox* • Kristina Loggia *Jojo* • Martha Quinn *Mae Clutter* • Don Calfa *Ralph Willum* • Lycia Naff *TC* ■ *Dir/Scr* Dan Hoskins

Chori Chori ★★★★U

Comedy 1956 · Ind · BW · 122min

Having been the mainstay of RK Films for eight years, the most popular romantic teaming in the history of Indian cinema parted company after this reworking of the Frank Capra classic *It Happened One Night*. As the heiress who defies her father and elopes to marry a heel, Nargis is suitably haughty, but it's only when she meets up with journalist Raj Kapoor that the picture catches light. A treat for fans and a fascinating insight into remakes, Bollywood style. DP In Hindi.

Nargis *Baby* • Raj Kapoor *Suman* • Master Bhagwan • Johnny Walker • Mukri ■ *Dir* Anant Thakur • *Scr* Aga Jani Kashmiri

A Chorus Line ★★★PG

Musical 1985 · US · Colour · 117min

The highly successful Broadway show was so relentlessly theatrical that it was generally considered impossible to film. The strength of the show remains, but, by incorporating flashbacks and, crucially, substituting songs and choreography, the original is undermined, not enhanced. Nevertheless, there is much of merit, especially Alyson Reed, touching as key dancer Cassie, and ex-*Dallas* regular Audrey Landers, who does well by one of the great showstoppers. Michael Douglas puts in a sharp performance as the show's producer. TS Swearing. *DVD* Blu

Michael Douglas (1) *Zach* • Alyson Reed *Cassie* • Terrence Mann *Larry* • Michael Blevins *Mark* • Yamil Borges *Morales* • Vicki Frederick *Sheila* • Audrey Landers *Val* • Jan Gan Boyd *Connie* • Sharon Brown *Kim* • Gregg Burge *Richie* • Cameron English *Paul* • Nicole Fosse *Kristine* ■ *Dir* Richard Attenborough • *Scr* Arnold Schulman, from the musical by Michael Bennett, Nicholas Dante, James Kirkwood

A Chorus of Disapproval ★PG

Comedy 1988 · UK · Colour · 95min

If you want to remove the comedy, pithy insights, energy and spirit from the work of stage maestro Alan Ayckbourn, your first choice of director should be Michael Winner. And, as expected, the director lumbers his way through a text from which odd moments of social satire escape untouched, but more by good luck than design. JM Swearing. *DVD*

C

Anthony Hopkins *Dafydd Ap Llewellyn* • Jeremy Irons *Guy Jones* • Richard Briers *Ted Washbrook* • Gareth Hunt *Ian Hubbard* • Patsy Kensit *Linda Washbrook* • Alexandra Pigg *Bridget Baines* • Prunella Scales *Hannah Ap Llewellyn* • Jenny Seagrove *Fay Hubbard* • Lionel Jeffries *Jarvis Huntley-Pike* • Sylvia Syms *Rebecca Huntley-Pike* ■ *Dir* Michael Winner • *Scr* Alan Ayckbourn, Michael Winner, from the play by Alan Ayckbourn

The Chosen ★★★ PG
Drama   1981 · US · Colour · 103min

Mannered or magnificent? Rod Steiger's performance as a Hasidic rabbi dominates the film, for good or bad. His son (Robby Benson) is venturing out of his restrictively religious range by becoming friends with the son of a Zionist professor (Maximilian Schell). Set in New York at the time of the founding of Palestine, director Jeremy Paul Kagan conjures the time's fervent atmosphere, but it's Steiger's risk-all exhibition you'll remember. TH

Maximilian Schell *Professor David Malter* • Rod Steiger *Reb Saunders* • Robby Benson *Danny Saunders* • Barry Miller *Reuven Malter* ■ *Dir* Jeremy Paul Kagan • *Scr* Edwin Gordon, from the novel by Chaim Potok

Chosen Survivors ★★
Science fiction   1974 · US/Mex · Colour · 98min

Jackie Cooper and Bradford Dillman are among a group of specially selected citizens who are carted off to a deep underground bunker to test individual reactions to probable nuclear war. Unfortunately a horde of killer vampire bats are sealed in with them, and it's supper time. Sutton Roley's ecological revenge thriller is clearly inspired by Hitchcock's *The Birds* and the bat effects are wholly convincing, but his protagonists are obvious clichés. RB

Jackie Cooper *Raymond Couzins* • Alex Cord *Steven Mayes* • Richard Jaeckel *Gordon Ellis* • Bradford Dillman *Peter Macomber* • Pedro Armendáriz Jr *Luis Cabral* • Diana Muldaur *Alana Fitzgerald* ■ *Dir* Sutton Roley • *Scr* HB Cross, Joe Reb Moffley, from a story by Cross

Chris & Don: a Love Story ★★★
Documentary   2007 · US · Colour · 90min

Diary entries, photos and interviews tell the 34-year love story of Christopher Isherwood (whose *Berlin Stories* inspired *Cabaret*) and famed portrait painter Don Bachardy. Their convention-defying affair is also the tale of LA's nascent – and back in the 1950s largely closeted – gay culture and is given a lively treatment in this 2007 documentary. Seeing the couple preserved like flies in amber on home-movies and mixing with talents like Tennessee Williams is fascinating. DvB

Don Bachardy *Narrator* • WH Auden • Ted Bachardy • Christopher Isherwood • Tennessee Williams ■ *Dir* Tina Mascara, Guido Santi

Christ Stopped at Eboli ★★★★ PG
Drama   1979 · It/Fr/W Ger · Colour · 145min

Francesco Rosi's adaptation of Carlo Levi's memoir divided critics between those who felt it sentimentalised his opposition to the fascist regime, and those who reckoned the director's almost neorealist use of everyday characters and the rural landscape helped the film capture the spirit of its source. Surprisingly, for such a literate work, Rosi doesn't delve too deeply into the causes of Italy's lurch to the right. Thanks to a monumental performance from Gian Maria Volonté, however, he does succeed in conveying both the writer's fears for his country and his unswerving faith in the decency of its population. DP Italian +subtitles. DVD

Gian Maria Volonté *Carlo Levi* • Paolo Bonacelli *Don Luigi Magalone* • Alain Cuny *Baron Rotundo* • Lea Massari *Luisa Levi* • Irene Papas *Giulia* • François Simon *Don Traiella* ■ *Dir* Francesco Rosi • *Scr* Francesco Rosi, Tonino Guerra, Raffaele La Capria, from the memoirs *Cristo Si é Fermato a Eboli* by Carlo Levi

The Christian Licorice Store ★★★
Drama   1971 · US · Colour · 84min

When did you last see a movie about a tennis champion who sells out to commercialism that boasts an acting role for Jean Renoir, one of the world's greatest directors? Add to this appearances by cult director Monte Hellman (*Two-Lane Blacktop*) and silent star Gilbert Roland, and you have a feast for buffs and a very arty, wacky piece of 1970s indulgence. The tennis player who "goes Hollywood" is played by Beau Bridges, while Bond girl Maud Adams is the photographer who covers his life story. AT

Beau Bridges *Franklin Cane* • Maud Adams *Cynthia Vicstrom* • Gilbert Roland *Jonathan Carruthers* • Allan Arbus *Monroe* • Anne Randall *Texas girl* • Monte Hellman *Joseph* • Jean Renoir ■ *Dir* James Frawley • *Scr* Floyd Mutrux

Christiane F ★★★★ 18
Drama   1981 · W Ger · Colour · 120min

Sending moral campaigners scrambling for their soapboxes and critics reaching for superlatives, this graphic depiction of the miseries of drug addiction is strewn with powerful images and provocative insights. Based on a bestselling book written by two reporters from *Der Stern*, the film traces one 13-year-old girl's descent into heroin dependency and prostitution. Natja Brunckhorst and Thomas Haustein give agonisingly authentic performances, but director Uli Edel occasionally over-indulges himself, notably at the David Bowie concert. Sketchy in its sociology, but undeniably powerful. DP German +subtitles. DVD

Natja Brunckhorst *Christiane F* • Thomas Haustein *Detlef* • Jens Kuphal *Axel* • Jan Georg Effler *Bernd* • Christiane Reichelt *Babsi* • Daniela Jaeger *Kessi* • Kerstin Richter *Stella* • David Bowie ■ *Dir* Ulrich Edel [Uli Edel] • *Scr* Herman Weigel, from a non-fiction book by Kai Hermann, Horst Rieck

Christine ★★★ 18
Horror   1983 · US · Colour · 105min

Adapted from the novel by Stephen King, this killer-car chiller is the ultimate in auto eroticism. The idea that a 1958 Plymouth Fury can turn into a jealous mistress is a cracker and, through his ingenious use of close-ups and seductive angles, director John Carpenter turns Christine into the sassiest thing on four wheels. He also gets a likeable performance out of Keith Gordon as the geek who becomes a dude the moment he inserts the key in the ignition. But it's overlong and more effective as dark comedy than horror. DP Violence, swearing. DVD

Keith Gordon *Arnie Cunningham* • John Stockwell *Dennis Guilder* • Alexandra Paul *Leigh Cabot* • Robert Prosky *Will Darnell* • Harry Dean Stanton *Rudolph Junkins* • Christine Belford *Regina Cunningham* ■ *Dir* John Carpenter • *Scr* Bill Phillips, from the novel by Stephen King

The Christmas Candle ★★ U
Seasonal fantasy   2013 · UK/US · Colour · 99min

This festive family offering will probably be remembered for Susan Boyle's acting bow as the singing wife of church warden James Cosmo, who welcomes a new vicar (Hans Matheson) to the Cotswold village of Gladbury some time in the late 19th century. Having had his beliefs tested in the big city, the vicar finds faith and fate conspire to teach him a yuletide lesson. That lesson might once have been taken to heart by British audiences, but it's hard to see it having much impact in our cynical times, especially as the script errs too frequently towards sentimental contrivance. DP

Hans Matheson *David Richmond* • Samantha Barks *Emily Barstow* • Lesley Manville *Bea Haddington* • Sylvester McCoy *Edward Haddington* • James Cosmo *Herbert Hopewell* • Susan Boyle *Eleanor Hopewell* ■ *Dir* John Stephenson • *Scr* Candace Lee, Eric Newman, from the novel by Max Lucado

The Christmas Card ★★
Romantic drama   2006 · US · Colour · 84min

This predictable romantic melodrama is so sugary that you could probably get cavities just from watching it. A relentless emotional button-pusher, it stars Alice Evans as a small-town girl whose Christmas card to a random soldier in Afghanistan (John Newton) gives the serviceman renewed strength and inspires him to go on a mission to find her. Only Ed Asner as Evans's protective father delivers any sense of realism, but his earnestness seems out of place amid all the greetings card-style cuteness. SF

John Newton (2) *Cody* • Alice Evans *Faith* • Edward Asner *Luke* • Brian Robinson (2) *Edo* • Lois Nettleton *Rosie* • Charlie Holliday *Rev Ives* ■ *Dir* Stephen Bridgewater • *Scr* Joany Kane

A Christmas Carol ★★★ U
Period drama   1938 · US · BW · 69min

Few would dispute the fact that Alastair Sim is the finest screen Scrooge (in 1951's *Scrooge*), but Lionel Barrymore would have given him a hard act to follow. Sadly, disability forced him to withdraw from this typically polished MGM version of Charles Dickens's yuletide favourite. Reginald Owen is a good substitute, however, impressing particularly during the visitations of Marley and the other Christmas ghosts. DP

Reginald Owen *Ebenezer Scrooge* • Gene Lockhart *Bob Cratchit* • Kathleen Lockhart *Mrs Cratchit* • Terry Kilburn *Tiny Tim* • Barry Mackay *Fred* • Lynne Carver *Bess* ■ *Dir* Edwin L Marin • *Scr* Hugo Butler, from the story by Charles Dickens

A Christmas Carol ★★★ U
Period drama   1984 · US · Colour · 96min

George C Scott is in towering form in this handsome adaptation of Dickens's Yuletide favourite. Rather than settling for easy reformation, Scott's Scrooge gives the ghosts as good as he gets and has to be dragged away from ideals forged during a difficult youth. Unfortunately, the members of a stellar supporting cast lack Scott's rigour and turn in sentimental caricatures that dishonour both source and star. However, director Clive Donner makes atmospheric use of his Shrewsbury locations. DP DVD

George C Scott *Ebenezer Scrooge* • Nigel Davenport *Silas Scrooge* • Frank Finlay *Marley's Ghost* • Angela Pleasence *Ghost of Christmas Past* • Roger Rees *Fred Holywell* • David Warner *Bob Cratchit* • Edward Woodward *Ghost of Christmas Present* • Susannah York *Mrs Cratchit* • Anthony Walters *Tiny Tim* ■ *Dir* Clive Donner • *Scr* Roger O Hirson, from the story by Charles Dickens

A Christmas Carol ★★ U
Animated drama   1997 · US · Colour · 66min

It's hard to arrive at a new approach to Charles Dickens's beloved yuletide tale. This isn't even the first animated adaptation, but it's certainly one of the most sentimental versions (courtesy of its ghastly songs), with the inspirational message of goodwill to all being given a determinedly contemporary consumerist feel. With a graphic style as flat as a TV cartoon, it's left to the vocal talents to enliven the action. DP

Tim Curry *Ebeneezer Scrooge* • Whoopi Goldberg *Spirit of Christmas Present* • Michael York *Bob Cratchit* • Edward Asner *Marley* • Frank Welker *Debit* • Kath Soucie *Mrs Cratchit* ■ *Dir* Stan Phillips • *Scr* Jymn Magon, from the story by Charles Dickens

A Christmas Carol ★★★ PG
Period drama   1999 · US · Colour · 89min

As Ebenezer Scrooge, Patrick Stewart proves himself worthy company for Alastair Sim, Albert Finney and George C Scott. This TV movie is not the most lavish or inventive adaptation of Charles Dickens's most-filmed tale, but Joel Grey and Desmond Barrit acquit themselves well as two of the spirits whose midnight promptings transform Stewart from a penny-pinching curmudgeon into a joyous reveller. There's even a nod towards modernity with the

casting of Richard E Grant and Saskia Reeves as the Cratchits. Stewart holds the piece together with a subtle performance. DP DVD

Patrick Stewart *Mr Ebenezer Scrooge* • Richard E Grant *Bob Cratchit* • Joel Grey *The Ghost of Christmas Past* • Ian McNeice *Mr Albert Fezziwig* • Saskia Reeves *Mrs Cratchit* • Desmond Barrit *The Ghost of Christmas Present* • Bernard Lloyd *Jacob Marley* ■ *Dir* David Jones (3) • *Scr* Peter Barnes, from the story by Charles Dickens

A Christmas Carol ★★ PG
Seasonal fantasy musical
2004 · US · Colour · 87min

Despite the fact that it was produced by the ever-saccharine Hallmark company, there's something rather crude about this musical adaptation of Charles Dickens's story. Traditionalists will wince at the sight of Jane Krakowski gyrating around Kelsey Grammer's bed as the Ghost of Christmas Past. The shoddiness of the special effects further detracts from any sense of ethereality – there are plenty of familiar faces here, including Jason Alexander, Jennifer Love Hewitt and Geraldine Chaplin, but they're marooned by this poor festive fare. DP DVD

Kelsey Grammer *Ebenezer Scrooge* • Jennifer Love Hewitt *Emily* • Jason Alexander *Jacob Marley* • Geraldine Chaplin *Ghost of Christmas Future/Blind beggar woman* • Jesse L Martin *Ghost of Christmas Present/Ticket seller* • Jane Krakowski *Ghost of Christmas Past/Streetlamp lighter* • Patrick David *Chest-in-safe ghost* • Steven Miller *Young Ebenezer Scrooge* • Edward Gower *Bob Cratchit* ■ *Dir* Arthur Allan Seidelman • *Scr* Lynn Ahrens, from a musical by Mike Ockrent, Ahrens, from the novel by Charles Dickens

A Christmas Carol ★★ PG
Seasonal animated fantasy
2009 · US · Colour · 95min

Jim Carrey spreads himself thin in this faithful animated adaptation of the Dickens classic, playing not only the miserly Scrooge but also the ghosts who visit him on a cold Christmas Eve. The star does a fair English accent, but it's difficult to see why director Robert Zemeckis cast such a zany actor only to put him in a straitjacket. Thankfully, the motion-capture technology doesn't have the same unnatural effect it did in the director's earlier *Polar Express*, but it doesn't do justice to the actors, either. SP DVD Blu-ray 3D

Jim Carrey *Ebenezer Scrooge/Ghost of Christmas Past/Ghost of Christmas Present/Ghost of Christmas Yet to Come* • Colin Firth *Fred* • Gary Oldman *Bob Cratchit/Marley/Tiny Tim* • Robin Wright Penn [Robin Wright] *Belle/Fan* • Bob Hoskins *Mr Fezziwig/Old Joe* • Cary Elwes *Dick Wilkins/Portly gentleman no 1/Mad fiddler/guest no 2/Businessman no 1* • Molly Quinn *Belinda Cratchit* ■ *Dir* Robert Zemeckis • *Scr* Robert Zemeckis, from the novel by Charles Dickens

Christmas Carol: the Movie ★ U
Part-animated seasonal drama
2001 · UK/Ger · Colour · 77min

Charles Dickens's classic ghost story suffers the indignity of being turned into a sentimental and unimaginatively drawn cartoon. Director Jimmy T Murakami ruins the classic tale by adding tangential storylines, presumably to appeal to a more juvenile audience. The whole is framed by a live-action scene depicting Dickens (Simon Callow) arriving in Boston to read his story to an assembled audience. AJ DVD

Simon Callow *Scrooge/Charles Dickens* • Kate Winslet *Belle* • Nicolas Cage *Jacob Marley* • Jane Horrocks *Ghost of Christmas Past* • Michael Gambon *Ghost of Christmas Present* • Rhys Ifans *Bob Cratchit* • Juliet Stevenson *Mrs Cratchit/Mother Gimlet* • Robert Llewellyn *Old Joe* ■ *Dir* Jimmy T Murakami • *Scr* Piet Kroon, Robert Llewellyn, from the story *A Christmas Carol* by Charles Dickens

Christmas Comes Home to Canaan ★★

Drama   2011 · US · Colour · 88min

Unresolved issues return to trouble widower Billy Ray Cyrus and his rural Texas clan in this flimsy sequel to TV-movie heart-tugger *Christmas in Canaan*. But though the story is about reawakened feelings, there's no emotional impact to the 1970s-set events, as Cyrus's farmer speedily falls for the physiotherapist (Gina Holden) assigned to help his young son try to walk again. The unnatural dialogue and inexpressive performances are no help, either. SF

Billy Ray Cyrus *Daniel Burton* • Gina Holden *Briony Adair* • Liam James *Bobber Burton* • Matt Ward *Rodney Freeman* ■ *Dir* Neill Fearnley • *Scr* Donald Davenport, from the novel by Davenport, Kenny Rogers

The Christmas Consultant ★★

Seasonal comedy   2012 · Can · Colour · 93min

An energetic David Hasselhoff plays on his eccentric public persona in this simplistic and undemanding comedy about the real meaning of Christmas. Wide-eyed and manic-looking, the former *Baywatch* star throws himself into his role as the titular organiser, who's hired by career-focused Caroline Rhea to handle every detail of her disconnected family's yuletide. The result is cheesily predictable. SF

David Hasselhoff *Owen* • Caroline Rhea *Maya Fletcher* • Barclay Hope *Jack Fletcher* • Jessica McLeod *Anna Fletcher* ■ *Dir* John Bradshaw • *Scr* Gregg Rossen, Brian Sawyer

Christmas Eve ★★

Comedy drama   1947 · US · BW · 90min

This sentimental film boasts an impressive cast but little else of note and basically consists of three interwoven stories, which culminate on Christmas Eve. They involve the three adopted sons of elderly Ann Harding who needs their help to escape the clutches of an avaricious nephew. The lost sons are a rodeo rider (Randolph Scott), an apparent criminal (George Raft) and a playboy (George Brent). BB

George Raft *Mario Torio* • George Brent *Michael Brooks* • Randolph Scott *Jonathan* • Joan Blondell *Ann Nelson* • Virginia Field *Claire* • Dolores Moran *Jean* • Ann Harding *"Aunt "Matilda" Reid* • Reginald Denny *Phillip Hastings* • Douglass Dumbrille *Doctor Bunyan* ■ *Dir* Edwin L Marin • *Scr* Laurence Stallings, from a stories by Laurence Stallings, from a stories by Richard H Landau [Richard Landau], from a stories by Robert B Altman [Robert Altman, uncredited]

The Christmas Gift ★★

Seasonal drama   2009 · US · Colour · 96min

In this flimsy heart-tugger, a couple desperate for children (Dean Cain and Jean Louisa Kelly) take in three troublesome orphans for the festive period. It's immediately obvious from Kelly's infatuated expression what the outcome of their stay will be, so the bulk of the film feels like padding in preparation for the happy-ever-after ending. Where the drama works best is in the scenes exploring the boys' vulnerability, adding moments of much-needed poignancy to an otherwise emotionally bland tale. SF

Dean Cain *Jack Green* • Jean Louisa Kelly *Cherie Green* • Mimi Kennedy *Rita Green* • Spencir Bridges *Ray* • Reginald VelJohnson *Rodney* ■ *Dir* David S Cass Sr • *Scr* Donald Martin, Mitchell Gabourie

Christmas Holiday ★★★PG

Film noir   1944 · US · BW · 88min

With that frothy title and Gene Kelly and Deanna Durbin starring, you could well expect a musical. However, this melodrama treads on the wilder shores of *film noir* in the hands of expert director Robert Siodmak and screenwriter Herman J Mankiewicz. A miscast Kelly never really convinces as a returned murderer, but Durbin is excellent in her only non-frivolous role. TS *DVD*

Deanna Durbin *Jackie Lamont/Abigail Martin Manette* • Gene Kelly *Robert Manette* • Richard Whorf *Simon Fenimore* • Dean Harens *Lt Charles Mason* • Gladys George *Valerie De Merode* • Gale Sondergaard *Mrs Manette* • David Bruce *Lt Gerald Tyler* • Minor Watson *Townsend* ■ *Dir* Robert Siodmak • *Scr* Herman J Mankiewicz, from the novel by W Somerset Maugham

Christmas in Canaan ★★

Drama   2009 · US · Colour · 90min

Love is the glue in this warm but idealistic family heart-tugger, based on a novel co-written by country singer Kenny Rogers. Opening in 1960s Texas, it sees Billy Ray Cyrus's principled widower initiate an unlikely friendsh p between his farmboy son and a bookish black classmate when he forces them to spend time together as punishment for fighting each other. One injured puppy and some clunky acting and dialogue later, and the lads have naturally bonded for life. From here, the film covers so much ground that it dilutes the impact of even the most dramatic moments. SF

Billy Ray Cyrus *Daniel Burton* • Tom Heaton *Wylie* • Jaishon Fisher *Young Rodney* • Zak Ludwig *Young DJ* • Jessica Mcleod *Young Sarah* ■ *Dir* Neill Fearnley • *Scr* Donald J Davenport, from the novel by Davenport, Kenny Rogers

Christmas in Connecticut ★★★

Comedy   1945 · US · BW · 101min

In this corny but enjoyable little piece, Barbara Stanwyck almost convinces as the oh-so-chic journalist whose column extols the virtues of home cooking and country living. As a promotional stunt, she is forced to look after a navy hero (Dennis Morgan) for Christmas – except, of course, she lives in the city, can't cook and has to rent a cottage in Connecticut. The idea is sound enough, but it becomes awfully sentimental. TS

Barbara Stanwyck *Elizabeth Lane* • Dennis Morgan *Jefferson Jones* • Sydney Greenstreet *Alexander Yardley* • Reginald Gardiner *John Sloan* • SZ Sakall *Felix Bassenak* • Robert Shayne *Dudley Beecham* • Jna O'Connor *Norah* • Frank Jenks *Sinkewicz* • Joyce Compton *Mary Lee* ■ *Dir* Peter Godfrey • *Scr* Lionel Houser, Adele Comandini, from the story by Aileen Hamilton

Christmas in Connecticut ★★U

Comedy   1992 · US · Colour · 89min

Arnold Schwarzenegger opted for an unusual change of pace for his directorial debut, a remake of a sugary old Christmas favourite from 1945. Sadly, it needs some of the firepower that Schwarzenegger brings to his blockbuster action movies, for this is routine fare, updated with too little imagination for the 1990s. Dyan Cannon is entertaining and believable as the TV presenter who decides to take heroic ranger Kris Kristofferson into her home for Christmas as a publicity stunt, but Schwarzenegger has upped the saccharine content of the ta e to unacceptable levels. JF

Dyan Cannon *Elizabeth Blane* • Kris Kristofferson *Jefferson Jones* • Tony Curtis *Alex Yardley* • Richard Roundtree *Mr Prescott* • Kelly Cinnante *Josie* • Gene Lythgow *Tyler* • Jimmy Workman *Kevin* ■ *Dir* Arnold Schwarzenegger • *Scr* Janet Brownell, from the 1945 film

Christmas in July ★★★U

Comedy   1940 · US · BW · 64min

Dick Powell stars as a young clerk who, mistakenly believing he's won $25,000 in a slogan-writing competition, goes on a manic spending spree. The second film from the uniquely inventive Preston Sturges is not in the same class as his first, *The Great McGinty*, or such subsequent classics, but it's beautifully played and peppered with brilliantly observed comedy cameos from a memorable supporting cast. A humane, funny and romantic romp. RK *DVD*

Dick Powell *Jimmy MacDonald* • Ellen Drew *Betty Casey* • Raymond Walburn *Mr Maxford* • Alexander Carr *Mr Schindel* • William Demarest *Mr Bildocker* • Ernest Truex *Mr Baxter* • Franklin Pangborn *Announcer* ■ *Dir/Scr* Preston Sturges

Christmas in Wonderland ★★12

Seasonal comedy   2007 · US/Can · Colour · 98min

This minor-league festive offering would have probably gone unnoticed had it not contained one of Patrick Swayze's final performances. High jinks of an all-too predictable nature ensue when Swayze's jobless parent is tasked with carrying out the Christmas shopping with his three children in tow, leading to the discovery of a bag of counterfeit cash and a run in with three bumbling crooks and some overeager cops. Tim Curry's shameless turn as a Royal Mountie with an inexplicable Scot's accent is sheer panto excess. JH *DVD*

Patrick Swayze *Wayne Saunders* • Matthew Knight *Brian Saunders* • Amy Schlagel *Mary Saunders* • Zoe Schlagel *Mary Saunders* • Tim Curry *Gordon McLoosh* • Cameron Bright *Danny Saunders* • Carmen Electra *Ginger Peachum* • Chris Kattan *Leonard "Leo" Cardoza* ■ *Dir* James Orr • *Scr* Wanda Birdsong Shope, James Orr, Jim Cruickshank

The Christmas Pageant ★★

Romantic comedy   2011 · US · Colour · 87min

Melissa Gilbert learns a few rushed lessons about what really matters in life in this contrived and predictable seasonal comedy. Gamely wading through the clichés, she plays a broke Broadway director who ends up in charge of a small-town pageant after getting fired yet again for her temperamental behaviour. Unfortunately, for a film about following your heart, events are not very affecting. SF

Melissa Gilbert *Vera Parks* • Robert Mailhouse *Jack Harmon* • Edward Herrmann *Garrett Clark* • Lennon Wynn *Kristen* ■ *Dir* David S Cass Sr • *Scr* Mark Valenti

A Christmas Star ★★★U

Seasonal drama   2015 · UK · Colour · 81min

A young girl born at Christmas with a magical gift must find a way to stop her town being taken over by a ruthless developer. An independent British film with a sleigh-load of charm, this features a strong cast, making a rather slight storyline more engaging with warm performances, particularly from young lead Erin Galway-Kendrick. Former 007 Pierce Brosnan hams it up in a fleeting appearance as an irate businessman, while good humour cuts through the treacle to make an infectiously festive family movie. JL

Rob James-Collier *Pat McKerrod* • Suranne Jones *Miss Darcy* • Richard Clements *Joe O'Hanlon* • Bronagh Waugh *Maria O'Hanlon* • Liam Neeson *Narrator/Radio DJ* • Julian Fellowes ■ *Dir* Richard Elson • *Scr* Maire Campbell, Richard Elson

A Christmas Story ★★★★PG

Comedy   1983 · US · Colour · 89min

A much underrated look at what it's like to be an avaricious child with Christmas approaching, this witty, insightful, hugely enjoyable movie is riven with glorious home truths and a merciful lack of saccharine surrounding a topic that generally reduces directors to lachrymose morons. Even more surprising is that it comes from Bob Clark, director of the smutty teen comedy *Porky's*. Peter Billingsley plays Ralphie, and his quest for juvenile justice and a Red Ryder BB gun is an enormous joy. The follow-up, *It Runs in the Family* (1994), was a disappointment. SH *DVD*

Melinda Dillon *Mrs Parker* • Darren McGavin *Mr Parker* • Peter Billingsley *Ralphie* • Ian Petrella *Randy* • Scott Schwartz *Flick* • RD Robb *Schwartz* • Tedde Moore *Miss Shields* ■ *Dir* Bob Clark • *Scr* Jean Shepherd, Leigh Brown, Bob Clark, from the novel *In God We Trust, All Others Pay Cash* by Jean Shepherd

The Christmas Tale ★★★

Horror thriller   2005 · Sp · Colour · 71min

Written by *[Rec]* co-writer Luis Berdejo, this cruel yet pleasurable take on *Whistle down the Wind* follows a group of children out prowling the woods, who happen upon a wounded woman dressed in a Santa suit. Their first instinct is to help her, but then they discover she's carried out a robbery and proceed to torture her to get the stolen cash. *Pan's Labyrinth* star Ivana Baquero gives a great performance, and director Paco Plaza uses horror movie imagery to deliver a wickedly effective punch. Some fun Spanish pop culture references (including Baccara's *Yes Sir, I Can Boogie* on the soundtrack) help the action crackle along nicely. AJ Spanish +subtitles.

Maru Valdivielso *Rebecca* • Christian Casas *Koldo* • Roger Babia *Peti* • Daniel Casadellà *Eugenio* • Ivana Baquero *Moni* • Pau Poch *Tito* ■ *Dir* Paco Plaza • *Scr* Luis Berdejo

A Christmas Tale ★★★★15

Comedy drama   2008 · Fr · Colour · 145min

Director and co-writer Arnaud Desplechin's compelling and impeccably acted family saga sees ailing matriarch Catherine Deneuve's children arrive for a Christmas reunion. But her search for a bone marrow donor does not take over the film, as Desplechin is far more concerned with domestic issues than medical emergencies. He is particularly intrigued (and appalled) by prodigal son Mathieu Amalric's relationships with the waspishly serene Deneuve, embittered sister Anne Consigny and girlfriend Emmanuelle Devos, who is clearly as amused as she is disconcerted by the dysfunction raging politely around her. What this incisive comedy drama illustrates are the scandals and compromises, rituals and regrets that somehow keep even the most fractious families together. DP French +subtitles. *DVD*

Catherine Deneuve *Junon Vuillard* • Jean-Paul Roussillon *Abel Vuillard* • Mathieu Amalric *Henri* • Anne Consigny *Elizabeth* • Emmanuelle Devos *Faunia* • Chiara Mastroianni *Sylvia* • Melvil Poupaud *Ivan* ■ *Dir* Arnaud Desplechin • *Scr* Arnaud Desplechin, Emmanuel Bourdieu, from the non-fiction book *La Greffe* by Jacques Ascher, Jean-Pierre Jouet

The Christmas Tree ★★U

Drama   1969 · Fr/It · Colour · 107min

This marks a departure for Bond director Terence Young, who also scripted this heartfelt tale about a father's determination to make his son's last days as enjoyable as possible. Stricken with leukemia, Brook Fuller is presented with gifts as different as a tractor and wolves stolen from a zoo, as William Holden and his old army pal Bourvil pander to his every whim. Nicely photographed by Henri Alekan, but Georges Auric's score reinforces the film's gushing sentimentality. DP

William Holden (2) *Laurent* • Virna Lisi *Catherine* • Bourvil *Verdun* • Brook Fuller *Pascal* • Madeleine Damien *Marinette* • Friedrich Ledebur *Vernet* ■ *Dir/Scr* Terence Young

A Christmas Visitor ★★

Seasonal drama   2002 · US · Colour · 88min

In this gentle and undemanding mix of drama and fantasy, a grieving family hasn't celebrated Christmas for 11 years following the death of a son in the first Gulf War. But the festive season suddenly works its magic when dad William Devane decides it's time for them to embrace life again. Understated performances and a tender script enhance the film's old-fashioned charm, while the increasing poignancy of events makes some of the more far-fetched moments easier to swallow. SF

William Devane *George Boyajian* • Meredith Baxter *Carol Boyajian* • Dean McDermott *Matthew* • Reagan Pasternak *Jean Boyajian* • Aaron Ashmore *John Boyajian* ■ *Dir* Christopher Leitch • *Scr* David Saperstein

The Christmas Wish ★★

Seasonal drama   1998 · US · Colour · 78min

Surprisingly, Debbie Reynolds rates this as one of her favourite vehicles and she twinkles pleasingly enough as the widow who asks her doting grandson Neil Patrick Harris to track down the mysterious woman mentioned in her late husband's diary. This schmaltzy TV movie is amiable, but decidedly middling, fare. DP

Neil Patrick Harris *Will Martin* • Debbie Reynolds *Ruth "Gram" Martin* • Naomi Watts *Renee* • Alexandra Wilson *Julia* • Beverly Archer *Enid Cook* ■ *Dir* Ian Barry • *Scr* Greg Taylor, from a story by Beth Polson, from the novel by Richard Siddoway

Christmas with the Coopers ★★ 12A

Seasonal comedy　2015 · US · Colour · 106min

If you're dreaming of a grey Christmas, this seasonal comedy might be for you. Diane Keaton is on neurotic autopilot as the ashy-bloused Mrs Cooper and John Goodman is the husband who is in two minds about their impending divorce. It's a secret, of course, to be revealed before Christmas Ed Helms and Olivia Wilde after their big Christmas get-together. Inevitably, the festive spirit thaws things out towards the end, but it's too much of a dull slog getting there. The Coopers are, quite simply, bad company. SP Sexual references, some swearing.

Diane Keaton *Charlotte* • John Goodman *Sam* • Alan Arkin *Bucky* • Amanda Seyfried *Ruby* • Olivia Wilde *Eleanor* ■ *Dir* Jessie Nelson • *Scr* Steven Rogers

Christmas with the Kranks ★ PG

Seasonal comedy　2004 · US · Colour · 94min

This soulless tale raises so few laughs, it barely justifies its comedy label. Tim Allen and Jamie Lee Curtis play the Kranks, a Chicago couple who incur the wrath of their local community when they decide to forgo Christmas and its associated trappings in favour of a luxury cruise. Poorly scripted and lazily directed. SF *DVD*

Tim Allen *Luther Krank* • Jamie Lee Curtis *Nora Krank* • Dan Aykroyd *Vic Frohmeyer* • Erik Per Sullivan *Spike Frohmeyer* • Cheech Marin [Richard "Cheech" Marin] *Officer Salino* • Jake Busey *Officer Treen* • M Emmet Walsh *Walt Scheel* • Elizabeth Franz *Bev Scheel* ■ *Dir* Joe Roth • *Scr* Chris Columbus, from the novel *Skipping Christmas* by John Grisham

Christopher Columbus ★ U

Historical biography　1949 · UK · Colour · 105min

If you thought Gérard Depardieu missed the mark in Ridley Scott's *1492: Conquest of Paradise*, wait till you set eyes on this turkey. Fredric March looks noble and the 1940s Technicolor is fabulous. Alas, the pace is nonexistent and the action is little more than a series of wax tableaux sporting familiar faces. TS

Fredric March *Christopher Columbus* • Florence Eldridge *Queen Isabella* • Francis L Sullivan *Francisco de Bobadilla* • Kathleen Ryan *Beatriz* • Derek Bond *Diego de Arana* • Nora Swinburne *Juana de Torres* • Abraham Sofaer *Luis de Santangel* • Linden Travers *Beatriz de Peraza* ■ *Dir* David MacDonald • *Scr* Sydney Box, Muriel Box, Cyril Roberts

Christopher Columbus: the Discovery ★ PG

Historical adventure　1992 · US · Colour · 115min

This is not so much a milestone to mark the 500th anniversary of the discovery of America as a millstone round the neck of nearly everyone connected with it. George Corraface, as Columbus, bores for Spain and Rachel Ward's accent as Queen Isabella is almost as bizarre as Tom Selleck's wig. Marlon Brando, as Torquemada, resembles a tethered balloon. TH Violence.

George Corraface [Georges Corraface] *Christopher Columbus* • Marlon Brando *Torquemada* • Tom Selleck *King Ferdinand* • Rachel Ward *Queen Isabella* • Robert Davi *Martin Pinzon* • Catherine Zeta-Jones *Beatriz* • Oliver Cotton *Harana* • Benicio Del Toro *Alvaro* • Mathieu Carrière *King John* ■ *Dir* John Glen • *Scr* John Briley, Cary Bates, Mario Puzo, from a story by Mario Puzo

Christopher Strong ★★★

Romantic melodrama　1933 · US · BW · 77min

Katharine Hepburn's sturdy performance and an abundance of intriguing ideas go some way to compensate for Dorothy Arzner's uneven direction of this romantic drama. Extremely advanced for its years, the film examines female independence and society's demands on women through the story of gutsy flier Hepburn and her affair with a married politician. JM *DVD*

Katharine Hepburn *Lady Cynthia Darrington* • Colin Clive *Christopher Strong* • Billie Burke *Elaine Strong* • Helen Chandler *Monica Strong* ■ *Dir* Dorothy Arzner • *Scr* Zoe Akins, from the novel by Gilbert Frankau

Chromophobia ★★ 15

Drama　2005 · Fr/US/UK · Colour · 133min

Onegin director Martha Fiennes's belated second feature is a patchy ensemble drama that touches on a range of contemporary issues. Set mainly in London, it stars her brother Ralph Fiennes as Stephen, a gay art historian who's friends with the well-heeled but dysfunctional Iona (Kristin Scott Thomas) and her lawyer husband, Marcus (Damian Lewis). Throw in an ambitious reporter (Ben Chaplin) and a dying prostitute (Penélope Cruz) and you have a set of storylines that cover everything from political malfeasance to breast implants and paedophilia. The film is certainly ambitious in scope, but it feels a good half an hour too long. Nevertheless, there is still enough here to mark Fiennes as a writer/director of promise. DA *DVD*

Ben Chaplin *Trent Masters* • Penélope Cruz *Gloria* • Ralph Fiennes *Stephen Tulloch* • Ian Holm *Edward Aylesbury* • Rhys Ifans *Colin* • Damian Lewis *Marcus Aylesbury* • Kristin Scott Thomas *Iona Aylesbury* • Clem Tibber *Orlando Aylesbury* • Harriet Walter *Penelope Aylesbury* • Anthony Higgins *Geoffrey Wharton* ■ *Dir/Scr* Martha Fiennes

Chronic ★★★★ 15

Drama　2015 · Mex/US · Colour · 93min

In a career-reviving performance, Tim Roth is mesmeric in this bleak but audacious drama as a hospice nurse who gives home care to three dying people through the course of the film. Composed mostly from long, static takes that evoke the drudgery of care and witness the agony of the afflicted, it's a gruelling work in many respects, reminiscent in some ways of Michael Haneke's *Amour* but with even more arthouse austerity. Michel Franco's commitment to exploring mortality and terminal care is laudable, but the shock ending is unnecessary. LF

Tim Roth *David* • Sarah Sutherland *Nadia* • David Dastmalchian *Bernard* • Bitsie Tulloch *Lidia* • Claire van der Boom *Alice* ■ *Dir/Scr* Michel Franco

Chronicle ★★★★ 15

Science-fiction drama　2012 · US · Colour · 80min

Three teens gain extraordinary powers in this fabulous addition to the "found footage" subgenre (*Cloverfield*, *Trollhunter*). Grounded very much in the everyday, it follows a troubled nerd (Dane DeHaan), his much cooler cousin (Alex Russell) and the big man on campus (Michael B Jordan) as they explore powers assimilated while investigating a local cave. Initially using their telekinesis for pranks, the three teen titans exhibit an infectious sense of wonder as they revel in their astonishing abilities. But absolute power corrupts, as one of their number discovers, and things take a darker turn, leading to a jaw-dropping smackdown worthy of any blockbuster. JA Violence, swearing. *DVD*

Michael B Jordan *Steve Montgomery* • Dane DeHaan *Andrew Detmer* • Michael Kelly (2) *Richard Detmer* • Ashley Hinshaw *Casey Letter* • Anna Wood *Monica* • Alex Russell *Matt Garetty* ■ *Dir* Josh Trank • *Scr* Max Landis, from a story by Landis, Josh Trank

Chronicle of a Death Foretold ★★★★ 15

Drama　1987 · It/Fr · Colour · 105min

Sumptuously photographed by Pasqualino De Santis, this is a mesmerising (if occasionally sluggish) adaptation of Gabriel García Márquez's novel of family honour, revenge and murder in a small Colombian town. Director Francesco Rosi deftly intercuts between flashbacks and reminiscences, as doctor Gian Maria Volonté attempts to uncover the facts behind a 20-year-old crime. While Rupert Everett is overly languid as the wealthy suitor who abandons deflowered bride Ornella Muti, the other members of the cast provide the ring of authenticity you'd expect from Italy's finest latter-day realist. DP Spanish +subtitles.

Rupert Everett *Bayardo San Roman* • Ornella Muti *Angela Vicario* • Gian Maria Volonté *Cristo Bedoia* • Irene Papas *Angela's mother* ■ *Dir* Francesco Rosi • *Scr* Francesco Rosi, Tonino Guerra, from the novel by Gabriel Garcia Marquez

Chronicle of a Love ★★★ PG

Drama　1950 · It · BW · 97min

Departing from the neorealism of his postwar documentaries, Michelangelo Antonioni made his feature debut with this atypically conventional tale of suspicion and snobbery, adultery and guilt. Clearly, though, he is already employing those trademark long takes and making symbolic use of the physical environment to explore the recurrent themes of urban alienation, social displacement and the impermanence of relationships. Yet this reliance on inanimates for psychological revelation somewhat devalues the contribution of the cast. DP In Italian.

Lucia Bosé *Paola Molon Fontana* • Massimo Girotti *Guido* • Ferdinando Sarmi *Enrico Fontana* • Gino Rossi *Carloni, the detective* • Marika Rowsky *Joy, the model* • Rosi Mirafiore *Barmaid* • Rubi D'Alma *Paola's friend* ■ *Dir* Michelangelo Antonioni • *Scr* Michelangelo Antonioni, Danièle D'Anza, Silvio Giovaninetti, Francesco Maselli, Piero Tellini, from a story by Michelangelo Antonioni

Chronicle of the Burning Years ★★★★

Political drama　1975 · Alg · Colour · 177min

Throughout the period covered in this epic account of Algerian history (1939-54), the indigenous film industry was dominated by so-called "cinema mudjahad", or "freedom fighter cinema". It's ironic, therefore, that Mohammed Lakhdar-Hamina's film should belong to the tradition that succeeded it: "cinema djidid", or "new cinema". Couching a family drama in terms of a Hollywood melodrama and employing a diversity of symbolic character types, the film shows how the attempt to suppress cultural as well as political aspirations resulted in the politicisation of ordinary people and the FLN revolt against the colonial government. Imposing but impersonal. DP In Arabic.

Yorgo Voyagis *Achmed* • Mohammed Lakhdar-Hamina *Milhoud* • Cheik Nourredine *Friend* ■ *Dir* Mohammed Lakhdar-Hamina • *Scr* Mohammed Lakhdar-Hamina, Rachid Boujedra

The Chronicles of Narnia: The Lion, the Witch and the Wardrobe ★★★ PG

Fantasy adventure　2005 · US · Colour · 137min

This ambitious, old-fashioned adaptation retains much of the magical allure of the popular children's classic. The four Pevensie siblings are evacuated from London to a country manor house during the Second World War. There they discover an enchanted wardrobe that leads to a wintry, fairy-tale realm, populated by talking animals and mythical creatures, but under the malevolent spell of Tilda Swinton's imperious White Witch – setting the scene for a climactic battle between good and evil. The film is perhaps more low-key than many modern youngsters are used to, with some plot hints, but there's still plenty to delight. SF *DVD* CS

Tilda Swinton *Jadis, the White Witch* • Georgie Henley *Lucy Pevensie* • Skandar Keynes *Edmund Pevensie* • Anna Popplewell *Susan Pevensie* • William Moseley *Peter Pevensie* • James McAvoy *Mr Tumnus* • Jim Broadbent *Prof Digory Kirke* • Liam Neeson *Aslan* • Ray Winstone *Mr Beaver* • Dawn French *Mrs Beaver* • Rupert Everett *Fox* ■ *Dir* Andrew Adamson • *Scr* Ann Peacock, Andrew Adamson, Christopher Markus, Stephen McFeely, from the novel by CS Lewis

The Chronicles of Narnia: Prince Caspian ★★★ PG

Fantasy adventure　2008 · US · Colour · 143min

Andrew Adamson returns as director for the second instalment in CS Lewis's *Narnia* series and the tone is darker. It's a year after the events of the first film, but time has moved on 1,300 years in Narnia, where the repressive Telmarines have all but driven out the magical natives. The four Pevensie children are summoned by Prince Caspian (Ben Barnes), the rightful Telmarine heir, who wants to overthrow his nasty uncle Miraz (Sergio Castellitto). Although this is fantasy adventure at its blandest, there's plenty of camp court intrigue, quaint pantomime action and epic CGI battles between fabled creatures, talking animals and massive armies. And there's even a lovable sword-fighting mouse (voiced by Eddie Izzard). It all makes for fun, lively – if patently safe – swashbuckling spectacle. AJ *DVD* Blu

Ben Barnes *Prince Caspian* • Georgie Henley *Lucy Pevensie* • Skandar Keynes *Edmund Pevensie* • William Moseley *Peter Pevensie* • Anna Popplewell *Susan Pevensie* • Sergio Castellitto *Miraz* • Liam Neeson *Aslan* • Warwick Davis *Nikabrik* • Peter Dinklage *Trumpkin* • Tilda Swinton *Jadis, the White Witch* • Eddie Izzard *Reepicheep* ■ *Dir* Andrew Adamson • *Scr* Andrew Adamson, Christopher Markus, Stephen McFeely, from the novel by CS Lewis

The Chronicles of Narnia: The Voyage of the Dawn Treader ★★★★ PG

Action fantasy adventure　2010 · US/Aus · Colour · 112min

Wonderful escapist fantasy flows nonstop in the best instalment in the Narnia series to date. Seasoned director Michael Apted deploys the usual mix of adolescent derring-do, impressive special effects and sledgehammer moral lessons with a captivating dynamism that refreshes the mythic underpinnings of CS Lewis's adventure. In what is the most Tolkienesque of the tales, the two younger Pevensie siblings, Lucy (Georgie Henley) and Edmund (Skandar Keynes), and their insufferable cousin Eustace (an absolutely brilliant Will Poulter) are whisked aboard the buccaneering ship of King Caspian (Ben Barnes) as he searches for the seven lost lords of Narnia. It's a thrilling and swashbuckling spellbinder. AJ Some violence. *DVD* Blu

Ben Barnes *King Caspian* • Skandar Keynes *Edmund Pevensie* • Georgie Henley *Lucy Pevensie* • Will Poulter *Eustace Clarence Scrubb* • Simon Pegg *Reepicheep* • Liam Neeson *Aslan* • Gary Sweet *Drinian* • Bill Nighy *Reepicheep* ■ *Dir* Michael Apted • *Scr* Christopher Markus, Stephen McFeely, Michael Petroni, from the novel by CS Lewis

The Chronicles of Riddick ★★ 15

Science-fiction thriller　2004 · US · Colour · 114min

A sci-fi movie with a tremendous sense of scale and visual splendour, this is ambitious but disappointing. David Twohy takes his monosyllabic antihero from *Pitch Black* and thrusts him into an imaginative universe full of sleek spacecraft and war-ravaged cities. Vin Diesel grunts his way through endless fights with bounty hunters, prison guards and an army of religious supermen. Unfortunately, Twohy forgets to provide a compelling story, and it all comes across as an overblown and pompous space opera. GM Violence. *DVD* Blu

Vin Diesel *Riddick* • Thandie Newton *Dame Vaako* • Karl Urban *Vaako* • Colm Feore *Lord Marshal* • Linus Roache *Purifier* • Keith David *Imam* • Yorick van Wageningen *The Guv* • Alexa Davalos *Kyra* • Nick Chinlund *Toombs* • Judi Dench *Aereon* ■ *Dir* David Twohy • *Scr* David Twohy, from the character created by Jim Wheat, Ken Wheat

Chu Chin Chow ★★★ U

Musical fantasy　1934 · UK · BW · 103min

This legendary and massively popular British stage musical by Oscar Asche, complete with its unimaginative Frederick Norton score, finally reached the screen with all its faults revealed. George Robey's performance as Ali Baba is forever enshrined here, and there's some interesting period casting, with Anna May Wong as Zahrat the slave girl and villain Fritz Kortner as boss of the 40 thieves. The uninspired choreography is by ballet great Anton Dolin. TS

George Robey *Ali Baba* • Fritz Kortner *Abu Hassan* • Anna May Wong *Zahrat* • John Garrick *Nur-al-din* • Pearl Argyle *Marjanah* • Dennis Hoey *Rakham* ■ *Dir* Walter Forde • *Scr* Sidney Gilliat, L DuGarde Peach, Edward Knoblock, from the musical by Oscar Asche, Frederic Norton

Chuck & Buck ★★★★ 15
Comedy drama   2000 · US · Colour · 91min

Essentially a film about stalking, this excellent independent feature confounds expectations by opting for the creepy and the quirky. This surprise tack keeps the viewer intrigued and allows sympathy for both stalked and stalker, and it's rounded off with a delicious twist in the tale. Chris Weitz and Mike White are former schoolfriends who've drifted apart, but remain bonded by a single act of homosexual dabbling. When the childlike White's mum dies, he renews contact with Weitz, but the latter has a new life with fiancée Beth Colt. It's nicely scripted, skilfully directed, beautifully acted and, considering its subject matter, surprisingly warm and likeable. DA Swearing, sex scenes. *DVD*

Mike White *Buck O'Brien* • Chris Weitz *Charlie "Chuck" Sitter* • Lupe Ontiveros *Beverly* • Beth Colt *Carlyn* • Paul Weitz *Sam* • Maya Rudolph *Jamila* ■ *Dir* Miguel Arteta • *Scr* Mike White

CHUD ★ 18
Horror   1984 · US · Colour · 83min

Thanks to toxic waste dumped in the Manhattan sewage system, tramps and derelicts have mutated into "Cannibalistic Humanoid Underground Dwellers". That's according to this lamentable urban horror movie, which is neither gory nor exciting enough to merit much attention. Ridiculous monsters and unappealing main characters only add insult to injury in this crass exploiter. AJ

John Heard *George Cooper* • Kim Greist *Lauren Daniels* • Daniel Stern *The Reverend* • Christopher Curry *Captain Bosch* • George Martin (1) *Wilson* • John Ramsey *Commissioner* ■ *Dir* Douglas Cheek • *Scr* Parnell Hall

CHUD II: Bud the Chud ★ 15
Horror comedy   1989 · US · Colour · 84min

Sequel in name only to the 1984 turkey, this sees a bunch of teenagers steal a corpse from a government research facility, only for it to turn cannibalistic and run amok in a small town. One look at the script, no doubt, prompted director David Irving to play this for broad laughs, but nobody saw the joke. RS

Brian Robbins *Steve* • Bill Calvert *Kevin* • Tricia Leigh Fisher *Katie* • Gerrit Graham *Bud the Chud* • Robert Vaughn (1) *Masters* ■ *Dir* David Irving • *Scr* M Kane Jeeves [Ed Naha]

A Chump at Oxford ★★★ U
Comedy   1940 · US · BW · 62min

Rewarded for foiling a bank robbery, Laurel and Hardy find themselves among the "dreaming spires" in this agreeable comedy. While the film reunites the boys with fabled producer Hal Roach, it also saddles them with third-rate director Alfred Goulding, who allows this loose collection of gags to ramble. Beside such stale situations as settling into the dean's lodgings, there are some classic moments, including the trek around the "haunted maze", Stan's glorious transformation into college hero Lord Paddington, and Ollie's demotion to the role of butler. DP

Stan Laurel *Stan* • Oliver Hardy *Ollie* • James Finlayson *Baldy Vandevere* • Peter Cushing *Jones* ■ *Dir* Alfred Goulding • *Scr* Felix Adler, Harry Langdon, Charles Rogers

The Chumscrubber ★★★ 15
Satirical comedy drama   2005 · US/Ger · Colour · 103min

Arie Posin's ultimately silly but slyly engaging feature debut is a cautionary tale. Troubled teen Jamie Bell tries to make sense of his drug-dealing best friend's suicide within his laughably self-obsessed sit-com community. Veering between magical realism, stark shock horror, whimsical soap opera and generation gap angst, Posin gets the balance of caustic comedy and quirky drama nearly right. It only falters in the focal plot mechanism of a kidnap scheme carried out to acquire the deceased's stash of happy pills. AJ Swearing, violence, drug abuse. *DVD*

Jamie Bell *Dean Stiffle* • Glenn Close *Mrs Johnson* • Ralph Fiennes *Mayor Michael Ebbs* • Lauren Holly *Boutique owner* • Allison Janney *Mrs Stiffle* • Carrie-Anne Moss *Jerri Falls* • Rita Wilson *Terri Bratley* • Camilla Belle *Crystal Falls* • Rory Culkin *Charlie Stiffle* • John Heard *Officer Lou Bratley* ■ *Dir* Arie Posin • *Scr* Zac Stanford, from a story by Stanford, Arie Posin

Chung King Express ★★★★ 12
Romantic comedy   1994 · HK · Colour · 101min

Quentin Tarantino declared this film to be a masterpiece, and he's not far wrong, for director Wong Kar-Wai's exceptional control over the two disparate storylines is awe-inspiring. The first, shorter episode concerns a jilted cop's encounter with a blonde-wigged heroin trafficker, while the second focuses on a waitress's preoccupation with another cop, who doesn't appreciate her passion until it's too late. Established stars Tony Leung and Brigitte Lin are upstaged somewhat by newcomers Takeshi Kaneshiro and Faye Wong, but the performances as a whole are a joy. DP Cantonese, Mandarin +subtitles. Violence, swearing *DVD*

Qingxia Lin [Brigitte Lin] *The drug dealer* • Takeshi Kaneshiro *He Qiwu, Cop 223* • Tony Chiu-Wai Leung [Tony Leung (2)] *Cop 663* • Faye Wong *Faye* • Valerie Chow *Air hostess* ■ *Dir/Scr* Wong Kar-Wai

Chunky Monkey ★★ 15
Black comedy   2001 · UK · Colour · 88min

British writer/director Greg Cruttwell's low-budget black comedy debut is as intriguing as it is daft. A cross between a stage play and an offbeat sitcom, it's so outlandish that it keeps you hooked just to see where all the idiocy is leading. David Threlfall plays a psychopathic loner who's in the middle of clearing up his flat after committing a murder, getting ready for an appointment with a Julie Andrews lookalike and a tub of Chunky Monkey ice cream. However, his work is disturbed by a succession of bizarre visitors. SF Violence, swearing, sexual references. *DVD*

David Threlfall *Donald* • Alison Steadman *Beryl* • Nicola Stapleton *Mandy* • David Schofield *Frank* • Colin McFarlane *Trevor* • Danny Nussbaum *Nuggett* ■ *Dir/Scr* Greg Cruttwell

The Church ★★★ 18
Horror   1988 · It · Colour · 97min

Originally slated to complete Dario Argento's *Demons* trilogy, this gothic horror was turned over to Michele Soavi. Opening with a medieval witch-hunt which results in a cathedral being built on the mass grave of some suspected Satanists, the story jumps forward in time to show bibliophile Tomas Arana and caretaker's daughter Asia Argento investigating the fiendish mechanical devices the architect installed to prevent malevolent spirits escaping into the world. Soavi's film is ingeniously designed, but the intriguing concept is wasted. DP In Italian.

Asia Argento *Lotte* • Thomas Arana [Tomas Arana] *Evald* • Feodor Chaliapin [Feodor Chaliapin Jr] *Bishop* • Hugh Quarshie *Father Gus* • Barbara Cupisti *Lisa* ■ *Dir* Michele Soavi • *Scr* Dario Argento, Franco Ferrini, Michele Soavi, from a story by Dario Argento, Franco Ferrini

Churchill: the Hollywood Years ★★ 15
Satirical comedy   2004 · UK/Ire · Colour · 80min

Peter Richardson's blunt satire on Hollywood's habit of rewriting history stars Christian Slater as the "real" Winston Churchill, a gung-ho American GI, and Neve Campbell as a spirited Princess Elizabeth, heir to the British throne. The Anglo-American twosome team up to foil a dastardly plot by Hitler (Antony Sher) to topple the monarchy. It's an amusingly bizarre notion, but Richardson's film fails to deliver on the promise of its premise, despite game performances. DA Swearing. *DVD*

Christian Slater *Winston Churchill* • Neve Campbell *Princess Elizabeth* • Antony Sher *Adolf Hitler* • Jessica Oyelowo *Princess Margaret* • Mackenzie Crook *Jim Charoo* • Miranda Richardson *Eva Braun* • Leslie Phillips *Lord W'ruff* • Rik Mayall *Baxter* • Bob Mortimer *Potter* • Vic Reeves *Bendle* • Harry Enfield *King George V* ■ *Dir* Peter Richardson • *Scr* Peter Richardson, Peter Richens

Ciao, Federico! ★★★★ 15
Documentary   1970 · US/It · Colour · 57min

One critic said Fellini's films ceased to be art when Fellini himself became a work of art. That self-aggrandisement is evident in this documentary about the Italian maestro, caught while directing his exotic Roman tale, *Satyricon*. The great man proves to be impossible to interview: an evasive, chronic liar and sly keeper of his own image. But he's such a marvellous raconteur, you can't help loving him and admiring Gideon Bachmann for colluding so graciously. AT

■ *Dir* Gideon Bachmann

Ciao! Manhattan ★★★ 18
Drama   1973 · US · Colour and BW · 91min

It's somehow fitting that this patchwork portrait of model-actress Edie Sedgwick has been cobbled together from such sharply contrasting footage. One of the many who found her 15 minutes of fame with Andy Warhol, she exudes elfin charm in Chuck Wein's 1967 monochrome study. But by the time David Weisman and John Palmer caught up with the 28 year-old at her parents home three years later, it was clear that this drug-addled, silicon-implanted Barbie was not long for this world. DP

Edie Sedgwick *Susan* • Wesley Hayes *Butch* • Isabel Jewell *Mummy* • Paul America *Paul* • Viva *Fashion editor* • Roger Vadim *Dr Braun* • Christian Marquand *Entrepreneur* ■ *Dir/Scr* John Palmer, David Weisman

El Cid ★★★★★ U
Epic historical adventure   1961 · US/It · Colour · 180min

The epic was in danger of losing its audience when this lavish account of the career of Spanish patriot Rodrigo Díaz de Vivar was first released. It gave Charlton Heston the chance to carry the weight of a nation on his shoulders again, as he takes on the occupying Moors. Director Anthony Mann avoids a mere history lesson, effectively handling the court intrigue and the feud between Heston and estranged wife Sophia Loren. But it's the astonishing action sequences produced by Yakima Canutt's second-unit crew that give the picture its Super Technirama impact. With outstanding supporting performances, a literate script and a superlative, Oscar-nominated score by Miklos Rozsa, this is 1960s Hollywood at its spectacular best. DP *DVD* *Blu-ray*

Charlton Heston *Rodrigo Díaz de Vivar/El Cid* • Sophia Loren *Chimene* • John Fraser *King Alfonso* • Raf Vallone *Count Ordonez* • Genevieve Page *Queen Urraca* • Gary Raymond *King Sancho* • Herbert Lom *Ben Yussuf* • Massimo Serato *Fanez* • Douglas Wilmer *Moutamin* • Frank Thring *Al Kadir* • Hurd Hatfield *Count Arias* • Ralph Truman *King Ferdinand* • Andrew Cruickshank *Count Gomez* • Michael Hordern *Don Diego* ■ *Dir* Anthony Mann • *Scr* Philip Yordan, Fredric M Frank, Ben Barzman (uncredited), from a story by Fredric M Frank • *Music* Miklos Rozsa • *Cinematographer* Robert Krasker

The Cider House Rules ★★★★★ 12
Period drama   1999 · US · Colour · 120min

The third John Irving novel to reach the screen (after *The World According to Garp* and *The Hotel New Hampshire*), this is a rich, evocative period piece that makes the most of its New England locations. Tobey Maguire plays Homer Wells, a foundling who, having spent all his young life at an orphanage run by Michael Caine's kindly abortionist, decides to seek new pastures. Alas, he finds the codes he lives by of little use in the real world. Although drastically slimmed down from Irving's original (Homer's 15-year odyssey is reduced to a mere 15 months), Lasse Hallström's film has a simple integrity that fills every frame, while Caine won an Oscar for his performance. NS *DVD* *Blu-ray*

Tobey Maguire *Homer Wells* • Charlize Theron *Candy Kendall* • Delroy Lindo *Arthur Rose* • Paul Rudd *Wally Worthington* • Michael Caine *Dr Wilbur Larch* • Jane Alexander *Nurse Edna* • Kathy Baker *Nurse Angela* • Kate Nelligan *Olive Worthington* ■ *Dir* Lasse Hallström • *Scr* John Irving, from his novel

Il Cielo è Sempre Più Blu ★★★ 15
Drama   1995 · It · Colour · 109min

With over 130 speaking parts and 30 different storylines, there's little wonder Antonello Grimaldi's ambitious film was dubbed "a Roman *Short Cuts*". Yet the roving style of Robert Altman is not the only influence on a picture that most vividly recalls the portmanteau compilations of short stories that were so popular in the 1960s. The action is naturally fragmented and some characters pass us by before we've even noticed them. There are neat vignettes, however, featuring Dario and Asia Argento, Margherita Buy (as a vindictive traffic warden) and Enrico Lo Verso as a lovesick postman. DP Italian +subtitles. Violence, swearing, sex scenes.

Asia Argento *Teenage cousin* • Luca Barbareschi *Shyster* • Margherita Buy *Traffic warden* • Roberto Citran *Businessman* • Enrico Lo Verso *Postman* • Ivano Marescotti *Jogger* • Dario Argento *Man confessing to Franciscan monk* • Silvio Orlando *Mechanic* ■ *Dir* Antonello Grimaldi • *Scr* Daniele Cesarano, Paolo Marchesini

La Ciénaga ★★★ 18
Comedy drama   2001 · Arg/Sp/US · Colour · 99min

Former documentary director Lucrecia Martel makes an impressive feature film debut with this dark domestic melodrama set in the stifling provincial backwoods of northern Argentina. Events tumble out of control after wealthy drunk Graciela Borges has an accident during a stagnant pool party. Middle-class Borges's recovery brings her into contact with down-at-heel suburban cousin Mercedes Morán and her unruly family. Martel draws painfully persuasive performances from her ensemble cast. DP Spanish +subtitles.

Mercedes Morán *Tali* • Graciela Borges *Mecha* • Martín Adjemian *Gregorio* • Diego Baenas *Joaquín* • Sofia Bertolotto *Momi* ■ *Dir/Scr* Lucrecia Martel

Cimarron ★★★★
Epic western   1931 · US · BW · 122min

Richard Dix, newspaper owner and maverick campaigner for human rights, is also a restless wanderer who disappears for long periods, leaving his indomitable wife Irene Dunne to carry on the paper and the fight for justice. This sprawling epic cost RKO the unprecedented sum of $1,433,000. The studio was rewarded with Oscars for best picture – the only western to get the award until *Dances with Wolves* six decades later – art direction and screenplay. A little dated now, but otherwise excellent. RK

Richard Dix *Yancey Cravat* • Irene Dunne *Sabra Cravat* • Estelle Taylor *Dixie Lee* • Nance O'Neil *Felice Venable* • William Collier Jr *The Kid* ■ *Dir* Wesley Ruggles • *Scr* Howard Estabrook, from the novel by Edna Ferber • *Cinematographer* Edward Cronjager • *Art Director* Max Ree

C

Cimarron ★★ U
Epic western   1960 · US · Colour · 147min

This remake of the classic 1931 version of Edna Ferber's novel about the Oklahoma Land Rush, is, sadly, a misfire. It's the very least of director Anthony Mann's works, marred by MGM's insistence on studio filming when locations were imperative, and by a hopelessly inept and miscast Maria Schell in the key role. Glenn Ford delivers a strong performance, but the film remains little more than an insubstantial melodrama. **TS**

Glenn Ford *Yancey Cravet* • Maria Schell *Sabra Cravet* • Anne Baxter *Dixie Lee* • Arthur O'Connell *Tom Wyatt* • Russ Tamblyn *Cherokee Kid* • Mercedes McCambridge *Sarah Wyatt* ■ *Dir* Anthony Mann • *Scr* Arnold Schulman, from the novel by Edna Ferber

The Cimarron Kid ★★★ U
Western   1951 · US · Colour · 83min

The Dalton gang rides again in a serviceable western that, unusually, has Audie Murphy in the role of outlaw. Released on parole, he hides out with Noah Beery Jr and his gang after being falsely accused of a train heist. But, while the prospect of a new life with Beverly Tyler is enticing, Murphy is determined to take on one last job before he hangs up his guns. Better known for his psychological westerns, Budd Boetticher handles this programme filler with intelligent efficiency, drawing a thoughtful performance from Murphy. **DP**

Audie Murphy *Cimarron Kid* • Yvette Dugay *Rose of Cimarron* • Beverly Tyler *Carrie Roberts* • John Hudson (1) *Dynamite Dick* • James Best *Bitter Creek* • Leif Erickson *Marshal Sutton* • Noah Beery [Noah Beery Jr] *Bob Dalton* ■ *Dir* Budd Boetticher • *Scr* Louis Stevens, from a story by Louis Stevens, Kay Lenard

The Cincinnati Kid ★★★ PG
Drama   1965 · US · Colour · 97min

Intended as a *Hustler* for poker players, this started out with Steve McQueen as the young hotshot and Spencer Tracy as his older, poker-faced adversary. Sam Peckinpah was the director and Paddy Chayefsky the screenwriter. Tracy was the first to go, being replaced by Edward G Robinson. Six days into shooting, Peckinpah was fired because he was working too slowly. Enter new writers and a new director, Norman Jewison. The result, considering the production's chequered history, is not at all bad. **AT** *DVD*

Steve McQueen (1) *Cincinnati Kid* • Edward G Robinson *Lancey Howard* • Ann-Margret *Melba* • Karl Malden *Shooter* • Tuesday Weld *Christian* • Joan Blondell *Lady Fingers* • Rip Torn *Slade* • Jack Weston *Pig* ■ *Dir* Norman Jewison • *Scr* Ring Lardner Jr, Terry Southern, from the novel by Richard Jessup

Cinderella ★★★★ U
Animated romantic fantasy
1950 · US · Colour · 74min

Industrial-strength Disney animation reinforces all the coy clichés of Charles Perrault's story, though not the sexual ones. There are some delightful singing mice, a sadistically erotic stepmother and a languidly cruel cat called Lucifer. The songs are what give it an extra dimension, though: the Oscar-nominated *Bibbidi-Bobbidi-Boo*, sung by Verna Felton, and the winsome *A Dream Is a Wish Your Heart Makes*, performed by Ilene Woods. **TH** *DVD* Blu

Ilene Woods *Cinderella* • William Phipps *Prince Charming* • Eleanor Audley *Stepmother* • Verna Felton *Fairy Godmother* • James MacDonald *Jacques/Gus-Gus* • Rhoda Williams *Anastasia* ■ *Dir* Wilfred Jackson, Hamilton Luske, Clyde Geronimi • *Scr* William Peet, Ted Sears, Homer Brightman, Kenneth [Ken] Anderson, Erdman Penner, Winston Hibler, Harry Reeves, Joe Rinaldi, from the story *Cinderella* by Charles Perrault

Cinderella II: Dreams Come True ★★ U
Animated romance   2002 · US · Colour · 70min

Disney's made-for-video sequel to the 1950 classic takes over where its predecessor finished, with Cinders finding it hard adjusting to her new life as a princess. The main pleasure, as before, comes from lovable mice Gus and Jaq, who write a storybook that creates the film's three short segments. Ultimately, despite a couple of cute moments, the ordinary animation and terrible tunes suggest that Disney should have quit at the original fairy-tale ending. **JC** *DVD*

Jennifer Hale *Cinderella* • Tress MacNeille *Anastasia* • Rob Paulsen *Jaq/Baker/Sir Hugh* • Corey Burton *Gus* • Russi Taylor *Fairy Godmother/Mary Mouse/Beatrice/Daphne/Drizella* • Holland Taylor *Prudence* ■ *Dir* John Kafka • *Scr* Tom Rogers, Jill E Blotevogel, Jule Selbo

Cinderella ★★ U
Musical fantasy   1965 · US · Colour · 83min

An energetic Rodgers and Hammerstein score brings frothiness to a fairy-tale favourite in this second version of their made-for-television musical. Introducing a young, sweet-voiced Lesley Ann Warren in the title role, the production is shot like a stage show, putting the focus on the performances, which feel true to the original source story, yet may seem stilted by today's standards. Playful support from the likes of Ginger Rogers adds a touch of vintage Hollywood to the proceedings. **SF**

Lesley Ann Warren *Cinderella* • Stuart Damon *Prince* • Ginger Rogers *Queen* • Walter Pidgeon *King* • Celeste Holm *Fairy godmother* • Jo Van Fleet *Stepmother* • Pat Carroll *Prunella* • Barbara Ruick *Esmerelda* ■ *Dir* Charles S Dubin • *Scr* Joseph Schrank, from the story *Cinderella* by Charles Perrault • *Music/lyrics* Richard Rodgers, Oscar Hammerstein II

Cinderella ★★★★ U
Fantasy   2015 · US · Colour · 101min

The most famous rags-to-riches fairy tale gets a wonderful Disney makeover under director Kenneth Branagh, using a light touch with elaborate stylisation, stunning chocolate box production values and ravishing costume design. Lily James is perfect as Ella, breathing touching, credible sweetness into the role, and Cate Blanchett is exceptional, too, as her sumptuously outfitted, vindictive stepmother – think Bette Davis does Cruella De Vil. With respectful links to the original (Lucifer the cat, a rendition of "Bibbidi-Bobbidi-Boo") and storybook tweaks to add freshness, it's an opulent, magical, timeless enchantment in its own right. **AJ** *DVD* Blu

Lily James *Cinderella* • Cate Blanchett *Stepmother* • Helena Bonham Carter *Fairy Godmother* • Richard Madden *Prince* • Stellan Skarsgård *Grand Duke* • Hayley Atwell *Cinderella's mother* • Ben Chaplin *Cinderella's father* ■ *Dir* Kenneth Branagh • *Scr* Chris Weitz • *Costume Designer* Sandy Powell

Cinderella Jones ★★ U
Musical comedy   1946 · US · BW · 83min

This amiable but dated Warner Bros fable was shot during the war but held back so long that all wartime references had to be removed and some rather bland linking material filmed especially. The director of this modest trifle is, surprisingly, the great choreographer Busby Berkeley. **TS**

Joan Leslie *Judy Jones* • Robert Alda *Tommy Coles* • SZ Sakall *Gabriel Popik* • Edward Everett Horton *Keating* • Julie Bishop *Camille* • William Prince *Bart Williams* • Charles Dingle *Minland* • Ruth Donnelly *Cora Elliott* ■ *Dir* Busby Berkeley • *Scr* Charles Hoffman, from a story by Philip Wylie

Cinderella Liberty ★★★ 15
Drama   1973 · US · Colour · 111min

Macho sailor James Caan docks in Seattle for the night and gets involved with hooker Marsha Mason in this urban fairy tale from director Mark Rydell. The set up is intriguing enough as Caan plays pool against Mason with her body as the prize, and Rydell manages to give the ending a satisfyingly ironic twist, but the saccharine level may be unacceptably high for more cynical viewers. **TH** Swearing, brief nudity.

James Caan *John Baggs* • Marsha Mason *Maggie* • Kirk Calloway *Doug* • Eli Wallach *Lynn Forshay* • Allyn Ann McLerie *Miss Watkins* • Burt Young *Master-at-arms* • Bruno Kirby Jr [Bruno Kirby]

Alcott • Dabney Coleman *Executive officer* ■ *Dir* Mark Rydell • *Scr* Darryl Ponicsan, from the novel by Darryl Ponicsan

Cinderella Man ★★★★ 12
Biographical sports drama
2005 · US · Colour · 138min

This boxing picture may echo the basic plot of *Rocky* – a no-hoper unexpectedly gets the chance to fight for the heavyweight championship of the world – but it has the added impact of being a true story, set during the Great Depression of the 1930s. Jim Braddock (Russell Crowe) was a decent boxer who is reduced to labouring in the docks to feed his family. A comeback fight is the beginning of his journey towards a title clash with Max Baer (played here by Craig Bierko). Crowe is perfectly cast as a pugilist who doesn't know when he is beaten, and the film captures the power, majesty and sheer brutality of the toughest of sports. **BP** Swearing, violence. *DVD* Blu

Russell Crowe *Jim Braddock* • Renée Zellweger *Mae Braddock* • Paul Giamatti *Joe Gould* • Craig Bierko *Max Baer* • Bruce McGill *Jimmy Johnston* • Paddy Considine *Mike Wilson* ■ *Dir* Ron Howard • *Scr* Cliff Hollingsworth, Akiva Goldsman, from a story by Cliff Hollingsworth

A Cinderella Story ★★ PG
Romantic comedy   2004 · US · Colour · 91min

Orphaned student Hilary Duff is smitten by an anonymous, online sweet-talker (Chad Michael Murray, a modern-day Prince Charming), who's a dreamy diversion from the cruel demands of her self-obsessed stepmother (Jennifer Coolidge) and spiteful stepsisters. Duff and Murray make a cute but not particularly charismatic couple. Unfortunately their performances are undermined by corny dialogue and a hackneyed plotline that updates the original story too literally. **SF** *DVD*

Hilary Duff *Sam Montgomery* • Jennifer Coolidge *Fiona* • Chad Michael Murray *Austin Ames* • Dan Byrd *Carter* • Regina King *Rhonda* • Julie Gonzalo *Shelby* • Lin Shaye *Mrs Wells* • Madeline Zima *Brianna* ■ *Dir* Mark Rosman • *Scr* Leigh Dunlap

Cinderfella ★★★ U
Comedy   1960 · US · Colour · 84min

This amiable retelling stars Jerry Lewis as the put-upon stepson and winsome Anna Maria Alberghetti as a demure "Princess Charming". As producer, Lewis affords himself some notable set pieces, especially the entrance at the ball, zigzagging down a seemingly endless stairway to Count Basie's beat. Non-Lewis fans may find the ballads and interminable goofing tiresome. **TS** *DVD*

Jerry Lewis *Fella* • Judith Anderson *Wicked stepmother* • Ed Wynn *Fairy godfather* • Anna Maria Alberghetti *Princess Charmein* • Henry Silva *Maximilian* • Robert Hutton *Rupert* • Count Basie ■ *Dir/Scr* Frank Tashlin

Cinema Komunisto ★★★
Documentary
2010 · Ser/Neth/Gr · Colour · 100min

This account of the development of Yugoslavian cinema between 1946 and 1980 concentrates on the role played by Avala Studios, which was formed under the guidance of film fanatic Marshall Josip Broz Tito. The leader wanted movies to help create a myth of the fledgeling republic, and also set up massive Hollywood co-productions, including 1969's *The Battle of Neretva*, which starred Yul Brynner and Orson Welles, and *Sutjeska* (1973), in which Richard Burton took the Tito role. Critical assessment of Avala's 700-odd features is noticeably lacking, but the clips of Tito hobnobbing with the likes of Alfred Hitchcock and Sophia Loren, and the interview with his projectionist Leka Konstantinovic provide an intriguing insight into the mechanics of state-controlled cinema. **DP** Serbo-Croat +subtitles. *DVD*

■ *Dir/Scr* Mila Turajlic

Cinema Paradiso ★★★★★ PG
Drama   1988 · It/Fr · Colour · 118min

Winner of the Oscar for best foreign language film, this is both an unashamedly sentimental rite-of-passage picture and a charming reminder of the lost magic of cinema-going. The stars are projectionist Philippe Noiret and his adorable young assistant, Salvatore Cascio, but it's the patrons of the village cinema in Sicily who give the film its irresistible flavour, entering into the spirit of each and every movie. The 1994 director's cut contains 32 minutes that were removed from Giuseppe Tornatore's original following a lukewarm domestic response, making it even more of a wonderfully nostalgic experience. **DP** Italian, French +subtitles. *DVD* Blu

Philippe Noiret *Alfredo* • Jacques Perrin *Salvatore as an adult* • Salvatore Cascio *Toto (Salvatore as a child)* • Marco Leonardi *Salvatore as a teenager* • Agnese Nano *Elena* ■ *Dir* Giuseppe Tornatore • *Scr* Giuseppe Tornatore, Vanna Paoli

Cinema Verite ★★★★ 12
Drama based on a true story
2011 · US · Colour · 86min

The directors of *American Splendor*, Shari Springer Berman and Robert Pulcini, once again look back to the 1970s with this visually seductive drama about the making of the ground-breaking reality TV show *An American Family*. The series made waves in 1973, focusing on the seemingly sunny yet fractured Loud family, headed by hippyish mum Pat (Diane Lane, a stand-out) and philandering dad Bill (Tim Robbins). James Gandolfini lends twinkly-eyed charm to film-maker Craig Gilbert, who we are led to believe manipulated Pat and Bill to increase the series' dramatic weight. As an exploration of the process of documentary-making it doesn't quite work, but as a simmering family drama it certainly does. **DC** Sexual references, brief swearing.

Tim Robbins *Bill Loud* • Diane Lane *Pat Loud* • James Gandolfini *Craig Gilbert* • Patrick Fugit *Alan Raymond* • Kathleen Quinlan *Mary* • Lolita Davidovich *Val* ■ *Dir* Shari Springer Berman, Robert Pulcini • *Scr* David Seltzer

The Circle ★★★★ PG
Drama   2000 · Iran/It/Swi · Colour · 90min

Iranian director Jafar Panahi's award-winning movie highlights such contentious issues as divorce, abortion and prostitution to demonstrate the universal discrimination against women in modern Iranian society. An almost Hitchcockian tension develops as eight women suffer male oppression in everyday scenarios ranging from childbirth to buying a bus ticket, all in the space of 24 hours. The raw, hand-held camerawork captures the backstreet ambience of durability and despair. But it's the courageous naturalism of the non-professional cast that provides the drama with its poignancy and power. **DP** Farsi +subtitles. *DVD*

Fereshteh Sadr Orafai *Pari* • Maryiam Palvin Almani *Arezou* • Nargess Mamizadeh *Nargess* • Solmaz Gohlami *Solmaz* ■ *Dir* Jafar Panahi • *Scr* Kambuzia Partovi, from an idea by Jafar Panahi • *Cinematographer* Bahram Badakhshani

The Circle ★★★ 15
Drama documentary
2014 · Swi · Colour and BW · 101min

Switzerland was one of the few places where homosexuality was legal in the late 1950s and Stefan Haupt's docudrama impeccably and meticulously re-creates the scene centred on a nightclub/advice bureau/publication called The Circle that was founded by actor Karl Meier in 1942. The primary focus is on the romance between teacher Ernst Ostertag (Matthias Hungerbühler) and 18-year-old drag artist Röbi Rapp (Sven Schelker), and Haupt incorporates interview footage of the elderly real-life Ostertag and Rapp. It's an intriguing insight into a little-known aspect of LGBT history. **DP** German, French +subtitles. Swearing, sex scenes, nudity.

U SUITABLE FOR ALL   **Ua** SUITABLE ESPECIALLY FOR YOUNG CHILDREN (DVD ONLY)   **PG** PARENTAL GUIDANCE   **12A** UNDER 12s TO BE ACCOMPANIED (CINEMA ONLY)

Röbi Rapp • Ernst Ostertag • Sven Schelker *Young Röbi* • Matthias Hungerbühler *Young Ernst* • Anatole Taubman *Felix* • Marianne Sägebrecht *Erika Rapp* ■ *Dir* Stefan Haupt • *Scr* Stefan Haupt, Christian Felix, Urs Frey, Ivan Madeo

Circle of Danger ★★★U
Drama 1950 · UK · BW · 82min

The clever plot here has Ray Milland investigating the death of his commando brother in the Second World War, only to find that things aren't quite what they seem to be. Despite the talented Jacques Tourneur in the director's chair and Alfred Hitchcock collaborator Joan Harrison as co-producer, the movie isn't quite what it seems to be either. Still, Tourneur does what he can with all those red herrings and makes the whole watchable enough. TS

Ray Milland *Clay Douglas* • Patricia Roc *Elspeth Graham* • Marius Goring *Sholto Lewis* • Hugh Sinclair *Hamish McArran* • Naunton Wayne *Reggie Sinclair* • Dora Bryan *Bubbles* ■ *Dir* Jacques Tourneur • *Scr* Philip MacDonald, from his novel *White Heather*

Circle of Deceit ★★
Drama 1981 · Fr/W Ger · Colour · 108min

West German journalist Bruno Ganz, beset by marital woes, is on assignment in the Lebanon with his photographer Jerzy Skolimowski. Once there, he gets caught up in events – among them an affair with Hanna Schygulla – that compromise both his professional and personal integrity. A sobering but somewhat confused film from Germany's Volker Schlöndorff, this mix of the personal and the political is uneasy, and is compounded by a hero whose inadequacy and self-preoccupation render him deeply tiresome. RB In German.

Bruno Ganz *Georg Laschen* • Hanna Schygulla *Arianna Nassar* • Jerzy Skolimowski *Hoffmann* • Gila Von Weitershausen *Greta Laschen* • Jean Carmet *Rudnik* ■ *Dir* Volker Schlöndorff • *Scr* Volker Schlöndorff, Jean-Claude Carrière, Margarethe von Trotta, Kai Hermann, from the novel *Die Fälschung* by Nicolas Born

Circle of Deception ★★★
Second World War drama
1960 · UK · BW · 99min

During the Second World War, a nervy and sensitive Canadian officer (Bradford Dillman) is made a fall guy by British intelligence, who drop him in Normandy with false information, confident he'll be captured by the Germans and crack under pressure. Well-directed by Jack Lee, with convincing performances from Dillman and a host of first-class English stage and TV actors, this is a decent espionage drama. RK

Suzy Parker *Lucy Bowen* • Bradford Dillman *Paul Raine* • Harry Andrews *Captain Rawson* • Paul Rogers *Major Spence* • John Welsh *Major Taylor* • Robert Stephens *Captain Stein* ■ *Dir* Jack Lee (2) • *Scr* Nigel Balchin, Robert Musel, from the story *Small Back Room in St Marylebone* by Alec Waugh in *Esquire* magazine

Circle of Friends ★★★★15
Romantic drama 1995 · US/Ire · Colour · 98min

As feature debuts go, they don't come much better than Minnie Driver's. She not only holds together this amiable adaptation of Maeve Binchy's novel, but she positively lights up the screen as Benny, the country girl who has to abandon her Dublin education (and rugby star Chris O'Donnell) to work in the family shop and fight off the unwanted attentions of the wonderfully smarmy Alan Cumming. Colin Firth is overly mannered as the Protestant landlord, and Pat O'Connor slips in too many emerald vistas, but this is witty and charming. DP Swearing, sex scenes. *DVD*

Chris O'Donnell *Jack* • Minnie Driver *Benny* • Geraldine O'Rawe *Eve* • Saffron Burrows *Nan* • Alan Cumming *Sean* • Colin Firth *Simon Westward* • Aidan Gillen *Aidan* • Mick Lally *Dan Hogan* • Ciaran Hinds *Professor Flynn* ■ *Dir* Pat O'Connor • *Scr* Andrew Davies, from the novel by Maeve Binchy

Circle of Friends ★★
Mystery thriller 2006 · Can/US · Colour · 88min

Dexter star Julie Benz plays amateur detective in this unconvincing whodunnit. Returning to her home town, the young widow becomes sure that the sudden deaths of a number of her old schoolfriends were actually down to murder. Cue lots of ominous music and an irritating pair of rambling flashbacks, as director Stefan Pleszczynski struggles to create an air of suspense. SF

Julie Benz *Maggie Dale* • Chris Kramer *Harry Salinger* • Venus Terzo *Susan Jennings* • Paula Costain *Joan Salinger* • Adrianne Richards *Emily Howard* ■ *Dir* Stefan Pleszczynski • *Scr* Joyce Heft Brotman

Circle of Passion ★★★
Romantic drama 1996 · US/UK · Colour · 110min

Writer/director Charles Finch takes a leading role as an unhappily married banker who has a fling with hat-maker Sandrine Bonnaire during a business trip to Paris. He has to decide where to hang *his* hat when he falls in love with her. Jane March plays the banker's less than amorous other half, and the emotion of her performance is a revelation after her rather flat performances in such films as *The Lover* and *The Color of Night*. DA English, French +subtitles.

Sandrine Bonnaire *Katherine Beaufort* • Jane March *Amanda Murray* • James Fox *Arthur Trevane* • Charles Finch *Thomas Murray* • Jean Rochefort *Gerard Panier* • Julian Sands *Roderick* ■ *Dir/Scr* Charles Finch

Circle of Two ★
Drama 1980 · Can · Colour · 98min

Sixteen-year-old student Tatum O'Neal goes to see a porno movie. Who should we spot in the audience but a haggard-looking Richard Burton! What follows is an inordinate amount of slush, with Burton urging O'Neal to become a writer and she urging him to resume his career as an artist. Burton received $750,000 for the role and delivered a bored performance that was hardly worth a single cent. AT Violence, nudity. *DVD*

Richard Burton *Ashley St Clair* • Tatum O'Neal *Sarah Norton* • Nuala Fitzgerald *Claudia Aldrich* • Robin Gammell *Mr Norton* • Patricia Collins *Mrs Norton* • Donann Cavin *Smitty* • Michael Wincott *Paul* • Kate Reid *Dr Emily Reid* ■ *Dir* Jules Dassin • *Scr* Thomas Hedley, from the story *A Lesson in Love* by Marie Terese Baird

The Circuit ★★
Action drama 2008 · Can/US · Colour · 88min

This so-so TV movie stars *Gossip Girl*'s Michelle Trachtenberg as a stock car driver on the verge of becoming the next big thing. When she's offered the chance to compete with the pros, she jumps at it, but lands directly in the path of her estranged father, who is a legend of the sport. Old resentments resurface, threatening to put her off course, but she finds other distractions in the shape of a hotshot young driver. Veering between earnest and brash, this drama just never finds the right tone. CM

Michelle Trachtenberg *Kylie Shines* • Bill Campbell [Billy Campbell] *Al Shines* • Drew Fuller *Kid Walker* • Paul Rae *Robin Cates* • Tommy Lioutas *Jake Milley* • Maurice Dean Wint *Andy "Crash" Davis* ■ *Dir* Peter Werner • *Scr* Quinton Peeples, Bill Hanley

Circuitry Man ★★15
Science-fiction thriller
1990 · US · Colour · 88min

More time spent at the typewriter and a little less playing with special effects might have resulted in a better and certainly more coherent movie than this futuristic patchwork. As it is, Dana Wheeler-Nicholson's flight from the villainous Lu Leonard, carrying a case full of pleasure-inducing computer chips, is little more than a string of clichés and pompous pronouncements. Followed by a sequel, *Plughead Rewired: Circuitry Man II*. DP Swearing, violence.

Jim Metzler *Danner* • Dana Wheeler-Nicholson *Lori* • Lu Leonard *Juice* • Vernon Wells *Plughead* • Barbara Alyn Woods *Yoyo* • Dennis Christopher *Leech* ■ *Dir* Steven Lovy • *Scr* Steven Lovy, Robert Lovy

Circumstantial Evidence ★★★
Crime drama 1945 · US · BW · 67min

This is a neat and unpretentious 20th Century-Fox second feature about the fallibility of memory, in particular that of eyewitnesses in a murder trial. The witnesses see, or think they see, Michael O'Shea kill a grocer with whom he is fighting, resulting in his being accused of murder. That fine actor Lloyd Nolan brings his *Michael Shayne, Private Detective* persona to bear on this thoughtful plot, but O'Shea is a rather bland lead. Nevertheless, John Larkin's direction is assured, and the moral uncertainties make for compulsive viewing. TS

Michael O'Shea (1) *Joe Reynolds* • Lloyd Nolan *Sam Lord* • Trudy Marshall *Agnes Hannon* • Billy Cummings *Pat Reynolds* • Ruth Ford *Mrs Simms* • Reed Hadley *Prosecutor* • Roy Roberts *Marty Hannon* • Scotty Beckett *Freddy Hanlon* • Byron Foulger *Bolger* ■ *Dir* John Larkin • *Scr* Robert Metzler, Samuel Ornitz, from a story by Nat Ferber, Sam Duncan

The Circus ★★★★U
Silent comedy 1928 · US · BW · 71min

Charles Chaplin's theme of despondent love all but ovewhelms the brilliant slapstick set pieces (a chase through a hall of mirrors, being trapped in a lion's cage) when the Tramp, on the run from the police, joins the circus and falls for a bare-back rider (Merna Kennedy). Chaplin got a special award for acting, writing, directing and producing the film, but the best moments are the least self-conscious and hark back to his music hall origins (walking a tightrope with falling trousers and a clinging monkey, for example). Not the best Chaplin, but still pretty sensational. TH *DVD*

Charlie Chaplin [Charles Chaplin] *Tramp* • Allan Garcia *Circus proprietor* • Merna Kennedy *Girl* • Harry Crocker *Rex* • George Davis *Magician* • Stanley J Stanford [Tiny Sanford] *Head property man* • Henry Bergman *Old clown* ■ *Dir/Scr* Charles Chaplin

Circus ★18
Comedy thriller 1999 · UK/US · Colour · 91min

Set in Brighton, this clueless crime comedy in the Tarantino mould features a collection of unappealing crooks who repeatedly stab each other in the back and a ludicrous story that makes no sense. Bad casting abounds: John Hannah is far too wimpy to convince as a tough, wily killer, while comedian Brian Conley is embarrassing as the least menacing crime lord in movie history. JC *DVD*

John Hannah *Leo Garfield* • Famke Janssen *Lily Garfield* • Peter Stormare *Julius Harvey* • Eddie Izzard *Troy Cabrara* • Fred Ward *Elmo Somerset* • Brian Conley *Bruno Maitland* • "Tiny" Lister Jr [Tom "Tiny" Lister Jr] *George "Moose" Marley* ■ *Dir* Rob Walker • *Scr* David Logan

Circus Friends ★★U
Drama 1956 · UK · BW · 64min

Although it doesn't add up to much today, this little picture deserves its place in British screen history as the first project brought to completion by producer Peter Rogers and director Gerald Thomas, the godfathers of the *Carry On* series. There's a sentimental charm to this rural tale in which Alan Coleshill and Carol White rescue their pet pony from farmer Meredith Edwards after their penurious father, John Horsley, sells it to help pay his circus bills. DP

Alan Coleshill *Nicky* • Carol White *Nan* • David Tilley *Martin* • Pat Belcher *Beryl* • Meredith Edwards *Farmer Beasley* • John Horsley *Bert Marlow* • Sam Kydd *George* ■ *Dir* Gerald Thomas • *Scr* Peter Rogers

Circus of Fear ★★PG
Horror thriller 1967 · UK · Colour · 82min

Christopher Lee wears a black woolly hood for nearly all of his scenes in this lame whodunnit. He's the facially scarred lion tamer in Barberini's Circus, and one of many suspects in a murder case investigated by Scotland Yard's Leo Genn. John Moxey's disappointing direction accents the cops-and-robbers elements over any marginal terror, but the stalwart efforts of the cast act as a safety net for the shaky plot. AJ *DVD*

Christopher Lee *Gregor* • Leo Genn *Inspector Elliott* • Anthony Newlands *Barberini* • Heinz Drache *Carl* • Eddi Arent *Eddie* • Klaus Kinski *Manfred* • Margaret Lee *Gina* • Suzy Kendall *Natasha* ■ *Dir* John Moxey [John Llewellyn Moxey] • *Scr* Peter Welbeck [Harry Alan Towers], from the novel *Again the Three Just Men* by Edgar Wallace

Circus of Horrors ★★★15
Horror thriller 1960 · UK · Colour · 88min

Definitely a film to make your flesh creep, this nifty British horror is more in keeping with the gimmicky style of Roger Corman or William Castle than your average Hammer. Anton Diffring is perfectly cast as an incompetent plastic surgeon who takes refuge under Donald Pleasence's big top after the knife slips once too often. Director Sidney Hayers makes superb use of the circus locale, dreaming up wonderfully grotesque ways of bumping off the outcasts that Diffring has remodelled when they try to escape his barbarous regime. DP *DVD*

Anton Diffring *Dr Schuler* • Erika Remberg *Elissa* • Yvonne Monlaur *Nicole* • Donald Pleasence *Vanet* • Jane Hylton *Angela* • Kenneth Griffith *Martin* • Conrad Phillips *Inspector Ames* • Jack Gwillim *Superintendent Andrews* ■ *Dir* Sidney Hayers • *Scr* George Baxt • *Cinematographer* Douglas Slocombe

Cirque du Freak: the Vampire's Assistant ★★12
Fantasy horror 2009 · US · Colour · 109min

Director Paul Weitz fails to capture any plausible magic or teen angst in this unevenly toned treatment of the first trilogy in Darren Shan's popular coming-of-age fantasy book series for young adults. The casting of bland Chris Massoglia is no help, either; he plays Darren Shan, the small-town youth who unknowingly breaks a 200-year-old truce between warring vampire factions. At least John C Reilly brings some class to his role as Shan's undead mentor. But there's so much plot and so many colourful characters crammed in, it seems more about setting up the sequels than making a decent original. AJ Violence, swearing. *DVD*

John C Reilly *Larten Crepsley* • Ken Watanabe *Mr Tall* • Josh Hutcherson *Steve* • Chris Massoglia *Darren Shan* • Salma Hayek *Madame Truska* • Willem Dafoe *Gavner Purl* • Ray Stevenson *Murlaugh* • Patrick Fugit *Evra the Snake Boy* ■ *Dir* Paul Weitz • *Scr* Brian Helgeland, Paul Weitz, from the *Cirque du Freak* novels by Darren Shan

Cirque du Soleil: Worlds Away ★★★PG
Fantasy 2012 · US · Colour · 91min

The celebrated Canadian circus company takes viewers on a journey through several of their well-known shows, linked here by a story of one girl's search for a trapeze artist, who is magically sucked into a mysterious underworld. Cue a series of excerpts from such Cirque "greatest hits" as *Zumanity* and a lengthy sequence from *The Beatles Love*. It's all beautifully choreographed, the performers are remarkable and the set design is wonderful, but even in 3D, writer/director Andrew Adamson's film lacks the exhilarating thrill of seeing the shows live. TeS *DVD*

Erica Linz *Mia* • Igor Zaripov *The Aerialist* ■ *Dir/Scr* Andrew Adamson

The Cisco Kid ★★
Western 1931 · US · BW · 60min

The huge success of the early talkie *In Old Arizona* (1929) prompted the Fox company to produce this lightweight follow-up with Warner Baxter and Edmund Lowe repeating their roles. Baxter's suave Mexican bandit robs a bank to save the ranch of a widow with young children and is again pursued by

Lowe's Irish-American lawman. Mobile camerawork and a short running time aid this sentimental tale. He reprised the role in 1939's *The Return of the Cisco Kid.* AE

Warner Baxter *The Cisco Kid* • Edmund Lowe *Sgt Patrick "Mickey" Dunn* • Conchita Montenegro *Carmencita* • Nora Lane *Sally Benton* ■ *Dir* Irving Cummings • *Scr* Al Cohn, from the character created by O Henry in his short story *Caballero's Way* in *Everybody's Magazine* (July 1907)

C

The Cisco Kid and the Lady
★★★ U

Western   1939 · US · BW · 73min

This is a deeply charming if fluffily slight outing for Cesar Romero as the Cisco Kid. The plot is a curious combination of boggling complexity and wafer-thin skimming: gold prospecting, abandoned babies, murder, weddings and funerals are all thrown helter-skelter into the tale and regurgitated as a delightful madcap romp. Overall good fun. SH

Cesar Romero *Cisco Kid* • Marjorie Weaver *Julie Lawson* • Chris-Pin Martin *Gordito* • George Montgomery *Tommy Bates* • Robert Barrat *Jim Harbison* • Virginia Field *Billie Graham* • Harry Green *Teasdale* • Ward Bond *Walton* ■ *Dir* Herbert I Leeds • *Scr* Frances Hyland, from a story by Stanley Rauh, from characters by O Henry

Cisco Pike
★★★

Crime drama   1971 · US · Colour · 94min

In order to create a sense of the emptiness at the centre of 1970s pop and drug culture, writer/director Bill L Norton decided here to dispense with any plot, with the result that his evocation of Los Angeles occasionally borders on the flabby. The film is awash with anti-establishment attitudes and creates an atmosphere that is still affecting, despite Norton's penchant for distracting showy touches. Kris Kristofferson, as the has-been rock star, and Gene Hackman, as the corrupt cop, supply plenty of electricity. JM Swearing.

Kris Kristofferson *Cisco Pike* • Gene Hackman *Holland* • Karen Black *Sue* • Harry Dean Stanton *Jesse* • Viva *Merna* • Joy Bang *Lynn* • Roscoe Lee Browne *Music store owner* • Antonio Fargas *Buffalo* ■ *Dir/Scr* Bill L Norton

The Citadel
★★★★

Drama   1938 · US/UK · BW · 112min

An idealistic young doctor (Robert Donat) battling the slum conditions of a Welsh mining village marries the local schoolteacher (Rosalind Russell) and moves to London, where he is corrupted by the moneyed ease of a society practice. Adapted from AJ Cronin's bestseller, this solid MGM drama makes for thoroughly satisfactory viewing. Donat is perfectly cast, as are Ralph Richardson as his friend and Cecil Parker as a bungling surgeon. Impeccably directed by King Vidor, the picture was voted the year's best by the New York Film Critics. RK

Robert Donat *Andrew Manson* • Rosalind Russell *Christine Manson* • Ralph Richardson *Denny* • Rex Harrison *Dr Lawford* • Emlyn Williams *Owen* • Francis L Sullivan *Ben Chenkin* • Mary Clare *Mrs Orlando* • Cecil Parker *Charles Every* ■ *Dir* King Vidor • *Scr* Ian Dalrymple, Elizabeth Hill, Frank Wead, from the novel by AJ Cronin

The Citadel
★★★ PG

Comedy drama   1989 · Alg · Colour · 98min

Algerian director Mohamed Chouikh seeks to expose the iniquities of polygamy by presenting us with a stark portrait of life within a strict Muslim community. However, while he elicits sympathy for Khaled Barkat, the orphan adopted by decadent merchant Djilali Ain-Tedeles, and for the trio of wives the latter exploits, Chouikh fails to weave the characters into a satisfying dramatic whole. Still, courageous and visually haunting. DP Arabic +subtitles.

Khaled Barkat *Kaddour* • Djilali Ain-Tedeles *Sidi* • Fettouma Ousliha *Helima* • Momo *Aissa* • Fatima Belhadj *Nedjama* ■ *Dir/Scr* Mohamed Chouikh

Citadel
★★ 15

Horror   2012 · Ire/UK · Colour · 84min

Ciaran Foy's low-budget debut feature stars Aneurin Barnard as a widowed, agoraphobic new father who is tormented by a gang of feral hoodies. Events become increasingly improbable after kindly nurse Wunmi Mosaku tries to reach out to the youths and foul-mouthed priest James Cosmo coerces Barnard into helping him destroy the brood's lair. Foy makes adept use of tight framing to keep the focus on Barnard's mounting terror, but the storytelling and characterisation are markedly less impressive. DP Violence, swearing.

Aneurin Barnard *Tommy* • James Cosmo *Priest* • Wunmi Mosaku *Marie* • Amy Shiels *Joanne* • Jake Wilson *Danny* ■ *Dir/Scr* Ciaran Foy

LANDMARK FILM
Orson Welles's unmissable debut challenges the conventions of storytelling using flashbacks, overlapping dialogue, deep focus, long takes, ceilinged sets and psychologically dense characterisation

Citizen Kane
★★★★★ U

Classic drama   1941 · US · BW · 114min

Acclaimed by critics and film-makers alike, *Citizen Kane* has topped *Sight & Sound*'s decennial "all-time top ten" since 1962. Not bad for the feature film debut of 25-year-old Orson Welles, whose experience lay in theatre and radio (most of the actors in *Kane* were colleagues from his Mercury Theatre company), and who claimed his sole preparation was to watch John Ford's *Stagecoach* 40 times. Unhindered by preconceptions, he proceeded to experiment with sound, camera angles and movement and deep focus in a way few had even conceived of. Aided by cinematographer Gregg Toland, he brought visual drama to every shot, brilliantly disguising the picture's shoestring budget (it required a record 116 sets). In addition, Welles also turned in a magnificent performance as Charles Foster Kane, the press baron whose torrid life was so similar to that of William Randolph Hearst that the latter broke the film at the box office through negative publicity. Utterly unmissable. DP *DVD* *Blu-ray*

Orson Welles *Charles Foster Kane* • Joseph Cotten *Jedediah Leland/Man in projection room* • Dorothy Comingore *Susan Alexander Kane* • Agnes Moorehead *Mary, Kane's mother* • Ruth Warrick *Emily Monroe Norton Kane* • Ray Collins *Jim W Gettys* • Erskine Sanford *Herbert Carter/Man in projection room* • Everett Sloane *Mr Bernstein* • William Alland *Jerry Thompson/Narrator of "News on the March"* • Paul Stewart *Raymond, head butler* • George Coulouris *Walter Parks Thatcher* • Fortunio Bonanova *Matiste* • Gus Schilling *John, head waiter/Man in projection room* ■ *Dir* Orson Welles • *Scr* Herman J Mankiewicz, Orson Welles • *Music* Bernard Herrmann • *Editor* Robert Wise • *Art Directors* Van Nest Polglase, Perry Ferguson • *Special Effects* Vernon L Walker

Citizen Ruth
★★★

Black comedy   1996 · US · Colour · 105min

Laura Dern carries this issue-based film single-handedly as Ruth Stoops, a homeless, pregnant drug abuser who triggers a violent debate between pro-lifers and abortion rights campaigners following her arrest for sniffing patio sealant. The range of characters includes Swoosie Kurtz, her lesbian lover Kelly Preston, Burt Reynolds's pro-lifer and Tippi Hedren's pro-choice harpy. Director Alexander Payne manages to satirise as well as explain. LH

Laura Dern *Ruth Stoops* • Swoosie Kurtz *Diane Sieglar* • Kurtwood Smith *Norm Stoney* • Mary Kay Place *Gail Stoney* • Kelly Preston *Rachel* • MC Gainey *Harlan* • Kenneth Mars *Dr Charlie Rollins* • Tippi Hedren *Jessica Weiss* • Burt Reynolds *Blaine Gibbons* • Diane Ladd *Ruth's mother* ■ *Dir* Alexander Payne • *Scr* Alexander Payne, Jim Taylor

Citizen X
★★★ 18

Thriller based on a true story
1995 · US/Hun · Colour · 98min

The true story of the Soviet Union's most famous serial killer makes absorbing

viewing. Former schoolteacher Chikatilo (Jeffrey DeMunn) murdered and mutilated 52 children over an eight-year period, yet managed to evade capture because of government corruption, ineffectual police procedures and the fact that the authorities couldn't admit to such western depravity polluting their culture. Stephen Rea is subtly convincing as the forensic expert who doggedly pursued the killer, while Donald Sutherland deservedly won numerous awards as the military man who finally backed his hunches. AJ Violence, swearing.

Stephen Rea *Detective Viktor Burakov* • Donald Sutherland *Colonel Fetisov* • Max von Sydow *Dr Aleksandr Bukhanovsky* • Jeffrey DeMunn *Andre Chikatilo* • John Wood (2) *Gorbunov* • Joss Ackland *Bondarchuk* ■ *Dir* Chris Gerolmo • *Scr* Chris Gerolmo, from the non-fiction book *The Killer Department* by Robert Cullen

Citizenfour
★★★★ 15

Documentary   2014 · Ger/US · Colour · 112min

Hong Kong, 2013: Edward Snowden, a former employee of the American National Security Agency, tells a select group of journalists (whom he has contacted under the handle Citizenfour) about the mass surveillance and gross abuses of power used by his organisation. Film-maker Laura Poitras is there to film the meetings. Flagrant abuses of power are unveiled by the affable yet sincere whistleblower, whose awareness of the danger he is in only furthers the thriller-like feel of the documentary. While the film loses some urgency in its final third, it's a thrilling, shocking snapshot of a moment in time that will live in history, a reminder of the very real threat that those in power can pose to the citizens they have sworn to protect. JL English, Portuguese, German +subtitles. Swearing.

Edward Snowden • Glenn Greenwald ■ *Dir* Laura Poitras

Citizens Band
★★★★

Comedy   1977 · US · Colour · 95min

This highly amusing and raunchy comedy is about CB radio enthusiasts (remember that craze?) in a small midwestern town, eavesdropping on one another with hilarious results. An excellent script, on-the-button performances from Paul Le Mat and Candy Clark, and a great soundtrack featuring Richie Havens and Joe Cocker brighten this charming slab of suburban American graffiti. AJ

Paul Le Mat *Blaine Lovejoy, Spider* • Candy Clark *Pam, Electra* • Ann Wedgeworth *Joyce Rissley, Dallas Angel* • Marcia Rodd *Connie Rissley, Portland Angel* • Charles Napier *Harold Rissley, Chrome Angel* • Roberts Blossom *Papa Thermodyne* • Bruce McGill *Dean Lovejoy, Blood* ■ *Dir* Jonathan Demme • *Scr* Paul Brickman

City across the River
★★★

Drama   1949 · US · BW · 90min

This depicts the exploits of a teenage gang in New York, focusing in particular on one member (Peter Fernandez) and demonstrating how a petty criminal, driven by circumstance, can become a killer. Directed by Maxwell Shane in tough, semi-documentary style, the movie grips with its pace and its graphic depiction of the harsh conditions of tenement life. A very young Tony Curtis appears as a gang member. RK

Stephen McNally *Stan Albert* • Thelma Ritter *Mrs Cusack* • Peter Fernandez *Frank Cusack* • Luis Van Rooten *Joe Cusack* • Jeff Corey *Lt Macon* • Anthony Curtis [Tony Curtis] *Mitch* ■ *Dir* Maxwell Shane • *Scr* Dennis Cooper, Irving Schulman, Maxwell Shane, from the novel *The Amboy Dukes* by Irving Schulman

City beneath the Sea
★★★ U

Adventure   1953 · US · Colour · 86min

This is one of those highly Technicolored Universal programme co-features that we all took for granted when they appeared in double bills, and which are now a positive joy. Robert Ryan and Anthony Quinn star in an underwater adventure romp, snarling at

each other over hidden treasure. Love interest is provided by Mala Powers and Suzan Ball, Lucille Ball's cousin, who would continue to act after her leg was amputated due to cancer, and who died tragically young in 1955. TS

Robert Ryan *Brad Carlton* • Mala Powers *Terry* • Anthony Quinn *Tony Bartlett* • Suzan Ball *Venita* • George Mathews *Captain Meade* • Karel Stepanek *Dwight Trevor* • Lalo Rios *Calypso* • Woody Strode *Djion* ■ *Dir* Budd Boetticher • *Scr* Jack Harvey, Ramon Romero, from the story *Port Royal – Ghost City beneath the Sea* by Harry E Riesberg

City beneath the Sea
★★ U

Science-fiction adventure
1971 · US · Colour · 89min

Irwin Allen, Mr Disaster Movie himself, took a dive in this pilot for a TV series that was never made. It's easy to see why, as each crisis facing the vast submerged 21st-century metropolis of Pacifica had been done better in previous Allen shows. Asteroids on a collision course, sea monsters, internal dissension and bullion robberies are piled on in the desperate effort to build excitement. Wooden and waterlogged. AJ

Stuart Whitman *Admiral Michael Matthews* • Robert Wagner *Brett Matthews* • Rosemary Forsyth *Lia Holmes* • Robert Colbert *Commander Woody Patterson* • Susana Miranda *Elena* • Burr DeBenning *Dr Aguila* • Richard Basehart *President* • Joseph Cotten *Dr Ziegler* ■ *Dir* Irwin Allen • *Scr* John Meredyth Lucas, from a story by Irwin Allen

City by the Sea
★★★ 18

Police drama based on a true story
2002 · US · Colour · 104min

This performance-driven action drama is a poignant and powerful reflection on human weakness and the potential agonies of emotional attachment. Robert De Niro plays a respected New York City homicide detective who is torn between familial and professional notions of duty when a drug dealer's murder is attributed to his estranged son (James Franco). De Niro delivers a fine, heart-rending performance, and benefits from some weighty support. SF Violence, swearing, drug abuse, sex scenes. *DVD*

Robert De Niro *Lt Vincent LaMarca* • Frances McDormand *Michelle* • James Franco *Joey LaMarca* • Eliza Dushku *Gina* • William Forsythe *Spyder* • George Dzundza *Reg Duffy* • Patti LuPone *Maggie* • Anson Mount *Dave Simon* ■ *Dir* Michael Caton-Jones • *Scr* Ken Hixon, from the article *Mark of a Murderer* by Michael McAlary

City for Conquest
★★★★ PG

Melodrama   1940 · US · BW · 94min

Director Anatole Litvak tells a tough tale as truck driver-turned-prize fighter James Cagney tries to protect his sensitive composer brother, superbly played by Arthur Kennedy in his adult movie debut. Check out future director Elia Kazan, here playing a hood, and watch sexy and sympathetic Ann Sheridan interact with a young Anthony Quinn. A worthy follow-up to the Warner Bros social dramas of the 1930s. TS

James Cagney *Danny Kenny* • Ann Sheridan *Peggy Nash* • Frank Craven *"Old Timer"* • Donald Crisp *Scotty McPherson* • Arthur Kennedy *Eddie Kenny* • Elia Kazan *"Googi"* • Anthony Quinn *Murray Burns* ■ *Dir* Anatole Litvak • *Scr* John Wexley, from the novel by Aben Kandel

The City Girl
★★ 18

Drama   1984 · US · Colour · 81min

The drama in Martha Coolidge's follow-up to *Valley Girl* derives from the opposing forces that pull struggling photographer Laura Harrington apart at the seams. Trying to assert her independence, she dumps her long-time partner to play the field. Things backfire badly when a pimp she is secretly snapping scares the living daylights out of her by trashing her apartment. Harrington impresses in this tale of a modern woman trying to survive in the big wide world. FL

Laura Harrington *Anne* • Joe Mastroianni *Joey* • Carole McGill *Gracie* • Peter Riegert *Tim* • James Carrington *Steve* • Lawrence Phillips *The stripper* • Geraldine Baron *Monica* ■ *Dir* Martha Coolidge • *Scr* Judith Thompson, Leonard-John Gates, from a story by Martha Coolidge, John MacDonald

City Hall ★★★★ 15

Political drama   1996 · US · Colour · 106min

This is reminiscent of one of those Warner Bros gangster films of the 1930s, but director Harold Becker's update is even more violent and exciting. Al Pacino is the New York mayor, rabble-rousing as he plots a path to the White House, but finding himself thwarted in his political ambition when a child is killed in the crossfire between a cop and a drug dealer. His naive deputy, John Cusack, investigates the crime with the help of attorney Bridget Fonda, only to find the perpetrators are uncomfortably close to home. Not particularly original, but superbly acted and entertaining. TH Violence, swearing. *DVD*

Al Pacino *Mayor John Pappas* • John Cusack *Kevin Calhoun* • Bridget Fonda *Marybeth Cogan* • Danny Aiello *Frank Anselmo* • Martin Landau *Judge Walter Stern* • David Paymer *Abe Goodman* • Tony Franciosa [Anthony Franciosa] *Paul Zapatti* • Lindsay Duncan *Sydney Pappas* ■ *Dir* Harold Becker • *Scr* Ken Lipper, Paul Schrader, Nicholas Pileggi, Bo Goldman

City Heat ★★★ 15

Comedy thriller   1984 · US · Colour · 93min

Clint Eastwood and Burt Reynolds were dream casting, but this got off to a bad start. Originally called *Kansas City Jazz*, it had been written by Blake Edwards, who was also to direct. But Eastwood and Edwards disliked each other from the first, so Edwards left and Richard Benjamin took over. Despite the on-set problems, the movie is a nostalgic sprint through Prohibition-era Kansas City, with Eastwood as a cop and Reynolds as a private eye, who team up and clear the town of gangsters. AT Swearing, violence.

Clint Eastwood *Lieutenant Speer* • Burt Reynolds *Mike Murphy* • Jane Alexander *Addy* • Madeline Kahn *Caroline Howley* • Rip Torn *Primo Pitt* • Irene Cara *Ginny Lee* • Richard Roundtree *Dehl Swift* • Tony LoBianco *Leon Coll* ■ *Dir* Richard Benjamin • *Scr* Sam O Brown [Blake Edwards], Joseph C Stinson, from a story by Sam O Brown [Blake Edwards]

The City Is Dark ★★★

Film noir   1954 · US · BW · 73min

Ex-con Gene Nelson on parole in Los Angeles attempts to go straight with the support of his wife Phyllis Kirk, but soon finds himself up against hostile forces. Nelson is excellent; so is Sterling Hayden as a vengeful and sadistic cop. Solid and pacey, Andre De Toth's movie takes a gritty look at police methods, the criminal world and the difficulties crooks face when they try to escape their former lives. RK

Sterling Hayden *Detective Sergeant Sims* • Gene Nelson *Steve Lacey* • Phyllis Kirk *Ellen* • Ted De Corsia *"Doc" Penny* • Charles Buchinsky [Charles Bronson] *Ben Hastings* • Jay Novello *Dr Otto Hessler* • James Bell *Daniel O'Keefe* ■ *Dir* Andre De Toth • *Scr* Crane Wilbur, Bernard Gordon, Richard Wormser, from the story *Criminals Mark* by John Hawkins, Ward Hawkins

City Island ★★★★ 12

Comedy drama   2009 · US/Pol · Colour · 99min

A small island off Manhattan is the setting for this low-key comedy drama of secrets and family ties, starring Andy Garcia as wannabe actor Vince Rizzo. Writer/director Raymond De Felitta lets the comedy spring naturally from the friction between characters and, in particular, a burgeoning love affair between newcomer Tony (Steven Strait) and Vince's wife (a wonderfully mouthy Julianna Margulies). It's occasionally contrived, but the underlying affection between the Rizzos (including a wickedly funny Ezra Miller and Garcia's real-life daughter Dominik García-Lorido) keeps the film grounded. And Garcia's gift for comedy is a true revelation. SP *DVD*

Andy Garcia *Vince Rizzo* • Julianna Margulies *Joyce Rizzo* • Alan Arkin *Michael Malakov* • Emily Mortimer *Molly Charlesworth* • Steven Strait *Tony Nardella* ■ *Dir/Scr* Raymond De Felitta

City Lights ★★★★★ U

Silent comedy romance   1931 · US · BW · 82min

A consummate storyteller, Charles Chaplin could reduce his audience to fits of laughter and, without warning, plunge them to the depths of pathos. With this masterpiece, telling the story of a tramp and the blind flower girl (Virginia Cherrill) he falls in love with, Chaplin went against the incoming tide of talking pictures by using only music, sound effects, subtitles and his own inestimable pantomime skills. He told Sam Goldwyn: "If it's a failure, I believe it will strike a deeper blow than anything else that has ever happened to me in this life." It was a resounding success. TH *DVD* *BL*

Charlie Chaplin [Charles Chaplin] *Tramp* • Virginia Cherrill *Blind girl* • Florence Lee *Her grandmother* • Harry Myers *Eccentric millionaire* • Allan Garcia *His butler* • Jean Harlow *Guest* ■ *Dir/Scr* Charles Chaplin • *Music* Charles Chaplin

City of Angels ★★★ 12

Romantic fantasy drama   1998 · US · Colour · 109min

A semi-remake of Wim Wenders's *Wings of Desire*, this Hollywood version has Nicolas Cage as an angel inhabiting Los Angeles who falls for heart surgeon (yes, really) Meg Ryan . Will he give up his otherworldly delights so he can "fall" to earth and be with her? And will they both drown in the slushy sentimentality of it all? Happily, not quite, thanks to a well-chosen soundtrack and a winning performance from Cage. JB Violence, swearing, brief nudity. *DVD*

Nicolas Cage *Seth* • Meg Ryan *Dr Maggie Rice* • Dennis Franz *Nathaniel Messinger* • André Braugher *Cassiel* • Colm Feore *Jordan* ■ *Dir* Brad Silberling • *Scr* Dana Stevens

City of Ember ★★ PG

Fantasy adventure   2008 · US · Colour · 90min

Young leads Saoirse Ronan (*Atonement*) and Harry Treadaway (*Control*) shine among the established talent of Bill Murray, Tim Robbins and Martin Landau in this flawed but watchable post-apocalypse fantasy. Based on the first book in Jeanne DuPrau's bestselling trilogy, the story is set some 200 years after an unspecified disaster has driven the few survivors underground. The two youngsters believe that the outside world holds the key to survival, but must first piece together clues left by the city's founders. This second film from *Monster House* director Gil Kenan is brimming with ideas but is hampered by a plodding storyline and below-par visual effects. DA *DVD* *BL*

Saoirse Ronan *Lina Mayfleet* • Harry Treadaway *Doon Harrow* • Bill Murray *Mayor Cole* • Tim Robbins *Loris Harrow* • Martin Landau *Sul* • Toby Jones *Barton Snode* • Mary Kay Place *Mrs Murdo* • Marianne Jean-Baptiste *Clary* ■ *Dir* Gil Kenan • *Scr* Caroline Thompson, from the novel *The City of Ember* by Jeanne DuPrau

City of Fear ★★

Thriller   1959 · US · BW · 74min

Following their collaboration on *Murder by Contract*, action man Vince Edwards and director Irving Lerner reteamed for this tense little thriller that boasts photography by Lucien Ballard and a score by Jerry Goldsmith. It follows Edwards as he tries to get rid of a canister that he thinks contains heroin, but is, in fact, loaded with a radioactive material. Hardly heart-stopping stuff, and Edwards isn't the most gifted of actors, but it's not bad. DP

Vince Edwards *Vince Ryker* • Lyle Talbot *Chief Jensen* • John Archer *Lieutenant Mark Richards* • Steven Ritch *Dr Wallace* • Patricia Blair *June* • Joe Mell *Crown* ■ *Dir* Irving Lerner • *Scr* Steven Ritch, Robert Dillon

City of Ghosts ★★★ 15

Thriller   2002 · US · Colour · 111min

Matt Dillon's directorial debut plays like a dark love letter to Cambodia. In this slow-burning thriller, the actor also takes the lead as a conman who flees the US for Cambodia following an insurance scam. Here, passionately detailed visuals present a snapshot of an alien culture, populated by quirky characters who add colour to Dillon's hunt for his shadowy associate James Caan. The picture lacks the complexity and pacing to really grip, but it's still an admirable effort. SF Swearing, violence, sex scenes, drug abuse. *DVD*

Matt Dillon *Jimmy Cremmins* • James Caan *Marvin* • Natascha McElhone *Sophie* • Gérard Depardieu *Emile* • Sereyvuth Kem *Sok* • Stellan Skarsgård *Kaspar* • Rose Byrne *Sabrina* • Shawn Andrews *Robbie* • Chalee Sankhavesa *Sideth* ■ *Dir* Matt Dillon • *Scr* Matt Dillon, Barry Gifford

City of God ★★★★★ 18

Crime thriller   2002 · Bra/Ger/Fr · Colour · 124min

Inspired by Paulo Lins's fact-based novel, this three-act chronicle of gangland rivalry on the streets of Rio de Janeiro resists the temptation to glamorise crime, as so many New York Mob movies have done. Yet director Fernando Meirelles's audacious visual style may disconcert those expecting a neorealistic approach to the story of a teenage hoodlum's rise and fall. It invites comparisons with *GoodFellas*, as the often explosive and meticulously designed action spans the late 1960s to the early 80s. But the no-holds-barred authenticity of the non-professional juvenile cast and Meirelles's edgy social commitment make it a wholly unique experience. DP Portuguese +subtitles. Violence, swearing, sex scenes, drug abuse, nudity. *DVD* *BL*

Alexandre Rodrigues *Buscapé, "Rocket"* • Leandro Firmino da Hora *Zé Pequeño, "Li'l Ze"* • Phellipe Haagensen *Bené, "Beny"* • Douglas Silva *Dadinho, "Li'l Dice"* • Jonathan Haagensen *Cabeleira, "Shaggy"* • Matheus Nachtergaele *Sandro Cenoura, "Carrot"* ■ *Dir* Fernando Meirelles • *Scr* Braulio Mantovani, from the novel by Paulo Lins

City of Hope ★★★★★ 15

Drama   1991 · US · Colour · 124min

The title is ironic to the point of sarcasm, but that's just what you expect from director John Sayles, the greatest of Hollywood independents. This hugely impressive film brilliantly portrays the conflicts and corruption inherent within a New Jersey community as fault-lines upon which the community is built. It's how these seeming abstractions affect people's lives that concerns Sayles and, while there's no central star to light up the dark places, the cast's ensemble acting is vivid enough for an epic that winds down to a bleak finale. TH Violence, swearing, drug abuse.

Vincent Spano *Nick Rinaldi* • Joe Morton *Wynn* • Tony LoBianco *Joe Rinaldi* • Barbara Williams (2) *Angela* • Stephen Mendillo *Yoyo* • Chris Cooper *Riggs* • Charlie Yanko *Stavros* • Jace Alexander *Bobby* • Angela Bassett *Reesha* ■ *Dir/Scr* John Sayles

City of Industry ★★ 18

Crime thriller   1996 · US · Colour · 92min

This dour revenge thriller stars Harvey Keitel as a crook tracking down an associate who got greedy after a lucrative robbery. The solid, if unexceptional performances from Keitel and Stephen Dorff (as the scumbag he pursues), combined with John Irvin's no-frills direction and a by-the-numbers plot lend this the appearance of a tough TV movie. JC Swearing, violence. *DVD*

Harvey Keitel *Roy Egan* • Stephen Dorff *Skip Kovich* • Timothy Hutton *Lee Egan* • Famke Janssen *Rachel Montana* • Wade Dominguez *Jorge Montana* • Michael Jai White *Odell Williams* • Elliott Gould *Gangster* ■ *Dir* John Irvin • *Scr* Ken Solarz

City of Joy ★★★ 15

Drama   1992 · Fr/UK · Colour · 129min

A much derided movie on its release, Roland Joffé's overlong and occasionally muddled tale of life in a Calcutta slum actually has much to recommend it. Patrick Swayze turns in a credible performance as the dedicated if emotionally constipated doctor, and Pauline Collins is far from clichéd as the gutsy, confrontational nurse. Joffé brings the abject squalor of the overpopulated alleys to vibrant, atmospheric life. SH Violence, swearing.

Patrick Swayze *Max Lowe* • Pauline Collins *Joan Bethel* • Om Puri *Hasari Pal* • Shabana Azmi *Kamla Pal* • Art Malik *Ashoka* • Ayesha Dharker [Ayesha Dharkar] *Amrita Pal* • Santu Chowdhury *Shambu Pal* • Imran Badsah Khan *Manooj Pal* ■ *Dir* Roland Joffé • *Scr* Mark Medoff, from the novel by Dominique LaPierre

City of Life ★★

Drama   2009 · UAE · Colour · 130min

Ali F Mostafa's place in screen history is assured, as the director of the first feature from the United Arab Emirates. But this Dubai-set melodrama is decidedly clichéd and underwhelming, suffering from thin characterisation and woeful dialogue. The exception to this is a provocative peek behind the glitz and glamour of the burgeoning resort. Conscious of his state funding, however, Mostafa packs the picture with shots of luxurious buildings and fast cars, when more might have been made of this insight into the restrictions placed upon the rich. DP Arabic, English, Hindi +subtitles.

Alexandra Maria Lara *Natalia Moldovan* • Sonu Sood *Basu* • Saoud Al Kaabi *Faisal* • Jason Flemyng *Guy Berger* ■ *Dir* Ali F Mostafa • *Scr* Ali F Mostafa, Jonny Brown, Gerry Sherard, Tim Smythe, from a story by Mostafa

City of Life and Death ★★★★ 15

Historical war drama   2009 · Chi/HK · BW · 130min

While Florian Gallenberger's *John Rabe* focused on the foreigners trapped in the 1937 Siege of Nanking, Lu Chuan's magisterial reconstruction views events from the perspective of the persecuted Chinese and their Japanese conquerors. This is a defiantly non-melodramatic epic that centres on Japanese sergeant Hideo Nakaizumi, who witnesses events with a sense of horror that is compounded by his terror of disobeying orders. His Chinese counterpart is Fan Wei, who does whatever it takes to survive within the embassy enclave. Superbly designed and photographed, this is hugely impressive and emotionally wrenching. DP Mandarin +subtitles. *DVD* *BL*

Liu Ye *General Lu* • Gao Yuanyuan *Miss Jiang* • Hideo Nakaizumi *Kadokawa* • Wei Fan *Mr Tang* ■ *Dir/Scr* Lu Chuan

The City of Lost Children ★★★★ 15

Fantasy adventure   1995 · Fr/Sp/Ger · Colour · 107min

Ron Perlman stars in this sinister fantasy adventure from French directors Jean-Pierre Jeunet and Marc Caro who, with their extraordinary *Delicatessen*, set new standards for dark fables. From its nightmare opening to the climactic battle, this surreal tale is an astonishing eye-opener as carnival strongman One (Perlman) leads the fight against the evil Krank (Daniel Emilfork), who steals children's dreams. If you think films can do nothing new, prepare to be surprised. Also available in a dubbed version. TH French +subtitles. *DVD* *BL*

Ron Perlman *One* • Daniel Emilfork *Krank* • Judith Vittet *Miette* • Dominique Pinon *Clones/Diver/Stocle* • Jean-Claude Dreyfus *Marcello, the flea tamer* • Mireille Mossé *Mademoiselle Bismuth* ■ *Dir* Marc Caro, Jean-Pierre Jeunet • *Scr* Gilles Adrien, Jean-Pierre Jeunet, Marc Caro, Guillaume Laurant

City of Men ★★★ 15

Crime drama   2007 · Bra/US · Colour · 102min

A companion piece to the excellent *City of God*, this crime drama is once again set against the backdrop of a Rio de Janeiro shanty town where gang warfare is rife, and features some of the same young actors. Here, two teenage friends – Ace (Douglas Silva) and Wallace (Darlan Cunha) – find themselves taking different paths following the revelation of a shattering event that connects their families. More a tale of hope in adversity than rage in chaos, this is not the cinematic kick in the teeth that *City of God* was, but the performances still have an authentic and compelling feel about them. DA Portuguese +subtitles. Swearing. DVD BL

Douglas Silva *Acerola "Ace"* • Darlan Cunha *Laranjinha "Wallace"* ■ *Dir* Paulo Morelli • *Scr* Elena Soarez, from a story by Soarez, Paulo Morelli

The City of No Limits
★★★ 12A

Thriller 2002 · Sp/Arg · Colour · 120min

An old man's regrets and his family's guilty secrets intersect in Antonio Hernández's intriguing study of loyalty, memory and the consequences of momentous actions. Leonardo Sbaraglia avoids his romantic responsibilities towards both Argentinian girlfriend Leticia Bredice and sister-in-law Ana Fernández by embarking on a mission to lay Fernando Fernán Gómez's Civil War ghosts. DP French, Spanish +subtitles.

Leonardo Sbaraglia *Victor* • Fernando Fernán Gómez *Max* • Geraldine Chaplin *Marie* • Ana Fernández *Carmen* • Adriana Ozores *Pilar* • Leticia Bredice *Eileen* • Roberto Alvarez *Luis* ■ *Dir* Antonio Hernández • *Scr* Enrique Brasó, Antonio Hernández

A City of Sadness ★★★★ 12

Drama 1989 · Tai · Colour · 151min

The winner of the Golden Lion at Venice, this epic of intimate details puts a human face on the momentous events that buffeted Taiwan between the Japanese surrender in 1945 and the arrival of Chiang Kai-Shek's Nationalists four years later. There's a sense of microcosm about the deteriorating widower's household, with one son working as a translator during the occupation, another a deaf mute fighting for independence, the third a petty gangster and the fourth a soldier presumed killed in action. Hou Hsiao-Hsien's subtle compositions and meticulous pacing draw the viewer into the drama. DP Mandarin, Hokkien +subtitles.

Tony Chiu-Wai Leung [Tony Leung (2)] *Lin Wen-Ching* • Xin Shufen *Hinomi* • Chen Sown-Yung *Lin Wen-Heung* • Kao Jai *Lin Wen-Leung* • Li Tianlu *Lin Ah-Lu* • Wu Yi-Fang *Hinoe* ■ *Dir* Hou Hsiao-Hsien • *Scr* Wu Nien-Jen, Chu Tien-Wen

The City of the Dead
★★★ 15

Horror 1960 · UK · BW · 77min

Also known as *Horror Hotel*, this cheap and chilling supernatural thriller reeks of atmospheric horror and benefits enormously from its stagebound sets and black-and-white photography. A young history student goes to a remote Massachusetts village to research black magic and falls prey to a reincarnated witch burned at the stake 250 years earlier. Professor Christopher Lee is part of the modern coven holding the hamlet in a grip of sacrificial terror. AJ DVD

Christopher Lee *Professor Driscoll* • Venetia Stevenson *Nan Barlow* • Patricia Jessel *Elizabeth Selwyn/Mrs Newless* • Betta St John *Patricia Russell* • Valentine Dyall *Jethrow Keane* • Dennis Lotis *Richard Barlow* • Norman Macowan *Reverend Russell* • Ann Beach *Lottie* ■ *Dir* John Moxey [John Llewellyn Moxey] • *Scr* George Baxt, from a story by Milton Subotsky

City of Tiny Lights

Crime drama 2016 · UK · Colour

This is a preview – no prints were available to review prior to publication: Cricket-loving private eyes with a Ugandan-Asian background are a bit thin on the ground on the big screen, something this adaptation of Patrick Neate's best-selling crime novel sets out to correct. Riz Ahmed, impressive in a string of films including *Shifty*, *Four Lions* and *Ill Manors*, plays the boozy West London gumshoe searching for a missing prostitute, in a Chandleresque walk down the mean multicultural streets of modern Britain. SvM

Riz Ahmed [Rizwan Ahmed] *Tommy Akhtar* • Cush Jumbo *Melody Chase* • Roshan Seth • Billie Piper • Danny Webb ■ *Dir* Pete Travis • *Scr* Patrick Neate, from his novel

The City of Violence ★★★ 18

Action revenge thriller 2006 · S Kor · Colour · 89min

Films from the Far East are in fashion. This revenge thriller from Korea is maybe not the best of them. But nor is it, by any stretch of the imagination, the worst. Instead, *The City of Violence* is a good, solid example of the calibre of Far East film that is now arriving in the West. The plot is standard genre stuff: a big-city detective returns to his home town and, with the help of one old friend, gets his own back on the local hoodlums who have killed another old friend. The talky bits are, well, talky. The chop-socky fight scenes are in between are brisk and exciting. DA Korean +subtitles. DVD

Jung Doo-hong *Jung Tae-soo* • Ryoo Seung-wan *Ryoo Suk-hwan* • Lee Beom-soo *Jang Pil-ho* • Joeng Soek-yong *Ryoo Dong-hwan* • An Kil-kang *Oh Wang-jae* • Lee Joo-sil *Suk-hwan's mother* • Kim Seo-hyung *Jang Mi-ran* ■ *Dir* Ryoo Seung-wan • *Scr* Lee Won-jae, Ryoo Seung-wan, Kim Jeong-min

City of War: the Story of John Rabe ★★★ 15

Biographical drama 2009 · Fr/Chi/Ger · Colour · 128min

Although never as devastatingly powerful as Lu Chuan's *City of Life and Death*, this is still a harrowing account of the 1937 Nanking Massacre from the viewpoint of those trapped within the International Security Zone. When the Japanese army conquered the city, German factory manager John Rabe organised a neutral area in the embassy district in an attempt to protect 200,000 refugees. With Ulrich Tukur excelling as Rabe, this is an old-fashioned tribute to a reluctant hero that frustratingly marginalises other key characters. DP Cantonese, Mandarin, German, Japanese, English +subtitles. DVD BL

Ulrich Tukur *John Rabe* • Daniel Brühl *Dr Georg Rosen* • Steve Buscemi *Dr Robert Wilson* • Anne Consigny *Valérie Duprès* • Dagmar Manzel *Dora Rabe* • Zhang Jingchu *Langshu* ■ *Dir* Florian Gallenberger • *Scr* Florian Gallenberger, from a diary by John Rabe

City of Women ★★★★ 18

Fantasy drama 1980 · It/Fr · Colour · 139min

Intended as Federico Fellini's contribution to a collaboration with Ingmar Bergman entitled *Love Duet* and briefly touted as a Dustin Hoffman vehicle, this is a sexual variation on the Scrooge theme. Marcello Mastroianni returns as Fellini's alter ego to embark on a revelatory journey through a gynocentric hell. There's little wonder feminist commentators decried the picture, but this phantasmagoria of flesh also contains priceless moments of parody, autobiography and satire. DP Italian +subtitles. DVD BL

Marcello Mastroianni *Snaporaz* • Anna Prucnal *Elena* • Bernice Stegers *Woman on train* • Jole Silvani *Motorcyclist* • Donatella Damiani *Feminist on roller skates* • Ettore Manni *Dr Katzone* ■ *Dir* Federico Fellini • *Scr* Federico Fellini, Bernardino Zapponi, Brunello Rondi

City on Fire ★★

Disaster movie 1979 · Can · Colour · 105min

Leslie Nielsen plays it straight in this disaster movie, so it does at least provide some unintentional giggles. For the most part, though, it's minor stuff, with a collection of vaguely familiar TV faces along with such movie legends as Henry Fonda and Ava Gardner almost being burned to a cinder after gasoline seeps into the city's sewer system. JF

Barry Newman *Frank Whitman* • Susan Clark *Diana Brockhurst-Lautrec* • Shelley Winters *Nurse Andrea Harper* • Leslie Nielsen *Mayor William Dudley* • James Franciscus *Jimbo* • Ava Gardner *Maggie Grayson* • Henry Fonda *Fire chief* ■ *Dir* Alvin Rakoff • *Scr* Jack Hill, David P Lewis, Celine La Freniere

City on Fire ★★★★ 18

Action thriller 1987 · HK · Colour · 101min

In this violent Hong Kong thriller, the inspiration for Quentin Tarantino's *Reservoir Dogs*, Oriental superstar Chow Yun-Fat stars as an undercover cop who works his way into a gang planning a jewel heist. When it all goes wrong, the gang returns to its warehouse rendezvous, where the recriminations begin. Director Ringo Lam accelerates the violence with skill, though it lacks the poignancy that Tarantino was to inject into his ground-breaking crime drama. TH Cantonese +subtitles. Violence, nudity. DVD

Chow Yun-Fat *Ko Chow* • Lee Sau Yin [Danny Lee] *Ah Foo* • Sun Yueh *Inspector Lau* • Carrie Ng *Hung* ■ *Dir* Ringo Lam • *Scr* Tommy Sham, from a story by Ringo Lam

City Rats ★ 15

Black comedy drama 2008 · UK · Colour · 93min

Director Steve M Kelly's ponderous look at loneliness and despair in the big city is a micro-budget soap opera showcasing good actors wasting their talent. There's nothing here that hasn't been seen a thousand times before, as eight lost London souls struggle for an emotional connection in a collection of intermingled tales. The characters are largely stereotypes, including alcoholic ex-con Danny Dyer and disabled prostitute Susan Lynch. Only the story involving Kenny Doughty trying to get his deaf-mute gay brother James Lance a hot date rings true and avoids being mawkish. AJ DVD

Tamer Hassan *Jim* • Danny Dyer *Pete* • Ray Panthaki *Dean* • Susan Lynch *Gina* • Kenny Doughty *Olly* • James Lance *Chris* • MyAnna Buring *Sammy* • Natasha Williams *Carol* ■ *Dir* Steve M Kelly • *Scr* Simon Fantauzzo

City Slickers ★★★★ 15

Comedy western 1991 · US · Colour · 109min

Billy Crystal and chums Daniel Stern and Bruno Kirby are the city folk who get the chance to play at *Rawhide* in this winning comedy blockbuster. Seeking to stave off middle age, the trio join a motley group who have volunteered to drive cattle across the range under the eye of irascible old cowboy Jack Palance. Despite some sentimental moments, this is an engaging piece that gently pokes fun at both midlife crises and the Wild West. Palance won a best supporting actor Oscar for his performance. JF Swearing. DVD

Billy Crystal *Mitch Robbins* • Daniel Stern *Phil Berquist* • Bruno Kirby *Ed Furillo* • Patricia Wettig *Barbara Robbins* • Helen Slater *Bonnie Rayburn* • Jack Palance *Curly* • Noble Willingham *Clay Stone* • Tracey Walter *Cookie* ■ *Dir* Ron Underwood • *Scr* Lowell Ganz, Babaloo Mandel, from a story by Billy Crystal

City Slickers II: the Legend of Curly's Gold ★★ 12

Comedy western 1994 · US · Colour · 110min

Producers always rush out sequels to sleepers (or surprise box-office hits), hoping to cash in while the audience is still in the right mood. Unfortunately, sleepers are by definition films no one initially had much confidence in, and film-makers often struggle to repeat the inexplicably successful formula. This is a case in point. Jack Palance briefly reprises his Oscar-winning role, but a hit comedy needs more than cameos, cattle and scenery. DP Some swearing. DVD

Billy Crystal *Mitch Robbins* • Daniel Stern *Phil Berquist* • Jon Lovitz *Glen Robbins* • Jack Palance *Duke/Curly Washburn* • Patricia Wettig *Barbara Robbins* • Pruitt Taylor Vince *Bud* • Bill McKinney *Matt* • Lindsay Crystal *Holly Robbins* • Beth Grant *Lois* ■ *Dir* Paul Weiland • *Scr* Billy Crystal, Lowell Ganz, Babaloo Mandel

City Streets ★★★

Crime melodrama 1931 · US · BW · 73min

This is the story of mobster's daughter Sylvia Sidney, jailed for a crime she didn't commit, and her romance with carnival worker Gary Cooper, who finds himself in trouble as a result of their involvement. One of the key offerings of its period, the film introduced Sylvia Sidney, the brilliantly understated stage actress with the born-to-suffer face, and made her an instant star at Paramount. Although this gangster melodrama seems very dated now, the stars and Rouben Mamoulian's innovative, atmospheric direction provide much to enjoy. RK

Gary Cooper *The Kid* • Sylvia Sidney *Nan Cooley* • Paul Lukas *Big Fellow Maskal* • Guy Kibbee *Pop Cooley* • William Boyd (1) *McCoy* • Wynne Gibson *Agnes* • Betty Sinclair *Pansy* • Stanley Fields *Blackie* ■ *Dir* Rouben Mamoulian • *Scr* Max Marcin, Oliver HP Garrett, from a story by Dashiell Hammett

City That Never Sleeps ★★

Detective drama 1953 · US · BW · 90min

Chicago cop Gig Young plans to quit the force, and his wife, for nightclub dancer Mala Powers. To finance his desertion, he accepts an offer from crooked lawyer Edward Arnold to escort gangster William Talman to safety. This moderately entertaining, competently performed crime drama gives an authentic picture of night-time police work in Chicago. RK

Gig Young *Johnny Kelly* • Mala Powers *Sally Connors* • William Talman *Hayes Stewart* • Edward Arnold *Penrod Biddel* • Chill Wills *Joe Chicago* • Marie Windsor *Lydia Biddel* • Paula Raymond *Kathy Kelly* • Otto Hulett *Sgt John Kelly Sr* ■ *Dir* John H Auer • *Scr* Steve Fisher

City under the Sea ★★★ U

Science-fiction adventure 1965 · UK/US · Colour · 83min

Tenuously based on Edgar Allan Poe, with Jules Verne being the main uncredited inspiration, this fanciful mix of comedy adventure and submarine suspense was director Jacques Tourneur's final feature. Vincent Price enjoyably camps it up as the immortal underwater leader of a Cornish contingent of smugglers-turned-gill-men, and the whole subterranean soufflé is highly watchable even if, sadly, it does slide from the poetic to the pathetic. AJ

Vincent Price *Captain, Sir Hugh Tregathion* • David Tomlinson *Harold Tiffin-Jones* • Tab Hunter *Ben Harris* • Susan Hart *Jill Tregellis* • John Le Mesurier *Rev Jonathan Ives* • Henry Oscar *Mumford* • Derek Newark *Dan* ■ *Dir* Jacques Tourneur • *Scr* Charles Bennett, Louis M Heyward, from the poems *The Doomed City (City in the Sea)* and *A Descent into the Maelstrom* by Edgar Allan Poe

A Civil Action ★★★ 15

Courtroom drama based on a true story 1998 · US · Colour · 110min

John Travolta stars as an ambulance chasing attorney who takes on potentially lucrative cases so he can settle out of court and collect his cut. Writer/director Steven Zaillian's film isn't entirely credible, even if the events did actually happen. Travolta's metamorphosis from cynical manipulator to self-destructive righter of wrongs is hard to swallow, and even harder to empathise with. Classy performances all round, though, with a brilliant turn from Robert Duvall. JC Swearing.

John Travolta *Jan Schlichtmann* • Robert Duvall *Jerome Facher* • Tony Shalhoub *Kevin Conway* • William H Macy *James Gordon* • Zeljko Ivanek *Bill Crowley* • Bruce Norris *William Cheeseman* • John Lithgow *Judge Skinner* • Kathleen Quinlan *Anne Anderson* • James Gandolfini *Al Love* • Stephen Fry *Pinder* • Dan Hedaya *John Riley* • Sydney Pollack *Al Eustis* • Kathy Bates *Judge* ■ *Dir* Steven Zaillian • *Scr* Steven Zaillian, from the novel by Jonathan Harr

Civilization ★★★

Silent drama 1916 · US · BW · 102min

Widely considered to be both the father of the western and the founder of the studio system, Thomas Ince was a major player in Hollywood. But his celluloid reputation rests on this pacifist tract – although it's now believed such directors as Raymond West and Reginald Barker actually called the shots. Produced during the First World War, it is set in the kingdom of Wredpryd and has the spirit of Christ possessing a militaristic inventor who persuades the king to terminate a conflict after a tour of the battlefield. Though now deemed naive, it is nonetheless a valuable record of early movie allegory. DP

Herschel Mayall *The King of Wredpryd* • Lola May *Queen Eugenie* • Howard Hickman *Count Ferdinand* • Enid Markey *Katheryn Haldemann* • George Fisher (1) *The Christus* ■ *Dir* Thomas Harper Ince [Thomas Ince], Raymond B West, Reginald Barker • *Scr* C Gardner Sullivan

The Claim ★★★★ 15
Period drama
2000 · UK/Can/Fr · Colour · 115min

This ambitious drama, inspired by *The Mayor of Casterbridge* and set in a gold-rush town, boasts some superb performances. Peter Mullan sells his wife and baby daughter to a gold prospector in return for the claim to a gold mine. Years later, he has built the town of Kingdom Come and enjoys a relationship with a brothel owner (Milla Jovovich), but the past returns to haunt him in the form of his dying wife (Nastassja Kinski) and grown daughter (Sarah Polley). This is beautifully filmed by cinematographer Alwin Kuchler and, despite some underdeveloped characters, is an often haunting tale. JB Violence, swearing, nudity. *DVD*

Peter Mullan *Daniel Dillon* • Milla Jovovich *Lucia* • Wes Bentley *Dalglish* • Nastassja Kinski *Elena Dillon* • Sarah Polley *Hope Dillon* • Shirley Henderson *Annie* ■ *Dir* Michael Winterbottom • *Scr* Frank Cottrell Boyce, from the novel *The Mayor of Casterbridge* by Thomas Hardy • *Cinematographer* Alwin Kuchler • *Music* Michael Nyman

Claire Dolan ★★★ 18
Drama
1998 · US/Fr · Colour · 95min

Lodge H Kerrigan's debut study of a haunted schizophrenic is a visually ambitious and boldly ambiguous film about a prostitute who seeks to start a new life away from her chillingly vicious pimp. Approaching her duties with a clinical detachment, Claire is played with an authentic mixture of suppressed loathing, quiet self-worth and sheer terror by the excellent Katrin Cartlidge, whose determination to escape on her own terms underscores her emotional reserve. DP

Katrin Cartlidge *Claire Dolan* • Vincent D'Onofrio *Elton Garrett* • Colm Meaney *Roland Cain* • Patrick Husted *George* ■ *Dir/Scr* Lodge H Kerrigan

Claire's Knee ★★★★ PG
Comedy
1970 · Fr · Colour · 101min

The fifth of Eric Rohmer's "Six Moral Tales", this is a hypnotic study of temptation, sumptuously shot by Nestor Almendros in the shimmering Annecy sunshine. Although events unfold from the viewpoint of the diplomat Jean-Claude Brialy, the attention, as so often in Rohmer's films, is focused firmly on the emotions of young women, in this case, of the sisters (Laurence De Monaghan and Béatrice Romand) he has been encouraged to flirt with in a bid to experience passion before his wedding. Entertaining and provocative. DP French +subtitles. *DVD*

Jean-Claude Brialy *Jérôme* • Aurora Cornu *Aurora* • Béatrice Romand *Laura* • Laurence De Monaghan *Claire* • Michèle Montel *Madame Walter* • Gérard Falconetti *Gilles* ■ *Dir/Scr* Eric Rohmer • *Producers* Barbet Schroeder, Pierre Cottrell

The Clairvoyant ★★★
Drama
1934 · UK · BW · 80min

Claude Rains was the villain or victim of many a Hollywood melodrama. This underused British actor gets a crack at the lead in this creaky drama from director Maurice Elvey, in which he peddles fake predictions at a music hall until he suddenly starts hitting nails on the head. Rains is impressive throughout, whether faking on the stage, pleading to be taken seriously or explaining his friendship with Jane Baxter to wife Fay Wray. TS

Claude Rains *Maximus* • Fay Wray *Rene* • Jane Baxter *Christine* • Mary Clare *Mother* • Ben Field *Simon* • Athole Stewart *Lord Southwood* • Felix Aylmer *Counsel* • Donald Calthrop *Derelict* ■ *Dir* Maurice Elvey • *Scr* Charles Bennett, Bryan Edgar Wallace, from the novel by Ernst Lothar

Clambake ★ U
Musical
1967 · US · Colour · 97min

Elvis Presley's 25th film – a reworking of *The Prince and the Pauper* – looks like it cost next to nothing, and probably did. It features a perfunctory performance from the King, who has less screen time than his co-star Will Hutchins. The colour is garish, the back projection looks phoney and the songs are below par. TS *DVD*

Elvis Presley *Scott Heyward* • Shelley Fabares *Dianne Carter* • Will Hutchins *Tom Wilson* • Bill Bixby *James Jamison III* • Gary Merrill *Sam Burton* • James Gregory *Duster Heyward* • Amanda Harley *Ellie* • Suzie Kaye *Sally* ■ *Dir* Arthur Nadel • *Scr* Arthur Browne Jr

Le Clan ★★ 15
Drama
2004 · Fr/Swi · Colour · 89min

This offers an often visually striking but relentlessly grim look at masculinity through the story of three young brothers living in Annecy in France after the death of their mother. It's effectively a three-parter, following small-time drug dealer Nicolas Cazalé's feud with a drugs gang, his attempts to rope older brother and ex-con Stéphane Rideau into his plans for revenge, and the affair between youngest brother Thomas Dumerchez and one of Cazalé's male friends. The camera lingers lovingly on male flesh, but the result is neither lyrical nor provocative. LF French +subtitles. Swearing, sexual references, nudity.

Nicolas Cazalé *Marc* • Stéphane Rideau *Christophe* • Thomas Dumerchez *Olivier* • Salim Kechiouche *Hicham* • Bruno Lochet *Father* • Jackie Berroyer *Robert* • Vincent Martinez *Teacher* • Aure Atika *Emilie* ■ *Dir* Gaël Morel • *Scr* Gaël Morel, Chr stophe Honoré

The Clan ★★★★
Crime drama based on a true story
2015 · Arg/Sp · Colcur · 110min

The biggest hit in Argentine cinema history, this gripping film from local hero director Pablo Trapero tells the true story of Arquimedes Puccio (an ice-cold Guillermo Francella) whose government job kidnapping supposed dissidents (dubbed The Disappeared as many victims were never found) ended when the Videla dictatorship collapsed in 1981. Related in gritty Scorsese fashion with striking Hollywood style, this reveals Trapero's storytelling prowess and technical flair, with the tension building to a truly stunning climax. AJ In Spanish. *DVD*

Antonia Bengoechea *Adriana Puccio* • Gastón Cocchiarale *Maguila Puccio* • Guillermo Francella *Arquimedes Puccio* ■ *Dir* Pablo Trapero • *Scr* Pablo Trapero, Esteban Student, Julian Loyala

The Clan of the Cave Bear ★★ 15
Fantasy drama
1986 · US · Colour · 94min

Daryl Hannah is the strange blond prehistoric human who is taken in by a gang of grunting Neanderthals and proceeds to make her own small contribution to the evolution of the species. This boasts a script by acclaimed film-maker John Sayles, but in the end it falls into the worthy but dull category. JF Violence, nudity. *DVD*

Daryl Hannah *Ayla* • Pamela Reed *Iza* • James Remar *Creb* • Thomas G Waites *Broud* • John Doolittle *Brun* • Curtis Armstrong *Goov* • Martin Doyle *Grod* • Adel C Hammoud *Vorn* ■ *Dir* Michael Chapman • *Scr* John Sayles, from the novel by Jean M Auel

Clan of the White Lotus ★★★
Martial arts drama
1980 · HK · Colour · 95min

The year after entering *The 36th Chamber of Shaolin*, Gordon Liu galvanised his position among the most revered old-school kung fu artists in this, one of the most enjoyable examples of the genre. Liu plays a Shaolin warrior who swears to avenge the death of his brother at the hands of the arrogant head of the White Lotus clan; a character affectionately pastiched by Quentin Tarantino in *Kill Bill Vol 2*. The methods employed to counteract his foe's elusiveness are as unexpected as they are elegant. GR Cantonese dubbed.

Chia Hui Liu [Gordon Liu] *Wei-Ting* ■ *Dir* Lo Lieh

The Clandestine Marriage ★★ 15
Period comedy drama
1999 · UK · Colour · 87min

Though gamely directed by Christopher Miles, this 18th-century period piece is a mismatched mating of British talents. Nigel Hawthorne heads the cast as a drunken lord trying to get his family entwined with the nouveau riche, while Joan Collins puts her best bosoms forward as a domineering snob. Alas, they can't convince us there's much wit in the piece. The film's walking waxworks look is impeccable, but it doesn't make us care about the characters. TH Sex scenes.

Nigel Hawthorne *Lord Ogleby* • Joan Collins *Mrs Heidelberg* • Timothy Spall *Sterling* • Tom Hollander *Sir John Ogleby* • Paul Nicholls *Lovewell* • Natasha Little *Fanny* • Cyril Shaps *Canton* ■ *Dir* Christopher Miles • *Scr* Trevor Bentham, from the play by George Coleman the Elder, David Garrick

Clara's Heart ★★★ 15
Melodrama
1988 · US · Colour · 108min

Jamaican resort-hotel maid Clara (Whoopi Goldberg) gives comfort and wise counsel to a grieving couple (Kathleen Quinlan and Michael Ontkean) on vacation after the death of their baby. They then take her back with them to Baltimore to run their lives and that of their "rich kid" son (Neil Patrick Harris). Unashamedly old-fashioned and sentimental, this is a manipulative weepie-cum-feel good movie, expertly assembled by director Robert Mulligan. RK

Whoopi Goldberg *Clara Mayfield* • Michael Ontkean *Bill Hart* • Kathleen Quinlan *Leona Hart* • Neil Patrick Harris *David Hart* • Spalding Gray *Dr Peter Epstein* • Beverly Todd *Dora* • Hattie Winston *Blanche Loudon* ■ *Dir* Robert Mulligan • *Scr* Mark Medoff, from the novel by Joseph Olshan • *Cinematographer* Freddie Francis • *Music* Dave Grusin

Clarence, the Cross-Eyed Lion ★★★ U
Adventure
1965 · US · Colour · 87min

This pilot for the TV series *Daktari* is entertaining, but only hints at the superb blend of comedy and adventure that made the show such a big hit in the 1960s. Marshall Thompson and Cheryl Miller play the heads of an animal behaviour centre deep in the African jungle, going on to become TV regulars. Here, they are upstaged – not only by the wonderful Clarence, but also by movie veterans Richard Haydn and Betsy Drake. DP

Marshall Thompson *Dr Marsh Tracy* • Betsy Drake *Julie Harper* • Cheryl Miller *Paula* • Richard Haydn *Rupert Rowbotham* • Alan Caillou *Carter* • Rockne Tarkington *Juma* ■ *Dir* Andrew Marton • *Scr* Alan Caillou, from a story by Art Arthur, Marshall Thompson

Clash by Night ★★★
Melodrama
1952 · US · BW · 104min

Tough Barbara Stanwyck returns to her seaside home town, marries straight Paul Douglas, but hankers after smooth projectionist Robert Ryan. The top-billed stars are of secondary interest today, however, as this movie features an early appearance by Marilyn Monroe, giving an intelligent and astoundingly sexy performance. What is surprising is that this inexpensive RKO melodrama is from revered émigré director Fritz Lang, who fails to disguise the inherent dullness of the material. TS

Barbara Stanwyck *Mae Doyle* • Paul Douglas *Jerry D'Amato* • Robert Ryan *Earl Pfeiffer* • Marilyn Monroe *Peggy* • J Carrol Naish *Uncle Vince* • Keith Andes *Joe Doyle* ■ *Dir* Fritz Lang • *Scr* Alfred Hayes, David Dortort, from the play by Clifford Odets

Clash by Night ★
Crime drama
1963 · UK · BW · 75min

This British crime drama was released in the US as *Escape by Night* to avoid confusion with the 1952 Fritz Lang melodrama of the same name. The only interesting thing about this bargain-basement tale of escaped prisoners is the sight of Peter Sallis gleefully torching a barn that has already been doused in paraffin. DP

Terence Longdon *Martin Lord* • Jennifer Jayne *Nita Lord* • Harry Fowler *Doug Roberts* • Peter Sallis *Victor Lush* • Alan Wheatley *Ronald Grey-Simmons* • Vanda Godsell *Mrs Grey-Simmons* ■ *Dir* Montgomery Tully • *Scr* Maurice J Wilson, Montgomery Tully, from the novel by Rupert Croft-Brooke

Clash of the Titans ★★★ 12
Fantasy adventure
1981 · US/UK · Colour · 113min

This stodgy rerun of *Jason and the Argonauts* has Perseus, Andromeda and assorted giant livestock going through their mythological paces. Harry Hamlin and Judi Bowker make anaemic lovers, Laurence Olivier overacts as Zeus, but Ray Harryhausen's stop-motion special effects are as wonderfully wobblesome as ever. Fans of the genre will find plenty to enjoy. AT *DVD* *BD*

Laurence Olivier *Zeus* • Harry Hamlin *Perseus* • Claire Bloom *Hera* • Maggie Smith *Thetis* • Ursula Andress *Aphrodite* • Judi Bowker *Andromeda* • Jack Gwillim *Poseidon* • Susan Fleetwood *Athena* • Pat Roach *Hephaestus* • Burgess Meredith *Ammon* • Sian Phillips *Cassiopeia* • Tim Pigott-Smith *Thallo* ■ *Dir* Desmond Davis • *Scr* Beverley Cross

Clash of the Titans ★★★ 12
Fantasy action adventure
2010 · US · Colour · 101min

Hot on the heels of *Percy Jackson and the Lightning Thief* comes this bigger budget mythological adventure, a remake of the 1981 original. *Avatar's* Sam Worthington builds on his action-man credentials as Perseus, the demi-god who must kill the fearsome Kraken to save Andromeda and gain revenge on Hades (Ralph Fiennes), who murdered his family. Perseus's (mostly) human allies – including Mads Mikkelsen and Nicholas Hoult – bring a little humour to the mix, and the film takes pains to squeeze a little character into the action. From the opening harpie attack, through giant scorpions and a wonderfully sinuous Medusa, there's a barrage of spectacle. A sequel, *Wrath of the Titans*, reached cinemas in 2012. AC Violence. *DVD* *BD*

Sam Worthington *Perseus* • Liam Neeson *Zeus* • Ralph Fiennes *Hades* • Gemma Arterton *Io* • Alexa Davalos *Andromeda* • Danny Huston *Poseidon* • Jason Flemyng *Calibos/Acrisius* • Mads Mikkelsen *Draco* ■ *Dir* Louis Leterrier • *Scr* Travis Beacham, Phil Hay, Matt Manfredi, from the 1981 film

Class ★★ 15
Comedy drama
1983 · US · Colour · 94min

This typical sexual rites-of-passage movie is overlaid with dubious 1980s concerns about making money and wearing the right designer clothes. There is something queasily tacky about Jacqueline Bisset debagging her son's schoolfriend in a glass-sided lift, and the rest of this distinctly self-satisfied movie is full of the kind of selfishness that takes you back to the decade of materialism. SH Violence, swearing, drug abuse, sex scenes, nudity. *DVD*

Rob Lowe *Skip* • Andrew McCarthy *Jonathan* • Jacqueline Bisset *Ellen* • Cliff Robertson *Mr Burroughs* • Stuart Margolin *Balaban* • John Cusack *Roscoe* ■ *Dir* Lewis John Carlino • *Scr* Jim Kouf, David Greenwalt

The Class ★★★★ 15
Social drama
2008 · Fr · Colour · 124min

Laurent Cantet's account of a year in the life of a teacher at a tough Paris school was the first French film to win the Palme d'Or since 1987. The film stars real-life teacher François Bégaudeau and is based on his own semi-autobiographical novel *Entre les Murs*. Although Bégaudeau is basically playing himself, the kids were recruited from a real junior high school and improvised their roles around pupils Bégaudeau had taught. *The Class's* undeniable power comes from the film's sly observations of the complex relationship between a (good) teacher and a classroom full of challenging pupils from a variety of ethnic backgrounds. It's subtle, moving and undeniably great cinema. **AS** French +subtitles. *DVD*

François Bégaudeau *François Marin* • Nassim Amrabt *Nassim* • Laura Baquela *Laura* • Cherif Bounaidja Rachedi *Cherif* • Juliette Demaille *Juliette* • Dalla Doucoure *Dalla* ■ *Dir* Laurent Cantet • *Scr* Laurent Cantet, Robin Campillo, François Bégaudeau, from the book *Entre les Murs* by Bégaudeau

Class ★★
Romantic drama 2010 · US · Colour · 100min

Clichés and stereotypes provide an uninspired foundation for this contrived tale of love across the social divide. Rich law student Justin Bruening reluctantly mentors jobless single mum Jodi Lyn O'Keefe for a college project. As the antagonism between them dissipates, the romantic tension increases, but the leads just look awkward. Exaggerated support from Eric Roberts as Bruening's hideously judgemental dad compounds the lack of realism. **SF**

Jodi Lyn O'Keefe *Kylie Burch* • Justin Bruening *Whitt Sheffield* • Eric Roberts *Benjamin Sheffield* • Constance Marie *Victoria* • Catherine Mary Stewart *Julia* ■ *Dir* David S Cass Sr • *Scr* Pamela Wallace

Class Act ★★15
Comedy 1992 · US · Colour · 93min

There's trouble in the high school classroom when a tough street hood and an intellectual nerd swap identities. That's the premise behind this blunt comedy vehicle, built around the talents of one-time rap sensations Kid 'n' Play (Christopher Reid and Christopher Martin). The stars' winning personalities just about make this bearable, despite the fact that the film suffers from in-joke fatigue. **AJ**

Christopher Reid *Duncan Pinderhughes* • Christopher Martin (2) *Blade* • Andre Rosey Brown *Jail burn* • Meshach Taylor *Duncan's dad* • Mariann Aalda *Duncan's mum* ■ *Dir* Randall Miller • *Scr* John Semper, Cynthia Freidlob, from a story by Michael Swerdlick, Wayne Rice, Richard Brenne

Class Action ★★★15
Courtroom drama 1991 · US · Colour · 104min

Gene Hackman and Mary Elizabeth Mastrantonio play dad-and-daughter lawyers in this powerful courtroom drama from British director Michael Apted. Hackman is the concerned, scruffy liberal, while Mastrantonio is the thrusting achiever, with ambition and power suits hiding an essential decency. Unfortunately, the whiff of contrivance takes the edge off several scenes, as the lawyers' personal antipathy invades their working lives, but otherwise this is classy stuff that showcases two actors on top form. **JM** Swearing. *DVD*

Gene Hackman *Jedediah Tucker Ward* • Mary Elizabeth Mastrantonio *Maggie Ward* • Joanna Merlin *Estelle Ward* • Colin Friels *Michael Grazier* • Jonathan Silverman *Brian* • Donald Moffat *Quinn* • Laurence Fishburne *Nick Holbrook* • Jan Rubes *Pavel* • Matt Clark *Judge Symes* ■ *Dir* Michael Apted • *Scr* Carolyn Shelby, Christopher Ames, Samantha Shad

Class of '44 ★★15
Drama 1973 · US · Colour · 95min

It's graduation time at a Brooklyn high school, and three close friends must part; Oliver Conant goes off to war, while Jerry Houser and Gary Grimes enrol in college. This is a recycled version of Robert Mulligan's hugely successful *Summer of '42*, using the same screenwriter, characters and lead actors. Made with evocative attention to period detail and trading on the

charm of Grimes and his co-stars, it's OK, but not more. **RK**

Gary Grimes *Hermie* • Jerry Houser *Oscy* • Oliver Conant *Benjie* • William Atherton *Fraternity president* • Sam Bottoms *Marty* • Deborah Winters *Julie* • Joe Ponazecki *Professor* • Murray Westgate *Principal* ■ *Dir* Paul Bogart • *Scr* Herman Raucher

The Class of Miss MacMichael ★★★15
Comedy drama 1978 · UK · Colour · 94min

This chalkface bungle features two watchable, hyperactive performances by Glenda Jackson and Oliver Reed. At a special needs school, he's the headmaster who's a brute to the kids but a charmer with the parents, while she's a dedicated teacher whose caring integrity manages to break through student hostility. There's more sexual permissiveness unleashed here than in other teenage dramas of the time but, when Jackson and Reed are absent, this doesn't make it any more watchable. **TH** Some swearing, violence.

Glenda Jackson *Conor MacMichael* • Oliver Reed *Terence Sutton* • Michael Murphy (1) *Martin* • Rosalind Cash *Una Ferrar* • John Standing *Fairbrother* • Riba Akabusi *Gaylord* • Phil Daniels *Stewart* • Patrick Murray *Boysie* • Sylvia O'Donnell *Marie* • Sharon Fussey *Belinda* ■ *Dir* Silvio Narizzano • *Scr* Judd Bernard, from the novel by Sandy Hutson

Class of 1984 ★★18
Drama 1982 · Can · Colour · 93min

This ultra-violent, ultra-cynical thriller built up something of a cult following: it spawned two equally nasty sequels, and continues to inspire bigger-budgeted imitators (*The Principal*, *The Substitute*). Perry King stars as the dedicated teacher who takes the law into his own hands to wrest control of his school back from psycho Timothy Van Patten and his chums, who are terrorising students and staff alike. Director Mark L Lester stages the set pieces with ruthless efficiency. **JF** *DVD*

Perry King *Andy Norris* • Timothy Van Patten *Peter Stegman* • Merrie Lynn Ross *Diane Norris* • Roddy McDowall *Terry Corrigan* • Al Waxman *Detective Stawiski* • Lisa Langlois *Patsy* • Michael J Fox *Arthur* ■ *Dir* Mark L Lester • *Scr* John Saxton, Mark L Lester, from a story by Tom Holland

Class of 1999 ★★18
Science fiction 1990 · US · Colour · 92min

This sequel to *Class of 1984* - directed, like the original, by Mark L Lester - presents the high school of the future as a violent battleground. It's so bad the teachers have been replaced by robots who can supposedly handle the psychopathic kids. Brutal and camp at the same time, this tale fails because Lester thinks he can insert a message into the mayhem. A further sequel followed. **JB** *DVD*

Malcolm McDowell *Dr Miles Langford* • Bradley Gregg *Cody Culp* • John P Ryan *Mr Hardin* • Pam Grier *Ms Connors* • Stacy Keach *Dr Bob Forrest* • Traci Lin [Traci Lind] *Christine Langford* ■ *Dir* Mark L Lester • *Scr* C Courtney Joyner, from a story by Mark L Lester

The Class of '92 ★★★★12
Documentary 2013 · UK · Colour · 95min

This unique documentary tells the story of six young football players - David Beckham, Ryan Giggs, Paul Scholes, Nicky Butt and the Neville brothers - who were brought through the Manchester United ranks at the same time, and charts the careers that have made them club legends. With the glorious 1998-99 Treble season as its backbone, an unbelievable journey is relived through old footage and narrated by famous football names. **JL** Swearing.

David Beckham • Ryan Giggs • Phil Neville • Gary Neville • Paul Scholes ■ *Dir* Benjamin Turner, Gabe Turner

Class of Nuke 'Em High ★18
Science-fiction horror 1986 · US · Colour · 81min

This typically bargain-basement production from Troma, the no-frills company who

brought us the cult-ish *Toxic Avenger* movies, follows a bunch of high school kids who suffer radiation mutation from a local nuclear plant. It's awfully acted, insanely scripted and cluelessly directed. Two sequels followed. **JC** *DVD* *BL*

Janelle Brady *Chrissy* • Gilbert Brenton *Warren* • Robert Prichard *Spike* • RL Ryan *Mr Paley* • James Nugent Vernon *Eddie* • Brad Dunker *Gonzo* • Gary Schneider *Pete* ■ *Dir* Richard W Haines, Samuel Weil [Lloyd Kaufman] • *Scr* Richard W Haines, Mark Rudnitsky, Samuel Weil [Lloyd Kaufman], Stuart Strutin, from a story by Richard W Haines

La Classe de Neige ★★★15
Psychological thriller 1998 · Fr · Colour · 97min

This potentially gripping drama suffers from indifferent handling, despite a heroic performance from Clément Van Den Bergh as the anxiety-ridden outsider at a school ski camp. Director Claude Miller makes effective use of the wintry light and the stunning snowscapes, which help get across the central theme of imagination and reality becoming dangerously intertwined. But Miller can't disguise the gaping holes in the screenplay. **DP** French +subtitles. .

Clément Van Den Bergh *Nicolas* • Lokman Nalcakan *Hodkann* • François Roy *The father* • Yves Verhoeven *Patrick* • Emmanuelle Bercot *Miss Grimm* ■ *Dir* Claude Miller • *Scr* Claude Miller, Emmanuel Carrère, from a novel by Emmanuel Carrère • *Cinematographer* Guillaume Schiffman

Classe Tous Risques ★★★12
Crime drama 1959 · Fr/It · BW · 108min

This very early feature by Claude Sautet is clearly influenced as much by the gangster thrillers of Jean-Pierre Melville as Hollywood genre fare. Lino Ventura plays a mobster hiding out in Nice with his two children. His former associates in Paris hire a hitman to kill him, but the two men become friends. Ventura is a sort of French Bogart and carries a romantic sense of doomy heroism. As the killer who switches allegiances, Jean-Paul Belmondo is all youth and recklessness. **AT** In French. *DVD* *BL*

Lino Ventura *Abel Davos* • Sandra Milo *Liliane* • Jean-Paul Belmondo *Eric Stark* • Marcel Dalio *Arthur Gibelin* • Jacques Dacqmine *Blot* • Claude Cerval *Raoul Fargier* ■ *Dir* Claude Sautet • *Scr* José Giovanni, Claude Sautet, Pascal Jardin, from Giovanni's novel

Claudia ★★★★
Comedy drama 1943 · US · BW · 91min

Dorothy McGuire makes an enchanting film debut here, reprising the title role she played on Broadway in Rose Franken's popular play. Her performance as a young woman coming to terms with married life is the highlight of a film that's unusually frank for its time about domestic issues. Robert Young is perfectly cast as McGuire's husband and Ina Claire does well as her ailing mother. A less effective but equally well-acted sequel, *Claudia and David*, followed. **TS**

Dorothy McGuire *Claudia* • Robert Young (1) *David Naughton* • Ina Claire *Mrs Brown* • Reginald Gardiner *Jerry Seymour* • Olga Baclanova *Madame Daruska* • Jean Howard *Julie* ■ *Dir* Edmund Goulding • *Scr* Morrie Ryskind, from the play by Rose Franken

Claudia and David ★★★
Comedy drama 1946 · US · BW · 77min

This follow-up to 1943's charming *Claudia* continues the ever-so-slight tale of the titular couple as they have a son and discover what really matters in life. Keeping sentiment at bay, Dorothy McGuire and her underrated screen partner Robert Young turn in suitably enthusiastic performances. Effortlessly directed by talented Walter Lang, this lacks the then-daring plotline of its predecessor, but is engaging nevertheless. **TS**

Dorothy McGuire *Claudia* • Robert Young (1) *David* • Mary Astor *Elizabeth Van Doren* • John Sutton *Phil Dexter* • Gail Patrick *Julia Naughton* • Rose Hobart *Edith Dexter* • Harry Davenport *Dr*

Harry • Florence Bates *Nancy Riddle* ■ *Dir* Walter Lang • *Scr* Rose Franken, William Brown Meloney, from the story by Franken

Claudine ★★★
Drama 1974 · US · Colour · 92min

This looks at the tribulations of a single black mother, attempting to rear six children in an urban environment, and her relationship with her refuse collector boyfriend. Well directed by John Berry, this engaging drama is beautifully played by Diahann Carroll (who was nominated for a best actress Oscar), James Earl Jones and an excellent cast of youngsters. Devoid of the usual dose of drugs and crime, the film points up the problems of the working-class black community. **RK**

Diahann Carroll *Claudine* • James Earl Jones *Roop* • Lawrence Hilton-Jaques [Lawrence-Hilton Jacobs] *Charles* • Tamu *Charlene* • David Kruger *Paul* • Yvette Curtis *Patrice* ■ *Dir* John Berry • *Scr* Tina Pine [Tina Rome], Lester Pine

The Clay Bird ★★★PG
Period political drama 2002 · Fr/Ban · Colour · 98min

Despite lacking the budget to fully re-create the tide of social unrest that swept through East Pakistan in the late 1960s, director Tareque Masud nevertheless succeeds in conveying the tensions and prejudices that led to the foundation of an independent Bangladesh by focusing on the trials of one divided family. Homeopath Jayanto Chattopadhyay's rigid adherence to traditional Muslim beliefs may seem overly melodramatic, while his son Nuril Islam Bablu's contrasting school experiences smack of contrivance. But the discussion of how unthinking religious belief and political commitment can provoke violent extremism remains valid. **DP** Bengali +subtitles.

Nuril Islam Bablu *Anu* • Russell Farazi *Rokon* • Jayanto Chattopadhyay *Kazi* • Rokeya Prachy *Ayesha* • Soaeb Islam *Milon* ■ *Dir* Tareque Masud • *Scr* Tareque Masud, Catherine Masud

The Clay Pigeon ★★★
Thriller 1949 · US · BW · 63min

This bracingly efficient thriller from stalwart director Richard Fleischer stars Bill Williams as the amnesiac sailor who wakes from a coma to find himself accused of informing on his comrades in a Japanese PoW camp. With a taut screenplay from *High Noon* writer Carl Foreman, and crisp photography from Robert De Grasse, Williams's gradual enlightenment is made more gripping by the knowledge that it was based on an actual incident in southern California. **DP**

Bill Williams *Jim Fletcher* • Barbara Hale *Martha Gregory* • Richard Quine *Ted Niles* • Richard Loo *Ken Tokoyama* • Frank Fenton *Lt Cmdr Prentice* • Martha Hyer *Miss Harwick* ■ *Dir* Richard O Fleischer [Richard Fleischer] • *Scr* Carl Foreman, from his story

Clay Pigeons ★★★15
Black comedy 1998 · US · Colour · 103min

Joaquin Phoenix, Janeane Garofalo and Vince Vaughn embark on an entertaining and harrowing road trip in director David Dobkin's psychological comedy about double-double-cross and serial killing in Montana. Phoenix is a young man with a past who is befriended by a serial killer - and every woman he introduces to him seems to wind up dead. Bringing a satirical edge to the weather-beaten sleazy crime genre, this features a great Golden Oldie soundtrack. **AJ** Violence, swearing, sex scenes, drug abuse, nudity. *DVD*

Joaquin Phoenix *Clay* • Vince Vaughn *Lester* • Janeane Garofalo *Agent Shelby* • Gregory Sporleder *Earl* • Georgina Cates *Amanda* • Scott Wilson *Sheriff Mooney* ■ *Dir* David Dobkin • *Scr* Matthew Healy • *Cinematographer* Eric Edwards [Eric Alan Edwards]

Clean ★★★★15
Drama 2004 · Fr/UK/Can · Colour · 106min

This moving and elegiac overview of the present and possible future of a drug-addled former rock celebrity (played by Maggie Cheung) is beautifully paced with brilliant perfomances. After the death of her equally addicted rock-singer husband, Cheung sets out to find a better, cleaner life that will include her son (James Dennis). Now in the custody of her husband's parents (Nick Nolte and Martha Henry) in Canada, the child barely knows his mother and what he does know, he hates. Shot in a confident and unhurried style, this is a mature piece of work from director Olivier Assayas. KK English, French, Cantonese +subtitles. Swearing, drug abuse. **DVD**

Maggie Cheung *Emily Wang* • Nick Nolte *Albrecht Hauser* • Béatrice Dalle *Elena* • Jeanne Balibar *Irene Paolini* • Don McKellar *Vernon* • Martha Henry *Rosemary Hauser* • James Johnston *Lee* • James Dennis *Jay* ■ *Dir* Olivier Assayas • *Scr* Olivier Assayas

Clean and Sober ★★★ 15
Drama 1988 · US · Colour · 118min

Although he made his name as a comic, Michael Keaton has always impressed in dramatic roles, particularly those with a darker tinge. This was his first real foray into straight territory, and he delivers a mesmerising performance as a cynical, bitter drug addict in rehab who slowly learns to face up to his responsibilities. Although Glenn Gordon Caron's direction is too small-scale, there's no denying this film's power. JF

Michael Keaton *Daryl Poynter* • Kathy Baker *Charlie Standers* • Morgan Freeman *Craig* • M Emmet Walsh *Richard Dirks* • Luca Bercovici *Lenny* • Tate Donovan *Donald Towle* • Henry Judd Baker *Xavier* • Claudia Christian *Iris* ■ *Dir* Glenn Gordon Caron • *Scr* Tod Carroll

Clean Slate ★★★ 12
Comedy 1994 · US · Colour · 102min

Wayne's World star Dana Carvey plays a detective with a rare form of amnesia in this mildly amusing comedy. Every morning he wakes up with his memory wiped completely clean of the previous day's events – a particularly unfortunate occurrence seeing he's the key witness in a Mob trial. Chuckles may be thin on the ground during Carvey's constant manic memory refreshment, but the endearingly dotty premise proves compelling. AJ **DVD**

Dana Carvey *Maurice Pogue* • Valeria Golino *Sarah/Beth* • James Earl Jones *Dolby* • Kevin Pollak *Rosenheim* • Michael Gambon *Cornell* • Michael Murphy (1) *Dr Doover* • Jayne Brook *Paula* • Vyto Ruginis *Hendrix* • Olivia D'Abo *Judy* ■ *Dir* Mick Jackson • *Scr* Robert King

Cleaner ★★ 15
Thriller 2007 · US · Colour · 85min

Renny Harlin is not a director known for subtlety or in-depth characterisation and that's just fine when it to comes to making gleefully over-the-top action movies such as *Die Hard 2* and *The Long Kiss Goodnight*. With *Cleaner*, he seems to have tried to stretch himself and it looks as if it hurt. It's a self-consciously gloomy thriller starring Samuel L Jackson as a former cop who now runs a company that cleans up the mess after a body has been taken away. After one particularly unpleasant job, he becomes mixed up in a mystery involving his ex-partner (Ed Harris, who spends the entire movie looking as if he's about to burst into flames), a beautiful woman (Eva Mendes) whose husband has gone missing, and a brutish detective who starts asking tough questions (Luiz Guzman). JnC **DVD**

Samuel L Jackson *Tom Cutler* • Ed Harris *Eddie Lorenzo* • Eva Mendes *Ann Norcut* • Luis Guzman *Jim Vargas* • Keke Palmer *Rose Cutler* ■ *Dir* Renny Harlin • *Scr* Matthew Aldrich

Cleanskin ★★★ 15
Thriller 2012 · UK · Colour · 103min

This is a rough, tough and often very violent picture that sees Sean Bean play a British secret service agent who's ordered to track down some missing Semtex explosive and the home-grown Islamist suicide cell that possesses it. The title is spy-speak for terrorists with no criminal record who are almost impossible to trace. Bean is his usual gruffly minimalist self, and the film certainly

has ambition – and some memorable fight scenes – but it also lacks the extra oomph that could have done for Bean's action-movie career what *Taken* did for Liam Neeson's. DA Violence, swearing, sex scenes, nudity. **DVD** **Blu**

Sean Bean *Ewan* • Abhin Galeya *Ash* • Charlotte Rampling *Charlotte McQueen* • Peter Polycarpou *Nabil* • Tuppence Middleton *Kate* • Tom Burke *Mark* ■ *Dir/Scr* Hadi Hajaig

Clear and Present Danger ★★★ 12
Political thriller 1994 · US · Colour · 135min

It's no wonder that three first-rank screenwriters were hired to adapt this sequel to *Patriot Games*, as there is so much plot in Tom Clancy's original novel that it's a minor miracle they squeezed it all into 135 minutes. It takes the picture some time to gather momentum, but, once the links between the Colombian drugs barons and some top US officials are established, it's action all the way, with Harrison Ford on commanding form for his second outing as CIA troubleshooter Jack Ryan. Ben Affleck took over the role in 2002 for *The Sum of All Fears*. DP Violence, swearing. **DVD** **Blu**

Harrison Ford *Jack Ryan* • Willem Dafoe *Clark* • Anne Archer *Cathy Ryan* • Joaquim de Almeida *Felix Cortez* • Henry Czerny *Robert Ritter* • Harris Yulin *James Cutter* • Donald Moffat *President Bennett* • Miguel Sandoval *Ernesto Escobedo* ■ *Dir* Phillip Noyce • *Scr* Donald Stewart, Steven Zaillian, John Milius, from the novel by Tom Clancy

Clear History ★★★
Comedy 2013 · US · Colour · 100min

It's a terrible title but try to overlook that. This feature-length comedy is what Larry David has been doing instead of making a ninth series of *Curb Your Enthusiasm*. It's not quite *Curb the Movie* but the riffs and rhythms are very similar. David plays Nathan Flomm, a top marketing guy who becomes a national laughing stock when he blows his chance of a fortune. So he starts a new life in Martha's Vineyard, where years later his billionaire former boss (Jon Hamm) shows up in the same neighbourhood with a gorgeous wife (Kate Hudson) and plans to build a mansion. From there, a deliciously stupid revenge tragedy unfolds, with some weepingly funny moments and a nice cameo from Michael Keaton. DB

Larry David *Nathan Flomm/Rolly DaVore* • Jon Hamm *Will Haney* • Bill Hader *Rags* • Philip Baker Hall *McKenzie* • Kate Hudson *Rhonda* • Michael Keaton *Joe Stumpo* ■ *Dir* Greg Mottola • *Scr* Larry David, Alec Berg, David Mandel, Jeff Schaffer

Clearcut ★★★ 18
Thriller 1992 · Can · Colour · 97min

Since *Dances with Wolves*, Graham Greene has been steadily building up an impressive body of work. As the volatile member of a band of Canadian Indians battling to keep a lumber company off their land, Greene gives a quietly imposing performance that suggests a deep commitment to the cause at issue. The film's subplot, about the corruption of the judicial system, is also handled with restraint, making the sudden outburst of violence even more shocking. DP Violence, swearing.

Ron Lea *Peter Maguire* • Graham Greene (2) *Arthur* • Rebecca Jenkins *Female reporter* • Michael Hogan (3) *Bud Rickets* • Floyd Red Crow Westerman *Wilf Redwing* • Tia Smith *Polly* ■ *Dir* Richard Bugajski [Ryszard Bugajski] • *Scr* Rob Forsyth, from the novel *A Dream Like Mine* by MT Kelly

The Clearing ★★★ 12
Thriller 2004 · US · Colour · 90min

A mature Robert Redford is joined by Helen Mirren and Willem Dafoe in this intriguing, understated kidnap drama. Redford plays a used-car magnate who is kidnapped by Dafoe. The relationship between Redford and Dafoe is marked by subtle shifts in power and knowledge, and is central to the story. However, the suffering of those at home is given equal weight, as wife Mirren muses on marriage and Redford's infidelity.

The acting is solid, as are the production values, but this doesn't quite fulfil its promise. LB Swearing, violence. **DVD**

Robert Redford *Wayne Hayes* • Helen Mirren *Eileen Hayes* • Willem Dafoe *Arnold Mack* • Alessandro Nivola *Tim Hayes* • Matt Craven *Agent Ray Fuller* • Melissa Sagemiller *Jill Hayes* • Wendy Crewson *Louise Miller* • Larry Pine *Tom Finch* • Diana Scarwid *Eva Finch* ■ *Dir* Pieter Jan Brugge • *Scr* Justin Haythe, from a story by Pieter Jan Brugge, Justin Haythe

Cleo from 5 to 7 ★★★★★★ PG
Drama 1961 · Fr · BW and Colour · 85min

This remarkable feature typifies all that was good in French film-making during its celebrated New Wave. Beneath her cool exterior, Corinne Marchand as Cleo manages to convey a range of emotions in the two hours she has to fill waiting for the results of a test for cancer. Writer/director Agnès Varda introduces the unexpected into both the central story and its many diversions, cinematographer Jean Rabier's images of Paris are uncomplicated, and the performances are cleverly stylised. Watch out for a film within the film, featuring Jean-Luc Godard and other New Wave luminaries. DP French +subtitles. **DVD**

Corinne Marchand *Cleo* • Antoine Bourseiller *Antoine* • Dorothée Blanck *Dorothee* • Michel Legrand *Bob, the pianist* • Dominique Davray *Angele* • José-Luis De Villalonga *The Lover* • Jean-Claude Brialy *Actor in comedy film* • Anna Karina *Actor in comedy film* • Eddie Constantine *Actor in comedy film* • Sami Frey *Actor in comedy film* • Danièle Delorme *Actor in comedy film* • Jean-Luc Godard *Actor in comedy film* • Yves Robert *Actor in comedy film* ■ *Dir/Scr* Agnès Varda

Cleopatra ★★★ PG
Historical drama 1934 · US · BW · 101min

Cecil B DeMille's film about Caesar, Anthony and Cleopatra isn't really a historical epic at all; it's a 1930s sex comedy about two guys and a gal who also happen to rule the world. DeMille can't quite jump the major hurdle – that Cleopatra never two-timed Caesar – and thus ends up with two separate stories, but the movie has real charm, if little substance. Colbert is sexy, but both Warren William and Henry Wilcoxon are lummoxes. AT **DVD** **Blu**

Claudette Colbert *Cleopatra* • Warren William *Julius Caesar* • Henry Wilcoxon *Marc Antony* • Gertrude Michael *Calpurnia* • Joseph Schildkraut *Herod* • Ian Keith *Octavian* • C Aubrey Smith *Enobarbus* • Ian MacLaren *Cassius* • Arthur Hohl *Brutus* ■ *Dir* Cecil B DeMille • *Scr* Waldemar Young, Vincent Lawrence, Bartlett McCormick

Cleopatra ★★★ PG
Historical drama 1963 · US · Colour · 240min

Taking inflation into account, *Cleopatra* remains one of the most expensive films ever made: around $40m at the time, roughly $250m in today's money. So why did it cost so much? Well, starting production in wintry England with Peter Finch, Stephen Boyd and director Rouben Mamoulian didn't help matters. Cranking up again in Rome – this time with Joseph L Mankiewicz shooting by day and writing by night – Elizabeth Taylor's frequent illnesses gave the accountants nightmares, even if her on-set romance with Richard Burton was a publicist's dream. The spectacle is the thing, yet the film does succeed in making some sense of an extraordinary moment in history. AT **DVD** **Blu**

Elizabeth Taylor *Cleopatra* • Richard Burton *Mark Antony* • Rex Harrison *Julius Caesar* • Pamela Brown *High priestess* • George Cole *Flavius* • Hume Cronyn *Sosigenes* • Cesare Danova *Apollodorus* • Kenneth Haigh *Brutus* • Andrew Keir *Agrippa* • Martin Landau *Rufio* • Roddy McDowall *Octavian* ■ *Dir* Joseph L Mankiewicz • *Scr* Joseph L Mankiewicz, Ranald MacDougall, Sidney Buchman, from the works of Plutarch, Suetonius and Appian, and the novel *The Life and Times of Cleopatra* by Carlo Mario Franzero • *Costume Designers* Irene Sharaff, Vittorio Nino Novarese, Renie • *Cinematographer* Leon Shamroy • *Production Designer* John De Cuir • *Special Effects* Emil Kosa

Cleopatra Jones ★★ 15
Blaxploitation action drama 1973 · US · Colour · 84min

After napalming opium fields in Turkey, statuesque narcotics agent Tamara Dobson returns to LA to confront Shelley Winters, lesbian queen of the drug underworld. Jack Starrett handles the action well, though clumsy martial arts and comic book theatrics conspire against his vigorous direction. Yet the meld of funky exuberance, urban angst and camp performances make this a heady, badass cocktail. AJ **DVD**

Tamara Dobson *Cleopatra Jones* • Bernie Casey *Reuben* • Brenda Sykes *Tiffany* • Antonio Fargas *Doodlebug* • Bill McKinney *Officer Purdy* • Dan Frazer *Detective Crawford* • Stafford Morgan *Sergeant Kert* • Shelley Winters *Mommy* ■ *Dir* Jack Starrett • *Scr* Max Julien, from a story by Max Julien, Sheldon Keller

Cleopatra Jones and the Casino of Gold ★★ 15
Blaxploitation action drama 1975 · US/HK · Colour · 92min

Super-foxy Tamara Dobson is sent to Hong Kong to free two CIA agents caught in the Chinatown underworld clutches of the evil Dragon Lady (Stella Stevens). The result is more glossy high camp and low-grade action, with the statuesque Dobson piling on the silver eye shadow and changing into increasingly outlandish outfits. Slick and outrageous fun. AJ **DVD**

Tamara Dobson *Cleopatra Jones* • Stella Stevens *Dragon Lady* • Tanny *Mi Ling* • Norman Fell *Stanley Nagel* • Albert Popwell *Matthew Johnson* • Caro Kenyatta *Melvin* ■ *Dir* Chuck Bail • *Scr* William Tennant, from characters by Max Julien

Clerks ★★★★ 18
Comedy 1994 · US · BW · 88min

Director Kevin Smith's prize-winning debut feature is a micro-budget marvel that showcases his dry wit and wonderful sense of the absurd. It focuses on a day in the life of a New Jersey convenience store, where the double act of Brian O'Halloran and Jeff Anderson amuses, charms and offends as they lounge around discussing sex, videos, food prices, sex, *Star Wars* and sex. Their counterculture diatribes are by turn screamingly funny and wincingly accurate, although those of a sensitive nature should be warned. Smith's direction is as delightful as it is often unreliable. AJ Swearing. **DVD** **Blu**

Brian O'Halloran *Dante Hicks* • Jeff Anderson *Randal* • Marilyn Ghiglotti *Veronica* • Lisa Spoonauer *Caitlin* • Jason Mewes *Jay* • Kevin Smith (2) *Silent Bob* ■ *Dir/Scr* Kevin Smith (2)

Clerks II ★★★ 15
Comedy 2006 · US · Colour and BW · 93min

Kevin Smith gets back to his roots with this amiable sequel that's set ten years after his breakthrough movie. On the surface, nothing much has changed: slacker icons Dante and Randal are still stuck in a dead-end job – this time in a fast-food restaurant – and Jay and Silent Bob (played by Smith himself) are still hanging around outside. Dante is about to get married, but his boss (Rosario Dawson) may also be in love with him. The romantic entanglements stretch credibility and a big dance number is worryingly straight-faced. But the joyfully obscene dialogue and set pieces prove that Smith, thankfully, is still growing old disgracefully. JF Swearing. **DVD**

Brian O'Halloran *Dante Hicks* • Jeff Anderson (1) *Randal Graves* • Rosario Dawson *Becky Scott* • Trevor Fehrman *Elias Grover* • Jennifer Schwalbach *Emma* • Jason Mewes *Jay* • Kevin Smith (2) *Silent Bob* • Ben Affleck *Gawking guy* ■ *Dir/Scr* Kevin Smith (2) • *Cinematographer* David Klein

Click ★★ 12
Fantasy comedy drama 2006 · US · Colour · 103min

Adam Sandler reteams with director Frank Coraci (*The Waterboy*, *The Wedding Singer*) in this high-concept comedy that's undermined by queasy sentimentality.

C

Sandler plays a workaholic architect who acquires a universal remote control that allows him to fast-forward through things that peeve him. But he soon realises that skipping life's little obstacles means he misses out on a lot more besides. This is Sandler at his least likeable, and the starry supporting cast struggles to make much headway. JF Swearing, sexual references. **DVD** Blu

Adam Sandler *Michael Newman* • Kate Beckinsale *Donna Newman* • Christopher Walken *Morty* • David Hasselhoff *Mr Ammer* • Henry Winkler *Ted Newman* • Julie Kavner *Trudy Newman* • Sean Astin *Bill* • Jennifer Coolidge *Janine* ■ *Dir* Frank Coraci • *Scr* Steve Koren, Mark O'Keefe • *Cinematographer* Dean Semler

The Client ★★★★ 15
Thriller 1994 · US · Colour · 115min

Lawyer Susan Sarandon takes on the case of her career when young Brad Renfro, who has inadvertently witnessed a Mob-related suicide, asks her to represent him. She soon finds herself up against the full might of the legal establishment led by ambitious federal attorney Tommy Lee Jones while at the same time trying to protect her youthful client from vengeful Mafia hitman Anthony LaPaglia. Director Joel Schumacher isn't noted for his subtlety, but he makes a pretty good go of producing a believable relationship between the stubborn but lonely Sarandon and the rebellious Renfro. JF Violence, swearing. **DVD**

Susan Sarandon *Reggie Love* • Tommy Lee Jones *Roy Foltrigg* • Mary-Louise Parker *Dianne Sway* • Anthony LaPaglia *Barry Muldano* • JT Walsh *McThune* • Anthony Edwards *Clint Von Hooser* • Brad Renfro *Mark Sway* • Will Patton *Sergeant Hardy* ■ *Dir* Joel Schumacher • *Scr* Akiva Goldsman, Robert Getchell, from the novel by John Grisham

Client-9: the Rise and Fall of Eliot Spitzer ★★★ 15
Documentary 2010 · US · Colour · 117min

In this slick documentary, director Alex Gibney (*Enron: the Smartest Guys in the Room*) focuses on the charismatic politician whose involvement with a prostitution ring led to his resignation as Governor of New York in 2008. It is amusing and somewhat sad that a man of Spitzer's energy and repute would succumb to purchasing "girlfriend experiences" for $1,000 per hour, and he relates the sorry tale himself with candour and a certain amount of shame-faced grace. KK Swearing, nudity.

Eliot Spitzer ■ *Dir/Scr* Alex Gibney

Client Seduction ★★
Crime thriller 2014 · Can · Colour · 90min

An attempt to improve her tarnished public image backfires on lawyer Ally Sheedy when she takes up the case of a homeless teen (Rhys Ward) accused of murder in this far-fetched tale of lies, manipulation and mother-daughter conflict. She soon finds everything that she holds dear at risk as her rebellious offspring (a suitably stroppy Annie Clark) falls under the street Svengali's spell. What keeps the TV movie watchable is the shifting power balance between Sheedy and Ward, leading to a reasonable if tension-free climax. SF

Ally Sheedy *Melissa Eco* • Rhys Ward *Greg Milles* • Annie Clark *Abby Eco* • John Ralston *Detective Mike* ■ *Dir* Penelope Buitenhuis • *Scr* Al Kratina

Cliffhanger ★★★★ 15
Action thriller 1993 · US/Neth · Colour · 108min

High adventure and vertigo blend with blood and bullets to make this tension-packed tall tale a spectacular avalanche of escapism. Sylvester Stallone is the rock-climbing "Rocky" clone who loses his nerve during the opening peak rescue and must find it again when a gang of desperate criminals crash-lands during a blizzard on his mountain manor. Nail-biting stunts and photography that's close to the edge are the true stars of this alpine *Die Hard*, directed with breathless energy by Renny Harlin. AJ Swearing, violence. **DVD** Blu

Sylvester Stallone *Gabe Walker* • John Lithgow *Qualen* • Michael Rooker *Hal Tucker* • Janine Turner *Jessie Deighan* • Rex Linn *Travers* • Caroline Goodall *Kristel* • Leon *Kynette* • Craig Fairbrass *Delmar* • Paul Winfield *Walter Wright* ■ *Dir* Renny Harlin • *Scr* Michael France, Sylvester Stallone, from a story by Michael France, from an idea by John Long • *Cinematographers* Alex Thomson, Adam Dale

Clifford's Really Big Movie ★★ U
Animated adventure 2004 · US · Colour · 71min

Clifford the Big Red Dog gets his own big-screen adventure in this spin-off from the children's cartoon series, based on the books by Norman Bridwell. It sees the inexplicably humongous canine (voiced by the late John Ritter) and his regular-sized pals T-Bone and Cleo run away from home to join a floundering troupe of carnival animals. With its unsophisticated plot and flat, simplistic animation, this is an undemanding film that will appeal only to little ones. SF **DVD**

John Ritter *Clifford* • Wayne Brady *Shackelford* • Grey DeLisle *Emily Elizabeth/Mrs Howard* • Jenna Elfman *Dorothy* • John Goodman *George Wolfsbottom* • Jess Harnell *Dirk* • Kel Mitchell *T-Bone* • Judge Reinhold *Larry* ■ *Dir* Robert Ramirez [Robert C Ramirez] • *Scr* Robert Ramirez [Robert C Ramirez], Rhett Reese, from characters by Norman Bridwell

Climates ★★★★ 15
Relationship drama 2006 · Tur/Fr · Colour · 97min

Turkish writer/director Nuri Bilge Ceylan follows up the award-winning *Uzak* (2003) with another masterly but desperately sad study of the difficulties that people have in communicating and committing in an increasingly insular world. Here, the director also stars as Isa, a dour chauvinist academic whose fractured relationship with the younger Bahar (played by real-life spouse Ebru Ceylan) is charted over the course of the changing seasons. Nazan Kesal appears as Isa's ex-lover, whose willingness to tolerate rough treatment sums up the film's contention that even a bad relationship is better than none. Their skilled performances generate a sense of ironic melancholy, while Gokhan Tiryaki's stylish HD cinematography reinforces the mood. DP Turkish +subtitles. A sex scene. **DVD**

Nuri Bilge Ceylan *Isa* • Ebru Ceylan *Bahar* • Nazan Kesal [Nazan Kirilmis] *Serap* • Mehmet Eryilmaz *Mehmet* • Arif Asci *Arif* • Fatma Ceylan *Isa's mother* • Emin Ceylan *Isa's father* ■ *Dir/Scr* Nuri Bilge Ceylan • *Cinematographer* Gokhan Tiryaki

Climbing High ★★ U
Romantic comedy 1938 · UK · BW · 78min

Carol Reed was fortunate to produce anything at all on this occasion, bearing in mind the tensions behind the scenes. Imported American star Kent Taylor quit because of a delayed start, while Jessie Matthews disliked so many of the songs that they were dropped. It speaks volumes for Reed that the end result is not only watchable but rather entertaining, thanks, primarily, to Taylor's replacement, Michael Redgrave, playing a wealthy socialite who falls for penniless Matthews. DP

Jessie Matthews *Diana* • Michael Redgrave *Nicky Brooke* • Noel Madison *Gibson* • Alastair Sim *Max* • Margaret Vyner *Lady Constance* • Mary Clare *Lady Emily* • Francis L Sullivan *Madman* • Enid Stamp-Taylor *Winnie* ■ *Dir* Carol Reed • *Scr* Stephen Clarkson, from a story by Lesser Samuels, Marion Dix

Clive of India ★★★
Biographical drama 1935 · US · BW · 95min

A very famous film of its day, this expensively produced but drearily directed epic offered the perfect role to the immaculately spoken Ronald Colman: Robert Clive, one of Britain's great folk heroes. Colman is marvellous in the role, securing India for Britain at the cost of his own happiness, and it really doesn't matter at all that the real Clive led a completely different life. TS

Ronald Colman *Robert Clive* • Loretta Young *Margaret Maskelyne Clive* • Colin Clive *Captain Johnstone* • Francis Lister *Edmund Maskelyne* • Vernon Downing *Stringer* • Peter Shaw (1) *Miller* • Neville Clark *Vincent* • Ian Wolfe *Kent* ■ *Dir* Richard Boleslawski • *Scr* WP Lipscomb, RJ Minney, from their play *Clive*

Cloak and Dagger ★★★ PG
Spy thriller 1946 · US · BW · 106min

Director Fritz Lang here turns a run-of-the-mill Second World War espionage tale into a gripping thriller that drips with nail-biting tension and brilliantly evokes the bleak atmosphere of the time. Gary Cooper plays the American nuclear research scientist who is sent to learn the secrets of Germany's atomic bomb programme. In hiding with the Resistance in war-torn, Nazi-occupied Italy, he is put in the care of violently anti-Fascist and embittered Lilli Palmer. Cooper is fine, and Palmer, making her American film debut, shows an admirable grasp of a complex character. RK **DVD**

Gary Cooper *Professor Alvah Jesper* • Lilli Palmer *Gina* • Robert Alda *Pinkie* • Vladimir Sokoloff *Dr Polda* • J Edward Bromberg *Trenk* • Marjorie Hoshelle *Ann Dawson* • Charles Marsh *Erich* ■ *Dir* Fritz Lang • *Scr* Albert Maltz, Ring Lardner Jr, from a story by Boris Ingster, John Larkin, from a non-fiction book by Corey Ford, Alastair MacBain

Cloak and Dagger ★★ PG
Adventure thriller 1984 · US · Colour · 96min

ET star Henry Thomas witnesses enemy agents trying to steal government secrets in this contrived update of the 1949 suspense classic, *The Window*. No one believes him apart from the evil spies themselves, so he goes on the run helped by imaginary superhero playmate Jack Flack (Dabney Coleman, who also plays the boy's father). Franklin lurches from tongue-in-cheek humour to exciting espionage, but undercuts any palpable menace by unsuccessfully shuffling the two tones together. AJ

Henry Thomas *Davey Osborne* • Dabney Coleman *Jack Flack/Hal Osborne* • Michael Murphy (1) *Rice* • Christina Nigra *Kim Gardener* • John McIntire *George MacCready* • Jeanette Nolan *Eunice MacCready* ■ *Dir* Richard Franklin • *Scr* Tom Holland

Clochemerle ★★★
Comedy 1948 · Fr · Colour · 94min

Considered indelicate in some quarters on its release, this quaintly bawdy adaptation provides a priceless memoir of provincial France in the 1940s. At issue is whether mayor Jean Brochard has the right to install a new *vespasienne* (or open-air urinal) in the centre of his Beaujolais village. Gently lampooning the national character, director Pierre Chenal dilutes the political satire, but this knowingly played romp is still amusing. DP French +subtitles.

Jean Brochard *Mayor Piéchut* • Simone Michels *Judith Toumignon* • Maximilienne *Justine Putet* • Paul Demange *François Toumignon* • Félix Oudart *Le curé Ponosse* • Cri-Cri Muller [Christiane Muller] *Adele Torbayon* ■ *Dir* Pierre Chenal • *Scr* Pierre Laroche, Gabriel Chevallier, from Chevallier's novel

The Clock ★★★★ U
Romantic drama 1945 · US · BW · 91min

This charming MGM romance contains a beguiling performance from the great Judy Garland, looking radiant and near her professional peak. She and soldier Robert Walker enjoy a brief encounter in New York, and director Vincente Minnelli cleverly makes the city the third character in the movie. There are also some minor players worthy of note: a drunken Keenan Wynn, a sympathetic James Gleason and a speechless Marshall Thompson. A little gem of a movie. TS

Judy Garland *Alice Mayberry* • Robert Walker *Corporal Joe Allen* • James Gleason *Al Henry* • Keenan Wynn *Drunk* • Marshall Thompson *Bill* • Lucile Gleason *Mrs Al Henry* ■ *Dir* Vincente Minnelli • *Scr* Robert Nathan, Joseph Schrank, from a story by Paul Gallico, Pauline Gallico

Clockers ★★★ 18
Crime thriller 1995 · US · Colour · 123min

Spike Lee's urban drama has cop Harvey Keitel investigating a killing. Low-level drug-dealer Mekhi Phifer is the prime suspect, though Phifer's brother Isaiah Washington has confessed to the crime. Not Lee's best work – some critics were distinctly cool about the stark imagery and idiosyncratic cinematography – but for once, at least, the director lets the story deliver the message, instead of imposing it from above. TH Violence, swearing. **DVD**

Harvey Keitel *Rocco Klein* • John Turturro *Larry Mazilli* • Delroy Lindo *Rodney* • Mekhi Phifer *Strike* • Isaiah Washington *Victor* • Keith David *Andre the Giant* • Pee Wee Love *Tyrone* • Regina Taylor *Iris Jeeter* • Tom Byrd [Thomas Jefferson Byrd] *Errol Barnes* ■ *Dir* Spike Lee • *Scr* Richard Price, Spike Lee, from the novel by Richard Price

Clockmaker ★★ U
Science-fiction adventure 1999 · US/Rom · Colour · 82min

In this derivative but genial time-travel adventure, young Anthony Medwetz discovers a collection of clocks controlling the past, present and future in the apartment of an eccentric neighbour. But it takes Zachary McLemore pushing a tempting button for the trouble to start, as he disturbs the time-space continuum and the boys and their 15-year-old friend, Katie Johnston, have to travel to the 19th century to prevent the computer revolution from happening too soon and changing history forever. Owing more to Robert Zemeckis than HG Wells, this sci-fi jaunt should keep undemanding young audiences amused. DP **DVD**

Anthony Medwetz *Henry* • Katie Johnston *Marybeth* • Zachary McLemore *Devon* • Pierrino Mascarino *Markham* • Daisy Nystul *Betty* • Tom Gulager *Bankwell* ■ *Dir* Christopher Remy • *Scr* Benjamin Carr

Clockstoppers ★★ PG
Science-fiction comedy adventure 2002 · US · Colour · 90min

This adventure produced by the children's TV channel Nickelodeon shouldn't have made it past the small screen. Teenager Jesse Bradford discovers a watch among his father's possessions that can stop time, while the wearer can move around unseen. However, Bradford doesn't do anything naughty or novel with it. Instead he impresses the new girl at school (Paula Garcés), gives some bullies a lesson they'll never forget and helps a friend win a contest. StH **DVD**

Jesse Bradford *Zak Gibbs* • Paula Garcés *Francesca* • French Stewart *Dr Earl Dopler* • Michael Biehn *Gates* • Robin Thomas *Dr Gibbs* • Julia Sweeney *Jenny Gibbs* • Garikayi Mutambirwa *Meeker* ■ *Dir* Jonathan Frakes • *Scr* Rob Hedden, J David Stem, David N Weiss, from a story by Rob Hedden, Andy Hedden, J David Stem, David N Weiss

Clockwatchers ★★ 12
Comedy drama 1997 · US · Colour · 91min

In seeking to capture the ennui of office life, director Jill Sprecher succeeds all too well with a film as repetitive and monotonous as its subject. There is much potential in this cast, but they're merely required to do the dramatic equivalent of licking envelopes. As the quartet of temps whose friendship is tested by an outbreak of petty pilfering, they each have moments of inspiration. For the most part, however, they seem subdued by the banality of the script and the slow pace. DP **DVD**

Toni Collette *Iris* • Parker Posey *Margaret* • Lisa Kudrow *Paula* • Alanna Ubach *Jane* • Helen FitzGerald *Cleo* • Stanley DeSantis *Art* • Jamie Kennedy *Eddie* ■ *Dir* Jill Sprecher • *Scr* Jill Sprecher, Karen Sprecher

Clockwise ★★★ PG
Comedy 1986 · UK · Colour · 91min

John Cleese stars as a headmaster with a mania for punctuality who has to travel to Norwich for a conference. When he boards the wrong train, the result is an increasingly frenzied cross-country dash with a

U SUITABLE FOR ALL Uc SUITABLE ESPECIALLY FOR YOUNG CHILDREN (DVD ONLY) PG PARENTAL GUIDANCE 12A UNDER 12s TO BE ACCOMPANIED (CINEMA ONLY)

schoolgirl and a former girlfriend in tow. Cleese finds it difficult to be unfunny, and he unravels here much like Basil Fawlty, from a simmering starting point to a climax of epic proportions. JF Swearing. **DVD**

John Cleese *Brian Stimpson* • Alison Steadman *Gwenda Stimpson* • Penelope Wilton *Pat* • Stephen Moore *Mr Jolly* • Sharon Maiden *Laura* • Constance Chapman *Mrs Wheel* • Joan Hickson *Mrs Trellis* • Ann Way *Mrs Way* • Pat Keen *Mrs Wisely* • Geoffrey Hutchings *Mr Wisely* ■ *Dir* Christopher Morahan • *Scr* Michael Frayn

Clockwork Mice ★★★ 15
Drama   1994 · UK · Colour · 94min

Director Vadim Jean skirts the harsher side of life in a special needs school to concentrate on the unlikely friendship between unruly Ruaidhri Conroy and Ian Hart, the novice teacher convinced he can make a difference. The staffroom romance makes for a pleasing diversion and there are expert cameos from John Alderton and James Bolam. With its heart a little too determinedly on its sleeve, this is still an involving, amusing and rather sad film. DP Swearing, brief nudity. **DVD**

Ian Hart *Steve Drake* • Ruaidhri Conroy *Conrad James* • Catherine Russell *Polly* • Art Malik *Laney* • Claire Skinner *Fairy* • Nigel Planer *Parkey* • John Alderton *Swaney* • James Bolam *Wackey* • Lilly Edwards *Mrs Charlton* • Robin Soans *Millwright* ■ *Dir* Vadim Jean • *Scr* Rod Woodruff

LANDMARK FILM
Highly provocative, this important work of art is so powerful that countless images from it are still familiar today

A Clockwork Orange
★★★★ 18
Futuristic drama   1971 · UK · Colour · 130min

Withdrawn from release by director Stanley Kubrick in 1974 and officially unseen until 1999 (after his death), *A Clockwork Orange* suffers from an artificially inflated degree of mythology. Adapted from the 1962 Anthony Burgess novel about anarchic yobs in a grey, dystopian future, it was shocking then and remains shocking today, particularly the scenes of rape and sadistic violence in the first half. But such unpleasant excesses make important points about the dangers of two-tier totalitarianism, and the scenes in which ringleader Malcolm McDowell is relentlessly brainwashed into submission send an ambiguous message. Kubrick's vision is a thing to behold; whether it's an actual masterpiece remains up for debate. AC Violence, swearing, sex scenes, nudity. **DVD**

Malcolm McDowell *Alex* • Patrick Magee *Mr Alexander* • Warren Clarke *Dim* • James Marcus *Georgie* • Adrienne Corri *Mrs Alexander* • Miriam Karlin *Cat Lady* • Aubrey Morris *Deltoid* • Michael Bates *Chief guard* • Michael Tarn *Pete* • Steven Berkoff *Constable* • David Prowse [Dave Prowse] *Julian* • Carl Duering *Dr Brodsky* ■ *Dir* Stanley Kubrick • *Scr* Stanley Kubrick, from the novel by Anthony Burgess • *Cinematographer* John Alcott • *Editor* Bill Butler • *Production Designer* John Barry (2) • *Music* Walter Carlos [Wendy Carlos]

Clone ★★ 15
Romantic science-fiction drama
2010 · Ger/Hun/Fr · Colour · 107min

The path of true love takes a macabre turn for Eva Green (*Casino Royale*) and *Doctor Who's* Matt Smith in this unsettling romantic drama. Long-lost childhood friends Rebecca and Tommy fall in love when they are reunited as adults. After a fatal car accident, the devastated Rebecca decides to give birth to and raise her lover's clone. But will the line between maternal love and desire become blurred? It's taboo-challenging stuff that's given substance by Benedek Fliegauf's art house direction. But the languid mood borders on the tedious as the story twists and turns towards its inevitable but long-winded all-will-be-revealed ending. JA **DVD**

Matt Smith *Thomas* • Eva Green *Rebecca* • Lesley Manville *Judith* • Peter Wight *Ralph* • Istvan Lenart *Henry* • Hannah Murray *Monica* ■ *Dir/Scr* Benedek Fliegauf

Close Encounters of the Third Kind ★★★★★ PG
Science-fiction drama
1977 · US · Colour · 126min

Steven Spielberg's brilliantly realised suburban sci-fi saga reverses years of flying saucer attacks with the notion that visitors from outer space just might be friendly. Richard Dreyfuss strikes the perfect note of childlike inquisitiveness as the man "chosen" to make contact with alien lifeforms, despite obstruction by family and government. Spielberg confirms his genius for painting a convincing picture of mundane domestic life, subsequently shattered by extraordinary events (notably the terrifying kidnap of a young boy and Dreyfuss's slide into apparent insanity). The special effects are spectacular, John Williams's score is emotionally charged, and it's impossible not to get caught up in the protracted climax. AC **DVD**

Richard Dreyfuss *Roy Neary* • François Truffaut *Claude Lacombe* • Teri Garr *Ronnie Neary* • Melinda Dillon *Jillian Guiler* • Bob Balaban *David Laughlin* • J Patrick McNamara *Project leader* • Warren Kemmerling *Wild Bill* • Roberts Blossom *Farmer* ■ *Dir/Scr* Steven Spielberg • *Cinematographer* Vilmos Zsigmond • *Music* John Williams • *Production Designer* Joe Alves • *Art Director* Dan Lomino • *Set Designer* Phil Abramson • *Special Effects* Douglas Trumbull, Roy Arbogast, Gregory Jein, Matthew Yuricich, Richard Yuricich

Close My Eyes ★★★ 18
Drama   1991 · UK · Colour · 104min

In this overwrought and claustrophobic drama, Saskia Reeves and Clive Owen star as siblings who become a little too close for comfort. Stephen Poliakoff, as both writer and director, handles the controversial subject matter with sensitivity and he is rewarded with two heart-rendingly intense performances from his leads. However, the best playing comes from Alan Rickman as Reeves's husband, who delivers a witty yet melancholic performance. JF Swearing, sex scenes, nudity. **DVD**

Alan Rickman *Sinclair Bryant* • Clive Owen *Richard Gillespie* • Saskia Reeves *Natalie Gillespie* • Karl Johnson (2) *Colin* • Lesley Sharp *Jessica* ■ *Dir/Scr* Stephen Poliakoff

Close to Home ★★★★ 15
Political satire   2005 · Is · Colour · 94min

A slyly subversive insight into the role of women in the Israeli military, this is a surprisingly compassionate satire that makes its political points without resorting to caricature. Indeed, debuting writer/directors Vidi Bilu and Dalia Hager impose such a matter-of-fact tone on the episodic, fact-based proceedings that the dangers faced by two feckless conscripts and the harassment of Palestinians they encounter seem almost routine. While Bilu and Hager concentrate more on the small acts of rebellion that the two commit against their superiors, they also use a shocking downtown bomb attack to reveal the threat posed to national security by the ineptitude of such disaffected troops. DP Hebrew, Arabic +subtitles. **DVD**

Naama Schendar *Mirit* • Smadar Sayar *Smadar* ■ *Dir/Scr* Dalia Hager, Vidi Bilu

Close to My Heart ★★★
Drama   1951 · US · BW · 90min

The beautiful Gene Tierney and the dependable Ray Milland star as a couple in the process of adopting a baby from an orphanage, run by Fay Bainter. When they discover that the baby's father was a murderer, they nevertheless proceed with the adoption. Written and directed by William Keighley, this is a serviceable tale that combines drama with soap opera sentimentality and suggests environment is ultimately more important than heredity. RK

Ray Milland *Brad Sheridan* • Gene Tierney *Midge Sheridan* • Fay Bainter *Mrs Morrow* • Howard St John *EO Frost* • Mary Beth Hughes *Arlene* • Ann Morrison *Mrs Barker* • James Seay *Heilner* ■

Dir William Keighley • *Scr* James R Webb, from his story *A Baby for Midge* • *Cinematographer* Robert Burks • *Music* Max Steiner

Close-Up ★★★★ U
Experimental documentary drama
1989 · Iran · Colour · 93min

Dazzling in its simple ingenuity, this fantasy on a true story is widely regarded as Abbas Kiarostami's masterpiece. The premise sounds complicated, with the action constantly cross-cutting between Hossain Sabzian's trial for impersonating celebrated Iranian director Mohsen Makhmalbaf, and reconstructions of the way in which he duped a family into believing their son was to star in one of his films. However, such is Kiarostami's mastery of his material and his delicious sense of mischief in exploring the contrasts between art and life that everything slots into place with awesome precision. DP Farsi +subtitles. **DVD**

Hossain Sabzian *Himself* • Mohsen Makhmalbaf *Himself* • Abolfazl Ahankhah *Father* • Mehrdad Ahankhah *Son* • Manoochehr Ahankhah *Son* • Mahrokh Ahankhah *Daughter* • Nayer Mohseni Zonoozi *Daughter* • Abbas Kiarostami ■ *Dir/Scr* Abbas Kiarostami

A Closed Book ★★ 15
Thriller   2009 · UK · Colour · 84min

In this disappointing thriller, Tom Conti plays a blind author and art critic whose seclusion in his palatial country home is ended when he hires an assistant to help him write an autobiography. Enter Daryl Hannah, whose helpful demeanour soon fades to reveal a sinister secret agenda. Essentially a claustrophobic two-handed psycho-drama (like *Sleuth*), the film benefits from the all-too-rare starring role from Conti, but the cat-and-mouse plot fizzles out long before its lacklustre finale. JA

Tom Conti *Sir Paul* • Daryl Hannah *Jane Ryder* • Miriam Margolyes *Mrs Kilbride* • Simon MacCorkindale *Andrew Boles* • Elaine Paige *Canvasser* ■ *Dir* Raoul Ruiz • *Scr* Gilbert Adair, from his novel

Closed Circuit ★★ 15
Thriller   2013 · UK/US · Colour · 96min

After a bomb in London leaves many dead, barrister Eric Bana defends the sole surviving suspect. However, when Bana's ex-lover Rebecca Hall is appointed as special advocate to the case, the pair find both their careers and lives in jeopardy as they unravel a far-reaching conspiracy. On paper, the film has the makings of a taut and clever thriller, but director John Crowley is forced to spend so much screen time explaining the legal complexities of terrorist trials that the pace never gets into top gear. The clunky dialogue makes the leads appear wooden, with only Jim Broadbent as a government bigwig with a hidden agenda making any real impact. TeS Violence, swearing. **DVD**

Eric Bana *Martin Rose* • Rebecca Hall *Claudia Simmons-Howe* • Ciarán Hinds [Ciaran Hinds] *Devlin* • Jim Broadbent *Attorney General* • Riz Ahmed [Rizwan Ahmed] *Nazrul Sharma* • Kenneth Cranham *Cameron Fischer* ■ *Dir* John Crowley • *Scr* Steven Knight

Closely Observed Trains ★★★★ 15
Second World War comedy drama
1966 · Cz · BW · 88min

One of the key pictures of the Czech New Wave of the mid-1960s, this is a superbly controlled piece of cinema that deserved its Oscar for best foreign language film. Set during the Nazi occupation, the film follows the bungled efforts of a bashful young apprentice railway guard to lose his virginity, seduce the stationmaster's wife and commit suicide. After a variety of misadventures, he meets a beautiful resistance fighter who finally offers him the chance to prove himself. Employing a complex, episodic structure, Jiří Menzel - making his feature debut - seamlessly dovetails satire, romance, heroism and the horror of war to devastating tragicomic effect. DP Czech +subtitles. **DVD**

Vaclav Neckar *Milos Hrma* • Jitka Bendova *Masa* • Vladimir Valenta *Stationmaster* • Josef Somr [Josef Sommer] *Hubicka* • Libuse Havelkova *Stationmaster's wife* ■ *Dir* Jiří Menzel • *Scr* Jiří Menzel, Bohumil Hrabal

Closer ★★★ 15
Relationship drama   2004 · US · Colour · 99min

Adapted by Patrick Marber from his own achingly modish hit play, this follows a quartet of London urbanites (played by Julia Roberts, Jude Law, Natalie Portman and Clive Owen) as their love lives intertwine and they inflict emotional damage on each other. The performances are as warm as the deliberately stagey dialogue will allow, with Owen the standout as aggressive consultant Larry, while Mike Nichols's superficial but elegant direction and Stephen Goldblatt's glossy photography give the story a sheen of sophistication. AS Swearing. **DVD BD**

Julia Roberts *Anna* • Jude Law *Dan* • Natalie Portman *Alice* • Clive Owen *Larry* ■ *Dir* Mike Nichols • *Scr* Patrick Marber, from his play • *Cinematographer* Stephen Goldblatt

Closer to the Moon ★★ 12A
Heist comedy based on a true story
2014 · Rom/US · Colour · 112min

It's Romania, 1959. As a kick against Jewish oppression under the Communist regime, five idealists decide to rob the state bank to fund their dissident activities - under the pretence of making a heist movie. Caught by the authorities, they're bizarrely forced to re-stage their robbery for a propaganda film. The story is so quintessentially Romanian, it should have been made in Romanian, with Romanian actors. Instead, it has Mark Strong and Vera Farmiga and, though decently made, it won't have much impact. DA Violence, swearing, sex scenes.

Vera Farmiga *Alice* • Mark Strong *Max Rosenthal* • Harry Lloyd *Virgil* • Anton Lesser *Holban* ■ *Dir/Scr* Nae Caranfil

The Closer We Get ★★★ PG
Documentary   2015 · UK/Eth · Colour · 91min

When her elderly mother's stroke leaves her needing constant care, Scottish film-maker Karen Guthrie returns to the family nest. In this hour of crisis, her father also moves back in, and Guthrie takes the opportunity to reveal his past misadventures. Other people's families are, of course, endlessly fascinating, and the Guthrie saga is certainly a dramatic one. This small-scale documentary offers a tender, intimate portrayal, though it's never quite bereft of the feeling that Guthrie is taking advantage of her family. That misgiving aside, it is a compelling watch. TJ Some swearing.

■ *Dir/Scr* Karen Guthrie

The Closer You Get ★★★ 12
Comedy   2000 · Ire/UK · Colour · 88min

Uberto Pasolini, producer of *The Full Monty*, strays into *Waking Ned* territory with this ribald piece of Oirish whimsy. Screenwriter William Ivory has concocted an amiable fable about the sexual frustrations of a small Donegal community, which would rather resort to Florida beach babes and Spanish trawlermen than see beneath the workaday façade of their neighbours. Ian Hart excels as the crotch-obsessed butcher, while Ewan Stewart impresses as a mammy's boy. DP **DVD**

Ian Hart *Kieran* • Sean McGinley *Ian* • Niamh Cusack *Kate* • Ruth McCabe *Mary* • Ewan Stewart *Pat* • Sean McDonagh *Sean* ■ *Dir* Aileen Ritchie • *Scr* William Ivory, from a story by Herbie Wave

The Closet ★★★ 15
Comedy   2001 · Fr · Colour · 81min

With its mix of high camp and mocking machismo, this is a resolutely unreconstructed farce that targets political correctness in France. Daniel Auteuil pretends to be gay in order to avoid redundancy from Jean Rochefort's condom company, and Thierry Lhermitte's mischievous executive dupes the boorish Gérard Depardieu into befriending him to save his own skin. DP French +subtitles. **DVD**

Daniel Auteuil *François Pignon* • Gérard Depardieu *Félix Santini* • Thierry Lhermitte *Guillaume* • Michèle Laroque *Mademoiselle Bertrand* • Jean Rochefort *Kopel, company director* • Alexandra Vandernoot *Christine* ■ *Dir/Scr* Francis Veber

Closet Land ★★★
Political drama 1991 · US · Colour · 95min

Co-executive produced by Ron Howard, with guidance from Amnesty International, this intense drama stars Alan Rickman as an interrogator-cum-torturer and Madeleine Stowe as his victim, an author of children's stories who is accused of subversion. Using a single set – a gleaming, hi-tech interrogation chamber – the drama is heavily allegorical: there are no names, no countries, just a universal symbol of oppression and a nod or two towards Franz Kafka. The sense of claustrophobia is overwhelming, and so are the performances, but Radha Bharadwaj's direction is perhaps better than her script. AT Swearing.

Madeleine Stowe *Woman* • Alan Rickman *Man* ■ *Dir/Scr* Radha Bharadwaj

Closing the Ring ★★★ 12
Romantic drama
2006 · UK/Can/US · Colour · 113min

In 1990s Michigan, Ethel Ann (Shirley MacLaine) attends the funeral of her husband Chuck, accompanied by his old friend Jack (Christopher Plummer). But her tears are not shed for Chuck, and her wartime secret is at the core of director Richard Attenborough's tale of love lost and found again. Mischa Barton shines as the young Ethel Ann in the Second World War flashbacks, though Neve Campbell as Ethel Ann's modern-day daughter is weighed down with moralistic dialogue. The contemporary Belfast-set subplot about the discovery of a gold ring takes a long time to make itself relevant to all the buried emotions, but the performances as a whole are good, and the movie is moving despite being rather corny. KK **DVD**

Shirley MacLaine *Ethel Ann Roberts* • Christopher Plummer *Jack Etty* • Mischa Barton *Young Ethel Ann* • Pete Postlethwaite *Quinlan* • Brenda Fricker *Grandma Reilly* • Neve Campbell *Marie* • Gregory Smith *Young Jack* • Stephen Amell *Teddy Gordon* ■ *Dir* Richard Attenborough • *Scr* Peter Woodward

Cloud Atlas ★★★ 15
Science-fiction fantasy epic
2012 · Ger/US/Chi/HK/Sing/UK/Sp · Colour · 164min

David Mitchell's 2004 source novel was deemed unfilmable because of its elaborate structure – it interweaves six apparently unrelated but obliquely overlapping stories that span 600 years, beginning in the mid-19th century. But directors Andy and Lana Wachowski (*The Matrix*), and Tom Tykwer (*Run Lola Run*) have done a commendable job of bringing this hugely ambitious book to the screen. The sci-fi elements of the story fare best, notably the story of a rebel leader in a Seoul of the future, but the less visually flashy sections (an ageing publisher is imprisoned in an old folks' home) have an eccentric appeal, too. Nevertheless, the film is not helped by its epic length and also problematic is that its stars (including Tom Hanks, Halle Berry and Hugh Grant) in numerous roles each are frequently unrecognisable under wigs and heavy make-up. As an experiment in offbeat blockbuster film-making, however, this has a certain maverick élan. DW Violence, swearing, sex scenes. **DVD BL**

Tom Hanks *Dr Henry Goose/Hotel manager/Isaac Sachs/Dermot Hoggins/Cavendish lookalike actor/Zachry* • Halle Berry *Native woman/Jocasta Ayrs/Luisa Rey/Indian party guest/Ovid/Meronym* • Jim Broadbent *Captain Molyneux/Vyvyan Ayrs/Timothy Cavendish/Korean musician/Prescient 2* • Hugo Weaving *Haskell Moore/Tadeusz Kesselring/Bill Smoke/Nurse Noakes/Boardman Mephi/Old Georgie* • Jim Sturgess *Adam Ewing/Poor hotel guest/Megan's dad/Highlander/Hae-Joo Chang/Zachry's brother-in-law* • Hugh Grant *Reverend Giles*

Horrox/Hotel heavy/Lloyd Hooks/Denholme Cavendish/Seer Rhee/Kona chief • Ben Whishaw *Cabin boy/Robert Frobisher/Store clerk/Georgette/Tribesman* • Susan Sarandon *Madame Horrox/Older Ursula/Yusouf Suleiman/Abbess* ■ *Dir* Tom Tykwer, Andy Wachowski [Lilly Wachowski], Lana Wachowski • *Scr* Tom Tykwer, Andy Wachowski, Lana Wachowski [Larry Wachowski], from David Mitchell's novel

The Cloud Capped Star ★★★★ PG
Drama 1960 · Ind · BW · 121min

Director Ritwik Ghatak combines social realism with stylised expressionism in this audacious melodrama, which also evokes Bengali myth and the "selfless sister" pictures of the great Japanese director Kenji Mizoguchi. Sacrificing her health and happiness to fulfil the ambitions of her siblings, Supriya Choudhury gives a performance of determination and dignity. While this first part of Ghatak's Calcutta trilogy was acclaimed for its political conviction and cinematic invention, the concluding instalments, *E Flat* (1961) and *The Golden Thread* (1962), caused such a furore that he made no further features for a decade. DP Bengali +subtitles. **DVD**

Supriya Choudhury *Nita* • Anil Chatterjee *Shankar* • Bijon Bhattacharya *Father* • Gita Dey *Mother* • Dwiju Bhawal *Montu, younger brother* • Niranjan Roy *Sanat* ■ *Dir* Ritwik Ghatak • *Scr* Ritwik Ghatak, from a story by Shaktipada Rajguru

Cloud Cuckoo Land ★★ 12A
Drama 2004 · UK · Colour · 94min

With few companies willing to back a project co-scripted by and starring an actor with cerebral palsy, the sheer fact that this inspirational drama was made at all is its crowning achievement. Steve Varden turns in a spirited performance as the 20-something who heads for the Lake District in a bid to establish his independence on learning that his beloved grandfather (Derek Jacobi) has cancer. However, the search for the wreckage of a valuable Second World War plane is not without its melodramatic moments, and Varden's romance with waitress Boo Pearce doesn't always ring true. DP

Steve Varden *Sandy Kenyon* • Derek Jacobi *Victor Kenyon* • Boo Pearce *Lucy* • Kriss Dosanjh *Vijay* • Billy Fane *Trevor* • Jane Wall *Jasmine* • Fuman Dar *Surgeon* • Sarah Beauvoisin *Irene* ■ *Dir* Matt Dickinson • *Scr* Matt Dickinson, Steve Varden

Cloud Dancer ★★
Drama 1979 · US · Colour · 91min

Flying ace David Carradine thrills the crowd with his daredevil antics, but seems to have little time for his friends and family – until he helps drug-addicted pilot Joseph Bottoms kick his habit. Meanwhile, on the ground, Jennifer O'Neill fears for his safety. What he doesn't know is that she's just had his baby. Good aerial stunt work almost makes this melodrama worth watching. AJ

David Carradine *Bradley Randolph* • Jennifer O'Neill *Helen St Clair* • Joseph Bottoms *Tom Loomis* • Albert Salmi *Ozzie Randolph* ■ *Dir* Barry Brown (2) • *Scr* William Goodhart, from a story by William Goodhart, Brown, Daniel Tamkus

Cloud 9 ★★★ 15
Romantic drama 2008 · Ger · Colour · 99min

The romantic and sexual possibilities of old age are explored in frank yet tender detail in German director Andreas Dresen's thoughtful drama. Acknowledging that advancing years are no barrier to all-consuming emotion, the leisurely tale sees married 60-something Inge (Ursula Werner) abruptly turn their previously happy life upside down by embarking on a passionate affair with vigorous septuagenarian Karl (Horst Westphal), in sharp contrast to her dependable relationship with her husband. The only false note comes in the feature's hurried final act, when a contrived resolution replaces the low-key realism with melodrama. SF German +subtitles. Swearing, sex scenes, nudity.

Ursula Werner *Inge* • Horst Rehberg *Werner* • Horst Westphal *Karl* • Steffi Kühnert *Petra* ■ *Dir* Andreas Dresen • *Scr* Andreas Dresen, Jörg Hauschild, Laila Stieler, Cooky Ziesche

Cloudburst ★★
Thriller 1951 · UK · BW · 83min

The dynamic American stage and screen actor Robert Preston, yet to find stardom, is at the centre of this British-made thriller, directed by Francis Searle and co-starring Elizabeth Sellars. Preston is a code-cracking expert at the Foreign Office who uses the skills and contacts he accrued during the war to track down the hit-and-run criminals who killed his wife. The plot may strain credibility a little, but this bleak and violent potboiler is quite involving. RK

Robert Preston *John Graham* • Elizabeth Sellars *Carol Graham* • Colin Tapley *Inspector Davis* • Sheila Burrell *Lorna* • Harold Lang *Mickie* • Mary Germaine *Peggy* ■ *Dir* Francis Searle • *Scr* Francis Searle, Leo Marks, from the play by Leo Marks

The Clouded Yellow ★★★ PG
Crime drama 1950 · UK · BW · 81min

This competent thriller has disgraced spy Trevor Howard involved with Jean Simmons and a case of murder after he becomes curator of a butterfly collection. As the cops close in, the couple head for a boat to Mexico with special agent Kenneth More in hot pursuit. The plot has too few tricks up its sleeve to engross, but director Ralph Thomas teases it out effectively by making good use of such images as the unnerving display cabinets and the Liverpool waterfront. DP **DVD**

Jean Simmons *Sophie Malraux* • Trevor Howard *David Somers* • Sonia Dresdel *Jess Fenton* • Barry Jones *Nicholas Fenton* • Maxwell Reed *Nick* • Kenneth More *Willy* • André Morell *Chubb* ■ *Dir* Ralph Thomas • *Scr* Eric Ambler, from a story by Janet Green • *Cinematographer* Geoffrey Unsworth

Clouds of Sils Maria ★★★★ 15
Drama
2014 · Fr/Swi/Ger · Colour and BW · 118min

Juliette Binoche takes centre stage as a French movie star who is on her way to Switzerland for a tribute to the theatre director who discovered her, when she receives news of the great man's death. She is accompanied by her long-suffering PA (Kristen Stewart) and they decide to stay on in the Alps to allow Binoche to prepare for a revival of the play in which she made her name. Director Olivier Assayas's comedy drama is a wise, playful work that pivots on a clutch of knockout naturalistic performances, especially the increasingly impressive Stewart. LF English, French, German +subtitles. Swearing, brief nudity. **DVD BL**

Juliette Binoche *Maria Enders* • Kristen Stewart *Valentine* • Chloë Grace Moretz *Jo-Ann Ellis* • Lars Eidinger *Klaus Diesterweg* • Johnny Flynn *Christopher Giles* • Brady Corbet *Piers Roaldson* ■ *Dir/Scr* Olivier Assayas

Cloudy with a Chance of Meatballs ★★★★ U
Animated comedy fantasy
2009 · US · Colour · 89min

Based on the bestselling children's book by Judi and Ron Barrett, this is a colourful and clever animated romp, with Bill Hader voicing a nerdy scientist whose inventions normally end in failure. But then he makes a machine that turns water into food and soon it starts raining cheeseburgers. A TV weathergirl (Anna Faris) covers the story and tries to help him avert a junk food disaster. The vocal talents of Hader and Faris – and an unmissable turn from Mr T as the town's cop – make the characters funny and believable, with not a wasted moment in this surprising and entertaining visual treat. A sequel was released in 2013. KK **DVD**

Bill Hader *Flint Lockwood* • Anna Faris *Sam Sparks* • James Caan *Tim Lockwood* • Neil Patrick Harris *Steve the Monkey* • Bruce Campbell *Mayor Shelbourne* • Andy Samberg

---

"Baby" Brent • Mr T *Earl Devereaux* • Benjamin Bratt *Manny* ■ *Dir* Phil Lord, Christopher Miller [Chris Miller] • *Scr* Phil Lord, Christopher Miller [Chris Miller], from the illustrated children's book by Judi & Ron Barrett

Cloudy with a Chance of Meatballs 2 ★★★ U
Animated comedy fantasy
2013 · US · Colour · 90min

Jurassic Park meets *Saturday Kitchen* in this charmingly surreal sequel about the nerdy inventor who designed a water-into-food machine. Bill Hader again voices Flint Lockwood, who discovers that the machine he thought he had destroyed is still causing chaos, turning his home town into a jungle populated by food monsters like shrimpanzees, tacodiles and slightly scary cheespiders. The frenetic action is peppered with ecological messages and, while not as spontaneous or consistently delightful as its predecessor, the film's bright, frame-filling visuals provide another smartly tasty spectacle. AJ **DVD BL SP CS**

Bill Hader *Flint Lockwood* • Anna Faris *Sam Sparks* • James Caan *Tim Lockwood* • Will Forte *Chester V* • Benjamin Bratt *Manny* • Neil Patrick Harris *Steve the monkey* • Terry Crews *Earl Devereaux* ■ *Dir* Cody Cameron, Kris Pearn • *Scr* John Francis Daley, Jonathan M Goldstein, from characters by Judi & Ron Barrett

Cloverfield ★★★ 15
Science-fiction action thriller
2008 · US · Colour · 81min

A gigantic creature of unknown origin pulverises its way through Manhattan in this YouTube-style monster mash-up co-produced by *Lost* creator JJ Abrams. There are clever dashes of *The Beast from 20,000 Fathoms* and *The Host*, but the characters – partygoers filming a going-away do – lack emotional depth and stumble a little too carelessly into danger. The interesting gimmick here is the intimate approach to epic disaster provided by the action unfolding via an amateur camcorder. This *Blair Witch* flair often creates a gripping, up-close-and-personal portrait of events, and the shaky-cam terrors meld effectively with loud bangs and glimpses of the HP Lovecraft-inspired behemoth. AJ **DVD BL**

Lizzy Caplan *Marlena Diamond* • Jessica Lucas *Lily Ford* • TJ Miller *Hudson "Hud" Platt* • Michael Stahl-David *Rob Hawkins* • Mike Vogel *Jason Hawkins* • Odette Yustman *Beth McIntyre* • Margot Farley *Jenn* • Theo Rossi *Antonio* ■ *Dir* Matt Reeves • *Scr* Drew Goddard

The Clown ★★
Drama 1952 · US · BW · 90min

Red Skelton is now a forgotten clown, and this reworking of *The Champ* shows us why. He plays an alcoholic old vaudevillian, idolised by his son (Tim Considine), who dreams of making a comeback on television. Alas, he's flawed, and floored, by his own weak character. Some moments suggest what Skelton was capable of, but there aren't enough to rescue director Robert Z Leonard's mawkish melodrama from bathos. TH

Red Skelton *Dodo Delwyn* • Tim Considine *Dink Delwyn* • Jane Greer *Paula Henderson* • Loring Smith *Goldie* • Fay Roope *Dr Strauss* • Philip Ober *Ralph Z Henderson* • Walter Reed *Joe Hoagley* ■ *Dir* Robert Z Leonard • *Scr* Martin Rackin, from a story by Frances Marion, Leonard Praskins

Clown ★★ 18
Horror 2014 · US/Can · Colour · 95min

Director Jon Watts's demon-curse horror in which a clown suit possesses an unfortunate dad (Andy Powers) after he entertains at his son's birthday party is not on the splatter level of producer Eli Roth's more excessive work, *Hostel* for instance. Expanded from a fake trailer, it's efficiently put together if a little sedate, and Powers does prove a tragic figure, even after the suit transmogrifies him into a demonic jester driven to feast on children. JA Violence, swearing. **DVD**

Andy Powers *Kent* • Laura Allen *Meg* • Peter Stormare *Karlsson* • Christian Distefano *Jack* • Eli Roth *Frowny the Clown* ■ *Dir* Jon Watts • *Scr* Jon Watts, Christopher D Ford

Clownhouse ★★ 15
Horror 1988 · US · Colour · 78min

If viewers can somehow distance themselves from the behind-the-scenes scandal surrounding this movie (director Victor Salva molested one of his child actors), they will discover a genuinely spooky exercise in horror. In this incredibly atmospheric chiller, three escaped lunatics disguise themselves as clowns and terrorise three young brothers left home alone. The stalking sequences are nail-biting, though the lack of action makes things a little tedious. KB

Nathan Forrest Winters *Casey* • Brian McHugh *Geoffrey* • Sam Rockwell *Randy* • Tree *Evil Cheezo* ■ *Dir/Scr* Victor Salva

The Clowns ★★★★ U
Documentary 1970 · It/Fr/W Ger · Colour · 91min

Italy's great ringmaster of the cinema returns to the source of his inspiration – the circus – and skilfully absorbs it into his own personal vision. Remembering the Rimini of his childhood when the circus came to town, Federico Fellini has stated: "My films owe an enormous amount to the circus. For me the clowns were always a traumatic visual experience, ambassadors of a vocation of a showman." Here, the maestro not only reveals their comedic craft by watching and talking to exponents of the profession. He also sends up the documentary-making process itself. RB Italian +subtitles. *DVD* *SD*

■ *Dir* Federico Fellini • *Scr* Federico Fellini, Bernardino Zapponi • *Music* Nino Rota

The Club ★★★
Comedy drama 1980 · Aus · Colour · 96min

This is a bracing look behind the scenes at the personal and power politics involved in the running of an Australian Rules football club. It is based on an equally rumbustious stage play from David Williamson. This may not be as polished a film as Bruce Beresford's later success *Driving Miss Daisy*, but it makes up for what it lacks in finesse with rude energy and muscular acting. PF Swearing, drug abuse, brief nudity.

Jack Thompson *Laurie Holden* • Graham Kennedy *Ted Parker* • Frank Wilson (2) *Jock Riley* • Harold Hopkins *Danny Rowe* • John Howard (2) *Geoff Hayward* ■ *Dir* Bruce Beresford • *Scr* David Williamson, from his play

The Club ★★★ 18
Drama 2015 · Chil · Colour · 97min

The uneasy quiet of a remote hideaway for disgraced Catholic priests and nuns is shattered by the ranting arrival of an abuse victim in this powerful and topical drama from Chile. To sort out the kerfuffle and keep a lid on things, the Church sends in a crisis counsellor.*TheClub* is told in an understated style that depicts these priests and nuns as flawed human beings, many in denial. It loses its vice-like grip a little in a last half hour, but it's still a worthwhile if sometimes tough watch. DA Spanish +subtitles. *DVD* *SD*

Alfredo Castro *Father Vidal* • Roberto Farías *Sandokan* • Antonia Zegers *Sister Mónica* • Jaime Vadell *Father Silva* • Alejandro Goic *Father Ortega* ■ *Dir* Pablo Larraín • *Scr* Guillermo Calderón, Pablo Larraín, Daniel Villalobos

Club de Femmes ★★★★ 12
Comedy drama 1936 · Fr · BW · 95min

This recently rediscovered melodrama is an enticing mix of social comment, sexual suggestion and screwball comedy. Gliding his camera around the mod-con hostel, with its swimming pool and gleaming sub-Deco furnishings, direcor Jacques Deval showcases the exuberance and beauty of youth, without neglecting either the doubts and desires simmering beneath the antiseptic veneer or the implicit chauvinism of the unseen male world outside. Danielle Darrieux shines as a boy-mad dancer, but

Betty Stockfeld's corrupted innocent, Josette Day's blonde bombshell and Else Argal's tormented lesbian also impress. DP French +subtitles.

Danielle Darrieux *Claire Derouve* • Betty Stockfeld *Greta Kremmer* • Else Argal *Alice Hermin* • Raymond Galle *Robert* • Eve Francis *Mme Fargeton* • Josette Day *Juliette* ■ *Dir/Scr* Jacques Deval

Club le Monde ★★★ 18
Comedy drama 2001 · UK · Colour · 78min

Director Simon Rumley's take on club culture works only fitfully, with its blend of drama and offbeat comedy. Subplots involving a conflicted bouncer, two underage toffs and a gossipy, coke-sniffing duo who refuse to leave the ladies' loo end up proving more diverting than the central plot strand involving Alison McKenzie and Brad Gorton's broken romance. However, the film does re-create the atmosphere of a club night successfully, while giving the episodes an "overheard" feel that's totally in keeping with the setting. DP *DVD*

Danny Nussbaum *Mr Sunglasses* • Emma Pike *Yas* • Tania Emery *Kelly* • Lee Oakes *Chas* • Emma Handy *Ra* • Tom Connolly *Anthony* • Tom Halstead *Patrick* • Daniel Ainsleigh *Steve* ■ *Dir/Scr* Simon Rumley

Club Paradise ★★ 15
Comedy 1986 · US · Colour · 91min

Harold Ramis has matured into a fine comedy director – *Groundhog Day, Multiplicity* – but during the 1980s he specialised in crass efforts such as this early Robin Williams vehicle. Williams plays the host of a run-down Caribbean resort who has to cope with noisy American tourists and a brewing rebellion. The cast is eclectic, but the gags are about as sparse as the hotel's "luxury" facilities. JF Swearing, drug abuse.

Robin Williams *Jack Moniker* • Peter O'Toole *Governor Anthony Croyden Hayes* • Rick Moranis *Barry Nye* • Jimmy Cliff *Ernest Reed* • Twiggy *Phillipa Lloyd* • Adolph Caesar *Prime Minister Solomon Gundy* • Eugene Levy *Barry Steinberg* • Joanna Cassidy *Terry Hamlin* ■ *Dir* Harold Ramis • *Scr* Harold Ramis, Brian Doyle-Murray, from a story by Ed Roboto, Tom Leopold, Chris Miller, David Standish

Clubbed ★★ 18
Crime drama 2008 · UK · Colour · 94min

This muddled piece of 1980s gangland lore follows Midlands factory worker Danny (Mel Raido) as he takes up boxing to prevent a repeat of the battering that he suffered in front of his kids, and becomes a nightclub doorman. But his new sense of self is jeopardised by a drugs baron, who is determined to get his dealers into the establishment. There are provocative points about masculinity and the role of the community in countering crime. But director Neil Thompson is unsure whether to celebrate or avoid the lazy shorthand of recent British crime flicks, and ends up delivering a glorified TV episode studded with moments of sickening violence. DP Violence, swearing.

Mel Raido *Danny* • Colin Salmon *Louis* • Shaun Parkes *Rob* • Scot Williams *Sparky* • Maxine Peake *Angela* • Ronnie Fox *Billy Hennessy* • Neil Morrissey *Simon* ■ *Dir* Neil Thompson (2) • *Scr* Geoff Thompson

Clubbed to Death ★★ 18
Romantic drama 1996 · Fr/Por/Neth · Colour · 84min

This strange, dark and narrative-less film from director Yolande Zauberman stars Elodie Bouchez as a girl who falls asleep on a bus and awakes to find herself on the outskirts of Paris. Stumbling around, she ends up in a nightclub where she encounters Roschdy Zem. Few words are spoken in this pop video-style foray into Parisian rave culture. LH French +subtitles. Drug abuse, swearing, violence.

Elodie Bouchez *Lola Monnet* • Roschdy Zem *Emir Areski* • Béatrice Dalle *Saïda* • Richard Courcet *Ismael* ■ *Dir* Yolande Zauberman • *Scr* Yolande Zauberman, Noémie Lvovsky, Emmanuel Salinger, D Belloc

Clubland ★★ 15
Comedy drama 2006 · Aus · Colour · 101min

Australia's variety club scene is the setting for this dysfunctional family drama. Brenda Blethyn stars as Jean, an ex-pat comedian whose bawdy routines seem more suited to working men's clubs than the neo-Vegas niteries of Sydney. With her husband, a crooner-turned-security guard, out of the picture, Jean begins to rely heavily on her two sons, with 20-year-old Tim (Khan Chittenden) assuming much of the responsibilty for a younger brother with cerebral palsy. Blethyn can do this kind of well-meaning but overbearing blue-collar mum stuff in her sleep, and Cherie Nowlan's film offers no more than its low-key status suggests. DW *DVD*

Brenda Blethyn *Jean Dwight* • Khan Chittenden *Tim Dwight* • Emma Booth *Jill* • Richard Wilson (4) *Mark Dwight* • Frankie J Holden *John Dwight* • Rebecca Gibney *Lana* • Philip Quast *Ronnie Stubbs* ■ *Dir* Cherie Nowlan • *Scr* Keith Thompson • *Cinematographer* Mark Wareham

Clue ★★ PG
Period comedy 1985 · US · Colour · 92min

Based on the board game Clue (known as Cluedo in the UK), this is a perfect example of a gimmick movie. The plot (an amalgam of various Agatha Christie clichés) involves a number of guests invited to dinner at a spooky mansion, where they endure a murderous evening. Scripted and written by British sitcom stalwart Jonathan Lynn in his first Hollywood venture, this is a broad, somewhat camp comedy. It was originally released with three different endings, though there was only one version in the UK. DF *DVD*

Tim Curry *Wadsworth* • Madeline Kahn *Mrs White* • Christopher Lloyd *Professor Plum* • Eileen Brennan *Mrs Peacock* • Martin Mull *Mr Green* • Martin Mull *Colonel Mustard* • Lesley Ann Warren *Miss Scarlett* ■ *Dir* Jonathan Lynn • *Scr* Jonathan Lynn, from the board game devised by Anthony E Pratt

Clueless ★★★★ 12
Romantic comedy 1995 · US · Colour · 93min

Would you believe a loose adaptation of Jane Austen's *Emma* plonked down squarely in *Beverly Hills 90210*? Well, that's the idea behind this screamingly funny satire-cum-parody, which perfectly captures the inanities of 1990s teen America. Alicia Silverstone is a delight as Cher, the chic but dippy blonde who's devoted to improving the love lives of her Rodeo Drive-shopping high-school girlfriends, even though she can't sort out her own. Her lawyer father Dan Hedaya and intellectual stepbrother Paul Rudd look on in total bemusement. Director Amy Heckerling's smart satire sharpens its comedic scalpel on the manners and mores of self-centred fashion victims. AJ Some swearing. *DVD*

Alicia Silverstone *Cher* • Stacey Dash *Dionne* • Paul Rudd *Josh* • Brittany Murphy *Tai* • Donald Adeosun Faison [Donald Faison] *Murray* • Elisa Donovan *Amber* • Wallace Shawn *Mr Hall* • Twink Caplan *Miss Geist* • Dan Hedaya *Mel* ■ *Dir* Amy Heckerling • *Scr* Amy Heckerling, from the novel *Emma* by Jane Austen

Cluny Brown ★★★ PG
Romantic comedy 1946 · US · BW · 96min

No longer quite what *Variety* called a "smasheroo", this somewhat outmoded satirical soufflé on British upper-class mores is nonetheless diverting. A comedy romance from director Ernst Lubitsch, whose famous "touch" is still very much in evidence, it stars Jennifer Jones as a lady plumber doubling up as a maid for an English family who are all vague to the point of imbecility. Charles Boyer is a Czech writer who arrives in the household having fled the Nazis. RK *DVD*

Jennifer Jones *Cluny Brown* • Charles Boyer *Adam Belinski* • Peter Lawford *Andrew Carmel* • Helen Walker *Betty Cream* • Reginald Gardiner *Hilary Ames* • Reginald Owen *Sir Henry Carmel* • C Aubrey Smith *Col Duff-Graham* ■ *Dir* Ernst Lubitsch • *Scr* Samuel Hoffenstein, Elizabeth Reinhardt, from the novel by Margery Sharp

Coach Carter ★★★ 12
Sports drama based on a true story
2005 · Ger/US · Colour · 130min

Samuel L Jackson's barnstorming performance is the main reason to watch this solidly entertaining "true story". He plays a high-school basketball coach who took the unheard of step of benching his players and jeopardising their shot at the state title when he discovered they were failing academically. This, needless to say, didn't sit at all well with the students. Clichéd it may be, but the movie is involving and well acted. AS Swearing. *DVD*

Samuel L Jackson *Coach Ken Carter* • Robert Ri'chard *Damien Carter* • Rob Brown *Kenyon Stone* • Ashanti *Kyra* • Debbi Morgan *Tonya Carter* • Rick Gonzalez *Timo Cruz* • Antwon Tanner *Worm* • Nana Gbewonyo *Junior Battle* • Channing Tatum *Jason Lyle* • Denise Dowse *Principal Garrison* ■ *Dir* Thomas Carter • *Scr* Mark Schwahn, John Gatins

Coal Miner's Daughter ★★★★ PG
Biographical drama 1980 · US · Colour · 119min

Sissy Spacek won a best actress Oscar for her heartfelt portrayal of country singer Loretta Lynn in this movie biopic from British director Michael Apted. Based on Lynn's autobiography, the film charts the singer's life from poverty in deepest Kentucky to her success as the queen of country music. It's a fascinating, no-holds-barred adaptation that includes her battle with drugs, a rocky marriage and the death of friend Patsy Cline. JB Swearing, violence. *DVD*

Sissy Spacek *Loretta Lynn* • Tommy Lee Jones *Doolittle Lynn* • Levon Helm *Ted Webb* • Phyllis Boyens *Clara Webb* • William Sanderson *Lee Dollarhide* • Beverly D'Angelo *Patsy Cline* ■ *Dir* Michael Apted • *Scr* Tom Rickman, from the autobiography by Loretta Lynn, George Vescey

Coast of Skeletons ★★★ U
Adventure 1964 · UK · Colour · 90min

Richard Todd returns as redoubtable cop Harry Sanders in this watchable adventure, only here he's out to nab insurance fraudsters rather than smugglers in the African jungle (as in *Death Drums along the River* released the previous year). This mystery sees Sanders out to snoop on a smooth-talking Texas wheeler-dealer (played by TV western star Dale Robertson), who's dredging for diamonds off the infamous Coast of Skeletons in West Africa (or Namibia, as it's now known). Todd is suitably phlegmatic and quite handy in a fight, and the Namibian locations are certainly diverting. JA

Richard Todd *Inspector Harry Sanders* • Dale Robertson *AJ Magnus* • Heinz Drache *Janny von Koltze* ■ *Dir* Robert Lynn • *Scr* Anthony Scott Veitch, from a story by Peter Welbeck [Harry Alan Towers], from the novel *Sanders of the River* by Edgar Wallace

Coast to Coast ★★
Comedy 1980 · US · Colour · 94min

Ever since *It Happened One Night* swept the Oscars in 1934, the runaway odd couple has been a comic staple in Hollywood. Here Dyan Cannon plays the screwball "fugitive" hitting the road to escape a conniving husband. But Cannon never really sparks with Robert Blake as the trucker who agrees to take her coast to coast in a bid to shake the brutal debt collector on his own tail. DP

Dyan Cannon *Madie Levrington* • Robert Blake *Charlie Callahan* • Quinn Redeker *Benjamin Levrington* • Michael Lerner *Dr Froll* • Maxine Stuart *Sam Klinger* ■ *Dir* Joseph Sargent • *Scr* Stanley Weiser

Cobain: Montage of Heck ★★★★ 15
Part-animated documentary
2015 · US · Colour · 131min

An exhaustive, haunting but suitably punk-rock hagiography of Kurt Cobain, doomed leader of US grunge superstars Nirvana, who sold 100 million records worldwide. It's a chronological telling of the frontman's foreshortened, 27-year life story from peripatetic Pacific Northwest childhood to suicide, via international superstardom and was made with the full co-operation of his estate – his daughter, Frances Bean Cobain, is an executive producer. Though the abrasively primal music may not be to everybody's taste, the casual observer ought to be convinced of Cobain's innate creative talent and the tragedy of his demise. AC *DVD* *BL*

Courtney Love • Kimberley Cobain • Krist Novoselic • Don Cobain ■ *Dir/Scr* Brett Morgen

Cobb ★★★★ 18

Biographical sports drama
1994 · US · Colour and BW · 122min

This portrait of the sports hero as warped monster gives Tommy Lee Jones the chance to deliver a grandstand performance as Ty Cobb, the real-life baseball ace known as the "Georgia Peach". Soured by a lifetime of bigotry and bullying, Cobb is seen trying to camouflage past sins as he dictates his autobiography to a sports writer (Robert Wuhl). Director Ron Shelton, whose *Bull Durham* and *White Men Can't Jump* were jokey tales of disillusionment set in the sporting world, here redefines the life of an idol with honest savagery. TH Violence, swearing, nudity.

Tommy Lee Jones *Ty Cobb* • Robert Wuhl *Al Stump* • Lolita Davidovich *Ramona* • Ned Bellamy *Ray* • Scott Burkholder *Jimmy* • Allan Malamud *Mud* ■ *Dir* Ron Shelton • *Scr* Ron Shelton, from the biography by Al Stump

The Cobbler ★★ 12

Comedy drama   2014 · US · Colour · 108min

This high-concept comedy stars Adam Sandler as Max, a dissatisfied cobbler who gets in over his head when he discovers a stitching machine that allows him to turn into the person whose shoes he puts on. This premise and much of the first act are quirky and fun, and Sandler heads up the film with a subtle, convincing performance; however, the plot does get progressively stranger. JL In English, Yiddish. Some violence, swearing, sexual references. *DVD*

Adam Sandler *Max Simkin* • Method Man *Ludlow* • Ellen Barkin *Elaine Greenawalt* • Dan Stevens *Dance club DJ* • Steve Buscemi *Jimmy* • Dustin Hoffman *Abraham Simkin* ■ *Dir* Thomas McCarthy • *Scr* Thomas McCarthy, Paul Sado

Cobra ★★ 18

Action thriller   1986 · US · Colour · 83min

"Crime is the disease and I'm the cure," claims cop Sylvester Stallone in a practically plotless mix of shooting and stabbing. It's unfortunate his idea of characterisation is mirror shades and a penchant for chewing matches. The relentless sequences of murder and mayhem are competently filmed by director George Pan Cosmatos. JC Violence, swearing. *DVD* *BL*

Sylvester Stallone *Marion "Cobra" Cobretti* • Brigitte Nielsen *Ingrid* • Reni Santoni *Gonzales* • Andrew Robinson *Detective Monte* • Lee Garlington *Nancy Stalk* ■ *Dir* George Pan Cosmatos • *Scr* Sylvester Stallone, from the novel *Fair Game* by Paula Gosling

Cobra Verde ★★ PG

Period drama   1988 · W Ger · Colour · 110min

Although again depicting the exploits of an obsessive outsider in an inhospitable environment, this is the least cohesive of the epic collaborations between Klaus Kinski and Werner Herzog. Filmed under typically arduous conditions in Ghana, the action follows the fortunes of an exiled Brazilian bandit whose attempts to revive the slave trade are dashed by the insane ruler of Dahomey. Herzog succeeds in anthropologically dissecting the civilisation under his gaze, but his take on the evils of colonialism and the majesty of Africa is uninspired. DP German +subtitles. Violence, swearing, nudity. *DVD*

Klaus Kinski *Francisco Manoel da Silva* • Taparica *King Ampaw* • José Lewgoy *Don Octavio Coutinho* • Salvatore Basile *Captain Fraternidade*

• Bossa Ahadee *Kwame II of Nsein* ■ *Dir* Werner Herzog • *Scr* Werner Herzog, from the novel *The Viceroy of Ouidah* by Bruce Chatwin

Cobra Woman ★★

Fantasy adventure   1944 · US · Colour · 70min

High camp thrills abound in this richly dumb jungle melodrama about a bride-to-be kidnapped and taken to a mysterious island. There she discovers her evil twin sister is high priestess of a cobra-worshipping cult. Maria Montez is something of a cult figure today, and her performance here as the dual protagonists is considered a career best. Alas, Robert Siodmak directs this bunkum with too straight a face. RS

Maria Montez *Tollea/Naja* • Jon Hall *Ramu* • Sabu *Kado* • Lon Chaney Jr *Hava* • Edgar Barrier *Martok* • Mary Nash *Queen* • Lois Collier *Veeda* • Samuel S Hinds *Father Paul* • Moroni Olsen *MacDonald* ■ *Dir* Robert Siodmak • *Scr* Gene Lewis, Richard Brooks, from a story by W Scott Darling

The Cobweb ★★★

Drama   1955 · US · Colour · 123min

It's literally curtains for credibility as this wondrous tosh, one of the last of Hollywood's postwar psychiatric trilogy, concerns the choosing of new drapes for the library of a psychiatric clinic, which causes as many problems for the staff as it does for the patients. The adaptation of William Gibson's novel becomes too wordy, but when you have the benefit of stars such as Richard Widmark, Lauren Bacall, Gloria Grahame, Lillian Gish and Charles Boyer, who cares? TH

Richard Widmark *Dr Stewart McIver* • Lauren Bacall *Meg Faversen Rinehart* • Charles Boyer *Dr Douglas N Devanal* • Gloria Grahame *Karen McIver* • Lillian Gish *Victoria Inch* • John Kerr *Steven W Holte* • Susan Strasberg *Sue Brett* ■ *Dir* Vincente Minnelli • *Scr* John Paxton, from the novel by William Gibson

The Coca-Cola Kid ★★★ 15

Comedy   1985 · Aus · Colour · 94min

The political and sexual themes that Serbian director Dusan Makavejev explored in his earlier works are only quaintly challenging in this offbeat comedy about corporate ideals. Eric Roberts is the Coca-Cola go-getter sent to Australia to test the market, where he comes into oddly engaging conflict with a wacky soft drinks manufacturer (Bill Kerr). The result is a laid-back, culture-clash whimsy full of incidental pleasures, the main one being Greta Scacchi burning up the screen as a sexy secretary. AJ

Eric Roberts *Becker* • Greta Scacchi *Terri* • Bill Kerr *T George McDowell* • Max Gilles *Frank* • Kris McQuade *Juliana* • Tony Barry *Bushman* • Chris Haywood *Kim* ■ *Dir* Dusan Makavejev • *Scr* Frank Moorhouse, from his short stories

A Cock and Bull Story ★★★★ 15

Satirical comedy drama
2005 · UK · Colour · 90min

Michael Winterbottom directs this extremely clever comedy based on Laurence Sterne's supposedly unfilmable 18th-century novel. Structured as a film within a film, it presents both choice extracts of Tristram Shandy's non-linear autobiography and the journey of a modern movie crew as they try to re-create it on a shoestring budget. Steve Coogan plays Shandy (with echoes of Sterne) and Shandy's father, as well as a fictionalised version of himself. What unfolds is a neat parody of English period dramas wrapped up in a hilarious "making of" mockumentary. Coogan and his bickering co-star Rob Brydon are brilliant, while quirky supporting characters add depth to the multilayered piece. SF Swearing, sex scenes. *DVD*

Steve Coogan *Tristram Shandy/Walter Shandy/Steve Coogan* • Rob Brydon *Uncle Toby/Rob Brydon* • Keeley Hawes *Elizabeth Shandy* • Shirley Henderson *Susannah/Shirley Henderson* • Dylan Moran *Dr Slop* • David Walliams *Parson* • Jeremy Northam *Mark, the director* • Naomie Harris *Jennie* • Stephen Fry *Patrick Wildgust the curator/Parson Yorick* • Gillian Anderson *Widow*

Wadman/Gillian Anderson ■ *Dir* Michael Winterbottom • *Scr* Martin Hardy [Frank Cottrell Boyce, Michael Winterbottom], from the novel *The Life and Opinions of Tristram Shandy, Gentleman* by Laurence Sterne

The Cock-Eyed World ★★★

Comedy musical   1929 · US · BW · 115min

This early talkie from Raoul Walsh – who went on to be one of the best directors of such gangster movies as *White Heat* – is a rollicking adventure comedy about the further exploits of Sergeants Flagg and Quirt (Victor McLaglen and Edmund Lowe), the heroes of *What Price Glory?* (1926). Always trying to one-up each other, they unite with their fists in adversity. It holds the interest, though the narrative technique looks dated. TH

Victor McLaglen *Sgt Flagg* • Edmund Lowe *Sgt Harry Quirt* • Lili Damita *Elenita* • Lelia Karnelly *Olga* • Bobby Burns *Connors* • Jean Bary *Fanny* ■ *Dir* Raoul Walsh • *Scr* Raoul Walsh, William K Wells, from a play by Maxwell Anderson, Laurence Stallings

Cockles & Muscles ★★★ 15

Musical comedy romance
2004 · Fr · Colour · 94min

Olivier Ducastel and Jacques Martineau co-direct this delightful sexual romp, which makes splendid use of both its Côte d'Azur locations and its engaging ensemble cast. However, while the emphasis is supposed to be on teenager Romain Torres's holiday crushes on best pal Edouard Collin and local plumber Jean-Marc Barr, it's Valéria Bruni-Tedeschi who effortlessly steals the film with an effervescent display of liberated sensuality. DP French +subtitles. Swearing, drug abuse, sex scenes.

Valéria Bruni-Tedeschi *Béatrix* • Gilbert Melki *Marc* • Jean-Marc Barr *Didier* • Jacques Bonnaffé *Mathieu* • Edouard Collin *Martin* • Romain Torres *Charly* • Sabrina Seyvecou *Laura* • Yannick Baudin *Michaël* ■ *Dir/Scr* Olivier Ducastel, Jacques Martineau

The Cockleshell Heroes ★★★★ U

Second World War drama
1955 · UK · Colour · 93min

Crisply directed by José Ferrer, this tremendously exciting film sees Royal Marines go on a secret mission to destroy enemy shipping. Ferrer also leads the fine cast and commands the nightime raid on the Bordeaux docks. Ferrer and Trevor Howard strike well against each other as the unorthodox major and resentful captain, and the training scenes are imaginative and effective. The movie was a big hit, and was reissued as the top half of a double bill with *From Here to Eternity*; this necessitated the optical adjustment of the latter into a widescreen format so that it wouldn't look too shabby alongside this film! TS *DVD*

José Ferrer *Major Stringer* • Trevor Howard *Captain Thompson* • Victor Maddern *Sergeant Craig* • Anthony Newley *Clarke* • David Lodge *Ruddock* • Peter Arne *Stevens* • Percy Herbert *Loman* • Graham Stewart *Booth* ■ *Dir* José Ferrer • *Scr* Bryan Forbes, Richard Maibaum, from a story by George Kent

Cockneys vs Zombies ★★ 15

Comedy horror   2011 · UK · Colour · 87min

George A Romero meets Guy Ritchie for some lame laughs in this East End riff on *Shaun of the Dead*. Harry Treadaway and Rasmus Hardiker play brothers who rob a bank to stop the closure of grandad Alan Ford's retirement home just as a zombie outbreak occurs. While the young cast are likeable, it's the kick-ass older generation – Richard Briers, Honor Blackman, Dudley Sutton – who really add spark to the cheap and cheerful proceedings. However, despite some nice creative flashes from director Matthias Hoene, the one-joke set-up quickly pales. AJ Violence, swearing. *DVD* *BL*

Harry Treadaway *Andy McGuire* • Rasmus Hardiker *Terry McGuire* • Michelle Ryan *Katy McGuire* • Ashley "Bashy" Thomas *Mental Mickey* • Alan Ford *Ray McGuire* • Honor Blackman *Peggy* • Richard Briers *Hamish* • Dudley Sutton *Eric* ■ *Dir* Matthias Hoene • *Scr* James Moran

---

Cocktail ★★ 15

Romantic drama   1988 · US · Colour · 99min

Having turned fighter pilots and pool players into sex objects, Tom Cruise did the same service for bartenders, learning the meaning of life by mixing drinks under the tutelage of Martini-mentor Bryan Brown. Cruise's technique is impressive; but then along comes Elisabeth Shue, who makes him re-assess his lifestyle. A bland concoction mixed with agents and the studio. AT Swearing, nudity.

Tom Cruise *Brian Flanagan* • Bryan Brown *Doug Coughlin* • Elisabeth Shue *Jordan Mooney* • Lisa Banes *Bonnie* • Laurence Luckinbill *Mr Mooney* • Kelly Lynch *Kerry Coughlin* • Gina Gershon *Coral* • Ron Dean *Uncle Pat* ■ *Dir* Roger Donaldson • *Scr* Heywood Gould, from his novel

Coco avant Chanel ★★★★ 12

Biographical drama
2009 · Fr/Bel · Colour · 105min

An icon of French cinema (Audrey Tautou) meets an icon of French fashion in this arresting chronicle of the formative years of Coco Chanel. The emotional core of the story is the personal sacrifice Coco made in pursuit of success, determined to remain her own woman in a world shaped by wealthy men. Anne Fontaine's engrossing, thoroughly elegant film slightly falters in its scrappy final stages, yet its subtle insights are still worth celebrating. TJ French +subtitles. *DVD* *BL*

Audrey Tautou *Coco Chanel* • Benoît Poelvoorde *Étienne Balsan* • Alessandro Nivola *Arthur "Boy" Capel* • Marie Gillain *Adrienne Chanel* • Emmanuelle Devos *Emilienne d'Alençon* ■ *Dir* Anne Fontaine • *Scr* Anne & Camille Fontaine, Christopher Hampton, Jacques Fieschi, from non-fiction books by Edmonde Charles-Roux • *Cinematographer* Christophe Beaucarne

Coco Chanel & Igor Stravinsky ★★★ 15

Romantic drama
2009 · Fr · BW and Colour · 113min

The tempestuous affair between Russian composer Igor Stravinsky and French couturier Coco Chanel is recalled with abundant polish but little passion in Jan Kounen's rigidly refined melodrama. Elena Morozova's sulky silence as Catherine Stravinsky is a suitable counterpoint to the imperious performance of Anna Mouglalis as Chanel. But Mads Mikkelsen can't capture the great man's restless genius and adopts a stuffy stoicism that also seems to suffuse the cinematography and score. DP French, English, Russian +subtitles. Some sex scenes, nudity. *DVD* *BL*

Anna Mouglalis *Coco Chanel* • Mads Mikkelsen *Igor Stravinsky* • Elena Morozova *Catherine Stravinsky* • Natacha Lindinger *Misia Sert* • Grigori Manoukov [Grigori Manukov] *Sergei Diaghilev* • Rasha Bukvic *Grand Duke Dimitri* ■ *Dir* Jan Kounen • *Scr* Chris Greenhalgh, Jan Kounen, Carlo de Boutiny, from the novel *Coco & Igor* by Greenhalgh • *Music* Gabriel Yared • *Cinematographer* David Ungaro

The Cocoanuts ★★★ U

Comedy   1929 · US · BW · 75min

With an energy that bursts through any attempts at sophistication, this is the first film the Marx brothers made for Paramount. It's adapted – though you'd scarcely know it – from their Broadway stage hit, written by George S Kaufman and Irving Berlin. Groucho is the seedy manager of a Florida hotel, which has hot and cold running Harpo and Chico, besides jewel thieves and the matronly Margaret Dumont, a monument Groucho is always trying to climb or put down. Dated it may be, but still lots of fun. TH *DVD*

Groucho Marx *Hammer* • Harpo Marx *Harpo* • Chico Marx *Chico* • Zeppo Marx *Jamison* • Mary Eaton *Polly* • Oscar Shaw *Bob* • Katherine Francis *Penelope* • Margaret Dumont *Mrs Potter* ■ *Dir* Robert Florey, Joseph Santley • *Scr* Morris Ryskind, from the play by George S Kaufman, Irving Berlin

Cocoon ★★★★ PG

Science-fiction fantasy
1985 · US · Colour · 112min

Director Ron Howard hit the big time with this blockbuster about pensioners finding a new lease of life after stumbling across aliens on a rescue mission from another planet. What saves it from a complete wallow in sentimentality is the sharp and sassy playing of a distinguished cast of Hollywood legends – Oscar-winning Don Ameche, Wilford Brimley, real-life husband and wife Hume Cronyn and Jessica Tandy – all of whom easily steal the show from the bland Steve Guttenberg and Tahnee Welch. Howard handles the human drama and sci-fi with equal aplomb. JF Swearing, brief nudity. DVD BD

Steve Guttenberg *Jack Bonner* • Brian Dennehy *Walter* • Don Ameche *Art Selwyn* • Wilford Brimley *Ben Luckett* • Hume Cronyn *Joe Finley* • Jack Gilford *Bernie Lefkowitz* • Maureen Stapleton *Mary Luckett* • Jessica Tandy *Alma Finley* • Gwen Verdon *Bess McCarthy* • Herta Ware *Rose Lefkowitz* • Tahnee Welch *Kitty* • Barret Oliver *David* ■ *Dir* Ron Howard • *Scr* Tom Benedek, from a story by David Saperstein

Cocoon: the Return ★★ PG

Science-fiction fantasy
1988 · US · Colour · 114min

Straining far too hard to recapture the touching whimsy of Ron Howard's original film, director Daniel Petrie has succeeded only in producing a mawkish melodrama. Here, the rejuvenated elderly couples return with their alien guardians to see how their family and friends are doing back on Earth. Although the ever-dapper Don Ameche reprises his Oscar-winning role, there is much less of a spring in his step, and the script is glum. DP Swearing. DVD

Don Ameche *Art Selwyn* • Hume Cronyn *Joe Finley* • Wilford Brimley *Ben Luckett* • Courteney Cox *Sara* • Jack Gilford *Bernie Lefkowitz* • Steve Guttenberg *Jack Bonner* • Maureen Stapleton *Mary Luckett* • Elaine Stritch *Ruby* • Jessica Tandy *Alma Finley* • Gwen Verdon *Bess McCarthy* ■ *Dir* Daniel Petrie • *Scr* Stephen McPherson, from a story by Stephen McPherson, Elizabeth Bradley, from characters by David Saperstein

Code 46 ★★ 15

Futuristic romantic drama
2003 · UK/US · Colour · 89min

In a gloomy future with human cloning and genetic manipulation, Tim Robbins is a fraud investigator who's sent to Shanghai to find the source of some counterfeit travel documents. There, he is mysteriously drawn to Samantha Morton, who is also his chief suspect. Despite the intriguing premise, the film is rather tedious, the storyline plodding and obscure, and matters are not helped by the limited budget. The film is partly salvaged by a terrific performance from Samantha Morton, but Robbins lacks spark. DA Sex scenes, nudity. DVD

Tim Robbins *William Geld* • Samantha Morton *Maria* • Jeanne Balibar *Sylvie Geld* • Om Puri *Backland* • Essie Davis *Doctor* ■ *Dir* Michael Winterbottom • *Scr* Frank Cottrell Boyce

Code Name: Emerald ★★ PG

Second World War thriller
1985 · US · Colour · 91min

This is a polished piece of film-making. So polished, in fact, that any trace of originality or enterprise has been scrupulously wiped away. Surely the only excuse for making a Second World War espionage adventure in 1985 was to divulge the secrets of some hitherto hush-hush true-life operation. Not, as here, to take elements from any number of wartime thrillers and form them into yet another collage of double agents, decent Nazis and Gestapo sadists. DP Swearing.

Ed Harris *Gus Lang* • Max von Sydow *Jurgen Brausch* • Horst Buchholz *Walter Hoffman* • Helmut Berger *Ernst Ritter* • Cyrielle Claire *Claire Jouvet* • Eric Stoltz *Andy Wheeler* • Patrick Stewart *Colonel Peters* • Graham Crowden *Sir Geoffrey Macklin* ■ *Dir* Jonathan Sanger • *Scr* Ronald Bass, from his novel *The Emerald Illusion*

Code Name: the Cleaner ★★ PG

Spy spoof
2007 · US · Colour · 89min

Cedric the Entertainer stars in this stale spy spoof as an amnesiac who suspects he's an undercover agent but may be just a humble janitor. The jarring mix of lowest-common-denominator laughs and serious thriller elements makes it feel like you're watching two different films – both of them substandard. Meanwhile, the inane, stereotyped characters are beneath even buffoonish Cedric, with Lucy Liu, Nicollette Sheridan and Mark Dacascos wasted in underwritten roles. SF DVD BD

Cedric the Entertainer *Jake Rogers* • Lucy Liu *Gina* • Nicollette Sheridan *Diane* • Mark Dacascos *Eric Hauck* • Callum Keith Rennie *Shaw* • Niecy Nash *Jacuzzi* • DeRay Davis *Ronnie* • Will Patton *Riley* ■ *Dir* Les Mayfield • *Scr* Robert Adetuyi, George Gallo

Code of Silence ★★ 18

Action thriller
1985 · US · Colour · 96min

Even with the rather wooden Chuck Norris in the lead, director Andrew Davis still manages to generate a fair bit of mindless excitement here. Norris is the maverick cop who gets caught up in a drug war. He's boring, but there are some great action set pieces. JF Swearing, drug abuse. DVD

Chuck Norris *Eddie Cusack* • Henry Silva *Luis Comacho* • Bert Remsen *Commander Kates* • Mike Genovese *Tony Luna* • Nathan Davis *Felix Scalese* • Ralph Foody *Cragie* ■ *Dir* Andrew Davis • *Scr* Michael Butler, Dennis Shryack, Mike Gray, from a story by Michael Butler, Dennis Shyrack

Code Unknown ★★★★ 15

Drama
2000 · Fr/Ger/Rom · Colour · 112min

Opening with an audacious nine-minute tracking shot, Michael Haneke returns to the territory of *71 Fragments of a Chronology of Chance* (1994) to accuse us of becoming both desensitied to both the world around us and lazy in our film watching. Set in a microcosmic Paris, the various stories involving a Romanian refugee, a teenage runaway, an abused African liberal and a disillusioned actress are interwoven with a facility that demonstrates a total mastery of both sound and image. If some of the political theorising is somewhat naive and the direction is occasionally manipulative, the acting is superb. DP French, Malinke, Romanian, German, English, Arabic +subtitles. DVD

Juliette Binoche *Anne* • Thierry Neuvic *Georges* • Sepp Bierbichler *The farmer* • Alexandre Hamidi *Jean* ■ *Dir/Scr* Michael Haneke

CodeBreakers ★★

Period drama based on a true story
2005 · US · Colour · 88min

This dull period drama based on a scandal that rocked 1950s America explores how cadets at the West Point Military Academy – including the son of the football coach (Scott Glenn) – were found to have cheated on their exams and the furore that followed. The feature is efficiently constructed, with solid performances and an evocative retro look. But while its themes are as relevant today as they were in 1951, the story is so slow-paced and uninspiring that it's hard to stay awake, let alone care. SF

Scott Glenn *Coach Earl "Red" Blaik* • Jeff Roop *George Holbrook* • Zachery Bryan *[Zachery T›* Bryan] *Brian Nolan* • Corey Sevier *Bob Blaik* • Theo Rossi *Desantis* • Jake Busey *Straub* ■ *Dir* Rod Holcomb • *Scr* G Ross Parker, from the non-fiction book *A Return to Glory* by Bill McWilliams

Codename Wildgeese ★★ 15

Action adventure
1984 · UK/It · Colour · 88min

This ridiculous commando movie bears absolutely no relation to the Richard Burton/Roger Moore action classic, *The Wild Geese*. What we get instead is a very sullen Lewis Collins leading a motley crew of mercenaries in a fight against an opium warlord in South East Asia. Plenty of explosions and car chases ensue, plus a fair quota of brutality. RS

Lewis Collins *Wesley* • Lee Van Cleef *China* • Ernest Borgnine *Fletcher* • Klaus Kinski *Charlton* • Manfred Lehmann *Klein* • Mimsy Farmer *Kathy* • Thomas Danneberg *Arbib* • Frank Glaubrecht *Stone* • Wolfgang Pampel *Baldwin* ■ *Dir* Anthony Dawson [Antonio Margheriti] • *Scr* Michael Lester

Cody the Robosapien ★★ PG

Science-fiction adventure
2012 · US · Colour · 82min

Director Sean McNamara's brisk tale is harmless, undemanding fun. Bobby Coleman plays a New Orleans youngster who finds robot boy Cody in a dumpster after inventor David Eigenberg helps him evade evil tycoon Kim Coates. There's little actual novelty on show, but there's a decent degree of craftsmanship, as the CGI is well integrated into the action, and the cute robot's rapport with Coleman is creditably done. But the story gets sidetracked by subplots, and there are too many cornball montages and ill-judged break-dancing sequences. DP DVD

Bobby Coleman *Henry* • Penelope Ann Miller *Joanna* • David Eigenberg *Allan* • Holliston Coleman *Meagan* • Joaquim de Almeida *Esperenza* • Kim Coates *Porter* • Jae Head *Cody/ Robosapien* ■ *Dir* Sean McNamara • *Scr* Max Botkin

Un Coeur en Hiver ★★★★ 15

Drama
1992 · Fr · Colour · 100min

Few film-makers are capable of producing such incisive studies of intimate relationships as Claude Sautet, yet it was only with this intense picture that he first received the international acclaim he so richly deserved. This subtle and superbly crafted film is so naturalistic and touches on so many raw emotional nerves that, at times, it is almost unbearable to watch. Daniel Auteuil and Emmanuelle Béart are exceptional as the violin-maker and the musician whose fated attraction intrudes calamitously upon a world of order and beauty. DP French +subtitles. DVD

Daniel Auteuil *Stéphane* • Emmanuelle Béart *Camille* • André Dussollier *Maxime* • Elisabeth Bourgine *Hélène* • Brigitte Catillon *Régine* ■ *Dir* Claude Sautet • *Scr* Claude Sautet, Jacques Fieschi, Jérôme Tonnerre

Coffee and Cigarettes ★★ 15

Comedy
2003 · US · BW · 92min

Jim Jarmusch's movie consists of 11 vignettes featuring a cast of famous actors and musicians chatting over the two titular vices, seeing what sparks might fly from the unusual pairings. Shot starkly in black and white (repeatedly using the same three or four angles) there's a nagging sense of *déjà vu*. With the exception of Cate Blanchett's double act playing against herself, there's rarely a moment to get the heart pumping. However, the wittiest episode features Steve Coogan and Alfred Molina, while the ever-reliable Bill Murray has a surreal encounter with hip-hop giants GZA and RZA. Punctuated by sporadic moments of pleasure, the film leaves you slightly irritated and in need of something more substantial. GM DVD

Roberto Benigni *Roberto* • Steven Wright *Steven* • Joie Lee *Good Twin* • Cinqué Lee *Evil Twin/ Kitchen guy* • Steve Buscemi *Waiter* • Iggy Pop *Iggy* • Tom Waits *Tom* • Joe Rigano *Joe* • Vinny Vella *Vinny* • Vinny Vella Jr *Vinny Jr* • Renee French *Renee* • EJ Rodriguez *Waiter* • Alex Descas *Alex* • Isaach de Bankole *Isaach* • Cate Blanchett *Cate/Shelly* • Mike Hogan *Waiter* • Jack White (3) *Jack* • Meg White *Meg* • Alfred Molina *Alfred* • Steve Coogan *Steve* • Katy Hansz *Katy* • GZA • RZA • Bill Murray • Bill Rice *Bill* • Taylor Mead *Taylor* ■ *Dir/Scr* Jim Jarmusch

Coffin Rock ★★★ 15

Thriller
2009 · UK/Aus · Colour · 88min

It takes a while for writer/director Rupert Glasson's quirky feature debut to get into its stride and summon up an uneasy atmosphere. But once the film gets past its soap opera beginning and moves into "obsessive psycho" territory, the slick suspense becomes palpable, frightening and gruesome. Sam Parsonson gives a terrifyingly unhinged performance as the drifter who targets a married woman desperate to conceive a child. Parsonson's delusional reasons for his actions are skillfully woven throughout the main narrative, making the core issues of this topical shocker zing with a chilling authenticity. The title refers to a small Australian coastal town where everyone knows each other's business. AJ Violence, swearing, sex scenes.

Robert Taylor (4) *Rob Willis* • Lisa Chappell *Jess Willis* • Sam Parsonson *Evan* • Geoff Morrell *George* • Terry Camilleri *Tony* • Jodie Dry *Megan* ■ *Dir* Rupert Glasson

Coffy ★★★ 18

Blaxploitation action drama
1973 · US · Colour · 86min

Nurse Pam Grier masquerades as a junkie to infiltrate a drug cartel and take revenge on the Mob who turned her little sister into an addict. Jack Hill's extremely violent, blaxploitation classic made the halter-topped, Capri-panted Grier, in her first leading role, queen of the genre, while plenty of nudity and nasty blood-letting keep the action bubbling along. Thanks to strong roles like this, and acting smarts to match, Grier became a cult star. AJ DVD BD

Pam Grier *Coffy* • Booker Bradshaw *Brunswick* • Robert DoQui *King George* • William Elliott *Carter* • Allan Arbus *Vitroni* • Sid Haig *Omar* • Barry Cahill *McHenry* ■ *Dir/Scr* Jack Hill

Cohen and Tate ★★ 18

Crime thriller
1988 · US · Colour · 82min

Scoring a cult hit with *The Hitcher*, writer/director Eric Red sticks with the road movie format for this low-budget thriller about a boy who witnesses a gangland murder and gets kidnapped by a pair of hitmen, played by Roy Scheider and Adam Baldwin. High on humour and muscular doses of violence, the action is clumsily confined to the interior of a car, lending it a theatrical style. RS

Roy Scheider *Cohen* • Adam Baldwin *Tate* • Harley Cross *Travis Knight* • Cooper Huckabee *Jeff Knight* • Suzanne Savoy *Martha Knight* ■ *Dir/Scr* Eric Red

Coherence ★★★ 15

Science-fiction thriller
2013 · US/UK · Colour · 87min

This inventive low-budget sci-fi yarn begins as four couples gather for a dinner party. But their plans for a quiet night in are interrupted by a comet that is passing perilously close to Earth. It causes a blackout, and without power, the internet or electricity, how will they cope? While it's unlikely that the quantum physics would stand up to rigorous analysis, the philosophical questions about alternative worlds, identity and fate provide some food for thought, and there are some tense moments and whispers of a sinister atmosphere. LB DVD

Emily Foxler *Em* • Nicholas Brendon *Mike* • Maury Sterling *Kevin* • Lorene Scafaria *Lee* • Hugo Armstrong *Hugh* • Elizabeth Gracen *Beth* ■ *Dir* James Ward Byrkit • *Scr* James Ward Byrkit, from a story by Byrkit, Alex Manugian

Cold Comes the Night ★★★ 15

Crime thriller
2013 · US · Colour · 90min

The very title reeks of *film noir*, and so, too, does the content of Tze Chun's dark and intermittently brutal thriller. Alice Eve plays the owner of a struggling roadside motel; *Breaking Bad* star Bryan Cranston plays a Mob deliveryman who holes up there after his cash-filled car is impounded by a corrupt local cop. Cranston's eyesight is failing, and he needs Eve and her young daughter to be his eyes as he bids to get the car, and the money, back. Cranston is suitably sinister, but it's Eve who impresses as she evolves from timid motel mouse to empowered action-taker. The film works a touch too hard but on the whole, it's a very watchable drama. DA Violence, swearing. DVD BD

C

Alice Eve *Chloe* • Bryan Cranston *Topo* • Logan Marshall-Green *Billy* • Ursula Parker *Sophia* • Leo Fitzpatrick *Donnie* • Erin Cummings *Amber* ■ *Dir* Tze Chun • *Scr* Tze Chun, Osgood Perkins [Oz Perkins], Nick Simon

Cold Comfort ★★★ U
Thriller   1989 · Can · Colour · 88min

There are echoes of Stephen King's *Misery* in this chilling tale, but who's going to hear them out in the Canadian wilderness? A classic example of why you should never accept lifts from strangers, the story turns on the relationship that develops between teenager Margaret Langrick and the travelling salesman her father brings home as her birthday present. Maury Chaykin is splendidly malevolent as the deranged dad, while Paul Gross gives an astute performance as the lamb brought to the slaughter. Vic Sarin directs with a sure hand, leaving events tantalisingly open-ended. DP Swearing, nudity.

Maury Chaykin *Floyd* • Paul Gross *Stephan* • Margaret Langrick *Dolores* ■ *Dir* Victor Sarin [Vic Sarin] • *Scr* Richard Beattie, L Elliott Simms, from a play by James Garrard

Cold Creek Manor ★ 15
Suspense thriller   2003 · US/UK · Colour · 113min

Absolutely ludicrous from its hokey start to senseless finish, this haunted house thriller boasts only one shock – the fact that Mike Figgis (*Leaving Las Vegas*) considered it worth directing. When city slickers Dennis Quaid and Sharon Stone move to a dilapidated country mansion, they face sinister threats from former owner and ex-con Stephen Dorff, who wants to keep a dark family secret buried there. AJ Swearing, some violence. DVD

Dennis Quaid *Cooper Tilson* • Sharon Stone *Leah Tilson* • Stephen Dorff *Dale Massie* • Juliette Lewis *Ruby* • Kristen Stewart *Kristen Tilson* • Ryan Wilson *Jesse Tilson* • Dana Eskelson *Sheriff Ferguson* • Christopher Plummer *Mr Massie* ■ *Dir* Mike Figgis • *Scr* Richard Jefferies

Cold Dog Soup ★★ 15
Black comedy   1989 · US · Colour · 84min

A sexually inexperienced young innocent, promised a close encounter by a tempting young lass if he agrees to bury her mother's dog, meets a disturbed cab driver who demands they form a team and sell the dog. Equally inexperienced (and it shows) is director Alan Metter, who has a clutch of good ideas about surreal black comedy, but seems unable to produce the right tone to put them across to his audience. Randy Quaid, as the cabbie, squeezes some milage from one-note psychosis. JM DVD

Randy Quaid *Jack Cloud* • Frank Whaley *Michael Latchmer* • Christine Harnos *Sarah Hughes* • Sheree North *Mrs Hughes* • Nancy Kwan *Mme Chang* • Seymour Cassel *JoJo* ■ *Dir* Alan Metter • *Scr* Thomas Pope from a novel by Stephen Dobyns

Cold Feet ★★ 15
Comedy   1989 · US · Colour · 88min

This bizarre tale of western eccentrics has a brilliant but undisciplined cast who wander off into Method acting overdrive because there is no firm hand on the directorial tiller. Based on a script by Jim Harrison and the terribly hip Thomas McGuane and featuring a narrative that doesn't so much rove as list from side to side, this is a small cult hit which charmed some on its release while massively infuriating others. SH Violence, swearing.

Keith Carradine *Monte* • Sally Kirkland *Maureen* • Tom Waits *Kenny* • Bill Pullman *Buck* • Rip Torn *Sheriff* • Kathleen York *Laura* • Jeff Bridges *Bartender* ■ *Dir* Robert Dornhelm • *Scr* Thomas McGuane, Jim Harrison

Cold Fever ★★★★ 15
Drama   1994 · Ice/Ger/Swi/US · Colour · 81min

Considering its size, the Icelandic film industry produces films of a remarkably high quality, and Fridrik Thor Fridriksson's road movie is a case in point. In his bid to perform a traditional burial service for his geologist parents who died in Iceland seven years earlier, Japanese businessman Masatoshi Nagase encounters all manner of eccentric locals who make his odyssey a truly memorable experience. Fridriksson makes magnificent use of the island's snowy wastes and distinctive settlements, and only the contrived appearances of American "tourists" Lili Taylor and Fisher Stevens jar. DP Japanese, Icelandic +subtitles. DVD

Masatoshi Nagase *Atsushi Hirata* • Lili Taylor *Jill* • Fisher Stevens *Jack* • Gisli Halldorsson *Siggi* • Laura Hughes [Laura Leigh Hughes] *Laura* • Seijun Suzuki *Hirata's grandfather* • Hiromasa Shimada *Suzuki* • Mayayuki Sasaki *Higashino* ■ *Dir* Fridrik Thor Fridriksson • *Scr* Jim Stark, Fridrik Thor Fridriksson

Cold Fish ★★★ 18
Black comedy horror thriller
2010 · Jpn · Colour · 146min

A milksop finds himself trapped in a pact with a madman in Sion Sono's macabre black comedy. Keen to offload his troublesome teenage daughter (Hikari Kajiwara) so he can get to know his new bride (Megumi Kagurazaka), a tropical fish shop owner (Mitsuru Fukikoshi) agrees to let her board with a rival trader (Denden) and his younger wife (Asuka Kurosawa). But, rather than being benefactors, the couple turn out to be ruthless killers. The knowing performances, perceptive cinematography and clever production design help make up for the director's overindulgent moments. DP Japanese +subtitles. Violence, sex scenes, brief swearing. DVD

Mitsuru Fukikoshi *Nobuyuki Shamoto* • Denden *Yukio Murata* • Asuka Kurosawa *Aiko Murata* • Megumi Kagurazaka *Taeko Shamato* • Hikari Kajiwara *Mitsuko Shamoto* ■ *Dir* Sion Sono • *Scr* Sion Sono, Yoshiki Takahashi

Cold Front ★★★ 15
Spy thriller   1989 · US/Can · Colour · 89min

This sturdy crime thriller makes up for what it lacks in originality with two strong performances from Martin Sheen and Michael Ontkean (still best known as the sheriff in television's *Twin Peaks*). The pair play a US Drug Enforcement Agency officer and a plain-clothes Canadian Mountie respectively, who find themselves reluctantly teamed together when they get dragged into the world of espionage. It's simple, undemanding stuff, and the violent mayhem is ably held together by director Paul Bnarbic. JF Swearing. DVD

Martin Sheen *John Hyde* • Michael Ontkean *Derek MacKenzie* • Kim Coates *Mantha* • Beverly D'Angelo *Amanda* • Yvan Ponton *Inspector Duchesne* ■ *Dir* Paul Bnarbic • *Scr* Sean Allan, Stefan Arngrim

Cold Heaven ★★★ 15
Psychological thriller
1992 · US · Colour · 102min

Barely released to cinemas because the financing company ran into problems, this Nicolas Roeg mystery drama stars his wife, Theresa Russell, as a doctor's wife who starts an affair with another doctor only to discover her husband has been killed in a boating accident. What a coincidence! But then things start to get decidedly weird. Based on a novel by Brian Moore, the picture never quite delivers the zingers it promises but the Mexican locations are splendid, and Russell is alluring. AT

Theresa Russell *Marie Davenport* • Mark Harmon *Alex Davenport* • James Russo *Daniel Corvin* • Will Patton *Father Niles* • Richard Bradford *Monsignor Cassidy* • Talia Shire *Sister Martha* • Julie Carmen *Anna Corvin* ■ *Dir* Nicolas Roeg • *Scr* Allan Scott, from the novel by Brian Moore

Cold in July ★★★★ 15
Thriller   2014 · US/Fr · Colour · 105min

Mullet hairstyles and gruesome twists abound in this 1980s-set pulp tale from director Jim Mickle and regular screenwriting partner Nick Damici. After accidentally killing an unarmed intruder, small-town Texas family man Michael C Hall (*Dexter*) must contend with the dead man's vengeful father (Sam Shepard), until both begin to suspect there's more going on than meets the eye. Mickle's seedy hardcore thriller fires on all retro cylinders, with powerhouse performances from Hall, Shepard and Don Johnson (as a private eye), and one of the best-executed shoot-outs in recent memory. AJ Violence, swearing. DVD Blu

Michael C Hall *Richard Dane* • Sam Shepard *Ben Russell* • Don Johnson *Jim Bob Luke* • Vinessa Shaw *Ann Dane* ■ *Dir* Jim Mickle • *Scr* Nick Damici, Jim Mickle, from Joe R Lansdale's novel

The Cold Light of Day ★★ 15
Action thriller   2012 · US/Sp · Colour · 89min

Kidnappers turn an American family's Spanish holiday into a nightmare, but even more shocking for eldest son Will (Henry Cavill) is what he learns about his stern father (Bruce Willis) in this fish-out-of-water thriller. It's pacey, the plot never gets too stupid, and the Madrid locations look the part, but Cavill proves an identikit square-jawed hero and Sigourney Weaver's clearly coasting as a CIA handler who may not be all she seems. A time-passer for all concerned, the audience included. TJ Violence, swearing. DVD Blu

Bruce Willis *Martin Shaw* • Henry Cavill *Will Shaw* • Sigourney Weaver *Jean Carrack* • Jim Piddock *Meckler* • Caroline Goodall *Laurie Shaw* ■ *Dir* Mabrouk El Mechri • *Scr* Scott Wiper, John Petro

Cold Mountain ★★★ 15
Wartime romantic drama
2003 · US/UK/Rom/It · Colour · 147min

Jude Law and Nicole Kidman play southern sweethearts who become separated when he heads off to fight for the Confederacy during the US Civil War. The film then follows both his odyssey back from the front, with all the people and perils he encounters en route, and her struggle to survive on the mountain of the title. Along the way, Kidman is helped out by a drifter, played rather over-tetchily by Renée Zellweger. Director Anthony Minghella's film is beautifully shot by John Seale and has some great moments, but these are too few and far between. DA Violence, sex scenes. DVD Blu

Jude Law *WP Inman* • Nicole Kidman *Ada Monroe* • Renée Zellweger *Ruby Thewes* • Donald Sutherland *Reverend Monroe* • Ray Winstone *Teague* • Brendan Gleeson *Stobrod Thewes* • Philip Seymour Hoffman *Reverend Veasey* • Natalie Portman *Sara* • Kathy Baker *Sally Swanger* • James Gammon *Esco Swanger* • Giovanni Ribisi *Junior* ■ *Dir* Anthony Minghella • *Scr* Anthony Minghella, from the novel by Charles Frazier

Cold Sassy Tree ★★★
Romantic drama   1989 · US · Colour · 95min

An above average made-for-TV movie starring the redoubtable Faye Dunaway in a role which is positively enhanced by her chronic overacting. She stars with the excellent Richard Widmark in this tale of a couple who outrage the sensibilities of a parochial one-horse town. Dunaway gives it her all, and is aided by a decent, thoughtful script and gentle, appropriate direction by Joan Tewkesbury. SH

Faye Dunaway *Love Simpson* • Richard Widmark *E Rucker Blakeslee* • Neil Patrick Harris *Will Tweedy* • Frances Fisher *Loma* • Lee Garlington *Mary Willis* • John Jackson [John M Jackson] *Hoyt* • Jay O Sanders *Clayton McAllister* ■ *Dir* Joan Tewkesbury • *Scr* Joan Tewkesbury, from the novel by Olive Ann Burns

Cold Souls ★★★ 12A
Fantasy comedy drama
2008 · US/Fr · Colour · 101min

Though it initially promises to follow the lead of Spike Jonze's dark and zany 1999 comedy *Being John Malkovich* by casting *Sideways* star Paul Giamatti as himself in far-from-real circumstances, this clever, surreal comedy is closer to the more whimsical work of a young Woody Allen. Working on an off-Broadway production of Chekhov's *Uncle Vanya*, Giamatti finds his neuroses getting in the way of his performance, so he arranges for his soul to be removed and kept in storage. It's a witty and engaging film, though it becomes needlessly complicated with the addition of a subplot about Russian soul-trafficking. DW Swearing, nudity.

Paul Giamatti • David Strathairn *Dr Flintstein* • Dina Korzun *Nina* • Katheryn Winnick *Sveta* • Lauren Ambrose *Stephanie* ■ *Dir/Scr* Sophie Barthes

Cold Steel ★★ 18
Action drama   1987 · US · Colour · 86min

An interesting cast of disparate acting talent isn't enough to save this standard action film from director Dorothy Ann Puzo, daughter of *Godfather* novelist Mario Puzo. Brad Davis is utterly wasted as an LA cop out to avenge the murder of his father. Lower down the billing is 1980s pop icon Adam Ant, who turns in a decent performance. Worth catching only if you're curious to see a pre-*Basic Instinct* Sharon Stone. RS

Brad Davis *Johnny Modine* • Sharon Stone *Kathy* • Adam Ant *Mick* • Jonathan Banks *Iceman* • Jay Acovone *Cookie* • Eddie Egan *Lieutenant Hill* • Sy Richardson *Rashid* ■ *Dir* Dorothy Ann Puzo • *Scr* Michael Sonye, Moe Quigley, from a story by Lisa M Hansen, Dorothy Ann Puzo, Michael Sonye

Cold Sweat ★★ 15
Action thriller   1971 · Fr/It · Colour · 89min

Stone-faced Charles Bronson takes time off from his busy urban vigilante schedule to head for the French Riviera, only to be forced into drug smuggling by crime boss James Mason. James Bond director Terence Young's overly familiar revenge tale relies on turgid violence and Bronson's laid-back, tough-guy persona. AJ Some violence, swearing, sex scenes, nudity.

Charles Bronson *Joe Martin* • Liv Ullmann *Fabienne Martin* • James Mason *Ross* • Jill Ireland *Moira* • Michel Constantin *Whitey* ■ *Dir* Terence Young • *Scr* Shimon Wincelberg, Albert Simonin, from the novel *Ride the Nightmare* by Richard Matheson

Cold Weather ★★★ 15
Mystery drama   2010 · US · Colour · 103min

Director Aaron Katz's follow-up to the excellent but little seen *Quiet City* and *Dance Party, USA* is a teasing blend of melodrama, whodunnit mystery and domestic comedy. Cris Lankenau plays the Sherlock Holmes-obsessed Doug who, assisted by his sister (Trieste Kelly Dunn) and workmate (Raúl Castillo), searches for clues after his ex-girlfriend disappears. Despite being satisfyingly baffling, the case proves something of a MacGuffin, as Katz is actually more interested in the interaction between Doug and his indulgent sibling. Nevertheless, Andrew Reed's shadowy cinematography reinforces the mood, as Katz plays delightfully droll games with genre convention. DP Swearing, nudity.

Cris Lankenau *Doug* • Trieste Kelly Dunn *Gail* • Raúl Castillo *Carlos* • Robyn Rikoon *Rachel* • Jeb Pearson *Jim Warden* • Brendan McFadden *Swen* ■ *Dir* Aaron Katz • *Scr* Aaron Katz, from a story by Katz, Brendan McFadden, Ben Stambler

Coldblooded ★★ 18
Black comedy crime drama
1995 · US · Colour · 89min

Jason Priestley is cast here as a nerdy Mafia bookie who gets promoted by his boss Robert Loggia to the rank of *Pulp Fiction*-style assassin, only to discover he has a natural talent for killing. This potentially novel spoof of hitman movies is smothered under a welter of unfunny gags and Priestley's charmless performance, though Michael J Fox, who co-produced the film, turns in an amusing cameo. RS Violence, swearing.

Jason Priestley *Cosmo* • Kimberly Williams *Jasmine* • Peter Riegert *Steve* • Robert Loggia *Gordon* • Janeane Garofalo *Honey* • Josh Charles *Randy* • Michael J Fox *Tim Alexander* ■ *Dir/Scr* M Wallace Wolodarsky [Wallace Wolodarsky]

The Coldest City
Thriller   2017 · US · Colour

This is a preview – no prints were available to review as we went to press: Berlin in the late 1980s is the setting for this thriller based on the graphic novel by Antony Johnston. Charlize Theron headlines as an MI6 spy who is tasked with hunting down double agents after the murder of one of her colleagues, and just as the ball is set in motion to bring down the Berlin Wall. Expect more action thrills than political chicanery, though, as the job of directing falls to first-timer/former stunt co-ordinator David Leitch. SP

James McAvoy *Percival* • Charlize Theron *Lorraine Broughton* • Toby Jones *Gray* • Eddie Marsan *Spyglass* • John Goodman ■ *Dir* David Leitch • *Scr* Kurt Johnstad, from Antony Johnston's graphic novel

The Colditz Story ★★★★ U
Second World War drama
1954 · UK · BW · 93min

One of seemingly dozens of PoW dramas made in the mid-1950s, this is set in the infamous German fortress of the title. The story about the daring escapes undertaken by Allied prisoners has little time for the psychology of imprisonment, but the action is still well-played – tense at times, music-hall jolly at others. John Mills plays Pat Reid, on whose first-hand account the film is based, and Eric Portman, Ian Carmichael, Lionel Jeffries and Bryan Forbes are the other inmates of heroic hue. AT *DVD* *BD*

John Mills *Pat Reid* • Eric Portman *Colonel Richmond* • Christopher Rhodes *Mac* • Lionel Jeffries *Harry* • Bryan Forbes *Jimmy* • Ian Carmichael *Robin* • Richard Wattis *Richard* ■ *Dir* Guy Hamilton • *Scr* Guy Hamilton, Ivan Foxwell, from the non-fiction book by PR Reid

Colette
Biographical period drama 2018 · UK · Colour

This is a preview – no prints were available to review as we went to press: Keira Knightley once bemoaned the amount of time she spent in corsets, but her strongest roles have seen her in period costume from *Pride & Prejudice* to *Anna Karenina*. In this biographical portrait, she'll be in costume again, all be it 20th-century, as French novelist Sidonie-Gabrielle Colette – the brain behind *Chéri* and *Gigi*. Yorkshire-born director Wash Westmoreland (*Still Alice*) has the task of trying to keep it from slipping into soap opera. SP

Keira Knightley *Colette* ■ *Dir* Wash Westmoreland • *Scr* Wash Westmoreland, Richard Glatzer

Colin ★★★ 18
Horror 2008 · UK · Colour · 97min

With an alleged £45 budget and actors recruited via the likes of Facebook, you'd expect this bargain-basement British horror to be terrible. But beneath the shaky camcorder visuals and amateur dramatics, there's actually a watchable little film. A tale of a UK zombie apocalypse told unusually from the flesh-muncher's perspective, it centres on the eponymous Londoner (Alastair Kirton), as he joins the rising ranks of suburban undead and provides the link between a series of grisly and inventively shot vignettes. Debut writer/director Marc Price works wonders with his limited resources, concentrating on atmosphere rather than narrative. So, while the material is too flimsy for its running time, the sound design is good and the effects look surprisingly realistic. SF Violence, swearing.

Alastair Kirton *Colin* • Daisy Aitkens *Linda, Colin's sister* • Kate Alderman *False Laura* • Leanne Pammen *Laura* • Tat Whalley *Marlen, Linda's friend* • Kerry Owen *Colin's mother* ■ *Dir/Scr* Marc Price

Collapse ★★★
Documentary 2009 · US · Colour · 82min

This sombre documentary predicts grim times ahead for a planet overreliant on fossil fuels, as oil companies continue to wield untold power over governments. Director Chris Smith trains his camera on investigative journalist Michael Ruppert, who warns that "the speed at which things are falling apart" may be too fast to arrest, as the world's resources are perilously depleted and alternative energy sources are not up to the job. There are clear parallels

with former US vice-president Al Gore's arguments in *An Inconvenient Truth*, only Smith's film makes less use of showbiz-style graphics and its overall message has a more ominous tone. TeS

Michael Ruppert ■ *Dir* Chris Smith

Collateral ★★★★ 15
Action crime thriller 2004 · US · Colour · 114min

Tom Cruise stars as a cold-blooded hitman in this effective, edgy thriller from director Michael Mann. After hijacking a taxi and its driver, Cruise embarks on a series of ruthlessly efficient assassinations across night-time LA while the hapless cabbie (Jamie Foxx) tries to work out ways to escape. Cruise is well cast against type and is surprisingly effective as the killer, but it's Mann's astonishing style that really marks the film out. Shot on a mixture of film and digital video, the night-time lights of LA look alternately moody, surreal and dangerous. AS Swearing, violence. *DVD* *BD*

Tom Cruise *Vincent* • Jamie Foxx *Max Durocher* • Jada Pinkett Smith *Annie* • Mark Ruffalo *Fanning* • Peter Berg *Richard Weidner* • Bruce McGill *Pedrosa* • Irma P Hall *Ida* • Barry Shabaka Henley [Barry "Shabaka" Henley] *Daniel* • Javier Bardem *Felix* ■ *Dir* Michael Mann • *Scr* Stuart Beattie

Collateral Beauty
Drama 2016 · US · Colour

This is a preview – no prints were available to review as we went to press: Will Smith leads a starry line-up that includes British beauties Keira Knightley, Kate Winslet and Helen Mirren in a hopefully life-affirming drama from *The Devil Wears Prada* director David Frankel. There's clearly a strong feminine edge to the story of Smith's ad executive who falls into a spiral of depression following a personal tragedy, so his colleagues try to bring him back from the brink. SP

Will Smith *Howard Iniet* • Kate Winslet *Claire* • Keira Knightley *Aimee Moore* • Helen Mirren *Brigitte* • Edward Norton *Whit Tardsham* • Naomie Harris *Madeleine* ■ *Dir* David Frankel • *Scr* Allan Loeb

Collateral Damage ★★ 15
Action thriller 2001 · US · Colour · 104min

Arnold Schwarzenegger plays a vengeful firefighter hunting the Colombian terrorists who've blown up an embassy building, killing his wife and child. The film's start and finish have plenty of bang for your buck but the flabby middle section sees Schwarzenegger's one-man army collecting a woman and child to protect, which muddles both the action and the revenge theme. DA Swearing, violence. *DVD* *BD*

Arnold Schwarzenegger *Gordy Brewer* • Elias Koteas *Agent Brandt* • Francesca Neri *Selena Perrini* • Cliff Curtis *Claudio, "El Lobo" Perrini* • John Leguizamo *Felix* • John Turturro *Sean Armstrong* ■ *Dir* Andrew Davis • *Scr* David Griffiths, Peter Griffiths, from a story by David Griffiths, Peter Griffiths, Ronald Roose

The Collection ★★ 18
Horror thriller 2011 · US · Colour · 78min

The insidious saga of the maniac who collects survivors of his home-invasion killing sprees continues with this even grislier follow-up to *The Collector* (2009). Here, the masked mystery man starts with a vicious cull of clubbers at a backstreet venue where he grabs tycoon's daughter Elena (Emma Fitzpatrick) and spirits her back to his charnel-house lair. If you like horror to be a lethal labyrinth with elaborate traps around every corner, then this should be right up your alley. JA Violence.

Josh Stewart *Arkin* • Emma Fitzpatrick *Elena* • Tergesen, Lee *Lucello* • Christopher McDonald *Mr Peters* ■ *Dir* Marcus Dunstan • *Scr* Marcus Dunstan, Patrick Melton

La Collectionneuse ★★★★ 15
Drama 1967 · Fr · Colour · 82min

This is the third of Eric Rohmer's "Six Moral Tales", and the first of feature length.

Winner of the special jury prize at Berlin, it tells of the summer encounter between sexually liberated teenager Haydée Politoff, antique dealer Patrick Bauchau and his friend Daniel Pommereulle. Attracted and unnerved by Politoff's amorous exploits, they attempt to reform her without becoming part of her collection of lovers. As you would expect of Rohmer, there is plenty of amusing and insightful chat, as his young cast flirt and succumb, resist and reproach. DP French, English +subtitles. *DVD*

Patrick Bauchau *Adrien* • Haydée Politoff *Haydée* • Daniel Pommereulle *Daniel* • Seymour Hertzberg [Eugene Archer] *Sam* • Mijanou Bardot *Carole* • Annik Morice *Carole's friend* ■ *Dir* Eric Rohmer • *Scr* Eric Rohmer, Patrick Bauchau, Haydée Politoff, Daniel Pommereulle

The Collector ★★★★ 15
Thriller 1965 · US/UK · Colour · 114min

This is a genuinely disturbing chunk of *Grand Guignol* about a maladjusted, butterfly-collecting young man who kidnaps an art student and keeps her in his cellar. Based on an equally disturbing and complex novel by John Fowles, this was in its day a fashionable shocker and X-certificated. Now it comes across as a fascinating period piece, featuring two quintessential 1960s stars in possibly their best roles – painfully handsome Terence Stamp as the collector, and beautiful auburn-haired Samantha Eggar as the victim of his attentions. Kenneth More was also cast as Eggar's older lover, but his whole role was removed in the final edit. TS

Terence Stamp *Freddie Clegg* • Samantha Eggar *Miranda Grey* • Mona Washbourne *Aunt Annie* • Maurice Dallimore *Neighbour* • William Beckley *Crutchley* • Gordon Barclay *Clerk* ■ *Dir* William Wyler • *Scr* Stanley Mann, John Kohn, from the novel by John Fowles

The Collector ★★★ 18
Horror thriller 2009 · US · Colour · 86min

Feast trilogy co-writers Marcus Dunstan and Patrick Melton reconceived their script (originally a *Saw* prequel) as a home invasion torture game chiller, as burglar Josh Stewart, who's out to steal a rare gem, finds a demented psycho has already broken in and put the captive inhabitants through bloody hell. Dunstan makes his directorial debut with this classy, suspenseful scare machine. And it contains the obligatory grungy lighting, industrial rock soundtrack and extreme mutilation via pliers, chisel, acid, fishhooks and bladed chandelier that any *Saw* franchise gore fan could wish for. AJ Violence *DVD* *BD* *CS*

Josh Stewart *Arkin* • Michael Reilly Burke *Michael Chase* • Andrea Roth *Victoria Chase* • Madeline Zima *Jill Chase* • Juan Fernández [Juan Fernandez] *The Collector* ■ *Dir* Marcus Dunstan • *Scr* Marcus Dunstan, Patrick Melton

Colleen ★★
Musical comedy 1936 · US · BW · 90min

When eccentric millionaire Hugh Herbert puts gold-digger Joan Blondell in charge of his dress shop, his family is outraged. Complications ensue when his nephew, Dick Powell, brings Ruby Keeler in to take over. A feeble script and forgettable score make this a disappointing final outing for Powell and Keeler, paired for the sixth and last time in a Warner Bros musical. RK

Dick Powell *Donald Ames III* • Ruby Keeler *Colleen* • Jack Oakie *Joe Cork* • Joan Blondell *Minnie Hawkins* • Hugh Herbert *Cedric Ames* • Louise Fazenda *Alicia Ames* • Paul Draper *Paul* • Luis Alberni *Carlo* ■ *Dir* Alfred E Green • *Scr* Peter Milne, Frederick Hugh Herbert [F Hugh Herbert], Sig Herzig, from a story by Robert Lord • *Music Director* Leo Forbstein [Leo F Forbstein]

College ★★★★★ U
Silent romantic comedy 1927 · US · BW · 66min

Buster Keaton's running, jumping but rarely standing-still film is a story about his going to college and trying to transcend athletically his bookworm exterior to win the heart of student Anne Cornwall. She's surrounded by admiring jocks, but he's determined to flatten them in a decathlon

of sports, though he gets it all wrong – knocking down hurdles, or being thrown by the hammer instead of the other way around. There's one spectacular sequence in which he apes a soda-jerk to disastrous effect, and the final pole-vault to rescue the girl is balletically brilliant. TH *DVD*

Buster Keaton *Ronald* • Ann Cornwall *Mary Haines, the girl* • Flora Bramley *Mary's friend* • Harold Goodwin (1) *Jeff Brown, a rival* • Grant Withers *Jeff's friend* • Buddy Mason *Jeff's friend* • Snitz Edwards *Dean Edwards* ■ *Dir* James W Horne • *Scr* Carl Harbaugh, Bryan Foy

College Road Trip ★ U
Comedy 2008 · US · Colour · 79min

The increasingly unfunny Martin Lawrence plays an overly protective father who is determined that daughter Raven-Symoné will end up at a university close to home. However, she has other ideas so Lawrence decides to take her on a road trip and talk her around. It's hard to decide what is the worst thing about this film: the shrill antics of Symoné or the desperate mugging of Lawrence. But in the end Donny Osmond's excruciating turn as a parent with a penchant for show-tune duets takes that particular honour. JF *DVD*

Martin Lawrence *Chief James Porter* • Raven-Symoné *Melanie Porter* • Donny Osmond *Doug Greenhut* • Brenda Song *Nancy* • Will Sasso *Deputy O'Mally* • Eshaya Draper *Trey Porter* ■ *Dir* Roger Kumble • *Scr* Emi Mochizuki, Carrie Evans, Cinco Paul, Ken Daurio

College Swing ★★ PG
Musical 1938 · US · BW · 86min

Despite having three writers on the movie, including an uncredited Preston Sturges, and Raoul Walsh as director, this is little more than an excuse for a variety show. The silly plot, such as it is, has bird-brained Gracie Allen inheriting a college and hiring vaudevillians as professors. Allen does a few turns with husband George Burns, Martha Raye yells a number of songs, Bob Hope cracks corny jokes and Betty Grable shakes her legs. RB *DVD*

George Burns *George Jonas* • Gracie Allen *Gracie Alden* • Martha Raye *Mabel* • Bob Hope *Bud Brady* • Edward Everett Horton *Hubert Dash* • Florence George *Ginna Ashburn* • Ben Blue *Ben Volt* • Betty Grable *Betty* • Jackie Coogan *Jackie* • John Payne *Martin Bates* ■ *Dir* Raoul Walsh • *Scr* Walter DeLeon, Francis Martin, from a story by Ted Lesser

Collision Course ★★ 18
Comedy 1987 · US · Colour · 96min

This thoroughly unremarkable variation on the Arnold Schwarzenegger vehicle *Red Heat* was shelved for three years after it was made, because of the lawsuit that followed the bankruptcy of its production company, DEG. It wasn't until 1992 that it was released on video in the US – something of an embarrassment for Jay Leno, who had just assumed the host's chair of that famous US chatfest *The Tonight Show*. As the detective teamed with visiting Japanese inspector Pat Morita, Leno reveals why this is his sole starring role to date. A disappointment. DP

Noriyuki "Pat" Morita [Pat Morita] *Investigator Fujitsuka Natsuo* • Jay Leno *Detective Tony Costas* • Ernie Hudson *Shortcut* • Chris Sarandon *Philip Madras* • John Hancock *Lieutenant Ryerson* • Tom Noonan *Scully* • Al Waxman *Dingman* ■ *Dir* Lewis Teague • *Scr* Frank Darius Namei, Robert Resnikoff

Colombiana ★★ 15
Action adventure 2011 · US/Fr · Colour · 103min

The setting (Latin America's drug wars) and shapely star (Zoë Saldana), plus the involvement of cult French director Luc Besson, promise a level of thrills, raunchiness and brutality that this surprisingly tame action flick never quite delivers. It makes a refreshing change to see a woman handling the artillery, as Saldana wages a one-woman war against the gangs who killed her parents, and a man as the purely decorative love interest. The story itself, however, sticks to the usual formula, as Saldana leads the clueless FBI officer (Lennie James) on a merry dance

C

while he investigates her ever more elaborate assassinations. **DW** English, Spanish +subtitles. *DVD* *BL*

Zoe Saldana [Zoë Saldana] *Cataleya Restrepo* • Cliff Curtis *Emilio* • Lennie James *Special Agent Ross* • Michael Vartan *Danny Delaney* • Amandla Stenberg *Young Cataleya Restrepo* • Callum Blue *Richard* ■ *Dir* Olivier Megaton • *Scr* Luc Besson, Robert Mark Kamen

Le Colonel Chabert ★★★ 12
Period drama   1994 · Fr · Colour · 106min

Cinematographer Yves Angelo made his directorial debut with this handsome adaptation of one of the novels making up Balzac's *Comédie Humaine*. Gérard Depardieu is typically bullish as the Napoleonic veteran returning ten years after his supposed death to discover his wife (Fanny Ardant) has remarried, taking his fortune with her. The war scenes are magnificent, the intrigue compelling and the sense of period faultless. However, Angelo occasionally gets so carried away by the grandeur and gravitas of the production that the pace drops to a crawl. **DP** French +subtitles. *DVD*

Gérard Depardieu *Chabert* • Fanny Ardant *Countess Ferraud* • Fabrice Luchini *Derville* • André Dussollier *Count Ferraud* • Daniel Prévost *Boucard* • Olivier Saladin *Huré* ■ *Dir* Yves Angelo • *Scr* Jean Cosmos, Yves Angelo, Véronique Legrange, from the novel by Honoré de Balzac

Colonel Effingham's Raid
★★★ U
Comedy drama   1945 · US · BW · 70min

Bluff Charles Coburn's 1943 supporting Oscar for *The More the Merrier* helped elevate him to lead status, and here he's well cast in this minor 20th Century-Fox rustic comedy drama about a returning army officer fighting a one-man battle to preserve his southern town's heritage. He seldom played leads again, but was Oscar-nominated for his subsequent movie, *The Green Years*. **TS** *DVD*

Charles Coburn *Colonel Effingham* • Joan Bennett *Ella Sue Dozier* • William Eythe *Al* • Allyn Joslyn *Earl Hoats* • Elizabeth Patterson *Emma* ■ *Dir* Irving Pichel • *Scr* Kathryn Scola, from the novel by Barry Fleming

Colonel March Investigates
★★
Crime mystery   1953 · UK · BW · 70min

Boris Karloff runs a Scotland Yard division called the "Department of Queer Complaints", wears an eye-patch and carries a swordstick. These three short stories proving his investigative brilliance were actually glued together from Karloff's British TV show, *Colonel March of Scotland Yard*. Threadbare production values don't help. **AT**

Boris Karloff *Colonel March* • Ewan Roberts *Inspector Ames* • Richard Wattis *Cabot* • John Hewer *John Parrish* • Sheila Burrell *Joan Forsythe* • Joan Sims *Marjorie Dawson* ■ *Dir* Cyril Endfield [Cy Endfield] • *Scr* Leo Davis, from the TV series by Carter Dickson

Colonel Redl
★★★★ 15
Period drama
1984 · Hun/W Ger/Austria · Colour · 143min

This is a compelling study of the decaying Austro-Hungarian empire and the social, racial and political tensions that eventually undermined it. Klaus Maria Brandauer excels as the railwayman's son whose casual facility for deceit and obsessive devotion to honour enable him to rise through the ranks of the Imperial Army until both his background and his bisexuality become an embarrassment to the establishment. Armin Mueller-Stahl's ruthless Franz Ferdinand is equally impressive, but it's the chilling way director István Szabó charts the complex web of events that makes this sumptuous picture so memorable. **DP** German +subtitles. Some violence, swearing, sex scenes, nudity. *DVD*

Klaus Maria Brandauer *Alfred Redl* • Hans Christian Blech *Colonel von Roden* • Armin Mueller-Stahl *Archduke Franz Ferdinand* • Gudrun Landgrebe *Katalin Kubinyi* • Jan Niklas

Christoph Kubinyi ■ *Dir* István Szabó • *Scr* István Szabó, Peter Dobai, from the play *A Patriot for Me* by John Osborne

Colonia
★★★ 15
Thriller based on a true story
2015 · Ger/Lux/Fr · Colour · 109min

Under the rule of General Pinochet in the early 1970s, the "Colonia Dignidad" was a compound used to torture political prisoners and other unspeakable acts. German Florian Gallenberger makes this the setting of a thriller that doubles as a prison-break movie, with Emma Watson as an air stewardess who finds out that her lover (Daniel Brühl) is being held at the camp. Michael Nyqvist is suitably monstrous as cult leader Paul Schäfer, although sadly the film doesn't do justice to his real-life victims. **SC** In English, Spanish. Violence, swearing, child abuse references.

Emma Watson *Lena* • Daniel Brühl *Daniel* • Michael Nyqvist *Paul Schäfer* • Richenda Carey *Gisela* ■ *Dir* Florian Gallenberger • *Scr* Florian Gallenberger, Torsten Wenzel

The Colony
★★ 18
Science-fiction horror
2013 · Can · Colour · 90min

Survivors of an ice age are reduced to living in underground bunkers, where catching the common cold is as deadly as having the plague - a mere sniffle earns ejection with extreme prejudice. However, the chilling status quo is disturbed when contact with a neighbouring settlement is lost, forcing Laurence Fishburne and young volunteer Kevin Zegers to investigate. This subzero sci-fi tale has the odd tense moment, but it's just too derivative to really raise the temperature. **JA** Violence. *DVD* *BL*

Laurence Fishburne *Briggs* • Bill Paxton *Mason* • Kevin Zegers *Sam* • Charlotte Sullivan *Kai* ■ *Dir* Jeff Renfroe • *Scr* Jeff Renfroe, Svet Rouskov, Patrick Tarr, Pascal Trottier, from a story by Tarr, Trottier

Color Me Blood Red
★★ 18
Horror   1965 · US · Colour · 79min

This is a surprisingly restrained schlocker, with Don Joseph (aka Gordon Oas-Heim) playing an egomaniacal artist who kills to maintain the stocks of red "paint" that have helped establish his reputation with the pretentious critic who had previously spurned him. Mostly acting with his eyes on stalks, Joseph conveys tortured self-delusion rather well, but the remainder of the cast are less effective. **DP** *DVD*

Don Joseph [Gordon Oas-Heim] *Adam Sorg* • Candi Conder *April* • Elyn Warner *Gigi* • Scott H Hall *Farnsworth* • Jerome Eden *Rolf* ■ *Dir/Scr* Herschell G Lewis [Herschell Gordon Lewis]

Color of a Brisk and Leaping Day
★★★
Period drama   1996 · US · BW · 85min

Fight your way through the title and you will find an American indie production about a man who wants to rebuild and reopen the railroad that once ran through Yosemite national park. This majestic wilderness was made world famous by Ansel Adams's photographs; Christopher Münch's film mirrors Adams's imagery while the Chinese-American hero, played by Peter Alexander, sets about realising his obsession. Like the story itself the movie is a labour of love, set in the 1940s, incorporating archive footage and full of remarkable detail. **AT**

Peter Alexander *John Lee* • Jeri Arredondo *Nancy* • Henry Gibson *Robinson* • Michael Stipe *Skeeter* • David Chung *Mr Lee* • Diana Larkin *Wendy* ■ *Dir/Scr* Christopher Münch • *Cinematographer* Rob Sweeney

The Color of Money
★★★★ 15
Sports drama   1986 · US · Colour · 114min

Paul Newman reprises the role of "Fast" Eddie Felson, the pool shark he played in 1961's *The Hustler*, and deservedly won the best actor Oscar. Here, the ageing Felson takes on pushy pupil Vincent (Tom Cruise)

and both learn a trick or two as Felson prepares his prodigy for a national tournament in Atlantic City. The confrontational climax never quite convinces, but Richard Price's knockout script is one to treasure and director Martin Scorsese brings his trademark visual style to bear on the production. **TH** Violence, swearing, nudity. *DVD*

Paul Newman *"Fast" Eddie Felson* • Tom Cruise *Vincent Lauria* • Mary Elizabeth Mastrantonio *Carmen* • Helen Shaver *Janelle* • John Turturro *Julian* • Forest Whitaker *Amos* ■ *Dir* Martin Scorsese • *Scr* Richard Price, from the novel by Walter Tevis

Color of Night
★ 18
Erotic thriller   1994 · US · Colour · 134min

Richard Rush was once a half-decent film-maker but he came a cropper with this atrocity, which became notorious after some full-frontal shots of Bruce Willis were snipped by the censors. So even though we don't get the Full Brucey, we do get a lousy whodunnit, in which every member of a therapy group goes out of their way to prove they're madder than the rest. This is so awful it can't be missed. **DP** Swearing, violence, sex scenes, nudity. *DVD*

Bruce Willis *Dr Bill Capa* • Jane March *Rose* • Rubén Blades *Martinez* • Lesley Ann Warren *Sondra* • Scott Bakula *Dr Bob Moore* • Brad Dourif *Clark* • Lance Henriksen *Buck* • Kevin J O'Connor *Casey* • Andrew Lowery *Dale* ■ *Dir* Richard Rush • *Scr* Matthew Chapman, Billy Ray, from a story by Billy Ray

The Color of Paradise
★★★★ PG
Drama   1999 · Iran · Colour · 86min

Majid Majidi's follow-up to his Oscar-nominated delight, *The Children of Heaven*, combines a fairy-tale atmosphere with sensual imagery to produce a gentle parable on the dangers of social ambition and spiritual hypocrisy. There's a *Kikujiro* feel to the relationship between miner Hossein Mahjub and his eight-year-old son, Mohsen Ramezani, as the rascally widower comes to reappraise his priorities after a prestigious betrothal falls through. But leaving a deeper impression is Majidi's depiction of the blind boy's sensitivity to both his family (particularly his beloved grandmother) and the natural world around him. Simple but cinematic, moving and inspiring. **DP** Farsi +subtitles.

Hossein Mahjub *Hashem, the father* • Mohsen Ramezani *Mohammad* • Salime Feizi *Grandmother* ■ *Dir/Scr* Majid Majidi

The Color Purple ★★★★ 15
Period drama   1985 · US · Colour · 147min

On this film's release, it was fashionable to castigate director Steven Spielberg for his somewhat glossy, sugar-coated version of Alice Walker's celebrated Pulitzer Prize-winning novel about a young black woman's struggle for self- and racial identity. Yet this is actually an impressive, dignified attempt to turn a radical and often difficult book into mainstream entertainment with a message. Whoopi Goldberg is wonderful in the lead, Danny Glover and Margaret Avery are sublime, and watch out for Oprah Winfrey playing *very* out of character. **SH** Violence, swearing. *DVD* *BL*

Whoopi Goldberg *Celie* • Danny Glover *Albert Johnson* • Margaret Avery (2) *Shug Avery* • Oprah Winfrey *Sofia* • Willard Pugh *Harpo* • Akosua Busia *Nettie* • Desreta Jackson *Young Celie* • Adolph Caesar *Old Mister* • Rae Dawn Chong *Squeak* ■ *Dir* Steven Spielberg • *Scr* Menno Meyjes, from the novel by Alice Walker

Colorado Territory ★★★
Western   1949 · US · BW · 94min

This is an exciting westernised remake of the Humphrey Bogart classic *High Sierra*, with an identical plot and the same director in Raoul Walsh. Walsh manages to create a superbly sweaty atmosphere, with Joel McCrea this time as the outlaw on the run, hiding out in the desert. The themes are adult and the tension is beautifully sustained. **TS**

Joel McCrea *Wes McQueen* • Virginia Mayo *Colorado Carson* • Dorothy Malone *Julie Ann* • Henry Hull *Winslow* • John Archer *Reno Blake* • James Mitchell *Duke Harris* • Morris Ankrum *US marshal* • Basil Ruysdael *Dave Rickard* • Frank Puglia *Brother Tomas* ■ *Dir* Raoul Walsh • *Scr* John Twist, Edmund H North, from the novel *High Sierra* by WR Burnett

Colors
★★★ 18
Crime drama   1988 · US · Colour · 126min

With *Dragnet*-style gravity, this movie informs us of the 600 gangs, the 70,000 gang members and the 400 gang-related murders in LA County each year. Then cops Robert Duvall and Sean Penn take to the streets to apprehend the troublesome youths. Directed by Dennis Hopper with some urgency, the picture is tense and unpleasant, with sympathy for both sides of the war. Duvall and Penn make a fine combination of old sage and high-octane rookie, but this is so grim it's hard to enjoy. **AT** Violence, swearing. *DVD* *BL*

Sean Penn *Danny McGavin* • Robert Duvall *Bob Hodges* • Maria Conchita Alonso *Louisa Gomez* • Randy Brooks *Ron Delaney* • Don Cheadle *Rocket* ■ *Dir* Dennis Hopper • *Scr* Michael Schiffer, from a story by Michael Schiffer, Richard DiLello

The Colossus of New York
★
Science-fiction horror   1958 · US · BW · 71min

When Otto Kruger stays late at the lab to transplant his brother's brain into a robot, he ends up with a combination of Frankenstein's monster and *The Wrong Trousers*. The big lad is soon biting chunks out of the Big Apple. The dialogue and effects are wretched and the direction is more leaden than the creature's footwear. **DP**

Ross Martin *Dr Jeremy Spensser* • Mala Powers *Anne Spensser* • Charles Herbert *Billy Spensser* • John Baragrey *Dr Henry Spensser* • Otto Kruger *Dr William Spensser* • Robert Hutton *Professor John Carrington* • Ed Wolff *Colossus* ■ *Dir* Eugène Lourié • *Scr* Thelma Schnee, from a story by Willis Goldbeck

The Colossus of Rhodes
★★★
Period adventure
1961 · It/Fr/Sp · Colour · 127min

Before he went on to make spaghetti westerns with such fierce artistry, and after several credits as screenwriter on historical epics, Sergio Leone made this spectacular adventure, his official debut as a director. Rory Calhoun stars as Athenian soldier Dario, who joins a slave uprising against oppressive ruler King Xerxes. There are some explicit torture and battle scenes, and touches of Leone irony to lighten the rather lumpen load. **TH**

Rory Calhoun *Dario* • Lea Massari *Diala* • Georges Marchal *Peliocles* • Conrado San Martin *Thar* • Angel Aranda *Koros* • Mabel Karr *Mirte* ■ *Dir* Sergio Leone • *Scr* Ennio De Concini, Sergio Leone, Cesare Seccia, Luciano Martino, Duccio Tessari, Age Gavioli, Carlo Gualtieri, Luciano Chittarini

Colossus: the Forbin Project ★★★
Science-fiction thriller
1969 · US · Colour · 99min

The years have been kind to Joseph Sargent's thinking man's sci-fi entry, which imagines a time when one super computer has total control over all western defence systems. When it decides to link terminals with its Soviet counterpart in a bid for world domination, its human masters discover they can't switch the damn thing off. Cleverly playing up the thriller aspects of the story and cannily making the computer the film's central character, this is a well-acted and utterly persuasive shocker. **RS**

Eric Braeden *Dr Charles Forbin* • Susan Clark *Dr Cleo Markham* • Gordon Pinsent *The President* • William Schallert *Grauber* • Leonid Rostoff *1st Chairman* • Georg Stanford Brown *Fisher* • Tom Basham *Harrison* ■ *Dir* Joseph Sargent • *Scr* James Bridges, from the novel *Colossus* by DF Jones

U SUITABLE FOR ALL   Uc SUITABLE ESPECIALLY FOR YOUNG CHILDREN (DVD ONLY)   PG PARENTAL GUIDANCE   12A UNDER 12s TO BE ACCOMPANIED (CINEMA ONLY)

The Colour of Lies ★★★★ 15

Suspense thriller 1999 · Fr · Colour · 112min

Couching the old-fashioned whodunnit in a deliciously modern form, Claude Chabrol brings an acute sense of character and place to this teasing mystery. Cameraman Eduardo Serra's views of Brittany are expertly alternated with tight close-ups, as police inspector Valéria Bruni-Tedeschi investigates the rape and murder of a ten-year-old girl. Jacques Gamblin's performance as the brooding artist – and prime suspect – is balanced neatly by his breezy nursing wife Sandrine Bonnaire, while the petty preoccupations of the locals are slyly contrasted with the opinions of media luvvie Antoine de Caunes. DP French +subtitles.

Sandrine Bonnaire *Viviane Sterne* · Jacques Gamblin *René Sterne* · Antoine de Caunes *Germain-Roland Desmot* · Valéria Bruni-Tedeschi *Frederique Lesage* · Bulle Ogier *Yvelyne Bordier* ■ *Dir* Claude Chabrol · *Scr* Claude Chabrol, Odile Barski

The Colour of Pomegranates ★★★★★ U

Biographical drama
1969 · USSR · Colour · 69min

Ostensibly this is a fantasy on the life of the 18th-century Armenian poet Arutiun Sayadin, the carpet weaver's apprentice who rose to become first the court minstrel Sayat Nova ("the king of song"), and then an archbishop. Yet the sumptuous tableaux devised by director Sergei Paradjanov are only vaguely concerned with the depiction of actual events. Instead, they are a breathtaking amalgam of subversive symbols drawn from both religious iconography and nationalist folklore. Much of the meaning will be indecipherable to those without specialist knowledge, but you can still surrender yourself to the rhythm and beauty of this remarkable film. DP Armenian +subtitles. *DVD*

Sofiko Chiaureli *Young Poet/Poet's Love/Nun/ Angel/Mime* · V Galestyan *Poet in the Cloister* · M Aleksanian *Poet as a Child* · G Gegechkori *Poet as an Old Man* ■ *Dir/Scr* Sergei Paradjanov

Colt .45 ★★★ U

Western 1950 · US · Colour · 72min

Craggy Randolph Scott stars in this successful western as a gun salesman whose deadly wares are stolen by Zachary Scott and used in a series of hold-ups. Apart from a romantic interlude with Ruth Roman that's totally unconvincing, it's fast-moving, though conventional, and benefits from the use of 1950s Technicolor and the iconic charm of Scott. TS

Randolph Scott *Steve Farrell* · Ruth Roman *Beth Donovan* · Zachary Scott *Jason Brett* · Lloyd Bridges *Paul Donovan* · Alan Hale *Sheriff Harris* · Ian MacDonald *Miller* · Chief Thundercloud *Walking Bear* ■ *Dir* Edwin L Marin · *Scr* Thomas Blackburn, from his story

Column South ★★★ U

Western 1953 · US · Colour · 84min

This beautifully photographed Universal western stars fresh-faced former war hero Audie Murphy. He plays a cavalry officer sympathetic to the Indians, perceptively pointing out that helping the dispossessed native Americans would ultimately strengthen the Union. Don't worry, the politics don't get in the way of the well-staged action sequences. TS

Audie Murphy *Lieutenant Jed Sayre* · Joan Evans *March Whitlock* · Robert Sterling *Captain Lee Whitlock* · Ray Collins *Brig Gen Storey* · Dennis Weaver *Menguito* ■ *Dir* Frederick De Cordova · *Scr* William Sackheim · *Cinematographer* Charles P Boyle

Coma ★★★★ 15

Thriller 1977 · US · Colour · 108min

Doctor Geneviève Bujold and sinister surgeon Richard Widmark clash memorably in this taut medical thriller, faithfully adapted from Robin Cook's bestseller by doctor-turned-novelist Michael Crichton. The *ER/Jurassic Park* creator also directs and expertly turns the suspense screws in

the gripping way that has become his trademark. Crichton's assured sense of creepy paranoia gives an extra disturbing edge to the hospital horrors. AJ Violence, swearing, brief nudity.

Geneviève Bujold *Dr Susan Wheeler* · Michael Douglas (1) *Dr Mark Bellows* · Richard Widmark *Dr George A Harris* · Rip Torn *Dr George* · Elizabeth Ashley *Mrs Emerson* · Lois Chiles *Nancy Greenly* · Harry Rhodes [Hari Rhodes] *Dr Morelind* · Tom Selleck *Sean Murphy* ■ *Dir* Michael Crichton · *Scr* Michael Crichton, from the novel by Robin Cook

Comanche ★★ U

Western 1956 · US · Colour · 87min

This very routine western, allegedly based on fact, is made interesting by the fact that it introduced glamorous South American star Linda Cristal to an English-speaking audience. In the lead is the past-his-prime Dana Andrews, grim-faced and having trouble with his lines, playing a frontier scout who attempts to end the fighting between the Comanche and the US Cavalry. TS

Dana Andrews *Read* · Kent Smith *Quanah Parker* · Linda Cristal *Margarita* · Nestor Paiva *Puffer* · Henry Brandon *Black Cloud* · John Litel *General Miles* · Reed Sherman *French* · Stacy Harris *Downey* · Lowell Gilmore *Ward* ■ *Dir* George Sherman · *Scr* Carl Krueger

Comanche Station ★★★★ PG

Western 1960 · US · Colour · 70min

This final film in the series of Ranown westerns from director Budd Boetticher and co-producer/star Randolph Scott is a fine meditation on ageing. It's a companion piece thematically to John Ford's *The Searchers*, but arguably bleaker and more realistic – this austere work strips the genre to its bare essentials. Supporting the craggy Scott is the well-cast Claude Akins as a flamboyant bounty hunter, and their final confrontation is especially effective. Particularly notable is Burt Kennedy's screenplay, which utilises the western's emotive iconography brilliantly. TS

Randolph Scott *Jefferson Cody* · Nancy Gates *Mrs Lowe* · Claude Akins *Ben Lane* · Skip Homeier *Frank* · Richard Rust *Dobie* · Rand Brooks *Station man* · Dyke Johnson *Mr Lowe* ■ *Dir* Budd Boetticher · *Scr* Burt Kennedy

Comanche Territory ★★ U

Western 1950 · US · Colour · 75min

American folk legend Jim Bowie (he of the knife fame) has been portrayed several times on the movie screen, perhaps most notably by Richard Widmark in *The Alamo* and Alan Ladd in *The Iron Mistress*. This, alas, is one of the more lacklustre versions of Bowie's exploits. Macdonald Carey fails to convey any sense of destiny as he tries to stop lovely Maureen O'Hara and her evil brother Charles Drake from mining on Indian territory. TS

Maureen O'Hara *Katie* · Macdonald Carey *James Bowie* · Will Geer *Dan'l Seeger* · Charles Drake *Stacey Howard* · Pedro de Cordoba *Quisima* · Ian MacDonald *Walsh* · Rick Vallin *Pakanah* · Parley Baer *Boozer* ■ *Dir* George Sherman · *Scr* Oscar Brodney, Lewis Meltzer, from a story by Lewis Meltzer

The Comancheros ★★★★ PG

Western 1961 · US · Colour · 102min

This was a marvellous swan song for *Casablanca* director Michael Curtiz, who died the following year. Indeed, much of this handsome western was actually directed by star John Wayne, in tandem with second unit director Cliff Lyons. Wayne plays a Texas Ranger on the trail of a gang of outlaws who are supplying arms and liquor to the Comanches. The scale is substantial, and Curtiz fills the screen with rip-roaring action. The score is one of Elmer Bernstein's best and most elegiac, and there's a terrific star-building performance from Lee Marvin. TS *DVD*

John Wayne *Captain Jake Cutter* · Stuart Whitman *Paul Regret* · Ina Balin *Pilar* · Nehemiah Persoff *Graile* · Lee Marvin *Tully Crow* · Michael Ansara *Amelung* · Patrick Wayne *Tobe* · Bruce Cabot *Major Henry* · Henry Daniell *Gireaux* ■

Dir Michael Curtiz · *Scr* James Edward Grant, Clair Huffaker, from the novel by Paul I Wellman · *Cinematographer* William Clothier

Comandante ★★★ PG

Documentary 2002 · US/Sp · Colour · 95min

Writer/director Oliver Stone makes an accomplished documentary debut with this portrait of Cuban revolutionary leader Fidel Castro. Given three days access, Stone peppers the ever-alert 75-year-old with questions about everything from the Bay of Pigs affair and the subsequent Missile Crisis to Ché Guevara and the Soviet alliance, and is only obviously sidestepped on such topics as his love life, religion, homosexuality and Cuba's role in Vietnam. The mix of archive footage and scenes of Castro touring Havana suggest his undiminished popularity, but Stone clearly isn't convinced of the extent or permanence of his achievement. DP Spanish, English +subtitles. *DVD*

■ *Dir* Oliver Stone · *Scr* from an idea by José Ibañez, Alvaro Longoria

Les Combattants ★★★ 15

Romantic comedy 2014 · Fr · Colour · 98min

Despite winning three Césars, Thomas Cailley's debut feature never quite delivers on its promise. Set in the south-western region of Aquitaine, it opens in droll fashion with siblings Arnaud and Manu (played by Kévin Azaïs and Antoine Laurent) deciding to take over their late father's lumber business. But the former is smitten after he is bested in a fight by a tomboy (Adèle Haenel). The leads are splendid, but Cailley's direction is a little wayward, while the charm of the screenplay is undermined by a disappointing dénouement. DP French +subtitles. Swearing, a sex scene, brief nudity.

Adèle Haenel *Madeleine Beaulieu* · Kévin Azaïs *Arnaud Labrède* · Antoine Laurent *Manu Labrède* · Brigitte Roüan *Hélène Labrède* ■ *Dir* Thomas Cailley · *Scr* Thomas Cailley, Claude Le Pape

Come and Get It ★★ PG

Period drama 1936 · US · BW · 95min

This is the story of humble young lumberjack Edward Arnold who becomes a wealthy and powerful tycoon. Sacrificing the woman he loves (Frances Farmer) to ambition along the way, he has to face the bitter disillusion of old age. Adapted from Edna Ferber's novel and co-directed by heavyweights William Wyler and Howard Hawks, this is a curate's egg of a period piece, while the film, beautifully mounted, runs out of steam halfway through. RK

Edward Arnold *Barney Glasgow* · Joel McCrea *Richard Glasgow* · Frances Farmer *Lotta Morgan/Lotta Bostrom* · Walter Brennan *Swan Bostrom* · Andrea Leeds *Evvie Glasgow* · Frank Shields (1) *Tony Schwerke* ■ *Dir* Howard Hawks, William Wyler · *Scr* Jules Furthman, Jane Murfin, from the novel by Edna Ferber

Come and See ★★★★ 15

Epic wartime drama
1985 · USSR · Colour and BW · 140min

Set in Byelorussia in 1943, director Elem Klimov's harrowing wartime odyssey follows the exploits of a peasant boy who falls in with partisans as they battle the Nazis. There's a bucolic beauty to this coming-of-age epic but that's only a minor diversion from the countless atrocities that take a toll on the young hero. Rarely has innocence destroyed been so utterly unrelenting. JA Russian +subtitles. *DVD*

Alexei Kravchenko *Florya* · Olga Mironova *Glasha* · Liubomiras Laucevicius · Vladas Bagdonas ■ *Dir* Elem Klimov · *Scr* Elem Klimov, Ales Adamovich, from *The Khatyn Story* and *A Punitive Squad* by Ales Adamovich

Come as You Are ★★★★ 15

Comedy drama 2011 · Bel/Neth · Colour · 109min

Warmly humorous and uplifting, this tale about the triumph of human spirit over disability is a true treat. Belgians Philip, Lars and Jozef are best buddies. Philip is quadriplegic, Lars has terminal cancer and uses a wheelchair, while Jozef is blind.

When they hear of a Spanish brothel that specialises in catering for the disabled, the friends hire a minibus, secure the services of a larger-than-life lady driver-cum-nurse, then head south in search of sun, sea, sand and sex. Mirth, mayhem and some sadness ensue. *Come as You Are* is part road movie, part romance and part tale of friendship – and all worth watching. DA Dutch, French, English, Spanish +subtitles. Swearing. *DVD* *Blu*

Robrecht Vanden Thoren *Philip* · Gilles De Schryver *Lars* · Tom Audenaert *Jozef* · Isabelle De Hertogh *Claude* ■ *Dir* Geoffrey Enthoven · *Scr* Pierre De Clercq, from a story by Mariano Vanhoof, from an idea by Asta Philpot

Come Back, Little Sheba ★★★★ PG

Drama 1952 · US · BW · 91min

Sheba is a little pooch and surrogate child that's gone missing; Shirley Booth is its owner desperate for its return. Her husband, meanwhile, a failed doctor, is so provoked by the cavortings of two virile student lodgers that he hits the bottle after a year on the wagon. Based on a Broadway hit, this is a classic slice of Americana, oscillating between comedy and tragedy and performed by actors who squeeze the text until not a drop of drama remains on the page. The showstopper, though, is Booth, who won an Oscar for her screen debut. AT *DVD*

Burt Lancaster *Doc Delaney* · Shirley Booth *Lola Delaney* · Terry Moore *Marie Buckholder* · Richard Jaeckel *Turk Fisher* · Philip Ober *Ed Anderson* · Lisa Golm *Mrs Goffman* · Walter Kelley *Bruce* ■ *Dir* Daniel Mann · *Scr* Ketti Frings, from the play by William Inge

Come Back to the Five and Dime, Jimmy Dean, Jimmy Dean ★★★★ 15

Drama 1982 · US · Colour · 109min

Robert Altman drops his usual scattergun approach to direct a wholly focused adaptation of Ed Graczyk's play about a group of women who gather to commemorate the death of their beloved Jimmy Dean. Sandy Dennis, Cher and Karen Black are among the beautiful losers who are now slightly older and bitchier than they were when they originally formed the fan club. Altman brilliantly conveys their changes of mood via a wall mirror in what is one of the better variations on a stage theme. TH

Sandy Dennis *Mona* · Cher *Sissy* · Karen Black *Joanne* · Sudie Bond *Juanita* · Marta Heflin *Edna Louise* · Kathy Bates *Stella May* · Mark Patton *Joe Qualley* ■ *Dir* Robert Altman · *Scr* Ed Graczyk, from his play

Come Blow Your Horn ★★

Comedy 1963 · US · Colour · 111min

The first of playwright Neil Simon's Broadway comedy successes to be filmed, this is not quite as funny on screen as it thinks it is. There's sterling work from Frank Sinatra as an unrepentant Jewish bachelor, but the problem lies in the overacting of Lee J Cobb and the great Yiddish comedian Molly Picon as Frankie's parents. It's one of those incredibly glossy 1960s productions from Paramount, but all the dressing can't hide the moralistic trifle that lies underneath. TS

Frank Sinatra *Alan Baker* · Lee J Cobb *Mr Baker* · Molly Picon *Mrs Baker* · Barbara Rush *Connie* · Jill St John *Peggy* · Tony Bill *Buddy Baker* · Dan Blocker *Mr Eckman* · Phyllis McGuire *Mrs Eckman* · Dean Martin *Bum* ■ *Dir* Bud Yorkin · *Scr* Norman Lear, from the play by Neil Simon · *Art Directors* Hal Pereira, Roland Anderson

Come Fill the Cup ★★★

Drama 1951 · US · BW · 110min

A reporter loses his job as a result of his drinking problem but rehabilitates himself with the help of a reformed alcoholic friend and goes on to give similar assistance to his boss's son. Although this descends into the maudlin and improbable somewhere along the way, a strong cast and Gordon Douglas's gritty direction make for an attention-holding melodrama that also involves gangster elements. The always mesmerising James Cagney stars as the reporter, with James Gleason, Raymond Massey and an Oscar-nominated Gig Young. **RK**

James Cagney *Lew Marsh* • Phyllis Thaxter *Paula Copeland* • Raymond Massey *John Ives* • James Gleason *Charley Dolan* • Gig Young *Boyd Copeland* • Selena Royle *Dolly Copeland* ∎ *Dir* Gordon Douglas • *Scr* Ivan Goff, Ben Roberts, from the novel by Harlan Ware

Come Fly with Me ★★ U
Comedy   1962 · US/UK · Colour · 108min

The romantic adventures and entanglements of three air hostesses (Dolores Hart, Pamela Tiffin, Lois Nettleton) make up this empty flimflam, more interesting as a glossy travelogue than a romantic comedy. The plotless waffle never becomes airborne, however. **RK**

Dolores Hart *Donna Stuart* • Hugh O'Brian *First Officer May* • Karl Boehm [Karlheinz Böhm] *Baron Franz von Elzingen* • Karl Malden *Walter Lucas* • Pamela Tiffin *Carol Brewster* • Lois Nettleton *Hilda "Bergie" Bergstrom* • Dawn Addams *Katie* • Richard Wattis *Oliver Garson* • Lois Maxwell *Gwen* ∎ *Dir* Henry Levin • *Scr* William Roberts, from his story, from the novel *Girl on a Wing* by Bernard Glemser

Come Live with Me ★★★★
Romantic comedy   1941 · US · BW · 86min

Penniless writer James Stewart marries beautiful refugee Hedy Lamarr so she won't be deported from America in this finely mounted and intelligently made MGM movie from Hollywood's golden era. Watch it for its star power alone, and marvel at how convincing and likeable the two leads are, as director Clarence Brown skilfully creates an atmosphere that allows you to care deeply about Lamarr's plight. The playing is exemplary, the mood sublime, and this deserves to be better known. **TS**

James Stewart *Bill Smith* • Hedy Lamarr *Johnny Jones* • Ian Hunter *Barton Kendrick* • Verree Teasdale *Diana Kendrick* • Donald Meek *Joe Darsie* • Barton MacLane *Barney Grogan* • Edward Ashley *Arnold Stafford* ∎ *Dir* Clarence Brown • *Scr* Patterson McNutt, from a story by Virginia Van Upp

Come Next Spring ★★★ U
Drama   1956 · US · Colour · 87min

Long-absent Arkansas farmer Steve Cochran, cured of his drinking problems and restlessness, returns home to his understandably wary wife Ann Sheridan, his daughter Sherry Jackson (who lost the power of speech during one of his drinking bouts) and the son born after his departure. How he regains the love and respect of his family and the community forms the stuff of this rural tale. Directed by RG Springsteen, it's a whole lot better than it sounds. **RK**

Ann Sheridan *Bess Ballot* • Steve Cochran *Matt Ballot* • Walter Brennan *Jeff Storys* • Sherry Jackson *Annie* • Richard Eyer *Abraham* • Edgar Buchanan *Mr Canary* • Sonny Tufts *Leroy Hytower* ∎ *Dir* RG Springsteen • *Scr* Montgomery Pittman

The Come On ★★
Romantic thriller   1956 · US · BW · 83min

Anne Baxter, looking great but struggling against the odds with an unconvincing script and Russell Birdwell's uncertain direction, is the star of this less than compelling melodrama. She plays an unhappily married woman who tries to persuade honest fisherman Sterling Hayden to kill her husband after he falls for her on a Mexican beach. Although he refuses, the involvement leads to further plot complications. **RK**

Anne Baxter *Rita Kendrick* • Sterling Hayden *Dave Arnold* • John Hoyt *Harley Kendrick* • Jesse White *JJ McGonigle* • Wally Cassell *Tony Margoli* • Alex Gerry *Chalmers* • Tiger McVey *Hogan* • Theodore Newton *Captain Getz* ∎ *Dir* Russell Birdwell • *Scr* Warren Douglas, Whitman Chambers, from a novel by Whitman Chambers

Come On George ★★★ U
Comedy   1939 · UK · BW · 85min

The remarkable thing about George Formby's film career is that he managed to make around 20 features, used a similar storyline in every single one, and nobody minded! He always played an eager beaver whom everyone thought was a dead loss apart from the girl whose smile inspired him to become a world-beater. Here, the object of his affections is Pat Kirkwood, and the sphere in which he gets to prove his unsuspected prowess is horse racing. **DP**

George Formby *George* • Pat Kirkwood *Ann Johnson* • Joss Ambler *Sir Charles Bailey* • Meriel Forbes *Monica Bailey* • Cyril Raymond *Jimmy Taylor* • George "Gabby" Hayes *Bannerman* ∎ *Dir* Anthony Kimmins • *Scr* Anthony Kimmins, Leslie Arliss, Val Valentine

Come Out and Play ★★★ 18
Horror   2012 · Mex · Colour · 82min

Children are little monsters – literally – in this effective remake of cult Euro-horror *Who Can Kill a Child?*. Director Makinov has not veered from the plot of the chilling 1976 Spanish original, in which a man and his pregnant partner head off to a remote island paradise for a bit of peace and quiet, only to discover a resort devoid of adults (well, living ones anyway). The sense of foreboding is palpable in a slow-burn horror that benefits from an ominous (but not obtrusive) electronic score, and from having much of the action staged in dazzling daylight. **JA** English, Spanish +subtitles. Violence, swearing.

Vinessa Shaw *Beth* • Ebon Moss-Bachrach *Francis* • Daniel Giménez Cacho [Daniel Gimenez Cacho] *Misael* • Gerardo Taracena *Felipe* ∎ *Dir* Makinov • *Scr* Makinov, from Juan José Plans's novel *El Juego de los Niños*

Come Out Fighting ★★
Comedy   1945 · US · BW · 62min

This was the last of producer Sam Katzman's 22 *East Side Kids* B-movies; after this entry, star Leo Gorcey turned them into the Bowery Boys, under which moniker they made another 48 pictures. Considering the paltry plot – a police commissioner wants his nerdish son toughened up by the kids – you can see why Gorcey chose to rethink his position. The pace never lets up under veteran William "One Shot" Beaudine's direction, but the clowning is non-existent. **TS**

Leo Gorcey *Muggs* • Huntz Hall *Glimpy* • Billy Benedict *Skinny* • Gabriel Dell *Pete* • June Carlson *Jane* • Amelita Ward *Rita* ∎ *Dir* William Beaudine • *Scr* Earl Snell

Come Play with Me ★ 18
Sex comedy   1977 · UK · Colour · 90min

This atrocious sex comedy is one of the worst ever made, but was hyped to incredible box-office success by its producer and adult magazine publisher, David Sullivan. The plot – forgers take refuge on a health farm – marks time for a crude song-and-dance routine and turns by several well-known British character actors. However, the sex scenes, clearly added later, feature fleeting appearances by Sullivan's protegée, Mary Millington, then known as "Britain's Linda Lovelace". **DM** *DVD*

Irene Handl *Lady Bovington* • Alfie Bass *Kelly* • George Harrison Marks *Clapworthy* • Ronald Fraser *Slasher* • Mary Millington *Sue* • Tommy Godfrey *Blitt* • Cardew Robinson *McIvor* • Toni Harrison Marks *Miss Dingle* ∎ *Dir/Scr* George Harrison Marks

Come See the Paradise ★★★ 15
Period drama   1990 · US · Colour · 127min

Never comfortable with the period or its implications, writer/director Alan Parker has an uphill struggle on his hands with this story about the treatment of America's Japanese population during the Second World War. His depiction of the romance between Dennis Quaid and Tamlyn Tomita is successful, although he doesn't always

keep Quaid's exuberant style in check. **DP** Violence, swearing, nudity.

Dennis Quaid *Jack McGurn* • Tamlyn Tomita *Lily Kawamura* • Sab Shimono *Mr Kawamura* • Shizuko Hoshi *Mrs Kawamura* • Stan Egi *Charlie Kawamura* • Ronald Yamamoto *Harry Kawamura* • Akemi Nishino *Dulcie Kawamura* ∎ *Dir/Scr* Alan Parker

Come September ★★★
Romantic comedy   1961 · US · Colour · 113min

When wealthy American businessman Rock Hudson visits his Italian villa in July, instead of September as usual, he discovers it is being run as a hotel in his absence. His major-domo (Walter Slezak), glamorous Gina Lollobrigida and young marrieds Bobby Darin and Sandra Dee (just married in real life, too) become involved in the comic confusions that follow. Directed with appropriate insouciance by Robert Mulligan and played with easy charm by Hudson. **RK**

Rock Hudson *Robert Talbot* • Gina Lollobrigida *Lisa Fellini* • Sandra Dee *Sandy* • Bobby Darin *Tony* • Walter Slezak *Maurice* • Rossana Rory *Anna* ∎ *Dir* Robert Mulligan • *Scr* Stanley Shapiro, Maurice Richlin

Come to the Stable ★★★ U
Comedy drama   1949 · US · BW · 94min

Unless you have an aversion to nun movies, there's a great deal of pleasure to be had from watching Loretta Young and Celeste Holm as they arrive in the New England town of Bethlehem and set about their charitable work, initially aided by Elsa Lanchester as a bohemian artist. (All three actresses were Oscar-nominated for their work in this film.) Director Henry Koster handles the tale well, without lapsing into schmaltz. **TS**

Loretta Young *Sister Margaret* • Celeste Holm *Sister Scolastica* • Hugh Marlowe *Robert Mason* • Elsa Lanchester *Miss Potts* • Thomas Gomez *Luigi Rossi* • Dorothy Patrick *Kitty* • Basil Ruysdael *Bishop* • Dooley Wilson *Anthony James* ∎ *Dir* Henry Koster • *Scr* Oscar Millard, Sally Benson, from a story by Clare Boothe Luce

The Comeback ★ 18
Horror   1977 · UK · Colour · 96min

1970s crooner Jack Jones starring in a horror movie? That's about the scariest thing in this far-fetched gothic tale about an American singer recording a new album in an isolated English country manor full of dead bodies, including his ex-wife's. Director Pete Walker's heavy-handed crossbreed of rock and horror draws on numerous genre clichés, but offers up no decent chills of its own. **RS** Violence, swearing. *DVD*

Jack Jones (2) *Nick Cooper* • Pamela Stephenson *Linda Everett* • David Doyle *Webster Jones* • Bill Owen *Mr B* • Sheila Keith *Mrs B* • Holly Palance *Gail Cooper* ∎ *Dir* Pete Walker • *Scr* Murray Smith

The Comedian ★★ 15
Comedy drama   2012 · UK · Colour · 78min

British realism gets a European polish in this well-intentioned but unsatisfying debut feature from Tom Shkolnik. Edward Hogg plays a failed stand-up whose routine we only ever see once in a scene that suggests he will never break into the mainstream. On the night bus home he meets Nathan Stewart-Jarrett and the pair begin an affair, but Hogg finds it hard to commit to the relationship. The ensemble performances are excellent, especially in a series of long, clearly improvised scenes, but sadly there's not enough of a story to sustain the film through its frequent lulls. **DW** Swearing, sex scenes.

Edward Hogg *Ed* • Elisa Lasowski *Elisa* • Nathan Stewart-Jarrett *Nathan* ∎ *Dir/Scr* Tom Shkolnik

The Comedians ★★★ PG
Drama   1967 · Fr/US · Colour · 146min

What a temptation it must have been for Elizabeth Taylor and Richard Burton to star in this Graham Greene adaptation of his own novel about the despairing turmoil of life in Haiti under the tyrannical Papa Doc Duvalier – a duet for two dramatic hands. Peter Glenville's leaden direction, however, generates little heat as Taylor, playing the

wife of ambassador Peter Ustinov, has an affair with hotel owner Burton. Alec Guinness, as an arms dealer, makes the most profound contribution to an all-star cast. **TH**

Richard Burton *Brown* • Alec Guinness *Major Jones* • Elizabeth Taylor *Martha Pineda* • Peter Ustinov *Ambassador Pineda* • Paul Ford *Mr Smith* • Lillian Gish *Mrs Smith* • Georg Stanford Brown *Henri Philipot* • James Earl Jones *Dr Magiot* ∎ *Dir* Peter Glenville • *Scr* Graham Greene, from his novel

Comédie de l'Innocence ★★★ PG
Drama   2000 · Fr · Colour · 98min

This story of bourgeois Parisian mother Isabelle Huppert who indulges her son in his claim that he belongs to another woman sets an ominous tone that recalls the sub-Hitchcock style of French master Claude Chabrol. In fact, this is the handiwork of the ever-perplexing director Raúl Ruiz, who mischievously underpins the mystery with larger questions of identity and individuality to create an unsettling domestic drama in which the actions of the characters are sometimes not only illogical but also plainly unfathomable. **DP** French +subtitles. *DVD*

Isabelle Huppert *Ariane d'Orville* • Jeanne Balibar *Isabella Stirner* • Charles Berling *Serge* • Edith Scob *Laurence* • Nils Hugon *Camille d'Orville* ∎ *Dir* Raúl Ruiz [Raúl Ruiz] • *Scr* Françoise Dumas, Raoul Ruiz [Raúl Ruiz], from the novel *Il Figlio di Due Madri* by Massimo Bontempelli

The Comedy Man ★★★ 15
Comedy drama   1964 · UK · BW · 87min

A struggling middle-aged rep actor, dreaming of the big break, finds fortune through a TV commercial, but walks away from the high life to pursue his career. Written by Peter Yeldham with a nice balance between irony and drama, and directed by Alvin Rakoff with an accurate eye for the brave bonhomie of unemployed actors, this modest British film boasts a superior cast. **RK**

Kenneth More *Chick Byrd* • Cecil Parker *Rutherford* • Dennis Price *Tommy Morris* • Billie Whitelaw *Judy* • Norman Rossington *Theodore* • Angela Douglas *Fay* • Frank Finlay *Prout* • Edmund Purdom *Julian* ∎ *Dir* Alvin Rakoff • *Scr* Peter Yeldham, from the novel by Douglas Hayes

A Comedy of Power ★★★ 12
Drama   2006 · Fr/Ger · Colour · 105min

Claude Chabrol's seventh collaboration with Isabelle Huppert is a sly satire based on the Elf affair that rocked the French business community in the 1990s. Ultimately, the charges brought against the various corrupt tycoons and oleaginous politicians prove something of a MacGuffin, as the ever Hitchcock-inspired auteur is far more interested in the impact the case has on magistrate Huppert's marriage to sulky Robin Renucci and her curious relationship with slacker nephew Thomas Chabrol (son of the director). Sadly, neither subplot engrosses as it might. But Huppert is still splendidly haughty while dismissing the arrogance of those she interrogates, and thornily vulnerable when she realises that the chauvinists in the upper echelons resent her gatecrashing their club. **DP** French +subtitles. *DVD*

Isabelle Huppert *Judge Jeanne Charmant-Killman* • François Berléand *Michel Humeau* • Patrick Bruel *Sibaud* • Robin Renucci *Philippe* • Maryline Canto *Erika* • Thomas Chabrol *Félix* • Jean-François Balmer *Boldi* • Pierre Vernier *Presiding Judge Martino* ∎ *Dir* Claude Chabrol • *Scr* Odile Barski, Claude Chabrol

The Comedy of Terrors ★★ 15
Horror comedy   1964 · US · Colour · 79min

Undertakers Vincent Price and Peter Lorre (in one of his last films) drum up business by murdering potential customers in a lesser effort from Jacques Tourneur, director of such classics as *Cat People* and *Curse of the Demon*. Boris Karloff and Basil Rathbone complete a fearsome foursome who try hard to extract every ounce of humour from the regrettably dull script.

This is a marginally interesting failure. AJ Violence. *DVD* *BL*

Vincent Price *Waldo Trumbull* • Peter Lorre *Felix Gillie* • Boris Karloff *Amos Hinchley* • Basil Rathbone *John F Black* • Joe E Brown *Cemetery keeper* • Joyce Jameson *Amaryllis Trumbull* • Beverly Powers *Mrs Phipps* ■ *Dir* Jacques Tourneur • *Scr* Richard Matheson

Comes a Bright Day ★★ 15
Romantic crime thriller
2012 · UK · Colour · 87min

Commercials director Simon Aboud gets off to a patchy start in features with this ambitious but flawed heist-cum-love story. The conceit about hotel porter Craig Roberts pretending to be grander than he is to impress jewellery shop assistant Imogen Poots is nicely done. But, from the moment that thieves take Roberts, Poots and her boss, Timothy Spall, hostage during a bungled raid, Aboud struggles to cope with the shifts in tone between over coy romance and gun-toting thriller. Nevertheless, Roberts and Poots make a quaint couple, while Spall is typically engaging. DP Violence, swearing. *DVD*

Craig Roberts *Sam Smith* • Imogen Poots *Mary Bright* • Kevin McKidd *Cameron* • Timothy Spall *Charlie* ■ *Dir/Scr* Simon Aboud

Comes a Horseman ★★ 15
Western
1978 · US · Colour · 113min

Montana has never looked more beautiful than in this interesting but mightily flawed attempt at a Fordian western from Alan J Pakula. Despite some valiant performances from Jane Fonda as a hard-bitten ranch boss and Jason Robards as a land-grabbing cattle baron, the movie ultimately plods through its paces. SH *DVD*

James Caan *Frank Athearn* • Jane Fonda *Ella Connors* • Jason Robards *Jacob "JW" Ewing* • George Grizzard *Neil Atkinson* • Richard Farnsworth *Dodger* • Jim Davis (1) *Julie Blocker* • Mark Harmon *Billy Joe Meynert* ■ *Dir* Alan J Pakula • *Scr* Dennis Lynton Clark • *Cinematographer* Gordon Willis

Comet ★★★★ 15
Romantic science-fiction drama
2014 · US · Colour · 91min

This bittersweet, time-hopping relationship drama follows bickering couple Dell (Justin Long), an anxious sceptic able to make Sherlock Holmes-like deductions about everyone he speaks to, and Kimberly (Emmy Rossum), who proceeds to challenge his pessimistic attitudes towards life and love. The story flashes between various points in their six-year relationship, which may or may not be playing out across several parallel universes. It's reminiscent of films like *(500) Days Of Summer* and *Annie Hall*, but it's still a great watch in its own right. SC

Justin Long *Dell* • Emmy Rossum *Kimberly* ■ *Dir/Scr* Sam Esmail

Comfort and Joy ★★★★ PG
Comedy
1984 · UK · Colour · 100min

A Glaswegian radio station holds a pin-up contest, even though listeners cannot see the contestants. The story, which is full of such felicities, involves local disc jockey Bill Paterson who has been abandoned by his partner Eleanor David. His redemption comes about when he finds he's mediating in an ice-cream war between two branches of the "Scotia Nostra". Bill Forsyth's film works well as an urban fairy tale and has a few quirky surprises. TH *DVD* *BL*

Bill Paterson *Alan "Dickie" Bird* • Eleanor David *Maddy* • CP Grogan *[Clare Grogan] Charlotte* • Alex Norton *Trevor* • Patrick Malahide *Colin* • Rikki Fulton *Hilary* • Roberto Bernardi *Mr McCool* • George Rossi *Bruno* • Peter Rossi *Paolo* ■ *Dir/Scr* Bill Forsyth

The Comfort of Strangers ★★ 18
Drama
1991 · It/UK · Colour · 100min

The novels of Ian McEwan have proved irresistible to film-makers, but so far few have transferred to the screen with any degree of success. This brooding drama – about a couple (Rupert Everett and Natasha Richardson) drawn into Christopher Walken's sinister trap – lacks both the elegance and the bite of McEwan's prose. Paul Schrader is one of American cinema's most literate directors, but his over-deliberate approach means this drips with pretension. DP *DVD*

Christopher Walken *Robert* • Natasha Richardson *Mary* • Rupert Everett *Colin* • Helen Mirren *Caroline* • Manfredi Aliquo *Concierge* ■ *Dir* Paul Schrader • *Scr* Harold Pinter, from the novel by Ian McEwan

The Comic ★★★★
Comedy drama
1969 · US · Colour · 95min

This is an underrated, little-seen tragicomedy about a silent film comic, magnificently played by Dick Van Dyke, who uses people and abuses himself in his struggle to get to the top. Written and directed by Carl Reiner, its Hollywood insights are many and brutal, while the acting is exceptional – Mickey Rooney is a standout. It only goes to show that comedy is no laughing matter. TH

Dick Van Dyke *Billy Bright* • Michele Lee *Mary Gibson* • Mickey Rooney *Cockeye* • Cornel Wilde *Frank Powers* • Nina Wayne *Sybil* • Pert Kelton *Mama* • Steve Allen ■ *Dir* Carl Reiner • *Scr* Carl Reiner, Aaron Ruben

Comic Book Confidential ★★★ 15
Documentary
1988 · Can · Colour · 85min

It's hard to know how to approach this documentary tracing the history of American comics from the 1930s onwards. The discussion by the country's leading cartoonists (including Marvel Comics' Stan Lee and the amazing Robert Crumb) of how the style and content of their work has changed is fascinating, and the comic books themselves are so irresistible that you find yourself longing to read them from cover to cover. But director Ron Mann presents his material in such a sloppy way that the energy and invention of the illustrations are frittered away. DP *DVD*

Jack Kirby • Robert Crumb • Will Eisner • Stan Lee • Art Spiegelman • Bill Griffith ■ *Dir/Scr* Ron Mann

Coming Home ★★★★ 18
Drama
1978 · US · Colour · 122min

High-powered, Oscar-winning performances by Jon Voight and Jane Fonda are the big attraction of this post-Vietnam melodrama. The film is set on the home front, and centres on the romance between an embittered paraplegic and a marine captain's wife, working as a volunteer in a veteran's hospital. Bruce Dern is also top-notch as Fonda's husband. The screenplay skirts close to sentimentality, if not soap opera at points. But it too won an Oscar, and only a hard heart would remain unmoved. PF Swearing, sex scenes. *DVD*

Jane Fonda *Sally Hyde* • Jon Voight *Luke Martin* • Bruce Dern *Captain Bob Hyde* • Robert Ginty *Sergeant Dink Mobley* • Penelope Milford *Viola Munson* • Robert Carradine *Billy Munson* • Charles Cyphers *Pee Wee* ■ *Dir* Hal Ashby • *Scr* Waldo Salt, Robert C Jones, from a story by Nancy Dowd

Coming to America ★★★ 15
Romantic comedy
1988 · US · Colour · 111min

Eddie Murphy teams up once again with his *Trading Places* director John Landis for a comedy that at least requires him to do more than just chuckle. Murphy plays a pampered African prince who rebels against his father (James Earl Jones) and comes to America, with sidekick Arsenio Hall in tow, to find a wife. Landis aims for a 1930s-style feel but the script isn't as clever as it thinks it is, so it's left to Murphy to carry the picture. JF Swearing, nudity. *DVD* *BL*

Eddie Murphy *Prince Akeem/Clarence/Saul/Randy Watson* • Arsenio Hall *Semmi/Morris/Extremely ugly girl/Reverend Brown* • James Earl Jones *King Jaffe Joffer* • Shari Headley *Lisa McDowell* • Madge Sinclair *Queen Aoleon* • Calvin Lockhart *Colonel Izzi* • John Amos *Cleo McDowell* • Allison Dean *Patrice McDowell* • Eriq La Salle *Darryl Jenks* • Don Ameche *Mortimer Duke* •

Ralph Bellamy *Randolph Duke* ■ *Dir* John Landis • *Scr* David Sheffield, Barry W Blaustein, from a story by Eddie Murphy

The Command ★★★ U
Western
1954 · US · Colour · 93min

This now-forgotten western was important in its day for being the first Warner Bros film to be made in CinemaScope. It was also filmed, though never released, in 3D. Because two versions were filmed simultaneously, involving twice as much work for a single fee, the cast is relatively undistinguished. The colourless Guy Madison plays an inexperienced army doctor who has to lead a civilian wagon train through Indian territory. The action sequences, when they arrive, are spectacular. TS

Guy Madison *Capt MacClaw* • Joan Weldon *Martha* • James Whitmore *Sergeant Elliot* • Carl Benton Reid *Colonel Janeway* • Harvey Lembeck *Gottschalk* • Ray Teal *Dr Trent* • Bob Nichols *O'Hirons* • Don Shelton *Major Gibbs* ■ *Dir* David Butler • *Scr* Russell Hughes, Samuel Fuller, from the novel *Rear Guard* by James Warner Bellah

Command Decision ★★★★ U
Second World War drama
1948 · US · BW · 107min

Should the commander of American bomber squadrons in Britain send his crews deeper into Germany to try to destroy a factory making long-range aircraft, knowing full well that such forays are effectively suicide missions? The unlikely bearer of this harrowing moral dilemma is Clark Gable, brilliantly anguished in a role given added resonance as a result of his own wartime flying experience on bombing missions. Underrated director Sam Wood makes you forget that this was once a major Broadway theatrical hit, and a terrific cast gives Gable superb back-up. TS *DVD*

Clark Gable *Brig Gen KC "Casey" Dennis* • Walter Pidgeon *Major Gen Roland G Kane* • Van Johnson *Tech Sgt Immanuel T Evans* • Brian Donlevy *Brig Gen Clifton L Garnet* • Charles Bickford *Elmer Brockhurst* • John Hodiak *Col Edward R Martin* • Edward Arnold *Congressman Arthur Malcolm* • Cameron Mitchell *Lt Ansel Goldberg* ■ *Dir* Sam Wood • *Scr* William R Laidlaw, George Froeschel, from the play by William Wister Haines

Command Performance ★ U
Musical
1937 · UK · BW · 80min

This is another of the feeble British vehicles that attempted to make a film star out of Arthur Tracy, popular on radio as "The Street Singer". Here he plays an entertainer who, suffering from stage fright, takes up with a band of nomads and falls in love with a gypsy girl. It's an unconvincing tale, awash with sentimentality and treacly ballads. RK *DVD*

Arthur Tracy *Street Singer* • Lilli Palmer *Susan* • Mark Daly *Joe* • Rae Collett *Betty* • Finlay Currie *Manager* ■ *Dir* Sinclair Hill • *Scr* George Pearson, Michael Hankinson, Sinclair Hill, from the play by C Stafford Dickens

Commandments ★★ 15
Comedy drama
1996 · US · Colour · 84min

Losing his wife, his house and his job in a series of disasters, Aidan Quinn decides to test God by systematically breaking every one of his Ten Commandments, in the hope of receiving some sort of sign as to The Lord's plan. Perhaps commandment number 11 should be "Thou Shalt Not Waste Good Actors On Material Like This." JB Swearing, sexual references, some violence.

Aidan Quinn *Seth Warner* • Courteney Cox *Rachel Luce* • Anthony LaPaglia *Harry Luce* • Shirl Bernheim *Sylvia* • Peter Jacobson *Banker* • Patrick Garner *Banker* • Marcia DeBonis *Receptionist* • Amy Sedaris *Scholar* ■ *Dir/Scr* Daniel Taplitz

Commando ★★★ 18
Action adventure
1985 · US · Colour · 86min

Arnold Schwarzenegger gets the good-guy role here, in his first movie after finding cult success with *The Terminator*. Although he still looks a little awkward with dialogue, he makes for a spectacularly destructive hero, playing a former commando called back into action when his daughter is kidnapped by an old adversary. Dan Hedaya is an engaging chief villain, and there's a spirited turn from Rae Dawn Chong as Arnie's unwilling partner. JF Swearing, violence. *DVD* *BL*

Arnold Schwarzenegger *Colonel John Matrix* • Rae Dawn Chong *Cindy* • Dan Hedaya *General Arius* • Vernon Wells *Bennett* • James Olson *General Kirby* • David Patrick Kelly *Sully* • Alyssa Milano *Jenny* • Bill Duke *Cooke* ■ *Dir* Mark L Lester • *Scr* Steven E de Souza, from a story by Joseph Loeb III, Matthew Weisman, Steven E de Souza

The Commandos Strike at Dawn ★★
Second World War drama
1942 · US · BW · 99min

Paul Muni plays a Norwegian fisherman fighting Nazi tyranny alongside a team of British commandos. When his daughter is held hostage by the Nazis he escapes to England and leads a sabotage mission to Norway. Based on a yarn by *Hornblower* writer CS Forester and adapted by Irwin Shaw, it's a bit plodding for a flag-waver, getting bogged down with romance supplied by Anna Lee, but boasts an interesting cast. AT

Paul Muni *Erik Toreson* • Anna Lee *Judith Bowen* • Lillian Gish *Mrs Bergesen* • Sir Cedric Hardwicke *[Cedric Hardwicke] Admiral Bowen* • Robert Coote *Robert Bowen* • Ray Collins *Bergesen* ■ *Dir* John Farrow • *Scr* Irwin Shaw, from a story by CS Forester

La Commare Secca ★★ 12
Crime drama
1962 · It · BW · 88min

Bernardo Bertolucci's first feature was based on a five-page outline by Pier Paulo Pasolini, whom the young man had assisted on *Accattone* the previous year. But Bertolucci had less interest in the Roman proletariat than Pasolini, and the film, which follows an investigation into the murder of a prostitute seen from different perspectives, is merely an interesting cinematic exercise. RB Italian +subtitles. *DVD*

Francesco Ruiu *Luciano Maialetti, "Canticchia"* • Giancarlo De Rosa *Nino* • Vincenzo Ciccora *Mayor* • Alvaro D'Ercole *Francolicchio* • Romano Labate *Pipito* ■ *Dir* Bernardo Bertolucci • *Scr* Bernardo Bertolucci, Sergio Citti, Pier Paolo Pasolini, from a story by Pasolini

Comment J'ai Tué Mon Père ★★★ 15
Psychological drama
2001 · Fr/Sp · Colour · 94min

This is a simmering, but largely superficial, study of bourgeois manners. Charles Berling is suitably uptight as the successful Parisian physician whose confidence is dented by the return of his father, Michel Bouquet, who abandoned the family years before to tend the sick in the Third World. Director Anne Fontaine captures the mix of envy, respect and animosity that fuels the relationship, but she leaves Berling's wife, Natacha Régnier, on the periphery, when her hesitant reaction might have provided an emotional counterbalance to the psychological posturing. DP French +subtitles. *DVD*

Michel Bouquet *Maurice* • Charles Berling *Jean-Luc* • Natacha Régnier *Isa* • Stéphane Guillon *Patrick* • Amira Casar *Myriem* • Hubert Koundé *Jean-Toussaint* ■ *Dir* Anne Fontaine • *Scr* Jacques Fieschi, Anne Fontaine

The Commissar ★★★★ PG
Drama
1967 · USSR · BW · 103min

The winner of the Silver Bear at Berlin, 20 years after it was banned by the Kremlin, this allegory on the birth of the Soviet state is also one of the few films of the Communist era to deal with anti-Semitism and revolutionary womanhood. Consciously evoking the visual style of the great silent montagists, the story of Red Army commissar Nonna Mordyukova's stay with an impoverished Jewish family during the last days of her pregnancy overflows with a tolerance and humanity utterly at odds with the Civil War raging outside. Director Alexander Askoldov's courageous stance meant he never worked again. DP Russian +subtitles. **DVD**

Nonna Mordyukova *Claudia Vavilova* • Rolan Bykov *Yefim* • Raisa Niedashkovskaya *Maria* • Vasily Shukshin *Commander* ■ *Dir/Scr* Alexander Askoldov

The Commitments★★★★ 15
Musical drama   1991 · UK · Colour · 112min

The soundtrack album sold like hot cakes, it walked away with Bafta awards for best film, best direction and best adapted screenplay, and it should have made bigger stars of its cast. Alan Parker's film also brought the work of future Booker Prize-winning author Roddy Doyle to the attention of the chattering classes. Laced with Irish charm and blessed with some superb music sung with passion by Andrew Strong, Bronagh Gallagher, Angeline Ball and Maria Doyle, it's also very funny. DP Swearing. **DVD**

Robert Arkins *Jimmy Rabbitte* • Michael Aherne *Steven Clifford* • Angeline Ball *Imelda Quirke* • Maria Doyle [Maria Doyle Kennedy] *Natalie Murphy* • Dave Finnegan *Mickah Wallace* • Bronagh Gallagher *Bernie McGloughlin* • Felim Gormley *Dean Fay* • Glen Hansard *Outspan Foster* • Dick Massey *Billy Mooney* • Johnny Murphy *Joey "The Lips" Fagan* • Kenneth McCluskey *Derek Scully* • Andrew Strong *Deco Cuffe* ■ *Dir* Alan Parker • *Scr* Dick Clement, Ian La Frenais, Roddy Doyle, from the novel by Roddy Doyle

Committed   ★★ 15
Romantic comedy   2000 · US · Colour · 93min

In Lisa Krueger's spectacularly miscalculated treatise on marital fidelity, Heather Graham is woefully miscast as the New Yorker who takes her wedding vows so seriously that when her husband (Luke Wilson) abandons her to pursue his photographic career, she crosses the States to win him back. The trip here is an excuse to pack the action with quirky characters in the hope that no one notices the fact the story is going nowhere. DP Swearing. **DVD**

Heather Graham *Joline* • Casey Affleck *Jay* • Luke Wilson *Carl* • Goran Visnjic *Neil* • Patricia Velasquez *Carmen* • Alfonso Arau *Grampy* • Mark Ruffalo *T-Bo* ■ *Dir/Scr* Lisa Krueger

Common-Law Cabin ★★★ 18
Cult crime melodrama
1967 · US · Colour · 69min

This is one of sexploitation director Russ Meyer's early breast-obsessed, mock morality melodramas that put him on the cult map. Using his familiar theme of sexually frustrated men and top-heavy women flung together in a weird setting and succumbing to temptation before paying the price for their illicit lust, this is the most existential item Meyer ever made. Stripper Babette Bardot (no relation) plays the "housekeeper" of a dilapidated inn where customers "relax". AJ Violence, swearing, nudity. **DVD**

Ken Swofford *Barney Rickert* • Alaina Capri *Shelia Ross* • Jack Moran *Dewey Hoople* • Adele Rein *Coral Hoople* • Andrew Hagara *Laurence Talbot III* • Franklin Bolger *Cracker* • Babette Bardot *Babette* • John Furlong *Dr Martin Ross* ■ *Dir* Russ Meyer • *Scr* Jack Moran

Common People   ★★★ 12A
Comedy drama   2013 · UK · Colour · 89min

Kerry Skinner and Stewart Alexander's directorial debut has nothing to do with the Pulp song, but is a genial mesh of stories taking place across Tooting Common in South London. The linking device of an escaped parrot is a touch contrived, but it allows the film to flit between a cash-strapped single father, an expectant mother, a couple of devoted pensioners, an alcoholic in love with a Muslim, a taciturn homeless man and a troop of young adventurers. Nothing remarkable happens but Alexander's script deftly captures a strong sense of community. DP

Sam Kelly *Derrick* • Diana Payan *Pam* • Iarla McGowan *Ian Baxter* • Kerry Skinner *Jenny* • Stewart Alexander *Harry* • Michael Ballard *Homeless* ■ *Dir* Stewart Alexander, Kerry Skinner • *Scr* Stewart Alexander

A Common Thread
★★★★ 12

Drama   2004 · Fr · Colour · 84min

Pregnant teenager Lola Naymark and Ariane Ascaride, grieving for the loss of her son, seem to have nothing in common. But as they embroider fabric for a Parisian fashion house, they discover shared hopes and fears that surmount their generational differences. The intense silences allow director Eléonore Faucher and cinematographer Pierre Cottereau to concentrate on the intricate handicraft that is as mesmerising as the contrasts between Naymark's bubbly country girl and the ever-excellent Ascaride's world-weary loner. DP French +subtitles. **DVD**

Lola Naymark *Claire* • Ariane Ascaride *Madame Mélikian* • Thomas Laroppe *Guillaume* • Jackie Berroyer *M Lescuyer* • Marie Félix *Lucile* • Anne Canovas *Madame Lescuyer* ■ *Dir* Eléonore Faucher • *Scr* Eléonore Faucher, Gaëlle Macé

Common Threads: Stories from the Quilt   ★★★★
Documentary   1989 · US · Colour · 75min

This Oscar-winning documentary, narrated by Dustin Hoffman, highlights the heartache and sorrow behind many of the embroidered panels that made up the Aids quilt laid out on the Mall in Washington DC at the height of the tragic epidemic. The personal stories of loss are often unbearably moving and have a sizeable emotional impact as key social issues are raised and ill-informed perceptions are quashed. An important film in increasing awareness of a medical condition wrongly thought at the time to be just a gay problem. AJ

Dustin Hoffman *Narrator* ■ *Dir* Robert Epstein [Rob Epstein], Jeffrey Friedman • *Scr* Jeffrey Friedman, Robert Epstein

The Common Touch ★★★ U
Drama   1941 · UK · BW · 111min

This London drama builds on the themes of poverty and deprivation explored in John Baxter's 1933 directorial debut, *Doss House*. The action follows teenage tycoon Geoffrey Hibbert, as he disguises himself as a derelict to discover the dark schemes being hatched by his company's ambitious managing director, Raymond Lovell. Seeking to expose the iniquities of slum housing and the corruption of big business may seem an odd topic for a wartime film, but it typifies Baxter's uncompromisingly socialist approach to cinema. DP

Greta Gynt *Sylvia Meadows* • Geoffrey Hibbert *Peter Henderson* • Joyce Howard *Mary Weatherby* • Harry Welchman *Porter, Lincoln's Inn* • Edward Rigby *Tich* • Raymond Lovell *Cartwright* ■ *Dir* John Baxter • *Scr* Barbara K Emary, Geoffrey Orme, from a novel by Herbert Ayres

The Commune   ★★★★ 15
Drama   2016 · Den · Colour · 111min

Though set in the 1970s, this intimate drama isn't a retroactive critique of its time. Instead, it's a poignant, bittersweet study of a marriage in decline, from director Thomas Vinterberg (*Festen*). A populous cast moves in with a lecturer (Ulrich Thomsen) and his TV presenter wife (Trine Dyrholm) to share the costs of his inherited mansion house. The people in this commune serve as a Greek chorus of sorts, as the couple – beautifully portrayed by Thomsen and Dyrholm – wilfully sabotage their suburban utopia. DW In Danish. Sex scenes.

Ulrich Thomsen *Erik* • Trine Dyrholm *Anna* • Fares Fares *Allon* ■ *Dir* Thomas Vinterberg • *Scr* Thomas Vinterberg, Tobias Lindholm

Communion   ★★ 15
Science-fiction thriller
1989 · US · Colour · 104min

Was author Whitley Strieber abducted by aliens as outlined in his bestselling book *Communion*? Or was his close encounter and subsequent medical probing just a bizarre hallucination, or even a cynical marketing ploy? You really won't be any the wiser after watching this ponderous and pompous quasi-documentary, despite an enormous amount of conviction from Christopher Walken as the traumatised novelist. AJ Violence, swearing. **DVD**

Christopher Walken *Whitley Strieber* • Lindsay Crouse *Anne Strieber* • Joel Carlson *Andrew Strieber* • Frances Sternhagen *Dr Janet Duffy* • Andreas Katsulas *Alex* • Terri Hanauer *Sara* • Basil Hoffman *Dr Friedman* • John Dennis Johnston *Fireman* • Dee Dee Rescher *Mrs Greenberg* ■ *Dir* Philippe Mora • *Scr* Whitley Strieber, from his book

Company   ★★★ 15
Crime drama   2001 · Ind · Colour · 155min

Director Ram Gopal Varma takes a sturdy approach in this uncompromising exposé of how criminal gangs have taken control of every aspect of Indian life – from politics and commerce, to the running of Bollywood itself. But, with Ajay Devgan and Vivek Oberoi flexing their muscles as the mortal foes and Mohan Lal impressing as a crusading police inspector, this makes for revealing and riveting viewing. DP Hindi +subtitles. **DVD**

Ajay Devgan *Malik* • Vivek Oberoi *Chandu* • Mohan Lal *Srinivasan* • Manisha Koirala *Saroja* • Antara Mali *Kannu* ■ *Dir* Ram Gopal Varma • *Scr* Jaideep Sahni

The Company   ★★★★ 12
Dance drama
2003 · US/Ger/UK · Colour · 107min

Director Robert Altman's latest look at a microcosmic community is more an interested glance than his usual penetrating glare. Yet it's still another seductive spellbinder, with Altman expertly choreographing his film to match the concepts of Chicago's Joffrey Ballet. This jettisons soap-opera histrionics for revealing glimpses of the sheer craft and commitment involved. It focuses on the progress of a promising ingénue (Neve Campbell) from chorus to featured ballerina, under the watchful eye of mercurial company director Malcolm McDowell. Best known as queen of the *Scream* films, Campbell acquits herself surprisingly well. AJ **DVD**

Neve Campbell *Ry* • Malcolm McDowell *Alberto Antonelli* • James Franco *Josh* • Barbara Robertson *Harriet* • William Dick *Edouard* • Susie Cusack *Susie* • Marilyn Dodds Frank *Ry's mother* • John Lordan *Ry's father* ■ *Dir* Robert Altman • *Scr* Barbara Turner, from a story by Neve Campbell, Barbara Turner

Company Business   ★★ 15
Comedy thriller   1991 · US · Colour · 94min

While this is a competent enough spy caper, it went straight to video in the UK. Gene Hackman plays a former CIA agent who is drawn back into the world of espionage for a spy swap involving Russian agent Mikhail Baryshnikov. Hackman more than covers for any deficiencies in the acting department from his co-star, however, this lacks verve and imagination. JF Some violence, swearing. **DVD**

Gene Hackman *Sam Boyd* • Mikhail Baryshnikov *Pyiotr Grushenko* • Kurtwood Smith *Elliot Jaffe* • Terry O'Quinn *Colonel Grissom* • Daniel Von Bargen *Mike Flinn* ■ *Dir/Scr* Nicholas Meyer

Company Limited   ★★★★ U
Drama   1971 · Ind · BW · 113min

Although he had a huge following abroad, the Bengali director Satyajit Ray was often accused by Indian critics of ignoring the subcontinent's myriad of social and political problems. This mild attack on the educated middle classes is the kind of film Frank Capra might have made, had he allowed his head to rule his heart. As the sales manager prepared to brook a little corruption to secure privilege, Barun Chanda is quite superb. Subtle, satirical and sharp as a tack. DP Bengali +subtitles.

Barun Chanda *Shyamal Chatterjee* • Sharmila Tagore *Tutul* • Parumita Chowdhary *Shyamal's sister-in-law* • Harindranath Chattopadhyay *Sir Baren* ■ *Dir* Satyajit Ray • *Scr* Satyajit Ray, from the novel *Seemabaddha* by Sankar

Company Man   ★ 15
Comedy   2000 · US · Colour · 82min

This film has a really impressive cast, and one can only assume that co-writer/co-director/star Douglas McGrath (who has appeared in several Woody Allen movies) convinced his players that he really was Woody Allen and that he was remaking *Bananas*. Instead, this comedy – about a teacher in the 1960s who becomes a spy and gets involved in a plot to overthrow Castro – is a mess. JB **DVD**

Sigourney Weaver *Daisy Quimp* • Douglas McGrath *Allen Quimp* • John Turturro *Crocker Johnson* • Anthony LaPaglia *Fidel Castro* • Ryan Phillippe *Rudolph Petrov* • Denis Leary *Fry* • Woody Allen *Lowther* • Alan Cumming *General Batista* ■ *Dir/Scr* Peter Askin, Douglas McGrath

The Company Men   ★★★ 15
Drama   2010 · US · Colour · 100min

The fallout from the 2008 financial crisis is explored in this well-intentioned but ill-gauged study of men dealing with redundancies at a multinational company. Directed by *The West Wing/ER* writer John Wells, this Boston-set drama has the air of a superior TV soap about it, with Ben Affleck leading a stellar cast as a high-flying executive unexpectedly thrown on the scrapheap when his firm downsizes. As an issue movie, it just about passes muster, but it's hard to imagine too many people believing in Kevin Costner as Affleck's salt-of-the-earth carpenter brother-in-law, who teaches Affleck that honest toil is as worthwhile as chasing big bucks. AC Swearing. **DVD** **BD**

Ben Affleck *Bobby Walker* • Tommy Lee Jones *Gene McClary* • Chris Cooper *Phil Woodward* • Kevin Costner *Jack Dolan* • Maria Bello *Sally Wilcox* • Rosemarie DeWitt *Maggie Walker* • Craig T Nelson *James Salinger* ■ *Dir/Scr* John Wells • Cinematographer Roger Deakins

The Company of Strangers
★★★★ PG

Drama   1990 · Can · Colour · 100min

The sisterhood of women is lovingly proclaimed by this Canadian movie in which non-actors play themselves in a fictitious situation: in this case, seven elderly women who are stranded in a remote farmhouse when their touring bus breaks down. Each woman's story illuminates the experience of being female and being human as the group waits to be picked up. Paced by director Cynthia Scott with patient care, it has a rare distinction – it actually likes people. TH

Alice Diabo *Alice* • Constance Garneau *Constance* • Winifred Holden *Winnie* • Cissy Meddings *Cissy* • Mary Meigs *Mary* • Catherine Roche *Catherine* • Michelle Sweeney *Michelle* • Beth Webber *Beth* ■ *Dir* Cynthia Scott • *Scr* Gloria Demmers, Cynthia Scott, David Wilson, Sally Bochner

The Company of Wolves
★★★ 18

Supernatural fantasy   1984 · UK · Colour · 91min

Dark variations on the *Little Red Riding Hood* theme are adeptly explored by director Neil Jordan, co-writing with Angela Carter, in this arresting visual treat that at times resembles a pretentious Hammer horror. Dreams within dreams build up a psychological fright mosaic, as young Sarah Patterson goes through the broad spectrum of emotions generally known as adolescence. Angela Lansbury is super-eccentric form as the granny. A fine exercise in art design, lyrical mood and sinister allegory. AJ Violence. **DVD** **BD**

Angela Lansbury *Grandmother* • David Warner *Father* • Sarah Patterson *Rosaleen* • Stephen Rea *Young groom* • Graham Crowden *Old priest* • Shane Johnstone *Amorous boy* • Brian Glover *Boy's father* • Susan Porrett *Boy's mother* ■ *Dir* Neil Jordan • *Scr* Angela Carter, Neil Jordan, from the short stories by Angela Carter • *Cinematographer* Bryan Loftus • *Art Director* Anton Furst

The Company She Keeps ★★★

Drama 1950 · US · BW · 82min

This is the jaunty tale of an ex-con, played with convincing guile by Jane Greer, who dearly wishes to go straight but is not helped to that end when she falls for her parole officer's boyfriend. Greer is excellent, as is Dennis O'Keefe, and the two interact with just the right pinch of spice. There's sizeable amount of charm inserted into the rather lame script, saving the day. SH

Lizabeth Scott *Joan* • Jane Greer *Diane* • Dennis O'Keefe *Larry* • Fay Baker *Tilly* • John Hoyt *Judge Kendall* • James Bell *Mr Neeley* • Don Beddoe *Jamieson* • Bert Freed *Smitty* ■ *Dir* John Cromwell • *Scr* Ketti Frings

The Company You Keep ★★★15

Thriller 2012 · US · Colour · 116min

Robert Redford's political thriller shows us what happens to some old radicals of the 60s: the fire burns within them still, even if there's snow on the roof. Featuring a baker's dozen of stars, this is an interesting if earnest take on the discrepancies between activism and civic duty, as a former activist goes on the run when his cover is blown. A lumpen screenplay hamstrings the drama but big thrills are to be had seeing remarkable performers strutting their stuff. KK Swearing. *DVD*

Robert Redford *Jim Grant* • Shia LaBeouf *Ben Shepard* • Julie Christie *Mimi Luri* • Nick Nolte *Donal* • Terrence Howard *Cornelius* • Stanley Tucci *Ray Fuller* • Brendan Gleeson *Henry Osborne* • Sam Elliott *Mac McLeod* ■ *Dir* Robert Redford • *Scr* Lem Dobbs, from Neil Gordon's novel

Les Compères ★★★★

Comedy drama 1983 · Fr · Colour · 92min

Slickly scripted according to the rhythms of French stage farce, this was the second of three collaborations between director Francis Veber and actors Pierre Richard and Gérard Depardieu. As the journalist tricked into believing he is the father of teenage runaway Stéphane Bierry, Depardieu essentially plays stooge to the manic-depressive Richard, who has been told the same fib by ex-girlfriend Anny Duperey. Less sentimental and more authentic than the Hollywood remake, *Fathers' Day*. DP French +subtitles.

Pierre Richard *François Pignon* • Gérard Depardieu *Jean Lucas* • Anny Duperey *Christine Martin* • Michel Aumont *Paul Martin* • Stéphane Bierry *Tristan Martin* • Roland Blanche *Jeannot* ■ *Dir/Scr* Francis Veber

The Compleat Beatles ★★★PG

Music documentary 1982 · US · Colour and BW · 115min

Beatles fans are not fond of this patchy US documentary about the Fab Four, but there is still much to interest the casual viewer. Director Patrick Montgomery does a thorough job with the early years and has tracked down Allan Williams ("the man who sold the Beatles") and Tony Sheridan (who used the Beatles as a backing band) among others. The film was made without the co-operation of the Beatles and their wives. DM

Malcolm McDowell *Narrator* ■ *Dir* Patrick Montgomery • *Scr* David Silver

A Complete History of My Sexual Failures ★★★18

Documentary 2007 · UK · Colour · 89min

British film-maker Chris Waitt's highly personal confessional may have been inspired by personality-led documentaries like Morgan Spurlock's *Super Size Me*, as Waitt tries to figure out why he can't hold down a steady relationship. It starts promisingly enough, as he contacts a string of ex-girlfriends who emphatically refuse to be interviewed. But once it's established that he's not going to have much material to work with, Waitt embarks on a series of bizarre quests that see him visit a dominatrix, overdose on Viagra and finally take to the streets to find a woman who will sleep with him. Waitt himself is an engagingly shabby hero, and there are some hilarious moments, but on the whole this probably says more about one man's idiocy than human nature. DW *DVD*

Chris Waitt • Hilary Waitt ■ *Dir* Chris Waitt • *Cinematographer* Steven Mochrie

Complex of Fear ★★★18

Thriller 1993 · US · Colour · 90min

Chelsea Field lives in a creepy apartment block and feels threatened in this nifty little TV chiller, which focuses on a residential complex plagued by a series of vicious rapes. Field is a potential victim, Hart Bochner a resident rookie cop and the ever-reliable Joe Don Baker the investigating detective. The plotting is a mite predictable, but director Brian Grant still summons up an air of claustrophobic suspense. JF Violence, swearing. *DVD*

Hart Bochner *Ray Dolan* • Chelsea Field *Michelle Dolan* • Joe Don Baker *Detective Frank Farrel* • Brett Cullen *Ed Wyle* • Farrah Forke *Vicki* • Ashley Gardner *Doreen Wylie* • Jordan Williams *Lee Harrison* ■ *Dir* Brian Grant • *Scr* Dyanne Asimow, Matt Dorff

Compliance ★★★15

Thriller based on a true story 2012 · US · Colour · 90min

Ostensibly a kind of moral maze movie, this well-made but ultimately rather queasy American indie puts the audience through an ordeal that almost matches that of its characters. The setting is a small-town burger joint, where the manager, Ann Dowd, receives a phone call from a man claiming to be a cop and accusing worker Dreama Walker of stealing money from a customer. Dowd resolves to settle the matter, putting all her faith in the voice at the end of the phone, and from here on in the investigation takes a darker and more sexual turn. Viewers who stick with this may wonder if such a serious matter warrants slightly less prurient treatment. DW Violence, swearing. *DVD*

Ann Dowd *Sandra* • Dreama Walker *Becky* • Pat Healy *Officer Daniels* • Bill Camp *Van* • Philip Ettinger *Kevin* • James McCaffrey *Detective Neals* ■ *Dir/Scr* Craig Zobel

Complicity ★18

Thriller 1999 · UK · Colour · 95min

You'd be better off going back to Iain Banks's original novel than waste your time with this unsatisfactory adaptation. Jonny Lee Miller stars as Banks's journalist antihero Cameron and, despite support from Brian Cox and Bill Paterson, he's endlessly bland. Director Gavin Millar seems all at sea with this Scotland-based tale, which involves sex, drugs and murderous atrocities. LH *DVD*

Jonny Lee Miller *Cameron* • Keeley Hawes *Yvonne* • Brian Cox (1) *Detective Chief Inspector McDunn* • Paul Higgins *Andy Gould* • Jason Hetherington *William* • Rachael Stirling *Claire Gould* • Bill Paterson *Wallace Byatt* ■ *Dir* Gavin Millar • *Scr* Brian Elsley, from the novel by Iain Banks

Compromising Positions ★15

Comedy thriller 1985 · US · Colour · 94min

Thelma & Louise star Susan Sarandon does her best with one of her few ropey roles in this uneven farce, about a woman who starts investigating the death of her dentist only to get caught up in a world of ex-mistresses and pornography. It's silly in the extreme, and Sarandon and her co-stars (Raul Julia, Joe Mantegna, Edward Herrmann) look distinctly uncomfortable. JB

Susan Sarandon *Judith Singer* • Raul Julia *Lieutenant David Suarez* • Edward Herrmann *Bob Singer* • Judith Ivey *Nancy Miller* • Mary Beth Hurt *Peg Tuccio* • Joe Mantegna *Bruce Fleckstein*

• Anne De Salvo *Phyllis Fleckstein* ■ *Dir* Frank Perry • *Scr* Susan Isaacs, from a novel by Susan Isaacs

Compulsion ★★★★12

Period crime drama 1959 · US · BW · 98min

Bradford Dillman and Dean Stockwell, two wealthy, homosexual college students, murder a boy in cold blood to prove that the perfect crime is possible. Adapted from Meyer Levin's book and brilliantly directed by Richard Fleischer in semi-documentary style, this is a thinly veiled account of the notorious 1924 Leopold and Loeb case. Dillman's sneering psychopath is superb, as is Stockwell's more human, less confident counsel, modelled on the famous Clarence Darrow who saved Leopold and Loeb from the chair, is a tour de force. RK *DVD* *BD*

Orson Welles *Jonathan Wilk* • Dean Stockwell *Judd Steiner* • Bradford Dillman *Artie Straus* • EG Marshall *Horn* • Diane Varsi *Ruth Evans* • Martin Milner *Sid* • Richard Anderson *Max* ■ *Dir* Richard Fleischer • *Scr* Richard Murphy, from the novel by Meyer Levin

Computer Chess ★★★15

Comedy 2013 · US · BW and Colour · 91min

In this experimental exercise in analogue nostalgia, writer/director Andrew Bujalski affectionately spoofs aspects of early 1980s life, while also exploring the dangers of becoming over-reliant on soon-to-be obsolete technology. While the gadgetry jokes are amusing and the discussion of artificial intelligence is intriguing, the human elements of the scattershot storyline are only fitfully engaging – although Patrick Riester does make an appealing antihero. DP *DVD* *BD*

Wiley Wiggins *Martin Beuscher* • Patrick Riester *Peter Bishton* • Myles Paige *Michael Papageorge* • Robin Schwartz *Shelly Flintic* • Gordon Kindlmann *Schoesser* ■ *Dir/Scr* Andrew Bujalski

The Computer Wore Tennis Shoes ★★U

Comedy 1969 · US · Colour · 86min

What might have been a nifty idea for a half-hour TV show is stretched to breaking point in this Disney comedy. Kurt Russell stars as the teenager who becomes a genius after a computer downloads its memory system into his brain. Suddenly, our hero is winning game shows and taking on Cesar Romero's stupendously inept crime ring. Russell returned for a follow-up film, *Now You See Him, Now You Don't*, in 1972. DP *DVD*

Cesar Romero *AJ Arno* • Kurt Russell *Dexter* • Joe Flynn *Dean Higgins* • William Schallert *Professor Quigley* • Alan Hewitt *Dean Collingsgood* • Richard Bakalyan *Chillie Walsh* ■ *Dir* Robert Butler • *Scr* Joseph L McEveety

Comrade X ★★★U

Romantic comedy 1940 · US · BW · 89min

Hedy Lamarr was seldom more glamorous than as the Russian tram-driver who falls for hunky American journalist Clark Gable. You might expect more than just froth from master director King Vidor, but he was shrewd enough to know that wartime audiences wanted, and just let his two great stars get on with it. TS

Clark Gable *McKinley B Thompson* • Hedy Lamarr *Theodora* • Oscar Homolka *Vasiliev* • Felix Bressart *Vanya* • Eve Arden *Jane Wilson* • Sig Rumann [Sig Ruman] *Emil Von Hofer* • Natasha Lytess *Olga* • Vladimir Sokoloff *Michael Bastakoff* ■ *Dir* King Vidor • *Scr* Ben Hecht, Charles Lederer, from a story by Walter Reisch

Comrades: a Lanternist's Account of the Tolpuddle Martyrs and What Became of Them ★★★★15

Historical drama 1986 · UK · Colour · 174min

Bill Douglas struggled to finance this epic tribute to those pioneer trades unionists. Although set in Dorset in the 1830s, the story of the farm labourers who were deported to Australia for protesting against their harsh conditions and meagre wages had a contemporary resonance as, 150 years later, the Thatcher government sought to break union power. However, while Douglas is keen to highlight the continued existence of exploitation, the superb performances keep it rooted in its period. DP *DVD*

Robin Soans *George Loveless* • William Gaminara *James Loveless* • Stephen Bateman *Old Tom Stanfield* • Philip Davis *Young Stanfield* • Keith Allen *James Hammett* • Alex Norton *Lanternist* • James Fox *Norfolk* • Michael Hordern *Mr Pitt* • Vanessa Redgrave *Mrs Carlyle* ■ *Dir/Scr* Bill Douglas

La Comunidad ★★★15

Comedy thriller 2000 · Sp · Colour · 108min

Alex de la Iglesia is in Chabrol territory with this mischievously macabre thriller. Carmen Maura throws herself into the role of an estate agent who discovers a lottery win stashed in a Madrid tenement, only to realise that the other occupants have no intention of letting her take it. From the feline credits to the high-rise finale, the pace is unrelenting as Maura fends off the attentions of murderous neighbours. Excess wins out over invention before the end, but the sheer bravura of the exercise sweeps you along. DP Spanish +subtitles. Violence, swearing.

Carmen Maura *Julia* • Eduardo Antuña *Charly* • Jesús Bonilla *Ricardo* • Paca Gabaldón *Hortensia* • Sancho Gracia *Castro* • Emilio Gutiérrez Caba *Emilio* • Terele Pávez *Ramona* ■ *Dir* Alex de la Iglesia • *Scr* Jorge Guerricaechevarría, Alex de la Iglesia

The Con ★★12

Romantic crime drama 1998 · US · Colour · 88min

Before you ask what William H Macy is doing in a whimsical TV movie such as this, he co-wrote it with director Steven Schachter. More puzzling is why he devised such a dull character and then set him in such a stock situation. Macy's too skilled an actor wholly to alienate our affections, here playing a simple-minded southerner who comes into an unexpected fortune, with gold-digging Rebecca De Mornay planning to marry, then murder, him. Eager to please but rather uninspired. DP

Rebecca De Mornay *Barbara/Nancy* • William H Macy *Bobby Sommerdinger* • Frances Sternhagen *Hadabelle* • Mike Nussbaum *Harry* ■ *Dir* Steven Schachter • *Scr* William H Macy, Steven Schachter

Con Air ★★★★18

Action thriller 1997 · US · Colour · 110min

This is a top-notch thrill-athon, with Nicolas Cage as an ex-Army Ranger jailed for a murder he committed in self-defence, whose release is interrupted when his flight home is hijacked by a bunch of America's most dangerous felons. Cage's impossibly cool macho posturing is irresistible, as is John Malkovich's tongue-in-cheek turn as a super criminal. John Cusack and Ving Rhames lend snappy support, while Steve Buscemi steals nearly every scene he is in with an inspired pastiche of Hannibal Lecter. JC Violence, swearing. *DVD* *BD*

Nicolas Cage *Cameron Poe* • John Cusack *Vince Larkin* • John Malkovich *Cyrus "the Virus" Grissom* • Steve Buscemi *Garland Greene* • Ving Rhames *Diamond Dog* • Colm Meaney *Duncan Malloy* • Rachel Ticotin *Sally Bishop* • Nick Chinlund *Billy Bedlam* ■ *Dir* Simon West • *Scr* Scott Rosenberg

The Con Artists ★PG

Comedy 1976 · It · Colour · 89min

Versatile director Sergio Corbucci turns his attention to the crime world with this clumsily plotted caper, but he lacks the lightness of touch to bring much life to this bovine variation on *The Sting*. Always prone to overplaying comedy, Anthony Quinn milks every gag as an escaped convict. DP Italian dubbed.

Anthony Quinn *Philippe Bang* • Adriano Celentano *Felix* • Capucine *Belle Duke* • Corinne Cléry *Charlotte* ■ *Dir* Sergio Corbucci • *Scr* Arnold Maury, Max D'Rita

C

Conan the Barbarian
★★★ 15

Fantasy action adventure
1982 · US · Colour · 125min

Arnold Schwarzenegger took a musclebound step closer to superstardom with this entertaining sword-and-sorcery epic. Director/co-writer John Milius quotes Nietzsche and ladles on the fantasy with a Wagnerian flourish as Arnie's Nordic superman ventures forth to avenge his parents' death at the hands of James Earl Jones's warlord. He's aided in his quest by thief Sandahl Bergman and would-be comic sidekick Gerry Lopez. It's all too humourless for its own good, but looks fabulous. A remake is due in 2011, with Jason Momoa in the title role. TH Violence, swearing, nudity. DVD Blu-ray

Arnold Schwarzenegger *Conan* · James Earl Jones *Thulsa Doom* · Max von Sydow *King Osric* · Sandahl Bergman *Valeria* · Ben Davidson *Rexor* · Cassandra Gaviola *Witch* · Gerry Lopez *Subotai* · Mako *Wizard* ■ *Dir* John Milius · *Scr* John Milius, Oliver Stone, from characters by Robert E Howard

Conan the Destroyer ★★ 15

Fantasy action adventure
1984 · US · Colour · 96min

Arnold Schwarzenegger returns to his breakthrough role as the mythical hero but the kitsch magic of the John Milius original is missing this time around. However, the requisite number of ugly villains, beautiful temptresses and doe-eyed heroines are present and correct, Schwarzenegger doesn't have to do too much acting and director Richard Fleischer keeps the often violent action flowing smoothly. JF Violence. DVD

Arnold Schwarzenegger *Conan* · Grace Jones *Zula* · Wilt Chamberlain *Bombaata* · Mako *Akjiro, the "Wizard"* · Tracey Walter *Malak* · Sarah Douglas *Queen Taramis* · Olivia D'Abo *Princess Jehnna* ■ *Dir* Richard Fleischer · *Scr* Stanley Mann, from a story by Roy Thomas, Gerry Conway, from characters by Robert E Howard

Conan the Barbarian ★★ 15

Action fantasy
2011 · US · Colour · 107min

This update for the sword-and-sorcery hero sees TV actor Jason Momoa (*Stargate: Atlantis*) encroaching on Arnie territory, with more blood and less humour. Adopting the barest elements from writer Robert E Howard's novelettes, the plot sees Conan seeking Stephen Lang, the warlord who killed his noble father (Ron Perlman) and set his village alight. Lang and daughter Rose McGowan are deliciously evil without being entirely callous, but it's Perlman who steals the show. KK Violence, a sex scene. DVD Blu-ray

Jason Momoa *Conan* · Rachel Nichols *Tamara* · Ron Perlman *Corin, Conan's father* · Stephen Lang *Khalar Zym* · Rose McGowan *Marique* ■ *Dir* Marcus Nispel · *Scr* Thomas Dean Donnelly, Sean Hood, Joshua Oppenheimer, from a character by Robert E Howard

Concerning Violence
★★★★ 15

Documentary
2014 · Swe/Den/Fin/US/Nor/Ger · Colour and BW · 89min

This is a compelling treatise on the use of physical and psychological violence in the oppression of Africa between the 1960s and 80s. Extracts from psychiatrist Frantz Fanon's provocative denunciation of colonialism, *The Wretched of the Earth*, are read with measured emphasis by singer-activist Lauryn Hill. Some of the most disconcerting imagery involves the casual racism of white Africans in British outposts like Rhodesia, while the human cost of struggle is chillingly shown in the sight of a breast-feeding mother and baby who have both lost limbs in a bomb blast. DP In English, Swedish, French, Portuguese. Violence, sexual/racist references.

Lauryn Hill *Narrator* · Gayatri Chakravorty Spivak *Preface* ■ *Dir* Goran Hugo Olsson · *Scr* from the non-fiction book *The Wretched of the Earth* by Frantz Fanon

The Concert ★★★ 15

Comedy drama
2009 · Fr/It/Bel/Rom/Rus · Colour · 117min

This feel-good comedy drama stars Alexei Guskov as a Russian conductor who was sacked mid-concert 30 years previously for using Jewish musicians and is now reduced to working as the Bolshoi's janitor. But when he intercepts a fax offering the orchestra a concert in Paris he sees the opportunity for a comeback. A charming Mélanie Laurent (*Inglourious Basterds*) plays the superstar violinist Guskov hires for the occasion. It's corny at times but, by and large, this is symphonic fun with a nicely filmed climax of Tchaikovsky's *Concerto for Violin and Orchestra in D major*. DA French, Russian +subtitles. Swearing. DVD

Alexei Guskov *Andrei Filipov* · Mélanie Laurent *Anne-Marie Jacquet* · Dimitri Nazarov *Sacha Grossman* · Valeri Barinov *Ivan Gavrilov* · François Berléand *Olivier Morne Duplessis* · Miou-Miou *Guylène de la Rivière* ■ *Dir* Radu Mihaileanu · *Scr* Radu Mihaileanu, Matthew Robbins, Alain-Michel Blanc, from a story by Héctor Cabello Reyes,Thierry Degrandi

The Concert for Bangladesh
★★★ U

Concert documentary
1972 · US · Colour · 94min

This is an unfussy documentary of one of the major media events of 1971: the twin benefit concerts held at Madison Square Garden for the starving refugee children of Bangladesh organised by George Harrison and noted sitar player Ravi Shankar. Press conferences and rehearsals are intercut with performances by Harrison (singing Beatles classics and solo hits), Shankar, Ringo Starr, Billy Preston, Leon Russell and Eric Clapton. The highlight is Bob Dylan, then making his first public appearance in two years, singing *Blowin' in the Wind* and *Just like a Woman*. AJ DVD

George Harrison · Bob Dylan · Mick Jagger · Ringo Starr · Ravi Shankar · Eric Clapton ■ *Dir/Scr* Saul Swimmer · *Producers* George Harrison, Allen Klein

Concert for George ★★★★

Concert movie 2003 · UK/US · Colour · 104min

Staged at the Royal Albert Hall on 29 November 2002 – exactly a year after George Harrison's death – and unfussily filmed by David Leland and Chris Menges using over a dozen cameras, this celebration of Harrison's music proves that the "quiet Beatle" was a consummate songwriter in his own right. Surviving Beatles Ringo Starr and Paul McCartney (whose ukulele introduction to *Something* is a showstopper), Travelling Wilburys Jeff Lynne and Tom Petty, and key musical collaborators Eric Clapton and Ravi Shankar join Harrison's son Dhani in an all-star update of the first rock aid gig, *The Concert for Bangladesh*. DP DVD

■ *Dir* David Leland · *Cinematographer* Chris Menges

Concrete Canyons ★★

Police drama 2010 · Can · Colour · 95min

An understated yet expressive lead performance distracts from all the clichés in this watchable crime drama about parenting and second chances. Scott Patterson adds depth to his small-town stereotype, playing a Rocky Mountains ex-sheriff and expert tracker who takes to the mean streets of Chicago to try to clear his estranged son of murder. It's the subtle handling of the emotional and family issues behind this contrived detective work that keeps the film interesting. SF Some swearing.

Scott Patterson *Ben Sloane* · Polly Shannon *Detective Susan Kincaid* · Emilie Ullerup *Maggie* · Andrew Dunbar *Nick* ■ *Dir* Terry Ingram

Concussion ★★★ 15

Drama 2013 · US · Colour · 96min

In this intense drama, Robin Weigert plays lesbian Abby, a bored housewife and mother married to a successful female

lawyer. After a blow to the head, Abby develops an alter ego as Eleanor, a prostitute for women. However, her double life takes its toll and the lines between fantasy and reality become blurred. Although the premise may sound like a salacious porn scenario, writer/director Stacie Passon's film is an intelligent, thought-provoking examination of female desire and the consequences of duplicity. TeS Swearing, sex scenes.

Robin Weigert *Abby Ableman/Eleanor* · Maggie Siff *Sam Bennet* · Daniel London *Evan* · Ben Shenkman *Graham Bennet* ■ *Dir/Scr* Stacie Passon

Concussion ★★★ 12

Sports drama
2015 · US/Aus/UK · Colour · 117min

The story of Dr Bennet Omalu, the Nigerian pathologist whose 2002 autopsy on American football hero Mike Webster revealed previously undisclosed levels of brain trauma in the US's most popular game. It's a strange subject for an awards-hopeful movie, but Will Smith gives it his best shot in one of his more grounded performances, portraying Omalu as a decent, religious man driven by duty and respect for the dead. As a two-hour feature, it's something of a mixed bag, but there are flashes of what made the story interesting in the first place. DW Some swearing. DVD Blu-ray

Will Smith *Dr Bennet Omalu* · Alec Baldwin *Dr Julian Bailes* · Gugu Mbatha-Raw *Prema Mutiso* · Arliss Howard *Dr Joseph Maroon* · Paul Reiser *Dr Elliot Pellman* ■ *Dir* Peter Landesman · *Scr* Landesman, from the article *Game Brain* by Jeanne Marie Laskas · *Music* James Newton Howard

Condemned ★★ U

Drama 1929 · US · BW · 82min

Oscar history was made within the best actor category of 1930. Ronald Colman, George Arliss and Maurice Chevalier all received two separate nominations, but only Arliss emerged triumphant. Colman is great fun in *Bulldog Drummond*, but it's harder to fathom why he was nominated for this creaky early talkie about a prisoner who falls in love with the warden's wife (Ann Harding). Directed by Wesley Ruggles, it's a clumsy mix of action adventure, drippy romance and an exposé of the iniquities of the infamous Devil's Island. DP

Ronald Colman *Michel Oban* · Ann Harding *Mme Vidal* · Dudley Digges *Warden Jean Vidal* · Louis Wolheim *Jacques Duval* · William Elmer *Pierre* · William Vaughn *Vidal's orderly* ■ *Dir* Wesley Ruggles · *Scr* Sidney Howard

The Condemned ★★ 18

Action thriller 2007 · US · Colour · 108min

It's kill or die in this gritty yet absurdly message-heavy vehicle for former wrestling star Steve Austin. Armed with bulldozer fists and predictably pithy dialogue, he plays one of ten death-row convicts fighting for their lives and freedom in a sadistic *Battle Royale*-style internet reality show. Grimy, shaky-cam visuals and a pumping soundtrack accentuate the brainless barrage of sweat, blood and rage that follows, but what begins as an enjoyably exaggerated action flick sours in the clumsy final act. SF In English, German. Violence, swearing. DVD Blu-ray

Steve Austin (2) *Jack Conrad* · Vinnie Jones *McStarley* · Rick Hoffman *Goldman* · Robert Mammone *Breckel* ■ *Dir* Scott Wiper · *Scr* Rob Hedden, Scott Wiper, from a story by Wiper, Hedden, Andy Hedden

Condemned Women ★★★

Prison drama 1938 · US · BW · 76min

A 1930s version of *Prisoner: Cell Block H*, minus the cardboard sets but heavy on the melodrama. There's no messing with these ladies of the slammer as they fight, eat, fight, sleep and fight again all the way to lights out, with surly Sally Eilers striking up a less than wholesome relationship with prison psychiatrist Louis Hayward. Nothing overly subtle here, but there are some cracking performances. SH

Sally Eilers *Linda Wilson* · Louis Hayward *Phillip Duncan* · Anne Shirley *Millie Anson* · Esther Dale *Matron Glover* · Lee Patrick *Big Annie* ■ *Dir* Lew Landers · *Scr* Lionel Houser

El Condor ★★

Western 1970 · US · Colour · 101min

Director John Guillermin came unstuck with this western about a pair of mercenaries raiding a Mexican fort for its gold. The Spanish-shot movie contains none of the tongue-in-cheek humour that's often the salvation of the European western. Lee Van Cleef and Jim Brown look good, but the constant brutality and slow pace make this very hard to enjoy. TS Violence, swearing, nudity.

Lee Van Cleef *Jaroo* · Jim Brown *Luke* · Patrick O'Neal (1) *Chavez* · Mariana Hill [Marianna Hill] *Claudine* · Iron Eyes Cody *Santana* · Imogen Hassall *Dolores* · Elisha Cook Jr *Old convict* · Gustavo Rojo *Colonel Aguinaldo* ■ *Dir* John Guillermin · *Scr* Larry Cohen, Steven Carabatsos

Condorman ★ U

Comedy 1981 · US · Colour · 86min

Disney, for all its ability to create animated magic, regularly churned out live-action pictures that would embarrass a camcorder enthusiast. This is worse than most. Michael Crawford stars, but surely both he and Oliver Reed (as the KGB agent trying to stop Crawford rescuing spy Barbara Carrera) could have found something better to do? DP DVD

Michael Crawford *Woody* · Oliver Reed *Krokov* · Barbara Carrera *Natalia* · James Hampton *Harry* · Jean-Pierre Kalfon *Morovich* · Dana Elcar *Russ* · Vernon Dobtcheff *Russian agent* ■ *Dir* Charles Jarrott · *Scr* Marc Stirdivant, Glen Caron, Mickey Rose, from the novel *The Game of X* by Robert Sheckley

Conduct Unbecoming ★★ PG

Period drama 1975 · UK · Colour · 106min

Trevor Howard and Richard Attenborough almost redeem this dull, studio-bound drama set at the height of the British Raj. As the widow of the regimental hero, Susannah York accuses a newly arrived lieutenant of assaulting her, leading to his court martial, a lot of twitching moustaches and an exposure of Victorian moral hypocrisy. AT DVD

Michael York *Second Lieutenant Arthur Drake* · Richard Attenborough *Major Lionel Roach* · Trevor Howard *Colonel Benjamin Strang* · Stacy Keach *Captain Rupert Harper* · Christopher Plummer *Major Alastair Wimbourne* · Susannah York *Mrs Marjorie Scarlett* ■ *Dir* Michael Anderson · *Scr* Robert Enders, from the play by Barry England

The Conductor ★★★★

Musical drama 1980 · Pol · Colour · 102min

After decades spent in the United States, a famous classical maestro (John Gielgud) returns to his birthplace in Poland as a guest conductor with the provincial town's struggling orchestra. Although in frail health and nearing the end of his life, he is able to inject new life into the musicians. Made by the great Andrzej Wajda, this poignant film is redolent with atmosphere and tension, but disappointingly hints at deeper significance without conveying much. Gielgud, however, is absolutely superb, despite being dubbed into Polish. RK Polish +subtitles.

John Gielgud *John Lasocki* · Krystyna Janda *Marta* · Andrzej Seweryn *Adam Pietryk* ■ *Dir* Andrzej Wajda · *Scr* Andrzej Kijowski

Cone of Silence ★★★★

Drama 1960 · UK · BW · 76min

Former Hitchcock editor Charles Frend directs this expertly made, taut British movie. It contains some fine heart-stopping moments, while Peter Cushing, George Sanders and character actor Bernard Lee give superb performances. Some of the technical details and hardware have inevitably dated in this aeronautical drama about the investigation into a plane crash in India, but the striking compositions and beautifully paced editing remain very impressive. TS

Michael Craig *Captain Hugh Dallas* • Peter Cushing *Captain Clive Judd* • Bernard Lee *Captain George Gort* • Elizabeth Seal *Charlotte Gort* • George Sanders *Sir Arnold Hobbes* • André Morell *Captain Edward Manningham* • Gordon Jackson *Captain Bateson* ■ *Dir* Charles Frend • *Scr* Robert Westerby, from the novel by David Beaty • *Cinematographer* Arthur Grant • *Editor* Max Benedict

Coneheads ★★ PG
Comedy 1993 · US · Colour · 86min

The American satirical series *Saturday Night Live* has spawned some blockbuster movies – *The Blues Brothers* and *Wayne's World*, for instance – but this Dan Aykroyd creation sank without trace. Aykroyd is reunited with old TV colleagues Jane Curtin and Laraine Newman for this dismal comedy about a family of aliens trying to get to grips with life on Earth, but the characters are long past their sell-by date. **JF** Swearing, sex scenes. DVD

Dan Aykroyd *Beldar* • Jane Curtin *Prymaat* • Michael McKean *Seedling* • Michelle Burke *Connie* • David Spade *Turnball* • Chris Farley *Ronnie* • Jason Alexander *Larry Farber* • Lisa Jane Persky *Lisa Farber* • Sinbad *Otto* • Jon Lovitz *Dr Rudolf* • Phil Hartman *Marlax* • Laraine Newman *Laarta* • Ellen DeGeneres *Coach* ■ *Dir* Steve Barron • *Scr* Tom Davis, Dan Aykroyd, Bonnie Turner, Terry Turner

Coney Island ★★★ U
Musical comedy 1943 · US · Colour · 96min

Here's Betty Grable at the peak of her wartime career, singing period songs like *Put Your Arms around Me, Honey* in gloriously garish, 20th Century-Fox Technicolor. It's a piece of tosh about saloon-keeper George Montgomery wanting to turn her into a big star, despite rival hotelier Cesar Romero, who wants her for himself. Familiar stuff, but vastly entertaining in its unsophisticated, mindless way. **TS**

Betty Grable *Kate Farley* • George Montgomery *Eddie Johnson* • Cesar Romero *Joe Rocco* • Charles Winninger *Finnigan* • Phil Silvers *Frankie* ■ *Dir* Walter Lang • *Scr* George Seaton

Confession ★★★★
Melodrama 1937 · US · BW · 88min

This splendid melodrama, told in flashback, stars the elegant Kay Francis as a singer who kills her seducer, pianist Basil Rathbone. (He'd taken a shine to her daughter, the swine!) This is a stunner, with design and camerawork very reminiscent of a classy German feature (it's based on a 1935 Pola Negri vehicle), while émigré director Joe May pulls out all the stops and weaves a wonderfully flamboyant Hollywood tapestry. **TS**

Kay Francis *Vera* • Ian Hunter *Leonide Kilrow* • Basil Rathbone *Michael Michailow* • Jane Bryan *Lisa* • Donald Crisp *Presiding judge* • Mary Maguire *Hildegard* • Dorothy Peterson *Mrs Koslov* ■ *Dir* Joe May • *Scr* Julius J Epstein, Margaret LaVino, Stanley Logan, from the film *Mazurka* by Hans Hameau • *Cinematographer* Sid Hickox • *Art Director* Anton Grot

Confession ★★ PG
Crime thriller 1955 · UK · BW · 86min

The confidentiality of the confessional is a well-worn movie theme, and Ken Hughes finds nothing new to say about the subject here. A priest hears a voice confess to murder and then finds his world collapsing around him as his vow of silence prevents him from passing on the information that will nail the killer. The film gives viewers a rare chance to see Charlie Chaplin's son, Sydney, in a leading role. **DP**

Sydney Chaplin *Mike Nelson* • Audrey Dalton *Louise* • John Bentley *Inspector Kessler* • Peter Hammond *Alan* • John Welsh *Father Neil* • Jefferson Clifford *Pop* • Patrick Allen *Corey* • Pat McGrath *Williams* ■ *Dir* Ken Hughes • *Scr* Ken Hughes, from a play by Don Martin

The Confession ★★★
Political drama 1970 · Fr/It · Colour · 139min

This film *à clef* is a thinly disguised account of the 1951 show trial in which Czech foreign minister Artur London and 13 other party officials were charged by the Communist regime with being American-backed, pro-Zionist spies. Clearly intent on demonstrating that extremism knows no boundaries, Costa-Gavras presents a grinding insight into Stalinist brutality. However, this works better as a portrait of a man under pressure than as a political argument. **DP** French +subtitles.

Yves Montand *"Gerard"/Artur London* • Simone Signoret *Lise* • Gabriele Ferzetti *Kohoutek* • Michel Vitold *Smola* • Jean Bouise *Man in factory* • Laszlo Szabo *Secret policeman* ■ *Dir* Costa-Gavras • *Scr* Jorge Semprun, from the non-fiction book *L'Aveu* by Lise London, Artur London

The Confession ★★
Courtroom drama 1999 · US · Colour · 114min

A top-notch cast can't stop this well-meaning courtroom drama from toppling into uncomfortable melodrama. Alec Baldwin is the slick lawyer who finds his conscience pricked when he is hired to defend Ben Kingsley, who's accused of murdering the people he thinks are responsible for the accidental death of his son. The capable cast make the most of the emotionally charged material, but it's too strident for its own good. **JF**

Alec Baldwin *Roy Bleakie* • Ben Kingsley *Harry Fertig* • Amy Irving *Sarah Fertig* • Ryan Marsini *Stevie Fertig* • Boyc Gaines *Liam Clarke* ■ *Dir* David Jones (3) • *Scr* David Black, from the novel *Fertig* by Sol Yurick

Confession of a Child of the Century ★ 15
Period drama 2011 · Fr · Colour · 115min

Rock singer Pete Doherty is wildly miscast in this 1830s-set drama, which is as dull and cumbersome as its title. Doherty plays Octave, a well-to-do young Parisian who sinks into debauchery and despair when he finds his mistress with another man. Later, following the death of his father, Octave retires to the country, where he falls for the widowed, slightly older Brigitte (Charlotte Gainsbourg). Doherty looks the part (hairstyle aside), but he can't act for toffee, while the film strives too hard to be deep and meaningful. **DA** Sex scenes. DVD

Charlotte Gainsbourg *Brigitte* • Pete Doherty *Octave* • Lily Cole *Elise* • August Diehl *Desgenais* ■ *Dir* Sylvie Verheyde • *Scr* Sylvie Verheyde, from the novel *La Confession d'un Enfant du Siècle* by Alfred de Musset

The Confessional ★★★★ 15
Thriller 1995 · Can/UK/Fr · Colour and BW · 96min

The filming in the 1950s of Hitchcock's *I Confess*, the Quebec-based thriller about the sanctity of a priest's confessional, provides the background to this intricate story of an adopted brother seeking his real father. It marks the film directorial debut of Robert Lepage, a noted Canadian theatre director whose style is as compelling as it is sumptuous. The story seesaws between 1989, and the hunt for paternal identity, and 1952, when Hitchcock (played by Ron Burrage) arrives in Quebec and blames his assistant (Kristin Scott Thomas) for letting the Catholic Church make too many cuts in his film. **TH** English, French +subtitles.

Lothaire Bluteau *Pierre Lamontagne* • Patrick Goyette *Marc Lamontagne* • Jean-Louis Millette *Raymond Massicotte* • Kristin Scott Thomas *Hitchcock's secretary* • Ron Burrage *Alfred Hitchcock* • Richard Fréchette *André* • François Papineau *Lamontagne* • Anne-Marie Cadieux *Manon* ■ *Dir/Scr* Robert Lepage

Confessions ★★★★ 15
Psychological thriller 2010 · Jpn · Colour · 106min

Memories of Matsuko director Tetsuya Nakashima's adaptation of Kinae Minato's novel is a tale of dark deeds and muddled motives that's an audacious exhibition of cinematic ingenuity and control. He shows how a young child's death sets in motion a terrible train of events that involves the girl's grieving mother, the students she holds responsible and their horribly fascinated classmate. The director boldly confronts such contentious issues as domestic dysfunction, bullying and the alienating effects of technology, while also continually confounding audience expectations by gradually revealing more of the truth – and the pitiless acts of revenge it inspires. DP Japanese +subtitles. Violence. DVD BD

Takako Matsu *Yuko Moriguchi* • Yukito Nishii *Shuya* • Kaoru Fujiwara *Naoki* • Ai Hashimoto *Mizuki* • Masaki Okada *Yoshiteru Terada* • Yoshino Kimura *Naoki's mother* • Dir Tetsuya Nakashima • Scr Tetsuya Nakashima, from the novel *Kokuhaku* by Kanae Minato

Confessions from a Holiday Camp ★ 18
Sex comedy 1977 · UK · Colour · 84min

The *Confessions* films relied on a blend of saucy humour and "What the Butler Saw"-style smut. This was the fourth and last of these cheap comedies, with Robin Askwith as an over-sexed entertainments officer at a camp run by an ex-prison officer. DP Swearing, nudity. DVD

Robin Askwith *Timothy Lea* • Anthony Booth *Sidney Noggett* • Doris Hare *Mum* • Bill Maynard *Dad* • Sheila White *Rosie* • Colin Crompton *Roughage* • Liz Frazer *Mrs Whitemonk* • Linda Hayden *Brigitte* ■ *Dir* Norman Cohen • *Scr* Christopher Wood, from a novel by Timothy Lea [Christopher Wood]

Confessions of a Dangerous Mind ★★★★ 15
Biographical comedy drama 2002 · US/Ger/UK · Colour · 108min

For his remarkably accomplished debut behind the camera, George Clooney tackles the unreliable memoirs of Chuck Barris, the host and creator of influential US TV shows *The Dating Game* and *The Gong Show*, who also claims to have killed 33 people as a hitman for the CIA. Charlie Kaufman contributes a sharp, deadpan script, while the film's gleefully erratic tone and style fluctuates between gaudy 1960s psychedelia and muted Cold War grit, enriched by Clooney's fluency with a camera. Sam Rockwell is believable and entertaining as Barris, and Drew Barrymore is on good form as his girlfriend. **JC** Sex scenes, violence, swearing. DVD

Sam Rockwell *Chuck Barris* • Drew Barrymore *Penny Pacino* • George Clooney *Jim Byrd* • Julia Roberts *Patricia Watson* • Rutger Hauer *Keeler* • Maggie Gyllenhaal *Debbie* • Kristen Wilson *Loretta* • Jennifer Hall *Georgia* ■ *Dir* George Clooney • *Scr* Charlie Kaufman, from the autobiography *Confessions of a Dangerous Mind: an Unauthorized Autobiography* by Chuck Barris

Confessions of a Driving Instructor ★ 18
Sex comedy 1976 · UK · Colour · 85min

The third in the series of smutty comedies based on the novels of Timothy Lea is something of an embarrassment for all concerned. The mix of double entendres and soft-core gropings can only be described as abysmal. Robin Askwith mugs like a trouper, but it's sad that accomplished comedy actresses Irene Handl and Liz Fraser signed up for this rubbish. DP Swearing, nudity. DVD

Robin Askwith *Timothy Lea* • Anthony Booth *Sidney Noggett* • Windsor Davies *Mr Truscott* • Sheila White *Rosie* • Doris Hare *Mum* • Bill Maynard *Dad* • Liz Fraser *Mrs Chalmers* • Irene Handl *Miss Slenderparts* • George Layton *Tony Bender* ■ *Dir* Norman Cohen • *Scr* Christopher Wood, from a novel by Timothy Lea [Christopher Wood]

Confessions of a Nazi Spy ★★★ U
Spy drama 1939 · US · BW · 110min

Warner Bros declared war on Germany long before America itself and this documentary-style spy drama, showing G-men searching out Nazis rallying undercover in America, is one of its most blatant pieces of propaganda. Paul Lukas and Edward G Robinson blend into the woodwork well enough, but there's a whole casting directory of scar-faced villains to make you wonder how they ever got through immigration. **TH**

Edward G Robinson *Ed Renard* • Francis Lederer *Schneider* • George Sanders *Schlager* • Paul Lukas *Dr Kassel* • Henry O'Neill *DA Kellogg* • Lya Lys *Erika Wolff* • Grace Stafford *Mrs Schneider* ■ *Dir* Anatole Litvak • *Scr* Milton Krims, John Wexley, from a story by Milton Krims, John Wexley, from the article *Storm over America* by Leon G Turrou

Confessions of a Pop Performer ★ 18
Sex comedy 1975 · UK · Colour · 87min

Robin Askwith abandons his window-cleaning round to help organise a tour for a band of no-hopers and finds himself knee-deep in groupies (the finale at the Palladium has to be seen to be believed). Askwith struggles with a dismal script and comes off much better than Tony Blair's father-in-law, Anthony Booth. DP Swearing, sex scenes, nudity. DVD

Robin Askwith *Timothy Lea* • Anthony Booth *Sidney Noggett* • Bill Maynard *Mr Lea* • Doris Hare *Mrs Lea* • Sheila White *Rosie* • Bob Todd *Mr Barnwell* • Jill Gascoine *Mrs Barnwell* • Peter Cleall *Nutter Normington* ■ *Dir* Norman Cohen • *Scr* Christopher Wood, from a novel by Timothy Lea [Christopher Wood]

Confessions of a Serial Killer ★★★★ 15
Crime drama 1987 · US · Colour · 95min

Savage yet brilliant, this minor masterpiece will inevitably be compared to the similar *Henry: Portrait of a Serial Killer*, made around the same time. In police custody, serial killer Daniel Ray Hawkins (extremely well-played by Robert A Burns) begins a series of confessions about his life and crimes. The flaw in this narrative device is outweighed by the movie's virtues, which include gritty location shooting that lends an authenticity to the proceedings. **KB** DVD

Robert A Burns *Daniel Ray Hawkins* • Dennis Hill Moon *Lawton* • Berkley Garrett *Sheriff Will Gaines* • Sidney Brammer *Molly* • DeeDee Norton *Monica* ■ *Dir/Scr* Mark Blair

Confessions of a Shopaholic ★★★ PG
Romantic comedy 2009 · US · Colour · 99min

Star Isla Fisher (*Wedding Crashers*) proves to be the most precious commodity in this chick flick based on the bestselling novels by Sophie Kinsella. The action is relocated from London to New York, with Fisher playing heroine Rebecca Bloomwood, an aspiring fashion journalist who has run up massive credit-card debts in the shops on Fifth Avenue. She takes a job on a dull financial publication in a bid to advance her career, but struggles to curb her shopaholic tendencies. Hugh Dancy channels Hugh Grant as her boss – the man who competes with Gucci shoes for Rebecca's attention. It's a fresh and funny premise, but the way the action plays out is often unconvincing. Thankfully, Fisher proves to have rare star quality, throwing herself into the role with perfect comic timing. SP DVD BD

Isla Fisher *Rebecca Bloomwood* • Hugh Dancy *Luke Brandon* • Krysten Ritter *Suze Cleath-Stewart* • Joan Cusack *Jane Bloomwood* • John Goodman *Graham Bloomwood* • John Lithgow *Edgar West* • Kristin Scott Thomas *Alette Naylor* • Julie Hagerty *Hayley* ■ *Dir* PJ Hogan • *Scr* Kayla Alpert, Tim Firth, Tracey Jackson, from the novels *The Secret Dreamworld of a Shopaholic*, *Shopaholic Abroad* by Sophie Kinsella

Confessions of a Teenage Drama Queen ★★★ PG
Comedy 2004 · US/Ger · Colour · 85min

Lindsay Lohan plays a popular New York teenager who is transferred to a suburban New Jersey school where bitchy Megan Fox rules the roost. Instant rivals, they both set out to snatch the lead role in a musical version of *Pygmalion* and light up the life of rock star Adam Garcia. Candyfloss colours and some animation give the proceedings a little extra sparkle, which helps when the film takes itself too seriously. Lohan emerges as a real contender for grown-up stardom. TH *DVD*

Lindsay Lohan *Lola Cep* • Adam Garcia *Stu Wolff* • Glenne Headly *Karen Cep* • Alison Pill *Ella Gerard* • Carol Kane *Miss Baggoli* • Eli Marienthal *Sam* • Megan Fox *Carla Santini* • Sheila McCarthy *Mrs Gerard* ■ *Dir* Sara Sugarman • *Scr* Gail Parent, from the novel by Dyan Sheldon

Confessions of a Trickbaby ★★ 18

Black comedy thriller
1999 · US/Fr/Can · Colour · 93min

The second film (after *Freeway*) in Matthew Bright's proposed trilogy of radically reworked fairy tales is so over-the-top, it's halfway down the other side. In this outrageous spin on *Hansel and Gretel*, Natasha Lyonne and Maria Celedonio play damaged teens who break out of detention and strike out on a murderous road trip to Mexico for a climactic confrontation with transvestite nun Vincent Gallo. Directed in the style of the sexploitation films it spoofs, this could earn cult status. DA *DVD*

Natasha Lyonne *White Girl (Crystal)* • Maria Celedonio *Angela (Cyclona)* • Vincent Gallo *Sister Gomez* ■ *Dir/Scr* Matthew Bright

Confessions of a Window Cleaner ★ 18

Sex comedy 1974 · UK · Colour · 86min

This is the first of the four saucy comedies adapted from the bestselling novels of Timothy Lea. In addition to introducing us to Robin Askwith and his shiftless brother-in-law (played by Tony Blair's father-in-law, Anthony Booth), the film also wastes some of Britain's finest comic talent, who vainly try to wring a laugh out of the smutty situations and limp jokes. DP Swearing, sex scenes, nudity. *DVD*

Robin Askwith *Timothy Lea* • Anthony Booth *Sidney Noggett* • Sheila White *Rosie Noggett* • Dandy Nichols *Mrs Lea* • Bill Maynard *Mr Lea* • Linda Hayden *Elizabeth Radlett* • John Le Mesurier *Inspector Radlett* • Joan Hickson *Mrs Radlett* ■ *Dir* Val Guest • *Scr* Christopher Wood, Val Guest, from a novel by Timothy Lea [Christopher Wood]

Confessions of an American Bride ★★

Romantic comedy 2005 · US · Colour · 90min

Although director Douglas Barr exploits *American Pie* alumna Shannon Elizabeth's physique to the full, he also lets her show off her comic talents in this routine but amiable romantic comedy. She may struggle to convince as the career girl who lands boy-next-door Eddie McClintock, and then frets about every detail of their dream wedding, but Elizabeth handles the showy shifts between situation comedy, surreal reveries and speeches to camera with aplomb. It's a shame, therefore, that Adam Horowitz and Edward Kitsis's screenplay seeks to tempt her by a lame 11th-hour fling with her high-school idol (Geoff Stults). DP

Shannon Elizabeth *Samantha Hoyt* • Eddie McClintock *Ben Rosen* • Geoff Stults *Luke Stinson* • Roz Michaels *Sheila Rosen* • Amy Rutherford *Kirsten* • Reagan Pasternak *Anne* ■ *Dir* Douglas Barr (2) • *Scr* Edward Kitsis, Adam Horowitz

Confessions of an Opium Eater ★★★

Melodrama 1962 · US · BW · 79min

For years, Albert Zugsmith's deliriously sensational melodrama, with its scenes of slave trafficking and opium smoking, thrilled America's "midnight matinée" crowd. In Britain it was available only in an excessively censored version called *Evils of Chinatown*. Neither version bears any relation to Thomas De Quincey's memoir, except that the hero (Vincent Price) is described as a descendant of the author. Price is a seaman who lands in San Francisco and helps rescue abducted women. There is a lot of dross to endure, but the weird atmosphere is often startling and Price's narration is also notable. DM

Vincent Price *De Quincey* • Linda Ho *Ruby Low* • Philip Ahn *Ching Foon* • Richard Loo *George Wah* • June Kim *Lotus* ■ *Dir* Albert Zugsmith • *Scr* Robert Hill, Seton I Miller, from Thomas De Quincey's story

The Confessions of Thomas Quick ★★★★ 15

Documentary 2015 · UK/Swe · Colour · 93min

This thriller is no piece of Scandi-*noir* but is ripped from the real-life headlines that exposed the lurid exploits of Sweden's most notorious serial killer. Given the name Sture Bergwall but taking the moniker of Thomas Quick, as it sounded more like a serial killer, the now elderly subject of director Brian Hill's chilling but fascinating documentary confessed to having murdered 39 people after being committed to a progressive psychiatric institution. An utterly absorbing film, it delivers something entirely unexpected about the human condition. JA In English, Swedish. References to sexual violence.

■ *Dir* Brian Hill

Confetti ★★ 15

Romantic comedy
2006 · UK/US · Colour · 95min

Musical fans Martin Freeman and Jessica Stevenson play one of three couples battling it out to stage a wedding magazine's most original nuptials. Robert Webb is an ardent naturist who proposes a nude wedding. Stephen Mangan finds a good slant as a washed-up tennis player bent on victory, but even this storyline flounders as the big day dawns and the action takes off into bizarre realms. This provides a few funny moments, but too often feels meandering and obvious. SP Swearing, nudity. *DVD*

Martin Freeman *Matt* • Jessica Stevenson *Sam* • Stephen Mangan *Josef* • Meredith MacNeill *Isabelle* • Robert Webb *Michael* • Olivia Colman *Joanna* • Vincent Franklin *Archie Heron* • Jason Watkins *Gregory Hough* • Jimmy Carr *Antoni* • Alison Steadman *Sam's mother* ■ *Dir/Scr* Debbie Isitt

Confidence ★★★★ U

Drama 1979 · Hun · Colour · 105min

Although the underlying theme of this intense drama is the mutual confidence civilisation needs to survive, István Szabó's, for once, less concerned with the momentous events of history than the simple interaction of individuals. Forced to pose as a married couple during the Nazi occupation of Budapest, Ildiko Bansagi and Peter Andorai progress from fear and superstition to implicit trust and passion as they realise their interdependence. It's the claustrophobic exchanges that give it a power and truth that owes as much to Szabó and cinematographer Lajos Koltai as to the superlative leads. DP Hungarian +subtitles.

Ildiko Bansagi *Kata* • Peter Andorai *Janos* • O Gombik *Old woman* • Karoly Csaki *Old man* ■ *Dir* István Szabó • *Scr* István Szabó, from a story by Erika Szanto, István Szabó

Confidence ★★★ 15

Crime thriller 2002 · US/Ger · Colour · 93min

Grifter Edward Burns is co-opted by eccentric crime boss Dustin Hoffman into scamming a banker through a complex scheme involving corporate loans, wire transfers and offshore accounts. Burns gives an appealing turn and the film is packaged as a classy *film noir*, but what makes this merely good rather than great is its inability to make its characters come off as real human beings rather than ciphers designed to ignite plot fireworks. IF Violence, swearing, sex scenes, nudity. *DVD*

Edward Burns *Jake Vig* • Rachel Weisz *Lily* • Andy Garcia *Gunther Butan* • Dustin Hoffman *Winston King* • Paul Giamatti *Gordo* • Donal Logue *Whitworth* • Luis Guzmán [Luis Guzman] *Omar Manzano* • Brian Van Holt *Miles* ■ *Dir* James Foley • *Scr* Doug Jung

Confidences Trop Intimes ★★★★ 15

Comedy drama 2004 · Fr · Colour · 99min

Diametric opposites forge an unlikely link in Patrice Leconte's subtle and literate comedy of sexual manners. Initially, there's a gulf between Fabrice Luchini's fastidious tax lawyer and the mysterious Sandrine Bonnaire, who mistakes his office for that of her new psychiatrist. But as Bonnaire continues to seek him out to impart her sensual despair, Luchini comes to appreciate that his entire existence is based upon a misconception of his true self. The consultations are occasionally racy, but it's enchantment rather than lust that inspires Luchini's devotion and so his deceit never seems sinister. DP French +subtitles. Swearing. *DVD*

Fabrice Luchini *William Faber* • Sandrine Bonnaire *Anna Delambre* • Michel Duchaussoy *Dr Monnier* • Anne Brochet *Jeanne* • Gilbert Melki *Marc* • Laurent Gamelon *Luc* • Hélène Surgère *Madame Mulon* ■ *Dir* Patrice Leconte • *Scr* Jérôme Tonnerre, Patrice Leconte

Confidential ★★★

Crime drama 1935 · US · BW · 67min

This fast-moving gangster movie dates from the period when prolific director Edward L Cahn was still making half-decent films. It stars Donald Cook as a G man who infiltrates the Mob and falls for sexy Evalyn Knapp while tangling with nasty sadist J Carrol Naish. It moves along at a fine rate as a good programme filler should, and doesn't outstay its welcome. TS

Donald Cook *Dave Elliot* • Evalyn Knapp *Maxine* • Warren Hymer *Midget* • J Carrol Naish *Lefty* • Herbert Rawlinson *JW Keaton* • Theodore von Eltz *Walsh* • Morgan Wallace *Van Cleve* ■ *Dir* Edward L Cahn • *Scr* Weilyn Totman, Olive Cooper, from a story by John Rathmell, Scott Darling

Confidential Agent ★★

Thriller 1945 · US · BW · 117min

This is a Warner Bros version of the novel by Graham Greene about a former Spanish musician who gives up his career to fight the Fascists and goes to Britain to stop the English selling coal to Franco's troops. Charles Boyer makes an engaging hero, but the Hollywood England takes some swallowing. Villains Peter Lorre and Katina Paxinou do their best to stop Boyer, but Lauren Bacall fails to convince as a British coal baron's daughter. This movie isn't uneventful, just uninvolving. TS

Charles Boyer *Denard* • Lauren Bacall *Rose Cullen* • Victor Francen *Licata* • Wanda Hendrix *Else* • George Coulouris *Captain Currie* • Peter Lorre *Contreras* • Katina Paxinou *Mrs Melandey* • John Warburton *Neil Forbes* ■ *Dir* Herman Shumlin • *Scr* Robert Buckner, from the novel by Graham Greene

Confidential Report ★★ PG

Film noir 1955 · Sp/Swi · BW · 93min

Also known as *Mr Arkadin*, this fascinating picture is a fearful mess that betrays, all too clearly, the financial and production problems with which Orson Welles had to contend. As in *Citizen Kane*, the subject is a mysterious, all-powerful man, but this time around the approach is one of self-parody and self-indulgence. Welles filmed it in his beloved place of exile, Spain, with a fancy cast and fanciful camera angles. AT *DVD*

Orson Welles *Gregory Arkadin* • Robert Arden *Guy Van Stratten* • Paola Mori *Raina Arkadin* • Michael Redgrave *Burgomil Trebitsch* • Patricia Medina *Mily* • Akim Tamiroff *Jakob Zouk* • Mischa Auer *Professor* • Katina Paxinou *Sophie* ■ *Dir* Orson Welles • *Scr* Orson Welles, from his novel

Confidentially Yours ★★★ PG

Comedy mystery thriller
1983 · Fr · BW · 106min

As he did with *Shoot the Pianist* and *The Bride Wore Black*, François Truffaut took an American pulp novel as the basis for this rather self-regarding, mildly amusing comedy thriller. Shot in black and white by

Nestor Almendros in an attempt to capture the style of the 1940s *film noir*, it tells of real estate agent Jean-Louis Trintignant who, accused of the murder of his wife and her lover, goes into hiding while his secretary Fanny Ardant tries to prove his innocence. RB French +subtitles. *DVD*

Fanny Ardant *Barbara Becker* • Jean-Louis Trintignant *Julien Vercel* • Philippe Laudenbach *M Clement* • Caroline Sihol *Marie-Christine Vercel* • Xavier Saint-Macary *Bertrand Fabre* • Jean-Pierre Kalfon *Massoulier* ■ *Dir* François Truffaut • *Scr* François Truffaut, Suzanne Schiffman, Jean Aurel, from the novel *The Long Saturday Night* by Charles Williams

Confine ★★ 15

Thriller 2012 · UK · Colour · 80min

There are distant echoes of Nic Roeg's *Performance* and even Roman Polanski's *Repulsion* in this thriller about a reclusive, disfigured ex-model whose home is targeted by intruders. But, as the tortured agoraphobic who gets caught up in the felonious schemes of Eliza Bennett, real-life model Daisy Lowe has little of the charisma of Mick Jagger or Catherine Deneuve. The film looks nice enough (someone has a lovely flat) but the battle of wills between Lowe and an impressive Bennett is not one of acting equals, which undermines the increasingly unbelievable story. JA English, French +subtitles. *DVD*

Daisy Lowe *Pippa* • Eliza Bennett *Kayleigh* • Alfie Allen *Henry* • Richard Wellings-Thomas *Neil* ■ *Dir/Scr* Tobias Tobbell

Confirm or Deny ★★★

Second World War drama
1941 · US · BW · 73min

A top-flight cast who know their way around a Second World War spy thriller and a decent script (from a story co-written by Samuel Fuller) make this a cut above the ordinary blitzkrieg saga. The Ministry of Disinformation plotline gets a trifle convoluted in the middle, but the movie is saved from disappearing under its own self-importance by the effective playing of Don Ameche and Joan Bennett. TS

Don Ameche *Mitch* • Joan Bennett *Jennifer Carson* • Roddy McDowall *Albert Perkins* • John Loder *Captain Channing* • Raymond Walburn *H Cyrus Sturtevant* • Arthur Shields *Jeff* • Eric Blore *Mr Hobbs* • Helene Reynolds *Dorothy* • Claude Allister [Claud Allister] *Williams* ■ *Dir* Archie Mayo • *Scr* Jo Swerling, from a story by Henry Wales, Samuel Fuller

Conflagration ★★★★

Tragedy 1958 · Jpn · BW · 96min

Adapted from Yukio Mishima's novel, *The Temple of the Golden Pavilion*, which was itself based on actual events, Kon Ichikawa's painstaking study of disillusion and misguided devotion has often been accused of being a clinical enterprise, obsessed with textured imagery and surface symbolism. However, Raizo Ichikawa poignantly conveys the pain experienced by the student priest, whose dismay at what he sees as the desecration of his temple prompts him to preserve its beauty and integrity by destroying it. DP Japanese +subtitles.

Raizo Ichikawa *Mizoguchi* • Tatsuya Nakadai • Ganjiro Nakamura *Tayama* • Yoko Uraji • Michiyo Aratama • Tamao Nakamura ■ *Dir* Kon Ichikawa • *Scr* Natto Wada, Keiji Hasebe, Kon Ichikawa, from the novel *The Temple of the Golden Pavillion* by Yukio Mishima • *Cinematographer* Kazuo Miyagawa

Conflict ★★★ PG

Thriller 1945 · US · BW · 81min

From a great period in *film noir*, this is a slightly substandard Warner Bros melodrama, despite a story co-written by Robert Siodmak. It is held together by Humphrey Bogart, who occasionally looks as though he'd rather be somewhere else, even when he's plotting to do away with his wife in order to marry her sister. The censor was pretty tough in those days, but the mood's still dark and tense, even if the conclusion is obvious. TS

Humphrey Bogart *Richard Mason* • Alexis Smith *Evelyn Turner* • Sydney Greenstreet *Dr Mark Hamilton* • Rose Hobart *Katherine Mason* • Charles Drake *Professor Norman Holdsworth* • Grant Mitchell *Dr Grant* • Patrick O'Moore *Detective Lieutenant Egan* • Ann Shoemaker *Nora Grant* • Frank Wilcox *Robert Freston* ■ *Dir* Curtis Bernhardt • *Scr* Arthur T Horman, Dwight Taylor, from a story by Robert Siodmak, Alfred Neumann

Conflict of Wings ★★★ U
Comedy   1953 · UK · Colour · 85min

The borrowings come thick and fast in this sentimental rural drama about the residents of a Norfolk village trying to stop the RAF turning a local bird sanctuary into a firing range. But, while it never lives up to the great Ealing comedies, this is still a pleasing little picture, with the Norfolk Broads looking lovely in Arthur Grant and Martin Curtis's washed-out colour photography. The folklore behind the tale is charming, there are a couple of tear-jerking moments and a rousing rally-round finale. DP

John Gregson *Bill Morris* • Muriel Pavlow *Sally* • Kieron Moore *Squadron Leader Parsons* • Niall MacGinnis *Harry Tilney* • Harry Fowler *Buster* • Guy Middleton *Adjutant* • Sheila Sweet *Fanny Bates* • Campbell Singer *Flight Sergeant Campbell* ■ *Dir* John Eldridge • *Scr* Don Sharp, John Pudney, from the novel by Don Sharp

The Conformist ★★★★★ 15
Period drama
1970 · It/Fr/W Ger · Colour · 108min

A masterful blend of Freud and Fascism, Bernardo Bertolucci's adaptation of Alberto Moravia's novel examines the link between sexual and political repression in order to assess the impact of Italy's authoritarian past on its deeply divided present. Aided by Vittorio Storaro's luscious cinematography, Bertolucci perfectly captures the false sense of wellbeing exuded by Mussolini's regime. Jean-Louis Trintignant is superb as the conformist of the title, a victim of child abuse who has grown up with a desperate desire to belong. Trintignant is ably supported by Stefania Sandrelli and Dominique Sanda in this disturbing, visually imposing and influential movie. DP Italian +subtitles. Violence, swearing, nudity. *DVD* *Blu*

Jean-Louis Trintignant *Marcello Clerici* • Stefania Sandrelli *Giulia* • Gastone Moschin *Manganiello* • Enzo Tarascio *Quadri* • Pierre Clémenti *Lino Semirama* • Dominique Sanda *Anna Quadri* • Christian Alegny *Raoul* ■ *Dir* Bernardo Bertolucci • *Scr* Bernardo Bertolucci, from a novel by Alberto Moravia

Confucius ★★★ 15
Historical biographical drama
2010 · Chi · Colour · 119min

Action star Chow Yun-Fat goes for a real change of pace here, playing the Chinese sage whose musings on ethics, justice and civility would make him one of the world's most influential philosophers. Set at a time when China was made up of warring territories, the film begins with Confucius becoming a minister for the ruler of the Lu kingdom. But he soon falls foul of jealous rivals and is forced into exile for nearly two decades. Fans of *Crouching Tiger, Hidden Tiger* and *Hero* will no doubt be disappointed by the lack of swordfights or long battle scenes, but it is beautifully shot and contains a magnetic central performance from the ever-charismatic Chow. JA Mandarin +subtitles. Violence. *DVD* *Blu*

Chow Yun-Fat *Confucius (Long Qiu)* • Zhou Xun *Nanzi* • Chen Jianbin *Ji-Sun Si* • Yao Lu *Ruler of Lu* • Zhang Xingzhe *Gongshan Niu* ■ *Dir* Hu Mei • *Scr* Khan Chan, He Yanjiang • *Cinematographer* Peter Pau

Congo ★ 12
Adventure   1995 · US · Colour · 103min

The plot here, combining a lost civilisation, a highly intelligent gorilla and venal scientists after diamonds for a laser gun, is a lacklustre *Boys' Own* no-brainer, and the movie scrapes the bottom of the fantasy barrel with dire acting and clichéd special effects. AJ Swearing.

Dylan Walsh *Peter Elliot* • Laura Linney *Dr Karen Ross* • Ernie Hudson *Monroe Kelly* • Tim Curry *Herkermer Homolka* • Grant Heslov *Richard* • Joe Don Baker *RB Travis* • Mary Ellen Trainor *Moira* • Stuart Pankin *Boyd* ■ *Dir* Frank Marshall • *Scr* John Patrick Shanley, from the novel by Michael Crichton

The Congress ★★★ 15
Part-animated fantasy
2013 · Is/Ger/Pol/Lux/Fr/Bel · Colour · 118min

The concept of stars selling their souls to the studio becomes a futuristic reality in this surreal black comedy directed by Ari Folman – Oscar-nominated for his 2009 animated war film *Waltz with Bashir*. Robin Wright stars as Hollywood actress Robin Wright, whose agent (Harvey Keitel) convinces her to accept a proposition from an oily film executive (Danny Huston) that will see her handing over all rights to her image for two decades. The humour here is dark and incisive, with an especially bold front from Wright. She bears the brunt of some very brutal dialogue in what turns into an anarchic riot of animation, throwing up some dazzling ideas but never quite fulfilling its satirical promise. DW Violence, swearing, a sex scene, nudity. *DVD* *Blu*

Robin Wright • Harvey Keitel *Al* • Jon Hamm *Dylan Truliner* • Danny Huston *Jeff Green* • Paul Giamatti *Dr Barker* ■ *Dir* Ari Folman • *Scr* Ari Folman, from the novel *The Futurological Congress* by Stanislaw Lem

Congress Dances ★★★
Musical   1931 · Ger · BW · 92min

In Vienna for the 1814 Congress, Tsar Alexander of Russia (Willy Fritsch) falls for a shop assistant (Lillian Harvey) rather than the countess (Lil Dagover) put his way by the devious Prince Metternich (Conrad Veidt). Delicately directed by Erik Charell from a soufflé-light script, this early German musical largely ignores the political implications of the setting. Filmed in three different versions – English, French and German, with Henri Garat replacing Fritsch for the French market – its charm has faded with time, though its lightweight approach and opulent settings proved hugely influential throughout the decade. RK

Lillian Harvey [Lilian Harvey] *Christel Weinzinger* • Conrad Veidt *Prince Metternich* • Lil Dagover *The Countess* • Willy Fritsch *Tsar Alexander of Russia/Uralsky* • Gibb McLaughlin *Bibikoff, the Czar's adjutant* • Reginald Purdell *Pepi, his secretary* ■ *Dir* Erik Charell • *Scr* Norman Falk, Robert Liebmann

The Conjuring ★★★ 15
Horror   2013 · US · Colour · 111min

Before they investigated the Amityville Horror, real-life demonologist Ed Warren and his clairvoyant wife Lorraine supported the Perron family through a supernatural onslaught at their remote Rhode Island farmhouse in 1971. The fact that director James Wan knows his way round a haunted house initially makes this "true" story a superbly produced, wonderful looking and potent tale of things that go bump in the night. Wan's prowling camera expertly stages jolts for their maximum shock value, but the fright takes flight when the unseen turns more visible. AJ Violence.

Vera Farmiga *Lorraine Warren* • Patrick Wilson *Ed Warren* • Lili Taylor *Carolyn Perron* • Ron Livingston *Roger Perron* • Joey King *Christine Perron* • Mackenzie Foy *Cynthia Perron* ■ *Dir* James Wan • *Scr* Chad & Carey Hayes

The Conjuring 2 ★★★★ 15
Horror   2016 · US · Colour · 133min

Anyone who likes to be frightened will be covered in gooseflesh watching this spooky sequel. Mixing fact (the famous Enfield Poltergeist case from the 1970s) with fantasy, this again features Patrick Wilson and Vera Farmiga as real-life ghostbusters Ed and Lorraine Warren – the couple who give a damn about the damned. They race to the North London home of single mum Peggy (Frances O'Connor), who is tormented by a banquet of inexplicable events. Like its predecessor, this solid, big-budget horror is incredibly beautiful, and

the detail is correct even if it's been heavily elaborated. KK Violence, swearing.

Vera Farmiga *Lorraine Warren* • Patrick Wilson *Ed Warren* • Frances O'Connor *Peggy Hodgson* • Madison Wolfe *Janet Hodgson* • Simon McBurney *Maurice Grosse* • Franka Potente *Anita Gregory* ■ *Dir* James Wan • *Scr* James Wan, Chad Hayes, Carey Hayes, David Leslie Johnson

A Connecticut Yankee ★★★
Comedy   1931 · US · BW · 95min

Will Rogers stars as a man who dreams that he is back in the middle ages, where he brings his foreign influence to bear on the manners and morals of King Arthur's court. Mark Twain's classic satirical fantasy had been the basis of a 1921 silent, and would resurface in 1949 as a Bing Crosby musical. This version is witty and agreeable, but somewhat dated. RK

Will Rogers (1) *Hank* • William Farnum *King Arthur* • Myrna Loy *Queen Morgan Le Fay* • Maureen O'Sullivan *Alisande* • Frank Albertson *Clarence* • Mitchell Harris *Merlin* ■ *Dir* David Butler • *Scr* William Conselman, Owen Davis, from the novel *A Connecticut Yankee in King Arthur's Court* by Mark Twain

A Connecticut Yankee in King Arthur's Court ★★★ U
Musical   1949 · US · Colour · 102min

Bing Crosby stars in this musical adaptation of Mark Twain's fantasy about a 20th-century American who dreams himself back to medieval times. Arriving at Camelot, he is regarded as something of a wizard at King Arthur's court. The film substitutes broad comedy for wit, and the musical numbers – with the exception of *Busy Doing Nothing* – are pretty forgettable. The Technicolor production is lavish, though, while Tay Garnett directs with spirit. RK *DVD*

Bing Crosby *Hank Martin* • William Bendix *Sir Sagramore* • Rhonda Fleming *Sandy* • Cedric Hardwicke *King Arthur* • Murvyn Vye *Merlin* • Henry Wilcoxon *Sir Lancelot* • Richard Webb *Sir Galahad* ■ *Dir* Tay Garnett • *Scr* Edmund Beloin, from the novel by Mark Twain

Connecting Rooms ★★ 15
Romantic drama   1969 · UK · Colour · 100min

This slightly bonkers drama has schoolteacher Michael Redgrave on the run from child abuse charges and near to suicide. Then there's a female cellist (Bette Davis) who claims to be a solo artist but is in fact a street busker. Together they share rooms in a shabby Bayswater B&B run by Kay Walsh. It's all very 1930s, except for the "Swinging London" appendages of pop stars and an air of kookiness. AT Nudity. *DVD*

Bette Davis *Wanda Fleming* • Michael Redgrave *James Wallraven* • Alexis Kanner *Mickey* • Kay Walsh *Mrs Brent* • Gabrielle Drake *Jean* ■ *Dir* Franklin Gollings • *Scr* Franklin Gollings, from the play *The Cellist* by Marion Hart

The Connection ★★★ 15
Crime thriller based on a true story
2014 · Fr/Bel · Colour · 124min

This fact-based thriller tells the story of *The French Connection* from the Gallic perspective, focusing on the attempts by police in the 1970s and 80s to stop the export of heroin through Marseilles. *The Artist's* Jean Dujardin plays it straight as the committed cop who embarks on an Eliot Ness-style crusade to bring down charismatic kingpin Gilles Lellouche. The sun-bleached locations act in stark contrast to the bleak Big Apple portrayed in William Friedkin's 1971 film but, despite sympathetic performances, this sprawling crime epic fails to deliver enough tension to hold the interest. JH French, English +subtitles. *DVD*

Jean Dujardin *Pierre Michel* • Gilles Lellouche *Gaëtan Zampa* • Céline Sallette *Christiane Zampa* • Mélanie Doutey *Christiane Zampa* • Guillaume Gouix *José Alvarez* • Bruno Todeschini *The Banker* ■ *Dir* Cédric Jimenez • *Scr* Audrey Diwan, Cédric Jimenez

Connie and Carla ★★ 12
Comedy   2004 · US · Colour · 93min

Writer Nia Vardalos's insipid follow-up to 2002's surprise hit *My Big Fat Greek Wedding* has her and Toni Collette playing wannabe singers who decide to disguise themselves as performers in a West Hollywood drag club after accidentally witnessing a Mob murder. Weakly plotted gender-confusion comedy follows as Connie (Vardalos) falls for a drag queen's straight brother (a charm-free David Duchovny) who doesn't realise that she's a woman. Woefully underwritten and lacking fizz. AS *DVD*

Nia Vardalos *Connie* • Toni Collette *Carla* • David Duchovny *Jeff* • Stephen Spinella *Robert/ "Peaches"* • Alec Mapa *Lee/"N'Cream"* • Christopher Logan *Brian/"Brianna"* • Robert Kaiser *Paul* • Ian Gomez *Stanley* • Debbie Reynolds ■ *Dir* Michael Lembeck • *Scr* Nia Vardalos

The Conqueror ★★★ PG
Historical adventure 1956 · US · Colour · 106min

This splendid hokum is rendered ludicrous today by the casting of John Wayne as Genghis Khan, but it doesn't deserve its reputation as one of the worst movies ever made. Splendidly directed by Dick Powell, it is best viewed dubbed into any foreign language as the dialogue is silly beyond belief. TS *DVD*

John Wayne *Temujin* • Susan Hayward *Bortai* • Pedro Armendáriz *Jamuga* • Agnes Moorehead *Hunlun* • Thomas Gomez *Wang Kahn* • John Hoyt *Shaman* • William Conrad *Kasar* • Ted De Corsia *Kumlek* • Lee Van Cleef *Chepei* ■ *Dir* Dick Powell • *Scr* Oscar Millard

Conquest ★★★★ U
Historical romantic drama
1937 · US · BW · 115min

"Sire, you stand in the sun," says Greta Garbo's Marie to Charles Boyer's Napoleon, perhaps aware for once of finding herself playing opposite a suitably talented co-star. Garbo, as you would expect, is simply superb as Bonaparte's Polish mistress, and the Great Lover himself makes an endearingly vulnerable Napoleon in this finely mounted MGM production. Clarence Brown – surely a film craftsman who deserves more appreciation – shows why he was Garbo's favourite director, enhancing her striking features and presenting her as a warm and tender woman fit for the Emperor of France. TS

Greta Garbo *Marie Walewska* • Charles Boyer *Napoleon* • Reginald Owen *Talleyrand* • Alan Marshal *Captain D'Ornano* • Henry Stephenson *Count Walewska* • Leif Erickson *Paul Lachinski* • Dame May Whitty *Laetitia Bonaparte* • C Henry Gordon *Prince Poniatowski* • Maria Ouspenskaya *Countess Pelagia* ■ *Dir* Clarence Brown • *Scr* Samuel Hoffenstein, Salka Viertel, SN Behrman, from a play by Helen Jerome, from the novel *Pani Walewska* by Waclaw Gasiorowski

The Conquest of Everest ★★★★ U
Documentary   1953 · UK · Colour · 74min

Ever since Herbert G Ponting recorded Captain Scott's ill-fated bid to reach the South Pole, the movie camera has been accompanying heroic ventures. Shot in even more arduous conditions, this is a remarkable account of the expedition that saw Edmund Hillary and Sherpa Tenzing become the first to reach the peak of the world's highest mountain. It's a pity the camera couldn't make the final ascent, but the various stages of the climb, with their difficulties and dangers, make gripping viewing thanks to some inspired editing, Louis MacNeice's literate commentary and Arthur Benjamin's rousing score. DP *DVD*

Meredith Edwards *Narrator* ■ *Dir* George Lowe • *Scr* Louis MacNeice • *Editor* Adrian de Potier

Conquest of Space ★★★ U
Science-fiction drama
1955 · US · Colour · 77min

Paramount slashed the budget and added soap-opera bubbles to George Pal's sequel to *Destination Moon*. With the accent more

C

on science than on fiction, this aims to offer an accurate reflection of what a trip to Mars would be like technically, and how it would affect the crew psychologically. Despite an out-of-sync religious tone, the reverential approach still evokes a sense of wonder. AJ
Walter Brooke *Samuel Merritt* • Eric Fleming *Barney Merritt* • Mickey Shaughnessy *Mahoney* • Phil Foster *Siegle* • William Redfield *Cooper* • William Hopper *Fenton* • Ross Martin *Fodor* ■ *Dir* Byron Haskin • *Scr* Philip Yordan, Barre Lyndon, George Worthing Yates, from the book *The Mars Project* by Chesley Bonestell, Willy Ley

Conquest of the Air ★★ U
Documentary drama 1936 · UK/US · BW · 62min

This was to be the first instalment of an ambitious trilogy on the development of land, sea and air transport planned by producer Alexander Korda as part of his assault on the American market. However, this untidy collage of history lesson and dramatic reconstruction was an age in production and looked no better in the screening room. Zoltan Korda shared the directorial credit with several others, which can't have helped. DP *DVD*
Frederick Culley *Roger Bacon* • Franklin Dyall *Jerome de ascoli* • Alan Wheatley *Borelli* • Hay Petrie *Tiberius Cavallo* • John Abbott *Derozier* • Laurence Olivier *Vincent Lunardi* • Bryan Powley *Sir George Cayley* • Henry Victor *Otto Lilienthal* • John Trumbull *Von Zeppelin* ■ *Dir* Zoltan Korda, Alexander Esway, Alexander Shaw, John Monk Saunders • *Scr* Hugh Gray, Peter Bezencenet, from stories by John Monk Saunders, Antoine de St Exupery

Conquest of the Planet of the Apes ★★★ 15
Science-fiction adventure
1972 · US · Colour · 86min

The fourth film in the sci-fi saga illustrates how the ape revolt happened in the first place. Caesar, played by series regular Roddy McDowall, gains the power of speech, forms enslaved fellow simians into guerrilla groups and leads them against the evil human race. J Lee Thompson provides gritty direction and there's plenty of fun philosophising. *Battle for the Planet of the Apes* (1973) concluded the series. AJ Violence. *DVD* *BL*
Roddy McDowall *Caesar* • Don Murray *Breck* • Ricardo Montalban *Armando* • Natalie Trundy *Lisa* • Hari Rhodes *MacDonald* • Severn Darden *Kolp* • Lou Wagner *Busboy* • John Randolph *Commission chairman* ■ *Dir* J Lee Thompson • *Scr* Paul Dehn, from characters by Pierre Boulle

Conquest of the South Pole ★★★ 12
Drama 1989 · UK · Colour · 95min

Manfred Karge's allegorical fantasy was a huge hit for the Traverse Theatre in Edinburgh, so it's fitting that the film version should be shot in and around the now-defunct docks of the Scottish capital. Though hampered by an ultra-low budget, debutant director Gilles MacKinnon exploits the visual potential of this story of a group of unemployed youths who ward off despair by re-creating Amundsen's journey to the South Pole in their own back yard. NS
Stevan Rimkus *Sloopianek* • Ewen Bremner *Penguin* • Leonard O'Malley *Butcher* • Laura Girling *Louise* • Gordon Cameron *Brown* • Alastair Galbraith *Frankieboy* • Julie-Kate Oliver *Rosie* ■ *Dir* Gilles MacKinnon • *Scr* Gareth Wardell, from the play by Manfred Karge

Consenting Adults ★★★ 15
Psychological thriller 1992 · US · Colour · 94min

Kevin Kline and Mary Elizabeth Mastrantonio are the ordinary husband and wife whose lives are turned upside down when a couple-from-hell move in next door. Extremely plodding action from *All the President's Men* director Alan J Pakula and a rather wooden Kline slow things down somewhat, but the day is saved by a mesmerising performance from Kevin Spacey as the creepy neighbour. JB Violence, swearing, nudity. *DVD*
Kevin Kline *Richard Parker* • Mary Elizabeth Mastrantonio *Priscilla Parker* • Kevin Spacey *Eddy Otis* • Rebecca Miller *Kay Otis* • Forest

Whitaker *David Duttonville* • EG Marshall *George Gordon* ■ *Dir* Alan J Pakula • *Scr* Matthew Chapman

The Consequences of Love ★★★★ 15
Crime drama 2004 · It · Colour · 99min

Paolo Sorrentino's meticulous drama stars Toni Servillo as a secretive businessman who has been living for eight years in a quiet Swiss hotel near the Italian border. His routine consists of weekly trips to the local bank, the occasional card game and a regular heroin fix. But Servillo's growing affection for barmaid Olivia Magnani causes him to cross the mobsters who exiled him from his family following a financial indiscretion. There is little action here, but it still generates great suspense, thanks to impeccable performances and the work of cinematographer Luca Bigazzi. DP Italian +subtitles. Swearing, drug abuse. *DVD*
Toni Servillo *Titta Di Girolamo* • Olivia Magnani *Sofia* • Adriano Giannini *Valerio* • Angela Goodwin *Isabella* • Raffaele Pisu *Carlo* • Enzo Vitagliano *Pippo D'Anto* • Vittorio Di Prima *Nitto Lo Riccio* ■ *Dir/Scr* Paolo Sorrentino

Consolation Marriage ★★★
Comedy drama 1931 · US · BW · 82min

Irene Dunne and Pat O'Brien, both on the rebound, meet and marry for solace and companionship. They carve out a decent life for themselves and have a child, but their equilibrium is threatened when their former flames (Lester Vail and Myrna Loy) reappear. Director Paul H Sloane offers a measure of charm and humour to balance the sentimentality. RK
Irene Dunne *Mary Brown Porter* • Pat O'Brien *Steve Porter* • John Halliday *Jeff* • Myrna Loy *Elaine Brandon* • Lester Vail *Aubrey* • Matt Moore *Colonel* • Pauline Stevens *Baby* ■ *Dir* Paul Sloane [Paul H Sloane] • *Scr* Humphrey Pearson, from a story by William Cunningham

Conspiracy ★★★ 15
Second World War historical drama
2001 · US/UK · Colour · 95min

This admirably dispassionate cable TV movie exposes the cold calculation that went into the planning of the Final Solution. Based on minutes from a meeting chaired by SS security chief Reinhard Heydrich, it's an open indictment of the sheer evil that underpinned the Nazi regime. But while every effort has been made to avoid caricature, the performances do occasionally seem mannered. The distinction is best seen in the contrast between Kenneth Branagh's charismatic Heydrich and Stanley Tucci's display of ruthless vanity as Eichmann. DP *DVD*
Stanley Tucci *Adolf Eichmann* • Kenneth Branagh *Reinhard Heydrich* • Colin Firth *Dr Wilhelm Stuckart* • Barnaby Kay *SS Major Rudolph Lange* • Ben Daniels *Dr Josef Buhler* • David Threlfall *Dr Wilhelm Kritzinger* • Jonathan Coy *Dr Erich Neumann* • Brendan Coyle *SS General Heinrich Muller* • Ian McNeice *Gerhard Klopfer* • Owen Teale *Dr Roland Freisler* ■ *Dir* Frank Pierson • *Scr* Loring Mandel

Conspiracy of Hearts ★★★★ PG
Second World War drama
1960 · UK · BW · 108min

This moving and underrated tale about nuns helping Jewish children escape the Nazis in war-torn Italy was made with sincerity and feeling by Ralph Thomas. The movie boasts an immensely talented cast, headed by the luminous Lilli Palmer as the Mother Superior, with Sylvia Syms and Yvonne Mitchell as caring nuns and David Kossoff as a rabbi. This thoughtful casting lends the film resonance, and it's far better than its potentially mawkish plot combination of children and nuns would suggest. TS *DVD*
Lilli Palmer *Mother Katherine* • Sylvia Syms *Sister Mitya* • Ronald Lewis *Major Spoletti* • Albert Lieven *Colonel Horsten* • Yvonne Mitchell *Sister Gerta* • Peter Arne *Lt Schmidt* • Nora Swinburne *Sister Tia* • Michael Goodliffe *Fr Desmaines* • David Kossoff *Rabbi* ■ *Dir* Ralph Thomas • *Scr* Robert Presnell Jr, from material by Dale Pitt (front for Adrian Scott)

Conspiracy Theory ★★★ 15
Action mystery thriller
1997 · US · Colour · 129min

Mel Gibson plays a neurotic New York cabbie consumed by wild conspiracy theories in director Richard Donner's uneven thriller. It's the newsletter Gibson produces that intensifies interest in him from ominous parties such as creepy Patrick Stewart, who may work for the CIA. But that's only the half of it, because when he turns to Justice Department attorney Julia Roberts for help, the *Manchurian Candidate*-like plot kicks off. AJ Violence, swearing. *DVD*
Mel Gibson *Jerry Fletcher* • Julia Roberts *Alice Sutton* • Patrick Stewart *Dr Jonas* • Cylk Cozart *Agent Lowry* • Stephen Kahan [Steve Kahan] *Wilson* • Terry Alexander *Flip* • Alex McArthur *Cynic* ■ *Dir* Richard Donner • *Scr* Brian Helgeland

Conspirator ★ U
Spy drama 1949 · UK · BW · 86min

A dire, anti-communist tract that fitted in with Hollywood's postwar paranoia is transposed to Britain where Guards Officer Robert Taylor seems to be passing military secrets to the Russians. He's also married to Elizabeth Taylor, which makes matters even worse, because he's ordered to kill her. AT
Robert Taylor (1) *Maj Michael Curragh* • Elizabeth Taylor *Melinda Greyton* • Robert Flemyng *Capt Hugh Ladholme* • Harold Warrender *Col Hammersbrook* • Honor Blackman *Joyce* • Marjorie Fielding *Aunt Jessica* • Thora Hird *Broaders* • Wilfrid Hyde White *Lord Pennistone* ■ *Dir* Victor Saville • *Scr* Sally Benson, Gerard Fairlie, from a novel by Humphrey Slater

The Conspirator ★★★ 12
Historical drama 2010 · US · Colour · 122min

Robert Redford directs James McAvoy and Robin Wright in this worthy, wordy American Civil War drama set in the aftermath of President Abraham Lincoln's assassination. Wright plays Confederate widow and mother Mary Surratt, the only woman arrested and tried for alleged collusion in the conspiracy surrounding the killing. McAvoy plays the Union army officer forced reluctantly to conduct her defence. It's a solid historical courtroom drama based firmly in fact, with fine acting from a top-notch cast. But with too much period detail, the whole thing is just a little dry and ponderous. DA Violence. *DVD* *BL*
James McAvoy *Frederick Aiken* • Robin Wright *Mary Surratt* • Kevin Kline *Secretary Edwin M Stanton* • Tom Wilkinson *Reverdy Johnson* • Evan Rachel Wood *Anna Surratt* • Danny Huston *Joseph Holt* • Justin Long *Nicholas Baker* ■ *Dir* Robert Redford • *Scr* James Solomon, from a story by Solomon, Gregory Bernstein

The Conspirators ★★
Spy drama 1944 · US · BW · 101min

Is this an unofficial sequel to *Casablanca*? Resistance fighter Paul Henreid is finally in Lisbon after escaping from Holland, hunted by the Nazis but finding shelter with Sydney Greenstreet, Peter Lorre and exotic Hedy Lamarr who are all resistance underground members. The cast is familiar, but they compensate for the formulaic plotting and the patriotic slogans that pass for a script, and for the lethargic direction. AT
Hedy Lamarr *Irene* • Paul Henreid *Vincent* • Sydney Greenstreet *Quintanilla* • Peter Lorre *Bernazsky* • Victor Francen *Von Mohr* • Joseph Calleia *Capt Pereira* • Carol Thurston *Rosa* • Vladimir Sokoloff *Miguel* • George Macready *The Con Man* ■ *Dir* Jean Negulesco • *Scr* Vladimir Pozner, Leo Rosten, from a novel by Frederic Prokosch

Conspirators of Pleasure ★★★★ 18
Experimental fantasy comedy
1996 · Cz Rep/Swi/UK · Colour · 82min

Focusing on the antics of some lonely Prague neighbours, Jan Svankmajer's dark satire explores everything from de Sade and Freud to the nature of political freedom, the influence of the media and the possibility of happiness in a world primed to

prevent it. From the man making papier-mâché chickens out of porn mags and umbrellas to the woman with a bagful of breadcrumbs, the gallery of eccentrics is both sinister and sympathetic; the performances are all the more remarkable considering each fantasy is acted out in silence. DP Nudity, violence. *DVD*
Petr Meissel *Mr Peony* • Gabriela Wilhelmova *Mrs Loubalova* • Barbara Hrzanova *Mrs Malkova the postmistress* • Anna Wetlinska *Mrs Beltinska the newscaster* • Jiri Labus *Mr Kula the news vendor* • Pavel Novy *Mr Beltinska the police commissioner* ■ *Dir/Scr* Jan Svankmajer

Constance ★★★★ 15
Drama 1984 · NZ · Colour · 98min

The debuting Donogh Rees is outstanding in this inspired exploration of the relationship between the Hollywood "woman's picture" and real life in 1940s Auckland. Tempering the nostalgia evoked by his knowing visuals, director Bruce Morrison makes Rees's disastrous attempt to behave like a movie heroine truly excruciating. Although the dialogue is occasionally too self-conscious, the references to the films of Garbo, Dietrich, Davis and Crawford are splendidly staged, making their ironic commentary on the hapless Constance's existence all the more prescient. DP
Donogh Rees *Constance Elsworthy* • Shane Briant *Simon Malyon* • Judie Douglass *Sylvia Elsworthy* • Martin Vaughan *Alexander Elsworthy* • Donald MacDonald *John Munroe* • Mark Wignall *Richard Lewis* • Graham Harvey *Errol Barr* ■ *Dir* Bruce Morrison • *Scr* Jonathan Hardy, Bruce Morrison

The Constant Factor ★★
Drama 1980 · Pol · Colour · 90min

Physicist, multilinguist and serious film-maker Krzysztof Zanussi often deals with complex themes but sometimes fails to engage audiences in his cinema of ideas and argument. Not least here because of a distinct lack of activity in the actual shooting. This film obviously resonated in contemporary Poland in its dissection of a society where corruption in the work place contradicted the equality promised by a Communist regime. Tadeusz Bradecki finds his ambitions frustrated as much by bureaucracy as his own inadequacies. BB Polish +subtitles.
Tadeusz Bradecki *Witold* • Zofia Mrozowska *Witold's mother* • Malgorzata Zajaczkowska *Grazyna* • Cezary Morawski *Stefan* ■ *Dir/Scr* Krzysztof Zanussi

The Constant Gardener ★★★★ 15
Political thriller
2005 · UK/Ger · Colour · 123min

City of God director Fernando Meirelles brings his distinctive visual style to this moving political thriller, based on the novel by John le Carré. Ralph Fiennes plays a Foreign Office diplomat in Kenya, whose activist wife (an Oscar-winning Rachel Weisz) is found murdered. The story is then played out in a series of flashbacks, as Fiennes tries to understand his wife's motives and the events that led to her death. Drug company profiteering, conspiracy and murder are at the core of this film, but it's also a touching love story that will break your heart. SuR Violence, nudity. *DVD* *BL*
Ralph Fiennes *Justin Quayle* • Rachel Weisz *Tessa Quayle* • Danny Huston *Sandy Woodrow* • Bill Nighy *Sir Bernard Pellegrin* • Pete Postlethwaite *Lorbeer* • Richard McCabe *Arthur Hammond* • Donald Sumpter *Tim Donohue* • Juliet Aubrey *Gloria Woodrow* ■ *Dir* Fernando Meirelles • *Scr* Jeffrey Caine, from the novel by John le Carré

The Constant Husband ★★★★ U
Comedy 1955 · UK · Colour · 88min

Rex Harrison is superbly cast as an amnesiac philanderer in this jolly romp from British film-makers Frank Launder and Sidney Gilliat. Giving Harrison a run for his money are Kay Kendall (whom he later married), Margaret Leighton and French actress Nicole Maurey. The 1950s Technicolor photography gives the film a very pleasant period sheen, while the witty screenplay by Gilliat and Val Valentine ensures this comedy is a delight. **TS**

Rex Harrison *Charles Hathaway* • Margaret Leighton *Miss Chesterman* • Kay Kendall *Monica* • Cecil Parker *Llewellyn* • Nicole Maurey *Lola* • George Cole *Luigi Sopranelli* • Raymond Huntley *JF Hassett* ■ *Dir* Sidney Gilliat • *Scr* Sidney Gilliat, Val Valentine • *Cinematographer* Ted Scaife

The Constant Nymph ★
Silent drama   1928 · UK · BW · 110min

This British-made silent version of a bestselling 1920s novel and a hit West End play is the first of three screen adaptations. It's by far the least successful, despite the presence of matinée idol Ivor Novello in the starring role as a composer breaking the heart of schoolgirl Mabel Poulton, who remains in love with him into her adulthood. Overlong and under-characterised. **RK**

Mary Clare *Linda Sanger* • Ivor Novello *Lewis Dodd* • Mabel Poulton *Tessa Sanger* • Benita Hume *Antonia Sanger* • Dorothy Boyd *Pauline Sanger* ■ *Dir* Adrian Brunel • *Scr* Margaret Kennedy, Basil Dean, Alma Reville, from the play by Margaret Kennedy, Basil Dean, from the novel by Margaret Kennedy

The Constant Nymph ★★★
Drama   1933 · UK · BW · 97min

After the ineptitude of the 1928 silent version of the hit play by Basil Dean and Margaret Kennedy (based on her popular novel), eminent theatre director Dean made this first sound version, starring Brian Aherne as the composer struggling for inspiration and Victoria Hopper as the young girl whose constant love provides it, only for events to end in tragedy. A fragile piece, somewhat sedately played, it's probably too delicate for present-day audiences, but remains a stylish and poignant offering. **RK**

Victoria Hopper *Tess Sanger* • Brian Aherne *Lewis Dodd* • Leonora Corbett *Florence* • Lyn Harding *Albert Sanger* • Mary Clare *Linda Sanger* • Jane Baxter *Antonia Sanger* ■ *Dir* Basil Dean • *Scr* Margaret Kennedy, Basil Dean, Dorothy Farnum, from the play by Margaret Kennedy, Basil Dean, from the novel by Margaret Kennedy

The Constant Nymph ★★★
Drama   1943 · US · BW · 111min

Already filmed twice in Britain, this Warner Bros version is sensitively directed for maximum emotional impact by Edmund Goulding. Charles Boyer stars as the composer loved by schoolgirl Joan Fontaine (Oscar-nominated), whose constancy accompanies her into adulthood. Interminably slow to get going, it nevertheless succeeds in tugging the heartstrings and it boasts a terrific supporting cast. **RK**

Charles Boyer *Lewis Dodd* • Joan Fontaine *Tessa Sanger* • Alexis Smith *Florence Creighton* • Charles Coburn *Charles Creighton* • Brenda Marshall *Toni Sanger* • Dame May Whitty *Lady Longborough* • Peter Lorre *Bercovi, Fritz* • Joyce Reynolds *Paula Sanger* ■ *Dir* Edmund Goulding • *Scr* Kathryn Scola, from the play by Margaret Kennedy, Basil Dean, from the novel by Margaret Kennedy

Constantine ★★★ 15
Supernatural action fantasy
2005 · Ger/US/Aus · Colour · 115min

This diluted but visually arresting comic book adaptation stars Keanu Reeves as the chain-smoking John Constantine, a cancer-ridden exorcist who's condemned to save souls and take on all manner of vile demons on Earth. Rachel Weisz co-stars as a police detective who teams up with Constantine after her apparently loony twin sister (also played by Weisz) takes a swan dive off a high ledge. The script feels like little more than sticky tape holding together the visual effects, but they're very impressive effects indeed. **LF** DVD 🔵 CS

Keanu Reeves *John Constantine* • Rachel Weisz *Angela Dodson/Isabel Dodson* • Shia LaBeouf *Chas* • Tilda Swinton *Gabriel* • Pruitt Taylor Vince *Father Hennessy* • Djimon Hounsou *Midnite* • Gavin Rossdale *Balthazar* • Peter Stormare

Satan ■ *Dir* Francis Lawrence • *Scr* Kevin Brodbin, Frank Cappello, from a story by Kevin Brodbin, from the comic book *Hellblazer* by Jamie Delano, Garth Ennis, from the character created by Alan Moore in *Swamp Thing*

Constantine and the Cross ★★★
Historical drama   1961 · It · Colour · 116min

Cornel Wilde stars as the crusading warrior-protector of persecuted Christians, who became emperor of the Holy Roman Empire. This Italian-made historical epic is packed with the obligatory ingredients of the genre, including political intrigue, romance, and much blood-letting, with no punches pulled in scenes of battle, torture and Christians being thrown to the lions. Christine Kaufmann (a future Mrs Tony Curtis) is a doomed Christian maid, and there's a stand-out performance from Massimo Serato as a scheming politico. **RK** Italian dubbed.

Cornel Wilde *Constantine* • Christine Kaufmann *Livia* • Belinda Lee *Fausta* • Elisa Cegani *Helena* • Massimo Serato *Maxentius* • Fausto Tozzi *Hadrian* ■ *Dir* Lionello De Felice • *Scr* Ennio De Concini, Ernesto Guida, Lionello De Felice, Diego Fabbri, Fulvio Palmieri, Franco Rossetti, Guglielmo Santangelo

Consuming Passions ★★ 15
Comedy   1988 · UK/US · Colour · 94min

Based on a play by Michael Palin and Terry Jones, of Monty Python fame, Giles Foster's comedy is not exactly a masterpiece. A floundering chocolate factory has its fortunes improve dramatically when three workers are accidentally knocked into a mixing vat. Suddenly the nation starts clamouring for their "special" chocolate with its mystery ingredient. Vanessa Redgrave delivers a strange performance as a litigating widow. **LH**

Vanessa Redgrave *Mrs Garza* • Jonathan Pryce *Mr Farris* • Tyler Butterworth *Ian Littleton* • Freddie Jones *Graham Chumley* • Sammi Davis *Felicity* • Prunella Scales *Ethel* • Thora Hird *Mrs Gordon* • William Rushton *Big Teddy* ■ *Dir* Giles Foster • *Scr* Paul D Zimmerman, Andrew Davies, from the play *Secrets* by Michael Palin, Terry Jones

Contact ★★★ PG
Science-fiction drama
1997 · US · Colour · 143min

A rather over-zealous take on new age spirituality mars this otherwise impressive adaptation of Carl Sagan's bestselling novel. Jodie Foster stars as the dedicated astronomer who receives a message from extraterrestrials explaining how humble humans can build a spacecraft and go to meet them. The digital effects are stunning and director Robert Zemeckis is at home with the action sequences; if only he had stuck to the sci-fi. However, the climactic scene of Foster's pod journey features one of the transcendent performances in all of cinema. **JF** DVD

Jodie Foster *Dr Eleanor "Ellie" Arroway* • Matthew McConaughey *Palmer Joss* • Tom Skerritt *Dr David D'umlin* • Angela Bassett *Rachel Constantine* • John Hurt *SR Hadden* • David Morse *Theodore "Ted" Arroway* • Rob Lowe *Richard Rank* • James Woods *Michael Kitz* ■ *Dir* Robert Zemeckis • *Scr* James V Hart, Michael Goldenberg, from a story by Ann Druyan, Carl Sagan, from the novel by Carl Sagan

Contagion ★ 15
Science-fiction thriller
2000 · UK/US/Ger · Colour · 93min

Germ unit security guard Peter Weller becomes the carrier of a fast-acting virus that kills anyone he touches within minutes. Scientist William Hurt is immune to the strain and he's sent to track him down with the help of Natascha McElhone. Anthony Hickox directs with his usual aplomb but is let down by a contrived, barely convincing script and Weller's absolutely terrible performance. **AJ** DVD

William Hurt *David Whitman* • Peter Weller *Joseph Müller* • Natascha McElhone *Holly Anderson* • Katja Woywood *Karin Schiffer* • Michael Brandon *Wyles* • Christopher Cazenove

President of Clarion • Geraldine McEwan *Lilian Rodgers* ■ *Dir* Anthony Hickox • *Scr* John Penney

Contagion ★
Drama   2001 · US · Colour · 95min

Babylon 5's Bruce Boxleitner is woefully miscast as the US president in this appalling world-in-peril drama. But Lin Shaye (*Dead End*) and Jeffrey Combs (*Re-Animator*) also overact spectacularly as the terrorists responsible for unleashing a particularly lethal form of the Ebola virus. It's down to doctor Megan Gallagher to predictably save the day – in a preposterously tension-free, almost casual style. **SF** Violence.

Bruce Boxleitner *President Howard* • Megan Gallagher *Dr Diane Landis* • Lin Shaye *Laura Crowley* • Thomas Wright [Tom Wright] *Tom Brenner* • Dan Lauria *General Ryker* • Jeffery Combs [Jeffrey Combs] *Brown* ■ *Dir* John Murlowski • *Scr* Russell V Manzatt

Contagion ★★★ 12
Disaster thriller   2011 · US/UAE · Colour · 101min

A virus triggers a global pandemic in this taut and intelligent thriller. Gwyneth Paltrow's Hong Kong business trip soon appears to be key to the virus's path, as eco-scientists Laurence Fishburne, Kate Winslet and Jennifer Ehle struggle to contain the bug. Their efforts are hampered, however, by a sensationalist blogger (Jude Law). Director Steven Soderbergh's subplot-hopping ensemble piece is reminiscent of his earlier Oscar-winning *Traffic*, but never quite delivers the same level of drama or tension. The cast is exemplary, however, with Matt Damon standing out as Paltrow's seemingly immune husband. **TeS** DVD 🔵

Marion Cotillard *Dr Leonora Orantes* • Matt Damon *Mitch Emhoff* • Kate Winslet *Dr Erin Mears* • Jude Law *Alan Krumwiede* • Laurence Fishburne *Dr Ellis Cheever* • Gwyneth Paltrow *Beth Emhoff* • Jennifer Ehle *Dr Ally Hextall* ■ *Dir* Steven Soderbergh • *Scr* Scott Z Burns • *Cinematographer* Peter Andrews [Steven Soderbergh]

Container ★★★ 15
Experimental drama   2006 · Swe · BW · 71min

Swedish director Lukas Moodysson's previous effort, *A Hole in My Heart*, featured hardcore pornography and documentary footage of genital surgery. *Container* doesn't have any particularly shocking images, but aesthetically it's Moodysson's most extreme film. There's no plot to mention, just gritty, black-and-white images of an obese, often naked man cavorting around dumps, abandoned buildings and assorted debris-filled rooms. For fans of experimental cinema, the effect is mesmerising. Others might find it duller than dishwater. **LF** Swearing, nudity. DVD

Peter Lorentzon *Man* • Mariha Aberg *Woman* • Jena Malone *Voice* ■ *Dir/Scr* Lukas Moodysson • *Cinematographers* Jesper Kurlandsky, Lukas Moodysson

Containment ★★★ 15
Horror thriller   2015 · UK · Colour · 76min

In this low-budget contagion thriller from first-time director Neil Mcenery-West, the residents of a Southampton tower block wake to find their doors and windows sealed and people in orange hazmat suits erecting tent hospitals down below. Mcenery-West does well with limited resources, wringing tension from claustrophobia and paranoia until a crisis point is reached. Resourcefulness and sincerity are the heroes of the hour here. **AC** Swearing, violence.

Lee Ross *Mark* • Sheila Reid *Enid* • Andrew Leung *Sergei* • Gabriel Senior *Nicu* • Louise Brealey *Sally* ■ *Dir* Neil Mcenery-West • *Scr* David Lemon, from a story by Neil Mcenery-West

The Contender ★★★ 15
Political drama   2000 · US/Fr · Colour · 121min

Former film critic Rod Lurie makes an assured second feature (his debut was 1999's *Deterrence*) with this streetwise insight into both the predatory nature of Washington power-broking and the

increasingly base motives of contemporary journalism. In a part written especially for her, Joan Allen gives an Oscar-nominated performance as the senator selected by popular president Jeff Bridges (also nominated) to succeed his recently deceased vice-president. **DP** DVD

Gary Oldman *Shelly Runyon* • Joan Allen *Laine Hanson* • Jeff Bridges *President Jackson Evans* • Christian Slater *Reginald Webster* • William Petersen [William L Petersen] *Jack Hathaway* • Saul Rubinek *Jerry Toliver* • Sam Elliott *Kermit Newman* • Philip Baker Hall *Oscar Billings* ■ *Dir/Scr* Rod Lurie

Continental Divide ★★★ PG
Romantic comedy   1981 · US · Colour · 98min

This underrated romantic comedy demonstrated that John Belushi possessed subtler gifts than just gross clowning. In a not entirely successful attempt to re-create the golden age of Tracy and Hepburn, Belushi plays a slobbish, urbanised journalist who falls in and out of love with nature scientist Blair Brown. The leads work well together and, although the pacing and tone is a little uneasy, the film is very watchable. **JF** DVD

John Belushi *Ernie Souchak* • Blair Brown *Nell Porter* • Allen Garfield *Howard* • Carlin Glynn *Sylvia* • Tony Ganios *Possum* • Val Avery *Yablonowitz* • Bill Henderson *Train conductor* • Liam Russell *Deke* ■ *Dir* Michael Apted • *Scr* Lawrence Kasdan

Contraband ★★★ U
Second World War spy thriller
1940 · UK · BW · 91min

Directed by Michael Powell from a story by Emeric Pressburger, this is a neat wartime espionage thriller that depicts a London crawling with spies, rather in the manner of Alfred Hitchcock's *Sabotage* and *The Man Who Knew Too Much*. Powell makes brilliant use of the blackouts and includes one cheeky sequence when hundreds of unwanted plaster casts of Neville Chamberlain get shot to pieces. This would have been Deborah Kerr's first feature film, but all her scenes were left on the cutting-room floor. **AT**

Conrad Veidt *Captain Andersen* • Valerie Hobson *Mrs Sorensen* • Hay Petrie *Axel Skold/Erik Skold* • Esmond Knight *Mr Pidgeon* • Raymond Lovell *Van Dyne* ■ *Dir* Michael Powell • *Scr* Michael Powell, Brock Williams, from a story by Emeric Pressburger

Contraband ★★★ 15
Thriller   2012 · US/UK/Ice/Fr · Colour · 105min

Mark Wahlberg is back in action-man mode in this skilfully shot if slightly uneven thriller. Set in a murky New Orleans, it has a former expert smuggler (Wahlberg) dragged back into the business to save his dimwit brother-in-law from the attentions of mobsters led by the terrifyingly twitchy (and barely recognisable) Giovanni Ribisi. Wahlberg gives a solid performance, while Icelandic director Baltasar Kormakur (here remaking his own 2008 film *Reykjavik-Rotterdam*) shows visual flair and handles the action scenes well. But you can't help feeling that, pacing-wise, this could have done with the likes of Tony Scott to give it the kick it needs. **AS** English, Spanish +subtitles. Violence, swearing, drug abuse. DVD 🔵

Mark Wahlberg *Chris Farraday* • Kate Beckinsale *Kate Farraday* • Ben Foster *Sebastian Abney* • Giovanni Ribisi *Tim Briggs* • JK Simmons *Captain Camp* • Lukas Haas *Danny Raymer* ■ *Dir* Baltasar Kormakur • *Scr* Aaron Guzikowski, from the film *Reykjavik-Rotterdam* by Arnaldur Indrioason, Oskar Jonasson

Contraband Spain ★★ U
Mystery   1955 · UK · Colour · 82min

Richard Greene headlines this mediocre thriller as an American agent intent on rounding up a gang of smugglers operating out of Barcelona. Clearly aiming for a Graham Greene sort of entertainment, writer/director Lawrence Huntington is hampered more by the paucity of his imagination than the meagreness of his

resources. The acting is disappointing considering the calibre of the cast. DP
Richard Greene *Lee Scott* • Anouk Aimée *Elena Vargas* • Michael Denison *Ricky Metcalfe* • José Nieto *Pierre* • John Warwick *Bryan* • Philip Saville *Martin Scott* • Alfonso Estella *Marcos* • GH Mulcaster *Colonel Ingleby* ■ *Dir/Scr* Lawrence Huntington

The Contract ★★★
Drama   1980 · Pol · Colour · 111min

A Warsaw doctor arranges the civil marriage of his son but his young wife refuses to go through with the subsequent church service. Nevertheless, her father-in-law goes ahead with the wedding reception, where sex, alcohol and family divisions crash the party. This is film-maker Krzysztof Zanussi at his most straightforward, making an ironic, sometimes funny film that examines a wealthy strata of Polish society on the brink of its collapse. Interesting and entertaining, it features a stand-out performance as Leslie Caron as a kleptomaniac ballerina. RB Polish, French, English, German, Swedish +subtitles.
Maja Komorowska *Dorota* • Tadeusz Lomnicki *Adam* • Magda Jaroszowna *Lilka* • Krzysztof Kolberger *Piotr* • Nina Andrycz *Olga* • Zofia Mrozowska *Maria* • Beata Tyszkiewicz *Nina* • Janusz Gajos *Boleslaw* • Leslie Caron *Penelope Wilson* ■ *Dir/Scr* Krzysztof Zanussi

The Contract ★★ 15
Crime thriller   2006 · Ger/US · Colour · 92min

Despite the A-list involved, this is a depressingly ordinary action caper, which unsurprisingly went straight to video in most countries. John Cusack plays a former cop turned teacher who heads into the wild to bond with his surly teenage son (Jamie Anderson). Unfortunately, they have the misfortune to stumble across a dying FBI agent, who was in the process of escorting master assassin Morgan Freeman into custody and they resolve to finish the job. Director Bruce Beresford's brisk and economical direction is a plus, while the two leads are their usual reliable selves. However, the fact that the Freeman character is such a sympathetic soul means there is little tension between guard and captor, while plot logic is in short supply. JF
DVD Blu
Morgan Freeman *Frank Carden* • John Cusack *Ray Keene* • Jamie Anderson (2) *Chris Keene* • Alice Krige *Miles* • Megan Dodds *Sandra* • Corey Johnson *Davis* • Jonathan Hyde *Turner* ■ *Dir* Bruce Beresford • *Scr* Stephen Katz, John Darrouzet

The Contractor ★★ 15
Action thriller
2007 · US/UK/Bul · Colour · 94min

A betrayed Wesley Snipes broods his way through this understated though predictable thriller. He plays a retired CIA marksman who finds himself on the run from both British police and his US bosses after he's called on to assassinate a terrorist in London. Solid performances offset the feature's direct-to-DVD status, with *Inkheart*'s Eliza Bennett impressive as the young truant whose befriending of Snipes evokes Luc Besson's *Leon*. SF DVD
Wesley Snipes *James Dial* • Eliza Bennett *Emily Day* • Lena Headey *DI Annette Ballard* • Ralph Brown *Jeremy Collins* • Charles Dance *DCS Andrew Windsor* • Gemma Jones *Mrs Day* ■ *Dir* Josef Rusnak • *Scr* Robert Foster, Joshua Michael Stern, from a story by Robert Katz, Andre Farwagi

Control ★★★★ 15
Biographical music drama
2007 · UK/Aus/Jpn · BW · 116min

Dutch photographer Anton Corbijn's long-term love affair with 1970s Manchester rock band Joy Division bears rich fruit in his intimate and affecting biopic of their tragic lead singer Ian Curtis. Based on the memoirs of Curtis's widow Deborah (portrayed with poignant resilience by Samantha Morton), the monochrome feature traces the iconic star's short life, from his David Bowie-fixated teens and early marriage, to his debilitating struggle with fame, depression and ill-health that led

to his suicide, aged 23. *Brighton Rock*'s Sam Riley is uncannily convincing as Curtis, capturing both his hyperactive stage persona and his tortured private side, while beautifully framed visuals enhance the excellent performances. But the picture's biggest surprise is its earthy humour, which further dismantles the myth behind the man. SF DVD Blu
Sam Riley *Ian Curtis* • Samantha Morton *Deborah Curtis* • Alexandra Maria Lara *Annik Honore* • Joe Anderson (1) *Peter "Hooky" Hook* • James Anthony Pearson *Bernard Sumner* • Toby Kebbell *Rob Gretton* • Craig Parkinson *Tony Wilson* • Harry Treadaway *Steve Morris* • Andrew Sheridan *Terry* • Robert Shelly *Twinny* ■ *Dir* Anton Corbijn • *Scr* Matt Greenhalgh, from the memoirs *Touching from a Distance* by Deborah Curtis • *Cinematographer* Martin Ruhe

The Convent ★★
Mystery drama   1995 · Fr/Por · Colour · 90min

The legend of Faust is cloaked in the conventions of the gothic novel in this intriguing if baffling curio from Portuguese maestro Manoel de Oliveira. Strewing the action with casual literary references, the veteran director prompts us to muse on the nature of good and evil as he lures us into the cavernous convent of Arrabida. John Malkovich is the scholar seeking to prove that Shakespeare was a Hispanic Jew, but for once he is outshone by Luis Miguel Cintra as the sinister guardian who tempts the professor with intellectual immortality in order to seduce his wife (Catherine Deneuve). DP English, French, Portuguese +subtitles.
Catherine Deneuve *Helene* • John Malkovich *Michael Padovic* • Luis Miguel Cintra *Baltar* • Leonor Silveira *Piedade* • Duarte D'Almeida *Baltazar* • Heloisa Miranda *Berta* ■ *Dir* Manoel de Oliveira • *Scr* Manoel de Oliveira, from an idea by Augustina Bessa-Luis

The Conversation ★★★★★ 12
Psychological thriller
1974 · US · Colour · 109min

In this small masterpiece from director Francis Ford Coppola, Gene Hackman gives a superb performance as the lonely surveillance expert tracking the movements and voices of Frederic Forrest and Cindy Williams, only to find that marital infidelity could be part of a murder plot. Coppola tweaks the idea to surreal effect, while editor Walter Murch orchestrates eavesdropping into a uniquely baffling wall of sound. This haunting thriller skilfully taps into post-Watergate paranoia resulting in an intensely fascinating study of a perpetrator turned victim of the surveillance society. TH Violence, brief nudity. DVD Blu
Gene Hackman *Harry Caul* • John Cazale *Stan* • Allen Garfield *"Bernie" Moran* • Frederic Forrest *Mark* • Cindy Williams *Ann* • Michael Higgins *Paul* • Elizabeth MacRae *Meredith* • Teri Garr *Amy* • Harrison Ford *Martin Stett* • Mark Wheeler *Receptionist* • Robert Shields *Mime* • Robert Duvall *The Director* ■ *Dir/Scr* Francis Ford Coppola • *Sound* Walter Murch, Arthur Rochester

Conversation Piece ★★★ 18
Drama   1974 · It/Fr · Colour · 116min

Luchino Visconti, having suffered a major stroke that confined him to a wheelchair, concocted this story about an ageing, homosexual professor who lives surrounded by art and books. Cut off from the real world, he finds his ivory tower invaded when a countess and her jet-setting brood rent the apartment upstairs. Visconti's usual themes - the collision of cultures, the clash between old and new, the imminence of death - are covered in opulent fashion. AT Swearing, sex scenes. DVD Blu
Burt Lancaster *Professor* • Helmut Berger *Konrad Hubel* • Claudia Marsani *Lietta Brumonti* • Silvana Mangano *Bianca Brumonti* • Stefano Patrizi *Stefano* • Elvira Cortese *Erminia* • Claudia Cardinale *Professor's wife* ■ *Dir* Luchino Visconti • *Scr* Suso Cecchi D'Amico, Luchino Visconti, from a story by Enrico Medioli

Conversations with My Gardener ★★★★ 12A
Comedy drama   2006 · Fr · Colour · 108min

Veteran actors Daniel Auteuil and Jean-Pierre Darroussin are at the top of their game in this charmingly intimate French drama. Auteuil plays a Parisian artist in the throes of a midlife crisis, who returns to his late parents' country house. He hires a worldly-wise gardener (Darroussin), who turns out to be an old schoolfriend, to plant a vegetable garden for him. The two men bond over their work, with class differences reduced to ironic name tags, "Gardener" and "Dauber". Wisely, director Jean Becker (son of famed French film-maker Jacques Becker) doesn't force the drama, as "Dauber"'s art is gradually rejuvenated by craft. A sedate and enchanting pleasure. JR French +subtitles.
Daniel Auteuil *Painter* • Jean-Pierre Darroussin *Gardener* • Fanny Cottençon *Hélène* • Alexia Barlier *Magda* • Hiam Abbass *Gardener's wife* • Elodie Navarre *Carole* • Roger Van Hool *Tony* • Michel Lagueyrie *René* ■ *Dir* Jean Becker • *Scr* Jean Becker, Jean Cosmos, Jacques Monnet, from the novel by Henri Cueco

Conversations with Other Women ★★★ 15
Relationship comedy drama
2005 · US · Colour · 81min

Helena Bonham Carter and Aaron Eckhart meet at a wedding, and over the course of the day - and night - their shared history is revealed. Indie film-maker Hans Canosa isn't interested in a rosy-hued picture of soulmates passing in the night, as much as a mournful dissection of the relationship between two people who were once in love. Canosa's use of split screen offers some revealing contrasts between past and present, but using the technique for every scene becomes rather wearisome. At times the jaded outlook is a little oppressive, but thankfully there are plenty of moments of wit and whimsy to balance things out. SP Swearing, sex scenes. DVD
Helena Bonham Carter *Woman* • Aaron Eckhart *Man* • Nora Zehetner *Young woman* • Erik Eidem *Young man* ■ *Dir* Hans Canosa • *Scr* Gabrielle Zevin • *Cinematographer* Steve Yedlin

Convict 99 ★★ U
Comedy   1938 · UK · BW · 84min

Who else but Will Hay could apply for the headship of a school only to find himself appointed a prison governor and then get mistaken for the most dangerous inmate? Sadly, the film loses its way once Hay assumes power and introduces a regime so liberal that the lags take over. The great man is somewhat below par in this muddled and overlong comedy. DP DVD
Will Hay *Benjamin Twist* • Moore Marriott *Jerry the Mole* • Graham Moffatt *Albert* • Googie Withers *Lottie* • Garry Marsh *Johnson* • Peter Gawthorne *Sir Cyril Wagstaffe* • Basil Radford *Governor* ■ *Dir* Marcel Varnel • *Scr* Marriott Edgar, Val Guest, Jack Davies, Ralph Smart, from a story by Cyril Campion

Convicted ★★
Prison drama   1950 · US · BW · 90min

Jailed for manslaughter after killing a man in a bar-room brawl, Glenn Ford becomes romantically entangled with Dorothy Malone, the daughter of governor Broderick Crawford. Ford's situation worsens, however, when he sees convict Millard Mitchell kill another inmate. Although strongly cast, well played and competently directed, this prison melodrama is monumentally routine. RK
Glenn Ford *Joe Hufford* • Broderick Crawford *George Knowland* • Millard Mitchell *Malloby* • Dorothy Malone *Kay Knowland* • Carl Benton Reid *Capt Douglas* • Frank Faylen *Ponti* ■ *Dir* Henry Levin • *Scr* William Bowers, Fred Niblo Jr, Seton I Miller, from the play *The Criminal Code* by Martin Flavin

Conviction ★★★ 15
Biographical drama
2010 · US/UK · Colour · 102min

Hilary Swank is given a gutsy role in this solid true-story drama. She plays an unmarried working mum whose brother (Sam Rockwell) is imprisoned for murder. Believing him to be innocent, she then dedicates her life to learning to practise law in a bid to get him freed. Swank and Rockwell are as good as you'd expect as the chalk-and-cheese siblings, while there's dependable support from the likes of Minnie Driver and Juliette Lewis. There's a whiff of "TV movie of the week" about this tale of one woman's crusade against injustice, but, like the similarly themed *Erin Brockovich*, there's also much to recommend it. DA Swearing. DVD
Hilary Swank *Betty Anne Waters* • Sam Rockwell *Kenny Waters* • Minnie Driver *Abra Rice* • Melissa Leo *Nancy Taylor* • Peter Gallagher *Barry Scheck* • Juliette Lewis *Roseanna Perry* ■ *Dir* Tony Goldwyn • *Scr* Pamela Gray

Convicts ★★★
Period drama   1991 · US · Colour · 110min

There's a major theme here - the dying days of the Old South - but it's compressed by playwright/screenwriter Horton Foote into almost allegorical terms. Robert Duvall acts his socks off as the senile plantation owner who fights in the Civil War and then hires black convicts to work the place, thus preserving slavery. It's this shadowy history that is recalled by Lukas Haas in the film's rather peculiar dramatic structure. Duvall's portrayal of senility makes the film worth seeing. AT
Robert Duvall *Soll Gautier* • Lukas Haas *Horace Robedaux* • Starletta DuPois *Martha Johnson* • James Earl Jones *Ben Johnson* • Carlin Glynn *Asa* • Gary Swanson *Billy* • Mel Winkler *Jackson* ■ *Dir* Peter Masterson • *Scr* Horton Foote, from his play

Convicts Four ★★
Prison drama   1962 · US · BW · 105min

Also known as *Reprieve*, this dour prison drama takes a turn for the better when a convict is granted a stay of execution and takes up painting, a pastime that changes his uncaring character and leads to his eventual rehabilitation. Millard Kaufman's film is well-meaning and sincere, while Ben Gazzara, Vincent Price and Rod Stieger deliver strong performances. After a while, though, it becomes a bit dull. TH
Ben Gazzara *John Resko* • Stuart Whitman *Principal Keeper* • Ray Walston *Iggy* • Vincent Price *Carl Carmer* • Rod Steiger *Tiptoes* • Broderick Crawford *Warden* • Dodie Stevens *Resko's sister* • Sammy Davis Jr *Wino* ■ *Dir* Millard Kaufman • *Scr* Millard Kaufman, from the non-fiction book *Reprieve* by John Resko

Convoy ★★★ PG
Second World War drama
1940 · UK · BW · 85min

A convoy of ships, led by captain Clive Brook, is intercepted in the North Sea by a German battleship. Its firepower destroys Brook's cruiser and kills the first officer (John Clements), who had been the lover of the skipper's wife. A taut, realistic and emotionally involving flag-waver, well directed by the highly regarded Pen Tennyson, tragically killed in 1941 before he could fulfil his potential. RK
Clive Brook *Captain Armitage* • John Clements *Lieutenant Crawford* • Edward Chapman *Captain Eckersley* • Judy Campbell *Lucy Armitage* • Edward Rigby *Mr Mathews* • Charles Williams (1) *Shorty Howard* • Allan Jeayes *Commander Blount* • John Laurie *Gates* • Stewart Granger *Sutton* • Michael Wilding *Dot* • Penelope Dudley Ward *Mabel* ■ *Dir* Pen Tennyson • *Scr* Pen Tennyson, Patrick Kirwan

Convoy ★★★ 12
Comedy adventure   1978 · US · Colour · 106min

This film remains the epitome of trucking movies. Kris Kristofferson is the heroic driver who thumbs his nose at authority and collects a disparate group of truckers in an epic journey across the US, which sees him cross the roadblocks of sheriff Ernest

Borgnine. It's pretty lightweight fare for director Sam Peckinpah, but he builds an unstoppable momentum that makes you forget the weak performances. The appalling title song, which is actually the source of the movie, was a massive hit at the time. JF Swearing. *DVD* *BL*

Kris Kristofferson *Martin Penwald, "Rubber Duck"* • Ali MacGraw *Melissa* • Ernest Borgnine *Lyle Wallace, "Dirty"* • Burt Young *Bobby, "Pig Pen"* • Madge Sinclair *"Widow Woman"* • Franklyn Ajaye *"Spider Mike"* • Brian Davies *Chuck Arnoldi* • Seymour Cassel *Governor Gerry Haskins* ■ *Dir* Sam Peckinpah • *Scr* BWL Norton, from the song by CW McCall

Les Convoyeurs Attendent ★★★★ 🔟

Comedy drama 1999 · Bel/Fr/Swi · BW · 89min

Having impressed as the serial killer in *Man Bites Dog*, Benoît Poelvoorde surpasses himself in this bizarre black comedy from Belgium. As the ambulance-chasing photojournalist bullying his son to break the world door-opening record in order to win a car in a contest, he combines tough love, class consciousness and repressed self-loathing to create a truly unique character whose muddled motives almost excuse his eccentric excesses. An astute mix of melodrama and macabre humour. DP French +subtitles.

Benoît Poelvoorde *Roger* • Morgane Simon *Luise* • Bouli Lanners *Coach* • Dominique Baeyens *Mother* • Philippe Grand'Henry *Felix* • Jean-François Devigne *Michel* • Lisa LaCroix *Jocelyne* ■ *Dir* Benoît Mariage • *Scr* Benoît Mariage, Emmanuelle Bada, Jean-Luc Seigle • *Cinematographer* Philippe Guilbert

Coogan's Bluff ★★★ 🔟

Crime drama 1968 · US · Colour · 90min

Clint Eastwood still wore a cowboy hat in his first attempt to move from the western landscape into the contemporary urban setting, but under Don Siegel's taut direction he carried off the switch successfully. In many ways the forerunner of Dirty Harry, Eastwood's laconic Arizona sheriff tracking down a murderer in Manhattan was his first character to get upset by big city sleaze and escalating crime. This stylish and gritty crime drama set the seal on Eastwood's screen persona for decades to come. AJ Violence, swearing. *DVD* *BL*

Clint Eastwood *Walt Coogan* • Lee J Cobb *Sheriff McElroy* • Susan Clark *Julie* • Tisha Sterling *Linny Raven* • Don Stroud *Ringerman* • Betty Field *Mrs Ringerman* • Tom Tully *Sheriff McCrea* • Melodie Johnson *Millie* ■ *Dir* Don Siegel • *Scr* Herman Miller, Dean Reisner, Howard Rodman, from a story by Herman Miller

Cook & Peary: the Race to the Pole ★★

Historical adventure 1983 · US · Colour · 100min

Richard Chamberlain and Rod Steiger play rival explorers at loggerheads over their expeditions to the North Pole in this biased and sadly undynamic true-life drama that certainly shows its age. Stilted and stodgy, the flashback-centred tale sees Chamberlain's aggrieved Dr Frederick Cook challenge the officially recognised view that it was unscrupulous naval commander Robert E Peary (a terse Steiger) who reached the Pole first. The bleakly beautiful landscapes and the historically revealing interaction with indigenous people add a sense of authenticity to a predominantly unconvincing TV movie. SF

Richard Chamberlain *Frederick Cook* • Rod Steiger *Robert E Peary* • Diane Venora *Marie Fidele Hunt* • Michael Gross *James Troth* • Samm-Art Williams *Matt Henson* ■ *Dir* Robert Day • *Scr* IC Rapoport

The Cook, the Thief, His Wife and Her Lover ★★★★ 🔞

Black comedy drama 1989 · UK/Fr · Colour · 118min

One of avant-garde director Peter Greenaway's most accessible films is a truly elegant, shocking and transfixing experience. A Jacobean drama in contemporary clothing, this savage indictment of greed, power and control in today's wannabe society finds Helen Mirren memorably strutting her stuff in another risky, and risqué, performance, while manic Michael Gambon portrays evil personified. Memorably scored by Michael Nyman, Greenaway's stunning "designer dream" is sick, sexy and rude in about equal provocative proportions and totally unforgettable. AJ Violence, swearing, sex scenes, nudity. *DVD* *BL*

Richard Bohringer *Richard Borst, the Cook* • Michael Gambon *Albert Spica, the Thief* • Helen Mirren *Georgina Spica, the Wife* • Alan Howard *Michael, the Lover* • Tim Roth *Mitchel* • Gary Olsen *Spangler* • Liz Smith *Grace* • Alex Kingston *Adele* • Ian Dury *Terry Fitch* ■ *Dir/Scr* Peter Greenaway • *Cinematographer* Sacha Vierny • *Costume Designer* Jean-Paul Gaultier

Cookie ★★ 🔟

Crime comedy 1989 · US · Colour · 89min

Emily Lloyd is the mobster's daughter trying to keep dad out of trouble in this uneven comedy. Unfortunately, despite the talents on board, director Susan Seidelman still manages to make a bland, unfunny mess of a movie whose behind-the-scenes stories (Peter Falk allegedly slapped Lloyd, who annoyed him, during a scene when he was supposed to fake it) are much more interesting than what's going on in front of the camera. JB Violence, swearing.

Peter Falk *Dominick "Dino" Capisco* • Dianne Wiest *Lenore* • Emily Lloyd *Carmella "Cookie" Voltecki* • Michael V Gazzo *Carmine Taratino* • Brenda Vaccaro *Bunny* • Adrian Pasdar *Vito* • Lionel Stander *Enzo Della Testa* • Jerry Lewis *Arnold Ross* ■ *Dir* Susan Seidelman • *Scr* Nora Ephron, Alice Arlen

Cookie's Fortune ★★★ 🔢

Comedy drama 1999 · US · Colour · 112min

Director Robert Altman has a bizarre collection of hits and misses in his oeuvre, and this falls somewhere in the middle. The ensemble piece finds Glenn Close and Julianne Moore hamming it up as two sisters trying to cover up the "disgraceful" suicide of ageing relative Cookie, while simultaneously attempting to inherit her worldly goods. Cookie's more worthy heirs, rebel Liv Tyler and long-standing handyman Charles S Dutton, cotton on to their shenanigans. LH Some sex scenes. *DVD*

Glenn Close *Camille* • Julianne Moore *Cora Duvall* • Liv Tyler *Emma Duvall* • Chris O'Donnell *Jason Brown* • Charles S Dutton *Willis Richland* • Patricia Neal *Jewel Mae "Cookie" Orcutt* • Ned Beatty *Lester Boyle* ■ *Dir* Robert Altman • *Scr* Anne Rapp

Cool and Crazy ★★★★ 🔟

Music documentary 2000 · Nor/Swe/Fin · Colour · 100min

The prospect of spending 105 minutes in the company of a Norwegian male voice choir may not sound that inviting, but Knut Erik Jensen's documentary portrait of the Berlevåg choristers is a delight. The members of the choir reside in a remote fishing town that's been badly hit by recession, and their music and cheerful camaraderie play an important part in sustaining morale. Whether depicting the choir rehearsing outdoors in the face of a blizzard or excitedly making their way to the Russian city of Murmansk for a recital, the film conveys the warmth of community that insulates these gloriously eccentric characters from their icy surroundings. DP Norwegian +subtitles. *DVD*

■ *Dir* Knut Erik Jensen • *Cinematographers* Svein Krøvel, Aslaug Holm

The Cool and the Crazy ★★★ 🔢

Drama 1958 · US · BW · 77min

Take a walk on the jive side with this cheap and cheerful juvenile delinquent classic starring James Dean wannabe Scott Marlowe. It's all here: seedy pushers, flaming car crashes, wild ones "hooked on smoke," service station hold-ups and rebels without a cause resorting to violence to feed their addictions. Originally banned in Britain, this high school dope exposé is remarkably well acted, fast paced and realistic. AJ *DVD*

Scott Marlowe *Bennie Saul* • Gigi Perreau *Amy* • Dick Bakalyan [Richard Bakalyan] *Jackie Barzan* • Dick Jones [Dickie Jones] *Stu Summerville* • Shelby Storck *Lt Sloan* ■ *Dir* William Witney • *Scr* Richard C Sarafian

Cool as Ice ★★ 🅿🅶

Crime drama 1991 · US · Colour · 87min

Just what is it that makes singers think they can act? Here rapper Vanilla Ice (remember him?) proves that he hasn't mastered the thespian art, as he tries and fails to translate his musical persona to the screen. Ice rides into town with his posse like *The Wild One*, and he's soon romancing the kind of girl whose daddy wouldn't approve of anyone. Still, the music's catchy. JB Brief swearing. *DVD*

Vanilla Ice *Johnny Van Owen* • Kristin Minter *Kathy* • Michael Gross *Gordon Winslow* • Sydney Lassick *Roscoe McCallister* • Dody Goodman *Mae McCallister* • Naomi Campbell *Singer at first club* • Candy Clark *Grace Winslow* ■ *Dir* David Kellogg • *Scr* David Stenn

Cool Blue ★ 🔟

Romantic comedy 1988 · US · Colour · 86min

This is an early film role for Woody Harrelson, better known at the time for playing dumb barman Woody Boyd in the TV sitcom *Cheers*. Here he plays an aspiring painter who loves, then loses a girl (Ely Pouget). A straight-to-video cheapie, notable only for featuring an uncredited cameo from Sean Penn. FL

Woody Harrelson *Dustin* • Ely Pouget *Christiane* • Gloria LeRoy *Ida* • Hank Azaria *Buzz* • Sean Penn *Phil the plumber* ■ *Dir/Scr* Richard Shepard, Mark Mullin

A Cool, Dry Place ★★★ 🔟

Drama 1998 · US · Colour · 94min

Not many people saw this vastly underrated drama about a single father who puts his career as a high-powered lawyer on hold to raise his five-year-old son in a small town. Vince Vaughn is awe-inspiring in the lead, and the rest of the cast, which includes Joey Lauren Adams as his new girlfriend and Monica Potter as his ex-wife, is also terrific. This may not be as showy as some dramas, but it has heart. ST

Vince Vaughn *Russell Durrell* • Monica Potter *Kate* • Joey Lauren Adams *Beth* • Devon Sawa *Noah* ■ *Dir* John N Smith • *Scr* Matthew McDuffie, from the novel *Dance Real Slow* by Michael Grant Jaffe

Cool Hand Luke ★★★★ 🔟

Prison drama 1967 · US · Colour · 121min

Chiming perfectly with the "Summer of Love" in which it was released, this subtle blend of acknowledging the needs of the individual and respecting a freedom of spirit was one of the key American films of the 1960s. It's basically an old-fashioned chain-gang movie, told in stunning Technicolor. Paul Newman is superb, and both the prologue and the egg-eating scene have become screen classics. The religious symbolism does get a little tiresome, but the movie is clearly the career high point of director Stuart Rosenberg. TS Violence, brief nudity. *DVD* *BL*

Paul Newman *Luke Jackson* • George Kennedy *Dragline* • JD Cannon *Society Red* • Lou Antonio *Koko* • Robert Drivas *Loudmouth Steve* • Strother Martin *Captain* • Jo Van Fleet *Arletta* • Clifton James *Carr* • Dennis Hopper *Babalugats* ■ *Dir* Stuart Rosenberg • *Scr* Donn Pearce, Frank R Pierson, from a novel by Donn Pearce • *Cinematographer* Conrad Hall

Cool Money ★★ 🔟

Crime drama based on a true story 2005 · US · Colour · 87min

James Marsters (who is best known as Spike in *Buffy the Vampire Slayer* and *Angel*) plays a genial jewel thief in this fact-based TV movie. Bored with family life in Miami, Marsters hooks up with John Cassini and Wayne Robson to hit New York's swankiest hotels. And though wife Robin

Brule wants him to go straight, she gets a taste for the high life he provides. With Marsters oozing charm and Margot Kidder cameoing knowingly as his mother, this should have been a breezy romp. But the robberies lack ingenuity and even the climactic heist (one of the biggest in US criminal history) falls flat. DP *DVD*

James Marsters *Bobby Comfort* • John Cassini *Sammy Nalo* • Larry Manetti *Detective Ed O'Connor* • Wayne Robson *Doc* • Robin Brule *Stephanie Comfort* • Jason Schombing *Phil Parris* • Margot Kidder *Peggy Comfort* • Dan Warry-Smith *Country* ■ *Dir* Gary Burns • *Scr* Shelley Evans, from the short story *Unlucky Pierre* by Marvin J Wolf, Katherine Mader, from the non-fiction book *Rotten Apples: Chronicles of New York Crime and Mystery: 1689 to the Present* by Wolf, Mader • *Cinematographer* Luc Montpellier

The Cool Ones ★★ 🅄

Musical comedy 1967 · US · Colour · 95min

If you can endure its antiquated humour, this pop musical, one of several directed by former actor Gene Nelson, has some delights. By chance, the plot hasn't dated at all: fading pop singer Gil Peterson and go-go dancer Debbie Watson are persuaded by publicist Roddy McDowall to pretend to be a romantic item. Frivolous, and 20 minutes too long. DM

Roddy McDowall *Tony* • Debbie Watson *Hallie* • Gil Peterson *Cliff* • Robert Coote *Stan* • Phil Harris *MacElwaine* • Nita Talbot *Dee Dee* • Mrs Elva Miller *Mrs Miller* • Glen Campbell *Patrick* • Teri Garr *Hallie's friend* ■ *Dir* Gene Nelson • *Scr* Robert Kaufman, Gene Nelson, from a story by Joyce Geller

Cool Runnings ★★★★ 🅿🅶

Sports comedy based on a true story 1993 · US · Colour · 94min

If someone had invented the story of a Jamaican bobsleigh team entering the Olympics, they'd have been laughed out of the room. But, as the story is true and Disney knows how to produce feel-good material better than most, what results is a hugely entertaining comedy guaranteed to have you cheering on the underdogs. Admittedly, it's a little predictable at times, but the eager performances of John Candy and his Olympic hopefuls carry the day. DP Some violence, swearing. *DVD*

Leon *Derice Bannock* • Doug E Doug *Sanka Coffie* • Rawle D Lewis *Junior Bevil* • Malik Yoba *Yul Brenner* • John Candy *Irving Blitzer* • Raymond J Barry *Kurt Hemphill* • Peter Outerbridge *Josef Grool* • Paul Coeur *Roger* ■ *Dir* Jon Turteltaub • *Scr* Michael Goldberg, Tommy Swerdlow, Lynn Siefert, from a story by Lynn Siefert, Michael Ritchie

The Cool World ★★★★

Drama 1963 · US · BW · 105min

A semi-underground movie and a near-classic, this depicts the lives of street gangs in the black ghetto of Harlem. Director Shirley Clarke had been born into affluent Park Avenue society and seemed destined to be a choreographer before she started making movies. Her first feature, *The Connection*, dealt frankly with heroin addiction, and this, her second, has the same documentary style and poetic rawness. Using non-professional actors, it shows life on the streets, with compassion but without condescension. It became an international art house hit. AT

Hampton Clanton *Duke* • Carl Lee *Priest* • Yolanda Rodriguez *Luanee* • Clarence Williams III *Blood* • Marilyn Cox *Miss Dewpoint* • Georgia Burke *Grandma* • Gloria Foster *Mrs Custis* • Bostic Felton *Rod* ■ *Dir* Shirley Clarke • *Scr* Shirley Clarke, Carl Lee, from the play by Robert Rossen, from the novel by Miller

Cool World ★★ 🔟

Part-animated comedy fantasy 1992 · US · Colour · 97min

Gabriel Byrne is the creator of the comic *Cool World*, who discovers that his fictional creation - femme fatale Holli Would (voiced by Kim Basinger) - actually exists. She wants to be real; all that stands in her way is Brad Pitt, the human detective of the cartoon world. Although director Ralph Bakshi has come up with some stunning animated characters, they are not always seamlessly integrated with their live-action counterparts, and the script is confusing and unfunny. JF Violence, swearing. **DVD**

Kim Basinger *Holli Would* • Gabriel Byrne *Jack Deebs* • Brad Pitt *Detective Frank Harris* • Michele Abrams *Jennifer Malley* • Janni Brenn-Lowen *Mom Harris* • William Frankfather *Cop* • Greg Collins *Cop* • Murray Podwal *Store patron* ■ *Dir* Ralph Bakshi • *Scr* Mark Victor, Michael Grais, Larry Gross, from a story by Ralph Bakshi, Frank Mancuso Jr • *Animation* Bruce Woodside

The Cooler ★★★★15

Romantic drama 2002 · US · Colour · 97min

Is luck a product of fate or psychology? That's the question posed by director Wayne Kramer's wonderfully quirky film in which unlucky William H Macy is employed by casino manager Alec Baldwin to make high rollers to lose, simply by his presence. But when he falls in love with waitress Maria Bello, Macy's "cooling" abilities subside. By turn a tender love story about two lost souls finding their perfect match, a lament for the fading glamour of Rat Pack-era Las Vegas and a vaguely mystical parable about chance and destiny, this sexually frank tale is consistently smart, amusing and intriguing. AJ Violence, swearing. **DVD**

William H Macy *Bernie Lootz* • Maria Bello *Natalie Belisario* • Alec Baldwin *Shelly Kaplow* • Shawn Hatosy *Mikey* • Ron Livingston *Larry Sokolov* • Paul Sorvino *Buddy Stafford* • Estella Warren *Charlene* • Arthur J Nascarella [Arthur Nascarella] *Nicky "Fingers" Bonnatto* ■ *Dir* Wayne Kramer • *Scr* Frank Hannah, Wayne Kramer

A Cooler Climate ★★★15

Drama 1999 · US · Colour · 95min

Revelling in the opportunity to demonstrate their contrasting acting styles, Sally Field and Judy Davis each earned an Emmy nomination for their work in Susan Seidelman's assertive TV adaptation. Guilty about the affair that ended her 26-year marriage, Field accepts a housekeeping post in Davis's Maine home and soon seeks solace from her employer's fastidious snootiness in the arms of artist Winston Rekert. Seidelman refuses to succumb to touchy-feely platitudes and keeps the tone bullish, while steering her divas away from overt scene stealing. DP

Judy Davis *Paula* • Sally Field *Iris* • Winston Rekert *Jack* • Jerry Wasserman *Leo* • Carly Pope *Beth* ■ *Dir* Susan Seidelman • *Scr* Marsha Norman, from the novel by Zena Collier

Cooperstown ★★★★

Sports drama 1993 · US · Colour · 100min

You don't need to know much about baseball to enjoy the performances of Alan Arkin and Graham Greene in this wisecracking, superior TV movie about memory, friendship and regret. Having never forgiven recently deceased catcher Greene for the play that cost their team a big game, Arkin's forgotten pitcher sets out for the Cooperstown Hall of Fame to set the record straight. Beautifully written by playwright Lee Blessing, the banter between Arkin and Greene is as sharp as it's priceless. DP

Alan Arkin *Harry Willette* • Ed Begley Jr *Dave Cormeer* • Josh Charles *Jody* • Paul Dooley *Sid Wiggins* • Graham Greene (2) *Raymond Maracle* • Charles Haid *Little Eddie McVee* ■ *Dir* Charles Haid • *Scr* Lee Blessing

Cooties ★★★15

Comedy horror 2014 · US · Colour · 84min

Just about what you'd expect from the writers of *Glee* and *Saw*, this comedy horror plays agreeably fast and loose with its twisted gags and bad taste gore. Chicken nuggets made from tainted meat infect an elementary school's cafeteria, transforming the kids into cannibal zombies. It's up to wannabe novelist/substitute teacher Elijah Wood to lead the oddball faculty to safety. Sadly, co-directors Jonathan Milott and Cary Murnion lose their imaginative grip halfway and this unabashed colourful

fantasy turns distinctly lukewarm. AJ Violence, swearing, drug abuse. **DVD** **Blu**

Elijah Wood *Clint* • Rainn Wilson *Wade* • Alison Pill *Lucy* • Jack McBrayer *Tracy* • Leigh Whannell *Doug* ■ *Dir* Jonathan Milott, Cary Murnion • *Scr* Ian Brennan, Leigh Whannell, from a story by Josh C Waller

Le Cop ★★★★18

Comedy 1985 · Fr · Colour · 102min

The wonderful Philippe Noiret is the French equivalent to Walter Matthau or an over-lunched great dane. Here he stars as a Parisian cop who lives with a tart in Montmartre, bets on the gee-gees, readily accepts bribes and buys lavish meals with the ill-gotten gains. More small-time crook than cop, in fact, especially when he inducts his rookie partner Thierry Lhermitte into the joys of crime. Noiret makes this skate along the moral edge, a balancing act to marvel at. AT French +subtitles.

Philippe Noiret *René* • Thierry Lhermitte *François* • Régine *Simone* • Grace De Capitani *Natacha* • Julien Guiomar *Bloret* • Pierre Frag *Pierrot* • Claude Brosset *Inspector Vidal* • Albert Simono *Inspector LeBlanc* ■ *Dir* Claude Zidi • *Scr* Claude Zidi, Didier Kaminka

Le Cop II ★★★15

Comedy drama 1989 · Fr · Colour · 102min

Claude Zidi's *Le Cop* was a huge hit in France, so sequel was inevitable. Philippe Noiret and Thierry Lhermitte reprise their roles as the dirty cop and his idealistic young apprentice. The story revolves around the latter's decision to go straight – an appalling prospect for his partner, who takes bribes and drugs race horses. Once again the low life of Paris is beautifully observed. In 2003, Zidi made a belated second sequel, *Part-Time Cop*. AT French +subtitles.

Philippe Noiret *René* • Thierry Lhermitte *François* • Guy Marchand *Felix Brisson* • Line Renaud *Simone* • Grace De Capitani *Natacha* • Michel Aumont *Commissioner Bloret* • Jean-Pierre Castaldi *Guy Portal* • Jean-Claude Brialy *Banker* ■ *Dir* Claude Zidi • *Scr* Claude Zidi, Simon Michael, Didier Kaminka

Cop ★★★★18

Crime thriller 1988 · US · Colour · 105min

James Woods gives a dazzling performance here and lifts what could have been merely another variation on the *Dirty Harry* theme into a different league altogether. Woods plays an obsessive homicide detective, bordering on the psychotic, who becomes convinced there is a serial killer on the loose in Los Angeles. The only common link appears to be feminist book shop manager Lesley Ann Warren. Director James B Harris fails to capture the twisted sickness of James Ellroy's source novel, but more than compensates by cranking up the tension. JF Swearing, violence, sex scenes, nudity. **DVD**

James Woods *Lloyd Hopkins* • Lesley Ann Warren *Kathleen McCarthy* • Charles Durning *Dutch Pelz* • Charles Haid *Whitey Haines* • Raymond J Barry *Fred Gaffney* • Randi Brooks *Joanie Pratt* • Steven Lambert *Bobby Franco* • Christopher Wynne *Jack Gibbs* ■ *Dir* James B Harris • *Scr* James B Harris, from the novel *Blood on the Moon* by James Ellroy

Cop and a Half ★PG

Comedy thriller 1993 · US · Colour · 88min

This feeble comedy thriller is the perfect yardstick for measuring just how far Burt Reynolds had fallen from grace since his peak in the 1970s. It wastes the talents of a star normally at ease with such frivolity, and the efforts of the rest of the cast are sunk by a heavy script and ponderous direction from former *Happy Days* star Henry Winkler. JM Swearing, violence. **DVD**

Burt Reynolds *Nick McKenna* • Norman D Golden II *Devon Butler* • Ruby Dee *Rachel* • Holland Taylor *Captain Rubio* • Ray Sharkey *Fountain* • Sammy Hernandez *Raymond* • Frank Sivero *Chu* • Rocky Giordani *Quintero* ■ *Dir* Henry Winkler • *Scr* Arne Olsen

Cop au Vin ★★★★15

Drama 1984 · Fr · Colour · 104min

There's usually a slap-up meal in every Claude Chabrol movie, so how typical of him to name one after a cornerstone of French cuisine, *Poulet au Vinaigre*, but the English title is even wittier. The story involves a contentious property deal, a clutch of corpses, a postman and his crippled mother, played by Stéphane Audran. Yet the movie is dominated by Jean Poiret, who is an out-of-town detective with a nose for a suspect and the stomach for a big dinner. As ever, the combination of Chabrol's mordant tone and a certain technical flair produces a delectable dish. A sequel, *Inspector Lavardin* followed in 1986. AT French +subtitles. **DVD**

Jean Poiret *Inspector Lavardin* • Stéphane Audran *Mme Cuno* • Michel Bouquet *Hubert Lavoisier* • Jean Topart *Philippe Morasseau* • Lucas Belvaux *Louis Cuno* • Pauline Lafont *Henriette Uriel* ■ *Dir* Claude Chabrol • *Scr* Dominique Roulet, Claude Chabrol, from the novel *Une Mort en Trop* by Dominique Roulet

Cop Car ★★★★15

Thriller 2015 · US · Colour · 84min

Two runaway boys find an abandoned police car, quickly figure out how to drive it, and are soon kangaroo-ing down empty Colorado backroads, unaware that its corrupt cop driver wants it back...with extreme prejudice. Here's a high-concept B-movie of real distinction, the sheer guile of this malign cop – another great bad-guy role for Kevin Bacon – contrasting beautifully with the innocence of the boys. One scene with a defibrillator is so gripping, you might need one yourself. SvM Violence, swearing, drug abuse. **DVD**

Kevin Bacon *Sheriff Kretzer* • James Freedson-Jackson *Travis* • Hays Wellford *Harrison* • Kyra Sedgwick *Dispatch* ■ *Dir* Jon Watts • *Scr* Jon Watts, Christopher D Ford

Cop Land ★★★★18

Police drama 1997 · US · Colour · 110min

This is a real change of pace for Sylvester Stallone, in a touching role as an out-of-shape New Jersey cop with a hearing disability and no self-esteem, who uncovers police corruption among his friends. Stallone gives it his all (including a dramatic weight gain for the role) and is easily the match of the terrific cast, which includes Robert De Niro, Harvey Keitel and a really nasty Ray Liotta. Writer/director James Mangold's urban western succumbs to a few clumsy contrivances, but the quality of acting and a riveting climax are recommendation enough. JC Swearing, violence, nudity. **DVD** **Blu**

Sylvester Stallone *Sheriff Freddy Heflin* • Robert De Niro *Moe Tilden* • Harvey Keitel *Ray Donlan* • Ray Liotta *Gary Figgis* • Peter Berg *Joey Randone* • Janeane Garofalo *Deputy Cindy Betts* • Robert Patrick *Jack Rucker* • Michael Rapaport *Murray Babitch* • Annabella Sciorra *Liz Randone* • Cathy Moriarty *Rose Donlan* ■ *Dir/Scr* James Mangold

Cop Out ★★15

Comedy 2010 · US · Colour · 103min

Bruce Willis and stand-up comedian Tracy Morgan buddy up as New York police detectives for this 1980s-inspired cop movie. The sketchy plot sees Willis's veteran Jimmy Monroe caught up in the pursuit of a valuable baseball card that could pay for his daughter's wedding. This is supposed to make us care, but only emphasises the silly macho mindset that has Monroe pitted against his ex-wife's new husband (Jason Lee). It's a surprising change of pace for director Kevin Smith; more frantic than the bawdy, dialogue-led comedies he's known for and lacking in the trademark irony. Like Willis, the formula just comes across as old and tired. SP Violence, swearing, sexual references. **DVD** **Blu**

Bruce Willis *Jimmy Monroe* • Tracy Morgan *Paul Hodges* • Adam Brody *Mangold* • Kevin Pollak *Hunsaker* • Ana de la Reguera *Gabriela* • Guillermo Diaz *Poh Boy* • Michelle Trachtenberg

Ava • Seann William Scott *Dave* • Jason Lee *Roy* ■ *Dir* Kevin Smith (2) • *Scr* Mark Cullen, Robb Cullen

Copacabana ★U

Musical comedy 1947 · US · BW · 91min

A staggeringly unscintillating pairing of two stars whose careers were all behind them: the great Groucho Marx and Carmen Miranda, who has difficulty accommodating her usual headgear on this cheapie's pathetic budget. Unless you're a fan of the stars, this turkey's a non-starter. TS

Groucho Marx *Lionel Q Devereaux* • Carmen Miranda *Carmen Navarro/Fifi* • Steve Cochran *Steve Hunt* • Gloria Jean *Anne* • Ralph Sanford *Liggett* • Andy Russell ■ *Dir* Alfred E Green • *Scr* Laslo Vadnay, Alan Boretz, Howard Harris, Sydney P Zelinka, from a story by Laslo Vadnay

Copper Canyon ★★★U

Western 1950 · US · Colour · 83min

1940s beauty Hedy Lamarr had just made something of a comeback in the blockbuster *Samson and Delilah* when Paramount put her in this intriguing western, set just after the Civil War and directed by John Farrow. Beautiful colour photography by Oscar-winning Charles Lang enhances the action, while Ray Milland is well cast as a Confederate officer working undercover to foil crooks out to exploit festering north-south antagonisms. TV

Ray Milland *Johnny Carter* • Hedy Lamarr *Lisa Roselle* • Macdonald Carey *Lane Travis* • Mona Freeman *Caroline Desmond* • Harry Carey Jr *Lt Ord* • Frank Faylen *Mullins* ■ *Dir* John Farrow • *Scr* Jonathan Latimer, from a story by Richard English

Cops and Robbers ★★★

Crime caper 1973 · US · Colour · 88min

This rattling crime caper is taken at such a lick by director Aram Avakian that you don't notice the inconsistencies and contrivances in the plot. Cliff Gorman and Joseph Bologna give winning performances as a couple of New York cops who use a parade for returning astronauts as cover for an audacious Wall Street raid. The frantic action is given extra zip by the splendid score. DP

Cliff Gorman *Tom* • Joseph Bologna *Joe* • Dick Ward [Richard Ward] *Paul Jones* • Shepperd Strudwick *Eastpoole* • Ellen Holly *Mrs Wells* • John Ryan [John P Ryan] *Patsy O'Neill* • Nino Ruggeri *Mr Joe* ■ *Dir* Aram Avakian • *Scr* Donald E Westlake, from his novel

Cops and Robbersons ★★PG

Comedy 1994 · US · Colour · 88min

Jack Palance is the grouchy cop on surveillance duty, who is forced to move in with dysfunctional suburbanites the Robbersons, headed up by TV cop-show fan Chevy Chase. Chase, in amiable buffoon mode, makes a nice foil for Palance and there are creditable supporting turns from Robert Davi and Dianne Wiest, but director Michael Ritchie's heart doesn't appear to be in it. JF

Chevy Chase *Norman Robberson* • Jack Palance *Jack Stone* • Dianne Wiest *Helen Robberson* • Robert Davi *David Barry Gray Tony Moore* • Jason James Richter *Kevin Robberson* • Fay Masterson *Cindy Robberson* ■ *Dir* Michael Ritchie • *Scr* Bernie Somers

Copycat ★★★★18

Suspense thriller 1995 · US · Colour · 122min

In this inventive, stylish and gripping thriller, tough detective Holly Hunter teams up with agoraphobic criminal psychologist Sigourney Weaver in the hunt for a serial killer duplicating the crimes of his most notorious predecessors. Thanks to the unbearable suspense created by Jon Amiel's imaginative direction – the bathroom-set climax is a crackerjack shocker – the super-smart script and the confident performances of the two stellar leads, this mimic murder mystery is one of the best crafted chillers of the 1990s. AJ Swearing, violence. **DVD**

Sigourney Weaver *Helen Hudson* • Holly Hunter *MJ Monahan* • Dermot Mulroney *Ruben Goetz* • William McNamara *Peter Foley* • Harry Connick

Jr *Daryll Lee Cullum* • Will Patton *Nicoletti* • John Rothman *Andy* • Shannon O'Hurley *Susan Schiffer* ■ *Dir* Jon Amiel • *Scr* Ann Biderman, David Madsen

Copying Beethoven ★★★ 12
Period romantic drama
2006 • Ger/UK/Hun/US • Colour • 111min
Director Agnieszka Holland's handsome take on composer Ludwig van Beethoven's final years feels surprisingly authentic. Ed Harris's Beethoven is a witty yet cruel egocentric, tormenting young, female copyist and aspiring composer Anna Holtz (a strong Diane Kruger) after he employs her to transcribe his latest work. Though the film's plodding remainder never matches the high point of Beethoven conducting his Ninth Symphony, there's still enough creative energy to keep events engaging, while Holland's eye for detail helps distract from the continual bending of the truth. SF *DVD* *SL*

Ed Harris *Ludwig van Beethoven* • Diane Kruger *Anna Holtz* • Matthew Goode *Martin Bauer* • Ralph Riach *Wenzel Schlemmer* • Phyllida Law *Mother Canisius* • Joe Anderson (1) *Karl van Beethoven* • Angus Barnett *Krenski* ■ *Dir* Agnieszka Holland • *Scr* Stephen J Rivele, Christopher Wilkinson • *Cinematographer* Ashley Rowe

Coquette ★★★
Melodrama
1929 • US • BW • 75min
Back in the silent era, Mary Pickford's little-girl mannerisms earned her the title of "The World's Sweetheart". This was her first talkie, in which she plays a southern belle whose flirtation with handsome beau Johnny Mack Brown gets her into big trouble. Pickford won an Oscar for the film, though it was really in recognition of her previous work; the public weren't quite ready to see her as a Deep South damsel. TH

Mary Pickford *Norma Besant* • Johnny Mack Brown *Michael Jeffery* • Matt Moore *Stanley Wentworth* • John St Polis *Dr John Besant* ■ *Dir* Sam Taylor • *Scr* Sam Taylor, John Grey, Allen McNeil, from the play by George Abbott, Anne P Bridges

Coraline ★★★★ PG
Animated fantasy
2008 • US • Colour • 96min
Henry Selick's stop-motion animation version of Neil Gaiman's celebrated children's book is just as darkly original as the director's earlier feature *The Nightmare before Christmas*. Here, stuck in dreary rural Oregon, 11-year-old Coraline (voiced by Dakota Fanning) discovers a parallel world that offers more thrills and surprises than her own seemingly dull life. However, her near-perfect "Other Mother" (a deliciously wicked pantomime turn by Teri Hatcher) has a hidden agenda. The sinister plot, coupled with the eye-popping set design, makes for a menacing universe that provides excitement and thrills, but maybe a little too intense for younger viewers used to more sanitised fare. TeS *DVD* *Blu-ray* *3D*

Dakota Fanning *Coraline Jones* • Teri Hatcher *Mother/Other Mother* • Jennifer Saunders *Miss Spink* • Dawn French *Miss Forcible* • Keith David *Cat* • John Hodgman *Father/Other Father* • Robert Bailey Jr *Wybie Lovat* • Ian McShane *Mr Bobinsky* ■ *Dir* Henry Selick • *Scr* Henry Selick, from the novel by Neil Gaiman

The Core ★★★ 12
Science-fiction action thriller
2002 • US/UK • Colour • 129min
Having exhausted the more traditional threats to human existence, the Hollywood disaster movie now moves on to positively esoteric cataclysms: in this case the Earth's core ceasing to rotate. While international landmarks explode and surface-dwellers face terminal sunburn, a secret team of top scientists builds a burrowing machine designed to penetrate the core and set it spinning again. This is by-the-numbers movie-making, but it has enough excitingly staged set pieces to offset the daft plot. AS *DVD* *Blu-ray*

Aaron Eckhart *Dr Josh Keyes* • Hilary Swank *Major Rebecca "Beck" Childs* • Delroy Lindo *Dr Ed "Braz" Brazzelton* • Stanley Tucci *Dr Conrad*

Zimsky • DJ Qualls *Taz "Rat" Finch* • Richard Jenkins *Gen Thomas Purcell* • Tcheky Karyo *Dr Serge Leveque* • Bruce Greenwood *Commander Robert Iverson* • Alfre Woodard *Dr Talma "Stick" Stickley* ■ *Dir* Jon Amiel • *Scr* Cooper Layne, John Rogers

Coriolanus ★★★ 15
Political drama
2010 • UK • Colour • 122min
Ralph Fiennes makes a strong directorial debut with this full-blooded contemporary restaging of Shakespeare's Roman tragedy set in a conflict-ravaged city (it was shot in Belgrade, Serbia). Having previously played the title role on stage, a brooding, sinewy, imperious Fiennes sports shaven head and military fatigues as the wartime general who seeks political office, is forced into exile and grows "from man to dragon". While Gerard Butler is less convincing as his blood enemy and Vanessa Redgrave occasionally overcooked as his controlling mother, Brian Cox strikes the right tone as an influential senator and Jessica Chastain brings a tenderness to Fiennes's spouse. AC Violence. *DVD* *Blu-ray*

Ralph Fiennes *Caius Martius, "Coriolanus"* • Gerard Butler *Tullus Aufidius* • Brian Cox (1) *Menenius* • Vanessa Redgrave *Volumnia* • Jessica Chastain *Virgilia* • John Kani *General Cominius* ■ *Dir* Ralph Fiennes • *Scr* John Logan, from the play by William Shakespeare

Corky ★ U
Drama
1972 • US • Colour • 88min
Robert Blake, a grease monkey from the Deep South who is more in love with his car than his long-suffering wife (Charlotte Rampling), becomes insanely jealous when she gets a job. There's a fight here and a car chase there, but no drama. Bruce Geller was so incensed at the way his central character was treated that he had his screenwriting credit removed, though he was still billed as producer. FL

Robert Blake *Corky* • Charlotte Rampling *Corky's wife* • Patrick O'Neal (1) *Randy* • Christopher Connelly *Billy* • Pamela Payton-Wright *Rhonda* • Ben Johnson (1) *Boland* ■ *Dir* Leonard Horn • *Scr* Eugene Price, Bruce Geller (uncredited)

Corky Romano ★ 12
Comedy
2001 • US • Colour • 82min
In this is a lazy, lame Mob comedy, Chris Kattan plays the forgotten son of Mob boss Peter Falk, who is asked to infiltrate the FBI to retrieve some damning evidence against the family. Despite his persistent bungling he soon becomes regarded as a super-agent and finds his loyalties divided. Kattan mugs his way through the feeble slapstick set pieces and the talented supporting cast tries not to look embarrassed. JF *DVD*

Chris Kattan *Corky Romano* • Vinessa Shaw *Agent Kate Russo* • Peter Falk *Pops* • Peter Berg *Paulie* • Chris Penn *Peter* • Fred Ward *Leo Corrigan* • Richard Roundtree *Howard Schuster* ■ *Dir* Rob Pritts • *Scr* David Garrett, Jason Ward

Corman's World: Exploits of a Hollywood Rebel
★★★★ 15
Documentary
2011 • US • Colour • 86min
"Very polite, almost British." "Hip, cool." These are just a few of the observations uttered about producer/director Roger Corman, the doyen of low-budget independent cinema and the engaging subject of this terrific documentary. It charts his six decade-long career from creature feature *Monster from the Ocean Floor* (1954), via his opulent Edgar Allan Poe adaptations, through to cult LSD drama *The Trip* in the 1960s. In the 70s the focus turns to violent exploitation flicks such as *Death Race 2000* and the film then follows Corman's singular career all the way up to 2010 monster mash-up *Dinoshark*. The archive material and priceless anecdotes are a treat, but it's the quality of the interviewees (whose careers he often kick-started) that makes the film such a joy. Among them, Martin Scorsese, an unusually cheerful Robert De Niro, Ron Howard and Jack Nicholson at his most effusive (and emotional) are great value. JA *DVD* *Blu-ray*

Roger Corman • Martin Scorsese • Quentin Tarantino • Robert De Niro • Jack Nicholson • Peter Fonda • Peter Bogdanovich • Ron Howard ■ *Dir* Alex Stapleton

The Corn Is Green ★★★
Period drama
1945 • US • BW • 113min
Bette Davis stars as spinster schoolteacher Lilly Moffat in a very Warner Bros version of Emlyn Williams's distinguished play. Unfortunately, this film seriously betrays its theatrical origins, not just in its hokey plot about Davis trying to send her star pupil (John Dall, far too callow) to Oxford, but also in its relentlessly phoney Hollywood studio/Welsh village setting. Nevertheless, Davis is mighty fine and the supporting cast is excellent, particularly Nigel Bruce as the local squire. TS

Bette Davis *Lilly Moffat* • John Dall *Morgan Evans* • Joan Lorring *Bessie Watty* • Nigel Bruce *Squire* • Rhys Williams *Mr Jones* • Rosalind Ivan *Mrs Watty* • Mildred Dunnock *Miss Ronberry* • Arthur Shields *Will Davis* ■ *Dir* Irving Rapper • *Scr* Casey Robinson, Frank Cavett, from the play by Emlyn Williams

Cornered ★★★
Crime drama
1945 • US • BW • 102min
This is a pleasant little toughie, not quite a thriller and a shade too bright for a *film noir*, and directed with consummate skill by Edward Dmytryk. Dick Powell delivers a high-octane performance, chasing down his wife's murderer in Second World War Argentina, in a Buenos Aires peopled with veteran character actors. The women are a shade uninteresting, but Powell's tough demeanour more than compensates. TS

Dick Powell *Gerard* • Walter Slezak *Incza* • Micheline Cheirel *Madame Jarnac* • Nina Vale *Senora Camargo* • Edgar Barrier *DuBois* • Morris Carnovsky *Santana* • Steven Geray *Senor Camargo* • Jack La Rue [Jack LaRue] *Diego* ■ *Dir* Edward Dmytryk • *Scr* John Paxton, from a story by John Wexley, from a title by Ben Hecht

Coroner Creek ★★ U
Western
1948 • US • Colour • 89min
Randolph Scott is out for revenge in this no-nonsense western from Ray Enright, one of seven they worked on together. When Scott's bride-to-be dies in a stagecoach raid, he begins a search for the man behind the robbery (George Macready), who has started his own ranch with his ill-gotten gains. The veteran cast can't rise above the stodgy script. SF

Randolph Scott *Chris Danning* • Marguerite Chapman *Kate Hardison* • George Macready *Younger Miles* • Sally Eilers *Della Harms* • Edgar Buchanan *Sheriff O'Hea* • Barbara Reed [Barbara Read] *Abbie Miles* • Wallace Ford *Andy West* • Forrest Tucker *Ernie Combs* ■ *Dir* Ray Enright • *Scr* Kenneth Gamet, from the novel by Luke Short

The Corporation ★★★★ PG
Documentary
2003 • Can • Colour • 144min
Mark Achbar and Jennifer Abbott's epic documentary tackles everything from the constitutional protection afforded American companies to the bullying tactics of multinationals and the "nag factor" built into children's television advertising. With executives from the likes of Shell and Goodyear so willing to shoot themselves in the foot, the eloquence of Noam Chomsky, Naomi Klein and Michael Moore is almost redundant. The corruption, exploitation and eco-ignorance of big business has never been so damningly exposed. DP *DVD*

■ *Dir* Mark Achbar, Jennifer Abbott • *Scr* Joel Bakan, Harold Crooks (narration), Mark Achbar (narration), from the non-fiction book *The Corporation: the Pathological Pursuit of Profit and Power* by Joel Bakan

The Corpse ★★★★
Horror
1969 • UK • Colour • 93min
In this effectively spooky thriller, a tyrannical stockbroker (Michael Gough at his beastliest) torments his wife and daughter to such a degree that they decide to murder him. Those who have seen *Les Diaboliques* will recognise the remainder of the plot. Writer Olaf Pooley (who also plays

a nosey neighbour) does not play fair when it comes to the explanation, but director Viktors Ritelis wrings such tension out of every shocking development that one is prepared to forgive the underhandedness. DM

Michael Gough *Walter Eastwood* • Yvonne Mitchell *Edith Eastwood* • Sharon Gurney *Jane Eastwood* • Simon Gough *Rupert Eastwood* • Olaf Pooley *Reid* • David Butler *Gregson* • Mary Hignett *Mrs Roberts* ■ *Dir* Viktors Ritelis • *Scr* Olaf Pooley

Corridors of Blood ★★★ 15
Horror drama
1962 • UK • BW • 83min
Surgeon Boris Karloff is forced to sign false death certificates when he gets involved with two loathsome grave robbers (Christopher Lee and Francis de Wolff) during his work on an experimental anaesthetic. Boasting beautiful black-and-white photography, this 19th-century-set tale has a great combination of gas-lit melodrama, pseudo-historic science and body-snatcher gruesomeness. It also marked the first time Karloff and Lee worked together. AJ *DVD*

Boris Karloff *Dr Bolton* • Betta St John *Susan* • Christopher Lee *Resurrection Joe* • Finlay Currie *Supt Matheson* • Adrienne Corri *Rachel* ■ *Dir* Robert Day • *Scr* Jean Scott Rogers • *Cinematographer* Geoffrey Faithfull

Corrina, Corrina ★★★ U
Romantic drama
1994 • US • Colour • 110min
Ray Liotta here provides the single-parent contrivance that enables housekeeper Whoopi Goldberg to bond with Tina Majorino, a sad little seven-year-old who has stopped speaking since the death of her mother. Goldberg and Majorino make one of the most appealing double acts of recent years. As the action is set in 1959, there are also some barbed comments about interracial love and the obstacles facing educated black women. DP *DVD*

Whoopi Goldberg *Corrina Washington* • Ray Liotta *Manny Singer* • Tina Majorino *Molly Singer* • Wendy Crewson *Jenny Davis* • Larry Miller *Sid* • Erica Yohn *Grandma Eva* • Jenifer Lewis *Jevina* • Joan Cusack *Jonesy* • Harold Sylvester *Frank* • Don Ameche *Grandpa Harry* ■ *Dir/Scr* Jessie Nelson

The Corrupt Ones ★★★
Thriller
1966 • Fr/It/W Ger • Colour • 92min
This old-fashioned quest adventure is so sexist and racially dismissive that it wouldn't pass muster today. But, back in the mid-1960s, two-fisted mavericks were all the rage and Robert Stack's gung-ho photographer is presented with an ancient Chinese medallion containing clues to the location of an emperor's treasure trove. Elke Sommer has less to do as his pouting sidekick, but the action is pacey and slickly staged. DP

Robert Stack *Cliff Wilder* • Elke Sommer *Lily Mancini* • Nancy Kwan *Tina* • Christian Marquand *Joey Brandon* • Maurizio Arena *Danny Mancini* ■ *Dir* James Hill • *Scr* Brian Clemens

Corruption ★★★
Horror
1968 • UK • Colour • 90min
Unanimously slated by the press as cheap and nasty when it was first shown, this horrific thriller is actually a minor masterpiece of *Grand Guignol* and underrated director Robert Hartford-Davis's best film by far. It stars Peter Cushing as a surgeon, who goes to desperate lengths to get the pituitary glands he needs to restore fiancée Sue Lloyd's disfigured face. Cushing and Lloyd both throw themselves into their roles with gusto and are aided by a fast-moving script. Released in other countries as *Laser Killer*, though with more graphic material, the final scene remains one of the most demented ever filmed. DM

Peter Cushing *Sir John Rowan* • Sue Lloyd *Lynn Nolan* • Trevor Trevarthen *Steve Harris* • Kate O'Mara *Val Nolan* • David Lodge *Groper* • Anthony Booth *Mike Orme* ■ *Dir* Robert Hartford-Davis • *Scr* Donald Ford, Derek Ford

The Corruptor ★★ 18

Action crime thriller 1999 · US · Colour · 105min

With muscle man Mark Wahlberg and cool Hong Kong star Chow Yun-Fat on board, you'd expect this tale of police corruption, Chinese gangs and murder in New York's Chinatown to be action-packed. Instead, this is a surprisingly plodding and confusing thriller that's low on interesting set pieces. Both stars have charisma to spare, but they're bogged down by the unnecessarily convoluted plot. JB Violence. **DVD**

Chow Yun-Fat *Nick Chen* · Mark Wahlberg *Danny Wallace* · Ric Young *Henry Lee* · Paul Ben-Victor *Schabacker* · Andrew Pang *Willy Ung* · Byron Mann *Bobby Vu* · Elizabeth Lindsey *Louise Deng* · Brian Cox (1) *Sean Wallace* ■ *Dir* James Foley · *Scr* Robert Pucci

The Corsican Brothers ★★★ U

Swashbuckling adventure
1941 · US · BW · 95min

Douglas Fairbanks Jr summons up some of the swashbuckling bravado associated with his father in this adaptation of the Alexandre Dumas story. Fairbanks gets the dual role of separated Siamese twins, Mario and Lucien - one rich, the other poor - who reunite to seek out those who killed their relatives. It dawdles in places, Akim Tamiroff is more laughable than villainous and it lacks a proper heroine. Yet Fairbanks is worth watching, if only for his imitation of his father's mannerisms. AT

Douglas Fairbanks Jr *Mario Franchi/Lucien Franchi* · Ruth Warrick *Isabelle* · Akim Tamiroff *Colorra* · HB Warner *Dr Paoli* · Henry Wilcoxon *Count Franchi* · J Carrol Naish *Lorenzo* ■ *Dir* Gregory Ratoff · *Scr* George Bruce, from the novel by Alexandre Dumas

Corvette K-225 ★★ U

Second World War drama
1943 · US · BW · 98min

This wartime flag-waver is an unabashed tribute to the crews of the Corvettes, the nimble craft that escorted freighters across the Atlantic, taking on the U-boats that preyed on them. Randolph Scott is the skipper who falls in love with Ella Raines, whose brother is on Scott's ship and whose other brother has already been killed in action. Below decks, Robert Mitchum takes a minor role in one of the 18 movies he made in 1943. AT

Randolph Scott *Lt Cmdr MacClain* · James Brown (1) *Paul Cartwright* · Ella Raines *Joyce Cartwright* · Barry Fitzgerald *Stooky O'Meara* · Andy Devine *Walsh* · Walter Sande *Evans* · Richard Lane *Admiral* · James Flavin *Gardner* · Robert Mitchum *Shepard* ■ *Dir* Richard Rosson · *Scr* John Rhodes Sturdy

Corvette Summer ★★★

Comedy adventure drama
1978 · US · Colour · 104min

The directing debut of Matthew Robbins is a youth movie very much in the mould of *American Graffiti*. Mark Hamill, then fresh from the original *Star Wars*, stars as a young man who spends most of his time fondling, stroking and polishing the love of his life: a restored and customised Chevrolet Corvette. When the car is stolen, Hamill goes looking for it with the help of trainee prostitute Annie Potts. Robbins's directing career proved to be fairly undistinguished after this promising first feature. AT

Mark Hamill *Kent Dantley* · Annie Potts *Vanessa* · Eugene Roche *Ed McGrath* · Kim Milford *Wayne Lowry* · Richard McKenzie *Principal* · William Bryant *Police PR* · Philip Bruns *Gil* ■ *Dir* Matthew Robbins · *Scr* Hal Barwood, Matthew Robbins

Cosh Boy ★★★

Crime drama 1952 · UK · BW · 72min

Packed with incidents that scandalised middle-class moralists, Lewis Gilbert's film claimed to be a realistic portrait of juvenile delinquency. It may have seemed daring at the time, but today this overwrought study of alienation and rebellion looks tame and stands only as a testament to an innocent age when people were more easily shocked. James Kenney seems the most gentle thug

ever to terrorise the streets of London, but Joan Collins comes closer to life as the nice girl doomed to a life of misery. DP

James Kenney *Roy Walsh* · Joan Collins *Rene Collins* · Betty Ann Davies *Elsie Walsh* · Robert Ayres *Bob Stevens* · Hermione Baddeley *Mrs Collins* · Hermione Gingold *Queenie* · Nancy Roberts *Gran Walsh* · Stanley Escane *Pete* ■ *Dir* Lewis Gilbert · *Scr* Lewis Gilbert, Vernon Harris, from the play *Master Crook* by Bruce Walker

Cosi ★★★

Comedy 1996 · Aus · Colour · 100min

Slacker Ben Mendelsohn takes a job as dramatic director at a mental hospital in this typically broad Australian comedy. One of the inmates is obsessed with staging the Mozart opera *Cosi Fan Tutte*, which Mendelsohn directs against all the odds and the wishes of the hospital's administrators. Mark Joffe's film is quite funny most of the way through, but it veers into cheap sentimentality towards the end. ST Swearing.

Ben Mendelsohn *Lewis* · Barry Otto *Roy* · Toni Collette *Julie* · Aden Young *Nick* · Rachel Griffiths *Lucy* · Pamela Rabe *Ruth* · Colin Friels *Errol* ■ *Dir* Mark Joffe · *Scr* Louis Nowra, from his play

The Cosmic Man ★ U

Science-fiction drama 1959 · US · BW · 69min

John Carradine is the mysterious creature from another planet who arrives on Earth in a huge weightless globe. His presence unleashes a debate between the military authorities who want to blow him up, and the scientific establishment who want to keep him alive. This dismal science-fiction programme filler is mercifully short in length and equally short of action and ideas. RK

Bruce Bennett *Dr Karl Sorenson* · John Carradine *Cosmic man* · Angela Greene *Kathy Grant* · Paul Langton *Colonel Mathews* · Scotty Morrow *Ken Grant* · Lyn Osborn *Sergeant Gray* · Walter Maslow *Dr Richie* ■ *Dir* Herbert Greene · *Scr* Arthur C Pierce

Cosmopolis ★★ 15

Drama 2012 · Fr/Can/Por/It · Colour · 104min

Don DeLillo's novel dissecting the American Dream comes to the screen in a highbrow intellectual exercise, too faithfully adapted by director David Cronenberg. Expressionless Robert Pattinson is the financial whizzkid who must watch his empire crumble over the course of one day in Manhattan, and finds momentary distraction in sexual encounters with three women. It's a good-looking movie, but the immersion in the psychosis of cyber-capitalism soon becomes boring, despite the supporting presence of Juliette Binoche, Mathieu Amalric and Paul Giamatti. AJ Violence, swearing, sex scenes, nudity. **DVD** **Blu**

Robert Pattinson *Eric Packer* · Juliette Binoche *Didi Fancher* · Sarah Gadon *Elise Shifrin* · Mathieu Amalric *Andre Petrescu* · Jay Baruchel *Shiner* · Kevin Durand *Torval* · Paul Giamatti *Benno Levin* ■ *Dir* David Cronenberg · *Scr* David Cronenberg, from Don DeLillo's novel

The Cottage ★★ 18

Black comedy horror
2008 · UK · Colour · 87min

Films walk a fine line when they blend horror with humour. Features like *Shaun of the Dead* manage it successfully. Unfortunately, *The Cottage* does not. In the second film from director Paul Andrew Williams, Andy Serkis and Reece Shearsmith play the comically inept crooks who hold gangster's daughter Jennifer Ellison to ransom in a remote country cottage. However, also in the vicinity is a maniac farmer who looks like an axe-wielding refugee from *The Texas Chain Saw Massacre*. Williams's debut was the highly regarded crime drama *London to Brighton*. Yet, despite spirited performances from its principal actors, this coarsely humorous horror will only appeal to more undiscerning genre fans. DA **DVD**

Andy Serkis *David* · Reece Shearsmith *Peter* · Jennifer Ellison *Tracey* · Steve O'Donnell *Andrew* · Doug Bradley *Old man* · Simon Schatzberger *Steven* ■ *Dir/Scr* Paul Andrew Williams

A Cottage on Dartmoor ★★★★ PG

Silent drama 1929 · UK · BW · 87min

Planned as a silent, but released as a part-talkie (the sound discs have since been lost), this has all the expressionist fluidity of late-1920s European cinema. It's a striking visual experience and never less than compelling, even if the story of a barber whose obsession with a manicurist lands him in jail for attempted murder is pure melodrama. Director Anthony Asquith's gliding camera movements, colour tints and intricate montages are testimony to his stylish technique, and the film is rightly regarded as one of the best late-British silents. DP **DVD**

Norah Baring *Sally* · Uno Henning *Joe* · Hans Schlettow *Farmer Harry Stevens* · Judd Green *Customer* ■ *Dir* Anthony Asquith · *Scr* Anthony Asquith, from a story by Herbert C Price

Cottage to Let ★★★ U

Second World War thriller
1941 · UK · BW · 86min

The American release title *Bombsight Stolen* is a clue to what Alfred Hitchcock would call the MacGuffin (or plot device) that drives this lively wartime propaganda piece from director Anthony Asquith. The story of a Nazi kidnap plot in the wilds of Scotland is pretty much par for the course, but what sets this picture apart is the truly extraordinary cast. Michael Wilding and John Mills have to settle for supporting roles behind Leslie Banks and Alastair Sim, but stealing everyone's thunder is debutant George Cole (a protégé of Sim's) as the cockney evacuee who becomes a hero. DP **DVD**

Leslie Banks *John Barrington* · Alastair Sim *Charles Dimble* · John Mills *Lieutenant George Perrey* · Jeanne de Casalis *Mrs Barrington* · Carla Lehmann *Helen Barrington* · George Cole *Ronald Mittsby* · Michael Wilding *Alan Trentley* ■ *Dir* Anthony Asquith · *Scr* Anatole de Grunwald, JOC Orton, from the play by Geoffrey Kerr

The Cotton Club ★★★ 15

Period crime drama 1984 · US · Colour · 123min

Richard Gere gets a chance to reveal his cornet-playing abilities in this tale of music and the Mob in toe-tappin' 1920s Harlem. Sadly, Gere's musical talents far outshine his performance, which seems almost trance-like in places. The blame must lie with director Francis Coppola, who, in expending his energy on visual clout and showbiz set pieces (some of which are fabulous), under-directs his actors and forgets about the plot. JM Violence, swearing, nudity. **DVD**

Richard Gere *Dixie Dwyer* · Gregory Hines *Sandman Williams* · Diane Lane *Vera Cicero* · Bob Hoskins *Owney Madden* · Lonette McKee *Lila Rose Oliver* · James Remar *Dutch Schultz* · Nicolas Cage *Vincent Dwyer* · Allen Garfield *Abbadabba Berman* · Fred Gwynne *Frenchy Demange* · Gwen Verdon *Tish Dwyer* · Larry Fishburne [Laurence Fishburne] *Bumpy Rhodes* ■ *Dir* Francis Coppola [Francis Ford Coppola] · *Scr* William Kennedy, Francis Ford Coppola, from a story by William Kennedy, Francis Ford Coppola, Mario Puzo, from a pictorial history by James Haskins

Cotton Comes to Harlem ★★★★

Crime comedy thriller
1970 · US · Colour · 96min

Although a respected actor and civil rights activist, Ossie Davis put much more than his reputation on the line when he directed this abrasive crime comedy on the streets of Harlem. Residents and militant campaigners alike were appalled that he should choose to further the cause with such a seemingly flippant picture. But the script gives Raymond St Jacques plenty of scope to make social statements as he and Godfrey Cambridge investigate preacher Calvin Lockhart's dodgy pan-African association. A

sequel, *Come Back Charleston Blue*, followed this huge commercial success. DP

Godfrey Cambridge *Gravedigger Jones* · Raymond St Jacques *Coffin Ed Johnson* · Calvin Lockhart *Rev Deke O'Malley* · Judy Pace *Iris* · Redd Foxx *Uncle Bud* · Cleavon Little *Lo Boy* ■ *Dir* Ossie Davis · *Scr* Ossie Davis, Arnold Perl, from a novel by Chester Himes

Cotton Mary ★★ 15

Period drama 1999 · UK · Colour · 118min

This handsomely mounted study of the socio-racial rifts that divided India in the years after Independence proves once again that, while Ismail Merchant is a producer of exemplary taste, his approach to direction stifles potentially interesting ideas with ponderous performances and rarified aestheticism. Co-director Madhur Jaffrey's snobbish Anglo-Indian nurse overwhelms a drama already awash with unsympathetic characters. DP

Greta Scacchi *Lily MacIntosh* · Madhur Jaffrey *Cotton Mary* · James Wilby *John MacIntosh* · Sarah Badel *Mrs Evans* · Riju Bajaj *Mugs* · Gerson Da Cunha *Doctor Correa* · Joanna David *Mrs Smythe* · Neena Gupta *Blossom* ■ *Dir* Ismail Merchant, Madhur Jaffrey · *Scr* Alexandra Viets

Cotton Queen ★★ U

Comedy 1937 · UK · BW · 84min

Long regarded as a mere journeyman, German-born director Bernard Vorhaus has enjoyed something of a renaissance of late. This was the last film he made in this country before relocating to Hollywood, although it's hard to see why the studio executives would have been impressed by this underfunded production, a creaky comedy in which mill owner's daughter Mary Lawson goes snooping into a rival's factory and falls for his son. DP

Will Fyffe *Bob Todcastle* · Stanley Holloway *Sam Owen* · Mary Lawson *Joan* · Helen Haye *Margaret Owen* · Jimmy Hanley *Johnny Owen* · Gibson Gowland *Jailor* ■ *Dir* Bernard Vorhaus · *Scr* Louis Golding, Scott Pembroke, from a story by Syd Courtnenay, Barry Peake

The Couch Trip ★★★ 15

Comedy 1988 · US · Colour · 95min

In this often too slack offering, director Michael Ritchie is thankfully well served by the infectious comic nonsense of Dan Aykroyd, as a mental patient who carries out a nifty scam and becomes a celebrity therapist in LA. It is Aykroyd's wild, high-flying invention that turns this skinny offering into a one-man party at which the star has the most fun. Even Walter Matthau, typically lugubrious and crusty, is dull by comparison. JM Swearing. **DVD**

Dan Aykroyd *John W Burns Jr* · Walter Matthau *Donald Becker* · Charles Grodin *Dr George Maitlin* · Donna Dixon *Dr Laura Rollins* · Richard Romanus *Harvey Michaels* · Mary Gross *Vera Maitlin* · David Clennon *Dr Lawrence Baird* · Arye Gross *Perry Kovin* · Chevy Chase *Condom father* ■ *Dir* Michael Ritchie · *Scr* Steven Kampmann, Will Porter, Sean Stein, from a novel by Ken Kolb

The Counsellor ★★★ 18

Thriller 2013 · US/UK · Colour · 112min

Ridley Scott's curious thriller stars Michael Fassbender as a lawyer who gets his hands dirty in a drug-trafficking deal with shady underworld figures Javier Bardem and Brad Pitt. When a rival organisation hijacks a huge shipment on the US-Mexican border, both Fassbender and his glamorous fiancée Penélope Cruz find their lives in danger. Novelist Cormac McCarthy's first original screenplay is an oblique morality tale of love and greed populated by outlandish characters, while the enigmatic performances and stylistically violent set pieces gloss over a stuttering narrative that only partially delivers. TeS Violence, swearing, sex scenes. **DVD** **Blu**

Michael Fassbender *The Counsellor* · Penélope Cruz *Laura* · Cameron Diaz *Malkina* · Javier Bardem *Reiner* · Brad Pitt *Westray* · Rosie Perez *Ruth* ■ *Dir* Ridley Scott · *Scr* Cormac McCarthy

Counsellor-at-Law ★★★

Drama 1933 · US · BW · 77min

Adapted by Elmer Rice from his own successful Broadway play, and impeccably directed by William Wyler, the movie details the professional and personal crises that beset a brilliant, self-made Jewish lawyer (John Barrymore) whose future is affected by the surfacing of a past indiscretion. Barrymore gives a compelling performance, with excellent support from Doris Kenyon as his unsympathetic Gentile wife and Bebe Daniels as the secretary who loves him. Solid, substantial drama. RK

John Barrymore *George Simon* • Bebe Daniels *Regina Gordon* • Doris Kenyon *Cora Simon* • Onslow Stevens *John P Tedesco* • Isabel Jewell *Bessie Green* • Melvyn Douglas *Roy Darwin* • Thelma Todd *Lillian La Rue* • Marvin Kline *Weinberg* • John Qualen *Breitstein* ■ *Dir* William Wyler • *Scr* Elmer Rice, from his play

Count Dracula ★★⑫

Horror 1970 · Sp/It/W Ger/UK · Colour · 96min

Fed up by Hammer playing fast and loose with the famous vampire figure, Christopher Lee joined forces with Spanish schlock-meister Jesus Franco to make the one of the most faithful adaptations of Bram Stoker's 1897 novel. The end result falls way short of those good intentions thanks to the low budget, numerous script inconsistencies, camera shadows in full view and Franco's usual deadly direction. AJ Violence.

Christopher Lee *Dracula* • Herbert Lom *Van Helsing* • Klaus Kinski *Renfield* • Soledad Miranda *Lucy Westenra* • Maria Rohm *Mina Harker* • Fred Williams *Jonathan Harker* • Jack Taylor *Quincy Morris* • Paul Muller *Dr Seward* ■ *Dir* Jesus Franco • *Scr* Jesus Franco, August Finochi, Harry Alan Towers, Carlo Fadda, Milo G Cuccia, Dietmar Behnke, from the novel *Dracula* by Bram Stoker

Count Five and Die ★★★

Second World War spy drama 1957 · UK · BW · 91min

When plans to peddle false information to the Nazis about the whereabouts of the forthcoming D-Day invasion begin to come unstuck, British intelligence officer Nigel Patrick is made alert to the possibility of their being a traitor in his team. The obvious suspect is glamorous new radio operator Annemarie Düringer, with whom Patrick's second-in-command (Jeffrey Hunter) is in love. Though familiar, this is still suspenseful. RK

Jeffrey Hunter *Ranson* • Nigel Patrick *Howard* • Anne-Marie Düringer [Annemarie Düringer] *Rolande* • David Kossoff *Mulder* • Claude Kingston *Willem* • Philip Bond *Piet* • Rolf Lefebvre *Faber* • Larry Burns *Martins* • Arthur Gross *Jan* ■ *Dir* Victor Vicas • *Scr* Jack Seddon, David Pursall

The Count of Monte Cristo ★★★★

Period adventure 1934 · US · BW · 113min

Although written for Fredric March, who pulled out ahead of filming, Robert Donat stamped his mark as the Napoleonic sailor who is framed and imprisoned in the appalling Chateau d'If, supposedly to languish there for the rest of his days. However, he uses his time wisely, coolly plotting to escape and wreak his revenge on those who betrayed him. This handsomely mounted swashbuckler is the best of the adaptations of Alexandre Dumas's celebrated tale and showcases Donat at his charming, romantic best. AT

Robert Donat *Edmond Dantès* • Elissa Landi *Mercedes* • Louis Calhern *Raymond de Villefort Jr* • Sidney Blackmer *Mondego* • Raymond Walburn *Danglars* • OP Heggie *Abbé Faria* • William Farnum *Captain Leclere* ■ *Dir* Rowland V Lee • *Scr* Philip Dunne, Dan Totheroh, Rowland V Lee, from the novel by Alexandre Dumas

The Count of Monte Cristo ★★★ Ⓤ

Period adventure 1974 · UK · Colour · 98min

Richard Chamberlain is a sturdy Edmond Dantes in this lavish adaptation of the classic Alexandre Dumas tale about the disguised nobleman who exacts revenge on those who had him imprisoned. Director David Greene struggles with the more static jail sequences, but once the action switches to Paris he makes the most of the plush settings to bring the picture to life. Louis Jourdan does well as De Villefort, but Tony Curtis confuses behaving like a star with acting. DP

Richard Chamberlain *Edmond Dantes* • Tony Curtis *Mondego* • Trevor Howard *Abbé Faria* • Louis Jourdan *De Villefort* • Donald Pleasence *Danglars* • Kate Nelligan *Mercedes* ■ *Dir* David Greene • *Scr* Sidney Carroll, from the novel by Alexandre Dumas

The Count of Monte Cristo ★★★ ⑫

Period adventure 2001 · US/UK/Ire · Colour · 125min

Kevin Reynolds's stylistic excesses are mostly absent here, to the benefit of this old-fashioned, handsomely mounted version of the enduring adventure. Jim Caviezel plays Edmond Dantès, who, through the devious scheming of his best friend (Guy Pearce), is thrown into a desolate island prison. But after 13 years of incarceration, he escapes, adopts a dashing new identity and proceeds to exact his revenge. Caviezel is both credible and sympathetic, while Pearce's sneering rogue avoids falling into caricature. JC **DVD**

Jim Caviezel *Edmond Dantès* • Guy Pearce *Fernand Mondego* • Richard Harris *Abbé Faria* • James Frain *Villefort* • Dagmara Dominczyk *Mercedes Iguanada* • Michael Wincott *Dorleac* • Luis Guzman *Jacopo* • Helen McCrory *Valentina Villefort* ■ *Dir* Kevin Reynolds • *Scr* Jay Wolpert, from the novel by Alexandre Dumas

The Count of the Old Town ★★★

Comedy 1935 · Swe · BW · 84min

This film marked Ingrid Bergman's screen debut, although she is pretty much a peripheral character in a freewheeling tour around Stockholm's bohemian quarter. Valdemar Dahlquist topped the bill as the leader of a group of amiable wastrels. Playing a maid in one of their watering holes, Bergman also has some love scenes with Edvin Adolphson, but contemporary critics paid more attention to her puppy fat than her acting. DP Swedish +subtitles.

Valdemar Dahlquist *The Count* • Sigurd Wallen *The Gherkin* • Eric Abrahamsson *Borstis* • Weyler Hildebrand *Detective Goransson* • Artur Cederborgh *Engstrom* • Ingrid Bergman *Elsa Edlund* ■ *Dir* Edvin Adolphson, Sigurd Wallen • *Scr* Arthur Natorp, Siegfried Fischer

Count the Hours ★★

Crime drama 1953 · US · BW · 76min

When an itinerant farm worker is sentenced to death for murder, his wife and a lawyer, who shows more than a passing interest in her, battle to prove his innocence and bring the true culprit to book. MacDonald Carey, Teresa Wright, John Craven and Dolores Moran (as Carey's rich fiancée) star in an efficient directorial exercise for Don Siegel, who maintains the tension in what is essentially no more than a so-so programme filler. RK

Macdonald Carey *Doug Madison* • Teresa Wright *Ellen Braden* • John Craven *George Braden* • Dolores Moran *Paula Mitchener* • Edgar Barrier *Gillespie* • Jack Elam *Max Verne* ■ *Dir* Don Siegel • *Scr* Doane R Hoag, Karen De Wolf, from a story by Doane R Hoag

Count Three and Pray ★★★

Period drama 1955 · US · Colour · 102min

This grim, bucolic period drama marked the screen debut of Broadway and TV actress Joanne Woodward, soon-to-be Mrs Paul Newman, as a tough-minded orphan gal caught up in the mayhem caused by new preacher in town Van Heflin, a pastor with a past. Notable today for its early use of CinemaScope, the movie benefits from fine acting from Heflin and Woodward, and a noteworthy typecast villain in Raymond Burr. TS

Van Heflin *Luke Fargo* • Joanne Woodward *Lissy* • Phil Carey [Philip Carey] *Albert Loomis* • Raymond Burr *Yancey Huggins* • Allison Hayes *Georgina Decrais* • Myron Healey *Floyd Miller* ■ *Dir* George Sherman • *Scr* Herb Meadow

Count Yorga, Vampire ★★★

Horror 1970 · US · Colour · 89min

Robert Quarry entered the "Horror Hall of Fame" thanks to his convincing turn here as an amoral Californian bloodsucker in this low-budget gross-out, blending crude horror with macabre wit. Originally planning to make a sex film (hence the inclusion of numerous soft-core starlets as vampire brides in the cast), director Bob Kelljan saw the light when *Night of the Living Dead* mopped up at the box office. So in came the ashen-faced undead feasting on cat's intestines, plus other moments of shock sleaze. An even better sequel, *The Return of Count Iorga*, followed. DP

Robert Quarry *Count Iorga* • Roger Perry *Dr Hayes* • Michael Murphy (1) *Paul* • Michael Macready *Michael* • Donna Anders *Donna* • Judy Lang [Judith Lang] *Erica* ■ *Dir/Scr* Bob Kelljan

Count Your Blessings ★★ Ⓤ

Romantic comedy 1959 · US · Colour · 102min

As fatuous as its title, this soft-focus MGM confection has one of those plots that everyone hates: a loathsome child brings together an estranged couple, in this case hard-working Deborah Kerr and perpetually wooden Rossano Brazzi. Jean Negulesco directs this soggy romance, which not even Maurice Chevalier can help. TS

Deborah Kerr *Grace Allingham* • Rossano Brazzi *Charles-Edouard de Valhubert* • Maurice Chevalier *Duc de St Cloud* • Martin Stephens *Sigismond* • Tom Helmore *Hugh Palgrave* ■ *Dir* Jean Negulesco • *Scr* Karl Tunberg, from the novel *The Blessing* by Nancy Mitford

Countdown ★★★★ Ⓤ

Drama 1967 · US · Colour · 97min

This fascinating early work from Robert Altman is about the planning of a mission to the Moon and its effect on the lives of those involved. There are early signs of what would become Altman trademarks (the large cast; the cool, documentary air) and he coaxes fine, naturalistic performances from James Caan and Robert Duvall as the two astronauts, only one of whom will go on the mission. JF

James Caan *Lee Stegler* • Joanna Moore *Mickey Stegler* • Robert Duvall *Chiz* • Barbara Baxley *Jean* • Charles Aidman *Gus* • Steve Ihnat *Ross* • Michael Murphy (1) *Rick* ■ *Dir* Robert Altman • *Scr* Loring Mandel, from the novel *The Pilgram Project* by Hank Searls

Countdown to Zero ★★★ ⑫

Documentary 2010 · US · Colour · 89min

This campaigning documentary offers a sobering warning that the possibility of nuclear destruction is still very much with us. Lucy Walker's film is a conventional, perhaps slightly dry assemblage of archive footage and sage opinion from scientists, politicians, activists and intelligence experts, but the fact the film-makers were granted interviews with Jimmy Carter, Mikhail Gorbachev, former US Secretary of Defense Robert McNamara and Tony Blair gives some sense of its clout and credibility. The overall approach is still somewhat didactic but there's no denying the importance of the issues. TJ **DVD**

Tony Blair • Jimmy Carter • Mikhail Gorbachev • Robert S McNamara ■ *Dir* Lucy Walker

Counter-Attack ★★★

Second World War drama 1945 · US · BW · 90min

This worthy piece of pro-Soviet propaganda was one of the productions used to denounce screenwriter John Howard Lawson during Hollywood's postwar communist witch-hunt. It's hardly the most subtle of stories, yet it effectively conveys the bitter enmity that existed between Marxists and Nazis. It also serves as an involving psychological thriller, with Russians Paul Muni and Marguerite Chapman battling for the upper hand with seven enemy soldiers in a besieged factory cellar. DP

Paul Muni *Alexei Kulkov* • Marguerite Chapman *Lisa Elenko* • Larry Parks *Kirichenko* • Harro Meller *Ernemann* • Roman Bohnen *Kostyuk* • George Macready *Colonel Semenov* ■ *Dir* Zoltan Korda • *Scr* John Howard Lawson, from the play *Pobyeda* by Ilya Vershinin, Mikhail Ruderman

Counterblast ★★

Thriller 1948 · UK · BW · 99min

Among the first films to consider Nazi experiments into germ warfare, this brisk British thriller boasts the interesting premise of turning a wanted war criminal into an accidental hero. Having killed an Australian doctor to escape a death camp, Mervyn Johns arrives in England to develop a lethal serum. However, a fondness for lab assistant Nova Pilbeam and the growing suspicions of scientist Robert Beatty cause him to rethink his tactics. This was an ambitious picture for its time. DP

Robert Beatty *Dr Rankin* • Mervyn Johns *Dr Bruckner* • Nova Pilbeam *Tracy Shaw* • Margaretta Scott *Sister Johnson* • Sybilla Binder *Martha* ■ *Dir* Paul L Stein • *Scr* Jack Whittingham, from a story by Guy Morgan

The Counterfeit Killer ★★ ⑫

Crime drama 1968 · US · Colour · 89min

Joseph Leytes adapted this serviceable crime thriller from his own *The Faceless Man*, a 1966 episode of Chrysler Theatre TV dramas. Its main appeal lies in the casting, as it provides meaty roles for Jack Weston (playing a conniving fence) and Joseph Wiseman (a ruthless gang boss). But Hawaii Five-O fans will be tuning in to see future star Jack Lord play the government gunman who is ordered to go undercover. DP

Jack Lord *Don Owens* • Shirley Knight *Angie Peterson* • Jack Weston *Randolph Riker* • Charles Drake *Dolan* • Joseph Wiseman *Rajeski* • Don Hanmer *O'Hara* ■ *Dir* Josef Leytes [Joseph Leytes] • *Scr* Steven Bochco, Harold Clements [Harold Clemens], from TV play *The Faceless Man* by Joseph Leytes

The Counterfeit Traitor ★★★

War drama based on a true story 1962 · US · Colour · 140min

Adapted from Alexander Klein's book about the true-life exploits of a Swedish undercover agent, this is a slickly-made espionage story, but with too few moments of nail-biting tension to justify its excessive running time. As the oil importer posing as a Nazi sympathiser, William Holden hurtles across northern Europe with some conviction, and is well supported by his endeavours by the likes of Lilli Palmer, Eva Dahlbeck and Klaus Kinski. But while writer/director George Seaton keeps the dialogue terse and credible, he too often dawdles when the action demands a bit of dash. DP

William Holden (2) *Eric Erickson* • Lilli Palmer *Marianne Mollendorf* • Hugh Griffith *Collins* • Ernst Schröder *Baron Von Oldenbourg* • Eva Dahlbeck *Ingrid Erickson* • Ulf Palme *Max Gumpel* • Carl Raddatz *Otto Holtz* ■ *Dir* George Seaton • *Scr* George Seaton, from the non-fiction book by Alexander Klein

The Counterfeiters ★★★★ ⑮

Second World War drama based on a true story 2007 · Ger/Austria/Fr · Colour · 94min

This astonishing Second World War drama tells the true story of Salomon "Sally" Sorowitsch (Karl Markovics), a Jewish counterfeiter who is ensnared in a Nazi plot while incarcerated in a concentration camp. Arrested in pre-war Berlin, Sally survives long enough to be sent to Sachsenhausen, centre of a scheme to produce enough forged Allied currency to destabilise the US and UK economies. In return for their expertise, the forgers are granted privileges such as clean beds, cigarettes and food, but one of their number, Adolf Burger (on whose memoir this is based), attempts to sabotage the project. Writer/director Stefan

Ruzowitzky doesn't foreground the Nazi brutality, while the compelling screenplay wrestles with the moral agonies surrounding collaboration. **AS** German +subtitles. *DVD*

Karl Markovics *Salomon "Sally" Sorowitsch* • August Diehl *Adolf Burger* • Devid Striesow *Sturmbannführer Friedrich Herzog* • Martin Brambach *Hauptscharführer Holst* • August Zirner *Dr Klinger* • Veit Stübner *Atze* • Sebastian Urzendowsky *Kolya* • Andreas Schmidt *Zilinsky* • Tilo Prückner *Dr Viktor Hahn* • Lenn Kudrjawizki *Loszek* ■ *Dir* Stefan Ruzowitzky • *Scr* Stefan Ruzowitzky, from the memoirs *The Devil's Workshop* by Adolf Burger

Counterpoint ★★
Second World War drama
1967 · US · Colour · 106min

Charlton Heston plays an American conductor who, along with his 70-strong orchestra, is captured by the Germans in Belgium during the Battle of the Bulge. Nazi general Maximilian Schell has orders to shoot all prisoners, but will spare the lives of the musicians if they play a concert. The musical extracts are by far the most convincing moments in an otherwise implausible story. **TH** Some swearing.

Charlton Heston *Lionel Evans* • Maximilian Schell *General Schiller* • Kathryn Hays *Annabelle Rice* • Leslie Nielsen *Victor Rice* • Anton Diffring *Colonel Arndt* • Linden Chiles *Lieutenant Long* ■ *Dir* Ralph Nelson • *Scr* Joel Oliansky, James Lee, from the novel *The General* by Alan Sillitoe

Counterspy ★★PG
Comedy thriller   1953 · UK · BW · 66min

Typical "quota quickie" about a ring of spies who use an innocuous nursing home as their hideout. Some topicality is given to the otherwise threadbare plot – the spies are after plans for jet engines, and there's a chase through one of London's newest tourist attractions, the Festival Gardens on London's South Bank. **AT** *DVD*

Dermot Walsh *Manning* • Hazel Court *Clare Manning* • Hermione Baddeley *Del Mar* • Alexander Gauge *Smith* • James Vivian *Larry* • Archie Duncan *Jim* • Frederick Schrecker *Plattnauer* • Hugh Latimer *Barlow* • Bill Travers *Rex* • Beryl Baxter *Girl* ■ *Dir* Vernon Sewell • *Scr* Gary Elmes, Michael Lefevre

Countess Dracula ★★★18
Horror   1970 · UK · Colour · 89min

In order to masquerade as her own daughter, an ageing countess begins bathing in the blood of virgins to restore her youth. Ingrid Pitt, the first lady of British horror movies, excels in this colourful hokum based on the legend of notorious Hungarian countess Elizabeth Bathory. The film atones for its lack of terror with a brittle atmosphere of decay. **DP** Violence, nudity. *DVD* *SD*

Ingrid Pitt *Countess Elisabeth Nadasdy* • Nigel Green *Captain Dobi* • Sandor Eles *Imre Toth* • Maurice Denham *Master Fabio* • Lesley-Anne Down *Ilona* • Patience Collier *Julia* ■ *Dir* Peter Sasdy • *Scr* Jeremy Paul, from a story by Alexander Paal, Peter Sasdy, Gabriel Ronay

A Countess from Hong Kong ★★
Romantic comedy   1967 · UK · Colour · 122min

Director Charles Chaplin sadly disappointed fans eagerly awaiting his first film in ten years, completely misjudging Sophia Loren and Marlon Brando in this clumsy romantic comedy. The result is hugely embarrassing, with Brando surly instead of suave as the diplomat who finds Russian émigrée aristocrat Loren stowed away in his cabin. **TH**

Marlon Brando *Ogden Mears* • Sophia Loren *Natascha* • Sydney Chaplin *Harvey Crothers* • Tippi Hedren *Martha* • Patrick Cargill *Hudson* • Margaret Rutherford *Miss Gaulswallow* • Michael Medwin *John Felix* • Oliver Johnston *Clark* ■ *Dir/Scr* Charles Chaplin

The Countess of Monte Cristo ★★U
Musical   1948 · US · BW · 76min

This marks the last screen appearance of Norwegian Olympic ice-skating champion

Sonja Henie, who made several successful films in the late 1930s and early 1940s when her competitive days were over. Not one of her better movies, the one-joke plot has Henie and Olga San Juan as barmaids posing as a countess and her maid at a luxury hotel. **RK**

Sonja Henie *Karen Kirsten* • Olga San Juan *Jenny Johnsen* • Michael Kirby *Paul von Cram* • Dorothy Hart *Peg Manning* • Arthur Treacher *Managing director* ■ *Dir* Frederick De Cordova • *Scr* William Bowers, from the film by Walter Reisch

Country ★★★PG
Drama   1984 · US · Colour · 105min

Iowa farmers Jessica Lange and Sam Shepard survive a twister, but face foreclosure and bankruptcy when the US government demands the full and immediate return on a huge loan. Very much a personal project for Lange, this social drama may beat its "big message" drum a little too loudly, but it also provides a convincing portrait of how harsh country life can be. It was the second on-screen pairing (after *Frances*) of real-life partners Shepard and Lange, the latter winning an Oscar nomination for her down-to-earth performance. **AT**

Jessica Lange *Jewell Ivy* • Sam Shepard *Gil Ivy* • Wilford Brimley *Otis* • Matt Clark *Tom McMullen* • Therese Graham *Marlene Ivy* • Levi L Knebel *Carlisle Ivy* • Jim Haynie *Arlon Brewer* • Sandra Seacat *Louise Brewer* ■ *Dir* Richard Pearce • *Scr* William D Wittliff

The Country Bears ★★PG
Musical comedy   2002 · US · Colour · 84min

Christopher Walken's performance as a vengeful banker saves the day in this lacklustre family comedy. Based on a Disney theme park attraction, it's a simplistic morality tale about love, loyalty and friendship. The stars are the washed-out country-and-western bear group of the title (actually actors in unconvincing fuzzy suits). When a deliciously theatrical Walken threatens to repossess their Country Bear Hall, the quarrelling performers are persuaded to reform by an ardent young fan (another ursine critter, voiced by Haley Joel Osment). This lacks the magic to charm. **SF** *DVD* *CS*

Haley Joel Osment *Beary* • Christopher Walken *Reed Thimple* • Stephen Tobolowsky *Norbert Barrington* • Daryl "Chill" Mitchell [Daryl Mitchell] *Officer Hamm* • MC Gainey *Roadie* • Diedrich Bader *Ted Bedderhead/Officer Cheats* • Megan Fay *Mrs Barrington* • Eli Marienthal *Dex Barrington* • Candy Ford *Trixie St Clair* • James Gammon *Big Al* ■ *Dir* Peter Hastings • *Scr* Mark Perez, based on the theme park attraction "Walt Disney's Country Bear Jamboree"

Country Dance ★★★
Drama   1970 · UK · Colour · 112min

Peter O'Toole is ideally cast as Sir Charles Henry Arbuthnot Pinkerton Ferguson, a dipsomaniac Scots aristocrat who once canoodled with his sister in the barn and has been besotted by her ever since. But the sister, Susannah York, is now married to Michael Craig. Incest as a theme has always been a risky business and this accordingly bombed at the box office, perhaps because this title – it was originally *Brotherly Love* – threatened clogs and bagpipes. **AT**

Peter O'Toole *Sir Charles Henry Arbuthnot Pinkerton Ferguson* • Susannah York *Hilary Dow* • Michael Craig *Douglas Dow* • Harry Andrews *Brigadier Crieff* • Cyril Cusack *Dr Maitland* • Judy Cornwell *Rosie* • Brian Blessed *Jock Baird* • Robert Urquhart *Auctioneer* ■ *Dir* J Lee Thompson • *Scr* James Kennaway

The Country Doctor ★★
Drama   1936 · US · BW · 93min

Jean Hersholt is his usual solid, sympathetic self in this backwoods drama set in Canada, which involves a diphtheria outbreak, the fight to build a hospital and the birth of quintuplets. Inspired by the famous Dionne quintuplets, this version features real newsreel footage and the quins themselves playing their fictional counterparts. Folksy and worthy. **RK**

Jean Hersholt *Dr John Luke* • June Lang *Mary MacKenzie* • George "Slim" Summerville [Slim Summerville] *Constable Jim Ogden* • Michael Whalen *Tony Luke* • Dorothy Peterson *Nurse Katherine Kennedy* • Robert Barrat *MacKenzie* • Jane Darwell *Mrs Graham* ■ *Dir* Henry King • *Scr* Sonya Levien, from a story by Charles E Blake

The Country Girl ★★★PG
Drama   1954 · US · BW · 99min

Grace Kelly won a Best Actress Oscar for putting on glasses and looking after alcoholic hubby Bing Crosby in this version of Clifford Odets's turgid play, which also won director George Seaton an Academy Award for his screenplay. William Holden plays the theatre director who becomes embroiled with Kelly. With hindsight, and the demise of all three principles, the film has an extra piquancy if the viewer knows that in real life Kelly was romantically involved with both Crosby and Holden. **TS** *DVD*

Bing Crosby *Frank Elgin* • Grace Kelly *Georgie Elgin* • William Holden (2) *Bernie Dodd* • Anthony Ross *Phil Cook* • Gene Reynolds *Larry* • Eddie Ryder *Ed* ■ *Dir* George Seaton • *Scr* George Seaton, from the play by Clifford Odets

The Country Girls ★★★PG
Period drama   1983 · UK · Colour · 102min

Most rite of passage pictures focus on teenage lads, so it makes a refreshing change to follow a couple of girls discovering the pleasures and pitfalls of life. Adapted from the novel by Edna O'Brien, this engaging account of growing up in 1950s Ireland takes us along the familiar route from convent school to the big city. However, director Desmond Davis succeeds in presenting each act of rebellion and stolen moment of innocent passion as something exhilaratingly new. **DP**

Sam Neill *Mr Gentleman* • Maeve Germaine *Kate* • Jill Doyle *Baba Brennan* • Britta Smith *Lil* • John Olohan *Hickey* • Patricia Martin *Martha* • Des Nealon *Mr Brennan* • John Kavanagh *James* ■ *Dir* Desmond Davis • *Scr* Edna O'Brien, from the novel by Edna O'Brien

Country Life ★★★★12
Period drama   1994 · Aus · Colour · 112min

This drawn-out but absorbing take on Chekhov's *Uncle Vanya* was adapted by Michael Blakemore and transplanted to post-First World War Australia. A failed writer (Blakemore himself) returns to a New South Wales sheep farm with new wife Greta Scacchi, who becomes the object of desire of drunken doctor Sam Neill and nervy landowner John Hargreaves. Neatly capturing the inherent comedy in people's everyday life, the film's vein of melancholy sets off that humour to real effect. **TH**

Sam Neill *Dr Max Askey* • Greta Scacchi *Deborah Voysey* • Kerry Fox *Sally Voysey* • John Hargreaves *Jack Dickens* • Michael Blakemore *Alexander Voysey* • Googie Withers *Hannah* • Patricia Kennedy *Maud Dickens* ■ *Dir* Michael Blakemore • *Scr* Michael Blakemore, from the play *Uncle Vanya* by Anton Chekhov

Country Strong ★★12
Music drama   2010 · US · Colour · 112min

Sparks fly between a young, recovering-addict country singer (Gwyneth Paltrow) and her husband/manager (real-life country star Tim McGraw) in this creaky melodrama that's full of the typical clichés associated with the musical genre. Writer/director Shana Feste is clearly indebted to the Oscar-winning *Crazy Heart* and Robert Altman's epic *Nashville*, but the script all too often stumbles into mediocre soap-opera territory. Paltrow again proves she's no slouch as a singer, although even her undeniable on-screen charisma fails to elevate proceedings above predictable tear-jerker status. **TeS** *DVD* *SD*

Gwyneth Paltrow *Kelly Canter* • Tim McGraw *James Canter* • Garrett Hedlund *Beau Hutton* • Leighton Meester *Chiles Stanton* • Marshall Chapman *Winnie* • Jeremy Childs *JJ* ■ *Dir/Scr* Shana Feste

County Hospital ★★U
Comedy   1932 · US · BW · 18min

Who else but Stan Laurel would visit someone in traction and offer them hard-boiled eggs and nuts? Unfortunately, that's about as funny as this two-reeler gets. There are a couple of good moments as Ollie's plastered leg heads ceilingward, but once they head home, the action lapses back to the earliest days of silent slapstick as Stan careers through the streets causing all manner of chaos. **DP** *DVD*

Stan Laurel *Stan* • Oliver Hardy *Ollie* • William Austin *Englishman* • Baldwin Cooke *Orderly* • Billy Gilbert *Doctor* • Belle Hare *Nurse* ■ *Dir* James Parrott • *Scr* HM Walker

Coup de Torchon ★★★★12
Drama   1981 · Fr · Colour · 123min

In transferring Jim Thompson's novel *Pop 1280* from the American Deep South to equatorial Africa in 1938, Bertrand Tavernier passes comment on imperialism, appeasement and the corrupting nature of power, as well as exploring the psychology of a weak man pushed to his limits. For all the script's dark deliberations, however, the film's bite is provided by Philippe Noiret's dissemblingly shambolic performance as the scorned cop who abuses his position to cover up a murderous vendetta against everyone who's slighted him. **DP** French +subtitles. Violence, swearing. *DVD*

Philippe Noiret *Lucien Cordier* • Isabelle Huppert *Rose* • Jean-Pierre Marielle *Le Peron/His brother* • Stéphane Audran *Huguette Cordier* • Eddy Mitchell *Nono* • Guy Marchand *Chavasson* ■ *Dir* Bertrand Tavernier • *Scr* Jean Aurenche, Bertrand Tavernier, from the novel *Pop 1280* by Jim Thompson

Coupe de Ville ★★★15
Comedy drama   1990 · US · Colour · 97min

This is funny, endearing and very unlike director Joe Roth's earlier films. Three estranged brothers are ordered by their father, Alan Arkin, to drive across America with a car for their mother's 50th birthday. Cue much argument and a particularly memorable scene where they all dispute the significance of hit song *Louie, Louie*. With decent comic gags throughout, this is slight but entertaining. **LH**

Patrick Dempsey *Bobby Libner* • Arye Gross *Buddy Libner* • Daniel Stern *Marvin Libner* • Annabeth Gish *Tammy* • Rita Taggart *Betty Libner* • Joseph Bologna *Uncle Phil* • Alan Arkin *Fred Libner* • James Gammon *Doc Sturgeon* ■ *Dir* Joe Roth • *Scr* Mike Binder

Couple in a Hole ★★★12
Thriller   2015 · UK/Bel/Fr · Colour · 100min

This unusual drama is a study of grief and loss. Set in a French forest, it tells the story of John (Paul Higgins) and Karen (Kate Dickie), a married couple who are living in a small cave. Having suffered a tragedy, they are now shunning the outside world, avoiding human contact and living in isolation. But then Karen is bitten by a spider... Some viewers won't accept the premise, given that it's somewhat bizarre, but Higgins and Dickie combine to create a haunting, downbeat film about two people consumed by sorrow. **SC** English, French +subtitles. Violence, swearing. *DVD*

Paul Higgins *John* • Kate Dickie *Karen* • Jérôme Kircher *André* • Corinne Masiero *Céline* ■ *Dir/Scr* Tom Geens

Couples Retreat ★★15
Relationship comedy
2009 · US/Jpn · Colour · 108min

A holiday in a luxury South Pacific resort turns out to involve a chastening programme of marital therapy in this ensemble frolic, co-written by and co-starring *Swingers* duo Vince Vaughn and Jon Favreau. The trip has been organised by Jason Bateman and Kristen Bell in a last ditch attempt to save their marriage, but the compulsory ministrations of Jean Reno's self-styled "couples whisperer" also highlights the tensions within the relationships of their friends. Although Vaughn is appealing in an uninspiring "regular guy" role, and Favreau's game for sundry humiliations as the 40-something lecher in the group, there's more midlife crisis than rollicking wit. TJ Sexual references. *DVD* *BL*

Vince Vaughn *Dave* • Jason Bateman *Jason* • Jon Favreau *Joey* • Faizon Love *Shane* • Kristin Davis *Lucy* • Malin Akerman *Ronnie* • Kristen Bell *Cynthia* • Jean Reno *Marcel* ■ *Dir* Peter Billingsley • *Scr* Vince Vaughn, Jon Favreau, Dana Fox

Courage Mountain ★★ U
Adventure drama 1989 · US/Fr · Colour · 94min

Continuing Johanna Sypri's much loved story about joy-bringing Swiss mountain girl Heidi, this lovingly staged but impossibly contrived adventure will doubtless appeal to adolescent females. Juliette Caton leads her classmates to safety across the Alps when the First World War encroaches on their patch. Charlie Sheen gives a mortifying performance as Peter the goatherd. DP

Juliette Caton *Heidi* • Charlie Sheen *Peter* • Leslie Caron *Jane Hillary* • Yorgo Voyagis *Signor Bonelli* • Laura Betti *Signora Bonelli* • Jan Rubes *Grandfather* • Joanna Clarke *Ursula* • Nicola Stapleton *Ilsa* ■ *Dir* Christopher Leitch • *Scr* Weaver Webb, from a story by Fred Brogger, Mark Brogger, from characters by Johanna Spyri

Courage of Lassie ★★★ U
Second World War drama
1946 · US · Colour · 88min

The title of this moving tale of wartime doggie heroism is misleading, as Lassie actually plays a collie called Bill. Humans on board include the lovely young Elizabeth Taylor (from *Lassie Come Home*) and the always likeable Frank Morgan. Tom Drake is also effective as the "boy next door", but the real star – apart from the mutt – is the sumptuous Technicolor. TS *DVD*

Elizabeth Taylor *Kathie Merrick* • Frank Morgan *Harry MacBain* • Tom Drake *Sgt Smitty* • Selena Royle *Mrs Merrick* • Harry Davenport *Judge Payson* • George Cleveland *Old man* ■ *Dir* Fred M Wilcox • *Scr* Lionel Houser

Courage under Fire ★★★ 15
War drama 1996 · US · Colour · 111min

This is a big, self-important Gulf War movie that looks good, sounds noble but rings rather hollow. Meg Ryan is a pilot due to get a posthumous medal for bravery, but has there been a cover-up of the real events? This is a *Rashomon* for the 1990s, with war hero Denzel Washington searching for the truth. The subject matter, strong performances and stylish direction combine to make the movie seem more incisive than it really is. AT Violence, swearing. *DVD* *BL*

Denzel Washington *Nat Serling* • Meg Ryan *Karen Walden* • Lou Diamond Phillips *Monfriez* • Michael Moriarty *General Hershberg* • Matt Damon *Ilario* • Bronson Pinchot *Bruno* • Seth Gilliam *Altameyer* • Regina Taylor *Meredith Serling* • Scott Glenn *Tony Gartner* ■ *Dir* Edward Zwick • *Scr* Patrick Sheane Duncan

The Courageous Heart of Irena Sendler ★★★ 12
Biographical war drama
2009 · US · Colour · 91min

In 1942 in the Warsaw Ghetto, Polish social worker Irena Sendler (Anna Paquin) dares to take a stand against the abuse of her Jewish neighbours. As rumours of mass extermination in Auschwitz begin to circulate, she hatches a plan to ferry children out of the ghetto and re-house them with sympathetic Catholic families. This earnest TV movie lets the maudlin score, and Paquin's troubled face, do all the emotional heavy lifting. It's an honourable effort, paying tribute to the real Sendler's incredible achievement, yet inevitably suffers in comparison to its obvious inspiration, *Schindler's List*. JR In English, Russian, German, Latvian.

Anna Paquin *Irena Sendler* • Marcia Gay Harden *Janina Sendler* • Goran Visnjic *Stefan Zgrzembski* • Nathaniel Parker *Dr Majkowski* ■ *Dir* John Kent Harrison • *Scr* John Kent Harrison, Larry

Spagnola, from the non-fiction book *Irena Sendler: Mother of the Children of the Holocaust* by Anna Mieszkowska

Cours du Soir ★★★ U
Comedy 1967 · Fr · Colour · 27min

Taking the form of an evening class and shot on the set of *Playtime*, this may not be Jacques Tati's most innovative film, but it provides an invaluable record of the vaudeville sketches with which he made his name. Starting with a demonstration of smoking styles, Tati trots out his famous tennis, fishing and horse-riding techniques, as well as a brief reprise of his beloved postman routine. But you only have to look at how badly his besuited students cope with the simple slapstick task of tripping on a step to realise how deceptively easy Tati makes each mime appear. DP French +subtitles.

Jacques Tati ■ *Dir* Nicolas Ribowski • *Scr* Jacques Tati

The Court Jester ★★★★ U
Comedy 1956 · US · Colour · 96min

This medieval spoof, produced, written and directed by the formidable team of Norman Panama and Melvin Frank, gave Danny Kaye one of his finest roles, as the meek and mild valet who saves a kingdom from its tyrannical ruler. Basil Rathbone cuts an elegant figure of villainy, while Glynis Johns, Cecil Parker and Angela Lansbury get almost as many laughs as Kaye by playing it straight. It's as much horseplay as swordplay and, altogether, a witty delight. TH *DVD*

Danny Kaye *Hawkins* • Glynis Johns *Maid Jean* • Basil Rathbone *Sir Ravenhurst* • Angela Lansbury *Princess Gwendolyn* • Cecil Parker *King Roderick* • Mildred Natwick *Griselda* • Robert Middleton *Sir Griswold* ■ *Dir/Scr* Norman Panama, Melvin Frank

The Court-Martial of Billy Mitchell ★★★★ U
Biographical courtroom drama
1955 · US · Colour · 100min

This true-life courtroom drama is given enormous impact by director Otto Preminger and his Oscar-nominated writers, Milton Sperling and Emmet Lavery. The film is based on events in 1925, when US Army general Mitchell (played by Gary Cooper) dared to question bureaucracy and argue for a separate Air Force. He also predicted that America and Japan would one day go to war, years before Pearl Harbor. Cooper's languid sincerity makes its mark, but it's Rod Steiger as a venomous prosecutor who gets all the best lines. TH

Gary Cooper *General Billy Mitchell* • Rod Steiger *Major Allan Guillion* • Charles Bickford *General Guthrie* • Ralph Bellamy *Congressman Frank Reid* • Elizabeth Montgomery *Margaret Lansdowne* • Jack Lord *Commander Zachary Lansdowne* • Peter Graves (2) *Captain Elliott* • Darren McGavin *Russ Peters* ■ *Dir* Otto Preminger • *Scr* Milton Sperling, Emmet Lavery, from their story

The Court-Martial of Jackie Robinson ★★★★
Biographical drama 1990 · US · Colour · 100min

This TV movie about Jackie Robinson, who went on to become the first black player in big-time baseball and a full-blown national hero, homes in on an incident early in his life when he endured bigotry as a GI. André Braugher supplies ample energy as Robinson while Bruce Dern stands out in an impressive supporting cast that also includes Ruby Dee, who played Robinson's wife in 1950's *The Jackie Robinson Story*, and who returns here as his mum. Director Larry Peerce cleverly avoids any self-conscious analysing of issues, thereby maintaining the power of the piece. JM

André Braugher *Jackie Robinson* • Ruby Dee *Mallie Robinson* • Stan Shaw *Joe Louis* • Daniel Stern *William Cline* • Bruce Dern *Ed Higgins* • Kasi Lemmons *Rachel Isum Robinson* ■ *Dir* Larry Peerce • *Scr* L Travis Clark, Steve Duncan, Clayton Frohman, Dennis Lynton Clark, from a story by Dennis Lynton Clark

The Courtneys of Curzon Street ★★★ U
Period drama 1947 · UK · BW · 120min

Although it now seems twee, it's easy to see why this class-divide drama would have been so popular in postwar Britain. With an egalitarian theme and plenty of period gaiety to distract from the austerity of the time, this box-office smash perfectly demonstrates director Herbert Wilcox's ability to gauge public taste. Here, Michael Wilding's aristocrat shocks Victorian society by falling for Anna Neagle's spirited maid. DP

Anna Neagle *Catherine O'Halloran* • Michael Wilding *Sir Edward Courtney* • Gladys Young *Lady Courtney* • Michael Medwin *Edward Courtney* • Coral Browne *Valerie* • Daphne Slater *Cynthia* • Jack Watling *Teddy Courtney* ■ *Dir* Herbert Wilcox • *Scr* Nicholas Phipps, from a story by Florence Tranter

The Courtship of Andy Hardy ★★ U
Comedy drama 1942 · US · BW · 94min

The Andy Hardy series clocked up a dozen episodes with this offering which gave all-American families role models and reassurance while father was away fighting the war. In this story, Judge Hardy (Lewis Stone) uses his son Mickey Rooney to help a married couple reconcile themselves to their tearaway daughter. AT

Mickey Rooney *Andy Hardy* • Lewis Stone *Judge James K Hardy* • Donna Reed *Melodie Nesbitt* • Fay Holden *Mrs Emily Hardy* • Cecilia Parker *Marian Hardy* • Ann Rutherford *Polly Benedict* • William Lundigan *Jeff Willis* • Sara Haden *Aunt Milly* ■ *Dir* George B Seitz • *Scr* Agnes Christine Johnston, from characters by Aurania Rouverol

The Courtship of Eddie's Father ★★★★ U
Comedy drama 1963 · US · Colour · 118min

This absolutely charming and unfairly neglected film is directed by Vincente Minnelli, beautifully filmed by veteran cinematographer Milton Krasner, and features a simply swell performance from the excellent Glenn Ford. Ronny Howard (now better known as director Ron Howard) keeps sentimentality at bay as the six-year-old Eddie, as do the dynamic Stella Stevens and Shirley Jones; there's also a terrific cameo from Dick Van Dyke's underrated brother, Jerry. This is a warm-hearted treat, far superior to the TV series that followed. TS

Glenn Ford *Tom Corbett* • Ronny Howard [Ron Howard] *Eddie Corbett* • Shirley Jones *Elizabeth Marten* • Dina Merrill *Rita Behrens* • Stella Stevens *Dollye Daly* • Roberta Sherwood *Mrs Livingston* • Jerry Van Dyke *Norman Jones* ■ *Dir* Vincente Minnelli • *Scr* John Gay, from a novel by Mark Toby

Couscous ★★★ 15
Social drama 2007 · Fr · Colour · 154min

The themes tackled in director Abdellatif Kechiche's slice-of-life drama (infidelity, relationship conflict, the quest for a better existence) are pure soap opera, but there's a real intelligence at work here. When Arab shipbuilder Slimane (Habib Boufares) is made redundant from his job in a French port, he takes a gamble by opening a restaurant on a renovated boat. Boufares's performance in the lead is a snapshot of uncommunicative exhaustion and quiet dignity; yet it's the energetic supporting cast that captures the imagination as enjoyably protracted dinner scenes let them chatter incessantly. It's through these deceptively simple sequences that the film offers an implicit commentary on Franco-Arab identity and the casual racism endured by immigrants who want nothing more than to better themselves. JR French +subtitles.

Habib Boufares *Slimane* • Hafsia Herzi *Rym* • Faridah Benkhetache *Karima* • Aktouche Abdelhamid *Hamid* • Bouraouissa Marzouk *Souad* ■ *Dir/Scr* Abdellatif Kechiche [Abdel Kechiche]

Cousin Bette ★★★ 15
Period drama 1997 · US/UK · Colour · 104min

This version of Balzac's novel has Jessica Lange in the title role, plotting revenge on her family who have virtually abandoned her while lavishing everything on her cousin. Its story of social upheaval is mirrored by the political chaos of mid-19th-century France, but the picture suffers rather from international casting and other compromises brought on by trans-Atlantic financing. However, Lange gives a wonderful portrait of malice and Elisabeth Shue has fun as a flirtatious actress. AT Nudity, sex scenes, swearing, violence.

Jessica Lange *Bette Fisher* • Elisabeth Shue *Jenny Cadine* • Geraldine Chaplin *Adeline Hulot* • Bob Hoskins *Mayor Cesar Crevel* • Hugh Laurie *Baron Hector Hulot* • Laura Fraser *Mariette* • Toby Stephens *Victorin Hulot* • Kelly Macdonald *Hortense Hulot* ■ *Dir* Des McAnuff • *Scr* Lynn Siefert, Susan Tarr, from the novel by Honoré de Balzac

Cousin Bobby ★★★ PG
Documentary 1992 · US · Colour · 70min

Jonathan Demme directs this absolutely fascinating documentary about his cousin Robert Castle, an Episcopalian priest in Harlem. The Oscar-winning director follows the outspoken radical activist as he goes about his daily ministering and builds up a riveting portrait of the man, his life and the dedicated work he does among his adoring flock. The use of race riot footage is heavy-handed, but otherwise this is a nicely crafted valentine from one proud relative to another. AJ

■ *Dir* Jonathan Demme

Cousin, Cousine ★★★ 12
Comedy 1975 · Fr · Colour · 91min

The problem with accessible art house movies is that they often feel empty. That's certainly the case in this gentle satire on middle-class mores, which was so successful in the States that it was remade as *Cousins*. Fondly mocking the morality of his characters, Jean-Charles Tacchella refuses to rip into them as Buñuel would have done, choosing instead to make the romance between wronged wife Marie-Christine Barrault and Victor Lanoux seem rather sweet. DP French +subtitles.

Marie-Christine Barrault *Marthe* • Victor Lanoux *Ludovic* • Marie-France Pisier *Karine* • Guy Marchand *Pascal* • Ginette Garcin *Biju* • Sybil Maas *Diane* • Jean Herbert *Sacy* ■ *Dir* Jean-Charles Tacchella • *Scr* Jean-Charles Tacchella, Danièle Thompson

Les Cousins ★★★★ 12
Drama 1959 · Fr · BW · 109min

Winner of the Golden Bear at the 1959 Berlin film festival, this is an intriguing variation on the "town mouse and country mouse" theme which cynically asserts that just desserts are simply pie in the sky. Gérard Blain skilfully charts the descent from wide-eyed wonder to self-pitying despair as the student from the sticks who slaves at the Sorbonne, only to fail his exams and lose his girlfriend to his indolent but ultimately successful cousin (Jean-Claude Brialy). Parisian Claude Chabrol presents his home town with evident enthusiasm, though the scenes of student excess have dated badly. DP French +subtitles. *DVD* *BL*

Gérard Blain *Charles* • Jean-Claude Brialy *Paul* • Juliette Mayniel *Florence* • Claude Cerval *Clovis* • Genevieve Cluny *Genevieve* • Michèle Meritz *Yvonne* • Corrado Guarducci *Italian Count* • Guy Decomble *Librarian* ■ *Dir* Claude Chabrol • *Scr* Claude Chabrol, Paul Gegauff

Cousins ★★★ 15
Romantic comedy 1989 · US · Colour · 108min

A remake of the French film *Cousin, Cousine*, this glossy romance features Isabella Rossellini and Ted Danson as relatives-by-marriage who find themselves falling in love during a succession of family gatherings. He's married to ice-cold Sean Young, who in turn is having an affair with Rossellini's hubby, William Petersen. Danson gives one of his most likeable movie performances, while Young steals the show by playing the role of bitchy cheating wife to the max. JB Swearing, sexual references. *DVD*

Ted Danson *Larry Kozinski* • Isabella Rossellini *Maria Hardy* • Sean Young *Tish Kozinski* • William L Petersen *Tom Hardy* • Lloyd Bridges *Vince Kozinski* • Norma Aleandro *Edie Costello* • Keith Coogan *Mitch Kozinski* ■ *Dir* Joel Schumacher • *Scr* Stephen Metcalfe, from the film *Cousin, Cousine* by Jean-Charles Tacchella, Danièle Thompson

The Cove ★★★★ 12
Documentary   2009 · US · Colour · 87min

This moving documentary may be about dolphins, but it's oceans away from the fluffiness of *Flipper*, the US TV series that brought the creature to international attention back in the 1960s. Ironically it is Ric O'Barry, the man who trained the dolphins for that show, who's the driving force here. He leads an expedition (including underwater cameramen, marine explorers and divers) that uses guerrilla filming techniques and *Mission Impossible*-style subterfuge in an attempt to expose the annual slaughter of thousands of dolphins by the fishermen of a remote Japanese village. To compound that scandal, there's also an issue with toxins in the animals' flesh that constitute a serious health hazard. Not all documentaries are natural material for the big screen, but this shocking exposé really packs a punch and is occasionally as thrilling as any fictional big-budget offering. DA

■ *Dir* Louie Psihoyos • *Scr* Mark Monroe

The Covenant ★ 12
Supernatural horror thriller
2006 · US · Colour · 93min

Revamping teen-witch movie *The Craft* for boys, this brash and empty horror film lacks magic. At an elite public school in Massachusetts, four teenagers (led by *Sky High's* Steven Strait) struggle to cope with their supernatural powers. This plays like something brainstormed in a marketing meeting, with director Renny Harlin desperately trying to appeal to the core demographic with a thrash-metal soundtrack, petulant teen angst, and some subversive humour. He fails miserably. JR Violence. *DVD* *BD*

Steven Strait *Caleb Danvers* • Sebastian Stan *Chase Collins* • Laura Ramsey *Sarah Wenham* • Taylor Kitsch *Pogue Parry* • Toby Hemingway *Reid Garwin* • Jessica Lucas *Kate Tunney* • Wendy Crewson *Evelyn Danvers* • Stephen McHattie *James Danvers* ■ *Dir* Renny Harlin • *Scr* JS Cardone

Cover Girl ★★★★ U
Musical romantic comedy
1944 · US · Colour · 102min

This Technicolor treat features a score by Jerome Kern and the ravishing Rita Hayworth as a New York chorus girl whose career takes off after she appears on a magazine cover. Columbia borrowed the young Gene Kelly from MGM and gave him free rein with his own sections of the movie, for what turned out to be a milestone in the history of glossy film musicals. Kelly knocked down soundstage walls to create a continuous street scene for himself, Hayworth and Phil Silvers to dance through without any need for cuts. A little dated, a little corny, but still a pleasure. TS *DVD*

Rita Hayworth *Rusty Parker/Maribelle Hicks* • Gene Kelly *Danny McGuire* • Phil Silvers *Genius* • Lee Bowman *Noel Wheaton* • Jinx Falkenburg *Jinx* • Leslie Brooks *Maurine Martin* • Eve Arden *Cornelia Jackson* • Otto Kruger *John Coudair* • Jess Barker *John Coudair as a young man* • Anita Colby *Anita* ■ *Dir* Charles Vidor • *Scr* Virginia Van Upp, Marion Parsonnet, Paul Gangelin, from a story by Erwin Gelsey • *Cinematographers* Rudolph Maté, Allen M Davey • *Music Director* MW Stoloff [Morris Stoloff] • *Orchestration* Carmen Dragon • *Art Directors* Lionel Banks, Gary Odell • *Set Designer* Fay Babcock

Cover Girl Killer ★★★
Crime drama   1959 · UK · BW · 61min

Apart from a handful of low-budget movies, writer/director Terry Bishop spent much of his career in TV, which would appear to have been the British cinema's loss if this clipped little thriller is anything to go by. The dialogue does strike a false note every now and then, but Bishop succeeds in re-creating a world of tawdry glamour that is a far cry from the glitz of today's supermodels as a serial killer targets a magazine's pin-ups. DP

Harry H Corbett *The man* • Felicity Young *June Rawson* • Spencer Teakle *John Mason* • Victor Brooks *Inspector Brunner* • Tony Doonan *Sergeant* • Bernadette Milnes *Gloria* • Christina Gregg *Joy* • Charles Lloyd Pack *Captain Adams* ■ *Dir/Scr* Terry Bishop

The Covered Wagon ★★★★★
Silent western   1923 · US · BW · 98min

Shot on a lavish scale in Utah and Nevada, this was the first truly epic western and one of the biggest-grossing silent movies ever made. It also created the imprint for countless movies and TV series with its story of pioneers facing redskins and ruffians on the wagon trail westwards. Directed by James Cruze - with, it's said, John Ford as his assistant - the film's many highlights include a buffalo hunt and a dramatic river crossing, though the vapid romance between J Warren Kerrigan and Lois Wilson tends to diminish the storyline. With terrific camerawork from Karl Brown, it set the standard for future westerns. TH

Lois Wilson *Molly Wingate* • J Warren Kerrigan *Will Banion* • Ernest Torrence *Jackson* • Charles Ogle *Mr Wingate* • Ethel Wales *Mrs Wingate* • Alan Hale *Sam Woodhull* • Tully Marshall *Bridger* • Guy Oliver *Kit Carson* ■ *Dir* James Cruze • *Scr* Jack Cunningham

The Cow ★★★★
Drama   1969 · Iran · BW · 104min

Dariush Mehrjui's hugely influential drama has the duel distinction of having been both part-funded (and then banned) by the Shah of Iran and the primary reason why the Ayatollah Khomeini allowed film-making after the Islamic Revolution. For all its dense symbolism, the plotline couldn't be simpler, as villager Ezzatollah Entezami feels the unexpected death of his cherished cow - the only one in the village - so personally that he gradually becomes convinced that he himself is a cow. This astute insight into rural poverty and the superstition and paranoia of village life has lost none of its power. DP Farsi +subtitles.

Ezzatollah Entezami *Masht Hassan* • Mahmoud Dowlatabadi • Parviz Fanizadeh • Jamshid Mashayekhi *Abbas* • Ali Nassirian *Islam* • Esmat Safavi ■ *Dir* Dariush Mehrjui • *Scr* Dariush Mehrjui, from a play by Gholam-Hossein Saedi

The Cow and the President ★★★ PG
Comedy   2000 · Fr · Colour · 92min

Inspired by a photograph of Bill Clinton and a Thanksgiving turkey, yet also recalling the 1951 Paul Gallico adaptation, *Never Take No for an Answer*, this is a charming example of the old movie adage that children invariably know better than grown-ups. Having both lost their mothers at birth, eight-year-old Mehdi Ortelsberg and a calf called Maéva strike up an unlikely friendship that looks set to be terminated by a BSE scare. Director Philippe Muyl challenges society's increasingly callous treatment of animals, yet avoids sentimentality in having the boy appeal to Paris for a reprieve. Nicely done. DP French +subtitles.

Bernard Yerles *Romain* • Florence Pernel *Sarah* • Mehdi Ortelsberg *Lucas* • Christian Bujeau *Jean-René* • Bernard Bloch *Bichon* ■ *Dir/Scr* Philippe Muyl

Cowboy ★★★ PG
Western   1958 · US · Colour · 88min

This grim and gripping western reunited the star and director from the previous year's *3:10 to Yuma*, taciturn Glenn Ford and talented Delmer Daves. It's the story of a young tenderfoot (the excellent Jack Lemmon) and his relationship with tough trail boss Ford. The atmosphere is thoroughly authentic - listen to Ford's acute description of the intelligence of a cowboy's horse - and the Technicolor photography is sharp. TS *DVD*

Glenn Ford *Tom Reece* • Jack Lemmon *Frank Harris* • Anna Kashfi *Maria Vidal* • Brian Donlevy *Doc Bender* • Dick York *Charlie* • Victor Manuel Mendoza *Mendoza* • Richard Jaeckel *Paul Curtis* ■ *Dir* Delmer Daves • *Scr* Edmund H North, from the non-fiction book *My Reminiscences as a Cowboy* by Frank Harris • *Cinematographer* Charles Lawton Jr

The Cowboy and the Lady ★★★ U
Romantic comedy   1938 · US · BW · 87min

Producer Samuel Goldwyn teamed Merle Oberon and Gary Cooper for this romantic comedy about the daughter of a presidential candidate who meets a rodeo cowboy on a blind date. She lies about her background, and complications arise when he proposes marriage. To compensate for what is a very slight story, Goldwyn had the good sense to hire some of the period's cleverest writers. The screen never ignites, but Merle and Coop make a handsome couple. TS

Gary Cooper *Stretch* • Merle Oberon *Mary Smith* • Patsy Kelly *Katie Callahan* • Walter Brennan *Sugar* • Fuzzy Knight *Buzz* • Mabel Todd *Elly* • Henry Kolker *Mr Smith* • Harry Davenport *Uncle Hannibal Smith* • Emma Dunn *Ma Hawkins* ■ *Dir* HC Potter • *Scr* SN Behrman, Sonya Levien, from a story by Leo McCarey, Frank R Adams

Cowboy Bebop: the Movie ★★ 12
Animated action fantasy
2001 · Jpn · Colour · 110min

This flatly drawn and tediously plotted futuristic thriller is a spin-off from a supposedly popular TV cartoon. A small group of bounty hunters is trying to thwart a dastardly bio-terrorism plot. Despite a late 21st-century setting, this has an odd, out-of-date look. JC Japanese +subtitles. Violence. *DVD*

Koichi Yamadera *Spike Spiegel* • Unsho Ishizuka *Jet Black* • Megumi Hayashibara *Faye Valentine* • Aoi Tada *Ed* • Yasuku Yara *Hoffman* ■ *Dir* Shinichiro Watanabe • *Scr* Keiko Nobumoto, from a story by Hajime Yatate

The Cowboy Way ★★ 12
Action comedy   1994 · US · Colour · 102min

Woody Harrelson, with a gleeful disregard for restraint, whoops and hollers his way through the picture, as he and rodeo partner Kiefer Sutherland stalk the Big Apple in search of their Mexican buddy's kidnapped daughter. Harrelson does at least try to make something out of the hugely derivative script, but it's all rather coarse and clumsy. DP Swearing. *DVD*

Woody Harrelson *Pepper* • Kiefer Sutherland *Sonny* • Dylan McDermott *Stark* • Ernie Hudson *Officer Sam Shaw* • Cara Buono *Teresa* • Marg Helgenberger *Margarette* ■ *Dir* Gregg Champion • *Scr* Bill Wittliff, from a story by Bill Wittliff, Rob Thomson

The Cowboys ★★ 12
Western   1972 · US · Colour · 128min

John Wayne hires a group of schoolboys to help him on a cattle drive in this morose, awkwardly paced and overlong would-be epic western. In truth, this rite-of-passage saga just doesn't work, owing to a cumbersome structure and a rather nauseating pro-violence, revenge-is-good message. On the plus side, Bruce Dern and Slim Pickens are good to watch, and Roscoe Lee Browne and Colleen Dewhurst add dignity. TS *DVD* *BD*

John Wayne *Wil Andersen* • Roscoe Lee Browne *Jebediah Nightlinger* • Bruce Dern *Long Hair* • Colleen Dewhurst *Kate* • Slim Pickens *Anse* • Lonny Chapman *Preacher* ■ *Dir* Mark Rydell • *Scr* Irving Ravetch, Harriet Frank Jr, William Dale Jennings, from Jennings's novel

Les Cowboys ★★★ 12A
Drama   2015 · Fr · Colour · 105min

A contemporary reworking of John Ford's western *The Searchers*, this is set in modern France with the focus on a cowboy-loving father who embarks on a quest to find his teenage daughter after she abruptly disappears from a local fête to run off with a Muslim lad. Its unfair to call this meandering drama a remake of Ford's 1956 film, as Bidegain uses it as a template to contemplate themes that resonate as powerfully in the early 21st century as they did back in the 50s. JA In English, French. Drug abuse, some violence, swearing.

François Damiens *Alain Balland* • Finnegan Oldfield *Georges Balland, "Kid"* • Agathe Dronne *Nicole Balland* • Ellora Torchia *Shazhana* • John C Reilly *The American* • Antonia Campbell-Hughes *Emma* ■ *Dir* Thomas Bidegain • *Scr* Thomas Bidegain, Noé Debré, from an idea by Bidegain, Laurent Abitbol

Cowboys & Aliens ★★★★ 12
Science-fiction western adventure
2011 · US · Colour · 113min

Mysterious cowboy Daniel Craig must join forces with tyrannical cattle baron Harrison Ford to make a stand against a fistful of giant mole monsters from outer space in this surprisingly successful hybrid of *The Searchers* and *Independence Day*. Iron Man director Jon Favreau's solid adaptation of a popular 2006 graphic novel is a rousing winner, remaining true to both genres, and boasts genuine surprise, scary jolts and terrific camouflaged spacecraft effects, while the teaming of Craig and Ford works like a charm. AJ Violence. *DVD* *BD*

Daniel Craig *Jake Lonergan* • Harrison Ford *Col Woodrow Dolarhyde* • Olivia Wilde *Ella* • Sam Rockwell *Doc* • Noah Ringer *Emmett* • Keith Carradine *Sheriff Taggart* ■ *Dir* Jon Favreau • *Scr* Roberto Orci, Alex Kurtzman, Damon Lindelof, Mark Fergus, Hawk Ostby, from a comic book by Scott Mitchell Rosenberg

Coyote Ugly ★★ 12
Romantic comedy drama
2000 · US · Colour · 96min

Think *Flashdance* meets *Cocktail* and you'll have a good idea what this flashy Jerry Bruckheimer production is all about. Cute girl Piper Perabo leaves her toll-booth-worker dad (John Goodman) and the safety of the New Jersey suburbs for the bright lights of New York City to pursue her dream of being a songwriter. In the meantime she lands a job at a notorious bar, Coyote Ugly (inspired by a real-life NYC watering hole). A glossy, pop-music-filled piece of fluff. JB *DVD* *BD*

Piper Perabo *Violet Sanford* • Adam Garcia *Kevin O'Donnell* • John Goodman *Bill* • Maria Bello *Lil* • Izabella Miko *Cammie* • Tyra Banks *Zoe* ■ *Dir* David McNally • *Scr* Gina Wendkos

Crack House ★★ 18
Crime drama   1989 · US · Colour · 86min

In 50 years, this movie will be rediscovered and appreciated in the same way that *Reefer Madness* is now. Like that camp classic, this movie is an anti-drug pamphlet dressed up in exploitation clothing, though it's considerably more violent and sexually explicit. Drugs lord Jim Brown has everyone in his LA neighborhood on drugs except for one teenage Hispanic couple. This needs time to reach its full laugh potential. KB

Jim Brown *Steadman* • Richard Roundtree *Lieutenant Johnson* • Anthony Geary *Dockett* • Angel Tompkins *Mother* • Cheryl Kay *Melissa* • Gregg Gomez Thomsen *Rick Morales* ■ *Dir* Michael Fischa • *Scr* Blake Schaeffer, from a story by Jack Silverman

A Crack in the Floor ★ 18
Horror   2000 · US · Colour · 89min

A group of dope-smoking, sex mad city kids go on a camping trip, find an old cabin in the woods they think is uninhabited and spend the rest of movie running from a psycho-killer. Co-director Corby Timbrook does nothing to elevate his bloodbath above the rest of the standard hack-and-thwack pack. Terminally unbalanced by its narrative flaws. AJ *DVD*

Mario Lopez *Lehman* • Gary Busey *Tyler Trout* • Bo Hopkins *Sheriff Talmidge* • Rance Howard *Floyd Fryed* • Tracy Scoggins *Jeremiah's mother* • Justine Priestley *Kate* • Daisy McCrackin *Heidi* • Bentley Mitchum *Johnny* ■ *Dir* Corby Timbrook, Sean Stanek • *Scr* Sean Stanek

Crack in the Mirror ★★★
Crime drama   1960 · US · BW · 96min

A working-class woman of a certain age (Juliette Greco) murders her construction worker husband (Orson Welles) with the help of her virile young lover (Bradford Dillman). The couple are brought to trial, where she is defended by an ambitious young lawyer (Dillman again), who is having an affair with the wife (Greco) of the young man's elderly counsel (Welles). An ingenious idea, directed with pace and style by Richard Fleischer, and with excellent performance from the dual role-playing principals. The message is simplistic and obvious, however, and all six characters are cold, heartless and unsympathetic. RK

Orson Welles *Hagolin/Lamoriciere* • Juliette Greco *Exponine/Florence* • Bradford Dillman *Larnier/Claud* • Alexander Knox *President* • Catherine Lacey *Mother Superior* • William Lucas *Kerstner* • Maurice Teynac *Doctor* ■ *Dir* Richard Fleischer • *Scr* Mark Canfield [Darryl F Zanuck], from the novel *Drama in the Mirror* by Marcel Haedrich

Crack in the World ★★**U**
Science-fiction thriller
1964 · US · Colour · 95min

Scientists attempt to harness the inner energy of the earth and get it all wrong in this moderate sci-fi thriller. Director Andrew Marton knows how to milk this kind of thing, and no one looks more worried about the end of the world than tight-lipped Dana Andrews. The effects just about pass muster, though they may look familiar to fans of the genre. TS

Dana Andrews *Dr Stephen Sorensen* • Janette Scott *Mrs Maggie Sorensen* • Kieron Moore *Ted Rampion* • Alexander Knox *Sir Charles Eggerston* • Peter Damon *Masefield* • Gary Lasdun *Markov* ■ *Dir* Andrew Marton • *Scr* Jon Manchip White, Julian Halevy [Julian Zimet], from a story by Jon Manchip White

Crack-Up ★★**U**
Spy drama   1936 · US · BW · 70min

This very routine programme filler is made far livelier than it has any right to be by the solid acting of an adept supporting cast. Brian Donlevy is a test pilot bribed to steal the design plans of a revolutionary new war plane. Peter Lorre, always watchable even in below-par formula espionage material such as this, is the airport's dumb, bugle-blowing mascot who's really a double agent with his bug-eyes on the same blueprints. AJ

Peter Lorre *Colonel Gimpy* • Brian Donlevy *Ace Martin* • Helen Wood *Ruth Franklin* • Ralph Morgan *John Fleming* • Thomas Beck *Joe Randall* • Kay Linaker *Mrs Fleming* • Lester Matthews *Sidney Grant* ■ *Dir* Malcolm St Clair • *Scr* Charles Kenyon, Sam Mintz, from a story by John Goodrich

Crack-Up ★★
Thriller   1946 · US · BW · 93min

In this dark thriller, Pat O'Brien plays an art lecturer and curator who suffers, or appears to suffer, a nervous breakdown when an international consortium of villains reckons he's too close to exposing a forgery racket. This is an unusual role for O'Brien who stars alongside Claire Trevor, as his loyal girlfriend, and classy Herbert Marshall as a Scotland Yard investigator posing as an art expert. Directed with real flair by Irving Reis, the movie gets off to a terrific start but promises more than it delivers. RK

Pat O'Brien *George Steele* • Claire Trevor *Terry* • Herbert Marshall *Traybin* • Ray Collins *Dr Lowell* • Wallace Ford *Cochrane* • Dean Harens *Reynolds* • Damian O'Flynn *Stevenson* • Erskine Sanford *Barton* • Mary Ware *Mary* ■ *Dir* Irving Reis • *Scr* John Paxton, Ben Bengal, Ray Spencer, from the short story *Madman's Holiday* by Fredric Brown

The Cracker Factory ★★★★
Drama   1979 · US/UK · Colour · 100min

Natalie Wood excels in this made-for-TV movie, imbuing this distinguished drama with both class and dignity as a depressed suburban housewife committed to care after a failed suicide bid. There's a marvellous supporting cast on hand in this prestige production: watch for Vivian Blaine, who played Adelaide in the screen version of *Guys and Dolls*, plus Juliet Mills and a pre-*Cheers* appearance from Shelley Long. The men are negligible, but doctor Perry King is suitably sympathetic. TS

Natalie Wood *Cassie Barrett* • Perry King *Dr Edwin Alexander* • Peter Haskell *Charlie Barrett* • Shelley Long *Clara* • Vivian Blaine *Helen* • Marian Mercer *Eleanor* • Juliet Mills *Tinkerbell* • John Harkins *Father Dunhill* ■ *Dir* Burt Brinckerhoff • *Scr* Richard A Shapiro, from the novel by Joyce Rebeta-Burditt

Crackerjack ★★**U**
Comedy drama   1938 · UK · BW · 76min

Tom Walls, well-loved star of the Aldwych farces during the 1920s, here plays burglar Jack Drake, a sort of "Robbing Hood" who lifts from the rich to help the poor. His success makes other local crooks jealous, and thereby hangs this awfully thin tale, enlivened only by the youthful presence of the lovely Lilli Palmer as co-star. It takes a long time to get up to speed, and today seems very dated indeed. TS

Tom Walls *Jack Drake* • Lilli Palmer *Baroness von Haltse* • Noel Madison *Sculpie* • Edmond Breon [Edmund Breon] *Tony Davenport* • Leon M Lion *Hambro Golding* ■ *Dir* Albert de Courville • *Scr* AR Rawlinson, Michael Pertwee, Basil Mason, from a novel by WB Ferguson

Cracks ★★★★**15**
Coming-of-age drama
2009 · Ire/UK/Sp/US/Fr · Colour · 99min

Director Jordan Scott (daughter of Ridley Scott) shows a sure touch in this, her debut feature. It's a sensual, erotically charged 1930s-set melodrama that has a passing similarity in theme to *The Pride of Miss Jean Brodie*. Eva Green is compelling as Miss G, an inspirational and unorthodox teacher at a girls' boarding school. She dazzles her favoured charges, led by Juno Temple, with tales of foreign travel and adventure, and encourages them to realise their potential. But trouble arrives with the appearance of a mysterious Spanish pupil (Maria Valverde), and what follows is a mesmerising tale of infatuation, jealousy and betrayal. AS Violence, sexual references, nudity. *DVD* *Blu-ray*

Eva Green *Miss G* • Juno Temple *Di Radfield* • Maria Valverde *Fiamma* • Imogen Poots *Poppy* • Ellie Nunn *Lily* • Adele McCann *Laurel* • Zoe Carroll *Rosie* • Clemmie Dugdale *Fuzzy* • Sinead Cusack *Miss Nieven* ■ *Dir* Jordan Scott • *Scr* Ben Court, Caroline Ip, Jordan Scott, from the novel by Sheila Kohler

The Cracksman ★★**U**
Crime comedy   1963 · UK · Colour · 107min

This is far and away Charlie Drake's finest hour on the big screen. Sadly, that's not saying much. He also co-scripted this average crime comedy, in which he plays a locksmith whose devotion to duty lands him in jail. A muddle of slapstick and pathos, the film is ridiculously overlong and needlessly opulent. DP *DVD*

Charlie Drake *Ernest Wright* • George Sanders *The Guv'nor* • Dennis Price *Grantley* • Nyree Dawn Porter *Muriel* • Eddie Byrne *Domino* • Finlay Currie *Feathers* • Percy Herbert *Nosher* ■ *Dir* Peter Graham Scott • *Scr* Lew Schwartz, Mike Watts, Charlie Drake

Cradle of Fear ★★★**18**
Portmanteau horror   2001 · UK · Colour · 119min

Drenched in blood and bad taste, this chronicles the crimes of a cannibalistic hypnotist and his lugubrious henchman. Shot on high-resolution video against the backdrop of some quintessentially British locations, this gore quartet revels in its scabrous portrait of a decadent society in which no depravity is deemed excessive

and no one is immune from an obsession with self-gratification. DP *DVD*

Dani Filth *The man* • Eileen Daly *Natalie* • Emily Bouffante *Melissa* • Stuart Laing *Richard* • David McEwen *Kemper* • Louie Brownsell *Nick* • Emma Rice *Emma* • Edmund Dehn *Detective Neilson* ■ *Dir/Scr* Alex Chandon

Cradle 2 the Grave ★★★**15**
Martial arts crime thriller
2003 · US · Colour · 97min

Romeo Must Die duo Jet Li and rapper DMX here reunite with director Andrzej Bartkowiak for another frenetic slice of cultural fusion. Combining eastern martial arts with western urban grit, this plays with the clichés of the buddy movie. DMX's streetwise entrepreneur is forced into an uneasy alliance with Taiwanese intelligence agent Li after his young daughter is kidnapped by Li's former partner (Mark Dacascos). Witty and unpretentious. SF Violence, swearing, sex scenes. *DVD*

Jet Li *Su* • DM X *Tony Fait* • Anthony Anderson *Tommy* • Kelly Hu *Sona* • Tom Arnold *Archie* • Mark Dacascos *Ling* • Gabrielle Union *Daria* ■ *Dir* Andrzej Bartkowiak • *Scr* John O'Brien, Channing Gibson, from a story by John O'Brien

Cradle Will Rock ★★★**15**
Political drama based on a true story
1999 · US · Colour · 128min

Set during the anti-communist witch-hunts of the 1930s, this dense and rather gruelling political drama focuses on the efforts of a bunch of New York theatre folk, including Orson Welles, to stage a left-wing play. When the powers that be block the project, all involved decide the show must go on. Tim Robbins marshals the material with skill, convincingly evoking the vibrancy of both place and period. Yet he over-eggs the pudding by cramming in too many storylines. DA *DVD*

Hank Azaria *Marc Blitzstein* • Rubén Blades *Diego Rivera* • Joan Cusack *Hazel Huffman* • John Cusack *Nelson Rockefeller* • Cary Elwes *John Houseman* • Philip Baker Hall *Gray Mathers* • Cherry Jones *Hallie Flanagan* • Angus MacFadyen *Orson Welles* • Bill Murray *Tommy Crickshaw* • Vanessa Redgrave *Countess LaGrange* • Susan Sarandon *Margherita Sarfatti* • John Turturro *Aldo Silvano* • Emily Watson *Olive Stanton* ■ *Dir/Scr* Tim Robbins

The Craft ★★★**15**
Supernatural horror thriller
1996 · US · Colour · 100min

Four schoolfriends find that sorcery is a real help when it comes to relationship problems and dealing with their various physical and emotional worries. Until one of them seeks real power, that is. This skilfully mixes a brew of plausible characters, neat visual effects and a few creepy moments. The attractive cast of stars-to-be coupled with the film's glossy visual style lift this above your average genre fare, as does a smarter-than-expected script. JC Violence, swearing. *DVD*

Robin Tunney *Sarah* • Fairuza Balk *Nancy* • Neve Campbell *Bonnie* • Rachel True *Rochelle* • Skeet Ulrich *Chris* • Christine Taylor *Laura Lizzie* • Breckin Meyer *Mitt* • Nathaniel Marston *Trey* • Cliff De Young *Mr Bailey* ■ *Dir* Andrew Fleming • *Scr* Peter Filardi, Andrew Fleming, from a story by Peter Filardi

The Craic ★★★**15**
Comedy   1999 · Aus · Colour · 85min

Stand-up comic Jimeoin McKeown stars as a Belfast shirker, who has to flee with his mate Alan McKee after they fall foul of IRA leader Robert Morgan. Things get no better in Sydney, where his appearance on a TV dating game results in immigration officials, secret service agents and Morgan pursuing him through the outback. The winning personality of the star and the perfect pitch and pace of Ted Emery's direction ensured its place among the biggest box-office hits in Australian cinema history. DP Swearing.

Jimeoin [Jimeoin McKeown] *Fergus* • Alan McKee *Wesley* • Robert Morgan *Colin* • Jane Hall *Alice* • Kate Gorman *Margo* ■ *Dir* Ted Emery • *Scr* Jimeoin [Jimeoin McKeown]

Craig's Wife ★★
Drama   1936 · US · BW · 74min

This was the movie that turned actress Rosalind Russell into a fully fledged box-office name: a turgid tale about a housewife who cares more for material things than for her husband. Overrated cult director Dorothy Arzner, a former editor and scriptwriter, tries to add hidden depths to the source material, an intractable play by Grace Kelly's uncle, George. TS

Rosalind Russell *Harriet Craig* • John Boles *Walter Craig* • Billie Burke *Mrs Frazier* • Jane Darwell *Mrs Harold* • Dorothy Wilson *Ethel Landreth* • Alma Kruger *Miss Austen* ■ *Dir* Dorothy Arzner • *Scr* Mary C McCall Jr, from the play by George Kelly

The Cranes Are Flying ★★★★**PG**
Romantic drama   1957 · USSR · BW · 91min

One of the first Soviet films made after a political "thaw" which seemed to herald a new artistic freedom in the country's cinema, this prize-winning love story, directed by Mikhail Kalatozov, concerns a young hospital worker (Tatyana Samoilova) who contracts a loveless marriage following reports that her soldier fiancé has been killed. An unpretentious and poetic movie about love and the Second World War that benefits from some majestic camerawork and a sensitive performance by Samoilova. The film received the Palme d'Or at Cannes in 1958. RB *DVD*

Tatyana Samoilova *Veronica* • Alexei Batalov *Boris* • Vasili Merkuriev *Byodor Ivanovich* • Aleksandr Shvorin *Mark* • S Kharitonova *Irina* ■ *Dir* Mikhail Kalatozov • *Scr* Victor Rosov, from a play by Victor Rosov • *Cinematographer* Sergei Urusevsky

Crank ★★**18**
Action thriller   2006 · US · Colour · 84min

Mark Neveldine and Brian Taylor betray their roots in commercials with this nonstop barrage of flashy tricks and breakneck action in which visual and narrative absurdity vie with each other on an insanely epic scale. Jason Statham plays a retired hitman injected with poison who will die if his adrenaline level drops. To keep his heart rate up he ingests every drug going and, in a hilarious highlight, has public sex in Chinatown with girlfriend Amy Smart. It's *Speed* with a man instead of a bus, but taken seriously it's just a violent and vulgar distraction. AJ Violence, swearing, drug abuse, a sex scene, nudity. *DVD* *Blu-ray* *CS*

Jason Statham *Chev Chelios* • Amy Smart *Eve* • Efren Ramirez *Kaylo* • Dwight Yoakam *Doc Miles* • Jose Pablo Cantillo *Verona* • Carlos Sanz *Carlito* ■ *Dir/Scr* Mark Neveldine, Brian Taylor

Crank: High Voltage ★★**18**
Action thriller   2009 · US · Colour · 91min

An ageing Chinese mobster gets a new lease of life by stealing Jason Statham's virtually indestructible heart in the identikit sequel to the 2006 speed-freak cult movie. Returning co-directors Mark Neveldine and Brian Taylor's philosophy is "if it ain't broke don't fix it" in their continuation of the preposterously frenetic franchise – here, Statham's Chev Chelios has to constantly recharge his replacement battery-operated organ to keep himself alive. With the core cast also back, everything is jacked-up to the max in an insanely violent, live-action cartoon with beyond-bad-taste slurs towards every race and gender, outrageous sexual offensiveness and rapid-fire swearing. AJ Violence, swearing, sex scenes, nudity. *DVD* *Blu-ray*

Jason Statham *Chev Chelios* • Amy Smart *Eve* • Clifton Collins Jr *El Huron* • Efren Ramirez *Venus* • Bai Ling *Ria* • David Carradine *Poon Dong* • Dwight Yoakam *Doc Miles* ■ *Dir* Mark Neveldine, Brian Taylor • *Scr* Mark Neveldine, Brian Taylor, from characters by Neveldine, Taylor

Crash! ★
Horror   1977 · US · Colour · 89min

Sue Lyon brings home a supernatural relic whose spirit possesses anything with wheels, including the family auto. When her

C

crippled husband (José Ferrer) tries to kill her, the demonic vehicle tries to kill him in return. A low-budget, confusing wreck. **AJ**

José Ferrer *Marc Denne* • John Carradine *Dr Edwards* • Sue Lyon *Kim Denne* • John Ericson *Greg* • Leslie Parrish *Kathy* ■ *Dir* Charles Band • *Scr* Marc Marais

Crash ★★★★★ 18
Drama 1996 · Can · Colour · 96min

How the giving and receiving of love, and the sexual act that usually communicates those primal feelings, will evolve in our increasingly technological world, is at the core of this controversial masterpiece from director David Cronenberg. Based on JG Ballard's cult novel, this uncompromising film is set among a group of urban sophisticates so morally exhausted that they need to invent perversions to keep what sensuality they have left alive. Car accidents become sadomasochistic turn-ons and bodily injury becomes a metaphor for how we must reshape our eroded humanity to exist in the hi-tech future. In no way pornographic or exploitative, and containing the most astonishing performance from Deborah Kara Unger, Cronenberg's daring, intellectual wake-up call is potent food for thought and a landmark 1990s fantasy. **AJ** Swearing, sex scenes, nudity, violence. *DVD*

James Spader *James Ballard* • Holly Hunter *Dr Helen Remington* • Elias Koteas *Vaughan* • Deborah Kara Unger *Catherine Ballard* • Rosanna Arquette *Gabrielle* • Peter MacNeil [Peter MacNeill] *Colin Seagrave* ■ *Dir* David Cronenberg • *Scr* David Cronenberg, from the novel by JG Ballard

Crash ★★★★ 15
Drama 2004 · US/Ger/Aus · Colour · 107min

Los Angeles provides the setting for writer/director Paul Haggis's finely tuned ensemble drama about interconnected lives, which ambitiously weaves several narrative strands into a short time frame, in this case, just 36 hours. A raft of fully developed characters – among them a corrupt cop (Matt Dillon), a highly-strung wife (Thandie Newton) and a sharp detective (Don Cheadle) – are linked by chance, criminal acts and simmering racial tensions. As events unfold, even the most seasoned moviegoer will find something here to surprise and shock. **KK** Swearing, violence. *DVD* *Blu*

Sandra Bullock *Jean* • Don Cheadle *Graham Walters* • Matt Dillon *Officer Ryan* • Jennifer Esposito *Ria* • William Fichtner *Flanagan* • Brendan Fraser *Rick* • Terrence Howard *Cameron* • Chris "Ludacris" Bridges *Anthony* • Thandie Newton *Christine* • Ryan Phillippe *Officer Hansen* ■ *Dir* Paul Haggis • *Scr* Paul Haggis, Bobby Moresco, from a story by Paul Haggis

Crash Dive ★★ U
Second World War adventure
1943 · US · Colour · 101min

On board a US submarine, lieutenant Tyrone Power (in his last movie before his own Second World War service) and commander Dana Andrews are rivals for the love of Anne Baxter. Stick with this adventure (it's dull in patches) to witness Hollywood propaganda at its most blatant. The special effects won an Oscar (Fred Sersen for visuals, Roger Heman for sound). **TS** *DVD*

Tyrone Power USMCR [Tyrone Power] *Lt Ward Stewart* • Anne Baxter *Jean Hewlett* • Dana Andrews *Lt Comm Dewey Connors* • James Gleason *McDonnell* • Dame May Whitty *Grandmother* ■ *Dir* Archie Mayo • *Scr* Jo Swerling, from a story by WR Burnett

The Crash Reel ★★★★ 12
Documentary 2013 · US · Colour · 108min

Director Lucy Walker's sensitive study follows Kevin Pearce, the 23-year-old snowboarder who was training to represent the United States at the Vancouver Winter Olympics when a horrific crash on a practice run left him with serious injuries to his brain. Putting Pearce's long road to recovery in the context of his epic rivalry with Shaun White, Walker captures the addictive thrill of extreme sports that

prompts Pearce to attempt an audacious comeback. But with his parents and brothers urging caution, Walker's film becomes less a study of athletic excellence than of domestic intimacy, and deeply moving it is, too. **DP** Swearing.

Kevin Pearce • Shaun White ■ *Dir* Lucy Walker

Crash: the Mystery of Flight 1501 ★★★ PG
Drama 1990 · US · Colour · 91min

A nearly-but-not-quite fascinating American TV movie, starring Cheryl Ladd and centring on the crash of a plane that goes down with no clear explanation. The in-flight scenes avoid most of the clichés of the airplane disaster genre, but the attempt to solve the mystery of the film's title gets a spot mired in the excessive detail provided about the life of one of the crash's two survivors. **PF**

Cheryl Ladd *Diane Halstead* • Jeffrey DeMunn *Scott Cody* • Doug Sheehan *Greg Halstead* • Frederick Coffin *Wes Goddard* • Peter Jurasik *Bob Stanton* • Jim Metzler *Spense Zolman* ■ *Dir* Philip Saville • *Scr* E Arthur Kean

Crashout ★★★ 15
Crime drama 1955 · US · BW · 84min

This tough crime drama follows six escaped convicts as they spend three days holed up in a cave before going after buried loot. The usual fall-outs and double crosses steadily reduce their number, but telling characterisations and clever plot developments maintain the interest. All credit to the usually undistinguished director and co-writer, Lewis R Foster, who has the benefit of some terrific black-and-white photography by Russell Metty. **AE**

William Bendix *Van Duff* • Arthur Kennedy *Joe Quinn* • Luther Adler *Pete Mendoza* • William Talman *Swanee Remsen* • Gene Evans *Monk Collins* • Marshall Thompson *Billy Lang* • Beverly Michaels *Alice Mosher* • Gloria Talbott *Girl on train* ■ *Dir* Lewis R Foster • *Scr* Lewis R Foster, Hal E Chester

Crawl ★★★ 15
Crime thriller 2011 · Aus · Colour · 77min

Claustrophobic heat and brooding terror are effectively evoked in this homage to *film noir*, Alfred Hitchcock and the Coen brothers. In a rural Australian town, a seedy bar owner hires a Croatian hitman (George Shevtsov) to murder a garage owner after a business deal goes bad, but the simple plan backfires and an innocent waitress is taken hostage. It's a slow-burning exercise in tightly wound tension, crafted with graceful skill, atmospheric lighting and fluid camerawork. Writer/director Paul China could not have been better served by leads Shevtsov and Georgina Haig, the latter playing a character called Marilyn Burns in a nod to the heroine of the original *Texas Chain Saw Massacre*. **AJ** Violence, swearing, drug abuse. *DVD*

Georgina Haig *Marilyn Burns* • George Shevtsov *The Stranger* • Paul Holmes *Slim Walding* • Lauren Dillon *Holly* ■ *Dir/Scr* Paul China

Craze ★ 15
Horror 1973 · UK · Colour · 91min

Jack Palance gives his eye-rolling all as a mad antique collector who plans to increase his wealth by sacrificing London dolly birds to his favourite African idol. Trashy, endless rubbish from producer Herman Cohen, with an amazingly eclectic cast, this infernal nonsense even defeats veteran horror director Freddie Francis. **AJ** *DVD*

Jack Palance *Neal Mottram* • Diana Dors *Dolly Newman* • Julie Ege *Helena* • Edith Evans *Aunt Louise* • Trevor Howard *Superintendent Bellamy* • Suzy Kendall *Sally* • Michael Jayston *Detective Sergeant Wall* • Hugh Griffith *Solicitor* ■ *Dir* Freddie Francis • *Scr* Aben Kandel, Herman Cohen, from the novel *Infernal Idol* by Henry Seymour

The Crazies ★★★ 18
Science-fiction horror
1973 · US · Colour · 98min

This is a commendable, if unsuccessful, attempt by director George A Romero to

repeat the success of his revolutionary horror classic *Night of the Living Dead*. Here, panic and paranoia prevail when an army plane carrying a biochemical virus crashes in Pennsylvania and turns the locals into killers. Shifting points of view keep involvement to a minimum and greatly undercut the suspense, despite some effective gore moments. Remade in 2010. **AJ** Violence, swearing. *DVD*

Lane Carroll *Judy* • WG McMillan [Will MacMillan] *David* • Harold Wayne Jones *Clank* • Lloyd Hollar *Col Pockem* • Richard Liberty *Artie* • Lynn Lowry *Kathie* • Richard France *Dr Watts* ■ *Dir* George A Romero • *Scr* George A Romero, from a story by Paul McCollough

The Crazies ★★★★ 15
Horror 2010 · US · Colour · 97min

This upgrade of horror maestro George A Romero's 1973 cult favourite from *Sahara* director Breck Eisner is a much more worthwhile remake than most. In an expert reinvention, sheriff Timothy Olyphant and his pregnant wife Radha Mitchell try to escape the deadly virus that's turning the local population into zombie-like psychopathic killers. Eisner puts the suspenseful action on a far bigger canvas by using wide-open spaces to superbly creepy effect. The horror moments are equally well staged and sustained, with the car-wash attack a particular highlight. Not only is the film effective in making points about potential quarantine dangers, but also in how they could be horribly mishandled, and it's all frighteningly underlined by the shocking finale. **AJ** Violence, swearing. *DVD* *Blu*

Timothy Olyphant *Sheriff David Dutton* • Radha Mitchell *Dr Judy Dutton* • Danielle Panabaker *Becca Darling* • Joe Anderson (1) *Russell Clank* • Christie Lynn Smith *Deardra Farnum* ■ *Dir* Breck Eisner • *Scr* Scott Kosar, Ray Wright, from the 1973 film

CRAZY ★★★ 15
Coming-of-age comedy drama
2005 · Can · Colour · 127min

This vibrant rite-of-passage tale from Canadian director Jean-Marc Vallée is a pop culture-soaked journey through the first 20 years of a sexually confused Montreal boy's life. It takes well-trodden themes and delivers them in an irreverently fresh way. From his early 1960s childhood to his rebellious, Bowie-obsessed teens, Zac's existence is upbeat and idiosyncratic. The family conflicts that unfold swing from darkly comic to painfully raw. It's only in the final third that the picture loses momentum, overstretching itself by tackling too many issues. **SF** French +subtitles. Swearing, sex scenes, drug abuse. *DVD*

Michel Côté *Gervais Beaulieu* • Marc-André Grondin *Zachary Beaulieu (15-21 years old)* • Danielle Proulx *Laurianne Beaulieu* • Emile Vallée *Zachary Beaulieu (6-8 years old)* • Pierre-Luc Brillant *Raymond Beaulieu (22-28 years old)* • Maxime Tremblay *Christian Beaulieu (24-30 years old)* • Alex Gravel *Antoine Beaulieu (21-27 years old)* • Natacha Thompson *Michelle (15-22 years old)* • Johanne Lebrun *Doris* ■ *Dir* Jean-Marc Vallée • *Scr* Jean-Marc Vallée, François Boulay

crazy/beautiful ★★★ 12
Romantic drama 2001 · US · Colour · 94min

Director John Stockwell's sexy teen drama is predictable from beginning to end, but fortunately the journey is made bearable by the refreshing charm of Kirsten Dunst who illuminates even the most witless lines of dialogue. She plays a spoilt little rich girl who's constantly getting into drink and drug trouble. Deprived Hispanic Jay Hernandez, on the other hand, is a model student who takes his career goals seriously. They fall in love and wreak havoc on each other's differing lives. **AJ** *DVD*

Kirsten Dunst *Nicole Oakley* • Jay Hernandez *Carlos Nunez* • Bruce Davison *Tom Oakley* • Herman Osorio *Luis* • Miguel Castro *Eddie* • Tommy De La Cruz *Victor* ■ *Dir* John Stockwell • *Scr* Phil Hay, Matt Manfredi

Crazy for Christmas ★★ PG
Seasonal drama 2005 · US · Colour · 89min

In this flimsy festive diversion, cash-strapped single mum Andrea Roth is hired to chauffeur an eccentric rich man (Howard Hesseman) around town on Christmas Eve. The syrupy seasonal sentiments come thick and fast, as the Santa-like millionaire spreads holiday cheer while mysteriously trying to bond with his reluctant driver. **SF** *DVD*

Andrea Roth *Shannon McManus-Johnson* • Howard Hesseman *Fred Nickells* • Jason Spevack *Trevor McManus-Johnson* • Yannick Bisson *Peter Archer* ■ *Dir* Eleanor Lindo • *Scr* Rick Bitzelberger, Michael A Simpson

Crazy from the Heart ★★★★ PG
Romantic comedy 1991 · US · Colour · 90min

The consistently underrated Christine Lahti gives a glorious performance as a schoolteacher who falls for janitor Rubén Blades, causing all sorts of ructions in her small town. Lahti's real-life husband Thomas Schlamme directs with a sure, delicate touch that lifts this potentially ordinary story, revealing considerable character insight. The pace is nigh on perfect, the leading actors are believable and the charge generated between them keeps the audience guessing to the very end. **SH** Swearing.

Christine Lahti *Charlotte Bain* • Rubén Blades *Ernesto Ontiveros* • William Russ *Coach Dewey Whitcomb* • Louise Latham *Mae Esther Bain* • Tommy Muñiz *Tomas Ontiveros* • Mary Kay Place *Merrilee Payton* • Robyn Lively *Franny Payton* ■ *Dir* Thomas Schlamme • *Scr* Linda Voorhees

Crazy Heart ★★★★ 15
Music drama 2009 · US · Colour · 106min

Music is the food of love, and love feeds the muse itself, in this intimate drama starring Jeff Bridges. Like the approach of first-time writer/director Scott Cooper, Bridges's turn is modest, though jokingly brash in places – and the more compelling because of those contradictions. Playing craggy faded country singer Bad Blake, he quietly works his way into the affections of a journalist (a tough yet tender Maggie Gyllenhaal) and becomes caught between his need for her and a long-held booze addiction. The script is creaky in places, and Colin Farrell is miscast as Bad's big-name protégé. But Bridges's iconic, Oscar-winning performance makes it easy to forget the imperfections. **SP** Swearing. *DVD* *Blu*

Jeff Bridges *Bad Blake* • Maggie Gyllenhaal *Jean Craddock* • Robert Duvall *Wayne Kramer* • Tom Bower *Bill Wilson* • Colin Farrell (2) *Tommy Sweet* • James Keane *Manager* ■ *Dir* Scott Cooper • *Scr* Scott Cooper, from Thomas Cobb's novel

Crazy in Alabama ★★★ 12
Comedy drama 1999 · US · Colour · 108min

Antonio Banderas makes an accomplished directorial debut with this engaging mix of quirky comedy and civil rights drama that gives his partner, Melanie Griffith, her best role in years. While downtrodden housewife Lucille (Griffith) heads for Hollywood with her husband's head in a hatbox, her young nephew Peejoe (Lucas Black) becomes a key witness in the murder of a black protester. Robert Wagner and Rod Steiger shine in supporting roles. **NS** Violence, swearing. *DVD*

Melanie Griffith *Lucille* • David Morse *Dove* • Lucas Black *Peejoe* • Cathy Moriarty *Earlene* • Meat Loaf Aday [Meat Loaf] *Sheriff John Doggett* • Rod Steiger *Judge Mead* • Robert Wagner *Harry Hall* • Elizabeth Perkins *Joan Blake* ■ *Dir* Antonio Banderas • *Scr* Mark Childress, from his novel

Crazy in Love ★★★★ PG
Romantic drama 1992 · US · Colour · 89min

Here's one for those who usually give TV movies a miss. Director Martha Coolidge conjures up a winning drama in which she gets the balance between comedy and sentiment just about right. Holly Hunter plays a wife anxious about the faithfulness of her husband (Bill Pullman). Hunter and her one-time flatmate Frances McDormand give lovely performances, but the film belongs to Gena Rowlands who makes acting look easy. This is the sort of frothy romance Hollywood made to order before someone mislaid the formula. DP

Holly Hunter *Georgie Symonds* • Gena Rowlands *Honora* • Frances McDormand *Clare* • Bill Pullman *Nick Symonds* • Julian Sands *Mark Constable* • Herta Ware *Pem* • Joanne Baron *Mona Tuchman* • Diane Robin *Jean Snizort* ■ *Dir* Martha Coolidge • *Scr* Gerald Ayres, from the novel by Luanne Rice

Crazy Mama ★★★

Crime road movie   1975 · US · Colour · 79min

This rough-hewn road movie from director Jonathan Demme tracks three generations of women, plus their partners, on a lunatic trans-American crime spree. Cloris Leachman, Ann Sothern, Jim Backus and Stuart Whitman head the eclectic cast of an upbeat celebration of 1950s Americana that stems from Demme's so-called "exploitation" period. Worth seeing as an indication of where a top talent learns his trade. DA

Cloris Leachman *Melba* • Stuart Whitman *Jim Bob* • Ann Sothern *Sheba* • Jim Backus *Mr Albertson* • Donny Most *Shawn* • Linda Purl *Cheryl* • Bryan England *Snake* • Dennis Quaid ■ *Dir* Jonathan Demme • *Scr* Robert Thom, from a story by Frances Doel

Crazy Moon ★★★ 15

Comedy drama   1986 · Can · Colour · 85min

This comic tale originally went by the rather hideous name of *Huggers*, but don't let either title put you off: this sweet, if somewhat clichéd romance has a lot to recommend it. Kiefer Sutherland is moving as the wealthy high-school outsider who falls for a deaf girl (Vanessa Vaughan) and encounters opposition from family and peers. JB DVD

Kiefer Sutherland *Brooks* • Peter Spence *Cleveland* • Vanessa Vaughan *Anne* • Ken Pogue *Alec* • Eve Napier *Mimi* • Harry Hill (1) *Dr Bruno* ■ *Dir* Allan Eastman • *Scr* Tom Berry, Stefan Wodoslawsky

Crazy People ★ 15

Comedy   1990 · US · Colour · 87min

This embarrassingly bungled comedy started life with the best of intentions (to satirise the glossy excesses of the advertising industry) but slipped heavily on its own banana skin. Dudley Moore, is the ad man who is thrown into a luxury sanatorium after he launches a campaign of slogans which tell the truth. Inept and offensive. SH Swearing. DVD

Dudley Moore *Emory Leeson* • Daryl Hannah *Kathy Burgess* • Paul Reiser *Stephen Bachman* • JT Walsh *Charles F Drucker* • Bill Smitrovich *Bruce* • Alan North *Judge* • David Paymer *George* • Mercedes Ruehl *Dr Liz Baylor* ■ *Dir* Tony Bill • *Scr* Mitch Markowitz

Crazy, Stupid, Love

★★★★ 12

Romantic comedy drama
2011 · US · Colour · 124min

In this disarming comedy drama, Steve Carell and Ryan Gosling share the majority of the screen-time in a multi-stranded story, with Carell on form as a happily married man – until wife Julianne Moore asks for a divorce. Gosling is the womaniser who offers to help restore Carell's manhood, and for a while this plays like *Pygmalion* in shiny suits. Another subplot involving Carell's son and the babysitter slows the pace, and a contrived finale somewhat undermines the realism, but there's more than enough charm and good humour here. SP Some swearing, sexual references. DVD BL

Steve Carell *Cal Weaver* • Ryan Gosling *Jacob Palmer* • Julianne Moore *Emily Weaver* • Emma Stone *Hannah* • Analeigh Tipton *Jessica Riley* • Jonah Bobo *Robbie* • Joey King *Molly* • Marisa Tomei *Kate* ■ *Dir* Glenn Ficarra, John Requa • *Scr* Dan Fogelman

Creation ★★ PG

Biographical drama   2009 · UK · Colour · 103min

Paul Bettany and his real-life wife Jennifer Connelly reteam eight years after *A Beautiful Mind* in another story about a troubled genius. Bettany stars as 19th-century naturalist Charles Darwin, whose ground-breaking work on evolution, *On the Origins of Species*, puts him at odds with the church and his deeply religious wife (Connelly). The scenes of domestic life are well handled by director Jon Amiel (*Sommersby*), but the film quickly descends from historical drama into a banal ghost story, with Darwin haunted by the memory of his daughter (Martha West). SP DVD BL

Paul Bettany *Charles Darwin* • Jennifer Connelly *Emma Darwin* • Jeremy Northam *Reverend Innes* • Toby Jones *Thomas Huxley* • Benedict Cumberbatch *Joseph Hooker* • Jim Carter *Parslow* • Bill Paterson *Dr Gully* ■ *Dir* Jon Amiel • *Scr* John Collee, from a story by Jon Amiel, Collee, from the biography *Annie's Box: Charles Darwin, His Daughter and Human Evolution* by Randal Keynes

Creator ★★ 15

Romantic comedy drama
1985 · US · Colour · 103min

This jumbled comedy drama involves a Nobel Prize-winning scientist turned college professor who tries to resurrect his long-dead wife via cloning. Peter O'Toole brings his customary God-like grandeur to the lead role, complemented by a young, amiable supporting cast. The film's chief handicap is an excess of soap opera-style plot strands. JC DVD

Peter O'Toole *Dr Harry Wolper* • Mariel Hemingway *Meli* • Vincent Spano *Boris* • Virginia Madsen *Barbara Spencer* • David Ogden Stiers *Sid Kuhlenbeck* • John Dehner *Paul* • Karen Kopins *Lucy Wolper* • Kenneth Tigar *Pavlo* ■ *Dir* Ivan Passer • *Scr* Jeremy Leven, from his novel

Creature from the Black Lagoon ★★★★ PG

Horror   1954 · US · BW · 79min

It's horribly dated, the acting's lousy, the 3D effects are worthless and the monster is a man in a rubber suit. Yet this remains one of the all-time classic monster movies. The by-the-numbers plot – explorers encounter a half-man, half-fish that has the hots for Julia Adams – is enlivened by director Jack Arnold's atmospheric use of the Florida Everglades locations and a sympathetic portrait of the "Gill-Man". The underwater sequences are particularly memorable, while the scene where Adams swims alone with the creature watching from below plays upon all our fears. Avoid the two turgid sequels that followed: *Revenge of the Creature* (1955) and *The Creature Walks among Us* (1956). RS DVD BL 3D

Richard Carlson *David Reed* • Julia Adams [Julie Adams] *Kay Lawrence* • Richard Denning *Mark Williams* • Antonio Moreno *Carl Maia* • Nestor Paiva *Lucas* • Whit Bissell *Edwin Thompson* • Ben Chapman *Gill-Man* • Ricou Browning *Gill-Man (underwater sequences only)* ■ *Dir* Jack Arnold • *Scr* Harry Essex, Arthur Ross, from a story by Maurice Zimm

Creature from the Haunted Sea ★ 12

Horror   1961 · US · BW · 74min

This is another in the long line of Roger Corman quickies geared around a cheaply constructed monster. Playboy conman Anthony Carbone kills loyalists planning a counter-revolution in the Caribbean for their funds and blames the murders on a mythical sea creature. AJ DVD

Antony Carbone *Renzo Capetto* • Betsy Jones-Moreland *Mary-Belle* • Edward Wain [Robert Towne] *Sparks Moran* • Edmundo Rivera Alvarez *Tostada* • Robert Bean *Jack* • Sonya Noemi Mango ■ *Dir* Roger Corman • *Scr* Charles B Griffith

The Creature Walks among Us ★★

Horror   1956 · US · BW · 78min

The third and final outing for *The Creature from the Black Lagoon* (after 1955's *Revenge of the Creature*). Captured in the Everglades by scientists Jeff Morrow and Rex Reason, the famous Gill Man is mutated so he can live on land. Blamed for a crime he didn't commit, the transformed semi-human breaks out of his cage to bring his tormentors to justice while falling under the spell of Leigh Snowden. A disappointment. AJ

Jeff Morrow *Dr William Barton* • Rex Reason *Dr Thomas Morgan* • Leigh Snowden *Marcia Barton* • Gregg Palmer *Jed Grant* • Maurice Manson *Dr Borg* • Don Megowan *Creature (on land)* ■ *Dir* John Sherwood • *Scr* Arthur Ross

Creature with the Atom Brain ★

Science-fiction crime horror
1955 · US · BW · 69min

"He comes from beyond the grave!" hailed the poster, and you'll feel like crawling into one after watching this laboured hokum. Here a suitably bonkers Richard Denning uses atomic energy to create zombie-like robots as instruments of his tortured revenge. Curt Siodmak, who wrote the classic *I Walked with a Zombie* in 1943, really seems to be slumming it here. RS

Richard Denning *Dr Chet Walker* • Angela Stevens *Joyce Walker* • S John Launer *Captain Dave Harris* • Michael Granger *Frank Buchanan* • Gregory Gaye *Professor Steigg* ■ *Dir* Edward L Cahn • *Scr* Curt Siodmak

Les Créatures ★★★★

Drama   1966 · Fr/Swe · Colour and BW · 91min

Agnès Varda's most avant-garde film begins with an inverted homage to the scene in Robert Bresson's *Pickpocket*, as items are slipped into pockets rather as ideas unwittingly pop into heads. Following a car crash, as a result of which hard-boiled novelist Michel Piccoli is scarred and wife Catherine Deneuve is left mute, the action switches to the island of Noirmoutier, where Piccoli finds inspiration for his latest book by walking among the eccentric inhabitants. This is an often surreal experience, but its optimistic conclusion shifts it back from fairy tale into something approaching life. DP French +subtitles.

Catherine Deneuve *Mylène* • Michel Piccoli *Edgar* • Eva Dahlbeck *Michèle Quellec* • Jacques Charrier *René de Montyon* • Nino Castelnuovo *Jean Modet* • Ursula Kubler *Vamp* ■ *Dir/Scr* Agnès Varda

Creatures the World Forgot ★★ 18

Adventure   1971 · UK · Colour · 91min

Hammer's fourth exotic excursion back to One Million Years BC skips monster dinosaurs and special effects to concentrate on sexy cavewomen. Buxom Julie Ege is the daughter of a tribal chief given to the leader of a rival clan, in a thin story that's just an excuse for the former Miss Norway to slip into a revealing wardrobe of leather bikinis and skimpy furs. AJ Nudity.

Julie Ege *Nala* • Brian O'Shaughnessy *Mak* • Tony Bonner *Toomak* • Robert John *Rool* • Marcia Fox *Dumb girl* • Rosalie Crutchley *Old crone* • Don Leonard *Old leader* ■ *Dir* Don Chaffey • *Scr* Michael Carreras

Creed ★★★★ 12

Sports drama   2015 · US · Colour · 133min

Forty years after the original, the seventh instalment in the *Rocky* franchise is one of its best – a fresh-faced crowd-pleaser for fans and the uninitiated alike. Michael B Jordan plays Adonis Johnson, son of the late Apollo Creed, who seeks out a coach in his father's nemesis and friend Rocky Balboa (Sylvester Stallone). A perfect transition of old and new, Stallone and Jordan are a credible screen partnership, and judicious use of the *Rocky* theme still brings tears to the eyes. Pure entertainment – this is one fine boxing movie with a hero for young and old. KK Violence, swearing, sexual references. DVD BL

Sylvester Stallone *Rocky Balboa* • Michael B Jordan *Adonis Creed* • Tessa Thompson *Bianca* • Phylicia Rashad *Mary Anne Creed* ■ *Dir* Ryan Coogler • *Scr* Ryan Coogler, Aaron Covington, from characters by Sylvester Stallone

Creep ★★★ 18

Horror thriller   2004 · UK/Ger · Colour · 81min

Christopher Smith's debut feature is an entertaining ghost-train ride through subterranean hazards. A late journey on the London Underground turns into a nightmare for Franka Potente when she falls asleep on a platform and finds herself trapped underground. Tautly directed by Smith and well-anchored by a barnstorming turn from Potente, this often brutal tale creeps you out with sudden shocks, eerie atmospherics and gory thrills. AJ Violence. DVD

Franka Potente *Kate* • Sean Harris *Craig* • Vas Blackwood *George* • Ken Campbell *Arthur* • Jeremy Sheffield *Guy* • Paul Rattray *Jimmy* • Kelly Scott *Mandy* • Debora Weston *Mya* • Emily Gilchrist *Karen* ■ *Dir/Scr* Christopher Smith

The Creeping Flesh ★★★ 15

Horror   1972 · UK · Colour · 88min

Scientist Peter Cushing discovers a giant skeleton in Borneo, which grows flesh when touched by water, in this over-complicated Victorian morality fable given a classy Hammer-style sheen by director Freddie Francis. Don't try to make sense of it: just enjoy the gloomily disturbing dark tone and some neat shocks provided by the prehistoric perambulating bones. Co-star Christopher Lee is bloodcurdling as an envious brother, while Cushing's sympathetic performance ranks with his best screen work. AJ DVD

Christopher Lee *James Hildern* • Peter Cushing *Emmanuel Hildern* • Lorna Heilbron *Penelope* • George Benson *Waterlow* • Kenneth J Warren *Lenny* • Duncan Lamont *Inspector* • Harry Locke *Barman* • Hedger Wallace *Dr Perry* • Michael Ripper *Carter* ■ *Dir* Freddie Francis • *Scr* Peter Spenceley, Jonathon Rumbold

Creepshow ★★★ 15

Portmanteau horror   1982 · US · Colour · 115min

Director George A Romero and top terror writer Stephen King neatly capture the ironic spirit of those forbidden 1950s horror comics in a lively anthology of ghoulishly funny fear tales. Zombie fathers, green space fungus, caged ancient creatures and the walking dead adroitly come alive from the pages of a comic book thrown away by a concerned parent. Stylishly scary stuff. AJ Swearing, violence. DVD BL

Hal Holbrook *Henry* • Adrienne Barbeau *Wilma* • Fritz Weaver *Dexter* • Leslie Nielsen *Richard* • EG Marshall *Upson* • Ed Harris *Hank* • Ted Danson *Harry* • Stephen King *Jordy* ■ *Dir* George A Romero • *Scr* Stephen King

Creepshow 2 ★ 18

Horror   1987 · US · Colour · 85min

Penny-dreadful in every respect, this three-part anthology is one of the worst vehicles off the Stephen King production line. A comic-crazed kid opens the latest issue of *Creepshow* and delves into tales concerning a murderous cigar store Indian, a killer oil slick and a zombie hitch-hiker. This slapdash dud is devoid of any imagination. AJ DVD

Tom Savini *The Creep* • Domenick John *Boy Billy* • Dan Kamin *Old Chief Wood'nhead* • George Kennedy *Ray Spruce* • Dorothy Lamour *Martha Spruce* • Frank S Salsedo [Frank Salsedo] *Ben Whitemoon* • Paul Satterfield *Deke* ■ *Dir* Michael Gornick • *Scr* George A Romero, from stories by Stephen King

Cremaster 4 ★★ 12A

Experimental fantasy
1994 · US/UK/Fr · Colour · 42min

American artist Matthew Barney here turns cinema into art with this first instalment in his ambitious five-part film project, the *Cremaster* cycle. Curiously beginning with *Cremaster 4* (episodes 1,5,2 and 3 follow

C

respectively), this dreamy slice of abstract weirdness is simultaneously beguiling and bewildering. Everything unfolds so differently to conventional film-making that Barney immediately captures attention with a series of bizarre, dialogue-free scenarios that loosely centre around the Isle of Man TT races and Manx folklore. The repetitive nature of these scenes and their languorous pace makes it hard to maintain this initial fascination. SF

Matthew Barney *Loughton candidate* • Dave Molyneux *Ascending hack, Team Molyneux* • Graham Molyneux *Ascending hack, Team Molyneux* • Steve Sinnot *Descending hack, Team Sinnot* • Karl Sinnot *Descending hack, Team Sinnot* • Sharon Marvel *Loughton faerie* ∎ *Dir/Scr* Matthew Barney

Cremaster 1 ★★★ PG

Experimental musical 1995 · US · Colour · 41min

Artist Matthew Barney's second instalment in his five-part *Cremaster* cycle is a cool and refined lesson in abstract image making, and is easier to fathom than its predecessor. Though the film's dialogue-free surrealism is still entirely bizarre, the symbolism is clearer, based on obvious themes of female fertility and reproduction. Mixing a retro vibe with sci-fi-style sterility, Barney uses two Goodyear airships floating above an American football stadium as the centrepiece to his celluloid art. Inside the craft, immaculately groomed air stewardesses flaunt their elegance, while on the pitch below dazzlingly dressed women perform synchronised dance routines à la Busby Berkeley. Hypnotically compelling. SF

Marti Domination *Goodyear* • Gemma Bourdon Smith *Goodyear hostess in Green Lounge* • Kathleen Crepeau *Goodyear hostess in Green Lounge* • Nina Kotov *Goodyear hostess in Green Lounge* • Jessica Sherwood *Goodyear hostess in Green Lounge* • Tanyth Berkeley *Goodyear hostess in Red Lounge* • Miranda Brooks *Goodyear hostess in Red Lounge* • Kari McKahan *Goodyear hostess in Red Lounge* • Catherine Mulchahy *Goodyear hostess in Red Lounge* ∎ *Dir/Scr* Matthew Barney

Cremaster 5 ★★★ 12A

Experimental opera 1997 · US · Colour · 54min

There's actually something of a conventional storyline in the third of artist Matthew Barney's sumptuous *Cremaster* cycle instalments. But the film offers far too much dazzling exotica to be concerned with such commonplace triviality. Ursula Andress plays the Queen of Chain, who sings mournful arias to her dead magician lover (Barney) in an alternate 19th-century Budapest, while flashbacks reveal his fate and a weird giant (Barney again) trots about in the waters of the city's famous Gellert Baths. Richly brought to life, with beautiful attention to detail, this is a baroque, colour-saturated marvel that luxuriates in warmth and passion. SF

Ursula Andress *Queen of Chain* • Matthew Barney *Diva/Giant/Magician* • Joanne Rha *Queen's Usher/Fudor Sprite* • Susan Rha *Queen's Usher/Fudor Sprite* ∎ *Dir/Scr* Matthew Barney

Cremaster 2 ★★★ 18

Experimental drama 1999 · US · Colour · 79min

The biological and reproductive themes that snake through American artist Matthew Barney's five-part cycle go from implicit to explicit in this, the penultimate instalment. An eccentric and challenging mishmash of surreal imagery and outright weirdness, the film artistically re-interprets the life of murderer Gary Gilmore, who received the death penalty for his crimes in 1977. The film mixes the polished sophistication of *Cremaster 1* with the grimy, incessant vulgarity of thrash metal music and the mystery of Houdini (played by Norman Mailer). This is the most forceful and confrontational of the five films. SF

Norman Mailer *Harry Houdini* • Matthew Barney *Gary Gilmore* • Anonymous *Baby Fay La Foe* • Lauren Pine *Bessie Gilmore* • Scott Ewalt *Frank Gilmore* • Patty Griffin *Nicole Baker* • Michael Thomson *Max Jensen* ∎ *Dir/Scr* Matthew Barney

Cremaster 3 ★★★★ 15

Experimental fantasy 2002 · US · Colour · 179min

US artist Matthew Barney concludes his epic five-part film project with this sumptuous visual feast. An exotic and immaculately constructed celluloid experience, it's the most accessible of the cycle – an ambitious and provocative attempt to create pure cinematic art. Though all the films lack traditional narrative structures, *3* uses the imposing New York landmarks the Chrysler Building and the Guggenheim Museum as a centrepiece for a dream-like episode involving Masonic ritual, Celtic mythology, a demolition derby and the artist's signature molten Vaseline. The dazzling imagery may be practically impossible to decipher, but Barney's ability to turn abstract ideas into animated tableaux still makes his work spellbinding viewing. SF **DVD**

Richard Serra *Hiram Abiff* • Matthew Barney *Entered Apprentice* • Aimee Mullins *Entered Novitiate/Oonagh MacCumhail* • Paul Brady *Cloud Club maitre d'* • Terry Gillespie *Cloud Club barman* ∎ *Dir/Scr* Matthew Barney • *Cinematographer* Peter Strietmann

The Cremator ★★★★

Black comedy drama 1968 · Cz · BW · 99min

A prime example of Czech gothic, this is not only a chilling study of psychological collapse, but also a disturbing insight into the seductive power of totalitarianism. As the Nazi-era undertaker who is convinced that he can save humanity by fire, Rudolf Hrusinsky gives a performance that irresistibly recalls Peter Lorre at his most pathetically unhinged. His distorted expressions are emphasised by Juraj Herz's insistent use of close-ups, notably during the scenes at the fairground. DP Czech +subtitles.

Vlasta Chramostova *Lakmé* • Rudolf Hrusinsky *Kopfrkingl* • Jirí Menzel *Dvorzak* • Ilja Prachar *Walter Reineke* ∎ *Dir* Juraj Herz • *Scr* Juraj Herz, Ladislav Fuks, from the novel by Ladislav Fuks

Crescendo ★★★

Horror 1970 · UK · Colour · 95min

This "mini-Hitchcock" thriller from Hammer Films borrows as much from *Psycho* as it does from the studio's own series of early 1960s whodunnits (*Paranoiac*, for example). Touted as a new departure for the "House of Horror", this demented tale of dead composers, lunatic twins and drug-addicted cripples merely adds sex and discreet nudity to the tried-and-tested shocker formula. If you can swallow Stefanie Powers as a PhD music student, this one's for you. AJ

Stefanie Powers *Susan* • James Olson *Georges* • Margaretta Scott *Danielle* • Jane Lapotaire *Lillianne* • Joss Ackland *Carter* • Kirsten Betts *Catherine* ∎ *Dir* Alan Gibson • *Scr* Jimmy Sangster, Alfred Shaughnessy

Le Cri du Coeur ★★★

Drama 1994 · Fr/Burkina Faso · Colour · 86min

Idrissa Ouedraogo's seventh feature follows 11-year-old Said Diarra and his mother as they leave their village in Mali to join his father in Paris, where he has recently bought a garage. However, hopes that Diarra will one day study medicine are jeopardised after he suffers a series of nightmares about a wild hyena. Measured, thoughtful and earnestly played. DP French +subtitles.

Richard Bohringer *Paulo* • Said Diarra *Moctar* • Félicité Wouassi *Saffi* • Alex Descas *Ibrahim Sow* • Clémentine Célarié *Deborah* ∎ *Dir* Idrissa Ouedraogo • *Scr* Idrissa Ouedraogo, Robert Gardner, Jacques Akchoti

Le Cri du Hibou ★★★★ 15

Black comedy thriller 1987 · Fr/It · Colour · 104min

Patricia Highsmith's novel has been transposed from the USA to France, where Christophe Malavoy has left Paris, and his psychologically abusive wife, for Vichy. In the middle of a screaming-match divorce, he obsessively watches the beautiful

Mathilda May, who responds by neglecting her dreary fiancé. When he disappears, the death-obsessed Malavoy becomes a suspect. Typically, Claude Chabrol is less concerned with narrative than with his characters and clinically dissecting the French middle classes. Elegantly acted by Malavoy, this is also notable for winning Mathilda May a César as most promising young actress. BB French +subtitles.

Christophe Malavoy *Robert* • Mathilda May *Juliette* • Virginie Thévenet *Veronique* • Jacques Penot *Patrick* • Jean-Pierre Kalfon *Commissioner* ∎ *Dir* Claude Chabrol • *Scr* Odile Barski, Claude Chabrol, from the novel *The Cry of the Owl* by Patricia Highsmith

Cría Cuervos ★★★ 12

Drama 1975 · Sp · Colour · 104min

Although it became something of a totem of post-Franco optimism, this elliptical chronicle of a young woman's tormented inner life is really about the passivity of a population disenfranchised by fascism and the guilt it would have to endure before Spain's painful memories could be assuaged. As the child who believes she has power over death after witnessing the demise of her father, Ana Torrent superbly conveys that mix of terror and innocence that is unique to childhood. But having Geraldine Chaplin play both Ana's mother and Ana as an adult muddles matters. DP Spanish +subtitles. Sexual references. **DVD** **BLU**

Geraldine Chaplin *Ana as an adult/Maria* • Ana Torrent *Ana* • Conchita Perez *Irene* • Maite Sanchez *Juana* • Monica Randall *Paulina* ∎ *Dir/Scr* Carlos Saura

Cries and Whispers ★★★★★ 18

Drama 1972 · Swe · Colour · 87min

Focusing on the failure of love and the agony of loss, this is one of Ingmar Bergman's finest achievements. Combining memories, fantasies and moments of intense family drama, this harrowing study of pain, passion, sisterhood and death brought Bergman a hat-trick of Oscar nominations, although it was Sven Nykvist who won the award for his luscious cinematography. However, it's the stunning art direction of Marik Vos that provides this disturbing chamber drama with its unforgettable manor house setting and its mesmerising red colour scheme. Harriet Andersson, Ingrid Thulin and Liv Ullmann dominate proceedings as the well-heeled sisters, but Kari Sylwan is every bit as impressive as the peasant maid. DP Swedish +subtitles. Violence. **DVD**

Ingrid Thulin *Karin* • Liv Ullmann *Maria* • Harriet Andersson *Agnes* • Kari Sylwan *Anna* • Erland Josephson *Doctor* • George Arlin *Karin's husband* • Henning Moritzen *Joakin* ∎ *Dir/Scr* Ingmar Bergman

Cries in the Dark ★★

Crime thriller 2006 · Can · Colour · 90min

In this predictable but highly watchable crime drama, Eva La Rue delivers a sympathetic performance as a cop trying to solve the grisly killing of her pregnant sister. Yet while the investigative puzzle fits together far too easily, it's still surprisingly compelling. Part of this is down to the disturbing nature of the murder and its twisted aftermath, which collectively give the film a harder edge than your usual made-for-TV fare. SF

Eva LaRue *Callahan* [Eva La Rue] *Carrie Macklin* • Adam Harrington *Scott* • Gina Chiarelli *Rosa* • Adrian Holmes *Detective Wynn* ∎ *Dir* Paul Schneider (1) • *Scr* Kraig Wenman

Crime and Passion ★

Comedy drama 1976 · US/W Ger · Colour · 92min

Shady investment banker Omar Sharif convinces his mistress/secretary Karen Black to marry tycoon Bernhard Wicki, to whom he's heavily in debt. Sharif and Black do their utmost to make the daft plot of this slight comedy drama fly, but it's an uphill battle, especially as they have no really

suspenseful or amusing moments to back them up. AJ

Omar Sharif *Andre* • Karen Black *Susan* • Joseph Bottoms *Larry* • Bernhard Wicki *Rolf* ∎ *Dir* Ivan Passer • *Scr* Jesse Lasky Jr, Pat Silver, from the novel *An Ace Up Your Sleeve* by James Hadley Chase

Crime and Punishment ★★★★

Crime drama 1935 · Fr · BW · 110min

Pierre Blanchar walked away with the best actor prize at Venice for his portrayal of Raskolnikov, the angst-ridden student whose killing of a pawnbroker brings police inspector Porphyre (Harry Baur) down on his head. Blanchar is matched all the way by the brilliant Baur, but this is as much a triumph of art direction as it is of acting, with the doom-laden sets superbly capturing the poverty and despair that make Raskolnikov the most sympathetic of murderers. DP French +subtitles.

Harry Baur *Porphyre* • Pierre Blanchar *Raskolnikov* • Madeleine Ozeray *Sonia* • Marcelle Géniat *Madame Raskolnikov* • Lucienne Lemarchand *Dounia* • Alexandre Rignault *Raxoumikhine* • Magdelaine Berubet *Aliona* ∎ *Dir* Pierre Chenal • *Scr* Marcel Ayme, Pierre Chenal, Christian Stengal, Wladimir Strijewski, from the novel by Feodor Dostoyevsky • *Art Director* Eugène Lourié

Crime and Punishment ★★★★

Crime drama 1935 · US · BW · 87min

Made on a relatively low budget at Columbia, this dark, semi-expressionist version of the Dostoyevsky classic is pared to the bone with an austerity and religious purity. Peter Lorre, in a rare leading role and appearing unusually beautiful, is subtly compelling as the university graduate struggling to overcome his spiritual arrogance, while Edward Arnold is well cast as the resolute inspector who pokes and prods at Lorre's guilt. DO

Peter Lorre *Roderick Raskolnikov* • Edward Arnold *Inspector Porfiry* • Marian Marsh *Sonya* • Tala Birell *Antonya "Toni" Raskolnikov* • Elisabeth Risdon *Mrs Raskolnikov* • Robert Allen *Dmitri* • Douglass Dumbrille *Grilov* • Mrs Patrick Campbell *Pawnbroker* ∎ *Dir* Josef von Sternberg • *Scr* SK Lauren, Joseph Anthony, from the novel by Feodor Dostoyevsky

Crime and Punishment ★★★ 12

Crime drama 1983 · Fin · Colour · 89min

This was the remarkably assured feature debut of Finnish director Aki Kaurismäki. He has made something of a speciality of updating literary classics, but this reworking of Dostoyevsky's harrowing novel is perhaps his most audacious. Markku Toikka stars as Rahikainen, a suitably dissolute-looking latter-day Raskolnikov, whose descent into crime is laid firmly at the door of 1980s Finnish society. DP Finnish +subtitles. **DVD**

Markku Toikka *Rahikainen* • Aino Seppo • Esko Nikkari • Hannu Lauri • Olli Tuominem ∎ *Dir* Aki Kaurismäki • *Scr* Aki Kaurismäki, Paul Pentti, from the novel by Feodor Dostoyevsky

Crime + Punishment in Suburbia ★★ 15

Drama 2000 · US · Colour · 94min

With its designer nihilism and new-wave gimmickry, director Rob Schmidt's reworking of Dostoyevsky is the darkest of a spate of teens-meet-classics pictures. But this dour diatribe has little else to recommend it. Abandoned by her mother Ellen Barkin and abused by her stepfather Michael Ironside, high-school student Monica Keena is driven to bloody revenge. This essay in grunge-spattered melancholy lacks both suburban authenticity and insight. DP **DVD**

Monica Keena *Roseanne Skolnik* • Vincent Kartheiser *Vincent* • Jeffrey Wright *Chris* • James DeBello *Jimmy* • Michael Ironside *Fred Skolnik* • Ellen Barkin *Maggie Skolnik* ∎ *Dir* Rob Schmidt • *Scr* Larry Gross

U SUITABLE FOR ALL Uc SUITABLE ESPECIALLY FOR YOUNG CHILDREN (DVD ONLY) PG PARENTAL GUIDANCE 12A UNDER 12s TO BE ACCOMPANIED (CINEMA ONLY)

Crime and Punishment, USA ★★★

Crime drama   1959 · US · BW · 80min

This is a genuine curio from American independent director Denis Sanders, who is now best remembered for his superb but atypical rockumentary, *Elvis: That's the Way It Is*. An update of Dostoyevsky's novel, it stars a debuting George Hamilton as the young law student involved in murder, and he gives an impressive performance that is totally at odds with his later "celebrity" status. TS

George Hamilton *Robert* • Mary Murphy (1) *Sally* • Frank Silvera *Lt AD Porter* • Marian Seldes *Debbie Cole* • John Harding *Swanson* • Wayne Heffley *Rafe* • Toni Merrill *Mrs Cole* • Lew Brown (2) *Samuels* ■ *Dir* Denis Sanders • *Scr* Walter Newman, from the novel by Feodor Dostoyevsky

Le Crime de Monsieur Lange ★★★★ PG

Black comedy   1935 · Fr · BW · 80min

This black comedy belongs to the optimistic phase of French film-making in the 1930s known as "poetic realism". It shows how the workers successfully take over a pulp publishing house on the reported death of its exploitative owner. Jules Berry, as the brutal boss, and René Lefèvre, as the writer whose "Arizona Jim" westerns revive the company's fortunes, are exceptional. However, the film's greatness rests on director Jean Renoir's masterly use of deep focus photography, which brings vibrant life to every corner of the magnificent studio set. DP French +subtitles. *DVD*

René Lefèvre *Lange* • Jules Berry *Batala* • Florelle *Valentine* • Nadia Sibirskaia *Estelle* • Sylvia Bataille *Edith* • Henri Guisol *Meunier* • Maurice Baquet *Charles* • Marcel Levesque *Concierge* ■ *Dir* Jean Renoir • *Scr* Jacques Prévert, Jean Renoir, Jean Castanier, from a story by Jean Castanier • *Cinematographer* Jean Bachelet

Crime Doctor ★★

Horror mystery   1943 · US · BW · 65min

Based on Max Marcin's popular radio series, this launched a ten-film franchise that was very much in the Columbia tradition of briskly buzzing B-movies. Warner Baxter takes the title role as the former gangster whose bout of amnesia prompts him to embark on a new life as a psychiatrist specialising in the criminal mind. His expertise, rather than his past, becomes the key to cases involving ghosts, twins, typhoid, dreams, art dealers and arsonists, as well as a good mixture of adroit and doltish cops. DP

Warner Baxter *Robert Ordway/Phil Morgan* • Margaret Lindsay *Grace Fielding* • John Litel *Emilio Caspari* • Ray Collins *Dr John Carey* • Harold Huber *Joe Dylan* • Don Costello (1) *Nick Ferris* • Leon Ames *Captain William Wheeler* • Constance Worth *Betty* ■ *Dir* Michael Gordon • *Scr* Graham Baker, Louis Lantz, Jerome Odlum, from the radio series by Max Marcin

Crime in the Streets ★★★★

Crime drama   1956 · US · BW · 90min

This terrific, intense early Don Siegel movie is a quintessential 1950s teen angst flick that started life as a television play in the heyday of US TV drama. John Cassavetes, who played the role on TV, may seem a little old for the role of embittered teenage gang leader, but Sal Mineo and future director Mark Rydell are superb as his sidekicks in his plan to execute a man who slighted him. These juvenile delinquents may try your patience, but they demand attention in this razor-sharp depiction of street violence. TS

James Whitmore *Ben Wagner* • John Cassavetes *Frankie Dane* • Sal Mineo *Baby Gioia* • Mark Rydell *Lou Macklin* • Denise Alexander *Maria Gioia* • Malcolm Atterbury *Mr McAllister* • Peter Votrian *Richie Dane* • Virginia Gregg *Mrs Dane* ■ *Dir* Don Siegel • *Scr* Reginald Rose, from his TV play

Crime of Passion ★★★★

Film noir   1957 · US · BW · 85min

In a role tailor-made for her, Barbara Stanwyck stars as the wife of decent cop Sterling Hayden. Ruthlessly ambitious for her husband, she sleeps with about-to-retire police chief Raymond Burr. When he names somebody else as his successor, however, the enraged Stanwyck pulls a gun on him. A skilful suspense drama in the *film noir* mould, this is well directed by Gerd Oswald and played for all its worth by both the principals and the supporting cast. RK

Barbara Stanwyck *Kathy Ferguson* • Sterling Hayden *Bill Doyle* • Raymond Burr *Inspector Tony Pope* • Fay Wray *Alice Pope* • Royal Dano *Captain Alidos* • Virginia Grey *Sara* ■ *Dir* Gerd Oswald • *Scr* Jo Eisinger

Crime of the Century ★★★ 15

Drama based on a true story   1996 · US · Colour · 110min

This interesting if rather downbeat movie focuses on the 1932 Lindbergh baby kidnapping and the German immigrant, Bruno Richard Hauptmann, who was arrested for the crime. The film stars Stephen Rea as the unfortunate Hauptmann, while Isabella Rossellini plays Hauptmann's wife, who stood by him when he was accused of the crime that shocked America and for which the authorities desperately needed a culprit. Gripping stuff, but don't expect all the ends to be tied up by the final credits. JB

Stephen Rea *Bruno Richard Hauptmann* • Isabella Rossellini *Anna Hauptmann* • JT Walsh *Colonel Norman Schwarzkopf Sr* • Michael Moriarty *Governor Harold Hoffman* • Allen Garfield *Lieutenant James Finn* ■ *Dir* Mark Rydell • *Scr* William Nicholson, from the non-fiction book *The Airman and the Carpenter* by Ludovic Kennedy

Crime on the Hill ★★ PG

Crime drama   1933 · UK · BW · 63min

When a member of the landed gentry is murdered, his estate is expected to go to his niece Sally Blane. But then Phyllis Dare reveals that she and the victim were secretly married. Local vicar Lewis Casson and his friend, doctor Nigel Playfair, decide to investigate further, with the finger of suspicion pointing at Blane's fiancé, Anthony Bushell. A creaky, sub-Agatha Christie murder mystery. RK *DVD*

Sally Blane *Sylvia Kennett* • Nigel Playfair *Dr Moody* • Lewis Casson *Rev Michael Gray* • Anthony Bushell *Tony Fields* • Phyllis Dare *Claire Winslow* • Judy Kelly *Alice Green* ■ *Dir* Bernard Vorhaus • *Scr* Michael Hankinson, Vera Allinson, EM Delafield, Bernard Vorhaus, from a play by Jack de Leon, Jack Celestin

Crime Spree ★★★ 15

Crime comedy   2002 · Can/US/UK · Colour · 95min

Gérard Depardieu and ageing pop idol Johnny Hallyday star as the leaders of a crew of bumbling French crooks who are sent to Chicago to carry out a major jewellery heist, only to accidentally rob Mafia boss Harvey Keitel. While the film is predictable and derivative, it still works well, thanks in part to the actors' strong chemistry. The bawdy slapstick in the first half is particularly hilarious, although the humour occasionally sits uneasily with the violence. SF French, English +subtitles. Swearing, sex scenes, violence. *DVD*

Gérard Depardieu *Daniel Foray* • Harvey Keitel *Frankie Zammeti* • Johnny Hallyday *Marcel Burot* • Renaud *Zero* • Richard Bohringer *Laurant Bastaldi* • Saïd Taghmaoui *Sami Zerhouni* • Albert Dray *Raymond Gayet* • Stéphane Freiss *Julien Labesse* ■ *Dir/Scr* Brad Mirman

Crime Story ★★★ 18

Martial arts action thriller   1993 · HK · Colour · 102min

Although Jackie Chan's new Hollywood fans know him chiefly for such light-hearted romps as *Rush Hour*, when he was in Hong Kong he didn't shy away from harder-edged material. This is a prime example: an action-packed thriller, based loosely on the real-life epidemic of kidnapping that once plagued the former colony. Chan, playing a copy hunting for a missing businessman, comes up trumps in some dazzling martial arts action, less fancy but more realistic than some of his later films. JF Cantonese +subtitles. *DVD*

Jackie Chan *Inspector Eddie Chan* • Kent Cheng *Inspector Hung* • Lo Ka-Ying *Wong Yat-Fei* ■ *Dir* Kirk Wong • *Scr* Cheun Tin-nam, Chan Man-keung, Cheung Tsi-sing, Chan Tak-sam

Crime without Passion ★★★

Crime drama   1934 · US · BW · 67min

So successful was the writing partnership of Ben Hecht and Charles MacArthur – the creators of *The Front Page* – that Paramount gave them carte blanche to produce, direct and write this tale about a celebrated lawyer who murders his mistress when he falls for another woman. There's a nice twist in store, though, and a silky smooth Claude Rains unravels most effectively. It's smart, gripping and doesn't hang about. AT

Claude Rains *Lee Gentry* • Margo *Carmen Brown* • Whitney Bourne *Katy Costello* • Stanley Ridges *Eddie White* • Paula Trueman *Buster Malloy* • Leslie Adams *O'Brien* • Greta Granstedt *Della* • Esther Dale *Miss Keeley* • Charles MacArthur ■ *Dir/Scr* Ben Hecht, Charles MacArthur

El Crimen del Padre Amaro ★★★ 15

Religious drama   2002 · Mex/Sp/Arg/Fr · Colour · 113min

This tale of a young Catholic priest led into temptation during his new countryside posting has photogenic appeal, if limited depth, thanks to its soap-opera level script. Gael García Bernal has narrow scope for characterisation as the lustful priest, but the powerful finale does reveal a tougher side to his amiable personality. Bernal's union with attractive churchgoer Ana Claudia Talancón is the film's primary concern, the eccentric supporting characters and the exposé of political corruption within the town are what really fuel the story. JC Spanish +subtitles. *DVD*

Gael García Bernal *Father Amaro* • Sancho Gracia *Father Benito* • Ana Claudia Talancón *Amelia* • Angélica Aragón *Sanjuanera* • Luisa Huertas *Dionisia* • Damián Alcázar *Father Natalio* • Ernesto Gómez Cruz *Bishop* • Pedro Armendáriz [Pedro Armendáriz Jr] *Municipal president* ■ *Dir* Carlos Carrera • *Scr* Vicente Leñero, from the novel by Eça de Queirós • *Cinematographer* Guillermo Granillo

Crimes and Misdemeanors ★★★★★ 15

Comedy drama   1989 · US · Colour · 99min

Woody Allen is the finest practitioner of screen comedy since the collapse of the studio system. He is also more than capable of tackling weightier topics in the manner of his idol, Ingmar Bergman. In one of his most ambitious films, Allen combines his archetypal wisecracking style with his more serious moral preoccupations, and the result is a compelling piece of cinema that is as troubling as it is hilarious. The excellent Martin Landau plays an eye surgeon whose lover (Anjelica Huston) threatens to expose his private and professional indiscretions to his loyal wife (Claire Bloom). Allen, as a documentary film-maker, is also at war with himself, although he has a convenient scapegoat for his failures in his brother-in-law (Alan Alda), a TV sitcom director with a gleeful lack of taste and a talent for seducing women. DP Swearing. *DVD*

Martin Landau *Judah Rosenthal* • Mia Farrow *Halley Reed* • Alan Alda *Lester* • Woody Allen *Clifford Stern* • Anjelica Huston *Dolores Paley* • Claire Bloom *Miriam Rosenthal* • Joanna Gleason *Wendy Stern* • Sam Waterston *Ben* ■ *Dir/Scr* Woody Allen

Crimes at the Dark House ★★★ PG

Crime melodrama   1939 · UK · BW · 65min

Tod Slaughter was one of the first cult stars of British cinema. Even at the height of his popularity, his rolling-eye acting style was the last thing in prime ham, yet the barnstorming melodramas in which he appeared make for marvellous entertainment and deserve their place in the hallowed halls of turkeydom. Who cares if this reworking of Wilkie Collins's classic *The Woman in White* creaks so loudly you can scarcely hear the dialogue? It's a rattling good yarn, played with amateur theatrical gusto. DP *DVD*

Tod Slaughter *Sir Percival Glyde* • Hilary Eaves *Marian Fairlie* • Sylvia Marriott *Laura Fairlie* • Hay Petrie *Dr Fosco* • Geoffrey Wardwell *Paul Hartwright* • David Horne *Mr Fairlie* • Margaret Yarde *Mrs Bullen* ■ *Dir* George King • *Scr* Edward Dryhurst, Frederick Hayward, HF Maltby, from the novel *The Woman in White* by Wilkie Collins

Crimes of Passion ★★★★ 18

Erotic drama   1984 · US · Colour · 102min

Ken Russell's stylish satire stars Kathleen Turner as a frigid fashion designer by day and prostitute China Blue by night. However, her double life is turned upside down when she encounters private eye John Laughlin, who ends up falling for the troubled woman, and deranged street preacher Anthony Perkins (brilliantly evoking Norman Bates), who's out to save her, dead or alive. As you'd expect from Russell, no punches are pulled when it comes to the lurid sex scenes, but the film looks terrific and Turner gives a bravura performance. JA Violence, swearing, sex scenes, nudity. *DVD* *Blu*

Kathleen Turner *Joanna Crane/China Blue* • Anthony Perkins *Reverend Peter Shayne* • John Laughlin *Bobby Grady* • Annie Potts *Amy Grady* • Bruce Davison *Donny Hopper* • Norman Burton *Lou Bateman* • James Crittenden *Tom Marshall* • Peggy Feury *Adrian* ■ *Dir* Ken Russell • *Scr* Barry Sandler

Crimes of Passion ★★

Mystery thriller   2005 · Can/US · Colour · 90min

Dina Meyer gives an enjoyable performance as a seductive schemer in this serpentine tale of deceit and betrayal. Teaming up with a cocksure, married co-worker (Jonathan Higgins), she cons her boss out of millions by filing a fictitious sexual harassment suit. But the duo's perfect crime soon turns into a mess of blackmail and murder. You're likely to guess some of the final act surprises, though their melodramatic execution makes them fun to watch. SF Swearing, a sex scene.

Dina Meyer *Rebecca Walker* • Jonathan Higgins *Jerry Dennings* • Amy Sloan *Shannon Dennings* • John H Brennan *Frank Schaffer* ■ *Dir* Richard Roy • *Scr* Brad Mirman

The Crimes of Stephen Hawke ★★★

Period melodrama   1936 · UK · BW · 69min

Tod Slaughter throws himself with gusto into a gloriously over-the-top performance as a monstrous Regency supervillain, rolling the worst of Jack the Ripper, Frankenstein's monster and Jekyll and Hyde into one. Outwardly a kind-at-heart moneylender, he has, in fact, gained his wealth by murder, viciously snapping the spines of his victims. The only outlet for his humanity is his adopted daughter. This is a joyously hammy melodrama. PF

Tod Slaughter *Stephen Hawke* • Marjorie Taylor *Julia Hawke* • Eric Portman *Matthew Trimble* • Gerald Barry *Miles Archer* • Ben Soutten *Nathaniel* • DJ Williams *Joshua Trimble* • Charles Penrose *Sir Franklyn* • Norman Pierce *Landlord* ■ *Dir* George King • *Scr* HF Maltby, from a story by Jack Celestin

Crimes of the Future ★★

Science-fiction horror   1970 · Can · BW · 62min

Canadian cult director David Cronenberg's second underground feature – a companion piece to his debut *Stereo* (1969) – deals with deadly cosmetics wiping out the female race, and how the male population sublimate their sexual desires by becoming paedophiles. All the diverse themes Cronenberg subsequently expands on in his later works are here in seminal form, but the film is rather pretentious, eccentric and over-stylised. AJ *DVD*

Ronald Mlodzik *Adrian Trilpod* • Jon Lidolt • Tania Zolty • Jack Messinger • William Haslam ■ *Dir/Scr* David Cronenberg

Crimes of the Heart ★★★★ 15
Comedy drama 1986 · US · Colour · 100min

Beth Henley, adapting her own Pulitzer Prize-winning play, serves up three meaty parts for a trio of Hollywood's leading actresses – Jessica Lange, Diane Keaton and Sissy Spacek – and they certainly make the most of it. The story is pretty slight – three sisters are reunited after one of them is released from prison – and the stage origins are very apparent. However, all three actresses deliver stunning performances and the result is a warm, rewarding tragicomedy. JF Swearing.
DVD

Diane Keaton *Lenny Magrath* • Jessica Lange *Meg Magrath* • Sissy Spacek *Babe Magrath* • Sam Shepard *Doc Porter* • Tess Harper *Chick Boyle* • David Carpenter *Barnette Lloyd* • Hurd Hatfield *Old Grandaddy* • Beeson Carroll *Zackery Botrelle* ■ *Dir* Bruce Beresford • *Scr* Beth Henley, from her play

Crimewave ★★★ PG
Crime comedy 1985 · US · Colour · 82min

Opening with a car filled with nuns speeding through Detroit and ending with an extended chase sequence, this never slows down enough to pick up our interest, even though it wants to take us for a ride. It's a slapstick attempt at *film noir* by director Sam Raimi, who also co-wrote the script with Joel and Ethan Coen. The end result, however, is too simplistic, and its story of a security-systems installer caught between a couple of hitmen is rather patronising, but there are some splendidly eccentric moments. TH *DVD*

Louise Lasser *Helene Trend* • Reed Birney *Vic Ajax* • Paul L Smith [Paul Smith] *Faron Crush* • Brion James *Arthur Coddish* • Sheree J Wilson *Nancy* • Edward R Pressman *Ernest Trend* • Bruce Campbell *Renaldo "The Heel"* • Antonio Fargas *Blind man* • Wiley Harker *Governor* ■ *Dir* Sam Raimi • *Scr* Joel Coen, Ethan Coen, Sam Raimi

The Criminal ★★★ PG
Prison drama 1960 · UK · BW · 93min

This steely crime thriller, scripted by Alun Owen from a story by Jimmy Sangster, unflinchingly explores the cut-throat nature of urban crime and the cold realities of prison life. Stanley Baker is outstanding as the tough villain whose contempt for authority of any sort makes him a target for both monstrous prison officer Patrick Magee and racketeer Sam Wanamaker after he refuses to disclose the whereabouts of the loot snatched during a racecourse heist. Director Joseph Losey punctuates the simmering tension with eruptions of violence that still shock today. DP

Stanley Baker *Johnny Bannion* • Sam Wanamaker *Mike Carter* • Grégoire Aslan *Frank Saffron* • Margit Saad *Suzanne* • Jill Bennett *Maggie* • Rupert Davies *Mr Edwards* • Patrick Magee *Chief Warder Barrows* ■ *Dir* Joseph Losey • *Scr* Alun Owen, from a story by Jimmy Sangster

The Criminal ★★★ 15
Mystery drama 1999 · UK/US · Colour · 95min

The opening sequence, in which musician Steven Mackintosh (bearing the Kafka-esque name J) is lured into a one-night stand with Natasha Little, is quite mesmerising. Yet from the moment he wakes to find himself up to his neck in conspiracy, the action follows an all-too-familiar route. Mackintosh admirably conveys the everyman's terror at finding his head above the parapet. The best moments, however, are provided by cops Bernard Hill and Holly Aird. DP *DVD*

Steven Mackintosh *"J"* Jasper Rawlins • Eddie Izzard *Peter Hume* • Natasha Little *Sarah Maitland* • Yvan Attal *Mason* • Holly Aird *Detective Sergeant Rebecca White* • Andrew Tiernan *Harris* • Justin Shevlin *Barker* • Barry Stearn *Noble* • Bernard Hill *Inspector Walker* ■ *Dir/Scr* Julian Simpson

Criminal ★★★ 15
Crime drama 2004 · US · Colour · 83min

Steven Soderbergh's long-time collaborator Gregory Jacobs makes his directorial debut with this worthy remake of the Argentinian crime drama *Nine Queens*. A twisting tale of two small-town con artists who stumble upon the scam of a lifetime, it's slick and stylish entertainment. In an enjoyably sleazy turn, John C Reilly plays unscrupulous mentor to Diego Luna's inexperienced grifter. This caper is seductive, but falters in its reliance on coincidence. SF Swearing. *DVD*

John C Reilly *Richard Gaddis* • Diego Luna *Rodrigo* • Maggie Gyllenhaal *Valerie* • Peter Mullan *William Hannigan* • Jonathan Tucker *Michael* • Enrico Colantoni *Bookish man* • Zitto Kazann *Ochoa* ■ *Dir* Gregory Jacobs • *Scr* Gregory Jacobs, Sam Lowry [Steven Soderbergh], from the film *Nine Queens* by Fabian Bielinsky

Criminal ★★★ 15
Crime action thriller 2016 · US · Colour · 113min

An identity crisis is at the heart of this peppy thriller that's anchored by Kevin Costner as a convicted sociopath. The plot sees science whizz Tommy Lee Jones implanting Costner's faulty frontal lobe with the memories of recently deceased CIA operative Ryan Reynolds in order to find a cyber terrorist. But soon Costner is on the lam. Director Ariel Vromen adopts a Euro-grit, *Bourne*-like aesthetic that is slightly at odds with the *Face/Off*-style high concept, but in amidst the rollicking violence and obvious softer scenes, there's a good dose of wink-wink humour. SP Violence, swearing.

Kevin Costner *Jericho Stewart* • Gary Oldman *Quaker Wells* • Tommy Lee Jones *Dr Franks* • Gal Gadot *Jill Pope* • Ryan Reynolds *Bill Pope* • Alice Eve *Marta Lynch* ■ *Dir* Ariel Vromen • *Scr* Douglas Cook [Douglas S Cook], David Weisberg

The Criminal Code ★★★
Prison drama 1930 · US · BW · 98min

This was the film that elevated Boris Karloff to stardom and led to his portrayal of Frankenstein's monster. He'd played Ned Galloway on stage and the role was enlarged for this movie. Master draughtsman director Howard Hawks doesn't allow the theatrical origins to show, although the tragic ending has disappeared as Karloff now snarls: "That kid don't take no rap from me." Cell life is well evoked, and the film convinces as long as you believe warden Walter Huston would hire his daughter's lover, trusted convict Phillips Holmes, to be his personal driver! TS

Walter Huston *Warden Brady* • Phillips Holmes *Robert Graham* • Constance Cummings *Mary Brady* • Boris Karloff *Ned Galloway* • Mary Doran *Gertrude Williams* • DeWitt Jennings *Gleason* • John Sheehan *McManus* • Otto Hoffman *Fales* ■ *Dir* Howard Hawks • *Scr* Fred Niblo Jr, Seton I Miller, from the play by Martin Flavin

Criminal Court ★★
Crime drama 1946 · US · BW · 62min

Tom Conway is a defence lawyer with political ambitions, and nightclub singer Martha O'Driscoll is his fiancée. Conway, however, has accidentally killed someone, and O'Driscoll is blamed for it because she found the body. Conway defends her in court, finds time to get married *and* elected as district attorney. All this in about an hour's running time – and there's still time for a few songs! AT

Tom Conway *Steve Barnes* • Martha O'Driscoll *Georgia Gale* • June Clayworth *Joan Mason* • Robert Armstrong *Vic Wright* • Addison Richards *District Attorney Gordon* • Pat Gleason *Joe West* • Steve Brodie *Frankie* ■ *Dir* Robert Wise • *Scr* Lawrence Kimble, from a story by Earl Felton

Criminal Law ★★ 18
Thriller 1988 · US · Colour · 109min

British actor Gary Oldman's first major Hollywood movie sees him in one of his oh-so-rare good guy roles. He's a defence attorney who gets suspected killer Kevin Bacon off, only to discover later that he's guilty. Despite director Martin Campbell's efficiency at creating tension, this starts off as fairly implausible and gets sillier as it goes on. JC

Gary Oldman *Ben Chase* • Kevin Bacon *Martin Thiel* • Tess Harper *Detective Stillwell* • Karen Young *Ellen Faulkner* • Joe Don Baker *Detective Mesel* • Ron Lea *Gary Hull* • Karen Woolridge *Claudia Curwen* ■ *Dir* Martin Campbell • *Scr* Mark Kasdan

Criminal Lawyer ★★★
Crime drama 1937 · US · BW · 71min

Lee Tracy stars as a lawyer whose successful ascent up the power ladder comes to a halt when he confesses to his criminal associations. He brings gangland supremo Eduardo Ciannelli down with him, winning the heart of Margot Grahame in the process. Christy Cabanne directs this programme filler from RKO, drawing first-class performances from his cast – in particular Tracy – to make for a tight and absorbing addition to the popular legal-political genre. RK

Lee Tracy *Brandon* • Margot Grahame *Madge Carter* • Eduardo Ciannelli *Larkin* • Erik Rhodes *Bandini* • Betty Lawford *Molly Walker* • Frank M Thomas *William Walker* • Wilfred Lucas *Brandon's assistant* ■ *Dir* Christy Cabanne • *Scr* GV Atwater, Thomas Lennon (1), from a story by Louis Stevens

The Criminal Life of Archibaldo de la Cruz ★★★
Crime black comedy 1955 · Mex · BW · 72min

This was Luis Buñuel's response to his first return to Europe in almost a decade. His target was the kind of seemingly solid citizen who maintains the iniquitous status quo while proclaiming moral superiority. Buñuel shoots away his pedestal by portraying him as an inhibited transvestite whose childhood experience of death inspires a spree of fetishistic murder attempts. Employing a naturalism that makes Ernesto Alonso's imagined crimes all the more grotesquely amusing, this is an audacious but flawed black comedy. DP Spanish +subtitles.

Miroslava *Lavinia* • Ernesto Alonso *Archibaldo de la Cruz* • Rita Macedo *Patricia Terrazas* • Ariadna Welter *Carlota* • Rodolfo Landa *Alejandro Rivas* • Andrea Palma *Senor Cervantes, mother of Carlota* ■ *Dir* Luis Buñuel • *Scr* Luis Buñuel, Eduardo Ugarte, from a novel by Rodolfo Usigli

Criminal Lovers ★★★ 18
Crime drama 1999 · Fr/Jpn · Colour · 91min

François Ozon attempts to turn a fairy tale into an urban myth in this stylish and highly manipulative melodrama. The action moves from the grimy reality of the school showers, where Natacha Régnier and Jérémie Rénier kill the youngster she claims raped her, to the storybook realm of the forest, where they bury the body. Then, in a nod to the tale of Hansel and Gretel, they encounter sinister woodsman, Miki Manojlovic, who imprisons them in his cellar. Ambitious and stylish, but despite the often unbearable suspense, the disparate elements fail to gel. DP French +subtitles. *DVD*

Natacha Régnier *Alice* • Jérémie Rénier *Luc* • Miki Manojlovic *The woodsman* • Salim Kechiouche *Saïd* • Yasmine Belmadi *Karim* ■ *Dir/Scr* François Ozon

The Crimson Curtain★★★★
Period romance 1952 · Fr · BW · 46min

Novelist and film critic Alexandre Astruc, renowned for coining the phrase *caméra-stylo*, wrote that cinema should be "a means of writing as supple and as subtle as that of written language". Practising what he preaches in this, his debut film as a director, he unfolds the tale of a young officer's illicit, silent and nocturnal affair with the daughter of the household where he's billeted. Stylish and unusual, the narrative takes the place of the dialogue, with the camera and mute presence of the actors conveying the drama. This jewel of a short feature demonstrates that, for movies, less can sometimes be more. RB English narration.

Jean-Claude Pascal *The officer* • Anouk Aimée *Albertine* • Madeleine García *Her mother* • Jim Gérald *Her father* ■ *Dir* Alexandre Astruc • *Scr* Alexandre Astruc, from the short story *Le Rideau Cramoisi* by Jules Barbey d'Aurevilly

Crimson Gold ★★★★ 12
Drama 2003 · Iran · Colour · 92min

This riveting and often amusing drama reveals the shifting social attitudes that are slowly taking hold in modern Tehran. Flashing back from a jewellery store robbery, the action focuses on the unlikely events and chance encounters that prompt mild-mannered pizza delivery man Hossain Emadeddin to snap. This is potent, poignant and soberingly credible. DP Farsi +subtitles. *DVD*

Hossain Emadeddin *Hussein* • Pourang Nakhael *Pourang* • Azita Rayeji *The Bride* • Sheisi Ali Kamyar • Shahram Vaziri *Jeweller* ■ *Dir* Jafar Panahi • *Scr* Abbas Kiarostami

The Crimson Kimono ★★★
Crime drama 1959 · US · BW · 81min

This is an oddly poignant excursion into maverick American independent director Sam Fuller's underworld. Two detectives in the Little Tokyo district of Los Angeles fall for the same woman who's involved in their investigation into a stripper's murder. Characters range from the hard-boiled to the plain mushy, but Fuller's energetic methods stir up a sympathy not normally present in his movies. Low-key and sometimes banal, but still a stylish work. TH

Victoria Shaw *Christine Downs* • Glenn Corbett *Detective Sergeant Charlie Bancroft* • James Shigeta *Detective Joe Kojaku* • Anna Lee *Mac* ■ *Dir/Scr* Samuel Fuller

Crimson Peak ★★ 15
Romantic horror drama 2015 · US · Colour · 113min

The combination of director Guillermo del Toro's flair for supernatural horror and gothic melodrama would appear to be a match made in heaven. And with Mia Wasikowska as the Jane Eyre-like American innocent swept off her feet by Tom Hiddleston's brooding baronet and taken to his spooky ancestral pile in England, how could it go wrong? But this predictable if occasionally gruesome tale is a huge disappointment considering the talent in front of and behind the camera. JA Violence, a sex scene. *DVD* *Blu*

Mia Wasikowska *Edith Cushing* • Jessica Chastain *Lady Lucille Sharpe* • Tom Hiddleston *Sir Thomas Sharpe* • Charlie Hunnam *Dr Alan McMichael* • Jim Beaver *Carter Cushing* ■ *Dir* Guillermo del Toro • *Scr* Lucinda Coxon, Guillermo del Toro, Matthew Robbins

The Crimson Pirate ★★★★ U
Swashbuckling adventure 1952 · US · Colour · 104min

This is a gorgeous swashbuckler, with Burt Lancaster and his diminutive former circus colleague Nick Cravat swinging through the rigging with sharpened blades clamped between their perfect teeth. Encouraged by the success of *The Flame and the Arrow*, Lancaster and his partner Harold Hecht persuaded Warner Bros to a big budget, and shooting got under way on European locations without a finished script. Lancaster designed the terrific action sequences and puts in a mesmerising star turn. AT

Burt Lancaster *Vallo* • Nick Cravat *Ojo* • Eva Bartok *Consuelo* • Torin Thatcher *Humble Bellows* • James Hayter *Prudence* • Leslie Bradley *Baron Gruda* • Margot Grahame *Bianca* • Christopher Lee *Attache* ■ *Dir* Robert Siodmak • *Scr* Roland Kibbee

The Crimson Rivers ★★★ 15
Crime thriller 2000 · Fr · Colour · 101min

An elusive killer terrorises a remote alpine university in this grisly but absorbing thriller that owes much to *Se7en*. Stars Jean Reno and Vincent Cassel bring their Gallic charisma to bear as the chalk-and-cheese cop duo brought together when their seemingly unconnected cases collide –

U SUITABLE FOR ALL   Uc SUITABLE ESPECIALLY FOR YOUNG CHILDREN (DVD ONLY)   PG PARENTAL GUIDANCE   12A UNDER 12s TO BE ACCOMPANIED (CINEMA ONLY)

Reno, the cerebral veteran inspector; Cassel the impulsive action-man cop. The plot occasionally has too much going on for its own good, but the fantastic locations and the star chemistry more than compensate. JA French +subtitles. Violence, swearing. *DVD*

Jean Reno *Commissaire Pierre Niémans* • Vincent Cassel *Max Kerkerian* • Nadia Farès *Fanny Fereira* • Jean-Pierre Cassel *Dr Bernard Chernezé* • Karim Belkhadra *Capt Dahmane* ■ *Dir* Mathieu Kassovitz • *Scr* Mathieu Kassovitz, Jean-Christophe Grangé, from a novel by Jean-Christophe Grangé

Crimson Tide ★★★★15
Action thriller   1995 · US · Colour · 117min

An American nuclear submarine is ordered to make a pre-emptive strike on Russian rebels who have taken over a missile base, then receives a second, incomplete, radio message suggesting it holds off the attack. Captain Gene Hackman is determined to use his nuclear capability, whatever the consequences. However, his mutinous executive officer (Denzel Washington) stands between him and the horribly alluring Doomsday button. Propelled at full throttle by fast pacing and a palpable friction between the two leads, this riveting thriller is further fuelled by a slick score from Hans Zimmer. AT Violence, swearing. *DVD* *BD*

Denzel Washington *Lt Cdr Ron Hunter* • Gene Hackman *Capt Ramsey* • George Dzundza *Cob* • Viggo Mortensen *Lt Peter "Weps" Ince* • Matt Craven *Lt Roy Zimmer* • James Gandolfini *Lt Bobby Dougherty* • Rocky Carroll *Lt Darik Westergaurd* ■ *Dir* Tony Scott • *Scr* Michael Schiffer, from a story by Michael Schiffer, Richard P Henrick

The Crimson Wing ★★★PG
Wildlife documentary
2008 · US/UK/Fr · Colour · 74min

Why are flamingos pink? That's just one of the questions answered in this visually stunning documentary about the flamingo colony that flocks each year to the breeding grounds of Lake Natron in northern Tanzania. The unique ecosystem of this body of water provides an algae that not only turns their feathers pink but also nourishes their young. Directors Matthew Aeberhard and Leander Ward have assembled some priceless footage, but unfortunately the images are often brought down to earth by the intrusively would-be philosophical commentary – and an ill-suited choice of narrator in Mariella Frostrup. But the sight of the flamingos in flight remains a marvel to behold. TJ *DVD* *BD*

Mariella Frostrup *Narrator* ■ *Dir* Matthew Aeberhard, Leander Ward • *Scr* Melanie Finn

La Crise ★★★★15
Comedy   1992 · Fr · Colour · 91min

Coline Serreau's study of social exclusion continues her search to find genuine emotion beneath the masculine veneer of invulnerability. Sacked for being too good at his job and shocked by the infidelity of both his wife and his mother, bourgeois Parisian Vincent Lindon finds his glib idealism repeatedly shattered by the realities of modern life. Solace comes via an unlikely friendship with orphan Patrick Timsit. A dark satire with a distinctly Voltairean morality about it, the film's exposure of class snobbery and liberal hypocrisy eventually gives way to sentimentality, but the performances are first-rate. DP French +subtitles.

Vincent Lindon *Victor* • Patrick Timsit *Michou* • Zabou *Isabelle* • Maria Pacôme *Victor's mother* • Yves Robert *Victor's father* • Annick Alane *Mamie* • Valerie Alane *Thérèse* • Gilles Privat *Laurent* ■ *Dir/Scr* Coline Serreau

Crisis ★★★
Silent drama   1928 · Ger · BW · 98min

Exploring the ennui of bourgeois marriage and the scandalous temptations of the Berlin underground, this least known of GW Pabst's silent classics is both a compelling human drama and an invaluable record of socio-cultural life in Weimar Germany. Its depiction of decadence now seems rather quaint, but there's a sting in the tail, as bored housewife Brigitte Helm agrees to remarry Gustav Diessl, the stuffed shirt of a lawyer whose neglect drove her to dalliance and divorce. DP

Gustav Diessl *Thomas Beck* • Brigitte Helm *Irene* • Hertha von Walther *Liana* • Jack Trevor *Walter Frank* • Nico Turoff *Sam Taylor* ■ *Dir* GW Pabst • *Scr* Adolf Lantz, Ladislaus Vajda, Helen Gosewisch, from an idea by Fritz Schulz

Crisis ★★★12
Melodrama   1945 · Swe · BW · 88min

Ingmar Bergman's directorial debut is overbalanced by the importation of a character from one of his own plays. Played by Stig Olin, the city cad shifts the focus away from country teenager Inga Landgré, who leaves foster mother Dagny Lind to work in birth mother Marianne Löfgren's beauty salon. Consequently, her seduction comes to matter less than his suicide, thus rendering her return to boy-next-door Allan Bohlin something of an anticlimax. However, there are nascent flashes of trademark Bergman, notably in his use of mirrors, dreams and expressionist symbolism. DP Swedish +subtitles. *DVD*

Inga Landgré *Nelly* • Stig Olin *Jack* • Dagny Lind *Ingeborg* • Marianne Löfgren *Jenny* • Allan Bohlin *Ulf* ■ *Dir* Ingmar Bergman • *Scr* Ingmar Bergman, from the radio play *Moderhjertet/Mother Heart* by Leck Fischer

Crisis ★★
Melodrama   1950 · US · BW · 95min

Cary Grant, the smooth embodiment of American decency in scores of Hollywood productions, strolls through this misfiring melodrama as a brain surgeon forced to perform a dangerous operation on a South American dictator. Ideas concerning repression and freedom are rather too obviously put forward in Richard Brooks's flawed directorial debut. JM

Cary Grant *Dr Eugene Norland Ferguson* • José Ferrer *Raoul Farrago* • Paula Raymond *Helen Ferguson* • Signe Hasso *Senora Isabel Farrago* • Ramon Navarro *Colonel Adragon* • Gilbert Roland *Gonzales* ■ *Dir* Richard Brooks • *Scr* Richard Brooks, from the story *The Doubters* by George Tabori

Criss Cross ★★★★
Film noir   1949 · US · BW · 87min

This classic *film noir* stars Burt Lancaster as a decent armoured car guard who starts courting his ex-wife, Yvonne De Carlo, now engaged to rich mafioso Dan Duryea. Lancaster is trapped into robbing his own firm, leading to much double-crossing and murder. Having all the *noir* trappings one needs – fateful flashbacks, a drab urban setting, doom-laden Miklos Rozsa music – this also contains a lot of sexual energy and a thrillingly shot robbery. Steven Soderbergh remade it in 1995 as *The Underneath*. AT

Burt Lancaster *Steve Thompson* • Yvonne De Carlo *Anna* • Dan Duryea *Slim* • Stephen McNally *Ramirez* • Richard Long *Slade Thompson* • James Curtis [Tony Curtis] *Gigolo* ■ *Dir* Robert Siodmak • *Scr* Daniel Fuchs, from the novel by Don Tracy

CrissCross ★★15
Drama   1992 · US · Colour · 96min

After all the acclaim for *A World Apart*, Chris Menges came horribly unstuck with this, his second stab at directing. While he admirably captures the sights and sounds of Key West in the late 1960s, he fails to inject any life into an all-too-predictable tale of a waitress who turns to stripping to support her son after they're abandoned by her Vietnam-scarred husband. Goldie Hawn is hopelessly miscast as the mother. DP Violence, swearing, nudity.

Goldie Hawn *Tracy Cross* • Arliss Howard *Joe* • James Gammon *Emmett* • David Arnott *Chris Cross* • Keith Carradine *John Cross* • JC Quinn *Jetty* • Steve Buscemi *Louis* • Paul Calderon *Blacky* ■ *Dir* Chris Menges • *Scr* Scott Sommer, from his novella

Critical Care ★★★15
Medical drama   1997 · US · Colour · 102min

James Spader is on top form as a young resident doctor, supervising a man on life support and attempting to assist his two daughters, who disagree on the choice of treatment. Kyra Sedgwick wants to pull the plug; Margo Martindale wants to maintain a vegetative state as long as possible. The hospital, meanwhile, is content to keep the patient alive as long as his insurance money swells their coffers. LH *DVD*

James Spader *Dr Werner Ernst* • Kyra Sedgwick *Felicia Potter* • Helen Mirren *Stella* • Anne Bancroft *Nun* • Albert Brooks *Dr Butz* • Margo Martindale *Connie Potter* • Wallace Shawn *Furnaceman* ■ *Dir* Sidney Lumet • *Scr* Steven S Schwartz, from the novel by Richard Dooling

Critical Condition ★15
Comedy   1987 · US · Colour · 93min

Director Michael Apted must have been having a bad day when he agreed to direct this unamusing vehicle for Richard Pryor. Pryor plays a hustler who feigns insanity to stay out of prison and, after a series of ludicrous misadventures, ends up running the institution into which he has been committed. JB Swearing. *DVD*

Richard Pryor *Eddie* • Joe Mantegna *Chambers* • Rubén Blades *Louis* • Rachel Ticotin *Rachel* • Bob Dishy *Dr Foster* • Sylvia Miles *Maggie* • Joe Dallesandro *Stucky* • Randall "Tex" Cobb *Box* ■ *Dir* Michael Apted • *Scr* Denis Hamill, John Hamill, from a story by Alan Swyer

Critic's Choice ★★★
Comedy   1963 · US · Colour · 99min

This started life as a Broadway in-joke as to whether theatre critic Walter Kerr should review his wife Jean's play, but became diluted en route to the movies and fetched up as a vehicle for Bob Hope and Lucille Ball. It's not very funny, though director Don Weis paints a sharp picture of the waspish New York theatre milieu. TS

Bob Hope *Parker Ballantine* • Lucille Ball *Angela Ballantine* • Marilyn Maxwell *Ivy London* • Rip Torn *Dion Kapakos* • Jessie Royce Landis *Charlotte Orr* • John Dehner *SP Champlain* ■ *Dir* Don Weis • *Scr* Jack Sher, from the play by Ira Levin

Critters ★★★15
Horror comedy   1986 · US · Colour · 82min

Stephen Herek directs a cheeky smash-and-grab raid on *Gremlins* and comes up with a crude but entertaining horror comedy. The "critters" of the title are a race of nasty hedgehog-like alien creatures who invade a small American town and proceed to wreak havoc until two intergalactic bounty hunters arrive to save the day. The cast remains stoically straight-faced, the creatures nab the best lines (in subtitles), and Herek keeps his tongue stuck firmly in his cheek. Three sequels followed, with the second featuring one Leonardo DiCaprio. JF Violence, swearing. *DVD*

Dee Wallace Stone *Helen Brown* • M Emmet Walsh *Harv* • Billy Green Bush *Jay Brown* • Scott Grimes *Brad Brown* • Nadine Van Der Velde *April Brown* • Don Opper *Charlie McFadden* • Terrence Mann *Johnny Steele* • Billy Zane *Steve Elliot* ■ *Dir* Stephen Herek • *Scr* Stephen Herek, Dominic Muir

Crocodile ★15
Horror adventure   2000 · US · Colour · 90min

Has the director of *The Texas Chain Saw Massacre* really been reduced to ripping off mediocre monster movies? Sadly, Tobe Hooper is at the helm of this stalk 'n' scoff farrago, in which a stereotypical gaggle of college kids are preyed upon by a fiend who has more in common with a junior art-class project than a cutting-edge special effect. Appalling. DP *DVD*

Mark McLaughlin *Brady* • Caitlin Martin *Claire* • Chris Solari *Duncan* • Julie Mintz *Annabelle* • Sommer Knight *Sunny* ■ *Dir* Tobe Hooper • *Scr* Jace Anderson, Adam Gierasch, Michael D Weiss

"Crocodile" Dundee ★★★★15
Comedy adventure
1986 · Aus/US · Colour · 92min

The first, and best, of the tales about the Australian outback's living legend, who can wrestle crocodiles with bare hands and subdue ladies with naked charisma. Paul Hogan took his lager-commercial he-man into the big time, and the big city, and the result is as agreeable as if it were Tarzan coping in a concrete jungle. Director Peter Faiman's languid pace gives us time to appreciate this particular Wizard from Oz as he survives sophisticates' taunts and outwits street villains. A pity Hogan couldn't keep the momentum going for later movies, but for this, he created a totally likeable superhero. TH Swearing. *DVD*

Paul Hogan *Michael J "Crocodile" Dundee* • Linda Kozlowski *Sue Charlton* • John Meillon *Walter Reilly* • David Gulpilil *Neville Bell* • Mark Blum *Richard Mason* • Michael Lombard *Sam Charlton* • Ritchie Singer *Con* ■ *Dir* Peter Faiman • *Scr* Paul Hogan, Ken Shadie, John Cornell, from a story by Paul Hogan

"Crocodile" Dundee II ★★★PG
Comedy adventure
1988 · US/Aus · Colour · 111min

Having scored a massive box-office hit with the first movie, Paul Hogan could be forgiven for reprising the role of Mick "Crocodile" Dundee. Less excusable, however, is the misguided attempt to blend the inspired comedy of the original with the kind of rescue adventure that was old hat in the long-gone days of the film serial. But Hogan is as amiable as before and there are funny moments, mostly in the attitudes of the outback residents towards the city slickers who have kidnapped Linda Kozlowski. JM Violence, swearing. *DVD*

Paul Hogan *Michael J "Crocodile" Dundee* • Linda Kozlowski *Sue Charlton* • John Meillon *Walter Reilly* • Hechter Ubarry *Rico* • Juan Fernandez *Miguel* • Ernie Dingo *Charlie* • Charles Dutton [Charles S Dutton] *Leroy Brown* • Mark Blum *Richard Mason* • Steve Rackman *Donk* • Gerry Skilton *Nugget* • Gus Mercurio *Frank* ■ *Dir* John Cornell • *Scr* Paul Hogan, Brett Hogan, from characters by Paul Hogan

Crocodile Dundee in Los Angeles ★PG
Comedy adventure
2001 · US/Aus · Colour · 91min

Quite what drove Paramount Studios to bankroll a third instalment in the "Crocodile" Dundee franchise will be beyond anyone unlucky enough to sit through it. Characteristics that once seemed charming in star Paul Hogan are now as weathered as his face. The story concerns a Hollywood backlot art heist uncovered by Dundee. The direction borders on the soporific and, at 62, Hogan seems to know he is too old for this schtick. AC *DVD*

Paul Hogan *Michael J "Crocodile" Dundee* • Linda Kozlowski *Sue Charleton* • Jere Burns *Arnan Rothman* • Jonathan Banks *Milos Drubnik* • Alec Wilson *Jacko* • Serge Cockburn *Mikey Dundee* • Gerry Skilton *Nugget O'Cass* ■ *Dir* Simon Wincer • *Scr* Matthew Berry, Eric Abrams, from characters by Paul Hogan

The Crocodile Hunter: Collision Course ★★★PG
Comedy adventure
2002 · Aus/US · Colour · 85min

This good-natured romp stars eccentric Australian wildlife expert Steve Irwin, who died in 2006 at the age of 44 when a stingray barb pierced his heart while he was filming in Australia's Great Barrier Reef. It's something of an oddity – a combination of documentary-style close encounters with various outback inhabitants and a lightweight thriller plot about the race to retrieve a fallen satellite gizmo. The so-called storyline – incorporating one-dimensional CIA agents and an aggressive female cattle rancher – is so slight it barely exists, but Irwin's enthusiastic one-on-one duels with deadly snakes, spiders and, of course, crocodiles (punctuated by educational addresses to the audience) are a scream. JC **DVD**

Steve Irwin • Terri Irwin • Magda Szubanski *Brozzie Drewitt* • David Wenham *Sam Flynn* • Lachy Hulme *Agent Robert Wheeler* • Aden Young *Ron Buckwhiler* • Kenneth Ransom *Agent Vaughan Archer* • Kate Beahan *Jo Buckley* ■ *Dir* John Stainton • *Scr* Holly Goldberg Sloan, from a story by John Stainton

Cromwell ★★★★ PG
Historical drama 1970 · UK · Colour · 133min

Richard Harris's warts-and-all Oliver Cromwell and Alec Guinness's unyielding Charles I make this historic double act very watchable. They bring past politics to vivid life and put paid to the idea that right and grace were on the side of royalist Cavaliers as opposed to the Puritan Roundheads. The usually undervalued Ken Hughes was given an enormous budget for a British film at the time, and the result is a long-winded but compelling tale with some mightily well-staged battles. TH **DVD**

Richard Harris *Oliver Cromwell* • Alec Guinness *King Charles I* • Robert Morley *Earl of Manchester* • Dorothy Tutin *Queen Henrietta Maria* • Frank Finlay *John Carter* • Timothy Dalton *Prince Rupert* • Patrick Wymark *Earl of Strafford* • Patrick Magee *Hugh Peters* • Nigel Stock *Sir Edward Hyde* ■ *Dir* Ken Hughes • *Scr* Ken Hughes, Ronald Harwood • *Cinematographer* Geoffrey Unsworth • *Costume Designer* Vittorio Nino Novarese

Cronos ★★★★ 18
Horror 1992 · Mex · Colour · 92min

This is a compelling and wonderfully atmospheric film from Mexican director Guillermo del Toro. Although thematically profound, stately in pace and largely devoid of the kind of blood-letting beloved of schlock fans, this is still a highly effective chiller. Federico Luppi is superb as the antiques dealer who becomes enslaved by the Cronos device, a mysterious mechanical insect that forces its victims into acts of vampirism. DP English, Spanish +subtitles. Violence, swearing. **DVD** Blu

Federico Luppi *Jesus Gris* • Ron Perlman *Angel de la Guardia* • Claudio Brook *Dieter de la Guardia* • Margarita Isabel *Mercedes Gris* ■ *Dir/Scr* Guillermo del Toro

The Croods ★★★ U
Animated comedy adventure 2013 · US · Colour · 94min

Croods by name, but sophisticated by nature, this *Flintstones*-esque slice of CGI-animated family fun has Nicolas Cage and Emma Stone voicing the dad and daughter of a not-so-modern Stone Age family. Fleeing impending apocalypse in the company of a more evolved teenager (Ryan Reynolds) from another tribe, they seek safety, shelter and enlightenment through a colourful and weirdly trippy landscape of land whales, elephant mice and piranha parrots. *The Croods* sometimes mistakes frantic for fun, and its emotional complexities and all-over-the-place ending may baffle younger viewers. But there's enough prehistorical slapstick to keep the kids entertained and adults amused. DA **DVD** Blu **cs**

Nicolas Cage *Grug* • Emma Stone *Eep* • Ryan Reynolds *Guy* • Catherine Keener *Ugga* • Cloris Leachman *Gran* • Clark Duke *Thunk* ■ *Dir* Chris Sanders (2), Kirk De Micco • *Scr* Chris Sanders (2), Kirk De Micco, from a story by Sanders, De Micco, John Cleese

Crooked Hearts ★★★ 15
Drama 1991 · US · Colour · 107min

This thoughtful low-budget movie disappeared swiftly on release but was revived some time later when word got around that it is rather good. Peter Coyote is solid in a pivotal role as an unfaithful patriarch causing ripples in the family pond. There are many strands to this intelligent, well paced film that evolve delicately on screen, aided by strong performances. SH Swearing, sex scenes, nudity.

Peter Berg *Tom* • Vincent D'Onofrio [Vincent D'Onofrio] *Charley* • Jennifer Jason Leigh *Marriet* • Noah Wyle *Ask* • Peter Coyote *Edward* •

Cindy Pickett *Jill* • Juliette Lewis *Cassie* ■ *Dir* Michael Bortman • *Scr* Michael Bortman, from the novel by Robert Boswell

The Crooked Road ★★
Thriller 1964 · UK/Yug · BW · 94min

This thriller is a story of Balkan intrigue starring Robert Ryan as a US reporter investigating a corrupt dictator. Stewart Granger plays the dictator with his tongue in his cheek, but the sad script, derived from a Morris West novel, lets the cast down badly. It was filmed in Yugoslavia, which President Tito was then promoting as the next Almeria. AT

Robert Ryan *Richard Ashley* • Stewart Granger *Duke of Oragna* • Nadia Gray *Cosima* • Marius Goring *Harlequin* • George Coulouris *Carlos* • Catherine Woodville *Elena* • Robert Rietty *Police chief* ■ *Dir* Don Chaffey • *Scr* Jay Garrison, Don Chaffey, from the novel *The Big Story* by Morris West

The Crooked Sky ★★ U
Crime thriller 1957 · US · BW · 76min

This crime quickie is notable primarily because it was scripted by Norman Hudis, who went on to become a key scribe in both the *Carry On* and *Man from UNCLE* series. American actor Wayne Morris plays a detective flown over to help Scotland Yard smash an international counterfeit ring. Morris turns in a no-nonsense performance, but is easily upstaged by that master of menace, Anton Diffring. DP

Wayne Morris *Mike Conklin* • Karin Booth *Sandra Hastings* • Anton Diffring *Fraser* • Bruce Seton *Mac* • Sheldon Lawrence *Bill* • Collette Barthrop *Penny* • Frank Hawkins *Robson* • Murray Kash *Lewis* ■ *Dir* Henry Cass • *Scr* Norman Hudis, from a story by Lance Z Hargreaves, Maclean Rogers

Crooklyn ★★★ 12
Comedy drama 1994 · US · Colour · 109min

An African-American family living in 1970s Brooklyn struggles to recover from the racial turmoil of the 1960s in Spike Lee's semi-autobiographical tale, inspired by his youth. Alfre Woodard and Delroy Lindo are excellent as the middle-class Carmichaels, whose household is a reflection of the outside tensions tearing at the fabric of society. Not as confrontational as Lee's other films, *Crooklyn* still suffers slightly from the director's choppy narrative style. That said, this is a sure and mature work. AJ

Alfre Woodard *Carolyn Carmichael* • Delroy Lindo *Woody Carmichael* • David Patrick Kelly *Tony Eyes* • Zelda Harris *Troy Carmichael* • Spike Lee *Snuffy* • Vondie Curtis-Hall *Uncle Brown* ■ *Dir* Spike Lee • *Scr* from a story by Joie Susannah Lee, Spike Lee, Joie Susannah Lee, Cinqué Lee

Crooks and Coronets ★★ U
Comedy crime thriller 1969 · UK · Colour · 104min

An old-style English caper comedy, this has Edith Evans, Hattie Jacques and Harry H Corbett improbably joined by Hollywood heavies Telly Savalas and Warren Oates. This strange casting gives the film a certain interest, not to mention eccentricity, as the cast are involved in a plot to rob a British stately home of its silver and art treasures. Dame Edith owns the stately pile and does her doddery old dowager act to perfection, but the this is far too frantic and full of those terribly dated Swinging Sixties fads and fashions. AT

Telly Savalas *Herbie Hassler* • Edith Evans *Lady Sophie Fitzmore* • Warren Oates *Marty Miller* • Cesar Romero *Nick Marco* • Harry H Corbett *Frank Finley* • Nicky Henson *Lord Fitzmore* • Hattie Jacques *Mabel* • Arthur Mullard *Perce* ■ *Dir/Scr* Jim O'Connolly

Crooks Anonymous ★★ U
Comedy 1962 · UK · BW · 83min

Playing a stripper was hardly the most auspicious start to Julie Christie's career, but she manages to cover herself in some glory in this amiable if unremarkable comedy. It's an amusing but limited idea: what else would the members of a villains'

self-help group do but put their individual expertise to collective misuse? Stanley Baxter and Leslie Phillips run through their usual tricks, while Wilfrid Hyde White, James Robertson-Justice and Robertson Hare steal scenes at will. DP

Leslie Phillips *Dandy Forsdyke* • Stanley Baxter *RS Widdowes* • Wilfrid Hyde White *Montague* • Julie Christie *Babette* • James Robertson-Justice *Sir Harvey Russelrod* • Michael Medwin *Ronnie* • Pauline Jameson *Prunella* • Robertson Hare *Grimsdale* ■ *Dir* Ken Annakin • *Scr* Jack Davies, Henry Blyth

Crooks in Cloisters ★★★ U
Comedy 1963 · UK · Colour · 93min

Anything but a pseudo-*Carry On*, this cosy bungled crime comedy is much more a product of the post-Ealing school. The emphasis is firmly on character as Ronald Fraser and his gang lie low in a monastery to throw the cops off their trail. Bernard Cribbins is in fine fettle as one of Fraser's gormless colleagues and Barbara Windsor is funnier than the *Carry Ons* ever allowed her to be. DP **DVD**

Ronald Fraser *Walt* • Barbara Windsor *Bikini* • Grégoire Aslan *Lorenzo* • Bernard Cribbins *Squirts* • Davy Kaye *Specs* • Melvyn Hayes *Willy* • Wilfrid Brambell *Phineas* • Joseph O'Connor *Father Septimus* • Corin Redgrave *Brother Lucius* • Francesca Annis *June* ■ *Dir* Jeremy Summers • *Scr* TJ Morrison, Mike Watts, from a story by Mike Watts

Crooks' Tour ★★ U
Spy comedy 1940 · UK · BW · 81min

Basil Radford and Naunton Wayne reprise the Charters and Caldicott characters first seen in Alfred Hitchcock's *The Lady Vanishes* in this slight comic flag-waver, adapted from a radio serial produced by that film's screenwriters, Frank Launder and Sidney Gilliat. Once again it's espionage all the way for the cricket-mad duo, who this time around are mistaken for Nazi spies in Baghdad. Director John Baxter maintains a jaunty pace throughout. DP

Basil Radford *Charters* • Naunton Wayne *Caldicott* • Greta Gynt *La Palermo* • Abraham Sofaer *Ali* • Charles Oliver *Sheik* • Gordon McLeod *Rossenger* ■ *Dir* John Baxter • *Scr* John Watt, Max Kester

Cross Creek ★★ U
Biographical drama 1983 · US · Colour · 115min

Beautifully filmed by John A Alonzo, this biographical drama suggests how Marjorie Kinnan Rawlings might have got the inspiration for her sentimental classic, *The Yearling*. Yet in devoting so much of his energy to capturing the atmosphere of the Florida backwoods in the late 1920s, director Martin Ritt leaves little room for anything other than loosely connected vignettes. As the would-be author who leaves New York to learn her craft, Mary Steenburgen is passive, and not even her encounters with bullish Rip Torn shake her serenity. DP

Mary Steenburgen *Marjorie Kinnan Rawlings* • Rip Torn *Marsh Turner* • Peter Coyote *Norton Baskin* • Dana Hill *Ellie Turner* • Alfre Woodard *Geechee* • Malcolm McDowell *Maxwell Perkins* ■ *Dir* Martin Ritt • *Scr* Dalene Young, from the memoirs by Marjorie Kinnan Rawlings

Cross My Heart ★★★ 18
Comedy 1987 · US · Colour · 86min

This thoroughly amiable and underrated romantic comedy makes up for what it lacks in wit with charming central performances. Intended as a vehicle for Martin Short, the picture is stolen out from under him by Annette O'Toole, who surely deserves to be a bigger star than she is. Barriers and pretences predictably come tumbling down as newly sacked Short and single mum O'Toole stumble through a date. Sadly the contrived ending is a disappointing fudge. DP

Martin Short *David* • Annette O'Toole *Kathy* • Paul Reiser *Bruce* • Joanna Kerns *Nancy* • Jessica Puscas *Jessica* • Lee Arenberg *Parking attendant* ■ *Dir* Armyan Bernstein • *Scr* Armyan Bernstein, Gail Parent

Cross My Heart ★★★★ PG
Comedy drama 1990 · Fr · Colour · 104min

Sylvain Copans is hugely impressive as the 12-year-old whose friends rally round to keep his mother's death a secret so that the authorities can't pack him off to an orphanage. The ingenious methods to which they resort to deflect suspicion have both an innocence and a black comedic edge that makes this such a treat for both the young and those who might have forgotten how troubling and invigorating childhood can be. DP French +subtitles.

Sylvain Copans *Martin* • Nicolas Parodi *Jérôme* • Cécilia Rouaud *Marianne* • Delphine Gouttman *Hélène* • Olivier Montiège *Antoine* • Lucie Blossier *Claire* • Kaldi El Hadj *Dédé* ■ *Dir/Scr* Jacques Fansten

Cross of Honour ★★★ 15
Second World War drama 2012 · Nor/Swe · Colour · 99min

Harry Potter's Rupert Grint is the only real "name" actor in this decent war film. Two planes shoot each other down over Norway in 1940. Three Germans and two Brits survive, and all five are forced to set their differences aside when they find themselves sharing the same hunter's cabin, which provides the only shelter from the harsh Norwegian winter. The film is long on words, a little light on action and occasionally succumbs to corn and cliché, but it does do the whole camaraderie-through-crisis thing with some skill and likeability. DA English, German, Norwegian +subtitles. Swearing. **DVD** Blu

Florian Lukas *Horst Schopis* • Rupert Grint *Robert Smith* • David Kross *Josef Schwartz* ■ *Dir* Petter Naess • *Scr* Ole Meldegaard, Dave Mango, Petter Naess

Cross of Iron ★★★★ 18
Second World War drama 1977 · UK/W Ger · Colour · 127min

Director Sam Peckinpah switches from westerns such as *The Wild Bunch* to another kind of savagery – Germans in retreat on the Russian Front during the Second World War – and makes this as graphic an anti-war film as anything since *All Quiet on the Western Front*. James Coburn is the disillusioned sergeant, sickened by slaughter and the double dealings of officers such as Maximilian Schell. This exercise in macho ideals is bloody action, elegantly choreographed to chilling effect. Forget the dire 1978 sequel, *Breakthrough*. TH Violence, swearing, nudity. **DVD** Blu

James Coburn *Steiner* • Maximilian Schell *Stransky* • James Mason *Brandt* • David Warner *Kiesel* • Klaus Lowitsch [Klaus Löwitsch] *Kruger* • Vadim Glowna *Kern* • Roger Fritz *Triebig* ■ *Dir* Sam Peckinpah • *Scr* Herbert Asmodi, Julius J Epstein, from the novel *The Willing Flesh* by Willi Heinrich

The Cross of Lorraine ★★★
Second World War drama 1943 · US · BW · 90min

This sincere and well-made wartime tribute to the French Resistance tells the story of a group of PoWs held in a Nazi concentration camp. Yet, despite MGM's top-notch production values and a fine cast, it is difficult to accept the likes of Gene Kelly, Cedric Hardwicke and Peter Lorre in such a grim drama; only dashing Jean-Pierre Aumont and nasty Hume Cronyn really convince. As a piece of propaganda, though, the movie did its job well. TS

Jean-Pierre Aumont *Paul* • Gene Kelly *Victor* • Sir Cedric Hardwicke [Cedric Hardwicke] *Father Sebastian* • Richard Whorf *François* • Joseph Calleia *Rodriguez* • Peter Lorre *Sergeant Berger* • Hume Cronyn *Duval* • Billy Roy *Louis* ■ *Dir* Tay Garnett • *Scr* Michael Kanin, Ring Lardner Jr, Alexander Esway, Robert D Andrews, from a story by Lilo Damert, Robert Aisner, from the book *A Thousand Shall Fall* by Hans Habe

Crossed Over ★★
Drama based on a true story 2002 · Can/US · Colour · 120min

Though it has all the ingredients of a quality redemptive drama, this true-story tale about a friendship between a death-row prisoner and a bereaved mother continually squanders its potential. Jennifer Jason Leigh stars as murderess Karla Faye Tucker, the first woman to be executed in Texas since the American Civil War. But while she coasts along predictably, co-star Diane Keaton lacks sincerity, never ringing true as the writer who befriends Tucker as a means of facing up to her own son's hit-and-run demise. **SF** Brief violence, swearing, sexual references.

Diane Keaton *Beverly Lowry* • Jennifer Jason Leigh *Karla Faye Tucker* • Maury Chaykin *Ethan Lowry* • Connor Price *Young Peter* • Nick Roth *Peter Lowry* ■ *Dir* Bobby Roth • *Scr* John Wierick, from the memoirs *Crossed Over: a Murder/a Memoir* by Beverly Lowry

Crossed Swords ★★🅤
Swashbuckling adventure
1954 · It/US · Colour · 83min

One of the films Errol Flynn made in Europe during his flight from debts and marriage in America. A dyspeptic-looking Flynn strutting his stuff in a tinpot dukedom called Sidonia, which has decreed bachelorhood to be illegal. Of the dozens of women on offer it's Gina Lollobrigida, playing the duke's daughter, who lays down the law at Flynn's feet, threatening to put an end to his "wandering". **AT**

Errol Flynn *Renzo* • Gina Lollobrigida *Francesca* • Cesare Danova *Raniero* • Nadia Gray *Fulvia* • Paola Mori *Tomasina* • Roldano Lupi *Pavoncello* • Alberto Rabagliati *Gennarelli* • Silvio Bagolini *Buio* ■ *Dir* Milton Krims, Vittorio Vassarotti • *Scr* Milton Krims

Crossfire ★★★★🅿🅖
Film noir
1947 · US · BW · 86min

This terrific thriller tells the story of four GIs, just back from the Second World War, who become involved in a murder. The original novel made the victim a homosexual, but in the movie he's a Jew - at the time, not only a safer choice as far as censorship was concerned, but also more resonant in the aftermath of the war and considering Hollywood's own racial mix. Directed by Edward Dmytryk and produced by Adrian Scott (both of whom were later blacklisted in the Communist witch-hunt), it's an impressive and gripping film, superbly performed. **AT**

Robert Young (1) *Finlay* • Robert Mitchum *Keeley* • Robert Ryan *Montgomery* • Gloria Grahame *Ginny* • George Cooper (2) *Mitchell* • Steve Brodie *Floyd* • William Phipps *Leroy* • Sam Levene *Joseph Samuels* • Paul Kelly (1) *Man* • Jacqueline White *Mary Mitchell* ■ *Dir* Edward Dmytryk • *Scr* John Paxton, from the novel *The Brick Foxhole* by Richard Brooks

Crossing Delancey ★★★★🅿🅖
Romantic comedy 1988 · US · Colour · 92min

Adapted by Susan Sandler from her own play, this charismatic comedy about 30-something New Yorkers proves that love is not only blind, but also has a poor sense of smell. Peter Riegert makes the unlikeliest romantic hero as the pickle maker who tries to convince pretentious bookseller Amy Irving that they are made for one another, in spite of her interest in hack novelist Jeroen Krabbé. Lovingly capturing the sights and sounds of the Jewish neighbourhood situated south of Delancey Street, director Joan Micklin Silver never allows emotion to descend into sentiment. **DP**

Amy Irving *Isabelle Grossman* • Peter Riegert *Sam Posner* • Jeroen Krabbé *Anton Maes* • Reizl Bozyk *Bubbie Kantor* • Sylvia Miles *Hannah Mandelbaum* ■ *Dir* Joan Micklin Silver • *Scr* Susan Sandler, from her play

The Crossing Guard ★★★★🄸🄵
Drama 1995 · US · Colour · 106min

This forceful drama, written and directed by Sean Penn, features Jack Nicholson as the father of a drink-driving victim who vows to kill the man responsible (David Morse). What follows is not a plot-heavy revenge thriller, but a poignant and believable study of a tragedy that has sucked the life out of its tormented protagonists. A slow-burning pace, fine performances and an intelligent script make this drama feel painfully real. **JC** Violence, swearing, a sex scene, nudity. **DVD** **Blu**

Jack Nicholson *Freddy Gale* • David Morse *John Booth* • Anjelica Huston *Mary* • Robin Wright *JoJo* • Piper Laurie *Helen Booth* • Priscilla Barnes *Verna* • Robbie Robertson *Roger* ■ *Dir/Scr* Sean Penn

Crossing Over ★★🄸🄸
Drama 2008 · US · Colour · 108min

The lives of illegal immigrants hoping to remain in the US and the attempts of Los Angeles authorities trying to prevent it shape this provocative ensemble drama. The spotlight falls on a Mexican single mother (Alice Braga) caught working without papers, an Australian actress (Alice Eve) with an expired visa and a dodgy Brit (Jim Sturgess) passing as a Jewish religious teacher. Deciding their fates are a Homeland Security cop (Harrison Ford) and an immigration lawyer (Ashley Judd) who wear their hearts on their sleeve, while a green-card adjudicator (Ray Liotta) has few moral scruples. It all makes for a bustling two hours, but writer/director Wayne Kramer relies too heavily on clunky coincidences without ever really managing to surprise us. **TJ** Violence, swearing, nudity. **DVD** **Blu**

Harrison Ford *Max Brogan* • Jim Sturgess *Gavin Kossef* • Ray Liotta *Cole Frankel* • Ashley Judd *Denise Frankel* • Summer Bishil *Taslima Jahangir* • Cliff Curtis *Hamid Baraheri* • Alice Eve *Claire Sheperd* ■ *Dir/Scr* Wayne Kramer

Crossplot ★★🄿🄶
Thriller 1969 · UK · Colour · 92min

Roger Moore wasn't James Bond when he made this, just a TV star with some time to kill between *The Saint* and *The Persuaders*. Set in swinging London, the plot has Moore as an advertising executive looking for the ideal girl for a campaign, who just happens to be mixed up with a sinister political organisation. *Variety* condemned the film's listlessness, though they lacked prescience by saying, "Moore is not wholly convincing as a man of action." **AT** **DVD**

Roger Moore *Gary Fenn* • Martha Hyer *Jo Grinling* • Claudie Lange *Marla Kogash* • Alexis Kanner *Tarquin* • Francis Matthews *Ruddock* • Bernard Lee *Chilmore* ■ *Dir* Alvin Rakoff • *Scr* Leigh Vance, John Kruse, from a story by Leigh Vance

Crossroads ★★
Mystery 1942 · US · BW · 83min

William Powell stars as an amnesiac diplomat in Paris who becomes the target of blackmailers. He is then accused of being a wanted criminal in court and, because of his amnesia, cannot prove otherwise. Filmed on a studio backlot version of Paris, its chief virtues are in the cast: Hedy Lamarr as Powell's wife, Basil Rathbone as his blackmailer and Claire Trevor as a nightclub singer. **AT**

William Powell *David Talbot* • Hedy Lamarr *Lucienne Talbot* • Claire Trevor *Michelle Allaine* • Basil Rathbone *Henri Sarrow* • Felix Bressart *Dr Andre Tessier* • Margaret Wycherly *Mme Pelletier* • Reginald Owen *Concierge* ■ *Dir* Jack Conway • *Scr* Gus Trosper

Crossroads ★★🄸🄵
Road movie 1986 · US · Colour · 94min

Based on the myth that blues legend Robert Johnson sold his soul to the Devil, this is essentially a musical version of *The Karate Kid*. Joe Seneca plays as an old compadre of Johnson's who persuades the young guitarist to take him home to Mississippi. Only Seneca's yarns and Ry Cooder's lazy score make the trek tolerable, though it's infinitely more entertaining than the ludicrous finale, in which Macchio trades riffs with Frank Zappa's old axeman, Steve Vai. **DP**

Ralph Macchio *Eugene Martone* • Joe Seneca *Willie Brown* • Jami Gertz *Frances* • Robert Judd *Scratch* • Joe Morton *Scratch's assistant* • Steve Vai *Jack Butler* • Dennis Lipscomb *Lloyd* ■ *Dir* Walter Hill • *Scr* John Fusco

Crossroads ★★★🄿🄶
Romantic comedy drama
2002 · US · Colour · 91min

Despite its naive, picture-postcard view of America, this showcase for teen singing sensation Britney Spears is hard to dislike. Simplistic in the extreme but not without charm, the film sees Spears and childhood friends Zoë Saldana and Taryn Manning on a road trip of discovery. If you can cope with the high cheese factor, director Tamra Davis's rose-tinted movie will be an engaging journey. **JC**

Britney Spears *Lucy* • Anson Mount *Ben* • Zoë Saldana *Kit* • Taryn Manning *Mimi* • Kim Cattrall *Caroline* • Dan Aykroyd *Pete* • Justin Long *Henry* ■ *Dir* Tamra Davis • *Scr* Shonda Rhimes

Crossworlds ★★★🄸🄵
Science-fiction adventure
1996 · US · Colour · 87min

Cheap and cliché-ridden it may be, but this *Stargate* meets *Star Wars* hybrid is an enjoyably unpretentious fantasy romp. All-American Josh Charles learns from a mysterious stranger that the crystal around his neck is the key to a trans-dimensional portal where time and space have no meaning. In this "crossworld", he teams up with Rutger Hauer in a battle for survival against megalomaniac Stuart Wilson. If you can get over the slow start, this is an entertaining experience. **AJ** Violence, swearing. **DVD**

Rutger Hauer *AT* • Josh Charles *Joe Talbot* • Stuart Wilson (1) *Ferris* • Andrea Roth *Laura* • Perry Anzilotti *Rebo* ■ *Dir* Krishna Rao • *Scr* Krishna Rao, Raman Rao

LANDMARK FILM
Ang Lee's breathtakingly beautiful film takes the Chinese martial arts genre to an international mainstream audience

Crouching Tiger, Hidden Dragon ★★★★★🄸🄵
Period action romance
2000 · US/Chi/Tai · Colour · 115min

Exhibiting cinematic influences ranging from John Ford and Akira Kurosawa to *The Matrix*, Ang Lee's handsome epic puts the art back into martial arts. Those familiar with the works of King Hu and Tsui Hark will revel in the unhurried way he reworks the conventions of the swordplay genre to explore the perennial themes of love and loyalty, duty and sacrifice. But Lee also combines brilliant stunt work with special effects to create such memorable sequences as the rooftop pursuit and the treetop battle. Chow Yun-Fat and Michelle Yeoh excel as the warriors seeking the stolen sword of Green Destiny, but the most electrifying performance is Zhang Ziyi's teenage thief. **DP** Mandarin +subtitles. **DVD** **Blu**

Chow Yun-Fat *Li Mu Bai* • Michelle Yeoh *Yu Shu Lien* • Zhang Ziyi *Jen* • Chang Chen *Lo* • Cheng Pei Pei *Jade Fox* ■ *Dir* Ang Lee • *Scr* James Schamus, Wang Hui-Ling, Tsai Kuo-Jung, from the novel by Wang Du Lu • *Cinematographer* Peter Pau • *Choreographer* Yuen Wo Ping [Yuen Woo-Ping]

Crouching Tiger, Hidden Dragon: Sword of Destiny ★★★🄸🄵
Martial arts action adventure
2016 · US · Colour and BW · 100min

A Chinese *wuxia* adventure performed in English? That's the novel proposition of this easily digestible sequel to Ang Lee's martial arts masterpiece from 2000. Not that it lacks authenticity: the original film's action choreographer, Yuen Wo-Ping, assumes directorial duties here, while Michelle Yeoh reprises her role as the contemplative Yu Shu Lien. The film lacks the romantic yearning that made its predecessor so emotionally resonant, and it also plays out on a less epic canvas (those verdant New Zealand locations notwithstanding). But it's hard not to be caught up in the excitement. **JH** Some violence.

Donnie Yen *Silent Wolf* • Michelle Yeoh *Yu Shu Lien* • Harry Shum Jr *Wei Fang* • Natasha Liu Bordizzo *Snow Vase* • Jason Scott Lee *Hades* •

Dai ■ *Dir* Yuen Wo-Ping [Yuen Woo-Ping] • *Scr* John Fusco, from the novel *Crane Iron Pentalogy* by Wang Du Lu

Croupier ★★🄸🄵
Thriller 1998 · Fr/Ger/UK · Colour · 90min

This account of double-dealing in a London casino is fascinating in its detail, but the improbable romantic backdrop given to the story by scriptwriter Paul Mayersberg does director Mike Hodges no favours. Clive Owen plays a croupier-turned-writer who is prompted by his buccaneering father (Nicholas Ball) to return to the tables. Owen's poker-faced acting doesn't involve us, while the story strands never properly intertwine. **TH** Violence, swearing, sex scenes, nudity. **DVD**

Clive Owen *Jack Manfred* • Alex Kingston *Jani de Villiers* • Kate Hardie *Bella* • Nicholas Ball *Jack Manfred Sr* • Gina McKee *Marion Neil* ■ *Dir* Mike Hodges • *Scr* Paul Mayersberg

The Crow ★★★★🄸🄵
Action fantasy 1994 · US · Colour · 97min

In this dark, surreal version of James O'Barr's 1980s cult comic book, Brandon Lee (son of Bruce) plays a rock musician returning from the grave to take revenge on the notorious street gang who murdered him and his fiancée. It's a stunningly designed fantasy with *Grand Guignol* gloominess at a jolting premium. The comic book origins may be too obvious at times, but the dynamic action scenes and the bravura kinetic style of director Alex Proyas mean it always grips and thoroughly entertains. This dark fable about life after death was given a poignant spin when Lee was tragically killed during an on-set stunt accident. **AJ** Violence, swearing, drug abuse, brief nudity. **DVD** **Blu**

Brandon Lee *Eric Draven* • Michael Wincott *Top Dollar* • Rochelle Davis *Sarah* • Ernie Hudson *Albrecht* • David Patrick Kelly *T Bird* • Angel David *Skank* ■ *Dir* Alex Proyas • *Scr* David J Schow, John Shirley, from the comic book by James O'Barr • *Cinematographer* Dariusz Wolski • *Art Director* Simon Murton

The Crow: City of Angels ★🄸🄵
Supernatural action fantasy
1996 · US · Colour · 90min

Vincent Perez replaces the late Brandon Lee as a murder victim resurrected from the dead to confront his killers in this shameless rehash of the original. Lacking the tragic resonance and strong performances of its predecessor, director Tim Pope's sequel is ponderous, dull and mechanical. **AJ** Sex scenes, swearing, violence. **DVD** **Blu**

Vincent Perez *Ashe* • Mia Kirshner *Sarah* • Richard Brooks (2) *Judah* • Iggy Pop *Curve* • Thuy Trang *Kali* • Ian Dury *Noah* • Thomas Jane *Nemo* • Vincent Castellanos *Spider Monkey* ■ *Dir* Tim Pope • *Scr* David S Goyer, from the comic book by James O'Barr

The Crow: Wicked Prayer ★🄸🄵
Fantasy horror 2005 · US · Colour · 95min

An over-acting cast do their best to out-weird each other in this lame addition to the tired horror franchise. The lead offender is Edward Furlong who mistakes crazy eyes for tortured emotion. He stars as a murdered ex-con who returns from the dead to avenge his sweetheart's ritualistic slaying. David Boreanaz and Tara Reid play the Satanist lovers that he targets. **SF** Violence, swearing, drug abuse, sexual references. **DVD**

Edward Furlong *Jimmy Cuervo/The Crow* • Tara Reid *Lola Byrne* • David Boreanaz *Luc Crash* • Danny Trejo *Harold* • Dennis Hopper *El Niño* • Emmanuelle Chriqui *Lily* ■ *Dir* Lance Mungia • *Scr* Lance Mungia, Jeff Most, Sean Hood, from the novel by Norman Partridge, from the comic book by James O'Barr

The Crowd ★★★★★
Silent drama 1928 · US · BW · 104min

In this powerful silent drama from director King Vidor, James Murray gives a

C

superlative performance as an idealistic young man trapped in a dead-end job whose ambitions are dogged by tragedy. Such was the film's influence that its depiction of regimented office life and the palliative power of mass laughter were later referenced by such eminent directors as Billy Wilder and Preston Sturges. Murray was plucked from a crowd of extras to star in the film. Sadly, he was unable to cope with celebrity and died in his mid-30s after falling into the Hudson River. Vidor continued the story in 1934's *Our Daily Bread*. AE

Eleanor Boardman *Mary* • James Murray (1) *John* • Bert Roach *Bert* • Estelle Clark *Jane* • Daniel G Tomlinson *Jim* • Dell Henderson *Dick* ■ *Dir* King Vidor • *Scr* King Vidor, John VA Weaver, Harry Behn, Joe Farnham [Joseph Farnham] (titles), from a story by King Vidor • *Cinematographer* Henry Sharp

The Crowd Roars ★★★
Sports drama 1932 · US · BW · 84min

This dated motor-racing melodrama is redeemed by a knockout performance from a cocky James Cagney, acting away on all cylinders despite the rather obvious back projection and model shots. The film has all the fast-paced style Warner Bros fans expect, speedy dialogue and a batch of regulars in the cast. However, it's a far cry from Howard Hawks's best work and those studio racetrack shots really let it down. The same shots were used in the 1939 remake, *Indianapolis Speedway*. TS

James Cagney *Joe Greer* • Joan Blondell *Anne* • Eric Linden *Eddie Greer* • Ann Dvorak *Lee* • Guy Kibbee *Dad Greer* • Frank McHugh *Spud Connors* • Regis Toomey *Dick Wilbur* • William Arnold *Bill Arnold* ■ *Dir* Howard Hawks • *Scr* John Bright, Niven Busch, Kubec Glasmon

The Crowd Roars ★★
Sports drama 1938 · US · BW · 90min

Robert Taylor plays a boxer who is soured on life after he accidentally kills an opponent. Becoming a pawn of Edward Arnold's racketeer, he falls in love with the man's daughter (Maureen O'Sullivan). Frank Morgan does one of his tipsy turns as Taylor's alcoholic father, while Richard Thorpe directs competently. Alas, the film lacks any real punch. Mickey Rooney starred in a 1947 remake, *Killer McCoy*. AE

Robert Taylor (1) *Tommy McCoy* • Edward Arnold *Jim Cain* • Frank Morgan *Brian McCoy* • Maureen O'Sullivan *Sheila Carson* • William Gargan *Johnny Martin* • Lionel Stander *"Happy" Lane* • Jane Wyman *Vina* • Nat Pendleton *"Pug" Walsh* ■ *Dir* Richard Thorpe • *Scr* Thomas Lennon (1), George Bruce, George Oppenheimer, from a story by George Bruce

The Crowded Sky ★★★
Drama 1960 · US · Colour · 105min

Progenitor of the group jeopardy movie, with a pre-*Airport* collection of second-string movie stars slightly past their prime, this typically glossy Warner Bros melodrama has a week that virtually enshrines its year. The plot is satisfyingly and classically simple – an airliner and a navy jet are on a collision couse – and the whole is skilfully directed by craftsman Joseph Pevney. A camp treat, maybe, but a treat nonetheless. TS

Dana Andrews *Dick Barnett* • Rhonda Fleming *Cheryl Heath* • Efrem Zimbalist Jr *Dale Heath* • John Kerr *Mike* • Anne Francis *Kitty Foster* • Keenan Wynn *Nick Hyland* • Troy Donahue *McVey* • Patsy Kelly *Gertrude* ■ *Dir* Joseph Pevney • *Scr* Charles Schnee, from the novel by Hank Searls

Crows and Sparrows ★★★★
Political drama 1949 · Chi · BW · 113min

Already established as one of China's finest film-makers with *Spring River Flows East* (1947), Zheng Junli had to change his political tune for a paean to Maoist ideology that confirmed his status within the communist film industry. There are similarities in this tale of tenement folk to Jean Renoir's Popular Front picture, *Le Crime de Monsieur Lange*, as various residents struggle to stay the right side of their avaricious landlord while also trying to

pick a path through the minefield of political affiliations. DP Mandarin +subtitles.

Zhao Dan *Little Broadcast* • Wu Yin *Mrs Xiao* • Wei Heling *Mr Kong* • Sun Daolin *Teacher Hua* • Shangguan Yunzhu *Mrs Hua* • Li Tianji *Mr Hou* ■ *Dir* Zheng Junli • *Scr* Baichen Chen, Lingu Wang, Tao Xu, Dan Zhao, Junli Zheng, Fu Shen

The Crucible ★★★★ 12
Period drama 1996 · US · Colour · 118min

Arthur Miller's emotionally raw play about suspected witchcraft in 17th-century Massachusetts – a veiled attack on the McCarthy-inspired communist witch-hunts of the 1950s – is here brilliantly brought to the screen by director Nicholas Hytner. Hytner brilliantly captures both a believable period flavour and the stifling atmosphere of fear and suspicion in Salem. Daniel Day-Lewis is characteristically intense as the married man caught in the middle, but the real fireworks come from Winona Ryder, as the wicked young girl whose manipulative behaviour is the story's catalyst, and Paul Scofield's commanding presence as the trial's judge. JC Violence, brief nudity.
DVD

Daniel Day-Lewis *John Proctor* • Winona Ryder *Abigail Williams* • Paul Scofield *Judge Danforth* • Joan Allen *Elizabeth Proctor* • Bruce Davison *Reverend Parris* • Rob Campbell *Reverend Hale* • Jeffrey Jones *Thomas Putnam* • Peter Vaughan *Giles Corey* ■ *Dir* Nicholas Hytner • *Scr* Arthur Miller, from his play

Crucible of Terror ★ 18
Horror 1971 · UK · Colour · 85min

Former disc jockey Mike Raven turned actor to appear in this kooky *House of Wax* variant. He shouldn't have given up his day job! Woodenly playing an insane sculptor, Raven covers the dead bodies of his murder victims in bronze after being possessed by an evil spirit. Longer on talk than terror, with stilted direction and ridiculous dialogue. AJ Violence, nudity.

Mike Raven *Victor Clare* • Mary Maude *Millie* • James Bolam *John Davies* • Ronald Lacey *Michael* • Betty Alberge *Dorothy* • John Arnatt *Bill* • Beth Morris *Jane Clare* ■ *Dir* Ted Hooker • *Scr* Ted Hooker, Tom Parkinson

The Crucified Lovers
★★★★★ PG
Romantic period drama 1954 · Jpn · BW · 102min

Originally written as a piece for marionettes by the 16th-century playwright Monzaemon Chikamatsu and subsequently adapted for the kabuki stage, this tale of doomed defiance has been filmed with a painterly yet wholly cinematic realism by the master Japanese director, Kenji Mizoguchi. Subtly depicting passion without any physical contact between merchant's wife Kyoko Kagawa and besotted clerk Kazuo Hasegawa, he retains the human element of the story in spite of his unceasing attention to period detail. He also makes expert use of the landscape (sublimely photographed by Kazuo Miyagawa) to contrast their innocent devotion with the brutality of shogunate society. DP Japanese +subtitles.
DVD

Kazuo Hasegawa *Mohei* • Kyoko Kagawa *Osan* • Eitaro Shindo *Ishun* • Sakae Ozawa [Eitaro Ozawa] *Sukeemon* • Yoko Minamida *Otama* • Haruo Tanaka *Doki* • Chieko Naniwa *Oko* • Ichiro Sugai *Genbee* ■ *Dir* Kenji Mizoguchi • *Scr* Yoshikata Yoda, Matsutaro Kawaguchi, from the play *The Legend of the Grand Scroll Makers* by Monzaemon Chikamatsu

Crude ★★★
Documentary 2009 · US · Colour · 105min

This documentary about a long-running ecological lawsuit has an unmissable target – oil giant Chevron – and a sympathetic victim – 30,000 indigenous Ecuadorians – but balances its political commitment with a welcome human warmth. Film-maker Joe Berlinger's sympathies evidently lie with the natives whose lands have been ruined by carcinogenic chemicals, but he allows the corporate bods to have their say. Berlinger's purpose is not to cheerlead or simply to show genial Ecuadorian lawyer

Pablo Fajardo rubbing shoulders with celebrity activists like Trudie Styler and Sting, but to highlight how easily money can tilt the scales of justice. DP English, Spanish, A'ingae, Secoya +subtitles.

■ *Dir* Joe Berlinger

A Crude Awakening: the Oil Crash ★★★★ PG
Documentary 2006 · Swi · Colour · 82min

Doubtless the tycoons controlling the world's major oil companies will denounce as green scaremongering Basil Gelpke and Ray McCormack's darkly ironic survey of the future of fossil fuel and the damage it has already done to the environment. But when one-time Opec bigwigs, Iraqi energy ministers and former advisers to the Bush administration all confirm the statistics and projections being made by the scientists, it's difficult not to be both impressed and dismayed. The optimism of the wonderfully glib 1950s promo films contrasts chillingly here with the catalogue of unheeded warnings and the alarming immediacy of some of the worst predictions that will be fulfilled if we fail to act. Neither strident nor patronising, this is common-sense advocacy that we'd be foolish to disregard. DP **DVD**

■ *Dir/Scr* Basil Gelpke, Ray McCormack

The Crude Oasis ★★★
Psychological drama 1995 · US · Colour · 80min

Filmed in a fortnight for just $25,000, Alex Graves's directorial debut failed to make much impact during the indie boom of the mid-1990s. There's a hard-boiled *film noir* feel to its steamy storyline, which sees a small-town housewife meeting the man who's been haunting her nightmares when she goes to buy petrol to fuel her suicide bid after her husband's infidelity. Helped by a taut script and snappy dialogue, lead actors Jennifer Taylor, Aaron Shields and Robert Peterson are suitably shifty. But it's Graves's slow-building of suspense and his menacing use of the Kansas settings that sharpen this movie. DP Swearing.

Jennifer Taylor *Karen Webb* • Aaron Shields *Harley* • Robert Peterson *Jim* • Mussef Sibay *Earp* ■ *Dir/Scr* Alex Graves

Cruel Intentions ★★★ 15
Drama 1999 · US · Colour · 93min

Dangerous Liaisons for the under-20s is the basic premise of this sexed-up, revved-up teen picture. Sarah Michelle Gellar and Ryan Phillippe star as the contemporary Merteuil and Valmont, machinating round New York and laying their bet as to whether or not Phillippe can bed Reese Witherspoon. You can understand why director Roger Kumble saw the classic novel as an apt metaphor for teenage sexuality and exploration, but with the depth gone, this is simply an entertaining romp. LH Swearing, sex scenes, drug abuse. **DVD**

Sarah Michelle Gellar *Kathryn Merteuil* • Ryan Phillippe *Sebastian Valmont* • Reese Witherspoon *Annette Hargrove* • Selma Blair *Cecile Caldwell* • Louise Fletcher *Helen Rosemond* • Joshua Jackson *Blaine Tuttle* ■ *Dir* Roger Kumble • *Scr* Roger Kumble, from the novel *Les Liaisons Dangereuses* by Choderlos de Laclos

Cruel Intentions 2 ★★ 15
Drama 2000 · US · Colour · 83min

Following the success of *Cruel Intentions*, Roger Kumble signed to direct a TV series entitled *Manchester Prep*. However, the show was cancelled before its first two episodes were even aired. So Kumble has stitched them together to make this shamelessly steamy prequel to his teen pic reworking of *Dangerous Liaisons*, in which a feckless playboy has to choose between true love and impressing his cynical stepsister. It atones in nastiness for what it lacks in star wattage. A second, straight-to-video sequel followed in 2004. DP Swearing, nudity. **DVD**

Robin Dunne *Sebastian Valmont* • Amy Adams *Kathryn Merteuil* • Sarah Thompson *Danielle Sherman* • Keri Lynn Pratt *Cherie* • Barry Flatman *Sherman* • Mimi Rogers *Tiffany Merteuil-Valmont* ■ *Dir* Roger Kumble • *Scr* Roger

Kumble, from characters by Roger Kumble, from the novel *Les Liasions Dangereuses* by Choderlos de Laclos

The Cruel Sea ★★★★ PG
Second World War drama 1952 · UK · BW · 120min

Charles Frend's *San Demetrio London* was one of the finest naval combat films made anywhere during the Second World War. Here, Frend's insight into the conditions endured and the emotions experienced by embattled sailors of all ranks is very much to the fore in this stirring adaptation. It is a prime example of the docudramatic style that, spurning the gung-ho heroics of Hollywood, characterised the best British war films. DP **DVD** **BD**

Jack Hawkins *Ericson* • Donald Sinden *Lockhart* • John Stratton *Ferraby* • Denholm Elliott *Morrell* • Stanley Baker *Bennett* • John Warner *Baker* • Bruce Seton *Tallow* • Liam Redmond *Watts* • Virginia McKenna *Julie Hallam* • Glyn Houston *Phillips* • Alec McCowen *Tonbridge* ■ *Dir* Charles Frend • *Scr* Eric Ambler, from Nicholas Monsarrat's novel

Crumb ★★★★ 18
Documentary 1995 · US · Colour · 120min

Robert Crumb became a hero of the American underground in the mid-1960s for such cartoon strips as *Fritz the Cat* and *Keep on Truckin'*. Yet, as Terry Zwigoff's documentary opens, the cult cartoonist was packing his bags to settle in France and abandon not just a legion of fans, but also the various feminist groups who denounced him for the sexism of his work and the chauvinism of his private life. This is anything but hagiography, with Crumb coming across as a highly resistible character, while his brothers Charles and Maxon prove every bit as fascinating. This is an often shocking, sometimes horrifying portrait of an artist and his world. DP **DVD**

Robert Crumb ■ *Dir* Terry Zwigoff

The Crusades ★★
Historical drama 1935 · US · BW · 123min

Another episode in *The History of the World* by Cecil B DeMille. This time Cecil tackles the Crusades, following Richard I and the Christians as they set forth from Europe to attack Saladin's Muslim hordes. Loretta Young is Richard's lady love, whom he agrees to marry in exchange for food and horses; he absents himself from their wedding, sending his sword in his place. This was a box-office disaster, though the siege of Jerusalem is as juicy as one expects from this legendary director. AT

Loretta Young *Berengaria* • Henry Wilcoxon *Richard* • Ian Keith *Saladin* • Katherine DeMille *Alice* • C Aubrey Smith *The Hermit* • Joseph Schildkraut *Conrad of Montferrat* ■ *Dir* Cecil B DeMille • *Scr* Harold Lamb, Waldemar Young, Dudley Nichols, from the non-fiction book *The Crusade: Iron Men and Saints* by Harold Lamb

Crush ★★★ 18
Drama 1992 · NZ · Colour · 92min

Alison Maclean makes an arresting feature debut with this dark treatise on sexual ambiguity, power games and identity crises. The mercenary Marcia Gay Harden exploits literary critic Donogh Rees's incapacity to move in on author William Zappa and his impressionable daughter, Caitlin Bossley. The bubbling mud of New Zealand's top tourist site Rotorua symbolises the seething emotions underlying the increasingly sinister events, while Harden's ruthless opportunism represents the threat of American cultural imperialism. This erotic psychological thriller eventually boils over into melodrama. DP **DVD**

Marcia Gay Harden *Lane* • Donogh Rees *Christina* • Caitlin Bossley *Angela* • William Zappa *Colin* • Pete Smith *Horse* • Jon Brazier *Arthur* ■ *Dir* Alison Maclean • *Scr* Alison Maclean, Anne Kennedy

The Crush ★★★ 15
Thriller 1993 · US · Colour · 85min

Fatal Attraction meets *Lolita* in this derivative thriller. Alicia Silverstone, making her film debut, is the precocious 14-year-old whose flirtation with Cary Elwes's journalist becomes a campaign of terror when he rejects her overtures in favour of a grown-up woman. There's some nastily unnerving fun, while Silverstone's poisonous performance displays star quality. AME Violence, swearing, sex scenes, nudity.

Cary Elwes *Nick Eliot* • Alicia Silverstone *Darian* • Jennifer Rubin *Amy* • Kurtwood Smith *Cliff Forrester* • Gwynyth Walsh *Liv Forrester* ■ *Dir/Scr* Alan Shapiro

Crush ★★15
Romantic comedy drama
2001 · UK/Ger/US · Colour · 107min

The plot centres on three 40-something single women – Andie MacDowell's way-too-glamorous headmistress, Anna Chancellor's swearing doctor and Imelda Staunton's frumpy policewoman – who meet to drink and commiserate with each other over their love lives. When MacDowell embarks on an affair with a 25-year-old former pupil (Kenny Doughty), the bonds of friendship begin to unravel. This is sabotaged by weak characterisation and an uneasy mix of comedy and tragedy. AC Swearing, sex scenes. *DVD*

Andie MacDowell *Kate* • Imelda Staunton *Janine* • Anna Chancellor *Molly* • Kenny Doughty *Jed* • Bill Paterson *Rev Gerald Farquhar Marsden* ■ *Dir/Scr* John McKay

Crusoe ★★★15
Period adventure 1988 · US · Colour · 90min

Daniel Defoe's classic allegory gets another makeover, this time with Aidan Quinn as the shipwrecked hero. His Robinson Crusoe is a slave trader whose moral failings are reversed first by his pet dog, then by an escaped slave whom he saves, and finally by a cannibal. Directed by Caleb Deschanel, better known as a cameraman, and superbly shot in the Seychelles, it's a generally impressive achievement that pushes its message home without undue force. AT

Aidan Quinn *Crusoe* • Ade Sapara *The Warrior* • Elvis Payne *Runaway Slave* • Richard Sharp *Colcol* • Colin Bruce *Clerk* • Jimmy Nail *Tarik* • Timothy Spall *Reverend Milne* • Warren Clarke *Captain Lee* ■ *Dir* Caleb Deschanel • *Scr* Walon Green, Christopher Logue, from the novel *The Life and Adventures of Robinson Crusoe* by Daniel Defoe

Cry-Baby ★★★15
Musical parody 1989 · US · Colour · 87min

John Waters's hilarious send-up of *Grease* and *Jailhouse Rock* revolves around juvenile delinquent Johnny Depp having the hots for square Amy Locane. A superb soundtrack mixes real throbbing golden oldies with wonderful rock 'n' roll parodies, and the usual hip cast (including Iggy Pop and porn queen Traci Lords) pushes the vivid cartoon caricatures as close to the edge as possible. The nostalgic delights in Waters's reform school drool are often more subtle than his other period offering, *Hairspray*, but it's still a polished debunking of pop culture from the "Pope of Trash". AJ Swearing. *DVD* *BL*

Johnny Depp *Wade "Cry-Baby" Walker* • Amy Locane *Allison Vernon-Williams* • Susan Tyrrell *Ramona* • Polly Bergen *Mrs Vernon-Williams* • Iggy Pop *Belvedere* • Ricki Lake *Pepper* • Traci Lords *Wanda* • Kim McGuire *Hatchet-Face* • Troy Donahue *Hatchet's father* • Mink Stole *Hatchet's mother* • Joe Dalesandro *Milton's father* • Patricia Hearst *Wanda's mother* • Willem Dafoe *Hateful guard* • Mary Vivian Pearce *Picnic mother* ■ *Dir/Scr* John Waters (2)

The Cry Baby Killer ★★
Crime drama 1958 · US · BW · 61min

Jack Nicholson's first big break – and his last for some time – was gaining the title role in this low-budget contribution to the juvenile delinquency cycle of the time. Nicholson made his film debut as the frightened teenager who shoots two bullies and barricades himself in a storeroom with some hostages. The siege that follows is well handled by director Jus Addiss, but Nicholson's part is too underwritten. AE

Harry Lauter *Porter* • Jack Nicholson *Jimmy* • Carolyn Mitchell *Carole* • Brett Halsey *Manny* • Lynn Cartwright *Julie* • Ralph Reed *Joey* • John Shay *Gannon* • Barbara Knudson *Mrs Maxton* ■ *Dir* Jus Addiss • *Scr* Melvin Levy, Leo Gordon, from a story by Gordon

Cry Danger ★★★
Crime drama 1951 · US · BW · 79min

A former child actor and film editor, Robert Parrish made an impressive directorial debut with this tough thriller starring one-time crooner Dick Powell as an ex-convict on a quest to free a pal still in jail. The film is set in the ghetto area of Los Angeles, to allow Powell to hole up in a seedy trailer camp to stake out said friend's wife (played by Rhonda Fleming). Hot on atmosphere and tight on suspense, this was an auspicious debut from an underrated director. TS

Dick Powell *Rocky Malloy* • Rhonda Fleming *Nancy* • Richard Erdman *Delong* • William Conrad *Castro* • Regis Toomey *Cobb* • Jean Porter *Darlene* • Jay Adler *Williams* ■ *Dir* Robert Parrish • *Scr* William Bowers, from a story by Jerome Cady

Cry for Happy ★
Romantic comedy 1961 · US · Colour · 110min

A quartet of American navy photographers, on leave in Japan during the Korean War, become romantically entangled with four geisha girls who are attempting to found an orphanage. This is predictable, witless and desperately unfunny, while the portrayal of the girls is deeply patronising. RK

Glenn Ford *Andy Cyphers* • Donald O'Connor *Murray Prince* • Miiko Taka *Chiyoko* • James Shigeta *Suzuki* • Miyoshi Umeki *Harue* • Michi Kobi *Hanakichi* • Howard St John *Admiral Bennett* ■ *Dir* George Marshall • *Scr* Irving Brecher, from the novel by George Campbell

Cry for Me Billy ★★
Western 1972 · US · Colour · 87min

Long in post-production and never properly released, this post-hippy western is not entirely without interest. Cliff Potts plays an alienated gunfighter who rescues an Indian girl after being appalled at the white man's treatment of the native American. When she's raped, he sets out on a violent quest for revenge. TS

Cliff Potts *Billy* • Oaxchil *Indian girl* • Harry Dean Stanton *Luke Todd* • Don Wilbanks *Sergeant* • Woodrow Chambliss *Prospector* • Roy Jenson *Blacksmith* ■ *Dir* William A Graham • *Scr* David Markson

Cry Freedom ★★★★PG
Biographical drama 1987 · UK · Colour · 151min

This ambitious, worthy attempt by Richard Attenborough to re-create the success of *Gandhi* with another epic biographical portrait tells the story of the doomed South African civil rights leader Steve Biko. Attenborough is well served by the charismatic playing of Denzel Washington as the black activist and Kevin Kline as the liberal newspaper editor Donald Woods. The early scenes, in which the comfortably middle class Woods gradually has his eyes opened to the true horrors of the apartheid system, are sharply observed. The film loses its way a little when the attention switches to the plight of the Woods family, but their final attempts at flight are genuinely suspenseful. JF Some violence, swearing. *DVD*

Kevin Kline *Donald Woods* • Denzel Washington *Steve Biko* • Penelope Wilton *Wendy Woods* • John Hargreaves *Bruce* • Alec McCowen *Acting High Commissioner* • Kevin McNally *Ken* • Zakes Mokae *Father Kani* • Ian Richardson *State prosecutor* • Josette Simon *Dr Ramphele* • John Thaw *Kruger* • Timothy West *Captain de Wet* • Miles Anderson *Lemick* ■ *Dir* Richard Attenborough • *Scr* John Briley, from the non-fiction books *Biko* and *Asking for Trouble* by Donald Woods

A Cry from the Streets ★★★U
Drama 1957 · UK · BW · 100min

Dogmatic social worker Barbara Murray, who deals with underprivileged children,

enlists the help of Max Bygraves as an assistant. He saves the day when a child whose mother commits suicide goes on the run with the kids of a murderer – and a gun. Neither as melodramatic as it sounds, nor all doom and gloom, this is a decent attempt at realism, directed in quasi-documentary style. RK

Max Bygraves *Bill Lowther* • Barbara Murray *Ann Fairlie* • Colin Petersen *Georgie* • Dana Wilson *Barbie* • Kathleen Harrison *Mrs Farrer* • Mona Washbourne *Mrs Daniels* ■ *Dir* Lewis Gilbert • *Scr* Vernon Harris, from the novel *The Friend in Need* by Elizabeth Coxhead

Cry Havoc ★★★
Second World War melodrama
1943 · US · BW · 97min

An interesting, accomplished cast does the *Tenko* routine as the likes of Joan Blondell and Ann Sothern pitch up on the island of Bataan during the height of Second World War hostilities. The material originated on the stage, and it shows in the movie's enclosed, claustrophobic look. However, despite the rather hackneyed dialogue and abundance of realistic make-up, this is a stirring, emotive tale. SH

Margaret Sullavan *Lieutenant Smith* • Ann Sothern *Pat* • Joan Blondell *Grace* • Fay Bainter *Captain Marsh* • Marsha Hunt *Flo Norris* • Ella Raines *Connie* • Frances Gifford *Helen* • Diana Lewis *Nydia* ■ *Dir* Richard Thorpe • *Scr* Paul Osborne, from the play *Proof Thro' the Night* by Allen R Kenward

A Cry in the Dark ★★★★15
Biographical drama
1988 · US/Aus · Colour · 116min

This is an absolutely riveting and at times harrowing telling of the bizarre real-life story of Lindy Chamberlain, who claimed her baby was killed by a dingo at Ayers Rock in 1980. The movie covers a huge amount of ground: Aboriginal myths, the Chamberlains' Seventh Day Adventism, the media circus and the way the case challenged the legal system and obsessed Australians for years. Meryl Streep gives one of her best performances: a portrait of a tough, humourless woman who eventually earns our sympathy and pity. Sam Neill as her morose preacher husband is equally impressive. AT Swearing, brief nudity. *DVD*

Meryl Streep *Lindy Chamberlain* • Sam Neill *Michael Chamberlain* • Bruce Myles *Barker* • Charles Tingwell *Justice Muirhead* • Nick Tate *Charlwood* • Neil Fitzpatrick *Phillips* ■ *Dir* Fred Schepisi • *Scr* Robert Caswell, Fred Schepisi, from the non-fiction book *Evil Angels* by John Bryson

A Cry in the Night ★
Crime drama 1956 · US · BW · 75min

Alan Ladd's Jaguar company made this sordid melodrama, with Ladd himself delivering the brief narration. Young Natalie Wood can't stand being at home with her domineering policeman father (Edmond O'Brien), and Raymond Burr's middle-aged Peeping Tom has been messed up by a possessive mother. The trouble starts when Burr kidnaps her. There's never any doubt how it will end. AE

Edmond O'Brien *Taggart* • Brian Donlevy *Bates* • Natalie Wood *Liz* • Raymond Burr *Loftus* • Richard Anderson *Owen* • Irene Hervey *Helen* • Carol Veazie *Mrs Loftus* • Mary Lawrence *Madge* • Alan Ladd *Narrator* ■ *Dir* Frank Tuttle • *Scr* David Dortort, from the novel *All Through the Night* by Whit Masterson

Cry of the Banshee ★★15
Horror 1970 · UK · Colour · 87min

The last period horror Vincent Price made finds the flamboyant villain back in *Witchfinder General* territory as an obsessed 16th-century witch-hunting magistrate hounded by demonic forces. Veteran actress Elisabeth Bergner (her name was misspelt on the original credits) plays the witch who unleashes werewolf-in-disguise Patrick Mower on the hedonistic patriarch. Director Gordon Hessler's lightweight chiller is a rather coy affair

that's neither sexy nor spooky enough. AJ Violence, nudity. *DVD*

Vincent Price *Lord Edward Whitman* • Elisabeth Bergner *Oona* • Essy Persson *Lady Patricia* • Hugh Griffith *Mickey* • Patrick Mower *Roderick* • Hilary Dwyer *Maureen* • Carl Rigg *Harry* ■ *Dir* Gordon Hessler • *Scr* Tim Kelly, Christopher Wicking, from a story by Tim Kelly

Cry of the City ★★★★12
Film noir 1948 · US · BW · 91min

One of the toughest and most uncompromising examples from that great period of 20th Century-Fox *film noir*, this is an emotive and exciting study of the relationship between one-time boyhood pals, gangster Richard Conte and cop Victor Mature. Richard Murphy's screenplay is adult and clever, and expressionist émigré director Robert Siodmak knows exactly how to paint this particular ultra-urban picture. For those who have been unable to take Mature seriously as an actor, this ranks with his best work: it's a finely etched and undeniably sympathetic performance. TS *DVD*

Victor Mature *Lt Vittorio Candella* • Richard Conte *Martin Rome* • Fred Clark *Lt Jim Collins* • Shelley Winters *Brenda* • Betty Garde *Miss Florence Pruett* • Berry Kroeger *Niles* • Tommy Cook *Tony Rome* • Debra Paget *Teena Riconti* • Hope Emerson *Rose Given* • Roland Winters *Ledbetter* ■ *Dir* Robert Siodmak • *Scr* Richard Murphy, from the novel *The Chair for Martin Rome* by Henry Edward Helseth

Cry of the Hunted ★★★
Drama 1953 · US · BW · 78min

Italian heart-throb Vittorio Gassman is an escaped convict being pursued through the boggy Louisiana bayous by officer Barry Sullivan. The few scenes with Polly Bergen – playing Sullivan's wife – were added later in an attempt to attract the female audience. But this is really a suspenseful chase movie, shot on authentically swampy locations. AT

Vittorio Gassman *Jory* • Barry Sullivan *Lt Tunner* • Polly Bergen *Janet Tunner* • William Conrad *Goodwin* • Mary Zavian *Ella* • Robert Burton *Warden Keeley* • Harry Shannon *Sheriff Brown* • Jonathan Cott *Deputy Davis* ■ *Dir* Joseph H Lewis • *Scr* Jack Leonard, from the story by Jack Leonard, Marion Wolfe

The Cry of the Owl ★★15
Thriller 2009 · Can/UK/Ger/Fr · Colour · 95min

Nothing quite gels in this awkward take on the suspense novel by Patricia Highsmith. Going from far-fetched to ridiculous, the sluggish thriller sees troubled, divorced Paddy Considine abruptly begin a relationship with neighbour Julia Stiles after she catches him spying on her. Then her violent ex disappears. Unfortunately, while Considine nails his character's twitchy discomfort, he's let down by his distractingly poor American accent and some clunky dialogue. With neither realism nor tension to support it, the climax is particularly flat, squandering the drama of the final deadly moments. SF Violence, swearing, some gore. *DVD*

Paddy Considine *Robert Forrester* • Julia Stiles *Jenny Thierolf* • Caroline Dhavernas *Nickie Grace* • Charlotte Sullivan *Sally Neilson* • James Gilbert (3) *Greg Wyncoop* ■ *Dir* Jamie Thraves • *Scr* Jamie Thraves, from the novel by Patricia Highsmith

Cry of the Werewolf ★
Horror 1944 · US · BW · 62min

Mild even by 1940s horror standards and utterly conventional in every respect, director Henry Levin's debut feature stars Nina Foch as queen of the Troiga gypsies. She murders a New Orleans museum curator to cover up the fact that she has inherited the curse of lycanthropy from her dead mother. Feeling far longer than it is, this banal potboiler lacks rudimentary suspense. AJ

Nina Foch *Celeste LaTour* • Stephen Crane *Bob Morris* • Osa Massen *Elsa Chauvet* • Blanche Yurka *Bianca* • Barton MacLane *Lt Barry Lane* ■ *Dir* Henry Levin • *Scr* Griffin Jay, Charles O'Neal, from a story by Griffin Jay

Cry Terror ★★★
Crime thriller   1958 · US · BW · 96min

Low budget meets high suspense in this adroit thriller from writer/director Andrew L Stone, in which TV repairman James Mason, his wife Inger Stevens and his daughter Terry Ann Ross are held hostage by Rod Steiger, Angie Dickinson and Jack Klugman, who are plotting an extortion coup. Inventively contrived and executed, the action grips as it accelerates. **TH**

James Mason *Jim Molner* • Rod Steiger *Paul Hoplin* • Inger Stevens *Joan Molner* • Neville Brand *Steve* • Angie Dickinson *Kelly* • Kenneth Tobey *Frank Cole* • Jack Klugman *Vince* • Jack Kruschen *Charles Pope* • Terry Ann Ross *Pat Molner* ■ *Dir/Scr* Andrew L Stone

Cry, the Beloved Country ★★★★ PG
Drama   1951 · UK · BW · 103min

Made in those grievous days of apartheid in South Africa, this adaptation of Alan Paton's stirring bestseller – with Canada Lee as the country minister looking for a lost son in Johannesburg – so obviously had its heart in the right place that it was hard to criticise. It still is, even in the post-apartheid era, because Zoltan Korda's direction, though naive, has a passionate directness that is timeless. One of the acting delights is Sidney Poitier as a preacher who forgives all, but forgets nothing. **TH** *DVD*

Canada Lee *Stephen Kumalo* • Charles Carson *James Jarvis* • Sidney Poitier *Reverend Maimangu* • Joyce Carey *Margaret Jarvis* • Edric Connor *John Kumalo* • Geoffrey Keen *Father Vincent* ■ *Dir* Zoltan Korda • *Scr* Alan Paton, John Howard Lawson (uncredited), from the novel by Alan Paton

Cry, the Beloved Country ★★★★
Drama   1995 · S Afr/US · Colour · 111min

This powerful adaptation of Alan Paton's 1940s-set racial drama centres on the converging lives of a black minister in rural South Africa and his white landowner neighbour. The first major feature to be shot in South Africa after the abolition of apartheid, Darrell James Roodt's film gains emotional resonance from the gentle, softly spoken sincerity of James Earl Jones as the pastor, devastated by the fate of his family in Johannesburg. Even if it occasionally feels a little manipulative (John Barry's score, for example), it is hard not to be affected. **JC** Violence, swearing.

James Earl Jones *Reverend Stephen Kumalo* • Richard Harris *James Jarvis* • Charles S Dutton *John Kumalo* • Vusi Kunene *Father Msimangu* • Leleti Khumalo *Katie* • Dambisa Kente *Gertrude Kumalo* • Eric Miyeni *Absolom Kumalo* • Dolly Rathebe *Mrs Kumalo* ■ *Dir* Darrell James Roodt • *Scr* Ronald Harwood, from the novel by Alan Paton

Cry Vengeance ★★★
Crime drama   1954 · US · BW · 81min

Mark Stevens, the handsome if rather bland leading man of Fox pictures of the 1940s, took on a tougher image in the 1950s. In this gripping crime drama, the first of five films he directed, Stevens plays a former detective who, after three years in prison, seeks revenge on the man he thinks framed him for a crime he didn't commit. A pulsating score and rapid editing helps give the film a lively pace, though the plot is somewhat convoluted and contrived. **RB**

Mark Stevens *Vic Barron* • Martha Hyer *Peggy Harding* • Skip Homeier *Roxey* • Joan Vohs *Lily Arnold* • Douglas Kennedy *Tino Morelli* • Don Haggerty *Lt Ryan* ■ *Dir* Mark Stevens • *Scr* Warren Douglas, George Bricker • *Editor* Elmo Veron • *Music* Paul Dunlap

Cry Wolf ★★ PG
Mystery   1947 · US · BW · 80min

Screen icons Barbara Stanwyck and Errol Flynn were both past their box-office prime when they teamed up for this dour Warner Bros drama. When her husband kicks the bucket, Stanwyck returns to the old estate to find Flynn up to no good in the west wing. Very little fun, thanks to Peter Godfrey's turgid direction. **TS**

Errol Flynn *Mark Caldwell* • Barbara Stanwyck *Sandra Marshall* • Geraldine Brooks *Julie Demarest* • Richard Basehart *James Demarest* • Jerome Cowan *Senator Charles Caldwell* • John Ridgely *Jackson Laidell* • Patricia White [Patricia Barry] *Angela* ■ *Dir* Peter Godfrey • *Scr* Catherine Turney, from the novel by Marjorie Carleton

Cry_Wolf ★★★ 12
Horror thriller   2005 · US · Colour · 90min

A cyber-prank goes horribly wrong for the pupils of a posh prep school in Jeff Wadlow's all-stalk no-slash horror. British student Julian Morris and class sexpot Lindy Booth send a group email crediting a local murder to a fictitious serial killer. But their fabrication becomes reality when a real ski-masked maniac starts roaming the campus. Ably co-written and stylishly directed by Wadlow, this is a convoluted whodunnit, relying on practical jokes, red herrings, bogus bogeymen and false scares rather than anything of a gory nature. **AJ** Violence. *DVD* *BL*

Lindy Booth *Dodger* • Julian Morris *Owen* • Jared Padalecki *Tom* • Kristy Wu *Regina* • Sandra McCoy *Mercedes* • Paul James *Lewis* • Jon Bon Jovi *Rich Walker* • Jesse Janzen *Randall* • Gary Cole *Mr Matthews* ■ *Dir* Jeff Wadlow • *Scr* Jeff Wadlow, Beau Bauman

Crying Freeman ★★★ 18
Action drama
1995 · Fr/Jpn/Can/US · Colour · 97min

Hong Kong-style action meets James Bond in a beautifully crafted adaptation of the cult Japanese comic strip. Enigmatic Mark Dacascos is the latest in a long line of human killing machines programmed by the Sons of the Dragon Society to respond to hypnotic signals. Because he sheds a tear after each contract killing, he earns the nickname "Crying Freeman." How he keeps his identity a secret fuels the cranked-up plot packed with inventive explosions, balletic gunplay, hyperkinetic stunts and forbidden love. **AJ** Violence, swearing, sex scenes, nudity. *DVD*

Mark Dacascos *Yo Hinomura/Freeman* • Julie Condra *Emu O'Hara* • Rae Dawn Chong *Detective Forge* • Byron Mann *Koh* • Mako *Shudo Shimizaki* • Tcheky Karyo *Detective Netah* ■ *Dir* Christophe Gans • *Scr* Christophe Gans, Thierry Cazals, from the comic book by Kazuo Koike, Ryoichi Ikegami

The Crying Game ★★★★ 18
Drama   1992 · UK · Colour · 107min

Virtually ignored on its release, this offbeat tale went on to become a monster hit in America and even earned an Oscar for best original screenplay for writer/director Neil Jordan. It's a beguiling, eccentric blend of romantic drama and political thriller, and at its centre is a charismatic performance from Stephen Rea. He plays an IRA terrorist who flees to London after the botched kidnapping of a British soldier, played somewhat unconvincingly by Forest Whitaker. Ridden with guilt he locates the dead man's former lover (an extraordinary Oscar-nominated performance from Jaye Davidson) and finds himself falling in love. **JF** Violence, swearing, nudity. *DVD*

Stephen Rea *Fergus* • Miranda Richardson *Jude* • Jaye Davidson *Dil* • Forest Whitaker *Jody* • Adrian Dunbar *Maguire* • Breffini McKenna [Breffni McKenna] *Tinker* • Jim Broadbent *Col* • Tony Slattery *Deveroux* • Shar Campbell *Bar performer* • David Crionelly *Security man* ■ *Dir/Scr* Neil Jordan

Crying with Laughter ★★★ 18
Psychological thriller
2009 · UK · Colour · 93min

Justin Molotnikov's brutal and uncompromising Scottish memory game sees Stephen McCole in his first lead role as Joey Frisk, a foul-mouthed Scottish stand-up on the verge of the big time, who seems to go out of his way to alienate everyone. One day an old schoolfriend turns up and leads Joey towards the source of his alienation and self-loathing. McCole delivers a breakthrough performance in a hard-edged, uncompromising role, and some of the twists are well done, but the film is not without flaws – the comedy is not funny and the storyline teeters uncertainly on the edge of credibility when it moves into Hitchcockian psycho-thriller territory. **BP**

Stephen McCole *Joey Frisk* • Andrew Neil *Jonathan Meldrick* • Jo Hartley *Karen* • Malcolm Shields *Frank Archer* • Micaiah Dring *Colette* • Tom Jude *DS Burns* ■ *Dir/Scr* Justin Molotnikov

The Crystal Ball ★★★ U
Comedy   1943 · US · BW · 81min

When gorgeous Texan Paulette Goddard fails to win a beauty contest, she takes up fake fortune-telling to earn a buck and gets involved with a bunch of swindlers. All ends happily when her shenanigans lead her to Ray Milland, the man of her dreams. An innocuous, slightly fantastical, and reasonably diverting comedy with a slapstick finale, this is nicely played and directed. **RK**

Ray Milland *Brad Cavanaugh* • Paulette Goddard *Toni Gerard* • Gladys George *Mme Zenobia* • Virginia Field *Jo Ainsley* • Cecil Kellaway *Pop Tibbets* • William Bendix *Biff Carter* • Mary Field *Foster* • Ernest Truex *Mr Martin* ■ *Dir* Elliott Nugent • *Scr* Virginia Van Upp, from a story by Steven Vas

Crystal Fairy and the Magical Cactus ★★★ 18
Road movie   2013 · Chil · Colour · 98min

Indie star Michael Cera played an arrogant, self-obsessed version of himself in *This Is the End*, and he further subverts his image here. He plays a young student in Santiago, who initiates a trip to the desert to find a legendary hallucinogenic cactus. By itself, Cera's obnoxious turn would soon run out of steam, but paired with Gaby Hoffmann's irritating yet strangely empathetic Crystal Fairy – a wild and wacky hippie chick – it provides the dynamic for an amiable, atmospheric road movie that's refreshingly free of cynicism. **DW** English, Spanish +subtitles. Swearing, sexual references, drug abuse, nudity.

Michael Cera *Jamie* • Gaby Hoffmann *Crystal Fairy* ■ *Dir/Scr* Sebastián Silva

Crystal Voyager ★★ U
Documentary   1972 · US/Aus · Colour · 75min

While not quite of the calibre of Bruce Brown's *The Endless Summer*, this documentary portrait of inventor extraordinaire George Greenough should keep armchair surf fans happy. Having already devised both the short board and the knee board, Greenough became a sports movie legend when he successfully pioneered a method of on-board filming to capture at first hand the intense experience of riding deep inside a breaker. **DP** *DVD*
■ *Dir* David Elfick • *Scr* George Greenough

Cub ★★★ 15
Horror   2014 · Bel · Colour · 82min

A cute play on words suggests a supernatural dimension that never really materialises in this inventive Belgian coming-of-age chiller. Although a local werewolf myth is an integral part of the story, the cub of the title is a bullied 12-year-old boy named Sam (Maurice Luijten), who joins his scout group on an ill-fated camping trip to the woods. The kills are surprisingly gruesome, but the suddenly manic tone breaks faith with the thoughtful intensity of the build-up and its intriguing eco-revenge theme goes, like many of its young cast, under the bus. **DW** In Flemish and French +subtitles. *DVD*

Maurice Luijten *Sam* • Stef Aerts *Peter* • Evelien Bosmans *Jasmijn* • Titus De Voogdt *Kris* ■ *Dir* Jonas Govaerts • *Scr* Jonas Govaerts, Roel Mondelaers

Cuba ★★★★ 12
Period satirical drama
1979 · US · Colour · 117min

In this hugely underrated drama, Sean Connery stars as a British security adviser who washes up in Cuba during the last weeks of the Batista regime. He's been hired by the losing side and his growing doubts are set beside his love for a woman he first met in 1942, in Casablanca. This bracing satire features a great performance from Connery, while subplots spin off with a wealth of secondary characters as director Richard Lester weaves a fascinating tale about a country where romance, revolution and bombs co-exist. **AT** *DVD*

Sean Connery *Robert Dapes* • Brooke Adams *Alexandra Pulido* • Jack Weston *Gutman* • Hector Elizondo *Ramirez* • Denholm Elliott *Skinner* • Martin Balsam *General Bello* • Chris Sarandon *Juan Pulido* ■ *Dir* Richard Lester • *Scr* Charles Wood

Cuban Fury ★★★ 15
Romantic comedy   2014 · UK · Colour · 93min

Nick Frost shakes off the accusation that he and Simon Pegg are joined at the hip by playing the romantic lead in this good-natured comedy. Frost carries himself very well as a one-time salsa prodigy who returns to the floor after years in a dead-end job. But when it comes to the actual dancing, he quickly finds himself in over his head. There's plenty of rib-tickling banter between Frost and his co-stars, who include Rashida Jones as Frost's boss, Ian McShane as his mentor, Chris O'Dowd as a greasy love rival and a scene-stealing Kayvan Novak (*Four Lions*) as a flamboyant fellow dancer. **SP** Swearing, sexual references. *DVD* *BL*

Nick Frost *Bruce Garrett* • Rashida Jones *Julia* • Chris O'Dowd *Drew* • Olivia Colman *Sam* • Kayvan Novak *Bejan* • Rory Kinnear *Gary* ■ *Dir* James Griffiths • *Scr* Jon Brown, from an idea by Nick Frost

Cubbyhouse ★★ 15
Horror   2001 · Aus · Colour · 84min

This tongue-in-cheek Aussie horror is a throwback to the 1980s slew of possessed building stories. The oddly unmenacing centre of demonic power is a shed in a quiet suburb, where single mother Belinda McClory hopes to start a new life with her three children. Its old fashioned innocence may amuse, but it barely delivers any shocks or suspense. **JC** *DVD*

Joshua Leonard *Danny* • Belinda McClory *Lynn Graham* • Jerome Ehlers *Harrison/Harrow* • Lauren Hewett *Bronwyn* • Craig McLachlan ■ *Dir* Murray Fahey • *Scr* Ian Coughlan, Murray Fahey

Cube ★★★★ 15
Science-fiction thriller
1997 · Can · Colour · 86min

Six strangers wake up to find themselves in a 14ft by 14ft cube. When they try to get out, they find they are snared in a seemingly endless maze of interlocking cubicles armed with lethal booby traps. How did they get there? Why have they been incarcerated? Director Vincenzo Natali's extraordinary debut feature takes a unique idea and milks its potential to the maximum with panache and visual dexterity. Genuinely creepy and gory, this sci-fi horror puzzle is awash with bold ideas and unsettling tension. Two sequels (to date) followed. **AJ** Swearing, violence. *DVD* *BL*

Nicole de Boer *Leaven* • Nicky Guadagni *Holloway* • David Hewlett *Worth* • Andrew Miller *Kazan* • Julian Richings *Alderson* • Wayne Robson *Rennes* • Maurice Dean Wint *Quentin* ■ *Dir* Vincenzo Natali • *Scr* Vincenzo Natali, André Bijelic, Graeme Manson

The Cuckoo ★★★ 12
War comedy drama   2002 · Rus · Colour · 97min

Writer/director Alexander Rogozhkin's sincere and often witty treatise on the futility of war and the barrier of language opens with an intense sequence in which Ville Haapasalo, a Finnish conscript in the Nazi army, breaks the shackle tethering him to a rock (he's been left as prey for Soviet snipers as punishment for his pacifism). But he's no safer once he reaches the hut of Lapp peasant Anni-Kristiina Juuso, as wounded Red Army trooper Viktor Bychkov mistakes him for a fascist that he's duty bound to kill. Beautifully photographed, this astute blend of satire, romance and mysticism cuts to the very heart of human nature. DP Russian, Finnish, Sami +subtitles. Violence. *DVD*

Ville Haapasalo *Veiko* • Anni-Kristiina Juuso *Anni* • Viktor Bychkov *Ivan* ■ *Dir/Scr* Aleksandr Rogozhkin • *Cinematographer* Andrei Zhegalov

Cuckoo ★15
Thriller   2009 · UK · Colour · 88min

Writer/director Richard Bracewell's clunky thriller stars Laura Fraser as Polly, a student who fears she's going mad when mysterious voices start surrounding her. So she turns to the one person she thinks she can trust, professor Richard E Grant. Unfortunately, he has a dark secret of his own, in this substandard tale of "sounds and lies". Bracewell's lofty ambitions are clear to see in what is an obvious labour of love, but they simply don't come off in a mess of clichés and barely adequate performances. AJ Swearing. *DVD* *Blu*

Richard E Grant *Professor Julius Greengrass* • Laura Fraser *Polly* • Antonia Bernath *Jimi* • Adam Fenton *Chapman* ■ *Dir/Scr* Richard Bracewell

A Cuckoo in the Nest ★★★
Comedy   1933 · UK · BW · 87min

Ben Travers's farces have dated badly on screen, though they still play perfectly well in their various theatre versions. So the main pleasure in watching this stagey British talkie lies in its preservation of the original Aldwych company interpretation, as directed by chief *farceur* Tom Walls. Walls co-stars with Ralph Lynn in a slight but appealing saga about newlyweds at a country inn. The most durable member of the cast is the still very funny Robertson Hare as a parson on a visit. TS

Tom Walls *Major Bone* • Ralph Lynn *Peter Wyckham* • Yvonne Arnaud *Marguerite Hickett* • Robertson Hare *Reverend Sloley-Jones* • Mary Brough *Mrs Spoker* • Veronica Rose *Barbara Wyckham* • Gordon James *Noony* ■ *Dir* Tom Walls • *Scr* Ben Travers, AR Rawlinson, from the play by Ben Travers

Cujo ★★18
Horror   1983 · US · Colour · 89min

A rabid St Bernard traps spirited Dee Wallace and her son Danny Pintauro in a Ford Pinto and terrorises them for days in director Lewis Teague's predictable Stephen King adaptation, which sports a half-baked script and an altered, upbeat ending. The car siege should be a harrowing ordeal, but the suspense becomes laughably static, despite all the visual trickery thrown in to generate interest. AJ Swearing, violence. *DVD*

Dee Wallace [Dee Wallace Stone] *Donna Trenton* • Christopher Stone *Steve Kemp* • Danny Pintauro *Tad Trenton* • Daniel Hugh-Kelly *Vic Trenton* • Ed Lauter *Joe Camber* ■ *Dir* Lewis Teague • *Scr* Don Carlos Dunaway, Lauren Currier, from the novel by Stephen King

Cul-de-Sac ★★★15
Psychological comedy thriller
1966 · UK · BW · 100min

In this surreal, macabre thriller, recluse Donald Pleasence strives to keep his young wife Françoise Dorléac cloistered for himself in a Holy Island castle, despite the attentions of gangsters-on-the-run Lionel Stander and Jack MacGowran. Fetishes abound in this, the most Buñuelian of all Roman Polanski's work, but weird slapstick comedy often undermines the deeply serious kinkiness. The result is an acquired taste. TH *DVD*

Donald Pleasence *George* • Françoise Dorléac *Teresa* • Lionel Stander *Richard* • Jack MacGowran *Albert* • Iain Quarrier *Christopher* • Geoffrey Sumner *Christopher's father* • Renee Houston *Christopher's mother* • William Franklyn *Cecil* • Trevor Delaney *Nicholas* ■ *Dir* Roman Polanski • *Scr* Gérard Brach, Roman Polanski

The Culpepper Cattle Co
★★★★
Western   1972 · US · Colour · 92min

This grim rite-of-passage western is superbly directed by Dick Richards, whose subsequent career failed to live up to such

early promise. The extreme violence (tame by today's standards) earned it an X certificate in the UK. Gary Grimes plays the 16 year-old who sets out on a cattle drive alongside authentic western types such as Luke Askew and Bo Hopkins, both from Sam Peckinpah's repertory company. There are also superb performances from Billy "Green" Bush, the hardy trail boss of the title, and Clint Eastwood regular Geoffrey Lewis. TS

Gary Grimes *Ben Mockridge* • Billy "Green" Bush [Billy Green Bush] *Frank Culpepper* • Luke Askew *Luke* • Bo Hopkins *Dixie Brick* • Geoffrey Lewis *Russ* • Wayne Sutherlin *Missoula* • Charles Martin Smith *Tim Slater* ■ *Dir* Dick Richards • *Scr* Eric Bercovici, Gregory Prentiss, from a story by Dick Richards

Cult of the Cobra ★★
Horror thriller   1955 · US · BW · 79min

This is one of those inexplicable cases of a humdrum potboiler achieving cult recognition in later life. This is a war movie with a difference, in that American GIs face death, not from Nazi bullets, but an ancient curse. When a group of overly curious soldiers enter an Indian temple during a secret ceremony, they're followed home by an exotic serpent woman who starts bumping them off. RS

Faith Domergue *Lisa* • Richard Long *Paul Able* • Marshall Thompson *Tom Markel* • Kathleen Hughes *Julia* • Jack Kelly *Carl Turner* • Walter Coy *Inspector* • Myrna Hansen *Marian* • David Janssen *Rico Nardi* ■ *Dir* Francis D Lyon • *Scr* Jerry Davis, Cecil Maiden, Richard Collins, from a story by Jerry Davis

The Cup ★★★★PG
Comedy   1999 · Bhutan/Aus · Colour · 90min

Directed by Khyentse Norbu, one of the most revered incarnate lamas in the Tibetan Buddhist hierarchy, this is Bhutan's first ever feature film. Played exclusively by non-professionals, it follows mischievous novice monk Jamyang Lodro in his bid to watch his hero Ronaldo play for Brazil in the 1998 World Cup final. Using shadow puppetry and satellite TV to highlight the need for tradition and progress to co-exist, this charmingly humorous tale also celebrates the exuberance of youth and the sagacity of the elderly, as Jamyang finds an unlikely ally in his venerable abbot. Beautifully shot in glowing colours, this is simply inspirational cinema. DP Hindi, Tibetan +subtitles.

Jamyang Lodro *Orgyen* • Orgyen Tobgyal *Geko* • Neten Chokling *Lodo* ■ *Dir/Scr* Khyentse Norbu • *Cinematographer* Paul Warren

The Cup ★★PG
Horse racing drama based on a true story
2011 · Aus · Colour · 101min

This Australian horse-racing drama is based on the true story of Damien Oliver (Stephen Curry), a jockey spurred on by personal tragedy to compete for the prestigious Melbourne Cup. Taking its cue from almost every underdog sports movie that came before it, the film unashamedly dives for the heartstrings, to the point where you may find yourself genuinely swept up in the final stages. However, this emotional investment is short-lived, as on the whole the plot forgoes depth and genuine conflict in favour of exhausted clichés. JL Some swearing.

Stephen Curry *Damien Oliver* • Brendan Gleeson *Dermot Weld* • Daniel MacPherson *Jason Oliver* • Alice Parkinson *Jenny* ■ *Dir* Simon Wincer • *Scr* Eric O'Keefe, Simon Wincer

Cup Final ★★★★15
War drama   1991 · Is · Colour · 104min

Set against the political complexities of the Middle East, this simple tale of war, humanity and football explores the relationship that develops between a Jewish soldier and his Arab jailer during the 1982 World Cup finals. The scenes depicting the Israeli invasion of Lebanon are rather tentatively handled, but director Eran Riklis is on much surer ground with the interaction between the two men, whose loathing turns to respect as the tournament

progresses. Thoughtful and accomplished. DP Arabic, Hebrew +subtitles.

Moshe Ivgi *Cohen* • Muhamad Bacri [Muhamad Bakri] *Ziad* • Salim Dau *Mussa* • Basam Zuamut *Abu Eyash* • Yussef Abu Warda *George* ■ *Dir* Eran Riklis • *Scr* Eyal Halfon, from an idea by Eran Riklis

Cupcakes ★★★12
Comedy   2013 · Is/Fr · Colour · 88min

Director Eytan Fox's enjoyably kitsch Israeli confection celebrates and satirises TV song contests. Efrat Dor plays the frustrated songwriter persuading her pals to form a group to show the executives running a Eurovision-style show how it's done. Amazingly, the Cupcakes get selected to go to the final, but first each member has a problem to resolve. There are too many plotlines and too little depth of character, but the ensemble hams it up with glee, and the catchy key song (composed by Scissor Sister Scott Hoffman) helps. DP Hebrew, French, English +subtitles. Swearing, sexual references, drug abuse, brief nudity. *DVD*

Dana Ivgy *Dana* • Keren Berger *Keren* • Yael Bar-Zohar *Yael* • Efrat Dor *Efrat* • Anat Waxman *Anat* ■ *Dir* Eytan Fox • *Scr* Eli Bijaoui, Eytan Fox

Curdled ★★18
Black comedy thriller 1995 · US · Colour · 85min

This began life as a short film that inspired part of Quentin Tarantino's *Pulp Fiction*. He then turned executive producer to help director and co-writer Reb Braddock expand the original into a full-length movie. Itinerant cleaning maid Angela Jones discovers the identity of a serial killer from the debris left behind in his flat, but has difficulty proving it. The result has some neat touches, but it might have been better had it kept to its original duration. TH Swearing, violence. *DVD*

Angela Jones *Gabriela* • William Baldwin *Paul Guell* • Bruce Ramsay *Eduardo* • Lois Chiles *Katrina Brandt* • Barry Corbin *Lodger* • Mel Gorham *Elena* ■ *Dir* Reb Braddock • *Scr* John Maass, Reb Braddock

The Cure ★★★★U
Silent comedy   1917 · US · BW · 23min

Charles Chaplin's 1917 short is a ruthlessly comic and inventive frolic. When Charlie goes to stay at a spa for recovering alcoholics, gallons of liquor get dumped into the resort's water and change everyone into hyperactive lunatics. Our hero falls for Edna Purviance, as usual, and comes up against the massive Eric Campbell. This contains some remarkable comedy routines that Chaplin later said were derived from his days in music hall. TH

Charles Chaplin *Alcoholic gentleman at spa* • Edna Purviance *Fellow guest at spa* • Eric Campbell *Man with gout* • John Rand *Male Nurse* • Albert Austin *Male Nurse* • Frank J Coleman *Proprietor* • James T Kelley *Ancient Bell Boy* ■ *Dir/Scr* Charles Chaplin

The Cure ★★★12
Drama   1995 · US · Colour · 94min

This thoughtful drama deals with the friendship between two boys, one of whom has contracted Aids from a blood transfusion. Directed by actor Peter Horton, this small, insightful movie deals with big issues and benefits enormously from a talented cast. Tough kid Brad Renfro and the poorly Joseph Mazzello are first-rate, skilfully supported by Annabella Sciorra as Mazzello's mother and Bruce Davison as his doctor. Believable and affecting. JC

Joseph Mazzello *Dexter* • Brad Renfro *Erik* • Diana Scarwid *Gail* • Bruce Davison *Dr Stevens* • Annabella Sciorra *Linda* • Aeryk Egan *Tyler* • Delphine French *Tyler's girlfriend* • Andrew Broder *Tyler's buddy* ■ *Dir* Peter Horton • *Scr* Robert Kuhn

The Cure for Love ★★U
Romantic comedy drama
1949 · UK · BW · 99min

Adapted from a successful West End stage play, this English romantic comedy was a strange and awkward choice for revered actor Robert Donat, who produced, directed

and starred. It concerns a soldier hero who, while on leave in his home town in Lancashire, falls in love with a London evacuee (real-life wife to be, Renée Asherson) and has difficulty finding the courage to tell his fiancée Dora Bryan. Stagey and dated. RK

Robert Donat *Jack* • Renée Asherson *Milly* • Marjorie Rhodes *Mrs Hardacre* • Charles Victor *Henry* • Thora Hird *Mrs Dorbell* • Dora Bryan *Jenny* • Gladys Henson *Mrs Jenkins* • John Stratton *Sam* ■ *Dir* Robert Donat • *Scr* Robert Donat, Albert Fennell, Alexander Shaw, from the play by Walter Greenwood

The Curious Case of Benjamin Button ★★★★12
Romantic fantasy drama
2008 · US · Colour · 159min

After the darkness and savagery of *Fight Club* and *Se7en*, director David Fincher's third collaboration with Brad Pitt represents a major shift in style and tone. Adapted from F Scott Fitzgerald's short story, the action begins in the 21st century and then flashes back to 1918 when baby Benjamin (Pitt) is born with the physiology of a geriatric. As the years pass he proceeds to "grow" younger, but the teenage Benjamin still resembles an elderly man when he first meets Daisy, the girl who will become the love of his life (in the form of Cate Blanchett). It's their attempts to consummate those romantic feelings that form the backbone of the film, although time, inevitably, works against them. Make-up and state-of-the-art CGI special effects show Pitt's journey from old age to youth, but what's remarkable here is that the computer wizardry doesn't overshadow the heartfelt story. JR *DVD* *Blu*

Brad Pitt *Benjamin Button* • Cate Blanchett *Daisy* • Tilda Swinton *Elizabeth Abbott* • Elle Fanning *Daisy, aged 6* • Jason Flemyng *Thomas Button* • Elias Koteas *Monsieur Gateau* • Julia Ormond *Caroline* ■ *Dir* David Fincher • *Scr* Eric Roth, from a story by Roth, Robin Swicord, from the short story by F Scott Fitzgerald

Curious Dr Humpp ★★★18
Cult erotic horror   1967 · Arg · BW · 103min

This real oddity is one of the most bizarre mixes of sex, horror and sci-fi ever made. Forget the story about a voyeuristic mad scientist giving kidnapped girls aphrodisiacs; it's the fusion of paranoid fantasy, horrific morality play and soft-core banality that makes this Argentinian movie such a gobsmacker. Striking imagery, misshapen monsters, black-faced mutants, a talking brain from Italy and creatures playing weird musical instruments in foggy courtyards surrounded by zombies make this drama curiously unforgettable. AJ Spanish dubbed. Sex scenes. *DVD*

Richard Bauleo [Ricardo Bauleo] *George* • Gloria Prat *Rachel* • Aldo Barbero *Dr Humpp* • Susan Beltran [Susana Beltran] *Enfermera* • Justin Martin *Barman* • Michel Angel • Mary Albano • Al Bugatti ■ *Dir* Emilio Vieyra • *Scr* Emilio Vieyra, Raul Zorrilla

Curious George ★★★U
Animated comedy adventure
2006 · US · Colour · 83min

Margret and HA Rey's mischievous monkey creation leaps onto the big screen in this animated reworking of the classic children's books. A short and sunny confection aimed at the under-sevens, it explores how jungle-dwelling George ends up in the big city, after becoming fascinated with Ted, "The Man with the Yellow Hat" (voiced by Will Ferrell), a museum guide hunting for an ancient idol to save his workplace from closure. Though the tale has been updated for contemporary audiences, the original spirit of the books remains. An inferior animated sequel, *Curious George 2: Follow that Monkey!* was produced in 2009. SF *DVD*

Will Ferrell *Ted, the Man with the Yellow Hat* • Drew Barrymore *Maggie* • David Cross (2) *Bloomsberry Jr* • Eugene Levy *Clovis* • Joan Plowright *Miss Plushbottom* • Dick Van Dyke *Bloomsberry* • Frank Welker *George* ■ *Dir* Matthew O'Callaghan • *Scr* Ken Kaufman, from a story by Ken Kaufman, Mike Werb, from the illustrated children's books by Margret Rey, HA Rey

Curly Sue ★★ PG

Comedy   1991 · US · Colour · 97min

Director John Hughes unexpectedly misses the target with this sentimental comedy about a young girl and her con artist travelling companion (James Belushi) who attempt to take Chicago lawyer Kelly Lynch for a ride. Belushi is always watchable, but even he can't make up for the cutesy performance of Alisan Porter in the title role. **JB** Some swearing.

James Belushi *Bill Dancer* · Kelly Lynch *Grey Ellison* · Alisan Porter *Curly Sue* · John Getz *Walker McCormick* · Fred Dalton Thompson *Bernard Oxbar* ■ *Dir/Scr* John Hughes

Curly Top ★★★ U

Musical   1935 · US · BW · 76min

Shirley Temple is at her exquisite best here: a dimpled moppet playing Cupid to her sister Rochelle Hudson and John Boles, who adopts Temple and Hudson from an orphanage. This kind of movie made Temple a top movie star across the world and saved her studio, 20th Century-Fox, from bankruptcy. She's as good as she ever was in this unoriginal musical, revealing a talent and a surety of poise that's positively frightening in one so young. **TS**

Shirley Temple *Elizabeth Blair* · John Boles *Edward Morgan* · Rochelle Hudson *Mary Blair* · Jane Darwell *Mrs Denham* · Rafaela Ottiano *Mrs Higgins* · Esther Dale *Aunt Genevieve Graham* · Etienne Girardo *Mr Wyckoff* · Maurice Murphy *Jimmie Rogers* ■ *Dir* Irving Cummings · *Scr* Patterson McNutt, Arthur Beckhard, from a story by Jean Webster

The Curse ★★★ 18

Horror   1987 · US · Colour · 82min

Take method actor-turned-director David Keith, put him together with Italian rip-off producer Ovidio G Assonitis, and the result is very grisly food for thought. A glowing meteor crash lands near the Tennessee farm of redneck Claude Akins, mutating his produce and livestock before affecting the local community. There's a lot going on in this cynical chiller, though it's undercut once the film degenerates into formula zombie territory. **AJ**

Wil Wheaton *Zachary Hayes* · Claude Akins *Nathan Hayes* · Malcolm Danare *Cyrus* · Cooper Huckabee *Dr Alan Forbes* · John Schneider *Carl Willis* · Amy Wheaton *Alice Hayes* · Steve Carlisle *Charley Davidson* ■ *Dir* David Keith · *Scr* David Chaskin, from the story *The Colour Out of Space* by HP Lovecraft

Curse II: The Bite ★★ 18

Horror thriller
1989 · US/It/Jpn · Colour · 93min

Although his film has absolutely nothing to do with *The Curse*, opportunist Italian producer Ovidio G Assonitis tacked on the title to this insanely stupid snake spectacular. Jill Schoelen and boyfriend J Eddie Peck are driving through a nuclear testing ground in Arizona when a radioactive rattler bites Peck on the arm, turning the limb into a snake. Daft glove-puppet special effects defuse the gore factor, but this is still entertaining trash. **AJ**

Jill Schoelen *Lisa* · J Eddie Peck *Clark* · Jamie Farr *Harry* · Savina Gersak *Iris* · Bo Svenson *Sheriff* · Marianne Muellerleile *Big Flo* ■ *Dir* Fred Goodwin [Federico Prosperi] · *Scr* Fred Goodwin, Susan Zelouf

Curse III: Blood Sacrifice ★ 18

Horror   1991 · US · Colour · 87min

Completely unrelated to the previous two *Curse* movies, this catchpenny chiller (originally titled *Panga*) is set in early 1950s East Africa and concerns a plantation owner's pregnant wife (Jennilee Harrison) interrupting a witch doctor's black magic ceremony. For her sin, she is earmarked as sacrificial victim to a rubber monster. Christopher Lee lends gravity to the poorly shot production. **AJ**

Christopher Lee *Doctor Pearson* · Jenilee Harrison *Elizabeth Armstrong* · Henry Cele *Mletch* · Andre Jacobs *Geoff Armstrong* · Zoe Randall *Anthea Steed* ■ *Dir* Sean Barton · *Scr* John Hunt, Sean Barton, from a story by Richard Haddon Haines

Curse of Chucky ★★★ 18

Horror   2013 · US · Colour · 92min

Nearly ten years after his last appearance (in *Seed of Chucky*), the dastardly doll possessed by a serial killer returns to cut a swathe through another herd of hapless grown-ups. Initially eerie and foreboding, the film soon sees heads begin to roll as Chucky's ghoulish antics run the gloriously gory gamut of death by axe, electrocution and kitchen knife, all done in the best possible distaste. **JA** Violence, swearing.

DVD BLU CS

Fiona Dourif *Nica* · Brad Dourif *Charles Lee Ray/Chucky* · Danielle Bisutti *Barb* · Brennan Elliott *Ian* · A Martinez *Father Frank* · Jennifer Tilly *Tiffany* ■ *Dir* Don Mancini · *Scr* Don Mancini, from his characters

The Curse of Frankenstein ★★★★ 12

Horror   1957 · UK · Colour · 79min

This was the classic that single-handedly revived traditional British gothic and firmly placed the "Hammer House of Horror" on the global gore map. Peter Cushing is the demented Baron who yearns to resurrect the dead, while Christopher Lee plays the hideous creature who proves his mad theories correct. With its gruesome atmosphere, unflinching direction and outstanding design, this phenomenally successful film was the first colour version of Mary Shelley's gallows fairy tale, setting a standard Hammer found it hard to live up to. The series continued with *The Revenge of Frankenstein*. **AJ** Violence. DVD BLU

Peter Cushing *Baron Victor Frankenstein* · Christopher Lee *The Creature* · Hazel Court *Elizabeth* · Robert Urquhart *Paul Krempe* · Valerie Gaunt *Justine* · Noel Hood *Aunt Sophia* ■ *Dir* Terence Fisher · *Scr* Jimmy Sangster, from the novel *Frankenstein* by Mary Shelley · *Art Director* Bernard Robinson

The Curse of the Cat People ★★★★ U

Horror fantasy   1944 · US · BW · 66min

Producer Val Lewton originally wanted to call this picture *Aimée and Her Friend*, but RKO executives were so determined to cash in on Lewton's 1942 success, *Cat People*, that he was persuaded to change the title. Inspired by a Robert Louis Stevenson short story, it is more a study of child psychology than a horror film, but the brooding lighting, the all-pervading sense of menace and the occasional shock make for tense viewing. Simone Simon is superb as Irena, the cursed panther-woman who inspires pity rather than fear. A charming chiller. **DP**

Simone Simon *Irena* · Kent Smith *Oliver Reed* · Jane Randolph *Alice Reed* · Ann Carter *Amy* · Elizabeth Russell *Barbara* · Julia Dean *Julia Farren* · Eve March *Miss Callahan* · Erford Gage *Captain of the guard* ■ *Dir* Robert Wise, Gunther von Fritsch · *Scr* DeWitt Bodeen · *Cinematographer* Nicholas Musuraca

Curse of the Crimson Altar ★★ 15

Horror   1968 · UK · Colour · 83min

With a title like this you'd expect sacrifices galore, but none was as great as that made by its star, Boris Karloff. The horror legend makes one of his final screen appearances in this lacklustre offering about devil worship in an old dark house. Not that Karloff cared much about quality, as he was enjoying the pleasure of being back in England. Christopher Lee co-stars, along with Barbara Steele as a 300-year-old witch. **TH** Brief nudity, violence. DVD BLU

Boris Karloff *Professor Marsh* · Christopher Lee *JD Morley* · Mark Eden *Robert Manning* · Virginia Wetherell *Eve* · Barbara Steele *Lavinia* · Rupert Davies *Vicar* · Michael Gough *Elder* · Rosemarie Reede *Esther* ■ *Dir* Vernon Sewell · *Scr* Mervyn Haisman, Henry Lincoln

The Curse of the Dragon ★★★ 15

Documentary
1993 · US · BW and Colour · 85min

Narrated by *Star Trek*'s George Takei, this documentary tribute to Bruce Lee packs in plenty of information and insight. There are home movies of his early competition victories, interviews with fellow actors such as James Coburn and Chuck Norris and behind-the-scenes footage of stunt sequences from *Enter the Dragon*. Sadly, there are also shots of the funerals of both Bruce and his actor son Brandon, who was killed on the set of *The Crow*, which spark off a discussion about whether the family was cursed. Intriguing viewing. **DP**

George Takei *Narrator* ■ *Dir* Fred Weintraub, Tom Kuhn

Curse of the Fly ★★ PG

Horror   1965 · UK · BW · 82min

Brian Donlevy takes over from Vincent Price as the mad doctor experimenting with teleportation through the fourth dimension in this average second sequel to monster hit *The Fly*. Unfortunately, he still can't get the matter transmissions right, and the mutant results of his labours are locked in a closet. Journeyman director Don Sharp's talent for shock effects gets lost amid the stiff acting, slow pacing and cheap production values, but the odd moment of eerie atmosphere does surface. **AJ** DVD

Brian Donlevy *Henri Delambre* · George Baker *Martin Delambre* · Carole Gray *Patricia Stanley* · Yvette Rees *Wan* · Bert Kwouk [Burt Kwouk] *Tai* · Michael Graham *Albert Delambre* · Jeremy Wilkin *Inspector Ronet* ■ *Dir* Don Sharp · *Scr* Harry Spalding, from characters by George Langelaan

Curse of the Golden Flower ★★★★ 15

Period romantic drama
2006 · Chi/HK · Colour · 109min

The third action film from Chinese director Zhang Yimou (following *Hero* and *House of Flying Daggers*) is a visually stunning and emotionally charged experience. Set in 10th-century China, the plot is part Shakespeare, part *Dynasty*-style soap opera. As the Emperor (Chow Yun-Fat) and his younger wife (Gong Li) engage in a bitter power struggle, three princes get caught up in their Machiavellian games. The Chinese superstars are terrific as the power-hungry parents, the choreographed massed-battle scenes are gloriously over the top and the sumptuous, Oscar-nominated costumes alone make the movie worth watching. **DA** Mandarin +subtitles. Violence. DVD BLU

Chow Yun-Fat *The Emperor* · Gong Li *The Empress* · Jay Chou *Prince Jai* · Liu Ye *Crown Prince Wan* · Chen Jin *Imperial doctor's wife* · Ni Dahong *Imperial doctor* · Li Man *Chan* · Qin Junjie *Prince Yu* ■ *Dir* Zhang Yimou · *Scr* Zhang Yimou, Wu Nan, Bian Zhihong, from the play *Thunderstorm* by Cao Yu · *Cinematographer* Zhao Xiaoding · *Costume Designer* Yee Chung Man

The Curse of the Jade Scorpion ★★ 12

Period comedy   2001 · US/Ger · Colour · 97min

Woody Allen is in nostalgic mood for this handsome tribute to the 1940s crime B-movie. However, he misses the timbre of hard-boiled argot and allows his pastiche plot to meander. But what really prevents a potentially diverting project from taking off is the love/hate mismatch between Allen's hapless gumshoe and efficiency expert Helen Hunt, who have both been hypnotised into doing the bidding of nefarious showman David Ogden Stiers. Dan Aykroyd and Charlize Theron gamely boost underwritten supporting roles, but can't disguise the lethal lack of inspiration. **DP** DVD

Woody Allen *CW Briggs* · Helen Hunt *Betty Ann Fitzgerald* · Dan Aykroyd *Chris Magruder* · Charlize Theron *Laura Kensington* · Brian

Markinson *Al* · Wallace Shawn *George Bond* · David Ogden Stiers *Eli Voytak "Voltan" Polgar* · Elizabeth Berkley *Jill* ■ *Dir/Scr* Woody Allen

The Curse of the Living Corpse ★

Horror   1964 · US · BW · 83min

A millionaire vows to murder all his spiteful relatives if he is buried alive. When he is, a hooded maniac starts assassinating everyone in nasty ways. A drab attempt to emulate Roger Corman's Edgar Allan Poe adaptations, this laughably bad early gore movie has little to recommend it, besides the fact that it features Roy Scheider's film debut. **AJ**

Helen Warren *Abigail Sinclair* · Roy Scheider *Philip Sinclair* · Margot Hartman *Vivian Sinclair* · Robert Milli *Bruce Sinclair* · Hugh Franklin *James Benson* ■ *Dir/Scr* Del Tenney

The Curse of the Mummy's Tomb ★★ 15

Horror   1964 · UK · Colour · 76min

After moderate success with *The Mummy* (1959), Hammer made several more films featuring the bandaged monster, though all lacked inspiration. In this, the second, there's the customary tomb opening, followed by the customary resurrection of its occupant. The mummy takes an unconscionably long time to go on his customary killing spree, though when it comes it does produce a few tense moments. **DM**

Terence Morgan *Adam Beauchamp* · Ronald Howard *John Bray* · Fred Clark *Alexander King* · Jeanne Roland *Annette Dubois* · John Paul *Inspector Mackenzie* · Jack Gwillim *Sir Giles* · George Pastell *Hashmi Bey* · Dickie Owen *Mummy* ■ *Dir* Michael Carreras · *Scr* Henry Younger [Michael Carreras]

The Curse of the Pink Panther ★★ PG

Comedy mystery   1983 · UK · Colour · 105min

Without Peter Sellers, this seventh instalment in the comedy series produces negligible humour. The search for the amiable but idiotic Inspector Clouseau wavers when the inspector's vindictive boss (Herbert Lom) programmes the computer to select the world's worst detective for the job. A bumbling Ted Wass is chosen and sets about interviewing characters from previous movies. *Son of the Pink Panther* concluded the series in 1993. **TH**

David Niven *Sir Charles Litton* · Ted Wass *Clifton Sleigh* · Rich Little *Sir Charles Litton (voice)* · Robert Wagner *George Litton* · Herbert Lom *Dreyfus* · Joanna Lumley *Chandra* · Capucine *Lady Litton* · Robert Loggia *Bruno* · Harvey Korman *Professor Balls* · Burt Kwouk *Cato* · Leslie Ash *Juleta Shane* · Roger Moore *Jacques Clouseau* ■ *Dir* Blake Edwards · *Scr* Blake Edwards, Geoffrey Edwards

The Curse of the Werewolf ★★ 12

Horror   1961 · UK · Colour · 87min

Hammer's stab at the werewolf legend may look tame compared to later computerised transformations, but this was shocking stuff in its day, and much horrid imagery was censored. Today the scenes with villagers muttering in the inn look like parody, and everything is so brightly lit there's not much atmosphere. There's also a long prologue that has little to do with the story of Oliver Reed, who goes on a killing spree every full moon. When Reed does appear, however, he gives a riveting performance. **DM**

Oliver Reed *Leon* · Clifford Evans *Alfredo* · Yvonne Romain *Servant girl* · Catherine Feller *Cristina* · Anthony Dawson *Marques Siniestro* · Josephine Llewellyn *Marquesa* · Richard Wordsworth *Beggar* ■ *Dir* Terence Fisher · *Scr* John Elder [Anthony Hinds], from the novel *The Werewolf of Paris* by Guy Endore

The Curse of the Wraydons ★★

Crime melodrama   1946 · UK · BW · 99min

There was a time when Tod Slaughter was considered the scariest actor alive. It's hard to imagine that now, judging from his ultra-stagey performance in this dull adaptation of Maurice Sandoz's Victorian play *Springheeled Jack, the Terror of London*, which freely embroiders on the 19th-century legend of a leaping prowler. Larger-than-life Slaughter is always fun to watch, though, slicing the ham thick as a mad inventor who commits murder with a diabolical gizmo. A quaint diversion. AJ

Tod Slaughter *Philip Wraydon* • Bruce Seton *Captain Jack Clayton* • Gabriel Toyne *Lieutenant Payne* • Andrew Laurence *George Heeningham* • Lorraine Clews *Helen Sedgefield* • Pearl Cameron *Rose Wraydon* ■ *Dir* Victor M Gover • *Scr* Michael Barringer, from the play *Springheeled Jack, the Terror of London* by Maurice Sandoz

Cursed ★★ 15
Horror thriller 2005 · US/Ger · Colour · 95min

Christina Ricci and Jesse Eisenberg star as siblings who are infected by a lycanthrope after a road accident. The events that follow, as the two slowly begin to transform, aren't so much scary as darkly amusing, with scriptwriter Kevin Williamson's adolescent witticisms to the fore. However, Wes Craven's direction is surprisingly clumsy and the CGI effects are so appalling that they overshadow everything else, spoiling the creepy fun and turning a guilty pleasure into groan-worthy rubbish. SF DVD

Christina Ricci *Ellie* • Joshua Jackson *Jake* • Jesse Eisenberg *Jimmy* • Judy Greer *Joannie* • Scott Baio • Milo Ventimiglia *Bo* • Kristina Anapau *Brooke* • Portia de Rossi *Zela* ■ *Dir* Wes Craven • *Scr* Kevin Williamson

Curtain Call ★★★ U
Romantic comedy 1940 · US · BW · 62min

Some three decades before Mel Brooks's *The Producers* (1968), this breezy RKO programmer has a theatre impresario and his go-to director seek to use a small-town hopeful's dismal play to keep a restless star under contract. As played by Donald MacBride and Alan Mowbray, the pair soon find themselves in a jam when diva Helen Vinson declares that she adores Barbara Read's scenario. Dalton Trumbo (one of the Hollywood Ten during the Communist witch-hunt) provides the engaging cast with plenty of zesty dialogue, while MacBride and Mowbray would be reunited the following year for *Footlight Fever*. DP

Alan Mowbray *Donald Avery* • Donald MacBride *Geoffrey "Jeff" Crandall* • Barbara Read *Helen Middleton* • Helen Vinson *Charlotte Morley* • John Archer *Ted Palmer* ■ *Dir* Frank Woodruff • *Scr* Dalton Trumbo, from a story by Howard J Green

Curtain Call ★★
Supernatural comedy 1997 · US · Colour · 91min

James Spader moves into a New York apartment, unaware that his new home already has two tenants: the quarreling ghosts of two former Broadway stars, Michael Caine and Maggie Smith. When they realise their new flatmate is having girlfriend troubles, the pair (whom only Spader can see and hear) decide to meddle, with supposedly hilarious results. Despite all-out efforts from the heavyweight cast, this is never more than mildly amusing. JB

James Spader *Stevenson Lowe* • Polly Walker *Julia Winston* • Michael Caine *Max Gale* • Maggie Smith *Lilly Marlowe* • Buck Henry *Charles Van Allsburg* • Sam Shepard *Will Dodge* • Frank Whaley *Brett Conway* • Marcia Gay Harden *Michelle Tippet* • Frances Sternhagen *Amy* • Valerie Perrine *Monica* ■ *Dir* Peter Yates • *Scr* Todd Alcott, from a story by Andrew Karsch [Andrew S Karsch]

Curtain Up ★★★ U
Comedy 1952 · UK · BW · 78min

There's a nice irony in the fact that a film about a play in which the author refuses to sacrifice a single word of her text has been loosely adapted from the original stage show. Margaret Rutherford is in fine fettle as the persistent playwright, while Robert Morley gives a performance of polished petulance as the director of the down-at-heel stock company who insists on wholesale changes. This amusing dig at showbiz preciousness is most agreeable. DP

Robert Morley *Harry* • Margaret Rutherford *Catherine* • Olive S oane *Maud* • Joan Rice *Avis* • Charlotte Mitchell *Daphne* • Kay Kendall *Sandra* • Liam Gaffney *Norwood* • Margaret Avery (1) *Mary* ■ *Dir* Ralph Smart, from the play *On Monday Next* by Philip King

Custer of the West ★★★ U
Western 1967 · US/Sp · Colour · 135min

Intended as an epic spectacle, this became a miscasting mistake. British star Robert Shaw as the general is at odds with both accent and character, and the great *film noir* director Robert Siodmak has to make do with an inferior script that mixes fact with fiction. There are some fine battle sequences, though, and Custer's "Last Stand" makes a poignant finale, while Robert Ryan, as an army deserter, brands the screen with white-hot style. TH DVD

Robert Shaw *General George Custer* • Mary Ure *Elizabeth Custer* • Jeffrey Hunter *Lieutenant Benteen* • Ty Hardin *Major Marcus Reno* • Robert Ryan *Sergeant Mulligan* • Charles Stalnaker *Lieutenant Howells* • Robert Hall *Sergeant Buckley* • Lawrence Tierney *General Philip Sheridan* ■ *Dir* Robert Siodmak • *Scr* Bernard Gordon, Julian Halevy [Julian Zimet]

The Custodian ★★★ 15
Crime thriller 1993 · Aus · Colour · 105min

Anthony LaPaglia adds an extra layer of class to an already impressive Australian corruption thriller, as a machiavellian cop playing the internal affairs department and his ruthless, bent colleagues off against each other. Part of the film's appeal is that you're never quite sure which side LaPaglia is on, and so much of the credit for that must go writer/director John Dingwall's intelligent script. The supporting performances are first rate, too. JF DVD

Anthony LaPaglia *Quinlan* • Hugo Weaving *Church* • Barry Otto *Ferguson* • Kelly Dingwall *Reynolds* • Essie Davis *Jilly* • Bill Hunter *Managing director* • Skye Wansey *Claire* ■ *Dir/Scr* John Dingwall

Custody of the Heart ★★ PG
Drama 2000 · US · Colour · 87min

An accomplished cast is wasted on this unexceptional TV movie, with Lorraine Bracco as the careerist whose spare time is divided between her family and disabled mother. Martin Donovan is miscast as the husband so emasculated by his wife's competence that he sues for divorce, while Bracco's decision to abandon her life and begin again in a renovated lighthouse detaches the plot from its semblance of reality and leaves it to drift into fanciful melodrama. DP DVD

Lorraine Bracco *Claire Raphael* • Martin Donovan (2) *Dennis Raphael* • Dennis Boutsikaris *Nick Brody* • Michael Cera *Johnny Raphael* • Charlotte Arnold *Kiki Raphael* ■ *Dir* David Hugh Jones [David Jones (3)] • *Scr* Marsha Norman, from the novel *A Woman's Place* by Barbara Delinsky

Cut ★★ 18
Horror spoof 2000 · Aus · Colour · 79min

Those *Scream* sequels have so much to answer for, with their penchant for generic in-jokes and the paraphernalia of movie-making. Contributing a passable Parker Posey impression, Molly Ringwald plays the temperamental American star of a low-budget horror whose cast and crew keep falling victim to a masked, shears-wielding maniac. The odd gore gag pays off, but the filmic references are lame and the closing emphasis on the supernatural is as redundant as Kylie Minogue's cameo. DP

Molly Ringwald *Vanessa Turnbull* • Jessica Napier *Raffy Carruthers* • Sarah Kants *Hester Ryan* • Geoff Revell *Lossman* • Frank Roberts *Brad/Scar Man* • Kylie Minogue *Hilary Jacobs* • Stephen Curry *Rick Stephens* ■ *Dir* Kimble Rendall • *Scr* Dave Warner

The Cut ★★★ 15
Historical drama 2014 · Ger/Fr/Pol/It/Can/Tur · Colour · 133min

This harrowing tale begins in 1915, with Nazaret (Tahar Rahim), an Armenian blacksmith living with his wife and twin daughters, who one night is taken away by Turkish authorities and forced into slavery. Eventually, realising that his daughters have survived, he sets out on an odyssey to find them. Sadly, as he travels from country to country, the film starts to feel repetitive, while Nazaret's muteness forces Rahim to convey emotions with facial expressions. It's still affecting in places, however, and by highlighting the Armenian genocide, it tells a story that deserves to be told. SC
Armenian, Arabic, Turkish, Kurdish, Spanish, English +subtitles. DVD

Tahar Rahim *Nazaret Manoogian* • Simon Abkarian *Krikor* • Makram Khouri *Omar Nasreddin* ■ *Dir* Fatih Akin • *Scr* Fatih Akin, Mardik Martin

A Cut Above ★★★ 15
Comedy drama 1989 · US · Colour · 105min

This lightweight *ER*-style frolic focuses on a group of young students getting to grips with grown-up medicine. Matthew Modine is the charismatic underachiever who refuses to play the competitive games set by harsh tutor Christine Lahti; Daphne Zuniga supplies the romantic interest and Zakes Mokae pops up as a wise old doctor. Director Thom Eberhardt does his best, but the script uneasily mixes slapstick with sentimentality. Released in the UK on DVD under its American title, *Gross Anatomy*. JF Swearing. DVD

Matthew Modine *Joe Slovak* • Daphne Zuniga *Laurie Rorbach* • Christine Lahti *Dr Rachel Woodruff* • Todd Field *David Schreiner* • John Scott Clough *Miles Reed* • Alice Carter *Kim McCauley* • Robert Desiderio *Dr Banks* ■ *Dir* Thom Eberhardt • *Scr* Ron Nyswaner, Mark Spragg, Ron Nyswaner, Mark Spragg, from a story by Howard Rosenman, Alan Jay Glueckman, Stanley Isaacs, Mark Spragg

Cutaway ★★ 12
Action drama 2000 · US · Colour · 100min

Director Guy Manos is a former skydiving world champion, so the aerial sequences on show here are absolutely stunning. Unfortunately, as a writer (he co-scripted this with brother Greg) Manos is a brilliant parachutist. The lazy plot sees Stephen Baldwin going undercover with a champion skydiving team whose members he suspects of drug-running. An uncomfortable mix of sporting clichés and psychobabble. JF DVD

Tom Berenger *Redline* • Stephen Baldwin *Agent Vic Cooper* • Dennis Rodman *Turbo* • Ron Silver *Margate* • Maxine Bahns *Star* ■ *Dir* Guy Manos • *Scr* Greg Manos, Guy Manos

Cutie and the Boxer ★★★
Documentary 2013 · US · Colour · 82min

Zachary Heinzerling's film is a revealing insight into a creative partnership. Artist Ushio Shinohara was already a renowned member of the Japanese avant-garde when he decamped to America in 1969. His wife Noriko is 21 years his junior and produces semi-autobiographical drawings, in which her Cutie character tries to cope with her pugnacious partner, Bullie. Somehow, the pair have stayed together and Heinzerling follows them and artist son Alex over a five-year period, as they prepare for separate exhibitions. It's an affectionate and occasionally charming movie, but the overwhelming emotion it evokes is sadness. DP English, Japanese +subtitles. Some swearing, nudity. DVD

■ *Dir* Zachary Heinzerling

Cutter's Way ★★★★ 15
Crime drama 1981 · US · Colour · 104min

This underrated thriller, while occasionally overwrought, is also an engaging study in moral responsibility. Disabled Vietnam veteran Cutter (John Heard) teams up with his gigolo friend Bone (Jeff Bridges) in a bid to expose tycoon Stephen Elliott as the murderer of a hitch-hiker. Cutter and Bone are seriously unlikeable characters, yet director Ivan Passer and writer Jeffrey Alan Fiskin make us see light in these hearts of darkness. Misunderstood at the time, it's now a worthy melodrama. Its original title, *Cutter and Bone*, was changed because the studio thought it sounded too much like surgery. TH Swearing. DVD

Jeff Bridges *Richard Bone* • John Heard *Alex Cutter* • Lisa Eichhorn *Maureen "Mo" Cutter* • Ann Dusenberry *Valerie Duran* • Stephen Elliott (1) *JJ Cord* • Arthur Rosenberg *George Swanson* • Nina Van Pallandt *Woman in hotel* ■ *Dir* Ivan Passer • *Scr* Jeffrey Alan Fiskin, from the novel *Cutter and Bone* by Newton Thornburg

CutThroat Island ★★ PG
Action adventure 1995 · US · Colour · 117min

Renny Harlin's pirate picture has all the ingredients to shiver the timbers and it also boasts the best treasure map ever seen on screen, yet it has gone down in history as one of the biggest box-office disasters of recent times. Geena Davis and Matthew Modine swagger with suitable bravado, but their performances are sunk by the predictability of the action. Polished entertainment, but with a little more imagination it could have been exhilarating. DP Violence, swearing. DVD

Geena Davis *Morgan Adams* • Matthew Modine *William Shaw* • Frank Langella *Captain Dawg Brown* • Maury Chaykin *John Reed* • Patrick Malahide *Ainslee* • Stan Shaw *Glasspoole* • Rex Linn *Mr Blair* • Paul Dillon *Snelgrave* ■ *Dir* Renny Harlin • *Scr* Robert King, Marc Norman, from a story by Michael Frost Beckner, James Gorman, Bruce A Evans, Raynold Gideon

Cutting Class ★★ 18
Comedy horror 1989 · US · Colour · 87min

Notable only for featuring a very early performance from Brad Pitt, this is for shlock horror fans only. Jill Schloelen stars as an all-American cutie who has school jock Pitt for a boyfriend. When pupils start mysteriously dying, blame automatically falls on nutcase Donovan Leitch. But then Schloelen starts noticing Pitt isn't all he seems. Lines like "I am a murderer. Not as prestigious as a lawyer or a doctor, but the hours are good!" will have you reaching for the remote. LH DVD

Donovan Leitch *Brian Woods* • Jill Schloelen *Paula Carson* • Brad Pitt *Dwight Ingalls* • Roddy McDowall *Dr Dante* • Martin Mull *William Carson III* ■ *Dir* Rospo Pallenberg • *Scr* Steve Slavkin

The Cutting Edge ★★★ PG
Romantic sports drama 1992 · US · Colour · 97min

DB Sweeney plays a macho ice-hockey player who is paired with snooty ice-skating hopeful Moira Kelly in a bid to win gold at the Olympics. Sweeney and Kelly spark off each other nicely and they are ably supported by the likes of Terry O'Quinn and Roy Dotrice. The skating scenes are splendidly staged, and director Paul Michael Glaser only loses his footing during with some *Rocky*-style histrionics. JF DVD

DB Sweeney *Doug Dorsey* • Moira Kelly *Kate Moseley* • Roy Dotrice *Anton Pamchenko* • Terry O'Quinn *Jack Moseley* • Dwier Brown *Hale* • Chris Benson *Walter Dorsey* • Kevin Peeks *Brian* ■ *Dir* Paul M Glaser [Paul Michael Glaser] • *Scr* Tony Gilroy

Cutting It Short ★★★
Comedy 1980 · Cz · Colour · 98min

Although a prize winner at Venice, this chronicle of the early married life of screenwriter Bohumil Hrabal's parents ranks among Jiří Menzel's least trenchant satires on the Czech establishment. Effortlessly blending small-town period detail with whimsical character comedy, it charts brewery manager Jiri Schmitzer's attempts to curb the progressive inclinations of his beautiful, liberated wife (Magda Vasaryova) and the antics of his eccentric brother (Jaromir Hanzlik). Charmingly played and filmed, but rather lacking in bite. DP

Jiri Schmitzer *Francin* • Magda Vasaryova *Marja* • Jaromir Hanzlik *Pepin* • Rudolf Hrusinsky *Dr Gruntorad* • Oldrich Vlach *Ruzicka* • Frantisek Rehak *Vejvoda* • Petr Cepek • Oldrich Vizner *Barber* ■ *Dir* Jiří Menzel • *Scr* Jiří Menzel, Bohumil Hrabal

C

Cyborg ★★★ 18
Science-fiction adventure
1989 · US · Colour · 79min

Director Albert Pyun's cheap sci-fi adventure features characters all named after electric guitars. Jean-Claude Van Damme is a futuristic mercenary hired to escort a cyborg carrying the antidote to a deadly plague that has almost wiped out mankind in the 21st century. Pyun piles on the trash, panache and gratuitous violence with style. AJ *DVD*

Jean-Claude Van Damme *Gibson Rickenbacker* • Deborah Richter *Nady Simmons* • Vincent Klyn *Fender Tremolo* • Alex Daniels *Marshall Strat* • Dayle Haddon *Pearl Prophet* • Blaise Loong *Furman Vox* • Rolf Muller *Brick Bardo* ■ *Dir* Albert Pyun • *Scr* Kitty Chalmers

Cyborg 2: Glass Shadow
★★★ 18
Science-fiction adventure
1993 · US · Colour · 95min

A martial arts-fighting cyborg (Angelina Jolie) is created by a sinister US corporation to destroy a Japanese rival in an action-packed futuristic adventure with a fun cast. Hero Elias Koteas falls for the sexy humanoid, and together they fight bounty hunter Billy Drago and mercenary storm troopers. Michael Schroeder keeps things bubbling along in this violent fantasy, which has flashbacks to the original. AJ *DVD*

Elias Koteas *Colson "Colt" Ricks* • Angelina Jolie *Casella "Cash" Reese* • Billy Drago *Danny Bench* • Jack Palance *Mercy* • Allen Garfield *Martin Dunn* ■ *Dir* Michael Schroeder • *Scr* Ron Yanover, Mark Gelman, Michael Schroeder, from a story by Ron Yanover, Mark Gelman

Cyborg 3: The Recycler
★★★ 18
Science-fiction adventure
1994 · US · Colour · 87min

This has a more thought-provoking script and better delineated characters than others in the series. Despicable "recycler" (bounty hunter) Richard Lynch preys on the comfort of benevolent humanoids. Scientist Zach Galligan and reproductive replicant Khrystyne Haje are caught up in the battle between bloodthirsty mankind and innocent robots for the right to procreate. Lynch takes magnetic evil to a new level of villainy. AJ *DVD*

Zach Galligan *Evans* • Malcolm McDowell *Lord Talon* • Michael Bailey Smith *Donovan* • Rebecca Ferratti *Elexia* • Khrystyne Haje *Cash* • Andrew Bryniarski *Jocko* • Richard Lynch *Lewellyn* ■ *Dir* Michael Schroeder • *Scr* Barry Victor, Troy Bolotnick

Cyborg Cop ★ 18
Science-fiction action thriller
1993 · US · Colour · 92min

David Bradley heads off to a Caribbean island in search of his missing brother. There he uncovers a secret organisation run by John Rhys-Davies that kidnaps innocent people and converts them into killer cyborgs. Seemingly filmed in abandoned buildings or vacant lots, this is a cheesy *Terminator* rip-off with unexceptional action scenes. The only reason there's a sequel is that both were filmed back to back. KB *DVD*

David Bradley (4) *Jack Ryan* • John Rhys-Davies *Kessel* • Alonna Shaw *Cathy* • Todd Jensen *Phillip* • Rufus Swart *Cyborg* • Ron Smerczak *Callan* • Anthony Fridjohn *Hogan* ■ *Dir* Sam Firstenberg • *Scr* Greg Latter

Cycling with Molière
★★★★ 15
Comedy drama
2013 · Fr · Colour · 105min

Fabrice Luchini's fourth collaboration with director Philippe Le Guay is a droll study of the thespian temperament that's full of acidic asides on the chasm between high and lowbrow culture. Lambert Wilson is impressive as a hammy soap actor intent on luring his reclusive friend Luchini back to the boards for a production of Molières *The Misanthrope*. Some of the slapstick feels forced, but the witty script is as sharp as

the performances. DP French, Italian +subtitles.

Fabrice Luchini *Serge Tanneur* • Lambert Wilson *Gauthier Valence* • Maya Sansa *Francesca* • Camille Japy *Christine* ■ *Dir* Philippe Le Guay • *Scr* Philippe Le Guay, from an idea by Le Guay, Fabrice Luchini

Cyclo ★★★★★ 18
Crime drama   1995 · Fr/Viet · Colour · 123min

In total contrast to the elegiac *Scent of Green Papaya*, this is a quite stunning achievement from Vietnamese director Tran Anh Hung. Tackling such complex themes as paternity, mother-child affinity and spiritual twinship, it is also an uncompromising portrait of life on the streets of Ho Chi Minh City. Le Van Loc is sensational as the teenage pedicab driver who falls in with gangster-pimp Tony Leung when his cycle is stolen. The camerawork is exceptional, with long, energetic takes arranged alongside slow, poetic images. Bold and brave, determined and disturbing. DP Vietnamese +subtitles.

Le Van Loc *The cyclo* • Tony Chiu-Wai Leung [Tony Leung (2)] *The poet* • Tran Nu Yen-Khe *The sister* • Nguyen Nhu Quynh *The madam* ■ *Dir* Tran Anh Hung • *Scr* Tran Anh Hung, Nguyen Trung Bing

The Cyclops ★
Science fiction   1957 · US · BW · 64min

Even by Bert I Gordon's low standards, this is a seriously dumb film. Gloria Talbott plays a woman searching for her fiancé, who goes missing after his plane crashes in a radiation-polluted area. He subsequently turns up as a 50ft tall, one-eyed mutant. Bargain basement tosh. RS

James Craig *Russ Bradford* • Gloria Talbott *Susan Winter* • Lon Chaney Jr *Martin Melville* • Tom Drake *Lee Brand* • Duncan "Dean" Parkin [Dean Parkin] *Bruce Barton/The Cyclops* • Vincente Padula [Vincent Padula] *The Governor* ■ *Dir/Scr* Bert I Gordon

Cymbeline ★★
Crime drama   2014 · US · Colour · 98min

Ethan Hawke and Ed Harris headline an ill-advised modern version of one of Shakespeare's more obscure and less highly rated plays, with its action transposed from anti-Roman unease in Ancient Britain to a turf war in a modern-day US city. The relocation is unconvincing, and so, too, are most of the performances. Harris, watchable in whatever he appears in, copes best with his bits of Bard; Hawke less so. This won't quite have Shakespeare spinning in his grave – at least it's proof there's more to US movie-making than blockbusters. DA

Ethan Hawke *Iachimo* • Ed Harris *Cymbeline* • Milla Jovovich *The Queen* • John Leguizamo *Pisanio* • Penn Badgley *Posthumus* • Dakota Johnson *Imogen* ■ *Dir* Michael Almereyda • *Scr* Michael Almereyda, from Shakespeare's play

Cynara ★★ PG
Melodrama   1932 · US · BW · 74min

Directed by King Vidor, this story of marital infidelity has Ronald Colman's London barrister betraying his wife, Kay Francis, by falling for shopgirl Phyllis Barry. It's a tragedy, though the real drama was on the set, when Colman's dislike of the role led to press reports of his drunkenness. Colman sued Goldwyn for $1 million, dropped the case and brazenly announced his retirement. AT

Ronald Colman *Jim Warlock* • Kay Francis *Clemency Warlock* • Phyllis Barry *Doris Lea* • Henry Stephenson *John Tring* • Viva Tattersall *Milly Miles* • Florine McKinney *Garla* ■ *Dir* King Vidor • *Scr* Frances Marion, Lynn Starling, from the play by HM Harwood, Robert Gore-Brown, from the novel *An Imperfect Lover* by Robert Gore-Brown

Cynthia ★★ U
Comedy drama   1947 · US · BW · 98min

Fifteen-year-old Elizabeth Taylor, already blossoming into sensuous young womanhood, is the eponymous heroine of this light domestic drama, directed by the expert Robert Z Leonard. It's the facile but reasonably involving tale of an adolescent

girl fighting to loosen the controlling bonds of an over-protective mother (Mary Astor) and be allowed to go on her first date (with Jimmy Lydon). RK

Elizabeth Taylor *Cynthia Bishop* • George Murphy *Larry Bishop* • SZ Sakall *Prof Rosenkrantz* • Mary Astor *Louise Bishop* • Gene Lockhart *Dr Fred I Jannings* • Spring Byington *Carrie Jannings* • Jimmy Lydon [James Lydon] *Ricky Latham* • Scotty Beckett *Will Parker* ■ *Dir* Robert Z Leonard • *Scr* Charles Kaufman, Harold Buchman, from the play *The Rich, Full Life* by Vina Delmar

Cypher ★★★ 15
Science-fiction action thriller
2002 · US · Colour and BW · 91min

Director Vincenzo Natali's film features creative special effects and an amazingly sleek look, all elegantly presented with tricksy élan and stylish bravura. When accountant Jeremy Northam exchanges his dull grind for an excitement-filled existence as an industrial spy, he uncovers a sinister brainwashing operation. Natali plays with the boundaries between reason and madness, dreams and reality, and flashbacks and flash-forwards with some aplomb. AJ *DVD*

Jeremy Northam *Morgan Sullivan* • Lucy Liu *Rita* • Nigel Bennett *Ed Finster* • Timothy Webber *Frank Calloway* • David Hewlett *Vergil Dunn* ■ *Dir* Vincenzo Natali • *Scr* Brian King

Cyrano de Bergerac ★★★ U
Period drama   1950 · US · BW · 112min

Edmond Rostand's famous classic about the French army officer whose oversized nose prevents him declaring his love for the beautiful Roxane. Instead he woos her with poetic love letters on behalf of his young friend. This respectful screen translation stars José Ferrer as a dignified, moving Cyrano, a part he had played on Broadway and which here won him an Oscar for best actor. Michael Gordon directs in journeyman fashion, while William Prince and Mala Powers are adequate as the young lovers. RK

José Ferrer *Cyrano* • Mala Powers *Roxane* • William Prince *Christian* • Morris Carnovsky *Le Bret* • Ralph Clanton *de Guiche* • Lloyd Corrigan *Ragueneau* • Virginia Farmer *Duenna* ■ *Dir* Michael Gordon • *Scr* Carl Foreman, from the play by Edmond Rostand

Cyrano de Bergerac
★★★★★ U
Romantic drama   1990 · Fr · Colour · 137min

An exceptional performance by Gérard Depardieu lights up this sumptuous adaptation of Edmond Rostand's classic play from director Jean-Paul Rappeneau. He thoroughly deserved his best actor prize at Cannes for the passion, wit and finesse he displays here as the noted swordsman and poet, whose search for happiness is hindered by his exceptionally large nose. Novelist Anthony Burgess supplied the English translation, brilliantly utilising the original's lyrical verse and treating audiences to subtitles of exquisite poetry. DP French +subtitles. *DVD*

Gérard Depardieu *Cyrano de Bergerac* • Anne Brochet *Roxane* • Vincent Perez *Christian de Neuvillette* • Jacques Weber *Comte de Guiche* • Roland Bertin *Ragueneau* • Philippe Morier-Genoud *Le Bret* • Pierre Maguelon *Carbon de Castel-Jaloux* • Josiane Stoleru *Duenna* ■ *Dir* Jean-Paul Rappeneau • *Scr* Jean-Claude Carrière, Jean-Paul Rappeneau, from the play by Edmond Rostand

Cyrus ★★★★ 15
Romantic comedy   2010 · US · Colour · 87min

A love triangle of the weirdest kind lies at the heart of this dark but refreshingly kind-hearted romantic comedy. John C Reilly plays the underdog lead, a man still pining for his ex-wife (Catherine Keener) who falls for a single mother (Marisa Tomei) at a party. The relationship is tested when Reilly meets Tomei's 20-something son, Cyrus (Jonah Hill). At first, the boy seems welcoming, but Reilly begins to suspect that he has a hidden agenda. The battle of wits that follows is both funny and human, with

a rewarding and emotional pay-off that makes a welcome change from the increasingly irony-enriched fare we've come to expect. DW Swearing. *DVD* *BD*

John C Reilly *John* • Jonah Hill *Cyrus* • Marisa Tomei *Molly* • Catherine Keener *Jamie* • Matt Walsh *Tim* ■ *Dir/Scr* Jay Duplass, Mark Duplass

D2: the Mighty Ducks ★★ U
Sports comedy   1994 · US · Colour · 102min

The original *Mighty Ducks* was a bit of a surprise package, and it has gone on to spawn a couple of equally inoffensive if bland sequels. Emilio Estevez is once again the coach of the ragbag misfits, leading them to the Goodwill Games only to get seduced by the trappings of fame. Sam Weisman stages the ice-hockey games with some flair. JF *DVD*

Emilio Estevez *Gordon Bombay* • Kathryn Erbe *Michele* • Michael Tucker *Tibbles* • Jan Rubes *Jan* • Carsten Norgaard *Wolf* ■ *Dir* Sam Weisman • *Scr* Steven Brill

D3: the Mighty Ducks ★★ PG
Sports comedy   1996 · US · Colour · 99min

Original star Emilio Estevez makes a brief appearance in this third instalment in the successful but unremarkable franchise about the junior hockey team. In Robert Lieberman's contribution to the series, the Mighty Ducks - slightly more grown-up this time around - are bonafide champs, but they still find it difficult to adapt at their snooty new school. JF *DVD*

Emilio Estevez *Gordon Bombay* • Jeffrey Nordling *Coach Orion* • David Selby *Dean Buckley* • Heidi Kling *Casey* • Joshua Jackson *Charlie* • Joss Ackland *Hans* ■ *Dir* Robert Lieberman • *Scr* Steven Brill, from a story by Kenneth Johnson, Jim Burnstein, from characters by Brill

DC Cab ★★ 15
Comedy   1983 · US · Colour · 99min

This uneasy mix of blue collar laughs and drama focuses on the battle between two rival groups of cabbies. There's an interesting cast, but it's unremarkable stuff and is only of note as a career marker for fans of Joel Schumacher. JF

Max Gail *Harold* • Adam Baldwin *Albert* • Mr T *Samson* • Charlie Barnett *Tyrone* • Gary Busey *Dell* • DeWayne Jessie *Bongo* • Gloria Gifford *Miss Floyd* • Marsha Warfield *Ophelia* • Irene Cara ■ *Dir* Joel Schumacher • *Scr* Joel Schumacher, from a story by Topper Carew, Schumacher

DC Sniper: 23 Days of Fear ★★ 12
Crime drama based on a true story
2003 · US · Colour · 85min

Made with indecent haste after the Washington sniper killings of October 2002, this TV movie predated the trial that saw John Allen Muhammad and his teenage accomplice, John Lee Malvo, found guilty of the murders. As a result, the action has been put together from news bulletins and press reports and so feels like a hack job – which is bitingly ironic, given that the theme of director Tom McLoughlin's reconstruction is the media's lack of responsibility in reporting a sensational story. Charles S Dutton attempts to instil some gravitas as the police chief, but he's fighting a losing battle. DP *DVD*

Charles S Dutton *Charles Moose* • Jay O Sanders *Douglas Duncan* • Bobby Hosea *John Muhammad* • Trent Cameron *John Lee Malvo* • Helen Shaver *Sandy Moose* • Tom O'Brien *Lieutenant Jacobs* • Charlayne Woodard *Mildred Muhammad* ■ *Dir* Tom McLoughlin • *Scr* Dave Erickson

D-Day the Sixth of June ★★★ PG
Second World War romantic drama
1956 · US · Colour · 101min

This stirring and well-played romantic drama set at the time of the Normandy landings in 1944 shows the personal problems of officers encroaching on their work. Robert Taylor stars as the American serviceman who recalls his affair with Dana Wynter, while her fiancé Richard Todd was fighting in Africa. Aside from the familiar "stiff-upper-lip" heroics, this offers some fine acting and action sequences. SH *DVD*

Robert Taylor (1) *Brad Parker* • Richard Todd *John Wynter* • Dana Wynter *Valerie* • Edmond O'Brien *Colonel Timmer* • John Williams *Brigadier Russell* • Jerry Paris *Raymond Boyce* • Robert Gist *Dan Stenick* • Richard Stapley *David Archer* • Alex Finlayson *Colonel Harkens* ■ *Dir* Henry Koster • *Scr* Ivan Moffat, Harry Brown, from the novel by Lionel Shapiro

DOA ★★★ PG
Film noir   1949 · US · BW · 83min

This may not be the best *film noir* of the immediate postwar period, but it's one of the most unusual - how many people get to hunt for their own murderer? Edmond O'Brien responds to that unenviable challenge with grim determination in this slow-burning thriller. Once the scene is set, director Rudolph Maté takes us on a tortuous journey through the less salubrious parts of Los Angeles. Moodily shot by Ernest Laszlo and with a cracking score by Dimitri Tiomkin, it stands up well to the 1988 remake. DP *DVD*

Edmond O'Brien *Frank Bigelow* • Pamela Britton *Paula Gibson* • Luther Adler *Majak* • Beverly Campbell [Beverly Garland] *Miss Foster* • Lynn Baggett [Lynne Baggett] *Mrs Philips* • William Ching *Halliday* • Henry Hart *Stanley Philips* • Neville Brand *Chester* ■ *Dir* Rudolph Maté • *Scr* Russell Rouse, Clarence Greene

DOA ★★★ 18
Music documentary   1980 · US · Colour · 89min

This chaotic rockumentary details punk music's assault on comfortable America, set against the bleak backdrop of British daily life that spawned the movement. Extensive coverage of the Sex Pistols' US tour combines with rare footage of X-Ray Spex, Generation X, Sham 69 and the Rich Kids, plus a harrowing interview with a spaced-out Sid Vicious and Nancy Spungen, to give an overview of why punk scared the establishment so much. As a film, it's a complete shambles with some shining moments of frenzied energy and excitement. In other words, the perfect record of its subject matter. AJ

■ *Dir* Lech Kowalski

DOA ★★★★ 15
Crime thriller   1988 · US · Colour · 93min

Dennis Quaid's gripping performance is just one reason why Rocky Morton and Annabel Jankel's smart and snappy retread of the memorable 1949 *film noir* is ripe for reappraisal. The *Max Headroom* creators begin their psycho thriller with the now famous exchange: "I wanna report a murder." "Whose?" "Mine!", and dress up the action with a smashing visual flash. Particularly impressive is the gimmick allying Quaid's deteriorating health to the colour draining out of the film, ending up in monochrome. A terrific touch in a thoroughly enjoyable remake. AJ Violence, swearing. *DVD*

Dennis Quaid *Dexter Cornell* • Meg Ryan *Sydney Fuller* • Charlotte Rampling *Mrs Fitzwaring* • Daniel Stern *Hal Petersham* • Jane Kaczmarek *Gail Cornell* • Christopher Neame (2) *Bernard* • Robin Johnson *Cookie Fitzwaring* • Rob Knepper [Robert Knepper] *Nicholas Lang* • Brion James *Detective Ulmer* ■ *Dir* Rocky Morton, Annabel Jankel • *Scr* Charles Edward Pogue, from a story by Pogue, Clarence Greene, Russell Rouse • *Cinematographer* Yuri Neyman

DOA: Dead or Alive ★★★ 15
Action adventure
2006 · Ger/UK · Colour · 82min

The screen incarnation of Tecmo's bestselling video game is a messy, unpretentious and entertaining romp that finds the planet's most hard-bodied martial artists invited to the world's greatest fight tournament. Of course, the contest is just a ruse for the sinister (and scenery-chewing) Eric Roberts to exploit the participants. Terrific special effects, exciting CGI-enhanced stunt choreography and scantily clad heroines take the mind off the ludicrous and ruthlessly edited plot. And the target audience for this "so-bad-it's-good" fluff won't care anyway. AJ Violence. *DVD*

Jaime Pressly *Tina Armstrong* • Holly Valance *Christie Allen* • Devon Aoki *Kasumi* • Sarah Carter *Helena Douglas* • Kane Kosugi *Ryu Hayabusa* • Natassia Malthe *Ayane* • Matthew Marsden *Maximillian Marsh* • Eric Roberts *Donovan* ■ *Dir* Corey Yuen • *Scr* JF Lawton

D-Tox ★ 18
Action thriller
2001 · US/Ger/Can · Colour · 91min

After failing to catch the vicious serial killer responsible for the death of his girlfriend, detective Sylvester Stallone goes on an alcoholic bender and ends up in a detox programme for cops at a remote, snowbound facility in Wyoming. And, surprise, that's where the sadistic assassin is masquerading as one of the Betty Ford-style boozehounds. Derivative, nasty and just plain stupid. AJ *DVD* Blu

Sylvester Stallone *Jake Malloy* • Tom Berenger *Hank* • Charles S Dutton *Hendricks* • Kris Kristofferson *Dr John "Doc" Mitchell* • Polly Walker *Jenny* • Sean Patrick Flanery *Connor* • Christopher Fulford *Frank Slater* ■ *Dir* Jim Gillespie • *Scr* Ron L Brinkerhoff, Patrick Kelly, from the novel *Jitter Joint* by Howard Swindle

The D Train ★★★ 15
Comedy   2015 · UK/US · Colour · 100min

This bromantic comedy has more edge than you might expect. The title refers to an unpopular family man struggling to organise a high school reunion, who convinces himself that people will turn up if he goes to LA to secure the attendance of coolest guy in school James Marsden. Happily, there are several funny moments along the way, while Marsden is perfect as the chiselled hunk who peaked before graduation. At times, the film is broader than it needs to be, but there are just enough laughs to compensate. SC Swearing, sex scenes, drug abuse.

Jack Black *Dan Landsman* • James Marsden *Oliver Lawless* • Kathryn Hahn *Stacey Landsman* • Jeffrey Tambor *Bill* ■ *Dir/Scr* Andrew Mogel, Jarrad Paul

Da ★★★ PG
Fantasy comedy drama
1988 · US · Colour · 97min

Irish-American writer Martin Sheen returns to Ireland for the funeral of his father Barnard Hughes. However, no sooner is Sheen back on the old sod than the old sod materialises by his elbow, only too keen to reminisce about the old days. Adapted by Hugh Leonard from his own play, the film's theatrical roots are all too visible. Nevertheless, this is an unashamed heartstring-tugger that manages to be both funny and touching. SR *DVD*

Barnard Hughes *Da* • Martin Sheen *Charlie* • William Hickey *Drumm* • Doreen Hepburn *Mother* • Karl Hayden *Young Charlie* • Hugh O'Conor *Boy Charlie* • Ingrid Craigie *Polly* • Joan O'Hara *Mrs Prynne* ■ *Dir* Matt Clark • *Scr* Hugh Leonard, from his play and from his novel *Home before Night*

The Da Vinci Code ★★★ 12
Mystery thriller   2006 · US · Colour · 142min

Fans of author Dan Brown's blockbuster novel will not be disappointed by this faithful adaptation. Tom Hanks stars as the Harvard professor whose expertise in symbology sees him ensnared in an unusual Parisian murder case - one that spirals into a search for the Holy Grail and, by extension, a secret that could threaten the foundations of the Christian religion. Joined in his investigations by enigmatic French cryptologist Audrey Tautou, Hanks is soon the object of a cat-and-mouse chase. The action is a tad dry and precise with an emphasis on plot rather than breakneck pace. KK English, French +subtitles. *DVD* Blu

Tom Hanks *Robert Langdon* • Audrey Tautou *Sophie Neveu* • Ian McKellen *Sir Leigh Teabing* • Alfred Molina *Bishop Aringarosa* • Jürgen Prochnow *André Vernet* • Paul Bettany *Silas* • Jean Reno *Bezu Fache* • Etienne Chicot *Lt Collet* ■ *Dir* Ron Howard • *Scr* Akiva Goldsman, from the novel by Dan Brown

Dad ★★ PG
Drama   1989 · US · Colour · 112min

This tries to provoke and uplift, but ends up being nothing more than an utterly false and manipulative melodrama. This is a shame because it starts well, yet from the moment Jack Lemmon falls ill, the film falls apart. Although his performance is not without its merits, it doesn't atone for the wild overplaying of Ted Danson as his son and the sloppy turn of Ethan Hawke as his grandson. DP

Jack Lemmon *Jake Tremont* • Ted Danson *John Tremont* • Olympia Dukakis *Bette Tremont* • Kathy Baker *Annie* • Kevin Spacey *Mario* • Ethan Hawke *Billy Tremont* • Zakes Mokae *Dr Chad* • JT Walsh *Dr Santana* • Peter Michael Goetz *Dr Ethridge* ■ *Dir* Gary David Goldberg • *Scr* Gary David Goldberg, from the novel by William Wharton

Dad and Dave: on Our Selection ★★★ PG
Period comedy drama
1995 · Aus · Colour and Sepia · 102min

Since they were adapted by Raymond Longford in the silent era and Ken G Hall in the 1930s, the cod memoirs of Steele Rudd (written pseudonymously by Arthur Hoey) have fallen out of favour with Australian film-makers. Lampooning the caricature of the ocker Aussie, this revival not only reflects the nation's burgeoning self-image, but also reveals just how far cinema Down Under has come since the original series were produced. Leo McKern and Geoffrey Rush are ideally teamed as the Queenslanders striving to make the most of their farm, while Joan Sutherland provides the sense betwixt the bluster. DP *DVD*

Leo McKern *Dad Rudd* • Joan Sutherland *Mother Rudd* • Geoffrey Rush *Dave* • David Field *Dan* • Noah Taylor *Joe* • Essie Davis *Kate* • Celia Ireland *Sarah* ■ *Dir* George Whaley • *Scr* George Whaley, from stories by Steele Rudd [Arthur Hoey]

Dad Savage ★★ 18
Crime thriller   1997 · UK · Colour · 99min

This is a downright strange British stab at a *Reservoir Dogs*-style crime thriller. Patrick Stewart is entirely unconvincing as the titular flower grower who has a hidden "pension fund" accrued from various illegal activities. His gang members' desire for the loot leads to murder, double-cross and all the other clichés of the genre. Alternately boring and confusing. JC Violence, swearing.

Patrick Stewart *Dad Savage* • Kevin McKidd *H* • Helen McCrory *Chris* • Joseph McFadden *Bob* • Marc Warren (1) *Vic* • Jake Wood *Sav* ■ *Dir* Betsan Morris Evans • *Scr* Steven Williams

Daddy and Them ★★★ 15
Black comedy   1999 · US · Colour · 97min

Billy Bob Thornton's third directorial outing is reminiscent of Frank Capra's 1938 screwball comedy *You Can't Take It with You*, as it packs a bunch of eccentrics into its affectionate discussion of Deep South family life. However, the pacing couldn't be more different and the Miramax suits were so bemused by this leisurely whimsy that they shelved the movie for three years. The emphasis here is firmly on performance, as the dysfunctional Arkansas kinfolk of Thornton and wife Laura Dern respond to uncle Jim Varney's arrest for murder. Consequently, narrative pace matters much less than allowing stalwart players like Andy Griffith, Diane Ladd and Brenda Blethyn to revel in their off-the-wall characters. DP *DVD*

Billy Bob Thornton *Claude* • Laura Dern *Ruby* • Diane Ladd *Jewel* • Kelly Preston *Rose* • Andy Griffith *OT* • Jim Varney *Hazel* • Brenda Blethyn *Julia* • Ben Affleck *Lawrence Bowen* • Jamie Lee Curtis *Elaine Bowen* ■ *Dir/Scr* Billy Bob Thornton

Daddy Day Care ★★ PG
Comedy   2003 · US · Colour · 88min

What this lacks in originality it makes up for in cuteness and verve. Eddie Murphy and

Jeff Garlin play sacked advertising executives who decide to set up a children's day-care centre; cue major mishaps as a house full of angel-faced youngsters turn into marauding monsters - much to the delight of rival childcare provider Anjelica Huston. Simplistic, and too sweet for mass appeal. SF *DVD*

Eddie Murphy *Charlie Hinton* • Jeff Garlin *Phil* • Steve Zahn *Marvin* • Regina King *Kim Hinton* • Kevin Nealon *Bruce* • Jonathan Katz *Mr Dan Kubitz* • Siobhan Fallon Hogan [Siobhan Fallon] *Peggy* • Anjelica Huston *Miss Harridan* ■ *Dir* Steve Carr • *Scr* Geoff Rodkey

Daddy Day Camp ★ PG
Comedy   2007 · US · Colour · 85min

A half-hearted sequel to box-office hit *Daddy Day Care*, *Daddy Day Camp* quickly squanders whatever goodwill its predecessor generated. It's bad enough that Eddie Murphy, star of the 2003 original, is replaced by the infinitely less funny Cuba Gooding Jr; what's unforgivable is the slapdash plotting, trite sermonising and complete dearth of entertainment in this truly appalling follow-up. Gooding Jr takes over the character of Charlie Hinton, who here decides to purchase a run-down summer camp. A battle with a rival camp is the extent of the plot, while the desperate screenwriters do their best to earn the PG rating (though not many laughs) with lots of toilet humour. JR *DVD* (Blu-ray)

Cuba Gooding Jr *Charlie Hinton* • Lochlyn Munro *Lance Warner* • Richard Gant *Colonel Buck Hinton* • Tamala Jones *Kim Hinton* • Paul Rae *Phil Ryerson* • Brian Doyle-Murray *Uncle Morty* • Joshua McLerran *Dale* • Spencir Bridges *Ben Hinton* ■ *Dir* Fred Savage • *Scr* Geoff Rodkey, J David Stem, David N Weiss, from a story by Rodkey, Joel Cohen, Alec Sokolow, from characters by Rodkey

Daddy Long Legs ★★★★
Silent comedy drama   1919 · US · BW · 85min

In pigtails rather than her customary curls, 27-year-old Mary Pickford plays the rebellious youngster who leads a revolt against the prison-like conditions in her orphanage. There is much honest emotion along with the humour, while Marshall Neilan shows why he was her favourite director. (He also appears as a prospective suitor.) The girl's rich benefactor, the mysterious Daddy Long Legs, would register more importantly in later versions of the story, most notably the 1955 musical with Leslie Caron and Fred Astaire. AE

Mary Pickford *"Judy" Abbott* • Milla Davenport *Mrs Lippert* • Wesley Barry *Her pal* • Marshall Neilan *Jimmie McBride* ■ *Dir* Marshall Neilan • *Scr* Agnes Christine Johnston, from the novel and play by Jean Webster

Daddy Long Legs ★★★ U
Comedy drama   1931 · US · BW · 80min

Mary Pickford's silent hit metamorphosed into one of 20th Century-Fox's hardy perennials, but this tale of a secret guardian falling for his young ward needed to be handled with extreme care on the grounds of taste. In this version, pretty Janet Gaynor, though a shade too old for the part, makes a charming foundling, Warner Baxter is a handsomely sturdy patron of at least a convincing age, and the whole story of their May-December relationship is deeply satisfying. TS

Janet Gaynor *Judy Abbott* • Warner Baxter *Jervis Pendleton* • Una Merkel *Sally McBride* • John Arledge *Jimmy McBride* • Claude Gillingwater Sr [Claude Gillingwater] *Riggs* • Kathlyn Williams *Mrs Pendleton* ■ *Dir* Alfred Santell • *Scr* Sonya Levien, SN Behrman, from the novel and play by Jean Webster

Daddy Long Legs ★★★★ U
Romantic musical comedy
1955 · US · Colour · 121min

The third American screen version of Jean Webster's novel features a perfectly cast Fred Astaire, who literally glides his way through the tissue-thin plot about an orphan falling for her playboy benefactor. This could be tasteless, bearing in mind the vast age gap, but it's a musical and the delightful Leslie Caron is the girl.

Interestingly, this was released when rock 'n' roll was at its peak, and features the great Astaire doing the *Sluefoot*. A charming, old-fashioned musical. TS *DVD*

Fred Astaire *Jervis Pendleton* • Leslie Caron *Julie* • Terry Moore *Linda* • Thelma Ritter *Miss Pritchard* • Fred Clark *Griggs* ■ *Dir* Jean Negulesco • *Scr* Phoebe Ephron, Henry Ephron, from the novel and play by Jean Webster • *Music/lyrics* Johnny Mercer

Daddy-O ★ PG
Musical drama   1959 · US · Colour · 70min

Here's an early embarrassment in the career of composer John Williams: a cheap and awful slice of teen schlock, its catchpenny title derived from then-contemporary slang. The negligible plot follows truck driver Dick Contino as he fights hoodlums and smashes a drugs ring, all the while singing forgettable tunes. This was already dated when it was made. TS *DVD*

Dick Contino *Phil Sandifer* • Sandra Giles *Jana Ryan* • Bruno VeSota *Sidney Chillas* • Gloria Victor *Marcia* • Ron McNeil *Duke* • *Dir* Lou Place • *Scr* David Moessinger

Daddy's Dyin'... Who's Got the Will? ★★★ 15
Comedy drama   1990 · US · Colour · 92min

Every now and then a director has to concede defeat and admit that a play with crackling dialogue and eccentric characters can get by without cinematic flourishes. Jack Fisk makes all the right choices in this adaptation of Del Shores's hit play and the result is an often hilarious comedy of dysfunctional family life. Beau Bridges has rarely been better as a loudmouth, bullying his chalk-and-cheese sisters, who are played to perfection by Amy Wright, Tess Harper and Beverly D'Angelo. DP Swearing, drug abuse.

Beau Bridges *Orville Turnover* • Beverly D'Angelo *Evalita Turnover* • Tess Harper *Sara Lee* • Judge Reinhold *Harmony* • Amy Wright *Lurlene* • Patrika Darbo *Marlene Turnover* • Bert Remsen *Buford Turnover* • Molly McClure *Mama Wheelis* • Keith Carradine *Clarence* • Newell Alexander *Sid Cranford* ■ *Dir* Jack Fisk • *Scr* Del Shores, from his play

Daddy's Gone A-Hunting ★★
Thriller   1969 · US · Colour · 107min

As both editor and director for ace horror producer Val Lewton, you would have expected Mark Robson to have made a better fist of this chiller. The thrills he concentrates on, however, are those of a sexual, rather than a suspenseful, nature and so the action is not as tense as it should be. Still, there are a couple of black comic touches, and Scott Hylands is convincingly deranged as he seeks revenge on Carol White for the abortion she kept secret from him. DP Swearing.

Carol White *Cathy Palmer* • Scott Hylands *Kenneth Daly* • Paul Burke *Jack Byrnes* • Mala Powers *Meg Stone* • Rachel Ames *Dr Parkington's nurse* • Barry Cahill *FBI agent Crosley* • James Sikking [James B Sikking] *FBI Agent Menchell* ■ *Dir* Mark Robson • *Scr* Lorenzo Semple Jr, Larry Cohen

Daddy's Home ★★ 12
Comedy   2015 · US · Colour · 95min

They got on like a house on fire in *The Other Guys*, but Will Ferrell and Mark Wahlberg only kindle a few lukewarm laughs in this comedy. Ferrell is the gawky suburban stepdad who does little except look on in envy when the children's biological father, Wahlberg, rolls back into town. Ferrell's funniest characters have a little bit of guile and a lot of pomp to balance out the idiocy, but there's no fun in laughing at a character this pathetic, while Wahlberg is never more irritating than in the saccharine finale. SP Some swearing, sexual references. *DVD* (Blu-ray)

Will Ferrell *Brad* • Mark Wahlberg *Dusty* • Linda Cardellini *Sarah* • Thomas Haden Church *Leo* ■ *Dir* Sean Anders • *Scr* John Morris (2), Brian Burns, Sean Anders, from a story by Burns

Dad's Army ★★★ U
Comedy   1971 · UK · Colour · 90min

Dad's Army remains one of the best loved of all British comedy series. As with so many other TV spin-offs, the producers couldn't resist tinkering with the winning formula, and here we are treated to a Nazi invasion of Walmington-on-Sea that is somewhat at odds with the cosy incompetence that made the series so irresistible. But this is still great fun and it's always a pleasure to see such gifted character actors at work. DP *DVD*

Arthur Lowe *Captain Mainwaring* • John Le Mesurier *Sergeant Wilson* • Clive Dunn *Corporal Jones* • John Laurie *Private Frazer* • James Beck *Private Walker* • Arnold Ridley *Private Godfrey* • Ian Lavender *Private Pike* • Liz Fraser *Mrs Pike* • Bernard Archard *General Fuller* • Derek Newark *RSM* • Bill Pertwee *Hodges* • Frank Williams *Vicar* • Edward Sinclair *Verger* • Anthony Sager *Police sergeant* • Pat Coombs *Mrs Hall* ■ *Dir* Norman Cohen • *Scr* Jimmy Perry, David Croft, from their TV series

Dad's Army ★★★ PG
Wartime comedy   2016 · UK · Colour · 95min

Director Oliver Parker revives another iconic comedy series following his reboot of the *St Trinian's* franchise in 2007. Here, he takes command of the second big-screen outing for the BBC's beloved Home Guard warhorse, in which Toby Jones's deluded Captain Mainwaring and Michael Gambon's smiley Private Godfrey are the standouts in an impressive parade of British character actors. It's an all-out laugh attack, expanding the action from parochial intrigue to espionage and actual conflict. Annette Crosbie and Julia Foster are a delight as Godfrey's sisters but, while the new *Dad's Army* is celebratory in tone, not all the gags/plotlines honour the spirit of the series. MB Swearing, violence. *DVD* (Blu-ray)

Toby Jones *Captain Mainwaring* • Bill Nighy *Sergeant Wilson* • Catherine Zeta-Jones *Rose Winters* • Michael Gambon *Private Godfrey* • Tom Courtenay *Lance Corporal Jones* • Bill Paterson *Private Fraser* • Daniel Mays *Private Walker* • Blake Harrison *Private Pike* • Sarah Lancashire *Mrs Pike* • Alison Steadman *Mrs Fox* • Mark Gatiss *Colonel Theakes* • Ian Lavender *Brigadier Pritchard* ■ *Dir* Oliver Parker • *Scr* Hamish McColl, from the TV series by Jimmy Perry, David Croft • *Cinematographer* Christopher Ross

Daens ★★★★ 15
Biographical period drama
1992 · Bel/Fr/Neth · Colour · 132min

This is an Oscar-nominated journey through the life and hard times of a 19th-century Catholic priest in Flanders, who took on a political role in order to speak up for the downtrodden mill workers in the textile town of Aalst. The struggle between Father Adolf Daens and the establishment is spelled out in simple, didactic fashion. But the growling performance of Jan Decleir, as Daens, and a narrative anger that threatens immediate revolution help to turn this into something to savour. TH Flemish +subtitles.

Jan Decleir *Adolf Daens* • Gérard Desarthe *Charles Woeste* • Antje De Boeck *Nette Scholliers* • Michael Pas *Jan De Meeter* ■ *Dir* Stijn Coninx • *Scr* François Chevallier, Stijn Coninx, from the novel *Pieter Daens* by Louis Paul Boon

Daffy Duck's Movie: Fantastic Island ★★★ U
Animated compilation
1983 · US · Colour · 74min

Directed by the legendary Friz Freleng and with voices by the great Mel Blanc, this is yet another collection of old Warner Bros cartoons combined and released under a new title. It's a veritable Who's Who of *Looney Tunes/Merrie Melodie* favourites, with Sylvester and Tweety, Yosemite Sam (as a pirate), Foghorn Leghorn, Pepe LePew and Speedy Gonzales all putting in an appearance. However, there's the odd classic tucked away here, notably *Mutiny on the Bunny*, starring Bugs himself. DP

Mel Blanc • June Foray • Les Tremayne ■ *Dir* Friz Freleng • *Scr* John Dunn, David Detiege, Friz Freleng

Daffy Duck's Quackbusters ★★★ U
Animated compilation
1988 · US · Colour · 75min

Disney is the undoubted master of the animated feature, but when it comes to the five-minute cartoon, however, Warner Bros clearly has the edge. The best thing about compilation films like this one is that each component is a classic in its own right. In this neat spoof of *Ghostbusters*, Daffy, Bugs Bunny and Porky Pig join forces to rid the world of spooks. Younger viewers might not get all the subtle references to classic horror films, but *The Night of the Living Duck* and *The Duxorcist* are hilarious. DP

Mel Blanc • Roy Firestone • BJ Ward ■ *Dir* Greg Ford, Terry Lennon

Dahmer ★★ 15
Biographical crime drama
2002 · US · Colour · 97min

Exploring the adult life and motivations of notorious 1990s American serial killer Jeffrey Dahmer, David Jacobson avoids sensationalising the gruesome events that cost many young men their lives. He endeavours to rationalise Dahmer's deeds by balancing brief physical violence with the psychological turmoil that allegedly preceded it, but it's made less effective by Jeremy Renner's insipid central performance. SF Swearing, nudity. *DVD*

Jeremy Renner *Jeffrey Dahmer* • Bruce Davison *Lionel Dahmer* • Artel Kayaru *Rodney* • Matt Newton *Lance Bell* • Dion Basco *Khamtay* • Kate Williamson *Grandma* ■ *Dir/Scr* David Jacobson

Daisies ★★★★ 15
Comedy   1966 · Cz · Colour · 72min

The two most significant female artists of the Czech New Wave collaborated on this anarchic assault on materialism. In addition to designing the stylised visuals, Ester Krumbachova co-wrote the screenplay with director Vera Chytilova, whose husband, Jaroslav Kucera, served as cinematographer. Employing collage, superimposition, symbolic *mise en scène* and prismatic distortion, they concoct a surrealist fantasy of the banality and conformity of Czech society as two girls, both named Marie, dupe several boorish males before indulging in an orgy of gleeful destruction. DP Czech +subtitles. *DVD*

Jitka Cerhova *Marie I* • Ivana Karbonova *Marie II* ■ *Dir* Vera Chytilova • *Scr* Vera Chytilova, Ester Krumbachova

The Daisy Chain ★★
Horror thriller   2008 · Ire/UK · Colour · 89min

The wilds of Ireland provide an imposing and suitably bleak backdrop for this otherwise uninspiring twist on the "evil kid" movie. Combined with a mournful score, they alone give the slow and predictable horror thriller its atmosphere, as bland couple Samantha Morton and Steven Mackintosh become embroiled in a series of strange occurrences after taking in a troubled local orphan (impressive youngster Mhairi Anderson) who's believed to be a fairy changeling. SF

Samantha Morton *Martha Conroy* • Steven Mackintosh *Tomas Conroy* • Mhairi Anderson *Daisy Gahan* • David Bradley (2) *Sean Cryan* ■ *Dir* Aisling Walsh • *Scr* Lauren Mackenzie

Daisy Kenyon ★★★★
Romantic melodrama   1947 · US · BW · 98min

Beginning with *Laura*, director Otto Preminger served up a dark and sinister series of movies throughout the 1940s, today labelled *film noir* but then just called thrillers. They're really melodramas at heart, served up with all the seaminess the censors and 20th Century-Fox would allow, and hold up well today as a consistently fine body of work. Here, Joan Crawford is Daisy, torn between Dana Andrews and Henry Fonda. There's also a surprisingly daring (for its day) subplot about child abuse. TS

Joan Crawford *Daisy Kenyon* • Dana Andrews *Dan O'Mara* • Henry Fonda *Peter* • Ruth Warrick *Lucile O'Mara* • Martha Stewart *Mary Angelus* • Peggy Ann Garner *Rosamund* • John Garfield

U SUITABLE FOR ALL   Ua SUITABLE ESPECIALLY FOR YOUNG CHILDREN (DVD ONLY)   PG PARENTAL GUIDANCE   12A UNDER 12s TO BE ACCOMPANIED (CINEMA ONLY)

Man in restaurant ■ *Dir* Otto Preminger • *Scr* David Hertz, from the novel by Elizabeth Janeway

Daisy Miller ★★★ U
Period drama 1974 · US · Colour · 87min

One of the key themes of Henry James's writings was the clash between American and European culture. So it's fascinating to watch a story in which surface actions are almost irrelevant being related by a director steeped in the storytelling traditions of John Ford and Howard Hawks. Peter Bogdanovich captures the styles, the manners and the atmosphere of late 19th-century Italy, but never comes close to conveying the inner life of the characters. The director was criticised for casting then-girlfriend Cybill Shepherd in the title role, and this marked the beginning of her decline. DP *DVD*

Cybill Shepherd *Annie P "Daisy" Miller* • Barry Brown *Frederick Winterbourne* • Cloris Leachman *Mrs Ezra B Miller* • Mildred Natwick *Mrs Costello* • Eileen Brennan *Mrs Walker* • Duilio Del Prete *Mr Giovanelli* • James McMurtry *Randolph C Miller* • Nicholas Jones *Charles* ■ *Dir* Peter Bogdanovich • *Scr* Frederic Raphael, from the novel by Henry James

Dakota ★★ PG
Western 1945 · US · BW · 81min

Big John Wayne found himself working out his Republic contract in this western directed by a studio hack, which despite a strong support cast, is fairly typical of that minor studio's output. Wayne rides to the rescue of farmers whose valuable land is targeted by crooks, but his heart doesn't seem to be in it. TS

John Wayne *John Devlin* • Vera Hruba Ralston [Vera Ralston] *Sandy* • Walter Brennan *Captain Bounce* • Ward Bond *Jim Bender* • Ona Munson *"Jersey" Thomas* • Hugo Haas *Marko Poli* ■ *Dir* Joseph Kane • *Scr* Lawrence Hazard, Howard Estabrook, from a story by Carl Foreman

Dakota ★★ U
Drama 1988 · US · Colour · 91min

Lou Diamond Phillips plays a teenager on the run, with all the usual adolescent hang-ups, who gets to grips with his life while working on a Texas ranch. Phillips smoulders away effectively enough and there are good supporting turns from a largely unknown cast, while Fred Holmes handles the directorial chores with some skill. JF

Lou Diamond Phillips *Dakota* • Eli Cummins *Walt* • DeeDee Norton *Molly* ■ *Dir* Fred Holmes • *Scr* Darryl Kuntz, Sara Lynn Kuntz

Dakota Incident ★ U
Western 1956 · US · Colour · 88min

A dire western, this has an adequate cast – headed by Dale Robertson and Linda Darnell – hamstrung by pretentious dialogue and fuzzy characterisations. After interminable scenes in town setting up these boring characters, they set off on the stage to be attacked by Cheyenne Indians, but this only leads to more excessive gabbing after the group takes cover in a dry waterhole. AE

Dale Robertson *John Banner* • Linda Darnell *Amy Clarke* • John Lund *Carter Hamilton* • Ward Bond *Senator Blakely* ■ *Dir* Lewis R Foster • *Scr* Frederic Louis Fox

Daleks – Invasion Earth 2150 AD ★★★ U
Science-fiction adventure 1966 · UK · Colour · 80min

The second feature (after 1965's *Doctor Who and the Daleks*) starring Peter Cushing as the Doctor has the BBC's world-famous Time Lord aiding human survivors in their future guerrilla war against the diabolical Daleks. *Independence Day* it's not, but director Gordon Flemyng keeps the colourful action moving swiftly along to cheerful effect. Through all the mindless mayhem roll the impressive Daleks, one of science fiction's greatest creations. AJ *DVD* Blu-ray

Peter Cushing *Doctor Who* • Bernard Cribbins *Tom Campbell* • Ray Brooks *David* • Jill Curzon *Louise* • Roberta Tovey *Susan* • Andrew Keir *Wyler* • Godfrey Quigley *Dortmun* ■ *Dir* Gordon Flemyng • *Scr* Milton Subotsky

Dallas ★★ PG
Western 1950 · US · Colour · 90min

Before his Oscar-winning role in *High Noon*, Gary Cooper's career was heading for the doldrums. Ageing and thought to be past his prime, he had become hard to cast. In this very average Warner Bros western, Coop has little to do as a former Confederate officer seeking revenge by pretending to be a lawman, and looks uncomfortable doing it. TS

Gary Cooper *Blayde "Reb" Hollister* • Ruth Roman *Tonia Robles* • Steve Cochran *Bryant Marlow* • Raymond Massey *Will Marlow* • Barbara Payton *Flo* • Leif Erickson *Martin Weatherby* • Antonio Moreno *Felipe* • Jerome Cowan *Matt Coulter* • Reed Hadley *Wild Bill Hickok* ■ *Dir* Stuart Heisler • *Scr* John Twist, from his story

Dallas Buyers Club ★★★★ 15
Drama based on a true story 2013 · US · Colour · 111min

Featuring a superb central performance by Matthew McConaughey, this fact-based tale takes a refreshingly unsentimental view of the 1980s Aids crisis. McConaughey plays Ron Woodroof, a fast-living Texas redneck who becomes infected after a fling with a junkie. When he realises that his hospital treatment isn't helping, Woodroof begins a series of schemes to bring alternative medicines to his fellow patients. Director Jean-Marc Vallée smartly keeps things low-key and subtle, allowing Woodruff to blossom quite plausibly from a racist homophobe into a noble civil-rights crusader, aided in his cause by Jared Leto's fragile transsexual. DW Swearing, sexual references, nudity, drug abuse. *DVD* Blu-ray

Matthew McConaughey *Ron Woodroof* • Jennifer Garner *Dr Eve Saks* • Jared Leto *Rayon* • Denis O'Hare *Dr Sevard* • Steve Zahn *Tucker* ■ *Dir* Jean-Marc Vallée • *Scr* Craig Borten, Melisa Wallack • *Editors* Martin Pensa, Jean-Marc Vallée

Dallas Doll ★★ 18
Comedy drama 1994 · US · Colour · 100min

Australian director Ann Turner came seriously unstuck with this comedy drama, an unacknowledged reworking of Pier Paolo Pasolini's 1968 classic *Theorem*. Sandra Bernhard stars as a golf guru who disrupts the ordinary life of a middle-class Sydney family by raising their expectations of life and fulfilling their sexual fantasies. Bernhard has none of the mystery and charm Terence Stamp brought to *Theorem* and is never allowed to go into her customary overdrive. DP

Sandra Bernhard *Dallas Adair* • Victoria Longley *Rosalind* • Frank Gellacher *Stephen* • Jake Blundell *Charlie* • Rose Byrne *Rastus* • Jonathan Leahy *Eddy* • Douglas Hedge *Mayor Tonkin* • Melissa Thomas *Margaret* • Elaine Lee *Mrs Winthrop* • Alethea McGrath *Aunt Mary* • John Frawley *Mr Fellowes* • Roy Billing *Dave Harry* ■ *Dir/Scr* Ann Turner

The Daltons Ride Again ★★
Western 1945 · US · BW · 72min

Five years after *When the Daltons Rode*, here they are again in a virtual remake. This time, though, it's a resolutely B-grade cast taking over from Randolph Scott and co, with the four outlaw brothers being played by Alan Curtis, Kent Taylor, Lon Chaney Jr and Noah Beery Jr. The quartet wreak havoc throughout Kansas before the all-action climactic bank raid. Efficient enough entertainment. TS

Alan Curtis *Emmett Dalton* • Kent Taylor *Bob Dalton* • Lon Chaney Jr *Grat Dalton* • Noah Beery Jr *Ben Dalton* • Martha O'Driscoll *Mary* • Jess Barker *Jeff* • Thomas Gomez *McKenna* ■ *Dir* Ray Taylor • *Scr* Roy Chanslor, Paul Gangelin, Henry Blankfort

The Dam Busters ★★★★★ U
Classic Second World War drama 1954 · UK · BW · 119min

This thrilling drama about the bouncing-bomb raid on the dams of the Ruhr valley is truly compelling viewing and stands among the best British movies about the Second World War. Indeed, thanks to its potent blend of scientific suspense and aerial action, accompanied by that stirring soundtrack, it has convinced generations of movie-watchers that the mission was a major turning point in the war rather than a risky venture that the brass hats considered something of a sideshow. Michael Redgrave puts a pinch too much bumbling boffin into his Barnes Wallis, but Richard Todd was never better as Wing Commander Guy Gibson, who led the raid. DP *DVD* Blu-ray

Richard Todd *Wing Commander Guy Gibson* • Michael Redgrave *Dr Barnes N Wallis* • Ursula Jeans *Mrs Wallis* • Basil Sydney *Sir Arthur Harris* • Patrick Barr *Captain Joseph Summers* • Ernest Clark *AVM Ralph Cochrane* • Derek Farr *Group Captain Whitworth* • Charles Carson *Doctor* • Stanley Van Beers *Sir David Pye* • Colin Tapley *Dr WH Glanville* • John Fraser *Flight Lieutenant Hopgood* • George Baker *Flight Lieutenant Maltby* • Robert Shaw *Flight Sergeant Pulford* ■ *Dir* Michael Anderson • *Scr* RC Sherriff, from the non-fiction book *The Dam Busters* by Paul Brickhill, from the story *Enemy Coast Ahead* by Wing Commander Guy Gibson

Damage ★★★ 18
Erotic drama 1992 · UK/Fr · Colour · 111min

Louis Malle, directing his first English-language film since his return from America to France, employs an almost leisurely (but always exact) camera to highlight the emotional centre of this traumatic tale. Taken from Josephine Hart's bestseller by scriptwriter David Hare, the explosion of emotion is muted by moments of implausibility, caused by some widely varying acting styles. Whereas Miranda Richardson crumbles believably as the spurned wife, Juliette Binoche, as the object of an MP's lust, simply pouts seductively, while Jeremy Irons, as the politician, spends too much time behaving like a startled rabbit. JM Swearing, sex scenes, nudity. *DVD*

Jeremy Irons *Stephen Fleming* • Juliette Binoche *Anna Barton* • Miranda Richardson *Ingrid Fleming* • Rupert Graves *Martyn Fleming* • Leslie Caron *Elizabeth Prideaux* • Ian Bannen *Edward Lloyd* • Gemma Clarke *Sally Fleming* • Peter Stormare *Peter* • Julian Fellowes *Donald Lindsay* ■ *Dir* Louis Malle • *Scr* David Hare, from the novel by Josephine Hart

Dames ★★★
Musical comedy 1934 · US · BW · 91min

This is a super Depression-era musical, with wonderfully kaleidoscopic choreography from maestro Busby Berkeley. The dialogue is as witty as ever, but the blackmail-cum-putting-on-a-show storyline is contrived, and the whole lacks the dazzle of stablemates *42nd Street* and the first two Berkeley *Gold Diggers*. No matter – the production numbers are sensational, and the cast, featuring witty Joan Blondell and wacky ZaSu Pitts, is compulsively watchable. TS

Joan Blondell *Mabel Anderson* • Dick Powell *Jimmy Higgens* • Ruby Keeler *Barbara Hemingway* • ZaSu Pitts *Mathilda Hemingway* • Hugh Herbert *Ezra Ounce* • Guy Kibbee *Horace* • Arthur Vinton *Bulger* • Phil Regan *Jimmy Harris* • Busby Berkeley *Choreography* ■ *Dir* Ray Enright • *Scr* Delmer Daves, from a story by Robert Lord, Delmer Daves

Les Dames du Bois de Boulogne ★★★★★ PG
Drama 1946 · Fr · BW · 81min

Robert Bresson's second feature, his last to use professional actors and be filmed in a studio, takes an anecdote from Diderot's *Jacques le Fataliste* and moves it to a 20th-century setting. When a man tells his girlfriend that he no longer loves her, she wreaks revenge by arranging a meeting between him and an ex-prostitute, only revealing her history after they marry. Jean Cocteau's screenplay brilliantly dissects the fable's ethical issues, while the director's austerity enhances the dramatic tension. RB French +subtitles. *DVD*

Paul Bernard *Jean* • Maria Casarès *Hélène* • Elina Labourdette *Agnès* • Lucienne Bogaert *Agnès's mother* • Jean Marchat *Jacques* ■ *Dir* Robert Bresson • *Scr* Robert Bresson, Jean Cocteau, from the novel *Jacques le Fataliste et Son Maître* by Denis Diderot

Damien – Omen II ★★★ 18
Horror 1978 · US · Colour · 102min

The Antichrist becomes an adolescent evil-doer in the second part of the satanic saga, which relies too openly on the same shock suspense tricks that made *The Omen* (1976) such a huge success. Here, Damien reads the Book of Revelation and discovers all about his true past. Don Taylor's direction is banal, but William Holden and Lee Grant handle their roles as Damien's marked foster parents with skill. The saga continued in 1980 with *The Final Conflict*. AJ Violence, swearing. *DVD* Blu-ray

William Holden (2) *Richard Thorn* • Lee Grant *Ann Thorn* • Jonathan Scott-Taylor *Damien Thorn* • Robert Foxworth *Paul Buher* • Nicholas Pryor *Charles Warren* • Lew Ayres *Bill Atherton* • Sylvia Sidney *Aunt Marion* • Lance Henriksen *Sergeant Neff* ■ *Dir* Don Taylor • *Scr* Stanley Mann, Michael Hodges, from characters by David Seltzer

Damn Yankees ★★★ U
Musical 1958 · US · Colour · 105min

After the success of *The Pajama Game*, Broadway's George Abbott and Hollywood's Stanley Donen teamed up again for this second show by the same writing team. Despite this talent, this time round the show didn't quite transfer, despite a supporting cast comprised entirely of the stage cast, and the retention of the original Bob Fosse choreography. The problem lies with Tab Hunter in the difficult leading role: to put it mildly, he lacks pizzazz. There's still a lot of fun to be gleaned, though: Gwen Verdon (Mrs Fosse) is a knockout, and Ray Walston is arguably the definitive movie Devil. TS

Tab Hunter *Joe Hardy* • Gwen Verdon *Lola* • Ray Walston *Applegate* • Russ Brown *Van Buren* • Shannon Bolin *Meg Boyd* • Nathaniel Frey *Smokey* • Jimmie Komack *Rocky* • Rae Allen *Gloria* • Robert Shafer *Joe Boyd* • Jean Stapleton *Sister* • Albert Linville *Vernon* • Bob Fosse *Mambo dancer* ■ *Dir* George Abbott, Stanley Donen • *Scr* George Abbott, from the play *Damn Yankees!* by Douglas Wallop, George Abbott, from the novel *The Year The Yankees Lost the Pennant* by Douglas Wallop

Damnation ★★★ 15
Drama 1988 · Hun · BW · 114min

Long after Gabor Medvigy's meandering monochrome images have faded, the unrelenting bleakness of Bela Tarr's study of an all-encompassing obsession will linger in the mind. Whether it's the sight of outcast Miklos B Szekely peering through the rain to watch his married lover (Vali Kerekes) singing at the Titanic Bar or the shocking finale, the film exercises a compulsion that is never diminished by its pessimism. This intense picture could almost be called an apocalyptic *noir*. DP Hungarian +subtitles. *DVD*

Miklos B Szekely *Karrer* • Vali Kerekes *The singer* ■ *Dir* Bela Tarr • *Scr* Bela Tarr, Laszlo Krasznahorkai

Damnation Alley ★ 12
Science-fiction adventure 1977 · US · Colour · 87min

An utterly pedestrian adaptation of Roger Zelazny's much-admired novel, this takes place after a nuclear holocaust and features psychedelic visual effects that are really quite awful. Five survivors cross America in a futuristic tank driven by George Peppard, looking for others after receiving mystery radio signals. Lacklustre acting, tedious exposition and laughable rubber monsters damn this regrettable misfire. AJ Violence, swearing. *DVD*

Jan-Michael Vincent *Tanner* • George Peppard *Denton* • Dominique Sanda *Janice* • Paul Winfield *Keegan* • Jackie Earle Haley *Billy* ■ *Dir* Jack Smight • *Scr* Alan Sharp, Lukas Heller, from the novel by Roger Zelazny

The Damned ★★12

Science-fiction thriller   1961 · UK · BW · 91min

A downbeat financial disaster from Hammer, this clearly reflects the troubled shoot, the creative differences between director Joseph Losey and the cost-conscious House of Horror, and the delayed release in butchered form. While on holiday in Weymouth, and after being mugged by biker gang leader Oliver Reed, American boat owner Macdonald Carey stumbles on a secret government programme in which radioactive children are being schooled to repopulate the planet after a nuclear war. The plot never really fuses to create the powerful Orwellian fable the film was once acclaimed as. AJ *DVD*

Macdonald Carey *Simon Wells* • Shirley Anne Field *Joan* • Viveca Lindfors *Freya Nelson* • Alexander Knox *Bernard* • Oliver Reed *King* • Walter Gotell *Major Holland* • Brian Oulton *Mr Dingle* • Kenneth Cope *Sid* ■ *Dir* Joseph Losey • *Scr* Evan Jones, from the novel *The Children of Light* by HL Lawrence

The Damned ★★★★18

Period drama   1969 · It/W Ger · Colour · 146min

The rise of fascism in the 1930s is mirrored by the antics of an upper-class German family (clearly based on the real-life Krupps) in director Luchino Visconti's Wagnerian-style drama. Dirk Bogarde plays the general manager of an armaments factory who becomes embroiled in a power struggle as his employers, the Essenbecks, murder and blackmail each other for the ownership of the company. Bogarde turns in an accomplished performance, while Helmut Berger is also excellent as the son who rapes his mother, setting in motion a series of events that lead to tragedy. Condemned by some as ponderous, this is still remarkable. TH Italian dubbed. Violence, sex scenes. *DVD*

Dirk Bogarde *Friedrich Bruckmann* • Ingrid Thulin *Baroness Sophie von Essenbeck* • Helmut Griem *Aschenbach* • Helmut Berger *Martin von Essenbeck* • Charlotte Rampling *Elisabeth Thallman* ■ *Dir* Luchino Visconti • *Scr* Luchino Visconti, Nicola Badalucco, Enrico Medioli • *Cinematographers* Pasqualino De Santis, Armando Nannuzzi

The Damned Don't Cry ★★★PG

Crime drama   1950 · US · BW · 98min

This is a splendidly titled but resolutely low-rent Joan Crawford vehicle, despite the production values of Warner Bros. It's a steamy crime drama, in which director Vincent Sherman fails to rein in Crawford's excesses. She chews the scenery and her men as only she can, but is as splendid as ever, but the males (colourless David Brian, mean Steve Cochran, bland Kent Smith) are rather a let down. TS *DVD*

Joan Crawford *Ethel Whitehead* • David Brian *George Castleman* • Steve Cochran *Nick Prenta* • Kent Smith *Martin Blackford* • Hugh Sanders *Grady* • Selena Royle *Patricia Longworth* ■ *Dir* Vincent Sherman • *Scr* Harold Medford, Jerome Weidman, from a story by Gertrude Walker

Damned River ★18

Action adventure   1989 · US · Colour · 91min

This crude exploitation effort is directed by Michael Schroeder, who made his directing debut with the funny *Out of the Dark*. This second effort about a bunch of young Americans shooting the rapids in Zimbabwe isn't up to par, being a rip-off of *Deliverance*. AT

Stephen Shellen *Ray* • Lisa Aliff *Anne* • John Terlesky *Carl* • Marc Poppel *Luke* • Bradford Bancroft *Jerry* • Louis Van Niekerk *Von Hoenigen* ■ *Dir* Michael Schroeder, John Crowther • *Scr* Bayard Johnson

The Damned United ★★★★15

Sports drama   2009 · UK/US · Colour · 93min

Director Tom Hooper gleefully re-creates the hairy, fag-smoking, pre-Premiership days of English club football in telling the story of manager Brian Clough's unhappy 44-day tenure at Leeds United in 1974. Michael Sheen follows up *Frost/Nixon* with another pitch-perfect performance, showing how the arrogant, outspoken, grudge-fuelled Clough tried to take on the club, its players, fans and revered former manager Don Revie (a well-cast Colm Meaney). In adapting David Peace's dense novel, Peter Morgan (*The Queen*) lightens the tone and (mercifully) keeps the footballing action to a minimum, focusing on what happens in the dugout, the boardroom and behind the weatherbeaten façade of Elland Road. AC Swearing. *DVD* *Blu-ray*

Michael Sheen *Brian Clough* • Timothy Spall *Peter Taylor* • Colm Meaney *Don Revie* • Jim Broadbent *Sam Longson* • Stephen Graham *Billy Bremner* • Peter McDonald *Johnny Giles* ■ *Dir* Tom Hooper • *Scr* Peter Morgan, from the novel by David Peace

A Damsel in Distress ★★★U

Musical comedy   1937 · US · BW · 100min

Adapted by PG Wodehouse from a play that was based on his own novel, this was Fred Astaire's second film without Ginger Rogers. But he's in sparkling form as a dance star attempting to trip the light fantastic with aristocratic Joan Fontaine. Hermes Pan's choreography won an Oscar, but every step is pure Astaire, and Fontaine (who was better known as a dramatic actress) never misses a beat. George Burns and Gracie Allen show why they are so fondly remembered. DP *DVD*

Fred Astaire *Jerry Halliday* • George Burns • Gracie Allen • Joan Fontaine *Lady Alyce Marshmorton* • Reginald Gardiner *Keggs* • Ray Noble *Reggie* • Constance Collier *Lady Caroline Marshmorton* • Montagu Love *Lord John Marshmorton* ■ *Dir* George Stevens • *Scr* PG Wodehouse, SK Lauren, Ernest Pagano, from a play by PG Wodehouse, Ian Hay, from a novel by PG Wodehouse

Damsels in Distress ★★★12

Comedy   2011 · US · Colour · 95min

Female students at an Ivy League college take it upon themselves to save their colleagues from depression and falling standards of decorum in this comedy of manners, which marks the return of writer/director Whit Stillman (*Metropolitan*) after a 13-year hiatus. Setting the agenda is the domineering Violet (Greta Gerwig), whose forthright opinions are far from conventional. But does she have the right to organise everyone else's love lives when her own relationships are far from perfect? With its ever-so-elegant dialogue and squeaky-clean surroundings, this is light years away from the usual raunchy frat-house frolics. The result is an undeniably witty and intelligent affair. TJ *DVD*

Greta Gerwig *Violet Wister* • Adam Brody *Charlie* • Analeigh Tipton *Lily* • Megalyn Echikunwoke *Rose* • Carrie MacLemore *Heather* • Hugo Becker *Xavier* ■ *Dir/Scr* Whit Stillman

Dan Candy's Law ★★★

Historical western   1973 · Can · Colour · 90min

Donald Sutherland shines as Dan Candy, the rangy Mountie who always gets his man. This is based on the true story of Almighty Voice (Gordon Tootoosis), a Cree Indian fugitive who evaded the Canadian Mounties for more than a year. The plot may not be up to much, but it's most interesting as a chance to see how conflict between white police and native American Indians was dealt with back in the 1970s and for Claude Fournier's stunning photography, evoking the brutality of the rugged Canadian landscape. FL

Donald Sutherland *Sgt Dan Candy* • Kevin McCarthy *Sgt Malcolm Grant* • Chief Dan George *Sounding Sky* • Gordon Tootoosis *Almighty Voice* ■ *Dir* Claude Fournier • *Scr* George Malko

Dan in Real Life ★★★★PG

Romantic comedy drama   2007 · US · Colour · 94min

Steve Carell and Juliette Binoche make an unlikely romantic pairing in this uplifting comedy drama from director Peter Hedges. Dan (Carell) is a middle-aged widower bringing up three daughters, while writing a family advice column for a city newspaper. They all think he's resigned to being single forever until a chance meeting in a bookshop with the alluring Marie (Binoche). But as luck would have it, Marie is already involved with Dan's brother Mitch (Dane Cook), leaving Dan to sweep his new-found love under the carpet during a boisterous get-together at his parents' house. Milking the socially awkward set-up for tears as well as laughs, Hedges delivers a tender delight. Of course, nothing here bears much relation to "real life"; instead, it's a genteel fantasy about love, second chances and the healing power of family. JR *DVD* *SD*

Steve Carell *Dan Burns* • Juliette Binoche *Marie* • Dane Cook *Mitch Burns* • John Mahoney *Poppy Burns* • Emily Blunt *Ruthie Draper* • Dianne Wiest *Nana Burns* • Norbert Leo Butz *Clay Burns* • Alison Pill *Jane Burns* ■ *Dir* Peter Hedges • *Scr* Peter Hedges, Pierce Gardner • *Cinematographer* Lawrence Sher

Dance Flick ★★★15

Spoof comedy   2009 · US · Colour · 84min

With their *Scary Movie* franchise well established, the Wayans family has cut a thin if inventive groove in the parody genre. This well-produced debut feature from Damien Dante Wayans spoofs the likes of *High School Musical*, *Fame* and other teen dance films. The familiar plot follows a young interracial couple (Damon Wayans Jr and Shoshana Bush) as they join forces to win a dance competition, providing the excuse for a series of film and TV in-jokes that are high on comic invention if rather low on taste. It's silly, smart and confident, but those who act their age, and not their shoe size, may not get it. KK Swearing, sexual references. *DVD*

Damon Wayans Jr *Thomas* • Shoshana Bush *Megan* • Affion Crockett *A-Con* • Craig Wayans *Truck* • Essence Atkins *Charity* • Amy Sedaris *Ms Cameltoe* • Shawn Wayans *Baby Daddy* • Marlon Wayans *Mr Moody* ■ *Dir* Damien Dante Wayans [Damien Wayans] • *Scr* Damien Dante Wayans, Keenen Ivory Wayans, Shawn Wayans, Marlon Wayans, Craig Wayans

Dance, Fools, Dance ★★★

Crime drama   1931 · US · BW · 81min

Joan Crawford - young, bright-eyed and light years away from the monster image for which she is more familiar - stars in this Depression-era drama as the spoilt daughter of a stockbroker who loses everything when the market crashes. Left with nothing, Crawford becomes a cub reporter and goes undercover to investigate bootlegging gangster Clark Gable. Tightly directed by Harry Beaumont, this is compact, suspenseful and entertaining. RK

Joan Crawford *Bonnie Jordan* • Lester Vail *Bob Townsend* • Cliff Edwards *Bert Scranton* • William Bakewell *Rodney Jordan* • William Holden (1) *Stanley Jordan* • Clark Gable *Jake Luva* • Earle Foxe *Wally Baxter* ■ *Dir* Harry Beaumont • *Scr* Aurania Rouverol, Richard Schayer, from a story by Aurania Rouverol

Dance, Girl, Dance ★★

Musical   1940 · US · BW · 89min

Lucille Ball and Maureen O'Hara are ambitious chorus girls in Maria Ouspenskaya's dance troupe. While O'Hara aspires to being a classical ballerina, Ball is happy to become a successful stripper. Both are in love with Louis Hayward. Pioneering female director Dorothy Arzner, who took over at short notice after filming commenced, does her best with an inadequate script and a miscast O'Hara; she

manages to bring the film to life from time to time - usually when Ball is on screen. RK

Lucille Ball *Bubbles* • Maureen O'Hara *Judy* • Louis Hayward *Jimmy Harris* • Ralph Bellamy *Steve Adams* • Virginia Field *Elinor Harris* • Maria Ouspenskaya *Madame Basilova* • Mary Carlisle *Sally* • Katherine Alexander *Miss Olmstead* • Edward Brophy *Dwarfie* ■ *Dir* Dorothy Arzner • *Scr* Tess Slesinger, Frank Davis, from a story by Vicki Baum

Dance Hall ★★PG

Drama   1950 · UK · BW · 77min

Several of Ealing's biggest talents collaborated on this downbeat drama, which fully captures the sense of austerity that pervaded postwar Britain. With Alexander Mackendrick among the screenwriters, Douglas Slocombe behind the camera, Seth Holt at the editing desk and Michael Balcon producing, one can't question the film's pedigree. However, director Charles Crichton settles for too many caricatures in this story of four women who assert the independence they gained doing war work. DP *DVD*

Donald Houston *Phil* • Bonar Colleano *Alec* • Petula Clark *Georgie Wilson* • Natasha Parry *Eve* • Jane Hylton *Mary* • Diana Dors *Carol* • Gladys Henson *Mrs Wilson* • Sydney Tafler *Manager* • Douglas Barr (1) *Peter* • Kay Kendall *Doreen* • Eunice Gayson *Mona* • Dandy Nichols *Mrs Crabtree* ■ *Dir* Charles Crichton • *Scr* EVH Emmett, Diana Morgan, Alexander Mackendrick

Dance Little Lady ★★U

Drama   1954 · UK · Colour · 84min

Terence Morgan made something of a habit of being horrid to little Mandy Miller on screen in the mid-1950s. He was her father in *Mandy*, the moving Ealing drama about deafness, and here he is the unscrupulous stage father who is determined to see her name in lights. The dance sequences are fine, but the poor production values ruin the look of the film. DP *DVD*

Terence Morgan *Mack Gordon* • Mai Zetterling *Nina Gordon* • Guy Rolfe *Dr John Ransome* • Mandy Miller (1) *Jill Gordon* • Eunice Gayson *Adele* • Reginald Beckwith *Poldi* • Ina De La Haye *Madame Bayanova* • Harold Lang *Mr Bridson* • Richard O'Sullivan *Peter* • Jane Aird *Mary* ■ *Dir* Val Guest • *Scr* Val Guest, Doreen Montgomery, from a story by R Howard Alexander, Alfred Dunning

Dance Me Outside ★★★

Drama   1994 · US/Can · Colour · 84min

Thankfully avoiding the cinematic clichés of the past about native North Americans, this movie examines their lives in a contemporary context with seriousness and wit. Ryan Rajendra Black and Adam Beach are the young men on a Canadian reservation constantly diverted from fulfilling their ambitions by booze and drugs, while the racist killer of a dance-hall girl gets off with a light sentence, angering the community. The mix of quirky humour and sententious drama doesn't always blend, but this look at a nation within a nation still has power. TH Violence, swearing.

Ryan Rajendra Black *Silas Crow* • Adam Beach *Frank Fencepost* • Jennifer Podemski *Sadie Maracle* • Michael Greyeyes *Gooch* • Lisa Lacroix [Lisa LaCroix] *Illiana* • Kevin Hicks *Robert McVay* • Rose Marie Trudeau *Ma Crow* ■ *Dir* Bruce McDonald • *Scr* Bruce McDonald, Don McKellar, John Frizzell, from the novel by WP Kinsella

The Dance of Death ★★

Drama   1969 · UK · Colour · 148min

One of Sir Laurence Olivier's last stage performances is captured on film in this static version of the National Theatre production of August Strindberg's classic play. Cantankerous sea captain Olivier and wife Geraldine McEwan continuously bicker on their island home and turn what's left of their marriage into a war zone. As a record of Olivier's mesmerising stagecraft, it's a must. As a film, though, it's a torpid bore, with the camera placed in one position throughout the angst-ridden action. AJ

Laurence Olivier *Edgar* • Geraldine McEwan *Alice* • Robert Lang *Kurt* • Janina Faye *Judith* • Malcolm Reynolds *Allan* • Carolyn Jones *Jenny* • Maggie Riley *Kristin* ■ *Dir* David Giles • *Scr* CD Locock, from the play by August Strindberg

The Dance of Reality
★★★★ 18

Biographical drama 2013 · Chil · Colour · 132min

Alejandro Jodorowsky (director of quintessential 1970 cult flick *El Topo*) returns to his childhood in 1930s Chile for this striking semi-autobiographical drama. Shot in Tocopilla, the actual village of his youth, this surreal blend of truth and fantasy is a story of two halves – the first about the young Alejandro and the second following his martinet father, Jaime. It won't be to all tastes (graphic nudity, full-frontal urination) and is more hallucinatory memory book than straight autobiography, but what a journey it is. JA Spanish +subtitles. Violence, nudity.

Alexandro Jodorowsky *Alexandro as an adult* • Brontis Jodorowsky *Jaime* • Pamela Flores *Sara* • Jeremias Herskovits *Alexandro as a child* ■ *Dir/Scr* Alexandro Jodorowsky

Dance of the Dwarfs
★★

Horror action adventure
1983 · US/Phil · Colour · 93min

Anthropologist Deborah Raffin hires drunken loser helicopter pilot Peter Fonda to fly her in the jungle to find a missing scientist investigating reports of a lost tribe of pygmy reptile men. Ignore the unremarkable special effects and there are some acting sparks to enjoy between the mismatched couple, but this is generally cut-rate fare. AJ

Deborah Raffin *Dr Evelyn Howard* • Peter Fonda *Harry Bediker* • John Amos *Esteban* ■ *Dir* Gus Trikonis • *Scr* GW King, Larry H Johnson, Michael Viner, from the novel by Geoffrey Household

Dance with a Stranger
★★★★ 15

Biographical drama 1984 · UK · Colour · 96min

Miranda Richardson is incandescent as Soho nightclub hostess Ruth Ellis, the last woman to be hanged in Britain, in this absorbing, brutal account of the infamous 1955 murder case. Sticking closely to the facts about why she shot her aristocratic lover, racing driver David Blakely (Rupert Everett), this film from director Mike Newell has a great sense of period and strikes the exact balance between fascination and luridness. AJ Sex scenes, violence, swearing, nudity. *DVD*

Miranda Richardson *Ruth Ellis* • Rupert Everett *David Blakely* • Ian Holm *Desmond Cussen* • Matthew Carroll *Andy* • Tom Chadbon *Anthony Findlater* • Jane Bertish *Carole Findlater* • David Troughton *Cliff Davis* • Paul Mooney *Clive Gunnel* • Stratford Johns *Morrie Conley* • Joanne Whalley *Christine* • Susan Kyd *Barbara* • Lesley Manville *Maryanne* ■ *Dir* Mike Newell • *Scr* Shelagh Delaney

Dance with Me
★★ PG

Romantic drama 1998 · US · Colour · 121min

Think *Strictly Ballroom* with a mambo beat and you'll easily figure out the entire plot of this easy on the eye dance drama from director Randa Haines. Chayanne plays a Cuban youngster who gets a job as a handyman at a Houston dance studio working for Kris Kristofferson, whom he believes to be his father. There he meets Vanessa L Williams, and it's not long before the two of them are steaming up the dance floor with their stunningly choreographed Latin numbers. Forget the clichéd plot and performances and just enjoy those salsa dance moves. JB *DVD*

Vanessa L Williams *Ruby* • Chayanne *Rafael* • Kris Kristofferson *John* • Joan Plowright *Bea* • Jane Krakowski *Patricia* • Beth Grant *Lovejoy* ■ *Dir* Randa Haines • *Scr* Daryl Matthews • *Choreographers* Daryl Matthews, Liz Curtis

Dance with Me
★★

Drama 2008 · UK · Colour · 82min

Writer/director Sasha C Damjanovski takes the "tango nuevo" dance as his inspiration for this underwhelming micro-budget Brit

flick. Choreographer Johanne Murdock and her husband Adam Napier, a lawyer, have retreated to an idyllic lakeside cottage: he to recover from a mysterious psychological condition; she to rehearse with her dancers. The film examines the role of intimacy and physicality in relationships, and whether a lack of them can become a barrier to true love. This idea is well handled early on, as the pair's distance is magnified by the closeness of the dance interludes, but it becomes muddled by a misjudged second-act twist. Yet Damjanovski's debut feature is not without merit, with Murdock's performance in particular one to watch. JoC

Johanne Murdock *Alice* • Adam Napier *Neil* • Jane Stanton *Lizzie* ■ *Dir/Scr* Sasha C Damjanovski

Dance with Me Henry ★★ U

Comedy 1956 · US · BW · 80min

This was Bud Abbott and Lou Costello's last film together, and it's obvious that their comic partnership had reached the end of its tether. Here Lou plays the owner of an amusement park who becomes involved in Bud's gambling debts. When a district attorney is murdered, Lou finds he's being pursued by the police *and* the mob. The boys strive hard to make it work, and the strain shows. TH

Lou Costello *Lou Henry* • Bud Abbott *Bud Flick* • Gigi Perreau *Shelley* ■ *Dir* Charles Barton • *Scr* Devery Freeman, from a story by William Kozlenko, Leslie Kardos

Dancehall Queen ★★ 15

Musical dance drama
1996 · Jam · Colour · 96min

Knowing patois is a useful skill when it comes to understanding this Jamaican street film. Audrey Reid stars as a single mother, struggling to survive by selling drinks outside popular dance halls, while predatory men are after her 15-year-old daughter. Adopting a mystery persona, Reid starts wowing in the dance halls. The soundtrack is as atmospheric as walking through the Notting Hill Carnival, but the sudden shift from Reid's extremely grim life into comedy doesn't quite hang together. LH *DVD*

Audrey Reid *Marcia* • Carl Davis *Uncle Larry* • Paul Campbell (2) *Priest* • Pauline Stone-Myrie *Mrs Gordon* ■ *Dir* Don Letts, Rick Elgood • *Scr* Suzanne Fenn, Don Letts, Ed Wallace, from an idea by Don Letts, Ed Wallace

Dancer in the Dark ★★★ 15

Musical drama
2000 · Den/Fr/Swe/It/Ger/Nor/Neth/Ice/Fin/UK · Colour · 134min

Lars von Trier is an excellent director of shocking and innovative material, and here he combines that ability with an old-fashioned musical subplot. Pop singer Björk wavers between raw and amateurish as a Czech immigrant in 1960s small-town America. Suffering from an inherited condition of encroaching blindness, she works to earn the money for an operation that will save her ten-year-old son from the same fate. The elfin Björk is every inch the victim, but von Trier's unremittingly fatalistic narrative does not make this easy viewing. AC Violence. *DVD*

Björk *Selma Jezková* • Catherine Deneuve *Kathy* • David Morse *Bill* • Peter Stormare *Jeff* • Udo Kier *Dr Pokorny* • Joel Grey *Oldrich Novy* ■ *Dir/Scr* Lars von Trier

Dancer, Texas Pop 81
★★★ PG

Comedy drama 1998 · US · Colour · 97min

Since they were 11, a group of small-town Texans have vowed to explore the wider world. But when it comes to leaving, everyone has an excuse to stay. Shot in just 25 days by debutant Tim McCanlies, this rites-of-passage picture deserves to reach a much wider audience. It's funny without being trite and moving without being corny. Moreover, it's spiritedly performed by the teenage cast. DP

Breckin Meyer *Keller Coleman* • Ethan Embry *Squirrel* • Peter Facinelli *Terrell Lee Lusk* • Eddie Mills *John Hemphill* • Ashley Johnson *Josie* • Patricia Wettig *Mrs Lusk* • Alexandra Holden *Vivian* • Michael O'Neil *Mr Lusk* ■ *Dir/Scr* Tim McCanlies

The Dancer Upstairs
★★★ 15

Political thriller 2002 · US/Sp · Colour · 127min

Vivified by José Luis Alcaine's predatory camerawork, John Malkovich's directorial debut owes a sizeable debt to the brand of political thriller perfected by Costa-Gavras. Javier Bardem excels as the Latin American lawyer-turned-cop who is constantly hindered by official corruption and public indifference as he agonisingly comes to realise that ballet teacher Laura Morante is associated with the perpetrators of a series of terrorist attacks. Despite a surfeit of contrivances, it's an arresting blend of *policier* and sociological treatise. DP *DVD*

Javier Bardem *Agustin Rejas* • Laura Morante *Yolanda* • Juan Diego Botto *Sucre* • Elvira Minguez *Llosa* • Alexandra Lencastre *Sylvina* • Oliver Cotton *General Merino* ■ *Dir* John Malkovich • *Scr* Nicholas Shakespeare, from his novel

Dancers ★★ PG

Drama 1987 · US · Colour · 94min

The flowing blond locks of Mikhail Baryshnikov tumble over both stage and boudoir in this infamous raunchy ballet movie. Director Herbert Ross's version of a dance soap works moderately well on a light, inconsequential level, with Julie Kent making a bright debut as the latest ingénue to get Baryshnikov's tights in a twist. Despite all that, the dancing throughout is a marvellous treat. SH Some swearing.

Mikhail Baryshnikov *Anton (Tony)* • Alessandra Ferri *Francesca* • Leslie Browne *Nadine* • Thomas Rall [Tommy Rall] *Patrick* • Lynn Seymour *Muriel* • Victor Barbee *Wade* ■ *Dir* Herbert Ross • *Scr* Sarah Kernochan

Dances with Wolves
★★★★★ 15

Epic western 1990 · US · Colour · 173min

Kevin Costner's directorial debut, the first western to win the best picture Oscar for 60 years, is a heartfelt attempt to create a frontier epic and to atone for Hollywood's shameful depiction of native American life. Costner himself plays the depressed, battle weary Union officer, a Civil War hero who, given the choice, opts for a remote posting in South Dakota to see the frontier before it disappears. Costner directs with a clear passion for the subject, and proves that epic westerns can still work if their heart is in the right place, the characters are real and the cinematography is stunning. DP English, Sioux +subtitles. Sex scenes, nudity, violence. *DVD* ▷

Kevin Costner *Lieutenant John Dunbar/Dances with Wolves* • Mary McDonnell *Stands with a Fist* • Graham Greene (2) *Kicking Bird* • Rodney A Grant *Wind in his Hair* • Floyd Red Crow Westerman *Chief Ten Bears* • Tantoo Cardinal *Black Shawl* • Robert Pastorelli *Timmons* • Charles Rocket *Lieutenant Elgin* • Maury Chaykin *Major Fambrough* ■ *Dir* Kevin Costner • *Scr* Michael Blake, from the novel by Michael Blake • *Cinematographer* Dean Semler

Dancin' thru the Dark
★★★ 15

Comedy drama 1989 · UK · Colour · 90min

Director Mike Ockrent takes a minor Willy Russell play and turns it into a pleasant screen diversion. On the eve of Claire Hackett and Con O'Neill's wedding, both her hen party and his stag "do" end up at the same nightclub. Cue an avalanche of scouse home truths and tart comedy, especially when it's revealed the bride's ex-boyfriend is in the house band. AJ *DVD*

Claire Hackett *Linda* • Con O'Neill *Peter* • Colin Welland *Manager* • Willy Russell *Sourface* • Julia Deakin *Bernadette* • Angela Clarke *Maureen* • Sandy Hendrickse *Carol* • Louise Duprey *Frances* • Simon O'Brien *Kav* • Conrad Nelson *Dave* •

Mark Womack *Eddie* • Andrew Naylor *Billy* • Peter Watts *Robbie* ■ *Dir* Mike Ockrent • *Scr* Willy Russell, from his play *Stags and Hens*

Dancing at Lughnasa
★★★ PG

Period drama 1998 · UK/Ire · Colour · 90min

Director Pat O'Connor stumbles a little with this rather meandering adaptation of Brian Friel's acclaimed play about five unmarried sisters living in rural Ireland in the 1930s, with Meryl Streep as Kate, the eldest. Into this secluded world comes their elder brother Michael Gambon, a missionary in Africa who has been seduced by "heathen" ways, and Rhys Ifans, sister Catherine McCormack's ex-lover and the father of her child. However, O'Connor spends too much time dwelling on the beautiful Irish countryside for the pace ever to move above a slow crawl. JB Some swearing. *DVD*

Meryl Streep *Kate Mundy* • Michael Gambon *Father Jack Mundy* • Catherine McCormack *Christina Mundy* • Kathy Burke *Maggie Mundy* • Sophie Thompson *Rose Mundy* • Brid Brennan *Agnes Mundy* • Rhys Ifans *Gerry Evans* • Darrell Johnston *Michael Mundy* • Lorcan Cranitch *Danny Bradley* ■ *Dir* Pat O'Connor • *Scr* Frank McGuinness, from the play by Brian Friel

Dancing at the Blue Iguana
★★ 18

Drama 2000 · US/UK · Colour · 118min

The most credible scenes in Michael Radford's film about the lives of Los Angeles strippers are those that feature the disrobing of his committed female cast. This ensemble drama, created through an improvisational workshop, has some shining performances, notably Daryl Hannah as the dizzy Angel and Jennifer Tilly's brassy Jo. However, there's nowhere near enough material for a full-length movie, and this too often veers from depressing authenticity to unconvincing caricature. JC *DVD*

Daryl Hannah *Becky Willow, "Angel"* • Jennifer Tilly *Ellen Taylor, "Jo"* • Sandra Oh *Cathy, "Jasmine"* • Charlotte Ayanna *Jessie* ■ *Dir* Michael Radford • *Scr* Michael Radford, David Linter, from improvisational workshops

Dancing at the Harvest Moon
★★

Romantic drama 2002 · US · Colour · 95min

In this lachrymose TV melodrama, Jacqueline Bisset discovers that her husband of 25 years has been cheating on her and realises that she's falling in love with the son of her first love (who is half her age). Bisset's performance is lifeless and Eric Mabius offers little but looks as her toyboy, but Valerie Harper brings some welcome edge as her sassy friend. DP Swearing.

Jacqueline Bisset *Maggie* • Eric Mabius *John Fleming* • Valerie Harper *Claire* ■ *Dir* Bobby Roth • *Scr* Peter Nelson, from the novel by KC McKinnon

Dancing Co-Ed ★★

Musical comedy 1939 · US · BW · 82min

The co-ed of the title is 19-year-old Lana Turner, at the gateway to major stardom at MGM, playing a college student with show biz ambitions who triumphs in both classroom and theatre. Flimsy nonsense, but one which serves its purpose as a star vehicle for the "sweater girl". RK

Lana Turner *Patty Marlow* • Richard Carlson *Pug Braddock* • Artie Shaw • Ann Rutherford *Eve* • Lee Bowman *Freddie Tobin* • Leon Errol *Sam "Pops" Marlow* • Roscoe Karns *Joe Drews* • Monty Woolley *Prof Lange* • Thurston Hall *HW Workman* ■ *Dir* S Sylvan Simon • *Scr* Albert Mannheimer, from a story by Albert Treynor

Dancing in Jaffa ★★★★ PG

Dance documentary 2013 · US · Colour · 89min

In this observational documentary, former champion ballroom dancer Pierre Dulaine returns to his native Jaffa in Israel to teach dance and cross-cultural understanding to the mixed local community. As the child of Palestinian-Irish parents forced to leave during the formation of Israel, this mission carries deep personal significance for the pixie-ish yet determined dance tutor, whose methods have found great success within the New York public school system. The film engrossingly shows the innocence of children transforming attitudes on both sides when traditional social barriers are removed. TJ English, Arabic, Hebrew +subtitles.

Pierre Dulaine • Yvonne Marceau ■ *Dir* Hilla Medalia • *Scr* Philip Shane, Hilla Medalia

Dancing in the Dark ★★★ U
Musical comedy 1949 · US · Colour · 89min

Former vaudeville star George Jessel forged a later career as producer of musicals at 20th Century-Fox, of which this is an interesting example, since it's set in the Fox studio itself (glamorous, and also cheap). Debonair William Powell is most welcome as a former star, now down on his luck and working as a talent scout, who discovers pert Betsy Drake in a plot twist that will have you hollering "enough!". But the real joke for insiders is Adolphe Menjou's uncanny impersonation of Fox boss Darryl F Zanuck. A pleasing time-waster. TS

William Powell *Emery Slide* • Mark Stevens *Bill Davis* • Betsy Drake *Julie* • Adolphe Menjou *Grossman* • Randy Stuart *Rosalie* • Lloyd Corrigan *Barker* • Hope Emerson *Mrs Schlaghammer* ■ *Dir* Irving Reis • *Scr* Mary C McCall Jr, Marion Turk, Jay Dratler, from the musical *Bandwagon* by George S Kaufman, Howard Dietz, Arthur Schwartz

Dancing in the Dark ★★★ 15
Drama 1986 · Can · Colour · 98min

The mundane existence of a middle-class housewife begins to take its toll on her sanity in this dour Canadian drama. Recalled through confessions to a psychiatrist in flashback, Martha Henry's 20-year marriage to Neil Munro seems like a life sentence, as each meal and chore is greeted with the same self-centred boorishness. Lifting mannerisms from Jack Lemmon in full midlife crisis, Munro comes across as thoughtless, but he has none of the maliciousness that drives nosey neighbour Carole Galloway to destroy their far from happy home. DP Violence.

Martha Henry *Edna* • Neil Munro *Harry* • Rosemary Dunsmore *Nurse* • Richard Monette *Doctor* • Elena Kudaba *Edna's roommate* • Brenda Bazinet *Susan* ■ *Dir* Leon Marr • *Scr* Leon Marr, from the novel by Joan Barfoot

Dancing Lady ★★★
Musical 1933 · US · BW · 92min

This vintage MGM musical melodrama teams two of the great sex symbols of their day, Joan Crawford and Clark Gable; they were real-life lovers off screen, and it shows. The *ménage à trois* is aptly completed by suave Franchot Tone, a future Mr Joan Crawford. Fred Astaire makes his movie debut, playing himself and bringing some dignity to the ridiculously tasteless production number, *Let's Go Bavarian*. There's also an appearance by the Three Stooges, though they are nothing short of embarrassing. TS

Joan Crawford *Janie Barlow* • Clark Gable *Patch Gallagher* • Franchot Tone *Tod Newton* • Fred Astaire • Nelson Eddy • May Robson *Dolly Todhunter* • Winnie Lightner *Rosette Henrietta La Rue* • Robert Benchley *Ward King* • Ted Healy *Steve* ■ *Dir* Robert Z Leonard • *Scr* Allen Rivkin, PJ Wolfson, from the novel by James Warner Bellah

The Dancing Masters ★★ PG
Comedy 1943 · US · BW · 63min

One of the decidedly non-vintage films that Laurel and Hardy made for 20th Century-Fox in the 1940s. Considerably below their best, they play struggling dance school patrons, whose client Trudy Marshall is in love with would-be inventor Robert Bailey. The boys stage some madcap schemes in a bid to raise money for Bailey, but the drippy lovers are given far too much screen time. Not even the presence of Margaret Dumont and Robert Mitchum in a bit part can liven it up. DP

Stan Laurel *Stan* • Oliver Hardy *Ollie* • Trudy Marshall *Mary Harlan* • Robert Bailey *Grant Lawrence* • Matt Briggs *Wentworth Harlan* • Margaret Dumont *Mrs Harlan* • Bob Mitchum [Robert Mitchum] *Mickey* ■ *Dir* Mal St Clair [Malcolm St Clair] • *Scr* W Scott Darling, from a story by George Bricker

Dancing with Crime ★★ PG
Crime drama 1946 · UK · BW · 79min

Real-life newlyweds Richard Attenborough and Sheila Sim co-star in this stark crime quickie, which also marks the feature debut of Dirk Bogarde as a bobby on the beat. Attenborough is a cabbie who becomes the scourge of black marketeers when he investigates the suspicious death of an army pal (Bill Owen). With Sim going undercover at the local dance hall, the film will evoke memories of Saturday nights gone by. DP *DVD*

Richard Attenborough *Ted* • Sheila Sim *Joy* • Barry K Barnes *Paul* • Garry Marsh *Sergeant Murray* • John Warwick *Inspector Carter* • Judy Kelly *Toni* • Barry Jones *Gregory* • Bill Owen *Dave* • Diana Dors *Hostess* • Dirk Bogarde *Policeman* ■ *Dir* John Paddy Carstairs • *Scr* Brock Williams, Peter Fraser

The Dancing Years ★★ U
Musical drama 1949 · UK · Colour · 98min

A love affair between young composer Dennis Price and star of the musical stage Giselle Preville falters through a misunderstanding which leads her to leave him and marry prince Anthony Nicholls. Directed by Harold French, this screen transfer of a musical by Ivor Novello is outmoded, sickly sweet and devoid of what charm the original stage show offered. The debonair Price is hardly a natural for the genre, but the titles does offer plenty of Novello's melodies. RK

Dennis Price *Rudi Kleiber* • Gisèle Préville *Maria Zeitler* • Patricia Dainton *Grete* • Anthony Nicholls *Prince Reinaldt* ■ *Dir* Harold French • *Scr* Warwick Ward, Jack Whittingham, from an operetta by Ivor Novello

Dandin ★★★★
Comedy 1988 · Fr · Colour · 116min

Based on Molière's comedy *Georges Dandin*, this rumbustious tale of greed, suspicion and debasement is a lesser-known example of the playwright's genius for exposing the complexities and absurdities of human nature. Roger Planchon keeps this cruellest of comedies racing along, drawing an excellent performance from Claude Brasseur as the peasant who suffers an endless round of humiliations after he takes a wife to improve his social standing. He is ably supported by Zabou as his spouse, and Daniel Gélin as the father-in-law who is the chief architect of his misery. DP French +subtitles.

Claude Brasseur *Georges Dandin* • Zabou *Angélique* • Daniel Gélin *M de Sotenville* • Nelly Borgeaud *Mme de Sotenville* ■ *Dir* Roger Planchon • *Scr* Roger Planchon, from the play *Georges Dandin* by Molière

Danger by My Side ★
Crime thriller 1962 · UK · BW · 63min

The road to justice leads to a Soho nightclub in this tawdry British B-movie. The hit-and-run murder, the sleazy club scenes, the heist and the motor-launch finale are all executed with the minimum of imagination as Maureen Connell puts her personal safety on the line while helping the police catch her detective-brother's killers. Charles Saunders's poor pacing leaves the cast high and dry. DP

Anthony Oliver *Inspector Willoughby* • Maureen Connell *Lynne* • Alan Tilvern *Venning* • Bill Nagy *Sam Warren* • Sonya Cordeau *Francine Dumont* ■ *Dir* Charles Saunders • *Scr* Ronald C Liles, Aubrey Cash

Danger: Diabolik ★★★ 12
Crime comedy 1967 · It/Fr · Colour · 96min

Based on a cult comic strip, this mix of fantasy and madcap criminality is directed with mischievous glee by horror specialist Mario Bava. Utilising stylised sets and encouraging his multinational cast to camp

it, Bava arrives at a *Barbarella*-style romp, a comparison that is reinforced by the presence of John Phillip Law as the master criminal who curries favour with the populace by destroying Italy's tax records. The press conference given by pompous minister Terry-Thomas, under the influence of laughing gas, is riotously funny. DP *DVD*

John Phillip Law *Diabolik* • Marisa Mell *Eva Kant* • Michel Piccoli *Inspector Ginko* • Adolfo Celi *Ralph Valmont* • Terry-Thomas *Minister of Finance* ■ *Dir* Mario Bava • *Scr* Mario Bava, Dino Maiuri, Brian Degas, Tudor Gates, from a story by Angela Giussani, Luciana Giussani, Dino Maiuri, Adriano Baracco

Danger Lights ★★
Comedy drama 1930 · US · BW · 87min

Beefy Louis Wolheim and dapper Robert Armstrong lock in conflict over Jean Arthur, against a background of problems in running a railway. A melange of romance, melodrama and macho tension, this mediocre movie is of interest in that it saw the short-lived launch (by RKO) of a new "wide stereoscopic" process. The technique and Karl Struss's cinematography do add a dimension of depth to the proceedings, but the huge costs involved made this the first and last time it was used. RK

Louis Wolheim *Dan Thorn* • Robert Armstrong *Larry Doyle* • Jean Arthur *Mary Ryan* • Hugh Herbert *Professor* • Frank Sheridan *Ed Ryan* ■ *Dir* George B Seitz • *Scr* James Ashmore Creelman, Hugh Herbert

Danger – Love at Work ★★★ U
Comedy 1937 · US · BW · 78min

The Viennese-born Otto Preminger had only directed one film in Germany when he was given a contract at 20th Century-Fox. This enjoyable screwball comedy was the second picture he made for the studio. The inconsequential plot involves Jack Haley as a lawyer sent to a small town to buy up a piece of property owned by an eccentric family, but the cast makes the movie: Mary Boland at her most scatterbrained, pert Ann Sothern, fussy Edward Everett Horton and demented John Carradine. RB *DVD*

Ann Sothern *Toni Pemberton* • Jack Haley *Henry MacMorrow* • Mary Boland *Mrs Alice Pemberton* • Edward Everett Horton *Howard Rogers* • John Carradine *Herbert Pemberton* • Walter Catlett *Uncle Alan* ■ *Dir* Otto Preminger • *Scr* James Edward Grant, Ben Markson, from a story by James Edward Grant

Danger Patrol ★★ U
Adventure 1937 · US · BW · 59min

This RKO second feature looks at the foolhardy men who transport dangerous nitroglycerin to oil fields to quench fires. Because of the pedestrian direction by the prolific journeyman Lew Landers, the potentially explosive material fails to catch alight. However, it's good to see veteran character actor Harry Carey in a leading role. He is a driver who is opposed to his daughter (pretty Sally Eilers) marrying a man in the same dangerous profession. RB

Sally Eilers *Cathie Street* • John Beal *Dan Loring* • Harry Carey *Sam "Easy" Street* • Frank M Thomas *Rocky Sanders* • Edward Gargan *Gabby Donovan* ■ *Dir* Lew Landers • *Scr* Sy Bartlett, from a story by Helen Vreeland, Hilda Vincent

Danger Route ★
Spy thriller 1967 · UK · Colour · 92min

This is a sloppily constructed spy thriller that aims for the gloss, levity and excitement of a Bond movie and misses by a mile. Director Seth Holt goes off on so many tangents that the central plot – about agent Richard Johnson's mission to kill a Soviet scientist before he can pass secrets to the Americans – is completely obscured. Dismal. DP

Richard Johnson *Jonas Wilde* • Carol Lynley *Jocelyn* • Barbara Bouchet *Mari* • Sylvia Syms *Barbara Canning* • Gordon Jackson *Stern* • Harry Andrews *Canning* • Diana Dors *Rhoda Gooderich* • Maurice Denham *Peter Ravenspur* • Sam

Wanamaker *Lucinda* ■ *Dir* Seth Holt • *Scr* Meade Roberts, from the novel *The Eliminator* by Andrew York

Danger Within ★★★ U
Second World War drama 1958 · UK · BW · 96min

Anyone who has seen Billy Wilder's PoW-camp classic *Stalag 17* will find this workmanlike British imitation somewhat predictable. The story has a whodunnit element that is cleverly and wittily plotted, but prisoners and guards alike are cardboard cutouts and it takes some competent character acting to make them even half credible. Richard Attenborough and Bernard Lee come off best, while Richard Todd trots out all his gruff officer mannerisms. Director Don Chaffey sustains the suspense with unfussy ease. DP

Richard Todd *Lt Col David Baird* • Bernard Lee *Lt Col Huxley* • Michael Wilding *Maj Charles Marquand* • Richard Attenborough *Capt Bunter Phillips* • Dennis Price *Capt Rupert Callender* • Donald Houston *Capt Roger Byford* • Michael Caine *Prisoner with pin-up* ■ *Dir* Don Chaffey • *Scr* Bryan Forbes, Frank Harvey, from the novel by Michael Gilbert

Danger Zone ★★ 18
Action adventure 1996 · US · Colour · 88min

In this fairly routine straight-to-video adventure, Billy Zane plays a mine inspector in a small African state who is duped into carrying the can for a catastrophic spillage of lethal toxic waste supplied by CIA agent and former buddy Robert Downey Jr. Or is the plot thicker than it seems? The two leads are charismatic and the action rattles along nicely, but the ecological message begins to grate. JF Violence. *DVD*

Billy Zane *Rick Morgan* • Robert Downey Jr *Jim Scott* • Ron Silver *Dupont* • Cary-Hiroyuki Tagawa *Chang* • Lisa Collins *Dr Kim Woods* ■ *Dir* Allan Eastman • *Scr* Jeff Albert

Dangerous ★★★★ PG
Melodrama 1935 · US · BW · 75min

Bette Davis won her first Oscar for this fine melodrama about a fading alcoholic star who gets a chance to resurrect her career. At the time it was felt that the Academy Award was a compensatory one for Davis not winning the previous year as the spiteful Mildred in *Of Human Bondage*. Seen today, Davis's performance here is truly magnificent and splendidly overblown, with all those mannerisms well under control as Warner Bros veteran director Alfred E Green hands the movie to her on a platter. TS

Bette Davis *Joyce Heath* • Franchot Tone *Don Bellows* • Margaret Lindsay *Gail Armitage* • Alison Skipworth *Mrs Williams* • John Eldredge *Gordon Heath* • Dick Foran *Teddy* • Pierre Watkin *George Sheffield* ■ *Dir* Alfred E Green • *Scr* Laird Doyle

Dangerous Afternoon ★★ U
Crime drama 1961 · UK · BW · 61min

Former editor Charles Saunders turned out a series of unexceptional movies after taking to directing, including this negligible crime drama. The story – about an escaped convict whose refuge for former women prisoners is threatened by a blackmailer – began life on stage, and Saunders does little to open out the forgotten play. DP

Ruth Dunning *Miss Frost* • Nora Nicholson *Mrs Sprule* • Joanna Dunham *Freda* • Howard Pays *Jack Loring* • May Hallatt *Miss Burge* ■ *Dir* Charles Saunders • *Scr* Brandon Fleming, from a play by Gerald Anstruther

Dangerous Attraction ★★
Crime thriller based on a true story 2012 · US · Colour · 95min

The physical and psychological impact of stalking is explored in this thought-provoking TV movie. Based on real events, it's enhanced by Amanda Righetti's convincing turn as an outgoing coffee shop worker whose entire life is adversely affected when pasty-faced barista Will Estes becomes obsessed with her. Righetti (who plays Grace Van Pelt in TV hit *The Mentalist*) completely nails her character's vulnerability, adding emotional meat to the simple and action-light narrative. The rather sedate climax may disappoint some people, though it is in keeping with the film's sober approach. SF

Amanda Righetti *Casey Cooper* • Harry Hamlin *Richard* • Will Estes *Morgan Pierce* • Eric Szmanda *Detective Dominic Leary* ■ *Dir* Michael Lohmann • *Scr* Stacey K Pantazis

Dangerous Beauty ★★★ 15
Period romance 1997 · US · Colour · 107min

Catherine McCormack co-stars with the glamorous city of Venice in this picturesque feminist fable, based on the biography of real-life 16th-century courtesan and poet Veronica Franco. McCormack lusts after impoverished aristocrat Rufus Sewell and an education, but is denied both by the prejudices of the time. Director Marshall Herskovitz splashes out on atmosphere and McCormack delivers her witty lines with aplomb, but the climax is too melodramatic to be credible. Also known as *The Honest Courtesan*. TH Violence, swearing, sex scenes, nudity. **DVD**

Catherine McCormack *Veronica Franco* • Rufus Sewell *Marco Venier* • Oliver Platt *Maffio Venier* • Moira Kelly *Beatrice Venier* • Fred Ward *Domenico Venier* • Jacqueline Bisset *Paola Franco* ■ *Dir* Marshall Herskovitz • *Scr* Jeannine Dominy, from the biography by Margaret Rosenthal

Dangerous Corner ★★
Mystery melodrama 1934 · US · BW · 66min

The only reason for sticking with this – and it's a long wait – is the double ending retained from JB Priestley's play. Starring Virginia Bruce, Conrad Nagel and Melvyn Douglas, this abridged screen version makes heavy weather of an after-dinner discussion between a publisher and friends about the apparent suicide of one of their group and the disappearance of valuable bonds. Director Phil Rosen's handling of the drama is dreary. AE

Melvyn Douglas *Charles* • Conrad Nagel *Robert* • Virginia Bruce *Olwen* • Erin O'Brien-Moore *Freda* • Ian Keith *Martin* • Betty Furness *Betty* ■ *Dir* Phil Rosen • *Scr* Anne Morrison Chapin, Madeleine Ruthven, from JB Priestley's play

Dangerous Exile ★★★ PG
Swashbuckling adventure
1957 · UK · Colour · 87min

Stylishly shot by Geoffrey Unsworth and featuring a rousing score by Georges Auric, this historical adventure makes up for its cumbersome plot with some slick swashbuckling and an unrelenting pace. Louis Jourdan is the aristocrat who smuggles the son of Louis XVI across the channel to prevent the rabid revolutionaries from getting their egalitarian mitts on him. This kind of romp wasn't really Irish director Brian Desmond Hurst's strong suit, but he keeps the action rattling along. DP

Louis Jourdan *Duc de Beauvais* • Belinda Lee *Virginia Traill* • Keith Michell *Colonel St Gerard* • Richard O'Sullivan *Louis* • Martita Hunt *Aunt Fell* • Finlay Currie *Mr Patient* • Anne Heywood *Glynis* ■ *Dir* Brian Desmond Hurst • *Scr* Robin Estridge, Patrick Kirwan, from the novel *A King Reluctant* by Vaughan Wilkins

Dangerous Female ★★★★
Crime drama 1931 · US · BW · 80min

This is the first film version of *The Maltese Falcon*, retitled for release in Britain and subsequent TV screenings to avoid confusion with John Huston's 1941 Humphrey Bogart classic. There's another version as well, called *Satan Met a Lady*, released in 1936, in which the legendary falcon became a ram's horn. This early Warner Bros melodrama is faithful to the great Dashiell Hammett novel, and Ricardo Cortez is a much more womanising Sam Spade than Bogie. TS

Bebe Daniels *Ruth Wonderly* • Ricardo Cortez *Sam Spade* • Dudley Digges *Kaspar Gutman* • Una Merkel *Effie Perine* • Robert Elliott *Detective Dundy* • J Farrell MacDonald *Polhouse* ■ *Dir* Roy Del Ruth • *Scr* Maude Fulton, Lucien Hubbard, Brown Holmes, Dashiell Hammett, from the novel *The Maltese Falcon* by Dashiell Hammett

Dangerous Game ★ 18
Drama 1993 · US · Colour · 104min

Abel Ferrara aimed to give us an unadorned insight into the film-making process and show how on-set tensions can often result in great art. Instead, he came up with a pretentious folly, in which an over-indulged cast bandy expletives and gorge themselves in an orgy of grandiloquence and gesturing. DP Violence, swearing, sex scenes, drug abuse, nudity. **DVD**

Madonna *Sarah Jennings* • Harvey Keitel *Eddie Israel* • James Russo *Francis Burns* • Nancy Ferrara *Madlyn Israel* • Reilly Murphy *Tommy* • Victor Argo *Director of photography* • Leonard Thomas *Prop guy* • Christina Fulton *Blonde* ■ *Dir* Abel Ferrara • *Scr* Abel Ferrara, Nicholas St John

A Dangerous Game ★★★ PG
Documentary 2014 · UK · Colour · 101min

Anthony Baxter's follow-up to *You've Been Trumped* again looks at the effect that Donald Trump's luxury golf course has on various Aberdeenshire homeowners. In addition, the film-maker looks at similar golf developments in other parts of the world – including Croatia and Nevada – and manages to secure a one-to-one interview with Trump himself. Some truly damning statistics are served up, but while Trump is clearly the villain here, the film itself is often too righteous and one-sided for its own good. SC

Donald Trump ■ *Dir* Anthony Baxter • *Scr* Richard Phinney

Dangerous Ground ★★ 18
Crime thriller
1996 · S Afr/US · Colour and BW · 91min

This is a well-meaning but botched study of crime in post-apartheid Johannesburg. Sex, drugs and corruption in the new South Africa is an interesting concept, but the potentially fascinating political undercurrents aren't explored. Darrell James Roodt's film suffers from unconvincing characters, over-ripe dialogue and ineffectual stabs at social comment. JC Violence, swearing, drug abuse, nudity.

Ice Cube *Vusi* • Elizabeth Hurley *Karin* • Sechaba Morojele *Ernest* • Ving Rhames *Muki* • Thokozani Nkosi *Young Vusi* • Ron Smerczac [Ron Smerczak] *Interrogation policeman* ■ *Dir* Darrell Roodt [Darrell James Roodt] • *Scr* Greg Latter, Darrell James Roodt

Dangerous Liaisons ★★★★ 15
Period drama 1988 · US · Colour · 114min

Stephen Frears's richly textured production of the scandalous 18th-century "sex as power play" novel is a handsome homage to the idea that women lose out in a man's world even where they at first appear to be in control. The extraordinary performances of Glenn Close, as the vindictive Marquise de Merteuil, and Michelle Pfeiffer, as the pure wife despoiled by the slimy Valmont (John Malkovich) on a wager, help make this chilling depiction of an era's corruption totally believable. Malkovich, though, seems ill-cast, with none of the necessary seduction in his portrayal. That aside, this remains a treat for eye and mind. TH Sex scenes, nudity. **DVD**

Glenn Close *Marquise de Merteuil* • John Malkovich *Vicomte de Valmont* • Michelle Pfeiffer *Madame de Tourvel* • Swoosie Kurtz *Madame de Volanges* • Keanu Reeves *Chevalier Dancény* • Mildred Natwick *Madame de Rosemonde* • Uma Thurman *Cécile de Volanges* • Peter Capaldi *Azolan* • Joe Sheridan *Georges* ■ *Dir* Stephen Frears • *Scr* Christopher Hampton, from his play *Les Liaisons Dangereuses*, from the novel by Choderlos de Laclos • *Production Designer* Stuart Craig • *Set Designer* Gerard James • *Costume Designer* James Acheson (1)

The Dangerous Lives of Altar Boys ★★ 15
Part-animated drama
2001 · US · Colour · 100min

Director Peter Care, making his feature debut, reveals his rock video roots at every turn in this sketchy rites-of-passage tale that mixes live action and comic book-style animation. It follows four 1970s Catholic schoolboys (including Kieran Culkin and Emile Hirsch) as they rebel against their lives and the strict educational regime of nun Sister Assumpta (co-producer Jodie Foster). The film tries hard to be edgy, but the story is too fragmented to support such jarring techniques and the characters are underdeveloped. SF Swearing, drug abuse. **DVD**

Kieran Culkin *Tim Sullivan* • Jena Malone *Margie Flynn* • Emile Hirsch *Francis Doyle* • Vincent D'Onofrio *Father Casey* • Jodie Foster *Sister Assumpta* • Jake Richardson *Wade* • Tyler Long *Joey* ■ *Dir* Peter Care

A Dangerous Man ★★ 18
Action thriller 2009 · Can/US · Colour · 90min

Steven Seagal and director Keoni Waxman up their game considerably with this intense and brutal crime thriller. Re-teaming following the atrocious *The Keeper*, they turn a hackneyed plotline into a fast-paced fan-pleaser, as Seagal's ex-Special Forces operative comes out of prison fighting after wrongly serving six years for murder. It's all rather preposterous and increasingly confusing, but it's delivered with a gung ho energy that's riotously entertaining. SF Violence, brief nudity. **DVD**

Steven Seagal *Shane Daniels* • Marlaina Mah *Tia* • Vitaliy Kravchenko *Vlad* • Jesse Hutch *Sergey* • Terry Chen *Chen* ■ *Dir/Scr* Keoni Waxman

A Dangerous Method ★★★ 15
Period drama based on a true story
2011 · Ger/Can/UK · Colour · 95min

The feud between Sigmund Freud and Carl Jung, the fathers of modern psychoanalysis, provides the backdrop to this intelligent and sexually charged tale, centring on an unlikely affair between the idealistic Jung (Michael Fassbender) and a hysterical patient turned assistant, then mistress, then peer (Keira Knightley). Its stage origins show, and Knightley isn't up to carrying such a demanding role, but at the core of the script by Christopher Hampton (*Dangerous Liaisons*) lurks a provocative story about the delicate dividing lines between mind, body and soul. DW **DVD** **Blu-ray**

Keira Knightley *Sabina Spielrein* • Viggo Mortensen *Sigmund Freud* • Michael Fassbender *Carl Jung* • Vincent Cassel *Otto Gross* • Sarah Gadon *Emma Jung* • André Hennicke [Andre Hennicke] *Professor Eugen Bleuler* ■ *Dir* David Cronenberg • *Scr* Christopher Hampton, from his play *The Talking Cure*, from the non-fiction book *A Most Dangerous Method* by John Kerr

Dangerous Minds ★★★ 15
Biographical drama 1995 · US · Colour · 94min

With an entire romantic subplot involving Andy Garcia ending up on the cutting-room floor, this schoolroom drama may have gained a singularity of purpose, but it definitely lost a much-needed release from the intensity of the classroom crusade. Although not a convincing ex-marine, Michelle Pfeiffer turns in a solid performance as she tries to give her deprived students some sort of chance in life. Screenwriter Ronald Bass pushes his luck linking Bob Dylan and Dylan Thomas, and the results-by-reward policy will have many teachers up in arms. DP Swearing, some violence. **DVD**

Michelle Pfeiffer *LouAnne Johnson* • George Dzundza *Hal Griffith* • Courtney B Vance *Mr George Grandey* • Robin Bartlett *Ms Carla Nichols* • Bruklin Harris *Callie Roberts* • Renoly Santiago *Raul Sanchero* ■ *Dir* John N Smith • *Scr* Ronald Bass, Elaine May (uncredited), from the book *My Posse Don't Do Homework* by LouAnne Johnson

Dangerous Mission ★ U
Crime thriller 1954 · US · Colour · 74min

Originally filmed in 3D, this is widely acknowledged as one of the worst films made during the great stereoscopic experiment of the early 1950s. Victor Mature gives one of his most convincing impressions of a cardboard cutout as a New York lawman who treks into Montana's Glacier National Park to prevent hoodlum Vincent Price from rubbing out Piper Laurie, the runaway witness to a gangland shooting. DP 30

Victor Mature *Matt Hallett* • Piper Laurie *Louise Graham* • William Bendix *Joe Parker* • Vincent Price *Paul Adams* • Betta St John *Mary Tiller* ■ *Dir* Louis King • *Scr* Horace McCoy, WR Burnett, Charles Bennett, from a story by Horace McCoy, James Edmiston

Dangerous Money ★
Mystery 1946 · US · BW · 65min

Sidney Toler rings up his 21st and penultimate appearance as Earl Derr Biggers's Oriental sleuth Charlie Chan. The slim plot has the duo trying to figure out who bumped off a government agent. Terry Morse was no great shakes as a director, but with its caricatured suspects and stock whodunnit situations, the script would have defeated even Hitchcock. DP

Sidney Toler *Charlie Chan* • Gloria Warren *Rona Simmonds* • Victor Sen Yung *Jimmy Chan* • Rick Vallin *Tao Erickson* • Joseph Crehan *Capt Black* • Willie Best *Chattanooga* ■ *Dir* Terry Morse • *Scr* Miriam Kissinger, from characters by Earl Derr Biggers

Dangerous Moonlight ★★★ PG
Second World War drama
1941 · UK/US · BW · 81min

This is the wartime movie remembered for its Richard Addinsell score, which introduced to the world the massively popular (and ultra-corny) *Warsaw Concerto*, as irredeemably romantic pianist Anton Walbrook never stops playing it. The impossibly lovely Sally Gray is the American journalist Walbrook marries and who helps the musician recover his memory after a brush with a German bomber. It's dull and not particularly well directed, but it's still potent tosh. TS **DVD**

Anton Walbrook *Stefan Radetzky* • Sally Gray *Carole Peters* • Derrick de Marney *Mike Carroll* • Percy Parsons *Bill Peters* • Keneth Kent *De Guise* ■ *Dir* Brian Desmond Hurst • *Scr* Shaun Terence Young [Terence Young], Brian Desmond Hurst, Rodney Ackland, from a story by Young

Dangerous Moves ★★★ PG
Drama 1984 · Swi · Colour · 100min

Richard Dembo's directorial debut may have landed the best foreign film Oscar, but it scarcely ranks among the worthiest winners of the award. Somewhat labouring the strategic comparisons, he uses the World Chess Championship in Geneva as a metaphor for the Cold War. Ailing Soviet Grand Master Michel Piccoli (in imperious form) enjoins battle with Alexandre Arbatt, a Russian who defected to the west. While there's a sly wit underlying the suspense, what stands out is the way ruthless cunning impinges on the cerebral jousting. DP French +subtitles.

Michel Piccoli *Akiva Liebskind* • Alexandre Arbatt *Pavius Fromm* • Leslie Caron *Henia* • Liv Ullmann *Marina* • Daniel Olbrychski *Tac-Tac* • Michel Aumont *Kerossian* ■ *Dir/Scr* Richard Dembo

Dangerous Offender: the Marlene Moore Story ★★★
Drama based on a true story
1996 · Can · Colour · 92min

The Sweet Hereafter's Brooke Johnson delivers an intense performance in this powerful award winner about the controversial landmark case of Marlene Moore, the first female to be designated a dangerous offender under Canadian law – making her subject to indefinite imprisonment. Despite their relentlessly downbeat nature, the tragic events remain gripping thanks to Johnson, who takes a violent, outwardly unsympathetic character and exposes the emotionally disturbed young woman inside. SF Violence, brief nudity.

Brooke Johnson *Marlene Moore* • Patricia Gage *Maureen Woodcock* • Jayne Eastwood *Mrs Moore* • David Fox *Superintendent Kerr* ■ *Dir* Holly Dale • *Scr* Janis Cole

Dangerous Parking ★★ 18
Drama 2007 · UK · Colour · 109min

Writer/director Peter Howitt leaves behind the cosy comedy stylings of films like *Sliding Doors* and *Laws of Attraction* with this adaptation of Stuart Browne's cult novel. Howitt also stars here as Noah Arkwright, a boozy film-maker who is forced to take stock after a drunken encounter with recovering alcoholic Kirstin (Rachael Stirling). His subsequent half-hearted stab at rehabilitation is just the first step along the road to sobriety. Noah's skewed outlook on the world does provide some laughs, but the overall effect is downright depressing, with the lead character's rampant egocentricity making it difficult to empathise with him. SP
Swearing.

Peter Howitt *Noah Arkwright* • Saffron Burrows *Clare* • Sean Pertwee *Ray* • Rachael Stirling *Kirstin* • Alice Evans *Etta* • Dervla Kirwan *Noah's mum* • Tom Conti *Dr Baker* ■ *Dir* Peter Howitt • *Scr* Peter Howitt, from the novel by Stuart Browne

A Dangerous Pledge ★★★
Silent drama 1920 · Swe · BW · 78min

A scarcity of prints has caused Victor Sjöström's reputation as a director to be dimmed. But, as anyone familiar with Ingmar Bergman's *Wild Strawberries* will know, he has a formidable screen presence. So the restoration of this droll melodrama presents an overdue opportunity to study him in action on both sides of the camera. As the miserly pawnbroker presented with a waif as a loan bond, Sjöström achieves a curmudgeonly compassion that is enlivened by the occasional twinkle in the eye. Not the masterpiece some have claimed, but still impressive. DP

Victor Sjöström *Master Sammel Eneman* • Concordia Selander *Mother Boman* • Greta Almroth *Tora, her daughter* • Harald Schwenzen *Knut, sailor* ■ *Dir* Victor Sjöström • *Scr* Hjalmar Bergman

A Dangerous Profession ★★
Crime drama 1949 · US · BW · 79min

This fast-moving, comfortably familiar and thoroughly forgettable crime programme filler has ex-cop George Raft, now a partner in a bail bond company with Pat O'Brien, deciding to investigate the mysterious death of a suspect (Bill Williams) he has bailed out. Could his interest in the dead man's pretty widow (Ella Raines) have anything to do with his determination to solve the crime? RK

George Raft *Kane* • Pat O'Brien *Farley* • Ella Raines *Lucy* • Bill Williams *Brackett* • Jim Backus *Ferrone* • Roland Winters *McKay* • Betty Underwood *Elaine* ■ *Dir* Ted Tetzlaff • *Scr* Martin Rackin, Warren Duff

Dangerous When Wet ★★★ U
Musical comedy 1953 · US · Colour · 95min

This is one of Esther Williams's most amiable musical comedies, in which she and her whole health-nut family are persuaded to swim the English Channel. There's a super live/animated sequence featuring Tom and Jerry, and a marvellous moment when the film stops for a number by Barbara Whiting, playing Esther's peppy younger sister. Williams married her leading man in this movie in reality, and became Mrs Fernando Lamas. TS

Esther Williams *Katy* • Fernando Lamas *André Lanet* • Jack Carson *Windy Webbe* • Charlotte Greenwood *Ma Higgins* • Denise Darcel *Gigi Mignon* • William Demarest *Pa Higgins* • Donna Corcoran *Junior Higgins* • Barbara Whiting *Suzie Higgins* ■ *Dir* Charles Walters • *Scr* Dorothy Kingsley

A Dangerous Woman ★★★ 18
Thriller 1993 · US · Colour · 97min

Directed with sensitivity by Stephen Gyllenhaal, and given greater depth than the Hollywood norm by his writer-wife, Naomi Foner, this is a slow-burning drama with a surprisingly subtle starring performance from Debra Winger as an emotionally disturbed woman trying to come to terms with life in small-town America. A chain of events involving her aunt Barbara Hershey, failed writer Gabriel Byrne and sleazy local petty criminal David Strathairn pushes the childlike Winger to the edge in a mannered, yet affecting tale. AJ

Debra Winger *Martha Horgan* • Barbara Hershey *Frances Beecham* • Gabriel Byrne *Colin Mackey* • Chloe Webb *Birdie* • David Strathairn *Getso* • John Terry *Steve Bell* • Laurie Metcalf *Anita Bell* • Maggie Gyllenhaal *Patsy* • Jacob Gyllenhaal [Jake Gyllenhaal] *Edward* ■ *Dir* Stephen Gyllenhaal • *Scr* Naomi Foner, from a novel by Mary McGarry Morris

Dangerous Years ★★★
Crime 1947 · US · BW · 62min

Marilyn Monroe has an early role in this interesting little movie that broached the subject of teenage delinquency, a growing problem in the postwar years. Former "Dead End Kid" William (Billy) Halop is a disoriented youth, raised in an orphanage, who turns to crime and is ultimately tried for murder. TV

Billy Halop *Danny Jones* • Ann E Todd *Doris Martin* • Jerome Cowan *Weston* • Anabel Shaw *Connie Burns* • Richard Gaines *Edgar Burns* • Marilyn Monroe *Evie* ■ *Dir* Arthur Pierson • *Scr* Arnold Belgard

Dangerously Close ★★ 18
Crime thriller 1986 · US · Colour · 90min

What begins as an intriguing suspense movie, about student vigilantes who take their self-appointed enforcement policies too far, degenerates into a sloppy thriller once the bodies of low-income pupils start piling up. John Stockwell, who also co-wrote the poorly conceived script, stars as the leader of "The Sentinels", a bunch of neo-Nazi bully boys who patrol their affluent high school rooting out "undesirables". RS

John Stockwell *Randy McDevitt* • J Eddie Peck *Donny Lennox* • Carey Lowell *Julie* • Bradford Bancroft *Krooger Raines* • Don Michael Paul *Ripper* • Thom Mathews *Brian Rigletti* • Jerry Dinome *Lang Bridges* • Madison Mason *Corrigan* • Dedee Pfeiffer *Nikki* ■ *Dir* Albert Pyun • *Scr* Scott Fields, John Stockwell, Marty Ross, from a story by Marty Ross

Dangerously They Live ★★★
Second World War spy drama 1942 · US · BW · 76min

The great John Garfield is wasted in a routine role as a doctor caught up in kidnapped Allied secret agent Nancy Coleman in this melodramatic wartime mixture of spies and medicine from Warner Bros. It's tosh, of course, but entertaining, nevertheless, and it helped wake up American audiences to the fact that there was a war on. TS

John Garfield *Dr Michael Lewis* • Nancy Coleman *Jane* • Raymond Massey *Dr Ingersoll* • Moroni Olsen *Mr Goodwin* • Esther Dale *Dawson* • Lee Patrick *Nurse Johnson* • John Ridgely *John* ■ *Dir* Robert Florey • *Scr* Marion Parsonnet, from story

Daniel Boone, Trail Blazer ★★ PG
Adventure 1957 · US · Colour · 75min

This lively film has its own little place in movie history as the final picture shot in Hollywood using two-colour stock (modern films are three-colour). Bruce Bennett, who made his name as Tarzan in the mid-1930s, stars as the legendary frontiersman guiding a wagon train from North Carolina to Kentucky. Lon Chaney Jr is on form as his sidekick, but the performances merit a better script. DP DVD

Bruce Bennett *Daniel Boone* • Lon Chaney Jr *Blackfish* • Faron Young *Faron Callaway* • Kem Dibbs *Girty* • Damian O'Flynn *Andy Callaway* • Jacqueline Evans *Rebecca Boone* • Nancy Rodman *Susannah Boone* • Freddy Fernandez *Israel Boone* • Carol Kelly *Jemima Boone* ■ *Dir* Albert C Gannaway, Ismael Rodriguez • *Scr* Tom Hubbard, John Patrick

Daniel Defoe's Robinson Crusoe ★★ 12
Adventure drama 1996 · US · Colour · 86min

Pierce Brosnan makes an unconvincing job of playing Daniel Defoe's famous castaway in this dismally dumbed-down screen bowdlerisation. Ian Hart cameos as the novelist to set up the tale of shipwreck and survival, but the events that unfold in this dramatisation often bear little resemblance to those in the novel. William Takaku's Friday is almost completely a figment of the screenwriters' imaginations. DP

Pierce Brosnan *Robinson Crusoe* • William Takaku *Patek* • Polly Walker *Mary* • Ian Hart *Daniel Defoe* • James Frain *Robert* • Damian Lewis *Patrick* ■ *Dir* Rod Hardy, George Miller (1) • *Scr* Christopher Lofren, Tracy Keenan Wynn, Christopher Canaan, David Stevens, from the novel *The Life and Strange Surprising Adventures of Robinson Crusoe* by Daniel Defoe

Danielle Steel's Mixed Blessings ★★ 12
Romantic drama 1995 · US · Colour · 86min

Three couples deal with pregnancy, adoption and infertility in this weepie based on the Danielle Steel novel. The plot is predictable, but the TV-based cast gives its all. Director Bethany Rooney makes sure every moment is a three-hankie one. JB DVD

Gabrielle Carteris *Diana Douglas* • Bruce Greenwood *Andy Douglas* • Scott Baio *Charlie Winwood* • Julie Condra *Barbie Winwood* • Alexandra Paul *Beth* • Bess Armstrong *Pilar Coleman* • James Naughton *Brad Coleman* • Bruce Weitz *Dr Alex Johnson* ■ *Dir* Bethany Rooney • *Scr* L Virginia Browne, Rebecca Soladay, from the novel by Danielle Steel

Danielle Steel's No Greater Love ★★ PG
Period romantic drama
1996 · US · Colour · 86min

This frothy melodramatic confection takes in cataclysmic world news (the sinking of the *Titanic*) and reduces it to a facile excuse for showing us yet another of Steel's strong, brave and well turned-out women battling the odds. The cast has been wheeled out on castors and it runs through its hand-wringing paces as if the script is being relayed by hidden short-wave radio. SH DVD

Kelly Rutherford *Edwina Winfield* • Chris Sarandon *Sam Horowitz* • Nicholas Campbell *Stone* • Daniel Hugh-Kelly *Ben Jones* • Simon MacCorkindale *Patrick Kelly* • Michael Landes *George Winfield* ■ *Dir* Richard Heffron [Richard T Heffron] • *Scr* Carmen Culver from the novel by Danielle Steel

Danielle Steel's Once in a Lifetime ★★★ PG
Romantic drama 1994 · US · Colour · 87min

Get out those hankies, this is one of the weepier movie adaptations of a Danielle Steel novel. Lindsay Wagner plays an author reluctant to love again after her husband and daughter are killed in a fire. On top of all this, her young son is deaf. There's no prize for guessing who rescues our heroine from all this – TV-movie king Barry Bostwick. JB DVD

Lindsay Wagner *Daphne Fields* • Barry Bostwick *Dr Matthew Dane* • Duncan Regehr *Justin* • Amy Aquino *Barbara* • Rex Smith *Jeffrey Fields* • Jessica Sinegal *Aimee* ■ *Dir* Michael Miller (2) • *Scr* Syrie Astrahan James, from the novel by Danielle Steel

Danielle Steel's Palomino ★★ PG
Romantic drama 1991 · US · Colour · 91min

There's enough corn to fill you up for a lifetime in this TV adaptation of Danielle Steel's novel. Lindsay Frost plays the photographer who retreats to a ranch after her marriage ends, and subsequently falls in love with rough-and-ready ranch hand Lee Horsley, from the wrong side of the tracks. Featuring Eva Marie Saint and Rod Taylor, both of whom should have known better. JB DVD

Lindsay Frost *Samantha Taylor* • Lee Horsley *Tate* • Eva Marie Saint *Caroline* • Rod Taylor *Bill* ■ *Dir* Michael Miller (2) • *Scr* Karol Ann Hoeffner, from the novel by Danielle Steel

Danielle Steel's A Perfect Stranger ★★ 12
Romantic drama 1994 · US · Colour · 87min

From the moment you see the author's name in the title, you know what to expect of this glitzy TV melodrama. Luxury, deception and no little passion are all to the fore here as ambitious attorney Robert Urich finds himself falling for Stacy Haiduk, the trophy wife of terminally ill millionaire Darren McGavin. Strictly for soap fans and Steel readers only. DP DVD

Robert Urich *Alex Hale* • Stacy Haiduk *Raphaella Phillips* • Marion Ross *Charlotte Brandon* • Darren McGavin *John Henry Phillips* • Susan Sullivan *Kaye* • Holly Marie Combs *Amanda* ■ *Dir* Michael Miller (2) • *Scr* Jan Worthington, from the novel by Danielle Steel

Danielle Steel's Remembrance ★★ PG
Romantic drama 1996 · US · Colour · 87min

Eva LaRue may not be in the same league as Joan Crawford and Barbara Stanwyck, but she suffers nobly as the Italian wife of an American army officer frozen out of the family by hellish mother-in-law Angie Dickinson. Directed with exemplary overstatement by Bethany Rooney, this is undemanding. DP DVD

Angie Dickinson *Margaret Fullerton* • Eva LaRue *Serena Fullerton* • Jeffrey Nordling *Brad Fullerton* • James Calvert *Teddy Fullerton* ■ *Dir* Bethany Rooney • *Scr* David Ambrose, from the novel by Danielle Steel

Danielle Steel's Star ★★ 15
Romantic melodrama 1993 · US · Colour · 92min

Jennie Garth plays a rising young star of the entertainment world who has put her personal tragedies behind her, but remains haunted by her first love Craig Bierko. Director Michael Miller revels in the melodramatic clichés, and the result is an undemanding slice of romantic tosh. JF DVD

Jennie Garth *Crystal Wyatt* • Craig Bierko *Spencer Hill* • Ted Wass *Ernie* • Terry Farrell *Elizabeth* ■ *Dir* Michael Miller (2) • *Scr* Claire Labine, Danielle Steel, from the novel by Danielle Steel

Danielle Steel's Zoya ★★ PG
Period romantic drama
1995 · US · Colour · 170min

Distilled from a four-hour mini-series, but still quite a marathon, this costume melodrama can't be accused of stinting on period detail. However, the storyline is riddled with romanticised clichés and historical stereotypes, as revolution forces Melissa Gilbert's Russian royal to flee to Paris with resourceful grandmother Diana Rigg. It's undemanding stuff, but fans of airport page-turners will have few complaints. DP DVD

Melissa Gilbert *Zoya Ossipov* • Bruce Boxleitner *Clayton Andrews* • Denise Alexander *Axelle* • Taryn Davis *Young Sasha* • David Warner *Vladimir* • Diana Rigg *Evgenia* ■ *Dir* Richard A Colla • *Scr* L Virginia Browne, from the novel by Danielle Steel

The Danish Girl ★★★★ 15
Biographical drama 2015 · US · Colour · 115min

The story of how Danish landscape painter Einar Wegener became a woman named Lili Elbe is the focus of this tasteful, no doubt sanitised yet emotionally powerful biopic. But, even though Eddie Redmayne gets top billing as the tragic Wegener, director Tom Hooper's follow-up to *Les Misérables* is actually focused on his artist wife Gerda (Alicia Vikander). The facts might be moot, but Vikander is sensational in that rarest of things: a love story about a woman who finds her inner strength while letting go. DW
Sexual references. DVD BD

Eddie Redmayne *Einar Wegener/Lili Elbe* • Alicia Vikander *Gerda Wegener* • Ben Whishaw *Henrik* • Amber Heard *Ulla* • Matthias Schoenaerts

Hans ■ *Dir* Tom Hooper • *Scr* Lucinda Coxon, from David Ebershoff's novel • *Music* Alexandre Desplat

Danny Boy ★ U

Drama 1941 · UK · BW · 79min

What on earth was someone of Ann Todd's stature doing in a piece of sentimental nonsense like this? She is woefully miscast as a singer hitting the road to find her estranged husband and son, who have become buskers. DP

Ann Todd *Jane Kay* • Wilfrid Lawson *Jack Newton* • John Warwick *Nick Carter* • Grant Tyler *Danny* • David Farrar *Harold Martin* ■ *Dir* Oswald Mitchell • *Scr* Vera Allinson

Danny Collins ★★★ 15

Comedy drama 2015 · US · Colour · 102min

Al Pacino does his best work in years playing a fading rock star who takes a sentimental journey after receiving a letter from John Lennon – four decades after it was sent. Collins has lost himself in drink, drugs and fan expectations, but buttoned-up hotelier Annette Bening provides a room and piano to facilitate his creative rebirth. It's a joy to watch the mischievous banter between them, although that relationship is overtaken by Collins's efforts to get to know his son (Bobby Cannavale), prompting predictable emotional outpourings. Thankfully, Collins keeps his sense of humour, and Pacino even outshines his razzle-dazzle zoot suits. SP *DVD* Blu

Al Pacino *Danny Collins* • Annette Bening *Mary Sinclair* • Jennifer Garner *Samantha Leigh Donnelly* • Bobby Cannavale *Tom Donnelly* • Christopher Plummer *Frank Grubman* • Nick Offerman *Guy DeLoach* ■ *Dir/Scr* Dan Fogelman

Danny Deckchair ★★★

Comedy 2003 · Aus · Colour · 101min

This contrived yet genial Aussie comedy benefits from the charming chemistry between Rhys Ifans and Miranda Otto. As plot devices go, a life-changing journey in a deckchair attached to helium balloons must rank among the oddest. But accident-prone lorry driver Ifans's transportation from a dead-end existence in the Sydney suburbs to romantic bliss in a New South Wales backwater just about works – in an Ealing sort of way. However, you consistently have to suspend disbelief to accept some of the plot contrivances, most notably traffic cop Otto's charmed acceptance of Ifans's bizarre arrival and the complete inability of Ifans's partner (Justine Clarke) to track him down. DP Swearing, sexual situations.

Rhys Ifans *Danny Morgan* • Miranda Otto *Glenda Lake* • Justine Clarke *Trudy Dunphy* • Rhys Muldoon *Sandy Upman* • Frank Magree *Sgt Dave Mackie* • Anthony Phelan *Jim Craig* ■ *Dir/Scr* Jeff Balsmeyer • *Cinematographer* Martin McGrath

Danny, the Champion of the World ★★★ U

Comedy drama 1989 · UK/US · Colour · 94min

Jeremy Irons and his real-life son Samuel play a happy single-parent family in the 1950s who clash with obnoxious squire Robbie Coltrane over poaching and ownership of land. Samuel saves the day in a well-observed comedy drama in the Ealing style, with fleshed-out characterisations provided by a great supporting cast of British actors. Solid family entertainment. AJ *DVD*

Jeremy Irons *William Smith* • Samuel Irons *Danny Smith* • Cyril Cusack *Dr Spencer* • Robbie Coltrane *Victor Hazell* • Lionel Jeffries *Mr Snoddy* • Ronald Pickup *Captain Lancaster* • Jimmy Nail *Rabbetts* • William Armstrong *Springer* • Michael Hordern *Lord Claybury* • Jean Marsh *Miss Hunter* • John Woodvine *Tallon* ■ *Dir* Gavin Millar • *Scr* John Goldsmith, from Roald Dahl's illustrated children's book

La Danse: the Paris Opera Ballet ★★★ PG

Documentary 2009 · US/Fr/Jpn/Fin · Colour · 158min

Having already profiled La Comédie-Française and the American Ballet Theatre

in the mid-1990s, Frederick Wiseman returns to the arts for this typically detached but ever-acute study of the Paris Opera Ballet. Those unfamiliar with the likes of *The Nutcracker*, *Romeo and Juliet* and more modern works like Mats Ek's *The House of Bernarda Alba* may find the lengthy rehearsal passages less engrossing than the behind-the-scenes activities of the opera staff and their tireless artistic director, Brigitte Lefèvre. Nevertheless, the climactic performance sequences are mesmerising, with John Davey's camera capturing the kinetic energy and athletic grace of the dancers with Degas-like reverence. DP French, English +subtitles.

■ *Dir* Frederick Wiseman • *Cinematographer* John Davey

Dante's Inferno ★★★

Drama 1935 · US · BW · 89min

As the title implies, there is an absolutely super vision of hell, replete with nudity. Most of the screen time, however, is taken up with a Spencer Tracy-Claire Trevor romance; the two Broadway actors acquit themselves well, assuring themselves of future Hollywood success. Tracy's bombast suits his role as a carnival barker owner who gets too big for his boots, and watch closely for a young dancer called Rita Cansino, before she altered her hairline and changed her surname to Hayworth. TS

Spencer Tracy *Jim Carter* • Claire Trevor *Betty McWade* • Henry B Walthall *Pop McWade* • Scotty Beckett *Sonny* • Alan Dinehart *Jonesy* • Rita Cansino [Rita Hayworth] *Speciality dancer* ■ *Dir* Harry Lachman • *Scr* Philip Klein, Robert Yost, from a story by Cyrus Wood, adapted by Edmund Goulding

Dante's Peak ★★★ 12

Disaster action adventure 1997 · US · Colour · 108min

Pierce Brosnan's vulcanologist sees the warning signs for major lava problems in a small mountainside town but no one will believe him. This has some corking digital magma and a lot of cardboard in its path. Director Roger Donaldson papers over dialogue and character deficiencies with some exciting set pieces. Brosnan and Linda Hamilton offer serviceable performances. JC Violence, swearing.

DVD Blu

Pierce Brosnan *Harry Dalton* • Linda Hamilton *Rachel Wando* • Jamie Renee Smith *Lauren Wando* • Jeremy Foley *Graham Wando* • Elizabeth Hoffman *Ruth* • Charles Hallahan *Paul Dreyfus* • Grant Heslov *Greg* ■ *Dir* Roger Donaldson • *Scr* Leslie Bohem

Danton ★★★★ PG

Historical drama 1982 · Fr/Pol · Colour · 130min

With Agnieszka Holland among the scriptwriting team and the great Polish director Andrzej Wajda behind the camera, it's easy to read this passionate account of the political ambushing of one of the key figures of the French Revolution as an allegorical study of the Solidarity movement. Gérard Depardieu gives arguably the finest performance of his career as the corrupt but committed man of the people, impressing both with his public oratory and his bitter ideological feuds with Wojciech Pszoniak's Robespierre. Although Wajda's free with the facts, he captures the fervour and fury of the period superbly. DP French +subtitles. Violence, brief nudity.

Gérard Depardieu *Georges Danton* • Wojciech Pszoniak *Maximilien Robespierre* • Patrice Chéreau *Camille Desmoulins* • Angela Winkler *Lucile Desmoulins* ■ *Dir* Andrzej Wajda • *Scr* Jean-Claude Carrière, Andrzej Wajda, Agnieszka Holland, Boleslaw Michalek, Jacek Gasiorowski, from the play *The Danton Affair* by Stanislawa Przybyszewska

Daratt ★★★★ PG

Drama 2006 · Fr/Chad/Bel/Austria/UK · Colour · 95min

Chad's leading film-maker Mahamat-Saleh Haroun follows the excellent *Abouna* with this compelling blend of Mozart's *La Clemenza di Tito* and Shakespeare's *Hamlet*. Ordered by his blind grandfather to murder

the man who killed his father during the 40-year civil war, teenager Ali Bacha Barkaï tracks Youssouf Djaoro to a backstreet bakery and becomes his apprentice. Exploiting confused emotions and glowering silences to explore the themes of forgiveness and reconciliation, Haroun captures the grim ironies of a riven society. Also functioning as a seethingly subtle thriller, this consistently forces us to reassess our attitude to the frightened youth fighting a battle that is not really his own, and the lonely warrior left to live with the futility of his crimes. DP Chad Arabic, French +subtitles.

Ali Bacha Barkaï *Atim* • Youssouf Djaoro *Nassara* • Aziza Hisseine *Aïcha* • Khayar Oumar Défallah *Atim's grandfather* ■ *Dir/Scr* Mahamat-Saleh Haroun

Darby O'Gill and the Little People ★★★ U

Fantasy 1959 · US · Colour · 86min

Tall-tale teller extraordinaire Albert Sharpe does a deal with the leprechauns (led by Jimmy O'Dea) to ensure daughter Janet Munro's happiness with the Sean Connery. Although Connery looks a little uneasy at having to sing, the performances are largely fine. But this is all about special effects, ranging from the mischievous imps on horseback to the terrifying arrival of the ghostly Costa Bower or Death Coach. DP

Albert Sharpe *Darby O'Gill* • Jimmy O'Dea *King Brian* • Janet Munro *Katie* • Sean Connery *Michael McBride* • Kieron Moore *Pony Sugrue* • Estelle Winwood *Sheelah* • Walter Fitzgerald *Lord Fitzpatrick* ■ *Dir* Robert Stevenson • *Scr* Lawrence E Watkin, from the Darby O'Gill stories by HT Kavanagh

Darby's Rangers ★★

Second World War drama 1958 · US · BW · 105min

This overlong, routine, dreary-looking drama follows American commandos in frontline action in north Africa and Italy during the Second World War. Charlton Heston signed up for the lead, but Jack L Warner apparently reneged on the deal. Veteran director William A Wellman had to settle for young TV stars James Garner and Edd Byrnes and European newcomer Etchika Choureau, who struggle to make an impression. AE

James Garner *Major William Darby* • Etchika Choureau *Angelina De Lotta* • Jack Warden *Master Sergeant Saul Rosen* • Edward Byrnes [Edd Byrnes] *Lieutenant Arnold Dittman* • Venetia Stevenson *Peggy McTavish* • Torin Thatcher *Sergeant McTavish* • Peter Brown *Rollo Burns* • Joan Elan *Wendy Hollister* • Stuart Whitman *Hank Bishop* ■ *Dir* William A Wellman • *Scr* Guy Trosper, from a book by Major James Altieri

Daredevil ★★ 15

Action fantasy 2003 · US · Colour · 99min

There are redeeming features to this Marvel comic adaptation – not least its strong visuals and attractive cast – but these do not add up to a satisfying whole. As a child, Matt Murdock is blinded by radioactive waste that simultaneously heightens his other senses. He grows up to be a New York lawyer (played by Ben Affleck) who doubles as a nocturnal crime-fighter. The flabby narrative introduces a soppy love story involving Jennifer Garner and a cursory game of cat-and-mouse against Colin Farrell's poorly sketched villain. AC Violence, swearing. *DVD* Blu

Ben Affleck *Matthew "Matt" Murdock/Daredevil* • Jennifer Garner *Elektra Natchios* • Michael Clarke Duncan *Wilson Fisk/Kingpin* • Colin Farrell (2) *Bullseye* • Joe Pantoliano *Ben Urich* • Jon Favreau *Franklin "Foggy" Nelson* • David Keith *Jack Murdock* • Kevin Smith (2) *Jack Kirby, lab assistant* • Stan Lee *Old man at crossing* ■ *Dir* Mark Steven Johnson • *Scr* Mark Steven Johnson, from stories and characters by Stan Lee, Bill Everett, Frank Miller

The Darjeeling Limited ★★★★ 15

Adventure comedy drama 2007 · US · Colour · 87min

Writer/director Wes Anderson (*Rushmore*, *The Royal Tenenbaums*) has created his own stilted, downbeat magical-realist world, in which characters often stare straight ahead and sit in uniform rows. From that rich seam comes a grand, spiritual "rail movie" in which three brothers unite for a trip across India, a year after the death of their father. Owen Wilson is the controlling eldest son, Adrien Brody the middle child (and a beatific father-to-be), while co-writer Jason Schwartzman's the angst-ridden, randy youngest. *The Darjeeling Limited* may be largely set and shot in India but we are unmistakeably in Anderson country. Less maddeningly esoteric than his previous film, *The Life Aquatic with Steve Zissou*, it's a handsome, intriguing and subtly funny character study that almost leads to enlightenment. AC Swearing, sex scenes.

DVD Blu

Owen Wilson *Francis* • Adrien Brody *Peter* • Jason Schwartzman *Jack* • Anjelica Huston *Patricia* • Amara Karan *Rita* • Camilla Rutherford *Alice* • Irrfan Khan [Irfan Khan] *The father* • Bill Murray *The businessman* ■ *Dir* Wes Anderson • *Scr* Wes Anderson, Roman Coppola, Jason Schwartzman • *Cinematographer* Robert Yeoman

The Dark ★★ 15

Science-fiction horror 1979 · US · Colour · 86min

This disjointed sci-fi horror movie was started by director Tobe Hooper as a fully fledged horror, then completed by John "Bud" Cardos when something more *Alien*-inspired was required. A confusing mix of supernatural slasher and intergalactic monster movie, this features a murderous alien stalking LA. Little happens in the attacks, all predicted by a mystic, and the murders themselves have minimal impact. AJ Violence, swearing, a sex scene.

William Devane *Ray Warner* • Cathy Lee Crosby *Zoe Owens* • Richard Jaeckel *Detective Mooney* • Warren Kemmerling *Captain Speer* • Biff Elliot *Bresler* ■ *Dir* John "Bud" Cardos • *Scr* Stanford Whitmore

The Dark ★★★ 15

Horror thriller 2005 · Ger/UK · Colour · 89min

Director John Fawcett mixes Welsh mythology with maternal guilt and some very scary sheep to create a highly unusual supernatural horror. Maria Bello brings her young daughter Sophie Stuckey to a remote Welsh farmhouse in a last-ditch attempt to reconcile with her husband (Sean Bean). Then tragedy strikes, and Bello becomes obsessed with the belief that Sarah is not dead but trapped in a kind of distorted parallel world. Fawcett's gripping and atmospheric chiller offers a fascinating look at ancient religious beliefs, as it slowly builds towards a brilliantly realised and heart-rending finale. AJ Violence. *DVD*

Sean Bean *James* • Maria Bello *Adelle* • Richard Elfyn *Rowan* • Maurice Roëves *Dafydd* • Abigail Stone *Ebrill* • Sophie Stuckey *Sarah* ■ *Dir* John Fawcett • *Scr* Stephen Massicotte, from the novel *Sheep* by Simon Maginn

Dark Alibi ★

Mystery 1946 · US · BW · 61min

The first eight entries in the Charlie Chan series after it transferred from Fox to Monogram were bashed out by journeyman writer George Callahan and the strain is readily evident by his swan song, in which as much emphasis is placed on humour as on the clues. Sidney Toler investigates who is responsible for leaving fake fingerprints at the scenes of crimes to implicate innocent people. DP

Sidney Toler *Charlie Chan* • Mantan Moreland *Birmingham* • Ben Carter *Carter* • Benson Fong *Tommy Chan* • Teala Loring *June* ■ *Dir* Phil Karlson • *Scr* George Callahan, from characters by Earl Derr Biggers

The Dark Angel ★★★ U
Romantic drama 1935 · US · BW · 101min

One of the great four-hankie melodramas, this is the talkie remake of a famous Guy Bolton play originally filmed in 1925 with Ronald Colman and Vilma Banky. Here Merle Oberon gives an Oscar-nominated performance as Kitty Vane, loved by upright Herbert Marshall and war-blinded Fredric March. This is an expertly crafted "woman's picture" in which Oberon, shorn of her trademark fashionable hairstyles and expensive wardrobes, is a revelation. The creaky theatrical origins seep through now and then, but acerbic co-scriptwriter Lillian Hellman keeps bathos at bay. **TS**

Fredric March *Alan Trent* · Merle Oberon *Kitty Vane* · Herbert Marshall *Gerald Shannon* · Janet Beecher *Mrs Shannon* · John Halliday *Sir George Barton* · Henrietta Crosman *Granny Vane* ■ *Dir* Sidney Franklin · *Scr* Lillian Hellman, Mordaunt Shairp, from the play by Guy Bolton

Dark Angel ★★★ 18
Science-fiction thriller 1989 · US · Colour · 87min

Dolph Lundgren gives one of his best performances as a Houston detective on the trail of an intergalactic drug dealer in this smartly scripted and crisply directed science-fiction spin on the buddy cop movie. The alien pusher has come to Earth to obtain a substance produced within the human body that is much sought after as a narcotic on their planet. The stock ingredients are all well proportioned in a cracking yarn that's exciting and full of extra twists. **AJ** *DVD*

Dolph Lundgren *Jack Caine* · Brian Benben *Laurence Smith* · Betsy Brantley *Diane Pollon* · Matthias Hues *Talec* · David Ackroyd *Switzer* · Jim Haynie *Captain Malone* ■ *Dir* Craig R Baxley · *Scr* Jonathan Tydor, Leonard Maas Jr

The Dark at the Top of the Stairs ★★
Period drama 1960 · US · Colour · 123min

The William Inge play on which this memoir of life in 1920s Oklahoma is based won the Pulitzer Prize. Unfortunately, whatever merit the original might have had as a theatrical experience has been dissipated here by Delbert Mann's reverential approach to its themes of sexual awakening, family discord, class snobbery and anti-Semitism. Its attitudes have become so outdated that they are likely to breach even the most flexible code of political correctness. **DP**

Robert Preston *Rubin Flood* · Dorothy McGuire *Cora Flood* · Eve Arden *Lottie* · Angela Lansbury *Mavis Pruitt* · Shirley Knight *Reenie Flood* · Lee Kinsolving *Sammy Golden* ■ *Dir* Delbert Mann · *Scr* Irving Ravetch, Harriet Frank Jr, from the play by William Inge

The Dark Avenger ★★★ U
Swashbuckling drama 1955 · US/UK · Colour · 84min

Before he stiffened up into arthritic gestures that passed for acting, Errol Flynn made this final parry-and-lunge costumed swashbuckler. Its story - about an English prince fighting off Peter Finch and his unmerry French conspirators and safeguarding Joanne Dru in the process - is no history lesson, but tuition on how to get away with Flynn's kind of daredevilry. It's a small-scale epic that no discredit, for he was, indeed, a class act. **TH**

Errol Flynn *Prince Edward* · Joanne Dru *Lady Joan Holland* · Peter Finch *Count de Ville* · Yvonne Furneaux *Marie* · Patrick Holt *Sir Ellys* · Michael Hordern *King Edward III* · Moultrie Kelsall *Sir Bruce* · Robert Urquhart *Sir Philip* ■ *Dir* Henry Levin · *Scr* Daniel B Ullman, Phil Park (uncredited) · *Cinematographer* Guy Green

Dark Blue ★★★ 15
Police thriller 2002 · US/Ger/UK · Colour · 113min

This routine thriller is given some much needed impact by a muscular performance from Kurt Russell. Set in the run-up to the LA riots, it follows Russell's uncompromising cop as he keeps the peace with extreme prejudice, carrying on the corruption that has been handed down through generations in the face of a new breed of policeman (represented here by Ving Rhames). It's marred by obvious plotting, grating dialogue and a lack of rounded characterisations, but this comes to life when Russell is on the screen. **IF** Violence, swearing, sex scenes. *DVD*

Kurt Russell *Eldon Perry* · Scott Speedman *Bobby Keough* · Michael Michele *Beth Williamson* · Brendan Gleeson *Jack Van Meter* · Ving Rhames *Arthur Holland* · Lolita Davidovich *Sally Perry* · Dash Mihok *Gary Sidwell* ■ *Dir* Ron Shelton · *Scr* David Ayer, from a story by James Ellroy

Dark Blue World ★★★ 12
Second World War romantic drama 2001 · Cz Rep/UK/Ger · Colour · 108min

Jan Sverak, director of the Oscar-winning *Kolya*, reunites with his screenwriter father Zdenek for this engaging memoir about the Czech pilots who flew alongside the RAF during the Second World War. Neatly dovetailing dogfights with domestic drama, the film avoids stereotype and sentiment, as Ondrej Vetchy and his rookie pal discover that their mutual attraction to sailor's wife Tara FitzGerald is infringing on their mission. **DP** Czech, English, German +subtitles. Violence. *DVD*

Ondrej Vetchy *Lt Frantisek "Franta" Slama* · Krystof Hadek *Karel Vojtisek* · Tara FitzGerald *Susan Whitmore* · Oldrich Kaiser *Machaty* · Hans-Jorg Assmann *Doctor Blaschke* · Charles Dance *Wing Commander Bentley* ■ *Dir* Jan Sverak · *Scr* Zdenek Sverak

Dark City ★★★
Mystery drama 1950 · US · BW · 97min

Don DeFore loses all the company cash in a rigged poker game, then hangs himself. It's a fabulous *noir* opening, but director William Dieterle fails to maintain the tight suspense as Charlton Heston, here making his feature debut, is stalked by DeFore's psychopathic brother. That said, it's a typically well-crafted Paramount production, and Lizabeth Scott smoulders seductively. **TS**

Charlton Heston *Danny Haley* · Lizabeth Scott *Fran* · Don DeFore *Arthur Winant* · Jack Webb *Augie* · Ed Begley *Barney* · Henry Morgan [Harry Morgan] *Soldier* · Mark Keuning *Billy Winant* · Mike Mazurki *Sidney Winant* ■ *Dir* William Dieterle · *Scr* Larry Marcus, John Meredyth Lucas, from a story by Larry Marcus

Dark City ★★★★ 15
Science-fiction fantasy thriller 1998 · US · Colour · 96min

Director Alex Proyas lends a potent gothic atmosphere to this dream-like fantasy about a race of mysterious bald figures who continually reconfigure a surreal, gloomy city and its inhabitants as some sort of weird experiment. As with *The Crow*, Proyas employs every striking camera angle in his visual vocabulary, breathing dread into the overhanging *Batman*-style architecture. The effects are impressively realised, too, as buildings stretch and widen before our eyes. Although overshadowed by the film's visual flair, the eclectic cast adds a splash of colour to the shadowy surroundings. **JC** *DVD*

Rufus Sewell *John Murdoch* · Kiefer Sutherland *Dr Daniel Schreber* · Jennifer Connelly *Emma Murdoch* · William O'Brien *Mr Hand* · Ian Richardson *Mr Book* · Colin Friels *Walenski* · Mitchell Butel *Husselbeck* · Frank Gallacher *Stromboli* · Melissa George *May* · William Hurt *Inspector Frank Bumstead* ■ *Dir* Alex Proyas · *Scr* Alex Proyas, Lem Dobbs, David S Goyer, from a story by Alex Proyas · *Cinematographer* Dariusz Wolski

Dark Command ★★ U
Western 1940 · US · BW · 89min

After John Wayne's success in *Stagecoach*, his home studio, Republic, promoted him from B-westerns to this big-budget effort. Wayne is the simple cowpoke who successfully runs for marshal to impress his girl and, as a result, the much better qualified other candidate, Walter Pidgeon, turns to a life of crime. The film lurches between static dialogue scenes and bursts of action. **AE** *DVD*

John Wayne *Bob Seton* · Claire Trevor *Mary McCloud* · Walter Pidgeon *William Cantrell* · Roy Rogers *Fletch McCloud* · George "Gabby" Hayes *Doc Grunch* · Porter Hall *Angus McCloud* ■ *Dir* Raoul Walsh · *Scr* Grover Jones, Lionel Hauser, F Hugh Herbert, from the novel by WR Burnett

The Dark Corner ★★★ PG
Film noir 1946 · US · BW · 95min

Although relatively unknown, this is a rattlingly good and cleverly plotted *film noir*, skilfully directed by Henry Hathaway. It's marred only by too-obvious studio sets and a bland leading man in Mark Stevens, who's not quite tough enough as the private eye framed by his former partner. Still, there's a nicely etched performance from Lucille Ball (of all people) as a hard-boiled secretary. **TS** *DVD*

Mark Stevens *Bradford Galt* · Lucille Ball *Kathleen* · Clifton Webb *Hardy Cathcart* · William Bendix *White Suit* · Kurt Kreuger *Tony Jardine* · Cathy Downs *Mari Cathcart* · Reed Hadley *Lt Frank Reeves* · Constance Collier *Mrs Kingsley* ■ *Dir* Henry Hathaway · *Scr* Jay Dratler, Bernard Schoenfeld, from a short story by Leo Rosten · *Cinematographer* Joseph MacDonald [Joe MacDonald]

The Dark Crystal ★★★★ PG
Fantasy adventure 1982 · UK · Colour · 89min

Few film-makers feel at home in the realms of fantasy, but Jim Henson had an affinity with the magical. Although *The Dark Crystal* emerged from the darker side of his imagination, it's still a mesmerising picture that will enchant older children and adults alike. The story is a basic slice of sword and sorcery, following Jen and Kira as they attempt to restore a splinter of a crystal that will free the "Mystics" from the tyranny of the "Skeksis". However, there is a liberal sprinkling of Muppet-style humour to enliven the adventure, and, with the exception of the "Gelflings", the creatures are inspired. **DP** *DVD* *Blu*

Stephen Garlick *Jen* · Billie Whitelaw *Aughra* · Lisa Maxwell *Kira* · Barry Dennen *Chamberlain* · Michael Kilgarriff *General* · Percy Edwards *Fizzgig* ■ *Dir* Jim Henson, Frank Oz · *Scr* David Odell, from a story by Jim Henson

Dark Days ★★★ 15
Documentary 2000 · US · BW · 78min

British film-maker Marc Singer spent two years underground shooting his debut feature, a compassionate documentary about the inhabitants of the Amtrak tunnel network beneath New York's Pennsylvania Station. With his monochrome imagery evoking Depression-era photojournalism, Singer makes the distinction between homeless and hopeless, as he captures the ingenious ways his articulate subjects survive in their subterranean world. Yet there is also genuine pain in the frank discussion of the way in which drugs robbed some of life, if not hope. Less convincing, however, is the "happy ending", when the Amtrakers are resettled in above-ground accommodation. **DP** *DVD*

■ *Dir* Marc Singer · *Cinematographer* Marc Singer · *Editor* Melissa Neidich · *Music* DJ Shadow

Dark Eyes ★★ PG
Romantic comedy 1987 · It · Colour · 112min

In addition to winning the best actor prize at Cannes, Marcello Mastroianni landed an Oscar nomination for his bravura performance in this self-conscious amalgamation of four Chekhov short stories. Directing with a fine eye for period detail, Nikita Mikhalkov robs the action of its social and pyschological subtlety by calling for grandiloquent gestures and stereotypical characterisations, which turn delicate situations into potboiler set pieces. As an ageing playboy, the ever astute Mastroianni is able to give a shaded performance. **DP** Italian +subtitles.

Marcello Mastroianni *Romano* · Silvana Mangano *Elisa* · Marthe Keller *Tina* · Elena Sofonova *Anna* · Pina Cei *Elisa's mother* ■ *Dir* Nikita Mikhalkov · *Scr* Alexander Adabashian, Nikita Mikhalkov, Suso Cecchi D'Amico, from the short stories *Anna around the Neck, The Lady with the Little Dog, My Wife, The Name-Day Party* by Anton Chekhov

Dark Eyes of London ★★★ PG
Horror 1939 · UK · BW · 72min

In one of the most effective examples of screen *Grand Guignol*, Bela Lugosi is at his evil best as the director of an insurance company who kills his clients so he can collect on their policies. Disguised as the kindly old proprietor of a home for the blind, he carries out his nefarious swindles with the assistance of a hideous giant. Based on an Edgar Wallace novel, this British-made shocker, directed by Walter Summers, is both bleak and remarkably scary for the time. **AJ**

Bela Lugosi *Dr Orloff* · Hugh Williams *Inspector Holt* · Greta Gynt *Diana Stuart* · Edmond Ryan [Edmon Ryan] *Lt O'Reilly* · Wilfrid Walter *Jake, the Monster* · Alexander Field *Grogan* ■ *Dir* Walter Summers · *Scr* Patrick Kirwan, Walter Summers, John Argyle, from a novel by Edgar Wallace

Dark Habits ★★★ 15
Comedy 1983 · Sp · Colour · 110min

Pedro Almodóvar's third feature is a Buñuelian satire on religious hypocrisy bedecked in the most gloriously tacky Catholic kitsch. Seeking sanctuary after her lover's overdose, hard-nosed chanteuse Cristina Sánchez Pascual is shocked by what she finds inside the Convent of Humble Redeemers. But while it's tempting to mock the nuns in Julieta Serrano's charge - with Carmen Maura devoting herself to a menagerie, Marisa Paredes experiencing ecstatic visions and Chus Lampreave devouring pulp fiction - the film is as much about the irredeemable decadence of the secular world as it is about the sins committed beyond the cloisters. **DP** Spanish +subtitles. *DVD*

Cristina Sánchez Pascual *Yolanda Bell* · Willmore [Will More] *Jorge* · Julieta Serrano *Mother Julia* · Marisa Paredes *Sister Estiércol* · Mary Carrillo *Marquesa* · Carmen Maura *Sister Perdida* · Chus Lampreave *Sister Rata de Callejón* ■ *Dir/Scr* Pedro Almodóvar

The Dark Half ★★★ 18
Horror 1991 · US · Colour · 116min

Timothy Hutton does his finest work in years in this Stephen King adaptation. He plays a bestselling writer whose emerging supernatural side manifests itself in the form of a brutal serial killer who starts stalking the New England family home. George A Romero makes this both possible and frightening by twisting the usual slasher genre conventions, but spoils it with an overblown ending. **AJ** Violence, swearing. *DVD*

Timothy Hutton *Thad Beaumont/George Stark* · Michael Rooker *Sheriff Alan Pangborn* · Amy Madigan *Liz Beaumont* · Julie Harris (2) *Reggie Delesseps* · Robert Joy *Fred Clawson* · Rutanya Alda *Miriam Cowley* · Chelsea Field *Annie Pangborn* · Kent Broadhurst *Mike Donaldson* ■ *Dir* George A Romero · *Scr* George A Romero, from the novel by Stephen King

Dark Harbor ★★
Thriller 1998 · US · Colour · 90min

Polly Walker and Alan Rickman star in this average thriller, directed by Adam Coleman Howard. They play a squabbling couple, struggling through a storm to reach the ferry that will take them to their island home. However, their problems *really* begin when they pick up a battered boy (Norman Reedus). Walker and Rickman are fine as the icy marrieds. For all that, this is one of those films that just doesn't hang together. **LH**

Alan Rickman *David Weinberg* · Polly Walker *Alexis Chandler Weinberg* · Norman Reedus *Young man* ■ *Dir* Adam Coleman Howard · *Scr* Adam Coleman Howard, Justin Lazard

Dark Horse ★★ 15
Drama 1992 · US · Colour · 70min

After her mother dies, teenager Ari Meyers goes out of her way to get into trouble to get some attention from her workaholic dad played by Ed Begley Jr. Ordered to do community service at a local horse ranch, she learns to love horses with the help of ranch owner Mimi Rogers. The kid's a brat, Rogers is sleepwalking, and who told Ed Begley Jr he could act? There's a twist at the end, but only lovers of weepies will make it that far. ST

Mimi Rogers *Dr Susan Hadley* • Ed Begley Jr *Jack Mills* • Ari Meyers *Allison Mills* • Samantha Eggar *Mrs Curtis* • Tab Hunter *Perkins* • Chad Smith *Clint* ■ *Dir* David Hemmings • *Scr* JE MacLean, from a story by Tab Hunter

Dark Horse ★★ 15
Comedy drama 2011 · US · Colour · 85min

Despite an interesting cast, its unlikely that anyone other than fans of Todd Solondz (*Happiness*) will be satisfied by this offering from the tabco-breaking director. Jordan Gelber is a nerdish man-child who lives with his mother and father. Selma Blair is also back at home the victim of her own mysterious, self-destructive past. They meet, he proposes, and after a sudden courtship she begins to think: "Well, why not?" The characters are all awful, and what seems to aspire to being a modern comedy of manners is simply a mean-spirited satire. DW Swearing, sexual references. DVD

Jordan Gelber *Abe* • Selma Blair *Miranda (formerly "Vi")* • Justin Bartha *Richard* • Mia Farrow *Phyllis* • Christopher Walken *Jackie* • Zachary Booth *Justin* ■ *Dir/Scr* Todd Solondz

The Dark Horse ★★★★ 15
Drama based on a true story 2014 · NZ · Colour · 124min

Kiwi star Cliff Curtis makes a triumphant return to his homeland with this multi-award-winning true story after *Whale Rider* propelled him to a career in Hollywood in 2002. He plays a brilliant speed chess player with bipolar disorder who takes a group of troubled kids under his wing for an unlikely tilt at the national chess championships. Director James Napier Robertson manages to avoid most of the sentimental clichés usually associated with these sorts of true stories, giving the film a gritty sheen that ultimately makes its inspirational message all the more uplifting. JF

Cliff Curtis *Genesis Potini* • James Rolleston *Mana* • Kirk Torrance *Noble* • Xavier Horan *Jedi* ■ *Dir/Scr* James Napier Robertson

Dark Horse ★★★ PG
Drama documentary 2014 · UK · Colour · 86min

Everyone's a sucker for an underdog story and director Louise Osmond recounts the tale of racing outsider Dream Alliance with a judicious blend of sentiment, wit and inspiration. The plucky horse bounces back from serious injury at Aintree to win the Welsh Grand National in 2009, but this is also a poignant study of a disenfranchised mining community pulling together in the depths of a recession. Osmond might have delved deeper into the morality of National Hunt racing, but with editor Joby Gee she ably relates the account with archive footage, photographs and a few blurry re-constructions. DP

■ *Dir/Scr* Louise Osmond

Dark Intruder ★★★
Horror 1965 · US · BW · 58min

Murders occurring in turn-of-the-century San Francisco are traced back to Sumerian devil creatures by a psychic investigator in this pilot for a horror series. (The show, to be called *Black Cloak*, never materialised, so the pilot was given a theatrical release.) Superior make-up effects and a nifty HP Lovecraft-style atmosphere add power to the supernatural shocks, while future *Naked Gun* star Leslie Nielsen proves once again what a loss he was to straight melodrama. AJ

Leslie Nielsen *Brett Kingsford* • Gilbert Green *Harvey Misbach* • Charles Bolender *Nikola* • Mark Richman [Peter Mark Richman] *Robert Vandenburg* • Judi Meredith *Evelyn Lang* • Werner Klemperer *Prof Malaki* ■ *Dir* Harvey Hart • *Scr* Barre Lyndon

The Dark Is Rising ★★ 12
Fantasy action adventure 2007 · US · Colour · 94min

The success of Harry Potter has reinvigorated children's fantasy cinema and this lacklustre outing is just one of several attempts to cash-in on the wizards and witches boom. Its pedigree is impressive, at least, being based on the second of British author Susan Cooper's five-book cycle of Arthurian fantasy novels about the battle between the forces of Light and Dark. This hurried, far-from-faithful adaptation follows American teen in England Will Stanton (Alexander Ludwig) as he discovers that he's the last of a group of immortal warriors, led by Merriman (Ian McShane) and Miss Greythorne (Frances Conroy). To defeat The Rider (Christopher Eccleston) and restore the power of Light, Will must hunt for six mythical signs scattered across time - but these journeys to the Viking era and beyond prioritise special effects at the expense of coherent plotting. JR DVD

Alexander Ludwig *Will Stanton* • Christopher Eccleston *The Rider* • Ian McShane *Merriman Lyon* • Frances Conroy *Miss Greythorne* • Gregory Smith *Max* • Amelia Warner *Maggie Barnes* • James Ccsmo *Dawson* • Jim Piddock *Old George* ■ *Dir* David L Cunningham • *Scr* John Hodge, from Susan Cooper's novel • *Cinematographer* Joel Ransom

Dark Journey ★★★ U
First World War spy drama 1937 · UK · BW · 80min

Vivien Leigh runs a Stockholm dress shop during the First World War. In reality, though, she's a double agent working for the Allies. Complications ensue when she becomes emotionally involved with a German baron (the silkily threatening Conrad Veidt) who cottons on to the truth. Producer Alexander Korda brought out all the big guns for this spy drama: Victor Saville directs, Georges Périnal and Harry Stradling provide some beautiful photography, while Richard Addinsell supplies the score. The result is meticulously wrought tosh. RK

Conrad Veidt *Baron Karl Von Marwitz* • Vivien Leigh *Madeleine Goddard* • Joan Gardner *Lupita* • Anthony Bushell *Bob Carter* • Ursula Jeans *Gertrude* • Margery Pickard *Colette* • Eliot Makeham *Anatole* • Austin Trevor *Dr Muller* ■ *Dir* Victor Saville • *Scr* Arthur Wimperis, from a story by Lajos Biró

The Dark Knight ★★★★★ 12
Action fantasy 2008 · US · Colour · 145min

If *Batman Begins* was the classy hors d'oeuvre in Christopher Nolan's blockbuster trilogy, then this awesome follow-up is a main course that delivers on all levels. Christian Bale is back as Gotham City's nocturnal guardian, but just as Batman has the bad guys on the run, he's soon in the fight of his life with the ultimate opponent, the Joker (Heath Ledger). In the performance that earned him a posthumous Oscar, Ledger creates a villain who's smart, charismatic, vicious and very, very scary. But this is no simple face-off between two iconic opponents. Ledger's scarred schemer wants to bring everything crashing down – the city, the police, even the criminal underworld, itself. A Joker for our times, perhaps. Nolan revels in their physical and psychological jousting, and there are plenty of fights, chases and explosive set pieces for action junkies. But this is a blockbuster with ambition, as well being one of the best action yarns of the noughties. JA Violence. DVD

Christian Bale *Bruce Wayne/Batman* • Heath Ledger *The Joker* • Aaron Eckhart *Harvey Dent/Two-Face* • Michael Caine *Alfred Pennyworth* • Gary Oldman *Lieutenant James Gordon* • Morgan Freeman *Lucius Fox* • Maggie Gyllenhaal *Rachel*

Dawes • Eric Roberts *Salvatore "The Boss" Maroni* • Anthony Michael Hall *Engel* ■ *Dir* Christopher Nolan • *Scr* Christopher Nolan, Jonathan Nolan, from a story by Christopher Nolan, David S Goyer, from characters by Bob Kane, Jerry Robinson (the Joker) • *Cinematographer* Wally Pfister

The Dark Knight Rises ★★★★ 12
Action fantasy 2012 · US · Colour · 157min

Christopher Nolan concludes his Batman franchise with another ambitious epic, · which sees Christian Bale's caped crime-fighter taken to hell and back. Eight years on from events in the last film, Bruce Wayne has become a recluse. But when nefarious masked terrorist Bane (a beefed-up Tom Hardy) infiltrates the city and Wayne encounters slinky cat burglar Selina Kyle (Anne Hathaway), it's time for the tortured tycoon to suit up and get back in the game. Nolan produces some superb set pieces and gets terrific performances from his cast, both regular and new (nods to Joseph Gordon-Levitt as an idealistic young cop and Hathaway, who's spot on as a sexy but no-nonsense Catwoman). This is a long haul and does sag occasionally, but Nolan can still be credited with producing a superhero franchise unmatched for its mood, menace and quality. JA In English, French. DVD Blu

Christian Bale *Bruce Wayne/Batman* • Anne Hathaway *Selina Kyle* • Tom Hardy *Bane* • Michael Caine *Alfred Pennyworth* • Gary Oldman *Commissioner Gordon* • Morgan Freeman *Lucius Fox* • Joseph Gordon-Levitt *John Blake* • Marion Cotillard *Miranda Tate* • Matthew Modine *Foley* ■ *Dir* Christopher Nolan • *Scr* Christopher Nolan, Jonathan Nolan, from a story by Christopher Nolan, David S Goyer, from characters by Bob Kane

The Dark Light ★
Crime thriller 1951 · UK · BW · 66min

Imagine *Shallow Grave* shot in a lighthouse with a cast of no-hopers and the budget of a public information film, and you'll have some idea of what this dismal Hammer offering is like. "Quota quickie" veteran Vernon Sewell gets matters off to a promising start as a desperate gang of bank robbers are rescued from the stormy sea by a lighthouse crew, but tosses away the dramatic possibilities of the claustrophobic setting. DP

Albert Lieven *Mark* • David Greene *Johnny* • Norman Macowan *Rigby* • Martin Benson *Luigi* • Catherine Blake *Linda* • Jack Stewart *Matt* ■ *Dir/Scr* Vernon Sewell

The Dark Mirror ★★★★ PG
Psychological thriller 1946 · US · BW · 81min

This near-classic thriller from director Robert Siodmak stars Lew Ayres as a psychologist trying to discover which twin sister is a killer. Nunnally Johnson's script springs few real surprises, raiding the textbooks of Freud, but Siodmak pulls out all the melodramatic stops with low-key lighting and weird camera angles. Dimitri Tiomkin's music, meanwhile, heaves like an ocean in a bad mood, and, as the two sisters, Olivia de Havilland seems to be saying, "Bette Davis, eat your heart out." AT DVD

Olivia de Havilland *Terry Collins/Ruth Collins* • Lew Ayres *Dr Scott Elliott* • Thomas Mitchell *Detective Stevenson* • Richard Long *Rusty* • Charles Evans *District Attorney Girard* ■ *Dir* Robert Siodmak • *Scr* Nunnally Johnson, from the novel by Vladimir Pozner • *Cinematographer* Milton Krasner

Dark of the Sun ★★ 15
Adventure 1967 · UK · Colour · 96min

This tough colonial adventure follows Rod Taylor and Jim Brown as they become entangled in the civil war in the Congo in 1960. Taylor is the man of no principle, until the script's sermonising gets to him, while Brown, as his buddy, plays the Congo native with a conscience. Directed on location by Jack Cardiff, the film's schoolboy heroics sit awkwardly beside its political rhetoric. AT Some violence, swearing.

Rod Taylor *Captain Bruce Curry* • Yvette Mimieux *Claire* • Jim Brown *Sergeant Ruffo* • Kenneth More *Dr Wreid* • Peter Carsten *Henlein* • Olivier Despax *Surrier* ■ *Dir* Jack Cardiff • *Scr* Quentin Werty, Adrian Spies, from the novel by Wilbur A Smith

Dark Passage ★★★ 15
Film noir thriller 1947 · US · BW · 101min

Escaped convict Humphrey Bogart changes his appearance with plastic surgery and hides out with artist Lauren Bacall while he attempts to prove he is innocent of his wife's murder. The third Bogart/Bacall outing, written and directed by Delmer Daves, is slick and efficient, yet somewhat disappointing. The first 40 minutes or so are ingeniously photographed from Bogart's subjective point of view, tantalisingly keeping us waiting for the star's appearance. Otherwise, the movie is a low-key affair. RK DVD

Humphrey Bogart *Vincent Parry* • Lauren Bacall *Irene Jansen* • Bruce Bennett *Bob* • Agnes Moorehead *Madge Rapf* • Tom D'Andrea *Sam* • Clifton Young *Baker* ■ *Dir* Delmer Daves • *Scr* Delmer Daves, from the novel *Dark Passage* by David Goodis

The Dark Past ★★★ PG
Crime drama 1948 · US · BW · 71min

This is a moody remake of 1939's *Blind Alley*, the melodrama about a demented thug holding the local psychologist hostage while the latter tries to talk the convict into reasoning out why he turned bad. It always was a good plot, and here skilled director Rudolph Maté brings light and shade to bear on this once trail-blazing subject. William Holden makes a brave stab at the killer, but Lee J Cobb brings real Method intensity to the understanding psychiatrist. TS

William Holden (2) *Al Walker* • Nina Foch *Betty* • Lee J Cobb *Dr Andrew Collins* • Adele Jergens *Laura Stevens* • Stephen Dunne [Steve Dunne] *Owen Talbot* • Lois Maxwell *Ruth Collins* • Berry Kroeger *Mike* • Steven Geray *Professor Fred Linder* • Wilton Graff *Frank Stevens* • Robert Osterloh *Pete* ■ *Dir* Rudolph Maté • *Scr* Philip MacDonald, Michael Blankfort, Albert Duffy, Malvin Wald, Oscar Saul, from the play *Blind Alley* by James Warwick

Dark Places ★
Horror 1973 · UK · Colour · 90min

Asylum administrator Robert Hardy inherits a supposedly haunted mansion where some grisly deaths occurred and a great deal of money is hidden. Psychiatrist Christopher Lee and his sister, Joan Collins, plot to cheat him out of his estate, despite the murderous spiritual presence of its previous owner. Leaden sub-Hammer horror, directed with little flair by veteran Don Sharp and containing inert performances. AJ

Christopher Lee *Dr Mandeville* • Joan Collins *Sarah* • Robert Hardy *Edward/Andrew* • Herbert Lom *Prescott* • Jane Birkin *Alta* • Carleton Hobbs *Old Marr* ■ *Dir* Don Sharp • *Scr* Ed Brennan, Joseph Van Winkle

Dark Places ★★★ 15
Thriller 2015 · UK/Fr/US · Colour and BW · 107min

This dark, downbeat thriller involves plenty of twists and turns. Adapted from the novel by Gillian Flynn (*Gone Girl*), it has Charlize Theron as a damaged, hostile 30-something whose mother and sisters were murdered when she was seven years old. Swept along by lawyers and press hounds, she testified that her older brother (Tye Sheridan) was responsible for the murders...but now believing that his conviction was a miscarriage of justice, she revisits the events that ruined her life. Theron is solid enough in the lead, and the central mystery is reasonably intriguing before the beans are spilled. SC Swearing, violence, drug abuse. DVD Blu

Charlize Theron *Libby Day* • Nicholas Hoult *Lyle* • Chloë Grace Moretz *Young Diondra* • Christina Hendricks *Patty Day* ■ *Dir* Gilles Paquet-Brenner • *Scr* Gilles Paquet-Brenner, from Gillian Flynn's novel

Dark Prince – the Legend of Dracula ★★★ 18

Horror   2000 · US · Colour · 87min

A highly romanticised, yet basically accurate, telling of how 15th-century Romanian warlord Vlad Tepes became the brutal blood-drinking tyrant of Eastern European folklore and the basis for Bram Stoker's Dracula character. All the infamous atrocities are present and correct in this swashbuckling horror telemovie and B-movie maestro Joe Chappelle makes the most out of its low budget and Romanian locations. The final shift into fantasy is a little awkwardly done but overall it's impressive. AJ *DVD*

Rudolf Martin *Vlad the Impaler* • Michael Sutton *Radu* • Christopher Brand *Bruno* • Peter Weller *Father Stefan* • Jane March *Lidia* • Roger Daltrey *King Janos* ■ *Dir* Joe Chappelle • *Scr* Tom Baum [Thomas Baum]

The Dark Road ★★

Drama   1948 · UK · BW · 74min

This was Alfred Goulding's first feature after directing Laurel and Hardy in *A Chump at Oxford* in 1940. With his background in comedies, he struggles with this grim tale tracing the life and crimes of a surly borstal boy. To his credit, he achieves a certain cheap realism and catches the argot of postwar criminality. But neither Charles Stuart, as the delinquent who drifts from petty larceny to jewel robbery, nor Joyce Linden, as the girl he exploits, are up to the task. DP

Charles Stuart *Sidney Robertson* • Joyce Linden *Ann* • Antony Holles • Roddy Hughes • Patricia Hicks ■ *Dir* Alfred Goulding

Dark Shadows ★★★ 12

Horror comedy drama   2012 · US · Colour · 114min

Director Tim Burton layers on the signature quirkiness in this mannered gothic farce based on the 1960s supernatural soap opera. In his eighth Burton collaboration, Johnny Depp plays vampire Barnabas Collins, who returns to his Maine stately pile in 1972 after two centuries of witch-enforced hibernation and sets about restoring his family's fortunes. The actors certainly throw themselves into the nonsense, and Burton's style is a visual treat, but in trying to capture the cult TV show's blend of eccentric comedy and melodrama, the film's sense of madcap fun is often left high and dry. AJ Some violence, sexual references, drug abuse. *DVD*

Johnny Depp *Barnabas Collins* • Eva Green *Angelique Bouchard* • Michelle Pfeiffer *Elizabeth Collins Stoddard* • Helena Bonham Carter *Dr Julia Hoffman* • Chloë Grace Moretz *Carolyn Stoddard* • Jonny Lee Miller *Roger Collins* • Christopher Lee *Clarney* • Alice Cooper ■ *Dir* Tim Burton • *Scr* Seth Grahame-Smith, from a story by John August, Grahame-Smith, from the TV series by Dan Curtis • *Music* Danny Elfman

Dark Skies ★★★ 15

Science-fiction horror   2013 · US · Colour · 93min

Sinister goings-on in suburbia make life a living hell for Keri Russell, Josh Hamilton and their two sons in this taut shocker, which sees unseen forces invade the family home. Writer/director Scott Stewart delivers some pleasing jolts in a story that owes much to *Poltergeist*, but tends to signpost too many of its scares and plot twists. Russell and Hamilton convince as the initially sceptical parents who come under suspicion from neighbours, but are eclipsed by the subtle performance of Dakota Goyo as their troubled eldest son. TeS Swearing. *DVD*

Keri Russell *Lacy Barrett* • Josh Hamilton *Daniel Barrett* • JK Simmons *Edwin Pollard* • Dakota Goyo *Jesse Barrett* • Kadan Rockett *Sam Barrett* ■ *Dir/Scr* Scott Stewart

Dark Star ★★★★ PG

Cult science fiction   1973 · US · Colour · 79min

In director John Carpenter's impressive feature debut, hippy spacemen fight boredom on a 20-year mission to seek out and destroy unstable planets. Produced as a film project at the University of Southern California for just $60,000, this sly parody begins as a satire on *2001: a Space Odyssey*. However, it quickly moves into original territory as the cabin-fevered crew cope with a vicious alien stowaway, a nagging computer and a thermo-nuclear device that's all set to explode. Witty, profound and cleverly scored by Carpenter with a selection of electronic country and western tunes. AJ *DVD*

Brian Narelle *Doolittle* • Andreijah Pahich *Talby* • Carl Kuniholm *Boiler* • Dan O'Bannon *Pinback* • Joe Sanders *Powell* ■ *Dir* John Carpenter • *Scr* John Carpenter, Dan O'Bannon

Dark Summer ★★ 12

Drama   1994 · UK · Colour · 70min

As the familiar scouse skyline recedes, to be replaced by sobering images of urban decay, there's a glimmer that Charles Teton's debut feature is going to deal with the real Liverpool, rather than the melodramatised *Brookside* version. But the social implications of the relationship between black labourer Steve Ako and Joeline Garnier-Joel, his white boss's daughter, are soon forgotten, as Ako embarks on a boxing career that will cost him everything. Director Teton's advertising background is proclaimed in almost every self-consciously grubby shot. DP

Steve Ako *Abraham Wilson* • Joeline Garnier-Joel *Jess Shepherd* • Bernie Deasy *Amateur coach* • Chris Darwin *Alan Shepherd* • Dermott Mulholland ■ *Dir* Charles Teton • *Scr* Charles Teton, with additional material from Bernie Deasy, Steve Cheers, Bernd Lubke

Dark Tide ★★ 15

Adventure thriller   2012 · US/S Afr · Colour · 108min

Director John Stockwell is no stranger to aquatic adventures, having already made *Blue Crush* and *Into the Blue*, but this shark-attack flick is brimming with clichés and caricatures. Traumatised after seeing her assistant savaged by a great white, shark expert Halle Berry has broken up with her cameraman boyfriend (Olivier Martinez) and allowed her boat trip business to decline. But a wealthy Brit (Ralph Brown) makes her an offer she can't refuse to let him and his son swim outside a shark cage, with all-too-predictable consequences. DP *DVD*

Halle Berry *Kate Mathieson* • Olivier Martinez *Jeff Le Grange* • Ralph Brown *William Brady* • Luke Tyler *Luke Brady* • Mark Elderkin *Tommy* ■ *Dir* John Stockwell • *Scr* Ronnie Christensen, Amy Sorlie

Dark Tower ★ 18

Supernatural horror thriller   1989 · US · Colour · 91min

Michael Moriarty plays an investigator called in when a supernatural force starts bumping off people in a skyscraper. This appalling mix of *Omen*-style operatic deaths and *Poltergeist* scares ran into production problems, and Hammer veteran Freddie Francis was replaced as director. RS

Michael Moriarty *Dennis Randall* • Jenny Agutter *Carolyn Page* • Carol Lynley *Tilly Ambrose* • Theodore Bikel *Dr Max Gold* • Anne Lockhart *Elaine* • Kevin McCarthy *Sergie* ■ *Dir* Freddie Francis • *Scr* Robert J Avrech, Ken Wiederhorn, Ken Blackwell, from a story by Robert J Avrech

The Dark Tower

Fantasy horror western   2017 · US · Colour

This is a preview – no prints were available to review as we went to press: From the fertile imagination of Stephen King comes a story set in the Old West – except this is a mystical version of that land. Idris Elba rides upfront as the last "Gunslinger", a knight of the frontier and part of an ancient order, while Matthew McConaughey is the sinister "Man in Black" who stalks him in search of the eponymous tower. The question is whether the sense of mystery in King's series of eight books can be teased out for a film audience – there could be too much going on, or not enough. SP

Idris Elba *Roland Deschain/The Gunslinger* • Matthew McConaughey *Man in Black* • Jackie Earle Haley *Sayre* ■ *Dir* Nikolaj Arcel • *Scr* Nikolaj Arcel, Akiva Goldsman, Anders Thomas Jensen, Jeff Pinkner, from Stephen King's novel

A Dark Truth ★★ 15

Action thriller   2012 · Can · Colour · 106min

This would-be eco-thriller has a lot of potential, but it is not nearly as engaging as it could be. The cast, led by Andy Garcia and co-starring Forest Whitaker, is certainly strong, while writer/director Damian Lee's story about the privatisation of water resources by global conglomerates remains a topical and relatively underreported issue. The talent works hard, but the script suffers thanks to its hackneyed polemics on the nature of man and the value of truth, which drain the plot of what excitement it musters. ReP English, Spanish + subtitles.

Andy Garcia *Jack Begosian* • Forest Whitaker *Francisco Francis* • Eva Longoria *Mia Francis* • Kim Coates *Bruce Swinton* • Deborah Kara Unger *Morgan Swinton* • Kevin Durand *Tor* ■ *Dir/Scr* Damian Lee

Dark Victory ★★★★ PG

Melodrama   1939 · US · BW · 100min

This Bette Davis vehicle boasts one of her best performances as an heiress tragically stricken with a brain tumour. The condition means that she will go blind before dying, and so paves the way for a death scene so memorably heart-rending (aided by a knockout Max Steiner score which the star loathed) that it took Davis to the number one female movie star slot in the US. All of those classy Warner Bros production values are well in evidence, hiding the fact that this is really a load of old codswallop. Humphrey Bogart performs as though he knows he's been miscast. Remade in Britain in 1963 as *Stolen Hours*, starring Susan Hayward. TS *DVD*

Bette Davis *Judith Traherne* • George Brent *Dr Frederick Steele* • Humphrey Bogart *Michael O'Leary* • Geraldine Fitzgerald *Ann King* • Ronald Reagan *Alec Hamin* • Henry Travers *Dr Parsons* • Cora Witherspoon *Carrie Spottswood* • Virginia Brissac *Martha* ■ *Dir* Edmund Goulding • *Scr* Casey Robinson, from the play by George Emerson Brewer Jr, Bertram Bloch

Dark Victory ★★

Romantic drama   1976 · US · Colour · 90min

In this TV-movie remake of the classy 1939 Bette Davis/George Brent version, Elizabeth Montgomery stars as a cancer-stricken TV producer with no time for a personal life, who falls for the doctor who discovers the seriousness of her condition. While competent, she's not in Davis's class and director Robert Butler's funereal pacing doesn't help matters. Anthony Hopkins surpasses the efforts of Brent, playing the solicitous doctor, but it's hardly a stretch for him. DP

Elizabeth Montgomery *Katherine Merrill* • Anthony Hopkins *Dr Michael Grant* • Michele Lee *Dolores Marsh* • Janet MacLachlan *Eileen* • Michael Lerner *Manny* • John Elerick *Jeremy* • Herbert Berghof *Dr Kassiter* • Vic Tayback *Archie* ■ *Dir* Robert Butler • *Scr* M Charles Cohen, from the play by George Emerson Brewer Jr, Bertram Bloch

Dark Water ★★★★ 15

Supernatural horror   2002 · Jpn · Colour · 96min

Hideo Nakata's nerve-fraying film about a mother's desperate search for a missing child reclaims the horror movie from the slasher antics that prevail on either side of the Pacific. Hitomi Kuroki is outstanding as the divorcee whose paranoia on learning that a kidnapper once inhabited an upstairs room increases in proportion to the oozing stain on her ceiling. But the real star is the run-down Tokyo tenement whose scuffed colours and enveloping shadows are eerily evoked in Junichiro Hayashi's lowering photography. Stylish, atmospheric and very disturbing. DP Japanese +subtitles. *DVD*

Hitomi Kuroki *Yoshimi Matsubara* • Rio Kanno *Ikuko Matsubara, aged six* • Mirei Oguchi *Mitsuko Kawai* • Asami Mizukawa *Ikuko Hamada, aged*

16 ■ *Dir* Hideo Nakata • *Scr* Yoshihiro Nakamura, Ken-ichi Suzuki, from the novel *Honogurai Mizu No Soko Kara* by Koji Suzuki

Dark Water ★★★ 15

Supernatural horror   2005 · US/Jpn · Colour · 100min

Jennifer Connelly works up a convincing sweat here, playing a single mother whose daughter (Ariel Gade) makes friends with the ghostly little girl upstairs, as a sinister damp patch appears on the ceiling of their apartment. Initially filmed in 2002 by Japanese horror maestro Hideo Nakata, this tale is put through the Hollywood wringer and all the really scary stuff is taken out in the process. What saves the film is the tenderly drawn bond between mother and daughter. SP Swearing, violence. *DVD*

Jennifer Connelly *Dahlia Williams* • John C Reilly *Mr Murray* • Tim Roth *Jeff Platzer* • Dougray Scott *Kyle* • Pete Postlethwaite *Mr Veeck* • Camryn Manheim *Teacher* • Ariel Gade *Ceci* ■ *Dir* Walter Salles • *Scr* Rafael Yglesias, from the film by Yoshihiro Nakamura, Ken-ichi Suzuki, from the novel *Honogurai Mizu No Soko Kara* by Koji Suzuki

Dark Waters ★★ U

Drama   1944 · US · BW · 85min

Merle Oberon lends her exotic allure to this Andre De Toth-directed melodrama set in the Louisiana bayou. Oberon plays an heiress traumatised by the shipping accident in which her parents died, while Thomas Mitchell plays the malcontent who, sensing her incipient madness, hopes to push her over the edge and collect the money. Franchot Tone is the kindly medic who also takes a fancy to his patient. It's juicily acted when the script allows, with some good moments. AT

Merle Oberon *Leslie Calvin* • Franchot Tone *Dr George Grover* • Thomas Mitchell *Mr Sydney* • Fay Bainter *Aunt Emily* • John Qualen *Uncle Norbert* • Elisha Cook Jr *Cleeve* • Rex Ingram (2) *Pearson Jackson* ■ *Dir* Andre De Toth • *Scr* Joan Harrison, Marian Cockrell, Arthur Horman, from the novel by Frank Cockrell, Marian Cockrell

The Dark Wind ★★★ 15

Crime mystery   1991 · US · Colour · 106min

Rookie native American cop Lou Diamond Phillips tracks down a group of murderous drug dealers operating on the Navajo reservations in this intermittently fascinating adaptation of Tony Hillerman's novel. Despite much artistic licence taken with the book's characters, director Errol Morris makes superb use of the magnificent Arizona and New Mexico locations and gives this unusual thriller an intensely brooding atmosphere. Although Indian leaders objected to the ancient rites depicted, they're an intriguing aspect which sets the film apart from other similarly-styled cop adventures. AJ

Lou Diamond Phillips *Officer Jim Chee* • Fred Ward *Lieutenant Joe Leaphorn* • Gary Farmer *Sheriff Albert "Cowboy" Dashee* • John Karlen *Jake West* • Lance Baker *Mr Archer* • Gary Basaraba *Larry* ■ *Dir* Errol Morris • *Scr* Eric Bergren, Neal Jimenez, Mark Horowitz, from the novel by Tony Hillerman

Darker than Amber ★★

Crime thriller   1970 · US · Colour · 97min

Thriller writer John D MacDonald's detective Travis McGee (in his only cinematic outing, though a series was mooted) is incarnated by likeable Rod Taylor, and glossily filmed on exotic Caribbean and Miami locations. Watch for Jane Russell's penultimate screen appearance. TS

Rod Taylor *Travis McGee* • Suzy Kendall *Vangie/Merrimay* • Theodore Bikel *Meyer* • Jane Russell *Alabama Tiger* • James Booth *Burk* ■ *Dir* Robert Clouse • *Scr* Ed Waters, from the novel by John D MacDonald

The Darkest Hour ★★ 12

Science-fiction horror thriller   2011 · US/Rus · Colour · 85min

Moscow is the setting for this Hollywood alien-invasion yarn from director Chris Gorak. Following in the wake of such

noughties nightmares as *War of the Worlds* and *Cloverfield*, Gorak's sci-fi thriller tracks software entrepreneurs Emile Hirsch and Max Minghella as they hide out with tourists Olivia Thirlby and Rachael Taylor after invisible beasties with a ruthless line in molecular disintegration lay waste to planet Earth. Although efficiently made, the movie is burdened with a perfunctory script and sadly lacks the stylish imagination that co-producer Timur Bekmambetov brought to his supernatural epics *Night Watch* and *Day Watch*. **JA** Some violence, swearing. **DVD**
Blu-ray

Emile Hirsch *Sean* • Olivia Thirlby *Natalie* • Max Minghella *Ben* • Rachael Taylor *Anne* • Joel Kinnaman *Skylar* ■ *Dir* Chris Gorak • *Scr* Jon Spaihts, from a story by Spaihts, MT Ahern, Leslie Bohem

The Darkest Light ★★★ 12
Drama 1999 · UK · Colour · 90min

This post-millennial downer outlines the never-ending misfortunes of Stephen Dillane and Kerry Fox's Yorkshire family. It's only when their daughter (Keri Arnold) and her Indian schoolmate think they've seen a vision of the Virgin Mary on the moors that Simon Beaufoy's contemplation on the true meaning of faith gathers momentum. The film is well acted, but the subject matter is so depressing that even those with patience to wallow in misery will find it a long haul. **AJ** Swearing. **DVD**

Keri Arnold *Catherine* • Stephen Dillane *Tom* • Kerry Fox *Sue* • Kavita Sungha *Uma* • Jason Walton *Matthew* • Nisha K Nayar *Nisha* • Nicholas Hope *Father Mark* ■ *Dir* Simon Beaufoy, Billie Eltringham • *Scr* Simon Beaufoy

Darklands ★★★ 18
Horror thriller 1996 · UK · Colour · 86min

Although it's a virtual rip-off of *The Wicker Man*, this shocker is an impressively dark and reasonably frightening tale of pagan ritual and human sacrifice. Journalist Craig Fairbrass investigates a series of killings in south Wales and learns, too late, that he has a terrifying part to play in blood-soaked rites aimed at regenerating an ancient religion. While Fairbrass lacks the range to milk his part for every shaded nuance, Julian Richards's feature debut proves the spirit of Hammer lives on. **AJ** Swearing, nudity, violence.

Craig Fairbrass *Frazer Truick* • Rowena King *Rachel Morris* • Jon Finch *David Keller* • David Duffy *Carver* • Roger Nott *Dennis Cox* • Richard Lynch *Salvy* • Nicola Branson *Becky* ■ *Dir/Scr* Julian Richards

Darkman ★★★★ 18
Fantasy horror 1990 · US · Colour · 91min

Independent director Sam Raimi's first studio movie is a splashy amalgam of *The Phantom of the Opera* and *Doctor X*, with a perfectly cast Liam Neeson donning synthetic flesh masks to take revenge on the mobsters who disfigured him. Pathos and tragedy are always lurking beneath the horrific surface of this take on classic 1930s *Grand Guignol*, given a nifty 1990s spin by exaggerated camera moves and psychedelic visuals. A tasty buffet of gothic moodiness, startling make-up effects and expressionistic artifice, this is Raimi on virtuoso form. **AJ** Swearing, violence. **DVD**

Liam Neeson *Peyton Westlake/Darkman* • Frances McDormand *Julie Hastings* • Colin Friels *Louis Strack Jr* • Larry Drake *Robert G Durant* • Nelson Mashita *Yakitito* • Jessie Lawrence Ferguson *Eddie Black* • Rafael H Robledo *Rudy Guzman* • Danny Hicks *Skip* • Theodore Raimi [Ted Raimi] *Rick* ■ *Dir* Sam Raimi • *Scr* Chuck Pfarrer, Sam Raimi, Ivan Raimi, Daniel Goldin, Joshua Goldin, from a story by Sam Raimi • *Cinematographer* Bill Pope

Darkman II: the Return of Durant ★★★ 18
Fantasy horror 1995 · US/Can · Colour · 88min

This direct-to-video sequel is as dynamic and fast-paced as its predecessor, thanks to director Bradford May taking more than a few leaves out of the Sam Raimi style book. Arnold Vosloo takes over from Liam Neeson as the synthetic mask-wearing Dr

Peyton Westlake.The formula is 1940s pulp fiction with a twist of black comedy and some superior special effects, and it all works like a charm. **AJ** Violence, swearing. **DVD**

Arnold Vosloo *Dr Peyton Westlake/Darkman* • Larry Drake *Robert G Durant* • Renee O'Connor *Laurie Brinkman* • Kim Delaney *Jill Randall* • Lawrence Dane *Dr Alfred Hathaway* • Jesse Collins *Dr David Brinkman* • David Ferry *Eddie* ■ *Dir* Bradford May • *Scr* Steve McKay, Chuck Pfarrer, from a story by Robert Eisele, Lawrence Hertzog, from characters by Sam Raimi

Darkman III: Die Darkman Die ★★★ 15
Fantasy horror 1996 · US · Colour · 83min

In this second sequel, the "Urban Bigfoot" is pitted against evil drug baron Jeff Fahey, who is determined to learn the secret of deformed superhero Peyton Westlake's strength. With executive producer Sam Raimi and returning director/cameraman Bradford May maintaining the quality and integrity of both previous adventures, and with a well-realised script accenting character as much as explosive gimmicks, this comic-strip horror escapade is a worthwhile addition to the series. **AJ** Violence, swearing. **DVD**

Jeff Fahey *Peter Rooker* • Arnold Vosloo *Dr Peyton Westlake/Darkman* • Roxann Biggs-Dawson [Roxann Biggs] *Angela Rooker* • Darlanne Fluegel *Dr Bridget Thorne* • Alicia Panetta *Jenny Rooker* ■ *Dir* Bradford May • *Scr* Mike Werb, Michael Colleary, from characters by Sam Raimi

Darkness ★★ 15
Horror mystery 2002 · Sp/US · Colour · 84min

This is a messy and muddled supernatural tale about an American family moving into a Spanish country house that seems to be haunted by the ghosts of six local children who disappeared 40 years earlier. The solid cast tries its best to invoke shuddery suspense as the silly and repetitive plot unfolds, but the slow pace of this formula horror defeats them at every bland turn. **AJ** Violence, swearing. **DVD**

Anna Paquin *Regina* • Lena Olin *Maria* • Iain Glen *Mark* • Giancarlo Giannini *Albert Rua* • Fele Martínez *Carlos* • Stephan Enquist *Paul* • Fermí Reixach *Villalobos* ■ *Dir* Jaume Balagueró • *Scr* Jaume Balagueró, Fernando de Felipe

The Darkness ★★ 15
Horror thriller 2016 · US · Colour · 92min

After a family trip to former native American territories near the Grand Canyon, a sinister presence seems to have entered the household of fractious couple Kevin Bacon and Radha Mitchell, in this LA-set spookfest with echoes of *Poltergeist*. It's a decently acted, competently mounted but fairly tame affair. After a watchable first-hour, though, the movie's played most of its cards, and the finale's startlingly bland, given the sheer ferocity of director Greg McLean's breakthrough shocker *Wolf Creek*. **TJ** Swearing.

Kevin Bacon *Peter Taylor* • Radha Mitchell *Bronny Taylor* • David Mazouz *Michael Taylor* • Lucy Fry *Stephanie Taylor* ■ *Dir* Greg Mclean [Greg McLean] • *Scr* Greg Mclean, Shayne Armstrong, Shane Krause

Darkness Falls ★ 15
Psychological thriller 1998 · UK · Colour · 87min

Ray Winstone and Sherilyn Fenn co-star in this poorly directed, badly acted drama. Winstone plays a man teetering on the edge of insanity following a car crash which has left his pregnant wife in a coma. Tricking his way into the Isle of Man home of obnoxious businessman Tim Dutton and his neglected wife (Fenn), Winstone holds them at gunpoint. Clunkingly awful. **JB** Swearing. **DVD**

Sherilyn Fenn *Sally Driscoll* • Ray Winstone *John Barrett* • Tim Dutton *Mark Driscoll* • Anita Dobson *Mrs Hayter* • Bryan Pringle *Clive Hayter* • Robin McCaffrey *Jane Barrett* • Michael Praed *Hit man* • Oliver Tobias *Simpson* ■ *Dir* Gerry Lively • *Scr* John Howlett, from the play *Dangerous Obsession* by NJ Crisp

Darkness Falls ★ 15
Horror 2003 · US · Colour · 82min

This risible slice of low-grade horror hokum has two attractive 20-somethings and a nine-year-old terrorised by the "Tooth Fairy", the legendary witch of the small New England town, Darkness Falls. The airborne harridan can only survive in the dark – cue much lurking in the shadows. The biggest shock of the film is that the limp effects are by the usually excellent Stan Winston. Laughably bad. **AS** **DVD**

Chaney Kley *Kyle Walsh* • Emma Caulfield *Caitlin* • Lee Cormie *Michael* • Grant Piro *Larry* • Sullivan Stapleton *Matt* • Steve Mouzakis *Dr Murphy* ■ *Dir* Jonathan Liebesman • *Scr* John Fasano, James Vanderbilt, Joe Harris, from a story by Joe Harris, from his short film *Tooth Fairy*

Darkness in Tallinn ★★★★ 15
Crime thriller 1993 · Fin/Est/Swe/US · BW and Colour · 95min

If you can excuse the transition from monochrome to colour and Ilkka Jarvilaturi's determination to include every conceivable directorial flourish, then you're in for a treat with this Estonian heist movie. As the power-station worker persuaded by his pregnant wife to assist in the theft of the national treasury on its return from safe-keeping in Paris, Ivo Uukkivi gives a wonderfully bemused performance that gains a harder edge as the blood begins to flow. But this isn't just a quirky *film noir*. It's also a fascinating portrait of a long-oppressed country still not sure of its fate despite regaining independence. **DP** Estonian, Russian +subtitles.

Ivo Uukkivi *Toivo* • Milena Gulbe *Maria* • Monika Mager *Terje* • Enn Klooren *Mihhail "Misha"* • Vaino Laes *Andres* ■ *Dir* Ilkka Jarvilaturi • *Scr* Ilkka Jarvilaturi, Paul Kolsby

Darling ★★★★ 15
Drama 1965 · UK · BW · 122min

At every turn of his Oscar-winning script, Frederic Raphael invites us to admire just how clever he's been in dissecting the shallowness of celebrity and the gullibility of the public. Yet no matter how much we want to resist falling under the spell of such a self-congratulatory piece of work, there's no denying that this is both an astute snapshot of a moment in time and a wicked insight into the national character that still has relevance today. Julie Christie thoroughly merited her Oscar as the model hellbent on fame and Dirk Bogarde is equally splendid. **DP** **DVD** **Blu-ray**

Laurence Harvey *Miles Brand* • Dirk Bogarde *Robert Gold* • Julie Christie *Diana Scott* • Roland Curram *Malcolm* • José-Luis De Villalonga *Cesare* • Alex Scott (1) *Sean Martin* ■ *Dir* John Schlesinger • *Scr* Frederic Raphael, from a story by Frederic Raphael, John Schlesinger, Joseph Janni

Darling, How Could You! ★★
Comedy 1951 · US · BW · 95min

This adaptation was to be Gloria Swanson's follow-up to *Sunset Blvd*. When she refused to test for the role, however, it was given to Joan Fontaine. Quickly shot using the Washington Square sets left over from *The Heiress*, this tale of a daughter who erroneously thinks her mother is having an affair is not one of director Mitchell Leisen's better efforts. Despite some funny lines, the pace is too lethargic, while the playing is more cute than charming. **TV**

Joan Fontaine *Alice Grey* • John Lund *Dr Robert Grey* • Mona Freeman *Amy* • Peter Hanson *Dr Steve Clark* • David Stollery *Cosmo* • Virginia Farmer *Fanny* ■ *Dir* Mitchell Leisen • *Scr* Dodie Smith, Lesser Samuels, from the play *Alice-Sit-by-the-Fire* by JM Barrie

Darling Lili ★★★ U
First World War spy drama 1970 · US · Colour · 135min

This lengthy First World War charade is an underrated and utterly charming valentine from director Blake Edwards to his wife, Julie Andrews, who takes the lead role of a Mata Hari-type figure. The star is

marvellously supported by dashing air ace Rock Hudson and British satirist Lance Percival in his best film role. The film was shot by *Red River* cinematographer Russell Harlan, and also boasts some marvellous aerial dogfight sequences. It does take itself too seriously at times, though, and non-Andrews fans should avoid it. **TS**

Julie Andrews *Lili Smith* • Rock Hudson *Major William Larrabee* • Jeremy Kemp *Kurt von Ruger* • Lance Percival *TC* • Michael Witney *Youngblood Carson* • Jacques Marin *Major Duvalle* • André Maranne *Lt Liggett* ■ *Dir* Blake Edwards • *Scr* Blake Edwards, William Peter Blatty

D'Artagnan's Daughter ★★★ 15
Period adventure 1994 · Fr · Colour · 124min

Costume adventures might not be what we expect from Bertrand Tavernier, but his enthusiasm for this spirited romp is evident in the panache of his direction. Sophie Marceau leaves her convent to coax father Philippe Noiret out of retirement in order to save Louis XIV's throne. With Claude Rich and Charlotte Kady providing disdainful villainy, this is fun, but prone to longueurs and odd slapstick. **DP** French +subtitles. Violence, nudity. **DVD**

Sophie Marceau *Eloise* • Philippe Noiret *D'Artagnan* • Claude Rich *Duke of Crassac* • Sami Frey *Aramis* • Jean-Luc Bideau *Athos* • Raoul Billerey *Porthos* • Charlotte Kady *Scarlet woman* • Nils Tavernier *Quentin* ■ *Dir* Bertrand Tavernier • *Scr* Michel Leviant, from the novel *Vingt Ans Après* by Alexandre Dumas

The Darwin Adventure ★★ U
Biographical drama 1972 · UK · Colour · 90min

A biopic about Charles Darwin, whose voyages to South America and the Galapagos Islands aboard HMS *Beagle* fuelled his theory of natural selection, a theory that shocked the religious establishment of the Victorian world. In a subject far more suited to the television drama or mini-series, this is a sketchy effort that convinces us of Darwin's importance but turns his romantic life into soap opera. **AT**

Nicholas Clay *Charles Darwin* • Susan Macready *Emma Wedgewood* • Ian Richardson *Captain Fitzroy* • Robert Flemyng *Professor Henslow* ■ *Dir* Jack Couffer • *Scr* William Fairchild, from a story by Jack Couffer, Max Bella

DARYL ★★★ PG
Science-fiction drama 1985 · US · Colour · 96min

Although highly derivative, this New Age fairy tale is a charming, lightweight diversion about a Florida couple whose lives are transformed after fostering a young boy suffering from what they believe to be amnesia. When they learn DARYL actually stands for Data Analysing Robot Youth Lifeform, the real drama unfolds as they fight to stop his termination by Pentagon intelligence agents. The plot's formulaic, but this is nicely written and well acted. **AJ** **DVD**

Mary Beth Hurt *Joyce Richardson* • Michael McKean *Andy Richardson* • Barret Oliver *Daryl* • Colleen Camp *Elaine Fox* • Kathryn Walker *Ellen Lamb* • Josef Sommer *Dr Jeffrey Stewart* ■ *Dir* Simon Wincer • *Scr* David Ambrose, Allan Scott, Jeffrey Ellis

Date Movie ★★ 15
Romantic comedy spoof 2006 · US · Colour · 81min

After spoofing teen slasher flicks with the *Scary Movie* franchise, writers Jason Friedberg and Aaron Seltzer now turn their attention to romantic comedies. Alyson Hannigan is the heroine whose parents disapprove of her relationship with Adam Campbell because he's not of their Greek-African-American-Indian-Japanese heritage. The odd, decent gag aside, Friedberg and Seltzer are too often content to go for the cheap laughs. **SP** Swearing. **DVD**

Alyson Hannigan *Julia Jones* • Adam Campbell *Grant Funkyerdoder* • Jennifer Coolidge *Roz Funkyerdoder* • Tony Cox *Hitch* • Fred Willard *Bernie Funkyerdoder* • Eddie Griffin *Frank Jones*

D

• Sophie Monk *Andy* • Marie Matiko *Betty* ■ *Dir* Aaron Seltzer • *Scr* Jason Friedberg, Aaron Seltzer

Date Night ★★★★ 15
Comedy   2010 · US · Colour · 84min

Director Shawn Levy (*Night at the Museum*) keeps the action wacky and tight in this outrageous – yet plausible – screwball comedy. Tina Fey (*Baby Mama, 30 Rock*) and Steve Carell (*The 40 Year Old Virgin*) are hilarious as the married couple whose little white lie transforms a romantic "date night" into a hysterically hellish evening of endless mayhem. Twistily plotted while also subtly knowing, this has nimble wisecracks with which couples everywhere can readily identify among the action and slapstick. The comic chemistry between Fey and Carell couldn't be better, but Mark Wahlberg very nearly steals the show as the security expert who doesn't seem to own a shirt. KK
DVD BL

Tina Fey *Claire Foster* • Steve Carell *Phil Foster* • Mark Wahlberg *Holbrooke* • Taraji P Henson *Detective Arroyo* • Jimmi Simpson *Armstrong* • Mila Kunis *Whippit* • Leighton Meester *Katy* • James Franco *Taste* ■ *Dir* Shawn Levy • *Scr* Josh Klausner

A Date with a Dream ★★ U
Comedy   1948 · UK · BW · 58min

In only his second credited role, Terry-Thomas starred in this feeble comedy with brothers Len and Bill Lowe, playing the members of an Ensa trio who reunite after the war to revive their hopes of showbiz success. The nightclub routines are pretty awful and director Dicky Leeman hasn't a clue how to structure a narrative. But Jean Carson spares everyone's blushes as the girl they all fall for, and Norman Wisdom makes his feature debut. DP *DVD*

Terry-Thomas *Terry* • Jean Carson [Jeannie Carson] *Jean* • Len Lowe *Len* • Bill Lowe *Bill* • Wally Patch *Uncle* • Norman Wisdom *Shadow boxer* ■ *Dir* Dicky Leeman • *Scr* Robert S Baker, Monty Berman, Dicky Leeman

Date with Darkness ★
Drama based on a true story
2003 · US · Colour · 95min

The ink was still wet on the judgement when this true-story drama went into production. Having jumped bail and fled the country, Max Factor cosmetics heir Andrew Luster was convicted in his absence of 86 counts of rape and sentenced to 124 years in jail. As the movie was about to wrap, Luster was apprehended in the Mexican town of Puerto Vallarta by bounty hunter Duane "Dog" Chapman, and this shamefully opportunistic enterprise had its happy ending. Jason Gedrick plays the wealthy predator who used the drug GHB to date-rape and video his victims, and the film's prurient fascination with his crimes is decidedly distasteful. DP

Jason Gedrick *Andrew Luster* • Marla Sokoloff *Connie* • Lisa Edelstein *Maeve Fox* • Sarah Carter *Sarah* • Stefanie von Pfetten *Teri* • Winston Rekert *Fred* • Samantha Ferris *Detective Melissa Smith* ■ *Dir* Bobby Roth • *Scr* Chris Canaan

A Date with Judy ★★★ U
Musical comedy   1948 · US · Colour · 113min

This utterly charming musical dates from MGM's greatest period, though it may be a little overlong and twee for today's tastes. Sweet Jane Powell plays the title role, but Richard Thorpe's film also gives the young and oh-so-beautiful Elizabeth Taylor a chance to shine. Wallace Beery is top-billed, but he was near the end of this life and Technicolor wasn't too kind to him. Still, at least he gets to perform with Carmen Miranda. The song *It's a Most Unusual Day* was a huge hit. TS

Wallace Beery *Melvin R Foster* • Jane Powell *Judy Foster* • Elizabeth Taylor *Carol Pringle* • Carmen Miranda *Rosita Conchellas* • Xavier Cugat *Cugat* • Robert Stack *Stephen Andrews* ■ *Dir* Richard Thorpe • *Scr* Dorothy Cooper, Dorothy Kingsley, Aleen Leslie

A Date with the Falcon ★★
Detective mystery   1941 · US · BW · 63min

Following *The Gay Falcon*, this was the second film in the 16-episode *Falcon* series, with which RKO followed their *Saint* movies. Here the suave investigator (George Sanders) and his nervy sidekick (Allen Jenkins) get involved in the case of a kidnapped scientist. Typical of the plethora of "gentleman sleuth" second features popular in the 1930s and 40s, it's of little interest now, though Sanders is always a pleasure to watch. RK *DVD*

George Sanders *Falcon* • Wendy Barrie *Helen Reed* • James Gleason *O'Hara* • Allen Jenkins *Goldy* • Mona Maris *Rita Mara* • Victor Kilian *Max* • Frank Moran *Dutch* ■ *Dir* Irving Reis • *Scr* Lynn Root, Frank Fenton, from the character created by Michael Arlen

The Daughter ★★★ 15
Drama   2016 · Aus · Colour · 94min

This moody drama follows two families who are torn apart by a dark secret. The setting is a small logging town, where wealthy mill owner Geoffrey Rush is about to remarry. In the days leading up to the ceremony, his estranged son (Paul Schneider) reconnects with a childhood friend, Ewen Leslie. From here, the story unfolds gradually, building to a devastating revelation that involves Leslie's beloved wife (Miranda Otto) and his teenage daughter (Odessa Young). The ending will be too abrupt for some, but the story is involving, detailing how some secrets can have tragic consequences. SC
Swearing, sex scenes.

Geoffrey Rush *Henry* • Ewen Leslie *Oliver* • Paul Schneider (2) *Christian* • Miranda Otto *Charlotte* • Odessa Young *Hedvig* • Sam Neill *Walter* ■ *Dir* Simon Stone • *Scr* Simon Stone, from his adaptation of Henrik Ibsen's play *The Wild Duck*

Daughter of Darkness ★★
Crime drama   1948 · UK · BW · 91min

This brooding, violent melodrama concerns an Irish servant girl (Siobhan McKenna) who is not only a nymphomaniac, but also a psychopathic killer given to murdering her admirers. Directed by Lance Comfort, this British offering is an opportunity to see McKenna, one of the most compelling of Irish stage actresses, portraying a maniac with full-blooded commitment. Little else to recommend it, though. RK

Anne Crawford *Bess Stanforth* • Maxwell Reed *Dan* • Siobhan McKenna *Emily Beaudine* • George Thorpe *Mr Tallent* • Barry Morse *Robert Stanforth* • Liam Redmond *Father Cocoran* • Honor Blackman *Julie Tallent* ■ *Dir* Lance Comfort • *Scr* Max Catto, from his play *They Walk Alone*

Daughter of Dr Jekyll ★
Horror   1957 · US · BW · 69min

Dr Jekyll doesn't actually appear in this unusual take on the gothic classic. Instead, the film tells of his less well-known daughter, who, upon landing in England to claim her father's inheritance, is blamed for a series of grisly murders. The result is a hotch-potch of vampire, werewolf and Jekyll-and-Hyde elements, all searching in vain for a coherent storyline. A masterclass of abysmal acting. RS

John Agar *George Hastings* • Gloria Talbott *Janet Smith* • Arthur Shields *Dr Lomas* • John Dierkes *Jacob* • Martha Wentworth *Mrs Merchant* ■ *Dir* Edgar G Ulmer • *Scr* Jack Pollexfen

The Daughter of Rosie O'Grady ★★★ U
Musical comedy   1950 · US · Colour · 103min

This unpretentious, charming Warner Bros period musical has an attractive cast, headed by June Haver, a former Fox blonde who married Fred MacMurray and whose talent and appeal tend to be forgotten nowadays. Debonair singer Gordon MacRae and talented dancer Gene Nelson provide solid support, but look out for that young teenager: it's Debbie Reynolds, making her movie musical debut. TS

June Haver *Patricia O'Grady* • Gordon MacRae *Tony Pastor* • James Barton *Dennis O'Grady* • Debbie Reynolds *Maureen O'Grady* • SZ "Cuddles" Sakall [SZ Sakall] *Miklos Teretzky* • Gene Nelson *Doug Martin* • Sean McClory *James Moore* • Marsha Jones *Katie O'Grady* • Jane Darwell *Mrs Murphy* ■ *Dir* David Butler • *Scr* Jack Rose, Melville Shavelson, Peter Milne, from a story by Jack Rose, Melville Shavelson • *Music Director* Ray Heindorf

Daughter of the Nile ★★★ PG
Drama   1987 · Tai · Colour · 83min

The least typical entry in Hou Hsiao-Hsien's filmography, this Taipei tale of family in-fighting and social frustration dazzles with its urban iconography. Schoolgirl Yang Lin tries to tend house, hold down a fast-food job and prevent her cop father and gangster brother from tearing each other apart. Hou blends wit with warmth in exploring both the complex web of relationships and the ambitions that drive his superbly realised characters. DP
Mandarin, Hokkien +subtitles.

Yang Lin *Lin Hsiao-yang* • Kao Jai *Lin Hsiao-fang* • Yang Fan *Ah-sang* ■ *Dir* Hou Hsiao-Hsien • *Scr* Zhu Tianwen

Daughters Courageous ★★★
Drama   1939 · US · BW · 106min

Wandering Claude Rains returns to his cosy home town just in time to stop wife Fay Bainter marrying Donald Crisp and to deal with daughter Priscilla Lane's engagement to John Garfield. Put over with fluent ease, this sentimental and lightweight movie is almost as charming as its blockbusting predecessor, *Four Daughters*, which had made an instant star of Warner Bros newcomer Garfield the previous year. Rushing to capitalise on that success, the studio recycled the formula, re-employing the same director (Michael Curtiz) and cast. *Four Wives* continued the story. RK

Claude Rains *Jim Masters* • John Garfield *Gabriel Lopez* • Jeffrey Lynn *Johnny Heming* • Fay Bainter *Nan Masters* • Donald Crisp *Sam Sloane* • May Robson *Penny* • Frank McHugh *George* • Dick Foran *Eddie Moore* • George Humbert *Manuel Lopez* • Berton Churchill *Judge Hornsby* • Priscilla Lane *Buff Masters* • Rosemary Lane *Tinka Masters* • Lola Lane *Linda Masters* ■ *Dir* Michael Curtiz • *Scr* Julius J Epstein, Philip C Epstein, from the play *Fly Away Home* by Irving White, Dorothy Bennett

Daughters of Darkness ★★★★ 18
Horror   1970 · Bel/Fr/W Ger · Colour · 95min

The legend of Elizabeth Bathory (who Hammer lionised in *Countess Dracula*) provides the inspiration for this lyrically erotic, art house shocker, expertly directed by the Belgian Harry Kümel. Delphine Seyrig is the well-preserved *haute couture* vampire who insinuates her evil self on an unsuspecting honeymoon couple at a luxurious seaside hotel in Ostend. Explicitly sexual and violent, the haunting atmosphere, Seyrig's brilliant performance and the always striking imagery make this European chiller a stunning masterwork. AJ
In French. *DVD*

Delphine Seyrig *Countess Bathory* • Daniele Ouimet *Valerie* • John Karlen *Stefan Chiltern* • Andrea Rau *Ilona Harczy* ■ *Dir* Harry Kümel • *Scr* Harry Kümel, Pierre Drouot, JJ Amiel • *Cinematographer* Van Der Enden

Daughters of Satan ★ 18
Horror   1972 · US · Colour · 86min

A bottom-of-the-barrel horror, notable only for putting future *Magnum PI* star Tom Selleck on the road to fame. He's an art collector whose wife buys a painting of three witches being burned at the stake and gradually becomes possessed by the one she resembles. Featuring terrible dialogue and soap-opera dramatics. AJ *DVD*

Tom Selleck *James Robertson* • Barra Grant *Chris Robertson* • Tani Phelps Guthrie [Tani Guthrie] *Kitty Duarte* • Vic Silayan *Dr Dangal* ■ *Dir* Hollingsworth Morse • *Scr* John C Higgins, from a story by John Bushelman

Daughters of the Dust ★★★★ PG
Experimental period drama
1991 · US · Colour · 107min

Completed over several years, Julie Dash's low-budget feature debut is a poetic tribute to African culture, the oral tradition and the spirit of the Gullah people, who owe their descent to the freed slaves who settled on the islands off the coasts of South Carolina and Georgia. Set in 1902, the film uses a gathering that precedes the mainland odyssey of five women to explore questions of race, sex and family as well as nationality and exile. The imagery impresses, with the naturally-lit colours given a sense of history remembered by Dash's stylised use of slow motion. DP

Adisa Anderson *Eli Peazant* • Cheryl Lynn Bruce *Viola* • Cora Lee Day *Nana Peazant* • Kaycee Moore *Haagar* • Alva Rogers *Eula Peazant* • Bahni Turpin *Iona Peazant* • Trula Hoosier *Trula* ■ *Dir/Scr* Julie Dash

Dave ★★★★ 15
Romantic political comedy
1993 · US · Colour · 105min

Part-time presidential impersonator Kevin Kline is called into the White House when the real president suffers a stroke. However, he soon begins to get a taste for the job, much to the horror of shifty White House aide Frank Langella. Kline is excellent as both the naive stand-in and the ruthless president, while Sigourney Weaver is fine as the bitter First Lady who begins to see her "husband" in a new light. Look out for Oliver Stone, playing himself, trying to convince a disbelieving chat-show host that there is another conspiracy afoot. A delightful, gentle satire on the Washington scene. JF *DVD*

Kevin Kline *Dave Kovic/President Bill Mitchell* • Sigourney Weaver *Ellen Mitchell* • Frank Langella *Bob Alexander* • Kevin Dunn *Alan Reed* • Ving Rhames *Duane Stevenson* • Ben Kingsley *Vice-President Nance* • Charles Grodin *Murray Blum* • Faith Prince *Alice* ■ *Dir* Ivan Reitman • *Scr* Gary Ross

Dave Chappelle's Block Party ★★★ 15
Comedy music documentary
2005 · US · Colour · 98min

Director Michel Gondry returns to his music-video roots in this hip-hop variation on the old "let's put on a show" format. Gondry may occasionally fawn over comic Dave Chappelle as he invites folks from his Ohio home town to a free gig in Brooklyn and hobnobs with the talent backstage. But he uses his battery of Super 16 cameras ably to capture the energy and excitement of the event. Aficionados will appreciate turns by Kanye West, dead prez, Erykah Badu, Kool G Rap and Big Daddy Kane, but the highlights are Chappelle's homage to James Brown and the reunion of The Fugees for a splendid rendition of *Killing Me Softly*. DP *DVD*

Dave Chappelle *Dave Chappelle/Host* • Mos Def • Lauryn Hill • Wyclef Jean ■ *Dir* Michel Gondry • *Scr* Dave Chappelle

David ★★★★ U
Drama   1979 · W Ger · Colour · 125min

One of the most powerful films ever made about the Holocaust, this adaptation of Joel Konig's fact-based book isn't primarily about courage or heroic charity. Instead, it's a harrowing study of the gnawing terror that was part of everyday life for Jews living under the Nazi tyranny. Director Peter Lilienthal refuses to sentimentalise the humanity of the decent few, or reduce the endless round of concealment and escape to mere action set pieces. With Mario Fischel's determination born out of fear as the hunted teenager and Walter Taub outstanding as his Rabbi father, this thoroughly merited its Golden Bear at Berlin. DP German +subtitles.

Walter Taub *Rabbi Singer* • Irena Vrkljan *Wife* • Eva Mattes *Toni* • Mario Fischel *David* ■ *Dir* Peter Lilienthal • *Scr* Jurek Becker, Ulla Ziemann, Peter Lilienthal, from the novel by Joel Konig

David and Bathsheba ★★ U
Biblical drama   1951 · US · Colour · 110min

Gregory Peck is the King of Israel, who spots Susan Hayward's red-headed Bathsheba going about her ablutions and is instantly smitten, subsequently incurring the wrath of God and having to atone for his sins. More of a plodding, pompous moral debate than an epic, Henry King's movie eschews a lot of the DeMille-style orgies and battles one would expect. AT *DVD*

Gregory Peck *David* • Susan Hayward *Bathsheba* • Raymond Massey *Nathan* • Kieron Moore *Uriah* • James Robertson-Justice *Abishai* • Jayne Meadows *Michal* ■ *Dir* Henry King • *Scr* Philip Dunne

David and Lisa ★★★ 12
Drama based on a true story
1962 · US · BW · 93min

David and Lisa are mental patients. He's autistic, obsessively tidy and hates being touched; she's a schizophrenic who talks only in gobbledegook rhymes, or else doesn't talk at all. On the one hand, this seems like a typical slice of American psychobabble about misunderstood kids. The acting, however, raises the story to an entirely different level – the performances of Keir Dullea and Janet Margolin are totally sincere and deeply touching. AT *DVD*

Keir Dullea *David* • Janet Margolin *Lisa* • Howard Da Silva *Dr Swinford* • Neva Patterson *Mrs Clemens* • Clifton James *John* • Richard McMurray *Mr Clemens* • Nancy Nutter *Maureen* • Matthew Anden *Simon* ■ *Dir* Frank Perry • *Scr* Eleanor Perry, from a non-fiction book by Dr Theodore Isaac Rubin

David and Lisa ★★★ PG
Drama   1998 · US · Colour · 86min

This is a well-meaning TV remake of the 1962 original, but what was innovative back then now feels very dated and similar to countless other dysfunctional teen movies. At a boarding school for emotionally disturbed adolescents, a hostile loner who detests being touched falls in love with a childlike girl who only speaks in rhyme. Sidney Poitier gives a sympathetic performance as the caring psychiatrist, and the film, while slow-paced, is moving. MC *DVD*

Sidney Poitier *Dr Jack Miller* • Lukas Haas *David* • Brittany Murphy *Lisa* • Debi Mazar *Maggie* • Allison Janney *Alix* • Kim Murphy *Natalie* ■ *Dir* Lloyd Kramer • *Scr* Lloyd Kramer, from the 1962 film

David Bowie Is Happening Now ★★★ PG
Documentary   2013 · UK · Colour · 98min

Since the unexpected death of David Bowie in January 2016, this informative walk through the Victoria & Albert Museum's acclaimed 2013 retrospective may provide something of an acceptable substitute. Curators Victoria Broackes and Geoffrey Marsh combine expertise with fandom as they guide us through the best of more than 300 exhibits, with special emphasis on the exhaustive parade of original, often iconic, outfits. AC

■ *Dir* Hamish Hamilton, Katy Mullan

David Brent: Life on the Road ★★★ 15
Comedy   2016 · UK · Colour · 95min

Ricky Gervais slips back into his *The Office* role of David Brent with ease, using the same mockumentary style to showcase his musical talents, as Brent hires a tour bus to ferry his band around Reading. There isn't a plot as such, just a series of toe-curling stage turns while pressure builds backstage. It could have been *This Is Spinal Tap* meets Alan Partridge, but it doesn't quite catch fire. Yet as a snigger-inducing portrait of a tragicomic hero, it's heart-warming chilled entertainment. SP Swearing, sexual references.

Ricky Gervais *David Brent* • Doc Brown [Ben Bailey Smith] *Dom* • Tom Basden *Dan* • Tom Bennett *Nigel* • Jo Hartley *Pauline* ■ *Dir/Scr* Ricky Gervais

David Copperfield ★★★★★ U
Classic period drama   1935 · US · BW · 124min

This immaculately cast and designed David O Selznick production for MGM remains the definitive version of Charles Dickens's vaguely autobiographical classic novel. While Basil Rathbone is Mr Murdstone to a T, and there couldn't possibly be any other Aunt Betsey Trotwood than Edna May Oliver, the real casting coups are Lennox Pawle's perfect Mr Dick and Roland Young's Uriah Heep. If the great WC Fields makes Micawber a star turn, it's no bad thing, and both Freddie Bartholomew and Frank Lawton as the young and the grown-up David, respectively, could not be bettered. This film is a richly entertaining reminder of what Hollywood did best. TS

WC Fields *Mr Micawber* • Lionel Barrymore *Dan Peggotty* • Freddie Bartholomew *David as a child* • Maureen O'Sullivan *Dora* • Madge Evans *Agnes* • Edna May Oliver *Aunt Betsey* • Lewis Stone *Mr Wickfield* • Frank Lawton *David as a man* • Elizabeth Allan *Mrs Copperfield* • Roland Young *Uriah Heep* • Basil Rathbone *Mr Murdstone* • Elsa Lanchester *Clickett* • Jean Cadell *Mrs Micawber* • Jessie Ralph *Nurse Peggotty* • Lennox Pawle *Mr Dick* • Una O'Connor *Mrs Gummidge* ■ *Dir* George Cukor • *Scr* Howard Estabrook, Hugh Walpole, from the novel by Charles Dickens • *Cinematographer* Oliver T Marsh • *Editor* Robert J Kern

David's Mother ★★★ PG
Drama   1994 · US · Colour · 92min

Kirstie Alley proves herself a capable dramatic actress in this sensitive TV movie, as a mother who devotes her life to the care of her autistic son. Alley won an Emmy for her performance, as did Michael Goorjian, who plays David as a teenager. The script presents genuine situations and emotions without resorting to platitudes or easy sentiment, and gives the powerhouse cast plenty to get its teeth into. DP *DVD*

Kirstie Alley *Sally Goodson* • Sam Waterston *John* • Stockard Channing *Bea* • Michael Goorjian *David aged 17* • Chris Sarandon *Phillip* • Phylicia Rashad *Gladys* • Steve Ivany *David aged 59* ■ *Dir* Robert Allan Ackerman • *Scr* Bob Randall, from the play by Walt Lloyd

Davy ★★ U
Comedy drama   1958 · UK · Colour · 85min

Michael Relph directs his father in what turned out to be Ealing's fourth from last feature. It's a shamelessly sentimental affair that gave Harry Secombe an opportunity to prove there was life outside *The Goon Show*, as he has to decide whether to stick with the family's struggling music-hall act or seize his chance by auditioning for opera supremo Alexander Knox at Covent Garden. Secombe's spirited rendition of Puccini's *Nessun Dorma* demonstrates what a fine singer he was, but he seems less comfortable with the more melodramatic aspects of the picture. DP *DVD*

Harry Secombe *Davy Morgan* • Ron Randell *George* • George Relph *Uncle Pat Morgan* • Susan Shaw *Gwen* • Bill Owen *Eric* • Alexander Knox *Sir Giles Manning* ■ *Dir* Michael Relph • *Scr* William Rose

Davy Crockett, King of the Wild Frontier ★★★ U
Western adventure   1955 · US · Colour · 88min

The first of two cinema features, both adapted from a TV series produced by the Disney studio, about the legendary backwoodsman who became a congressman and died at the Alamo. Crockett is one of America's most bizarre, contradictory and elusive historical personages, but this movie simply prints the legend. Fess Parker, a jovial, athletic type, plays Crockett and successfully turned the coonskin hat into the fashion accessory most demanded by children in the mid-1950s, plus there's that hit theme song to hum along with as well. AT

Fess Parker *Davy Crockett* • Buddy Ebsen *George Russel* • Basil Ruysdael *Andrew Jackson* • Hans Conried *Thimblerig* • William Bakewell *Tobias Norton* • Kenneth Tobey *Colonel Jim Bowie* • Pat Hogan *Chief Red Stick* • Helene Stanley *Polly Crockett* ■ *Dir* Norman Foster • *Scr* Tom Blackburn

Davy Crockett and the River Pirates ★★★ U
Western adventure   1956 · US · Colour · 86min

Davy Crockett was a phenomenon of the 1950s. Originally intended only for Disney's US TV shows, the noble buckskin-clad frontiersman swept the world after Uncle Walt strung some episodes together and released them in cinemas. This was the second theatrical outing, a feast of fun that falls clearly into two halves. The more enjoyable first part pits Crockett (Fess Parker) against self-styled "King of the River", splendidly hammed by Jeff York, while the second half deals with Indian confrontations. TS

Fess Parker *Davy Crockett* • Buddy Ebsen *George Russel* • Jeff York *Mike Fink* • Kenneth Tobey *Jocko* • Clem Evans *Cap'n Cobb* • Irving Ashkenazy *Moose* • Mort Mills *Sam Mason* ■ *Dir* Norman Foster • *Scr* Norman Foster, Tom Blackburn

Dawg ★★ 15
Romantic comedy   2001 · US · Colour · 80min

Denis Leary plays a disreputable likely lad in this over-calculating hybrid of *The Bachelor* and *Liar, Liar*. He mugs knowingly as a playboy who will inherit his grandmother's millions if he succeeds in apologising personally to each and every woman he's wronged. Unfortunately, Victoria Hochberg is clearly striving to make an impression on her feature debut and pushes too hard with both the character comedy and the innuendo. DP *DVD*

Denis Leary *Doug "Dawg" Munford* • Elizabeth Hurley *Anna Lockheart* • Steffani Brass *Lindsay Anne Wickman* • Eddie Adams (2) *Young Dawg* ■ *Dir* Victoria Hochberg • *Scr* Ken Hastings

Dawn Anna ★★ PG
Drama based on a true story
2005 · US · Colour · 84min

Although not quite as prevalent as before, "disease of the week" tear-jerkers have long been a staple of American TV. But, while this doesn't deviate too far from the tried and tested formula, this is a cut above most thanks to a gritty, unsentimental turn from Debra Winger. She plays Dawn Anna Townsend, a single mother, teacher and high school volleyball coach, who has to completely rebuild her life following life-threatening surgery to remove a brain tumour. Sympathetically directed by Winger's husband, Arliss Howard (under a pseudonym), this is still a little treacly at times, although it's hard not to be moved by the story or Winger's committed performance. JF *DVD*

Debra Winger *Dawn Anna Townsend* • Alex Van Bink • Sam Howard *Josh* • Stephen Warner *Matt* • Krista Rae *Kristin* • Tatiana Maslany *Lauren (age 12)* ■ *Dir* Less R Howard [Arliss Howard] • *Scr* Arliss Howard, Albert T Lemme [Robert Munic], James Howard [Jim Howard]

Dawn at Socorro ★★★
Western   1954 · US · Colour · 80min

This is one of the last western co-features in rich Technicolor, and jolly splendid it looks, too, with glistening saloon interiors and bright location exteriors. But veteran director George Sherman brings his usual lack of style to bear and fails to get the best out of the sexually charged pairing of rugged Rory Calhoun and fiery Piper Laurie, both of whom are excellent in what is basically a routine plot about a reformed gunslinger. TS

Rory Calhoun *Brett Wade* • Piper Laurie *Rannah Hayes* • David Brian *Dick Braden* • Kathleen Hughes *Clare* • Alex Nicol *Jimmy Rapp* • Edgar Buchanan *Sheriff Cauthen* • Lee Van Cleef *Earl Ferris* ■ *Dir* George Sherman • *Scr* George Zuckerman • *Cinematographer* Carl Guthrie

Dawn of the Dead ★★★★★ 18
Horror   1978 · US · Colour · 126min

With its shopping mall setting, some see this astoundingly violent sequel to the classic *Night of the Living Dead* as a satirical attack on American consumerism and shallow materialistic values. Others merely see it as a great zombie fantasy, as the reawakened dead resume their cannibalistic stalking of the living. Cynical, devastating and relentless, Romero's masterpiece about the American Dream turning into a terrifying nightmare is an ideal blend of black comedy and harrowing carnage. Romero continued his series with 1985's *Day of the Dead*. AJ Swearing, violence. *DVD* ▶

David Emge *Stephen* • Ken Foree *Peter* • Scott H Reiniger *Roger* • Gaylen Ross *Francine* • David Crawford *Dr Foster* • David Early *Mr Berman* • George A Romero *TV director* ■ *Dir/Scr* George A Romero • *Music* Dario Argento and the Goblins

Dawn of the Dead ★★★ 18
Horror   2004 · US/Jpn/Fr · Colour · 95min

Director Zack Snyder's remake of George A Romero's 1978 zombie horror is an efficient exercise in recycling. Romero's original screenplay acts as the flesh and bones for James Gunn's updated script, in which a group of survivors, including a nurse (Sarah Polley) and a police officer (Ving Rhames), finds refuge from a plague of zombies in a shopping precinct. This is a gruesome but entertaining big-budget take on the horror classic, but Snyder's film lacks the satirical edge that gave Romero's original so much bite. TH *DVD* CS

Sarah Polley *Ana Clark* • Ving Rhames *Kenneth* • Jake Weber *Michael* • Mekhi Phifer *Andre* • Ty Burrell *Steve* • Michael Kelly (2) *CJ* • Kevin Zegers *Terry* • Lindy Booth *Nicole* ■ *Dir* Zack Snyder • *Scr* James Gunn (2), from the film by George A Romero

Dawn of the Mummy ★ 18
Horror   1981 · US · Colour · 88min

The bright arc lights used for a photo shoot in an Egyptian tomb revive the ancient pharaoh and his slave army in this dispiriting mix of Hammer horror and extreme zombie violence. Completely vapid, with ham acting and shameless mugging galore, this can only be recommended to splatter addicts. AJ *DVD*

Brenda King *Lisa* • Barry Sattels *Bill* • George Peck *Rick* • John Salvo *Gary* • Joan Levy *Jenny* • Diane Beatty *June* ■ *Dir* Frank Agrama [Farouk Agrama] • *Scr* Daria Price, Ronald Dobrin, Frank Agrama, from a story by Dobrin, Price

Dawn of the Planet of the Apes ★★★★ 12
Science-fiction action adventure
2014 · US · Colour · 125min

In this sequel to 2011's *Rise of the Planet of the Apes*, most of the human population has been wiped out by simian flu. While superintelligent chimpanzee Caesar (Andy Serkis), now the leader of a large ape colony, feels compassion for the beleaguered humans, right-hand-ape Koba (Toby Kebbell) determines to show him the error of mixing with mankind. What follows is an epic tale of betrayal, deception and brutality that plays out like a Greek tragedy – with a touch of *Animal Farm* thrown in. The script is superb as is the ape characterisation – the acting of Serkis et al, coupled with the magic of the visual effects, means there's no sense that what you're seeing is constructed on a computer. A storming, soulful blockbuster that's got both brains and heart. LB Violence, some swearing. *DVD* ▶ 3D

Jason Clarke (2) *Malcolm* • Gary Oldman *Dreyfus* • Andy Serkis *Caesar* • Keri Russell *Ellie* • Toby Kebbell *Koba* • Kodi Smit-McPhee *Alexander* ■ *Dir* Matt Reeves • *Scr* Mark Bomback, Rick Jaffa, Amanda Silver, from the novel *Planet of the Apes* by Pierre Boulle

The Dawn Patrol ★★
First World War drama   1930 · US · BW · 105min

This famous flying picture was Howard Hawks's first talkie. The story concerns a squadron of British flyers stoically running near-suicidal bombing raids over Germany during the First World War. Hawks later made far better flying pictures; this one is hampered by the primitive talkie technology, the artificiality of the dialogue and the wooden performances. AT

Richard Barthelmess *Dick Courtney* • Douglas Fairbanks Jr *Douglas Scott* • Neil Hamilton *Major Brand* • William Janney *Gordon Scott* • James

The Dawn Patrol ★★★★ 🅤
First World War melodrama
1938 · US · BW · 98min

A marvellously unsentimental First World War melodrama, this remake of the Howard Hawks movie is actually better cast (Errol Flynn, David Niven and Basil Rathbone all on top form) and better directed (by Edmund Goulding) than the original. It incorporates library material and action sequences from Hawks's movie, and there is a very real sense of the passion and futility of war in the gripping screenplay that realistically conveys horror among comrades and grace under pressure. **TS**

Errol Flynn *Captain Courtney* • David Niven *Lieutenant Scott* • Basil Rathbone *Major Brand* • Donald Crisp *Phipps* • Melville Cooper *Sergeant Watkins* • Barry Fitzgerald *Bott* • Carl Esmond *Von Mueller* • Peter Willes *Hollister* • Morton Lowry *Donnie Scott* • Michael Brooke *Squires* • James Burke *Flaherty* ■ *Dir* Edmund Goulding • *Scr* Seton I Miller, Dan Totheroh, from the story *The Flight Commander* by John Monk Saunders

The Dawn Rider ★★ 🅤
Western   1935 · US · BW · 55min

This uninspiring John Wayne programme filler dates from that period when he was trapped in Lone Star westerns before his resurrection in *Stagecoach* nine years later. The Duke is chasing his father's murderer, who turns out to be Denny Meadows, who later changed his name to Dennis Moore and propped up many a B-movie. Cinematographer Archie Stout ended his career with Wayne, working on some of the Duke's more famous Warner Bros movies, but his work here is purely functional. **TS** 📀

John Wayne *John Mason* • Marion Burns *Alice* • Yakima Canutt *Barkeeper* • Reed Howes *Ben* • Denny Meadows [Dennis Moore] *Rudd* • Bert Dillard *Buck* • Jack Jones (1) *Black* ■ *Dir* RN Bradbury [Robert N Bradbury] • *Scr* RN Bradbury, from a story by Lloyd Nosler

The Dawning ★★★★ 🅟🅖
Period drama   1988 · UK · Colour · 93min

Rebecca Pidgeon made her debut in this striking film about pre-Partition Ireland. Pidgeon, stifled by living with aunt Jean Simmons and disabled grandfather Trevor Howard (in his last role), falls in love with bumbling city boy Hugh Grant. When she meets an enigmatic stranger (Anthony Hopkins), however, suddenly her world begins to turn on its head. Avoiding heavy-handedness or didacticism, director Robert Knights depicts the rise of the Irish Republican Army through Pidgeon's own progression from naive teenager to adult. **LH**

Anthony Hopkins *Major Angus Barry/Cassius* • Rebecca Pidgeon *Nancy Gulliver* • Jean Simmons *Aunt Mary* • Trevor Howard *Grandfather* • Tara MacGowran *Maeve* • Hugh Grant *Harry* • Ronnie Masterson *Bridie* ■ *Dir* Robert Knights • *Scr* Moira Williams, from the novel *The Old Jest* by Jennifer Johnston

The Day after Tomorrow ★★★★ 🅒
Disaster movie   2004 · US · Colour · 118min

This jaw-dropping disaster movie makes director Roland Emmerich's previous outings feel like expensive dress rehearsals. The cautionary tale piles on Hollywood excess to deliver a US-centred thrill-ride in which global warming abruptly pushes the planet into a new ice age during one incredible worldwide superstorm. Though there's a human element, focusing on climatologist Dennis Quaid's cross-country journey to Manhattan to rescue his trapped son, Jake Gyllenhaal, it's the weather effects that take centre stage. Never mind that the dialogue is often cheesy and the performances melodramatic, what counts here is the enormous entertainment factor. **SF** Some swearing. 📀 🔵

Dennis Quaid *Professor Jack Hall* • Jake Gyllenhaal *Sam Hall* • Ian Holm *Professor Terry Rapson* • Emmy Rossum *Laura Chapman* • Sela Ward *Doctor Lucy Hall* • Dash Mihok *Jason Evans* • Jay O Sanders *Frank Harris* • Austin Nichols *JD* • Arjay Smith *Brian Parks* • Tamlyn Tomita *Janet Tokada* • Glenn Plummer *Luther* • Adrian Lester *Simon* • Kenneth Welsh *Vice President Becker* ■ *Dir* Roland Emmerich • *Scr* Jeffrey Nachmanoff, Roland Emmerich, from a story by Roland Emmerich

A Day at the Races ★★★ 🅤
Comedy   1937 · US · BW · 104min

The Marx Brothers' second film for MGM was hidebound by the decision to overload the mayhem with mediocre musical interludes that the studio bigwigs believed would give the picture more class. The inconsistent support playing similarly saps much of the action's energy, undoing the sterling work of the wonderful Margaret Dumont. As ever, the trio's own performances are splendid, with the "Tootsie frootsie ice cream" sketch standing as the best of the Chico/Groucho routines. **DP** 📀

Groucho Marx *Dr Hugo Z Hackenbush* • Chico Marx *Tony* • Harpo Marx *Stuffy* • Allan Jones *Gil* • Maureen O'Sullivan *Judy* • Margaret Dumont *Mrs Upjohn* • *Dir* Sam Wood • *Scr* Robert Pirosh, George Seaton, George Oppenheimer, from a story by Robert Pirosh, George Seaton

Day Dreams 🅤🅤🅤🅤🅤 🅤
Silent comedy   1922 · US · BW · 21min

Whether he's being pursued by an army of policemen on to a ferry, or walking round and round a ship's paddle-wheel like a hamster, Buster Keaton is just trying to prove his love for Renée Adorée. He wants to show her he can get – and keep – a job in the city. But since the jobs include working as a street-sweeper and as a nurse in a pet hospital, it takes a lot of persuasion. An early Keaton three-reeler, this manages to insert elements of surreality into even the humdrum. **TH** 📀

Buster Keaton *The young man* • Renée Adorée *The girl* • Joe Keaton *Her father* • Edward F Cline [Edward Cline] *Stage manager* ■ *Dir* Buster Keaton, Eddie Cline [Edward Cline] • *Scr* Buster Keaton, Edward F Cline

Day for Night 🅤🅤🅤🅤🅤 🅟🅖
Satirical drama   1973 · Fr · Colour · 110min

The winner of the best foreign language film Oscar, this is an exhilarating celebration of the movie-making process. Everything that could possibly go wrong on François Truffaut's film-within-the-film, *Meet Pamela*, does so in spades. Yet Truffaut's character battles on in the search for meaningful art. Regular collaborator Jean-Pierre Léaud is on cracking form as the actor who falls in love with leading lady Jacqueline Bisset, who spoofs her own image to perfection. There are also lovely supporting turns from Valentina Cortese and Nathalie Baye, while novelist Graham Greene (billed as Henry Graham) pops up in a cameo that was something of a practical joke at Truffaut's expense. **DP** French, English +subtitles. 📀

François Truffaut *Ferrand* • Jacqueline Bisset *Julie* • Jean-Pierre Léaud *Alphonse* • Valentina Cortese *Severine* • Jean-Pierre Aumont *Alexandre* • Jean Champion *Bertrand* • Dani *Lilianne* • Alexandra Stewart *Stacey* • Bernard Menez *Bernard* • Nike Arrighi *Odile* • Nathalie Baye *Assistant* • Bernard Menez *Bernard* ■ *Dir* François Truffaut • *Scr* François Truffaut, Suzanne Schiffman, Jean-Louis Richard

The Day I Became a Woman ★★★★ 🅟🅖
Drama   2000 · Iran · Colour · 74min

A short story trilogy using the three stages of womanhood as its basis, Marziyeh Meshkini's first feature examines the restraints Iranian society places upon its women. Each has its own distinctive tone: the heartfelt simplicity of a young girl's last hour of play before taking the chador contrasts with the frantic satire of a husband's bid to prevent his wife from competing in a cycle race and, in the final surreal story, the disarming irony of an old lady atoning for a lifetime's drudgery by spending her savings on household gadgets. Infused with a graceful naturalism, this is a truly touching film. **DP** Farsi +subtitles. 📀

Fatemeh Cherag Akhar *Hava* • Shabnam Toloui *Ahoo* • Azizeh Sedighi *Hoora* ■ *Dir* Marziyeh Meshkini • *Scr* Mohsen Makhmalbaf, Marziyeh Meshkini, from short stories by Mohsen Makhmalbaf

A Day in October ★★★ 🄸🄴
Second World War drama   1991 · US/Den · Colour · 96min

Such was Denmark's antipathy to the invading Nazis and its sense of indivisible nationhood that only a relatively small percentage of its Jewish population was consigned to concentration camps. This melodrama concentrates on the heroism of a single family whose protection of a wounded partisan led to the mass exodus of Danish Jews to Sweden. Kenneth Madsen's uplifting film is given additional power by the understated performances of DB Sweeney and Daniel Benzali. **DP**

DB Sweeney *Niels Jensen* • Kelly Wolf *Sara Kublitz* • Tovah Feldshuh *Emma Kublitz* • Daniel Benzali *Solomon Kublitz* • Ole Lemmeke *Larson* • Kim Romer *Arne* ■ *Dir* Kenneth Madsen • *Scr* Damian F Slattery

A Day in the Death of Joe Egg ★★★★ 🄸🄴
Black comedy drama   1971 · UK · Colour · 101min

The fate of a child with cerebral palsy might not appear suitable material for a black comedy. Yet Peter Nichols's adaptation of his own hit play is less concerned with euthanasia than with the very human emotions being experienced by the girl's angst-ridden parents. Faced with constant shifts in tone, director Peter Medak prevents the action from becoming either tasteless or sentimental, thanks, largely, to the exceptional performances of Alan Bates and Janet Suzman. Free of the Brechtian devices that characterised the stage version, this is a provocative look at people under pressure and the transience of love. **DP** Swearing, nudity. 📀

Alan Bates *Brian* • Janet Suzman *Sheila* • Peter Bowles *Freddie* • Sheila Gish *Pam* • Joan Hickson *Grace* • Elizabeth Robillard *Jo* • Murray Melvin *Doctor* ■ *Dir* Peter Medak • *Scr* Peter Nichols, from his play

The Day Lincoln Was Shot ★★★
Historical drama   1998 · US · Colour · 95min

The basic facts are well-known, but director John Gray digs a bit deeper and comes up with a very modern political thriller. His made-for-TV film also features audacious against-type casting, with Lance Henriksen surprisingly convincing as the war-weary Lincoln, and *Northern Exposure*'s Rob Morrow believably psychotic as John Wilkes Booth. **JF**

Rob Morrow *John Wilkes Booth* • Lance Henriksen *Abraham Lincoln* • Donna Murphy *Mary Todd Lincoln* • Jean Louisa Kelly *Lucy Halle* • Wil Wheaton *Robert Lincoln* ■ *Dir* John Gray • *Scr* John Gray, Tim Metcalfe, from the non-fiction book by Jim Bishop

A Day of Fury ★★
Western   1956 · US · Colour · 77min

Rebel Dale Robertson finds himself outside civic convention in a conservative frontier town. This moody little western, very much of its time, has its moments, but Robertson is both too bland and too old for the role, and the direction is very average. **TS**

Dale Robertson *Jagade* • Mara Corday *Sharman Fulton* • Jock Mahoney *Marshal Allan Burnett* • Carl Benton Reid *Judge John J McLean* ■ *Dir* Harmon Jones • *Scr* James Edmiston, Oscar Brodney, from a story by James Edmiston

Day of the Animals ★★★ 🄸🄴
Horror   1977 · US · Colour · 92min

One of the best movies made by horror hack William Girdler, who died in a tragic helicopter accident just as he was about to hit the big time with *The Manitou*. Ecological erosion of the ozone layer causes wild creatures to attack a group of Californian hikers in this creditable effort. Bears, wolves, vultures, snakes, dogs and rats (in a truly amazing forest ranger attack) all get in on the menacing act that's beautifully photographed and directed for lively shock value. **AJ**

Christopher George *Steve Buckner* • Leslie Nielsen *Paul Jensen* • Lynda Day George *Terry Marsh* • Richard Jaeckel *Taylor MacGregor* • Michael Ansara *Daniel Santee* ■ *Dir* William Girdler • *Scr* William Norton, Eleanor Norton, from a story by Edward E Montoro

Day of the Bad Man ★★
Western   1958 · US · Colour · 82min

The majestic photography of Irving Glassberg gives this small routine western a certain grandeur. Ageing Fred MacMurray stars as a judge who's trying to maintain law and order until the hour arrives when a condemned outlaw goes to the gallows. Director Harry Keller pays far too much attention to MacMurray's grim features, but there is the compensation of some irresistible western stalwarts in the cast. **TS**

Fred MacMurray *Judge Jim Scott* • Joan Weldon *Myra Owens* • John Ericson *Sheriff Barney Wiley* • Robert Middleton *Charlie Hayes* • Marie Windsor *Cora Johnson* • Edgar Buchanan *Sam Wyckoff* • Skip Homeier *Howard Hayes* • Lee Van Cleef *Jake Hayes* ■ *Dir* Harry Keller • *Scr* Lawrence Roman, from a story by John M Cunningham

The Day of the Beast ★★★★ 🄸🄸
Black comedy horror   1995 · Sp/It · Colour · 99min

Spanish director Alex de la Iglesia's highly engaging continental smash hit is a wicked parody of doom prophecy movies such as *The Omen*, with a dash of *Die Hard* thrown in. This scintillating and original spoof effortlessly mixes the sinister with the absurd, as three very unusual wise men search for the birth place of the Antichrist in Madrid on Christmas Eve. A screwball horror that's packed with demons, demises and diverting detail, it's as much a serious indictment of the way the media distorts reality as it is a clever genre satire. **AJ** Spanish +subtitles. Violence, swearing, nudity.

Alex Angulo *Angel Berriatua* • Armando De Razza *Ennio Lombardi* • Santiago Segura *Jose Maria* • Terele Pávez *Rosario* • Nathalie Sesena *Mina* • Jaime Blanch *Toyota 1* • Maria Grazia Cucinotta *Susana* ■ *Dir* Alex de la Iglesia • *Scr* Alex de la Iglesia, Jorge Guerricaechevarría

Day of the Dead ★★★★ 🄸🄴
Horror   1985 · US · Colour · 96min

After *Night of the Living Dead* (1968) and *Dawn of the Dead* (1978), George A Romero continued his series in a sophisticated, disturbing and horrifying way. Scientists in an underground missile base try to make ways of domesticating and controlling the cannibalistic zombie hordes so they can be re-integrated into society. Investing the living, rotting corpses with human touches (they shave and listen to personal stereos) is a stroke of genius on Romero's part, and one that makes his unnervingly bleak world vision both an intellectual and terrifying shock to the system. Followed by *George A Romero's Land of the Dead* (2005). **AJ** Violence, swearing. 📀 🔵

Lori Cardille *Sarah* • Terry Alexander *John* • Joseph Pilato *Captain Rhodes* • Jarlath Conroy *McDermott* • Antone DiLeo Jr [Anthony DiLeo Jr] *Miguel* • Richard Liberty *Dr Logan* • Howard Sherman [Sherman Howard] *Bub* ■ *Dir/Scr* George A Romero

Day of the Dead ★★ 🄸🄴
Horror   2008 · US · Colour · 82min

With zombie classic *Dawn of the Dead* slickly rebooted by director Zack Snyder back in 2004, it was only a matter of time before the third part of George A Romero's seminal saga would be remade. It's just a pity that Steve Miner was unable to maintain the undoubted quality Snyder brought to his offering. Little of the original 1985 Romero movie remains apart from the

🅤 SUITABLE FOR ALL   🅤ᵉ SUITABLE ESPECIALLY FOR YOUNG CHILDREN (DVD ONLY)   🅟🅖 PARENTAL GUIDANCE   🄸🄰 UNDER 12s TO BE ACCOMPANIED (CINEMA ONLY)

involvement of military folk (Mena Suvari and Ving Rhames among them) trying to survive a zombie outbreak in a small town. Gorily efficient rather than spectacular. JA Violence. **DVD** **BL**

Ving Rhames *Captain Rhodes* • Mena Suvari *Sarah Bowman* • Nick Cannon *Salazar* • Ian McNeice *Paul* • Michael Welch *Trevor Bowman* ■ *Dir* Steve Miner • *Scr* Jeffrey Reddick, from the 1985 film

The Day of the Dolphin ★★★**PG**

Drama   1973 · US · Colour · 100min

George C Scott takes on one of the biggest challenges of his career by conducting meaningful conversations with dolphins, but succeeds in making this odd set up believable. But while teaches his pet dolphin endearments like "Fa" and "Pa", this isn't a Flipperish, Disney-pic. Indeed, things get decidedly bleak when it's revealed that Scott's dolphins are destined to be used as sentient torpedoes in a plot to assassinate the President aboard his yacht. Georges Delerue's score is a high point. AT **DVD**

George C Scott *Dr Jake Terrell* • Trish Van Devere *Maggie Terrell* • Paul Sorvino *Mahoney* • Fritz Weaver *Harold DeMilo* • Jon Korkes *David* • Edward Herrmann *Mike* • Leslie Charleson *Maryanne* ■ *Dir* Mike Nichols • *Scr* Buck Henry, from a novel by Robert Merle

Day of the Evil Gun ★★**PG**

Western   1968 · US · Colour · 89min

Originally planned as a TV movie, this western starts out as an unofficial and wholly competent remake of *The Searchers*. Glenn Ford and Arthur Kennedy bond surprisingly well as they survive all manner of perils in a bid to rescue Ford's family from the Apache, and there's solid support from the underrated Dean Jagger as an untrustworthy trader. But the action takes an unexpected and rather improbable turn, which rather spoils the film. DP

Glenn Ford *Lorn Warfield* • Arthur Kennedy *Owen Forbes* • Dean Jagger *Jimmy Noble* • John Anderson *Captain Jefferson Addis* • Paul Fix *Sheriff Kelso* • Nico Minardos *DeLeon* • Dean Stanton [Harry Dean Stanton] *Sergeant Parker* ■ *Dir* Jerry Thorpe • *Scr* Charles Marquis Warren, Eric Bercovici, from the novel by Charles Marquis Warren

Day of the Fight ★★★

Sports documentary   1951 · US · BW · 16min

Adapting his 1949 *Prizefighter* photographic spread for *Look* magazine, Stanley Kubrick made his debut with this deceptively simple profile of middleweight Walter Cartier. While it seems as though Kubrick is merely chronicling Cartier's efforts to pass the time, he is actually showing how he psyches himself up to beat his opponent. Kubrick captures a sense of immediacy with his innovative angles and handheld exuberance. Yet for all its accomplishments, this 16-minute short didn't prove to be the director's breakthrough, even though it was acquired for RKO's *This Is America* series. DP

Douglas Edwards *Narrator* ■ *Dir* Stanley Kubrick • *Scr* Robert Rein • *Cinematographers* Stanley Kubrick, Alexander Singer

Day of the Flowers ★★**15**

Comedy drama 2012 · UK/Cub · Colour · 99min

Acclaimed ballet dancer Carlos Acosta shows off his thespian moves in this good-looking if lightweight story about two chalk-and-cheese Scots sisters exploring their family's connection with Castro's Cuba. Acosta smoulders alluringly alongside uptight Glasgow leftie Eva Birthistle and her fashion-victim sibling Charity Wakefield (providing bubbly comedic contrast). But the movie leans much too heavily on Latin stereotypes and makes Birthistle's heroine so exasperating that it's hard to buy into her romantic progress. TJ Swearing.

Eva Birthistle *Rosa* • Charity Wakefield *Ailie* • Carlos Acosta *Tomas* • Bryan Dick *Conway* • Chris Simpson [Christopher Simpson] *Ernesto* ■ *Dir* John Roberts • *Scr* Eirene Houston

The Day of the Jackal ★★★★★**15**

Thriller   1973 · UK/Fr · Colour · 136min

A magnificent script from Kenneth Ross and a masterly central performance from Edward Fox form the backbone of this big-screen version of Frederick Forsyth's bestselling novel, but it's Fred Zinnemann's matchless direction that makes it such compelling viewing. The pacing of the picture is superb, a methodical accumulation of detail that is as fastidious as Fox's preparation for his mission to assassinate General de Gaulle. Although the action crisscrosses Europe, there's no postcard prettiness, just a sure grasp of the atmosphere of each place before getting down to the business of the scene. Remade in 1997 as *The Jackal*, starring Bruce Willis. DP Violence, swearing, brief nudity. **DVD**

Edward Fox *The Jackal* • Michel Lonsdale *Claude Lebel* • Alan Badel *Minister* • Tony Britton *Inspector Thomas* • Adrien Cayla-Legrand *President General Charles de Gaulle* • Cyril Cusack *Gunsmith* • Donald Sinden *Mallinson* • Derek Jacobi *Caron* • Eric Porter *Colonel Rodin* • Delphine Seyrig *Colette de Montpelier* • Timothy West *Berthier* ■ *Dir* Fred Zinnemann • *Scr* Kenneth Ross, from the novel by Frederick Forsyth

The Day of the Locust ★★★★**18**

Period drama   1975 · US · Colour · 137min

This chronicle of Hollywood losers, eaten up by ambition but possessing no talent, gets lavish coverage from British director John Schlesinger. Karen Black stars as a would-be starlet, the daughter of drunken vaudevillian Burgess Meredith, who takes Donald Sutherland for a ride and almost snares sketch artist William Atherton as well. Adapted from Nathanael West's famous novel about early Tinseltown, the film sprawls too indulgently but remains enormously watchable throughout. TH Violence, nudity, sex scenes. **DVD**

Donald Sutherland *Homer Simpson* • Karen Black *Faye Greener* • Burgess Meredith *Harry Greener* • William Atherton *Tod Hackett* • Geraldine Page *Big Sister* ■ *Dir* John Schlesinger • *Scr* Waldo Salt, from the novel by Nathanael West

Day of the Outlaw ★★★**PG**

Western   1959 · US · BW · 88min

In this fine bleak western, veteran director Andre De Toth manages to emphasise every nuance of rage in anti-McCarthyite screenwriter Philip Yordan's bitter isolationist allegory. Rugged Robert Ryan is the rancher who finally makes a stand against Burl Ives's gang of renegade cut-throats. The snow-covered landscape (beautifully photographed in stark black and white by Russell Harlan) makes the tale seem even bleaker, with the climactic gunfight in a blizzard quite remarkable. TS **DVD** **BL**

Robert Ryan *Blaise Starrett* • Burl Ives *Jack Bruhn* • Tina Louise *Helen Crane* • Alan Marshal *Hal Crane* • Nehemiah Persoff *Dan* • Venetia Stevenson *Ernine* • Donald Elson *Vic* ■ *Dir* Andre De Toth • *Scr* Philip Yordan

The Day of the Triffids ★★**15**

Science-fiction horror
1962 · UK · Colour · 93min

A meteor shower blinds all but a few Earthlings, leaving society at the mercy of carnivorous plants from outer space in this rather disappointing version of John Wyndham's classic sci-fi novel. The Triffids themselves are bizarrely menacing, though, and Freddie Francis directed the lighthouse scenes that were added later in a bravura effort to beef up the chills and thrills. AJ **DVD**

Howard Keel *Bill Masen* • Janette Scott *Karen Goodwin* • Nicole Maurey *Christine Durrant* • Kieron Moore *Tom Goodwin* • Mervyn Johns *Mr Coker* • Alison Leggatt *Miss Coker* ■ *Dir* Steve Sekely • *Scr* Bernard Gordon [Philip Yordan], from the novel by John Wyndham

Day of Wrath ★★★★★**PG**

Period drama   1943 · Den · BW · 92min

Put to the stake for witchcraft, Anna Svierkier places a curse on the pastor (Thorkild Roose) who condemned her. Disaster and death are then visited upon Roose and his family, beginning with his discovery that his wife Lisbeth Movin is having an affair with a younger man (Preben Lerdoff Rye). Made by Denmark's great genius of the cinema, Carl Th Dreyer, this is an uncompromising vision of human frailty, stupidity, bigotry and cruelty, made all the more horrifying by the startling beauty of its images. Not easy, but rewarding. RK Danish +subtitles. **DVD**

Thorkild Roose *Absalon Pedersson* • Lisbeth Movin *Anne, his wife* • Sigrid Neiiendam *Merete, his mother* • Preben Lerdorff Rye *Martin, his son* ■ *Dir* Carl Th Dreyer • *Scr* Carl Th Dreyer, Mogens Skot-Hansen, Poul Knudsen, from the play and novel *Anne Pedersdotter* by Hans Wiers-Jenssens

Day One ★★★★

Second World War drama
1989 · US · Colour · 141min

The spectre of nuclear warfare is made real and immediate in this TV movie based on the true story of the Second World War Manhattan Project's race to build the first atomic bomb. David W Rintels's taut script, veteran Joseph Sargent's insightful direction and a splendid cast make this Emmy-winning production gleam with the feeling of living history. Moving, frightening and richly rewarding. MC

John McMartin *Dr Arthur Compton* • Brian Dennehy *General Leslie Groves* • Richard Dysart *President Harry S Truman* • Michael Tucker *Leo Szilard* • Hume Cronyn *James F Byrnes* • Hal Holbrook *General George Marshall* ■ *Dir* Joseph Sargent • *Scr* David W Rintels, from the book *Day One: Before Hiroshima and After* by Peter Wyden

The Day the Earth Caught Fire ★★★**PG**

Science-fiction drama   1961 · UK · BW · 99min

Atomic explosions at the two poles put the planet on a collision course with the Sun in this bleak British doomsday vision. With the emphasis on the reactions of some London journalists to the impending catastrophe rather than elaborate special effects, this tautly intelligent sci-fi thriller hits all the right buttons, helped by a script full of fatalistic quips and cynicism. Engrossing, with a memorable fade-out on two possible newspaper headlines. AJ **DVD** **BL**

Leo McKern *Bill Maguire* • Janet Munro *Jeannie* • Edward Judd *Peter Stenning* • Michael Goodliffe *Night editor* • Bernard Braden *News editor* • Reginald Beckwith *Harry* • Gene Anderson *May* • Austin Trevor *Sir John Kelly* • Renée Asherson *Angela* • Michael Caine *Policeman* ■ *Dir* Val Guest • *Scr* Val Guest, Wolf Mankowitz

The Day the Earth Stood Still ★★★★★**U**

Classic science-fiction drama
1951 · US · BW · 88min

Coming just four months after Christian Nyby and Howard Hawks had unleashed *The Thing from Another World* upon a petrified Cold War public, director Robert Wise's sci-fi classic was a welcome sign of hope, as a mysterious spaceship from an unknown planet brings a message of peace rather than destruction. From Bernard Herrmann's otherworldly score to Lyle Wheeler and Addison Hehr's simple designs, this has had an incalculable influence on big screen science fiction. For all its philosophical solemnity and heavy-handed religious symbolism, Edmund H North's script deftly pokes fun at the Red-baiters who had done so much to foster the nuclear scare, while his notion that children accept without question what grown-ups are too cynical to see has continued to resurface throughout the blockbuster era. DP **DVD** **BL**

Michael Rennie *Klaatu* • Patricia Neal *Helen Benson* • Hugh Marlowe *Tom Stevens* • Sam Jaffe *Dr Barnhardt* • Billy Gray *Bobby Benson* •

Frances Bavier *Mrs Barley* • Lock Martin *Gort* ■ *Dir* Robert Wise • *Scr* Edmund H North, from the short story *Farewell to the Master* by Harry Bates

The Day the Earth Stood Still ★★**12**

Science-fiction drama
2008 · US · Colour · 99min

Robert Wise's alien-invasion original, released in 1951, is an iconic entry in the canon of 1950s sci-fi, thanks in part to its muted parable of Christian redemption. Fifty-seven years on, this fatuous remake ditches the Cold War/religious subtext – and even the flying saucers – in its attempt to deliver a more contemporary allegory, as spaceman Keanu Reeves arrives with a warning for humanity. At his best when dealing with the CGI-heavy action, director Scott Derrickson fumbles the plotting and loses sight of what made the original so unique. JR **DVD** **BL**

Keanu Reeves *Klaatu* • Jennifer Connelly *Dr Helen Benson* • Kathy Bates *Regina Jackson* • John Cleese *Professor Barnhardt* • Jaden Smith *Jacob Benson* • Jon Hamm *Michael Granier* ■ *Dir* Scott Derrickson • *Scr* David Scarpa, from the 1951 film, from the short story *Farewell to the Master* by Harry Bates

The Day the Fish Came Out ★★

Satire   1967 · UK/Gr · Colour · 108min

Michael Cacoyannis's follow-up to his highly acclaimed *Zorba the Greek* couldn't have been more different, or more of a disappointment: a ham-fisted satire that falls prisoner to the modish mood of its time. Tom Courtenay and Colin Blakely play Nato airmen whose plane, carrying a pair of H-bombs and a doomsday weapon, ditches in the sea near a Greek island. Cacoyannis struggles to integrate the clashing styles of farce and realism into any coherent whole. RS

Tom Courtenay *Navigator* • Sam Wanamaker *Elias* • Colin Blakely *Pilot* • Candice Bergen *Electra* • Ian Ogilvy *Peter* ■ *Dir/Scr* Michael Cacoyannis

The Day the Sun Turned Cold ★★★★**12**

Murder mystery drama based on a true story
1994 · HK · Colour · 100min

Taken as a political allegory or an Oedipal melodrama, Ho Yim's award-winning film is both troubling and compelling. It scarcely matters whether Si Ching Gao Wa (a powerful Mongolian actress who also starred in the director's 1984 breakthrough, *Homecoming*) actually killed her husband. What is so intriguing is why her son (Tao Chung Wa) would betray her to the authorities, and why he would wait a decade before doing so. Based on true events and told in a measured, unsettlingly realistic manner, this provocative picture will linger long in the mind. DP Mandarin +subtitles.

Si Ching Gao Wa *Pu Fengying, the mother* • Tao Chung Wa *Guan Jian, the son* • Ma Jingwu *Guan Shichang, the father* ■ *Dir* Ho Yim • *Scr* Ho Yim, Wang Xing Dong

The Day the World Ended ★★**PG**

Science fiction drama   1956 · US · BW · 78min

The first science-fiction film from cult director Roger Corman has seven survivors of a nuclear war fighting off atomic radiation mutants from their mountain retreat. Not much else happens in this cheesy yet ludicrously entertaining fright flick, which transposes the Garden of Eden myth into an uncertain future. The ads at the time promised "a new high in naked shrieking terror", but the only shrieks to be heard now will be ones of laughter at the three-eyed, four-armed monster suits. AJ **DVD**

Richard Denning *Rick* • Lori Nelson *Louise* • Adele Jergens *Ruby* • Touch Connors [Mike Connors] *Tony* • Paul Birch *Maddison* ■ *Dir* Roger Corman • *Scr* Lou Rusoff, from his story

The Day the World Ended
★★ 15

Science-fiction horror
2001 · US · Colour · 86min

Despite taking its title from Roger Corman's 1956 B-movie about radiation-induced mutants, this TV remake is most indebted to *Invasion of the Body Snatchers*. No one believes youngster Bobby Edner's claims that recent murders are the work of his biological father, who he believes is an extraterrestrial. Predictable and one-dimensional. DP *DVD*

Randy Quaid *Dr Michael McCann* • Bobby Edner *Benjamin James McCann* • Nastassja Kinski *Dr Jennifer Stillman* • Harry Groener *Sheriff* • Lee DeBroux *Harlan* • Stephen Tobolowsky *Ed Turner* ■ *Dir* Terence Gross • *Scr* Max Enscoe, Annie de Young, from a story by Brian King

The Day They Gave Babies Away
★★ U

Period drama
1957 · US · Colour · 102min

A rather curious account of the hardships and tragedies faced by a mid-19th-century Scottish immigrant family in the American backwoods, this stars the unlikely pairing of Britain's Glynis Johns and the hunky Cameron Mitchell. The result is little more than a plodding seasonal tear-jerker, but, despite the weak characterisation and mediocre direction, it's good to see the famously husky-voiced Johns as a doughty pioneer wife. RK

Glynis Johns *Mamie Eunson* • Cameron Mitchell *Robert Eunson* • Rex Thompson *Robbie Eunson* • Patty McCormack *Annabelle Eunson* ■ *Dir* Allen Reisner • *Scr* Dale Eunson, Katherine Eunson

The Day They Robbed the Bank of England
★★★ U

Crime caper
1960 · UK · BW · 84min

In 1901, Irish nationalists plot to rob the Old Lady of Threadneedle Street of its gold bullion, taking it through the sewers and down the River Thames. Both a heist thriller and a sophisticated political drama, this was directed by John Guillermin, who makes the most of the planning and features some clever use of locations, but most eyes will be on Peter O'Toole as the young security guard Fitch. David Lean saw his performance and cast him in *Lawrence of Arabia*. AT

Aldo Ray *Norgate* • Elizabeth Sellars *Iris Muldoon* • Hugh Griffith *O'Shea* • Peter O'Toole *Fitch* • Kieron Moore *Walsh* • Albert Sharpe *Tosher* • John Le Mesurier *Green* • Joseph Tomelty *Cohoun* ■ *Dir* John Guillermin • *Scr* Howard Clewes, Richard Maibaum, from the novel by John Brophy

The Day Time Ended
★

Science-fiction adventure
1980 · US/Sp · Colour · 80min

Jim Davis's family moves into a solar-powered desert home, only to find they're slap-bang in the middle of a time vortex that lures visiting aliens to warn them about Earth's imminent destruction. A nonsensical blend of cardboard special effects, this is a crudely assembled affair. AJ

Jim Davis (1) *Grant* • Christopher Mitchum *Richard* • Dorothy Malone *Ana* • Marcy Lafferty *Beth* • Scott Kolden *Steve* • Natasha Ryan *Jenny* ■ *Dir* John "Bud" Cardos • *Scr* Wayne Schmidt, J Larry Carroll, David Schmoeller, from a story by Steve Neill

A Day to Remember
★★ U

Drama
1953 · UK · BW · 91min

This mix of poignant drama and postcard comedy follows Cockney darts captain Stanley Holloway as he leads his team on a day trip to Boulogne. A host of familiar faces take caricature cameos. However, the stories that linger longest in the mind are those owing least to contrivance: notably widower James Hayter's return to his honeymoon hotel, and ex-soldier Donald Sinden's reunion with Odile Versois, the beauty he'd known as a child during the war. DP

Stanley Holloway *Charley Porter* • Donald Sinden *Jim Carver* • Joan Rice *Vera Mitchell* • Odile Versois *Martine Berthier* • James Hayter *Fred*

Collins • Harry Fowler *Stan Harvey* • Edward Chapman *Mr Robinson* • Peter Jones *Percy Goodall* • Bill Owen *Shorty Sharpe* • Meredith Edwards *Bert Tripp* • George Coulouris *Captain* • Vernon Gray *Marvin* • Thora Hird *Mrs Trott* • Theodore Bikel *Henri Dubot* ■ *Dir* Ralph Thomas • *Scr* Robin Estridge, from the novel *The Hand and the Flower* by Jerrard Tickell

Day Watch
★★★ 15

Fantasy horror thriller
2006 · Rus · Colour · 139min

Emulating its predecessor *Night Watch* with its state-of-the-art visuals, *Day Watch* finds hero Anton Gorodetsky (Konstantin Khabensky) firmly embroiled in the battle between the supernatural forces of Light and Darkness when he is framed for murder. The two sides each have a "Great Other" – one is Svetlana, the love of Anton's life, while the other is his embittered son Yegor, who has aligned himself with the forces of evil. A clash between these powerful beings could bring an end to the centuries-long truce between the Night Watch and the Day Watch, and cause the end of the world. Director Timur Bekmambetov populates his movie with some quite breathtaking stunts and special effects (a car careering up the side of a multistorey building is a particular stand-out), which make up for the somewhat dense narrative. JA Russian, Chagatai, English +subtitles. *DVD* Blu

Konstantin Khabensky *Anton Gorodetsky* • Maria Poroshina *Svetlana* • Vladimir Menshov *Boris Geser* • Galina Tunina *Olga* • Viktor Verzhbitsky *Zavulon* • Zhanna Friske *Alisa* • Dima Martynov *Yegor* • Valery Zolotukhin *Kostya's father* • Alexei Chadov *Kostya* ■ *Dir* Timur Bekmambetov • *Scr* Timur Bekmambetov, Sergei Lukyanenko, Alexander Talal, from the novel by Lukyanenko, Vladimir Vasiliev

The Day Will Dawn
★★★ U

Second World War romance
1942 · UK · BW · 94min

Markedly less restrained than many other British tales of wartime resistance, this well-meaning flag-waver is still far more effective than the majority of have-a-go Hollywood movies on the same theme. The story of a British journalist liaising with the Norwegian underground to help destroy a German U-boat base is merely par for the course. What sets this apart is a remarkable cast of British stalwarts, not one of whom puts a foot wrong. DP *DVD*

Ralph Richardson *Lockwood* • Deborah Kerr *Kari Alstead* • Hugh Williams *Colin Metcalfe* • Griffith Manes *Inspector Gunter* • Francis L Sullivan *Wettau* • Roland Culver *Naval Attaché* • Niall MacGinnis *Olaf* • Finlay Currie *Alstead* ■ *Dir* Harold French • *Scr* Terence Rattigan, Anatole de Grunwald, Patrick Kirwan, from a story by Frank Owen

Daybreak
★★

Period romance
1931 · US · BW · 72min

Ramon Novarro stars as a handsome Austrian guardsman who falls in love with the appealing Helen Chandler in this period romance. Although the film is elegantly and sensitively directed by Frenchman Jacques Feyder, with a supporting cast that includes the redoubtable C Aubrey Smith, it failed to appeal to the public then and is unlikely to do so now. RK

Ramon Novarro *Willi* • Helen Chandler *Laura* • Jean Hersholt *Herr Schnabel* • C Aubrey Smith *Gen von Hartz* ■ *Dir* Jacques Feyder • *Scr* Ruth Cummings, Cyril Hume, Zelda Sears, from the play by Arthur Schnitzler

Daybreak
★★ PG

Crime drama
1946 · UK · BW · 77min

At the time, the producers Muriel and Sydney Box complained that their British melodrama had been held up by censorship and ruined by cuts. It is hard to see how it could have worked, even in its entirety, as Eric Portman portrays an unemployed hangman seeking revenge on the Swedish lover (Maxwell Reed) of his wife (Ann Todd). Despite Portman's usual magnetism, the result is quite laughable. TH

Eric Portman *Eddie* • Ann Todd *Frankie* • Maxwell Reed *Olaf* • Edward Rigby *Bill Shackle* • Bill Owen *Ron* • Jane Hylton *Doris* • Eliot Makeham *Mr Bigley* • Margaret Withers *Mrs Bigley* • John Turnbull *Superintendent* • Maurice Denham *Inspector* ■ *Dir* Compton Bennett • *Scr* Muriel Box, Sydney Box, from a play by Monckton Hoffe

Daybreakers
★★★ 18

Horror thriller
2008 · Aus/US · Colour · 93min

Humans are the hunted minority in a near-future world populated by vampires in this intriguingly weird sci-fi/horror hybrid. Principled vampire scientist Ethan Hawke creates a synthetic plasma substitute to ensure mankind's survival, although his boss (Sam Neill) is making a fortune out of harvesting blood at inflated prices. This skilful blend of John Carpenter, Bram Stoker and Philip K Dick features smart takes on the vampire mythos (sun-proofed cars and video mirrors), inventively engineered shocks and copious blood loss. Hawke is terrific, while Willem Dafoe ramps up the fun factor as a Van Helsing-type with a big secret. AJ Violence, swearing, brief nudity. *DVD* Blu

Ethan Hawke *Edward Dalton* • Willem Dafoe *Lionel "Elvis" Cormac* • Michael Dorman *Frankie Dalton* • Claudia Karvan *Audrey Bennett* • Sam Neill *Charles Bromley* • Isabel Lucas *Alison Bromley* ■ *Dir* The Spierig Brothers [Michael Spierig], The Spierig Brothers [Peter Spierig] • *Scr* The Spierig Brothers [Michael Spierig, Peter Spierig]

Daydream Believer
★★ 15

Romantic comedy drama
1991 · Aus · Colour · 81min

Beginning with unpleasant scenes of child abuse, Kathy Mueller's film lurches forward in time to find the child in question has grown into the timid Miranda Otto, whose tactic in times of stress is to imagine she's a horse. There is some heavy-handed satire at the expense of wealthy businessman Martin Kemp and a last-minute rescue worthy of a silent melodrama. DP Violence, swearing, brief nudity.

Miranda Otto *Nell* • Martin Kemp *Digby* • Anne Looby *Margot* • Alister Smart *Ron* • Gia Carides *Wendy* • Bruce Venables *Stu* ■ *Dir* Kathy Mueller • *Scr* Saturday Rosenberg

Daylight
★★★ 12

Disaster movie
1996 · US · Colour · 114min

This is an involving tale about a group of motorists who become trapped in a New York tunnel under the Hudson River following a freak accident. Director Rob Cohen's classy contribution to the 1990s disaster movie resurgence is less reliant on slick visual effects than most, and Sylvester Stallone displays more vulnerability than expected as the leader of an escape party. Cohen's orchestration of the requisite action scenes is impressive. JC Violence, swearing. *DVD* Blu

Sylvester Stallone *Kit Latura* • Amy Brenneman *Madelyne Thompson* • Viggo Mortensen *Roy Nord* • Dan Hedaya *Frank Kraft* • Jay O Sanders *Steven Crighton* • Karen Young *Sarah Crighton* • Claire Bloom *Eleanor Trilling* • Sage Stallone *Vincent* ■ *Dir* Rob Cohen • *Scr* Leslie Bohem

Daylight Robbery
★★ 15

Crime thriller
2007 · UK · Colour · 95min

Bank robbers use the 2006 World Cup in Germany as a cover for their heist in this low-budget thriller that feels like a belated addition to the raft of mockney British gangster movies inspired by *Lock, Stock and Two Smoking Barrels*. First-time writer/director Paris Leoni depicts the heist itself with rigour, the ingenious use of an airport check-in desk supposedly giving the gang a watertight alibi. But the robbery itself is fraught with problems, as greed, incompetence and sheer bad luck take their toll on ringleaders Alex (Geoff Bell) and Norman (Justin Salinger). Despite marshalling his ensemble cast with military precision, Leonti's workmanlike direction isn't helped by his limitations as a writer. JR *DVD*

Geoff Bell *Alex* • Paul Nicholls *Chubby* • Justin Salinger *Norman* • Robert Boulter *Jay* • Vas Blackwood *Lucky* • Johnny Harris *Terry* • Leo Gregory *Matty* • Shaun Williamson *Police chief* ■ *Dir/Scr* Paris Leonti

Days and Nights in the Forest
★★★★

Drama
1969 · Ind · BW · 115min

Satyajit Ray was encouraged in his early film career by the great French director Jean Renoir, and his influence is clearly evident in this Bengali reworking of the classic featurette *Une Partie de Campagne*. Seeking to escape from the stress of Calcutta, four friends travel to the forest, where their encounters and misadventures cause them to take stock of their lives. Supremely capturing the glow of a summer's day and taking sly shots at the bourgeois mentality, Ray draws inspired performances from his leads. DP Bengali +subtitles.

Soumitra Chatterjee *Ashim* • Subhendu Chatterjee *Sanjoy* • Samit Bhanja *Harinath* • Robi Ghosh *Sekhar* ■ *Dir* Satyajit Ray • *Scr* Satyajit Ray, from the novel by Suil Ganguly

Days of Being Wild
★★★★ 12

Drama
1990 · HK · Colour · 90min

This stylish, intricately structured drama not only harks back to the 1960s, but also explores the fears attending Hong Kong's handover to China. Leslie Cheung excels as a rebel with the cause of tracing his Filipino mother, callously leaving the broken hearts of waitress Maggie Cheung and showgirl Carina Lau in his wake. Two years in production and strikingly shot by Christopher Doyle, Wong Kar-Wai's second feature was such a flop at the domestic box office that a sequel was abandoned. However, internationally, it confirmed Wong's reputation as a rising art house star. DP Cantonese +subtitles. *DVD*

Leslie Cheung *Yuddy* • Maggie Cheung *Su Lizhen* • Tony Chiu-Wai Leung [Tony Leung (2)] *Smirk* • Carina Lau *Fung-Ying* ■ *Dir/Scr* Wong Kar-Wai

Days of Glory
★★ PG

Second World War romantic drama
1944 · US · BW · 85min

Gregory Peck made his Hollywood debut in this, playing a Russian patriot fighting the Nazi invaders in this wartime flag-waver. Designed to show how friendly Uncle Sam was with Uncle Joe Stalin, it's never more than a B-picture, efficiently directed by Jacques Tourneur and co-starring Tamara Toumanova, a prima ballerina who grandly resisted Hollywood's efforts to turn her into a star. AT

Gregory Peck *Vladimir* • Tamara Toumanova *Nina* • Lowell Gilmore *Semyon* • Maria Palmer *Yelena* • Alan Reed *Sasha* • Hugo Haas *Fedor* ■ *Dir* Jacques Tourneur • *Scr* Casey Robinson, from a story by Melchior Lengyel

Days of Glory
★★★★ 12

Second World War drama
2006 · Fr/Bel/Mor/Alg · Colour · 118min

Rachid Bouchareb's *Days of Glory* is a complex and affecting movie that handles a thorny subject with sensitivity. It begins in 1943 and introduces us to a small team of North African soldiers whose lives will be changed by the Second World War. Not only do they face death in the gunsights of the Nazis, but they struggle to gain the respect of a French army that despises them while both needing and expecting their loyalty. The camaraderie of the men is believable, thanks to a superb ensemble cast headed by comedian Jamel Debbouze, who here gives a serious performance rich with pathos and dignity. DW French, Arabic +subtitles. Swearing, some violence. *DVD* Blu

Jamel Debbouze *Said* • Samy Naceri *Yassir* • Roschdy Zem *Messaoud Souni* • Sami Bouajila *Abdelkader* • Bernard Blancan *Martinez* • Mathieu Simonet *Leroux* • Benoît Giros *Captain Durieux* ■ *Dir* Rachid Bouchareb • *Scr* Rachid Bouchareb, Olivier Lorelle • *Cinematographer* Patrick Blossier

---

U SUITABLE FOR ALL   Uc SUITABLE ESPECIALLY FOR YOUNG CHILDREN (DVD ONLY)   PG PARENTAL GUIDANCE   12A UNDER 12s TO BE ACCOMPANIED (CINEMA ONLY)

Days of Grace ★★★ 15

Crime drama 2011 · Mex/US/Fr · Colour · 131min

Director Everardo Valerio Gout makes an instant impression with a dynamic debut that owes much to 1990s Hong Kong crime flicks like *Hard-Boiled*. Gout capably interweaves a trio of storylines across three football World Cups between 2002 and 2010. But his preoccupation with kinetic imagery and violent set pieces keeps the audience at a distance from honest cop Tenoch Huerta, delinquent Kristyan Ferrer and abducted businessman Carlos Bardem. The score, by Nick Cave among others, helps it maintain its grip. DP Spanish +subtitles. Violence, swearing, sex scenes, drug abuse, nudity. *DVD*

Tenoch Huerta [Tenoch Huerta Mejia] *Lupe Esperanza, "Teacher"* • Dolores Heredia *Susana* • Carlos Bardem *Victim X* ■ *Dir/Scr* Everardo Valerio Gout

Days of Heaven ★★★★ PG

Period drama 1978 · US · Colour · 89min

This truly extraordinary visual treat from director Terrence Malick and Oscar-winning cinematographer Nestor Almendros may not have been a great commercial success, but its look has been much copied since. Malick takes a couple of disenfranchised labourers, Richard Gere and Brooke Adams, and Gere's little sister, Linda Manz, and sets them down in the golden vastness of the Texas wheat fields. A tragedy-strewn love triangle develops between Gere, Adams and their employer, Sam Shepard, though Malick steps back from the narrative to give us a curiously disembodied elegy on poverty and freedom. SH *DVD*

Richard Gere *Bill* • Brooke Adams *Abby* • Sam Shepard *Farmer* • Linda Manz *Linda* • Robert Wilke [Robert J Wilke] *Farm foreman* • Jackie Shultis *Linda's friend* • Stuart Margolin *Mill foreman* ■ *Dir/Scr* Terrence Malick

Days of Jesse James ★★ U

Western 1939 · US · BW · 52min

Republic packed singing cowboy Roy Rogers into nine horse operas in 1939 and this surprisingly violent affair is easily the most memorable, if only for its revisionist frontier history. Hired by banker Arthur Loft to recover the loot lifted in a daring robbery, Rogers joins Frank and Jesse James's gang, only to discover that they have been framed for the crime and he defends them against bounty-hunting railroad detective, Harry Woods. DP *DVD*

Roy Rogers • George "Gabby" Hayes *Gabby Whittaker* • Don Barry [Donald Barry] *Jesse James* • Pauline Moore *Mary Whittaker* • Harry Woods *Captain Worthington* • Arthur Loft *Sam Wyatt* • Wade Boteler *Dr Samuels* • Ethel Wales *Martha Samuels* • Scotty Beckett *Buster Samuels* • Michael Worth [Harry Worth] *Frank James* ■ *Dir* Joseph Kane • *Scr* Earl Snell, from a story by Jack Natteford

Days of Thrills and Laughter ★★★ U

Comedy compilation 1961 · US · BW · 89min

Film purists baulk at these Robert Youngson compilations but they did achieve a cinema release, and as a result became, for many, an introduction to the wonderful world of silent cinema. At the time, it was difficult, or more accurately, impossible to see pre-sound movies in anywhere near decent copies with proper projection. This is a fine selection (albeit with added commentary by Jay Jackson, music and a little juggling with projection speeds) and includes the work of such geniuses as Charlie Chaplin, Harry Langdon, Laurel and Hardy, Douglas Fairbanks (Sr, of course!) and queen of the serials, Pearl White. For those who have never seen them, this is a good introduction and will fuel the desire to view more from this fabulous period when the movies were young. TS

Jay Jackson *Narrator* ■ *Dir/Scr* Robert Youngson

Days of Thunder ★★★ 15

Sports drama 1990 · US · Colour · 102min

This flashy action picture resulted in Tom Cruise's marital union with co-star Nicole Kidman. Motor sport movies have a lousy track record at the box office and this cliché-ridden stock car action movie was a costly flop. Reworking many of the themes in Howard Hawks's *The Crowd Roars*, Robert Towne's script must have looked a sure-fire winner, and there's little wrong with Tony Scott's zippy race sequences or Robert Duvall's performance as Cruise's manager. DP Swearing. *DVD* *Blu*

Tom Cruise *Cole Trickle* • Robert Duvall *Harry Hogge* • Nicole Kidman *Dr Claire Lewicki* • Randy Quaid *Tim Daland* • Cary Elwes *Russ Wheeler* • Michael Rooker *Rowdy Burns* • Fred Dalton Thompson *Big John* • John C Reilly *Buck Bretherton* • JC Quinn *Waddell* ■ *Dir* Tony Scott • *Scr* Robert Towne, from a story by Robert Towne, Tom Cruise

Days of Wine and Roses ★★★★ PG

Drama 1962 · US · BW · 112min

For those who know Jack Lemmon only as one half of *The Odd Couple*, or as a Grumpy Old Man, this will be a revelation: he's in heart-rending dramatic mode as an advertising executive, driven to drink by his work and taking wife Lee Remick along for the alcoholic ride. Adapted by JP Miller from his own TV play, the film is directed by Blake Edwards with a poignancy you don't expect, and acted by Lemmon and Remick with a force that remains memorable long after viewing. TH *DVD*

Jack Lemmon *Joe Clay* • Lee Remick *Kirsten Arnesen* • Charles Bickford *Ellis Arnesen* • Jack Klugman *Jim Hungerford* • Alan Hewitt *Leland* • Tom Palmer *Ballefoy* • Debbie Megowan *Debbie* ■ *Dir* Blake Edwards • *Scr* JP Miller, from his television play

A Day's Pleasure ★★★ U

Silent comedy drama 1919 · US · BW · 18min

In this Charlie Chaplin two-reeler, the comedy is condensed into a chaotic family outing on the river, where sea-sickness afflicts every passenger on a crowded cruiser. Edna Purviance is along for the ride, while Jackie Coogan makes his first appearance with Chaplin; he would later co-star with the great man in *The Kid*. TH

Charles Chaplin *Father* • Edna Purviance *Mother* • Tom Wilson *Cop* • Sydney Chaplin [Syd Chaplin] *Father* • Jackie Coogan *Boy* ■ *Dir/Scr* Charles Chaplin

The Daytrippers ★★★★ 15

Comedy 1998 · US · Colour · 83min

All of the mother-in-law-from-hell jibes that comedians used to make are on display in this sparky story about relationships among a family of oddballs. Led by dominating mother Anne Meara, the clan drives to the city to track down the husband (Stanley Tucci) whom Hope Davis thinks has been unfaithful. Davis is fairly sane about the whole issue, which is more than can be said about the rest of the family, with Meara being the wackiest of the lot. Writer/ director Greg Mottola has contrived some great one-liners, but his one flaw is that the mother-in-law is almost too obnoxious. TH Swearing. *DVD*

Hope Davis *Eliza* • Stanley Tucci *Louis D'Amico* • Parker Posey *Jo Malone* • Liev Schreiber *Carl* • Anne Meara *Rita Malone* • Pat McNamara *Jim Malone* • Campbell Scott *Eddie* ■ *Dir/Scr* Greg Mottola

Dazed and Confused ★★★★ 15

Comedy drama 1993 · US · Colour · 98min

Some of Hollywood's hottest young talent cut their teeth on this ultra-hip movie, among them Matthew McConaughey and Ben Affleck. But it's Jason London and Rory Cochrane who carry this freewheeling story, as a couple of high school wasters on the last day of the summer term. Director Richard Linklater employs a pseudo-documentary style to expose teenage life in the raw, with all the attendant angst, arrogance, aggression and amorousness. This honest and incisive portrait is both funny and scary. AJ Swearing, drug abuse. *DVD* *Blu*

Jason London *Randy "Pink" Floyd* • Sasha Jenson *Don Dawson* • Rory Cochrane *Slater* • Wiley Wiggins *Mitch Kramer* • Michelle Burke *Jodi Kramer* • Shawn Andrews *Pickford* • Anthony Rapp *Tony* • Adam Goldberg *Mike* • Christin Hinojosa *Sabrina* • Milla Jovovich *Michelle* • Matthew McConaughey *Wooderson* • Ben Affleck *O'Bannion* ■ *Dir/Scr* Richard Linklater

De Sade ★★

Biographical drama 1969 · US/W Ger · Colour · 107min

Begun by director Cy Endfield and completed by Roger Corman (uncredited), this is a beautiful-looking muddle of historical fact and hysterical fiction, with fuzzy fantasy and soft-core orgies punctuating the hopelessly contrived flow. Keir Dullea does his best as the marquis, but the Eurotrash supporting cast and John Huston's embarrassing turn as de Sade's cruel father places this squarely in the "interesting flop" category. AJ

Keir Dullea *Marquis de Sade* • Senta Berger *Anne de Montreuil* • Lilli Palmer *Mme de Montreuil* • John Huston *Abbé de Sade* • Anna Massey *Renée de Montreuil* • Ute Levka *Rose Keller* ■ *Dir* Cy Endfield • *Scr* Richard Matheson, Peter Berg

The Dead ★★★★ U

Period drama 1987 · US/UK · Colour · 79min

This beautifully judged adaptation of James Joyce's story about a family Christmas party in turn-of-the-century Dublin is a fitting swan song to director John Huston's distinguished career. Huston captures the national character with a deft economy that few film-makers could hope to emulate. But it's the quality of the ensemble acting that makes this warm, nostalgic and intimate drama such a moving experience. Anjelica Huston is superb, while Donal McCann also impresses as her regretful husband. DP *Blu*

Anjelica Huston *Gretta Conroy* • Donal McCann *Gabriel Conroy* • Rachael Dowling *Lily* • Cathleen Delaney *Aunt Julia Morkan* • Helena Carroll *Aunt Kate Morkan* • Ingrid Craigie *Mary Jane* • Dan O'Herlihy *Mr Browne* • Frank Patterson *Bartell D'Arcy* • Donal Donnelly *Freddy Malins* ■ *Dir* John Huston • *Scr* Tony Huston, from the short story by James Joyce

Dead Again ★★★ 15

Thriller 1991 · US · Colour and BW · 103min

The present is tense because the past is imperfect in Kenneth Branagh's determinedly old-fashioned thriller in the Hitchcock tradition. He's a cynical LA private detective hired to research the background of amnesiac mystery woman Emma Thompson, who's obsessed by scissors and tormented by nightmares from someone else's life. An enjoyably overdone, stylish mix of *film noir* trivia and eccentric plotting, Branagh's dark reincarnation parody will keep you guessing right up until the OTT finale. AJ Swearing, violence. *DVD*

Kenneth Branagh *Mike Church/Roman Strauss* • Emma Thompson *Grace/Margaret Strauss* • Derek Jacobi *Franklyn Madson* • Andy Garcia *Gray Baker* • Wayne Knight *"Piccolo" Pete* • Hanna Schygulla *Inge* • Campbell Scott *Doug* • Gregor Hesse *Frankie* • Robin Williams *Dr Cozy Carlisle* ■ *Dir* Kenneth Branagh • *Scr* Scott Frank

The Dead and the Deadly ★★★★ 18

Supernatural comedy drama 1983 · HK · Colour · 97min

Rightly considered one of the best supernatural comedies ever made in Hong Kong, this is a mix of kung fu, Chinese spiritualism and knockabout fun. Diminutive Wu Ma (who also directs) is killed while attempting an inheritance swindle, and his ghost takes over the body of hulking martial arts superstar Samo Kam-Bo Hung to get his revenge. It takes Cherry Cho-Hung Chung's battle with some supernatural powers, however, to put things right. Played for laughs rather than thrills, Wu's film has a seductively mystic feel. DP Cantonese, Mandarin +subtitles.

Samo Kam-Bo Hung [Sammo Hung] *Wah Li* • Cherry Cho-Hung Chung [Cherie Chung] *Miss Yuen* ■ *Dir* Wu Ma • *Scr* Samo Kam-Bo Hung [Sammo Hung], Barry Ping-Yiu Wong

Dead Babies ★★★ 18

Black comedy 2000 · UK · Colour · 100min

Adapted from the cult novel by Martin Amis, this is a quirky effort about the extremes society will go to for new thrills and kicks. Updating the novel's action from the early 1970s, Marsh sets his movie in the near future where a group of upper-class misfits performs a controlled experiment with a new superdrug invented by a Charles Manson-style chemistry professor (played by director William Marsh). Loaded with disturbing imagery, gruesome special effects and startling sex scenes, this somewhat heavy-handed social critique raises provocative questions. AJ

Paul Bettany *Quentin* • Olivia Williams *Diana* • Charlie Condou *Giles* • Alexandra Gilbreath *Celia* • Cristian Solimeno *Andy* • Andy Nyman *Keith* • William Marsh *Marvel* ■ *Dir* William Marsh • *Scr* William Marsh, from the novel by Martin Amis

Dead-Bang ★★★ 18

Detective action thriller 1989 · US · Colour · 101min

Don Johnson stars in this thriller as a cop with the usual hang-ups – divorced, kids, workaholic, hot temper, tendency to kill people. On the trail of a cop killer, he winds up in Nowhere, Oklahoma, home of white supremacists who plan the overthrow of the US government. Director John Frankenheimer pumps this up nicely, orchestrating some clever twists. AT

Don Johnson *Jerry Beck* • Bob Balaban *Elliot Webly* • William Forsythe *Arthur Kressler* • Penelope Ann Miller *Linda* • Frank Military *Bobby Burns* • Tate Donovan *John Burns* • Antoni Stutz *Ray* • Mickey Jones *Sleepy* ■ *Dir* John Frankenheimer • *Scr* Robert Foster

Dead Beat ★★★

Crime thriller 1994 · US · Colour · 93min

This serial killer chiller, set in New Mexico in 1965, has Bruce Ramsay playing an Elvis-fixated psychopath whose band of disciples include little lost rich girl Natasha Gregson Wagner and snivelling acolyte Balthazar Getty. Adam Dubov's directorial debut was co-produced by the actor Christopher Lambert, while the casting of Natalie Wood's daughter and J Paul Getty's great-grandson add a certain *frisson* to the proceedings. AT

Bruce Ramsay *Kit* • Balthazar Getty *Rudy* • Natasha Gregson Wagner *Kirsten* • Meredith Salenger *Donna* • Deborah Harry *Mrs Kurtz* • Sara Gilbert *Martha* • Max Perlich *Jimmie* • Alex Cox *English teacher* ■ *Dir* Adam Dubov • *Scr* Adam Dubov, Janice Shapiro

Dead Birds ★★★ 15

Period horror thriller 2004 · US · Colour · 87min

In this low-budget but effectively atmospheric American Civil War-set horror, Henry Thomas and Patrick Fugit star as part of a motley outlaw band consisting of Confederate deserters, an escaped slave and an army nurse, on the run after a bungled robbery. They take refuge in a seemingly abandoned mansion, but the old house has a rather unsavoury past and a supernatural presence soon begins to manifest itself – in increasingly macabre ways – over the course of a long night. The South's racist legacy is an obvious allusion here, but the film also works well simply as a brooding shocker. RR

Henry Thomas *William* • Patrick Fugit *Sam* • Isaiah Washington *Todd* • Michael Shannon *Clyde* • Mark Boone Junior *Joseph* • Nicki Aycox *Annabelle* ■ *Dir* Alex Turner (1) • *Scr* Simon Barrett

Dead Bodies ★★

Black comedy 2003 · Ire · Colour · 85min

There's an air of *Shallow Grave* about this slow-burning black comedy from first-time director Robert Quinn. A slickly shot exploration of the darker side of humanity, it stars Andrew Scott as a young Dubliner whose life spirals out of control following his girlfriend's accidental death. Attempting to bury her corpse, he becomes entangled in an unsolved murder case. Though the underdeveloped plotline lacks credibility, it remains intriguing thanks to the quirky tone and frequent twists. Quinn shows impressive visual flair and there's solid support from Kelly Reilly as Scott's eager new love interest. Ultimately, the abrupt finale is irritatingly ambiguous, but for a low-budget debut this film's enjoyable enough. SF Violence, swearing, a sex scene, nudity.

Andrew Scott *Tommy* • Kelly Reilly *Viv* • Sean McGinley *Detective Inspector Wheeler* • Gerard McSorley *Gordon Ellis* • Darren Healy *Noel* • Katy Davis *Jean* ■ *Dir* Robert Quinn • *Scr* Derek Landy

Dead Bolt Dead ★★ 15

Crime drama   1999 · UK · Colour · 89min

This low-budget crime thriller, framed around two simultaneous sieges after a botched hit, is weighed down at first by self-consciously snappy dialogue, but later settles into a reasonably interesting battle of wills between captor and hostages. Neil Stuke is well cast as a laid-back assassin and there's some palpable friction as crime boss James Laurenson awaits his fate. JC **DVD**

Ariyon Bakare *Thug* • Monique de Villiers *Wife* • James Laurenson *Boss* • Neil Stuke *Assassin* • Ronnie McCann *Driver* ■ *Dir* James Rogan • *Scr* Paul de Villiers

Dead Calm ★★★★ 15

Thriller   1988 · Aus · Colour · 96min

Nicole Kidman and director Phillip Noyce were catapulted into the Hollywood frontline by this scary revel. It's an ingenious psychological thriller in the grand Hitchcock tradition, with a very simple premise: a couple (Kidman and Sam Neill) take a yachting trip to try to recover from the death of their young son, but when they rescue the sole survivor (Billy Zane) from a sinking schooner, things take a very nasty turn. Noyce expertly cranks up the tension to fever pitch and you'll be screaming with delicious panic in one of the best ocean-going shockers since *Jaws*. AJ Swearing, violence, nudity. **DVD**

Sam Neill *John Ingram* • Nicole Kidman *Rae Ingram* • Billy Zane *Hughie Warriner* • Rod Mullinar *Russell Bellows* • Joshua Tilden *Danny* ■ *Dir* Phillip Noyce • *Scr* Terry Hayes, from the novel by Charles Williams

The Dead Can't Lie ★★★ 15

Supernatural thriller   1988 · US · Colour · 93min

Playboy Colin Bruce is being pursued by his dead wife, the immaculately groomed Virginia Madsen, and hires hard-boiled private eye Tommy Lee Jones to give her back the jewels that she was buried with, in order to be left alone. Naturally, the detective falls for the ghost. There's Frederic Forrest as a Russian Orthodox priest and some smart dialogue about Lillian Gish, but it's probably too pretentious for some tastes. TS Swearing, nudity.

Tommy Lee Jones *Eddie Martel* • Virginia Madsen *Rachel Carlyle* • Colin Bruce *Charlie Rand* • Kevin Jarre *Tim* • Denise Stephenson *Debbie* • Frederic Forrest *Father George* ■ *Dir/Scr* Lloyd Fonvielle

Dead Cert ★★

Sports drama   1974 · UK · Colour · 99min

Co-adapted from Dick Francis's runaway bestseller by former racing pundit John Oaksey, this tale of death and doping on the eve of the Grand National is a desperate stab for a box-office hit by director Tony Richardson. The authentic atmosphere of stableyards and racecourses that characterises Francis's thrillers has been missed by a lot more than a short head here. DP

Judi Dench *Laura Davidson* • Michael Williams *Sandy* • Scott Antony *Alan* • Ian Hogg *Bill Davidson* • Nina Thomas *Penny* • Mark Dignam

Clifford Tudor • Julian Glover *Lodge* ■ *Dir* Tony Richardson • *Scr* Tony Richardson, John Oaksey, from the novel by Dick Francis

The Dead Don't Dream ★★

Western   1948 · US · BW · 62min

The splendid title can't disguise the fact that this is a rather routine Hopalong Cassidy programme filler, actually the penultimate of that 66-strong series. Here, Cassidy investigates a series of murders in a frontier hotel. A whole new audience discovered Hoppy on television reruns and advertising promotions, and silver-haired William Boyd became popular all over again. TS

William Boyd (1) *Hopalong Cassidy* • Andy Clyde *California Carlson* • Rand Brooks *Lucky Jenkins* • John Parrish *Jeff Potter* • Leonard Penn *Earl Wesson* • Mary Tucker *Mary Benton* ■ *Dir* George Archainbaud • *Scr* Francis Rosenwald, from characters by Clarence E Mulford

Dead End ★★★★ PG

Crime drama   1937 · US · BW · 88min

This marvellously evocative, albeit resolutely studio-bound, version of Sidney Kingsley's fine play is brilliantly directed by William Wyler from an adaptation by Lillian Hellman. The streets and gutters of production designer Richard Day's magnificent set are a little too clean, a little too well lit, but this is a fine work with brilliant performances, particularly from Sylvia Sidney and then new face Humphrey Bogart. Though Joel McCrea is a shade too bland as the worthy hero, the youngsters in the movie went on to their own series success, initially as the Dead End Kids and, eventually, as the Bowery Boys. TS **DVD**

Sylvia Sidney *Drina* • Joel McCrea *Dave* • Humphrey Bogart *Baby Face Martin* • Wendy Barrie *Kay* • Claire Trevor *Francie* • Allen Jenkins *Hunk* • Marjorie Main *Mrs Martin* • Billy Halop *Tommy* • Huntz Hall *Dippy* • Bobby Jordan *Angel* • Gabriel Dell *TB* • Bernard Punsley *Milty* • Charles Peck *Philip Griswold* • Leo Gorcey *Spit* ■ *Dir* William Wyler • *Scr* Lillian Hellman, from the play by Sidney Kingsley • *Cinematographer* Gregg Toland

Dead End ★★★ 15

Supernatural horror thriller
2003 · Fr · Colour · 79min

This horror film twists a traditional Christmas drive to visit in-laws into a ghostly nightmare of death and terror, after dad Ray Wise decides to take his family on an unfamiliar short cut. Wise draws together the mishmash of schlock, chills and dark comedy with a delightfully over-the-top performance. His melodramatic outbursts, as his loved-ones fall prey to a mysterious woman in white, are as unnerving as they are humorous. SF Swearing, violence. **DVD**

Ray Wise *Frank Harrington* • Alexandra Holden *Marion Harrington* • Lin Shaye *Laura Harrington* • Mick Cain *Richard Harrington* • Billy Asher *Brad Miller* • Amber Smith *Lady in white* ■ *Dir/Scr* Jean-Baptiste Andrea, Fabrice Canepa

Dead Europe ★★★ 18

Drama   2012 · Aus/UK · Colour · 80min

Based on a novel by Christos Tsiolkas (author of *The Slap*), *Dead Europe* is half ghost story, half European travelogue, and while its lashings of atmosphere and grimy tone will delight some, its deliberately baffling plot and ambiguous conclusion will irritate many others. After his father's unexplained suicide, Australian photographer Isaac (Ewen Leslie) embarks on a trip to Greece, his father's homeland, to scatter his ashes. But on his journey he finds not the Europe of picture postcards, but a rotten, violent and seedy world peopled by porn merchants and drug addicts. It's a strange but compelling story, and the theme of the dangers of returning ignorantly to the past is powerfully explored. AS In English, Greek, French, Hungarian, Hebrew. Violence, swearing, sex scenes, drug abuse, nudity.

Ewen Leslie *Isaac* • Marton Csokas *Nico* • Kodi Smit-McPhee *Josef* • Jean-François Balmer *Gerry* • Igal Naor *Syd* ■ *Dir* Tony Krawitz • *Scr* Louise Fox, from Christos Tsiolkas's novel

Dead Funny ★★★

Comedy mystery   1995 · US/UK · Colour · 91min

At the start of this comedy, Andrew McCarthy lies dead on the kitchen table, impaled by a samurai sword. When his girlfriend (Elizabeth Peña) comes home and discovers him, she opens a bottle of champagne and calls a friend over. That's when the flashbacks begin, showing how McCarthy's practical joker reached such a pretty pass. The slightly nerdy McCarthy is well-cast here, and Peña makes her museum employee a very wacky character. AT

Elizabeth Peña *Vivian Saunders* • Andrew McCarthy *Reggie Barker* • Paige Turco *Louise* • Blanche Baker *Barbara* • Allison Janney *Jennifer* • Adelle Lutz *Mari* • Lisa Jane Persky *Sarah* ■ *Dir* John Feldman • *Scr* John Feldman, Cindy Oswin

Dead Heart ★★ 18

Detective thriller   1996 · Aus · Colour · 101min

When it comes to depicting the Aborigines on screen, the infringement of tribal rights seems to be the only topic producers consider worth tackling. Consequently, what we have here is another thriller in which the clash of progress and tradition results in a murder, which is investigated by a well-intentioned white cop. Bryan Brown uncovers evidence of bootlegging, adultery and black magic with grim determination. DP Swearing, violence, nudity.

Bryan Brown *Ray Lorkin* • Ernie Dingo *David* • Angie Milliken *Kate* • Aaron Pedersen *Tony* • Lewis Fitz-Gerald *Les* • John Jarratt *Charlie* ■ *Dir/Scr* Nicholas Parsons

Dead Heat ★★★ 18

Comedy horror   1988 · US · Colour · 80min

Just when you thought nothing original could be made of the buddy-cop genre, along comes Mark Goldblatt's outlandish horror comedy. Treat Williams and Joe Piscopo star as cops who uncover a scheme by batty old Vincent Price to resuscitate the dead. In a movie that's imaginative and disgusting in equal measure, a butcher shop full of meat comes alive to do battle with the heroes, while Williams himself hilariously turns into a zombie and has 12 hours to solve the case before decomposition sets in. RS

Treat Williams *Roger Mortis* • Joe Piscopo *Doug Bigelow* • Darren McGavin *Dr Ernest McNab* • Lindsay Frost *Randi James* • Vincent Price *Arthur P Loudermilk* • Clare Kirkconnell *Rebecca Smythers* • Keye Luke *Mr Thule* ■ *Dir* Mark Goldblatt • *Scr* Terry Black

Dead Heat ★★ 15

Crime drama   2002 · Can · Colour · 93min

The plot of this horse-racing thriller is more than a little convoluted, as Kiefer Sutherland's weak-hearted Boston cop comes up against mobster Daniel Benzali when he falls in with Anthony LaPaglia's idea of buying a horse. The banter between Sutherland and LaPaglia is brisk, but this is essentially an old-fashioned B-movie. DP Swearing. **DVD**

Kiefer Sutherland *Pally LaMarr* • Radha Mitchell *Charlotte LaMarr* • Anthony LaPaglia *Ray LaMarr* • Lothaire Bluteau *Tony LaRoche* • Daniel Benzali *Frank Finnegan* ■ *Dir/Scr* Mark Malone

Dead Heat on a Merry-Go-Round ★★ PG

Crime caper   1966 · US · Colour · 102min

There's little to distinguish this crime caper from others of its ilk, though it does give Harrison Ford fans the opportunity to see their hero make his big-screen debut. Few could carry off the wisecracking tough guy act better than James Coburn, but even he seems to be going through the motions here as he robs the bank at Los Angeles airport during the arrival of the Russian premier. Bernard Girard can't sustain either momentum or interest. DP **DVD**

James Coburn *Eli Kotch* • Camilla Sparv *Inger Knudson* • Aldo Ray *Eddie Hart* • Nina Wayne *Frieda Schmid* • Robert Webber *Milo Stewart* •

Rose Marie *Margaret Kirby* • Todd Armstrong *Alfred Morgan* • Harrison Ford *Bellhop* ■ *Dir/Scr* Bernard Girard

The Dead Lands ★★★★ 15

Action epic   2014 · NZ/UK · Colour · 102min

Looking for a dynamic action fantasy with honour codes, violent battle scenes and a total lack of product placement? Try this atmospheric New Zealand production, set in the period of that country's history before the arrival of the first white settlers. James Rolleston stars as Hongi, who is accused by a passing tribe – led by the devious Wirepa (Te Kohe Tuhaka) – of desecrating a holy burial ground. Though he's innocent of the crime, it looks bad for the young man. But when he is spared, Wirepa's apparent leniency causes Hongi's trusting family to drop their guard. Filmed entirely in the Maori language, this is an exotic and satisfying alternative to the average Hollywood punch-'em-up, an offbeat war story with a neat sideline in ancient magic-realist philosophy. DW Maori +subtitles. Violence. **DVD**

James Rolleston *Hongi* • Lawrence Makoare *The Warrior* • Te Kohe Tuhaka *Wirepa* • Xavier Horan *Rangi* • George Henare *Tane* • Raukura Turei *Mehe* ■ *Dir* Toa Fraser • *Scr* Glenn Standring

Dead Letter Office ★★★

Drama   1998 · Aus · Colour · 95min

John Ruane's surreal, often lyrical drama is both sad and uplifting. Set in an office for undeliverable mail that is under threat of mechanisation, this tale of damaged people and indefatigable hope turns on the unlikely relationship between new employee Mirando Otto (who still writes to her long-absent father) and her Chilean boss George DelHoyo, who was driven from his homeland because of his political views. Both powerful and poignant. DP English, Spanish +subtitles. Swearing, a sex scene.

George DelHoyo *Frank Lopez* • Miranda Otto *Alice* • Nicholas Bell *Kevin* • Georgina Naidu *Mary* • Syd Brisbane *Peter* • Barry Otto *Gerald Urquhart* • Vanessa Steele *Carmen* ■ *Dir* John Ruane • *Scr* Deborah Cox

Dead Man ★★★ 18

Western   1995 · US/Ger · BW · 116min

Johnny Depp stars as a mundane clerk who arrives in the shoot-'em-up Wild West town of Machine to take a job as an accountant, only to find the position has been filled. Things go from bad to worse when he accidentally kills a man and is pursued as a gunslinger. Independent director Jim Jarmusch's black-and-white take on the cowboy movie is as bizarre and deadpan as his usual work, but it's enlivened by the eclectic supposting cast. TH Swearing, brief nudity. **DVD** **BD**

Johnny Depp *William Blake* • Crispin Glover *Train fireman* • Gibby Haines *Man with gun in alley* • George Duckworth *Man at end of street* • Richard Boes *Man with wrench* • John Hurt *John Scholfield* • John North *Mr Olafsen* • Robert Mitchum *John Dickinson* • Mili Avital *Thel Russell* • Gabriel Byrne *Charlie Dickinson* • Lance Henriksen *Cole Wilson* • Gary Farmer *Nobody* • Iggy Pop *Salvatore "Sally" Jenko* ■ *Dir/Scr* Jim Jarmusch

Dead Man Down ★★★ 15

Crime thriller   2013 · US · Colour · 112min

This two-pronged revenge thriller stars Colin Farrell as a man who infiltrates the gang responsible for the deaths of his wife and daughter. When neighbour Noomi Rapace witnesses Farrell murder one of the bad guys, she threatens to go to the cops unless he also help her grisly plan for justice. Danish director Niels Arden Oplev adds a few European flourishes to a solid *noir* premise, and Farrell is relatively charismatic as the numbed but determined avenger. Yet the constant need for dialogue to fill in an unnecessarily complicated backstory tends to interrupt the pace of the film. TeS English, French, Hungarian, Albanian, Spanish +subtitles. Violence, swearing, a sex scene. **DVD** **BD**

D

Colin Farrell (2) *Victor* • Noomi Rapace *Beatrice* • Terrence Howard *Alphonse* • Dominic Cooper *Darcy* • Isabelle Huppert *Valentine* • Armand Assante *Lon Gordon* • F Murray Abraham *Gregor* ■ *Dir* Niels Arden Oplev • *Scr* JH Wyman

Dead Man on Campus ★★15
Comedy   1998 · US · Colour · 90min

Tom Everett Scott and Mark-Paul Gosselaar are on the verge of being kicked out of school because of low grades. When they discover a clause in the school constitution saying they will get automatic As if a roommate commits suicide, they set about finding a suitably depressed person to share with. It's amiably played, but the direction lacks bite. JF Swearing, sexual references.

Tom Everett Scott *Josh* • Mark-Paul Gosselaar *Cooper* • Poppy Montgomery *Rachel* • Lochlyn Munro *Cliff* • Randy Pearlstein *Buckley* • Corey Page *Matt* • Alyson Hannigan *Lucy* • Dave Ruby *Zeke* ■ *Dir* Alan Cohn • *Scr* Michael Traeger, Mike White, from a story by Adam Larson Broder, Anthony Abrams

Dead Man Running ★15
Crime drama   2009 · UK · Colour · 87min

In writer/director Alex De Rakoff's uninspired British gangster film, American loan shark Mr Thigo (rapper Curtis "50 Cent" Jackson) flies to London to give reformed villain Nick (Tamer Hassan) 24 hours to repay the £100,000 he borrowed – or his dear old mum gets "taken out". Neither Hassan nor co-star Danny Dyer have the acting chops to pull off the light-hearted buddy-movie elements, and old hands Brenda Blethyn (as Nick's mum) and Phil Davis (as her would-be killer) struggle to bring any weight to a movie that misfires at every turn. TeS Violence, swearing, sexual references, drug abuse. *DVD* *Blu-ray*

Tamer Hassan *Nick* • Danny Dyer *Bing* • Brenda Blethyn *Nick's mum* • Curtis "50 Cent" Jackson *Mr Thigo* • Monet Mazur *Frankie* • Ashley Walters *Fitzroy* • Phil Davis [Philip Davis] *Johnny Sands* ■ *Dir* Alex De Rakoff • *Scr* Alex De Rakoff, from a story by John Luton

Dead Man Walking ★★★★15
Biographical prison drama
1995 · US · Colour · 117min

Sean Penn gives a chilling and mesmerising portrayal of sociopathy, as Matthew Poncelet, a multiple killer on death row with no sense of remorse. His sparring partner is Susan Sarandon, in an Oscar-winning performance as Sister Helen Prejean, the nun who became Poncelet's spiritual adviser during his final countdown, and whose book about the experience was the inspiration for the film. Sarandon's nun is a sort of social worker with faith, whose sexually charged chats with Penn take us into the heart of the debate about capital punishment. But director Tim Robbins's refusal to make a clear judgement on the issue is frustrating. AT Violence, swearing, brief nudity. *DVD*

Susan Sarandon *Sister Helen Prejean* • Sean Penn *Matthew Poncelet* • Robert Prosky *Hilton Barber* • Raymond J Barry *Earl Delacroix* • R Lee Ermey *Clyde Percy* • Celia Weston *Mary Beth Percy* • Lois Smith *Helen's mother* ■ *Dir* Tim Robbins • *Scr* Tim Robbins, from the book by Sister Helen Prejean

Dead Man's Curve ★★★★15
Black comedy   1997 · US · Colour · 86min

This twisted comedy thriller becomes addictive viewing, thanks to the mesmerising performance from Matthew Lillard. Three roommates (Lillard, Michael Vartan and Randall Batinkoff) learn that their college has an unspoken rule that, should a student commit suicide, the students sharing their room are awarded perfect grades because they have had to suffer such a trauma. So, it's not long before Vartan and Lillard have offed their best pal and this is only the beginning of the double-crossing, back-stabbing and murder. JB Swearing, sex scenes. *DVD*

Matthew Lillard *Tim* • Michael Vartan *Chris* • Randall Batinkoff *Rand* • Keri Russell *Emma* • Tamara Craig Thomas *Natalie* • Anthony Griffith *Detective Schipper* • Bo Dietl *Detective Amato* ■ *Dir/Scr* Dan Rosen

Dead Man's Evidence ★★U
Spy drama   1962 · UK · BW · 67min

This provides a sobering insight into how the rest of the British film industry was handling espionage thrillers while Terence Young was making *Dr No*. With his heyday as TV's William Tell already behind him, Conrad Phillips stars as a spy sent to investigate when the body of a defector is washed up on an Irish beach. The direction is as perfunctory as the script. DP

Conrad Phillips *David Baxter* • Jane Griffiths *Linda Howard* • Veronica Hurst *Gay Clifford* • Ryck Rydon *Fallon* ■ *Dir* Francis Searle • *Scr* Arthur La Bern, Gordon Wellesley, from a story by Arthur La Bern

Dead Man's Eyes ★★
Mystery   1944 · US · BW · 64min

Lon Chaney Jr returns for another in Universal's *Inner Sanctum* series, this time as a struggling artist whose sudden blindness threatens his engagement to Jean Parker and leads to a double murder. Dwight Babcock's screenplay introduces a sinister sci-fi element, as surgeon Jonathan Hale offers Chaney the hope of restored sight through a pioneering cornea transplant. The direction is steady instead of taut, but Chaney is typically sympathetic. DP

Lon Chaney [Lon Chaney Jr] *Dave Stuart* • Jean Parker *Heather "Brat" Hayden* • Paul Kelly (1) *Dr Alan Bittaker* • Thomas Gomez *Captain Drury* • Jonathan Hale *Dr Sam Welles* • Edward Fielding *Dr Stanley "Dad" Hayden* • Acquanetta *Tanya Czoraki* ■ *Dir* Reginald Le Borg • *Scr* Dwight V Babcock

Dead Man's Folly ★★★PG
Murder mystery   1986 · US · Colour · 89min

While not perhaps among Agatha Christie's best mysteries, this slick TV movie will still keep you guessing whodunnit. As the fastidious Belgian detective Hercule Poirot, Peter Ustinov is invited to organise a murder hunt for a village fête only to find himself confronted with the real thing. In a case where nearly everybody is a thoroughly nasty piece of work, there is plenty of scope for the supporting cast to ham it up. DP

Peter Ustinov *Hercule Poirot* • Jean Stapleton *Mrs Oliver* • Constance Cummings *Mrs Folliat* • Tim Pigott-Smith *Sir George Stubbs* • Jonathan Cecil *Hastings* • Kenneth Cranham *Inspector Bland* • Susan Wooldridge *Miss Brewis* • Christopher Guard *Alec Legge* • Jeff Yagher *Eddie South* ■ *Dir* Clive Donner • *Scr* Rod Browning, from the novel by Agatha Christie

Dead Man's Shoes ★★★18
Crime thriller   2004 · UK · Colour · 86min

This morally ambiguous shocker features an uncomfortably matter-of-fact performance from co-writer Paddy Considine. He plays a tortured ex-army man who returns to the rural Midlands village of his youth to take revenge on a drugs gang who used and abused his younger, mentally disabled brother (Toby Kebbell). With many of the cast being non-actors and much of the dialogue improvised, there's a strong sense of realism that makes the violence portrayed so much more horrific, and edgy laughs soon degenerate into grim brutality. SF Swearing, drug abuse. *DVD* *Blu-ray*

Paddy Considine *Richard* • Gary Stretch *Sonny* • Toby Kebbell *Anthony* • Stuart Wolfenden *Herbie* • Neil Bell *Soz* • Paul Sadot *Tuff* ■ *Dir* Shane Meadows • *Scr* Paddy Considine, Shane Meadows

Dead Men Can't Dance ★★15
War action adventure 1997 · US · Colour · 93min

They can't act, either, and the same can be said for the cast of this war drama about the first women to be accepted into the ranks of the US Rangers. Borrowing heavily from *Full Metal Jacket*, director Stephen M

Anderson charts the progress of a group of women through the Rangers training programme to action in the demilitarised zone outside North Korea. Some good action scenes, but nothing to keep you on the edge of your seat. ST *DVD*

Michael Biehn *Hart* • Kathleen York *Victoria Elliot* • Adrian Paul *Shooter* • R Lee Ermey *Pullman T Fowler* • Shawnee Smith *Sgt Addie Cooper* • Joel McKinnon Miller *Bearclaw* • John Carroll Lynch *Sgt Plonder* • Grace Zabriskie *Brig Gen Burke* ■ *Dir* Stephen M Anderson [Steve Anderson (1)] • *Scr* Bill Kerby, Mark Sevi, Paul Sinor

Dead Men Don't Die ★PG
Black comedy   1991 · US · Colour · 94min

Elliott Gould stars in this dire comedy about a newsreader who is shot dead and then brought back to life by his voodoo-chanting cleaning lady. It's all completely silly and rather childish, with Gould lumbering from one pratfall to another, looking uncomfortable throughout. JB Violence, swearing.

Elliott Gould *Barry Barron* • Melissa Anderson [Melissa Sue Anderson] *Dulcie Niles* • Mark Moses *Jordan Penrose* ■ *Dir/Scr* Malcolm Marmorstein

Dead Men Don't Wear Plaid ★★★★PG
Detective spoof   1982 · US · BW · 84min

Steve Martin's early collaborations with director and co-writer Carl Reiner still rank among his best. This ingenious spoof finds Martin as a hard-boiled private eye with a dangerous phobia about cleaning women who gets involved in a supremely silly story involving a cheese professor and sinister Nazis. However, this provides the slenderest of excuses for Martin to be spliced into an array of classic movies and swap dumb dialogue with stars such as Bette Davis, Burt Lancaster, Barbara Stanwyck, Ray Milland in some of their most famous roles. Martin is on inspired form and Rachel Ward is a revelation in a rare comic role, and there are some wonderful moments for film buffs. JF Swearing. *DVD*

Steve Martin *Rigby Reardon* • Rachel Ward *Juliet Forrest* • Carl Reiner *Field Marshal Von Kluck* • Reni Santoni *Carlos Rodriguez* • George Gaynes *Dr Forrest* ■ *Dir* Carl Reiner • *Scr* George Gipe, Carl Reiner, Steve Martin

Dead of Night ★★★★★PG
Portmanteau horror 1945 · UK · BW · 99min

Ealing will for ever be associated with its celebrated comedies, but this chilling quintet deserves to be considered among the studio's finest achievements. Including stories penned by HG Wells and EF Benson, *Dead of Night* illustrates how ghost stories should be filmed. Alberto Cavalcanti's "The Ventriloquist's Dummy" episode has lost none of its shocking power, thanks largely to Michael Redgrave's astonishing performance, which ranks among the best of his career. There's also much to raise the hair on the back of the neck in Robert Hamer's "The Haunted Mirror", while the linking story involving architect Mervyn Johns brings it all to a nightmarish conclusion. DP *DVD* *Blu-ray*

Mervyn Johns *Walter Craig* • Roland Culver *Eliot Foley* • Mary Merrall *Mrs Foley* • Anthony Baird *Hugh Grainger* • Judy Kelly *Joyce Grainger* • Sally Ann Howes *Sally O'Hara* • Michael Allen (1) *Jimmy Watson* • Googie Withers *Joan Courtland* • Ralph Michael *Peter Courtland* • Michael Redgrave *Maxwell Frere* ■ *Dir* Alberto Cavalcanti, Basil Dearden, Robert Hamer, Charles Crichton • *Scr* John Baines, Angus MacPhail, TEB Clarke, from stories by HG Wells, EF Benson, John Baines, Angus MacPhail

Dead of Night ★★★15
Horror   1972 · Can/UK/US · Colour · 84min

This cross between *The Monkey's Paw* and *Night of the Living Dead* is a tense low-budget horror gem. Distraught mother Lynn Carlin wishes her son Richard Backus would return from an unspecified war, clearly Vietnam. But when he does, it's as a walking corpse who syringes blood from his victims to sate his grisly appetite. With chilling make-up effects by writer Alan

Ormsby and Tom Savini, it's a brilliantly sick and unpretentious allegory. AJ

John Marley *Charles Brooks* • Lynn Carlin *Christine Brooks* • Henderson Forsythe *Dr Philip Allman* • Richard Backus *Andy Brooks* • Anya Ormsby *Cathy Brooks* • Jane Daly *Joanne* ■ *Dir* Bob Clark • *Scr* Alan Ormsby

Dead of Winter ★★★15
Thriller   1987 · US · Colour · 96min

It's slightly disconcerting to see Arthur Penn, the highly distinctive director of *Bonnie and Clyde* and *Alice's Restaurant*, switching to formula. That said, it's a pleasure to see a film where suspense is sustained by craft rather than through wham-bam action or gore. Penn allows Mary Steenburgen to relish no less than three roles, while Roddy McDowall is an unnerving study in controlled evil as the assistant to Jan Rubes's eccentric doctor. JM

Mary Steenburgen *Katie McGovern/Julie Rose/Evelyn* • Roddy McDowall *Thomas Franklin Murray* • Jan Rubes *Dr Joseph Lewis* • William Russ *Rod Sweeney* • Mark Malone *Roland McGovern* • Ken Pogue *Officer Mullavy* • Wayne Robson *Officer Huntley* ■ *Dir* Arthur Penn • *Scr* Marc Shmuger, Mark Malone

Dead Pigeon on Beethoven Street ★★15
Detective mystery
1972 · W Ger · Colour · 86min

Near the end of a long career, veteran maverick director Samuel Fuller managed to put together this turgid hotch-potch of half-baked ideas, funded by German television and filmed entirely in Germany. Hard to tell if this is genuine tongue-in-cheek spy stuff or just inept movie storytelling, but Fuller's fans seem eager to accord Sam the benefit of the doubt. There's no excusing the wooden performances from Glenn Corbett or Christa Lang (Mrs S Fuller) in the leading roles, though. TS

Glenn Corbett *Sandy* • Christa Lang *Christa* • Sieghardt Rupp *Kessin* • Anton Diffring *Mensur* • Alex D'Arcy *Novka* • Anthony Chinn *Fong* ■ *Dir/Scr* Samuel Fuller

Dead Poets Society ★★★★PG
Coming-of-age period drama
1989 · US · Colour · 123min

Peter Weir's warm, touching tale struck a chord with audiences around the world. Robin Williams is the unconventional teacher at a stuffy boys' school in late-1950s America, who awakens a love of poetry and writing among a disparate group of troubled adolescents headed by Robert Sean Leonard and Ethan Hawke. However, the individualism he fosters eventually leads to tragedy. The two young leads turn in subtle performances and, if Tom Schulman's Oscar-winning screenplay does lurch occasionally into mawkish melodrama, it's lusciously photographed and genuinely moving. JF *DVD* *Blu-ray*

Robin Williams *John Keating* • Robert Sean Leonard *Neil Perry* • Ethan Hawke *Todd Anderson* • Josh Charles *Knox Overstreet* • Gale Hansen *Charlie Dalton* • Dylan Kussman *Richard Cameron* • Allelon Ruggiero *Steven Meeks* • James Waterston *Gerard Pitts* • Norman Lloyd *Mr Nolan* • Kurtwood Smith *Mr Perry* ■ *Dir* Peter Weir • *Scr* Tom Schulman • *Cinematographer* John Seale

The Dead Pool ★★18
Crime thriller   1988 · US · Colour · 87min

"Dirty" Harry Callahan's fifth outing finds the San Francisco detective looking decidedly ropey around the edges. Clint Eastwood goes through his iconic paces and directs the film in all but name; the actual credit, however, goes to Buddy Van Horn, Clint's stuntman. It's a flaccid, silly and extremely sadistic tale involving a demented movie fan who bumps off minor celebrities, with Liam Neeson co-starring as a British horror film director. TS Violence, swearing. *DVD* *Blu-ray*

D

D

Clint Eastwood *Inspector Harry Callahan* • Patricia Clarkson *Samantha Walker* • Evan C Kim [Evan Kim] *Al Quan* • Liam Neeson *Peter Swan* • David Hunt *Harlan Rook* ■ *Dir* Buddy Van Horn • *Scr* Steve Sharon, from a story by Steve Sharon, Durk Pearson, Sandy Shaw, from the character created by Harry Julian Fink, RM Fink

Dead Presidents ★★★ 18
Crime drama   1995 · US · Colour · 114min

Bronx boy Larenz Tate returns from a tour of duty in Vietnam to find his urban life just as messed up as the war. Armed robbery seems the only solution. It's interesting to see the "coming home" story told from a black perspective, and there are some stunning sequences, but the film's tone is so grim, and the characters so superficial, that it never quite sucks you in. JC Sex scenes, swearing, violence. DVD

Larenz Tate *Anthony Curtis* • Keith David *Kirby* • Chris Tucker *Skip* • Freddy Rodriguez *Jose* • Rose Jackson *Juanita Benson* • N'Bushe Wright *Delilah Benson* • Alvaletah Guess *Mrs Benson* • James Pickens Jr *Mr Curtis* ■ *Dir* Albert Hughes, Allen Hughes • *Scr* Michael Henry Brown, from a story by Albert Hughes, Allen Hughes, Michael Henry Brown, from the story *Specialist No 4 Haywood T "The Kid" Kirkland* by Wallace Terry

Dead Reckoning ★★★★ U
Film noir   1947 · US · BW · 96min

Humphrey Bogart stars in this hard-boiled thriller, with sultry Lizabeth Scott as the duplicitous dame. The plot is very ordinary – war veteran Bogart trying to find out who killed his buddy – but the dialogue is as sharp as a razor: in one scene, Bogie confides of chanteuse Scott, "Maybe she was all right, and maybe Christmas in July." Watch out for Morris Carnovsky in one of his last roles before he was blacklisted during the McCarthy witch-hunt, here playing a villainous nightclub owner. Director John Cromwell steps back and just lets his cast get on with it. TS DVD

Humphrey Bogart *Rip Murdock* • Lizabeth Scott *Coral Chandler* • Morris Carnovsky *Martinelli* • Charles Cane *Lt Kincaid* • William Prince *Johnny Drake* • Marvin Miller *Krause* • Wallace Ford *McGee* ■ *Dir* John Cromwell • *Scr* Oliver HP Garrett, Steve Fisher, Allen Rivkin (adaptation), from an unpublished story by Gerald Adams [Gerald Drayson Adams], Sidney Biddell

Dead Ringer ★★★ PG
Melodrama   1964 · US · BW · 111min

This is a late Bette Davis vehicle in which she stars as twins. Under the gritty direction of her *Now, Voyager* co-star Paul Henreid she's in post-*Baby Jane* mode, as one sister kills the other and takes her place in the mansion on the hill. It's good to see 1960s stalwarts like Peter Lawford and Karl Malden with something to get their teeth into. TS

Bette Davis *Margaret/Edith* • Karl Malden *Sergeant Jim Hobbson* • Peter Lawford *Tony Collins* • Philip Carey *Sergeant Ben Hoag* • Jean Hagen *Dede* • George Macready *Paul Harrison* • Estelle Winwood *Matriarch* ■ *Dir* Paul Henreid • *Scr* Albert Beich, Oscar Millard, from the story *La Otra* by Rian James

Dead Ringers ★★★★ 18
Psychological thriller
1988 · Can · Colour · 110min

This finely wrought urban horror tale was inspired by the true story of identical twin gynaecologists who were found dead on New York's Upper East Side in 1975. Here, with the setting transposed to Toronto, Jeremy Irons expertly plays both Beverly and Elliot Mantle, with Geneviève Bujold as the internationally famous, infertile actress who, quite literally, can't choose between them. Director David Cronenberg here demonstrates a uniquely distressing and subtle talent, and the result is enough to put you off visiting fertility clinics for ever. TS Violence, swearing, a sex scene, nudity. DVD

Jeremy Irons *Beverly/Elliot Mantle* • Geneviève Bujold *Claire Niveau* • Heidi Von Palleske *Dr Cary Weiler* • Barbara Gordon *Danuta* • Shirley Douglas *Laura* • Stephen Lack *Anders Wolleck* • Nick Nichols *Leo* • Lynne Cormack *Arlene* ■

Dir David Cronenberg • *Scr* David Cronenberg, Norman Snider, from the book *Twins* by Bari Wood, Jack Geasland

Dead Run ★★ U
Spy comedy   1967 · Fr/W Ger/It · Colour · 96min

This tongue-in-cheek spy thriller has CIA agent Peter Lawford and the Mafia both chasing a petty thief who has run off with an attaché case containing top, top-secret papers. In fact, the papers are just our old friend the MacGuffin, since the movie is really all about Lawford's smarmy womanising and gentle spoofing from French director Christian-Jaque. AT French dubbed.

Georges Geret *Carlos* • Peter Lawford *Dain* • Ira von Fürstenberg *Suzanne* • Maria Grazia Buccella *Anna* • Horst Frank *Manganne* • Werner Peters *Bardieff* • Jean Tissier *Adelgate* ■ *Dir* Christian-Jaque • *Scr* Michel Levine, Christian-Jaque, Pascal Jardin, Dany Tyber, from the novel by Robert Scheckley

Dead Sexy ★★ 18
Erotic thriller   2001 · US · Colour · 85min

This is a by-the-numbers retread of *Basic Instinct*, with Shannon Tweed as a cop tracking a serial killer who's targeting high-class prostitutes. The plot, which sees Tweed going undercover and falling for the enigmatic chief suspect, offers nothing new, although the handful of bedroom sequences are far more explicit than many of its kind. JC DVD

Shannon Tweed *Kate McBain* • John Enos *Blue* • Kenneth White *Capt Snyder* • Eric Keith *Billy Trainer* ■ *Dir* Robert Angelo • *Scr* Elroy Canton, Anthony Laurence Greene

Dead Silence ★★ 15
Horror   2007 · US · Colour · 87min

Saw director James Wan and writer Leigh Whannell resurrect the concept of the malevolent dummy in this deliberately retro horror. The backstory reveals the fate of ventriloquist Mary Shaw, who went mad and was sadistically murdered by vengeful locals. But when the wife of former resident Ryan Kwanten is brutally slain, he returns to his still-cursed home town – convinced that Shaw's vengeful doll is the culprit. Detective Donnie Wahlberg isn't so sure. Old-fashioned scares and elegant visual style might suggest a homage to Universal's golden age of horror – the studio's famous monochrome logo makes an appearance – but sadly, this is fatally undermined by its predictable plotting and bland acting. AJ DVD Blu-ray

Ryan Kwanten *Jamie Ashen* • Amber Valletta *Ella Ashen* • Donnie Wahlberg *Detective Lipton* • Michael Fairman *Henry Walker* • Joan Heney *Marion Walker* • Bob Gunton *Edward Ashen* • Judith Roberts (1) *Mary Shaw* ■ *Dir* James Wan • *Scr* Leigh Whannell, from a story by James Wan, Whannell • *Cinematographer* John R Leonetti

Dead Snow ★★★ 18
Horror   2009 · Nor · Colour · 87min

Nazi zombies come out to feed in this tongue-in-cheek horror, set among the stunning, snow-covered mountains of Norway. Following the eerie beginning, this crisp-looking film sees a group of young medical students travel to an isolated cabin for a ski break, only to encounter the ravenous cohorts. Director Tommy Wirkola certainly knows the work of his predecessors – Sam Raimi, John Carpenter, George A Romero – so his second movie is by no means original, but it does benefit from the sheer gusto of the cast and some fabulously gruesome moments. JA Norwegian +subtitles. DVD Blu-ray

Vegar Hoel *Martin* • Lasse Valdal *Vegard* • Charlotte Frogner *Hanna* • Stig Frode Henriksen *Roy* ■ *Dir* Tommy Wirkola • *Scr* Tommy Wirkola, Stig Frode Henriksen

The Dead Zone ★★★★ 15
Horror   1983 · US · Colour · 103min

In this engrossing yet strangely unembellished adaptation of Stephen King's bestseller by director David Cronenberg, Christopher Walken plays the teacher who wakes from a coma to find he has

---

acquired the ability to foresee the future. As his value to society increases, his life crumbles, especially when he envisions the horrifying truth of mankind's destiny under the possible control of evil politician Martin Sheen. While it has none of Cronenberg's usual bracing style, it is thoughtful and moving at times, with Walken, Sheen and Brooke Adams giving top-notch performances. AJ Violence, swearing, brief nudity. DVD

Christopher Walken *Johnny Smith* • Brooke Adams *Sarah Bracknell* • Tom Skerritt *Sheriff George Bannerman* • Herbert Lom *Dr Sam Weizak* • Anthony Zerbe *Roger Stuart* • Colleen Dewhurst *Henrietta Dodd* • Martin Sheen *Greg Stillson* ■ *Dir* David Cronenberg • *Scr* Jeffrey Boam, from the novel by Stephen King

Deadfall ★ 12
Crime thriller   1968 · UK · Colour · 114min

This insufferably pretentious twaddle from Bryan Forbes masquerades as a heist movie, as Michael Caine teams up with husband-and-wife Eric Portman and Giovanna Ralli for an audacious robbery. Sadly, the film doesn't provide any workaday thrills, and also fatally lacks a sense of humour. AT DVD

Michael Caine *Henry Clarke* • Giovanna Ralli *Fe Moreau* • Eric Portman *Richard Moreau* • Nanette Newman *Girl* • David Buck *Salinas* • Carlos Pierre *Antonio* • Leonard Rossiter *Fillmore* ■ *Dir* Bryan Forbes • *Scr* Bryan Forbes, from the novel by Desmond Cory • *Music* John Barry (1)

Deadfall ★★★ 15
Crime thriller   2012 · US · Colour · 90min

This well-paced thriller stars Eric Bana and Olivia Wilde as sibling crooks on the run from a botched casino heist. The pair decide to split up and head for the Canadian border, with Wilde hitching a ride with just released ex-con Charlie Hunnam. Director Stefan Ruzowitzky skilfully juggles the family-conflict subplots, although the string of coincidences is, arguably, a little contrived. However, Bana's marvellously psychotic turn steals the show, while old hands Kris Kristofferson and Sissy Spacek, as Hunnam's parents, add gravitas to proceedings. TeS Violence, swearing, sex scenes. DVD

Eric Bana *Addison* • Charlie Hunnam *Jay Mills* • Olivia Wilde *Liza* • Kris Kristofferson *Chet Mills* • Sissy Spacek *June Mills* • Kate Mara *Hanna* • Treat Williams *Sheriff Marshall Becker* ■ *Dir* Stefan Ruzowitzky • *Scr* Zach Dean

Deadhead Miles ★★
Comedy road movie   1972 · US · Colour · 93min

After making the sublime cult movie *The Unholy Rollers*, director Vernon Zimmerman tried to match it with this offbeat road movie about a long-distance trucker and the wacky people he meets en route. Despite an inspired and often hilarious script by Terrence Malick, and Alan Arkin acting his socks off, the end result is a meandering muddle that remained unreleased for over ten years. Eminently watchable and absolutely terrible by turns. AJ

Alan Arkin *Cooper* • Paul Benedict *Tramp* • Hector Elizondo *Bad character* • Oliver Clark *Durazno* • Charles Durning *Red ball rider* • Lawrence Wolf *Pineapple* • Barnard Hughes *Old man* • William Duell *Auto parts attendant* • Loretta Swit *Woman with glass eye* • John Milius *2nd state trooper* • Ida Lupino *She* • George Raft ■ *Dir* Vernon Zimmerman • *Scr* Terrence Malick

Deadlier than the Male ★★★ 12
Mystery adventure   1966 · UK · Colour · 96min

This was the first of two 1960s adventures for HC "Sapper" McNeile's debonair hero "Bulldog" Drummond, updated to capitalise on the James Bond phenomenon. Richard Johnson gives a good account of himself as the bachelor insurance man investigating the untimely ends of a friend and several high rollers. The perpetrators of said crimes are played with mischievous glee by Elke Sommer and Sylva Koscina, whose bickering exchanges and bitchy one-upmanship are a twisted joy. Johnson

---

reprised his role in 1969's *Some Girls Do*. JH DVD

Richard Johnson *Hugh "Bulldog" Drummond* • Elke Sommer *Irma Eckman* • Sylva Koscina *Penelope* • Nigel Green *Carl Petersen* • Suzanna Leigh *Grace* • Steve Carlson (2) *Robert Drummond* ■ *Dir* Ralph Thomas • *Scr* Jimmy Sangster, David Osborn, Liz Charles-Williams, from a story by Jimmy Sangster, from the novels by Sapper [HC McNeile]

Deadline ★★ 15
Supernatural horror thriller
2009 · US/Malaysia · Colour · 81min

Poor Brittany Murphy certainly deserved better than this hackneyed haunted-house tale. In one of her last films before her death in 2009, she looks wan and suitably fragile as a troubled writer who makes a disturbing discovery after retreating to a remote Victorian mansion to work. The movie's supposed meat involving the house's former occupants leads to predictable revelations, while bad scripting is conveniently explained away by the mental instability of Murphy's character. Finally, a head-scratching twist will only add to viewer aggravation. SF Violence, suicide. DVD

Brittany Murphy *Alice* • Thora Birch *Lucy* • Tammy Blanchard *Rebecca* • Marc Blucas *David* ■ *Dir/Scr* Sean McConville

Deadline at Dawn ★★
Mystery   1946 · US · BW · 83min

This was the only movie directed by the Group Theater of New York's influential left-winger Harold Clurman, and dismayingly pretentious it is, too, despite a sterling performance from Susan Hayward as a dancer trying to clear a sailor (the undercast Bill Williams) of murder. The picture has a screenplay by Clifford Odets, who knew the theatre milieu well. Clurman turned out to be an inept director in this medium, failing to make much of the opportunities to hand. TS

Susan Hayward *June Goff* • Paul Lukas *Gus* • Bill Williams *Alex Winkley* • Joseph Calleia *Bartelli* • Osa Massen *Helen Robinson* • Lola Lane *Edna Bartelli* • Jerome Cowan *Lester Brady* • Marvin Miller *Sleepy Parsons* ■ *Dir* Harold Clurman • *Scr* Clifford Odets, from a novel by William Irish [Cornell Woolrich]

Deadline – USA ★★★
Crime drama   1952 · US · BW · 86min

A clever but improbable tale has Humphrey Bogart lending his formidable presence to the role of a hard-boiled newspaper editor trying to persuade proprietor Ethel Barrymore not to sell her Pulitzer Prize-winning journal, while he simultaneously confronts the Mob and argues before the bench over the obligations of the press to its readers. It's an interesting subject, shot in the offices of the New York *Daily News*, but dully filmed. TS

Humphrey Bogart *Ed Hutcheson* • Ethel Barrymore *Mrs Garrison* • Kim Hunter *Nora* • Ed Begley *Frank Allen* • Warren Stevens *Burrows* • Paul Stewart *Thompson* • Martin Gabel *Rienzi* • Joseph De Santis [Joe De Santis] *Schmidt* ■ *Dir/Scr* Richard Brooks

Deadlocked ★★ 12
Crime drama   2000 · US · Colour · 86min

There's a hint of the storyline that informed the Denzel Washington vehicle *John Q* in this courtroom TV drama, in which anxious father Charles S Dutton takes both the jury and the victim's husband hostage to ensure his son gets a fair trial. The problem is that while Dutton gives a typically imposing performance, the remainder of the cast is unable to attain the same level of conviction. DP DVD

David Caruso *Ned Stark* • Charles S Dutton *Jacob Doyle* • Jo D Jonz *Demond Doyle* • John Finn *Jake Fisque* • Diego Wallraff *Sergeant DeLucca* • Malcolm Stewart *Richard Castlemore* ■ *Dir* Michael W Watkins [Michael Watkins] • *Scr* David Rosenfelt, Erik Jendresen, from a story by David Rosenfelt

A Deadly Adoption ★★
Thriller   2015 · US · Colour · 85min

In an unusual move, Will Ferrell and Kristen Wiig star as a couple whose dream turns into a nightmare when a woman hired to be their surrogate mother (Jessica Lowndes) comes to stay with them. The film is pitched as a pastiche of Lifetime's original movies and their reputation for melodrama. However, it's executed so earnestly that the tone becomes unclear, which simply produces a low-quality thriller with famous names in the lead roles, as Wiig, Ferrell and Lowndes all get the prolonged pauses and dramatic stares just right, fitting into the TV-movie style perfectly. JL

Will Ferrell *Robert Benson* • Jessica Lowndes *Bridgette* • Kristen Wiig *Sarah Benson* • Debra Christofferson *Ellen* ■ *Dir* Rachel Goldenberg • *Scr* Andrew Steele

Deadly Advice ★15
Black comedy   1993 · UK · Colour · 86min

Sadly, this dreary farce starring Jane Horrocks is low on laughs as the spirits of infamous British murderers such as Dr Crippen dole out advice to henpecked Horrocks on how best to kill her domineering mother, Brenda Fricker. This semi-detached suburban shocker misses by miles. AJ *Violence, swearing, nudity.*

Jane Horrocks *Jodie Greenwood* • Brenda Fricker *Iris Greenwood* • Imelda Staunton *Beth Greenwood* • Jonathan Pryce *Dr Ted Philips* • Edward Woodward *Major Herbert Armstrong* • Billie Whitelaw *Kate Webster* • Hywel Bennett *Dr Crippen* • Jonathan Hyde *George Joseph Smith* • John Mills *Jack the Ripper* • Ian Abbey *Bunny* • Eleanor Bron *Judge* ■ *Dir* Mandie Fletcher • *Scr* Glenn Chandler

The Deadly Affair ★★★★15
Spy drama   1966 · UK · Colour · 106min

James Mason worked regularly with Sidney Lumet on both stage and television, but this gripping adaptation of a John le Carré novel was their first film collaboration. Mason gives a studied performance as the intelligence officer investigating the suspicious suicide of a diplomat, with the ever-dependable Harry Andrews also on bristling form as a no-nonsense copper. Director Lumet expertly weaves Mason's deplorable domestic situation into the equation, coaxing an unsympathetic portrayal from Harriet Andersson as Mason's promiscuous wife. DP

James Mason *Charles Dobbs* • Simone Signoret *Elsa Fennan* • Maximilian Schell *Dieter Frey* • Harriet Andersson *Ann Dobbs* • Harry Andrews *Inspector Mendel* • Kenneth Haigh *Bill Appleby* • Lynn Redgrave *Virgin* • Roy Kinnear *Adam Scarr* ■ *Dir* Sidney Lumet • *Scr* Paul Dehn, from the novel *Call for the Dead* by John le Carré

The Deadly Bees ★
Horror   1967 · UK · Colour · 83min

Suzanna Leigh plays the pop singer who visits a remote island to recover from exhaustion. There she meets an insane beekeeper who breeds a strain of mutant bee that attacks a certain scent. This is one of the worst films Oscar-winning cinematographer-turned-director Freddie Francis ever made for Hammer rivals Amicus - a lacklustre plod through obvious red herrings and banal dialogue. AJ

Suzanna Leigh *Vicki Robbins* • Frank Finlay *Manfred* • Guy Doleman *Hargrove* • Catherine Finn *Mrs Hargrove* • John Harvey *Thompson* • Michael Ripper *Hawkins* • Anthony Bailey *Compere* • Tim Barrett *Harcourt* ■ *Dir* Freddie Francis • *Scr* Robert Bloch, Anthony Marriott, from the novel *A Taste for Honey* by HF Heard

Deadly Blessing ★★★18
Horror   1981 · US · Colour · 97min

This early nerve-jangler from horrormeister Wes Craven turns an everyday woman-in-peril terror tale into an epic of vindictive evil. In the rural serenity of eastern Pennsylvania, young widow Maren Jensen is persecuted by a religious cult led by Ernest Borgnine backed up by demonic forces that not even Sharon Stone can withstand. Snake-haters should beware of one shock scene, but it engenders a chilling despair that makes the ending all the more scary. TH *Violence, swearing, sex scenes, brief nudity.*

Ernest Borgnine *Isaiah* • Maren Jensen *Martha* • Susan Buckner *Vicky* • Sharon Stone *Lana* • Jeff East *John Schmidt* • Lisa Hartman *Faith* • Lois Nettleton *Louisa* • Coleen Riley *Melissa* ■ *Dir* Wes Craven • *Scr* Wes Craven, Glenn M Benest, Matthew Barr

The Deadly Companions ★★★PG
Western   1961 · US · Colour · 93min

Sam Peckinpah made his debut as a movie director with this often gripping psychological western, which concentrates on the interaction of its quartet of key characters before it bursts into violent life on the streets of a ghost town. As the rose among three thorns, Maureen O'Hara is excellent, but it's the posturing between gunmen Brian Keith, Chill Wills and Steve Cochran that holds the attention. The direction is tentative at times, but the script is rock solid. DP *DVD*

Maureen O'Hara *Kit* • Brian Keith *Yellowleg* • Steve Cochran *Billy* • Chill Wills *Turk* • Strother Martin *Parson* • Will Wright *Doctor* • Jim O'Hara *Cal* ■ *Dir* Sam Peckinpah • *Scr* AS Fleischman, from his novel

Deadly Friend ★★18
Horror   1986 · US · Colour · 86min

In this daft horror yarn from Wes Craven, Matthew Laborteaux is the teen genius whose robot is destroyed shortly before his girlfriend is killed. Naturally, he decides to plant the robot's brain into his girl's head - but things don't go as planned. The plot bears a remarkable resemblance to the cult shocker *Re-Animator*, made the year before, but this is still an enjoyable, if unscary piece of entertainment. JB

Matthew Laborteaux *Paul* • Kristy Swanson *Samantha* • Anne Twomey *Jeannie Conway* • Michael Sharrett *Tom* • Richard Marcus *Harry* • Anne Ramsey *Elvira Williams* • Russ Marin *Dr Johanson* • Andrew Roperto *Carl Denton* ■ *Dir* Wes Craven • *Scr* Bruce Joel Rubin, from the novel *Friend* by Diana Henstell

The Deadly Game ★★★12
Drama   1986 · US · Colour · 112min

That superb character actor John Lithgow is here given the chance to get his teeth into a decent leading role in co-writer/director Marshall Brickman's wry drama, which is also known as *The Manhattan Project*. Lithgow is entirely persuasive as the nuclear physicist slowly emerging from the protective cocoon of his intellect and beginning to understand the ramifications of his work when his girlfriend's son enters a home-made bomb for a science fair. DP *DVD*

John Lithgow *John Mathewson* • Christopher Collet *Paul Stephens* • Cynthia Nixon *Jenny Anderman* • Jill Eikenberry *Elizabeth Stephens* • John Mahoney *Lt Col Conroy* ■ *Dir/Scr* Marshall Brickman

Deadly Honeymoon ★★
Crime mystery   2009 · US · Colour · 89min

Appearances are deceptive in this otherwise routine mystery thriller in which a honeymooning male passenger goes missing during a Hawaiian cruise. Conveniently, a holidaying FBI agent is on board to investigate. What follows is a superficial and rather unexciting affair, with heavy-handed character stereotyping providing a few, obligatory red herrings, only for the film's supposed twists to become increasingly obvious. SF *Some swearing, drug abuse.*

Summer Glau *Lindsey* • Chris Carmack *Trevor* • Zoe McLellan *Gwen Merced* • Erik Palladino *Sherrick* ■ *Dir* Paul Shapiro • *Scr* Ron McGee

The Deadly Mantis ★★
Science-fiction thriller   1957 · US · BW · 78min

The dawning of the atomic age gave rise to an invasion of big bug movies, but this perfunctorily-directed, would-be sci-fi epic from Nathan Juran isn't in the same league as *Them!* or *Tarantula*. Still, there's something cathartic about watching a giant praying mantis, awoken from its arctic slumber by nuclear testing, laying waste to tourist attractions in New York and Washington DC. Starring Craig Stevens, then famous as television's Peter Gunn. RS

Craig Stevens *Colonel Joe Parkman* • William Hopper *Dr Ned Jackson* • Alix Talton *Marge Blaine* • Donald Randolph *General Mark Ford* ■ *Dir* Nathan Juran • *Scr* Martin Berkeley, from a story by William Alland

Deadly Nightshade ★★PG
Crime drama   1953 · UK · BW · 59min

In spite of its penury, this typical 1950s British crime quickie - about an escaped convict who unwittingly assumes the identity of a spy - is curiously engaging. Director John Gilling throws in a few Cornish coastal views, but he's mostly confined to unconvincing sets. The cheapskate look only adds to the charm. DP *DVD*

Emrys Jones *Robert Matthews/John Barlow* • Zena Marshall *Ann Farrington* • John Horsley *Inspector Clements* • Joan Hickson *Mrs Fenton* • Hector Ross *Canning* ■ *Dir* John Gilling • *Scr* Lawrence Huntington

Deadly Pursuit ★★★15
Action thriller   1988 · US · Colour · 105min

This solid thriller treads too much familiar ground to stand out from the pack. Sidney Poitier stars as a lawman saddled with a mismatched partner (Tom Berenger) who gives him as much trouble as the bad guy. The fact that Berenger's girlfriend Kirstie Alley is directly in danger from the crazed killer comes as no surprise, either. The performances are pretty good, while British director Roger Spottiswoode makes the most of the great outdoors and stages a couple of pulsating action sequences. DP *Swearing, violence.* *DVD*

Sidney Poitier *Warren Stantin* • Tom Berenger *Jonathan Knox* • Kirstie Alley *Sarah* • Clancy Brown *Steve* • Richard Masur *Norman* ■ *Dir* Roger Spottiswoode • *Scr* Harv Zimmel, Michael Burton, Daniel Petrie Jr, from a story by Zimmel

The Deadly Trackers ★★★15
Western   1973 · US · Colour · 100min

Richard Harris stars as a peace-loving sheriff who becomes a vengeance-seeking animal after his wife and son are killed by Rod Taylor and his vile gang. Rated PG in America but given an X certificate on its release in Britain, the picture has an intense physicality as Harris undergoes his usual sadomasochistic, Brando-esque voyage of self-denial, self-discovery and self-parody. Samuel Fuller began the film in Spain, but the footage was scrapped and the film was restarted in Mexico with Barry Shear as director. A fascinating rag-bag of a movie. AT

Richard Harris *Kilpatrick* • Rod Taylor *Brand* • Al Lettieri *Gutierrez* • Neville Brand *Choo Choo* • William Smith *Schoolboy* • Paul Benjamin *Jacob* • Pedro Armendáriz Jr *Blacksmith* ■ *Dir* Barry Shear • *Scr* Lukas Heller, from the story *Riata* by Samuel Fuller

The Deadly Trap ★
Psychological spy thriller   1971 · Fr/It · Colour · 97min

Neorealist French director René Clément was well past his prime when he tackled this lacklustre thriller, a hotch-potch of soap-opera dramatics, murder and espionage. Faye Dunaway and Frank Langella try to give the sub-Hitchcock plot an edge, but the leisurely pace and colour-supplement locations do little to inspire any tension or suspension of disbelief. AJ *DVD*

Faye Dunaway *Jill Hallard* • Frank Langella *Philip Hallard* • Barbara Parkins *Cynthia* • Michèle Lourié *Kathy* • Patrick Vincent *Patrick* ■ *Dir* René Clément • *Scr* Sidney Buchman, Eleanor Perry, from the novel *The Children Are Gone* by Arthur Cavanaugh, adapted by Daniel Boulanger, René Clément

Deadly Visions ★★12
Thriller   2004 · Can · Colour · 94min

Former *Desperate Housewives* star Nicollette Sheridan takes the lead in this far-fetched yarn, giving an emotionally uneven performance as a cornea transplant patient who suffers horrific visions of her donor's last moments. Unsurprisingly, she turns detective to prove her theory that the dead woman was murdered, encountering an assortment of lazy character stereotypes during her all-too-easy investigation. But while the storyline is as unrealistic as the acting and dialogue, there's enjoyment and just enough intrigue in watching such an unlikely heroine nail a killer. SF *Some violence, swearing.* *DVD*

Nicollette Sheridan *Ann Culver* • Gordon Currie *John Culver* • Sarah Deakins *Cara Tapper* • Phil Granger [Philip Granger] *Lt Austin Burke* • Haili Page *Sandy* ■ *Dir* Michael Scott • *Scr* John Murlowski

Deadly Weapons ★18
Crime drama   1974 · US · Colour · 71min

The talk of the town in 1974, this diabolically bad crime drama is little more than a freak show designed to exhibit the 73-inch bust of its star, credited as Zsa Zsa on the film and as Chesty Morgan in the advertising. Chesty tracks down the racketeers who killed her boyfriend and takes revenge by smothering them with her mammoth mammaries. DM *DVD*

Zsa Zsa [Chesty Morgan] *Crystal Davies* • Harry Reems *Tony* • Greg Reynolds *Larry* ■ *Dir* Doris Wishman • *Scr* JJ Kendall

Deadly Whispers ★★15
Thriller   1995 · US · Colour · 90min

This TV movie deals with the familiar phenomenon of a loved one at a police press conference becoming the prime suspect in the murder investigation. Tony Danza stars as the father who vows to apprehend his daughter's killer, only for the evidence to begin stacking up against him. Directed with some skill, but unrelentingly melodramatic. DP *DVD*

Tony Danza *Tom Acton* • Pamela Reed *Carol Acton* • Ving Rhames *Detective Jackson* • Heather Tom *Kathy Acton* • Sean Haberle *Jim* ■ *Dir* Bill Norton [Bill L Norton] • *Scr* Dennis Turner, from the novel by Ted Schwarz

Deadpool ★★★15
Fantasy action adventure   2016 · US · Colour · 103min

In this refreshingly oddball if uneven X-Men spin-off, Ryan Reynolds is in his element as the grudging mutant whose tongue is as sharp as the swords that he uses to dispatch the bad guys. His target is Ajax (Ed Skrein) who uses a cruel and unusual treatment to cure our antihero of cancer and alter his genes, giving him the power of self-healing but also unsightly burns. Director Tim Miller, making his feature debut, sometimes struggles with the balance of extreme black comedy, violence and lovey-dovey stuff, but that's part of the film's charm. *Deadpool 2* is due in 2017. SP *Violence, swearing, sex scenes, nudity.* *DVD* *Blu-ray* *CS*

Ryan Reynolds *Wade/Deadpool* • Morena Baccarin *Vanessa* • Ed Skrein *Ajax* • TJ Miller *Weasel* • Gina Carano *Angel Dust* ■ *Dir* Tim Miller • *Scr* Rhett Reese, Paul Wernick, from the comic book by Fabian Nicieza (writer), Rob Liefeld (artist)

Deal of the Century ★★15
Satirical black comedy   1983 · US · Colour · 94min

Given the talent on show, this brackish political satire has to go down as a major disappointment. Chevy Chase, Sigourney Weaver and Gregory Hines are the trio who luck into the weapons deal of the century, only to find things go horribly wrong. The performances are likeable enough, but the screenplay by Paul Brickman lacks focus and William Friedkin's direction never strikes the right tone. JF

Chevy Chase *Eddie Muntz* • Sigourney Weaver *Mrs De Voto* • Gregory Hines *Ray Kasternak* • Vince Edwards *Frank Stryker* • William Marquez *General Cordosa* ■ *Dir* William Friedkin • *Scr* Paul Brickman

Dealers ★★★ 15

Drama 1989 · UK · Colour · 87min

This somewhat impoverished imitation of *Wall Street* would have been a much better movie had it stuck to the clinical, cynical depiction of life in the City rather than veering off into the realms of predictable thrillerdom. Rebecca De Mornay and Paul McGann might be the headliners, but there's nothing new about the way their love/hate relationship shifts once they start pulling in the big bucks. Derrick O'Connor, on the other hand, gives a compelling performance as the former whizzkid hooked on the devil's dandruff. DP Violence, swearing. *DVD*

Paul McGann *Daniel Pascoe* • Rebecca De Mornay *Anna Schuman* • Derrick O'Connor *Robby Barrell* • John Castle *Frank Mallory* • Paul Guilfoyle (2) *Lee Peters* • Rosalind Bennett *Bonnie* • Adrian Dunbar *Lennox Mayhew* • Nicholas Hewetson *Jamie Dunbar* • Sara Sugarman *Elana* • Dikran Tulaine *Wolfgang* • Douglas Hodge *Patrick Skill* ■ *Dir* Colin Bucksey • *Scr* Andrew MacLear

Dean Koontz's Sole Survivor ★★ 15

Thriller 2000 · Can · Colour · 164min

Edited down from a four-hour mini-series, this supernatural thriller sticks so closely to the tried-and-trusted Dean Koontz formula that you may find yourself experiencing a little *déjà vu*. Billy Zane and John C McGinley face off bullishly as the grieving husband of a plane crash victim and the troubleshooter for a sinister paranormal organisation intent on mastering death. But no matter how far you suspend your disbelief, the plot keeps coming back with yet more clichés and contrivances. However, what's most disappointing here is the fact that a gifted cinematographer like Mikael Salomon is wasting his talent directing such mediocre pulp. DP *DVD*

Billy Zane *Joe Carpenter* • John C McGinley *Yates* • Isabella Hofmann *Barbara Chrisman* • Gloria Reuben *Rose* • Rachel Victoria *21-21* • Mitchell Kosterman *Becker* • Wally Dalton *Jeff Ealing* • Christine Willes *Mercy Ealing* ■ *Dir* Mikael Salomon • *Scr* Richard Christian Matheson, from the novel by Dean Koontz

Dean Spanley ★★★★ U

Period comedy drama 2008 · NZ/UK/Cay · Colour · 96min

Based on Lord Dunsany's novel, this shaggy dog story effortlessly puts forward the notion that dapper clergyman Dean Spanley (Sam Neill) is the reincarnation of the beloved childhood pet of a testy patriarch played by Peter O'Toole. Set in Edwardian London, the impossibly refined action feels rather like an after-dinner anecdote. Beautifully played by the impeccable cast, charmingly scripted by Alan Sharp and directed by Toa Fraser with a subtlety that's matched by Leon Narbey's cinematography, this is a demure delight. DP

Jeremy Northam *Henslowe Fisk "Fisk Jr"* • Sam Neill *Dean Walter Arthur Graham Spanley* • Bryan Brown *JJ Wrather* • Peter O'Toole *Horatio Fisk "Fisk Sr"* • Judy Parfitt *Mrs Brimley* • Art Malik *Swami Prash* ■ *Dir* Toa Fraser • *Scr* Alan Sharp, from the novel *My Talks with Dean Spanley* by Lord Dunsany • *Cinematographer* Leon Narbey

Dear America: Letters Home from Vietnam ★★★★★ PG

Documentary 1987 · US · Colour and BW · 82min

Rarely has the horror of the Vietnam War been brought home with such immediacy and power. Director Bill Couturie ploughed through thousands of missives for this highly personal history, appositely and soberingly illustrated by footage gleaned from the archives of NBC and the Department of Defense, much of it

previously unseen. Read with selfless sincerity and dramatic simplicity by the likes of Robert De Niro, Sean Penn, Michael J Fox and Kathleen Turner, the letters heart-rendingly demonstrate how the naive optimism turned into grim disenchantment of senseless slaughter and humiliating defeat. DP

Robert De Niro *Narrator* • Sean Penn *Narrator* • Michael J Fox *Narrator* • Kathleen Turner *Narrator* ■ *Dir* Bill Couturie • *Scr* from the non-fiction book *Dear America: Letters Home from Vietnam* by Bernard Edelman

Dear Brigitte ★★★ U

Comedy 1966 · US · Colour · 100min

Directed by Henry Koster, veteran of light-hearted family entertainment, this incident-packed comedy stars James Stewart and Glynis Johns and features a charming cameo from Brigitte Bardot, playing herself. Pro-arts professor Stewart has an eight-year-old son (Billy Mumy) who, much to his father's annoyance, is revealed to be a mathematical genius. The boy also writes love letters to Bardot and dreams of going to France to meet her. Lots of twists and turns ensue, with Stewart and Johns giving typically expert performances. RK

James Stewart *Robert Leaf* • Fabian *Kenneth* • Glynis Johns *Vina* • Cindy Carol *Pandora* • Billy Mumy [Bill Mumy] *Erasmus* • John Williams *Upjohn* • Ed Wynn *Captain* • Brigitte Bardot ■ *Dir* Henry Koster • *Scr* Hal Kanter, from the novel *Erasmus with Freckles* by John Haase

Dear Diary ★★★★★ 15

Biographical comedy drama 1994 · It/Fr · Colour · 96min

Nanni Moretti is the maverick genius of modern Italian cinema. Here he abandons the formulas of traditional film-making and embarks upon a personal journey that takes him to a movie theatre, the site of Pier Paolo Pasolini's murder, the Aeolian Islands and his own doctor's surgery. The side swipes at Roman architecture, *Henry: Portrait of a Serial Killer*, teenagers, television and the Italian health service are as sharp as they are quirky. Each section of this three-part pseudo-documentary contains a memorable moment, whether it's Moretti's encounter with Jennifer Beals or the relaying of soap-opera plotlines across Stromboli. Unhurried, unusual and unmissable. DP Italian, French +subtitles.

Nanni Moretti • Giovanna Bozzolo *Actor in Italian film* • Sebastiano Nardone *Actor in Italian film* • Antonio Petrocelli *Actor in Italian film* • Giulio Base *Car driver* • Jennifer Beals ■ *Dir/Scr* Nanni Moretti

Dear Frankie ★★★★ 12

Drama 2003 · UK · Colour · 100min

Single mum Emily Mortimer tries to protect her young deaf son from the truth about his abusive father in this poignant Scottish drama from first-time feature director Shona Auerbach. Jack McElhone is wonderfully natural as nine-year-old Frankie, who corresponds with his absentee dad, unaware that it's his devoted mother who's picking up the letters and faking the replies. Mortimer is appealing, while Gerard Butler has magnetic allure as the stranger she pays to masquerade as Frankie's father. SF Swearing. *DVD*

Emily Mortimer *Lizzie* • Gerard Butler *The Stranger* • Jack McElhone *Frankie* • Sharon Small *Marie* • Mary Riggans *Nell* • Jayd Johnson *Catriona* • Sean Brown *Ricky Monroe* ■ *Dir* Shona Auerbach • *Scr* Andrea Gibb

Dear God ★★ PG

Comedy 1996 · US · Colour · 107min

Comedian Greg Kinnear – who was nominated for an Oscar for his work in *As Good As It Gets* – got his first leading role in this lightweight comedy about a petty criminal who takes it upon himself to read and reply to the many letters written to God when he's made to work for the post office. Cute, inoffensive stuff, perfect for a rainy afternoon and enlivened by Kinnear's enjoyable performance. JB *DVD*

Greg Kinnear *Tom Turner* • Laurie Metcalf *Rebecca Frazen* • Maria Pitillo *Gloria McKinney* • Tim Conway *Herman Dooly* • Hector Elizondo *Vladek Vidov* • Jon Seda *Handsome* • Roscoe Lee Browne *Idris Abraham* • Anna Maria Horsford *Lucille* • Rue McClanahan *Mom Turner* ■ *Dir* Garry Marshall • *Scr* Warren Leight, Ed Kaplan

Dear Heart ★★★★

Romantic comedy 1964 · US · BW · 96min

Forlorn small-town postmistress Geraldine Page – in New York for a post office convention – causes trouble when she falls for delegate Glenn Ford, who's betrothed to, but not enamoured of, widow Angela Lansbury. Written by Tad Mosel, a great name from early American TV, it's properly sentimental without being mawkish, while Page, clutching isolation to herself as steadfastly as a security blanket, is touchingly true as a middle-aged woman teetering on the edge of the eccentricity. TH

Glenn Ford *Harry Monk* • Geraldine Page *Evie Jackson* • Michael Anderson Jr *Patrick* • Barbara Nichols *June* • Patricia Barry *Mitchell* • Charles Drake *Frank Taylor* • Angela Lansbury *Phyllis* ■ *Dir* Delbert Mann • *Scr* Tad Mosel, from his story *The Out-of-Towners*

Dear John ★★★

Romantic drama 1964 · Swe · BW · 110min

Nominated for a best foreign film Oscar, this was Lars Magnus Lindgren's fourth feature. Yet for all its success, he would make only three more films. It has sea captain Jarl Kulle's romance with waitress Christina Schollin skilfully interspersed with flashbacks detailing their pre-stories – he was abandoned by his wife and she was so hurt by the man who left her pregnant that she is now suspicious of Kulle's eager intentions. Watchfully played. DP Swedish +subtitles.

Jarl Kulle *John* • Christina Schollin *Anita* • Helena Nilsson *Helena* • Morgan Andersson *Raymond* ■ *Dir* Lars Magnus Lindgren • *Scr* Lars Magnus Lindgren, from the novel by Olle Lansberg

Dear John ★★★★ 12

Romantic drama 2010 · US · Colour · 103min

Lasse Hallström's deft direction turns the weepie bestseller by Nicholas Sparks into a timely and emotive depiction of two young people struggling to overcome the obstacles in the way of their love. Channing Tatum stars as John Tyree, an American soldier who falls for a beautiful, good-hearted student (Amanda Seyfried) while on leave. However, the course of true love does not run smoothly for the pair. Tatum and Seyfried are credible and wonderfully matched, while Richard Jenkins's portrayal of Tyree senior is heart-rending but realistic. It may be mawkish in places, but *Dear John* is genuinely sincere throughout the story's unpredictable twists and turns. Despite its flaws, this is a wonderfully filmed romance that will have even the toughest of guys dabbing away the tears. KK Violence, sexual situations. *DVD* *Blu*

Channing Tatum *John Tyree* • Amanda Seyfried *Savannah Curtis* • Henry Thomas *Tim Wheddon* • Scott Porter *Randy* • Richard Jenkins *Mr Tyree* • DJ Cotrona *Noodles* • David Andrews (2) *Mr Curtis* • Keith Robinson *Captain Stone* ■ *Dir* Lasse Hallström • *Scr* Jamie Linden, from the novel by Nicholas Sparks

Dear Mr Prohack ★★★ U

Romantic comedy 1949 · UK · BW · 85min

Cecil Parker, one of Britain's best and most distinctive stiff-upper-lip character actors, takes a title role tailor-made for his screen persona. He plays an adept government Treasury official who comes into a fortune, but proves rather less competent at handling his own money. His unwise investments and the foolish extravagances of his family make for a one-joke comedy that eventually runs out of steam, but there's fun to be had along the way. RK

Cecil Parker *Arthur Prohack* • Glynis Johns *Mimi Warburton* • Hermione Baddeley *Eve Prohack* • Dirk Bogarde *Charles Prohack* • Sheila Sim *Mary Prohack* • Heather Thatcher *Lady Maslam* • Denholm Elliott *Oswald Morfey* • Ian Carmichael

Hatter ■ *Dir* Thornton Freeland • *Scr* Ian Dalrymple, Donald Bull, from the play *Mr Prohack* by Edward Knoblock, Arnold Bennett, from the novel by Arnold Bennett

Dear Murderer ★★ PG

Crime thriller 1947 · UK · BW · 90min

When wealthy London businessman Eric Portman learns his wife Greta Gynt has had an affair during his absence, he murders the man. When he discovers she has a new lover (Maxwell Reed), he frames him for the crime. A nifty but thoroughly unpleasant British thriller, in which the protagonists are so vile we can only rejoice when they get their comeuppance. RK

Eric Portman *Lee Warren* • Greta Gynt *Vivien Warren* • Dennis Price *Richard Fenton* • Jack Warner *Inspector Pembury* • Maxwell Reed *Jimmy Martin* ■ *Dir* Arthur Crabtree • *Scr* Muriel Box, Sydney Box, Peter Rogers, from the play *Dear Murderer* by St John L Clowes

Dear Ruth ★★★

Comedy 1947 · US · BW · 95min

William Holden co-stars with Paramount's briefly popular Joan Caulfield in this adaptation of Norman Krasna's hit Broadway play about a pen-pal relationship with a difference. Mayhem ensues as a result of a recalcitrant, precocious and idealistic schoolgirl (bouncy Mona Freeman) corresponding with a soldier on active duty, using elder sister Caulfield's name. Director William D Russell deftly controls the polished cast in this endearing and delightful comedy. Two inferior sequels, *Dear Wife* and *Dear Brat*, followed. RK

Joan Caulfield *Ruth Wilkins* • William Holden (2) *Lt William Seacroft* • Edward Arnold *Judge Harry Wilkins* • Mary Philips *Edith Wilkins* • Mona Freeman *Miriam Wilkins* • Billy De Wolfe *Albert Kummer* • Virginia Welles *Martha Seacroft* ■ *Dir* William D Russell • *Scr* Arthur Sheekman, from the play by Norman Krasna

Dear Wendy ★★★★ 15

Satirical drama 2004 · Den/Ger/UK/Fr/Nor/Swe · Colour · 100min

America's love affair with guns is cleverly satirised in this thought-provoking drama from Thomas Vinterberg. In a mature and convincing performance, Jamie Bell plays a fervent pacifist in a poor American mining town who sets up a secret gun-worshipping club. The flamboyantly styled gun-organisation becomes a means of mental empowerment for other local outcasts. It's quirky and imaginatively constructed, with every element from soundtrack to costumes serving a vital function. Yet most crucially the picture is also a stinging comment on individuality and intolerance, resulting in a shocking and tragic climax. SF Swearing, violence. *DVD*

Jamie Bell *Dick* • Bill Pullman *Krugsby* • Michael Angarano *Freddie* • Danso Gordon *Sebastian* • Novella Nelson *Clarabelle* • Chris Owen *Huey* • Alison Pill *Susan* • Mark Webber *Stevie* ■ *Dir* Thomas Vinterberg • *Scr* Lars von Trier

Dear White People ★★★★ 15

Satirical comedy drama 2014 · US · Colour · 103min

Stylish, sleek and sharp, this terrific debut by writer/director Justin Simien is a streamlined satire that swaps subtlety for jaw-dropping honesty. *Dear White People* is the title of a controversial campus radio show where a student host (Tessa Thompson) takes smart swipes at race and culture in a fictional American Ivy League college. By examining America's social ills in microcosm using a seriously talented cast, succulent photography and a snappy pace, Simien has crafted a small film that's kind of a big deal. KK *DVD*

Tyler James Williams *Lionel Higgins* • Tessa Thompson *Sam White* • Brandon P Bell *Troy Fairbanks* • Dennis Haysbert *Dean Fairbanks* • Teyonah Parris *Colandrea "Coco" Conners* • Kyle Gallner *Kurt Fletcher* ■ *Dir/Scr* Justin Simien

Dear Wife ★★ U

Comedy 1949 · US · BW · 88min

This sequel to the successful comedy *Dear Ruth* (1947) was directed by Richard Haydn with the same leading players. The plot finds William Holden married to Joan Caulfield and running against his father-in-law Edward Arnold for the state senate, while her younger sister Mona Freeman continues on her socially conscious way. Freeman almost steals the show from the more seasoned players. *Dear Brat* concluded the series in 1951. RK

William Holden (2) *Bill Seacroft* • Joan Caulfield *Ruth Seacroft* • Billy De Wolfe *Albert Kummer* • Mona Freeman *Miriam Wilkins* • Edward Arnold *Judge Wilkins* ■ *Dir* Richard Haydn • *Scr* Arthur Sheekman, N Richard Nash, from characters by Norman Krasna

Death & Life of Charlie St Cloud ★★12
Drama 2010 · US · Colour · 95min

Yachtsman Zac Efron sees dead people – especially his younger brother, whose death he feels responsible for. That's why he's put his life on hold and is working in a cemetery. Under Burr Steers's earnest direction, this blatant tear-jerker is more maudlin than subtle, more schmaltzy than emotionally true. Former Disney poster boy Efron isn't up to the lightweight demands made on him, and Kim Basinger is underused as his mother. AJ Swearing.
DVD ◗

Zac Efron *Charlie St Cloud* • Amanda Crew *Tess Carroll* • Kim Basinger *Claire St Cloud* • Dave Franco *Sully* • Donal Logue *Tink Weatherbee* • Charlie Tahan *Sam St Cloud* • Ray Liotta *Florio Ferrente* ■ *Dir* Burr Steers • *Scr* Lewis Colick, Craig Pearce, from Ben Sherwood's novel

Death and the Maiden ★★★★18
Drama 1994 · UK/US/Fr · Colour · 99min

Adapted for the screen by Rafael Yglesias and Ariel Dorfman from Dorfman's play, this is an anguished tour de force, in which a traumatised woman turns her living room into a court to try the neighbour she believes raped and tortured her during a previous fascist dictatorship. Outstandingly played by Sigourney Weaver and Ben Kingsley (as her possible tormentor), the effective three-hander succeeds because of a dreadful electricity sparking between the two leads. TH Violence, swearing, nudity.

Sigourney Weaver *Paulina Escobar* • Ben Kingsley *Dr Roberto Miranda* • Stuart Wilson (1) *Gerardo Escobar* • Krystia Mova *Dr Miranda's wife* • Rodolphe Vega *Dr Miranda's son* ■ *Dir* Roman Polanski • *Scr* Rafael Yglesias, Ariel Dorfman, from the play by Ariel Dorfman

Death at a Funeral ★15
Black comedy drama 2007 · Ger/UK/US · Colour · 87min

Estranged brothers Daniel (Matthew Macfadyen) and Robert (Rupert Graves) are reunited for their father's funeral. Their extended – and dysfunctional – family, which includes Keeley Hawes, Jane Asher and Kris Marshall, comes together for the event. After a mysterious stranger (Peter Dinklage) appears, skeletons soon begin to fall from closets, and nothing and no one is spared embarrassment in the ensuing "hilarity". This ludicrous and offensive farce contains some particularly repellent and vulgar scenes. Director Frank Oz really should have known better. DA **DVD**

Matthew Macfadyen *Daniel* • Rupert Graves *Robert* • Peter Dinklage *Peter* • Daisy Donovan *Martha* • Alan Tudyk *Simon* • Kris Marshall *Troy* • Andy Nyman *Howard* • Ewen Bremner *Justin* • Keeley Hawes *Jane* • Jane Asher *Sandra* ■ *Dir* Frank Oz • *Scr* Dean Craig

Death at a Funeral ★★★15
Comedy 2010 · US/UK · Colour · 88min

This American remake of the 2007 UK-set farce is superior in every way. Chris Rock stars as the responsible brother who locks horns with successful younger sibling Martin Lawrence during their father's funeral. But that's just the start. Middle-class family tensions abound: Zoë Saldana calms her anxious boyfriend (James Marsden) with a pill that turns out to be a hallucinogenic; a man appears (Peter Dinklage, reprising his role from the original

movie) who claims to have known the deceased very well; a widow harangues her daughter-in-law for not supplying a grandchild. The hugely tangled web is teased out with sizzle from a fantastic cast and snap from director Neil LaBute (*In the Company of Men*). This may not be top-notch comedy but it moves at a cracking pace and high production values add gloss to the broad slapstick antics. KK Swearing, nudity. **DVD** ◗

Zoë Saldana *Elaine* • Danny Glover *Uncle Russell* • James Marsden *Oscar* • Luke Wilson *Derek* • Martin Lawrence *Ryan Barnes* • Chris Rock *Aaron Barnes* • Peter Dinklage *Frank* • Regina Hall *Michelle* • Loretta Devine *Cynthia* • Tracy Morgan *Norman* ■ *Dir* Neil LaBute • *Scr* Dean Craig

Death Becomes Her ★★★★PG
Black comedy 1992 · US · Colour · 99min

Meryl Streep and Goldie Hawn enliven this special-effects laden, extremely dark comedy from Robert Zemeckis. Superbitch actress Streep and novelist Hawn are the present and former loves of plastic surgeon-turned-mortician Bruce Willis, whose talents can't compete with witch Isabella Rossellini and her devilish gift of eternal youth. Zemeckis's under-rehearsed direction is at odds with a savagely delicious script and inspired casting. Both leading ladies are superbly acerbic as they try to outbitch each other, while Willis is a pleasant surprise as the put-upon hubby in this most enjoyable oddity. SH Violence, swearing, nudity. **DVD**

Meryl Streep *Madeline Ashton* • Bruce Willis *Ernest Menville* • Goldie Hawn *Helen Sharp* • Isabella Rossellini *Lisle Von Rhuman* • Ian Ogilvy *Chagall* • Adam Storke *Dakota* • Nancy Fish *Rose* ■ *Dir* Robert Zemeckis • *Scr* Martin Donovan, David Koepp

Death by Hanging ★★★★
Black comedy based on a true story 1968 · Jpn · BW · 117min

If Akira Kurosawa was Japan's most American director, then Nagisa Oshima is its most European. The influence of Brecht, Buñuel, Godard and Dusan Makavejev can all be felt in this stylised account of a true story, which typifies Oshima's combative approach to both film-making and politics. Charged with the murder and rape of two girls, a first-generation Korean student (Yun Yun-Do) survives the noose but loses his memory. So his jailers subject him to a macabre and increasingly menacing reconstruction of his alleged crimes. A scathing denunciation of capital punishment and Japan's almost institutionalised hatred of the Korean community. DP Japanese +subtitles.

Yun Yun-Do *R* • Kei Sato *Head Of Execution Ground* • Fumio Watanabe *Education officer* • Toshio Ishido *Chaplain* • Masao Adachi *Security officer* • Mutsuhiro Toura *Doctor* • Nagisa Oshima *Narrator* ■ *Dir* Nagisa Oshima • *Scr* Tsutomu Tamura, Mamoru Sasaki, Michinori Fukao, Nagisa Oshima

Death Collector ★★★15
Crime drama 1976 · US · Colour · 89min

Joe Cortese gets a job as a debt collector and gets caught up in the Mafia lifestyle, with suitably violent consequences. Although considered nothing more than a *Mean Streets* clone at the time, in retrospect director Ralph DeVito's gritty drama foreshadows many of the themes Martin Scorsese would later explore in *GoodFellas* and *Casino*. (Look out for Joe Pesci, the star of those two movies, in one of his earliest roles.) Great goon dialogue and quirky details set this apart. AJ **DVD**

Joe Cortese *Jerry Bolanti* • Lou Criscuolo *Anthony Iadavia* • Joe Pesci *Joey* • Bobby Alto *Serge* • Frank Vincent *Bernie Feldshuh* • Keith Davis *Marley* • Jack Ramage *Herb Greene* • Anne Johns *Paula* • Bob D'Andrea *Neil* ■ *Dir/Scr* Ralph DeVito

Death Defying Acts ★★★PG
Period romantic drama 2007 · UK/Aus · Colour · 92min

At first glance, *Death Defying Acts* seems a fairly conventional romantic drama about a confidence trickster – a music-hall psychic played by Catherine Zeta-Jones – who falls for Harry Houdini (Guy Pearce), the target of one of her cons. But it becomes something darker in the hands of Australian director Gillian Armstrong (*Mrs Soffel*). Houdini is an escapologist, international celebrity and himself a showbiz trickster. He has offered a big reward to contact his dead mother, and he is attracted to Zeta-Jones not just for her supposed psychic powers, but also for her resemblance to mum. The historic Edinburgh backdrop looks rather theatrical at times, and the blend of fact and fiction is a little contrived. But a more serious flaw is the lack of chemistry between the two stars. However, Armstrong's mix of darkness and light, life and death, marks the film out as highly unusual at the very least. BP Some violence, swearing, sexual references. **DVD**

Guy Pearce *Harry Houdini* • Catherine Zeta-Jones *Mary McGarvie* • Timothy Spall *Mr Sugarman* • Saoirse Ronan *Benji* • Frankey Martyn *Rose* • Malcolm Shields *Leith Romeo* • Leni Harper *Leith Romeo's wife* • Ralph Riach *Mr Robertson* ■ *Dir* Gillian Armstrong • *Scr* Tony Grisoni, Brian Ward • *Cinematographer* Haris Zambarloukos

Death Drives Through ★★U
Motor racing drama 1935 · UK · BW · 64min

Most notable on its release for the racing sequences filmed at the famous Brooklands circuit, this is now primarily of interest because the story was concocted by a young John Huston, in conjunction with Katherine Strueby. There's a hint of Howard Hawks's *The Crowd Roars* about the scenario, as Chili Bouchier pleads with inventor Robert Douglas not to risk his life at the wheel to prove a point to her motor tycoon father, Percy Walsh, and rival Miles Mander. This ably conveys the danger of motor sport but, while Mander is suitably caddish and Bouchier is her typically ebullient self, Douglas lacks the dash of a daredevil hero. DP **DVD**

Robert Douglas *Kit Woods* • Chili Bouchier *Kay Lord* • Miles Mander *Garry Ames* • Percy Walsh *Mr Lord* • Lillian Gunns *Binnie* ■ *Dir* Edward L Cahn • *Scr* Gordon Wellesley, from a story by John Huston, Katherine Strueby

Death Drums along the River ★★PG
Crime mystery 1963 · UK · Colour · 79min

British veteran director Lawrence Huntington fetched up in South Africa in the days when it wasn't politically kosher to do so and delivered this strangely appealing update of the hoary old Edgar Wallace imperialist saga *Sanders of the River*. The film features Richard Todd attempting to resuscitate his career by playing the police inspector. He reprised the role in 1965's *Coast of Skeletons*. TS

Richard Todd *Inspector Harry Sanders* • Marianne Koch *Dr Inge Jung* • Vivi Bach *Marlene* • Walter Rilla *Dr Schneider* • Jeremy Lloyd *Hamilton* ■ *Dir* Lawrence Huntington • *Scr* Harry Alan Towers, Nicolas Roeg, Kevin Kavanagh, Lawrence Huntington, from the novel *Sanders of the River* by Edgar Wallace

Death Game ★★
Thriller 1976 · US · Colour · 86min

San Francisco architect Seymour Cassel lets two hitch-hikers, Sondra Locke and Colleen Camp, into his house where they proceed to seduce, bind and torture him. This is an unnerving psychodrama, with sleazy sex and compelling depravity oozing from every exploitative frame. A prime example of 1970s post-Manson paranoia, the ridiculous twist ending lets this down. AJ

Sondra Locke *Jackson* • Colleen Camp *Donna* • Seymour Cassel *George Manning* • Beth Brickell *Karen Manning* • Michael Kalmansohn *Delivery*

boy • Ruth Warshawsky *Mrs Grossman* ■ *Dir* Peter S Traynor • *Scr* Anthony Overman, Michael Ronald Ross

Death Game ★★★15
Horror mystery 2010 · Jpn · Colour · 102min

Five men and five women are forced to get down and dirty to obtain a lucrative job in a suspenseful thriller from Hideo Nakata (whose *Ring* movies did so much to turn the West on to Japanese horror). At first, this survival-of-the-nastiest yarn seems like *Battle Royale* (particularly with Tatsuya Fujiwara as lead actor). However, it's evidently Agatha Christie's *Ten Little Indians* that's the real inspiration and that whodunnit aspect may appeal to those who prefer their thrillers twisty rather than gory. JA Japanese +subtitles. Violence. **DVD**

Tatsuya Fujiwara *Rikuhiko Yuki* • Kin'ya Kitaôji *Yoshi Ando* • Nagisa Katahira *Sawako Fuchi* • Shinji Takeda *Sousuke Iwai* ■ *Dir* Hideo Nakata • *Scr* Satoshi Suzuki, from the novel *The Incite Mill* by Honobu Yonezawa

Death Hunt ★★★18
Thriller adventure based on a true story 1981 · US · Colour · 97min

Charles Bronson is up to his macho tricks again in this violent adventure that trades on his *Death Wish* persona. He plays a trapper in the Canadian Rockies who is wrongly accused of murder and goes on the run, pursued by Mountie Lee Marvin. Director Peter Hunt does a decent job of shaping the borderline exploitation thrills into a highly watchable form, and the crisp photography helps enormously. AJ Violence, swearing.

Charles Bronson *Albert Johnson* • Lee Marvin *Sergeant Edgar Millen* • Angie Dickinson *Vanessa McBride* • Andrew Stevens *Alvin Adams* • Carl Weathers *Sundog* • William Sanderson *Ned Warren* • Jon Cedar *Hawkins* ■ *Dir* Peter Hunt • *Scr* Michael Grais, Mark Victor • *Cinematographer* James Devis

Death in a French Garden ★★★★18
Thriller 1985 · Fr · Colour · 97min

Teasing and dripping with style, this is that rare blend of form and content that engages both the eye and the mind. Through elliptical editing and arch manipulation of his characters, director Michel Deville leaves us as baffled as his hero, a young guitar teacher played by Christophe Malavoy. Not only does he discover his affair with his pupil's mother (Nicole Garcia) is being filmed; he also learns he's being stalked by the gay assassin who's been hired to kill his employer (Michel Piccoli). The ambiguity and elegance may not be to all tastes, but the performances, especially Piccoli's, are excellent. DP French +subtitles. **DVD**

Michel Piccoli *Graham Tombsthay* • Nicole Garcia *Julia Tombsthay* • Anémone *Edwige Ledieu* • Christophe Malavoy *David Aurphet* • Richard Bohringer *Daniel Forest* ■ *Dir* Michel Deville • *Scr* Michel Deville, Rosalinde Damamme, from the novel *Sur la Terre comme au Ciel* by René Belletto

Death in Brunswick ★★★★15
Black comedy 1990 · Aus · Colour · 103min

Now here is a Sam Neill you won't have seen before. He's on cracking form as a down-at-heel cook in a sleazy restaurant in the Brunswick area of Melbourne, who hopes that an affair with waitress Zoe Carides will help him escape his domineering mother. But the only bodily contact he gets is with the corpse of his Turkish colleague in this black comedy that works best during the restaurant scenes where the dialogue fizzes and the racial mix bubbles. DP Violence, swearing, nudity. **DVD**

Sam Neill *Carl Fitzgerald* • Zoe Carides *Sophie Papafagos* • John Clarke (2) *Dave* • Yvonne Lawley *Mrs Fitzgerald* • Nico Lathouris *Mustafa* • Nicholas Papademetriou *Yanni Voulgaris* ■ *Dir* John Ruane • *Scr* John Ruane, Boyd Oxlade, from the novel by Boyd Oxlade

D

A Death in Canaan ★★★
Drama based on a true story
1978 · US · Colour · 125min

Police manipulation and lies lead to a disturbing miscarriage of justice in Tony Richardson's Emmy-nominated crime drama, based on a real-life 1970s murder case. Adapted from Joan Barthel's bestseller (she's played here by Stefanie Powers), this superior though largely one-sided TV movie sees locals in a small Connecticut town rallying to help naive teen Paul Clemens after he's accused of killing his mother. Strong acting increases the realism and bolsters a courtroom-centred second half. SF

Stefanie Powers *Joan Barthel* · Paul Clemens *Peter Reilly* · Brian Dennehy *Barney Parsons* ■ *Dir* Tony Richardson · *Scr* Thomas Thompson, Scott Eastman, from the non-fiction book *A Death in Canaan* by Joan Barthel

Death in the Garden ★★★
Thriller 1956 · Fr/Mex · Colour · 95min

This jungle western was originally to be scripted by Jean Genet as a vehicle for Yves Montand. Luis Buñuel accepted the directorial reins with reluctance, yet he manages to explore his key themes of bourgeois avarice, religious hypocrisy and sexual repression while following a motley crew as it escapes across hostile terrain after a South American uprising. The perils encountered are drearily generic, but Buñuel transforms this gloriously photographed Eden into a gruellingly perilous place. DP French +subtitles.

Simone Signoret *Djin* · Georges Marchal *Shark* · Charles Vanel *Castin* · Tito Junco *Chenko* · Michel Piccoli *Father Lisardi* ■ *Dir* Luis Buñuel · *Scr* Luis Buñuel, Luis Alcoriza, Raymond Queneau, Gabriel Arout, from a novel by José André Lacour · *Cinematographer* Jorge Stahl

Death in the Shadows: the Sam Sheppard Story ★★★ 15
Drama based on a true story
1998 · US · Colour · 90min

Believe it or not, *The Fugitive* – about an innocent doctor wrongly accused of murder – was actually based on a real story. In this TV movie, however, events have moved on and are now seen through the eyes of the physician's grown-up son. Peter Strauss plays the brilliant but arrogant surgeon Sam Sheppard, while Henry Czerny is his son, who starts digging into his father's case with the help of a local lawyer. An intriguing spin on a now-familiar tale. JF *DVD*

Peter Strauss *Dr Sam Sheppard* · Henry Czerny *Sam "Chip" Reese Sheppard* · Lindsay Frost *Marilyn Sheppard* ■ *Dir* Peter Levin · *Scr* Adam Greenman, from the non-fiction book *Memory of Justice: the True Story of the Sam Sheppard Murder Case* by Cynthia L Cooper, Sam Reese Sheppard

Death in the Sun ★
Action adventure
1975 · W Ger/S Afr · Colour · 95min

Trevor Howard and Christopher Lee put in fine cameo performances in an otherwise amateur exploitation thriller shot in Zimbabwe with a stupid script, inept direction and mediocre photography. In an East African British colony under threat from a Mau-Mau style uprising, farmer Howard's daughter is graphically raped by an albino native (Horst Frank in a totally unconvincing coat of whitewash). AJ

Christopher Lee *Bill* · James Faulkner *Terrick* · Trevor Howard *Johannes* · Horst Frank *Whispering Death* · Sybil Danning *Sally* · Sascha Hehn *Peter* · Sam Williams *Katchemu* ■ *Dir* Jürgen Goslar · *Scr* Scot Finch, from the novel *Whispering Death* by Daniel Carney

Death in Venice ★★★★★ 15
Period drama 1971 · It/Fr · Colour · 125min

Former matinée idols Dirk Bogarde and Silvana Mangano increased their standing with art house audiences after this sumptuous reworking of Thomas Mann's novella. Bogarde's composer (an author in the original) arrives in Venice amid rumours of a cholera epidemic, troubled that he can no longer experience emotion, but the sight of Mangano's teenage son, Bjorn Andresen, stirs long dormant feelings. Luchino Visconti was a master of colour composition and here he has created a haunting work that is as operatic as it is cinematic. It is perhaps too sedate in places, but the shimmering photography more than compensates. DP *DVD*

Dirk Bogarde *Gustav von Aschenbach* · Bjorn Andresen *Tadzio* · Silvana Mangano *Tadzio's mother* · Marisa Berenson *Frau von Aschenbach* · Mark Burns *Alfred* ■ *Dir* Luchino Visconti · *Scr* Luchino Visconti, Nicola Badalucco, from the novella by Thomas Mann · *Cinematographer* Pasquale De Santis [Pasqualino De Santis] · *Art Director* Ferdinando Scarfiotti · *Costume Designer* Piero Tosi

Death Japanese Style ★★★★ 18
Black comedy
1984 · Jpn · Colour and BW · 123min

The high cost of dying in Japan is shrewdly, albeit sometimes crudely, satirised by director Juzo Itami, whose deconstruction of a three-day wake for a bad-tempered elder by his daughter and son-in-law is as wild as it is witty. Seemingly inspired by his own experiences, Itami establishes the samurai-slash style of film-making railing at a society that has lost touch with its traditions – a style he was to reinforce with his subsequent, better-known comedy *Tampopo*. TH Japanese +subtitles.

Tsutomu Yamazaki *Wabisuke Inoue* · Nobuko Miyamoto *Chizuko Amamiya* · Kin Sugai *Kikue Amamiya* · Shuji Otaki *Shokichi Amamiya* · Ichiro Zaitsu *Satomi* ■ *Dir/Scr* Juzo Itami

The Death Kiss ★★★
Mystery 1933 · US · BW and Tinted · 74min

Director Edwin L Marin's potboiler is an old-fashioned Hollywood thriller in every sense. Bela Lugosi plays the manager of Tinseltown's Tiffany Studios where a murder is committed on the set of a new production. While no great shakes in the mystery department, this is an intriguing behind-the-scenes look at the motion picture mechanics of the era. AJ

David Manners *Franklyn Drew* · Adrienne Ames *Marcia Lane* · Bela Lugosi *Joseph Steiner* · John Wray *Detective Lieut Sheehan* · Vince Barnett *Officer Gulliver* · Alexander Carr *Leon A Grossmith* · Edward Van Sloan *Tom Avery* ■ *Dir* Edwin L Marin · *Scr* Gordon Kahn, Barry Barringer, Joe Traub, from the novel by Madelon St Denis

Death Line ★★★★ 18
Horror 1972 · UK · Colour · 83min

Reactionary cop Donald Pleasence investigates mysterious disappearances in the London Underground and makes the startling discovery that a colony of cannibals has existed in the creepy tunnels since a Victorian cave-in disaster. Strong stuff in its day, Gary Sherman never directed a better movie than this grisly chiller, which provides dark scares while presenting an effective commentary on violence. Highly recommended. AJ

Donald Pleasence *Inspector Colquhoun* · Christopher Lee *Stratton-Villiers* · Norman Rossington *Detective Rogers* · David Ladd *Alex Campbell* · Sharon Gurney *Patricia Wilson* ■ *Dir* Gary Sherman · *Scr* Ceri Jones, from the story *Death Line* by Gary Sherman

Death Machine ★★★ 18
Science-fiction horror
1994 · UK · Colour · 111min

Home-grown director Stephen Norrington fashions a distinctly un-British but hugely entertaining techno-thriller. Set in the near future, the story pits hi-tech weapons firm executive Ely Pouget and a gang of terrorists against barmy scientist Brad Dourif and his bone-crunching killing machine in a deserted office building. There's little in the way of character development, but former effects man Norrington never lets the pace slacken for a minute and designs some ingenious action sequences. DP

Brad Dourif *Jack Dante* · Ely Pouget *Hayden Cale* · William Hootkins *John Carpenter* · John Sharian *Sam Raimi* · Martin McDougall *Yutani* · Richard Brake *Scott Ridley* · Rachel Weisz *AN Other personnel manager* ■ *Dir/Scr* Stephen Norrington

Death of a Bureaucrat ★★★★
Black comedy 1966 · Cub · BW · 84min

Tomás Gutiérrez Alea achieved international acclaim with this deliciously macabre comedy. Produced for the state-run ICAIC, it reveals an unexpected tolerance on the part of the Castro regime, as the satire at its expense is both funny and far from flattering. Frustrated at every turn by red tape, Salvador Wood has to resort to grave robbing to retrieve the union card his recently widowed aunt requires for her pension. Shot through with a Buñuelian strain of humour. DP Spanish +subtitles.

Salvador Wood *Nephew* · Silvia Planas *Aunt* · Manuel Estanillo *Bureaucrat* · Gaspar De Santelices *Nephew's boss* ■ *Dir* Tomás Gutiérrez Alea · *Scr* Alfredo Del Cueto, Ramón Suárez, Tomás Gutiérrez Alea

Death of a Cheerleader ★★★ 12
Mystery drama 1994 · US · Colour · 87min

This isn't in the same league as the witty 1993 Holly Hunter film *The Positively True Adventures of the Alleged Texas Cheerleader-Murdering Mom*, but still provides a gripping portrait of high-school politics. Student Tori Spelling delights in tormenting the school's geeks, including bright-but-plain Kellie Martin, but then turns up dead. Director William A Graham sympathetically chronicles the complex pressures of adolescent life. JF Swearing, violence, drug abuse. *DVD*

Kellie Martin *Angela Delvecchio* · Tori Spelling *Stacy Lockwood* · Valerie Harper *Mrs Delvecchio* · Terry O'Quinn *Ed Saxe* · James Avery *Agent Gilwood* · Andy Romano *Mr Delvecchio* · Margaret Langrick *Jill Anderson* ■ *Dir* William A Graham · *Scr* Dan Bronson, from a story by Dan Bronson, Randall Sullivan, from an article by Randall Sullivan

Death of a Gentleman ★★★★ 12A
Sports documentary 2015 · UK · Colour · 98min

Some four years in the making, this is a powerful, if somewhat scattershot indictment of the governance of international cricket. With even some of its staunchest supporters calling for four-day matches, Test cricket is clearly approaching a crossroads. But journalists Sam Collins and Jarrod Kimber suggest that the direction currently being plotted by the International Cricket Council (ICC) is ruinous in the extreme. Ultimately, the pair fail to nail the suspected conspiracy, but they ask enough awkward questions to disconcert all cricket lovers. DP Some swearing. *DVD*

Narayanaswami Srinivasan · Giles Clarke · Gideon Haigh · Kevin Pietersen · Tony Greig · Jonathan Agnew ■ *Dir* Johnny Blank, Sam Collins, Jarrod Kimber · *Scr* Sam Collins, Jon Hotten, Jarrod Kimber

Death of a Gunfighter ★★★
Western 1969 · US · Colour · 94min

This fine, grim western bears all the hallmarks of its uncredited director, the great Don Siegel, who took over from Robert Totten after Totten fell out with star Richard Widmark. The credit was given to that alias agreed by the Directors Guild, one Allen Smithee (this was, in fact, the first feature to bear the name). Widmark is once again compulsively watchable as a former gunman-turned-marshal while Lena Horne is brilliantly cast as his woman. This may be too downbeat and slow for many tastes, but the casting of Widmark and Horne makes it an interesting collector's item. TS

Richard Widmark *Marshal Frank Patch* · Lena Horne *Claire Quintana* · Carroll O'Connor *Lester Locke* · David Opatoshu *Edward Rosenbloom* · Kent Smith *Andrew Oxley* ■ *Dir* Allen Smithee [Robert Totten], Allen Smithee [Don Siegel] · *Scr* Joseph Calvelli, from the novel by Lewis B Patten

Death of a Salesman ★★★★
Drama 1951 · US · BW · 111min

This powerful and generally faithful film version of Arthur Miller's hit Broadway play – the tragedy of a mediocre individual trying to understand his life of failure – replaced the original stage star, Lee J Cobb, with screen veteran Fredric March. Sad for Cobb when some other members of the stage production – Mildred Dunnock as the wife, Cameron Mitchell as one of his two sons – were retained, but March is superb as the despairing salesman and gained an Oscar nomination. (He lost to Humphrey Bogart in *The African Queen*.) The theatrical transitions to flashbacks might have been avoided, but this is highly commendable work by director Laslo Benedek. AE

Fredric March *Willy Loman* · Mildred Dunnock *Linda Loman* · Kevin McCarthy *Biff* · Cameron Mitchell *Happy* · Howard Smith *Charley* · Royal Beal *Ben* ■ *Dir* Laslo Benedek · *Scr* Stanley Roberts, from the play by Arthur Miller

Death of a Salesman ★★★ PG
Drama 1985 · US · Colour · 130min

In director Volker Schlöndorff's fascinating version of Arthur Miller's play, Dustin Hoffman re-creates his Broadway role as Willy Loman, the ageing commercial traveller trapped in his vision of the go-getting American Dream. Hoffman starts at the top of his voice and continues in the same vein, as if still playing to the back row, though Kate Reid, as Loman's long-suffering wife, and Stephen Lang and Emmy-winning John Malkovich as their sons, give more subtle performances. TH *DVD*

Dustin Hoffman *Willy Loman* · Kate Reid *Linda Loman* · John Malkovich *Biff Loman* · Stephen Lang *Happy Loman* · Charles Durning *Charley* · Louis Zorich *Ben* ■ *Dir* Volker Schlöndorff · *Scr* Arthur Miller, adapted from the original Broadway production staged by Michael Rudman

Death of a Schoolboy ★★★ PG
Biographical drama
1990 · Austria · Colour · 89min

Austrian director Peter Patzak's film about the assassination of Archduke Franz Ferdinand in Sarajevo was full of possibilities. The spark that ignited the "tinderbox of Europe" was provided by Gavrilo Princip, a member of the Black Hand freedom fighters, but this biopic gives us too few insights into either the tense political situation in the summer of 1914 or the convictions that drove the boy to murder. It's handsomely mounted and the performances are earnest, but also too ponderous. DP Some German dubbed.

Reuben Pillsbury *Gavrilo* · Christopher Chaplin *Trifco* · Robert Movic *Cabri* · Sinolicka Trpkova *Sophia* · Hans Michael Rehberg *School director* · Philippe Léotard *Dr Levin* · Alexis Arquette *Milan* · Alan Cox *Anarchist* ■ *Dir* Peter Patzak · *Scr* David Anthony, Peter Patzak, from the book by Hans Konig

Death of a Scoundrel ★★
Crime drama 1956 · US · BW · 119min

This film *à clef* on the life of Serge Rubenstein is something of a family affair, with George Sanders getting the chance to betray real-life brother Tom Conway and seduce then wife Zsa Zsa Gabor. Overlong and repetitive, the action follows Sanders as he treads the familiar path from stony-broke immigrant to spendthrift playboy. DP

George Sanders *Clementi Sabourin* · Yvonne De Carlo *Bridget Kelly* · Zsa Zsa Gabor *Mrs Ryan* · Victor Jory *Leonard Wilson* · Nancy Gates *Stephanie North* · John Hoyt *Mr O'Hara* · Coleen Gray *Mrs Van Renassalear* · Lisa Ferraday *Zina Monte* · Tom Conway *Gerry Monte* ■ *Dir/Scr* Charles Martin

U SUITABLE FOR ALL   Uc SUITABLE ESPECIALLY FOR YOUNG CHILDREN (DVD ONLY)   PG PARENTAL GUIDANCE   12A UNDER 12s TO BE ACCOMPANIED (CINEMA ONLY)

Death of a Soldier ★★ 18

War drama based on a true story
1985 · Aus · Colour · 92min

This is something of a departure for French-born, Australian-raised film-maker Philippe Mora. Although there are some expressionistic touches, the action is much less stylised than in his earlier documentaries. Rugged performances from James Coburn and Bill Hunter convey some of the tensions that arise between the US Army and the authorities Down Under during the hunt for a GI (Reb Brown) suspected of strangling several Melbourne women. DP Violence, swearing, nudity.

James Coburn *Major Patrick Danneberg* • Reb Brown *Private Edward J Leonski* • Bill Hunter *Detective Sergeant "Bluey" Adams* • Maurie Fields *Detective Sergeant Ray Martin* • Belinda Davey *Margot Saunders* • Max Fairchild *Major William Fricks* ■ *Dir* Philippe Mora • *Scr* William Nagle

Death of an Angel ★★★ 12

Drama
1985 · US · Colour · 91min

Cult indoctrination and its attendant psychological problems are snapped into sharp focus in this psychological thriller. Bonnie Bedelia goes to Mexico to wrest her impressionable daughter, Pamela Ludwig, from the evil clutches of a religious sect and its charismatic leader, Nick Mancuso. The superior cast and intelligent treatment of religious power-plays elevate this thriller above the norm. AJ DVD

Bonnie Bedelia *Grace* • Nick Mancuso *Father Angel* • Pamela Ludwig *Vera* • Alex Colon *Robles* ■ *Dir/Scr* Petru Popescu

The Death of Mario Ricci ★★★★ PG

Mystery romance
1983 · Fr/Swi · Colour · 100min

A Swiss investigative journalist comes to a remote mountain village to interview an expert on famine. The man appears to be on the edge of a nervous breakdown, which is somehow connected with the mystery surrounding the death of Mario Ricci, an Italian immigrant worker. Brilliantly assembled by Swiss director Claude Goretta, with a central performance by Gian Maria Volonté that deservedly won him the best actor award at Cannes, the film is redolent with atmosphere, tension and visual flair. RK French +subtitles.

Gian Maria Volonté *Bernard Fontana* • Magali Noël *Solange* • Heinz Bennent *Henri Kremer* • Mimsy Farmer *Cathy Burns* • Jean-Michel Dupuis *Didier Meylan* ■ *Dir* Claude Goretta • *Scr* Claude Goretta, Georges Haldas

The Death of Mr Lazarescu ★★★★ 15

Black comedy drama
2005 · Rom · Colour · 154min

Director Cristi Puiu launches his series "Six Stories from the Bucharest Suburbs" with this epic, but always engrossing and frequently enraging exposé of the flaws in both the Romanian health service and modern humanity. Following cantankerous 60-something widower Ion Fiscuteanu on his odyssey around the city's hospitals with a complaint that only over-worked and under-motivated paramedic Luminta Gheorghiu takes seriously, Puiu explores everything from the breakdown of community to the arrogance of the medical profession and the incompetence of the post-Communist bureaucracy. However, he laces this bleak satire with moments of genuine amusement and compassion. DP Romanian +subtitles. Swearing. DVD

Luminta Gheorghiu *Mioara* • Ion Fiscuteanu *Dante Remus Lazarescu* • Gabriel Spahiu *Leo* • Doru Ana *Sandu* • Dana Dogaru *Miky* • Serban Pavlu *Gelu* • Florin Zamfirescu *Dr Ardelean* • Clara Voda *Dr Gina Filip* ■ *Dir* Cristi Puiu • *Scr* Cristi Puiu, Razvan Radulescu

The Death of the Incredible Hulk ★★ PG

Action adventure
1990 · US · Colour · 94min

One of a number of TV movie spin-offs from the wearisome series, this has Bill Bixby still searching for a way of ridding himself of the alter ego who ruins all his clothes. Here he finds a sympathetic scientist (Philip Sterling) to help reverse the genetic process only to find himself the target of evil terrorists. Green-dyed Lou Ferrigno once again ripples his muscles, but the playing and the direction are as bland as usual. JF DVD

Bill Bixby *Dr David Banner* • Lou Ferrigno *The Hulk* • Elizabeth Gracen *Jasmin* • Philip Sterling *Dr Ronald Pratt* • Andreas Katsulas *Kasha* • Carla Ferrigno *Bank clerk* ■ *Dir* Bill Bixby • *Scr* Gerald DiPego, from characters by Stan Lee, Jack Kirby

Death on the Nile ★★★ PG

Murder mystery
1978 · UK · Colour · 133min

Peter Ustinov takes over from Albert Finney as pernickety Belgian sleuth Hercule Poirot in this solid, star-studded dramatisation of Agatha Christie's paddle-steamer mystery. The plot is suitably tricky, the Egyptian locations dazzling and all the actors onboard seem to be having a terrific time – especially Angela Lansbury as a drunken writer and Maggie Smith as an acid-tongued nurse. It's only in comparison with 1974's *Murder on the Orient Express* that the film inevitably suffers – the solution just isn't quite as satisfying. DvB DVD

Peter Ustinov *Hercule Poirot* • Jane Birkin *Louise Bourget* • Lois Chiles *Linnet Ridgeway* • Bette Davis *Mrs Van Schuyler* • Mia Farrow *Jacqueline de Bellefort* • Jon Finch *Mr Ferguson* • Olivia Hussey *Rosalie Otterbourne* • IS Johar *Manager of the Karnak* • George Kennedy *Andrew Pennington* • Angela Lansbury *Mrs Salome Otterbourne* • Simon MacCorkindale *Simon Doyle* • David Niven *Colonel Rice* • Maggie Smith *Miss Bowers* • Jack Warcen *Dr Bessner* • Harry Andrews *Barnstaple* • Sam Wanamaker *Rockford* ■ *Dir* John Guillermin • *Scr* Anthony Shaffer, from the novel by Agatha Christie

Death Proof ★★ 18

Crime action thriller
2007 · US · Colour and BW · 109min

Writer/director Quentin Tarantino pays tribute to 1970s exploitation cinema with this stylistically authentic, though overly talky, twist on the psycho killer tale. Originally released Stateside as part of the *Grindhouse* double bill alongside Robert Rodriguez's *Planet Terror*, it fuses the slasher and chase genres with variable success. Plotwise, there's scarcely enough material, with two distinct sets of female friends falling victim to a murderous stalker (a superb Kurt Russell) whose weapon of choice is his specially reinforced – and hence "death proof" – car. Extensive stretches of Tarantino's trademark, smart-mouthed dialogue clumsily plug the gaps and slow the pace, yet there are some genuinely exhilarating chase sequences. SF Violence. DVD BD

Kurt Russell *Stuntman Mike* • Rose McGowan *Pam* • Sydney Poitier [Sydney Tamiia Poitier] *Jungle Julia* • Vanessa Ferlito *Arlene/Butterfly* • Jordan Ladd *Shanna* • Rosario Dawson *Abernathy* • Mary Elizabeth Winstead *Lee* • Zoë Bell ■ *Dir/Scr* Quentin Tarantino • *Editor* Sally Menke

Death Race ★★★ 15

Futuristic action thriller
2008 · US/UK · Colour · 106min

Privatised prisons make a killing forcing inmates into pay-per-view car races to the death in director Paul WS Anderson's bluntly violent take on the future for extreme sports and reality TV. Jason Statham does his charismatic moody loner turn as ex-Nascar champion Jensen Ames, who's framed for murder to become a pawn in the machinations of sadistic warden Joan Allen. Unlike the 1975 cult flick *Death Race 2000*, this is less a political satire than a frenetically edited set of epic crashes, spectacular explosions and bloody revenge. It's Ian McShane who impresses the most, playing a genius mechanic who provides Statham with his weapons-customised vehicle. AJ Violence, swearing. DVD BD

Jason Statham *Jensen Ames* • Tyrese Gibson *Machine Gun Joe* • Ian McShane *Coach* • Joan Allen *Hennessey* • Natalie Martinez *Case* • Max Ryan *Slovo "Angel Wings" Pachenko* ■ *Dir* Paul WS Anderson [Paul Anderson (1)] • *Scr* Paul WS Anderson [Paul Anderson], from a story by Anderson, from the film *Death Race 2000*, from the short story *The Racer* by Ib Melchior

Death Race 2000 ★★★ 18

Futuristic action satire
1975 · US · Colour · 76min

This ultra-violent, action-packed satire is set in the future showing the fascist American government sponsoring a nationally televised road race where drivers score points for ramming pedestrians. The event is staged to pacify the ravenous public's lust for blood and stop them from getting involved with revolutionaries determined to overthrow the President. Although very graphic, light-hearted direction by Paul Bartel keeps the subversive demolition derby on an amusing track. AJ Swearing, brief nudity. DVD

David Carradine *Frankenstein* • Simone Griffeth *Annie* • Sylvester Stallone *Machine Gun Joe Viterbo* • Mary Woronov *Calamity Jane* • Roberta Collins *Mathilda the Hun* • Martin Kove *Nero the Hero* • Louisa Moritz *Myra* • Don Steele *Junior Bruce* ■ *Dir* Paul Bartel (1) • *Scr* Robert Thom, Charles B Griffith, from a story by Ib Melchior

Death Rides a Horse ★★★ 15

Spaghetti western
1967 · It · Colour · 110min

This overlong but spirited spaghetti western confidently uses the tried and tested clichés of the genre: the greenhorn gunfighter joining forces with a master marksman; the baddies turned upstanding leaders of the community; and the duellist with an empty gun. John Phillip Law is the youth searching for his parents' murderers, the same people Lee Van Cleef is hunting after they put him in jail. With stylish direction and a neat twist in the tale, this is an efficient horse opera. AJ Italian dubbed. DVD

John Phillip Law *Bill* • Lee Van Cleef *Ryan* • Luigi Pistilli *Wolcott* • Anthony Dawson [Antonio Margheriti] *Manina* • José Torres (1) *Pedro* ■ *Dir* Giulio Petroni • *Scr* Luciano Vincenzoni

Death Sentence ★★★ 18

Revenge action thriller
2007 · US · Colour · 101min

In a powerful, remarkably shaded performance, Kevin Bacon turns from mild-mannered executive to *Taxi Driver*-style vigilante when his son is slaughtered in a gang initiation. With ethical and moral issues unusually well drawn considering the often far-fetched plot, the tit-for-tat retribution swings compellingly from righteous side to venal side in ever-increasing tension-laden circles before believably blurring. John Goodman's chilling cameo as the gang leader's sleazy father creates further involving conflict and James Wan's crafty, gritty direction sustains suspense throughout the gory action. AJ Violence, swearing. DVD BD

Kevin Bacon *Nick Hume* • Kelly Preston *Helen Hume* • John Goodman *Bones Darley* • Garrett Hedlund *Billy Darley* • Aisha Tyler *Detective Wallis* • Leigh Whannell *Spink* ■ *Dir* James Wan • *Scr* Ian Jeffers, from the novel by Brian Garfield • *Cinematographer* John R Leonetti

Death Takes a Holiday ★★★

Romantic fantasy
1934 · US · BW · 79min

A witty and sophisticated Paramount fable with a clever, though wordy, screenplay, this stars Fredric March as a very urbane Grim Reaper visiting Earth to learn how he is perceived and discover why humans are so scared of him. He takes the form of a handsome prince, only to fall in love during a palazzo house party. Director Mitchell Leisen keeps this bubbling along at a very healthy 79 minutes, which really makes you wonder how the 1998 remake *Meet Joe Black* clocked in at a grim three hours. TS

Fredric March *Prince Sirk* • Evelyn Venable *Grazia* • Sir Guy Standing [Guy Standing] *Duke Lambert* • Katherine Alexander *Alda* • Gail Patrick *Rhoda* • Helen Westley *Stephanie* • Kathleen Howard *Princess Maria* • Kent Taylor *Corrado* ■ *Dir* Mitchell Leisen • *Scr* Maxwell Anderson, Gladys Lehman, Walter Ferris, from the play by Alberto Casella

Death to Smoochy ★★ 15

Black comedy drama
2002 · US/UK · Colour · 105min

This odd mix of comedy and drama stars Robin Williams as a sleazy, mean-spirited children's entertainer on TV who finds himself sacked for taking backhanders. In his place, young, idealistic Edward Norton is hired, who dresses up as a Barney-like character named Smoochy. The darkly comic elements work brilliantly, but someone obviously got nervous about such a dark look at children's TV and decided to make it as cute and fluffy as Smoochy by the end. JB DVD

Robin Williams *Rainbow Randolph* • Edward Norton *Sheldon Mopes/Smoochy the Rhino* • Catherine Keener *Nora Wells* • Danny DeVito *Burke Bennett* • Jon Stewart *Marion Frank Stokes* • Harvey Fierstein *Merv Green* • Pam Ferris *Tommy Cotter* ■ *Dir* Danny DeVito • *Scr* Adam Resnick

Death Train ★★ 15

Action thriller
1993 · UK/Cro/US · Colour · 94min

In this minor TV movie, based on the Alistair MacLean novel, renegade Russian general Christopher Lee is exporting nuclear weapons to Iraq to start a revolution and Patrick Stewart is in charge of the UN army task force deciding to call in drunken ex-SAS officer Pierce Brosnan to head the mission. Cue ripe dialogue, very tepid thrills and typical low-rent action in a would-be tough thriller. The stellar cast doesn't help much. AJ Swearing, violence. DVD

Pierce Brosnan *Mike Graham* • Patrick Stewart *Malcolm Philpott* • Alexandra Paul *Sabrina Carver* • Ted Levine *Alex Tierney* • Christopher Lee *General Benin* • John Abineri *Leitzig* • Nic D'Avirro *Rodenko* • Clarke Peters *Whitlock* ■ *Dir* David S Jackson • *Scr* David S Jackson, from the novel by Alistair MacLean

Death Valley ★★ 18

Crime thriller
1982 · US · Colour · 84min

This low-grade "stalk and slash" movie focuses on a young boy visiting his mother in Arizona who unwittingly becomes the target of a psychopath. Director Dick Richards succeeds in creating a low quota of suspense, but he allows the predictable plot to be hampered by inferior acting. RS

Paul Le Mat *Mike* • Catherine Hicks *Sally* • Stephen McHattie *Hal* • A Wilford Brimley [Wilford Brimley] *Sheriff* • Peter Billingsley *Billy* • Edward Herrmann *Paul* • Jack O'Leary *Earl* ■ *Dir* Dick Richards • *Scr* Richard Rothstein

Death Vengeance ★★★ 18

Action crime drama
1982 · US · Colour · 91min

As *Death Wish* rip-offs go, Lewis Teague's film is fairly close to the cream of the crop. Tom Skerritt is excellent as a Philadelphia shopkeeper who organises a vigilante group to crack down on local deviants, becoming a media celebrity by default. The pace is lively, but Teague tries to have his cake and eat it, denouncing violent retribution on the one hand while succumbing to crowd-pleasing mayhem on the other. RS

Tom Skerritt *John D'Angelo* • Patti LuPone *Lisa D'Angelo* • Michael Sarrazin *Vince Morelli* • Yaphet Kotto *Ivanhoe Washington* • David Rasche *Michael Taylor* • Donna DeVarona *Sara Rogers* • Gina DeAngelis *Vera D'Angelo* • Jonathan Adam Sherman *Danny D'Angelo* ■ *Dir* Lewis Teague • *Scr* Tom Hedley, David Zelag Goodman

Death Warrant ★★★ 18

Action thriller
1990 · US/Can · Colour · 85min

Even for a Jean-Claude Van Damme movie, this is an excessively violent, if clinically efficient, exercise in body pulverising. Van Damme stars as a maverick Royal Canadian Mountie, sent to a prison where there's been a series of grisly unsolved murders. There he comes face to face with an old foe: the psychopathic "Sandman", played with zealous enthusiasm by Patrick Kilpatrick. To some extent this marked a career breakthrough for Van Damme, who got to play not just a kickboxer, but – hey! – an undercover kickboxer. Deran Sarafian's direction is brutally efficient, but fans won't be disappointed. **RS** *DVD*

Jean-Claude Van Damme *Louis Burke* • Cynthia Gibb *Amanda Beckett* • Robert Guillaume *Hawkins* • George Dickerson *Tom Vogler* • Art LaFleur *Sergeant DeGraf* • Patrick Kilpatrick *Naylor, "The Sandman"* ■ *Dir* Deran Sarafian • *Scr* David S Goyer

Death Watch ★★★ 🔞
Science-fiction satire
1980 · Fr/W Ger/UK · Colour · 125min

This futuristic discourse on the intrusiveness of TV is much bleaker than either Didier Grousset's *Kamikaze* or *The Truman Show*. With Glasgow providing the desolate backdrop, this shows how easy it is to commit acts of psychological trespass, as Harvey Keitel uses a miniature camera implanted in his skull to record the final days of the terminally ill Romy Schneider for unscrupulous Harry Dean Stanton's reality show. **DP** In English, French, German. Swearing. *DVD* *BL*

Romy Schneider *Katherine Mortenhoe* • Harvey Keitel *Roddy* • Harry Dean Stanton *Vincent Ferriman* • Thérèse Liotard *Tracey* • Max von Sydow *Gerald Mortenhoe* ■ *Dir* Bertrand Tavernier • *Scr* Bertrand Tavernier, David Rayfiel, from the novel *The Continuous Katherine Mortenhoe (The Unsleeping Eye)* by David Compton

Death Wish ★★★ 🔞
Crime thriller   1974 · US · Colour · 93min

This is the highly controversial sleaze epic that finally made Charles Bronson a star in America, and set a regrettable trend for ultra-violent vigilante thrillers. Bronson mechanically plays liberal architect Paul Kersey, who takes matters into his own hands after his wife is killed and his daughter is raped by a Manhattan gang (led by Jeff Goldblum in his film debut). Director Michael Winner's blood-lusting shocker is as intense and upsetting as it is morally reprehensible, and was very influential in its day, but spawned a series of dismal sequels. **AJ** Violence, swearing, nudity. *DVD*

Charles Bronson *Paul Kersey* • Hope Lange *Joanna Kersey* • Vincent Gardenia *Frank Ochoa* • Steven Keats *Jack Toby* • William Redfield *Sam Kreutzer* • Stuart Margolin *Aimes Jainchill* • Jeff Goldblum *Mugger* ■ *Dir* Michael Winner • *Scr* Wendell Mayes, from the novel by Brian Garfield

Death Wish II ★ 🔞
Crime thriller   1981 · US · Colour · 84min

Charles Bronson takes his lone vigilante act to Los Angeles in this crudely exploitative, belated first sequel to Michael Winner's trend-setting trash thriller. Beginning as it means to go on with the rape and murder of Bronson's Spanish maid, it would be offensive if it weren't so laughably over the top. **AJ** Swearing, violence, nudity. *DVD*

Charles Bronson *Paul Kersey* • Jill Ireland *Geri Nichols* • Vincent Gardenia *Frank Ochoa* • JD Cannon *New York DA* • Anthony Franciosa *LA Police Commissioner* • Ben Frank *Lieutenant Mankiewicz* • Robin Sherwood *Carol Kersey* ■ *Dir* Michael Winner • *Scr* David Engelbach, from characters by Brian Garfield

Death Wish 3 ★ 🔞
Crime thriller   1985 · US · Colour · 86min

With any remaining shred of political subtlety erased by the appallingly exploitative *Death Wish II*, director Michael Winner continues his freelance vigilante saga in ludicrously over-the-top mode. This time a pack of punks and gay Hell's Angels terrorises a Manhattan apartment block. Ridiculous and revolting. **AJ**

Charles Bronson *Paul Kersey* • Deborah Raffin *Kathryn Davis* • Ed Lauter *Richard Shriker* • Martin Balsam *Bennett* • Gavan O'Herlihy *Fraker* • Kirk Taylor *Giggler* • Alex Winter *Hermosa* ■ *Dir* Michael Winner • *Scr* Don Jakoby, Michael Edmonds, from characters by Brian Garfield

Death Wish 4: the Crackdown ★ 🔞
Crime thriller   1987 · US · Colour · 95min

Crusading vigilante architect Charles Bronson cleans up three crack-dealing LA

syndicates after one causes the death of his girlfriend's (Kay Lenz) daughter in this shoddily staged sequel. J Lee Thompson takes over the directing reins from Michael Winner and incredibly does an even lousier job marshalling the inept plot, inane dialogue and senseless violence. Awful. **AJ** Violence, swearing.

Charles Bronson *Paul Kersey* • Kay Lenz *Karen Sheldon* • John P Ryan *Nathan White* • Perry Lopez *Ed Zacharias* • Soon-Teck Oh *Detective Nozaki* • George Dickerson *Detective Reiner* • Jesse Dabson *Randy Viscovich* • Dana Barron *Erica Sheldon* ■ *Dir* J Lee Thompson • *Scr* Gail Morgan Hickman, from characters by Brian Garfield

Death Wish V: the Face of Death ★ 🔞
Crime thriller   1994 · US · Colour · 91min

Charles Bronson's one-man crusade against lowlifes continues when his girlfriend, fashion designer Lesley-Anne Down, is slaughtered by her mobster ex-lover Michael Parks. Transvestite henchmen and acid attacks barely liven up the formulaic violence in this absolute dross. **AJ** Swearing, nudity.

Charles Bronson *Paul Kersey* • Lesley-Anne Down *Olivia Regent* • Michael Parks *Tommy O'Shea* • Saul Rubinek *Brian Hoyle* • Erica Lancaster *Chelsea Regent* ■ *Dir* Allan Goldstein [Allan A Goldstein] • *Scr* Stephen Peters, from characters by Brian Garfield

Deathsport ★★ 🔞
Futuristic action horror
1978 · US · Colour · 82min

Ranger guides David Carradine and Claudia Jennings battle the evil Statesmen, futuristic Hell's Angels who ride cycles called Death Machines, in a banal reworking of *Death Race 2000*. It's set in the post-apocalyptic year 3000, and mixes cheap *Star Wars* tricks and cannibal mutants into the vehicular violence. There's lots of fiery crashes and gory comedy, but little sense in a movie shot separately by directors Henry Suso and Allan Arkush and then literally stuck together. **AJ** *DVD*

David Carradine *Kaz Oshay* • Claudia Jennings *Deneer* • Richard Lynch *Ankar Moor* • William Smithers *Doctor Karl* • David McLean *Lord Zirpola* • Jesse Vint *Polna* ■ *Dir* Henry Suso, Allan Arkush • *Scr* Henry Suso, Donald Steward, from a story by Frances Doel

Deathtrap ★★ 🄿🄶
Thriller   1982 · US · Colour · 111min

The play by Ira Levin was a particularly clever piece of stagecraft that, like *Sleuth*, was heavily dependent on the theatre itself to make its tricks work. Here, Michael Caine stars as a playwright in search of a hit, while Christopher Reeve is the former student who sends him a script. No matter how well director Sidney Lumet manages to disguise the theatricality, the basic plot devices sink the project cinematically. **TS** Some swearing.

Michael Caine *Sidney Bruhl* • Christopher Reeve *Clifford Anderson* • Dyan Cannon *Myra Elizabeth Maxwell Bruhl* • Irene Worth *Helga Ten Dorp* • Henry Jones *Porter Milgrim* ■ *Dir* Sidney Lumet • *Scr* Jay Presson Allen, from the play by Ira Levin

Deathwatch ★★★
Drama   1966 · US · BW · 88min

In the 1960s, an awkward translation of Jean Genet's difficult play, about the rivalries and tensions between three convicts (one awaiting execution) in a prison cell, had a surprisingly successful run in Los Angeles. This film is basically a record of that production with a new prologue and flashbacks added. It is still heavy going, but the Method-influenced performances are good. One of the inmates is played by Leonard Nimoy, just before he found fame in *Star Trek*, another by Paul Mazursky, who went on to write and direct films such as *Down and Out in Beverly Hills* and *Bob & Carol & Ted & Alice*. **DM**

Leonard Nimoy *Jules LeFranc* • Michael Forest *Greeneyes* • Paul Mazursky *Maurice* • Robert Ellenstein *Guard* • Gavin Macleod *Emil* ■ *Dir* Vic

Morrow • *Scr* Barbara Turner, Vic Morrow, from the play *Haute Surveillance* by Jean Genêt and translated by Bernard Frechtman as *Deathwatch*

Deathwatch ★ 🔟5
Supernatural horror
2002 · UK/Ger · Colour · 91min

If war is hell, this combat-themed chiller from debutant writer/director Michael J Bassett isn't much better. *Billy Elliot's* Jamie Bell plays the youngest recruit of a First World War platoon that's lost deep in enemy territory, but takes refuge in an uncharted trench where the men are systematically picked off by a seemingly supernatural assassin. Bassett's lumbering direction blasts any horror or suspense clean out of the target area. **AJ** *DVD*

Jamie Bell *Charlie Shakespeare* • Hugo Speer *Sergeant Tate* • Matthew Rhys *"Doc" Fairweather* • Andy Serkis *Private Quinn* • Laurence Fox *Captain Jennings* • Dean Lennox Kelly *McNess* ■ *Dir/Scr* Michael J Bassett

The Debt ★★★ 🔟5
Spy drama
2010 · US/UK/Hun/Is · Colour · 113min

A decent but unspectacular war crimes tale is elevated above the ordinary here by the sheer calibre of its cast – including Helen Mirren, Sam Worthington, Tom Wilkinson and rising star Jessica Chastain (*Tree of Life*). The story flits back and forth between 1966, when three Israeli agents are sent in to East Berlin to kidnap a Nazi war criminal, and 30 years later, when a book is published about the mission. Other than a distracting disparity in looks between two of the three pairs of characters, the movie is an entertaining addition to the recent wave of retro spy films. **DA** Violence, swearing. *DVD* *BL*

Helen Mirren *Rachel Singer* • Sam Worthington *Young David* • Jessica Chastain *Young Rachel Singer* • Tom Wilkinson *Stephan Gold* • Marton Csokas *Young Stephan* • Ciaran Hinds *David Peretz* ■ *Dir* John Madden • *Scr* Jane Goldman, Peter Straughan, Matthew Vaughn, from the film *Ha-Hov* by Assaf Bernstein, Ido Rosenblum

The Debt Collector ★★★★ 🔞
Drama   1999 · UK · Colour · 105min

As hard-hitting as a kick in the stomach, this gritty Scottish drama is outstanding on all fronts. First-time director Anthony Neilson has crafted a visceral and cathartic tale with virtuoso skill, combining tragedy on a Shakespearean scale with vibrant colour and superb camera control. Billy Connolly stars as a reformed ex-con and now successful sculptor whose violent past comes back to haunt him in the shape of his arresting officer, Ken Stott. Stott takes it upon himself to deal Connolly true retribution for his crimes, and in the process both they and their families suffer severe repercussions. **LH** Violence, sexual threat, swearing. *DVD*

Billy Connolly *Nickie Dryden* • Ken Stott *Gary Keltie* • Francesca Annis *Val Dryden* • Iain Robertson *Flipper* • Annette Crosbie *Lana* • Alastair Galbraith *Colquhoun* ■ *Dir/Scr* Anthony Neilson • *Music* Adrian Johnston • *Cinematographer* Dick Pope

Los Debutantes ★★★ 🔞
Crime thriller   2003 · Chil · Colour · 114min

Director Andrés Waissbluth demonstrates the camera's talent for deception in this simmering thriller. By revealing events from the viewpoint of each of his three main protagonists, Waissbluth withholds the significance of seemingly minor events until we are as deeply embroiled in underworld danger as Néstor Cantillana and Juan Pablo Miranda, the shanty-town brothers who have fallen for Antonella Ríos, the slinky dancer lover of Santiago mobster Alejandro Trejo. Although it doesn't always gel, this is still satisfyingly nasty. **DP** Spanish +subtitles. Sex scenes, drug abuse. *DVD*

Antonella Ríos *Gracia* • Néstor Cantillana *Silvio* • Juan Pablo Miranda *Victor* • Alejandro Trejo *Don Pascual* • Eduardo Barril *Don Marco* • Victor Montero *Marcelo* • Roberto Farías *Danilo* • Anita Alvarado *Solange* ■ *Dir* Andrés Waissbluth • *Scr* Andrés Waissbluth, Julio Rojas

Decadence ★ 🔞
Comedy   1993 · UK/Ger · Colour · 113min

This pretentious film version of his own play is a virtual textbook on how not to make the transition from stage to screen. Stephen Berkoff, who both directs and stars alongside Joan Collins, can't bear to excise a single rhyming couplet, resulting in interminable monologues interspersed with bouts of lame slapstick, plus bizarre cameos. The leads play dual roles from different ends of the social spectrum, but plot comes a poor second to the author's laboured satire on the privileged classes. **NS**

Steven Berkoff *Steve/Les/Helen's "Couturier"* • Joan Collins *Helen/Sybil* • Christopher Biggins *Entourage* • Michael Winner *Entourage* • Marc Sinden *Entourage* ■ *Dir* Steven Berkoff • *Scr* Steven Berkoff, from his play

The Decameron ★★★★ 🔞
Period drama
1970 · It/Fr/W Ger · Colour · 106min

This was the first film in Pier Paolo Pasolini's trilogy based on famous medieval story cycles – *The Canterbury Tales* and *Arabian Nights* being the others. The director himself plays Giotto, seen working on a fresco while around him revolve eight of Boccaccio's bawdy tales of sexual deception, which involve lascivious nuns, a false saint and three brothers who kill their sister's lover. Untrammelled by any Freudian or religious guilt, this episodic movie captures much of the spirit of the original. **RB** Italian +subtitles.

Franco Citti *Ciappelletto* • Ninetto Davoli *Andreuccio of Perugia* • Angela Luce *Peronella* • Patrizia Capparelli *Alibech* • Jovan Jovanovic *Rustico* • Gianni Rizzo *Head friar* • Pier Paolo Pasolini *Giotto* ■ *Dir* Pier Paolo Pasolini • *Scr* Pier Paolo Pasolini, from the stories by Giovanni Boccaccio • *Cinematographer* Tonino Delli Colli • *Art Director* Dante Ferretti

Decameron Nights ★★★
Period adventure   1953 · UK · Colour · 93min

Suave Louis Jourdan plays both yarnspinner Boccaccio and the leads in a trio of stories, framed by a device whereby he and Joan Fontaine flee 14th-century Florence to escape the plague, holing up in her villa. Unsurprisingly, Fontaine co-stars in the three tales as well. The result is diverting and mildly risqué tosh, beautifully photographed in rich Technicolor by talented cameraman Guy Green. Director Hugo Fregonese knows how to get the most out of this kind of flamboyant material. **TS**

Joan Fontaine *Fiametta/Ginevra/Isabella/Bartolomea* • Louis Jourdan *Boccaccio/Paganino/Giulio/Bertrando* • Binnie Barnes *Contessa/Old witch/Nerina* • Godfrey Tearle *Ricciardo/Bernabo* • Joan Collins *Pampinea/Maria* • Mara Lane *Girl in Villa* • George Bernard Messenger • Bert Bernard *Messenger* ■ *Dir* Hugo Fregonese • *Scr* George Oppenheimer, from the stories by Giovanni Boccaccio

Decasia ★★★ 🄤
Experimental movie   2002 · US · BW · 67min

Exploring the fragility of nitrate film stock and the transience of the human endeavours it records, Bill Morrison's experimental feature is both a fascinating study of decay and a visually arresting display of melancholic beauty. Originally commissioned for a multimedia stage show, this moving collage of old film footage occasionally suffers from the relentless drone of Michael Gordon's score. But the manner in which the mottled patches of corrupted celluloid obscure or reveal objects, change the nature and/or pace of the imagery or simply achieve their own abstract patterns, becomes as entrancing as it is entertaining. **DP**

■ *Dir/Scr* Bill Morrison

Deceived ★★★ 🔟5
Psychological thriller 1991 · US · Colour · 103min

Goldie Hawn is happily married to John Heard, only to discover after his accidental death that she knew very little about him. Despite her best efforts, Hawn lacks credibility in the pivotal role, so it's left to the ever-excellent Heard to make the most of what is one of his rare leading roles. Director Damian Harris generates some suspense, but the climax is just plain silly. JF Swearing, some violence. **DVD**

Goldie Hawn *Adrienne Saunders* • John Heard *Jack Saunders* • Ashley Peldon *Mary Saunders* • Robin Bartlett *Charlotte* • Tom Irwin *Harvey Schwartz* • Amy Wright *Evelyn Wade* • Kate Reid *Rosalie* ■ *Dir* Damian Harris • *Scr* Mary Agnes Donoghue, Derek Saunders [Bruce Joel Rubin], from a story by Mary Agnes Donoghue

The Deceivers ★★ 15

Period drama 1988 · UK · Colour · 98min

In the absence of regular partner James Ivory, producer Ismail Merchant has managed to miss both the rousing adventure and the intriguing ideas contained in John Masters's novel of cultism and culture clash. Part of the problem lies with director Nicholas Meyer, who is unsure whether to opt for mini-series glossiness or schlock goriness as a secret cult is linked to a spate of murders that disturb the peace of 1820s India. DP **DVD**

Pierce Brosnan *William Savage* • Saeed Jaffrey *Hussein* • Shashi Kapoor *Chandra Singh* • Helen Michell *Sarah Wilson* • Keith Michell *Colonel Wilson* • David Robb *George Angelsmith* • Tariq Yunus *Feringea* ■ *Dir* Nicholas Meyer • *Scr* Michael Hirst, from the novel by John Masters

December Boys ★★ 12

Coming-of-age drama
2007 · Aus/UK/US/Ger · Colour · 100min

Harry Potter star Daniel Radcliffe proves there's life beyond Hogwarts in this coming-of-age drama set in 1960s Australia. He plays Maps, the eldest of four orphaned boys who are dispatched from their Catholic convent to spend the holidays in a small seaside village. As the summer unfolds, they encounter the quirky local residents and see their long-established friendship slide into rivalry as they compete to be adopted by a childless young couple. This plodding adaptation of Michael Noonan's 1963 novel sees director Rod Hardy prop up the whimsical drama with occasional forays into childhood fantasy involving a gigantic CGI fish and cartwheeling nuns. It's insufferably mawkish and terribly unambitious, yet Radcliffe tackles his central role with impressive sensitivity. JR Sex scenes, nudity. **DVD**

Daniel Radcliffe *Maps* • Lee Cormie *Misty* • Christian Byers *Spark* • James Fraser *Spit* • Jack Thompson *Bandy McAnsh* • Teresa Palmer *Lucy* ■ *Dir* Rod Hardy • *Scr* Marc Rosenberg, from a story by Ronald Kinnoch, from the novel by Michael Noonan

December Bride ★★★ PG

Period drama 1990 · UK · Colour · 84min

This tale of undisclosed paternity from the Emerald Isle is also a careful and sincere study of the problems that have divided the Irish people throughout the 20th century. Saskia Reeves impresses as the maid whose simultaneous affairs with brothers Donal McCann and Ciaran Hinds scandalise the God-fearing members of an isolated farming community. But what elevates this film above the average melodrama is French cinematographer Bruno de Keyzer's brooding views of the austere Northern Ireland coastline and director Thaddeus O'Sullivan's avoidance of sensationalism. DP

Saskia Reeves *Sarah* • Donal McCann *Hamilton Echlin* • Ciaran Hinds *Frank Echlin* • Patrick Malahide *Sorleyson* • Brenda Bruce *Martha* • Michael McKnight *Fergus* • Dervla Kirwan *Young Martha* • Peter Capaldi *Young Sorleyson* • Geoffrey Golden *Andrew Echlin* ■ *Dir* Thaddeus O'Sullivan • *Scr* David Rudkin, from the novel by Sam Hanna Bell

The Decent One ★ 15

Documentary
2014 · Austria/Is · BW and Colour · 96min

It is rare to find a documentary so efficient in nullifying the intrigue of its subject matter, which in this case is the life of Heinrich Himmler, architect of the Nazi's

"Final Solution" and, in his own estimation, a decent, upstanding family man. Vanessa Lapa directs like an uninspiring history teacher, composing the film entirely of archival footage and a newly available cache of letters and personal diaries that are read aloud in a relentless monotone. A wholly misconceived, hopelessly leaden slog. AS In English, German. Distressing scenes.

Tobias Moretti *Heinrich Himmler* • Sophie Rois *Marga Himmler* • Antonia Moretti *Gudrun Himmler* ■ *Dir* Vanessa Lapa • *Scr* Vanessa Lapa, Ori Weisbrod

A Decent Proposal ★★

Mystery thriller 2006 · Can · Colour · 90min

A marriage of convenience is built on dark secrets in this ineffective TV thriller. Jessica Tuck plays the pregnant career woman who weds her boss following her boyfriend's reported death, only to discover that the unscrupulous tycoon may be linked to the tragedy. Tuck's performance makes it hard to empathise with her character's dilemma and the listless pacing and lack of drama don't help matters. SF

Jessica Tuck *Tia McLealand* • Spencer Rochfort *Nick Marsh* • Andrew Airlie *John Bleekham* • Jennifer Spence *Gwen Stathis* • Hrothgar Mathews *Tony Evans* ■ *Dir* Neill Fearnley • *Scr* Debra & Morgan Gendel

Deception ★★★★ PG

Melodrama 1946 · US · BW · 107min

In one of the great "concerto" movies, film composer Eric Wolfgang Korngold's music receives as much of a showcase here as does star Bette Davis, who plays a pianist whose patron is suave composer/conductor Claude Rains. This is splendid stuff, brilliantly orchestrated in both senses, as Davis lies to her husband, refugee cellist Paul Henreid, about her former relationship with Rains. Rains gets the best lines, and delivers them quite superbly, but Davis is at her best in what was to be one of her last great melodramas for Warner Bros. TS

Bette Davis *Christine Radcliffe* • Paul Henreid *Karel Novak* • Claude Rains *Alexander Hollenius* • John Abbott *Bertram Gribble* • Benson Fong *Manservant* • Richard Walsh *Porter* ■ *Dir* Irving Rapper • *Scr* John Collier, Joseph Than, from the play *Jealousy (Monsieur Lamberthier)* by Louis Verneuil

Deception ★★★ 15

Thriller 2000 · US · Colour · 99min

This entertaining thriller benefits greatly from a few fun plot twists and a colourful cast. Ben Affleck is an ex-con who assumes the identity of his dead cellmate in order to hook up with the guy's gorgeous pen-pal girlfriend (Charlize Theron). They share a few passionate moments before her nasty brother, sleazy Gary Sinise, coerces Affleck into robbing a casino. Sinise plays his role with just the right touch of menace and humour, but Affleck is out of his league as an action hero. ST Violence, swearing, sex scenes. **DVD**

Ben Affleck *Rudy Duncan* • Charlize Theron *Ashley* • Gary Sinise *Gabriel* • Clarence Williams III *Merlin* • Dennis Farina *Jack Bangs* • James Frain *Nick* • Donal Logue *Pug* ■ *Dir* John Frankenheimer • *Scr* Ehren Kruger

Deception ★★ 15

Erotic thriller 2008 · US · Colour · 102min

Hugh Jackman and Ewan McGregor really should know better than to be associated with this lacklustre so-called thriller. McGregor plays a workaholic auditor who is enticed by urbane lawyer Jackman into the secret world of "The List", an up-market club where all his sexual fantasies can be realised. Naturally, there's a catch, and McGregor finds himself blackmailed into siphoning off funds from the company he is auditing. The film desperately tries to persuade you that it is twisty and turny, but the viewer is always ten minutes ahead of any supposed plot revelation. Despite its star power and surface gloss, the only deception this plodding, predictable film practises is self-deception. DA **DVD** **Blu-ray**

Hugh Jackman *Wyatt Bose* • Ewan McGregor *Jonathan McQuarry* • Michelle Williams *"S"* • Lisa Gay Hamilton *Detective Russo* • Maggie Q *Tina* • Natasha Henstridge *Wall Street analyst* ■ *Dir* Marcel Langenegger • *Scr* Mark Bomback

Deception ★★★ 15

Crime thriller 2013 · It · Colour · 125min

Cinema Paradiso director Guiseppe Tornatore goes the Hitchcockian romantic thriller route with this classy mystery set in Europe's big stakes art world. Geoffrey Rush is splendid as an eccentric auctioneer who is asked to evaluate a priceless antique collection - and ends up falling in love with the secretive seller (Sylvia Hoeks). Tornatore overdoes the symbolism somewhat, but this is still a reasonably absorbing confection of neuroses, glamour and hustle in the old school tradition of *Charade* and *Vertigo*. AJ Violence, swearing, a sex scene, nudity. **DVD**

Geoffrey Rush *Virgil Oldman* • Sylvia Hoeks *Claire Ibbetson* • Jim Sturgess *Robert* • Donald Sutherland *Billy Whistler* • Philip Jackson *Fred* ■ *Dir/Scr* Giuseppe Tornatore

Decision at Sundown ★★ PG

Western 1957 · US · Colour · 77min

Western star Randolph Scott hit a winning streak when he teamed up with director Budd Boetticher and writer Burt Kennedy on such gems as *The Tall T* and *Comanche Station*. This is visually less impressive, set in town rather than out in the wide-open spaces, and the plot - about Scott's personal feud with local bigwig John Carroll - is rather verbose. AE

Randolph Scott *Bart Allison* • John Carroll *Tate Kimbrough* • Karen Steele *Lucy Summerton* • Valerie French *Ruby James* • Noah Beery [Noah Beery Jr] *Sam* • John Archer *Dr Storrow* • Andrew Duggan *Sheriff Swede Hansen* ■ *Dir* Budd Boetticher • *Scr* Charles Lang, from a story by Vernon L Fluharty

Decision before Dawn ★★★ PG

Spy drama 1951 · US · BW · 117min

This is a long and distinctly sombre spy drama, with Oskar Werner playing a German PoW who agrees to spy against his own people, apparently motivated by the belief that he can help shorten the war and save lives. The Americans send him back home loaded up with espionage tricks, giving rise to a moral conundrum: is he a traitor, a hero or simply a martyr-in-waiting? The most impressive aspect of the film is the location shooting in a bombed-out postwar Germany. AT **DVD**

Richard Basehart *Lt Rennick* • Gary Merrill *Colonel Devlin* • Oskar Werner *Happy* • Hildegarde Neff *Hilde* • Dominique Blanchar *Monique* • OE Hasse *Oberst Von Ecker* • Wilfried Seyfert [Wilfried Seyferth] *SS Man Scholtz* • Hans Christian Blech *Tiger* ■ *Dir* Anatole Litvak • *Scr* Peter Viertel, from the novel *Call It Treason* by George Howe • *Cinematographer* Frank Planer [Franz Planer]

Deck the Halls ★★ PG

Seasonal comedy 2006 · US · Colour · 89min

There's little Christmas cheer on offer in this mean-spirited and largely unfunny sleigh ride through seasonal cliché. Uptight yuletide fanatic Matthew Broderick finds his Mr Christmas title challenged by new happy-go-lucky neighbour Danny DeVito, whose ambition is to decorate his house with so many fairy lights it can be seen via satellite. Awkward pacing, wayward comic timing and jarring changes in tone don't help the short-supply laughs. But the colourful winter wonderland settings and adept performances keep boredom at bay - especially from *Wicked* Broadway star Kristin Chenoweth as DeVito's spouse. AJ Some swearing. **DVD**

Danny DeVito *Buddy Hall* • Matthew Broderick *Steve Finch* • Kristin Davis *Kelly Finch* • Kristin Chenoweth *Tia Hall* • Alia Shawkat *Madison Finch* • Dylan Blue *Carter Finch* ■ *Dir* John Whitesell • *Scr* Chris Ord, Matt Corman, Don Rhymer

The Decks Ran Red ★★

Crime 1958 · US · BW · 84min

James Mason plays the captain of a rusty old freighter whose crew unscrupulous deckhand Broderick Crawford is planning to murder so he can scuttle the ship and claim the salvage money. Mason, however, foils the plan with a little help from the cook's wife (beautiful Dorothy Dandridge). Director Andrew Stone maintains the tension here, but the film is sunk by his banal dialogue. RB

James Mason *Capt Edwin Rumill* • Dorothy Dandridge *Mahia* • Broderick Crawford *Henry Scott* • Stuart Whitman *Leroy Martin* • Katharine Bard *Joan Rumill* • Jack Kruschen *Alex Cole* • John Gallaudet *"Bull" Pringle* ■ *Dir/Scr* Andrew Stone [Andrew L Stone]

Decline and Fall... of a Birdwatcher ★

Satire 1968 · UK · Colour · 123min

Ex-documentary director John Krish has a stab at Evelyn Waugh's partly autobiographical 1928 work, *Decline and Fall*. It was a vainglorious attempt, as the joys of this hilarious comedy of upper-class manners lie solely on the page; neither Krish nor his trio of scriptwriters have the satirical wit or irreverent verve to translate them to the screen. They're not helped by Robin Phillips's ghastly performance. DP

Robin Phillips *Paul Pennyfeather* • Donald Wolfit *Dr Fagan* • Genevieve Page *Margot Beste-Chetwynde* • Robert Harris *Prendergast* • Leo McKern *Captain Grimes* • Colin Blakely *Philbrick* • Rodney Bewes *Arthur Potts* • Donald Sinden *Prison governor* ■ *Dir* John Krish • *Scr* Ivan Foxwell, Alan Hackney, Hugh Whitemore, from the novel *Decline and Fall* by Evelyn Waugh

The Decline of the American Empire ★★★★ 18

Comedy drama 1986 · Can · Colour · 97min

Nominated for a best foreign film Oscar, this sophisticated satire on the sexual mores of a group of ageing intellectuals is superbly structured by Québecois director Denys Arcand. Having shown us the quartet of history tutors and their four female friends separately expressing their forthright views on physical pleasure, he then brings them together for a dinner party at which bourgeois discretion is soon forgotten amid the seepage of guilty secrets. As revealing as the bristling dialogue, flashbacks punctuate the action to shade in the characters. DP French +subtitles. **DVD**

Pierre Curzi *Pierre* • Rémy Girard *Remy* • Yves Jacques *Claude* • Daniel Briere *Alain* • Dominique Michel *Dominique* • Louise Portal *Diane* • Dorothée Berryman *Louise* • Genevieve Rioux *Danielle* • Gabriel Arcand *Mario* ■ *Dir/Scr* Denys Arcand

The Decline of Western Civilization ★★★★

Music documentary 1980 · US · Colour · 100min

Penelope Spheeris's cult documentary takes an unflinching and non-judgemental look at the Los Angeles punk scene at the fag end of the 1970s. She blends live performances from anonymous bands such as Circle Jerks, Black Flag and Fear (who were a particular favourite of John Belushi) with revealing contributions from managers, fans and the group members themselves. While most use the camera as a mirror for their preening, some are surprisingly articulate about their lifestyle - the downside of which is illustrated in the interview with Darby Crash, lead singer of the Germs, who ended up on a mortuary slab before the film was even released. This is the first in a trilogy of rock documentaries made by Spheeris that, viewed today, seem like valuable cultural documents. RS **DVD** **Blu-ray**

■ *Dir/Scr* Penelope Spheeris

D

The Decline of Western Civilization Part II: the Metal Years ★★★ 18
Music documentary · 1988 · US · Colour · 89min

A great companion piece to *This Is Spinal Tap*, Penelope Spheeris's documentary follow-up to her revealing record of the Los Angeles punk scene at the end of the 1970s exposes the less than blemish-free world of Heavy Metal music. MTV-style concert footage is mixed with unplugged, warts-and-all interviews with the likes of Kiss, Ozzy Osbourne and Alice Cooper; Guns N' Roses declined to appear. Unsurprisingly, common themes broached are groupies, booze and drugs: Steve Tyler of Aerosmith freely admits "millions went up my nose". Utterly compelling, insightful and often hilarious. RS *DVD* *Blu-ray*

■ *Dir* Penelope Spheeris

The Decline of Western Civilization Part III ★★★ 15
Music documentary · 1997 · US · Colour · 82min

The searing final chapter in Penelope Spheeris's trilogy of music documentaries, this focuses not on the rock personalities, but on the disenfranchised Hollywood waifs who make up the dwindling audience of Los Angeles's contemporary punk/metal scene. Grimmer in tone than its two predecessors, it maps out a generation of no-hopers with a bleak vision of the future. Despite Spheeris's exploitative interview techniques, this deservedly won the Freedom of Expression award at Robert Redford's Sundance film festival. RS *DVD* *Blu-ray*

■ *Dir* Penelope Spheeris

Decoding Annie Parker ★★ 15
Drama based on a true story
2013 · US · Colour · 95min

Samantha Morton stars as dogged real-life cancer sufferer Annie Parker. After the demise of several of her loved ones, Parker refuses to believe that diet or environmental factors are causing their disease. In a parallel story, Helen Hunt plays a geneticist researching the link between genetics and breast cancer. Eventually, the two women's stories intertwine, albeit not in a satisfying way, as Hunt phones in her performance, leaving Morton to carry the film. But this is still a poignant independent film for breast cancer sufferers and those who love them. KK Swearing, sex scenes, nudity.

Samantha Morton *Annie Parker* · Helen Hunt *Mary-Claire King* · Aaron Paul *Paul* · Alice Eve *Louise* · Maggie Grace *Sarah* ■ *Dir* Steven Bernstein · *Scr* Steven & Adam Bernstein, Michael Moss

Deconstructing Harry ★★★ 18
Comedy drama · 1997 · US · Colour · 91min

Woody Allen's tumultuous private life seems to spill sourly into this bad-taste story about a novelist, Harry Block (Allen), whose friends and relatives are used as thinly-disguised characters in his books, despite screams of protest from those he exploits. Block is suffering from a lack of inspiration for his latest book and is as out of focus with life as actor Robin Williams is – literally – out of focus in one of the film's funniest ideas. Rarely has Allen's use of a movie as a psychiatrist's couch been quite so evident. TH Swearing, sex scenes. *DVD*

Caroline Aaron *Doris* · Woody Allen *Harry Block* · Kirstie Alley *Joan* · Bob Balaban *Richard* · Richard Benjamin *Ken* · Eric Bogosian *Burt* · Billy Crystal *Larry* · Judy Davis *Lucy* · Hazelle Goodman *Cookie* · Mariel Hemingway *Beth Kramer* · Amy Irving *Jane* · Julie Kavner *Grace* · Julia Louis-Dreyfus *Leslie* · Demi Moore *Helen* · Elisabeth Shue *Fay* · Stanley Tucci *Paul Epstein* · Robin Williams *Mel* ■ *Dir/Scr* Woody Allen

The Decoy Bride ★★ 12
Romantic comedy · 2011 · UK · Colour · 85min

A Hollywood star (Alice Eve) attempts to marry her writer fiancé (David Tennant) away from the prying eyes of the world's press in this less-than-original romantic comedy. But when the couple escape to a remote Scottish island and still find paparazzi in pursuit, it's up to Kelly Macdonald's unlucky-in-love local girl to help them out by acting as a marital stand-in. Director Sheree Folkson's feature debut owes much to *It Happened One Night* and the Ealing comedies, but without doing justice to either. Sadly the script is just too ordinary and predictable to raise anything but a slight smile. JA *DVD*

Kelly Macdonald *Katie* · David Tennant *James* · Alice Eve *Lara Tyler* · Dylan Moran *Charley* · Michael Urie *Steve Korbitz* · Sally Phillips *Emma* ■ *Dir* Sheree Folkson · *Scr* Sally Phillips, Neil Jaworski, from a story by Phillips

The Deep ★★★ 15
Adventure · 1977 · US · Colour · 119min

Jacqueline Bisset in a wet T-shirt, Donna Summer's titular disco hit and *Jaws* author Peter Benchley co-scripting from his own novel were enough to make this soggy sea saga of rival divers after shipwrecked drugs a major box-office hit. With 40 per cent of his action taking place underwater in creepy depths, director Peter Yates doesn't have to do much to keep tension on an even keel. But slick photography aside, the silly script and two-dimensional characterisations succeed in sinking plausibility. AJ Violence, swearing, brief nudity. *DVD*

Robert Shaw *Romer Treece* · Jacqueline Bisset *Gail Berke* · Nick Nolte *David Sanders* · Louis Gossett [Louis Gossett Jr] *Henri Cloche* · Eli Wallach *Adam Coffin* · Robert Tessier *Kevin* ■ *Dir* Peter Yates · *Scr* Peter Benchley, Tracey Keenan Wynn, from the novel by Peter Benchley

The Deep ★★★★ 12
Drama based on a true story
2012 · Ice/Nor · Colour · 92min

This unbelievable true story from Iceland dramatises the 1984 incident of a fishing trawler that capsized in a freak accident and deposited its crew in the North Atlantic swell. One man, Gulli, managed to swim ashore, surviving longer in the water than was thought possible. Gulli is believably played by burly Olafur Darri Olafsson, and director Baltasar Kormakur re-creates the confounding circumstances effectively. He takes a thoughtful, even quizzical approach to depicting what it must be like to be touched by the miraculous. TJ Icelandic +subtitles. Swearing. *DVD*

Olafur Darri Olafsson *Gulli* · Johann G Johannsson *Palli* · Bjorn Thors *Hannes* ■ *Dir* Baltasar Kormakur · *Scr* Baltasar Kormakur, Jon Atli Jonasson

Deep Blue ★★★★
Documentary · 2003 · UK/Ger · Colour · 90min

Filmed over three years off the Maldives, Azores, Caymans, Bermuda and Antarctica, this off-shoot of David Attenborough's BBC television series *The Blue Planet* provides a visually striking and occasionally harrowing insight into the staggering diversity of marine life. A sense of ever-present danger pervades the footage of dolphins, penguins, seals and baby whales. But it's the inhabitants of the seemingly more tranquil world 5000 metres below the surface that catch the eye and it's a shame that Michael Gambon's commentary couldn't have been more informative, especially as some of the more ethereal ocean-bed species had never been seen before, let alone photographed. DP *DVD*

Michael Gambon *Narrator* ■ *Dir/Scr* Alastair Fothergill, Andy Byatt

The Deep Blue Sea ★★★
Drama · 1955 · UK · Colour · 98min

Beautiful, middle-aged Vivien Leigh leaves her husband, a judge, and the comfort of her home to live in drab digs and continue an affair with Kenneth More, an attractive younger man. An ex-RAF pilot, Moore is unable to adjust to postwar life, and he is also losing interest in Leigh, which leads her to a suicidal crisis. Terence Rattigan's famous and oft-revived play is a sharply observed and emotionally searing period piece. All the more pity, then, that the film fails to capture the emotion of the original. RK

Vivien Leigh *Hester* · Kenneth More *Freddie Page* · Eric Portman *Miller* · Emlyn Williams *Sir William Collyer* · Moira Lister *Dawn Maxwell* · Alec McCowen *Ken Thompson* · Dandy Nichols *Mrs Elton* · Arthur Hill *Jackie Jackson* · Miriam Karlin *Barmaid* · Sidney James *Man in street* ■ *Dir* Anatole Litvak · *Scr* Terence Rattigan, from his play

Deep Blue Sea ★★★ 15
Science-fiction action thriller
1999 · US · Colour · 100min

Three genetically mutated, super-intelligent sharks stalk the marooned members of an underwater research facility. A B-movie cast struggles gamely with the hopelessly mundane dialogue, but director Renny Harlin's film remains afloat through sheer nerve, technical prowess and some spectacular shock moments. AJ Violence, swearing. *DVD* *Blu-ray*

Saffron Burrows *Dr Susan McAlester* · Thomas Jane *Carter Blake* · LL Cool J *Sherman "Preacher" Dudley* · Jacqueline McKenzie *Janice Higgins* · Michael Rapaport *Tom "Scog" Scoggins* · Stellan Skarsgård *Jim Whitlock* · Samuel L Jackson *Russell Franklin* ■ *Dir* Renny Harlin · *Scr* Duncan Kennedy, Donna Powers, Wayne Powers

The Deep Blue Sea ★★★★ 12
Romantic drama · 2011 · UK · Colour · 94min

In this beautifully acted relationship drama, an adaptation of Terence Rattigan's 1952 play, Rachel Weisz is stunning form as the suicidal middle-class wife who drops out of a loveless but dependable marriage, only to find that life with her new, much younger lover (Tom Hiddleston) isn't really enough for her. Fans of director Terence Davies will see his sure, steady signature in its gold-burnished visions of peeling paint, wartime bomb shelters and and jaunty pub singalongs, but the fragmented first 20 minutes may put off some of Rattigan's admirers. DW Swearing. *DVD* *Blu-ray*

Rachel Weisz *Hester Collyer* · Tom Hiddleston *Freddie Page* · Simon Russell Beale *Sir William Collyer* ■ *Dir* Terence Davies · *Scr* Terence Davies, from the play by Terence Rattigan

Deep Cover ★★★★ 18
Crime thriller · 1992 · US · Colour · 103min

One of the most underrated cop thrillers of the 1990s, this is an exhilarating and intelligent examination of blurred lines between those who break the law and those who enforce it. A suitably intense Laurence (still being billed as Larry) Fishburne is the undercover detective who sets out to unravel a major drugs ring by forming a curious alliance with shady, neurotic lawyer Jeff Goldblum. It's their relationship that forms the heart of the movie and both deliver superb performances. However, director Bill Duke doesn't stint on the action sequences and delivers some stunningly choreographed slices of screen mayhem. JF *DVD*

Larry Fishburne [Laurence Fishburne] *Russell Stevens Jr/John Q Hull* · Jeff Goldblum *David Jason* · Victoria Dillard *Betty McCutcheon* · Charles Martin Smith *Carver* · Sydney Lassick *Gopher* · Clarence Williams III *Taft* ■ *Dir* Bill Duke · *Scr* Henry Bean, Michael Tolkin, from Tolkin's story

Deep Crimson ★★★ 18
Crime drama
1996 · Mex/Fr/Sp · Colour · 109min

Dedicated to Leonard Kastle, who covered the same true-life case in *The Honeymoon Killers*, this is notable for both the genuine passion of its grotesque protagonists and the muted savagery of their crimes. Posing as brother and sister, corpulent nurse Regina Orozco and temperamental gigolo Daniel Gimenez Cacho prey on lonely heart widows with an insouciance that is hideous in its pitilessness. DP Spanish +subtitles. Violence, swearing, sex scenes.

Daniel Gimenez Cacho *Nicolas Estrella* · Regina Orozco *Coral Fabre* · Marisa Paredes *Irene Gallardo* · Veronica Merchant *Rebeca Sampedro* · Julieta Egurrola *Juanita Norton* · Rosa Furman *Mrs Silberman* ■ *Dir* Arturo Ripstein · *Scr* Paz Alicia Garciadiego

Deep End ★★★★ 15
Drama · 1970 · US/W Ger · Colour · 91min

This is one of the strangest movies to come out of the Swinging Sixties. Directed by Polish émigré Jerzy Skolimowski, it's set in the grottily dank Chelsea public baths. John Moulder-Brown – a callow, haunted-looking 15-year-old – and Jane Asher are the employees, who swap changing rooms so he can please the ladies (including bosomy football fanatic Diana Dors) and she can pleasure the gents. The pool provides the film's central metaphor and some bizarre, shocking things happen in it. AT Nudity. *DVD*

Jane Asher *Susan* · John Moulder-Brown *Mike* · Karl Michael Vogler *Swimming instructor* · Christopher Sandford *Fiancé* · Diana Dors *Lady client* ■ *Dir* Jerzy Skolimowski · *Scr* Jerzy Skolimowski, Jerzy Gruza, Boleslaw Sulik

The Deep End ★★★ 15
Drama · 2001 · US · Colour · 96min

In spite of her association with the British avant-garde (mainly thanks to her collaboration with the late Derek Jarman), Tilda Swinton is particularly convincing as a white-collar American housewife under duress. While her husband is away on naval duties, she finds it's actually her son who's in deep water as he dabbles in underage sex with an older man. Her attempts to intervene result in disaster; Swinton ends up with blood on her hands and Goran Visnjic's blackmailer at her door. Swinton's icy demeanour adds to this chilly thriller, which attacks the steely veneer of American middle-class life with a sledgehammer. LH *DVD*

Tilda Swinton *Margaret Hall* · Goran Visnjic *Alek Spera* · Jonathan Tucker *Beau Hall* · Peter Donat *Jack Hall* · Josh Lucas *Darby Reese* ■ *Dir* Scott McGehee, David Siegel · *Scr* Scott McGehee, David Siegel, from the novel *The Blank Wall* by Elizabeth Sanxay Holding

The Deep End of the Ocean ★★ 12
Drama · 1999 · US · Colour · 108min

Michelle Pfeiffer plays the mother whose life is turned upside down after her toddler son goes missing, never, it seems, to be seen again. How she and her family (including older son Jonathan Jackson and husband Treat Williams) cope or, more to the point, *don't* cope is really the stuff of TV movies, and there's little here to raise this above that status. Whoopi Goldberg, as the cop in charge of the case, adds little interest. JB Swearing. *DVD*

Michelle Pfeiffer *Beth Cappadora* · Treat Williams *Pat Cappadora* · Jonathan Jackson *Vincent Cappadora, aged 16* · John Kapelos *George Karras* · Ryan Merriman *Sam* · Whoopi Goldberg *Candy Bliss* ■ *Dir* Ulu Grosbard · *Scr* Stephen Schiff, from the novel by Jacquelyn Mitchard

Deep Impact ★★★★ 12
Science-fiction drama
1998 · US · Colour · 116min

A huge comet is on a collision course with Earth in director Mimi Leder's disaster movie, which gains a certain amount of credibility by highlighting the human side of the impending catastrophe. The frightening scenario focuses on TV reporter Téa Leoni, who stumbles upon the story, and astronaut Robert Duvall, who leads a mission to intercept the threat in space. Using her trademark documentary-style realism and frenzied camerawork, Leder gives this a gripping immediacy. AJ Swearing. *DVD*

Robert Duvall *Spurgeon Tanner* · Téa Leoni *Jenny Lerner* · Elijah Wood *Leo Biederman* · Vanessa Redgrave *Robin Lerner* · Maximilian Schell *Jason Lerner* · Morgan Freeman *President Tom Beck* · James Cromwell *Alan Rittenhouse* ■ *Dir* Mimi Leder · *Scr* Michael Tolkin, Bruce Joel Rubin

Deep in My Heart ★★★ U

Musical biography   1954 · US · Colour · 126min

Underrated in its day, this is the fictionalised biopic of composer Sigmund Romberg, of *The Student Prince* and *Desert Song* fame, featuring a cast of MGM contract stars performing magnificently. Most of it was directed by Stanley Donen, though ace choreographers Robert Alton and Jack Donohue helped out, and the whole is held together by the bravura performance of José Ferrer as Romberg. Good fun all round, and quite moving, too. TS *DVD*

José Ferrer *Sigmund Romberg* • Merle Oberon *Dorothy Donnelly* • Helen Traubel *Anna Mueller* • Doe Avedon *Lillian Romberg* • Walter Pidgeon *JJ Shubert* • Paul Henreid *Florenz Ziegfeld* • Tamara Toumanova *Gaby Deslys* • Paul Stewart *Bert Towsend* • Rosemary Clooney • Gene Kelly • Fred Kelly • Jane Powell • Vic Damone • Ann Miller • Cyd Charisse • Howard Keel • Tony Martin (1) *Tony Martin* ■ *Dir* Stanley Donen • *Scr* Leonard Spigelgass, from the biography by Elliott Arnold

Deep Red ★★★ 18

Murder mystery   1975 · It · Colour · 120min

Playing sinister games with doubles and mirrors, Dario Argento draws on a wealth of movie references to give this stylised chiller its unnerving atmosphere. What's most striking, however, is his incessant use of a fluid camera that fills each meticulously constructed sequence with unease. David Hemmings becomes obsessed with tracking down a killer, only for his classical musician to soon find himself being pursued as both suspect and target. Argento's delight in eccentric props and angular angles, together with his reliance on pop psychology, help make this a fascinating odyssey into psychosis, despite its flaws. DP Italian +subtitles. *DVD* *Blu*

David Hemmings *Marcus Daly* • Daria Nicolodi *Gianna* • Gabriele Lavia *Carlo* • Clara Calamai *Marta* • Macha Méril *Helga* ■ *Dir* Dario Argento • *Scr* Dario Argento, Bernardino Zapponi

Deep Rising ★★★ 15

Futuristic action horror
1998 · US · Colour · 101min

This dopey sea-monster movie from Stephen Sommers is a tepid horror tale in which a hi-tech pleasure cruiser on its maiden voyage is overrun by modern-day pirates, then attacked by a multi-tentacled, Hydra-like creature. The film navigates an ocean of hilarious monster-movie clichés and derivative special-effects sequences. AJ Violence, swearing. *DVD*

Treat Williams *John Finnegan* • Famke Janssen *Trillian* • Anthony Heald *Simon Canton* • Kevin J O'Connor *Joey Pantucci* • Wes Studi *Hanover* • Derrick O'Connor *Captain* • Jason Flemyng *Mulligan* • Cliff Curtis *Mamooli* ■ *Dir/Scr* Stephen Sommers

The Deep Six ★★ U

Second World War drama
1958 · US · Colour · 108min

When Alan Ladd turned producer/star through his Jaguar company just after his career peaked with *Shane*, he stuck to formula film-making with old cronies. *The Deep Six* is a wartime drama set on a cruiser in the Pacific, the main complication being whether Ladd's Quaker beliefs will get in the way of his duties as the ship's gunnery officer. The issue is never properly resolved, but the film is slickly made and quite watchable. AE

Alan Ladd *Alec Austen* • Dianne Foster *Susan Cahill* • William Bendix *Frenchy Shapiro* • Keenan Wynn *Lt Cdr Edge* • James Whitmore *Cdr Meredith* • Efrem Zimbalist Jr *Lt Blanchard* • Jeanette Nolan *Mrs Austen* ■ *Dir* Rudolph Maté • *Scr* John Twist, Harry Brown, Martin Rackin, from the novel by Martin Dibner

Deep Throat ★★★ 18

Erotic comedy   1972 · US · Colour · 50min

The most infamous, commercially successful and influential hard-core movie ever produced made Linda Lovelace an overnight sensation and director Gerard Damiano the leading light of fashionable "porno chic". Ground-breaking because it made watching porn acceptable, the film itself is badly made and full of stupid humour and dull stretches. It's important to note that Lovelace is not a sexual object being used by male abusers, but a take-charge, independent woman pursuing pleasure for her own needs. AJ *DVD*

Linda Lovelace • Harry Reems • Dolly Sharp • Carol Connors • William Love • Ted Street ■ *Dir/Scr* Gerard Damiano

Deep Valley ★★★

Drama   1947 · US · BW · 103min

This is one of director Jean Negulesco's better movies, with Ida Lupino as a parent-dominated farm girl who shelters a convict (played by Dane Clark) after he escapes from a chain gang. Clark's scenes with Lupino are extremely touching, in a screenplay which boasts added dialogue by William Faulkner. There's a fine Max Steiner score, and a special bonus comes from some attractive location shooting. TS

Ida Lupino *Libby* • Dane Clark *Barry* • Wayne Morris *Barker* • Fay Bainter *Mrs Saul* • Henry Hull *Mr Saul* • Willard Robertson *Sheriff* • Rory Mallinson *Foreman* • Jack Mower *Supervisor* ■ *Dir* Jean Negulesco • *Scr* Salka Viertel, Stephen Morehouse Avery, from the novel by Dan Totheroh

Deep Water ★★★★ PG

Documentary
2006 · UK · Colour and BW · 89min

This compelling account of Donald Crowhurst's ill-fated attempt to win the 1968 round-the-world yacht race is told with unobtrusive skill by Louise Osmond and Jerry Rothwell. A self-effacing amateur, Crowhurst captured the public's imagination when he embarked on the voyage in a trimaran of his own design, *Teignmouth Electron*. However, they knew nothing of his bid to cheat his fellow competitors (and avoid bankruptcy) by lingering in the Atlantic after the *Electron* became unseaworthy, hoping to dash for Britain and receive a hero's welcome. The interviewees (his family and rivals) are largely sympathetic to Crowhurst's plight, but the real revelations come from his logbooks, tape recordings and home-movie footage. DP Some swearing. *DVD*

Simon Russell Beale *Donald Crowhurst* • Jean Badin *Bernard Moitessier* • Tilda Swinton *Narrator* • Donald Crowhurst • Robin Knox-Johnston ■ *Dir* Louise Osmond, Jerry Rothwell

DeepStar Six ★ 15

Science-fiction horror
1989 · US · Colour · 94min

An experimental underwater colony disturbs a prehistoric sea creature in this shallow combination of *Alien* and *Jaws*. Directed by Sean S Cunningham, this soggy farrago sinks fast in an ocean of technical mumbo jumbo, murky model work and outrageously bad acting. AJ *DVD*

Taurean Blacque *Laidlaw* • Nancy Everhard *Joyce Collins* • Greg Evigan *McBride* • Miguel Ferrer *Snyder* • Nia Peeples *Scarpelli* • Matt McCoy *Richardson* • Cindy Pickett *Diane Norris* • Marius Weyers *Van Gelder* ■ *Dir* Sean S Cunningham • *Scr* Lewis Abernathy, Geof Miller, from a story by Lewis Abernathy

The Deer Hunter ★★★★★ 18

War drama   1978 · US/UK · Colour · 176min

This multi-Oscar winner from Michael Cimino remains one of the finest and most controversial movies about the Vietnam War. Starring Robert De Niro, Christopher Walken, John Savage and John Cazale, this is a modern version of the Second World War drama *The Best Years of Our Lives*, showing how men and America itself cope

with the horrors of war and its aftermath. With its mournful guitar theme, this intense drama lingers long in the memory. AT Violence, swearing. *DVD* *Blu*

Robert De Niro *Michael Vronsky* • John Cazale *Stan, "Stosh"* • John Savage *Steven* • Christopher Walken *Nick* • Meryl Streep *Linda* • George Dzundza *John* • Chuck Aspegren *Axel* • Shirley Stoler *Steven's mother* • Rutanya Alda *Angela* ■ *Dir* Michael Cimino • *Scr* Deric Washburn, from a story by Michael Cimino, Deric Washburn, Louis Garfinkle, Quinn K Redeker • *Cinematographer* Vilmos Zsigmond • *Editor* Peter Zinner • *Music* Stanley Myers

The Deerslayer ★★ U

Historical adventure   1957 · US · Colour · 76min

This adaptation of James Fenimore Cooper's classic adventure has Lex Barker as the hunter who teams up with his Mohican blood brother, Chingachgook (Carlos Rivas), to rescue a trapper and his two daughters from nasty Indians. A dead duck as far as suspense is concerned, back projection and indoor sets make this seem as artificial as the acting. TH

Lex Barker *The Deerslayer* • Rita Moreno *Hetty* • Forrest Tucker *Harry Marsh* • Cathy O'Donnell *Judith* • Jay C Flippen *Old Tom Hutter* • Carlos Rivas *Chingachgook* • John Halloran *Old warrior* ■ *Dir* Kurt Neumann • *Scr* Carroll Young, Kurt Neumann, from the novel by James Fenimore Cooper

Def by Temptation ★★ 18

Horror   1990 · US · Colour · 94min

Producer, director and writer James Bond III (really!) also stars as a redneck divinity student, in New York for a final fling before entering the ministry. He soon falls prey to Cynthia Bond, a demon who cruises uptown singles bars. Daft special effects and formula blood-letting are jazzed up with perverse sexual twists and a great soundtrack. AJ *DVD*

James Bond III *Joel* • Cynthia Bond *Temptress* • Kadeem Hardison *K* • Bill Nunn *Dougy* • Minnie Gentry *Grandma* • Samuel L Jackson *Minister Garth* • Melba Moore *Madam Sonya* ■ *Dir/Scr* James Bond III • *Cinematographer* Ernest R Dickerson

Def-Con 4 ★★★ 15

Futuristic action adventure
1984 · US · Colour · 84min

This post-apocalyptic action film doesn't have the budget to provide too many futuristic thrills, yet what it lacks in hardware trappings it more than makes up for in imaginative staging. While radiation-ravaged America is overrun by sadistic punks and militant cannibals, this low-rent *Mad Max* remains a watchable enough potboiler before it degenerates into a routine cat-and-mouse chase. AJ Violence. *DVD*

Lenore Zann *JJ* • Maury Chaykin *Vinny* • Kate Lynch *Jordan* • Kevin King *Gideon Hayes* • John Walsch *Walker* • Tim Choate *Howe* • Jeff Pustil *Lacey* ■ *Dir/Scr* Paul Donovan

The Defector ★★

Spy drama   1966 · W Ger/Fr · Colour · 68min

This muddled European spy drama was the last film of the great Montgomery Clift, here looking tired and displaying little of the talent that illuminated *From Here to Eternity* and *A Place in the Sun*. A hackneyed Cold War drama, which was heavily truncated for its British release, it also stars Clift's loyal friend Roddy McDowall, who was on board to guide him through his barbiturate and alcohol-induced haze, and ends up giving the better performance. TS

Montgomery Clift *Professor James Bower* • Hardy Kruger *Peter Heinzman* • Roddy McDowall *CIA Agent Adams* • Macha Méril *Frieda Hoffman* • Christine Delaroche *Ingrid* • David Opatoshu *Orlovsky* • Hannes Messemer *Dr Saltzer* • Jean-Luc Godard *Orlovsky's friend* ■ *Dir* Raoul Lévy • *Scr* Robert Guenette, Lewis Gannet, Peter Francke, Raoul Lévy, from the novel *The Spy* by Paul Thomas

Defence of the Realm ★★★★ PG

Thriller   1985 · UK · Colour · 91min

The role of the sozzled veteran reporter who for once finds himself involved in a meaningful story is brought wonderfully to life by Denholm Elliott, here trying to clear the name of an MP who's forced to resign after a sex scandal. Gabriel Byrne, as Elliott's ambitious young colleague, is less effective, but the film has plenty of tension and co-star Greta Scacchi proves a worthy accomplice. This unsettling movie proves the truth of the maxim that *all* governments are up to no good. A remake from BBC Films is currently in production. TH *DVD*

Gabriel Byrne *Nick Mullen* • Greta Scacchi *Nina Beckman* • Denholm Elliott *Vernon Bayliss* • Ian Bannen *Dennis Markham* • Fulton Mackay *Victor Kingsbrook* • Bill Paterson *Jack Macleod* • David Calder *Harry Champion* • Robbie Coltrane *Leo McAskey* ■ *Dir* David Drury • *Scr* Martin Stellman

The Defender ★★ 18

Martial arts action drama
1994 · HK · Colour · 88min

Jet Li's Hong Kong movies tend to be all-action affairs showcasing his extraordinary martial arts skills. However, director Corey Yuen decides to throw some romantic melodrama and a couple of moments of ill-advised comic relief into this story. As a result, Li often looks uncomfortable as the impassive elite Red Army officer detailed to protect murder witness Christy Chung. DP Cantonese, Mandarin dubbed. Violence, swearing. *DVD*

Jet Li *John Chang* • Christy Chung *Michelle Yeung* • Ngai Sing *Wong* • Kent Cheng *Charlie Leung* • Leung Wing-Chung *Ken* ■ *Dir* Corey Yuen • *Scr* Gordon Chan

Defending Our Kids: the Julie Posey Story ★★

Drama based on a true story
2003 · US · Colour · 100min

Plot holes and overacting dilute the impact of this thought-provoking real-life tale about a housewife who collaborates with police to help catch internet paedophiles. Former *Ghostbusters* actress Annie Potts exaggerates every emotion in the title role, a stylistic miscalculation that makes the often clichéd yet obviously heartfelt storyline seem even more contrived. It's left to voiceover statistics at the end to pack the most punch. SF Some violence, swearing.

Annie Potts *Julie Posey* • Michael O'Keefe *Mike Harris* • Carl Marotte *Jerry Posey* • Janet Kidder *Cassandra Harris* • Ksenia Solo *Kristyn Posey* ■ *Dir* Joanna Kerns • *Scr* Eric Tuchman

Defending Your Life ★★ PG

Comedy drama   1991 · US · Colour · 106min

Director/star Albert Brooks takes a ham-fisted run at judgement after demise, one of the most abused movie concepts since the glorious *A Matter of Life and Death*, with heaven portrayed as a large shopping mall complete with shuttle trucks and revolving doors. This is an "ordinary Joe" version of the tale, and Brooks's ensuing "trial" for entry through the non-pearly gates is an example of movie-making at its most tedious. SH Swearing.

Albert Brooks *Daniel Miller* • Meryl Streep *Julia* • Rip Torn *Bob Diamond* • Lee Grant *Lena Foster* • Buck Henry *Dick Stanley* ■ *Dir/Scr* Albert Brooks

Defendor ★★ 15

Crime comedy drama
2009 · Can/US/UK · Colour · 97min

A low-key comedy drama, this has much in common with *Kick-Ass* (ordinary citizen dons home-made costume to clear up crime), but here Woody Harrelson's good-hearted crime fighter is no lovestruck adolescent, but an emotionally damaged adult whose clottish attempts to cleanse the streets bring agony rather than ecstasy. Harrelson is a perfect fit for the role; gleefully utilising an oddball arsenal of weapons (marbles, lime juice, wasps) against a crime kingpin. However, a lull in the pacing hampers things somewhat, despite the best efforts of a decent cast. JA Violence, swearing, drug abuse.

Woody Harrelson *Arthur Poppington/Defendor* • Elias Koteas *Sgt Chuck Dooney* • Michael Kelly *Paul Carter* • Sandra Oh *Dr Ellen Park* • Kat Dennings *Katerina Debrofkowitz* • Clark Johnson *Captain Roger Fairbanks* ■ *Dir/Scr* Peter Stebbings

Defenseless ★★★ 18
Thriller 1991 · US · Colour · 99min

Barbara Hershey stars as a lawyer who is drawn into a murderous conspiracy when her former lover and client (JT Walsh) is found dead. With Sam Shepard, Mary Beth Hurt and Sheree North offering strong support, the playing of the classy cast can't be faulted, and director Martin Campbell skilfully sustains the suspense throughout. JF Violence, swearing, brief nudity.

Barbara Hershey *TK Katwuller* • Sam Shepard *George Beutel* • Mary Beth Hurt *Ellie Seldes* • JT Walsh *Steven Seldes* • Kellie Overbey *Janna Seldes* • Jay O Sanders *Bull Dozer* ■ *Dir* Martin Campbell • *Scr* James Hicks, from the story by Jeff Burkhart, James Hicks

Defiance ★★★ 15
Action drama 1979 · US · Colour · 102min

Jan-Michael Vincent is pitted against a vicious New York street gang in this weirdly engaging, if violent action drama. No prizes for guessing who tames who, though. The old-fashioned "man against the world" plot gains extra interest from the strong supporting cast, gritty dialogue and John Flynn's atmospheric direction. AJ Violence, swearing.

Jan-Michael Vincent *Tommy Gamble* • Theresa Saldana *Marsha Bernstein* • Fernando Lopez *"Kid"* • Danny Aiello *Carmine* • Art Carney *Abe* • Santos Morales *Paolo* • Rudy Ramos *Angel Cruz* ■ *Dir* John Flynn • *Scr* Thomas Michael Donnelly, from a story by Thomas Michael Donnelly, Mark Tulin

Defiance ★★ 15
Fact-based Second World War drama 2008 · US · Colour · 131min

Daniel Craig leads a Jewish resistance movement against the Nazis in this worthy Second World War drama from *Blood Diamond* director Edward Zwick. Set in Belarus in 1941, the story follows the Bielski brothers - Tuvia (Craig), Zus (Liev Schreiber) and Asael (Jamie Bell) - as they flee the German invaders and local collaborators following the murder of their parents. Their forest refuge eventually becomes a launch pad for attacks on the enemy and daring rescue missions. As the group's leader, a moody Craig clashes with Schreiber (a forceful screen presence here), but it's Jamie Bell who is most effective, conveying budding maturity in the face of constant danger. AJ English, Russian, German +subtitles. Violence, swearing. DVD Blu

Daniel Craig *Tuvia Bielski* • Liev Schreiber *Zus Bielski* • Jamie Bell *Asael Bielski* • Alexa Davalos *Lilka Tictin* • Allan Corduner *Shimon Haretz* • Mark Feuerstein *Isaac Malbin* • Jodhi May *Tamara Skidelsky* ■ *Dir* Edward Zwick • *Scr* Edward Zwick, Clayton Frohman, from the non-fiction book *Defiance: the Bielski Partisans* by Nechama Tec

The Defiant Ones ★★★★ U
Crime drama 1958 · US · BW · 96min

This still powerful drama was, in its day, a superb cinematic strike for racial equality. Two convicts, one black, one white, find themselves shackled together in their escape from a chain gang in the Deep South. Tony Curtis plays the bigoted "Joker" Jackson, and Sidney Poitier leapt to stardom as the angry, articulate Noah Cullen. This is one of underrated Stanley Kramer's finest movies, and the Oscar-winning story and screenplay were co-written by the blacklisted Nedrick Young. TS DVD

Tony Curtis *John "Joker" Jackson* • Sidney Poitier *Noah Cullen* • Theodore Bikel *Sheriff Max Muller* • Charles McGraw *Captain Frank Gibbons* • Lon Chaney Jr *Big Sam* • King Donovan *Solly* •

Claude Akins *Mac* ■ *Dir* Stanley Kramer • *Scr* Nathan E Douglas [Nedrick Young], Harold Jacob Smith

Déficit ★★ 15
Drama 2007 · Mex · Colour · 79min

Gael García Bernal makes a competent directorial debut with this low-key drama, and also stars as Cristobal, a rich kid who takes advantage of his parents being away to have a party in their plush home in Mexico. But his sister (Camila Sodi) has had the same idea, and she's joined by her own set of hippy pals. Sadly, it's hard to warm to any of the characters, and when night descends and the drink and drugs kick in, it all inevitably ends up a bit of an emotional mess. Devandra Banhart's bewitching theme is perhaps what lingers most, but Bernal still demonstrates that he has a future behind the camera as well as in front of it. JH Spanish +subtitles. DVD

Gael García Bernal *Cristobal* • Camila Sodi *Elisa* • Tenoch Huerta Mejía *Adan* • Luz Cipriota *Dolores* ■ *Dir* Gael García Bernal • *Scr* Kyzza Terrazas

Definitely, Maybe ★★ 12
Romantic comedy 2008 · US/UK · Colour · 107min

Ryan Reynolds needs every ounce of his considerable charm in this long-winded and lethargic romantic comedy. Reynolds plays a New York advertising executive who, on the eve of his divorce, is asked by his precocious ten-year-old (*Little Miss Sunshine's* Abigail Breslin) to tell all about his love life before his marriage. So, in one of those scenarios beloved of Hollywood movies, he decides to spill the beans about his three serious girlfriends, but alters their names in the process. We have to guess which girl dad actually married: was it girl-next-door Emily (Elizabeth Banks); buddy April (Isla Fisher); or free spirit Summer (Rachel Weisz)? As the seemingly interminable series of flashbacks and flash-forwards unfolds, you may find it hard to care. DA Swearing, sexual references. DVD Blu

Ryan Reynolds *Will Hayes* • Elizabeth Banks (2) *Emily* • Rachel Weisz *Summer Hartley* • Isla Fisher *April* • Kevin Kline *Hampton Roth* • Abigail Breslin *Maya Hayes* ■ *Dir/Scr* Adam Brooks

Le Défroqué ★★★★
Religious drama 1953 · Fr · BW · 93min

Having already won best actor at Venice for his performance in *Monsieur Vincent* (1947), Pierre Fresnay plays a very different kind of priest in this cogent if melodramatic treatise on faith and the nature of goodness, which earned Léo Joannon the best director prize at Berlin. Abandoning his vocation after his experiences in a Nazi prison camp, Fresnay is guided back towards Catholicism by Pierre Trabaud, who was inspired to his calling by his friend's essential humanity. It's an intense and often traumatic experience, heightened by Fresnay's honest performance. DP French +subtitles.

Pierre Fresnay *Maurice Morand* • Pierre Trabaud *Gérard Lacassagne* • Nicole Stéphane *Catherine Grandpré* • Marcelle Géniat *Mme Morand* • Léo Joannon *Canon Jousseaume* • Jacques Fabbri *Soldier* ■ *Dir* Léo Joannon • *Scr* Léo Joannon, Denys de La Patellière

Déjà Vu ★ 15
Supernatural thriller 1984 · UK · Colour · 90min

This is an apt title for a movie sporting the age-old soul transference plot, but with nothing tweaked to make it unique or remotely interesting. The ghost of a prima ballerina is upsetting writer Nigel Terry and his wife Jaclyn Smith. When tarot card reader Shelley Winters regresses Terry back to the 1930s, it turns out that he was a choreographer in love with the dancer, and that Smith is her reincarnation. Hokey and unconvincing. AJ

Jaclyn Smith *Maggie Rogers/Brooke Ashley* • Nigel Terry *Gregory Thomas/Michael Richardson* • Claire Bloom *Eleanor Harvey* • Shelley Winters *Olga Nabokov* • Richard Kay *William Tanner in 1935* • Frank Gatliff *William Tanner in 1984* •

Michael Ladkin *Willmer* ■ *Dir* Anthony Richmond [Tonino Ricci] • *Scr* Ezra D Rappaport, Anthony Richmond [Tonino Ricci], Arnold Schmidt, Joane A Gil, from the novel *Always* by Trevor Meldal-Johnson

Déjà Vu ★★ 15
Romance 1997 · US/UK · Colour · 117min

Henry Jaglom's study of love perhaps owes more to his own sudden bliss than to his success in shaping some recalcitrant material into a screenplay. Since he met and married Victoria Foyt, Jaglom admits to toning down the autobiographical content of his films, sadly depriving them of the idiosyncracies that made them so fascinating. In this love letter to Foyt, Stephen Dillane takes the Jaglom part of the man whose world is turned upside down by an encounter with a woman he feels he's known forever. DP Swearing.

Stephen Dillane *Sean Elias* • Victoria Foyt *Dana Howard* • Vanessa Redgrave *Skelly* • Glynis Barber *Claire Stoner* • Michael Brandon *Alex* • Vernon Dobtcheff *Konstantine* ■ *Dir* Henry Jaglom • *Scr* Henry Jaglom, Victoria Foyt

Déjà Vu ★★★ 12
Science-fiction action thriller 2006 · US · Colour · 121min

Denzel Washington reteams with his *Crimson Tide* and *Man on Fire* director Tony Scott for this sci-fi thriller about manipulating the past to save lives in the future. Washington plays a federal agent investigating a bombing, who is given access to a top-secret government team experimenting with the link between the present and the past. He believes he can use their discoveries to prevent the crime from happening. This is a gloriously dumb thriller that teases with some serious themes, but Scott is far more interested in crash, bang, wallop pyrotechnics - in particular, a freeway car chase that occurs simultaneously in the past and the present - so doesn't quite follow them through. JR Some violence. DVD Blu

Denzel Washington *Doug Carlin* • Paula Patton *Claire Kuchever* • Val Kilmer *Agent Pryzwarra* • James Caviezel [Jim Caviezel] *Carroll Oerstadt* • Adam Goldberg *Denny* • Elden Henson *Gunnars* • Erika Alexander *Shanti* • Bruce Greenwood *Jack McCready* ■ *Dir* Tony Scott • *Scr* Bill Marsilii, Terry Rossio • *Cinematographer* Paul Cameron

Delicacy ★★★★ 12
Romantic comedy drama 2011 · Fr · Colour · 106min

This quietly affecting French comedy drama stars Audrey Tautou as Nathalie, a young widow who throws herself into her work following the untimely death of her perfect partner, only to cause a sensation by throwing herself at an unlikely colleague. Author David Foenkinos adapts his own bestseller for the screen along with his brother Stéphane and, as co-directors, their sensitivity to the characters shines through. That's helped in no small measure by Tautou's nuanced performance and the many little touches that speak of Nathalie's gradual healing. Poignant and charming, this romance will strike a chord with anyone who has loved and lost, and its optimistic message lingers fondly in the memory. JH French, Swedish +subtitles. Swearing. DVD Blu

Audrey Tautou *Nathalie* • François Damiens *Markus* • Bruno Todeschini *Charles* • Mélanie Bernier *Chloé* • Joséphine de Meaux *Sophie* • Pio Marmaï *François* ■ *Dir* David Foenkinos, Stéphane Foenkinos • *Scr* David Foenkinos, from his novel *La Délicatesse*

A Delicate Balance ★★★ PG
Drama 1973 · US/UK · Colour · 128min

Despite an extraordinary cast, this version of Edward Albee's Pulitzer Prize-winning play - directed by Tony Richardson for TV's American Film Theatre - is a stiff narrative about a neurotic Connecticut family that goes to war with itself. Katharine Hepburn, Paul Scofield, Lee Remick, Joseph Cotten and Betsy Blair pull out the dramatic stops, but the result remains defiantly stagebound. TH DVD

Katharine Hepburn *Agnes* • Paul Scofield *Tobias* • Lee Remick *Julia* • Kate Reid *Claire* • Joseph Cotten *Harry* • Betsy Blair *Edna* ■ *Dir* Tony Richardson • *Scr* Edward Albee, from his play

The Delicate Delinquent ★★★ U
Comedy 1957 · US · BW · 96min

Although mooted as a Dean Martin and Jerry Lewis vehicle, the strain was beginning to show in *Pardners* (1956). So Lewis went solo for the first time, with Darren McGavin in the cop role earmarked for Martin. As the titular "teenager", Lewis's mix of schmaltz and slapstick ensured he maintained his public popularity. Today both subject and title have lost their resonance, but in the days of *The Blackboard Jungle* these antics passed for satire. TS DVD

Jerry Lewis *Sidney Pythias* • Darren McGavin *Mike Damon* • Martha Hyer *Martha Henshaw* • Robert Ivers *Monk* • Horace McMahon *Captain Riley* • Richard Bakalyan *Artie* • Joseph Corey *Harry* • Mary Webster *Patricia* ■ *Dir/Scr* Don McGuire

Delicatessen ★★★★ 15
Black comedy fantasy 1990 · Fr · Colour · 95min

Jean-Pierre Jeunet and Marc Caro made their feature debut with this gloriously surreal comedy, set in a run-down city of the future. Rarely can a film have had so many disparate influences. In addition to the visual inspiration of French comic books and the eccentricity of Heath Robinson, there are references to the poetic realism of Marcel Carné and René Clair, as well as the darker visions of David Lynch and Terry Gilliam. With society on the verge of collapse, butcher Jean-Claude Dreyfus prospers by killing his employees and selling their flesh as meat to his hungry tenants. The gallery of grotesques participates in some of the funniest set pieces of recent years. DP French +subtitles. Violence, nudity. DVD Blu

Dominique Pinon *Louison* • Marie-Laure Dougnac *Julie Clapet* • Jean-Claude Dreyfus *The Butcher* • Karin Viard *Mademoiselle Plusse* • Ticky Holgado *Monsieur Tapioca* • Anne-Marie Pisani *Madame Tapioca* • Jacques Mathou *Roger Cube* • Rufus *Robert Cube* • Jean-François Perrier *Monsieur Interligator* • Sylvie Laguna *Madame Interligator* ■ *Dir/Scr* Jean-Pierre Jeunet, Marc Caro

Delicious ★★★ U
Musical romantic comedy 1931 · US · BW · 102min

Silent superstars Charles Farrell and Janet Gaynor teamed for the ninth time in this romantic comedy directed by David Butler, which marked the first occasion that George and Ira Gershwin composed directly for the screen. The musical highlight is undoubtedly the extract from George's *New York Rhapsody*, but the fantasy sequence in which Gaynor's Scottish immigrant is welcomed by the Statue of Liberty and Swedish valet El Brendel's parodic love song are good fun. DP

Janet Gaynor *Heather Gordon* • Charles Farrell (1) *Larry Beaumont* • El Brendel *Jansen* • Raul Roulien *Sascha* • Lawrence O'Sullivan *O'Flynn* • Manya Roberti *Olga* • Virginia Cherrill *Diana* • Olive Tell *Mrs Van Bergh* • Mischa Auer *Mischa* ■ *Dir* David Butler • *Scr* Guy Bolton, Sonya Levien, from a story by Guy Bolton

Delicious ★★★ 15
Romantic drama 2013 · UK · Colour · 82min

There may be a whiff of *Amélie* about Tammy Riley-Smith's feature debut, but it rapidly becomes clear that *Delicious* is not your standard romance. Louise Brealey stars as Stella, who has an unspecified eating disorder, with Nico Rogner as budding chef Jacques, who moves into the flat above. Sheila Hancock supplies the light relief as the pair's internet-dating neighbour. The film may be slight and a little predictable but it does pack a surprising punch - largely thanks to Brealey's anguished turn in the lead. CW Swearing, sexual references.

U SUITABLE FOR ALL   Uc SUITABLE ESPECIALLY FOR YOUNG CHILDREN (DVD ONLY)   PG PARENTAL GUIDANCE   12A UNDER 12s TO BE ACCOMPANIED (CINEMA ONLY)

Louise Brealey *Stella* • Nico Rogner *Jacques* • Sheila Hancock *Patti* • Adrian Scarborough *Victor* • Nicholas Rowe *Adolf* • Finty Williams *Sully* ■ *Dir/Scr* Tammy Riley-Smith

The Delinquents ★
Drama   1957 · US · BW · 72min

Robert Altman's first feature, directed in his beloved home town of Kansas City, is a fascinating, if cheesy relic of its era. Tom Laughlin plays a good boy who gets mixed up in a street gang with his girlfriend (Rosemary Howard), whose parents think she is not old enough to go steady. Julia Lee sings *The Dirty Rock Boogie* – and sadly, that's as good as it gets. **TH**

Tom Laughlin *Scotty* • Peter Miller (1) *Cholly* • Richard Bakalyan *Eddy* • Rosemary Howard *Janice* • Helene Hawley *Mrs White* • Leonard Belove *Mr White* • Lotus Corelli *Mrs Wilson* • James Lantz *Mr Wilson* • Christine Altman *Sissy* ■ *Dir/Scr* Robert Altman

The Delinquents ★★ 15
Romantic drama   1989 · Aus · Colour · 100min

At the height of her soap opera/pop singer fame, *Neighbours* star Kylie Minogue made her feature film debut in this passable tale of teenage torment set in 1950s Australia. Minogue and Charlie Schlatter co-star as the misunderstood young lovers ignoring adult condemnation in director Chris Thomson's tear-jerker, based on the novel by Criena Rohan, tennis player Pat Cash's aunt. **AJ**

Kylie Minogue *Lola Lovell* • Charlie Schlatter *Brownie Hansen* • Desirée Smith *Mavis* • Todd Boyce *Lyle* • Angela Punch McGregor *Mrs Lovell* • Lynette Curran *Mrs Hansen* ■ *Dir* Chris Thomson • *Scr* Mac Gudgeon, Clayton Frohman, Dorothy Hewitt, from a novel by Criena Rohan

Delirious ★★ PG
Comedy   1991 · US · Colour · 91min

Soap opera scriptwriter John Candy is knocked unconscious, wakes up inside his own fictional TV serial *Beyond Our Dreams*, and watches in comic horror as his own romantic plotlines backfire. Written by former James Bond screenwriter Tom Mankiewicz, this tediously strained fiasco hinges on lovelorn Candy's magical ability to manipulate lathered events by typing them out seconds before they happen. A game cast is wasted in this painfully unfunny affair. **AJ** 📀

John Candy *Jack Gable* • Emma Samms *Rachel Hedison/Laura* • Mariel Hemingway *Janet Dubois/Louise* • Raymond Burr *Carter Hedison* • Dylan Baker *Blake Hedison* • Charles Rocket *Ty Hedison* • David Rasche *Dr Paul Kirkland/Dennis* • Jerry Orbach *Lou Sherwood* • Robert Wagner *Jack Gates* ■ *Dir* Tom Mankiewicz • *Scr* Fred Freeman, Lawrence J Cohen

Deliver Us from Evil ★★★ 15
Documentary   2006 · US · Colour · 98min

This sobering, Oscar-nominated documentary chronicles one Irish-American priest's persistent abuse of children in California during the 1970s and the Catholic Church's complicity in the cover-up of his crimes. Film-maker Amy Berg's approach to serial abuser Oliver O'Grady and the Church superiors who opted to move him from parish to parish rather than remove him is non-hysterical and non-judgemental – O'Grady's "confession", in which he details his shocking crimes in a matter-of-fact fashion, makes for compelling if uncomfortable viewing. **DA** 📀

Oliver O'Grady • Adam • Jeff Anderson (2) • Pope Benedict XVI • Monsignor Cain ■ *Dir/Scr* Amy Berg

Deliver Us from Evil ★★★ 15
Action horror   2014 · US · Colour · 113min

South Bronx detective Eric Bana (playing real-life cop-turned-demonologist Ralph Sarchie) teams up with rebel Jesuit priest Edgar Ramirez to halt a series of possessions striking New York in this supernatural police procedural inspired by Sarchie's writing. Early on, there's too much creeping around in dark spaces leading to standard issue scares, but then the unsettling atmosphere really kicks in when the primal force starts terrorising Bana's family. **AJ** Violence, swearing. 📀 🔵

Eric Bana *Ralph Sarchie* • Edgar Ramirez *Mendoza* • Olivia Munn *Jen* • Chris Coy *Jimmy* • Dorian Missick *Gordon* ■ *Dir* Scott Derrickson • *Scr* Scott Derrickson, Paul Harris Boardman, from the non-fiction books *Beware the Night* by Ralph Sarchie and *Deliver Us from Evil: A New York City Cop Investigates the Supernatural* by Sarchie and Lisa Collier Cool

Deliverance ★★★★★ 18
Thriller   1972 · US · Colour · 104min

Though best, if most uncomfortably, remembered for townie Ned Beatty's shocking encounter with the hillbillies in the Appalachian mountains, John Boorman's provocative thriller is about more than shock tactics. It charts the gradual erosion of "civilisation" by the elements, as four men on a back-to-nature canoe holiday, led by the macho Burt Reynolds, meet with disaster and destiny. It works as a piece of straightforward suspense cinema, with an uneasy atmosphere conjured from the start by the iconic "duelling banjos" scene, but it also resonates as a metaphor about masculinity under threat. **AC** Swearing, violence. 📀

Jon Voight *Ed Gentry* • Burt Reynolds *Lewis Medlock* • Ned Beatty *Bobby Trippe* • Ronny Cox *Drew Ballinger* • Bill McKinney *Mountain man* • Herbert "Cowboy" Coward *Toothless man* • James Dickey *Sheriff Bullard* ■ *Dir* John Boorman • *Scr* James Dickey, from his novel • *Cinematographer* Vilmos Zsigmond • *Editor* Tom Priestley

The Delivery ★★★ 18
Crime thriller   1998 · Neth/Bel · Colour · 95min

While Roel Reiné's flashy thriller has neither the gloss of *Nikita* nor the innovation of *Run Lola Run*, it still makes for energetic entertainment. The pulsing sex scenes and the explosive finale are disingenuously derivative of generic Hollywood fodder. But it's the unpredictability of the plotting that gives small-time losers Freddy Douglas and Fedja van Huet's Ecstasy-smuggling trip from the Netherlands to Spain its edge. **DP** Dutch, French, Spanish +subtitles. 📀

Fedja Van Huet *Alfred* • Freddy Douglas *Guy* • Aurélie Meriel *Loulou* • Esmée de la Bretonière *Anna* • Jonathan Harvey *Marc* ■ *Dir* Roel Reiné • *Scr* David Hilton, from a story by Roel Reiné

Delivery Man ★★ 12
Comedy   2013 · US · Colour · 100min

A sperm donor's past catches up with him in director Ken Scott's Hollywood remake of his own serio-comic Canadian movie, *Starbuck*. That was the nickname David (Vince Vaughn) used during his frequent visits to a sperm bank in his cash-strapped youth, but now he finds he's the biological father of 533 children, 142 of whom have joined in a lawsuit to reveal his identity. The results are mildly diverting, but outright belly laughs are in short supply. It's warm-hearted, certainly, but ultimately undone by a would-be feelgood premise that makes less sense the more you think about it. **TJ** Swearing, sexual references. 📀 🔵

Vince Vaughn *David Wozniak* • Cobie Smulders *Emma* • Chris Pratt *Brett* • Britt Robertson [Brittany Robertson] *Kristen* • Dave Patten *Adam* ■ *Dir* Ken Scott (2) • *Scr* Ken Scott, from the 2011 film *Starbuck* by Scott, Martin Petit

De-Lovely ★★ PG
Musical biographical drama   2004 · US/Lux · Colour and BW · 119min

This biopic opens with ailing composer Cole Porter (an admirable Kevin Kline) being transported to a theatre where a stage musical based on his life is apparently in rehearsal. Flashbacks then move the action from the expat scene in Paris to Broadway and Hollywood, and the homosexual Porter's complicated marriage to wealthy socialite Linda Lee (an adequate Ashley Judd). A pretentious folly, but it looks fabulous. **AJ**

Kevin Kline *Cole Porter* • Ashley Judd *Linda Porter* • Kevin McNally *Gerald Murphy* • Allan Corduner *Monty Woolley* • Sandra Nelson *Sara Murphy* • Keith Allen *Irving Berlin* • James Wilby *Edward Thomas* • John Barrowman *Night and*

Day performer • Kevin McKidd *Bobby Reed* • Peter Polycarpou *Louis B Mayer* • Jonathan Pryce *Gabe* ■ *Dir* Irwin Winkler • *Scr* Jay Cocks

The Delta Factor ★
Adventure   1970 · US · Colour · 91min

Mickey Spillane himself backed this adaptation of one of his lesser-known novels, but Christopher George is a poor man's James Bond as an adventurer recruited by the CIA to head an undercover mission. Stingy on the action, this would-be international drama is more confusing than intriguing, while a ridiculous subplot about an imprisoned scientist seems tacked on. **RS**

Christopher George *Morgan* • Yvette Mimieux *Kim Stacy* • Diane McBain *Lisa Gordot* • Ralph Taeger *Art Keefer* • Yvonne De Carlo *Valerie* • Sherri Spillane *Rosa* ■ *Dir* Tay Garnett • *Scr* Tay Garnett, Raoul Walsh, from the novel by Mickey Spillane

The Delta Force ★★ 15
Action adventure   1986 · US · Colour · 123min

Middle-Eastern terrorists menace a planeload of Hollywood has-beens in an exploitative version of the actual 1985 skyjacking of a TWA flight in Athens. The surprisingly accurate first half supplies some swift-paced tension before low-rent action hero Chuck Norris arrives on the scene, riding a rocket-armed motorcycle and destroying all credibility along with the baddies. **AJ** 📀 🔵

Chuck Norris *Major Scott McCoy* • Lee Marvin *Colonel Nick Alexander* • Martin Balsam *Ben Kaplan* • Joey Bishop *Harry Goldman* • Robert Forster *Abdul* • Lainie Kazan *Sylvia Goldman* • George Kennedy *Father O'Malley* • Hanna Schygulla *Ingrid* • Susan Strasberg *Debra Levine* • Bo Svenson *Captain Campbell* • Robert Vaughn (1) *General Woolbridge* • Shelley Winters *Edie Kaplan* ■ *Dir* Menahem Golan • *Scr* Menahem Golan, James Bruner

Delta Force 2 ★ 18
Action adventure   1990 · US · Colour · 105min

At least the original had Lee Marvin in the cast; for this clumsy sequel we're left with just stone-face Chuck Norris, whose neck muscles do most of the acting. Where the original explored the theme of political terrorism, the follow-up has Norris leading his marines against the drug cartels of Colombia. A second sequel, without Norris, followed in 1991. **RS** 📀

Chuck Norris *Colonel Scott McCoy* • Billy Drago *Ramon Cota* • John P Ryan *General Taylor* • Richard Jaeckel *John Page* • Begona Plaza *Quinquina* • Paul Perri *Major Bobby Chavez* • Hector Mercado *Miguel* • Mark Margolis *General Olmedo* ■ *Dir* Aaron Norris • *Scr* Lee Reynolds, from characters by James Bruner, Menahem Golan

Delta of Venus ★★ 18
Erotic drama   1995 · Fr/US · Colour · 94min

Soft-core king Zalman King is only interested in the salacious element in Anaïs Nin's oeuvre, so the result here is a beautifully packaged but stunningly dull tale set in 1940s Paris, punctuated by pop promo-style sex scenes. Audie England plays the writer who discovers a profitable sideline in writing rude stories. The performers look good but struggle to bring even a touch of credibility to their roles. **JF** Swearing, sex scenes, drug abuse, nudity. 📀

Audie England *Elena* • Costas Mandylor *Lawrence* • Eric Da Silva *Marcel* • Marek Vasut *Luc* • Emma Louise Moore *Ariel* ■ *Dir* Zalman King • *Scr* Elisa Rothstein, Patricia Louisiana Knop, from the novel by Anaïs Nin

Delta Pi ★ 18
Comedy   1985 · US · Colour · 84min

Possibly the only feature-length film ever devoted to the noble sport of mud wrestling, this sploshed on to the UK market as *Mugsy's Girls*. The plot focuses on a group of female students who take to the mucky ring in a bid to save their sorority. Among those getting dirty are Laura Branigan, a one-hit American rock wonder in the late 1980s and – more mind-

bogglingly – veteran Oscar-winning actress Ruth Gordon. Unspeakably bad. **JF**

Ruth Gordon *Mugsy* • Eddie Deezen *Lane* • James Marcel *Shawn* • Steve Brodie *Jack Enoff* • Laura Branigan *Monica* ■ *Dir/Scr* Kevin Brodie

Deluge ★★★
Disaster movie   1933 · US · BW · 68min

Long believed lost, director Felix E Feist's feature debut was rediscovered in 1987 and immediately hailed as one of Hollywood's earliest "disaster" movies. It combines special effects work with footage of an actual Californian earthquake to depict the tidal wave that engulfs the Eastern seaboard and leaves Sidney Blackmer to romance Peggy Shannon in the belief that his wife and family have perished. **DP**

Peggy Shannon *Claire Arlington* • Lois Wilson *Helen Webster* • Sidney Blackmer *Martin Webster* • Matt Moore *Tom* • Fred Kohler *Jephson* • Ralf Harolde *Norwood* • Edward Van Sloan *Prof Carlyle* • Samuel Hinds [Samuel S Hinds] *Chief prosecutor* ■ *Dir* Felix E Feist [Felix Feist] • *Scr* John Goodrich, Warren B Duff [Warren Duff], from the novel *Deluge; a Romance* by S Fowler Wright

Delusions of Grandeur ★★★
Period comedy   1971 · Fr · Colour · 108min

Gérard Oury casts restraint aside in this bawdy lampoon. Louis De Funès gleefully overplays every scene as the jilted noble seeking revenge on the King of Spain by arranging for his wife to commit adultery with valet Yves Montand, who bears a striking resemblance to the monarch's cousin. Beautifully shot by Henri Decaë and lavishly designed by Georges Wakhevitch, this is still something of an acquired taste. **DP** French dubbed.

Yves Montand *Blaze* • Louis De Funès *Salluste* • Alberto de Mendoza *King* • Karin Schubert *Queen* • Gabriele Tinti *Cesar* • Alice Sapritch *Dona Juna* • Don Jaime De Mora *Priego* ■ *Dir* Gérard Oury • *Scr* Gerard Oury, Marcel Jullian, Daniele Thompson, from the play *Ruy Blas* by Victor Hugo

Dementia 13 ★★★ 15
Horror   1963 · US · BW · 74min

A series of axe murders marks the anniversary of a little girl's drowning at an eerie Irish castle. This is a passable horror whodunnit, directed by Francis Ford Coppola, aged 24, on a $22,000 budget. The future leading light of Hollywood convinced Ireland's prestigious Abbey Players to appear for minimum wages, begged William Campbell and Patrick Magee to star and used the same sets as the Roger Corman production he was assisting on. Those sets give an atmospheric patina to the proceedings, despite numerous continuity errors and poor production values. A seminal minor classic. **AJ** 📀

William Campbell *Richard Haloran* • Luana Anders *Louise Haloran* • Bart Patton *Billy Haloran* • Mary Mitchel *Kane* • Patrick Magee *Justin Caleb* • Eithne Dunn *Lady Haloran* • Peter Read *John Haloran* • Karl Schanzer *Simon* ■ *Dir/Scr* Francis Ford Coppola

Demetrius and the Gladiators ★★★ PG
Epic   1954 · US · Colour · 96min

In this sequel to *The Robe*, Victor Mature – the custodian of Christ's bloodstained piece of homespun – tries to keep it from falling into the clutches of Caligula. Forced to become a gladiator, Mature's antics in the arena arouse the passion of Messalina (Susan Hayward), the wife of stuttering Claudius (Barry Jones), and antagonise Caligula, played by the deliriously camp Jay Robinson. The result is a juicy excursion into ancient Rome that lacks the oppressive religiosity of the first film. **AT** 📀

Victor Mature *Demetrius* • Susan Hayward *Messalina* • Michael Rennie *Peter* • Debra Paget *Lucia* • Anne Bancroft *Paula* • Jay Robinson *Caligula* • Barry Jones *Claudius* • Ernest Borgnine *Strabo* ■ *Dir* Delmer Daves • *Scr* Philip Dunne, from characters by Lloyd C Douglas

The Demi-Paradise ★★★ U
Second World War drama
1943 · UK · BW · 114min

In this wartime propaganda piece from director Anthony Asquith, Laurence Olivier stars as a heavily accented Russian visitor who comes to England and finds a country stuffed to the brim with national stereotypes. In his wisdom, however, he manages to see beyond the peculiarities and, after falling in love with Penelope Dudley Ward, appreciates England for what it really is. This being wartime, and him being the inventor of a new type of ship's propeller, it's all jolly timely and actually quite charming. TS

Laurence Olivier *Ivan Dimitrevitch Kouzenetsoff* · Penelope Dudley Ward *Ann Tisdall* · Marjorie Fielding *Mrs Tisdall* · Margaret Rutherford *Rowena Ventnor* · Felix Aylmer *Mr Runalow* · Edie Martin *Aunt Winnie* · Joyce Grenfell *Mrs Pawson* · Wilfrid Hyde White *Waiter* ■ *Dir* Anthony Asquith · *Scr* Anatole de Grunwald

Demolition ★★ 15
Romantic drama
2015 · US · Colour · 100min

Jake Gyllenhaal earns no sympathy here as an emotionally stunted investment banker, left reeling but unable to show it by the death of his wife. Grieving father-in-law Chris Cooper is rightly outraged by Gyllenhaal's odd behaviour, which includes fixating on Naomi Watts. Director Jean-Marc Vallée (*Dallas Buyers Club*) loses the character in a jumble of quirks, and as a result this just doesn't hang together. SP Swearing.

Jake Gyllenhaal *Davis Mitchell* · Naomi Watts *Karen Moreno* · Chris Cooper *Phil* · Polly Draper *Margot* ■ *Dir* Jean-Marc Vallée · *Scr* Bryan Sipe

Demolition Man ★★★★ 15
Science-fiction thriller
1993 · US · Colour · 110min

Sylvester Stallone wisely keeps his tongue stuck firmly in his cheek in this slick, futuristic thriller. He plays a tough cop whose unconventional methods land him in a cryogenic prison. Decades later, he is defrosted to hunt down an old sparring partner, the spectacularly psychopathic Wesley Snipes, who has escaped from his deep frozen state and is creating havoc in the now crime-free Los Angeles (renamed San Angeles). The writers have a lot of fun sending up modern-day political correctness, while director Marco Brambilla delivers the goods when it comes to the action set pieces. JF Swearing, violence.
DVD BL

Sylvester Stallone *John Spartan* · Wesley Snipes *Simon Phoenix* · Sandra Bullock *Lenina Huxley* · Nigel Hawthorne *Dr Raymond Cocteau* · Benjamin Bratt *Alfredo Garcia* · Bob Gunton *Chief George Earle* · Glenn Shadix *Associate Bob* · Denis Leary *Edgar Friendly* ■ *Dir* Marco Brambilla · *Scr* Daniel Waters, Robert Reneau, Peter M Lenkov, from a story by Lenkov, Reneau

Demon House ★ 18
Horror
1997 · US · Colour · 81min

The second sequel to *Night of the Demons* reverts back to the gory stupidity of the cheap original rather than the imaginatively delirious outrage of its immediate predecessor. The floating demon Angela (played once more by Amelia Kinkade) returns to annihilate another group of dumb teenagers who hide out in her ancestral home. Gratuitous nudity, derivative violence and amateurish acting condemn this to the bottom of the barrel. AJ DVD

Amelia Kinkade *Angela* · Kris Holdenreid *Vince* · Gregory Calpakis *Nick* · Stephanie Bauder *Holly* · Patricia Rodriguez *Abbie* · Larry Day *Larry* ■ *Dir* Jimmy Kaufman [Jim Kaufman] · *Scr* Kevin S Tenney

Demon Seed ★★★★ 15
Science-fiction horror
1977 · US · Colour · 90min

This literate sci-fi take on *Rosemary's Baby* is as weird, provocative and compelling as you would expect from Donald Cammell, the co-director of *Performance*. Julie Christie is dazzling as the victim of a power-crazed computer that decides it's greater than its genius creator and malfunctions to conceive a child. This claustrophobic cautionary tale shrouds its incredible special effects in a powerful hallucinatory atmosphere, with Robert Vaughn providing the creepily compelling voice of the machine. AJ Violence, swearing, nudity.
DVD

Julie Christie *Dr Susan Harris* · Fritz Weaver *Dr Alex Harris* · Gerrit Graham *Walter Gabler* · Berry Kroeger *Petrosian* · Lisa Lu *Dr Soon Yen* · Larry J Blake *Cameron* · John O'Leary *Royce* · Robert Vaughn (1) *Proteus IV* ■ *Dir* Donald Cammell · *Scr* Robert Jaffe, Roger O Hirson, from the novel by Dean R Koontz

Demonlover ★★
Thriller
2002 · Fr/Jpn/Mex/US · Colour · 130min

This combination of cyber-thriller and capitalist condemnation begins inticingly, as Paris-based executive Connie Nielsen displays a ruthless streak in negotiating a lucrative deal with a Japanese animation studio specialising in 3D pornography. But the narrative spirals out of control following an eye-popping sampling of *anime* ingenuity. DP French, English, Japanese +subtitles. Violence, swearing, sex scenes.

Connie Nielsen *Diane de Monx* · Charles Berling *Hervé Le Millinec* · Chloë Sevigny *Elise Lipsky* · Gina Gershon *Elaine Si Gibril* · Jean-Baptiste Malartre *Henri-Pierre Volf* · Dominique Reymond *Karen* · Edwin Gerard *Edward Gomez* · Thomas M Pollard *Rodney LaCruz, American lawyer* ■ *Dir/Scr* Olivier Assayas

Demons Never Die ★ 15
Horror
2011 · UK · Colour · 102min

Friday the 13th in inner-city London is the best description for director Arjun Rose's debut, which fails to convince on any level. Eight teenagers, including Robert Sheehan (TV's *Misfits*), sign a suicide pact because of bullying, eating disorders, errant parents and so on, only to be targeted by a masked killer. Ashley Walters and Reggie Yates play the least credible detectives in history, and *Luther* star Idris Elba executive produced - but wisely doesn't appear in - this under-par horror, with little in the way of gore, chills or logic. AJ DVD BL

Robert Sheehan *Archie* · Jennie Jacques *Jasmine* · Ashley Walters *Bates* · Tulisa Contostavlos *Amber* · Jason Maza *Kenny* · Reggie Yates *Mason* ■ *Dir/Scr* Arjun Rose

Demons of the Mind ★★★ 18
Psychological horror 1971 · UK · Colour · 84min

As the 1970s dawned, Hammer tried different avenues of horror to survive the chilling competition. This was an experiment by director Peter Sykes to foster the artier side of the genre by delving deep into the psychological roots of the madness afflicting a troubled aristocratic family and the dark reasons why the baron keeps his children locked up in his Bavarian castle. Acted with a conviction by a strong cast, it's ambitious, difficult and often intelligent stuff. AJ Swearing.

Paul Jones *Carl Richter* · Gillian Hills *Elizabeth Zorn* · Robert Hardy *Baron Frederic Zorn* · Michael Hordern *Priest* · Patrick Magee *Dr Falkenberg* · Shane Briant *Emil Zorn* · Yvonne Mitchell *Aunt Hilda* ■ *Dir* Peter Sykes · *Scr* Christopher Wicking, from a story by Frank Godwin, Wicking

Denial
Drama 2016 · US/UK · Colour

This is a preview - no prints were available to review as we went to press: In 1996, British historian David Irving sued US academic Deborah Lipstadt, claiming she had libelled him by calling him a Holocaust denier, falsifier and bigot in her book *Denying the Holocaust*. *Denial* tells the story of that court case, and should be an interesting test of the talents of Rachel Weisz as Lipstadt and Timothy Spall as Irving. David Hare has adapted Lipstadt's book, and since he also adapted *The Reader* for the screen, a thoughtful but politically engaged experience seems guaranteed. SvM

Rachel Weisz *Deborah E Lipstadt* · Tom Wilkinson *Richard Rampton* · Timothy Spall *David Irving* · Andrew Scott *Anthony Julius* · Mark Gatiss *Professor Robert Jan van der Pelt* · *Dir* Mick Jackson · *Scr* David Hare, from the non-fiction book *History on Trial: My Day in Court with a Holocaust Denier* by Deborah Lipstadt · *Music* Howard Shore

Denise Calls Up ★★★ 15
Romantic comedy 1995 · US · Colour · 79min

People fall in love without holding hands; women have babies without a mate; and friends stay close for years without ever seeing each other. Hal Salwen's sophisticated cautionary fable is bound to strike a communication chord with those who feel technology has a lot to answer for. This perceptive and consistently funny look at lifestyles today shows a small group of workaholic New Yorkers conducting their lives over the telephone to such an extent that they have forgotten how to interact on a human level. AJ

Tim Daly [Timothy Daly] *Frank Oliver* · Caroleen Feeney *Barbara* · Dan Gunther *Martin Wiener* · Dana Wheeler-Nicholson *Gale* · Liev Schreiber *Jerry* · Aida Turturro *Linda* · Alanna Ubach *Denise* ■ *Dir/Scr* Hal Salwen

Dennis ★★★ PG
Comedy 1993 · US · Colour · 91min

This adaptation of Hank Ketcham's comic strip was released as *Dennis the Menace* in the USA, but shortened simply to *Dennis* in this country to avoid confusion with *The Beano*'s tousle-haired terror. Often very funny, but just as often painfully poor, the film was co-written and produced by John Hughes, who seems to have cobbled it together from ideas left over from *Home Alone*. Mason Gamble just gets by as the mischievous imp; Walter Matthau, however, is brilliant as his long-suffering victim, Mr Wilson. DP Some violence.

Walter Matthau *Mr Wilson* · Mason Gamble *Dennis Mitchell* · Joan Plowright *Martha Wilson* · Christopher Lloyd *Switchblade Sam* · Lea Thompson *Alice Mitchell* · Robert Stanton *Henry Mitchell* · Amy Sakasitz *Margaret Wade* · Kellen Hathaway *Joey* · Paul Winfield *Chief of Police* · Natasha Lyonne *Polly* ■ *Dir* Nick Castle · *Scr* John Hughes, from characters by Hank Ketcham

Dennis the Menace Strikes Again ★★ U
Comedy 1998 · US · Colour · 71min

This treacly sequel lines up Don Rickles and Betty White as the long-suffering neighbours of Dennis the Menace (Justin Cooper). If the first five minutes - featuring a menagerie of escaped animals and Rickles's wagon ride down a flight of stairs half-naked - don't send you off screaming, then perhaps you'll enjoy the appearance of George Kennedy as Dennis's grandfather. ST

Justin Cooper *Dennis Mitchell* · Don Rickles *Mr Wilson* · George Kennedy *Grandpa* · Brian Doyle-Murray *Professor* · Carrot Top *Sylvester* · Betty White *Mrs Wilson* · Dwier Brown *George Mitchell* · Heidi Swedberg *Alice Mitchell* ■ *Dir* Charles T Kanganis · *Scr* Tim McCanlies, from a story by Tim McCanlies, Jeff Schechter, from characters by Hank Ketcham

The Dentist ★★★★ U
Comedy 1932 · US · BW · 20min

Based on a sketch first performed in the Earl Carroll Vanities, this marked WC Fields's debut for slapstick supremo Mack Sennett. Having forbidden his daughter to marry the ice man and endured golfing hell, Fields is next tormented by a bearded patient and Elise Cavanna's stubborn tooth. (The shots in which she throws her legs around his waist to assist his merciless assault with the dental pliers were excised for TV screenings until the 1970s.) The film established the Fields persona that would serve him to the end of his career. DP
DVD

WC Fields *Dentist* · "Babe" Kane [Marjorie Kane] *Daughter* · Arnold Gray *Arthur the iceman* · Dorothy Granger *Patient (Miss Peppitone)* · Elise Cavanna *Patient (Miss Mason)* ■ *Dir* Leslie Pearce · *Scr* WC Fields

The Dentist ★★★ 18
Horror 1996 · US · Colour · 88min

In director Brian Yuzna's gory oral scare-fest, Corbin Bernsen is the Beverly Hills dentist who goes murderously crazy when his professional and private lives stop conforming to his impossibly high standards. As paranoia sets in, he fights the moral decay contaminating his world with the sharp tools of his trade. The dental torture that follows is both grisly and hilariously funny, though the sequel is even better. Spawned two years later. AJ Violence. DVD

Corbin Bernsen *Dr Feinstone* · Linda Hoffman *Brooke* · Molly Hagan *Jessica* · Ken Foree *Detective Gibbs* · Virginya Keehne *Sarah* · Patty Toy *Karen* · Jan Hoag *Candy* · Christa Sauls *April Reign* · Tony Noakes *Detective Sunshine* · Earl Boen *Marvin Goldblum* · Michael Stadvec *Matt* ■ *Dir* Brian Yuzna · *Scr* Stuart Gordon, Dennis Paoli, Charles Finch

Dentist in the Chair ★★ U
Comedy 1960 · UK · BW · 75min

Bob Monkhouse co-wrote and stars in this unremarkable little comedy, which will only have viewers in fits if they have been subjected to laughing gas. If the flimsy plot about stolen instruments at a dental training school isn't bad enough, the ghastly gags will set your teeth on edge. Numbing the pain, however, are the willing performances of Monkhouse and Kenneth Connor. DP DVD

Bob Monkhouse *David Cookson* · Peggy Cummins *Peggy Travers* · Kenneth Connor *Sam Field* · Eric Barker *The Dean* · Ronnie Stevens *Brian Dexter* · Vincent Ball *Michaels* ■ *Dir* Don Chaffey · *Scr* Val Guest, Bob Monkhouse, George Wadmore, from the novel by Matthew Finch

Dentist on the Job ★ PG
Comedy 1961 · UK · BW · 84min

A year after cutting his teeth on *Dentist in the Chair*, Bob Monkhouse returned in this disappointing sequel with a script that's so full of cavities you'll soon be wincing with pain and crying out for laughing gas. Newly qualified Monkhouse beams his way through a series of gags that could easily have been extracted from the *Doctor in the House* reject file. DP

Bob Monkhouse *David Cookson* · Kenneth Connor *Sam Field* · Ronnie Stevens *Brian Dexter* · Shirley Eaton *Jill Venner* · Eric Barker *Colonel JJ Proudfoot/Dean* · Richard Wattis *Macreedy* · Reginald Beckwith *Duff* · Charles Hawtrey *Pharmacist* · Graham Stark *Man* ■ *Dir* CM Pennington-Richards · *Scr* Hazel Adair, Hugh Woodhouse, Bob Monkhouse

Denver & Rio Grande ★★★ U
Western 1952 · US · Colour · 88min

Renowned for the climactic head-on collision involving a pair of antique steam trains, this solid programmer succeeds in overcoming its clichés and stereotypes to produce a rattling good yarn. The feud between Edmond O'Brien of the titular railroad and Sterling Hayden of the Canyon City and San Juan runs along predictable lines, with the latter devoting more time to sabotaging his rival's efforts than concentrating on his own. But director Byron Haskin keeps the pace brisk and allows dependable supports to ply their stalwart trade. DP

Edmond O'Brien *Jim Vesser* · Sterling Hayden *McCabe* · Dean Jagger *General Palmer* · Laura Elliott [Laura Elliot] *Linda Prescott* · Lyle Bettger *Johnny Buff* · J Carrol Naish *Harkness* · ZaSu Pitts *Jane* ■ *Dir* Byron Haskin · *Scr* Frank Gruber

The Departed ★★★★ 18
Crime drama 2006 · US · Colour · 145min

After a run of solid but ultimately underwhelming efforts (*Gangs of New York*, *The Aviator*), *The Departed* finds Martin Scorsese returning to form with a superior crime drama, based on the Hong Kong movie *Infernal Affairs*. Rookie Boston cop Billy Costigan (Leonardo DiCaprio) goes undercover to help catch local Mafia godfather Frank Costello (Jack Nicholson).

Meanwhile, Costello has groomed Colin Sullivan (Matt Damon) to be his spy on the force. The leads are luminous (especially Nicholson, doing his best work in years), but supporting players Mark Wahlberg, Alec Baldwin and Ray Winstone all steal scenes with glee. **LF** Violence, swearing, sex scenes, nudity, drug abuse. *DVD* *BL*

Leonardo DiCaprio *Billy Costigan* • Matt Damon *Colin Sullivan* • Jack Nicholson *Frank Costello* • Mark Wahlberg *Dignam* • Martin Sheen *Queenan* • Ray Winstone *Mr French* • Vera Farmiga *Madolyn* • Alec Baldwin *Ellerby* ▪ *Dir* Martin Scorsese • *Scr* William Monahan, from the film *Infernal Affairs* by Alan Mak, Felix Chong • *Editor* Thelma Schoonmaker

Departure ★★★ 15
Romantic drama   2015 · UK/Fr · Colour · 108min

Theatre director Andrew Steggall makes a decent feature-film debut with this sincere if overly familiar tale of adolescent self-obsession and sexual confusion. Alex Lawther stars as 15-year-old Elliot, who's in southern France to help his mother (Juliet Stevenson) clear out their holiday home before his father flies in to finalise the sale. That is until Elliot allows himself to become distracted by older teen Clément (Phénix Brossard). Steggall overdoes the aquatic imagery, but he makes evocative use of Brian Fawcett's shimmering vistas, and the performances are admirable. **DP** English, French +subtitles. Swearing, sex scenes.

Juliet Stevenson *Beatrice* • Alex Lawther *Elliot* • Phénix Brossard *Clément* • Finbar Lynch *Philip* • Niamh Cusack *Sally* ▪ *Dir/Scr* Andrew Steggall

Departures ★★★★ 12
Drama   2008 · Jpn · Colour · 125min

Death informs life in this elegantly simple Japanese film. Unemployed cellist Daigo (Masahiro Motoki) finds himself apprentice to a terse undertaker (Tsutomu Yamazaki) and learning how to prepare the bodies of the dead for their journeys to the next world. Daigo proves adept at the work – it's a pity his wife (Ryoko Hirosue) is repulsed by his new profession. Winner of the 2009 Oscar for best foreign film, *Departures's* whimsical take on the Japanese funeral industry proves surprisingly funny. Director Yojiro Takita delights in playing with the squeamish qualities of his subject, as the undertakers deal with deceased transvestites and shoot ill-conceived corporate videos. Yet it's also gently uplifting, as Daigo's journey of self-discovery is fired by his new-found appreciation of the end that awaits us all. **JR** Japanese +subtitles. *DVD* *BL*

Masahiro Motoki *Daigo Kobayashi* • Ryoko Hirosue *Mika Kobayashi* • Tsutomu Yamazaki *Ikuei Sasaki* • Kimiko Yo *Yuriko Kamimura* ▪ *Dir* Yojiro Takita • *Scr* Kundo Koyama

Derailed ★ 15
Action thriller   2002 · US · Colour · 85min

Jean-Claude Van Damme looks musclebound and leaden here, as his Nato agent tries to prevent Tomas Arana's terrorists from stealing a top-secret bio-weapon from thief Laura Elena Harring. There's nothing new about the train-board premise, and the dialogue and special effects are lamentable. **DP** In English, German. Violence, swearing. *DVD*

Jean-Claude Van Damme *Jacques Kristoff* • Tomas Arana *Mason Cole* • Laura Elena Harring [Laura Harring] *Galina Konstantin* • Susan Gibney *Madeline Kristoff* • Lucy Jenner *Natasha* • Jessica Bowman *Bailey Kristoff* • Kristopher Van Varenberg *Ethan Kristoff* ▪ *Dir* Bob Misiorowski • *Scr* Jace Anderson, Adam Gierasch

Derailed ★★ 15
Thriller   2005 · US · Colour · 102min

Swedish director Mikael Hafstrom makes his English language debut with this neo-noir thriller that boasts plenty of sharp turns. Sadly, the plotting is all too predictable, as fellow commuters Jennifer Aniston and Clive Owen indulge in an extramarital flirtation. Apart from having zero chemistry, the pair are placed in the most contrived of circumstances to get talking, and as a result all the Hitchcockian devices that follow are rendered futile. **SP** Swearing, violence. *DVD*

Clive Owen *Charles Schine* • Jennifer Aniston *Lucinda Harris* • Melissa George *Deanna Schine* • Vincent Cassel *LaRoche* • RZA *Winston Boyko* • Xzibit *Dexter* • Addison Timlin *Amy Schine* • Giancarlo Esposito *Detective Church* • David Morrissey *Sam Griffin* • Tom Conti *Elliot Firth* ▪ *Dir* Mikael Hafstrom • *Scr* Stuart Beattie, from the novel by James Siegel

Deranged ★★★ 18
Horror   1974 · US · Colour · 79min

Based on the abhorrent real-life crimes of cannibal killer Ed Gein, who inspired *Psycho* and *The Texas Chain Saw Massacre*, this ghoulish shocker was disowned by its producer for being too repellently realistic. Roberts Blossom plays a sexually repressed mummy's boy who preserves the old dear's corpse and murders people to keep her company. Blossom gives a stand-out central performance, managing the near-impossible feat of making a sympathetic character out of a psychopath killer. **RS** Violence, some swearing. *DVD*

Roberts Blossom *Ezra Cobb* • Cosette Lee *Ma Cobb* • Robert Warner *Harlan Kootz* • Marcia Diamond *Jenny Kootz* • Robert McHeady *Sheriff* • Marian Waldman *Maureen Selby* • Jack Mather *Drunk* ▪ *Dir* Jeff Gillen, Alan Ormsby • *Scr* Alan Ormsby

Derby Day ★★★ U
Drama   1952 · UK · BW · 81min

This is an engaging, absorbing look at the various flotsam and jetsam that pit themselves against the Fates at Epsom Downs on Derby Day. The British class system was firmly rooted and unassailable in the early 1950s, and director Herbert Wilcox nicely milks its rituals and nuances at a great cultural event. The portmanteau cast effortlessly goes through its paces with aplomb and confidence. We have been here many times before, but it's still fun. **SH**

Anna Neagle *Lady Helen Forbes* • Michael Wilding *David Scott* • Googie Withers *Betty Molloy* • John McCallum *Tommy Dillon* • Peter Graves (1) *Gerald Berkeley* • Suzanne Cloutier *Michele Jolivet* • Gordon Harker *Joe Jenkins* • Gladys Henson *Gladys* ▪ *Dir* Herbert Wilcox • *Scr* Monckton Hoffe, John Baines, Alan Melville, from a story by Arthur Austie

Dersu Uzala ★★★ U
Period adventure
1975 · USSR/Jpn · Colour · 134min

Anxious to appear open to cultural exchange, the Soviet Union gave Japanese maestro Akira Kurosawa untold roubles and all of Siberia's wilderness to play with for this eco-epic. It's a vast tone poem, set in the early 20th century when an expedition led by Yuri Solomin sets out to map the icy wastes. And that's it, really: a collection of episodes showing man's attempts to come to terms with nature at its toughest. There are some great moments, but there are also long periods when the camera just stares meaningfully at nothing. **AT** Russian +subtitles. *DVD*

Maxim Munzuk *Dersu Uzala* • Yuri Solomin *Captain Arseniev* • A Pyatkov *Olentiev* • V Kremena *Turtygin* • S Chokmorov *Chang-Bao* • S Danilchenko *Anna* ▪ *Dir* Akira Kurosawa • *Scr* Akira Kurosawa, Yuri Nagibin, from the novel by Vladimir Arseniev

The Descendants ★★★★ 15
Comedy drama   2011 · US/UK · Colour · 110min

Director Alexander Payne has past form (*Sideways*, *About Schmidt*) finding moving pathos in older men coping with stasis. Here, it's George Clooney's Hawaii-based lawyer, whose unfaithful wife is in a coma after a boating accident. Playing against his usual dashing persona, Clooney is greying, baggy and uncool in tucked-in shirts and pumps, a remote husband and hands-off father. Payne's skilfully rationed moments of humorous relief play out against a precipitous, verdant landscape, gorgeously shot by *Sideways* cinematographer Phedon Papamichael. Warm, subtle and gentle, *The Descendants* demonstrates what can happen when indie talent is nurtured to

mainstream success. **AC** Swearing. *DVD* *BL*

George Clooney *Matt King* • Shailene Woodley *Alexandra King* • Beau Bridges *Cousin Hugh* • Robert Forster *Scott Thorson* • Judy Greer *Julie Speer* • Matthew Lillard *Brian Speer* • Nick Krause *Sid* ▪ *Dir* Alexander Payne • *Scr* Alexander Payne, Nat Faxon, Jim Rash, from the novel by Kaui Hart Hemmings

The Descent ★★★★ 18
Horror   2005 · UK · Colour · 95min

An all-female caving expedition goes horribly wrong when six friends end up in an uncharted system and encounter a monstrous cannibal race in Neil Marshall's brilliantly constructed panic attack. Desperation, betrayals and imploding relationships prove as fatal to the girls as the subterranean threat. From the high-impact opening shock to the poignantly bleak ending, this is super-scary and vicious – edgy British horror at its very best. **AJ** *DVD* *BL*

Shauna Macdonald *Sarah* • Natalie Mendoza *Juno* • Alex Reid *Beth* • Saskia Mulder *Rebecca* • Nora-Jane Noone *Holly* • MyAnna Buring *Sam* ▪ *Dir/Scr* Neil Marshall

The Descent: Part 2 ★★★ 18
Horror thriller   2009 · UK · Colour · 89min

Picking up exactly where Neil Marshall's chilling original left off, this less frightening companion piece sees traumatised Sarah Carter (Shauna Macdonald) emerge from the Appalachian mountain caves, only to be forced back into the subterranean depths by a suspicious police force that wants her help in locating her five missing girlfriends. Unlike Sarah, who gradually regains her memory and realises how futile the mission is, the rescue party has no idea what horrors lie in store. The plot is heavily contrived and anyone who has seen the first film will find the claustrophobic atmosphere and sudden scares familiar, but there are some well-staged action highlights featuring all the required cliff-hanging, rock falls and underwater scenes. **AJ** Violence. *DVD* *BL*

Shauna Macdonald *Sarah Carter* • Natalie Mendoza *Juno* • Douglas Hodge *Dan* • Krysten Cummings *Deputy Elen Rios* • Gavan O'Herlihy *Sheriff Vaines* • Joshua Dallas *Greg* • Norah-Jane Noone *Holly* • Anna Skellern *Cath* ▪ *Dir* Jon Harris • *Scr* J Blakeson, James McCarthy, James Watkins, from characters by Neil Marshall

Descent into Hell ★★★
Crime thriller   1986 · Fr · Colour · 90min

This is a tidy enough thriller, but it lacks both the hard-boiled edge and star credibility that would raise it above the average. Claude Brasseur is sufficiently world-weary as the alcoholic author who accidentally kills a petty thief while vacationing in Haiti. But Sophie Marceau, as the trophy wife who helps conceal his crime, is short on *femme* fatality. **DP** French dubbed.

Claude Brasseur *Alan Kolber* • Sophie Marceau *Lola Kolber* • Sidiki Bakaba [Sijiri Bakaba] *Theophile Bijou* • Hyppolyte Girardot *Philippe Devignat* • Gérard Rinaldi *Elvis* • Marie Dubois *Lucette Beulemans* • Betsy Blair *Mrs Burns* ▪ *Dir* Francis Girod • *Scr* Francis Girod, Jean-Loup Dabadic, from the novel *The Wounded and the Slain* by David Goodis

Desert Bloom ★★★★ PG
Period drama   1985 · US · Colour · 101min

In this period piece, director Eugene Corr splendidly captures the simmering, underlying tensions and almost childlike incredulity of a 1950s America heralding in the nuclear age. The bigger issues of the Bomb are used to add colour to an enclosed tale of dysfunctional family life, wonderfully played by Jon Voight as the drunken stepfather of young Annabeth Gish and Ellen Barkin as her sexy aunt. Corr takes an age to establish his characters and plot, but once up and running there isn't a more atmospheric film about pre-Kennedy America. **SH** Some swearing.

Annabeth Gish *Rose* • Jon Voight *Jack* • JoBeth Williams *Lily* • Ellen Barkin *Starr* • Jay Underwood *Robin* • Desiree Joseph *Dee Ann* • Dusty Balcerzak *Barbara Jo* • Allen Garfield *Mr Mosol* • Tressi Loria *Shelly* ▪ *Dir* Eugene Corr • *Scr* Eugene Corr, from a story by Linda Remy, Eugene Corr

Desert Blue ★★★ 15
Comedy drama   1998 · US · Colour · 86min

Two travellers, father John Heard and daughter Kate Hudson, get trapped in a rural backwater after a chemical truck spillage. Their encounters with the town's restless youth expose personal prejudices and result in an unlikely romance between snobbish Hudson and bad boy Brendan Sexton III. Christina Ricci and Ben Affleck's brother Casey also appear. **LH**

Brendan Sexton III *Blue Baxter* • Kate Hudson *Skye* • John Heard *Father* • Christina Ricci *Ely* • Casey Affleck *Pete* • Sara Gilbert *Sandy* • Ethan Suplee *Cale* • Michael Ironside *Agent Bellows* ▪ *Dir/Scr* Morgan J Freeman

Desert Dancer ★★ 15
Biographical drama   2014 · UK · Colour · 99min

Richard Raymond's well-meaning, but off-puttingly naïve biopic of dancer Afshin Ghaffarian sees him first as a boy, growing up in a country where dancing is outlawed. Later, as a university student, Afshin (Reece Ritchie) teams with classmate Elaheh (Freida Pinto) to create a piece in support of reformist presidential candidate Mir-Hossein Mousavi. Unfortunately, there is little political depth and dramatic tension in the leaden script, and Raymond shoots Akram Khan's kinetic choreography with little flair or dynamism. **DP** Drug abuse, some violence. *DVD*

Reece Ritchie *Afshin Ghaffarian* • Freida Pinto *Elaheh* • Nazanin Boniadi *Parisa Ghaffarian* • Tom Cullen *Ardavan* ▪ *Dir* Richard Raymond • *Scr* Jon Croker

The Desert Fox ★★★ PG
Second World War action drama
1951 · US · BW · 84min

James Mason stars as Field Marshal Erwin Rommel, who was known as a professional soldier rather than a Nazi sadist. Henry Hathaway's film begins as a wartime adventure, then turns into a study of disenchantment as Rommel, beaten by Montgomery's 8th Army, returns to Germany and joins the plot against Hitler. There's a good supporting cast and Hathaway directs with solid assurance. Mason reprised his role in the sequel, *The Desert Rats*. **AT** *DVD*

James Mason *Erwin Rommel* • Cedric Hardwicke *Dr Karl Strolin* • Jessica Tandy *Frau Rommel* • Luther Adler *Hitler* • Everett Sloane *General Burgdorf* • Leo G Carroll *Field Marshal Von Rundstedt* • George Macready *General Fritz Bayerlein* ▪ *Dir* Henry Hathaway • *Scr* Nunnally Johnson, from the biography by Desmond Young

Desert Fury ★★★
Drama   1947 · US · Colour · 96min

Lizabeth Scott runs away from school and heads home to Nevada where her mom, Mary Astor, runs a gambling house and where the men get very steamed up indeed. There's widowed gambler John Hodiak, his henchman Wendell Corey and the most virile cop west of the Pecos, Burt Lancaster, in his third screen outing. It's really a western in modern dress, a display of macho posturing that's ridiculous and gripping at the same time. **AT**

John Hodiak *Eddie Bendix* • Lizabeth Scott *Paula Haller* • Burt Lancaster *Tom Hanson* • Wendell Corey *Johnny Ryan* • Mary Astor *Fritzie Haller* • Kristine Miller *Claire Lindquist* • William Harrigan *Judge Berle Lindquist* • James Flavin *Pat Johnson* ▪ *Dir* Lewis Allen • *Scr* Robert Rossen, from the novel *Desert Town* by Ramona Stewart

Desert Gamble ★★★
Romantic comedy drama
1996 · US · Colour · 97min

Oscar nominees Stockard Channing (*Six Degrees of Separation*) and Jennifer Tilly (*Bullets over Broadway*) join forces for this hilarious romantic comedy. They play two

D

very different women, in Reno for quickie divorces, who find they have more in common than they could ever have imagined. Scott Glenn, Randy Travis and Stuart Wilson provide the beef in a TV movie written and produced by Victoria Tennant, the English actress better known as Steve Martin's ex-wife. NS

Stockard Channing *Pen* • Jennifer Tilly *Edie* • Scott Glenn *Harry* • Stuart Wilson (1) *Victor* • Randy Travis *Pony Cobb* • Martin Mull *Johnnie Sparkle* • Chris Sarandon *Max* • Louise Fletcher *Judge* • Beverly D'Angelo *Barlady* ■ *Dir* Matthew Irmas • *Scr* Victoria Tennant

Desert Hearts ★★★★ 18

Drama   1985 · US · Colour · 87min

One of the very few truly risk-taking movies to come out of the mid-1980s, this tale of lesbian love in Reno was a deserved critical success at the time. Natalie Cooper's intriguing, intelligent screenplay gives great roles to Helen Shaver and Patricia Charbonneau, and the resulting juxtaposition – of a disillusioned older woman falling for a younger, freer spirit – works a treat. What scenes of carnal knowledge there are – for this is a film about relationships and prejudice – are deftly handled without sensationalism. This is one of those seminal pictures that show what Hollywood can do when it casts fear aside. SH

Helen Shaver *Vivian Bell* • Patricia Charbonneau *Cay Rivvers* • Audra Lindley *Frances Parker* • Andra Akers *Silver Dale* • Dean Butler *Darrell* • Gwen Welles *Gwen* ■ *Dir* Donna Deitch • *Scr* Natalie Cooper, from the novel *Desert of the Heart* by Jane Rule

Desert Heat ★★ 18

Action drama   1999 · US · Colour · 91min

This violent variation on *High Plains Drifter* confirmed suspicions of Jean-Claude Van Damme's commercial decline. Pat Morita mugs shamelessly as the eccentric handyman who helps Van Damme's suicidal, motorbiking former hitman rid a desert town of a gang of vicious drug dealers. Laced with native American mysticism and crude comedy, the story follows predictable lines. DP *DVD*

Jean-Claude Van Damme *Eddie Lomax* • Nikki Bokal *Carol* • Larry Drake *Ramsey Hogan* • Bill Erwin *Eli Hamilton* • Neil Delama *Lester* ■ *Dir* Danny Mulroon [John G Avildsen] • *Scr* Tom O'Rourke

Desert Legion ★★ U

Swashbuckling adventure   1953 · US · Colour · 85min

Alan Ladd stars in this B-grade swashbuckler as a soldier in the Foreign Legion who survives an ambush and is nursed back to health by the alluring Arlene Dahl. Dahl lives in a hidden city called Madara, and enlists Ladd to help keep it from the clutches of villain Richard Conte. Comic relief comes from Ladd's buddy, Akim Tamiroff. AT

Alan Ladd *Paul Lartel* • Richard Conte *Crito/Calif* • Arlene Dahl *Morjana* • Akim Tamiroff *Private Plevko* • Leon Askin *Major Vasil* • Oscar Beregi (2) *Khalil* • Anthony Caruso *Lieutenant Messaoud* • Don Blackman *Kumbaba* ■ *Dir* Joseph Pevney • *Scr* Irving Wallace, Lewis Meltzer, from the novel *The Demon Caravan* by George Arthur Surdez

Desert Mice ★★ U

Second World War comedy   1959 · UK · BW · 80min

The feeble title pun on "Desert Rats" (the nickname given to the British troops who fought against Rommel in North Africa) rather sets the tone for this overlookable comedy from director Michael Relph. Full of predictable characters, humdrum incidents and gags that would have lowered the morale of even the most battle-hardened tommy, it accompanies an Ensa concert party on its tour of army camps. DP *DVD*

Alfred Marks *Major Poskett* • Sidney James *Bert Bennett* • Dora Bryan *Gay* • Dick Bentley *Gavin O'Toole* • Reginald Beckwith *Fred* • Irene Handl *Miss Patch* • Liz Fraser *Edie* ■ *Dir* Michael Relph • *Scr* David Climie

The Desert Rats ★★★ U

Second World War action drama 1953 · US · BW · 84min

This rather aloof desert-stormer, meant as a follow-up to *The Desert Fox*, again boasts James Mason as Field Marshal Rommel, this time ordering the Battle of Tobruk against Allied forces that include Richard Burton commanding Aussie troops. Burton has his own problems with his cowardly old schoolteacher-turned-volunteer Robert Newton, but still manages to bring down Rommel's forces. TH *DVD*

Richard Burton *Captain MacRoberts* • Robert Newton *Bartlett* • Robert Douglas *General* • Torin Thatcher *Barney* • Chips Rafferty *Smith* • Charles Tingwell *Lieutenant Carstairs* • James Mason *Rommel* • Charles Davis (1) *Pete* ■ *Dir* Robert Wise • *Scr* Richard Murphy

The Desert Song ★★

Musical   1929 · US · BW and Colour · 125min

This is an early sound version of the operetta about a seemingly wimpish Briton who, as the mysterious "Red Shadow", leads a revolt against villainous Arabs. Remade in 1944 and 1953, this rendition is worth seeing, not for its competence, but for its unintentional laughs. John Boles sings adequately, despite his stiff upper lip, while Carlotta King has a certain winsome banality as the girl who despises him at first. TH

John Boles *The Red Shadow* • Carlotta King *Margot* • Louise Fazenda *Susan* • Johnny Arthur *Benny Kidd* • Edward Martindel *Gen Bierbeau* • Jack Pratt *Pasha* • Myrna Loy *Azuri* ■ *Dir* Roy Del Ruth • *Scr* Harvey Gates, from the operetta by Sigmund Romberg, Otto Harbach, Lawrence Schwab, Frank Mandel, Oscar Hammerstein II

The Desert Song ★★★ U

Musical   1944 · US · Colour · 94min

The second of three screen versions of the operetta about the romantic, heroic leader of a band of Riffs in North Africa who fight off their evil oppressors. This version was given contemporary relevance by having the villains as Nazis and the hero (Dennis Morgan) an American in disguise who, with his band of men, sabotages the building of a railway track. Directed by Robert Florey, this romantic nonsense can't miss for fans of Romberg's lush and rousing melodies, which include *One Alone* and *The Riff Song*. RK

Dennis Morgan *Paul Hudson* • Irene Manning *Margot* • Bruce Cabot *Col Fontaine* • Victor Francen *Caid Yousseff* • Lynne Overman *Johnny Walsh* • Gene Lockhart *Pere FanFan* • Faye Emerson *Hajy* • Marcel Dalio *Tarbouch* ■ *Dir* Robert Florey • *Scr* Robert Buckner, from the operetta by Sigmund Romberg, Otto Harbach, Lawrence Schwab, Frank Mandel, Oscar Hammerstein II

The Desert Song ★★★ U

Musical   1953 · US · Colour · 105min

This handsomely mounted Warner Bros remake of Sigmund Romberg's popular operetta is easy enough on the eye, and easier still on the ear. But the good-looking Gordon MacRae is miscast as the young American anthropologist doubling by night as El Khobar, avenger of the desert Riffs. Still, Kathryn Grayson sings *One Alone* as if her life depended on it, and Raymond Massey is perfect as the cruel and villainous sheik. TS

Kathryn Grayson *Margot* • Gordon MacRae *Paul Bonnard/El Khobar* • Steve Cochran *Captain Fontaine* • Raymond Massey *Yousseff* • Dick Wesson *Benjy Kidd* • Allyn McLerie [Allyn Ann McLerie] *Azuri* • Ray Collins *General Birabeau* ■ *Dir* Bruce Humberstone [H Bruce Humberstone] • *Scr* Roland Kibbee, from the operetta by Sigmund Romberg, Otto Harbach, Lawrence Schwab, Frank Mandel, Oscar Hammerstein II

Desert Thunder ★★ 15

Action thriller   1998 · US · Colour · 82min

Set in the aftermath of Operation Desert Storm, this gung-ho action thriller pits retired flyboy Daniel Baldwin and a *Dirty Dozen*-style squadron against a top-secret chemical weapons plant with thuddingly predictable consequences. The macho

posturing is hard to swallow, but the flying sequences are surprisingly effective. DP *DVD*

Tim Abell *Bobby "Jet "Burkett* • Richard Tyson *Streets* • Daniel Baldwin *Lee Miller* • Ari Barak *General Ali Aziz* • Stevie Johnson *Johnny V Jones* • Melissa Brasselle *Michele Parker* • Marc Casabani *Hassim* • Stacy Haiduk *Ally "Al" Malone* ■ *Dir* Jim Wynorski • *Scr* Lenny Juliano

The Desert Trail ★★ U

Western   1935 · US · BW · 54min

Trapped at Monogram Studios and contracted to a seemingly relentless series of B-westerns, John Wayne managed to hone his persona and learn screencraft in routine films such as this one. Director Cullin Lewis (Lewis Collins) does what he can with the desperately average "mistaken identity" plot, but there's not much to work with. TS *DVD*

John Wayne *John Scott* • Mary Kornman *Anne* • Paul Fix *Jim* • Eddy Chandler *Kansas Charlie* • Carmen Laroux *Juanita* • Lafe McKee *Sheriff Barker* • Al Ferguson *Pete* ■ *Dir* Cullen Lewis [Lewis D Collins] • *Scr* Lindsley Parsons

The Deserted Station ★★★★

Drama   2002 · Iran/Fr/Neth · Colour · 93min

Ali Reza Raisian's third feature reverberates with the preoccupations of Iran's most pre-eminent film-maker, Abbas Kiarostami, upon whose story it is based. A car breakdown sets up a trademark Kiarostami investigation of town and country mores, in which the wife's minding of the nearby shanty school (while the teacher goes off to help her husband fix the car) permits a revealing insight into the impact of rural poverty on the virtually forgotten local women and children. Leila Hatami produces a touching display of compassion and shame, as she explores a near-dormant desert railway line, but Raisian also injects plenty of humour into his humanistic approach to the subject matter. DP Farsi +subtitles.

Leila Hatami *The Wife* • Nezam Manouchehri *The Husband* • Mehran Rajabi *Feizollah* ■ *Dir* Ali Reza Raisian • *Scr* Kambozia Partovi, from a short story by Abbas Kiarostami

The Deserter ★★ 15

Western   1971 · It/Yug · Colour · 94min

A lot of familiar western faces are in this cavalry versus Indians epic, but since this is a Euro-western, shot in Yugoslavia, there are also several Italians, plus Yugoslavian heart-throb Bekim Fehmiu in the title role. Hollywood director Burt Kennedy – noted for maintaining a sharp pace and no messing about – somehow talked John Huston into a cameo appearance. AT

Bekim Fehmiu *Captain Victor Kaleb* • John Huston *General Miles* • Richard Crenna *Major Wade Brown* • Chuck Connors *Reynolds* • Ricardo Montalban *Natachai* • Ian Bannen *Crawford* • Brandon de Wilde *Ferguson* • Slim Pickens *Tattinger* • Albert Salmi *Schmidt* • Woody Strode *Jackson* • Patrick Wayne *Bill Robinson* ■ *Dir* Burt Kennedy • *Scr* Clair Huffaker, from a story by Stuart J Byrne, William H James

Design for Living ★★★

Romantic comedy drama   1933 · US · BW · 86min

A famous Noël Coward play becomes a minor work in the canon of the great Ernst Lubitsch. His usually witty visual style is seemingly cramped by having to rely too much on the master's witticisms, as translated into movietalk by ace scenarist Ben Hecht. Of course, in this famous *ménage à trois* tale, Gary Cooper and Fredric March are super fun. But why on earth are they both in such a dither over the self-regarding Miriam Hopkins? TS

Fredric March *Tom Chambers* • Gary Cooper *George Curtis* • Miriam Hopkins *Gilda Farrell* • Edward Everett Horton *Max Plunkett* • Franklin Pangborn *Mr Douglas* • Isabel Jewell *Lisping Stenographer* • Harry Dunkminson *Mr Egelbauer* • Helena Phillips *Mrs Egelbauer* ■ *Dir* Ernst Lubitsch • *Scr* Ben Hecht, from the play by Noël Coward

Design for Scandal ★★★ U

Romantic comedy   1941 · US · BW · 84min

The last movie the fabulous Rosalind Russell made under her MGM contract is a deft romantic comedy based on a clever idea: ace newshound Walter Pidgeon is sent out to dish some dirt on squeaky-clean judge Russell, and falls for her. Screenwriter Lionel Houser provides some sparkling repartee, and director Norman Taurog keeps the froth moving along at a brisk pace. Mix in those glossy MGM production values and you have a very watchable time-filler. TS

Rosalind Russell *Judge Cornelia Porter* • Walter Pidgeon *Jeff Sherman* • Edward Arnold *Judson M Blair* • Lee Bowman *Walter Caldwell* • Jean Rogers *Dotty* • Donald Meek *Mr Wade* • Guy Kibbee *Judge Graham* ■ *Dir* Norman Taurog • *Scr* Lionel Houser

The Designated Mourner ★★

Drama   1997 · UK · Colour · 94min

This chat-fest is a lament for the passing of high art in an age of middlebrow mediocrity. Set in an unnamed country on the edge of revolution, the action centres around the discussions between intellectual Mike Nichols, his wife Miranda Richardson, and her poet father, David De Keyser. Focusing on the dialogue rather than seeking ways to open out Wallace Shawn's stage play, director David Hare slams the door shut on all but the cognoscenti. DP Swearing.

Mike Nichols *Jack* • Miranda Richardson *Judy* • David De Keyser *Howard* ■ *Dir* David Hare • *Scr* Wallace Shawn, from his play

Designing Woman ★★★★ U

Romantic comedy   1957 · US · Colour · 117min

This has a nicely punning title, plus a witty Oscar-winning screenplay by George Wells that seems to have missed its decade, despite having sophisticated and assured comedy direction from MGM ace Vincente Minnelli. With its plot about a fashion designer and crusading sports columnist getting married, it's reminiscent of a Spencer Tracy/Katharine Hepburn comedy. Lauren Bacall gives good value, but Gregory Peck lacks the lightness of touch required. TS

Gregory Peck *Mike Hagen* • Lauren Bacall *Marilla Hagen* • Dolores Gray *Lori Shannon* • Sam Levene *Ned Hammerstein* • Tom Helmore *Zachary Wilde* • Mickey Shaughnessy *Maxie Stulz* • Jesse White *Charlie Arneg* ■ *Dir* Vincente Minnelli • *Scr* George Wells, from an idea by Helen Rose

Desire ★★★★ U

Romantic comedy   1936 · US · BW · 91min

To evade detection at the Spanish border, a glamorous lady jewel thief hides the pearls she stole in Paris by dropping them into the pocket of an unsuspecting American motor car designer. In the course of her manoeuvrings to retrieve them, she falls in love with him. Marlene Dietrich and Gary Cooper star in this witty, scintillating romantic comedy, produced by Ernst Lubitsch and glowing with signs of his "touch". RK *DVD*

Marlene Dietrich *Madeleine de Beaupré* • Gary Cooper *Tom Bradley* • John Halliday *Margoli, Carlos* • William Frawley *Mr Gibson* • Ernest Cossart *Aristide Duval* • Akim Tamiroff *Police Official* • Alan Mowbray *Dr Edouard Pauquet* ■ *Dir* Frank Borzage • *Scr* Edward Justus Mayer, Waldemar Young, Samuel Hoffenstein, from the play *Die Schönen Tage von Aranjuez* by Hans Szekely, RA Stemmle

Desire & Hell at Sunset Motel ★★★ 15

Comedy thriller   1991 · US · Colour · 95min

1950s nostalgia meets oddball *film noir* when bombshell Sherilyn Fenn and her toy salesman husband (Whip Hubley) shack up in a dingy motel on the way to Disneyland. The deliberately convoluted plot involves Hubley hiring David Hewlett to spy on Fenn and her new lover, while the latter (David Johansen) plots to kill her spouse.

Corkscrew twists abound, but for all its attempts to be wacky, erotic and offbeat, Alan Castle's crafty nightmare comedy remains little more than an interesting diversion. AJ

Sherilyn Fenn *Bridey DeSoto* • Whip Hubley *Chester DeSoto* • David Hewlett *Deadpan Winchester* • David Johansen *Auggie March* • Paul Bartel (1) *Manager* • Kenneth Tobey *Captain Holiday* • Parker Whitman *Boss* • Shannon Sturges *Louella* ■ *Dir/Scr* Alan Castle

Desire in the Dust ★★
Drama　　　1960 · US · BW · 102min

This tale of lust, death and madness in the Deep South generates much heat but little light. Shot in black-and-white CinemaScope by Lucien Ballard, this good-looking film involves ex-convict Ken Scott who, having taken a manslaughter rap for his lover Martha Hyer, returns home to put the cat among the pigeons. These include Hyer's father Raymond Burr, a political bigwig with ambitions, and her mother Joan Bennett, who has gone insane. Decently enough acted. RK

Raymond Burr *Colonel Ben Marquand* • Martha Hyer *Melinda Marquand* • Joan Bennett *Mrs Marquand* • Ken Scott (1) *Lonnie Wilson* • Brett Halsey *Dr Ned Thomas* • Edward Binns *Luke Connett* ■ *Dir* William F Claxton • *Scr* Charles Lang, from the novel by Harry Whittington

Desire Me ★★
Drama　　　1947 · US · BW · 90min

The first MGM film to be released with no director credit is pretty silly, but it's no worse and a good deal glossier than most Hollywood pap. Greer Garson is told by buddy Richard Hart that hubby Robert Mitchum was killed in the war; naturally, he wasn't. The director who took his name off the film was George Cukor, and both Mervyn LeRoy and Jack Conway allegedly directed bits. Not that bad. TS

Greer Garson *Marise Aubert* • Robert Mitchum *Paul Aubert* • Richard Hart *Jean Renaud* • Morris Ankrum *Martin* • George Zucco *Father Donnard* • Cecil Humphreys *Dr Andre Leclair* • David Hoffman *Postman* • Florence Bates *Mrs Lannie, "Joo-Lou"* ■ *Scr* Marguerite Roberts, Zoe Akins

Desire under the Elms ★★ PG
Drama　　　1958 · US · BW · 106min

In Eugene O'Neill's gloomy drama, New Englander Burl Ives's young wife (a miscast and virtually incomprehensible Sophia Loren) falls for his son (an overtly sensitive Anthony Perkins). This is overblown melodrama, but director Delbert Mann opts for realism, despite that fact that Daniel Fapp's crystal-clear VistaVision photography reveals every phoney set and emotion for what it is. TS DVD

Sophia Loren *Anna Cabot* • Anthony Perkins *Eben Cabot* • Burl Ives *Ephraim Cabot* • Frank Overton *Simeon Cabot* • Pernell Roberts *Peter Cabot* • Rebecca Welles *Lucinda* • Jean Willes *Florence* ■ *Dir* Delbert Mann • *Scr* Irwin Shaw, from the play by Eugene O'Neill

Desiree ★★★ U
Historical romance　1954 · US · Colour · 105min

Marlon Brando as Napoleon may seem like ideal casting – indeed, the "Great Mumbler" looks and sounds splendid – but it's clear from his sleepwalking performance that the star himself regarded this as a chore. In fact, it was, being Fox boss Darryl F Zanuck's settlement for Brando walking off *The Egyptian*. Nevertheless, there is a splendid coronation sequence and some elegant costumes, plus a lovely Josephine played by Merle Oberon, while the title role went to Jean Simmons. TS

Marlon Brando *Napoleon Bonaparte* • Jean Simmons *Desiree Clary* • Merle Oberon *Josephine* • Michael Rennie *Bernadotte* • Cameron Mitchell *Joseph Bonaparte* • Elizabeth Sellars *Julie* • Charlotte Austin *Paulette* • Cathleen Nesbitt *Madame Bonaparte* • Evelyn Varden *Marie* ■ *Dir* Henry Koster • *Scr* Daniel Taradash, from the novel by Annemarie Selinko • *Costume Designers* André Hubert, Charles Le Maire

Desk Set ★★★★ U
Romantic comedy　1957 · US · Colour · 99min

The wit of the original title was lost in the UK when it was released as *His Other Woman*. But the sparkle in this penultimate pairing of the great Spencer Tracy and the wonderful Katharine Hepburn still endures, even if the slight plot – Tracy plays an efficiency expert hired to automate Hepburn's office – seems stretched. Watching their on-screen clash from the sidelines are splendid comic players Gig Young and Joan Blondell, and director Walter Lang sensibly lets the stars get on with it. TS DVD

Spencer Tracy *Richard Sumner* • Katharine Hepburn *Bunny Watson* • Gig Young *Mike Cutler* • Joan Blondell *Peg Costello* • Dina Merrill *Sylvia* • Sue Randall *Ruthie* • Neva Patterson *Miss Warringer* ■ *Dir* Walter Lang • *Scr* Phoebe Ephron, Henry Ephron, from the play by William Marchant

Desolation Canyon ★★
Western drama　2006 · US · Colour · 96min

This western may be pretty innocuous, but it can't be accused of stinting on plot. Patrick Duffy stars as the sheriff who teams up with retired gunslinger and old Civil War buddy Stacy Keach to track down a gang of bank robbers that includes Keach's wayward son, Victor Browne, who has kidnapped his own son as an insurance gambit. Added to the mix are a couple of bounty hunters who want the outlaws for crimes committed in Mexico. Sadly, the action lacks generic grit and guts and always feels like a showcase for stars of yesteryear. DP

Patrick Duffy *Tomas "Swede" Lundstrom* • Stacy Keach *Samuel Kendrick* • David Rees Snell *Edwin* • Kenny Johnson *Press Reynolds* • Drake Johnston *Abe Kendrick* • A Martinez *Arturo Zetta* • Kelly Overton *Olivia* ■ *Dir* David S Cass Sr • *Scr* Dan Fitzsimons

Despair ★★★ 15
Drama　　　1978 · W Ger · Colour · 114min

A whiff of *Satan's Brew* pervades Rainer Werner Fassbinder's dark drama of dual identity and the desire for death. However, there's none of the grubbiness of that showy experiment in this tale, set in pre-Nazi Germany, which – as you would expect of a screenplay adapted by Tom Stoppard from a novel by Vladimir Nabokov – has an ingenuity to match its erudition. Warning of the perils of confusing life with art, Fassbinder uses Dirk Bogarde's failed bid to pass himself off as a murdered tramp to explore the inevitability of fascism and the indolence of the individual. DP DVD BD

Dirk Bogarde *Hermann Herman* • Andréa Ferréol *Lydia Herman* • Volker Spengler *Ardalion* • Klaus Löwitsch *Felix Weber* • Alexander Allerson *Mayer* • Bernhard Wicki *Orlovius* • Peter Kern *Muller* ■ *Dir* Rainer Werner Fassbinder • *Scr* Tom Stoppard, from a novel by Vladimir Nabokov

Desperado ★★★★ 18
Action adventure　1995 · US · Colour · 104min

The quirky no-budget charm of *El Mariachi* may have gone, but director Robert Rodriguez revels in the chance to splash out with the backing of a studio to reimagine his modest debut feature. Antonio Banderas assumes the mantle of the mysterious guitar-playing stranger who arrives south of the border seeking vengeance against an evil drugs baron and keeps his tongue wedged firmly in cheek as he carries out his acrobatic slaughter of bad guys. The result is joyful mayhem. Banderas reprised his role in the 2003 sequel, *Once upon a Time in Mexico*. JF Sex scenes, swearing, drug abuse, nudity. DVD

Antonio Banderas *El Mariachi* • Joaquim de Almeida *Bucho* • Sa ma Hayek *Carolina* • Steve Buscemi *Buscemi* • Cheech Marin [Richard "Cheech" Marin] *Short bartender* • Quentin Tarantino *Pick-up guy* ■ *Dir/Scr* Robert Rodriguez

The Desperadoes ★★ U
Western　　　1943 · US · Colour · 86min

Historically important as Columbia's first feature in Technicolor, this large-scale western has the dubious benefits of some rather garish art direction and some strangely-lit night sequences. The star teaming of Randolph Scott and Glenn Ford makes this routinely plotted tale very watchable, though neither had fully developed their screen persona: Scott isn't quite taciturn enough, and Ford is still very much the juvenile in a role that calls for more maturity. TS

Randolph Scott *Sheriff Steve Upton* • Glenn Ford *Cheyenne Rogers* • Claire Trevor *The Countess* • Evelyn Keyes *Allison McLeod* • Edgar Buchanan *Uncle Willie McLeod* • Guinn "Big Boy" Williams *Nitro Rankin* • Raymond Walburn *Judge Cameron* • Porter Hall *Banker Stanton* ■ *Dir* Charles Vidor • *Scr* Robert Carson, from a story by Max Brand

Desperate ★★★★
Film noir　　　1947 · US · BW · 71min

Director Anthony Mann made a knockout series of B-thrillers in the 1940s that were notable for their cracking pace and economic use of sets and lighting. In this fine example, Steve Brodie plays an honest trucker who is forced to flee the Mob after he gets caught up in a warehouse caper and the killing of a cop. The movie is one virtually continuous flight and has a terrific twist at the end, while there's real directorial skill on screen. TS

Steve Brodie *Steve Randall* • Audrey Long *Anne Randall* • Raymond Burr *Walt Radak* • Douglas Fowley *Pete* • William Challee *Reynolds* • Jason Robards [Jason Robards Sr] *Ferrari* • Freddie Steele *Shorty* ■ *Dir* Anthony Mann • *Scr* Harry Essex, Martin Rackin, from a story by Dorothy Atlas, Anthony Mann

Desperate Characters ★★★
Drama　　　1971 · US · Colour · 87min

Shirley MacLaine heads a cast of little-known screen actors in a nightmare glimpse into the horrors of Manhattan life, as perceived, written and directed by Broadway playwright Frank D Gilroy. Covering 48 hours in the life of MacLaine and her husband (Kenneth Mars), there's no conventional narrative, just a series of incidents that reflect the breakdown of urban life and the struggle to live with it. Downbeat, yet beautifully constructed and acutely observed. RK

Shirley MacLaine *Sophie* • Kenneth Mars *Otto* • Gerald S O'Loughlin *Charlie* • Sada Thompson *Claire* • Jack Somack *Leon* • Chris Gampel *Mike* • Mary Ellen Hokanson *Flo* • Robert Bauer *Young man* • Carol Kane *Young girl* ■ *Dir* Frank D Gilroy • *Scr* Frank D Gilroy, from the novel by Paula Fox

Desperate Escape ★★★
Crime drama mystery　2009 · Can · Colour · 86min

This atmospheric TV movie might be light on action, but it certainly knows how to hold the attention. Part of that's down to former *Law & Order* regular Elisabeth Röhm, who nails her role as an amnesiac trying to piece together the events that left her in a coma. Violent flashbacks and a carefully engineered air of unease make her confusion and increasing panic feel even more convincing. Though there are ultimately no surprises, director George Mendeluk keeps the pacing taut and drip-feeds facts to maintain interest. SF

Elisabeth Röhm *Brooke Harris* • Michael Shanks *Michael Coleman* • Serinda Swan *Melissa* • Françoise Robertson *Detective Jean Wagner* ■ *Dir* George Mendeluk • *Scr* Shane Bitterling, Natalie Kiwi

The Desperate Hours ★★★★ PG
Thriller　　　1955 · US · BW · 107min

Superbly directed by William Wyler, this searing adaptation of author Joseph Hayes's Broadway hit features the last great villainous performance of Humphrey Bogart, playing an escaped convict holding Fredric March and his family hostage in their own home. It's unbearably claustrophobic as March summons up hidden strengths to protect his loved ones from a criminal who has no redeeming features. This was the first movie to be filmed in black-and-white VistaVision ("motion picture high fidelity"), and the depth of field and quality of Lee Garmes's photography is superb. TS DVD

Humphrey Bogart *Glenn* • Fredric March *Dan Hilliard* • Arthur Kennedy *Jesse Bard* • Martha Scott *Eleanor Hilliard* • Dewey Martin *Hal* • Gig Young *Chuck* • Mary Murphy (1) *Cindy* • Richard Eyer *Ralphie* ■ *Dir* William Wyler • *Scr* Joseph Hayes, from his novel and play

Desperate Hours ★★★ 15
Thriller　　　1990 · US · Colour · 100min

Michael Cimino's combustible thriller stars Mickey Rourke as the brutal gangster who invades the suburban home of Anthony Hopkins and Mimi Rogers. Cimino breaks free of the story's stage origins (there are some vivid scenes in the Colorado wilderness) and updates William Wyler's 1955 film version by having Hopkins's marriage on the verge of collapse. The result bristles with drama and visual spectacle. AT Violence, swearing.

Mickey Rourke *Michael Bosworth* • Anthony Hopkins *Tim Cornell* • Mimi Rogers *Nora Cornell* • Lindsay Crouse *Chandler* • Kelly Lynch *Nancy Breyers* • Elias Koteas *Wally Bosworth* • Mike Nussbaum *Mr Nelson* ■ *Dir* Michael Cimino • *Scr* Lawrence Konner, Mark Rosenthal, Joseph Hayes, from the film, novel and play by Joseph Hayes • *Cinematographer* Douglas Milsome

Desperate Journey ★★★ PG
Second World War adventure　1942 · US · BW · 103min

Superstar Errol Flynn was medically unfit for military service, but fought the Second World War memorably on screen in a series of Warner Bros action adventures, invariably directed with great pace by Raoul Walsh. Here, Australian Flynn and four other RAF recruits crash-land in Germany and attempt to make their way back to England in *Boys' Own* fashion. "Now for Australia and a crack at the Japs!" says our Errol. A rattlingly good adventure. TS

Errol Flynn *Flight Lieutenant Terrence Forbes* • Ronald Reagan *Flying Officer Johnny Hammond* • Raymond Massey *Major Otto Baumeister* • Nancy Coleman *Kaethe Brahms* • Alan Hale *Flight Sergeant Kirk Edwards* • Arthur Kennedy *Flying Officer Jed Forrest* • Sig Rumann [Sig Ruman] *Preuss* ■ *Dir* Raoul Walsh • *Scr* Arthur T Horman, from his story *Forced Landing*

Desperate Justice ★★★ PG
Drama　　　1993 · US · Colour · 88min

Aside from a charismatically blunt role in *Victor/Victoria* (which scooped her an Oscar nomination), Lesley Ann Warren has more often been at the centre of efficient yet mundane offerings. This is a surprisingly hard-edged TV outing, in which she plays a mother so distraught over her daughter's assault that she shoots the suspected attacker. Director Armand Mastroianni is admirably unsentimental in his approach. JM DVD

Lesley Ann Warren *Carol Sanders* • Bruce Davison *Bill Sanders* • Missy Crider *Jill Sanders* • Allison Mack *Wendy Sanders* • Annette O'Toole *Ellen Wells* • David Byron *Frank Warden* • Shirley Knight *Bess Warden* ■ *Dir* Armand Mastroianni • *Scr* John Robert Bensink, from the novel by Richard Speight

Desperate Living ★★★★ 18
Satirical melodrama　1977 · US · Colour · 90min

This lurid ensemble melodrama is John Waters's most "serious" work. Mink Stole is a highly strung, bourgeois housewife whose quest for self-actualisation and liberation leads her to a fascistic royal kingdom ruled by the very pink and vulgar Queen Carlotta (Edith Massey). The villagers are commanded to walk and dress backwards, while sex changes, rabies and auto-castration all work their magic into the plot. A woman's picture par bizarre excellence, this relentless screechfest may look cheap and cluttered, but it comes with a poignant ending that is endearingly apocalyptic. DO

Liz Renay *Muffy St Jacques* • Mink Stole *Peggy Gravel* • Susan Lowe *Mole McHenry* • Edith Massey *Queen Carlotta* • Mary Vivian Pearce *Princess Coo-Coo* • Jean Hill *Grizelda Brown* • Cookie Mueller *Flipper* ■ *Dir/Scr* John Waters (2)

Desperate Measures ★★ 15
Thriller 1998 · US · Colour · 96min

A good premise, a great cast and an excellent director (Barbet Schroeder) amount to very little in a dumb thriller that rapidly goes downhill. Andy Garcia stars as a policeman who needs the rare bone marrow of the very unhinged Michael Keaton in order to save his ill son. Initially a intriguing, this disappointingly develops into an implausible action thriller as the overacting Keaton runs amok in a hospital. JC **DVD**

Michael Keaton *Peter McCabe* • Andy Garcia *Frank Connor* • Brian Cox (1) *Captain Jeremiah Cassidy* • Marcia Gay Harden *Dr Samantha Hawkins* • Erik King *Nate Oliver* • Efrain Figueroa *Vargus* • Joseph Cross *Matthew Conner* • Janel Moloney *Sarah Davis* ■ *Dir* Barbet Schroeder • *Scr* David Klass

Desperate Moment ★★★ U
Mystery thriller 1953 · UK · BW · 88min

This was one of several films in which handsome young Dirk Bogarde played a fugitive on the run, prior to consolidating his popularity and stardom with the following year's *Doctor in the House*. The meaningless title conceals a ludicrous plot in which Bogarde, believing girlfriend Mai Zetterling is dead, confesses to a murder he did not commit. When he discovers she is still alive, they go off to catch the real villain. The stars make it entertaining enough. TS

Dirk Bogarde *Simon von Halder* • Mai Zetterling *Anna de Burgh* • Philip Friend *Robert Sawyer* • Albert Lieven *Paul* • Frederick Wendhousen *Grote* • Carl Jaffe *Becker* • Gerard Heinz *Bones* • André Mikhelson *Inspector* ■ *Dir* Compton Bennett • *Scr* Patrick Kirwan, George H Brown, from the novel by Martha Albrand

The Desperate Ones ★★
Second World War drama 1967 · US/Sp · Colour · 104min

Alexander Ramati, a novelist turned film-maker, displayed a deep social conscience and interest the Second World War, especially the experiences of its Jewish and gypsy victims. Regrettably his sturdy movies, such as this and *The Assisi Underground*, lack filmic quality, despite having international star casts. This tells of prisoners who escape a Siberian prison camp and make a perilous journey to join the Polish army. BB

Maximilian Schell *Marek* • Raf Vallone *Victor* • Irene Papas *Ajmi* • Theodore Bikel *Kisielev* • Maria Perschy *Marusia* • Fernando Rey *Ibram* ■ *Dir* Alexander Ramati • *Scr* Alexander Ramati, from his novel *Beyond the Mountains*

Desperate Remedies ★★★ 18
Period drama 1993 · NZ · Colour · 89min

The liaisons are more dangerous, the ladies more wicked and the obsessions even more magnificent in this extraordinary historical (not to say hysterical) soap opera from New Zealand. Fabulously stylised sets, amazing design and deafening opera music accompany this gaudy Brontë-esque tale about the fall of high society draper Jennifer Ward-Lealand when she hires a penniless immigrant to marry her opium-addicted sister. AJ Violence, swearing, drug abuse, nudity.

Jennifer Ward-Lealand *Dorothea Brook* • Kevin Smith (1) *Lawrence Hayes* • Lisa Chappell *Anne Cooper* • Cliff Curtis *Fraser* • Michael Hurst *William Poyser* • Kiri Mills *Rose* ■ *Dir* Stewart Main, Peter Wells • *Scr* Stewart Main, Peter Wells • *Production Designer* Michael Kane • *Set Designer* Shane Radford

Desperate Search ★★★
Adventure drama 1952 · US · BW · 71min

This is a tight little drama, beautifully directed by Joseph H Lewis, who became the cult director of such terrific films as *Gun Crazy* and *The Big Combo*. The always underrated Howard Keel, a major star over this period, said that this unheralded little black-and-white movie was his personal favourite among his films, and he and Jane

Greer are exceptionally fine as the parents of two children who are missing after a plane crash. TS

Howard Keel *Vince Heldon* • Jane Greer *Julie Heldon* • Patricia Medina *Nora Stead* • Keenan Wynn *"Brandy"* • Robert Burton *Wayne* • Lee Aaker *Don* ■ *Dir* Joseph Lewis [Joseph H Lewis] • *Scr* Walter Doniger, from the novel by Arthur Mayse

Desperately Seeking Susan ★★★★ 15
Screwball comedy thriller 1985 · US · Colour · 99min

This smart and utterly charming movie is most notable for the fact that Madonna is actually very good in it. She's the free-living, wildly dressed Susan who trades messages with her lover in the *New York Times*, while Rosanna Arquette plays Roberta, the bored housewife who follows the ads until a bump on the head leads her to believe she actually is Susan. The two lead women are tough and desirable at the same time, and they are ably supported by Mark Blum as Roberta's moronic husband and Aidan Quinn as the man even the strongest woman could not resist being rescued by. JB Swearing. **DVD**

Rosanna Arquette *Roberta Glass* • Madonna *Susan* • Aidan Quinn *Dez* • Mark Blum *Gary Glass* • Robert Joy *Jim* • Laurie Metcalf *Leslie Glass* • Will Patton *Wayne Nolan* • Steven Wright *Larry Stillman* • John Turturro *Ray* ■ *Dir* Susan Seidelman • *Scr* Leora Barish

Despicable Me ★★★★ U
Animated comedy 2010 · US · Colour · 90min

This wonderfully inventive animated yarn tells the story of ruthless baddie Gru (voiced by Steve Carell), who finds his position as the world's greatest villain threatened by an up-and-coming rival. Together with his boffin sidekick Dr Nefario (Russell Brand), Gru hatches a plot to steal the Moon, using a trio of young sisters from the local orphanage to obtain a shrink-ray gun. But a growing bond with the orphans threatens to soften Gru's resolve. The film is constantly laugh-out-loud funny, the voice cast (including Julie Andrews as Gru's disapproving mother) is exemplary, and prepare to fall head-over-heels in love with Gru's diminutive yellow helpers, the minions. A sequel hit cinemas in 2013 and the minions got their own spin-off in 2015. TeS Some swearing. **DVD** **Blu** **CS**

Steve Carell *Gru* • Jason Segel *Vector* • Russell Brand *Dr Nefario* • Kristen Wiig *Miss Hattie* • Miranda Cosgrove *Margo* • Will Arnett *Mr Perkins* • Julie Andrews *Gru's mom* • Dana Gaier *Edith* • Elsie Fisher *Agnes* ■ *Dir* Pierre Coffin, Chris Renaud • *Scr* Ken Daurio, Cinco Paul, from a story by Sergio Pablos

Despicable Me 2 ★★★★ U
Animated comedy 2013 · US · Colour · 93min

This sequel finds the no-longer-despicable super-criminal Gru (voiced by Steve Carell) wallowing in domestic bliss with the trio of orphan girls he adopted in the first movie – until he's faced with a new evil threat. Gru has to call upon his cunning of old to scupper the plans of a mysterious, shady figure intent on world domination. Gru's little yellow helpers, the Minions, are centre stage, and at one point even turn against their beloved master. It's a nifty twist that brings added jeopardy to an already exciting plot, while the retro-futuristic designs and inventive gadgets add further texture to a spectacular romp brimming with laughs. *Minions* was released in 2015 and *Despicable Me 3* is due in 2017. TeS **DVD** **Blu** **CS**

Steve Carell *Gru* • Kristen Wiig *Lucy Wilde* • Benjamin Bratt *Eduardo* • Miranda Cosgrove *Margo* • Russell Brand *Dr Nefario* • Steve Coogan *Silas Ramsbottom* • Elsie Fisher *Agnes* • Dana Gaier *Edith* ■ *Dir* Pierre Coffin, Chris Renaud • *Scr* Ken Daurio, Cinco Paul, from characters by Daurio, Paul and Sergio Pablos • *Music* Pharrell Williams

Despicable Me 3
Animated comedy 2017 · US · Colour

This is a preview – no prints were available to review as we went to press: With the first two films grossing $1.5 billion and spin-off *Minions* another hit, the third proper movie in Universal's popular series will be a hot ticket when it opens in July 2017. We left Gru and his girls with a wife and mother, as Gru (Steve Carell) and Lucy (Kristen Wiig) got married. But you can be sure it won't be plain sailing for the former super-criminal, as Pamela Walker is slated to voice Margo, Edith and Agnes's natural mother... no doubt leading to tears as well as excitement and laughs. TF

Steve Carell *Gru/Dru* • Miranda Cosgrove *Margo* • Trey Parker *Balthazar Bratt* • Dana Gaier *Edith* • Nev Scharrel *Agnes* • Pierre Coffin *Minions Kevin/Bob/Stuart* ■ *Dir* Kyle Balda, Pierre Coffin • *Scr* Ken Daurio, Cinco Paul, from their characters

Despite the Falling Snow ★★★ 12A
Romantic thriller 2016 · UK/Serbia · Colour · 93min

Beginning in Moscow during the frostiest days of the Cold War, this small but nicely formed romantic pot-boiler stars Rebecca Ferguson as a young idealist working within the communist establishment, spying for the Americans. She strikes up a relationship with a politician to pass on his secrets. Decades after defecting, that same politician (Charles Dance) is determined to solve the mystery of Ferguson's disappearance. This taut and talky film is well played by all concerned, but given the big themes, it's a rather small affair. DA Sex scenes.

Rebecca Ferguson *Katya/Lauren* • Charles Dance *Old Alexander* • Anthony Head *Old Misha* • Antje Traue *Marina* ■ *Dir/Scr* Shamim Sarif • *Music* Rachel Portman

Destination Gobi ★★ PG
Second World War drama 1953 · US · Colour · 85min

A US Navy contingent sent to observe weather conditions in the Gobi desert joins forces with the Mongol hordes to fight the Japanese. Richard Widmark delivers his usual no-nonsense performance in this load of old nonsense, which claims to be a true story. Robert Wise keeps the desert scenery shifting while the story remains fairly static. AT **DVD**

Richard Widmark *CPO Sam McHale* • Don Taylor *Jenkins* • Casey Adams [Max Showalter] *Walter Landers* • Murvyn Vye *Kengtu* • Darryl Hickman *Wilbur Cohen* • Martin Milner *Elwood Halsey* ■ *Dir* Robert Wise • *Scr* Everett Freeman, from a story by Edmund G Love

Destination Moon ★★★ U
Science-fiction adventure 1950 · US · Colour · 91min

Intended to be the first realistic film about space exploration, producer George Pal's fun effort was beaten into cinemas by the exploitation quickie *Rocketship X-M*. But that didn't have an animated lecture on the principles of space travel hosted by Woody Woodpecker! Co-scripted by science-fiction great Robert A Heinlein, the pedestrian tale of man's first lunar landing has dated badly. Yet the enthralling look, taken straight from the pulp fiction illustrations of the day, is enchanting and colourful and the special effects (which won an Oscar) are impressive for the era. AJ **DVD**

Warner Anderson *Dr Charles Cargreaves* • John Archer *Jim Barnes* • Tom Powers *Gen Thayer* • Dick Wesson *Joe Sweeney* • Erin O'Brien-Moore *Emily Cargreaves* • Ted Warde *Brown* ■ *Dir* Irving Pichel • *Scr* Rip van Ronkel, Robert A Heinlein, James O'Hanlon • *Special Effects* Lee Zavitz • *Cartoon Sequence* Walter Lantz • *Production Designer* Ernst Fegte

Destination Murder ★★
Thriller 1950 · US · BW · 72min

Stanley Clements had played young thug roles in some decent movies (notably *Going My Way*), but he never managed to turn his teenage toughness into adult charm. This is

an average B-movie, of interest only to collectors, though Joyce MacKenzie makes a pert co-star, playing the daughter of a murder victim who hooks up with Clements. TS

Joyce MacKenzie *Laura Mansfield* • Stanley Clements *Jackie Wales* • Hurd Hatfield *Stretch Norton* • Albert Dekker *Armitage* • Myrna Dell *Alice Wentworth* • James Flavin *Lt Brewster* ■ *Dir* Edward L Cahn • *Scr* Don Martin

Destination Tokyo ★★★ U
Second World War drama 1943 · US · BW · 129min

Cary Grant and John Garfield steer their submarine towards Tokyo, their mission to land a meteorologist secretly in Japan to tell an aircraft carrier's bombers when the weather will be clear enough for an attack. Getting there is the real story as the sub runs the underwater gauntlet of depth charges and the usual on-board mishaps. Grant, as the captain, does his best in a cardboard role, though Garfield does better as the womaniser with no women around. AT

Cary Grant *Captain Cassidy* • John Garfield *Wolf* • Alan Hale *Cookie* • John Ridgely *Reserve* • Dane Clark *Tin Can* • Warner Anderson *Executive* • William Prince *Pills* • Robert Hutton *Tommy* • Tom Tully *Mike* ■ *Dir* Delmer Daves • *Scr* Albert Maltz, Delmer Daves, from a story by Steve Fisher

Les Destinées Sentimentales ★★★★ 12
Period drama 2000 · Fr/Swi · Colour · 172min

Adapted with literary respect and cinematic assurance, Olivier Assayas's condensation of Jacques Chardonne's three-volume novel is a remarkable achievement. The visual style is wholly modern, yet never detracts from either the sense of period or the gravity of the themes. The story follows pastor Charles Berling from his desertion of both the church and his adulterous wife (Isabelle Huppert), through his marriage to the inexperienced Emmanuelle Béart and his ongoing obsession with reviving the family porcelain business. Epic, elegant and expertly acted. DP French +subtitles. **DVD**

Emmanuelle Béart *Pauline* • Charles Berling *Jean Barnery* • Isabelle Huppert *Nathalie* • Olivier Perrier *Philippe Pommerel* • ' [Dominique Reymond] *Julie Desca* • André Marcon *Paul Desca* • Alexandra London *Louise Desca* • Julie Depardieu *Marcelle* ■ *Dir* Olivier Assayas • *Scr* Jacques Fieschi, Olivier Assayas, from a novel by Jacques Chardonne

Destiny ★★★★
Silent fantasy drama 1921 · Ger · BW · 79min

Luis Buñuel once claimed that *Destiny* "opened my eyes to the poetic expressiveness of the cinema". This dark and mystical allegory was Fritz Lang's first notable critical success, and it remains impressive for its range of mood, the mastery of its visual composition, its extravagant settings and its special effects. Written by Lang with Thea von Harbou (whom he married in 1924), it's the story of a wife (Lil Dagover) who begs Death to spare her husband's life. RB

Lil Dagover *Fiancée/Zobeide/Fiametta/Tiao Tsien* • Walter Janssen *Fiancé/European/Liang* • Bernhard Goetzke *Death/El Mot/Archer* • Rudolf Klein-Rogge *Girolamo* • Lewis Brody *The Moor* ■ *Dir* Fritz Lang • *Scr* Fritz Lang, Thea von Harbou

Destiny of a Man ★★★★ PG
Second World War drama 1959 · USSR · BW · 96min

Having left his wife and children to fight on the Front during the Second World War, Sergei Bondarchuk is taken prisoner by the Nazis and sent to a concentration camp. He escapes and returns home to find that his family is dead. A powerfully realistic and much acclaimed Russian film, this marks the directing debut of the legendary actor Bondarchuk. He gives a searing portrayal of an ordinary man's despair and courage, and he captures all too graphically the horror of the war as experienced by the Russians. RK Russian dubbed. **DVD**

Sergei Bondarchuk *Andrei Sokolov* • Zinaida Kirienko *Irina* • Pavlik Boriskin *Vanyushka* • Pavel Volkov *Ivan Timofeyevich* • Yuri Averin *Myuller* ■ *Dir* Sergei Bondarchuk • *Scr* Yuri Lukin, Fyodor Shakhmagonov, from a novel by Mikhail Sholokhov

Destiny Turns on the Radio ★ 15

Comedy fantasy 1995 · US · Colour · 98min

This self-consciously quirky comedy has a clumsy dollop of mysticism dumped on top. Dylan McDermott stars as an escaped convict returning to Las Vegas to reclaim his stolen cash; Nancy Travis plays his singer ex-girlfriend. Both give charmless performances, while Quentin Tarantino's turn as a supernatural stalker could be the worst acting work by a director ever. JC

Dylan McDermott *Julian* • James LeGros *Thoreau* • Quentin Tarantino *Johnny Destiny* • Nancy Travis *Lucille* • James Belushi *Tuerto* • Janet Carroll *Escabel* ■ *Dir* Jack Baran • *Scr* Robert Ramsey, Matthew Stone

Destricted ★ 18

Sex anthology 2006 · UK/US · Colour · 115min

Seven directors illuminate their personal meeting points between art and sexuality in this anthology of provocative short films. In the best and most entertaining episode, *kids* director Larry Clark videotapes auditions of young men dreaming of adult movie stardom. Whatever its pretensions, this isn't so much a film as a tedious, laughable, desperate-to-shock art installation. AJ Some subtitles. Sex scenes. *DVD*

■ *Dir* Matthew Barney, Richard Prince, Larry Clark, Marco Brambilla, Sam Taylor-Wood, Marina Abramovic, Gaspar Noé

Destroy All Monsters ★★★ PG

Science-fiction fantasy 1968 · Jpn · Colour · 85min

Alien Kilaakis unleash Toho Studios' entire repertory company of rubber-suited, scaly behemoths to raze a selection of capital cities in this, the ultimate Japanese monster movie. Godzilla attacks New York, Mothra invades Peking and Rodan obliterates Moscow, while Wenda, Baragon and Spigas, the mega-spider from *Son of Godzilla*, all make appearances. This mighty marathon features a zany comic-strip plot, hilariously wooden acting and atrocious special effects miniatures. AJ Japanese dubbed.

Akira Kubo *Capt Katsuo Yamabe* • Jun Tazaki *Dr Yoshido* • Yoshio Tsuchiya *Dr Otani* • Kyoko Ai *Queen of the Kilaaks* ■ *Dir* Ishiro Honda [Inoshiro Honda] • *Scr* Kaoru Mabuchi, Ishiro Honda

The Destructors ★

Science-fiction spy adventure 1968 · US · Colour · 96min

There's little doubt that the low-budget nature of this feeble sci-fi thriller undermines its credibility, while the rabid Cold War xenophobia does nothing for its contemporary appeal. But it's equally obvious that special agent Richard Egan's heart isn't in the search for a consignment of laser rubies that have been stolen from a top-secret lab. Michael Ansara valiantly attempts some sinister villainy, but how seriously can you take a swimsuit tycoon masquerading as a spy? DP

Richard Egan *Dan Street* • Patricia Owens *Charlie* • John Ericson *Dutch Holland* • Michael Ansara *Count Mario Romano* • Joan Blackman *Stassa* • David Brian *Hogan* ■ *Dir* Francis D Lyon • *Scr* Larry E Jackson, Arthur C Pierce

Destry ★★★

Western 1954 · US · Colour · 94min

Good fun, especially for fans of baby-faced Audie Murphy and lovers of Universal westerns of the 1950s, until you realise this is a remake of the superb James Stewart/ Marlene Dietrich film *Destry Rides Again*. It isn't up to its distinguished predecessors, and shouldn't really be judged against them as it was made for a whole new generation of film-goers. TS

Audie Murphy *Tom Destry* • Mari Blanchard *Brandy* • Lyle Bettger *Decker* • Lori Nelson *Martha Phillips* • Thomas Mitchell *Rags Barnaby* • Edgar Buchanan *Mayor Hirim Sellers* • Wallace Ford *Doc Curtis* • Alan Hale Jr *Jack Larson* ■ *Dir* George Marshall • *Scr* Edmund H North, DD Beauchamp, from a story by Felix Jackson, from the novel *Destry Rides Again* by Max Brand

Destry Rides Again ★★★★★ PG

Western comedy drama 1939 · US · BW · 90min

Remembered today for its rollicking good humour and the fabulous Marlene Dietrich performing *See What the Boys in the Back Room Will Have*, this comedy has a universal appeal. Here's lanky and lovable James Stewart as Tom Destry, who manages to clean up the lawless town of Bottleneck by using a slow drawl rather than a quick draw. Dietrich, cast against type, and Stewart, in his first western lead, strike sparks off one another (and in real life, too!), and the catfight between Dietrich and Una Merkel has never been bettered. TS *DVD*

Marlene Dietrich *Frenchy* • James Stewart *Tom Destry* • Mischa Auer *Boris* • Charles Winninger *Washington "Wash" Dimsdale* • Brian Donlevy *Kent* • Allen Jenkins *Gyp Watson* • Warren Hymer *Bugs Watson* • Una Merkel *Lily Belle Callahan* ■ *Dir* George Marshall • *Scr* Felix Jackson, Henry Meyers, Gertrude Purcell, from the novel by Max Brand

Detachment ★★★ 15

Drama 2011 · US · Colour · 93min

Adrien Brody is the quiet centre of a ferocious storm in this drama from provocative British director Tony Kaye (*American History X*). He plays a disillusioned supply teacher who copes with the everyday grind by remaining emotionally detached. But he's surrounded by chaos and rage, powerfully expressed here in confrontational close-ups and in the scathing sarcasm of school counsellor James Caan. Still, the loudest voice belongs to Kaye, whose head-on approach is sure to ruffle feathers. Admittedly, the film is heavy-handed in places, but it still makes you sit up and take notice. SP Swearing, sex scenes, suicide theme. *DVD* *Blu*

Adrien Brody *Henry Barthes* • Christina Hendricks *Ms Sarah Madison* • Marcia Gay Harden *Principal Carol Dearden* • James Caan *Mr Charles Seaboldt* • Blythe Danner *Ms Perkins* • Lucy Liu *Dr Doris Parker* • Tim Blake Nelson *Mr Wiatt* • Bryan Cranston *Mr Dearden* ■ *Dir* Tony Kaye • *Scr* Carl Lurd

The Detective ★★★ 12

Crime drama 1968 · US · Colour · 109min

Cynical New York police detective Frank Sinatra is called upon to solve a case involving the brutal murder of a gay man. What follows is a hard-hitting, well-paced drama that takes swipes at slipshod policing and corruption in City Hall and features one of Sinatra's best performances. Sadly, the film's attitude towards homosexuality and sex in general – considered daring back in 1968 – is very dated. SR Violence. *DVD*

Frank Sinatra *Joe Leland* • Lee Remick *Karen Leland* • Ralph Meeker *Curran* • Jack Klugman *Dave Schoenstein* • Jacqueline Bisset *Norma Maclver* • Horace McMahon *Farrell* • Lloyd Bochner *Dr Roberts* • William Windom *Colin Maclver* • Robert Duvall *Nestor* • Sugar Ray Robinson *Kelly* ■ *Dir* Gordon Douglas • *Scr* Abby Mann, from the novel by Roderick Thorp

Detective ★★★ 15

Detective thriller 1985 · Fr · Colour · 93min

It's rare that one of French director Jean-Luc Godard's movies actually aims to entertain, but this does, being a jokey movie about detective movies in which various characters try to solve a murder committed in a Paris hotel two years earlier. The plot sprouts myriad subplots and Godard dedicates the picture to Clint Eastwood, John Cassavetes and cult 1940s director Edgar G Ulmer. AT French +subtitles. Swearing. *DVD*

Claude Brasseur *Emile Chenal* • Nathalie Baye *Francoise Chenal* • Johnny Hallyday *Jim Fox-Warner* • Laurent Terzieff *Detective William*

Prospero • Jean-Pierre Léaud *Nephew* • Alain Cuny *Old Mafioso* • Stephane Ferrara *Tiger Jones* • Emmanuelle Seigner *Princess of the Bahamas* • Julie Delpy *Wise young girl* ■ *Dir* Jean-Luc Godard • *Scr* Alain Sarde, Philippe Setbon, Anne-Marie Mieville, Jean-Luc Godard

Detective Dee and the Mystery of the Phantom Flame ★★★★ 12

Period action adventure 2010 · Chi/HK · Colour · 118min

Forensic science, mystical forces and electrifying action combine to thrilling effect in this Asian hit set in the seventh century. Andy Lau stars as the brilliant but treasonous lawman who's put in charge of the investigation by Empress Wu when two of her officials die after spontaneously bursting into flame. It's the supernatural elements of this medieval mystery that are the most interesting, while seasoned director Tsui Hark blends ravishing scenery with skilfully choreographed set pieces, and keeps the story bounding along. JH Mandarin +subtitles. Violence. *DVD* *Blu*

Andy Lau *Detective Dee* • Li Bingbing *Shangguan Jing'er* • Carina Lau *Wu Zeitian, the Empress* • Deng Chao *Pei Donglai* • Tony Leung Ka Fai [Tony Leung (1)] *Shatuo Zhong* ■ *Dir* Tsui Hark • *Scr* Zhang Jialu • *Action director* Sammo Hung

Detective Story ★★★★ 12

Crime drama 1951 · US · BW · 98min

Sidney Kingsley's smash-hit play about the ugliness of life as seen from the squad room of a drab police station loses none of its claustrophic intensity on screen under William Wyler's resourceful direction. Kirk Douglas is memorable as the cop who despises weakness and wrongdoing, only to find that his intolerance is his undoing. But many others are equally good, including William Bendix (fellow cop), Eleanor Parker (Douglas's wife) and George Macready (despicable abortionist). AE *DVD*

Kirk Douglas *Det James McLeod* • Eleanor Parker *Mary McLeod* • William Bendix *Det Lou Brody* • Lee Grant *Shoplifter* • Bert Freed *Det Dakis* • Frank Faylen *Det Gallagher* • Horace McMahon *Lt Monaghan* • Craig Hill *Arthur Kindred* • George Macready *Karl Schneider* • Joseph Wiseman *Charley Gennini* • Cathy O'Donnell *Susan Carmichael* ■ *Dir* William Wyler • *Scr* Philip Yordan, Robert Wyler, from the play by Sidney Kingsley

Determination of Death ★★

Crime drama 2001 · US · Colour · 100min

Everywhere you look in Michael Miller's unoriginal crime drama, there's a familiar face. If only he'd found something more productive for them to do. There's an element of suspense in the storyline, which sees Marc Singer, the abusive husband of Michele Greene, seemingly meeting a sticky end on a hunting trip. DP

Michele Greene *Katie Williams* • Marc Singer *Reese Williams* • Veronica Hamel *Virginia "Ginny" Halloran* • John Ratzenberger *Charlie Halloran* • William Katt *John Logan* • George Dzundza *Mac* ■ *Dir* Michael Miller (2) • *Scr* Sharon Barry McTigue, James Hirsch, from a story by Sharon Barry McTigue

Deterrence ★★★ 15

Political thriller 1999 · US/Fr · Colour · 99min

In this bomb-crisis thriller, Kevin Pollak stars as the harassed US President, stranded in a diner in the Colorado backwoods and attempting to avert a nuclear catastrophe. Writer/director Rod Lurie cleverly leads us into a gradual acceptance of the unlikely situation through excellent use of the claustrophobic setting. Sheryl Lee Ralph and Timothy Hutton give steady performances as the security advisers who seek to persuade Pollak to disengage his sensibilities in dealing with a rampant Iraq. DP

Kevin Pollak *President Walter Emerson* • Timothy Hutton *Marshall Thompson* • Sean Astin *Ralph* • Sheryl Lee Ralph *Gayle Redford* • Clotilde Courau *Katie* • Badja Djola *Harvey* ■ *Dir/Scr* Rod Lurie

The Detonator ★★ 15

Action thriller 2006 · US/Rom · Colour · 92min

Wesley Snipes stars as a loose-cannon American agent in eastern Europe who is punished for his mishandling of a mission by being sent on thankless escort duty. But he's forced to go on the run with Romanian Mafia widow Silvia Colloca after her safe house is blown. The dialogue may be banal, but the set pieces are spectacular – particularly if you're a fan of predictable, low-budget action movies. SuR *DVD*

Wesley Snipes *Sonni Griffith* • Silvia Colloca *Nadia Cominski* • Tim Dutton *Jozef Bostanescu* • William Hope *Michael Shepard* • Matthew Leitch *Dimitru Ilinca* ■ *Dir* Po Chih Leong • *Scr* Martin Wheeler

Detour ★★★★ U

Cult thriller 1945 · US · BW · 67min

This remarkably pacey and stylish B-movie thriller is now rightly recognised as a minor classic. It's a fitting tribute to skilled director Edgar G Ulmer, who made this hard-boiled little gem in just six days. Lead Tom Neal's lack of acting ability actually helps the stark tale of a hitch-hiker buffeted by fate, and the remarkable Ann Savage creates the kind of *femme fatale* you wouldn't want to meet in the dark. The clever use of night shooting and a score seemingly made up from Chopin's out-takes enhance the deeply satisfying, grimy tale. TS *DVD*

Tom Neal *Al Roberts* • Ann Savage *Vera* • Claudia Drake *Sue* • Edmund MacDonald *Charles Haskell Jr* • Tim Ryan *Diner proprietor* • Esther Howard *Hedy* • Roger Clark *Dillon* ■ *Dir* Edgar G Ulmer • *Scr* Martin Goldsmith

Detroit 9000 ★★ 18

Blaxploitation crime thriller 1973 · US · Colour · 102min

This is a crudely photographed and relentlessly violent cops-and-robbers thriller, blaxploitation style. Jewel thieves make off with $400,000 of loot from attendees at a black congressman's fundraiser in Detroit, the murder capital of the world. Two cops - one black, the other white - are assigned to the case, which plonks the usual clichés (pimps, thugs, hookers and racial hatreds) into a mediocre police procedural. AJ

Alex Rocco *Lieutenant Danny Bassett* • Hari Rhodes *Sergeant Jesse Williams* • Vonetta McGee *Roby Harris* • Ella Edwards *Helen* • Scatman Crothers *Reverend Markham* ■ *Dir* Arthur Marks • *Scr* Orville Hampton, from a story by Arthur Marks, Orville Hampton

Detroit Rock City ★★★ 15

Comedy 1999 · US · Colour · 90min

High school and the 1970s have always been popular topics in Hollywood. Here they meet head on, with a bit of road movie and country mouse comedy thrown in for good measure. With only the soundtrack to nail down the period, there's a universality about the adventures of four lads bunking off to Motown for a rock concert. The inevitabilities are given nostalgic bravura by the pace and idiosyncrasy of Adam Rifkin's direction. DP Swearing. *DVD* CS

Edward Furlong *Hawk* • Giuseppe Andrews *Lex* • James DeBello *Trip* • Sam Huntington *Jeremiah "Jam" Bruce* • Gene Simmons • Paul Stanley • Shannon Tweed *Amanda Finch* ■ *Dir* Adam Rifkin • *Scr* Carl V Dupré • *Producers* Gene Simmons, Barry Levine, Kathleen Haase

Deuce Bigalow: Male Gigolo ★★ 15

Comedy 1999 · US · Colour · 84min

Pitched low and hitting even lower, this bad-taste comedy will either have you laughing like a drain or looking for the "off" button. Rob Schneider plays an idiot aquarist who, while fish-sitting for a male escort, gets hooked into servicing a clientele of his own. His customers embrace every conceivable imperfection, from Tourette syndrome to missing limbs. Add an extra star if you find pratfalling pensioners funny. DA *DVD*

Rob Schneider *Deuce Bigalow* • Arija Bareikis *Kate* • William Forsythe *Detective Chuck Fowler* • Eddie Griffin *TJ* • Oded Fehr *Antoine LeConte*

Gail O'Grady *Claire* • Richard Riehle *Bob Bigalow* ■ *Dir* Mike Mitchell • *Scr* Harris Goldberg, Rob Schneider

Deuce Bigalow: European Gigolo ★ 15

Comedy   2005 · US · Colour · 79min

Rob Schneider returns as the unwilling, cut-price gigolo. He's lured by his erstwhile "man-pimp" (Eddie Griffin) to Amsterdam, where the disjointed plot throws in a bunch of freaky clients and a serial killer whose identity is obvious from the outset. This badly scripted, low-budget follow-up feels gritty, dirty and perverse. **KK** Swearing, drug abuse. *DVD*

Rob Schneider *Deuce Bigalow* • Eddie Griffin *TJ Hicks* • Jeroen Krabbé *Gaspar Voorsboch* • Til Schweiger *Heinz Hummer* • Hanna Verboom *Eva Voorsboch* • Douglas Sills *Chadsworth Buckingham III* • Carlos Ponce *Rodrigo* • Charles Keating *Gian-Carlo* • Rachel Stevens *Louisa, the dirty girl* ■ *Dir* Mike Bigelow • *Scr* Rob Schneider, David Garrett, Jason Ward, from a story by Schneider, from the character created by Schneider, Harris Goldberg

Le Deuxième Souffle ★★★

Crime thriller   1966 · Fr · BW · 149min

From the opening homage to *A Man Escaped*, the influence of Robert Bresson can be felt throughout this intense investigation into that old cliché about honour among thieves. Yet this *noirish* mix of poetic realism and police procedural also bears the imprint of Jean-Pierre Melville, even though the thrilling mountain heist is less typical of his precise style than the cat-and-mouse confrontation between escaped gangster Lino Ventura and circumspect detective Paul Meurisse. **DP** French +subtitles.

Lino Ventura *Gustave Minda* • Paul Meurisse *Inspector Blot* • Raymond Pellegrin *Paul Ricci* • Christine Fabrega *Manouche* • Pierre Zimmer *Orloff* • Marcel Bozzuffi *Ricci* ■ *Dir* Jean-Pierre Melville • *Scr* Jean-Pierre Melville, José Giovanni, from a novel by José Giovanni

Dev ★★★ 15

Drama   2004 · Ind · Colour · 164min

Director Govind Nihalani virtually guarantees success to this project by bringing together Indian cinema legends Amitabh Bachchan and Om Puri. Unemployed law graduate Fardeen Khan singles out Bachchan's police commissioner as his target for revenge after his father falls victim to political violence. With Puri trying to prevent Bachchan from jeopardising his career by engaging in a personal feud and Kareena Kapoor seeking to channel her boyfriend's rage, this is a hard-hitting political drama. **DP** Hindi +subtitles. *DVD*

Amitabh Bachchan *Dev Pratap Singh* • Om Puri *Tejinder Khosla* • Amrish Puri *Chief Minister Bhandarker* • Fardeen Khan *Farhaan* • Kareena Kapoor *Aaliya* ■ *Dir* Govind Nihalani • *Scr* Meenakshi Sharma

Devdas ★★★★ PG

Romantic drama   1955 · Ind · Colour · 161min

Twenty years after serving as cinematographer on PC Barua's 1935 adaptation of Saratchandra Chatterjee's 1917 novella, Bimal Roy directed this stylish remake. It features a masterly performance from Dilip Kumar, who redeems the deeply flawed character of Devdas with some affecting human frailty. Spurning the opportunity to elope with his childhood sweetheart (Suchitra Sen), Devdas heads for Calcutta where his kindness towards a prostitute (Vyjayanthimala) earns her undying devotion. However, he loses her love, too, and embarks on an epic train journey to conquer his demons. **DP** Hindi, Urdu +subtitles. *DVD*

Dilip Kumar *Devdas* • Vyjayanti Mala [Vyjayanthimala] *Chandramukhi* • Motilal *Chunni Babu* • Suchitra Sen *Parvati* • Nasir Hussain (1) *Dharamdas* ■ *Dir* Bimal Roy • *Scr* Rajinder Singh Bedi, Nabendu Ghosh, from the novella by Saratchandra Chatterjee

Devdas ★★★ PG

Musical romantic drama   2002 · Ind · Colour · 184min

There have been numerous adaptations of Sarat Chandra Chatterjee's novel, but this is flattered by the exhilarating presence of Madhuri Dixit. She revels in the role of the Calcutta courtesan who attempts to console country boy Shah Rukh Khan, as he battles with the bottle and his remorse at leaving behind childhood sweetheart Aishwarya Rai. The magnificent sets and costumes made this version one of the most expensive Hindi films ever produced. **DP** Hindi +subtitles. *DVD*

Shah Rukh Khan *Devdas Mukherjee* • Aishwarya Rai *"Paro" Parvati* • Madhuri Dixit *Chandramukhi* • Jackie Shroff *Chunnilal* ■ *Dir* Sanjay Leela Bhansali • *Scr* Prakash Kapadia, Sanjay Leela Bhansali, from the novella by Saratchandra Chatterjee • *Music/Lyrics* Ismail Darbar

Devi ★★★★

Drama   1960 · Ind · BW · 100min

Examining religious fanaticism, Satyajit Ray's first film after the completion of the Apu trilogy was briefly banned for being disrespectful towards the goddess Kali. But this is as much a study of rural superstition and the passing of a traditional way of life as a calculated assault on the Hindu faith. Exceptionally played, if occasionally melodramatic, it also explores the position of women in Indian society, as Chhabi Biswas destroys his 17-year-old daughter-in-law (Sharmila Tagore) after becoming convinced she is a divine reincarnation. Ray enhances this powerful story with some hauntingly stylised imagery. **DP** Bengali +subtitles.

Chhabi Biswas *Kalikinkar Roy* • Sharmila Tagore *Doyamoyee* • Soumitra Chatterjee *Umaprasad* • Karuna Bannerjee *Harasundari* ■ *Dir/Scr* Satyajit Ray

Devil ★★★ 15

Horror thriller   2010 · US · Colour · 76min

Based on a story by M Night Shyamalan, this passable chiller is the first movie in the proposed *Night Chronicles* trilogy – supernatural stories set in the modern urban world. Here, five strangers find themselves trapped in a lift in a Philadelphia office building. So far, so claustrophobic. But it soon emerges (thanks to a Mexican security guard who knows his folklore) that the Devil is also among them and wants to claim their souls. True, it's all a bit spooky rather than gory, but the cinematography by Tak Fujimoto (*The Silence of the Lambs*) is effective, especially the disorientating opening credits sequence. **JA** Violence. *DVD* Blu-ray

Chris Messina *Detective Bowden* • Geoffrey Arend *Salesman/Vince* • Bojana Novakovic *Young woman/Sarah* • Logan Marshall-Green *Mechanic/Tony* ■ *Dir* John Erick Dowdle • *Scr* Brian Nelson, from a story by M Night Shyamalan

The Devil and Daniel Webster ★★ U

Fantasy drama   1941 · US · BW · 101min

Variously known as *All That Money Can Buy* and *The Devil and Daniel Webster*, this features a fine musical score that rightly won an Academy Award for composer Bernard Herrmann. Would that the rest of the movie were as good. New England farmer James Craig (inadequate and charmless) sells his soul to scene-stealing, wicked Walter Huston's Mr Scratch. Lawyer Daniel Webster (Edward Arnold) is hijacked into the story to plead Craig's case. Rigidly humourless and prosaic. **TS** *DVD*

Edward Arnold *Daniel Webster* • Walter Huston *Mr Scratch* • James Craig *Jabez Stone* • Jane Darwell *Ma Stone* • Simone Simon *Belle* • Gene Lockhart *Squire Slossum* • John Qualen *Miser Stevens* ■ *Dir* William Dieterle • *Scr* Dan Totheroh, from the story *The Devil and Daniel Webster* by Stephen Vincent Benet

The Devil and Max Devlin ★★ PG

Comedy   1981 · US · Colour · 91min

Despite a wicked turn from Bill Cosby as Satan, this mawkish tale has little in the way of uplifting charm. The hell sequences are easily the most inspired thanks to their devilish design, and the dastardly dialogue between Cosby and sinner Elliott Gould also entertains. But the rest centres on the wishes Gould grants the gullible in return for their souls and is short on laughs and awash with sentiment. **DP** *DVD*

Elliott Gould *Max Devlin* • Bill Cosby *Barney Satin* • Susan Anspach *Penny Hart* • Adam Rich *Toby Hart* • Julie Budd *Stella Summers* • David Knell *Nerve Nordlinger* • Sonny Shroyer *Big Billy* • Charles Shamata [Chuck Shamata] *Jerry* ■ *Dir* Steven Hilliard Stern • *Scr* Mary Rodgers, from a story by Mary Rodgers, Jimmy Sangster

The Devil and Miss Jones ★★★ U

Comedy   1941 · US · BW · 92min

Jean Arthur's smart, sassy brittleness can brighten up any comedy – including this one, which has a touch of Frank Capra in its bogus courting of socialist issues. Arthur plays a shopgirl who suddenly comes face to face with the big boss, zillionaire Charles Coburn, when he decides to get a taste of real life by posing as a shop assistant himself. It has its moments, but what it really needs is a proper leading man. Instead it has Robert Cummings, whose main interest is forming a union. **AT**

Jean Arthur *Mary Jones* • Robert Cummings *Joe* • Charles Coburn *John P Merrick* • Edmund Gwenn *Hooper* • Spring Byington *Elizabeth* • SZ Sakall *George* • William Demarest *First detective* • Walter Kingsford *Allison* • Montagu Love *Harrison* ■ *Dir* Sam Wood • *Scr* Norman Krasna

Devil and the Deep ★★

Drama   1932 · US · BW · 72min

Submarine commander Charles Laughton (in his first American film) is consumed with jealousy every time anybody so much as glances in the direction of his glamorous wife Tallulah Bankhead. When he discovers she has formed a more-than-friendly alliance with Gary Cooper, Laughton takes extreme measures that backfire on him. Boasting an appearance by newcomer Cary Grant, this melodrama contrives to be both overheated and undernourished. **RK**

Tallulah Bankhead *Diana Sturm* • Gary Cooper *Lt Sempter* • Charles Laughton *Cmdr Charles Sturm* • Cary Grant *Lt Jaeckel* • Paul Porcasi *Hassan* • Juliette Compton *Mrs Planet* ■ *Dir* Marion Gering • *Scr* Benn W Levy, from a story by Harry Hervey, from the novel *Sirènes et Tritons, le Roman du Sous-marin* by Maurice Larrouy

The Devil and the Nun ★★★★ PG

Historical drama   1960 · Pol · BW · 101min

The winner of the Special Jury prize at Cannes, this intensely disturbing drama is based on the same occurrences at the French convent of Loudun that inspired Ken Russell's *The Devils*. While certainly a stylised representation, director Jerzy Kawalerowicz's version exhibits considerably more restraint in depicting the demonic possession of Ursuline superior Lucyna Winnicka, whose lusts not only consume the other sisters, but also drive devout exorcist Mieczyslaw Voit to murder in a bid to win her favour. **DP** Polish +subtitles. *DVD*

Lucyna Winnicka *Mother Joan of the Angels* • Mieczyslaw Voit *Father Jozef Suryn/Rabbi* • Anna Ciepielewska *Sister Malgorzata* • Maria Chwalibog *Awdosia* • Kazimierz Fabisiak *Father Brym* ■ *Dir* Jerzy Kawalerowicz • *Scr* Tadeusz Konwicki, Jerzy Kawalerowicz, from a story by Jaroslaw Iwaszkiewicz

The Devil at Four o'Clock ★★★ PG

Disaster adventure   1961 · US · Colour · 121min

Director Mervyn LeRoy always enjoyed an exotic location, and this overlong Pacific island-set hokum was probably more fun to make than it is to watch. Our advice is to park your brain and enjoy old-fashioned Hollywood as it lurches into the 1960s, exploding volcano and all. Cast as an agnostic convict, Frank Sinatra gets a chance to act with his idol Spencer Tracy, who never turned down an opportunity to play a priest, his original calling. Compulsively viewable because of the sheer star power on display. **TS** *DVD*

Spencer Tracy *Father Matthew Doonan* • Frank Sinatra *Harry* • Kerwin Mathews *Father Joseph Perreau* • Jean-Pierre Aumont *Jacques* • Grégoire Aslan *Marcel* • Alexander Scourby *Governor* • Barbara Luna *Camille* • Cathy Lewis *Matron* ■ *Dir* Mervyn LeRoy • *Scr* Liam O'Brien, from the novel by Max Catto

Devil Bat ★★ U

Horror   1940 · US · BW · 72min

One of the better-known films from Bela Lugosi's sad years on Poverty Row, this tedious and predictable shocker has the *Dracula* star in his other customary role, playing a mad scientist who takes revenge on his enemies by setting his giant killer bats on them. Although he is laughably hammy, fans rate his performance better than those he would later give for Monogram. **DM** *DVD*

Bela Lugosi *Dr Paul Carruthers* • Suzanne Kaaren *Mary Heath* • Dave O'Brien *Johnny Layton* • Guy Usher *Henry Morton* ■ *Dir* Jean Yarbrough • *Scr* John Thomas Neville, from a story by George Bricker

The Devil Commands ★★★

Horror   1941 · US · BW · 61min

Boris Karloff grabs the attention in one of the weirdest movies he made, playing an unhinged scientist trying to communicate with the dead via a brain-wave recording contraption and stolen corpses. Time has been kind to director Edward Dmytryk's vastly underrated macabre miniature. Today, the quaint surrealist touches of wired-up bodies in diving suits give it a quirky atmosphere, while Anne Revere's evil spiritualist adds further chills. **AJ**

Boris Karloff *Dr Julian Blair* • Richard Fiske (1) *Dr Richard Sayles* • Amanda Duff *Anne Blair* • Anne Revere *Mrs Walters* • Ralph Penney *Karl* • Dorothy Adams *Mrs Marcy* ■ *Dir* Edward Dmytryk • *Scr* Robert D Andrews, Milton Gunzberg, from the novel *The Edge of Running Water* by William Sloane

The Devil Dared Me to ★★★

Action comedy   2007 · NZ · Colour · 77min

Cult Kiwi TV comedy series *Back of the Y* is New Zealand's answer to *Jackass* and this big-screen spin-off is juvenile, crude and moronic – and that's intended as a compliment. Gormless stuntman Randy Cambell (Chris Stapp) sets out to emulate the exploits of his late father by joining the stunt team of the obnoxious Dick Johansonson (Matt Heath). Subtlety doesn't come into it, but Stapp and Heath's brand of cheerful tastelessness can be very refreshing. **JF**

Chris Stapp *Randy Cambell* • Matt Heath *Dick Johansonson* • Bonnie Soper *Tracy "Tragedy" Jones* • Phil Brough *Spanners Watson* • Floyd Alexander-Hunt *Cindy Cockburn* ■ *Dir* Chris Stapp • *Scr* Chris Stapp, Matt Heath

Devil Dogs of the Air ★★ U

Drama   1935 · US · BW · 86min

This is a very average piece of Marine Flying Corps hokum, with James Cagney and Pat O'Brien striking sparks off each other and air sequences that are a combination of back projection and library shots. It moves fast and looks good, but relies too much on the personalities of its stars. **TS**

James Cagney *Thomas Jefferson "Tommy" O'Toole* • Pat O'Brien *Lt Bill Brannigan* • Margaret Lindsay *Betty Roberts* • Frank McHugh *Crash Kelly* • Helen Lowell *Ma Roberts* ■ *Dir* Lloyd Bacon • *Scr* Malcolm Stuart Boylan, Earl Baldwin

The Devil-Doll ★★★ PG

Horror   1936 · US · BW · 78min

The sight of Lionel Barrymore in drag adds a note of merriment to this engagingly bizarre tale of terror, which was the penultimate movie from director Tod Browning, Hollywood's first master of the macabre. Barrymore plays a wrongly convicted criminal who escapes from prison and poses as a sweet old dollmaker, exacting his revenge by using a serum that shrinks people to Barbie size. The scares may be dated, but the special effects are still enthralling, as is the offbeat fantasy atmosphere. AJ

Lionel Barrymore *Paul Lavond, "Madame Mandelip"* • Maureen O'Sullivan *Lorraine Lavond* • Frank Lawton *Toto* • Robert Greig *Emil Coulvet* • Lucy Beaumont *Madame Lavond* • Henry B Walthall *Marcel* ■ *Dir* Tod Browning • *Scr* Garret Fort, Guy Endore, Erich von Stroheim, from a story by Tod Browning, from the novel *Burn, Witch, Burn!* by Abraham Merritt

Devil Doll ★★15
Horror   1964 · UK · BW · 76min

This cheap British shocker owes more than a little to the classic ventriloquist episode in *Dead of Night*. Surprisingly highly regarded in some quarters, this low budget exploitation movie features Bryant Halliday as the Great Vorelli, who can transfer souls into his ventriloquist's dummy. TS

Bryant Halliday *The Great Vorelli* • William Sylvester *Mark English* • Yvonne Romain *Marianne* • Sandra Dorne *Vorelli's assistant* • Karel Stepanek *Dr Heller* • Francis De Wolff *Dr Keisling* • Nora Nicholson *Aunt Eva* • Philip Ray *Uncle Walter* ■ *Dir* Lindsay Shonteff • *Scr* George Barclay [Ronald Kinnoch], Lance Z Hargreaves, from a story by Frederick E Smith

Devil in a Blue Dress ★★★★15
Period crime thriller   1995 · US · Colour · 97min

After his brilliant thriller *One False Move*, director Carl Franklin makes all the right moves with this atmospheric thriller. It's a supremely stylish movie, with Denzel Washington as a man with time on his hands who's hired to find a politician's girlfriend (Jennifer Beals), and in the process is framed for murder. The film has a timberyard full of sawn-off dialogue and enough high-voltage tension to work an electric chair. TH Violence, swearing, sex scenes, nudity. DVD

Denzel Washington *Ezekial "Easy" Rawlins* • Tom Sizemore *Dewitt Albright* • Jennifer Beals *Daphne Monet* • Don Cheadle *Mouse* • Maury Chaykin *Matthew Terell* • Terry Kinney *Todd Carter* • Mel Winkler *Joppy* • Albert Hall *Odell* • Lisa Nicole Carson *Coretta James* ■ *Dir* Carl Franklin • *Scr* Carl Franklin, from the novel by Walter Mosley

Devil in the Flesh ★★★
Romance   1947 · Fr · BW · 77min

Set during the last months of the First World War, this once controversial love story stars Micheline Presle as a young wife who embarks on an affair with a 17-year-old schoolboy (Gérard Philipe) while her husband is fighting at the Front. Directed by the Claude Autant-Lara, the film sparked outrage in certain quarters for its uncritically sympathetic portrayal of lovers betraying a soldier away at war. Viewed now, it can be seen as a richly romantic and sensuous tale, supported by two touching lead performances. RB In French.

Micheline Presle *Marthe Grangier* • Gérard Philipe *François Jaubert* • Jean Debucourt *M Jaubert* • Denise Grey *Mme Grangier* • Pierre Palau *M Marin* • Jean Varas *Jacques Lacombe* • Jeanne Pérez *Mme Marin* • Jacques Tati *Soldier in blue* ■ *Dir* Claude Autant-Lara • *Scr* Jean Aurenche, Pierre Bost, from the novel *Le Diable au Corps* by Raymond Radiguet

The Devil Inside ★15
Supernatural horror thriller
2011 · US · Colour · 83min

This drab shocker stars Fernanda Andrade as an American woman who journeys to Rome to discover whether her mother was possessed by demons or simply mentally ill when she brutally killed three people. Combining the found-footage style of *The Last Exorcism* with the narrative arc of *The Rite*, the increasingly derivative events play out more histrionically than scarily. The

abrupt cliffhanging cheat ending adds insult to injury. AJ Violence, swearing.

Fernanda Andrade *Isabella Rossi* • Simon Quarterman *Father Ben Rawlings* • Evan Helmuth *Father David Keith* • Ionut Grama *Michael Schaefer* • Suzan Crowley *Maria Rossi* • Bonnie Morgan *Rosa Sorlini* ■ *Dir* William Brent Bell • *Scr* William Brent Bell, Matthew Peterman

The Devil Is a Sissy ★★
Drama   1936 · US · BW · 91min

Three New York schoolboys – rich kid Freddie Bartholomew, middle-class Jackie Cooper, and slum child Mickey Rooney – team up and get into trouble. Deftly directed by WS Van Dyke, this was designed to showcase three members of MGM's impressive roster of juvenile actors. Cooper was already an established star, Bartholomew was on the way up and Rooney was then the least-known. RK

Freddie Bartholomew *Claude* • Jackie Cooper *"Buck" Murphy* • Mickey Rooney *"Gig" Stevens* • Ian Hunter *Jay Pierce* • Peggy Conklin *Rose* • Katherine Alexander *Hilda Pierce* • Gene Lockhart *Mr Murphy* ■ *Dir* WS Van Dyke • *Scr* John Lee Mahin, Richard Schayer, from a story by Rowland Brown

The Devil Is a Woman ★★★★★U
Satirical romantic drama
1935 · US · BW · 76min

The film that archivist John Kobal described as "a shower of diamonds" and the one that Marlene Dietrich felt best captured her beauty was the final of seven vehicles engineered for her by director Josef von Sternberg, the "Leonardo of the lenses". She plays a seductress who, during carnival week in the south of Spain, finds her two most devoted infatuees in a duel for her attentions. A triumph of lighting, make-up and design, this is high camp stylisation of an unusually luxuriant kind, relentlessly amusing but not remotely silly. Even bemused viewers will delight at Dietrich's sublimely ridiculous costumes as well as some of Hollywood's most awe-inspiring imagery. The unobtainable object of desire has never been more sumptuously captured. DO DVD

Marlene Dietrich *Concha Perez* • Lionel Atwill *Don Pasqual* • Cesar Romero *Antonio Galvan* • Edward Everett Horton *Don Paquito* • Alison Skipworth *Señora Perez* • Don Alvarado *Morenito* • Tempe Pigott *Tuerta* • Paco Moreno *Secretary* ■ *Dir* Josef von Sternberg • *Scr* John Dos Passos, SK Winston, from the novel and play *La Femme et le Pantin (The Woman and the Puppet)* by Pierre Louys • *Cinematographers* Josef von Sternberg, Lucien Ballard • *Costume Designer* Travis Banton • *Art Directors* Josef von Sternberg, Hans Dreier

The Devil Makes Three ★★U
Thriller   1952 · US · BW · 90min

This so-so thriller, filmed in Bavaria, enabled MGM to satisfy the "I must do non-musicals" clause in Gene Kelly's contract and use up their postwar frozen Deutschmarks. Andrew Marton directs with verve but little regard for genre; he also fails to stop a miscast Kelly mugging as a counterintelligence officer who returns to Munich to find the German family who saved his life during the war. Pier Angeli brightens up the grim proceedings. TS

Gene Kelly *Capt Jeff Eliot* • Pier Angeli *Wilhelmina Lehrt* • Richard Rober *Col James Terry* • Richard Egan *Lt Parker* • Claus Clausen *Heisemann* • Wilfried Seyferth *Hansig* ■ *Dir* Andrew Marton • *Scr* Jerry Davis, from the story by Lawrence Bachmann [Lawrence P Bachmann]

Devil on Horseback ★★U
Drama   1954 · UK · BW · 93min

Juvenile star Jeremy Spenser plays the young son of a miner who becomes a successful jockey, but his cruel tendency to flog the horses has disastrous consequences. Directed by Cyril Frankel, this is well acted, strong on atmosphere and story, but lacks pace and the racing sequences are disappointing. RK

Googie Withers *Mrs Jane Cadell* • John McCallum *Charles Roberts* • Jeremy Spenser *Moppy Parfitt* • Meredith Edwards *Ted Fellowes* • Liam Redmond *"Scarlett" O'Hara* • Sam Kydd *Darky* • Malcolm Knight *Squib* ■ *Dir* Cyril Frankel • *Scr* Neil Paterson, Montagu Slater, from a story by James Curtis

The Devil, Probably ★★18
Drama   1977 · Fr · Colour · 91min

Although it won a prestigious award at Berlin, Robert Bresson's most earnest film is also his least engaging. In having 20-year-old student Antoine Monnier pay a junkie to stage his "suicide" in Père Lachaise cemetery, Bresson is clearly lamenting the death of individualism in an indifferent world. However, he is unable to find a suitable motive for the crime. Militant ecologist Henri de Maublanc blames society's ills on pollution and famine, but others seek political, spiritual, cultural and psychological causes. DP French +subtitles. DVD

Antoine Monnier *Charles* • Tina Irissari *Alberte* • Henri de Maublanc *Michel* • Laelita Carcano *Edwige* • Regis Hanrion *Dr Mime* • Nicolas Deguy *Valentin* • Geoffroy Gaussen *Bookseller* ■ *Dir/Scr* Robert Bresson

The Devil Rides Out ★★★15
Horror   1968 · UK · Colour · 91min

As a Satanic spectacular, this is the business, even if, for once in a Hammer horror, Christopher Lee is on the side of virtue. Director Terence Fisher searches for credibility in Dennis Wheatley's trashy tale of the Duc de Richleau (Lee) trying to save Patrick Mower's soul from the clutches of Charles Gray, a rotted limb of Satan. Whatever cynical giggles this might cause are soon flattened by the deadpan approach, some seriously orgiastic production numbers and a scary script from the ever-reliable Richard Matheson. TH DVD

Christopher Lee *Duc de Richleau* • Charles Gray *Mocata* • Nike Arrighi *Tanith* • Leon Greene *Rex* • Patrick Mower *Simon* • Gwen Ffrangcon-Davies *Countess* • Sarah Lawson *Marie* • Paul Eddington *Richard* ■ *Dir* Terence Fisher • *Scr* Richard Matheson, from the novel by Dennis Wheatley

The Devil-Ship Pirates ★★★PG
Period swashbuckling drama
1964 · UK · Colour · 82min

Christopher Lee received top-billing for the first time in this agreeable Hammer excursion into swashbuckling costume drama. He's the Spanish captain looting the English coast during the Armada era, who hits on a daring plan to save his crew when his ship runs aground – seal off the area and convince the locals Spain has conquered England. Hammer delivers its usual top-notch production values and Lee indulges in some splendid swordfighting. AJ DVD

Christopher Lee *Captain Robeles* • Andrew Keir *Tom* • John Cairney *Harry* • Duncan Lamont *Bosun* • Michael Ripper *Pepe* • Ernest Clark *Sir Basil* • Barry Warren *Manuel* ■ *Dir* Don Sharp • *Scr* Jimmy Sangster

The Devil Thumbs a Ride ★★★
Thriller   1947 · US · BW · 62min

Short and sharp, writer/director Felix Feist's low-budget gem features a no-nonsense performance from Lawrence Tierney. Here he plays a hitch-hiker, picked up by innocent motorist Ted North, who soon reveals himself to be an amoral killer. Tierney's electrifying presence overcomes the talky script and lifts this rarely seen thriller to the status of minor classic. AJ

Lawrence Tierney *Steve* • Ted North *Jimmy* • Nan Leslie *Carol* • Betty Lawford *Agnes* • Andrew Tombes *Joe Brayden* • Harry Shannon *Owens* • Glenn Vernon *Jack* • Marian Carr *Diane* ■ *Dir* Felix Feist • *Scr* Felix Feist, from the novel by Robert C DuSoe

The Devil to Pay ★★★U
Comedy   1930 · US · BW · 69min

Ronald Colman's dashing good looks made him a star in the silent era, but what really catapulted him to the ranks of the all-time movie greats was the coming of sound. It revealed an elegant speaking voice that became every male's ideal. Here Colman plays the son of a wealthy man who falls for a beautiful socialite (Loretta Lynn). It creaks a bit now, but confirms Colman's magnetic presence. TS

Ronald Colman *Willie Leeland* • Loretta Young *Dorothy Hope* • Florence Britton *Susan Leeland* • Frederick Kerr *Lord Leeland* • David Torrence *Mr Hope* • Mary Forbes *Mrs Hope* • Paul Cavanagh *Grand Duke Paul* • Myrna Loy *Mary Carlyle* ■ *Dir* George Fitzmaurice • *Scr* Benjamin Glazer, Frederick Lonsdale, from a play by Frederick Lonsdale

The Devil Wears Prada ★★★PG
Comedy drama   2006 · US · Colour · 104min

Meryl Streep is the boss from hell in this glossy but shallow fashion industry satire, quietly stealing every scene as the formidable editor of New York style magazine *Runway*. It's a delicious, precise performance that reduces Anne Hathaway's aspiring journalist to a crudely drawn, sitcom cliché, as she goofily struggles to meet Streep's increasingly difficult demands. Though the trials here are never quite as cruel as in ex-US *Vogue* staffer Lauren Weisberger's source book, they're still as entertaining, boasting a similar exuberance to director David Frankel's earlier project, *Sex and the City*. Yet for all its colourful and catty observations, the film lacks genuine bite, making a morally triumphant conclusion feel like a cop-out. SF Mild swearing. DVD

Meryl Streep *Miranda Priestly* • Anne Hathaway *Andy Sachs* • Stanley Tucci *Nigel* • Emily Blunt *Emily* • Simon Baker (1) *Christian Thompson* • Adrian Grenier *Nate* • Tracie Thoms *Lilly* • Rich Sommer *Doug* ■ *Dir* David Frankel • *Scr* Aline Brosh McKenna, from the novel by Lauren Weisberger • *Costume Designer* Patricia Field

The Devils ★★★★18
Historical horror   1971 · UK · Colour · 106min

Ken Russell's adaptation of Aldous Huxley's *The Devils of Loudun* is repulsive, hysterical, disturbing, overwhelming, stunning, compelling and fascinating. For once, Russell's surreal hallucinogenic style matches his frenzied material and, while condemned as being anti-religious, this is in fact a highly moral tale of absolute faith. In one of the most controversial and censored films of all time, Oliver Reed gives his best performance as the 17th-century French priest destroyed by political manipulators, and Vanessa Redgrave is almost as good as a humpbacked nun; Derek Jarman's sets are nearly a match for them both, however. AJ Violence, swearing, sex scenes, drug abuse, nudity. DVD

Oliver Reed *Father Urbain Grandier* • Vanessa Redgrave *Sister Jeanne* • Dudley Sutton *Baron de Laubardemont* • Max Adrian *Ibert* • Gemma Jones *Madeleine* • Murray Melvin *Mignon* • Michael Gothard *Father Barre* • Georgina Hale *Philippe* ■ *Dir* Ken Russell • *Scr* Ken Russell, from the play by John Whiting, from the novel *The Devils of Loudun* by Aldous Huxley

The Devil's Advocate ★★PG
Drama   1977 · W Ger · Colour · 104min

Based on the novel by Morris West, who also wrote the script, this moral fable stars John Mills as a terminally ill Catholic priest who comes to Rome in 1958 to decide if a man executed 14 years earlier deserves canonisation. This is strangely uninvolving, due mainly to having English actors play Italian characters. Tackling the persecution of the Jews as well as homosexuality within the priesthood, Guy Green's movie is also overloaded with would-be significance. AT

John Mills *Monsignor Blaise Meredith* • Stéphane Audran *Contessa* • Jason Miller *Dr Meyer* • Paola Pitagora *Nina* • Leigh Lawson *Nerone* • Timothy

D

West *Anselmo* • Patrick Mower *Il Lupo* • Raf Vallone *Aurelio* • Daniel Massey *Black* ■ *Dir* Guy Green • *Scr* Morris West, from his novel

The Devil's Advocate ★★ 18

Supernatural thriller 1997 · US · Colour · 143min

Keanu Reeves plays a hotshot lawyer lured to a New York law firm run by Al Pacino, whose character, John Milton, is an unsubtle signpost to the diabolical turn of events. The heavy-handed dropping of clues, including visions from Reeves's wife, Charlize Theron, makes the eventual revelation a very tardy one. It's not remotely believable and is directed with po-faced urgency. AT Swearing, violence, sex scenes. *DVD* *SL*

Keanu Reeves *Kevin Lomax* • Al Pacino *John Milton* • Charlize Theron *Mary Ann Lomax* • Jeffrey Jones *Eddie Barzoon* • Judith Ivey *Mrs Lomax* • Connie Nielsen *Christabella* • Craig T Nelson *Alexander Cullen* • Don King • *Dir* Taylor Hackford • *Scr* Jonathan Lemkin, Tony Gilroy, Andrew Neiderman

The Devil's Arithmetic ★★★ 12

Second World War fantasy drama 1999 · US · Colour · 91min

Modern teenager Kirsten Dunst, who only grudgingly accepts the Jewish faith, finds herself swept into the life of a Nazi death camp prisoner when she is asked to "open the front door" at a Seder feast. There, like a refugee Dorothy in *The Wizard of Oz*, she experiences all the Holocaust horrors first hand and learns to understand why traditions are so important to her people. Gritty and raw, if sometimes over-preachy, this packs a punch. AJ *DVD*

Kirsten Dunst *Hannah Stern* • Brittany Murphy *Rivkah* • Paul Freeman *Rabbi* • Mimi Rogers *Lenore Stern* • Louise Fletcher *Aunt Eva* • Nitzan Sharron *Ariel* • Shelly Skandrani *Leah* ■ *Dir* Donna Deitch • *Scr* Robert J Avrech, from the novel by Jane Yolen

The Devil's Backbone ★★★★ 15

Period supernatural horror 2001 · Sp/Mex · Colour · 107min

This allegorical ghost story is set near the end of the Spanish Civil War when ten-year-old Fernando Tielve is sent to a remote orphanage, reputedly haunted by the ghost of a dead boy. There Tielve uncovers a secret involving sadistic young caretaker Eduardo Noriega, who surely represents fascism in the film's vivid metaphor for the war. Mexican director Guillermo del Toro relies on the power of suggestion and sound for the chilling, ever-present horror as the fates of the orphans and their guardians become tragically inter-linked. AC Spanish +subtitles. Violence, sex scenes, swearing. *DVD* *BL*

Marisa Paredes *Carmen* • Eduardo Noriega (2) *Jacinto* • Federico Luppi *Casares* • Fernando Tielve *Carlos* • Iñigo Garcés *Jaime* ■ *Dir* Guillermo del Toro • *Scr* Guillermo del Toro, Antonio Trashorras, David Munoz • *Cinematographer* Guillermo Navarro

Devil's Canyon ★★

Western 1953 · US · Colour · 89min

Originally filmed in 3D, this RKO western is actually more of a thriller, as psychotic killer Stephen McNally attempts to wreak revenge on fellow inmate Dale Robertson, a former US marshal serving ten years for his involvement in a fatal shoot-out. Virginia Mayo helps McNally escape from jail, but no prizes for guessing who she ends up with. The period realism of the Arizona Territorial Prison setting makes this an unusual time-passer, but it's all a bit grim, and a stronger cast would have helped. TS *SD*

Dale Robertson *Billy Reynolds* • Virginia Mayo *Abby Nixon* • Stephen McNally *Jesse Gorman* • Arthur Hunnicutt *Frank Taggert* • Robert Keith (1) *Steve Morgan* • Jay C Flippen *Captain Wells* ■ *Dir* Alfred Werker • *Scr* Frederick Hazlitt Brennan, Harry Essex, from a story by Bennett R Cohen, Norton S Parker • *Cinematographer* Nicholas Musuraca

Devil's Cargo ★★

Detective mystery 1948 · US · BW · 63min

Two years after RKO dropped the Falcon franchise, it was snapped up by Poverty Row unit Film Classics, who changed the amateur sleuth's name to Michael Waring and installed professional magician John Calvert in the role. While this enabled Calvert to slip in a couple of conjuring tricks, it did little to bridge the charisma gap left by his predecessors. The formula remained unchanged, however, with Rochelle Hudson's husband facing jail for the murder of her putative lover. *Appointment with Murder* was the next instalment. DP

John Calvert *Michael Waring/The Falcon* • Rochelle Hudson *Margo Delgado* • Roscoe Karns *Lieutenant Hardy* • Lyle Talbot *Johnny Morello* • Theodore von Eltz *Thomas Mallon* ■ *Dir* John F Link • *Scr* Don Martin, from a story by Robert Tallman, Jason James, from the character created by Michael Arlen

Devil's Doorway ★★★ U

Western 1950 · US · BW · 84min

Robert Taylor gives one of his best performances as the Shoshone Indian who fights with distinction in the Civil War but is deprived of his valuable Wyoming spread by racists taking advantage of new homesteading laws. The contrived introduction of an inexperienced female lawyer to argue his case does little to lighten the mood of stark hopelessness. This is a visually powerful film thanks to the keen eye of director Anthony Mann and his cameraman John Alton. AE

Robert Taylor (1) *Lance Poole* • Louis Calhern *Verne Coolan* • Paula Raymond *Orrie Masters* • Marshall Thompson *Rod MacDougall* • James Mitchell *Red Rock* • Edgar Buchanan *Zeke Carmody* • Rhys Williams *Scotty MacDougall* • Spring Byington *Mrs Masters* ■ *Dir* Anthony Mann • *Scr* Guy Trosper

The Devil's Double ★★ 18

Drama based on a true story 2011 · Bel · Colour · 103min

Dominic Cooper tackles a demanding twin role in this drama based on the real-life exploits of the Iraqi army lieutenant forced to become the body double for Saddam Hussein's sadistic son Uday. As Latif Yahia, the soldier who knows his family will be killed unless he follows orders, Cooper seethes with indignation, but he is if anything even better as the terrifying Hussein Jr, playing him as a spoiled child with very grown-up appetites for sex and torture. The film's essentially superficial approach has little fresh insight to offer once it's established that Uday was indeed a monster and former 007 director Lee Tamahori manages only a few flickers of suspense. TJ Violence, swearing, drug abuse, sex scenes, nudity. *DVD* *BL*

Dominic Cooper *Uday Hussein/Latif Yahia* • Ludivine Sagnier *Sarrab* • Raad Rawi *Munem* • Philip Quast *Saddam Hussein/Faoaz* • Mimoun Oaissa *Ali* ■ *Dir* Lee Tamahori • *Scr* Michael Thomas, from the autobiography by Latif Yahia

Devil's Due ★★ 15

Horror 2014 · US · Colour · 88min

Devil's Due is a modest addition to the spawn-of-Satan genre, and the tired and over-familiar found-footage format does it few favours. Allison Miller and Zach Gilford honeymoon in the Dominican Republic and after a wild night out they both experience a mystery blackout. Back at home, they discover that they are going to have a baby. The film flirts brazenly with the clichés of the genre, from covens to creepy clairvoyants, and is contrived and inconsistent. But there are just about enough jumpy bits to keep the more easily pleased horror fan happy. DA Swearing.

Allison Miller *Samantha McCall* • Zach Gilford *Zach McCall* • Sam Anderson *Father Thomas* • Robert Belushi *Mason* • Catherine Kresge *Tina* • Aimee Carrero *Emily* ■ *Dir* Matt Bettinelli-Olpin, Tyler Gillett • *Scr* Lindsay Devlin

The Devil's Eye ★★ PG

Comedy 1960 · Swe · BW · 83min

This laboured comedy is one of Ingmar Bergman's poorest pictures. From the moment Gunnar Bjornstrand appears to introduce the methodology, theatricality rests heavily on both the staging and the performances. Jarl Kulle injects a little verve as the playboy released from Hell to seduce parson's daughter Bibi Andersson, thus removing the sty her purity has caused in the devil's eye. DP Swedish +subtitles. *DVD*

Jarl Kulle *Don Juan* • Bibi Andersson *Britt-Marie* • Axel Duberg *Jonas, her fiancé* • Nils Poppe *Pastor, her father* • Gertrud Fridh *Pastor's wife* • Sture Lagerwall *Pablo* • Stig Järrel *Satan* • Gunnar Björnstrand *Actor* ■ *Dir* Ingmar Bergman • *Scr* Ingmar Bergman, from the radio play *Don Juan Returns* by Oluf Bang

Devil's Gate ★★★ 12A

Mystery drama 2002 · UK · Colour · 99min

This old-fashioned melodrama is steeped in gothic bleakness, thanks to the Shetland locations. Laura Fraser reluctantly returns to the island of Devil's Gate after receiving a phone call from ex-boyfriend Callum Blue, who tells her that her estranged father (Tom Bell) is dying. Furious to discover the injuries have been exaggerated, she finds herself caught in a web of secrets and intrigue. Director Stuart St Paul's otherworldly tale may be a little overwrought at times, but its careful plotting and attention to character detail make for refreshing viewing. BP

Laura Fraser *Rachael* • Callum Blue *Rafe* • Luke Aikman *Matt* • Tom Bell *Jake* • Roger Ashton-Griffiths *Eagle* • Patrick Gordon *Clem* • Lynda Bellingham *Marlene* ■ *Dir* Stuart St Paul • *Scr* Stuart St Paul, Trevor Todd

The Devil's General ★★★

War drama 1955 · W Ger · BW · 96min

Featuring an award-winning performance from Curt Jurgens and based on a play by Carl Zuckmayer, this West German-made drama was inspired by the life of Ernst Udets, the highest-ranking German air ace to have survived the Great War, who took his own life just prior to the Second World War because of his disgust with Hitler. Jurgens is the loyal patriot and officer, driven to extremes by his abhorrence of the Nazi regime. Well made and engrossing. RB German +subtitles.

Curt Jurgens *General Harras* • Victor de Kowa *Schmidt-Lausitz* • Karl John *Oderbruch* • Eva-Ingeborg Scholz *Fräulein Mohrungen* • Marianne Koch *Dorothea Geiss* • Albert Lieven *Oberst Eilers* • Helmut Kautner • *Scr* Georg Hurdalek, Helmut Käutner, from a play by Carl Zuckmayer

The Devil's Hairpin ★★

Sports drama 1957 · US · Colour · 83min

In his second film as director, Cornel Wilde plays a washed-up racing champ who runs a bar and has a drunken girlfriend (Jean Wallace, the star's real-life wife). Goaded into making a comeback, Wilde has to fight his inner demons, which stem from the time when he almost killed his brother. It's a corny story, but petrol-heads should enjoy the racing footage and the sight of some lovely 1950s cars. AT

Cornel Wilde *Nick Jargin* • Jean Wallace *Kelly* • Arthur Franz *Rhinegold* • Mary Astor *Mrs Jargin* • Paul Fix *Doc* • Larry Pennell *Johnny* ■ *Dir* Cornel Wilde • *Scr* James Edmiston, Cornel Wilde, from Edmiston's novel *The Fastest Man on Earth*

The Devil's Holiday ★★★

Drama 1930 · US · BW · 80min

A young manicurist (Nancy Carroll) on the make is rescued from amorality and transformed by the strength of a young man's love. A morality play for its time that has little bearing on real life now, this nonetheless remains a tender love story and is sensitively directed by Edmund Goulding, who also wrote it. The film boasts a genuinely affecting performance by Carroll, who narrowly lost the 1929/30 best actress Oscar to Norma Shearer. RK

Nancy Carroll *Hallie Hobart* • Phillips Holmes *David Stone* • James Kirkwood *Mark Stone* • Hobart Bosworth *Ezra Stone* • Ned Sparks *Charlie Thorne* • Morgan Farley *Monkey McConnell* • Jed Prouty *Kent Carr* • Paul Lukas *Dr Reynolds* ■ *Dir* Edmund Goulding • *Scr* Edmund Goulding, from his story

Devil's Island ★★

Drama 1940 · US · BW · 65min

After treating a wounded political revolutionary, respected brain surgeon Boris Karloff is unjustly sentenced to ten years imprisonment on the notorious Devil's Island. There he must survive barbaric conditions and preserve his humanity in the shadow of the guillotine. Condemned by the French government on its first outing, the film was heavily censored and re-released a year later. Karloff's convincing performance holds this together. AJ

Boris Karloff *Dr Charles Gaudet* • Nedda Harrigan *Mme Lucien* • James Stephenson *Colonel Armand* • Adia Kuznetzoff *Pierre* • Rolla Gourvitch *Colette* • Will Stanton *Bobo* • Edward Keane *Dr Duval* • Robert Warwick *Demontre* • Pedro De Cordoba *Marcal* ■ *Dir* William Clemens • *Scr* Kenneth Garnet, Don Ryan, from the story *The Return of Doctor X* by Anthony Coldeway, Raymond Schrock

Devil's Knot ★★★ 15

Crime drama based on a true story 2013 · US · Colour · 113min

In a notorious case in Arkansas in 1993, a trio of teenagers who became known as the "West Memphis Three" were jailed for the murder of three young boys. The teens were convicted on highly questionable evidence, amid claims of a witch hunt and a tabloid frenzy, and director Atom Egoyan sets much of this dramatic retelling around the initial court case. However, the film runs the risk of fogging the truth by moulding the narrative into an exercise in emotional button-pushing. Although beautifully shot and with powerful performances from Colin Firth (as a private investigator) and Reese Witherspoon (as the mother of one of the boys), the film feels incomplete, the script ending long before the subsequent appeals and revelations that continued to grab headlines. TeS Swearing. *DVD* *BL*

Reese Witherspoon *Pam Hobbs* • Colin Firth *Ron Lax* • Dane DeHaan *Chris Morgan* • Mireille Enos *Vicki Hutcherson* • Bruce Greenwood *Judge Burnett* • Elias Koteas *Jerry Driver* • Stephen Moyer *John Fogelman* • Alessandro Nivola *Terry Hobbs* • Kevin Durand *John Mark Byers* ■ *Dir* Atom Egoyan • *Scr* Paul Harris Boardman, Scott Derrickson, from the non-fiction book *Devil's Knot: The True Story of the West Memphis Three* by Mara Leveritt

Devils of Darkness ★ 15

Horror 1964 · UK · Colour · 84min

The first British vampire movie to use a contemporary setting finds undead Hubert Noel posing as an artist in Brittany. Here he heads a cult of devil worshippers who indulge in orgies with exotic snake dancers and sacrifice innocent tourists on their graveyard crypt altar. Little sense of terror, or even atmosphere, is raised in this undistinguished, stilted dud. AJ *DVD*

William Sylvester *Paul Baxter* • Hubert Noel [Hubert Noël] *Count Sinistre/Armond du Moliere* • Tracy Reed *Karen* • Carole Gray *Tania* • Diana Decker *Madeline Braun* • Rona Anderson *Anne Forest* • Peter Illing *Inspector Malin* ■ *Dir* Lance Comfort • *Scr* Lyn Fairhurst

Devils on the Doorstep ★★★★

Second World War black comedy drama 2000 · Chi · Colour and BW · 162min

Treading the fine line between collaboration and resistance, Jiang Wen's sprawling study of life in an isolated Chinese village in the last days of the Japanese occupation provides a fascinating insight into a forgotten aspect of the Second World War. The director also stars as the nobody who suddenly becomes the centre of attention after two prisoners – a Japanese soldier and a Chinese translator – are billeted in his house for interrogation. However, it soon becomes clear the hostages have been

U SUITABLE FOR ALL   Uc SUITABLE ESPECIALLY FOR YOUNG CHILDREN (DVD ONLY)   PG PARENTAL GUIDANCE   12A UNDER 12s TO BE ACCOMPANIED (CINEMA ONLY)

abandoned and Jiang is forced to make the unenviable choice between disposing of them or risking his own neck to save them. DP Mandarin, Japanese +subtitles.

Jiang Wen *Ma Dasan* • Jiang Hongbo *Yu'er* • Teruyuki Kagawa *Kosaburo Hanaya* • Yuan Ding *Dong Hanchen* ■ *Dir* Jiang Wen • *Scr* You Fengwei, Shi Jianquan, Shu Ping, Jiang Wen, from a story by Jiang, Shu, from the novella *Shengcun* by You Fengwei

The Devil's Own ★★ 15
Thriller   1997 · US · Colour · 106min

Bedevilled by production problems (constant script changes, disenchanted Brad Pitt wanting to quit, changes in the political situation while shooting), it's hardly surprising that director Alan J Pakula's IRA thriller is a fudged disappointment. Harrison Ford is the New York cop who takes Irish émigré Pitt into his home without realising he's a terrorist on a missile-buying mission for the Republican cause. AJ Swearing, violence. *DVD* *BD*

Harrison Ford *Tom O'Meara* • Brad Pitt *Frankie McGuire, "Rory Devaney"* • Margaret Colin *Sheila O'Meara* • Rubén Blades *Edwin "Eddie" Diaz* • Treat Williams *Billy Burke* • George Hearn *Peter Fitzsimmons* • Mitchell Ryan *Chief Jim Kelly* • Natascha McElhone *Megan Doherty* • David O'Hara *Martin MacDuff* ■ *Dir* Alan J Pakula • *Scr* David Aaron Cohen, Vincent Patrick, Kevin Jarre

The Devil's Playground ★★ U
Western   1946 · US · BW · 65min

This was the first of 12 Hopalong Cassidy features to be produced by their star, silver-haired William Boyd. Boyd ensured his character operated according to a rigid ethical code, unusual considering that Hopalong dressed entirely in black, the clothing usually worn by the western villain, and rode a lone range. Here, he's accompanied by sidekick Andy Clyde and his trusty steed Topper. This story, which sees Cassidy set out to foil an evil sheriff, is an excellent example of a series western, and a fine introduction to Clarence E Mulford's gentleman cowboy. TS

William Boyd (1) *Hopalong Cassidy* • Andy Clyde *California Carlson* • Rand Brooks *Lucky Jenkins* • Elaine Riley *Mrs Evans* • Robert Elliott *Judge Morton* • Joseph J Greene *Sheriff* ■ *Dir* George Archainbaud • *Scr* Doris Schroeder, from a story by Ted Wilson, from characters by Clarence E Mulford

The Devil's Playground ★★★ 15
Drama   1976 · Aus · Colour · 94min

This is a nicely structured, if a tad po-faced look at the awkward sexual awakenings of boys at a Roman Catholic boarding school, made by Australian writer/director Fred Schepisi and based on his childhood experiences. Schepisi's intelligent screenplay gives the little-known cast a chance to indulge in a great deal of breast-beating. But he doesn't take us any deeper into the issue than a legion of others before. SH

Arthur Dignam *Brother Francine* • Nick Tate *Brother Victor* • Simon Burke *Tom Allen* • Charles McCallum *Brother Sebastian* • John Frawley *Brother Celian* • Jonathan Hardy *Brother Arnold* • Gerry Duggan *Father Hanrahan* ■ *Dir/Scr* Fred Schepisi

The Devil's Rain ★★★
Horror   1975 · US/Mex · Colour · 85min

This colourful, if confusing satanic shocker has coven leader Ernest Borgnine searching for an ancient book that will enable him to deliver a fresh batch of souls to the prince of darkness. Worth persevering through the muddled set-up for the effects-laden climax where most of the cast members are reduced to screaming, oozing slime. Also notable for the sight of *Star Trek*'s William Shatner tied naked to a sacrificial altar, and a brief appearance from John Travolta. AJ

Ernest Borgnine *Jonathan Corbis* • Eddie Albert *Dr Richards* • Ida Lupino *Mrs Preston* • William Shatner *Mark Preston* • Keenan Wynn *Sheriff Owens* • Tom Skerritt *Tom Preston* • Joan

Prather *Julie Preston* • John Travolta *Danny* ■ *Dir* Robert Fuest • *Scr* Gabe Essoe, James Ashton, Gerald Hopman

The Devil's Rejects ★★★ 18
Horror   2005 · US/Ger/Can · Colour · 104min

Rob Zombie follows up his 2001 debut *House of 1000 Corpses* with a pitch-black sequel that's bigger and nastier in every way. The film swaps the original's flashy visuals and surreal atmosphere for unflinching brutality and ultra-gritty realism. The crimes of the depraved Firefly family finally catch up with them, forcing the serial-killing Otis (Bill Moseley), Baby (Sheri Moon Zombie) and Captain Spaulding (Sid Haig) to run for their lives. This boasts grainy, 1970s-style cinematography and an evocative period soundtrack. SF *DVD*

Sid Haig *Captain Soaulding* • Bill Moseley *Otis* • Sheri Moon Zombie [Sheri Moon] *Baby* • Matthew McGrory *Tiny* • William Forsythe *Sheriff John Wydell* • Leslie Easterbrook *Mother Firefly* • Dave Sheridan *Officer Ray Dobson* ■ *Dir* Rob Zombie • *Scr* Rob Zombie, from his characters

The Devil's Rock ★★★ 18
Horror   2011 · NZ · Colour · 82min

A Nazi, a Kiwi soldier and a demon are the main characters in this horror chamber piece set during the Second World War. Arriving to blow up an enemy gun encampment, Captain Grogan (Craig Hall) discovers the bloody remains of German troops, ripped apart by a demon (Gina Varela) unleashed as part of the Nazis' research into the black arts. What follows is, by turns, silly and scary, with Varela seductively alluring as the she-beast from hell. Undemanding horror fans should be entertained. JR violence, swearing

Craig Hall *Captain Ben Grogan* • Matthew Sunderland *Col Klaus Meyer* • Gina Varela *Helena* • Karlos Drinkwater *Sergeant Joseph Tane* ■ *Dir* Paul Campion • *Scr* Paul Finch, Brett Ihaka, from a story by Paul Campion

The Devil's Teardrop ★★
Crime drama   2010 · US/Can · Colour · 89min

Strip away the tense soundtrack and there's little to get excited about in this mediocre crime thriller, in which Natasha Henstridge's special agent teams up with a retired FBI handwriting analyst (Tom Everett Scott) to stop a killer following a machine gun attack in a Washington DC train station. Adapted from the novel by *The Bone Collector* author Jeffery Deaver, it's a predictable tale that's littered with plot holes and continually reflects its TV movie-status despite earnest performances from its likeable leads. SF

Tom Everett Scott *Parker Kincaid* • Natasha Henstridge *Margaret Lukas* • Rena Sofer *Joan* • Gabriel Hogan *Len Hardy* • Jonathan Higgins *Cage* • Jake Goodman *Robby Kincaid* ■ *Dir* Norma Bailey • *Scr* Ron Hutchinson, from Jeffery Deaver's novel

The Devil's Wanton ★★★
Drama   1949 · Swe · BW · 80min

Based on his own script, Ingmar Bergman's first important film contains many of his later philosophical preoccupations, particularly his view of a Godless, loveless universe. Over-ambitious, though interesting in the light of its creator's entire oeuvre, it tells of a director and writer who become embroiled in the wretched life of a suicidal prostitute. Made very cheaply and using sets from another movie, it made no profit but enhanced Bergman's reputation in Sweden. However, he had to wait six years for *Smiles of a Summer's Night* to make his name internationally. RB Swedish +subtitles. *DVD*

Doris Svedlund *Birgitta-Carolina Soderberg* • Birger Malmsten *Thomas* • Eva Henning *Sofi* • Hasse Ekman *Martin Grande* • Stig Olin *Peter* • Irma Christenson *Linnea* • Anders Henrikson *Paul* ■ *Dir/Scr* Ingmar Bergman

Devotion ★★★★ U
Biographical drama   1946 · US · BW · 106min

Writers are notoriously difficult to portray on film: since writing is an intellectual concept and cinema a visual medium, how

does one convey what makes a writer write? Director Curtis Bernhardt doesn't bother with such ramifications, though. Olivia de Havilland and Ida Lupino play Charlotte and Emily Brontë, both of whom lust after Paul Henreid, while Arthur Kennedy is excellent as the alcoholic Bramwell. This romanticised saga could be about anybody, but it's still a splendid period melodrama. TS

Ida Lupino *Emily Brontë* • Olivia de Havilland *Charlotte Brontë* • Nancy Coleman *Anne Brontë* • Paul Henreid *Nicholls* • Sydney Greenstreet *Thackeray* • Arthur Kennedy *Branwell Brontë* • Dame May Whitty *Lady Thornton* ■ *Dir* Curtis Bernhardt • *Scr* Keith Winter, from a story by Theodore Reeves

Dharam Veer ★★★ PG
Fantasy adventure   1977 · Ind · Colour · 154min

Take a deep breath before settling down with this swashbuckling fairy tale because the action is as spectacular as it is complicated. Wild tigers, wise hawks, wicked princes and heroic gypsies all have their part to play here, but the core plotline concerns Dharmendra and Jeetendra as twin boys separated at birth. One is raised in luxury, the other as a woodcutter's son, but romance and a court conspiracy bring them together. DP Hindi +subtitles. *DVD*

Dharmendra *Dharam* • Jeetendra *Veer* • Pran *Hunter* • Zeenat Aman *Princess* ■ *Dir* Manmohan Desai • *Scr* Prayag Raj, KB Pathak

Dheepan ★★★ 15
Crime drama   2015 · Fr · Colour · 114min

Though it won the Palme D'Or at the 2015 Cannes film festival, Jacques Audiard's seventh feature is the weakest of his four films to premiere there. *Dheepan* is the story of an immigrant in modern France, with Jesuthasan Antonythasan as a Sri Lankan fighter who escapes the horrors of the civil war by teaming up with a woman and child to take on the identities and passports of a real family. The set-up works well, but the final explosion into violence seems too pat for such a slick, sophisticated storyteller. DW French +subtitles. Violence, swearing

Jesuthasan Antonythasan *Dheepan* • Kalieaswari Srinivasan *Yalini* • Claudine Vinasithamby *Illayaal* • Vincent Rottiers *Brahim* ■ *Dir* Jacques Audiard • *Scr* Jacques Audiard, Thomas Bidegain, Noé Debré

Dhoom ★★★ 12
Action thriller   2004 · Ind · Colour · 128min

Director Sanjay Gadhvi places the emphasis in this rousing adventure firmly on adrenaline action, as detective Abhishek Bachchan enlists the help of motorcycle rebel Uday Chopra to nab suave crook John Abraham. Consequently, Esha Deol and Rimi Sen are confined to love-interest musical interludes, as Gadhvi glorifies the speeding machines and their photogenic riders. Style unashamedly triumphs over substance throughout, but the story rattles along and the set pieces are very slickly staged. DP Hindi +subtitles. *DVD*

Abhishek Bachchan *Jai Dixit* • John Abraham *Kabir* • Uday Chopra *Ali* • Esha Deol *Sheena* • Rimi Sen *Sweety Dixit* ■ *Dir* Sanjay Gadhvi • *Scr* Vijay Krishna Acharya

Dhoom: 2 ★★★ 12
Action thriller   2006 · Ind · Colour · 151min

Pop video meets shampoo ad in director Sanjay Gadhvi's energetic and ultra-glossy sequel to his 2004 Bollywood action thriller, *Dhoom*. A vacuous but entertaining genre-hopper, it sees Abhishek Bachchan and Uday Chopra reprise their roles as the chalk-and-cheese Mumbai cops – this time, they are on the trail of a master-of-disguise thief (Hrithik Roshan), whose hi-tech heists provide the stunt-packed centre pieces for an otherwise rambling picture. Hunky Roshan and his wannabe accomplice (played by Aishwarya Rai) sizzle, and help to hide the many plot holes with their strong chemistry and model looks. SF English, Hindi +subtitles. *DVD*

Hrithik Roshan *Aryan Singh/Mr A* • Aishwarya Rai *Sunehri* • Abhishek Bachchan *Jai Dixit* • Bipasha Basu *Sonali Bose/Monali Bose* • Uday Chopra *Ali Akbar Fateh Khan* ■ *Dir* Sanjay Gadhvi • *Scr* Vijay Krishna Acharya, from a story by Aditya Chopra

Les Diables ★★★★ 15
Drama   2002 · Fr/Sp · Colour · 105min

By opening with the song from Charles Laughton's *The Night of the Hunter*, director Christophe Ruggia here alerts us to the fact that Adèle Haenel and Vincent Rottiers are children in peril. However, there's no single villain in the mould of Robert Mitchum's manic preacher, but an entire society that has failed the mentally traumatised girl and her tougher brother, who were abandoned by their mother and now seek to survive either inside institutions or on the run. The strength of this affecting film lies in its authenticity, sensitivity and the intensity of the performances. DP French +subtitles.

Adèle Haenel *Chloé* • Vincent Rottiers *Joseph* • Rochdy Labidi *Karim* • Jacques Bonnaffé *Doran* • Aurélia Petit *Joseph's mother* • Galamelah Lagraa *Djamel* ■ *Dir* Christophe Ruggia • *Scr* Christophe Ruggia, Olivier Lorelle

The Diabolical ★★★ 15
Horror   2015 · US · Colour · 82min

Despite facing foreclosure, Ali Larter resists the threats of a tech company representative (Patrick Fischler) and copes with the anxiety of a social worker (Merrin Dungey) over her daughter's anger-management issues. But her primary concern is that her kids' veins turn black when they try to leave the property... The performances are capable and the paranormal effects flashily effective, but director Alistair Legrand fails to generate any palpable terror and the ending feels rather rushed. DP Violence.

Ali Larter *Madison* • Arjun Gupta *Nikolai* • Max Rose *Jacob* • Chloe Perrin *Haley* ■ *Dir* Alistair Legrand • *Scr* Alistair Legrand, Luke Harvis

Diabolically Yours ★★★
Psychological thriller   1967 · Fr · Colour · 93min

Diabolically dubbed, more like. This excellent Gallic thriller, the last film made by master director Julien Duvivier (*Pépé le Moko*), was distributed worldwide in a version that saddled handsome Alain Delon and sexy Senta Berger with bland American accents, a poor decision that seriously affects the credibility of their characters. Not that it really matters, for this is one of those glossy French thrillers where the goodies are good-looking, the baddies are slimy and all the plot twists unravel by the end. TS French dubbed.

Alain Delon *Pierre* • Senta Berger *Christiane* • Sergio Fantoni *Freddie* • Peter Mosbacher *Kim* ■ *Dir* Julien Duvivier • *Scr* Julien Duvivier, Paul Gégauff, from the novel by Louis Thomas

Diabolique ★★ 18
Thriller   1996 · US · Colour · 102min

If ever a film didn't need a Hollywood remake, it's Henri-Georges Clouzot's superb, twist-packed 1954 thriller *Les Diaboliques*, about a corpse that refuses to stay dead. Director Jeremiah Chechik hasn't got the foggiest idea how to create atmosphere, relying instead on melodramatic performances and the odd thunderstorm. JC Violence, swearing, nudity. *DVD*

Sharon Stone *Nicole Horner* • Isabelle Adjani *Mia Baran* • Chazz Palminteri *Guy Baran* • Kathy Bates *Shirley Vogel* • Spalding Gray *Simon Veatch* • Shirley Knight *Edie Danziger* • Allen Garfield *Leo Kaztman* ■ *Dir* Jeremiah Chechik • *Scr* Don Roos, from the 1954 film *Les Diaboliques*

LANDMARK FILM
Brimming with original tricks and a heady atmosphere, Henri-Georges Clouzot's moody thriller inspires many imitations

Les Diaboliques ★★★★★ 15

Thriller 1954 · Fr · BW · 112min

In this brilliantly nasty thriller from Henri-Georges Clouzot, the wife (Vera Clouzot) and mistress (Simone Signoret) of a sadistic headmaster (Paul Meurisse) plot together to kill him – but then find his body is missing. The film's graveyard gloom is typified by the oppressive atmosphere of neglect and despair at Meurisse's school, while the final shot marvellously suggests unpleasantness to come – the climax here is one of cinema's most diabolical scenes. This is a masterpiece that easily matches the best of Hitchcock. TH French +subtitles.

DVD **BL**

Simone Signoret *Nicole Horner* • Vera Clouzot *Christina Delassalle* • Paul Meurisse *Michel Delassalle* • Charles Vanel *Inspector Fichet* • Pierre Larquey *M Drain* • Noël Roquevert *M Herboux* • Jean Brochard *Plantiveau* • Thérèse Dorny *Mme Herboux* • Michel Serrault *Raymond* ■ *Dir* Henri-Georges Clouzot • *Scr* Henri-Georges Clouzot, Jérôme Géromini, Frédéric Grendel, René Masson, from the novel *Celle Qui N'Etait Plus* by Pierre Boileau, Thomas Narcejac • *Cinematographer* Armand Thirard

Diabolo Menthe ★★★★ 12

Romantic drama 1977 · Fr · Colour · 96min

Director Diane Kurys also wrote the script for this highly rated French film, an insightful portrayal of early adolescence that was extensively based on her own experiences. The film follows a rebellious schoolgirl through her spell at a stuffy French lycée. It's a rollercoaster ride whose ups and downs encompass sadistic teachers and first periods, parental divorce and first love. DA French +subtitles.

Eléonore Klarwein *Anne Weber* • Odile Michel *Frederique Weber* • Anouk Ferjac *Madame Weber* • Coralie Clément *Perrine Jacquet* • Marie Véronique Maurin *Muriel Cazau* • Valérie Stand *Martine Dubreuil* ■ *Dir/Scr* Diane Kurys

Diagnosis: Murder ★★

Crime thriller 1974 · UK · Colour · 90min

Psychiatrist Christopher Lee is suspected of murdering his wife after she disappears. The twist is that he was planning to murder her anyway so he could be with his mistress. This tepid made-for-television thriller received a brief theatrical release thanks to its star cast. A stoic performance from Lee and a few whodunnit wrinkles along the way make it of passing interest. AJ

Jon Finch *Inspector Lomax* • Judy Geeson *Helen* • Christopher Lee *Dr Stephen Hayward* • Tony Beckley *Sergeant Green* • Dilys Hamlett *Julia Hayward* • Jane Merrow *Mary Dawson* • Colin Jeavons *Bob Dawson* ■ *Dir* Sidney Hayers • *Scr* Philip Levene

Dial M for Murder ★★★★ PG

Thriller 1954 · US · Colour · 101min

Alfred Hitchcock only took on this version of Frederick Knott's play to fulfil his Warners contract, and such was his lack of interest in the project that he claimed he could have phoned in his direction and that the action wouldn't have been any less interesting if he had staged it in a phone box. But as Ray Milland plots to bump off wife Grace Kelly there are plenty of deft touches that loudly proclaim "genius at work". Milland's sinister sophistication catches the eye, but Kelly's subtly shaded suffering is superb. Remade with Michael Douglas and Gwyneth Paltrow in 1998 as *A Perfect Murder*. DP **DVD** **SD**

Ray Milland *Tony Wendice* • Grace Kelly *Margot Wendice* • Robert Cummings *Mark Halliday* • John Williams *Chief Inspector Hubbard* • Anthony Dawson *Captain Lesgate* • Patrick Allen *Pearson* • George Leigh *William* • George Alderson *Detective* • Robin Hughes *Police sergeant* ■ *Dir* Alfred Hitchcock • *Scr* Frederick Knott, from his play

Diameter of the Bomb ★★★ 12

Documentary 2005 · UK/Can · Colour · 82min

This well-meaning, but slightly overbearing, documentary examines the aftermath of the bombing of a Jerusalem bus in June 2002. The film looks at how this atrocity not only ended the lives of the victims and the Hamas suicide bomber who detonated the device, but also shaped the lives of many others, from the victims' families to the emergency workers who were at the scene or treated the injured later. The title is inspired by a poem by Yehuda Amichai, which speaks of the concentric waves of repercussion that emanate from a single act of political violence to encompass the world itself. Unfortunately, the documentary's reach is more limited than that, and while the film-makers strive for even-handedness, there's little attempt to draw a bigger picture. LF English, Hebrew, Arabic +subtitles.

■ *Dir* Andrew Quigley, Steven Silver

The Diamond ★★

Crime drama 1954 · UK · BW · 83min

A rare UK venture into 3D, this crime programme filler was shot in a process called Spacemaster. The action follows American detective Dennis O'Keefe as he teams with British bobby Philip Friend to uncover how a batch of synthetic diamonds links two seemingly unconnected incidents – a bullion robbery and the disappearance of an atomic scientist. Mostly shown in its flat format, the film was jointly directed by its star and Montgomery Tully, who was something of a dab hand at atmosphere-free mysteries. DP

Dennis O'Keefe *Treasury Agent Joe Dennison* • Margaret Sheridan *Marlene Miller* • Philip Friend *Chief Inspector McClaren* • Alan Wheatley *Thompson Blake* • Francis De Wolff *Yeo* ■ *Dir* Dennis O'Keefe, Montgomery Tully • *Scr* John C Higgins, from the novel *Rich Is the Treasure* by Maurice Procter

Diamond City ★★ PG

Drama 1949 · UK · BW · 85min

This is a mediocre attempt by the British film industry to transplant the wide-open spaces, excitement and gunslinging of the American western to the veldts of South Africa. Stolid David Farrar tries to bring law and order to the titular diamond-mining town, which takes some doing as the movie was shot at Denham Studios in London. A lacklustre oddity. AJ **DVD**

David Farrar *Stafford Parker* • Honor Blackman *Mary Hart* • Diana Dors *Dora* • Niall MacGinnis *Hans Muller* • Andrew Crawford *David Raymond* • Mervyn Johns *Hart* ■ *Dir* David MacDonald • *Scr* Roland Pertwee, from a story by Roger Bray

Diamond Head ★★★

Melodrama 1962 · US · Colour · 106min

Charlton Heston plays a powerful landowner with ambitions to be Hawaii's senator. When his sister Yvette Mimieux plans to marry Polynesian James Darren (in heavy make-up), Heston does everything he can to prevent it – despite having a Hawaiian mistress who's pregnant with his child. This isn't the Hawaii of grass skirts, ukeleles, hula-hula and aloha. Instead it's the exotic setting for a no-holds-barred melodrama, with Heston simmering impressively like the Diamond Head volcano of the title. AT

Charlton Heston *Richard Howland* • Yvette Mimieux *Sloan Howland* • George Chakiris *Dr Dean Kahana* • France Nuyen *Mei Chen* • James Darren *Paul Kahana* • Aline MacMahon *Kapiolani Kahana* ■ *Dir* Guy Green • *Scr* Marguerite Roberts

The Diamond Queen ★★ U

Period adventure 1953 · US · Colour · 76min

This swashbuckler has French adventurer Fernando Lamas going to India in search of a jewel fit for the crown of Louis XIV. There he finds a big, fat, sparkly diamond attached to Maya, queen of Nepal (Arlene Dahl), who is herself attached to the Great Mogul, a jealous cove played by Sheldon Leonard. As

usual with these essays in exotica, there's a lot of silly dialogue, lavish costumes and lascivious dance routines. Lamas and Dahl married shortly after the film was completed. AT

Fernando Lamas *Jean Tavernier* • Arlene Dahl *Maya* • Gilbert Roland *Baron Paul de Cabannes* • Sheldon Leonard *Great Mogul* • Jay Novello *Gujar* • Michael Ansara *Jumla* • Richard Hale *Gabriel Tavernier* ■ *Dir* John Brahm • *Scr* Otto Englander, from his story

Diamond Skulls ★★★ 18

Drama 1989 · UK · Colour · 83min

Gabriel Byrne stars in this picture that offers him a chance to extend his already considerable range of characters, playing an aristocrat who tries to cover up a hit-and-run accident. In a rare venture into fictional films, documentary specialist Nick Broomfield only scratches the surface of his themes of class responsibility and dangerous obsession. Yet he maintains the dramatic tension more than adequately. DP Violence, swearing, sex scenes.

Gabriel Byrne *Lord Hugo Buckton* • Amanda Donohoe *Ginny Buckton* • Douglas Hodge *Jamie* • Sadie Frost *Rebecca* • Matthew Marsh *Raul* • Michael Hordern *Lord Crewne* • Judy Parfitt *Lady Crewne* • Ralph Brown (2) *Jack* • Ian Carmichael *Exeter* ■ *Dir* Nick Broomfield • *Scr* Tim Rose Price, from an idea by Nick Broomfield, Tim Rose Price

Diamonds ★ PG

Crime drama 1975 · US/Is · Colour · 103min

Robert Shaw in a dual role in this heist picture as two brothers: one a jewel thief, the other a security expert. This sort of set-up is both technically cumbersome and rather tiresome, and the film does not disappoint on either count, being very tedious and shoddily made. Shelley Winters contributes an excruciating cameo. AT

Robert Shaw *Charles/Earl Hodgson* • Richard Roundtree *Archie* • Barbara Seagull [Barbara Hershey] *Sally* • Shelley Winters *Zelda Shapiro* • Shai K Ophir *Moshe* • Gadi Yageel *Gaby* ■ *Dir* Menahem Golan • *Scr* Menaham Golan, David Paulsen, from a story by Menaham Golan

Diamonds ★★

Comedy drama 1999 · US/Ger · Colour · 91min

To see Kirk Douglas slowed by both his own physical disability and a banal script is sad indeed. The 83-year-old actor plays a man who, like himself, is suffering from the after effects of a stroke. His son (Dan Aykroyd) wants him to go into a home, but Dad, who used to be a boxer, wants to stay independent. Deciding to pick up the gems he was once paid to throw a fight, Douglas, his son and grandson (Corbin Allred) drive to Reno. The dialogue is tedious and the ideas are older than Douglas himself. TH

Kirk Douglas *Harry* • Lauren Bacall *Sin-Dee* • Dan Aykroyd *Lance* • Corbin Allred *Michael* • Jenny McCarthy *Sugar* • Kurt Fuller *Moses* • Mariah O'Brien *Tiffany* • John Landis *Gambler* ■ *Dir* John Asher [John Mallory Asher] • *Scr* Allan Aaron Katz

Diamonds Are Forever ★★ 12

Spy adventure 1971 · UK · Colour · 120min

After *You Only Live Twice*, Sean Connery said "Never again", but after George Lazenby's sole effort in *On Her Majesty's Secret Service*, Connery was lured back for a fee of more than $1 million, which he donated to the Scottish International Educational Trust. One of the weakest Bonds, its plot about diamond smuggling develops rather tiresomely, while Connery simply goes through the motions. AT **DVD** **BL**

Sean Connery *James Bond* • Jill St John *Tiffany Case* • Charles Gray *Blofeld* • Lana Wood *Plenty O'Toole* • Jimmy Dean *Willard Whyte* • Bruce Cabot *Saxby* • Putter Smith *Mr Kidd* • Bruce Glover *Mr Wint* • Norman Burton *Felix Leiter* • Joseph Furst *Dr Metz* • Bernard Lee *"M"* • Desmond Llewelyn *"Q"* • Leonard Barr *Shady Tree* • Lois Maxwell *Miss Moneypenny* ■ *Dir* Guy Hamilton • *Scr* Richard Maibaum, Tom Mankiewicz, from the novel by Ian Fleming

Diamonds for Breakfast ★★ U

Crime caper 1968 · UK · Colour · 102min

Marcello Mastroianni sleepwalks through this dotty crime caper that, like so many 1960s co-productions, sought to reproduce the suave heroism of the Bond movies. He plays a shop-owner who is fourth in line to the Russian throne. Debutant director Christopher Morahan fails to invest much fun or excitement into this tale of an impoverished nobleman's bid to swipe the Romanov gems with the help of seven sexy assistants. DP

Marcello Mastroianni *"Nicky", Grand Duke Nicholas* • Rita Tushingham *Bridget* • Elaine Taylor *Victoria* • Maggie Blye *Honey* • Francesca Tu [Francisca Tu] *Jeanne* • Warren Mitchell *Popov* • Leonard Rossiter *Inspector* ■ *Dir* Christopher Morahan • *Scr* Pierre Rouve, NF Simpson, Ronald Harwood

Diana ★★ 12

Drama based on a true story 2013 · UK/US/Swe · Colour · 107min

Director Oliver Hirschbiegel (Oscar-nominated for Hitler portrait *Downfall*) struggles to add anything new or insightful in this dramatisation of the two years in the life of Princess Diana that led up to 1997's fatal car crash in Paris. Naomi Watts's Diana is a bundle of mannerisms, using fluttering eyelashes and winsome tactics to woo Pakistani heart surgeon Hasnat Khan (a saint-like Naveen Andrews). Evidently, Hirschbiegel and Watts are wary of probing too deeply into the mindset of the "Queen of people's hearts", making the end result pure fluff. SP Swearing. **DVD** **BL**

Naomi Watts *Princess Diana* • Naveen Andrews *Dr Hasnat Khan* • Douglas Hodge *Paul Burrell* • Geraldine James *Oonagh Toffolo* • Charles Edwards *Patrick Jephson* • Juliet Stevenson *Sonia* • Cas Anvar *Dodi Fayed* ■ *Dir* Oliver Hirschbiegel • *Scr* Stephen Jeffreys

Diana & Me ★★

Romantic comedy 1997 · Aus · Colour · 97min

Toni Collette plays a frumpy Australian innocent whose name, Diana Spencer, wins her a trip to London. There her efforts to meet her namesake lead to much crossing of paths, misadventures with paparazzi Dominic West and her transformation from geek to chic. Written and produced before the Princess of Wales's death, this reeks of bad taste, despite the addition of an opening scene that turns the rest of the movie into a flashback. AME

Toni Collette *Diana Spencer* • Dominic West *Rob Naylor* • Malcolm Kennard *Mark Fraser* • Victoria Eagger *Carol* • John Simm *Neil* • Serena Gordon *Lady Sarah Myers-Booth* • Roger Barclay *Richard* • Tom Hillier *Neville* • Jerry Hall • Bob Geldof • Kylie Minogue ■ *Dir* David Parker • *Scr* Matt Ford, from a screenplay (unproduced) by Elizabeth Coleman

Diane ★★ U

Historical romance 1955 · US · Colour · 110min

"Sweater girl" Lana Turner is in period costume as Diane de Poitier, the love consultant to French king Pedro Armendáriz who nevertheless falls for the king's son, Roger Moore. Stuffed to the frills with Hollywood detail, this lavish production does benefit from its majestic score by the great Miklos Rozsa. The dialogue, however, betrays none of the usual wit and grace of its writer, Christopher Isherwood. TH

Lana Turner *Diane* • Roger Moore *Prince Henri* • Pedro Armendáriz *Francis I* • Marisa Pavan *Catherine de Medici* • Cedric Hardwicke *Ruggieri* • Torin Thatcher *Count de Breze* • Taina Elg *Alys* ■ *Dir* David Miller (1) • *Scr* Christopher Isherwood, from the novel *Diane de Poitier* by John Erskine

Diary for My Children ★★★★ 12

Political biographical drama 1982 · Hun · BW · 102min

Winner of the special jury prize at Cannes, this is the first part of Marta Mészáros's superb *Diary* trilogy. Based on her own experiences in Budapest after her family returned from exile in the Soviet Union, the

U SUITABLE FOR ALL   Uc SUITABLE ESPECIALLY FOR YOUNG CHILDREN (DVD ONLY)   PG PARENTAL GUIDANCE   12A UNDER 12s TO BE ACCOMPANIED (CINEMA ONLY)

film gives such a precise portrait of a nation coming to terms with the strictures of communism that it was not shown in the west until 1984. Although time and place are established with great skill, the direction is curiously dispassionate for an autobiography. DP Hungarian +subtitles. **DVD**

Zsuzsa Czinkoczi *Juli* • Anna Polony *Magda* • Jan Nowicki *Janos* • Tamas Toth *Janos's son* • Mari Szemes *Grandmother* • Pal Zolnay *Grandfather* ■ *Dir/Scr* Marta Mészáros

Diary for My Loves ★★★★ PG

Political biographical drama
1987 · Hun · Colour and BW · 130min

The sequel to *Diary for My Children* takes events from the death of Stalin to the 1956 Hungarian uprising. Again, Marta Mészáros humanises this momentous period by focusing on Zsuzsa Czinkoczi, the 18-year-old girl whose determination to use her Moscow film scholarship to trace her imprisoned father results in a relationship with activist Jan Nowicki. Acted with integrity and probing the psychological depths of its characters, this is a highly personal yet acutely political film. DP Hungarian +subtitles.

Zsuzsa Czinkoczi *Juli* • Anna Polony *Magda* • Jan Nowicki *Janos* • Pal Zolnay *Grandfather* • Mari Szemes *Grandmother* • Irina Kouberskaya *Anna Pavlova* • Adel Kovats *Natacha* ■ *Dir* Marta Mészáros • *Scr* Marta Mészáros, Eva Pataki

Diary for My Father and Mother ★★★

Political biographical drama
1990 · Hun · Colour and BW · 110min

The concluding part of director Marta Mészáros's autobiographical trilogy, which began with *Diary for My Loves* and continued with *Diary for My Loves*. Tracing the course and consequences of the 1956 uprising in Hungary, the film is more focused on historical events than its predecessors. So, while those familiar with the central characters will have an advantage, the action should still be comprehensible to new viewers. Mészáros spins her complex web of shifting loyalties, dubious motives and personal crises with great skill. DP Hungarian +subtitles.

Zsuzsa Czinkoczi *Juli* • Jan Nowicki *Janos* • Mari Torocsik *Vera* • Ildiko Bansagi *Ildi* • Anna Polony *Magda* ■ *Dir* Marta Mészáros • *Scr* Marta Mészáros, Eva Pataki

Diary of a Chambermaid ★★★ 15

Satirical period drama 1946 · US · BW · 83min

Although ostensibly a vehicle for Paulette Goddard, penned and co-produced by her then-husband, Burgess Meredith, this is also a bold attempt by Jean Renoir to make a comedy of domestic manners in the style of his own *La Règle du Jeu*, within the strictures of the Hollywood system. While his intentions are undermined by the inconsistent playing of a seemingly well-chosen cast, Meredith's adaptation and Renoir's direction are not without merit. DP

Paulette Goddard *Celestine* • Burgess Meredith *Capt Mauger* • Hurd Hatfield *Georges* • Francis Lederer *Joseph* • Judith Anderson *Mme Lanlaire* • Florence Bates *Rose* • Irene Ryan *Louise* ■ *Dir* Jean Renoir • *Scr* Burgess Meredith, from the novel by Octave Mirbeau

The Diary of a Chambermaid ★★★★ 12

Drama 1964 · Fr/It · BW · 93min

Shifting the action from the turn of the century to 1928, Luis Buñuel's reworking of Octave Mirbeau's novel is far more savage than Jean Renoir's 1946 version. Buñuel scathingly reveals the fascist tendencies of the French bourgeoisie, while simultaneously presenting a hilarious gallery of grotesques for us to laugh at. Jeanne Moreau plays Célestine as a cooly calculating customer, while Michel Piccoli's rakish husband and Georges Géret's bigoted gamekeeper are both suitably loathsome. A mercilessly bitter film,

undeservedly overshadowed by the director's other masterpieces. DP French +subtitles. **DVD**

Jeanne Moreau *Célestine* • Georges Géret [Georges Geret] *Joseph* • Michel Piccoli *M Monteil* • Françoise Lugagne *Mme Monteil* • Daniel Ivernel *Capitaine Mauger* • Jean Ozenne *M Rabour* • Gilberte Géniat *Rose* • Jean-Claude Carrière *Curé* ■ *Dir* Luis Buñuel • *Scr* Luis Buñuel, Jean-Claude Carrière, from the novel by Octave Mirbeau

Diary of a City Priest ★★

Biographical drama 2001 · US · Colour · 78min

Based on the autobiography of Catholic priest Father John McNamee, this worthy drama owes an obvious debt to Georges Bernanos's *Diary of a Country Priest*, which was memorably filmed in 1950 by Robert Bresson. David Morse's inner-city cleric feels the agony of loneliness and the demands on his faith as he ministers to his Philadelphia parishioners. Director Eugene Martin tries to emulate Bresson's pared down approach, but the decision to animate some of the saints in the stained-glass windows of St Malachy's church to turn Morse's deliberations into dialogue was a miscalculation. DP

David Morse *Father John McNamee* • John Ryan *Father Dave Hagan* • Phillip Goodwin *St Francis of Assisi* • Ana Reeder *St Therese* • Robert Sella *St Malachy* • Judy Bauerlein *Sister Mary* ■ *Dir* Eugene Martin • *Scr* Eugene Martin, from the autobiography by Father John McNamee

Diary of a Country Priest ★★★★★ PG

Drama 1950 · Fr · BW · 110min

One of the most influential films ever made, this sublime masterpiece shows how an adaptation can remain faithful to its source while still being wholly cinematic. Building atmosphere, character and content through the gradual accumulation of detail, director Robert Bresson minutely captures the agony, humility and despair suffered by a dying priest who feels he has failed in his mission to increase the holiness of his flock. Claude Laydu, whose first film this was, is utterly convincing in the lead role, and the result is an almost spiritual experience. Although Bresson was forced to cut 40 minutes, this is nonetheless a glorious example of the power that cinema can attain. DP French +subtitles. **DVD**

Claude Laydu *Priest of Ambricourt* • Nicole Ladmiral *Chantal* • Nicole Maurey *Mademoiselle Louise* • Marie-Monique Arkell *Countess* • Armand Guibert *Priest of Torcy* • Jean Riveyre *Count* • Jean Danet *Olivier* ■ *Dir* Robert Bresson • *Scr* Robert Bresson, from the novel by Georges Bernanos • *Cinematographer* Léonce-Henri Burel

Diary of a Hitman ★★ 18

Crime thriller 1992 · US · Colour · 86min

This ambitious but gloomy existential thriller never really shakes off its stage origins despite an impressive cast. Forest Whitaker plays a world-weary assassin who has an attack of conscience when he is hired to kill Sherilyn Fenn and her Aids-afflicted child. The performances are impressively low-key, but it's just a little too talky and static. JF

Forest Whitaker *Dekker* • Sherilyn Fenn *Jain* • Sharon Stone *Kiki* • Seymour Cassel *Koenig* • James Belushi *Shandy* • Lewis Smith *Zidzyk* ■ *Dir* Roy London • *Scr* Kenneth Pressman, from his play *Insider's Price*

Diary of a Lost Girl ★★★★★ PG

Silent drama 1929 · Ger · BW · 115min

It took German director GW Pabst to recognise the unique qualities of Louise Brooks, ill-used by Hollywood. Having made the exquisite bob-haired actress into an enduring icon with *Pandora's Box*, charting the decline and fall of the amoral Lulu, this followed immediately. This time Brooks's heroine descends into degradation as an innocent victim of circumstance, suffering harsh and painful cruelties at the hands of a social order dominated by sex, money and hypocrisy. Massacred by the censors –

apparently almost half the film was excised before its release – but what remains is an absorbing masterpiece of silent cinema. RK **DVD** **Blu**

Louise Brooks *Thymiane Henning* • Josef Rovensky *Robert Henning* • Fritz Rasp *Meinert* • Edith Meinhard *Erika* • Vera Pawlowa *Aunt Frieda* • André Roanne *Count Osdorff* • Arnold Korff *Elder Count Osdorff* • Andrews Engelmann *Director of reform school* ■ *Dir* GW Pabst • *Scr* Rudolf Leonhardt, from the novel *Das Tagebuch einer Verlorenen* by Margarethe Boehme

Diary of a Mad Housewife ★★★★

Drama 1970 · US · Colour · 94min

This is an acerbic, witty and perceptive peek at the world of American housewife Carrie Snodgress, married to snob Richard Benjamin and locked into an affair with suave author Frank Langella. Snodgress was never this good again (she was nominated for an Oscar for her performance). Benjamin virtually repeated his smarmy performance in *Marriage of a Young Stockbroker* the following year. TS

Richard Benjamin *Jonathan Balser* • Frank Langella *George Prager* • Carrie Snodgress *Tina Balser* • Lorraine Cullen *Sylvie Balser* • Frannie Michel *Liz Balser* • Lee Addoms *Mrs Prinz* ■ *Dir* Frank Perry • *Scr* Eleanor Perry, from the novel by Sue Kaufman

Diary of a Madman ★★ 15

Horror 1963 · US · Colour · 92min

French magistrate Vincent Price inherits an invisible evil spirit when he accidentally kills a condemned murderer in prison. This entity then forces him to slash to death Nancy Kovack, the opportunistic model who has been posing for his amateur sculptures. Standard horror fare, with a neat 19th-century period atmosphere and Price having another shuddery field day in a tailor-made histrionic role. AJ Violence.

Vincent Price *Simon Cordier* • Nancy Kovack *Odette* • Chris Warfield *Paul* • Elaine Devry *Jeanne* • Stephen Roberts *Rennedon* • Lewis Martin *Priest* ■ *Dir* Reginald Le Borg • *Scr* Robert E Kent, from the story *La Horla* by Guy de Maupassant

Diary of a Serial Killer ★ 18

Thriller 1997 · US · Colour · 88min

While investigating transvestite nightlife, a struggling freelance writer stumbles across a serial killer in action. But rather than report the crime to the driven detective in charge of the case, he strikes up a bizarre deal to document the killer's motives and handiwork. A promising concept is ruined by the soap opera approach and the miscast lead actors. AJ Swearing, violence. **DVD**

Gary Busey *Nelson Keece* • Michael Madsen *Haynes* • Arnold Vosloo *Stefan* • Julia Campbell *Juliette* • Reno Wilson *Larou* ■ *Dir* Joshua Wallace, Alan Jacobs • *Scr* Jennifer Badham-Stewart, Christopher Koefoed

Diary of a Sex Addict ★★★ 18

Erotic thriller 2001 · US · Colour · 93min

Less trashy than the title suggests, this is actually a frank and troubling attempt to seriously tackle a genuine addiction. Michael Des Barres offers just the right combination of charm and sleaze as the English married restaurant owner who leads a voracious double life, while Rosanna Arquette and Nastassja Kinski add further credibility as wife and psychiatrist, respectively. Shot on digital video with jump cuts that emphasise Des Barres mounting mental anxiety, this is a fairly convincing portrait of a rarely tackled psychological problem. JC **DVD**

Rosanna Arquette *Grace Horn* • Nastassja Kinski *Jane Bordeaux* • Michael Des Barres *Sammy Horn* • Ed Begley Jr *Dr Aaron Spencer* • Alexandra Paul *Katherine* ■ *Dir* Joseph Brutsman • *Scr* Tony Peck, Joseph Brutsman

The Diary of a Teenage Girl ★★★★ 18

Drama 2015 · US/Bel · Colour · 97min

Explicit but never exploitative, this sensitive and entertaining take on Phoebe Gloeckner's novel dares to tell of smart 15-year-old Minnie (Bel Powley from TV's *Benidorm*) who wants to have sex but fears it will never ever happen. A tricky topic but credible, especially in San Francisco in 1976, where her mother (Kristen Wiig) parties hard and dates a simplistic 35-year-old (Alexander Skarsgård). Powley, Wiig and Skarsgård turn in finely observed turns, as Minnie follows her instincts and learns from her mistakes. KK **DVD**

Bel Powley *Minnie* • Alexander Skarsgård *Monroe* • Kristen Wiig *Charlotte* • Christopher Meloni *Pascal* • Margarita Levieva *Tabatha* ■ *Dir* Marielle Heller • *Scr* Marielle Heller, from the novel *The Diary of a Teenage Girl: an Account in Words and Pictures* by Phoebe Gloeckner

Diary of a Wimpy Kid ★★ PG

Comedy 2010 · US · Colour · 88min

Based on the bestselling "novel in cartoons" by Jeff Kinney, this weak comedy focuses on misfit pre-teen Greg (Zachary Gordon) as he negotiates his first year at middle school – a world of cliques, bullying and embarrassment. Director Thor Freudenthal punctuates the live action with animations based on Kinney's work, but whereas Greg's adventures in book form are full of subtlety and wry observation, the movie is swamped by sledgehammer clichés. TeS Some swearing. **DVD** **Blu**

Zachary Gordon *Greg Heffley* • Robert Capron *Rowley Jefferson* • Rachael Harris *Susan Heffley* • Steve Zahn *Frank Heffley* • Devon Bostick *Rodrick Heffley* • Chloë Grace Moretz *Angie Steadman* ■ *Dir* Thor Freudenthal • *Scr* Jeff Filgo, Jackie Filgo, Gabe Sachs, Jeff Judah, from the illustrated novel by Jeff Kinney

Diary of a Wimpy Kid: Rodrick Rules ★★★ U

Comedy 2011 · US · Colour · 95min

This marks the second live-action dramatisation of Jeff Kinney's popular "cartoon novels" about a smart-aleck American schoolboy, his friends and family. Zachary Gordon and Devon Bostick return as feuding siblings Greg and older brother Rodrick, here bribed into bonding by their desperate, peace-seeking parents (Rachael Harris, Steve Zahn, both pitch-perfect). The parenting styles here may not resonate quite so well this side of the pond, but the pre-teen angst, sibling squabbles and broad comedy should guarantee a welcome from younger viewers. DA Some swearing. **DVD** **Blu**

Zachary Gordon *Greg Heffley* • Devon Bostick *Rodrick Heffley* • Rachael Harris *Susan Heffley* • Robert Capron *Rowley Jefferson* • Steve Zahn *Frank Heffley* • Peyton List *Holly Hills* ■ *Dir* David Bowers • *Scr* Jeff Judah, Gabe Sachs, from the illustrated novel by Jeff Kinney

Diary of a Wimpy Kid 3: Dog Days ★★ U

Comedy 2012 · US/Can · Colour · 90min

This is the third film based on Jeff Kinney's wildly popular pre-teen books (here combining two in the series, *Dog Days* and *The Last Straw*). It's the summer holidays, and schoolboy hero Greg (Zachary Gordon again) is determined to avoid the activities his dad (Steve Zahn) has planned for the summer in his bid to hang out at the country club with class dream girl Holly. This is certainly not the best entry in the series, but the pre-teen-pleasing mix of japes, scrapes and sibling shenanigans should ensure that "Dog Days" does the business for Wimpy Kid fans everywhere. DA **DVD** **Blu**

Zachary Gordon *Greg Heffley* • Steve Zahn *Frank Heffley* • Devon Bostick *Rodrick Heffley* • Rachael Harris *Susan Heffley* • Robert Capron *Rowley Jefferson* • Peyton List *Holly Hills* ■ *Dir* David Bowers • *Scr* Maya Forbes, Gabe Sachs, Wallace Wolodarsky, from *Diary of a Wimpy Kid* illustrated novels *Dog Days* and *The Last Straw* by Jeff Kinney

D

The Diary of Anne Frank ★★★★★ U

Biographical drama 1959 · US · BW · 176min

This is a marvellous screen version of the most moving stories to emerge from the tragedy of the Second World War, about a Jewish girl forced to hide from the Nazis in occupied Amsterdam. It's beautifully directed by George Stevens in claustrophobic black-and-white CinemaScope, and superbly cast, with doe-eyed Millie Perkins near-perfect as Anne. Shelley Winters garnered a best supporting Oscar, and Academy Awards also rightly went to the camerawork and art direction. Underrated on its release, this is compulsively gripping. TS DVD

Millie Perkins *Anne Frank* • Joseph Schildkraut *Otto Frank* • Shelley Winters *Mrs Van Daan* • Ed Wynn *Mr Dussell* • Richard Beymer *Peter Van Daan* • Gusti Huber *Mrs Frank* • Lou Jacobi *Mr Van Daan* • Diane Baker *Margot Frank* ■ *Dir* George Stevens • *Scr* Frances Goodrich, Albert Hackett, from their play, from the diary by Anne Frank • *Cinematographer* William C Mellor • *Art Directors* Lyle Wheeler, George W Davis • *Music* Alfred Newman

The Diary of Anne Frank ★★★

Drama based on a true story 1980 · US · Colour · 100min

In 1959, George Stevens's adaptation of Anne Frank's celebrated diary drew eight Oscar nominations, with Shelley Winters winning a statuette for a best supporting actress. Doris Roberts steps into her shoes for this TV-movie remake and turns in a creditable performance, as does Melissa Gilbert in the title role previously played by Millie Perkins. Director Boris Sagal sensibly retained the services of Frances Goodrich and Albert Hackett, who wrote the prize-winning Broadway version of the tale. DP

Melissa Gilbert *Anne Frank* • Maximilian Schell *Otto Frank* • Joan Plowright *Edith Frank* • James Coco *Mr Van Daan* • Doris Roberts *Mrs Van Daan* • Clive Revill *Mr Dussel* • Scott Jacoby *Peter Van Daan* • Melora Marshall *Margot Frank* ■ *Dir* Boris Sagal • *Scr* Frances Goodrich, Albert Hackett, from their play, from the diary by Anne Frank

The Diary of Major Thompson ★★★ U

Comedy 1955 · Fr · BW · 87min

The last outing for Hollywood writer/director Preston Sturges, who by the time he made this in France seemed more interested in running restaurants than making films. Britain's debonair Jack Buchanan, at the end of his career, still sparkles and is remarkably well-cast as the title character trying to settle to life in a foreign land. There's much to enjoy in this semi-sophisticated farce with a genuinely Gallic air, faithfully based on author Pierre Daninos's very popular book. But be warned: crude dubbing mars the American version. TS In French.

Jack Buchanan *Major Thompson* • Martine Carol *Martine* • Noël-Noël *Taupin* ■ *Dir* Preston Sturges • *Scr* Preston Sturges, from the novel *Les Carnets du Major Thompson* by Pierre Daninos

Diary of the Dead ★★★★ 18

Horror 2007 · US/Can · Colour and BW · 91min

Horror icon George A Romero once again uses the undead to comment on the ills of contemporary US society in this fifth entry in his landmark horror series. This time, in a nod to *The Blair Witch Project*, the leader of a group of Pennsylvania film students turns documentarist when the news breaks of a zombie outbreak. This film-within-a-film records the students' struggle for survival - fittingly titled *The Death of Death*. The target of Romero's satire is the media: anyone holding a camcorder, writing a blog or texting their experiences is willing to compromise safety to sensationalise facts. Yet Romero never allows his message to get in the way of his usual innovative splatter and visceral excitement. *George A Romero's Survival of the Dead* followed in 2009. AJ DVD

Josh Close [Joshua Close] *Jason Creed* • Philip Riccio *Ridley* • Michelle Morgan *Debra* • Shawn Roberts *Tony* • Amy Lalonde [Amy Ciupak Lalonde] *Tracy* • Joe Dinicol *Eliot* • Scott Wentworth *Maxwell* ■ *Dir/Scr* George A Romero

Dick ★★★ 12

Comedy 1999 · US · Colour · 90min

Kirsten Dunst and Michelle Williams play two dim teens who stumble into the Watergate break-in and soon find themselves working as presidential dogwalkers for "Tricky Dick". It playfully tweaks at the Watergate myths, with the girls becoming fixtures in the Nixon White House and eventually serving as "Deep Throat". Williams's taped confession of her crush on the president is a high point, as is Dan Hedaya as a foul-mouthed Nixon. ST DVD

Kirsten Dunst *Betsy Jobs* • Michelle Williams *Arlene Lorenzo* • Dan Hedaya *President Richard M Nixon* • Dave Foley *Bob Haldeman* • Harry Shearer *G Gordon Liddy* • Ana Gasteyer *Rosemary Woods* • Will Ferrell *Bob Woodward* • Bruce McCulloch *Carl Bernstein* • Teri Garr *Helen Lorenzo* ■ *Dir* Andrew Fleming • *Scr* Andrew Fleming, Sheryl Longin

Dick Tracy ★★ PG

Detective adventure 1945 · US · BW · 58min

This was the first Dick Tracy feature, though cartoonist Chester Gould's square-jawed detective had previously appeared in four superb serials, incarnated by rugged Ralph Byrd. This flick isn't terribly good; the detective is played by Morgan Conway, who completed two features before public demand had him replaced with Byrd. More cheap but cheerful. TS

Morgan Conway *Dick Tracy* • Anne Jeffreys *Tess Trueheart* • Mike Mazurki *Splitface* • Jane Greer *Judith Owens* • Lyle Latell *Pat Patton* • Joseph Crehan *Chief Brandon* ■ *Dir* William Berke • *Scr* Eric Taylor, from the comic strip by Chester Gould

Dick Tracy vs Cueball ★★ PG

Detective adventure 1946 · US · BW · 62min

The second of RKO's Dick Tracy B-movies, with the detective portrayed by the vapid Morgan Conway; Ralph Byrd, who had played the role more convincingly for Republic, would return to the part in the last two RKO films. This is an apprentice work for director Gordon M Douglas and he keeps the pace up well. Sadly, the production values are shoddy. TS DVD

Morgan Conway *Dick Tracy* • Anne Jeffreys *Tess Trueheart* • Lyle Latell *Pat Patton* • Rita Corday *Mona Clyde* • Ian Keith *Vitamin Flintheart* • Dick Wessel *Cueball* • Douglas Walton *Priceless* • Esther Howard *Filthy Flora* ■ *Dir* Gordon M Douglas [Gordon Douglas] • *Scr* Dane Lussier, Robert E Kent, from a story by Luci Ward, from the comic strip by Chester Gould

Dick Tracy's Dilemma ★★ PG

Detective adventure 1947 · US · BW · 59min

For the penultimate feature in the RKO series, the studio at last realised the wisdom of casting Ralph Byrd as Chester Gould's comic-strip detective. Byrd, who had previously played Tracy in four Republic serials, seemed born to play the role, and audiences warmed to him. Unadventurous, but perfectly respectable. TS DVD

Ralph Byrd *Dick Tracy* • Kay Christopher *Tess Trueheart* • Lyle Latell *Pat Patton* • Jack Lambert *The Claw* • Ian Keith *Vitamin Flintheart* • Bernadene Hayes *Longshot Lillie* ■ *Dir* John Rawlins • *Scr* Robert Stephen Brode, from the comic strip by Chester Gould

Dick Tracy Meets Gruesome ★★ PG

Detective adventure 1947 · US · BW · 65min

A rare instance of one of those weirdly named cartoon creations sharing title billing with our hero, and rightly so, since Gruesome is played by the great Boris Karloff, top-billed over Ralph Byrd's Dick Tracy. This was the last Tracy movie until Warren Beatty donned the fedora four decades later, and the plot's a hoot: Karloff uses deep-freeze gas to hold people in place while he robs banks. TS DVD

Boris Karloff *Gruesome* • Ralph Byrd *Dick Tracy* • Anne Gwynne *Tess Trueheart* • Edward Ashley *LE Thal* • June Clayworth *Dr IM Learned* • Lyle Latell *Pat Patton* • Tony Barrett *Melody* • Skelton Knaggs *X-Ray* ■ *Dir* John Rawlins • *Scr* Robertson White, Eric Taylor, from a story by William H Graffis, Robert E Kent, from the comic strip by Chester Gould

Dick Tracy ★★★★ PG

Detective adventure 1990 · US · Colour · 100min

Warren Beatty nurtured this marvellous-looking rendition of the 1940s comic strip for several years and through many rewrites. He takes the title role as the laconic and almost monosyllabic detective surrounded by villains of a more colourful hue, such as Al Pacino as Big Boy. The film was received with reverential praise at the time - it is a great technical and ensemble achievement - but Beatty fails to inject the enterprise with any great depth or warmth. It's a near-perfect example, however, of how to bring florid characters off the page and on to the screen. SH DVD

Warren Beatty *Dick Tracy* • Madonna *Breathless Mahoney* • Al Pacino *Big Boy Caprice* • Glenne Headly *Tess Trueheart* • Charlie Korsmo *Kid* • Mandy Patinkin *88 Keys* • Charles Durning *Chief Brandon* • Paul Sorvino *Lips Manlis* • William Forsythe *Flattop* • Dustin Hoffman *Mumbles* • James Caan *Spaldoni* • Kathy Bates *Mrs Green* • Dick Van Dyke *Da Fletcher* • Estelle Parsons *Mrs Trueheart* • Jim Wilkey *Stooge* ■ *Dir* Warren Beatty • *Scr* Jim Cash, Jack Epps Jr, from the comic strip by Chester Gould • *Cinematographer* Vittorio Storaro • *Art Directors* Richard Sylbert, Rick Simpson

Dick Turpin - Highwayman ★★ U

Period drama 1956 · UK · Colour · 26min

There may not be a lot to detain the casual viewer in this brisk tale of highway robbery, which sees Philip Friend stealing the golden dowry of Diane Hart, only for a mutual attraction to develop between them. However, David Paltenghi's slickly directed short is significant in that it launched Hammer Films' very own widescreen process, Hammerscope, which would be used on such prestige projects as *The Abominable Snowman* (1957). DP

Philip Friend *Dick Turpin* • Diane Hart *Liz* • Allan Cuthbertson *Redgrove* • Gabrielle May *Genevieve* • Hal Osmond *Mac* • Raymond Rollett *Hawkins* • Norman Mitchell *Rooks* ■ *Dir* David Paltenghi • *Scr* Joel Murcott

Dickie Roberts: Former Child Star ★★★ 12

Comedy 2003 · US · Colour · 94min

There are more laughs than you might expect in this light-hearted vehicle for David Spade. He plays a washed-up former child star who, having missed his real-life childhood, is unable to generate the emotion necessary to clinch a possible movie comeback. To solve the problem, he moves in with an all-American family. The screenplay degenerates into schmaltz occasionally but Spade creates an unusual character who, despite being self-obsessed, is oddly vulnerable and likeable. AS DVD CS

David Spade *Dickie Roberts* • Mary McCormack *Grace Finney* • Jon Lovitz *Sidney Wernick* • Craig Bierko *George Finney* • Alyssa Milano *Cyndi* • Rob Reiner • Scott Terra *Sam Finney* • Jenna Boyd *Sally Finney* • Edie McClurg *Mrs Gertrude* ■ *Dir* Sam Weisman • *Scr* Fred Wolf, David Spade

The Dictator ★★ PG

Period romance 1935 · UK/Ger · BW · 82min

Among the most expensive pictures then produced in Britain, this costume drama had prestige written all over it. It boasted lavish sets by the Russian designer André Andreyev and sumptuous cinematography by Franz Planer. It even had a fascinating story to tell, as Denmark's 18th-century ruler Charles VII is deposed by his wife, Caroline Mathilde, and a German doctor who falls in love with her on a medical visit. But under the direction of Victor Saville, the action is suffocated by too much pomp. DP DVD

Clive Brook *Struensee* • Madeleine Carroll *Queen Caroline* • Emlyn Williams *King Charles VII* • Alfred Drayton *Brandt* • Nicholas Hannen *Goldberg* • Helen Haye *Queen Mother Juliana* ■ *Dir* Victor Saville • *Scr* Benn Levy, Hans Wilhelm, HG Lustig, Michael Logan, from a story by Lustig, Logan

The Dictator ★★★ 15

Satirical comedy 2012 · US · Colour · 83min

Sacha Baron Cohen aggressively reinvented the principles of clowning with the double whammy of mockumentaries *Borat* and *Brüno*. However, on this occasion he's opted out of that approach and reverted to the fiction format of his debut, the now rather quaint *Ali G indahouse*. Here, Baron Cohen plays Arab despot Admiral General Aladeen, who comes to New York to defend his North African country's nuclear weapons programme from investigation by the UN. But after a coup, he is forced to join forces with right-on health food store owner Anna Faris. The jokes may be dark and Aladeen shares many of Borat's non-PC concerns - sexism and anti-Semitism, mostly - but otherwise this is standard gross-out comedy fare and surprisingly formulaic by Baron Cohen's usual standards. DW Swearing, sexual references. DVD Blu

Sacha Baron Cohen *Admiral General Aladeen* • Megan Fox • Anna Faris *Zoey* • John C Reilly *Government agent* • Ben Kingsley *Tamir* ■ *Dir* Larry Charles • *Scr* Sacha Baron Cohen, Alec Berg, David Mandel, Jeff Schaffer

Did You Hear about the Morgans? ★★ PG

Romantic comedy drama 2009 · US · Colour · 99min

Sarah Jessica Parker and Hugh Grant headline this tale of marital mishap, playing two estranged New Yorkers clumsily trying to repair their marriage. After witnessing an organised crime hit, they are bustled off to Wyoming in the witness protection programme and have to contend with gun-toting locals, uncomfortable digs and being exposed as Democrats. Despite a high-quality cast and production, writer/director Marc Lawrence (*Music and Lyrics*) presents nothing new in what could have been a classy fish-out-of-water farce, while Parker and Grant sleepwalk their way through the whole affair. KK Some violence, swearing. DVD Blu

Hugh Grant *Paul Morgan* • Sarah Jessica Parker *Meryl Morgan* • Sam Elliott *Marshall Clayton* "*Clay*" *Wheeler* • Mary Steenburgen *Deputy Emma Wheeler* • Elisabeth Moss *Jackie Drake, Merly's PA* • Michael Kelly *Vincent* ■ *Dir/Scr* Marc Lawrence (2)

Die Another Day ★★★ 12

Spy adventure 2002 · UK/US · Colour · 126min

Director Lee Tamahori's fluid style and the relentless pace effortlessly propel this 20th James Bond adventure's intense action around the globe. Pierce Brosnan is on fine form (though he's let down by some poor CGI) as a betrayed and vengeful 007, combining the secret agent's usual charm and throwaway wit with true toughness and a streak of venom. Such character-broadening traits ensure that the format never feels stale, while the introduction of Halle Berry as a genuinely equal, if underdeveloped, female sidekick is a coup. There are only two "cons" to the movie and both involve Madonna - firstly, the singer's grating theme song and, secondly, her dire cameo as a fencing instructor. SF DVD Blu

Pierce Brosnan *James Bond* • Halle Berry *Jinx* • Toby Stephens *Gustav Graves* • Rosamund Pike *Miranda Frost* • Rick Yune *Zao* • Judi Dench *M* • John Cleese *Q* • Michael Madsen *Damian Falco* • Will Yun Lee *Colonel Moon* • Kenneth Tsang *General Moon* • Samantha Bond (2) *Miss Moneypenny* • Madonna *Verity, fencing instructor* ■ *Dir* Lee Tamahori • *Scr* Neal Purvis, Robert Wade, from characters by Ian Fleming

Die! Die! My Darling ★★★ 15

Horror thriller 1964 · UK · Colour · 92min

For its first suspense thriller in colour, Hammer turned to specialist genre screenwriter Richard (*The Incredible Shrinking Man*) Matheson and asked Tallulah Bankhead to star as a *Baby Jane*-inspired mad matron. Despite being intoxicated throughout the entire shoot, the legendary Broadway diva (in her last screen performance) produced a venomous characterisation of terrifying intensity as the religious fanatic keeping her dead son's fiancée (Stefanie Powers) a prisoner in her rambling mansion. AJ **DVD**

Tallulah Bankhead *Mrs Trefoile* • Stefanie Powers *Pat Carroll* • Peter Vaughan *Harry* • Maurice Kaufman *Alan Glentower* • Yootha Joyce *Anna* • Donald Sutherland *Joseph* • Robert Dorning *Ormsby* ■ *Dir* Silvio Narizzano • *Scr* Richard Matheson, from the novel *Nightmare* by Anne Blaisdell

Die Hard ★★★★★ 18
Action thriller 1988 · US · Colour · 131min

This is the action thriller that minted Bruce Willis's career, launched a franchise and still stands as a giant of the genre. It places a group of people in peril (office workers at a Christmas party in an otherwise empty Los Angeles skyscraper) when suave Alan Rickman's Euro-terrorists take them hostage. One man (Willis, naturally) is charged with saving them. Director John McTiernan handles the bravura, vertigo-inducing set pieces with aplomb and the script oozes dry wit, but the star of the show is Willis, as a resourceful but world-weary off-duty cop, who just wants to get home for Christmas. AC Violence, swearing, drug abuse, nudity. **DVD** **BD**

Bruce Willis *John McClane* • Alan Rickman *Hans Gruber* • Bonnie Bedelia *Holly Gennaro McClane* • Reginald VelJohnson *Sergeant Al Powell* • Paul Gleason *Dwayne T Robinson* • De'Voreaux White *Argyle* • William Atherton *Thornburg* • Hart Bochner *Harry Ellis* • James Shigeta *Takagi* • Alexander Godunov *Karl* ■ *Dir* John McTiernan • *Scr* Jeb Stuart, Steven E de Souza, from the novel *Nothing Lasts Forever* by Roderick Thorp

Die Hard 2: Die Harder ★★★★ 18
Action thriller 1990 · US · Colour · 118min

Bruce Willis wonders aloud how it could happen to him again, but dons the white singlet anyway for another hugely entertaining slice of action hokum. Director Renny Harlin makes no attempt to re-create the intriguing battle of wits in the original, and instead piles on increasingly grander explosions and set pieces. This time around Willis uncovers a terrorist plot on the ground and in the air as he waits for his wife to fly in to a snowbound Washington airport. JF Swearing, violence, brief nudity. **DVD** **BD**

Bruce Willis *John McClane* • Bonnie Bedelia *Holly McClane* • William Atherton *Dick Thornberg* • Reginald VelJohnson *Al Powell* • Franco Nero *General Ramon Esperanza* • William Sadler *Colonel Stuart* • John Amos *Captain Grant* • Dennis Franz *Carmine Lorenzo* • Art Evans *Barnes* ■ *Dir* Renny Harlin • *Scr* Steven E de Souza, Doug Richardson, from the novel *58 Minutes* by Walter Wager

Die Hard with a Vengeance ★★★★ 15
Action thriller 1995 · US · Colour · 122min

Mad bomber Jeremy Irons keeps Bruce Willis and Samuel L Jackson on their toes in this third instalment of the series, with a set of Simple Simon tasks that give a high-speed 20th-century labours-of-Hercules twist to the plot. Jackson and Willis trade quips and insults at a pace that matches the breathless action, while John McTiernan directs with a gleeful disregard for narrative logic. Cracking entertainment, though. DP **DVD** **BD**

Bruce Willis *John McClane* • Jeremy Irons *Simon* • Samuel L Jackson *Zeus Carver* • Graham Greene *Joe Lambert* • Colleen Camp *Connie Kowalski* • Larry Bryggman *Arthur Cobb* • Anthony Peck *Ricky Walsh* • Nick Wyman *Targo* ■ *Dir* John McTiernan • *Scr* Jonathan Hensleigh, from characters by Roderick Thorp

Die Hard 4.0 ★★★★ 12
Action thriller 2007 · US · Colour · 123min

Twelve years after he last wore the white vest in *Die Hard with a Vengeance*, Bruce Willis stars as John McClane again in this unabashedly retro blockbuster. As cyber-terrorists led by Timothy Olyphant (*Deadwood*) threaten to hack America to a complete standstill, McClane is once more the wrong guy in the wrong place at the wrong time. Will's returns to the role that made him an action star with unexpected ease, striking up a witty, odd-couple partnership with Justin Long's cowardly hacker. Aware of its own ridiculousness but unwilling to slip into outright parody, it instead channels the laughs into some immaculately polished quips for its ever-lugubrious hero. Loud, relentless and thoroughly entertaining, it's an enjoyable throwback to the 1980s. *A Good Day to Die Hard* is due in 2013. JR **DVD** **BD**

Bruce Willis *John McClane* • Timothy Olyphant *Thomas Gabriel* • Justin Long *Matt Farrell* • Maggie Q *Mai* • Cliff Curtis *Bowman* • Jonathan Sadowski *Trey* • Andrew Friedman *Casper* • Kevin Smith (2) *Warlock* • Mary Elizabeth Winstead *Lucy McClane* ■ *Dir* Len Wiseman • *Scr* Mark Bomback, from a story by Bomback, David Marconi, from the article *A Farewell to Arms* by John Carlin, from characters by Roderick Thorp • *Cinematographer* Simon Duggan

Die, Monster, Die! ★★ 12
Horror 1965 · US/UK · Colour · 75min

Former Roger Corman art director Daniel Haller's feature debut is a creditable genre effort in spite of itself. Scientist Nick Adams turns up at a remote village to visit his fiancée Suzan Farmer and her crippled father Boris Karloff only to find that a recently crash-landed meteorite is causing strange mutations. Haller gets the most chills from the visual components of his terror tale, rather than from the muddled script and weak acting. AJ **DVD**

Boris Karloff *Nahum Witley* • Nick Adams *Stephen Reinhart* • Freda Jackson *Letitia Witley* • Suzan Farmer *Susan Witley* ■ *Dir* Daniel Haller • *Scr* Jerry Sohl, from the novel *The Colour out of Space* by HP Lovecraft

Die Watching ★★★ 18
Thriller 1993 · US · Colour · 81min

B-movie king Tim Thomerson is underused here as the detective in charge of a serial murder investigation; somehow we're supposed to believe that Christopher Atkins can carry the film as the antisocial murderer. Atkins's character makes erotic videos and occasionally strangles the women who star in them. The police start to suspect him about the same time he falls in love with a local artist. Trashy but titillating, with some hilariously absurd fright effects. ST

Christopher Atkins *Michael Terrence* • Vali Ashton *Nola Carlisle* • Tim Thomerson *Detective Lewis* • Carlos Palomino *Detective Barry* • Mike Jacobs Jr *Adam Parker* ■ *Dir* Charles Davis (2) • *Scr* Kenneth J Hall

Different for Girls ★★★ 15
Romantic comedy drama 1996 · UK · Colour · 92min

What's Rupert Graves to do? His best mate (Steven Mackintosh) has had a sex change since they last met, and now he's finding himself attracted to her. That's the dilemma in director Richard Spence's decidedly offbeat romantic comedy. What follows is sometimes awkward, sometimes emotionally remote but, because of Graves and Mackintosh's fine acting, always watchable. AJ Violence, swearing, nudity.

Steven Mackintosh *Kim Foyle* • Rupert Graves *Paul Prentice* • Miriam Margolyes *Pamela* • Saskia Reeves *Jean Payne* • Charlotte Coleman *Alison* • Neil Dudgeon *Neil Payne* ■ *Dir* Richard Spence • *Scr* Tony Marchant

Dig! ★★★ 15
Music documentary 2004 · US · Colour · 108min

In 1996, Ondi Timoner planned a low-budget film about ten unknown bands. She wound up focusing on two, the Brian Jonestown Massacre and the Dandy Warhols. The resulting film, assembled from 1,500 hours of footage shot over seven years, makes a compelling, instructive and rough-edged documentary about the vagaries of underground rock crossing over to the mainstream. This becomes apparent as the Warhols find chart success, while the BJM descend into violence, recrimination and drug abuse. By turns hilarious and shocking. AC Swearing, drug abuse. **DVD**

Courtney Taylor (2) *Narrator* ■ *Dir* Ondi Timoner

Digby, the Biggest Dog in the World ★★ U
Comedy fantasy 1973 · UK · Colour · 84min

While Peter Sellers was a natural before a movie camera, his fellow Goons never really found a screen niche. Spike Milligan, for example, looks singularly lost in this children's comedy about a nosey pooch who guzzles down a sample of miracle plant food and just keeps growing. Even the versatile Jim Dale struggles to make a go of Michael Pertwee's script, which is essentially a one-gag shaggy dog story. DP

Jim Dale *Jeff Eldon* • Spike Milligan *Dr Harz* • Angela Douglas *Janine* • John Bluthal *Jerry* • Norman Rossington *Tom* • Milo O'Shea *Dr Jameson* • Richard Beaumont *Billy White* • Dinsdale Landen *Colonel Masters* • Garfield Morgan *Rogerson* • Victor Spinetti *Professor Ribart* ■ *Dir* Joseph McGrath • *Scr* Michael Pertwee, from a story by Charles Isaacs, from the book *Hazel* by Ted Key

Digging to China ★★ PG
Drama 1998 · US · Colour · 94min

Evan Rachel Wood plays Harriet, a ten-year-old girl who dreams of escaping her suffocating life with her alcoholic mother (Cathy Moriarty) and promiscuous sister (Mary Stuart Masterson) in this drama, the directorial debut of actor Timothy Hutton. Things perk up when Wood forms an unlikely friendship with the mentally disabled Kevin Bacon, though some scenes between the two are unbearably sentimental. LH

Kevin Bacon *Ricky Schroth* • Mary Stuart Masterson *Gwen Frankovitz* • Cathy Moriarty *Mrs Frankovitz* • Evan Rachel Wood *Harriet Frankovitz* • Marian Seldes *Leah Schroth* ■ *Dir* Timothy Hutton • *Scr* Karen Janszen

Digimon the Movie ★★ PG
Animated adventure 1999 · Jpn/US · Colour · 88min

Digimon are digital monsters – Pokémon-type cartoon characters who inhabit the computer world and can evolve into powerful warriors. The Digimon are linked to the real world via a bunch of "digidestined" youngsters who join forces with them to defeat the forces of evil. Originally in a TV series, this is their first cinema outing, and it loosely links together three tales of peril. The animation is rather better than Pokémon – although that isn't saying much. DA **DVD**

Lara Jill Miller *Kari/Young Kari* • Joshua Seth *Young Tai/Tai* • Bob Papenbrook *Red Greymon* ■ *Dir* Mamoru Hosoda, Shigeyasu Yamauchi • *Scr* Reiko Yoshida, Jeff Nimoy, Bob Buchholz

Dil Se... ★★★ 12
Musical romantic drama 1998 · Ind · Colour · 159min

Proving that mainstream Indian cinema doesn't necessarily have to be dressed up in Bollywood razzmatazz, this stylish melodrama uses a doomed romance to analyse the subcontinent's political heritage. Director Mani Rathnam may utilise songs to explore his characters' emotions, but he refuses to allow the escapist elements to dominate the story of radio journalist Shahrukh Khan's obsession with provincial girl Manisha Koirala who, unbeknown to him, is a key figure in a terrorist plot. DP Hindi +subtitles. **DVD**

Shahrukh Khan [Shah Rukh Khan] *Amar* • Manisha Koirala *Meghna* ■ *Dir* Mani Rathnam • *Scr* Mani Rathnam, from a story by Mani Ratnam

Dilemma ★
Drama 1962 · UK · BW · 67min

What would you do if you came home and found your wife missing and a dead body in the bath? Bury the corpse beneath the floorboards? Surely not. Then again, if you were the returning wife, would you condone your husband's actions and spend the rest of your life confined to the house for fear of discovery? No wonder British B-movies of the 1960s have such an awful reputation. DP

Peter Halliday *Harry Barnes* • Ingrid Hafner *Jean Barnes* • Patricia Burke *Mrs Jones* • Patrick Jordan *Inspector Murray* • Joan Heath *Mrs Barnes* • Robert Dean *Doctor* ■ *Dir* Peter Maxwell • *Scr* Pip Baker, Jane Baker

The Dilemma ★★ 12
Comedy 2011 · US · Colour · 106min

Good intentions lead to little of consequence in this underwhelming comedy. Vince Vaughn adopts the slick salesman approach as Ronny Valentine, the business partner and best buddy of Nick (a typically soppy Kevin James). Winona Ryder is lumbered with playing the wedge that is driven between them – married to Nick but spied by Ronny canoodling with another man (Channing Tatum). So begins a gradual nervous breakdown as Ronny frets over the best course of action to take. Sadly, the story lacks credibility and insight, and the gags are often incongruous. SP Swearing, sexual references. **DVD** **BD**

Vince Vaughn *Ronny Valentine* • Kevin James *Nick Brannen* • Jennifer Connelly *Beth* • Winona Ryder *Geneva* • Channing Tatum *Zip* • Queen Latifah *Susan Warner* ■ *Dir* Ron Howard • *Scr* Allan Loeb

Dillinger ★★★★ PG
Crime biography 1945 · US · BW · 69min

This is an extraordinarily effective Monogram B-movie, very successful in its day and still playing theatrically over 20 years later in a double-bill with the 1959 film, *Al Capone*. Budget limitations are obvious, but a tough, tight, Oscar-nominated screenplay by Phil Yordan more than compensates. The persuasive direction is by Max Nosseck, while Lawrence Tierney wields a tight lip as public enemy John Dillinger. TS **DVD**

Lawrence Tierney *Dillinger* • Anne Jeffreys *Helen* • Edmund Lowe *Specs* • Eduardo Ciannelli *Marco Minnelli* • Marc Lawrence (1) *Doc* • Elisha Cook Jr *Kirk* • Ralph Lewis *Tony* • Ludwig Stossel *Otto* ■ *Dir* Max Nosseck • *Scr* Leon Charles, Phil Yordan

Dillinger ★★★★ 18
Crime biography 1973 · US · Colour · 106min

Warren Oates gives a wonderfully slimy performance as gangster John Dillinger in this bullet-laced biography from director John Milius. Dillinger blazed his way to notoriety during the 1930s and was the first man to be tagged Public Enemy Number one, and here he's pursued across America by FBI man Ben Johnson. The movie was a coup for debut director John Milius, a hoodlum history that is small-scale but devastating all the same. TH Violence, swearing.

Warren Oates *John Dillinger* • Ben Johnson (1) *Melvin Purvis* • Michelle Phillips *Billie Frechette* • Cloris Leachman *Anna Sage* • Harry Dean Stanton *Homer Van Meter* • Geoffrey Lewis *Harry Pierpont* • John Ryan [John P Ryan] *Charles Mackley* • Richard Dreyfuss *George "Baby Face" Nelson* • Steve Kanaly *Lester "Pretty Boy" Floyd* ■ *Dir/Scr* John Milius

Dillinger and Capone ★★★ 15
Period crime drama 1995 · US · Colour · 90min

What could have been a run-of-the-mill gangster picture is given a boost by an interesting and intriguing plot. In 1934, criminal John Dillinger was gunned down by the Feds outside the Biograph Theater in Chicago. In this film, though, it's not Dillinger who gets killed but his brother, and the FBI are unaware of their error. A few years later, Al Capone, who knows the former bank robber's secret, holds John

D

Dillinger's family hostage to get him to recover money Capone has stashed in a Chicago hotel. The film moves briskly along, mainly due to the talented cast. JB *DVD*

Martin Sheen *John Dillinger* • F Murray Abraham *Al Capone* • Catherine Hicks *Abigail Dalton* • Michael Oliver *Sam Dalton* • Don Stroud *George* • Anthony Crivello *Lou Gazzo* • Stephen Davies *Cecil* • Clint Howard *Bobo* ■ *Dir* Jon Purdy • *Scr* Michael B Druxman

Dilwale Dulhania Le Jayenge ★★★ PG
Romantic drama 1995 · Ind · Colour · 181min

Some of the locations may be European, but this is as traditional a Bollywood masala as you could wish for. Shahrukh Khan and Kajol star as Londoners who fall in love during a month's vacation on the continent, but standing in the way of their happiness is an arranged marriage. With his father (acclaimed director Yash Chopra) acting as producer, Aditya Chopra could hardly go wrong with this debut outing. It's lively and packed with mischievous contrivance. DP Hindi +subtitles. *DVD*

Shahrukh Khan [Shah Rukh Khan] *Raj Malhotra* • Kajol *Simran* • Amrish Puri *Chaudhry Baldev Singh* • Farida Jalal *Lajwanti* ■ *Dir/Scr* Aditya Chopra

Dim Sum: a Little Bit of Heart ★★★★ PG
Comedy 1985 · US · Colour · 80min

Delicate but deceptively spicy, this delicious film shows just how easy it is to appear selfless while acting purely out of self-interest. Taking his stylistic cue from Yasujiro Ozu, director Wayne Wang allows the story to develop in its own time and space while drawing us into the world of San Francisco's Chinese community. This enables us to appreciate more fully the emotional games being played out by the elderly Kim Chew, her westernised daughter Laureen Chew and her roguish uncle Victor Wong, all of whom dissemble in their relationships to avoid making difficult decisions. DP *DVD*

Laureen Chew *Geraldine Tam* • Kim Chew *Mrs Tam* • Victor Wong (2) *Uncle Tam* • Ida FO Chung *Auntie Mary* • Cora Miao *Julia* • John Nishio *Richard* • Amy Hill *Amy Tam* • Keith Choy *Kevin Tam* ■ *Dir* Wayne Wang • *Scr* Terrel Seltzer, from an idea by Terrel Seltzer, Laureen Chew, Wayne Wang

Diminished Capacity ★★ 15
Comedy 2007 · US · Colour · 88min

Veteran actor Alan Alda's powers remain reassuringly intact in this otherwise bland sub-*Rain Man* character comedy. Here he plays Alzheimer's-affected Rollie, who may spend his time communing with the fish in his garden but is still determined that the sale of an ultra-rare baseball card will keep him out of residential care. The uninspired TV movie-style direction brings little to the proceedings. But at least there is an able supporting cast that includes Matthew Broderick as Alda's nephew, Virginia Madsen as Broderick's spiky love interest, and Dylan Baker and Bobby Cannavale in scene-stealing turns as rival sports-memorabilia dealers. TJ Swearing.

Matthew Broderick *Cooper* • Virginia Madsen *Charlotte* • Alan Alda *Rollie* • Dylan Baker *Mad Dog McClure* • Louis CK *Big Stan* • Bobby Cannavale *Lee Vivyan* ■ *Dir* Terry Kinney • *Scr* Sherwood Kiraly, Doug Bost, from the novel by Kiraly

Dimples ★★★ U
Period musical drama 1936 · US · BW · 75min

This was one of Shirley Temple's biggest hits and a good of example of why she became the world's biggest box-office draw. Here she sings *Oh Mister Man up in the Moon* and *Hey, What Did the Bluebird Say?* with great aplomb, and swaps dialogue with screen grandad Frank Morgan like the seasoned trouper she is. As a well-meaning kiddie in mid-19th century New York, she's irresistible. TS *DVD*

Shirley Temple *Sylvia Dolores Appleby, "Dimples"* • Frank Morgan *Professor Eustace Appleby* • Helen Westley *Mrs Caroline Drew* • Robert Kent

Diner ★★★★ 15
Comedy drama 1982 · US · Colour · 105min

This gentle, warm-hearted film about a group of young men in 1950s Baltimore was director Barry Levinson's debut feature and it remains among his finest work. It's a sympathetic portrait of youth on the threshold of adulthood that's episodic in structure; it also happens to be rather funny. In addition, Levinson shows a remarkable eye for talent. At the time, most of the performers were far from being household names; Steve Guttenberg, Mickey Rourke, Ellen Barkin, Kevin Bacon, Daniel Stern and Paul Reiser all boosted their careers after appearing in this movie. JF Swearing. *DVD*

Steve Guttenberg *Eddie* • Mickey Rourke *Boogie* • Ellen Barkin *Beth* • Kevin Bacon *Fenwick* • Daniel Stern *Shrevie* • Timothy Daly *Billy* • Paul Reiser *Modell* • Kathryn Dowling *Barbara* ■ *Dir/Scr* Barry Levinson

Le Dîner de Cons ★★★★ 15
Comedy 1998 · Fr · Colour · 76min

Despite betraying its stage origins, Francis Veber's splutteringly funny farce is a model of snowball comedy. From the moment publisher Thierry Lhermitte agrees to exhibit matchstick model-maker Jacques Villeret at one of his clique's "idiot dinners", his idyllic existence begins to fall apart as this balding bundle of good intentions dismantles his deceptions with devastating artlessness. Lhermitte is selfless as the despicable straight man, and Villeret has fashioned a masterly creation: a buffoonish descendant of Stan Laurel and Inspector Clouseau, whose every gesture has catastrophic consequences. DP French +subtitles. *DVD*

Jacques Villeret *François Pignon* • Thierry Lhermitte *Pierre Brochant* • Francis Huster *Leblanc* • Alexandra Vandernoot *Christine* • Daniel Prévost *Cheval* • Catherine Frot *Marlène* • Edgar Givry *Cordier* • Christian Pereira *Sorbier* ■ *Dir* Francis Veber • *Scr* Francis Veber, from his play

Dingo ★★
Drama 1991 · Aus/Fr · Colour · 109min

Miles Davis and Michel Legrand are the true stars here for producing a jazz score that, for all its geniality, this Australian drama scarcely deserves. Rolf De Heer attempts to impart a fantastical element to this middling meditation on dreams and destiny, in which a chance meeting with a legendary trumpeter transforms the life of a Poona Flats wannabe. Colin Friels impresses as he strives to fulfil his ambition, but co-star Davis gives a one-note performance. DP

Colin Friels *John "Dingo" Anderson* • Miles Davis *Billy Cross* • Helen Buday *Jane Anderson* • Joe Petruzzi *Peter* • Bernadette Lafont *Angie Cross* • Steve Shaw *Archie* • Helen Doig *Ruth* • Daniel Scott *Young John* ■ *Dir* Rolf De Heer • *Scr* Marc Rosenberg

Dinner at Eight ★★★★ PG
Comedy drama 1933 · US · BW · 106min

This sumptuously produced all-star MGM extravaganza is based on the witty George S Kaufman/Edna Ferber Broadway success, but with an even smarter screenplay by Frances Marion, Herman J Mankiewicz and the mordant Donald Ogden Stewart. Among the guests at socialite Billie Burke's grand dinner party are Marie Dressler, Wallace Beery and a couple of Barrymores, but it's blonde bombshell Jean Harlow who really shines. Director George Cukor proved himself highly skilled at handling this kind of super-production, and, in its day, this was a popular and critical hit. TS

Marie Dressler *Carlotta Vance* • John Barrymore *Larry Renault* • Wallace Beery *Dan Packard* • Jean Harlow *Kitty Packard* • Lionel Barrymore *Oliver Jordan* • Lee Tracy *Max Kane* • Edmund Lowe *Dr Wayne Talbot* • Billie Burke *Mrs Oliver Jordan* • Madge Evans *Paula Jordan* • Jean Hersholt *Joe Stengel* ■ *Dir* George Cukor • *Scr*

Frances Marion, Herman J Mankiewicz, Donald Ogden Stewart, from the play by George S Kaufman, Edna Ferber

Dinner at Eight ★★★ 15
Comedy drama 1989 · US · Colour · 93min

Lauren Bacall, Marsha Mason and Harry Hamlin head a prestige cast in this updated TV remake of George Cukor's classic 1933 comedy of New York social manners, itself based on the Broadway hit by George S Kaufman and Edna Ferber. The writing and direction may lack the sparkle of the Cukor version, but Bacall turns on the style as the acid-tongued pulp novelist Carlotta Vance. PF

Lauren Bacall *Carlotta Vance* • Marsha Mason *Millicent Jordan* • Charles Durning *Dan Packard* • Ellen Greene *Kitty Packard* • Harry Hamlin *Larry Renault* • John Mahoney *Oliver Jordan* • Stacy Edwards *Paula Jordan* ■ *Dir* Ron Lagomarsino • *Scr* Tom Griffin, from the 1933 film, from the play by George S Kaufman, Edna Ferber • *Executive Producer* Shelley Duvall

Dinner at the Ritz ★★★ U
Romantic thriller 1937 · UK · BW · 77min

Despite the enchanting presence of French actress Annabella (the future Mrs Tyrone Power), this thriller suffers from slack pacing and a hackneyed plot. Annabella plays the daughter of a murdered banker who comes to London to find the men responsible, with a little help from David Niven's government agent. A period artefact now, this was once considered the epitome of chic. TS *DVD*

David Niven *Paul de Brack* • Annabella *Ranie Racine* • Paul Lukas *Philip de Beaufort* • Romney Brent *Jimmy Rane* • Francis L Sullivan *Brogard* • Stewart Rome *Racine* ■ *Dir* Harold D Schuster [Harold Schuster] • *Scr* Roland Pertwee, from a story by Roland Pertwee, Romney Brent

Dinner for Schmucks ★ 12
Comedy 2010 · US/Ind · Colour · 108min

Sneering French comedy *Le Dîner de Cons* is given the Hollywood treatment here, and the results aren't pretty. Paul Rudd plays a corporate type hoping for promotion when he accepts an invitation to dinner at the boss's house. The cruel catch is that guests must bring along someone who will provide the after-dinner entertainment – to see who is the biggest idiot. As if this wasn't off-putting enough, Steve Carell plays the hapless plus-one like a borderline psychopath. The script is strung together with gags drawn out to excruciating length, and the result is a dog's dinner. SP Sexual references, brief swearing. *DVD*

Steve Carell *Barry Speck* • Paul Rudd *Tim Conrad* • Jemaine Clement *Kieran Vollard* • Jeff Denham *Lewis the ventriloquist* • Bruce Greenwood *Lance Fender* • Ron Livingston *Caldwell* • Stephanie Szostak *Julie* • Zach Galifianakis *Therman* ■ *Dir* Jay Roach • *Scr* David Guion, Michael Handelman, from the film and play *Le Dîner de Cons* by Francis Veber

Dinner Rush ★★★★ 15
Comedy drama 2000 · US · Colour · 94min

Director Bob Giraldi displays a mastery of texture and character in this delightful comedy drama set in a fashionable Manhattan restaurant. Danny Aiello exudes understated charm as the prosperous owner, who's dismayed that his family trattoria is forgoing traditional food for the flashy nouvelle cuisine that is the trademark of his talented chef son (star-in-the-making Edoardo Ballerini). During one fraught night, he and his staff must deal with mobsters wanting a piece of the action, a demanding food critic (played by an irresistible Sandra Bernhard), a lengthy power cut and various other diversions. Filmed in Giraldi's own restaurant, this is a finely polished gem. JC Violence, swearing, sex scenes. *DVD*

Danny Aiello *Louis* • Edoardo Ballerini *Udo* • Vivian Wu *Nicole* • Mike McGlone *Carmen* • Kirk Acevedo *Duncan* • Sandra Bernhard *Jennifer Freeley* • Summer Phoenix *Marti* ■ *Dir* Bob Giraldi • *Scr* Rick Shaughnessy, Brian Kalata

Dinner with Friends ★ 15
Drama 2001 · US · Colour · 90min

Director Norman Jewison trades subtle observations for ham-fisted showiness in this made-for-cable adaptation of a Pulitzer Prize-winning play. Applying over simplistic rationale to the idiosyncrasies of human relationships, he ploughs into the intimate nitty-gritty of romance and betrayal like an intrusive voyeur. This emotionally hollow melodrama throws up cliché after cliché, as idyllic couple Dennis Quaid and Andie MacDowell find their friends' divorce threatening their own perfect marriage. SF *DVD*

Dennis Quaid *Gabe* • Andie MacDowell *Karen* • Greg Kinnear *Tom* • Toni Collette *Beth* ■ *Dir* Norman Jewison • *Scr* Donald Margulies, from his play

Dino Time ★★ PG
Animated comedy adventure 2012 · US/S Kor · Colour · 81min

The voices of Melanie Griffith and Rob Schneider feature in a cartoon cute enough for dino-mad younger kids, though not one that will likely linger long in their memories, nor those of grown-ups. Three kids get hurled back 65 million years, and discover that the dinosaurs are like *Jurassic Park* than *Land before Time*. Driven by some half-decent action scenes, it will comfortably while away a wet afternoon. DA *DVD*

Pamela Adlon *Ernie* • Tara Strong *Julia* • Jane Lynch *Sue* • Melanie Griffith *Tyra* • Rob Schneider *Dodger* ■ *Dir* Choi Yoon-suk, John Kafka • *Scr* Adam Beechen, James Greco, Jae Woo Park, Zachary Rosenblatt

Dinosaur ★★★ PG
Animated adventure 2000 · US · Colour · 82min

While the story isn't exactly Kafka – abandoned baby dinosaur is raised by lemurs until they have to flee during a fiery meteor storm and join other dinosaurs on a treacherous trek to a new land – the animation is excellent. DB Sweeney and Julianna Margulies give life to their characters and there is solid vocal support from the rest of the cast in this ambitious Disney movie. JB *DVD* *Blu-ray*

DB Sweeney *Aladar* • Alfre Woodard *Plio* • Ossie Davis *Yar* • Samuel E Wright *Kron* • Julianna Margulies *Neera* • Joan Plowright *Baylene* • Della Reese *Eema* ■ *Dir* Eric Leighton, Ralph Zondag • *Scr* John Harrison, Robert Nelson Jacobs, from a screenplay (unproduced) by Walon Green, from a story by Thom Enriquez, John Harrison, Robert Nelson Jacobs, Ralph Zondag

The Dinosaur Project ★★★ 12
Adventure 2012 · UK · Colour · 79min

This is testament to what can be done on a budget if you have access to computer special effects programs and a certain amount of know-how. A group of scientists, and the inevitable camera-toting teen, head deep into the jungle to prove the truth or otherwise of legends about a living dinosaur. It's British, it's kind of fun and, at barely 80 minutes, it doesn't outstay its welcome. DA *DVD* *Blu-ray*

Natasha Loring *Dr Liz Draper* • Matt Kane *Luke Marchant* • Richard Dillane *Jonathan Marchant* ■ *Dir* Sid Bennett • *Scr* Sid Bennett, Jay Basu, from a story by Bennett, Tom Pridham

Dinosaur 13 ★★★ PG
Documentary 2014 · US · Colour · 94min

In the early 1990s a commercial fossil-hunting company excavating in the Badlands of South Dakota unearthed an almost complete T rex, only for it to be seized by the FBI, kicking off a complex legal battle involving Federal, state and Indian tribal law. This unfussily directed documentary tells the story from the point of view of the dinosaur's original discoverers, which is perhaps why the movie overlooks any discussion of the notion of unearthing fossils for profit. But as a David and Goliath tale of the picked-on little guy battling big government, it resonates powerfully. **AS** Some swearing. *DVD*

■ *Dir* Todd Douglas Miller • *Scr* From the book *Rex Appeal: The Amazing Story of Sue, the Dinosaur That Changed Science, the Law, and My Life* by Peter Larson, Kristin Donnan

Dinosaurus! ★★
Fantasy 1960 · US · Colour · 82min

Jurassic Park this ain't! A caveman, a friendly apatosaurus and a nasty T rex are disturbed from their slumber on a tropical island by construction workers in one of the funniest monster movies ever made. Best described as a prehistoric take on the Three Stooges' brand of comedy, viewers will shake their heads in dismay at the cheap mindlessness. Still, lousy special effects and worse acting make it hilariously compulsive viewing. **AJ**

Ward Ramsey *Bart Thompson* • Paul Lukather *Chuck* • Kristina Hanson *Betty Piper* • Alan Roberts *Julio* • Gregg Martell *Prehistoric man* • Fred Engelberg *Mike Hacker* ■ *Dir* Irvin S Yeaworth Jr • *Scr* Jean Yeaworth, Dan E Weisburd, from an idea by Jack H Harris

Dinoshark ★★15
Monster horror 2010 · US · Colour · 90min

By rights, this cheap companion to a slew of other water-monster movies (*Sharktopus, Dinocroc vs Supergator*) should be dreadful, but with Roger Corman producing and a better than average cast, it's actually moderately watchable. *Skyline* star Eric Balfour's attempts to involve the police are scuppered when his friend dies a gruesome death. Balfour's acting runs the gamut from A to B, but Iva Hasperger gives a performance worthy of a much better movie, and there are some decent shocks along the way. **SuR** *DVD*

Eric Balfour *Trace McGraw* • Iva Hasperger *Carol Brubaker* • Aarón Díaz *Luis* • Humberto Busto *Calderon* • Roger Corman *Dr Frank Reeves* ■ *Dir* Kevin O'Neill • *Scr* Frances Doel, Guy Prevost

Dionysus in '69 ★★★
Documentary 1970 · US · BW · 90min

At the outset of his career, Brian De Palma operated on the fringes of the New York avant-garde. Consequently, a self-conscious straining for effect informs this documentary as it seeks to match in visual terms the experimental nature of the Performance Group's adaptation of Euripides's *Bacchae*. Devised by Richard Schechner, the production encouraged audiences at the Performing Garage to participate in the play to achieve "total theatre". By using hand-held cameras and gimmicky devices like split screens, De Palma and fellow film-makers Robert Fiore and Bruce Joel Rubin attempt to capture the energy of the experience, but only partially succeed. **DP**

William Finley *Dicnysus* • William Shephard *Pentheus* • Joan MacIntosh *Agave* ■ *Dir* Brian De Palma, Bruce Fiore, Bruce Rubin [Bruce Joel Rubin] • *Scr* from the play *Dionysus in 69* by Richard Schechner, from the play *Bacchae* by Euripedes

Dior and I ★★★12A
Documentary 2014 · Fr · Colour · 89min

A highly informative and engrossing look behind the runway as a legendary fashion brand modernises while trying to honour its heritage. Belgian menswear wunderkind Raf Simons moves to the House of Dior and is expected to produce his first haute-couture line in just eight weeks. Featuring celebrity clips of Marlene Dietrich, Marion Cotillard, Sharon Stone and *Vogue* editor Anna Wintour, this is put together with all the style and elegance expected from such an atelier-driven subject. **AJ** In English, French, Italian.

Raf Simons • Marion Cotillard • Anna Wintour • Jennifer Lawrence (2) *Jennifer Lawrence* • Sharon Stone ■ *Dir/Scr* Frédéric Tcheng

Diplomacy ★★★★12
Wartime drama 2014 · Fr/Ger · Colour and BW · 80min

Niels Arestrup and André Dussollier reprise their stage roles of General Dietrich von Choltitz and Raoul Nordling in this fascinating account of the overnight meeting that saved Paris from destruction by the Nazis on 25 August 1944. In fact the discussions between the occupied capital's German governor and the Paris-born Swedish diplomat took days, but Cyril Gely's clever dialogue (from his own play) will quickly convince any sceptics that such witty, pithy exchanges could have happened, as Nordling pleaded for his home town and von Choltitz weighed his duty against the fate of his family and his posthumous reputation. **DP** In French, German. *DVD*

André Dussollier *Raoul Nordling* • Niels Arestrup *General von Choltitz* • Burghart Klaussner *Hauptmann Werner Ebernach* • Robert Stadlober *Lieutenant Bressensdorf* ■ *Dir* Volker Schlöndorff • *Scr* Volker Schlöndorff, Cyril Gely, from Gely's play

Diplomatic Courier ★★★U
Spy drama 1952 · US · BW · 97min

This rattlingly good Cold War thriller was shot on European locations, with Tyrone Power's blandness offset by his female co-stars: Soviet agent Hildegarde Neff and American tourist Patricia Neal. Look out too for Karl Malden, Lee Marvin and Charles Bronson on their respective paths to stardom. With hindsight, the "secret agenda" plot seems chillingly appropriate. Underrated and well worth a look. **TS**

Tyrone Power *Mike Kells* • Patricia Neal *Joan Ross* • Stephen McNally *Colonel Cagle* • Hildegarde Neff *Janine* • Karl Malden *Ernie* • James Millican *Sam Carew* • Stefan Schnabel *Platov* ■ *Dir* Henry Hathaway • *Scr* Casey Robinson, Liam O'Brien, from the novel *Sinister Errand* by Peter Cheyney

Diplomatic Siege ★★15
Action thriller 1999 · US · Colour · 90min

This boasts a better than average cast although that's probably more about the stars' current standing in Hollywood than the class of this bog-standard straight-to-video actioner. The reality-defying plot has Peter Weller and Daryl Hannah trapped in a US embassy taken over by terrorists. Tom Berenger, playing a US general, turns up to do little more than pick up his wages, leaving Weller and Hannah to wrestle with an illogical plot and lame dialogue. **JF** *DVD*

Peter Weller *Steve Mitchell* • Daryl Hannah *Erica Long* • Tom Berenger *Buck Swain* • Adrian Pintea *Goran* ■ *Dir* Gustavo Graef-Marino • *Scr* Mark Amin, Sam Bernard, Kevin Bernhardt, Robert Boris

Dirigible ★★★
Adventure 1931 · US · BW · 104min

Made some years before his sentimental association with small-town America transformed him into a Hollywood great, this reminds us that Frank Capra also worked in other genres. Two navy pilots experiment with airships, one of which crashes in the Antarctic, resulting in a three-way tug of war between the fame-seeking pilot, his wife and a colleague who covets her. Capra knows how to build and sustain action, but he is less sure with the mush of romance that, at times, sets the film in cement. **JM**

Jack Holt *Jack Bradcn* • Ralph Graves *Frisky Pierce* • Fay Wray *Helen* • Hobart Bosworth *Rondelle* • Roscoe Karns *Sock McGuire* • Harold Goodwin (1) *Hansen* • Clarence Muse *Clarence* ■ *Dir* Frank Capra • *Scr* Jo Swerling, Dorothy Howell, from a story by Lieutenant Commander Frank W Weed

The Dirt Bike Kid ★★★PG
Fantasy comedy 1986 · US · Colour · 86min

Fans of the Herbie movies should enjoy this similar tale of a boy with a bike that has a mind of its own. Peter Billingsley is the young teen in question, and he seems to have fun playing a character who is continually getting into the sorts of trouble only his wonder bike can get him out of. Not exactly memorable, but this is an amusing diversion. **JB**

Peter Billingsley *Jack Simmons* • Stuart Pankin *Mr Hodgkins* • Anne Bloom *Janet Simmons* • Patrick Collins *Mike* • Sage Parker *Miss Clavell* • Chad Sheets *Bo* • Gavin Allen *Max* • Danny Breen *Flaherty* ■ *Dir* Hoite C Caston • *Scr* David Brandes, Lewis Colick, from a story by J Halloran [Julie Corman]

The Dirties ★★★15
Black comedy drama 2013 · Can · Colour · 82min

Director/star Matt Johnson blurs fact and fiction in this disconcerting faux high-school documentary. Bullying victims Johnson and Owen Williams decide to make a vérité account of their treatment that will culminate in the pair taking vicious revenge on "the dirties". Jared Raab's camerawork is suitably jerky, while Johnson often seems to be riffing more on Jean-Luc Godard than Quentin Tarantino. But, for all its black comedic bravura, this is a touch too self-conscious to amuse. **DP** Violence, swearing, brief nudity. *DVD*

Matthew Johnson [Matt Johnson (3)] *Matt* • Owen Williams *Owen* • Krista Madison *Chrissy H* • Brandon Wickens *Jackman* ■ *Dir* Matthew Johnson [Matt Johnson (3)] • *Scr* Matthew Johnson, Matthew Miller (2), Evan Morgan, from a story by Josh Boles

Dirty Dancing ★★★★12
Romantic drama 1987 · US · Colour · 95min

This feel-good dance drama works a curious charismatic magic and catapulted the then-unknown Patrick Swayze to stardom. It was intended as a low-budget filler, a tale of sexual awakening at a Jewish holiday camp in 1963, but it became a much loved blockbuster. The casting is perfect, with ex-dancer Swayze as the sexy bad boy dancing coach and Jennifer Grey as the middle-class teenager, but what really makes the film unmissable is the fabulous dancing which, despite being highly erotic, is never tacky. A remake directed by Kenny Ortega is in production. **SH** Swearing. *DVD* *Blu*

Jennifer Grey *Frances "Baby" Houseman* • Patrick Swayze *Johnny Castle* • Jerry Orbach *Dr Jake Houseman* • Cynthia Rhodes *Penny Johnson* • Jack Weston *Max Kellerman* • Jane Brucker *Lisa Houseman* • Kelly Bishop *Marjorie Houseman* • Lonny Price *Neil Kellerman* ■ *Dir* Emile Ardolino • *Scr* Eleanor Bergstein • *Choreographers* Kenny Ortega, Miranda John Pritchett

Dirty Dancing 2 ★★PG
Romantic drama 2003 · US · Colour · 82min

This tale of polar opposites brought together by dance is a thematic reworking, rather than a sequel, to the 1987 hit. Set in Havana in 1958, it sees Romola Garai's American teen falling for fancy-footed local waiter Diego Luna. Though the two are attractive, their dancing lacks fire and there's no sense of the sexual tension that ignited the original. **SF** *DVD*

Diego Luna *Javier Suarez* • Romola Garai *Katey Miller* • Sela Ward *Jeannie Miller* • John Slattery *Bert Miller* • Jonathan Jackson *James Phelps* • January Jones *Eve* • Mika Boorem *Susie Miller* • Patrick Swayze *Dance instructor* ■ *Dir* Guy Ferland • *Scr* Boaz Yakin, Victoria Arch, from a story by Kate Gunzinger, Peter Sagal

Dirty Deeds ★★18
Crime comedy 2002 · Aus/UK · Colour · 93min

This follows the travails of an Australian crime boss (Bryan Brown) as he attempts to ward off the Chicago Mafia (in the corpulent shape of John Goodman) who are in town to muscle in on his slot-machine racket. Director David Caesar's uncertain direction and hectic editing obscure the film's strengths, particularly the always entertaining Brown and Goodman. **AS** *DVD*

Bryan Brown *Barry Ryan* • Toni Collette *Sharon Ryan* • John Goodman *Tony Testano* • Sam Neill *Det-Sgt Ray Murphy* • Sam Worthington *Darcy* • Kestie Morassi *Margaret* • Felix Williamson *Sal Cassela* • William McInnes *Hollywood* ■ *Dir/Scr* David Caesar

Dirty Dingus Magee ★★PG
Comedy western 1970 · US · Colour · 86min

Frank Sinatra plays a literally lousy outlaw in this vulgar, gross and bawdy comedy western, but he only succeeds in looking anachronistically stupid. There's a nice cast of old western reliables on hand to keep director Burt Kennedy's film watchable, plus a gem of a performance from the underrated Lois Nettleton. **TS**

Frank Sinatra *Dingus Magee* • George Kennedy *Hoke Birdsill* • Anne Jackson *Belle Kops* • Lois Nettleton *Prudence* • Jack Elam *John Wesley Hardin* • Michele Carey *Anna Hotwater* • John Dehner *General* • Harry Carey Jr *Stuart* ■ *Dir* Burt Kennedy • *Scr* Frank Waldman, Tom Waldman, Joseph Heller, from the novel *The Ballad of Dingus Magee* by David Markson

The Dirty Dozen ★★★★15
Second World War action adventure 1967 · US/UK · Colour · 143min

One of the smash hits of its year, this action-packed war movie is violent and amoral, and fans would say all the better for it. Whatever your tastes, there's no denying director Robert Aldrich's consummate skill with such material or the powerhouse impact of the starry all-male cast headed by Lee Marvin, factors that have helped maintain the film's popularity. The violence is in fact mild by today's standards, but it nevertheless leaves a nasty taste in the mouth as a group of sociopaths are released from jail on a suicide mission to murder Nazis, and the movie rightly earned its original X certificate. John Poyner won the best sound effects Oscar for his superb soundtrack. **TS** *DVD*

Lee Marvin *Major Reisman* • Ernest Borgnine *General Worden* • Charles Bronson *Joseph Wladislaw* • Jim Brown *Robert Jefferson* • John Cassavetes *Victor Franko* • Richard Jaeckel *Sgt Bowren* • George Kennedy *Maj Max Armbruster* • Trini Lopez *Pedro Jiminez* • Ralph Meeker *Capt Stuart Kinder* • Robert Ryan *Col Everett Dasher Breed* • Telly Savalas *Archer Maggott* • Donald Sutherland *Vernon Pinkley* • Clint Walker *Samson Posey* • Robert Webber *Colonel Denton* ■ *Dir* Robert Aldrich • *Scr* Lukas Heller, Nunnally Johnson, from the novel by EM Nathanson

The Dirty Game ★★
Portmanteau spy drama 1965 · Fr/It/W Ger · BW · 91min

This deglamorising spy compendium is patchy in the extreme. The first section has Vittorio Gassman going undercover in Rome to kidnap a jet fuel specialist; the second involves rival detachments of frogmen doing battle beneath the Gulf of Aden. The Le Carré-esque conclusion affords Henry Fonda the opportunity to demonstrate what a superb actor he is – even though he utters no more than a couple of lines of dialogue. **DP**

Henry Fonda *Kourlov* • Robert Ryan *General Bruce* • Vittorio Gassman *Perego* • Annie Girardot *Nanette* • Bourvil *Laland* • Robert Hossein *Dupont* • Peter Van Eyck *Berlin CIA head Petchatkin* • Maria Grazia Buccella *Natalia* ■ *Dir* Terence Young, Christian-Jaque, Carlo Lizzani, Werner Klinger • *Scr* Jo Eisinger, Jacques Laborie, Jacques Remy, Ennio De Concini, Christian-Jaque, from a screenplay (unproduced) by Philippe Bouvard

Dirty Grandpa ★★★15
Comedy 2016 · US · Colour · 97min

Zac Efron plays a conservative, about-to-be-wed young man who's fooled into taking his recently bereaved but hedonistic grandfather (Robert De Niro) to Florida for spring break. With drug use, nudity and lots of swearing, this comedy directed by Dan Mazer (writer of *Borat* and *Brüno*) could have been a mess of crass gags if not for the chemistry of the cast, particularly the two leads who have a rapport that wins you back even when the jokes inevitably stray over the line. **JL** Swearing, nudity, drug abuse. *DVD* *Blu*

Robert De Niro *Dick Kelly* • Zac Efron *Jason Kelly* • Zoey Deutch *Shadia* • Aubrey Plaza *Lenore* • Dermot Mulroney *David Kelly* ■ *Dir* Dan Mazer • *Scr* John Phillips (5)

D

Dirty Harry ★★★★★ 18
Crime thriller 1971 · US · Colour · 102min

This is the first and best outing for Clint Eastwood's San Francisco police inspector, in which he tramples on the American Constitution to bring gibbering psycho Andrew Robinson to justice. Directed by Don Siegel with his usual toughness and crisp efficiency, this is a masterpiece of action movie-making. Eastwood displays all the characteristic hard-boiled traits that are now part of his screen persona and cinema folklore. Making good use of Golden Gate locations, and armed with a smart and darkly cynical script, this original generates an excitement that none of the four sequels (*Magnum Force*, *The Enforcer*, *Sudden Impact* and *The Dead Pool*) could match. AJ Violence, swearing, brief nudity. *DVD* Blu

Clint Eastwood *Harry Callahan* · Harry Guardino *Lieutenant Bressler* · Reni Santoni *Chico* · John Vernon *Mayor* · Andy Robinson [Andrew Robinson] *Killer* · John Larch *Chief* · John Mitchum *DeGeorgio* · Mae Mercer *Mrs Russell* ■ *Dir* Don Siegel · *Scr* Harry Julian Fink, Rita M Fink, Dean Riesner, from a story by Harry Julian Fink, Rita M Fink · *Cinematographer* Bruce Surtees

Dirty Little Billy ★★★
Western 1972 · US · Colour · 92min

Rarely has a myth been so muddied as that of Billy the Kid in this early revisionist western, in which the lad is seen before notoriety gave him outlaw celebrity. Director Stan Dragoti's often surreal visuals mesmerise, with Coffeyville, Kansas, seen as a slop-bucket community from which Billy is only too happy to escape. The fictionalised antihero of the Wild West is played here by Michael J Pollard as a mentally challenged eccentric, which tends to subtract some sympathy from his situation. TH Swearing.

Michael J Pollard *Billy Bonney* · Lee Purcell *Berle* · Richard Evans *Goldie Evans* · Charles Aidman *Ben Antrim* · Dran Hamilton *Catherine McCarty* · Willard Sage *Henry McCarty* · Josip Elic *Jawbone* · Mills Watson *Ed* ■ *Dir* Stan Dragoti · *Scr* Stan Dragoti, Charles Moss · *Cinematographer* Ralph Woolsey

Dirty Oil ★★★ U
Documentary 2009 · Can/Ire · Colour · 75min

Despite the odd disputable claim and an occasional tendency to sentimentalise, this is a trenchant exposé of the damage being done to the landscape (and the people who occupy it) by the strip-mining of Canada's Alberta tar sands. An area the size of Florida has been ripped open to help meet the USA's need for a reliable supply of affordable oil. Narrator Neve Campbell and a number of experts reveal doom-laden pronouncements and grimly overwhelming statistics, but director Leslie Iwerks also wisely lets the views of post-apocalyptic devastation speak for themselves. DP

Neve Campbell *Narrator* ■ *Dir/Scr* Leslie Iwerks

Dirty Pretty Things ★★★ 15
Drama 2002 · UK/US · Colour · 93min

Stephen Frears here provides a distinctive insight into illegal immigrants living a hidden, knife-edge existence in London. Chiwetel Ejiofor is all soulful integrity as a Nigerian taxi driver who moonlights as a night porter in a hotel, while *Amélie's* Audrey Tautou elicits sympathy as a downtrodden Turkish asylum seeker. Aided by accomplished cinematographer Chris Menges, Frears's depiction of a seedy London is impressive, though the script's intrusive thriller elements dent the film's credibility. JC Sex scenes, violence, swearing. *DVD* Blu

Chiwetel Ejiofor *Okwe* · Audrey Tautou *Senay* · Sergi Lopez *Sneaky* · Sophie Okonedo *Juliette* · Benedict Wong *Guo Yi* · Sotigui Kouyate *Shinti* · Abi Gouhad *Shinti's son* ■ *Dir* Stephen Frears · *Scr* Steven Knight

Dirty Rotten Scoundrels ★★★ PG
Comedy 1988 · US · Colour · 105min

This proficient remake of the old David Niven/Marlon Brando caper movie *Bedtime*

Story cruises by on star power alone. Michael Caine is the veteran conman making a comfortable living on the Riviera, who takes brash American Steve Martin under his wing. However, the pair fall out when they compete to take rich heiress Glenne Headly to the cleaners. Caine more than holds his own against the manic Martin and, if the script offers few surprises, the south of France looks great and director Frank Oz ensures the action slips along smoothly. Frothy fun. JF Swearing. *DVD* Blu

Michael Caine *Lawrence Jamieson* · Steve Martin *Freddy Benson* · Glenne Headly *Janet Colgate* · Anton Rodgers *Inspector André* · Barbara Harris *Fanny Eubanks* · Ian McDiarmid *Arthur* · Dana Ivey *Mrs Reed* ■ *Dir* Frank Oz · *Scr* Dale Launer, Stanley Shapiro, Paul Henning

Dirty Sanchez: the Movie ★★ 18
Comedy 2006 · UK · Colour · 96min

Now, here's a movie that definitely belongs in the "don't try this at home" category. Those overgrown schoolboys from the cult MTV series receive the big-screen treatment here as they trawl the world in search of ever more stupid pranks. The paper-thin premise is that the daredevil quartet are killed during a stunt but are then challenged by the Devil to re-enact the Seven Deadly Sins. Think *Jackass*, only much, much more extreme. It's all thoroughly irresponsible, of course, but for those who enjoy a bit of good-natured self-inflicted pain and humiliation, this is for you. Those of a more sensitive disposition probably won't like it, which is doubtless some sort of recommendation. DA Swearing, crude sexual behaviour. *DVD*

Lee Dainton *Dainton* · Dan Joyce *Joycey* · Mike Locke *Pancho* · Matthew Pritchard *Pritchard* · Howard Marks *The Devil* ■ *Dir* Jim Hickey

A Dirty Shame ★★★ 18
Satirical comedy 2004 · US · Colour · 85min

It's filthy! It's disgusting! It's another film by John Waters. After the Hollywood satire *Cecil B Demented*, Waters is back to subvert suburbia with another bad-taste comedy. Tracey Ullman stars as a repressed woman who resists the advances of her husband (Chris Isaak) and locks her daughter (Selma Blair, with comically distended breasts) in her room to prevent her working in a strip club. Then she's involved in an accident, wakes with uncontrollable lust and falls in with sex guru Johnny Knoxville. John Waters's desire to outrage is as strong as ever, but can't compensate for a patchy script. TH Sexual references. *DVD*

Tracey Ullman *Sylvia Stickles* · Johnny Knoxville *Ray-Ray Perkins* · Selma Blair *Caprice Stickles* · Chris Isaak *Vaughn Stickles* · Suzanne Shepherd *Big Ethel* · Mink Stole *Marge the Neuter* · Patricia Hearst *Paige* ■ *Dir/Scr* John Waters (2)

Dirty Wars ★★★★ 15
Documentary 2013 · US/Afg/Iraq/Ken/Somalia/Yemen · Colour and BW · 86min

Murky secrets of the War on Terror are uncovered in this stark and ominous documentary fronted by investigative journalist Jeremy Scahill. He searches for proof of the "American Taliban", an elite, covert military unit, through Afghanistan, Yemen, Somalia and Kenya. It's a riveting film, made in a detective story-cum-thriller style, with a constant, looming sense of danger. And it widens out to examine the War itself, Islamic radicalisation, ever-expanding kill lists (that controversially include US citizens) and the game-changing death of bin Laden. JA English, Pashtu, Somali, Dari +subtitles.

■ *Dir* Richard Rowley · *Scr* David Riker, Jeremy Scahill

Dirty Weekend ★★ 18
Thriller 1992 · UK · Colour · 96min

Directed by Michael Winner, this was released to a crescendo of controversy concerning its gross violence, regarded as a sort of *Death Wish* in a skirt. Lia Williams plays a much-abused young woman who is

---

egged on by a Brighton clairvoyant to take her revenge on all men. She takes the advice very much to heart, using the knife he gives her to gruesome effect. JF Sex scenes, violence, swearing. *DVD*

Lia Williams *Bella* · Ian Richardson *Nimrod* · David McCallum (1) *Reggie* · Rufus Sewell *Tim* · Miriam Kelly *Marion* · Sylvia Syms *Mrs Crosby* · Shaughan Seymour *Charles* · Christopher Adamson *Serial Killer* · Sean Pertwee ■ *Dir* Michael Winner · *Scr* Michael Winner, from the novel by Helen Zahavi

Dirty Work ★★★ 12
Comedy 1998 · US · Colour · 78min

Norm MacDonald and Artie Lange play a couple of losers who discover their vocation in life: being paid to play humiliating pranks on behalf of wronged victims. Chevy Chase pops up as a cheerfully amoral surgeon, and there's a nicely grumpy turn from Jack Warden as MacDonald's dad. Despite losing its nerve by the end, this is for the most part a crudely nasty treat. JF Swearing.

Norm MacDonald *Mitch* · Artie Lange *Sam* · Christopher McDonald *Travis Cole* · Traylor Howard *Kathy* · Chevy Chase *Dr Farthing* · Don Rickles *Hamilton* · Jack Warden *Pops* · Chris Farley · Gary Coleman · Adam Sandler ■ *Dir* Bob Saget · *Scr* Fred Wolf, Norm Macdonald, Frank Sebastiano

The Disappearance ★★★ 15
Crime drama 1977 · Can/UK · Colour · 87min

There is much to admire in this tale of a hitman, played by a suitably haunting Donald Sutherland, pondering the disappearance of his wife while planning his next job. Beautifully shot on location in icy Canada, a symbol of the assassin's frozen emotions, the British supporting cast shine. Only Stuart Cooper's somewhat arty approach to Paul Mayersberg's admittedly confusing script lets the side down. RS *DVD*

Donald Sutherland *Jay* · Francine Racette *Celandine* · David Hemmings *Edward* · Virginia McKenna *Catherine* · Christopher Plummer *Deverell* · John Hurt *Atkinson* · David Warner *Burbank* ■ *Dir* Stuart Cooper · *Scr* Paul Mayersberg, from the novel *Echoes of Celandine* by Derek Marlowe · *Cinematographer* John Alcott

The Disappearance of Aimee ★★★★
Mystery drama 1976 · US · Colour · 110min

Based on a true story, this fascinating TV movie involves the disappearance of evangelist Aimee Semple McPherson (played by Faye Dunaway) in 1926. When she returned, Aimee claimed she had been abducted. Her mother, however, believed she had run off to have an affair, and the events became a national scandal. The story is handled in a gripping manner by director Anthony Harvey, but it's the performances that keep you pinned to your seat. JB

Faye Dunaway *Sister Aimee McPherson* · Bette Davis *Minnie Kennedy* · James Sloyan *District Attorney Asa Keyes* · James Woods *Assistant DA Joseph Ryan* · John Lehne *Captain Cline* · Lelia Goldoni *Emma Shaffer* ■ *Dir* Anthony Harvey · *Scr* John McGreevey

The Disappearance of Alice Creed ★★★ 18
Thriller 2009 · UK · Colour · 95min

A meticulously planned kidnap rapidly becomes a violent mess in writer/director J Blakeson's unremarkable feature debut. The stage-bound setting might have served to focus attention on some key emotional fireworks between capable lead Gemma Arterton and her equally serviceable co-stars Eddie Marsan and Martin Compston. Sadly, even if you do manage to concentrate on the twists, they more often come across as clunky rather than credible. LB Violence, swearing, sex scenes and nudity. *DVD* Blu

Gemma Arterton *Alice Creed* · Martin Compston *Danny* · Eddie Marsan *Vic* ■ *Dir/Scr* J Blakeson

---

The Disappearance of Finbar ★★★ 15
Drama 1996 · Ire/UK/Swe/Fr · Colour · 100min

The title refers to the vanishing act of a failed young Irish footballer from his home on a Dublin housing estate. Initially a mournful study of the repercussions of Finbar's (Jonathan Rhys) departure, the film takes on an altogether more humorous tone when his best friend (Luke Griffin) embarks on a Scandinavian odyssey to seek some answers. There are a few oddly appealing moments, although the film looks like two different movies spliced together. JC Swearing, a sex scene. *DVD*

Luke Griffin *Danny Quinn* · Jonathan Rhys Meyers *Finbar Flynn* · Sean McGinley *Detective Roche* · Fanny Risberg *Abbi* · Marie Mullen *Ellen Quinn* · Lorraine Pilkington *Katie Dunnigan* · Sean Lawlor *Michael Flynn* ■ *Dir* Sue Clayton · *Scr* Sue Clayton, Dermot Bolger, from the novel *The Disappearance of Rory Brophy* by Carl Lombard

The Disappearance of Garcia Lorca ★★★
Mystery thriller 1997 · US/Fr · Colour · 114min

After a teenage encounter with Spanish writer Federico Garcia Lorca (Andy Garcia), Esai Morales grows up determined to return to Spain and uncover the truth behind the great man's disappearance and untimely death. His amateur murder investigation suggests that, while a dead poet can be a national hero, a live one can be a national threat. Based on the speculations of author Ian Gibson, this is an interesting study of Lorca and the Spanish civil war. LH

Andy Garcia *Federico Garcia Lorca* · Esai Morales *Ricardo* · Edward James Olmos *Roberto Lozano* · Jeroen Krabbé *Colonel Aguirre* · Giancarlo Giannini *Taxi* · Miguel Ferrer *Centeno* · Marcela Walerstein *Maria Eugenia* · Eusebio Lázaro *Vicente Fernandez* ■ *Dir* Marcos Zurinaga · *Scr* Marcos Zurinaga, Juan Antonio Ramos, Neil Cohen, from the non-fiction books *The Assassination of Federico Garcia Lorca*, *Federico Garcia Lorca: A Life* by Ian Gibson

The Disappearance of Kevin Johnson ★★★ 15
Mystery thriller 1995 · US/UK · Colour · 101min

A whodunit thriller set in the movie world featuring Pierce Brosnan, Dudley Moore and James Coburn playing themselves. Filmed in mock-documentary style and unfolding like a real-life piece of investigative journalism, the twists and turns come thick and fast, with the suspense increasing as the surprise ending veers into view. Fascinating, original and hugely entertaining. AJ Swearing, sexual references.

Pierce Brosnan · James Coburn · Dudley Moore · Alexander Folk *Police detective* · Carl Sundstrom *Security guard* · Bridget Baiss *Gayle Hamilton* · Ian Ogilvy *Gary* · Charlotte Brosnan *Amy* ■ *Dir/Scr* Francis Megahy

The Disappeared ★★★★ 15
Horror 2008 · UK · Colour · 92min

Shot in washed out greys under overcast skies, director Johnny Kevorkian's debut is a disturbing slice of Brit-horror miserablism that follows teenage Matthew (Harry Treadaway) as he's haunted by sightings of his missing (presumed dead) younger brother. It's no glossy *Sixth Sense*, but rather a grim and grimy take on grief, the story of its hoodie stoner hero's breakdown. Carefully crafting its slow-burning shocks, this is an atmospheric chiller that inches under the skin. If Ken Loach made fright flicks, they'd probably look like this. JR Violence, swearing. *DVD*

Harry Treadaway *Matthew Ryan* · Greg Wise *Jake Ryan* · Alex Jennings *Adrian Ballan* · Tom Felton *Simon* · Georgia Groome *Sophie Pryor* ■ *Dir* Johnny Kevorkian · *Scr* Johnny Kevorkian, Neil Murphy

Disappearing Acts ★★★ 15
Romantic drama 2000 · US · Colour · 110min

Another classy HBO production, this emotionally complex drama follows the glorious ups and moving downs in the

---

relationship between builder Wesley Snipes and aspiring singer Sanaa Lathan. The two leads are superb, and neither they nor director Gina Prince-Bythewood flinch from the raw truths of love and relationships in the modern age. JF DVD

Wesley Snipes *Franklin Swift* • Sanaa Lathan *Zora Banks* • John Amos *Mr Swift* • CCH Pounder *Mrs Swift* • Regina Hall *Portia* ■ *Dir* Gina Prince-Bythewood • *Scr* Lisa Jones, from the novel by Terry McMillan

Disaster Movie ★ 12
Spoof comedy 2008 · US · Colour · 83min

Once upon a time the movie parody genre could be relied on to deliver laughs – *Airplane!*, *The Naked Gun* series and Mel Brooks's early movies always had a fair quotient of giggles. These days, though, the genre has been taken hostage by writer/directors Jason Friedberg and Aaron Seltzer, whose cinematic conveyor belt continues to crank out execrable dross like *Date Movie* and *Meet the Spartans* with alarming regularity. *Disaster Movie* follows the same tired formula by loosely apeing a major movie plot (in this case *Cloverfield*), then packing in references to other, entirely unconnected, recent movies in the mistaken belief this constitutes humour. JR Sexual, drug references. DVD

Matt Lanter *Will* • Vanessa Minnillo *Amy* • Gary "G Thang" Johnson [G Thang] *Calvin* • Nicole Parker *Enchanted princess* • Crista Flanagan *Juney* • Kimberly Kardashian [Kim Kardashian] *Lisa* • Carmen Electra *Beautiful assassin* ■ *Dir/Scr* Jason Friedberg, Aaron Seltzer

Disclosure ★★ 18
Thriller 1994 · US · Colour · 122min

Demi Moore plays Michael Douglas's former lover, who is promoted above him in a computer corporation. When Moore seeks to rekindle their passion, the now-married Douglas has second thoughts at a vital moment, and the much-miffed Moore accuses him of sexual harassment. This is a self-important and unintentionally funny thriller about corporate power and sexual equality, though there is too much emphasis on computer gizmos and cyber-babble. AT Swearing, sex scenes. DVD

Michael Douglas (1) *Tom Sanders* • Demi Moore *Meredith Johnson* • Donald Sutherland *Bob Garvin* • Roma Maffia *Catherine Alvarez* • Caroline Goodall *Susan Hendler* • Dennis Miller *Mark Lewyn* • Rosemary Forsyth *Stephanie Kaplan* • Dylan Baker *Philip Blackburn* • Nicholas Sadler *Don Cherry* ■ *Dir* Barry Levinson • *Scr* Paul Attanasio, from the novel by Michael Crichton

Disco Pigs ★★ 15
Coming-of-age drama
2001 · UK/Ire · Colour · 89min

This twisted rites-of-passage tale is an overwrought drama that doesn't quite come up with the goods. Inseparable since birth, next-door neighbours outsiders Cillian Murphy and Elaine Cassidy have grown up together as though they were twins – even having their own special language. But when they are prised apart on their 17th birthday, all hell breaks loose. Kirsten Sheridan's already precarious feature debut then collapses into a mêlée of sickening violence. DP DVD

Elaine Cassidy *Sinead, "Runt"* • Cillian Murphy *Darren, "Pig"* • Brian F O'Byrne *Runt's dad* • Eleanor Methven *Pig's mam* • Geraldine O'Rawe *Runt's mam* • Darren Healy *Marky* ■ *Dir* Kirsten Sheridan • *Scr* Enda Walsh, from her play

Disconnect ★★★ 15
Drama 2012 · US · Colour · 111min

The internet age comes under the microscope in this portmanteau film that, perhaps inevitably given its technological focus, became dated as soon as it wrapped. Cyber-bullying, internet fraud and online porn all come under the spotlight and, as is usual with multi-storyline projects, some strands are better than others. Still, there are insightful moments, and a section concerning a schoolboy who is hounded by thoughtless but not evil bullies retains its relevance – just as the film, as a whole,

reminds us of the necessity of human contact. DW DVD

Jason Bateman *Rich Boyd* • Hope Davis *Lydia Boyd* • Frank Grillo *Mike Dixon* • Paula Patton *Cindy Hull* • Andrea Riseborough *Nina Dunham* • Alexander Skarsgård *Derek Hull* ■ *Dir* Henry Alex Rubin • *Scr* Andrew Stern

The Discreet Charm of the Bourgeoisie ★★★★★ 15
Comedy drama 1972 · Fr · Colour · 97min

Brilliantly interweaving a sequence of disrupted dinners, three diversionary tales and a quartet of awakenings that alert us to the fact we have been sharing a dream, this sharply satirical and teasingly structured picture is one of Luis Buñuel's finest achievements as both film-maker and social commentator. At once a delightful comedy and a clinical assault on the bastions and behaviour of the bourgeoisie, it touches on all the director's favourite themes: sexual repression, religious hypocrisy and patriarchal paranoia. The playing is exceptional, though Fernando Rey, Delphine Seyrig and Michel Piccoli merit special mention. DP French +subtitles. DVD Blu

Fernando Rey *Ambassador* • Delphine Seyrig *Mme Simone Thévenot* • Stéphane Audran *Mme Alice Sénéchal* • Bulle Ogier *Florence* • Jean-Pierre Cassel *M Sénéchal* • Paul Frankeur *M Thévenot* • Julien Bertheau *Bishop Dufour* • Claude Piéplu *Colonel* • Michel Piccoli *Home Secretary* ■ *Dir* Luis Buñuel • *Scr* Luis Buñuel, Jean-Claude Carrière

Disgrace ★★★★ 15
Drama 2008 · Aus · Colour · 113min

JM Coetzee's Booker Prize-winning novel followed a Cape Town lecturer's fall from grace after an affair with a mixed-race student. In this handsome adaptation, John Malkovich giving a blistering performance as the tragic antihero who is sacked from his post and travels into the bush to join his daughter (Jessica Haines) on her remote farm. What follows next – land seizures, rape, violence and victimhood – uncoils with tragic inevitability and pushes Lurie to confront his own moral bankruptcy. Superbly handled by director Steve Jacobs and strikingly shot on location, *Disgrace* is riveting and harrowing viewing. JR Violence, sex scenes. DVD

John Malkovich *David Lurie* • Jessica Haines *Lucy* • Eriq Ebouaney *Petrus* • Fiona Press *Bev Shaw* • Antoinette Engel *Melanie Isaacs* ■ *Dir* Steve Jacobs • *Scr* Anna Maria Monticelli [Anna Jemison], from the novel by JM Coetzee

The Dish ★★★★ 12
Comedy drama 2000 · Aus · Colour · 96min

When Neil Armstrong became the first man to walk on the Moon on 20 July 1969, he was watched by a global TV audience of 600 million people. But how many of them had even heard of the Australian town of Parkes in New South Wales, whose radio telescope transmitted the pictures? Not many, and that's the arresting premise of this gentle, human comedy. A heart-warming tale of small-town folk getting on with the business of making history, it's full of self-deprecating, irreverent Aussie humour. AC DVD

Sam Neill *Cliff Buxton* • Kevin Harrington *Ross "Mitch" Mitchell* • Tom Long *Glenn Latham* • Patrick Warburton *Al Burnett* • Genevieve Mooy *May McIntyre* • Tayler Kane *Rudi Kellerman* • Billie Brown *Prime minister* • Roy Billing *Mayor Bob McIntryre* ■ *Dir* Rob Sitch • *Scr* Santo Cilauro, Tom Gleisner, Jane Kennedy, Rob Sitch

Dishonored ★★★★★ PG
First World War spy drama
1931 · US · BW · 87min

An erotic dream doubling as a First World War espionage drama, this extraordinary work was the third of director Josef von Sternberg's celebrated collaborations with Marlene Dietrich, and casts the latter as "Agent X-27" and Victor McLaglen as her rival and sexual plaything, "Agent H-14". Rivalling Garbo's *Mata Hari*, which was released the same year, it was a huge box-office hit, luring audiences with its promise of sex and spying. As the sultry spy doomed

by her predatory nature, Dietrich is radiant and poised in a performance that is at once controlled and all over the place, the result of von Sternberg's exactitude. DO DVD

Marlene Dietrich *Magda/X-27* • Victor McLaglen *Colonel Kranau* • Gustav von Seyffertitz *Secret Service head* • Warner Oland *Colonel von Hindau* • Lew Cody *Colonel Kovrin* • Barry Norton *Young lieutenant* • Davison Clark *Court-martial officer* • Wilfred Lucas *General Dymov* ■ *Dir* Josef von Sternberg • *Scr* Daniel N Rubin, from the story *X-27* by Josef von Sternberg • *Cinematographer* Lee Garmes

Dishonored Lady ★★
Crime drama 1947 · US · BW · 85min

Produced by Hedy Lamarr herself, this screen version of a Broadway hit finds her playing a neurotic magazine editor who goes off the rails and attempts to kill herself by driving her car into a garden wall. Luckily for her, said wall belongs to a psychiatrist! Alas, her shady past catches up with her and she's accused of murder. The wordy script and Robert Stevenson's pedestrian direction are drawbacks, but Lamarr does reasonably well. AT

Hedy Lamarr *Madeleine Damien* • Dennis O'Keefe *Dr David Cousins* • John Loder *Felix Courtland* • William Lundigan *Jack Garet* • Morris Carnovsky *Dr Caleb* • Paul Cavanagh *Victor Kranish* • Douglass Dumbrille *District attorney* ■ *Dir* Robert Stevenson • *Scr* Edmund H North, from the play by Edward Sheldon, Margaret Ayer Barnes

Disney's The Kid ★★★ PG
Comedy fantasy 2000 · US · Colour · 99min

Bruce Willis here returns to *The Sixth Sense* territory, starring alongside youngster Spencer Breslin in a film that has a tinge of the supernatural about it. Willis plays a heartless image consultant in need of redemption. Initially puzzled by the child who seems to be following him, Willis comes to realise that Breslin is in fact his younger self. Confronted by the past, the gruff adult has a chance to change his present-day existence for the better. The story is unalloyed by sentimentality and rings as true as a school bell. TH DVD

Bruce Willis *Russ Duritz* • Spencer Breslin *Rusty Duritz* • Emily Mortimer *Amy* • Lily Tomlin *Janet* • Chi McBride *Kenny* • Jean Smart *Deirdre Lafever* • Dana Ivey *Dr Alexander* ■ *Dir* Jon Turteltaub • *Scr* Audrey Wells

Disorder ★★★★ 15
Thriller 2015 · Fr /Bel · Colour · 94min

French writer/director Alice Winocour's discomforting second feature traps us in the head of a soldier suffering from hearing loss and PTSD, ingeniously illuminating his damaged psyche through music, sound and twitchy, edgy camerawork from cinematographer Georges Lechaptois. The sinister detachment of surveillance footage is nicely contrasted with the intimacy of the overall presentation, while Matthias Schoenaerts – for whom the part was written – is captivating in his intensity. EAS French +subtitles. Violence, swearing. DVD Blu

Matthias Schoenaerts *Vincent* • Diane Kruger *Jessie* • Paul Hamy *Denis* • Zaïd Errougui-Demonsant *Ali* ■ *Dir* Alice Winocour

Disorderlies ★ PG
Comedy 1987 · US · Colour · 82min

Rappers the Fat Boys' attempt to break into the movies is unlikely to stand the test of time. This Three Stooges-influenced screwball comedy sees the boys coming to the aid of millionaire Ralph Bellamy, who's about to be murdered by an evil nephew. Bellamy's career survived this turkey unscathed but the Fat Boys' bumbling soon wears thin. RS

Damon Wimbley *Kool Rock* • Darren Robinson *Buffy* • Mark Morales *Markie* • Ralph Bellamy *Albert Dennison* • Tony Plana *Miguel* • Anthony Geary *Winslow Lowry* • Marco Rodriguez *Luis Montana* • Troy Beyer *Carla* ■ *Dir* Michael Schultz • *Scr* Mark Feldberg, Mitchell Klebanoff

The Disorderly Orderly ★★★ U
Comedy 1964 · US · Colour · 89min

Jerry Lewis's comic genius is very much a matter of taste. In France he's virtually canonised; elsewhere, though, he has admirers and detractors in equal parts. This is exactly the type of movie that tends to infuriate both parties. It's very, very funny, with a wonderful climactic chase and a particularly hysterical moment where Lewis has sympathy pains with the choleric Alice Pearce. However, the film also contains some of the most melancholy and cloying sentiment in the whole of Lewis's oeuvre. TS

Jerry Lewis *Jerome Littlefield* • Glenda Farrell *Dr Jean Howard* • Everett Sloane *Mr Tuffington* • Karen Sharpe *Julie Blair* • Kathleen Freeman *Maggie Higgins* • Del Moore *Dr Davenport* • Susan Oliver *Susan Andrews* • Alice Pearce *Talkative patient* • Jack E Leonard *Fat Jack* ■ *Dir* Frank Tashlin • *Scr* Frank Tashlin, from a story by Norm Liebmann, Ed Haas

Disorganized Crime ★★ 15
Crime comedy 1989 · US · Colour · 97min

In what could have been a jolly rollercoaster ride, a group of criminals mooch about expectantly as they wait for the mastermind behind their latest heist to show up, but the movie deteriorates all too swiftly. Still, the assembled actors, including Corbin Bernsen and Lou Diamond Phillips, fight gamely with the lousy script, managing to create the occasional flicker of interest. SH Violence, swearing.

Hoyt Axton *Sheriff Henault* • Corbin Bernsen *Frank Salazar* • Rubén Blades *Carlos Barrios* • Fred Gwynne *Max Green* • Ed O'Neill *George Denver* • Lou Diamond Phillips *Ray Forgy* ■ *Dir/Scr* Jim Kouf

A Dispatch from Reuters ★★★ U
Biographical drama 1940 · US · BW · 98min

In the last of its series of high-minded historical biographies, Warner Bros squeezes a surprising amount of tense drama out of the story of Julius Reuter, whose passion for spreading the news goes from pigeon post to establishing his famous impartial wire service. Relishing a peaceful character part for once, Edward G Robinson is watchable as Reuter, while director William Dieterle and ace cameraman James Wong Howe give the film pace and visual distinction. AE

Edward G Robinson *Julius Reuter* • Edna Best *Ida Magnus* • Albert Basserman *Franz Geller* • Gene Lockhart *Bauer* • Otto Kruger *Dr Magnus* • Nigel Bruce *Sir Randolph Persham* ■ *Dir* William Dieterle • *Scr* Milton Krims

Disraeli ★★
Biographical drama 1929 · US · BW · 90min

This stolid biopic of the prime minister and Victorian novelist stars a monocled George Arliss. The real Mrs Arliss, Florence, gets to play Mrs Disraeli as well. On the political front, it's the race to purchase the Suez Canal in front of the Russians that commands the PM's attention, but on the domestic front it's romantic matchmaking. AT

George Arliss *Disraeli* • Joan Bennett *Lady Clarissa Pevensey* • Florence Arliss *Lady Mary Beaconfield* • Anthony Bushell *Charles, Lord Deeford* • David Torrence *Sir Michael, Lord Probert* ■ *Dir* Alfred E Green • *Scr* Julien Josephson, from the play by Louis Napoleon Parker

Distant Drums ★★ U
Period adventure 1951 · US · Colour · 99min

This Warner Bros adventure can't technically be termed a western – it's set in Florida – but deals with a familiar theme, as Seminole Indians go on the warpath against an expeditionary force in 1840. The supporting cast is way below par, and the whole thing is held together by the sheer star power of Cooper. If it all seems a little familiar, that's because director Raoul Walsh has reworked his own controversial

Second World War drama *Objective, Burma!*. **TS**

Gary Cooper *Captain Quincy Wyatt* • Mari Aldon *Judy Beckett* • Richard Webb *Richard Tufts* • Ray Teal *Private Mohair* • Arthur Hunnicutt *Monk* • Robert Barrat *General Zachary Taylor* • Clancy Cooper *Sergeant Shane* ■ *Dir* Raoul Walsh • *Scr* Niven Busch, Martin Rackin, from a story by Niven Busch

Distant Thunder ★★★★
Drama   1973 · Ind · Colour · 101min

This harrowing drama, set during the famine that ravaged Bengal in the early 1940s, is one of Satyajit Ray's most politically committed films. Yet it retains the humanism and concern for character that makes his work so compelling. While the railings at the caste system and government corruption make for powerful viewing, it's the slow realisation of a Brahmin and his wife that people matter more than rigid rules that makes this an unmissable experience. **DP** Bengali +subtitles.

Soumitra Chatterjee *Gangacharan* • Babita *Ananga* • Sandhya Roy *Chutki* • Ramesh Mukherjee *Biswas* • Chitra Bannerjee ■ *Dir/Scr* Satyajit Ray

Distant Thunder ★★★ 18
Drama   1988 · Can/US · Colour · 109min

This co-production casts the admirable John Lithgow as a traumatised Vietnam vet who has abandoned society for life in the wilds. Karate Kid Ralph Macchio plays the teenage son he deserted as a toddler. Thanks mainly to Lithgow, who doesn't know how to give a bad performance, this occasionally violent film holds the attention, despite struggling at times to keep its maudlin elements in check. **PF** Swearing.

John Lithgow *Mark Lambert* • Ralph Macchio *Jack Lambert* • Kerrie Keane *Char* • Reb Brown *Harvey Nitz* • Janet Margolin *Barbara Lambert* • Denis Arndt *Larry* • Jamey Sheridan *Moss* • Tom Bower *Louis* ■ *Dir* Rick Rosenthal • *Scr* Robert Stitzel, from a story by Robert Stitzel, Deedee Wehle

A Distant Trumpet ★★★★
Western   1964 · US · Colour · 117min

The last film from veteran director Raoul Walsh is impressive: a handsome, intelligent cavalry western, superbly scored by Max Steiner and ravishingly shot by William Clothier. Walsh makes partial reparation to the hordes of Indians slaughtered in previous westerns by using subtitles in an attempt to preserve their dignity, and the complex military themes are well handled. What lets this fine movie down, though, is the casting. Newlyweds Troy Donahue and Suzanne Pleshette are just too 1960s to convince us they belong in Walsh's Old West. **TS** Some native American dialogue +subtitles.

Troy Donahue *Second Lt Matthew Hazard* • Suzanne Pleshette *Kitty Mainwaring* • Diane McBain *Laura Greenleaf* • James Gregory *General Alexander Quait* • William Reynolds *Lt Mainwaring* • Claude Akins *Seely Jones* ■ *Dir* Raoul Walsh • *Scr* John Twist, Richard Fielder, Albert Beich, from the novel by Paul Horgan

Distant Voices, Still Lives ★★★★★ 15
Drama   1988 · UK · Colour · 80min

Never has song been used so poignantly as in Terence Davies's painful, yet curiously fond recollection of postwar Liverpool. The popular tunes that punctuate the ritualistic round of family gatherings and boozer sing-songs jarringly counterpoint the irrational violence perpetrated by Pete Postlethwaite's short-fused father. Unflinchingly depicting both the beatings and their consequences, Davies brings a bruising realism to the stylised series of vignettes, which adeptly avoid the patronising tone that jaundices so many portraits of working-class life. **DP** Violence, swearing. *DVD*

Freda Dowie *Mother* • Pete Postlethwaite *Father* • Angela Walsh *Eileen* • Dean Williams *Tony* • Lorraine Ashbourne *Maisie* • Marie Jelliman *Jingles* • Sally Davies *Eileen as a child* • Nathan Walsh *Tony as a child* • Susan Flanagan *Maisie as a child* • Michael Starke *Dave* ■ *Dir/Scr* Terence Davies

The Distinguished Gentleman ★★★ 15
Comedy   1992 · US · Colour · 107min

Eddie Murphy plays a smooth talking grifter who sets his sights on the ultimate con-politics. However, on his election as a senator, he quickly learns that the biggest villains are in Washington. Director Jonathan Lynn, of *Yes, Minister* fame, is a lot gentler on the American political scene than he was with our own, but there are some neat satirical jibes and he gives free rein to Murphy, who delivers a relaxed performance. **JF** Swearing, nudity. *DVD*

Eddie Murphy *Thomas Jefferson Johnson* • Lane Smith *Dick Dodge* • Sheryl Lee Ralph *Miss Loretta* • Joe Don Baker *Olaf Andersen* • Kevin McCarthy *Terry Corrigan* • Charles S Dutton *Elijah Hawkins* • Noble Willingham *Zeke Bridges* • James Garner *Jeff Johnson* ■ *Dir* Jonathan Lynn • *Scr* Marty Kaplan, from a story by Marty Kaplan, Jonathan Reynolds

District 9 ★★★★ 15
Science-fiction action drama
2009 · NZ/US/S Afr · Colour · 107min

Seemingly helpless extraterrestrials arrive on Earth and are treated like any other vulnerable minority – as if they're sub-human – in this startling mix of sci-fi action and trenchant social drama. By framing events as a mock-documentary set in his native Johannesburg, writer/director Neill Blomkamp makes obvious reference to the shadow of apartheid, but the film never seems preachy. Sharlto Copley delivers a remarkable performance as the glib bureaucrat heading up a brutal relocation operation, who's forced by escalating events into realising the error of his ways. It may give way to (admittedly effective) shoot-'em-up fare, but this remains a textbook example of fantasy cinema's ability to tackle thorny moral issues while splattering the screen with gloopy creature effects. **TJ** English, Nyanja, Afrikaans, Zulu, Xhosa, Sotha +subtitles. Violence, swearing, sexual references. *DVD*

Sharlto Copley *Wikus van de Merwe* • David James *Koobus Venter* • Jason Cope *Christopher Johnson/Grey Bradnam* • Vanessa Haywood *Tania van de Merwe* • Mandla Gaduka *Fundiswa Mhalanga* • Kenneth Nkosi *Thomas* ■ *Dir* Neill Blomkamp • *Scr* Neill Blomkamp, Terri Tatchell

District 13 ★★★ 15
Futuristic action thriller
2004 · Fr · Colour · 81min

The bare-bones plot of this Luc Besson-scripted concoction has a police undercover agent (played by Cyril Raffaelli) infiltrating a suburban crime enclave in a near-future Paris. But really, the film is a cinematic showcase for "free running" – an eye-popping, all-action blend of running, jumping and climbing in which urban landscapes are acrobatically scaled like assault courses. There's also an endearing tongue-in-cheekiness about the bits in between, too. Hugely entertaining. **DA** French +subtitles. Swearing, violence, drug abuse. *DVD*

Cyril Raffaelli *Damien* • David Belle *Leïto* • Tony D'Amario *K2* • Larbi Naceri *[Bibi Naceri] Taha* • Dany Verissimo *Lola* • Marc Andréoni *Carlos* • François Chattot *Krüger* • Alain Rimoux *Superintendent* ■ *Dir* Pierre Morel • *Scr* Luc Besson, Bibi Naceri

District 13: Ultimatum ★★★ 15
Action thriller   2009 · Fr · Colour · 96min

This hyper-kinetic joy ride is a follow-up to the action-packed 2004 French thriller *District 13*. The scene, once again, is a Paris of the near-future, where a walled-off district is both an outlaw enclave and a police no-go area. However, when unscrupulous property speculators plan to raze and redevelop the district, cop-and-crook heroes Damien and Leïto (played by the returning Cyril Raffaelli and David Belle) join forces to stop them. The original is now best known as the movie that introduced cinema audiences to the adrenaline rush of Parkour or "free running". There's plenty of that breathtaking physical discipline here, but it's just one aspect of a movie that's entertaining from start to finish. **DA** French +subtitles. Violence, swearing. *DVD* *BL*

Cyril Raffaelli *Capt Damien Tomaso* • David Belle *Leïto* • Philippe Torreton *President of the Republic* • Daniel Duval *Walter Gassman* • Elodie Yung *Tao* • Moussa Maaskri *Roland* ■ *Dir* Patrick Alessandrin • *Scr* Luc Besson

Disturbed ★★ 18
Psychological horror thriller
1990 · US · Colour · 93min

This low-budget thriller from director Charles Winkler, son of *Rocky* producer Irvin, stars a blond Malcolm McDowell as a psychiatrist who probably needs more treatment than the whole ward of stereotypical nuts he treats, especially when a patient he murdered returns to haunt him. McDowell's broad brush strokes are in tune with the demented camerawork. **RS**

Malcolm McDowell *Dr Derek Russell* • Geoffrey Lewis *Michael* • Priscilla Pointer *Nurse Francine* • Pamela Gidley *Sandy Ramirez* • Irwin Keyes *Pat Tuel* • Clint Howard *Brian* ■ *Dir* Charles Winkler • *Scr* Charles Winkler, Emerson Bixby

Disturbia ★★★ 15
Thriller   2007 · US · Colour · 100min

Taking Lives director DJ Caruso returns to the thriller genre with this engaging teen flick that plays like *Rear Window* for the MySpace generation. Shia LaBeouf (*Transformers*) plays a troubled adolescent who's put under house arrest for punching his teacher. After he befriends the cute newcomer next door (Sarah Roemer), the duo pass their time spying on their neighbours. However, an innocent game turns nasty when they begin to suspect that one of them (David Morse) is a serial killer. After a slow-burning set-up that milks the comedy value of home incarceration, the film swings slickly into suspense mode. LaBeouf is particularly affable, with an emotional honesty that papers over many of the plot cracks. But it's Morse who quietly steals the show, walking the fine line between shy and sinister with commendable ease. **SF** English, Spanish +subtitles. *DVD* *BL*

Shia LaBeouf *Kale* • David Morse *Mr Turner* • Sarah Roemer *Ashley* • Carrie-Anne Moss *Julie* • Aaron Yoo *Ronnie* • Jose Pablo Cantillo *Officer Gutierrez* ■ *Dir* DJ Caruso • *Scr* Christopher Landon, Carl Ellsworth, from a story by Landon

Disturbing Behavior ★★ 15
Thriller   1998 · US · Colour · 80min

Bad kids in a small town are turning good after undergoing experimental psychological treatment in this tepid teen variation on *The Stepford Wives*. Trouble is, they turn homicidal when sexually aroused, and it seems high-school student James Marsden is the only one to notice. Director David Nutter brings some moodiness to the material, but he can't seem to decide what sort of film he's making. **AJ** Swearing. *DVD*

Bruce Greenwood *Dr Caldicott* • James Marsden *Steve Clark* • Katie Holmes *Rachel Wagner* • Nick Stahl *Gavin Strick* • William Sadler *Dorian Newberry* • Steve Railsback *Officer Cox* • Tobias Mehler *Andy Effkin* ■ *Dir* David Nutter • *Scr* Scott Rosenberg

Diva ★★★★ 15
Cult crime drama   1981 · Fr · Colour · 112min

Considered one of the masterpieces of *cinéma du look* (the name given to French films of the 1980s in which style took precedence over content), *Diva* marked the directorial debut of Jean-Jacques Beineix. It's a dazzling job, brimful with bravura camera movements and ultra-chic images. The tale of two tapes (one a bootlegged recording of an opera star, the other incriminating evidence against a police inspector) rather gets lost as Beineix experiments with styles ranging from the Feuillade serials of the early years of the last century to the New Wave of the 1950s and 1960s. Yet this remains compelling viewing, if only for the amazing performance of Dominique Pinon. **DP** French +subtitles. Violence, swearing, nudity. *DVD*

Frédéric Andrei *Jules* • Wilhelmenia Wiggins Fernandez *Cynthia Hawkins* • Richard Bohringer *Gorodish* • Thuy An Luu *Alba* • Jacques Fabbri *Inspector Jean Saporta* • Chantal Deruaz *Nadia Kalonsky* • Roland Bertin *Simon Weinstadt* • Gérard Darmon *Spic* • Dominique Pinon *Le Curé* ■ *Dir* Jean-Jacques Beineix • *Scr* Jean-Jacques Beineix, Jean Van Hamme, from the novel by Delacorta • *Cinematographer* Philippe Rousselot

Dive Bomber ★★★ PG
Wartime drama   1941 · US · Colour · 126min

This wonderful flying drama features Errol Flynn and Fred MacMurray in fine fettle for a *Boys' Own* treat directed by Michael Curtiz. Ostensibly a piece of serious research into pilot blackout, it gives all concerned a roaring excuse to slap each other about in friendly fashion in a flurry of patched leather elbows. If your idea of a good film is the wind in your hair and aerial thrills, this is for you. **SH** *DVD*

Errol Flynn *Lieutenant Doug Lee* • Fred MacMurray *Commander Joe Blake* • Ralph Bellamy *Dr Lance Rogers* • Alexis Smith *Linda Fisher* • Regis Toomey *Tim Griffin* • Robert Armstrong *Art Lyons* • Allen Jenkins *Lucky Dice* ■ *Dir* Michael Curtiz • *Scr* Frank Wead, Robert Buckner, from the story *Beyond the Blue Sky* by Wead

Divergent ★★★ 12
Science-fiction romantic drama
2014 · US · Colour · 133min

Teens who inhabit a ruined, post-apocalyptic Chicago are tested to determine their personalities before being separated into warring factions in this respectable *Hunger Games* clone based on Veronica Roth's bestselling trilogy. Shailene Woodley plays Tris, a so-called Divergent, who doesn't fit into any one group and is therefore a danger to society. Information overload afflicts this first episode, before it becomes a moralistic slog through Tris's brutal initiation trials, and a romantic subplot (involving Theo James) doesn't add much intrigue. It's mostly familiar genre fare, but there is menace and suspense, and director Neil Burger (*Limitless*) delivers a rousing finale. Sequel *Insurgent* is due in 2015. **AJ** Some violence, swearing. *DVD* *BL*

Shailene Woodley *Beatrice "Tris" Prior* • Kate Winslet *Jeanine Matthews* • Theo James *Four* • Ashley Judd *Natalie Prior* • Tony Goldwyn *Andrew Prior* • Ansel Elgort *Caleb Prior* ■ *Dir* Neil Burger • *Scr* Evan Daugherty, Vanessa Taylor, from Veronica Roth's novel

The Divergent Series: Allegiant ★★ 12
Science-fiction action adventure
2016 · US · Colour · 115min

The latest adaptation of Veronica Roth's young adult series sees Tris (Shailene Woodley) and her lover Four (Theo James) break out of Chicago, only to find that an uncertain reality awaits them. Following the dreary *Insurgent*, this third instalment of the franchise throws a lot of impressive effects and action at the screen, but achieves just as little. While the new cast members are fun (Jeff Daniels is a particular highlight), this is a confusing addition to a muddled saga. The next in the series, *Ascendant*, is due in summer 2017. **JL** Some violence, swearing. *DVD* *BL*

Shailene Woodley *Tris* • Theo James *Four* • Zoë Kravitz *Christina* • Miles Teller *Peter* • Jeff Daniels *David* • Naomi Watts *Evelyn* ■ *Dir* Robert Schwentke • *Scr* Noah Oppenheim, Adam Cooper, Bill Collage, Steve Chbosky, from Veronica Roth's novel

The Divide ★★★★ 18
Horror thriller
2011 · Ger/US/Can · Colour · 107min

In this bleak, survival-of-the-fittest thriller from Xavier Gens (*Frontier(s)*, *Hitman*), that old Cold War staple of nuclear annihilation signals the end is nigh for the human race. Following a breathtaking beginning, Gens goes for an intimate rather than epic depiction of the end of civilisation, as eight people (including Rosanna Arquette and *Heroes* star Milo Ventimiglia) seek shelter in the underground bunker of their building's paranoid caretaker (played with glowering intensity by genre favourite Michael Biehn). The descent into savagery may not exactly be original, but the mystery of who is outside trying to get in and the labyrinthine confines of the shelter elevate the intrigue. Gens's skilful direction and the throat-grabbing performances from the cast add to the tension. JA Violence, swearing, a sex scene. **DVD** 🔵

Lauren German *Eva* • Michael Biehn *Mickey* • Milo Ventimiglia *Josh* • Courtney B Vance *Delvin* • Iván González *Sam* • Michael Eklund *Bobby* • Rosanna Arquette *Marilyn* ■ *Dir* Xavier Gens • *Scr* Karl Mueller, Eron Sheean

The Divide ★★★ 12A
Documentary 2016 · UK/US · Colour · 77min

What happens when the rich get richer? How did the income gap become so large? How does it affect the people who barely make enough money to survive? These are the questions that drive this timely documentary that examines economic inequality in the modern world. Casting an eye across the income spectrum, it follows seven individuals from different backgrounds. There's little doubt that the film's sympathies lie with the underprivileged, but director Katharine Round gives us plenty to think about. SC Swearing.

Noam Chomsky • Max Hastings ■ *Dir* Katharine Round

The Divided Heart ★★ U
Drama based on a true story
1954 · UK · BW · 89min

This British melodrama would be dismissed as sentimental tosh if it wasn't based on a true story that hit the headlines following the end of the Second World War. Drawing on the actual records of the case, director Charles Crichton uses a series of artful flashbacks to pad out the courtroom battle at the centre of the action, as biological mother Yvonne Mitchell fights Cornell Borchers for custody of the child Borchers adopted. Crichton lays on the pathos so thickly that the emotional drama never really tugs at our heartstrings. DP

Cornell Borchers *Inga* • Yvonne Mitchell *Sonja* • Armin Dahlen *Franz* • Alexander Knox *Chief Justice* • Geoffrey Keen *Marks* • Michel Ray *Toni* • Martin Keller *Toni* • Liam Redmond *First Justice* • Eddie Byrne *Second Justice* ■ *Dir* Charles Crichton • *Scr* Jack Whittingham, Richard Hughes

Divided We Fall ★★★★ PG
Second World War drama
2000 · Cz Rep · Colour · 117min

Inspired by a true story, Jan Hrebejk's film takes a darkly comic approach to the hideous events of the Holocaust. Any hope married couple Boleslav Polivka and Anna Siskova may have of keeping a low profile during the German occupation of their small Czech town is shattered by the sudden reappearance of a Jewish friend who had been sent to a concentration camp earlier in the war. They decide to hide the refugee in their larder, despite the fact their nosey neighbour is a Nazi lackey. The performances are first rate in a film in which only fact could be this fantastic while managing to be comic, appalling and poignant. DP Czech +subtitles. Violence. **DVD**

Boleslav Polivka *Josef Cizek* • Anna Siskova *Marie Cizkova* • Jaroslav Dusek *Horst Prohaska* • Csongor Kassai *David Wiener* • Jiri Kodet *Dr Fiser-Rybar* ■ *Dir* Jan Hrebejk • *Scr* Petr Jarchovsky, from his novel *Musime si Pomahat*

Divine ★★★
Comedy drama 1935 · Fr · BW · 82min

Colette provided the original story for this engaging work, plus some dialogue for the adaptation by Jean-Georges Auriol and director Max Ophüls. It tells of a young girl who leaves the countryside hoping to become a successful singer in Paris. She suffers problems and heartaches along the way, especially in the handsome form of Georges Rigaud as a milkman. The central theme - so beloved by Colette - shows the transformation of Simone Berriau into a woman of the world. BB French +subtitles.

Simone Berriau *Ludivine, "Divine" Jarisse* • Catherine Fonteney *Mme Jarisse* • Yvette Lebon *Roberte* • Jorge Rigaud [Georges Rigaud] *Antonin* • Philippe Hériat *Lutuf Allah, the fakir* ■ *Dir* Max Ophüls • *Scr* Colette, Jean-Georges Auriol, Max Ophüls, from the novel *L'Envers du Music-Hall* by Colette

The Divine Comedy ★★
Psychological drama
1992 · Por · Colour · 140min

This densely symbolic tract has little in common with Dante's medieval masterpiece, even though it shares such themes as faith and truth, sin and delusion. Veteran Portuguese director Manoel de Oliveira also scripted this portrait of an asylum where every patient believes themselves to be a character from the Bible or from *Crime and Punishment*. This is a wordy picture that is rarely enlightening or engrossing. DP Portuguese +subtitles.

Maria de Medeiros *Sonya* • Miguel Guilherme *Raskolnikov* • Luis Miguel Cintra *The prophet* • Mario Viegas *The philosopher* • Leonor Silveira *Eve* • Diogo Doria *Ivan* • Paulo Matos *Jesus* • Carlos Gomes *Adam* • Ruy Furtado *The director* ■ *Dir/Scr* Manoel de Oliveira

Divine Intervention ★★★ 15
Political comedy drama
2002 · Fr/Ger/Mor/Neth · Colour · 89min

Subtitled *A Chronicle of Love and Pain*, writer/director Elia Suleiman's quirky take on life in the occupied territories is strewn with poignant insights into coping in a divided society. The Nazareth-set opening vividly illustrates a number of neighbourhood tensions that serve as a backdrop to the romantic trysts between Suleiman and his Palestinian girlfriend, Manal Khader. However, for every astute incident, there are gross misfires. DP Arabic, Hebrew +subtitles. Swearing, violence. **DVD**

Elia Suleiman *ES* • Manal Khader *Woman* • Nayef Fahoum Daher *Father* • George Ibrahim *Santa Claus* • Jamal Daher *Jamal* • Amer Daher *Auni* ■ *Dir/Scr* Elia Suleiman

The Divine Lady ★★★
Silent historical drama 1928 · US · BW · 100min

Director Frank Lloyd won an early Oscar for this story of Emma, Lady Hamilton, Nelson's mistress and one of the most notorious women in English history. Corinne Griffith has a generous sweep of personality as Emma, though her performance pales in comparison with Vivien Leigh's in *That Hamilton Woman* (1941). The historical detail is taken very much for granted, and the film's appeal at the time was mainly due to its novelty. TH

Corinne Griffith *Emma, Lady Hamilton* • Victor Varconi *Lord Nelson* • HB Warner *Sir William Hamilton* • Ian Keith *Greville* • William Conklin *Romney* • Marie Dressler *Mrs Hart* ■ *Dir* Frank Lloyd • *Scr* Harry Carr (titles), Edwin Justus Mayer (titles), Forrest Halsey, from the novel *The Divine Lady: a Romance of Nelson and Emma Hamilton* by E Barrington

Divine Madness ★★★ 15
Concert movie 1980 · US · Colour · 82min

Shot over four days using up to 20 cameras, Michael Ritchie's record of Bette Midler's shows at the Pasadena Civic Auditorium broke the mould for concert films in terms of look and technique. Backed by the Harlettes, Midler blazes through songs and comic routines with the kind of unfettered energy that is sometimes the undoing of her feature work. She has an amazing range as a singer, but there's nothing particularly new in her interpretations, unlike her mix of stand-up and sketches that are as varied as her outlandish costumes. DP Swearing.

■ *Dir* Michael Ritchie • *Scr* Jerry Blatt, Bette Midler, Bruce Vilanch

Divine Secrets of the Ya-Ya Sisterhood ★★ 12
Comedy drama 2002 · US · Colour · 111min

Sandra Bullock plays the writer who has issues with her mother, so her mother's friends (Shirley Knight, Fionnula Flanagan and Maggie Smith) kidnap her so they can explain all the things her mother went through that turned her into the hard-drinking, bitchy woman she is now. Ashley Judd and Ellen Burstyn are terrific as the past and present version of Bullock's mum, but the story doesn't flow and is let down by a final revelation that isn't much of a surprise. JB Swearing, violence. **DVD**

Sandra Bullock *Sidda Lee Walker* • Ellen Burstyn *Vivi* • Fionnula Flanagan *Teensy* • James Garner *Shep Walker* • Ashley Judd *Younger Vivi* • Shirley Knight *Necie* • Angus MacFadyen *Connor McGill* • Maggie Smith *Caro* • Gina McKee *Genevieve* ■ *Dir* Callie Khouri • *Scr* Mark Andrus, from the novels *Divine Secrets of the Ya-Ya Sisterhood/Little Altars Everywhere* by Rebecca Wells

The Divine Woman
Silent romantic drama 1928 · US · BW · 85min

A long-lost treat for Greta Garbo fans, this film is now one of the American Film Institute's "most wanted" movies. The divine Greta starts out as a Breton peasant girl and ends up taking Paris - and lover Lars Hanson - by storm. Directed by Garbo's fellow Swede, Victor Seastrom. TS

Greta Garbo *Marianne* • Lars Hanson *Lucien* • Lowell Sherman *Legrand* • Polly Moran *Mme Pigonier* • Dorothy Cumming *Mme Zizi Rouck* • John Mack Brown [Johnny Mack Brown] *Jean Lery* ■ *Dir* Victor Seastrom [Victor Sjöström] • *Scr* Dorothy Farnum, John Colton (titles), from the play *Starlight* by Gladys Unger

The Diving-Bell and the Butterfly ★★★★ 12
Biographical drama
2007 · Fr/US · Colour · 107min

This biographical drama is based on the remarkable memoir of journalist Jean-Dominique Bauby, the editor of French *Elle*, who in 1995 woke from a coma in a state of almost total paralysis. Julian Schnabel's film dramatises the extraordinary efforts of Bauby (played by Mathieu Amalric) to dictate his story by blinking his left eye, as a speech therapist (Marie-Josée Croze) runs through a specially devised alphabet. Schnabel and screenwriter Ronald Harwood (both Oscar-nominated) break up these painstaking and (inevitably) slow scenes of the writing process with flashbacks of Bauby's earlier life. His plight and his attempts to communicate are moving and beautifully filmed, and there are superb performances from a cast that includes Emmanuelle Seigner (as his partner) and Max von Sydow (as his father). Yet the film struggles to do full justice to the author's unique achievement. BP French +subtitles. Nudity, brief swearing. **DVD**

Mathieu Amalric *Jean-Dominique Bauby* • Emmanuelle Seigner *Céline Desmoulin* • Jean-Pierre Cassel *Father Lucien* • Max von Sydow *Papinou* • Marie-Josée Croze *Henriette Durand* • Anne Consigny *Claude* • Patrick Chesnais *Dr Lepage* ■ *Dir* Julian Schnabel • *Scr* Ronald Harwood, from the memoir by Jean-Dominique Bauby

Il Divo ★★★★ 15
Political drama based on a true story
2008 · It/Fr · Colour · 117min

This chronicle of the remarkable career of Italian political titan Giulio Andreotti is a film that needs to be seen twice: once to take in the wealth of historical detail, and again to marvel in the brilliance of Paolo Sorrentino's direction. The rock on which Italy's Christian Democracy was founded and a prime minister many times over, Andreotti was ruthlessly ambitious and pitilessly pragmatic in the pursuit of power. However, his true genius lay in extricating himself from potentially ruinous scandals until the *tangentopoli* investigations of the early 1990s when the links between the Mafia and the political system were fully exposed. It's this episode that brings out the best in Sorrentino and star Toni Servillo (*Gomorrah*), who conveys the unremitting determination of an experienced political operator. DP Italian +subtitles. Violence.

Toni Servillo *Giulio Andreotti* • Anna Bonaiuto *Livia Andreotti* • Giulio Bosetti *Eugenio Scalfari* • Flavio Bucci *Franco Evangelisti* • Carlo Buccirosso *Paolo Cirino Pomicino* • Giorgio Colangeli *Salvo Lima* • Fanny Ardant *French ambassador's wife* ■ *Dir/Scr* Paolo Sorrentino

Le Divorce ★★★ 12
Romantic comedy drama
2003 · US/UK · Colour · 112min

This romantic comedy drama from director James Ivory and producer Ismail Merchant is a convoluted look at French and American sexual attitudes. Kate Hudson arrives in Paris just as her pregnant stepsister Naomi Watts is deserted by husband Melvil Poupaud. Hudson then starts an affair with his uncle Thierry Lhermitte. Glenn Close contributes to the proceedings as an expatriate American writer and Leslie Caron has a callously disapproving eye for everyone. More shallow than profound, but there are some satisfying moments. TH **DVD**

Kate Hudson *Isabel Walker* • Naomi Watts *Roxeanne "Roxy" de Persand* • Glenn Close *Olivia Pace* • Stockard Channing *Margreeve Walker* • Sam Waterston *Chester Walker* • Thierry Lhermitte *Edgar Cosset* • Leslie Caron *Suzanne de Persand* • Bebe Neuwirth *Julia Manchevering* • Matthew Modine *Tellman* • Stephen Fry *Piers Janely* • Melvil Poupaud *Charles-Henri de Persand* ■ *Dir* James Ivory • *Scr* Ruth Prawer Jhabvala, James Ivory, from the novel by Diane Johnson

Divorce American Style ★★★
Satirical comedy 1967 · US · Colour · 109min

This sophisticated, brilliantly cast comedy is compulsive viewing. The title, taken from the 1961 Italian original, masks a witty tale of contemporary mores in which separating spouses Dick Van Dyke and Debbie Reynolds take a baleful look at the effects of divorce on their friends. Jason Robards is brilliant as a man so crippled by alimony payments he's desperate to pair off ex-wife Jean Simmons, while Van Johnson makes even a used car salesman seem boyishly beguiling. TS

Dick Van Dyke *Richard Harmon* • Debbie Reynolds *Barbara Harmon* • Jason Robards *Nelson Downes* • Jean Simmons *Nancy Downes* • Van Johnson *Al Yearling* • Joe Flynn *Lionel Blandsforth* • Shelley Berman *David Grieff* • Martin Gabel *Dr Zenwinn* ■ *Dir* Bud Yorkin • *Scr* Norman Lear, from a story by Robert Kaufman

Divorce - Italian Style ★★★★
Black comedy 1961 · It · BW · 103min

It's not often that a foreign language film takes a mainstream Oscar, so the success of Pietro Germi and his fellow screenwriters suggests this wicked black comedy is doubly special. For all the ingenuity of the script, though, it's Marcello Mastroianni that makes these sinister Sicilian shenanigans so memorable. He plays the lovesick husband who opts to kill his shrewish wife (Daniella Rocca) rather than divorce her; in Italy, that's the easier option! Mastroianni expertly combines deadpan suavity with impeccable comic timing, while Germi directs with flair. DP In Italian.

Marcello Mastroianni *Ferdinando Cefalu* • Daniela Rocca *Rosalie Cefalu* • Stefania Sandrelli *Angela* • Leopoldo Trieste *Carmelo Patane* • Odoardo Spadaro *Don Gaetano* ■ *Dir* Pietro Germi • *Scr* Pietro Germi, Ennio DeConcini, Alfredo Giannetti

The Divorce of Lady X ★★★ U
Comedy 1938 · UK · Colour · 87min

Producer Alexander Korda used marvellous early three-strip Technicolor to give this piece of screwball whimsy a special lustre. The film starred his wife-to-be Merle

Oberon, who plays a party-goer trapped in a London hotel by one of those fogs so beloved of Americans. The Technicolor works, but Oberon doesn't: comedy wasn't her forte. The film's quite amusing, though, in its daffy way. TS

Merle Oberon *Leslie Steele* • Laurence Olivier *Logan* • Binnie Barnes *Lady Mere* • Ralph Richardson *Lord Mere* • Morton Selten *Lord Steele* • JH Roberts *Slade* • Gertrude Musgrove *Saunders* • Gus McNaughton *Waiter* • Eileen Peele *Mrs Johnson* ■ *Dir* Tim Whelan • *Scr* Ian Dalrymple, Arthur Wimperis, Lajos Biró, Robert Sherwood [Robert E Sherwood], from the play *Counsel's Opinion* by Gilbert Wakefield

Divorce Wars ★★★★
Drama　　　　　1982 · US · Colour · 100min

This cleverly scripted and insightful domestic drama about a divorce lawyer who can't solve the problems within his own marriage is co-written and directed by the talented Donald Wrye, whose work includes the Jack Lemmon version of *The Entertainer*. As the high-powered attorney, Tom Selleck proves yet again what a personable actor he is, and he's well teamed here with Jane Curtin. This made-for-TV drama is also worth catching for the last screen appearance of Joan Bennett. TS

Tom Selleck *Jack Kaiser* • Jane Curtin *Vickey Kaiser* • Candy Azzara *Sylvia Bemous* • Joan Bennett *Adele Burgess* • Maggie Cooper *Leslie Fields* • Charles Haid *Fred Bemous* ■ *Dir* Donald Wrye • *Scr* Donald Wrye, Linda Elstad, from a story by Linda Elstad

The Divorcee ★★★
Romantic drama　　1930 · US · BW · 83min

Norma Shearer won her best actress Academy Award for the spunky, sexy performance on display here. This may surprise viewers who only recall her as the grand queen of the lot in her later roles at a prestige-conscious MGM run by her husband, Irving Thalberg. In fact, this movie was based on a novel so racy that the author published it anonymously, and much of that substance (though not the actual plot) is on screen in those halcyon pre-Code days. Shearer plays a woman having an affair with a man loved by another woman. All a bit creaky now. TS

Norma Shearer *Jerry* • Chester Morris *Ted* • Conrad Nagel *Paul* • Robert Montgomery *Don* • Florence Eldridge *Helen* • Helene Millard *Mary* • Robert Elliott *Bill* • Mary Doran *Janice* ■ *Dir* Robert Z Leonard • *Scr* Nick Grinde, Zelda Sears, John Meehan, from the novel *Ex-Wife* by Ursula Parrott

Divorcing Jack ★★★ 15
Comedy thriller　1998 · UK/Fr · Colour · 105min

Virtuoso character actor David Thewlis utterly dominates this chase thriller set in Northern Ireland, in which he plays a drunken, foul-mouthed reporter whose life is in ruins. Robert Lindsay co-stars as an ambitious politician and Rachel Griffiths is great as a nun with a gun. The picture barely stops for breath, while Thewlis, with his grotty wardrobe, filthy hair and unshaven face, is a very different action hero. AT Swearing, violence, sex scenes. DVD

David Thewlis *Dan Starkey* • Rachel Griffiths *Lee Cooper* • Robert Lindsay *Michael Brinn* • Jason Isaacs *"Cow Pat" Keegan* • Laura Fraser *Margaret* • Richard Gant *Charles Parker* • Laine Megaw *Patricia Starkey* • Kitty Aldridge *Agnes Brinn* ■ *Dir* David Caffrey • *Scr* Colin Bateman, from his novel

Dixie ★★★ U
Musical biographical drama
1943 · US · Colour · 89min

A big hit in its day, this Bing Crosby vehicle purports to be the biography of Daniel Decatur Emmett, the man who wrote the South's most famous marching song. With its corny sentiment and minstrel shows, it's rather difficult, especially if you don't warm to Bing. But there's a notable screen debut from comedian Billy de Wolfe, and the 1940s Technicolor is simply sumptuous. TS

Bing Crosby *Dan Emmett* • Dorothy Lamour *Millie Cook* • Billy De Wolfe *Mr Bones* • Marjorie Reynolds *Jean Mason* • Lynne Overman *Mr*

Whitlock • Eddie Foy Jr *Mr Felham* • Raymond Walburn *Mr Cook* • Grant Mitchell *Mr Mason* ■ *Dir* A Edward Sutherland • *Scr* Darrell Ware, Claude Binyon, from the story by William Rankin

Dixie Dynamite ★
Action crime drama　1976 · US · Colour · 88min

This "good ol' boy" nonsense from director Lee Frost is punishment for the eyes, while the soundtrack, which includes songs by Duane Eddy, gives the ears a bashing too. Warren Oates stars as a motorcycle racer enlisted by two sisters to exact revenge upon the trigger-happy sheriff who killed their moonshiner father. Exuberant action, risible dialogue. RS

Warren Oates *Mack* • Christopher George *Sheriff Phil Marsh* • Jane Anne Johnstone *Dixie* • Kathy McHaley *Patsy* ■ *Dir* Lee Frost • *Scr* Lee Frost, Wes Bishop

Django ★★★★ 15
Spaghetti western　1966 · It/Sp · Colour · 87min

Switching effortlessly from the gritty realism of the mud-splattered streets to the stylised violence of the machine-gun shoot-outs, this superior spaghetti western from Sergio Corbucci owes as much to the Japanese samurai film as it does to the Hollywood horse opera. Franco Nero stars as the avenging angel who uses the armoury he keeps in a coffin to settle the feud between Mexican general Angel Alvarez and Civil War veteran Jose Bodalo and his red-hooded horsemen. The 30-plus *Django* movies truly represent the foundation of the genre. DP Italian dubbed. DVD

Franco Nero *Django* • Loredana Nusciak *Maria* • Jose Bodalo *Major Jackson* • Angel Alvarez *General Hugo Rodrigues* ■ *Dir* Sergio Corbucci • *Scr* Sergio Corbucci, Bruno Corbucci, Franco Rossetti, Jose G Maesso

Django, Prepare a Coffin
★★★ 15
Spaghetti western　1968 · It · Colour · 88min

This spaghetti western was one of many follow-ups to try to capitalise on the success of *Django*, but has a better claim than most, given that it was set to feature original star Franco Nero. In fact, it's a prequel of sorts, with Nero lookalike Terence Hill out for revenge after being ambushed during a transport of gold bullion. It's when Django's plan goes awry that Ferdinando Baldi's film gets more interesting. Clad in executioner's garb, Hill strikes an imposing figure – a far cry from the clowning cowboy he'd become famous for in the *Trinity* films. JH DVD

Terence Hill *Django* • Horst Frank *David Barry* • George Eastman [Luigi Montefiori] *Lucas* • José Torres (1) *Garcia* • Pinuccio Ardia *Horace* ■ *Dir* Ferdinando Baldi • *Scr* Franco Rossetti, Ferdinando Baldi, from a story by Rossetti

Django the Bastard ★★★ 12
Western　　　　　1970 · It · Colour · 94min

This is among the best films in this seminal spaghetti series. Antonio de Teffe (who also co-wrote) stars as the Civil War veteran who takes revenge on the Confederate officers who slaughtered his comrades. Stately, stylish and prone to sudden eruptions of violence (most notably the massacre of a band of Mexican desperados), this Wild West ghost story was clearly an influence on *High Plains Drifter*. DP Italian dubbed.

Antonio de Teffe *Django* • Rada Rassimov *Alethea* • Paolo Gozlino *Rod Murdoch* • Lu Kanante *Luke Murdoch* ■ *Dir* Sergio Garrone • *Scr* Anthony de Teffe, Sergio Garrone

Django Unchained ★★★★ 18
Western　　　　　2012 · US · Colour · 158min

Director Quentin Tarantino follows his Oscar-winning war homage *Inglourious Basterds* with this audacious and thrilling swagger through the good, bad and ugly sides of slavery, with Jamie Foxx as the slave-turned-bounty hunter who's on a mission to rescue his wife from a brutal plantation owner (Leonardo DiCaprio on top villainous form). The film is blessed with

enthralling, Academy Award-winning dialogue, surreal plot twists and a film buff's dream of a supporting cast. Oscar winner Christoph Waltz gives a brilliant performance of ruthless charm as Django's German mentor, but the real surprise is Samuel L Jackson's skin-crawling portrayal of DiCaprio's manipulative head servant. AJ Violence, swearing, nudity. DVD Blu

Jamie Foxx *Django* • Christoph Waltz *Dr King Schultz* • Leonardo DiCaprio *Calvin Candie* • Samuel L Jackson *Stephen* • Kerry Washington *Broomhilda von Shaft* • Don Johnson *Big Daddy* ■ *Dir/Scr* Quentin Tarantino • *Cinematographer* Robert Richardson

Djomeh ★★★★
Romantic drama　　2000 · Iran · Colour · 94min

Hassan Yektapanah was a former assistant director to acclaimed Iranian film-maker Abbas Kiarostami and invests his debut feature with the affecting humanism that makes his mentor's work so sincere. The film follows the day-to-day life of Djomeh (Jalil Nazari), an Afghan immigrant who has moved to Iran for reasons of the heart rather than war or poverty. Although primarily a treatise on exile and local schisms within Islam, this is also a charming tale of doomed devotion, as Djomeh quaintly pays court to an Iranian shopgirl. DP Farsi +subtitles.

Jalil Nazari *Djomeh* • Mahmoud Behraznia *Mr Mahmoud* • Mahbobeh Khalili *Setareh* • Rashid Akbari *Habib* ■ *Dir/Scr* Hassan Yektapanah

Do Bigha Zameen ★★★ U
Drama　　　　　1953 · Ind · BW · 124min

This is a fascinating hybrid of Bollywood musical and postwar European film-making. It's a shamelessly emotive melodrama, and Balraj Sahni gives the performance of his career as the peasant drawn to the city to save his home from unscrupulous speculators. The key inspiration is that of the Italian neorealist Vittorio De Sica, not only in the authentic use of location and the resort to sentimental humanism, but also in the plot borrowings from *Bicycle Thieves* and *Shoeshine*. DP Hindi +subtitles.

Balraj Sahni *Shambhu* • Ratan Kumar *Kanhaiya* • Murad *Sapru* • Nirupa Roy *Paro* ■ *Dir* Bimal Roy • *Scr* Hrishikesh Mukherjee, from a story by Salil Choudhury

Do Elephants Pray? ★★ 15
Drama　　　　　2009 · UK · Colour · 107min

The fourth feature from Paul Hills (*Boston Kickout*) is a bold attempt to mix screwball comedy with mystical melodrama. Frank Capra attempted something similar with *Lost Horizon* in 1937, but Hills and his writer/star Jonnie Hurn fall a long way short with their rites-of-passage tale. Hurn plays a stressed London advertising man who is persuaded to ditch his addictive luxuries in order to join her on an expedition to discover his true self in Brittany's mythical Brocéliande forest. A handsome and ambitious work, but it comes across as being overly florid and muddled. DP In English, French, Breton. Swearing, drug abuse, sex scenes, nudity.

Jonnie Hurn *Callum* • Julie Dray *Malika* • Marc Warren (1) *Marrien* • Rosie Fellner *Emma* • Grace Vallorani *Sark* • John Last *Jode* ■ *Dir* Paul Hills • *Scr* Jonnie Hurn

Do I Love You? ★★ 18
Romantic comedy drama
2003 · UK · Colour · 72min

Focusing on an interlocking group of young London lesbians, writer/director Lisa Gornick's debut is a mischievous and occasionally perceptive take on modern-day love, life and sexuality. Marina (Gornick herself) is pushed into an emotional crisis when her girlfriend (Raquel Cassidy) starts to get uncomfortably serious about their romance. Gornick paints a picture of queer culture that humorously reassesses popular misconceptions, while the wooden actors at least deliver their cheeky dialogue with enthusiasm. SF Swearing.

Lisa Gornick *Marina, woman on bike* • Raquel Cassidy *Romy, Marina's girlfriend* • Ruth Posner *Paula, Marina's mother* • Brendan Gregory *Stefan, Marina's father* • Sarah Patterson *Louise, a columnist* • Kemal Sylvester *Greg, Louise's boyfriend* • Kate McGoldrick *Alice, a photographer* • Harri Alexander *Lois, Alice's girlfriend* • Caitlin Morrow *Susie, Marina's ex-girlfriend* ■ *Dir/Scr* Lisa Gornick

Do Not Disturb ★★★ PG
Comedy　　　　　1965 · US · Colour · 97min

By the time this movie was made, the 1960s were swinging and sunny Doris Day had developed a chic and slightly risqué image, promoted by her producer/husband Martin Melcher. Here, Day and screen husband Rod Taylor suspect each other of varying infidelities abroad, but the pair deserve much better. Taylor was capable in his prime of enlivening mediocre material, and here he proves a worthy successor to Rock Hudson as a foil for Day. TS DVD

Doris Day *Janet Harper* • Rod Taylor *Mike Harper* • Hermione Baddeley *Vanessa Courtwright* • Sergio Fantoni *Paul Bellari* • Reginald Gardiner *Simmons* • Maura McGiveny *Claire Hackett* • Aram Katcher *Culkos* • Leon Askin *Langsdorf* • Pierre Salinger *American consul* ■ *Dir* Ralph Levy • *Scr* Milt Rosen, Richard Breen [Richard L Breen], from the play *Some Other Love* by William Fairchild

---

LANDMARK FILM

After this, movies can no longer be the sole preserve of white men

Do the Right Thing
★★★★ 18
Drama　　　　　1989 · US · Colour · 114min

Spike Lee's fierce racial drama concentrates on one sweltering day in New York where simmering racial tensions are about to explode. The focal point becomes a pizza parlour run by Danny Aiello, who refuses to replace his old Italian photographs with pictures of black heroes. Lee himself is excellent as Aiello's delivery boy, but the playing of the ensemble cast is exemplary and, although there are a dozen different storylines, Lee effortlessly meshes them together without losing sight of his central theme. Add to that Ernest Dickerson's bright, vibrant cinematography and the superb soundtrack, and the result is an exhilarating, passionate and often very funny modern classic. JF Swearing. DVD

Danny Aiello *Sal* • Spike Lee *Mookie* • John Turturro *Pino* • Richard Edson *Vito* • Ossie Davis *Da Mayor* • Ruby Dee *Mother Sister* • Giancarlo Esposito *Buggin' Out* • Bill Nunn *Radio Raheem* • Rosie Perez *Tina* • John Savage *Clifton* • Sam Jackson [Samuel L Jackson] *Mister Señor Love Daddy* ■ *Dir/Scr* Spike Lee

Do You Love Me? ★★★ U
Musical　　　　　1946 · US · Colour · 90min

The 1940s Technicolor of this charming 20th Century-Fox musical shows off Maureen O'Hara's flowing red tresses a treat. She's a college dean and she's loved by band vocalist Dick Haymes, who proves yet again that he was one of the greatest ever singers of slow-tempo ballads. Harry James, a big band star of the period, also appears, while Reginald Gardiner provides the laughs. TS

Maureen O'Hara *Katherine Hilliard* • Dick Haymes *Jimmy Hale* • Harry James *Barry Clayton* • Reginald Gardiner *Herbert Benham* • Richard Gaines *Ralph Wainwright* • Stanley Prager *Dilly* • BS Pully *Taxi driver* • Chick Chandler *Earl Williams* • Alma Kruger *Mrs Crackleton* ■ *Dir* Gregory Ratoff • *Scr* Robert Ellis, Helen Logan, Dorothy Bennett, from a story by Bert Granet

Do You Remember Love
★★★★ PG
Drama　　　　　1985 · US · Colour · 92min

Joanne Woodward won an Emmy for her role in this made-for-TV movie about how the family of a middle-aged college professor copes when she contracts Alzheimer's. Scriptwriter Vickie Patik also walked away with an award for her moving script, which pulls no punches and steers clear of melodrama, However, most plaudits should go to director Jeff Bleckner and the cast. JB

Joanne Woodward *Barbara Wyatt-Hollis* • Richard Kiley *George Hollis* • Geraldine Fitzgerald *Lorraine Wyatt* • Jim Metzler *Tom Hollis* • Jordan Charney *Marvin Langdon* • Ron Rifkin *Gerry Kaplan* • Susan Ruttan *Julie Myers* ■ *Dir* Jeff Bleckner • *Scr* Vickie Patik

The Doberman Gang ★★
Crime caper   1972 · US · Colour · 86min

Some bungling bank robbers come up with the idea of training a pack of dogs to do the job for them in this low-budget comedy. They even name the pooches after legendary gangsters: Dillinger, Bonnie and Clyde and so on. It's not Shakespeare, but once you've bought the premise it has its moments. Two sequels (*The Daring Dobermans* and *The Amazing Dobermans* with Fred Astaire) followed. PF

Byron Mabe *Eddie Newton* • Hal Reed *Barney Greer* • Julie Parrish *June* • Simmy Bow *Sammy* • Jojo D'Amore *Jojo* • John Tull *Pet shop owner* ■ Jay Paxton *Bank manager* • Diane Prior *Sandy* ■ *Dir* Byron Ross Chudnow • *Scr* Louis Garfinkle, Frank Ray Perilli

Dobermann ★★★★ 18
Crime thriller   1997 · Fr · Colour · 98min

Wildly stylish, this tongue-in-cheek cops and robbers tale bursts with dazzling technical trickery, explosive action scenes and deranged performances, particularly from Tcheky Karyo as the scariest cop who ever lived. Jan Kounen's comic-strip concoction has a fairly simplistic plot, but slick, sexy camerawork and editing, plus supercool criminal posturing from Vincent Cassel and Monica Bellucci give the film a dynamic edge. JC French +subtitles. Violence, sex scenes, drug abuse. DVD

Vincent Cassel *Yann LePentrec, "Le Dob"* • Monica Bellucci *Nathalie, "Nat la gitane"* • Tcheky Karyo *Chief Inspector Sauveur Christini* • Antoine Basler *Jean-Claude Ayache, "Mosquito"* ■ *Dir* Jan Kounen • *Scr* Jan Kounen, Joël Houssin, from the novels by Houssin

Doc ★★★★ 15
Western   1971 · US · Colour · 91min

This flawed but fascinating account of the famous gunfight at the OK Corral has Stacy Keach as Doc Holliday, Faye Dunaway as his girlfriend Katie Elder, and Harris Yulin especially impressive as the political opportunist Wyatt Earp. The shoot-out, when it comes, is impressively handled by director Frank Perry, who successfully avoids mimicking previous versions. Shorn of many of the familiar trappings, this account may disappoint traditional western fans, but its focus on Holliday's disenchantment seems to be a little parable about the moral bankruptcy of Nixon's America. AT DVD

Stacy Keach *Doc Holliday* • Faye Dunaway *Kate Elder* • Harris Yulin *Wyatt Earp* • Mike Witney [Michael Witney] *Ike Clanton* • Denver John Collins *Kid* ■ *Dir* Frank Perry • *Scr* Pete Hamill

Doc Hollywood ★★★ 12
Romantic comedy   1991 · US · Colour · 99min

In this diverting, folksy comedy, Michael J Fox plays an ambitious California-bound intern who finds himself press-ganged into becoming a doctor in a small South Carolina community. Revelling in local idiosyncrasies, director Michael Caton-Jones gives the film a lovely golden glow and produces a Capra-like hymn to the small town. There are fine performances from Fox and a talented supporting cast; look out for a neat cameo from George Hamilton. JF Swearing, nudity. DVD

Michael J Fox *Dr Benjamin Stone* • Julie Warner *Lou* • Barnard Hughes *Dr Hogue* • Woody Harrelson *Henry "Hank" Gordon* • David Ogden Stiers *Nick Nicholson* • Frances Sternhagen *Lillian* • George Hamilton *Dr Halberstrom* • Bridget Fonda *Nancy Lee* • Mel Winkler *Melvin* ■ *Dir* Michael Caton-Jones • *Scr* Jeffrey Price, Peter S Seaman, Daniel Pyne, from the novel *What?...Dead Again* by Neil B Shulman

Doc Savage: the Man of Bronze ★★ PG
Fantasy adventure   1975 · US · Colour · 96min

George Pal was a legendary figure in the worlds of sci-fi and fantasy, but this, his swan song film as a producer, is not the best way to remember him. The story is taken from the ever-popular Doc Savage books of the 1930s, with television's Tarzan, Ron Ely, in the title role. Despite director Michael Anderson's attempts to insert some knowing humour, this remains a rather tame and routine adventure. JF Violence.

Ron Ely *Doc Savage* • Paul Gleason *Long Tom* • Bill Lucking [William Lucking] *Renny* • Michael Miller (1) *Monk* • Eldon Quick *Johnny* • Darrell Zwerling *Ham* • Paul Wexler *Captain Seas* • Janice Heiden *Andriana* ■ *Dir* Michael Anderson • *Scr* George Pal, Joe Morhaim, from the novel by Kenneth Robeson

The Docks of New York ★★★★
Silent drama   1928 · US · BW · 60min

Josef von Sternberg's movie flopped in America, mainly because it was previewed the same week as the first talkie, *The Jazz Singer*. (A singular case of bad timing.) Over the years, though, the picture has been rediscovered as a highly effective melodrama about a ship's stoker who saves a streetwalker from suicide, marries her and then takes the blame when she's accused of murder. The film's romantic fatalism is compelling, and von Sternberg creates some stunning imagery. AT

George Bancroft *Bill Roberts* • Betty Compson *Sadie* • Olga Baclanova *Lou* • Clyde Cook *"Sugar" Steve* • Mitchell Lewis *Third engineer* • Gustav von Seyffertitz *"Hymn Book" Harry* • Guy Oliver *The Crimp* • May Foster *Mrs Crimp* ■ *Dir* Josef von Sternberg • *Scr* Jules Furthman • *Cinematographer* Harold Rosson

Docks of New York ★★
Crime comedy drama   1945 · US · BW · 61min

One of the last gasps of the *East Side Kids*, made shortly before star Leo Gorcey picked up the franchise and continued the series as *The Bowery Boys*. It's the same mixture as usual, involving some mayhem around stolen jewellery, while Huntz Hall's mugging over-compensates for the absence of series regulars Gabriel Dell and Bobby Jordan, both off working for Uncle Sam. Movie buffs should note that the Carlyle Blackwell Jr who appears here is *not* the infamous fashion critic "Mr Blackwell", as has been claimed. TS

Leo Gorcey *Muggs McGinnis* • Huntz Hall *Glimpy* • Billy Benedict *Skinny* • Bud Gorman *Danny* • Mende Koenig *Sam* • Gloria Pope *Saundra* • Carlyle Blackwell Jr *Marty* ■ *Dir* Wallace Fox • *Scr* Harvey Gates

Docteur Petiot ★★★★ 15
Biographical drama   1990 · Fr · Colour and BW · 97min

While most people are now familiar with the Holocaust heroics of Raoul Wallenberg and Oskar Schindler, the hideous crimes of Marcel Petiot have largely gone unrecorded. This chilling film recounts the career of one of France's most notorious serial killers, who conned Jews into believing he could smuggle them to Argentina before murdering them and incinerating their bodies. Michel Serrault is quite superb, whether reassuring loved ones or hurtling round the darkened streets. Christian de Chalonge's flamboyant direction exploits every cinematic trick in the book to create an authentic and genuinely horrific atmosphere. DP French +subtitles.

Michel Serrault *Docteur Petiot* • Pierre Romans *Ivan Drezner* • Zbigniew Horoks *Nathan Guzik* • Bérangère Bonvoisin *Georgette Petiot* • Aurore Prieto *Madame Guzik* ■ *Dir* Christian de Chalonge • *Scr* Dominique Garnier, Christian de Chalonge

The Doctor ★★★★ 15
Drama   1991 · US · Colour · 117min

William Hurt stars as a glib, egotistical doctor who's forced to re-appraise his life when he's diagnosed as suffering from cancer. When the tables are turned and he becomes a patient, he begins to realise the shortcomings of his profession. As moral issues come under the microscope (a rare enough event in Hollywood), Hurt makes a credible transition from blunt medical hard-nut to "born again" doctor with a conscience, and the probing script and first-class performances (from Hurt and Elizabeth Perkins as a fellow patient) prevent this harrowing drama from becoming an empty exercise in Hollywood schmaltz. JM DVD

William Hurt *Dr Jack McKee* • Christine Lahti *Anne McKee* • Elizabeth Perkins *June* • Mandy Patinkin *Murray* • Adam Arkin *Eli* • Charlie Korsmo *Nicky* • Wendy Crewson *Dr Leslie Abbott* ■ *Dir* Randa Haines • *Scr* Robert Caswell, from the memoirs *A Taste of My Own Medicine* by Ed Rosenbaum

The Doctor and the Devils ★★★ 15
Historical crime drama   1985 · UK · Colour · 88min

This rather earnest resurrection of the Burke and Hare bodysnatchers tale is pitched more as a dark moral fable than a horror film. Based on a script written by Dylan Thomas in the 1940s (unproduced because of censor problems), producer Mel Brooks got veteran Hammer horror director/cinematographer Freddie Francis to rework it. The result is high on period detail, but low on *Grand Guignol* chills. AJ Violence, swearing, nudity, sex scenes.

Timothy Dalton *Dr Thomas Rock* • Jonathan Pryce *Robert Fallon* • Twiggy *Jenny Bailey* • Julian Sands *Dr Murray* • Stephen Rea *Timothy Broom* • Phyllis Logan *Elizabeth Rock* • Lewis Fiander *Thornton* • Beryl Reid *Mrs Flynn* • TP McKenna *O'Connor* • Patrick Stewart *Professor Macklin* • Sian Phillips *Annabella Rock* ■ *Dir* Freddie Francis • *Scr* Ronald Harwood, from a screenplay (unproduced) by Dylan Thomas

The Doctor and the Girl ★★
Medical drama   1949 · US · BW · 97min

MGM, the studio that brought us the *Dr Kildare* series, returned to the hospital for Glenn Ford's first picture with the studio. Under the competent direction of Curtis Bernhardt, Ford plays an idealistic medic who eschews the rewards of becoming a specialist in order to help the underprivileged. RK

Glenn Ford *Dr Michael Corday* • Charles Coburn *Dr John Corday* • Gloria De Haven [Gloria DeHaven] *Fabienne Corday* • Janet Leigh *Evelyn Heldon* • Bruce Bennett *Dr Alfred Norton* • Nancy Davis *Mariette* ■ *Dir* Curtis Bernhardt • *Scr* Theodore Reeves, from the novel *Bodies and Souls* by Maxence van der Meersch

Doctor at Sea ★★ PG
Comedy   1955 · UK · Colour · 89min

Appearing in her first British film and still a year away from taking world cinema by storm in *And God Created Woman*, Brigitte Bardot here provides Dirk Bogarde with a welcome distraction from the miserable seasickness he experiences away from the terra firma of St Swithin's. Despite the lively rapport between the stars, however, the second of Rank's popular series is short on truly comic incident, and the shipboard location is rather limiting. DP DVD

Dirk Bogarde *Simon Sparrow* • Brigitte Bardot *Helene Colbert* • Brenda de Banzie *Muriel Mallet* • James Robertson-Justice *Captain Hogg* • Maurice Denham *Easter* • Michael Medwin *Trail* • Hubert Gregg *Archer* ■ *Dir* Ralph Thomas • *Scr* Nicholas Phipps, Richard Gordon, Jack Davies, from the novel by Richard Gordon

Doctor at Large ★★★ U
Comedy   1957 · UK · Colour · 94min

In this third entry in the series inspired by the novels of Richard Gordon, Dirk Bogarde, as accident-prone houseman Simon Sparrow, once again escapes the confines of St Swithin's in order to explore pastures new, in this case a country practice where nothing goes right. But it's only once he's back under the beady gaze of James Robertson-Justice that the film comes to life. This is amiable enough, but everyone is just a touch off colour, and the film shows signs of the terminal decline that would set in after Bogarde quit the series. DP DVD

Dirk Bogarde *Simon Sparrow* • Muriel Pavlow *Joy* • Donald Sinden *Benskin* • James Robertson-Justice *Sir Lancelot Spratt* • Shirley Eaton *Nan* • Derek Farr *Dr Potter-Shine* • Michael Medwin *Bingham* • Lionel Jeffries *Dr Hackett* ■ *Dir* Ralph Thomas • *Scr* Nicholas Phipps, Richard Gordon, from the novel by Richard Gordon

Doctor Blood's Coffin ★★ 15
Horror   1960 · UK · Colour · 91min

Director Sidney J Furie cut his teeth on such British programme fillers as this cheap and cheerful *Frankenstein*-flavoured tale. Doctor Kieron Moore experiments in bringing the dead back to life while his fetching nurse (Hazel Court) screams a lot amid the lurid, Hammer Horror-style glossiness. Enhanced by its Cornish tin-mine setting, Furie's cardboard suspense shocker is hardly a classic, but still great fun. AJ DVD

Kieron Moore *Dr Peter Blood* • Hazel Court *Linda Parker* • Ian Hunter *Dr Robert Blood* • Fred Johnson *Tregaye (Morton)* • Kenneth J Warren *Sergeant Cook* • Andy Alston *Beale* • Paul Stockman *Steve Parker* • John Ronane *Hanson* • Gerald C Lawson *Morton (Sweeting)* ■ *Dir* Sidney J Furie • *Scr* Jerry Juran, James Kelly, Peter Miller, from a story by Jerry Juran

Dr Broadway ★★
Crime comedy drama   1942 · US · BW · 68min

Anthony Mann's first feature film is a tight little thriller revolving around a Times Square medic who finds himself becoming a detective in a murder mystery. The second-league cast is headed by the competent Macdonald Carey and Jean Phillips, usually Ginger Rogers's stand-in. Various Broadway characters people the plot, there is some good location work and Mann keeps the action moving smartly. RB

Macdonald Carey *Dr Timothy "Doc" Kane* • Jean Phillips *Connie Madigan* • J Carrol Naish *Jack Venner* • Richard Lane *Patrick Doyle* • Edward Ciannelli [Eduardo Ciannelli] *Vic Telli* ■ *Dir* Anthony Mann • *Scr* Art Arthur, from the short story by Borden Chase

Dr Bull ★★★ U
Drama   1933 · US · BW · 79min

The folksy wisdom and whimsical humour of Will Rogers seem hopelessly old-fashioned today, but in the first third of the last century he was one of the biggest stars in the States. Rogers plays a small-town GP making light of his limited resources and the suspicions of would-be patients. Director John Ford, who was a sucker for this brand of homespun philosophising, loved the film, although modern audiences will probably find it somewhat twee. DP

Will Rogers (1) *Dr Bull* • Vera Allen *Janet Cardmaker* • Marian Nixon *May Tripping* • Howard Lally *Joe Tripping* • Berton Churchill *Herbert Banning* • Louise Dresser *Mrs Banning* • Andy Devine *Larry Ward* • Rochelle Hudson *Virginia Banning* ■ *Dir* John Ford • *Scr* Paul Green, Jane Storm, from the novel *The Last Adam* by James Gould Cozzens

Dr Crippen ★★ PG
Biographical crime drama   1962 · UK · BW · 94min

Considering the notoriously sordid subject matter, director Robert Lynn's true-crime case history should have been a far more riveting affair than this so-so account. Donald Pleasence is at his sinister best playing the monstrous doctor who murders his persecuting wife in order to elope with his typist lover. However, this remains remote and uninvolving because of the deliberately austere quasi-documentary stance. AJ DVD

Donald Pleasence *Dr Hawley Harvey Crippen* • Coral Browne *Belle Crippen* • Samantha Eggar *Ethel Le Neve* • Donald Wolfit *RD Muir* • James Robertson-Justice *Captain Kendall* • Geoffrey Toone *Mr Tobin* • Oliver Johnston *Lord Chief Justice* ■ *Dir* Robert Lynn • *Scr* Leigh Vance • *Cinematographer* Nick Roeg [Nicolas Roeg]

D

Dr Cyclops ★★★
Science-fiction thriller
1940 · US · Colour · 78min

Ernest B Schoedsack, co-director of the original *King Kong*, returns to the fantasy genre with this wonderfully weird tale of a mad scientist (Albert Dekker) who miniaturises explorers in his Amazon jungle laboratory. Borrowing ideas from *Kong* special effects man Willis O'Brien, Schoedsack crafts a well-mounted science-fiction thriller, the first of its kind in vivid Technicolor. The standard plot now looks hackneyed, but the impressive props make this a lot of fun. AJ

Albert Dekker *Dr Thorkel* · Janice Logan *Dr Mary Mitchell* · Thomas Coley *Bill Stockton* · Charles Halton *Dr Bulfinch* · Victor Kilian *Steve Baker* · Frank Yaconelli *Pedro* · Bill Wilkerson *Silent Indian* · Allen Fox *Cab driver* · Paul Fix *Dr Mendoza* · Frank Reicher *Prof Kendall* ■ *Dir* Ernest B Schoedsack · *Scr* Tom Kilpatrick · *Special Effects* Farciot Edouard

Doctor Detroit ★★ 15
Comedy
1983 · US · Colour · 86min

Featuring Dan Aykroyd in his first leading role after the death of his partner John Belushi, this comedy is only a partial success. The plot, which finds Aykroyd's mild-mannered college teacher getting mixed up with some hookers, gives him full rein to showcase all of his comic talents, and he is particularly good as a ludicrously OTT pimp. However, he is let down by a loose script and crude direction by Michael Pressman. JF

Dan Aykroyd *Clifford Skridlow* · Howard Hesseman *Smooth Walker* · TK Carter *Diavolo Washington* · Donna Dixon *Monica McNeil* · Lynn Whitfield *Thelma Cleland* · Lydia Lei *Jasmine Wu* · Fran Drescher *Karen Blittstein* ■ *Dir* Michael Pressman · *Scr* Carl Gottlieb, Robert Boris, Bruce Jay Friedman, from the novel *Detroit Abe* by Bruce Jay Friedman

Doctor Dolittle ★★★ U
Musical fantasy adventure
1967 · US · Colour · 138min

Children will revel in this musical comedy based on Hugh Lofting's stories, but this was an infamous costly disaster that almost killed off 20th Century-Fox. Its longevity belies the leaden affair, with a squeakily embarrassing Rex Harrison as the dotty doc. There are some good tunes, including the Oscar-winning *Talk to the Animals*, and the effects also won an Academy Award, but overall it is rather a bore – to adults, that is. SH *DVD*

Rex Harrison *Doctor John Dolittle* · Anthony Newley *Matthew Mugg* · Peter Bull *General Bellowes* · William Dix *Tommy Stubbins* · Portia Nelson *Sarah Dolittle* · Samantha Eggar *Emma Fairfax* · Richard Attenborough *Albert Blossom* · Norma Varden *Lady Petherington* ■ *Dir* Richard Fleischer · *Scr* Leslie Bricusse, from the stories by Hugh Lofting · *Music/Lyrics* Leslie Bricusse

Doctor Dolittle ★★★ PG
Fantasy comedy
1998 · US · Colour · 81min

After the success of *The Nutty Professor*, Eddie Murphy completed the transformation from foul-mouthed, fast-talking comic to all-round family entertainer with this high-grossing film. Murphy plays a doctor whose life is turned upside down when his old childhood gift – the ability to "talk to the animals" – is the cue for lots of juvenile gags from a host of guest voices. JF Swearing. *DVD*

Eddie Murphy *Dr John Dolittle* · Ossie Davis *Archer Dolittle* · Oliver Platt *Dr Mark Weller* · Peter Boyle *Calloway* · Richard Schiff *Dr Gene Reiss* · Kristen Wilson *Lisa* · Jeffrey Tambor *Dr Fish* · Kyla Pratt *Maya* · Paul Giamatti *Dr Betty Thomas* · *Scr* Nat Mauldin, Larry Levin, from stories by Hugh Lofting

Dr Dolittle 2 ★★ PG
Fantasy comedy
2001 · US · Colour · 83min

The tedious central plot of this sequel sees Eddie Murphy coaching a slovenly circus bear (voiced by Steve Zahn) to be an alpha male, attract a mate and save an endangered forest from destruction. The parade of supporting species with human characteristics is much the same as its far funnier predecessor, but the main story is flat and charmless. JC *DVD*

Eddie Murphy *Dr John Dolittle* · Kristen Wilson *Lisa Dolittle* · Jeffrey Jones *Joseph Potter* · Kevin Pollak *Jack Riley/Crocodile* · Raven-Symoné *Charisse Dolittle* · Kyla Pratt *Maya Dolittle* · Steve Zahn *Archie* · Lisa Kudrow *Ava* · Isaac Hayes *Possum* · Richard C Sarafian *God Beaver* ■ *Dir* Steve Carr · *Scr* Larry Levin, from the stories by Hugh Lofting

Dr Dolittle 3 ★★ PG
Fantasy comedy
2006 · US · Colour · 90min

Eddie Murphy is wisely absent from this flimsy and rather pointless second sequel to his 1998 hit comedy. Instead, his doctor character's daughter Maya (a returning Kyla Pratt) takes centre stage as a teen who resents inheriting her dad's ability to communicate with animals. Slapstick, jibes and a procession of repetitive and unfunny pratfalls replace a proper narrative, and the conclusion is so unexciting it scarcely matters. Two further sequels followed. SF Brief swearing. *DVD*

Kyla Pratt *Maya Dolittle* · Kristen Wilson *Lisa Dolittle* · Walker Howard *Bo Jones* · John Amos *Jud Jones* · Tommy Snider *Clayton* ■ *Dir* Rich Thorne · *Scr* Nina Colman, from the stories by Hugh Lofting

Dr Dolittle: Million Dollar Mutts ★★
Fantasy comedy
2009 · Can/US · Colour · 87min

Hollywood's eccentricities are the source of weak laughs here, as Dr Dolittle's daughter Maya (a returning Kyla Pratt) takes her animal-talking skills to LA for her third solo adventure. But while the goofy-looking critters she encounters (an obese, tutu-wearing pig, a rap-hating rabbit) will have younger viewers fitfully giggling, they don't give the already two-dimensional 17-year-old much to do. SF

Kyla Pratt *Maya Dolittle* · Tegan Moss *Tiffany Monaco* · Norm McDonald *Lucky* ■ *Dir* Alex Zamm · *Scr* Daniel & Steven Altiere

Dr Dolittle: Tail to the Chief ★★ PG
Comedy
2008 · US/Can · Colour · 83min

Dr Dolittle's teenage daughter (a returning Kyla Pratt) stands in for her famous father a second time in this skimpy fourth addition to the lowbrow family franchise. Here it's the US President (Peter Coyote) who needs her inherited animal-communication skills to sort out his pet pooch (distinctively voiced by Jennifer Coolidge). As with all of Pratt's minimally plotted solo adventures, it's the wisecracking and sadly underused creatures that stand out. SF *DVD*

Kyla Pratt *Maya Dolittle* · Peter Coyote *President Sterling* · Malcolm Stewart *Chief Dorian* · Niall Matter *Cole Fletcher* ■ *Dir* Craig Shapiro · *Scr* Matt Lieberman, Kathleen Laccinole

Dr Ehrlich's Magic Bullet ★★★
Biographical drama
1940 · US · BW · 102min

Edward G Robinson plays the German doctor who discovered a cure for syphilis – not celibacy but the drug Salvarsan – and won a Nobel Prize in 1908. A tricky subject for a Warner Bros biopic in 1940, but everything is done in the most tasteful manner. The original story by Norman Burnside was thoroughly rewritten with the help of John Huston and Heinz Herald, cutting out all the romantic twaddle to concentrate on Ehrlich peering through a microscope. It's absorbing viewing, and Robinson later regarded it as his finest performance. AT

Edward G Robinson *Dr Paul Ehrlich* · Ruth Gordon *Mrs Ehrlich* · Otto Kruger *Dr Emil von Behring* · Donald Crisp *Minister Althoff* · Maria Ouspenskaya *Franziska Speyer* · Montagu Love *Professor Hartmann* · Sig Rumann [Sig Ruman] *Dr Hans Wolfert* · Albert Bassermann *Dr Robert Koch* ■ *Dir* William Dieterle · *Scr* John Huston, Heinz Herald, Norman Burnside, from a story by Burnside

Doctor Faustus ★★★ PG
Drama
1967 · UK/It · Colour · 88min

Christopher Marlowe's play – about the man who sold his soul to the devil – was a favourite of Richard Burton's, who may have looked at Faust and seen himself, the great stage actor who willingly sold out to Hollywood and celebrity. Casting himself as Faust and his wife Elizabeth Taylor as Helen of Troy, Burton put the play on at Oxford and then used all his box-office clout to produce and co-direct this screen version. To his credit, Burton took with him his co-director and the Oxford cast, though the result is more a fascinating record of the stage production – Burton's reading of Marlowe's verse is magnificent – than a fully realised film. AT

Richard Burton *Doctor Faustus* · Elizabeth Taylor *Helen of Troy* · Andreas Teuber *Mephistopheles* · Ian Marter *Emperor* · Elizabeth O'Donovan *Empress* · David McIntosh *Lucifer* · Jeremy Eccles *Beelzebub* · Ram Chopra *Valdes* · Richard Carwardine *Cornelius* ■ *Dir* Richard Burton, Nevill Coghill · *Scr* Nevill Coghill, from the play by Christopher Marlowe

Doctor Françoise Gailland ★★★
Drama
1975 · Fr · Colour · 100min

Annie Girardot won a César (the French equivalent of an Oscar) for her performance in this three-hankie weepie. Also known as *No Time for Breakfast*, the film sticks pretty closely to the classic "women's picture" formula of the careerist whose professional ambitions are compromised by events in her personal life. Girardot skilfully captures first the anger, then the courage of the eponymous cancer victim, while Jean-Pierre Cassel and Isabelle Huppert offer selfless support. DP French dubbed.

Annie Girardot *Françoise Gailland* · Jean-Pierre Cassel *Daniel Letessier* · François Périer *Gérard Gailland* · Isabelle Huppert *Elisabeth Gailland* · William Coryn *Julien Gailland* ■ *Dir* Jean-Louis Bertucelli · *Scr* André G Brunelin, Jean-Louis Bertucelli, from the novel *Un Cri* by Noelle Loriot

Dr Giggles ★ 18
Horror
1992 · US · Colour · 91min

Heard the one about the kid sent mad by his father's surgical obsessions, who escapes from an asylum years later and turns up in his home town to wreak vengeance? Of course you have. An ultra-derivative medical *Halloween*, this hasn't one iota of originality on display and it's a comatose collection of "Dr Kill-Dare" clichés. AJ Swearing, violence.

Larry Drake *Evan Rendell* · Holly Marie Combs *Jennifer Campbell* · Glenn Quinn *Max Anderson* · Cliff De Young *Tom Campbell* · Richard Bradford *Officer Hank Magruder* · Keith Diamond *Officer Joe Reitz* · Michelle Johnson *Tamara* ■ *Dir* Manny Coto · *Scr* Manny Coto, Graeme Whifler

Dr Gillespie's Criminal Case ★★★
Medical drama
1943 · US · BW · 88min

With James Craven stepping into the shoes vacated by Phil Brown, this 12th entry in MGM's popular medical series continues the plotline started in *Calling Dr Gillespie*. Upset by former fiancée Donna Reed's romance with sergeant Michael Duane, Craven's homicidal maniac reduces Blair General to chaos, and the venerable senior surgeon is forced to call on junior doctors Van Johnson and Keye Luke for assistance. DP

Lionel Barrymore *Dr Leonard Gillespie* · Van Johnson *Dr Randall Adams* · Donna Reed *Marcia Bradburn* · Keye Luke *Dr Lee Wong How* · James Craven *Roy Todwell* · Nat Pendleton *Joe Wayman* · Alma Kruger *Molly Byrd* · Margaret O'Brien *Margaret* · Walter Kingsford *Dr Walter Carew* · Nell Craig *Nurse Parker* · Michael Duane *Sergeant Orisin* ■ *Dir* Willis Goldbeck · *Scr* Martin Berkeley, Harry Ruskin, Lawrence P Bachmann, from characters by Max Brand

Dr Gillespie's New Assistant ★★★
Medical drama
1942 · US · BW · 87min

Bereft of Dr Kildare, MGM entrusted new director Willis Goldbeck with the task of resuscitating its long-running medical series in this 11th film by contriving a contest to find a personable assistant to crotchety surgeon Lionel Barrymore. In setting three interns each a tricky case to diagnose, the studio sought to showcase star-in-waiting Van Johnson, while Goldbeck aimed to add a touch of topicality by having Keye Luke decamp partway through to join the Chinese nationalist army. DP

Lionel Barrymore *Dr Leonard Gillespie* · Van Johnson *Dr Randall Adams* · Susan Peters *Mrs Howard Young* · Richard Quine *Dr Dennis Lindsey* · Keye Luke *Dr Lee Wong How* · Nat Pendleton *Joe Wayman* · Alma Kruger *Molly Byrd* · Horace McNally [Stephen McNally] *Howard Young* · Nell Craig *Nurse Parker* ■ *Dir* Willis Goldbeck · *Scr* Martin Berkeley, Harry Ruskin, Lawrence P Bachmann, from characters by Max Brand

Doctor Glas ★★★
Drama
1968 · Den · BW · 83min

This is the bleakest of Mai Zetterling's directorial ventures. Collaborating on both screenplay and staging with husband David Hughes, she has created an unflinching study of isolation, despair and the contrast between physical and spiritual love. The triangle that forms between doctor Per Oscarsson, pastor Ulf Palme and his loyally chaste wife Lone Hertz will ultimately end in murder. DP

Per Oscarsson *Dr Glas* · Ulf Palme *Pastor Gregorius* · Lone Hertz *Helga Gregorius* · Nils Eklund *Markel* · Bente Dessau *Eva Martens* · Lars Lunoe *Klas Recke* ■ *Dir* Mai Zetterling · *Scr* Mai Zetterling, David Hughes, from the novel *Doktor Glas* by Hjalmar Soderberg

Dr Goldfoot and the Bikini Machine ★★ PG
Comedy
1965 · US · Colour · 84min

Very much a product of the Swinging Sixties, this slice of tosh combines several of the elements that made AIP films so popular at the drive-ins. Vincent Price plays the eponymous doctor, who creates female robots so they can marry rich men and line his coffers. Susan Hart plays the female lead, and Frankie Avalon and Dwayne Hickman are along for the ride. Even Annette Funicello drops in! It's all a little too daft, though, and the humour is positively leaden. TS

Vincent Price *Dr Goldfoot* · Frankie Avalon *Craig Gamble* · Dwayne Hickman *Todd Armstrong* · Susan Hart *Diane* · Jack Mullaney *Igor* · Fred Clark *DJ Pevney* · Annette Funicello *Girl in the Stock* ■ *Dir* Norman Taurog · *Scr* Elwood Ullman, Robert Kaufman, from a story by James Hartford

Dr Goldfoot and the Girl Bombs ★★
Comedy
1966 · US/It · Colour · 85min

Only in the mid-1960s could you have got away with a film like this! Thanks to cult Italian horror director Mario Bava, this sequel to *Dr Goldfoot and the Bikini Machine* piles on the style, but rather loses out in the fun stakes. Still, Vincent Price is his usual hammy self as Dr Goldfoot, who gets backing from China to start a war between the Americans and the Soviets using sexy robot girls with bombs implanted in their navels. RS

Vincent Price *Dr Goldfoot* · Fabian *Bill Dexter* · Franco Franchi *Franco* · Ciccio Ingrassia *Ciccio* · Laura Antonelli *Rosanna* ■ *Dir* Mario Bava · *Scr* Louis M Heyward, Castellano Pipolo, Robert Kaufman, from a story by James Hartford

Dr Heckyl & Mr Hype ★★
Comedy
1980 · US · Colour · 97min

Oliver Reed tackles the title role in a clumsy comedy that mixes the Jekyll and Hyde idea with elements of *The Nutty Professor*. Reed is engagingly grotesque – bulbous nose, mangy skin, the works – as a scientist who overdoses on an experimental diet formula and transforms into a dashing playboy with a predilection for killing. Reed enters into the rollicking spirit of the piece, but director Charles B Griffith ruins it with laboured dialogue and stilted slapstick. RS

Oliver Reed *Dr Heckyl/Mr Hype* • Sunny Johnson *Coral Careen* • Maia Danziger *Miss Finebum* • Virgil Frye *Lieutenant Mack Druck "Il Topo"* • Mel Welles *Dr Hinkle* • Kedrick Wolfe *Dr Lew Hoo* • Jackie Coogan *Sergeant Fleacollar* ■ *Dir/Scr* Charles B Griffith

Doctor in the House
★★★★ U

Comedy   1954 · UK · Colour · 87min

This film launched the popular St Swithin's series and made a matinée idol out of Dirk Bogarde. Following a class of students through their training, it delights in the dark side of hospital humour, with the medical misadventures providing much better entertainment than the romantic interludes. Kenneth More, Donald Sinden and Donald Houston are on top form as the duffers doing retakes, while Bogarde oozes charm and quiet comic flair. But stealing all their thunder is James Robertson-Justice as Sir Lancelot Spratt. Followed by *Doctor at Sea* and *Doctor at Large*. DP DVD

Dirk Bogarde *Simon Sparrow* • Muriel Pavlow *Joy* • Kenneth More *Grimsdyke* • Donald Sinden *Benskin* • Kay Kendall *Isobel* • James Robertson-Justice *Sir Lancelot Spratt* • Donald Houston *Taffy* • Suzanne Cloutier *Stella* ■ *Dir* Ralph Thomas • *Scr* Nicholas Phipps, from the novel by Richard Gordon

Doctor in Love
★★ PG

Comedy   1960 · UK · Colour · 92min

Though a box-office hit in its day, this comedy is even more episodic than others in the long-running series and comes over now as a thin excuse for a series of risqué encounters and double entendres. Leslie Phillips is impeccable as a philandering doctor finding the country air conducive to consultancies of the canoodling kind, and the supporting cast is as solid as ever. The film fails, however, because of Michael Craig, who is not only no Dirk Bogarde, but also no comedian. DP DVD

Michael Craig *Dr Richard Hare* • Virginia Maskell *Dr Nicola Barrington* • Leslie Phillips *Dr Tony Burke* • James Robertson-Justice *Sir Lancelot Spratt* • Carole Lesley *Kitten Strudwick* • Liz Fraser *Leonora* • Joan Sims *Dawn* • Nicholas Parsons *Dr Hinxman* • Irene Handl *Professor MacRitchie* ■ *Dir* Ralph Thomas • *Scr* Nicholas Phipps, from characters by Richard Gordon

Doctor in Distress
★★ PG

Comedy   1963 · UK · Colour · 98min

What a cast! What a letdown! After a one-film absence, Dirk Bogarde reluctantly returned to the role of Simon Sparrow in this muddled comedy and immediately announced he'd never step inside St Swithin's again. Faced with a script that reads like a medical school rag mag, the cast plods through the picture as though under anaesthetic. DP DVD

Dirk Bogarde *Dr Simon Sparrow* • Samantha Eggar *Delia* • James Robertson-Justice *Sir Lancelot Spratt* • Mylène Demongeot *Sonja* • Donald Houston *Major French* • Barbara Murray *Iris* • Dennis Price *Blacker* • Peter Butterworth *Ambulance driver* • Leo McKern *Heilbronn* ■ *Dir* Ralph Thomas • *Scr* Nicholas Phipps, Ronald Scott Thorn, from characters by Richard Gordon

Doctor in Clover
★★ PG

Comedy   1966 · UK · Colour · 96min

The penultimate entry in the seven-film series based on the comic novels of Richard Gordon is possibly the least strong in terms of incident, but there are some pleasing performances. Demonstrating his flair for the debonair, Leslie Phillips just about makes the whole thing worthwhile, but even he struggles with the anaemic story in which a romance and a new wonder drug complicate his hectic love life. DP DVD

Leslie Phillips *Dr Gaston Grimsdyke* • James Robertson-Justice *Sir Lancelot Spratt* • Shirley Anne Field *Nurse Bancroft* • John Fraser *Dr Miles Grimsdyke* • Joan Sims *Matron Sweet* • Fenella

Fielding *Tatiana Rubikov* ■ *Dir* Ralph Thomas • *Scr* Jack Davies, from characters by Richard Gordon

Doctor in Trouble
★★ PG

Comedy   1970 · UK · Colour · 86min

The seventh and last movie to be culled from Richard Gordon's bestselling series was based on a book called *Doctor on Toast*, which would have been a pretty apt title for this innocently smutty film, as it feels as if it has been warmed up from the leftovers of *Doctor at Sea*. Any enjoyment there is comes from the bullish performance of Leslie Phillips as the medic-turned-steward on board a luxury liner. DP DVD

Leslie Phillips *Dr Burke* • Harry Secombe *Llewellyn Wendover* • James Robertson-Justice *Sir Lancelot Spratt* • Angela Scoular *Ophelia O'Brien* • Irene Handl *Mrs Dailey* • Robert Morley *Captain George Spratt* • Freddie Jones *Master-at-Arms* • Joan Sims *Russian captain* • John Le Mesurier *Purser* • Simon Dee *Basil Beauchamp* • Graham Chapman *Roddy* ■ *Dir* Ralph Thomas • *Scr* Jack Davies, from the novel *Doctor on Toast* by Richard Gordon

Dr Jekyll and Mr Hyde
★★★ PG

Silent horror   1920 · US · Tinted · 82min

Based on Thomas Russell Sullivan's Victorian stage adaptation and steeped in the attitudes of that era, this is generally considered to be the best silent version of Robert Louis Stevenson's classic story. It's hopelessly dated by modern standards, though, while John Barrymore slices the ham far too thickly. His Jekyll isn't the villain of the piece so much as his girlfriend's father, played by Brandon Hurst. It's Hurst who suggests idealist Jekyll experiments with the good and evil sides of human nature, and he's also the one who deliberately leads him into temptation with silent goddess Nita Naldi. AJ DVD

John Barrymore *Dr Henry Jekyll/Mr Edward Hyde* • Martha Mansfield *Millicent Carew* • Nita Naldi *Gina* • Brandon Hurst *Sir George Carew* • Charles Lane (1) *Dr Richard Lanyon* • Louis Wolheim *Music hall proprietor* ■ *Dir* John S Robertson • *Scr* Clara S Beranger, from the novel *The Strange Case of Dr Jekyll and Mr Hyde* by Robert Louis Stevenson

Dr Jekyll and Mr Hyde
★★★★ 12

Horror   1931 · US · BW · 91min

Robert Louis Stevenson's oft-told split personality tale receives its most stylish, erotic and exciting treatment under Rouben Mamoulian's sure direction. Fredric March deservedly won the best actor Oscar – shared with Wallace Beery in *The Champ* – for his tormented performance; the single-take transformation scenes are particularly impressive. Also memorable is the smouldering sensuality of Miriam Hopkins as the prostitute who's the object of his evil attentions. This enduring adaptation is totally satisfying. AJ DVD

Fredric March *Dr Henry Jekyll/Mr Hyde* • Miriam Hopkins *Ivy Pearson* • Rose Hobart *Muriel Carew* • Holmes Herbert *Dr Lanyon* • Halliwell Hobbes *Brig Gen Carew* • Edgar Norton *Poole* • Arnold Lucy *Utterson* • Colonel McDonnell *Hobson* • Tempe Pigott *Mrs Hawkins* ■ *Dir* Rouben Mamoulian • *Scr* Samuel Hoffenstein, Percy Heath, from the novel *The Strange Case of Dr Jekyll and Mr Hyde* by Robert Louis Stevenson • *Cinematographer* Karl Struss • *Art Director* Hans Dreier • *Make-up* Wally Westmore

Dr Jekyll and Mr Hyde
★★★ 12

Horror   1941 · US · BW · 108min

Director Victor Fleming's first film after *Gone with the Wind* was this lavish MGM treatment of Robert Louis Stevenson's classic cautionary tale. With the accent on the bad doctor's emotional turmoil rendered in complex Freudian terms to little dramatic effect, it's a poor, if at times scary relation to the superior 1931 version. Spencer Tracy adds scant shading to either side of his split personality, despite an impressive and sinister transformation

montage. Worth seeing for the production standards and the luminescent Ingrid Bergman. AJ DVD

Spencer Tracy *Dr Harry Jekyll/Mr Hyde* • Ingrid Bergman *Ivy Peterson* • Lana Turner *Beatrix Emery* • Donald Crisp *Sir Charles Emery* • Ian Hunter *Dr John Lanyon* • Barton MacLane *Sam Higgins* • C Aubrey Smith *The bishop* • Peter Godfrey *Poole* ■ *Dir* Victor Fleming • *Scr* John Lee Mahin, from the novel *The Strange Case Of Dr Jekyll and Mr Hyde* by Robert Louis Stevenson

Dr Jekyll and Ms Hyde
★ 12

Comedy   1995 · US · Colour · 86min

This dire, unfunny and completely unnecessary comic twist on Robert Louis Stevenson's classic tale stars Tim Daly as Jekyll's descendant, a gormless fellow who has the unhappy knack of turning into trampy vamp Helen Hyde (Sean Young). The only really scary thing in the movie is Young's bad acting. JB Swearing, nudity.

Sean Young *Helen Hyde* • Tim Daly [Timothy Daly] *Dr Richard Jacks* • Lysette Anthony *Sarah Carver* • Stephen Tobolowsky *Oliver Mintz* • Harvey Fierstein *Yves DuBois* • Thea Vidale *Valerie* • Jeremy Piven *Pete Walston* • Polly Bergen *Mrs Unterveldt* ■ *Dir* David F Price • *Scr* Tim John, Oliver Butcher, William Davies, William Osborne, from a story by David F Price, from the novel *The Strange Case of Dr Jekyll and Mr Hyde* by Robert Louis Stevenson

Dr Jekyll & Sister Hyde
★★★ 15

Horror   1971 · UK · Colour · 93min

Written by Brian Clemens (longtime writer and producer of *The Avengers* TV series), this bizarre bisexual take on the split personality classic even includes the grave robbers Burke and Hare and a Jack the Ripper subplot. While not quite living up to its initial hype – "the transformation of a man into a woman will take place before your very eyes", warned the ads – it's still mid-range Hammer horror with extra heat supplied by solid Ralph Bates and Martine Beswick as the good and evil flip sides. AJ Violence, brief nudity. DVD

Ralph Bates *Dr Jekyll* • Martine Beswick *Sister Hyde* • Gerald Sim *Professor Robertson* • Lewis Fiander *Howard* • Dorothy Alison *Mrs Spencer* • Neil Wilson *Older policeman* • Ivor Dean *Burke* • Paul Whitsun-Jones *Sergeant Danvers* • Philip Madoc *Byker* • Tony Calvin *Hare* • Susan Brodrick *Susan* ■ *Dir* Roy Ward Baker • *Scr* Brian Clemens, from the novel *The Strange Case of Dr Jekyll and Mr Hyde* by Robert Louis Stevenson

Dr Kildare's Strange Case
★★★

Medical drama   1940 · US · BW · 76min

An even bigger hit than the previous three pictures in the Dr Kildare series (*Young Dr Kildare*, *Calling Dr Kildare*, *The Secret of Dr Kildare*), this fourth film concerns the use of electric shock therapy to cure a mental patient. The medical techniques might be somewhat dated, but the ethical questions remain valid in this snappy entry. Lew Ayres is again the perfect foil for Lionel Barrymore's irascible Dr Gillespie, who is bossed about in turn by Alma Kruger's nurse. RK

Lew Ayres *Dr James Kildare* • Lionel Barrymore *Dr Leonard Gillespie* • Laraine Day *Mary Lamont* • Shepperd Strudwick *Dr Gregory Lane* • Samuel S Hinds *Dr Stephen Kildare* • Emma Dunn *Martha Kildare* • Alma Kruger *Molly Byrd* • Nat Pendleton *Wayman* ■ *Dir* Harold S Bucquet • *Scr* Harry Ruskin, Willis Goldbeck, from a story by Max Brand, Willis Goldbeck

Dr Kildare Goes Home
★★★ U

Medical drama   1940 · US · BW · 78min

The fifth entry in MGM's popular hospital series is one of the few to move the action away from Blair General. Lew Ayres is impeccable as the idealistic young medic, who this time around sacrifices his chances of promotion by going off to help his country doctor father set up a clinic. Veteran character actor Samuel S Hinds plays Kildare's father. RK

Lew Ayres *Dr James Kildare* • Lionel Barrymore *Dr Leonard Gillespie* • Laraine Day *Mary Lamont* • Samuel S Hinds *Dr Stephen Kildare* • Gene Lockhart *George Winslow* • Nat Pendleton *Wayman* ■ *Dir* Harold S Bucquet • *Scr* Harry Ruskin, Willis Goldbeck, from a story by Max Brand, Goldbeck

Dr Kildare's Crisis
★★★

Medical drama   1940 · US · BW · 74min

The "crisis" in the sixth movie in the long-running medic series is one that personally affects young Dr James Kildare (Lew Ayres): his future brother-in-law may be suffering from epilepsy, a disease which could run in the family. Unusually for this B-movie series, the unfortunate patient is played by Robert Young, a star from MGM's A-company. Otherwise the regulars are in place. RK

Lew Ayres *Dr James Kildare* • Robert Young (1) *Douglas Lamont* • Lionel Barrymore *Dr Leonard Gillespie* • Laraine Day *Mary Lamont* • Emma Dunn *Mrs Martha Kildare* • Nat Pendleton *Joe Wayman* • Bobs Watson *Tommy* ■ *Dir* Harold S Bucquet • *Scr* Harry Ruskin, Willis Goldbeck, from a story by Max Brand, Willis Goldbeck

Dr Kildare's Wedding Day
★★★

Medical drama   1941 · US · BW · 82min

Laraine Day was gaining a large following as Mary Lamont, the dedicated nurse and fiancée of Dr Kildare (Lew Ayres), when MGM, who had been grooming her for bigger pictures, decided to have her killed by a truck. The elegant brunette, who had featured in eight Kildare episodes, was never again able to find a distinctive screen image. Up-and-coming comic Red Skelton provides some comic relief in this ironically titled and somewhat gloomy episode. RK

Lew Ayres *Dr James Kildare* • Lionel Barrymore *Dr Leonard Gillespie* • Laraine Day *Mary Lamont* • Red Skelton *Vernon Briggs* • Fay Holden *Mrs Bartlett* • Walter Kingsford *Dr Walter Carew* • Samuel S Hinds *Dr Stephen Kildare* • Nils Asther *Constanzo Labardi* ■ *Dir* Harold S Bucquet • *Scr* Willis Goldbeck, Harry Ruskin, from a story by Ormond Ruthven, Lawrence P Bachmann, from characters by Max Brand

Dr Kildare's Victory
★★★

Medical drama   1941 · US · BW · 92min

His fiancée having been killed off in the previous movie, *Dr Kildare's Wedding Day*, the eponymous medic seeks solace by falling for socialite patient Ann Ayars. This was the only picture in the 15-film series directed by WS Van Dyke, although the style differs not a jot from the others. It was released just before the news broke of Lew Ayres's conscientious objection to the war, which led him to be dropped by MGM. Blair General functioned without him for a further six titles. RK

Lew Ayres *Dr James Kildare* • Lionel Barrymore *Dr Leonard Gillespie* • Robert Sterling *Dr Roger Winthrop* • Ann Ayars *Edith "Cookie" Charles* • Jean Rogers *Annabelle Kirke* • Alma Kruger *Molly Byrd* • Walter Kingsford *Dr Walter Carew* • Nell Craig *Nurse Parker* ■ *Dir* Major WS Van Dyke II [WS Van Dyke] • *Scr* Harry Ruskin, Willis Goldbeck, from a story by Joseph Harrington, from characters by Max Brand

Dr M
★★ 18

Horror thriller   1989 · W Ger/It/Fr · Colour · 111min

Even Claude Chabrol's failures make for more interesting and compelling viewing than the latest bland Hollywood offering. This is a case in point. Set in a futuristic Berlin, the action centres on the evil schemes of Alan Bates, a media mogul who has obviously been modelled on Fritz Lang's hypnotising hoodlum Dr Mabuse. The story is jumbled and the acting unrestrained, but it's worth a look. DP Violence, swearing.

Alan Bates *Dr Marsfeldt* • Jennifer Beals *Sonja Vogler* • Jan Niklas *Klaus Hartmann* • Hanns Zischler *Moser* • Benoît Régent *Stieglitz* • William Berger *Penck* • Alexander Radszun *Engler* ■ *Dir* Claude Chabrol • *Scr* Sollace Mitchell, from a story by Thomas Bauermeister, from the novel *Dr Mabuse, der Spieler* by Norbert Jacques

D

Dr Mabuse, the Gambler
★★★★ PG

Silent crime thriller 1922 · Ger · BW · 270min

Director Fritz Lang's famous anti-totalitarianism silent allegory about a mad professor (Rudolf Klein-Rogge) trying to take over the world could be hard work for today's audiences. Despite being superbly designed, the plots-within-plots, characters in disguises and weird coincidental plot twists might prove childish and tiresome to some. Many, though, will attest to Lang's wit and cleverness at putting one over on the future Nazis by satirising the ideas of fascism. This was originally shown in two halves; the first is the more entertaining. **TS**
DVD BL

Rudolf Klein-Rogge *Dr Mabuse* · Alfred Abel *Graf Told* · Aud Egede Nissen *Cara Carozza* · Gertrude Welcker *Graefin Told* · Paul Richter *Edgar Hull* · Bernhard Goetzke *von Wenk* · Hans Adalbert von Schlettow *Georg* · Georg John *Pesch* ■ *Dir* Fritz Lang · *Scr* Fritz Lang, Thea von Harbou, from the novel *Dr Mabuse, der Spieler* by Norbert Jacques

Dr Morelle – the Case of the Missing Heiress
★

Detective drama 1949 · UK · BW · 73min

The first (and last) of an intended series based on a popular radio detective, this undistinguished B-feature murder mystery is typical of the early postwar output of Hammer before it discovered horror. Directed by Godfrey Grayson, it stars Valentine Dyall as Doctor Morelle, the sleuth who solves the murder of an heiress. **AE**

Valentine Dyall *Dr Morelle* · Julia Lang *Miss Frayle* · Philip Leaver *Samuel Kimber* · Jean Lodge *Cynthia Mason* · Peter Drury *Peter* ■ *Dir* Godfrey Grayson · *Scr* Ambrose Grayson, Roy Plomley, from a radio series by Ernest Dudley and a play by Wilfred Burr

LANDMARK FILM
The first James Bond film premieres on the day the first Beatles single comes out

Dr No
★★★★★ PG

Spy adventure 1962 · UK · Colour · 105min

The James Bond series started in great style with this cleverly conceived dose of sheer escapism that, unlike later episodes, remained true to the essence of Ian Fleming's super-spy novels. Director Terence Young set the 007 standard with terrific action sequences, highly exotic atmosphere and witty humour. There was also the sex, of course, and bikini-clad Ursula Andress couldn't have asked for a better star-making entrance. Looking back, it's understandable why this caused so much excitement as it was entirely different from anything else. Sean Connery is perfect as the debonair and ruthless secret agent with a licence to kill. **AJ** Violence. DVD
BL

Sean Connery *James Bond* · Ursula Andress *Honey* · Joseph Wiseman *Dr No* · Jack Lord *Felix Leiter* · Bernard Lee *"M"* · Anthony Dawson *Professor Dent* · John Kitzmiller *Quarrel* · Zena Marshall *Miss Taro* · Eunice Gayson *Sylvia* · Lois Maxwell *Miss Moneypenny* · Lester Prendergast *Puss Feller* · Reggie Carter *Jones* · Peter Burton *Major Boothroyd* ■ *Dir* Terence Young · *Scr* Richard Maibaum, Johanna Harwood, Berkely Mather, from the novel by Ian Fleming

Dr Phibes Rises Again
★★★ 15

Horror 1972 · UK · Colour · 87min

Vincent Price returns as the ingenious doctor, now in Egypt searching for the elixir of life, but continuing to outwit enemies with macabre murders, each grislier and funnier than the last. While it's not as splendid as *The Abominable Dr Phibes*, this sequel is mounted with lavish care by Robert Fuest, director of several classic episodes of *The Avengers*, and still scores high in the squirm and chuckle departments, thanks to Price's perfect timing and grandiose camp relish. **AJ** DVD
BL

Vincent Price *Dr Anton Phibes* · Robert Quarry *Biederbeck* · Valli Kemp *Vulnavia* · Hugh Griffith *Ambrose* · John Thaw *Shavers* · Keith Buckley

Stuart · Lewis Fiander *Baker* ■ *Dir* Robert Fuest · *Scr* Robert Fuest, Robert Blees, from characters by James Whiton, William Goldstein

Doctor Rhythm
★★ U

Musical comedy 1938 · US · BW · 81min

On the surface, this is a vapid, well below-average Bing Crosby flick. Connoisseurs should note, however, that the wondrous Beatrice Lillie co-stars as one Lorelei Dodge-Blodgett and performs her famous stage and record sketch, *Two Dozen Double Damask Dinner Napkins*. The silly plot, based on a story by O Henry, has Crosby as a doctor pretending to be a cop to stop Lillie's niece marrying a fortune-hunter. **TS**

Bing Crosby *Bill Remsen* · Mary Carlisle *Judy* · Beatrice Lillie *Lorelei Dodge-Blodgett* · Andy Devine *O'Roon* · Laura Hope Crews *Mrs Twombling* ■ *Dir* Frank Tuttle · *Scr* Jo Swerling, Richard Connell, from the story *The Badge of Policeman O'Roon* by O Henry

Dr Seuss' The Cat in the Hat
★★ PG

Fantasy comedy adventure 2003 · US · Colour · 78min

The much-loved children's book gets turned into big-screen mush in this colourful but lifeless adaptation, which makes scant use of Dr Seuss's wonderful rhymes and pacing, instead delivering a horribly self-aware vehicle for Mike Myers's ego. There's little magic or charm here as youngsters Dakota Fanning and Spencer Breslin find a rainy day at home lifted by the mysterious appearance of a giant talking feline. **SF**
DVD

Mike Myers *The Cat* · Alec Baldwin *Quinn* · Kelly Preston *Mom* · Dakota Fanning *Sally* · Spencer Breslin *Conrad* · Amy Hill *Mrs Kwan* · Sean Hayes *Mr Humberfloob/The Fish* · Dan Castellaneta *Thing 1/Thing 2* · Victor Brandt *Narrator* ■ *Dir* Bo Welch · *Scr* Alec Berg, David Mandel, Jeff Schaffer, from the story by Dr Seuss

Dr Seuss' Horton Hears a Who!
★★★★ U

Animated adventure 2008 · US · Colour · 82min

Adapted from a Dr Seuss story, this classy animated fable from the makers of *Ice Age* is a real treat for all ages. Horton the elephant (voiced by Jim Carrey) discovers a speck-sized world on a grain of pollen that is home to the city of Whoville, inhabited by the microscopic Whos. But Whoville is threatened with imminent destruction and, before Horton can even begin to save it, he must convince his fellow jungle folk that the place exists, and that he is not just suffering from some jumbo-sized delusion. The Mayor (voiced by Steve Carell) is the only Who able to communicate with Horton, and in addition to alerting his community to their peril, he also must convey to them that their salvation lies in a bigger, broader world that only he is aware of. This is terrific stuff – colourful, fast and fun. **DA**
DVD BL

Jim Carrey *Horton* · Steve Carell *Mayor of Whoville* · Carol Burnett *Kangaroo* · Dan Fogler *Councilman/Yummo Wickersham* · Laura Ortiz *Jessica* · Seth Rogen *Morton* · Jaime Pressly *Mrs Quilligan* · Isla Fisher *Dr Mary Lou Larue* ■ *Dir* Jimmy Hayward, Steve Martino · *Scr* Ken Daurio, Cinco Paul, from the illustrated children's book by Dr Seuss

Dr Seuss' The Lorax ★★★ U

Animated comedy adventure 2012 · US · Colour · 82min

Set in an entirely artificial world, this psychedelic Dr Seuss story sees a young boy (voiced by Zac Efron) venture outside the city limits to bring back a real tree for the girl of his dreams. There, he encounters the hermit-like Once-ler who destroyed the forest, despite the best efforts of woodland guardian the Lorax (a pleasantly cranky Danny DeVito). The eco-message of the book was ahead of its time when it was published in 1971, but stretching a short tale to feature length means the simplicity of the story is lost. Nevertheless, the catchy songs and heartfelt message mean this is still an enjoyable concoction. **LB** DVD BL
3D

Danny DeVito *The Lorax* · Ed Helms *The Once-ler* · Zac Efron *Ted Wiggins* · Taylor Swift *Audrey* · Betty White *Grammy Norma* ■ *Dir* Chris Renaud, Kyle Balda · *Scr* Ken Daurio, Cinco Paul, from Dr Seuss's illustrated children's book

Dr Socrates
★★★

Crime drama 1935 · US · BW · 71min

Paul Muni was the Marlon Brando of the 1930s, in technique if not in looks. His method of character establishment from the inside out earned him starring roles in many worthy biographies, so this was a welcome change of pace: a gangster thriller in which he plays the small-town doctor who is forced to treat wounded mobsters. There's wonderfully brisk direction by William Dieterle and a blustering performance by Barton MacLane as the gang leader. Remade in 1939 as *King of the Underworld*, starring Humphrey Bogart. **TH**

Paul Muni *Dr Caldwell* · Ann Dvorak *Josephine Gray* · Barton MacLane *Red Bastian* · Raymond Brown *Ben Suggs* · Ralph Remley *Bill Payne* · Hal K Dawson *Mel Towne* ■ *Dir* William Dieterle · *Scr* Robert Lord, Mary C McCall Jr, from a story by WR Burnett

Doctor Strange

Fantasy adventure 2016 · US · Colour

This is a preview – no prints were available to review prior to publication: *Sherlock* star Benedict Cumberbatch will make his much-anticipated debut as Earth's Sorcerer Supreme when the supernatural realm of the Marvel Universe is revealed in 2016. Bursting from the imagination of Spider-Man co-creators Stan Lee and Steve Ditko, Stephen Strange is a brilliant surgeon whose arrogance ruins his career and compels him to seek out mystical aid. Longtime comic-book foes Baron Mordo and Dormammu are rumoured to be the villains but who cares with Cumberbatch weaving spells as Marvel's master of mystic arts. **JA**

Benedict Cumberbatch *Doctor Stephen Strange* · Tilda Swinton *The Ancient One* · Chiwetel Ejiofor *Baron Karl Mordo* · Rachel McAdams *Surgeon* · Mads Mikkelsen *Sorcerer* ■ *Dir* Scott Derrickson · *Scr* Jon Spaihts, Scott Derrickson, C Robert Cargill, from the comic book by Stan Lee (writer), Steve Ditko (artist)

Dr Strangelove, or How I Learned to Stop Worrying and Love the Bomb
★★★★★ PG

Satirical comedy 1963 · UK · BW · 90min

Is this the way the world ends – not with a bang but a simper? Stanley Kubrick's ferocious Cold War satire makes us smile through gritted teeth as unhinged general Sterling Hayden sends a squadron of nuclear bombers to attack Russia and trigger an apocalypse-laden doomsday machine. Peter Sellers's three performances (bemused airman, confused president and crazed US Nazi adviser, re-armed by the prospect of world annihilation) spirals from gentle humour to surreal horror. The scenes in which Hayden raves about "bodily fluids" and Pentagon general George C Scott rants about statistical deaths were obviously inspired by Sellers's genius. Kubrick's unsparing disgust with our warlike instincts was never so obvious nor so grimly comic. **TH** Swearing.
DVD BL

Peter Sellers *Group Captain Lionel Mandrake/President Merkin Muffley/Dr Strangelove* · George C Scott *General "Buck" Turgidson* · Sterling Hayden *General Jack D Ripper* · Keenan Wynn *Colonel "Bat" Guano* · Slim Pickens *Major TJ "King" Kong* · Peter Bull *Ambassador de Sadesky* · Tracy Reed *Miss Scott* · James Earl Jones *Lieutenant Lothar Zogg* ■ *Dir* Stanley Kubrick · *Scr* Stanley Kubrick, Terry Southern, Peter George, from the novel *Red Alert* by Peter George · *Cinematographer* Gilbert Taylor · *Art Director* Ken Adam · *Editor* Anthony Harvey

Dr Syn
★★★ U

Period adventure 1937 · UK · BW · 77min

George Arliss retired from movies after starring in this sprightly 19th-century smuggling adventure. By day the respected vicar of Dymchurch, Arliss uses the cover of darkness to masquerade as the ruthless Dr Syn, daredevil brigand and scourge of the Kent coast. Defying his 69 years and reputation for stuffiness, Arliss gives a rousing performance. **DP**

George Arliss *Dr Syn* · John Loder *Denis Cobtree* · Margaret Lockwood *Imogene* · Roy Emerton *Captain Howard Cobtree* · Graham Moffatt *Jerry Jerk* · Frederick Burtwell *Rash* · George Merritt (1) *Mipps* ■ *Dir* Roy William Neill · *Scr* Roger Burford, Michael Hogan, from the novel by Russell Thorndike

Dr Syn, Alias the Scarecrow
★★★ U

Adventure 1963 · US · Colour · 97min

Patrick McGoohan sails through this Disney frolic as the kindly vicar of Dymchurch by day who becomes the notorious smuggler Dr Syn by night. A host of British acting stalwarts adds to the quaint Georgian atmosphere, augmented by some nice photography (by Paul Beeson) of authentic Kentish locations. Made for American TV, the film was originally shown in three episodes as *The Scarecrow of Romney Marsh* but was released theatrically overseas. **AT**

Patrick McGoohan *Dr Syn* · George Cole *Mr Mipps* · Michael Hordern *Squire Banks* · Tony Britton *Bates* · Geoffrey Keen *General Pugh* · Eric Flynn *Philip Brackenbury* · Kay Walsh *Mrs Waggett* ■ *Dir* James Neilson · *Scr* Robert Westerby, from the novel *Christopher Syn* by Russell Thorndike, William Buchanan

Dr T & the Women ★★ 12

Satirical romance 2000 · US · Colour · 116min

The usually excellent Robert Altman stumbles with this disappointing tale of a gynaecologist who adores women, despite the fact that all the females he knows make his life worse rather than better. While Richard Gere gives a nice, understated performance, the accomplished actresses are stuck with trying to make the best out of some badly written caricatures. **JB** Nudity, sexual references. DVD

Richard Gere *Dr Sullivan "Dr T" Travis* · Helen Hunt *Bree Davis* · Farrah Fawcett *Kate Travis* · Laura Dern *Peggy* · Shelley Long *Carolyn* · Tara Reid *Connie Travis* · Kate Hudson *Dee Dee Travis* · Liv Tyler *Marilyn* ■ *Dir* Robert Altman · *Scr* Anne Rapp

The Doctor Takes a Wife
★★★

Screwball comedy 1940 · US · BW · 88min

A delectable Loretta Young and an amiable Ray Milland co-star in this entertaining screwball comedy. She is a writer and feminist who's opposed to marriage; he teaches at medical school but is angling for promotion to professor. When a publicity stunt leads to their being mistaken for a newly married couple, she smells a new bestseller in the situation, while he discovers that the supposed change in his marital status will bring him his desired professional status. **RK**

Loretta Young *June Cameron* · Ray Milland *Dr Timothy Sterling* · Reginald Gardiner *John Pierce* · Gail Patrick *Marilyn Thomas* · Edmund Gwenn *Dr Lionel Sterling* · Frank Sully *Slapcovitch* ■ *Dir* Alexander Hall · *Scr* George Seaton, Ken Englund, from a story by Aleen Leslie

Dr Terror's House of Horrors
★★★ PG

Horror 1964 · UK · Colour · 93min

Vampires, werewolves, crawling hands, voodoo curses and creeping vines – they're all present and enjoyably correct in the first, and best, fun fright anthology from the Amicus horror factory, Hammer's only real 1960s rival. Peter Cushing is the tarot card reader telling five men on a train their grim fortunes. Director Freddie Francis delivers a fair quota of entertaining shocks with his trademark visual flair, and it's a joy to see DJ-turned-actor Alan Freeman at the mercy of that peculiar writhing plant. **AJ** DVD
BL

Peter Cushing *Dr Schreck* • Christopher Lee *Franklyn Marsh* • Roy Castle *Biff Bailey* • Donald Sutherland *Bob Carroll* • Neil McCallum *Jim Dawson* • Alan Freeman *Bill Rogers* • Max Adrian *Dr Blake* • Edward Underdown *Tod* ■ *Dir* Freddie Francis • *Scr* Milton Subotsky

Dr Who and the Daleks
★★★ U

Science-fiction adventure
1965 · UK · Colour · 79min

The first big-screen outing for the BBC's ever-popular sci-fi TV series has Peter Cushing playing the time-travelling Doctor with amiable aplomb as he pits his wits against those mobile knobbly tin cans forever shrieking "Exterminate". Lacking the bite and inventiveness that set the landmark series apart, this spin-off unwisely injects humour into its sparse scenario. Despite the many faults, it's still a slick slice of enjoyable mayhem. *Daleks - Invasion Earth 2150AD* followed in 1966. AJ *DVD*

Peter Cushing *Dr Who* • Roy Castle *Ian* • Jennie Linden *Barbara* • Roberta Tovey *Susan* • Barrie Ingham *Alydon* • Geoffrey Toone *Temmosus* • Mark Peterson *Elydon* • John Bown *Antodus* • Michael Coles *Ganatus* ■ *Dir* Gordon Flemyng • *Scr* Milton Subotsky, from the BBC TV series by Sydney Newman, from characters by Terry Nation

Doctor X
★★★

Horror
1932 · US · Colour · 76min

This is a weird mix of effective horror, creaky haunted house clichés and dated comic relief, the latter single-handedly disrupting the sombre mood created by director Michael Curtiz as police hunt for the "Full Moon Killer" among a group of eccentric medics. Considered a classic mainly for the scary "synthetic flesh" sequence, the film's more tiresome moments are masked by energetic lead performances. This was the first horror film to be shot in colour. AJ

Lionel Atwill *Dr Xavier* • Fay Wray *Joan Xavier* • Lee Tracy *Lee Taylor* • Preston Foster *Dr Wells* • John Wray *Dr Haines* • Harry Beresford *Dr Duke* • Arthur Edmund Carewe *Dr Rowitz* ■ *Dir* Michael Curtiz • *Scr* Robert Tasker, Earl Baldwin, from a play by Howard W Comstock, Allen C Miller

Doctor Zhivago
★★★★★ PG

Romantic epic
1965 · US · Colour · 191min

This adaptation of Boris Pasternak's classic novel has all the sweep and stateliness that characterised David Lean's mastery of the epic. At its centre is the star-crossed romance between married physician and poet Omar Sharif and dressmaker's daughter Julie Christie, whose passionate encounters are played out against the backdrop of the Great War and the Russian Revolution. The scene is set superbly, thanks largely to John Box's brilliant designs for both the plush and the poverty-ridden quarters of Moscow, and to Freddie Young's atmospheric cinematography. Moreover, the ever-meticulous Lean retains the intimacy of the love story within the sweep of momentous historical events. DP
DVD

Omar Sharif *Yuri Zhivago* • Julie Christie *Lara* • Geraldine Chaplin *Tonya Gromeko* • Rod Steiger *Komarovsky* • Alec Guinness *Yevgraf Zhivago* • Tom Courtenay *Pasha Antipov/Strelnikov* • Ralph Richardson *Alexander* • Siobhan McKenna *Anna Gromeko* • Rita Tushingham *Girl* • Bernard Kay *Bolshevik* • Klaus Kinski *Kostoyed* ■ *Dir* David Lean • *Scr* Robert Bolt, from the novel by Boris Pasternak

The Doctor's Dilemma ★★ U

Comedy
1958 · UK · Colour · 99min

Anthony Asquith fails to breathe life into this fast-fading satire on the foibles of Harley Street. Self-obsessed artist Dirk Bogarde improves the worse his tuberculosis becomes, but Leslie Caron never captures the stubborn devotion that inspires her fight to save him. George Bernard Shaw's comedy might have been scalpel-sharp back in 1903, but the foundation of the National Health Service rather blunted its edge. DP

Leslie Caron *Mrs Jennifer Dubedat* • Dirk Bogarde *Louis Dubedat* • Alastair Sim *Cutler Walpole* • Robert Morley *Sir Ralph Bloomfield-Bonington* • John Robinson (1) *Sir Colenso Ridgeon* • Felix Aylmer *Sir Patrick Cullen* • Peter Sallis *Picture gallery secretary* ■ *Dir* Anthony Asquith • *Scr* Anatole de Grunwald, from the play by George Bernard Shaw

Doctor's Orders
★★ U

Comedy
1934 · UK · BW · 69min

John Mills stars as a medical student whose romantic plans are complicated when his father (Leslie Fuller), a travelling medicine man, is revealed to be a carnival confidence trickster. The result is a flimsy, music hall-style comedy which gives the then-popular Leslie Fuller plenty of opportunities to deliver his trademark bombast as the quack whose heart turns out to be in the right place. AT

Leslie Fuller *Bill Blake* • John Mills *Ronnie Blake* • Marguerite Allan *Gwen Summerfield* • Mary Jerrold *Mary Blake* • Ronald Shiner *Miggs* • Georgie Harris *Duffin* • Felix Aylmer *Sir Daniel Summerfield* • William Kendall *Jackson* ■ *Dir* Norman Lee • *Scr* Clifford Grey, RP Weston, Bert Lee, from a story by Clifford Grey, Syd Courtenay, Lola Harvey

A Doctor's Story
★★★

Drama
1984 · US · Colour

The treatment of the elderly is addressed in this thought-provoking 1984 hospital drama about an ultra-dedicated doctor and his various vulnerable patients. Though dated, the gently engaging TV movie tackles issues that are sadly still relevant today and centres on a physician (Howard E Rollins Jr) who faces friction at home and work as he battles to prove a confused pensioner (Art Carney) isn't senile. The film's so warm and compassionate that some stilted acting and lack of realism scarcely matter. SF

Howard E Rollins Jr *Dr Zack Williams* • Art Carney *Harry Wickes* • Jodi Thelen *Dr Edie Farmer* • Viveca Lindfors *Mrs Kristina Karlberg* ■ *Dir* Peter Levin • *Scr* Ronald Rubin

Doctors' Wives
★★★ 18

Medical drama
1970 · US · Colour · 97min

Based on the principle that "if you can't beat 'em, join 'em", this attempts to be a super-sudsy soap opera like the ones TV was using to gnaw away at cinema attendances. Like *Peyton Place*, it's built around a community going through the usual rituals (neurosis, adultery, murder), though the acting is considerably classier: a young Gene Hackman, Dyan Cannon, Rachel Roberts and Carroll O'Connor. Distinguished screenwriter Daniel Taradash (*Rancho Notorious*) does not distinguish himself. TH

Dyan Cannon *Lorrie Dellman* • Richard Crenna *Pete Brennan* • Gene Hackman *Dave Randolph* • Carroll O'Connor *Joe Gray* • Rachel Roberts (1) *Della Randolph* • Janice Rule *Amy Brennan* • Diana Sands *Helen Straughn* • Ralph Bellamy *Jake Porter* ■ *Dir* George Schaefer • *Scr* Daniel Taradash, from the novel by Frank G Slaughter

Dodes'ka-Den
★★★★ 12

Fantasy drama
1970 · Jpn · Colour · 134min

After a five-year break (during which time he bailed on *Tora! Tora! Tora!*), Akira Kurosawa returned to make his first film in colour. Adapted from a collection of short stories, this affecting study of the hopes, fears and bitter realities of a group of slum dwellers originally ran for 244 minutes. Sensitively played and demonstrating an instinctive genius for colour, the gently paced mix of fantasy and melodrama typifies Kurosawa's essential humanity. Despite receiving an Oscar nomination for best foreign film, it was dismissed by the critics. Soon afterwards, the director attempted suicide. DP Japanese +subtitles. *DVD*

Yoshitaka Zushi *Rokuchan* • Kin Sugai *Rokuchan's mother* • Junzaburo Ban *Yukichi Shima* • Hisashi Igawa *Masuo Masuda* • Hideko Okiyama *Masuda's wife* ■ *Dir* Akira Kurosawa • *Scr* Akira Kurosawa, Hideo Oguni, Shinobu Hashimoto, from a short story collection by Shugoro Yamamoto

Dodge City
★★★★ PG

Western
1939 · US · Colour · 99min

Errol Flynn rides into Dodge, sees that "knavery is rampant" (as *Variety* described it in 1939) and sets about cleaning up the town with military precision. Why Warner Bros couldn't come clean and call him Wyatt Earp is a mystery. It's knockabout stuff, exuberantly directed in lush early Technicolor by Michael Curtiz, and is in sharp contrast to John Ford's later *My Darling Clementine* as well as more recent, revisionist trawls through the Earp legend. Flynn is in swashbuckling mode and Olivia de Havilland, as usual, is the woman in his life. AT

Errol Flynn *Wade Hatton* • Olivia de Havilland *Abbie Irving* • Ann Sheridan *Ruby Gilman* • Bruce Cabot *Jeff Surrett* • Frank McHugh *Joe Clemens* • Alan Hale *Rusty Hart* • John Litel *Matt Cole* • Henry Travers *Dr Irving* ■ *Dir* Michael Curtiz • *Scr* Robert Buckner

Dodgeball: a True Underdog Story
★★★ 12

Sports comedy
2004 · US/Ger · Colour · 88min

This slight and silly comedy features a hyper-energetic Ben Stiller and an almost catatonic Vince Vaughn. Vaughn owns a run-down gym and Stiller wants to take it over. Only by forming a dodgeball team and going to Las Vegas to win $50,000 in the national championships can Vaughn and his ragtag band of under-achievers save the day. Along the way the underdogs are whipped into shape by Rip Torn's insane coach. It's daft, but delivered with a good-natured spirit. GM Swearing, sexual references. *DVD*

Vince Vaughn *Peter La Fleur* • Ben Stiller *White Goodman* • Christine Taylor *Kate Veatch* • Rip Torn *Patches O'Houlihan* • Justin Long *Justin* • Stephen Root *Gordon* • Chris Williams *Dwight* • Hank Azaria *Young Patches O'Houlihan* ■ *Dir/Scr* Rawson Marshall Thurber

Dodsworth
★★★★★ PG

Romantic drama
1936 · US · BW · 96min

William Wyler's masterly film of Sinclair Lewis's novel has Walter Huston, Ruth Chatterton, Mary Astor and David Niven giving wonderful performances. It's a full-blown romance with a darker edge, gleamingly shot and nominated for seven Oscars, winning one for art direction. Producer Sam Goldwyn was offered the book for $20,000 and turned it down, thinking it would make a lousy movie. Sidney Howard subsequently adapted it into a Broadway hit starring Huston and Fay Bainter, and Goldwyn ended up buying the screen rights for $165,000. AT

Walter Huston *Sam Dodsworth* • Ruth Chatterton *Fran Dodsworth* • Paul Lukas *Arnold Iselin* • Mary Astor *Edith Cortright* • David Niven *Lockert* • Gregory Gaye *Kurt von Obersdorf* • Maria Ouspenskaya *Baroness von Obersdorf* • Odette Myrtil *Madame de Penable* ■ *Dir* William Wyler • *Scr* Sidney Howard, from his play, from the novel by Sinclair Lewis • *Art Director* Richard Day

Dog Day Afternoon
★★★★ 15

Crime drama
1975 · US · Colour · 119min

This is a film about a bank robbery, the proceeds of which are needed to pay for a sex-change operation. Weird but apparently true. From this material, Sidney Lumet creates a marvellous patchwork of a movie, cutting through the inept but passionate bank robbers (Al Pacino and John Cazale) whose bungled heist turns into a hostage situation, the corpulent cop leading the police siege (Charles Durning) and the mob that gathers outside the bank. Pacino's performance (which earned him a fourth Oscar nomination) is a multilayered display. AT Violence, swearing. *DVD*

Al Pacino *Sonny Wortzik* • John Cazale *Sal* • Charles Durning *Moretti* • Chris Sarandon *Leon Shermer* • Sully Boyar *Mulvaney* • Penelope Allen *Sylvia* • James Broderick *Sheldon* • Carol Kane *Jenny* • Beulah Garrick *Margaret* ■ *Dir* Sidney Lumet • *Scr* Frank Pierson, from an article by BF Kluge, Thomas Moore • *Cinematographer* Victor J Kemper

Dog Days
★★★ 18

Drama
2001 · Austria/Ger · Colour · 121min

Filmed over three hot Viennese summers, director Ulrich Seidl's award-winning debut feature draws heavily on his documentary experience to give fictional events an unnervingly authentic feel. Bleak humour underlies some of the improvised situations, most notably those involving compulsive hitch-hiker Maria Hofstätter and ageing widower Erich Finsches and his housekeeper, Gerti Lehner. As each vignette is played out before the remorseless camera, a scathing picture of contemporary Austria emerges. DP German +subtitles. *DVD*

Maria Hofstätter *Anna, the hitch-hiker* • Alfred Mrva *Hruby, the alarm systems man* • Erich Finsches *Walter, the old man* • Gerti Lehner *Walter's housekeeper* • Franziska Weiss *Klaudia, the young girl* • Rene Wanko *Mario, Klaudia's boyfriend* ■ *Dir* Ulrich Seidl • *Scr* Ulrich Seidl, Veronika Franz

Dog Eat Dog
★★ 15

Comedy drama
2000 · UK/Ger · Colour · 89min

Director Moody Shoaibi's low-budget film focuses on four cash-strapped Londoners who concoct a scheme to kidnap a celebrity writer's pet dog. But their get-rich-quick scheme goes literally to the dogs when they inadvertently petnap the pooch of a local crime boss (overplayed by Gary Kemp). This young black leads do their best, but this is not as quirky and original as it thinks it is. DA *DVD*

Mark Tonderai *Rooster* • Nathan Constance *Jess* • David Oyelowo *CJ* • Crunski *Chang* • Gary Kemp *Jesus* • Alan Davies *Phil* • Melanie Blatt *Kelly* • Steve Toussaint *Darcy* • Ricky Gervais *Bouncer* ■ *Dir* Moody Shoaibi • *Scr* Moody Shoaibi, Mark Tonderai

A Dog of Flanders
★★ U

Period drama
1999 · US · Colour · 96min

This is the fourth film version of Ouida's famous story, but never before has it been adapted with such disregard for its humbling simplicity. Director Kevin Brodie's bid to make the trials of an orphan artist accessible for today's youngsters is laudable enough and he makes splendid use of the Flemish locations. However, the cast (with the honorable exception of Jack Warden's grandfather) singularly fails to invest the action with human warmth. DP

Jon Voight *Michel La Grande* • Jack Warden *Jehan Daas* • Steven Hartley *Carl Cogez* • Bruce McGill *William the blacksmith* • Jeremy James Kissner *Older Nello* • Jesse James *Young Nello* • Cheryl Ladd *Anna Cogez* ■ *Dir* Kevin Brodie • *Scr* Kevin Brodie, Robert Singer, from the story by Ouida

Dog Park
★★

Romantic comedy
1998 · Can · Colour · 91min

It's a well-known fact that the best way to meet people is by walking the dog, and Bruce McCulloch's film is built around just such a premise. Luke Wilson stars as a recently dumped bloke who gets the hots for Natasha Henstridge in the park; sadly, she only has eyes for her dog. Meanwhile, Wilson's angst at being chucked by Kathleen Robertson is affecting their dog. Fluffy fare. LH

Natasha Henstridge *Lorna* • Luke Wilson *Andy* • Kathleen Robertson *Cheryl* • Janeane Garofalo *Jeri* • Bruce McCulloch *Jeff* • Kristin Lehman *Keiran* • Amie Carey *Rachel* • Gordon Currie *Trevor* ■ *Dir/Scr* Bruce McCulloch

Dog Pound
★★★ 18

Drama
2009 · Fr/Can/UK · Colour · 87min

There have been plenty of films set in prisons, but far fewer concerning incarceration in youth-offender institutions. The 1979 British drama *Scum*, starring a young Ray Winstone, is one notable exception, and it provides the inspiration for this updated, Americanised retread. Set in the harsh environs of a correctional facility for youth offenders in Montana, the story brutally follows the trials and tribulations of three new inmates: drug dealer Davis, car thief Angel and violent offender Butch. The cast of relative unknowns may put off audiences, but it certainly adds a much-needed air of authenticity to proceedings. **DA** Violence. **DVD** **BL**

Adam Butcher *Butch* • Shane Kippel *Davis* • Mateo Morales *Angel* • Taylor Poulin *Banks* • Dewshane Williams *Frank* ■ *Dir* Kim Chapiron • *Scr* Kim Chapiron, Jeremie Delon, from the film *Scum* by Roy Minton

Dog Soldiers ★★★★ 15

Horror   2001 · UK/Lux · Colour · 100min

This British horror is as scary, funny and exhilarating as any Hollywood fright-fest. A bunch of jaded British soldiers on weekend manoeuvres (and hence with limited live ammunition) stumble across the scene of a savage werewolf attack and hightail it to a secluded farmhouse, battling to make it through till dawn against wave after wave of lupine assaults. This is a sensational debut from writer/director Neil Marshall, which explodes into life in the first 20 minutes and rarely pauses for breath. JC **DVD**

Sean Pertwee *Sgt Harry Wells* • Kevin McKidd *Lawrence Cooper* • Liam Cunningham *Capt Richard Ryan* • Emma Cleasby *Megan* • Darren Morfitt *Spoon* • Chris Robson *Joe Kirkley* ■ *Dir/Scr* Neil Marshall

Dog Star Man ★★★★

Experimental silent drama
1964 · US · Colour and BW · 78min

The most brilliant work produced by avant-gardist Stan Brakhage is a masterpiece of superimpositional editing that recalls the pioneering work of Dziga Vertov. Following a prelude, the four parts of the piece (approximating the seasons) trace the stages of human life from cradle to grave, while also frequently alluding to the evolution of artistic endeavour. Utterly devoid of narrative, this dazzling silent collage of frantic camera movements, boldly coloured fragments and poetic diversions is impossible to appreciate in a single viewing. Brakhage later unravelled the multiple imagery for a 270-minute exposition, *The Art of Vision.* DP

Stan Brakhage *Dog Star Man* • Jane Brakhage *Woman* ■ *Dir/Scr* Stan Brakhage

The Dog Who Stopped the War ★★★ U

Drama   1984 · Can · Colour · 85min

This is the story a snowball fight that escalates into a neighbourhood war. Director André Melançon coaxes spirited performances from his young cast, with Cédric Jourde doing well as the cunning peace envoy, but, as you might expect, the hound steals every scene. Glorious photography adds to the enjoyment of this lovely little film from Quebec. DP French dubbed. **DVD**

Cédric Jourde *Luke* • Julien Elie *Mark* • Maripierre Arseneau-d'Anou *Sophie* • Duc Minh Vu *Warren* • Luc Boucher *Johnny* • Gilbert Monette *George* ■ *Dir* André Melançon • *Scr* Danyèle Patenaude • *Cinematographer* François Protat

Dogfight ★★★★ 15

Romantic drama   1991 · US · Colour · 89min

Barely seen on its original release, this poignant drama only emphasises what cinema lost with the death of River Phoenix. Most young actors could have carried off the role of the rookie marine who squires sensitive peacenik Lili Taylor to a pre-Vietnam "ugly date" party. But few would have brought such truth to a story so dependent on genuine emotion. Taylor is equally impressive, swallowing her hurt to discover what lies beneath an exterior necessarily toughened by boot camp. Directed by Nancy Savoca with an impeccable grasp of the mood of Kennedy's America, this is a must for more than just Phoenix fans. DP Violence, swearing

River Phoenix *Birdlace* • Lili Taylor *Rose* • Richard Panebianco *Berzin* • Anthony Clark *Oakie* • Mitchell Whitfield *Benjamin* • Holly Near *Rose Snr* • EG Daily [Elizabeth Daily] *Marcie* ■ *Dir* Nancy Savoca • *Scr* Bob Comfort

Do99ing: a Love Story ★★ 18

Comedy   2009 · UK · Colour · 103min

This tawdry sex comedy starts bullishly, with wannabe journalist Luke Treadaway conducting vox pops around Newcastle as he researches an article on dogging. But the slick intercutting between grainy camcorder footage and night-vision views of gyrating torsos is quickly supplanted by clumsy contrivance, as Treadaway goes snooping with randy cousin Richard Riddell. Rob Hardy's Tyneside vistas splendidly set the scene, but the uninvolving subplots tip the movie into a smutty mix of laugh-free sitcom and softcore 1970s romp. DP Swearing, sex scenes.

Luke Treadaway *Dan* • Kate Heppell *Laura* • Richard Riddell *Rob* • Sammy Dobson [Sammy T Dobson] *Tanya* • Justine Glenton *Sarah* • Michael Socha *Jim* ■ *Dir* Simon Ellis • *Scr* Brock Norman Brock, Michael Groom • *Cinematographer* Robert Hardy [Rob Hardy]

Doghouse ★★★ 15

Comedy horror   2009 · UK · Colour · 85min

A gang of unreconstructed males out to cheer up a divorced pal find their rural bolt hole's been swamped by "man-hating feminist cannibals" in this surprisingly entertaining romp. Although similar in outline to *Lesbian Vampire Killers*, this amusing splatter-fest has more going for it – Dan Schaffer's clever script unfalteringly sends up our heroes' chauvinistic attitudes to womankind in general, not just the scantily clad, virus-infected *femmes fatales* thirsting for their blood. True, it's not quite as satirically sharp as *Shaun of the Dead*, yet it's certainly a smarter outing than its premise would lead you to expect. TJ Violence. swearing. **DVD** **BL**

Danny Dyer *Neil* • Stephen Graham *Vince* • Noel Clarke *Mikey* • Keith-Lee Castle *Patrick* • Emil Marwa *Graham* • Lee Ingleby *Matt* • Terry Stone *Sergeant Gavin Wright* ■ *Dir* Jake West • *Scr* Dan Schaffer

Dogma ★★★★ 15

Religious satire   1999 · US · Colour · 123min

Kevin Smith tackles the subject of religion with a wickedly humorous touch that unsurprisingly offended some Catholic groups when the film was released. Matt Damon and Ben Affleck star as two fallen angels who discover there's a loophole that will allow them back into heaven, obliterating the Earth in the process. Non-believer Linda Fiorentino is called upon to stop them, with the help of two guardians (recurring characters Jay and Silent Bob, played by Jason Mewes and Smith himself). While the film does not work on every level, Smith again delivers a unique script and some terrifically funny performances. JB **DVD**

Ben Affleck *Bartleby* • George Carlin *Cardinal Glick* • Matt Damon *Loki* • Linda Fiorentino *Bethany* • Salma Hayek *Serendipity* • Jason Lee *Azrael* • Jason Mewes *Jay* • Alan Rickman *Metatron* • Chris Rock *Rufus* • Bud Cort *John Doe Jersey* • Alanis Morissette *God* • Kevin Smith (2) *Silent Bob* • Janeane Garofalo *Clinic girl* ■ *Dir/Scr* Kevin Smith (2)

Dogpound Shuffle ★★★

Comedy drama   1974 · Can · Colour · 100min

So often a scene-stealing character actor, Ron Moody gets a rare crack at a lead in this amiable piece of family entertainment. As the one-time vaudevillian desperate to raise $30 to get his beloved pet out of the dog pound, he demonstrates some of the soft-shoe style that made him such a hit as Fagin in *Oliver!* There's also some unselfish support from David Soul, who calls on his experiences as a pop singer for his tuneful turn as the washed-up prizefighter who becomes Moody's song-and-dance partner. DP

Ron Moody *Steps* • David Soul *Pritt* • Pamela McMyler *Pound lady* • Ray Strickland *Mr Lester Jr* • Raymond Sutton *Pound Attendant* ■ *Dir/Scr* Jeffrey Bloom

Dogs ★

Horror   1976 · US · Colour · 89min

This low-budget howler fails to convince with its tale of a pack of killer hounds on the loose in an isolated college campus. David McCallum struggles gamely as a biology professor whose students end up as Winalot chunks. If movies were dogs, this would be a shih tzu. RS

David McCallum (1) *Harlan Thompson* • George Wyner *Michael Fitzgerald* • Eric Server *Jimmy Goodmann* • Sandra McCabe *Caroline Donoghue* • Sterling Swanson *Dr Martin Koppelman* • Holly Harris *Mrs Koppelman* ■ *Dir* Burt Brinckerhoff • *Scr* O'Brian Tomalin

Dogs in Space ★★★★ 18

Drama   1986 · Aus · Colour · 102min

This appealingly quirky snapshot of punk life Down Under in the late 1970s marked the film debut of the INXS singer Michael Hutchence, who plays a heroin-taking wannabe rock star. The film focuses on struggling band Dogs in Space, led by Hutchence, plus their friends and hangers-on as they drift from party to gig to another party. The soundtrack, which mixes Aussie punk with Iggy Pop and Brian Eno, is superb, while the direction – from pop promo man Richard Lowenstein – is surprisingly unflashy. JF **DVD**

Michael Hutchence *Sam* • Saskia Post *Anna* • Nique Needles *Tim* • Deanna Bond *Girl* • Tony Helou *Luchio* • Chris Haywood *Chainsaw man* • Peter Walsh *Anthony* • Laura Swanson *Clare* • *Dir/Scr* Richard Lowenstein

A Dog's Life ★★★ U

Silent comedy   1918 · US · BW · 34min

Fresh from signing cinema's first million-dollar contract, Charlie Chaplin embarked on bringing a little sophistication to the frantic slapstick style that Mack Sennett had devised at Keystone. However, his debut three-reeler is an inconsistent affair, with cloying sentimentality debasing the moments of acute social critique and inspired hilarity. What does emerge, however, is the Tramp's indefatigability, as he and an abandoned mongrel set about stealing sausages from Syd Chaplin's lunch wagon and then delivering Edna Purviance from her dance-hall misery. It's not vintage, but it's amusing nonetheless. DP

Charles Chaplin *Tramp* • Edna Purviance *Bar singer* • Chuck Reisner [Charles Reisner] *Employment agency clerk* • Henry Bergman *Dance hall lady* • Albert Austin *Crook* • Sydney Chaplin [Syd Chaplin] *Lunch wagon owner* ■ *Dir/Scr* Charles Chaplin

The Dogs of War ★★ 15

Action drama   1980 · UK/US · Colour · 102min

Unleashed upon the big screen from Frederick Forsyth's thriller, these hounds unfortunately have been muzzled and boast too few snarls. Christopher Walken plays the disillusioned mercenary caught up in a dastardly plot to take over a West African state, but any possible thrills are overpowered by too much explanation. John Irvin's direction of the macho passions on display is both predictable and unfocused. TH Violence, swearing. **DVD**

Christopher Walken *Jamie Shannon* • Tom Berenger *Drew* • Colin Blakely *North* • Hugh Millais *Endean* • Paul Freeman *Derek* • JoBeth Williams *Jessie* ■ *Dir* John Irvin • *Scr* Gary DeVore, George Malko, from the novel by Frederick Forsyth

Dogtanian – the Movie ★★ U

Animated adventure   1989 · Sp · Colour · 93min

This full-length version of the popular Spanish cartoon series sticks closely to the familiar Dumas story. Like most other animated spin-offs, however, characters who are comfortable companions for 20 minutes become insufferable after an hour. A brash, yappy pup, Dogtanian is the least likeable of the Muskehounds, and we don't get nearly enough of the foxy Cardinal Richelieu as he plots an alliance with England. DP

■ *Dir* Luis Ballester • *Scr* from characters by Claudio Biem Boyd, from the novel *The Three Musketeers* by Alexandre Dumas

Dogtooth ★★★★ 18

Drama   2009 · Gr · Colour · 92min

This enigmatic little Greek nightmare about a dysfunctional family is pitched halfway between horror and satire. Three "children" (they look to be in their early 20s) are confined to an expansive villa, where they are constantly fed misinformation by their parents, until a woman brought into the home by "Father" to provide sex for "Son" upsets the weird dynamic. Reminiscent of the work of Michael Haneke and Lars von Trier, director Yorgos Lanthimos's disquieting, provocative film will strike some as frustratingly ambiguous, others as richly allegorical. AS Greek +subtitles. Violence, sex scenes, incest theme. **DVD** **BL**

Christos Stergioglou *Father* • Michelle Valley *Mother* • Aggeliki Papoulia *Older daughter* • Christos Passalis *Son* • Mary Tsoni *Younger daughter* • Anna Kalaitzidou *Christina* ■ *Dir* Yorgos Lanthimos • *Scr* Yorgos Lanthimos, Efthimis Filippou

Dogtown and Z-Boys ★★★ 15

Documentary   2001 · US · Colour · 90min

Narrated by Sean Penn and recalling the reverential style that characterised Bruce Brown's 1960s surf movies, this is a fond, but fatally self-mythologising memoir of the Zephyr skateboarding team. Known as the Z-Boys, these kids from the run-down LA neighbourhood of Dogtown rode their boards to national celebrity in the mid-1970s and revolutionised this distinctive urban sport. The unfussy contemporary footage of the team performing gravity-defying stunts in both local competitions and drained swimming pools is priceless. Less valuable, however, are the nostalgic insights provided by Jay Adams, Tony Alva and director Stacy Peralta, with the latter in particular suffering from an overblown sense of his own significance. DP Swearing. **DVD**

Sean Penn *Narrator* ■ *Dir* Stacy Peralta • *Scr* Stacy Peralta, Craig Stecyk • *Cinematographer* Peter Pilafian

Dogville ★★★★ 15

Drama
2003 · Den/Swe/UK/Fr/Neth/Ger/Fin/Nor · Colour · 170min

Director Lars von Trier abandons the restrictions that he devised for Dogme 95 and sets himself a new batch of creative dilemmas in this defiantly stylised picture that's played out on a single sound stage, with buildings and landmarks being suggested by outlines and props rather than existing as authentic sets. The ensemble cast is excellent, but it's Nicole Kidman who fixes the attention, playing the Depression-era runaway who places herself at the disposal of the residents of a Rocky Mountain backwater in return for their protection from the Mob. A sobering study in human frailty. (Made with additional funding from Norway, Germany and Finland.) DP Violence. **DVD**

Nicole Kidman *Grace* • Harriet Andersson *Gloria* • Lauren Bacall *Ma Ginger* • Jean-Marc Barr *The man with the big hat* • Paul Bettany *Tom Edison* • Blair Brown *Mrs Henson* • James Caan *The big man* • Patricia Clarkson *Vera* • Jeremy Davies *Bill Henson* • Ben Gazzara *Jack McKay* • Philip Baker Hall *Tom Edison Sr* • Udo Kier *The man in the coat* • Chloë Sevigny *Liz Henson* • Stellan Skarsgård *Chuck* ■ *Dir/Scr* Lars von Trier

Doing Time for Patsy Cline ★★★ 15

Comedy road movie   1997 · Aus · Colour · 92min

Miranda Otto teams up with real-life paramour Richard Roxburgh in a genial Aussie road movie with a country and western twang. Matt Day is a young innocent off to seek fame and fortune in Nashville. En route he hooks up with drug-dealing rogue Roxburgh and his redheaded girlfriend Otto, who harbours her own dreams of stardom. Things go pear-shaped when the trio get busted by the police. Attractively played by the three leads, the end result has a rich vein of self-mocking humour that leavens the rather heavy-handed stab at third-act pathos. NS **DVD**

Matt Day *Ralph* • Richard Roxburgh *Boyd* • Miranda Otto *Patsy* • Gus Mercurio *Tyrone* • Tony Barry *Dwayne* • Kiri Paramore *Ken* ■ *Dir/Scr* Chris Kennedy (1)

La Dolce Vita ★★★★★ 15
Classic drama 1960 · It/Fr · BW · 167min

Winner of the Palme d'Or at Cannes, this sprawling, scathing satire on the decadence of contemporary Italy and the hypocrisy of the Catholic Church confirmed Federico Fellini's reputation for flamboyant, controversial imagery. Marcello Mastroianni is outstanding as the journalist who, by day, jostles with the paparazzi in the hunt for movie stars, miraculous visitations and flying statues of Christ. By night, he indulges his passion for intellectual pretension and the indolent delights of the jet set. A dire warning that Italy was still politically and socially prone to the false promises of fascism, this almost Dante-esque odyssey so drained its Oscar-nominated director, he did not make another feature for three years. DP Italian +subtitles. Violence, swearing. **DVD** **BD**

Marcello Mastroianni *Marcello Rubini* • Anita Ekberg *Sylvia* • Anouk Aimée *Maddalena* • Yvonne Furneaux *Emma* • Magali Noël *Fanny* • Alain Cuny *Steiner* • Nadia Gray *Nadia* • Lex Barker *Robert* • Annibale Ninchi *Marcello's father* ■ *Dir* Federico Fellini • *Scr* Federico Fellini, Ennio Flaiano, Tullio Pinelli, Brunello Rondi, from a story by Federico Fellini, Ennio Flaiano, Tullio Pinelli

Dolina Mira ★★★
Second World War drama
1956 · Yug · BW · 82min

John Kitzmiller was still a GI when he was first cast in such neorealist classics as Roberto Rossellini's *Paisà* (1946), but it was the African-American's performance in this Yugoslav drama that earned him the best actor prize at Cannes. Again playing a Second World War soldier, Kitzmiller strikes up a charming relationship with Evelyne Wohlfeiler and the other waifs he encounters on their search for a valley that has escaped the Nazi blight. DP In Slovenian.

John Kitzmiller • Evelyne Wohlfeiler *Lotti* • Tugo Stiglic *Marko* • Boris Kralj *Strumfuhrer* • Maks Furijan *Scharfuhrer* • Cuk Janez *Vodnik* ■ *Dir* France Stiglic • *Scr* Ivan Ribic

Dollar ★★★
Comedy 1938 · Swe · BW · 88min

Having found stardom in romantic melodramas, Ingrid Bergman took a bit of a risk making this frantic comedy. As usual, she carried it off with the ease and grace that made her one of the finest actresses in cinema history. What with illicit romances, false suspicions, gambling debts, stock market crashes, secret pacts and mysterious illnesses, the plot concocted by Gustaf Molander takes credibility to its elastic limit. DP Swedish +subtitles.

Georg Rydeberg *Kurt Balzar* • Ingrid Bergman *Julia Balzar* • Kotti Chave *Louis Brenner* • Tutta Rolf *Sussi Brenner* • Håkan Westergren *Ludvig von Bathwyhl* • Birgit Tengroth *Katja* • Elsa Burnett *Mary Jonstone* • Edvin Adolphson *Dr Jonsson* ■ *Dir* Gustaf Molander • *Scr* Stina Bergman, Gustaf Molander, from the play by Hjalmar Bergman

Dollar for the Dead ★★ PG
Western 1998 · US · Colour · 94min

This is a commendable but flawed attempt to re-create the spaghetti western style of Sergio Leone, right down to shooting on the same Spanish sets Leone used. Director Gene Quintano also recalls John Woo in the two-fisted action and nonstop gunplay that feature throughout. Emilio Estevez comes to the aid of a crippled Civil War veteran (William Forsythe), and the pair hitch up to re-assemble a treasure map embossed on four leather holsters. Out to stop them are

"The Regulators" and a renegade troop of US cavalry. JF **DVD**

Emilio Estevez *The Cowboy* • William Forsythe *Dooley* • Howie Long *Reager* • Joaquim de Almeida *Friar Ramon* • Jonathan Banks *Skinner* • Ed Lauter *Colby* • Lance Kinsey *Tracker* • Jordi Mollà *Federal Captain* ■ *Dir/Scr* Gene Quintano

Dollars ★★★ 15
Crime comedy 1971 · US · Colour · 120min

Never anything less than hugely enjoyable, this often frantic caper stars Warren Beatty as a bank security expert dedicated to crime and Goldie Hawn as his happy hooker accomplice. Although there is little chemistry between the leads and the direction is occasionally over-elaborate, the thefts from the deposit boxes of three criminal heavies are conducted with training-manual precision, while the finale has all the intricacy of a Buster Keaton chase. DP

Warren Beatty *Joe Collins* • Goldie Hawn *Dawn Divine* • Gert Fröbe *Mr Kessel* • Robert Webber *Attorney* • Scott Brady *Sarge* • Arthur Brauss *Candy Man* • Robert Stiles *Major* ■ *Dir/Scr* Richard Brooks

The Dollmaker ★★★★ PG
Drama 1984 · US · Colour · 137min

This was Jane Fonda's first venture into small-screen movies, and she won an Emmy for her performance. After her husband lands a key wartime job in Detroit, Fonda's only escape from the trials of raising five children away from their Kentucky home comes from carving wooden dolls. The star reveals an intensity which has often been missing in the latter part of her career, although it helps that she's working with superior material. DP

Jane Fonda *Gertie Nevels* • Levon Helm *Clovis Nevels* • Geraldine Page *Mrs Kendrick* • Amanda Plummer *Marnie Childers* • Susan Kingsley *Sophronie* • Ann Hearn *Max* • Bob Swan *Victor* • Nikki Creswell *Cassie Nevels* • David Dawson *Amos Nevels* ■ *Dir* Daniel Petrie • *Scr* Susan Cooper, Hume Cronyn, from the novel by Harriette Arnow

Dolls ★★ 18
Comedy horror 1987 · US · Colour · 74min

A novel variation on the 1980s "stalk and slash" movie, replacing the usual lone killer with knife-wielding mannequins. Director Stuart Gordon carved out something of a niche for himself as a gore fiend with such films as *Re-Animator*, but this film – about a disparate group of travellers holed up in a spooky mansion inhabited by an ageing couple who make homicidal puppets – is fairly restrained and has a perverse sense of humour. RS **DVD**

Ian Patrick Williams *David Bower* • Carolyn Purdy-Gordon *Rosemary Bower* • Carrie Lorraine *Judy Bower* • Guy Rolfe *Gabriel Hartwicke* • Hilary Mason *Hilary Hartwicke* • Bunty Bailey *Isabel Prange* • Cassie Stuart *Enid Tilley* • Stephen Lee *Ralph Morris* ■ *Dir* Stuart Gordon • *Scr* Ed Naha

Dolls ★★★★ 12
Drama 2002 · Jpn · Colour · 108min

Opening with a traditional *bunraku* puppet production of 18th-century playwright Monzaemon Chikamatsu's *The Courier for Hell*, this highly stylised and mournfully elegiac study of doomed romance recalls director Takeshi Kitano's previous production, *Hana-Bi*. Cinematographer Katsumi Yanagijima gloriously captures the colours of the changing seasons, as Kitano links three tales that demonstrate the exquisite agony of love: a young careerist seeks to atone for his jilted fiancée's maddening grief; an elderly yakuza hopes to re-ignite a forgotten passion; and a fan endures blindness to prove his fidelity to a disfigured pop star. The stately pacing may dissuade some, but the subtle symbolism and exquisite staging will have most viewers falling under its hypnotic spell. DP Japanese +subtitles. **DVD**

Miho Kanno *Sawako* • Hidetoshi Nishijima *Matsumoto* • Tatsuya Mihashi *Hiro, the boss* • Chieko Matsubara *Ryoko, the woman in the park*

• Kyoko Fukada *Haruna Yamaguchi, the pop star* • Tsutomu Takeshige *Nukui, the fan* ■ *Dir/Scr* Takeshi Kitano

A Doll's House ★★★
Drama 1973 · US · Colour · 95min

Derived from the 1971 Broadway production directed by Patrick Garland, this version of Ibsen's classic play about the way marriage straitjackets women stars Claire Bloom as Nora, the flirtatious child-wife who gradually takes on an independence of spirit that resounds like the final slam of the symbolic door. She has some fine support by Anthony Hopkins and Ralph Richardson, though the result is a bit too earnest. TH

Claire Bloom *Nora Helmer* • Anthony Hopkins *Torvald Helmer* • Ralph Richardson *Dr Rank* • Denholm Elliott *Krogstad* • Anna Massey *Kristine Linde* • Edith Evans *Anne-Marie* ■ *Dir* Patrick Garland • *Scr* Christopher Hampton, from the play by Henrik Ibsen

A Doll's House ★★★★ PG
Drama 1973 · UK · Colour · 102min

This adaptation (by playwright David Mercer) of Ibsen's play appeared at the same time as the other 1973 version. Directed by Joseph Losey, however, it's the more cinematic, with its use of location (Norway) and camerawork (a mobile witness of events). Jane Fonda as Nora speaks up a little too blatantly for early women's liberation, but David Warner and Trevor Howard sustain Ibsen's then-revolutionary arguments with a subtlety that carries the play's message across time. TH **DVD**

Jane Fonda *Nora* • David Warner *Torvald* • Trevor Howard *Dr Rank* • Delphine Seyrig *Kristine Linde* • Edward Fox *Krogstad* • Anna Wing *Anne-Marie* ■ *Dir* Joseph Losey • *Scr* David Mercer, from the play by Henrik Ibsen

The Dolly Sisters ★★★ PG
Musical biography 1945 · US · Colour · 109min

Produced by vaudeville legend George Jessel, this zesty biopic of Hungarian singing sensations Jenny and Rosie Dolly was tailor-made for the talents of Betty Grable and June Haver. The story follows a predictable route as the girls bid farewell to cuddly uncle SZ Sakall to make it big the world over and romance John Payne and Frank Latimore respectively. Blending period and newly penned tunes (including the Oscar-nominated *I Can't Begin to Tell You*), this colourful turn-of-the-century romp became one of 20th Century-Fox's most profitable musicals. DP **DVD**

Betty Grable *Jenny* • June Haver *Rosie* • John Payne *Harry Fox* • SZ Sakall *Uncle Latsie* • Reginald Gardiner *Duke* • Frank Latimore *Irving Netcher* ■ *Dir* Irving Cummings • *Scr* John Larkin, Marian Spitzer

Dolores Claiborne ★★★★ 18
Mystery drama 1995 · US · Colour · 126min

Kathy Bates, who won an Oscar for her performance in the film version of Stephen King's novel *Misery*, here stars in another King adaptation, this time as a housekeeper accused of killing her elderly employer. Jennifer Jason Leigh co-stars as Bates's daughter, who suspects her mother is guilty of more than one killing. There are magnificent portrayals all round, especially from Christopher Plummer as a retired and vengeful cop, but Bates steals every scene. TH Violence, swearing. **DVD**

Kathy Bates *Dolores Claiborne* • Jennifer Jason Leigh *Selena St George* • Judy Parfitt *Vera Donovan* • Christopher Plummer *Detective John Mackey* • David Strathairn *Joe St George* • Eric Bogosian *Peter* • John C Reilly *Constable Frank Stamshaw* • Ellen Muth *Young Selena* ■ *Dir* Taylor Hackford • *Scr* Tony Gilroy, from the novel by Stephen King

Dolphin Tale ★★★ U
Drama based on a true story
2011 · US · Colour · 107min

Inspired by unlikely real-life events, this uplifting drama follows an introverted schoolboy (Nathan Gamble) through a life-changing summer. He discovers an injured dolphin stranded on the beach and his

decision to help marks the beginning of a journey of recovery for both animal and boy. Morgan Freeman is his usual entertaining self as a prosthetics expert, with Harry Connick Jr and Kris Kristofferson offering solid support as Gamble's widowed father and old-salt grandfather. There's little point in berating director Charles Martin Smith for milking every moving moment for maximum emotion: the dolphin's battle to survive is an affecting one, so maybe the film can be forgiven for occasionally ladling on the schmaltz. SuR **BD**

Nathan Gamble *Sawyer Nelson* • Harry Connick Jr *Dr Clay Haskett* • Ashley Judd *Lorraine Nelson* • Kris Kristofferson *Reed Haskett* • Morgan Freeman *Dr Cameron McCarthy* ■ *Dir* Charles Martin Smith • *Scr* Karen Janszen, Noam Dromi

Dolphin Tale 2 ★★★ U
Drama based on a true story
2014 · US · Colour · 107min

The true-life story of a dolphin named Winter and her prosthetic tail continues in this sweet and satisfying follow-up to the surprise 2011 family hit. Like the first film, this sequel's infectiously upbeat tone and laudable message is hard not to fall for, as Winter and the marine biologists who saved her face new problems. All the original cast return (including Harry Connick Jr, Ashley Judd, Morgan Freeman and Sawyer Nelson), but in the end, it's the feel-good animal antics that really appeal. JL **DVD** **BD**

Harry Connick Jr *Dr Clay Haskett* • Ashley Judd *Lorraine Nelson* • Morgan Freeman *Dr Cameron McCarthy* • Nathan Gamble *Sawyer Nelson* • Kris Kristofferson *Reed Haskett* • Cozi Zuehlsdorff *Hazel Haskett* ■ *Dir* Charles Martin Smith • *Scr* Charles Martin Smith, from characters by Karen Janszen, Noam Dromi

Dom Hemingway ★★★★ 15
Black comedy crime drama
2013 · UK · Colour · 89min

Jude Law trashes his slick matinee-idol image once and for all as the title character in this uneven but sporadically hilarious black comedy that finds him as a violent, podgy, balding safecracker released after serving 12 years inside. He heads to the south of France to collect a reward for keeping his mouth shut in prison, but fate has other plans for him. Despite some cartoonish scenes, Law commands the screen throughout, even rallying the film to an emotional climax involving his far-from-thrilled-to-see-him daughter (*Game of Thrones* star Emilia Clarke). DW Violence, swearing, drug abuse, a sex scene, nudity. **DVD** **BD**

Jude Law *Dom Hemingway* • Richard E Grant *Dickie Black* • Demián Bechir [Demian Bichir] *Mr Fontaine* • Emilia Clarke *Evelyn* • Kerry Condon *Melody* • Jumayn Hunter *Lestor* ■ *Dir/Scr* Richard Shepard • *Cinematographer* Giles Nuttgens

Domestic Disturbance ★★★ 12
Thriller 2001 · US · Colour · 85min

Vince Vaughn plays a monstrous stepfather with such finger-licking menace that even good-guy John Travolta has a job keeping up with his sinister machinations. Travolta plays the divorced father who is drawn into ex-wife Teri Polo's life with wealthy new husband Vaughn when son Matt O'Leary witnesses his stepdad's particular brand of murder and mayhem. This keeps up the suspense quotient, but can't overcome its stereotypical treatment of characters and events. TH **DVD**

John Travolta *Frank Morrison* • Vince Vaughn *Rick Barnes* • Teri Polo *Susan Morrison Barnes* • Matt O'Leary *Danny Morrison* • Ruben Santiago-Hudson *Sgt Edgar Stevens* • Susan Floyd *Diane* • Angelica Torn *Patty* • Steve Buscemi *Ray Coleman* ■ *Dir* Harold Becker • *Scr* Lewis Colick, from a story by Lewis Colick, William S Comanor, Gary Drucker

Dominick and Eugene ★★★ 15

Drama 1988 · US · Colour · 104min

Have the Kleenex handy when you watch this heart-rending tale of brotherly love, originally known here as *Nicky and Gino*. In a welcome change from his more usual villainous roles, Ray Liotta is a bright medical student devoted to his mentally disabled twin, Tom Hulce. But, if Liotta pursues his career, who will look after his brother? Overly sentimental perhaps, but compassionate and superbly played by the two leads. AJ Violence, swearing.

Tom Hulce *Dominick "Nicky" Luciano* · Ray Liotta *Eugene "Gino" Luciano* · Jamie Lee Curtis *Jennifer Reston* · Todd Graff *Larry "Snake" Higgins* · Bill Cobbs *Jesse Johnson* · David Strathairn *Martin Chernak* ■ *Dir* Robert M Young · *Scr* Alvin Sargent, Corey Blechman, from a story by Danny Porfirio

Dominion: Prequel to the Exorcist ★★ 15

Horror thriller 2005 · US · Colour · 111min

When director Paul Schrader screened his cut of this *Exorcist* prequel to studio executives they were so appalled by what they saw as its "lack of horror" they fired him and reshot the film from scratch with action director Renny Harlin at the helm (the resulting film was released under the title *Exorcist: the Beginning*). Schrader's version is only marginally better than Harlin's, and the plot details are similar: Stellan Skarsgård plays a young Father Merrin who, wracked with guilt over his inability to prevent a Nazi massacre, winds up in East Africa where he confronts the demon Pazuzu for the first time. The pace is slightly slower and a little creepier, but it's still a plodding, mostly unscary rehash. AS
DVD

Stellan Skarsgård *Father Lankester Merrin* · Gabriel Mann *Father Francis* · Clara Bellar *Rachel Lesno* · Ralph Brown (2) *Sergeant Major* · Billy Crawford *Cheche* · Israel Adurama *Jomo* · Andrew French *Chuma* · Antonie Kamerling *Kessel* · Julian Wadham *Major Granville* · Eddie Osei *Emekwi* ■ *Dir* Paul Schrader · *Scr* Caleb Carr, William Wisher

Dominique ★★

Thriller 1978 · UK · Colour · 99min

This daft thriller – about a husband who drives his crippled wife mad and then has to cope with her ghostly presence after she dies – is a variation on the old haunted house routine that offers few surprises and a lot of padding. The cast, however, is good, but action movie director Michael Anderson denies us the jolts the story promises. AT

Cliff Robertson *David Ballard* · Jean Simmons *Dominique Ballard* · Jenny Agutter *Ann Ballard* · Simon Ward *Tony Calvert* · Ron Moody *Doctor Rogers* · Judy Geeson *Marjorie Craven* · Michael Jayston *Arnold Craven* · Flora Robson *Mrs Davis* · David Tomlinson *Solicitor* · Jack Warner *George* ■ *Dir* Michael Anderson · *Scr* Edward Abraham, Valerie Abraham

Domino ★★ 15

Action thriller 2005 · Fr/US · Colour · 122min

Tony Scott takes his overblown style of film-making to new levels of superficiality in this frenetic film inspired by the true story of the late Domino Harvey, daughter of actor Laurence Harvey. Harvey (played by Keira Knightley) swapped her privileged life for bounty hunting. The initial set-up is slick and exciting, with Knightley enjoyably tongue-in-cheek as the sultry bad girl. Unfortunately, the characters and plotline remain underdeveloped. SF Swearing, violence. *DVD* Blu-ray

Keira Knightley *Domino Harvey* · Mickey Rourke *Ed Moseby* · Edgar Ramirez *Choco* · Lucy Liu *Taryn Miles* · Mena Suvari *Kimmie* · Christopher Walken *Mark Heiss* · Jacqueline Bisset *Sophie Wynn* · Jerry Springer · Rizwan Abbasi [Riz Abbasi] *Alf* ■ *Dir* Tony Scott · *Scr* Richard Kelly, from a story by Kelly, Steve Barancik

The Domino Principle ★★ 15

Political thriller 1977 · US · Colour · 97min

This feeble thriller – also known as *The Domino Killings* – has Gene Hackman as an expert marksman sprung from prison by an unnamed government agency and assigned to shoot an international bigwig. Adam Kennedy adapts his own novel, while director Stanley Kramer assembles a first-rate cast. The result, however, is a third-rate intrigue that is neither deep nor complex – just obscure. TH

Gene Hackman *Roy Tucker* · Candice Bergen *Ellie* · Richard Widmark *Tagge* · Mickey Rooney *Spiventa* · Edward Albert *Ross Pine* · Eli Wallach *General Tom Reser* · Ken Swofford *Warden Ditcher* ■ *Dir* Stanley Kramer · *Scr* Adam Kennedy, from his novel

Don Giovanni ★★★ 12

Opera 1979 · Fr/It/W Ger · Colour · 169min

Joseph Losey spent much time in France towards the end of his career, and it was there that he made this labour of love. Mozart's opera tells of a libertine who is offered redemption by the father of one of his conquests; it has been filmed many times, though never as sumptuously as this. Beautiful scenery and voices make this ideal for those who love opera but can't afford Covent Garden prices. FL Italian +subtitles.
DVD

Ruggero Raimondi *Don Giovanni* · John Macurdy *The Commander* · Edda Moser *Donna Anna* · Kiri Te Kanawa *Donna Elvira* · Kenneth Riegel *Don Ottavio* · José Van Dam *Leporello* · Teresa Berganza *Zerlina* · Malcolm King *Masetto* ■ *Dir* Joseph Losey · *Scr* Patricia Losey, Joseph Losey, Frantz Salieri, from the opera *Don Giovanni* by Wolfgang Amadeus Mozart, Lorenzo Da Ponte

Don Jon ★★★★ 18

Comedy 2013 · US · Colour · 90min

Former *Third Rock from the Sun* child star Joseph Gordon-Levitt shows his indie influences in his surprisingly full-on directing debut, the raunchy but deftly handled tale of a modern Don Juan with a major internet porn addiction. Gordon-Levitt is the pumped-up gym bunny who meets his match, and tries to mend his ways, after meeting a pneumatic Scarlett Johansson. It's a very unusual comedy, and Gordon-Levitt goes surprisingly far with the boorish but oddly likeable antihero, but he produces a final twist with a satisfyingly positive note that doesn't feel forced or preachy. DW Swearing, sex scenes, nudity, drug abuse.

Joseph Gordon-Levitt *Jon Martello, "Don Jon"* · Scarlett Johansson *Barbara* · Julianne Moore *Esther* · Rob Brown *Bobby* · Glenne Headly *Angela* · Brie Larson *Monica* · Tony Danza *Jon Sr* ■ *Dir/Scr* Joseph Gordon-Levitt

Don Juan ★★★★

Silent romantic drama 1926 · US · BW · 93min

Historically important, this was Warner Bros' (and indeed Hollywood's) first synchronised sound movie. No dialogue or songs – they would come the following year with *The Jazz Singer* – the film has a synchronised score and some pointed (though shamefully non-synchronised) sound effects. Yet this would have been a spectacular success with or without sound, the title role being tailor-made for the great John Barrymore, who clearly revels in the part. The beautiful young Mary Astor reforms the Don, while Estelle Taylor makes a super Lucretia Borgia. The expensive production is exceptionally well directed by Alan Crosland. TS

John Barrymore *Don Juan* · Mary Astor *Adriana Della Varnese* · Willard Louis *Perdillo* · Estelle Taylor *Lucretia Borgia* · Helene Costello *Rena, Adriana's maid* · Myrna Loy *Maria, Lucretia's maid* · Jane Winton *Beatrice* · John Roche *Leandro* · Warner Oland *Caesar Borgia* ■ *Dir* Alan Crosland · *Scr* Bess Meredyth, from the poem by Lord Byron

Don Juan DeMarco ★★★★ 15

Romantic drama 1995 · US · Colour · 93min

Lunatics take over the asylum in this enchanting feel-good fable that showcases Johnny Depp as the world's greatest lover on the verge of suicide. Burnt-out shrink Marlon Brando must prick the cod Casanova's fantasy bubble in therapy sessions, where his exaggerated Mexican past and hopelessly romantic conquests are revealed in mythic flashback, or have him committed. Instead, through Depp's grandiose, poetic delusions, Brando re-examines the importance of passion in his own marriage to Faye Dunaway. A scintillating lyrical tone makes this film a wonderfully funny, touching odyssey. AJ Swearing, nudity. *DVD*

Marlon Brando *Jack Mickler* · Johnny Depp *Don Juan DeMarco* · Faye Dunaway *Marilyn Mickler* · Géraldine Pailhas *Dona Ana* · Bob Dishy *Dr Paul Showalter* · Rachel Ticotin *Dona Inez* · Talisa Soto *Dona Julia* ■ *Dir* Jeremy Leven · *Scr* Jeremy Leven, from a character created by Lord Byron

Don Juan 73, or If Don Juan Were a Woman ★★ 18

Drama 1973 · Fr/It · Colour · 89min

Brigitte Bardot still looks stunning at 39, but her films were not getting much better; this was one of the last she made before vanishing from showbusiness altogether. Roger Vadim's movie centres on three traumatic affairs involving the same libertine woman. Notorious for a lesbian bed scene between Bardot and British actress Jane Birkin, this marked the first time the French superstar had ever appeared full-frontal before cameras. RS French dubbed.

Brigitte Bardot *Jeanne* · Jane Birkin *Clara* · Maurice Ronet *Pierre* · Mathieu Carrière *Paul* · Robert Hossein *Prevost* · Michèle Sand *Leporella* · Robert Walker Jr *Young Spaniard* ■ *Dir* Roger Vadim · *Scr* Jean Cau, Roger Vadim, Jean-Pierre Petrolacci

Don King: Only in America ★★★

Biographical drama 1997 · US · Colour · 116min

Ving Rhames gives a Golden Globe-winning performance in this TV biopic. Don King overcame countless obstacles in his bid to become the most flamboyant and, possibly, the most powerful promoter in the fight game. However, while director John Herzfeld is prepared to explore King's dealings with organised crime, white supremacists and various other self-seekers, he doesn't always show how King managed to turn situations to his advantage. Thus, King emerges as an all-American maverick whose success matters more than his methods. DP

Ving Rhames *Don King* · Vondie Curtis-Hall *Lloyd Price* · Jeremy Piven *Hank Schwartz* · Darius McCrary *Muhammad Ali* · Keith David *Herbert Muhammad* ■ *Dir* John Herzfeld · *Scr* Kario Salem, from the non-fiction book *Only In America: The Life and Crimes of Don King* by Jack Newfield

Don Q, Son of Zorro ★★★

Silent swashbuckling adventure 1925 · US · BW · 111min

Here's an early version of the Zorro tale, with the original swashbuckling hero, Douglas Fairbanks, playing both father and son. In fact, Fairbanks had already played the swish swordsmith in *The Mark of Zorro* in 1920, but this time round he had more money and Mary Astor as his co-star. While due allowance should be made for the histrionic acting, this remains a key Fairbanks adventure, with spectacular sets and rousing action. AT

Douglas Fairbanks *Don Cesar de Vega/Zorro* · Mary Astor *Dolores de Muro* · Donald Crisp *Don Sebastian* · Stella de Lanti *The Queen* · Warner Oland *Archduke Paul of Austria* · Jean Hersholt *Don Fabrique* · Albert MacQuarrie *Col Matsado* · Lottie Pickford Forrest *Lola* ■ *Dir* Donald Crisp · *Scr* Jack Cunningham · *Art Director* Edward M Langley

Don Quixote ★★★ U

Musical adventure drama 1932 · UK/Fr · BW · 78min

Cervantes's epic novel had already been adapted nine times before the exiled GW Pabst shot this rather stilted version with the great Russian vocalist Feodor Chaliapin. The supporting cast depended on the language you spoke: George Robey played the English Sancho Panza, while Dorville was his French counterpart. Chaliapin, who occasionally exceeds his thespian limitations, still produces moments of real pathos. Pabst is ill-served by song composer Jacques Ibert, but the cinematography is sublime. DP

Feodor Chaliapin *Don Quixote* · George Robey *Sancho Panza* · Sidney Fox *The Niece* · Miles Mander *The Duke* · Oscar Asche *Police Captain* · Dannio Carrasco · Emily Fitzroy *Sancho's wife* · Frank Stanmore *Priest* ■ *Dir* GW Pabst · *Scr* Paul Morand, Alexandre Arnoux, from the novel *El Ingenioso Hidalgo Don Quijote de la Mancha* by Miguel de Cervantes Saavedra · *Cinematographers* Nikolas Farkas [Nicolas Farkas], Paul Portier

Don Quixote ★★★★★ PG

Adventure 1957 · USSR · Colour · 101min

Having already played Alexander Nevsky and Ivan the Terrible for Eisenstein, Nikolai Cherkassov confirmed his status as one of Soviet cinema's finest actors by playing Cervantes's eccentric knight. With the Crimea standing in for the Spanish plains, the film achieves a picaresque sweep through Grigori Kozintsev's majestic use of widescreen colour. Assuredly staging such classic episodes as the encounter with the windmills, he wisely prevents the finale from becoming too maudlin. Yet it's the delightful performances that sustain the novel's wit and warmth, with Cherkassov expertly conveying Quixote's delusional pride and naive idealism, and Yuri Tolubeyev bringing an earthy loyalty to Sancho Panza. DP Russian dubbed. *DVD*

Nikolai Cherkassov *Don Quixote* · Yuri Tolubeyev *Sancho Panza* · T Agamirova *Altisidora* · V Freindlich *Duke* · L Vertinskaya *Duchess* · G Vitsin *Carrasco* · L Kasyanova *Aldonsa* ■ *Dir* Grigori Kozintsev · *Scr* Yevgeni Shvarts, from the novel *El Ingenioso Hidalgo Don Quijote de la Mancha* by Miguel de Cervantes Saavedra

Don Quixote ★★★ U

Dance 1973 · Aus · Colour · 111min

Co-directed by Robert Helpmann and Rudolf Nureyev, this film of Marius Petipa's light-hearted romantic ballet doesn't have much to do with tilting windmills. Instead it deals with a barber (Nureyev) who woos and wins his sweetheart with the aid of Helpmann's misguided knight and Sancho Panza (Ray Powell). Cinematographer Geoffrey Unsworth uses overhead shots to capture the full scale of the action; as a result, you feel as if you're in the frame instead of just watching it. FL

Robert Helpmann *Don Quixote* · Ray Powell *Sancho Panza* · Rudolf Nureyev *Basilio* · Francis Croese *Lorenzo* · Lucette Aldous *Kitri* · Colin Peasley *Gamache* · Marilyn Rowe *Street dancer* · Kelvin Coe *Espada* ■ *Dir* Rudolf Nureyev, Robert Helpmann

Don Quixote ★★★ PG

Adventure drama 2000 · US · Colour · 139min

John Lithgow and Bob Hoskins headline Peter Yates's marathon TV feature. Lithgow is quite magnificent in a role he'd long hoped to play. He invites genuine pathos as the delusional knight whose undimmed sense of chivalry is responsible for sending devoted squire Sancho Panza in search of challenges to please the fair Dulcinea. The Spanish locations are exploited to the full, but Yates finds no solution to the fragmentary nature of the novel. DP *DVD*

John Lithgow *Don Quixote/Don Alonso* · Bob Hoskins *Sancho Panza* · James Purefoy *Sampson Carrasco* · Lambert Wilson *Duke* · Isabella Rossellini *Duchess* · Vanessa L Williams *Dulcinea/Aldonza* · Amelia Warner *Antonia* ■ *Dir* Peter Yates · *Scr* John Mortimer, from the novel *El Ingenioso Hidalgo Don Quijote de la Mancha* by Miguel de Cervantes Saavedra

Doña Herlinda and Her Son
★★★★ 15

Comedy 1986 · Mex · Colour · 89min

Mexican director Jaime Humberto Hermosillo's gay comedy is a low-budget satire of sexual manners, as doctor Marco Antonio Trevino marries to placate his matchmaking mother, Guadalupe Del Toro, while still cohabiting with his music student lover, Arturo Meza. Mocking machismo, romance, sexual duplicity and social snobbery, the picture benefits from some adroit playing and a sharp script based on Hermosillo's own experiences. DP Spanish +subtitles.

Guadalupe Del Toro *Doña Herlinda* · Arturo Meza *Ramon* · Marco Antonio Trevino *Rodolfo* · Leticia Lupersio *Olga* · Angelica Guerrero *Ramon's mother* · Donato Castaneda *Ramon's father* · Guillermina Alba *Billy* ■ *Dir/Scr* Jaime Humberto Hermosillo

Le Donk & Scor-Zay-Zee
★★★★ 15

Spoof documentary 2009 · UK · Colour · 71min

Shot in five days, with no script and a budget of under £50,000, this deadpan mockumentary from British director Shane Meadows marks a return to his low-budget roots. Paddy Considine steals the show as Le Donk, a thick, slightly seedy but likeable Nottingham roadie whose estranged girlfriend is about to have their first child. Le Donk, though, still has dreams of rock stardom, and has recently attached himself to clown-like local white rapper Scor-Zay-Zee (Dean Palinczuk). Their strange chemistry provides the heart of what follows - a ribald, frequently hilarious and often unexpectedly moving buddy movie set in the run-up to an Arctic Monkeys concert. It's a deceptively rich, if silly, character piece. DW Swearing, sexual references. DVD

Paddy Considine *Le Donk* · Dean Palinczuk *Scor-Zay-Zee* · Olivia Colman *Olivia* · Richard Graham *Olivia's boyfriend* · Seamus O'Neill *Le Donk's lodger* · Nigel Reeks *Big Nige* · Alex Turner (2) *Alex Turner* · Shane Meadows ■ *Dir* Shane Meadows · *Scr* from an idea by Paddy Considine, Shane Meadows

Donkey Punch
★★★★ 18

Thriller 2007 · UK · Colour · 95min

The hedonistic Ibiza generation gets its own scary movie in this ingenious, low-budget British shocker that transfers claustrophobic "old dark house" chills to the open sea. In a Mallorca nightclub, three northern girls are befriended by three male deck hands who invite them back to an expensive yacht to party. Drink and drugs lead to risqué talk of a bizarre sex practice called the "Donkey Punch", and when the party becomes an anything-goes orgy, an overeager reveller tries it out with unforeseen results. What follows is an edge-of-the-seat, helter-skelter plunge into madness, as the boys try to cover up the incident, the girls become nervous wrecks and a bloody fight for survival ensues. DW Violence, swearing, sex scenes, drug abuse. DVD SD

Jaime Winstone *Kim* · Robert Boulter *Sean* · Sian Breckin *Lisa* · Tom Burke *Bluey* · Nichola Burley *Tammi* · Julian Morris *Josh* · Jay Taylor *Marcus* ■ *Dir* Olly Blackburn · *Scr* Olly Blackburn, David Bloom · *Cinematographer* Nanu Segal

Donkeys
★★ 15

Comedy drama 2010 · UK/Den · Colour · 76min

In 2003, Lars von Trier launched the "Advance Party" project to enable three directors to fashion their first feature-length tales around the same group of characters. Andrea Arnold got the ball rolling with *Red Road* (2006) and Morag McKinnon continued with this quirky drama about a Glaswegian 60-something (James Cosmo) whose life is shaken up when he's diagnosed with a terminal illness. McKinnon's direction lacks nuance and the film's critical and commercial failure perhaps explains why Mikkel Norgaard's concluding episode remains in development hell. DP Swearing, a sex scene. DVD

James Cosmo *Alfred* · Kate Dickie *Jackie* · Martin Compston *Stevie* · Brian Pettifer *Brian* · Natalie Press *April Hayley* ■ *Dir* Morag McKinnon · *Scr* Colin McLaren, based on characters by Lone Scherfig, Anders Thomas Jensen

Donnie Brasco
★★★★ 18

Crime drama 1997 · US · Colour · 121min

In this 1970s-set crime drama, Al Pacino stars as a sleazeball who inducts young Brasco, played by Johnny Depp, into the codes and "family" values of organised crime. In fact, Depp is an FBI undercover agent whose job threatens his marriage to Anne Heche as well as his life. Directed by Mike Newell, the film develops nicely as Depp finds himself becoming rather fond of his monstrous mentor. The period setting - a world of tacky shirts, fur collars and plastic lawns - is also beautifully evoked. AT Swearing, violence, a sex scene. DVD

Al Pacino *Lefty Ruggiero* · Johnny Depp *Joe Pistone/"Donnie Brasco"* · Michael Madsen *Sonny Black* · Bruno Kirby *Nicky* · James Russo *Paulie* · Anne Heche *Maggie Pistone* · Zeljko Ivanek *Tim Curley* · Gerry Becker *Dean Blandford* ■ *Dir* Mike Newell · *Scr* Paul Attanasio, from a non-fiction book by Joseph D Pistone, Richard Woodley

Donnie Darko
★★★★ 15

Psychological fantasy drama
2001 · US · Colour · 108min

Jake Gyllenhaal is an introverted student in therapy who keeps having visions of a 6ft tall rabbit that tells him the end of the world is imminent and forces him to commit acts of vandalism while sleepwalking. Director Richard Kelly's powerfully affecting meditation on parallel universes, time travel and paranoid schizophrenia is a stunningly crafted and hypnotic masterwork that opens up intriguing new genre avenues. The additional material included in the director's cut has divided critics. Some feel that adding to the coherence of the narrative has compromised the teasing mystery, while others have welcomed the chance to see the film as Kelly intended. AJ Drug abuse, violence, swearing. DVD SD

Jake Gyllenhaal *Donnie Darko* · Jena Malone *Gretchen Ross* · Drew Barrymore *Karen Pomeroy* · Mary McDonnell *Rose Darko* · Holmes Osborne *Eddie Darko* · Katharine Ross *Dr Lilian Thurman* · Patrick Swayze *Jim Cunningham* · Noah Wyle *Dr Monnitoff* · Maggie Gyllenhaal *Elizabeth Darko* ■ *Dir/Scr* Richard Kelly

Donor Unknown
★★★ 12A

Documentary
2010 · Bel/UK/Neth/Nor/US · Colour · 80min

Like many of the best documentaries, Jerry Rothwell's film tells a story that's stranger than fiction. It follows 20-year-old JoEllen Marsh as she attempts to trace her biological father, an anonymous sperm donor known enigmatically as Donor 150. However, when JoEllen turns to an organisation known as the Donor Sibling Registry, she manages to track down a half-sister and the story is taken up by the *New York Times*. What emerges is a moving, very human story about the search for belonging and identity. TP Brief drug abuse, nudity.

■ *Dir* Jerry Rothwell

Donovan's Brain
★★★ PG

Science-fiction drama 1953 · US · BW · 80min

Directed with unnerving seriousness by MGM journeyman Felix Feist, this is the most faithful and easily the best adaptation of Curt Siodmak's fiendish novel. The tale of doctor Lew Ayres's struggle with the maniacal powers of a dead industrialist's transplanted brain is given chilling credibility by the extraordinary range of expressions Ayres assumes whenever he's gripped by the millionaire's insane desire to destroy his family and former associates. DP DVD

Lew Ayres *Dr Patrick J Corey* · Gene Evans *Dr Frank Schratt* · Nancy Davis *Janice Cory* · Steve Brodie *Herbie Yocum* · Lisa K Howard *Chloe Donovan* ■ *Dir* Felix Feist · *Scr* Felix Feist, from the novel by Curt Siodmak

Donovan's Reef
★★★ U

Comedy drama 1963 · US · Colour · 104min

This ramshackle but enjoyable South Sea island romp was the last teaming of the great director John Ford and his friend John Wayne. Elizabeth Allen co-stars as the prim Bostonian whose presence on a Pacific island disturbs the drinking and brawling lifestyle of the Duke and his crony Lee Marvin. There's a seasonal touch involving Dorothy Lamour and a children's Christmas, though the best thing here is the Technicolor photography by William Clothier. TS DVD

John Wayne *"Guns" Donovan* · Lee Marvin *"Boats" Gilhooley* · Jack Warden *"Doc" Dedham* · Elizabeth Allen *Amelia Dedham* · Cesar Romero *Andre de Lage* · Dorothy Lamour *Fleur* · Jacqueline Malouf *Lelani* · Mike Mazurki *Sergeant Menkowicz* ■ *Dir* John Ford · *Scr* Frank Nugent, James Edward Grant, from a story by Edmund Beloin, from material by James Michener (uncredited)

Don's Party
★★★★ 18

Black comedy 1976 · Aus · Colour · 86min

Set on election night, 1969, this savage black comedy lifts the lid off suburban Australia and exposes all the prejudice and resentment simmering underneath. The dialogue crackles with offensive opinions and lacerating insults as the 11 guests throw off their ill-fitting gentility and let rip at one another as the beer flows and the results come in. Bruce Beresford paces the descent into uncivil war to perfection, while the cast are uniformly excellent in turning grotesque caricatures into credible specimens of boorish humanity. Look out for then-prime minister, John Gorton, in a cameo. DP

Ray Barrett *Mal* · Claire Binney *Susan* · Pat Bishop *Jenny* · Graeme Blundell *Simon* · John Hargreaves *Don Henderson* · Harold Hopkins *Cooley* · John Gorton ■ *Dir* Bruce Beresford · *Scr* David Williamson, from his play

Don't Be a Menace to South Central while Drinking Your Juice in the Hood
★ 15

Comedy 1996 · US · Colour · 85min

It's a great title, and there's no denying that the ghetto drama genre is ripe for send-up, but this is dire. It squanders its comic potential through lazy spoofing, ramshackle plotting and tasteless jokes. Not even the presence of what appears to be the entire Wayans family can save this sorry mess. JF DVD SD

Shawn Wayans *Ashtray* · Marlon Wayans *Loc Dog* · Tracey Cherelle Jones *Dashiki* · Chris Spencer [Christopher Spencer (1)] *Preach* · Suli McCullough *Crazy Legs* · Helen Martin *Grandma* · Isaiah Barnes *Doo Rag* · Lahmard Tate *Ashtray's father* · Keenen Ivory Wayans *Mailman* · Craig Wayans *First thug* ■ *Dir* Paris Barclay · *Scr* Shawn Wayans, Marlon Wayans, Phil Beauman

Don't Be Afraid of the Dark
★★

Thriller 1973 · US · Colour · 74min

Despite an immensely watchable cast, this TV movie suffers from a dumb and overly familiar premise. Kim Darby (*True Grit*) and Jim Hutton (father of Timothy) play a couple who move into a strange house. Unfortunately, it's full of odd little creatures who want to make Darby (totally wasted, as is Hutton) one of their own. John Newland's directing career never really took off, though his television work included episodes of *The Man from UNCLE*, *Hawaii Five-O* and *Alfred Hitchcock Presents*. Veteran actor William Demarest registers strongly, though. TS

Jim Hutton *Alex Farnham* · Kim Darby *Sally Farnham* · Barbara Anderson *Joan* · William Demarest *Harris* · Pedro Armendáriz Jr *Francisco Perez* · Lesley Woods *Ethel* · Sterling Swanson *Policeman* · JH Lawrence *George* · William Sylvester *Tom* · Don Mallon *Bob* ■ *Dir* John Newland · *Scr* Nigel McKeand

Don't Be Afraid of the Dark
★★★ 15

Horror 2010 · US/Aus · Colour · 95min

From its atmospheric opening, this remake of the 1973 film bears producer/writer Guillermo del Toro's unmistakable touch of class. Architect Guy Pearce's young daughter arrives to live with him and new girlfriend Katie Holmes at the 19th-century Rhode Island mansion they are restoring. Stumbling upon a hidden basement, the daughter unleashes an ancient force putting everyone's life - hers especially - in grave danger. The mix of tense playfulness and sudden shocks is an unnerving flight of dark fantasy. AJ DVD SD

Guy Pearce *Alex Hurst* · Katie Holmes *Kim* · Bailee Madison *Sally Hurst* · Jack Thompson *Harris* · Alan Dale (2) *Charles Jacoby* ■ *Dir* Troy Nixey · *Scr* Guillermo del Toro, Matthew Robbins, from the 1973 film

Don't Bother to Knock
★★★ PG

Thriller 1952 · US · BW · 76min

Marilyn Monroe was just a year away from stardom when she made this hysterical melodrama, which finds her trading twitches with that master of mannered mania, Richard Widmark. As the suicidal babysitter confronted by Widmark's leering hotel guest, Monroe occasionally looks close to the edge. Alas, this lacks both the psychological depth and the necessary suspense to distract us from the stilted acting and laboured direction. Anne Bancroft impresses in her feature debut, but it's the cast-against-type Monroe who catches the eye. DP

Richard Widmark *Jed Towers* · Marilyn Monroe *Nell* · Anne Bancroft *Lyn Leslie* · Donna Corcoran *Bunny* · Jeanne Cagney *Rochelle* · Lurene Tuttle *Ruth Jones* · Elisha Cook Jr *Eddie* · Jim Backus *Peter Jones* · Verna Felton *Mrs Ballew* ■ *Dir* Roy Baker [Roy Ward Baker] · *Scr* Daniel Taradash, from the novel by Charlotte Armstrong

Don't Bother to Knock
★★ PG

Comedy 1961 · UK · Colour · 84min

This is a leaden romp that starts out smug and ends up tasteless. Richard Todd looks uncomfortable as the philandering travel agent who discovers, to girlfriend June Thorburn's horror, that all his European flirtations have arrived at his Edinburgh home at once. Thanks to Geoffrey Unsworth and Anne V Coates respectively, it has better photography and editing than it deserves. DP

Richard Todd *Bill Ferguson* · Nicole Maurey *Lucille* · Elke Sommer *Ingrid* · June Thorburn *Stella* · Rik Battaglia *Giulio* · Judith Anderson *Maggie* · Dawn Beret *Harry* · Scott Finch *Perry* · Eleanor Summerfield *Mother* · John Le Mesurier *Father* · Warren Mitchell *Waiter* ■ *Dir* Cyril Frankel · *Scr* Denis Cannan, Frederick Gotfurt, Frederic Raphael, from the novel *Love from Everybody* by Clifford Hanley

Don't Come Knocking ★★ 15

Road movie drama
2005 · Ger/Fr/UK/US · Colour · 106min

Like their superior 1984 collaboration *Paris, Texas*, director Wim Wenders and screenwriter Sam Shepard here focus on a man struggling to put the pieces of his life back together. Shepard also takes the starring role as an ageing cowboy actor who discovers a son (Gabriel Mann) whom he'd never met. There's a seductively surreal quality to the dustbowl setting, but a series of confrontations becomes more affected and less credible with every knock on the door. SP Swearing. DVD

Sam Shepard *Howard Spence* · Jessica Lange *Doreen* · Tim Roth *Sutter* · Gabriel Mann *Earl* · Sarah Polley *Sky* · Fairuza Balk *Amber* · Eva Marie Saint *Howard's mother* · James Gammon *Old ranch hand* ■ *Dir* Wim Wenders · *Scr* Sam Shepard, from a story by Shepard, Wim Wenders

Don't Drink the Water ★★

Comedy 1969 · US · Colour · 98min

Woody Allen's sharp and angry stage play is bloated to portly buffoonery to suit comic

D

actor Jackie Gleason, with Allen's words rewritten for the screen by RS Allen and Harvey Bullock. Gleason stars as a Jewish caterer who is forced to take refuge in the American embassy in Vulgaria. He's suspected of spying by East European officials when he takes some snaps at the airport, and then tries to flee the fictional Iron Curtain country. TH

Jackie Gleason *Walter Hollander* • Estelle Parsons *Marion Hollander* • Ted Bessell *Axel Magee* • Joan Delaney *Susan Hollander* • Michael Constantine *Krojack* • Howard St John *Ambassador Magee* • Danny Meehan *Kilroy* • Richard Libertini *Father Drobney* ■ *Dir* Howard Morris • *Scr* RS Allen, Harvey Bullock, from the play by Woody Allen

Don't Drink the Water ★★★
Comedy   1994 · US · Colour

Woody Allen conceived the original play about Americans abroad and all things foreign when he was in Paris filming *What's New, Pussycat?*. It was performed on Broadway in 1966 with Lou Jacobi in the leading role, and in 1969 it was made with Jackie Gleason as the caterer accused of spying in an East European hell-hole. Allen always had a soft spot for the play, perhaps because he had based the main role on his own father. As he disliked Gleason's performance, he welcomed the chance to direct this remake for TV, casting himself and several of his friends. AT

Woody Allen *Walter Hollander* • Michael J Fox *Axel Magee* • Julie Kavner *Marion Hollander* • Mayim Bialik *Susan Hollander* • Dom DeLuise *Father Drobney* • Josef Sommer *Ambassador Magee* • Edward Herrmann *Mr Kilroy* • Austin Pendleton *Chef Oscar* ■ *Dir* Woody Allen • *Scr* Woody Allen, from his play

Don't Ever Leave Me ★★U
Comedy   1949 · UK · BW · 80min

Petula Clark is on typically ebullient form, playing the spoiled daughter of a star actress who is kidnapped by a wily old crook, only to fall for his grandson and refuse to go home. Jimmy Hanley simply has to look fetching in the latter role, but as the older man veteran character actor Edward Rigby relishes the chance to display a little Dickensian devilment. Arthur Crabtree's direction fails to hit a consistent tone. DP

Petula Clark *Sheila Farlaine* • Jimmy Hanley *Jack Denton* • Hugh Sinclair *Michael Farlaine* • Linden Travers *Mary Lamont* • Anthony Newley *Jimmy Knowles* ■ *Dir* Arthur Crabtree • *Scr* Robert Westerby, from the novel *The Wide Guy* by Anthony Armstrong

Don't Give Up the Ship
★★★U
Comedy   1959 · US · BW · 88min

This very funny Jerry Lewis vehicle comes from the period when Lewis had just split with Dean Martin and was still trying to establish his solo style. The wonderful wacky plot involves Jerry and sidekick Mickey Shaughnessy looking for a naval battleship that Lewis commanded during the Second World War and is now lost. (Don't ask!) Classy rich girl Dina Merrill turns in a mighty cute performance that makes you regret that she semi-retired from the screen in 1989 in order to run RKO Pictures with her husband, Ted Hartley. TS

Jerry Lewis *John Paul Steckler* • Dina Merrill *Ensign Benson* • Diana Spencer *Prudence Trabert* • Mickey Shaughnessy *Stan Wychinski* • Robert Middleton *Admiral Bludde* • Gale Gordon *Congressman Mandeville* • Mabel Albertson *Mrs Trabert* ■ *Dir* Norman Taurog • *Scr* Herbert Baker, Edmund Beloin, Henry Garson, from a story by Ellis Kadison

Don't Go Breaking My Heart
★★★PG
Romantic comedy   1999 · UK · Colour · 89min

Jenny Seagrove stars with *ER* heart-throb Anthony Edwards in this feel-good romantic comedy. She plays a widowed gardening expert who, through accident and misadventure, becomes involved with visiting American sports therapist Edwards. The only fly in the ointment is Charles

Dance in a ridiculously over-the-top role as Edwards's love rival. Viewed as a superficial piece of fluffy nonsense, the film is enjoyable. SuR Swearing.

Anthony Edwards *Tony Dorfman* • Jenny Seagrove *Suzanne Brody* • Charles Dance *Frank* • Jane Leeves *Juliet* • Tom Conti *Doctor Fiedler* • Linford Christie • Ben Reynolds *Ben* ■ *Dir* Willi Patterson • *Scr* Geoff Morrow

Don't Go near the Water
★★★U
Comedy   1957 · US · Colour · 106min

Patchy but always amiable and sometimes hilarious, this slapstick comedy deals with the problems faced by a naval public relations unit on a South Pacific island in attempting to promote a wholesome image of the service with little or no experience of ever having been at sea. Glenn Ford and Gia Scala are top-billed, but the standouts are Fred Clark, on top form as the irascible commanding officer, and burly Mickey Shaughnessy as a most unfortunate choice of sailor to thrust into the spotlight. AE

Glenn Ford *Lieutenant Max Siegel* • Gia Scala *Melora* • Earl Holliman *Adam Garrett* • Anne Francis *Lieutenant Alice Tomlen* • Keenan Wynn *Gordon Ripwell* • Fred Clark *Lieutenant Commander Clinton Nash* • Russ Tamblyn *Ensign Tyson* ■ *Dir* Charles Walters • *Scr* Dorothy Kingsley, George Wells, from the novel by William Brinkley

Don't Just Lie There, Say Something!
★PG
Comedy   1973 · UK · Colour · 87min

The Whitehall farces may have delighted London theatre-goers from the 1950s to the 1970s, but they have never worked on the screen. This film reduces the precise timing of the double entendres, the bedroom entrances and exits, and the dropped-trouser misunderstandings to the level of clumsy contrivance. Few *farceurs* are as practised as Leslie Phillips and Brian Rix, but they are powerless to save this. DP
DVD

Leslie Phillips *Sir William* • Brian Rix *Barry Ovis* • Joanna Lumley *Miss Parkyn* • Joan Sims *Birdie* • Derek Royle *Wilfred Potts* • Peter Bland *Inspector Ruff* • Katy Manning *Damina* ■ *Dir* Bob Kellett • *Scr* Michael Pertwee, from his play

Don't Just Stand There
★★★
Comedy   1968 · US · Colour · 99min

The pairing of the extremely likeable Robert Wagner and Mary Tyler Moore give this comedy added appeal. They join forces to search for novelist Glynis Johns, who has only managed to pen the first half of her new book. Harvey Korman pops up en route to great effect, and director Ron Winston papers over the holes in the script by keeping the pace at fever pitch. Glossy production values, period Technicolor and Techniscope lensing lend this artefact a quaint charm. TS

Robert Wagner *Lawrence Colby* • Mary Tyler Moore *Martine Randall* • Glynis Johns *Sabine Manning* • Barbara Rhoades *Kendall Flanagan* • Harvey Korman *Merriman Dudley* • Vincent Beck *Painter* • Joseph Perry *Jean-Jacques* ■ *Dir* Ron Winston • *Scr* Charles Williams, from his novel *The Wrong Venus*

Don't Knock the Rock ★★U
Musical   1956 · US · BW · 84min

Quickie producer Sam Katzman's follow-up to the enormously successful *Rock around the Clock* also features the airwave-shattering Bill Haley and the Comets. There's great period value in this movie: kiss-curled Haley and his great line-up playing numbers such as *Hook, Line and Sinker*, and the fabulous Little Richard at his peak performing *Long Tall Sally* and *Tutti Frutti*. But it lacks the innocence of its predecessor and looks as if it was thrown together in a hurry. TS

Bill Haley • Little Richard • Alan Dale (1) *Arnie Haines* • Alan Freed • The Treniers • Patricia Hardy *Francine MacLaine* • Fay Baker *Arlene MacLaine* ■ *Dir* Fred F Sears • *Scr* Robert E Kent, James B Gordon

Don't Look Back   ★★★★
Music documentary   1967 · US · BW · 95min

Fans of Bob Dylan will need no encouragement to watch this brilliantly filmed record of his British tour in 1965, the year of *Subterranean Homesick Blues*. But film enthusiasts should note that this is also a fine example of the craft of director/cameraman DA Pennebaker, one of the masters of *cinéma vérité*. Pennebaker just followed Dylan around, picking up truthful insights along the way, including revelatory moments with Joan Baez, Alan Price and, particularly, Dylan's manager Albert Grossman. The end result, edited down from over 20 hours of material, is a telling portrait of a unique performer at the height of his powers. TS DVD

Bob Dylan ■ *Dir* DA Pennebaker

Don't Look Now ★★★★★★15
Supernatural thriller
1973 · UK/It · Colour · 105min

A fiercely erotic scene of love-making between Donald Sutherland and Julie Christie forms the sensual core of this supernatural chiller, which offers a time-distorted vision of terror set in wintertime Venice, portrayed here as a hostile city of brooding silences and fog-shrouded canals. After the death of their young daughter, church restorer Sutherland and wife Christie take their grief with them to Italy, where the spectral presence of their child draws them into a labyrinth of cryptic signs and doom-laden portents. This is director Nicolas Roeg's masterpiece – the fear-drenched mood of alienation is sustained right up until the unforgettable final shot. TH Violence, swearing, nudity. DVD

Donald Sutherland *John Baxter* • Julie Christie *Laura Baxter* • Hilary Mason *Heather* • Clelia Matania *Wendy* • Massimo Serato *Bishop Barbarrigo* • Renato Scarpa *Inspector Longhi* • David Tree *Anthony Babbage* ■ *Dir* Nicolas Roeg • *Scr* Allan Scott, Chris Bryant, from a short story by Daphne du Maurier • *Cinematographer* Anthony Richmond [Anthony B Richmond] • *Editor* Graeme Clifford • *Music* Pino Donaggio

Don't Make Waves   ★★★
Comedy   1967 · US · Colour · 97min

Ealing expatriate Alexander Mackendrick, better known for *Whisky Galore!* and *Sweet Smell of Success*, directs this good-natured satire on Californian lifestyles. Tony Curtis gives a clever performance as a tourist who gets a job selling swimming pools. However, the real revelation is the witty comic playing of Sharon Tate, tragically murdered by the Manson "family" two years later. TS

Tony Curtis *Carlo Cofield* • Claudia Cardinale *Laura Califatti* • Sharon Tate *Malibu* • Robert Webber *Rod Prescott* • Joanna Barnes *Diane Prescott* • David Draper *Harry Hollard* • Mort Sahl *Sam Lingonberry* • Edgar Bergen *Madame Lavinia* • Ann Elder *Millie Gunder* ■ *Dir* Alexander Mackendrick • *Scr* Ira Wallach, George Kirgo, Maurice Richlin, from the novel *Muscle Beach* by Ira Wallach

Don't Move   ★★★15
Drama   2004 · It/Sp/UK · Colour · 116min

Penélope Cruz puts in an unglamorous but moving performance in this powerful and challenging drama. Co-writer/director Sergio Castellitto himself takes the lead role as a wealthy surgeon who's forced to remember a secret and tragic past when his daughter is involved in a road accident. As the girl lies comatose, he reflects on an extramarital affair that he enjoyed with downtrodden, working-class patient (Cruz). The film is difficult to watch but brilliantly acted, though the tacky soundtrack lowers the tone. SF Italian +subtitles. Swearing, sex scenes. DVD

Sergio Castellitto *Timoteo* • Penélope Cruz *Italia* • Claudia Gerini *Elsa* • Angela Finocchiaro *Ada* • Marco Giallini *Manlio* • Pietro De Silva *Alfredo* • Elena Perino *Angela* ■ *Dir* Sergio Castellitto • *Scr* Margaret Mazzantini, Sergio Castellitto, from the novel *Non ti muovere* by Margaret Mazzantini

Don't Move, Die and Rise Again
★★★★12
Period drama   1989 · USSR · BW · 102min

Winner of the Caméra d'Or at Cannes for the best debut feature, this is a bleak study of the way Japanese POWs were treated by their Soviet captors in the Stalinist era of the mid-1940s. Faithfully re-creating the ghastly conditions in which everyone lived and worked in a remote mining town, director Vitaly Kanevsky is keen to point out that the Russian miners were as much in captivity as the prisoners, and they wouldn't be able to go home once hostilities ended. The presence of two children, playing happily amid the degradation, only reinforces Kanevsky's depressing but well-made point. Sobering and provocative. DP Russian +subtitles.

Dinara Drukarova *Galiia* • Pavel Nazarov *Valerka* • Elena Popova *Nina* • Valery Ivchenko • Vyacheslav Bambushek • Vadim Ermolaev ■ *Dir/Scr* Vitaly Kanevsky

Don't Raise the Bridge, Lower the River
★★U
Comedy   1968 · UK · Colour · 95min

Jerry Lewis is quite hopelessly adrift and desperately unfunny in an awkward UK adaptation of humorist Max Wilk's novel. It's ham-fistedly directed by former actor Jerry Paris, and concerns Lewis's plans to steal a high-speed oil drill and peddle the plans to oil-rich Arabs. The Brits acquit themselves well, yet both pace and tone are uncertain, and Lewis's performance is embarrassingly undirected. TS

Jerry Lewis *George Lester* • Terry-Thomas *H William Horner* • Jacqueline Pearce *Pamela Lester* • Bernard Cribbins *Fred Davies* • Patricia Routledge *Lucille Beatty* • Dudley Heath • Michael Bates *Dr Spink* • Colin Gordon *Mr Hartford* ■ *Dir* Jerry Paris • *Scr* Max Wilk, from his novel

Don't Say a Word   ★★★15
Thriller   2001 · US/Aus · Colour · 108min

Michael Douglas plays a psychiatrist, whose comfortable existence is shattered when his young daughter is kidnapped. The ransom for her return is a six-digit number, locked in the memory of near-catatonic mental patient Brittany Murphy. Douglas must therefore delve into the girl's damaged psyche, retrieve the number and deliver it to kidnapper Sean Bean – and he has one day to do it. While the premise is ludicrous and some of the plot developments heavily signposted, thanks to compelling performances and pacey direction, this adds up to an enjoyable ride. JB Violence, swearing. DVD

Michael Douglas (1) *Dr Nathan Conrad* • Sean Bean *Patrick B Koster* • Brittany Murphy *Elisabeth Burrows* • Skye McCole Bartusiak *Jessie Conrad* • Guy Torry *Martin J Dolen* • Jennifer Esposito *Det Sandra Cassidy* • Shawn Doyle *Russel Maddox* • Famke Janssen *Aggie Conrad* • Oliver Platt *Dr Louis Sachs* ■ *Dir* Gary Fleder • *Scr* Anthony Peckham, Patrick Smith Kelly, from the novel by Andrew Klavan

Don't Take It to Heart
★★★U
Supernatural comedy   1944 · UK · BW · 86min

Written and directed by Jeffrey Dell, this haunted house comedy is a triumph of eccentricity over substance. It was made during wartime, but only the British could find propaganda value in a film in which the aristocracy triumphs over the beastly nouveaux riches thanks to an alliance between a ghost and a lawyer. Although Richard Greene and Patricia Medina are the leads, the supporting cast takes the acting honours, with Alfred Drayton hissable as the tycoon trying to land Brefni O'Rorke's stately pile at a knockdown price. DP

Richard Greene *Peter Hayward* • David Horne *Sir Henry Wade* • Patricia Medina *Lady Mary* • Alfred Drayton *Mr Pike* • Joan Hickson *Mrs Pike* • Richard Bird *Ghost Arthur* • Wylie Watson *Harry Bucket* • Brefni O'Rorke *Lord Chaunduyt* ■ *Dir/Scr* Jeffrey Dell

Don't Talk to Strange Men ★★ 12

Thriller 1962 · UK · BW · 63min

This worthy little thriller with a social message is more interesting now for its depiction of early 1960s Britain, but still has relevance today. Christina Gregg is the young girl in trouble after disobeying the instruction of the title, while Gillian Lind and Cyril Raymond are her very middle-class parents. TS *DVD*

Christina Gregg *Jean Painter* • Janina Faye *Ann Painter* • Conrad Phillips *Ron* • Dandy Nichols *Molly* • Cyril Raymond *Mr Painter* • Gillian Lind *Mrs Painter* • Gwen Nelson *Mrs Mason* ■ *Dir* Pat Jackson • *Scr* Gwen Cherrell

Don't Talk to Strangers ★★ 12

Thriller 1994 · US · Colour · 89min

Now that Pierce Brosnan has achieved superstar status, it's easy to forget that just a few years ago he could be found in run-of-the-mill TV movies such as this. Brosnan is about to sweep Shanna Reed off to a new life in California when her nine-year-old son is kidnapped. Suspicion falls on Reed's ex-husband, Terry O'Quinn, a cop putting up a bitter custody battle. The plot hardly bears close scrutiny, but there are enough twists to keep you guessing. DP Violence, some swearing.

Shanna Reed *Jane Bonner* • Pierce Brosnan *Patrick Brody* • Terry O'Quinn *Bonner* • Keegan Macintosh *Eric Bonner* • Michael MacRae *Detective Sandstrum* • Roger R Cross *Detective Barrett* ■ *Dir* Robert Lewis [Robert Michael Lewis] • *Scr* Neill D Hicks, Jon George, Nevin Schreiner

Don't Tell Mom the Babysitter's Dead ★★ 15

Comedy 1991 · US · Colour · 100min

The five Crandell children are forced to fend for themselves when their elderly and decidedly crotchety babysitter drops dead while their mother is on holiday in Australia. This reasonably engaging comedy from Stephen Herek veers uneasily from slightly adult comedy to farcical teenage wish-fulfilment, but remains remarkably good-humoured throughout the awkward shifts in tone. AJ Swearing. *DVD*

Christina Applegate *Sue Ellen "Swell" Crandell* • Joanna Cassidy *Rose Lindsey* • John Getz *Gus Brandon* • Josh Charles *Bryan* • Keith Coogan *Kenny Crandell* • Concetta Tomei *Mom Crandell* • David Duchovny *Bruce* • Kimmy Robertson *Cathy* ■ *Dir* Stephen Herek • *Scr* Neil Landau, Tara Ison

Don't Touch the Axe ★★★★ PG

Period drama 2006 · Fr/It · Colour · 131min

Despite being part of the provocative band of French critics-turned-directors who emerged from *Cahiers du Cinéma* in the 1950s, Jacques Rivette (*Celine and Julie Go Boating*) has always demonstrated a respect for text and theatricality. Indeed, this adaptation of Balzac's novel *La Duchesse de Langeais* could almost be accused of straying into the traditional territory that Rivette so despised. Here he portrays the emotional battles being fought by Napoleonic general Guillaume Depardieu and married beauty Jeanne Balibar in the salons of Restoration Paris. Balibar excels as the haughty temptress using her command of the rules of aristocratic society to torment Depardieu, but she's even more compelling after the spurned Depardieu goes on the counterattack and she retires to a nunnery to repent her pride. This intimate human story is imbued with insight and intensity by a master auteur. DP French +subtitles. *DVD*

Jeanne Balibar *Antoinette de Langeais* • Guillaume Depardieu *Armand de Montriveau* • Anne Cantineau *Clara de Sérizy* • Mathias Jung *Julien* • Julie Judd *Lisette* • Marc Barbé *Marquis de Ronquerolles* • Nicolas Bouchard *De Trailles* • Thomas Durand *De Marsay* ■ *Dir* Jacques Rivette • *Scr* Christine Laurent, Pascal Bonitzer, from Honoré de Balzac's novel *La Duchesse de Langeais*

Don't Worry about Me ★★★ 15

Romantic drama 2009 · UK · Colour · 79min

With Stuart Nicholas White's camera venerating the Liverpool skyline, actor David Morrissey's first feature as director is an exile's love letter to his home city. Switching adroitly between luminous vistas and forlorn backstreets, this is very much an actors' piece, following James Brough's cocky southerner as his trek north to follow up a one-night stand leads to a meeting with Helen Elizabeth's soft-hearted bookie's clerk. Made for just £100,000, the movie does betray its stage origins, but Morrissey clearly empathises with the characters and elicits laudably naturalistic performances from his leads. DP *DVD*

James Brough *David* • Helen Elizabeth *Tina* ■ *Dir* David Morrissey • *Scr* David Morrissey, Helen Elizabeth, James Erough, from the play *The Pool* by Elizabeth, Brough

Doom ★★ 15

Science-fiction action horror 2005 · US/Cz Rep/Ger/UK · Colour · 108min

In this *Aliens* knock-off, tough-talking Sarge (The Rock) leads an elite marine outfit to Mars to find out what has happened to a group of scientists working on an anthropological dig. Director Andrzej Bartkowiak resists the joy-stick approach to direction until right to the end - although that will probably be regarded as a negative by fans of the computer game on which this is based. JF Swearing, violence. *DVD* *Blu-ray*

Karl Urban *John Grimm, "Reaper"* • The Rock [Dwayne Johnson] *Sarge* • Rosamund Pike *Dr Samantha Grimm* • DeObia Oparei [Deobie Oparei] *Destroyer* • Ben Daniels *Goat* • Raz Adoti [Razaaq Adoti] *Duke* • Richard Brake *Portman* • Al Weaver *The Kid* • Dexter Fletcher *Pinky* ■ *Dir* Andrzej Bartkowiak • *Scr* David Callaham, Wesley Strick, from a story by Callaham, from the computer game by ID Software

Doom Generation ★★★ 18

Road movie 1995 · US/Fr · Colour · 80min

Gregg Araki succeeds triumphantly in both shocking the prudish and exhibiting his technical mastery in what he describes as his first heterosexual outing. This is a self-satisfied affair that too often thinks a cinematic in-joke or a cheap shot at middle American mores is more important than expanding the characters of teenage lovers Rose McGowan and James Duval and their maniacal mentor, Johnathon Schaech. Araki glamorises the sex as much as the violence, but the sight of a shopkeeper's severed head continuing to scream will be most people's abiding memory. DP *DVD*

James Duval *Jordan White* • Rose McGowan *Amy Blue* • Johnathon Schaech *Xavier Red, "X"* • Cress Williams *Peanut* • Skinny Puppy *Gang of goons* • Dustin Nguyen *Quickiemart clerk* • Margaret Cho *Clerk's wife* • Lauren Tewes *TV anchorwoman* • Christopher Knight (2) *TV anchorman* ■ *Dir/Scr* Gregg Araki

Doomsday ★★★ 18

Futuristic action horror 2008 · UK/US/S Afr · Colour · 112min

Director Neil Marshall's third film (after *Dog Soldiers* and *The Descent*) is a muscular melange of *Escape from New York*, the *Mad Max* trilogy and plague movies like *I Am Legend*. Following the outbreak of the deadly Reaper virus north of the border, Scotland is walled up and the population left to die. But decades later, the disease returns to threaten London. Enter hard-case heroine Rhona Mitra who's assigned to enter the quarantined dead zone with a crack team of specialists to seek a cure. There are breathtaking stunts, grisly splatter horror and eye-catching performances from Bob Hoskins, Malcolm McDowell and David O'Hara. However, Marshall fails to stay in control of his narrative or develop his characters. It's a pity, because there are plenty of sequences that could have made *Doomsday* the must-see blockbuster of the year. JA Violence, swearing. *DVD* *Blu-ray*

Rhona Mitra *Eden Sinclair* • Malcolm McDowell *Kane* • Bob Hoskins *Bill Nelson* • Adrian Lester *Norton* • David O'Hara *Michael Canaris* • Alexander Siddig *John Hatcher* • Sean Pertwee *Dr Talbot* • Darren Morfitt *Dr Ben Stirling* ■ *Dir/Scr* Neil Marshall

Doomsday Man ★★

Futuristic thriller 1998 · US · Colour · 89min

This futuristic thriller hits all the right buttons but still fails to excite. Yancy Butler plays the spirited soldier assigned to track down mad researcher James Marshall, who has made off with a lethal biological weapon from a top-secret base. Director William Greenblatt scores in the action sequences, but this is predictable fare. JF

Yancy Butler *Kate* • Esai Morales *Mike Banks* • James Marshall *Tom Banks* • Renee Griffin *Jill* ■ *Dir* William R Greenblatt • *Scr* Andrew Stein

Doomwatch ★★ 12

Mystery thriller 1972 · UK · Colour · 88min

As a spin-off from an ecological BBC TV series, this crash-landed in the swamp of horror instead of on the firmer ground of science fact or fiction. John Paul, Ian Bannen and Judy Geeson look suitably intense as an investigation is mounted into the effects of a sunken oil tanker on the inhabitants of an island off the Cornish coast only to discover something nastily mutated in the biological woodshed. Risibly alarmist, but the environmental dangers it pinpoints are only too topical. TH *DVD*

Ian Bannen *Dr Del Shaw* • Judy Geeson *Victoria Brown* • John Paul *Dr Quist* • Simon Oates *Dr Ridge* • George Sanders *Admiral* • Percy Herbert *Hartwell* • Geoffrey Keen *Sir Henry Layton* • Joseph O'Conor *Vicar* ■ *Dir* Peter Sasdy • *Scr* Clive Exton, from the TV series by Kit Pedler, Gerry Davis

The Door ★★★ 15

Science-fiction mystery thriller 2009 · Ger · Colour · 99min

Danish star Mads Mikkelsen (*Casino Royale*) brings his brooding charisma to bear in this intriguing sci-fi thriller. He plays a successful artist whose extracurricular activities while his wife is at work and his daughter is playing by a pool lands him in *Don't Look Now* territory. Five years later, he comes across the door of the title, a portal of possibilities that could be the solution to all that ails him. This is understated science fiction with a chilling edge - the magnetic Mikkelsen anchors this unexpected gem, but there's solid support, too, from Jessica Schwarz as his wife and Thomas Thieme as a neighbour who knows more than you think. JA German, English +subtitles. Violence, swearing, sex scenes. *DVD*

Mads Mikkelsen *David Andernach* • Jessica Schwarz *Maja Andernach* • Valeria Eisenbart *Leonie Andernach* • Thomas Thieme *Siggi Butschma* ■ *Dir* Anno Saul • *Scr* Jan Berger, from the novel *Die Damalstür* by Akif Pirinçci

The Door in the Floor ★★★★ 15

Drama 2004 · US · Colour · 106min

Jeff Bridges and Kim Basinger star as a couple whose teenage sons died in an accident some years ago. The tragedy has crushed the marriage and not even the couple's four-year-old daughter (Elle Fanning, sister of Dakota) can ease their sorrow. Bridges has descended into drinking and womanising, while Basinger begins a relationship with her husband's 16-year-old assistant (Jon Foster). Subtle, mature and surprising. KK Swearing, sex scenes. *DVD*

Jeff Bridges *Ted Cole* • Kim Basinger *Marion Cole* • Jon Foster (1) *Eddie O'Hare* • Mimi Rogers *Evelyn Vaughn* • Elle Fanning *Ruth Cole* • Bijou Phillips *Alice* • Louis Arcella *Eduardo Gomez* ■ *Dir* Tod Williams • *Scr* Tod Williams, from the novel *A Widow for One Year* by John Irving

Door to Door ★★★

Drama based on a true story 2002 · US · Colour · 91min

This inspirational biopic chronicles the remarkable working life of Bill Porter - a cerebral palsy sufferer who overcame all odds to become a door-to-door salesman in 1950s America. Saved from mawkishness by co-writer William H Macy's honest lead performance, the drama explores how patience, persistence and a wicked sense of humour gradually transformed a social reject into a neighbourhood cornerstone and his company's top salesperson. The drama benefits from some quality acting, with Helen Mirren in particular complementing Macy's affecting turn as his devoted mother. SF

William H Macy *Bill Porter* • Helen Mirren *Mrs Porter* • Kyra Sedgwick *Shelly Soomky Brady* • Kathy Baker *Gladys Sullivan* ■ *Dir* Steven Schachter • *Scr* William H Macy, Steven Schachter

Door-to-Door Maniac ★

Crime thriller 1961 · US · BW · 75min

Country-and-western singer Johnny Cash does himself few favours by appearing in this turgid and trashy thriller as a guitar-toting thug who extorts money from a bank president while holding his wife for ransom. Cash sings two songs: the extraordinary *I've Come to Kill* and *Five Minutes to Live*. The latter doubled as the movie's original title. AJ

Johnny Cash *Johnny Cabot* • Donald Woods *Ken Wilson* • Cay Forrester *Nancy Wilson* • Pamela Mason [Pamela Kellino] *Ellen* • Midge Ware *Doris* • Vic Tayback *Fred* • Ronnie Howard [Ron Howard] *Bobby* • Merle Travis *Max* ■ *Dir* Bill Karn • *Scr* MK Forrester, Robert L Joseph, from a story by Palmer Thompson

The Doors ★★★ 18

Musical biography 1991 · US · Colour · 134min

Although the title would have you believe that this is a biopic of the entire band, we learn next to nothing about Ray Manzarek, John Densmore or Robby Krieger, as the emphasis is so firmly on the Doors' charismatic, enigmatic frontman, Jim Morrison. Unfortunately, co-writer/director Oliver Stone is so preoccupied with exploring the native American influences on Morrison's music and re-creating the sights and sounds of the 1960s that we discover precious little about Morrison either. Val Kilmer does, however, pull off a remarkable impression of the vocalist. DP Violence, swearing, sex scenes, drug abuse, nudity. *DVD* *Blu-ray*

Val Kilmer *Jim Morrison* • Meg Ryan *Pamela Courson* • Kyle MacLachlan *Ray Manzarek* • Kevin Dillon *John Densmore* • Frank Whaley *Robby Krieger* • Billy Idol *Cat* • Dennis Burkley *Dog* • Josh Evans *Bill Siddons* • Michael Madsen *Tom Baker* • Kathleen Quinlan *Patricia Kennealy* ■ *Dir* Oliver Stone • *Scr* Oliver Stone, J Randall Johnson, Randy Johnson, Ralph Thomas, from the non-fiction book *Riders on the Storm* by John Densmore

Dope ★★★★ 15

Comedy drama 2015 · US · Colour · 98min

All the clichés of the African-American 'hood movie are turned on their head in this joyously fast-paced crime caper, in which three friends from the mostly black area of Inglewood, Los Angeles, horrify their posturing peers with their squeaky-clean behaviour. The clans connect at a birthday party for drug dealer Dom (rapper A$ap Rocky), where bright student Malcolm (Shameik Moore) is unwittingly saddled with a stash of top-grade narcotics after an attack by rival gang members. The stakes are high, but *Dope* is far from grim: it's a fast, funky and good-hearted take on the urban heist movie. DW Violence, swearing, sex scenes, drug abuse. *DVD*

Shameik Moore *Malcolm* • Tony Revolori *Jib* • Kiersey Clemons *Diggy* • Kimberly Elise *Lisa* ■ *Dir/Scr* Rick Famuyiwa

Doppelganger ★★ 18

Horror 1993 · US · Colour · 100min

Three years before becoming one of the first victims of the *Scream* franchise, Drew Barrymore was the star of her own hokey slasher flick, playing a young woman terrorised by an evil alter ego who's killing off her family in New York. Moving out to

Los Angeles, Drew begins an affair with her new roommate. But is it her or her doppelganger that he's fallen in love with? This intriguing premise is stifled by Avi Nesher's predictable and at times crass direction. RS *DVD*

Drew Barrymore *Holly Gooding* • George Newbern *Patrick Highsmith* • Dennis Christopher *Dr Heller* • Sally Kellerman *Sister Jan* • Leslie Hope *Elizabeth* • George Maharis *Wallace* ■ *Dir/Scr* Avi Nesher

Dorian Gray ★★★ 15
Period horror drama
2009 · UK/Cay/Can · Colour · 107min

Hesitantly falling between chintzy Hammer horror and cosy costume drama, director Oliver Parker's third Oscar Wilde adaptation (after *The Importance of Being Earnest* and *An Ideal Husband*) is a sumptuous but bland affair. Ben Barnes stars as the titular handsome socialite who's lured by mentor Henry Wotton (Colin Firth) into wanton ways, while his portrait bears the scars of his misdeeds. The infamous portrait is depicted as a living entity, whose sudden CGI movements provide the odd frisson, but dissolves from jam scenes to (tamely depicted) S&M orgies perfectly sum up the quaint awkwardness of this chocolate-box confection. AJ Violence, sex scenes, nudity, drug abuse. *DVD* *BL*

Ben Barnes *Dorian Gray* • Colin Firth *Lord Henry Wotton* • Ben Chaplin *Basil Hallward* • Rebecca Hall *Emily Wotton* • Fiona Shaw *Agatha* • Emilia Fox *Lady Victoria Wotton* • Rachel Hurd-Wood *Sybil Vane* • Maryam d'Abo [Maryam D'Abo] *Gladys* ■ *Dir* Oliver Parker • *Scr* Toby Finlay, from the novel *The Picture of Dorian Gray* by Oscar Wilde

Doss House ★★
Detective drama
1933 · UK · BW · 52min

John Baxter, an unsung hero of British cinema, made quota quickies and immensely popular regional comedies. His "serious" films began in tandem with the great 1930s documentary movement and introduced realist fiction. This feature debut tells of a journalist and a detective who infiltrate a doss house to trap a criminal taking refuge among the down and outs. Heavily atmospheric, it was described as a "descent into hell" story, Baxter remade it, indifferently, as *Judgment Deferred* (1951). BB

Frank Cellier *Editor* • Arnold Bell *Reporter* • Herbert Franklyn *Detective* • Mark Daly *Shoeblack* • Edgar Driver *Catsmeat Man* ■ *Dir* John Baxter • *Scr* Herbert Ayres

Dot and the Kangaroo ★★ U
Part-animated adventure
1976 · Aus · Colour · 71min

Based on the children's character created by Ethel Pedley, this is the first of Yoram Gross's series of live-action/animation films about the little red-headed girl who can talk to animals. There isn't much to get excited about in the story, in which Dot gets lost in the Australian bush and is helped out by a kindly kangaroo, and the songs will hardly set toes a-tapping, but the blend of cartoon characters and real wildlife footage is neatly done. Seven further films followed. DP

Robyn Moore (1) *Dot* ■ *Dir* Yoram Gross • *Scr* Yoram Gross, John Palmer, from a character created by Ethel Pedley

The Dot and the Line ★★★★★ U
Animated romantic comedy
1965 · US · Colour · 10min

Such is Chuck Jones's genius, there's no doubting the emotional depth of the three protagonists in this charming short: an immature pink dot, the straight black line who loves her and the coarse, hairy squiggle she prefers. This masterpiece remains unique in his output, with layout artist Maurice Noble's colourful designs contributing enormously in suggesting character mood. There's another superb soundtrack, this time with elegant music by Eugene Poddany and subtle narration by the great Robert Morley. CLP

Robert Morley *Narrator* ■ *Dir* Chuck Jones • *Scr* Juster Norton, from his story

Dot the i ★★ 15
Romantic thriller
2003 · UK/Sp · Colour · 87min

This curious mix of romance and psychological chills stars Gael García Bernal as a wannabe actor-cum-waiter in London who falls for Natalia Verbeke on the eve of her marriage to the staid but wealthy James D'Arcy. As she agonises over the choice between love and security, she also has the unsettling feeling that she is being watched by a mysterious stranger. You will probably think that you have it all figured out half way through, but then director Matthew Parkhill pulls out a far-fetched twist that derails all the good work that went before. JF *DVD*

Gael García Bernal *Kit* • Natalia Verbeke *Carmen* • James D'Arcy *Barnaby* • Tom Hardy *Tom* • Charlie Cox *Theo* ■ *Dir/Scr* Matthew Parkhill

The Double ★★ 12
Spy thriller
2011 · US · Colour · 94min

Retired CIA agent Richard Gere and young rookie Topher Grace team up to track down a Soviet assassin, in a spy thriller that's as dated and clichéd as it sounds. It's perfectly serviceable, however, and Grace brings the smart-assed charm that made him so watchable in *That '70s Show*, but there's nothing in here we've not seen before, and done better, too. Gere looks bored, but he and Grace, with a bit of help from Martin Sheen's CIA director, pull the movie over the finish line. DnM Some violence.

Richard Gere *Paul Shepherdson* • Topher Grace *Ben Geary* • Martin Sheen *Tom Highland* • Stephen Moyer *Brutus* ■ *Dir* Michael Brandt • *Scr* Michael Brandt, Derek Haas

The Double ★★★★ 15
Psychological drama
2013 · UK/US · Colour · 89min

Richard Ayoade's second outing as a director is an adaptation of a Dostoyevsky novella, switched to an Orwellian setting that's both retro and futuristic. The hero is Simon James (Jesse Eisenberg), an office drone whose feelings for fellow worker Mia Wasikowska go unrequited. Simon's life takes a turn for the worse with the arrival of new colleague James Simon (Eisenberg again), who is an exact physical double, but – being successful and sexually confident – his opposite in personality. Ayoade bravely avoids lightening the tone, instead utilising impressive sound editing and cinematography to craft an utterly compelling psychological fantasy. LB *DVD* *BL*

Jesse Eisenberg *Simon James/James Simon* • Mia Wasikowska *Hannah* • Wallace Shawn *Mr Papadopoulos* • Noah Taylor *Harris* • James Fox *The Colonel* ■ *Dir* Richard Ayoade • *Scr* Richard Ayoade, Avi Korine, from Korine's story, from Fyodor Dostoyevsky's novella

Double Bunk ★★ PG
Comedy
1961 · UK · BW · 88min

There's more pleasure to be had from spotting the support cast than from following the stars in some vintage British movies, and this under-directed comedy about honeymooners racing their houseboat is no exception. The nominal lead is Ian Carmichael, displaying his usual dottiness, but he had lost his ability to carry a picture by this point, and lovely though Janette Scott may be, she's no great shakes as an actress. TS *DVD*

Ian Carmichael *Jack Goddard* • Janette Scott *Peggy Deeley* • Liz Fraser *Sandra* • Sidney James *Sid Randall* • Dennis Price *Leonard Watson* • Reginald Beckwith *Alfred Harper* • Irene Handl *Mrs Harper* • Noel Purcell *O'Malley* • Miles Malleson *Reverend Thomas* ■ *Dir/Scr* CM Pennington-Richards

Double Cross ★★ U
Spy drama
1955 · UK · BW · 71min

This benefits from its Cornish locations and director Anthony Squire's tight use of the cramped conditions on board a fishing boat. Otherwise, it's B-business as usual, as salmon poacher Donald Houston realises mysterious passengers Anton Diffring and Delphi Lawrence have tricked him into ferrying Cold War secrets. DP

Donald Houston *Albert Pascoe* • Fay Compton *Alice Pascoe* • Anton Diffring *Dmitri Krassin* • Delphi Lawrence *Anna Krassin* • Allan Cuthbertson *Clifford* • William Hartnell *Whiteway* • Frank Lawton *Chief Constable* • Raymond Francis *Inspector Harris* ■ *Dir* Anthony Squire • *Scr* Anthony Squire, Kern Bennett, from the novel *The Queer Fish* by Kern Bennett

Double Crossbones ★★★ U
Satire
1951 · US · Colour · 75min

This smashing Donald O'Connor vehicle uses all of Universal's pirate-ship sets and costumes in a jolly tale of an apprentice shopkeeper who is mistaken for a famous buccaneer. Alan Napier makes a splendid Captain Kidd, and Hope Emerson is a fearsome Ann Bonney. However, the real pleasure is the sumptuous Technicolor, which makes the whole shebang seem rather better than it is. Fans of *Against All Flags* will have fun recognising props, while the narration is by Jeff Chandler, star of *Yankee Pasha*. TS

Donald O'Connor *Davy Crandell* • Helena Carter *Lady Sylvia Copeland* • Will Geer *Tom Botts* • John Emery *Governor Elden* • Hope Emerson *Mistress Ann Bonney* • Charles McGraw *Capt Ben Wickett* • Alan Napier *Capt Kidd* • Jeff Chandler *Narrator* ■ *Dir* Charles T Barton [Charles Barton] • *Scr* Oscar Brodney

Double Dare ★★★
Comedy thriller
1981 · Fr · Colour · 100min

Miou-Miou and Gérard Lanvin, who first worked together in *café-théâtre*, are here reunited by veteran director Georges Lautner for this sprightly comedy thriller. It's a frothy story that has Lanvin steal a judge's robes to escape his trial, only for Miou-Miou to insist he accompanies her to Nice and solve a murder mystery. There's plenty of spark between the leads and screen legend Renée Saint-Cyr (the director's mother) contributes a neat cameo. DP French dubbed.

Miou-Miou *Julie Boucher* • Gérard Lanvin *Gerard Louvier* • Renée Saint-Cyr *Madame Bertillon* • Julien Guiomar *Raymond* • Michel Galabru *Bailiff* ■ *Dir* Georges Lautner • *Scr* Jean-Marie Poiré

Double Deal ★★ 15
Romantic crime drama
1981 · Aus · Colour · 86min

This self-consciously smart-aleck thriller sat on the shelf for three years, and it's easy to see why. Brian Kavanagh tries desperately to deceive us as bored fashion model Angela Punch McGregor and criminal biker Warwick Comber play an increasingly far-fetched game of cat and mouse with her tycoon husband (Louis Jourdan) and his secretary (Diana Craig). Banal. DP

Louis Jourdan *Peter Sterling* • Angela Punch McGregor *Christina Sterling* • Diane Craig *June Stevens* • Warwick Comber *Young man* • Peter Cummins *Detective Mills* • Bruce Spence *Doug Mitchell* • June Jago *Mrs Coolidge* ■ *Dir/Scr* Brian Kavanagh

Double Dragon ★★★ 12
Martial arts adventure
1994 · US · Colour · 91min

In the ravaged, flooded Los Angeles of 2007, Mark Dacascos and Scott Wolf are streetwise youths who come upon one half of an ancient Chinese talisman, which gives awesome power to whoever possesses both halves. Unfortunately, the other portion is owned by unscrupulous gang boss Robert Patrick and his phalanx of gigantic henchmen. Decent effects and a wisecracking screenplay lift James Yukich's movie above the usual futuristic fare. JF *DVD* *BL*

Robert Patrick *Koga Shuko* • Mark Dacascos *Jimmy Lee* • Scott Wolf *Billy Lee* • Kristina Malandro Wagner *Linda Lash* • Julia Nickson [Julia Nickson-Soul] *Sartori Imada* • Alyssa Milano *Marian Delario* ■ *Dir* James Yukich • *Scr* Michael Davis, Peter Gould, from a story by Neal Shusterman, Paul Dini

Double Dynamite ★★ U
Comedy
1951 · US · BW · 77min

Thanks to a favour from a bookie (Nestor Paiva), a decent young bank clerk (Frank Sinatra) wins a fortune on a race. When $75,000 goes missing from the bank, however, the clerk's fiancée (Jane Russell) and unconventional waiter friend (Groucho Marx) are convinced he stole his new-found wealth. Apart from an occasional laugh supplied by Groucho, this is a thin and unfunny comedy. RK *DVD*

Jane Russell *Mildred "Mibs" Goodhug* • Groucho Marx *Emil J Keck* • Frank Sinatra *Johnny Dalton* • Don McGuire *Bob Pulsifer Jr* • Howard Freeman *RB Pulsifer Sr* • Harry Hayden *JL McKissack* • Nestor Paiva *"Hot Horse" Harris* • Lou Nova *Max* ■ *Dir* Irving Cummings • *Scr* Melville Shavelson, Harry Crane, from a story by Leo Rosten, from a character created by Mannie Manheim

Double Edge ★★
Political drama
1992 · Is · Colour · 86min

Assigned to Israel for three weeks, intrepid reporter Faye Dunaway finds herself drawn to both sides in the Arab/Israeli conflict. But when she writes about a family of Palestinian resistance fighters, the story gets her into trouble both politically and emotionally. Dunaway isn't at her most charismatic here, but the film is interesting enough and the ending has a nice punch. ST

Faye Dunaway *Faye Milano* • Amos Kollek *David* • Muhamad Bacri [Muhamad Bakri] *Mustafa Shafik* • Makram Khouri *Ahmed Shafik* • Michael Schneider *Max* • Shmuel Shiloh *Moshe* • Anat Atzmon *Censor* ■ *Dir/Scr* Amos Kollek

Double Impact ★★★ 18
Action thriller
1991 · US · Colour · 105min

Yet to handle one role convincingly, Jean-Claude Van Damme was a tad ambitious to take on two in this otherwise straightforward action thriller. In a performance that adds a new meaning to the term identical twins, Van Damme is equally wooden as the two brothers – one good, one a bit of a rogue – who are reunited to avenge the death of their parents. However, there's plenty of biffing, kicking and explosions for those who like that sort of thing. JF Swearing, violence, drug abuse, sex scenes, nudity. *DVD*

Jean-Claude Van Damme *Chad Wagner/Alex Wagner* • Geoffrey Lewis *Frank Avery* • Alan Scarfe *Nigel Griffith* • Alonna Shaw *Danielle Wilde* • Cory Everson *Kara* • Philip Yan Kin Chan [Philip Chan] *Raymond Zhang* • Bolo Yeung *Moon* ■ *Dir* Sheldon Lettich • *Scr* Sheldon Lettich, Jean-Claude Van Damme, from a story by Lettich, Van Damme, Steve Meerson, Peter Krikes

Double Indemnity ★★★★★ PG
Classic film noir
1944 · US · BW · 103min

Billy Wilder's classic thriller, with its crackling screenplay co-written by Raymond Chandler, is one of the best-loved examples of *film noir* ever made. Based on a short story by James M Cain (author of *The Postman Always Rings Twice*), it follows definitive *femme fatale* Barbara Stanwyck as she seduces insurance salesman Fred MacMurray into murdering – then feigning the accidental death of – her husband Tom Powers, before claiming the premium on the latter's life. However, dogged insurance investigator Edward G Robinson smells a rat and suspects Stanwyck of murder. Wilder was nominated for an Oscar, as was John F Seitz's cinematography and Miklos Rozsa's atmospheric score, while in the best actress category Stanwyck lost out to Ingrid Bergman for *Gaslight*. TS *DVD* *BL*

Fred MacMurray *Walter Neff* • Barbara Stanwyck *Phyllis Dietrichson* • Edward G Robinson *Barton Keyes* • Porter Hall *Mr Jackson* • Jean Heather *Lola Dietrichson* • Tom Powers *Mr Dietrichson* • Byron Barr *Nino Zachette* ■ *Dir* Billy Wilder • *Scr* Billy Wilder, Raymond Chandler, from the novella by James M Cain, as serialised in *Liberty* magazine

Double Indemnity ★★ PG
Crime thriller 1973 · US · Colour · 74min

This is a decidely tame made-for-TV take on Billy Wilder's classic 1944 thriller about a *femme fatale* who lures a hapless insurance investigator into murdering her husband and declaring the death an accident so they can make a claim on his policy. Samantha Eggar lacks the simmering sexuality of Barbara Stanwyck, leaving the viewer unconvinced by Richard Crenna's decision to risk everything for her love. DP DVD

Richard Crenna *Walter Neff* • Lee J Cobb *Barton Keyes* • Samantha Eggar *Phyllis Dietrichson* • Robert Webber *Edward Norton* ■ *Dir* Jack Smight • *Scr* Steven Bochco, from the 1944 film

Double Jeopardy ★★★ 15
Action thriller 1999 · US/Ger · Colour · 100min

This revenge thriller was a big hit in the US, where women lined up to see wronged wife Ashley Judd get her own back on her evil, cheating partner. What starts off as a romantic sailing trip turns into a nightmare when she wakes up one morning surrounded by coastguards with her spouse (Bruce Greenwood) missing and pools of blood all over the boat. Sent to prison for his murder, she discovers he faked his own death and has run off with their child and her best friend. Judd gives a believable performance, but Tommy Lee Jones gives a sub-*Fugitive* turn as the federal officer on her trail. Completely preposterous. JB DVD

Ashley Judd *Libby Parsons* • Tommy Lee Jones *Travis Lehman* • Bruce Greenwood *Nick Parsons* • Annabeth Gish *Angie* • Benjamin Weir *Matty aged 4* ■ *Dir* Bruce Beresford • *Scr* David Weisberg, Douglas S Cook

A Double Life ★★★ PG
Crime drama 1947 · US · BW · 99min

Debonair Ronald Colman won his only Oscar for his performance in this overtly theatrical melodrama about an actor who becomes dangerously absorbed with his stage roles in real life. As Colman is about to play Othello, Signe Hasso is the Desdemona who's under threat. Colman is an unlikely Moor, but he cleverly manages to convince, aided by George Cukor's adroit direction and the brilliant Oscar-winning score. The story, however, remains resolutely silly as Colman becomes increasingly unhinged. TS

Ronald Colman *Anthony John* • Signe Hasso *Brita* • Edmond O'Brien *Bill Friend* • Shelley Winters *Pat Kroll* • Ray Collins *Victor Donlan* • Philip Loeb *Max Lasker* • Millard Mitchell *Al Cooley* ■ *Dir* George Cukor • *Scr* Ruth Gordon, Garson Kanin • *Music* Miklos Rozsa

The Double Life of Véronique ★★★★ 15
Drama 1991 · Fr/Pol · Colour · 93min

A slight but mesmerising tale from Polish director Krzysztof Kieslowski, this disappointed some critics on its release after the scope of his monumental *Ten Commandments*. However, this is also a work of great intelligence, with its discussion of the fragility of humanity, the perils of ambition and the possibility that we may all have a spiritual twin somewhere in the world. Irène Jacob won the best actress prize at Cannes for her subtle dual performance as two woman, born in different countries, who are identical in appearance and in their gift for music. DP Polish, French +subtitles. Nudity. DVD BD

Irène Jacob *Weronika/Véronique* • Philippe Volter *Alexandre Fabbri* • Halina Gryglaszewska *Aunt* • Kalina Jedrusik *Gaudy woman* • Aleksander Bardini *Orchestra conductor* • Wladyslaw Kowalski *Weronika's father* ■ *Dir* Krzysztof Kieslowski • *Scr* Krzysztof Kieslowski, Krzysztof Piesiewicz

The Double Man ★★ PG
Spy thriller 1967 · UK · Colour · 100min

A miscast Yul Brynner plays two characters, one American and one German, and makes both of these tight-lipped agents equally dull. The real surprise is that this Swiss-located Elstree-based murk is directed by the redoubtable Franklin J Schaffner, best remembered for *Patton* and *Planet of the Apes*. Goes to show that, no matter how talented a director is, if it's not in the script it'll never be on the screen. TS

Yul Brynner *Dan Slater/Kalmar* • Britt Ekland *Gina* • Clive Revill *Frank Wheatley* • Anton Diffring *Col Berthold* • Moira Lister *Mrs Carrington* • Lloyd Nolan *Edwards* • David Bauer *Miller* ■ *Dir* Franklin J Schaffner • *Scr* Henry S Maxfield

Double Platinum ★★ PG
Musical drama 1999 · US · Colour · 86min

Diana Ross, one of the most successful female recording artists of all time, here stars with teen sensation Brandy, a pretender to her crown. Ross is a struggling lounge singer who abandons her daughter Brandy to pursue her showbiz dream. Flash forward 18 years, and Ross is now a massive star to whom Brandy – ignorant of her origins and just embarking on her own warbling career – goes to for advice. Fans will enjoy the tunes, but not the creaking melodrama. JF DVD

Diana Ross *Olivia King* • Brandy Norwood [Brandy] *Kayla Harris* • Christine Ebersole *Peggy* • Allen Payne *Ric Crtega* • Brian Stokes Mitchell *Adam Harris* • Roger Rees *Marc Reckler* • Samantha Brown *Poyana* ■ *Dir* Robert Allan Ackerman • *Scr* Nina Shengold

Double Take ★★★★ 12A
Fantasy documentary 2009 · Bel/Ger/Neth/It/Fr/US/UK · Colour and BW · 82min

This mischievous documentary examines the work of Alfred Hitchcock against the backdrop of the Cold War. Cunningly conceived by Belgian visual artist Johan Grimonprez and British novelist Tom McCarthy, the montage of existing footage and new material is thematically linked by Hitchcock's obsession with doubles. But, for all the originality of the concept and the ingenuity of the assemblage, this says less about media-generated paranoia (both then and now) than it does about Hitchcock's teasing attitude to his work and how badly US cinema currently needs somebody of his genius. DP Disturbing images.

Ron Burrage *Hitchcock double* • Mark Perry *Hitchcock voice* • Delfine Bafort *Tippi double* ■ *Dir* Johan Grimonprez • *Scr* Johan Grimonprez, from a story by Tom McCarthy, from the article *essay: 24 August, 1983* by Jorge Luis Borges

Double Team ★★ 18
Action adventure 1997 · US · Colour · 89min

Here Tsui Hark supplies a hyper-realistic surface sheen and loads of slow-motion violence, but gets no closer to drawing out a convincing performance from the Belgian star Jean-Claude Van Damme. Tsui also has to cope with another non-actor, in the shape of basketball legend Dennis Rodman. His ludicrous hair and clothes do at least deflect attention from his unfunny performance as a mysterious gunrunner who helps Van Damme track down master criminal Mickey Rourke. JF Violence, swearing. DVD

Jean-Claude Van Damme *Jack Quinn* • Dennis Rodman *Yaz* • Mickey Rourke *Stavros* • Paul Freeman *Goldsmythe* • Natacha Lindinger *Kath* • Valeria Cavalli *Dr Maria Trifioli* ■ *Dir* Tsui Hark • *Scr* Don Jakoby, Paul Mones, from a story by Don Jakoby

Double Trouble ★ U
Musical drama 1967 · US · Colour · 87min

Arguably the worst of the stream of pap movies the great Elvis Presley found himself trapped in by dint of manager Colonel Tom Parker's wheeling and dealing, this substandard frolic is actually set in a nonexistent London (filmed on a badly designed MGM set in Culver City) in a pathetic nod to the shift in musical culture at the time. Elvis sings one decent rock number, *Long-Legged Girl (with the Short Dress on)*, but this is truly lame-brained nonsense. TS DVD

Elvis Presley *Guy Lambert* • Annette Day *Jill Conway* • John Williams *Gerald Waverly* • Yvonne Romain *Claire Dunham* • Harry Wiere • Herbert Wiere • Sylvester Wiere • Chips Rafferty *Archie*

Brown • Norman Rossington *Arthur Babcock* ■ *Dir* Norman Taurog • *Scr* Jo Heims, from a story by Marc Brandel

Double Vision ★★ 18
Thriller 2002 · Tai/HK · Colour · 108min

One-time critic Chen Kuo-fu attempts to cross the divide between art house and the mainstream with this serial killer thriller only to come up way short. The opening segment, in which world-weary Taipei cop Tony Leung Ka-fai investigates a series of inventively grisly murders, is darkly intriguing. But once he's teamed with FBI agent David Morse, the story spirals into culture-clashing caricature and fantasy. DP Mandarin, Hokkien, English +subtitles. DVD

Tony Leung Ka-fai [Tony Leung (1)] *Huang Huo-tu* • David Morse *Kevin Richter* • Rene Lui *Ching-fang* • Leon Dai *Li Feng-bo* • Yang Kuei-Mei *Coroner* ■ *Dir* Chen Kuo-fu • *Scr* Chen Kuo-fu, Su Chao-Bin • *Cinematographer* Arthur Wong

Double Wedding ★★★ U
Screwball comedy 1937 · US · BW · 86min

This wonderfully wacky farce stars William Powell as an eccentric artist and Myrna Loy as a bossy designer, bent on forcing her feisty, movie-mad sister (Florence Rice) to marry conservative John Beal. At the time, several reviewers thought this frolic too European in tone – hardly surprising, since it's loosely based on Ferenc Molnar's play, *Great Love*. TS

William Powell *Charlie Lodge* • Myrna Loy *Margit Agnew* • Florence Rice *Irene Agnew* • John Beal *Waldo Beaver* • Jessie Ralph *Mrs Kensington Bly* • Edgar Kennedy *Spike* • Sidney Toler *Keough* ■ *Dir* Richard Thorpe • *Scr* Jo Swerling, Waldo Salt, from the play *Great Love* by Ferenc Molnar

Double Wedding ★★
Romantic comedy 2010 · US · Colour · 105min

In this sprightly but contrived romantic comedy, former teen stars Tia and Tamera Mowry play twin sisters who unwittingly date the same man. But charming beau OT Fagbenle (from BBC TV's *Material Girl*) is too lovestruck to notice that they're different women, despite Tamera's delightful pastry chef being passionate and impulsive, while Tia's lawyer is uptight and hesitant. Fortunately director Craig Pryce manages to keep the sentimentality sweet rather than sickly in the predictable resolutions that follow. SF

Tia Mowry *Deanna Warren* • Tamera Mowry *Danielle Warren* • Fagbenle O T *Tate* • Chad Connell *Jasper Cooper* • Laura DeCarteret *Elle Greenford* ■ *Dir* Craig Pryce • *Scr* Jennifer Maisel

Double Whammy ★ 15
Black comedy drama 2001 · US/Ger · Colour · 96min

The quirky charm of writer/director Tom DiCillo has deserted him in this grating comedy. Denis Leary gives a typically one-note performance as a cop whose debilitating back pain has made him a New York laughing stock, while a decorative Elizabeth Hurley as his chiropractor (and love interest) suggests that her *Austin Powers* comic assurance was a fluke. A total misfire from start to finish. JC DVD

Denis Leary *Det Ray Pluto* • Elizabeth Hurley *Dr Ann Beamer* • Steve Buscemi *Jerry Cubbins* • Luis Guzman *Juan Benitez* • Chris Noth [Christopher Noth] *Chick Dmitri* • Keith Knobbs *Duke* ■ *Dir/Scr* Tom DiCillo

Double X: the Name of the Game ★ 15
Crime drama 1991 · UK · Colour · 93min

Even in the darkest days of the low-budget crime drama, few films plumbed the depths reached by this atrocity. Norman Wisdom does his best to convince as a petty crook trying to keep his daughter out of the clutches of a criminal gang, but such is the awfulness of director Shani S Grewal's dialogue that Wisdom raises more laughs than he used to get in his sentimental comedies. DP Violence, swearing.

Simon Ward *Edward Ross* • William Katt *Michael Cooper* • Norman Wisdom *Arthur Clutton* • Bernard Hill *Iggy Smith* • Gemma Craven *Jenny Eskridge* • Leon Herbert *Ollie* • Derren Nesbitt *Minister* ■ *Dir* Shani S Grewal • *Scr* Shani S Grewal, from the short story *Vengeance* by David Fleming

Doubt ★★★ 15
Period drama 2008 · US · Colour · 99min

John Patrick Shanley here writes and directs an austere adaptation of his own Pulitzer Prize-winning play. Set in a Catholic boys' school in the Bronx in 1964, it's essentially a claustrophobic three-hander in which a priest (Philip Seymour Hoffman) is suspected of misconduct with the school's only black pupil. His chief accuser is the principal (Meryl Streep), whose religious certainty sets her on a collision course with Hoffman's modernising tendencies. Amy Adams completes this powerhouse trio as an innocent young nun. Shanley's dialogue is honed and articulate, but he is never quite able to overcome the piece's theatricality. AC DVD BD

Meryl Streep *Sister Aloysius Beauvier* • Philip Seymour Hoffman *Father Brendan Flynn* • Amy Adams *Sister James* • Viola Davis *Mrs Miller* • Alice Drummond *Sister Veronica* • Audrie Neenan *Sister Raymond* • Susan Blommaert *Mrs Carson* ■ *Dir* John Patrick Shanley • *Scr* John Patrick Shanley, from his play

Dougal and the Blue Cat ★★★ U
Animated adventure 1970 · Fr · Colour · 78min

Did you know that Dougal was called Pollux in the original French version of *The Magic Roundabout*? In this awesomely weird feature spin-off, the cynical shaggy dog is the only creature who can prevent the devious double act of Buxton the Cat and Madame Blue from stealing Zebedee's moustache and taking control of the Magic Garden. Directed with typically surreal inventiveness by Serge Danot, this zany adventure is made all the more hilarious by the crackling dialogue penned and delivered by Eric Thompson, father of Emma. DP DVD

Eric Thompson *Narrator/Dougal/Zebedee/Florence/Dylan/Buxton* • Fenella Fielding *Madame Blue* ■ *Dir* Serge Danot, Eric Thompson • *Scr* Serge Danot, Jacques Josselin, Eric Thompson

Doughboys ★★
First World War comedy 1930 · US · BW · 80min

Buster Keaton, the comic genius who made his reputation in the silent era, took quite a risk with this, his first talkie. It's the tale of a rich man joining the army by mistake, and was based on Keaton's own experiences during the First World War. Directed by Edward Sedgwick, the film works reasonably well, though sound was never Buster's natural medium. TH

Buster Keaton *Elmer* • Sally Eilers *Mary* • Cliff Edwards *Nescopeck* • Edward Brophy *Sgt Brophy* • Victor Potel *Svendenburg* • Arnold Korff *Gustave* • Frank Mayo *Capt Scott* ■ *Dir* Edward Sedgwick • *Scr* Al Boasberg, Sidney Lazarus, Richard Schayer, from a story by Al Boasberg, Sidney Lazarus

The Doughgirls ★★★
Wartime comedy 1944 · US · BW · 101min

This bowdlerised screen version of Joseph A Fields's Broadway hit about the wartime housing shortage in Washington DC is still very funny, but it's a long way behind other movies on the same subject (*The More the Merrier*, for example). Warner Bros contract players get a chance to shine in this ensemble comedy, particularly Ann Sheridan, Alexis Smith and Jane Wyman (then married to Ronald Reagan). Once again, however, the priceless Eve Arden – here playing a Russian – effortlessly walks away with every scene she's in. TS

Jack Carson *Arthur Halstead* • Jane Wyman *Vivian Halstead* • John Ridgely *Julian Cadman* • Ann Sheridan *Edna Stokes* • Charles Ruggles *Slade* • Alexis Smith *Nan* • Craig Stevens *Tom* • Eve Arden *Natalia* ■ *Dir* James V Kern • *Scr* James V Kern, Sam Hellman, from a play by Joseph A Fields

D

Doug's 1st Movie ★★★ U
Animated adventure 1999 · US · Colour · 77min

As an introduction to a much loved American children's TV character for wider audiences, this full-length Disney animation does a fairly successful job, with a tale hingeing on a now-familiar eco-message. A squidgy, pollution-induced monster (named after *Moby Dick* writer Herman Melville) is found by oddball high-school student Doug Funnie and his friend Skeeter in a lake owned by wicked tycoon Bill Bluff. The cautionary conclusion will be easily understood by the three-to-eight-year-olds at whom it's aimed. TH

Thomas McHugh *Doug Funnie/Lincoln* • Fred Newman *Skeeter/Mr Dink/Porkchop/Ned* • Chris Phillips *Roger Klotz/Boomer/Larry/Mr Chiminy* • Constance Shulman *Patti Mayonnaise* • Frank Welker *Herman Melville* ■ *Dir* Maurice Joyce • *Scr* Ken Scarborough

Le Doulos ★★★ 12
Crime drama 1962 · Fr · BW · 106min

Jean-Pierre Melville's flawed but fascinating crime thriller – a tribute to the classic American gangster movies of the 1930s and 1940s – casts Jean-Paul Belmondo as an underworld figure and police informer for whom treachery is a religion. First he helps an ex-con plan a heist; then he betrays him. Then he plans the man's escape from prison. Oh, and he kills his girlfriend, too. Look out for the famous nine-minute take in the policeman's office: Melville insisted the camera crew wore black and donned face masks to eliminate the risk of reflection in the windows and mirrors. AT French +subtitles. Violence. DVD

Jean-Paul Belmondo *Silien* • Serge Reggiani *Maurice* • Monique Hennessy *Therese* • René Lefèvre *Gilbert* • Jean Desailly *Inspector* • Michel Piccoli *Leader* • Carl Studer *Kern* ■ *Dir* Jean-Pierre Melville • *Scr* Jean-Pierre Melville, from the novel by Pierre Lesou

The Dove ★★★ PG
Biographical adventure
1974 · US/UK · Colour · 99min

Gregory Peck produced this beautifully shot film, based on a true story, in which a 16-year-old boy comes of age during a five-year solo circumnavigation of the globe in a small boat. Part travelogue, part adventure, the film makes you yearn for the days when not every beach and seaside town was over-developed, and features accomplished performances from a young Joseph Bottoms as the intrepid sailor, Deborah Raffin and Dabney Coleman. JB

Joseph Bottoms *Robin Lee Graham* • Deborah Raffin *Patti Ratteree* • John McLiam *Lyle Graham* • Dabney Coleman *Charles Huntley* • John Anderson *Mike Turk* • Colby Chester *Tom Barkley* • Ivor Barry *Kenniston* ■ *Dir* Charles Jarrott • *Scr* Peter Beagle, Adam Kennedy, from the non-fiction book by Robin Lee Graham, Derek Gill

Down among the Z-Men ★ U
Comedy 1952 · UK · BW · 67min

Although Peter Sellers, Harry Secombe and Spike Milligan co-starred in *Penny Points to Paradise* (1951), this was the only time all four founders of *The Goon Show* appeared together on celluloid. However, Michael Bentine's turn as a mad professor is just one of many space-fillers in this dismal army romp. Gone is the zany humour that made the radio show essential listening and, in its place, comes crude slapstick. DP DVD

Peter Sellers *Major Bloodnock* • Harry Secombe *Harry Jones* • Spike Milligan *Private Eccles* • Michael Bentine *Professor Osrick Purehart* • Carole Carr *Carole Gayley* ■ *Dir* Maclean Rogers • *Scr* Jimmy Grafton, Francis Charles

Down and Dirty ★★★ 15
Comedy 1976 · It · Colour · 111min

Ettore Scola directs this raucous comedy, which exploits the conventions of neorealism to mock its sentimental attitude to poverty. Set in a crumbling shanty town on the outskirts of Rome, the film introduces us to a gallery of grotesques, none more revolting than Nino Manfredi's one-eyed patriarch, whose vulgarity and greed bring out the darker side of his desperate relations. Although graphic in his depiction of their squalor, Scola refuses to portray the poor as innocent victims, but also refrains from cruelty in satirising their low expectations and boorish behaviour. DP Italian +subtitles.

Nino Manfredi *Giacinto* • Francesco Anniballi *Domizio* • Maria Bosco *Gaetana* • Giselda Castrini *Lisetta* ■ *Dir* Ettore Scola • *Scr* Ruggero Maccari, Ettore Scola

Down and Out in Beverly Hills ★★★ 15
Comedy 1986 · US · Colour · 103min

This box-office smash hit provided Nick Nolte with a choice comic role, and he makes the most of it. But there's something a shade too frantic and nervy about the film's pace and the performances of Bette Midler and Richard Dreyfuss as the nouveau riche Beverly Hills couple who find themselves giving house room to Nolte's hobo. Some very funny set pieces and the occasional unerring spotlight on snobbery make it a movie worth watching, but it's not a patch on the classic French original *Boudu, Saved from Drowning*. SH Some swearing, nudity. DVD

Nick Nolte *Jerry Baskin* • Bette Midler *Barbara Whiteman* • Richard Dreyfuss *Dave Whiteman* • Little Richard *Orvis Goodnight* • Tracy Nelson *Jenny Whiteman* • Elizabeth Peña *Carmen* • Evan Richards *Max Whiteman* • Donald F Muhich *Dr Von Zimmer* ■ *Dir* Paul Mazursky • *Scr* Paul Mazursky, Leon Capetanos, from the film *Boudu, Saved from Drowning* by Jean Renoir, from the play by René Fauchois

Down Argentine Way ★★★ U
Romantic musical 1940 · US · Colour · 85min

When this movie was first shown in cinemas, Argentina was as alien to American movie audiences as Mars, and the kind of Latin music presented here by Carmen Miranda was tremendously exciting. It's important to bear that in mind as you watch this witless farrago set in an Argentina that never gets off the 20th Century-Fox backlot. Betty Grable, playing the American girl who falls in love with rich horse breeder Don Ameche. The 1940s Technicolor is nice, but the supporting cast leaves a lot to be desired. TS DVD

Don Ameche *Ricardo Quintana* • Betty Grable *Glenda Crawford* • Carmen Miranda • Charlotte Greenwood *Binnie Crawford* • J Carrol Naish *Casiano* • Henry Stephenson *Don Diego Quintana* • Katharine Aldridge *Helen Carson* ■ *Dir* Irving Cummings • *Scr* Darrell Ware, Karl Tunberg, from a story by Rian James, Ralph Spence

Down by Law ★★★★ 15
Black comedy 1986 · US · BW · 106min

Jim Jarmusch's uneven but stylish *comédie noire* is an astute mixture of prison picture, road movie and downbeat screwball. Posturing hard men Tom Waits and John Lurie find themselves sharing a cell after they are framed for transporting a corpse and corrupting a minor respectively. Their petty feuding is interrupted by chatty new cellmate Roberto Benigni, who soon devises an escape plan. As the excellent soundtrack testifies, Waits and Lurie are more effectively paired as songwriters than performers, but they offer solid support to the brilliant Benigni, whose prattling is a joy. DP Swearing. DVD Blu

Tom Waits *Zack* • John Lurie *Jack Romano* • Roberto Benigni *Roberto* • Nicoletta Braschi *Nicoletta* • Ellen Barkin *Laurette* • Billie Neal *Bobbie* ■ *Dir/Scr* Jim Jarmusch

Down Dog ★★ 15
Comedy 2014 · UK · Colour · 96min

There are moments during this uneven comedy co-written by Simon Nye (TV's *Men Behaving Badly*) where you genuinely fear for the British film industry. In a bid to shock her ex-husband Frank (Jason Durr) into taking greater parenting responsibility, Rachel (Orla O'Rourke) cons Frank into thinking he has only months to live. Predictably, it's a life-changing revelation. One or two of the more serious father/son scenes pass muster, but emotional truths are few and far between. DA

Jason Durr *Frank Clayton* • Nick Moran *Bill* • Orla O'Rourke *Rachel/Harriet/Flora* • Tom Goodman-Hill *Dr Hill* ■ *Dir* Andres Dussan • *Scr* Simon Nye, Andres Dussan, Lawrence Tallis

Down in the Delta ★★★
Drama 1997 · US · Colour · 111min

Any film with the wonderful Alfre Woodard is worth catching, so don't miss this moving drama directed by the poet Maya Angelou. Woodard is the Chicago mother packed off with her children to a Mississippi backwater to escape the perils of the inner-city streets. While Angelou loads on the family values theme a little thickly in places, this is nonetheless an enjoyable and heart-rending picture, given extra weight by some classy performances from Loretta Devine, Esther Rolle and Wesley Snipes. JB

Alfre Woodard *Loretta* • Al Freeman Jr *Earl* • Mary Alice *Rosa Lynn* • Esther Rolle *Annie* • Loretta Devine *Zenia* • Wesley Snipes *Will* • Mpho Koaha *Thomas* • Kulani Hassen *Tracy* ■ *Dir* Maya Angelou • *Scr* Myron Goble

Down in the Valley ★★★ 15
Romantic drama 2004 · US · Colour · 112min

David Jacobson's haunting and ambitious drama centres on a richly nuanced turn from Edward Norton as a cowboy-obsessed drifter who sweeps high-school senior Evan Rachel Wood off her feet with his curiously naive charm. The love affair that follows is fuelled by an admiration that makes both the teenager and her neurosis-filled younger brother (Rory Culkin) oblivious to the gradual emotional cracks appearing in their new friend. This darkness beneath the sweetness explodes into startling violence. While beautifully performed, events become increasingly implausible. SF Swearing, violence. DVD

Edward Norton *Harlan Fairfax Carruthers* • Evan Rachel Wood *Tobe Sommers* • David Morse *Wade Sommers* • Rory Culkin *Lonnie Sommers* • Bruce Dern *Charlie* • John Diehl *Steve* • Geoffrey Lewis *Sheridan* • Elizabeth Peña *Gale* ■ *Dir/Scr* David Jacobson

Down Mexico Way ★★ U
Western 1941 · US · BW · 79min

A popular Gene Autry feature, this western has a little more action than most, plus a fair amount of well-known songs. Maybe that's why Joseph Santley, better known for musicals than westerns, was hired to direct. The plot's a nothing about Autry chasing some conmen who are posing as movie-makers. TS

Gene Autry *Gene* • Smiley Burnette *Frog* • Fay McKenzie *Maria Elena* • Harold Huber *Pancho Grande* • Sidney Blackmer *Gibson* • Joe Sawyer *Allen* • Andrew Tombes *Mayor Tubbs* • Murray Alper *Flood* • Paul Fix *Davis* • Duncan Renaldo *Juan* ■ *Dir* Joseph Santley • *Scr* Olive Cooper, Albert Duffy, from the story by Stuart McGowan, Dorrell McGowan

Down Periscope ★★ 12
Comedy 1996 · US · Colour · 88min

Frasier star Kelsey Grammer here plays a useless submarine commander who will be kicked out of the navy unless he can train a hapless crew in an old boiler of a sub how to outmanoeuvre the entire fleet. Director David S Ward has done this type of slapstick so many times before that he's run out of ideas. Still, Grammer tries his best, and he's well supported by the comic turns from the rest of the quality cast. JB Swearing. DVD

Kelsey Grammer *Lt Commander Thomas Dodge* • Lauren Holly *Lt Emily Lake* • Rob Schneider *Executive Officer Martin Pascal* • Harry Dean Stanton *Howard* • Bruce Dern *Admiral Yancy Graham* • William H Macy *Captain Knox* • Ken Hudson Campbell *Buckman* • Toby Huss *Nitro* • Rip Torn *Admiral Winslow* ■ *Dir* David S Ward • *Scr* Hugh Wilson, Eliot Wald, Andrew Kurtzman, from a story by Hugh Wilson

Down Terrace ★★★ 15
Crime comedy drama
2009 · UK · Colour · 89min

Offbeat comedy drama about a family of villains who suspect one of their gang is secretly working as a police informant. Patriarch Bill (Robert Hill) is relieved when his son Karl (Robin Hill) avoids a prison sentence, and returns to his modest Brighton semi to try to discover who the traitor might be. Director Ben Wheatley's low-key curiosity recalls both the domestic mundanity of *The Royle Family* and the more sinister themes of betrayal and revenge in *The Sopranos*. It's an audacious balancing act, by turns shocking and comical. TeS Violence, swearing, drug abuse.

Robin Hill *Karl* • Robert Hill (3) *Bill* • Julia Deakin *Maggie* • David Schaal *Eric* • Kerry Peacock *Valda* • Tony Way *Garvey* • Mark Kempner *Berman* • Michael Smiley *Pringle* ■ *Dir* Ben Wheatley • *Scr* Ben Wheatley, Robin Hill

Down Three Dark Streets ★★★ U
Detective crime drama 1954 · US · BW · 85min

When an FBI agent dies, a colleague takes on his caseload and finds himself caught up in three different crimes involving car theft, a gangster on the run and an extortion racket. Broderick Crawford stars as the investigator, while Martha Hyer makes an excellent gangster's moll. Ruth Roman and Marisa Pavan also appear, as a widow under threat and a blind girl respectively. In the best tradition of gritty, low-key crime thrillers, Arnold Laven's movie keeps the suspense going all the way to the final fade. RK

Broderick Crawford *Ripley* • Ruth Roman *Kate Martel* • Martha Hyer *Connie Anderson* • Marisa Pavan *Julie Angelino* • Casey Adams [Max Showalter] *Dave Millson* • Kenneth Tobey *Zack Stewart* • Gene Reynolds *Vince Angelino* • William Johnstone *Frank Pace* ■ *Dir* Arnold Laven • *Scr* Bernard C Schoenfeld, The Gordons [Gordon Gordon, Margaret Gordon], from their novel *Case File FBI*

Down to Earth ★★★ U
Musical fantasy 1947 · US · Colour · 96min

Along the same lines as the following year's *One Touch of Venus*, and incorporating a couple of characters directly from 1941's *Here Comes Mr Jordan*, this Columbia musical boasts two significant assets: Rita Hayworth and Technicolor. Some may find this whimsy about the goddess of dance (Hayworth) landing on Earth to help Larry Parks jazz up a musical show tiresome, but there's still much pleasure to be had. TS

Rita Hayworth *Terpsichore/Kitty Pendleton* • Larry Parks *Danny Miller* • Marc Platt *Eddie Marin* • Roland Culver *Mr Jordan* • James Gleason *Max Corkle* • Edward Everett Horton *Messenger 7013* • Adele Jergens *Georgia Evans* • George Macready *Joe Mannion* ■ *Dir* Alexander Hall • *Scr* Edwin Blum, Don Hartman, from the play *Heaven Can Wait* by Harry Segall

Down to Earth ★★ 12
Fantasy comedy 2001 · US · Colour · 83min

Chris Rock plays an unfunny stand-up comedian who is taken before his time and has to be returned to Earth by Mr King (Chazz Palminteri, playing God's right-hand man like a Mafia consiglieri). Trouble is, the comedian's original body has been cremated, and the only alternative has just been vacated by a fat-cat white businessman who's been bumped off by his wife and her lover. Rock tries hard – too hard at times. DA DVD

Chris Rock *Lance Barton* • Regina King *Sontee* • Chazz Palminteri *King* • Eugene Levy *Keyes* • Whitney Daniels *Frankie Faison* • Mark Addy *Cisco* • Greg Germann *Sklar* • Jennifer Coolidge *Mrs Wellington* ■ *Dir* Chris Weitz, Paul Weitz • *Scr* Chris Rock, Lance Crouther, Ali Le Roi, Louis CK, from the film *Heaven Can Wait* by Elaine May, Warren Beatty, from the play *Heaven Can Wait* by Harry Segall

Down to the Sea in Ships
★★★ PG
Adventure   1949 · US · BW · 115min

Henry Hathaway keeps this rousing whaling adventure firmly on course. Lionel Barrymore is his cantankerous self as a 19th-century seafarer whose grandson (Dean Stockwell) is torn between the old methods of the family firm and the modern techniques of first mate Richard Widmark. Hathaway makes the most of the set pieces, but the real highlight is the playing of such stalwarts as Cecil Kellaway, Gene Lockhart and Harry Davenport. DP **DVD**

Richard Widmark *Dan Lunceford* · Lionel Barrymore *Captain Bering Joy* · Dean Stockwell *Jed Joy* · Cecil Kellaway *Slush Tubbs* · Gene Lockhart *Andrew Bush* · Berry Kroeger *Manchester* · John McIntire *Thatch* · Henry Morgan [Harry Morgan] *Britton* · Harry Davenport *Mr Harris* ■ *Dir* Henry Hathaway · *Scr* John Lee Mahin, Sy Bartlett, from a story by Sy Bartlett, from the film by John LE Pell

Down to You
★★ 12
Romantic comedy   2000 · US · Colour · 87min

This teenage romance details the relationship between two New York college kids. Freddie Prinze Jr and Julia Stiles make attractive leads, but Kris Isacsson's film is marred by irritating voiceovers, asides to camera and loads of cracker-barrel philosophising about life and love. There's a fine supporting performance from Henry Winkler, but the picture would have benefited from a less smart-aleck approach. DA Sexual references, swearing. **DVD**

Freddie Prinze Jr *Al Connelly* · Julia Stiles *Imogen* · Shawn Hatosy *Eddie Hicks* · Selma Blair *Cyrus* · Zak Orth *Monk Jablonski* · Ashton Kutcher *Jim Morrison* · Rosario Dawson *Lana* · Henry Winkler *Chef Ray* ■ *Dir/Scr* Kris Isacsson

Down with Love
★★★ 12
Period romantic comedy
2003 · US/Ger · Colour · 97min

This frothy confection satirises and celebrates the sex comedies of the late 1950s and 60s. Renée Zellweger and Ewan McGregor aren't the most obvious stand-ins for Doris Day and Rock Hudson, but both hit the mark amusingly. Zellweger plays the new writing sensation who has produced a bestseller claiming that women can consign romance to the garbage heap, while McGregor's cocky journalist plots to disprove her claims publicly. This is shot in faux Technicolor with sublimely kitsch decor and a soundtrack choreographed to every accentuated footstep. JC **DVD**

Renée Zellweger *Barbara Novak* · Ewan McGregor *Catcher Block* · Sarah Paulson *Vikki Hiller* · David Hyde Pierce *Peter "Mac" MacMannus* · Rachel Dratch *Gladys* · Jack Plotnick *Maurice* · Tony Randall *Theodore Banner* · Jeri Ryan *Gwendolyn* ■ *Dir* Peyton Reed · *Scr* Eve Ahlert, Dennis Drake

Downfall
★★★★ 15
Second World War historical drama
2004 · Ger/Austria/It · Colour · 149min

The final days of the Third Reich are claustrophobically re-created in this acutely observed, Oscar-nominated drama. Made by German director Oliver Hirschbiegel, it's a ground-breaking attempt to confront the ghosts of his country's Nazi past. It's grotesquely surreal, as key personnel – among them Hitler's mistress Eva Braun (Juliane Köhler) – plot and party underground, while outside ordinary Berliners face the Allied advance. Such chilling matter-of-factness makes for a gripping experience, with Bruno Ganz's uncomfortably humanised Hitler particularly riveting. Rich period detail complements the superb acting, adding extra depth to a feature that's so eerily realistic, it's like watching history being replayed. SF German +subtitles. **DVD** **Blu-ray**

Bruno Ganz *Adolf Hitler* · Alexandra Maria Lara *Traudl Junge* · Corinna Harfouch *Magda Goebbels* · Ulrich Matthes *Joseph Goebbels* · Juliane Köhler *Eva Braun* · Heino Ferch *Albert Speer* · Christian Berkel *Professor Ernst-Gunther Schenck* · Matthias Habich *Professor Werner*

Haase* · Thomas Kretschmann *Hermann Fegelein* ■ *Dir* Oliver Hirschbiegel · *Scr* Bernd Eichinger, from the non-fiction book *Inside Hitler's Bunker: the Last Days of the Third Reich* by Joachim Fest and from the memoirs *Until the Final Hour: Hitler's Last Secretary* by Traudl Junge, Melissa Müller

The Downfall of Osen
★★★
Drama   1935 · Jpn · BW · 78min

Kenji Mizoguchi made 55 films between 1922 and 1935, of which only six have survived. However, while the director dismissed many of the pictures completed in this period, this moving drama is not only predicative of his recurrent themes, but also demonstrates considerable technical innovation. The story of servant girl Isuzu Yamada's bid to help Daijiro Natsukawa enter medical school by becoming a prostitute echoes the sacrifice of Mizoguchi's own geisha sister. The stylised realism and the inventive use of flashbacks give the film its historical value. DP In Japanese.

Isuzu Yamada *Osen* · Daijiro Natsukawa *Sokichi Hata* · Mitsusaburo Ramon *Ukiki* · Shin Shibata *Kumazawa* · Genichi Fujii *Matsuda* · Mitsuru Tojo *Kanya* · Junichi Kitamura *Sakazuki no Keishiro* ■ *Dir* Kenji Mizoguchi · *Scr* Tatsunosuke Takashima, from the short story *Baishoku Kamonanban* by Kyoka Izumi · *Cinematographer* Shigeto Miki [Minoru Miki]

Downhill
★★★ U
Silent drama   1927 · UK · BW · 82min

Many were disappointed by Alfred Hitchcock's reunion with Ivor Novello following their triumph with *The Lodger*. Yet this adaptation of a play Novello co-penned perfectly exploits his matinée status as it depicts his decline from public school hero to Marseille bum – all in the name of honour. Exploring social hypocrisy and the chasm that separates the classes, Hitchcock proves himself again the master of psychological insight, while his use of location is impeccable. DP **DVD**

Ivor Novello *Roddy Berwick* · Lilian Braithwaite *Lady Berwick* · Ian Hunter *Archie* · Robin Irvine *Tim Wakely* · Isabel Jeans *Julia* · Sybil Rhoda *Sybil Wakely* · Ben Webster *Dr James* ■ *Dir* Alfred Hitchcock · *Scr* Eliot Stannard, from the play by David L'Estrange [Ivor Novello], Constance Collier

Downhill
★★★ 15
Comedy drama   2014 · UK · Colour · 97min

As the film's tagline says, this British comedy drama is a road movie, only on foot! And it's a small delight. Four former school friends, now middle-aged, meet up again to tackle a near 200-mile coast-to-coast walk across northern England. But assorted midlife crises mess up their bid to re-bond, and comic incompatibilities within the group are exposed. Deftly played by a cast headed by Irish character actor Ned Dennehy, with well-written roles and gorgeous scenery to boot, *Downhill* is a home-grown treat. DA Swearing, sexual references, drug abuse.

Ned Dennehy *Julian* · Richard Lumsden *Gordon* · Karl Theobald *Keith* · Jeremy Swift *Steve* · Katie Lyons *Caroline* ■ *Dir* James Rouse · *Scr* Torben Betts, from a story by Betts, James Rouse, Benjamin Howell

Downhill Racer
★★ PG
Action drama   1969 · US · Colour · 97min

The first project from Robert Redford's own production company Wildwood, this skiing potboiler – low or plot, high on downhill racing - has the whiff of vanity about it. Redford stars as a handsome if egocentric skier being groomed as Olympic champion by hard-headed coach Gene Hackman, who later complained of feeling like "a high-priced extra". Inevitably, there is a girl, but the sport takes precedence and the appeal of the film, directed by Michael Ritchie (making his feature debut) lies in the well handled action sequences. AC **DVD**

Robert Redford *David Chappellet* · Gene Hackman *Eugene Caire* · Camilla Sparv *Carole Stahl* · Joe Jay Jalbert *Tommy Erb* · Timothy Kirk *DK Bryan* · Dabney Coleman *Mayo* · Jim

McMullan *Johnny Creech* ■ *Dir* Michael Ritchie · *Scr* James Salter, from the novel *The Downhill Racers* by Oakley Hall

Downtime
★ 15
Romantic thriller   1997 · UK/Fr · Colour · 86min

Two people from totally different backgrounds fall in love while trapped in a dangerously derelict lift in a Newcastle high rise. Even dafter than it sounds, this ludicrous fiasco switches between low-rent suspense and glib, socially-aware drama. No one acts sensibly, and the hostage crisis finale defies belief. AJ Swearing, some violence. **DVD**

Paul McGann *Rob* · Susan Lynch *Chrissy* · Tom Georgeson *Jimmy* · David Roper *Mike* · Denise Bryson *Jan* · David Horsefield *Kevin* · Stephen Graham *Jacko* ■ *Dir* Bharat Nalluri · *Scr* Caspar Berry

Downtown
★★★ 18
Action comedy   1990 · US · Colour · 91min

Comedy specialist Richard Benjamin is perhaps not the best director for a tough crime picture and there's nothing new or profound about his slant on white liberalism versus black realism. At least Anthony Edwards and co-star Forest Whitaker give their characters some depth. Edwards is the suburban cop transferred to a tough downtown neigbourhood, with Whitaker his streetwise new partner. DP Swearing, violence. **DVD**

Anthony Edwards *Alex Kearney* · Forest Whitaker *Dennis Curren* · Penelope Ann Miller *Lori Mitchell* · Joe Pantoliano *White* · David Clennon *Jerome Sweet* · Art Evans *Henry Coleman* · Kimberly Scott *Christine Curren* ■ *Dir* Richard Benjamin · *Scr* Nat Mauldin

Downtown 81
★★ 15
Documentary drama   1981 · US · Colour · 71min

Started by fashion photographer Edo Bertoglio back in 1980, only to be abandoned through lack of funds, this snapshot of Manhattan subculture was rediscovered by producer Maripol in the late 1990s, who attempted to tidy up the disjointed narrative by adding a voiceover from Slam star Saul Williams. Some may question whether this often aimless and frequently pretentious picture was worth the effort. But it does afford the opportunity to see Jean Michel Basquiat in a quasi-autobiographical tale about a struggling artist whose wish is granted by bag lady Debbie Harry. Moreover, it also provides performance records of several then-critical bands, including Tuxedomoon, Kid Creole and the Coconuts and James White and the Blacks. DP

Jean-Michel Basquiat *Jean* · Deborah Harry *Fairy godmother/Bag lady* · Anna Schroeder *Beatrice, the Love Interest* · Saul Williams *Narrator* ■ *Dir* Edo Bertoglio · *Scr* Glenn O'Brien

Dracula
★★★★ PG
Classic horror   1931 · US · BW · 74min

One of the most famous horror movies ever made, director Tod Browning's seminal classic is, by today's standards, rather talky, stagebound and bloodless, with most of its important chills occurring off-screen. However, it remains the most subtly romantic and highly atmospheric rendition of Bram Stoker's tale about the Transylvanian count, with Browning orchestrating the opening scenes to macabre perfection. Bela Lugosi's star turn (he'd been in the stage version since 1927) is an impressive film debut. A neglected sequel, *Dracula's Daughter*, followed five years later. AJ **DVD** **Blu-ray**

Bela Lugosi *Count Dracula* · Helen Chandler *Mina Seward* · David Manners *Jonathan Harker* · Dwight Frye *Renfield* · Edward Van Sloan *Dr Van Helsing* · Herbert Bunston *Dr Seward* · Frances Dade *Lucy Weston* ■ *Dir* Tod Browning · *Scr* Garrett Fort, from the play by Hamilton Deane, John Balderston, from the novel by Bram Stoker · *Cinematographer* Karl Freund · *Art Director* Charles D Hall · *Make-up* Jack Pierce

Dracula
★★★★★ 15
Classic horror   1958 · UK · Colour · 78min

Bram Stoker's terrifying vampire creation becomes a modern classic in the adept hands of the House of Hammer. The film was epoch-making in its impact, due to the fabulous gothic atmosphere, Terence Fisher's stylish direction and the fact that the undead tale was shot in vivd, gory colour for the first time. Christopher Lee's interpretation of Dracula is astonishingly fresh, heroic and powerful, while Peter Cushing makes an ideal Van Helsing. The latter's climactic battle with his bloodsucking nemesis is justly acclaimed as a magic movie moment in the history of the horror genre. AJ **DVD** **Blu-ray**

Peter Cushing *Van Helsing* · Michael Gough *Arthur Holmwood* · Melissa Stribling *Mina Holmwood* · Christopher Lee *Count Dracula* · Carol Marsh *Lucy Holmwood* · John Van Eyssen *Jonathan Harker* · Miles Malleson *Marx, the undertaker* ■ *Dir* Terence Fisher · *Scr* Jimmy Sangster, from the novel by Bram Stoker

Dracula
★★★ 15
Horror   1974 · US · Colour · 93min

Originally made for American television, this adaptation of the Bram Stoker classic was given a theatrical release overseas, albeit in a pared-down version. Jack Palance gives one of his better performances as a sympathetic, Byronic Dracula, a Transylvanian count motivated by love as much as bloodlust. Veteran screenwriter Richard Matheson scripts this underrated and adaptation, which offers refreshing new slants on the usual undead clichés. AJ

Jack Palance *Count Dracula* · Simon Ward *Arthur Holmwood* · Murray Brown *Jonathan Harker* · Nigel Davenport *Dr Van Helsing* · Pamela Brown *Mrs Westerna* · Fiona Lewis *Lucy Westerna* · Penelope Horner *Mina Murray* · Murray Brown *Jonathan Harker* ■ *Dir* Dan Curtis · *Scr* Richard Matheson, from the novel by Bram Stoker

Dracula
★★★★ 15
Horror   1979 · US · Colour · 104min

Like the 1931 version of Bram Stoker's tale, this streamlined remake is based on the hoary 1920s stage play, with the emphasis less on the supernatural horror and more on the Transylvanian count's seduction techniques. Frank Langella, fresh from the hit Broadway version, turns on the sensuality to great effect in director John Badham's stylishly atmospheric retread, with Laurence Olivier passionately histrionic as his nemesis, Van Helsing. While it's crafted as mainstream melodrama, there are enough chills to satisfy horror fans. AJ **DVD** **Blu-ray**

Frank Langella *Dracula* · Laurence Olivier *Van Helsing* · Donald Pleasence *Seward* · Kate Nelligan *Lucy* · Trevor Eve *Harker* · Jan Francis *Mina* · Janine Duvitski *Annie* · Tony Haygarth *Renfield* · Teddy Turner *Swales* ■ *Dir* John Badham · *Scr* WD Richter, from the play by Hamilton Deane, John Balderston, from the novel by Bram Stoker

Dracula AD 1972
★★ 15
Horror   1972 · UK · Colour · 91min

For this entry in their enduring *Dracula* series, Hammer relocated the count to swinging Chelsea, where he's holed up in a deconsecrated King's Road church and putting the bite on hippy layabouts. Derided at the time as a monumental misjudgement on the House of Horror's part, this slice of bell-bottomed phoniness can now be enjoyed as a camp period piece. AJ Violence, swearing. **DVD**

Christopher Lee *Count Dracula* · Peter Cushing *Professor Van Helsing* · Stephanie Beacham *Jessica* · Christopher Neame (2) *Johnny* · Michael Coles *Inspector* · Marsha A Hunt *Gaynor* · Caroline Munro *Laura* ■ *Dir* Alan Gibson · *Scr* Don Houghton, from characters by Bram Stoker

Dracula: Dead and Loving It
★ PG
Comedy horror   1995 · US · Colour · 90min

Mel Brooks's run of cinematic disappointments continued with this woeful spoof on vampire movies. Leslie Nielsen is dreadfully miscast as the count, although most of the blame must be levelled at director Brooks and his co-writers, who not only show no understanding of the genre they're sending up but who also seem to have forgotten how to write a gag. JF

Leslie Nielsen *Dracula* • Peter MacNicol *Renfield* • Steven Weber *Jonathan Harker* • Amy Yasbeck *Mina* • Lysette Anthony *Lucy* • Harvey Korman *Dr Seward* • Mel Brooks *Professor Van Helsing* • Mark Blankfield *Martin* ■ *Dir* Mel Brooks • *Scr* Mel Brooks, Rudy DeLuca, Steve Haberman, from a story by Rudy DeLuca, Steve Haberman, from characters by Bram Stoker

Dracula Has Risen from the Grave ★★★ 15
Horror 1968 · UK · Colour · 88min

A weak priest provides the blood that revives the evil Count Dracula and becomes his servant in a typical dose of vampire flesh-creeping from the Hammer House of Horror. A minor triumph of style over content, the third sequel to Hammer's 1958 classic succeeds by virtue of Freddie Francis's adventurous direction and his ability to extract religious irony from the formulaic script. Moody red filters are used to enhance the sanguinary motifs, while the ever-reliable Christopher Lee evokes supernatural menace. AJ *DVD*

Christopher Lee *Count Dracula* • Rupert Davies *Monsignor* • Veronica Carlson *Maria* • Barbara Ewing *Zena* • Barry Andrews *Paul* • Ewan Hooper *Priest* • Michael Ripper *Max* • Marion Mathie *Anna* ■ *Dir* Freddie Francis • *Scr* John Elder [Anthony Hinds], from characters by Bram Stoker

Dracula: Pages from a Virgin's Diary ★★★ 12
Silent dance horror
2002 · Can · BW and Colour · 74min

Bram Stoker's *Dracula* is re-interpreted as a gothic ballet in cult Canadian director Guy Maddin's sumptuous take on the classic vampire novel. Beautifully performed by the Royal Winnipeg Ballet, it's stylishly shot as a silent movie in black and white with occasional tints of colour. By sticking closely to the original text, Maddin's storyline is more full-bodied than many other Stoker adaptations, while the cinematography and art direction complement company choreographer Mark Godden's elegant dance movements. SF *DVD*

Zhang Wei-Qiang *Dracula* • Tara Birtwhistle *Lucy Westenra* • David Moroni *Dr Van Helsing* • CindyMarie Small *Mina Murray* • Johnny Wright *Jonathan Harker* ■ *Dir* Guy Maddin • *Scr* from the ballet by Mark Godden, from the novel by Bram Stoker • *Cinematographer* Paul Suderman

Dracula – Prince of Darkness ★★★★ 15
Horror 1965 · UK · Colour · 86min

Two couples dare to go travelling through the Carpathians in one of the best in the Hammer Dracula series. Veteran director Terence Fisher brings out the innate sexuality in the tightly plotted story and Christopher Lee (who died in 2015 at the age of 93) is awesome as the dreaded count, despite having no dialogue. The gruesome sequence where the infamous bloodsucker is resurrected in a perverse religious ritual remains shocking. AJ *DVD* ⬛

Christopher Lee *Count Dracula* • Barbara Shelley *Helen Kent* • Andrew Keir *Father Sandor* • Francis Matthews *Charles Kent* • Diana Kent *Charles Tingwell* *Alan Kent* • Thorley Walters *Ludwig* • Walter Brown *Brother Mark* ■ *Dir* Terence Fisher • *Scr* John Sansom, from characters by Bram Stoker

Dracula, Prisoner of Frankenstein ★
Horror 1972 · Sp · Colour · 86min

Spanish hack director Jesus Franco intended to make a parody of horror myths, but had neither the talent nor the budget to pull off the conceit. This sorry spectacle has Dr Frankenstein (a slumming Dennis Price) reviving Dracula (Franco regular Howard Vernon) with a nightclub singer's blood, so

that he can use his vampire acolytes to conquer the world. Featuring lousy make-up and shoddy special effects. AJ Spanish dubbed.

Dennis Price *Dr Frankenstein* • Howard Vernon *Dracula* • Alberto Dalbes • Genevieve Deloir ■ *Dir/Scr* Jesus Franco

Dracula 2001 ★★ 15
Horror 2000 · US · Colour · 95min

Count Dracula (Gerard Butler) crosses the Atlantic to New Orleans, seeking Van Helsing's Basin Street-based daughter, Justine Waddell. It's up to antique dealer Jonny Lee Miller and Virgin store sales assistant Waddell to thwart the Count's family reunion plans. Patrick Lussier's attempt to inject hip life into vampire mythology by giving it a *Scream* spin is plodding and schematic, tarted up with rock video imagery and camera trickery. Released in the US as *Dracula 2000*. AJ *DVD*

Jonny Lee Miller *Simon* • Christopher Plummer *Abraham Van Helsing/Matthew Van Helsing* • Justine Waddell *Mary* • Gerard Butler *Dracula* • Jennifer Esposito *Solina* • Omar Epps *Marcus* • Colleen Ann Fitzpatrick [Colleen Fitzpatrick] *Lucy* • Sean Patrick Thomas [Trick] ■ *Dir* Patrick Lussier • *Scr* Joel Soisson, from a story by Joel Soisson, Patrick Lussier

Dracula Untold ★★ 15
Action horror 2014 · US · Colour · 92min

Like *I, Frankenstein* before it, *Dracula Untold* seeks to reinvent one of cinema's most famous monsters. One part history lesson to several parts Hollywood spectacle, it stars Luke Evans (*The Hobbit* series) as Vlad III, Prince of Wallachia, who turns to the dark side to save his land from invading Turkish baddie Dominic Cooper. Mildly entertaining without offering any great quality, the movie is a half-decent action showcase for the talented Evans. DA Violence, sex scenes, some swearing. *DVD* Blu

Luke Evans *Vlad* • Dominic Cooper *Mehmed* • Sarah Gadon *Mirena* • Charles Dance *Master vampire* • Zach McGowan *Shkelgim* ■ *Dir* Gary Shore • *Scr* Matt Sazama, Burk Sharpless

Dracula vs Frankenstein ★ 15
Horror 1970 · US · Colour · 90min

Director Al Adamson surely ranks alongside Ed Wood as one of the genre's true incompetents. This is arguably his crowning glory – a hilarious mix of bad music, teenage dopeheads, beach parties and unconvincing monsters. Horror veterans J Carrol Naish and Lon Chaney Jr (who both never made another film) look thoroughly embarrassed, while the plot is a complete shambles. RS *DVD*

J Carrol Naish *Dr Frankenstein* • Lon Chaney Jr *Groton, the Mad Zombie* • Regina Carrol *Judith* • John Bloom (1) *The Monster* • Anthony Eisley *Mike Howard* • Russ Tamblyn *Rico* • Jim Davis (1) *Sgt Martin* • Zandor Vorkov *Count Dracula* ■ *Dir* Al Adamson • *Scr* William Pugsley, Samuel M Sherman

Dracula's Daughter ★★★ PG
Horror 1936 · US · BW · 68min

Edward Van Sloan returns as Von Helsing to face the undead once more in the neglected sequel to the 1931 *Dracula*. Gloria Holden became the first female vampire star, stalking the streets looking for a cure for her nocturnal agitations. In another first for the genre, she looks for young model Nan Grey with more than bloodsucking in mind. Moody and beautifully shot, this is saturated with bleak hopelessness. AJ

Otto Kruger *Dr Jeffrey Garth* • Gloria Holden *Countess Marya Zaleska* • Marguerite Churchill *Janet Blake* • Irving Pichel *Sandor* • Edward Van Sloan *Dr Von Helsing* • Nan Grey *Lili* • Hedda Hopper *Lady Esme Hammond* ■ *Dir* Lambert Hillyer • *Scr* Garrett Fort, from a story by John Balderston, Oliver Jeffries [David O Selznick], from the short story *Dracula's Guest* by Bram Stoker • *Cinematographer* George Robinson

Dracula's Widow ★ 18
Horror 1988 · US · Colour · 81min

Emmanuelle star Sylvia Kristel makes a poor and remarkably unsexy vampire in an anaemic addition to the undead genre from director Christopher Coppola, Francis Ford's nephew. As "the true wife of Dracula", Kristel arrives in Hollywood and takes up residence in a wax museum, whose owner (Lenny Von Dohlen) she enslaves. Pathetic. AJ *DVD*

Sylvia Kristel *Vanessa* • Josef Sommer *Lieutenant Lannon* • Lenny Von Dohlen *Raymond Everett* • Marc Coppola *Brad* • Stefan Schnabel *Von Helsing* • Rachel Jones *Jenny* ■ *Dir* Christopher Coppola • *Scr* Kathryn Ann Thomas, Christopher Coppola

Draft Day ★★ 15
Sports drama 2014 · US · Colour · 105min

Kevin Costner brings easy charm to yet another movie about US sport in this watchable American football drama from *Ghost Busters* director Ivan Reitman. However, don't expect any on-pitch action; this is all about the back-room machinations of draft day, when teams in the NFL get their pick of the best rookies on offer. It's no *Field of Dreams*, but Costner is a rock-solid presence and is well supported by a cast chock-full of recognisable faces. However, at nearly two hours in length, it could be a bit of a drag if your knowledge of the game is basic. JA Swearing, sexual references.

Kevin Costner *Sonny Weaver Jr* • Jennifer Garner *Ali* • Denis Leary *Coach Penn* • Frank Langella *Anthony Molina* • Sam Elliott *Coach Moore* • Sean Combs *Chris Crawford* ■ *Dir* Ivan Reitman • *Scr* Scott Rothman, Rajiv Joseph

Drag Me to Hell ★★★★ 15
Supernatural horror thriller
2009 · US · Colour · 94min

Spider-Man director Sam Raimi returns to his *Evil Dead* roots in this yucky, energetic and consistently entertaining fright movie. It's a glorious throwback to the EC Comics horror tradition of the 1950s, in which young mortgage broker Christine (Alison Lohman) becomes the victim of a curse after evicting glassy-eyed crone Lorna Raver from her house. Pursued by a demon, Christine only has three days before she's dragged – you guessed it – to hell. It's pure horror hokum, but the joy lies in the gleefully vindictive execution. JR Violence. *DVD* Blu

Alison Lohman *Christine Brown* • Justin Long *Clay Dalton* • Lorna Raver *Mrs Ganush* • Jessica Lucas *Ellen* • David Paymer *Mr Jacks* • Dileep Rao *Rham Jas* • Adriana Barraza *Shaun San Dena* ■ *Dir* Sam Raimi • *Scr* Ivan & Sam Raimi

The Dragnet
Silent crime drama 1928 · US · BW · 85min

This lost film by Josef von Sternberg features George Bancroft as a duped chief of detectives and lovely Evelyn Brent, who leaves gang boss William Powell for the dogged Bancroft. The screenplay was partly the work of two men who would help shape the style of Hollywood storytelling over the next few decades – Jules Furthman (*Shanghai Express*, *The Big Sleep*) and Herman J Mankiewicz (*Citizen Kane*). The camerawork is by the great Harold Rosson (*Singin' in the Rain*). TS

George Bancroft *Two-Gun Nolan* • Evelyn Brent *The Magpie* • William Powell *Dapper Frank Trent* • Fred Kohler *"Gabby" Steve* • Francis McDonald *Sniper Dawson* • Leslie Fenton *Shakespeare* ■ *Dir* Josef von Sternberg • *Scr* Jules Furthman, Charles Furthman, Herman J Mankiewicz (titles), from the story *Nightstick* by Oliver HP Garrett • *Editor* Helen Lewis

Dragnet ★★★ PG
Police drama 1954 · US · Colour · 88min

This spin-off from the famous American radio and TV series finds Jack Webb directing himself as Sergeant Joe Friday of the LAPD. The main problem with TV spin-offs is what works at 30 minutes doesn't always work at three times the length. This is certainly true of *Dragnet*, with its emphasis on police procedure making it

look like a "How to Be a Detective" recruitment film. Nevertheless, it offers a nostalgic look at the days before *Dirty Harry* and *The French Connection* came along. AT

Jack Webb *Sergeant Joe Friday* • Ben Alexander *Officer Frank Smith* • Richard Boone *Captain Hamilton* • Ann Robinson *Grace Downey* • Stacy Harris *Max Troy* • Virginia Gregg *Ethel Marie Starkie* • Victor Perrin *Adolph Alexander* • Georgia Ellis *Belle Davitt* ■ *Dir* Jack Webb • *Scr* Richard L Breen

Dragnet ★★ PG
Spoof police drama 1987 · US · Colour · 101min

It's a trawl through the comic depths for this parody of Jack Webb's 1950s TV series. Dan Aykroyd is the deadpan nephew of Webb's Sergeant Joe Friday, lumbered with an amoral, dishevelled partner in Tom Hanks and battling with porn king Dabney Coleman and Satanist Christopher Plummer. A virgin sacrifice is the most of it, as far as laughs are concerned. TH *DVD*

Dan Aykroyd *Det Sgt Joe Friday* • Tom Hanks *Pep Streebek* • Christopher Plummer *Rev Jonathan Whirley* • Harry Morgan *Captain Bill Gannon* • Alexandra Paul *Connie Swail* • Jack O'Halloran *Emil Muzz* • Dabney Coleman *Jerry Caesar* • Bruce Gray *Mayor Parvin* ■ *Dir* Tom Mankiewicz • *Scr* Dan Aykroyd, Alan Zweibel, Tom Mankiewicz

Dragon ★★★ 15
Action drama 2011 · HK/Chi · Colour · 98min

This is an ambitious attempt to cross the martial arts genre with *film noir*. The tension crackles between papermill worker Donnie Yen and detective Takeshi Kaneshiro after the latter comes to suspect that Yen's dispatch of two thugs robbing the local store was anything but the fluke he claims. The big showdown recalls golden age *wuxia* classics like Chang Cheh's *One-Armed Swordsman* (1967) but, while Yen's fight choreography is suitably explosive, the byplay between his humble family man and Kaneshiro's forensic sleuth is much more compelling. DP Mandarin +subtitles. Violence.

Donnie Yen *Liu Jin-xi/Tang Long* • Takeshi Kaneshiro *Xu Bai-jiu* • Tang Wei *Ayu* • Jimmy Wang Yu [Wang Yu (1)] *The Master* ■ *Dir* Peter Ho-Sun Chan • *Scr* Aubrey Lam, Joyce Chan

Dragon Blade ★★ 15
Period action adventure
2015 · Chi · Colour · 99min

Hollywood stars John Cusack and Adrien Brody join Jackie Chan in this Chinese-made action epic about rival Romans battling it out at the far end of the Silk Road. Chan brings martial artistry to the fight, Cusack his siege skills, but overall the film is a mishmash of languages, styles and tones. There's been a lot of money thrown at the movie, and there are some genuinely spectacular moments, but it's a film more likely to get watched for its curiosity value. DA Mandarin, English +subtitles. Violence, brief nudity. *DVD* Blu

Jackie Chan *Huo An* • John Cusack *Lucius* • Adrien Brody *Tiberius* • Sharni Vinson *Lady Crassus* ■ *Dir/Scr* Daniel Lee

Dragon Seed ★★
War drama 1944 · US · BW · 147min

This MGM version of life in China during the 1937 Japanese invasion couldn't have been more weirdly cast if they'd put all the studio contract players' names in a hat and just shaken them out. But if you can believe a Chinese, Bryn Mawr-accented Katharine Hepburn, you'll probably accept her extended family of Walter Huston, Akim Tamiroff and Aline MacMahon. The last credit of MGM's great contract director Jack Conway, this is one of Hollywood's most misconceived movies. TS

Katharine Hepburn *Jade* • Walter Huston *Ling Tan* • Aline MacMahon *Mrs Ling Tan* • Akim Tamiroff *Wu Lien* • Turhan Bey *Lao Er* • Hurd Hatfield *Lao San* • Frances Rafferty *Orchid* • Agnes Moorehead *3rd cousin's wife* • Lionel Barrymore *Narrator* ■ *Dir* Jack Conway, Harold S Bucquet • *Scr* Marguerite Roberts, Jane Murfin, from the novel by Pearl S Buck

Dragon: the Bruce Lee Story ★★★★ 15
Biographical drama   1993 · US · Colour · 114min

Adapted from the book by Lee's wife, Linda Lee Cadwell (played in the film by Lauren Holly), this is a curious mix of traditional Hollywood biography and Hong Kong ghost story. Jason Scott Lee (no relation) captures Bruce's exuberance and finesse with considerable skill. Directed with panache by Rob Cohen, the rags-to-riches tale sees Lee rise from street kid to martial arts master. Yet what's so fascinating is the insight into the private torment that the film suggests led to Lee's death. DP Violence. **DVD**

Jason Scott Lee *Bruce Lee* • Lauren Holly *Linda Lee* • Robert Wagner *Bill Krieger* • Michael Learned *Vivian Emery* • Nancy Kwan *Gussie Yang* • Lim Kay Tong *Philip Tan* • Ric Young *Bruce's father* • Wang Luoyong *Yip Man* • Sterling Macer Jr *Jerome Sprout* ■ *Dir* Rob Cohen • *Scr* Edward Khmara, John Raffo, Rob Cohen, from the non-fiction book *Bruce Lee: The Man Only I Knew* by Linda Lee Cadwell

Dragonard ★ 18
Period drama   1987 · US · Colour · 85min

Part bodice ripper, part slave drama, this 18th-century tale is a tough movie to figure out. On a British island in the Caribbean, the governor is killed the same night his daughter seduces a slave. The slave is accused of murder; when he can't be found, new governor Oliver Reed (even more over-the-top than usual) begins torturing the island's black population. Every now and then a rape scene is thrown in, just to make this disgusting display more intolerable. ST

Oliver Reed *Captain Shanks* • Eartha Kitt *Naomi* • Annabel Schofield *Honore* • Claudia Udy *Arabella* • Patrick Warburton *Richard Abdee* • Drummond Marais *Pierre* • Dennis Folbigge *Governor* ■ *Dir* Gérard Kikoine • *Scr* Peter Welbeck [Harry Alan Towers], Rick Marx, from a novel by Rupert Gilchrist

Dragonball Evolution ★ PG
Fantasy action adventure   2009 · US · Colour · 80min

It's hard to see why Akira Toriyama's *manga* franchise ever became such a multimedia phenomenon from director James Wong's simplistic live-action version. A band of young warriors led by geeky teen Goku (Justin Chatwin) try to bring together seven powerful dragonballs to stop evil Lord Piccolo (James Marsters) destroying earth. From *The Karate Kid* to *Star Wars*, there's nothing here that hasn't been seen before. And trying to re-create the *anime* cartoon look with real actors just doesn't work: the bad wigs, unconvincing make-up, cheesy dialogue and cheap special effects all underline the film's two-dimensional origins. AJ **DVD** **Blu-ray**

Justin Chatwin *Goku* • Emmy Rossum *Bulma* • Chow Yun-Fat *Master Roshi* • Jamie Chung *Chi Chi* • James Marsters *Lord Piccolo* • Joon Park *Yamcha* ■ *Dir* James Wong • *Scr* Ben Ramsey, from the graphic novel series *Dragonball* by Akira Toriyama

Dragonflies ★★★ 15
Psychological drama   2001 · Nor/Swe · Colour · 104min

This shoestring Norwegian drama offers a refreshing, rural variation on a well-worn theme. Kim Bodnia is an ex-con whose simply idyll with pregnant lover Maria Bonnevie is disrupted by the unexpected arrival of a ghost from his past, an old "friend" (played by Mikael Persbrandt) recently released from jail. But director Marius Holst seems uncertain whether to stage this as a psychological drama or a thriller; a dilemma that's exacerbated by his decision to allow the cast to improvise much of the dialogue. DP Norwegian +subtitles. **DVD**

Maria Bonnevie *Maria* • Kim Bodnia *Eddie* • Mikael Persbrandt *Kullman* • Tord Peterson [Tord Pettersson] *Sven* • Skarpjordet, Thomas *Thomas* ■ *Dir* Marius Holst • *Scr* Nicolaj Frobenius, Marius Holst, from the short story *Natt til Mork Morgen* by Ingvar Ambjornsen

Dragonfly ★★ 12
Supernatural romantic drama   2002 · US · Colour · 99min

Kevin Costner stars as an ER doctor who is devastated by the death of his pregnant wife (Susanna Thompson) while on a Red Cross mission in Venezuela. Costner becomes convinced that she is trying to contact him from "beyond", and an encounter with Linda Hunt's eccentric nun sends him off on a jungle adventure. Sadly, the understated performance of Costner can't rescue this schmaltzy misfire. LH Violence, swearing, nudity **DVD**

Kevin Costner *Joe Darrow* • Joe Morton *Hugh Campbell* • Ron Rifkin *Charlie Dickinson* • Linda Hunt *Sister Madeline* • Susanna Thompson *Emily Darrow* • Kathy Bates *Miriam Belmont* ■ *Dir* Tom Shadyac • *Scr* Dav d Seltzer, Brandon Camp, Mike Thompson, from a story by Brandon Camp, Mike Thompson

DragonHeart ★★★ PG
Fantasy adventure   1996 · US · Colour · 98min

Sean Connery lends his distinctive burr to Draco, a 10th-century dragon who joins forces with an itinerant knight (Dennis Quaid). The resu t is a likeable, if a tad over-eager mix of derring-do and special effects, which has everything from wicked kings and poetic monks to romantic encounters and revolting peasants. Quaid gives a rousing performance, but David Thewlis's dastardly despot belongs in a pantomime. DP **DVD** **Blu-ray**

Dennis Quaid *Bowen* • Sean Connery *Draco* • David Thewlis *Einon* • Pete Postlethwaite *Gilbert* • Dina Meyer *Kara* • Jason Isaacs *Felton* • Brian Thompson *Brok* • Lee Oakes *Young Einon* • Julie Christie *Aislinn* • John Gielgud *King Arthur* ■ *Dir* Rob Cohen • *Scr* Charles Edward Pogue, from a story by Patrick Read Johnson, Charles Edward Pogue

Dragonheart: a New Beginning ★★ PG
Fantasy adventure   1999 · US · Colour · 80min

In this sequel, the stable lad (Chris Masterson) with ambitions of knighthood is largely overshadowed by the presence of Drake, the junior dragon who was hatched and nurtured in the crypt of a monastery. As in the original, the CGI work is impressive, although Robby Benson is no substitute for Sean Connery in the voiceover department. Lots of action, but it's the byplay between boy and beast that kids will most enjoy. DP **DVD**

Chris Masterson *Geoff* • Harry Van Gorkum *Osric/Old Bowen* • Rona Figueroa *Princess Lian* • Matt Hickey *Mansel* • Henry O *Kwan* • Robby Benson *Drake the dragon* ■ *Dir* Doug Lefler • *Scr* Shari Goodhartz, from characters by Charles Edward Pogue, Patrick Read Johnson

Dragonslayer ★★★ PG
Fantasy adventure   1981 · US · Colour · 104min

The early 1980s brought a rash of fantasy adventures, ranging from the camp fun of *Conan the Barbarian* to such dire examples as *The Sword and the Sorcerer*. This film, which follows a magician's assistant on his quest to kill a dragon, is aimed more at a family audience, though it's not without its violent moments, and it benefits from a good cast that includes Ralph Richardson. The effects aren't bad either. JF **DVD**

Peter MacNicol *Galen* • Caitlin Clarke *Valerian* • Ralph Richardson *Ulrich* • John Hallam *Tyrian* • Peter Eyre *Casiodorus* • Albert Salmi *Greil* • Chloe Salaman *Princess Elspeth* • Roger Kemp *Horsrik* • Ian McDiarmid *Brother Jacopus* ■ *Dir* Matthew Robbins • *Scr* Hal Barwood, Matthew Robbins

Dragonworld ★★ U
Fantasy   1994 · US · Colour · 82min

Although the setting looks suspiciously like the eastern European castle cult horror producer Charles Band used for his more adult films, this is a charming if slight tale of a boy's friendship with a baby dragon. The effects aren't up too much, but it is a curiously innocent affair, and John Woodvine and Andrew Keir add a bit of class. A made-for-TV sequel followed in 1997. JF

Sam Mackenzie *John McGowan* • Brittney Powell *Beth Armstrong* • John Calvin *Bob Armstrong* • Courtland Mead *Young Johnny McGowan* • Lila Kaye *Mrs Cosgrove* • John Woodvine *Lester MacIntyre* • Andrew Keir *Angus McGowan* ■ *Dir* Ted Nicolaou • *Scr* Suzanne Glazener Naha, Ted Nicolaou, from a story by Charles Band

Dragonwyck ★★★ PG
Gothic melodrama   1946 · US · BW · 98min

This preposterous old tosh, a sort of Manderley-on-the-Hudson, marked distinguished film-maker Joseph L Mankiewicz's directorial debut. He does well by the material, but the casting leaves a lot to be desired. Top-billed Gene Tierney is a lovely governess, but Vincent Price hams quite extraordinarily as the sadistic master of the estate, while Glenn Langan is truly hopeless as the local doctor. There's pleasure to be had from watching these ludicrous performances on phoney sets, but you can't escape the feeling that it was meant to be taken seriously. TS **DVD**

Gene Tierney *Miranda Wells* • Walter Huston *Ephraim Wells* • Vincent Price *Nicholas Van Ryn* • Glenn Langan *Dr Jeff Turner* • Anne Revere *Abigail Wells* • Spring Byington *Magda* ■ *Dir* Joseph L Mankiewicz • *Scr* Joseph L Mankiewicz, from the novel by Anya Seton

Dragoon Wells Massacre ★★ PG
Western   1957 · US · Colour · 82min

This brisk, good-looking western benefits greatly from CinemaScope and the camerawork of William Clothier. The plot is routine, but Barry Sullivan and Katy Jurado make the most of their roles: he's a killer, she's a hooker. They are forced to join together to protect themselves from marauding Apaches. TS

Barry Sullivan *Link Ferris* • Dennis O'Keefe *Captain Matt Riordan* • Mona Freeman *Ann Bradley* • Katy Jurado *Mara Fay* • Jack Elam *Tioga* • Sebastian Cabot *Jonah* • Casey Adams [Max Showalter] *Phillip Scott* • Trevor Bardette *Marshal Bill Haney* ■ *Dir* Harold Schuster • *Scr* Warren Douglas, from a story by Oliver Drake

Dragstrip Girl ★★ PG
Drama   1957 · US · BW · 66min

Only the smouldering presence of 1950s cult sexpot Fay Spain in the title role makes this AIP cheapie at all watchable. Spain showed better form in higher-budgeted movies such as *Al Capone* and *God's Little Acre*, but she did not achieve lasting fame. Here she transcends the material in this banal flick about hot-rod racing. TS **DVD**

Fay Spain *Louise Blake* • Steven Terrell *Jim Donaldson* • John Ashley *Fred Armstrong* • Tommy Ivo *Rick Camden* • Frank Gorshin *Tommy* • Judy Bamber *Rhoda, the blonde* ■ *Dir* Edward L Cahn • *Scr* Lou Rusoff

Dramatic School ★★★ U
Drama   1938 · US · BW · 80min

Luise Rainer, a fragile and hard-to-cast talent, made precious few movies after her back-to-back best actress Oscars for *The Great Ziegfeld* (1936) and *The Good Earth* (1937). In all of them, however, she was superb. In this MGM drama reminiscent of the popular *Stage Door*, her co-stars are the up-and-coming Lana Turner and the lovely Paulette Goddard – but it's Rainer's movie through and through. TS

Luise Rainer *Louise* • Paulette Goddard *Nana* • Lana Turner *Mado* • Alan Marshal *Andre D'Abbencourt* • Anthony Allan [John Hubbard] *Fleury* • Henry Stephenson *Pasquel Sr* • Genevieve Tobin *Gina Bertier* • Gale Sondergaard *Madame Charlot* • Ann Rutherford *Yvonne* • Margaret Dumont *Teacher* • Dick Haymes *Student* ■ *Dir* Robert B Sinclair • *Scr* Ernst Vadja, Mary C McCall Jr, from the play *School of Drama* by Hans Szekely, Zoltan Egyed

The Draughtsman's Contract ★★★★★ 15
Period drama   1982 · UK · Colour · 103min

Peter Greenaway's first commercially released feature film is a calling card of dazzling virtuosity. A 17th-century draughtsman (Anthony Higgins) is hired to make 12 drawings of a country estate, and is paid in sexual favours by the landowner's wife and daughter (Janet Suzman and Anne Louise Lambert). The possibility of his drawings being an artistic witness to murder is deftly, tantalisingly displayed and his ultimate downfall from arrogant posturing is a lesson in class-distinction, only to be expected from the aristocratic world he's tried to enter. Michael Nyman's minimalist music reinforces the remarkable visuals in this clever and witty ground-breaking debut. TH Violence, sex scenes, nudity. **DVD**

Anthony Higgins *Mr Neville* • Janet Suzman *Mrs Herbert* • Anne Louise Lambert *Mrs Talmann* • Neil Cunningham *Mr Noyes* • Hugh Fraser *Mr Talmann* • Dave Hill *Mr Herbert* ■ *Dir/Scr* Peter Greenaway

D

Dread ★★★ 18
Horror   2009 · US/UK · Colour · 90min

A short story by British horror maestro Clive Barker is the basis for this compact and efficient psychological chiller, in which three college students, including *Twilight's* Jackson Rathbone, begin documenting people's deepest fears. But a traumatic past prompts the project's manipulative ringleader (a multi-faceted Shaun Evans) to take things to terrifying extremes. Although the plot's nothing new, impressive first-time writer/director Anthony DiBlasi achieves maximum impact via his largely sympathetic characters, stylishly murky visuals and judicious use of gore. SF

Jackson Rathbone *Stephen Grace* • Shaun Evans *Quaid* • Hanne Steen *Cheryl* ■ *Dir* Anthony DiBlasi • *Scr* Anthony DiBlasi, from Clive Barker's short story

Dream a Little Dream ★ 15
Comedy drama   1989 · US · Colour · 110min

Yet another body-swap movie with nothing new to offer. Here Jason Robards ends up in the body of spotty 16-year-old Corey Feldman after the latter crashes into his meditation session on a bicycle. The problem is that Feldman is utterly incapable of acting like an elderly man in a youngster's body, thus defeating the entire premise of the film. A sequel followed six years later. LH

Corey Feldman *Bobby Keller* • Corey Haim *Dinger* • Jason Robards *Coleman Ettinger* • Piper Laurie *Gena Ettinger* • Harry Dean Stanton *Ike Baker* • Meredith Salenger *Lainie Diamond* ■ *Dir* Marc Rocco • *Scr* Daniel Jay Franklin, Marc Rocco, DE Eisenberg, from a story by Daniel Jay Franklin

Dream Demon ★ 18
Fantasy thriller   1988 · UK · Colour · 85min

This tragic British answer to Freddy Krueger – "A Nightmare on Sloane Street" – is about as scary as a trip to Harvey Nichols. Jemma Redgrave is the upper-class socialite hunted by the press and suffering dream premonitions about her friends dying. A pointless terror exercise with awful performances. AJ

Jemma Redgrave *Diana Markham* • Kathleen Wilhoite *Jenny Hoffman* • Timothy Spall *Peck* • Jimmy Nail *Paul* • Mark Greenstreet *Oliver* • Susan Fleetwood *Deborah* • Annabelle Lanyon *Little Jenny* • Nickolas Grace *Jenny's father* ■ *Dir* Harley Cokliss • *Scr* Harley Cokliss, Christopher Wicking

Dream for an Insomniac ★★★ 15
Romantic comedy   1996 · US · BW and Colour · 83min

This charming, feel-good romantic comedy is admittedly about as solid as a grass hut in a hurricane. Ione Skye is the sleep-disordered romantic who, with best friend Jennifer Aniston, is determined to make it big in Hollywood. But her life gets complicated by the arrival of hunky kindred spirit MacKenzie Astin, who has a girlfriend. Filmed in a mixture of black and white and colour, this has enough good lines to keep you smiling and the young cast members deliver attractive performances. JF Swearing, sexual references. **DVD**

Ione Skye *Frankie* • Jennifer Aniston *Allison* • MacKenzie Astin *David Schrader* • Michael Landes *Rob* • Robert Kelker-Kelly *Trent* •

D

Seymour Cassel *Uncle Leo* • Sean San Jose Blackman *Juice* • Michael Sterk *BJ* • Leslie Stevens (3) *Molly* ■ *Dir/Scr* Tiffanie DeBartolo

Dream Girl ★★
Comedy 1948 · US · BW · 85min

Elmer Rice's Broadway satire, a vehicle for his wife Betty Field, is turned into a fun-fest for Paramount's reigning laff queen Betty Hutton. She hams every line and milks every gag as a daydreamer who imagines she's an understudy to an opera star or a broken-hearted whore. Hutton was immensely popular in the 1940s, but as a distaff version of *The Secret Life of Walter Mitty* this doesn't cut it. **TS**

Betty Hutton *Georgina Allerton* • Macdonald Carey *Clark Redfield* • Patric Knowles *Jim Lucas* • Virginia Field *Miriam Allerton Lucas* • Walter Abel *George Allerton* • Peggy Wood *Lucy Allerton* • Carolyn Butler *Claire* • Lowell Gilmore *George Hand* ■ *Dir* Mitchell Leisen • *Scr* Arthur Sheekman, from the play by Elmer Rice • *Music* Victor Young

Dream Home ★★★18
Horror 2010 · HK · Colour · 92min

This nightmarish satire on the more cut-throat aspects of the Hong Kong property market manages to be both a thoughtful social commentary and gory slasher without any real awkwardness in tone. Josie Ho plays a telemarketer working all hours to afford a harbour view apartment. But when real estate prices soar, she resorts to murder to drive the value of her dream home down. The film is told in fragmented flashback from the night she turns homicidal, which often dissipates the suspense, and though the horror element is inventive and cleverly staged, many will find the bloody violence graphic in the extreme. **AJ** Cantonese +subtitles. Violence. *DVD*

Josie Ho *Cheng Lai Sheung* • Eason Chan *Siu To* • Derek Tsang *Cheung Jai* • Lawrence Chou *On Jai* ■ *Dir* Pang Ho-Cheung • *Scr* Pang Ho-Cheung, Derek Tsang, Jimmy Wan, from a story by Pang

Dream House ★★★15
Mystery thriller 2011 · US · Colour · 88min

Daniel Craig and Rachel Weisz escape New York to a rural idyll where he intends to write. But a shocking truth about the house's history lies in store. The big-impact twist is revealed much earlier than tradition dictates, but there's quality support from Naomi Watts and Elias Koteas, and enough jumps and surprises to keep you interested. And, hey, it's got Daniel Craig in it! **AC** Violence, swearing. *DVD* *Blu*

Daniel Craig *Will Atenton* • Naomi Watts *Ann Patterson* • Rachel Weisz *Libby* • Elias Koteas *Boyce* • Jane Alexander *Dr Greeley* ■ *Dir* Jim Sheridan • *Scr* David Loucka

The Dream Life of Angels ★★★★18
Drama 1998 · Fr · Colour · 108min

Elodie Bouchez and Natacha Régnier shared the best actress prize at Cannes for their work in Erick Zonca's painfully realistic debut. Bouchez particularly impresses as the optimistic drifter whose creativity and resourcefulness see her through the daily crises that consistently floor her cynical new friend, who has become morbidly dependent on a doomed love affair with a rich man. Although prone to disconcerting moments of melodrama, this is still a provocative study of dislocation and isolation. **DP** French +subtitles. Sex scenes. *DVD*

Elodie Bouchez *Isa* • Natacha Régnier *Marie* • Grégoire Colin *Chriss* • Patrick Mercado *Charly* • Jo Prestia *Fredo* • Francine Massenhave *Attendant* • Zivko Niklevski *Yugoslav patron* ■ *Dir* Erick Zonca • *Scr* Erick Zonca, Roger Bohbot, Virginie Wagon, Pierre Schöller, Frederic Carpentier, Pierre Chosson, Jean-Daniel Magnin

Dream Lover ★15
Psychological thriller 1986 · US · Colour · 99min

This dreadful mess of a movie purports to explore the repercussions of extensive "dream therapy" on a young girl desperate

to rid herself of a recurring nightmare. The cast does its best to pick its way through a minefield of psychobabble and histrionics, but Alan J Pakula directs with a leaden hand. **SH** Violence, swearing, nudity.

Kristy McNichol *Kathy Gardner* • Ben Masters *Michael Hansen* • Paul Shenar *Ben Gardner* • Justin Deas *Kevin McCann* • John McMartin *Martin* • Gayle Hunnicutt *Claire* ■ *Dir* Alan J Pakula • *Scr* Jon Boorstin

Dream Lover ★★■
Thriller 1993 · US · Colour · 99min

Successful architect James Spader meets Mädchen Amick, the woman of his dreams and after a whirlwind romance they get married. But slowly (very slowly) he begins to wonder about her real motives in director Nicholas Kazan's low-key suspense thriller. While Kazan has fun setting up the stock situations and spinning plot threads off in surprising directions, this lethargically paced drama lacks flair. **AJ** Violence, sex scenes, swearing, nudity. *DVD*

James Spader *Ray Reardon* • Mädchen Amick *Lena Reardon* • Bess Armstrong *Elaine* • Fredrick Lehne [Fredric Lehne] *Larry* • Larry Miller *Norman* • Kathleen York *Martha* • Kate Williamson *Mrs Sneeder* ■ *Dir/Scr* Nicholas Kazan

A Dream of Kings ★★★★
Drama 1969 · US · Colour · 110min

Anthony Quinn gives a powerful portrayal of a Graeco-American paterfamilias in this neglected, marvellous, warm-hearted movie. Quinn is exceptionally fine as the gambler-philosopher trying to raise the money to send his dying son to Greece. Irene Papas is well cast as his wife, but tragic beauty Inger Stevens steals the film as the young widow Quinn has an affair with. It's a beautifully observed movie, excellently directed by Daniel Mann. **TS**

Anthony Quinn *Matsoukas* • Irene Papas *Caliope* • Inger Stevens *Anna* • Sam Levene *Cicero* • Val Avery *Fatsas* • Tamara Daykarhanova *Mother-in-law* • Peter Mamakos *Falconis* ■ *Dir* Daniel Mann • *Scr* Harry Mark Petrakis, Ian Hunter, from the novel by Harry Mark Petrakis

A Dream of Passion ★18
Drama 1978 · Gr · Colour · 101min

A thick pall of pretension hangs over this rancid cocktail of Greek myth and art house angst. Melina Mercouri gnaws her way through the scenery with a voracious appetite as the Greek actress who sees Ellen Burstyn's murderous American mother as the perfect publicity ruse for her new production of *Medea*. So far so ghastly. But once the women begin to merge emotionally (à la Ingmar Bergman's *Persona*), the entire edifice comes tumbling down. **DP** In English, Greek.

Melina Mercouri *Maya* • Ellen Burstyn *Brenda* • Andreas Voutsinas *Kostas* • Despo Diamantidou *Maria* • Dimitris Papamichael *Dimitris/Jason* • Yannis Voglis *Edward* ■ *Dir* Jules Dassin • *Scr* Jules Dassin, from the play *Medea* by Euripides

Dream Street ★★
Silent drama 1921 · US · BW · 102min

This is a heavily melodramatic outing from the great silent movie maestro DW Griffith. It's inspired by two *Limehouse Nights* short stories by *Broken Blossoms* author Thomas Burke. The result is uncomfortably racist and shows few signs of Griffith's undoubted picture-making genius, as dancer Carol Dempster inadequately serves as an obsessive sex object, whose very existence causes death, mayhem and destruction. **TS**

Carol Dempster *Gypsy Fair* • Ralph Graves *James "Spike" McFadden* • Charles Emmett Mack *Billy McFadden* • Edward Peil [Edward Peil Sr] *Swan Way* • WJ Ferguson *Gypsy's father* • Porter Strong *Samuel Jones* ■ *Dir* DW Griffith • *Scr* Roy Sinclair [DW Griffith], from the short stories *Gina of the Chinatown* and *The Sign of the Lamp* by Thomas Burke

The Dream Team ★★★★15
Comedy 1989 · US · Colour · 107min

This light-hearted spin on *One Flew over the Cuckoo's Nest* has a group of inmates from a psychiatric hospital slipping the leash

while on a day trip to New York. For Michael Keaton, in the year he became a superstar in *Batman*, the role offered the chance to return to what he does best - the silver-tongued, lovable rogue. He also benefits from a gallery of accomplished supporting players, most notably an anally retentive Christopher Lloyd. Director Howard Zieff makes an occasional attempt at seriousness, but keeps the laughs flowing smoothly. **JF** Violence, swearing, drug abuse, brief nudity. *DVD*

Michael Keaton *Billy Caulfield* • Christopher Lloyd *Henry Sikorsky* • Peter Boyle *Jack McDermott* • Stephen Furst *Albert Ianuzzi* • Dennis Boutsikaris *Dr Weitzman* • Lorraine Bracco *Riley* • Milo O'Shea *Dr Newald* • Philip Bosco *O'Malley* ■ *Dir* Howard Zieff • *Scr* Jon Connolly, David Loucka

Dream Wife ★★U
Comedy 1953 · US · BW · 98min

Cary Grant and Deborah Kerr dull? Well, they certainly are in this feeble slapstick concoction, a rare excursion into directing from screenwriter Sidney Sheldon. Grant's engaged to Kerr but falls for Betta St John, who has been trained to please men. Grant and Kerr teamed up again to far better effect in *An Affair to Remember*, but Sidney Sheldon made an even more wretched film (*The Buster Keaton Story*) before becoming a novelist. **TS**

Cary Grant *Clemson Reade* • Deborah Kerr *Effie* • Walter Pidgeon *Walter McBride* • Betta St John *Tarji* • Eduard Franz *Khan* • Buddy Baer *Vizier* • Les Tremayne *Ken Landwell* • Gloria Holden *Mrs Landwell* • Steve Forrest *Louis* ■ *Dir* Sidney Sheldon • *Scr* Sidney Sheldon, Herbert Baker, Alfred Lewis Levitt, from a story by Alfred Lewis Levitt

Dream with the Fishes ★★★18
Black comedy drama 1996 · US · Colour · 92min

Darkly melancholic, but also charmingly offbeat, Finn Taylor's directorial debut offers a moving study of loss and obsession. David Arquette, who also co-produced, plays a grieving, voyeuristic loner who gradually comes out of his shell when he gets mixed up with the dying Brad Hunt. Hunt is determined to live his final days to the full, which in his case means nude bowling, nude bank robbery and giving LSD to policemen. All the performances are good, and Taylor's vision is quirky and lyrical. **JF** Swearing, nudity, violence.

David Arquette *Terry* • Brad Hunt *Nick* • Cathy Moriarty *Aunt Elise* • Kathryn Erbe *Liz* • Patrick McGaw *Don* • JE Freeman *Joe, Nick's father* • Timi Prulhiere *Michelle* • Anita Barone *Mary* ■ *Dir* Finn Taylor • *Scr* Finn Taylor, from a story by Jeffrey Brown, Finn Taylor

Dreamboat ★★★U
Satirical comedy 1952 · US · BW · 83min

This very funny satire on the early days of television was made when TV was a novelty newcomer and not yet a threat to cinemas. Ginger Rogers is delightful as a silent-movie queen who revives her popularity by presenting her old movies on TV, annoying her former co-star Clifton Webb, now ensconced in "the groves of Academe". Rogers and Webb are particularly fetching, while Elsa Lanchester is a joy as Webb's lustful superior. **TS**

Clifton Webb *Thornton Sayre* • Ginger Rogers *Gloria* • Anne Francis *Carol Sayre* • Jeffrey Hunter *Bill Ainslee* • Elsa Lanchester *Dr Coffey* • Fred Clark *Sam Levitt* • Paul Harvey *Harrington* ■ *Dir* Claude Binyon • *Scr* Claude Binyon, from a story by John D Weaver

Dreamcatcher ★★15
Science-fiction horror 2003 · US/Aus · Colour · 128min

Four childhood friends on a hunting trip rescue a deranged oddball who, it soon emerges, is host to some sort of alien parasite. While they attempt to evade the monster, the military - in the shape of Morgan Freeman - arrives, determined to eradicate all trace of the shape-shifting beastie. Despite a screenplay co-written by William Goldman, initially effective

atmospherics and creditable performances, this is soon hobbled by poor quality CGI and an abysmally incoherent final act. **AS** *DVD*

Morgan Freeman *Colonel Abraham Curtis* • Thomas Jane *Dr Henry "H" Devlin* • Jason Lee *Jim "Beaver" Clarendon* • Damian Lewis *Professor Gary "Jonesy" Jones* • Timothy Olyphant *Pete Moore* • Tom Sizemore *Captain Owen Underhill* • Donnie Wahlberg *Douglas "Duddits" Cavell* ■ *Dir* Lawrence Kasdan • *Scr* Lawrence Kasdan, William Goldman, from the novel by Stephen King

Dreamcatcher ★★★★15
Documentary 2015 · UK/US/Neth · Colour · 98min

Director Kim Longinotto's immensely rewarding documentary follows charity worker Brenda Myers-Powell around Chicago's mean streets, schools and women's prisons as she endeavours to help women and girls at risk escape prostitution and its traps. A former sex worker herself, the ebullient Myers-Powell comes across as a force of nature with her tireless energy, radiant warmth and fabulous array of wigs, listening patiently to her clients' problems and helps them find hope, even in the darkest of circumstances. **LF** *DVD*

■ *Dir/Scr* Kim Longinotto

Dreamchild ★★★PG
Fantasy drama 1985 · UK · Colour · 94min

This is fascinating and imaginative, if seriously flawed exploration of the real-life person on whom the Reverend Charles Dodgson (aka Lewis Carroll) allegedly based his fictional character Alice. Coral Browne gives a deeply layered performance as the 80-year-old Alice Hargreaves, traumatised by her recollections of the famous relationship, while Dennis Potter's screenplay is typically taut and riveting. **SH**

Coral Browne *Mrs Alice Hargreaves* • Ian Holm *Reverend Charles Dodgson* • Peter Gallagher *Jack Dolan* • Caris Corfman *Sally Mackeson* • Nicola Cowper *Lucy* • Jane Asher *Mrs Liddell* ■ *Dir* Gavin Millar • *Scr* Dennis Potter

Dreamer ★★★U
Horse racing drama based on a true story 2005 · US · Colour · 100min

Inspired by real events, this feel-good drama stars Kurt Russell as a gifted trainer whose refusal to put down a filly with a supposedly career-ending broken leg earns him ownership of the horse - and dismissal from his job. Broke, yet desperate to please his young daughter (Dakota Fanning), he agrees to try to restore the steed to her former glory. Though the outcome is not unexpected, the story is beautifully cast and touching. **SF** *DVD*

Kurt Russell *Ben Crane* • Dakota Fanning *Cale Crane* • Kris Kristofferson *Pop Crane* • Elisabeth Shue *Lilly Crane* • Luis Guzman *Balon* • Freddy Rodriguez *Manolin* • David Morse *Palmer* • Oded Fehr *Prince Sadir* ■ *Dir/Scr* John Gatins

The Dreamers ★★★★18
Period drama 2003 · Fr/It/UK/US · Colour and BW · 110min

During the revolutionary spring of 1968 in France, twins Louis Garrel and Eva Green invite American fellow student Michael Pitt to stay at their parents' Paris apartment. There they test each other's cinematic, emotional, sexual and political ideals to see how far they will go. The fact the trio are film fanatics enables director Bernardo Bertolucci to explore a cineaste edge to their passions, and the vintage film clips give the drama further stylish resonance. Erotically explicit, this is a stunning return to form from the taboo-challenging director. **AJ** English, French +subtitles. *DVD*

Michael Pitt *Matthew* • Eva Green *Isabelle* • Louis Garrel *Théo* • Robin Renucci *Father* • Anna Chancellor *Mother* • Florian Cadiou *Patrick* ■ *Dir* Bernardo Bertolucci • *Scr* Gilbert Adair, from his novel *The Holy Innocents*

Dreamgirls ★★★12
Musical drama 2006 · US · Colour · 124min

Showered with Oscar nominations and winner of the best musical Golden Globe, this backstage drama fulfils glamour and glitz expectations in spades. Jennifer Hudson excels as the lead singer of 1960s backing group the Dreamettes, who is sidelined by new manager Jamie Foxx when he decides to promote Beyoncé Knowles to head up the trio. Plot sound familiar? It is, of course, the thinly disguised story of Diana Ross and the Supremes. Although uplifting and moving by turns, the tale – based on the hit Broadway musical – too closely follows its real-life equivalent to make any sense as fiction. And, for fans of the Supremes, the admittedly rousing score is a frustration. However, keeping pace with Hudson, supporting star Eddie Murphy reveals a dramatic depth previously only hinted at. SuR Brief swearing, drug abuse references. *DVD* 🔷

Jamie Foxx *Curtis Taylor Jr* • Beyoncé Knowles *Deena Jones* • Eddie Murphy *James "Thunder" Early* • Jennifer Hudson *Effie White* • Keith Robinson *CC White* • Hinton Battle *Wayne* • Sharon Leal *Michelle Morris* • Anika Noni Rose *Lorrell Robinson* • Danny Glover *Marty Madison* • John Lithgow *Jerry Harris* ■ *Dir* Bill Condon • *Scr* Bill Condon, from the musical by Tom Eyen (lyrics), Henry Krieger (music), from the story by Eyen • *Costume Designer* Sharen Davis • *Art Directors* John Myhre, Nancy Haigh

Dreaming ★★ U

Comedy   1944 · UK · BW · 78min

Comedians Bud Flanagan and Chesney Allen from the Crazy Gang star in this gently naive comedy produced by Britain's Ealing Studios. It's about a soldier who gets a knock on his head and drifts into a dream world. The dreams feature appearances from music hall turns such as xylophonist Teddy Brown and violinist Alfredo Campoli, plus cameos from famous jockeys Gordon Richards and Dick Francis in an attempt to comfort wartime audiences. TH

Bud Flanagan *Bud* • Chesney Allen *Ches* • Hazel Court *Wren/Avalah/Miss Grey* • Dick Francis *Sir Charles Paddock* • Philip Wade *Dr Goebbels* • Gerry Wilmott *United States General* • Peter Bernard *American soldier* • Ian MacLean *General* • Gordon Richards ■ *Dir* John Baxter • *Scr* Bud Flanagan [Dennis O'Keefe], Reginald Purdell

Dreaming of Joseph Lees ★★ 12

Drama   1998 · US/UK · Colour · 88min

Filmed on the Isle of Man, standing in for 1950s Somerset, this rural melodrama is heavy going, despite some glowingly worthy performances. Samantha Morton falls in love with geologist Rupert Graves, her cousin; when he takes off, she marries pig farmer Lee Ross. Then Graves returns, re-igniting passions. Eric Styles's direction is overwrought, while Catherine Linstrum's script is declamatory and stagey. TH Violence, sexual references.

Samantha Morton *Eva Babbins* • Rupert Graves *Joseph Lees* • Lee Ross *Harry Flite* • Miriam Margolyes *Signora Caldoni* • Frank Finlay *Eva's father* • Holly Aird *Maria Flite, Harry's sister* • Nicholas Woodeson *Mr Dian* ■ *Dir* Eric Styles • *Scr* Catherine Linstrum

Dreams ★★★ PG

Drama   1955 · Swe · BW · 86min

Sophisticated fashion photographer Eva Dahlbeck and jaunty model Harriet Andersson go to Gothenberg where the former attempts to revive an affair with married man Ulf Palme, and the latter has a flirtation with rich, retired diplomat Gunnar Bjornstrand. The gap between illusion and reality in Ingmar Bergman's film is reflected in the literal translation of the original Swedish title, *Women's Dreams*, while the casting of the lead actresses mirrors the shifting moods of the piece, alternately light-hearted and sombre. RB In Swedish. *DVD*

Harriet Andersson *Doris* • Eva Dahlbeck *Susanne* • Gunnar Björnstrand *The consul* • Ulf Palme *Henrik Lobelius* • Inga Landgré *Marta Lobelius* • Sven Lindberg *Palle* • Naima Wifstrand *Mrs Aren* • Benkt-Ake Benktsson *Magnus* ■ *Dir/Scr* Ingmar Bergman

Dreams of a Life ★★★★

Drama documentary   2011 · UK/Ire · Colour · 94min

In 2006, the body of 38-year-old Joyce Vincent was discovered in a flat in north London. But this was no murder mystery. She had been dead for three years. Film-maker Carol Morley became obsessed with this tragic incident, spending several years attempting to find out how Joyce was, and how anyone could fall through the cracks so completely. This affecting portrait of a lost life features interviews with people who knew her, as well as some affecting reconstructions. Zawe Ashton gives a fine performance as Joyce, subtly portraying a beautiful, popular woman who was nonetheless disconnected and lonely. She may have been forgotten in life, but Joyce Vincent will haunt anyone who watches this astonishing film. LB Sexual references. *DVD*

Zawe Ashton *Joyce Carol Vincent* • Alix Luka-Cain *Young Joyce* • Cornell S John *Father* • Neelam Bakshi *Mother* ■ *Dir/Scr* Carol Morley

Dreams of Gold: the Mel Fisher Story ★★★

Drama based on a true story   1986 · US · Colour · 95min

A TV dramatisation of Mel Fisher's obsessive 17-year search for a treasure-laden 17th-century galleon off the Florida coast, which threatened his family unity and led to a battle through the courts. This tale of doggedness and derring-do, though inevitably episodic, is handled with quiet efficiency. Cliff Robertson, a lobster trapper in his youth, looks particularly at home at sea, while Loretta Swit fits the bill as his wife. JM

Cliff Robertson *Mel Fisher* • Loretta Swit *Deo Fisher* • Ed O'Ross *Trooper Hudley* • Scott Paulin *Don Kincaid* • Jennifer Runyon *Angel Fisher* • Judi Evans *Penelope Cabot* • Bruce Toms *Kane Fisher* • Kerry Remsen *Taffi Fisher* • Jonathan Hogan *David Horan* ■ *Dir* James Goldstone • *Scr* Stanford Whitmore

Dreams That Money Can Buy ★★★★ 12

Experimental portmanteau drama   1946 · US · Colour and BW · 79min

This intriguing experiment in psychoanalytical surrealism (which took three years to complete) represents the most astonishing avant-garde collaboration in film history. Corralled by German Dadaist Hans Richter, the creative team comprises Max Ernst, Marcel Duchamp, Man Ray, Alexander Calder and Fernand Léger, while Louis Applebuam, Paul Bowles, John Cage, David Diamond, John Latouche and Darius Milhaud contributed to the score. A mysterious young man discovers he has a gift for dreaming and begins selling his bizarre visions to needy clients. Strikingly photographed by Arnold Eagle, the various vignettes range from the eccentric and satirical to the dazzling and disturbing, and their visual and psychological impact is mesmerising. DP Nudity, violence.

Jack Bittner *Joe/"Narcissus"* • Dorothy Griffith *Girl* ■ *Dir* Hans Richter • *Scr* Hans Richter, Max Ernst, Fernand Léger, Man Ray, Marcel Duchamp, Alexander Calder

Dreamscape ★★ 15

Science-fiction thriller   1984 · US · Colour · 94min

Psychic Dennis Quaid enters the American president's guilt-plagued nuclear nightmares to save him from a paranormal assassin in this workmanlike fantasy thriller. The perfectly cast actors fly as high as they can with the intriguing concept, but the script is mediocre and lacks any real excitement. The main pleasure of this efficient piece of film-making comes from the dream sequences that punctuate the political thriller framework. AJ *DVD*

Dennis Quaid *Alex Gardner* • Max von Sydow *Dr Paul Novotny* • Christopher Plummer *Bob Blair* • Eddie Albert *President* • Kate Capshaw *Dr Jane Devries* • David Patrick Kelly *Tommy Ray Glatman* • George Wendt *Charlie Prince* ■

Dir Joseph Ruben • *Scr* Joseph Ruben, David Loughery, Chuck Russell, from a story by David Loughery

Dredd ★★★★ 18

Science-fiction fantasy adventure   2012 · US · Colour · 91min

This gritty and very violent reboot of the *2000 AD* comic-strip is the thrilling, visceral film Judge Dredd fans have been waiting for. Smartly written by long-time Dredd fan Alex Garland (*28 Days Later*), the film embraces the dark heart of the source material in a way that Sylvester Stallone's 1995 take on the character failed to do. The no-nonsense law enforcer (played by Karl Urban, who never removes his helmet) and rookie Olivia Thirlby are trapped in a 200-storey slum controlled by psychotic drug-dealing hoodlum Lena Headey. It's spectacular stuff, with plenty of intense action, as Dredd implacably blasts his way through each level of the tower block. AJ Violence, drug abuse. *DVD* 🔷 *Thirlby*

Karl Urban *Judge Dredd* • Olivia Thirlby *Cassandra Anderson* • Lena Headey *Madeline "Ma-Ma" Madrigal* • Wood Harris *Kay* • Domhnall Gleeson *Clan Techie* ■ *Dir* Pete Travis • *Scr* Alex Garland, from characters by Carlos Ezquerra, John Wagner • *Cinematographer* Anthony Dod Mantle

Dressed to Kill ★★ U

Mystery   1946 · US · BW · 71min

Sherlock Holmes sets out to track down three music boxes containing stolen Bank of England engraving plates in this mystery, which was Basil Rathbone's final outing as the great detective. Patricia Morison does well as the villainess, but she doesn't have the evil presence of Moriarty. Luckily, Nigel Bruce is on form as Dr Watson and his bumbling joviality lightens up the dour atmosphere. TH *DVD*

Basil Rathbone *Sherlock Holmes* • Nigel Bruce *Dr Watson* • Patricia Morison *Hilda Courtney* • Edmond Breon [Edmund Breon] *Gilbert Emery* • Frederick Worlock *Colonel Cavanaugh* • Carl Harbord *Inspector Hopkins* ■ *Dir* Roy William Neill • *Scr* Leonard Lee, Frank Gruber, from a story by Sir Arthur Conan Doyle

Dressed to Kill ★★★★ 18

Thriller   1980 · US · Colour · 100min

Brian De Palma does his witty Hitchcock imitation again, and adds his own trademark layers of macabre black comedy and visual ingenuity to the *Psycho*-influenced proceedings. Sex-starved housewife Angie Dickinson's attempt to grab a little excitement leads to a dangerous situation, into which her son Keith Gordon and prostitute Nancy Allen (then the director's wife) are dragged. An eyebrow-raising performance from Michael Caine keeps this clever shocker moving along nicely, as De Palma's brilliant sleight-of-hand direction pulls out all the suspense stops, providing some unforgettable jolts. AJ Swearing, violence, sex scenes, nudity. *DVD* 🔷

Michael Caine *Dr Robert Elliott* • Angie Dickinson *Kate Miller* • Nancy Allen *Liz Blake* • Keith Gordon *Peter Miller* • Dennis Franz *Detective Marino* • David Margulies *Dr Levy* ■ *Dir/Scr* Brian De Palma • *Editor* Jerry Greenberg • *Music* Pino Donaggio

The Dresser ★★★★ PG

Drama   1983 · UK · Colour · 113min

The inspiration for Ronald Harwood's play came from his own experiences as Sir Donald Wolfit's dresser in the 1950s. Wolfit was an actor/manager of enormous girth and even greater eccentricity. To play the Wolfit character, Albert Finney also borrowed from Laurence Olivier and Charles Laughton, creating a vivid composite of a man who had "flashes of greatness". Getting Finney into his costumes is Tom Courtenay, giving another splendid performance: small-scale, seedy and obsequious. Both Finney and Courtenay were rightly nominated for Oscars. AT Some swearing. *DVD*

Albert Finney *Sir* • Tom Courtenay *Norman* • Edward Fox *Oxenby* • Zena Walker *Her Ladyship* • Eileen Atkins *Madge* • Michael Gough *Frank*

Carrington* • Cathryn Harrison *Irene* • Betty Marsden *Violet Manning* • Sheila Reid *Lydia Gibson* ■ *Dir* Peter Yates • *Scr* Ronald Harwood, from his play

The Dressmaker ★★★★ 15

Second World War drama   1988 · UK · Colour · 87min

It is 1944, and Joan Plowright defends Merseyside against the Germans. This is an excellent example of what the British do best: honourable thespians acting their utility socks off. This adaptation of a novel by Beryl Bainbridge, about two very different aunts raising their teenage niece, is written with great skill and flair by the always interesting John McGrath. Courage, fear, repression and sex with GIs are all mixed into this glorious, tautly acted vehicle. It can all seem a trifle claustrophobic at times, but this is a minor quibble. SH

Joan Plowright *Nellie* • Billie Whitelaw *Margo* • Jane Horrocks *Rita* • Peter Postlethwaite [Pete Postlethwaite] *Jack* • Tim Ransom *Wesley* • Rosemary Martin *Mrs Manders* • Pippa Hinchley *Valerie* • Tony Haygarth *Mr Manders* • Michael James-Reed *Chuck* ■ *Dir* Jim O'Brien • *Scr* John McGrath, from the novel by Beryl Bainbridge

The Dressmaker ★★★★ 12

Comedy drama   2015 · Aus/UK · Colour · 113min

When an haute-coutured Kate Winslet, portable sewing machine in hand, returns to her dusty, gossip-ridden home town in the Aussie outback, expect fireworks. That's because Winslet's Parisian-trained seamstress is back to settle a score, though her mother (Judy Davis in a superbly nuanced performance) doesn't remember having a daughter. Admittedly, the townsfolk are surreal caricatures but, despite its levity and wild shifts in tone, director Jocelyn Moorhouse's spicy take on Rosalie Ham's novel is a heartbreaking tragicomedy. It's also imaginative, funny, poignant and unforgettable. KK Violence, swearing, drug abuse. *DVD* 🔷

Kate Winslet *Myrtle "Tilly" Dunnage* • Liam Hemsworth *Teddy McSwiney* • Judy Davis *Molly Dunnage* • Hugo Weaving *Sergeant Farrat* • Caroline Goodall *Elsbeth* ■ *Dir* Jocelyn Moorhouse • *Scr* Jocelyn Moorhouse, PJ Hogan, from Rosalie Ham's novel

Dreyfus ★★★ U

Historical drama   1931 · UK · BW · 96min

An extremely worthy British reworking of a notable German success, this makes a deliberate shifting of emphasis, since the Dreyfus case was not only a staggering miscalculation of justice but also a national manifestation of anti-Jewish feeling. The famous case tells of a Jew in the French general staff who is framed for treason and sent to Devil's Island. Later movie versions of the tale – most notably *The Life of Emile Zola* and the underrated *I Accuse!* – may be more accessible, but there's no doubting this film's sincerity. TS

Cedric Hardwicke *Alfred Dreyfus* • Charles Carson *Col Picquart* • George Merritt (1) *Emile Zola* • Sam Livesey *Labori* • Beatrix Thompson *Lucie Dreyfus* • Garry Marsh *Major Esterhazy* ■ *Dir* FW Kraemer, Milton Rosmer • *Scr* Reginald Berkeley, Walter C Mycroft, from the play *The Dreyfus Case* by Wilhelm Herzog, Hans Rehfisch

Drifting Clouds ★★★★ PG

Romance   1996 · Fin/Ger/Fr · Colour · 92min

Aki Kaurismäki considers this urban morality tale to be a mix of *Bicycle Thieves* and *It's a Wonderful Life*. Yet the bright colours and ironic soundtrack make it a Helsinki version of *The Umbrellas of Cherbourg*, as waitress Kati Outinen and and her ex-tram driver husband Kari Vaananen unite to overcome the humiliations of poverty and menial employment. Minutely observed, perfectly paced and beautifully underplayed by the director's stock company, this is an affectionate portrait of real people surviving slings and arrows with a decency and determination. DP Finnish +subtitles.

D

Kati Outinen *Ilona Koponen* • Kari Vaananen *Lauri Koponen* • Elina Salo *Mrs Sjoholm* • Sakari Kuosmanen *Melartin* • Markku Peltola *Lajunen* ■ *Dir/Scr* Aki Kaurismäki

Driftwood ★★★ U
Drama   1946 · US · BW · 84min

This is a charmingly bucolic tale about likeable doctor Walter Brennan, who looks after an orphan waif who's never before strayed from the backwoods, winsomely played by nine-year-old Natalie Wood. Though some may feel Wood's performance a tad calculated, she shows all the early glimmerings of that shining talent that made her a major star of the 1950s and 1960s. Director Allan Dwan keeps the sentimentality reined in. TS

Ruth Warrick *Susan* • Walter Brennan *Murph* • Dean Jagger *Dr Steve Webster* • Charlotte Greenwood *Mathilda* • Natalie Wood *Jenny* • Margaret Hamilton *Essie Keenan* ■ *Dir* Allan Dwan • *Scr* Mary Loos, Richard Sale

Driftwood ★ 18
Drama   1996 · Ire/UK · Colour · 96min

Alone on a windswept island, Anne Brochet gets to roll her eyes as the seemingly normal sculptress who helps amnesiac castaway James Spader. Her kindness is gradually replaced by violent hysteria as her new lover threatens to return to civilisation. Spader offers only distracted hesitancy, so the burden of dramatic impetus falls on Brochet, who responds with a display of desperate theatricality. DP Violence, swearing and sex scenes. *DVD*

James Spader *The Man* • Anne Brochet *Sarah* • Barry McGovern *McTavish* • Anna Massey *Mother* • Aiden Grenell *Father* • Kevin McHugh *Motorcycle driver* ■ *Dir* Ronan O'Leary • *Scr* Richard MN Waring, Ronan O'Leary

Drillbit Taylor ★★★ 12
Comedy   2007 · US · Colour · 97min

With his Texan drawl and broken nose, Owen Wilson's laid-back screen presence proves charismatic enough to carry this breezily entertaining and likeable comedy. He stars as the eponymous army veteran of dubious pedigree, who's hired as a bodyguard by three bullied high school kids (Troy Gentile, Nate Hartley and David Dorfman). Pretending to be a supply teacher, Drillbit infiltrates the school, romances a teacher (Leslie Mann) and gives his young protégés some unique lessons in survival techniques. Wilson's slyly self-mocking turn works a treat, while the kids display a comic talent well beyond their years (particularly the already seasoned Gentile). JR Some violence, swearing, sexual references. *DVD* Blu

Owen Wilson *Drillbit Taylor* • Leslie Mann *Lisa* • Nate Hartley *Wade* • Troy Gentile *Ryan* • David Dorfman *Emmit* • Alex Frost *Filkins* • Josh Peck *Ronnie* • Danny McBride (2) *Don* ■ *Dir* Steven Brill • *Scr* Seth Rogen, Kristofor Brown, from a story by Edmond Dantes, Rogen, Brown

The Driller Killer ★★ 18
Horror   1979 · US · Colour · 94min

Abel Ferrara's notorious contribution to Do-It-Yourself serial slaying is actually an amateurish, art house affair that hardly deserves the "video nasty" label it received in the early 1980s. A disturbed artist is continually thwarted in his career. Noisy neighbours are his first targets as he enforces his own brand of peace and quiet with his Black and Decker. When it was finally released on video in the UK in 1999, 54 seconds were cut, and some of the more gratuitous scenes of violence were toned down via optical editing. JF Swearing, violence, sex scenes. *DVD*

Jimmy Laine [Abel Ferrara] *Reno* • Carolyn Marz *Carol* • Baybi Day *Pamela* • Harry Schultz *Dalton Briggs* • Alan Wynroth *Landlord* • Maria Helhoski *Nun* • James O'Hara *Man in church* ■ *Dir* Abel Ferrara • *Scr* Nicholas St John

Drinking Buddies ★★★★ 15
Romantic comedy drama   2013 · US · Colour · 86min

Prolific indie director Joe Swanberg is a dab hand with low-budget relationship movies, but nothing so far has been as polished as this offering. The setting is a craft brewery in Chicago, where co-workers Kate (Olivia Wilde) and Luke (Jake Johnson) seem to be made for each other, except they are seeing other people. Despite a minimalist plot, Swanberg's semi-improvised story is so amazingly rich in character chemistry, especially between the self-assured Kate and the wisecracking Luke, that *Drinking Buddies* could easily be likened to a laid-back hipster version of a Mike Leigh movie. Praise can't get much better than that. DW Swearing. *DVD*

Olivia Wilde *Kate* • Jake Johnson *Luke* • Anna Kendrick *Jill* • Ron Livingston *Chris* • Jason Sudeikis *Gene Dentler* • Ti West *Dave* ■ *Dir/Scr* Joe Swanberg

Drive ★★★★ 18
Crime thriller   2011 · US · Colour · 96min

Ryan Gosling is a stunt performer who uses his skills moonlighting as a getaway driver in this stylish though very violent revenge drama. When attractive married neighbour Carey Mulligan is menaced by gangsters, he acts to protect her, leading to bloody warfare within the local criminal fraternity. Albert Brooks and Ron Perlman are on fine form as the terrifying heavies but it's Gosling who anchors the movie with a strong, silent (and undeniably pretty) act that's surprisingly convincing. This is compellingly nasty but for those with the stomach for it, *Drive* is a lot of fun. AS Violence, swearing, nudity. *DVD* Blu

Ryan Gosling *Driver* • Carey Mulligan *Irene* • Bryan Cranston *Shannon* • Albert Brooks *Bernie Rose* • Ron Perlman *Nino* • Oscar Isaac *Standard* • Kaden Leos *Benecio* • Christina Hendricks *Blanche* ■ *Dir* Nicolas Winding Refn • *Scr* Hossein Amini, from the novel by James Sallis

Drive a Crooked Road ★★★
Crime drama   1954 · US · BW · 82min

A prime example of a Hollywood B-melodrama, this was originally shown in the UK as the support to Alec Guinness's *Father Brown*. Director Richard Quine's first thriller is a tautly paced action tale that reminds us of what a talented film-maker he was and how underrated he is today. The style may be a little drawn-out for contemporary tastes, and star Mickey Rooney's tendency to chew the scenery has not worn well, but Dianne Foster is an attractive foil. TS

Mickey Rooney *Eddie Shannon* • Dianne Foster *Barbara Mathews* • Kevin McCarthy *Steve Norris* • Jack Kelly *Harold Baker* • Harry Landers *Ralph* • Jerry Paris *Phil* • Paul Picerni *Carl* • Dick Crockett *Don* ■ *Dir* Richard Quine • *Scr* Blake Edwards, Richard Quine (adaptation), from a story by James Benson Nablo

Drive Angry ★★★ 18
Action fantasy horror   2011 · US · Colour · 100min

A nonstop riot of gratuitous sex, full-on violence, gory gunfights and explosive car crashes makes this a high-energy trash extravaganza. Vengeance-fuelled John Milton (Nicolas Cage) escapes Hell to pursue the satanic cult who killed his daughter and is now set on sacrificing her baby in order to unleash the Devil. Cage keeps his performance deliberately one-note to anchor the flashy mayhem, while William Fichtner steals every scene as the enigmatic Accountant, charged with getting Milton back to Hades. Pumped up to the max, the sizzling dialogue, cartoon action and visual wildness provide plenty of laughs and thrills. AJ Violence, swearing, drug abuse, sex scenes, nudity. *DVD* Blu

Nicolas Cage *John Milton* • Amber Heard *Piper* • William Fichtner *The Accountant* • Billy Burke *Jonah King* • David Morse *Webster* • Tom Atkins *Cap* ■ *Dir* Patrick Lussier • *Scr* Patrick Lussier, Todd Farmer

Drive, He Said ★★★
Drama   1971 · US · Colour · 90min

In the mid-1960s Jack Nicholson took a shine to Jeremy Larner's novel, which fused basketball (one of Nicholson's obsessions) with the activities of campus radicals during the escalation of the Vietnam War. Five years later, Nicholson had become a star but realised he couldn't play a basketball star. So he turned director and delivered this funky piece, which has lofty ambitions but never quite comes together. AT

William Tepper *Hector* • Karen Black *Olive* • Michael Margotta *Gabriel* • Bruce Dern *Bullion* • Robert Towne *Richard* • Henry Jaglom *Conrad* ■ *Dir* Jack Nicholson • *Scr* Jack Nicholson, Jeremy Larner, from the novel by Jeremy Larner

Drive Me Crazy ★★★ 12
Romantic comedy   1999 · US · Colour · 87min

Tailor-made for teenage girls (it stars *Sabrina the Teenage Witch's* Melissa Joan Hart and has a title song by Britney Spears), this is slight but sweet, featuring some nice performances. Hart plays a high school senior who is looking for a date to take her to the prom. When the school jock directs his attentions elsewhere, she sets her sights on the brooding boy next door (Adrian Grenier), though he needs a major makeover. JB Swearing. *DVD*

Melissa Joan Hart *Nicole Maris* • Adrian Grenier *Chase Hammond* • Stephen Collins *Mr Maris* • Mark Metcalf *Mr Rope* • William Converse-Roberts *Mr Hammond* • Faye Grant *Mrs Maris* • Susan May Pratt *Alicia* • Kris Park *Ray Neeley* ■ *Dir* John Schultz • *Scr* Rob Thomas, from the novel *How I Created My Perfect Dream Date* by Todd Strasser

Driven ★★★ PG
Sports action drama   2001 · US/Can · Colour · 111min

In an attempt to regain pole position as an action man, Sylvester Stallone not only stars in this monument to racing cars and breakneck effects, but also wears his screenwriter/co-producer cap, too. He plays a veteran race driver who's brought out of retirement by wheelchair-bound buddy Burt Reynolds to help his hotshot protégé Kip Pardue beat German ace Til Schweiger to the world championship. The formulaic tale is directed with minimal imagination by Renny Harlin, but, if high speed chases, races and crashes are your thing, then the director delivers the goods with aplomb. TH *DVD*

Sylvester Stallone *Joe Tanto* • Burt Reynolds *Carl Henry* • Kip Pardue *Jimmy Bly* • Stacy Edwards *Lucretia "Luc" Jones* • Til Schweiger *Beau Brandenburg* • Gina Gershon *Cathy* ■ *Dir* Renny Harlin • *Scr* Sylvester Stallone, from a story by Sylvester Stallone, Jan Skrentny, Neal Tabachnick

Driven to Kill ★★ 18
Action crime thriller   2009 · US/Can · Colour · 94min

It's a good job that Steven Seagal is a man of few words because in this far-fetched revenge thriller, he's very hard to understand. He plays a Russian gangster-turned-novelist who returns to the American underworld to find the thugs that murdered his ex-wife and left his daughter for dead. Realism and logic take a back seat in the events that follow, while the violent action feels fake and flat, with ridiculous camerawork and poor editing sucking the tension out of even the extended gunfight/martial arts finale. SF Violence. *DVD* Blu

Steven Seagal *Ruslan Drachev* • Dmitry Chepovetsky *Stephan* • Igor Jijikine *Mikhail* • Robert Wisden *Terry* ■ *Dir* Jeff F King [Jeff King] • *Scr* Mark James (2)

The Driver ★★★★ 15
Crime thriller   1978 · US · Colour · 87min

The story of a getaway driver who has no life outside his work is pared down to its absolute existential essentials in Walter Hill's terrific thriller. Critics thought that the writer/director was paying tribute to Jean-Pierre Melville's 1967 classic *Le Samouraï*, though he denied he'd ever seen it. Ryan O'Neal wears the same trenchcoat as Alain Delon; he also has the same cool demeanour and ruthless tunnel vision. The car chases are amazing, but it's O'Neal's calm you remember, together with its unravelling, as Isabelle Adjani and cop Bruce Dern get under his skin. AT *DVD* Blu

Ryan O'Neal *The Driver* • Bruce Dern *The Detective* • Isabelle Adjani *The Player* • Ronee Blakley *The Connection* • Matt Clark *Red plain-clothes man* • Felice Orlandi *Gold plain-clothes man* • Joseph Walsh *Glasses* • Rudy Ramos *Teeth* ■ *Dir/Scr* Walter Hill

The Driver's Seat ★★ 15
Drama   1975 · It · Colour · 93min

"It's not sex I want," says Elizabeth Taylor at the outset of this obscure melodrama, "but death." She also says she has used up all her supply of happiness, a line that one of her biographers pounced upon, claiming the movie was deeply personal. It's a doom-laden affair, acted with such seriousness it rates as a camp send-up of Antonioni's meditations on urban alienation. Taylor is simply playing herself as a cultural icon; Andy Warhol makes an appropriately fleeting appearance. AT

Elizabeth Taylor *Lise* • Ian Bannen *Richard* • Guido Mannari *Carlo* • Mona Washbourne *Mrs Fiedke* • Maxence Mailfort *Bill* • Andy Warhol ■ *Dir* Giuseppe Patroni-Griffi • *Scr* Raffaele La Capria, Giuseppe Patroni-Griffi, from the novel by Muriel Spark

Driving Aphrodite ★★ 12
Romantic comedy   2008 · Sp/US · Colour · 94min

Lightning doesn't strike twice here for star Nia Vardalos, whose 2002 romantic comedy *My Big Fat Greek Wedding* was the undoubted sleeper hit of that year. Again capitalising on her Greek roots, Vardalos plays Georgia, an impossibly glamorous Greek-American academic forced to work as a second-class tour guide in Athens. She swears this is her last summer leading a group of motley tourists to the famous sights of Greece, but soon rediscovers her *joie de vivre*. Despite a game cast, this is a weak, predictable 1970s-style comedy travelogue that provides more hearty stereotypes than laughs. KK Sexual references. *DVD*

Nia Vardalos *Georgia* • Richard Dreyfuss *Irv* • Alexis Georgoulis *Poupi* • Alistair McGowan *Nico* • Harland Williams *Big Al* • Rachel Dratch *Kim* ■ *Dir* Donald Petrie • *Scr* Mike Reiss

Driving Lessons ★★★ 15
Road movie comedy   2006 · UK · Colour · 93min

Harry Potter sidekick Rupert Grint branches out here as a shy teenager with a provisional driving licence and an overly protective mother (played by Laura Linney with perfect English accent). He takes a summer job with an eccentric theatrical dame, Julie Walters, who forces him to take her for a drive and their subsequent adventures include a trip to Edinburgh. Writer/director Jeremy Brock drew on his own youthful experience of working for Peggy Ashcroft, but the protagonist may remind some of Dustin Hoffman's character in *The Graduate*. While *Driving Lessons* is never as incisive as that Mike Nichols classic, it's a pleasant enough diversion. BP Swearing. *DVD*

Julie Walters *Evie* • Rupert Grint *Ben* • Laura Linney *Laura* • Nicholas Farrell *Robert* • Jim Norton *Mr Fincham* • Michelle Duncan *Bryony* ■ *Dir/Scr* Jeremy Brock

Driving Me Crazy ★★ PG
Comedy   1991 · US · Colour · 103min

Released in the States as *Dutch*, this was the first sign that teen pic wunderkind John Hughes was beginning to run out of ideas. This story of a sulky kid travelling through America for Thanksgiving in the company of his mother's beau may well strike you as familiar – think *Planes, Trains and Automobiles*, also penned by Hughes. Long on contrivance and short on comedy, this film will soon drive you crazy, too. DP Swearing.

Ed O'Neill *Dutch Dooley* • Ethan Randall [Ethan Embry] *Doyle Standish* • JoBeth Williams *Natalie Standish* • Ari Meyers *Brock* • Christopher McDonald *Reed Standish* • EG Daily [Elizabeth Daily] *Halley* ■ *Dir* Peter Faiman • *Scr* John Hughes

Driving Miss Daisy ★★★★ U
Drama   1989 · US · Colour · 94min

This small, unassuming movie went up against the big guns of Hollywood and emerged with a best picture Oscar. It charts the deepening relationship between an elderly widow and her black chauffeur in Atlanta. Miss Daisy (Oscar winner Jessica Tandy) is an independent former schoolteacher with a will of iron, until she crashes her new car and cannot get insurance on another. So her son (Dan Aykroyd) arranges a chauffeur (Morgan Freeman). The story covers the years from 1948 until 1973 – a period of racial strife and the civil rights movement – attaining the status of allegory in the process. AT **DVD**

Jessica Tandy *Miss Daisy* Daisy Werthan · Morgan Freeman *Hoke* Colburn · Dan Aykroyd *Boolie Werthan* · Patti LuPone *Florine Werthan* · Esther Rolle *Idella* · Joann Havrilla *Miss McClatchey* · William Hall Jr *Oscar* · Alvin M Sugarman *Dr Weil* ■ *Dir* Bruce Beresford · *Scr* Alfred Uhry, from his play

Drôle de Drame ★★★★
Period black comedy   1937 · Fr · BW · 109min

Set in Edwardian London, this witty and anarchic farce was the second of director Marcel Carné's seven collaborations with screenwriter Jacques Prévert; they went on to make the classic *Les Enfants du Paradis* in 1945. Played to perfection by a superb cast, the film involves a mystery writer (Michel Simon) accused by a visiting bishop (Louis Jouvet) of murdering his wife (Françoise Rosay). Jean-Louis Barrault appears as an animal-lover who kills butchers. RB French +subtitles.

Louis Jouvet *Archibald Soper, Bishop of Bedford* · Françoise Rosay *Margaret Molyneux* · Michel Simon *Irwin Molyneux/Félix Chapel* · Jean-Louis Barrault *William Kramps* · Jean-Pierre Aumont *Billy* · Nadine Vogel *Eva* · Pierre Alcover *Inspector Bray* · Henri Guisol *Buffington* · Jean Marais *Fatigued reveller* ■ *Dir* Marcel Carné · *Scr* Jacques Prévert, from the novel *His First Offence* by J Storer-Clouston

Drôle de Félix ★★★ 15
Road movie   2000 · Fr · Colour · 91min

Writer/directors Olivier Ducastel and Jacques Martineau explore the nature of kinship and modern French attitudes to race and sexuality in this ambling road movie. Travelling from Dieppe to Marseille to meet the father he never knew, Sami Bouajila encounters anti-Arab prejudice and homophobic ignorance at every turn. But he also finds acceptance among diverse members of his wider "family", including a vibrantly rebellious "grandmother" (a scene-stealing turn from Patachou) and an independent-minded "sister" (the ever-feisty Ariane Ascaride). DP French +subtitles. **DVD**

Sami Bouajila *Félix* · Patachou *Mathilde* · Ariane Ascaride *Isabelle* · Pierre-Loup Rajot *Daniel* · Charly Sergue *Jules* · Maurice Bénichou *Fisherman* ■ *Dir/Scr* Olivier Ducastel, Jacques Martineau

The Drop ★★★ 15
Crime drama
2014 · US/UK/Aus · Colour · 106min

Before his untimely death in 2013, James Gandolfini had already laid the ghost of Tony Soprano to rest with his final film: this off-kilter but characterful gangster story. What threatens to become the usual heist-gone-wrong drama soon goes in another direction, with buttoned-up bartender Tom Hardy blundering into a dark love triangle with the enigmatic Noomi Rapace and the vicious Matthias Schoenaerts. The tone is uneven, and the end a little queasy, but *The Drop's* unusual chemistry keeps its minimal plot ticking over nicely. DW Violence, swearing. **DVD**

Tom Hardy *Bob Saginowski* · Noomi Rapace *Nadia* · James Gandolfini *Cousin Marv* · Matthias Schoenaerts *Eric Deeds* · John Ortiz (1) *Detective Torres* · Ann Dowd *Dottie* ■ *Dir* Michael R Roskam · *Scr* Dennis Lehane, from his short story *Animal Rescue*

Drop Dead Darling ★★★
Comedy   1966 · UK · Colour · 100min

British director Ken Hughes is an unsung British talent, responsible for, among other films, *The Trials of Oscar Wilde* and *Chitty Chitty Bang Bang*. This handsome Shepperton-shot farce, released in the USA as *Arrivederci, Baby!*, offers a bravura role to the terrific Tony Curtis, as a charming Bluebeard, and some plum lines and opportunities for grimacing to the irascible Lionel Jeffries. Tastelessness abounds, but for once it's deliberate, and the Panavision and Technicolor photography is extremely glossy. TS

Tony Curtis *Nick Johnson* · Zsa Zsa Gabor *Gigi* · Rosanna Schiaffino *Francesca* · Lionel Jeffries *Parker* · Nancy Kwan *Baby* · Fenella Fielding *Fenella* · Anna Quayle *Aunt Miriam* · Warren Mitchell *Count de Pienzi/Maximilian* · Mischa Auer *Romeo* ■ *Dir* Ken Hughes · *Scr* Ken Hughes, from a story by Ken Hughes, Ronald Harwood, suggested by the novel *The Careful Man* by Richard Deming · *Cinematographer* Denys N Coop [Denys Coop]

Drop Dead Fred ★★ 12
Fantasy comedy   1991 · US · Colour · 95min

A high-energy performance by Rik Mayall in the title role is the chief interest in this largely uninteresting and unfunny comedy. It's the story of a grown woman (Phoebe Cates) who is revisited by the imaginary friend of her childhood (Mayall), on a mission to cheer her up at a bad time. A nice idea falls between all available stools and ends up as a mess on the floor. PF Swearing. **DVD**

Phoebe Cates *Elizabeth Cronin* · Rik Mayall *Drop Dead Fred* · Marsha Mason *Polly* · Tim Matheson *Charles Cronin* · Bridget Fonda *Annabella* · Carrie Fisher *Janie* · Keith Charles *Murray* · Ashley Peldon *Young Elizabeth* · Daniel Gerroll *Nigel* ■ *Dir* Ate De Jong · *Scr* Carlos Davis, Anthony Fingleton, from a story by Elizabeth Livingston

Drop Dead Gorgeous
★★★ 15
Black comedy   1999 · US · Colour · 93min

A sophisticated black comedy in mockumentary style, this traces a small-town beauty pageant from the auditions to the glitz and glamour of the finals. Kirsten Dunst, a sweet girl from a trailer-trash background, is pitted against spoilt little rich bitch Denise Richards. Meanwhile, someone in town is knocking off their competition. Ellen Barkin and Kirstie Alley are both entertaining as the girls' cat-fighting moms, and overall this is a refreshing and ironic take on suburban American life. Better than your average Hollywood fare. LH Swearing. **DVD**

Kirstie Alley *Gladys Leeman* · Ellen Barkin *Annette Atkins* · Kirsten Dunst *Amber Atkins* · Denise Richards *Becky Leeman* · Allison Janney *Loretta* · Will Sasso *Hank Vilmes* · Mindy Sterling *Iris Clark* · Sam McMurray *Lester Leeman* · Brittany Murphy *Lisa Swenson* · Amy Adams *Leslie Miller* · Adam West ■ *Dir* Michael Patrick Jann · *Scr* Lona Williams

DROP Squad ★★ 15
Satirical drama   1994 · US · Colour · 83min

"DROP" stands for "Deprogramming and Restoration of Pride", and is the name of a group that attempts to persuade African-Americans that they have "sold-out" their culture. The tone of this drama from Spike Lee's production company is a tad strident, as advertising executive Eriq La Salle proves a tough nut for the group to crack. Not as balanced as it should be, given the controversial subject matter, but well performed. JF

Eriq La Salle *Bruford Jamison Jr* · Vondie Curtis-Hall *Rocky* · Ving Rhames *Garvey* · Leonard Thomas *XB* · Michael Ralph *Trevor* · Billy Williams *Huey* · Eric A Payne [Eric Payne] *Stokeley* · Vanessa Williams *Mali* ■ *Dir* David Johnson · *Scr* David Johnson, Butch Robinson, David Taylor from the short film *The Session* by David Taylor

Drop Zone ★★★ 15
Thriller   1994 · US · Colour · 101min

This skydiving movie is an exhilarating ride, directed by action specialist John Badham with his usual flair and eye for spectacular set pieces. Wesley Snipes exudes charisma as the US marshal who sets out to hunt down the parachuting crooks whose airborne antics cost Snipes's brother his life. Gary Busey delivers another entertainingly villainous performance, while Yancy Butler is equally good as Snipes's reluctant partner. JF Swearing, violence. **DVD**

Wesley Snipes *Pete Nessip* · Gary Busey *Ty Moncrief* · Yancy Butler *Jessie Crossman* · Michael Jeter *Earl Leedy* · Corin Nemec *Selkirk* · Kyle Secor *Swoop* · Luca Bercovici *Jagger* · Malcolm-Jamal Warner *Terry Nessip* ■ *Dir* John Badham · *Scr* Peter Barsocchini, John Bishop, from a story by Tony Griffin

Drowning by Numbers
★★★★ 15
Black comedy drama   1988 · UK · Colour · 114min

In one of writer/director Peter Greenaway's darkest comedies, three generations of womenfolk, all named Cissie Colpitts, drown their menfolk with the acquiescence of local coroner Bernard Hill. Joan Plowright, Juliet Stevenson and Joely Richardson are delightfully lethal as the scheming trio, while Greenaway indulges his obsessions with word games, lists and the ache of mortality. Michael Nyman's score builds momentum, even though there isn't any, and it's luminous and lurid in equal measure. TH **DVD** **Blu-ray**

Bernard Hill *Madgett* · Joan Plowright *Cissie Colpitts 1* · Juliet Stevenson *Cissie Colpitts 2* · Joely Richardson *Cissie Colpitts 3* · Jason Edwards *Smut* · Bryan Pringle *Jake* · Trevor Cooper *Hardy* · David Morrissey *Bellamy* ■ *Dir/Scr* Peter Greenaway

Drowning Mona ★★ 12
Black comedy   2000 · US · Colour · 92min

This lame comedy starts out in a promising fashion by having Bette Midler killed during the opening credits. Alas, it quickly goes downhill. Police chief Danny DeVito is dealing with a much bigger mystery than discovering who offed Midler, the most hated resident of Verplanck, NY: he has to find someone who *didn't* want her dead. Nick Gomez's movie desperately wants to be a quirky black farce, but ends up more like an episode of "Trailer Trash Family Feud". You want to be amused by these characters, but they're just too stupid to be funny. ST **DVD**

Danny DeVito *Chief Wyatt Rash* · Bette Midler *Mona Dearly* · Neve Campbell *Ellen Rash* · Jamie Lee Curtis *Rona Mace* · Casey Affleck *Bobby Calzone* · William Fichtner *Phil Dearly* · Will Ferrell *Cubby* ■ *Dir* Nick Gomez · *Scr* Peter Steinfeld

The Drowning Pool ★★★ 12
Mystery thriller   1975 · US · Colour · 103min

Paul Newman's second outing (after 1966's *Harper*) as novelist Ross MacDonald's private detective Lew Harper sees him plunging into a swamp of Deep South greed and murder when he's called to oil baroness Joanne Woodward's bayou home to investigate a blackmail plot. The title refers to a hydrotherapy bath in an abandoned mental home, which is typical of the oddball eccentricity of the film and its characters. It's a pity that Stuart Rosenberg's direction is so straightforward because the impenetrable plot needs a more bizarre approach. TH

Paul Newman *Lew Harper* · Joanne Woodward *Iris Devereaux* · Tony Franciosa [Anthony Franciosa] *Chief Broussard* · Murray Hamilton *JJ Kilbourne* · Gail Strickland *Mavis Kilbourne* · Melanie Griffith *Schuyler Devereaux* · Linda Haynes *Gretchen* · Richard Jaeckel *Lieutenant Franks* ■ *Dir* Stuart Rosenberg · *Scr* Tracy Keenan Wynn, Lorenzo Semple Jr, Walter Hill, from the novel by Ross MacDonald

Drugstore Cowboy ★★★★ 18
Drama   1989 · US · Colour · 97min

This provocative drama set in early 1970s Oregon looks at the sordid life of four junkies who rob pharmacies to support their habits. Director Gus Van Sant brings an extraordinary visual style to this credible, non-judgemental portrayal of addiction, which is based on an unpublished semi-autobiographical novel by prisoner James Fogle. Matt Dillon gives a compelling performance and *The Naked Lunch* author William S Burroughs appears in a cameo as a priest turned dope fiend. There's a good oldies soundtrack, too. AJ Violence, swearing, drug abuse. **DVD**

Matt Dillon *Bob Hughes* · Kelly Lynch *Dianne Hughes* · James Remar *Gentry* · James LeGros *Rick* · Heather Graham *Nadine* · Beah Richards *Drug counsellor* · Grace Zabriskie *Bob's mother* · Max Perlich *David* · William S Burroughs *Tom the Priest* · Eric Hull *Druggist* ■ *Dir* Gus Van Sant · *Scr* Gus Van Sant, Daniel Yost, from a novel by James Fogle

Druids ★ 12
Period epic   2001 · Fr/Can/Bel · Colour · 109min

It is 60 BC, ancient France, a time of alarming fright wigs and even dodgier accents. Well, at least that's the case in this hilariously bad historical epic, which finds proud Gallic tribal leader Christopher Lambert trying to unite his squabbling countrymen against the devious Julius Caesar (a spectacularly miscast Klaus Maria Brandauer). Director Jacques Dorfmann stages the battle scenes with an astounding lack of inspiration. JF

Christophe Lambert [Christopher Lambert] *Vercingétorix* · Klaus Maria Brandauer *Caesar* · Max von Sydow *Guttuart* · Inés Sastre *Epona* · Bernard-Pierre Donnadieu *Dumnorix* ■ *Dir* Jacques Dorfmann · *Scr* Rospo Pallenberg, Norman Spinrad, Jacques Dorfmann, from a story by Anne de Leuselec, Jacques Dorfmann

The Drum ★★★★ U
Period adventure   1938 · UK · Colour · 89min

AEW Mason, author of *The Four Feathers*, wrote this story especially for producer Alexander Korda as a vehicle for talented 14-year-old star Sabu. The youngster delivers a truly beguiling performance as Prince Azim, forced from his inheritance by his uncle, the swinish villain Raymond Massey. It's ravishingly photographed in three-strip Technicolor, this is a stirring reminder of what British cinema was once about: telling a tale of the courageous struggle between right and wrong with an unerring sense of patriotism. TS

Sabu *Prince Azim* · Raymond Massey *Prince Ghul* · Valerie Hobson *Mrs Carruthers* · Roger Livesey *Captain Carruthers* · Desmond Tester *Bill Holder* · Martin Walker *Herrick* · David Tree *Lieutenant Escott* · Francis L Sullivan *Governor* ■ *Dir* Zoltan Korda · *Scr* Arthur Wimperis, Patric Kirwan, Hugh Gray, Lajos Biró (adaptation), from the novel by AEW Mason · *Cinematographers* Georges Perinal, Robert Krasker, Osmond Borrodaile, Geoffrey Unsworth

Drum ★ 18
Period drama   1976 · US · Colour · 99min

While *Mandingo* walked the tightrope between exploitation and gothic melodrama, this wretched sequel has no pretensions at all. It's a real cheapo, with Warren Oates as a slave breeder and Yaphet Kotto as one of his purchases. Things get seriously bogged down in a plot about interbreeding, before Kotto turns into Spartacus and instigates a very bloody slave revolt. AT

Warren Oates *Hammond Maxwell* · Ken Norton *Drum* · Isela Vega *Marianna* · Pam Grier *Regine* · Yaphet Kotto *Blaise* · John Colicos *DeMarigny* · Fiona Lewis *Augusta Chauvet* ■ *Dir* Steve Carver · *Scr* Norman Wexler, from the novel by Kyle Onstott

Drum Beat ★★★ U
Western   1954 · US · Colour · 107min

Alan Ladd brings an end to the Indian Wars in this fact-based western, which gave Charles Bronson his first starring role. Writer/director Delmer Daves toiled away in the public record office in order to be as impartial as possible in his account of the 1869 Modoc uprising. The script has an intelligence that matches his earlier *Broken Arrow*, one of the first Hollywood features to see the Wild West from the native American perspective. J Peverell Marley's views of the Oregon/California landscape are stunning. DP

Alan Ladd *Johnny MacKay* • Charles Bronson *Captain Jack* • Audrey Dalton *Nancy Meek* • Marisa Pavan *Toby* • Robert Keith (1) *Bill Satterwhite* • Rodolfo Acosta *Scarface Charlie* • Warner Anderson *General Canby* • Elisha Cook Jr *Crackel* ■ Dir/Scr Delmer Daves

Drumline ★★ PG
Musical drama　　　2002 · US · Colour · 113min

The clichés are reeled out with depressingly rhythmic precision in this lame remix of *Fame* and *Bring It On*. Nick Cannon is the rebellious but intuitively brilliant drummer who shakes up a starchy college marching band that is battling to unseat the flashy reigning champions. The best bits are the admittedly brilliantly choreographed musical set pieces, but the non-musical antics will leave most just brassed off. JF
DVD

Nick Cannon *Devon Miles* • Zoë Saldana *Laila* • Orlando Jones *Dr Lee* • Leonard Roberts *Sean Taylor* • G Q *Jayson* • Jason Weaver *Ernest* • Earl C Poitier *Charles* • Candace Carey *Diedre* ■ Dir Charles Stone III • Scr Tina Gordon Chism, Shawn Schepps, from a story by Shawn Schepps

Drums across the River ★★ PG
Western　　　1954 · US · Colour · 74min

This very average Audie Murphy western is somewhat redeemed by nice 1950s Technicolor and a very short running time. The plot – about how devout whites stole gold from the native Americans – deserves a better treatment, but the baby-faced Murphy, a former war hero, makes a sympathetic leading man. Among the support, Hugh O'Brian shows signs of star quality. TS

Audie Murphy *Gary Brannon* • Lisa Gaye *Jennie Marlowe* • Lyle Bettger *Frank Walker* • Walter Brennan *Sam Brannon* • Mara Corday *Sue* • Hugh O'Brian *Morgan* • Jay Silverheels *Taos* • Regis Toomey *Sheriff Beal* ■ Dir Nathan Juran • Scr John K Butler, Lawrence Roman, from a story by John K Butler

Drums along the Mohawk ★★★★ PG
Western adventure　1939 · US · Colour · 99min

One of the most beautiful and distinguished achievements of early colour, this fine movie tends to be overlooked among the other highlights of 1939, Hollywood's *annus mirabilis*. This is effectively a pre-western, dealing with Indian raids against the early settlers during the American War of Independence. It contains a rather disturbing anti-British bias, not for the first time from ace director John Ford. Taken as a romantic action adventure, though, it rattles along. Claudette Colbert is a little too well groomed for the frontier, but Henry Fonda seems perfectly at home. TS *DVD*

Claudette Colbert *Lana "Magdelana" Martin* • Henry Fonda *Gilbert Martin* • Edna May Oliver *Mrs Sarah McKlennar* • Eddie Collins *Christian Reall* • John Carradine *Caldwell* • Dorris Bowdon *Mary Reall* • Jessie Ralph *Mrs Weaver* ■ Dir John Ford • Scr Lamar Trotti, Sonya Levien, from a novel by Walter D Edmonds • Cinematographers Bert Glennon, Ray Rennahan • Art Directors Richard Day, Mark-Lee Kirk

Drunken Angel ★★★★ PG
Crime drama　　　1948 · Jpn · BW · 93min

This is notable as the first major screen appearance of Toshiro Mifune, whom director Akira Kurosawa would cast in virtually every one of his subsequent films. He plays a volatile gangster who has a bullet removed by a drunken doctor. When the doctor, played by another Kurosawa favourite, Takashi Shimura, also discovers that Mifune is suffering from tuberculosis, he is inexorably drawn to his patient's underworld of crime and violence. Part

realist drama, part gangster movie, this is a gripping story that also casts an observant eye over the evolving postwar Japanese society. AT Japanese +subtitles. *DVD*

Toshiro Mifune *Matsunaga* • Takashi Shimura *Dr Sanada* • Reisaburo Yamamoto *Okada* • Michiyo Kogure *Nanse* • Chieko Nakakita *Miyo* • Noriko Sengoku *Gin* ■ Dir Akira Kurosawa • Scr Keinosuke Uegusa, Akira Kurosawa

Drunken Master ★★★★ 15
Martial arts action comedy
1978 · HK · Colour · 106min

This was the film that saw Jackie Chan crowned as the clown prince of kung fu. As the legendary folk hero, Wong Fei-Hung, who is forced to suffer the humiliations of uncle Yuen Hsiao Tian's pitiless training programme, Chan reveals why he's so often acclaimed as Hong Kong's answer to Buster Keaton. But not everything is gloriously knockabout, with the encounter with assassin Huang Cheng Li being particularly brutal. Two sequels were released in 1994. DP Cantonese dubbed. *DVD*

Jackie Chan *Wong Fei-Hung* • Yuen Hsiao Tian [Simon Yuen] *Sam Seed* • Huang Cheng Li [Hwang Jang Lee] *Thunderfoot* • Michelle Yeoh ■ Dir Yuen Woo-Ping • Scr Hsiao Lung, Ng See Yuen

Dry Rot ★★ U
Comedy　　　1956 · UK · BW · 85min

Maurice Elvey was one of the longest-serving of all British directors, claiming to have shot over 300 films. This was his penultimate picture and, in keeping with many of the comedies that occupied his twilight years, it's not very good. This tale of crooked bookies plods along more slowly than a doped horse. Expert *farceurs* Ronald Shiner, Brian Rix and Sid James give polished performances. DP

Ronald Shiner *Alf Tubbs* • Brian Rix *Fred Phipps* • Peggy Mount *Sgt Fire* • Lee Patterson *Danby* • Sidney James *Flash Harry* • Christian Duvaleix *Polignac* • Joan Sims *Beth* • Heather Sears *Susan* ■ Dir Maurice Elvey • Scr John Chapman, from his play

A Dry White Season ★★★ 15
Drama　　　1989 · US · Colour · 102min

This worthy drama sees Marlon Brando deliver one of his most passionate performances in a long time, even if it is in a supporting role; Brando is the liberal lawyer who helps him challenge the establishment. Aided by a star-studded support cast, director Euzhan Palcy succeeds in producing a compelling and disturbing portrait of the brutality in pre-Mandela South Africa. JF Violence, swearing.

Donald Sutherland *Ben du Toit* • Janet Suzman *Susan du Toit* • Zakes Mokae *Stanley Makhaya* • Jürgen Prochnow *Captain Stolz* • Susan Sarandon *Melanie Bruwer* • Marlon Brando *Ian McKenzie* • Winston Ntshona *Gordon Ngubene* • Thoko Ntshinga *Emily* ■ Dir Euzhan Palcy • Scr Euzhan Palcy, Colin Welland, from the novel by André Brink

Dual Alibi ★★★
Crime drama　　　1946 · UK · BW · 81min

Moodily photographed in murky monochrome by James Wilson, this low-budget programme filler manages to capture the sinister atmosphere of a French circus as four performers succumb to greed and retribution. In a rare leading role, Herbert Lom excels as the trapeze-artist twins who win a million francs on the lottery, only to have their ticket switched by the conniving Terence de Marney and his girlfriend (played by wartime Queen of the Striptease Phyllis Dixey in her only major film role). The split-screen effects are occasionally a little threadbare, but director Alfred Travers milks the lookalike angle to good effect, especially when the murderous siblings begin squabbling over their retrieved wealth and the amorous Dixey. DP

Herbert Lom *Jules de Lisle/Georges de Lisle* • Terence de Marney *Mike Bergen* • Phyllis Dixey *Penny* • Ronald Frankau *Vincent Barney* • Abraham Sofaer *French Judge* • Harold Berens *Ali* ■ Dir Alfred Travers • Scr Vivienne Ades, Stephen Clarkson, Alfred Travers, from a story by Renault Capes • Cinematographer James Wilson

DuBarry Was a Lady ★★★
Musical comedy　　1943 · US · Colour · 96min

Cole Porter's risqué musical play was a hit on Broadway in 1939, but arrived on the screen four years later as a bowdlerised Red Skelton/Lucille Ball vehicle. Lucy, MGM's resident chirpy redhead, never looked lovelier than here, and newcomer Gene Kelly learned from this film never to look down at his feet again while dancing. It's an amiable romp, officially credited to director Roy Del Ruth, though the choreography is by Charles Walters, who began a distinguished career with this movie. TS

Lucille Ball *May Daly/Madame DuBarry* • Red Skelton *Louis Blore/King Louis* • Gene Kelly *Alec Howe/Black Arrow* • Douglass Dumbrille *Willie/Duc De Rigor* • Rags Ragland *Charlie/Dauphin* • Donald Meek *Mr Jones/Duc De Choiseul* • George Givot *Cheezy/De Roqueford* • Zero Mostel *Rami the Swami/Cagliostro* ■ Dir Roy Del Ruth • Scr Irving Brecher, Nancy Hamilton, Wilkie Mahoney, Albert Mannheimer, Jack McGowan, Charles Sherman, Mary C McCall Jr, from a play by BG De Sylva, Herbert Fields • Music Cole Porter

Dublin Nightmare ★★ PG
Murder mystery　　1958 · UK · BW · 60min

A Canadian photographer in Dublin discovers that his "dead" wartime friend is really an IRA leader. Sounds familiar? It should: this is a totally shameless B-movie rip-off of *The Third Man*, with Dublin substituted for Vienna and the IRA taking the place of penicillin. William Sylvester and Marla Landi are perfectly adequate stand-ins for Joseph Cotten and Alida Valli. TS *DVD*

William Sylvester *John Kevin* • Marla Landi *Anna* • Richard Leech *Steven Lawlor* • William Sherwood *Edward Dillon* • Harry Hutchinson *"Vulture"* ■ Dir John Pomeroy • Scr John Tully

The Duchess ★★★ 12
Historical drama
2008 · UK/Fr/It/US · Colour · 105min

Much has been made of the parallels between the lives of Georgiana, Duchess of Devonshire (1757-1806) and her descendant Lady Diana, Princess of Wales. Both were married young into high society, and required to please a devoted public and a cheating husband. Thankfully there isn't too much nudge-nudge, wink-wink in this adaptation of Amanda Foreman's biography, and Keira Knightley – as well as having the air of an English rose – brings dignity to Georgiana's suffering. Still, it's disappointing that Saul Dibb (who directed *Bullet Boy*) only skims the surface of her political life, dwelling instead on the intrigues that compromised her marriage. SP *DVD* 🄱

Keira Knightley *Georgiana, Duchess of Devonshire* • Ralph Fiennes *Duke of Devonshire* • Hayley Atwell *Bess* • Charlotte Rampling *Lady Spencer* • Dominic Cooper *Charles Grey* • Simon McBurney *Charles James Fox* • Aidan McArdle *Richard Brinsley Sheridan* • Richard McCabe *Sir James Hare* ■ Dir Saul Dibb • Scr Jeffrey Hatcher, Anders Thomas Jensen, from the biography *Georgiana, Duchess of Devonshire* by Amanda Foreman

The Duchess and the Dirtwater Fox ★★ PG
Comedy western　　1976 · US · Colour · 99min

George Segal and Goldie Hawn co-star as a gambler and a dance hall girl thrown together in adversity who pull off a few judicious scams. They fight, they make up, they swindle each other, he tells an awful lot of old Jewish jokes and we laugh – but not for long. Segal often seems to think that all he has to do is stand around and wink at the camera a few times. Hawn remains an overrated actress for some, and this movie

will do nothing to change their opinion. SH *DVD*

George Segal *Charlie Malloy* • Goldie Hawn *Amanda Quaid* • Conrad Janis *Gladstone* • Thayer David *Widdicombe* • Jennifer Lee (1) *Trollop* • Roy Jenson *Bloodworth* • Pat Ast *Dance hall girl* • Sid Gould *Rabbi* ■ Dir Melvin Frank • Scr Barry Sandler, Jack Rose, Melvin Frank, from a story by Barry Sandler

Duchess of Idaho ★★★ U
Musical romantic comedy
1950 · US · Colour · 98min

This minor MGM musical has Esther Williams's Sun Valley carnival star agreeing to vamp playboy John Lund so that he will better appreciate his best friend, Paula Raymond. But her would-be bandleader beau Van Johnson isn't in on the secret. Williams's aqua-ballets are choreographed here with efficiency, if not Berkleyesque imagination by Jack Donohue. Guest appearances by Eleanor Powell and the shamefully underused Lena Horne add some extra pizzazz to this undemanding but polished entertainment DP

Esther Williams *Christine Riverton Duncan* • Van Johnson *Dick Layn* • John Lund *Douglas J Morrisen Jr* • Paula Raymond *Ellen Hallet* • Clinton Sundberg *Matson* • Connie Haines *Peggy Elliott* • Mel Tormé *Cyril* • Amanda Blake *Linda Kinston* • Lena Horne • Eleanor Powell ■ Dir Robert Z Leonard • Scr Jerry Davis, Dorothy Cooper

Duck Dodgers in the 24½ Century ★★★★★
Animated science-fiction comedy
1953 · US · Colour · 7min

One of Chuck Jones's best-remembered cartoons, this sci-fi spoof has Daffy Duck, in the guise of space explorer Duck Dodgers, sent to Planet X in search of Illudium Phosdex, the shaving cream atom. With "eager young space cadet" Porky Pig, Dodgers does battle for the planet with an effeminate alien (christened Marvin Martian in 1979's *The Bugs Bunny/Road Runner Movie*). This was one of a brilliant series of shorts in which Jones placed Daffy's inflated ego in various postmodernist, generic surroundings, yet it has become the most famous, probably thanks to the timelessness of its targets, the purity of its humour and the witty designs of layout artist Maurice Noble. CLP

Mel Blanc *Daffy Duck/Porky Pig/Marvin Martian* ■ Dir Chuck Jones • Scr Michael Maltese

Duck Season ★★★ 15
Comedy　　　2004 · Mex · BW · 83min

Rarely has boredom been so engagingly presented on screen as in this Mexican comedy. Adolescent friends Diego Cataño and Daniel Miranda are home alone and set for a perfect Sunday until impoverished pizza delivery man Enrique Arreola arrives – 11 seconds late so they refuse to pay him – and won't leave the high-rise apartment without his money. Director Fernando Eimbcke never forces the issues and subtly laces the standoff with moments of wry wit and touching humanity. DP Spanish +subtitles. Swearing, some drug abuse. *DVD*

Enrique Arreola *Ulises* • Diego Cataño *Moko* • Daniel Miranda *Flama* • Danny Perea *Rita* ■ Dir Fernando Eimbcke • Scr Fernando Eimbcke, Paula Markovitch, Felipe Cazals

Duck Soup ★★★★★ U
Comedy　　　1933 · US · BW · 65min

The Marx Brothers reached peaks of anarchic brilliance in this comedy masterpiece, which burst upon audiences four years after their primitive feature debut in *The Cocoanuts*. Groucho, Chico, Harpo and the uncharismatic Zeppo are all entangled in a runaway satire that finds Groucho as a Ruritanian leader going to war because he's paid a month's advance rent on the battlefield. What helps make this the funniest Marx Brothers' film – besides the absence of the romantic interludes which dogged later outings – are the exchanges between Groucho and Margaret Dumont, plus a stunningly surreal mirror sequence. Classic quips, classy delivery. TH *DVD*

Groucho Marx *Rufus T Firefly* • Harpo Marx *Pinky* • Chico Marx *Chicolini* • Zeppo Marx *Bob Roland* • Margaret Dumont *Mrs Gloria Teasdale* • Raquel Torres *Vera Marcal* • Louis Calhern *Ambassador Trentino of Sylvania* • Edmund Breese *Zander* • Leonid Kinskey *Agitator* • Charles B Middleton [Charles Middleton] *Prosecutor* ■ *Dir* Leo McCarey • *Scr* Burt Kalmar, Harry Ruby, Arthur Sheekman, Nat Perrin

Duck Tales: the Movie – Treasure of the Lost Lamp
★★★ U

Animated adventure 1990 · US · Colour · 70min

Scrooge McDuck and the ever-troublesome Huey, Dewey and Louie go in search of a genie's lamp before it falls into the evil clutches of Merlock in this Disney animated adventure with an *Indiana Jones* twist. Alan Young (who once chatted to Mr Ed, the talking horse) voices Uncle Scrooge, while Christopher Lloyd brings some menace to the villain. It all feels a touch rough-and-ready, but younger children will lap it up. DP *DVD*

Alan Young *Scrooge McDuck* • Terence McGovern [Terry McGovern] *Launchpad McQuack* • Russi Taylor *Huey/Dewey/Louie/ Webby* • Richard Libertini *Dijon* • Christopher Lloyd *Merlock* • June Foray *Mrs Featherby* • Chuck McCann *Duckworth* ■ *Dir* Bob Hathcock • *Scr* Alan Burnett

Dude, Where's My Car? ★ 15
Comedy 2000 · US · Colour · 79min

The daft title is the most amusing thing about this embarrassing, laugh-free exercise in teen idiocy. Seann William Scott and Ashton Kutcher are the dumb, pot-smoking chums, who awaken from a night of hedonism to discover Kutcher's car is missing and re-trace their movements. JC Swearing. *DVD*

Ashton Kutcher *Jesse* • Seann William Scott *Chester* • Kristy Swanson *Christie Boner* • Jennifer Garner *Wanda* • Marla Sokoloff *Wilma* • David Herman *Nelson* ■ *Dir* Danny Leiner • *Scr* Philip Stark

Dudes ★★★ 15
Comedy 1987 · US · Colour · 86min

Penelope Spheeris made her name chronicling the punk scene, but is now better known for mainstream comedies such as *Wayne's World*. Here, Jon Cryer and Daniel Roebuck play New York punks hunting the renegade biker gang, led by Lee Ving, who murdered their buddy Flea (later to find fame as a member of the Red Hot Chili Peppers). The western elements are clumsily crafted on to the tale, but it's still an enjoyably offbeat ride. JF

Jon Cryer *Grant* • Daniel Roebuck *Biscuit* • Flea *Milo* • Lee Ving *Missoula* • Billy Ray Sharkey *Blix* • Glenn Withrow *Wes* • Michael Melvin *Logan* • Axxel G Reese *Red* ■ *Dir* Penelope Spheeris • *Scr* Randall Johnson

Dudley Do-Right ★★ PG
Comedy 1999 · US · Colour · 73min

Brendan Fraser, who scored a surprise hit in 1997 with *George of the Jungle*, brings another of Jay Ward's cartoon favourites to life, though with considerably less success. Director Hugh Wilson seems to be aiming for an affectionate live-action tribute to the likeably dumb Mountie of the title (Fraser) as he does battle with his nemesis, Snidely Whiplash (Alfred Molina). The actors enthusiastically enter into the spirit of tomfoolery, but there's far too much reliance on slapdash slapstick. JF *DVD*

Brendan Fraser *Dudley Do-Right* • Sarah Jessica Parker *Nell Fenwick* • Alfred Molina *Snidely Whiplash* • Alex Rocco *The Chief* • Eric Idle *The Prospector* • Robert Prosky *Inspector Fenwick* ■ *Dir* Hugh Wilson • *Scr* Hugh Wilson, from characters by Jay Ward

Due Date ★★★ 15
Comedy 2010 · US · Colour · 91min

In this combination of road movie and odd-couple comedy, uptight architect Peter Highman (Robert Downey Jr) is desperate to get back to LA for the birth of his first child. An encounter with screwy Ethan Tremblay (Zach Galifianakis) at the airport leads to Peter being put on the no-fly list and, as a last resort, he has to drive across America with Ethan. Following a template already established by John Hughes's much-loved *Planes, Trains and Automobiles*, the film's humour comes from scornful fusspot Downey Jr's growing aggravation at his unpredictably imbecilic travelling companion and the sundry slapstick scrapes they get into en route. Although Galifianakis is essentially reprising his *Hangover* role as the loose-cannon man-child in a burly beardy bloke's body, Downey Jr simmers effectively and there are some surprisingly poignant moments amid the high jinks. TJ Swearing, drug abuse, sexual references. *DVD BD*

Robert Downey Jr *Peter Highman* • Zach Galifianakis *Ethan Tremblay* • Michelle Monaghan *Sarah Highman* • Jamie Foxx *Darryl* • Juliette Lewis *Heidi* • Danny McBride (2) *Lonnie* ■ *Dir* Todd Phillips • *Scr* Alan R Cohen, Alan Freedland, Adam Sztykiel, Todd Phillips, from a story by Cohen, Freedland

Duel ★★★★★ PG
Thriller 1971 · US · Colour · 85min

Made for TV by a 20-something Steven Spielberg, this thriller proved such a hit that it enjoyed a theatrical release in Europe and launched the young director's career in movies. The pitch is simplicity itself: businessman Dennis Weaver in his red Plymouth Valiant is terrorised by an anonymously driven truck on a stretch of Californian desert highway. There's barely any dialogue – it's all palm-moistening, tyre-squealing action – but once you've seen it, you'll never forget it. It works as a parable about urban paranoia or as a roller coaster thriller that never lets up. The truck itself prefigures Spielberg's shark in *Jaws* as a marauding screen monster with a personality of its own. AC *DVD BD*

Dennis Weaver *David Mann* • Jacqueline Scott *Mrs Mann* • Eddie F restone *Cafe owner* • Lou Frizzell *Bus driver* • Gene Dynarski *Man in cafe* • Lucille Benson *Lady at Snakarama* ■ *Dir* Steven Spielberg • *Scr* Richard Matheson, from his story

Duel at Diablo ★★★ 15
Western 1966 · US · Colour · 103min

Co-producer/director Ralph Nelson's well-intentioned attempt to liberalise the western explores racist themes using an international cast. Unfortunately, it doesn't quite succeed, partly because the eclectic casting gets in the way of the authenticity. There is plenty of action, however, and a considerable amount of violence, as a cavalry troop escorting a wagon train of explosives out west is beset by Indians and riven by internal racial conflict. TS *DVD*

James Garner *Jess Remsberg* • Sidney Poitier *Toller* • Bill Travers *Lieutenant McAllister, "Scotty"* • Bibi Andersson *Ellen Grange* • Dennis Weaver *Willard Grange* • William Redfield *Sergeant Ferguson* • John Hoyt *Chata* ■ *Dir* Ralph Nelson • *Scr* Marvin H Albert, Michael M Grilikhes, from the novel *Apache Rising* by Marvin H Albert

The Duel at Silver Creek ★★ U
Western 1952 · US · Colour · 73min

This minor and utterly unremarkable Audie Murphy western somewhat surprisingly bears the name of ace *Dirty Harry* director Don Siegel. Unfortunately, it's absolutely devoid of the personal style Siegel brought to such low-budget films as *Invasion of the Body Snatchers* and *Riot in Cell Block 11*. But Murphy and Siegel fans won't want to miss it, and the supporting cast, including a pre-stardom Lee Marvin, also makes it watchable. TS *DVD*

Audie Murphy *Silver Kid* • Faith Domergue *Opal Lacey* • Stephen McNally *Marshal Lightning Tyrone* • Susan Cabot *Dusty Fargo* • Gerald Mohr *Rod Lacey* • Eugene Iglesias *Johnny Sombrero* • Lee Marvin *Tinhorn Burgess* • Walter Sande *Pete Fargo* ■ *Dir* Don Siegel • *Scr* Gerald Adams [Gerald Drayson Adams], Joseph Hoffman, from a story by Gerald Adams [Gerald Drayson Adams]

Duel in the Jungle ★★★ PG
Adventure 1954 · UK · Colour · 97min

This entertaining, if a little simplistic, action adventure is a real tribute to its producer, Marcel Hellman. The Technicolor photography, shot on location in Rhodesia by Erwin Hillier, is thrilling, and the film reunites the co-stars of *State Fair* (1945), Dana Andrews and Jeanne Crain, in a tale about the death of a diamond dealer. David Farrar steals the acting thunder as the villain, while Hollywood veteran director George Marshall keeps the tension taut. TS

Dana Andrews *Scott Walters* • Jeanne Crain *Marian Taylor* • David Farrar *Perry Henderson/ Arthur Henderson* • Patrick Barr *Superintendent Roberts* • George Coulouris *Captain Malburn* • Charles Goldner *Martell* • Wilfrid Hyde White *Pitt* ■ *Dir* George Marshall • *Scr* Sam Marx, TJ Morrison, from a story by SK Kennedy

Duel in the Sun ★★★★ PG
Western melodrama 1946 · US · Colour · 124min

Producer David O Selznick intended this costly production to be the equal of his *Gone with the Wind*. What he ended up with was a lurid western that, in its day, managed to offend church leaders and censorship boards alike. (Unsurprisingly, it became a massive box office hit.) Jennifer Jones stars as mixed-race Pearl Chavez and Gregory Peck plays lewd Lewt McCanles – roles that must surely have embarrassed them in hindsight. The infamous finale is simultaneously ludicrous and stunning, while Dimitri Tiomkin's score is splendid, and the use of Technicolor is especially striking. TS *DVD*

Jennifer Jones *Pearl Chavez* • Joseph Cotten *Jesse McCanles* • Gregory Peck *Lewt McCanles* • Lionel Barrymore *Senator McCanles* • Herbert Marshall *Scott Chavez* • Lillian Gish *Laura Belle McCanles* • Walter Huston *Jubal Crabbe, the sinkiller* • Charles Bickford *Sam Pierce* • Butterfly McQueen *Vashti* • Otto Kruger *Mr Langford* • Orson Welles *Narrator* ■ *Dir* King Vidor • *Scr* David O Selznick, Oliver HP Garrett, from the novel by Niven Busch

Duel of the Titans ★★★ U
Period adventure 1961 · It · Colour · 105min

Two of the finest exponents of the spaghetti western join forces on this superior sword-and-sandal offering. Sergio Corbucci called the shots, while Sergio Leone was among the septet of screenwriters. There's also an impressive double act in front of the camera, with ex-Mr Universe Steve Reeves teaming with one-time Tarzan Gordon Scott as the founders of Rome, Romulus and Remus. Even the supporting cast is better than average, with Virna Lisi providing the glamour and Massimo Girotti the gravitas. DP Italian dubbed.

Steve Reeves *Romulus* • Gordon Scott *Remus* • Virna Lisi *Julia* • Massimo Girotti *Tazio* • Jacques Sernas *Curzio* ■ *Dir* Sergio Corbucci • *Scr* Sergio Corbucci, Sergio Leone, Luciano Martino, Sergio Prosperi, Franco Rossetti, Ennio De Concini, Duccio Tessari

Duelist ★★ 12
Martial arts mystery thriller 2005 · S Kor · Colour · 103min

South Korean director Lee Myung-se's take on the martial arts epic is certainly a visual feast – unfortunately, there are simply too many tastes and flavours competing against each other. Set in ancient Korea, the story revolves around a beautiful young policewoman's search for a gang of coin counterfeiters, seemingly linked to senior figures in the government. Lee stages some stunning sword fights and action pieces, but the tone is uneven: one minute, it's all poetic slow-motion choreography; the next, it veers into *Benny Hill* territory. JF Korean +subtitles. Some violence. *DVD*

Ha Ji-won *Namsoon* • Kang Dong-won *Sad Eyes* • Ahn Sung-kee *Detective Ahn* • Song Young-chang *Minister of Defence* ■ *Dir* Lee Myung-se • *Scr* Lee Myung-se, Lee Hae-jyung, from the comic book *Damo* by Bang Hak-ki

The Duellists ★★★★ PG
Period drama 1977 · UK · Colour · 96min

Set against the heavyweight hostilities of the Napoleonic Wars, the small-time conflict of hussars Harvey Keitel and Keith Carradine – challenging each other over the years to a series of duels – might seem ludicrously beside the point. But Keitel's manic man of honour is a character whose chilling fixation says something about the wider conflict and humankind's need to struggle. This was director Ridley Scott's first feature after graduating from commercials, and it comes across as a coldly brilliant portrait of obsession. TH *DVD*

Keith Carradine *Armand d'Hubert* • Harvey Keitel *Gabriel Feraud* • Albert Finney *Fouché* • Edward Fox *Colonel* • Cristina Raines *Adèle* • Robert Stephens *General Treillard* • Tom Conti *Dr Jacquin* • Diana Quick *Laura* ■ *Dir* Ridley Scott • *Scr* Gerald Vaughan-Hughes, from the novella *The Duel* by Joseph Conrad

Duet for One ★★★★ 15
Drama 1986 · UK · Colour · 102min

Julie Andrews gives a moving, unsentimental performance as a concert violinist whose life is shattered, in slow motion, by the onset of multiple sclerosis. Saccharine music aside, director Andrei Konchalovsky ensures the story, which echoes the real-life experience of cellist Jacqueline du Pré, has real conviction, with Alan Bates movingly surly as Julie's composer husband and Max von Sydow disagreeably callous as the psychotherapist. TH

Julie Andrews *Stephanie Anderson* • Alan Bates *David Cornwallis* • Max von Sydow *Dr Louis Feldman* • Rupert Everett *Constantine Kassanis* • Margaret Courtenay *Sonia Randvich* • Cathryn Harrison *Penny Smallwood* ■ *Dir* Andrei Konchalovsky • *Scr* Tom Kempinski, Jeremy Lipp, Andrei Konchalovsky, from the play by Tom Kempinski

Duets ★★★ 15
Comedy drama 2000 · US · Colour · 107min

Directed by Bruce Paltrow and starring his daughter Gwyneth, this follows six would-be singers as they travel across America to take part in a big-money karaoke competition. The movie takes its time fleshing out its characters, who range from a starstruck waitress to an escaped con, and there are some terrific performances, notably from Paul Giamatti as a burned-out rep and singer Huey Lewis as a veteran karaoke hustler. Ironically, the most insipid performance comes from Miss Paltrow, though she does display a decent, non-dubbed singing voice. Otherwise, mature and entertaining character-driven drama. DA *DVD*

Gwyneth Paltrow *Liv* • Maria Bello *Suzi Loomis* • Scott Speedman *Billy Hannon* • André Braugher *Reggie Kane* • Paul Giamatti *Todd Woods* • Huey Lewis *Ricky Dean* • Angie Dickinson *Blair* ■ *Dir* Bruce Paltrow • *Scr* John Byrum

The Duff ★★★ 12
Comedy 2015 · US · Colour · 96min

The latest entry in the *Pygmalion* with Clearasil genre may not bring anything new to the table, but it's still fun to hang out with for a while. It follows Mae Whitman, initially branded a "DUFF" (the Designated Ugly Fat Friend). But she is transformed into a prom princess under the tutelage of her jock best friend (a mostly likeable Robbie Amell). A film supposedly about "being yourself" still insists that, for teenage girls, the most important achievement in school is peer approval. But this lack of originality is compensated for by snappy dialogue, energetic direction and great support from, among others, *The West Wing*'s Allison Janney as Bianca's ditzy mom. AS Some sexual references, brief swearing. *DVD BD*

Mae Whitman *Bianca* • Robbie Amell *Wesley* • Bella Thorne *Madison* • Bianca A Santos [Bianca Santos] *Casey* ■ *Dir* Ari Sandel • *Scr* Josh A Cagan, from Kody Keplinger's novel

D

D

Duffy ★★
Crime caper 1968 · UK · Colour · 101min

Portraitist Donald Cammell broke into films as the co-author of this slipshod heist caper that would have you believe its anarchic chaos is really ultra-chic comedy. Compounding the script's lack of focus is director Robert Parrish's preoccupation with flashy visuals and the Mediterranean locations, which leaves his cast floundering. James Coburn is bemused as the hippy drifter hired by half-brothers James Fox and John Alderton to rob their mean-spirited millionaire father, James Mason. DP
James Coburn *Duffy* · James Mason *Calvert* · James Fox *Stefane* · Susannah York *Segolene* · John Alderton *Anthony* · Barry Shawzin *Bakirgian* · Carl Duering *Bonivet* ■ *Dir* Robert Parrish · *Scr* Donald Cammell, Harry Joe Brown Jr, from a story by Donald Cammell, Harry Joe Brown Jr, Pierre De La Salle

Duffy's Tavern ★ U
Musical comedy 1945 · US · BW · 97min

This revue-style aberration from a distinguished studio (Paramount) hangs dozens of embarrassed-looking contract stars performing second-rate songs and sketches on to a paper-thin excuse for a plot. They are supposedly putting on a benefit show for innkeeper Ed Gardner (whose popular radio show of the same title gave rise to the idea). RK
Bing Crosby · Betty Hutton · Paulette Goddard · Alan Ladd · Dorothy Lamour · Veronica Lake · Ed Gardner *Archie/Ed Gardner* ■ *Dir* Hal Walker · *Scr* Melvin Frank, Norman Panama, Abram S Burrows [Abe S Burrows], Barney Dean, George White, Eddie Davis, Matt Brooks, from the radio series by Ed Gardner

The Duke ★★ U
Adventure comedy drama
1999 · UK/Can · Colour · 84min

This lively shaggy dog story should keep young children entertained with its canine lead and host of pantomimic characters. James Doohan plays a haughty English butler, whose niece (Courtnee Draper) becomes legal guardian to a distinguished hound named Hubert when he inherits aristocrat John Neville's estate. However, Neville's conniving nephew (Oliver Muirhead) is determined to use fair means or foul to claim the title for himself. DP
DVD
John Neville *The Duke* · James Doohan *Clive Chives* · Oliver Muirhead *Cecil Cavendish* · Judy Geeson *Lady Fautblossom* · Courtnee Draper *Charlotte Chives* · Carolyn Sadowska *The Queen* ■ *Dir* Philip Spink · *Scr* Craig Detweiler, Anne Vince, Robert Vince, from a story by Craig Detweiler

The Duke of Burgundy ★★★★★ 18
Drama 2014 · UK · Colour · 100min

Inspired by the soft-core erotic eurotrash films of Jess Franco and others, but with an injection of hard-core art house weirdness, director Peter Strickland's *The Duke of Burgundy* is a specialist item that won't appeal to those with conservative tastes. However, for adventurous souls willing to board Strickland's freaky funhouse ride, this will be pure bliss: a funny, melancholy and peculiarly haunting exploration of an S&M relationship between two women. The latter half's descent into David Lynchian surrealism verges on mannerism, but it's still a tremendously potent, bewitching work. LF *DVD* *BD*
Sidse Babett Knudsen *Cynthia* · Chiara D'Anna *Evelyn* · Eugenia Caruso *Dr Fraxini* · Zita Kraszko *Dr Schuller* · Monica Swinn *Lorna* ■ *Dir/Scr* Peter Strickland

The Duke of West Point ★★ U
Drama 1938 · US · BW · 109min

Minor South African star Louis Hayward was as bland a leading man as they came. He made this feature between playing the Saint and the Man in the Iron Mask, in what could be considered the peak of his career. Co-star Joan Fontaine makes a charming ingénue, but the real star of the movie is America's military academy West Point, whose governors recognised the recruitment value of such films. TS
Louis Hayward *Steven Early* · Joan Fontaine *Ann Porter* · Tom Brown *Sonny Drew* · Richard Carlson *Jack West* · Alan Curtis *Cadet Strong* · Donald Barry *Cadet Grady* · Gaylord Pendleton [Steve Pendleton] *Cadet Rains* · Charles D Brown *Doc Porter* · Jed Prouty *Mr Drew* ■ *Dir* Alfred E Green · *Scr* George Bruce

The Duke Wore Jeans ★★ U
Musical 1958 · UK · BW · 86min

Where movies are concerned, a single Tommy Steele is usually one too many, but two are more than flesh and blood can bear. Here he plays a likely lad who helps a charmless lookalike noble to escape being married off to feisty princess June Laverick. The "trading places" plot is an old chestnut of drama and the jerry-built sets and fifth-rate pop songs that adorn this tosh considerably scuff the sheen. DP *DVD*
Tommy Steele *Tony Whitecliffe/Tommy Hudson* · June Laverick *Princess Maria* · Michael Medwin *Cooper* · Eric Pohlmann *Bastini* · Alan Wheatley *King of Ritallia* · Mary Kerridge *Queen* · Ambrosine Philpotts *Duchess* · Clive Morton *Lord Whitecliffe* ■ *Dir* Gerald Thomas · *Scr* Norman Hudis, from a story by Lionel Bart, Michael Pratt

The Dukes of Hazzard ★ 15
Action comedy 2005 · US · Colour · 102min

Burt Reynolds carries what passes for the plot in this lame-brained big-screen retread of the iconic TV series. He plays nefarious town commissioner Boss Hogg, who uses a celebrity auto race as a decoy for his plan to steal the farm where Uncle Jesse (Willie Nelson) and good ole boys Luke (Johnny Knoxville) and Bo (Seann William Scott) run their moonshine business. Jessica Simpson pouts woodenly as their scantily clad cousin, Daisy. Lowbrow and moronic. AJ Violence. *DVD*
Seann William Scott *Bo Duke* · Johnny Knoxville *Luke Duke* · Jessica Simpson *Daisy Duke* · Burt Reynolds *Boss Hogg* · Willie Nelson *Uncle Jesse* · Joe Don Baker *Governor Jim Applewhite* · MC Gainey *Roscoe P Coltrane* · Jack Polick *Deputy Cletus* · David Koechner *Cooter* ■ *Dir* Jay Chandrasekhar · *Scr* John O'Brien, from a story by O'Brien, Jonathan L Davis, from characters by Gy Waldron

Dulcima ★★ 15
Drama 1971 · UK · Colour · 94min

John Mills gives a rambunctious performance as the Gloucestershire farmer who risks losing his carefully stashed wealth when he falls in lust with gold-digging Carol White. Writer/director Frank Nesbitt indulges in a little crude comedy, and Mills can't quite manage to avoid caricature. By the time White seduces gamekeeper Stuart Wilson, however, the tone has descended to the level of penny-dreadful melodrama. DP *DVD*
Carol White *Dulcima Gaskain* · John Mills *Mr Parker* · Stuart Wilson (1) *Gamekeeper* · Bernard Lee *Mr Gaskain* · Sheila Raynor *Mrs Gaskain* · Dudley Foster *Symes* ■ *Dir* Frank Nesbitt · *Scr* Frank Nesbitt, from a story by HE Bates

Duma ★★★★ U
Adventure drama 2005 · US · Colour · 96min

This handsome adventure drama from *Black Stallion* director Carroll Ballard tells the story of a white South African boy (Alexander Michaletos) and Duma, the young cheetah he has grown up with. When they have to leave the family farm and move to the big city, the boy is determined to release the cheetah back into the wild and embarks on a hazardous trek across the desert, joined by the mysterious Eamonn Walker. The film benefits from some spectacular wildlife photography and solid acting, plus an unsentimental storyline. DA *DVD*
Alexander Michaletos *Xan* · Eamonn Walker *Rip* · Campbell Scott *Peter* · Hope Davis *Kristin* · Mary Makhatho *Thandi* · Nthabiseng Kenoshi *Lucille* · Jennifer Steyn *Aunt Gwen* ■ *Dir* Carroll Ballard · *Scr* Karen Janszen, Mark St Germain, from a story by Carol Flint, Janszen, from the non-fiction book *How It Was with Dooms: a True Story from Africa* by Carol Cawthra Hopcraft, Xan Hopcraft

Dumb and Dumber ★★★★ 12
Comedy 1994 · US · Colour · 102min

With Jim Carrey, there will be half measures. So you'll either love this as one of his finest moments or loathe it as a perfect example of mind-numbing Hollywood cinema. But even the harshest critic will find it hard to suppress a couple of chuckles during this cheerfully moronic mix of slapstick, sight gags and toilet humour. Carrey and Jeff Daniels play two of the world's stupidest people who set off on a chaotic road trip when they attempt to return Lauren Holly's missing briefcase. JF Violence, nudity. *DVD* *BD*
Jim Carrey *Lloyd Christmas* · Jeff Daniels *Harry Dunne* · Lauren Holly *Mary Swanson* · Mike Starr *Joe Mentalino* · Karen Duffy *JP Shay* · Charles Rocket *Nicholas Andre* · Victoria Rowell *Athletic beauty* · Teri Garr *Helen Swanson* ■ *Dir* Peter Farrelly · *Scr* Peter Farrelly, Bennett Yellin, Bobby Farrelly

Dumb and Dumber To ★ 15
Comedy 2014 · US · Colour · 105min

Two decades have passed since Jim Carrey and Jeff Daniels goofed their way to box-office success in the original, but reprising their roles is an exceedingly dumb move. It isn't just that the joke has gotten old – and the actors look tired – it's that the Farrelly brothers push too hard for jaw-dropping moments, robbing the characters of the innocence and spirit of camaraderie that once balanced the stupidness. Harry (Daniels) needs a kidney and aims to harvest one from long-lost daughter Penny (Rachel Melvin). Nostalgia may tempt fans of the 1994 film, but there are fewer laughs in this sequel than Harry and Lloyd have brain cells. SP *DVD* *BD*
Jim Carrey *Lloyd Christmas* · Jeff Daniels *Harry Dunne* · Kathleen Turner *Fraida Felcher* · Rob Riggle *Travis/Captain Lippincott* · Laurie Holden *Adele Pichlow* · Rachel Melvin *Penny* ■ *Dir* Bobby Farrelly, Peter Farrelly · *Scr* Bobby Farrelly, Peter Farrelly, Sean Anders, Mike Cerrone, John Morris, Bennett Yellin

Dumb and Dumberer: When Harry Met Lloyd ★★ 12
Comedy 2003 · US/Ger · Colour · 81min

This belated prequel boasts neither of the original stars; Eric Christian Olsen and Derek Richardson step into Lloyd and Harry's shoes and do a pretty decent job. The plot has the doltish duo meeting for the first time and going on to foil a plot by corrupt principal Eugene Levy to embezzle school funds. This sometimes stoops lower than a limbo dancer in its search for easy laughs but for the young audience it's aimed at, this is diverting enough tosh. A further sequel is due in late 2014. DA *DVD*
Eric Christian Olsen *Lloyd Christmas* · Derek Richardson *Harry Dunne* · Rachel Nichols *Jessica* · Cheri Oteri *Ms Heller* · Luis Guzman *Ray* · Eden Henson *Turk* · Mimi Rogers *Mrs Dunne* · Eugene Levy *Principal Collins* ■ *Dir* Troy Miller · *Scr* Troy Miller, Robert Brenner, from a story by Robert Brenner, from characters by Peter Farrelly, Bennett Yellin, Bobby Farrelly

Dumbo ★★★★★ U
Classic animated fantasy
1941 · US · Colour · 64min

Although it was directed by Ben Sharpsteen, every frame of this Disney tale about the outcast elephant with huge ears was personally approved by Uncle Walt himself. The film won an Oscar for its score, with songs such as *When I See an Elephant Fly* and *Baby of Mine* (from the heartbreaking mother-child reunion) lingering long in the memory. On the animation side, the highlight is the parade of pink elephants after Dumbo and Timothy Mouse get tipsy. Made for a fraction of the cost of previous Disney animations, this may be one of the studio's shortest features, but it's also among the best. DP *DVD* *BD*
Edward Brophy *Timothy Mouse* · Herman Bing *Ringmaster* · Verna Felton *Elephant* · Sterling Holloway *Stork* · Cliff Edwards *Jim Crow* ■ *Dir* Ben Sharpsteen · *Scr* Joe Grant, Dick Huemer, from a book by Helen Aberson, Harold Pearl · *Music/lyrics* Frank Churchill, Oliver Wallace, Ned Washington

Dummy ★★★ 15
Comedy drama 2002 · US · Colour · 101min

This potentially poor taste comedy confirmed Adrien Brody as an edgy actor who is willing to tackle unconventional projects. But good though he is as a slow-witted New Jerseyite who takes up ventriloquism to try to conquer his painful reticence, his efforts are restricted by director Greg Pritikin's screenplay, which lurches between quirky Jewish humour and cloying sentimentality. DP *DVD*
Adrien Brody *Steven* · Milla Jovovich *Fangora* · Illeana Douglas *Heidi* · Vera Farmiga *Lorena* · Jessica Walter *Fern* · Ron Leibman *Lou* · Jared Harris *Michael* ■ *Dir/Scr* Greg Pritikin

Dune ★★★ 15
Science-fiction drama
1984 · US · Colour · 130min

Frank Herbert's mammoth cult novel, about the competition between two warring families for control of a barren planet renowned for its mind-expanding "spice", is converted by director David Lynch into a dense, swirling mass of religious symbolism and mysticism. Lynch was, reportedly, unhappy with the final cut, but his film is visually stunning and many of the scenes are among the most memorable and original of the genre. Kyle MacLachlan stars as the "messiah" alongside an amazing cast. Unwieldy and confusing, it's not as bad as it seemed on release. AJ Violence, swearing. *DVD* *BD*
Kyle MacLachlan *Paul Atreides* · Francesca Annis *Lady Jessica* · Paul Dourif *Piter De Vries* · José Ferrer *Padishah Emperor Shaddam IV* · Linda Hunt *Shadout Mapes* · Freddie Jones *Thufir Hawat* · Richard Jordan *Duncan Idaho* · Virginia Madsen *Princess Irulan* · Silvana Mangano *Reverend Mother Ramallo* · Kenneth McMillan *Baron Vladimir Harkonnen* · Patrick Stewart *Gurney Halleck* · Sting *Feyd Rautha* · Dean Stockwell *Dr Wellington Yueh* · Max von Sydow *Dr Kynes* · Sean Young *Chani* ■ *Dir* David Lynch · *Scr* David Lynch, from the novel by Frank Herbert

Dungeons & Dragons ★ 12
Fantasy adventure
2000 · US/Cz Rep · Colour · 103min

This screen version of the popular role-playing game has Empress Savina (Thora Birch) wanting equality for all citizens in the mythical kingdom of Izmer, but villainous Jeremy Irons plots to establish his own tyrannical rule. Shifting uneasily from banal adventure and arch brutality to unintentional hilarity and pantomime camp, this dreary fantasy adventure is scuppered by some dire performances. AJ Violence. *DVD*
Jeremy Irons *Profion* · Justin Whalin *Ridley Freeborn* · Marlon Wayans *Snails* · Zoe McLellan *Marina Pretensa* · Thora Birch *Empress Savina* · Kristen Wilson *Norda* · Richard O'Brien *Xilus* · Tom Baker *Halvarth* · Lee Arenberg *Elwood Gutworthy* ■ *Dir* Courtney Solomon · *Scr* Topper Lilien, Carroll Cartwright

Dungeons & Dragons: Wrath of the Dragon God ★
Fantasy adventure
2005 · Ger/Lith/UK/US · Colour · 105min

This cheap sequel to fantasy adventure flop *Dungeons & Dragons* (2000) makes the abysmal original seem like a masterpiece. Pantomimic Bruce Payne returns as the sadistic Damodar, here promoted from henchman to vengeful head villain as he attempts to use a powerful and ancient orb to destroy the mythical kingdom of Izmer. Poor acting, clunky dialogue and the most woeful CGI emphasise the plot's flimsiness. SF
Mark Dymond *Berek* · Bruce Payne *Damodar* · Clemency Burton-Hill *Melora* · Ellie Chidzley [Ellie Chidzey] *Lux* ■ *Dir* Gerry Lively · *Scr* Robert Kimmel, Gerry Lively, Brian Rudnick

Dunkirk ★★★ PG
Second World War drama
1958 · UK · BW · 129min

This Ealing reconstruction of the evacuation of Dunkirk is impressive in its scale and authenticity, but slightly disappointing in its writing and execution. John Mills, Richard Attenborough and Bernard Lee scarcely have to act as their respective parts - a corporal lost on the beaches, a snivelling stay-at-home and a cynical reporter - are so cleverly tailor-made. Director Leslie Norman handles the manoeuvres with skill and does well to maintain the docudramatic feel, in spite of some shoddy dialogue. DP *DVD*

John Mills *Binns* • Bernard Lee *Charles Foreman* • Richard Attenborough *Holden* • Robert Urquhart *Mike* • Ray Jackson *Barlow* • Meredith Edwards *Dave Bellman* • Anthony Nicholls *Military spokesman* • Michael Shillo *Jouvet* ■ *Dir* Leslie Norman • *Scr* David Divine, WP Lipscomb, from the novel *The Big Pick-Up* by Elleston Trevor and the play *Dunkirk* by Lt Col Ewen Butler, Maj JS Bradford • *Producer* Michael Balcon

Dunkirk
Second World War drama
2017 · US/UK/Fr · Colour

This is a preview - no prints were available to review as we went to press: After creating the dark fantasy world of Batman and sci-fi thrillers like *Inception* and *Interstellar*, director Christopher Nolan comes back down to earth to re-create the evacuation of Dunkirk - or Operation Dynamo - during the Second World War. A sterling British line-up is headlined by Tom Hardy, Cillian Murphy, Mark Rylance, Kenneth Branagh and in his feature film debut, One Direction heartthrob Harry Styles. With a total of 338,226 soldiers being rescued by a fleet of over 800 boats, this is a story of grand scope that inspired Churchill's famous speech, "We shall fight on beaches...". SP In English, French.

Tom Hardy • Mark Rylance • Kenneth Branagh • Cillian Murphy • Harry Styles • Aneurin Barnard ■ *Dir/Scr* Christopher Nolan

Dunston Checks In ★★★ PG
Comedy   1996 · Can · Colour · 84min

Dunston is an orangutan acting as the unwilling sidekick to a snooty English peer (Rupert Everett) who wants to use him to burgle New York's Majestic Hotel. Manager Jason Alexander's son Eric Lloyd is the only one onto the scam. Dunston's antics are as delightfully appealing as Faye Dunaway's rudely ruthless proprietor is unattractive. TH *DVD*

Jason Alexander *Robert Grant* • Faye Dunaway *Mrs Dubrow* • Eric Lloyd *Kyle Grant* • Rupert Everett *Lord Rutledge* • Graham Sack *Brian* • Paul Reubens *La Farge* • Glenn Shadix *Lionel Spalding* • Nathan Davis *Victor* ■ *Dir* Ken Kwapis • *Scr* John Hopkins, Bruce Graham, from a story by John Hopkins

The Dunwich Horror ★★ 18
Horror   1970 · US · Colour · 84min

Lovers of HP Lovecraft's stories had to wait until *Re-Animator* to see justice done to his full-blooded *Necronomicon* tales. Back in the 1960s, fans made do with fun fiascos from the Roger Corman scrap heap. In this comic caper, a hopelessly miscast Sandra Dee plays a student who is the drugged victim of a fertility rite, set up by the hammy Dean Stockwell in his bid to restore ancient powers of evil. AJ Violence.

Sandra Dee *Nancy Walker* • Dean Stockwell *Wilbur Whateley* • Ed Begley *Dr Henry Armitage* • Sam Jaffe *Old Whateley* • Donna Baccala *Elizabeth Hamilton* • Joanne Moore *Jordan Lavinia* • Talia Coppola [Talia Shire] *Cora* ■ *Dir* Daniel Haller • *Scr* Curtis Lee Hanson, Henry Rosenbaum, Ronald Silkosky, from the story by HP Lovecraft

Duplicity ★★★ 12
Romantic caper 2009 · US/Ger · Colour · 119min

Old-fashioned star power from Julia Roberts and Clive Owen illuminates this snappy espionage caper, though it's never quite as clever as it should be. There are double-crosses, glamorous international locations and flirtatious dialogue aplenty, as the former spies try to outwit the feuding heads of rival multinationals that have hired them to protect their products. The film spins an entertaining web that offers a jazzy modern take on 1960s caper yarns (much like the *Ocean's Eleven* franchise). Unfortunately, the elaborate plotting by writer/director Tony Gilroy (the *Bourne* trilogy) rather crowds out the fizz the story needs. TJ Brief swearing, sexual references. *DVD* *BL*

Julia Roberts *Claire Stenwick* • Clive Owen *Ray Koval* • Paul Giamatti *Richard "Dick" Garsik* • Tom Wilkinson *Howard Tully* • Thomas McCarthy *Jeff Bauer* • Billy Bob Thornton ■ *Dir/Scr* Tony Gilroy

During One Night ★★
Second World War drama
1961 · UK · BW · 85min

Sidney J Furie's Second World War drama has a whiff of controversy about it, as it explores the then taboo topics of virginity and impotence. Don Borisenko headlines as the USAF pilot who goes AWOL after a buddy is castrated during a mission, but his brushes with the military police and a sympathetic padre are nowhere near as involving as his encounters with a young Susan Hampshire. DP

Susan Hampshire *Jean* • Don Borisenko *David* • Sean Sullivan *Major* • Joy Webster *Prostitute* • Jackie Collins *Girl* • Tom Busby *Sam* ■ *Dir/Scr* Sidney J Furie

Dust ★★★ 18
Drama   1985 · Fr/Bel · Colour · 85min

Adapted from JM Coetzee's novel *In the Heart of the Country*, this brooding South African drama gives Trevor Howard the opportunity to explore a fully rounded character after years of formulaic cameos. As the boorish farmer who seduces the wife of his black foreman, he chillingly conveys the arrogance of supremacy and the lust of isolation. Yet it's Jane Birkin, as the daughter who becomes increasingly jealous of her father's new flame, who provides both the film's emotional core and its shocking resolution. Directed with extreme care, this is stern stuff. DP

Jane Birkin *Magda* • Trevor Howard *Father* • John Matshikiza *Hendrik* • Nadine Uwampa *Klein Anna* • Lourdes Christina Sayo Momoboko *Old Anna* • René Diaz *Jacob* • Tom Vrebos *Piet* ■ *Dir* Marion Hänsel • *Scr* Marion Hänsel, from the novel *In the Heart of the Country* by JM Coetzee

Dust ★★ 18
Drama
2001 · UK/Ger/It/Mac/US/Sp/Swi · Colour · 119min

This brutal, depressing film alternates between a contemporary New York drama and an early-20th-century "Wild East" blood bath. This is an awkward combination, and is not aided by an unappealing quartet of protagonists. Its starting point is the apparent robbery of an apartment by petty thief Adrian Lester, who is wounded by owner Rosemary Murphy. For some reason, she decides to recall the origins of her ancestors, namely two brothers (a pair of shaky performances from David Wenham and Joseph Fiennes) who end up as adversaries in Macedonia. JC *DVD*

Joseph Fiennes *Elijah* • David Wenham *Luke* • Adrian Lester *Edge* • Anne Brochet *Lilith* • Nikolina Kujaca *Neda* • Rosemary Murphy *Angela* ■ *Dir/Scr* Milcho Manchevski

Dust Be My Destiny ★★
Crime drama   1939 · US · BW · 88min

This routine melodrama is redeemed by the ever-excellent John Garfield. He's ideally cast as an innocent on the run, fleeing a murder rap. In jail, he falls for Priscilla Lane, the work-farm boss's stepdaughter, while newspaper editor Alan Hale takes an interest in his case. The story's more than a mite overfamiliar, and little more originality wouldn't have gone amiss. TS

John Garfield *Joe Bell* • Priscilla Lane *Mabel* • Alan Hale *Mike Leonard* • Frank McHugh *Caruthers* • Billy Halop *Hank* • Bobby Jordan *Jimmy* • Charley Grapewin *Pop* • Henry Armetta *Nick* ■ *Dir* Lewis Seiler • *Scr* Robert Rossen, from a novel by Jerome Odlum

Dust Devil ★★★★ 15
Horror thriller 1992 · UK · Colour · 103min

Richard Stanley's surreal serial killer horror thriller is a landmark British film of the 1990s. Combining African tribal myths with spaghetti western folklore, the *Hardware* director's highly personal magical mystery tour through sweeping Namibian vistas is an embarrassment of cinematic riches. It's a hallucinogenic eye-popper, a political allegory - accent on the gory - that bursts with atmospheric moodiness. Robert Burke is a forbidding presence as "The Hitcher from Hell", spinning an illusory web of dream-like terror around his suicidal victims. AJ Violence, swearing, sex scenes, nudity. *DVD*

Robert Burke *Dust Devil/"Hitch"* • Chelsea Field *Wendy Robinson* • Zakes Mokae *Ben Mukurob* • John Matshikiza *Joe Niemand* • Rufus Swart *Mark Robinson* • William Hootkins *Captain Cornelius Beyman* • Marianne Sägebrecht *Dr Leidzinger* ■ *Dir/Scr* Richard Stanley

Dust in the Wind ★★★ 15
Romantic drama 1987 · Tai · Colour · 109min

While not Hou Hsiao-Hsien's most ambitious picture, this bittersweet tale of country mice finding love in the big city, only to drift apart when patriotic duty calls, is full of human foibles and shrewd observations. As the teenagers leaving their mining village to complete their studies in Taipei, Wang Ching-Won and Xin Shufen have an honesty that reinforces the film's social realism, while the director's command of their environment is impeccable. For all the implied criticisms of Taiwan and China, however, it's a fairly noncommital picture. DP Hokkien, Mandarin +subtitles.

Wang Ching-Won *Wan* • Xin Shufen *Huen* • Che'en Shu-Fang *Huen's mother* • Li Tianlu *Grandpa* ■ *Dir* Hou Hsiao-Hsien • *Scr* Wu Nien-Jen, Chu Tien-Wen

Dusting Cliff 7 ★★ 18
Action thriller   1996 · US · Colour · 88min

The budget for this action thriller precludes any eye-popping pyrotechnics, while the ham-fisted direction prevents either pace or palpable tension. However, the real problem is the script, which is not only strewn with dismal dialogue, but also fails to present the villainous Lance Henriksen with a credible motive for pinching the nuclear and chemical weapons buried somewhere in the desert beneath Cliff 7. DP Violence, swearing.

Lance Henriksen *Roger McBride* • Nancy Allen *Anna Bishop* • Scott Lincoln *Brock Daniels* • Dean Scofield *Mitch Stevens* • Ashley Buccille *Carrie Bishop* ■ *Dir* William H Molina • *Scr* Jim Menza, Charles Philip Moore, Justin J Stanley, William H Molina

Dusty ★★★
Drama   1982 · Aus · Colour · 90min

Bill Kerr made his name on radio as one of Tony Hancock's sidekicks. But, in later years, his grizzled features suited him for roles in a number of Australian outdoor dramas. Here he plays a bushman turned shepherd who trains an abandoned wild hound (Dusty) into a champion sheepdog. Kerr is superb as the outsider whose loyalties lie with the wilds. DP

Bill Kerr *Tom* • Noel Trevarthen *Harry* • Carol Burns *Clara* • John Stanton *Railey Jordan* ■ *Dir* John Richardson • *Scr* Sonia Borg, from a novel by Frank Dalby Davison

Dusty Ermine ★★
Crime drama   1936 · UK · BW · 85min

This is far from the best film made by the recently rediscovered director Bernard Vorhaus. However, detective Anthony Bushell's pursuit of criminal peer Ronald Squire is not without its moments of tension and droll humour. Jane Baxter provides the glamour, but the real interest lies in the supporting performances of Felix Aylmer and Margaret Rutherford. DP

Jane Baxter *Linda Kent* • Anthony Bushell *Inspector Forsyth* • Ronald Squire *Jim Kent* • Margaret Rutherford *Miss Butterby* • Davina Craig *Goldie* • Athole Stewart *Mr Kent* • Felix Aylmer *Assistant commissioner* ■ *Dir* Bernard Vorhaus • *Scr* L du Garde Peach, Michael Hankinson, Arthur Macrae, Paul Hervey Fox, H Fowler Mear, from the play by Neil Grant

Dutchman ★★
Drama   1966 · UK · BW · 54min

Ostensibly, this shows how sadistic white woman Shirley Knight persecutes and eventually assaults black man Al Freeman Jr on the New York subway. But while there are multiple layers of socio-political symbolism beneath the surface, the action is so slow and portentous you soon tire of searching for them. Editor Anthony Harvey made his directorial debut with this 54-minute film. DP

Shirley Knight *Lula* • Al Freeman Jr *Clay* • Frank Lieberman *Subway Rider* • Robert Calvert *Subway Rider* ■ *Dir* Anthony Harvey • *Scr* Anthony Harvey, from the play by LeRoi Jones

The Dyatlov Pass Incident ★★★ 15
Horror thriller
2013 · US/UK/Rus · Colour · 96min

Another group of happy-go-lucky young people are turned into shivering, quivering wrecks in this surprisingly watchable found-footage chiller from Renny Harlin. Here, it's five students who are out to solve the deaths of nine hikers in the Ural Mountains in 1959. This horror subgenre may be well worn but, like Barry Levinson with *The Bay*, Harlin has rooted his film in actual events and uses the well-documented incident to tease out an absorbing mystery situated in spectacular locations. JA English, Russian +subtitles. Violence.

Holly Goss *Holly King* • Matt Stokoe *Jenson Day* • Luke Albright *JP Hauser Jr* • Ryan Hawley *Andy Thatcher* • Gemma Atkinson *Denise Evers* ■ *Dir* Renny Harlin • *Scr* Vikram Weet

D'Ye Ken John Peel? ★★
Drama   1934 · UK · BW · 84min

This is a crusty old melodrama in which Leslie Perrins chews the scenery with a delicious lack of restraint, playing the dastardly rogue whose idea of payment for an outstanding debt is to marry the debtor's daughter. But fear not for Winifred Shotter: riding to the rescue is Waterloo veteran John Garrick, who knows a thing or two about delivering damsels from distress. Hardly a lost classic. DP

John Garrick *Major John Peel* • Winifred Shotter *Lucy Merrall* • Stanley Holloway *Sam Small* • John Stuart *Captain Moonlight* • Leslie Perrins *Mr Craven* • Mary Lawson *Toinette* ■ *Dir* Henry Edwards • *Scr* H Fowler Mear, from a story by Charles Cullum

Dying of the Light ★★ 18
Thriller   2014 · US/Bahamas · Colour · 89min

Nicolas Cage playing a spy with a type of dementia that inclines him towards unpredictable behaviour - doesn't that sound like a recipe for something unhinged and wonderful? Sadly, the finished product falls way short of expectation. But there is sport to be had trying to work out what writer/director Paul Schrader's original intentions were, before the studio recut his film and added a jarring sub-*Bourne* soundtrack. As it is, a classic case of "what might have been". SvM In English, Romanian, Arabic. *DVD* *BL*

Nicolas Cage *Evan Lake* • Anton Yelchin *Milton Schultz* • Alexander Karim *Muhammad Banir* • Irène Jacob *Michelle Zubarain* ■ *Dir/Scr* Paul Schrader

Dying Young ★★ 15
Romantic drama 1991 · US · Colour · 106min

Joel Schumacher's tear-jerker leaves one wishing that the terminally sick rich lad at the centre of this interminable nonsense had died before the cameras arrived. Campbell Scott tries hard in a thankless role, made all the more difficult by the fact that Schumacher only has eyes for Julia Roberts as the blowsy girl from the wrong side of the tracks who answers Scott's advert for a carer. DP Swearing, nudity. *DVD*

D

Julia Roberts *Hilary O'Neil* • Campbell Scott *Victor Geddes* • Vincent D'Onofrio *Gordon* • Colleen Dewhurst *Estelle Whittier* • David Selby *Richard Geddes* • Ellen Burstyn *Mrs O'Neil* • Dion Anderson *Cappy* • Daniel Beer *Danny* ■ *Dir* Joel Schumacher • *Scr* Richard Friedenberg, from the novel by Marti Leimbach

Dynamite ★★★ U
Drama   1929 · US · BW · 69min

The first talkie from producer/director Cecil B DeMille, one of the few directors (along with Hitchcock and Spielberg) whose name is always instantly recognised by the public. This is very typical of DeMille, with a love triangle involving a condemned murderer (Charles Bickford), a giddy socialite (Kay Johnson) and a noble hero (Conrad Nagel), all thrown together in a mammoth mine disaster. The cave-in is spectacular, the costumes are splendid and the bathrooms are lavish. TS

Conrad Nagel *Roger Towne* • Kay Johnson *Cynthia Crothers* • Charles Bickford *Hagon Derk* • Julia Faye *Marcia Towne* • Muriel McCormac *Katie Derk* • Tyler Brooke *Life of the Party* • Joel McCrea *Marco the Sheik* ■ *Dir* Cecil B DeMille • *Scr* Jeanie Macpherson, John Howard Lawson, Gladys Unger, from a story by Macpherson

Dynamite Chicken ★★ 18
Satirical documentary
1971 · US · Colour · 75min

Only the 1960s could have given birth to a concept like this: a "multi-media mosaic" of American pop culture that incorporates rock footage, animation, newsreels and nudity. By turns offensive and enlightening, there are all-too-brief glimpses of such 20th-century icons as Jimi Hendrix, John and Yoko, the Velvet Underground and Lenny Bruce, and far too many shots of hippies doing what hippies did back then. A pre-fame Richard Pryor provides ironic comedy links. RS

Joan Baez • Richard Pryor • Ron Carey • Marshall Efron • Lisa Ryan • Paul Krasner • Leonard Cohen • John Lennon • Ondine • Andy Warhol • Jimi Hendrix • Lenny Bruce ■ *Dir/Scr* Ernest Pintoff

Dynamite Man from Glory Jail ★★★
Western   1971 · US · Colour · 97min

James Stewart plays a habitual criminal who is released after 40 years in jail and wants to claim $25,000 of prison pay that he has banked legitimately. But the bank manager has run off with it, forcing Stewart back to his old ways. The star chews up the scenery, while George Kennedy, Strother Martin and a young Kurt Russell offer expert support. AT

James Stewart *Mattie Appleyard* • George Kennedy *Doc Council* • Anne Baxter *Cleo* • Strother Martin *Lee Cottrill* • Kurt Russell *Johnny Jesus* • William Windom *Roy K Sizemore* ■ *Dir* Andrew V McLaglen • *Scr* James Lee Barrett, from the novel by Davis Grubb

Dynasty: the Making of a Guilty Pleasure ★★
Satirical drama
2004 · US/Aus · Colour · 120min

Dynasty was the glamour soap of the 1980s, a delightfully camp series about a mega-rich Denver oil family. This affectionate retelling of the show's rise and fall nails the kitsch factor but comes across as being a little cheap – something the Carringtons and Colbys never were. The focus is on the show's creators, Richard and Esther Shapiro (Ritchie Singer and Pamela Reed), who soldier on even though the show bears little resemblance to their original idea. Alice Krige has fun as Joan Collins but the biggest problem is that this is just not bitchy enough. JF

Pamela Reed *Esther Shapiro* • Alice Krige *Joan Collins* • Ritchie Singer *Richard Shapiro* • Melora Hardin *Linda Evans* • Bartholomew John *John Forsythe* • Robert Coleby *Rock Hudson* • Holly Brisley *Heather Locklear* ■ *Dir/Scr* Matthew Miller (1)

E Flat ★★★★
Romantic drama   1961 · Ind · BW · 134min

Ritwik Ghatak's compelling drama is the pivotal segment of his trilogy on the ramifications of the Partition of India. It reflects his turbulent relationship with the communist Indian People's Theatre, and the movie's complex political subtext may prove difficult for anyone unfamiliar with Partition and its aftermath. The action chronicles the divisions within a performing troupe and focuses on actress Supriya Choudhury's conflicted feelings for radical Abanish Bandyopadhyay and her fiancé in France. The Communist Party was so disgusted by the film's political debate that it sabotaged screenings, and this box-office failure began Ghatak's decline. DP Bengali +subtitles.

Abanish Bandyopadhyay [Abanish Bannerjee] *Bhrigu* • Supriya Choudhury *Anasuya* • Bijon Bhattacharya *Gagan* • Anil Chattopadhyay [Anil Chatterjee] *Rishi* ■ *Dir/Scr* Ritwik Ghatak

EMR ★★★ 15
Thriller   2004 · UK · Colour · 86min

Urban myths and conspiracy theories combine to intriguing effect in this surprisingly good thriller from James Erskine and Danny McCullough, making their feature debut. A micro-budget tale of paranoid confusion, it skilfully captures the mental disintegration of a lonely Londoner (Adam Leese), whose nerdy obsession with internet rumours and beliefs appears vindicated when he unexpectedly wakes up in a Mexican hotel room missing a kidney. From then on fantasy and reality blur into a time-slipping nightmare. Despite a rough-and-ready feel, the feature maintains its grip with constant twists and sharp editing. SF *DVD*

Adam Leese *Adam Jones* • Whitney Cummings *Cyberbunnylilly* • Guy Henry *Head agent* • Tom Hardy *Henry* • Gil Bellows *Paramedic* ■ *Dir/Scr* James Erskine, Danny McCullough

ET the Extra-Terrestrial ★★★★★ U
Classic science-fiction adventure
1982 · US · Colour · 109min

Steven Spielberg's ode to aliens could also be seen as a tribute to all the loners of the world, as little ET, abandoned by his extraterrestrial pals, has to cope on Earth until they can come back and rescue him. Luckily, he's befriended by an equally lonely little boy, played by Henry Thomas, who proceeds to teach his alien chum how to talk, dress up in women's clothes and guzzle beer. Much has been made of the changes and additions to the anniversary edition, but this is no extended director's cut; the alterations are minimal. Some of ET's facial expressions have been enhanced with computer animation, there are five additional minutes of footage that were left out of the original and – significantly in the current political climate – the guns carried by the government agents have been digitally replaced by walkie-talkies. However, 20 years after its first release, this is still a special, delightful adventure. JB *DVD*

Henry Thomas *Elliott* • Dee Wallace [Dee Wallace Stone] *Mary* • Peter Coyote *Keys* • Robert MacNaughton *Michael* • Drew Barrymore *Gertie* • KC Martel *Greg* • Sean Frye *Steve* • Tom Howell [C Thomas Howell] *Tyler* • Erika Eleniak *Pretty girl* ■ *Dir* Steven Spielberg • *Scr* Melissa Mathison • *Cinematographer* Allen Daviau • *Music* John Williams • *Special Effects* Carlo Rambaldi

Each Dawn I Die ★★★ PG
Prison drama   1939 · US · BW · 87min

What's lacking in credibility is made up for in ferocious energy here, as James Cagney portrays a framed campaigning reporter who is sent to prison and brutalised into throwing in his lot with a crime boss. Sombre undercurrents run below the routine melodrama, with the reporter believing he's been betrayed by both life and fellow convict George Raft. Cagney gives it all he's got. TH

James Cagney *Frank Ross* • George Raft *"Hood" Stacey* • Jane Bryan *Joyce Conover* • George Bancroft *Warden John Armstrong* • Stanley Ridges *Meuller* • Alan Baxter *Polecat Carlisle* ■ *Dir* William Keighley • *Scr* Norman Reilly Raine, Warren Duff, Charles Perry, from the novel by Jerome Odlum

The Eagle ★★★★ U
Silent adventure   1925 · US · BW · 70min

A film of enormous curiosity value because Rudolph Valentino's penultimate surge before he died shows – in his smouldering-eyed, he-man presence – just what his attraction was to those women who formed a cult after his death. As a modern-day Robin Hood, the "Black Eagle", Valentino makes a sinewy play for Vilma Banky, while being ironically observed by Tsarina Louise Dresser, who puts herself about as much as the hero. Much parodied since its release, it still has charisma – and that's because of Valentino: his star quality was so great he only needed one to tango. TH *DVD*

Rudolph Valentino *Vladimir Dubrovsky* • Vilma Banky *Mascha Troekouroff* • Louise Dresser *Czarina* • Albert Conti *Kuschka* • James A Marcus *Kyrilla Troekouroff* • George Nichols *Judge* • Carrie Clark Ward *Aunt Aurelia* ■ *Dir* Clarence Brown • *Scr* Hans Kräly

The Eagle ★★★ 12
Historical drama
2010 · UK/US · Colour · 109min

A Roman commander ventures into the wilds beyond Hadrian's Wall to clear his family name in this historical drama adapted from Rosemary Sutcliff's 1954 novel *The Eagle of the Ninth*. Channing Tatum brings plenty of brawn but a rather one-note brooding to the key role of Marcus Aquila, whose posting to the Empire's furthest reaches presents him with an opportunity to reclaim the ceremonial eagle lost when his father marched a legion into unconquered Caledonia, never to return. The film delivers a convincingly rugged portrait of second-century life, but less persuasive is the central relationship between Tatum's Roman officer and the freed slave (Jamie Bell, on sinewy form) he takes along on his mission. There's plenty of grit and craft on display here, yet somehow the result is never quite as rousing as you'd hope. TJ Violence. *DVD*

Channing Tatum *Marcus Aquila* • Jamie Bell *Esca* • Donald Sutherland *Uncle Aquila* • Mark Strong *Guern* • Tahar Rahim *Seal Prince* • Denis O'Hare *Lutorius* ■ *Dir* Kevin Macdonald • *Scr* Jeremy Brock, from the novel *The Eagle of the Ninth* by Rosemary Sutcliff

The Eagle and the Hawk ★★★★
War drama   1933 · US · BW · 63min

This mordant and very bitter "lost generation" First World War tale has a quite superb cast to do it justice. You couldn't wish for better than Fredric March as the disaffected leader of a British flying squadron, Cary Grant as his truculent air gunner, Jack Oakie as his best mate and Carole Lombard as March's London society doll. Reissue prints give Mitchell Leisen his due as assistant director, but first time out the full credit went to Stuart Walker alone. TS

Fredric March *Jeremiah Young* • Cary Grant *Henry Crocker* • Jack Oakie *Mike Richards* • Carole Lombard *Beautiful lady* • Sir Guy Standing [Guy Standing] *Major Dunham* • Forrester Harvey *Hogan* • Kenneth Howell *John Stevens* ■ *Dir* Stuart Walker • *Scr* Bogart Rogers, Seton I Miller, from the story by John Monk Saunders

Eagle Eye ★★★★ 12
Action thriller
2008 · US/Ger/UK · Colour · 112min

DJ Caruso and Shia LaBeouf, the director and star of *Disturbia*, team up again for this fast and furious conspiracy thriller. In a Hitchcockian tale of ordinary people caught up in extraordinary situations, LaBeouf plays a slacker who, along with single mother Michelle Monaghan, is contacted by a mysterious female voice at the end of a phone line. The pair are framed as terrorists, and must do as the voice commands in order to survive. The film is well-played, with a paranoid, 1970s sensibility, and this, along with moments of heart-pounding suspense and impressive stunt work, makes it a stylish and often awe-inspiring thrill ride. AJ *DVD* *BL*

Shia LaBeouf *Jerry* • Michelle Monaghan *Rachel* • Rosario Dawson *Zoe Perez* • Ethan Embry *Grant* • Billy Bob Thornton *Morgan* • Madilyn Sweeten *Becky* ■ *Dir* DJ Caruso • *Scr* John Glenn, Dan McDermott, Hillary Seitz, Travis Adam Wright [Travis Wright], from a story by McDermott • *Cinematographer* Dariusz Wolski

The Eagle Has Landed ★★★ 15
Second World War adventure
1976 · UK · Colour · 118min

This far-fetched but entertaining thriller stars Michael Caine as an unlikely German colonel who leads a task force to infiltrate an English village in 1943, with the aim of kidnapping prime minister Winston Churchill. Even more unlikely is English-hating Donald Sutherland's Irish accent allied with the cut-glass tones of Jenny Agutter, who plays the local girl he falls for. As a lurking party, the Germans aren't very convincing, but director John Sturges puts some hefty action into the untidy package, while Donald Pleasence's impersonation of Heinrich Himmler is totally credible. TH Swearing, violence. *DVD* *BL*

Michael Caine *Colonel Kurt Steiner* • Donald Sutherland *Liam Devlin* • Robert Duvall *Colonel Max Radl* • Jenny Agutter *Molly Prior* • Donald Pleasence *Heinrich Himmler* • Anthony Quayle *Admiral Wilhelm Canaris* • Jean Marsh *Joanna Grey* • John Standing *Father Philip Verecker* • Judy Geeson *Pamela Verecker* ■ *Dir* John Sturges • *Scr* Tom Mankiewicz, from the novel by Jack Higgins

The Eagle Has Two Heads ★★★
Drama   1948 · Fr · BW · 94min

Jean Cocteau's film of his play, *L'Aigle à Deux Têtes*, has Jean Marais – the hero of Cocteau's *Orphée* and star of the stage version – as a 19th-century anarchist who falls in love with the king's widow when he plans to assassinate her. The fact that he's also a dead ringer for the deceased king complicates matters, as do the plans of the queen's enemies. Less of an achievement than Cocteau's better-known movies – such as *Blood of a Poet* (1930) – this has an exuberant romanticism that's hard to resist. AT French +subtitles.

Edwige Feuillère *The Queen* • Jean Marais *Stanislas* • Sylvia Monfort *Edith de Berg* • Jean Debucourt *Felix de Willenstein* • Jacques Varennes *Count de Foehn* • Abdallah *Tony* ■ *Dir* Jean Cocteau • *Scr* Jean Cocteau, from his play *L'Aigle à Deux Têtes*

Eagle in a Cage ★★★★
Historical drama   1971 · UK · Colour · 102min

Napoleon's frustrating last years in exile on the tiny, remote island of St Helena make for a compelling drama. Seizing one of the best roles of his career, Kenneth Haigh is superb as the unbowed Bonaparte, and he's beautifully supported by John Gielgud, Ralph Richardson and Billie Whitelaw. Producer/screenwriter Millard Lampell had already nursed this project into an Emmy Award-winning TV production starring Trevor Howard in 1965, and his bitter personal experience of exile, as a blacklisted writer during the McCarthy era, resonates in his understanding of Napoleon. AME

John Gielgud *Lord Sissal* • Ralph Richardson *Sir Hudson Lowe* • Billie Whitelaw *Madame Bertrand* • Kenneth Haigh *Napoleon Bonaparte* • Moses Gunn *General Gourgaud* • Ferdy Mayne *Count Bertrand* • Lee Montague *Cipriani* • Georgina Hale *Betty Balcombe* ■ *Dir* Fielder Cook • *Scr* Millard Lampell

Eagle vs Shark ★★★ 15
Romantic comedy 2006 · NZ/US · Colour · 83min

New Zealand director Taika Waititi was nominated for an Oscar for his short *Two Cars, One Night*; he didn't win, but attracted attention when he was caught dozing while the award was being announced. His first full-length feature is an equally irreverent affair, a likeably quirky comedy about a rather dislikeable posse of geeky losers. Co-writer Loren Horsley's Lily is probably the nicest of the bunch, a shy fast-food waitress who falls for a gaming nerd (Jemaine Clement). It's very much in the vein of the cult hit *Napoleon Dynamite*, and while it's hard to see why Lily is so keen on the obnoxious Clement, it still exudes a ramshackle charm. JF *DVD*

Loren Horsley *Lily* • Jemaine Clement *Jarrod* • Joel Tobeck *Damon* • Brian Sergent *Jonah* • Craig Hall *Doug* • Rachel House *Nancy* ■ *Dir* Taika Waititi • *Scr* Taika Waititi, from a screenplay by Loren Horsley, Waititi

Eagle's Wing ★★★ PG
Western 1978 · UK · Colour · 99min

Anthony Harvey's strange, myth-laden movie pits two deeply troubled men against each other in a spiritual and material battle for the prize of a white stallion named Eagle's Wing. Martin Sheen and Sam Waterston are both superb in their playing of traditional enemies who recognise in each other the same desire to acquit themselves bravely in the critical eyes of their communities. The movie loses a certain momentum as Harvey piles subplot upon subplot, but otherwise this intelligent western is a treat. SH *DVD*

Martin Sheen *Pike* • Sam Waterston *White Bull* • Harvey Keitel *Henry* • Stéphane Audran *Widow* • Caroline Langrishe *Judith* • John Castle *Priest* • Jorge Luke *Red Sky* • Jose Carlos Ruis *Lame Wolf* • Manuel Ojeda *Miguel* ■ *Dir* Anthony Harvey • *Scr* John Briley, from a story by Michael Syson

The Ear ★★★★ 12
Political thriller 1969 · Cz · BW · 91min

This is one of the films "banned forever" by the Czech government in 1969, which finally emerged to great acclaim following the Velvet Revolution 20 years later. Directed with awesome control by Karel Kachyna, it is a blistering combination of political allegory and domestic drama. Radoslav Brzobohaty is the epitome of paranoia as the minor official who arrives home from a blood-letting party function convinced that he is next in line for dismissal and arrest. His feuds with wife Jirina Bohdalova as they strip the house of incriminating evidence are excruciating in their bitterness. DP Czech +subtitles. *DVD*

Jirina Bohdalova *Anna* • Radoslav Brzobohaty *Ludvik* • Gustav Opocensky *Conrade* • Miloslav Holub [Miroslav Holub] *General* • Lubor Tokos *Minister* ■ *Dir* Karel Kachyna • *Scr* Karel Kachyna, Jan Prochazka, from a story by Jan Prochazka

Earl Carroll Vanities ★★ U
Musical 1945 · US · BW · 91min

Princess Drina (Constance Moore) comes to New York to try to raise some money for her impoverished country. Desperate situations call for desperate measures, and she finds herself starring on Broadway in one of Earl Carroll's musical extravaganzas and receiving the romantic attentions of Dennis O'Keefe. Directed by Joseph Santley and offering some lively production numbers, this is still a candidate for the "Most Idiotic Musical of All Time" award. RK

Dennis O'Keefe *Danny Baldwin* • Constance Moore *Drina* • Eve Arden *Tex Donnelly* • Otto Kruger *Earl Carroll* • Alan Mowbray *Grand Duke*

Paul • Stephanie Bachelor *Claire Elliott* ■ *Dir* Joseph Santley • *Scr* Frank Gill Jr, from a story by Cortland Fitzsimmons

The Earl of Chicago ★★
Comedy drama 1940 · US · BW · 87min

Robert Montgomery stars as a Chicago gangster who inherits a title - and a castle! Accompanied by crooked lawyer Edward Arnold, he visits a very backlot England where he encounters butler Edmund Gwenn and solicitor Reginald Owen. Directed by MGM regular Richard Thorpe, who does what he can, this wasn't amusing then and sorely tries the patience now. TS

Robert Montgomery *"Silky" Kilmount* • Edward Arnold *"Doc" Ramsey* • Reginald Owen *Gervase Gonwell* • Edmund Gwenn *Munsey* • EE Clive *Redwood* • Norma Varden *Maureen Kilmount* • Halliwell Hobbes *Lord Chancellor* ■ *Dir* Richard Thorpe • *Scr* Lesser Samuels, from a story by Charles de Grandcourt, Gene Fowler, Brock Williams

The Early Bird ★★ U
Comedy 1965 · UK · Colour · 93min

Well past his movie sell-by date, Norman Wisdom is powerless to prevent this dreary dairy comedy from turning sour. The satirical jibes at large-scale automation are nowhere near sharp enough, while the tribute to Britain's fast-fading family firms is too twee. Regular straight men Jerry Desmonde and Edward Chapman are as solid as rocks and longtime director Robert Asher gives his star plenty of leeway. DP *DVD*

Norman Wisdom *Norman Pitkin* • Edward Chapman *Mr Grimsdale* • Jerry Desmonde *Hunter* • Paddie O'Neil *Mrs Hoskins* • Bryan Pringle *Austin* • Richard Vernon *Sir Roger* • John Le Mesurier *Colonel Foster* ■ *Dir* Robert Asher • *Scr* Jack Davies, Norman Wisdom, Eddie Leslie, Henry Blyth

An Early Frost ★★★★ 15
Drama 1985 · US · Colour · 96min

One of the first dramas on TV to tackle the subject of Aids, this is a poignant and powerful movie about a son who has to tell his parents he is both homosexual and has an Aids-related disease. Aidan Quinn gives a moving performance as the son, while Gena Rowlands and Ben Gazzara are superb as his mum and dad. Subsequent movies on the subject, such as *Philadelphia*, have lapsed into sentimentality, but director John Erman successfully manages to keep the schmaltz in check and produce a touching and effective film. JB

Aidan Quinn *Michael Pierson* • Gena Rowlands *Katherine Pierson* • Ben Gazzara *Nick Pierson* • Sylvia Sidney *Beatrice McKenna* • DW Moffett *Peter Hilton* • John Glover *Victor Dimato* • Sydney Walsh *Susan Maracek* ■ *Dir* John Erman • *Scr* Ron Cowen, Daniel Lipman, from a story by Sherman Yellen

Early Man
Animated comedy adventure 2018 · UK/Fr · Colour

This is a preview - no prints were available to review prior to publication: Nick Park hasn't directed a feature-length animation since the 2005's *Curse of the Were-Rabbit*. And what with the *Shaun the Sheep Movie* showing there's renewed creative vigour at Aardman, hopes are high that a feature set in cave-dwelling times will bring home the prehistoric bacon. The plot centres on a caveman called Dug and his pet boar Hognob, so there are echoes of the Wallace and Gromit double act. SvM

Eddie Redmayne *Dug* ■ *Dir* Nick Park • *Scr* Mark Burton, John O'Farrell

Early Spring ★★★★
Drama 1956 · Jpn · BW · 144min

Stylistically and thematically, the postwar films of Yasujiro Ozu are very much alike - even their titles (*Late Spring, Early Summer, Late Autumn*) are confusingly similar - yet each one is a gem. In this mature work, young clerk Ryo Ikebe finds temporary respite from the boredom of his job and his marriage in a brief affair with the firm's flirt. The characteristically slight plot, involving a

modern Japanese couple, unravels slowly with great formal beauty, economy, lucidity and humour. The outdoor scenes are limited to brief glimpses or to pauses in the action. RB Japanese +subtitles.

Chikage Awashima *Masako* • Ryo Ikebe *Sugiyama* • Keiko Kishi *"Goldfish"* • Chishu Ryu *Onodera* • So Yamamura *Kawai* • Haruko Sugimura *Masako's mother* • Kuniko Miyake *Sakae* • Eijiro Tono *Hattori* ■ *Dir* Yasujiro Ozu • *Scr* Yasujiro Ozu, Kogo Noda

Early Summer ★★★★
Drama 1951 · Jpn · BW · 150min

Few could manipulate screen space and time better than director Yasujiro Ozu. Precious little appears to happen in these two-and-a-half hours, yet they seem to fly by as the director's deceptively inobtrusive style draws you ever more deeply into the lives of Setsuko Hara and her family. As the devoted daughter who suddenly refuses to accept her ageing parents' choice of husband, Hara gives a wonderfully nuanced performance of quiet determination and dignity. But it's the way in which Ozu slowly accumulates detail and gently forces the characters to reveal themselves that makes this simple human drama so compelling. DP Japanese +subtitles. *DVD* *Blu-ray*

Setsuko Hara *Noriko* • Chishu Ryu *Koichi* • Kuniko Miyake *Fumiko* • Chikage Awashima *Aya Tamura* • Chieko Higashiyama *Shige* • Zen Murase *Minoru* • Ichiro Sugai *Shukichi* • Haruko Sugimura *Tami Yabe* ■ *Dir* Yasujiro Ozu • *Scr* Yasujiro Ozu, Kogo Noda

Earth ★★★★★ U
Silent drama 1930 · USSR · BW · 83min

Among the most moving films ever made, director Alexander Dovzhenko's hymn of praise to his native Ukraine comes as close as any silent picture to achieving cinematic poetry. Paced to match the gentle rhythms of nature, the story of the feud between a family of wealthy kulaks and some idealistic collective farmers has a pronounced political purpose. But it's primarily a celebration of the unending cycle of birth, love and death, hence the funeral of the murdered village chairman ending with a life-giving shower of summer rain. Combining lyrical beauty with simple truth, this is a masterpiece with a soul. DP

Stepan Shkurat *Opanas Trubenko* • Semyon Savshenko *Vasil Trubenko* • Pyotr Masokha *Khoma Belokon* • Mikola Nademski *Grandfather Semion Trubenko* • Nikolai Mikhailov *Father Gerasim* • Yelena Maksimova *Natalka* ■ *Dir/Scr* Alexander Dovzhenko

Earth ★★★ 15
Political romantic drama 1998 · Ind/Can · Colour · 101min

This is a disturbing depiction of Muslims, Hindus and Sikhs literally tearing each other apart. Considering the complexity of the political situation in late-1940s India, Deepa Mehta admirably delineates the rivalries, though it's only when independence is declared and Lahore erupts into sickening violence that the extent of these enmities becomes apparent. The plot is provocative, the acting committed, but dramatically it's something of a disappointment. DP English, Hindi +subtitles. Swearing. *DVD*

Maaia [Maia Sethna] *Lenny Sethna* • Nandita Das *Shanta (Lenny's ayah)* • Aamir Khan *Dil Nawaz (Ice Candy man)* • Rahul Khanna *Hasan (Masseur)* • Kulbhushan Kharbanda *Imam Din* • Kitu Gidwani *Bunty Sethna* ■ *Dir* Deepa Mehta • *Scr* Deepa Mehta, from the autobiography *Cracking India* by Bapsi Sidhwa

Earth ★★★★ PG
Wildlife documentary 2007 · UK/Ger · Colour · 94min

This feature-length version of the hit BBC TV series *Planet Earth* gives us a unique insight into the precarious balance of life on our planet. The production team set a new benchmark in nature documentaries, shooting thousands of hours of sumptuous high-definition footage across 26 countries over five years. Truly breathtaking sequences include frolicking polar bears emerging from hibernation, a herd of elephants fighting off a night attack by

lions, and colourful birds of paradise dancing in verdant rainforests. As a truncated companion to *Planet Earth*, which used the same footage, this is inevitably rather less epic in scope. However, Patrick Stewart's narration deftly holds the seemingly disparate sections together while underscoring a timely ecological warning. JR *DVD* *Blu-ray*

Patrick Stewart ■ *Dir* Alastair Fothergill, Mark Linfield • *Scr* Alastair Fothergill, Mark Linfield, Leslie Megahey

The Earth Dies Screaming ★ PG
Science fiction thriller 1964 · UK · BW · 61min

Great title, boring movie, even though it's only an hour long! Veteran horror director Terence Fisher hit the bottom of the alien-invasion barrel with the first in his off-Hammer sci-fi trilogy that continued with the better *Island of Terror* and *Night of the Big Heat*. Test pilot Willard Parker returns to England and finds the entire population wiped out by robots that kill by touch and then reanimate their victims as eyeless zombies. A dud. AJ *DVD*

Willard Parker *Jeff Nolan* • Virginia Field *Peggy Taggett* • Dennis Price *Quinn Taggett* • Vanda Godsell *Violet Courtland* ■ *Dir* Terence Fisher • *Scr* Henry Cross [Harry Spalding]

Earth Girls Are Easy ★★★★ PG
Musical satire 1988 · US · Colour · 100min

Three randy aliens (Jeff Goldblum, Jim Carrey and Damon Wayans) crash-land in LA and are given a guided tour through Planet Hollywood's craziness by two beautician Valley Girls in this enormously entertaining musical comedy. Geena Davis and Julie Brown are terrific in a popcorn movie that's full of bitchy one-liners and frothy fantasy. There's no attempt at a reality check in this hairsprayed *Lost in Space*, just breezy glitz, garish glamour and *Grease*-type songs in a trash setting. AJ *DVD*

Geena Davis *Valerie Dale* • Jeff Goldblum *Mac* • Jim Carrey *Wiploc* • Damon Wayans *Zebo* • Julie Brown *Candy Pink* • Charles Rocket *Ted* • Michael McKean *Woody* ■ *Dir* Julien Temple • *Scr* Julie Brown, Charlie Coffey, Terrence E McNally

Earth to Echo ★★★ PG
Science-fiction adventure 2014 · US · Colour · 87min

On the eve of eviction from their homes, three boys find their mobile phones picking up mysterious interference, which leads them to an otherworldly thingamajig that's the key to a hidden spaceship. But there's a sinister group of grown-ups after the alien gizmo, too. The special effects are decent, the pacing is fast and frantic, and it makes good use of the "found footage" approach. Aside from some heavy-handed philosophising about how distance doesn't dilute friendship, this is a superior junior sci-fi yarn. DA *DVD* *Blu-ray*

Teo Halm *Alex* • Brian "Astro" Bradley *Tuck* • Reece Hartwig *Munch* • Ella Wahlestedt *Emma* • Jason Gray-Stanford *Dr Lawrence Madsen* ■ *Dir* Dave Green • *Scr* Henry Gayden, from a story by Gayden, Andrew Panay

Earth vs the Flying Saucers ★★ U
Science-fiction fantasy 1956 · US · BW · 80min

Commendable only for special effects genius Ray Harryhausen's flying saucers trashing Washington DC's landmarks, this routine potboiler lifts most of its plot from HG Wells's *The War of the Worlds*. Hero scientist Hugh Marlowe, back in the nation's capital after surviving *The Day the Earth Stood Still*, slows down the plodding story even further by embarking on a sluggish romantic interlude with Joan Taylor. For serious Harryhausen freaks only. AJ *DVD*

Hugh Marlowe *Dr Russell A Marvin* • Joan Taylor *Carol Marvin* • Donald Curtis *Major Huglin* • Morris Ankrum *General Hanley* • John Zaremba *Professor Kanter* • Tom Browne Henry [Thomas Browne Henry] *Admiral Enright* • Grandon Rhodes *General Edmunds* • Larry Blake [Larry J

Blake] *Motorcycle officer* ■ *Dir* Fred F Sears • *Scr* George Worthing Yates, Raymond T Marcus [Bernard Gordon], from a story by Curt Siodmak, from the article *Flying Saucers from Outer Space* by Major Donald E Keyhoe

Earth vs the Spider ★ PG
Science-fiction horror 1958 · US · BW · 72min

A high-school biology teacher finds a "dead" giant spider and puts it in the gym. But when the local rock 'n' roll band starts practising for the prom, the mutation wakes up and rampages around town sucking the vital fluids from terrified teenagers. It sounds like trashy fun, and it is for about five minutes, then the dreadful special effects and awful performances lose their camp lustre. AJ *DVD*

Edward Kemmer *Mr Kingman* • June Kenny *Carol Flynn* • Gene Persson *Mike Simpson* • Gene Roth *Sheriff Cagle* • Hal Torey *Mr Simpson* • June Jocelyn *Mrs Flynn* ■ *Dir* Bert I Gordon • *Scr* Laszlo Gorog

Earth vs the Spider ★★ 15
Science-fiction horror
2001 · US · Colour · 86min

The 1958 sci-fi feature gets a passable TV-movie makeover in this tale of a wannabe superhero who mutates into a killer spider. Devon Gummersall plays the comic book obsessed security guard who injects himself with an experimental serum only to discover that his new-found superpowers run out of control. Dan Aykroyd gives a restrained performance as the cop on Gummersall's tail. The effects (from *Jurassic Park*'s Stan Winston) are better than the film deserves. JA Violence, swearing. *DVD*

Dan Aykroyd *Det Jack Grillo* • Theresa Russell *Trixie Grillo* • Devon Gummersall *Quentin Kemmer* • Amelia Heinle *Stephanie Lewis* • Christopher Cousins *Officer Williams* • Mario Roccuzzo *Nick Bezis* • John Cho *Han* ■ *Dir* Scott Ziehl • *Scr* Cary Solomon, Chuck Konzelman, Max Enscoe, Annie de Young, from a story by Mark "Crash" McCreary, Cary Solomon, Chuck Konzelman

The Earthling ★★ PG
Adventure drama 1980 · Aus · Colour · 96min

Terminally ill William Holden gives recently orphaned Ricky Schroder a crash course in life and survival techniques in the Australian outback. Overly sentimental, there is also an inordinate number of shots featuring cuddly koalas and loping kangaroos. Holden has an undeniable craggy charm, though Schroder isn't as cute as he could have been. AT

William Holden (2) *Patrick Foley* • Ricky Schroder [Rick Schroder] *Shawn Daley* • Jack Thompson *Ross Daley* • Olivia Hamnett *Bettina Daley* • Alwyn Kurts *Christian Neilson* • Redmond Phillips *Bobby Burns* ■ *Dir* Peter Collinson • *Scr* Lanny Cotler

Earthly Possessions ★★ 15
Drama 1999 · US · Colour · 98min

A trip to the local bank goes horribly wrong for preacher's wife Susan Sarandon when she's taken hostage by robber Stephen Dorff. Far from playing the victim, Sarandon manages to help Dorff escape and get his pregnant girlfriend Elisabeth Moss out of a home for unwed mothers. Sarandon does a great line in bored housewives, but her talents are smothered in this mediocre TV movie. LH *DVD*

Susan Sarandon *Charlotte Emery* • Stephen Dorff *Jake Simms Jr* • Jay O Sanders *Zack Emery* • Elisabeth Moss *Mindy* • Phoebe Lapine *Cheerleader No 1* • Anna Menken *Cheerleader No 2* ■ *Dir* James Lapine • *Scr* Steven Rogers, from the novel by Anne Tyler

Earthquake ★★★★ PG
Disaster movie 1974 · US · Colour · 117min

As usual in disaster movies, "the big one" hits Los Angeles at the worst possible moment for the cast in this highly enjoyable hokum. The first hour builds the tension with tremor suspense before the entire city is razed spectacularly to the ground; the dam-busting sequence inspired a Universal theme park favourite. Mark Robson's

extravaganza deservedly won a special achievement Oscar for best visual effects. An "8" on the entertainment Richter scale. AJ *DVD* *Blu-ray*

Charlton Heston *Stuart Graff* • Ava Gardner *Remy Graff* • George Kennedy *Lew Slade* • Lorne Greene *Sam Royce* • Geneviève Bujold *Denise Marshall* • Richard Roundtree *Miles Quade* • Marjoe Gortner *Jody* • Barry Sullivan *Dr Stockle* • Lloyd Nolan *Dr Vance* • Victoria Principal *Rosa* • Walter Matuschanskavasky [Walter Matthau] *Drunk* ■ *Dir* Mark Robson • *Scr* George Fox, Mario Puzo

Earthstorm ★
Disaster movie 2006 · US · Colour · 90min

There are echoes of *Armageddon* in this daft and cliché-riddled sci-fi thriller, in which Earth's future is threatened when a huge asteroid destabilises the Moon. Enter demolitions expert Stephen Baldwin, humanity's only salvation. B-movie lovers might get a kick out of some of the hilarious dialogue and implausible science, but few others will see a reason to bother. SF

Stephen Baldwin *John Redding* • Amy Price-Francis *Dr Lana Gale* • John Ralston *Dr Garth Pender* • Dirk Benedict *Victor Stevens* • Matt Gordon *Albert* • Anna Silk *Bryna* ■ *Dir* Terry Cunningham • *Scr* Michael Konyves

Easier with Practice ★★★ 15
Drama 2009 · US · Colour · 96min

This low-budget indie starts as a road movie, with Davy (*The Hurt Locker*'s Brian Geraghty) going on a cross-country reading tour in an attempt to flog his unpublished novel. But things take a sharp left turn when he receives an anonymous call from a mysterious *femme fatale*. The calls quickly become habit, opening the way for an unnerving and darkly amusing exploration of the fragile male ego. Director Kyle Patrick Alvarez keeps a cool distance, only zooming in when Davy is in the throes of passion with the unseen woman. Davy's real-life relationships with his brother (Kel O'Neill) and ex (Marguerite Moreau) aren't quite as involving as his telephone affair, and the finale veers into daytime chat-show territory. But this is still an engaging and moving tale. SP Swearing, sexual references. *DVD*

Brian Geraghty *Davy Mitchell* • Kel O'Neill *Sean Mitchell* • Marguerite Moreau *Samantha* • Jeanette Brox *Sarah* • Jenna Gavigan *Josie* • Kathryn Aselton *Nicole* ■ *Dir* Kyle Patrick Alvarez • *Scr* Kyle Patrick Alvarez, from the article *What Are You Wearing?* by Davy Rothbart

The East ★★★ 15
Thriller 2013 · US/UK · Colour · 111min

After their exceptional low-budget thriller *Sound of My Voice*, expectations were high for Zal Batmanglij and Brit Marling's second film. This tightly wound espionage eco-thriller is a more conventional affair, although it's just as well made. "The East" is a mysterious eco-collective that specialises in spectacular actions against enemies of the environment. Marling is a PI hired to infiltrate the group, but she finds herself drawn to Alexander Skarsgård for more than his politics. The love story feels a bit forced, but otherwise it's an intelligent examination of the dangers of both fanaticism and espionage. AS Violence, sex scenes, brief nudity, some swearing. *DVD*

Brit Marling *Sarah Moss* • Alexander Skarsgård *Benji* • Ellen Page *Izzy* • Toby Kebbell *Doc* • Shiloh Fernandez *Luca* • Julia Ormond *Paige Williams* • Patricia Clarkson *Sharon* ■ *Dir* Zal Batmanglij • *Scr* Zal Batmanglij, Brit Marling

East End Babylon ★★★ 18
Documentary
2012 · UK · Colour and BW · 100min

This is a rousing portrait of East End punks the Cockney Rejects. Brought up in Canning Town, teenage brothers Jeff and Mick Geggus had a sense of belonging that was key to their music. During the hectic years of the late 1970s and early 80s, the Rejects had hits with angry anthems like *The Greatest Cockney Rip Off* and *I'm Forever Blowing Bubbles*, but riotous gigs and right-wing associations undeservingly damaged their critical reputation. However, the

siblings recollect their heyday here with the same wit and realism that underpinned their dynamic and lastingly influential music. DP Violence, swearing. *DVD*

■ *Dir* Richard England

East Is East ★★★★ 15
Comedy drama 1999 · UK · Colour · 92min

This 1970s-set culture-clash comedy drama is thoroughly accessible and doesn't take itself too seriously as it follows the travails of a Pakistani dad, now married to an English woman, who is desperate that his teenage sons buckle under and accept arranged marriages. The boys, feeling "British" as opposed to "Asian", are resistant, and family wrangling ensues. This great little film is charming and refreshing. LH Swearing, violence. *DVD* *Blu-ray*

Om Puri *George Khan* • Linda Bassett *Ella Khan* • Jordan Routledge *Sajid Khan* • Archie Panjabi *Meenah Khan* • Emil Marwa *Maneer Khan* • Chris Bisson *Saleem Khan* • Jimi Mistry *Tariq Khan* • Raji James *Abdul Khan* ■ *Dir* Damien O'Donnell • *Scr* Ayub Khan-Din, from his play

East Lynne ★★★★
Melodrama 1931 · US · BW · 102min

One of the greatest Victorian melodramas becomes a surprisingly credible movie in the skilled hands of director Frank Lloyd, who has assembled an immaculate cast to bring conviction to a story that is, quite frankly, twaddle. Ann Harding is both beautiful and touching as the fallen woman struggling to regain her child, while Clive Brook and Conrad Nagel are both sturdy and excellent. Art director Joseph Urban's European re-creations on the backlot would be used again and again. TS

Ann Harding *Lady Isabella* • Clive Brook *Captain Levinson* • Conrad Nagel *Robert Carlyle* • Cecilia Loftus *Cornelia Carlyle* • Beryl Mercer *Joyce* • OP Heggie *Earl of Mount Severn* ■ *Dir* Frank Lloyd • *Scr* Bradley King, Tom Barry, from the novel by Mrs Henry Wood

East of Eden ★★★★ PG
Psychological drama 1955 · US · Colour · 112min

John Steinbeck's sprawling novel becomes a sprawling movie about two brothers vying for their father's love. It's Cain and Abel territory and the Biblical parallels are exploited well by Elia Kazan and writer Paul Osborn. The film has dated, but it's still worth seeing, for one main reason: James Dean's first starring role. Kazan was set on casting Marlon Brando, but when he met Dean – "a heap of twisted legs and denim rags, looking resentful for no particular reason" – he recognised the potential. AT *DVD* *Blu-ray*

James Dean (1) *Cal Trask* • Julie Harris (2) *Abra* • Raymond Massey *Adam Trask* • Jo Van Fleet *Kate Trask* • Burl Ives *Sheriff* • Richard Davalos *Aron Trask* • Albert Dekker *Will* • Lois Smith *Ann* • Harold Gordon *Albrecht* ■ *Dir* Elia Kazan • *Scr* Paul Osborn, from the novel by John Steinbeck

East of Elephant Rock ★★
Drama 1976 · UK · Colour · 92min

Judi Bowker guns down her lover in a jealous rage and pleads self-defence. Don Boyd's film is carried along by the momentum of a cracking story and an urge to see just how much lower it can descend. The Sri Lankan countryside, however, looks amazing. DP Some nudity.

John Hurt *Nash* • Jeremy Kemp *Harry Rawlins* • Judi Bowker *Eve Proudfoot* • Christopher Cazenove *Robert Proudfoot* • Anton Rodgers *Mackintosh* ■ *Dir* Don Boyd • *Scr* Don Boyd, from a story by Richard Boyle, James Atherton

East of Piccadilly ★★
Crime drama 1940 · UK · BW · 78min

This sordid murder mystery was an unusual offering to place before a country at war. Director Harold Huth paints a fascinating portrait of Soho in the late 1930s, but his handling of the whodunnit is much less assured. Red herrings abound as reporter Judy Campbell and crime writer Sebastian Shaw debate whether a waiter, an actor or

a Soviet spy is responsible for a series of murders. DP

Judy Campbell *Penny Sutton* • Sebastian Shaw *Tamsie Green* • Niall MacGinnis *Joe* • Henry Edwards *Inspector* • George Pughe *Oscar Juloff* • Martita Hunt *Ma* ■ *Dir* Harold Huth • *Scr* J Lee Thompson, Lesley Storym, from the novel by Gordon Beckles

East of Sudan ★★ U
Period adventure 1964 · UK · Colour · 84min

This lacklustre adventure is about a group who escape an outpost in the Sudan. The central characters are army regular Anthony Quayle and governess Sylvia Syms, and their relationship forms the subplot in this piece of hokum. Director Nathan Juran had the good sense to use British cameraman Wilkie Cooper on five films including this one and his contribution, in colour and Techniscope, enhances a rather dull movie. BB

Anthony Quayle *Richard Baker* • Sylvia Syms *Margaret Woodville* • Derek Fowlds *Murchison* • Jenny Agutter *Asua* • Johnny Sekka *Kimrasi* • Harold Coyne *Major Harris* ■ *Dir* Nathan Juran • *Scr* Jud Kinberg

East of Sumatra ★★ U
Action adventure 1953 · US · Colour · 81min

Set on the Pacific island of Tunga, this stars Jeff Chandler as a macho American mining engineer. Thanks to his boss John Sutton he soon falls foul of the island's ruler Anthony Quinn, whose alluring fiancée is played by actress Suzan Ball. Quinn and Ball also worked together on *City beneath the Sea* but the latter died tragically in 1955 of bone cancer. AT

Jeff Chandler *Duke Mullane* • Marilyn Maxwell *Lory Hale* • Anthony Quinn *Kiang* • Suzan Ball *Minyora* • John Sutton *Daniel Catlin* • Jay C Flippen *Mac* • Scatman Crothers *Baltimore* • Peter Graves (2) *Cowboy* ■ *Dir* Budd Boetticher • *Scr* Frank Gill Jr, Jack Natteford (adaptation), from a story by Louis L'Amour

East of the River ★★
Crime drama 1940 · US · BW · 73min

This is a lazy piece of backlot movie-making that did little for the burgeoning reputation of John Garfield. As the Italian-American wastrel, envious of adopted brother William Lundigan's looks and education, Garfield strikes a series of pseudo-Cagney poses as he struts around New York with his Mob buddies after a stretch at San Quentin prison. Things only begin to warm up when Lundigan pinches Garfield's girl, Brenda Marshall. DP

John Garfield *Joe Lorenzo* • Brenda Marshall *Laurie Romayne* • Marjorie Rambeau *Mama Teresa Lorenzo* • George Tobias *Tony* • William Lundigan *Nick Lorenzo* • Moroni Olsen *Judge Davis* ■ *Dir* Alfred E Green • *Scr* Fred Niblo Jr, from a story by John Fante, Ross B Willis

East Side of Heaven ★★★ U
Musical comedy 1939 · US · BW · 87min

Dripping in sentimentality, but nonetheless sweet-natured, this comedy marks the debut of 10-month-old Baby Sandy, a girl here cast as a boy (who would know!) who went on to become the star of her own series of movies. In this one, though, she is the excuse for star Bing Crosby to croon a handful of songs as a singing cab driver, saddled with the care of an abandoned baby. RK

Bing Crosby *Denny Martin* • Joan Blondell *Mary Wilson* • Mischa Auer *Nicky* • Irene Hervey *Mona* • Jerome Cowan *Claudius De Wolfe* • Robert Kent *Cyrus Barrett Jr* • C Aubrey Smith *Cyrus Barrett Sr* ■ *Dir* David Butler • *Scr* William Conselman, from a story by David Butler, Herbert Polesie

East Side, West Side ★★
Drama 1949 · US · BW · 107min

James Mason is married to Barbara Stanwyck, but unable to resist playing away with Ava Gardner. Stanwyck, meanwhile, does her best to be all saintly and forgive him, while war veteran Van Heflin offers her all the comfort he can muster. Smoothly performed by the appealing cast and smothered in Miklos Rozsa's syrupy music, this overcooked melodrama is an old-time soap opera. AT

Barbara Stanwyck *Jessie Bourne* • James Mason *Brandon Bourne* • Van Heflin *Mark Dwyer* • Ava Gardner *Isabel Lorrison* • Cyd Charisse *Rosa Senta* • Nancy Davis *Helen Lee* • Gale Sondergaard *Nora Kernan* • William Conrad *Lieutenant Jacobi* ■ *Dir* Mervyn LeRoy • *Scr* Isobel Lennart, from the novel by Marcia Davenport

East-West ★★★ 12
Period romantic drama
1999 • Fr/Rus/Sp/Bul • Colour • 119min

Régis Wargnier's Oscar-nominated period piece not only sheds light on a little-known episode in Soviet history, but also provides plenty of satisfyingly dramatic incident. The teaming of Oleg Menshikov and Sandrine Bonnaire is crucial, as they provide the emotional core of this stark exposé of the conditions that greet a White Russian exile and his French wife on accepting Stalin's duplicitous postwar amnesty. However, the secondary characters are also well delineated, particularly Catherine Deneuve's touring stage diva. DP French, Russian +subtitles. *DVD*

Sandrine Bonnaire *Marie* • Catherine Deneuve *Gabrielle Develay* • Oleg Menshikov *Alexei Golovin* • Sergei Bodrov Jr *Sasha* • Ruben Tapiero *Seryozha aged 7* • Erwan Baynaud *Seryozha aged 14* • Grigori Manukov *Pirogov* • Tatyana Dogilova *Olga* ■ *Dir* Régis Wargnier • *Scr* Régis Wargnier, Sergei Bodrov, Rustam Ibragimbekov, Louis Gardel

Easter Parade ★★★★★ U
Classic musical   1948 • US • Colour • 98min

Originally intended as a re-teaming of Judy Garland and Gene Kelly under Vincente Minnelli's direction after *The Pirate*, this turned out to be one of MGM's great seasonal delights. Producer Arthur Freed coaxed Fred Astaire out of retirement when Kelly broke his ankle, and entrusted the direction to the brilliant craftsman Charles Walters, and the result was simply wonderful. Aided by terrific Irving Berlin songs and radiant Technicolor design – all browns and greens – Astaire, Garland and Walters made an all-time classic, with Fred and Judy particularly outstanding in the perennial favourite *A Couple of Swells*. The screenplay is witty, co-star Ann Miller dances up a storm, and this is the one opportunity to enjoy the talents of Astaire and Garland on screen together. TS *DVD*

Judy Garland *Hannah Brown* • Fred Astaire *Don Hewes* • Peter Lawford *Jonathan Harrow III* • Ann Miller *Nadine Hale* • Jules Munshin *François* • Clinton Sundberg *Mike, the bartender* • Jeni LeGon *Essie* ■ *Dir* Charles Walters • *Scr* Frances Goodrich, Albert Hackett, Sidney Sheldon, Guy Bolton, from a story by Frances Goodrich, Albert Hackett • *Cinematographer* Harry Stradling • *Art Directors* Cedric Gibbons, Jack Martin Smith • *Music/lyrics* Irving Berlin

Eastern Boys ★★★★ 15
Drama   2012 • Fr • Colour • 129min

The term "melodrama" is rarely used as a compliment, but Robin Campillo goes some way to reclaiming it here. Well-heeled Parisian 50-something Olivier Rabourdin shows reckless naivety in picking up Ukrainian rent boy Kirill Emelyanov at the Gare du Nord. The boy and a gang of Russian thugs strip his plush apartment bare, but the story takes a twist when the pair do keep a date and the boy's illegal status becomes a threat to their hesitant romance. Campillo exposes the chasms between classes, races and generations with acerbic skill, but also coaxes superb performances from his leads. DP French, English, Russian +subtitles.

Olivier Rabourdin *Daniel* • Kirill Emelyanov *Marek/Rouslan* • Daniil Vorobyev [Danill Vorobyov] *Boss* • Edéa Darque *Chelsea* • Bislan Yakhiaev *Bislan* ■ *Dir/Scr* Robin Campillo • *Cinematographer* Jeanne Lapoirie

Eastern Promises ★★★★ 18
Thriller   2007 • UK/Can/US • Colour • 96min

Director David Cronenberg continues the exploration of violence and identity he started in his previous film *A History of*

Violence in this similarly gripping gangster thriller set among Russian mobsters in London. Anna (Naomi Watts) is a midwife whose attempt to track down the identity of a teenager who dies in childbirth leads her into the violent underworld of people-smuggling among the capital's Russian immigrant population. Viggo Mortensen is excellent as a Mob driver who babysits his temperamental boss (Vincent Cassel), while Armin Mueller-Stahl is suitably threatening asthe gang's leader. Production values are also high – Howard Shore provides the dramatic score and cinematographer Peter Suschitzky renders an atmospherically grimy view of London. Look out for a quite astonishingly staged fight scene in a Turkish baths. AS English, Russian +subtitles. Violence, swearing, a sex scene, nudity. *DVD*

Viggo Mortensen *Nikolai Luzhin* • Naomi Watts *Anna Khitrova* • Vincent Cassel *Kirill* • Armin Mueller-Stahl *Semyon* • Sinead Cusack *Helen* • Donald Sumpter *Yuri* • Jerzy Skolimowski *Stepan Khitrov* ■ *Dir* David Cronenberg • *Scr* Steve Knight [Steven Knight] • *Cinematographer* Peter Suschitzky • *Music* Howard Shore

Easy A ★★★★ 15
Comedy   2010 • US • Colour • 88min

Emma Stone delivers star-making charisma in this teen comedy as an anonymous high school student who becomes the centre of attention when her invented stories of sexual encounters start doing the rounds. There are stellar supporting contributions from Stanley Tucci and Patricia Clarkson as Stone's groovy parents, and Malcolm McDowell and Lisa Kudrow as members of the school staff. A deft, witty and sympathetic tale of adolescent confusions, this bravely references *The Scarlet Letter* and John Hughes teen pics of the 1980s – and gets away with it. TJ Sexual references. *DVD*

Emma Stone *Olive Penderghast* • Penn Badgley *Woodchuck Todd* • Amanda Bynes *Marianne* • Thomas Haden Church *Mr Griffith* • Patricia Clarkson *Rosemary Penderghast* • Cam Gigandet *Micah* • Lisa Kudrow *Mrs Griffith* • Malcolm McDowell *Principal Gibbons* • Stanley Tucci *Dill Penderghast* ■ *Dir* Will Gluck • *Scr* Bert V Royal

Easy Come, Easy Go ★★ U
Musical adventure   1967 • US • Colour • 90min

One of the weakest of Elvis Presley's later Paramount vehicles, this is almost as embarrassing for audiences as it clearly is for Elvis himself, dealing both with stupid and intractable material about finding lost treasure, and demeaning songs like *Yoga Is as Yoga Does*. The humour is feeble and invariably tasteless (anti-beatnik jokes in the 1960s?) and it's tough to watch Elsa Lanchester used as a figure of fun. The garish Technicolor just about makes this watchable. TS *DVD*

Elvis Presley *Ted Jackson* • Dodie Marshall *Jo Symington* • Elsa Lanchester *Madame Neherina* • Pat Priest *Dina Bishop* • Pat Harrington *Judd Whitman* • Skip Ward *Gil Carey* • Sandy Kenyon *Lt Schwartz* • Frank McHugh *Captain Jack* ■ *Dir* John Rich • *Scr* Allan Weiss, Anthony Lawrence

The Easy Life ★★★★
Drama   1962 • It • BW • 105min

Writer/director Dino Risi established himself as one of the most scathing critics of Italian complacency during the economic boom of the late 1950s. He was at his sharpest with this tragicomedy, in which cynical waster Vittorio Gassman sets about corrupting idealistic student Jean-Louis Trintignant. Risi gets the most out of his exceptional cast during Trintignant's meeting with Gassman's daughter, Catherine Spaak. DP Italian +subtitles.

Vittorio Gassman *Bruno Cortona* • Jean-Louis Trintignant *Roberto Mariani* • Catherine Spaak *Lilly, Bruno's daughter* • Luciana Angiolillo *Bruno's wife* • Linda Sini *Aunt Lidia* • Corrado Olmi *Alfredo* ■ *Dir* Dino Risi • *Scr* Dino Risi, Ettore Scola, Ruggero Maccari

Easy Living ★★★★ 15
Screwball comedy   1937 • US • BW • 87min

This is a smashing slapstick comedy, due mainly to the cracking script by Preston Sturges. The story is simple: a fur coat thrown out of a window gets stenographer Jean Arthur mistaken for a millionaire's mistress, leading to all sorts of misunderstandings. Arthur shows what a gifted comedian she was, coping beautifully with the wisecracks and pratfalls. Edward Arnold and Ray Milland also give spot-on performances, and there's a spectacular update on the old custard pie fight set in a New York automat. AT *DVD*

Jean Arthur *Mary Smith* • Edward Arnold *JB Ball* • Ray Milland *John Ball Jr* • Luis Alberni *Mr Louis Louis* • Mary Nash *Mrs Ball* • Franklin Pangborn *Van Buren* • William Demarest *Wallace Whistling* ■ *Dir* Mitchell Leisen • *Scr* Preston Sturges

Easy Living ★★★ PG
Romantic drama   1949 • US • BW • 76min

Based on an Irwin Shaw story, this tale of a retiring football player worried about his pension is smart, sassy and very satisfying. Victor Mature is cleverly cast as the New York Chiefs' ex-star halfback, and he gets terrific support from Lizabeth Scott as his overspending spouse and Lucille Ball as the team secretary who has the hots for him. Talented Jacques Tourneur makes this work far better than anyone could expect. TS

Victor Mature *Pete Wilson* • Lucille Ball *Anne* • Lizabeth Scott *Liza Wilson* • Sonny Tufts *Tim McCarr* • Lloyd Nolan *Lenahan* • Paul Stewart *Argus* • Jack Paar *"Scoop" Spooner* • Jeff Donnell *Penny McCarr* ■ *Dir* Jacques Tourneur • *Scr* Charles Schnee, from the story *Education of the Heart* by Irwin Shaw

Easy Money ★★ U
Portmanteau comedy drama
1947 • UK • BW • 89min

This portmanteau picture is based partly on a play by Arnold Ridley about four characters who dream of winning the pools in the era of postwar austerity, when thousands lived in hope of a windfall. Frankly, none of the tales is particularly original and the ones involving crooked Dennis Price and meek Mervyn Johns are decidedly ropey. But Edward Rigby's generosity towards his beloved band and the arguments that divide Jack Warner's family are rather neatly played. DP

Greta Gynt *Pat Parsons* • Jack Warner *Phillip Stafford* • Marjorie Fielding *Ruth Stafford* • Yvonne Owen *Carol Stafford* • Jack Watling *Dennis Stafford* • Petula Clark *Jackie Stafford* • Mabel Constanduros *Grandma* • Mervyn Johns *Herbert Atkins* • Joan Young *Agnes Atkins* • Dennis Price *Joe Henty* • Bill Owen *Mr Lee* ■ *Dir* Bernard Knowles • *Scr* Muriel Box, Sydney Box, from the play by Arnold Ridley (first story)

Easy Money ★★ 15
Comedy   1983 • US • Colour • 95min

The quick-fire vulgarity of Rodney Dangerfield isn't to everyone's taste, but even doubters will find to difficult to stifle the odd chuckle at this cheerfully crude comedy. The plot bears more than a passing resemblance to *Brewster's Millions*: slob-about-town Dangerfield has a year to clean up his act or face forfeiting millions from an inheritance. Joe Pesci scores in an early comic outing, and look out for Jennifer Jason Leigh in a small supporting role. JF

Rodney Dangerfield *Monty* • Joe Pesci *Nicky* • Geraldine Fitzgerald *Mrs Monahan* • Candy Azzara *Rose* • Taylor Negron *Julio* • Val Avery *Louie* • Jeffrey Jones *Clive* • Tom Ewell *Scrappleton* • Jennifer Jason Leigh *Allison* ■ *Dir* James Signorelli • *Scr* Rodney Dangerfield, Michael Endler, PJ O'Rourke, Dennis Blair

Easy Money ★★★★ 15
Crime thriller
2010 • Swe/Den/Ger/Nor/ Fr • Colour • 119min

This deftly plotted morality tale stars Joel Kinnaman as a Stockholm economics student who affects the persona of a high-flying jet-setter while living in digs and

driving an unlicensed cab. The bungled pick-up of an escaped Chilean drug dealer opens his eyes to the possibilities of organised crime, but Serbian hitman Dragomir Mrsic is soon closing in. As coolly atmospheric as the best in Scandi-drama, *Easy Money* matches every thrilling gunfight and tense drug deal with an insight into the humanity of its protagonists. AC Swedish, Serbian, Spanish, English, German +subtitles. Violence, swearing, drug abuse. *DVD* *BD*

Joel Kinnaman *Johan "JW" Westlund* • Matias Padin Varela *Jorge* • Dragomir Mrsic *Mrado* • Lisa Henni *Sophie* • Dejan Cukic *Radovan* ■ *Dir* Daniel Espinosa • *Scr* Maria Karlsson, Daniel Espinosa, Hassan Loo Sattarvandi, Fredrik Wikstrom, from the novel *Snabba Cash* by Jens Lapidus

Easy Money II ★★★★ 15
Crime thriller
2012 • Swe/Can/Ger • Colour • 96min

Joel Kinnaman once again plays social-climbing JW, and we pick up his story as he leaves prison only to discover that he's been swindled by his business partner on the outside, forcing him back into a life of crime. Remarkably, new director/co-writer Babak Najafi keeps up the energy of the original and juggles interlocking cross/double-cross plotlines with skill, while the rogue's gallery of supporting cast members lends the film an abrasive edge. SvM Swedish, Spanish, English, Serbian, Arabic, Croatian +subtitles. Violence, swearing, drug abuse *DVD* *BD*

Joel Kinnaman *Johan "JW" Westlund* • Matias Varela [Matias Padin Varela] *Jorge* • Dragomir Mrsic *Mrado* • Fares Fares *Mahmoud* ■ *Dir* Babak Najafi • *Scr* Maria Karlsson, Fredrik Wikstro°m Nicastro [Fredrik Wikstrom], Peter Birro, Babak Najafi, from the novels *Snabba cash, Aldrig fucka upp* by Jens Lapidus

Easy Money III: Life Deluxe ★★★★ 18
Crime thriller   2013 • Swe • Colour • 122min

Stockholm business studies whizz turned drug dealer Joel Kinnaman, who did time in the second film in this complex, steel-edged Swedish crime trilogy, is detrimentally sidelined here, while his likeable Chilean partner-in-crime Matias Varela dominates, planning the classic, heart-pounding one-last-heist. Under the slick direction of TV-schooled Jens Jonsson and with some surprising, sun-kissed excursions beyond Scandinavia, it's a suitably tense, bloody tale, tying up of strands whose emotional relationships are as key as the macho gunplay, swearing and Mafia-style philosophising. Anyone following the whole story will come away shocked and satisfied. AC Swedish, Spanish, English, Croatian, Arabic+subtitles. Violence, swearing *DVD* *BD*

Matias Varela [Matias Padin Varela] *Jorge Salinas Barrio* • Joel Kinnaman *Johan "JW" Westlund* • Martin Wallstrom *Martin Hägerström* ■ *Dir* Jens Jonsson • *Scr* Jens Jonsson, Maria Karlsson, from a story by Jonsson, Fredrik Wikström, from the novel *Livet Deluxe* by Jens Lapidus

LANDMARK FILM
Forces Hollywood to re-think its budgets, subject matter and audience

Easy Rider ★★★★★ 18
Cult road movie   1969 • US • Colour • 91min

As laid-back as the machines straddled by Dennis Hopper and Peter Fonda in their search for "the real America", and as hip as a whole drop-out generation, this magical mystery tour of the US has a casual conviction that outstrips Hopper's own on-the-run direction to touch a mythic nerve. Jack Nicholson's boozy lawyer successfully articulates the yearning of the alienated young. That the film ends in sullen and sudden death raises it to the power of allegory, and its success proved there was an audience and a need that the box-office pundits didn't even know existed. The studios tried desperately to repeat its low-budget magic, but couldn't. It just didn't equate with the usual Hollywood formula; it had created its own. TH Sex scenes, drug abuse, brief nudity. *DVD* *BL*

Peter Fonda *Wyatt/"Captain America"* • Dennis Hopper *Billy* • Jack Nicholson *George Hanson* • Phil Spector *Connection* • Antonio Mendoza *Jesus* • Warren Finnerty *Rancher* • Tita Colorado *Rancher's wife* • Robert Walker Jr *Jack* • Keith Green *Sheriff* • Toni Basil *Mary* • Karen Black *Karen* ■ *Dir* Dennis Hopper • *Scr* Dennis Hopper, Peter Fonda, Terry Southern • *Cinematographer* Laszlo Kovacs

Easy Riders, Raging Bulls ★★★ 15

Documentary 2003 • US/UK/Can • Colour • 113min

Based on Peter Biskind's bestseller and narrated by William H Macy, this is a solid survey of that brief golden age between the studio and blockbuster eras, when Hollywood permitted its auteurs to make films for adults that reflected the social, moral and political crises affecting America. Stripping away Biskind's penchant for gossip, Kenneth Bowser concentrates on the movies and the people who made them. He largely has to settle for archival contributions from such big guns as Francis Ford Coppola and Martin Scorsese, although the likes of Dennis Hopper and Peter Bogdanovich offer plenty of insights. DP *DVD*

William H Macy *Narrator* • Martin Scorsese • Francis Ford Coppola • Dennis Hopper • Peter Bogdanovich ■ *Dir* Kenneth Bowser • *Scr* Kenneth Bowser, from the non-fiction book by Peter Biskind

Easy to Love ★★★ U

Musical 1953 • US • Colour • 95min

There's not too much plot and few memorable songs (except for the Cole Porter title classic), but stunning Esther Williams needs no such help. This MGM musical is a perfectly constructed vehicle for the swimming star whose bossy, no-nonsense screen personality is well suited to this Florida-set satire on advertising. Lovers of high camp will cherish ace choreographer Busby Berkeley's contribution to the water ballets, stacking bodies upon water-skis with perfect symmetry. TS

Esther Williams *Julie Hallerton* • Van Johnson *Ray Lloyd* • Tony Martin (1) *Barry Gordon* • John Bromfield *Hank* • Edna Skinner *Nancy Parmel* • King Donovan *Ben* • Paul Bryar *Mr Barnes* • Carroll Baker *Clarice* ■ *Dir* Charles Walters • *Scr* Laslo Vadnay, William Roberts, from a story by Laslo Vadnay

Easy to Wed ★★★

Musical 1946 • US • Colour • 110min

Although it lacked the star power of the original, MGM could have no complaints about the performances in this remake of its 1936 screwball classic, *Libeled Lady*. Keenan Wynn is no substitute for Spencer Tracy, but he barks admirably as the editor who sends reporter Van Johnson to charm heiress Esther Williams out of a suit against their paper. The leads can't match the chemistry of William Powell and Myrna Loy, but they still look good together, while Lucille Ball, in one of her breakthrough roles, is every bit as sparky as Jean Harlow. DP

Van Johnson *Bill Stevens Chandler* • Esther Williams *Connie Allenbury* • Lucille Ball *Gladys Benton* • Keenan Wynn *Warren Haggerty* • Cecil Kellaway *JB Allenbury* • June Lockhart *Babs Norvell* ■ *Dir* Edward Buzzell • *Scr* Dorothy Kingsley, from the film *Libeled Lady* by Maurine Watkins, Howard Emmett Rodgers, George Oppenheimer

Easy Virtue ★★★ U

Silent drama 1927 • UK • BW • 80min

This early Alfred Hitchcock film sees him still developing his distinctive style. This is an adaptation of Noël Coward's play about a charming divorcee (Isabel Jeans) with a scandal in her past, who marries into a staid provincial family with predictable results. It's well scripted by Eliot Stannard, and captures the essence of the play even without Coward's witty dialogue. In one of the best scenes, when the hero is proposing

to the heroine over the telephone, Hitch cuts away from them and cleverly shows only the reactions on the face of the telephone operator. RB *DVD*

Isabel Jeans *Larita Filton* • Robin Irvine *John Whittaker* • Franklin Dyall *Mr Filton* • Enid Stamp-Taylor *Sarah* • Violet Farebrother *Mrs Whittaker* • Darcia Deane *Marion Whittaker* ■ *Dir* Alfred Hitchcock • *Scr* Eliot Stannard, from the play by Noël Coward

Easy Virtue ★★★ PG

Romantic comedy 2008 • UK/US • Colour • 92min

This elegant 1920s-set romantic comedy is loosely based on one of Noël Coward's less well-known plays that was first brought to the screen by Alfred Hitchcock in 1927. This version from director Stephan Elliott (*The Adventures of Priscilla, Queen of the Desert*) stars Ben Barnes as a naive young man who horrifies his upper-class mother (Kristin Scott Thomas) by returning from France with a wife (Jessica Biel) who's not only a racing driver but also (and even worse, it seems) an American. Meanwhile, his father (played by Colin Firth) seems to have other matters on his mind. The adaptation is witty and stylish, and there's a welcome dark undercurrent that offsets the more sugary moments. DA *DVD*

Jessica Biel *Larita* • Colin Firth *Mr Whittaker* • Kristin Scott Thomas *Mrs Whittaker* • Ben Barnes *John Whittaker* • Kris Marshall *Furber* • Kimberley Nixon *Hilda Whittaker* • Katherine Parkinson *Marion Whittaker* • Pip Torrens *Lord Hurst* • Christian Brassington *Phillip* • Charlotte Riley *Sarah* ■ *Dir* Stephan Elliott • *Scr* Stephan Elliott, Sheridan Jobbins, from the play by Noël Coward

Eat a Bowl of Tea ★★★ 15

Comedy drama 1989 • US • Colour • 98min

In his early films, Wayne Wang was more interested in the behaviour of his characters in specific cultural and social situations than he was in exploring their motives and emotions. While this made his work intriguing, it often lacked depth. Here the period atmosphere enhances a story about Chinese immigrants in postwar America, but again, beneath the layers of detail and quirky characterisation, there is scant substance. As a result this is engaging, but ultimately unsatisfying. DP English, Mandarin +subtitles.

Victor Wong (2) *Wah Gay* • Russell Wong *Ben Loy* • Cora Miao *Mei Oi* • Eric Chi Wai Tsang [Eric Tsang] *Ah Song* • Lau Siu-Ming *Lee Gong* • Wu Ming Yu *Mei Oi's mother* • Hui Fuan *Ben Loy's mother* ■ *Dir* Wayne Wang • *Scr* Judith Rascoe, from the novel by Louis Chu

Eat and Run ★★★ 15

Science-fiction comedy 1986 • US • Colour • 80min

This spoof on the "creature features" of the 1950s revolves around a king-sized alien whose favourite discovery on Earth turns out to be Italian food. Devouring an Italian sausage maker helps his appetite on its way, though it soon brings Irish cop Ron Silver on his trail. Certain humorous interludes are just too slack to hit home, but Silver, a much underused actor, acquits himself well at the centre of this amiable nonsense. JM *DVD*

Ron Silver *Mickey McSorely* • Sharon Schlarth *Judge Cheryl Cohen* • RL Ryan *Murray Creature* • John F Fleming *Police captain* • Derek Murcott *Sorely McSorely* • Robert Silver *Pusher* ■ *Dir* Christopher Hart • *Scr* Stan Hart, Christopher Hart

Eat Drink Man Woman ★★★★ PG

Comedy drama 1994 • Tai • Colour • 119min

Although the prime influence on Taiwanese director Ang Lee's stately style and several of the film's themes is the Japanese genius Yasujiro Ozu, there is more than a hint of Woody Allen in this complex ensemble comedy. The action flits between the problems facing each member of master chef Lung Sihung's family, and the performances are light and believable, while

the dialogue is full of wit and wisdom. DP Mandarin +subtitles.

Lung Sihung *Mr Chu* • Wang Yu-wen *Jia-ning* • Wu Chien-lien *Jia-chien* • Yang Kuei-Mei *Jia-jen* • Sylvia Chang *Jin-rong* • Winston Chao *Li Kai* • Chen Chao-jung *Guo Lun* ■ *Dir* Ang Lee • *Scr* Ang Lee, Wang Hui-ling, James Schamus

Eat My Dust! ★

Comedy action adventure 1976 • US • Colour • 88min

Charles B Griffith, the prolific writer of Roger Corman's best movies, turned director with this inept car crash comedy starring the famous Howard family of Ron, father Rance and brother Clint. Nothing more than a patchy excuse to destroy automobiles, trucks, boats and buildings on the cheap in a frantic demolition derby, while dumb cops and grease monkey Ron Howard's romantic interest look on in bemusement. AJ

Ron Howard *Hoover Niebold* • Chrissie Norris *Darlene* • Warren Kemmerling *Sheriff Harry Niebold* • Dave Madden *Big Bubba Jones* • Robert Broyles *Bud* • Evelyn Russel *Delores* • Rance Howard *Deputy Clark* • Clint Howard *Georgie* ■ *Dir/Scr* Charles B Griffith

Eat Pray Love ★★ 15

Biographical drama 2010 • US • Colour • 134min

This frilly but vivid travelogue, based on Elizabeth Gilbert's bestselling memoirs, is directed with verve by Ryan Murphy (creator of TV's *Glee*). It stars Julia Roberts as an American woman who abandons a failing marriage and impoverished love affair to spend a year eating in Italy, praying in India and loving in Bali. If you can swallow the guff about "Quest Physics" and the journey to "internal truth" you may find enlightenment in a true-life Mills & Boon romance with added guilt-free carbs. AC Brief swearing. *DVD* *BL*

Julia Roberts *Elizabeth "Liz" Gilbert* • James Franco *David Piccolo* • Javier Bardem *Felipe* • Billy Crudup *Stephen* • Richard Jenkins *Richard from Texas* • Viola Davis *Delia Shiraz* ■ *Dir* Ryan Murphy • *Scr* Ryan Murphy, Jennifer Salt, from memoirs by Elizabeth Gilbert

Eat the Peach ★★★ PG

Comedy drama 1986 • Ire • Colour • 91min

Armed with a true story, a tight budget and a video of the Elvis Presley vehicle *Roustabout*, director Peter Ormrod comes up with an engaging film whose main fault is its determination to be offbeat. As the jobless duo who set out to build a "Wall of Death", Stephen Brennan and Eamon Morrissey have a likeable loopiness. DP

Eamon Morrissey *Arthur* • Stephen Brennan *Vinnie Galvin* • Catherine Byrne *Nora Galvin* • Niall Toibin *Boots* • Joe Lynch *Boss Murtagh* • Tony Doyle *Sean Murtagh* • Takashi Kawahara *Bunzo* • Victoria Armstrong *Vicky Galvin* ■ *Dir* Peter Ormrod • *Scr* Peter Ormrod, John Kelleher, from an idea by Peter Ormrod

Eat the Rich ★★ 15

Comedy 1987 • UK • Colour • 84min

When a waiter loses his job at trendy London restaurant Bastards, he plots with a band of revolutionaries to put its customers on the menu. Peter Richardson's film is more of a student prank than a subversive satire. Of the main performers, Nosher Powell is memorable as a Home Secretary who behaves like a Kray brother. However, the movie's main fascination lies in its array of cameos, from Paul McCartney and Bill Wyman to Koo Stark and French and Saunders. AT

Lanah Pellay *Alex* • Nosher Powell *Nosher* • Fiona Richmond *Fiona* • Ronald Allen *Commander Fortune* • Lemmy *Spider* • Robbie Coltrane *Jeremy* • Kathy Burke *Kathy* • Miles Copeland *Derek* • Adrian Edmondson *Charles* • Dawn French *Debbie Draws* • Jools Holland *"Sun" Reporter* • Rik Mayall *Micky* • Shane McGowan *Terrorist* • Nigel Planer *DHSS manager* • Miranda Richardson *DHSS blonde* • Jennifer Saunders *Lady Caroline* • Sandie Shaw *Edgeley's girlfriend* • Koo Stark *Hazel* • Ruby Wax *Bibi de Coutts* • Bill Wyman *Toilet victim* • Paul McCartney ■ *Dir* Peter Richardson • *Scr* Peter Richens, Peter Richardson

Eaten Alive ★★ 18

Horror thriller 1976 • US • Colour • 81min

Tobe Hooper's little-seen follow-up to his seminal *Texas Chain Saw Massacre* is a heavily stylised tale that incorporates the shock value of the EC horror comics of the 1950s. Neville Brand stars as the psychopathic proprietor of a run-down hotel who feeds guests to his pet crocodile. While the film is perhaps guilty of perpetuating the myth that all backwoods yokels are a couple of strings short of a banjo, the goofy plot and impressive production design win the day. RS *DVD*

Neville Brand *Judd* • Mel Ferrer *Harvey Wood* • Carolyn Jones *Miss Hattie* • Marilyn Burns *Faye* • William Finley *Roy* • Stuart Whitman *Sheriff Martin* • Robert Englund *Buck* ■ *Dir* Tobe Hooper • *Scr* Alvin L Fast, Mardi Rustam, Kim Henkel

Eating ★★★

Comedy drama 1990 • US • Colour • 110min

A group of women talk about food and life at a birthday party, yet, fascinating though the interchanges and revelations are, they don't merit 110 minutes. The performances, however, are sparkling, with birthday girls Mary Crosby (30), Lisa Richards (40) and Marlena Giovi (50) revelling in a script exploring the ways in which women view food as both a comfort and a scourge. This is very much an ensemble piece, but mouthy Frances Bergen, mousy Daphna Kastner and bitchy Gwen Welles do stand out. DP

Lisa Richards *Helene* • Mary Crosby *Kate* • Marlena Giovi *Sadie* • Gwen Welles *Sophie* • Nelly Alard *Martine* • Frances Bergen *Mrs Williams* • Daphna Kastner *Jennifer* • Elizabeth Kemp *Nancy* • Rachelle Carson *Cathy* • Toni Basil *Jackie* • Marina Gregory *Lydia* ■ *Dir/Scr* Henry Jaglom

Eating Raoul ★★★★ 18

Black comedy 1982 • US • Colour • 79min

Paul and Mary Bland (brilliantly portrayed by director Paul Bartel and actress Mary Woronov) finance their dream restaurant by advertising for wealthy swingers and then killing them off during sex for their cash. Handyman Robert Beltran muscles in on the action by selling the bodies to a dog food factory. A cute black comedy, hilariously sending up California culture and executed with sadistic glee by all concerned. Bartel turned his cult sleeper into an off-Broadway musical in 1992. AJ *DVD*

Paul Bartel (1) *Paul Bland* • Mary Woronov *Mary Bland* • Robert Beltran *Raoul* • Susana Saiger *Doris the Dominatrix* • Ed Begley Jr *Hippy* • Dan Barrows *Bobbie R* • Richard Blackburn *James* • Ralph Brannen *Paco* • Buck Henry *Mr Leech* ■ *Dir* Paul Bartel (1) • *Scr* Paul Bartel, Richard Blackburn

L'Eau Froide ★★★★

Drama 1994 • Fr • Colour • 92min

This is a frank yet tender insight into troubled adolescence from director Olivier Assayas. Virginie Ledoyen gives a heart-rending performance as the mentally fragile product of a broken home who goes on the run with short-fused Parisian schoolboy Cyprien Fouquet after her father puts her in an institution. Shot with energy and authenticity, yet without condescension, the film not only captures the anxiety of youth, but also the feel of the early 1970s. DP French +subtitles.

Virginie Ledoyen *Christine* • Cyprien Fouquet *Gilles* • Laszlo Szabo *Gilles's father* • Jean-Pierre Darroussin *Inspector* • Dominique Faysse *Christine's mother* • Smail Mekki *Mourad* • Jackie Berroyer *Christine's father* ■ *Dir/Scr* Olivier Assayas

Eaux d'Artifice ★★★★ U

Experimental fantasy 1953 • US • Tinted • 12min

Having been frustrated in his attempts to direct again following the acclaim for *Fireworks* (1947), Kenneth Anger finally completed this elegiac companion piece in 1953. Part of the Magick Lantern Cycle and inspired by the ending to Ronald Firbank's novel, *Valmouth*, this baroque fantasy features the diminutive and fabulously dressed Carmillo Salvatorelli wandering through an ornate Italian garden to the strains of Vivaldi. The use of gargoyles, grottoes, staircases and fountains makes this a formally fascinating film, whose atmosphere is further enhanced by an inky blue tint that makes the play of light on water all the more mesmerising. DP

Carmillo Salvatorelli *Water Witch* ■ *Dir/Scr* Kenneth Anger • *Cinematographer* Kenneth Anger

Ebirah, Horror of the Deep ★★Ⓤ

Horror 1966 · Jpn · Colour · 83min

Or *Godzilla versus the Sea Monster*, as it was known everywhere else. In his sixth screen outing, the king of the monsters and his one-time arch enemy, Mothra, hiss and make up to battle the evil giant lobster Ebirah, being used as a p(r)awn by the nasty Red Bamboo gang seeking world domination. Typical Japanese monster fare featuring cardboard mayhem, laughable special effects and failed comedy sees Godzilla play football. Total trash? Naturally. Absolutely unmissable? Of course. AJ Japanese dubbed.

Akira Takarada *Yoshimura* • Toru Watanabe *Ryota Kane* • Hideo Sunazuka *Nita* • Kumi Mizuno *Daiyo* • Jun Tazaki *Red Bamboo commander* ■ *Dir* Jun Fukuda • *Scr* Shinichi Sekizawa

Eccentricities of a Blonde-Haired Girl ★★★★Ⓤ

Romantic drama 2009 · Por/Sp/Fr · Colour · 60min

Portuguese film-maker Manoel de Oliveira's career spans the silent and digital age; he celebrated his 101st birthday shortly before the release of this refined adaptation. Echoes of Luis Buñuel and Claude Chabrol abound as de Oliveira cuts between a train conversation involving Ricardo Trepa and Leonor Silveira, and the events that laid Trepa low. He is smitten with demure blonde Catarina Wallenstein, but his desperation to prove himself worthy lures him into some shady dealings. Luminously photographed by Sabine Lancelin, this is both deliciously old-fashioned and wittily wise in its satirical insights into our recessional times. DP Portuguese +subtitles. *DVD*

Ricardo Trepa *Macario* • Catarina Wallenstein *Luisa* • Diogo Doria *Francisco* • Leonor Silveira *Senhora* ■ *Dir* Manoel de Oliveira • *Scr* Manoel de Oliveira, from a short story by Eca de Queiros

Echo of Diana ★★Ⓤ

Spy drama 1963 · UK · BW · 61min

In this low-budget spy drama, the newshound leads are two Australian actors, Vincent Ball and Betty McDowall, which makes a refreshing change from the usual fading Hollywood stars. Their noses for a story begin to twitch when a mysterious death puts them on the track of one of the most alfresco covert operations you are ever likely to clap eyes on. Director Ernest Morris does well to sustain it for an hour. DP

Vincent Ball *Bill Vernon* • Betty McDowall *Joan Scott* • Geoffrey Toone *Colonel Justin* • Clare Owen *Pam Jennings* • Peter Illing *Kovali* ■ *Dir* Ernest Morris • *Scr* Reginald Hearne

Echo Park ★★★15

Comedy drama 1985 · Aus/US · Colour · 85min

This story of a trio of losers – Susan Dey as the aspiring actress reduced to working in a sleazy bar, Tom Hulce as a song-writing pizza boy and Michael Bowen body building himself up to disappointment – has moments of real truth and affection. As a study in human relationships it doesn't exactly resound with insight, but it almost – but not quite – reminds us of *Jules et Jim*. TH Swearing, sexual references. *DVD*

Tom Hulce *Jonathan* • Susan Dey *May* • Michael Bowen *August* • Christopher Walker *Henry Greer* • Shirley Jo Finney *Gloria* • Heinrich Schweiger *August's father* • Richard "Cheech" Marin *Syd* • John Paragon *Hugo* ■ *Dir* Robert Dornhelm • *Scr* Michael Ventura

Echo Park LA ★★★15

Coming-of-age drama 2005 · US · Colour · 86min

This touching rites-of-passage drama has undoubted charm, despite the shortcomings in its storytelling. Magdalena (Emily Rios) is a young Mexican-American girl whose 15th birthday festivities are thrown into turmoil when she reveals she is pregnant – without, she claims, having had sex. Banished by her ultra-religious father, Magdalena goes to live with her great-uncle Tomas. A heavy-handed gay subplot briefly skews the story's direction, but when the closing credits roll all that really matters is the young cast's passion and vivacity; shame we couldn't see more of it. DW Spanish, English +subtitles. Swearing, sexual references, drug abuse. *DVD*

Emily Rios *Magdalena* • Jesse Garcia *Carlos* • Chalo Gonzalez *Uncle Tomas* • JR Cruz *Herman* • Araceli Guzmán-Rico *Maria* • Jesus Castaños-Chima *Ernesto* • David W Ross *Gary* ■ *Dir/Scr* Richard Glatzer, Wash Westmoreland

Echoes of a Summer ★

Drama 1976 · US/Can · Colour · 99min

Jodie Foster assaults the tear ducts by playing a 12-year-old with a terminal heart condition. Facing certain death with startling courage, she makes life a little easier for her parents, played by Lois Nettleton and Richard Harris. Foster, who looks more like a boy than a girl in some scenes, is an odd blend of natural talent and applied emotion, although her love affair with Brad Savage is yucky. AT

Richard Harris *Eugene Striden* • Lois Nettleton *Ruth Striden* • Geraldine Fitzgerald *Sara* • William Windom *Doctor Halett* • Brad Savage *Phillip Anding* • Jodie Foster *Deirdre Striden* ■ *Dir* Don Taylor • *Scr* Robert L Joseph

The Eclipse ★★★★PG

Romantic drama 1962 · Fr/It · BW · 120min

This troubling, stylised film completed director Michelangelo Antonioni's "alienation trilogy". As in *L'Avventura* and *La Notte*, Monica Vitti is at the centre of events, here ending a passionless affair with the bookish Francisco Rabal to indulge in a fling with her mother's stockbroker, Alain Delon. Returning to his recurrent themes of the desensitising impact of urban life and the hopelessness of love, Antonioni presents his bleakest portrait of the modern age, with the famous seven-minute, 58-shot montage of cold, impersonal buildings symbolising the city's final victory over its inhabitants. DP Italian +subtitles. *DVD* *BL*

Monica Vitti *Vittoria* • Alain Delon *Piero* • Lilla Brignone *Vittoria's mother* • Francisco Rabal *Riccardo* • Louis Seignier *Ercoli* • Rossana Rory *Anita* • Mirella Riccia-di *Marta* ■ *Dir* Michelangelo Antonioni • *Scr* Michelangelo Antonioni, Tonino Guerra, Elio Bartoloni, Ottiero Ottieri

Eclipse ★★★★12

Romantic horror fantasy 2010 · US · Colour · 113min

There's more teen angst with a twist in this lively third instalment of the hit *Twilight* series, and the pressure is mounting on moody Bella (Kristen Stewart) to make a fangs-or-fur choice between vampire boyfriend Edward (Robert Pattinson) and werewolf boyfriend Jacob (Taylor Lautner). British director David Slade (*30 Days of Night*) balances the blend of action and romance far better than the directors of the two previous movies. And although *Eclipse* remains primarily for dedicated "Twihards", it's still easily accessible to series newcomers. A further instalment, *Breaking Dawn*, is being released in two parts in 2011 and 2012. DA Some violence. *DVD* *BL*

Kristen Stewart *Bella Swan* • Robert Pattinson *Edward Cullen* • Taylor Lautner *Jacob Black* • Bryce Dallas Howard *Victoria* • Billy Burke *Charlie Swan* • Dakota Fanning *Jane* • Ashley Greene *Alice Cullen* • Peter Facinelli *Dr Carlisle Cullen* • Nikki Reed *Rosalie Hale* ■ *Dir* David Slade • *Scr* Melissa Rosenberg, from the novel *Eclipse* by Stephenie Meyer

Ecoute le Temps ★★★12

Mystery crime drama 2005 · Fr · Colour · 95min

Voices from the past help solve a mystery in the present in writer/director Alanté Kavaïté's debut feature. Emilie Dequenne stars as a sound recordist who puts her equipment to distinctly unconventional use after her mother (Ludmila Mikaël) is murdered. Returning to her mother's crumbling farmhouse in the French countryside, she discovers that her microphones are inexplicably picking up sounds from the past. Set in an autumnal landscape populated by menacing townsfolk, this chiller evokes an unsettling feeling of unease and the central idea is ingenious and inherently creepy. But the film's supernatural sheen actually hides some disappointingly mundane secrets. JR French +subtitles. *DVD*

Emilie Dequenne *Charlotte* • Ludmila Mikaël *Charlotte's mother* • Mathieu Demy *Julien* • Jacques Spiesser *Charlotte's father* • Etienne Chicot *Monsieur Bourmel* • Eva Ionesco *Madame Bourmel* ■ *Dir/Scr* Alanté Kavaïté

Ecoute Voir... ★★★

Crime drama 1978 · Fr · Colour · 110min

Argentinian director Hugo Santiago is renowned for his rather strange political commentaries, and this film is no exception. The gracious Catherine Deneuve stars as a private detective hired to investigate and expose a sinister cult. Her trail leads to a mansion house in the middle of nowhere, where the group is attempting to interrupt radio waves with subliminal propaganda. Atmospheric and stylishly shot, the film's moodiness is compounded by a great soundtrack. LH French +subtitles.

Catherine Deneuve *Claude Alphand* • Sami Frey *Arnaud* • Anne Parillaud *Chole* • Florence Delay *Flora* • Antoine Vitez *Sect man* • Didier Haudepin *Secretary* ■ *Dir* Hugo Santiago • *Scr* Hugo Santiago, Claude Ollier

LANDMARK FILM
Hedy Lamarr outrages the censor with her scandalous nudity and sensuality – a first in a widely distributed film

Ecstasy ★★★★

Drama 1933 · Cz · BW · 68min

It's difficult to separate this Czech film from the furore it created at the time; it was banned outright in Germany and cut to ribbons by the rest of the world. However, it was shown intact privately all over Hollywood, where its star – the young Hedy Kiesler – would be imported and renamed Hedy Lamarr, becoming one of Tinseltown's loveliest love goddesses. And the reason for the furore: a famous sequence where Hedy is swimming in the nude and then runs starkers through the woods. In another, she discovers and demonstrates sexual pleasure in extreme close-up. Director Gustav Machaty creates a wonderful mood, and the overall (uncut) movie is one of cinema's great sensual masterpieces. TS Czech +subtitles.

Hedy Kiesler [Hedy Lamarr] *Eva* • Jaromir Rogoz *Emile* • Aribert Mog *Adam* • Leopold Kramer *Eva's father* ■ *Dir* Gustav Machaty • *Scr* Gustav Machaty, Franz Horky, Vitezslav Nezval, Jacques A Koerpel

The Ecstasy of Wilko Johnson ★★★★★15

Documentary 2015 · UK · Colour · 92min

In January 2013, 64-year-old guitarist Wilko Johnson, formerly of Canvey Island pub rock pioneers Dr Feelgood, was diagnosed with pancreatic cancer. Refusing chemotherapy, he embraced the clarity brought by his imminent demise and announced a farewell tour. Partisan director Julien Temple, whose documentaries have captured the Sex Pistols, Joe Strummer and Dr Feelgood (*Oil City Confidential*), employs his usual expressionistic blending of interview and archive to create a film both esoteric and down-to-earth. This incredible, personal story about an inspirational, no-nonsense figure resonates far beyond the music scene it also thrillingly depicts. AC Violence, swearing.

Wilko Johnson • Roger Daltrey ■ *Dir/Scr* Julien Temple

Ed ★PG

Sports comedy 1996 · US · Colour · 90min

Even the struggling actor Matt LeBlanc portrays in hit series *Friends* would have passed on this dim-witted family comedy, in which the star plays second fiddle to an ape. The Ed of the title is the chimpanzee mascot of a struggling baseball team who becomes the star player and helps LeBlanc out of his pitching slump. The primate gets the best lines – and all he does is grunt and shriek. JF

Matt LeBlanc *Jack Cooper* • Jayne Brook *Lydia* • Jack Warden *Chubb* • Bill Cobbs *Tippet* ■ *Dir* Bill Couturie • *Scr* David Mickey Evans, from a story by Janus Cercone, Ken Richards

Ed Gein ★★15

Biographical horror 2000 · US · Colour · 85min

In what is claimed to be the definitive true-life story of the Wisconsin farmer-turned-cannibal killer, whose 1957 case inspired a host of horror movies, director Chuck Parello has gone for simple storytelling rather than grit and gore. He delivers so many "spooky neighbour" clichés and shows so little of Gein's crimes that he never even scratches the surface of explaining what made the man actually tick. Steve Railsback in the title role has no depth or range, while the sporadic special effects are poor. SF *DVD*

Steve Railsback *Ed Gein* • Carrie Snodgress *Augusta Gein* • Sally Champlin *Mary Hogan* • Steve Blackwood *Eleanor* • Pat Skipper *Sheriff Jim Stillwell* ■ *Dir* Chuck Parello [Charles Parello] • *Scr* Stephen Johnston

Ed Wood ★★★★★15

Biographical drama 1994 · US · BW · 121min

Only one of cinema's finest directors could have so lovingly crafted this homage to one of its worst. Tim Burton's wonderful celebration of awful art, and the fascination it continues to exert, traces the weird career of Edward D Wood Jr, from his autobiographical exploitation quickie *Glen or Glenda* to his "masterpiece", the truly terrible *Plan 9 from Outer Space*. Johnny Depp is amazing as director Wood in Burton's black-and-white evocation of 1950s life in Grade Z-land, and Martin Landau deservedly won an Oscar for his uncanny impersonation of Wood's low-rent inspiration, Bela Lugosi. AJ Swearing, drug abuse. *DVD* *BL*

Johnny Depp *Ed Wood* • Martin Landau *Bela Lugosi* • Sarah Jessica Parker *Dolores Fuller* • Patricia Arquette *Kathy O'Hara* • Jeffrey Jones *Criswell* • GD Spradlin *Reverend Lemon* • Vincent D'Onofrio *Orson Welles* • Bill Murray *John "Bunny" Breckinridge* • Mike Starr *Georgie Weiss* ■ *Dir* Tim Burton • *Scr* Scott Alexander, Larry Karaszewski, from the book *Nightmare of Ecstasy* by Rudolph Grey

Eddie ★★★12

Sports comedy drama 1996 · US · Colour · 96min

The newly appointed basketball coach for the legendary New York Knicks is both an obsessive fan and a woman (motormouth Whoopi Goldberg). The Knicks' actual team doesn't appear, by the way, but the screen side does comprise various real-life hoop heroes. Not bad of its kind, with Goldberg taking no nonsense from the NBA stars, and there are also some stimulating slam-dunk sequences. JC Swearing.

Whoopi Goldberg *Edwina "Eddie" Franklin* • Frank Langella *Wild Bill Burgess* • Dennis Farina *Coach Bailey* • Richard Jenkins *Assistant Coach Zimmer* • Lisa Ann Walter *Claudine* • John Benjamin Hickey *Joe Nader* • Troy Beyer *Beth Hastings* ■ *Dir* Steve Rash • *Scr* John Connolly, David Loucka, Eric Champnella, Keith Mitchell, Steve Zacharias, Jeff Buhai, from a story by John Connolly, David Loucka, Steve Zacharias, Jeff Buhai

Eddie and the Cruisers ★★ PG

Drama 1983 · US · Colour · 91min

This intriguing if not completely successful spin on the rock movie provided an early platform for two actors on the verge of stardom. Tom Berenger plays a musician who, along with journalist Ellen Barkin, sets out to uncover the mystery behind the demise of his band Eddie and the Cruisers, the archetypal one-hit wonders who fell apart when the lead singer abruptly vanished. This sidesteps some of the more obvious rock clichés, but it falls apart near the end and, sadly, the music isn't very memorable. JF

Tom Berenger *Frank Ridgeway* • Michael Paré *Eddie Wilson* • Joe Pantoliano *Sal Amato* • Matthew Laurance *Sal Amato* • Helen Schneider *Joann Carlino* • David Wilson *Kenny Hopkins* • Michael "Tunes" Antunes *Wendell Newton* • Ellen Barkin *Maggie Foley* ■ *Dir* Martin Davidson • *Scr* Martin Davidson, Arlene Davidson, from the novel by PF Kluge

Eddie and the Cruisers II: Eddie Lives! ★★ PG

Drama 1989 · US/Can · Colour · 99min

The 1983 original was a big video hit, so this belated, cliché-ridden sequel brings Eddie (Michael Paré) back from the dead - or at least back from the blue-collar identity he's been hiding behind since his supposed fatal accident. Once again, Eddie's music has become popular and his cynical record company smells a money-making cash-in. JF

Michael Paré *Eddie Wilson/Joe West* • Marina Orsini *Diane* • Bernie Coulson *Rick* • Matthew Laurance *Sal* • Michael Rhoades *Dave Pagent* • Larry King • Bo Diddley • Martha Quinn *Music video hostess* ■ *Dir* Jean-Claude Lord • *Scr* Charles Zev Cohen, Rick Doehring, from characters by PF Kluge

The Eddie Cantor Story ★★ U

Biographical musical 1953 · US · Colour · 116min

The tale of how Israel Iskowitz, a poor Jewish boy from the Lower East Side of New York, became the rich and famous Hollywood star Eddie Cantor, has all the usual rags-to-riches ingredients and successfully invokes the atmosphere of vaudeville where Eddie started out as an entertainer. A number of his best songs (*If You Knew Susie*, *Making Whoopee*) are included, too, but the lack of a star personality, allied to a weak script, makes for an unengaging showbiz biopic. RK

Keefe Brasselle *Eddie Cantor* • Marilyn Erskine *Ida* • Aline MacMahon *Grandma Esther* • Arthur Franz *Harry Harris* • Alex Gerry *David Tobias* • Greta Granstedt *Rachel Tobias* • Gerald Mohr *Rocky* • William Forrest *Ziegfeld* ■ *Dir* Alfred E Green • *Scr* Sidney Skolsky, Ted Sherdeman, Jerome Weidman, from Skolsky's story

Eddie Macon's Run ★★ 15

Action crime drama 1983 · US · Colour · 90min

This uncomfortable late Kirk Douglas flick gives second billing to John Schneider, one of the stars of *The Dukes of Hazzard*. Like that TV show, this is little more than a prolonged celluloid chase, with a fair amount of crashes and smashes. Douglas shouldn't've been doing this kind of stuff at this stage of his career, but John Goodman does makes his movie debut here. TS

Kirk Douglas *Marzack* • John Schneider *Eddie Macon* • Lee Purcell *Jilly Buck* • Leah Ayres *Chris* • Lisa Dunsheath *Kay Potts* • Tom Noonan *Daryl Potts* • John Goodman *Hebert* ■ *Dir* Jeff Kanew • *Scr* Jeff Kanew, from the novel by James McLendon

Eddie Murphy Raw ★★ 18

Comedy concert 1987 · US · Colour · 86min

This overlong and poorly shot concert film of Eddie Murphy's one-man show is for die-hard fans only. Murphy may be a phenomenon as a movie star, but his stand-up routine leaves much to be desired - a foul-mouthed concoction trading on racial and sexual stereotypes that effortlessly offends majority tastes. His frenetic energy

and delivery are impressive, though, and his comic imitation of Bill Cosby is inspired. Watch for the uproarious fictional prologue set in a 1960s Murphy household. RS DVD

Eddie Murphy • Tatyana Ali *Singing child* • Billie Allen *Eddie's aunt* • Clebert Ford *Uncle Lester* • Geri Gibson *Second card player* • Samuel L Jackson *Eddie's uncle* ■ *Dir* Robert Townsend • *Scr* Eddie Murphy, Keenen Ivory Wayans

Eddie the Eagle ★★★★★ PG

Sports drama based on a true story
2016 · UK/US/Ger · Colour · 101min

They don't come any more crowd-pleasing than this quintessential underdog fable outlining the trials and tribulations of heroic failure Eddie "The Eagle" Edwards, who became an accidental ski-jumping record holder at the 1988 Calgary Winter Olympics. A terrific triumph over adversity tale told with deft assurance, energetic visuals and sharp observation, director Dexter Fletcher's rousing heart-warmer has you rooting for the lovable loser from frame one, while Taron Egerton in the title role gives this disarming biopic mass appeal. AJ Brief swearing. DVD BD

Taron Egerton *Michael "Eddie" Edwards* • Hugh Jackman *Bronson Peary* • Tim McInnerny *Target* • Jo Hartley *Janette* • Jim Broadbent *BBC commentator* • Christopher Walken *Warren Sharp* ■ *Dir* Dexter Fletcher • *Scr* Simon Kelton, Sean Macaulay

The Eddy Duchin Story ★★★★ U

Biographical drama 1956 · US · Colour · 117min

This is a deeply satisfying weepie, filmed in CinemaScope, about the New York society pianist struck down by leukaemia in his prime. Though the actual illness isn't named, the scenes in which Duchin, sympathetically portrayed by a mature Tyrone Power, takes leave of his son (Rex Thompson) are unbearably moving. This is a film strong on romance, and Power's relationship with the lovely Kim Novak is superbly orchestrated by director George Sidney against New York locations in autumnal colours. TS DVD

Tyrone Power *Eddy Duchin* • Kim Novak *Marjorie Oelrichs* • Victoria Shaw *Chiquita* • James Whitmore *Lou Sherwood* • Rex Thompson *Peter Duchin as a boy* • Shepperd Strudwick *Mr Wadsworth* • Frieda Inescort *Mrs Wadsworth* • Gloria Holden *Mrs Duchin* • Gregory Gaye *Philip* ■ *Dir* George Sidney (2) • *Scr* Samuel Taylor, from a story by Leo Katcher

Eden ★★★ 15

Crime drama based on a true story
2012 · US · Colour · 110min

Inspired by a real-life ordeal, this well-intentioned drama attempts to expose the hideous truths of the sex-trafficking industry. Director Megan Griffiths and her co-writer Richard B Phillips concentrate on the ingenuity and self-denial that enable a Korean-American teenager (played by Jamie Chung) to cope after she is abducted from a New Mexico bar. Staged with admirable restraint, the film is provocative without being prurient, but its credibility is strained towards the end. DP Violence, swearing, sexual references, drug abuse. DVD BD

Jamie Chung *Hyun Jae, "Eden"* • Matt O'Leary *Vaughan* • Beau Bridges *Bob Gault* • Scott Mechlowicz *Jesse* • Naama Kates *Svetlana* ■ *Dir* Megan Griffiths • *Scr* Megan Griffiths, Rick Phillips Jr, from a story by Chong Kim, Phillips Jr

Eden ★★★ 15

Biographical drama 2014 · Fr · Colour · 125min

A calm yet compulsive period piece about the "French touch" house music of the 1990s, *Eden* takes us on an experiential tour of the scene via its privileged protagonist Paul (Félix de Givry) who is at the heart of the movement. French film-maker Mia Hansen-Løve uses the experiences of her own brother Sven (who co-wrote the script) as a template for Paul, following him as he evolves from a fan in 1992 to an in-demand DJ. A soundtrack of 40 chosen tunes and sideline looks at Daft Punk's genesis makes Hansen-Løve's assured fourth feature a

heady trip for all ex-ravers. KK In French, English.

Félix de Givry *Paul Vallée* • Pauline Etienne *Louise* • Vincent Macaigne *Arnaud* • Hugo Conzelmann *Stan* ■ *Dir* Mia Hansen-Løve • *Scr* Mia Hansen-Løve, Sven Hansen-Løve • *Cinematographer* Denis Lenoir

Eden Lake ★★★ 18

Horror thriller 2008 · UK/Cay · Colour · 87min

This debut feature from director James Watkins gives a distinctively British twist to the staple American horror plot of a couple wandering off into the woods and falling foul of a bunch of crazies. Set fairly and squarely in Middle England, the movie pits Michael Fassbender and Kelly Reilly not against backwoods throwbacks but feral kids from a nearby town who violently interrupt the pair's camping weekend. A film about teen violence and youths with knives is bound to attract controversy, and many will deplore the film's graphic gore, especially in such a near-the-knuckle context. Fright fans, though, will applaud this fresh take on a hoary old horror plot. DA Violence. DVD

Kelly Reilly *Jenny* • Michael Fassbender *Steve* • Jack O'Connell (2) *Brett* • Thomas Turgoose *Cooper* • Tara Ellis *Abi* • Finn Atkins *Paige* ■ *Dir/Scr* James Watkins

Eden Valley ★★★ 15

Drama 1994 · UK · Colour · 40min

A slow, lyrical, almost impressionistic effort by the Amber film collective, this features famous harness racing family the Laidlers. You either find these working-class denizens of the North East fascinating, or you don't. Most of us uneasily straddle the two camps, one of which says that the work of Amber and its ilk is vital in keeping alive the drama and tension of dying ways of life, while the other says it is like watching paint dry, complete with impenetrable accents. SH

Brian Hogg *Hoggy* • Darren Bell *Billy* • Mike Elliot *Danker* • Jimmy Killeen *Probation officer* • Wayne Buck *Young lad* • Kevin Buck *Young lad* ■ *Dir/Scr* Richard Grassick, Ellen Hare, Sirkka Liisa Konttinen, Murray Martin, Pat McCarthy, Lorna Powell, Pete Roberts

The Edge ★★★ 15

Action adventure 1997 · US · Colour · 112min

A mediocre survival story is turned into an eminently watchable action adventure by the performances of Anthony Hopkins and Alec Baldwin. Hopkins plays a billionaire who suspects fashion photographer Baldwin covets his beautiful young wife (Elle Macpherson). When their plane crashes in the Alaskan wilderness, the rivals must learn to depend on each other to survive. This is enhanced by David Mamet's hard-boiled dialogue and Donald M McAlpine's awesome camerawork. TH DVD

Anthony Hopkins *Charles Morse* • Alec Baldwin *Robert Green* • Elle Macpherson *Mickey Morse* • Harold Perrineau *Stephen* • LQ Jones *Styles* • Kathleen Wilhoite *Ginny* ■ *Dir* Lee Tamahori • *Scr* David Mamet

Edge of Darkness ★★★ PG

Second World War drama
1943 · US · BW · 114min

This impressively grim Warner Bros war movie about the Norwegian Resistance features a stellar cast headed up by unlikely Scandinavians Errol Flynn, Ann Sheridan and Walter Huston. Flynn acquits himself well, and the film is expertly directed by veteran Lewis Milestone and superbly photographed by Sid Hickox. There's also fine support work, and this is stirring stuff, overtly propagandist when it was made but still pretty potent today. TS

Errol Flynn *Gunnar Brogge* • Ann Sheridan *Karen Stensgard* • Walter Huston *Dr Martin Stensgard* • Nancy Coleman *Katja* • Helmut Dantine *Captain Koenig* • Judith Anderson *Gerd Bjarnesen* • Ruth Gordon *Anna Stensgard* • John Beal *Johann Stensgard* • Morris Carnovsky *Sixtus Andresen* ■ *Dir* Lewis Milestone • *Scr* Robert Rossen, from the novel by William Woods

Edge of Darkness ★★★ 15

Conspiracy thriller
2009 · US/UK · Colour · 111min

Mel Gibson takes on the role first played so brilliantly by Bob Peck in this remake of the BBC's 1985 mini-series. He plays Thomas Craven, a detective whose adult daughter is shockingly, and inexplicably, gunned down on his doorstep. Craven's subsequent investigation sees him drawn into a terrifying conspiracy. The series is one of the undoubted high points of British TV drama, and fans are likely to be disappointed by the transposition to the big screen. Some of the plot's complexity and atmosphere are inevitably lost with the reduced running time, but Gibson is on good form and Martin Campbell (who also directed the original production) stages some effective action set pieces. AS Violence, swearing. DVD BD

Mel Gibson *Thomas Craven* • Ray Winstone *Darius Jedburgh* • Danny Huston *Jack Bennett* • Bojana Novakovic *Emma Craven* • Shawn Roberts *David Burnham* • David Aaron Baker *Millroy* • Jay O Sanders *Whitehouse* ■ *Dir* Martin Campbell • *Scr* Andrew Bovell, William Monahan, from the 1985 BBC TV series by Troy Kennedy Martin

Edge of Doom ★★ PG

Drama 1950 · US · BW · 93min

This is one of those "street punk" dramas that John Garfield used to swallow whole. Unfortunately, all Farley Granger can manage in the way of torment are a few scowls and sulks as he tries to prevent kindly priest Dana Andrews from discovering that he's guilty of murdering the cleric who denied his mother a decent funeral. Mark Robson's inconsistent direction is disappointing. DP

Dana Andrews *Father Roth* • Farley Granger *Martin Lynn* • Joan Evans *Rita Conroy* • Robert Keith (1) *Det Mandel* • Paul Stewart *Craig* • Mala Powers *Julie* ■ *Dir* Mark Robson • *Scr* Philip Yordan, from a novel by Leo Brady

The Edge of Dreaming ★★★

Documentary 2010 · UK · Colour · 73min

Amy Hardie's highly personal documentary traces her response to two dreams. On the first occasion, she dreams that her horse will die, and the animal promptly expires. That's spooky enough, but her subsequent vision sees her warned by her late former partner that she'll be dead within the year, which is followed by a very real slide into ill-health. Initially, Hardie's film risks seeming self-indulgent or inconsequential, yet the power of dreams to fill our waking hours with dread is a powerful subject matter. It may all work towards a resolution that seems a little too pat, but the reaction of Hardie and her family to the prospect of her mortality comes across as affecting and genuine. TJ

■ *Dir* Amy Hardie

Edge of Eternity ★★★ U

Western 1959 · US · Colour · 79min

This moderately exciting modern-day western has lawman Cornel Wilde pursuing murderer Mickey Shaughnessy towards the Grand Canyon and a cable-car climax. The overall effect is marred only by some cheap back projection that jars against the footage of the real thing. *Dirty Harry* director Don Siegel does wonders with the low budget and his short schedule, but even he can't get a performance out of Victoria Shaw. TS

Cornel Wilde *Les Martin* • Victoria Shaw *Janice Kendon* • Mickey Shaughnessy *Scotty O'Brien* • Edgar Buchanan *Sheriff Edwards* • Rian Garrick *Bob Kendon* • Jack Elam *Bill Ward* ■ *Dir* Donald Siegel [Don Siegel] • *Scr* Knut Swenson [Marion Hargrove], Richard Collins, from a story by Ben Markson, Knut Swenson [Marion Hargrove]

The Edge of Heaven ★★★★ 15

Drama 2007 · Ger/Tur/It · Colour · 115min

The winner of the best screenplay prize at Cannes, Fatih Akin's outstanding ensemble drama about the capriciousness of existence consistently recalls the great melodramas of Rainer Werner Fassbinder. It's no accident, then, that Fassbinder's muse Hanna Schygulla should feature so prominently here. She plays a German mother, who becomes involved in securing the release of Nurgul Yesilcay, the lesbian lover of her student daughter (Patrycia Ziolkowska), from a Turkish jail. Revelling in the coincidences of life and the contrasts between diametrically opposed cultures, Akin judges the tone and pace to perfection, while preventing the consciously contrived storylines from lapsing into soap operatics. DP Turkish, German, English +subtitles. *DVD*

Baki Davrak *Nejat Aksu* • Tuncel Kurtiz *Ali Aksu* • Nursel Kose *Yeter Ozturk* • Nurgul Yesilcay *Ayten Ozturk* • Hanna Schygulla *Susanne Staub* • Patrycia Ziolkowska *Lotte Staub* ■ *Dir/Scr* Fatih Akin

The Edge of Love ★★★ 15

Period drama based on a true story
2008 · UK · Colour · 106min

This emotionally charged drama loosely based on real events stars Keira Knightley as Vera, the childhood sweetheart of poet Dylan Thomas (Matthew Rhys), and tells the story of what happens when she runs into her married ex-lover in war-torn London. Thomas and his wife Caitlin (Sienna Miller) end up moving in with Vera – now working as a nightclub singer – but it soon becomes evident that three's a crowd. The situation doesn't improve when Vera marries her soldier boy lover (Cillian Murphy) on the eve of his posting overseas, and Thomas and the two women move to rural Wales. Director John Maybury's intense story of two women caught in the orbit of a remarkable man has its shortcomings, but it looks wonderful and contains a particularly effective performance from Knightley (who does her own singing). KK Swearing. *DVD*

Keira Knightley *Vera Phillips* • Sienna Miller *Caitlin Thomas* • Cillian Murphy *William Killick* • Matthew Rhys *Dylan Thomas* • Camilla Rutherford *Nicolette* • Alastair Mackenzie (2) *Anthony Devas* • Lisa Stansfield *Ruth Williams* ■ *Dir* John Maybury • *Scr* Sharman Macdonald

Edge of Sanity ★ 18

Psychological horror 1989 · UK · Colour · 87min

Anthony Perkins turns into a cocaine-snorting killer after experiments with a new drug backfire. Perkins, giving the most outrageous performance of his career, dwells more on the psychological change in his character than the physical one. No ghoulish make-up here, then; just a look that makes him come across like a hungover Iggy Pop. RS *DVD*

Anthony Perkins *Dr Henry Jekyll/Mr Jack Hyde* • Glynis Barber *Elisabeth Jekyll* • David Lodge *Gabriel Underwood* • Sarah Maur-Thorp *Susannah* • Ben Cole *Johnny* • Ray Jewers *Newcomen* ■ *Dir* Gérard Kikoine • *Scr* JP Felix, Ron Raley, from the novel *Dr Jekyll and Mr Hyde* by Robert Louis Stevenson

Edge of the City ★★★

Drama 1957 · US · BW · 85min

This is a dated and hectoring liberal drama about the destructive friendship between troubled loner John Cassavetes and hard-working labourer Sidney Poitier. Owing much to *On the Waterfront*, released three years earlier, the picture also followed teen dramas such as *Rebel without a Cause* and *The Blackboard Jungle* by taking delinquency out of the classroom and into the world of work. Despite its sledgehammer script and direction, it can still be enjoyed for the acting and the realistic location photography. AT

John Cassavetes *Axel North* • Sidney Poitier *Tommy Tyler* • Jack Warden *Charles Malik* • Kathleen Maguire *Ellen Wilson* • Ruby Dee *Lucy Tyler* • Robert F Simon *Mr Nordmann* • Ruth White *Mrs Nordmann* • Val Avery *Brother* ■ *Dir* Martin Ritt • *Scr* Robert Alan Aurthur, from his TV play *A Man Is Ten Feet Tall*

The Edge of the Horizon ★★★

Drama 1993 · Fr/Por · Colour · 91min

Portugal is the poor relation of European cinema; until recently, even its greatest film-maker, Manoel de Oliveira, struggled to find financial backing. Director Fernando Lopes accepted French funding for this atmospheric *film noir*, which stars Claude Brasseur as a pathologist whose life is transformed when he begins to delve into the criminal past of a corpse that appears to be his younger self. This is as much an exercise in style as it is a thriller, with Lopes bathing Lisbon's backstreets in shadow to keep us as much in the dark as Brasseur himself. DP Portuguese +subtitles.

Claude Brasseur *Spino* • Andréa Ferréol *Francesca* • Ana Padrão *Prostitute* • Antonio Valero *Alvaro* ■ *Dir* Fernando Lopes • *Scr* Christopher Frank, Jean Nachbaur, from the novel *Il Filo dell'Orizzonte* by Antonio Tabucchi

The Edge of the World ★★★★★ U

Drama 1937 · UK · BW · 71min

Made by Michael Powell, arguably the British cinema's most profoundly creative director, this is a fictional account of the harsh lives led by a dwindling community off the Scottish mainland. Filmed on the island of Foula, whose real-life inhabitants play the village people, it stars Niall MacGinnis, John Laurie, Finlay Currie and Belle Chrystall, all superb. But it is the landscape, and the spirit of a way of life being slowly but inevitably eroded, that dominate this poignant, elegiac tale of life, love and death. In 1978, Powell returned to the isle and shot a prologue and epilogue to the film, retitling the new version *Return to the Edge of the World*. RK *DVD* *BL*

John Laurie *Peter Manson* • Belle Chrystall *Ruth Manson* • Niall MacGinnis *Andrew Gray* • Finlay Currie *James Gray* • Eric Berry *Robbie Manson* • Michael Powell *Yachtsman* ■ *Dir/Scr* Michael Powell

Edge of Tomorrow ★★★ 12

Science-fiction action drama
2014 · US · Colour · 108min

Although it looks every inch the gung-ho alien-invasion blockbuster, this has a secret weapon: a time-loop device. Tom Cruise plays a cowardly global PR for the Allies who's sadistically packed off to the front. Instantly killed, he awakes 24 hours previously and endlessly relives this apocalyptic *Groundhog Day*, allowing him to second-guess the aliens and get to know Emily Blunt's special forces poster girl. It's a bloodless romance and the action builds to an anticlimax, but the story is adapted with surprising wit and director Doug Liman spins the reincarnation trope with thrilling momentum. AC Some violence, brief swearing. *DVD* *BL* *3D*

Tom Cruise *Major William Cage* • Emily Blunt *Rita Vrataski* • Bill Paxton *Master Sergeant Farell* • Brendan Gleeson *General Brigham* • Jonas Armstrong *Skinner* ■ *Dir* Doug Liman • *Scr* John-Henry Butterworth, Jez Butterworth, DW Harper, Joby Harold, Alex Kurtzman, Christopher McQuarrie, Roberto Orci, from the novel *All You Need Is Kill* by Hiroshi Sakurazaka

Edison ★★★ 15

Crime drama 2005 · Can · Colour · 91min

Despite the presence of stars such as Morgan Freeman and Kevin Spacey, this crime drama is notable mainly for teen idol Justin Timberlake's starring debut. He features in the pivotal role of a fledgling reporter getting in too deep while investigating police corruption. Timberlake tries almost too hard, but he's lacking that inner spark needed to make his character believable. As expected, however, Freeman and Spacey own the screen, while LL Cool J gives an honest performance of strength and subtlety. SuR *DVD*

Morgan Freeman *Ashford* • Kevin Spacey *Wallace* • Justin Timberlake *Pollack* • LL Cool J *Deed* • Dylan McDermott *Lazerov* • John Heard *Tilman* ■ *Dir/Scr* David J Burke [David Burke]

Edison, the Man ★★★ U

Biographical drama 1940 · US · BW · 106min

In a movie that contains almost as much sentimental invention as the practical kind, Thomas Alva Edison emerges as a sort of against-all-odds, American pioneer. Despite the sanitisation, Spencer Tracy offers a convincing study of the inventor, stubbornly fighting trials and tribulations and constructing the light bulb in a radiant sequence as exciting as any thriller. A sequel to Mickey Rooney's *Young Tom Edison*, Clarence Brown's film takes itself much more seriously. TH

Spencer Tracy *Thomas Alva Edison* • Rita Johnson *Mary Stilwell* • Lynne Overman *Bunt Cavatt* • Charles Coburn *General Powell* • Gene Lockhart *Mr Taggart* • Henry Travers *Ben Els* ■ *Dir* Clarence Brown • *Scr* Talbot Jennings, Bradbury Foote, from a story by Dore Schary, Bradbury Foote

Edith et Marcel ★ PG

Biographical romantic drama
1983 · Fr · Colour · 140min

When Patrick Dewaere killed himself early in the production, Marcel Cerdan Jr stepped up from technical adviser to play his famous boxing father in this account of his love affair with "the little sparrow", Edith Piaf. Claude Lelouch spends too much time on an irrelevant subplot involving a bibliophile and a prisoner of war. Lethargic, pretentious and wasteful. DP French +subtitles.

Evelyne Bouix *Edith Piaf/Margot de Villedieu* • Jacques Villeret *Jacques Barbier* • Francis Huster *Francis Roman* • Jean-Claude Brialy *Loulou Barrier* • Jean Bouise *Lucien Roupp* • Marcel Cerdan Jr *Marcel Cerdan* • Charles Aznavour ■ *Dir/Scr* Claude Lelouch

Edmond ★★★ 18

Black comedy drama
2005 · US/UK · Colour · 82min

With David Mamet seemingly concentrating on more mainstream action fare (the thriller *Spartan*, the TV series *The Unit*), this film version of his 1982 one-act play is a pleasing reminder of the dark power of his writing. Regular collaborator William H Macy stars as the title character, who is undergoing a rather extreme midlife crisis that causes him to leave his wife (Rebecca Pidgeon). On the advice of a stranger (Joe Mantegna), Edmond decides to investigate the city's sex joints, but his night on the town spirals wildly out of control. It's a little too episodic for its own good, but *Re-Animator* director Stuart Gordon – a respected theatre director in his own right – keeps things moving briskly along and sensibly doesn't try to disguise the picture's stage origins. And the cast of well-known faces, including Denise Richards, Bai Ling, Mena Suvari, Bokeem Woodbine and the *Re-Animator* himself Jeffrey Combs, delight in the rich rhythms of Mamet's provocative and profane dialogue. JF *DVD*

William H Macy *Edmond Burke* • Jeffrey Combs *Desk clerk* • Dulé Hill *Sharper* • Bai Ling *Girl* • Joe Mantegna *Man* • Denise Richards *B-girl* • Julia Stiles *Glenna* • Mena Suvari *Whore* • Dylan Walsh *Interrogator* • Rebecca Pidgeon *Edmond's wife* ■ *Dir* Stuart Gordon • *Scr* David Mamet, from his play • *Cinematographer* Denis Maloney

Ed's Next Move ★★★ 15

Romantic comedy 1996 · US · Colour · 83min

This is an engaging comedy about a Wisconsin nerd, Matt Ross (the Ed in question), going to the Big Apple and falling for musician Callie Thorne. Fortunately, Ross's worldly wise roommate Kevin Carroll is on hand to take him to diners and pump him with advice about women. Writer/director John Walsh makes an impressive debut with this low-budget feature. Romantic comedy is one of the toughest genres to crack; this one just about makes the grade. LH

Matt Ross *Eddie Brodsky* • Callie Thorne *Lee Nicol* • Kevin Carroll *Ray Obregon* • Ramsey Faragallah *Dr Banarjee* ■ *Dir/Scr* John Walsh

Edtv ★★★★ 12

Comedy 1999 · US · Colour · 117min

Director Ron Howard's delightfully soft-centred rumination on the excesses of television has suffered in the wake of *The Truman Show*, but comparisons are misplaced. Howard's movie is more concerned with feel-good laughs and formulaic romantic complications than hard-edged satire, and it doesn't disappoint in delivering sheer enjoyment. Matthew McConaughey gives a winning performance as the small-town video store assistant who agrees to be filmed 24 hours a day by a camera crew for a cable network. Hardly subtle yet highly entertaining. AJ Swearing. *DVD*

Matthew McConaughey *Ed Pekurny* • Ellen DeGeneres *Cynthia Topping* • Jenna Elfman *Shari* • Woody Harrelson *Ray Pekurny* • Sally Kirkland *Jeanette* • Martin Landau *Al* • Rob Reiner *Whitaker* • Dennis Hopper *Hank* • Elizabeth Hurley *Jill* • Michael Moore (2) *Panel member* • Clint Howard *Ken* ■ *Dir* Ron Howard • *Scr* Lowell Ganz, Babaloo Mandel, from the film *Louis XIX: Roi des Ondes* by Emile Gaudreault, Sylvie Bouchard

Educating Rita ★★★★ 15

Comedy drama 1983 · UK · Colour · 105min

This is a joy from start to finish, largely thanks to Willy Russell's crisp adaptation of his successful stage play and the lead players' divine suitability for the roles. Julie Walters is great as the sassy and streetwise heroine, eager for higher learning but smart enough to spot Michael Caine's foibles at a hundred paces, and Caine has one of his best ever roles as the drink-sodden, cynical lecturer. Some felt that Walters's portrayal patronised bright, working-class girls, but she brings genuine warmth to the part. SH Swearing. *DVD*

Michael Caine *Dr Frank Bryant* • Julie Walters *Rita "Susan" White* • Michael Williams *Brian* • Maureen Lipman *Trish* • Jeananne Crowley *Julia* • Malcolm Douglas *Denny* • Godfrey Quigley *Rita's father* ■ *Dir* Lewis Gilbert • *Scr* Willy Russell, from his play

An Education ★★★★★ 12

Coming-of-age drama
2008 · UK/US · Colour · 95min

Writer Nick Hornby's outstanding adaptation of excerpts from journalist Lynn Barber's coming-of-age memoir is a wonderful celebration of teenage intellectual and sexual curiosity. Set in a perfectly evoked pre-Swinging Sixties suburban London, it tells of the bittersweet emotional journey taken by a sheltered schoolgirl (Carey Mulligan), who jeopardises a place at Oxford for the "University of Life" offered by a man twice her age (the charmingly manipulative Peter Sarsgaard). Director Lone Scherfig brings the lightest touch and sureness of insights to a film that is smartly observant, fabulously funny (Alfred Molina's stuffy father, Rosamund Pike's bimbo socialite) and delightfully nonjudgemental. Mulligan's astonishing performance in particular captures an era's changing attitudes over female opportunity. AJ Sexual references. *DVD* *BL*

Carey Mulligan *Jenny* • Peter Sarsgaard *David* • Alfred Molina *Jack* • Dominic Cooper *Danny* • Rosamund Pike *Helen* • Olivia Williams *Miss Stubbs* • Emma Thompson *Headmistress* • Cara Seymour *Marjorie* ■ *Dir* Lone Scherfig • *Scr* Nick Hornby, excerpted from the memoir by Lynn Barber

The Education of Charlie Banks ★★★

Coming-of-age drama
2007 · US · Colour · 100min

Limp Bizkit frontman Fred Durst makes his directorial debut with this indie drama set at an Ivy League college in the 1980s. Jesse Eisenberg (*The Social Network*) plays nerdy freshman Charlie Banks, whose world is turned upside down when Mick (Jason Ritter), a violent thug he knew at high school, drops in to visit. Avoiding the obvious revenge plot, Durst takes this preppy tale of class and longing along a more engaging route as charming sociopath Mick begins to envy Charlie's campus lifestyle. Although it over-eggs its theme, the film is at least blessed with an affecting cast, especially Eisenberg, US cinema's current geek of choice. JR Violence, swearing, sex scenes, drug abuse.

Jesse Eisenberg *Charlie* • Jason Ritter *Mick* • Eva Amurri *Mary* • Chris Marquette *Danny* ■ *Dir* Fred Durst • *Scr* Peter Elkoff

The Education of Little Tree ★★ PG

Period drama 1997 · US/Can · Colour · 110min

This is the quiet, thoroughly tasteful account of a part-Cherokee boy (Joseph Ashton) struggling to come to terms with the white man's world when he goes to live with his grandparents in 1930s America. James Cromwell adds suitable moral authority to a moving tale, which is occasionally a touch too reverential. JF *DVD*

Joseph Ashton *Little Tree* • James Cromwell *Granpa* • Tantoo Cardinal *Granma* • Leni Parker *Martha* • Rebecca Dewey *Dolly* • William Rowat *Henry* • Robert Daviau *Ralph* • Graham Greene (2) *Willow John* ■ *Dir* Richard Friedenberg • *Scr* Richard Friedenberg, from the novel by Forrest Carter

Edward, My Son ★★

Drama 1949 · US/UK · BW · 112min

This reeks of theatricality, and the fault lies with the gimmick-ridden play on which it was based; co-written by actor Robert Morley as a vehicle for himself, it traced an ailing marriage and deliberately refrained from showing the eponymous Edward on stage. The film, which awkwardly preserves the same convention, features Hollywood import Spencer Tracy, uncomfortable as the despotic dad, and Deborah Kerr, unconvincing as his alcoholic missus. TS

Spencer Tracy *Arnold Boult* • Deborah Kerr *Evelyn Boult* • Ian Hunter *Dr Larry Woodhope* • Leueen MacGrath *Eileen Perrin* • James Donald *Bronton* • Mervyn Johns *Harry Simpkin* • Harriette Johns *Phyllis Mayden* • Felix Aylmer *Mr Hanray* • Walter Fitzgerald *Mr Kedner* ■ *Dir* George Cukor • *Scr* Donald Ogden Stewart, from the play by Robert Morley, Noel Langley

Edward Scissorhands ★★★★★ PG

Fantasy 1990 · US · Colour · 100min

Tim Burton's bewitchingly oddball "Beauty and the Beast" fairy tale is a masterpiece and one of the best fantasy films ever made. Its haunting power, exquisite charm and dark romance are a match for the spellbinding work of Hans Christian Andersen, while Johnny Depp's sensitive performance as scientist Vincent Price's "Punkenstein" creation is a revelation. Humanoid Edward's inability to touch the things he loves because of his razor and scissor appendages makes for potent symbolism of the highest mythic order. The finale packs an unforgettable emotional wallop, assisted by Danny Elfman's gloriously magical score. AJ Swearing, violence. *DVD* ◁Ɔ

Johnny Depp *Edward Scissorhands* • Winona Ryder *Kim Boggs* • Dianne Wiest *Peg Boggs* • Anthony Michael Hall *Jim* • Kathy Baker *Joyce Monroe* • Vincent Price *Inventor* • Alan Arkin *Bill Boggs* ■ *Dir* Tim Burton • *Scr* Caroline Thompson, from a story by Caroline Thompson, Tim Burton • *Cinematographer* Stefan Czapsky • *Art Director* Bo Welch

Edward II ★★ 15

Historical drama 1991 · UK · Colour · 86min

Director Derek Jarman's adaptation of Christopher Marlowe's play of court favouritism and lethal power games behind the throne is both a challenging and off-putting experience. Telling the admittedly compelling story of Britain's only acknowledged homosexual monarch, whose preference for his male lover rather than Queen Isabella led to a civil war, Jarman turns the grim 16th-century drama into a typically radical and confrontational polemic about the evils of homophobia,

stylishly staged in modern dress. AJ Violence, sex scenes.

Steven Waddington *Edward II* • Tilda Swinton *Isabella* • Andrew Tiernan *Gaveston* • Nigel Terry *Mortimer* • Dudley Sutton *Bishop of Winchester* • Kevin Collins *Lightborn* • Jerome Flynn *Kent* • Annie Lennox *Singer* ■ *Dir* Derek Jarman • *Scr* Derek Jarman, Stephen McBride, Ken Butler, from the play by Christopher Marlowe

The Eel ★★★ 18

Drama 1997 · Jpn · Colour · 111min

The joint winner of the 1997 Palme d'Or, this is a curious, sometimes powerful tale of one man's isolated existence, interlaced with fantasy, farce and a fish. Some will be touched by director Shohei Imamura's story of a reformed wife-killer whose only real friend is his pet eel. Others will be mystified by the near-silent central character, the dream-like moments and a bizarre comedy subplot involving unidentified flying objects. JC Japanese +subtitles. Violence, nudity. *DVD*

Koji Yakusho *Takuro Yamashita* • Misa Shimizu *Keiko Hattori* • Fujio Tsuneta *Jiro Nakajima* • Mitsuko Baisho *Misako Nakajima* ■ *Dir* Shohei Imamura • *Scr* Motofumi Tomikawa, Shohei Imamura, Daisuke Tengan, from the novel *Sparkles in the Darkness* by Akira Yoshimura

The Effect of Gamma Rays on Man-in-the-Moon Marigolds ★★

Drama 1972 · US · Colour · 100min

Although it won him a Pulitzer Prize, Paul Zindel's play feels like a clumsy pastiche of Tennessee Williams. So while it's possible to see why Paul Newman might be drawn to a film of the project, it's hard to see what he felt he could bring to the story of an unkempt widow struggling to raise her chalk-and-cheese daughters, given his refusal to explore its deeper emotional resonances. Clearly the chance of working with his wife Joanne Woodward and daughter Nell Potts was an incentive, but his stagey direction leaves them straining. DP

Joanne Woodward *Beatrice* • Nell Potts *Matilda* • Roberta Wallach *Ruth* • Judith Lowry *Nanny* • Richard Venture *Floyd* • Estelle Omens *Floyd's wife* ■ *Dir* Paul Newman • *Scr* Alvin Sargent, from the play by Paul Zindel

Effi Briest ★★★★ U

Period drama 1974 · W Ger · BW · 134min

Teenager Effi (Hanna Schygulla) is forced into an unsuitable marriage in Fassbinder's adaptation of Theodor Fontane's classic 19th-century novel. A lonely existence drives Effi to infidelity, and her husband's later discovery of the affair has tragic consequences. Despite an increasingly tempestuous professional relationship with Schygulla, Fassbinder has created a stylised but truly literary film. Using elegant monochrome photography and with mirrors reflecting the artifice of Effi's world, the director treats the original text with awed reverence. DP German +subtitles. *DVD* ◁

Hanna Schygulla *Effi Briest* • Wolfgang Schenck *Baron Geert von Instetten* • Ulli Lommel *Major Crampas* • Lilo Pempeit *Frau Briest* • Herbert Steinmetz *Herr Briest* • Hark Bohm *Gieshuebler* ■ *Dir* Rainer Werner Fassbinder • *Scr* Rainer Werner Fassbinder, from the novel by Theodor Fontane

Effie Gray ★★★★ 12

Period drama based on a true story 2014 · UK · Colour · 104min

Eminent critic John Ruskin, a key figure in the Victorian art scene, remains equally well known for his scandal-hit private life, which this period drama, written by Emma Thompson, explores from the perspective of his long-suffering spouse. Dakota Fanning looks every inch the pale-skinned Pre-Raphaelite heroine as the naive young bride who discovers her mother-dominated husband has little sexual interest in her. Note-perfect performances enhance this fascinating true story, with an excellent Greg Wise rendering the cruel but troubled Ruskin something of a tragic figure and

Fanning unexpectedly affecting in the lead. TJ Some sexual references. *DVD*

Dakota Fanning *Euphemia "Effie" Gray* • Emma Thompson *Lady Eastlake* • Tom Sturridge *John Everett Millais* • David Suchet *Mr Ruskin* • Julie Walters *Margaret Cox Ruskin* • Greg Wise *John Ruskin* • Claudia Cardinale *Viscountess* • Robbie Coltrane *Doctor* ■ *Dir* Richard Laxton • *Scr* Emma Thompson

The Egg and I ★★★ U

Comedy 1947 · US · BW · 107min

This massively popular film version of Betty MacDonald's autobiographical bestseller follows a couple of city slickers who buy a clapped-out old farmhouse and renovate it. Claudette Colbert is delightful as the newlywed who discovers on her wedding night that her husband, attractively played by a wry Fred MacMurray, wants to be a chicken farmer. Producer/director/ screenwriter Chester Erskine perhaps keeps events on too even a keel, but it still makes for a very pleasant, if undramatic, whole. TS

Claudette Colbert *Betty* • Fred MacMurray *Bob* • Marjorie Main *Ma Kettle* • Percy Kilbride *Pa Kettle* • Louise Allbritton *Harriet Putnam* • Richard Long *Tom Kettle* • Billy House *Billy* ■ *Dir* Chester Erskine • *Scr* Chester Erskine, Fred F Finklehoffe, from the autobiography by Betty MacDonald

The Egyptian ★★

Period epic 1954 · US · Colour · 138min

Even Michael Curtiz has difficulty in jollying up this solemn, overlong historical epic about the search for God in ancient Egypt. The dishy but wooden Edmund Purdom in the leading role doesn't help matters, and neither does hunky Victor Mature. The excellent music is a singular collaboration between Alfred Newman and Bernard Herrmann, while Leon Shamroy's colour CinemaScope photography was nominated for an Oscar. AT

Edmund Purdom *Sinuhe* • Jean Simmons *Merit* • Victor Mature *Horemheb* • Peter Ustinov *Kaptah* • Gene Tierney *Baketamon* • Michael Wilding *Akhnaton* ■ *Dir* Michael Curtiz • *Scr* Philip Dunne, Casey Robinson, from the novel by Mika Waltari

The Eiger Sanction ★★ 15

Spy thriller 1975 · US · Colour · 113min

In the weakest of his self-directed movies, Clint Eastwood plays a mountaineering art collector and spy who agrees to climb the Eiger and eliminate an agent in return for preferential tax status. It looks spectacular, but the lacklustre dialogue and performances let the film down. AT Violence, swearing, sex scenes, nudity. *DVD* ◁

Clint Eastwood *Jonathan Hemlock* • George Kennedy *Ben Bowman* • Vonetta McGee *Jemima Brown* • Jack Cassidy *Miles Mellough* ■ *Dir* Clint Eastwood • *Scr* Hal Dresner, Warren B Murphy, Rod Whitaker, from the novel by Trevanian

8½ ★★★★★ 15

Drama 1963 · It · BW · 132min

Having made six features and three short films, director Federico Fellini reckoned that this mesmerising insight into the creative process took his tally of movies to eight-and-a-half. The winner of the best foreign language film Oscar, this is a complex, painfully honest study of a man in a personal and professional crisis. After *La Dolce Vita*, Fellini was faced with the problem of repeating his success and this soul-searching film, with its mix of daydreams, memories, nightmares and frustrating confrontations, is a fantasy chronicle of his attempts to sustain his reputation as a cinematic genius. As the tormented film-maker, the exceptional Marcello Mastroianni is superbly supported by Anouk Aimée and Claudia Cardinale. DP Italian +subtitles. *DVD* ◁

Marcello Mastroianni *Guido Anselmi* • Claudia Cardinale *Claudia* • Anouk Aimée *Luisa Anselmi* • Sandra Milo *Carla* • Rossella Falk *Rossella* • Barbara Steele *Gloria Morin* • Mario Pisu *Mezzabotta* • Guido Alberti *Producer* ■ *Dir* Federico Fellini • *Scr* Federico Fellini, Tullio

Pinelli, Ennio Flajano, Brunello Rondi, from a story by Federico Fellini, Ennio Flajano • *Music* Nino Rota • *Costume Designer* Piero Gherardi

8½ Women ★★ 15

Comedy drama 1999 · Neth/UK/Lux/Ger · Colour · 115min

Intended as a tribute to Federico Fellini, Peter Greenaway's misfiring comedy seeks to explore man's tendency to idealise women. However, such is Greenaway's preoccupation with referencing cultural history that he fails to capitalise on the themes and relationships that arise when widowed businessman John Standing and son Matthew Delamere open their doors to various disaffected women. This is less misogynist than some have claimed, yet it's still unworthy of its auteur. DP *DVD*

John Standing *Philip Emmenthal* • Matthew Delamere *Storey Emmenthal* • Vivian Wu *Kito* • Shizuka Inoh *Simato* • Kirina Mano *Mio* • Toni Collette *Griselda* • Amanda Plummer *Beryl* • Polly Walker *Palmira* ■ *Dir/Scr* Peter Greenaway

Eight Below ★★★ PG

Adventure drama 2005 · Ger/US · Colour · 115min

Paul Walker gives a likeable performance as the guide to a group of Antarctic researchers who has developed a close bond with his eight sled dogs. He's devastated when treacherous weather conditions force the whole team to evacuate, leaving his "kids" stranded in the frozen wilds. Beautifully shot scenes unfold as the resourceful dogs battle to stay alive for more than six months. It's an exciting and enthralling mix, only slumping when the tale cuts back to Walker trying to put together a rescue mission in America. SF *DVD* ◁

Paul Walker *Jerry Shepard* • Bruce Greenwood *Davis McClaren* • Moon Bloodgood *Katie* • Jason Biggs *Charlie Cooper* • Gerard Plunkett *Dr Andy Harrison* • August Schellenberg *Mindo* • Wendy Crewson *Eve McClaren* • Belinda Metz *Rosemary* ■ *Dir* Frank Marshall • *Scr* David Digilio, from the 1983 film *Nankyoku Monogatari [Antarctica]* by Koreyoshi Kurahara, Toshiro Ishido, Kan Saji, Tatsuo Nogami

Eight Days a Week ★★★ 15

Comedy 1996 · US · Colour · 89min

Writer/director Michael Davis made his feature debut with this coming-of-age comedy. The story focuses on Joshua Schaefer's passion for his neighbour Keri Russell and the romantic vigil with which he hopes to win her heart. More a crash course in suburban living than a guide to successful courting, this often wincingly accurate insight into confused male adolescence may not be the ultimate teen pic, but it's far from being the worst. DP *DVD*

Joshua Schaefer *Peter* • Keri Russell *Erica* • RD Robb *Matt* • Mark Taylor *Peter's father* • Marcia Shapiro *Peter's mother* • Johnny Green (3) *Nick* • Buck Kartalian *Nonno* • Catherine Hicks *Ms Lewis* ■ *Dir/Scr* Michael Davis (3)

8 Heads in a Duffel Bag ★ 15

Black comedy 1997 · US · Colour · 94min

Tom Schulman makes his directorial debut with a lame comedy that doesn't have enough laughs. Joe Pesci plays a Mob hitman whose bag of heads gets mixed up with one belonging to a medical student. Pesci and most of the supporting cast simply mug their way through the proceedings. JB *DVD*

Joe Pesci *Tommy Spinelli* • Andy Comeau *Charlie* • Kristy Swanson *Laurie Bennett* • Todd Louiso *Steve* • George Hamilton *Dick Bennett* • Dyan Cannon *Annette Bennett* • David Spade *Ernie* • Anthony Mangano *Rico* ■ *Dir/Scr* Tom Schulman

800 Leagues down the Amazon ★★

Period adventure 1993 · US/Mex · Colour · 100min

This unprepossessing costume adventure was directed by Luis Llosa, who returned to the Amazon in 1997 for the laugh-a-minute

monster movie *Anaconda*. Barry Bostwick stars as a wealthy plantation owner escorting his daughter, Daphne Zuniga, to her wedding. However, they reckoned without the perils of the river and the schemes of bounty hunter Adam Baldwin. A bigger budget would have done nothing to improve the long-winded script. DP
Violence.

Daphne Zuniga *Minha* • Barry Bostwick *Garral* • Adam Baldwin *Koja* • Tom Verica *Monoel* • EE Ross *Frolgoso* ■ *Dir* Luis Llosa • *Scr* Laura Schiff, Jackson Barr, from the novel by Jules Verne

Eight Legged Freaks ★★12
Science-fiction horror comedy
2001 · US/Aus · Colour · 95min

David Arquette and Kari Wuhrer fight chemically mutated spiders in a rural mining town in this tongue-in-cheek take on the creature features of the 1950s and early 60s. With its blend of absurd set pieces, hammy acting and deliberately exaggerated dialogue, the movie works hard to capture the kitsch spirit of its predecessors. Though it's too self-conscious and heavy handed to succeed entirely, there's much to enjoy. SF
DVD

David Arquette *Chris McCormack* • Kari Wuhrer *Sheriff Sam Parker* • Scott Terra *Mike Parker* • Scarlett Johansson *Ashley Parker* • Doug E Doug *Harlan* • Rick Overton *Deputy Pete Willis* • Leon Rippy *Mayor Wade* ■ *Dir* Ellory Elkayem • *Scr* Jesse Alexander, Ellory Elkayem, from a story by Elkayem, Randy Kornfield

Eight Men Out ★★★15
Period drama based on a true story
1988 · US · Colour · 114min

John Cusack and Charlie Sheen star in a low-key and serious exposé of corruption in the American baseball game when, in 1919, the Chicago White Sox threw the World Series. When the truth became known, it was quickly dubbed the Black Sox Scandal. Written and directed by John Sayles, the picture details the social and economic stresses of the time that led the players into the clutches of hustlers and organised crime. It's a sad and compelling piece that is totally convincing and doesn't require a knowledge of baseball. AT *DVD*

John Cusack *Buck Weaver* • Charlie Sheen *Hap Felsch* • John Mahoney *Kid Gleason* • DB Sweeney *"Shoeless" Joe Jackson* • Clifton James *Charles Comiskey* • Eliot Asinof *Heydler* • David Strathairn *Eddie Cicotte* • John Sayles *Ring Lardner* ■ *Dir* John Sayles • *Scr* John Sayles, from the novel by Eliot Asinof

8 Mile ★★★★15
Drama   2002 · US/Ger · Colour · 105min

Director Curtis Hanson puts a new spin on the familiar "triumph against the odds" theme with this slick showcase for the talents of superstar rapper Eminem. Aspiring rap artist "Rabbit" hopes to escape his bleak life in Detroit's 8 Mile district. But, after losing his job and his (pregnant) girlfriend, he's forced to work in a soul-destroying factory and to live with his alcoholic mother (Kim Basinger) and her lover. While it doesn't break any new ground, the revelation here is Eminem, who delivers a likeable, honest performance. AS
Violence, swearing, drug abuse, sex scene, nudity. *DVD* *BL*

Eminem [Marshall Mathers] *Jimmy "Rabbit" Smith* • Kim Basinger *Stephanie* • Brittany Murphy *Alex* • Mekhi Phifer *Future* • Evan Jones *Cheddar Bob* • Omar Benson Miller *Sol George* • Eugene Byrd *Wink* • De'Angelo Wilson *DJ Iz* ■ *Dir* Curtis Hanson • *Scr* Scott Silver

8mm ★★18
Mystery thriller   1999 · US/Ger · Colour · 118min

Joel Schumacher directs this disappointing and depressing thriller. Honourable private detective Nicolas Cage is hired by a wealthy widow to uncover the identity of a teenage girl, whom the widow believes has been murdered in a reel of pornographic film found among her late husband's belongings. The trail leads a surprisingly bland Cage through LA's hard-core underworld, but the movie does have one saving grace in Joaquin Phoenix's jaded

sex-shop assistant. JF Violence, swearing, sex scenes, nudity. *DVD*

Nicolas Cage *Tom Welles* • Joaquin Phoenix *Max California* • James Gandolfini *Eddie Poole* • Peter Stormare *Dino Velvet* • Anthony Heald *Longdale* • Chris Bauer *Machine* • Catherine Keener *Amy Welles* ■ *Dir* Joel Schumacher • *Scr* Andrew Kevin Walker

8 Million Ways to Die
★★★18

Crime thriller   1986 · US · Colour · 110min

Oliver Stone wrote the original script of this urban thriller, intending to direct it himself. But financial problems led to a delay and, when Hal Ashby was brought in to direct, Robert Towne rewrote the script uncredited. Stone disowns it, Ashby was reportedly fired near the end of production and few people ever saw it. On the credit side, there are some vivid locations and a decent cast: Jeff Bridges as the cop with a drink problem, Rosanna Arquette as the mobster's moll and Andy Garcia as a drug dealer. AT *DVD*

Jeff Bridges *Matthew Scudder* • Rosanna Arquette *Sarah* • Alexandra Paul *Sunny* • Randy Brooks *Chance* • Andy Garcia *Angel Maldonado* • Lisa Sloan *Linda Scudder* ■ *Dir* Hal Ashby • *Scr* Oliver Stone, David Lee Henry, Robert Towne (uncredited), from the novel by Lawrence Block

8 minutes idle ★★★15
Comedy   2012 · UK · Colour · 118min

This modest charmer from BBC Films charts ten days in the life of a call-centre worker who finds himself turfed out of the family home. Affable but hopelessly ineffectual 20-something Dan (Tom Hughes) is left with no alternative but to sleep secretly in the store cupboard at work. Hughes gives a delightfully dozy performance and, although the comedy may be a trifle low-key for some, this captures the inconsequential nature of nine-to-five desk jockeying, while the Bristol backdrop lends it character. JH Swearing, sex scenes, nudity. *DVD*

Tom Hughes *Dan Thomas* • Ophelia Lovibond *Teri Walker* • Montserrat Lombard *Alice* • Antonia Thomas *Adrienne* • Paul Kaye *Steve Thomas* ■ *Dir* Mark Simon Hewis • *Scr* Nicholas Blincoe, Matt Thorne, from Thorne's novel

Eight o'Clock Walk ★★PG
Drama   1953 · UK · BW · 83min

Richard Attenborough finds himself on trial for his life in this lukewarm legal drama. Typically with courtroom pictures, there's too much chat and not enough action, although father-and-son barristers Ian Hunter and Derek Farr enjoy a few jousts before the verdict is returned. The problem is that, no matter how damning the evidence, you never believe for a second that cabbie Attenborough is guilty of murder. DP

Richard Attenborough *Tom Manning* • Derek Farr *Peter Tanner* • Cathy O'Donnell *Jill Manning* • Ian Hunter *Geoffrey Tanner* • Maurice Denham *Horace Clifford* • Bruce Seton *DCI* • Harry Welchman *Justice Herrington* • Kynaston Reeves *Mr Munro* ■ *Dir* Lance Comfort • *Scr* Katherine Strueby, Guy Morgan, from a story by Jack Roffey, Gordon Harbord

Eight on the Lam ★★U
Comedy   1967 · US · Colour · 107min

There was safety in numbers for Bob Hope at this stage of a career that wasn't just flagging but seemed at half-mast. A few years after *Seven Little Foys* this came along, with Bob as a nervous bank clerk accused of embezzlement who goes on the run with his seven children. Not even the acerbic wit of Phyllis Diller can cut through the bland sentimentality. TH

Bob Hope *Henry Dimsdale* • Phyllis Diller *Golda* • Jonathan Winters *Jasper Lynch* • Shirley Eaton *Ellie Barton* • Jill St John *Monica* • Stacey Maxwell *Linda* • Kevin Brody *Steve* ■ *Dir* George Marshall • *Scr* Albert E Lewin, Burt Styler, Bob Fisher, Arthur Marx, from a story by Fisher, Marx

8 Seconds ★★PG
Drama based on a true story
1994 · US · Colour · 100min

Bareback riding has never looked so easy as in this biopic of Lane Frost, whose brief career saw him become one of America's youngest ever rodeo champions. Such is the predictability of the bucking sequences that it's almost a relief to be plunged into Lane's marital misery and his search for the popularity. Luke Perry and Cynthia Geary are well matched as the ill-fated Frosts, but the action is just too tame to thrill. DP *DVD*

Luke Perry *Lane Frost* • Stephen Baldwin *Tuff Hedeman* • Cynthia Geary *Kellie Frost* • James Rebhorn *Clyde Frost* • Red Mitchell *Cody Lambert* • Carrie Snodgress *Elsie Frost* ■ *Dir* John G Avildsen • *Scr* Monte Merrick

8 Women ★★★★15
Musical murder mystery
2001 · Fr/It · Colour · 106min

This crackles with catty quips and also serves up an intriguing murder mystery in which eight women are trapped in an isolated country house with a murderer either on the loose or among their number. The costumes and sets both reference and satirise the styles of the 1950s, and are photographed in loving colour by Jeanne Lapoirie. The stellar cast is sublime, but Isabelle Huppert takes the honours as the dowdy sister of glamorous matriarch Catherine Deneuve. Holding it all together is the slick direction of François Ozon, whose blend of Agatha Christie and Douglas Sirk is as precise as it is mischievous. DP French +subtitles. Swearing. *DVD*

Danielle Darrieux *Mamy* • Catherine Deneuve *Gaby* • Isabelle Huppert *Augustine* • Emmanuelle Béart *Louise* • Fanny Ardant *Pierrette* • Virginie Ledoyen *Suzon* • Ludivine Sagnier *Catherine* • Firmine Richard *Mme Chanel* ■ *Dir* François Ozon • *Scr* François Ozon, from the play *8 Femmes* by Robert Thomas

18 Again! ★★PG
Comedy   1988 · US · Colour · 95min

George Burns did the majority of his best work on stage, radio and TV with his wife Gracie Allen. However, most viewers will remember him as a mischievous old man in films such as *The Sunshine Boys* and *Oh, God!* Those movies show off better the talents of the veteran trouper as he's given little screen time in this non-starting "body swap" comedy. DP

George Burns *Jack Watson* • Charlie Schlatter *David Watson* • Tony Roberts *Arnold* • Anita Morris *Madelyn* • Miriam Flynn *Betty* • Jennifer Runyon *Robin* • Red Buttons *Charlie* • George DiCenzo *Coach* ■ *Dir* Paul Flaherty • *Scr* Josh Goldstein, Jonathan Prince

The Eighteenth Angel ★★15
Horror   1997 · US · Colour · 84min

Soon after the unexplained death of his wife, Christopher McDonald accompanies his daughter, Rachael Leigh Cook, on a modelling assignment to Italy. There she becomes the target of a mysterious sect of priests preparing for the return of Satan. Some reasonable chills register along the way, despite the film's obvious contrivances and sloppy clichés. AJ Violence.

Christopher McDonald *Hugh Stanton* • Rachael Leigh Cook *Lucy Stanton* • Stanley Tucci *Todd Stanton* • Wendy Crewson *Norah Stanton* • Maximilian Schell *Father Simeon* ■ *Dir* William Bindley • *Scr* David Seltzer

The Eighth Day ★★★PG
Drama   1996 · Bel · Colour · 112min

This sentimental, life-affirming movie highlights the friendship between a corporate businessman who loathes his existence and a man with Down's syndrome who embraces life. Daniel Auteuil and Pascal Duquenne (who shared the best actor prize at Cannes) are both excellent, and their *Rain Man*-style relationship has some profoundly touching moments. However, director Jaco Van Dormael strives a little too hard for profundity,

decorating the film with poetic images of nature. JC French +subtitles.

Daniel Auteuil *Harry* • Pascal Duquenne *Georges* • Miou-Miou *Julie* • Isabelle Sadoyan *Georges's mother* • Henri Garcin *Company director* • Michele Maes *Nathalie* • Laszlo Harmati *Luis Mariano* • Helene Roussel *Julie's mother* ■ *Dir/Scr* Jaco Van Dormael

88 Minutes ★15
Crime thriller
2007 · Ger/US/Can · Colour · 102min

Longer and duller than its title promises, this clock-watching thriller sees Al Pacino shuffle his way through yet another rumpled hero. Forensic psychiatrist and lecturer by day, party animal by night, Pacino is waiting for the death-row execution of a vicious killer that his evidence helped convict when he receives a threatening phone call telling him he has just 88 minutes to live. Pacino's heavy-lidded performance barely registers concern, and his advanced years and hands-on approach to his pretty young students (including Alicia Witt and Leelee Sobieski) feels rather unseemly, especially since so many of them end up dead in their underwear. Creepy for all the wrong reasons. JR *DVD*

Al Pacino *Dr Jack Gramm* • Alicia Witt *Kim Cummings* • Leelee Sobieski *Lauren Douglas* • Amy Brenneman *Shelly Barnes* • William Forsythe *Frank Parks* • Deborah Kara Unger *Carol Lynn Johnson* ■ *Dir* Jon Avnet • *Scr* Gary Scott Thompson

84 Charing Cross Road
★★★★U

Biographical drama   1986 · UK · Colour · 95min

Adapted from Helene Hanff's bestselling account of her dealings with the staff of a London bookshop, this is an absolute delight. Building his film around the letters exchanged between Hanff and manager Frank Doel, director David Jones creates utterly credible characters, conveys something of the beauty of books and makes some telling comparisons between the gloomy reserve of postwar Britain and the effervescence of Cold War America. However, what makes this gentle drama so compelling are the performances of Anne Bancroft and Anthony Hopkins, who fashion a romance between two people who never meet. DP *DVD*

Anne Bancroft *Helene Hanff* • Anthony Hopkins *Frank Doel* • Judi Dench *Nora Doel* • Jean De Baer *Maxine Bellamy* • Maurice Denham *George Martin* • Eleanor David *Cecily Farr* • Mercedes Ruehl *Kay* • Daniel Gerroll *Brian* • Wendy Morgan *Megan Wells* ■ *Dir* David Jones (3) • *Scr* Hugh Whitemore, from the book by Helene Hanff

84 Charlie Mopic ★★★18
War drama   1989 · US · Colour · 90min

This eye-opening film about the Vietnam War has a viewpoint that neither waves flags nor wastes blame, as it follows a two-man documentary film crew accompanying a platoon "to record procedures peculiar to the combat situation". Such is the skill of writer/director Patrick Duncan that it all comes across as reality. The constant slang, though, is a barrier to our understanding, while the continual hand-held camera becomes too unsettling. TH Swearing. *DVD*

Jonathan Emerson *LT* • Nicholas Cascone *Easy* • Jason Tomlins *Pretty Boy* • Christopher Burgard *Hammer* • Glenn Morshower *Cracker* • Richard Brooks (2) *OD* • Byron Thomas *Mopic* ■ *Dir/Scr* Patrick S Duncan [Patrick Sheane Duncan]

Eighty Steps to Jonah ★★
Drama   1969 · US · Colour · 107min

Vegas vocalist Wayne Newton turns up in this sentimental tale of an innocent man on the run who poses as a handyman in a children's summer camp for the blind. The treatment of the story stays just a shade this side of saccharine. Several familiar faces, such as Mickey Rooney, turn up in small roles. JG

Wayne Newton *Mark Jonah Winters* • Jo Van Fleet *Nonna* • Keenan Wynn *Barney Glover* • Diana Ewing *Tracy* • Slim Pickens *Scott* • RG Armstrong *Mackray* • Brandon Cruz *Little Joe* • Erin Moran *Kim* • Mickey Rooney *Wilfred Bashford* • Sal Mineo *Jerry Taggart* ■ *Dir* Gerd Oswald • *Scr* Frederic Louis Fox, from a story by Gerd Oswald, Frederic Louis Fox

80,000 Suspects ★★ PG
Thriller   1963 · UK · BW · 104min

This epidemic movie seems to have everything going for it - a bit of cod science, millions being threatened by malevolent micro-organisms and a race against time involving the daredevil doctor and the unsuspecting carrier, but it doesn't come off. More emphasis is placed on repairing the hero's marriage than on preventing disaster, which should add a human dimension to the tale, but here deprives the picture of suspense. DP *DVD* *BL*

Claire Bloom *Julie Monks* • Richard Johnson *Steven Monks* • Yolande Donlan *Ruth Preston* • Cyril Cusack *Father Maguire* • Michael Goodliffe *Clifford Preston* • Mervyn Johns *Buckridge* • Kay Walsh *Matron* • Norman Bird *Mr Davis* • Basil Dignam *Medical officer* ■ *Dir* Val Guest • *Scr* Val Guest, from the novel *The Pillars of Midnight* by Elleston Trevor

Eisenstein in Guanajuato
★★★★ 18
Romantic drama based on a true story
2014 · Mex/Neth/Fin/Bel/Ger · Colour and BW · 105min

Director Peter Greenaway - a lifelong admirer of Sergei Eisenstein - mischievously opts to depict the revolutionary Russian at the most vulnerable point in his meteoric career, in this challenging treatise on art, faith, sexual identity and mortality. Finnish actor Elmer Bäck excels as the troubled genius facing creative block and a crisis of confidence over whether his trademark montage style can survive the coming of the talkies. As always with Greenaway, the dialogue tends towards the florid, but he remains a master image-maker. DP Sex scenes, nudity.

Elmer Bäck *Sergei Eisenstein* • Luis Alberti *Palomino Cañedo* • José Montini *Diego Rivera* • Cristina Velasco Lozano *Frida Kahlo* ■ *Dir/Scr* Peter Greenaway • *Cinematographer* Reinier van Brummelen

Ek Hi Rasta ★★★ U
Drama   1956 · Ind · BW · 153min

Baldev Raj Chopra was already one of India's most influential film critics when he turned director in 1951. This was one of the first features made for his own production company BR Films, which was renowned for tackling key social issues within the context of commercial pictures. With a title meaning "The Only Way", this is ostensibly an old-fashioned melodrama about revenge, murder and thwarted passion, with a villain straight out of a penny-dreadful. Yet it is also a heartfelt protest about the Hindu custom preventing the remarriage of widows. DP Hindi, Urdu +subtitles.

Ashok Kumar *Prakash Mehta* • Sunil Dutt *Amar* • Meena Kumari *Malti* • Daisy Irani • Jeevan *Munshi* ■ *Dir* BR Chopra

Eklavya: the Royal Guard
★★★★ 12
Period action adventure
2007 · Ind · Colour · 107min

Director Vidhu Vinod Chopra brings his trademark visual panache to this contemporary tale of intrigue, love, and betrayal set in Rajasthan. Amitabh Bachchan plays a royal guard to one of the kings of the ancient Ruritanian dynasty, whose loyalty is severely tested following the queen's death as the peasants suffer under the king's authority. Bolstered by a mighty performance from Bachchan, *Eklavya* delivers a particularly visceral kind of period spectacle that Bollywood audiences haven't seen in decades. OA Hindi +subtitles. Some violence. *DVD*

Amitabh Bachchan *Eklavya* • Sanjay Dutt *Pannalal Chohaar* • Saif Ali Khan *Harshwardhan* • Vidya Balan *Rajjo* • Jackie Shroff *Jyotiwardhan* • Jimmy Shergill *Udaywardhan* ■ *Dir* Vidhu Vinod Chopra • *Scr* Vidhu Vinod Chopra, Abhijit Joshi

El ★★★★
Black comedy drama   1953 · Mex · BW · 100min

Exploring Luis Buñuel's perennial themes of sexual terror, religious hypocrisy and bourgeois indolence, this seething melodrama was based on Mercedes Pinto's autobiographical novel. Buñuel also drew inspiration from his insanely jealous brother-in-law and his own emotional conflicts. Amazingly, the film was poorly received on its Mexican release, but the tale of 40-year-old Catholic virgin Arturo De Cordova's descent into paranoia after marrying the much younger Delia Garces is a probing study of moral and psychological collapse, stuffed with moments of inspired surrealism. DP In Spanish.

Arturo de Cordova *Francisco Galvan de Montemayor* • Delia Garces *Gloria* • Luis Beristain *Raul Conde* • Aurora Walker *Senora Esperanza Peralta* • Carlos Martinez Baena *Padre Velasco* • Manuel Donde *Pablo* ■ *Dir* Luis Buñuel • *Scr* Luis Buñuel, Luis Alcoriza, from the novel *Pensamientos* by Mercedes Pinto

El Dorado ★★★★★ PG
Western   1967 · US · Colour · 121min

"Ride, boldly ride..." sings George Alexander over the Remington-styled western paintings that accompany the titles to this elegiac masterwork, a fabulously entertaining tale from ace director Howard Hawks. Gunfighter John Wayne is a flawed hero, whose actions lead to a boy's suicide in a superbly staged preface to the plot, and whose resulting wounds dictate the pace and outcome of the movie. More than a match for the Duke is the great Robert Mitchum, in one of his best screen roles as an alcoholic sheriff. This film suffered on its release by comparison to Hawks's earlier western masterpiece *Rio Bravo*, but with the passing of time this screen meditation on ageing proves to be one of the most pleasurable of all Hollywood movies. TS *DVD*

John Wayne *Cole Thornton* • Robert Mitchum *JP Harrah* • James Caan *Mississippi* • Charlene Holt *Maudie* • Michele Carey *Joey MacDonald* • Arthur Hunnicutt *Bull Harris* • RG Armstrong *Kevin MacDonald* • Edward Asner *Bart Jason* • Johnny Crawford *Luke MacDonald* ■ *Dir* Howard Hawks • *Scr* Leigh Brackett, from the novel *The Stars in Their Courses* by Harry Brown

El Dorado ★★★ 15
Historical adventure
1988 · Sp/Fr · Colour · 122min

Director Carlos Saura's re-creation of the doomed 1560 expedition to find the fabled New World land of El Dorado is historically accurate, earnestly played and magnificently photographed by Teo Escamilla. Saura succeeds in conveying the mix of greed and reckless folly that inspired the conquistadors to risk all in the pursuit of wealth and power, but it never comes close to topping the achievement of *Aguirre, Wrath of God*, Werner Herzog's remarkable account of the same story made 16 years earlier. DP Spanish +subtitles. Violence.

Omero Antonutti *Lope de Aguirre* • Eusebio Poncela *Fernando de Guzman* • Lambert Wilson *Pedro de Ursua* • Gabriela Roel *Dona Ines* • José Sancho *Juan de la Bandera* • Féodor Atkine *Montoya* • Patxi Bisquert *Pedrarias* ■ *Dir/Scr* Carlos Saura

Election ★★★★ 15
Satirical comedy   1999 · US · Colour · 98min

Near the top of the league table for high-school movies, this is a dark and very funny twist on the popularity contest theme often central to the genre. The casting of Matthew Broderick as a devoted teacher trying to prevent manipulative overachiever Reese Witherspoon from becoming student president is inspired. Director/co-writer Alexander Payne is repaid by his star with a performance of sincere, if muddled idealism. Pitted against jock Chris Klein and his lesbian sister (Jessica Campbell making

a revelatory debut), Witherspoon's blend of corruption and compassion slyly satirises contemporary American politics, while George Washington Carver High serves as a microcosm of late-20th-century society. Astute, offbeat and uproarious. DP Swearing, sex scenes, nudity. *DVD* *BL*

Matthew Broderick *Jim McAllister* • Reese Witherspoon *Tracy Flick* • Chris Klein *Paul Metzler* • Phil Reeves *Walt Hendricks* • Mark Harelik *Dave Novotny* • Delaney Driscoll *Linda Novotny* • Molly Hagan *Diane McAllister* • Jessica Campbell *Tammy Metzler* ■ *Scr* Alexander Payne, Jim Taylor, from the novel by Tom Perrotta

Election ★★★★ 18
Crime drama   2005 · HK · Colour · 99min

With its simmering sense of latent violence and authentic insights into the workings of the Hong Kong underworld, this compelling crime drama makes twin virtues of its complexity and restraint. The struggle between Simon Yam and Tony Leung Ka-fai for the wooden baton that symbolises control over the territory's oldest and most powerful Triad, the Wo Sing Society, thrums with conspiratorial menace and corruption. DP Cantonese +subtitles. Violence. *DVD*

Simon Yam *Lok* • Tony Leung Ka-fai [Tony Leung (1)] *Big D* • Louis Koo *Jimmy* • Nick Cheung *Jet* • Cheung Siu Fai *Mr So* • Lam Suet *Big Head* • Lam Ka Tung *Kun* ■ *Dir* Johnnie To • *Scr* Yau Nai Hoi, Yip Tin Shing

Electra Glide in Blue ★★★ 15
Crime drama   1973 · US · Colour · 108min

A cult movie of its day, this abrasive mix of black comedy and satire made a one-hit wonder of its director, record producer James William Guercio. Robert Blake gives one of his best performances as a diminutive motorcycle cop who justifies his tough-guy act by claiming to be the exact same height as Alan Ladd. After some of the most graphic violence then seen on screen, the ending is something of a cop-out, but Conrad Hall's photography is outstanding. DP *DVD*

Robert Blake *John Wintergreen* • Billy Green Bush *Zipper Davis* • Mitchell Ryan *Harve Poole* • Jeannine Riley *Jolene* • Elisha Cook [Elisha Cook Jr] *Willie* • Royal Dano *Coroner* ■ *Dir* James William Guercio • *Scr* Robert Boris, Michael Butler, from a story by Robert Boris, Rupert Hitzig

Electric Boogaloo: the Wild, Untold Story of Cannon Films ★★★★ 18
Documentary
2014 · Aus/US/Is/UK · Colour and BW · 101min

Fans of bargain-basement cinema will find much to enjoy in this affectionate documentary about Cannon Films, the infamous production company best known for churning out schlocky, tasteless, low-budget motion pictures during the 1980s. Run by impulsive movie moguls Menahem Golan and Yoram Globus, Cannon was responsible for the poorly received *Death Wish* sequels, among others. Charting the company's rise and fall, *Electric Boogaloo* combines clips from these films (as well as many others) with anecdotal testimonies from various individuals, including Elliott Gould, Dolph Lundgren and Franco Zeffirelli. SC Violence, sex scenes, nudity. *DVD*

■ *Dir/Scr* Mark Hartley

Electric Dreams ★ PG
Romantic comedy
1984 · US/UK · Colour · 92min

"Computers are alive" is the theme of this daft romantic comedy. Lenny Von Dohlen plays a geeky architect whose new computer comes to life when champagne is spilt over it. Both owner and computer then fall for girl-next-door Virginia Madsen. Shot by director Steve Barron in the style of a pop promo, this starts brightly enough but soon disintegrates. LH *DVD*

Lenny Von Dohlen *Miles* • Virginia Madsen *Madeline* • Maxwell Caulfield *Bill* • Bud Cort *Edgar* • Don Fellows *Ryley* • Alan Polonsky *Frank* •

Wendy Miller *Computer clerk* • Harry Rabinowitz *Conductor* • Miriam Margolyes *Ticket girl* • Koo Stark *Soap opera girl* ■ *Dir* Steve Barron • *Scr* Rusty Lemorande

The Electric Horseman
★★ PG
Comedy western   1979 · US · Colour · 120min

Despite its title and fizzling lead performances by Robert Redford and Jane Fonda, this early eco-warning tale about mindless consumerism carries too little charge. Redford plays a down-on-his-luck rodeo rider who saves a thoroughbred horse from corporate greed and is chased into the desert by Fonda's TV newswoman. It's a solid romp, but it all becomes a bit preachy. TH *DVD*

Robert Redford *Sonny Steele* • Jane Fonda *Hallie Martin* • Valerie Perrine *Charlotta* • Willie Nelson *Wendell* • John Saxon *Hunt Sears* • Nicholas Coster [Nicolas Coster] *Fitzgerald* • Allan Arbus *Danny* • Wilford Brimley *Farmer* • Will Hare *Gus* ■ *Dir* Sydney Pollack • *Scr* Robert Garland, from a screenplay (unproduced) by Garland, Paul Gaer, from a story by Shelly Burton

Electric Man ★★★ 12A
Comedy   2012 · UK · Colour · 100min

Edinburgh provides the eye-catching backdrop to this micro-budget caper about the pursuit of a valuable comic. When the first issue of *Electric Man* accidentally ends up in Toby Manley and Mark McKirdy's cash-strapped comics shop, the dippy duo soon find themselves the target of an obsessed collector, a murderous hard man and a caped *femme fatale*. Director/co-writer David Barras's film may appeal more to comic-book geeks than superhero-movie fans, but if you're prepared to overlook its financial shortcomings, then this is an entertaining little yarn. JA Some swearing, sexual references.

Toby Manley *Jason Archer* • Mark McKirdy *Wolf* • Derek Dick [Fish] *Uncle Jimmy* • Jennifer Ewing *Lauren McCall* ■ *Dir* David Barras • *Scr* David Barras, Scott MacKay

Electric Moon ★★ 15
Satirical drama   1992 · UK · Colour · 102min

There's a distinct Ealing feel to this wry satire on themed holidays, which are seemingly designed to reinforce patronising perceptions of an idealised past. But there are also acerbic asides on India's colonial legacy and its predilection for bureaucratic pettifogging. Director Pradip Krishen reduces the western tourists to hideous stereotypes, yet he takes such a time doing so that the film fails to gain any momentum until rulebook martinet Naseeruddin Shah and duplicitous lodge manager Roshan Seth begin to feud over the latter's bogus safari operation. DP

Roshan Seth *Ranveer* • Naseeruddin Shah *Rambuhj Goswami* • Leela Naidu *Socks/Sukanya* • Gerson Da Cunha *Bubbles/Raja Ran Bikram Singh* • Raghubir Yadav [Raghuvir Yadav] *Boltoo* ■ *Dir* Pradip Krishen • *Scr* Arundhati Roy

Electricity ★★★★ 15
Drama   2014 · UK · Colour · 95min

Epilepsy and fractured family ties are the two main concerns of Bryn Higgins's naturalistic British drama. The person dealing with both is Lily (Agyness Deyn), a young woman who suffers from debilitating seizures that make it difficult for her to lead a normal life. In spite of this, however, she travels down from the north to London after the sudden death of her mother, deciding to track down her long-lost younger brother (Christian Cooke) to ensure he gets his share of the inheritance. The story itself isn't especially remarkable but the film is gifted with a fearless, revelatory, star-making performance by model-turned-actress Deyn. SC Swearing, a sex scene, some violence, brief nudity. *DVD*

Agyness Deyn *Lily O'Connor* • Lenora Crichlow *Mel* • Christian Cooke *Mikey O'Connor* • Paul Anderson (2) *Barry O'Connor* ■ *Dir* Bryn Higgins • *Scr* Joe Fisher, from Ray Robinson's novel

Electrick Children ★★★★ 15

Drama   2012 · US · Colour · 91min

This indie drama, the feature debut of writer/director Rebecca Thomas, is an original take on the fish-out-of-water scenario. A magnetic Julia Garner plays the naive 15-year-old Mormon who drives to Las Vegas with her brother (Liam Aiken) to track down the singer whom she believes made her pregnant when she listened to his band's cover of Blondie's *Hanging on the Telephone* on a forbidden tape recorder. Picked up by the sympathetic Rory Culkin and his grungy entourage, she and her brother soon experience drugs, drink and skateboarding for the first time. With its witty script, breezy, unforced performances and frequent surprises, *Electrick Children* announces a promising American talent. AC Swearing, drug abuse. *DVD*

Julia Garner *Rachel* • Rory Culkin *Clyde* • Liam Aiken *Mr Will* • Bill Sage *Tim* • Billy Zane *Paul* ■ *Dir/Scr* Rebecca Thomas

Elegy ★★ 15

Relationship drama   2008 · US · Colour · 107min

Ben Kingsley and Penélope Cruz share the screen and a bed in this pretentious adaptation of Philip Roth's novella *The Dying Animal*, charting the doomed affair between 60-something literature professor David Kepesh (Kingsley) and a much younger student (Cruz). Narrated from Kepesh's perspective, it's a melancholy tale of consuming passion in which the older man is convinced that he will be abandoned for someone younger and (presumably) less self-absorbed. Patricia Clarkson, Peter Sarsgaard and Dennis Hopper pad out the supporting roles brilliantly (though the latter stretches belief somewhat as a Pulitzer Prize-winning poet). They also add much needed diversion from all the navel-gazing and existential chatter about mortality, lust and the perfect curve of Cruz's breasts. JR Swearing, sex scenes, nudity. *DVD* Blu-ray

Penélope Cruz *Consuela Castillo* • Ben Kingsley *David Kepesh* • Dennis Hopper *George* • Patricia Clarkson *Carolyn* • Peter Sarsgaard *Kenneth Kepesh* • Deborah Harry *Amy* • Charlie Rose ■ *Dir* Isabel Coixet • *Scr* Nicholas Meyer, from the novella *The Dying Animal* by Philip Roth

Elektra ★★ 12

Martial arts action fantasy
2005 · US · Colour · 92min

Daredevil's lady friend Elektra gets a solo outing in this insipid adventure based on the spin-off Marvel comic book. Resuming events where the Ben Affleck vehicle ended, Jennifer Garner's warrior is literally back from the dead and working as a hired assassin. But when she's asked to kill a father and daughter on the run from a supernatural martial arts syndicate, Elektra's past and conscience catch up with her. The film is glossy and stylish, but Garner lacks charisma and the fight action is unimpressive. SF Violence. *DVD* Blu-ray

Jennifer Garner *Elektra Natchios* • Terence Stamp *Stick* • Goran Visnjic *Mark Miller* • Kirsten Prout *Abby Miller* • Cary-Hiroyuki Tagawa *Roshi* • Will Yun Lee *Kirigi* • Chris Ackerman *Tattoo* • Edson T Ribeiro *Kinkou* • Colin Cunningham *McCabe* ■ *Dir* Rob Bowman • *Scr* Raven Metzner, Zak Penn, Stuart Zicherman, from the Marvel character created by Frank Miller

The Element of Crime ★★★★ 15

Fantasy crime mystery
1984 · Den · Colour · 99min

Lars von Trier's debut feature is a ragbag of visual allusions to everything from German expressionism and Hollywood *noir* to the self-reflexivity of the *nouvelle vague* and the grim poetry of Andrei Tarkovsky. Yet shamus Michael Elphick's quest to unmask the mathematically minded serial perpetrator of the "Lotto murders" makes for compelling viewing. With Esmond Knight leading a first-rate multinational ensemble cast, this was rightly hailed as the work of a master-in-waiting. DP *DVD*

Michael Elphick *Fisher* • Esmond Knight *Osborne* • Me Me Lai *Kim* • Jerold Wells *Police Chief Kramer* • Ahmed El Shenawi *Therapist* • Astrid Henning-Jensen *Osborne's housekeeper* • Janos Hersko *Coroner* • Stig Larsson *Coroner's assistant* • Lars von Trier *Schmuck of Ages* ■ *Dir* Lars von Trier • *Scr* Lars von Trier, Niels Vorsel

Elementary School ★★★

Comedy   1991 · Cz · Colour · 100min

Jan Sverak made his feature debut with this powerful drama. Written by and starring Sverak's father, Zdenek, this largely autobiographical story focuses on life in Prague during the interlude between liberation from the Nazis and subjugation by the Communists. In addition to Zdenek and leading Czech actor Rudolf Hrusinsky, the cast also includes legendary film-makers Jirí Menzel and Karel Kachyna in cameo roles. The film was nominated for an Oscar, but the Sveraks were to go one better with the enchanting *Kolya*, which won the 1996 Academy Award for best foreign language film. DP Czech +subtitles.

Jan Triska *Igor Hnizdo* • Zdenek Sverak *Soucek* • Libuse Safrankova *Mrs Soucek* • Rudolf Hrusinsky *Schoolmaster* • Daniela Kolarova *Miss Maxova* • Vaclav Jakoubek *Eda* • Jirí Menzel *Doctor* • Karel Kachyna *School inspector* ■ *Dir* Jan Sverak • *Scr* Zdenek Sverak

Elena ★★★★ 12

Drama   2011 · Rus/Fr/US/Jpn · Colour · 104min

Financial tensions between a wealthy Russian businessman and his lower-class second wife (and former nurse) illustrate the country's changing social and economic realities in this absorbing drama from Andrey Zvyagintsev (*The Return*). Some viewers might find the pace a little too deliberate, but give it time and director Zvyagintsev's compelling purpose becomes clear; he asks probing questions, and the answers are not quite what we expect. It's certainly an unsettling vision of ruthless materialism in the new Russia, bolstered by a marvellous performance from Nadezhda Markina. TJ Russian +subtitles. *DVD*

Nadezhda Markina *Elena* • Andrey Smirnov *Vladimir* • Elena Lyadova *Katerina* • Alexey Rozin *Sergey* ■ *Dir* Andrey Zvyagintsev • *Scr* Andrey Zvyagintsev, Oleg Negin

Elena et les Hommes ★★★★ U

Period romantic drama
1956 · Fr/It · Colour · 94min

This deceptively lightweight period piece from writer/director Jean Renoir provides a glistening showcase for Ingrid Bergman. She plays a beautiful woman in Paris at the end of the 19th century looking for a wealthy meal ticket who gradually learns about the true meaning of love. Renoir's main concern is evoking the colour and gaiety of the time, and the result is an enchanting romantic fable. JF French +subtitles. *DVD*

Ingrid Bergman *Elena* • Mel Ferrer *Henri de Chevincourt* • Jean Marais *Rollan* • Jean Richard *Hector* • Magali Noël *Lolotte* • Juliette Greco *Miarka* • Pierre Bertin *Martin-Michaud* • Jean Castanier *Isnard* ■ *Dir/Scr* Jean Renoir

Eleni ★★★ PG

Biographical drama   1985 · US · Colour · 111min

What was uplifting on the page comes out flatly on film, in this re-creation of Nicholas Gage's book about his real-life search for the executioners of his peasant mother, who sacrificed herself to save her children from the communist faction that took over her Greek village. Kate Nelligan gives a poignant performance in flashback, but it's the search for truth by John Malkovich (as Gage) that holds what tension there is. TH *DVD*

Kate Nelligan *Eleni Gatzoyiannis* • John Malkovich *Nicholas Gage* • Linda Hunt *Katina* • Oliver Cotton *Katis* • Ronald Pickup *Spiro Skevis* • Glenne Headly *Joan* • Alfred Molina *Young Christos* ■ *Dir* Peter Yates • *Scr* Steve Tesich, from the book by Nicholas Gage

Elenya ★★★ PG

Second World War drama
1992 · UK · Colour · 78min

This tale about a young woman of Italian descent living with her aunt in the Welsh countryside feels dispiritingly familiar. Pascale Delafouge Jones superbly plays the ostracised girl, while Klaus Behrendt is utterly believable as the German pilot she befriends after he crashes in the woods. Skilfully portrayed and well photographed. SH

Margaret John *Old Elenya* • Pascale Delafouge Jones *Young Elenya* • Seiriol Tomos *Glyn* • Sue Jones-Davies *Maggie* • Iago Wynn Jones *Sidney* • Llio Millward *Schoolteacher* • Klaus Behrendt *Franz* ■ *Dir/Scr* Steve Gough

Elephant ★★★ 15

Drama   2003 · US · Colour · 78min

Director Gus Van Sant's Palme d'Or-winning film documents a normal day at an ordinary American high school. Except this day ends in a senseless massacre, much like the Columbine killings to which it alludes. The main characters are real students, and their casual encounters and improvised conversations are detailed in long travelling shots before Alex Frost and Eric Deulen enter school carrying assault weapons. Either a disturbingly poetic disaster movie or an arty view of a contemporary malaise, this raises more questions than it answers. AJ *DVD*

Alex Frost *Alex* • Eric Duelen *Eric* • John Robinson (3) *John McFarland* • Elias McConnell *Elias* • Jordan Taylor *Jordan* • Carrie Finklea *Carrie* • Nicole George *Nicole* • Brittany Mountain *Brittany* • Timothy Bottoms *Mr McFarland* ■ *Dir/Scr* Gus Van Sant

Elephant Boy ★★ U

Adventure   1937 · UK · BW · 78min

In 1936, the British-based movie mogul Alexander Korda dispatched the famed documentarist Robert Flaherty to India to make a version of Rudyard Kipling's *Toomai of the Elephants*. Flaherty discovered Sabu, who was a 12-year-old stable boy to a maharajah, and cast him in the leading role; he then shot some 50 hours of footage and returned to England with fine images but no story. Korda then put his brother Zoltan to work to patch things together. The result, predictably, is a bit of a mess, but it retains its exoticism. AT *DVD*

Sabu *Toomai* • Walter Hudd *Petersen* • Allan Jeayes *Machua Appa* • WE Holloway *Father* • Bruce Gordon (1) *Rham Lahl* • DJ Williams *Hunter* • Wilfrid Hyde White *Commissioner* • Iravatha *Kala Nag* ■ *Dir* Robert Flaherty, Zoltan Korda • *Scr* John Collier, Akos Tolnay, Marcia de Silva, from the novel *Toomai of the Elephants* by Rudyard Kipling

An Elephant Called Slowly ★★ U

Adventure   1969 · UK · Colour · 87min

Director James Hill tries to do for elephants what he did for lions in *Born Free* (1966), though with rather less success. The wildlife story again involves Virginia McKenna and Bill Travers, this time trying to protect three orphaned baby elephants. In the process they rub shoulders with the real-life Adamsons, the couple they played in the earlier film. Alas, the film failed to please audiences. FL

Virginia McKenna *Ginny* • Bill Travers *Bill* • Vinay Inambar *Mr Mophagee* • Joab Collins *Henry* • Ali Twaha *Mutiso* ■ *Dir* James Hill • *Scr* Bill Travers, James Hill

Elephant Juice ★★ 18

Comedy drama   1999 · US/UK · Colour · 83min

Pitched as a penetrating look at the relationship merry-go-round in modern-day London, this arch comedy drama is a banal bust. In her British film debut, French star Emmanuelle Béart plays a city whizzkid whose engagement to handsome artist Daniel Lapaine causes her close circle of friends to re-evaluate their own lives. Secret affairs, crises of conscience and a suicide attempt lead to a ho-hum happy ending. AJ Swearing, nudity. *DVD*

Emmanuelle Béart *Jules* • Sean Gallagher *Billy* • Daniel Lapaine *Will* • Mark Strong *Frank* • Daniela Nardini *Daphne* • Kimberly Williams *Dodie* • Lennie James *Graham* • Lee Williams *George* ■ *Dir* Sam Miller • *Scr* Amy Jenkins, from an idea by Amy Jenkins, Sam Miller

The Elephant Man

★★★★★ PG

Biographical drama   1980 · US · BW · 118min

This stylish, poignant drama is probably the closest director David Lynch has got to the mainstream. It's based on the true story of the horrifically disfigured John Merrick (a superb, unrecognisable John Hurt), who battled the prejudices of Victorian society. Full marks, too, for Freddie Francis's striking black-and-white cinematography and the excellent playing from a top-drawer cast. Made, surprisingly, given its weighty tone, by comic Mel Brooks's production company. JF *DVD* Blu-ray

John Hurt *John Merrick* • Anthony Hopkins *Frederick Treves* • Anne Bancroft *Mrs Madge Kendal* • John Gielgud *Carr Gomm* • Wendy Hiller *Mothershead* • Freddie Jones *Bytes* • Michael Elphick *Night porter* • Hannah Gordon *Mrs Treves* ■ *Dir* David Lynch • *Scr* Christopher de Vore, Eric Bergren, David Lynch, from the non-fiction books *The Elephant Man: A Study In Human Dignity* by Ashley Montagu and *The Elephant Man and Other Reminiscences* by Sir Frederick Treves • *Make-up* Christopher Tucker

Elephant Walk ★★★ U

Drama   1954 · US · Colour · 98min

Peter Finch marries Elizabeth Taylor and takes her back to Ceylon where his tea plantation has been established right in the path of commuting pachyderms. But domestic squabbles, an outbreak of typhoid and the promised elephant stampede do not prevent our heroes from producing a good, strong, freshly-brewed cuppa in this solid melodrama. AT *DVD*

Elizabeth Taylor *Ruth Wiley* • Dana Andrews *Dick Carver* • Peter Finch *John Wiley* • Abraham Sofaer *Appuhamy* • Abner Biberman *Dr Pereira* • Noel Drayton *Planter Atkinson* • Rosalind Ivan *Mrs Lakin* ■ *Dir* William Dieterle • *Scr* John Lee Mahin, from the novel by Robert Standish

Elevator Girl ★★

Romantic comedy   2010 · US · Colour · 105min

Love struggles across the social divide in this flimsy modern-day fairy tale, after hotshot lawyer Ryan Merriman falls for a free-spirited working-class girl (Lacey Chabert) that he meets in a lift. The usual romantic ups and downs ensue forcing the pair to re-evaluate their lives and expectations. But while the message-laden decisions they reach are as simplistic and predictable as the happy ending that follows, seasoned director Bradford May's light touch keeps proceedings cute rather than cloying. SF

Lacey Chabert *Liberty "Libby"* • Ryan Merriman *Jonathan* • Patty McCormack *Rosemary* ■ *Dir* Bradford May • *Scr* Amy Jenkins Notas

11:14 ★★★ 15

Black comedy drama
2003 · US/Can · Colour · 82min

The stars come out for a complex, clever and quirkily comic piece of film-making from writer/director director Greg Marcks. Hilary Swank, Patrick Swayze, Rachael Leigh Cook and Colin Hanks (son of Tom) are among the disparate suburbanites whose lives cross and collide before, during and after the freeway incident that takes place at the time of the title. Although the crash-centric jigsaw puzzle of a plot brings to mind *Crash*, this actually predates that film. DA Swearing, sex scenes. *DVD*

Hilary Swank *Buzzy* • Rachael Leigh Cook *Cheri* • Patrick Swayze *Frank* • Barbara Hershey *Norma* • Colin Hanks *Mark* • Henry Thomas *Jack* • Ben Foster *Eddie* • Shawn Hatosy *Duffy* ■ *Dir/Scr* Greg Marcks

11 Harrowhouse ★★

Crime comedy   1974 · UK · Colour · 108min

This overeager comedy foolhardily attempts to send up the heist caper. Only the bullish playing saves the day, as Aram

Avakian's direction is so slipshod that the enterprise has descended into low farce long before the extended chase finale. Hard though Charles Grodin and Candice Bergen try as the ingenious vacuuming jewel thieves, they're totally outclassed by a venerable supporting cast. DP

Charles Grodin *Chesser* • Candice Bergen *Maren* • John Gielgud *Meecham* • Trevor Howard *Clyde Massey* • James Mason *Watts* • Peter Vaughan *Coglin* • Helen Cherry *Lady Bolding* • Jack Watson *Miller* • Jack Watling *Fitzmaurice* ■ *Dir* Aram Avakian • *Scr* Jeffrey Bloom, Charles Grodin, from the novel *11 Harrowhouse Street* by Gerald A Browne

11'09''01 - September 11 ★★★ 12

Portmanteau documentary
2002 • Fr/Iran/Egy/Bosnia/Burkina Faso/UK/Mex/Is/Ind/US/Jpn • Colour and BW • 128min

Cinema seizes its responsibility to reflect reality, rather than simply provide an escape from it, in this laudably even-handed omnibus. While all involved express sympathy with those personally affected by the Twin Towers tragedy, more militant film-makers such as Ken Loach and Youssef Chahine challenge the ethics of postwar US foreign policy, while others including Amos Gitai and Danis Tanovic highlight the many local tragedies that were eclipsed by the media response to the attack. The project's sincerity is indisputable, but the quality of the contributions is mixed. DP **DVD**

■ *Dir* Samira Makhmalbaf, Claude Lelouch, Youssef Chahine, Danis Tanovic, Idrissa Ouedraogo, Ken Loach, Alejandro González Iñárritu, Amos Gitai, Mira Nair, Sean Penn, Shohei Imamura • *Scr* Samira Makhmalbaf, Claude Lelouch, Pierre Uytterhoeven, Youssef Chahine, Danis Tanovic, Idrissa Ouedraogo, Paul Laverty, Ken Loach, Vladimir Vega, Alejandro González Iñárritu, Amos Gitaï, Marie Josée Sanselme, Sabrina Dhawan, Sean Penn, Daisuke Tengan

The 11th Hour ★★ PG

Documentary   2007 • US • Colour • 88min

This earnest eco-documentary attempts to build on the crossover success of Al Gore's *An Inconvenient Truth*, but simply hammers home the same basic message but with less charm, subtlety and finesse. Produced and narrated by Leonardo DiCaprio, it aims to give a platform to environmental thinkers whose voices are excluded by the mainstream media. But in doing so it simply feels like a photo book stuffed with talking heads presenting facts and figures with little context. Still, if you're interested in things like sustainable architecture you may take on board at least something from the babble of doom-mongering. DW **DVD**

Leonardo DiCaprio *Narrator* • Mikhail Gorbachev • Stephen Hawking ■ *Dir/Scr* Nadia Conners, Leila Conners Petersen

Elf ★★★★ PG

Seasonal comedy fantasy
2003 • US • Colour • 92min

Director Jon Favreau's sweet seasonal comedy relies entirely on the talents of Will Ferrell, who plays an adult raised from a baby by Santa's little helpers. Ferrell discovers the existence of his birth father (James Caan in full-bore Scrooge mode) and heads for New York. Despite modern special effects trickery, this strives for the feel of vintage Disney through twee settings and storybook narration from Bob Newhart. Ferrell is the life and soul of an infectiously entertaining Christmas celebration. JC **DVD** **Blu**

Will Ferrell *Buddy* • James Caan *Walter* • Bob Newhart *Papa Elf* • Edward Asner *Santa* • Mary Steenburgen *Emily* • Zooey Deschanel *Jovie* • Daniel Tay *Michael* • Michael Lerner *Fulton* ■ *Dir* Jon Favreau • *Scr* David Berenbaum

Elfie Hopkins ★★ 15

Horror thriller   2011 • UK • Colour • 88min

Jaime Winstone's slacker turns amateur detective in this quirky yet underwhelming British chiller. Winstone is grunged up and annoyingly affected in the title role, as she and her fellow stoner pal (Aneurin Barnard) investigate a family of posh weirdos that's moved into their sleepy rural village.

Initially, the film is sluggish and uneventful, but picks up after Winstone's daftly scripted verbal suspicions are proven true, and creepy atmospherics turn to pure gore. Yet this over-the-top carnage only intensifies the feature's lack of depth and balance. SF Violence, swearing, drug abuse.

Jaime Winstone *Elfie Hopkins* • Aneurin Barnard *Dylan Parker* • Rupert Evans (2) *Mr Gammon* • Steven Mackintosh *Michael* • Ray Winstone *Butcher Bryn* • Kate Magowan *Mrs Gammon* ■ *Dir* Ryan Andrews • *Scr* Ryan Andrews, Riyad Barmania, from their story

The Elite Squad ★★★ 18

Action crime drama
2007 • Bra/US/Neth • Colour • 114min

This violent cop drama became a phenomenon as a pirated DVD, even before its official release in its native Brazil. Set in Rio de Janeiro in 1997, it focuses on agitated police chief Captain Nascimento (Wagner Moura), who is trying to find his replacement as head of the SWAT-style BOPE unit. There are only two likely candidates: the volatile Neto (Caio Junqueira) and the bookish Matias (Andre Ramiro). The scenes of torture are harsh and uncompromising as Nascimento ruthlessly cleans up his patch, making it easy to misread the film as sympathetic to the clearly rattled cop, while director José Padilha's shooting style is so frenetic that it's hard to tell whether he's just putting Brazil's messed-up law enforcement system into context or cheerleading for its death squads. DW Portuguese +subtitles. **DVD**

Wagner Moura *Captain Nascimento* • Caio Junqueira *Neto* • Andre Ramiro *Andre Matias* • Maria Ribeiro *Rosane* • Fernanda Machado *Nadia* • Fernanda de Freitas *Roberta* ■ *Dir* José Padilha • *Scr* Braulio Mantovani, José Padilha, Rodrigo Pimentel, from the non-fiction book *Elite da Tropa* by Andre Batista, Luiz Eduardo Soares

Elite Squad: the Enemy Within ★★★ 18

Action crime drama   2010 • Bra • Colour • 110min

This gritty anti-corruption drama follow-up has been a big hit in its native Brazil, as was the original, *The Elite Squad*, back in 2007. It's a wordier, more complex and less action-packed film than the first. But it's still a decent drama, as returning star Wagner Moura's no-nonsense Rio de Janeiro police commander discovers what filled the crime vacuum left by his crackdown on Rio de Janeiro's drugs trade a decade previously. DA Portuguese +subtitles. Violence. **DVD** **Blu**

Wagner Moura *Captain Nascimento* • Irandhir Santos *Fraga* • Andre Ramiro *Mathias* • Taina Muller *Clara* • Sandro Rocha *Russo* ■ *Dir* José Padilha • *Scr* José Padilha, Braulio Mantovani, from a story by Padilha, Mantovani, Rodrigo Pimentel

Elizabeth ★★★★ 15

Historical drama   1998 • UK • Colour • 118min

This Elizabethan political thriller charting the turbulent life and times of the self-proclaimed "Virgin Queen" is given a vivid contemporary focus by Indian director Shekhar Kapur's keen visual eye. A far cry from the usual "frock opera", this sumptuous biography is a thoughtful and dramatic triumph, with Australian actress Cate Blanchett revelatory as the strong-willed monarch who nimbly transforms from naive girlhood to true majesty, assisted by Sir Francis Walsingham (*Shine*'s Geoffrey Rush). Richard Attenborough, Joseph Fiennes and ex-footballer Eric Cantona flesh out an interesting cast. School history lessons were never this good! AJ Violence, sex scenes. **DVD** **Blu**

Cate Blanchett *Elizabeth I* • Geoffrey Rush *Sir Francis Walsingham* • Richard Attenborough *Sir William Cecil* • John Gielgud *The Pope* • Fanny Ardant *Mary of Guise* • Terence Rigby *Bishop Gardiner* • Christopher Eccleston *Duke of Norfolk* • Amanda Ryan *Lettice Howard* • Kathy Burke *Queen Mary Tudor* • Joseph Fiennes *Robert Dudley, Earl of Leicester* • Wayne Sleep *Dance tutor* • Angus Deayton *Woad, Chancellor of the Exchequer* • Eric Cantona *Monsieur de Foix* ■ *Dir* Shekhar Kapur • *Scr* Michael Hirst

Elizabeth: the Golden Age ★★★★ 12

Historical drama   2007 • UK/Fr • Colour • 110min

Almost ten years after her dazzling break-out role in *Elizabeth*, Cate Blanchett shows that she is still a force to be reckoned with as she reteams with director Shekhar Kapur. Queen Elizabeth I is now a little older and a lot wiser, as she faces potential conflict with Philip II of Spain (Jordi Mollà) and betrayal by her own cousin, Mary Stuart (Samantha Morton). It's only in her personal life that she's imprudent, flirting with Sir Walter Raleigh (a dashing Clive Owen), then growing jealous when he seduces one of her ladies-in-waiting. Kapur cleverly makes the dilemma of the 16th-century monarch relevant today, as Elizabeth is forced to sacrifice love for duty. And with a religious war brewing, the story resonates even more. Kapur plays fast and loose with history throughout, but the final scenes are both exciting and wildly romantic. SP **DVD** **Blu**

Cate Blanchett *Queen Elizabeth I* • Geoffrey Rush *Sir Francis Walsingham* • Clive Owen *Sir Walter Raleigh* • Rhys Ifans *Robert Reston* • Jordi Mollà *King Philip II of Spain* • Abbie Cornish *Bess Throckmorton* • Samantha Morton *Mary Stuart* • Tom Hollander *Sir Amyas Paulet* ■ *Dir* Shekhar Kapur • *Scr* Michael Hirst, William Nicholson • *Make-up* Jenny Shircore • *Costume Designer* Alexandra Byrne • *Cinematographer* Remi Adefarasin • *Production Designers* Guy Hendrix Dyas, Richard Roberts

Elizabeth of Ladymead ★★

Period drama   1948 • UK • Colour • 107min

This is a disappointing pageant, in which a concussed Anna Neagle imagines herself in various incarnations during a turbulent century of change. In 1854, she's a devotee of women's rights awaiting news of the conflict in the Crimea. By the post-Boer War era, she's become sufficiently independent to run the family estate. However, things take a sordid turn around the Treaty of Versailles, when her reckless behaviour drives her husband to suicide. DP

Anna Neagle *Elizabeth* • Hugh Williams *John, 1946* • Nicholas Phipps *John, 1854* • Michael Laurence (1) *John, 1919* • Bernard Lee *John, 1903* ■ *Dir* Herbert Wilcox • *Scr* Frank Harvey, Nicholas Phipps, from a play by Frank Harvey

Elizabethtown ★★ 12

Romantic comedy drama
2005 • US • Colour • 118min

This mawkish romantic comedy is a messy yarn in which Orlando Bloom's failed and suicidal shoe designer is taught to love again by the kooky air stewardess (Kirsten Dunst) he meets while flying to Kentucky to collect his dead father's body. An overlong lesson in love, loss and fear-management, the film preaches a message of emotional honesty yet its execution is often too contrived to swallow. SF Swearing. **DVD**

Orlando Bloom *Drew Baylor* • Kirsten Dunst *Claire Colburn* • Susan Sarandon *Hollie Baylor* • Alec Baldwin *Phil DeVoss* • Bruce McGill *Bill Banyon* • Judy Greer *Heather Baylor* • Jessica Biel *Ellen Kishmore* • Paul Schneider (2) *Jessie Baylor* • Loudon Wainwright [Loudon Wainwright III] *Uncle Dale* ■ *Dir/Scr* Cameron Crowe

Ella Enchanted ★★★ PG

Comedy fantasy adventure
2004 • US/UK/Ire • Colour • 92min

Fairy tales are engagingly deconstructed in director Tommy O'Haver's overly spiced-up adaptation. Spirited Anne Hathaway plays Ella of Frell, cursed at birth to obey every command, who navigates her way through a revisionist onslaught of villainous stepsisters, enslaved ogres and show-tune singing elves to conquer her fears and uncover a plot to kill the handsome Prince Charmont (Hugh Dancy). This is a camp mess but an appealing one. AJ **DVD**

Anne Hathaway *Ella of Frell* • Hugh Dancy *Prince Charmont* • Cary Elwes *Sir Edgar* • Aidan McArdle *Slannen of Pim* • Joanna Lumley *Dame Olga* • Minnie Driver *Mandy* • Jimi Mistry *Benny* • Eric Idle *Narrator* • Vivica A Fox *Lucinda Perriweather* • Patrick Bergin *Sir Peter* • Steve Coogan *Heston* ■ *Dir* Tommy O'Haver • *Scr* Laurie Craig,

Karen McCullah Lutz, Kirsten Smith, Jennifer Heath, Michelle J Wolff, from the novel by Gail Carson Levine

Ellery Queen Master Detective ★★

Detective mystery   1940 • US • BW • 67min

Ellery Queen, one of the most successful fictional detectives of all time, didn't have much luck with his movie incarnations, eventually finding his natural home on TV. Here, Queen is portrayed by an embarrassed Ralph Bellamy as a comic bumbling dolt. In this tale, the amateur detective is called in the solve the murder of a millionaire at a health spa. Bellamy only played Queen on four occasions, leaving the role to William Gargan in 1942 for three futher films. TS

Ralph Bellamy *Ellery Queen* • Margaret Lindsay *Nikki Porter* • Charley Grapewin *Inspector Queen* • James Burke *Sergeant Velie* • Michael Whalen *Dr James Rogers* • Marsha Hunt *Barbara Braun* • Fred Niblo *John Braun* ■ *Dir* Kurt Neumann • *Scr* Eric Taylor, from a story by Ellery Queen [Frederic Dannay, Manfred B Lee]

Elles ★★ 18

Drama   2011 • Fr/Pol/Ger • Colour • 95min

Polish director Malgoska Szumowska tackles the world of suburban prostition with this novel but not entirely successful approach to the *Belle de Jour* theme. Juliette Binoche plays the *Elle* magazine writer who leaves her cosy if dull existence to interview young sex workers in the underbelly of Paris. Binoche is her usual classy self, but Szumowska struggles to balance the sophisticated world of the journalist with the harsh life of her subjects, and the exploitatively graphic sex scenes don't help. DP French, Polish +subtitles. Violence, swearing, sex scenes, nudity. **DVD**

Juliette Binoche *Anne* • Anaïs Demoustier *Charlotte/"Lola"* • Joanna Kulig *Alicja* • Krystyna Janda *Alicja's mother* • Louis-Do de Lencquesaing *Patrick* • Andrzej Chyra *Sadist client* ■ *Dir* Malgoska Szumowska [Malgorzata Szumowska] • *Scr* Tine Byrckel, Malgoska Szumowska

Ellie ★ 15

Comedy   1984 • US • Colour • 85min

This soft-core sex comedy is somewhat dignified by the presence of Shelley Winters, but is mainly a pretext for *Penthouse* pet Sheila Kennedy to pose in any number of designer underwear outfits – and sometimes less. The latter is besieged by Winters's three sons after her wheelchair-bound father is murdered. AT

Sheila Kennedy *Ellie* • Shelley Winters *Cora* • Edward Albert *Tom* • Pat Paulsen *Sheriff* • George Gobel *Preacher* ■ *Dir* Peter Wittman • *Scr* Glenn Allen Smith

Ellie Parker ★★★ 15

Comedy   2005 • US • Colour • 95min

A splendid performance by Naomi Watts holds together this acerbic and astutely restrained insight into life in the Hollywood basement. The action expands upon a short that Watts made with writer/director Scott Coffey in 2001. But while her encounters with casting directors, agents and wannabe friends are consistently amusing, Watts comes into her own during the sequences in her car. Whether rehearsing accents, making calls or changing for her next audition, Watts makes Ellie irresistibly appealing. DP Swearing, drug abuse. **DVD**

Naomi Watts *Ellie Parker* • Rebecca Rigg *Sam* • Scott Coffey *Chris* • Mark Pellegrino *Justin* • Blair Mastbaum *Smash* • Chevy Chase *Dennis* ■ *Dir/Scr* Scott Coffey

Elling ★★★★ 15

Comedy drama   2001 • Nor • Colour • 82min

Nominated for the 2002 best foreign film Oscar, director Petter Naess's adaptation effectively combines offbeat comedy with poignant insight. Discovered hiding in a cupboard after the death of his mother, 40-something Elling (Per Christian Ellefsen) is taken to an institution where he meets the dull-witted Sven Nordin. Two years later, they are installed in an Oslo flat where Nordin's interest is diverted by pregnant neighbour Marit Pia Jacobsen, and Elling copes by writing poetry. Without a single patronising moment, this is a perceptive portrait of life on the margins. DP Norwegian +subtitles.

Per Christian Ellefsen *Elling* • Sven Nordin *Kjell Bjarne* • Per Christensen *Alfons Jorgensen* • Jørgen Langhelle *Frank Asli* • Marit Pia Jacobsen *Reidun Nordsletten* • Hilde Olausson *Gunn* • Ola Otnes *Hauger* • Eli-Anne Linnestad [Eli Anne Linnestad] *Johanne* ■ *Dir* Petter Naess • *Scr* Axel Hellstenius, from the novel *Brothers in Blood* by Ingvar Ambjornsen

Elmer Gantry ★★★★★ PG
Drama 1960 · US · Colour · 140min

Seldom does the cinema see such a perfect match of star and role as here, with Burt Lancaster as the conman who finds evangelism as easy to sell as vacuum cleaners. Lancaster rightly won the best actor Oscar for the finest performance of his career; the film also picked up Oscars for director Richard Brooks's screenplay and Shirley Jones's supporting turn as a vengeful prostitute. Also brilliantly cast is Jean Simmons as Sister Sharon Falconer, whose sincerity, like Gantry's, is never questioned. John Alton's colour photography is superb, but it's Brooks's handling of the key scenes that makes this film a Hollywood classic. TS *DVD*

Burt Lancaster *Elmer Gantry* • Jean Simmons *Sister Sharon Falconer* • Arthur Kennedy *Jim Lefferts* • Shirley Jones *Lulu Bains* • Dean Jagger *William L Morgan* • Patti Page *Sister Rachel* • Edward Andrews *George Babbitt* • John McIntyre [John McIntire] *Rev Pengilly* • Joe Maross *Pete* ■ *Dir* Richard Brooks • *Scr* Richard Brooks, from the novel by Sinclair Lewis

Eloge de l'Amour ★★★★★ PG
Experimental drama 2001 · Fr/Swi · BW and Colour · 94min

Already renowned for a career studded with memorable and revolutionary work, Jean-Luc Godard here produces an experimental meditation on the nature of love that ranks as one of his finest achievements. It's essentially a Teach Yourself Guide to the stylistic gimmicks – non-linear narrative, unusual editing techniques, varying visual textures – and ideological concerns – the "Hollywoodisation" of culture, the elusiveness of history and memory – that have pre-occupied the maverick maestro throughout his life. The consciously convoluted story concerns film-maker Bruno Putzulu's attempt to study the four stages of love – meeting, passion, separation and reconciliation – through the eyes of three couples. Godard's precise dissection of American cultural arrogance and the sly asides on the nature of heroism and the value of history lend a razor-sharp edge to this masterpiece. DP French +subtitles. *DVD*

Bruno Putzulu *Edgar* • Cécile Camp *The woman* • Jean Davy *Grandfather* • François Verny *Grandmother* • Philippe Lyrette *Philippe, Edgar's assistant* • Audrey Klebaner *Eglantine* ■ *Dir/Scr* Jean-Luc Godard • *Cinematographers* Christophe Pollock, Julien Hirsch

Eloise at the Plaza ★★
Comedy 2003 · US/UK · Colour · 89min

In this boisterous TV movie, Kay Thompson's popular literary creation Eloise proves the kind of on-screen heroine that young children love and adults endure. Portrayed with stage-school gusto by a smug Sofia Vassilieva, the interfering and bratty six-year-old turns New York's Plaza Hotel into her own personal playground. Over-the-top supporting performances add to the goofy air, allowing Julie Andrews to flaunt a laughable cockney accent in her wasted role as Eloise's long-suffering but adoring nanny. SF

Julie Andrews *Nanny* • Sofia Vassilieva *Eloise* • Jeffrey Tambor *Mr Salomone* • Kenneth Welsh *Sir Wilkes* • Debra Monk *Maggie* • Christine Baranski *Prunella Stickler* ■ *Dir* Kevin Lima • *Scr*

Janet Brownell, from the illustrated children's book by Kay Thompson (words), Hilary Knight (illustrations)

Elsa & Fred ★★★ 12
Romantic comedy drama 2014 · US · Colour and BW · 93min

Screen veterans Shirley MacLaine and Christopher Plummer rise above the patronising cuteness imposed by co-writer/director Michael Radford (*Il Postino*) in this tale of a late-blossoming love affair. As MacLaine projects her romantic whims – inspired by her favourite film, *La Dolce Vita* – onto her new next-door neighbour, the crotchety Plummer, the rapport between these two fine actors develops nicely. Although a touch of melodrama seems unavoidable, this is a romance characterised by light and whimsy. SP *DVD*

Shirley MacLaine *Elsa* • Christopher Plummer *Fred* • Marcia Gay Harden *Lydia* • Erika Alexander *Laverne* • Chris Noth [Christopher Noth] *Jack* ■ *Dir* Michael Radford • *Scr* Anna Pavignano, Michael Radford, from the film *Elsa y Fred* by Marcos Carnevale, Marcela Guerty, Lily Ann Martin • *Cinematographer* Michael McDonough

Elstree Calling ★★
Comedy musical 1930 · UK · BW · 86min

Hollywood had a ready produced several lavish musical revues to exploit sound and showcase contract artists when Britain's Elstree studio cobbled together this pathetically tatty-looking variety show, done against cardboard-looking sets. The production numbers are laughably bad, far funnier than the dire comedy sketches. There is historical interest in the fact that the really dreadful spoof of *The Taming of the Shrew* and other linking material were directed by Alfred Hitchcock. DM

Tommy Handley *Compère* ■ *Dir* Alfred Hitchcock, André Charlot, Jack Hubert, Paul Murray • *Scr* Adrian Brunel, Val Valentine, Walter Mycroft

The Elusive Pimpernel ★★ U
Period adventure 1950 · UK · Colour · 104min

This version of Baroness Orczy's *The Scarlet Pimpernel* is one of Michael Powell and Emeric Pressburger's lesser efforts; Powell had at one stage wanted the project to be a musical and called what he ended up with "a terrible mess". This is a little harsh, though, since the film is not without its moments of colour and excitement. David Niven is as suave as ever in the title role of the jaunty Englishman who, beneath his carefree exterior, dedicates himself to the task of saving French aristocrats from the revolutionary guillotine. PF

David Niven *Sir Percy Blakeney* • Margaret Leighton *Marguerite Blakeney* • Jack Hawkins *Prince of Wales* • Cyril Cusack *Chauvelin* • Robert Coote *Sir Andrew Ffoulkes* • Edmond Audran *Armand St Juste* • Danielle Godet *Suzanne de Tournai* ■ *Dir* Michael Powell, Emeric Pressburger • *Scr* Michael Powell, Emeric Pressburger, from the novel *The Scarlet Pimpernel* by Baroness Orczy

Elvira Madigan ★★★ PG
Romantic drama 1967 · Swe · Colour · 87min

This true tale of doomed love and flouted convention will either have you sobbing uncontrollably or wincing at its overt sentimentality. Director Bo Widerberg shot the illicit romance between a tightrope artist and a married soldier in hazy pastels, thus enhancing both the picturesque delights of the Swedish countryside and the beauty of Pia Degermark, who won the best actress prize at Cannes for her performance. DP Swedish +subtitles. *DVD*

Pia Degermark *Elvira* • Thommy Berggren *Sixten* • Lennart Malmer *Friend* • Nina Widerberg *Girl* • Cleo Jensen *Cook* ■ *Dir* Bo Widerberg • *Scr* Bo Widerberg, from the song *Visan om den sköna Konstberiderskan Elvira Madigans Kälek och Grymma Död* by Johan Lindström Saxon

Elvira, Mistress of the Dark ★ 15
Comedy 1988 · US · Colour · 91min

A distinctly American phenomenon, Elvira (real name Cassandra Peterson) is a camp vampette, an amalgam of Morticia Addams and Dolly Parton, who hosts horror movie nights on television. Graduating to her own feature movie, Peterson is cast as, well, a television horror movie host who inherits a haunted house. Horror buffs may get a kick out of the numerous references to the genre, but the rest of us will be bored by the predictable plot and unimpressed with the shoddy effects. RS *DVD*

Cassandra Peterson *Elvira* • W Morgan Sheppard [Morgan Sheppard] *Vincent Talbot* • Daniel Greene *Bob Redding* • Susan Kellermann *Patty* • Jeff Conaway *Travis* • Edie McClurg *Chastity Pariah* • Kurt Fuller *Mr Glotter* • Pat Crawford Brown *Mrs Meeker* • Lee McLaughlin *Earl Hooter* ■ *Dir* James Signorelli • *Scr* Sam Egan, John Paragon, Cassandra Peterson

Elvis & Nixon ★★★ 15
Comedy drama based on a true story 2016 · US · Colour · 85min

Given the enduring fascination with its eponymous icons it's no surprise that films continue to get made off the back of the reputations of Elvis Presley and Richard Nixon. On 21 December 1970, a meeting took place between the two which resulted in the most requested photo in the US National Archives. If the film has a vague grasp of Presley's demons, it's less sure about Nixon's. Regardless, the lighter touch is somewhat novel, even if it results in a film about two indelible figures that will itself be quickly forgotten. EAS Swearing.

Michael Shannon *Elvis Presley* • Kevin Spacey *Richard Nixon* • Alex Pettyfer *Jerry Schilling* • Johnny Knoxville *Sonny* • Colin Hanks *Egil Krogh* ■ *Dir* Liza Johnson • *Scr* Joey Sagal, Hanala Sagal, Cary Elwes

Elvis Has Left the Building ★★★ 15
Romantic comedy 2004 · US · Colour · 86min

Elvis impersonators are dropping like flies in this screwball comedy from *My Big Fat Greek Wedding* director Joel Zwick. It's the madcap story of a travelling cosmetics saleswoman (Kim Basinger, giving an endearingly sweet performance) who ends up on the run after being implicated in a series of fatalities involving Presley wannabes en route to a Las Vegas convention. Following a shaky start, the laughs come thick and fast, papering over an underdeveloped plot with unashamed absurdity and some surprising cameos. SF Violence, swearing. *DVD*

Kim Basinger *Harmony Jones* • John Corbett *Miles Taylor* • Annie Potts *Shirl* • Denise Richards *Belinda* • Sean Astin *Aaron* • Billy Ray Cyrus *Hank* • Angie Dickinson *Bobette* • Tom Hanks *Mailbox Elvis* ■ *Dir* Joel Zwick • *Scr* Mitchell Ganem, Adam-Michael Garber

Elvis on Tour ★★★ PG
Music documentary 1972 · US · Colour · 89min

Essential viewing for Elvis fans as the King goes on stage, but the raw energy of his 1950s performances and songs are long gone. The then-fashionable multiscreen technique here becomes tiresome: the King only needs one screen to himself. Still, the material is mesmerising for fans, and there's also a skilful trawl through Elvis's earlier life for non-devotees. Interesting to note that a youngster in the cutting rooms graduated from a similiar role on the multiscreen *Woodstock*: an assistant film editor named Martin Scorsese. TS

Elvis Presley ■ *Dir* Pierre Adidge, Robert Abel

Elvis: That's the Way It Is ★★★★ U
Music documentary 1970 · US · Colour · 103min

This magnificent record of the King's return to live performances was stunningly filmed in Las Vegas. More than just a documentary, it's a carefully-crafted Metro special, filmed in Panavision by the great

cameraman Lucien Ballard under the canny direction of Denis Sanders. The film is shot through with Presley's delicious sense of self-mockery, but the real pleasure comes from watching one of the greatest performers of the 20th century doing what he does best. Preserved here are great performances of such standards as *Suspicious Minds*, *You've Lost That Lovin' Feeling* and the electric *I Just Can't Help Believing*. TS *DVD*

Elvis Presley • James Burton • Glen Hardin • Charley Hodge • Jerry Scheff • Ronnie Tutt • John Wilkinson • Cary Grant ■ *Dir* Denis Sanders

Elvis – the Movie ★★★★ U
Biographical drama 1979 · US · Colour · 161min

John Carpenter's made-for-TV version of the Elvis Presley saga, which was sadly truncated on its cinema release in the UK, is a detailed and truthful account of one of the most potent myths of modern popular culture. Kurt Russell, though no lookalike, makes a fine job of playing Presley – as a child actor, he played alongside the King in a scene in *It Happened at the World's Fair* – while Shelley Winters is particularly moving as Elvis's tragic mother, Gladys. For those who don't know the story, this is a worthwhile introduction – a biopic made with respect and affection. TS *DVD* *BD*

Kurt Russell *Elvis Presley* • Shelley Winters *Gladys Presley* • Bing Russell *Vernon Presley* • Robert Gray *Red West* • Season Hubley *Priscilla Presley* • Pat Hingle *Colonel Tom Parker* • Abi Young *Natalie Wood* ■ *Dir* John Carpenter • *Scr* Anthony Lawrence

Elysium ★★★ 15
Science-fiction drama 2013 · US · Colour · 104min

District 9 writer/director Neill Blomkamp follows up with more of the same, except with star names and thrice the budget. The super-rich have decamped to man-made paradise Elysium, and terrestrial drone Matt Damon is determined to illegally enter this utopia for medical treatment. But assigned to stop him is chilling defence secretary Jodie Foster is *District 9*'s Sharlto Copley. Despite immaculate design and structure, this stirring fable about social inequality is ultimately lost under lock-and-load sci-fi bluster. AC Violence, swearing. *DVD* *BD*

Matt Damon *Max* • Jodie Foster *Secretary Delacourt* • Sharlto Copley *Kruger* • Wagner Moura *Spider* • Alice Braga *Frey* • Diego Luna *Julio* ■ *Dir/Scr* Neill Blomkamp

Embrace of the Serpent ★★★★ 12
Adventure 2015 · Arg/Col/Ven/Neth · BW and Colour · 119min

Colombian Ciro Guerra's epic, spiralling adventure takes a journey upriver through South American geography, history and myth to deliver one of the most ravishing films from the continent in years. Binding together stories from two different time periods, the Oscar-nominated movie shows how shaman Karamakate (the last of his tribe, played as young man and elder by different actors), engages with visitors from the developed world. David Gallego's cinematography is breathtaking and enhances an already magnetic experience. LF Spanish, Portuguese, German, Catalan, Latin +subtitles. Violence *DVD* *BD*

Jan Bijvoet *Théodor von Martius, "Théo"* • Brionne Davis *Evan* • Antonio Bolívar Salvador *Old Karamakate* • Nilbio Torres *Young Karamakate* ■ *Dir* Ciro Guerra • *Scr* Ciro Guerra, Jacques Toulemonde, from the diaries by Theodor Koch-Grunberg, Richard Evan Schultes

Embrace of the Vampire ★ 18
Erotic horror 1994 · US · Colour · 88min

Virginal Alyssa Milano falls under vampire Martin Kemp's spell in the days leading up to her 18th birthday, after which she must choose between a mortal existence or immortality with her undead lover. Poorly scripted with inane dialogue and virtually no

E

plot, the whole reason for this contrived fantasy's existence is to show Milano's nude body at every available opportunity. AJ *DVD*

Alyssa Milano *Charlotte* • Jennifer Tilly *Marika* • Martin Kemp *Vampire* • Harrison Pruett *Chris* • Charlotte Lewis *Sarah* • Jordan Ladd *Eliza* ■ *Dir* Anne Goursaud • *Scr* Nicole Coady, Halle Eaton, Rick Bitzelberger

Embryo ★ 12
Science-fiction drama
1976 · US · Colour · 103min

Frankenstein rides again in director Ralph Nelson's update. Rock Hudson gives one of his worst performances as the scientist who invents a hormone enabling foetuses to grow rapidly to maturity outside the womb. When he develops gorgeous Barbara Carrera, she turns into a homicidal maniac looking for the formula to stop her accelerated ageing. Embarrassing dialogue and nauseating special effects test the patience. AJ Violence, nudity. *DVD*

Rock Hudson *Dr Paul Holliston* • Diane Ladd *Martha* • Barbara Carrera *Victoria* • Roddy McDowall *Riley* • Anne Schedeen *Helen* • John Elerick *Gordon* ■ *Dir* Ralph Nelson • *Scr* Anita Doohan, Jack W Thomas

Emelie ★★★
Thriller
2015 · US · Colour

A parent's worst nightmare throbs at the heart of this devious little chiller. Sarah Bolger is all sweetness and light as the replacement babysitter who comes to the rescue of a couple keen to go out and celebrate their anniversary. That's unlucky for them because "Anna" only has evil plans in mind for their three children. Slowly, insidiously, Bolger forces her charges into terrified obedience. Proceedings do lurch into familiar territory, but Bolger is never less than menacing as the troubled child-minder. JA Violence, swearing.

Sarah Bolger *Emelie/"Anna"* • Joshua Rush *Jacob* • Carly Adams *Sally* • Thomas Bair *Christopher* ■ *Dir* Michael Thelin • *Scr* Richard Raymond Harry Herbeck, from a story by Herbeck, Thelin

The Emerald Forest ★★★ 12
Drama
1985 · UK · Colour · 109min

Director John Boorman teaches us a conservation lesson, with his son Charley as the boy kidnapped in the jungles of the Amazon. Found by his engineer father Powers Boothe, the wild child ponders whether a return to civilisation is worth it, while dad wonders if his dam-building is of any value. Such weighty matters are unbalanced by Charley's awkward acting and an over-earnest approach, though the film's appeal is strengthened by Philippe Rousselot's breathtakingly beautiful photography. TH Violence, drug abuse, nudity. *DVD*

Powers Boothe *Bill Markham* • Charley Boorman *Tommy* • Meg Foster *Jean Markham* • Estee Chandler *Heather* • Dira Paes *Kachiri* • William Rodriguez *Young Tommy* • Eduardo Conde *Uwe Werner* • Rui Polonah *Wanadi* ■ *Dir* John Boorman • *Scr* Rospo Pallenberg

Emergency ★★ U
Drama
1962 · UK · BW · 64min

Francis Searle's anaemic little movie re-creates the agony of an estranged couple and their young daughter who is in desperate need of a blood donor. Glyn Houston is the earnest Scotland Yard flatfoot looking for likely candidates while parents Zena Walker and Dermot Walsh look suitably in need of tranquillisers. Things get quite dramatic before the hour and the budget is up, in this remake of *Emergency Call* (1952). DP

Glyn Houston *Inspector Harris* • Zena Walker *Joan Bell* • Dermot Walsh *John Bell* • Colin Tapley *Dr Lloyd* • Garard Green *Professor Graham* • Antony Dawes *Sergeant Phillips* ■ *Dir* Francis Searle • *Scr* Don Nicholl, James O'Connolly, from the film *Emergency Call* by Lewis Gilbert, Vernon Harris

Emergency Call ★★ PG
Medical drama
1952 · UK · BW · 87min

A small child with a rare blood type needs a transfusion to pull through a critical operation, and the only donors available are a boxer at a career crossroads, a black sailor with attitude and a killer on the run. Director Lewis Gilbert takes this cliché-ridden mishmash and moulds it into a mildly diverting drama. Remade ten years later as *Emergency*. DP *DVD*

Jack Warner *Inspector Lane* • Anthony Steel *Dr Carter* • Joy Shelton *Laura Bishop* • Sidney James *Danny Marks* • Freddie Mills *Tim Mahoney* • Earl Cameron *George Robinson* • John Robinson (1) *Dr Braithwaite* • Thora Hird *Mrs Cornelius* • Eric Pohlmann *Flash Harry* • Sydney Tafler *Brett* ■ *Dir* Lewis Gilbert • *Scr* Lewis Gilbert, Vernon Harris

The Emigrants ★★★
Period epic
1971 · Swe · Colour · 150min

Oscar-nominated for best picture in 1972, this adaptation of Vilhelm Moberg's novels was followed by *The New Land* – which was also nominated, this time for best foreign film. Not content with co-scripting and directing this cross-continental epic, Jan Troell also shot and edited the imposing imagery that so powerfully conveys the pain of leaving Sweden for ever and the enormity of the challenge awaiting farmer Max von Sydow and his wife Liv Ullmann on the plains of Minnesota. It's often grindingly slow, but it's impossible not to be moved by the dangers and hardships they face en route to their new home. DP Swedish dubbed.

Max von Sydow *Karl Oskar* • Liv Ullmann *Kristina* • Eddie Axberg *Robert* • Pierre Lindstedt *Arvid* • Allan Edwall *Danjel* • Monica Zeterlund *Ulrika* • Hans Alfredson *Jonas Petter* ■ *Dir* Jan Troell • *Scr* Bengt Forslund, Jan Troell, from the novels by Vilhelm Moberg

Emil and the Detectives ★★ U
Crime comedy adventure
1964 · US · Colour · 92min

There's a Children's Film Foundation feel to this Disney version of Erich Kästner's ever-popular novel about a boy who stumbles across a master criminal's plan to rob Berlin's richest bank. Walter Slezak plays the Baron with an unnecessarily pantomimic brio, but most under-tens will be too busy identifying with the heroic Bryan Russell to notice. DP

Walter Slezak *Baron* • Bryan Russell *Emil* • Roger Mobley *Gustav* • Heinz Schubert *Grundeis* • Peter Ehrlich *Muller* • Cindy Cassell *Pony* • Elsa Wagner *Nana* ■ *Dir* Peter Tewksbury • *Scr* AJ Carothers, from the novel *Emil und die Detektiven* by Erich Kästner

Emile ★★★ 15
Drama
2003 · Can/UK/Nor · Colour · 88min

Centred on a subtle performance by Ian McKellen, this is a gentle and endearing tale about guilt, betrayal and resentment. McKellen's ageing professor is poignantly frail and flawed as he struggles with the ghosts of his past, stirred up during a trip from England to Canada to receive an honorary degree. Though his journey to redemption relies more on reflection than action, the emotional repercussions of his stay with his only living relatives (Deborah Kara Unger and newcomer Theo Crane) are thoroughly absorbing. SF *DVD*

Ian McKellen *Emile* • Deborah Kara Unger *Nadia/Nadia's mother* • Chris William Martin [Chris Martin (2)] *Carl* • Tygh Runyan *Freddy* • Ian Tracey *Tom* • Janet Wright *Alice* • Nancy Sivak *Superintendent* • Theo Crane *Maria/Nadia, aged 10* ■ *Dir/Scr* Carl Bessai

Emma ★★★ U
Melodrama
1932 · US · BW · 71min

This is a marvellous showcase for MGM superstar Marie Dressler, here cast as a long-suffering servant condemned to watch the family she has tended turn against her in her unuseful old age. In other hands this could be a recipe for gibbering bathos, but the great Dressler convinces with every single movement and gesture. (She was rightly nominated for an Academy Award.) Jean Hersholt is also excellent as the man of the house, and there's fine support from youngsters Richard Cromwell and Myrna Loy. TS

Marie Dressler *Emma Thatcher* • Richard Cromwell *Ronnie Smith* • Jean Hersholt *Mr Smith* • Myrna Loy *Isabelle* • John Miljan *District attorney* ■ *Dir* Clarence Brown • *Scr* Leonard Praskins, Zelda Sears

Emma ★★★★ U
Period romantic drama
1996 · UK/US · Colour · 116min

Gwyneth Paltrow made her mark as the quintessential Jane Austen heroine in this convincing period romance from writer/director Douglas McGrath. Paltrow stars as the strong-willed matchmaker who entangles her friend (Toni Collette) in hopeless passion while trying to uncover the identity of her own true soulmate. Laced with wit, sophistication and a host of fine supporting performances (Jeremy Northam, Alan Cumming, Juliet Stevenson), this bright drama weaves a magical spell, with Paltrow at its charming centre. AJ *DVD*

Gwyneth Paltrow *Emma* • Toni Collette *Harriet* • Alan Cumming *Mr Elton* • Jeremy Northam *Mr Knightley* • Ewan McGregor *Frank Churchill* • Greta Scacchi *Mrs Weston* • Juliet Stevenson *Mrs Elton* • Polly Walker *Jane Fairfax* • Sophie Thompson *Miss Bates* • Phyllida Law *Mrs Bates* • James Cosmo *Mr Weston* • Denys Hawthorne *Mr Woodhouse* ■ *Dir* Douglas McGrath • *Scr* Douglas McGrath, from the novel by Jane Austen

Emmanuelle ★★ 18
Erotic drama
1974 · Fr · Colour · 90min

Possibly the best-known porn film in the world, this made Sylvia Kristel an international star and spawned countless imitations. So is it any good? It's artfully shot by director Just Jaeckin, the Thailand locations are occasionally stunning and Kristel disrobes with some elegance. However, acting is far from her strong suit, and the dialogue and story, about the sexual awakening of a young woman, is banal. JF French +subtitles. *DVD*

Sylvia Kristel *Emmanuelle* • Alain Cuny *Mario* • Daniel Sarky *Jean* • Jeanne Colletin *Ariane* • Marika Green *Bee* • Christine Boisson *Marie-Ange* ■ *Dir* Just Jaeckin • *Scr* Jean-Louis Richard, from the novel by Emmanuelle Arsan

Emmanuelle 2 ★★ 18
Erotic drama
1975 · Fr · Colour · 87min

In this first sequel (one of eight starring Sylvia Kristel), the scene shifts from Bangkok to Hong Kong and then Bali – not that you'd notice, however, as most of the action takes place in soft-focus close-up. The Dutch actress invests the round of sexual encounters with a modicum of eroticism. *Goodbye Emmanuelle* followed in 1977. DP French dubbed. *DVD*

Sylvia Kristel *Emmanuelle* • Umberto Orsini *Jean* • Catherine Rivet *Anna-Maria* • Frédéric Lagache *Christopher* • Caroline Laurence *Ingrid* • Florence Lafuma *Laura* ■ *Dir* Francis Giacobetti • *Scr* Bob Elia, Francis Giacobetti, from the novel by Emmanuelle Arsan

Emma's War ★★ PG
Period drama
1985 · Aus · Colour · 92min

This is notable only for the fact that it was one of Lee Remick's last features before her tragic death from cancer at just 55. She plays a lonely, drunken mother who drags her daughters away from their blissful boarding school existence and deposits them in a run-down outback town where very little ever happens. The patchwork screenplay flits between episodes with no dramatic focus. DP *DVD*

Lee Remick *Anne Grange* • Miranda Otto *Emma Grange* • Bridey Lee *Laurel Grange* • Terence Donovan *Frank Grange* • Mark Lee (1) *John Davidson* • Pat Evison *Miss Arnott* • Donal Gibson *Hank* • Grigor Taylor *Dr Friedlander* • Noeline Brown *Mrs Mortimer* • Rebel Russell *Miss Gunz* ■ *Dir* Clytie Jessop • *Scr* Peter Smalley, Clytie Jessop

Emotional Backgammon ★ 15
Romantic drama
2003 · UK · Colour · 93min

Leon Herbert helms the first feature by a black British director for over a decade. He also plays the tough character who uses backgammon strategy to guide tailor Wil Johnson through his romantic entanglements with Brazilian girlfriend Daniela Lavender – who is being advised by her embittered best friend, Jacqueline de Peza. Misogyny informs the trite dialogue and the tone of the unpersuasive performances. DP

Wil Johnson *John* • Daniela Lavender *Mary* • Leon Herbert *Steve* • Jacqueline de Peza *Jane* • Bob Mercer *Paul* ■ *Dir* Leon Herbert • *Scr* Leon Herbert, Matthew Hope

Emperor ★★★ 12
Second World War drama
2012 · US/Jpn · Colour · 101min

Tommy Lee Jones stars as Douglas MacArthur, the victorious and imperious general in charge in Japan in the immediate aftermath of the Second World War. There's US pressure to have Japanese emperor Hirohito indicted for war crimes, and it's MacArthur's tricky job to decide. He assigns the investigation of Hirohito's culpability to a military subordinate (Matthew Fox, from TV's *Lost*), who's sensitive to Japanese sensibilities following a pre-war tryst with an exchange student. The film is beautifully made and finely acted, and a subplot about Fox's bid to find his lost love is just a spoonful of sugar to help some meaty military medicine go down. DA English, Japanese +subtitles. Violence, swearing. *DVD*

Matthew Fox *General Bonner Fellers* • Tommy Lee Jones *General Douglas MacArthur* • Eriko Hatsune *Aya Shimada* • Masayoshi Haneda *Takahashi* • Colin Moy *Major General Richter* • Toshiyuki Nishida *General Kajima* ■ *Dir* Peter Webber • *Scr* Vera Blasi, David Klass, from the book *His Majesty's Salvation* by Shiro Okamoto

The Emperor and the Assassin ★★ 12
Historical drama
1999 · Chi/Jpn/Fr · Colour · 154min

Despite four attempts at reworking this five-chaptered historical epic, Chen Kaige has again succumbed to the pictorialism that blighted *Temptress Moon* (1996). Embroidering the fragmentary facts known about Ying Zheng's unification of China in the late third century BC, Chen concocts a story of such complexity and specialised significance that it's difficult not only to keep track of events, but also to invest much emotional energy in the central characters. DP Mandarin +subtitles. *DVD*

Gong Li *Lady Zhao* • Zhang Fengyi *Jing Ke* • Li Xuejian *Ying Zheng, King of Qin* • Wang Zhiwen *Marquis Changxin* ■ *Dir* Chen Kaige • *Scr* Wang Peigong, Chen Kaige

The Emperor Jones ★★ PG
Drama
1933 · US · BW · 72min

The commanding presence and glorious voice of Paul Robeson dominate this screen version of Eugene O'Neill's play; indeed, it's an indication of his stature that he was given the lead at a time when few black actors starred in Hollywood movies. Scriptwriter DuBose Heyward opens out the play to include Jones's earlier life as a railroad porter before following him to the West Indies, where he becomes the tyrannical ruler of a remote isle. Despite a wealth of incident, the pacing is stilted and the film fails to capture the aura of fatalism that marked the original. TV *DVD*

Paul Robeson *Brutus Jones* • Dudley Digges *Smithers* • Frank Wilson (1) *Jeff* • Fredi Washington *Undine* • Ruby Elzy *Dolly* ■ *Dir* Dudley Murphy • *Scr* DuBose Heyward, from the play by Eugene O'Neill

Emperor of the North
★★★★ 15

Action adventure 1973 · US · Colour · 115min

This addictively tough action adventure follows a railway guard (Ernest Borgnine) who is proud of the fact that no tramp, especially not Lee Marvin, rides his train for free. Robert Aldrich's direction comes at the viewer like an express train and, typically fusing darkness with wit, creates a symbolic tale of the Depression, even if the drifter in this film is rather absurdly elevated to hero status. The Aldrich express does screech to a halt now and again with rather more chat than action, but there is enough pulsating drama and compelling detail to keep you glued. JM *DVD*

Lee Marvin *A-No 1* • Ernest Borgnine *Shack* • Keith Carradine *Cigaret* • Charles Tyner *Cracker* • Malcolm Atterbury *Hogger* • Simon Oakland *Policeman* • Harry Caesar *Coaly* ■ *Dir* Robert Aldrich • *Scr* Christopher Knopf

The Emperor Waltz ★★★ U

Musical comedy 1948 · US · Colour · 101min

Legend has it that this is Billy Wilder's worst movie, though it does have some delectably barmy moments. Set in the Austrian Tyrol, it stars Bing Crosby and his pet pooch, Buttons, peddling gramophones to the European nobility. Crosby falls for a countess, Joan Fontaine, while Buttons falls for a poodle. It's a fable about American enterprise and a lament for a Europe buried beneath the ruins of war. For collectors of kitsch, this all-yodelling comedy is essential viewing. AT *DVD*

Bing Crosby *Virgil H Smith* • Joan Fontaine *Countess Johanna Augusta Franziska Von Stolzenberg-Stolzenberg* • Roland Culver *Baron Holenia* • Lucile Watson *Princess Bitotska* • Richard Haydn *Emperor Franz Josef* • Harold Vermilyea *Chamberlain* • John Goldsworthy *Obersthofmeister* • Sig Ruman *Dr Zwieback* ■ *Dir* Billy Wilder • *Scr* Charles Brackett, Billy Wilder

The Emperor's Candlesticks ★★★ U

Period spy drama 1937 · US · BW · 88min

In the early 20th century, rival spies William Powell and Luise Rainer make the mistake of hiding their vital documents in a pair of candlesticks. This leads the stylish pair on a chase round Europe during which – of course – they fall in love. Lavishly mounted, acted as if the hokum were serious, and well directed by George Fitzmaurice, this is a charming, elegant tale of impeccably dressed and well-connected spies. RK

William Powell *Baron Stephan Wolensky* • Luise Rainer *Countess Olga Mironova* • Robert Young (1) *Grand Duke Peter* • Maureen O'Sullivan *Maria Orlech* • Frank Morgan *Col Baron Suroff* • Henry Stephenson *Prince Johann* • Bernadene Hayes *Mitzi Reisenbach* • Donald Kirke *Anton* • Douglass Dumbrille *Korum* ■ *Dir* George Fitzmaurice • *Scr* Monckton Hoffe, Harold Goldman, Herman Mankiewicz (uncredited), Hugh Mills (uncredited), John Meehan (uncredited), Erich von Stroheim (uncredited), from a story by Baroness Orczy, from her novel

The Emperor's Club ★★★ PG

Drama 2002 · US · Colour · 104min

This sentimental film about a committed but flawed teacher says nothing new about school life, but the acting makes it worthwhile. Posh prep school classics professor Kevin Kline is determined to inspire and mould the character of bad-boy new student Emile Hirsch. It's a tale of idealism, morality and betrayal, set in a privileged world. While this buckles under the weight of classroom clichés, its drama is well sustained by the cast, particularly by the ever excellent Kline. TH *DVD*

Kevin Kline *William Hundert* • Emile Hirsch *Sedgewick Bell* • Embeth Davidtz *Elizabeth* • Rob Morrow *James Ellerby* • Edward Herrmann *Headmaster Woodbridge* • Paul Dano *Martin Blythe* • Rishi Mehta *Deepak Mehta* • Jesse Eisenberg *Louis Masoudi* • Steven Culp *Older Martin Blythe* • Patrick Dempsey *Older Louis Masoudi* • Joel Gretsch *Older Sedgewick Bell* ■ *Dir* Michael Hoffman • *Scr* Neil Tolkin, from the short story *The Palace Thief* by Ethan Canin

The Emperor's New Clothes
★★★ PG

Period comedy 2001 · UK/It/Ger · Colour · 102min

Alan Taylor's period comedy recalls the offbeat charm of his debut *Palookaville*. But while it's literate and nimbly executed, it lacks the brio to match its conceit. Ian Holm revels in the dual role of the deposed emperor striving to regain his throne and the lookalike he's left in St Helena to disguise his flight. There are plenty of smiles as he treks across Europe, but once he reaches Paris and becomes enamoured of feisty melon-seller Iben Hjejle, the slick revisionism descends into historical cornball. DP *DVD*

Ian Holm *Napoleon Bonaparte/Eugene Lenormand* • Iben Hjejle *Pumpkin* • Tim McInnerny *Dr Lambert* • Nigel Terry *Montholon* • Hugh Bonneville *Bertrand* • Murray Melvin *Antommarchi* • Eddie Marsan *Marchand* • Clive Russell *Sgt Justin Bommel* ■ *Dir* Alan Taylor • *Scr* Kevin Molony, Alan Taylor, Herbie Wave, from the novel *The Death of Napoleon* by Simon Leys

The Emperor's New Clothes
★★★ 15

Documentary 2015 · US/UK/Fr · Colour · 96min

First things first. This isn't the old fairy tale, Disney version or otherwise. It's comedian Russell Brand in political activist mode, fronting a documentary rant against class inequality worldwide. Fatcat bankers come in for special criticism. Brand is a Marmite character... you either like him or you don't. As a frontman, he's no Michael Moore. But he is lively, handling serious stuff with a light touch. There's nothing here that will surprise the informed, but presumably Brand is hoping the film will pull in the kids that are his core audience. DA Swearing *DVD*

Russell Brand ■ *Dir* Russell Brand, Michael Winterbottom • *Scr* Michael Winterbottom

The Emperor's New Groove
★★★★ U

Animated comedy 2000 · US · Colour · 86min

In this refreshingly hip take on the mismatched buddy genre, Emperor Kuzco (David Spade) is the arrogant young ruler of a mythical South American kingdom, who is transformed into a llama by his power-hungry adviser, Yzma (Eartha Kitt), and cast into the jungle. Kuzco's only chance to reclaim his throne rests with affable peasant Pacha (John Goodman), whose picturesque village was due to be razed to accommodate the Emperor's new summer palace. Spade brings his rapier-like sarcasm, vocal dexterity and brilliant timing to the proceedings. This colourful, stylish and more adult endeavour has the character-driven pace missing from recent Disney animations. AJ *DVD* *Blu-ray*

David Spade *Kuzco/Kuzco Llama* • John Goodman *Pacha* • Eartha Kitt *Yzma* • Patrick Warburton *Kronk* • Wendie Malick *Chicha* ■ *Dir* Mark Dindal • *Scr* David Reynolds, from a story by Chris Williams, Mark Dindal • *Music* John Debney • *Music/Lyrics* Sting, David Hartley

Empire ★★ 15

Crime drama 2002 · US · Colour · 95min

Urban dramas don't get any more derivative than this hackneyed debut from Franc Reyes. Starring John Leguizamo, it tells the story of a South Bronx drugs dealer who teams up with a Wall Street hotshot to try to escape the ghetto. While Leguizamo runs rings around his co-stars, the mediocrity of the plot does him no favours. SF Swearing, violence, sex scenes, drug abuse. *DVD*

John Leguizamo *Victor Rosa* • Peter Sarsgaard *Jack* • Denise Richards *Trish* • Vincent Laresca *Jimmy* • Isabella Rossellini *La Colombiana* • Sonia Braga *Iris* • Delilah Cotto *Carmen* • Nestor Serrano *Rafael Menendez* ■ *Dir/Scr* Franc Reyes • *Cinematographer* Kramer Morgenthau

Empire of the Ants ★ 15

Science-fiction drama 1977 · US · Colour · 85min

This tacky tale of tepid terror is just another poverty-row, giant-insect tale from schlock director Bert I Gordon, featuring Joan Collins up to her designer khakis in mud fighting off laughably phoney mutant ants. She's the head swindler of a housing development consortium on a resort island where radiation waste has been dumped. AJ *DVD*

Joan Collins *Marilyn Fryser* • Robert Lansing *Dan Stokely* • John David Carson *Joe Morrison* • Albert Salmi *Sheriff Art Kincade* • Jacqueline Scott *Margaret Ellis* • Pamela Shoop *Coreen Bradford* • Robert Pine *Larry Graham* • Edward Power *Charlie Pearson* ■ *Dir* Bert I Gordon • *Scr* Jack Turley, from a story by Bert I Gordon, from a story by HG Wells

Empire of the Sun ★★★ PG

Second World War drama 1987 · US · Colour · 146min

Steven Spielberg's drama set in China during the Second World War is a glossy and rather tame affair, based on JG Ballard's semi-autobiographical novel. Bland Christian Bale plays 11-year-old Jim, who is separated from his family in Shanghai and ends up in a Japanese internment camp. The film has its heroic moments and scenes that depict the horror of war through the eyes of a child. However, despite the strong supporting cast, this seems a rather superficial look at life under occupation. JB Swearing, violence. *DVD*

Christian Bale *Jim Graham* • John Malkovich *Basie* • Miranda Richardson *Mrs Victor* • Nigel Havers *Dr Rawlins* • Joe Pantoliano *Frank Demerest* • Leslie Phillips *Maxton* • Robert Stephens *Mr Lockwood* • Burt Kwouk *Mr Chen* • Paul McGann *Lt Price* ■ *Dir* Steven Spielberg • *Scr* Tom Stoppard, from the novel by JG Ballard

Empire Records ★★★ 12

Comedy drama 1995 · US · Colour · 86min

This likeable if faintly preposterous teen flick is set around one day in the life of a small independent music store, run by Anthony LaPaglia, which is about to be taken over by a record giant. Liv Tyler looks suitably winsome but is overshadowed by co-stars Renee Zellweger and Rory Cochrane, while Maxwell Caulfield enjoys himself as a spoilt teen idol. Director Allan Moyle demonstrates a keen understanding of adolescent angst, though the film has a distinctly old-fashioned feel. JF Swearing, drug abuse. *DVD*

Anthony LaPaglia *Joe* • Rory Cochrane *Lucas* • Johnny Whitworth *A J* • Liv Tyler *Corey* • Renee Zellweger [Renée Zellweger] *Gina* • Robin Tunney *Debra* • Ethan Randall [Ethan Embry] *Mark* • Maxwell Caulfield *Rex* • Debi Mazar *Jane* ■ *Dir* Allan Moyle • *Scr* Carol Heikkinen

Employee of the Month
★★ 12

Romantic comedy 2006 · US · Colour · 103min

It isn't just the production values that are cut-price in this supermarket-set comedy. The laughs are cheap, and romantic leads Dane Cook and Jessica Simpson have barely enough charisma between them to sell a tube of toothpaste, let alone the flimsy plot. Cook plays a shiftless shelf-stacker who suddenly ups his game when it turns out that the good-looking new girl (Simpson) only dates guys who make employee of the month. Instead of sending up sales culture, director Greg Coolidge makes this just another half-baked comedy off the Hollywood conveyer belt. SP Swearing, some sexual references. *DVD*

Dane Cook *Zack* • Jessica Simpson *Amy* • Dax Shepard *Vince* • Efren Ramirez *Jorge* • Tim Bagley *Glen Gary* • Andy Dick *Lon* • Brian George *Iqbal* • Harland Williams *Russell* ■ *Dir* Greg Coolidge • *Scr* Don Calame, Chris Conroy, Greg Coolidge, from a story by Calame, Conroy

Employees' Entrance ★★★

Drama 1933 · US · BW · 74min

This rather daring film was one of many in the early 1930s that led to the introduction of the censorious Hay's Code. Warren William stars as the tyrannical owner of a huge New York department store, whose only concerns are power, money and women. He gives a job to Loretta Young, after she has slept with her future boss. When she falls in love and marries an ambitious salesman, matters are brought to a climax. Briskly directed, this is eventful, well-acted entertainment. BB

Warren William *Kurt Anderson* • Loretta Young *Madeline Walters* • Wallace Ford *Martin West* • Alice White *Polly Dale* • Hale Hamilton *Monroe* • Albert Gran *Denton Ross* ■ *Dir* Roy Del Ruth • *Scr* Robert Presnell, from a play by David Boehm

The Empty Canvas ★

Drama 1963 · Fr/It · BW · 104min

When Bette Davis met Damiano Damiani, the Italian cult director clearly lost. In one of her strangest roles, the bitch goddess does her utmost to save her artist son, Horst Buchholz, from his obsessive love for model Catherine Spaak. Davis is all at sea in an avant-garde melodrama, in which her determination to stay in front of 1960s cameras is her only steely motivation. AJ Some dialogue dubbed.

Bette Davis *Dino's mother* • Horst Buchholz *Dino* • Catherine Spaak *Cecilia* • Isa Miranda *Cecilia's mother* • Lea Padovani *Balestrieri's widow* • Daniela Rocca *Rita* • Georges Wilson *Cecilia's father* • Leonida Repaci *Balestrieri* ■ *Dir* Damiano Damiani • *Scr* Damiano Damiani, Tonino Guerra, Ugo Liberatore, from the novel *La Noia* by Alberto Moravia

The Empty Table ★★★★ PG

Drama 1985 · Jpn · Colour · 141min

A modest, tradition-minded Japanese family suddenly realise that their son is a terrorist and that they will be stigmatised because of his actions. Set in the 1970s, when the much-feared Japanese Red Army was committing outrages across the world, this Masaki Kobayashi picture (his last) is slow to unfold yet presents the world of the terrorist and his family with unusual insight, taking a real event – a televised police raid on the terrorists' mountain training centre in 1970 – as its starting point. AT Japanese +subtitles.

Tatsuya Nakadai *Nobuyuki Kidoji* • Mayumi Ogawa *Yukimo Kidoji* • Kie Nakai *Tamae Kidoji* • Kiichi Nakai *Otohiko Kidoji* • Takayuki Takemoto *Osamu Kidoji* • Shima Iwashita *Kiwa Nakahara* • Mikijiro Hira *Kawabe's lawyer* ■ *Dir* Masaki Kobayashi • *Scr* Masaki Kobayashi, from a story by Fumiko Enchi

En Equilibre ★★★ PG

Romantic drama 2015 · Fr · Colour · 83min

Denis Dercourt returns to form almost a decade after *The Page Turner* with a charming romance based on the experiences of French Paralympian Bernard Sachsé. Beautifully photographed in the glorious Breton countryside, the story would seem far-fetched if not rooted in fact. Paralysed in an accident on location, a stuntman (Albert Dupontel) befriends an insurance adjuster (Cécile de France) after his claim is contested. Dercourt avoids melodramatics, and even the inevitable romantic interlude is nicely judged. DP French +subtitles. Some swearing. *DVD*

Albert Dupontel *Marc Guermont* • Cécile de France *Florence Kernel* • Marie Baumer *Alexandra* • Patrick Mille *Julien Kernel* ■ *Dir* Denis Dercourt • *Scr* Denis Dercourt, from the non-fiction book *Sur mes quatre jambes* by Bernard Sachsé

En Plein Coeur ★★ 15

Drama 1998 · Fr · Colour · 97min

It's hard to believe this adaptation of Georges Simenon's novel was made by the same Pierre Jolivet who directed that intense morality tale, *Force Majeure*. In the absence of psychological truth, actorly earnestness scarcely atones. Yet Carole Bouquet is credibly crushed as her lawyer husband Gérard Lanvin defends wild child Virginie Ledoyen on a robbery charge, only to fall for her charms in the process. DA French +subtitles.

E

Gérard Lanvin *Michel* • Virginie Ledoyen *Cécile* • Carole Bouquet *Viviane* • Guillaume Canet *Vincent* • Aurelie Verillon *Samira* • Denis Podalydès *Martorel* ■ *Dir* Pierre Jolivet • *Scr* Roselyne Bosch, from the novel *En Cas de Malheur* by Georges Simenon

Enchanted ★★★★ PG

Part-animated romantic fantasy
2007 · US · Colour · 103min

This sweet and funny romantic fantasy stars Amy Adams (*Junebug*) as Giselle, who in the brief animated first segment is searching for her prince, and finds him in the form of Edward (James Marsden). But he has a wicked stepmother (Susan Sarandon) who has no intention of giving up her privileged place in the kingdom in favour of her future daughter-in-law, so (as animation gives way to live action) magics Giselle to a spot where there are no happy endings – New York, of course. Complete with an eye-popping production number in Central Park, sly digs at every established fairy-tale cliché and a witty script, this certainly boasts a wide-ranging appeal. If anything, the crash-bang-wallop CGI ending is rather overblown, but thankfully it's the simple charm and humour of the tale that lingers in the memory. SuR *DVD* Blu

Amy Adams *Giselle* • Patrick Dempsey *Robert Philip* • James Marsden *Prince Edward* • Timothy Spall *Nathaniel* • Idina Menzel *Nancy Tremaine* • Rachel Covey *Morgan Philip* • Susan Sarandon *Queen Narissa* • Julie Andrews *Narrator* ■ *Dir* Kevin Lima • *Scr* Bill Kelly

Enchanted April ★★★

Romantic comedy drama
1935 · US · BW · 65min

This amusing insight into Hollywood's view of polite Hampstead society owes more to the 1925 Kane Campbell stage adaptation than the original Elizabeth von Arnim novel. Rather too brief to allow the story to weave its magic, it's still an entertaining saga that sees neglected housewives Ann Harding (miscast) and Katherine Alexander rekindle the romance in their respective marriages to budding novelist Frank Morgan and pompous lawyer Reginald Owen. DP In English, Italian.

Ann Harding *Mrs Lotty Wilkins* • Frank Morgan *Mellersh Wilkins* • Katherine Alexander *Mrs Rose Arbuthnot* • Reginald Owen *Henry Arbuthnot* • Jessie Ralph *Phoebe Fisher* ■ *Dir* Harry Beaumont • *Scr* Samuel Hoffenstein, Ray Harris, from the play by Kane Campbell, from the novel *The Enchanted April* by Elizabeth von Arnim

Enchanted April ★★ U

Period romantic drama
1991 · UK · Colour · 95min

Genteel to the point of tedium, this British period piece relies on its four female stars – Miranda Richardson, Josie Lawrence, Polly Walker and Oscar-nominated Joan Plowright – who play four women bonding on an Italian holiday while waiting for their male partners. The women are worth the wait, but otherwise this has all the careful, itemised hallmarks of a made-for-TV movie. TH *DVD*

Miranda Richardson *Rose Arbuthnot* • Josie Lawrence *Lotty Wilkins* • Polly Walker *Lady Caroline Dester* • Joan Plowright *Mrs Fisher* • Alfred Molina *Mellersh Wilkins* • Michael Kitchen *George Briggs* • Jim Broadbent *Frederick Arbuthnot* • Davide Manuli *Beppo* ■ *Dir* Mike Newell • *Scr* Peter Barnes, from the novel by Elizabeth von Arnim

The Enchanted Cottage ★★★★ U

Romantic drama
1945 · US · BW · 92min

One of the great romances of the cinema, this tale of two society misfits depends very heavily on a serious suspension of disbelief from its audience. Writer Arthur Pinero referred to the original as a fable, and was very aware of its low credibility factor. But the First World War update works superbly, as disfigured veteran Robert Young and Dorothy McGuire retreat from the world to the cottage of the title, and director John Cromwell achieves a perfect tone. Give your heart to it, rather than your mind, and you'll love it. TS

Dorothy McGuire *Laura Pennington* • Robert Young (1) *Oliver Bradford* • Herbert Marshall *John Hillgrove* • Mildred Natwick *Mrs Abigail Minnett* • Spring Byington *Violet Price* • Hillary Brooke *Beatrice Alexander* • Richard Gaines *Frederick Price* • Alec Englander *Danny* • Mary Worth *Mrs Stanton* ■ *Dir* John Cromwell • *Scr* DeWitt Bodeen, Herman J Mankiewicz, from the play by Sir Arthur Wing Pinero [Arthur Wing Pinero]

Enchantment ★★★ U

Romantic drama
1948 · US · BW · 96min

Films following events in an English stately home have long held an attraction for American audiences. This one has the unusual distinction of being told by the ancestral pile itself. Based on a novel by Rumer Godden, it was advertised by RKO as "just about the most wonderful love story ever filmed". Of course it's nothing of the sort. However, David Niven gives a good account of himself as the hot-blooded lover in the first half and the wise old head in the second. DP

David Niven *General Sir Roland Dane* • Teresa Wright *Lark Ingoldsby* • Evelyn Keyes *Grizel Dane* • Farley Granger *Pilot Pax Masterson* • Jayne Meadows *Selina Dane* • Leo G Carroll *Proutie* • Philip Friend *Pelham Dane* ■ *Dir* Irving Reis • *Scr* John Patrick, from the novel *Take Three Tenses* by Rumer Godden

Encore ★★★

Portmanteau drama
1951 · UK · BW · 88min

Without ever really exerting a grip, this portmanteau picture, based on the stories of W Somerset Maugham, is a diverting collection of passable vignettes. The direction is pedestrian, but the performances of a fine cast of British stalwarts save the day. Nigel Patrick and Roland Culver give a polished demonstration of comic timing in *The Ant and the Grasshopper*, while Glynis Johns and Terence Morgan struggle to find the pathos in *Gigolo and Gigolette*. Best of all, however, is Kay Walsh, chattering in *Winter Cruise*. DP

Nigel Patrick *Tom Ramsey* • Roland Culver *George Ramsey* • Alison Leggatt *Freda Ramsey* • Kay Walsh *Miss Reid* • Noel Purcell *Captain* • Ronald Squire *Doctor* • Glynis Johns *Stella Cotman* • Terence Morgan *Syd Cotman* ■ *Dir* Harold French, Pat Jackson, Anthony Pelissier • *Scr* TEB Clarke, Arthur Macrae, Eric Ambler, from the short stories *The Ant and the Grasshopper*, *Gigolo and Gigolette* and *Winter Cruise* by W Somerset Maugham

Encounter at Raven's Gate ★★★★ 15

Science-fiction thriller
1988 · Aus · Colour · 85min

This stand-out Australian science-fiction thriller involves a paroled ex-convict, his brother, the brother's bored wife and the strange phenomena that occur at Raven's Gate farm – perhaps the work of visiting evil aliens. Director Rolf De Heer allows the viewer's imagination to go into overdrive thanks to creepy photography and evocative use of sound. Engrossing and packed with unusual incident (the sky raining dead birds), this atmospheric gem is a fine example of low-budget success. AJ

Steven Vidler *Eddie Cleary* • Celine Griffin *Rachel Cleary* • Ritchie Singer *Richard* • Vincent Gil *Felix Skinner* • Saturday Rosenberg *Annie* • Terry Camilleri *Dr Hemmings* ■ *Dir* Rolf De Heer • *Scr* Marc Rosenberg, Rolf De Heer, James Michael Vernon

Encounters at the End of the World ★★★ U

Documentary
2007 · US/Can · Colour · 96min

In this Oscar-nominated portrait of Antarctica's scientific community, film-maker Werner Herzog examines the often absurd daily mechanics of the McMurdo research station, enhancing his wry observations with the colourful stories of the "professional dreamers" based there. Juxtaposing their experiences with awe-inspiring footage that captures the surreal beauty of the Antarctic vistas, the director delivers another trademark meditation on human existence versus the savage

dynamism of nature. Although its languid pacing and rambling digressions won't suit everyone, those who appreciate Herzog's irreverent curiosity will find the documentary a delight. SF *DVD* Blu

Werner Herzog *Narrator* ■ *Dir* Werner Herzog

The End ★ 15

Comedy
1978 · US · Colour · 96min

Burt Reynolds directed himself in this tasteless mishmash so, presumably, Jerry Belson's script must have meant something to him. It means nothing to us, however, as a bearded Reynolds discovers he's medically doomed and starts to square his conscience with a life that has been totally selfish. Hamming is the order of the dying day – with Dom DeLuise coming a close second to the star. TH

Burt Reynolds *Wendell Sonny Lawson* • Dom DeLuise *Marlon Borunki* • Sally Field *Mary Ellen* • Strother Martin *Dr Waldo Kling* • David Steinberg *Marty Lieberman* • Joanne Woodward *Jessica* • Norman Fell *Dr Samuel Krugman* • Myrna Loy *Maureen Lawson* ■ *Dir* Burt Reynolds • *Scr* Jerry Belson

The End ★★★ 15

Documentary
2008 · US/Ger · BW and Colour · 80min

The brutal and practically extinct world of the old-school cockney gangster is laid bare in this gripping documentary from first-time writer/director Nicola Collins. Turning the camera on her own father, convicted armed robber Les Falco, and his equally hardcore friends, Collins (who appeared in *Snatch* with twin sister Teena) knits their unapologetic reminiscences into a chilling if one-sided portrait of East End gangland life. While their real-life experiences make Guy Ritchie crime movies look like children's fare, these self-proclaimed products of post-Second World War poverty are frighteningly charming, punctuating their horror stories with humour and wit, and filming in black and white automatically gives the men an air of cool sophistication. SF *DVD*

Les Falco *Dad* • Bobby Reading *"The guvnor"* • Jimmy Tibbs *Fight trainer* • Victor Dark *Bank robber* • Roy Shaw *Unlicenced fighter* • Mickey Ganella *Negotiator* ■ *Dir/Scr* Nicola Collins

End Game ★★ 12

Action thriller
2006 · US/Can · Colour · 92min

The most surprising thing about this proficient but unremarkable thriller is the quality of the talent on display. The plotting is standard straight-to-rental action fare, yet the cast (James Woods, Burt Reynolds, Peter Greene, Anne Archer) should lift it out of the ordinary. But sadly that's precisely what it is: ordinary. Cuba Gooding Jr is unconvincing as a Secret Service agent who is racked with guilt over his failure to prevent the assassination of the president (Jack Scalia); Angie Harmon plays the investigative journalist who smells a conspiracy. This marks the directorial debut of stunt expert Andy Cheng, and he stages the action sequences with some aplomb. But you never shake the feeling that Steven Seagal or Wesley Snipes is going to have to turn up at some stage to save the day. JF Some violence, brief swearing. *DVD*

Cuba Gooding Jr *Alex Thomas* • James Woods *Vaughn Stevens* • Angie Harmon *Kate Crawford* • Anne Archer *The First Lady* • Burt Reynolds *General Montgomery* • Jack Scalia *The President* • Peter Greene *Jack Baldwin* ■ *Dir* Andy Cheng • *Scr* Andy Cheng, JC Pollock

End of Days ★★★ 18

Supernatural action thriller
1999 · US · Colour · 127min

While Arnold Schwarzenegger's amateurish emoting never rings true in the role of a run-down, suicidal, alcoholic ex-cop, the "Devil searching for his bride" story provides some decent popcorn entertainment. Gabriel Byrne, meanwhile, rises above the clumsily structured and wholly derivative script to give an attention-grabbing performance as a very laid-back Prince of Darkness. JC Swearing, violence, nudity. *DVD*

Arnold Schwarzenegger *Jericho Cane* • Gabriel Byrne *The Man* • Kevin Pollak *Chicago* • Robin Tunney *Christine York* • CCH Pounder *Detective Marge Francis* • Rod Steiger *Father Kovak* • Miriam Margolyes *Mabel* ■ *Dir* Peter Hyams • *Scr* Andrew W Marlowe

The End of St Petersburg ★★★★ PG

Silent political drama 1927 · USSR · BW · 68min

Commissioned as part of the tenth anniversary celebrations of the Russian Revolution, the film was shot by the great Russian director Vsevolod Pudovkin at the same time and place (Leningrad) as Sergei Eisenstein's more famous *October* (1928). Both films dealt with the storming of the Winter Palace and the triumph of the Bolsheviks, but Pudovkin's film was shown two months before *October* and was the more popular version. The events were witnessed through the eyes of an uneducated peasant boy, someone with whom audiences could identify. Not as dazzling technically as *October*, it has some marvellous montage sequences and much emotional appeal. RB *DVD*

A Chistyakov *Worker* • Vera Baranovskaya *His wife* • Ivan Chuvelov *Ivan, a peasant* • V Chuvelov *Friend from the village* • A Gromov *Revolutionary* ■ *Dir* Vsevolod I Pudovkin • *Scr* Nathan Zarkhi, from the poem *The Bronze Horseman* by Vsevolod I Pudovkin, from the novel *St Petersburg* by Andrey Biely

The End of Summer ★★★★★ U

Drama 1961 · Jpn · Colour · 98min

Yasujiro Ozu's penultimate film shows a deep concern for the everyday life of his middle-class characters. An elderly widower, much to the dismay of his three daughters, decides to resume a relationship with his former mistress. Although the film is presented from the viewpoint of a Japanese family, it addresses universal themes governing relationships. Ozu uses delicate colour and shoots long scenes with his camera at a constant height to reveal both the inner truth and outer manifestation of life, which he depicts with rigour. BB Japanese +subtitles. *DVD*

Ganjiro Nakamura *Manbei Kohayagawa* • Setsuko Hara *Akiko Kohayagawa* • Yoko Tsukasa *Noriko Kohayagawa* • Michiyo Aratama *Fumiko Kohayagawa* • Yumi Shirakawa *Takako* ■ *Dir* Yasujiro Ozu • *Scr* Kogo Noda, Yasujiro Ozu • *Cinematographer* Asakazu Nakai

The End of the Affair ★★★★ PG

Wartime romantic drama
1954 · UK · BW · 101min

Graham Greene's mystical, semi-autobiographical novel of doomed romance is convincingly brought to life by director Edward Dmytryk and contains a trio of powerful star performances from Deborah Kerr, John Mills and the outstanding Peter Cushing. Only miscast lead Van Johnson fails to achieve the requisite Catholic angst, which is certainly suggested but not really explored by Stephen Murray as the all-important priest. TS

Deborah Kerr *Sarah Miles* • Van Johnson *Maurice Bendrix* • John Mills *Albert Parkis* • Peter Cushing *Henry Miles* • Michael Goodliffe *Smythe* • Stephen Murray *Father Crompton* ■ *Dir* Edward Dmytryk • *Scr* Lenore Coffee, from the novel by Graham Greene

The End of the Affair ★★★★ 18

Wartime romantic drama
1999 · US/UK · Colour · 97min

Graham Greene's literary style was always consciously cinematic, but he has been singularly ill-served by those translating his novels to the screen. However, Neil Jordan has made a laudable attempt at conveying the characters' inner lives in this second filming of Greene's most autobiographical fiction. The story of doomed adultery between writer Ralph Fiennes and married Julianne Moore has a delicious sense of stolen joy. With Ian Hart outstanding as the detective hired by the jealous Fiennes, and

Stephen Rea no less impressive as Moore's stuffy husband, this is an admirable study of adult emotion. DP Sex scenes. 𝗗𝗩𝗗

Ralph Fiennes *Maurice Bendrix* • Julianne Moore *Sarah Miles* • Stephen Rea *Henry Miles* • Ian Hart *Mr Parkis* • Jason Isaacs *Father Smythe* • James Bolam *Mr Savage* ∎ *Dir* Neil Jordan • *Scr* Neil Jordan, from the novel by Graham Greene

End of the Century: the Story of the Ramones ★★★ 15

Music documentary 2003 · US · Colour · 107min

Although hailed as the godfathers of punk, the Ramones never quite achieved the commercial success of the many British bands that followed in their wake. Consequently, Joey, Dee Dee, Johnny and Tommy were more familiar with the seedy underside of the rock dream, as they succumbed to the excesses of touring and growing creative differences. Michael Gramaglia and Jim Field's documentary uses archive material and exclusive interviews to explore the band's personal demons and assess their musical legacy. Almost a decade in the making, this is a comprehensive look at the band, albeit a touch short on previously unseen material. DP 𝗗𝗩𝗗

∎ *Dir* Michael Gramaglia, Jim Fields

The End of the Day ★★★★

Drama 1939 · Fr · BW · 93min

The least penetrating of the poetic realist allegories on the ruinous decadence of prewar France, this is still a superbly realised and desperately sad film. Director Julien Duvivier creates a tangible atmosphere of melancholy pride in which his exceptional cast essay the various retired actors who have lost their very identities after years of playing roles on and off the stage. Each performance is a gem, from failed classicist Victor Francen's attempts to insinuate himself into Madeleine Ozeray's affections, to the fury of ladies' man Louis Jouvet. But, as ever, it's Michel Simon, as a lifelong understudy, who steals the show. DP French +subtitles.

Michel Simon *Cabrissade* • Victor Francen *Gilles Marny* • Louis Jouvet *Raphaël Saint-Clair* • Madeleine Ozeray *Jeannette* • Arquillieres [Alexandre C Arquillière] *Monsieur Lucien* • Gabrielle Dorziat *Madame Chabert* • Sylvie *Madame Tusini* ∎ *Dir* Julien Duvivier • *Scr* Charles Spaak, Julien Duvivier

End of the Game ★★★

Mystery drama
1976 · W Ger/It · Colour · 106min

It's role reversal time, with actor Maximilian Schell taking the director's chair, and director Martin Ritt making a rare foray in front of the cameras. Ritt neatly plays a dying police commissioner who makes one last attempt to catch the master criminal he's been hunting for the last 30 years. Jon Voight, Robert Shaw and Donald Sutherland are the better-known acting names in a complicated but rewarding Euro-thriller. DA

Jon Voight *Walter Tschantz* • Jacqueline Bisset *Anna Crawley* • Martin Ritt *Hans Barlach* • Robert Shaw *Richard Gastman* • Helmut Qualtinger *Von Schwendi* • Gabriele Ferzetti *Dr Lutz* • Rita Calderoni *Nadine* • Friedrich Dürrenmatt *Friedrich* • Donald Sutherland *Corpse* ∎ *Dir* Maximilian Schell • *Scr* Friedrich Dürrenmatt, Bo Goldmann, Maximilian Schell, from the novel *The Judge and His Hangman* by Friedrich Dürrenmatt

The End of the Golden Weather ★★★ PG

Drama 1992 · NZ · Colour · 98min

This cult oddity may be too eccentric for some. Director Ian Mune and playwright Bruce Mason adapted Mason's one-man show about the imaginary world of a 12-year-old boy (Stephen Fulford). The gaggle of grotesques on parade lacks a single redeeming feature; meanwhile, the age gap between the adolescent boy and his father widens to a predictable chasm. Unlike the

curate's egg, this family drama really is good in parts. TH Some swearing.

Stephen Fulford *Geoff* • Stephen Papps *Firpo* • Paul Gittins *Dad* • Gabrielle Hammond *Mum* • David Taylor *Ted* • Alexandra Marshall *Molly* ∎ *Dir* Ian Mune • *Scr* Ian Mune, Bruce Mason, from Mason's play

End of the Line ★★★ PG

Drama 1987 · US · Colour · 103min

It's man versus the system time again in a warm and touching drama about tradition and doing the right thing. Shocked when they hear the news that their freight depot is about to be closed down, railway workers Wilford Brimley and Levon Helm steal a locomotive and head to corporate headquarters in Chicago to make their feelings known to the chairman, Henderson Forsyth. Beautifully played by the down-home lead duo, they don't come more graceful than this. AJ

Wilford Brimley *Will Haney* • Levon Helm *Leo Pickett* • Mary Steenburgen *Rose Pickett* • Barbara Barrie *Jean Haney* • Henderson Forsythe *Thomas Clinton* • Bob Balaban *Warren Gerber* • Kevin Bacon *Everett* • Holly Hunter *Charlotte* ∎ *Dir* Jay Russell • *Scr* Jay Russell, John Wohlbruck

The End of the Line ★★★ PG

Documentary 2009 · UK · Colour · 86min

It's a well-known fact that 70 per cent of the planet is covered with water. Less well-known is that an estimated 90 per cent of the large fish in that water have been wiped out because of overfishing. This disturbing but one-sided eco-documentary, based on *Daily Telegraph* environment editor Charles Clover's book, gives those scientists who are predicting a collapse of fish stocks a chance to speak out. The film's handsome underwater photography captures the fragility of the natural resource that man is destroying, but the upbeat ending preaching a message of sustainability and consumer choice seems somewhat contrived after all the earlier doom-mongering. JR

Charles Clover ∎ *Dir* Rupert Murray • *Scr* From the non-fiction book by Charles Clover

The End of the River ★★ U

Drama 1947 · UK · BW · 79min

This curio, produced by Michael Powell and Emeric Pressburger, was directed by Derek Twist, who had edited Powell's 1937 semi-documentary about Shetland islanders, *The Edge of the World*. The all-purpose exotic Sabu here plays Manoel, forced to leave his jungle home for the corrupt and dirty city and finding himself on trial for murder. Despite a good cast and the Brazilian locations, the result is disappointing. AT

Sabu *Manoel* • Bibi Ferreira *Teresa* • Esmond Knight *Dantos* • Robert Douglas *Mr Jones* • Antoinette Cellier *Conceicao* • Torin Thatcher *Lisboa* • Orlando Martins *Harrigan* • Raymond Lovell *Colonel Porpino* • James Hayter *Chico* ∎ *Dir* Derek Twist • *Scr* Wolfgang Wilhelm, from the novel *Death of a Common Man* by Desmond Holdridge

End of the Road ★

Comedy drama 1970 · US · Colour · 110min

One day, a visiting alien may alight upon a can of film containing this movie. After ten minutes, he'll switch it off and say to his alien comrade, "Fancy a beer, mate?" For few movies are as boringly awful as this one. It's a counterculture affair with psychedelic trips, mental illness and a graphic message about abortion. AT

Stacy Keach *Jake Horner* • Harris Yulin *Joe Morgan* • Dorothy Tristan *Rennie Morgan* • James Earl Jones *Doctor D* • Grayson Hall *Peggie Rankin* • Ray Brock *Sniper Man/Mrs Dockey* • James Coco *School Man* • Oliver Clark *Dog Man* ∎ *Dir* Aram Avakian • *Scr* Dennis McGuire, Terry Southern, Aram Avakian, from the novel *The End of the Road* by John Barth

The End of the Tour ★★★★ 15

Drama 2015 · US · Colour · 105min

For a masterclass in quality acting, look no further than this true story of the Rolling

Stone reporter who struck up a five-day interview friendship with reclusive US author David Foster Wallace. Jesse Eisenberg plays the reporter, toning down his trademark twitchiness. But the real surprise is Jason Segel as the author. Who would have thought that the pleasant but rather bland star of such comedies as *Knocked Up*, *This Is 40* and *Sex Tape* would have such a finely nuanced dramatic performance in him. DA 𝗗𝗩𝗗

Jesse Eisenberg *David Lipsky* • Jason Segel *David Foster Wallace* • Anna Chlumsky *Sarah* • Joan Cusack *Patty* • Mamie Gummer *Julie* • Ron Livingston *Lipsky's editor* ∎ *Dir* James Ponsoldt • *Scr* Donald Margulies, from the non-fiction book *Although of Course You End Up Becoming Yourself: A Road Trip with David Foster Wallace* by David Lipsky

End of the World ★

Science fiction 1977 · US · Colour · 88min

Space invaders use a Californian convent as a base of operations in their plot to blow up the Earth because mankind is polluting the universe. Christopher Lee lends a modicum of dignity to the incredibly tacky proceedings as a Catholic priest and his extraterrestrial double who is controlling the murderous alien nuns. Tedious junk with a has-been cast. AJ

Christopher Lee *Father Pergado/Zindar* • Sue Lyon *Sylvia Boran* • Kirk Scott *Professor Andrew Boran* • Dean Jagger *Ray Collins* • Lew Ayres *Beckerman* • Macdonald Carey *John Davis* • Liz Ross *Sister Patrizia* ∎ *Dir* John Hayes • *Scr* Frank Ray Perilli

The End of the World (in Our Usual Bed in a Night Full of Rain) ★★

Drama 1978 · It/US · Colour · 104min

The first in a four-picture deal with Warners, this turned out to be the only film controversial Italian director Lina Wertmuller made in the States. Despite working once more with her favourite star, Giancarlo Giannini, Wertmuller lets herself be weighed down by polemic in this talkative confrontation between old-world machismo (Italian journalist Giannini) and self-assertive feminism (American photographer Candice Bergen). The observations are worth making, but the flashback structure does little to make it accessible. DP Swearing.

Giancarlo Giannini *Paolo* • Candice Bergen *Lizzy* • Anne Byrne *Friend* • Flora Carabella *Friend* • Mario Scarpetta *Friend* ∎ *Dir/Scr* Lina Wertmuller

The End of Violence ★★★ 15

Thriller 1997 · US/Ger/Fr · Colour · 116min

As a mysterious figure (Gabriel Byrne) uses surveillance cameras to keep watch over the city, a Hollywood producer (Bill Pullman), who's become rich thanks to the public's thirst for blood, is kidnapped by inept gangsters. Escaping, he goes undercover and finds kindness on the streets; his wife (Andie MacDowell), meanwhile, tries to find him. The result is an uneasy mix of Fritz Lang determinism and Frank Capra optimism, but, in the hands of director Wim Wenders, it makes for a very watchable and oddly poignant film. TH Swearing.

Bill Pullman *Mike* • Andie MacDowell *Paige* • Gabriel Byrne *Ray* • Loren Dean *Doc* • Traci Lind *Cat* • Rosalind Chao *Claire* • K Todd Freeman *Six* • Chris Douridas *Technician* ∎ *Dir* Wim Wenders • *Scr* Nicholas Klein, from a story by Wim Wenders, Nicholas Klein

End of Watch ★★★ 15

Police drama 2012 · US · Colour · 104min

This is another effective cop movie from *Training Day* writer David Ayer, though it has none of that film's cynical wit. It has a shaven-headed Jake Gyllenhaal and Michael Peña as a pair of uniformed LA cops who stumble into a big-time drugs deal with tragic repercussions. The film is shot almost wholly on handheld cameras (Gyllenhaal being enrolled in a film course and documenting his job as part of a project) so the relentless shaky cam will irritate some

viewers. Much of the movie's appeal relies on the relationship between the wisecracking duo, and it is appealingly acted and well directed, but at times the tale becomes crudely manipulative and implausible. AS Violence, swearing, sexual references, drug abuse. 𝗗𝗩𝗗 🄱🄻

Jake Gyllenhaal *Officer Brian Taylor* • Michael Peña [Michael Pena] *Officer Mike Zavala* • America Ferrera *Officer Orozco* • Anna Kendrick *Janet* • Cody Horn *Officer Davis* ∎ *Dir/Scr* David Ayer

Ender's Game ★★★ 12

Science-fiction action adventure
2013 · US · Colour · 109min

Based on the sci-fi bestseller, this takes place in a future where Earth is under threat from aliens, and the military grooms children with exceptional computer gaming skills to fight back. The most talented wunderkind is Ender Wiggin (a assured Asa Butterfield), but is he too sensitive to lead a team of his peers into battle? The premise of a gifted boy thrown into a world of cliques and hierarchies may have the ring of Harry Potter in space, but director Gavin Hood imbues the tale with deeper moral dilemmas, while the special effects dazzle and veteran soldiers Harrison Ford and Ben Kingsley add gravitas. TeS Some violence. 𝗗𝗩𝗗 🄱🄻

Harrison Ford *Colonel Hyrum Graff* • Asa Butterfield *Ender Wiggin* • Ben Kingsley *Mazer Rackham* • Viola Davis *Major Gwen Anderson* • Hailee Steinfeld *Petra Arkanian* • Abigail Breslin *Valentine Wiggin* ∎ *Dir* Gavin Hood • *Scr* Gavin Hood, from Orson Scott Card's novel

Endless Love ★★ 15

Romantic drama 1981 · US · Colour · 110min

Vaguely interesting for causing controversy at the time, this tacky tale of illicit teenage romance hasn't aged particularly well. Martin Hewitt and Brooke Shields are the mismatched youngsters who fall in love, much to the disapproval of the latter's father (Don Murray). Director Franco Zeffirelli brings a modicum of class and style to the affair, but not enough to overcome the cloying sentimentality on show. Watch for Tom Cruise, making his feature debut. JF

Brooke Shields *Jade Butterfield* • Martin Hewitt *David Axelrod* • Shirley Knight *Anne Butterfield* • Don Murray *Hugh Butterfield* • Richard Kiley *Arthur Axelrod* • Beatrice Straight *Rose Axelrod* • James Spader *Keith* • Tom Cruise *Billy* ∎ *Dir* Franco Zeffirelli • *Scr* Judith Rascoe, from the novel by Scott Spencer

Endless Love ★★ 12

Romantic drama 2014 · US · Colour · 100min

First filmed by Franco Zeffirelli in 1981, this tale of obsessive teenage love has been toned down for today's youth audience. Gabriella Wilde plays Jade, a white-collar "good" girl, while Alex Pettyfer (*I Am Number Four*) is David, a blue-collar, mildly "bad" boy. They fall madly in love, much to the dismay of Jade's protective dad (Bruce Greenwood). Shana Feste's film is kind of fun if you're in the right mood for some undemanding candyfloss or a good old emotional wallow. DA Swearing, a sex scene, some violence. 𝗗𝗩𝗗

Alex Pettyfer *David Elliot* • Gabriella Wilde *Jade Butterfield* • Bruce Greenwood *Hugh Butterfield* • Joely Richardson *Anne Butterfield* • Robert Patrick *Harry Elliot* ∎ *Dir* Shana Feste • *Scr* Shana Feste, Joshua Safran, from Scott Spencer's novel

Endless Night ★★★ 15

Psychological thriller 1971 · UK · Colour · 95min

A torrid sex scene shatters the carefully established suspense in this dark thriller – hardly the kind of thing you'd expect in an Agatha Christie mystery. But then, this is not a typical offering from the queen of crime. Comedy specialist Sidney Gilliat keeps you guessing here as American heiress Hayley Mills becomes convinced that not even husband Hywel Bennett and friend Britt Ekland can protect her from a malevolent menace. DP

Hayley Mills *Ellie* • Hywel Bennett *Michael* • Britt Ekland *Greta* • George Sanders *Lippincott* • Per Oscarsson *Santonix* • Peter Bowles *Reuben* • Lois Maxwell *Cora* ■ *Dir* Sidney Gilliat • *Scr* Sidney Gilliat, from the novel by Agatha Christie

The Endless Summer

★★★ U

Documentary   1964 · US · Colour · 91min

Two surfers, Mike Hynson and Robert August, travel the world in search of the "perfect wave" in this classic surfing documentary put together by film-maker Bruce Brown. Capturing the subculture at the precise time it was having the most profound influence on popular music and Californian lifestyles, the duo visit the virgin beaches of Africa, Australia, New Zealand, Tahiti and Hawaii for time-elapsed sunsets and fabulous shots of them riding wild surf. Groovy music by the Sandals, a five-piece surfing outfit, accompany the beautiful images and Brown's hip surfer-speak is a history lesson in itself. AJ *DVD*

Bruce Brown *Narrator* ■ *Dir/Scr* Bruce Brown • *Cinematographer* Bruce Brown

The Endless Summer II

★★ U

Documentary   1994 · US · Colour · 105min

The search for the "perfect wave" continues, 28 years on, with beach boys Pat O'Connell and Robert "Wingnut" Weaver being followed around the world by all-round film-maker Bruce Brown. This time it's Alaska, Bali, Fiji, France and Java getting the photographic picture postcard treatment. Fans of the original will be equally impressed by this stunningly shot document, despite Brown's narration being slightly more pretentious and irritating. AJ *DVD*

■ *Dir* Bruce Brown • *Scr* Bruce Brown, Dana Brown

Endurance

★★★ U

Sports documentary drama
1998 · US/UK/Ger · Colour · 83min

Bud Greenspan may have supervised the Atlanta Olympic sequences, but this portrait of the veteran Ethiopian distance runner Haile Gebrselassie is very much the work of ethnographer Leslie Woodhead. The athlete's young nephew, Yonas Zergaw, plays him in a series of dramatic reconstructions showing how he ran 12 miles every day to the school nearest his home village of Asela and then relocated to Addis Ababa in the hope of emulating his 10,000-metre hero, Miruts Yifter. This is a stirring study of raw ambition and awesome dedication. DP In English, Amharic.

Haile Gebrselassie • Bekele Gebrselassie • Alem Tellahun • Yonas Zergaw *Young Haile Gebrselassie* • Shawanness Gebrselassie *Haile's mother* • Tedesse Haile *Haile's father* ■ *Dir* Leslie Woodhead, Bud Greenspan • *Scr* Leslie Woodhead

The Endurance: Shackelton's Legendary Antarctic Expedition

★★★ PG

Documentary
2000 · US/UK/Swe/Ger · Colour and BW · 93min

The intrepid durability of Ernest Shackleton's 1914 Antarctic expedition throughout its ill-fated bid to cross the polar continent on foot was captured first hand by Australian cameraman Frank Hurley. Much of his tinted footage appears in this blindly admiring account, but George Butler's documentary also draws heavily on Caroline Alexander's meticulous book to piece together an exact chronology. Narrator Liam Neeson links the archival clips, interviews, graphic sequences and dramatic reconstructions to paint a portrait of an inspired leader, while also considering the validity of exploration. DP *DVD*

Liam Neeson *Narrator* ■ *Dir* George Butler • *Scr* Caroline Alexander, Joseph Dorman, from a non-fiction book by Alexander

Enduring Love

★★★ 15

Psychological thriller
2004 · UK/US · Colour · 96min

A bizarre accident links two strangers in director Roger Michell's illogical and annoying metaphysical thriller. After attempting to halt a runaway hot-air balloon, which results in a man falling to his death, Daniel Craig is mercilessly stalked by fellow would-be rescuer Rhys Ifans, who believes himself in love with Craig. Wilfully obscure, this corrosive and bitter tale is bolstered by expert performances from Craig and Ifans. AC Swearing, violence. *DVD*

Daniel Craig *Joe Rose* • Rhys Ifans *Jed* • Samantha Morton *Claire* • Bill Nighy *Robin* • Susan Lynch *Rachel* • Helen McCrory *Mrs Logan* • Andrew Lincoln *TV producer* • Corin Redgrave *Professor* ■ *Dir* Roger Michell • *Scr* Joe Penhall, from the novel by Ian McEwan

Enemies, a Love Story

★★★★ 15

Comedy drama   1989 · US · Colour · 114min

This is a wonderfully lyrical and multilayered ensemble piece, about the painful, tangled relationships of a group of Jewish immigrants in postwar New York. The acting is sublime, particularly from Lena Olin as a disturbed but passionate Holocaust survivor and Ron Silver as her emotionally repressed, egocentric lover. Director Paul Mazursky has fashioned a deeply moving, thought-provoking movie that, despite suffering marginally from insufficient light and shade, challenges the mind and stirs the heart. SH Swearing, sex scenes, nudity.

Anjelica Huston *Tamara* • Ron Silver *Herman Broder* • Lena Olin *Masha* • Margaret Sophie Stein *Yadwiga* • Judith Malina *Masha's mother* • Alan King *Rabbi Lembeck* • Rita Karin *Mrs Schreier* ■ *Dir* Paul Mazursky • *Scr* Roger L Simon, Paul Mazursky, from the novel by Isaac Bashevis Singer

Enemies Closer

★★ 15

Action thriller   2013 · Can/US · Colour · 81min

Jean-Claude Van Damme's collaborations with director Peter Hyams have produced two of his best action movies in *Timecop* (1994) and *Sudden Death* (1995). Sadly, this 2013 cat-and-mouse thriller isn't in that class, though it's watchable enough if you're in an undemanding mood. Riffing on his villain from *The Expendables 2*, Van Damme plays the evil Xander, who's out to reclaim a drugs shipment from the waters off a tourist island. JA *DVD*

Jean-Claude Van Damme *Xander* • Tom Everett Scott *Henry* • Orlando Jones *Clay* • Linzey Cocker *Kayla* ■ *Dir* Peter Hyams • *Scr* Eric Bromberg, James Bromberg

Enemies of the People

★★★★

Documentary
2009 · UK/US/Camb · Colour and BW · 93min

Thet Sambath is an unlikely hero. The Cambodian journalist has spent his career attempting to understand the mentality that led the Khmer Rouge to order the brutal massacres in the killing fields of the 1970s. He regularly travels into the countryside to interview the peasants who committed the atrocities on behalf of Pol Pot's infamous regime. The confessions he hears in this documentary are chilling, especially as those involved aren't always penitent. The methodology employed by Thet and co-director Rob Lemkin is occasionally manipulative and the truth often remains elusive. But this is absolutely compelling, nonetheless. DP In English, Central Khmer.

Thet Sambath ■ *Dir/Scr* Rob Lemkin, Thet Sambath

The Enemy

★★

Action thriller   2000 · US/Lux · Colour · 101min

There's something uncomfortably old-fashioned about this thriller. It lacks the zip of today s modern action thrillers, and the casting doesn t help either, with neither Luke Perry nor Olivia D'Abo being memorable as the scientist and secret agent, out to rescue Perry's father (Horst Bucholtz) from terrorists who want him to hand over a lethal chemical weapon. JF

Luke Perry *Mike Ashton* • Olivia D'Abo *Penny Johnson* • Roger Moore *Robert Ogilvy* • Tom Conti *John Creger* • Horst Buchholz *George Ashton* ■ *Dir* Tom Kinninmont • *Scr* John Penney, from the novel *The Enemy* by Desmond Bagley

Enemy

★★★★ 15

Thriller   2013 · Can/Sp · Colour · 86min

In what appears to be an alternate, possibly totalitarian Toronto, Jake Gyllenhaal's soulless college lecturer chances upon his own duplicate (also Gyllenhaal) in a rented movie and proceeds to stalk him. While impending chaos seems to hover over the high-rise city and spiders are crushed for entertainment in a sex club, the two Jakes meet and their lives merge. Heavy with symbolism and the subconscious, Denis Villeneuve's remote style, de-saturated palate and lack of answers make *Enemy* difficult to love, but it will stay with you. AC Swearing, sex scenes, nudity *DVD*

Jake Gyllenhaal *Adam/Anthony* • Mélanie Laurent *Mary* • Sarah Gadon *Helen* ■ *Dir* Denis Villeneuve • *Scr* Javier Gullón, from the novel *The Double* by José Saramago

Enemy at the Gates

★★ 15

Second World War drama
2001 · US/Ger/UK/Ire · Colour · 125min

Featuring three miscast stars and a spectacularly awful script, director Jean-Jacques Annaud's uninspiring drama focuses on the battle for Stalingrad. According to Annaud's version of events, the lengthy conflict (summer 1942 to February 1943) boiled down to a sniper duel between legendary Russian shepherd Jude Law and German nobleman Ed Harris. Soviet propaganda genius Joseph Fiennes elevates Law to folk hero status, but they both fall in love with Rachel Weisz. AJ Violence, swearing. *DVD*

Jude Law *Vassily Zaitsev* • Joseph Fiennes *Danilov* • Rachel Weisz *Tania* • Bob Hoskins *Nikita Khrushchev* • Ed Harris *Major König* • Ron Perlman *Koulikov* • Eva Mattes *Mother Filipov* ■ *Dir* Jean-Jacques Annaud • *Scr* Alain Godard, Jean-Jacques Annaud, from the novel by William Craig, and from the novel *Vendetta* by Derek Lambert

The Enemy Below ★★★★ PG

Second World War drama
1957 · US · Colour · 93min

This is one of the best submarine movies, a stunning drama about a Second World War German U-boat and the US destroyer that's stalking it, whose captains only meet in the final reel. As the respective skippers, Curt Jurgens and Robert Mitchum turn in fine performances. The special effects won an Oscar, but it is the direction by Dick Powell that is really remarkable – his taut handling of the action makes this one of his finest movie achievements. The film was actually based on a real story, written into novel form by wartime submarine captain DA Rayner. TS *DVD*

Robert Mitchum *Captain Murrell* • Curt Jurgens *Von Stolberg* • Al Hedison [David Hedison] *Lieutenant Ware* • Theodore Bikel *Schwaffer* • Russell Collins *Doctor* • Kurt Kreuger *Von Holem* • Frank Albertson *Chief Petty Officer Crain* ■ *Dir* Dick Powell • *Scr* Wendell Mayes, from the novel by DA Rayner • *Special Effects (Audible)* Walter Rossi

Enemy Mine

★★★★ 12

Science-fiction fantasy
1985 · US · Colour · 103min

Earthman Dennis Quaid and lizard-like alien Louis Gossett Jr (virtually unrecognisable under very impressive scaly make-up) crash-land on an unknown planet and learn that co-operation equals survival. Director Wolfgang Petersen makes this racial tolerance plea in outer space disguise a satisfying blend of action spills and emotional thrills. It touches both the brain and heart, remaining true to its pulp science-fiction roots while never being anything less than engrossing. AJ Some violence, swearing. *DVD* *Blu*

Dennis Quaid *Willis Davidge* • Louis Gossett Jr *Jeriba Shigan* • Brion James *Stubbs* • Richard Marcus *Arnold* • Carolyn McCormick *Morse* • Bumper Robinson *Zammis* • Jim Mapp *Old Drac* • Lance Kerwin *Wooster* ■ *Dir* Wolfgang Petersen • *Scr* Edward Khmara, from a story by Barry Longyear

An Enemy of the People

★★★ U

Period drama   1977 · US · Colour · 102min

Action hero Steve McQueen peers through a thicket of beard to take on a much-coveted role as the doctor whose warning that the local spa is polluted leads to antagonism from the small town's inhabitants. George Schaefer's direction is as worthy as McQueen's performance, but Charles Durning's counterbalance to the doctor's righteous indignation shows us what real acting is, and how dull McQueen seems in comparison. TH

Steve McQueen (I) *Dr Thomas Stockmann* • Charles Durning *Peter Stockmann* • Bibi Andersson *Catherine Stockmann* • Eric Christmas *Morten Kiil* • Michael Cristofer *Hovstad* • Richard A Dysart [Richard Dysart] *Aslaksen* • Michael Higgins *Billing* ■ *Dir* George Schaefer • *Scr* Alexander Jacobs, from the play by Henrik Ibsen, adapted by Arthur Miller

An Enemy of the People

★★ U

Drama   1989 · Ind · Colour · 95min

In many ways this adaptation of Ibsen's play (also released as *Ganashatru*) was a courageous enterprise, as director Satyajit Ray was returning to work after a four-year hiatus following a heart attack and was forbidden to shoot on location by his doctors. However, while we can forgive the studio-bound feel, it's hard to ignore the fact that this is a dull film made almost interminable by the impossibly earnest performance of Soumitra Chatterjee as the doctor trying to close a temple following the contamination of its water supply. DP Bengali +subtitles.

Soumitra Chatterjee *Dr Ashok Gupta* • Ruma Guha-Thakurta *Maya Gupta* • Dhritiman Chatterjee *Nichit Gupta* • Mamata Shankar *Ranu Gupta* • Dipankar Dey *Haridas Bagchi* ■ *Dir* Satyajit Ray • *Scr* Satyajit Ray, from the play by Henrik Ibsen

Enemy of the State

★★★★ 15

Conspiracy thriller   1998 · US · Colour · 133min

Expert direction by Tony Scott and a winning central performance by Will Smith give this cracking hi-tech thriller extra edge and appeal. When an incriminating tape revealing the murder of congressman Jason Robards accidentally ends up in Smith's possession, he finds himself relentlessly pursued by corrupt Jon Voight and his posse of electronic trackers, who use spy satellites, transmitters and all manner of undercover gizmos to trace him. An exciting action adventure that's both intriguing and thought-provoking. AJ Swearing, violence. *DVD* *Blu*

Will Smith *Robert Clayton Dean* • Gene Hackman *Brill* • Jon Voight *Reynolds* • Lisa Bonet *Rachel Banks* • Regina King *Carla Dean* • Ian Hart *Bingham* • Jason Lee Zavitz • Gabriel Byrne "*Brill*" • Jason Robards *Hammersly* • Tom Sizemore *Pintero* ■ *Dir* Tony Scott • *Scr* David Marconi

The Enemy Within ★★★ 12

Conspiracy thriller   1994 · US · Colour · 86min

Would anyone dare to challenge the authority of Uncle Sam and overthrow an elected US government? That's the intriguing premise behind this efficient remake of the 1964 film *Seven Days in May*. By TV movie standards, a strong cast has been assembled here, and the performances are professional, but it lacks the power of the original. SuR Brief swearing, violence. *DVD*

Forest Whitaker *Col MacKenzie Casey* • Sam Waterston *President William Foster* • Dana Delany *Chief of Staff Betsy Corcoran* • Jason

Robards *General R Pendleton Lloyd* • Josef Sommer *Defense Secretary Charles Potter* • George Dzundza *Jake* ■ *Dir* Jonathan Darby • *Scr* Darryl Ponicsan, Ron Bass [Ronald Bass], from the film *Seven Days in May* by Rod Serling, from the novel *Seven Days in May* by Fletcher Knebel, Charles W Bailey II [Charles Waldo Bailey]

L'Enfance Nue ★★★ 15
Drama 1968 · Fr · Colour · 79min

Co-produced by François Truffaut, this is a remarkable first feature from director Maurice Pialat, especially since the participants are not professional actors. The sensitive yet unsentimental tale focuses on a ten-year-old boy who is abandoned by his mother. Handed over to the social services, he is treated with dispassion and becomes a teenage nightmare when placed with foster parents. This extremely well-observed docudrama takes all perspectives into account, while the relationship the child develops with his aged grandmother, Marie Marc, is particularly touching. LH French +subtitles. *DVD*

Michel Terrazon *François* • Linda Gutemberg *Simone* • Raoul Billerey *Roby* • Pierette Deplanque *Josette* • Marie-Louise Thierry *Mme Minguet* • Rene Thierry *M Minguet* • Henri Puff *Raoul* • Marie Marc *Meme* • Maurice Coussoneau *Letillon* ■ *Dir/Scr* Maurice Pialat

L'Enfant ★★★★ 12
Social drama 2005 · Bel/Fr · Colour · 91min

Brothers Luc and Jean-Pierre Dardenne won their second Palme d'Or for this uncompromising, compassionate study of the depths to which people can be driven by poverty and despair. Young Jérémie Renier wheels and deals in all manner of illicit goods with his schoolboy gang. While his teenage girlfriend Déborah François is in hospital he sublets their flat, and he later sells their newborn baby to traffickers. The Dardennes make life on the margins of Liège appear so hopeless that Renier's actions do seem more misguidedly well-intentioned than wilfully criminal. Complete with an intense chase sequence and a touchingly optimistic finale, this confirms the brothers as masters of edgy poetic realism. DP French +subtitles. Swearing, violence. *DVD*

Jérémie Renier [Jérémie Rénier] *Bruno* • Déborah François *Sonia* • Jérémie Segard *Steve* • Fabrizio Rongicne *Young thug* • Olivier Gourmet *Plainclothes officer* ■ *Dir/Scr* Luc Dardenne, Jean-Pierre Dardenne

L'Enfant Sauvage ★★★★ U
Period drama based on a true story 1970 · Fr · BW · 82min

This is a historical drama that eschews costume finery in favour of philosophical debate. The film tackles such complex notions as natural law, the supremacy of society, the right to resist injustice and the conflict between scientific research and emotional subjectivity, but it is also a very human tale. Set in 1798, it relates the true story of Victor (Jean-Pierre Cargol), the forest foundling who is introduced to the basics of civilisation by Dr Jean Itard (François Truffaut). Making pleasing use of antiquated cinematic devices and actual journal extracts, this has a documentary feel that makes it fascinating. DP French +subtitles. *DVD*

Jean-Pierre Cargol *Victor, the boy* • Paul Villé *Rémy* • François Truffaut *Dr Jean Itard* • Françoise Seigner *Madame Guérin* • Claude Miller *Monsieur Lemeri* • Annie Miller *Madame Lemeri* ■ *Dir* François Truffaut • *Scr* François Truffaut, Jean Gruault, from the non-fiction book *Mémoire et Rapport sur Victor de L'Aveyron* by Jean-Marc Gaspard Itard

Les Enfants de Lumière ★★★★★
Compilation 1995 · Fr · BW and Colour · 102min

Several fictional features and personal memoirs were commissioned to commemorate the centenary of cinema, but few celebrate film's unique ability to entertain, move, provoke or reminisce with such charm and intelligence as this superb French compilation. Divided thematically, this priceless collection of greatest clips

features a Who's Who of French film, with Gérard Philipe and Jean Marais rubbing shoulders with the great Jean Gabin and Jean-Louis Barrault, and Arletty, Michèle Morgan and Simone Signoret competing for the soft-focus spotlight. The brainchild of top producer Jacques Perrin, it also has the benefit of a spine-tingling score from Michel Legrand. DP English, French +subtitles.

Anthony Valentine *Narrator* ■ *Dir* André Asseo, Pierre Billard, Ala n Corneau, Claude Miller, Claude Sautet

Les Enfants du Paradis ★★★★★ PG
Classic period drama 1945 · Fr · BW · 182min

The most courageous and elegant act of defiance in cinema history, this beautiful tale of Parisian popular theatre in the early 19th century was shot under the noses of the Gestapo towards the end of the Second World War. Determined to premiere the picture in a liberated France, director Marcel Carné tolerated all manner of delays, including the absence of cast members sent on missions for the Resistance. On the surface, the film is a tale of unrequited love, but it is in fact a tribute to the indomitable spirit of Free France, as personified by Garance (Arletty), the legendary actress who resists all attempts to possess her. DP French +subtitles. *DVD* *Blu-ray*

Arletty *Garance* • Jean-Louis Barrault *Baptiste Debureau* • Pierre Brasseur *Frédérick Lemaître* • Marcel Herrand *Lacenaire* • Pierre Renoir *Jéricho, the old clothes man* • Maria Casarès *Natalie* • Etienne Decroux *Anselme Debureau* ■ *Dir* Marcel Carné • *Scr* Jacques Prévert, Marcel Carné, from their original idea • *Art Directors* Alexandre Trauner, Léon Barsacq, Raymond Gabutti

Les Enfants du Siècle ★★★ 15
Biographical period drama 1999 · Fr/UK · Colour · 108min

Diane Kurys examines the pre-Chopin love life of the 19th-century French writer George Sand. Juliette Binoche gives a steady performance as Sand (the pen name of Baroness Dudevant), a fiercely independent mother of two, who leaves her husband to pursue a career in literature. Much of the focus, however, falls on her passionate relationship with poet Alfred de Musset (Benoît Magimel), who is driven by self-doubt and family disapproval into a life of debauchery and regret. This was cut by almost half an hour for its belated UK release. DP French +subtitles.

Juliette Binoche *George Sand* • Benoît Magimel *Alfred de Musset* • Stefano Dionisi *Pietro Pagello* • Robin Renucci *François Buloz* • Karin Viard *Marie Dorval* • Isabelle Carré *Aimée d'Alton* • Patrick Chesnais *Gustave Planche* ■ *Dir* Diane Kurys • *Scr* Diane Kurys, Murray Head, François-Olivier Rousseau

Les Enfants Terribles ★★★★ 12
Drama 1949 · Fr · BW · 100min

Budgetary restraint goes a long way to explaining the effectiveness of this adaptation of Jean Cocteau's 1929 novel. By shooting much of the action in his own apartment and on the stage of the Théâtre Pigalle, director Jean-Pierre Melville was able to reproduce the simmering claustrophobia that makes the obsessive relationship between brother and sister Edouard Dermithe and Nicole Stéphane so intense. Although Cocteau narrates and directed the seaside scene, the film's erotic tension and visual poetry are down to Melville's finesse, which ensures that the tale becomes troubling tragicomedy instead of melodramatic high camp. DP French +subtitles. *DVD*

Nicole Stéphane *Elisabeth* • Edouard Dermithe *Paul* • Jacques Bernard *Gerad* • Renée Cosima *Dargelos/Agathe* • Roger Gaillard *Gerard's uncle* • Melvyn Martin *Michael* • Jean Cocteau *Narrator* ■ *Dir* Jean-Pierre Melville • *Scr* Jean Cocteau, Jean-Pierre Melville, from the novel by Jean Cocteau

L'Enfer ★★★ 15
Thriller 1993 · Fr · Colour · 97min

L'Enfer, or *Hell*, began in 1964 as a movie starring Romy Schneider and Serge Reggiani and directed by Henri-Georges Clouzot. Shortly after shooting started, Reggiani quit through illness; then Clouzot himself was felled by a heart attack. After Clouzot's death in 1977 the project passed to Claude Chabrol. It's a story about pathological jealousy, acted to the hilt by the sensuous Emmanuelle Béart, whose character is married to seething hotel owner François Cluzet. Things get out of control, tipping the picture into the realm of black comedy. AT French +subtitles. *DVD*

Emmanuelle Béart *Nelly* • François Cluzet *Paul* • Nathalie Cardone *Marylin* • André Wilms *Doctor Arnoux* • Marc Lavoine *Martineau* • Christiane Minazzoli *Madame Vernon* • Dora Doll *Madame Chabert* • Mario David *Duhamel* ■ *Dir* Claude Chabrol • *Scr* Henri-Georges Clouzot, José-André Lacour

L'Enfer ★★ 15
Drama 2005 · Fr/It/Bel/Jpn · Colour · 102min

The great Polish director Krzysztof Kieslowski roughed out scripts with longtime collaborator Krzysztof Piesiewicz for a trilogy of films but died before shooting could begin. Tom Tykwer was the first director to have a go at bringing these last works to the screen with 2002's sluggish *Heaven*; and now comes this flavourless fruit of Danis Tanovic's labour. Using a cool, wintry palette, the story follows the unhappy lives of three estranged sisters living in Paris. There's lots of symbolic visuals and tricksy crosscutting, but when the big revelation comes, it's really not worth the wait. LF French +subtitles. Violence, nudity.

Emmanuelle Béart *Sophie* • Karin Viard *Céline* • Marie Gillain *Anne* • Guillaume Canet *Sébastien* • Jacques Gamblin *Pierre* • Jacques Perrin *Frédéric* • Carole Bouquet *The mother* • Miki Manojlovic *The father* • Jean Rochefort *Louis* • Maryam D'Abo *Julie* ■ *Dir* Danis Tanovic • *Scr* Krzysztof Piesiewicz, from the idea for one part of the proposed film trilogy *Heaven, Hell and Purgatory* by Krzysztof Kieslowski, Krzysztof Piesiewicz

The Enforcer ★★★★ PG
Crime drama 1951 · US · BW · 84min

This terrific Warner Bros crime drama features Humphrey Bogart on the right side of the law for once, closing in on a gang of professional killers with the help of key witnesses, including Zero Mostel in one of his last movie roles before he was blacklisted during the communist witch-hunt. Bretaigne Windust takes the credit as director, though most of the film was actually directed by the uncredited Raoul Walsh. Unusually, there's no romance to slow down the action as it moves to a riveting finale. Also known as *Murder, Inc.* TS *DVD*

Humphrey Bogart *Martin Ferguson* • Zero Mostel *"Big Babe" Lazich* • Ted De Corsia *Joseph Rico* • Everett Sloane *Albert Mendoza* • Roy Roberts *Captain Frank Nelson* • Lawrence Tolan [Michael Tolan] *"Duke" Malloy* • King Donovan *Sergeant Whitlow* • Robert Steele [Bob Steele] *Herman* ■ *Dir* Bretaigne Windust • *Scr* Martin Rackin

The Enforcer ★★ 18
Crime thriller 1976 · US · Colour · 92min

The Identikit collection of corrupt cops and crazed killers confronting Clint Eastwood's Harry Callahan in this third film in the *Dirty Harry* series is hardly a match for the no-nonsense lawman's unique talents. Only Harry's new partner (played with spirit by Tyne Daly) has any depth, but this intriguing relationship is wasted in a welter of sexist one-liners. Fans would have to wait seven years for Harry's fourth outing, *Sudden Impact*. DP Violence, swearing, nudity. *DVD* *Blu-ray*

Clint Eastwood *Harry Callahan* • Tyne Daly *Kate Moore* • Bradford Dillman *Captain McKay* • Harry Guardino *Lieutenant Bressler* • DeVeren Bookwalter *Bobby Maxwell* • John Mitchum *DiGeorgio* • John Crawford *Mayor* ■ *Dir* James Fargo • *Scr* Stirling Silliphant, Dean Reisner, from characters by Harry Julian Fink, RM Fink

The Enforcer ★★ 18
Martial arts action thriller 1995 · HK · Colour · 100min

An early attempt by Jet Li to move on from the historical martial arts epics which made his name into more western-friendly action roles, this is a proficient but unconvincing thriller. Playing a Beijing cop who goes undercover to infiltrate a Hong Kong crime syndicate, Li's dazzling fight skills are well to the fore. However, the dubbing is atrocious and the screen time given over to the precocious Tse Miu, who plays his adoring son, is sentimental. JF Cantonese dubbed. *DVD*

Jet Li *Kung Wei* • Anita Mui *Anna* • Tse Mui *Johnny* • Yu Rong Guang *Po Kwong* ■ *Dir* Corey Yuen • *Scr* Sandy Shaw, Wong Jing

England Made Me ★★★★
Period drama 1973 · UK · Colour · 100min

Graham Greene's least-known novel was the inspiration behind this underrated film that, like *Cabaret* the year before, offers a fascinating glimpse of pre-Second World War Germany. Michael York plays a sponging Englishman whose dealings with Peter Finch's sinister financier almost lead him to become incestuously involved with his own sister (Hildegard Neil). The potential for atmosphere is vividly explored by director Peter Duffell. TH

Peter Finch *Erich Krogh* • Michael York *Anthony Farrant* • Hildegard Neil *Kate Farrant* • Michael Hordern *F Minty* • Joss Ackland *Hiller* • Tessa Wyatt *Liz Davidge* • Michael Sheard *Fromm* • William Baskiville [Bill Baskiville] *Stein* ■ *Dir* Peter Duffell • *Scr* Peter Duffell, Desmond Cory, from the novel by Graham Greene

English, August ★★★
Comedy drama 1994 · Ind · Colour · 118min

Based on the cult novel by Upamanyu Chatterjee, this was among the first Indian independent productions to score at the box-office and helped usher in a new generation of non-Bollywood, English-language movie-makers. What makes this all the more remarkable was that the film marked director Dev Benegal's feature debut. It's an iconoclastic comedy drama in which a civil servant struggles to find his niche in Madna (reputedly the subcontinent's hottest little town) against a backdrop of drugs, infidelity, pornography and corruption. DP Hindi, English +subtitles.

Tanvi Azmi *Malti Srivastava* • Rahul Bose *Agastya Sen* • Shivaji Satham *Govinde Sathe* • Salim Shah *Ravi Srivastava* • Yogendra Tikku *Kumar* ■ *Dir* Dev Benegal • *Scr* Dev Benegal, Upamanyu Chatterjee, from a novel by Upamanyu Chatterjee

The English Patient ★★★★★ 15
Second World War romantic drama 1996 · US · Colour · 155min

This skilful adaptation of Michael Ondaatje's difficult novel is at heart two love stories, one in the present, the other told in flashback. Ralph Fiennes is the hideously burned "English patient" tended to by Juliette Binoche's nurse in an Italian monastery at the end of the Second World War. His story, torrid and dangerous, is pieced together gradually, while Binoche falls in love with a bomb disposal officer (Naveen Andrews). Fiennes is in fact a Hungarian, a mapmaker charting the Sahara who got caught up in the war and in an affair with the unhappily married Kristin Scott Thomas. It's an ambitious film, and director Anthony Minghella's skill lies equally in his screenplay, which delivers explanation only in fragments but keeps us involved for what is an epic running time. AC Violence, swearing, sex scenes. *DVD* *Blu-ray*

Ralph Fiennes *Count Laszlo Almasy* • Juliette Binoche *Hana* • Willem Dafoe *Caravaggio* • Kristin Scott Thomas *Katharine Clifton* • Naveen Andrews *Kip* • Colin Firth *Geoffrey Clifton* • Julian Wadham *Madox* • Jürgen Prochnow *Major Müller* • Kevin Whately *Hardy* ■ *Dir* Anthony Minghella • *Scr* Anthony Minghella, from the novel by Michael Ondaatje

The English Teacher ★★★ 15

Comedy drama   2013 · US · Colour · 87min

Julianne Moore is the popular high-school teacher who has given up on romance, preferring instead to concentrate on her on-going love affair with literature. However, her cosy life is shaken up after a chance meeting with former star pupil Michael Angarano, who has failed to make it as a playwright in New York. Moore gives a beautifully understated performance as the sweet but hopelessly naive teacher, who causes ructions when she tries to stage his first play at the school. While there are some thoughtful points about the nature of artistic ambition and compromise, Craig Zisk's unfussy direction keeps things nice and light. JF Swearing, some sexual references. *DVD*

Julianne Moore *Linda Sinclair* • Greg Kinnear *Dr Tom Sherwood* • Michael Angarano *Jason Sherwood* • Lily Collins *Halle Anderson* • Nathan Lane *Carl Kapinas* • Fiona Shaw *Narrator* ■ Dir Craig Zisk • Scr Dan Chariton, Stacy Chariton

English without Tears ★★

Romantic comedy   1944 · UK · BW · 88min

Five years after screenwriters Terence Rattigan and Anatole de Grunwald and cinematographer Bernard Knowles collaborated on the witty comedy of manners *French without Tears*, they reunited for this less perceptive, but still amusing, satire on the leisured classes at war. While the romance between wealthy ATS girl Penelope Ward and butler Michael Wilding had its social significance, the attack on the League of Nations would have struck the loudest chord with contemporary audiences. DP

Michael Wilding *Tom Gilbey* • Lilli Palmer *Brigid Knudsen* • Penelope Ward *Joan Heseltine* • Claude Dauphin *Jean de Freyeinet* • Roland Culver *Sir Cosmo Brandon* • Peggy Cummins *Bobby Heseltine* • Margaret Rutherford *Lady Christabel Beauclerk* ■ Dir Harold French • Scr Terence Rattigan, Anatole de Grunwald

The Englishman Who Went up a Hill, but Came down a Mountain ★★★ PG

Romantic comedy   1995 · UK · Colour · 95min

Hugh Grant does what he does best – mildly bumbling, nice Englishness – in this engaging slice of whimsy that harks back to the Ealing comedies of old. Grant plays a cartographer who is called upon to rule on whether a Welsh village's beloved landmark is a hill or a mountain. The canny locals are determined it's the latter and proceed to run rings around the hapless Grant. The plot is about as slight as the slope in question, but the talented pairing of the cast makes it a modest treat. JF *DVD*

Hugh Grant *Reginald Anson* • Tara FitzGerald *Betty of Cardiff* • Colm Meaney *Morgan the Goat* • Ian Hart *Johnny Shellshocked* • Kenneth Griffith *Reverend Jones* • Ian McNeice *George Garrad* • Robert Blythe *Ivor the Grocer* • Robert Pugh *Williams the Petroleum* ■ Dir Christopher Monger • Scr Christopher Monger, from a story by Ifor David Monger, Ivor Monger

Enigma ★★ 15

Thriller   1982 · UK/Fr · Colour · 97min

This Cold War thriller is neither one thing nor another, and seems to have suffered some post-production rethinking plotwise. The classy cast pretends they know what's going on as the KGB try to kill five dissidents in the west, only to find their way barred by unlikely CIA agent Martin Sheen. The title of this Anglo-French co-production is rather apt. TS

Martin Sheen *Alex Holbeck* • Brigitte Fossey *Karen* • Sam Neill *Dimitri Vasilkov* • Derek Jacobi *Kurt Limmer* • Michel Lonsdale *Bodley* • Frank Finlay *Canarsky* • David Baxt *Melton* • Kevin McNally *Bruno* ■ Dir Jeannot Szwarc • Scr John Briley, from the novel *Enigma Sacrifice* by Michael Barak

Enigma ★★★ 15

Second World War romantic thriller
2001 · UK/US/Neth/Ger · Colour · 116min

This concentrates on the quiet, bookish pluck of British codebreakers at Bletchley Park. Dougray Scott plays the fragile but brilliant Tom Jericho, back at his desk after a nervous breakdown and drawn into a race against time to crack the latest German cipher. He also suspects that Saffron Burrows, with whom he is infatuated, is a spy. This well-acted wartime intrigue is commendable for the intelligence it assumes on the part of the audience, but the effect is spoiled somewhat by a superfluous, *Boys' Own* adventure ending. AC Violence, swearing, a sex scene. *DVD*

Dougray Scott *Tom Jericho* • Kate Winslet *Hester* • Saffron Burrows *Claire* • Jeremy Northam *Wigram* • Nikolaj Coster Waldau [Nikolaj Coster-Waldau] *"Puck" Pukowski* • Tom Hollander *Logie* • Corin Redgrave *Admiral Trowbridge* ■ Dir Michael Apted • Scr Tom Stoppard, from the novel by Robert Harris

The Enigma of Kaspar Hauser ★★★★ PG

Period biographical drama
1974 · W Ger · Colour · 109min

Nuremberg in the 1820s is here seen through the eyes of Kaspar Hauser, the real-life noble savage who was dumped in the town square after a lifetime of beatings and sensory deprivation. Werner Herzog's fact-based drama, though ostensibly the tale of one man's response to civilisation, is more a film about awakening than socio-political values. It's easy to be captivated by the eager expression of Bruno S as he drinks in sights and sounds like an excited child and to sneer at the smug bourgeois attitudes of the townsfolk. Manipulative, but powerful. DP German +subtitles. *DVD*

Bruno S *Kaspar* • Brigitte Mira *Kathe, the servant* • Willy Semmelrogge *Circus director* • Hans Musaus *Unknown man* • Michael Kroecher *Lord Stanhope* • Henry van Lyck *Captain* ■ Dir/Scr Werner Herzog

L'Ennui ★★★ 18

Erotic comedy drama   1998 · Fr · Colour · 116min

Director Cédric Kahn explores the struggle for power that underpins many relationships in this erotic comedy drama. However, with its repeated acts of perfunctory sex and the slow descent into manic envy by an intellectually moribund academic, this adaptation of Alberto Moravia's novel might have made for heavy going, were it not for the outstanding performances of Charles Berling and Sophie Guillemin. DP French +subtitles. *DVD*

Charles Berling *Martin* • Sophie Guillemin *Cécilia* • Arielle Dombasle *Sophie* • Robert Kramer *Leopold Meyers* • Alice Grey *Cécilia's mother* • Maurice Antoni *Cécilia's father* ■ Dir Cédric Kahn • Scr Cédric Kahn, Laurence Ferreira Barbosa, Gilles Taurand, from the novel *La Noia* by Alberto Moravia

Enough ★ 15

Thriller   2002 · US · Colour · 110min

The issue of domestic violence is exploited for cheap thrills in this tawdry cat-and-mouse thriller. Jennifer Lopez, lip-glossed to perfection, works through a catalogue of female stereotypes, from blushing bride to spousal punching bag to mother who fights back. For all its gut-churning brutality, the film remains a grotesque mockery of reality. SF *DVD*

Jennifer Lopez *Slim* • Billy Campbell [Bill Campbell] *Mitch* • Juliette Lewis *Ginny* • Dan Futterman *Joe* • Fred Ward *Jupiter* • Jim Toller *Bill Cobbs* • Tessa Allen *Gracie* • Noah Wyle *Robbie* ■ Dir Michael Apted • Scr Nicholas Kazan

Enough Said ★★★★ 12

Romantic comedy   2013 · US · Colour · 89min

James Gandolfini gives one of his final performances in this adult-skewed tale of love and loss. He plays an overweight charmer who meets a divorced masseuse (Julia Louis-Dreyfus) at a party. Fat bellies, slobby behaviour and lack of adequate bedroom furniture all play a role in making the course of true love as bumpy as possible. Dedicated to the late Gandolfini, it's written and directed by Nicole Holofcener (*Friends with Money*), and boasts laughs that are light and lilting, only occasionally veering into dangerous waters. KK Some swearing, sexual references. *DVD*

Julia Louis-Dreyfus *Eva* • James Gandolfini *Albert* • Catherine Keener *Marianne* • Toni Collette *Sarah* • Tavi Gevinson *Chloe* ■ Dir/Scr Nicole Holofcener

Enron: the Smartest Guys in the Room ★★★ 12

Documentary   2005 · US · Colour · 109min

This solidly but not over-imaginatively assembled documentary tells how Enron, one of the mightiest and most well-regarded corporations on Wall Street was revealed to be a house of trick cards, built on greed, deceit and political opportunity. Based on a bestseller co-written by Bethany McLean, the first reporter to break the scandal of Enron's misdeeds, the film traces how top executives Kenneth Lay and Jeff Skilling manipulated the energy market, embezzled employee pension funds, and engineered an "energy crisis" to push up the price of electricity. LF Swearing. *DVD*

Peter Coyote *Narrator* ■ Dir Alex Gibney • Scr Alex Gibney, from the non-fiction book *The Smartest Guys in the Room: the Amazing Rise and Scandalous Fall of Enron* by Bethany McLean, Peter Elkind

Ensign Pulver ★★

Second World War comedy drama
1964 · US · Colour · 104min

This is a prime example of how a bad idea can result in a worse movie. *Mister Roberts* had been an overwhelming triumph on stage and screen. So, spurred on by the fact that Jack Lemmon had won an Oscar as Ensign Pulver, Warner Bros decided to push out the boat once more. Robert Walker Jr tries valiantly to recapture the impishness of the wheeler-dealer Pulver, but never emerges from the shadow of his predecessor. DP

Robert Walker Jr *Ensign Pulver* • Burl Ives *Captain* • Walter Matthau *Doc* • Tommy Sands *Bruno* • Millie Perkins *Scotty* • Kay Medford *Head nurse* • Larry Hagman *Billings* • Gerald S O'Loughlin *LaSueur* • Sal Papa *Gabrowski* • James Coco *Skouras* • Jack Nicholson *Dolan* ■ Dir Joshua Logan • Scr Joshua Logan, Peter S Feibleman, from characters by Joshua Logan, Thomas Heggen

Enter Arsene Lupin ★★

Crime adventure   1944 · US · BW · 71min

Hungarian exile and one-time cinematographer Charles Korvin made his acting debut here as writer Maurice Leblanc's notorious gentleman thief. But for once, purloining gems and avoiding the clutches of inspector J Carrol Naish are nowhere near as important as stealing the heart of Ella Raines. Sloppily scripted by Bertram Millhauser and directed with little suspense by Ford Beebe. DP

Charles Korvin *Arsene Lupin* • Ella Raines *Stacie* • J Carrol Naish *Ganimard* • George Dolenz *Dubose* • Gale Sondergaard *Bessie Seagrave* • Miles Mander *Charles Seagrave* • Leyland Hodgson *Constable Ryder* ■ Dir Ford Beebe • Scr Bertram Millhauser, from characters by Maurice Leblanc

Enter Laughing ★★★ U

Comedy   1967 · US · Colour · 110min

...and exit giggling at director Carl Reiner's adaptation of the play based on his early career experiences. Reni Santoni is the young man who defies mother Shelley Winters and decides to become a professional actor. He goes through the usual rituals of acceptance before realising his dream. Very astute and witty stuff, with José Ferrer's turn as a pompous producer worth the price of admission alone. TH

Reni Santoni *David Kolowitz* • José Ferrer *Mr Marlowe* • Shelley Winters *Mrs Kolowitz* • Elaine May *Angela* • Jack Gilford *Mr Foreman* • Janet Margolin *Wanda* • David Opatoshu *Mr Kolowitz* •

Michael J Pollard *Marvin* ■ Dir Carl Reiner • Scr Joseph Stein, Carl Reiner, from the play by Joseph Stein, from the novel by Carl Reiner

Enter Madame! ★★

Musical comedy drama   1933 · US · BW · 81min

Cary Grant, the wealthy husband of tantrum-throwing opera star Elissa Landi, has to cope with playing second fiddle to both her career and her entourage of peculiar characters. This film version of a 1920 Broadway hit comedy fails to survive the transfer to another medium or the passage of time. The coolly lovely Landi was hardly the ideal choice for this extrovert role, but Grant exudes his usual easy charm. RK

Elissa Landi *Lisa Della Robbia* • Cary Grant *Gerald Fitzgerald* • Lynne Overman *Mr Farnum* • Sharon Lynne *Flora Preston* • Michelette Burani *Bice* • Paul Porcasi *Archimede* • Adrian Rosley *Doctor* • Cecilia Parker *Aline Chalmers* ■ Dir Elliott Nugent • Scr Charles Brackett, Gladys Lehman, from the play by Gilda Varesi Archibald, Dorothea Donn-Byrne

Enter the Dragon ★★★★ 18

Martial arts adventure
1973 · US · Colour · 99min

Bruce Lee, the "Fred Astaire of martial arts", is at his balletic, brilliant best in this kung fu classic that, tragically, proved to be his last completed film. When his sister commits suicide rather than succumb to the henchmen of a ruthless master criminal, Lee leaves the Shaolin temple where he teaches kung fu and spiritual discipline to become a James Bond-like secret agent. When he arrives at an island fortress to take part in a brutal martial arts tournament, he finds himself having to smash an opium ring and a white slavery racket. In the opinion of many aficionados, the intricate and athletic fight scenes have yet to be bettered. DP Violence, swearing, drug abuse, nudity. *DVD* *Blu-ray*

Bruce Lee *Lee* • John Saxon *Roper* • Jim Kelly *Williams* • Kien Shih *Han* • Bob Wall [Robert Wall] *Oharra* • Ahna Capri *Tania* • Angela Mao Ying *Su-Lin* • Betty Chung *Mei Ling* ■ Dir Robert Clouse • Scr Michael Allin

Enter the Ninja ★★★ 18

Martial arts action adventure
1981 · US · Colour · 94min

After the kung fu mania of the early 1970s came a spate of movies relishing the silent but lethal killing machine that is the Japanese ninja. Evil Filipino crime baron Christopher George is intimidating a farmer into giving him his precious land, but he reckons without visiting friend and ninja Franco Nero who makes short shrift of various henchmen until he is forced into a real ninja-style showdown with Sho Kosugi. Two sequels followed in 1983. JF Violence *DVD* *Blu-ray*

Franco Nero *Cole* • Susan George *Mary-Ann Landers* • Sho Kosugi *Hasegawa* • Alex Courtney *Frank Landers* • Will Hare *Dollars* • Zachi Noy *The "Hook"* • Dale Ishimoto *Komori* • Christopher George *Charles Venarius* ■ Dir Menahem Golan • Scr Dick Desmond

Enter the Void ★★★ 18

Supernatural drama
2010 · Fr/US/Ger/It/Jpn/Can · Colour · 154min

This dense, psychedelic collage of sounds and images – inspired by *The Tibetan Book of the Dead* – follows an American drug dealer (Nathaniel Brown) who is shot by Tokyo police during a raid. First we see flashbacks of his life, then move to the present day, where life is going on without him. The more adventurous will embrace its offbeat energy but for most, *Enter the Void* will be hard work, made especially challenging by sporadic, shocking bursts of explicit sex and violence. DW English, Japanese +subtitles. Sex scenes, drug abuse, violence. *DVD*

Paz de la Huerta *Linda* • Nathaniel Brown *Oscar* • Cyril Roy *Alex* • Olly Alexander *Victor* • Masato Tanno *Mario* • Ed Spear *Bruno* ■ Dir Gaspar Noé • Scr Gaspar Noé, Lucile Hadzihalilovic

The Entertainer ★★★ PG
Drama 1960 · UK · BW · 99min

John Osborne's follow-up to his ground-breaking *Look Back in Anger* brought Laurence Olivier to the world of kitchen sink drama. Olivier gives a stunning performance as music-hall has-been Archie Rice, a seedy vaudeville artist who brings misery to all who know him. It was a personal triumph for Olivier on stage but, in enshrining the legendary actor's performance on celluloid, director Tony Richardson laid bare Olivier's technique. The result was too mannered and flopped at the box office, yet now can be viewed as an enduring record of that great stage production. TS *DVD*

Laurence Olivier *Archie Rice* • Brenda de Banzie *Phoebe Rice* • Joan Plowright *Jean* • Roger Livesey *Billy* • Alan Bates *Frank* • Daniel Massey *Graham* • Albert Finney *Mick Rice* • Miriam Karlin *Soubrette* • Shirley Anne Field *Tina* • Thora Hird *Mrs Lapford* ■ *Dir* Tony Richardson • *Scr* John Osborne, Nigel Kneale, from the play by John Osborne

The Entertainer ★★★
Drama 1975 · US/Aus · Colour · 106min

Jack Lemmon boldly goes where few actors would dare to go – into the footsteps of Laurence Olivier as on-the-skids music hall comedian Archie Rice. John Osborne's play is switched from Britain to the US and from the Suez Crisis to 1944. Married Archie's young *femme fatale* this time is Bambi (Annette O'Toole), whose rich father could back a musical to revive Archie's fortunes, but it doesn't work out. Directed by Donald Wrye, this is a pointless remake that has none of the social savagery of Osborne's original, but Jack Lemmon contributes a fascinating reading of Archie. TH

Jack Lemmon *Archie Rice* • Ray Bolger *Billy Rice* • Sada Thompson *Phoebe Rice* • Tyne Daly *Jean* • Michael Cristofer *Frank* • Annette O'Toole *Bambi* • Mitchell Ryan *Mr Pasko* ■ *Dir* Donald Wrye • *Scr* Elliott Baker, from the play by John Osborne

Entertaining Angels: the Dorothy Day Story ★★★ 12
Period biographical drama
1996 · US · Colour · 106min

Moira Kelly (*Chaplin*) stars as Dorothy Day in this moving and well-played family film set during the Depression era. Day was a radical journalist who later became a Catholic and devoted her life to looking after the poor. While younger viewers will learn about helping others and older viewers will feel uplifted, film buffs should also tune in for the cast, which includes Martin Sheen and a pre-*Austin Powers* Heather Graham. JB

Moira Kelly *Dorothy Day* • Martin Sheen *Peter Maurin* • Lenny Von Dohlen *Forster* • Heather Graham *Maggie* • Paul Lieber *Mike Gold* • Geoffrey Blake *Floyd Dell* • James Lancaster *Eugene O'Neill* • Boyd Kestner *Lionel Moise* ■ *Dir* Michael Ray Rhodes • *Scr* John Wells

Entertaining Mr Sloane ★★★ 15
Black comedy 1969 · UK · Colour · 90min

The quintessential black comedy from Joe Orton, in which a brother and sister vie for the sexual favours of a muscle-bound stud, is brought to the screen with some panache by director Douglas Hickox. Clive Exton's semi-faithful script attempts to widen the play's rather enclosed feel, but Orton is a playwright who belongs on a small stage with one chintz sofa. The cast is superb, particularly Beryl Reid as Kath and Harry Andrews as her homosexual sibling. SH
DVD

Beryl Reid *Kath* • Peter McEnery *Mr Sloane* • Harry Andrews *Ed* • Alan Webb *Kemp* ■ *Dir* Douglas Hickox • *Scr* Clive Exton, from the play by Joe Orton

The Entity ★★★ 18
Horror 1981 · US · Colour · 119min

Barbara Hershey is being repeatedly raped by an invisible evil spirit. But is the widowed mother under constant demonic assault,

---

or is it all in her subconscious? Director Sidney J Furie's above-average supernatural thriller has a literate script by genre writer Frank De Felitta from his own novel. Horror aficionados may be disappointed by the lack of *Exorcist*-style special effects, but a tense, fearful atmosphere is maintained precisely because of this creative choice. A complex chiller. AJ Violence, swearing.

Barbara Hershey *Carla Moran* • Ron Silver *Phil Schneidermann* • David Labiosa *Billy* • George Coe *Dr Weber* • Margaret Blye [Maggie Blye] *Cindy Nash* • Jacqueline Brookes *Dr Cooley* • Richard Brestoff *Gene Kraft* ■ *Dir* Sidney J Furie • *Scr* Frank DeFelitta, from his novel

Entourage ★★★ 15
Comedy 2015 · US · Colour · 100min

The hit HBO comedy series gets a feature-length outing, as movie star Vincent Chase (Adrian Grenier) and his friends navigate life, love and fame while trying to finish off Vincent's ambitious directorial debut. From the opening credits to the numerous star cameos (including Mark Wahlberg and Liam Neeson), the film seems in every way like an extended episode of the series. It's about as lightweight a movie as you can imagine, but fans of the show will love this last bid for stardom from TV's favourite hangers-on. JL Violence, swearing, sex scenes, drug abuse.
DVD

Adrian Grenier *Vincent Chase* • Jeremy Piven *Ari Gold* • Kevin Dillon *Johnny Drama* • Kevin Connolly *Eric* • Billy Bob Thornton *Larsen McCredle* • Liam Neeson ■ *Dir* Doug Ellin • *Scr* Doug Ellin, from a story by Ellin, Rob Weiss, from Ellin's characters • *Cinematographer* Steven Fierberg

Entr'Acte ★★★
Silent experimental fantasy
1924 · Fr · Colour · 22min

In the early 1920s, the young actor-turned-director René Clair made two subversive shorts, *Paris Qui Dort* and this energetic fantasy, in which he illustrates his sense of the absurd and has fun at the expense of the bourgeoisie. This divertissement was premiered in Paris, between two acts of a controversial ballet, and is fascinating as an example of avant-garde cinema and for the famous contemporary figures who grace its frantic Dadaist attack on convention. Clair described it as "visual babbling", but it established his career. BB

Jean Börlin • Inge Fris • Man Ray • Erik Satie • Marcel Duchamp ■ *Dir* René Clair • *Scr* René Clair, from a story by Francis Picabia

Entrapment ★★ 12
Romantic thriller 1999 · US · Colour · 108min

Few 68-year-old actors would turn down a chance to enjoy old-fashioned heist high jinks with the beautiful Catherine Zeta-Jones. But surely Sean Connery must have had his doubts about whether the romantic undertones would be plausible. They aren't, but in a film where logic, intelligence and charm take a back-seat to the leading lady's tight trousers, that isn't particularly surprising. The robbery scenes are mechanical yet effective, but what's shocking is that the whole thing is played straight. JC *DVD*

Sean Connery *Robert "Mac" MacDougal* • Catherine Zeta-Jones *Virginia "Gin" Baker* • Ving Rhames *Thibadeaux* • Will Patton *Hector Cruz* • Maury Chaykin *Conrad Greene* • Kevin McNally *Haas* • Terry O'Neill *Quinn* • Madhav Sharma *Security chief* ■ *Dir* Jon Amiel • *Scr* Ronald Bass, William Broyles Jr, from a story by Ronald Bass, Michael Hertzberg

Entre Nous ★★★ 15
Romantic drama 1983 · Fr · Colour · 110min

Diane Kurys's absorbing third feature stars Miou-Miou as a former art student and Isabelle Huppert as a Jewish refugee, both bored with their lives and on the verge of walking out on their husbands and children. Kurys offers a frank and convincing story that's set in a superbly evoked Lyons in the early 1950s. The two leads are matched by Guy Marchand as Huppert's husband, also a

---

Jewish refugee whose only crime is his innate goodness. AT French +subtitles.

Miou-Miou *Madeleine* • Isabelle Huppert *Lena* • Guy Marchand *Michel* • Jean-Pierre Bacri *Costa* • Robin Renucci *Raymond* • Patrick Bauchau *Carlier* • Jacques Alric *Monsieur Vernier* • Jacqueline Doyen *Madame Vernier* ■ *Dir* Diane Kurys • *Scr* Diane Kurys, from the book by Olivier Cohen, Diane Kurys

Envy ★ 12
Comedy 2003 · US · Colour · 94min

This Barry Levinson-directed comedy was hanging around on the shelf until the success of Jack Black in *The School of Rock* freed it from potential obscurity. It's the tale of two best friends, Ben Stiller and Black. Black invents "Vapoorizer", a substance that makes dog excrement disappear into thin air; Stiller turns down the chance to invest in the product and is eaten up by an all-consuming envy when his buddy becomes a multi-millionaire. This offers titters rather than belly laughs, but the cast is strong. SP *DVD*

Ben Stiller *Tim Dingman* • Jack Black *Nick Vanderpark* • Rachel Weisz *Debbie Dingman* • Amy Poehler *Natalie Vanderpark* • Christopher Walken *J-Man* • Hector Elias *Eduardo* ■ *Dir* Barry Levinson • *Scr* Steve Adams

Epic ★★★ U
Animated adventure 2013 · US · Colour · 98min

Fast-paced, fun and fashionably "green", this piece of computer cartoonery is from the same stable as the *Ice Age* series and *Rio*, and has a voice cast to kill for. Amanda Seyfried plays teenager MK, who gets shrunk to insect size, and finds herself caught in a woodland war between the forces of life (Colin Farrell, Josh Hutcherson, Beyoncé Knowles) and decay (Christoph Waltz). After a rather sombre start, *Epic* finds a well-paced groove of alternating dark and light comic scenes, while director Chris Wedge doesn't let the eco-minded philosophy get in the way of some nicely animated action. DA *DVD*
Blu *3D*

Colin Farrell (2) *Ronin* • Josh Hutcherson *Nod* • Amanda Seyfried *Mary Katherine* • Christoph Waltz *Mandrake* • Beyoncé Knowles *Queen Tara* • Chris O'Dowd *Grub* ■ *Dir* Chris Wedge • *Scr* Tom J Astle, Matt Ember, James V Hart, William Joyce (2), Daniel Shere • *Music* Danny Elfman

Epic Movie ★ 15
Epic spoof 2007 · US · Colour · 89min

There's very little that's epic about this senseless parody, but then there's very little that's funny about it, either. Following on from the *Scary Movie* franchise and *Date Movie*, writers-turned-directors Jason Friedberg and Aaron Seltzer continue their hit-and-miss (but mostly miss) approach to comedy, spoofing such recent films as *Pirates of the Caribbean*, *The Chronicles of Narnia* and *The Da Vinci Code*. Scarily, this mind-numbingly unamusing film topped the box office on its cinema release in the US. JR Swearing, sexual references. *DVD*

Kal Penn *Edward* • Adam Campbell *Peter* • Jennifer Coolidge *White Bitch* • Jayma Mays *Lucy* • Faune Chambers *Susan* • Crispin Glover *Willy* ■ *Dir/Scr* Jason Friedberg, Aaron Seltzer

The Epic of Everest ★★★ U
Silent documentary
1924 · UK · Tinted and BW · 86min

Despite providing an invaluable record of the doomed 1924 bid to climb the world's highest mountain, as well as containing the first footage ever filmed of daily life in Tibet, Captain John Noel's pioneering documentary lacks the intimacy and immediacy of Frank Hurley's *South* (1919) and Herbert G Ponting's *The Great White Silence* (1924). Perhaps this is because lost climbers George Mallory and Andrew Irvine are less iconic than polar explorers Ernest Shackleton and Robert Falcon Scott. Although this is an exceptional technical achievement, Noel's failure to introduce the expedition members keeps the audience at

---

a distance and somehow diminishes the heroism of their sacrifice. DP *DVD* *Blu*

Andrew Irvine (1) *Andrew Irvine* • George Mallory ■ *Dir* JBL Noel

An Episode in the Life of an Iron Picker ★★★★ 12A
Drama
2013 · Bosnia/Fr/Slovenia/It · Colour · 74min

A Roma family in Bosnia play themselves in this dramatised re-creation of events. In a small rural community, Nazif (Nazif Mujic) feeds his family as best he can, but the household is thrown into crisis when wife Senada's (Senada Alimanovic) pregnancy goes awry and she needs an emergency operation. The hospital insists on a hefty upfront fee and director Danis Tanovic uses this incident to illustrate the point that inhumanity at best, prejudice at worst, is now in the ascendant as fallout from the conflict. Thanks to the straighforward, low-key direction, the family's struggles come across with a telling authenticity. TJ In Bosnian, Romany.

Nazif Mujic *Nazif* • Senada Alimanovic *Senada* • Semsa Mujic *Semsa* • Sandra Mujic *Sandra* ■ *Dir/Scr* Danis Tanovic • *Cinematographer* Erol Zubcevic

The Equalizer ★★★ 15
Crime thriller 2014 · US · Colour · 126min

In the hit 1980s TV show, British actor Edward Woodward played Robert McCall, the retired agent-turned-good Samaritan who equalised the odds for ordinary citizens beset by bad guys. In director Antoine Fuqua's slick reboot, it's his *Training Day* star Denzel Washington who initially appears to be just an ordinary blue collar stiff, until he befriends a young hooker (Chloë Grace Moretz) in thrall to a fearsome Russian syndicate, and his true identity emerges. Of course it's ludicrous, but this is *The Equalizer*, and Washington has the stellar charisma and mobility to keep total disbelief from the door. A sequel is due in September 2017. JA Violence, swearing.
DVD *Blu*

Denzel Washington *Robert McCall* • Marton Csokas *Teddy* • Chloë Grace Moretz *Teri* • David Harbour *Masters* • Bill Pullman *Brian Plummer* • Melissa Leo *Susan Plummer* ■ *Dir* Antoine Fuqua • *Scr* Richard Wenk, from the TV series by Michael Sloan, Richard Lindheim

Equilibrium ★★★ 15
Futuristic action thriller
2002 · US · Colour · 102min

In this sci-fi smorgasbord of borrowed clichés, an impressively pumped-up Christian Bale plays a futuristic cop whose job it is to enforce a law compelling the population to take an emotion-suppressing drug. But when he himself stops taking the medication, he falls in love with renegade "sense-offender" Emily Watson. Often preposterous and heavy-handed, but with enough slick visuals to offset the silliness. AS Violence, swearing. *DVD* *Blu*

Christian Bale *John Preston* • Emily Watson *Mary* • Taye Diggs *Brandt* • Angus MacFadyen *Dupont* • Sean Bean *Partridge* • Sean Pertwee *Father* • Matthew Harbour *Robbie Preston* • William Fichtner *Jurgen* • Dominic Purcell *Seamus* ■ *Dir/Scr* Kurt Wimmer

Equinox ★★★★ 15
Drama 1992 · US · Colour · 105min

Alan Rudolph is one of the most eclectic directors currently working in American cinema. This latter-day fairy tale offers the part of a lifetime to Matthew Modine as chalk-and-cheese twins: one a violent gangster who longs to settle down, the other a tongue-tied geek besotted with an equally bashful Lara Flynn Boyle, giving an exquisite portrayal of painful shyness. The dialogue is intelligent and provocative, and Rudolph handles his excellent cast with great finesse. DP Violence, swearing, nudity.

Matthew Modine *Henry Petosa/Freddy Ace* • Lara Flynn Boyle *Beverly Franks* • Fred Ward *Mr Paris* • Tyra Ferrell *Sonya Kirk* • Marisa Tomei *Rosie Rivers* • Kevin J O'Connor *Russell Franks* •

E

Lori Singer *Sharon Ace* • M Emmet Walsh *Pete Petosa* • Tate Donovan *Richie Nunn* ■ *Dir/Scr* Alan Rudolph

Equinox Flower ★★★★ U
Drama 1958 · Jpn · Colour · 112min

A film of parallel plotlines and elliptical shifts, this ranks among Yasujiro Ozu's most playful pictures, as well as being his first in colour. Exposing the ironic duality of the subservient "salaryman" who insists on being master in his own household, Ozu uses this two-act satire to espouse the emancipation of women and the emergence of youth. As the father dumbfounded by his daughter's decision to refuse an arranged liaison, Shin Saburi gives a fine display of stubborn impotence in the face of the quiet determination of the headstrong Ineko Arima and his prudent wife, Kinuyo Tanaka. DP In Japanese. **DVD BL**

Shin Saburi *Watara Hirayama* • Kinuyo Tanaka *Kiyoko Hirayama* • Ineko Arima *Setsuko Hirayama* • Miyuki Kuwano *Hisako Hirayama* ■ *Dir* Yasujiro Ozu • *Scr* Kogo Noda, Yasujiro Ozu, from a novel by Ton Satomi

Equus ★★★ 15
Psychological drama 1977 · US · Colour · 132min

Peter Shaffer's powerful play about a boy whose repressed emotions lead him to blind horses was so acclaimed that it was inevitable it would become a film. However, this is very much a theatrical piece, and the set pieces that work so well on stage lose much of their impact on screen. The long speeches delivered by psychiatrist Richard Burton hold theatre audiences spellbound, but here seem as flatly staged as a party political broadcast. Peter Firth is clearly in awe of Burton, and Sidney Lumet has too much respect for the text. DP **DVD**

Richard Burton *Martin Dysart* • Peter Firth *Alan Strang* • Colin Blakely *Frank Strang* • Joan Plowright *Dora Strang* • Harry Andrews *Harry Dalton* • Eileen Atkins *Hesther Saloman* • Jenny Agutter *Jill Mason* • Kate Reid *Margaret Dysart* ■ *Dir* Sidney Lumet • *Scr* Peter Shaffer, from his play

Eragon ★★ PG
Fantasy adventure 2006 · US · Colour · 99min

Set in a world of dragons and sorcery, *Eragon* fails to conjure the magic of Christopher Paolini's bestselling book. Ed Speleers stars (with some initial uncertainty) as the farm boy who becomes a "dragon rider", threatening the tyrannical rule of John Malkovich's king. Jeremy Irons employs a dry sense of humour as Eragon's mentor Brom, alleviating some of the tedium as the youngster considers his true mission. Rachel Weisz voices Saphira, the winged beast that carries Eragon into battle, and first-time director Stefen Fangmeier provides some distraction from the dithering script with fast-paced flying scenes. Sadly, the CGI effects aren't emotionally engaging enough, and the tale fails to spark. SP Mild violence. **DVD BL**

Ed Speleers *Eragon* • Jeremy Irons *Brom* • Sienna Guillory *Arya* • Robert Carlyle *Durza* • Djimon Hounsou *Ajihad* • Garrett Hedlund *Murtagh* • Joss Stone *Angela* • Rachel Weisz *Saphira* • John Malkovich *King Galbatorix* • Alun Armstrong *Uncle Garrow* ■ *Dir* Stefen Fangmeier • *Scr* Peter Buchman, from the novel by Christopher Paolini • *Cinematographer* Hugh Johnson

Eraser ★★ 15
Action thriller 1996 · US · Colour · 106min

Arnold Schwarzenegger is the "eraser" of the title – a federal marshal for the witness protection programme who protects witnesses by wiping out their identities. Of course, things don't go to plan, and he and damsel-in-distress Vanessa Williams have to dodge bullets, explosions and quips before our hero can save the day. This lacks the nonstop gung-ho action we've come to expect from Arnie's movies. JB Violence, swearing. **DVD**

Arnold Schwarzenegger *US Marshal John Kruger* • James Caan *Deguerin* • Vanessa Williams [Vanessa L Williams] *Lee* • James Coburn *Beller* • Robert Pastorelli *Johnny C* • James Cromwell *Donahue* • Danny Nucci *Monroe* • Andy Romano

Harper ■ *Dir* Charles Russell [Chuck Russell] • *Scr* Tony Puryear, Walon Green, from a story by Michael S Chernuchin, Tony Puryear, Walon Green

Eraserhead ★★★★ 18
Cult experimental horror
1976 · US · BW · 85min

Filmed over a five-year period, this is the legendary cult movie that put director David Lynch on the morbid mystery map. Lynch's surreal study in urban alienation, retarded sexuality and parental nightmare is a relentless assault on the senses (maternal ones especially) that recalls Luis Buñuel's ground-breaking *Un Chien Andalou* in its powerful graphic imagery and non-linear monochrome narrative. It's consistently creepy, arcane and unsettling, and many will find Lynch's intense mood piece increasingly uncomfortable to watch. AJ **DVD BL**

John Nance [Jack Nance] *Henry Spencer* • Charlotte Stewart *Mary* • Allen Joseph *Bill* • Jeanne Bates *Mary's mother* • Judith Anna Roberts *Beautiful girl across the hall* • Laurel Near *Lady in the radiator* • V Phipps-Wilson *Landlady* • Jack Fisk *Man in the planet* • Jean Lange *Grandmother* ■ *Dir/Scr* David Lynch

Erasing David ★★ 12
Documentary 2009 · UK · Colour · 79min

David Bond and Melinda McDougall's documentary investigates how much privacy has been curtailed as Britain becomes increasingly subjugated to surveillance. Bond decided to go off-grid for a month and hired a couple of private eyes to see if they could track him down by trawling the internet and following his paper trail. The fact that he chose to undertake this mission when his wife was pregnant will alienate many viewers, as will his unpersuasive video-diary pieces. But there are sufficient revelations to leave a lingering sense of unease about our snooping society. DP **DVD**

■ *Dir* David Bond (2), Melinda McDougall • *Music* Michael Nyman

Erik the Viking ★★ 15
Comedy adventure 1989 · UK · Colour · 75min

Tim Robbins would probably prefer to forget his role as a sort of "New Man" Viking who seeks to put an end to such traditional activities as raping and looting. Despite the presence of John Cleese and writer/director Terry Jones in a top-flight British cast, you can't escape the feeling that this was a lot more fun to make than it is to watch. A sadly wanting Nordic spoof. JF Swearing. **DVD**

Tim Robbins *Erik* • Mickey Rooney *Erik's grandfather* • Eartha Kitt *Freya* • Imogen Stubbs *Princess Aud* • John Cleese *Halfdan the Black* • Gary Cady *Keitel Blacksmith* • Antony Sher *Loki* • John Gordon-Sinclair *Ivar the Boneless* • Samantha Bond (2) *Helga* • Tim McInnerny *Sven the Berserk* • Terry Jones *King Arnulf* ■ *Dir/Scr* Terry Jones

Erin Brockovich ★★★★ 15
Biographical drama 2000 · US · Colour · 125min

This drama's ace in the hole is Julia Roberts, who earns every cent of her $20-million salary as the spirited heroine. A twice-divorced mother of three, Roberts lands a job in the office of small-time lawyer Albert Finney, where she stumbles across some misplaced medical records while filing real estate documents. Intrigued, she investigates, eventually uncovering evidence that a power company has wrecked the health of a local community with contaminated water. Based on a true story, Steven Soderbergh's emotionally rich drama is compulsive viewing, thanks to Roberts's performance, Finney's lovable turn and a perfectly pitched script. AJ Swearing. **DVD BL**

Julia Roberts *Erin Brockovich* • Albert Finney *Ed Masry* • Aaron Eckhart *George* • Marg Helgenberger *Donna Jensen* • Cherry Jones *Pamela Duncan* • Peter Coyote *Kurt Potter* • Erin Brockovich-Ellis *Waitress* ■ *Dir* Steven Soderbergh • *Scr* Susannah Grant

Ernest Goes to Camp ★ PG
Comedy 1987 · US · Colour · 88min

The appeal of American comedy star Jim Varney remains bewildering to British audiences, but he must have something going for him if the movie output of his Ernest P Worrell character is anything to go by. This is the one that launched the whole sorry saga, with gormless Ernest (Varney) causing havoc at a summer camp. The charmless mugging of the star grates, while the combination of childish slapstick and cornball sentimentality is unappetising. JF **DVD**

Jim Varney *Ernest P Worrell* • Victoria Racimo *Nurse St Cloud* • John Vernon *Sherman Krader* • Iron Eyes Cody *Old Indian Chief* • Lyle Alzado *Bronk Stinson* ■ *Dir* John R Cherry III • *Scr* John R Cherry III, Coke Sams

Ernest Saves Christmas ★ U
Fantasy 1988 · US · Colour · 87min

Designed very firmly to celebrate all things festive, this tale has the frenetic Jim Varney (as cab driver Ernest P Worrell) helping Santa Claus look for his successor. Everyone thinks Santa's a white-bearded old nuisance, apart from Varney, of course. SH

Jim Varney *Ernest P Worrell* • Douglas Seale *Santa* • Oliver Clark *Joe Carruthers* • Noelle Parker *Harmony* • Robert Lesser *Marty* • Gailard Sartain *Chuck* ■ *Dir* John Cherry [John R Cherry III] • *Scr* B Kline, Ed Turner, from a story by Ed Turner

Ernest Goes to Jail ★ PG
Comedy 1990 · US · Colour · 77min

Jim Varney reprises his "mad as a rat" routine as Ernest P Worrell, this time finding himself holed up in jail while an Ernest lookalike runs amok, sullying his already dubious reputation. Fans of Ernest come in two distinct categories: children under 14 who wish to suspend their brains, and those who were never in the habit of exercising their brains in the first place. SH

Jim Varney *Ernest P Worrell/Felix Nash/Auntie Nelda* • Gailard Sartain *Chuck* • Bill Byrge *Bobby* • Barbara Bush [Barbara Tyson] *Charlotte Sparrow* • Barry Scott *Rubin Bartlett* • Randall "Tex" Cobb *Lyle* • Dan Leegant *Oscar Pendlesmythe* • Charles Napier *Warden* ■ *Dir* John Cherry [John R Cherry III] • *Scr* Charlie Cohen

Ernest Scared Stupid ★ PG
Comedy horror 1991 · US · Colour · 88min

This entry in the long-running *Ernest* series harks back to the days when Laurel and Hardy or Abbott and Costello could spook each other with a white sheet. Jim Varney returns as the doltish Ernest P Worrell, accidentally waking up a troll he then has to stop making off with the town's children. Subtle it ain't. DP

Jim Varney *Ernest P Worrell* • Eartha Kitt *Old Lady Hackmore* • John Cadenhead *Tom Tulip* • Bill Byrge *Bobby Tulip* • Austin Nagler *Kenny* • Shay Astar *Elizabeth* • Jonas Moscartolo *Trantor* • Richard Woolf *Matt* ■ *Dir* John Cherry [John R Cherry III] • *Scr* Charles Gale, Coke Sams, from a story by Coke Sams, John Cherry [John R Cherry III]

Ernest Rides Again ★ PG
Comedy 1993 · US · Colour · 89min

Jim Varney must be a real glutton for punishment. He returns yet again as Ernest P Worrell in this silly children's comedy that falls so far short of funny it's pitiful. Only in an Ernest film would a nutty professor claim that the crown jewels were hidden inside a cannon from the American War of Independence and be correct! DP **DVD**

Jim Varney *Ernest P Worrell* • Ron K James *Abner Melon* • Linda Kash *Nan Melon* • Tom Butler *Dr Glencliff* ■ *Dir* John Cherry [John R Cherry III] • *Scr* John Cherry [John R Cherry III], William M Akers

Eroica ★★★ 12
Portmanteau wartime drama
1958 · Pol · BW · 80min

True to the ironic intent of its subtitle, this is *A Heroic Symphony in Two Movements*. The

first story, *Schzerzo alla Polacca*, focuses on a black-marketeer who blunders into the ranks of the Polish underground and becomes the voice of sanity in a mad world. *Ostinato Lugubre* centres on a group of concentration camp inmates who sustain their morale by believing one of their number has escaped. Andrzej Munk's sly feature infuriated the authorities. DP Polish +subtitles. Some swearing. **DVD**

Edward Dziewonski *Dzidzius* • Barbara Polomska *Zosia* • Leon Niemczyk *Lt Kolya* • Ignacy Machowski *Major* • Jozef Nowak *Kurzawa* • Roman Klosowski *Szpakowski* • Bogumil Kobiela *Dabecki* ■ *Dir* Andrzej Munk • *Scr* Jerzy Stefan Stawinski

Eros ★★★ 15
Portmanteau drama
2004 · HK/US/Fr/It/Lux · Colour and BW · 106min

The great Michelangelo Antonioni was 92 when he made his contribution to this three-part treatise on love and desire. However, *The Dangerous Thread of Things* feels like a grotesque parody of his once cutting-edge blend of enigmatic dialogue and elliptical structuring, offering a voyeuristic treatment of Christopher Buchholz's relationships with Regina Nemni and Luisa Ranieri. Mercifully, Christopher Doyle's lustrous cinematography ensures that Wong Kar-Wai's *The Hand* is infinitely more sensual in its chronicling of apprentice tailor Chang Chen's tactile fixation with courtesan Gong Li. But Peter Andrews's *noirish* monochrome is equally effective in *Equilibrium*, a mischievous exercise in neurotica by Steven Soderbergh, in which stressed executive Robert Downey Jr relates his recurrent fantasies of the elusive Ele Keats to twitchy shrink Alan Arkin. DP Mandarin, English, Italian +subtitles.

Gong Li *Miss Hua* • Chang Chen *Zhang* • Tin Fung *Master Jin* • Robert Downey Jr *Nick Penrose* • Alan Arkin *Dr Pearl/Hal* • Ele Keats *Woman/ Cecelia* • Christopher Buchholz *Christopher* • Regina Nemni *Cloe* • Luisa Ranieri *Girl/Linda* ■ *Dir* Wong Kar-Wai, Steven Soderbergh, Michelangelo Antonioni • *Scr* Wong Kar-Wai; Steven Soderbergh; Michelangelo Antonioni, Tonino Guerra, from stories in *Quel Bowling sul Tevere* by Michelangelo Antonioni

Erotic Tales ★
Erotic drama 1994 · Ger · Colour · 170min

Six directors, including Ken Russell, Bob Rafelson and Susan Seidelman, waste their time and talent telling sexy stories, each with unexpected endings. More silly than erotic, each tale is serviceable at best and has little sexual content or nudity. AJ

Arliss Howard *Bruce Lomann* • Cynda Williams *Davida Urked* • Mira Sorvino *Teresa* • John Turturro *Kim* • Robert Downey Jr *Nick Penrose* • Richard Barboza *Leroy* • Gosia Dobrowolska *Sarah* • Anu Arya *Aggarwal* ■ *Dir* Bob Rafelson, Susan Seidelman, Ken Russell, Melvin Van Peebles, Paul Cox, Mani Kaul • *Scr* Bob Rafelson, Jonathan Brett, Susan Seidelman, Ken Russell, Melvin Van Peebles, Paul Cox, Barry Dickins, Margot Wiburd

Erotique ★★ 18
Erotic comedy drama
1994 · US/Ger · Colour · 83min

Despite the intriguing concept – three women directors from the independent film sector offer up a trio of erotic tales from the female perspective – this has to go down as a noble failure. In *Let's Talk about Sex* Lizzie Borden provides a dry examination of an actress who works for a phone sex company, while Monika Treut offers up a stylish but uneven tale about a wealthy lesbian in *Taboo Parlor*. The pick of the three, though, is *Wonton Soup* from Clara Law, who delivers some laughs with a refreshing romp about a confused man trying to impress his partner with his knowledge of ancient Asian sex texts. JF

Kamala Lopez-Dawson [Kamala Dawson] *Rosie* • Bryan Cranston *Dr Robert Stern* • Ron Orbach *Nikki* • Priscilla Barnes *Claire* • Camilla Soeberg *Julia* • Michael Carr *Victor* • Marianne Sägebrecht *Hilde* • Tim Lounibos *Adrian* • Hayley Man Ann • Choi Hark-kin *Uncle* ■ *Dir* Lizzie Borden, Monika Treut, Clara Law • *Scr* Lizzie Borden (from her story), Susie Bright, Monika Treut, Eddie Ling-Ching Fong

The Errand Boy ★★★ U
Comedy   1961 · US · BW · 88min

Comic genius Jerry Lewis co-wrote, produced, directed and starred in this extremely funny satire of movie-making, filmed with great affection in his home studio Paramount. Lewis cast the film brilliantly, with veterans such as Brian Donlevy and the great Sig Ruman providing the perfect foil for the madcap comedian. If you don't care for him at all, you won't be converted. TS *Morty S Tashman* DVD

Jerry Lewis *Morty S Tashman* • Brian Donlevy *TP* • Howard McNear *Dexter Sneak* • Dick Wesson *The AD* • Pat Dahl *Miss Carson* • Sig Ruman *Baron Elston Carteblanche* ■ *Dir* Jerry Lewis • *Scr* Jerry Lewis, Bill Richmond

Escapade ★★
Period romance   1935 · US · BW · 87min

A somewhat stale comedy which marked the Hollywood debut of Luise Rainer, promoted as the "New Garbo". Rainer plays a naive young girl who falls under the spell of Viennese womaniser William Powell. Original release prints carried a two-minute epilogue in which Powell steps out of character and introduces the audience to Miss Rainer, promising a great career ahead of her. Three years later she'd won two Oscars; in another two years she was all but forgotten. AT

William Powell *Fritz Heideneck* • Luise Rainer *Leopoldine Major* • Frank Morgan *Karl Harrandt* • Virginia Bruce *Gerta Keller* • Reginald Owen *Paul Harrandt* • Mady Christians *Anita Keller* • Laura Hope Crews *Countess Feldon* ■ *Dir* Robert Z Leonard • *Scr* Herman J Mankiewicz, from the fiim *Maskerade* by Walter Reisch

Escapade in Japan ★★★ U
Adventure   1957 · US · Colour · 92min

Teresa Wright and Cameron Mitchell play the worried parents of a child who goes missing in Japan when his flight crash-lands. The story has something for the whole family and it's cleverly directed for maximum sentiment by veteran Arthur Lubin. Mitchell makes the most of a rare leading role, and youngsters Jon Provost and Roger Nakagawa give sound performances. Take a closer look at that rangy serviceman, the one called Dumbo - it's Clint Eastwood. TS

Teresa Wright *Mary Saunders* • Cameron Mitchell *Dick Saunders* • Jon Provost *Tony Saunders* • Roger Nakagawa *Hiko* • Kuniko Miyake *Michiko* • Susumu Fujita *Kei Tanaka* • Clint Eastwood *Dumbo* ■ *Dir* Arthur Lubin • *Scr* Winston Miller

The Escape ★★★
Silent drama   1914 · US · BW

A long-lost title from the great innovator DW Griffith's massive motion picture output, based on a stage melodrama about a tenement family from New York's East Side. Fred Turner is the father, while Mae Marsh and Blanche Sweet play his daughters. The former falls in with gangster "Bull" McGee (Donald Crisp), a wrong 'un if ever there was one, though the latter has a chance to get out of the ghetto when she falls for handsome Owen Moore. Sentimental tosh was dear to Griffith's heart, and his genius made it possible for him to transcend such material on occasion. TS

Donald Crisp *"Bull" McGee* • Fred Turner *Jim Joyce* • Robert Harron *Larry Joyce* • Blanche Sweet *Mae Joyce* • Mae Marsh *Jennie Joyce* • Owen Moore *Dr Von Eiden* • Ralph Lewis *Senator* • Tammany Young *McGee's henchman* ■ *Dir* DW Griffith • *Scr* DW Griffith, from the play by Paul Armstrong

Escape ★★ U
Drama   1930 · UK · BW · 67min

Impresario Basil Dean, who had taken only tentative steps into silent cinema, broke into talkies with this tale of a fugitive on Dartmoor. Unfortunately, his inexperience with both the camera and the primitive sound technology further compound the staginess of his own adaptation of John Galsworthy's tedious play. Sir Gerald du Maurier also struggles, often failing to rein in an effusiveness designed to hit the back of the stalls. DP DVD

Gerald du Maurier *Captain Matt Denant* • Edna Best *Shingled lady* • Gordon Harker *Convict* • Horace Hodges *Gentleman* • Madeleine Carroll *Dora* • Mabel Poulton *Girl of the town* • Lewis Casson *Farmer* ■ *Dir* Basil Dean • *Scr* Basil Dean, John Galsworthy, from the play by John Galsworthy

Escape ★★ U
Second World War drama   1940 · US · BW · 103min

Robert Taylor stars as an American travelling to Germany in a desperate bid to rescue his mother (Russian actress Alla Nazimova) from a Nazi concentration camp. He's helped by countess Norma Shearer, a German-American whose lover is the dastardly Conrad Veidt, a Nazi general. All very starry and, alas, all very phoney. AT

Norma Shearer *Countess Von Treck* • Robert Taylor (1) *Mark Preysing* • Conrad Veidt *Gen Kurt Von Kolb* • Alla Nazimova *Emmy Ritter* • Felix Bressart *Fritz Keller* • Albert Bassermann [Albert Basserman] *Dr Arthur Henning* • Philip Dorn *Dr Ditten* ■ *Dir* Mervyn LeRoy • *Scr* Arch Oboler, Marguerite Roberts, from a novel by Ethel Vance

The Escape Artist ★★ PG
Drama   1982 · US · Colour · 90min

Ryan O'Neal's son Griffin holds his own in this mishmash of vaudeville and small-town corruption. Bragging that he will escape a prison sentence within an hour cues a flashback for O'Neal about his childhood in theatre. Exploited by his aunt and uncle, who perform "the best escape act since Houdini" he hones his skills and escapes, lifting the wallet of the vindictive son of the local major, Raul Julia. A formulaic mess. LH DVD

Griffin O'Neal *Danny Masters* • Raul Julia *Stu Quinones* • Teri Garr *Arlene* • Gabriel Dell *Uncle Burke* • Desi Arnaz *Mayor Quinones* • John P Ryan *Vernon* • Elizabeth Daily *Sandra* • M Emmet Walsh *Fritz* • Jackie Coogan *Magic shop owner* ■ *Dir* Caleb Deschanel • *Scr* Melissa Mathison, Stephen Zito, from the novel by David Wagoner

Escape by Night ★★
Crime drama   1953 · UK · BW · 78min

Something of an improvement on the usual hokum churned out by low-budget expert John Gilling, this drama lacks any of the menace or desperation with which it would have been saturated by even the most pedestrian Hollywood B-movie director. Yet Sid James gives a solid performance as the vice boss on the run who holds a journalist hostage, and he is well supported by Bonar Colleano as a crusading reporter. DP

Bonar Colleano *Tom Buchan* • Andrew Ray *Joey Weston* • Sidney James *Gino Rossini* • Ted Ray *Mr Weston* • Simone Silva *Rosetta Mantania* • Patrick Barr *Inspector Frampton* ■ *Dir/Scr* John Gilling

Escape from Alcatraz ★★★★ 15
Prison drama based on a true story   1979 · US · Colour · 107min

Don Siegel directs this tough and compelling reconstruction of the only successful escape from San Francisco's notorious island prison in its 29-year history. Driven star crazy by the strictures of warden Patrick McGoohan's regime and the brutality of his fellow inmates, Clint Eastwood plans a bid for freedom with Fred Ward and Jack Thibeau. Blessed with expert performances, Siegel shoots the preparations with an attention to detail that exerts as strong a grip as the escape itself. DP DVD

Clint Eastwood *Frank Morris* • Patrick McGoohan *Warden* • Roberts Blossom *Chester "Doc" Dalton* • Jack Thibeau *Clarence Anglin* • Fred Ward *John Anglin* • Paul Benjamin *English* • Larry Hankin *Charley Butts* ■ *Dir* Don Siegel • *Scr* Richard Tuggle, from the book by J Campbell Bruce

Escape from Fort Bravo ★★★ PG
Western   1953 · US · Colour · 94min

Planned as a 3D movie but shown flat, this otherwise impressive early John Sturges western suffers from the use of obvious studio exteriors in many key sequences. On location, though, in the dust of the desert as Mescalero Indians menace escaped Confederate prisoners, the use of landscape is mighty fine. Union captain William Holden is suitably rugged, while lovely Eleanor Parker is charming. TS

William Holden (2) *Captain Roper* • Eleanor Parker *Carla Forester* • John Forsythe *Captain John Marsh* • William Demarest *Campbell* • William Campbell *Cabot Young* • Polly Bergen *Alice Owens* • Richard Anderson *Lieutenant Beecher* • Carl Benton Reid *Colonel Owens* ■ *Dir* John Sturges • *Scr* Frank Fenton, from a story by Michael Pate, Phillip Rock

Escape from LA ★★ 15
Futuristic action thriller   1996 · US · Colour · 96min

In John Carpenter's shambolic, big-budget sequel to his superior *Escape from New York*, Kurt Russell returns as macho hero Snake Plissken, who this time around is blackmailed into scouring the City of Angels for a doomsday device stolen by the president's daughter. Apart from the witty, face-lifted zombie section, this unexciting rehash lacks the sharp black comedy of the original. AJ DVD

Kurt Russell *Snake Plissken* • AJ Langer *Utopia* • Steve Buscemi *"Map to the Stars" Eddie* • George Corraface *[Georges Corraface] Cuervo Jones* • Stacy Keach *Malloy* • Michelle Forbes *Brazen* • Pam Grier *Hershe* • Jeff Imada *Saigon Shadow* • Cliff Robertson *President* • Peter Fonda *Pipeline* • Paul Bartel (1) *Congressman* ■ *Dir* John Carpenter • *Scr* John Carpenter, Debra Hill, Kurt Russell, from characters by John Carpenter, Nick Castle

Escape from New York ★★★ 15
Futuristic action thriller   1981 · US · Colour · 94min

Sullen Kurt Russell impersonates Clint Eastwood in director John Carpenter's tough futuristic western that never fulfils the ingenuity of its premise: the president's plane crashes in Manhattan, which is now a maximum security prison, and Russell has to go in and rescue him. This is certainly one of Carpenter's slickest looking films, with the presence of Lee Van Cleef reinforcing its Sergio Leone associations. But, despite a marvellous night-time opening sequence, this slice of escapism often disappoints, though it still rates higher than the poor sequel *Escape from LA*. AJ Swearing, violence. DVD Blu

Kurt Russell *Snake Plissken* • Lee Van Cleef *Bob Hauk* • Donald Pleasence *President* • Isaac Hayes *Duke of New York* • Adrienne Barbeau *Maggie* • Harry Dean Stanton *"Brain"* • Ernest Borgnine *Cabby* ■ *Dir* John Carpenter • *Scr* John Carpenter, Nick Castle

Escape from Planet Earth ★★★ U
Animated science-fiction comedy   2013 · US/Can · Colour · 80min

This lightweight tale introduces two blue-skinned brothers from the planet Baab. Scorch is an astronaut, reckless and egotistical. Brother Gary is head of mission control, a button pusher, more serious. But when Scorch is captured by humans, it's Gary who rides to the rescue. The movie takes a little time to get going, but picks up pace later on, and youngsters will enjoy the colourful design, while parents will recognise some period sci-fi references and the voice talents of William Shatner and Ricky Gervais (as a computer). DA DVD Blu 3D

Rob Corddry *Gary Supernova* • Brendan Fraser *Scorch Supernova* • Ricky Gervais *Mr James Bing* • William Shatner *General Shanker* • Sarah Jessica Parker *Kira Supernova* ■ *Dir* Cal Brunker • *Scr* Cal Brunker, Bob Barlen, from a story by Tony Leech, Cory Edwards

Escape from Polygamy ★★
Romantic drama   2013 · US · Colour

A Mormon-like compound in Utah is the setting for this extremely far-fetched yet fun tale of forbidden teen romance and corrupt authority. Entertainingly acted and attractively shot, the Romeo and Juliet-style melodrama captures the warmth and intensity of young love, as adolescents Haley Lu Richardson and boy band-handsome Jack Falahee fall head over heels after she moves to the ultra-restrictive community with her widowed mother. William Mapother's chilling turn as the predatory Prophet and some shock twists keeping interest levels high, despite the ever-increasing implausibility of proceedings. SF

Mary McCormack *Leann* • William Mapother *Ervil* • Haley Lu Richardson *Julina* • Jack Falahee *Ryder* ■ *Dir* Rachel Goldenberg • *Scr* Damon Hill

Escape from Sobibor ★★★★ 15
War drama based on a true story   1987 · UK/US · Colour · 142min

This is a compelling account of the escape from a Nazi death camp deep in the Polish countryside, concocted by a cabal of Jewish workers and Soviet soldiers. Given the horrifying number of people who died in the Sobibor gas chambers, the fact that more than 300 prisoners fled from this hellhole may seem slight. But their achievement remains one of the most audacious acts of courage in the entire Second World War. In a superb ensemble cast headed by Rutger Hauer and Joanna Pacula, Alan Arkin is excellent as the ringleader. Jack Gold directs with restraint and his TV film deservedly won two Golden Globes. DP Violence.

Alan Arkin *Leon Feldhendler* • Rutger Hauer *Sasha* • Joanna Pacula *Luka* • Emil Wolk *Samuel* • Hartmut Becker *Sgt Wagner* • Jack Shepherd *Itzhak* • Kurt Raab *Sgt Frenzel* ■ *Dir* Jack Gold • *Scr* Reginald Rose, from the non-fiction book by Richard Rashke

Escape from the Planet of the Apes ★★★★ PG
Science-fiction adventure drama   1971 · US · Colour · 93min

The third in the popular movie series sees Roddy McDowall and Kim Hunter land in present-day California after surviving the catastrophe that ended *Beneath the Planet of the Apes*. It's very much a film of two halves, the first being an amusing collection of observations on modern life, as seen through the eyes of the more advanced apes. The second half, is much darker, with the arrogant and fearful humans being driven to unspeakable cruelty to protect their future. An intelligent script and solid performances add up to a fine film. *Conquest of the Planet of the Apes* (1972) followed. DP DVD Blu

Roddy McDowall *Cornelius* • Kim Hunter *Zira* • Bradford Dillman *Dr Lewis Dixon* • Natalie Trundy *Dr Stephanie Branton* • Eric Braeden *Dr Otto Hasslein* • William Windom *The President* • Sal Mineo *Milo* • Albert Salmi *E-1* • Jason Evers *E-2* • John Randolph *Chairman* ■ *Dir* Don Taylor • *Scr* Paul Dehn, from characters by Pierre Boulle

Escape from Zahrain ★★ U
Action thriller   1962 · US · Colour · 93min

This well-upholstered but ultimately mundane would-be thriller is set in the Middle East. Yul Brynner leads a motley crew across the Panavisioned desert to find guest star James Mason. Such worthies as Sal Mineo and Jack Warden are along for the (underscripted) ride, but veteran director Ronald Neame shows little sense of dramatic pacing despite the handsome location photography. TS

Yul Brynner *Sharif* • Sal Mineo *Ahmed* • Madlyn Rhue *Laila* • Jack Warden *Huston* • James Mason *Johnson* ■ *Dir* Ronald Neame • *Scr* Robin Estridge, from a novel by Michael Barrett • *Cinematographer* Ellsworth Fredericks

Escape Me Never ★★★
Melodrama   1935 · UK · BW · 101min

The smash-hit play was especially written by Margaret Kennedy to exploit the considerable abilities of star Elisabeth Bergner. This unsurprising film version, directed by Bergner's husband Paul Czinner, is virtually a transcript of the show, even down to the same male smoothie

E

leads (Hugh Sinclair and Griffith Jones). The tale is pure tosh, involving unwed mother Bergner going nuts over no-good cad composer Sinclair. But it does reveal Bergner's range, and you'll be surprised at how charming, sexy and talented the lady is. **TS**

Elisabeth Bergner *Gemma Jones* • Hugh Sinclair *Sebastian Sanger* • Griffith Jones *Caryl Sanger* • Penelope Dudley Ward *Fenella McClean* • Irene Vanbrugh *Mrs McClean* • Leon Quartermaine *Mr McClean* ■ *Dir* Paul Czinner • *Scr* Carl Zuckmayer, Robert J Cullen, from the novel *The Fool of the Family* and the play *Escape Me Never* by Margaret Kennedy

Escape Me Never ★★
Melodrama   1947 · US · BW · 103min

This idiotically cast remake of the old Elisabeth Bergner vehicle has Ida Lupino as the Bergnerian waif (you're no waif, Ida) and Errol Flynn as the caddish composer she falls for. Only skilled Eleanor Parker really convinces as Flynn's fling after he marries Lupino. British expatriate director Peter Godfrey does what he can with this stale tosh, though the Erich Wolfgang Korngold score goes some way to mitigate the silliness. **TS**

Errol Flynn *Sebastian Dubrok* • Ida Lupino *Gemma Smith* • Eleanor Parker *Fenella MacLean* • Gig Young *Caryl Dubrok* • Reginald Denny *Ivor MacLean* • Isobel Elsom *Mrs MacLean* • Albert Basserman *Professor Heinrich* • Ludwig Stossel *Mr Steinach* ■ *Dir* Peter Godfrey • *Scr* Thomas Williamson, from the novel *The Fool of the Family* and the play *Escape Me Never* by Margaret Kennedy

Escape Plan ★★★ 15
Action thriller   2013 · US · Colour · 110min

Action titans Sylvester Stallone and Arnold Schwarzenegger join forces in this prison-set thriller with a twist. Stallone plays a security expert who tests the integrity of penitentiaries from the inside. When his latest assignment goes awry, Stallone teams up with fellow inmate Schwarzenegger to stage the daddy of all break-outs. Director Mikael Hafstrom relishes throwing newfangled gadgetry and sci-fi scares into the mix, while the stars' verbal sparring and carefully choreographed fisticuffs are just what their legions of fans will want. **TeS** Violence, swearing. *DVD* *Blu*

Sylvester Stallone *Ray Breslin* • Arnold Schwarzenegger *Emil Rottmayer* • Jim Caviezel *Willard Hobbes* • Curtis "50 Cent" Jackson *Hush* • Sam Neill *Dr Kyrie* • Vinnie Jones *Drake* ■ *Dir* Mikael Hafstrom • *Scr* Miles Chapman, Arnell Jesko [Jason Keller], from Chapman's story

Escape Route ★★ U
Spy thriller   1952 · UK · BW · 79min

George Raft gives a fair impression of a man who has had his arms welded to his sides in this dismissable quickie thriller. One of the handful of films Raft made in Europe after his Hollywood fortunes dipped, it's a lightweight affair in which he plays an FBI agent called in to discover who is smuggling scientists to the east. **DP**

George Raft *Steve Rossi* • Sally Gray *Joan Miller* • Clifford Evans *Michael Grand* • Reginald Tate *Colonel Wilkes* • Patricia Laffan *Miss Brooks* • Frederick Piper *Inspector Reid* • Roddy Hughes *Porter* • John Warwick *Brice* ■ *Dir* Seymour Friedman, Peter Graham Scott • *Scr* John V Baines, Nicholas Phipps

Escape to Athena ★★ PG
Second World War adventure   1979 · UK · Colour · 114min

Despite the best efforts and intentions of mogul Lew Grade, most of his film-producing legacy is, regrettably, underwhelming. This is a prime example: a slight plot combines an ancient treasure caper with a Second World War escape adventure and wastes the talents of such diverse names as David Niven, Elliott Gould, Claudia Cardinale and Sonny Bono. And they aren't even the leads! **TS** *DVD* *Blu*

Roger Moore *Major Otto Hecht* • Telly Savalas *Zeno* • David Niven *Professor Blake* • Claudia Cardinale *Eleana* • Stefanie Powers *Dottie Del Mar* • Richard Roundtree *Nat Judson* • Sonny

Bono *Bruno Rotelli* • Elliott Gould *Charlie Dane* • William Holden (2) *Prisoner* ■ *Dir* George Pan Cosmatos • *Scr* Richard S Lochte, Edward Anhalt, from a story by Richard S Lochte, George Pan Cosmatos

Escape to Burma ★★ PG
Adventure   1955 · US · Colour · 83min

One of the last films to be directed by Allan Dwan, this trite melodrama contributed to the decline of RKO. Barbara Stanwyck and Robert Ryan are wasted here as lovers in the jungle whose tryst is disturbed by David Farrar when he tries to arrest Ryan for murder. There's a final twist, but by then you'll be numb with boredom, despite the dutiful performances. **TS**

Barbara Stanwyck *Gwen Moore* • Robert Ryan *Jim Brecan* • David Farrar *Cardigan* • Murvyn Vye *Makesh* • Lisa Montell *Andora* • Robert Warwick *Sawbwa* ■ *Dir* Allan Dwan • *Scr* Talbot Jennings, Hobart Donavan, from the story *Bow Tamely to Me* by Kenneth Perkins

Escape to Victory ★★★ PG
Second World War sports drama   1981 · US · Colour · 111min

Can you imagine what this corny PoW picture would have been like if producer Freddie Fields had not secured the services of Michael Caine, Sylvester Stallone, Max von Sydow and a squad of international footballing legends? It's obvious that director John Huston didn't quite know what to make of it all, but his sure touch and Pelé's football choreography turn this into a rousing romp. **DP** Swearing. *DVD* *Blu*

Sylvester Stallone *Robert Hatch* • Michael Caine *John Colby* • Pelé *Luis Fernandez* • Bobby Moore *Terry Brady* • Osvaldo Ardiles *Carlos Rey* • Paul Van Himst *Michel Fileu* • Kazimierz Deyna *Paul Wolchek* • Hallvar Thoresen *Gunnar Hilsson* • Mike Summerbee *Sid Harmor* • Co Prins *Pieter Van Beck* • Russell Osman *Doug Clure* • John Wark *Arthur Hayes* • Soren Linsted *Erik Borge* • Kevin O'Calloghan *Tony Lewis* • Max von Sydow *Major Karl Von Steiner* • Daniel Massey *Colonel Waldron* • Tim Pigott-Smith *Rose* ■ *Dir* John Huston • *Scr* Evan Jones, Yabo Yablonsky, from a story by Yabo Yablonsky, Djordje Milicevic, Jeff Maguire

Escape to Witch Mountain ★★★ U
Science-fiction adventure   1975 · US · Colour · 93min

With actors such as Ray Milland, Eddie Albert and Donald Pleasence treating this Disney children's movie as seriously as any other adult-themed film they might tackle, the result is pacey, scary and sentimental. Milland is oozingly malevolent as the villain who wants to use the clairvoyant powers of two youngsters for his own nefarious ends. Plenty of thrills, even if it is a bit dated. Bette Davis appears in the follow-up movie, *Return from Witch Mountain*. **TH** *DVD*

Kim Richards *Tia Malone* • Ike Eisenmann *Tony Malone* • Ray Milland *Aristotle Bolt* • Eddie Albert *Jason O'Day* • Donald Pleasence *Lucas Deranian* • Walter Barnes *Sheriff Purdy* ■ *Dir* John Hough • *Scr* Robert Malcolm Young, from the novel by Alexander Key

Escape under Pressure ★★ 12
Action drama   2000 · US · Colour · 87min

Jean Pellerin takes an eternity to get Rob Lowe's army engineer, his classics professor wife Larissa Miller, diverse baddies and a statue of Artemis on to a boat travelling between Athens and Lesbos. Connoisseurs of crassness will enjoy the flashback to ancient Greece and the cheap imitations of *Titanic*. Released on video and DVD in the UK as *The Cruel Deep*. **DP** Swearing, violence. *DVD*

Rob Lowe *John Spencer* • Craig Wasson *Elgin Bates* • Larissa Miller *Chloe Spencer* • Harry Van Gorkum *Crowley* • Scott Anthony Viscomi *Nikos Gravas* ■ *Dir* Jean Pellerin • *Scr* Martin Lazarus

The Escapist ★★ 15
Thriller   2002 · UK · Colour · 86min

The perfect life of pilot Jonny Lee Miller is torn apart when psychopathic criminal

Andy Serkis breaks into his home and murders his pregnant wife. After faking his death, Miller packs a life of crime into a few months, getting sent to higher and higher security prisons until he and Serkis meet again. Despite a highly charged plot and great use of locations, this unconvincing thriller is full of stereotypical prison characters and revenge-movie clichés. **JF** Violence, swearing. *DVD*

Jonny Lee Miller *Denis* • Andy Serkis *Ricky Barnes* • Gary Lewis *Ron* • Jodhi May *Christine* • Paloma Baeza *Valerie* • Vas Blackwood *Vin* • Philip Barantini *Joey* ■ *Dir* Gillies MacKinnon • *Scr* Nick Perry

The Escapist ★★★ 15
Prison thriller   2007 · UK/Ire · Colour · 97min

Writer/director Rupert Wyatt's feature debut begins with lifer convict Frank Perry (Brian Cox) attempting a break-out to be with his critically ill daughter. But what separates this prison thriller from more traditional jailbreak movies is the use of time-shifting flashbacks. Unfortunately, the stylised, fractured structure tends to undercut the suspense, even though the redemptive finale reveals the unusual reason for its use. Nevertheless, Cox anchors the drama with a strong, silent mystique and there's sterling support from Steven Mackintosh (as a vindictive psycho) and Joseph Fiennes (as the muscle in Perry's crew). **AJ** *DVD*

Brian Cox (1) *Frank Perry* • Joseph Fiennes *Lenny Drake* • Liam Cunningham *Brodie* • Seu Jorge *Viv Batista* • Dominic Cooper *James Lacey* • Steven Mackintosh *Tony* • Damian Lewis *Rizza* ■ *Dir* Rupert Wyatt • *Scr* Rupert Wyatt, Daniel Hardy

Escobar: Paradise Lost ★★★ 15
Romantic thriller   2014 · Fr/Sp/Pan/Bel · Colour · 119min

This muscular account of a naive Canadian's relationship with Colombian drug lord Pablo Escobar may open sluggishly, but it builds to a tense finale. Josh Hutcherson abandons his surf business to romance Claudia Traisac - whose uncle just happens to be the most powerful and dangerous man in the entire country. Hutcherson's innocent abroad is hard to like, and Benecio Del Toro's Pablo Escobar over-channels Brando (as both Kurtz and Corleone), but the suspense grips once the authorities close in on Escobar's compound. **DP** English, Spanish +subtitles. Violence.

Benicio Del Toro *Pablo Escobar* • Josh Hutcherson *Nick* • Claudia Traisac *Maria* • Brady Corbet *Dylan* ■ *Dir* Andrea Di Stefano • *Scr* Andrea Di Stefano, Francesca Marciano (adaptation)

The Escort ★★★ 18
Drama   1999 · Fr/UK · Colour · 101min

Daniel Auteuil here plays a Frenchman in London who discovers he can make big bucks as a male escort. The action has a bitter tang of authenticity, as the opportunistic Auteuil preys on bored socialites, timid housewives and lonely hearts. But his relationships with fellow gigolo Stuart Townsend and single-mother hooker Liza Walker are less persuasive, diverting us into the realms of melodrama. **DP** English, French +subtitles. Swearing, sex scenes, violence. *DVD*

Daniel Auteuil *Pierre* • Stuart Townsend *Tom* • Liza Walker *Kim* • Noah Taylor *Gem* • Frances Barber *Jessica* • Claire Skinner *Patricia* ■ *Dir* Michel Blanc • *Scr* Michel Blanc, from an idea by Hanif Kureishi

Escort West ★★★ U
Western   1959 · US · BW · 76min

Produced by John Wayne's brother, Robert E Morrison, this was too modest a venture to interest the big man himself. So Victor Mature takes the lead as the ex-Confederate soldier heading west with his young daughter. Along the way he picks up two sisters (Elaine Stewart and Faith Domergue) and their wounded servant (Rex Ingram), all survivors of an Indian attack.

This is a cut above the average thanks to an eventful narrative and well-developed characters. **AE**

Victor Mature *Ben Lassiter* • Elaine Stewart *Beth Drury* • Faith Domergue *Martha Drury* • Reba Waters *Abbey Lassiter* • Noah Beery Jr *Jamison* • Leo Gordon *Vogel* • Rex Ingram (2) *Nelson* • John Hubbard *Lieutenant Weeks* • Harry Carey Jr *Travis* • Slim Pickens *Wheeler* ■ *Dir* Francis D Lyon • *Scr* Leo Gordon, Fred Hartsook, from a story by Steven Hayes

Eskiya ★★★★ 15
Drama   1996 · Tur · Colour · 127min

Turkey's biggest ever box-office hit, this astute drama exploits Hollywood convention to produce a film few in America would have the wit to make. Yavuz Turgul turns Istanbul into a hostile wilderness as Kurdish bandit Sener Sen returns from 35 years in jail to take his revenge on the friend who not only betrayed him, but also stole his girl. Rambling and brimming over with life, this is an engrossing mix of social comment, unassuming heroism, wry humour and shameless sentiment, with the relationship between the bandit and a brash street rogue symbolising what young and old can learn from each other. **DP** Turkish +subtitles. Violence, swearing, drug abuse.

Sener Sen *Baran* • Ugur Yucel *Cumali* • Sermin Sen *Keje* • Yasim Salkim *Emel* ■ *Dir/Scr* Yavuz Turgul

Esma's Secret ★★★ 15
Drama   2006 · Austria/Bosnia/Ger/Cro · Colour · 90min

Debuting director Jasmila Zbanic won the Golden Bear at the 2006 Berlin film festival for this intense, if rather laboured, Bosnian-set drama. Mirjana Karanovic excels as single mother Esma, who has convinced her teenage daughter Sara (Luna Mijovic) that her absent father is a "shaheed" - a martyr of the civil war. However, eventually Esma is forced to reveal the truth about her child's paternity. After spending a large part of the film establishing the storyline, Zbanic rushes the resolution and the tale loses credibility as a consequence. **DP** Bosnian +subtitles. Swearing. *DVD*

Mirjana Karanovic *Esma* • Luna Mijovic *Sara* • Leon Lucev *Pelda* • Kenan Catic *Samir* • Jasna Ornela Berry *Jasna Beri* • Dejan Acimovic *Cenga* ■ *Dir/Scr* Jasmila Zbanic

Les Espions ★★★ PG
Spy thriller   1957 · Fr/It · BW · 121min

While maybe not of the same calibre as *Les Diaboliques*, Henri-Georges Clouzot's adaptation is still clearly the work of a master of suspense. Everything about this tale of espionage and deception is open to question, whether it's the existence of a top-secret nuclear device, the intentions of the Soviet and American agents who come clamouring after it or the motives of a sanitorium director who allows the intriguing charade to be played out under his roof. Curt Jurgens and Peter Ustinov stand out in a splendid international cast, but the real star is the director. **DP** French +subtitles. *DVD*

Gérard Séty *Malic* • Curd Jürgens [Curt Jurgens] *Visitor* • Vera Clouzot *Patient* • Peter Ustinov *Russian agent* • Sam Jaffe *American agent* • Martita Hunt *Nurse* • OE Hasse *Vogel* ■ *Dir* Henri-Georges Clouzot • *Scr* Henri-Georges Clouzot, Jérôme Géromini, from the novel *Midnight Patient* by Egon Hostowsky

Essential Killing ★★ 15
Thriller   2010 · Pol/Nor/Ire/Hun · Colour · 81min

This impressionistic film from Polish director Jerzy Skolimowski looks at the current climate of war in the Middle East by focusing on an Arab warrior (Vincent Gallo), who is captured in a blazing desert by allied forces, tortured, and then sent to an internment camp. But he escapes and is forced to use his most basic instincts to survive. Gallo's intense performance is thankfully too weird to leave much room for unintentional comedy (although a fair bit seeps in), but for most, this will be hard to take, like a warped, nightmarish parody of

Mr Bean. DW English, Polish, Arabic +subtitles. Violence, swearing. **DVD BL**
Vincent Gallo *Mohammed* • Emmanuelle Seigner *Margaret* • David Price *Interrogation officer* ■ *Dir* Jerzy Skolimowski • *Scr* Ewa Piaskowska, Jerzy Skolimowski • *Cinematographer* Adam Sikora

Essex Boys ★★★ 18
Crime drama based on a true story
1999 · UK · Colour · 97min

This slick British crime thriller breaks no new ground and tries too hard to be tough. Yet interest is sustained by taut pacing, a nicely murky plot and spirited performances from Alex Kingston, Tom Wilkinson, Charlie Creed-Miles and a scenery-chewing Sean Bean. The story centres on a young minicab driver (Creed-Miles) who is hired by a hard man fresh out of prison. He finds himself in the firing line when a drug deal prompts a power struggle among rival elements of the Essex criminal fraternity. DA Violence, swearing, drug abuse, sex scenes. **DVD**
Sean Bean *Jason Locke* • Alex Kingston *Lisa Locke* • Charlie Creed-Miles *Billy Reynolds* • Tom Wilkinson *John Dyke* • Larry Lamb *Peter Chase* • Terence Rigby *Henry Hobbs* • Billy Murray *Perry Elley* • Amelia Lowdell *Nicole* ■ *Dir* Terry Winsor • *Scr* Jeff Pope, Terry Winsor

Esther and the King ★
Biblical drama 1960 · US/It · Colour · 109min

Biblical stuff and nonsense, with Joan Collins marrying the Persian king to stop the oppression of the Jews and save the throne from various plots and assassins. Shot in Italy like so many Hollywood epics, it veers between the laughable and the plodding, and you'd never guess that Hollywood action maestro Raoul Walsh directed it. AT
Joan Collins *Esther* • Richard Egan *King Ahasuerus* • Denis O'Dea *Mordecai* • Sergio Fantoni *Haman* • Rick Battaglia [Rik Battaglia] *Simon* • Renato Baldini *Klydrathes* ■ *Dir* Raoul Walsh • *Scr* Raoul Walsh, Michael Elkins • *Cinematographer* Mario Bava

Esther Kahn ★★ 15
Period drama 2000 · Fr/UK · Colour · 148min

Set in London at the turn of the 19th century, this drawn-out period tale charts the progress of a Jewish seamstress from East End backstreet to West End acclaim playing Hedda Gabler. In his first film in English, French director Arnaud Desplechin neither captures the imagination nor exploits such compelling themes as poverty, sexual betrayal and personal ambition. Even more fatally, he fails to coax any emotion out of his lead actress, Summer Phoenix. DP
Summer Phoenix *Esther Kahn* • Ian Holm *Nathan Quellen* • Frances Barber *Rivka Kahn* • Fabrice Desplechin *Philippe Haygard* • Ian Bartholomew *Norton, Shylock's director* • Emmanuelle Devos *Sylvia l'Italienne* • Anton Lesser *Sean* ■ *Dir* Arnaud Desplechin • *Scr* Arnaud Desplechin, Emmanuel Bourdieu, from a story by Arthur Symons

Esther Waters ★★ U
Period melodrama 1948 · UK · BW · 105min

This tawdry adaptation plunges between the two stools of heritage production and sensationalist melodrama. Dirk Bogarde is suitably scurrilous as a rascally footman, but the action slows fatally when he is off screen, with Kathleen Ryan facing all her trials (single motherhood, the workhouse and Bogarde's drinking) with sulkiness. DP
Kathleen Ryan *Esther Waters* • Dirk Bogarde *William Latch* • Cyril Cusack *Fred Parsons* • Ivor Barnard *Randal* • Fay Compton *Mrs Barfield* • Margaret Diamond *Sarah Tucker* • Morland Graham *Ketley* ■ *Dir* Ian Dalrymple, Peter Proud • *Scr* Michael Gordon, William Rose, from a novel by George Moore

The Eternal ★ 15
Horror 1998 · US · Colour · 95min

A ludicrous mixture of Irish whimsy, Druid folklore and zombie witches, this is a mind-boggling mistake. Allison Elliott plays an alcoholic New Yorker who returns to the Emerald Isle to visit her uncle (Christopher Walken) and becomes possessed by the spirit of a 2,000-year-old witch whose remains have been discovered in the local peat bog. This simple-minded shocker is one of the daftest horror movies ever made. AJ **DVD**
Alison Elliott (2) *Nora/Niamh* • Jared Harris *Jim* • Christopher Walken *Bill Ferriter* • Rachel O'Rourke *Alice* • Lois Smith *Mrs Ferriter* • Karl Geary *Sean* ■ *Dir/Scr* Michael Almereyda

Eternal Love ★★★
Silent romantic drama 1929 · US · BW · 71min

Set in 1812, this features John Barrymore and Camilla Horn as the Swiss couple who take to the Alps after being wrongfully accused of murdering her husband. Released in the midst of the talkie furore, Ernst Lubitsch's silent swan song comes complete with occasional sound effects, most notably during the climactic avalanche. It was ignored by contemporary audiences and hasn't been of much interest to critics since – perhaps because it stands in such stark contrast to the frothy farces that came to be seen as Lubitsch's trademark in Hollywood. DP
John Barrymore *Marcus Paltram* • Camilla Horn *Ciglia* • Victor Varconi *Lorenz Gruber* • Hobart Bosworth *Reverend Tass* • Bodil Rosing *Housekeeper* • Mona Rico *Pia* ■ *Dir* Ernst Lubitsch • *Scr* Hans Kraly, Katherine Hilliker (titles), HH Caldwell (titles), from the novel *Der König der Bernina, Roman aus dem Schweizerischen* by Jakob Christoph Heer

Eternal Love ★★★ PG
Romantic drama 1943 · Fr · BW · 107min

The subject of endless debates about whether this updating of the legend of Tristan and Isolde had pro-Nazi sympathies, this is also a film that leaves one wondering how much better it might have been had screenwriter Jean Cocteau also directed instead of the more literal Jean Delannoy. Permanently on set, Cocteau clearly influenced the fairy-tale setting, the dreamy atmosphere and the rather bloodless acting of doomed lovers Jean Marais and Madeleine Sologne. The result is pompous, perhaps, but unceniably arresting and affecting. DP French +subtitles.
Madeleine Sologne *Nathalie* • Jean Marais *Patrice* • Yvonne de Bray *Gertrude* • Jane Marken *Anne* • Jean Murat *Marc* • Pierre Piéral *Achille* • Roland Toutain *Lionel* ■ *Dir* Jean Delannoy • *Scr* Jean Cocteau

Eternal Sunshine of the Spotless Mind ★★★★ 15
Romantic comedy drama 2003 · US · Colour · 103min

In this inventive collaboration with music video director Michel Gondry, Jim Carrey and Kate Winslet meet by chance, and lose their minds over each other. Literally. After their affair ends, Winslet decides she can't live with the memories and goes to Lacuna Inc, a quirky, modest business that erases unwanted recollections. Carrey then discovers what she's done and decides to follow suit. This outing from Charlie Kaufman's oddball imagination is wonderfully intriguing, often touching and typically convoluted. The only minor quibbles are Carrey's understated performance and a slightly lacklustre ending. BP Swearing. **DVD BL**
Jim Carrey *Joel Barish* • Kate Winslet *Clementine Kruczynski* • Kirsten Dunst *Mary* • Mark Ruffalo *Stan* • Elijah Wood *Patrick* • Tom Wilkinson *Dr Howard Mierzwiak* • Jane Adams (2) *Carrie* • David Cross (2) *Rob* ■ *Dir* Michel Gondry • *Scr* Charlie Kaufman, from a story by Charlie Kaufman, Michel Gondry, Pierre Bismuth

Eternally Yours ★★★ PG
Romantic drama 1939 · US · BW · 87min

This lightweight but endearing romance is from an era when Hollywood really knew how to cook the recipe properly. The lovely Loretta Young is involved with magician David Niven in a vicissitude-strewn marriage. Director Tay Garnett brings his aerial knowledge to bear on some scenes, but seems generally content to let the movie coast along on the charms of the leading players. TS **DVD**
David Niven *Tony Halstead* • Loretta Young *Anita Halstead* • Broderick Crawford *Don Barnes* • Hugh Herbert *Benton* • Billie Burke *Aunt Abby* • C Aubrey Smith *Bishop Hubert Peabody* • ZaSu Pitts *Carrie Bingham* • Eve Arden *Gloria* ■ *Dir* Tay Garnett • *Scr* Gene Towne, Graham Baker, John Meehan

Eternity and a Day ★★★ PG
Drama 1998 · Gr/Fr/It/Ger · Colour · 127min

Winner of the Palme d'Or at Cannes, this meditation on memory and mortality follows dying writer Bruno Ganz around Salonika as he seeks to atone for a life of self-obsession by helping a young Albanian refugee. Switching lyrically between a sunlit past filled with missed opportunities and the murky moodiness of the poet's present, director Theo Angelopoulos is over-deliberate in both his pacing and symbolism. For all its epic scope and its sublime camera movements, this is never as provocative as Angelopoulos's impressive 1995 film, *Ulysses' Gaze*. DP Greek +subtitles.
Bruno Ganz *Alexandre* • Isabelle Renaud *Anna* • Fabrizio Bentivoglio *The Poet* • Despina Bebedeli *Mother* • Achileas Skevis *The Child* • Vassilis Seimenis *Son-in-law* ■ *Dir* Theo Angelopoulos • *Scr* Theo Angelopoulos, Petros Markaris, Tonino Guerra, Giorgio Silvagni

Ethan Frome ★★★
Period drama 1993 · US/UK · Colour · 107min

This adaptation of the Edith Wharton novel is a bleak, dark affair, but rewarding. Liam Neeson is the proud farmer trapped in a cold marriage with Joan Allen who finds love in the shape of her cousin, Patricia Arquette. The three leads bring resonance to the doom-laden story and, although it can be heavy going at times, it remains a moving experience. JF
Liam Neeson *Ethan Frome* • Patricia Arquette *Mattie Silver* • Joan Allen *Zeena Frome* • Tate Donovan *Reverend Smith* • Katharine Houghton *Ruth Hale* • Stephen Mendillo *Ned Hale* • Deborah Ayer *Young Ruth* • Jay Goede *Denis Eady* ■ *Dir* John Madden • *Scr* Richard Nelson, from the novel by Edith Wharton

Etre et Avoir ★★★★ U
Documentary 2002 · Fr · Colour · 99min

In this delightful documentary, 55-year-old teacher Georges Lopez reflects on his two decades at a tiny school in the rural Auvergne as he prepares his penultimate year group for their uncertain future. Lopez handles the various personality clashes, domestic crises and learning difficulties of the children in his care with patience, professionalism and pride. Capturing the sense of community and conveying the pivotal role Lopez has played in so many lives, director Nicolas Philibert's film is a fond and fascinating portrait of an unassuming local hero. DP French +subtitles. **DVD BL**
■ *Dir/Scr* Nicolas Philibert

Eu Sei Que Vou Te Amar ★★★
Drama 1986 · Bra · Colour · 110min

Fernanda Torres shared the best actress prize at Cannes for her work in this intense study of a marriage in crisis, which also reflects the political uncertainty of its time. Yet, without the counterbalancing performance of Thales Pan Chacon, this would have been as askew an enterprise as Vittorio De Sica's *Indiscretion of an American Wife*, in which Montgomery Clift's Method style completely overwhelms Jennifer Jones. In some ways, this is an inversion of that film, as an estranged Brazilian couple meet to discuss their problems and the chances of a reconciliation. DP Portuguese +subtitles.
Fernanda Torres • Thales Pan Chacon ■ *Dir/Scr* Arnaldo Jabor

Eureka ★★★ 18
Drama 1982 · UK · Colour · 124min

Nicolas Roeg has directed some great movies and though this torrid tale of greed, gold and gangsters isn't one of them, there's still enough of his distinctive style to grab the attention. Gene Hackman (in a scorching turn) stars as the prospector who finds a fortune but no joy, particularly when his daughter takes up with a playboy (Rutger Hauer). Confrontation is inevitable but then things turn nasty when mobsters come on the scene. It's a minor Roeg but a classy cast ensures it's never less than interesting. JA Violence **DVD BL**
Gene Hackman *Jack McCann* • Theresa Russell *Tracy* • Rutger Hauer *Claude Maillot Van Horn* • Jane Lapotaire *Helen McCann* • Mickey Rourke *Aurelio D'Amato* • Ed Lauter *Charles Perkins* • Joe Pesci *Mayakofsky* • Helena Kallianiotes *Frieda* • Corin Redgrave *Worsley* ■ *Dir* Nicolas Roeg • *Scr* Paul Mayersberg, from the novel *Who Killed Sir Harry Oakes?* by Marshall Houts

Eureka ★★★★ 15
Psychological road movie 2000 · Jpn · Sepia · 208min

Director Shinji Aoyama has called this extraordinary film "a prayer for modern man, who is searching for the courage to go on living." The story follows coach driver Koji Yakusho and siblings Aoi and Masaru Miyazaki, who are the only survivors of a tragic bus hijacking. Two years after the incident, Yakusho seeks out the traumatised teenagers and suggests a cross-country journey to save their damaged souls. Aoyama's meditation on redemption allows for a measured discussion of memory, regret and the erosion of cultural identity. DP Japanese +subtitles. **DVD**
Koji Yakusho *Makoto Sawai* • Aoi Miyazaki *Kozue Tamura* • Masaru Miyazaki *Naoki Tamura* • Yohichiroh Saitoh *Akihiko* • Sayuri Kokusho *Yumiko* • Ken Mitsuishi *Shigeo* ■ *Dir/Scr* Shinji Aoyama

Eureka Stockade ★★ PG
Adventure 1949 · UK · BW · 98min

This is the story of the clashes between police and miners during the Australian gold rush of the 1850s after the government tried to restrict the miners' freedom of movement. Chips Rafferty plays the sharpest thorn in the authorities' side, but despite the obvious research and the efforts at authenticity, it's a stodgy film that hasn't worn the years well. AT **DVD**
Chips Rafferty *Peter Lalor* • Jane Barrett *Alicia Dunne* • Jack Lambert *Commissioner Rede* • Peter Illing *Raffaello* • Gordon Jackson *Tom Kennedy* • Ralph Truman *Gov Hotham* • Sydney Loder *Vern* • John Fernside *Sly grog seller* ■ *Dir* Harry Watt • *Scr* Harry Watt, Walter Greenwood, from a story by Harry Watt

Europa ★★★★ 15
Political thriller 1991 · Den · Colour and BW · 107min

Lars von Trier's mesmerising study of a defeated nation is a bold and imaginative attempt to fuse Kafka-esque paranoia with a mix of visual styles. Max von Sydow's opening narration, when combined with hypnotic shots of a maze of railway tracks, creates an atmosphere of uncertainty that pervades the rest of the picture. Jean-Marc Barr gives a suitably wide-eyed performance as the American sleeping-car conductor caught between the occupying Allies, Nazi partisans and the railway company in postwar Germany. DP English, German +subtitles. Violence. **DVD**
Jean-Marc Barr *Leopold Kessler* • Barbara Sukowa *Katharina Hartmann* • Udo Kier *Lawrence Hartmann* • Ernst-Hugo Jaregard *Uncle Kessler* • Erik Merk *Pater* • Jørgen Reenberg *Max Hartmann* • Henning Jensen *Siggy* • Eddie Constantine *Colonel Harris* • Max von Sydow *Narrator* ■ *Dir* Lars von Trier • *Scr* Lars von Trier, Niels Vorsel

Europa Europa ★★★★ 15
Second World War biographical drama
1991 · Fr/Ger · Colour · 107min

This extraordinary story proves once again that truth is stranger than fiction. Marco Hofschneider is hugely impressive as Salomon Perel, the Jewish teenager who fled to Soviet-occupied Poland to escape the Nazi tyranny, only to become accepted as a loyal Aryan after he was captured by the advancing Germans. He becomes a hero of the Hitler Youth and even manages to romance rabid anti-Semite Julie Delpy. Agnieszka Holland's wonderfully understated direction allows the cruel ironies to bite hard. DP German +subtitles. Nudity. *DVD*

Marco Hofschneider *Young Salomon Perel* · Julie Delpy *Leni* · André Wilms *Robert* · Salomon Perel *Old Salomon Perel* · Ashley Wanninger *Gerd* · René Hofschneider *Isaak Perel* · Piotr Kozlowski *David Perel* ■ *Dir* Agnieszka Holland · *Scr* Agnieszka Holland, from the memoirs by Salomon Perel

Europa '51 ★★★
Drama　1952 · It · BW · 118min

This is probably the best of the four spiritual melodramas Ingrid Bergman made with her husband Roberto Rossellini. Bergman plays a superficial American society woman living in Rome who believes she is the cause of her young son's suicide. She seeks salvation by tending the poor and the sick, much to the incomprehension of her bourgeois husband (Alexander Knox). Rossellini's unfussy direction creates a genuine feeling of spirituality. RB Italian +subtitles.

Ingrid Bergman *Irene Girard* · Alexander Knox *George Girard* · Ettore Giannini *Andrea* · Giulietta Masina *Passerotto* · Sandro Franchina *Michele* · Teresa Pellati *Ines* ■ *Dir* Roberto Rossellini · *Scr* Roberto Rossellini, Sandro De Leo, Mario Pannunzio, Ivo Perilli, Brunello Rondi, Diego Fabbri, Donald Ogden Stewart (English dialogue)

The Europeans ★★★★ U
Period drama　1979 · UK · Colour · 87min

James Ivory came closer than anyone to translating the near-unfilmable Henry James to the screen in this beautifully-judged drama. Aided, as ever, by the impeccable production values of Ismail Merchant and the intelligent writing of Ruth Prawer Jhabvala, Ivory's take on cross-continental snobbery is deliciously played by an immaculate cast. Returning to 1850s Boston, Lee Remick expertly keeps the lid on a performance that begged extravagance, thus ensuring that her gold-digging countess remains sympathetic. DP *DVD*

Lee Remick *Eugenia* · Robin Ellis *Robert Acton* · Wesley Addy *Mr Wentworth* · Tim Choate *Clifford Wentworth* · Lisa Eichhorn *Gertrude Wentworth* · Nancy New *Charlotte Wentworth* · Kristin Griffith *Lizzie Acton* ■ *Dir* James Ivory · *Scr* Ruth Prawer Jhabvala, from the novel by Henry James

EuroTrip ★★★ 15
Comedy　2004 · US · Colour · 87min

There's something to offend almost everybody in this raucous and rude teen sex comedy in which an American student (Scott Mechlowitz) embarks on a trip across Europe in search of an internet friend he has accidentally dumped, believing her to be a he. In the process every European stereotype is wheeled out, but despite the gleefully crude xenophobia there are enough laughs in this good-natured follow-up to 2000's *Road Trip* to keep the less easily shocked amused. AS Swearing, nudity. *DVD*

Scott Mechlowicz *Scotty Thomas* · Michelle Trachtenberg *Jenny* · Jacob Pitts *Cooper Harris* · Travis Wester *Jamie* · Jessica Boehrs *Mieke* · Lucy Lawless *Madame Vandersexxx* · Vinnie Jones *Mad Maynard* · Matt Damon *Donny* · Kristin Kreuk *Fiona* ■ *Dir* Jeff Schaffer · *Scr* Alec Berg, David Mandel, Jeff Schaffer

Eva ★★★★ 15
Drama　1962 · Fr/It · BW · 104min

This simmering study of obsession provides Jeanne Moreau with one of the meatiest roles of her career. As the ruthless opportunist exploiting the weakness of successful novelist Stanley Baker, she presents in many ways the darker side of Catherine, the character she played the previous year in François Truffaut's *Jules et Jim* – a perfect woman whose middle name is trouble. It's as if Michelangelo Antonioni had decided to make a *film noir*, as Joseph Losey turns Venice into a city of lost souls. DP

Jeanne Moreau *Eva Olivier* · Stanley Baker *Tyvian* · Virna Lisi *Francesca Ferrara* · Giorgio Albertazzi *Braneo Maloni* · James Villiers *Arthur McCormick* · Riccardo Garrone *Michele* · Lisa Gastoni *The redhead* · Checco Rissone *Pieri* ■ *Dir* Joseph Losey · *Scr* Hugo Butler, Evan Jones, from the novel *Eve* by James Hadley Chase

Evan Almighty ★★★ PG
Comedy fantasy　2007 · US · Colour · 91min

Steve Carell's show-stopping turn in the 2003 Jim Carrey vehicle *Bruce Almighty* was the spark of creation for this biblically themed comedy. He returns as vain newscaster Evan Baxter, recently elected to Congress when he's visited by God (Morgan Freeman) and instructed to build an ark. Carell's everyman quality and impeccable comic timing serve him well as he struggles to convince the world that the end is nigh, although none of it is as riotously funny as that one "nervous breakdown" scene in the first film. This time he and director Tom Shadyac have less material to work with, but Carell's geeky charm, some great lines from Wanda Sykes and a bagful of CGI tricks just about keep this vessel afloat. SP Brief swearing. *DVD* *Blu-ray*

Steve Carell *Evan Baxter* · Morgan Freeman *God* · John Goodman *Congressman Long* · Wanda Sykes *Rita* · Lauren Graham *Joan Baxter* · John Michael Higgins *Marty* · Jimmy Bennett *Ryan Baxter* · Johnny Simmons *Dylan Baxter* ■ *Dir* Tom Shadyac · *Scr* Steve Oedekerk, from a story by Oedekerk, Joel Cohen, Alec Sokolow, from characters by Steve Koren, Mark O'Keefe

Eve and the Handyman ★ PG
Sex comedy　1961 · US · Colour · 64min

Sex film pioneer Russ Meyer's leering peep show features his then wife Eve in all the pin-up roles. She's a ribald detective shadowing comic handyman Anthony-James Ryan as he plies his trade. Barely watchable in these more enlightened times, this may be of quaint historical interest to those into glamour magazine nostalgia. AJ

Anthony-James Ryan *Handyman* · Eve Meyer *Eve* ■ *Dir/Scr* Russ Meyer

Eve of Destruction ★ 18
Science-fiction thriller
1991 · US · Colour · 95min

This female version of *The Terminator* features an eye-catching performance from Dutch star Renée Soutendijk as a scientist who creates a cyborg in her own image, which then runs amok with a thermonuclear bomb in its womb. Gregory Hines plays the cop tracking her down, while Duncan Gibbins directs with some verve. However, the interesting premise isn't explored amid the obligatory explosions and fifth-rate effects. RS *DVD*

Gregory Hines *Jim McQuade* · Renée Soutendijk *Dr Eve Simmons/Eve VIII* · Michael Greene *General Curtis* · Kurt Fuller *Schneider* · John M Jackson *Peter Arnold* · Loren Haynes *Steve the robot* ■ *Dir* Duncan Gibbins · *Scr* Duncan Gibbins, Yale Udoff

Eve of Destruction ★
Science-fiction disaster movie
2013 · US · Colour

A tiny plot is stretched beyond breaking point in this interminably dull disaster movie in which a prospective new power source has deadly repercussions. Favouring unnecessary padding over story development, the cut-down TV mini-series ends up mainly talk and no drama. Over-used shots of agitated keyboard tapping and excessively gloomy visuals compound the lack of excitement, and leave you desperate for the last-act destruction to begin. SF

Steven Weber *Dr Karl Dameron* · Christina Cox *Dr Rachel Bannister* · Treat Williams *Max Salinger* · Aleks Paunovic *Ruslan* ■ *Dir* Robert Lieberman · *Scr* Richard Beattie

The Eve of St Mark ★★★
Second World War drama
1944 · US · BW · 96min

Maxwell Anderson's flag-waving Broadway play was a key wartime work, written in a form of blank verse and extremely emotive for an audience with sons and relatives at war immediately after Pearl Harbor. To its credit, the movie doesn't greatly expand the piece, although it does expurgate some of the original dialogue. The barrack room scenes in particular convey the heartfelt feelings of the time, despite serious undercasting owing to the fact that 20th Century-Fox's top leading men were themselves in the forces. TS

Anne Baxter *Janet Feller* · William Eythe *Private Quizz West* · Michael O'Shea (1) *Private Thomas Mulveray* · Vincent Price *Private Francis Marion* · Ruth Nelson *Nell West* · Ray Collins *Deckman West* · Stanley Prager *Private Glinka* · Henry Morgan [Harry Morgan] *Private Shevlin* ■ *Dir* John M Stahl · *Scr* George Seaton, from the play by Maxwell Anderson

Evel Knievel ★★
Biographical drama　1971 · US · Colour · 88min

George Hamilton stars as the famed daredevil motorcyclist, reflecting on major events that have shaped his life in this mildly diverting film biography of one of the great cultural figures of the 1970s. The script is guilty of too much cod philosophising, but Marvin J Chomsky's film is redeemed by some truly wonderful stock footage of Knievel in action. This is not to be confused with *Viva Knievel!*, which appeared six years later and featured the man playing himself. RS

George Hamilton *Evel Knievel* · Sue Lyon *Linda* · Bert Freed *Doc Kincaid* · Rod Cameron *Charlie Kresson* · Dub Taylor *Turquoise Smith* ■ *Dir* Marvin J Chomsky · *Scr* Alan Caillou, John Milius

Evel Knievel ★★
Biographical drama　2004 · Can · Colour · 110min

Played by George Hamilton in *Evel Knievel* (1971) and appearing as himself in *Viva Knievel!* (1977), America's most famous stunt rider is portrayed by *CSI* star George Eads in this formulaic biopic. Veteran director John Badham handles the spectacle and the melodrama with equal aplomb, and Eads has an easy swagger as he dices with death at Caesar's Palace and Snake River Canyon. But not even the casting of Beau Bridges as Knievel's father-in-law or Jaime Pressly as his wife, Linda, can inject much life into this superficial account of the small-town rebel who became a hard-partying daredevil. DP

George Eads *Evel* · Beau Bridges *John Bork* · Jaime Pressly *Linda Bork* · Lance Henriksen *Knoffel* · Jake Brockman *Younger Bobby/Evel* · Fred Dalton Thompson *Jay Samo* ■ *Dir* John Badham · *Scr* Jason Horwitch, from a biography by Steve Mandich

Evelyn ★★★ PG
Social drama based on a true story
2002 · Ire/UK/US/Ger · Colour · 90min

Triumph-over-adversity stories don't come much more manipulative than this syrupy, true-life drama set in 1950s Ireland. A warm, if contrived, account of paternal love, this stars Pierce Brosnan as a charismatic single father struggling to bring up three children after his wife abandons them. Brosnan is devastated when the authorities force his brood into care and what follows is a poignant, albeit predictable, courtroom battle to get them back. SF *DVD*

Pierce Brosnan *Desmond Doyle* · Aidan Quinn *Nick Barron* · Julianna Margulies *Bernadette Beattie* · Sophie Vavasseur *Evelyn Doyle* · Alan Bates *Tom Connolly* · Hugh McDonagh *Maurice Doyle* · Frank Kelly *Henry Doyle* ■ *Dir* Bruce Beresford · *Scr* Paul Pender

Evelyn Prentice ★★★
Mystery melodrama　1934 · US · BW · 78min

Star power makes this overheated soap opera of infidelity, murder and courtroom revelations seem better than it is. William Powell and Myrna Loy were teamed for the third time in this tale of a lawyer, suspected of philandering by his wife, who promptly gets involved with a blackmailing gigolo. The plot convulsions stretch credibility to breaking point, but the film is saved by its cast. TV

William Powell *John Prentice* · Myrna Loy *Evelyn Prentice* · Una Merkel *Amy Drexel* · Rosalind Russell *Nancy Harrison* · Isabel Jewell *Judith Wilson* · Harvey Stephens *Lawrence Kennard* · Edward Brophy *Eddie Delaney* ■ *Dir* William K Howard · *Scr* Lenore Coffee, from WE Woodward's novel

Even Cowgirls Get the Blues ★★ 15
Comedy adventure　1993 · US · Colour · 92min

In this misfiring comedy, Uma Thurman is lumbered with the role of a fashion model with abnormally long thumbs, who takes to hitch-hiking and ends up at the Rubber Rose Ranch, which is inhabited by lesbian cowgirls. Adapted from a bizarre novel by Tom Robbins, it's a belated flower-power idea that's decidedly below par. A miscalculation for director Gus Van Sant. TH

Uma Thurman *Sissy Hankshaw* · Lorraine Bracco *Delores Del Ruby* · Noriyuki "Pat" Morita [Pat Morita] *The Chink* · Angie Dickinson *Miss Adrian* · Keanu Reeves *Julian Gitchie* · John Hurt *The Countess* · Rain Phoenix *Bonanza Jellybean* · Ed Begley Jr *Rupert* · Carol Kane *Carla* · Sean Young *Marie Barth* · Crispin Glover *Howard Barth* · Roseanne Arnold [Roseanne Barr] *Madame Zoe* · Buck Henry *Dr Dreyfus* · Grace Zabriskie *Mrs Hankshaw* · Heather Graham *Cowgirl Heather* ■ *Dir* Gus Van Sant · *Scr* Gus Van Sant, from the novel by Tom Robbins

Even Dwarfs Started Small ★★★ PG
Drama　1970 · W Ger · BW · 89min

With this, his second feature film, Werner Herzog joined the elite of the new German cinema. Like his debut, *Signs of Life* (1968), the movie is set on an island, here used as a penal colony, and the allegorical story illuminates Herzog's unflattering view of humankind. The volcanic terrain houses only dwarfs, who indulge in increasingly rebellious acts against authority. Herzog made better films and documentaries than this darkly comic attack on institutionalism, but this disturbing work foreshadows his later extremism. BB German +subtitles. *DVD*

Helmut Döring *Hombre* · Gerd Gickel *Pepe* · Paul Glauer *Deputy* · Erna Gschwendtner *Azucar* ■ *Dir/Scr* Werner Herzog

Even the Rain ★★★ 15
Drama　2010 · Sp/Mex/Fr · Colour · 98min

In Bolivia to make a revisionist biopic of Christopher Columbus, producer Luis Tosar and director Gael García Bernal find themselves moving in opposite directions after they cast a local militant in a supporting role and he becomes involved in a protest. Awash with post-colonial guilt and anti-capitalist fury, this is a film with its heart in the right place. But the screenplay pushes its political luck on occasion, so this works better as a satire on the compromises necessary to make movies than as a diatribe against multinational conglomerates. DP Spanish, Quechua, English +subtitles. Swearing, nudity.

Gael García Bernal *Sebastián* · Luis Tosar *Costa* · Juan Carlos Aduviri *Daniel/Hatuey* · Karra Elejalde *Anton/Christopher Columbus* · Carlos Santos *Alberto/Las Casas* · Raúl Arévalo *Juan/Montesinos* ■ *Dir* Iciar Bollain · *Scr* Paul Laverty

Evening ★★ 12
Romantic drama
2007 · Ger/US · Colour · 112min

This leaden screen adaptation of Susan Minot's delicate novel about the treacherousness of memory focuses on dying Vanessa Redgrave's remembrance of things past and how it affects her bickering daughters, Toni Collette and Natasha Richardson. Claire Danes plays the young Redgrave in the 1950s flashbacks that reveal the life-changing events at her best friend's Rhode Island wedding. The terrific female cast gamely tries to overcome the superficial emotional content and predictable storyline: Glenn Close oozes uptight old money as the bride's mother; Eileen Atkins makes her whimsical nurse-cum-angel role fly; and Meryl Streep's late arrival saves the maudlin third act. AJ Swearing. *DVD*

Claire Danes *Ann Grant* • Toni Collette *Nina Mars* • Vanessa Redgrave *Ann Lord* • Patrick Wilson *Harris Arden* • Hugh Dancy *Buddy Wittenborn* • Natasha Richardson *Constance Haverford* • Mamie Gummer *Lila Wittenborn* • Eileen Atkins *The night nurse* • Meryl Streep *Lila Ross* • Glenn Close *Mrs Wittenborn* ■ *Dir* Lajos Koltai • *Scr* Susan Minot, Michael Cunningham, from the novel by Minot • *Cinematographer* Gyula Pados

The Evening Star ★★★ 15
Drama 1996 · US · Colour · 123min

This disappointing but still interesting sequel to *Terms of Endearment* picks up the story more than a decade later. Shirley MacLaine returns as eccentric matriarch Aurora, now of pensionable age but just as feisty as she struggles to bring up her late daughter's children. Despite a brief cameo from MacLaine's fellow *Endearment* Oscar winner Jack Nicholson, and strong performances by Juliette Lewis and Miranda Richardson, this never truly sparkles, largely owing to a lacklustre script, but it does touch the heart. JB Swearing, nudity.

Shirley MacLaine *Aurora Greenway* • Bill Paxton *Jerry Bruckner* • Juliette Lewis *Melanie Horton* • Miranda Richardson *Patsy Carpenter* • Ben Johnson (1) *Arthur Cotton* • Jack Nicholson *Garrett Breedlove* • Scott Wolf *Bruce* • George Newbern *Tommy Horton* • Marion Ross *Rosie Dunlop* ■ *Dir* Robert Harling • *Scr* Robert Harling, from the novel by Larry McMurtry

Evensong ★★★ U
Musical drama 1934 · UK · BW · 81min

Evelyn Laye plays an Irish opera singer pursued by the likes of handsome Archduke Carl Esmond. Some may find this saga poignant; others will think it unbearably silly and slow. However, Fritz Kortner makes a powerful contribution as the impresario, and if you peer hard enough you'll spot Alec Guinness in a small role. It's impossible not to enjoy dialogue such as "My cousin has been assassinated at Sarajevo – God only knows what this is going to lead to!" TS

Evelyn Laye *Irela/Maggie O'Neil* • Fritz Kortner *Kober* • Alice Delysia *Mme Valmond* • Carl Esmond *Archduke Theodore* • Emlyn Williams *George Murray* • Muriel Aked *Tremlowe* • Patrick O'Moore *Bob McNeil* • Alec Guinness *Soldier* ■ *Dir* Victor Saville • *Scr* Edward Knoblock, Dorothy Farnum, from the play by Edward Knoblock, Beverley Nichols, from the novel by Beverley Nichols

Event Horizon ★★★ 18
Science-fiction horror
1997 · US/UK · Colour · 91min

This is an enjoyable slice of space splatter from British director Paul Anderson. The *Event Horizon* of the title is an experimental spacecraft that has been missing for years but has just been located. A rescue team, led by Laurence Fishburne, is sent to retrieve it, but it soon becomes apparent that it's in the grip of a malevolent force. Fishburne, Sam Neill, Joely Richardson and Sean Pertwee bring some class to the determinedly B-movie dialogue, and Anderson delivers some nasty sequences that will please horror fans. JF Violence, swearing, nudity. *DVD*

Laurence Fishburne *Miller* • Sam Neill *Weir* • Kathleen Quinlan *Peters* • Joely Richardson *Starck* • Richard T Jones *Cooper* • Jason Isaacs *DJ* • Sean Pertwee *Smith* ■ *Dir* Paul Anderson (1) • *Scr* Philip Eisner

Ever After: a Cinderella Story ★★★★ PG
Romantic fantasy 1998 · US · Colour · 121min

Andy Tennant brings new freshness and vitality to the Cinderella story in this delightful reworking that treats the legend as if it were hard historical fact. All the pantomime sorcery and comical sidekicks have been jettisoned, and the result allows the romance between Drew Barrymore's feisty servant girl and Dougray Scott's handsome prince to shine even brighter. Anjelica Huston re-interprets the evil stepmother role with deft assurance, and Leonardo da Vinci makes a surprising fairy godmother figure. A handsomely mounted epic. AJ Brief swearing. *DVD* *BL*

Drew Barrymore *Danielle* • Anjelica Huston *Baroness Rodmilla* • Dougray Scott *Prince Henry* • Patrick Godfrey *Leonardo da Vinci* • Megan Dodds *Marguerite* • Melanie Lynskey *Jacqueline* • Timothy West *King Francis* • Judy Parfitt *Queen Marie* ■ *Dir* Andy Tennant • *Scr* Andy Tennant, Susannah Grant, Rick Parks, from the story *Cinderella* by Charles Perrault

Ever in My Heart ★★
Drama 1933 · US · BW · 70min

This far-fetched weepie presents Barbara Stanwyck as an upper-crust New Englander defiantly marrying a good German who's forced by anti-Hun fervour to return home during the First World War. They meet again: she as a frontline canteen worker, he as a German spy. Ever-reliable Stanwyck gives it all she's got and almost manages to draw some warmth from Otto Kruger as the love of her life, but the cursory direction of Archie Mayo deprives it of any real impact. AE

Barbara Stanwyck *Mary Archer* • Otto Kruger *Hugo Wilbrandt* • Ralph Bellamy *Jeff* • Ruth Donnelly *Lizzie* • Laura Hope Crews *Grandma Archer* • Frank Albertson *Sam* • Ronnie Crosby *Teddy* • Clara Blandick *Anna* ■ *Dir* Archie Mayo • *Scr* Bertram Milhauser, from a story by Beulah Marie Dix, Bertram Milhauser

Everest ★★ 12
Adventure thriller based on a true story
2015 · US/UK · Colour · 116min

Based on tragic events from 1996, this story of survival on the world's highest mountain feels surprisingly small. Icelandic director Baltasar Kormakur assembles a big-name cast, including Jake Gyllenhaal, Keira Knightley and Emily Watson, but he doesn't give them the material to really dig deep into the terror-stricken souls of those caught at 29,000ft. Even the visual sweep you'd expect is lacking. The biggest obstacle, though, is the passive response of all involved – with so little introspection, their ordeal just leaves you stone cold. SP *DVD* *BL* *3D*

Josh Brolin *Beck Weathers* • Jake Gyllenhaal *Scott Fischer* • Robin Wright *Peach Weathers* • Emily Watson *Helen Wilton* • Keira Knightley *Jan Arnold* • Sam Worthington *Guy Cotter* • Clive Standen *Ed Viesturs* ■ *Dir* Baltasar Kormakur • *Scr* Simon Beaufoy, William Nicholson

Evergreen ★★★ U
Musical comedy 1934 · UK · BW · 89min

Unquestionably British musical star Jessie Matthews's most popular movie, this Michael Balcon-produced trifle is directed by Victor Saville. A girl poses as her own music-hall star mum, a situation which naturally evokes complications when romance arrives. Jessie is quite lovely, sumptuously photographed by Glen MacWilliams, and given to wearing endearing see-through gowns. TS *DVD*

Jessie Matthews *Harriet Green/Harriet's daughter* • Sonnie Hale *Leslie Benn* • Betty Balfour *Maudie* • Barry Mackay *Tommy Thompson* • Ivor MacLaren *Marquis of Staines* • Hartley Power *Treadwell* • Patrick Ludlow *Lord Shropshire* • Betty Shale *Mrs Hawkes* ■ *Dir* Victor Saville • *Scr* Emlyn Williams, Marjorie Gaffney, from the play by Benn W Levy

An Everlasting Piece ★★★★ 15
Comedy 2000 · US · Colour · 99min

Belfast in the 1980s is the somewhat unlikely setting for director Barry Levinson's eccentric comedy. Barry McEvoy (who also wrote the hilarious script) and Brian F O'Byrne work as hairdressers in a prison asylum, relieving their boredom with lame attempts at poetry. When deranged hairpiece kingpin Billy Connolly (an all-too-brief cameo) is incarcerated, the pair decide to go into business as the "Piece People". With much-needed help from McEvoy's mouthy girlfriend (an ebullient performance from Anna Friel), they soon find themselves in competition with some ludicrously named rivals. The action moves swiftly without descending into farce. SS Swearing. *DVD*

Barry McEvoy *Colm O'Neill* • Brian F O'Byrne *George* • Anna Friel *Bronagh* • Pauline McLynn *Gerty* • Billy Connolly *Scalper* ■ *Dir* Barry Levinson • *Scr* Barry McEvoy

Everly ★★ 18
Action thriller 2014 · US · Colour · 88min

In this over-the-top vengeance thriller, the bullets and blood fly as Salma Hayek fights to live long enough to protect her mother and daughter from the brutal gangster who imprisoned her as a sex slave. Hayek's performance, along with the slick, stylish direction, would be a winning combination, were it not for the startling amount of graphic violence on display. Director Joe Lynch revels in showing woundings and torture, to the point where even the most hardened action fans may find themselves wincing. JL English, Japanese +subtitles. Violence, swearing, nudity.

Salma Hayek *Everly* • Hiroyuki Watanabe *Taiko* • Laura Cepeda *Edith* • Akie Kotabe *The Dead Man* ■ *Dir* Joe Lynch • *Scr* Yale Hannon, from a story by Hannon, Joe Lynch

Eversmile, New Jersey ★★ PG
Road movie 1989 · Arg/UK · Colour · 87min

This production must rank as one of the most unusual entries on the CV of star Daniel Day-Lewis. He plays a bike-riding dentist preaching the gospel of good dental hygiene with missionary zeal in the most far-flung parts of Argentina. The film's quirkiness is initially rather appealing, but it rapidly palls. DA *DVD*

Daniel Day-Lewis *Fergus O'Connell* • Mirjana Jokovic *Estela* • Gabriela Acher *Celeste* • Ignacio Quiros *The "Boss"* • Boy Olmi *Radio announcer* • Alberto Benegas *Sheriff* • Ruben Patagonia *Butler* • Matias Puelles *Child* • Eduardo Santoro *Party guest* ■ *Dir* Carlos Sorin • *Scr* Jorge Goldenberg, Roberto Sheuer, Carlos Sorin

Every Day's a Holiday ★★★
Comedy 1937 · US · BW · 78min

Deprived of her salty dialogue by the censors, there's little Mae West can do but sing and flounce, but she still does it better than anybody else. In this average vehicle, she's a delight, disguised as a French singer to escape New York detective Edmund Lowe because she sold Herman Bing the Brooklyn Bridge. Lloyd Nolan plays Lowe's crooked boss and there's a rare glimpse of Louis Armstrong for good measure. TS

Mae West *Peaches O'Day* • Edmund Lowe *Captain Jim McCarey* • Charles Butterworth *Larmadou Graves* • Charles Winninger *Von Reighle Van Pelter Van Doon* • Walter Catlett *Nifty Bailey* • Lloyd Nolan *Honest John Quade* • Louis Armstrong • Herman Bing *Fritz Krausmeyer* ■ *Dir* A Edward Sutherland • *Scr* Mae West

Every Day's a Holiday ★★ U
Musical comedy 1964 · UK · Colour · 89min

Director James Hill's attempt to take the Swinging Sixties to the seaside is often laughably bad. John Leyton is the nominal star of this talent-show farrago, although the musical headliners are Freddie and the Dreamers, who were trying to match the movie achievements of the Beatles in *A Hard Day's Night*. However, no film with cinematography by Nicolas Roeg can be dismissed out of hand, and Ron Moody and Liz Fraser provide accomplished comic support. DP *DVD*

Freddie and the Dreamers *The Chefs* • John Leyton *Gerry Pullman* • Mike Sarne *[Michael Sarne]* • Timothy Gilbin • Ron Moody *Professor Bastinado* • Liz Fraser *Miss Slightly* • Grazina Frame *Christina Barrington de Witt* • Susan Baker *Susan* ■ *Dir* James Hill • *Scr* Anthony Marriott, Jeri Matos, James Hill, from the story by Anthony Marriott

Every Girl Should Be Married ★★ U
Romantic comedy 1948 · US · BW · 81min

This lightweight movie was the 55th of Cary Grant's 74 films, and the star used his considerable sway to cast his future wife Betsy Drake in the female lead. This film is an unworthy vehicle: it's not only the title that renders it desperately old-fashioned in today's post-feminist world, there's also a rather unpalatable plotline about a paediatrician (Grant) and a department store clerk (Drake) who wants to get married at all costs. TS

Cary Grant *Dr Madison Brown* • Betsy Drake *Anabel Sims* • Franchot Tone *Roger Sanford* • Diana Lynn *Julie Hudson* • Alan Mowbray *Mr Spitzer* • Elisabeth Risdon *Mary Nolan* ■ *Dir* Don Hartman • *Scr* Stephen Morehouse Avery, Don Hartman, from a story by Eleanor Harris

Every Home Should Have One ★ 15
Comedy 1970 · UK · Colour · 89min

This dismal comedy was co-scripted by Marty Feldman, Barry Took and Denis Norden, and it boasts a top-notch comic cast. But their efforts are totally overshadowed by a shambolic, leering performance from Feldman, making his second screen appearance, as a mad advertising executive who devises a series of steamy commercials for a brand of frozen porridge. DP Sex scenes, swearing, brief nudity. *DVD* *BL*

Marty Feldman *Teddy* • Shelley Berman *Nat Kaplan* • Judy Cornwell *Liz Brown* • Julie Ege *Inga Giltenberg* • Patrick Cargill *Wallace Trufitt MP* • Jack Watson *McLaughlin* • Patience Collier *Mrs Levin* • Penelope Keith *Lotte von Gelbstein* • Dinsdale Landen *Reverend Mellish* ■ *Dir* Jim Clark • *Scr* Marty Feldman, Barry Took, Denis Norden, from a story by Milton Shulman, Herman Kretzmer

Every Little Crook and Nanny ★★★
Comedy 1972 · US · Colour · 92min

A glorious piece of self-guying from Victor Mature illuminates this hit-and-miss Mob comedy, though we don't spend nearly enough time in his company. Instead we get Lynn Redgrave, mugging for all she's worth, as a nanny who abducts the son of a Mafia godfather (guess who?). If only Cy Howard had written himself a better script; he might not have had to direct with such frenetic energy. DP

Lynn Redgrave *Miss Poole, Nanny* • Victor Mature *Carmine Ganucci* • Paul Sand *Benny Napkins* • Maggie Blye *Stella* • Austin Pendleton *Luther* • John Astin *Garbugli* • Dom DeLuise *Azzecca* • Louise Sorel *Marie* • Phillip Graves *Lewis Ganucci* ■ *Dir* Cy Howard • *Scr* Cy Howard, Jonathan Axelrod, Robert Klane, from a novel by Ed McBain [Evan Hunter]

Every Sunday ★★★ U
Musical 1936 · US · BW · 10min

This enchanting featurette was designed by MGM as a screen test for young contractees Judy Garland and Deanna Durbin. They play a pair of teenage friends who save a Sunday afternoon park orchestra from closure by taking to the bandstand to modernise the repertoire, singing a song each and a duet. MGM ended up retaining Garland, while Durbin went off to Universal, where her string of hits saved the studio from bankruptcy. Historic, and a must for fans. RK

Judy Garland *Judy* • Deanna Durbin *Edna* ■ *Dir* Felix E Feist [Felix Feist] • *Scr* Mauri Grashin

E

Every Time We Say Goodbye ★★ 15

Period romantic drama
1986 · US/Is · Colour · 93min

After a string of comedy successes Tom Hanks took his first crack at something weightier in this modest romantic drama. He plays a Second World War pilot stationed near Jerusalem who falls for a local Jewish girl (Cristina Marsillach), much to the consternation of her family. Hanks looks a little uncomfortable in the lead role, but director Moshe Mizrahi does pull the right emotional strings. JF Swearing.

Tom Hanks *David* • Cristina Marsillach *Sarah* • Benedict Taylor *Peter* • Anat Atzmon *Victoria* • Gila Almagor *Lea* • Moni Moshanov *Nessin* ■ *Dir* Moshe Mizrahi • *Scr* Moshe Mizrahi, Rachel Fabien, Leah Appet, from a story by Moshe Mizrahi

Every Which Way but Loose ★★★ 12

Comedy drama
1978 · US · Colour · 109min

Clint Eastwood cruises through this coarse comedy as a travelling prizefighter whose best buddy is a beer-swilling, lowlife orangutan named Clyde. There are plenty of lively scenes to keep fans satisfied, and Eastwood just about manages to avoid being made a monkey of by his scene-stealing co-star. His romantic hankerings after country singer Sondra Locke don't add much to the brew, though. A feeble sequel, *Any Which Way You Can*, followed. DP Brief nudity, violence, swearing. *DVD*

Clint Eastwood *Philo Beddoe* • Sondra Locke *Lynn Halsey-Taylor* • Geoffrey Lewis *Orville* • Ruth Gordon *Ma* • Beverly D'Angelo *Echo* • Walter Barnes *Tank Murdock* • Sam Gilman *Fat man's friend* ■ *Dir* James Fargo • *Scr* Jeremy Joe Kronsberg

Everybody Does It ★★★ U

Comedy
1949 · US · BW · 97min

This very funny remake of *Wife, Husband and Friend* sensibly retains Nunnally Johnson's clever script almost word for word, but is far better cast than that 1939 Loretta Young vehicle. Celeste Holm is simply terrific as a woman who wants to sing opera but can't, while Paul Douglas is no less fine as her husband, who *can* sing opera but doesn't! Elsewhere Linda Darnell is lovely as the local neighbourhood diva. This trifle is consistently amusing. TS

Paul Douglas *Leonard Borland* • Linda Darnell *Cecil Carver* • Celeste Holm *Doris Borland* • Charles Coburn *Major Blair* • Millard Mitchell *Mike Craig* • Lucile Watson *Mrs Blair* • John Hoyt *Wilkins* • Leon Belasco *Hugo* ■ *Dir* Edmund Goulding • *Scr* Nunnally Johnson, from from the story *Career in C Major* by James M Cain in *American Magazine*

Everybody Has a Plan ★★★ 15

Crime drama
2012 · Arg/Sp/Ger · Colour · 113min

Viggo Mortensen may be best known as the hero of the *Lord of the Rings* trilogy, but in this Argentinian neo-noir drama he plays not one but two unsavoury characters – and in Spanish. Pedro lives a modest, criminal life down by the delta, while his estranged twin Agustín is a city doctor who is being pressured into adopting a baby by his wife. When Pedro unexpectedly comes to visit, Agustín sees a way out of his middle-class prison and decides to take his brother's identity. Debuting director Ana Piterbarg gets rather bogged down in the midlife-crisis elements of the story, but Mortensen's handling of the chalk-and-cheese brothers is superb. DW Spanish +subtitles. *DVD*

Viggo Mortensen *Agustín/Pedro* • Soledad Villamil *Claudia* • Daniel Fanego *Adrián* • Javier Godino *Rubén* • Sofía Gala Castiglione [Sofía Gala] *Rosa* ■ *Dir/Scr* Ana Piterbarg

Everybody Sing ★★★ U

Musical
1938 · US · BW · 91min

This sparkling young Judy Garland flick was one of those "crazy family" movies so popular in the 1930s. Garland is the second daughter of Reginald Owen and actress Billie Burke, who puts on a show with cook Fanny Brice and Allan Jones. Judy sings five numbers, all especially arranged for her by her mentor, the great Roger Edens, and reveals that magnificent talent that only a year later would make her an international star in *The Wizard of Oz*. TS

Allan Jones *Ricky Saboni* • Fanny Brice *Olga Chekaloff* • Judy Garland *Judy Bellaire* • Reginald Owen *Hillary Bellaire* • Billie Burke *Diana Bellaire* • Reginald Gardner *Jerrold Hope* • Lynne Carver *Sylvia Bellaire* • Monty Woolley *John Fleming* ■ *Dir* Edwin L Marin • *Scr* Florence Ryerson, Edgar Allan Woolf, James Gruen, from their story • *Music Director* Roger Edens

Everybody Wants Some!! ★★★★ 15

Comedy
2016 · US · Colour · 116min

The spiritual sequel to Richard Linklater's '70s-set classic *Dazed and Confused*, this seems at first to be nothing more than a wholesome examination of sexual freedom at college. But look past its 1980s details – Carl Sagan, vinyl and VHS – and you'll see the writer/director using a team of baseball players to examine the meaning of life via no particular plot. Although nostalgic for the beauty and confusion of youth as it tangles with the wider world, the film is overall a delicious, feel-good romp. Pacey and completely entertaining, this comedy rocks. KK Swearing, sexual references, drug abuse, nudity.

Blake Jenner *Jake* • Zoey Deutch *Beverly* • Wyatt Russell *Willoughby* • Tyler Hoechlin *McReynolds* ■ *Dir/Scr* Richard Linklater

Everybody Wins ★ 15

Mystery drama
1990 · UK · Colour · 92min

This is a sort of thriller, with Nick Nolte as a widowed private eye hired and then seduced by mysterious Debra Winger, who wants him to open up an old murder case. Winger is given reams of dialogue to declaim and some utterly unplayable scenes to wade through. Arthur Miller is a great playwright, but he can't write a decent screenplay. AT Swearing, nudity. *DVD*

Debra Winger *Angela Crispini* • Nick Nolte *Tom O'Toole* • Will Patton *Jerry* • Jack Warden *Judge Harry Murdoch* • Judith Ivey *Connie* • Frank Converse *Charlie Haggerty* • Kathleen Wilhoite *Amy* • Frank Military *Felix* ■ *Dir* Karel Reisz • *Scr* Arthur Miller

Everybody's All-American ★★★ 15

Drama
1988 · US · Colour · 121min

Dennis Quaid plays a legendary American football star in this saga of sporting success and failure that begins in the Eisenhower era of flash cars, material plenty and patriotism. Quaid marries a local beauty queen (Jessica Lange), and the film charts 25 turbulent years in their lives. It's over-plotted, though Lange's performance lifts the lightweight material. AT Violence, swearing, a sex scene, brief nudity.

Dennis Quaid *Gavin Grey* • Jessica Lange *Babs Rogers Grey* • Timothy Hutton *Donnie "Cake"* • John Goodman *Ed Lawrence* • Carl Lumbly *Narvel Blue* • Raymond Baker *[Ray Baker] Bolling Kiely* • Savannah Smith Boucher *Darlene Kiely* • Patricia Clarkson *Leslie Stone* ■ *Dir* Taylor Hackford • *Scr* Tom Rickman, from the novel by Frank Deford

Everybody's Fine ★★★ 12

Drama
1990 · It/Fr · Colour · 123min

Marcello Mastroianni has a ball as an elderly father of five who travels all over Italy to visit his now grown-up clan and gets some shocks when he discovers his children haven't quite turned out as he expected. There's a welcome appearance by Michèle Morgan as a Rimini widow, but this is predominantly a showcase for the delightful Mastroianni, who makes the most of the opportunity. Director/co-writer Giuseppe Tornatore finds room for sentimentality in an otherwise cynical tale. AT Italian +subtitles.

Marcello Mastroianni *Matteo Scuro* • Michèle Morgan *Woman on train* • Marino Cenna *Canio* • Roberto Nobile *Guglielmo* • Valeria Cavalli *Tosca* • Norma Martelli *Norma* ■ *Dir* Giuseppe Tornatore • *Scr* Giuseppe Tornatore, Tonino Guerra, Massimo De Rita, from a story by Giuseppe Tornatore

Everybody's Fine ★★ 12

Comedy drama
2009 · US/It · Colour · 95min

With a cast that includes Robert De Niro, Drew Barrymore, Kate Beckinsale and Sam Rockwell, and a premise that has echoes of Alexander Payne's *About Schmidt*, you could expect good things from this comedy drama. However, both are wasted on a routine remake of a much superior Italian original, *Stanno Tutti Bene* (1990). De Niro plays a widower who decides to make amends for past paternal indifference by paying his now grown-up kids surprise visits. Ultimately, the film seems less well suited to an American sensibility than the original was to a European one. DA *DVD*

Robert De Niro *Frank Goode* • Drew Barrymore *Rosie* • Kate Beckinsale *Amy* • Sam Rockwell *Robert* • Melissa Leo *Colleen* ■ *Dir* Kirk Jones • *Scr* Kirk Jones, from the 1990 film

Everyday ★★★★ 15

Drama
2012 · UK · Colour · 90min

A brood of kids sleepily go through their morning rituals before straggling out behind their exhausted mother for a lengthy succession of bus and train journeys. They're visiting their dad who's in prison. Filming in short bursts over five years, director Michael Winterbottom uses the repetition of daily life to show how an enforced separation affects a family. Shirley Henderson and John Simm are terrific as the parents, but the children are real-life siblings rather than actors and their natural performances accentuate the air of realism. The experience is emotionally draining but, ultimately, it is a rewarding story of survival and love. JnR Swearing. *DVD*

Shirley Henderson *Karen* • John Simm *Ian* • Shaun Kirk *Shaun* • Robert Kirk *Robert* • Katrina Kirk *Katrina* • Stephanie Kirk *Stephanie* ■ *Dir* Michael Winterbottom • *Scr* Michael Winterbottom, Laurence Coriat

Everyone Says I Love You ★★★★ 12

Musical comedy
1996 · US · Colour · 96min

This musical from Woody Allen dares to be different – none of the cast can sing. It's a comedy of frustrated emotions, in which Allen tries to woo Julia Roberts, his ex-wife (played by Goldie Hawn) takes charge of an ex-convict and her daughter (Drew Barrymore) is absorbed by teenage angst. Despite revisiting the usual Allen themes, this is a bold departure from the norm. Characters suddenly launch into songs and there's a wonderful dance sequence on the banks of the Seine, but the lack of musical skills can be a little distracting. The result, though, is strangely endearing. TH Swearing. *DVD*

Woody Allen *Joe* • Alan Alda *Bob* • Goldie Hawn *Steffi* • Julia Roberts *Von* • Drew Barrymore *Skylar* • Edward Norton *Holden* • Natasha Lyonne *DJ* • Gaby Hoffmann *Lane* • Natalie Portman *Laura* • Lukas Haas *Scott* • Tim Roth *Charles Ferry* ■ *Dir/Scr* Woody Allen

everything ★★★ 18

Psychological drama
2004 · UK · Colour · 91min

Writer/director Richard Hawkins makes an impressive debut with this clipped, compelling drama. Strong scripting is the key to the simmering relationship between ageing Geordie prostitute Jan Graveson and Ray Winstone's vacillating punter, which plays out over a series of intense but platonic encounters. However, the tension drops when the action shifts to scenes involving Winstone's wife (Lindy Sellars) and a terrified Belarussian hooker (Katherine Clisby). DP Swearing. *DVD*

Ray Winstone *Richard* • Jan Graveson *Naomi* • Lois Winstone *Anna* • Lindy Sellars *Richard's wife* • Katherine Clisby ■ *Dir/Scr* Richard Hawkins

Everything Is Illuminated ★★★ 12

Comedy drama
2005 · US · Colour · 101min

This whimsical story of a neurotic young writer's journey to Ukraine to delve into his grandfather's wartime past is the directorial debut of actor Liev Schreiber. Elijah Wood stars as the Jewish American author who takes a surreal road trip that brings him into contact with the Ukrainian lunatic fringe. This includes such characters as his guide Alex (beautifully played by Eugene Hutz) and Alex's apparently blind grandfather (Boris Leskin) who acts as the pair's driver, aided by his vicious seeing-eye dog. Told in a dreamy, painterly fashion, this quirky movie is occasionally too theatrical for its own good. KK English, Russian, Ukrainian +subtitles. Swearing, violence. *DVD*

Elijah Wood *Jonathan Safran Foer* • Eugene Hutz *Alex* • Boris Leskin *Grandfather* • Laryssa Lauret *Lista* • Jonathan Safran Foer *Leaf blower* • Stepan Samudovsky *Safran, Jonathan's grandfather* • Jana Hrabetova *Jonathan's grandmother* • Zuzana Hodkova *Alex's mother* ■ *Dir* Liev Schreiber • *Scr* Liev Schreiber, from the novel by Jonathan Safran Foer

Everything Is Thunder ★★★

First World War drama
1936 · UK/US · BW · 77min

This oddly titled film struck a chord with the great writer (and film critic) Graham Greene, who identified with the original novel's complicated plot involving disguises, human frailty and men in hiding, fearful of discovery by the police and betrayal. Constance Bennett is cast as a prostitute (only hinted at because of censorship rules) who helps Canadian officer and PoW Douglass Montgomery escape. There's a twist, involving her lover's sacrifice, that contributes to the pace of this intelligent entertainment. BB

Constance Bennett *Anna* • Douglass Montgomery *Hugh McGrath* • Oscar Homolka *Detective Goertz* • Roy Emerton *Kostner* • Frederick Lloyd *Muller* ■ *Dir* Milton Rosmer • *Scr* Marion Dix, John Orton, from a novel by Jocelyn L Hardy

Everything Must Go ★★★★ 15

Comedy drama
2010 · US · Colour · 92min

...or the living death of a salesman. Will Ferrell plays the sales executive whose job, marriage and finances are crumbling around him, thanks to his inability to stop drinking. Locked out of his house, Ferrell sets up camp on his front lawn, only to find an unlikely ally in a lonely youngster (a subtly confident turn from Christopher CJ Wallace). The friendship that forms between these two lost boys slowly but surely works a curious magic on both of them, giving each a new sense of purpose. It's no *Leaving Las Vegas*, but as a sombre study of human frailty, it works well, with Ferrell fitting his character like a glove. SuR Swearing, a sex scene. *DVD* *Blu*

Will Ferrell *Nick Porter* • Rebecca Hall *Samantha* • Christopher CJ Wallace [Christopher Jordan Wallace] *Kenny Loftus* • Michael Peña [Michael Pena] *Frank Garcia* • Laura Dern *Delilah* ■ *Dir* Dan Rush • *Scr* Dan Rush, from the short story *Why Don't You Dance?* by Raymond Carver

Everything or Nothing: the Untold Story of 007 ★★★★ 12

Documentary
2012 · US/UK · Colour and BW · 93min

James Bond fans may think they know everything about Britain's greatest secret agent, but this trawl through the history of the film franchise (released to coincide with the 50th anniversary of *Dr No*) still feels like a refreshing affair. Not the usual wallow in girls, gadgets and villains, this instead chronicles the cultural icon through the prism of the lives of creator Ian Fleming and original producers Albert "Cubby" Broccoli and Harry Saltzman. Director Stevan Riley (*Fire in Babylon*) skilfully illustrates the trio's relationship with a neat use of previously unseen archive, home movies and film clips.

All the 007s are interviewed (except for Connery, sadly), with the contributions from Lazenby, Moore and Brosnan being particularly humorous and insightful. Casual observers will be fascinated, and even Bond obsessives may find something new to chew on, during this revealing account of the genesis of cinema's most enduring series. JA Violence, swearing, sexual references, brief nudity. *DVD*

Roger Moore • George Lazenby • Timothy Dalton • Pierce Brosnan • Daniel Craig • Judi Dench • Robert Davi • Ken Adam • Lucy Fleming • Barbara Broccoli ■ Dir/Scr Stevan Riley

Everything That Rises
★★★★ PG

Western drama 1998 · US · Colour · 90min

This is a heart-warming and uplifting look at the harsh struggles faced by contemporary American farmers. Dennis Quaid and Mare Winningham are the credible heroes of this gritty TV movie, who face the challenges and seemingly insurmountable obstacles placed before them, including their son's disability and bank loan problems, with vim, vigour and personal sacrifice. Beautifully acted, this realistic drama makes for refreshing, thought-provoking and compelling viewing. AJ

Dennis Quaid *Jim Clay* • Mare Winningham *Kyle Clay* • Harve Presnell *Garth* • Meat Loaf *Red* • Ryan Merriman *Nathan Clay* • Bruce McGill *Alan Jamison* • Denise Durham *Red's wife* ■ Dir Dennis Quaid • Scr Mark Spragg

Everything You Always Wanted to Know about Sex ... but Were Afraid to Ask
★★★ 18

Comedy 1972 · US · Colour · 84min

Woody Allen's third outing as actor/writer/director, made in the days when his films were largely an excuse to string together a relentless series of gags, is one of his least satisfying pictures. But this seven-story sex-manual parody does have its redeeming features. The razor-sharp Michelangelo Antonioni spoof and Lou Jacobi's ill-timed experiment in cross-dressing are neatly done, but Gene Wilder's affair with a sheep is rather woolly and the "What's My Perversion?" panel game quickly runs out of steam. The best is left to last, as Woody and his fellow sperms prepare to parachute to glory. DP Sex scenes. *DVD* *Blu*

Woody Allen *Victor/Fabrizio/Fool/Sperm* • John Carradine *Doctor Bernardo* • Lou Jacobi *Sam* • Louise Lasser *Gina* • Anthony Quayle *King* • Tony Randall *Operator* • Lynn Redgrave *Queen* • Burt Reynolds *Switchboard* • Gene Wilder *Doctor Ross* • Jack Barry ■ Dir Woody Allen • Scr Woody Allen, from a non-fiction book by Dr David Reuben

Everywhere + Nowhere
★★★ 15

Drama 2011 · UK · Colour · 96min

Menhaj Huda's follow-up to *Kidulthood* is a coming-of-age tale that takes the clichés of British youth rebellion pictures since the 1950s and adds some slick visuals and banging beats. Changing the emphasis from class to ethnic conflict, Huda's film follows 20-something British Asian Ash (James Floyd), who struggles to reconcile the wishes of his traditional older brother (Alyy Khan) with his burning desire to become a DJ. Most of the action takes place over one wild night out, but putting aside the melodramatics, Huda draws fine performances from a solid ensemble and makes shrewd use of Brian Tufano's evocative camerawork to convey a palpable sense of place and community. DP Swearing, sex scenes, drug abuse.

James Floyd *Ash Khan* • Shivani Ghai *Sairah Khan* • Alyy Khan *Ahmed Khan* • Adam Deacon *Zaf* • Neet Mohan *Riz* • Elyes Gabel *Jaz* • James Buckley *Jamie* • Simon Webbe *Ronnie* ■ Dir Menhaj Huda • Scr Menhaj Huda, Gurpreet Kaur Bhatti, from a story by Huda

Eve's Bayou
★★★★ 15

Drama 1997 · US · Colour and BW · 104min

"The summer I killed my father, I was ten years old," begins this remarkable Louisiana-set drama, the promising debut of Kasi Lemmons. The hero/antihero is Dr Batiste (Samuel L Jackson), a loving father and womanising local physician who, one summer night in 1962, is not discreet enough in his philandering. Jackson is a charismatic presence, but the focus is on the women of the family, and Lemmons's impressive screenplay and direction allow her female cast to shine. TH Swearing.

Samuel L Jackson *Louis Batiste* • Lynn Whitfield *Roz Batiste* • Debbi Morgan *Mozelle Batiste Delacroix* • Vondie Curtis-Hall *Julian Grayraven* • Branford Marsalis *Harry Delacroix* • Lisa Nicole Carson *Matty Mereaux* • Meagan Good *Cisely Batiste* • Jurnee Smollett *Eve Batiste* ■ Dir/Scr Kasi Lemmons

The Evictors
★★ 18

Horror 1979 · US · Colour · 88min

When city newlyweds rent a lonely farm in an isolated village in Arizona, the locals view them with distrust, while it appears the previous owners are refusing to stay buried. Director Charles B Pierce generates a convincing sense of place and community amid the requisite splatter, and the final twist is just good enough to catch you off guard. RS

Vic Morrow *Jake Rudd* • Michael Parks *Ben Watkins* • Jessica Harper *Ruth Watkins* • Sue Ane Langdon *Olie Gibson* • Dennis Fimple *Bumford* • Bill Thurman *Preacher Higgins* • Jimmy Clem *Buckner* • Harry Thomasson *Wheeler* ■ Dir Charles B Pierce • Scr Charles B Pierce, Paul Fisk, Garry Rusoff

Evidence of Blood
★★★ 15

Mystery thriller 1998 · US · Colour · 104min

David Strathairn and Mary McDonnell, a memorable pairing in John Sayles's Oscar-nominated *Passion Fish*, are reunited for this fine made-for-TV thriller set in the Deep South. Award-winning writer Strathairn returns to his home town and finds himself involved in a 40-year-old murder case for which a local man was sent to the electric chair. Director Andrew Mondshein sets a leisurely pace and the film works all the better for it. JF

David Strathairn *Jackson Kinley* • Mary McDonnell *Dora Overton* • Sean McCann *Theodore Warfield* • Chris Wiggins *Horace Talbott* • Jackie Burroughs *Granny Dollar* ■ Dir Andrew Mondshein • Scr Dalene Young, from a novel by Thomas H Cook

Evidence of Love
★★★★ 18

Biographical crime drama 1990 · US · Colour · 90min

This TV movie tells the true tale about a supposedly kindly, decent, devout Texas housewife who beat her best friend to death with an axe. The build-up and backdrop to this grim event are filtered through the trial with tremendous insight and a hefty dramatic punch by director Stephen Gyllenhaal. However, it is Barbara Hershey's soulful performance you'll remember. JM *DVD*

Barbara Hershey *Candy Morrison* • Brian Dennehy *Ed Reivers* • John Terry *Stan Blankenship* • Richard Gilliland *Dale Morrison* • Lee Garlington *Peggy Blankenship* • Hal Holbrook *Dr Beardsley* • Matthew Posey *Norman Billings* ■ Dir Stephen Gyllenhaal • Scr Cynthia Cidre, from the non-fiction book by John Bloom, Jim Atkinson

Evil
★★★ 15

Period drama 2003 · Swe/Den · Colour · 108min

In 1950s Sweden, Andreas Wilson plays an unruly teenager who is sent by his mother to a strict boarding school. There he finds an institution run by a cadre of sadistic prefects whose violent bullying is all but ignored by the staff. Wilson is more than serviceable as the plucky teen who must stand up both for himself and his friend Henrik Lundstrom. But, while competently acted and directed, this doesn't reveal anything new. AS Swedish +subtitles. Violence, swearing. *DVD*

Andreas Wilson *Erik Ponti* • Henrik Lundstrom *Pierre Tanguy* • Gustaf Skarsgard *Otto Silverhielm* • Linda Zilliacus *Marja* • Jesper Salen *Dahlen* • Filip Berg *Johan* • Johan Rabaeus *Erik's stepfather* • Marie Richardson *Erik's mother* ■ Dir Mikael Hafstrom • Scr Mikael Hafstrom, Hans Gunnarsson, from the novel *Ondskan* by Jan Guillou

Evil Aliens
★ 18

Science-fiction horror comedy 2004 · UK · Colour · 93min

Jake West's carnage-strewn tale stars real-life presenter Emily Booth as a struggling cable TV host who takes her crew to a remote Welsh island to investigate a bizarre extraterrestrial abduction claim. The battle for ratings soon turns into a fight for their lives against alien invaders. Cheap and irrepressibly silly, the inept film falls over itself to get quick laughs, while Z-grade acting corrodes the picture further. SF Violence.

Emily Booth *Michelle Fox* • Jamie Honeybourne *Gavin Gorman* • Samuel Butler *Ricky Anderson* • Jodie Shaw *Candy Vixen* • Peter McNeil O'Connor *Jack Campbell* • Nick Smithers *Bruce Barton* • Jennifer Evans *Cat Williams* • Chris Adamson *Llyr Williams* ■ Dir/Scr Jake West

The Evil beneath Loch Ness
★ 15

Action fantasy 2001 · US · Colour · 82min

The Loch Ness Monster legend gets a farcically absurd overhaul in a rock-bottom monstrosity. Scientist Patrick Bergin is called in to investigate new sightings of Nessie and deals with the usual dire warnings from the locals and his ex-wife (Lysette Anthony). This tedious juvenile tosh has one pathetic special effect: the swimming monster repeated ad nauseam. AJ *DVD*

Patrick Bergin *Richard Blay* • Lysette Anthony *Elizabeth Borden* • Brian Wimmer *Case* • Lysa Apostle *Julie* • Dir Chuck Comisky • Scr Shane Bitterling, Justin Stanley

The Evil Dead
★★★★ 18

Horror 1981 · US · Colour · 79min

Director Sam Raimi burst onto the horror scene with this crude cult favourite that's short on story but long on excessive gore and innovative camerawork (future director Joel Coen was the assistant editor). An evil force tries to destroy five friends on vacation in a backwoods cabin when they discover an ancient Sumerian Book of the Dead. Cue all manner of vicious zombies, giggling ghouls and hideous demons going overboard in a relentless blood-splattering attack. The only way to kill them is to hack them to pieces, so sit back and watch the body parts and viscera fly in this essential 1980s horror. Currently being remade for a 2013 release. AJ Swearing, violence. *DVD* *Blu*

Bruce Campbell *Ash* • Ellen Sandweiss *Cheryl* • Betsy Baker *Linda* • Hal Delrich *Scott* • Sarah York *Shelly* ■ Dir/Scr Sam Raimi

Evil Dead II
★★★ 18

Horror comedy 1987 · US · Colour · 80min

Director Sam Raimi's thrill-packed heaven for gore-hounds starts with an embellished recap of the original film before spinning off into another possession tale, with hopeless hero Ash (Bruce Campbell) again trying to repel a nasty demonic onslaught. Flashy special effects, hysterical scare tactics and Three Stooges-style farce combine with Raimi's trademark dizzying camera angles and manic wit for a breathless rollercoaster ride through twisted genre conventions. A disappointing second sequel, *Army of Darkness*, followed. AJ *DVD* *Blu*

Bruce Campbell *Ash* • Sarah Berry *Annie* • Dan Hicks [Danny Hicks] *Jake* • Kassie Wesley *Bobby Joe* • Theodore Raimi [Ted Raimi] *Possessed Henrietta* • Denise Bixler *Linda* • Richard Domeier *Ed* • Jim Peaks *Professor Raymond Knowby* • Lou Hancock *Henrietta* ■ Dir Sam Raimi • Scr Sam Raimi, Scott Spiegel

Evil Dead
★★★★ 18

Horror 2013 · US/NZ · Colour · 87min

Fede Alvarez makes a terrific directing debut with a true reboot – not a slavish remake – of Sam Raimi's 1981 horror, which captures the spirit of the cult classic while tweaking the basic cabin-in-the-woods plot in all the right places. For starters, the five friends are in the remote forest to wean one of their number off drugs – her ravings about demons are seen as symptoms of cold turkey. Inspired as much by *The Exorcist* and recent Asian horror, while smartly embracing dialogue, humour and image similarities to (co-producer) Raimi's original, this maniacal nightmare pulls out all the stops in the top-drawer scare and hardcore gore departments. The energy drops off a little between the splatter but the twisted blood-storm climax makes this essential and memorable viewing for genre buffs. AJ Violence, swearing, brief nudity. *DVD* *Blu* *CS*

Jane Levy *Mia* • Shiloh Fernandez *David* • Lou Taylor Pucci *Eric* • Jessica Lucas *Olivia* ■ Dir Fede Alvarez • Scr Fede Alvarez, Rodo Sayagues, from the 1981 film

Evil of Frankenstein
★★ 12

Horror 1964 · UK · Colour · 83min

The third of Hammer's *Frankenstein* films (after *The Curse of Frankenstein* and *The Revenge of Frankenstein*) and the least interesting of all. Peter Cushing lends his usual conviction to the mad doctor part, this time bringing his brain-damaged creation back to life with the help of a mesmerist. Lumbering direction by Freddie Francis matches the gait of New Zealand wrestler Kiwi Kingston as the bolted one. *Frankenstein Created Woman* (1966) continued the series. AJ *DVD* *Blu*

Peter Cushing *Baron Frankenstein* • Peter Woodthorpe *Zoltan* • Sandor Eles *Hans* • Kiwi Kingston *Creature* • Duncan Lamont *Chief of Police* • Katy Wild *Beggar girl* ■ Dir Freddie Francis • Scr John Elder

Evil Roy Slade
★★★★

Comedy western 1971 · US · Colour · 97min

Penned by Garry Marshall and Jerry Belson, this underrated, made-for-TV western spoof is a splendid showcase for John Astin who, apart from his stint as Gomez in *The Addams Family* TV series, never quite fulfilled his comic potential. Timing every set piece and throwaway gag with equal precision, he revels in the role of the west's most loathsome bandit, who is determined to go straight and win the heart of schoolteacher Pamela Austin. Milton Berle and Mickey Rooney are standouts, while Dick Shawn nearly steals the show as a hilariously incompetent lawman. DP

Mickey Rooney *Nelson Stool* • Dick Shawn *Marshal Bing Bell* • Henry Gibson *Clifford Stool* • Dom DeLuise *Logan Delp* • Edie Adams *Flossie* • Pamela Austin *Betsy Potter* • Milton Berle *Harry Fern* • John Astin *Evil Roy Slade* • Pat Morita *Turhan* • Penny Marshall *Bank teller* • John Ritter *Minister* ■ Dir Jerry Paris • Scr Jerry Belson, Garry Marshall

Evil Spirits
★★

Mystery horror 1991 · US · Colour · 95min

Psycho undergoes a sex change, as batty landlady Karen Black is apparently bumping off her lowlife boarders and banking their social security cheques, while psychically conversing with her husband's wheelchair-bound, mummified corpse. Supposedly a gory black comedy, the only laughs to be had are unintentional ones, although the above-average celebrity horror cast will hold the interest of genre enthusiasts. AJ

Karen Black *Mrs Purdy* • Michael Berryman *Mr Balzac* • Arte Johnson *Lester Potts* • Virginia Mayo *Mrs Wilson* • Martine Beswick *Vanya* • Bert Remsen *Mr Wilson* • Mikel Angel *Willie* ■ Dir Gary Graver • Scr Mikel Angel

The Evil That Men Do
★ 18

Action thriller 1984 · US · Colour · 85min

With its numerous beatings and rapes, this repellent film surely ranks as Charles Bronson's most depraved picture – quite a feat! The stone-faced star plays a professional hitman coaxed out of retirement to deal with a torturer working in an oppressed South American country. Director J Lee Thompson suffers from muddled ethics – by taking the moral high ground, the film is guilty of revelling in the scenes of torture it supposedly decries. RS Violence, drug abuse, swearing, nudity. **DVD**

Charles Bronson *Holland* • Theresa Saldana *Rhiana Hidalgo* • Joseph Maher *Dr Clement Molloch* • José Ferrer *Dr Hector Lomelin* • Rene Enriquez *Max Ortiz* • John Glover *Briggs* • Raymond St Jacques *Randolph* • Antoinette Bower *Claire* ■ *Dir* J Lee Thompson • *Scr* David Lee Henry, John Crowther, from the novel by Lance R Hill

Evil under the Sun ★★★ PG
Murder mystery   1982 · UK · Colour · 111min

This is a typically polished whodunnit, which sees Peter Ustinov make his second appearance as the fussy Belgian detective Hercule Poirot. You won't use up too many little grey cells figuring out who is responsible for the murder of actress Diana Rigg, but there's enormous pleasure to be had from sitting through the picture while waiting to be proved right. Majorca looks hot, but it would have been nice if the producers had retained the original Cornish setting. DP **DVD**

Peter Ustinov *Hercule Poirot* • Colin Blakely *Sir Horace Blatt* • Jane Birkin *Christine Redfern* • Nicholas Clay *Patrick Redfern* • Maggie Smith *Daphne Castle* • Roddy McDowall *Rex Brewster* • Sylvia Miles *Myra Gardener* • James Mason *Odell Gardener* • Denis Quilley *Kenneth Marshall* • Diana Rigg *Arlena Marshall* ■ *Dir* Guy Hamilton • *Scr* Anthony Shaffer, from the novel by Agatha Christie

Evil Woman ★ 15
Comedy   2001 · US/Aus/Can · Colour · 92min

Released under the title *Saving Silverman* in the US, this crass comedy has a splendidly surreal premise: Neil Diamond is enlisted by flatmates Jack Black and Steve Zahn to save buddy Jason Biggs from the matrimonial clutches of bunny-boiling girlfriend Amanda Peet. All promise and precious little delivery, this is mean-spirited and overplayed. DA **DVD**

Jason Biggs *Darren Silverman* • Steve Zahn *Wayne* • Jack Black *J D* • Amanda Peet *Judith* • R Lee Ermey *Coach* • Amanda Detmer *Sandy* • Neil Diamond ■ *Dir* Dennis Dugan • *Scr* Hank Nelken, Greg DePaul

Evita ★★★ PG
Musical biography   1996 · US · Colour · 134min

Madonna's most successful foray into movies, taken from one of the most successful musicals of recent years, casts her as the woman who became mother-figure to Argentina through marriage to President Juan Perón (Jonathan Pryce). Director Alan Parker eschews explanatory dialogue to link the music, resulting in a curiously airless and enigmatic piece which never involves us in the traumas of Evita or Argentina. Antonio Banderas, meanwhile, co-stars as the Everyman revolutionary whose appearance and reappearance in Evita's life is never fully explained. TH **DVD**

Madonna *Eva Perón* • Antonio Banderas *Ché* • Jonathan Pryce *Juan Perón* • Jimmy Nail *Agustín Magaldi* • Victoria Sus *Doña Juana* • Julian Littman *Brother Juan* • Olga Merediz *Blanca* • Laura Pallas *Elisa* • Andrea Corr *Perón's mistress* ■ *Dir* Alan Parker • *Scr* Alan Parker, Oliver Stone, from the musical by Andrew Lloyd Webber, Tim Rice • *Cinematographer* Darius Khondji

Evolution ★★★ PG
Science-fiction action comedy   2001 · US · Colour · 97min

Ivan Reitman's lightweight but amiably daft science-fiction comedy features laid-back performances and a tongue-in-cheek approach, but it lacks wit and sparkle. Fortunately, it does boast the considerable comic charm of David Duchovny and Orlando Jones (as college professors), Seann William Scott (as an aspiring

fireman) and Julianne Moore (as a government scientist), while the loose Darwinian concept allows for an entertainingly mad menagerie of regenerated digital creatures. JC **DVD**

David Duchovny *Dr Ira Kane* • Orlando Jones *Dr Harry Block* • Seann William Scott *Wayne* • Julianne Moore *Allison* • Ted Levine *General Woodman* • Ethan Suplee *Deke* • Katharine Towne *Nadine* • Dan Aykroyd *Governor Lewis* ■ *Dir* Ivan Reitman • *Scr* David Diamond, David Weissman, Don Jakoby, from a story by Don Jakoby

Evolution ★★ 15
Horror mystery   2015 · Fr/Bel/Sp · Colour · 81min

Director Lucile Hadzihalilovic's aquatic fairy tale is a gender-swapped companion piece to her equally enigmatic and mystifying debut, *Innocence*. In a remote seaside village, pale-skinned mothers nurture their sons to pregnancy age with a strange diet and sinister hospital treatments. When ten-year-old Nicolas (Max Brebant) starts questioning this existence, his coming-of-age nightmare truly begins. Beautifully shot by Manuel Dacosse (*Amer*), this ambiguous odyssey piles on the ambient weirdness and avant-garde creepiness with little actual effect. AJ French +subtitles. Nudity.

Max Brebant *Nicolas* • Roxane Duran *Stella* • Julie-Marie Parmentier *La mère* • Mathieu Goldfeld *Victor* ■ *Dir* Lucile Hadzihalilovic • *Scr* Lucile Hadzihalilovic, Alante Kavaite [Alanté Kavaïté]

Ex-Lady ★
Drama   1933 · US · BW · 67min

Warners Bros gave Bette Davis her first "official" starring role, that of a woman with startlingly progressive attitudes to sex and marriage that moderate when love enters her life. Davis described the result as a shaming "piece of junk", critics and audiences agreed, and her official leading lady status was delayed for a year or two. RK

Bette Davis *Helen Bauer* • Gene Raymond *Don Peterson* • Frank McHugh *Hugo Van Hugh* • Monroe Owsley *Nick Malvyn* • Claire Dodd *Iris Van Hugh* • Kay Strozzi *Peggy Smith* ■ *Dir* Robert Florey • *Scr* David Boehm, from the story by Edith Fitzgerald, Robert Riskin

Ex Machina ★★★★ 15
Science-fiction thriller   2014 · UK/US · Colour · 103min

In the directorial debut of screenwriter Alex Garland (*The Beach*), computer programmer Domhnall Gleeson wins a competition to spend a week with the reclusive creator of the world's top search engine (Oscar Isaac). Gleeson's purpose once there is to perform a variation of the Turing test on an advanced AI (a strikingly sensitive Alicia Vikander) to see whether it has consciousness. The low-key set-up has the key players confined to an ultra-modern house and grounds, all beautifully rendered in a dreamy haze, and Garland keeps things compellingly cerebral, questioning in a satisfying way what it is to be human. EAS **DVD** **BL**

Domhnall Gleeson *Caleb* • Oscar Isaac *Nathan* • Alicia Vikander *Ava* • Sonoya Mizuno *Kyoko* • Claire Selby *Lily* ■ *Dir/Scr* Alex Garland

The Ex-Mrs Bradford ★★★
Comedy mystery   1936 · US · BW · 81min

A fast-moving screwball farce, this delightfully teams William Powell with the lovely Jean Arthur. The sophisticated Powell is a surgeon investigating a murder in which a black widow spider was the weapon. It's all good, clean fun, with a marvellous supporting cast of RKO regulars, notably cop James Gleeson and Eric Blore, typecast as a butler. It's not directed too well, but it's always a pleasure to view these stars. TS

William Powell *Dr Bradford* • Jean Arthur *Paula Bradford* • James Gleeson *Inspector Corrigan* • Eric Blore *Stokes* • Robert Armstrong *Nick Martel* • Lila Lee *Miss Prentiss* • Grant Mitchell *Mr Summers* ■ *Dir* Stephen Roberts • *Scr* Anthony Veiller, from a story by James Edward Grant

Exam ★★★ 15
Psychological thriller   2009 · UK · Colour · 96min

Eight job applicants face the selection test from hell in British writer/director Stuart Hazeldine's confident debut. A pressure-cooker exploration of the extremes of human ambition, it's a sci-fi tinged psychological thriller that plays like a dystopian take on TV's *The Apprentice*. Claustrophobic foreboding infuses the lean plot, as the disparate candidates (the most well-known face among them being Jimi Mistry) get 80 minutes in a guarded, windowless room to tackle a conundrum that unleashes the best – and worst – in their archetypal personalities. The overall result is an impressive calling card for Hazeldine, even if the climax lacks the impact promised by its ingenious set-up. SF Violence, swearing. **DVD** **BL**

Luke Mably *White* • Jimi Mistry *Brown* • Colin Salmon *The invigilator* • Nathalie Cox *Blonde* • Chuk Iwuji *Black* • Gemma Chan *Chinese girl* ■ *Dir* Stuart Hazeldine • *Scr* Stuart Hazeldine, from a story by Simon Garrity

Excalibur ★★★★ 15
Action fantasy   1981 · UK/US · Colour · 134min

Director John Boorman's vivid and passionate telling of the Arthurian legend is a thoroughly convincing visualisation of the Knights of the Round Table myth within Dark Ages history. Masterfully intermingling fable and magic with a gritty reality, Boorman explores the cosmic duality of good versus evil, paganism versus Christianity, mighty Merlin versus malevolent Morgana, with eccentric élan. The search for the Holy Grail and the final battle are simply stunning sequences, and, while the dizzying pace leaves scant time for proper characterisation. AJ Some violence, brief nudity. **DVD**

Nigel Terry *King Arthur* • Helen Mirren *Morgana* • Nicol Williamson *Merlin* • Nicholas Clay *Lancelot* • Cherie Lunghi *Guenevere* • Paul Geoffrey *Perceval* • Robert Addie *Mordred* • Gabriel Byrne *Uther Pendragon* • Liam Neeson *Gawain* • Corin Redgrave *Duke of Cornwall* • Patrick Stewart *Leondegrance* ■ *Dir* John Boorman • *Scr* Rospo Pallenberg, John Boorman, from the prose romance *Le Morte d'Arthur* by Thomas Malory

Excess Baggage ★ 12
Romantic comedy adventure   1997 · US · Colour · 96min

In the first film from her production company First Kiss, Alicia Silverstone stars as an annoying, spoiled brat who fakes her own kidnapping by locking herself in the trunk of her car. She then gets snatched for real when thief Benicio Del Toro steals it in this dire comedy adventure. Lacking in laughs, romance and action, the film plods along painfully, with only the reliable Christopher Walken injecting any entertaining moments. JB **DVD**

Alicia Silverstone *Emily* • Benicio Del Toro *Vincent* • Christopher Walken *Ray* • Jack Thompson *Alexander* • Harry Connick Jr *Greg* • Nicholas Turturro *Stick* • Michael Bowen *Gus* • Robert Wisden *Detective Sims* ■ *Dir* Marco Brambilla • *Scr* Max D Adams, Dick Clement, Ian La Frenais, from a story by Max D Adams

Excessive Force ★★★ 18
Thriller   1993 · US · Colour · 84min

Thomas Ian Griffith has always stood out from the ranks of action heroes as someone who can act a bit. He's never really crossed over into the mainstream but his thrillers usually deliver the goods, and this is no exception. He's helped by an outstanding supporting cast that includes Burt Young, as a gangster who murders Griffith's police colleagues in revenge for a drugs bust, prompting our moody hero to take the law into his own hands. JF **DVD**

Thomas Ian Griffith *Devlin* • Burt Young *Sal DiMarco* • James Earl Jones *Jake* • Charlotte Lewis *Anita Gilmour* • Tom Hodges *Dylan* • Tony Todd *Frankie Hawkins* • Randy Popplewell *Tony* ■ *Dir* Jon Hess • *Scr* Eric Rhodes

Excision ★★★ 18
Horror   2012 · US · Colour · 80min

Director Richard Bates Jr's high-gloss but surreal tragicomedy stars AnnaLynne McCord, who gives a raw performance as the awkward adolescent trying to fit into high school, please her demanding parents and find her place in life. She dreams of becoming a surgeon to help her younger sister who's dying of cystic fibrosis, but her angst-ridden delusions and medical fantasies eventually turn to psychosis, providing this challenging and creepy chiller with a nerve-shattering ending. With a cool cult cast (John Waters, Malcolm McDowell), smart cultural references, and graphic sex and gore, this suburban nightmare merrily runs the gamut from pitch black to ultra bizarre. AJ Swearing, sex scenes, nudity. **DVD** **BL**

AnnaLynne McCord *Pauline* • Traci Lords *Phyllis* • Ariel Winter *Grace* • Roger Bart *Bob* • Jeremy Sumpter *Adam* • John Waters (2) *Reverend William* • Malcolm McDowell *Mr Cooper* • Marlee Matlin *Amber* ■ *Dir/Scr* Richard Bates Jr

Execution of Justice ★★★ 15
Biographical crime drama   1999 · US · Colour · 98min

Anyone who's seen the Oscar-winning documentary *The Times of Harvey Milk* will not only know what a controversial impact he made on San Francisco after becoming its first openly gay supervisor in the mid-1970s, but will also be aware of the injustice that surrounded his murder. This is an earnest attempt to expose the "Twinkie Defense" miscarriage that enabled Dan White to get away with an eight-year sentence by proving he acted not from malice but the effects of a surfeit of junk food. It's necessarily verbose, but this TV movie is also played with conviction. DP

Timothy Daly *Dan White* • Peter Coyote *Harvey Milk* • Khalil Kain *Sister Boom Boom* • Tyne Daly *Goldie Judge* • Stephen Young *George Moscone* ■ *Dir* Leon Ichaso • *Scr* Michael Butler, from the play by Emily Mann

The Execution of Private Slovik ★★★★ 12
Second World War drama based on a true story   1974 · US · Colour · 116min

The 1970s was not only a golden age for American cinema but it wasn't a bad decade for TV movies, too, as demonstrated by this moving true-story drama about the first US soldier to be shot for desertion since the Civil War. Fresh from his break-out role in Terrence Malick's *Badlands*, Martin Sheen gives a heart-rending performance as personable petty thief Eddie Slovik, whose attempts to turn his life around through a job and marriage are thwarted when he's conscripted into fighting in Europe. This is heart-on-sleeve film-making from director Lamont Johnson, but it's Sheen's Emmy-nominated turn that firmly anchors the narrative. JA In English, French. **DVD**

Martin Sheen *Eddie Slovik* • Mariclare Costello *Antoinette Slovik* • Ned Beatty *Father Stafford* • Gary Busey *Jimmy Feedek* • Matt Clark *Dunn* • Ben Hammer *Lt Col Leacock* • Charlie Sheen *Kid at wedding* ■ *Dir* Lamont Johnson • *Scr* Richard Levinson, William Link, Lamont Johnson, from the non-fiction book by William Bradford Huie

The Executioner ★★ PG
Spy drama   1970 · UK · Colour · 105min

This convoluted spy drama finds George Peppard playing a British secret agent uncovering treachery within his department and collusion within the CIA. Peppard looks rather lost amid a cast of English stalwarts, while director Sam Wanamaker seems far more interested in scoring points about the British class system than concentrating on plot logic and suspense. AT

George Peppard *John Shay* • Joan Collins *Sarah Booth* • Judy Geeson *Polly Bendel* • Oscar Homolka *Racovsky* • Charles Gray *Vaughan Jones* • Nigel Patrick *Colonel Scott* • George Baker *Philip Crawford* ■ *Dir* Sam Wanamaker • *Scr* Jack Pulman, from a story by Gordon McDonell

The Executioner's Song
★★★ 15

Biographical crime drama
1982 · US · Colour · 135min

Tommy Lee Jones won an Emmy for his performance as Gary Gilmore, the murderous thief whose demand to be executed in mid-1970s Utah made him an unlikely anti-hero of the death penalty debate. Adapted by Norman Mailer from his own book, the action flits between Gilmore's life of crime, his romance with a teenage strumpet (Rosanna Arquette) and his courtroom battle to face a firing squad. But, for all its eloquence, the script fails to crack Gilmore's psyche. Moreover, director Lawrence Schiller struggles to reconcile the fact that his own part in this sorry saga is being re-enacted by a sensation-seeking showman. DP

Tommy Lee Jones *Gary Mark Gilmore* · Christine Lahti *Brenda Nicol* · Rosanna Arquette *Nicole Baker* · Eli Wallach *Uncle Vern Damico* · Steven Keats *Larry Samuels* · Walter Olkewicz *Pete Galovan* ■ *Dir* Lawrence Schiller · *Scr* Norman Mailer, from his non-fiction book

Executive Action ★★★★ PG

Political thriller
1973 · US · Colour · 86min

This drama about the Kennedy assassination in Dallas makes for absolutely riveting viewing. It shows how a shadowy group of businessmen and military leaders (including Robert Ryan and Burt Lancaster) plots to kill JFK, who has "gone soft on communism and the blacks". Brilliantly organised, the film describes how the shooters plan their kill as well as the search for a fall guy, Lee Harvey Oswald. It's as tense as *The Day of the Jackal*, only this time the question is not how does he fail, but how do they get away with it? AT

Burt Lancaster *Farrington* · Robert Ryan *Foster* · Will Geer *Ferguson* · Gilbert Green *Paulitz* · John Anderson *Halliday* · Paul Carr *Gunman Chris* · Colby Chester *Tim* · Ed Lauter *Operation chief, team A* ■ *Dir* David Miller (1) · *Scr* Dalton Trumbo, from a story by Donald Freed, Mark Lane

Executive Decision ★★★ 15

Action thriller
1996 · US · Colour · 127min

In this competent thriller, director Stuart Baird makes good use of the set pieces, diverting attention from the once far-fetched but now rather chilling plot in which David Suchet's gang of Arab terrorists is headed towards the US in a hijacked jumbo jet with enough stolen Russian nerve gas to kill millions of Americans. Steven Seagal and Kurt Russell share top billing as part of an elite team that sets out in a stealth bomber to defuse the situation. Mindless fun. JF Violence, swearing. DVD

Kurt Russell *David Grant* · Steven Seagal *Lt Col Austin Travis* · Halle Berry *Jean* · John Leguizamo *Rat* · Oliver Platt *Cahill* · Joe Morton *Cappy* · David Suchet *Nagi Hassan* · BD Wong *Louie* ■ *Dir* Stuart Baird · *Scr* Jim Thomas, John Thomas

Executive Suite ★★★★ U

Drama
1954 · US · BW · 104min

Cameron Hawley's novel about a boardroom battle for power seemed an unlikely subject for a glossy MGM movie. However, in the hands of editor-turned-director Robert Wise, this gritty drama is riveting, helped by an all-star cast. William Holden heads the corporate suits, and there's particularly strong support from Fredric March, Nina Foch and Walter Pidgeon. But what dignifies the whole proceedings is, uniquely for Hollywood, the absence of a music score. TS

William Holden (2) *McDonald Walling* · June Allyson *Mary Blemond Walling* · Barbara Stanwyck *Julia O Tredway* · Fredric March *Loren Phineas Shaw* · Walter Pidgeon *Frederick Y Alderson* · Shelley Winters *Eva Bardeman* · Paul Douglas *Josiah Walter Dudley* · Louis Calhern *George Nyle Caswell* · Nina Foch *Erica Martin* ■ *Dir* Robert Wise · *Scr* Ernest Lehman, from the novel by Cameron Hawley

Executive Target ★★★ 18

Action thriller
1996 · US · Colour · 91min

Essentially a series of increasingly spectacular car chases, this cheap and cheerful action thriller makes for entertainingly stupid viewing. Michael Madsen stars as the stunt driver who's sprung from prison by a shady organisation to help kidnap the president (Roy Scheider) when he's visiting Los Angeles. Keith David is splendidly over-the-top as the chief villain, while director Joseph Merhi just can't wait to smash up more vehicles. Great fun. JF Violence, swearing, nudity. DVD

Michael Madsen *Nick James* · Roy Scheider *President Carlson* · Keith David *Lamar Quentin* · Angie Everhart *Lacey* · Dayton Callie *Bela* ■ *Dir* Joseph Merhi · *Scr* Jacobsen Hart, Dayton Callie

Exhibition ★★★★ 15

Drama
2013 · UK · Colour · 104min

With this, her third movie, director Joanna Hogg is on home turf with a London-set story. Former punk rocker Viv Albertine and conceptual artist Liam Gillick play an artist couple, known only as D and H, who work from their austere modernist house. Tiny hints suggest the future is uncertain for these two, who seem to be selling the house in order to move on from something bad that happened. An uncompromisingly rarefied study, this takes patience, but for those inclined to embrace its minimalism it is haunting and brave. LF Swearing, sex scenes, nudity. DVD

Viv Albertine *D* · Liam Gillick *H* · Tom Hiddleston *Estate agent* · Harry Kershaw *Estate agent* · Christopher McWatters *Neighbour guest* · Mary Roscoe *Neighbour guest* ■ *Dir/Scr* Joanna Hogg

The Exile ★★ U

Historical drama
1947 · US · BW · 91min

Douglas Fairbanks Jr not only stars as the exiled Charles II; he also wrote the script and produced the picture. So what we see is evidence of a star's clout rather than his talent, since it's a poorly written piece of historical flummery that gives Fairbanks a number of women to romance while hiding from Cromwell's agents in Europe. As one would expect of director Max Ophüls, it contains some sensuous camerawork. AT

Douglas Fairbanks Jr *Charles Stuart* · Maria Montez *The Countess* · Paula Croset [Rita Corday] *Katie* · Henry Daniell *Colonel Ingram* · Nigel Bruce *Sir Edward Hyde* · Robert Coote *Pinner* · Otto Waldis *Jan* · Eldon Gorst *Seymour* ■ *Dir* Max Ophüls · *Scr* Douglas Fairbanks Jr, from the novel *His Majesty, the King* by Cosmo Hamilton

Exiled ★★★★ 15

Action crime drama
2006 · HK · Colour · 104min

Election director Johnnie To's action crime drama again revolves around Triad conflict, but is also close in spirit to the classic westerns of Sergio Leone and Sam Peckinpah. A sequel of sorts to his breakthrough hit *The Mission*, the story revolves around five gangster pals who are reunited in Macau. One of them (Nick Cheung) has been in hiding after a failed hit on his old boss (Simon Yam) and now has a price on his head. The other four have come either to kill or protect him. However, old loyalties eventually win out, setting the scene for a bloody showdown with their vengeful employer. Although To's direction is playful at times, the melancholy air recalls Peckinpah's *The Wild Bunch*, as do some of the stunning slow-motion set pieces. JF Cantonese +subtitles. DVD

Anthony Wong (1) *Blaze* · Francis Ng *Tai* · Roy Cheung *Cat* · Lam Suet *Fat* · Simon Yam *Boss Fay* · Richie Ren *Sergeant Chen* ■ *Dir* Johnnie To · *Scr* Szeto Kam-yuen, Yip Tin Shing

Exiles ★★★ 15

Road movie drama
2004 · Fr/Jpn · Colour · 98min

This amiable, exotic road movie won Tony Gatlif the best director prize at the 2004 Cannes film festival, but the film's spicy charms might not be to everyone's tastes. Romain Duris and Lubna Azabal are sitting round naked in their Paris flat one day and decide to make a pilgrimage to Algeria, where both their families hail from. En route, the two meet gypsies, seductive flamenco dancers and, once in Algeria, hostile locals. There's not really a lot of plot here, but Gatlif's camera lingers lovingly on his sexy stars and serves up big dollops of funky, world music on the soundtrack. LF French, Arabic, Romany, Spanish +subtitles. Nudity, sex scenes. DVD

Romain Duris *Zano* · Lubna Azabal *Naima* · Leila Makhlouf *Leila* · Habib Cheik *Habib* · Zouhir Gacem *Said* ■ *Dir/Scr* Tony Gatlif

eXistenZ ★★★★ 15

Futuristic thriller
1999 · Can/UK · Colour · 96min

It seems that David Cronenberg cannot shake off his obsession with "body horror". Though this futuristic virtual-reality thriller sidesteps the more explicit visceral gore of *The Fly* and *Videodrome*, it nonetheless involves pulsating computer-game consoles and handsets that plug directly into the flesh. Despite the usual high degree of visual invention and good lead performances from Jude Law (as a security guard) and Jennifer Jason Leigh (as creator of the eponymous game), the movie is not quite up there with Cronenberg's best. AC Violence, swearing. DVD

Jennifer Jason Leigh *Allegra Geller* · Jude Law *Ted Pikul* · Ian Holm *Kiri Vinokur* · Don McKellar *Yevgeny Nourish* · Callum Keith Rennie *Hugo Carlaw* · Sarah Polley *Merle* · Christopher Eccleston *Levi* · Willem Dafoe *Gas* ■ *Dir/Scr* David Cronenberg · *Cinematographer* Peter Suschitzky

Exit through the Gift Shop ★★★★★★ 15

Documentary
2010 · UK · Colour and BW · 82min

Whether he directed it or not, and whether it's even "true" or not, the film debut of guerrilla artist Banksy provides the perfect showcase for his dark, subversive wit. Using talking heads, archive footage and a voiceover from Rhys Ifans, this documentary-within-a-documentary finds a disguised Banksy recalling how he became involved with LA-based Frenchman and fan of street art Thierry Guetta. Slick, sharp and fantastically entertaining, this is a film that works not just as a cautionary tale about the pitfalls of helping strangers but also as a crafty meditation on art, its true value and our own gullibility. DW DVD Blu

Rhys Ifans *Narrator* · Thierry Guetta ■ *Dir* A Banksy Film [Banksy] · *Music* Geoff Barrow, Roni Size

Exit to Eden ★ 18

Sex comedy
1994 · US · Colour · 109min

This unfunny sex comedy is only worth catching if you can stomach the sight of Dan Aykroyd in bondage gear. Aykroyd and Rosie O'Donnell play a pair of investigators going "undercover" at an S&M resort run by Dana Delany, while *Strictly Ballroom* star Paul Mercurio wanders around in something resembling a nappy. A career low for all. JB DVD

Dana Delany *Lisa Emerson* · Paul Mercurio *Elliot Slater* · Rosie O'Donnell *Sheila* · Dan Aykroyd *Fred* · Hector Elizondo *Martin Halifax* · Stuart Wilson (1) *Omar* · Iman *Nina* ■ *Dir* Garry Marshall · *Scr* Deborah Amelon, Bob Brunner, from the novel by Anne Rice

Exit Wounds ★★ 18

Action drama
2001 · US/Aus · Colour · 97min

Action star Steven Seagal, looking far from the svelte fast-moving hero he should be, plays a disgraced cop who is transferred to a tough inner city precinct, where he discovers his new colleagues are selling heroin to drug dealers. Seagal's performance in this comeback film is typically wooden, and the Toronto locations are hardly convincing as Detroit. However, rapper DMX provides some relief from the usual shenanigans. JF Swearing, violence, nudity. DVD

Steven Seagal *Orin Boyd* · DM X *Latrell Walker* · Isaiah Washington *George Clark* · Anthony Anderson *TK* · Michael Jai White *Strutt* · Bill Duke *Hinges* · Jill Hennessy *Annette Mulcahy* · Tom Arnold *Henry Wayne* ■ *Dir* Andrzej Bartkowiak · *Scr* Ed Horowitz, Richard D'Ovidio, from the novel by John Westermann

Exodus ★★★★ PG

Epic drama
1960 · US · Colour · 199min

Leon Uris's bestseller gets the Otto Preminger treatment in this accomplished, epic retelling of events leading to the birth of Israel in 1948. With a script by former blacklistee Dalton Trumbo, this is a gritty, forthright and marvellously cinematic experience, if a long one. Some critics weren't happy about the all-star cast, though it's hard to imagine better than Paul Newman or Eva Marie Saint as nurse Kitty Fremont. Sal Mineo was nominated for best supporting actor as freedom fighter Dov Landau, but the Oscar went to Ernest Gold's grandiose music, which has achieved classic status. TS Some violence DVD

Paul Newman *Ari Ben Canaan* · Eva Marie Saint *Kitty Fremont* · Ralph Richardson *Gen Sutherland* · Peter Lawford *Maj Caldwell* · Lee J Cobb *Barak Ben Canaan* · Sal Mineo *Dov Landau* · John Derek *Taha* · Hugh Griffith *Mandria* · Gregory Ratoff *Lakavitch* ■ *Dir* Otto Preminger · *Scr* Dalton Trumbo, from the novel by Leon Uris

Exodus: Gods and Kings ★★★ 12

Biblical epic
2014 · UK/US · Colour · 144min

Gladiator meets *The Ten Commandments* in Ridley Scott's inconsistent slog through the Old Testament. But this grand-scale adventure lacks the awe of the pious epics of yesteryear thanks to laughable scripting and camp performances. Christian Bale is a commanding presence as Moses who is exiled from Egypt by King Ramses (an unconvincing Joel Edgerton). Ten spectacular plagues and the Passover later, the new prophet leads his people to the Promised Land. Scott gives the story a modern thriller edge and visually resplendent, high-end CGI but the excitement is dampened by a draggy middle and a tedious epilogue. AJ Some violence. DVD Blu

Christian Bale *Moses* · Joel Edgerton *Ramses* · John Turturro *Seti* · Aaron Paul *Joshua* · Ben Mendelsohn *Hegep* · Sigourney Weaver *Tuya* · Ben Kingsley *Nun* ■ *Dir* Ridley Scott · *Scr* Bill Collage, Adam Cooper, Steven Zaillian

The Exorcism of Emily Rose ★★★ 15

Horror drama based on a true story
2005 · US · Colour · 114min

Director Scott Derrickson's unusually intelligent chiller - loosely based on the 1970s case of German teenager Anneliese Michel - stars Laura Linney as an ambitious defence lawyer who takes on the case of a Catholic priest (Tom Wilkinson) charged with negligent homicide. Was Emily Rose (Jennifer Carpenter) demonically possessed when she died or was it just a psychotic-epileptic disorder as church-going prosecutor Campbell Scott claims? This believable spine-tingler is also a compelling courtroom drama. AJ DVD Blu

Laura Linney *Erin Bruner* · Tom Wilkinson *Father Richard Moore* · Campbell Scott *Ethan Thomas* · Colm Feore *Karl Gunderson* · Jennifer Carpenter *Emily Rose* · Mary Beth Hurt *Judge Brewster* · Henry Czerny *Dr Briggs* · Shohreh Aghdashloo *Dr Adani* ■ *Dir* Scott Derrickson · *Scr* Paul Harris Boardman, Scott Derrickson

LANDMARK FILM
With its ten Oscar nominations, William Friedkin's demonic frightener legitimises the horror genre overnight

The Exorcist ★★★★★ 18

Horror
1973 · US · Colour · 116min

One of the most talked-about and reviled horror movies of all time. Unbelievably scary when it first came out, its overall impact has been lessened by time and repeated genre duplication. But the macabre, obscene demonstrations of manifest evil still retain their power to startle and nauseate, particularly Linda Blair's "head-turning" antics as the possessed child. Aside from the graphic and revolutionary special effects, director William Friedkin dwells on the allegorical religious subtleties, making this a richly satisfying experience for horror aficionados. Special mention should go to Robert Knudson and Chris Newman, for their marvellous, Oscar-winning use of sound. AJ Violence, swearing, sexual references. **DVD** **BL**

Ellen Burstyn *Mrs MacNeil* • Max von Sydow *Father Merrin* • Lee J Cobb *Lieutenant Kinderman* • Jason Miller *Father Karras* • Linda Blair *Regan MacNeil* • Kitty Winn *Sharon* • Jack MacGowran *Burke Dennings* • Reverend William O'Malley *Father Dyer* • Wallace Rooney *Bishop* • Mercedes McCambridge *Voice of the Demon* ■ *Dir* William Friedkin • *Scr* William Peter Blatty, from his novel • *Cinematographer* Owen Roizman • *Art Director* Bill Malley • *Make-up* Dick Smith • *Sound* Robert Knudsen, Chris Newman (2)

Exorcist II: The Heretic ★★★ 18

Horror 1977 · US · Colour · 112min

The jury is still out on this critical and financial disaster, tampered with by the studio after audiences cracked up at the devilish finale. The focus here is on the quest of Father Richard Burton to quell the demon still present within Linda Blair, now in therapy to combat recurring nightmares. Yes, Burton overplays the doom-laden script. And, yes, all the African mumbo jumbo is bewildering. But director John Boorman deliberately accents the weighty mythological angles to create a film as complex and intellectual as it is visceral, and his daring approach is overdue for reappraisal. AJ **DVD**

Linda Blair *Regan MacNeil* • Richard Burton *Father Lamont* • Louise Fletcher *Dr Gene Tuskin* • Max von Sydow *Father Merrin* • Kitty Winn *Sharon* • Paul Henreid *The Cardinal* • James Earl Jones *Older Kokumo* • Ned Beatty *Edwards* ■ *Dir* John Boorman • *Scr* William Goodhart, from characters by William Peter Blatty

The Exorcist III ★★★ 15

Horror 1990 · US · Colour · 105min

Director William Peter Blatty's official sequel to his original story is an intellectual suspense chiller. Lieutenant Kinderman (George C Scott replacing Lee J Cobb from the original terror classic) investigates a series of sacrilegious murders by the Gemini Killer, who may be a servant of the Devil. Relying heavily on static shots, elongated close-ups and academic dialogue to convey the real horror of life, sin and unbelief, Blatty's film is full of unexpected surprises, quirkiness and one absolutely frightening moment of pure shock. AJ **DVD**

George C Scott *Lieutenant William Kinderman* • Ed Flanders *Father Dyer* • Brad Dourif *The Gemini Killer* • Jason Miller *Patient X* • Nicol Williamson *Father Morning* • Nancy Fish *Nurse Allerton* • Samuel L Jackson *Dream blind man* ■ *Dir* William Peter Blatty • *Scr* William Peter Blatty, from his novel *Legion*

Exorcist: the Beginning ★ 15

Horror 2004 · US · Colour · 108min

This sloppy prequel is the crudest of shockers. Paul Schrader was removed as director after his cut was deemed too cerebral, but could it have been worse than Renny Harlin's bad B-movie? Future Georgetown exorcist Father Merrin (Stellan Skarsgård) loses his faith during the Nazi occupation of Holland and rediscovers it in a remote area of Kenya in 1949. The cast fails to rise above the clichéd gruesomeness. Schrader's version was released in 2005 under the title *Dominion: Prequel to the Exorcist*. AJ Violence. **DVD**

Stellan Skarsgård *Father Lankester Merrin* • James D'Arcy *Father Francis* • Izabella Scorupco *Dr Sarah Novack* • Remy Sweeney *Joseph* • Julian Wadham *Major Granville* • Andrew French *Chuma* • Ralph Brown (2) *Sergeant Major* • Ben Cross *Semelier* • Alan Ford *Jeffries* ■ *Dir* Renny Harlin • *Scr* Alexi Hawley, from a story by William Wisher, Caleb Carr, from characters by William Peter Blatty

Exotica ★★★★ 18

Drama 1994 · Can · Colour · 99min

Prying behind the façade of the respectable is director Atom Egoyan's stock-in-trade. In this pulsating study of need, isolation and fantasy, he effortlessly slips between past and present to create myriad plot strands that he finally ties together with a mastery few can match. The scenes within the strip club of the title drip with erotic tension, reinforced by the sinister DJ-ing of Elias Koteas, the seductive dancing of Mia Kirshner and the disturbing willingness of auditor Bruce Greenwood to succumb to her charms. Add in a smuggling operation centred on a pet shop and you have a truly provocative movie. DP Swearing, nudity. **DVD** **BL**

Bruce Greenwood *Francis* • Mia Kirshner *Christina* • Elias Koteas *Eric* • Don McKellar *Thomas* • Arsinée Khanjian *Zoe* • David Hemblen *Inspector* • Sarah Polley *Tracey* • Victor Garber *Harold* ■ *Dir/Scr* Atom Egoyan

The Expatriate ★★ 15

Action thriller 2012 · US/Can/Bel/UK · Colour · 100min

This solid chase thriller uses a template that recalls *Taken*, without ever reaching the same heights. The always watchable Aaron Eckhart plays an ex-CIA agent and security systems specialist whose personal and professional life is suddenly erased. With his moody teenage daughter (Liana Liberato) in tow, he strives to find out who is behind this mess, and crosses paths with former Bond girl Olga Kurylenko along the way. The movie is unevenly paced and the plot overly complicated, but there are committed performances from Eckhart and the talented Liberato. DA Violence. **DVD** **BL**

Aaron Eckhart *Ben Logan* • Olga Kurylenko *Anna Brandt* • Liana Liberato *Amy* • Neil Napier *Derek Kohler* • Kate Linder *Principal Gibbins* ■ *Dir* Philipp Stölzl • *Scr* Arash Amel

The Expendables ★★ 18

Action adventure 2010 · US · Colour · 99min

Writer and director Sylvester Stallone recruits a who's-who of action hero pals for this over-the-top shoot-'em-up. When a mission in South America goes awry, mercenary Stallone enlists Jason Statham, Jet Li, Terry Crews and Randy Couture for an explosive showdown. The cast only temporarily distracts from the clichéd dialogue and a plot riddled with holes, while a fleeting joint cameo by Bruce Willis and Arnold Schwarzenegger does little to help. TeS Violence, swearing. **DVD** **BL**

Sylvester Stallone *Barney Ross* • Jason Statham *Lee Christmas* • Jet Li *Yin Yang* • Eric Roberts *James Munroe* • Dolph Lundgren *Gunnar Jensen* • Giselle Itie *Sandra* • Mickey Rourke *Tool* • Bruce Willis *Mr Church* • Arnold Schwarzenegger *Trench* ■ *Dir* Sylvester Stallone • *Scr* Sylvester Stallone, David Callaham, from a story by Callaham

The Expendables 2 ★★★ 15

Action adventure 2012 · US · Colour · 98min

With Simon West (*Con Air*) at the helm, and Jean-Claude Van Damme and Chuck Norris added to the action-man stew, this sequel is much better than the original film. A well-cast Van Damme plays the villain (called Jean Vilain) who plans to change the balance of world power by selling plutonium to the highest bidder. The nonstop mayhem includes cartoonish battles, geysers of CGI blood and seemingly impossible stunts. The laughs come thick and fast, too, mainly at Arnold Schwarzenegger's expense, though he does get one of the best jokes in the movie. AJ Violence. **DVD** **BL**

Sylvester Stallone *Barney Ross* • Jason Statham *Lee Christmas* • Jet Li *Yin Yang* • Dolph Lundgren *Gunnar Jensen* • Chuck Norris *Booker* • Liam Hemsworth *Billy "The Kid" Timmons* • Jean-Claude Van Damme *Jean Vilain* • Bruce Willis *Mr Church* • Arnold Schwarzenegger *Trench* ■ *Dir* Simon West • *Scr* Sylvester Stallone, Richard Wenk, from a story by Wenk, David Agosto, Ken Kaufman, based on David Callaham's characters

The Expendables 3 ★★★ 12

Action adventure 2014 · US · Colour · 121min

Mercenary Sylvester Stallone retires his ageing longtime crew and recruits youthful hotshots when hired to capture ruthless arms dealer Mel Gibson. But when the new kids on the Glock are captured, the "Grey Team" must come to the rescue. There are more than a few dull stretches, the climactic duel is lame and the finale errs on the tedious side, but, on the whole, this is a winning mix of wisecracking banter and macho, take-no-prisoners attitude. AJ Violence, swearing. **DVD** **BL**

Sylvester Stallone *Barney Ross* • Mel Gibson *Conrad Stonebanks* • Jason Statham *Lee Christmas* • Antonio Banderas *Galgo* • Harrison Ford *Drummer* • Arnold Schwarzenegger *Trench* ■ *Dir* Patrick Hughes (2) • *Scr* Sylvester Stallone, from a story by Stallone, from characters by David Callaham

The Experiment ★★★ 18

Psychological prison thriller 2000 · Ger · Colour · 113min

This taut German thriller was inspired by the notorious 1971 Stanford Prison Experiment, in which college students were asked to take part in a two-week simulation of prison life. Director Oliver Hirschbiegel builds the tension brilliantly, only to dilute its intensity with unnecessary diversions and an unimaginative all-action finale. The feud between former journalist Moritz Bleibtreu and latent fascist Justus von Dohnányi soon descends into generic macho posturing. DP German +subtitles. **DVD**

Moritz Bleibtreu *Tarek Fahd, No 77* • Edgar Selge *Professor Dr Klaus Thon* • Christian Berkel *Robert Steinhoff, No 38* • Justus von Dohnányi *Berus* • Maren Eggert *Dora* • Andrea Sawatzki *Dr Jutta Grimm* ■ *Dir* Oliver Hirschbiegel • *Scr* Mario Giordano, Christoph Darnstädt, Don Bohlinger, from the novel *Black Box* by Giordano

Experiment Perilous ★★★

Period melodrama 1944 · US · BW · 91min

This clever but wordy suspense drama is expertly directed by the talented Jacques Tourneur. Insane husband Paul Lukas and glamorous wife Hedy Lamarr are embroiled in a psychological battle of wits, with George Brent as the psychiatrist trying to rescue Lamarr. Written and produced by Warren Duff, the movie is helped by the Oscar-nominated 1903 period art direction. TS

Hedy Lamarr *Allida Bedereaux* • George Brent *Dr Huntington Bailey* • Paul Lukas *Nick Bedereaux* • Albert Dekker *Claghorne* • Carl Esmond *Maitland* • Olive Blakeney *Cissie* ■ *Dir* Jacques Tourneur • *Scr* Warren Duff, from the novel by Margaret Carpenter

Experimenter: the Stanley Milgram Story ★★★ 12

Drama based on a true story 2014 · US · Colour · 94min

Director Michael Almereyda delves into the controversial research of social psychologist Stanley Milgram (Peter Sarsgaard), beginning in 1961 with Milgram's notorious "obedience" experiments when ordinary people were asked to deliver electric shocks to strangers. The question of compliance to authority then went global a year later with the Eichmann trial, yet instead of fame and fortune, Milgram ended up with a reputation for deception. Although Almereyda adds some interesting touches, dramatically this is still a bit of an arid experience. JA Swearing **DVD**

Winona Ryder *Alex "Sasha" Milgram* • Peter Sarsgaard *Stanley Milgram* • Taryn Manning *Mrs Lowe* • Anton Yelchin *Rensaleer* • Kellan Lutz *William Shatner* • John Leguizamo *Taylor* ■ *Dir/Scr* Michael Almereyda

The Experts ★ 15

Spy comedy 1989 · US · Colour · 89min

John Travolta spent a long time in the wilderness before Quentin Tarantino rejuvenated his career in *Pulp Fiction*, and this is an excellent example of the drivel he was making. This part-screwball comedy,

part-Cold War satire stars Travolta, Arye Gross and Travolta's now-wife Kelly Preston in a tale of slick city types inveigled into aiding the dreaded "Ruskies" in their secret project to replicate American suburbia. SH

John Travolta *Travis* • Kelly Preston *Bonnie* • Arye Gross *Wendell* • Deborah Foreman *Jill* • James Keach *Yuri* • Charles Martin Smith *Cameron* ■ *Scr* Dave Thomas • *Scr* Nick Thile, Steven Greene, Eric Alter, from a story by Steven Greene, Eric Alter

Expired ★★

Romantic comedy drama 2007 · US · Colour · 100min

Samantha Morton experiences the cruelty of love in this flimsy romantic comedy. Delivering another quirkily understated turn, she elicits viewer sympathy as a big-hearted LA traffic warden who begins dating an abrasive co-worker. Played with relish by Jason Patric, he's a sweary, conceited and entirely unrealistic chauvinist pig, who's so mean you wonder why Morton bothers with him. Writer/director Cecilia Miniucchi offers no explanations, merely throwing her leads into absurdly awkward situations that are more about malicious laughs than emotional insight. SF

Samantha Morton *Claire Barney* • Jason Patric *Jay Caswell* • Teri Garr *Mother Barney/Aunt Tilde* • Illeana Douglas *Wilma* • Anthony John Crane *Blue car owner* ■ *Dir/Scr* Cecilia Miniucchi

Exploding Sun ★★

Science-fiction drama 2013 · Can · Colour

A slumming-it Julia Ormond is one of the few recognisable faces in this rambling and laughably unrealistic disaster movie, that's cut down from a two-part TV mini-series. Tediously convoluted, with a needless mess of globe-spanning subplots, the overlong tale throws in everything but the kitchen sink to cook up some drama, as the maiden voyage of the world's first commercial space shuttle goes tragically awry. SF

David James Elliott *Don Wincroft* • Anthony Lemke *Craig Bakus* • Natalie Brown *Cheryl Wincroft* • Mylène Dinh Robic *Denise Balaban* ■ *Dir* Michael Robison • *Scr* Jeff Schechter

Explorers ★★★ U

Science-fiction adventure 1985 · US · Colour · 104min

This is a minor entry in the Joe Dante canon, but an amusing family yarn all the same. A pre-fame Ethan Hawke and River Phoenix team up with Jason Presson as a trio of kids who build their own spacecraft and set off on the adventure of a lifetime. The youngsters are uniformly excellent, Mary Kay Place and Dante regular Dick Miller stand out among the grown-ups, and the tone is unpatronising and unsentimental. JF **DVD**

Ethan Hawke *Ben Crandall* • River Phoenix *Wolfgang Müller* • Jason Presson *Darren Woods* • Amanda Peterson *Lori Swenson* • Dick Miller *Charlie Drake* • James Cromwell *Mr Müller* • Dana Ivey *Mrs Müller* • Leslie Rickert *Neek* • Mary Kay Place *Mrs Crandall* ■ *Dir* Joe Dante • *Scr* Eric Luke

Exposé ★★★ 18

Erotic thriller 1975 · UK · Colour · 79min

Director James Kenelm Clarke's erotic thriller stars Udo Kier as the novelist whose attempts to meet his deadline are hampered by a sexy typist with a hidden agenda (Linda Hayden) and his former girlfriend (played by 1970s sex starlet Fiona Richmond). Without much competition, the film stood out as a well photographed and reasonably well written (although completely illogical) example of the genre. After being saddled with being a British "video nasty", it developed a cult following. DM Violence, swearing, sex scenes, nudity.

Udo Kier *Paul Martin* • Linda Hayden *Linda Hindstatt* • Fiona Richmond *Suzanne* • Patsy Smart *Mrs Aston* ■ *Dir/Scr* James Kenelm Clarke

Exposed ★★ 15
Drama   1983 · US · Colour · 95min

Before *Reservoir Dogs* star Harvey Keitel became cool he appeared in this tepid thriller as a terrorist who crosses paths with jet-set model Nastassja Kinski when she's not romancing violinist Rudolf Nureyev. Kinski has travelled to the big city to become a concert pianist. Supposedly sexy and arty, this is neither. JB

Nastassia Kinski [Nastassja Kinski] *Elizabeth Carlson* • Rudolf Nureyev *Daniel Jelline* • Harvey Keitel *Rivas* • Ian McShane *Greg Miller* • Bibi Andersson *Margaret* • Ron Randell *Curt* • Pierre Clémenti *Vic* • Dov Gottesfeld *Marcel* • James Russo *Nick* ▪ *Dir/Scr* James Toback

Exposed ★★ 15
Drama   2016 · US · Colour · 102min

Standard police story meets arthouse social study in this New York-set tale whose release version was disowned by writer/ director Gee Malik Linton. The studio allegedly cut 25 minutes, changed Linton's title (*Daughter of God*), and then credited him using the name Declan Dale. Be that as it may, what's on screen is an ungainly offering, with Keanu Reeves making heavy weather of it as a detective looking into his colleague's death. Mildly intriguing at first, it gets bogged down in a self-consciously mysterious gloom in which very little happens. TJ Violence, swearing *DVD*

Keanu Reeves *Detective Galban* • Ana de Armas *Isabel de la Cruz* • Mira Sorvino *Janine Cullen* • Christopher McDonald *Lieutenant Elway* ▪ *Dir* Declan Dale [Gee Malik Linton] • *Scr* Gee Malik Linton

The Express ★★★ PG
Biographical sports drama   2008 · US/Ger · Colour · 124min

This schmaltzy sports biopic from director Gary Fleder puts a racial spin on the usual triumph-over-adversity formula. In 1961 American footballer Ernie Davis (known as "The Elmira Express") became the first black athlete to be named the most outstanding college player. Showing Davis's rise from freshman to running-back star through dozens of bone-crunching matches, *The Express* centres on a fine performance by Rob Brown, who invests the footballer with proud vulnerability as he's jeered at by rednecks and even some of his white team-mates. However, the real heart of the film is provided by Dennis Quaid's coach, who struggles with his own prejudices while growling mantras about winning games not trophies. JR *DVD*

Dennis Quaid *Ben Schwartzwalder* • Rob Brown *Ernie Davis* • Omar Benson Miller *Jack Buckley* • Clancy Brown *Roy Simmons* • Charles S Dutton *Willie "Pops" Davis* ▪ *Dir* Gary Fleder • *Scr* Charles Leavitt, from the biography *Ernie Davis: the Elmira Express* by Robert Gallagher

Expresso Bongo ★★★★ 12
Musical   1959 · UK · BW · 101min

This isn't only a fascinating snapshot of Soho in the skiffle and coffee bar era, but it's also one of the best musicals ever produced in this country. Oozing the easy charm and shiftless opportunism that had just served him so well in *Room at the Top*, Laurence Harvey is perfectly cast as the talent agent hoping to get rich quick through rookie rocker Cliff Richard who, for all his raw appeal, is also very religious. Val Guest captures the fads and fashions of the late 1950s, but it's Wolf Mankowitz's crackling script that gives the film its authenticity. DP *DVD*

Laurence Harvey *Johnny Jackson* • Sylvia Syms *Maisie King* • Yolande Donlan *Dixie Collins* • Cliff Richard *Bongo Herbert* • Meier Tzelniker *Mayer* • Ambrosine Philpotts *Lady Rosemary* • Eric Pohlmann *Leon* ▪ *Dir* Val Guest • *Scr* Wolf Mankowitz, from a play by Julian More, Mankowitz

The Exquisite Sinner ★★
Silent romantic melodrama   1926 · US · BW · 60min

Renée Adorée is a gypsy girl and Myrna Loy a "living statue" in this starring vehicle for Conrad Nagel. He plays a young Frenchman who eschews conventional society to seek liberation with a band of wandering gypsies. This is a silent collector's piece for admirers of Josef von Sternberg, here directing his third Hollywood film and his first for MGM. The studio disliked the film and extensive retakes were filmed by Phil Rosen, but the film still bears the hallmarks of Hollywood's master visual stylist. RK

Conrad Nagel *Dominique Prad* • Renée Adorée *Silda, the gypsy maid* • Paulette Duval *Yvonne* • Frank Currier *Colcnel* • George K Arthur *His orderly* • Myrna Loy *The living statute* ▪ *Dir* Josef von Sternberg, Phil Rosen • *Scr* Josef von Sternberg, Alice DG Miller, Joe Farnham [Joseph Farnham] (titles), from the novel *Escape* by Alden Brooks

Extension du Domaine de la Lutte ★★★★ 18
Drama   1999 · Fr · Colour · 115min

Dismissed in France for lacking the literary precision of Michel Houellebecq's cult novel, this is, nevertheless, a deliciously melancholic insight into the psyche of the bourgeois male, caught between the last flickerings of professional and romantic ambition and the resigned acceptance of middle-aged mediocrity. The byplay between the world-weary Philippe Harel and José Garcia's overeager IT virgin is keenly observed and superbly controlled. Harel's misanthropic musings give the film its sardonic charm DP French +subtitles.

Philippe Harel *Our Hero* • José Garcia *Raphaël Tisserand* • Catherine Mouchet *Psychologist* • Cécile Reigher *Catherine Lechardey* ▪ *Dir* Philippe Harel • *Scr* Philippe Harel, Michel Houellebecq, from the novel *Extension du Domaine de la Lutte* by Michel Houellebecq

The Exterminating Angel ★★★★ 12
Satirical drama   1962 · Mex · BW · 88min

Luis Buñuel turns his attention to another of his favourite targets, the middle classes, in this searing condemnation of convention and outmoded morality. Clearly revealing its surrealist roots, this blackly comic film ingeniously uses a nightmare dinner party to make the terrifying assertion that the bourgeois lifestyle is every bit as hideous and limiting as any concentration camp regime. Brilliantly played, this is one of Buñuel's most pessimistic films, and its chilling ending will leave you dumbstruck. DP Spanish +subtitles. *DVD*

Silvia Pinal *Letitia* • Jacqueline Andere *Alicia Roc* • José Baviera *Leandro* • Augusto Benedico *Doctor* • Luis Beristain *Cristian Ugalde* • Antonio Bravo *Russell* • Claudio Brook *Julio, majordomo* • Cesar Del Campo *Colonel* • Rosa Elena Durgel *Silvia* ▪ *Dir* Luis Buñuel • *Scr* Luis Buñuel, Luis Alcoriza, from the play *Los Naufragos de la Calle de la Providencia* by José Bergamin

The Exterminating Angels ★★★
Erotic fantasy drama   2006 · Fr · Colour · 102min

Jean-Claude Brisseau's poetic and sensual erotic fantasy drama is a very French treatise on capturing physical frisson on screen. While holding auditions for a thriller, Frédéric van den Driessche's middle-aged director discovers that an actress's orgasm wasn't faked, but was achieved thanks to the presence of the camera. He then decides to explore further into the phenomenon, but how far is he entitled go in re-creating erotic encounters for his camera before he trespasses into temptation? With as much satirically pretentious chat as scenes of graphic nudity, this is a real curio. DP French +subtitles.

Frédéric van den Driessche [Frédéric Van Den Driessche] *François* • Maroussia Dubreuil *Charlotte* • Lise Bellynck *Julie* • Marie Allan *Stéphanie* • Raphaële Godin *Apparition* • Margaret Zenou *Apparition* ▪ *Dir/Scr* Jean-Claude Brisseau

The Exterminator ★★ 18
Crime drama   1980 · US · Colour · 97min

For a straightforward tale of violent revenge, this is a surprisingly influential film in straight-to-video circles. Avenging Vietnam vet Robert Ginty was henceforth known as Robert "Exterminator" Ginty, and became quite a draw in his own right. Here Ginty is on the trail of the murderous gang that beat up his comrade. He finds himself using his brutal combat skills to tackle the CIA, the cops and the crime families who are all after his blood. Followed by a speedily produced sequel released the same year. JF *DVD*

Christopher George *Detective James Dalton* • Samantha Eggar *Dr Megan Stewart* • Robert Ginty *John Eastland* • Steve James (1) *Michael Jefferson* • Tony DiBenedetto *Chicken Pimp* • Dick Boccelli *Gino Pontivini* • Patrick Farrelly *CIA Agent Shaw* • Michele Harrell *Maria Jefferson* ▪ *Dir/Scr* James Glickenhaus

The Extra Day ★★ PG
Portmanteau drama   1956 · UK · Colour · 80min

Had this portmanteau picture been shot in Italy or France in the same period, the five short stories about the mundane lives of some movie extras would have been made with *bona fide* bit players rather than with a cast comprising a second division Hollywood star, a faded French siren and umpteen ubiquitous British character actors. Sid James comes closest to convincing us he's a real human being, but the trite tales and the bogus behind-the-scenes atmosphere render this merely a disappointing curio. DP *DVD*

Richard Basehart *Joe Blake* • Simone Simon *Michele Blanchard* • George Baker *Steven Marlow* • Josephine Griffin *Toni Howard* • Colin Gordon *Sir George Howard* • Laurence Naismith *Kurt Vorn* • Charles Victor *Bert* • Sidney James *Barney West* • Joan Hickson *Mrs West* ▪ *Dir/Scr* William Fairchild

Extract ★★ 15
Comedy   2009 · US · Colour · 92min

Office Space director Mike Judge returns to the work place for this puzzling morality tale. Jason Bateman plays the owner of a flavour-extract factory who is frustrated by his sex life with his wife (Kristen Wiig). Urged on by his bartender pal (Ben Affleck), Bateman hires a gigolo for his wife so he can pursue a sexy – but duplicitous – new employee (Mila Kunis). Add to the mix a horrific factory accident and the impending sale of the company and you have a bemusing black comedy that is as unfocused as it is unbelievable. KK Swearing, sexual references, drug abuse.

Jason Bateman *Joel* • Mila Kunis *Cindy* • Kristen Wiig *Suzie* • Ben Affleck *Dean* • JK Simmons *Brian* • Clifton Collins Jr *Step* • Gene Simmons *Joe Adler* ▪ *Dir/Scr* Mike Judge

Extralarge: Moving Target ★★
Detective drama   1990 · It/US · Colour · 88min

Best known for his partnership with Terence Hill in spaghetti westerns and comedy action films, Bud Spencer here finds himself pounding a Florida beat with former *Miami Vice* star Philip Michael Thomas. As private eyes in possession of a nuclear secret wanted by both desperate assassins and crooked CIA agents, it doesn't take a genius to work out that much tyre tread will be lost before it's all quiet on the waterfront. This was the first in a series of seven *Extralarge* made-for-TV movies. DP

Bud Spencer *Jack "Extralarge" Costello* • Philip Michael Thomas *Dumas* • Juan Fernandez *Rashid* • Vivian Ruiz *Mrs Martinez* • Lou Bedford *Sam* • Jackie Davis *Harry* ▪ *Dir/Scr* Enzo G Castellari

The Extraordinary Adventures of Adèle Blanc-Sec ★★★ 12
Period fantasy adventure   2010 · Fr · Colour · 102min

There's certainly a hint of Hollywood blockbuster about Luc Besson's adaptation of Jacques Tardi's famed French comic strip about a female adventurer. But a strong injection of Gallic eccentricity ensures plenty of deviation from the usual formula. The action begins in Paris, 1912, with a pterodactyl hatching from its egg in a museum and going on to menace the city. Louise Bourgoin's indefatigable heroine blends Indiana Jones's guile with a certain head-girl hauteur, and though much of the knockabout comedy and verbal wit is lost in translation, the sheer whimsy, enchanting Paris locations and deliciously ornate design work add to the appeal of a film that marches defiantly to its own beat. TJ French +subtitles. Brief nudity. *DVD* *Blu-ray*

Louise Bourgoin *Adèle Blanc-Sec* • Mathieu Amalric *Professor Dieuleveult* • Gilles Lellouche *Inspector Caponi* • Jean-Paul Rouve *Justin de Saint-Hubert* ▪ *Dir* Luc Besson • *Scr* Luc Besson, from the comic books *Adèle et le Bête* and *Momies en Folie* by Jacques Tardi

Extraordinary Measures ★★ PG
Drama based on a true story   2010 · US · Colour · 104min

This fact-based drama would be little more than a disease-of-the-week special but for the A-list status of stars Brendan Fraser and Harrison Ford. The story follows a medical company executive and father of three (Fraser), whose two younger children have a debilitating genetic illness. When the medical establishment fails them, he seeks out an irascible scientist (Ford), whose pioneering research may point to a possible cure. Fraser convinces as the distraught parent, while Ford plays the scientist as an icy professional. Keri Russell also acquits herself well in the thankless role of put-upon wife and mother. The film is nicely balanced between weepie and thriller, but ultimately this is TV-movie material with Hollywood movie actors. KK

Harrison Ford *Dr Robert Stonehill* • Brendan Fraser *John Crowley* • Keri Russell *Aileen Crowley* • Jared Harris *Dr Kent Webber* • Courtney B Vance *Marcus Temple* • Dee Wallace [Dee Wallace Stone] *Sal* ▪ *Dir* Tom Vaughan (1) • *Scr* Robert Nelson Jacobs, from the non-fiction book *The Cure: How a Father Raised $100 million – and Bucked the Medical Establishment – in a Quest to Save His Children* by Geeta Anand

Extraordinary Rendition ★★ 15
Drama   2007 · UK · Colour · 77min

This drama ploughs much the same detention-without-trial furrow as the same year's Jake Gyllenhaal/Reese Witherspoon political thriller *Rendition*, only with a British slant, and with rather more emphasis on the detention's after-effects. A teacher of Middle East extraction is snatched off the streets of London by shadier elements of the British security forces, and whisked abroad to a hell-hole prison for interrogation and torture. As the detainee, Omar Berdouni suffers manfully for his art, while Andy Serkis (Gollum in the *Lord of the Rings* movies) is nicely understated as his interrogator. It's a decent enough film, but rather overshadowed by its starrier American counterpart. DA Violence, swearing, sex scenes, drug abuse, nudity. *DVD*

Omar Berdouni *Zaafir Ahmadi* • Andy Serkis *Maro, the interrogator* • Ania Sowinski *Ewa* • Jimmy Yuill *Dean* • Hugh Ross *Solicitor* • Ehti Aslam *University student* • Nick Bartlett *Sergei Illyich* ▪ *Dir/Scr* Jim Threapleton

The Extraordinary Seaman ★★ U
Second World War comedy   1969 · US · Colour · 79min

David Niven was going through a rough patch at this point in his career and with this movie he hit a positive thicket. Alan Alda, Mickey Rooney and Jack Carter, on the run from the Japanese, find Niven living on a beached ship in the Philippines. Faye Dunaway joins the crew, which is consolation for nobody but her agent, as director John Frankenheimer seems unable to get to grips with the action. TH

David Niven *Lieutenant Commander Finchhaven* • Faye Dunaway *Jennifer Winslow* • Alan Alda *Lieutenant JG Morton Krim* • Mickey Rooney *Cook 3rd Class WWJ Oglethorpe* • Jack Carter *Gunner's Mate Orville Toole* • Juano Hernandez *Ali Shar* • Manu Tupou *Seaman 1st Class*

Lightfoot Star • Barry Kelley *Admiral Barnwell* ■ *Dir* John Frankenheimer • *Scr* Phillip Rock, Hal Dresner, from a story by Rock

Extraterrestrial ★★ 15

Science-fiction horror
2014 · Can · Colour · 96min

In this half-hearted mash-up of *The X-Files*, *War of the Worlds* and *Communion*, five college friends go on holiday to a remote cabin in the woods. Naturally they are unaware the area is a close encounter hot spot, and end up whisked aboard a standard issue UFO populated by clichéd space invaders. Revelling in its B-movie conventions to little dramatic effect, this intergalactic slasher is often unintentionally hilarious and even the presence of veteran character actor Michael Ironside can't elevate the campy stodge. The final shot is undeniably ingenious and witty – but it's a long haul getting there. AJ DVD ◄►

Brittany Allen *April* • Freddie Stroma *Kyle* • Michael Ironside *Travis* • Gil Bellows *Sheriff Murphy* • Melanie Papalia *Melanie* • Jesse Moss *Seth* ■ *Dir* Colin Minihan • *Scr* The Vicious Brothers

Extreme Close-Up ★★

Drama   1973 · US · Colour · 80min

Television reporter James McMullan, working on a series about invasion of privacy, gets sucked into the kind of sexual voyeurism he's seeking to expose when he spies on a woman in the block opposite him. Although the script by *Jurassic Park*'s Michael Crichton cleverly plays with *Rear Window* and *Peeping Tom* motifs, Jeannot Szwarc's direction can't elevate the material from superficial, seedy exploitation. AJ

James McMullan [Jim McMullan] *John Norman* • Kate Woodville [Catherine Woodville] *Sally Norman* • James A Watson Jr *Cameraman* ■ *Dir* Jeannot Szwarc • *Scr* Michael Crichton

Extreme Measures ★★★ 15

Mystery thriller   1996 · US/UK · Colour · 113min

In this silly but enjoyable *Coma*-style medical thriller, Hugh Grant stars as a doctor who uncovers dastardly deeds involving homeless patients at a big city hospital. Grant is out-acted and outclassed at every turn by co-star Gene Hackman, who chews up the scenery and spits it out as the revered surgeon who is Grant's number one suspect. Director Michael Apted's film contains no surprises, but it does have a few laughs thanks to Grant and Hackman (unintentionally and intentionally, respectively). JB Violence, swearing. DVD

Hugh Grant *Dr Guy Luthan* • Gene Hackman *Dr Lawrence Myrick* • Sarah Jessica Parker *Jodie Trammel* • David Morse *Frank Hare* • Bill Nunn *Detective Burke* • John Toles-Bey *Bobby* • Paul Guilfoyle (2) *Dr Jeffery Manko* • David Cronenberg *Hospital lawyer* ■ *Dir* Michael Apted • *Scr* Tony Gilroy, from the novel by Michael Palmer

Extreme Ops ★★ 12

Action thriller
2003 · UK/Ger/US/Lux/Can · Colour · 89min

This flick aims to be the ultimate action movie – celebrating extreme snowboarding – but our attention gets swept away by an avalanche of clichés. A film-making crew led by Rufus Sewell is in the Austrian Alps to record the ski stylings of gold-medallist Bridgette Wilson-Sampras, but then they spot a Serbian war criminal. Director Christian Duguay's narrative loses out to the obvious – including some rather fake-looking CGI effects. TH DVD

Devon Sawa *Will* • Bridgette Wilson-Sampras [Bridgette Wilson] *Chloe* • Rupert Graves *Jeffrey* • Rufus Sewell *Ian* • Heino Ferch *Mark* • Joe Absolom *Silo* • Klaus Lowitsch [Klaus Löwitsch] *Pavle* ■ *Dir* Christian Duguay • *Scr* Michael Zaidan, from a story by Timothy Scott Bogart, Mark Mullin

Extreme Prejudice ★★★ 18

Action thriller   1987 · US · Colour · 100min

Director Walter Hill, initially revered for his unravelling of the male psyche and his lyrical expression of violence (à la Sam

Peckinpah), has in recent years simply settled for violent action. He pokes wry fun here at the central clichéd conflict between two old pals who each end up on opposite sides of the law. Hill is also aided by two actors who exude tough-guy behaviour with ease: Nick Nolte as the Texas Ranger and Powers Boothe as the chum-turned-drug lord. JM Violence, swearing, sex scenes, drug abuse, nudity. DVD

Nick Nolte *Jack Benteen* • Powers Boothe *Cash Bailey* • Michael Ironside *Major Paul Hackett* • Maria Conchita Alonso *Sarita Cisneros* • Rip Torn *Sheriff Hank Pearson* • Clancy Brown *Sergeant McRose* • Matt Mulhern *Sergeant Coker* • William Forsythe *Sergeant Atwater* ■ *Dir* Walter Hill • *Scr* Deric Washburn, Harry Kleiner, from a story by John Milius, Fred Rexer

Extremely Loud & Incredibly Close ★★★ 12

Drama   2012 · US · Colour · 124min

Director Stephen Daldry tackles the aftermath of 9/11 in this earnest adaptation of the best-selling novel. It follows a nine-year-old New Yorker (Thomas Horn) who may have Asperger's, as he goes to obsessive lengths to comprehend the death of his father (Tom Hanks) in the World Trade Center. Horn carries the film with his detailed portrayal of an irritatingly precocious boy, and Viola Davis and Jeffrey Wright are also exceptional as strangers he meets on his travels. However, Max von Sydow eclipses them all with a deft turn as the boy's curmudgeonly companion. The conclusions drawn may test your patience, but the performances do draw you in. KK DVD ◄►

Tom Hanks *Thomas Schell* • Thomas Horn *Oskar Schell* • Max von Sydow *The renter* • Sandra Bullock *Linda Schell* • Jim Goodman *Stan the doorman* • Viola Davis *Abby Black* ■ *Dir* Stephen Daldry • *Scr* Eric Roth, from Jonathan Safran Foer's novel • *Cinematographer* Chris Menges

Extremities ★★ 18

Drama   1986 · US · Colour · 84min

Is *Extremities* controversial or exploitative? There's a large helping of both as Farrah Fawcett escapes a would-be rapist (James Russo) only for him to return and terrorise her. The surprise comes when she turns the tables on him, but this leads to a relentless catalogue of brutality that never truly tackles the sensitive subject at hand. JB DVD

Farrah Fawcett *Marjorie* • James Russo *Joe* • Diana Scarwid *Terry* • Alfre Woodard *Patricia* • Sandy Martin *Officer Sudow* • Eddie Velez *1st officer* ■ *Dir* Robert M Young • *Scr* William Mastrosimone, from his play

The Eye ★★★★ 15

Psychological horror thriller
2002 · HK/Sing · Colour · 95min

Directors Danny and Oxide Pang focus on a blind violinist in this superbly controlled chiller. Tapping into the terror of anticipation, the brothers unnerve us from the off with Lee Sin-Je's first blurred images of the world following a corneal transplant. However, it's the succeeding nightmares, shifting scenes and ghostly apparitions that prove to be the most disturbing and send Lee and counsellor Lawrence Chou to the Thai village where her psychic donor met her grisly end. With eye-catching effects and a tingling score, this is a stylish blend of the psychological and the visceral. DP Cantonese, Mandarin, Thai +subtitles. Violence. DVD

Lee Sin-Je *Man* • Lawrence Chou *Dr Wah* • Chutcha Rujinanon *Ling* • Candy Lo *Man's sister* • Pierre Ping *Dr Eak* ■ *Dir* Oxide Pang, Danny Pang • *Scr* Jojo Yuet-Chun Hui, Oxide Pang, Danny Pang

The Eye 2 ★★★ 15

Psychological horror thriller
2004 · HK/Sing · Colour · 94min

The Pang brothers' follow-up delves into the very interesting creepy-crawl space between western urban legend and eastern Buddhist undercurrents. Shu Qi is the pregnant woman cursed with the ability to see ghosts. Featuring the now standard girl-

with-long-dark-hair-over-eyes Asian cliché, the Pangs take a far more novel approach in introducing the unexpected apparitions accompanied by surprise sound effects. It's a tad too long, but crisply shot. AJ Mandarin, Thai +subtitles. Violence. DVD

Shu Qi *Joey Cheng* • Jesdaporn Pholdee *Sam* • Eugenia Yuan *Yuen Chi-Kei* ■ *Dir/Scr* Pang Brothers [Oxide Pang], Pang Brothers [Danny Pang]

The Eye ★★★ 15

Supernatural horror thriller
2008 · US · Colour · 92min

Yet another Asian horror movie is given the Hollywood treatment in this slick reworking of the 2002 shocker from the Pang brothers. Jessica Alba stars as a blind violinist who receives a double corneal transplant, only to be plagued by ghostly visions. Alba is appealing in her own wooden way, but everything else has an overly familiar ring to it – from the repetitiously-in-your-face spectres to their screeching sounds. A good-looking compromise that will work its second-hand spell on those unfamiliar with the original. AJ DVD ◄►

Jessica Alba *Sydney Wells* • Alessandro Nivola *Dr Paul Faulkner* • Parker Posey *Helen Wells* • Rade Serbedzija *Simon McCullough* • Rachel Ticotin *Rosa Martinez* • Chloë Moretz [Chloë Grace Moretz] *Alicia* ■ *Dir* David Moreau, Xavier Palud • *Scr* Sebastian Gutierrez, from the 2002 film

An Eye for an Eye ★★ 15

Martial arts action thriller
1981 · US · Colour · 99min

When this was made, Chuck Norris just about ruled supreme in the martial arts stakes, and, though he was no Bruce Lee, this is a serviceable enough vehicle for his talents. He is his usual monosyllabic self as the former cop who launches a destructive private war against the Triads after the death of his partner. Quite what Christopher Lee is doing here is anybody's guess, but there are enough set pieces to keep fans contented. JF DVD

Chuck Norris *Sean Kane* • Christopher Lee *Morgan Canfield* • Richard Roundtree *Capt Stevens* • Matt Clark *Tom McCoy* • Mako *James Chan* • Maggie Cooper *Heather Sullivan* • Rosalind Chao *Linda Chan* ■ *Dir* Steve Carver • *Scr* William Gray, James Bruner, from a story by James Bruner

Eye for an Eye ★★★ 18

Thriller   1995 · US · Colour · 97min

The casting of Sally Field as a gun-toting vigilante and Kiefer Sutherland as an out-and-out baddie gives novelty value to this revenge thriller from director John Schlesinger. Field plays a woman who is catapulted into a world of terror when her daughter is raped and murdered. Forensic evidence points to Sutherland, but when he escapes jail on a legal technicality Field sets out to exact her own form of justice. Field is perhaps a touch too mumsy to convince, but Sutherland clearly relishes playing a lowlife killer. JF Violence, swearing. DVD

Sally Field *Karen McCann* • Ed Harris *Mack McCann* • Olivia Burnette *Julie McCann* • Alexandra Kyle *Megan McCann* • Kiefer Sutherland *Robert Doob* • Joe Mantegna *Detective Sergeant Denillo* • Beverly D'Angelo *Dolly Green* • Darrell Larson *Peter Green* ■ *Dir* John Schlesinger • *Scr* Amanda Silver, Rick Jaffa, from the novel by Erika Holzer

Eye in the Sky ★★★★ 15

War thriller   2015 · UK · Colour · 102min

With his seventh crack of the feature director's whip, South African film-maker Gavin Hood (*Tsotsi*, *Ender's Game*) confronts the hot topic of drone strikes. Helen Mirren's steely colonel is the remote commander of a joint UK/US mission aiming to capture key terror targets. All the legal restrictions, political implications, tactical arguments and moral quandaries relating to remote warfare are fashioned into a narrative of nail-biting suspense, and there's humour from Alan Rickman, in his final film role, as a general acting as an

exasperated intermediary. EAS Swearing. DVD ◄►

Helen Mirren *Colonel Katherine Powell* • Aaron Paul *Steve Watts* • Alan Rickman *Lieutenant General Frank Benson* • Barkhad Abdi *Jama Farah* • Jeremy Northam *Brian Woodale* • Iain Glen *Foreign Secretary James Willett* ■ *Dir* Gavin Hood • *Scr* Guy Hibbert

Eye of God ★★★ 15

Drama   1997 · US · Colour · 79min

This labyrinthine tale of passion, violence and religious fanaticism in small-town America is held together by a simmering performance from Kevin Anderson, who leaves jail to marry Martha Plimpton, the burger waitress who's been writing to him during his sentence for assault. But cutting across this uneasy romance is sheriff Hal Holbrook's attempt to coax the truth from terrified teenager Nick Stahl, found dazed and bloodied. This plays fast and loose with the narrative structure, but it's worth staying the course. DP DVD

Martha Plimpton *Ainsley Dupree* • Kevin Anderson *Jack Stillings* • Hal Holbrook *Sheriff Sam Rogers* • Nick Stahl *Tom Spencer* • Margo Martindale *Dorothy* • Mary Kay Place *Claire Spencer* • Richard Jenkins *Willard Sprague* ■ *Dir* Tim Blake Nelson • *Scr* Tim Blake Nelson, from his play

Eye of the Beholder ★ 18

Thriller
1999 · Can/UK/US/Aus · Colour · 100min

In this stodgy combination of ersatz James Bond and sub-Hitchcock thriller, Secret Service agent Ewan McGregor is assigned to follow serial killer Ashley Judd. However, because the seductive assassin reminds him of his long-lost daughter, he darts all over the world obsessively spying on her. Stephan Elliott's farcical potboiler paints itself into far too many ludicrous corners, while McGregor does little with a thankless role. AJ DVD

Ewan McGregor *The Eye* • Ashley Judd *Joanna Eris* • k d lang *Hilary* • Jason Priestley *Gary* ■ *Dir* Stephan Elliott • *Scr* Stephan Elliott, from the novel by Marc Behm

Eye of the Cat ★★★

Thriller   1969 · US · Colour · 100min

Riddled with laughable lines and so many plot potholes that the story forever teeters on the brink of collapse, it's hard to believe that this rickety chiller was penned by Joseph Stefano, the man who wrote the screenplay for *Psycho*. What keeps you watching are the performances of the three leads, who play it with earnest conviction. Eleanor Parker particularly enjoys herself as the disabled *grande dame*, whose house full of cats thwarts the gold-digging ambitions of nephew Michael Sarrazin and his accomplice, Gayle Hunnicutt. DP

Michael Sarrazin *Wylie* • Gayle Hunnicutt *Kassia* • Eleanor Parker *Aunt Danny* • Tim Henry *Luke* • Laurence Naismith *Dr Mills* • Jennifer Leak *Poor Dear* • Linden Chiles *Bendetto* • Mark Herron *Bellemondo* ■ *Dir* David Lowell Rich • *Scr* Joseph Stefano

Eye of the Devil ★★

Horror   1966 · UK · BW · 95min

Controversial in its day, and extensively cut for American release, director J Lee Thompson's daft occult thriller concerns a French nobleman sacrificing himself to the grape gods to improve the vintage of his faltering vineyard. David Niven and Deborah Kerr add considerable authority to the silly premise. Warlock David Hemmings and witch Sharon Tate have their moments turning a toad into a dove and hypnotising the locals. AJ

Deborah Kerr *Catherine de Montfaucon* • David Niven *Philippe de Montfaucon* • Donald Pleasence *Pere Dominic* • Edward Mulhare *Jean-Claude Ibert* • Flora Robson *Countess Estell* • Emlyn Williams *Alain de Montfaucon* • David Hemmings *Christian de Caray* • Sharon Tate *Odile* • John Le Mesurier *Dr Monnet* ■ *Dir* J Lee Thompson • *Scr* Robin Estridge, Dennis Murphy, from the novel *Day of the Arrow* by Philip Loraine

U SUITABLE FOR ALL   **Uc** SUITABLE ESPECIALLY FOR YOUNG CHILDREN (DVD ONLY)   **PG** PARENTAL GUIDANCE   **12A** UNDER 12s TO BE ACCOMPANIED (CINEMA ONLY)

Eye of the Killer ★★★ 15
Crime thriller 1999 · UK/Ger · Colour · 96min

Kiefer Sutherland doesn't disappoint in this straight-to-video thriller as a detective who develops psychic skills that come in handy when he has to track down a serial killer. Not the brainiest of scripts, and some of the cast just turned up to pick up their pay slips, but fans of the genre will enjoy guessing the outcome. Also known as *After Alice*. JB Swearing, violence. **DVD**

Kiefer Sutherland *Detective Mickey Hayden* • Henry Czerny *Harvey* • Polly Walker *Dr Vera Swann* • Gary Hudson *John Hatter* ■ *Dir* Paul Marcus • *Scr* Jeff Miller

Eye of the Needle ★★★ 15
Second World War spy thriller
1981 · UK · Colour · 108min

This is an entertaining film version of Ken Follett's novel about a lethal Nazi agent who has somehow managed to infiltrate the lower reaches of the railway network during the war. This might seem an unglamorous base of operations from which to subvert the Allied war effort, but Donald Sutherland as the Nazi keeps the suspenseful story of murder, romance and intrigue on the right track. It's essentially a 1980s version of a 1940s spy yarn. PF **DVD**

Donald Sutherland *Henry Faber* • Kate Nelligan *Lucy Rose* • Ian Bannen *Percy Godliman* • Christopher Cazenove *David Rose* • Faith Brook *Lucy's mother* • Barbara Ewing *Mrs Garden* • David Hayman *Canter* ■ *Dir* Richard Marquand • *Scr* Stanley Mann, from the novel by Ken Follett

The Eye of the Storm ★★★ 15
Drama 2011 · Aus/UK · Colour · 114min

Director Fred Schepisi makes a bold bid to translate Nobel laureate Patrick White's intricately seething family saga to the screen and the result is highly entertaining and deceptively sharp in its dissection of age, gender and class issues. Charlotte Rampling is typically imperious as the Sydney matriarch whose ailments have prompted feckless actor son Geoffrey Rush to return from London and gold-digging daughter Judy Davis to abandon Europe in the hope of landing a legacy. Judy Morris's screenplay valiantly tries to be true to its source and, even if the direction is a touch haphazard, the performances are splendid, with Rush and Davis camping it up hilariously as the hypocritical siblings. DP Swearing, sex scenes. **DVD**

Geoffrey Rush *Sir Basil Hunter* • Charlotte Rampling *Elizabeth Hunter* • Judy Davis *Dorothy de Lascabanes* • Alexandra Schepisi *Flora* • Helen Morse *Lotte* • John Gaden *Arnold Wyburd* ■ *Dir* Fred Schepisi • *Scr* Judy Morris, from the novel by Patrick White

Eye of the Stranger ★ 15
Action mystery 1993 · US · Colour · 96min

Writer/director/actor David Heavener casts himself in the Clint Eastwood role as the nameless stranger who wanders into a small town. Corrupt mayor Martin Landau seems to be calling all the shots, but the stranger sets about bringing him and his cronies to justice for an unsolved murder. Many fights and meaningful shots of the stranger's boots follow. Inept and cliché-ridden. ST

David Heavener *Stranger* • Martin Landau *Mayor Howard Baines* • Sally Kirkland *Lori* • Don Swayze *Rudy* • Stella Stevens *Doc* • Sy Richardson *Jeb* • Joe Estevez *Sheriff* • John Pleshette *Joe* • Thomas F Duffy *Ballack* ■ *Dir/Scr* David Heavener

Eye of the Tiger ★★ 18
Thriller 1986 · US · Colour · 87min

Framed for a crime he didn't commit, Vietnam veteran Gary Busey goes home after his release from jail to take vengeance on the real culprits, biker drug-dealers led by William Smith. Wire decapitations, dynamite stuck in people's orifices and Busey's RV customised with cannons are the various methods of dispatch in this violent and unpleasant thriller. AJ Violence, swearing.

Gary Busey *Buck Matthews* • Yaphet Kotto *JB Deveraux* • Seymour Cassel *Sheriff* • Bert Remsen *Father Healey* • Jorge Gil *Jamie* • William Smith *Blade* • Kimberlin Ann Brown *Dawn* • Denise Galik *Christie* ■ *Dir* Richard C Sarafian • *Scr* Michael Montgomery

Eye Witness ★★★
Courtroom drama 1949 · UK · BW · 105min

Also known as *Your Witness*, Robert Montgomery's fourth credited directorial outing is a compact courtroom drama, laced with a little amateur sleuthing. Just about every scene contains a venerable British character actor, from wrongly accused war hero Michael Ripper to judge Felix Aylmer. But it's Montgomery's hotshot American attorney who dominates the proceedings, as he searches for the mysterious poetry-loving woman who can corroborate Ripper's plea of self-defence. Slow in places, but steadily directed, well acted and satisfying. DP

Robert Montgomery *Adam Heyward* • Leslie Banks *Colonel Summerfield* • Patricia Wayne [Patricia Cutts] *Alex Summerfield* • Felix Aylmer *Judge* • Harcourt Williams *Beamish* • Andrew Cruickshank *Sir Adrian Horth, KC* • Wylie Watson *Widgery* • Michael Ripper *Sam Baxter* ■ *Dir* Robert Montgomery • *Scr* Hugo Butler, Ian McLellan Hunter, William Douglas Home, from a story by Hugo Butler

Eyes in the Night ★★★
Crime drama 1942 · US · BW · 79min

This superior MGM thriller is a bit too polished to be a *film noir*. Starring avuncular character actor Edward Arnold as a blind detective, it's one of those formula movies offered to gifted new directorial talent, in this case the young Fred Zinnemann. The nominal star is Ann Harding, but Donna Reed shows she has real star quality. A sequel, *The Hidden Eye*, was released in 1945. TS

Edward Arnold *Captain Duncan Maclain* • Ann Harding *Norma Lawry* • Donna Reed *Barbara Lawry* • Allen Jenkins *Marty* • John Emery *Paul Gerente* • Horace McNally [Stephen McNally] *Gabriel Hoffman* • Katherine Emery *Cheli Scott* ■ *Dir* Fred Zinnemann • *Scr* Guy Trosper, Howard Emmett Rogers, from the novel *Odor of Violets* by Baynard Kendrick

Eyes of a Stranger ★ 18
Horror 1980 · US · Colour · 79min

Jennifer Jason Leigh stars in this voyeuristic and distasteful horror as the blind and deaf sister of TV anchorwoman Lauren Tewes. During the Miami summer, serial killer John DiSanti has been raping and murdering local women. Tewes discovers the killer is her next-door neighbour, and attempts to prove his guilt before he comes after her and the defenceless Leigh. Extremely exploitative. LH

Lauren Tewes *Jane* • Jennifer Jason Leigh *Tracy* • John DiSanti *Stanley Herbert* • Peter DuPre *David* • Gwen Lewis *Debbie* • Kitty Lunn *Annette* ■ *Dir* Ken Wiederhorn • *Scr* Mark Jackson, Eric L Bloom

Eyes of an Angel ★★
Adventure crime drama
1991 · US · Colour · 91min

John Travolta stars as a single parent, struggling to bring up his daughter Ellie Raab. Only released on the coat-tails of its star's post-*Pulp Fiction* comeback, this violent story follows Raab as she nurses a mobster's injured Doberman back to health, not realising that her involvement with the pooch will have her and Travolta fleeing Chicago. It really is no surprise to learn Robert Harmon's movie failed to find a distributor for four years. LH

John Travolta *Bobby* • Ellie Raab *The Girl* • Tito Larriva *Cissy* • Richard Edson *Goon* • Vincent Guastaferro *Goon* • Jeffrey DeMunn *Georgie* • Jacqueline Pulliam *Gloria* ■ *Dir* Robert Harmon • *Scr* Robert Stitzel

Eyes of Laura Mars ★★★ 15
Psychological thriller 1978 · US · Colour · 99min

Designed as a vehicle for Barbra Streisand (she sings the theme song), this ended up starring Faye Dunaway as the photographer who develops a psychic link with a killer and witnesses his gruesome murders while they are being committed. Co-written by John Carpenter, it's a standard slasher melodrama with a glitzy face-lift (her gallery photos were actually taken by Helmut Newton). It's decently done, but the surface gloss always wins out over any deeper psychological substance. AJ Violence, swearing, nudity. **DVD**

Faye Dunaway *Laura Mars* • Tommy Lee Jones *Detective John Neville* • Brad Dourif *Tommy Ludlow* • René Auberjonois *Donald Phelps* • Raul Julia *Michael Reisler* • Frank Adonis *Sal Volpe* • Michael Tucker *Bert* • Lisa Taylor *Michele* ■ *Dir* Irvin Kershner • *Scr* John Carpenter, David Zelag Goodman

The Eyes of Tammy Faye ★★★ 12
Documentary 2000 · US/UK · Colour · 78min

Fenton Bailey and Randy Barbato's portrait of American TV evangelist Tammy Faye Bakker Messner is like the lady herself – kitsch, melodramatic and endearingly camp. Narrated by celebrity drag artist RuPaul, it's an absorbing exposé of how she and her ex-husband Jim Bakker became the biggest names in the "electric church", only for scandal in the 1980s to destroy their multi-million dollar empire. With heavily made-up eyes often brimming with tears, Tammy Faye emotes her way through her turbulent life story, turning it into pure soap opera. Though her viewpoint is central, she doesn't hijack proceedings entirely, and there's plenty of talking head interviews and archive footage for balance. SF **DVD**

RuPaul *Narrator* ■ *Dir* Fenton Bailey, Randy Barbato

Eyes Wide Open ★★★ 12
Drama 2009 · Is/Ger/Fr · Colour · 92min

The life of a husband and father in an Orthodox Jewish community in Jerusalem is turned upside down by homosexual passion in this intimate Israeli drama. A controversial film owing to its subject matter and milieu, Haim Tabakman's directorial debut is also a very clear-headed one, respectful to the community's spiritual life and traditions yet never trivialising the feelings that swamp its central character. Arguably the approach is too low-key for the audience to share the heat of passion, but the film's point about the need for understanding is made with dignity and an appreciable tinge of sorrow. TJ Hebrew, Yiddish +subtitles. Nudity. **DVD** **BD**

Zohar Strauss *Aaron* • Ran Danker *Ezri* • Tinkerbell *Rivka* • Tzahi Grad *Rabbi Vaisben* • Isaac Sharry *Mordechai* • Avi Grayinik *Israël Fischer* ■ *Dir* Haim Tabakman • *Scr* Merav Doster, from her story

Eyes Wide Shut ★★★ 18
Psychological drama
1999 · US/UK · Colour · 152min

Full of trademark themes and characteristic compositions, Stanley Kubrick's final film is also his most fascinatingly flawed. With its style often resembling 1970s European art house movies, it lacks the morbidity to pass as a Buñuelian satire, while it is far too stately and serious to succeed as a commercial enterprise. Tom Cruise – as the doctor recklessly seeking a means of avenging his wife's fantasised infidelity – is too controlled for his character's fraught nocturnal adventures to be plausible. Nicole Kidman as his wife is less visible, though she simmers with the potential for erotic danger. Despite expectations, this is a disappointingly conservative conclusion to a career spent pushing back cinematic boundaries. DP **DVD** **BD**

Tom Cruise *Dr William Harford* • Nicole Kidman *Alice Harford* • Sydney Pollack *Victor Ziegler* • Marie Richardson *Marion Nathanson* • Rade Serbedzija *Milich* • Todd Field *Nick Nightingale* • Vinessa Shaw *Domino* • Alan Cumming *Desk clerk* ■ *Dir* Stanley Kubrick • *Scr* Stanley Kubrick, Frederic Raphael, from the novella *Traumnovelle* by Arthur Schnitzler

Eyes without a Face ★★★★★ 15
Horror 1959 · Fr/It · BW · 86min

This is one of the most haunting horror films ever made. Director Georges Franju made his name with a series of inspired documentary shorts, and it's the realism of his approach that makes his "poetic fantasy" so unnerving. There's nothing of the hammy Hollywood mad scientist in Pierre Brasseur, as he and assistant Alida Valli resort to murder in order to rebuild the face of his daughter, Edith Scob. Franju's control of atmosphere is masterly, Eugen Schüfftan's photography is outstanding, and Auguste Capelier deserves a mention for designing Scob's unforgettable mask. DP French +subtitles. Violence. **DVD** **BD**

Pierre Brasseur *Professor Génessier* • Alida Valli *Louise* • Edith Scob *Christiane* • François Guérin *Jacques* • Juliette Mayniel *Edna Gruber* ■ *Dir* Georges Franju • *Scr* Jean Redon, Georges Franju, Jean Redon, Claude Sautet, Pierre Boileau, Thomas Narcejac, from the novel *Les Yeux sans Visage* by Jean Redon • *Music* Maurice Jarre

Eyewitness ★★★ PG
Crime drama 1956 · UK · BW · 79min

Donald Sinden, a rather bland leading man on both stage and screen before this was made, successfully attempts a rather different role, conveying all the ruthlessness of the heartless killer as he tries to rub out the witness to a crime. He is effectively supported by Muriel Pavlow (as his intended victim), while director Muriel Box unfurls the suspense with good timing. JM **DVD**

Donald Sinden *Wade* • Muriel Pavlow *Lucy Church* • Belinda Lee *Penny* • Michael Craig *Jay Church* • Nigel Stock *Barney* • Susan Beaumont *Probationer nurse* • David Knight *Mike* ■ *Dir* Muriel Box • *Scr* Janet Green

Eyewitness ★★ 15
Thriller 1970 · UK · Colour · 87min

Why did a playwright of the calibre of Ronald Harwood bother himself with this adaptation of Mark Hebden's minor "cry wolf" thriller? It's hardly original stuff, and the threadbare plot leaves players a lot more experienced than Mark Lester looking forlorn. Lester is wincingly wide-eyed as the fanciful child whose account of a murder is disbelieved by all and sundry. DP

Mark Lester (2) *Timothy, "Ziggy"* • Lionel Jeffries *Colonel* • Susan George *Pippa* • Tony Bonner *Tom* • Jeremy Kemp *Galleria* • Peter Vaughan *Paul* • Peter Bowles *Victor* • Betty Marsden *Madame Robiac* ■ *Dir* John Hough • *Scr* Ronald Harwood, from the novel by Mark Hebden

Eyewitness ★★★ 15
Thriller 1981 · US · Colour · 97min

Shy night janitor William Hurt foolishly pretends to know something about a murder at his building in order to get close to TV newswoman Sigourney Weaver in this sub-"Hitch" cocktail of New York paranoia and fairy-tale romance from director Peter Yates. It's a slick and enjoyable thriller, with Yates deftly moving his classy cast through one mind-bending plot contortion after another and the suspense becomes truly nail-biting. The film may be more familiar by its British title, *The Janitor*. AJ

William Hurt *Daryll Deever* • Sigourney Weaver *Tony Sokolow* • Christopher Plummer *Joseph* • James Woods *Aldo* • Irene Worth *Mrs Sokolow* • Kenneth McMillan *Mr Deever* • Pamela Reed *Linda* • Morgan Freeman *Lieutenant Black* ■ *Dir* Peter Yates • *Scr* Steve Tesich

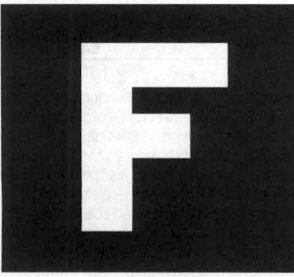

F
★★★★ 18

Horror thriller 2010 · UK · Colour · 75min

Writer/director Johannes Roberts's trim, tense and intricately constructed psychodrama derives its suspense from the sickening feelings of powerlessness he conjures for David Schofield's cynical, alcoholic English teacher. When he stays late at school one night, Schofield is forced to face his demons as the building comes under attack from a faceless threat intent on causing maximum bloody mayhem. The head-scratching climax aside, this is a chilling, if bleak, experience, with a superb central performance. AJ Violence, swearing. DVD Blu-ray

David Schofield *Robert Anderson* • Eliza Bennett *Kate Anderson* • Ruth Gemmell *Sarah Balham* • Juliet Aubrey *Helen Anderson* ■ *Dir/Scr* Johannes Roberts

The FBI Story
★★★★ PG

Crime drama 1959 · US · Colour · 142min

James Stewart gives tremendous credibility and heart to what is virtually a potted history of America's Federal Bureau of Investigation under its now notorious head, J Edgar Hoover. The device of telling the story through the eyes and exploits of one agent, who takes on everyone from the Klan to the Mob to the Nazi secret service, verges on the unlikely, but is colourfully told against the backdrop of Stewart's domestic life. Vera Miles is impressive as his wife, and there's a marvellous supporting cast. TS

James Stewart *Chip Hardesty* • Vera Miles *Lucy Hardesty* • Murray Hamilton *Sam Crandall* • Larry Pennell *George Crandall* • Nick Adams *John Graham* • Diane Jergens *Jennie, as an adult* • Jean Willes *Anna Sage* • Joyce Taylor *Anne, as an adult* ■ *Dir* Mervyn LeRoy • *Scr* Richard L Breen, John Twist, from the book by Don Whitehead

FDR: the Last Year
★★★

Biographical drama 1980 · US · Colour · 100min

Jason Robards stars in this reverential account of Franklin Delano Roosevelt's hectic final months, as he plays down a chronic heart condition to run for a fourth term as president, help co-ordinate the D-Day landings and plan for the postwar world with Churchill and Stalin at Yalta. The film really comes to life during the election battle, although the scenes with his super-efficient wife Eleanor (played by Eileen Heckart) and sympathetic mistress Lucy Rutherford (Kim Hunter) are also revealing. DP

Jason Robards *President Franklin Delano Roosevelt* • Eileen Heckart *Eleanor Roosevelt* • Edward Binns *General "Pa" Watson* • Augusta Dabney *Grace Tully* • Larry Gates *Admiral Leahy* • Michael Gross *Dr Howard Bruenn* • Kim Hunter *Lucy Rutherford* • James Karen *Admiral McIntire* • Nehemiah Persoff *Josef Stalin* ■ *Dir* Anthony Page • *Scr* Stanley R Greenberg, from the book *FDR's Last Year* by Jim Bishop

F for Fake
★★★ PG

Documentary
1973 · Fr/Iran/W Ger · Colour · 84min

Much of this sly treatise on deception was shot by François Reichenbach for a TV documentary on art forger supreme Elmyr de Hory. When news broke that his biographer, Clifford Irving, had also faked his life of Howard Hughes, Orson Welles jumped at the chance to use Reichenbach's footage and added to it sequences of prestidigitation, confessional pieces on his own chicanery and a marvellously convoluted story about Oja Kodar and some Picasso paintings. Welles opens the film by promising to tell the absolute truth for one hour. DP DVD

Oja Kodar *The Girl* • Orson Welles • Joseph Cotten *The Guest* ■ *Dir* Orson Welles • *Scr* Orson Welles

FM
★★

Music drama 1977 · US · Colour · 104min

It tells you something when a soundtrack album ends up being more popular than the film it's taken from. Such was the case for John A Alonzo's debut feature, a sketch-driven take on life at a progressive rock station in 1970s Los Angeles. Michael Brandon stars as a DJ determined to keep commercialism at bay, who leads a revolt when the playlist becomes too square for his liking. Amiable enough, but a deeply flawed product. RS

Michael Brandon *Jeff Dugan* • Eileen Brennan *Mother* • Alex Karras *Doc Holiday* • Cleavon Little *Prince* • Martin Mull *Eric Swan* • Cassie Yates *Laura Coe* • Norman Lloyd *Carl Billings* • James Keach *Lieutenant Reach* • Linda Ronstadt • Jimmy Buffett • Tom Petty ■ *Dir* John A Alonzo • *Scr* Ezra Sacks

FTA
★★

Political documentary
1972 · US · Colour · 96min

The makers of this documentary claimed the title stood for "Free the Army" or even, bearing in mind the project's collaborative nature, "Free Theatre Associates". But few doubted what the "F" signified, in light of Jane Fonda's well-publicised stance against the Vietnam War. She insisted that the shows were staged as a feminist response to the girlie entertainment being offered to the troops by the likes of Bob Hope, but the army saw only anti-war propaganda and kept the troupe off its bases. DP

Jane Fonda • Donald Sutherland • Pamela Donegan • Len Chandler • Rita Martinson • Holly Near ■ *Dir* Francine Parker • *Scr* Michael Alaimo, Pamela Donegan, Jane Fonda, Robin Menken, Holly Near, Donald Sutherland, Dalton Trumbo

FTW
★★★ 18

Crime thriller 1994 · US · Colour · 97min

The initials stand for Frank T Wells, the rodeo rider played by Mickey Rourke. After serving ten years for manslaughter, Wells is determined to revive his rodeo career and gets drawn into an affair with Lori Singer, who pays for his career on the proceeds of bank robberies. It's a peculiar mix, populated by assorted lowlifes and shot amid the spectacular scenery of Montana. AT Swearing, sex scenes. DVD

Mickey Rourke *Frank T Wells* • Lori Singer *Scarlett Stuart* • Brion James *Sheriff Rudy Morgan* • Peter Berg *Clem* ■ *Dir* Michael Karbelnikoff • *Scr* Mari Kornhauser, from a story by Kornhauser, "Sir" Eddie Cook [Mickey Rourke]

FX: Murder by Illusion
★★★★ 15

Crime thriller 1985 · US · Colour · 108min

In this compulsively watchable thriller set in the intriguing world of special effects, Bryan Brown stars as an ace film technician who's hired by the US government to stage the fake assassination of a mobster-turned-informant. When the assignment takes a number of violent twists, Brown ends up on the run, armed only with his bag of tricks to expose corruption in high places. For both action fans and gore hounds, this is fast-paced fun. AJ Violence, swearing. DVD

Bryan Brown *Rollie Tyler* • Brian Dennehy *Leo McCarthy* • Diane Venora *Ellen* • Cliff De Young *Lipton* • Mason Adams *Colonel Mason* • Jerry Orbach *Nicholas DeFranco* • Joe Grifasi *Mickey* ■ *Dir* Robert Mandel • *Scr* Robert T Megginson, Gregory Fleeman

FX 2
★★★ 15

Crime thriller 1991 · UK/US · Colour · 107min

Bryan Brown returns as the special effects whizz in this sequel, which, while lacking the fresh ingenuity of the original, remains a sly, entertaining thriller. This time Brown gets mixed up with crooked law enforcement officers, among others, but again runs rings around the crooks with the use of his incredible skills. Brian Dennehy once more provides solid support, while the underrated Richard Franklin directs with some style and an appropriate light touch. JF Violence, swearing, nudity. DVD

Bryan Brown *Rollie Tyler* • Brian Dennehy *Leo McCarthy* • Rachel Ticotin *Kim Brandon* • Joanna Gleason *Liz Kennedy* • Philip Bosco *Ray Silak* • Kevin J O'Connor *Matt Neely* ■ *Dir* Richard Franklin • *Scr* Bill Condon, from characters by Robert T Megginson, Gregory Freeman

The Fabulous Baker Boys
★★★★ 15

Romantic drama 1989 · US · Colour · 108min

This sophisticated salute to family, romance, friends and disillusionment is pure bliss from start to finish. Real-life brothers Jeff and Beau Bridges play the cocktail lounge piano players of the title whose volatile relationship explodes when they employ sultry torch singer Michelle Pfeiffer to revitalise their tired act. Sweetly directed by Steve Kloves, the film smoothly zeroes in on many universal truths along its delightful way, with the fabulous Bridges boys' faultless timing and underplaying allowing Pfeiffer to shine radiantly. AJ Swearing. DVD

Jeff Bridges *Jack Baker* • Michelle Pfeiffer *Susie Diamond* • Beau Bridges *Frank Baker* • Ellie Raab *Nina* • Jennifer Tilly *Monica Moran* • Xander Berkeley *Lloyd* • Dakin Matthews *Charlie* • Gregory Itzin *Vince Nancy* • Wendy Girard *Donna Baker* ■ *Dir/Scr* Steve Kloves

The Fabulous Dorseys
★★ U

Biographical musical 1947 · US · BW · 88min

Warring bandleaders Tommy and Jimmy Dorsey were stolid and ageing when they played themselves in this rather lacklustre biopic, which is best enjoyed simply as a visual record of their music. The storytelling is perfunctory and the Dorsey Brothers themselves are no actors. Perhaps the most telling fact about them is that they were prepared to portray themselves on screen constantly battling with each other, and that it took the death of their father to bring them together. TS DVD

Tommy Dorsey • Jimmy Dorsey • Janet Blair *Jane Howard* • Paul Whiteman • William Lundigan *Bob Burton* • Sara Allgood *Mrs Dorsey* • Arthur Shields *Mr Dorsey* • James Flavin *Gorman* ■ *Dir* Alfred E Green • *Scr* Richard English, Art Arthur, Curtis Kenyon

Face
★★★ 18

Crime thriller 1997 · UK · Colour · 101min

Robert Carlyle, who became a star after two movies and a TV series (*Trainspotting, The Full Monty, Hamish Macbeth*), here plays a thief seeking a traitor in his gang following a bungled robbery. The film is simple-mindedly clichéd and as predictable as a calendar. Still, there are terrific performances from Carlyle, Ray Winstone, Peter Vaughan and Sue Johnston, while director Antonia Bird shows that screen violence is not just a game that boys can play. TH Violence, swearing. DVD

Robert Carlyle *Ray* • Ray Winstone *Dave* • Steven Waddington *Stevie* • Philip Davis *Julian* • Damon Albarn *Jason* • Lena Headey *Connie* • Peter Vaughan *Sonny* • Sue Johnston *Alice* ■ *Dir* Antonia Bird • *Scr* Ronan Bennett

The Face at the Window
★★

Crime melodrama 1939 · UK · BW · 66min

Arguably barnstormer Tod Slaughter's best performance (surely no one ever called it acting?) was in this third version of a Parisian *Petit Guignol* about a revived presumed-dead body, revealing our hero and his mad brother to be serious bank robbers. Slaughter chews a good deal of scenery, while director George King sometimes lets the pace drag. TS

Tod Slaughter *Chevalier Del Gardo* • Marjorie Taylor *Cecile De Brisson* • John Warwick *Lucien Cortier* • Leonard Henry *Gaston* • Aubrey Mallalieu *De Brisson* ■ *Dir* George King • *Scr* AR Rawlinson, Randall Faye, from F Brooke Warren's play

The Face behind the Mask
★★★★

Horror 1941 · US · BW · 68min

Peter Lorre is ideally cast in this low-budget gem, as the watchmaker disfigured in a fire who turns to crime and romances a blind girl with tragic results. Robert Florey's subtle direction turns a stock horror situation on its head and gives threatening tension to the simmering, sinister undercurrent. A magical mood piece, this is a haunting expressionist B-movie garnished with gruesome poetry. AJ

Peter Lorre *Janos Szabo* • Evelyn Keyes *Helen Williams* • Don Beddoe *Jim O'Hara* • George E Stone *Dinky* • John Tyrell *Watts* • Stanley Brown *Harry* ■ *Dir* Robert Florey • *Scr* Allen Vincent, Paul Jarrico, from a story by Arthur Levinson, from a radio play by Thomas Edward O'Connell

A Face in the Crowd
★★★★ PG

Satirical drama 1957 · US · BW · 125min

Andy Griffith (*Matlock*) makes his big-screen debut here, giving the performance of his career as "Lonesome" Rhodes, the small-town philosopher who is discovered by a TV producer (Patricia Neal) and rocketed to fame and fortune. Director Elia Kazan and writer Budd Schulberg had previously collaborated for *On the Waterfront*, both winning Oscars. Although less celebrated, this film about the corrupting power of the media remains topical today. Watch out for a young Lee Remick, also in her first film. SuR

Andy Griffith *"Lonesome" Rhodes* • Patricia Neal *Marcia Jeffries* • Anthony Franciosa *Joey Kiely* • Walter Matthau *Mel Miller* • Lee Remick *Betty Lou Fleckum* • Percy Waram *Colonel Hollister* • Rod Brasfield *Beanie* • Charles Irving *Mr Luffler* ■ *Dir* Elia Kazan • *Scr* Budd Schulberg, from his short story *The Arkansas Traveler* • *Art Directors* Richard Sylbert, Paul Sylbert

Face of a Fugitive
★★★ U

Western 1959 · US · Colour · 80min

This intriguing minor western is particularly well directed by Paul Wendkos and stars Fred MacMurray as a bank robber trying to shake off his past and settle down in a new town. MacMurray is a shade too old and staid for his role (and, besides, his toupee never really convinces), but watch out for then-newcomer James Coburn, who takes over the screen every time he appears. Wendkos made a number of highly regarded low-budget films around this period before basing his career in television. TS

Fred MacMurray *Jim Larson/Ray Kincaid* • Lin McCarthy *Mark Riley* • Dorothy Green *Ellen Bailey* • Alan Baxter *Reed Williams* • Myrna Fahey *Janet* • James Coburn *Purdy* • Francis De Sales *Allison* ■ *Dir* Paul Wendkos • *Scr* David T Chantler, Daniel B Ullman, from the story *Long Gone* by Peter Dawson

The Face of an Angel
★★★★ 15

Drama 2014 · UK/It/Sp · Colour · 101min

Though it is not directly the subject of this film, the 2007 murder of British student Meredith Kercher provides the backdrop for this surprisingly sensitive meditation on the way our society and the media react to violent crime. Loosely split into three movements – the Hell, Purgatory and Paradise of Dante's *Inferno* – this finds its protagonist, a once-promising film-maker, coming to terms with the unthinkable: the death of a loved one in the most devastating circumstances. DW Swearing, sex scenes, drug abuse. DVD Blu-ray

Daniel Brühl *Thomas* • Kate Beckinsale *Simone Ford* • Cara Delevingne *Melanie* • Rosie Fellner *Katherine* ■ *Dir* Michael Winterbottom • *Scr* Paul Viragh, from the non-fiction book *Angel Face: Sex, Murder, and the Inside Story of Amanda Knox* by Barbie Latza Nadeau

The Face of Another

★★★★ 12

Drama 1966 · Jpn · BW · 121min

A compelling treatise on identity and the correlation between physique and personality, this was Hiroshi Teshigahara's first feature since *Woman of the Dunes*. Shades of Franju's *Eyes without a Face* fall upon the action, as Tatsuya Nakadai dons a mask to disguise the hideous disfigurement incurred in an industrial accident. But, is it the mask that prompts him to discard his wife on a spurious charge of adultery, or the same desperate feelings of alienation that drive scarred Miki Irie to commit incest with her devoted brother? Disturbing, but absorbing. DP Japanese +subtitles. *DVD*

Machiko Kyo *Mrs Okuyama* • Tatsuya Nakadai *Mr Okuyama* • Mikijiro Hira • Miki Irie • *Dir* Hiroshi Teshigahara • *Scr* Kobo Abe, from the novel *Tanin No Kao* by Kobo Abe

The Face of Fear

★★★★

Drama 1971 · US · Colour · 75min

You'll have some idea of the quality of this TV movie when you learn it was executive produced by Quinn Martin, the man responsible for such gems as *The Untouchables*, *The Fugitive* and *The Streets of San Francisco*. It stars Elizabeth Ashley as the leukemia-stricken Iowa teacher who hires a hitman to spare her the agonies of a slow death – only to discover she isn't fatally ill! Ashley seems genuinely terrified, but the acting honours go to Ricardo Montalban and Jack Warden as the cops racing against time to find her unknown assassin. DP

Ricardo Montalban *Sgt Frank Ortega* • Jack Warden *Lt George Coye* • Elizabeth Ashley *Sally Dillman* • Dane Clark *Fennington* • Roy Poole *Glenn Kennedy* • Charles Dierkop *Patsy Fain* • Burr DeBenning *Fennington* • Regis J Cordic *Dr Landsteiner* ■ *Dir* George McCowan • *Scr* Edward Hume, from the novel *Sally* by EV Cummingham

The Face of Fu Manchu

★★★ PG

Horror 1965 · UK · Colour · 92min

This is the first and best of Christopher Lee's portrayals of mystery writer Sax Rohmer's insidious East-Asian arch villain. Here he plans to conquer the world with a poison gas invented by a German professor held prisoner at his secret HQ under the Thames – very handy for those Chinese water tortures. Propelled by an eerie opening, this atmospheric comic-strip fantasy is skilfully assembled, and Nigel Green is superb as Fu Manchu's Scotland Yard nemesis, Nayland Smith. The series continued the following year with *The Brides of Fu Manchu*. AJ *DVD*

Christopher Lee *Fu Manchu* • Nigel Green *Nayland Smith* • James Robertson-Justice *Sir Charles Fortesque* • Howard Marion-Crawford *Dr Walter Petrie* • Tsai Chin *Lin Tang* • Joachim Fuchsberger *Carl Jansen* • Karin Dor *Maria* • Walter Rilla *Professor Muller* ■ *Dir* Don Sharp • *Scr* Harry Alan Towers, from characters by Sax Rohmer

The Face of Love

★★★ 12A

Romantic drama 2013 · US · Colour · 91min

In this well-played movie, Annette Bening plays a middle-aged widow who is taken aback when she sees an exact double of her late husband (Ed Harris). Feeling alive for the first time in years, she tracks down the doppelganger – a divorced art teacher (also Harris). Before long, they have entered into an intoxicating yet twisted relationship. From here, the story's plausibility becomes stretched in places, while Robin Williams is wasted in an underwritten role as Nikki's neighbour. But both Bening and Harris are utterly convincing, even when the film around them isn't. SC Some swearing, sexual references.

Annette Bening *Nikki Lostrom* • Ed Harris *Garrett Mathis/Tom Young* • Jess Weixler *Summer* • Amy Brenneman *Ann* • Robin Williams *Roger Stillman* • Linda Park *Jan* ■ *Dir* Arie Posin • *Scr* Matthew McDuffie, Arie Posin

Face/Off

★★★★ 18

Action thriller 1997 · US · Colour · 133min

Nicolas Cage has lost his face and now he wants it back. Problem is, it's attached to John Travolta whose own face has been stitched on to Cage. Cage is a terrorist who, having planted a bomb somewhere in LA, is put into a coma by his FBI agent nemesis (Travolta). This is when the plastic surgery comes in – it is the only way to dupe Cage's associates into revealing the bomb's location. The mix of bizarre plotting, high-octane thrills and sentimental drama doesn't always gel, but director John Woo more than delivers in the overblown action stakes. AT Swearing, violence, drug abuse. *DVD* ⊕

John Travolta *Sean Archer* • Nicolas Cage *Castor Troy* • Joan Allen *Eve Archer* • Alessandro Nivola *Pollux Troy* • Gina Gershon *Sasha Hassler* • Dominique Swain *Jamie Archer* • Nick Cassavetes *Dietrich Hassler* • Harve Presnell *Lazarro* ■ *Dir* John Woo • *Scr* Mike Werb, Michael Colleary

The Face on the Milk Carton

★★

Drama 1995 · US · Colour · 87min

In the US, pictures of missing children are placed on milk cartons, a practice that remarkably delivers results. This TV movie poses a fascinating question: what would you do if you learnt, from such a picture, that you were, in fact, a missing child? Kellie Martin stars as the confused teenager, but TV-movie veteran Waris Hussein doesn't make the most of the intriguing premise. JF

Kellie Martin *Janie Jessmon* • Jill Clayburgh *Miranda Jessmon* • Sharon Lawrence *Sada Sands* • Edward Herrmann *Frank Jessmon* • Johnny Green (3) *Reeve Shields* • Richard Masur *Jonathan Sands* ■ *Dir* Waris Hussein • *Scr* Nancy Isaak, from the book *The Face on the Milk Carton/Whatever Happened to Janie* by Caroline B Cooney

Face the Music

★★

Crime drama 1954 · UK · BW · 84min

This adequate mystery offers a rare nice guy outing to soulless screen villain Alex Nicol, slumming in Britain after his Hollywood career went into a decline. Looking nothing like a trumpeter, he goes underground to prove his innocence when he is accused of murdering a singer. In one of his last assignments before becoming Hammer's horror maestro, director Terence Fisher never manages to intrigue. DP

Alex Nicol *James Bradley* • Eleanor Summerfield *Barbara Quigley* • John Salew *Max Marguiles* • Paul Carpenter *Johnny Sutherland* • Geoffrey Keen *Maurice Green* ■ *Dir* Terence Fisher • *Scr* Ernest Borneman, from his novel

Face to Face

★★ U

Portmanteau drama 1952 · US · BW · 89min

Inspired by portmanteau movies, such as *Dead of Night* and *Forever and a Day*, which glued several short stories together, a young millionaire named Huntington Hartford somehow persuaded RKO to revive the format. John Brahm's section is a version of Joseph Conrad's *The Secret Sharer*, with James Mason hiding a murder suspect on his ship. Bretaigne Windust's film is *The Bride Comes to Yellow Sky*, based on a Stephen Crane story, with Robert Preston as a Texan sheriff whose fiancée is threatened by a long-time adversary. The fiancée is played by Marjorie Steele, who was married to Hartford. Both stories are effectively told on dime budgets, and audiences stayed away in droves. AT

James Mason *Captain* • Gene Lockhart *Capt Archbold* • Michael Pate *Swimmer* • Albert Sharpe *1st Mate* • Robert Preston *Sheriff* • Marjorie Steele *Bride* • Minor Watson *Bad man* • Dan Seymour *Drummer* • James Agee *Prisoner* ■ *Dir* John Brahm, Bretaigne Windust • *Scr* Aeneas MacKenzie, James Agee, from the short story *The Secret Sharer* by Joseph Conrad, from the short story *The Bride Comes to Yellow Sky* by Stephen Crane

Face to Face

★★★ 12

Western 1967 · It/Sp · Colour · 93min

This is less a spaghetti western than a political parable. Gian Maria Volonté gives a highly persuasive performance as a college professor who discovers a talent for banditry when sent to recover his health at a small western town. But the subtext is too often thrust to the fore, with the result that the exploits of the prof and his gang become an irrelevance as writer/director Sergio Sollima sermonises on the misuse of power and the rule of fear. Ennio Morricone contributes a typically poignant score. DP Italian dubbed. *DVD*

Gian Maria Volonté *Brad Fletcher* • Tomas Milian *Solomon "Beauregard" Bennett* • William Berger *Charles Siringo* • Jolanda Modio *Marie* • Carole Andre *Cattle Annie* • Gianni Rizzo *Williams* ■ *Dir/Scr* Sergio Sollima • *Music* Ennio Morricone

Face to Face

★★

Drama 1976 · Swe · Colour · 135min

Originally presented as a four-part TV series, this intense, personal drama suffers from its drastic truncation. After a string of successes, Ingmar Bergman allows introspection to get the better of him with this tiresome study of suppressed trauma, which is so riddled with familiar images and themes it often feels like a bad homage by a slavish acolyte. But while Bergman loses himself in unresolved homosexual subplots and stylised dream sequences, Liv Ullmann turns in a compelling performance as a psychiatrist. DP Swedish +subtitles.

Liv Ullmann *Dr Jenny Isaksson* • Erland Josephson *Dr Tomas Jacobi* • Gunnar Björnstrand *Grandfather* • Aino Taube-Henriksson [Aino Taube] *Grandmother* • Kari Sylwan *Maria* • Sif Raud *Elizabeth Wankel* • Sven Lindberg *Dr Erik Isaksson* • Tore Segelcke *The lady* ■ *Dir/Scr* Ingmar Bergman

A Face to Kill For

★ 12

Thriller 1999 · US · Colour · 87min

A soap opera-style melodrama disintegrates into a preposterous thriller in this dismal tale of betrayal and retribution. Former *Happy Days* actress Crystal Bernard overacts as the disfigured horse trainer who takes drastic action to get even, after being framed by her gold-digging husband (*Desperate Housewives*' Doug Savant). Sent to prison, she undergoes plastic surgery and plans an elaborate revenge. The absurd events are only made worse by an intrusive soundtrack and sluggish pacing. But the biggest disaster is Bernard's accent, which is so unconvincing that it detracts from her plight. SF Brief violence, swearing.

Crystal Bernard *Allison Bevens* • Billy Dean *Sam* • Doug Savant *Virgil* • Claire Rankin *Julia* • Bonnie Gallup *Marion* ■ *Dir* Michael Toshiyuki Uno • *Scr* David Venable, Andrew Laskos

Faces

★★★★ 15

Drama 1968 · US · BW · 124min

This challenging, gritty example of 1960s New American cinema from John Cassavetes combines Method acting with the cinematic techniques of the French New Wave. The marriage of Californian liberals John Marley and Lynn Carlin is on the rocks and after yet another row he storms out to spend the night with prostitute Gena Rowlands, while she finds solace in the arms of hippy Seymour Cassel. The picture originally lasted six hours and there are still places where some cutting would not go amiss, but the improvised performances are exceptional. DP *DVD* ⊕

John Marley *Richard Forst* • Gena Rowlands *Jeannie Rapp* • Lynn Carlin *Maria Forst* • Fred Draper *Freddie* • Seymour Cassel *Chet* • Val Avery *McCarthy* • Dorothy Gulliver *Florence* • Joanne Moore *Jordan Louise* • Darlene Conley *Billy Mae* ■ *Dir/Scr* John Cassavetes

Faces in the Dark

★★ PG

Thriller 1960 · UK · BW · 81min

This tale of blindness and rage should have been a real nail-biter, but ex-documentary director David Eady doesn't have the thriller instinct and throws away countless opportunities to make the tension unbearable. Mild-mannered John Gregson is the blind person under threat. DP

John Gregson *Richard Hammond* • Mai Zetterling *Christiane Hammond* • Michael Denison *David Merton* • John Ireland *Max Hammond* • Tony Wright *Clem* • Nanette Newman *Janet* • Valerie Taylor *Miss Hopkins* ■ *Dir* David Eady • *Scr* Ephraim Kogan, John Tully, from the novel by Pierre Boileau, Thomas Narcejac

Faces of Children

★★★

Silent drama 1925 · Swi/Fr · BW · 114min

Having experimented with expressionism in his early career, Belgian-born Jacques Feyder refined his poetic realist style in this sentimental tale of motherly love. But not even a director with his visual gifts could completely eradicate the melodramatic miming endemic in silent acting. Consequently, the performances work against the stylised authenticity of the sets, although the story itself is more than a little contrived. Child star Jean Forest is the pick of the cast, as the boy who resents his father's remarriage so torments his new stepsister, Arlette Peyran. DP

Jean Forest *Jean Amsler* • Rachel Devirys *Jeanne Dutois* • Victor Vina *Pierre Amsler* • Arlette Peyran *Arlette Dutois* • Pierrette Houyez *Pierrette Amsler* • Henri Duval *Canon Taillier* • Suzy Vernon *Jean's mother* ■ *Dir* Jacques Feyder • *Scr* Jacques Feyder, Françoise Rosay

The Facility

★★ 18

Horror 2012 · UK · Colour · 79min

It's a case of kill or cure for seven volunteers taking part in a trial for a new drug in director Ian Clark's low-budget first feature. With the guinea pigs confined to a remote medical facility, it's not long before they become convinced all is not as it seems, particularly when night falls and the meltdowns begin. The movie is unnerving rather than terrifying or excessively gory. Clark knows his horror set-ups, but it's a tried-and-tested formula and there's little that's unexpected taking place... which is a pity, as Clark shows promise and the cast give energetic performances. JA Violence, swearing, brief nudity. *DVD*

Alex Reid *Joni* • Steve Evets *Morty* • Aneurin Barnard *Adam* • Nia Roberts *Katie* • Skye Lourie *Carmen* ■ *Dir/Scr* Ian Clark

Facing Window

★★★ 15

Romantic drama 2003 · It/UK/Tur/Por · Colour · 102min

Director Ferzan Ozpetek has always exhibited an atmospheric sense of place and he makes the most of the backstreets of Rome in this sincere study of suppressed secrets and second chances. Evoking the fears and prejudices of Italy's fascist past, this focuses on discontented housewife Giovanna Mezzogiorno, who enlists the help of handsome neighbour Raoul Bova to solve the mystery of amnesiac camp survivor Massimo Girotti. Veteran actor Girotti, who first came to prominence in the neorealist era, manages a moving display of wounded bemusement, but the culinary symbolism occasionally feels strained. DP Italian +subtitles. Swearing. *DVD*

Giovanna Mezzogiorno *Giovanna* • Massimo Girotti *Davide* • Raoul Bova *Lorenzo* • Filippo Nigro *Filippo* • Serra Yilmaz *Emine* • Massimo Poggio *Younger Davide* ■ *Dir* Ferzan Ozpetek • *Scr* Gianni Romoli, Ferzan Ozpetek

The Factory

★★ 15

Thriller 2012 · US/Can/Fr · Colour · 100min

This tired compendium of serial killer clichés sees John Cusack playing a detective whose teenage daughter (Mae Whitman) becomes the latest victim of a serial killer. He starts taking the law into his own hands, placing even more strain on his relationship with his detective partner (Jennifer Carpenter). There are some stylish *Se7en*-like wintry visuals but the mechanical plotting and performances strip the movie of any genuine suspense. JF Violence, swearing, sex scenes. *DVD* ⊕

John Cusack *Mike* • Jennifer Carpenter *Kelsey* • Dallas Roberts *Carl* • Mae Whitman *Abby* ■ *Dir* Morgan O'Neill • *Scr* Morgan O'Neill, Paul A Leyden

F

Factory Girl ★★★ 15
Period biographical drama
2006 · US · Colour and BW · 95min

Sienna Miller stars as Edie Sedgwick, the US heiress and model who was Andy Warhol's muse and reputedly the inspiration for the Velvet Underground song *Femme Fatale* and Bob Dylan's *Just like a Woman*. She was only 28 when she died of a drugs overdose in 1971. Miller manages to elicit sympathy for the poor little rich girl, who could so easily be dismissed as over-privileged and weak-willed, while Guy Pearce's amusing portrayal of Warhol is one of the film's strengths – the artist as a self-indulgent mummy's boy. Sadly, Hayden Christensen is hopelessly miscast as Edie's rock star lover. Director George Hickenlooper shows a readiness to challenge the legacy of Warhol and the Factory set, yet some elements of this biographical drama still seem to be all about surface. **BP** Swearing, sex scenes, drug abuse. *DVD*

Sienna Miller *Edie Sedgwick* • Guy Pearce *Andy Warhol* • Hayden Christensen *Billy Quinn* • Jimmy Fallon *Chuck Wein* • Mena Suvari *Richie Berlin* • Shawn Hatosy *Syd Pepperman* • Illeana Douglas *Diana Vreeland* • Jack Huston *Gerard Malanga* • Beth Grant *Julia Warhol* • James Naughton *Fuzzy Sedgwick* ■ *Dir* George Hickenlooper • *Scr* Captain Mauzner, from a story by Mauzner, Simon Monjack, Aaron Richard Golub

Factotum (A Man Who Preforms Many Jobs) ★★★★ 15
Black comedy drama
2005 · Nor/US/Ger/It · Colour · 89min

Based on the mainly autobiographical prose works of cult author Charles Bukowski, director Bent Hamer's film features a career-best performance from Matt Dillon. He plays a drunkard who pursues women and booze with as much verve as his writing, while Lili Taylor and Marisa Tomei impress as the troubled women who share this booze-soaked existence. Dillon is the intoxicating centrepiece for a comedy that's raw and unflinching but lovingly crafted with bleak deadpan humour. **KK** Swearing, sex scenes. *DVD*

Matt Dillon *Henry "Hank" Chinaski* • Lili Taylor *Jan* • Marisa Tomei *Laura* • Fisher Stevens *Manny* • Didier Flamand *Pierre* • Adrienne Shelly *Jerry* • Karen Young *Grace* • Tom Lyons *Tony Endicott* ■ *Dir* Bent Hamer • *Scr* Bent Hamer, Jim Stark, from the novel *Factotum* and other works by Charles Bukowksi

The Facts of Life ★★★
Comedy
1960 · US · BW · 103min

This pairs two of the screen's greatest clowns (though both Bob Hope and Lucille Ball play virtually straight parts here) as married – but not to each other – lovers desperately trying to consummate their affair, and being thwarted at every turn. Naughty rather than raunchy, it was deemed suitable as a saucy dish to present to the Queen at that year's Royal Film Performance. Their engaging teamwork makes this little flick memorable. **TS**

Bob Hope *Larry Gilbert* • Lucille Ball *Kitty Weaver* • Ruth Hussey *Mary Gilbert* • Don DeFore *Jack Weaver* • Louis Nye *Charles Busbee* • Philip Ober *Doc Mason* • Marianne Stewart *Connie Mason* • Peter Leeds *Thompson* ■ *Dir* Melvin Frank • *Scr* Norman Panama, Melvin Frank • *Costume Designer* Edith Head

The Faculty ★★★ 15
Science-fiction horror thriller
1998 · US · Colour · 99min

Scream writer Kevin Williamson teams up with *From Dusk till Dawn* director Robert Rodriguez for this enjoyable reworking of alien invasion movies, bolstered by Williamson's patented in-jokes and genre subversions. This succeeds through assured performances from the teenage cast, zippy direction and the writer's refusal to take even the most tense moments seriously. Despite a disappointing reliance on digital effects in the final third, this is classy entertainment. **JC** Violence, swearing, drug abuse, nudity. *DVD* *BD*

Josh Hartnett *Zeke* • Elijah Wood *Casey Connor* • Clea DuVall *Stokely* • Jordana Brewster *Delilah* • Laura Harris *Marybeth* • Shawn Hatosy *Stan* • Salma Hayek *Nurse Harper* • Robert Patrick *Coach Willis* • Piper Laurie *Mrs Olson* • Famke Janssen *Miss Burke* ■ *Dir* Robert Rodriguez • *Scr* Kevin Williamson, from a story by David Wechter, Bruce Kimmel

Fade to Black ★★★ 18
Horror
1980 · US · Colour · 97min

When a movie fanatic's loser lifestyle tips him over the edge into insanity, he embarks on a killing spree disguised as his favourite film characters. Vernon Zimmerman turns in an intelligent and imaginative movie, with plenty of cinematic references and in-jokes to enjoy, but an excess of violence leaves a bitter aftertaste. **RS**

Dennis Christopher *Eric* • Linda Kerridge *Marilyn* • Tim Thomerson *Dr Moriarty* • Morgan Paull *Gary* • Hennen Chambers *Bart* • Marya Small *Doreen* • Mickey Rourke *Richie* ■ *Dir/Scr* Vernon Zimmerman

Fade to Black ★★ 15
Music documentary 2004 · US · Colour · 105min

Hip-hop megastar Jay-Z commemorated his brief 2003 retirement with this superficial music documentary. Cutting between his impressive "farewell" concert at Madison Square Garden and his *Black Album* studio sessions, it's an unimaginatively constructed PR exercise that's more self-indulgent than revelatory. Fans wanting a greatest hits package won't be disappointed – the concert footage is extensive, capturing the vitality of the celebrity-packed performance. But the rest of the material is badly edited and confusing. **SF** Swearing. *DVD*

Jay-Z • Memphis Bleek • Mary J Blige • Beyoncé Knowles • Sean "P Diddy" Combs [Sean Combs] *Sean P Diddy Combs* ■ *Dir* Pat Paulson, Michael John Warren

Fade to Black ★★ 15
Mystery thriller
2006 · UK/US/It/Lux · Colour · 104min

In 1948, Orson Welles was at Rome's Cinecittà studios filming *Black Magic* and getting over his break-up from his second wife, Rita Hayworth. The premise of Oliver Parker's playful mystery is that the great actor/director became embroiled there for real in a political murder plot to rival any of his fictional *films noirs*. As a fantasy, it certainly has promise. Danny Huston brings his customary charm and charisma to the role of the larger-than-life Welles, and there's solid support from Christopher Walken, Diego Luna and Paz Vega. But their best efforts struggle to overcome Parker's stodgy direction and a portrayal of postwar Italian politicking that most will find baffling. **DA** *DVD*

Danny Huston *Orson Welles* • Diego Luna *Tommaso* • Paz Vega *Lea Padovani* • Christopher Walken *Brewster* • Anna Galiena *Aida* • Nathaniel Parker *Viola* • Violante Placido *Stella* ■ *Dir* Oliver Parker • *Scr* Oliver Parker, from the novel by Davide Ferrario

Fading Gigolo ★★★ 15
Sex comedy drama 2013 · US · Colour · 86min

John Turturro writes, directs and stars in this feather-light New York tale about a middle-aged guy who decides to sell his body for sex. Woody Allen plays the shady friend who convinces him to give it a go, presenting him with his first client (a ball-busting Sharon Stone) for a cut of the action. It's a big leap for a quiet man who works in a florist, but Turturro makes a virtue of his enigmatic character. It's Turturro and Allen's scenes together, plus the rich sense of place, that really bring the film to life. **SP** *DVD* *BD*

John Turturro *Fioravante* • Woody Allen *Murray* • Vanessa Paradis *Avigal* • Liev Schreiber *Dovi* • Sharon Stone *Dr Parker* • Sofia Vergara *Selima* ■ *Dir/Scr* John Turturro

Fahrenheit 451 ★★★ 12
Science-fiction drama
1966 · UK · Colour · 107min

The only film François Truffaut directed in English, this adaptation of Ray Bradbury's deeply troubling novel promises much but is sadly flawed. Syd Cain's futuristic sets cleverly convey the menace and desperation of a society in which books are banned and burned, Cyril Cusack's fire chief is hugely resistible as he unquestioningly performs his duty and Julie Christie superbly judges the contrasts in her dual role. But Oskar Werner seems to have lost the plot and, as he's driving force, this is a major stumbling block. **DP** *DVD*

Oskar Werner *Montag* • Julie Christie *Linda/ Clarisse* • Cyril Cusack *Captain* • Anton Diffring *Fabian* • Jeremy Spenser *Man with apple* • Alex Scott (1) *Henry Brulard* ■ *Dir* François Truffaut • *Scr* François Truffaut, Jean-Louis Richard, David Rudkin, Helen Scott, from the novel by Ray Bradbury • *Cinematographer* Nicolas Roeg

Fahrenheit 9/11 ★★★★ 15
Political documentary
2004 · US · Colour · 122min

Michael Moore's controversial Palme d'Or winning documentary is a blistering attack on George W Bush's administration. The film investigates the legitimacy of Bush's presidency, his links to the Bin Laden family, the role oil played in the response to the World Trade Center attacks and how the pursuit of the Taliban led to the Iraq war. He even takes us up to the abuse of Iraqi prisoners by US soldiers that dominated the news in the first half of 2004. The assembled news footage and street interviews are always riveting, contentious and one-sided. This agitprop reflection on the dubious agenda of American foreign policy inevitably preaches to the converted, but it also uncovers or highlights many thought-provoking facts. **AJ** *DVD*

■ *Dir/Scr* Michael Moore (2)

Fail-Safe ★★★★ PG
Drama
1964 · US · BW · 107min

This follows the same flight path as *Dr Strangelove* as a squadron of US planes, loaded with nuclear bombs, accidentally sets off to devastate Moscow and cannot be halted from its doomsday mission. Director Sidney Lumet builds the tension from neurotic jitters (Larry Hagman as presidential interpreter) through to psychotic jeopardy (Walter Matthau's anti-Soviet professor urging the Armageddon sanction) when fail-safe devices fail and American president Henry Fonda has to warn his Soviet counterpart that the world is heading into nightmare. By telling it straight, the idea loses a certain satirical edge, but gains a hint of reality. **TH** *DVD*

Henry Fonda *The President* • Walter Matthau *Groeteschele* • Frank Overton *General Bogan* • Dan O'Herlihy *General Black* • Fritz Weaver *Colonel Cascio* • Larry Hagman *Buck* • Edward Binns *Colonel Grady* • William Hansen *Secretary Swenson* ■ *Dir* Sidney Lumet • *Scr* Walter Bernstein, from the novel by Eugene Burdick, Harvey Wheeler

Fail Safe ★★★ PG
Political thriller
2000 · US · BW · 84min

Remaking the 1964 Sidney Lumet Cold War classic about a president who nukes New York in atonement for a rogue missile's decimation of Moscow was a challenge in itself. But to do it in one take and in letterboxed black and white was asking a lot of even this talented cast. It was 40 years since live TV drama went out of vogue and the odd gaff here explains why. Yet, director Stephen Frears achieves a judicious blend of suspense and philosophising, as the various hawks and doves seek to sway Richard Dreyfuss while George Clooney's plane gets ever closer to its target. **DP** *DVD*

George Clooney *Col Grady* • Noah Wyle *Buck* • Richard Dreyfuss *President* • Hank Azaria *Professor Groeteschele* • Brian Dennehy *Gen Bogan* • Harvey Keitel *Warren Black* • Don Cheadle *Pierce* • James Cromwell *Gordon Knapp*

• Sam Elliott *Congressman Tom Raskob* ■ *Dir* Stephen Frears • *Scr* Walter Bernstein, from the novel by Harvey Wheeler, Eugene Burdick

Failure to Launch ★★ 12
Romantic comedy 2006 · US · Colour · 92min

This lumbering film pretends to address the trend of 30-something slackers who are unwilling to fly the nest. It is actually an excuse to have a character called Tripp (played by Matthew McConaughey) fall over in all manner of slapstick episodes. An under-used Kathy Bates plays the long-suffering mother who hires Sarah Jessica Parker to tempt him into moving out. **SP** *DVD*

Matthew McConaughey *Tripp* • Sarah Jessica Parker *Paula* • Zooey Deschanel *Kit* • Justin Bartha *Ace* • Bradley Cooper *Demo* • Terry Bradshaw *Al* • Kathy Bates *Sue* ■ *Dir* Tom Dey • *Scr* Tom J Astle, Matt Ember

Faintheart ★★ 12
Comedy
2008 · UK · Colour · 87min

The result of a unique experiment, *Faintheart* was developed on the MySpace social networking website, with users chipping in ideas and jokes. The end result is a comedy about a loser called Richard (Eddie Marsan) who spends too much time dressing up as a Viking and re-enacting battles, and not enough time on his personal relationships. The film plods along inoffensively and predictably, without inspiration or flair. Ewen Bremner does deliver a characteristically fine performance as Richard's Trekkie mate, but Anne Reid is wasted as his mother-in-law. **BP** *DVD*

Eddie Marsan *Richard* • Jessica Hynes [Jessica Stevenson] *Cath* • Ewen Bremner *Julian* • Anne Reid *Barbara* • Tim Healy *Geoff* • Paul Nicholls *Gary* • Bronagh Gallagher *Maggie* ■ *Dir* Vito Rocco • *Scr* David Lemon, Vito Rocco, from a story by Lemon

Fair Game ★★ 15
Action drama
1995 · US · Colour · 86min

T-shirt clad Cindy Crawford gets chased by baddies and falls into the water a lot, and that's about it. If you can believe supermodel Crawford (in her big Hollywood debut) is a high-powered lawyer then you will probably just about swallow the nonsensical story about Russian villains who are convinced she has some valuable information about their American operation. Some enjoyably destructive set pieces aside, the only fun to be had is Steven Berkoff's over-the-top performance. **JF** Swearing, violence, nudity. *DVD*

William Baldwin *Detective Max Kirkpatrick* • Cindy Crawford *Kate McQuean* • Steven Berkoff *Kazak* • Christopher McDonald *Lieutenant Mayerson* • Miguel Sandoval *Juantorena* • Salma Hayek *Rita* ■ *Dir* Andrew Sipes • *Scr* Charlie Fletcher, from the novel by Paula Gosling

Fair Game ★★★ 12
Political thriller based on a true story
2010 · US/UAE · Colour · 103min

Naomi Watts impresses, while the often impressive Sean Penn coasts, in this dramatised account of the Valerie Plame scandal. CIA operative Plame (Watts) had her cover deliberately blown by the Bush administration in 2003, apparently in response to a critical newspaper article about the reasons for invading Iraq by her ex-diplomat husband, Joe Wilson (Penn). The two-time Oscar winner hardly stretches himself as the outraged spouse, but the movie's driving force is Watts, whose attempts to negotiate a political minefield as well as hold her marriage together are thoroughly convincing. **AS** English, French +subtitles. Some swearing. *DVD* *BD*

Naomi Watts *Valerie Plame* • Sean Penn *Joseph "Joe" Wilson* • Sam Shepard *Sam Plame* • Noah Emmerich *Bill* • Michael Kelly (2) *Jack* • Bruce McGill *Jim Pavitt* ■ *Dir* Doug Liman • *Scr* Jez and John-Henry Butterworth, from the memoirs *Fair Game* by Valerie Plame Wilson and *The Politics of Truth* by Joseph Wilson • *Cinematographer* Doug Liman

Fair Warning ★★
Mystery   1937 · US · BW · 68min

One of those 20th Century-Fox programme fillers made swiftly and cheaply, invariably on existing sets, this was intended as little more than support for the main feature, but is fascinating to view today. John Howard Payne plays a swimming instructor involved in murder. Top-billed, however, is the excellent J Edward Bromberg, whose career would be tragically cut short by the communist witch-hunt (he was blacklisted and died in London in 1951 at the age of 48). TS

J Edward Bromberg *Matthew Jericho* • Betty Furness *Kay Farnham* • John Howard Payne [John Payne] *Jim Preston* • Victor Kilian *Sam* • Billy Burrud *Malcolm Berkhardt* • Gavin Muir *Herbert Willett* • Gloria Roy *Grace Hamilton* ■ *Dir* Norman Foster • *Scr* Norman Foster, Saul Elkins (uncredited), from the short story *Paradise Canyon Mystery* by Philip Wylie

Fair Wind to Java ★★★ PG
Adventure   1953 · US · Colour · 87min

Fred MacMurray stars as a seafaring skipper in this rip-roaring adventure, racing against time and pirate Robert Douglas to recover a hoard of diamonds before Krakatoa erupts, and romancing Vera Ralston along the way. Unfortunately, the film is spoiled by its cheap studio backdrops and hopeless effects - you'll fall about laughing when the volcano blows. Still, there's much to enjoy, including Victor McLaglen as a drunken sailor. TS

Fred MacMurray *Captain Boll* • Vera Ralston *Kim Kim* • Robert Douglas *Pulo Besar/St Ebenezer* • Victor McLaglen *O'Brien* • John Russell *Flint* • Buddy Baer *Kung* • Claude Jarman Jr *Chess* • Grant Withers *Jason Blue* • *Dir* Joseph Kane • *Scr* Richard Tregaskis, from the novel by Garland Roark

Fairfield Road ★★
Romantic drama   2010 · US · Colour · 100min

Desperate Housewives star Jesse Metcalfe is converted a little too quickly to the joys of small-town life in this flimsy yet pleasantly simplistic romantic drama. Delivering a performance based predominantly on his looks rather than acting range, he plays a US political aide who ends up licking his wounds in quaint Cape Cod after his career and relationship take a nose dive. Naturally, the place's welcoming atmosphere and slower pace work their magic - along with the charms of headstrong but sweet local bookshop owner Natalie Lisinska. SF

Jesse Metcalfe *Noah McManus* • Natalie Lisinska *Hailey Caldwell* • Derek McGrath *Sam Peabody* • Natalie Brown *Wendy Greenhill* • Brandon Firla *Randall Henderson* ■ *Dir* David Weaver • *Scr* Tracy Rosen

The Fairy ★★★★ PG
Romantic comedy   2011 · Fr/Bel · Colour · 90min

Slapstick aficionados rejoice, as Dominique Abel and Fiona Gordon deliver a charmingly off-kilter homage to Chaplin, Keaton and Tati. Gordon escapes from an asylum and convinces a hotel clerk (Abel) that she is a fairy who can grant him three wishes. The premise may be a simple one, but plot isn't the strong point of this team - they excel at absurdist set pieces that surprise and amuse with their unpredictability. With Bruno Romy's myopic bartender and Philippe Martz's fussy tourist adding to the fun, this is close to irresistible. DP French, English +subtitles. DVD

Dominique Abel *Dom* • Fiona Gordon *The fairy* • Philippe Martz *John the Englishman* • Bruno Romy *L'Amour Fiou barman* • Vladimir Zongo *Illegal immigrant* ■ *Dir/Scr* Dominique Abel, Fiona Gordon, Bruno Romy

FairyTale: a True Story ★★★★ U
Period drama based on a true story
1997 · US · Colour · 93min

Charles Sturridge lyrically directs this family tale, based on the true story of two young girls who, in 1917, produced photographs of a group of winged, fairy-like creatures they had taken at the bottom of their garden. The story follows the controversy that surrounded the photographs - were they real or were they faked? Luminaries such as Sir Arthur Conan Doyle (Peter O'Toole) and Harry Houdini (Harvey Keitel) debated the authenticity of the pictures. It's beautifully filmed, with nice special effects by Tim Webber, and Sturridge infuses the it with a sense of wonder and romanticism that contrasts with the more sombre backdrop of the First World War. JB

Florence Hoath *Elsie Wright* • Elizabeth Earl (2) *Frances Griffiths* • Paul McGann *Arthur Wright* • Phoebe Nicholls *Polly Wright* • Bill Nighy *Edward Gardner* • Bob Peck *Harry Briggs* • Harvey Keitel *Harry Houdini* • Peter O'Toole *Sir Arthur Conan Doyle* • Mel Gibson *Frances' father* ■ *Dir* Charles Sturridge • *Scr* Ernie Contreras, from a story by Ernie Contreras, Albert Ash, Tom McLoughlin

Faithful ★ 15
Comedy   1996 · US · Colour · 87min

Actor/scriptwriter Chazz Palminteri isn't so lucky with this adaptation of his stage play as he was with *A Bronx Tale*. In director Paul Mazursky's hands, Palminteri's three-hander turns into bland fare, showing little insight and featuring Cher in one of her worst performances. She plays the wife of Ryan O'Neal, who has hired hitman Palminteri to kill her on their 20th wedding anniversary. A depressingly flat, entertainment-free zone. AJ

Cher *Margaret O'Donnell* • Chazz Palminteri *Tony* • Ryan O'Neal *Jack O'Donnell* • Paul Mazursky *Dr Susskind* • Amber Smith *Debbie* • Elisa Leonetti *Maria* ■ *Dir* Paul Mazursky • *Scr* Chazz Palminteri

Faithless ★★★
Melodrama   1932 · US · BW · 76min

Made at the height of the Depression, this movie canters through a melodramatic story about a spoiled socialite who plumbs the depths before love saves the day. Tallulah Bankhead plays the daughter of a banker whose business has failed. She rejects Robert Montgomery despite the fact that she loves him, and sponges off acquaintances, eventually becoming mistress to one of them. This pre-Hays Code film ran into censorship problems in Britain because of its candour. BB

Tallulah Bankhead *Carol Morgan* • Robert Montgomery *Bill Wade* • Hugh Herbert *Mr Peter M Blainey* • Maurice Murphy *Anthony Wade* • Sterling Holloway *Reporter* • Charles Williams (1) *Reporter* ■ *Dir* Harry Beaumont • *Scr* Carey Wilson, from a story by Mildred Cram

Faithless ★★★★ 15
Drama   2000 · Swe/Nor/Fin · Colour · 147min

Given the history between director Liv Ullmann and screenwriter Ingmar Bergman, it's tempting to speculate on the autobiographical content of this intense study of infidelity and inspiration. It explores the impact of Lena Endre's affair with director Krister Henriksson on both her conductor husband, Thomas Hanzon, and their young daughter. Further blurring the line between fiction and reality, Bergman has Endre relate her story to Erland Josephson, a blocked scenarist whose relationship to the flashback events is never clarified. This is complex, mature and engrossing cinema. DP Swedish +subtitles. DVD

Lena Endre *Marianne Vogler* • Erland Josephson *Bergman* • Krister Henriksson *David* • Thomas Hanzon *Markus* • Michelle Gylemo *Isabelle* • Juni Dahr *Margareta* ■ *Dir* Liv Ullmann • *Scr* Ingmar Bergman

Fakers ★★ 15
Comedy crime caper   2004 · UK · Colour · 81min

There's something endearingly reminiscent of the 1960s about this watchable crime caper. Matthew Rhys plays a small-time conman who's in debt to London crime lord Art Malik. When Rhys stumbles across a lost sketch by an Italian master, he sees a way of wiping out his slate clean - he commissions several copies and seeks to flog them to some of London's less scrupulous art dealers over the course of a single morning. This is decently made, but lacks big-screen appeal. DA Swearing. DVD

Matthew Rhys *Nick Edwards* • Kate Ashfield *Eve Evans* • Tom Chambers *Tony Evans* • Art Malik *Foster Wright* • Tony Haygarth *Phil Norris* • Edward Hibbert *Edward Fisher* • Paul Clayton *Gordon Price* • Larry Lamb *Harvey Steed* • Rula Lenska *Sylvia Creat* ■ *Dir* Richard Janes • *Scr* Paul Gerstenberger

The Falcon and the Co-Eds ★★ PG
Detective mystery   1943 · US · BW · 65min

Logic was never the byword of this RKO series, but utter confusion reigns in this seventh entry. Tom Conway investigates the death of a professor at a girls' school and, while the screenwriters are adept at bumping off suspects, the motives are so obscure that repeated viewing of Conway's accusatory summation only reveals additional loose ends and inconsistencies. No wonder William Clemens directed at such a lick. DP DVD

Tom Conway *Tom Lawrence/The Falcon* • Jean Brooks *Vicky Gaines* • Rita Corday *Marguerita Serena* • Amelita Ward *Jane Harris* • Isabel Jewell *Mary Phoebus* • George Givot *Dr Anatole Graelich* • Cliff Clark *Timothy Donovan* • Ed Gargan [Edward Gargan] *Bates* ■ *Dir* William Clemens • *Scr* Ardel Wray, Gerald Geraghty, from the story by Ardel Wray, from the character created by Michael Arlen

The Falcon and the Snowman ★★★ 15
Spy drama based on a true story
1985 · US · Colour · 125min

This convoluted spy thriller stars Timothy Hutton as a college dropout who obtains US secrets and, with his drug-addicted buddy Sean Penn, passes them on to the Soviet embassy in Mexico. The movie is about the motives for treason and the loss of moral purpose in America, underlined by some heavy-handed flashbacks to Vietnam, the Kennedys, Martin Luther King and even John Lennon. Directed with customary visual flair by John Schlesinger, it's undeniably gripping, if a little long and unfocused. AT Violence, swearing. DVD

Timothy Hutton *Christopher Boyce* • Sean Penn *Daulton Lee* • Pat Hingle *Mr Boyce* • Richard Dysart *Dr Lee* • Lori Singer *Lana* • David Suchet *Alex* • Dorian Harewood *Gene* • Priscilla Pointer *Mrs Lee* ■ *Dir* John Schlesinger • *Scr* Steven Zaillian, from the book by Robert Lindsey

The Falcon in Danger ★★
Detective mystery   1943 · US · BW · 70min

When $100,000 in securities goes missing and two corpses show up, who better to solve the mystery than debonair detective the Falcon (Tom Conway)? The sixth entry in RKO's B-movie series is far from the most suspenseful. Indeed, apart from the opening sequence, in which an empty plane crashes at an airport and a couple of assassination attempts take place, the mystery is often forced to take a backseat to the Falcon's romance with Amelita Ward. DP DVD

Tom Conway *The Falcon* • Jean Brooks *Iris* • Elaine Shepard *Nancy* • Amelita Ward *Bonnie* • Cliff Clark *Donovan* • Ed Gargan [Edward Gargan] *Bates* • Clarence Klob *Palmer* • Felix Basch *Morley* • Richard Davies (1) *Ken* ■ *Dir* William Clemens • *Scr* Fred Niblo Jr, Craig Rice, from the character created by Michael Arlen

The Falcon in Hollywood ★★
Detective mystery   1944 · US · BW · 67min

Hooray for Hollywood, because without the trip around RKO's back lot and visits to such landmarks as the Hollywood Bowl, this whodunnit would have been over in two reels. The vacationing Tom Conway clearly revels in being surrounded by beautiful starlets as he tries to discover who killed the acting ex of a costume designer on the eve of her wedding to a hotshot director. This tenth outing for the RKO hero is a ploddingly predictable thriller. DP DVD

Tom Conway *Tom Lawrence/The Falcon* • Barbara Hale *Peggy Callahan* • Veda Ann Borg *Billie* • Jean Brooks *Roxanna* • Rita Corday *Lilli D'Allio* • John Abbott *Martin Dwyer* • Sheldon

Leonard *Louie* ■ *Dir* Gordon Douglas • *Scr* Gerald Geraghty, from the character created by Michael Arlen

The Falcon in Mexico ★★
Detective mystery   1944 · US · BW · 70min

According to Hollywood legend, the location footage used in this puzzling ninth series entry was borrowed from Orson Welles's infamously scuppered documentary, *It's All True*. Certainly, the Mexican vistas add to the appeal of this typical mystery, in which Tom Conway allies with artist's daughter Martha MacVicar to discover how her long-dead father could have painted a portrait of Cecilia Callejo. With a trio of murders, a couple of unnecessary musical interludes and one near miss, this is certainly a busy picture. DP DVD

Tom Conway *Tom Lawrence/The Falcon* • Mona Maris *Raquel* • Martha MacVicar *Barbara Wade* • Nestor Paiva *Manuel Romero* • Mary Currier *Paula Dudley* • Cecilia Callejo *Dolores Ybarra* ■ *Dir* William Berke • *Scr* Gerald Geraghty, George Worthing Yates, from the character created by Michael Arlen

The Falcon in San Francisco ★★★
Detective mystery   1945 · US · BW · 65min

Joseph H Lewis's sole entry in RKO's long-running crime series (the 11th) is undoubtedly the most stylish. It's also the funniest, with Tom Conway's doltish sidekick Edward Brophy spending as much time searching for a wife as he does looking for clues to solve the case. A murder on a train sparks this lively adventure, in which the Falcon plays nursemaid to orphaned Sharyn Moffett while trying to clear Rita Corday of involvement with a gang of silk smugglers. DP DVD

Tom Conway *Tom Lawrence/The Falcon* • Rita Corday *Joan Marshall* • Edward S Brophy [Edward Brophy] *Goldie Locke* • Sharyn Moffett *Annie Marshall* • Fay Helm *Doreen Temple* ■ *Dir* Joseph H Lewis • *Scr* Robert Kent, Ben Markson, from a story by Robert Kent, from the character created by Michael Arlen

The Falcon Out West ★★
Detective mystery   1944 · US · BW · 64min

Tom Conway finds himself in sagebrush country after millionaire Lyle Talbot collapses inexplicably on a New York dance floor. A trip to his ranch in Texas, in the unwelcome company of inspector Cliff Clark and his doltish sidekick Don Douglas, reveals the culprit, but not before Conway has survived two attempts on his life. The script coasts along. DP

Tom Conway *The Falcon* • Barbara Hale *Marion* • Don Douglas *Hayden* • Carole Gallagher *Vanessa* • Joan Barclay *Mrs Irwin* • Cliff Clark *Inspector Donovan* • Ed Gargan [Edward Gargan] *Bates* • Minor Watson *Caldwell* ■ *Dir* William Clemens • *Scr* Billy Jones, Morton Grant, from the character created by Michael Arlen

The Falcon Strikes Back ★★★
Detective mystery   1943 · US · BW · 65min

One of the finest slapstick stooges since the silent era, Edgar Kennedy steals the show here as a malevolent puppeteer caught up in the same war bond scam for which the police want to question our dapper hero, The Falcon (Tom Conway), after he is found unconscious alongside a very dead bank manager. Dashing off the playful dialogue with aplomb, Conway relishes his first solo outing as the crime-fighter in this fifth instalment of the long-running series. Clearly, the superior direction of Edward Dmytryk helped this slickly staged mystery. DP DVD

Tom Conway *The Falcon* • Harriet Hilliard [Harriet Nelson] *Gwynne Gregory* • Jane Randolph *Marcia Brooks* • Edgar Kennedy *Smiley Dugan* • Cliff Edwards *Goldie* • Rita Corday *Mia Bruger* • Erford Gage *Rickey Davis* ■ *Dir* Edward Dmytryk • *Scr* Edward Dein, Gerald Geraghty, from a story by Stuart Palmer, from the character created by Michael Arlen

F

The Falcon Takes Over
★★★

Detective mystery   1942 · US · BW · 63min

Raymond Chandler's *Farewell, My Lovely* was the inspiration for George Sanders's penultimate outing as Michael Arlen's suave sleuth. (Sanders handed over the role to his real-life brother Tom Conway in *The Falcon's Brother*). An escaped convict, a priceless necklace and a clever impostor are the plot strands that Irving Reis weaves together at breakneck speed. The third, and easily the best, entry in RKO's series. DP *DVD*

George Sanders *The Falcon* • Lynn Bari *Ann Riordan* • Allen Jenkins *Goldie Locke* • James Gleason *Inspector Mike O'Hara* • Helen Gilbert *Diana Kenyon* • Ward Bond *Moose Malloy* • Ed Gargan [Edward Gargan] *Bates* ■ *Dir* Irving Reis • *Scr* Lynn Root, Frank Fenton, from the character created by Michael Arlen and the novel *Farewell, My Lovely* by Raymond Chandler

Falcons
★★ 15

Drama
2002 · Ice/UK/Nor/Ger/Fr · Colour · 91min

Beautifully photographed by Harald Paalgard, but utterly lacking in logic and precision, this bizarre road movie never seems sure where it's heading. Initially, it appears as though American jailbird Keith Carradine has arrived in Iceland intent on either self-discovery or suicide. But he is then distracted by eccentric artist Margret Vilhjalmsdottir, who is taking care of a rescued falcon and so begins a meandering journey across the northlands. DP Icelandic, English +subtitles. *DVD*

Keith Carradine *Simon* • Margret Vilhjalmsdottir *Dua* • Ingvar E Sigurdsson *Cop* ■ *Dir* Fridrik Thor Fridriksson • *Scr* Fridrik Thor Fridriksson, Einar Karason

The Falcon's Adventure ★★

Detective mystery   1946 · US · BW · 61min

Considering the uninspiring job he did on *The Falcon in Mexico*, it's rather surprising that RKO executives let William Berke direct the 13th entry in this ever-lively series. It turned out to be the troubleshooter's final assignment for the studio, however, as Tom Conway cancels his vacation to keep both Madge Meredith and a formula for synthetic industrial diamonds out of the hands of the villains who have framed him for her father's murder. John Calvert took over the role of the Falcon for a further three adventures, beginning with *Devil's Cargo* (1948). DP *DVD*

Tom Conway *The Falcon* • Madge Meredith *Louisa Braganza* • Edward S Brophy [Edward Brophy] *Goldie* • Robert Warwick *Sutton* • Myrna Dell *Doris* • Steve Brodie *Benny* • Ian Wolfe *Denison* • Carol Forman *Helen* ■ *Dir* William Berke • *Scr* Aubrey Wisberg, Robert Kent, from the character created by Michael Arlen

The Falcon's Alibi
★★

Detective mystery   1946 · US · BW · 62min

This 12th entry is one of the weakest in the series, a tale of jewel theft and murders that leaves you doubting Tom Conway's powers of detection. A waiter, a hotel guest and sassy band singer Jane Greer all bite the dust before Conway finally twigs who's responsible for the theft of Esther Howard's pearls, which he was supposed to protect. DP *DVD*

Tom Conway *The Falcon* • Rita Corday *Joan* • Vince Barnett *Goldie* • Jane Greer *Lola* • Elisha Cook Jr *Nick* • Emory Parnell *Metcalf* • Al Bridge *Inspector Blake* • Esther Howard *Mrs Peabody* ■ *Dir* Ray McCarey • *Scr* Paul Yawitz, from a story by Dane Lussior, Manny Seff, from the character created by Michael Arlen

The Falcon's Brother
★★

Detective mystery   1942 · US · BW · 62min

George Sanders handed over the reins of RKO's popular B-franchise to his brother Tom Conway during this disappointing thriller, the fourth in the 16-film series. The war rears its ugly head for the only time in the series, as Conway arrives in South America in time to help Sanders track down some Fifth Columnists. Directed with brisk efficiency, but little imagination. Conway went on to star as the Falcon a further nine times, beginning with 1943's *The Falcon Strikes Back*. DP *DVD*

George Sanders *Gay Lawrence* • Tom Conway *Tom Lawrence* • Jane Randolph *Marcie Brooks* • Don Barclay *Lefty* • Cliff Clark *Inspector Timothy Donovan* ■ *Dir* Stanley Logan • *Scr* Stuart Palmer, Craig Rice, from the character created by Michael Arlen

The Fall
★ 15

Period fantasy adventure
2006 · US · Colour · 112min

Violent fantasy blurs with lovelorn reality in this epic folly from *The Cell* director Tarsem Singh (billed here simply as Tarsem). Set in 1920s Los Angeles, it stars Lee Pace as an injured silent-movie stuntman who spins an exotic fairy tale for child patient Catinca Untaru so that she'll help him commit suicide. Apart from the odd stunning image, it's a mind-numbing bore with ludicrous visual flash punctuating the arch posing and bad acting. AJ *DVD* *SD*

Lee Pace *Roy Walker* • Justine Waddell *Nurse Evelyn/Sister Evelyn* • Catinca Untaru *Alexandria* • Kim Uylenbroek *Doctor/Alexander the Great* • Aiden Lithgow *Alexander's messenger* • Sean Gilder *Walt Purdy* ■ *Dir* Tarsem [Tarsem Singh] • *Scr* Dan Gilroy, Nico Soultanakis, Tarsem, from the film *Yo Ho Ho* by Valeri Petrov

The Fall
★★★★ 12A

Documentary   2016 · UK/US · Colour · 95min

You forget just how vulnerable South African teenager Zola Budd was when she arrived in the UK clutching a gleaming new fast-tracked passport to compete under our flag at the 1984 LA Olympics. Meanwhile, across the Atlantic, her heroine Mary Decker was trying her best to avoid all the hype. Most will remember the calamitous outcome of that inaugural 3,000m for women, but what this brilliantly executed documentary does is not just bring the two together for the first time since that fateful day, but also look at the rubble-strewn route they took to get to the starting line. TrP

Mary Slaney • Zola Pieterse • Brooks Johnson • Richard Slaney • Ruth Wysocki ■ *Dir* Daniel Gordon

Fall into Darkness
★★ 15

Mystery thriller   1996 · US · Colour · 87min

The execution is pretty routine, but there is more intrigue than usual in this made-for-TV thriller. Tatyana Ali plays a brilliant music student who falls victim to a young socialite's plan to avenge her brother's death. The playing of Ali and her co-star Jonathan Brandis is bland, but there are enough twists and turns in the plot to keep the viewer guessing. JF Swearing, violence. *DVD*

Tatyana M Ali [Tatyana Ali] *Sharon McKay* • Jonathan Brandis *Chad Lear* • Charlotte Ross *Ann Price* • Sean Murray (2) *Jerry Price* • Paul Scherrer *Paul Lear* ■ *Dir* Mark Sobel • *Scr* JB White, from the novel by Christopher Pike

The Fall of Babylon
★★★

Silent historical epic   1919 · US · BW · 82min

DW Griffith's 1916 epic *Intolerance* contained four separate stories, virtually bankrupted Griffith, and audiences found it far too much to swallow in one gulp. So Griffith took out the juiciest story, about a mountain girl who loves Belshazzar and protects him against the evil high priest of Bel, added some new scenes and released the "new" film in 1919. There's lashings of sex and violence, and a staggering set filled with elephant statues and thousands of swirling semi-naked extras. The penalty is Griffith's overlay of moral indignation. AT

Tully Marshall *The High Priest of Bel* • Constance Talmadge *The mountain girl* • Elmer Clifton *The Rhapsode* • Alfred Paget *Prince Belshazzar* • Carl Stockdale *Nabonidus, King of Babylonia* • Seena Owen *Attarea, favorite of Belshazzar* ■ *Dir/Scr* DW Griffith • *Cinematographer* GW Bitzer [Billy Bitzer]

The Fall of the Essex Boys
★★ 18

Crime drama based on a true story
2012 · UK · Colour · 87min

This is the fourth film inspired by the 1995 Rettendon Range Rover murders since *Essex Boys* in 2000. The slaughter of three hard-nut drug dealers in an Essex country lane was national news at the time but this brutal, expletive-laden geezer-fest demonstrates that the story has been well and truly squeezed dry. The drama is competently put together but the rat-a-tat narration is intrusive and characterisation is perfunctory at best. JA Violence, swearing, drug abuse, sex scenes, nudity. *DVD*

Nick Nevern *Darren Nichols* • Robert Cavanah *Mickey Steele* • Kierston Wareing *Karen* • Ewan Ross *DI Philip Stone* • Peter Barrett *Pat Tate* • Kate Magowan *DC Jefferson* ■ *Dir* Paul Tanter • *Scr* Stephen Reynolds, from a story by Jonathan Sothcott, Reynolds

The Fall of the House of Usher
★★★★ 12

Horror   1960 · US · Colour · 78min

The huge success of this elegant tale of foreboding horror, based on an Edgar Allan Poe story of substance (unlike some later knock-offs), cemented director Roger Corman's artistic style and developed Vincent Price's "Master of the Macabre" persona. Price is superb as the white-haired, hypersensitive recluse Roderick Usher who has a demented obsession with his ancestors. Lavishly produced, visually gorgeous and still scary after all these years. AJ *DVD* *SD*

Vincent Price *Roderick Usher* • Mark Damon *Philip Winthrop* • Myrna Fahey *Madeline Usher* • Harry Ellerbe *Bristol* ■ *Dir* Roger Corman • *Scr* Richard Matheson, from the story by Edgar Allan Poe • *Cinematographer* Floyd Crosby

The Fall of the Roman Empire
★★★★ PG

Historical epic   1964 · US · Colour · 172min

Producer Samuel Bronston's legacy of six European-shot epics looks more cherishable as the years pass, and leaves one aching to see them once more in their full cinematic glory. This fine example has excellent chariot action and a wonderful, if brief, performance by Alec Guinness. Sophia Loren has seldom looked lovelier, and the screenplay with its nods to historian Edward Gibbon is resolutely intelligent. The distinguished support cast ensures that the long movie never palls, and Anthony Mann directs with his usual finesse. TS *DVD* *SD*

Sophia Loren *Lucilla* • Stephen Boyd *Livius* • Alec Guinness *Marcus Aurelius* • Christopher Plummer *Commodus* • James Mason *Timonides* • Omar Sharif *Sohamus* • Anthony Quayle *Verulus* • John Ireland *Ballomar* • Mel Ferrer *Cleander* • Eric Porter *Julianus* ■ *Dir* Anthony Mann • *Scr* Ben Barzman, Basilio Franchina, Philip Yordan • *Cinematographer* Robert Krasker • *Music* Dmitri Tiomkin

Fall Time
★★ 18

Crime thriller   1994 · US · Colour · 84min

Mickey Rourke's career decline continued with this daft, muddled crime thriller. He and Stephen Baldwin (wildly over the top) play two vicious bank robbers who kidnap a trio of prank-loving teenagers whom they mistakenly believe are planning to rob a bank they have already targeted. In director Paul Warner's hands the film lurches clumsily from one unlikely situation to the next. JF Violence, swearing.

Mickey Rourke *Florence* • Stephen Baldwin *Leon* • Sheryl Lee *Patty* • Sammy Kershaw *Officer Donny* • Jason London *Tim* • David Arquette *David* ■ *Dir* Paul Warner • *Scr* Steven Alden, Paul Skemp

Fallen
★★★ 15

Supernatural thriller   1998 · US · Colour · 119min

In this convoluted, *Omen*-esque chiller, Denzel Washington gives a strong central performance as a Philadelphia homicide detective pursuing a supernatural serial killer. The initial development of the tale is intriguing, with seemingly disparate strands of information gradually combining into the discovery of a vengeful ancient god. But the atmosphere is only fitfully scary because of writer/producer Nicholas Kazan's loose-ended, pretentiously unresolved script. AJ Swearing, violence. *DVD*

Denzel Washington *John Hobbes* • John Goodman *Jonesy* • Donald Sutherland *Lieutenant Stanton* • Embeth Davidtz *Gretta Milano* • James Gandolfini *Lou* • Elias Koteas *Edgar Reese* • Gabriel Casseus *Art* ■ *Dir* Gregory Hoblit • *Scr* Nicholas Kazan

Fallen Angel
★★★★ PG

Film noir   1945 · US · BW · 95min

This terrific Fox *film noir* was directed by Otto Preminger in the wake of his classic *Laura*. Slightly softened by the casting of Alice Faye, who was ill at ease in a leading role, it is greatly enhanced by the presence of Dana Andrews and Linda Darnell. They're a nervy opportunist and sexy paramour respectively in a knockout plot involving Andrews's wish to quit respectable Faye for bad girl Darnell. Watch Andrews – his quizzical, deadpan features always seemed more alert for Preminger than under any other director. TS *DVD* *SD*

Alice Faye *June Mills* • Dana Andrews *Eric Stanton* • Linda Darnell *Stella* • Charles Bickford *Mark Judd* • Anne Revere *Clara Mills* • Bruce Cabot *Dave Atkins* • John Carradine *Professor Madley* • Percy Kilbride *Pop* ■ *Dir* Otto Preminger • *Scr* Harry Kleiner, from the novel by Marty Holland

Fallen Angels
★★★★ 15

Comedy drama   1995 · HK · Colour · 94min

Asian film-maker Wong Kar-Wai always offers skewed and original views of a seemingly familiar world, accompanied by weirdly inappropriate pop music. Here the director takes his peripatetic camera on a vivid trip through the neon-soaked nightlife of Hong Kong as hitman Leon Lai comes into contact with three other frustrated lost souls. The multilayered story blends riveting philosophical musings on missed opportunities, the impermanence of memory and the inevitability of loneliness, brilliantly serving it all up in a *Pulp Fiction*-style wrapper. AJ Cantonese +subtitles. *DVD* *SD*

Leon Lai *Wong Chi-Ming* • Takeshi Kaneshiro *He Zhiwu* • Charlie Yeung *Cherry* • Michelle Reis *Agent* • Karen Mok *Blondie* ■ *Dir/Scr* Wong Kar-Wai

The Fallen Idol
★★★★ PG

Thriller   1948 · UK · BW · 91min

While working as a film critic in the 1930s, Graham Greene noticed Carol Reed's developing directorial talent. This was the first of their three collaborations as writer and director, and what a minor masterpiece it is. Bobby Henrey gives an exceptional performance as the ambassador's son whose attempts to help the butler he idolises only land the latter in hot water with the police after the suspicious death of the butler's wife. Credit is also due to Ralph Richardson and Michèle Morgan for allowing the boy to steal every scene in the interest of suspense. DP *DVD* *SD*

Ralph Richardson *Baines* • Michèle Morgan *Julie* • Bobby Henrey *Felipe* • Sonia Dresdel *Mrs Baines* • Denis O'Dea *Inspector Crowe* • Walter Fitzgerald *Dr Fenton* • Dandy Nichols *Mrs Patterson* • Bernard Lee *Detective Hart* • Jack Hawkins *Detective Lake* ■ *Dir* Carol Reed • *Scr* Graham Greene, Lesley Storm, William Templeton, from the short story *The Basement Room* by Graham Greene

The Fallen Sparrow ★★★ PG

Spy drama   1943 · US · BW · 93min

In this entertaining though sometimes unintelligible spy drama, there's a strong feeling of a left-leaning plot that's been knobbled by the studio. Tough guy John Garfield gives a great performance as the battle weary veteran who returns from the hell of an internment camp in the Spanish Civil War only to find he's being chased by Nazi agents in the US. Maureen O'Hara is on hand to help, but this *film noir*-like material needed a tighter hand on the tiller than studio hack Richard Wallace. TS *DVD*

John Garfield *Kit* • Maureen O'Hara *Toni Donne* • Walter Slezak *Dr Skaas* • Patricia Morison *Barby Taviton* • Martha O'Driscoll *Whitney Hamilton* • Bruce Edwards *Ab Parker* ■ *Dir* Richard Wallace • *Scr* Warren Duff, from the novel by Dorothy B Hughes

The Falling ★★★★ 15
Mystery thriller 2014 · UK · Colour · 97min

Fear of female sexuality is at the heart of this deliciously dreamy drama. Set in a strict English girls' school in 1969, it finds a group of teens, including Maisie Williams, under the spell of Florence Pugh, whose husky tones and promiscuity signal her maturity. When a tragedy occurs, it triggers a fainting epidemic among the pupils. Writer/director Carol Morley (*Dreams of a Life*) crafts a bewitching and immersive allegory that's beautifully shot by Agnès Godard. The influences of *Twin Peaks* and *Picnic at Hanging Rock* are evident but *The Falling* remains quintessentially, gloriously British. EAS *DVD*

Maisie Williams *Lydia Lamont* • Florence Pugh *Abbie Mortimer* • Greta Scacchi *Miss Mantel* • Monica Dolan *Miss Alvaro* • Maxine Peake *Eileen Lamont* • Mathew Baynton *Mr Hopkins* ■ *Dir/Scr* Carol Morley • *Cinematographer* Agnès Godard • *Music* Tracey Thorn

Falling Down ★★★★ 18
Satirical thriller 1992 · US/Fr · Colour · 107min

Made from a script rejected by every major Hollywood studio, this is a storming portrait of inner-city life in America. That stateside critics were virtually unanimous in condemning it as a dangerous and irresponsible fantasy says more about the insecurities of the world's sole remaining superpower than it does about the merits of Joel Schumacher's bold, believable and darkly funny film. As the headlines never cease to remind us, the idea that an ordinary Joe can snap and go on a violent spree is depressingly feasible. Michael Douglas gives a superb performance and he's matched by the excellent Robert Duvall. Courageous, mature film-making. DP Swearing, violence. *DVD* *Blu-ray*

Michael Douglas (1) *D-Fens, William Foster* • Robert Duvall *Prendergast* • Barbara Hershey *Beth* • Rachel Ticotin *Sandra* • Tuesday Weld *Mrs Prendergast* • Frederic Forrest *Surplus Store owner* • Lois Smith *D-Fens's mother* • Joey Hope Singer *Adele* ■ *Dir* Joel Schumacher • *Scr* Ebbe Roe Smith

Falling from Grace ★★ 15
Drama 1992 · US · Colour · 96min

Rock star John Mellencamp made his directorial debut with this tale of a country singer who discovers he has few fans in his home town. Larry McMurtry wrote the screenplay, but this is closer to *Texasville* than it is to *The Last Picture Show*, with such clichéd characters as a brutal father, an envious brother and an embittered old flame moping around a dead-end part of Indiana. The storyline is unlikely in the extreme, but this is still an astute portrait of the delusions that attend celebrity. DP

John Mellencamp *Bud Parks* • Mariel Hemingway *Alice Parks* • Claude Akins *Speck Parks* • Dub Taylor *Grandpa Parks* • Kay Lenz *PJ Parks* • Larry Crane *Ramey Parks* • Kate Noonan *Linda* ■ *Dir* John Mellencamp • *Scr* Larry McMurtry

Falling in Love ★★★ PG
Romantic drama 1984 · US · Colour · 101min

Robert De Niro and Meryl Streep are such dramatic heavyweights it's difficult to see them as ordinary people involved in a typical affair. Yet this succeeds thanks to their subtle performances, as the separately married Manhattan commuters whose daily contact becomes mutual obsession. Ulu Grosbard's stilted direction is a hindrance, but De Niro and Streep more than compensate. TH Swearing. *DVD*

Meryl Streep *Molly Gilmore* • Robert De Niro *Frank Raftis* • Harvey Keitel *Ed Lasky* • Jane Kaczmarek *Ann Raftis* • George Martin (1) *John Trainer* • David Clennon *Brian Gilmore* • Dianne Wiest *Isabelle* ■ *Dir* Ulu Grosbard • *Scr* Michael Christofer

Falling in Love Again ★★★ 12
Romantic comedy drama 1980 · US · Colour · 95min

Elliott Gould is perfectly cast as the New Yorker in midlife crisis, remembering the girl he loved and won when they were both much younger. Unfortunately, his wife Susannah York couldn't make a success of their married life. For all its spot-on observations, this comedy drama about an American hero who can't come to terms with the way things are is introspective and narcissistic. York's younger self is played by Michelle Pfeiffer with a glow that suggested stardom was ahead. TH *DVD*

Elliott Gould *Harry Lewis* • Susannah York *Sue Lewis* • Michelle Pfeiffer *Sue Wellington* • Kaye Ballard *Mrs Lewis* • Stuart Paul *Pompadour/Young Harry* • Robert Hackman *Mr Lewis* • Steven Paul *Stan the con* • Todd Helper *Alan Childs* ■ *Dir* Steven Paul • *Scr* Steven Paul, Ted Allan, Susannah York, from a story by Hank Paul, Steven Paul

Falling in Love with the Girl Next Door ★★
Romantic comedy 2006 · US · Colour · 92min

California's Catalina Island is the picturesque location for this light and innocuous romantic comedy, featuring a host of familiar TV talent. Shelley Long and Patty Duke play the long feuding neighbours whose one-upmanship during the annual Halloween party causes an emotional headache for their adult children (Crystal Allen and Ken Marino) after the duo secretly fall in love. Though the constant rivalry starts to feel a bit daft and overplayed, it does give the plot welcome colour and focus - especially since Allen and Marino's bland, developing relationship dominates the action. Ultimately, events are extremely predictable but they're warm-hearted enough to enjoy, with a suitably cosy finale to leave viewers on a high. SF

Patty Duke *Bridget Connolly* • Shelley Long *Betsy Lucas* • Crystal Allen *Theresa Connolly* • Ken Marino *Mark Lucas* • Patrick Duffy *James Connolly* • Bruce Boxleitner *Frank Lucas* ■ *Dir* Armand Mastroianni • *Scr* Sally Nemeth

The Falls ★★★★ PG
Science-fiction drama 1980 · UK · Colour · 186min

Peter Greenaway is at his most mischievously accessible and intellectually sophisticated in this pastiche documentary chronicling the impact of an unexplained phenomenon dubbed the "Violent Unknown Event" (VUE) on 92 people whose surnames all contain the word "Fall". The accompanying commentary, delineating the biographies of these eccentric unfortunates, is stuffed with literate wordplay, surreal concepts, numerical sequences and satirical asides, as Greenaway links the VUE with various bizarre ornithological and linguistic manifestations. The use of found footage and photography is equally inspired, as it enables Greenaway to demonstrate his visual acuity while reinforcing a Pythonesque absurdity. DP *DVD*

Colin Cantlie *Narrator* • Hilary Thompson *Narrator* • Sheila Canfield *Narrator* • Adam Leys *Narrator* • Serena MacBeth *Narrator* • Martin Burrows *Narrator* ■ *Dir/Scr* Peter Greenaway • *Cinematographers* Mike Coles, John Rosenberg • *Music* Michael Nyman, Brian Eno, John Hyde, Keith Pendlebury

False Identity ★★ 15
Thriller 1990 · US · Colour · 94min

James Keach directs his brother Stacy in this suspense thriller about a man who returns home after nearly 20 years in prison, unable to remember much of his past. Keach is terrific as the disturbed ex-con and is given impressive support from Geneviève Bujold (*Coma*) and Veronica Cartwright (*Alien*), but this is eventually spoiled by a badly fitting finale. Shame, because otherwise this is a well-played and interesting drama. JB

Stacy Keach *Harlan Errickson/Ben Driscoll* • Geneviève Bujold *Rachel Roux* • Tobin Bell *Marshall Errickson* • Veronica Cartwright *Vera Errickson* • Mimi Maynard *Audrey* • Mike Champion [Michael Champion] *Luther* ■ *Dir* James Keach • *Scr* Sandra K Bailey

Fame ★★★ 15
Musical drama 1980 · US · Colour · 128min

This musical drama from director Alan Parker might not be as much fun as *Bugsy Malone* and the songs aren't a patch on those in *The Commitments*, but it is, nevertheless, a thoroughly entertaining look at life in New York's High School for the Performing Arts (and, more to the point, it's miles better than the TV series that followed). Interestingly enough, none of the cast playing in a film all about making it big has gone on to become a movie star. A remake, with original cast member Debbie Allen, is released in September 2009. DP Swearing, drug abuse, a sex scene, brief nudity. *DVD*

Eddie Barth *Angelo* • Irene Cara *Coco Hernandez* • Lee Curreri *Bruno Martelli* • Laura Dean *Lisa Monroe* • Antonia Franceschi *Hilary Van Doren* • Boyd Gaines *Michael* • Albert Hague *Shorofsky* • Tresa Hughes *Naomi Finsecker* • Gene Anthony Ray *Leroy Johnson* • Debbie Allen *Lydia* ■ *Dir* Alan Parker • *Scr* Christopher Gore

Fame ★★ 12
Musical drama 2009 · US · Colour · 117min

A fresh intake of students at New York's School of Performing Arts sweat their way towards a start in showbiz in this makeover of Alan Parker's 1980 hit musical. The result is clearly pitched at an audience weaned on *High School Musical*, who may not notice that - despite the earnest efforts of faculty members Kelsey Grammer and Charles S Dutton - the plot is a string of clichés. There's nothing here as memorable as Irene Cara's original theme song - a fact we're reminded of when a grisly cover version seeps out over the closing credits. TJ *DVD* *Blu-ray*

Debbie Allen *Principal Angela Simms* • Charles S Dutton *Mr James Dowd* • Kelsey Grammer *Mr Martin Cranston* • Bebe Neuwirth *Ms Lynn Kraft* • Asher Brook *Marco* • Kherington Payne *Alice* • Kristy Flores *Rosie Martinez* • Kay Panabaker *Jenny Garrison* ■ *Dir* Kevin Tancharoen • *Scr* Allison Burnett, from the 1980 film

Fame Is the Spur ★★★
Drama 1947 · UK · BW · 115min

Labour's first prime minister, Ramsay MacDonald, was supposedly the inspiration for Howard Spring's bestseller, which is the source for director Roy Boulting's political drama. Yet Nigel Balchin's screenplay owes more to melodramatic contrivance than to historical fact, as Michael Redgrave rises from the north country slums to high office by waving his grandfather's trusty sword during his rabble-rousing speeches, and exploiting friends and foes alike. DP

Michael Redgrave *Hamer Radshaw* • Rosamund John *Ann Radshaw* • Bernard Miles *Tom Hanaway* • Hugh Burden *Arnold Ryerson* • Jean Shepeard *Mrs Radshaw* • Guy Verney *Grandpa* ■ *Dir* Roy Boulting • *Scr* Nigel Balchin, from a book by Howard Spring

La Famille Bélier ★★★★ 12A
Comedy drama 2014 · Fr/Bel · Colour · 100min

Karin Viard and François Damiens are the slightly eccentric, deaf, farming parents of hearing teenage daughter Louane Emera. But when Emera discovers she possesses an amazing soprano voice, tough decisions loom in a film that lures us in through good-natured knockabout comedy, but then delivers affecting emotions. Whatever the arguments about hearing performers in deaf roles, Viard and Damiens are utterly believable, while Emera was a deserved winner of a César on her debut. A real crowd-pleaser, this is well worth seeking out. TJ French, French sign language +subtitles. Sex references, some swearing

Karin Viard *Gigi* • François Damiens *Rodolphe* • Eric Elmosnino *Thomasson* • Louane Emera *Paula* ■ *Dir* Eric Lartigau • *Scr* Victoria Bedos,

Stanislas Carré de Malberg, with Eric Lartigau, Thomas Bidegain (adaptation), from an idea by Victoria Bedos

The Family ★★★★
Drama 1987 · It/Fr · Colour · 128min

Without once leaving the symbolically decorated apartment of an upper-middle-class Roman family, this increasingly static conversation piece explores 80 years of Italian national and domestic trauma through the eyes of one man and his quarrelsome kinsmen. Leading an ensemble cast of uniform excellence, Vittorio Gassman laments his decision to marry Stefania Sandrelli instead of her sister, Fanny Ardant, while director Ettore Scola shifts effortlessly between melodrama and comedy, while passing insightful comments on the national character. DP Italian +subtitles.

Vittorio Gassman *Carlo/Carlo's grandfather* • Fanny Ardant *Adriana* • Stefania Sandrelli *Beatrice* • Andrea Occhipinti *Carlo, as a young man* • Jo Champa *Adriana, as a young woman* ■ *Dir* Ettore Scola • *Scr* Ruggero Maccari, Furio Scarpelli, Ettore Scola

The Family ★★ 15
Action comedy thriller 2013 · US/Fr · Colour · 107min

Robert De Niro drowsily parodies his macho image in another Mob comedy, this time from French writer/director Luc Besson. De Niro plays a Mafia hood relocated from Brooklyn to Normandy in a wildly extravagant Witness Protection Program scheme with his wife (Michelle Pfeiffer) and kids. Pfeiffer at least makes the most of her part, but Besson mocks his compatriots, often using extreme violence instead of a sly punch line. And for the most part, the visuals are as cheap as the jokes. SP Violence, swearing, sex scenes. *DVD* *Blu-ray*

Robert De Niro *Fred Blake/Giovanni Manzoni* • Michelle Pfeiffer *Maggie Blake* • Tommy Lee Jones *Robert Stansfield* • Dianna Agron *Belle Blake* • John D'Leo *Warren Blake* ■ *Dir* Luc Besson • *Scr* Luc Besson, Michael Caleo, from the novel *Malavita* by Tonino Benacquista

A Family Affair ★★
Comedy 1937 · US · BW · 68min

Worthy of a modest footnote in cinema history as being the first in the long-running Andy Hardy series - 15 films in all. Mickey Rooney plays the small-town American teen whose father is the local judge, the role played here by Lionel Barrymore, later inherited by Lewis Stone. Rooney falls for a girl, while his dad has work-related problems. As per the series which followed, it's a hymn to all things American, land of the free and, it seems, of the cute and precocious. AT

Lionel Barrymore *Judge Hardy* • Mickey Rooney *Andy Hardy* • Cecilia Parker *Marian Hardy* • Eric Linden *Wayne Trenton* • Charley Grapewin *Frank Redmond* • Spring Byington *Mrs Hardy* • Julie Haydon *Joan Hardy* ■ *Dir* George B Seitz • *Scr* Kay Van Riper, from the play *Skidding* by Aurania Rouverol

Family Business ★★★ 15
Comedy drama 1989 · US · Colour · 109min

The line-up is mouthwatering (Sean Connery, Dustin Hoffman and Matthew Broderick, plus director Sidney Lumet), but the result is something of a disappointment. Connery plays an irascible, old-school thief and Hoffman is his bitter son who is now desperately trying to go straight. However, he is reluctantly drawn back into a life of crime when he learns that his own son (Broderick) is about to go to work with grandpa in the family business. The scenes between the leads are superb, but all three are poorly served by an ill-focused script and surprisingly sluggish direction. JF Swearing, violence. *DVD*

Sean Connery *Jessie McMullen* • Dustin Hoffman *Vito McMullen* • Matthew Broderick *Adam McMullen* • Rosana De Soto *Elaine McMullen* • Janet Carroll *Margie* • Victoria Jackson *Christine* • Bill McCutcheon *Doheny* • Deborah Rush *Michele Dempsey* ■ *Dir* Sidney Lumet • *Scr* Vincent Patrick, from his book

F

The Family Friend ★★★ 15

Drama   2006 · It/Fr · Colour · 102min

Despite a remarkable display of grasping misanthropy by stage veteran Giacomo Rizzo, writer/director Paolo Sorrentino's third feature lacks the wit and precision of his excellent *The Consequences of Love*. Rizzo revels in his role as the elderly tailor with a profitable sideline as a loan shark. When bride-to-be Laura Chiatti agrees to sleep with him to reduce the interest charged on her father's loan, his obsession clouds his judgement. Sorrentino's use of colour and composition is exemplary and Luca Bigazzi's photography is never less than painterly. But the contention that Rizzo's avarice and lechery are representative of a universal dishonesty and immorality proves unconvincing. DP
Italian +subtitles. Swearing, sex scenes.
DVD

Giacomo Rizzo *Geremia* • Fabrizio Bentivoglio *Gino* • Laura Chiatti *Rosalba* • Gigi Angelillo *Saverio* • Clara Bindi *Geremia's mother* • Barbara Valmorin *Bingo's grandmother* ■ *Dir/Scr* Paolo Sorrentino • *Cinematographer* Luca Bigazzi

Family Gathering ★★

Drama   2010 · US · Colour · 89min

In this contrived melodrama, Natasha Henstridge plays a New York designer who ends up neck-deep in clichés when she returns to her family farm for her mother's funeral. Father/daughter conflict erupts, exacerbated by a "business is struggling" subplot. You can easily guess what follows, as Henstridge's character adopts an allegedly useless sheepdog and the appropriately named Lucky proves the solution to the clan's problems – both financial and emotional. Everything's very convenient and reductive, but it could have been saved by a bit more genuine heart. SF

Natasha Henstridge *Lisa Rayborn* • Harry Hamlin *Jim Rayborn* • Lawrence Dane *Clay Rayborn* • Anthony Lemke *Don Lally* ■ *Dir* John Bradshaw • *Scr* Kevin Commins

The Family Jewels ★ U

Comedy   1965 · US · Colour · 95min

After the split with comedy partner Dean Martin, the unique talents of Jerry Lewis made him one of those performers you just couldn't ignore. But the man who influenced Jim Carrey and Adam Sandler began at one point to overreach himself and this movie is a sorry reminder of that period. Here, Lewis plays seven roles as potential guardians of precocious little Donna Butterworth, heiress to a fortune. He also directed this clumsy, unfunny load of old tripe. RS *DVD*

Jerry Lewis *Willard Woodward/Everett Peyton/ James Peyton/Eddie Peyton/Julius Peyton/ "Bugs" Peyton/Skylock Peyton* • Sebastian Cabot *Dr Matson* • Donna Butterworth *Donna Peyton* • Jay Adler *Attorney* ■ *Dir* Jerry Lewis • *Scr* Jerry Lewis, Bill Richmond

Family Life ★★★ 15

Drama   1971 · UK · Colour · 103min

This is a harrowing study of mental illness and the methods of treating it. Making only his third feature, director Ken Loach was already employing the uncompromisingly realistic style that has since become his trademark and some of the scenes in which teenager Sandy Ratcliff is subjected to electroconvulsive therapy are among the most traumatic of her career. Rarely has family life been presented in such a gloomy light, and Bill Dean and Grace Cave deserve much credit for depicting such thoroughly detestable parents. Over-manipulative, maybe, but still deeply disturbing. DP
Violence, swearing. *DVD*

Sandy Ratcliff *Janice Baildon* • Bill Dean *Mr Baildon* • Grace Cave *Mrs Baildon* • Malcolm Tierney *Tim* • Hilary Martyn *Barbara Baildon* • Michael Riddall *Dr Donaldson* • Alan MacNaughtan *Mr Carswell* • Johnny Gee *Man in garden* ■ *Dir* Ken Loach • *Scr* David Mercer, from his TV play *In Two Minds*

The Family Man ★★★ 12

Seasonal romantic fantasy
2000 · US · Colour · 129min

Nicolas Cage is the high-powered businessman who goes to bed in his designer Manhattan apartment on Christmas Eve, but wakes up in a suburban home on Christmas Day, complete with wife, dog and kids. It seems he's getting the chance to see what his life would have been like had he stayed with his college sweetheart Téa Leoni instead of pursuing a highly successful life in the fast lane. Cage is fun as the fish out of water trying to adapt to school runs and working at a local tyre company, and Leoni is spot-on as his harassed wife. JB *DVD*

Nicolas Cage *Jack Campbell* • Téa Leoni *Kate* • Don Cheadle *Cash* • Jeremy Piven *Arnie* • Saul Rubinek *Alan Mintz* • Josef Sommer *Lassiter* ■ *Dir* Brett Ratner • *Scr* David Diamond, David Weissman

Family Plan ★ PG

Comedy   1997 · US · Colour · 92min

Leslie Nielsen has persisted with the spoofery that relaunched his career, with patchy results. With this turkey, however, he hits a new low. After the death of an old friend, the bungling Nielsen finds himself in charge of a crumbling summer camp for orphans; Judge Reinhold is the slimeball out to convert the property into a holiday resort. JF Some swearing. *DVD*

Leslie Nielsen *Harry Haber* • Judge Reinhold *Jeffrey Shayes* • Eddie Bowz *Matt Nolan* • Emily Procter *Julie Rubins* ■ *Dir* Fred Gerber • *Scr* Paul Bernbaum

Family Plan ★★

Romantic comedy   2005 · US · Colour · 85min

Blatantly ripping off the plot of the classic farce *Christmas in Connecticut*, this romantic comedy couldn't have a better pedigree. However, it's closer in tone to Arnold Schwarzenegger's mediocre 1992 remake than Peter Godfrey's 1945 original. Tori Spelling tries hard as the single careerist who has to reapply for her own job when her company changes hands. Greg Germann (of *Ally McBeal* fame) mugs genially and there's an early glimpse of *Little Miss Sunshine's* Abigail Breslin as the "borrowed" daughter, but this is lacklustre fare. DP

Tori Spelling *Charlie McKenzie* • Jordan Bridges *Buck Maddox* • Greg Germann *Edward Walcott* • Kali Rocha *Stacy* • Kate Vernon *Victoria Walcott* • Christopher Cass *Troy* • Abigail Breslin *Nicole* ■ *Dir* David S Cass Sr • *Scr* Rick Gitelson [Richard Gitelson]

Family Plot ★★★★ PG

Comedy thriller   1976 · US · Colour · 115min

Fifty years after he made what he regarded as his directorial debut, Alfred Hitchcock signed off with this gently twisting thriller. Hitchcock coaxes along a deliciously contrived plot that sets kidnappers William Devane and Karen Black on a collision course with fake medium Barbara Harris and her partner Bruce Dern as they search for a missing heir. The performances are perfect, and it is to Hollywood's shame that it has not made better use of such gifted players since. DP *DVD* ⓑ

Karen Black *Fran* • Bruce Dern *Lumley* • Barbara Harris *Blanche* • William Devane *Adamson* • Ed Lauter *Maloney* • Cathleen Nesbitt *Julia Rainbird* • Katherine Helmond *Mrs Maloney* • Warren J Kemmerling [Warren Kemmerling] *Grandison* ■ *Dir* Alfred Hitchcock • *Scr* Ernest Lehman, from the book *The Rainbird Pattern* by Victor Canning

Family Sins ★★

Drama   2004 · US · Colour · 86min

In this fact-based TV movie, lawyer Will Patton seeks to convict seemingly respectable estate agent Kirstie Alley, who's charged with fronting a family *firm* that's involved in robbery, rape, arson, kidnapping and much more. Small-screen outings inspired by headlines tend to be sensationalist, but director Graeme Clifford just about keeps the lid on proceedings. He's helped by a splendidly multilayered performance from Alley, and steady contributions from Patton and Deanna Milligan, as the victim of Alley's "charity" who blows the whistle. DP

Kirstie Alley *Brenda Geck* • Deanna Milligan *Marie Devereaux* • Will Patton *Philip Rothman* • Kathleen Wilhoite *Nadine Devereaux* • Kevin McNulty *Kenneth Geck* • David Richmond-Peck *Joey Geck* • Patrick Gilmore *Scott Mathers* ■ *Dir* Graeme Clifford • *Scr* Donald Martin

The Family Stone ★★★ PG

Romantic comedy drama
2005 · US · Colour · 98min

Sarah Jessica Parker plays it admirably straight as the outsider who's brought home for Christmas by boyfriend Dermot Mulroney where he's planning to propose. But his family (headed by a steely Diane Keaton) are thrown into upheaval, and the reception they give Parker is as hard as their name suggests. The dearth of likeable characters make this an uneasy experience initially. Then writer/director Thomas Bezucha begins to unmask the monsters to reveal a disarming humanity beneath, resulting in a warm yet sharply funny family portrait. SP *DVD*

Sarah Jessica Parker *Meredith Morton* • Diane Keaton *Sybil Stone* • Dermot Mulroney *Everett Stone* • Rachel McAdams *Amy Stone* • Claire Danes *Julie Morton* • Luke Wilson *Ben Stone* • Craig T Nelson *Kelly Stone* ■ *Dir/Scr* Thomas Bezucha

A Family Thing ★★ 15

Comedy drama   1996 · US · Colour · 104min

Robert Duvall and James Earl Jones take centre stage in this charming if somewhat flimsy comedy drama. Duvall plays a good ole boy from Arkansas who is astonished to discover on his mother's death that his real mum was a black servant. He then reluctantly sets out to meet his half-brother, city cop Jones. The sparring of the two grumpy old men overcomes the deficiencies in plot and the sentimentality in a script co-written by Billy Bob Thornton. JF
Swearing, brief violence.

Robert Duvall *Earl Pilcher, Jr* • James Earl Jones *Ray Murdoch* • Michael Beach *Virgil* • Irma P Hall *Aunt T* • Grace Zabriskie *Ruby* • Regina Taylor *Ann* • Mary Jackson *Carrie* ■ *Dir* Richard Pearce • *Scr* Tom Epperson, Billy Bob Thornton

Family Viewing ★★★★ 15

Satirical drama   1987 · Can · Colour · 82min

Atom Egoyan makes inspired use of camcorder footage in this remarkable satire on dysfunctional nuclear family life. Delving into the darkest corners of society, Egoyan emerges with a story about a quiet teenager Aidan Tierney who finds refuge with his institutionalised grandmother away from the sexual obsessions of his seemingly respectable father and stepmother. Exploring themes that recur in all his films, this is a sly, sharp and often touching picture. DP *DVD* ⓑ

David Hemblen *Stan* • Aidan Tierney *Van* • Gabrielle Rose *Sandra* • Arsinée Khanjian *Aline* • Selma Keklikian *Armen* • Jeanne Sabourin *Aline's mother* • Rose Sarkisyan *Van's mother* ■ *Dir/Scr* Atom Egoyan

The Family Way ★★★★ 15

Comedy drama   1966 · UK · Colour · 110min

Considered somewhat risqué in its day, this gentle comedy can now be seen as a fond portrait of an era when sex was still taboo. Complete with a score by Paul McCartney, it recounts the experience of so many 1960s newlyweds who had to share a house with their in-laws for much of the early part of their married lives. Hywel Bennett is bang on form as the husband so wound up by cohabitation that he is unable to consummate his marriage to the equally impressive Hayley Mills. But it's her real-life dad, John Mills, who steals the show with a splendid study in working-class cantankerousness. DP *DVD*

Hayley Mills *Jenny Piper* • Hywel Bennett *Arthur Fitton* • John Mills *Ezra Fitton* • Marjorie Rhodes *Lucy Fitton* • Avril Angers *Liz Piper* • John Comer *Leslie Piper* • Wilfred Pickles *Uncle Fred* • Barry Foster *Joe Thompson* ■ *Dir* Roy Boulting • *Scr*
Bill Naughton, Roy Boulting, Jeffrey Dell, from the play *All in Good Time* by Bill Naughton • *Music* Paul McCartney

The Famous Sword ★★★

Period drama   1945 · Jpn · BW · 65min

Keen to keep working, but reluctant to shoot the kind of propaganda demanded by the government, Kenji Mizoguchi spent the Second World War making historical dramas. This was his last solo wartime project and scrupulously avoids any overtly political message. Instead, it serves up a tale of daughterly determination and loyal devotion, in which apprentice swordmaker Shotaro Hanayagi seeks the assistance of master craftsman Eijiro Yanagi in making the weapon that will enable Isuzu Yamada to avenge her murdered father. While nowhere near as impressive as his work either side of the war, this is anything but anodyne entertainment. DP Japanese +subtitles.

Shotaro Hanayagi *Kiyone Sakurai* • Isuzu Yamada *Sasae Onoda* • Ichijiro Oya *Kozaemon Onoda* • Eijiro Yanagi *Kiyohide Yamatomori* • Kan Ishii *Kiyotsugu* ■ *Dir* Kenji Mizoguchi • *Scr* Matsutaro Kawaguchi

The Fan ★★ PG

Period drama   1949 · US · BW · 76min

This is director Otto Preminger's rather dull, abridged version of Oscar Wilde's witty play, *Lady Windermere's Fan*. Although the screenplay was co-authored by famed wit Dorothy Parker, this is an updated and desecrated version of the plot, suffering from the heavy-handed directorial style. Jeanne Crain and Richard Greene are colourless Windermeres, George Sanders is a dull Lord Darlington, and, in her last movie, the lovely Madeleine Carroll a wan Mrs Erlynne. TS *DVD*

Jeanne Crain *Lady Windermere* • Madeleine Carroll *Mrs Erlynne* • George Sanders *Lord Darlington* • Richard Greene *Lord Windermere* • Martita Hunt *Duchess of Berwick* ■ *Dir* Otto Preminger • *Scr* Walter Reisch, Dorothy Parker, Ross Evans, from the play *Lady Windermere's Fan* by Oscar Wilde

The Fan ★★★ 18

Thriller   1981 · US · Colour · 90min

Fans of charismatic old-timers will enjoy this thriller about glamorous stage star Lauren Bacall being pursued by psychotic stalker Michael Biehn. The excellent James Garner appears as Bacall's ex-husband, and Maureen Stapleton plays her secretary. But it's Bacall's picture, and she has no problems convincing us she's a star of the first order. AT

Lauren Bacall *Sally Ross* • James Garner *Jake Berman* • Maureen Stapleton *Belle Goldman* • Hector Elizondo *Ralph Andrews* • Michael Biehn *Douglas Breen* • Anna Maria Horsford *Emily Stolz* • Kurt R Johnson *David Branum* ■ *Dir* Edward Bianchi • *Scr* Priscilla Chapman, John Hartwell, from the novel by Bob Randall

The Fan ★★ 15

Thriller   1996 · US · Colour · 111min

Robert De Niro is the psycho fan from hell and the object of his obsession is baseball star Wesley Snipes. It's when the San Francisco Giant team member hits a losing streak that the pitiful loser moves into action with fatal consequences. Despite being directed by Tony Scott with flash and dash, his over-vigorous use of mannered camera angles does nothing for this implausible plot that's short of both suspense and surprise. AJ *DVD*

Robert De Niro *Gil Renard* • Wesley Snipes *Bobby Rayburn* • Ellen Barkin *Jewel Stern* • John Leguizamo *Manny* • Benicio Del Toro *Juan Primo* • Patti D'Arbanville-Quinn [Patti D'Arbanville] *Ellen Renard* ■ *Dir* Tony Scott • *Scr* Phoef Sutton, from the story by Peter Abrahams

Fanboys ★★★ 15

Road movie comedy   2008 · US · Colour · 85min

If you're allergic to Wookies, Boba Fett or lightsabers, look away now. Set in 1998, this uber-geek comedy follows a bunch of 20-something *Star Wars* fans – Sam Huntington, Christopher Marquette, Dan

Fogler and Jay Baruchel – on a harebrained quest to break into Skywalker Ranch and steal a copy of the long-awaited *Star Wars Episode I: the Phantom Menace*. Full of in-jokes, it's aimed squarely at the comic-book store, memorabilia-collecting fraternity, but its sweet-natured jibes at sci-fi fandom only raise the odd chuckle. JR *DVD* 🔵

Sam Huntington *Eric* • Dan Fogler *Hutch* • Jay Baruchel *Windows* • Kristen Bell *Zoe* • Christopher George Marquette *Linus* • Carrie Fisher *Doctor* • William Shatner • Billy Dee Williams *Judge Reinhold* • Seth Rogen *Admiral Seasholtz/Alien/Roach* ■ *Dir* Kyle Newman • *Scr* Ernest Cline, Adam F Goldberg, from a story by Cline, Dan Pulick

Fancy Pants ★★★ U
Musical comedy 1950 · US · Colour · 92min

This riotous teaming of Bob Hope and Lucille Ball is yet another reworking of *Ruggles of Red Gap*. It finds Hope out West again, after his success as *The Paleface*. Hope makes not the slightest attempt to "buttle" in the English manner, but Ball is excellent as a rootin' tootin' tomboy heiress. Director George Marshall simply indulges them. TS

Bob Hope *Humphrey* • Lucille Ball *Agatha Floud* • Bruce Cabot *Cart Belknap* • Jack Kirkwood *Mike Floud* • Lea Penman *Effie Floud* • Hugh French *George Van-Basingwell* ■ *Dir* George Marshall • *Scr* Edmund Hartmann [Edmund L Hartmann], Robert O'Brien, from the story *Ruggles of Red Gap* by Harry Leon Wilson

Fandango ★★★ 15
Comedy drama 1985 · US · Colour · 86min

This gently quirky rites-of-passage comedy drama began life as a student project for director Kevin Reynolds, and follows five college friends in the early 1970s who set off on one last adolescent adventure before entering adulthood. Kevin Costner shines as the anarchic unofficial leader of the group, but he is more than matched by Judd Nelson, who turns in a powerful, mature performance. JF Swearing, brief nudity.

Kevin Costner *Gardner Barnes* • Judd Nelson *Phil Hicks* • Sam Robards *Kenneth Waggener* • Chuck Bush *Dorman* • Brian Cesak *Lester* • Elizabeth Daily *Judy* ■ *Dir* Kevin Reynolds • *Scr* Kevin Reynolds, from his short film

Fanfan la Tulipe ★★★★ 12
Satirical historical romance
1951 · Fr · BW · 95min

This glorious spoof on the Hollywood swashbuckler is beautifully designed and filmed with a real feel for both the period trappings and the energetic action by cinematographer Christian Matras. The plot is fabulously preposterous, as Gérard Philipe confounds bandits and the Austrian army to win the heart of princess Sylvie Pelayo. With a sparkling script, a dashing lead and solid support from the likes of Gina Lollobrigida as Fanfan's mentor, it's no wonder Christian-Jaque won the best director prize at Cannes. DP French +subtitles. *DVD*

Gérard Philipe *Fanfan la Tulipe* • Gina Lollobrigida *Adeline* • Noël Roquevert *Fier-à-Bras* • Olivier Hussenot *Tranche Montagne* • Marcel Herrand *Louis XV* • Jean-Marc Tennberg *Lebel* • Sylvie Pelayo *Henriette de France* ■ *Dir* Christian-Jaque • *Scr* Christian-Jaque, René Wheeler, Henri Jeanson, from a story by René Wheeler, René Fallet

Fanny ★★★★
Drama 1932 · Fr · BW · 126min

Coming between *Marius* and *César*, the central segment of writer Marcel Pagnol's Marseille trilogy is easily the best directed. However, not even Marc Allégret could get much of a performance out of Orane Demazis, Pagnol's wife at the time. The rest of the cast are impeccable, though, with Raimu outstanding as the wily bar owner who persuades seafaring son Pierre Fresnay to abandon all claim to the child who has now found a father in widowed sailmaker, Fernand Charpin. The perfectly observed ambience and subtly shaded characters make this a joy to behold. DP French +subtitles.

Orane Demazis *Fanny* • Raimu *César* • Fernand Charpin *Panisse* • Pierre Fresnay *Marius* • Alida Rouffe *Honorine* • Robert Vattier *Mr Brun* ■ *Dir* Marc Allégret • *Scr* Marcel Pagnol, from his play, from his books *Marseilles Trilogy*

Fanny ★★
Drama 1961 · US · Colour · 133min

Stripped of its songs, Joshua Logan's reworking of his own 1954 Broadway production might have the striking Technicolor photography of Jack Cardiff in its corner, but it is utterly devoid of the local colour that made the 1932 adaptation of Marcel Pagnol's Marseille trilogy so enchanting. Charles Boyer is slyly charming as the waterfront bar owner who competes with sailmaker Maurice Chevalier for the affections of waif Leslie Caron, after lover Horst Buchholz leaves her pregnant. DP

Leslie Caron *Fanny* • Maurice Chevalier *Panisse* • Charles Boyer *César* • Horst Buchholz *Marius* • Baccaloni [Salvatore Baccaloni] *Escartifique* • Lionel Jeffries *M Brun* • Raymond Bussires *Admiral* • Victor Francen *Louis Panisse* ■ *Dir* Joshua Logan • *Scr* Julius J Epstein, from a play by SN Behrman, Joshua Logan, from the play by Marcel Pagnol, from the books *Marseilles Trilogy* by Marcel Pagnol

Fanny ★★★★ PG
Drama 2013 · Fr · Colour · 101min

The second instalment in Daniel Auteuil's remake of the classic Marcel Pagnol Marseille trilogy follows directly on from the ending of *Marius*. Here the focus switches to Victoire Bélézy's shellfish stallholder, whose troubled relationship with bar owner's son Marius (Raphaël Personnaz) leaves her open to an offer from elsewhere. Done with expertise and affection, this is quite irresistible, especially the play between Auteuil's crotchety patron and the very touching Bélézy, who gives a performance full of youthful passion. TJ French +subtitles.

Daniel Auteuil *César* • Victoire Bélézy *Fanny* • Jean-Pierre Darroussin *Panisse* • Raphaël Personnaz *Marius* • Marie-Anne Chazel *Honorine* ■ *Dir* Daniel Auteuil • *Scr* Daniel Auteuil, from the play by Marcel Pagnol

Fanny and Alexander ★★★★★ 15
Period drama
1982 · Swe/Fr/W Ger · Colour · 188min

The warmth, humour and compassion of this wonderful out-of-the-century family saga make it one of the most accessible movies ever made by Sweden's greatest director Ingmar Bergman. The story, which covers two years in the life of a well-to-do household as seen through the eyes of a small boy, is rendered all the more fascinating by the autobiographical elements that Bergman has included and by Sven Nykvist's Oscar-winning photography. The film takes us on a magical tour of the child's encounters with his oppressive, puritanical stepfather, his loving mother and his extended family in an atmosphere that is both cosy and scary. The result is an unmissable experience from a master film-maker. TH Swedish +subtitles. *DVD*

Gunn Wallgren *Grandmother Helena Ekdahl* • Börje Ahlstedt *Professor Carl Ekdahl* • Christina Schollin *Lydia Ekdahl* • Allan Edwall *Oscar Ekdahl* • Ewa Fröling *Emilie Ekdahl* • Pernilla Allwin *Fanny Ekdahl* • Bertil Guve *Alexander Ekdahl* • Jarl Kulle *Gustav Adolf Ekdahl* • Mona Malm *Alma Ekdahl* • Pernilla Wallgren [Pernilla August] *Maj* • Gunnar Björnstrand *Filip Landahl* • Jan Malmsjö *Bishop Edvard Vergerus* • Erland Josephson *Isak Jacobi* ■ *Dir/Scr* Ingmar Bergman • *Cinematographer* Sven Nykvist

Fanny & Elvis ★★ 15
Romantic comedy
1999 · UK/Fr · Colour · 106min

This soppy second-chance romance marks the directorial debut of writer Kay Mellor (best know for TV's *Band of Gold*), in which a budding Barbara Cartland finds millennial love with a much-married car dealer. Were it not for the knowing performances of Kerry Fox and Ray Winstone, the stodginess of Mellor's staging and the laziness of her

script would be all the more apparent. DP Swearing, sex scenes. *DVD*

Kerry Fox *Kate* • Ray Winstone *Dave* • Ben Daniels *Andrew* • David Morrissey *Rob* • Jennifer Saunders *Roanna* • Colin Salmon *Alan* • Gaynor Faye *Samantha* • William Ash *Rick* ■ *Dir/Scr* Kay Mellor

Fanny by Gaslight ★★★ PG
Period drama 1944 · UK · BW · 102min

This Gainsborough picture is more luridly Hogarthian than usual. Despite being visually sanitised, director Anthony Asquith's film doesn't hesitate in drawing attention to the sleazier corners of Victorian society. Phyllis Calvert plays the politician's illegitimate daughter whose unfortunate childhood threatens her future happiness. James Mason as an evil aristocrat and Stewart Granger as Calvert's suitor swagger in appropriate fashion. It seems innocent now, but it caused quite a fuss in its day. TH *DVD*

Phyllis Calvert *Fanny* • James Mason *Lord Manderstoke* • Stewart Granger *Harry Somerford* • Wilfrid Lawson *Chunks* • Jean Kent *Lucy* • Margaretta Scott *Alicia* • Nora Swinburne *Mrs Hopwood* • Cathleen Nesbitt *Kate Somerford* ■ *Dir* Anthony Asquith • *Scr* Doreen Montgomery, Aimee Stuart, from a novel by Michael Sadleir

Fanny Hill ★★ 18
Period erotic romp 1983 · UK · Colour · 93min

Although considerably classier than Russ Meyer's 1964 version, this is still a disappointingly bawdy dramatisation of John Cleland's 1749 erotic classic. Director Gerry O'Hara sets out to titillate rather than explore the sordid events behind the transformation of Lisa Raines from a comely country girl into a practised woman of pleasure. Moreover, this rambunctious approach leaves the admirably willing Oliver Reed and Shelley Winters little option but to go for pantomimic caricature, while Raines's shortcomings are as apparent as her charms. DP *DVD*

Lisa Raines [Lisa Foster] *Fanny Hill* • Oliver Reed *Lawyer* • Wilfrid Hyde White *Mr Barville* • Shelley Winters *Mrs Cole* • Alfred Marks *Lecher* ■ *Dir* Gerry O'Hara • *Scr* Stephen Chesley, from the novel *Fanny Hill - Memoirs of a Woman of Pleasure* by John Cleland

Fanny Hill: Memoirs of a Woman of Pleasure ★
Period erotic romp
1964 · US/W Ger · BW · 104min

Hilariously hyped at the time as a "female *Tom Jones*", this is notorious flesh merchant Russ Meyer's brush with the classics. In this case Meyer characteristically exploits the bawdy 18th-century novel about a young woman who finds herself working in a brothel, but his direction lacks any style or discernible talent. This is amateurish drivel that fails as comedy, titillation or historical fiction. RS

Miriam Hopkins *Mrs Maude Brown* • Leticia Roman *Fanny Hill* • Walter Giller *Hemingway* • Alex D'Arcy *The Admiral* • Helmut Weiss *Mr Dinklespieler* • Chris Howland *Mr Norbert* • Ulli Lommel *Charles* • Cara Garnett *Phoebe* ■ *Dir* Russ Meyer • *Scr* Robert Hill, from John Cleland's novel *Fanny Hill; or, Memoirs of a Woman of Pleasure*

LANDMARK FILM
Classical music-inspired imagery fills every frame in this first American film to use stereophonic sound

Fantasia ★★★★★★ U
Classic animation 1940 · US · Colour · 119min

This was a mighty innovation in feature-length cartoons as a concert of classical music is made visually articulate. Beethoven's *Pastoral* gets the kitsch treatment with cute mythology, and Mussorgsky's *Night on Bald Mountain* is a *danse macabre* of opened graves and broom-riding witches. Mickey Mouse even appears as Dukas's *Sorcerer's Apprentice*. Most successful are Bach abstractions, while the dying dinosaurs of Stravinsky's *Rite of Spring* represent an affirmation of life. Walt Disney and conductor Leopold Stokowski won a special Oscar for this high-

voltage masterpiece, which showed what could be achieved with a marriage of the technical (multiplane cameras, stereo sound) and the creative. TH *DVD* 🔵

Deems Taylor • Leopold Stokowski conducting the Philadelphia Symphony Orchestra ■ *Dir* Samuel Armstrong, James Algar, Bill Roberts, Paul Satterfield, Hamilton Luske, Jim Handley, Ford Beebe, Norm Ferguson [Norman Ferguson], Wilfred Jackson

Fantasia 2000 ★★★ U
Animation 1999 · US · Colour · 71min

The first release of the 21st century, and the only animated feature to be made in the giant IMAX format, Disney's long-awaited follow-up to the 1940 classic *Fantasia* is something of a disappointment. For while the spectacle is impressive, the artistic content is regrettably lacklustre. An ecological theme informs the visuals for Beethoven's *Fifth Symphony*, Respighi's *Pines of Rome* and Stravinsky's *Firebird Suite*; and Mickey Mouse returns for a underwhelming digital remastering of *The Sorcerer's Apprentice*. Worth catching for the experience. DP *DVD* 🔵

James Levine conducting the Chicago Symphony Orchestra • Steve Martin • Itzhak Perlman • Quincy Jones • Bette Midler • James Earl Jones • Penn [Penn Jillette] *Penn Jillette* • Teller • Angela Lansbury ■ *Dir* Pixote Hunt, Hendel Butoy, Eric Goldberg, James Algar, Francis Glebas, Paul Brizzi, Gaetan Brizzi, Don Hahn

The Fantasist ★★ 18
Thriller 1986 · Ire · Colour · 94min

Quite why director Robin Hardy never managed to live up to the huge potential of cult classic *The Wicker Man* remains a perplexing mystery. His only other feature film is an intriguing but confused chiller about a young woman (Moira Harris) heading to the bright lights of Dublin, only to fall into the radar of a disturbed psychopath who is terrorising the city. The slasher elements of the tale just don't gel with the setting and the psychological musings don't ring true either. JF

Moira Harris *Patricia Teeling* • Christopher Cazenove *Inspector McMyler* • Timothy Bottoms *Danny Sullivan* • John Kavanagh *Robert Foxley* • Mick Lally *Uncle Lar* ■ *Dir* Robin Hardy • *Scr* Robin Hardy, from the novel *Goosefoot* by Patrick McGinley

Fantastic Beasts and Where to Find Them
Fantasy adventure 2016 · UK/US · Colour

This is a preview - no prints were available to review prior to publication: When auditions were held for the part of Melody, 14,000 young girls queued for hours hoping to be the chosen one, proof, if any was needed, that JK Rowling is still quite a draw. This spin-off from the Harry Potter franchise is based on the book that Rowling wrote under the pseudonym of Newt Scamander (played by Eddie Redmayne), the fictional author of a book Harry owned in his first adventure. With a Harry stage play breaking box-office records, there's no sign of the Rowling juggernaut slowing down. TP 3D

Eddie Redmayne *Newt Scamander* • Katherine Waterston *Porpentina Goldstein* • Dan Fogler *Jacob Kowalski* • Alison Sudol *Queenie Goldstein* • Colin Farrell (2) *Percival Graves* ■ *Dir* David Yates • *Scr* JK Rowling, from her illustrated children's book

A Fantastic Fear of Everything ★★ 15
Comedy 2012 · UK · Colour · 96min

This laboured comedy stars Simon Pegg as a disillusioned children's author striving for more respectability as a serious writer. While researching Victorian serial killers, his irrational fears, paranoia and suppressed childhood memories send him into a tailspin. Pegg, on screen for the full running time, is as likeable as ever, but debuting writer/director Crispian Mills and co-director Chris Hopewell deliver a stuttering, off-balance film that rarely gets above second gear. **TeS** Swearing. *DVD* *BL*

Simon Pegg *Jack* • Amara Karan *Sangeet* • Paul Freeman *Dr Friedkin* • Clare Higgins *Clair* • Alan Drake *Perkins* ■ *Dir* Crispian Mills, Chris Hopewell • *Scr* Crispian Mills

Fantastic Four ★★12
Fantasy action adventure
2015 · US · Colour · 99min

The first family of Marvel comics gets royally shafted again in the fourth attempt at putting their story on screen. Four outsiders teleport to another dimension where cosmic radiation gives them superpowers that they learn to harness in this reboot directed by Josh Trank. It's completely banal in set-up and execution, with perfunctory CG visuals of the now done-to-death variety, and even the capable young leads can't punch above the bog-standard myth-making. This is strictly cardboard cut-out stuff. **AJ** Some violence. *DVD* *BL* *3D*

Miles Teller *Reed Richards/Mr Fantastic* • Michael B Jordan *Johnny Storm/The Human Torch* • Kate Mara *Sue Storm/The Invisible Woman* • Jamie Bell *Ben Grimm/The Thing* • Toby Kebbell *Victor Von Doom/Dr Doom* ■ *Dir* Josh Trank • *Scr* Simon Kinberg, Josh Trank, Jeremy Slater, from a story by Slater, from characters by Stan Lee (writer), Jack Kirby (artist)

Fantastic Four ★★PG
Fantasy action adventure
2005 · US/Ger · Colour · 101min

The uninspired storyline in this comic book adaptation sees the members of a space expedition – Ioan Gruffudd, Michael Chiklis, Jessica Alba, Chris Evans, Julian McMahon – travel through a strange cosmic storm, which gives them all different superpowers. What should be colourful fun turns rather inert and lifeless. **IF** *DVD* *BL*

Ioan Gruffudd *Reed Richards/Mr Fantastic* • Jessica Alba *Sue Storm/Invisible Woman* • Chris Evans *Johnny Storm/Human Torch* • Michael Chiklis *Ben Grimm/The Thing* • Julian McMahon *Victor Von Doom/Dr Doom* • Hamish Linklater *Leonard* • Kerry Washington *Alicia Masters* • Kevin McNulty *Jimmy O'Hoolihan* • Stan Lee *Willie Lumpkin* ■ *Dir* Tim Story • *Scr* Michael France, Mark Frost, from characters by Stan Lee (writer), Jack Kirby (artist)

Fantastic Mr Fox ★★★★PG
Animated comedy adventure
2009 · US · Colour · 83min

Quirky comedy director Wes Anderson channels the darkly comic genius of Roald Dahl for this animated version of one of Dahl's best-loved children's stories. In his first full-length animation, Anderson opts for an unorthodox retro style that has old-fashioned stop-motion effects taking the place of modern CGI and lovingly echoes Dahl's own home in the small detail (including the armchair in his writing hut). George Clooney does a stand-up job as the voice of Mr Fox, who promises his wife that he'll mend his wily chicken-thieving ways, only for temptation to get the better of him. Sadly, the female characters (especially Meryl Streep's Mrs Fox) are given little to do but, that aside, this is an endearing take on the tale. **SuR** *DVD* *BL*

George Clooney *Mr Fox* • Meryl Streep *Mrs Felicity Fox* • Jason Schwartzman *Ash* • Bill Murray *Badger* • Wally Wolodarsky *Kylie* • Eric Anderson *[Eric Chase Anderson] Kristofferson* • Michael Gambon *Franklin Bean* • Willem Dafoe *Rat* • Owen Wilson *Coach Skip* • Jarvis Cocker *Petey* • Wes Anderson *Weasel* • Brian Cox (1) *Action 12 reporter* • Adrien Brody *Field mouse* ■ *Dir* Wes Anderson • *Scr* Wes Anderson, Noah Baumbach, from Roald Dahl's illustrated children's book

Fantastic Planet ★★★★PG
Animated science-fiction fantasy
1973 · Fr/Cz · Colour · 71min

This remarkable animated French/Czech science-fiction fantasy depicts the odd happenings on planet Yagam. There, humans, called Oms, are pets of the giant Draags, and numerous allegorical references are imaginatively drawn as a war breaks out between the two factions. A fascinating fable utilising impressive organic design, surreal composition and stunning visuals, this Cannes award-winner is highly intriguing and compulsive viewing. **AJ** French dubbed. *DVD* *BL*

Barry Bostwick • Marvin Miller • Olan Soule • Cynthia Alder • Nora Heflin • Hal Smith • Mark Gruner • Monika Ramirez • Janet Waldo ■ *Dir* René Laloux • *Scr* René Laloux, from the book *Oms en Serie* by Stefan Wul

Fantastic Voyage ★★★★U
Science-fiction adventure
1966 · US · Colour · 96min

Shrunken doctors in a mini-sub journeying through the body of a dying Czech scientist to perform interior brain surgery provide the plot for this wonderfully ludicrous 1960s sci-fi classic. An interesting cast includes secret agent Stephen Boyd, Raquel Welch in a tight diving suit and Donald Pleasence in danger from rampaging white corpuscles. Director Richard Fleischer's deft execution and tremendous special effects for the time make for an imaginative guided tour through the bloodstream, along with the requisite doses of sex, suspense and sabotage. **AJ** *DVD* *BL*

Stephen Boyd *Grant* • Raquel Welch *Cora Peterson* • Donald Pleasence *Dr Michaels* • Edmond O'Brien *General Carter* • Arthur O'Connell *Colonel Donald Reid* • William Redfield *Captain Bill Owens* • Arthur Kennedy *Dr Duval* ■ *Dir* Richard Fleischer • *Scr* Harry Kleiner, David Duncan, from the novel by Otto Klement, Jay Lewis Bixby • *Art Directors* Jack Martin Smith, Dale Hennesy • *Cinematographer* Ernest Laszlo

Le Fantôme de la Liberté ★★★★15
Surreal drama
1974 · Fr · Colour · 99min

Luis Buñuel's penultimate film shows him as mordantly comic and subversive as ever, but this series of loosely linked surreal sketches betrays a certain fatigue and laziness. The title refers to Karl Marx's phrase, and Buñuel's theme seems to be that most people are really afraid of freedom. The best-remembered sequence has elegant guests seated on individual lavatories around a table from which they excuse themselves to go and have a meal in a little room behind a locked door. Audacious, certainly, but it lacks the discreet charm of the other episodic French movies of his late period. **RB** French +subtitles. *DVD*

Michel Lonsdale *Hatter* • Jean-Claude Brialy *M Foucauld* • Michel Piccoli *Second Prefect of Police* • Adriana Asti *Prefect's sister* • Julien Bertheau *First Prefect of Police* • Adolfo Celi *Docteur Legendre* • Monica Vitti *Mme Foucauld* ■ *Dir* Luis Buñuel • *Scr* Luis Buñuel, Jean-Claude Carrière

Far and Away ★★15
Romantic period adventure
1992 · US · Colour · 134min

In this curious, frothy 19th-century period piece, Tom Cruise somewhat unbelievably earns his living as a bare knuckle fighter, while his co-star and then real-life wife Nicole Kidman flounces around. Directed with predictable gloss and visual panache by Ron Howard, and with a soundtrack featuring the stirring strains of Irish singer Enya, this is a movie that bounces along on a sea of ripped petticoats, horse whips and rotten teeth. **SH** Violence, swearing, brief nudity. *DVD* *BL*

Tom Cruise *Joseph Donelly* • Nicole Kidman *Shannon Christie* • Thomas Gibson *Stephen* • Robert Prosky *Daniel Christie* • Barbara Babcock *Nora Christie* • Cyril Cusack *Danty Duff* • Colm Meaney *Kelly* • Eileen Pollock *Molly Kay* • Michelle Johnson *Grace* ■ *Dir* Ron Howard • *Scr* Bob Dolman, from a story by Ron Howard, Bob Dolman

Far Away ★★★
Drama
2001 · Fr/Sp · Colour · 120min

André Téchiné explores the plight of the would-be immigrant in this credible, but unfocused drama. Employing a digi-video style for added immediacy, he concentrates on the human drama, while bringing unbearable tension to the drug smuggling and money laundering sequences. A surfeit of sub-plots distracts from the central premise, which sees trucker Stéphane Rideau promise to smuggle Mohamed Hamaidi from Tangiers to Spain if he can effect a reconciliation with Rideau's estranged girlfriend, Lubna Azabal. **DP** French, English, Arabic, Spanish +subtitles. *DVD* *BL*

Stéphane Rideau *Serge* • Lubna Azabal *Sarah* • Mohamed Hamaidi *Said* • Yasmina Reza *Emily* ■ *Dir* André Téchiné • *Scr* André Téchiné, Faouzi Bensaïdi, Faouzi, Mehdi Ben Attia

The Far Country ★★★U
Western
1954 · US · Colour · 93min

This is a beautifully made western, set in snowy gold rush territory. James Stewart's character is unusual for a movie hero of this period: he's basically self-absorbed, a ruthless loner, a contrast to the remarkably affable villain, played with relish by John McIntire. This concept of character reversal doesn't quite come off, but director Anthony Mann's striking use of landscape and the intense and satisfying fury of the action sequences compensate. **TS**

James Stewart *Jeff Webster* • Ruth Roman *Ronda Castle* • Corinne Calvet *Renee Vallon* • Walter Brennan *Ben Tatem* • John McIntire *Mr Gannon* • Jay C Flippen *Rube* • Henry Morgan [Harry Morgan] *Ketchum* • Jack Elam *Newberry* ■ *Dir* Anthony Mann • *Scr* Borden Chase

Far from Heaven ★★★★★12
Romantic drama
2002 · US/Fr · Colour · 102min

An exquisite evocation of the 1950s tear-jerkers of director Douglas Sirk, Todd Haynes's gorgeously designed, stunningly photographed, ravishingly scored and beautifully acted melodrama is an immaculate masterpiece. Julianne Moore plays a housewife in 1957 Connecticut who, reeling from the discovery of husband Dennis Quaid's homosexuality, develops an attraction to her black gardener (Dennis Haysbert). This is a perfectly pitched synthesis of Sirkian themes: middle-class conformity, hypocrisy and self-delusion. Without a trace of intrusive irony, lush images illustrate a taboo-breaking story without suffering the restrictions of that time. **AJ** *DVD*

Julianne Moore *Cathy Whitaker* • Dennis Quaid *Frank Whitaker* • Dennis Haysbert *Raymond Deagan* • Patricia Clarkson *Eleanor Fine* • Viola Davis *Sybil* • James Rebhorn *Dr Bowman* • Celia Weston *Mona Lauder* ■ *Dir/Scr* Todd Haynes • *Cinematographer* Edward Lachman [Ed Lachman] • *Music* Elmer Bernstein

Far from Home ★★18
Horror thriller
1989 · US · Colour · 85min

Drew Barrymore kicked off her Lolita phase (*Poison Ivy* was the highpoint) with this rather undistinguished straight-to-video thriller. While on a cross-country trip, Matt Frewer and daughter Barrymore are forced to take refuge in a run-down trailer park when their vehicle runs out of fuel. Barrymore shows that she possessed the talent to make the transition from child to grown-up star. **JF** Violence, swearing, sex scenes, nudity.

Matt Frewer *Charlie Cross* • Drew Barrymore *Joleen Cross* • Richard Masur *Duckett* • Karen Austin *Louise* • Susan Tyrrell *Agnes Reed* • Anthony Rapp *Pinky Sears* • Jennifer Tilly *Amy* ■ *Dir* Meiert Avis • *Scr* Tommy Lee Wallace, from a story by Theodore Gershuny

Far from Home: the Adventures of Yellow Dog ★★★U
Adventure
1994 · US · Colour · 77min

This adventure, in which a golden labrador sticks by his teenage master, Jesse Bradford, after their boat capsizes in the wilds of British Columbia, thankfully lacks the sentiment of the Lassie era. Some of the survival methods might prove too strong for youngsters (although many will revel in the insect eating), but there is enough exciting action to keep them amused. **DP** *DVD*

Mimi Rogers *Katherine McCormick* • Bruce Davison *John McCormick* • Jesse Bradford *Angus McCormick* • Tom Bower *John Gale* • Joel Palmer *Silas McCormick* • Josh Wannamaker *David Finlay* • Margot Finley *Sara* ■ *Dir/Scr* Phillip Borsos

Far from the Madding Crowd ★★★★U
Period romantic drama
1967 · UK · Colour · 160min

Director John Schlesinger had the cream of 1960s British acting talent at his disposal for this beautifully realised adaptation of Thomas Hardy's windswept Wessex romance. Julie Christie stars as Bathsheba, the headstrong country girl made good, who captivates shepherd Alan Bates, landowner Peter Finch and dashing soldier Terence Stamp. Christie may be more Swinging Sixties than 1860s, but her co-stars are all rather good. It won't be to every Hardy fan's taste but Nicolas Roeg's masterful photography is sublime. **JA** *DVD* *BL*

Julie Christie *Bathsheba Everdene* • Terence Stamp *Sergeant Troy* • Peter Finch *William Boldwood* • Alan Bates *Gabriel Oak* • Fiona Walker *Liddy* • Prunella Ransome *Fanny Robin* • Alison Leggatt *Mrs Hurst* ■ *Dir* John Schlesinger • *Scr* Frederic Raphael, from the novel by Thomas Hardy

Far from the Madding Crowd ★★★12
Period romantic drama
2015 · US/UK · Colour · 113min

Boisterous rural colour is jettisoned in favour of something more romantic in this spirited yet safe Thomas Hardy adaptation. Carey Mulligan is compelling as Bathsheba, whose beauty and capability attract the attention of three men in 1870s Dorset: landowner William Boldwood (Michael Sheen); devoted employee Gabriel Oak (Matthias Schoenaerts); and caddish Sergeant Troy (Tom Sturridge). All complexity is abandoned, yet the story remains gripping and the cast is wonderful. **EAS** *DVD* *BL*

Carey Mulligan *Bathsheba Everdene* • Matthias Schoenaerts *Gabriel Oak* • Michael Sheen *William Boldwood* • Tom Sturridge *Sergeant Francis Troy* • Juno Temple *Fanny Robin* • Jessica Barden *Liddy* ■ *Dir* Thomas Vinterberg • *Scr* David Nicholls, from Thomas Hardy's novel

Far from Vietnam ★★★
Experimental political documentary
1967 · Fr · BW and Colour · 120min

For all the rhetoric spouted in this passionate protest against American involvement in Vietnam, it's the dreadful simplicity of the combat footage that has the most powerful effect. The opening sequence, for example, which juxtaposes US preparations for an air raid and the terrified response it evokes in Hanoi, makes for chilling viewing over 30 years on. There's undoubted socio-artistic integrity in Jean-Luc Godard's emotive confession and Alain Resnais's assessment of the war's morality, while the film is edited with supreme propagandist skill by Chris Marker. **DP** French, English +subtitles.

■ *Dir* Alain Resnais, William Klein, Joris Ivens, Agnès Varda, Claude Lelouch, Jean-Luc Godard • *Editor* Chris Marker

The Far Frontier ★★U
Western
1949 · US · Colour · 68min

Routine Roy Rogers fodder is given a little more glitz than usual for being filmed in the cheap colour process Trucolor, and is notable for being the last time sidekick Andy Devine rode with the (self-styled) King of the Cowboys. The plot's not without interest either, dealing as it does with outlaws smuggled back into the US from Mexico. **TS**

Roy Rogers • Gail Davis *Susan Hathaway* • Andy Devine *Judge Cookie Bullflacher* • Francis Ford *Alf Sharper* • Roy Barcroft *Bart Carroll* • Clayton Moore *Tom Sharper* • Robert Strange *Willis Newcomb* • Holly Bane *Rocco* ■ *Dir* William Witney • *Scr* Sloan Nibley

The Far Horizons ★★ U
Historical adventure 1955 · US · Colour · 107min

Canoes replace horses in this American frontier saga that takes dramatic liberties with the real-life expedition of Lewis and Clark up the Missouri river into the Northwest. The journey goes on far too long but is often spectacularly beautiful to behold. Fred MacMurray is the stern-jawed Lewis while Charlton Heston plays the virile Clark who forgets the girl back home (Barbara Hale) when he runs into Donna Reed's Shoshone maiden. **AE**

Fred MacMurray *Meriwether Lewis* • Charlton Heston *William Clark* • Donna Reed *Sacajawea* • Barbara Hale *Julia Hancock* • William Demarest *Sergeant Gass* • Alan Reed *Charboneau* • Eduardo Noriega (1) *Cameahwait* ■ *Dir* Rudolph Maté • *Scr* Winston Miller, Edmund H North, from the novel *Sacajawea of the Shoshones* by Della Gould Emmons

Far North ★★ 15
Drama 1988 · US · Colour · 84min

Playwright Sam Shepard's feature film debut as director stars his real-life partner Jessica Lange. Despite Lange's abilities, this still manages to be a major head-banging exercise in dragging Freudian clichés through the farm dust of Minnesota. The cast is impeccable, but Shepard's tangled script and lumpen direction let it down. **SH** Swearing.

Jessica Lange *Kate* • Charles Durning *Bertrum* • Tess Harper *Rita* • Donald Moffat *Uncle Dane* • Ann Wedgeworth *Amy* • Patricia Arquette *Jilly* • Nina Draxten *Gramma* • Pearl Fuller *Older Nurse* ■ *Dir/Scr* Sam Shepard

Far North ★★★★ 15
Drama 2007 · UK/Fr/Nor · Colour · 83min

A petty power struggle unfolds against majestic Arctic wastelands in this spellbinding drama from writer/director Asif Kapadia. Like his Bafta-winning feature debut *The Warrior*, the hostile landscape is a key character and dialogue is just as sparse. Michelle Yeoh is outstanding as Saiva, an Inuit keeping big emotions under wraps. Her only company is Anja (Michelle Krusiec), a girl she's raised as her own. Each day is a struggle to survive, so when a weary Russian soldier (a typically macho Sean Bean) stumbles into their territory, it's both a blessing and a curse. Sweeping scenery heightens the claustrophobia and, while the resolution is shocking, it gives the film a creepy resonance. **SP** Violence. *DVD*

Michelle Yeoh *Saiva* • Michelle Krusiec *Anja* • Sean Bean *Loki* ■ *Dir* Asif Kapadia • *Scr* Asif Kapadia, Tim Miller, from the short story *True North* by Sara Maitland

A Far Off Place ★★ PG
Adventure 1993 · US · Colour · 102min

This is a disappointingly Disneyfied adaptation of two Laurens van der Post novels. As a highly acclaimed cinematographer, debuting director Mikael Salomon clearly knows where to place his camera. Yet, in dumbing down the ecological themes for his adolescent audience, he inadvertently patronises Sarel Bok, the Kalahari bush guide who leads imperilled teens Reese Witherspoon and Ethan Randall across the desert and out of the clutches of evil ivory hunter Jack Thompson. **DP** Violence.

Reese Witherspoon *Nonnie Parker* • Ethan Randall [Ethan Embry] *Harry Winslow* • Jack Thompson *John Ricketts* • Maximilian Schell *Colonel Mopani Theron* • Sarel Bok *Xhabbo* • Robert Burke *Paul Parker* • Patricia Kalember *Elizabeth Parker* • Daniel Gerroll *John Winslow* ■ *Dir* Mikael Salomon • *Scr* Robert Caswell, Jonathan Hensleigh, Sally Robinson, from the books *A Story Like the Wind* and *A Far Off Place* by Laurens van der Post • *Cinematographer* Juan Ruiz-Anchia

Faraway, So Close ★★★ 15
Fantasy drama
1993 · Ger · BW and Colour · 138min

Wim Wenders's sequel to *Wings of Desire* is as visually beautiful and sweet-natured as the original. Fallen angel Bruno Ganz now runs a pizza restaurant, which makes his ghostly pal Otto Sander want a slice of mortality for himself. Unfortunately, he ends up working for illegal arms dealer Horst Buchholz. Wenders's mix of recent German history with weighty metaphysical concerns again uses stark black and white to depict the angels' viewpoint. **AJ** English, German +subtitles. Violence, swearing.

Otto Sander *Cassiel* • Peter Falk • Horst Buchholz *Tony Baker* • Nastassja Kinski *Raphaela* • Heinz Ruhmann *Konrad* • Bruno Ganz *Damiel* • Solveig Dommartin *Marior* • Rüdiger Vogler *Phillip Winter* • Lou Reed • Willem Dafoe *Emit Flesti* • Mikhail Gorbachev ■ *Dir* Wim Wenders • *Scr* Wim Wenders, Ulrich Zieger, Richard Reitinger, from a story by Wim Wenders

Farewell ★★★★ 12A
Thriller based on a true story
2010 · Fr · Colour · 113min

In 1981, at the height of the Cold War, a disgruntled Soviet intelligence officer (Emir Kusturica, better known for his directing) uses a French intermediary to leak vital Soviet spy secrets to the US. Based on a true story, this gripping espionage thriller criss-crosses deftly between machinations in Moscow, Paris and Washington (with Fred Ward as Ronald Reagan, David Soul as his chief of staff and Willem Dafoe as the boss of the CIA). In the process, it shows how one disillusioned dealist helped change the world – and all for a Sony Walkman and some Queen cassettes! Enthralling. **DA** French, Russian, English +subtitles. Swearing.

Emir Kusturica *Grigoriev* • Guillaume Canet *Pierre* • Alexandra Maria Lara *Jessica* • Fred Ward *Reagan* • David Soul *Hutton* • Willem Dafoe *Feeney* ■ *Dir* Christian Carion • *Scr* Christian Carion, Eric Raynaud, from the non-fiction book *Bonjour Farewell* by Serguei Kostine

The Farewell – Brecht's Last Summer ★★ 12
Period biographical drama
2000 · Ger/Pol · Colour · 88min

An air of melancholy hangs heavily over this slow-moving memoir of Bertolt Brecht's final visit to his summer retreat. The intensity of director Jan Schütte's film - set in 1956, a time of political turmoil behind the Iron Curtain - compensates for a certain lack of humanity. Disappointingly, Brecht (Josef Bierbichler) is something of a marginal figure, with the focus instead on his devoted wife. **DP** German +subtitles. *DVD*

Josef Bierbichler *Bertolt Brecht* • Monica Bleibtreu *Helene Weigel* • Jeanette Hain *Käthe Reichel* • Elfriede Irrall *Elisabeth Hauptmann* • Margit Rogall *Ruth Berlau* • Samuel Fintzi *Wolfgang Harich* ■ *Dir* Jan Schütte • *Scr* Klaus Pohl

Farewell Mr Kringle ★★
Seasonal romantic drama
2010 · US · Colour · 96min

A Christmas-hating blogger re-learns the magic of the season in this clichéd TV movie. Christine Taylor is the widowed big-city cynic who's speedily swayed by a small town's charms when she's sent to profile a Santa impersonator celebrating 50 years in the job. The life lesson that follows just doesn't generate the feel-good atmosphere you'd expect. Instead, weak characters and plotting make every scene seem hollow and flat, and even supposedly poignant events have little impact. **SF**

Christine Taylor *Annabelle "Anna" Wall* • Christopher Wiehl *Mark Stafford* • William Morgan Sheppard [Morgan Sheppard] *Kris Kringle* • Vivica A Fox *Zoe Marsden* ■ *Dir* Kevin Connor • *Scr* Robert Tate Miller

Farewell My Concubine ★★★★★ 15
Epic drama 1993 · HK/Chi · Colour · 150min

Banned for a time in China, Oscar nominated and joint winner of the Palme d'Or at Cannes in 1993 with Jane Campion's *The Piano*, Chen Kaige's fifth feature sweeps impressively across 50 years of Chinese history to trace the shifting relationship between Peking opera singers Zhang Fengyi and Leslie Cheung. A reluctance to explore with any depth Cheung's gay love for his friend Zhang and a rather prosaic presentation of the political events that rocked China after 1925 are the only quibbles one can have with this majestic and often riveting piece of film-making. Both men give remarkable performances, as does the beguiling Gong Li as Zhang's put-upon wife. **DP** Mandarin +subtitles. *Blu-ray*

Leslie Cheung *Douzi/Cheng Dieyi (young man)* • Zhang Fengyi *Shitou/Duan Xiaolou (young man)* • Gong Li *Juxian* • Lu Qi *Guan Jifa* • Ying Da *Na Kun* • Ge You *Master Yuan* • Li Chun *Xiao Si (teenager)* • Lei Han *Xiao Si (adult)* • Ma Mingwei *Douzi (child)* • Yin Zhi *Douzi (teenager)* • Fei Yang *Shitou (child)* • Zhao Hailong *Shitou (teenager)* ■ *Dir* Chen Kaige • *Scr* Lillian Lee, Lu Wei, from the novel by Lillian Lee

Farewell My Lovely ★★★★★ PG
Classic film noir 1944 · US · BW · 91min

Also known by its American title *Murder, My Sweet*, this terrific adaptation of the Raymond Chandler novel was the movie that established former crooner Dick Powell's new hard-boiled image. He plays the impoverished private eye Philip Marlowe, caught up in two tough and nasty cases that eventually dovetail into one. Quintessential *film noir*, this is superbly directed by Edward Dmytryk, and an economic use of voiceover that now stands as a skilful example of the device. Mike Mazurki is a perfect Moose Malloy, but it's Claire Trevor as Velma that you'll remember. This tight masterpiece is as good as it gets. **TS** *DVD*

Dick Powell *Philip Marlowe* • Claire Trevor *Mrs Grayle/Velma Valento* • Anne Shirley *Ann Grayle* • Otto Kruger *Jules Amthor* • Mike Mazurki *Moose Malloy* • Miles Mander *Mr Grayle* • Douglas Walton *Lindsay Marriott* ■ *Dir* Edward Dmytryk • *Scr* John Paxton, from the novel by Raymond Chandler

Farewell, My Lovely ★★★★ 15
Detective drama 1975 · US · Colour · 91min

This is a richly atmospheric and affectionate tribute to Raymond Chandler and 1940s *film noir*, with Robert Mitchum as Philip Marlowe. It's amazing that Mitchum came so late to the role that he seems born to play. The corrupt mess of Los Angeles hangs on those rumpled eyelids as he gives a mesmeric performance of world-weariness. Also impressive is Charlotte Rampling as the alluring Velma, who gives Mitchum a smile that, he says, he can feel in his hip pocket. **AT** *DVD*

Robert Mitchum *Philip Marlowe* • Charlotte Rampling *Mrs Velma Grayle* • John Ireland *Lieutenant Nulty* • Sylvia Miles *Mrs Jessie Florian* • Jack O'Halloran *Moose Malloy* • Harry Dean Stanton *Billy Rolfe* • Sylvester Stallone *Kelly/Jonnie* ■ *Dir* Dick Richards • *Scr* David Zelag Goodman, from the novel by Raymond Chandler

A Farewell to Arms ★★★ PG
First World War romantic drama
1932 · US · BW · 78min

Time has not been terribly kind to this adaptation of Ernest Hemingway's First World War love story about an English nurse and an American ambulance driver. But, in 1932, Helen Hayes and Gary Cooper (accompanied by Wagner on the soundtrack) created tidal waves of tears in movie theatres. Still worth seeing for this classically romantic performances and for the Oscar-winning photography by Charles Lang. **AT** *DVD* *Blu-ray*

Gary Cooper *Lieutenant Frederic Henry* • Helen Hayes *Catherine Barkley* • Adolphe Menjou *Major Rinaldi* • Mary Philips *Helen Ferguson* • Jack LaRue *Priest* • Blanche Frederici *Head nurse* • Henry Armetta *Bonello* ■ *Dir* Frank Borzage • *Scr* Benjamin Glazer, Oliver HP Garret, from the novel by Ernest Hemingway

A Farewell to Arms ★★★ PG
First World War romantic drama
1957 · US · Colour · 145min

Ambulance driver Rock Hudson is wounded in Italy during the First World War and falls in love with nurse Jennifer Jones. Jones was married to the film's producer, David O Selznick, who not only wanted to pay adoring tribute to his wife's beauty, but also sought to repeat the huge success of his earlier blockbuster *Gone with the Wind*. As a result, this is overblown and enjoyable, even with its disturbing depiction of war. **AT** *DVD*

Rock Hudson *Lt Frederic Henry* • Jennifer Jones *Catherine Barkley* • Vittorio De Sica *Major Alessandro Rinaldi* • Mercedes McCambridge *Miss Van Campen* • Kurt Kasznar *Bonello* • Oscar Homolka *Dr Emerich* • Elaine Stritch *Helen Ferguson* • Alberto Sordi *Father Galli* ■ *Dir* Charles Vidor • *Scr* Ben Hecht, from the novel by Ernest Hemingway

Farewell to the King ★ PG
Second World War adventure
1988 · US · Colour · 112min

Captain Nigel Havers (poorly cast) treks into Borneo's heart of darkness and discovers jungle "King" Nick Nolte, who's gone native to the strains of Basil Poledouris's score. Unsurprisingly, this militaristic nonsense is written and directed by John Milius, co-screenwriter of *Apocalypse Now*, who completely fails to uncover any significant resonance in his own material. **TS** Some violence, swearing. *DVD*

Nick Nolte *Learoyd* • Nigel Havers *Captain Fairbourne* • Frank McRae *Sergeant Tenga* • James Fox *Colonel Ferguson* • Marilyn Tokuda *Yoo* • Marius Weyers *Conklin* ■ *Dir* John Milius • *Scr* John Milius, from the book *L'Adieu au Roi* by Pierre Shoendoerffer

Fargo ★★★★★ 18
Black comedy thriller 1995 · US · Colour · 94min

The Coen brothers (director/writer Joel, producer/writer Ethan) are on top form with this quirky, unconventional, comedy-tinged crime thriller set in snowy Minnesota. Amateur kidnappers Steve Buscemi and Peter Stormare leave a trail of dead bodies that is investigated, with rare instinct and understanding, by heavily pregnant police chief Frances McDormand (who won an Oscar for her performance). Supposedly inspired by a true story, the film sees the Coens neatly subvert thriller clichés for their own surreal and philosophical ends, while retaining the genre's old-fashioned virtues and screw-tightening tension. While sweet-natured mirth is combined with deliciously twisted malice, and gory horror merges with offbeat humour, the whole is set against an extraordinary winter wonderland. A modern masterpiece. **AJ** *DVD* *Blu-ray*

Frances McDormand *Marge Gunderson* • William H Macy *Jerry Lundegaard* • Steve Buscemi *Carl Showalter* • Peter Stormare *Gaear Grimsrud* • Harve Presnell *Wade Gustafson* • Kristin Rudrud *Jean Lundegaard* • Tony Denman *Scotty Lundegaard* • Kurt Schweickhardt *Car salesman* ■ *Dir* Joel Coen • *Scr* Ethan Coen, Joel Coen • *Producer* Ethan Coen • *Cinematographer* Roger Deakins

Farinelli il Castrato ★★★★ 15
Biographical drama
1994 · Bel/Fr/It · Colour · 106min

Not since *Amadeus* has a film made classical music so popular as this bizarre take on the musical past. Stéfano Dionisi stars as castrated singer Farinelli, one of a select band of 18th-century tonal high-fliers, whose emasculated voice can drive an audience of women wild with lust, and who is forever feuding with his more virile brother and arguing with the composer Handel. **TH** French, Italian +subtitles. Sex scenes. *DVD*

Stefano Dionisi *Farinelli/Carlo Broschi* • Enrico Lo Verso *Riccardo Broschi* • Elsa Zylberstein *Alexandra* • Caroline Cellier *Margaret Hunter* • Marianne Basler *Countess Mauer* • Jacques Boudet *Philip V* • Graham Valentine *The Prince of*

Wales • Jeroen Krabbé *Handel* ■ *Dir* Gérard Corbiau • *Scr* Andrée Corbiau, from a screenplay (unproduced) by Andrée Corbiau, Gérard Corbiau

The Farm: Angola, USA ★★★

Documentary　　　1996 · US · Colour · 90min

This acclaimed documentary focuses on Angola Prison, a facility that is home to 5,000 convicts facing life sentences, the majority of whom will never see the outside world again. It's essentially a day in the life of a number of the prisoners, with co-director Wilbert Rideau listening sympathetically to the sobering, thoughtful insights of the felons as they desperately cling to the remote hope of one day leaving the facility. JF

Bernard Addison *Narrator* ■ *Dir* Jonathan Stack, Liz Garbus, Wilbert Rideau

The Farmer Takes a Wife ★★★ U

Period romantic drama　1935 · US · BW · 93min

Henry Fonda made his movie debut in this charming romance set along the Erie Canal in the 1850s, and created a screen persona that would endure for five decades. Determined, caring and trustworthy, he was virtually the American ideal. Janet Gaynor and Fonda are well matched under the direction of Victor Fleming who, refreshingly, elects to shoot in the open, away from studio backdrops. TS

Janet Gaynor *Molly Larkins* • Henry Fonda *Dan Harrow* • Charles Bickford *Jotham Klore* • Slim Summerville *Fortune Friendly* • Andy Devine *Elmer Otway* • Roger Imhof *Sam Weaver* • Jane Withers *Della* • Siegfried Rumann [Sig Ruman] *Blacksmith* ■ *Dir* Victor Fleming • *Scr* Edwin Burke, from the play by Frank B Elser, Marc Connelly, from the novel *Rome Haul* by Walter D Edmonds

The Farmer Takes a Wife ★★ U

Period musical　　1953 · US · Colour · 80min

This is an ill-advised musical remake of the 1935 period romance. Dale Robertson steps into Henry Fonda's shoes as the 19th-century land-lover who signs on to a barge on the Erie Canal to raise the money to buy a farm. But he lacks the naivety of the young Fonda, while brassy Betty Grable has none of the wide-eyed idealism that made Janet Gaynor so persuasive. The blaring songs, garish photography and director Henry Levin's idea of cosy nostalgia don't help much either. DP

Betty Grable *Molly* • Dale Robertson *Daniel Harrow* • Thelma Ritter *Lucy Cashdollar* • John Carroll *Jotham Klore* • Eddie Foy Jr *Fortune Friendly* • Charlotte Austin *Pearl* ■ *Dir* Henry Levin • *Scr* Walter Bullock, Sally Benson, Joseph Fields, from the play by Frank B Elser, Marc Connelly, from the novel *Rome Haul* by Walter D Edmonds • *Music* Cyril Mockridge • *Music/lyrics* Harold Arlen, Dorothy Fields

The Farmer's Daughter ★★★ U

Comedy drama　　1946 · US · BW · 96min

Loretta Young picked up her best actress Oscar for this strangely accented, but utterly charming performance as Katrin Holstrom, a fictionalised Swede who comes to Washington as a lady's maid and ends up running for Congress opposing the man she loves. Holstrom's really an RKO mouthpiece for producer Dore Schary's Hollywood-liberal political views; eventually Schary took over MGM from the ousted reactionary Louis B Mayer, and Young became one of the brightest names in the early days of television. TS

Loretta Young *Katrin Holstrom* • Joseph Cotten *Glenn Morley* • Ethel Barrymore *Mrs Morley* • Charles Bickford *Clancy* • Rose Hobart *Virginia* • Rhys Williams *Adolph* ■ *Dir* HC Potter • *Scr* Allen Rivkin, Laura Kerr, from the play *Hulda, Daughter of Parliament* by Juhni Tervataa

The Farmer's Wife ★★★ U

Silent comedy　　1928 · UK · BW · 97min

Eden Phillpott's play had been a long-running hit in the West End before Alfred Hitchcock translated it to the screen. It's a comedy of rural manners, as widower Jameson Thomas alights on the village's eligible spinsters before coming to appreciate the charms of his loyal housekeeper, Lilian Hall-Davis. But Hitchcock adds a veneer of social suspense that renders the farmer's search as much a study in gender and class as a melodramatic romance. DP **DVD**

Jameson Thomas *Samuel Sweetland* • Lillian Hall-Davis *Araminta Dench* • Gordon Harker *Churdles Ash* • Gibb McLaughlin *Henry Coaker* • Maud Gill *Thirza Tapper* • Louie Pounds *Widow Windeatt* ■ *Dir* Alfred Hitchcock • *Scr* Eliot Stannard, from the play by Eden Phillpotts, from the novel *Widecombe Fair* by Eden Phillpott

Fashions of 1934 ★★★

Musical comedy　　1934 · US · BW · 78min

Smooth charmer William Powell and glamorous assistant Bette Davis play the visiting Americans who succeed in running rings around the snooty, fashion-conscious inhabitants of Paris. Director William Dieterle spares no expense in invoking a dizzying world of elegant artifice, and there's sharp playing from the two leads. JF

William Powell *Sherwood Nash* • Bette Davis *Lynn Mason* • Frank McHugh *Snap* • Verree Teasdale *Grand Duchess Alix* • Reginald Owen *Oscar Baroque* • Henry O'Neill *Duryea* • Philip Reed *Jimmy* • Hugh Herbert *Joe Ward* ■ *Dir* William Dieterle • *Scr* F Hugh Herbert, Gene Markey, Kathryn Scola, Carl Erickson, from a story by Harry Collins, Warren Duff

Fast and Furious ★★

Comedy mystery　　1939 · US · BW · 73min

This was the last of three features (after *Fast Company* and 1939's *Fast and Loose*) written for MGM by the clever and witty Harry Kurnitz, here starring suave Franchot Tone and sexy Ann Sothern as the rare book dealers. This particular episode proved a training ground for Busby Berkeley, best known for his ground-breaking flamboyant choreography, who had left his home studio Warner Bros to establish himself as a "serious" director over at MGM. Despite the sparseness of the budget, it was a competent enough effort. TS

Franchot Tone *Joel Sloane* • Ann Sothern *Garda Sloane* • Ruth Hussey *Lily Cole* • Lee Bowman *Mike Stevens* • Allyn Joslyn *Ted Bentley* • John Miljan *Erie Bartell* ■ *Dir* Busby Berkeley • *Scr* Harry Kurnitz

Fast and Loose ★★

Comedy　　　1930 · US · BW · 70min

Miriam Hopkins was to become one of the brightest stars of the 1930s, but few would have guessed from her screen debut in this comedic misfire. Despite a script co-written by Preston Sturges, the story is a conventional rich-girl-falls-for-poor-boy affair. Carole Lombard, in the smaller role of a chorus girl who reforms Hopkins's playboy brother, comes off better, though Fred C Newmeyer's stilted direction favours no one. TV

Miriam Hopkins *Marion Lenox* • Carole Lombard *Alice O'Neil* • Charles Starrett *Henry Morgan* • Henry Wadsworth *Bertie Lenox* • Winifred Harris *Carrie Lenox* • Herbert Yost *George Grafton* ■ *Dir* Fred C Newmeyer • *Scr* Doris Anderson, Jack Kirkland, Preston Sturges, from the play *The Best People* by David Gray, Avery Hopwood

Fast and Loose ★★

Comedy mystery　　1939 · US · BW · 79min

The sequel to *Fast Company*, which starred Melvyn Douglas and Florence Rice as married sleuths, this one stars Robert Montgomery trying to discover what's happened to a collection of manuscripts which vanish from a library, and Rosalind Russell as his wife who complicates the situation. An undemanding piece of fluff, with the stars on good form. MGM made a further film, *Fast and Furious*, before abandoning the format which was a rip-off of *The Thin Man* series. AT

Robert Montgomery *Joel Sloane* • Rosalind Russell *Garda Sloane* • Reginald Owen *Vincent Charlton* • Ralph Morgan *Nicholas Torrent* •

Etienne Girardot *Christopher Oates* • Alan Dinehart *David Hilliard* ■ *Dir* Edwin L Marin • *Scr* Harry Kurnitz

The Fast and the Furious ★★★★ 15

Action thriller　　2001 · US/Ger · Colour · 102min

Director Rob Cohen's pedal-to-the-metal thriller has fabulous customised cars, scantily clad babes, moody hunks, bare-knuckle brawls and a boot full of turbo-charged stunts to spare. Vin Diesel is the champion of LA's illegal street racing subculture, where gangs organise cash-prize races between souped-up cars. But is his crew of tuned-up misfits, including girlfriend Michelle Rodriguez, behind a spate of recent truck hijackings? That's what cop Paul Walker goes undercover to find out, falling in love with Diesel's sister Jordana Brewster in the process. Followed by *2 Fast 2 Furious* in 2003. AJ **DVD** **BL** **CS**

Paul Walker *Brian Earl Spilner/Officer Brian O'Conner* • Vin Diesel *Dominic Toretto* • Michelle Rodriguez *Letty* • Jordana Brewster *Mia Toretto* • Rick Yune *Johnny Tran* • Chad Lindberg *Jesse* ■ *Dir* Rob Cohen • *Scr* Gary Scott Thompson, Erik Bergquist, David Ayer, from a story by Gary Scott Thompson, from an article by Ken Li

The Fast and the Furious: Tokyo Drift ★★★ 12

Action thriller　　2006 · US · Colour · 99min

This third instalment of the pedal-to-the-metal franchise (after 2003's *2 Fast 2 Furious*) has Lucas Black taking the lead role as a bad-boy teenager who's dispatched to Japan to stay with his estranged dad in order to avoid jail for illegal street racing. On arrival, he quickly falls under the twin influences of the local yakuza and the new craze for drifting (handbrake-sliding at high speed around hairpin bends). Boy racers will love it. DA **DVD** **BL**

Lucas Black *Sean Boswell* • Brian Tee *DK* • Bow Wow *Twinkie* • Sung Kang *Han* • Nathalie Kelley *Neela* • Zachery Ty Bryan *Clay* ■ *Dir* Justin Lin • *Scr* Alfredo Botello, Chris Morgan, Kario Salem

Fast & Furious ★★ 12

Action thriller　　2009 · US · Colour · 102min

Running on empty when not on autopilot, the fourth film in the fast-car franchise sidelines its illegal street-racing base for an exhausted drug-running plot. A tragic death brings Vin Diesel out of exile and back to LA, where he is forced to join up with his former enemy, FBI agent Paul Walker, to nail the killer. What follows is a barely credible story punctuated by scantily clad babes, macho posturing and extreme drag racing. A predictable romantic sub-plot involving Walker and Diesel's sister (Jordana Brewster) is resurrected, along with every hot rod movie cliché going, in this tired turbo-drive through the action motions. AJ Violence, sexual references, drug references. **DVD** **BL**

Vin Diesel *Dominic Toretto* • Paul Walker *Brian O'Conner* • Michelle Rodriguez *Letty* • Jordana Brewster *Mia Toretto* • Laz Alonso *Fenix* • Gal Gadot *Gisele* ■ *Dir* Justin Lin • *Scr* Chris Morgan, from characters by Gary Scott Thompson

Fast Five ★★★★ 12

Action thriller　　2011 · US · Colour · 124min

In *The Expendables* of car chase movies, Vin Diesel leads an enormously enjoyable reunion of returning cast members from every chapter of the adrenaline-pumping *Fast and the Furious* franchise. Diesel and his bank-robbing cohorts plan one last mega-heist so they can disappear forever, while at the same time evading tenacious FBI agent Dwayne Johnson, who is closing in on their operation. Director Justin Lin overdoes the picturesque swooping shots, but that's the only blot on the high-velocity landscape. Impossible to take seriously, this is fantastic fun. AJ Some violence, brief swearing. **DVD** **BL** **CS**

Dwayne Johnson *Agent Luke Hobbs* • Vin Diesel *Dominic Toretto* • Paul Walker *Brian O'Conner* • Jordana Brewster *Mia Toretto* • Tyrese Gibson

Roman Pearce ■ *Dir* Justin Lin • *Scr* Chris Morgan, from characters by Gary Scott Thompson

Fast & Furious 6 ★★ 12

Action thriller　　2013 · US · Colour · 124min

Franchise fatigue is beginning to show in this fifth sequel in the technically proficient street-racing series, despite the return of original stars Vin Diesel and Paul Walker. This time, the cars and cast are transported to an unrecognisably traffic-free London for more tyre-squealing action. Between deafening set pieces (highlight: a preposterously inventive and witty daylight tank chase on a Spanish motorway), the larky pit-stop banter falls clangingly flat, while Welshman Luke Evans's ex-SAS baddie lacks the requisite boo-hiss villainy. AC Violence, swearing. **DVD** **BL**

Vin Diesel *Dominic Toretto* • Paul Walker *Brian O'Conner* • Dwayne Johnson *Luke Hobbs* • Michelle Rodriguez *Letty* • Luke Evans *Owen Shaw* • Jordana Brewster *Mia Toretto* • Tyrese Gibson *Roman Pearce* ■ *Dir* Justin Lin • *Scr* Chris Morgan, from characters by Gary Scott Thompson

Fast & Furious 7 ★★★★ 12

Action thriller　　2014 · US · Colour · 131min

The monster muscle-car franchise continues to assault the senses in this globe-trotting sequel, with horror maestro James Wan's direction adding extra high style to proceedings. After his brother (Luke Evans) was hospitalised by Vin Diesel's crew in the last episode, former black ops assassin Jason Statham wants revenge. From the parachuting car free-fall drop and mountain roadside raid to the jump between the Etihad Towers in Abu Dhabi and a super-drone battle in Los Angeles, the epic excitement is expertly rendered for the highest speed thrill-ride. The film is dedicated to Paul Walker, who died during production, and the send-off he receives from his movie "family" is both moving and fitting. *Fast 8* is due in spring 2017. AJ **DVD** **BL**

Vin Diesel *Dominic Toretto* • Paul Walker *Brian O'Conner* • Dwayne Johnson *Hobbs* • Jason Statham *Deckard Shaw* • Michelle Rodriguez *Letty Ortiz* • Tyrese Gibson *Roman Pearce* ■ *Dir* James Wan • *Scr* Chris Morgan, from characters by Gary Scott Thompson • *Cinematographer* Stephen F Windon

Fast Company ★★

Comedy mystery　　1938 · US · BW · 73min

Melvyn Douglas and Florence Rice star as amateur detectives who specialise in finding stolen and bogus books but find themselves also caught up in a murder. The background of book auctions has some interest and Douglas is always an exceptionally smooth performer, though Rice never had the star appeal MGM initially thought she had. It was the first in a three-part series about married detectives – *Fast and Loose* and *Fast and Furious* followed. AT

Melvyn Douglas *Joel Sloane* • Florence Rice *Garda Sloane* • Claire Dodd *Julia Thorne* • Shepperd Strudwick *Ned Morgan* • Louis Calhern *Elias Z Bannerman* • Nat Pendleton *Paul Torison* • Douglass Dumbrille *Arnold Stamper* ■ *Dir* Edward Buzzell • *Scr* Marco Page, Harold Tarshis, from a story by Marco Page, Harry Kurnitz

Fast Food ★★★ PG

Comedy　　1989 · US · Colour · 88min

Anything goes in the burger wars – including spiking the sauce with an aphrodisiac. Students and scam artists Clark Brandon and Randal Patrick take on ruthless burger king Jim Varney whose expansion plans threaten their friend Tracy Griffith's gas station. This good-natured comedy boasts some decent jokes and an eccentric cast that includes Melanie Griffith's half-sister, Tracy, Michael J Pollard from *Bonnie and Clyde* and ex-porn star Traci Lords. AT

Clark Brandon *Auggie* • Randal Patrick *Drew* • Tracy Griffith *Samantha* • Michael J Pollard *Bud* • Lanny Horn *Calvin* • Jim Varney *Wrangler Bob Bundy* • Blake Clark *EG McCormick* • Traci Lords

Dixie Love ■ *Dir* Michael A Simpson • *Scr* Randal Patrick, Clark Brandon, Lanny Horn, from a story by Scott B Sowers, Jim Bastille

Fast Food ★ 18

Comedy drama 1998 · UK · Colour · 95min

Stewart Sugg, in his directorial debut, dishes up an overcooked, indigestible mess that borrows indiscriminately from *A Clockwork Orange*, *Blue Velvet* and diverse Scorsese and Tarantino pictures. Of the five friends reunited after decades of disappointment, only Douglas Henshall comes remotely close to giving a performance as he tries to save blind hooker Emily Woof from his safe-blowing mates and her savage pimp. A new low for the home-grown crime movie. DP Violence, swearing, drug abuse.

Douglas Henshall *Benny* • Emily Woof *Letitia/Claudia* • Miles Anderson *Dwayne* • Gerard Butler *Jacko* • Danny Midwinter *Bisto* • Sean Hughes *Fish* ■ *Dir/Scr* Stewart Sugg

Fast Food Nation ★★★ 15

Drama 2006 · UK/US · Colour · 108min

Eric Schlosser's bestselling non-fiction book about the convenience-food industry is brought to the screen here by director Richard Linklater. The director valiantly attempts to illustrate the author's polemic by crafting a set of interlocking fictional stories to illustrate his points. And so a burger-chain executive (Greg Kinnear) sets out to discover how cow faeces are getting into the beef patties at one processing plant, while a restaurant employee (Ashley Johnson) discovers the anti-globalisation movement. Viewers with sensitive stomachs should be forewarned: this is gruesome stuff. One can't fault the movie's message, but as drama it's too baggy and undernourished to satisfy fully. LF *DVD*

Greg Kinnear *Don Henderson* • Ashley Johnson *Amber* • Catalina Sandino Moreno *Sylvia* • Bobby Cannavale *Mike* • Paul Dano *Brian* • Patricia Arquette *Cindy* • Kris Kristofferson *Rudy* • Bruce Willis *Harry* • Ethan Hawke *Pete* • Luis Guzman *Benny* • Avril Lavigne *Alice* • Esai Morales *Tony* ■ *Dir* Richard Linklater • *Scr* Eric Schlosser, Richard Linklater, from the non-fiction book by Eric Schlosser

Fast Girls ★★★ 12

Sports drama 2012 · UK · Colour · 87min

The class-clashing plot may be unoriginal, but this sporting take on a familiar theme is slickly done. The film centres on the spiky relationship between two members of a British sprint relay team in training for the athletics World Championships. Shania (Lenora Crichlow, from TV's *Being Human*) is sassy and streetwise. Lisa (Lily James) is middle class and snobby. *Fast Girls* is equal parts cheese, corn and cliché, but it's great fun – even the sports scenes, often a problem in this kind of film, more than pass muster. DA Swearing, some violence. *DVD* ᗷ

Lenora Crichlow *Shania Andrews* • Lily James *Lisa Temple* • Noel Clarke *Tommy* • Bradley James *Carl* • Rupert Graves *David Temple* • Lashana Lynch *Belle Newman* • Lorraine Burroughs *Trix Warren* • Phil Davis [Philip Davis] *Brian* ■ *Dir* Regan Hall • *Scr* Jay Basu, Noel Clarke, Roy Williams

The Fast Lady ★★★ PG

Comedy 1963 · UK · Colour · 91min

Despite driving up too many B roads, this story of a civil servant (Stanley Baxter), his car (a Bentley) and the girl on whom he dotes (Julie Christie) has such a degree of fresh-faced innocence that you appreciate the film's charm rather than notice the rambling plot. This Rank movie is tackled with relish by the cast: Christie is simpering and decent, Baxter is spot-on with his "gormless comic" style and James Robertson-Justice booms throughout. JM *DVD*

James Robertson-Justice *Charles Chingford* • Leslie Phillips *Freddy Fox* • Stanley Baxter *Murdoch Troon* • Kathleen Harrison *Mrs Staggers* • Julie Christie *Claire Chingford* • Dick Emery *Shingler* ■ *Dir* Ken Annakin • *Scr* Jack Davies, Helen Blyth, from a story by Howard Keble

Fast Times at Ridgemont High ★★★★ 18

Comedy 1982 · US · Colour · 85min

Amy Heckerling s insightful, sympathetic and still very funny foray into high school life is a stunning exception to the spate of dreadful post-*Animal House* teen sex comedies. Thoughtfully adapted by Cameron Crowe from his own novel, on the surface it's just another episodic story of high school students trying to lose their virginity – except: this also chronicles serious issues such as teenage pregnancy along with the usual high jinks. It also boasts a quite astonishing cast of then unknowns. JF Swearing, sex scenes, drug abuse, nudity. *DVD* ᗷ

Sean Penn *Jeff Spicoli* • Jennifer Jason Leigh *Stacy Hamilton* • Judge Reinhold *Brad Hamilton* • Robert Romanus *Mike Damone* • Brian Backer *Mark Ratner* • Phoebe Cates *Linda Barrett* • Forest Whitaker *Charles Jefferson* • Eric Stoltz *Stoner Bud* • Anthony Edwards *Stoner Bud* ■ *Dir* Amy Heckerling • *Scr* Cameron Crowe, from his novel

Fast-Walking ★★ 18

Comedy drama 1982 · US · Colour · 111min

This prison drama has James Woods in a typically amoral role as a guard who becomes involved in a plot to assassinate black activist Robert Hooks. There are some good performances from Tim McIntire, M Emmet Walsh and the ever-reliable Woods, but these accomplished actors can't hide the fact that this is a rather nasty and unpleasant film. JB Swearing, violence.

James Woods *Miniver* • Kay Lenz *Moke* • Tim McIntire *Wasco* • Robert Hooks *Galliot* • M Emmet Walsh *Sergeant Sanger* • Susan Tyrrell *Evie* • Charles Weldon *Jackson* ■ *Dir* James B Harris • *Scr* James B Harris. from the novel *The Rap* by Ernest Brawley

Faster ★★ 15

Revenge thriller 2010 · US · Colour · 93min

Fresh out of priscn, convicted bank robber Dwayne Johnson is a man on a mission. His motivation is revealed in the course of the story, but, essentially, if you're on his list of names, you're dead – unless, of course, burnt-out cop Billy Bob Thornton or perfectionist assassin Oliver Jackson-Cohen can stop him in his tracks. Despite appearing in a str ng of family-orientated films, the imposing Johnson shows he's still capable of playinç it mean and determined. Unfortunately, the movie starts taking itself way too seriously and bets too much on a final-reel twist that most viewers will spot coming a mile off. TJ Violence, swearing, drug abuse. *DVD* ᗷ

Dwayne Johnson *Driver* • Billy Bob Thornton *Cop* • Oliver Jackson-Cohen *Killer* • Carla Gugino *Cicero* • Maggie Grace *Lily* • Moon Bloodgood *Marina* • Adewale Akinnuoye-Agbaje *Evangelist* • Tom Berenger *Warden* ■ *Dir* George Tillman Jr • *Scr* Joe Gayton, Tony Gayton

LANDMARK FILM
Indie auteur Russ Meyer reinvents screen sex with his satirical, expertly edited pop-art melodramas involving man-crunching amazon women

Faster, Pussycat! Kill! Kill! ★★★★ 18

Cult satirical melodrama 1965 · US · BW · 83min

Three go-go dancers, led by *femme fatale* Tura Satana, go on a wild crime spree in California in Russ Meyer's cult favourite. After indulging in kidnapping, theft, murder and wanton exposure of their seemingly limitless cleavages, the crazy-for-kicks chicks take the Battle of the Sexes to the extreme, drawing some hapless males into a violently perverse cat-and-mouse game. This double-entendre parade through the seamier side of the Swinging Sixties is the definitive Meyer movie. AJ Violence, sex scenes. *DVD*

Tura Satana *Varla* • Haji *Rosie* • Lori Williams *Billie* • Susan Bernard [Sue Bernard] *Linda* • Stuart Lancaster *Old man* • Paul Trinka *Kirk* • Dennis Busch *Vegetaole* ■ *Dir* Russ Meyer • *Scr* Jack Moran, from a story by Russ Meyer

The Fastest Guitar Alive ★★ U

Musical comedy western 1966 · US · Colour · 87min

Roy Orbison is barely recognisable without his trademark shades in this shameless exploitation offering, but there's no mistaking that magical voice. A curious hybrid of matinée horse opera and teen drive-in picture, it casts him as a Confederate spy who becomes a fugitive after being trapped behind enemy lines at the end of the American Civil War. It's more a knockabout adventure than a genuine western, with the Big O (who hides a rifle behind his guitar) coming over as an uncomfortable throwback to such singing cowboys as Hopalong Cassidy and Roy Rogers. DP

Roy Orbison *Johnny Banner* • Sammy Jackson *Steve Menlo* • Maggie Pierce *Flo Chestnut* • Joan Freeman *Sue Chestnut* • Lyle Bettger *Charlie Mansfield* • John Doucette *Sheriff Max Cooper* • Patricia Donahue *Stella* ■ *Dir* Michael Moore (1) • *Scr* Robert E Kent

The Fastest Gun Alive ★★★ U

Western 1956 · US · BW · 85min

Glenn Ford is trying to live down his father's gunslinging past by working as a town storekeeper, when Broderick Crawford blasts in, exposing Ford and taunting him with his father's name. Russ Tamblyn has some knockabout moments at a barn dance, and Jeanne Crain is earnest and pretty as the pleading wife, but Ford shines, giving an outstanding performance in a taut, underrated western. TS

Glenn Ford *George Temple* • Jeanne Crain *Dora Temple* • Broderick Crawford *Vinnie Harold* • Russ Tamblyn *Eric Doolittle* • Allyn Joslyn *Harvey Maxwell* • Leif Erickson *Lou Glover* • Noah Beery Jr *Dink Wells* ■ *Dir* Russell Rouse • *Scr* Frank D Gilroy, Russell Rouse, Frank D Gilroy

Fat Albert ★★ U

Fantasy comedy adventure 2004 · US · Colour · 89min

This live action update of the 1970s cartoon series is probably too sugary for today's savvy youngsters. The original series, created by Bill Cosby (he serves as producer here and also pops up in a cameo), was centred around the feel-good antics of a gang of young black youths. Here the cartoon characters literally climb out of the TV set to help a lonely young teen (Kyla Pratt). Keenan Thompson makes a good fist of the fleshed out Fat Albert, but this is as much out of step with modern tastes as the cartoon characters are in the real world. JF *DVD*

Kenan Thompson *Fat Albert* • Kyla Pratt *Doris* • Shedrack Anderson III *Rudy* • Jermaine Williams *Mushmouth* • Keith Robinson *Bill* • Alphonso McAuley *Bucky* • Aaron A Frazier *Old Weird Harold* • Marques B Houston [Marques Houston] *Dumb Donald* • Bill Cosby ■ *Dir* Joel Zwick • *Scr* William H Cosby Jr [Bill Cosby], Charles Kipps

Fat City ★★★★

Sports drama 1972 · US · Colour · 96min

Strip away the sleaziness of the setting and you have that old Hollywood standby, *A Star Is Born*, recycled as a boxing picture. Stacy Keach (in a role offered first to Marlon Brando) is the boxer on the slide and Jeff Bridges is the one on the rise. John Huston, who directed wearing an oxygen mask owing to acute emphysema, shot the picture on skid row in Stockton, California, and aimed for a grimly realistic but not seedy, look. The result is a minor classic, necessarily brutal but with humanity and an underlying optimism. AT Violence, swearing.

Stacy Keach *Billy Tully* • Jeff Bridges *Ernie Munger* • Susan Tyrrell *Oma* • Candy Clark *Faye* • Nicholas Colasanto *Ruben* • Art Aragon *Babe* • Curtis Cokes *Earl* • Sixto Rodriguez *Lucero* • Billy Walker *Wes* ■ *Dir* John Huston • *Scr* Leonard Gardner, from his novel • *Cinematographer* Conrad Hall

Fat Slags ★ 15

Comedy 2004 · UK · Colour · 72min

This crude, one-note live-action adaptation of *Viz* comic's regular strip aims low and still manages to misfire. Fiona Allen and Sophie Thompson don fat suits to bring Sandra and Tracy, *Viz*'s booze-swilling, kebab-scoffing nymphos, to life. The girls' "star quality" is spotted by media baron Sean Cooley (Jerry O'Connell), after he receives a reality-altering bump on the head. IF Swearing. *DVD*

Sophie Thompson *Tracey* • Fiona Allen *Sandra* • Jerry O'Connell *Sean Cooley* • James Dreyfus *Fidor* • Anthony Head *Victor* • Michael Greco *Niarchos* • Geri Halliwell *Paige* • Tom Goodman-Hill *Baz* • Henry Miller *Dave* • Naomi Campbell *Sales assistant* • Angus Deayton *Maurice* • Dolph Lundgren *Randy* ■ *Dir* Ed Bye • *Scr* William Osborne, from characters by Chris Donald, Simon Donald [uncredited]

Fatal Attraction ★★★★ 18

Thriller 1987 · US · Colour · 114min

This is the movie that helped create a new genre: the crazed female from hell. Glenn Close is the obsessed woman driven to extreme lengths when she discovers that Michael Douglas is not going to leave his wife (Anne Archer) for her. Close is excellent in a thankless role, while Douglas established himself as the troubled icon of middle-class America. The movie's message (it's all right to have an affair as long as it's not with a nutcase) is more than a little dubious, but there is no denying its slick power and director Adrian Lyne milks the tension for all it's worth. However, he had to reshoot the movie's climax after test audiences gave the thumbs down to his first ending. Lyne later got the chance to reinstate the original ending with his director's cut. JF Violence, swearing, sex scenes, nudity. *DVD*

Michael Douglas (1) *Dan Gallagher* • Glenn Close *Alex Forrest* • Anne Archer *Beth Gallagher* • Ellen Hamilton Latzen *Ellen Gallagher* • Stuart Pankin *Jimmy* • Ellen Foley *Hildy* • Fred Gwynne *Arthur* • Meg Mundy *Joan Rogerson* ■ *Dir* Adrian Lyne • *Scr* James Dearden

Fatal Beauty ★★ 18

Comedy thriller 1987 · US · Colour · 99min

Director Tom Holland loses his humorous touch with this lukewarm vehicle for Whoopi Goldberg. She stars as a tough narcotics cop on the trail of some drug-dealing bad guys, which gives her an excuse to totter around in ill-advised prostitute disguise. Cheech Marin, Rubén Blades and Sam Elliott (as Goldberg's love interest) try their best to pretend they're in a movie worth sitting through. JB Swearing. *DVD*

Whoopi Goldberg *Rita Rizzoli* • Sam Elliott *Mike Marshak* • Rubén Blades *Carl Jimenez* • Harris Yulin *Conrad Kroll* • Brad Dourif *Leo Nova* • Cheech Marin [Richard "Cheech" Marin] *Bartender* ■ *Dir* Tom Holland (1) • *Scr* Hilary Henkin, Dean Riesner

Fatal Error ★★ 12

Science-fiction thriller 1999 · US · Colour · 87min

There's a lethal computer virus jumping from hardware to humans in this cautionary and topical conspiracy tale. Janine Turner plays the unconvincing US army agent who reluctantly teams up with disgraced doctor Antonio Sabato Jr in a race against time to shut down the deadly technology at its source. Though the concept is promising, it's weakly executed with increasingly implausible plotting hampered by hokey dialogue. SF *DVD*

Antonio Sabato Jr *Nick Baldwin* • Janine Turner *Samantha Carter* • Robert Wagner *Albert Teal* • Jason Schombing *Charlie* • Malcolm Stewart *Jack Doulan* • David Lewis (3) *Ned Henderson* ■ *Dir* Armand Mastroianni • *Scr* Rockne S O'Bannon, from the novel *Reaper* by Ben Mezrich

Fatal Honeymoon ★★

Crime drama based on a true story 2012 · US · Colour · 90min

Harvey Keitel adds interest but ultimately underperforms in this routine TV movie based on a true-life crime story. Playing a doting Alabama father, he gets to do his trademark anguished wailing when his unassertive daughter (Amber Clayton) drowns during her Australian honeymoon. Her cold and odious husband (Billy Miller) says it was a simple diving accident – though both Keitel and the cops suspect he killed her. While Miller's exaggerated villainy keeps you watching, it also makes the film feel flimsy and unrealistic. And even star Keitel doesn't quite seem real. SF

Harvey Keitel *Tommy Thomas* • Amber Clayton *Tina Watson* • Billy Miller *Gabe Watson* • Gary Sweet *Det Gary Campbell* ■ *Dir* Nadia Tass • *Scr* Teena Booth, Mac Gudgeon

Fatal Instinct ★★★ 15
Spoof thriller 1993 · US · Colour · 86min

Panned on its original release, this boasts some slick gags and several knowing performances. The problem is, it's often far too clever for its own good. Veteran director Carl Reiner has got the look and feel of latter-day *films noirs* off to a T, and he is well served by Armand Assante as a cop who doubles as a lawyer for the people he arrests, Kate Nelligan as his blatantly adulterous wife and Sherilyn Fenn and Sean Young as his *femmes fatales*. DP Swearing, sex scenes. *DVD*

Armand Assante *Ned Ravine* • Sherilyn Fenn *Laura* • Kate Nelligan *Lana Ravine* • Sean Young *Lola Cain* • Christopher McDonald *Frank Kelbo* • James Remar *Max Shady* ■ *Dir* Carl Reiner • *Scr* David O'Malley

Fatal Lady ★★
Murder mystery 1936 · US · BW · 75min

Walter Pidgeon returned to Hollywood from the Broadway stage to play opposite Mary Ellis in this ill-conceived attempt to turn the leading lady of stage musicals into a movie name. She plays an opera star suspected of murder, but the title of this hackneyed backstage drama proved sadly prophetic for Ellis, whose casting as a prima donna seemed both appropriate and unsympathetic. TS

Mary Ellis *Marion Stuart/Marla Delasano/Malevo* • Walter Pidgeon *David Roberts* • Ruth Donnelly *Melba York* • Norman Foster *Phillip Roberts* • Guy Bates Post *Feodor Glinka* • John Halliday *Romero Fontes* ■ *Dir* Edward Ludwig • *Scr* Samuel Ornitz, Horace McCoy, from a story by Harry Segall

Fatal Mission ★★
War drama 1990 · US · Colour · 84min

"Nothin's guaranteed in the 'Nam", or so declares American "black" operations agent Peter Fonda at the beginning of this movie. What is guaranteed is that you will have flashbacks to *Hell in the Pacific* about halfway through. Fonda assassinates a Communist leader, and while trying to escape, is taken prisoner by a Chinese agent, played by Tia Carrere. Together they find out that everyone's against them, and they have to rely on each other to survive. ST

Peter Fonda *Ken Andrews* • Tia Carrere *Mai Chong* • Mako *Trang* • Ted Markland *CIA Man* • Jim Mitchum [James Mitchum] *Captain Bauer* • Felind Obach *NVA Sergeant Tuong* • Joonee Gamboa *NVA Captain Hao* • Joe Mari *Vietnam general* ■ *Dir* George Rowe • *Scr* Anthony Gentile, John Gentile, George Rowe, Chosei Funahara, Peter Fonda, from a story by Erlinda Quiaoit Rowe

Fate ★★★ 15
Drama 2001 · Tur · Colour · 118min

Albert Camus's novel *L'Etranger* is the source for the first entry in Zeki Demirkubuz's *Tales of Darkness* trilogy. It's a measured and studiously played treatise on frailty, destiny and alienation that deftly combines moments of sobering drama with bleak comedy. Turkish shipping clerk Serdar Orcin's sanguine response to everything from his mother's death to imprisonment for a murder he didn't commit will frustrate some. But his curiously affectionate relationship with Zeynep Tokus, the wife who is also his boss's mistress, is more plausible than encounters with a vengeful neighbour and the verbose prison governor. DP Turkish +subtitles. Swearing.

Serdar Orcin *Musa Demircan* • Zeynep Tokus *Sinem* • Demir Karahan *Naim* • Engin Gunaydin *Necati* ■ *Dir* Zeki Demirkubuz • *Scr* Zeki Demirkubuz, from the novel *L'Etranger* by Albert Camus

Le Fate Ignoranti ★★★ 15
Drama 2001 · Fr/It · Colour · 105min

When medical worker Margherita Buy is widowed, she sets out to find the woman she suspects of having been her husband's mistress, but is confronted with Stefano Accorsi, a younger man with whom her husband had a long-term affair. Ferzan Ozpetek litters their relationship with contrived twists and facile resolutions, and the tension dissipates into cosiness. Well-meaning and earnestly played, but melodramatic and improbable. DP Italian, Turkish +subtitles. *DVD*

Margherita Buy *Antonia* • Stefano Accorsi *Michele* • Serra Yilmaz *Serra* • Andrea Renzi *Massimo* • Gabriel Garko *Ernesto* • Erica Blanc *Veronica* • Rosaria De Cicco *Luisella* ■ *Dir* Ferzan Ozpetek • *Scr* Gianni Romoli, Ferzan Ozpetek

Fate Is the Hunter ★★★ PG
Mystery drama 1964 · US · BW · 101min

Glenn Ford leads the investigation into an air crash for which his friend, pilot Rod Taylor, is thought to be responsible. Flashbacks show us what might have happened, until Ford and sole survivor Suzanne Pleshette restage the flight to solve the mystery. A lot of interesting detail and a surprising cast make this quite watchable, though Ford is fairly glum throughout. AT *DVD*

Glenn Ford *Sam McBane* • Nancy Kwan *Sally Fraser* • Rod Taylor *Capt Jack Savage* • Suzanne Pleshette *Martha Webster* • Jane Russell *Jane Russell, guest star* • Wally Cox *Ralph Bundy* • Mary Wickes *Mrs Llewelyn* • Dorothy Malone *Lisa Bond* ■ *Dir* Ralph Nelson • *Scr* Harold Medford, from the novel by Ernest K Gann

Fated ★★ 15
Romantic fantasy drama 2006 · UK · Colour · 98min

Despite making atmospheric use of Liverpool's iconic landmarks, Nicola Scott's adaptation of her own stage play too often feels like a travelogue rather than a fairy tale. The story of a nightclub bouncer who falls in love with an enchanted statue that has been granted a single night of life might have worked with a lighter touch. But the direction is as ponderous as the dialogue, and the performances of Brendan Mackey and Katrine de Candole are awkward in the extreme. Even familiar TV faces like Michael Angelis and Craig Charles struggle to make an impact amid the plethora of peripheral characters. DP Swearing.

Brendan Mackey *Joe* • Katrine de Candole *Amy (the statue)* • Michael Angelis *Tatty* • Craig Charles *Pedro* • Kate Robbins *Kathleen* • Lee Boardman *Jack* ■ *Dir* Nicola Scott • *Scr* Nicola Scott, from her play

Father ★★★
Drama 1990 · Aus · Colour · 106min

The father is Max von Sydow, a German living in Melbourne with his daughter (Carol Drinkwater), son-in-law and two grandchildren. A nice, happy family, until grandad is suddenly charged with committing wartime atrocities and is put on trial. While not in the same league as Costa-Gavras's *Music Box*, this is still a gripping drama, superbly played by von Sydow. The film explores the themes of guilt and the nature of truth with skill. AT Swearing, nudity.

Max von Sydow *Joe Mueller* • Carol Drinkwater *Anne Winton* • Julia Blake *Iya Zetnick* • Steve Jacobs *Bobby Winton* • Simone Robertson *Rebecca Winton* • Kahli Sneddon *Amy Winton* • Nicholas Bell *Paul Jamieson* ■ *Dir* John Power • *Scr* Tony Cavanaugh, Graham Hartley

Father and Son ★★★ PG

Drama 2003 · Rus/Ger/It/Fr/Neth/Swi · Colour · 82min

After the period exuberance of *Russian Ark*, Aleksandr Sokurov retreats into the more personal mood that characterised *Mother*

and Son in this awkward companion piece. Aleksandr Burov's glowing golden imagery is the film's undoubted glory. But despite the psychological estrangement that contrasts with their easy physicality, the relationship between war veteran Andrei Shetinin and his motherless soldier son Alexei Neimyshev is so intense that there's no room for onlookers. Moving, stylish, but frustratingly inaccessible. DP Russian +subtitles. *DVD*

Andrei Shetinin *Father* • Alexei Neimyshev *Son* • Aleksandr Razbash *Neighbour* • Marina Zasukhina *Girlfriend* ■ *Dir* Aleksandr Sokurov • *Scr* Sergei Potepalov

Father Brown ★★★★ U
Comedy thriller 1954 · UK · BW · 93min

Although occasionally overdoing the unworldliness, Alec Guinness brings GK Chesterton's sermonising sleuth to rich and vigorous life in this hugely enjoyable comedy thriller from director Robert Hamer. Fans of the original stories might be a tad aggrieved by the slight shift of period and the marked reduction in religious undertones, but the case of St Augustine's Cross is nevertheless packed with incident and intrigue. Peter Finch is languidly villainous as Flambeau and Joan Greenwood huskily seductive as the devout Lady Warren, but it's Cecil Parker's bishop and Ernest Thesiger's doddering librarian who stay longest in the memory. DP

Alec Guinness *Father Brown* • Joan Greenwood *Lady Warren* • Peter Finch *Flambeau* • Cecil Parker *Bishop* • Bernard Lee *Inspector Valentine* • Sidney James *Parkinson* • Gérard Oury *Inspector Dubois* • Ernest Thesiger *Vicomte* ■ *Dir* Robert Hamer • *Scr* Thelma Schnee, Maurice Rapf, Robert Hamer, from characters by GK Chesterton

Father Came Too ★★ PG
Comedy 1963 · UK · Colour · 88min

This is a disappointing outing, considering that it had all the makings of being an amusing inversion of the old mother-in-law joke. James Robertson-Justice stars as the father-in-law from hell who shatters the bliss of newlyweds Stanley Baxter and Sally Smith with his tactless intrusions and incessant hectoring. Such is his dominance of the action that there simply aren't enough gags to go round, leaving Leslie Phillips and Ronnie Barker twiddling their thumbs on the periphery. DP *DVD*

James Robertson-Justice *Sir Beverley Grant* • Leslie Phillips *Roddy Chipfield* • Stanley Baxter *Dexter Munro* • Sally Smith *Juliet Munro* • Ronnie Barker *Josh* • James Villiers *Benzil Bulstrode* ■ *Dir* Peter Graham Scott • *Scr* Jack Davies, Henry Blyth

Father Dear Father ★★ U
Comedy 1972 · UK · Colour · 94min

Based on the enduring sitcom first shown in 1968, this, as with most film versions of popular TV shows, lacks the cosy comic consistency of the original, even though it retains most of the cast. Guest stars Beryl Reid, Donald Sinden and Richard O'Sullivan are given too little to do as novelist Patrick Cargill's marriage to his agent is jeopardised by his trouble-prone daughters. DP

Patrick Cargill *Patrick Glover* • Natasha Pyne *Anna* • Ann Holloway *Karen* • Noel Dyson *Nanny* • Beryl Reid *Mrs Stoppard* • Donald Sinden *Philip* • Richard O'Sullivan *Richard* • Jack Watling *Bill Mossman* ■ *Dir* William G Stewart • *Scr* Johnnie Mortimer, from the TV series by Johnnie Mortimer, Brian Cooke

Father Goose ★★★ U
Second World War comedy drama 1964 · US · Colour · 116min

Cary Grant stars as a boozy beach bum caught up in Second World War heroics involving a gaggle of schoolgirls and their teacher, Leslie Caron. Grant is terrific, as ever, and his air of discomfort certainly helps the plot, but you have to wonder if a comedy about the Japanese invasion of the Pacific is actually a good idea. The Hollywood Academy thought so, and writers Peter Stone and Frank Tarloff won an Oscar for their screenplay. TS *DVD*

Cary Grant *Walter Eckland* • Leslie Caron *Catherine Freneau* • Trevor Howard *Frank Houghton* • Stephanie Berrington *Elizabeth* • Jennifer Berrington *Harriet* • Jack Good *Stebbings* ■ *Dir* Ralph Nelson • *Scr* Frank Tarloff, Peter Stone, from the story *A Place of Dragons* by SH Barnett

Father Hood ★ PG
Crime comedy 1993 · US · Colour · 91min

This dislikeable family comedy is really only for diehard Patrick Swayze fans. He plays the supposedly lovable rogue who sets off on the adventure of a lifetime with his two young kids who have been languishing in horrid foster care. The tone veers between naturalistic drama and simple-minded slapstick, and not even a talented cast can rescue this sinking ship. JF

Patrick Swayze *Jack Charles* • Halle Berry *Kathleen Mercer* • Sabrina Lloyd *Kelly Charles* • Brian Bonsall *Eddie Charles* • Michael Ironside *Jerry* • Diane Ladd *Rita* ■ *Dir* Darrell James Roodt • *Scr* Scott Spencer

The Father of My Children ★★★★ 12
Drama 2009 · Ger/Fr · Colour · 106min

In a poignant drama inspired by the real-life tragedy of prolific producer Humbert Balsan, Louis-Do de Lencquesaing plays genial workaholic Grégoire Canvel, whose passionate commitment descends into suicidal despair as his movie business fails. His state of mind is adroitly counterpointed by the determination of his wife, Chiara Caselli, to ensure that his legacy endures and that his three daughters think fondly of their father. The action is imbued with insight and intelligence. DP French +subtitles. *DVD*

Louis-Do de Lencquesaing *Grégoire Canvel* • Chiara Caselli *Sylvia Canvel* • Alice de Lencquesaing *Clémence Canvel* • Alice Gautier *Valentine Canvel* • Manelle Driss *Billie Canvel* • Eric Elmosnino *Serge* ■ *Dir/Scr* Mia Hansen-Løve

Father of the Bride ★★★★ U
Comedy 1950 · US · BW · 88min

Spencer Tracy has seldom been better than here in the title role. His gnarled face is peerless when confronted with so much frustration, and his retelling of the events leading up to the debris that was once his home is a joy. Joan Bennett co-stars as his wife and Elizabeth Taylor plays the bride whose impending nuptials lead to chaos. Director Vincente Minnelli keeps up a sprightly pace and gets the most out of the witty screenplay. This film was so successful that it inspired a sequel – *Father's Little Dividend* – and, four decades on, the inferior remake with its own follow-up. TS

Spencer Tracy *Stanley T Banks* • Joan Bennett *Ellie Banks* • Elizabeth Taylor *Kay Banks* • Don Taylor *Buckley Dunstan* • Billie Burke *Doris Dunstan* • Leo G Carroll *Mr Massoula* • Moroni Olsen *Herbert Dunstan* • Melville Cooper *Mr Tringle* ■ *Dir* Vincente Minnelli • *Scr* Albert Hackett, Francis Goodrich, from the novel by Edward Streeter

Father of the Bride ★★★★ PG
Comedy 1991 · US · Colour · 100min

The original 1950 marriage-go-round starring Spencer Tracy is given an amiable 1990s work-out by the *Baby Boom* and *Private Benjamin* husband-and-wife team of Charles Shyer and Nancy Meyers. Steve Martin shines as the anxious parent who can't find a single thing to like about his daughter's perfect fiancé, while continually counting the ceremony costs. Diane Keaton gives him sparkling back-up as the uncomplaining wife, but it's Martin Short who steals the entire movie as the camp wedding organiser. AJ *DVD*

Steve Martin *George Banks* • Diane Keaton *Nina Banks* • Kimberly Williams *Annie Banks* • Kieran Culkin *Matty Banks* • George Newbern *Bryan MacKenzie* • Martin Short *Franck Eggelhoffer* • BD Wong *Howard Weinstein* ■ *Dir* Charles Shyer

• *Scr* Nancy Meyers, Charles Shyer, from the film by Frances Goodrich, Albert Hackett, from the novel by Edward Streeter

Father of the Bride Part 2 ★★PG

Comedy   1995 · US · Colour · 101min

This loose version of 1951's *Father's Little Dividend* is full of false emotion, lame humour and pointless details. Steve Martin's peaceful life is upset this time by the simultaneous pregnancies of both his wife (Diane Keaton) and his newly-married daughter (Kimberly Williams). Although flashes of Martin's comic genius occasionally shine through the syrupy script, the verbal comedy on offer is dim-witted. AJ *DVD*

Steve Martin *George Banks* • Diane Keaton *Nina Banks* • Martin Short *Franck Eggelhoffer* • Kimberly Williams *Annie Banks-MacKenzie* • George Newbern *Bryan MacKenzie* • Kieran Culkin *Matty Banks* ■ *Dir* Charles Shyer • *Scr* Nancy Meyers, Charles Shyer, from the film *Father's Little Dividend* by Albert Hackett, Frances Goodrich, from characters by Edward Streeter

Father to Be ★★★

Comedy drama   1979 · Swe · Colour · 107min

This Swedish film takes a different slant on the expectant father scenario, as directed by Lasse Hallström. In the film's defence, it can be said that, through the use of live-action and animated daydreams, it does manage to be occasionally amusing before it goes off at a post-natal tangent. The big plus is Magnus Härenstam as the diligent father-to-be. DP Swedish +subtitles.

Magnus Härenstam *Bosse* • Anki Liden *Lena* • Micha Gabay *Bosse's pal* • Ulf Brunnberg *Bjorn* ■ *Dir/Scr* Lasse Hallström

Father Was a Fullback ★★★

Comedy   1949 · US · BW · 78min

This is one of those post-*Life with Father* movies, where the mother actually runs the household and the father manages to preserve his dignity and the illusion of being boss in his own home. Here, Maureen O'Hara rules the roost while Fred MacMurray buckles down on the gridiron as the football coach to a losing college team. Pleasant lightweight fare. TS

Fred MacMurray *George Cooper* • Maureen O'Hara *Elizabeth Cooper* • Betty Lynn *Connie Cooper* • Rudy Vallee *Mr Jessop* • Thelma Ritter *Geraldine* • Natalie Wood *Ellen Cooper* ■ *Dir* John M Stahl • *Scr* Aleen Leslie, Casey Robinson, Mary Loos, Richard Sale, from a play by Clifford Goldsmith

Fatherland ★★★15

Political drama   1986 · UK/Ger · Colour · 106min

To borrow a footballing cliché, this is a film of two halves. The opening section is classic Ken Loach, even though the setting might be unfamiliar. Making his screen debut, Gerulf Pannach is suitably despondent as the liberated East German folk singer whose creativity dries up after he exchanges the political restrictions of the Communist bloc for the capitalist demands of his new American record label. But the fascinating case study of clashing cultures is disappointingly sacrificed for a thriller subplot, as Pannach goes in search of his missing father in England. DP German, English +subtitles. *DVD*

Gerulf Pannach *Drittemann* • Fabienne Babe *Emma* • Cristine Rose *Lucy* • Sigfrit Steiner *James Dryden* • Robert Dietl *Lawyer* • Heike Schrotter *Marita* • Stephan Samuel *Max* ■ *Dir* Ken Loach • *Scr* Trevor Griffiths

Fathers and Daughters ★★15

Drama   2015 · US/It · Colour · 116min

Russell Crowe stars as a father suffering from post-traumatic stress disorder who's struggling to raise his daughter after the death of his wife. Amanda Seyfried plays the daughter as an adult, fighting her own demons as she begins a new relationship. Despite committed performances from the leads, equally unrealistic and sombre storylines unravel with maximum melodrama, thanks to overdramatic subplots and platitudes about love. The supporting cast is equally stranded, with Diane Kruger decidedly one dimensional as Seyfried's vindictive aunt. JL Sex references *DVD*

Russell Crowe *Jake Davis* • Amanda Seyfried *Katie* • Aaron Paul *Cameron* • Diane Kruger *Elisabeth* • Quvenzhané Wallis *Lucy* ■ *Dir* Gabriele Muccino • *Scr* Brad Desch

A Father's Betrayal ★★★15

Courtroom drama   1997 · US · Colour · 87min

Brian Dennehy both directs and stars in this high-quality, made-for-TV drama. He plays a ruthless attorney slowly rebuilding his relationship with his estranged son Reed Diamond. All that changes, however, when a friend of his son's (Alice Krige) accuses his father of raping her. Dennehy is in commanding form and his direction is equally dependable. He also draws good performances from a talented cast. DP Violence. *DVD*

Brian Dennehy *Ed Brannigan Sr* • Lynn Redgrave *Monica Brannigan* • Reed Diamond *Ed Brannigan Jr* • Alice Krige *Rebecca Daly* ■ *Dir* Brian Dennehy • *Scr* Joe Cacaci

Fathers' Day ★★12

Comedy   1997 · US · Colour · 95min

This surprisingly unfunny comedy stars Billy Crystal and Robin Williams as two men who are both told by Nastassja Kinski that they are the father of her wayward missing teenage son, in an attempt to get them to help her find him. This had the potential to be hilarious, but instead falls flat thanks to a weak script/ JB *DVD*

Robin Williams *Dale Putley* • Billy Crystal *Jack Lawrence* • Julia Louis-Dreyfus *Carrie Lawrence* • Nastassja Kinski *Collette Andrews* • Charlie Hofheimer *Scott Andrews* ■ *Dir* Ivan Reitman • *Scr* Lowell Ganz, Babaloo Mandel, from the film *Les Compères* by Francis Veber

Father's Doing Fine ★★★U

Comedy   1952 · UK · Colour · 83min

A certain bourgeois self-satisfaction permeates this superficial situation comedy. However, such is the precision of Henry Cass's direction and the exuberance of the performances that it's difficult not to be sucked into this frantic world of scatterbrained daughters, disastrous share deals and crooked butlers. Seemingly a door can't open without a fresh crisis breezing in, but Heather Thatcher's ennobled widow takes it all in her stride, unlike Richard Attenborough's nerve-jangled father-to-be. The pace disguises the fact that the humour has dated somewhat. DP

Richard Attenborough *Dougall* • Heather Thatcher *Lady Buckering* • Noel Purcell *Shaughnessy* • George Thorpe *Dr Drew* • Diane Hart *Doreen* • Susar Stephen *Bicky* • Mary Germaine *Gerda* • Virginia McKenna *Catherine* • Sidney James *Taxi driver* ■ *Dir* Henry Cass • *Scr* Anne Burnaby, from the play *Little Lambs Eat Ivy* by Noel Langley

Father's Little Dividend ★★★U

Comedy   1951 · US · BW · 81min

Director Vincente Minnelli was reunited with Spencer Tracy, Joan Bennett, Elizabeth Taylor and Don Taylor for this sequel to their 1950 smash hit *Father of the Bride*. The dividend, of course, is a grandchild, which leads Tracy into dialogue of the "coochy, coochy, coo" variety. Minnelli shot the film in only 22 days while the sets for the final ballet in *An American in Paris* were being constructed. AT *DVD*

Spencer Tracy *Stanley Banks* • Joan Bennett *Ellie Banks* • Elizabeth Taylor *Kay Dunstan* • Don Taylor *Buckley Dunstan* • Billie Burke *Doris Dunstan* • Moroni Olsen *Herbert Dunstan* ■ *Dir* Vincente Minnelli • *Scr* Frances Goodrich, Albert Hackett, from characters by Edward Streeter

Fathers of Girls ★★15

Drama   2010 · UK · Colour · 72min

Ray Winstone struggles manfully with a lugubrious and occasionally ludicrous screenplay by co-directors Ethem Cetintas and Karl Howman in this brooding tale of cynical revenge. Mourning the drug death of his student daughter (Lois Winstone), a Wiltshire solicitor plans a sinister form of payback for the nightclub owner and the doorman where his little princess bought her fatal overdose. Whether muttering threats and tips about tea-making under his breath or stalking his daughter's best friend, Winstone looks decidedly uncomfortable. But, as co-executive producer, he's really only got himself to blame. DP Swearing. *DVD*

Ray Winstone *Frank Horner* • Lois Winstone *Helen Horner* • Chloe Howman *Emma Salerno* • Luke Kempner *Simon* • James Hillier *Ron* ■ *Dir/Scr* Ethem Cetintas, Karl Howman

Fathom ★★★U

Spoof spy adventure   1967 · UK · Colour · 94min

This sprightly spoof combines the frenetic pace of a crime caper with the flashiness of a Bond movie. Shifting from the search for a lost H-bomb trigger to a race for a priceless statuette, the plot is almost an irrelevance as agents Raquel Welch and Tony Franciosa hurtle around the Mediterranean. Revelling in the sunny locations and the shenanigans, Welch gives one of her best performances in an often disappointing career. DP *DVD*

Raquel Welch *Fathom Harvill* • Tony Franciosa [Anthony Franciosa] *Peter Merriweather* • Ronald Fraser *Douglas Campbell* • Greta Chi *Jo-May Soon* • Richard Briers *Timothy* ■ *Dir* Leslie H Martinson • *Scr* Lorenzo Semple Jr, from the novel by Larry Forrester

Fatso ★★

Comedy   1979 · US · Colour · 93min

Anne Bancroft is such an attractively classy actress you'd expect her debut as feature director to be the same. Sadly, not. Following the death of an obese cousin, Dom DeLuise is trying to lose weight, hoping both to stay alive and impress Bancroft. The results are mawkish and crude, with enough jokes about excrement to fill a bucket. Bancroft should have known better, though she contributes a performance, to contrast with that of DeLuise, that is as elegant as the rest of the movie should have been. TH

Dom DeLuise *Dominick DiNapoli* • Anne Bancroft *Antoinette* • Ron Carey *Frankie* • Candice Azzara [Candy Azzara] *Lydia* • Michael Lombard *Charlie* ■ *Dir/Scr* Anne Bancroft

The Fault in Our Stars ★★★12

Romantic drama   2014 · US/Can/UK · Colour · 120min

Adapted from John Green's beloved young adult novel, this bittersweet tear-jerker alternates between mawkish melodrama and heartfelt sincerity. Shailene Woodley is utterly disarming as Hazel, a precocious teenager with thyroid cancer who meets an optimistic charmer named Gus (Ansel Elgort), who has lost one of his legs to bone cancer at a local support group. Woodley has a smile that lights up the screen and is utterly believable, even when the story isn't, while Elgort remains endearing despite being burdened with some mushy dialogue. SC Swearing. *DVD*

Shailene Woodley *Hazel Grace Lancaster* • Ansel Elgort *Augustus Waters* • Laura Dern *Frannie Lancaster* • Sam Trammell *Michael* • Nat Wolff *Isaac* • Willem Dafoe *Peter Van Houten* ■ *Dir* Josh Boone • *Scr* Scott Neustadter, Michael H Weber, from John Green's novel

Faust ★★★★★PG

Classic silent fantasy   1926 · Ger · BW · 115min

This is as much a masterpiece of design as a triumph for the director and his international cast. Inspired by the paintings of Caspar David Friedrich, Robert Herlth and Walter Röhrig brought all their Expressionist expertise to sculpting light, smoke and steam into the malevolent atmosphere that FW Murnau required for Faust's epic duel with Mephistopheles. Emil Jannings makes an imposing demon, Swedish star Gösta Ekman unassumingly transforms from decrepitude to youth and the untried Camilla Horn is suitably pure as the misused Marguerite (a role that was rejected by Lillian Gish). DP *DVD* 🅱

Gösta Ekman (1) *Faust* • Emil Jannings *Mephistopheles* • Camilla Horn *Marguerite* • Frida Richard *Marguerite's mother* • William Dieterle *Valentin, Marguerite's brother* • Yvette Guilbert *Marthe Schwerdtlein, Marguerite's aunt* • Eric Barclay *Duke of Parma* • Hanna Ralph *Duchess of Parma* ■ *Dir* Friedrich W Murnau [FW Murnau] • *Scr* Hans Kyser, from the play *The Tragical History of Doctor Faustus* by Christopher Marlowe, from the writings *Faust: eine Tragödie* by Johann Wolfgang von Goethe • *Cinematographer* Carl Hoffman

Faust ★★★★★12

Part-animated fantasy   1994 · UK/Cz Rep/Fr · Colour · 92min

Jan Svankmajer is the undisputed king of the puppet film, equally at ease with marionettes, claymation and stop-motion animation. His version of *Alice's Adventures in Wonderland* put a dark, disturbing slant on a much loved fantasy, and here he succeeds in adding a chilling new dimension to the legend of Faust. Largely set inside a timelessly magical theatre in modern-day Prague, the mind-bending action is littered with surreal images, satirical asides and serious messages. Petr Cepek gives a remarkable performance, never once betraying the fact that his co-stars are inanimates. This is beautiful, troubling and unmissable. DP

Petr Cepek *Faust* • Andrew Sachs ■ *Dir/Scr* Jan Svankmajer

Faust ★★★★15

Fantasy drama   2011 · Rus · Colour · 139min

Set in a timeless world in which God doesn't exist, but evil does, this reading of Goethe's play completes Russian auteur Aleksandr Sokurov's "tetralogy of power". Sokurov uses the fictional character of Faust to convey the avarice and lust that lies at the root of the global economic crisis. The triangle between Faust (Johannes Zeiler), Margarete (Isolda Dychauk) and the Mephistophelean moneylender (Anton Adasinskiy) is chillingly enacted, but this is really all about Sokurov's bleak vision of a doomed society. DP German +subtitles.

Johannes Zeiler *Heinrich Faust* • Anton Adasinskiy *Moneylender* • Isolda Dychauk *Margarete* • Georg Friedrich *Wagner* ■ *Dir* Aleksandr Sokurov • *Scr* Aleksandr Sokurov, Marina Koreneva, from a story by Yuri Arabov, from the play by Johann Wolfgang von Goethe

Faust: Love of the Damned ★18

Erotic horror   2001 · US/Sp · Colour · 96min

Brian Yuzna's shocker is an appallingly bad devil-in-disguise version of *The Crow*. Shattered after the murder of his girlfriend by a criminally demonic sect called The Hand, Mark Frost signs away his soul to the Devil in return for vengeance on her killers. But the satanic pact also means he's transformed into a sick superhero, armed with long metal claws, who must play a vital part in a black magic ritual. A crude dud. AJ *DVD*

Mark Frost *John Jaspers/Faust* • Isabel Brook *Dr Jade de Camp* • Andrew Divoff *M* • Jeffrey Combs *Lt Margolies* • Monica Van Campen *Claire* ■ *Dir* Brian Yuzna • *Scr* David Quinn, from the comic book *Faust* by Tim Vigil, David Quinn

Favela Rising ★★★12

Documentary   2005 · US · Colour · 78min

City of God graphically depicted the violence that pervades the slums of Rio de Janeiro, but there is a more positive side to life in the *favelas* (squatter settlements) as this uplifting documentary shows. Founded in the early 1990s, the AfroReggae Movement grew from a social and educational project to spawn a band that brings hope to the some of the city's poorest youths. The film shows how a sense of purpose and self-respect can keep kids away from drug and gun crime, but then the focus gradually shifts onto Anderson Sa, the reformed dealer who was inspired by his brother's murder to launch the group (with Jose Junior). As the tone leans increasingly towards hagiography, the movie rather loses sight of its wider sociological message. DP Portuguese +subtitles. Violence. **DVD**

■ *Dir* Matt Mochary, Jeff Zimbalist

The Favor ★★ 15
Romantic comedy 1994 · US · Colour · 93min

The main point of interest in this misguided romantic comedy is the appearance of Brad Pitt, before he established himself as one of Hollywood's leading pin-ups. The starring role goes to Harley Jane Kozak, who gets involved in all sorts of entanglements when she sets up best friend Elizabeth McGovern with old flame Ken Wahl. The supporting cast can't be faulted, but the script is short on gags and the direction clumsy. JF Swearing. **DVD**

Harley Jane Kozak *Kathy* • Elizabeth McGovern *Emily* • Bill Pullman *Peter* • Brad Pitt *Elliott* • Larry Miller *Joe Dubin* • Ken Wahl *Tom Andrews* • Ginger Orsi *Gina* • Leigh Ann Orsi *Hannah* ■ *Dir* Donald Petrie • *Scr* Sara Parriot, Josann McGibbon

Les Favoris de la Lune ★★★ 15
Comedy drama 1984 · Fr/It · Colour · 101min

Hurtling round Paris in pursuit of such artefacts as a priceless set of chinaware and a period nude, the various characters in Otar Iosseliani's frantic comedy don't have time to develop in the traditional sense. Nor does Iosseliani have the chance to dwell on his highly potent themes – the acquisitiveness of modern society and the consequent reduction of art to a lifestyle commodity. Yet the madcap interaction of the scheming gunsmith, the cuckolded locksmith and the burglar training his son remains hugely diverting in its own right. DP French +subtitles.

Alix de Montaigu *Delphine LaPlace* • Pascal Aubier *Monsieur LaPlace* • Gaspard Flori *Christian LaPlace* • Emilie Aubry *Lucie LaPlace* • Hans Peter Cloos *Monsieur Duphour-Paquet* • Maïté Nahyr *Madeleine Duphour-Paquet* • Julie Aubier *Sabine Duphour-Paquet* • Baptiste Blanchet *Marc Duphour-Paquet* • Katja Rupé *Clair* ■ *Dir* Otar Iosseliani • *Scr* Gérard Brach

The Favour, the Watch and the Very Big Fish ★★ 15
Comedy 1991 · Fr/UK · Colour · 84min

In this would-be surreal comedy, Bob Hoskins plays a photographer of religious tableaux involved with Natasha Richardson, who does orgiastic voiceovers for porn movies. When her ex-boyfriend Jeff Goldblum is released from jail, he agrees to pose for Hoskins as Christ, but the problems start when he tries to work miracles. Director Ben Lewin has a leaden approach to this Loony Toon-style farce. TH

Bob Hoskins *Louis Aubinard* • Jeff Goldblum *Pianist* • Natasha Richardson *Sybil* • Michel Blanc *Norbert* • Jacques Villeret *Charles* • Angela Pleasence *Elizabeth* • Jean-Pierre Cassel *Zalman* ■ *Dir* Ben Lewin • *Scr* Ben Lewin, from the short story *Rue Saint-Sulpice* by Marcel Aymé

Fazil ★★
Silent romantic drama 1928 · US · BW · 88min

Rudolph Valentino in *Son of the Sheik* inspired a flurry of exotic imitations, including this dated melodrama from the Fox studio, directed by Howard Hawks - his sixth silent movie. It features Charles Farrell as a petulant Arab prince who meets a pretty Parisienne, played by Norwegian actress Greta Nissen, and whisks her off to marriage and Mecca. However her liberated European ways clash with Arab tradition and his visits to his harem. Apparently this was quite sexy for its time, but is now only of interest as an early piece from a great American director. AT

Charles Farrell (1) *Prince Fazil* • Greta Nissen *Fabienne* • Mae Busch *Helene Debreuze* • Vadim Uraneff *Ahmed* • Tyler Brooke *Jacques Debreuze* • Eddie Sturgis *Rice* • Josephine Borio *Aicha* • John Boles *John Clavering* • John T Murray *Gondolier* ■ *Dir* Howard Hawks • *Scr* Seton I Miller, Philip Klein (adaptation), from the play *L'Insoumise* by Pierre Frondaie

Fear ★★★
Drama 1954 · It/W Ger · BW · 91min

A German industrialist's wife, who had an affair while her husband was in a PoW camp during the Second World War, finds herself blackmailed by her former lover's mistress. Ingrid Bergman stars in this German-Italian co-production, which marks the last of the six films she made with her writer/director husband, Roberto Rossellini, during her exile from Hollywood. A combination of psychological thriller and marital drama, the film is a rather lumbering affair but, thanks to the presence of the star, and the style of the director, it holds one's interest. RK German +subtitles.

Ingrid Bergman *Irene Wagner* • Mathias Wieman *Professor Albert Wagner* • Renate Mannhardt *Joanna Schultze* • Kurt Kreuger *Heinz Baumann* • Elise Aulinger *Martha* ■ *Dir* Roberto Rossellini • *Scr* Roberto Rossellini, Sergio Amidei, Franz Graf Treuberg, from the novel *Der Angst* by Stefan Zweig

Fear ★★ 18
Action adventure 1988 · US · Colour · 91min

Yet another therapy session for America on the Vietnam couch, it's just a shame the rest of us have to suffer. The movie runs a tiresomely predictable course as a family are held hostage in their isolated cabin by a gang of escaped cons, one of whom is played by Frank Stallone, brother of the more famous Sly. Fellow con Robert Factor turns out to be a psycho, but luckily dad (Cliff De Young) shares his Vietnam background and fights back thanks to various ingenious booby traps. Debut director Robert A Ferretti does his best with a restrictive budget but this is a lost cause. RS

Cliff De Young *Don Haden* • Kay Lenz *Sharon Haden* • Robert Factor *Jack Gracie* • Scott Schwartz *Brian Haden* • Geri Betzler *Jennifer Haden* • Frank Stallone *Robert Armitage* ■ *Dir* Robert A Ferretti • *Scr* Rick Scarry, Kathryn Connell, from a story by Robert A Ferretti

Fear ★★★ 18
Psychological thriller 1996 · US · Colour · 92min

Would you trust Mark Wahlberg with your 16-year-old daughter? Of course you wouldn't! But when the Walker family first meet her latest date, they think he's a saint with a great body. Alas, he soon turns into the "Boyfriend from Hell" in director James Foley's tautly constructed, albeit predictable thriller. The plot may be contrived, yet Foley adds a few more complexities than usual, while an excellent cast brings credibility to the relationships in crisis. AJ **DVD**

Mark Wahlberg *David McCall* • Reese Witherspoon *Nicole Walker* • William L Petersen *Steve Walker* • Amy Brenneman *Laura Walker* • Alyssa Milano *Margo Masse* ■ *Dir* James Foley • *Scr* Christopher Crowe

Fear and Desire ★ 12
War drama 1953 · US · BW · 61min

Stanley Kubrick believed his first feature - about a platoon of soldiers in an unspecified war fighting behind enemy lines - was "a serious effort, ineptly done", so he tried to suppress it. He was right to do so; for, despite some striking imagery, what wrecks the movie - made with money borrowed from relatives - are the uniformly terrible performances and the atrocious dialogue. AT Some violence. **DVD**

Frank Silvera *Mac* • Kenneth Harp *Lt Corby* • Virginia Leith *The Girl* • Paul Mazursky *Sidney* • Steve Coit *Fletcher* ■ *Dir* Stanley Kubrick • *Scr* Howard O Sackler, Stanley Kubrick

Fear and Loathing in Las Vegas ★★★ 18
Road movie 1998 · US · Colour · 113min

This was always going to be a challenging experiment, even for maverick director Terry Gilliam (who replaced Alex Cox in pre-production). Hunter S Thompson's distinctive prose survives nearly intact and, although Johnny Depp brings an amusingly twitchy energy to the role of gonzo journalist Raoul Duke, this brave film falls short of capturing the book's vibrancy. The pace is a bit too fast to allow the audience to clamber on board, so one can only watch in bemused admiration as it zooms past. DP Violence, swearing, drug abuse, brief nudity. **DVD**

Johnny Depp *Raoul Duke* • Benicio Del Toro *Dr Gonzo* • Tobey Maguire *Hitchhiker* • Ellen Barkin *North Star waitress* • Gary Busey *Highway patrolman* • Christina Ricci *Lucy* • Mark Harmon *Magazine reporter* • Cameron Diaz *Blonde TV reporter* • Lyle Lovett *Road person* ■ *Dir* Terry Gilliam • *Scr* Terry Gilliam, Tony Grisoni, Tod Davies, Alex Cox, from the novel by Hunter S Thompson

Fear and Trembling ★★★★ 12
Comedy 2003 · Fr · Colour · 102min

This is a stingingly satirical insight into Japanese corporate culture. Despite being born in Tokyo and still fluent in the language, Sylvie Testud's eager Belgian intern falls foul of her employers because of her inability to appreciate the rigidity of their hierarchical structure. Working predominantly in Japanese, Alain Corneau directs with a sly surety that reinforces the comic potential of the various cultural chasms without indulging in racial stereotyping. DP Japanese, French +subtitles. Violence, sexual references. **DVD**

Sylvie Testud *Amélie* • Kaori Tsuji *Miss Fubuki Mori* • Taro Suwa *Monsieur Saito* • Bison Katayama *Monsieur Omochi* • Yasunari Kondo *Monsieur Tenshi* • Sokyu Fujita *Monsieur Haneda* • Gen Shimaoka *Monsieur Unagi* ■ *Dir* Alain Corneau • *Scr* Alain Corneau, from the novel *Stupeur et Tremblements* by Amélie Nothomb

Fear, Anxiety, and Depression ★★
Comedy 1989 · US · Colour · 85min

Those familiar with Todd Solondz's *Welcome to the Dollhouse* and *Happiness* won't be entirely surprised by the tone of this earlier effort. The themes explored so successfully in the later films are all bubbling away under the surface of this loser romance. Solondz plays the Woody Allen-esque hero on the unblinking lookout for love but finding only ugliness and disappointment in his choice of partner. This film suffers from an overdose of wackiness and is too forced to be entirely believable. AJ

Todd Solondz *Ira Ellis* • Max Cantor *Jack* • Alexandra Gersten *Janice* • Jane Hamper *Junk* • Stanley Tucci *Donny* ■ *Dir/Scr* Todd Solondz

Fear City ★★★ 18
Crime drama 1984 · US · Colour · 94min

Melanie Griffith makes an early appearance in this vivid, exploitatitive shocker from director Abel Ferrara. The future star of *Working Girl* plays a stripper in mid-town Manhattan, helping out talent agent Tom Berenger just as a homicidal maniac is going about slaughtering professional striptease artists. Scenes of both straight and gay sex, not to mention the multiple murders, have a raw and visceral impact. TH **DVD**

Tom Berenger *Matt Rossi* • Billy Dee Williams *Al Wheeler* • Jack Scalia *Nicky Piacenza* • Melanie Griffith *Loretta* • Rossano Brazzi *Carmine* • Rae Dawn Chong *Leila* • Joe Santos *Frank* • Michael V Gazzo *Mike* ■ *Dir* Abel Ferrara • *Scr* Nicholas St John

Fear Eats the Soul ★★★★ 15
Romantic drama 1973 · W Ger · Colour · 89min

Rainer Werner Fassbinder's affecting film uses an unconventional love story to attack the prejudices inherent in German society in the early 1970s. As the widowed cleaner and the Moroccan mechanic whose cross-cultural age-gap romance is frowned upon by their family and friends, Brigitte Mira and El Hedi Ben Salem are so convincing it's easy to forget they are merely playing roles. Fassbinder also impresses as Mira's loathsome son-in-law, but it's the deceptive simplicity of his direction that elevates this incisive drama above the more popular period pieces of his later career. DP German +subtitles. **DVD**

Brigitte Mira *Emmi* • El Hedi Ben Salem *Ali* • Barbara Valentin *Barbara* • Irm Hermann *Krista* • Peter Gauhe *Bruno* • Karl Scheydt *Albert* • Rainer Werner Fassbinder *Eugen* ■ *Dir/Scr* Rainer Werner Fassbinder

Fear in the Night ★★★★ 12
Film noir 1947 · US · BW · 70min

A highly original thriller with a literally nightmarish quality, this B-movie is based on a book by *noir* specialist Cornell Woolrich (*Rear Window*), and the requisite *noir* elements of paranoia and uncertainty are evident in this tale of a man whose horrific dream seems to have truly taken place. The film's grip is maintained from the haunting opening, set in a room composed entirely of mirrored doors, and Jack Greenhalgh's stylised photography enhances the moody narrative. Director Maxwell Shane made the same story again, as *Nightmare*, in 1956. TV **DVD**

Paul Kelly (1) *Cliff Herlihy* • DeForest Kelley *Vince Grayson* • Ann Doran *Lil Herlihy* • Kay Scott *Betty Winters* • Robert Emmett Keane *Lewis* • Jeff York *Torrence* • Charles Victor *Capt Warner* ■ *Dir* Maxwell Shane • *Scr* Maxwell Shane, from the short story *Nightmare* by William Irish [Cornell Woolrich]

Fear in the Night ★★★ 12
Psychological horror 1972 · UK · Colour · 89min

This school chiller gets off to a cracking start with an eerie title sequence that concludes with a genuine shock. Peter Cushing, complete with an artificial arm and a genius for appearing when least expected, is on creepy form as a demented headmaster who plays sound effects records to re-create the atmosphere of his fire-damaged school. Judy Geeson is admirably ill at ease, while Ralph Bates and Joan Collins whip up some truly malevolent passion. More fun than frightening. DP Violence, swearing. **DVD**

Peter Cushing *Michael Carmichael* • Joan Collins *Molly Carmichael* • Ralph Bates *Robert Heller* • Judy Geeson *Peggy Heller* • James Cossins *Doctor* ■ *Dir* Jimmy Sangster • *Scr* Jimmy Sangster, Michael Syson

Fear Is the Key ★★★ 15
Action thriller 1972 · UK · Colour · 100min

This satisfying action thriller, based on an Alistair MacLean novel, has Barry Newman pursuing stolen jewels as well as vengeance for his wife and child who died aboard a hijacked plane. An excitingly staged car chase gets things off to a cracking start and Newman makes a convincingly hyped-up hero. It also marks the screen debut of Ben Kingsley. AT

Barry Newman *John Talbot* • Suzy Kendall *Sarah Ruthven* • John Vernon *Vyland* • Dolph Sweet *Jablonski* • Ben Kingsley *Royale* • Ray McAnally *Ruthven* • Peter Marinker *Larry* ■ *Dir* Michael Tuchner • *Scr* Robert Carrington, from the novel by Alistair MacLean

Fear No Evil ★★ 18
Supernatural horror 1980 · US · Colour · 94min

In director Frank LaLoggia's ambitious feature debut, Lucifer is reincarnated as an American high school student who does battle with two archangels in disguise. The acting is on the amateurish side, and the story loses its way in some aimless subplots. Yet this is still a strangely affecting vision of low-budget armageddon whose punk rock soundtrack is augmented by an elaborate symphonic score. AJ

Stefan Arngrim *Andrew* • Elizabeth Hoffman *Mikhail/Margaret Buchanan* • Frank Birney *Father Daly* • Kathleen Rowe McAllen *Gabrielle/Hulie* • Daniel Eden *Tony* • Jack Holland *Rafael/Father Damon* • Barry Cooper *Mr Williams* ■ *Dir/Scr* Frank LaLoggia

Fear of a Black Hat ★★★ 15

Spoof music documentary
1992 · US · Colour · 81min

Sampling freely from Rob Reiner's cult heavy metal comedy, this music-biz spoof could have been retitled "This Is Spinal Rap". Although it treads warily in places, the script spares countless direct hits as it follows the career of the rapping trio NWH (Niggaz with Hats). The blurred line between commercial success and social protest, the ludicrous press conference generalisations and the intrigues among the entourage are all keenly observed. Even the band members' names are spot-on – Tone-Def, Tasty Taste and Ice Cold. But the music can't hold a candle to the cod anthems of the mighty *Tap*. DP Sex scenes, swearing, nudity.

Rusty Cundieff *Ice Cold* • Kasi Lemmons *Nina Blackburn* • Mark Christopher Lawrence *Tone Def* • Larry B Scott *Tasty Taste* • Howie Gold *Guy Friesh* • G Smokey Campbell *First backstage manager* ■ *Dir/Scr* Rusty Cundieff

Fear of Fear ★★★★

Psychological drama
1976 · W Ger · Colour · 88min

Comfortable conformity is cited as the first sign of madness in this little-known film from Rainer Werner Fassbinder, originally made for television. Shot with a measured intensity, Margit Carstensen's slow decline into misery is charted with the apprehensive potency of a thriller. Will she commit suicide like her dishevelled neighbour? Or will she reconcile herself to her bourgeois ordinariness and resume her life without recourse to adulterous affairs or chemical solace? Challenging and irresistible. DP

Margit Carstensen *Margot* • Ulrich Faulhaber *Kurt* • Brigitte Mira *Mother* • Irm Hermann *Lore* • Armin Meier *Karli* • Adrian Hoven *Dr Merck* • Kurt Raab *Herr Bauer* • Ingrid Caven *Edda* • Lilo Pempeit *Mrs Schall* ■ *Dir* Rainer Werner Fassbinder • *Scr* Rainer Werner Fassbinder, from an idea by Asta Scheib • *Cinematographers* Jürgen Jüges, Ulrich Prinz

The Fear of 13 ★★★★ 15

Documentary   2015 · UK · Colour · 95min

Nicholas Yarris, a prisoner on death row in the US, who asked that his appeals process be terminated and his execution carried out, tells his own story in this fascinating, compelling and moving documentary portrait. With his sculpted cheekbones and thoughtful demeanour, he holds court with all the screen presence of a great actor, as British documentarist David Sington's cannily structured film unfolds a personal history where tragic circumstances, bitter injustice and unyielding determination all have their part to play. TJ Swearing.

Nick Yarris ■ *Dir* David Sington • *Cinematographer* Clive North

Fear on Trial ★★★★

Biographical drama   1975 · US · Colour · 100min

This outstanding TV movie tells the tragic true story of television personality John Henry Faulk, who fell victim to the McCarthyite blacklist in the 1950s and, with his career ruined, decided to sue for libel. William Devane gives a moving performance as Faulk and George C Scott is magnificent as his lawyer Louis Nizer. This riveting saga is expertly told by director Lamont Johnson. TV producers David Susskind and Mark Goodson play themselves, and Bruce Geller, the creator of TV series *Mission: Impossible*, plays his real-life father, the presiding judge in the case. TS

George C Scott *Louis Nizer* • William Devane *John Henry Faulk* • Dorothy Tristan *Laura Faulk* • William Redfield *Stan Hopp* • Bruce Geller *Judge Abraham N Geller* • David Susskind • Mark Goodson ■ *Dir* Lamont Johnson • *Scr* David W Rintels, from an autobiography by John Henry Faulk

Fear Strikes Out ★★★★

Biographical sports drama
1957 · US · BW · 102min

Director Robert Mulligan's feature film debut is a harrowing and intense biopic of Boston Red Sox baseball star Jim Piersall, superbly portrayed by Anthony Perkins, whose later mannerisms are held well in check as he movingly conveys Piersall's breakdown. Karl Malden has a tendency to over-emote but under Mulligan's direction, he gives a fine performance as the over-ambitious father, whose behaviour had such a devastating impact on his son. This is a touching and tragic tale, beautifully photographed in stunning black-and-white VistaVision by Haskell Boggs, and featuring a fine early score from Elmer Bernstein. TS

Anthony Perkins *Jimmy Piersall* • Karl Malden *John Piersall* • Norma Moore *Mary Teevan* • Adam Williams *Dr Brown* • Perry Wilson *Mrs John Piersall* • Peter Votrian *Jimmy Piersall as a boy* • Dennis McMullen *Phil* ■ *Dir* Robert Mulligan • *Scr* Ted Berkman, Raphael Blau, from the autobiography by James A Piersall, Albert S Hirshberg

Fear X ★★★ 12

Psychological thriller
2002 · Den/UK/Can/Nor · Colour · 87min

The American author of *Last Exit to Brooklyn* and *Requiem for a Dream* teams up with the Danish director of *Pusher* and *Bleeder* on this elusive search for truth. Intense yet measured, what makes this fascinating is the steely performance of John Turturro. He plays a Wisconsin security guard who's obsessed with discovering the reason for his wife's murder in the car park of the mall where he works. Guilty cop James Remar's torment is conveyed with equally brooding introspection, but this tense psychological thriller falls apart in the final act. DP Violence. **DVD**

John Turturro *Harry Cain* • Deborah Kara Unger *Kate* • Stephen McIntyre *Phil* • William Allen Young *Agent Lawrence* • Eugene M Davis *[Gene Davis] Ed* • Mark Houghton *Diner cop* • Jacqueline Ramel *Claire* • James Remar *Peter* ■ *Dir* Nicolas Winding Refn • *Scr* Nicolas Winding Refn, Hubert Selby Jr

FearDotCom ★ 18

Horror thriller
2002 · US/UK/Ger/Lux · Colour · 97min

Detective Stephen Dorff and public health inspector Natascha McElhone investigate a snuff torture website that brings death to all who log on in this nonsensical chiller. Director William Malone's *Ring* rip-off has a monochromatic murkiness stolen from *Se7en*. The real torture comes from having to sit through such ugly trash. AJ Violence, swearing, nudity. **DVD**

Stephen Dorff *Det Mike Reilly* • Natascha McElhone *Terry Huston* • Stephen Rea *Alistair Pratt, "The Doctor"* • Udo Kier *Polidori* • Amelia Curtis *Denise Stone* • Jeffrey Combs *Styles* • Nigel Terry *Turnbull* ■ *Dir* William Malone • *Scr* Josephine Coyle, from a story by Moshe Diamant

Fearless ★★★ 15

Drama   1993 · US · Colour · 116min

Containing sequences of astonishing power, this intense drama about the pain of loss and the stress of surviving a near-death experience struggles to live up to its breathtaking opening. Director Peter Weir has spent his career studying people trapped in unfamiliar environments, but here plane-crash survivor Jeff Bridges is a stranger to his own self. Yet Bridges and Rosie Perez give heart-rending performances as plane-crash survivors and the film remains a painful reminder of just how fragile life really is. DP Violence, swearing.

Jeff Bridges *Max Klein* • Isabella Rossellini *Laura Klein* • Rosie Perez *Carla Rodrigo* • Tom Hulce *Brillstein* • John Turturro *Dr Bill Perlman* • Benicio Del Toro *Manny Rodrigo* • Deirdre O'Connell *Nan Gordon* • John de Lancie *Jeff Gordon* ■ *Dir* Peter Weir • *Scr* Rafael Yglesias, from his novel

Fearless ★★★ 15

Biographical martial arts drama
2006 · HK/Chi · Colour · 99min

Jet Li stars in the true-life tale of a legendary Chinese martial arts master who dishonours himself by inadvertently killing the right enemy for the wrong reason. When members of his family are slaughtered in retribution, Li goes into self-imposed exile. The plot, true or not, may reek of rehashed Jean-Claude Van Damme, but Ronny Yu directs with considerable visual style and the fight scenes are long and physical. No wonder, then, that an aging Li has declared this to be his last martial arts movie, making it a must-see for both Li and fight-film fans. DA Cantonese, Mandarin, English, Japanese +subtitles.
DVD Blu

Jet Li *Huo Yuanjia* • Shidou Nakamura *Anno Tanaka* • Dong Yong *Nong Jinsun* • Betty Sun *Yueci* • Nathan Jones *[Nathan B Jones] Hercules O'Brien* • Collin Chou *Huo Yuanjia's father* • Bao Qijing *Granny Sun* • Masato Harada *Mr Mita* ■ *Dir* Ronny Yu • *Scr* Wang Bin, Chris Chow, Christine To, Li Feng

The Fearless Vampire Killers ★★★★ 12

Horror comedy   1967 · US · Colour · 103min

Want to know where *Interview with the Vampire* found most of its best ideas? Look no further than this lyrical exploration of undead myths that's poised on the knife edge of Hammer nightmare and *Carry On* farce. Eerie, funny, scary and brilliantly baroque, Roman Polanski's astoundingly beautiful tour de force features two genre firsts – a Jewish vampire unaffected by the crucifix and a gay vampire – plus his ill-fated wife-to-be Sharon Tate in her best role. It's worth seeing for the breathtaking ballroom mirror sequence alone. AJ Some violence.
DVD

Jack MacGowran *Professor Abronsius* • Roman Polanski *Alfred* • Alfie Bass *Shagal* • Jessie Robins *Mrs Shagal* • Sharon Tate *Sarah Shagal* • Ferdy Mayne *Count Von Krolock* • Iain Quarrier *Herbert Von Krolock* • Terry Downes *Koukol* ■ *Dir* Roman Polanski • *Scr* Gérald Brach, Roman Polanski

The Fearmakers ★

Political drama   1958 · US · BW · 84min

This preposterous right-wing melodrama has Dana Andrews returning to his Washington-based public relations firm only to find that his partner has mysteriously disappeared. The agency has been taken over by communists, whose agenda includes rigging opinion polls and promoting an end to the Cold War. A demeaning assignment for talented director Jacques Tourneur. AE

Dana Andrews *Alan Eaton* • Dick Foran *Jim McGinnis* • Mel Tormé *Barney Bond* • Marilee Earle *Lorraine Dennis* • Veda Ann Borg *Vivian Loder* • Kelly Thordsen *Harold Loder* ■ *Dir* Jacques Tourneur • *Scr* Elliot West, Chris Appley, from a novel by Darwin L Teilhet

Fear(s) of the Dark ★★★ 12

Animation   2007 · Fr/Bel · BW · 79min

Though films as diverse as *Shrek*, *Spirited Away* and *Toy Story* reinvented the popular concept of a cartoon feature at the turn of the millennium, adult animation hasn't been so quick to gain ground. Aimed at a squarely art house audience, this six-films-for-the-price-of-one compendium is a hit-and-miss study of terror whose better moments more than carry the bad. Best of the selection is Charles Burns's wonderfully dark sci-fi horror story about a college boy whose girlfriend becomes a predatory insect. And for sheer artistic innovation, Richard McGuire's closing section cannot be beaten. DW French +subtitles. **DVD**

Aure Atika *Laura* • Guillaume Depardieu *Eric* • Nicole Garcia *The woman* • Louisa Pili *Sumako* • Arthur H *The narrator* ■ *Dir* Marie Caillou, Blutch, Pierre Di Sciullo, Lorenzo Mattotti, Richard McGuire, Charles Burns • *Scr* Jerry Kramsky, Blutch, Charles Burns, Pierre Di Sciullo, Michel Pirus, Romain Slocombe, Richard McGuire

A Feast at Midnight ★★ PG

Comedy   1994 · UK · Colour · 102min

Stereotypes abound in this familiar rites-of-passage fantasy on the cruelty and camaraderie of public school life. Freddie Findlay attempts to win over the bullies by starting the secret "Scoffers Society"; its aim is to sample culinary delights denied them by the strict health food regime imposed by headmaster Robert Hardy. DP

Christopher Lee *Longfellow (Raptor)* • Robert Hardy *Headmaster* • Freddie Findlay *Magnus* • Aled Roberts *Goof* • Andrew Lusher *Tava* • Sam West *[Samuel West] Chef* • Lisa Faulkner *Miss Charlotte* • Edward Fox *Magnus's father* ■ *Dir* Justin Hardy • *Scr* Justin Hardy, Yoshi Nishio

Feast of July ★★ 15

Romantic period drama
1995 · UK · Colour · 111min

The title promises a feast, but this melancholy story set in late 19th-century England offers slim pickings. Embeth Davidtz plays a young woman deserted by her lover (Greg Wise) who is taken in by a rural family, headed by Tom Bell. She befriends his three sons and, when two of them go to war, falls for the youngest, simple-minded Ben Chaplin. Christopher Menaul directs this with an emphasis on melodramatic flourishes. TH **DVD**

Embeth Davidtz *Bella Ford* • Tom Bell *Ben Wainwright* • Gemma Jones *Mrs Wainwright* • James Purefoy *Jedd Wainwright* • Ben Chaplin *Con* • Kenneth Anderson *Matty Wainwright* • Greg Wise *Arch Wilson* ■ *Dir* Christopher Menaul • *Scr* Christopher Neame, from the novel by HE Bates • *Executive Producer* Ismail Merchant

Feast of Love ★★ 15

Romantic drama   2007 · US · Colour · 97min

American novelist Charles Baxter has a reputation for writing grown-up stories about love and loss. In this, the first film based on his work, a cast led by Morgan Freeman brings gravitas to the intertwined lives of several Portland residents. Greg Kinnear plays coffee-shop owner Bradley, who is dumped by his wife (Selma Blair) for another woman, and then jumps into marriage with Diana (Radha Mitchell), an icy estate agent. Meanwhile, ex-junkie Oscar (Toby Hemingway) and his girlfriend (Alexa Davalos) are being terrorised by his bullying dad (Fred Ward). All tell their stories to Harry (Freeman), a professor with a good listening ear and his own private grief. This is a solid, somewhat middlebrow drama, but it's not helped by director Robert Benton's overly reverent approach. JR **DVD**

Morgan Freeman *Harry Stevenson* • Greg Kinnear *Bradley Smith* • Radha Mitchell *Diana* • Billy Burke *David Watson* • Selma Blair *Kathryn* • Alexa Davalos *Chloe* • Toby Hemingway *Oscar* • Jane Alexander *Esther Stevenson* • Fred Ward *Bat* ■ *Dir* Robert Benton • *Scr* Allison Burnett, from the novel *The Feast of Love* by Charles Baxter

Federal Hill ★★★

Crime drama   1994 · US · BW · 100min

Boyz 'n the Hood Italian-style, as a gang of Rhode Island punks struggle to make sense of their lives as they hurtle down a drug-fuelled, self-destructive path. Nicholas Turturro (John's younger brother) stars as a jewel thief who specialises in random violence with his gang. Independent film-maker Michael Corrente's cutting edge black-and-white effort infuses the *Mean Streets* genre with a new raw, raucous and insightful energy helped enormously by a powerhouse performance from Turturro as a screwed-up psycho thief. AJ

Nicholas Turturro *Ralph* • Anthony DeSando *Nicky* • Libby Langdon *Wendy* • Michael Raynor *Frank* • Jason Andrews *Bobby* • Robert Turano *Joey* ■ *Dir/Scr* Michael Corrente

Federal Protection ★★ 18
Action thriller 2002 · US · Colour · 89min

This darkly comedic crime thriller demonstrates that Anthony Hickox has a knack for set pieces that he's not quite capable of carrying over into his general storytelling. Car thief Armand Assante's experiences under the witness protection programme are formulaic, as his relationship with new neighbour Angela Featherstone prompts her cheating husband and disloyal sister (David Lipper and Dina Meyer) to sell him out to the Mob for the bounty. DP DVD

Armand Assante *Frank Carbone/Howard Akers* · Angela Featherstone *Leigh Kirkindall* · Dina Meyer *Bootsie Cavander* · David Lipper *Denny Kirkindall* ■ *Dir* Anthony Hickox · *Scr* Craig Smith

Fedora ★★★★ PG
Drama 1978 · W Ger/Fr · Colour · 108min

This is director Billy Wilder's bittersweet tale about a fabled, Garbo-esque star of the 1930s who appears to have the secret of youth and lives in seclusion in Corfu. William Holden is the producer who worms his way into Marthe Keller's secret and tries to coax her out of retirement. Yes, there are flaws and some unintentional laughs – Michael York as a living screen legend? – but this is also a richly comic, deeply melancholy movie, enriched by Wilder's long perspective on the picture business. AT
DVD Blu

William Holden (2) *Barry Detweiler* · Marthe Keller *Fedora* · José Ferrer *Dr Vando* · Hildegarde Neff *Countess Sobryanski* · Frances Sternhagen *Miss Balfour* · Michael York · Henry Fonda ■ *Dir* Billy Wilder · *Scr* Billy Wilder, IAL Diamond, from the novel *Crowned Heads* by Thomas Tryon

Feds ★★ 15
Comedy 1988 · US · Colour · 79min

Before her searching, scorching performance in *The Hand That Rocks the Cradle*, Rebecca De Mornay made an unimpressive living playing anaemic, pretty blondes. As one of two female students who are aspiring FBI agents, she encounters male prejudice on a grand scale. All comic efforts in this direction seem to delight in the obvious, yet De Mornay herself has the right, light touch. JM Violence, swearing.

Rebecca De Mornay *Ellie DeWitt* · Mary Gross *Janis Zuckerman* · Ken Marshall *Brent Sheppard* · Fred Dalton Thompson *Bill Belecki* · Larry Cedar *Howard Butz* · James Luisi *Sperry* · Raymond Singer *Hupperman* ■ *Dir* Dan Goldberg · *Scr* Len Blum, Dan Goldberg

Feed ★★★ 18
Crime thriller 2005 · Aus · Colour · 96min

This gleefully twisted shocker from Down Under (though set mainly in the US) gives new meaning to the phrase "stomach-churning horror". Patrick Thompson plays a cyber-porn investigator obsessed with tracking down a pervert (Alex O'Loughlin) who he believes is literally fattening up obese women for the kill. This is pretty gross stuff and the bingeing segments – which feature a particularly brave performance from Gabby Millgate (*Muriel's Wedding*) – will leave even the most seasoned horror buff feeling slightly queasy. JF Violence, sex scenes. DVD

Alex O'Loughlin *Michael Turner/Feeder X* · Patrick Thompson *Phillip Jackson* · Gabby Millgate *Deirdre* · Jack Thompson *Richard* · Matthew Le Nevez *Nigel* · Rose Ashton *Abbey* · Sherly Sulaiman *Mary* · Marika Aubrey *Grace* · David Field *Father Turner* ■ *Dir* Brett Leonard · *Scr* Kieran Galvin, from an idea by Alex O'Loughlin, Patrick Thompson

Feeling Minnesota ★★ 18
Romantic comedy drama 1996 · US · Colour · 94min

In this quirky, low-budget film, Cameron Diaz plays the bride who ditches her husband-to-be (Vincent D'Onofrio) on her wedding day to run off with his estranged, wayward brother (Keanu Reeves), only to have her fiancé and an assortment of heavies come after them. Amusingly odd rather than hilariously funny – and with a liberal splattering of violence and bad language – this has its moments, but is perhaps of most appeal to fans of the two leads. JB Sex scenes. DVD

Keanu Reeves *Jjaks* · Vincent D'Onofrio *Sam* · Cameron Diaz *Freddie* · Delroy Lindo *Red* · Courtney Love *Rhonda, the waitress* · Tuesday Weld *Nora* · Dan Aykroyd *Ben* · Levon Helm *Bible salesman* ■ *Dir/Scr* Steven Baigelman

Feet First ★★ U
Comedy 1930 · US · BW · 69min

Harold Lloyd raids his own gag store to refloat this feeble comedy after it runs aground during an overlong sea voyage. Stowing away on a Honolulu liner to press his romantic suit with Barbara Kent, Lloyd's timid go-getter gets himself trapped in a mail sack, which just happens to land on a builder's hoist outside a skyscraper. The business with the gyrating fire hose is both inspired and hilarious. However, it comes too late to save a picture hamstrung by Lloyd's discomfort with dialogue. DP

Harold Lloyd *Harold Horne* · Robert McWade *John Tanner* · Lillianne Leighton *Mrs Tanner* · Barbara Kent *Mary* · Alec Francis [Alec B Francis] *Old timer* ■ *Dir* Clyde Bruckman · *Scr* Felix Adler, Lex Neal, Paul Gerard Smith, from a story by John Grey, Alfred A Cohn, Clyde Bruckman

Felicia's Journey ★★★★ 12
Psychological thriller 1999 · UK/Can · Colour · 111min

Pregnant Irish innocent Felicia (Elaine Cassidy) travels to Birmingham to find her lover, who has joined the British Army. There she is befriended by Hilditch (Bob Hoskins), a factory catering manager with a sinister interest in young girls. All the tabloid elements of a lurid thriller are here, but Canadian director Atom Egoyan avoids the obvious in his adaptation of William Trevor's novel. The result is a small masterpiece of atmosphere and insight that reveals the extraordinary in the everyday, with performances that transform the story into a scary fairy tale. TH DVD

Bob Hoskins *Hilditch* · Elaine Cassidy *Felicia* · Claire Benedict *Miss Calligary* · Brid Brennan *Mrs Lysaght* · Peter McDonald *Johnny* · Gerard McSorley *Felicia's father* · Arsinée Khanjian *Gala* ■ *Dir* Atom Egoyan · *Scr* Atom Egoyan, from the novel by William Trevor

Felix the Cat: the Movie ★ U
Animated fantasy 1989 · US · Colour · 78min

Felix the Cat made his debut as an animated short as far back as 1919, but this attempt to update the feline hero for a new generation is a monumental clanger and an insult to kids with even the merest of imaginations. Surrealism abounds as Felix goes on a quest to rescue a princess, encountering Mizards (mice with bodies of lizards) and a rhinoceros on a tightrope. Bland and uninspired. RS

Chris Phillips · Maureen O'Connell · Peter Neuman · Alice Playten · Susan Montanaro · Don Oriolo ■ *Dir* Tibor Hernadi · *Scr* Don Oriolo, Pete Brown, from a story and cartoon character created by Don Oriolo

Fellini's Roma ★★★ 15
Experimental comedy documentary 1972 · It/Fr · Colour · 116min

This mix of memories, fantasies and idle musings confirms Federico Fellini's visual genius, while also exposing his reckless lack of intellectual rigour. Beginning with youthful impressions of the Eternal City gained from his home town of Rimini, Fellini recalls people and place as the fancy takes him (hence the film's much-criticised shapelessness). Whether reminiscing or chatting to the likes of Marcello Mastroianni, Anna Magnani and Gore Vidal, he makes a companionable, if occasionally overbearing guide. DP Italian +subtitles.
DVD Blu

Federico Fellini · Peter Gonzales *Fellini, age 18* · Stefano Mayore *Fellini as a child* · Pia De Doses *Princess* · Renato Giovannelli *Cardinal Ottaviani* · Fiona Florence *Young prostitute* · Anna Magnani · Gore Vidal · Marcello Mastroianni ■ *Dir* Federico Fellini · *Scr* Federico Fellini, Bernardino Zapponi

Fellow Traveller ★★★★ 15
Political drama 1989 · UK/US · Colour · 97min

The title refers to someone with Communist sympathies, and this film deals with that terrible time in Hollywood when the blacklist was in force, a serious subject only rarely tackled by Hollywood itself. It's a genuinely political tale, directed (by the underrated Philip Saville) in anger, and played to perfection by the cast. The look and feel of the 1950s, and in particular the early birth pangs of commercial television in England are beautifully conjured up, and you'll never view Richard Greene's *The Adventures of Robin Hood* TV series in quite the same way again. TS

Ron Silver *Asa Kaufman* · Imogen Stubbs *Sarah Aitchison* · Daniel J Travanti *Jerry Leavy* · Hart Bochner *Clifford Byrne* · Katherine Borowitz *Joan Kaufman* · Julian Fellowes *D'Arcy* · Richard Wilson (3) *Sir Hugo Armstrong* ■ *Dir* Philip Saville · *Scr* Michael Eaton

Felon ★★★ 15
Prison drama 2008 · US · Colour · 99min

Men are reduced to animals in this brutal, exploitative prison drama. After killing a burglar, blue-collar family man Wade Porter (Stephen Dorff) is sent to a notoriously tough jail where he is mentored by a nihilistic, Shakespeare-spouting lifer (Val Kilmer, unrecognisably shaggy and tattooed). Writer/director Ric Roman Waugh shoots the incessant violence like gladiatorial cage fighting, salivating over each burst nose and fractured skull. It's nasty yet not without purpose, as it charts the desperation of an honest man forced into surviving by any means. JR Violence, swearing, nudity. DVD Blu

Stephen Dorff *Wade Porter* · Val Kilmer *John Smith* · Harold Perrineau *Lt Jackson* · Marisol Nichols *Laura* · Anne Archer *Maggie* · Sam Shepard *Gordon* ■ *Dir/Scr* Ric Roman Waugh

Felony ★★★ 15
Thriller 2013 · Aus/US · Colour · 101min

The cops may be heroes but they have feet of clay in this tense, flavoursome and complex Australian thriller written by and starring Joel Edgerton. After celebrating a lucky escape dodging a bullet in a raid, detective Edgerton knocks a paperboy off his bike as he drives home. Knowing he's finished if it gets out that he's been drinking, he starts to cover his tracks, a task made more difficult by the arrival on the scene of a pair of smart fellow detectives (Jai Courtney, Tom Wilkinson). If there's a criticism to be levelled, it's that director Matthew Saville isn't quite sure who is the focus, but Edgerton's haunted performance adds intensity. SvM Swearing. DVD

Joel Edgerton *Malcolm Toohey* · Tom Wilkinson *Detective Carl Summer* · Jai Courtney *Jim Melic* · Melissa George *Julie Toohey* ■ *Dir* Matthew Saville · *Scr* Joel Edgerton

Female ★★★
Romantic comedy drama 1933 · US · BW · 65min

A splendid starring vehicle for the largely forgotten Ruth Chatterton, this comedy drama presents her as an intelligent and liberated female who runs a car manufacturing company and seduces the better-looking male employees for amorous relief. Her astonishing mansion marks an early screen appearance for Frank Lloyd Wright's Ennis House in the Hollywood Hills. Skilfully directed by Michael Curtiz, the film rapidly loses conviction when dreary George Brent (Chatterton's real-life husband at the time) comes along and is supposed to bowl her over. AE

Ruth Chatterton *Alison Drake* · George Brent *Jim Thorne* · Lois Wilson *Harriet* · Johnny Mack Brown *George C Cooper* · Ruth Donnelly *Miss Frothingham* · Ferdinand Gottschalk *Pettigrew* ■ *Dir* Michael Curtiz · *Scr* Gene Markey, Kathryn Scola, from the novel by Donald Henderson Clarke

Female Agents ★★★ 15
Second World War thriller 2007 · Fr · Colour · 112min

Sophie Marceau heads the cast of this handsome Second World War yarn inspired by a real-life female Resistance agent. In 1944, Louise Desfontaines (Marceau) is recruited by Winston Churchill's Special Operations Executive (SOE) to rescue a British geologist before the Nazis extract vital information about the impending D-Day landings. The mission, which also involves Julie Depardieu, Marie Gillain, Déborah François and Maya Sansa, then evolves into an equally perilous plot to assassinate a German officer. Director Jean-Paul Salomé, whose previous films include the period romp *Arsène Lupin*, has created a well-mounted adventure that entertains from start to finish. DA French, German, English +subtitles. Violence, nudity.
DVD Blu

Sophie Marceau *Louise Desfontaines* · Julie Depardieu *Jeanne Faussier* · Marie Gillain *Suzy Desprez* · Déborah François *Gaëlle Lemenech* · Moritz Bleibtreu *Karl Heindrich* · Maya Sansa *Maria Luzzato* ■ *Dir* Jean-Paul Salomé · *Scr* Jean-Paul Salomé, Laurent Vachaud

The Female Animal ★
Romantic drama 1958 · US · BW · 82min

Saved from a serious injury by handsome George Nader, movie star Hedy Lamarr moves him into her beach house as both caretaker and lover. It's only a matter of time before her adopted daughter Jane Powell falls for him, too, as does former actress Jan Sterling. This inept movie is pulp melodrama of the worst kind. RK

Hedy Lamarr *Vanessa Windsor* · Jane Powell *Penny Windsor* · Jan Sterling *Lily Frayne* · George Nader *Chris Farley* · Jerry Paris *Hank Lopez* ■ *Dir* Harry Keller · *Scr* Robert Hill, from a story by Albert Zugsmith

The Female Bunch ★ 18
Drama 1969 · US · Colour · 80min

Women's Lib meets Russ Meyer-style sexploitation in this insane movie shot at the Spahn ranch, a disused film set occupied by the Manson "family" around the time of the notorious murders. A group of man-hating women live on a secluded farm who run drugs across the Mexican border. You'd think a movie filled with bouts of lesbianism, drug-taking, nudity, sadism and *tom thumb* actor Russ Tamblyn having his face branded would be fun – wrong! And spare a thought for poor old Lon Chaney Jr in his last ever role as a hired hand. RS

Russ Tamblyn *Bill* · Jennifer Bishop (1) *Grace* · Lon Chaney Jr *Monty* · Nesa Renet *Sandy* · Geoffrey Land *Jim* · Regina Carrol *Waitress* ■ *Dir* Al Adamson, John "Bud" Cardos · *Scr* Jale Lockwood, Brent Nimrod, from a story by Raphael Nussbaum

The Female Jungle ★ PG
Crime drama 1955 · US · BW · 70min

Lawrence Tierney stars as a police sergeant found drunk at the scene of an actress's murder in this below average whodunnit that's mainly of interest because it features the first significant role of 1950s sex bomb Jayne Mansfield. She was only paid $150 for her performance, but it typecast her as the dumb blonde/nymphomaniac for the rest of her tragically short life. AJ DVD

Lawrence Tierney *Sergeant Stevens* · John Carradine *Claude Almstead* · Jayne Mansfield *Candy Price* · Burt Kaiser *Alec Voe* · Kathleen Crowley *Peggy Voe* · James Kodl *Joe* ■ *Dir* Bruno VeSota · *Scr* Bruno VeSota, Burt Kaiser

Female Perversions ★★ 18
Drama 1996 · US/Ger · Colour · 108min

Tilda Swinton is a high-powered lawyer with judicial aspirations, who is outwardly a model of femininity but is plagued by neuroses. She has a stormy relationship with her sister Amy Madigan, a compulsive shoplifter. Secrets are unravelled and kit is taken off, but despite the promise of something interesting to come, it gets bogged down in pretentiousness. JB Swearing, sex scenes, violence. **DVD**

Tilda Swinton *Evelyn "Eve" Stephens* • Amy Madigan *Madelyn Stephens* • Karen Sillas *Renee* • Frances Fisher *Annunciata* • Laila Robins *Emma* • Paulina Porizkova *Langley Flynn* ■ *Dir* Susan Streitfeld • *Scr* Susan Streitfeld, Julie Hebert, from the non-fiction book *Female Perversions: the Temptations of Emma Bovary* by Louise J Kaplan

Female Trouble ★★★★18
Satirical melodrama 1974 · US · Colour · 95min

Along with *Pink Flamingos*, this is the film that gained cult director John Waters his trophy for spectacularly redefining melodrama. A twisted parallel of *Mildred Pierce*, it features the transvestite Divine on a perverse quest for self-realisation, following a disastrous Christmas morning in which her parents fail to deliver the requested cha-cha heels. The squeamish solo delivery of her baby is the first scene in what turns out to be a true mother-and-daughter-from-hell scenario, with Mink Stole as the insufferable brat. Also noteworthy is the overflowing, endearing Edith Massey in a category of acting all her own. In short, an unhinged celebration of bad taste (and the favourite of core Waters fans), with the director's customary disregard for the genteel in full force throughout. DO **DVD**

Divine *Dawn Davenport/Earl Peterson* • David Lochary *Donald Dasher* • Mary Vivian Pearce *Donna Dasher* • Mink Stole *Taffy Davenport* • Edith Massey *Aunt Ida Nelson* • Cookie Mueller *Concetta* • Susan Walsh *Chiclet* • Michael Potter *Gater* ■ *Dir/Scr* John Waters (2)

The Female Vampire ★18
Erotic horror 1973 · Fr/Bel/Por · Colour · 94min

In this ludicrous vampire tale, Lina Romay stars as a countess who seduces all and sundry. Jesus Franco dwells on badly executed bloodsucking, crass nudity and pointless zooms in what turned out to be one of his most popular poverty-row quickies. Ponderous and artlessly shot. AJ Violence.

Lina Romay (2) *Countess Irina Karlstein* • Jack Taylor *Baron Von Rathony* • Jess Franck [Jesus Franco] *Dr Roberts* • Jean-Pierre Bouyxou *Dr Orloff* ■ *Dir/Scr* Jesus Franco

The Feminine Touch ★★★
Comedy 1941 · US · BW · 97min

This entertaining Rosalind Russell comedy has a knockout central idea: Russell is the wife of writer Don Ameche, who's just penned a book on jealousy, and she thinks he's fooling around with the lovely Kay Francis. There's lots of MGM gloss, and star-to-be Van Heflin in sterling support as the publisher who has his eye on Russell. Director Woody Van Dyke II piles on the pace, and the cast simply couldn't be more glamorous – watch how both Francis and Russell are exquisitely back-lit, and not just in their close-ups. TS

Rosalind Russell *Julie Hathaway* • Don Ameche *John Hathaway* • Kay Francis *Nellie Woods* • Van Heflin *Elliott Morgan* • Donald Meek *Captain Makepeace Liveright* • Gordon Jones *Rubber-legs Ryan* ■ *Dir* WS Van Dyke II [WS Van Dyke] • *Scr* George Oppenheimer, Edmund L Hartmann, Ogden Nash

The Feminine Touch ★★U
Romantic drama 1956 · UK · Colour · 91min

This mediocre drama was among the last batch of films made at the famous Ealing Studios. Director Pat Jackson had made his name with realistic docudramas during the Second World War, but this tale of trainee nurses was a far cry from his earlier hospital picture *White Corridors*. Diana Wynyard stands out as Matron, but the five girls are a tepid bunch. DP

George Baker *Dr Jim Alcott* • Belinda Lee *Susan Richards* • Delphi Lawrence *Pat Martin* • Adrienne Corri *Maureen O'Brien* • Henryetta Edwards *Ann Bowland* • Barbara Archer *Liz Jenkins* • Diana Wynyard *Matron* ■ *Dir* Pat Jackson • *Scr* Ian McCormick, from the book *A Lamp Is Heavy* by Sheila Mackay Russell

Une Femme Est une Femme ★★★PG
Comedy drama 1961 · Fr · Colour · 79min

French New Wave director Jean-Luc Godard's third feature is often described as a homage to the Hollywood musical. Shot in colour and CinemaScope, it is also a love letter to its radiant star Anna Karina, whom Godard married shortly after the film was completed. She plays a stripper who badly wants a child, and when her boyfriend Jean-Claude Brialy won't give her one, so to speak, she turns to his best friend, Jean-Paul Belmondo. Back in 1961, its New Wave freshness took the breath away. AT French +subtitles. **DVD**

Anna Karina *Angéla* • Jean-Claude Brialy *Emile Recamier* • Jean-Paul Belmondo *Alfred Lubitsch* • Nicole Paquin *Suzanne* • Marie Dubois *First prostitute* • Marion Sarraut *Second prostitute* • Jeanne Moreau *Woman in bar* ■ *Dir* Jean-Luc Godard • *Scr* Jean-Luc Godard, from an idea by Geneviève Cluny

Femme Fatale ★★15
Thriller 1991 · US · Colour · 92min

Colin Firth plays an unbelievably naive Englishman abroad in Los Angeles who falls for the beautiful Lisa Zane, only for her to disappear suddenly. He then discovers she has a sinister past. Firth does his best with his material, but Ms Zane lacks the lure of a true *femme fatale*. There are some interesting ideas explored here, but the end result is a muddled mess. JF Swearing, violence, sex scenes.

Colin Firth *Joe Prince* • Lisa Zane *Elizabeth/Cynthia/Maura* • Billy Zane *Elijah* • Scott Wilson *Dr Beaumont* • Lisa Blount *Jenny* • Suzanne Snyder *Andrea* • Pat Skipper *Ted* ■ *Dir* Andre Guttfreund • *Scr* Michael Ferris, John D Brancato

Femme Fatale ★★★15
Crime thriller 2002 · Fr · Colour · 109min

Can reclusive French Ambassador's wife Rebecca Romijn-Stamos hide her former identity as a jewel thief when secret snaps taken by paparazzi photographer Antonio Banderas alert her former partners in crime into reclaiming stolen diamonds? Complete with a mind-bending last-act shift in reality many will find a complete cheat, Brian De Palma's audaciously seductive deception is a bold and imaginative exercise in film-making craft, with Romijn-Stamos a duplicitous blonde heroine in the best Hitchcock tradition. AJ English, French +subtitles. Violence, swearing, sex scenes, nudity. **DVD**

Rebecca Romijn-Stamos *Laure Ash/Lily* • Antonio Banderas *Nicolas Bardo* • Peter Coyote *Watts* • Gregg Henry *Shiff* • Rie Rasmussen *Veronica* • Eriq Ebouaney *Black Tie* • Edouard Montoute *Racine* • Thierry Frémont *Serra* ■ *Dir/Scr* Brian De Palma

Une Femme Française ★★18
Drama 1994 · Fr/UK/Ger · Colour · 94min

Daniel Auteuil and Emmanuelle Béart's off-screen relationship terminated during the production of this uninvolving story, set either side of the Second World War. The merest hint of their private tensions might have sparked this ponderous melodrama into life. He plays a PoW betrayed by his wife both during his incarceration and after their reconciliation. DP

Emmanuelle Béart *Jeanne* • Daniel Auteuil *Louis* • Gabriel Barylli *Mathias Behrens* • Jean-Claude Brialy *Arnoult* • Geneviève Casile *Solange* • Heinz Bennent *Andreas* • Michel Etcheverry *Charles* ■ *Dir* Régis Wargnier • *Scr* Régis Wagnier, Alain Le Henry

La Femme Infidèle ★★★★15
Thriller 1968 · Fr/It · Colour · 94min

Director Claude Chabrol's masterly thriller stars the stunning Stéphane Audran as the unfaithful wife of the title, whose husband kills her lover, then dumps him in a lake. Owing much to Hitchcock, this is an elegant, tense and wickedly funny satire on the middle classes, performed to perfection by Audran, Michel Bouquet as the decidedly creepy husband, and Maurice Ronet as the doomed lover. This was the first in a magnificent run of thrillers from Chabrol in which the main characters were always called Charles and Hélène. AT French +subtitles. **DVD**

Stéphane Audran *Hélène Desvallees* • Michel Bouquet *Charles Desvallees* • Maurice Ronet *Victor Pegala* • Serge Bento *Bignon* • Michel Duchaussoy *Police Officer Duval* • Guy Marly *Police Officer Gobet* ■ *Dir/Scr* Claude Chabrol

La Femme Publique ★★★★
Crime drama 1984 · Fr · Colour · 109min

Made shortly after he left his native Poland for France, Andrzej Zulawski's dazzling picture occasionally lacks focus, but there's no denying the ingenuity of its story, its Dostoyevskian preoccupations and its delirious style. There's a *Pygmalion* feel to tyrannical director Francis Huster's relationship with ambitious actress Valérie Kaprisky. But the more bizarre incidents occur, as Huster pursues the wife of Czech exile Lambert Wilson, who finds himself charged with the murder of a Lithuanian archbishop. DP French +subtitles.

Francis Huster *Lucas Kesling* • Valérie Kaprisky *Ethel* • Lambert Wilson *Milan Miiska* • Diane Delor *Elena* • Roger Dumas *Photographer* ■ *Dir* Andrzej Zulawski • *Scr* Andrzej Zulawski, Dominique Garnier

Fermat's Room ★★★15
Mystery thriller 2007 · Sp · Colour · 88min

Saw meets *Pi* in this sly Spanish thriller that manages to wring a few nifty twists out of what is now a familiar formula. Four eminent mathematicians (Lluís Homar, Alejo Sauras, Santi Millán and Elena Ballesteros) have been lured to an isolated house by a mysterious stranger (Federico Luppi) to solve a supposedly impossible paradox. However, their host abruptly departs, leaving behind a PDA that begins emitting a series of numerical puzzles; the catch is that the walls of the room contract each time a question goes unanswered, and the riddles become progressively harder. JF Spanish +subtitles. **DVD**

Lluís Homar *Hilbert* • Alejo Sauras *Galois* • Elena Ballesteros *Oliva* • Santi Millán *Pascal* • Federico Luppi *Fermat* ■ *Dir/Scr* Luis Piedrahita, Rodrigo Sopeña

FernGully: the Last Rainforest ★★U
Animated fantasy 1992 · Aus · Colour · 72min

Many critics felt this eco-worthy cartoon force-fed its tale of planet-saving too strenuously. The criticism was a bit unfair, as the story of a fairy, a fruit bat and a tiny lumberjack battling a malevolent spirit bent on destruction is well-meaning and thoroughly entertaining for youngsters. Its target audience won't mind the preachiness and adults can be sure of the film's good intentions. A sequel, *Ferngully 2: the Magical Rescue* followed in 1997. TH **DVD**

Samantha Mathis *Crysta* • Jonathan Ward *Zak* • Robin Williams *Batty Koda* • Christian Slater *Pips* • Tim Curry *Hexxus* • Grace Zabriskie *Magi Lune* • Geoffrey Blake *Ralph* • Robert Pastorelli *Tony* ■ *Dir* Bill Kroyer • *Scr* Jim Cox, from stories by Diana Young

The Ferragosto Dinner ★★★★U
Comedy 2008 · It · Colour · 72min

Gianni di Gregorio (co-writer of *Gomorrah*) makes an accomplished directorial debut with this minor delight, which will enchant anyone with an eye for exquisite detail, an ear for eloquently acerbic dialogue and a fascination with human nature. He also cuts an appealingly tragicomic figure, as the impoverished Roman fretting that he has wasted his life on his nonagenarian mother. His frustrations increase as he agrees to host venerable siblings Maria Calì and Marina Cacciotti only to have dotty Grazia Cesarini Sforza foisted on him, too. The movie pokes gentle fun at Italy's attitudes to family responsibility and its decaying infrastructure, and the quaint kookiness of the old dears makes it irresistible. DP Italian +subtitles. **DVD**

Gianni Di Gregorio *Giovanni* • Valeria De Franciscis *Giovanni's mother* • Marina Cacciotti *Luigi's mother* • Marina Calì *Aunt Maria* • Grazia Cesarini Sforza *Grazia* ■ *Dir* Gianni Di Gregorio • *Scr* Gianni Di Gregorio, from a story by Gregorio, Simone Riccardini

Ferris Bueller's Day Off ★★★★15
Comedy 1986 · US · Colour · 98min

Matthew Broderick – worshipped by students, scourge of teachers – decides to play truant with classmates chum Alan Ruck and girlfriend Mia Sara off to the big city for an adventure; uptight Dean of Students Jeffrey Jones is determined to catch him in the act. It's a simple story, but this remains the most fully rounded of writer/director John Hughes's teen comedies, although once again it's marred slightly by Hughes's familiar undercurrent of sentimentality. Broderick is likeable as the arrogant, spoilt brat, while Ruck is excellent as his melancholy friend. JF **DVD** **Blu** **CS**

Matthew Broderick *Ferris Bueller* • Alan Ruck *Cameron Frye* • Mia Sara *Sloane Peterson* • Jeffrey Jones *Ed Rooney* • Jennifer Grey *Jeanie Bueller* • Cindy Pickett *Katie Bueller* • Lyman Ward *Tom Bueller* • Edie McClurg *School secretary* • Charlie Sheen *Garth Volbeck* ■ *Dir/Scr* John Hughes

Ferry Cross the Mersey ★★★U
Musical 1965 · UK · BW · 89min

Impresario and Beatles manager Brian Epstein was keen to repeat the success of *A Hard Day's Night*, but director Jeremy Summers was no Richard Lester so this Gerry and the Pacemakers musical always feels highly imitative. The highlights are the anthemic title track and the sequence inside the Cavern, which captures the atmosphere of the cramped backstreet cellar where Merseybeat was born. DP **DVD**

Gerry Marsden *Gerry* • Freddie Marsden *Fred* • Leslie Maguire *Les* • Les Chadwick *Chad* • Cilla Black ■ *Dir* Jeremy Summers • *Scr* David Franden, from a story by Tony Warren

Ferry to Hong Kong ★★U
Drama 1958 · UK · Colour · 98min

Directed on location by Lewis Gilbert, the script was extensively rewritten and then ad-libbed by Orson Welles, who clashed loudly with co-star Curt Jurgens. For Welles, this "holiday" – he boycotted the premiere and never saw the finished film – was his first visit to Macao where he hatched the idea of filming Isak Dinesen's *The Immortal Story*. Welles hijacked Gilbert's camera equipment to shoot some background footage, which found its way into his 1968 film. AT

Curt Jurgens *Mark Conrad* • Orson Welles *Captain Hart* • Sylvia Syms *Liz Ferrers* • Jeremy Spenser *Miguel Henriques* • Noel Purcell *Joe Skinner* • Margaret Withers *Miss Carter* ■ *Dir* Lewis Gilbert • *Scr* Vernon Harris, Lewis Gilbert

The Ferryman ★★15
Horror thriller 2007 · UK/NZ · Colour · 96min

New Zealand has delivered a fair few cult horror classics over the years, but this one doesn't make the grade. Kerry Fox and Tamer Hassan play a couple taking four tourists on a chartered sailing trip, who are forced to make a diversion to rescue a sailor (John Rhys-Davies) from a stricken fishing boat. Unfortunately, Davies brings with him a malignant spirit, who, pretty soon, is leaping from body to body and causing bloody mayhem. The story quickly runs out of options and director Chris Graham doesn't generate much in the way of tension. JF **DVD**

John Rhys-Davies *The Greek* • Kerry Fox *Suze* • Sally Stockwell *Tate* • Amber Sainsbury *Kathy* • Tamer Hassan *Big Dave* • Craig Hall *Chris* ■ *Dir* Chris Graham • *Scr* Nick Ward, from a story by Matthew Metcalfe, Ward, from a story by Jesse Warn

F

Festen

The first Dogme 95 feature promotes its ideals of hand-held camerawork, natural lighting and uncompromising themes

Festen ★★★★ 15

Drama   1998 · Den · Colour · 100min

Dogme 95 was initiated with this ferocious filleting of middle-class hypocrisy from Thomas Vinterberg, who delivers the collective's "vow of chastity" (natural sound and light, hand-held camerawork, no post-production) with coruscating aplomb. It was deemed truth in cinema by Dogme film-makers and it's the airing of a shocking truth during a Danish patriarch's 60th birthday party and family reunion at a country house that takes the breath away here. The immediacy of the rough-and-ready style is perfect as a family secret is revealed with devastating effect. JA Danish +subtitles. *DVD*

Ulrich Thomsen *Christian* • Henning Moritzen *Helge* • Thomas Bo Larsen *Michael* • Paprika Steen *Helene* • Birthe Neuman *Elsa* • Trine Dyrholm *Pia* ■ *Dir* Thomas Vinterberg • *Scr* Thomas Vinterberg, Mogens Rukov

Festival ★★★

Music documentary
1967 · US · Colour and BW · 97min

A fan of folk music, or just want to know where the mockumentary *A Mighty Wind* got its inspiration? Look no further than this well-made, evocative documentary filmed by Murray Lerner at the Newport folk festival during the banner years 1963-66. It's practically a greatest hits compendium of the folk-rock boom: Judy Collins sings *Turn! Turn! Turn!*, Joan Baez and Donovan duet on *Colours*, and it captures Bob Dylan's first appearance at the event crooning *Mr Tambourine Man*, among others. The mutual appreciation bond between performers and their audience offers rare insight into what made the easy-going 1960s counterculture tick. Joan Baez's advice to one fan "Come out non-violently or I'll kill you!" is hilarious. AJ *DVD*

Bob Dylan • Johnny Cash • Pete Seeger • Joan Baez • Judy Collins • Donovan ■ *Dir/Scr* Murray Lerner

Festival ★★★ 18

Black comedy drama
2005 · UK · Colour · 102min

Annie Griffin makes her feature debut with this comedy that follows a motley band of stars and misfits in their attempts to survive the annual Edinburgh Fringe Festival. Griffin blends drama and black comedy, spiky Scottish characters and seemingly sophisticated foreigners, producing something that confounds expectations, challenges stereotypes and leaves viewers unsure whether to laugh or cry. For the most part the shifts in tone are uncomfortably frank. BP Swearing. *DVD*

Daniela Nardini *Joan Gerard* • Clive Russell *Brother Mike* • Lyndsey Marshal *Faith Myers* • Stephen Mangan *Sean Sullivan* • Amelia Bullmore *Micheline* • Chris O'Dowd *Tommy O'Dwyer* • Billy Carter *Conor* ■ *Dir/Scr* Annie Griffin

Festival Express ★★★★ 15

Music documentary
2003 · UK/Neth · Colour · 85min

This fascinating rock documentary belatedly puts together footage of the 1970 trans-Canada train tour undertaken by some of the world's top musicians, including The Band, Grateful Dead and Janis Joplin. The ramshackle tour, in which the musicians jammed en route and alighted to play a series of gigs, was a financial disaster. This had little effect on the morale of the performers, however, who treated the trip as a five-day party – an attitude that comes across in on- and off-stage footage that's surprisingly revealing, especially considering the on-the-hoof way in which it was filmed. Contemporary interviews with some of the surviving players give added insight, making this a must-see for fans of

the people involved and connoisseurs of rock lore. DA Swearing. *DVD*

■ *Dir* Bob Smeaton • *Cinematographers* Peter Biziou, Bob Fiore

Festival in Cannes ★★★

Romantic comedy drama
2001 · US/Fr · Colour · 99min

Filmed at Cannes during the 1999 festival and strewn with guest stars, this is an agile examination of the way in which an event designed to celebrate cinematic excellence has become a tawdry circus characterised by commercial frenzy. Director Henry Jaglom is well served here by a cast attuned to his method of unrehearsed improvisation. Greta Scacchi is particularly impressive as the star peddling a low-budget personal project, as is Anouk Aimée as a fading art house star undecided whether to headline Scacchi's indie or cameo in a blockbuster. DP

Anouk Aimée *Millie Marquand* • Greta Scacchi *Alice Palmer* • Maximilian Schell *Viktor Kovner* • Ron Silver *Rick Yorkin* • Zach Norman *Kaz Naiman* • Peter Bogdanovich *Milo* • Jenny Gabrielle *Blue* ■ *Dir* Henry Jaglom • *Scr* Henry Jaglom, Victoria Foyt

Fetishes ★★★ 18

Documentary
1996 · UK · Colour · 86min

Nick Broomfield's documentary about sadomasochism made its TV debut in defiance of the triumphant publicity tag "the film that Channel 4 dared not show". Having already made the controversial *Chicken Ranch*, which detailed the comings and goings at a real-life brothel, this wasn't the first time Broomfield had explored the sex sector. But the man who has also tackled Margaret Thatcher, Eugene Terreblanche and Courtney Love without batting an eyelid is clearly less than comfortable with Mistress Raven and the other occupants of New York's Pandora's Box club. Disturbingly compelling, this is a judgement-free, if graphic, insight into a highly singular world. DP Swearing, sex scenes. *DVD*

■ *Dir* Nick Broomfield

Le Feu Follet ★★★★ 12

Drama
1963 · Fr/It · BW · 103min

Released as *The Fire Within* in the States and sometimes called *Will o' the Wisp* in this country, Louis Malle's drama is widely regarded as one of his best. The story of an alcoholic who visits his friends in the hope of finding a reason to live could, in the wrong hands, have been an unbearably maudlin and melodramatic affair. But Malle shuns sentiment and turns this into a painfully truthful study of self-realisation. Maurice Ronet (the forgotten actor of the French New Wave) is outstanding as Alain Leroy, subtly earning our sympathy without ever really deserving it. DP French +subtitles. *DVD*

Maurice Ronet *Alain Leroy* • Léna Skerla *Lydia* • Yvonne Clech *Madamoiselle Farnoux* • Hubert Deschamps *D'Averseau* • Jean-Paul Moulinot *Dr La Barbinais* • Mona Dol *Madame La Barbinais* • Jeanne Moreau *Jeanne* ■ *Dir* Louis Malle • *Scr* Louis Malle, from the novel by Pierre Drieu la Rochelle

The Feud ★★★ 15

Comedy
1989 · US · Colour · 93min

In small-town America, the Beeler and the Bullard families start a feud when Dolf Beeler brandishes a cigar in the Bud Bullard's non-smoking hardware store. The row escalates and the hardware store becomes a smoking one – it's burned down in an arson attack. Then a car is bombed, people get killed and, of course, in the tradition of *Romeo and Juliet*, there's a love affair across the divide. Set in a sunny Eisenhower era of happy families, optimism and cars that look like spaceships, this is a deftly-made black comedy. AT

René Auberjonois *Reverton* • Joe Grifasi *Bud Bullard* • Ron McLarty *Dolf Beeler* • David Strathairn *The Stranger* • Gale Mayron *Bernice Beeler* • Scott Allegrucci *Tony Beeler* • Lynne

Killmeyer *Eva Bullard* ■ *Dir* Bill D'Elia • *Scr* Bill D'Elia, Robert Uricola, from the novel by Thomas Berger

Fever Pitch ★★ 15

Drama
1985 · US · Colour · 91min

Poor old Ryan O'Neal. In the 1970s he was the envy of Hollywood, but within a decade his career was seriously off the boil and only badly scripted roles, such as this as a sports writer who becomes addicted to gambling, seem to have popped through his letterbox. This film also marks a decline in fortunes for writer/director Richard Brooks. JB Swearing.

Ryan O'Neal *Taggart* • Catherine Hicks *Flo* • Giancarlo Giannini *Charley* • Bridgette Andersen *Amy* • Chad Everett *Dutchman* • John Saxon *Sports editor* • Hank Greenspun *Sun Publisher* • Keith Hefner *Casino boss* ■ *Dir/Scr* Richard Brooks

Fever Pitch ★★★★ 15

Romantic sports comedy
1996 · UK · Colour · 98min

This is a hugely entertaining reworking of Nick Hornby's runaway bestseller. Although the film is based on a football fanatic's memoir, there's much more to this romantic comedy than soccer. Colin Firth and best buddy Mark Strong buzz off to Highbury or are glued to the box, while girlfriend Ruth Gemmell and flatmate Holly Aird pass acerbic asides about how incapable the lads are of growing up. Football, fads, fashion aberrations and long-gone TV shows ensure this story is instantly recognisable to men of a certain age and also to their long-suffering female kin. The book got a Hollywood makeover in 2005 as *The Perfect Pitch*. DP Swearing. *DVD*

Colin Firth *Paul Ashworth* • Ruth Gemmell *Sarah Hughes* • Neil Pearson *Paul's dad* • Lorraine Ashbourne *Paul's mum* • Mark Strong *Steve* • Holly Aird *Jo* • Ken Stott *Ted, the headmaster* • Stephen Rea *Ray, the governor* • Luke Aikman *Young Paul* ■ *Dir* David Evans • *Scr* Nick Hornby, from his book

A Few Best Men ★★ 15

Comedy
2011 · UK/Aus · Colour · 92min

Like writer Dean Craig's *Death at a Funeral*, this comedy is set against the backdrop of a social function, in this case a wedding. Sadly, it's also a largely unfunny blend of frantic farce and gross-out humour. Xavier Samuel is the Londoner who heads Down Under to marry the Aussie backpacker (Laura Brent) he fell for on holiday. There's a naughty turn from Olivia Newton-John as the mother-in-law to be, but director Stephan Elliott struggles to bring any zip to the plodding script. JF Swearing, sexual references, nudity, drug abuse. *DVD*

Xavier Samuel *David* • Kris Marshall *Tom* • Kevin Bishop *Graham* • Tim Draxl *Luke* • Laura Brent *Mia* • Olivia Newton-John *Barbara* ■ *Dir* Stephan Elliott • *Scr* Dean Craig

A Few Days in September ★★ 15

Drama
2006 · Fr/It · Colour · 115min

Something certainly seems to have got lost in translation in Argentinean writer/director Santiago Amigorena's elegant-looking but confused tale of international espionage, set in the days leading up to 9/11. Juliette Binoche plays a French agent who is called on to babysit the two grown-up children (Sara Forestier and Tom Riley) of CIA agent Nick Nolte. The pair – one French, one American – were previously unaware of each other's existence. Nolte goes missing, presumably in possession of some extremely sensitive information, and is hunted by a neurotic assassin (an annoyingly quirky John Turturro) who pursues Binoche and her charges from Paris to Venice. Binoche fares the best of the talented cast, but even she struggles with the clumsy dialogue and plodding narrative. JF English, French, Italian, Arabic +subtitles.

Juliette Binoche *Irene* • John Turturro *William Pound* • Sara Forestier *Orlando* • Tom Riley *David* • Nick Nolte *Elliot* ■ *Dir/Scr* Santiago Amigorena

A Few Good Men ★★★★ 15

Courtroom drama   1992 · US · Colour · 132min

The ultimate rebel Jack Nicholson has a ball playing the ultimate establishment figure in this star-laden, rather old-fashioned courtroom drama, crisply directed by Rob Reiner. In fact, Nicholson's role of the obsessive, hard-nosed marine officer is little more than a scene-stealing cameo. The two leads are Tom Cruise and Demi Moore, who play naval lawyers trying to discover the truth behind the death of a marine. The climactic fireworks between Nicholson and Cruise make for compulsive viewing. JF Swearing, violence. *DVD*

Tom Cruise *Lt Daniel Kaffee* • Jack Nicholson *Col Nathan R Jessep* • Demi Moore *Lt Cmdr JoAnne Galloway* • Kevin Bacon *Capt Jack Ross* • Kiefer Sutherland *Lt Jonathan Kendrick* • Kevin Pollak *Lt Sam Weinberg* • James Marshall *Private First Class Louden Downey* • JT Walsh *Lt Col Matthew Markinson* ■ *Dir* Rob Reiner • *Scr* Aaron Sorkin, from his play

Fiddler on the Roof ★★★★ U

Musical comedy drama
1971 · US · Colour · 177min

Through the tale of Tevye and his search for husbands for his five daughters, director Norman Jewison describes the tragic background to the expulsion of the Jews from the Ukraine and the dissolution of their traditions. As Tevye the garrulous milkman, Topol is memorable, and to have his performance (he played the part on the London stage) preserved on film is a major plus. The generally unfamiliar supporting cast is exceptionally well chosen, but the real gem is the Oscar-winning soundtrack. It's quite long-winded, but is still a lasting memorial to one of the greatest, most heartbreaking of all Broadway shows. TS *DVD*

Topol *Tevye* • Norma Crane *Golde* • Leonard Frey *Motel* • Molly Picon *Yente* • Paul Mann *Lazar Wolf* • Rosalind Harris *Tzeitel* • Michele Marsh *Hodel* • Neva Small *Chava* • Michael Glaser [Paul Michael Glaser] *Perchik* • Raymond Lovelock *Fyedka* ■ *Dir* Norman Jewison • *Scr* Joseph Stein, from his book of the stage musical, from stories by Sholom Aleichem • *Cinematographer* Oswald Morris • *Music* Jerry Bock • *Lyrics* Sheldon Harnick

Fiddlers Three ★★

Comedy
1944 · UK · BW · 88min

The follow-up to *Sailors Three* is a cheap and cheerful reworking of Eddie Cantor's *Roman Scandals*. A bolt of lightning transports stars Tommy Trinder, Sonny Hale and Wren Diana Decker back to ancient Rome, where she takes the eye of the emperor Nero, and Tommy has to resort to a Carmen Miranda disguise to save her. The gags are poor and the songs are even worse, but any escape from the war was welcome. DP

Tommy Trinder *Tommy* • Frances Day *Poppaea* • Sonnie Hale *Professor* • Francis L Sullivan *Nero* • Diana Decker *Lydia* • Elisabeth Welch *Thora* ■ *Dir* Harry Watt • *Scr* Harry Watt, Diana Morgan, Angus MacPhail

La Fidélité ★★ 15

Drama
2000 · Fr · Colour · 166min

Andrzej Zulawski here directs his then real-life partner, Sophie Marceau, in a reckless updating of Madame de la Fayette's novel *La Princesse de Clèves*. What starts promisingly as a scathing dissection of modern cultural vacuity soon takes a turn for the worse as Marceau's Canadian photographer tumbles into bed with children's book publisher Pascal Greggory, forming a bond that compels her to reject the passionate advances of sexy colleague Guillaume Canet. DP French +subtitles.

Sophie Marceau *Clélia* • Pascal Greggory *Clève* • Guillaume Canet *Némo* • Magali Noël *Clélia's mother* ■ *Dir* Andrzej Zulawski • *Scr* Andrzej Zulawski, from the novel *La Princesse de Clèves* by Madame de La Fayette

The Field ★★★ 🔢

Drama 1990 · UK · Colour · 105min

Critics and audiences alike were rather underwhelmed by Jim Sheridan's follow-up to the phenomenally successful *My Left Foot*. Richard Harris received an Oscar nomination for his imposing performance as the grouchy farmer fighting to save "his" land, but it is the understated playing of John Hurt and Brenda Fricker that provides the real backbone of this handsome, if overbrewed production. DP Violence, swearing. **DVD**

Richard Harris *"Bull" McCabe* • Sean Bean *Tadgh McCabe* • Tom Berenger *Peter, the American* • Frances Tomelty *The widow* • Brenda Fricker *Maggie McCabe* • John Hurt *"Bird" O'Donnell* • Ruth McCabe *First tinker woman* ■ *Dir* Jim Sheridan • *Scr* Jim Sheridan, from a play by John B Keane

A Field in England ★★★ 🔢

Period horror 2013 · UK · BW · 90min

The League of Gentlemen's Reece Shearsmith plays an English Civil War deserter who has an extreme battlefield epiphany in this experimental horror from director Ben Wheatley (*Kill List*). Starkly beautiful random images prove equally demanding in what is, in effect, a head-scratching meditation on the true meaning of friendship in testing times. The centrepiece is a magic mushroom-induced psychedelic trip, which blows the minds of Shearsmith and his companions and reassembles certain facets of their personalities. AJ Violence, swearing, sexual references, nudity. **DVD**

Reece Shearsmith *Whitehead* • Michael Smiley *O'Neil* • Ryan Pope *Cutler* • Richard Glover *Friend* ■ *Dir* Ben Wheatley • *Scr* Amy Jump • *Cinematographer* Laurie Rose

Field of Dreams ★★★★ 🔢

Fantasy drama 1989 · US · Colour · 101min

This fantasy drama from director Phil Alden Robinson is a delightful blend of the blind-fate story and the more fanciful feel-good corn of Frank Capra. Kevin Costner, as an Iowa farmer, is the epitome of dignified determination as he accedes to a ghostly voice and turns the field on which the family depends for its livelihood into a baseball pitch. The underestimated Amy Madigan gives a good account of herself as his trusting wife, while Ray Liotta, Burt Lancaster and Frank Whaley represent the spirit world with distinction. DP **DVD**

Kevin Costner *Ray Kinsella* • Amy Madigan *Annie Kinsella* • Gaby Hoffman [Gaby Hoffmann] *Karin Kinsella* • Ray Liotta *"Shoeless" Joe Jackson* • Timothy Busfield *Mark* • James Earl Jones *Terence Mann* • Burt Lancaster *Dr "Moonlight" Graham* • Frank Whaley *Archie Graham* • Dwier Brown *John Kinsella* ■ *Dir* Phil Alden Robinson • *Scr* Phil Alden Robinson, from the novel *Shoeless Joe* by WP Kinsella

Fielder's Choice ★★

Drama 2005 · US · Colour · 85min

Family tragedy forces a career-obsessed advertising executive to reassess his life in this touching and gentle drama. Rob Lowe's younger brother Chad plays the titular Fielder who has to face a few home truths after reluctantly gaining custody of his sister's autistic son (K'Sun Ray). The plot is predictable but pleasingly well executed, making a simple human story consistently engaging. SF

Chad Lowe *Phillip Fielder* • George Segal *J D* • K'Sun Ray *Zach Fielder* • Marin Hinkle *Holly* • Bodhi Elfman *Lou* • Ellen Greene *Jill Fielder* ■ *Dir* Kevin Connor • *Scr* Scott Huebscher, Dan Roberts

The Fiend ★★★

Horror 1971 · UK · Colour · 91min

This unnerving stalk 'n' slash horror offering marries religious mania to *Peeping Tom*-style voyeuristic repression. With an opening in which a christening is cross-cut with a murder, it's clear that emotionally stunted Tony Beckley is not going to be fit to wear the policeman's uniform that he hides behind while pursuing his savage quest. Director Robert Hartford-Davis can't

be accused of subtlety, but this is still a disturbing film. DP

Ann Todd *Birdie Wemys* • Patrick Magee *Minister* • Tony Beckley *Kenny Wemys* • Madeline Hinde *Brigitte Lynch* • Suzanna Leigh *Paddy Lynch* • Percy Herbert *Commissionaire* • David Lodge *CID Inspector* ■ *Dir* Robert Hartford-Davis • *Scr* Brian Comport

Fiend without a Face ★★★ 🄿🄶

Science-fiction horror 1957 · UK · BW · 70min

Canadian atomic experiments cause human thoughts to transform into brain-sucking creatures in a grisly little 1950s number featuring unusually graphic special effects for the period. Arthur Crabtree's *Quatermass*-style shocker starts off pretty ordinarily but, once the flying spinal cords whip into throat-choking action, the screams you hear may well be your own! British to the core, despite the pseudo-American trappings and fading Hollywood actor Marshall Thompson taking centre stage. AJ **DVD**

Marshall Thompson *Major Jeff Cummings* • Terence Kilburn [Terry Kilburn] *Captain Chester* • Kynaston Reeves *Professor Walgate* • Stanley Maxted *Colonel Butler* • Michael Balfour *Sergeant Kasper* • Kim Parker *Barbara* ■ *Dir* Arthur Crabtree • *Scr* Herbert J Leder, from a story by Amelia Reynolds Long

The Fiendish Plot of Dr Fu Manchu ★ 🄿🄶

Comedy 1980 · US · Colour · 100min

There's no escaping the fact that the last film Peter Sellers made was also his worst (mercifully he didn't live to see two later *Pink Panther* out-take abominations). It was a bad idea in the first place to have Sellers play both the Oriental master villain and his dogged pursuer, Nayland Smith, but he spends so much time in disguise that it's sometimes hard to remember who he's supposed to be. DP

Peter Sellers *Dr Fu Manchu/Nayland Smith* • Helen Mirren *Alice Rage* • David Tomlinson *Sir Roger Avery* • Sid Caesar *Joe Capone* • Stratford Johns *Ismail* • John Le Mesurier *Perkins* ■ *Dir* Piers Haggard • *Scr* Jim Moloney, Rudy Dochtermann, from characters by Sax Rohmer

Fierce Creatures ★★ 🔢

Comedy 1997 · US/UK · Colour · 89min

John Cleese reassembled the team from *A Fish Called Wanda* for this soft-hearted caper. Cleese plays the new manager appointed by an Australian media mogul to jazz up a local zoo by adopting a "fierce creatures only" policy. Sadly, this follow-up lacks the magic of the original, and, despite the valiant efforts of a host of familiar faces, that vital spark is largely missing. JF **DVD**

John Cleese *Rollo Lee* • Jamie Lee Curtis *Willa Weston* • Kevin Kline *Vince McCain/Rod McCain* • Michael Palin *Bugsy Malone* • Ronnie Corbett *Reggie Sealions* • Carey Lowell *Cub Felines* • Robert Lindsay *Sydney Small Mammals* ■ *Dir* Fred Schepisi, Robert Young (2) • *Scr* John Cleese, Iain Johnstone, from an idea by Terry Jones, Michael Palin

The Fiercest Heart ★★ 🄴

Adventure 1961 · UK · Colour · 89min

This decidedly anti-colonial tale is really nothing more than a western transferred to the South African veld. Set in 1837, director George Sherman replaces wagon train adventure with a great Boer trek, while the usual fugitive outlaw figure becomes a political prisoner who escapes from a British internment camp and finds redemption in the arms of a pioneering woman. Stuart Whitman combines ruggedness and rigidity in about equal measure, and Juliet Prowse is just as inanimate. DP

Stuart Whitman *Bates* • Juliet Prowse *Francina* • Ken Scott (1) *Harry Carter* • Raymond Massey *Willem* • Geraldine Fitzgerald *Tante Maria* • Rafer Johnson *Nzobo* • Michael David *Barent* ■ *Dir* George Sherman • *Scr* Edmund H North, from the novel by Stuart Cloete

Fiesta ★★★

Musical 1947 · US · Colour · 102min

This sumptuous MGM production filmed on location down Mexico way and in glorious Technicolor, is little more than a starring vehicle for ultra-glamorous Esther Williams. She looks ravishing in a torero's outfit in a sort of Shakespearean plot in which she has to disguise herself as her twin brother – dashing screen newcomer Ricardo Montalban. Montalban falls for the equally ravishing Cyd Charisse, and the two of them get to indulge in a brace of fiery dance duets. Meanwhile, sister Esther finds romance with John Carroll. Tosh, of course, but simply fabulous to look at. TS

Esther Williams *Maria Morales* • Akim Tamiroff *Chato Vasquez* • Ricardo Montalban *Mario Morales* • John Carroll *Jose "Pepe" Ortega* • Mary Astor *Senora Morales* • Cyd Charisse *Conchita* ■ *Dir* Richard Thorpe • *Scr* George Bruce, Lester Cole

La Fièvre Monte à el Pao ★★★

Drama 1959 · Fr/Mex · BW · 100min

Part potboiler, part acute political analysis, this cynical drama unfolds on an island off the coast of a Latin American republic with a large population of jailbirds and political prisoners from the mainland. When the governor is assassinated, Gérard Philipe, his former secretary and a man of ideals, takes care of matters until a new governor (Jean Servais) is appointed. The director's cynical message – that individuals are forced to bow to systems – comes through loud and clear, but Philipe, making his last film before his early death, is unable to inject life into his ill-defined role. RB In French.

Gérard Philipe *Ramón Vásquez* • Maria Felix *Inés Rojas* • Jean Servais *Alejandro Gual* • Victor Junco *Indarte* • Roberto Cañedo *Coronel Olivares* • Andres Soler *Carlos Barreiro* • Domingo Soler *Juan Cárdenas* ■ *Dir* Luis Buñuel • *Scr* Luis Buñuel, Luis Alcoriza, Charles Dorat, Louis Sapin, Henry Castillou, from the novel by Henry Castillou

15 ★★★ 🔢

Drama 2003 · Sing · Colour · 96min

Royston Tan's uncompromising take on teenage ennui caused outrage in its native Singapore. The story of five young people living on the fringes of society is played out by actual street kids, who re-enact their own experiences of drug abuse, promiscuity and violence. Sequences containing an animated guide to suicide and a rap tribute to the Lion City's most feared street gangs reveal the director's outspoken support for these nonconformists. However, Tan's background in music videos lends the film a self-consciously modish look. DP Mandarin, Hokkien, Malay, Hindi +subtitles.

Shaun Tan *Shaun* • Melvin Chen *Melvin* • Erick Chun *Erick* • Melvin Lee *Armani* • Vynn Soh *Vynn* ■ *Dir/Scr* Royston Tan

15 Minutes ★★ 🔢

Thriller 2001 · US · Colour · 115min

This New York cop thriller with a social conscience teams old dog Robert De Niro with hip young gunslinger Edward Burns, throwing in *Frasier* star Kelsey Grammer for light relief. But while this purports to be a savage indictment of tabloid TV - De Niro's cop feeds crime exclusives to Grammer's news hack in return for exposure - it's merely a glossy sham. As the heroes pursue two eastern Europeans who are recording their murderous crime spree on videotape, any subtlety of message is swamped by the join-the-dots action. AC Violence, swearing. **DVD**

Robert De Niro *Eddie Flemming* • Edward Burns *Jordy Warsaw* • Kelsey Grammer *Robert Hawkins* • Avery Brooks *Leon Jackson* • Melina Kanakarades *Nicolette Karas* • Karel Roden *Emil Slovak* • Oleg Taktarov *Oleg Razgul* • Kim Cattrall *Cassandra* • Charlize Theron *Rose Hearn* ■ *Dir/Scr* John Herzfeld

5th Ave Girl ★★

Comedy 1939 · US · BW · 82min

The girl is poor-but-honest Ginger Rogers (a tad too old for the role) who's "adopted" by millionaire Walter Connolly for a night to be his companion, in order to compensate himself for familial neglect. There are some nice left-wing barbs here, but director Gregory La Cava's misanthropic view of human behaviour is unfamiliar and unsavoury. TS

Ginger Rogers *Mary Grey* • Walter Connolly *Mr Borden* • Verree Teasdale *Mrs Borden* • James Ellison *Michael* • Tim Holt *Tim Borden* • Kathryn Adams *Katherine Borden* ■ *Dir* Gregory La Cava • *Scr* Allan Scott

The Fifth Element ★★★★ 🄿🄶

Science-fiction action adventure 1997 · Fr · Colour · 121min

Ancient evil returns to destroy the galaxy in director Luc Besson's ultra-hip, socially conscious and clever film. Bruce Willis's laconic former government agent is forced to save the universe when the secret key to stopping this happening literally falls into his cab in 23rd-century New York. This superb flight of imagination soars into original terrain for an inventive rollercoaster ride; the satire is slick, the visuals unusual and the thrills futuristic. Gary Oldman is great as *haute-couture* corruption personified. AJ Violence, swearing, nudity. **DVD**

Bruce Willis *Korben Dallas* • Gary Oldman *Zorg* • Ian Holm *Cornelius* • Milla Jovovich *Leeloo* • Chris Tucker *Ruby Rhod* • Luke Perry *Billy* • Brion James *General Munro* • Lee Evans *Fog* ■ *Dir* Luc Besson • *Scr* Luc Besson, Robert Mark Kamen, from a story by Besson

The Fifth Estate ★★★★ 🔢

Drama based on a true story 2013 · US · Colour · 122min

The story of WikiLeaks founder Julian Assange (Benedict Cumberbatch) and his mission to expose the secrets of governments and the corporate world is recounted in a lively thriller in this engrossing film. Director Bill Condon references several other real-life screen dramas, most notably *All the President's Men*, *The Social Network* and *Zero Dark Thirty*, finding intrigue and tension in incidents that dominated world headlines. Cumberbatch gives a towering performance as Assange, although viewers may find themselves reminded of his Sherlock Holmes. TeS Violence, swearing, sexual references. **DVD**

Benedict Cumberbatch *Julian Assange* • Daniel Brühl *Daniel Domscheit-Berg* • Anthony Mackie *Sam Coulson* • David Thewlis *Nick Davies* • Laura Linney *Sarah Shaw* • Stanley Tucci *James Boswell* • Peter Capaldi *Alan Rusbridger* ■ *Dir* Bill Condon • *Scr* Josh Singer, from the non-fiction book *Inside WikiLeaks: My Time with Julian Assange at the World's Most Dangerous Website* by Daniel Domscheit-Berg and the non-fiction book *WikiLeaks: Inside Julian Assange's War on Secrecy* by David Leigh and Luke Harding

The 5th Monkey ★★

Adventure 1990 · US · Colour · 95min

Ben Kingsley's film career has taken some peculiar turns since his Oscar-winning portrayal of Gandhi in 1982. Here he finds himself deep in the Amazon rainforest attempting to sell some rare monkeys in order to make enough money to marry his true love. This meandering tale makes the most of the Brazilian landscape, but fails to sustain interest in Kingsley's ultimate goal, and its sermon on the need for conservation is overzealously preached. DP Violence.

Ben Kingsley *Cunda* • Mika Lins *Octavia* • Vera Fischer *Mrs Watts* • Silvia De Carvalho *Maria* • Carlos Kroeber *Mr Garcia* ■ *Dir* Eric Rochat • *Scr* Eric Rochat, from the novel *Le Cinquième Singe* by Jacques Zibi

The 5th Musketeer ★★ 🔢

Period adventure 1979 · Austria · Colour · 115min

Yet another rehash of *The Man in the Iron Mask*, with Beau Bridges rather poorly cast in the dual role as Louis XIV and his incarcerated twin brother. Sylvia Kristel – famous as the heroine of the soft-porn *Emmanuelle* films – plus Ursula Andress join an impressive roster of slumming veterans, including Rex Harrison, Olivia de Havilland and José Ferrer. Ken Annakin directs without fuss but the whole thing has the heaviness one expects from a Euro-pudding movie. **AT**

Beau Bridges *King Louis/Philippe* • Sylvia Kristel *Marie-Thérèse* • Ursula Andress *Madame De La Vallière* • Cornel Wilde *D'Artagnan* • Ian McShane *Fourquet* • Lloyd Bridges *Aramis* • Alan Hale Jr *Porthos* • Olivia de Havilland *Queen Anne* • José Ferrer *Athos* • Rex Harrison *Colbert* ■ *Dir* Ken Annakin • *Scr* David Ambrose, from a screenplay (unproduced) by George Bruce, from the novel *The Man in the Iron Mask* by Alexandre Dumas

The 5th Wave ★ 15

Science-fiction drama
2016 • US • Colour • 112min

Chloë Grace Moretz faces the alien equivalent of the biblical plagues of Egypt in this dreadful potboiler. Moretz gives it way more welly than the plot deserves as a high-school student who's searching for her younger brother after aliens arrive. Cue a global power outage, then earthquakes and floods, a bird-flu pandemic and infiltration in human guise as these aliens hope to rid the planet of its people. And the titular 5th wave? An all-out attack. It's director J Blakeson's first foray into sci-fi but he exhausts the so-so special effects in the first few minutes. **DA** Violence **DVD**

Chloë Grace Moretz *Cassie Sullivan* • Nick Robinson *Ben Parish* • Ron Livingston *Oliver Sullivan* • Maggie Siff *Lisa Sullivan* • Liev Schreiber *Colonel Vosch* ■ *Dir* J Blakeson • *Scr* Susannah Grant, from Rick Yancey's novel

Fifty Dead Men Walking
★★★ 15

Political thriller based on a true story
2008 • Can/UK/US • Colour • 112min

Director Kari Skogland's film is based on the autobiography of Martin McGartland, a police informant scaling the ranks of the IRA in the late 1980s. Jim Sturgess portrays McGartland as a well-meaning but confused youth in a divided Belfast where, as one character puts it, "you're not a man unless you've got a cause". Ben Kingsley, as McGartland's police "handler" Fergus, struggles with the task of providing the film with a moral compass – the title derives from the belief that McGartland's information saved the lives of at least 50 police and soldiers. However, Skogland's voyeuristic approach to the violence of the conflict tends to undermine any message. **TeS** Violence, swearing. **DVD**

Ben Kingsley *Fergus* • Jim Sturgess *Martin McGartland* • Kevin Zegers *Sean* • Natalie Press *Lara* • Rose McGowan *Grace* • Tom Collins *Mickey Adams* ■ *Dir* Kari Skogland • *Scr* Kari Skogland, from the autobiography by Martin McGartland, Nicholas Davies

Fifty/Fifty ★★★ 15

Action adventure   1991 • US • Colour • 96min

This decent little action adventure concerns two wisecracking mercenaries taking a job from the CIA to overthrow a South East Asian dictator. Along the way they have to train a guerrilla army and spar romantically for the favour of a pretty rebel soldier. The two tough guys are played by Peter Weller and Robert Hays, and they have a lot of chemistry together. The dialogue is good, but in the end the set-up is more fun than the payoff. **ST**

Peter Weller *Jake Wyer* • Robert Hays *Sam French* • Charles Martin Smith *Martin Sprue* • Ramona Rahman *Suleta* • Lim Kay Tong *Akhantar* ■ *Dir* Charles Martin Smith • *Scr* Michael Butler, Dennis Shryack, Jeff Levine, LeeAnn Lanctos, Chris Wood

50/50 ★★★★ 15

Comedy drama   2011 • Can/US • Colour • 95min

A diagnosis of cancer provides an unlikely launching pad for comedy in this beautifully played and surprisingly thoughtful fact-based buddy movie. Joseph Gordon-Levitt plays Adam, a 20-something whose life is rocked by the discovery of a malignant tumour. Adam soon finds, however, that being seriously ill causes strange reactions from his girlfriend (Bryce Dallas Howard), his mother (Anjelica Huston) and his best friend (Seth Rogen). Out of these elements emerges a touching, plausible and above all very funny story of human vulnerability, with the wonderful double act of Gordon-Levitt and Rogen at its core. **DW** Swearing, sex scenes. **DVD** **SL**

Joseph Gordon-Levitt *Adam Lerner* • Seth Rogen *Kyle* • Anna Kendrick *Katherine* • Bryce Dallas Howard *Rachael* • Anjelica Huston *Diane* • Philip Baker Hall *Alan* • Serge Houde *Richard* • Andrew Airlie *Dr Ross* ■ *Dir* Jonathan Levine • *Scr* Will Reiser

50 First Dates ★★★ 12

Romantic comedy   2004 • US • Colour • 94min

Only the grumpiest viewer could fail to be charmed by this sweet comedy. Featuring one of Adam Sandler's least goofy performances, it's a simple and undemanding story, with genuine warmth beneath the slapstick. Drew Barrymore plays a car-crash survivor whose short-term memory loss means she wakes up every morning with no knowledge of the day before. For laid-back, would-be suitor Sandler this means repeating their first date over and over again. It's an amusing concept, laced with poignancy. **SF** Drug abuse. **DVD** **SL**

Adam Sandler *Henry Roth* • Drew Barrymore *Lucy Whitmore* • Rob Schneider *Ula* • Sean Astin *Doug Whitmore* • Lusia Strus *Alexa* • Dan Aykroyd *Dr Keats* • Amy Hill *Sue* • Allen Covert *Ten Second Tom* • Blake Clark *Marlin Whitmore* ■ *Dir* Peter Segal • *Scr* George Wing

The 51st State ★★ 18

Action comedy drama
2001 • UK/Can • Colour • 88min

This glossy, visceral crime thriller from director Ronny Yu is a mere exercise in noisy excess, yet a few elements mark it out as something slightly unusual. The script about a master chemist trying to sell the ultimate in designer drugs was sent to Samuel L Jackson by a first-time writer and off-licence worker, and then given the go-ahead. It's set in less than glamorous Liverpool; streetwise Jackson's pharmacist hero wears a kilt and his sidekick Robert Carlyle is a rabid football fan. **JC** Drug abuse, violence, swearing. **DVD**

Samuel L Jackson *Elmo McElroy* • Robert Carlyle *Felix De Souza* • Emily Mortimer *"Dakota"* • Rhys Ifans *Iki* • Ricky Tomlinson *Durant* • Sean Pertwee *Virgil Kane* • Meat Loaf *The Lizard* ■ *Dir* Ronny Yu • *Scr* Stel Pavlou

55 Days at Peking ★★★★ U

Historical drama   1963 • US • Colour • 147min

This is an intelligent historical epic about the Boxer rebellion of 1900 when extremists besieged the compound of international diplomats. Charlton Heston stars in this Philip Yordan-scripted Chinese drama, filmed in a custom-built Peking, one of the most spectacular sets ever created. Switching smoothly between the wider political sphere and the personal dilemmas of the key players – Heston, David Niven, Ava Gardner – the movie is a carefully balanced study of principle and courage in action, partly directed by Nicholas Ray who suffered a heart attack during production and whose work was completed by second unit director Andrew Marton and an uncredited Guy Green. **AT** **DVD** **SL**

Charlton Heston *Major Matt Lewis* • Ava Gardner *Baroness Natalie Ivanoff* • David Niven *Sir Arthur Robertson* • Flora Robson *Dowager Empress Tzu Hsi* • John Ireland *Sergeant Harry* • Harry Andrews *Father de Bearn* ■ *Dir* Nicholas Ray • *Scr* Philip Yordan, Bernard Gordon, Robert Hamer

54 ★★★ 15

Drama   1998 • US • Colour • 89min

Vividly capturing the atmosphere of Studio 54 and the energy of the disco era, this ambitious chronicle of the notorious 1970s nightclub from writer/director Mark Christopher is only let down by a formulaic plot. Ryan Phillippe plays the hunky bartender from New Jersey who gains a surrogate family when he is sucked into the decadent, glitzy lifestyle of the spaced-out "in-crowd". Mike Myers is terrific as Steve Rubell, the club's permanently stoned, homosexual emcee. **AJ** Swearing, sex scenes, drug abuse. **DVD** **CS**

Ryan Phillippe *Shane O'Shea* • Salma Hayek *Anita* • Neve Campbell *Julie Black* • Mike Myers *Steve Rubell* • Sela Ward *Billie Auster* • Breckin Meyer *Greg Randazzo* • Sherry Stringfield *Viv* ■ *Dir/Scr* Mark Christopher

Fifty Shades of Black ★ 15

Spoof comedy   2016 • US • Colour • 88min

A *Fifty Shades of Grey* spoof telling the story of the relationship between a young student (Kali Hawk) and mysterious millionaire Christian Black. "Who wrote this, a third-grader?" exclaims star Marlon Wayans in a scene where he reads EL James's original book, but the question could very well be levelled at his own film. It's hard to imagine who would enjoy such a lowbrow feast of bad taste, whose only accomplishment is to prove that the classic movie spoof is well and truly dead. **JL** Swearing, sex scenes, nudity. **DVD**

Marlon Wayans *Christian* • Kali Hawk *Hannah* • Fred Willard *Gary* • Mike Epps *Ron* • Jane Seymour (2) *Claire* • Andrew Bachelor *Jesse* ■ *Dir* Michael Tiddes • *Scr* Marlon Wayans, Rick Alvarez

Fifty Shades of Grey ★★ 18

Erotic drama   2015 • US • Colour • 120min

Student Dakota Johnson is tempted to become a submissive sex slave to dominant mogul Jamie Dornan in this antiseptic adaptation of the first part of EL James's bestselling trilogy. Stripped back to basics by scriptwriter Kelly Marcel under the slick if mannered direction of Sam Taylor-Johnson, the pop-culture phenomenon emerges as a mere soap-opera romance. The kinkiness is fleeting, the nudity softcore, and the S&M more M&S than anything edgily erotic. **AJ** Sex scenes. **DVD** **SL**

Dakota Johnson *Anastasia Steele* • Jamie Dornan *Christian Grey* • Jennifer Ehle *Carla May Wilks* • Marcia Gay Harden *Dr Grace Trevelyan Grey* • Rita Ora *Mia Grey* • Callum Keith Rennie *Ray Steele* ■ *Dir* Sam Taylor-Johnson [Sam Taylor-Wood] • *Scr* Kelly Marcel, from EL James's novel

Fifty Shades Darker

Erotic drama   2017 • US • Colour

This is a preview – no prints were available to review prior to publication: The second instalment of the spankfest based on the novels by EL James, with Dakota Johnson and Jamie Dornan returning as the couple with the tangled relationship. In part two, Dornan's dominance extends from bedroom to boardroom when he buys the company she is working for. After the flaccid reviews of the first film, the press department has ramped things up by saying this could be more explicit. No Sam Taylor-Johnson to whip them into shape this time, though – the director clearly doesn't want to be seen to be trussing up another turkey. **TP**

Dakota Johnson *Anastasia Steele* • Jamie Dornan *Christian Grey* • Rita Ora *Mia Grey* • Kim Basinger *Elena Lincoln* ■ *Dir* James Foley • *Scr* Niall Leonard, from EL James's novel

52 Pick-Up ★★★ 18

Crime thriller   1986 • US • Colour • 103min

The 1980s saw two versions of Elmore Leonard's *52 Pick-Up*, both made by the same company. The first was *The Ambassador*, made in 1984; for the second, made two years later, they kept Leonard's original title and storyline and sensibly asked the novelist to write the script himself. Director John Frankenheimer is way below his best form but still keeps the plot simmering, while Roy Scheider is excellent as the man whose mistress has been murdered because he won't pay the blackmailers. Fans will not be disappointed. **AT** **DVD**

Roy Scheider *Harry Mitchell* • Ann-Margret *Barbara Mitchell* • Vanity *Doreen* • John Glover *Alan Raimy* • Robert Trebor *Leo Franks* • Lonny Chapman *Jim O'Boyle* • Kelly Preston *Cini* • Doug McClure *Mark Averson* ■ *Dir* John Frankenheimer • *Scr* John Steppling, Elmore Leonard, from the novel by Elmore Leonard

Fight Club ★★★★★ 18

Satirical drama   1999 • US • Colour • 133min

Chuck Palahniuk's bestseller is boldly brought to the screen by director David Fincher. The result is a shocking, provocative and highly amusing macho fantasy, as insomniac loser Edward Norton teams up with seditious soap salesman Brad Pitt to form a no-holds-barred fight club as an outlet for their directionless aggression. The growing cult's Project Mayhem takes subversive vandalism into the outside world with a series of ludicrous acts of sabotage. Fincher's satirical fable brilliantly plays with cinematic conventions and climaxes with a shock twist. This charged slice of nihilistic angst is a mesmerising ride through the 1990s male psyche, aided by elaborate production design, unconventional editing, startling images and superlative acting from the leads. **AJ** Violence, swearing, sex scenes. **DVD** **SL**

Brad Pitt *Tyler Durden* • Edward Norton *Narrator* • Helena Bonham Carter *Marla Singer* • Meat Loaf Aday [Meat Loaf] *Robert Paulsen* • Jared Leto *Angel Face* • Rachel Singer *Chloe* ■ *Dir* David Fincher • *Scr* Jim Uhls, from the novel by Chuck Palahniuk • *Cinematographer* Jeff Cronenweth • *Music* The Dust Brothers

The Fighter ★★★★★ 15

Biographical sports drama
2010 • US • Colour • 110min

Based on the career of welterweight boxing champ "Irish" Micky Ward, this rousing crowd-pleaser stars Mark Wahlberg as the fighter whose unlikely career took him from working-class poverty to the heights of pugilistic fame. Director David O Russell expertly handles the shift from gritty realism to the type of triumph-against-the-odds Hollywood finale that the material demands, delivering kinetic, exciting fight sequences and a peppering of humour along the way. Oscar-winning Christian Bale is a mass of crazy energy as Dicky Eklund, Micky's drug-addled half-brother and coach, but it's Wahlberg's lower-key performance as the good-natured scrapper torn between family loyalty and a desire to take a shot at glory that is the movie's real, and utterly irresistible, heart. **AS** Swearing, drug abuse. **DVD** **SL**

Mark Wahlberg *"Irish" Micky Ward* • Christian Bale *Dicky Eklund* • Amy Adams *Charlene Fleming* • Melissa Leo *Alice Ward* • Jack McGee *George Ward* • Miguel Espino *Alfonso Sanchez* • Peter Cunningham *Mike "Machine Gun" Mungin* • Anthony Molinari *Shea Neary* ■ *Dir* David O Russell • *Scr* Eric Johnson, Scott Silver, Paul Tamasy, from a story by Keith Dorrington, Tamasy, Johnson

Fighter Squadron ★★ U

Second World War drama
1948 • US • Colour • 94min

This routine Warner Bros war flick is of moderate interest in that it stars the ever-watchable Edmond O'Brien and Robert Stack as the flyboys struggling against both clichés and Technicolor make-up. It's of more interest today as it features the extremely gauche premiere appearance of superstar-to-be Rock Hudson, cast on looks alone, and whose single-line performance (requiring a phenomenal amount of takes to get right) is barely acceptable. The rest of the movie just about passes muster. **TS**

Edmond O'Brien *Maj Ed Hardin* • Robert Stack *Capt Stu Hamilton* • John Rodney *Col Bill Brickley* • Tom D'Andrea *Sgt Dolan* • Henry Hull *Brig Gen Mike McCready* • Rock Hudson *Lieutenant* ■ *Dir* Raoul Walsh • *Scr* Seton I Miller, Martin Rackin

Fighting ★★★ 15

Action drama 2009 · US/UK · Colour · 102min

A young hustler makes his way in the rough and tumble world of New York's illicit bare-knuckle boxing scene in this slightly-more-than-formulaic slugfest. The choreography's wincingly effective, yet the film's far more impressive when the boys aren't knocking seven bells out of one another. That's when we notice that leading man Channing Tatum (*Step Up*) can actually act, bringing credible sweetness to the romance subplot with waitress Zulay Henao. The result is closer to *Midnight Cowboy* than any number of Jean-Claude Van Damme movies. TJ *DVD* 🅱

Channing Tatum *Shawn MacArthur* · Terrence Howard *Harvey Boarden* · Luis Guzman *Martinez* · Brian White *Evan Hailey* · Zulay Henao *Zulay Velez* · Roger Guenveur Smith *Jack Dancing* · Flaco Navaja *Ray Ray* · Michael Rivera *Ajax* ■ *Dir* Dito Montiel · *Scr* Dito Montiel, Robert Munic

Fighting Caravans ★★★ U

Western 1931 · US · BW · 88min

This excellent, if dated, early Gary Cooper western features him as a young wagon train guide. Fresh from *Morocco* opposite Marlene Dietrich, he is here well paired with striking French actress Lili Damita. Ernest Torrence and Tully Marshall reprise the old-timers they played in *The Covered Wagon*, while Fred Kohler contributes some lively villainy that leads to a spectacular climactic attack by Indians as the travellers cross a river. AE

Gary Cooper *Clint Belmet* · Lili Damita *Felice* · Ernest Torrence *Bill Jackson* · Fred Kohler *Lee Murdock* · Tully Marshall *Jim Bridger* ■ *Dir* Otto Brower, David Burton (1) · *Scr* Edward E Paramore Jr, Keene Thompson, Agnes Brand Leahy, from a novel by Zane Grey

The Fighting Kentuckian ★★★ U

Historical adventure 1949 · US · BW · 94min

This is a genuine curio. Produced by the Duke himself, it details an interesting historical anomaly – the settling in America of Napoleon's exiled officers and their relatives immediately after the defeat at Waterloo. The political aspect isn't really explored, though, merely serving as a background for a rollicking romance with lots of fighting. Wayne's sidekick is Oliver Hardy, who acquits himself well without his usual partner, Stan Laurel; indeed, he's the best reason for viewing. TS

John Wayne *John Breen* · Vera Ralston *Fleurette DeMarchand* · Philip Dorn *Colonel Georges Geraud* · Oliver Hardy *Willie Paine* · Marie Windsor *Ann Logan* · John Howard (1) *Blake Randolph* · Hugo Haas *General Paul DeMarchand* ■ *Dir/Scr* George Waggner

Fighting Mad ★★

Action drama 1976 · US · Colour · 87min

This sleazy, low-budget effort from the Roger Corman factory stars Peter Fonda as an Arkansas rancher's son who declares war on big-business interests and does a Rambo when intimidation turns into murder. Paying a certain amount of lip service to environmental issues, this is really just an excuse to justify some vigilante violence and to allow novice writer/director Jonathan Demme a few opportunities to show off. AT Violence, swearing, nudity

Peter Fonda *Tom Hunter* · Lynn Lowry *Lorene Maddox* · John Doucette *Jeff Hunter* · Philip Carey *Pierce Crabtree* · Scott Glenn *Charlie Hunter* · Kathleen Miller *Carolee Hunter* ■ *Dir/Scr* Jonathan Demme

Fighting Man of the Plains ★★ U

Western 1949 · US · Colour · 93min

Randolph Scott stars as a former Quantrill's Raider, cleaning up a town with the help of outlaw Jesse James, in this sturdy Fox western from skilled producer Nat Holt. As James, Holt cast newcomer Dale Robertson, who later achieved fame in such TV series as *Tales of Wells Fargo* and The

Iron Horse. Look out for *Gone with the Wind*'s carpetbagger Victor Jory. TS

Randolph Scott *Jim Dancer* · Bill Williams *Johnny Tancred* · Victor Jory *Dave Oldham* · Jane Nigh *Florence Peel* · Douglas Kennedy *Ken Vedder* · Joan Taylor *Evelyn Slocum* · Dale Robertson *Jesse James* ■ *Dir* Edwin L Marin · *Scr* Frank Gruber, from his novel *Fighting Man*

The Fighting O'Flynn ★★★ U

Period swashbuckling adventure 1948 · US · BW · 94min

This rousing Napoleonic swashbuckler gives Douglas Fairbanks Jr copious opportunities to prove himself a chip off the old block. He certainly cuts a dash as the Irishman dividing his energies between thwarting the French and foiling obnoxious viceregal aide Richard Greene's plans to marry Helena Carter. But his co-written screenplay also contains elements of knowing humour at the expense of both the genre and the Fairbanks legend, as he ceaselessly jousts and duels, trysts and jests. DP

Douglas Fairbanks Jr *The O'Flynn* · Helena Carter *Lady Benedetta* · Richard Greene *Lord Sedgemouth* · Patricia Medina *Fancy Free* · Arthur Shields *Dooley* · JM Kerrigan *Timothy* · Lumsden Hare *Viceroy* ■ *Dir* Arthur Pierson · *Scr* Douglas Fairbanks Jr, Robert Thoeren, from the novel *The O'Flynn* by Justin Huntly McCarthy

The Fighting Prince of Donegal ★★ U

Swashbuckling adventure 1966 · UK · Colour · 105min

The title tells all – buckles swashed and derring-do done. Peter McEnery is the rebel in Ireland during Elizabethan times, wooing Susan Hampshire and battling a villainous Gordon Jackson, leader of the British troops who kidnaps McEnery's true love and mother. Aimed at youngsters, who may well overlook the cutout castle and the cast-offs dialogue. TH

Peter McEnery *Red Hugh* · Susan Hampshire *Kathleen* · Tom Adams *Henry O'Neill* · Gordon Jackson *Capt Leeds* · Andrew Keir *MacSweeney* · Norman Wooland *Sir John Perrott* ■ *Dir* Michael O'Herlihy · *Scr* Robert Westerby, from the novel *Red Hugh, Prince of Donegal* by Robert T Reilly

The Fighting Seabees ★★★ U

Second World War drama 1944 · US · BW · 99min

Although denied military service during the Second World War, John Wayne did his fair share of fighting on screen in propaganda movies such as this one, which is based on a true story. He stars as the boss of a construction company who orders his workers to take up arms against the invading Japanese. Wayne's hot-headedness causes his buddy's death, leading him to demolish all the enemy in sight, blasting his way to glory. Borden Chase's screenplay worked then, and it almost works now. TS *DVD*

John Wayne *Wedge Donovan* · Susan Hayward *Constance Chesley* · Dennis O'Keefe *Lt Cmdr Bob Yarrow* · William Frawley *Eddie Powers* · Leonid Kinskey *Johnny Novasky* · Jim Kerrigan [JM Kerrigan] *Sawyer Collins* ■ *Dir* Edward Ludwig · *Scr* Borden Chase, Aeneas MacKenzie, from a story by Borden Chase

The Fighting 69th ★★ PG

First World War drama 1940 · US · BW · 86min

James Cagney joins up for the First World War, but breaks down under fire in the trenches. His cowardice results in him sending up a star shell, giving away his regiment's position, causing many deaths. Fortunately there's a kindly, sympathetic priest at hand – good heavens, it's Pat O'Brien, what a surprise – who cures Cagney and gets him firing on all cylinders. A cynical piece of studio propaganda, efficiently directed by William Keighley. AT

James Cagney *Jerry Plunkett* · Pat O'Brien *Father Duffy* · George Brent *Wild Bill Donovan* · Jeffrey Lynn *Joyce Kilmer* · Alan Hale *Sgt Big*

Mike Wynn · Frank McHugh *"Crepe Hanger" Burke* ■ *Dir* William Keighley · *Scr* Norman Reilly Raine, Fred Niblo Jr, Dean Franklin

Fighting Stock ★★ PG

Comedy 1935 · UK · BW · 69min

While at film company Gainsborough, producer Michael Balcon demonstrated a highly catholic taste in comedy, including a yen for the Aldwych farces of Ben Travers, whom Balcon hired to write this comedy. This is not one of the strongest Balcon/Travers collaborations, but brigadier Tom Walls and bumbling nephew Ralph Lynn are on top of their game as they tackle a crotchety neighbour and deliver niece Marie Lohr from blackmailers during a stay in a country cottage. DP *DVD*

Tom Walls *Sir Donald Rowley* · Ralph Lynn *Sidney* · J Robertson Hare [Robertson Hare] *Duck* · Marie Lohr *Barbara Rivers* · Lesley Wareing *Eileen Rivers* · Veronica Rose *Diana Rivers* ■ *Dir* Tom Walls · *Scr* Ben Travers

The Fighting Sullivans ★★★★ U

Biographical drama 1944 · US · BW · 107min

This is the unbearably moving (because you know the outcome) true story of the five brothers of a single family who enlisted, fought, and died together in the Second World War (the American Navy consequently banned all family members from serving on the same ship). A superb cast does full justice to the tragedy of the brothers from Iowa, whose ship was sunk at Guadalcanal. Although the Sullivans are played by virtual unknowns, exceptionally fine acting is provided by Anne Baxter as the wife of Al Sullivan, the last to enlist, and in particular by Thomas Mitchell and Selena Royle as the boys' parents. TS *DVD*

Anne Baxter *Katherine Mary* · Thomas Mitchell *Thomas F Sullivan* · Selena Royle *Alleta Sullivan* · Edward Ryan *Albert Leo Sullivan* · Trudy Marshall *Genevieve "Gen" Sullivan* · John Campbell *Francis Henry Sullivan* · James Cardwell *George Thomas Sullivan* · John Alvin Madison *"Matt" Abel Sullivan* · George Offerman Jr *Joseph Eugene Sullivan* · Ward Bond *Commander Robinson* · Bobby Driscoll *Al as a child* ■ *Dir* Lloyd Bacon · *Scr* Mary C McCall Jr, from a story by Edward Doherty, Jules Schermer

The Fighting Temptations ★★ PG

Musical comedy 2003 · US · Colour · 117min

Director Jonathan Lynn (the co-creator of *Yes, Minister*) is rarely in control of the tone or pacing of this messy amalgam of African-American social attitudes and musical tastes. Cuba Gooding Jr clowns to excess as the cynical ad executive determined to galvanise the choristers at his aunt's church in order to inherit her fortune. But the diverse singing styles of Melba Moore, T-Bone and Beyoncé Knowles, and a feisty turn from LaTanya Richardson, provide some compensation. DP *DVD*

Cuba Gooding Jr *Darrin Hill* · Beyoncé Knowles *Lilly* · Mike Epps *Lucius* · Steve Harvey *Miles the DJ* · LaTanya Richardson *Paulina Pritchett* · Faith Evans *Maryann Hill* · Angie Stone *Alma* · Melba Moore *Bessie Cooley* ■ *Dir* Jonathan Lynn · *Scr* Elizabeth Hunter, Saladin K Patterson, from a story by Elizabeth Hunter

Figures in a Landscape ★★★ 15

Thriller 1970 · UK · Colour · 104min

A nightmare vision of a repressive future? A treatise on the survival of the fittest and the corruption of the innocent? Take your pick in Robert Shaw's reworking of Barry England's novel about two escaped prisoners (Shaw and Malcolm McDowell) who resort to violence to evade the dogged pursuit of a helicopter pilot. Director Joseph Losey cleverly uses the rugged landscape to show the hopelessness of their situation. By keeping the characters at a distance, however, he stops us sharing their plight. DP *DVD*

Robert Shaw *MacConnachie* · Malcolm McDowell *Ansell* · Henry Woolf *Helicopter pilot* · Christopher Malcolm *Helicopter observer* · Pamela Brown *Widow* · Andrew Bradford

Soldier ■ *Dir* Joseph Losey · *Scr* Robert Shaw, from the novel by Barry England · *Cinematographer* Henri Alekan

The File of the Golden Goose ★

Crime thriller 1969 · UK · Colour · 109min

Sam Wanamaker was talented in many fields, but he was not a good film director as this (the first of his five feature outings behind the camera) testifies. Admittedly the ponderous tale of American agent Yul Brynner's pursuit of international counterfeiters is hardly riveting material, but it would be markedly less irksome to watch if it had not been so baldly padded out with uninspired tableaux of the London landscape. This goose is a turkey. TS

Yul Brynner *Peter Novak* · Charles Gray *Nick "the Owl" Harrison* · Edward Woodward *Peter Thompson* · John Barrie *Sloane* ■ *Dir* Sam Wanamaker · *Scr* John C Higgins, James B Gordon, from a story by John C Higgins

The File on Thelma Jordon ★★★

Film noir 1949 · US · BW · 100min

Barbara Stanwyck is a murder suspect who works her spell on a hapless assistant DA, played to meek perfection by Wendell Corey. He has her acquitted, but discovers her true motives. Stanwyck has a terrific, deadly allure and the moody lighting and the music conspire with her, keeping the men fluttering around her like moths to a flame. A second-string *film noir* maybe, but director Robert Siodmak orchestrates it with flair. AT

Barbara Stanwyck *Thelma Jordon* · Wendell Corey *Cleve Marshall* · Paul Kelly (1) *Miles Scott* · Joan Tetzel *Pamela Marshall* · Stanley Ridges *Kingsley Willis* · Richard Rober *Tony Laredo* ■ *Dir* Robert Siodmak · *Scr* Ketti Frings, from a story by Marty Holland

La Fille Coupée en Deux ★★★★ 15

Drama 2007 · Ger/Fr · Colour · 114min

This drama from director Claude Chabrol may not be as pitilessly incisive as his past assaults on the narcissistic bourgeoisie, but it still brims with his trademark satirical savagery. There's a grim fascination in watching novelist François Berléand and indolent pharmaceutical heir Benoît Magimel competing for the affections of ingenuous TV weather presenter Ludivine Sagnier. Although the storytelling is impeccable, Sagnier is perhaps too sweet to play a *femme fatale*. That aside, Chabrol's insights are typically acute – maybe not a masterwork then, but clearly the work of a master. DP French +subtitles.

Ludivine Sagnier *Gabrielle Deneige* · Benoît Magimel *Paul Gaudens* · François Berléand *Charles Saint-Denis* ■ *Dir* Claude Chabrol · *Scr* Claude Chabrol, Cécile Maistre

Film ★★★

Experimental comedy drama 1965 · US · BW · 21min

Written by playwright Samuel Beckett of *Waiting for Godot* fame, this is notable not only for its ambiguity, but also for bringing Buster Keaton back from semi-retirement. Paring cinema down to its visual essentials, it's a parable of an old man fending off the futility of existence and his own obscurity. It hardly goes out of its way to explain itself but it's good to see Buster back again and wielding unusual silent power. TH

Buster Keaton *O* ■ *Dir* Alan Schneider · *Scr* Samuel Beckett · *Cinematographer* Boris Kaufman

Film Socialisme ★★★ PG

Drama 2010 · Swi/Fr · Colour · 97min

Jean-Luc Godard's trademark anger and iconoclasm are still present, as is his audiovisual ingenuity, but something is missing from what the director insists is his final film. Dispensing with subtitles in favour of brusque summations in so-called "Navajo English", Godard challenges non-French-speaking viewers to make what they can of the conversations among the passengers

F

F

aboard a cruise ship and the residents of a country garage. Devotees will be delighted by the dense difficulty, but this is really more idiosyncratic than insightful. DP French, English, German, Burkinabé +subtitles. *DVD*

Catherine Tanvier *The mother* • Christian Sinniger *The father* • Jean-Marc Stehlé *Otto Goldberg* • Patti Smith *The singer* • Robert Malouber *Nobody in real life* • Alain Badiou *The philosopher* ■ *Dir/Scr* Jean-Luc Godard

Un Filme Falado ★★★
Drama   2003 · Por/Fr/It · Colour · 96min

Language may be exclusive, but culture is universal according to Manoel de Oliveira in this engaging guided tour around the Mediterranean. With cinematographer Emmanuel Machuel providing picturesque views of the landmarks between Lisbon and Cairo, Leonor Silveira regales eight-year-old daughter Filipa de Almeida with the myths and mistakes of past civilisations, while casting aspersions on our own age of disposable art and crass celebrity. De Oliveira is less surefooted in the scenes centring on singer Irene Papas, businesswoman Catherine Deneuve and ex-model Stefania Sandrelli, who join captain John Malkovich at his table. DP Portuguese, French, Italian, English, Greek +subtitles.

Leonor Silveira *Rosa Maria* • John Malkovich *Captain John Walesa* • Catherine Deneuve *Delfina* • Stefania Sandrelli *Francesca* • Irene Papas *Helena* • Filipa de Almeida *Maria Joana* • Luis Miguel Cintra *Portuguese actor* ■ *Dir/Scr* Manoel de Oliveira

Filmed in Supermarionation
★★★★ PG
Documentary
2014 · UK · Colour and BW · 118min

Whether you are young or old, the impact of Gerry Anderson and his iconic TV puppet adventures will no doubt have made an impression. This fascinating documentary charts his career from the early basic puppetry of *Twizzle, Torchy the Battery Boy* and western show *Four Feather Falls* via the more sophisticated *Supercar* and *Fireball XL5* and peaks with spectacular colour extravaganzas like *Stingray* and especially *Thunderbirds*. Narrated by *Thunderbirds* characters Lady Penelope (voiced by Anderson's ex-wife, Sylvia) and Parker (David Graham), it's comprehensive, fun and brimming with anecdotes, trivia and intriguing insights. Fans couldn't ask for more. JA *DVD* CS

Gerry Anderson (1) *Gerry Anderson* • Sylvia Anderson • David Graham • Robert Easton ■ *Dir* Stephen La Rivière • *Scr* Stephen La Rivière, Andrew T Smith

Filth ★★★★ 18
Comedy drama
2013 · UK/Ger/Swe/Bel/US · Colour · 93min

Irvine Welsh's stream-of-semiconsciousness novel *Filth*, in which misanthropic, bipolar Edinburgh detective Bruce Robertson descends into a hell of drink, drugs and debasement, is moulded into a near-Shakespearean comic tragedy in the streamlining hand of writer/director Jon Baird. A top-flight supporting cast, including Jamie Bell, Jim Broadbent, Eddie Marsan, Imogen Poots and John Sessions, may just about get a broad-minded audience onside. And in the central role, James McAvoy gives a fearless performance that may be the crowning glory of his career, and further raises the palatability of what remains a deeply unpleasant journey. AC Violence, swearing, drug abuse, sex scenes, nudity. *DVD* *Blu*

James McAvoy *Detective Sergeant Bruce Robertson* • Jamie Bell *Ray "Raymundo" Lennox* • Imogen Poots *Amanda Drummond* • Joanne Froggatt *Mary* • Jim Broadbent *Dr Rossi* • Shirley Henderson *Bunty* • Ron Donachie *Hector* ■ *Dir* Jon S Baird • *Scr* Jon S Baird, from Irvine Welsh's novel

The Filth and the Fury
★★★ 15
Music documentary
2000 · UK/US · Colour · 103min

Director Julien Temple revisits *The Great Rock 'n' Roll Swindle* for a second look at the band with the gift of the gob: the Sex Pistols. Sidelining self-serving manager Malcolm McLaren, this punk retrospective combines comments from surviving band members with unseen archive footage and TV appearances, including the notorious encounter with Bill Grundy. The result is a more accurate and less sensationalised account of the era of safety-pinned, one-chord wonders. DA Swearing, drug abuse, sex scenes. *DVD*

■ *Dir* Julien Temple

The Final ★★★ 18
Horror thriller   2010 · US · Colour · 92min

Tormented students host a murder party to get their revenge on the bullying jocks and prom queens who have made their lives a misery, in a high-school horror liberally borrowing from other recent fright flicks. But a strong ensemble cast of unknowns, stylish photography, a neat vein of dark humour and understated direction mask the more familiar ingredients. There's way too much stagey exposition in the middle, but later this gets scarily nasty without going overboard on gore. The Columbine campus tragedy isn't overtly mentioned, yet it's clearly the motivation. AJ

Marc Donato *Dane* • Jascha Washington *Kurtis* • Whitney Hoy *Bridget* • Justin S Arnold *[Justin Arnold]* *Bradley* • Travis Tedford *Andy* • Julin Heather ■ *Dir* Joey Stewart • *Scr* Jason Kabolati

Final Analysis ★★ 15
Psychological thriller 1992 · US · Colour · 119min

With an alluring surface gloss that suggests more than is there, and a plot so clumsy that it regularly trips over itself, it is astonishing that the quality cast is able to salvage anything from the wreckage of this film. Uma Thurman is psychiatrist Richard Gere's patient and Kim Basinger is Thurman's married sister with whom he soon becomes involved. As the twists and turns in the story stretch credibility to breaking point, it's Basinger who brings character and determination to the heart of the film. JM Violence, swearing, nudity. *DVD*

Richard Gere *Isaac Barr* • Kim Basinger *Heather Evans* • Uma Thurman *Diana Baylor* • Eric Roberts *Jimmy Evans* • Paul Guilfoyle (2) *Mike O'Brien* • Keith David *Detective Huggins* ■ *Dir* Phil Joanou • *Scr* Wesley Strick, from a story by Robert Berger, Wesley Strick

Final Appointment ★★ U
Crime drama   1954 · UK · BW · 65min

Despite cutting a dash in low-budget fare such as this, John Bentley never quite made it as a movie star. Here he plays an reporter who links a series of killings to a wartime court martial. With help from assistant Eleanor Summerfield, he tracks down the sole surviving officer involved in the trial, but there's a sting in the tail. An undistinguished sequel followed. DP

John Bentley *Mike Billings* • Eleanor Summerfield *Jenny Drew* • Hubert Gregg *Hartnell* • Liam Redmond *Inspector Corcoran* • Meredith Edwards *Tom Martin* • Jean Lodge *Laura Robens* • Sam Kydd *Vickery* • Charles Farrell (2) *Percy* • Arthur Lowe *Barratt* ■ *Dir* Terence Fisher • *Scr* Kenneth Hayles, from a story by Sidney Nelson, Maurice Harrison

Final Approach ★ 15
Thriller   1991 · US · Colour · 96min

This *Twilight Zone*-style science-fiction thriller tries for zest, but lacks any originality. Debut director Eric Steven Stahl emphasises technology over content in this tale of a test pilot, played by the traditionally dour James B Sikking, who is interrogated after an accident involving a top-secret plane. The always reliable Hector Elizondo plays the psychiatrist probing his past. Gimmicky and uninvolving, this is

notable only for its pioneering use of digital sound. RS

James B Sikking *Colonel Jason J Halsey* • Hector Elizondo *Dr Dio Gottlieb* • Madolyn Smith Osborne *[Madolyn Smith]* *Casey Halsey* • Kevin McCarthy *General Geller* • Cameo Kneuer *Brooke Halsey* ■ *Dir* Eric Steven Stahl • *Scr* Eric Steven Stahl, Gerald Laurence

Final Combination ★★ 18
Crime thriller   1993 · US · Colour · 89min

A (failed) bid to turn former British light middleweight boxing champ Gary Stretch into a Hollywood action star, this sometimes unsavoury serial-killer outing also features hard working *Reservoir Dogs* cult actor Michael Madsen as the dogged cop on his trail. Stretch is actually quite menacing as the boxing obsessive who has left a trail of pulped faces across the USA. JF Swearing, violence, sex scenes.

Michael Madsen *Det Matt Dickson* • Lisa Bonet *Catherine Briggs* • Gary Stretch *Richard Welton* • Tim Russ *Det Chuck Rowland* • Damian Chapa *Donato* • Carmen Argenziano *Lt Stein* • Eric DaRe *Bouncer* • *Dir* Nigel Dick • *Scr* Larry Golin, Jonathan Tydor

The Final Comedown ★★
Blaxploitation thriller
1972 · US · Colour · 83min

This fairly average slice of blaxploitation has a stronger political slant than usual. It stars Billy Dee Williams as a young black man who gets mixed up with a Black Panther style organisation planning to make their mark in the cosy white middle-class suburbs. The political message is a little muddled and, as is often the case with these blaxploitation thrillers, the 1970s fashions provide the most entertainment. JF

Billy Dee Williams *Johnny Johnson* • D'Urville Martin *Billy Joe Ashley* • Celia Kaye *Rene Freeman* • Raymond St Jacques *Imir* ■ *Dir/Scr* Oscar Williams

The Final Countdown
★★★ PG
Science-fiction thriller
1980 · US · Colour · 98min

What would have happened if the Americans possessed modern aircraft carriers and nuclear weapons during the time of the attack on Pearl Harbor? That's the ingenious premise of this absorbing thriller as Kirk Douglas and Martin Sheen sail into a time warp, and have the power to alter history at the touch of a button. Reminiscent of the *Twilight Zone* but on a big budget, the film was given unprecedented access to film aboard the USS *Nimitz*. AT *DVD*

Kirk Douglas *Captain Matthew Yelland* • Martin Sheen *Warren Lasky* • Katharine Ross *Laurel Scott* • James Farentino *Commander Richard Owens* • Ron O'Neal *Commander Dan Thurman* • Charles Durning *Senator Samuel Chapman* • Victor Mohica *Black Cloud* ■ *Dir* Don Taylor • *Scr* David Ambrose, Gerry Davis, Thomas Hunter, Peter Powell

The Final Curtain ★★★ 15
Black comedy drama 2002 · UK · Colour · 79min

Director Patrick Harkins, in his debut, occasionally attempts to make too much of an impression in this satire on TV quiz shows, transient celebrity and the ruthlessness of showbusiness. However, Peter O'Toole is in bravura form as the veteran UK TV presenter whose decision to allow novelist Adrian Lester to pen his biography coincides with a battle to sell the concept of his family-friendly format to an American network in the face of fierce competition from his grotesque rival, Aidan Gillen. Barnstorming, if unsubtle, fun. DP *DVD*

Peter O'Toole *JJ Curtis* • Adrian Lester *Jonathan Stitch* • Aidan Gillen *Dave Turner* • Julia Sawalha *Karen* • Ralph Brown (2) *Timothy* • Henry Goodman *Ed Nbrezki* • Patrick Malahide *Dr Colworth* • Ian McNeice *Priest* ■ *Dir* Patrick Harkins • *Scr* John Hodge

Final Cut ★ 18
Drama   1998 · UK · Colour · 90min

This mock-docudrama was released, tellingly, at the height of "Cool Britannia", when a home-grown product, from pop to art, was greeted with exaggerated fanfare. Jude Law, then-spouse Sadie Frost and a bunch of stage schoolmates play themselves in a sleazy, North London-set chamber piece about backstabbing, drug-taking and deceit among a group of stage schoolmates. The material is thin and the net result is like watching someone else's home movie. AC Swearing. *DVD*

Ray Winstone *Ray* • Jude Law *Jude* • Sadie Frost *Sadie* • Holly Davidson *Holly* • John Beckett *John* • Mark Burdis *Mark* • Perry Benson *Tony* • Lisa Marsh *Lisa* ■ *Dir/Scr* Ray Burdis, Dominic Anciano

The Final Cut ★★ 12
Futuristic science-fiction thriller
2004 · Can/US/Ger · Colour · 90min

Robin Williams delivers here another performance of subtle understatement. He plays a "cutter", whose job is to splice together the memories of the recently deceased into a visual tribute of the dead person's life. However, an assignment to work on the life of one of the key executives involved in the controversial memory technology not only attracts the attention of opponents of the process – led by former cutter Jim Caviezel – but reawakens some buried secrets of his own. Omar Naim never really exploits the premise's full potential and this runs out of steam. JF Violence, swearing. *DVD*

Robin Williams *Alan Hakman* • Mira Sorvino *Delila* • Mimi Kuzyk *Thelma* • Thom Bishops *Hasan* • Jim Caviezel *Fletcher* • Brendan Fletcher *Michael* • Vincent Gale *Simon* ■ *Dir/Scr* Omar Naim

Final Destination ★★★ 15
Horror thriller   2000 · US · Colour · 93min

The X-Files veteran James Wong makes his feature debut with this entertaining thriller, in which the principals are named after movie horror legends. Devon Sawa's premonition of a midair disaster comes explosively true and Death begins to stalk those who escaped, thanks to Sawa's timely intervention. The premise is flawed and the exposition clumsy, but the methods of demise are as hilarious as they are ingenious. DP Violence, swearing. *DVD* *Blu*

Devon Sawa *Alex Browning* • Ali Larter *Clear Rivers* • Kerr Smith *Carter Horton* • Kristen Cloke *Valerie Lewton* • Seann William Scott *Billy Hitchcock* • Chad E Donella *Tod Waggner* • Amanda Detmer *Terry Chaney* ■ *Dir* James Wong • *Scr* Glen Morgan, James Wong, Jeffrey Reddick, Lara Fox, from a story by Jeffrey Reddick

Final Destination 2 ★★★ 15
Horror thriller   2002 · US · Colour · 86min

David R Ellis directs this effective sequel to the sleeper hit. This time around it's perturbed teenager AJ Cook who prompts Death to resume his stalking, after her premonitions save her and a group of motorists from a freeway pile-up. While the film is no more sophisticated than the original, it's a tense mix of innovative gore sequences and irony-laden dialogue, resulting in an over-the-top thrill-ride with no pretensions. SF *DVD* *Blu*

Ali Larter *Clear Rivers* • AJ Cook *Kimberly Corman* • Michael Landes *Officer Thomas Burke* • Terrence "T C" Carson *Eugene Dix* • Jonathan Cherry *Rory* • Keegan Connor Tracy *Kat* • Sarah Carter *Shaina* • Lynda Boyd *Nora Carpenter* ■ *Dir* David R Ellis • *Scr* J Mackye Gruber, Eric Bress, from a story by J Mackye Gruber, Eric Bress, Jeffrey Reddick, from characters by Jeffrey Reddick

Final Destination 3 ★★★ 15
Horror thriller   2006 · US · Colour · 88min

Like its predecessors, this delivers more gruesome deaths and ghoulish giggles. High-school graduate Mary Elizabeth Winstead is boarding the Devil's Flight rollercoaster ride when she has a terrifying premonition of a fatal accident. After she gets off, a scuffle breaks out and those classmates ejected from the ride then watch as disaster ensues. One by one they then fall victim to a series of elaborately structured and gory fatalities. AJ **DVD** ⬗

Mary Elizabeth Winstead *Wendy Christensen* • Ryan Merriman *Kevin Fischer* • Kris Lemche *Ian McKinley* • Alexz Johnson *Erin* • Sam Easton *Frankie Cheeks* • Jesse Moss *Jason Wise* ■ *Dir* James Wong • *Scr* James Wong, Glen Morgan, from a story by Jeffrey Reddick

The Final Destination ★★ 15

Horror thriller   2009 · US/Can · Colour · 78min

The fourth instalment in the grisly horror franchise sticks rigidly to the established death-premonition formula, to the point where viewers might reasonably think they've mistakenly sat down in front of one of its predecessors. David R Ellis, who also directed the second film in the series, pulls off a bravura opening set piece. But his efforts to top the gore content of the previous movies ultimately leads to bouts of gratuitous stomach-churning nastiness that quickly become wearisome. A further chapter was released in 2011. TeS Violence, swearing, sex scenes, nudity. **DVD** ⬗

Bobby Campo *Nick O'Bannon* • Shantel VanSanten *Lori Milligan* • Haley Webb *Janet Cunningham* • Nick Zano *Hunt Wynorski* • Mykelti Williamson *George Lanter* • Krista Allen *MILF/Samantha* ■ *Dir* David R Ellis • *Scr* Eric Bress, from characters by Jeffrey Reddick

Final Destination 5 ★★★ 15

Horror   2011 · US · Colour · 91min

The deaths are as elaborate and gory as ever in the fifth outing of the horror franchise. Here, a lucky few survive a bridge collapse, only to be told that they've merely delayed their grim reaping. Making his feature debut after assisting James Cameron on *Titanic* and *Avatar*, director Steven Quale keeps the slaughter visually impressive - the horrific opener being easily the most spectacular in the series. The turgid exposition doesn't help but fans will enjoy how it cleverly connects with the original movie, and replays every death from the series so far over the closing credits. AJ ⬗ ⬘

Nicholas D'Agosto *Sam Lawton* • Emma Bell *Molly* • Miles Fisher *Peter* • Courtney B Vance *Agent Block* • Arlen Escarpeta *Nathan* • David Koechner *Dennis* • Tony Todd *Bludworth* • PJ Byrne *Isaac* ■ *Dir* Steven Quale • *Scr* Eric Heisserer, from characters by Jeffrey Reddick

Final Fantasy: the Spirits Within ★★★ PG

Animated science-fiction adventure   2001 · Jpn/US · Colour · 101min

Japan's long-running computer-game franchise provides the bare, thematic bones for this 100-per-cent computer-animated movie. The film follows the quest of brilliant young scientist Dr Aki Ross (voiced by *ER's* Ming-Na) to find a peaceful end to the ongoing war between mankind and invading "phantoms" in 2065. The story is simple sci-fi stuff, but it's strong and intelligent enough to prevent this being merely an expensive exhibition match for the US-Japanese animators. AC **DVD** ⬗

Ming-Na *Dr Aki Ross* • Alec Baldwin *Capt Gray Edwards* • Ving Rhames *Ryan* • Steve Buscemi *Neil* • Peri Gilpin *Jane* • Donald Sutherland *Dr Sid* • James Woods *General Hein* • Keith David *Council member* • Jean Simmons *Council member* ■ *Dir* Hironobu Sakaguchi, Motonori Sakakibara • *Scr* Al Reinert, Jeff Vintar, from a story by Hironobu Sakaguchi

Final Girl ★★ 15

Action horror   2015 · Can/US · Colour · 80min

Sadistic teen killers meet their match when they terrorise Abigail Breslin's blue-eyed blonde in this disappointing thriller. The quartet, a sort of serial-killing version of the Riot Club, have a thing for hunting blondes in a nearby forest but unfortunately for them, their latest "victim" (Breslin) has been trained since childhood to be an instrument of vengeance for mystery man

Wes Bentley. Too mysterious for its own good. JA Violence, swearing. **DVD**

Abigail Breslin *Veronica* • Wes Bentley *Man* • Logan Huffman *Danny* • Alexander Ludwig *Chris* ■ *Dir* Tyler Shields • *Scr* Adam Prince, from a story by Stephen Scarlata, Alejandro Seri, Johnny Silver (2)

The Final Programme ★★ 15

Science-fiction fantasy   1973 · UK · Colour · 85min

The sight of the misshapen messiah will certainly send shudders down the spine of those who have stuck with the stylised imagery and apocalyptic incidents that comprise this baffling adaptation of one of Michael Moorcock's "Jerry Cornelius" stories. Jon Finch's bid to save both his sister and the planet is confounded by director Robert Fuest's preoccupation with look over logic. DP **DVD**

Jon Finch *Jerry Cornelius* • Jenny Runacre *Miss Brunner* • Hugh Griffith *Professor Hira* • Patrick Magee *Dr Baxter* • Sterling Hayden *Major Wrongway Lindbergh* • Graham Crowden *Dr Smiles* • George Coulouris *Dr Powys* ■ *Dir* Robert Fuest • *Scr* Robert Fuest, from the novel by Michael Moorcock

The Final Test ★★★ U

Comedy   1953 · UK · BW · 87min

Inspired by Don Bradman's famous second-ball dismissal in his final Test match, this charming film was adapted by Terence Rattigan from his own TV play. Jack Warner gives a no-nonsense performance as the old pro, only to be totally outplayed by Robert Morley as the poet who'd give anything to be a cricketer (much to the bewilderment of Warner's pretentious son, Ray Jackson). Anthony Asquith directs with a straight bat, producing a picture that is as quintessentially English as *Test Match Special*. Cricketing legends including Len Hutton, Denis Compton and Alec Bedser have cameos. DP **DVD**

Jack Warner *Sam Palmer* • Robert Morley *Alexander Whitehead* • Brenda Bruce *Cora* • Ray Jackson *Reggie Palmer* • George Relph *Syd Thompson* • Adrianne Allen *Aunt Ethel* • Len Hutton *Frank Jarvis* • Denis Compton • Alec Bedser ■ *Dir* Anthony Asquith • *Scr* Terence Rattigan, from his TV play

Find Me Guilty ★★★ 15

Biographical crime drama   2006 · US/Ger · Co our · 119min

Director Sidney Lumet's penultimate film stars Vin Diesel as Jackie DiNorscio, the oafish but charismatic mobster who decided to represent himself in one of the longest trials in US history. Lumet portrays this true story as a light comedy, although the film does have its serious moments, but the broad "wiseguy" stereotypes and courtroom setting become repetitive, especially given the long running time. Diesel's surprising comic timing gives the film a certain appeal, and he also handles the more dramatic final scenes capably. JL Swearing. **DVD**

Vin Diesel *Giacomo "Jackie Dee" DiNorscio* • Peter Dinklage *Ben Klandis* • Linus Roache *Sean Kierney* • Ron Silver *Judge Finestein* • Annabella Sciorra *Bella DiNorscio* ■ *Dir* Sidney Lumet • *Scr* Sidney Lumet, TJ Mancini, Robert J McCrea

Find the Lady ★ PG

Comedy   1976 · Can/UK · Colour · 85min

Hardly a film to boost the reputation of British or Canadian movie-making, this politically incorrect comedy is packed with the kind of raucous humour that rocks pubs towards last orders. John Candy and Lawrence Dane star as incompetent cops stomping their way through the upper classes in search of a missing socialite. DP **DVD**

Lawrence Dane *Detective Sergeant Roscoe Broom* • John Candy *Officer Kopek* • Mickey Rooney *Trigger* • Dick Emery *Leo-Hugo* • Peter Cook *JK Lewenhak* • Alexandra Bastedo *Victoria* ■ *Dir* John Trent • *Scr* Kenneth R Hughes

Finders Keepers ★ U

Musical comedy   1966 · UK · Colour · 85min

Five years after they made *The Young Ones*, Cliff Richard and Robert Morley were reunited for this dismal romp that, more significantly, marked the end of Cliff's screen collaboration with The Shadows. The story of a clean-cut combo who find an American atom bomb off the Spanish coast is too ridiculous to contemplate, and Cliff doesn't have any decent songs to distract us. DP

Cliff Richard *Cliff* • Robert Morley *Colonel Roberts* • Bruce Welch • Hank Marvin • Brian Bennett • John Rostill • John Le Mesurier *Mr X* ■ *Dir* Sidney Hayers • *Scr* Michael Pertwee, from a story by George H Brown • *Music/lyrics* The Shadows

Finders Keepers ★ 15

Comedy   1984 · US · Colour · 91min

A deeply depressing blip on Richard Lester's directorial career, this is a misguided, laugh-free comedy caper. Lightweights Michael O'Keefe and Beverly D'Angelo find themselves caught in an increasingly hysterical chase for a fortune hidden in a coffin. Pamela Stephenson is among those who bravely hide their embarrassment. Notable mainly for an early film appearance by Jim Carrey. JF

Michael O'Keefe *Michael Rangeloff* • Beverly D'Angelo *Standish Logan* • Pamela Stephenson *Georgiana Latimer* • Louis Gossett Jr *Century* • Ed Lauter *Josef Sirola* • Jim Carrey *Lane Biddlecoff* ■ *Dir* Richard Lester • *Scr* Ronny Graham, Terence Marsh, Charles Dennis, from the novel *The Next to Last Train Ride* by Charles Dennis

Finders Keepers, Lovers Weepers ★★ 18

Crime drama   1968 · US · Colour · 71min

This uncharacteristic crime drama from soft-core sex director Russ Meyer has too much moralising and a crueller edge than normal. Sleazy topless nightclub owner Paul Lockwood, his unfaithful wife and her bartender lover are held captive by two burglars employed by the tough brothel madam he's seeing on the sly. Sadly, this has little of Meyers's trademark titillation, sexual satire or broad humour. AJ Nudity. **DVD**

Anne Chapman *Kelly* • Paul Lockwood *Paul Lockwood, actor* • Gordon Wescourt *Ray* • Duncan McLeod *Cal* • Robert Rudelson *Feeny* • Lavelle Roby *Claire* • Jan Sinclair *Christiana* • Joey Duprez *Joy* • Nick Wolcuff *Nick* ■ *Dir* Russ Meyer • *Scr* Richard Zachary, from a story by Russ Meyer

Finding a Family ★★★ PG

Drama based on a true story   2011 · US · Colour · 88min

American teenager Jared Abrahamson seems to encounter nothing but bad luck in this intensely moving and inspirational true story. Consequently, viewers may need their hankies, as the immigrant's son battles to pursue his Harvard dream after his mum's escalating mental problems force him into care. It's all very manipulative but clearly heartfelt, driving home positive messages about education, perseverance and family. A likeable Abrahamson makes you really root for him, while Kim Delaney brings commendable pathos and dignity to her role as his struggling mother. SF

Kim Delaney *Ileana* • Jared Abrahamson *Alex Chivescu* • Sarah-Jane Redmond *Suzanne Bante* • Paul McGillion *Jim Bante* ■ *Dir* Mark Jean • *Scr* Pamela Wallace

Finding Forrester ★★★ 12

Drama   2000 · US/Can · Colour · 130min

Sean Connery stars in this drama from Gus Van Sant about literary aspirations. Connery (who also co-produced) plays an elderly, reclusive writer, a JD Salinger-like figure seemingly crippled by the success of his first novel. Living in the Bronx he befriends black teenager Rob Brown, a basketball ace with a brilliant literary streak, forced to downplay his intelligence. An unlikely friendship grows, as Connery

recognises and nurtures this talent - despite opposition from F Murray Abraham's malicious professor. This film has a mood and tempo that transcend manipulated cosiness. TH **DVD**

Sean Connery *William Forrester* • Rob Brown *Jamal Wallace* • F Murray Abraham *Professor Crawford* • Anna Paquin *Claire Spence* • Busta Rhymes *Terrell* • April Grace *Ms Joyce* • Michael Pitt *Coleridge* • Michael Nouri *Dr Spence* ■ *Dir* Gus Van Sant • *Scr* Mike Rich

Finding Graceland ★★ PG

Road movie   1999 · US · Colour · 92min

Depressed following the death of his wife, Johnathon Schaech takes to the road in his beaten-up car and picks up Harvey Keitel who insists he's the real Elvis. So do most of the awe-struck people they encounter on the road to Graceland in a whimsical saga about finding oneself and being true to your own feelings. Religious metaphor and *Blue Suede Shoes* nostalgia make for an uneasy mix and it does teeter on the edge of open-mouthed stupidity. But Elvis fans will love it, and Bridget Fonda is wonderful as a Marilyn Monroe impersonator. AJ **DVD**

Harvey Keitel *Elvis* • Bridget Fonda *Ashley* • Johnathon Schaech *Byron Gruman* • Gretchen Mol *Beatrice Gruman* • David Stewart *Purvis* ■ *Dir* David Winkler • *Scr* Jason Horwitch, from a story by David Winkler, Horwitch

Finding Mrs Claus ★★

Seasonal romantic comedy   2012 · Can · Colour · 89min

Mira Sorvino returns to *Romy and Michele* territory as Santa's romantically neglected wife, who magics herself into a bubbly hottie and then nips off to Las Vegas to provide some wish-fulfilment. But, as the innuendo-laden humour quickly emphasises, America's Sin City is a far cry from the North Pole. Fortunately, Mrs Claus's regret-filled husband (Will Sasso) is soon on her tail, adding a splash of fun to the convenient solutions and lessons of the heart. SF

Mira Sorvino *Jessica Claus* • Will Sasso *Kris Claus* • Laura Vandervoort *Noelle* • Aislyn Watson *Hope* ■ *Dir* Mark Jean • *Scr* Andrea Seybold, Kate Wharton, Andrea Stevens, from a story by Seybold, Wharton

Finding Nemo ★★★★★ U

Animated comedy adventure   2003 · US · Colour · 96min

This computer-generated animated feature is a rainbow-hued delight, overflowing with innovation and vitality. Australia's Great Barrier Reef provides a stunning starting point for this aquatic fable, as single-parent clownfish Marlin (voiced by Albert Brooks) sees his beloved only son, Nemo, snatched up by a scuba diver. From then on, it's a nonstop journey of visual excitement, as the distraught father sets off to rescue his offspring, encountering a host of colourful characters along the way. The voice casting is inspired, with Willem Dafoe, Geoffrey Rush and Eric Bana among those contributing supplementary texture to this marvellous sensory experience. SF **DVD** ⬗ **CS**

Albert Brooks *Marlin* • Ellen DeGeneres *Dory* • Alexander Gould *Nemo* • Willem Dafoe *Gill* • Geoffrey Rush *Nigel* • Barry Humphries *Bruce* • Austin Pendleton *Gurgle* • John Ratzenberger *Fish school voice* • Allison Janney *Peach* • Eric Bana *Anchor* ■ *Dir* Andrew Stanton, Lee Unkrich • *Scr* Andrew Stanton, Bob Peterson, David Reynolds, from a story by Andrew Stanton

Finding Dory ★★★★★ U

Animated adventure   2016 · US · Colour · 102min

Thirteen years on from Pixar's family adventure *Finding Nemo*, Dory, the plucky blue tang who helped Nemo's anxiety-wracked dad scour the oceans for his missing son, gets an origin story of her very own. But for Dory, the first step to retracing her own parents is remembering that she actually had any. The level of invention is simply dazzling, the comedy adeptly caters for parents and kids alike, while the story of a little fish learning to triumph over the disability that has thus far defined her sprinkles genuine tears amid the abundant laughter. TJ ▪ Sp CS

Ellen DeGeneres *Dory* • Albert Brooks *Marlin* • Hayden Rolence *Nemo* • Ed O'Neill *Hank* • Diane Keaton *Jenny* • Eugene Levy *Charlie* • Idris Elba *Fluke* ▪ *Dir* Andrew Stanton • *Scr* Victoria Strouse, Andrew Stanton, from a story by Stanton

Finding Neverland ★★★★ PG
Biographical period drama
2004 · US · Colour · 96min

Fantasy and reality combine to magical effect in this deeply affecting and beautifully crafted account of the creation and evolution of the children's classic *Peter Pan*. A perfectly cast Johnny Depp portrays the young-at-heart Scottish playwright JM Barrie, whose career is reinvigorated when he befriends the four fatherless Llewelyn Davies boys and their recently widowed mother Sylvia (Kate Winslet). Depp is magnificent, alternating between playful and sensitive as the joys and tragedies of this inspirational relationship unfold. It's a performance of genuine emotion, superbly complemented by Winslet's tender turn. SF
DVD Blu

Johnny Depp *Sir James Matthew Barrie* • Kate Winslet *Sylvia Llewelyn Davies* • Julie Christie *Mrs Emma du Maurier* • Radha Mitchell *Mary Ansell Barrie* • Dustin Hoffman *Charles Frohman* • Kelly Macdonald *"Peter Pan"* • Ian Hart *Sir Arthur Conan Doyle* • Eileen Essell *Mrs Snow* • Paul Whitehouse *Stage manager* • Freddie Highmore *Peter Llewelyn Davies* ▪ *Dir* Marc Forster • *Scr* David Magee, from the the play *The Man Who Was Peter Pan* by Allan Knee

Finding North ★★★ 15
Road movie
1997 · US · Colour · 90min

Tanya Wexler's feature debut takes an off-the-beaten-track approach to the road movie. Mixing gentle character comedy with life-affirming revelation, it features John Benjamin Hickey as a man with a mission – a Texan quest set by his dead lover – who is joined by Wendy Makkena as a just-sacked, 30-something Brooklynite desperate to escape the clutches of her shrewish Jewish mother. Played to the pleasingly melancholic strains of a country soundtrack, the film tackles the Aids issue with sensitivity and avoids unnecessary sentimentality. DP Swearing. *DVD*

Wendy Makkena *Rhonda Portelli* • John Benjamin Hickey *Travis Furlong* • Anne Bobby *Debi* • Rebecca Creskoff *Gina* • Angela Pietropinto *Mama Portelli* ▪ *Dir* Tanya Wexler • *Scr* Kim Powers

Finding Vivian Maier
★★★★ 12
Documentary
2014 · US · Colour and BW · 84min

This documentary about former nanny Vivian Maier who, after her death, was revealed to be a stunningly talented photographer, is both sympathetic and compelling. In 2007 director John Maloof bought an old box of negatives and, amazed by their quality, resolved to find out who took them. He and co-director Charlie Siskel reveal a complex, difficult character and hint at darker elements to Maier's personality as they try to bring this intensely private woman's life into focus. AS In English, French. *DVD* Blu

Vivian Maier • John Maloof ▪ *Dir/Scr* John Maloof, Charlie Siskel

A Fine Madness ★★★
Black comedy
1966 · US · Colour · 105min

This is probably the darkest screwball comedy ever made and it undoubtedly would have been bleaker still if studio boss Jack Warner hadn't demanded last-minute changes. Sean Connery gives a most vigorous performance as a poet devoid of inspiration and driven to distraction by the women in his life. Often painfully funny, but it's pretty misogynistic, with Joanne Woodward and Jean Seberg doing well with a script that has no time for them. DP

Sean Connery *Samson Shillitoe* • Joanne Woodward *Rhoda Shillitoe* • Jean Seberg *Lydia West* • Patrick O'Neal (1) *Dr Oliver West* • Colleen

Dewhurst *Dr Vera Kropotkin* • Clive Revill *Dr Menken* ▪ *Dir* Irvin Kershner • *Scr* Elliot Baker, from his novel

A Fine Mess ★ PG
Comedy
1986 · US · Colour · 86min

Had Blake Edwards swapped the word "hideous" for "fine", he would have been nearer the mark. Ted Danson hits an all-time career low as an actor who stumbles upon a plot to dope a horse before the big race, only to find himself hurtling around Los Angeles in some of the most shambolic chase sequences you've ever seen. Embarrassing to watch. DP

Ted Danson *Spence Holden* • Howie Mandel *Dennis Powell* • Richard Mulligan *Wayne "Turnip" Farragalla* • Stuart Margolin *Maurice "Binky" Dzundza* • Maria Conchita Alonso *Claudia Pazzo* • Jennifer Edwards *Ellen Frankenthaler* • Paul Sorvino *Tony Pazzo* • Dennis Franz *Phil* ▪ *Dir/Scr* Blake Edwards

A Fine Pair ★
Crime comedy drama   1968 · It · Colour · 89min

Director Francesco Maselli never comes to terms with the tone or the pacing of this crass crime caper. The basic premise is sound enough, with Claudia Cardinale suckering New York cop Rock Hudson into "returning" the priceless jewels that a thief of her acquaintance has stolen from an Austrian villa. Hudson looks bored and the romantic by-play between the leads is tiresome. DP Italian dubbed.

Rock Hudson *Captain Mike Harmon* • Claudia Cardinale *Esmeralda Marini* • Tomas Milian *Roger* • Leon Askin *Chief Wellman* ▪ *Dir* Francesco Maselli • *Scr* Francesco Maselli, Luisa Montagnana, Larry Gelbart, Virgil C Leone, from a story by Luisa Montagnana

The Finest Hour ★★ 15
War action thriller   1991 · US · Colour · 100min

Before Rob Lowe discovered there was more fun to be had in sending up his smoothie image than in playing it straight, he found himself relegated to straight-to-video fare such as this tired thriller. He plays a cocky young SEAL recruit who falls out with buddy Gale Hansen over a girl, in between fighting the Iraqis. JF Swearing, violence, brief nudity.

Rob Lowe *Hammer* • Gale Hansen *Dean* • Tracy Griffith *Barbara* • Eb Lottimer *Bosco* • Baruch Dror *Greenspan* • Daniel Dieker *Albie* • Michael Fountain *Carter* ▪ *Dir* Shimon Dotan • *Scr* Shimon Dotan, Stuart Schoffman

The Finest Hours ★★★ 12A
Action thriller based on a true story
2015 · US · Colour · 117min

A daring real-life sea rescue off Cape Cod in 1952 inspired this effects-enabled disaster movie, with Chris Pine as the square-jawed Coast Guard sailor who leads his men into the mountainous surf. Although the characterisation in this Disney production is just a little too safe and sanitised, the movie becomes surprisingly gripping. We're watching digital rather than genuine sea spray, but the historical basis makes the drama powerful, as does Casey Affleck's brooding turn as the engineer on board the stricken tanker. TJ Sp

Chris Pine *Bernie Webber* • Casey Affleck *Ray Sybert* • Ben Foster *Richard Livesey* • Eric Bana *Daniel Cluff* • Holliday Grainger *Miriam* ▪ *Dir* Craig Gillespie • *Scr* Eric Johnson, Paul Tamasy, Scott Silver, from the non-fiction book by Casey Sherman, Michael J Tougias

The Finger Points ★★
Crime drama   1931 · US · BW · 87min

Richard Barthelmess stars as a low-paid newspaper reporter who compromises his integrity by allowing gang leaders to buy his silence. This low-key crime drama is good in parts. Fay Wray is the girl who attempts to get Barthelmess to mend his ways, but Clark Gable appears as a gangster, and John Francis Dillon directs competently enough. RK

Richard Barthelmess *Breckenridge Lee* • Fay Wray *Marcia Collins* • Regis Toomey *Charlie "Breezy" Russell* • Clark Gable *Louis*

Blanco • Robert Elliott *City editor* ▪ *Dir* John Francis Dillon • *Scr* Robert Lord, from a story by John Monk Saunders, WR Burnett

Fingers ★★★★ 18
Psychological drama   1978 · US · Colour · 89min

James Toback's directorial debut is a strangely erotic and ominously threatening drama about a concert pianist who also collects debts for the Mob. The edgy direction and Harvey Keitel's compelling performance caught the attention of several major critics, including David Thomson and Pauline Kael, but the film did not find an audience. Toback is undeniably talented, but wayward, and his career has never really got going, but as studio-financed oddities go, this one is unmissable. Remade in 2005 as *The Beat That My Heart Skipped*. AT

Harvey Keitel *Jimmy Angelelli* • Tisa Farrow *Carol* • Jim Brown *Deems* • Michael V Gazzo *Ben Angelelli* • Marian Seldes *Mother* • Carole Francis *Christa* • Georgette Muir *Anita* • Danny Aiello *Butch* ▪ *Dir/Scr* James Toback

Fingers at the Window ★
Horror mystery   1942 · US · BW · 80min

Mad, bad Basil Rathbone impersonates the head of an asylum and hypnotises the inmates to carry out a string of axe murders. Actor Lew Ayres and his girlfriend Laraine Day (stars of the popular *Dr Kildare* series at the time) follow the trail of the "Robot Murders" (as the posters hyped it) and bring Rathbone to justice. Very dated and weakly directed. AJ

Lew Ayres *Oliver Duffy* • Laraine Day *Edwina Brown* • Basil Rathbone *Dr H Santelle* • Walter Kingsford *Dr Cromwell* • Miles Mander *Dr Kurt Immelman* ▪ *Dir* Charles Lederer • *Scr* Rose Caylor, Lawrence P Bachmann, from a story by Rose Caylor

Finian's Rainbow ★★★ U
Musical   1968 · US · Colour · 180min

It's tempting to suggest that the reason this satirical Broadway musical took 21 years to make it to the screen was because studio executives recognised that its magic works best on the stage. Even old hands would have struggled to balance the whimsical story of a leprechaun searching for his stolen gold with sharp insights into racism and greed. Directing his first film for a major studio, Francis Ford Coppola fumbles both fantasy and sermon. However, Fred Astaire is as charmingly watchable as ever. DP *DVD*

Fred Astaire *Finian McLonergan* • Petula Clark *Sharon McLonergan* • Tommy Steele *Og* • Don Francks *Woody* • Barbara Hancock *Susan the Silent* • Keenan Wynn *Judge Billboard Rawkins* ▪ *Dir* Francis Ford Coppola • *Scr* EY Harburg, Fred Saidy, from their play

Finishing School ★★
Drama   1934 · US · BW · 70min

Frances Dee has the leading role of the pupil at an exclusive girls' school who becomes pregnant, but most interest in this drama now resides in a perky performance by Ginger Rogers. She plays Dee's madcap roommate dispensing the wisecracks, and Billie Burke also has fun as Dee's selfish mother. RKO made the film a test of new directorial talent by teaming one of the film's writers, Wanda Tuchock, with an editor, George Nichols Jr. Only Nichols continued directing. AE

Frances Dee *Virginia Radcliff* • Billie Burke *Mrs Radcliff* • Ginger Rogers *Pony* • Bruce Cabot *MacFarland* • John Halliday *Mr Radcliff* • Beulah Bondi *Miss Van Alstyn* ▪ *Dir* Wanda Tuchock, George Nichols Jr • *Scr* Wanda Tuchock, Laird Doyle, from a story by David Hempstead, from the play *These Days* by Katherine Clugston

Fiorile ★★★★ 12
Drama   1993 · It/Fr/Ger · Colour · 113min

Tracing an ancestral curse over 200 years, the three stories in this elegant outing possess all the passion and wonderment we've come to expect from the Taviani brothers. Related by a father to his children as they visit their grandfather, the accounts are neatly woven into the journey and

punctuated by the kids' increasingly anxious questions. With the cast playing multiple roles, the action has a neorealist feel in spite of the period opulence, most evident in the Napoleonic episode. Magisterial filmmaking from one of cinema's most accomplished storytelling duos. DP Italian +subtitles.

Claudio Bigagli *Corrado/Alessandro* • Galatea Ranzi *Elisabetta/Elisa* • Michael Vartan *Jean/Massimo* • Lino Capolicchio *Luigi* • Constanze Engelbrecht *Juliette* • Athina Cenci *Gina* ▪ *Dir* Paolo Taviani, Vittorio Taviani • *Scr* Paolo Taviani, Vittorio Taviani, Sandro Petraglia, from a story by Paolo Taviani, Vittorio Taviani

Fire ★★★★ 15
Drama   1996 · Can/Ind · Colour · 107min

Parodying the traditions of the traditional masala melodrama and opening Deepa Mehta's controversial "elements" trilogy, this was one of the first Indian films to depict adultery, pornography, masturbation and lesbianism. Deprived of love in a patriarchal society, Shabana Azmi succumbs to the advances of her equally neglected sister-in-law, Nandita Das. With the exception of Ranjit Chowdhry's embittered servant, the males are rather crudely caricatured, but the female leads exhibit a courage that matches Mehta's bold discussion of such themes as arranged marriage, sexual emancipation, spiritual enslavement and disappointed ambition. DP English, Hindi +subtitles. Swearing, some sex scenes. *DVD*

Shabana Azmi *Radha* • Nandita Das *Sita* • Kulbhushan Kharbanda *Ashok* • Jaaved Jaaferi *Jatin* • Ranjit Chowdhry *Mundu* • Kushal Rekhi *Biji* ▪ *Dir/Scr* Deepa Mehta

Fire and Ice ★★ PG
Animated fantasy   1983 · US · Colour · 78min

Ralph Bakshi teams with legendary fantasy artist Frank Frazetta and comic book masters Roy Thomas and Gerry Conway for this showdown between good and evil set in mystical prehistoric times. With the figures being Rotoscoped (traced on to celluloid from live-action footage), the animation has a realistic feel, while the voice talents bring the multitude of characters to life. DP *DVD*

Susan Tyrrell *Juliana* • Maggie Roswell *Teegra* • William Ostrander *Taro/Larn* • Stephen Mendel *Nekron* • Clare Nono *Tutor* • Alan Koss *Envoy* • Hans Howes *Defender Captain* ▪ *Dir* Ralph Bakshi • *Scr* Roy Thomas, Gerry Conway, from a story and characters by Ralph Bakshi, Frank Frazetta

Fire at Sea ★★★★ 12A
Documentary   2016 · It/Fr · Colour · 113min

Winner of the Golden Lion at Venice and the Golden Bear at Berlin, this engrossing study looks at the impact of the migrant crisis on the Italian island of Lampedusa. During a year-long stay, Rosi witnessed several search-and-rescue operations for boatloads of refugees. This discreetly unflinching footage proves harrowing in the extreme, more so when juxtaposed with images of the islanders going about their daily lives. The two worlds barely seem to collide, but Rosi makes it abundantly clear this is an emergency that affects everyone. DP Italian, English +subtitles. Some swearing, distressing scenes *DVD*

▪ *Dir* Gianfranco Rosi • *Scr* Gianfranco Rosi, from an idea by Carla Cattani

Fire Down Below ★★
Romantic adventure   1957 · UK · Colour · 115min

Jack Lemmon and Robert Mitchum play smuggling partners who fall out over Rita Hayworth in this corny and only vaguely watchable melodrama. Hayworth is on board Mitchum's ship, trying to get to the West Indies so she can get a passport, when the boat catches fire, creating much back-projected action. The film wastes its top-rank cast and was shot in Britain on a tiny budget. AT

Rita Hayworth *Irena* • Jack Lemmon *Tony* • Robert Mitchum *Felix* • Herbert Lom *Harbour master* • Bonar Colleano *Lt Sellers* • Anthony Newley *Miguel* ■ *Dir* Robert Parrish • *Scr* Irwin Shaw, from a novel by Max Catto

Fire Down Below ★★ 18

Action adventure 1997 · US · Colour · 100min

Steven Seagal proves he is no tree-hugging peacenik in this eco-thriller. Joined by Harry Dean Stanton and a grizzled Kris Kristofferson in a tale of environmental mayhem in rural Tennessee, he plays a federal agent on a twin mission to track down the killer of a colleague and to destroy the industrialist who has been poisoning the local water supply. Fans will enjoy an unexpected treat as he warbles a folk song over the credits. JF Swearing, violence. **DVD**

Steven Seagal *Jack Taggart* • Marg Helgenberger *Sarah Kellogg* • Stephen Lang *Earl* • Brad Hunt *Orin Jr* • Kris Kristofferson *Orin Sr* • Harry Dean Stanton *Cotton* ■ *Dir* Felix Enriquez Alcala • *Scr* Jeb Stuart, Philip Morton, from a story by Jeb Stuart

A Fire Has Been Arranged ★★ U

Comedy 1935 · UK · BW · 66min

Bud Flanagan and Chesney Allen are on leave from most of the Crazy Gang, playing former convicts who go back to retrieve their plunder only to find that it's now covered by a building. The film's title suggests their possible solution to this problem. As comedy it relies too much on Flanagan and Allen's very fragile star-quality, though it does contain a "turn" by the magnificent Robb Wilton. TH **DVD**

Bud Flanagan *Bud* • Chesney Allen *Ches* • Mary Lawson *Betty* • Robb Wilton *Oswald* • Harold French *Toby* • Alastair Sim *Cutte* ■ *Dir* Leslie Hiscott • *Scr* H Fowler Mear, Michael Barringer, from a story by H Fowler Mear, James Carter

Fire, Ice and Dynamite ★★ PG

Action drama 1990 · W Ger · Colour · 101min

Having turned in his Walther PPK after 1985's *A View to a Kill*, Roger Moore found himself back in Bond territory - but only in terms of the daft plot and emphasis on stunts. Moore plays a wealthy man who fakes his own death and sets up an elaborate series of Olympic-type sports contests pitting his stepchildren against his creditors. The winners will get their hands on his fortune. This harmless time-waster is worth catching only for the stunning ski set pieces and for Moore's famous charm. RS **DVD**

Roger Moore *Sir George/McVay* • Connie de Groot *Lucy* • Geoffrey Moore *Dudley* • Simon Shepherd *Alexander* • Shari Belafonte-Harper [*Shari Belafonte*] *Serena* • Uwe Ochsenknecht *Victor* • Isaac Hayed ■ *Dir* Willy Bogner • *Scr* Tony Williamson, Willy Bogner

Fire in Babylon ★★★ 12

Sports documentary 2010 · UK · Colour · 87min

Director Stevan Riley charts the rise (and rise) of the West Indies cricket team from the trauma of touring Australia in 1975, when fast bowlers Dennis Lillee and Jeff Thomson were at their ferocious best, to the early 80s and beyond. Alongside revealing interviews with cricketing greats like Clive Lloyd, Michael Holding and the peerless Viv Richards, the turbulent state of race relations in South Africa, England and the Caribbean is never far away. It's a pity there are no testimonies from their opponents, but then this is a West Indian story of how a group of talented individuals became an unbeatable inspiration. JA Swearing. **DVD** **BLU-RAY**

■ *Dir/Scr* Stevan Riley

Fire in the Blood ★★★★ 12

Documentary 2012 · Ind/UK/Can · Colour · 87min

The best documentaries inform and provide insight into a subject, but when they also provoke moral outrage they can have a genuine, lasting impact on the viewer. Dylan

Mohan Gray's film chronicles how western pharmaceutical companies and governments blocked access to low-cost Aids drugs for populations in the developing world. His incisive and damning examination details how these institutions made use of draconian patent laws to maximise their profits at the expense of the lives of millions. Thanks to the testimonies of unsung heroes such as South African activist Zackie Achmat and Ugandan doctor Peter Mugyenyi, this film is utterly absorbing and impossible to forget. JA **DVD**

Bill Clinton • Desmond Tutu ■ *Dir/Scr* Dylan Mohan Gray

Fire in the Night ★★★★

Documentary 2013 · UK · Colour · 90min

On 6 July 1988, the North Sea oil rig Piper Alpha blew up. There were 226 men on it; 167 died, including two from the rescue boat. Anthony Wonke's powerful, patient film, made to commemorate the 25th anniversary of the disaster, takes a few of the 61 survivors back to that night. When the explosive fire broke out, few realised at first just how dangerous it was, but then the lights went out and metal began to melt. There are no interviews with families, no examination of the causes or the aftermath (other than a closing caption), nothing fancy about Wonke's film. But there is a real insight into the different ways people face death, and how those who do not die come to terms with their good fortune. BP

■ *Dir* Anthony Wonke

Fire in the Sky ★★★ 15

Science-fiction drama 1993 · US · Colour · 104min

A small-town lumberjack vanishes in the woods and his colleagues claim he was kidnapped by aliens. Problem is, the investigating officer here is sceptical James Garner and he suspects foul play. Director Robert Lieberman wisely concentrates on the emotional impact of the event on a close-knit circle of friends and family, although the eventual revelation of the abduction is genuinely scary. DB Sweeney shines in the lead role, although old pro Garner steals every scene. JF Swearing, violence, nudity. **DVD**

DB Sweeney *Travis Walton* • Robert Patrick *Mike Rogers* • Craig Sheffer *Allan Dallis* • Peter Berg *David Whitlock* • Henry Thomas *Greg Hayes* • Bradley Gregg *Bobby Cogdill* • James Garner *Lieutenant Frank Watters* ■ *Dir* Robert Lieberman • *Scr* Tracy Tormé, from the book *The Walton Experience* by Travis Walton

Fire Maidens from Outer Space ★ U

Science-fiction adventure 1956 · UK · BW · 79min

Life is such a trial for the female lost civilisation of Atlantis, stranded on the 13th moon of Jupiter. They wear bathing suits with little skirts, lie around in flames all day for extra energy, perform dances to Borodin's music and fight a lumpy-faced creature in ill-fitting tights. Bottom-of-the-barrel lunatic nonsense. AJ

Anthony Dexter *Luther Blair* • Susan Shaw *Hestia* • Paul Carpenter *Larson* • Harry Fowler *Sydney Stanhope* • Jacqueline Curtiss *Duessa* • Sidney Tafler [*Sydney Tafler*] *Dr Higgins* ■ *Dir/Scr* Cy Roth

Fire over England ★★★★ U

Historical adventure 1937 · UK · BW · 91min

This spectacular adventure, set in the Elizabethan past, is memorable not just for early sword- and word-play by Laurence Olivier, but for its political context - it's a call to arms against the growing forces of Nazism in Europe. Olivier is the young nobleman seeking revenge for the death of his father at the hands of the Spanish Inquisition, and warning Queen Elizabeth (Flora Robson) about the imminent Armada invasion. Raymond Massey sneers a lot as Philip II of Spain, while director William K Howard's lavish production design works hard to divert attention from uneven

dialogue matched to fervent jingoism. Great fun, though. TH

Flora Robson *Queen Elizabeth* • Raymond Massey *Philip of Spain* • Leslie Banks *Leicester* • Laurence Olivier *Michael Ingolby* • Vivien Leigh *Cynthia* • Morton Selten *Burleigh* • Tamara Desni *Elena* • Lyn Harding *Sir Richard Ingolby* • James Mason *Hillary Vane* ■ *Dir* William K Howard • *Scr* Clemence Dane, Sergei Nolbandov, from a novel by AEW Mason • *Cinematographer* James Wong Howe • *Costume Design* Rene Hubert

Fire Sale ★★

Comedy 1977 · US · Colour · 88min

Alan Arkin's second outing as a feature director is a wild farce that most contemporary critics denounced as distasteful. It's certainly on the dark side, with basketball coach Arkin adopting a troublesome black kid solely to secure him for his under-achieving team; meanwhile his brother Rob Reiner persuades crazed uncle Sid Caesar to torch the family department store by convincing him it's a Nazi stronghold. Arkin labours over too many misfiring gags and this clumsy comedy refuses to catch light. DP

Alan Arkin *Ezra Fikus* • Rob Reiner *Russel Fikus* • Vincent Gardenia *Benny Fikus* • Anjanette Comer *Marion Fikus* • Barbara Dana *Virginia* • Sid Caesar *Sherman* ■ *Dir* Alan Arkin • *Scr* Robert Klane, from his novel

Fire with Fire ★★ 15

Romantic drama 1986 · US · Colour · 99min

This dull tale of teenage angst is not as salacious as it first sounds. Prim Virginia Madsen's hormones go into overdrive when she catches sight of mean and moody junior convict Craig Sheffer, much to the disapproval of all those around her. Madsen and Sheffer do their best with the clichéd material and there's good support from Jon Polito, but the story has been better told elsewhere. JF

Virginia Madsen *Lisa Taylor* • Craig Sheffer *Joe Fisk* • Jon Polito *Boss* • Jeffrey Jay Cohen [*JJ Cohen*] *Mapmaker* • Kate Reid *Sister Victoria* • Jean Smart *Sister Marie* ■ *Dir* Duncan Gibbins • *Scr* Bill Phillips, Warren Skaaren, Paul Boorstin, Sharon Boorstin

Fire with Fire ★★ 15

Action crime drama 2012 · US · Colour · 93min

Although it's probably the biggest movie yet to emerge from rapper 50 Cent's production outfit, this damp squib still has "straight to DVD" stamped all over it (which is where the film ended up in the US). Josh Duhamel (*Transformers*) stars as a fireman who is placed in the witness protection programme after getting caught up in a gangland execution. But when he and his US marshal protector (Rosario Dawson) are tracked down by a hired assassin (Julian McMahon), he realises they will never be safe unless he takes the law into his own hands. Despite the efforts of a notable cast - Bruce Willis also plays a sympathetic detective - this fails to create the requisite sparks. JF Violence, swearing. **DVD** **BLU-RAY**

Josh Duhamel *Jeremy Coleman* • Bruce Willis *Lieutenant Mike Cella* • Rosario Dawson *Deputy Talia Durham* • Vincent D'Onofrio *David Hagan* • 50 Cent [*Curtis "50 Cent" Jackson*] *Lamar* • Julian McMahon *Robert* ■ *Dir* David Barrett • *Scr* Tom O'Connor

The Fireball ★★ U

Sports drama 1950 · US · BW · 83min

Multi-talented diminutive dynamo Mickey Rooney is the star of this unappealing drama about an orphan with a complex about his height who sets out to become a roller-skating champion, exhibiting ruthless ambition along the way. Rooney fans will be familiar with his brash, cocky brilliance but, although his presence enlivens this lacklustre movie, the character he plays is an unattractive one. Tay Garnett directs for 20th Century-Fox, whose relatively unknown contract player Marilyn Monroe appears. RK

Mickey Rooney *Johnny Casar* • Pat O'Brien *Father O'Hara* • Beverly Tyler *Mary Reeves* • James Brown [*JJ*] *Allen* • Marilyn Monroe *Polly* • Ralph Dumke *Bruno Crystal* ■ *Dir* Tay Garnett • *Scr* Tay Garnett, Horace McCoy

Fireball ★★★ 15

Action drama 2009 · Thai · Colour · 92min

Thai director Thanakorn Pongsuwan's action drama is a bone-crunching, eye-gouging blend of martial arts and basketball. There is a plot of sorts: ex-con Tai (played by Thai rock star Preeti Barameeanat) enters the world of fireball - an extremely violent underground sport that combines basketball and muay thai (Thai boxing) - to take revenge on the dirty slamdunker who put his twin brother into a coma. But the storyline is simply an excuse for a succession of viciously well-filmed scenes that mix fight sequences with basketball trickery. Despite a somewhat disappointing finale, this is a must-see for action fans. DA Thai +subtitles.

Preeti Barameeanat *Tai/Tan* • Arucha Tosawat *Ton* • 9 Million Sam *Zing* • Khanutra Chuchuaysuwan *Pang* • Kumpanat Oungsoongnern *Muk* ■ *Dir* Thanakorn Pongsuwan • *Scr* Thanakorn Pongsuwan, Kiat Sansanandana, Taweewat Wantha, Adirek Wattaleela

Fireball 500 ★★★ U

Action drama 1966 · US · Colour · 90min

This beach party movie has those icons of sand, sea and swimwear - Frankie Avalon, Fabian and the adorable Annette Funicello. The two boys are rivals for the girl as they race souped-up cars and get into hot water with illicit booze. The whole thing exudes an innocence and charm, as well as some very twangy, singalong tunes. Perhaps not quite up to the standards of previous William Asher beach epics, this is still unmissable for 1960s culture-vultures. AT

Frankie Avalon *Dave* • Annette Funicello *Jane* • Fabian *Leander* • Chill Wills *Big Jaw* • Harvey Lembeck *Charlie Bigg* • Julie Parrish *Martha* ■ *Dir* William Asher • *Scr* William Asher, Leo Townsend

Firecreek ★★★ 12

Western 1968 · US · Colour · 99min

James Stewart here succumbs to the notorious "yup-nope" syndrome, playing a monosyllabic part-time sheriff defending his fellow townsfolk from outlaw Henry Fonda and his gang of layabout thugs. Cast against type, Fonda obviously liked his role so much he became even more villainous for Sergio Leone's *Once upon a Time in the West*, released in Italy the same year. While this doesn't bear serious comparison with Leone's classic spaghetti western, it's entertaining enough. TH Violence.

James Stewart *Johnny Cobb* • Henry Fonda *Larkin* • Inger Stevens *Evelyn* • Gary Lockwood *Earl* • Dean Jagger *Whittier* • Ed Begley *Preacher Broyles* ■ *Dir* Vincent McEveety • *Scr* Calvin Clements

Fired Up! ★ 12

Comedy 2009 · US · Colour · 86min

If this cynical, misogynist teen comedy had been made by the adolescent boys it's aimed at, it would undoubtedly be less offensive. As it stands, the grown men behind this story about a pair of high-school jocks (Nicholas D'Agosto and Eric Christian Olsen) who ditch football practice to attend cheerleader camp should know better. This consists of nothing more than leering comments about the female cast's physical attributes and the odd homophobic gag - and that's definitely not worth leading a cheer for. JR Some swearing, sexual references. **DVD**

Nicholas D'Agosto *Shawn Colfax* • Eric Christian Olsen *Nick Brady* • Sarah Roemer *Carly* • Molly Sims *Diora* • Danneel Harris *Bianca* • David Walton *Dr Rick* • Philip Baker Hall *Coach Byrnes* • John Michael Higgins *Coach Keith* ■ *Dir* Will Gluck • *Scr* Freedom Jones

Fireflies in the Garden ★★★ 15

Melodrama 2007 · US/Ger · Colour · 95min

This quiet melodrama centres on writer Michael Taylor (Ryan Reynolds), who's heading home for a celebration involving his mother (Julia Roberts) when a fatal car accident shatters the family reunion. As the funeral plans get under way, Michael tries to make sense of his career, failing marriage and angry, combative relationship with his domineering father (Willem Dafoe). The narrative flashbacks show patterns within the Taylor clan repeating themselves, as secrets are unveiled and scenarios revisited with poignant attention. This isn't especially original, but does offer an unblinkered yet surprisingly positive examination of family dysfunction and reconciliation. KK *DVD*

Ryan Reynolds *Michael Taylor* • Julia Roberts *Lisa Taylor* • Willem Dafoe *Charles Taylor* • Emily Watson *Jane Lawrence* • Carrie-Anne Moss *Kelly* • Ioan Gruffudd *Addison* • Hayden Panettiere *Young Jane* • Cayden Boyd *Young Michael* ■ *Dir/Scr* Dennis Lee

The Firefly ★★★ U
Period musical 1937 · US · BW · 138min

"There's a song in the air, but the gay senorita doesn't seem to care..." Yes, it's the *Donkey Serenade* movie, with Allan Jones singing his heart out to vivacious Jeanette MacDonald, winning her from stern Warren William during the Spanish Peninsular War, as she takes a break from her regular singing swain Nelson Eddy. MGM's production is glossy and Robert Z "Pops" Leonard's direction classy, but the film's length is nearly unendurable. TS

Jeanette MacDonald *Nina Maria Azara* • Allan Jones *Don Diego Manrique De Lara* • Warren William *Colonel De Rougemont* • Douglass Dumbrille *Marquis De Melito* ■ *Dir* Robert Z Leonard • *Scr* Frances Goodrich, Albert Hackett, Ogden Nash, from the operetta by Otto A Harbach [Otto Harbach] • *Music* Rudolf Friml • *Music Director* Herbert Stothart

Firefox ★★ 15
Spy thriller 1982 · US · Colour · 119min

Given the level of his achievement since, it's hard to remember that in his early career as a director, Clint Eastwood delivered up one or two boring and emotionless films and this violent Cold War affair is hard going for even the most dedicated of fans. Eastwood plays a disillusioned flier who is sent across the Iron Curtain to steal a new Russian jet and bring it home. The supporting Britpack hams it up for all it's worth, but, while there are some decent flying sequences, Eastwood's heart doesn't appear to be in it. JF Swearing. *DVD*

Clint Eastwood *Mitchell Gant* • Freddie Jones *Kenneth Aubrey* • David Huffman *Buckholz* • Warren Clarke *Pavel Upenskoy* • Ronald Lacey *Semelovsky* ■ *Dir* Clint Eastwood • *Scr* Alex Lasker, Wendell Wellman, from the novel by Craig Thomas

Firehead ★★ 15
Science-fiction action adventure
1991 · US · Colour · 83min

Scientist Chris Lemmon (sounding and acting like his father Jack) and CIA agent Gretchen Becker team up to track down Soviet defector Brett Porter who can shoot laser beams from his eyes, move molecules and start fires. Christopher Plummer needs Porter to kill the president and start a Third World War, while Martin Landau is a retired admiral. A fuzzy muddle. AJ Violence, swearing.

Christopher Plummer *Colonel Garland Vaughn* • Chris Lemmon *Warren Hart* • Martin Landau *Admiral Pendleton* • Gretchen Becker *Melia Buchanan* • Brett Porter *Ivan Tibor* ■ *Dir* Peter Yuval • *Scr* Peter Yuval, Jeff Mandel

Firehouse Dog ★★ PG
Action comedy 2006 · US · Colour · 106min

Talented pets and fearless firefighters are both Hollywood staples, and this action comedy brings elements from both genres together in one child-friendly package. Canine action-movie star "Rexxx" falls from a plane and lands (literally) in the middle of a blaze. He's rescued by small-town fire chief Connor Fahey (Bruce Greenwood), who gives his stroppy son Shane (Josh Hutcherson) the task of finding the pooch's real owner. Attitude soon gives way to admiration, however, as Shane realises the dog has genuine stunt skills – but it's not long before Hollywood wants its star

performer back. With subplots about arson and father/son bonding, this is corny but competent entertainment for younger viewers. DA *DVD*

Josh Hutcherson *Shane Fahey* • Bruce Greenwood *Connor Fahey* • Dash Mihok *Trey Falcon* • Steven Culp *Zachary Hayden* • Bill Nunn *Joe Musto* • Bree Turner *Liz Knowles* • Scotch Ellis Loring *Lionel Bradford* ■ *Dir* Todd Holland • *Scr* Claire-Dee Lim, Mike Werb, Michael Colleary

Firelight ★★★ 15
Period romantic drama
1997 · US/UK · Colour · 99min

Tissues at the ready for this sugary 19th-century tale of a mother's love. Swiss governess Sophie Marceau agrees to conceive a child for English aristocrat Stephen Dillane, who takes the child back to his wife. A few years later the pair cross paths again when he takes her on as nanny to their daughter. The two leads seem uncomfortable with their roles, but the story is interesting enough and is enlivened by a strong performance by Dominique Belcourt as their daughter, and a supporting cast that includes Joss Ackland. JB Some swearing, a sex scene.

Sophie Marceau *Elisabeth Laurier* • Stephen Dillane *Charles Godwin* • Kevin Anderson *John Taylor* • Lia Williams *Constance* • Dominique Belcourt *Louisa Godwin* • Joss Ackland *Lord Clare* ■ *Dir/Scr* William Nicholson

Fireman Save My Child ★★ U
Comedy 1954 · US · BW · 80min

Abbott and Costello were the original stars of this slapdash comedy but their withdrawal made room for the less than stellar talents of Hugh O'Brian and Buddy Hackett. However, this silly tale set in an early 20th-century San Francisco fire department, is enlivened by the eccentric presence of Spike Jones and his City Slickers. The film bears no resemblance to the superior 1932 comedy of the same name. RB

Spike Jones *Lieutenant McGinty* • Buddy Hackett *Smokey* • Hugh O'Brian *Smitty* • Adele Jergens *Harry's wife* • Tom Brown *Captain Bill Peters* ■ *Dir* Leslie Goodwins • *Scr* Lee Loeb, John Grant

The Firemen's Ball ★★★★ PG
Political satire 1967 · Cz/It · Colour · 69min

Director Milos Forman's last film in Czechoslovakia before his American exile begins as a gently mocking comedy of small-town manners, but ends as a blazing allegorical satire on the incompetence, insularity and ideological idiocy of the state. Amid the wealth of comic detail that surrounds the ball held to celebrate a veteran fire chief's retirement, it's easy to forget that the real theme of this socialist realist parody is the Stalinist purges of the 1950s. But the chaotic beauty contest, the theft of the lottery prizes and the discomfort of the guest of honour can all be enjoyed without a deep knowledge of Czech politics. DP Czech +subtitles. *DVD*

Vaclav Stockel *Fire brigade commander* • Josef Svet *Old man* • Jan Vostrcil *Chairman of committee* • Josef Kolb *Josef* • Frantisek Debelka *First committee member* • Josef Sebanek *Second committee member* ■ *Dir* Milos Forman • *Scr* Milos Forman, Ivan Passer, Jaroslav Papousek

Firepower ★★★ 15
Action thriller 1979 · UK · Colour · 99min

One of the easiest jobs in film criticism is to knock the work of Michael Winner. But he's not always deserved the pannings he's received and this fast-moving (if admittedly empty-headed) thriller is no worse than many other luxury location jaunts that have escaped without censure. From the opening scene, in which Sophia Loren's husband is killed, to the highly predictable dénouement, there are explosions and car chases aplenty. On the plus side, Loren and James Coburn do make an attractive couple. Winner also edited the film under the pseudonym Arnold Crust. DP

Sophia Loren *Adele Tasca* • James Coburn *Jerry Fanon/Eddie* • OJ Simpson *Catlett* • Eli Wallach *Sal Hyman* • Anthony Franciosa *Dr Felix* • Vincent Gardenia *Frank Hull* • Victor Mature *Harold Everett* ■ *Dir* Michael Winner • *Scr* Gerald Wilson, from a story by Bill Kerby, Michael Winner

Fires on the Plain ★★★★★
Second World War drama
1959 · Jpn · BW · 107min

This is cinema's most terrifying study of the Second World War. Adapted by director Kon Ichikawa's wife, Natto Wada, from the novel by Shohei Ooka, Ichikawa's masterpiece has an otherworldly feel. Desperate, cannibalistic Japanese soldiers are left to fend for themselves on the Philippine island of Leyte, its desolate landscape littered with ominous fires. As the tubercular trooper who wanders the landscape in search of food and shelter, and whose infirmity delivers him from the hellish nightmare of survival, the almost wordless Eiji Funakoshi reacts to the atrocities he witnesses with such genuine horror that their impact becomes all the more immediate. DP Japanese +subtitles.

Eiji Funakoshi *Tamura* • Osamu Takizawa *Yasuda* • Mickey Curtis *Nagamatsu* • Mantaro Ushio *Sergeant* • Kyu Sazanka *Army surgeon* • Yoshihiro Hamaguchi *Officer* • Asao Sano *Soldier* • Masaya Tsukida *Soldier* • Hikaru Hoshi *Soldier* ■ *Dir* Kon Ichikawa • *Scr* Natto Wada, from the novel by Shohei Ooka

Fires Were Started ★★★★
Second World War documentary drama
1943 · UK · BW · 63min

Humphrey Jennings was the poet of the British Documentary Movement, but he reined in his imaginative impulses here to record the grim reality of the Blitz in what ranks among the finest Home Front films of the Second World War. As in all good propaganda, it's simplicity that makes the most impact. In depicting the Auxiliary Fire Service as a dedicated team, whose camaraderie is evident both at work and play, Jennings is able to inspire audience confidence in their quiet heroism, while also extolling their essential humanity. DP *DVD*

■ *Dir/Scr* Humphrey Jennings

Fires Within ★★ 15
Romantic drama 1991 · US · Colour · 83min

What makes this film, made by the talented Australian director Gillian Armstrong, disappointing is that its story of Cuban refugees in America throws up some fascinating political points, which are evaded by the pedestrian script. Greta Scacchi as a Cuban housewife is a rotten bit of casting, but she, Jimmy Smits and Vincent D'Onofrio (as her new lover) try to wring every ounce of significance out of the plot. DP Swearing. *DVD*

Jimmy Smits *Nestor* • Greta Scacchi *Isabel* • Vincent D'Onofrio *Sam* • Luis Avalos *Victor Hernandez* • Bertila Damas *Estella Sanchez* • Bri Hathaway *Maribi* ■ *Dir* Gillian Armstrong • *Scr* Cynthia Cidre, Peter Barsocchini

Firestarter ★★ 15
Supernatural drama 1984 · US · Colour · 109min

Stephen King's work has suffered mixed fortune at the hands of film-makers and this early folly is not one of the better adaptations. Drew Barrymore is the girl with very fiery thoughts that are connected to the sinister experiments dad and mum (David Keith and Heather Locklear) underwent. Despite a starry cast, there's little here in the way of frights or suspense. JF *DVD*

David Keith *Andrew McGee* • Drew Barrymore *Charlie McGee* • Freddie Jones *Dr Joseph Wanless* • Heather Locklear *Vicky McGee* • Martin Sheen *Captain Hollister* • George C Scott *John Rainbird* • Art Carney *Irv Manders* • Louise Fletcher *Norma Manders* ■ *Dir* Mark L Lester • *Scr* Stanley Mann, from the novel by Stephen King • *Music* Tangerine Dream

Firestorm ★★ 15
Action adventure 1998 · US · Colour · 85min

Former American football star Howie Long stars as a daredevil firefighter who finds himself caught up in a lethal forest blaze started by a group of escaped convicts hunting for their buried loot. Long is short on talent, William Forsythe effortlessly steals the show as a deranged robber, and director Dean Semler struggles away from the action sequences. JF Swearing, violence. *DVD*

Howie Long *Jesse* • Scott Glenn *Wynt* • William Forsythe *Shaye* • Suzy Amis *Jennifer* • Christianne Hirt *Monica* ■ *Dir* Dean Semler • *Scr* Chris Soth, Graham Yost (uncredited)

Firetrap ★★ 15
Disaster movie 2001 · US · Colour · 94min

Dean Cain headlines this competently made disaster movie. Director Harris Done efficiently reworks the *Towering Inferno* formula, thanks to some impressive effects. The opening segment, in which Cain's super-crook poses as a fireman in order to facilitate the purloining of a cutting-edge microchip, lacks suspense. But the action really begins to hot up once he's called upon to rescue his target's trapped employees. DP *DVD*

Dean Cain *Max Hooper* • Richard Tyson *Paul Brody* • Mel Harris *Cordelia* • Lori Petty *Lucy* • Harry Van Gorkum *Roger* ■ *Dir* Harris Done • *Scr* Diane Fine, Richard Preston Jr

Firewalker ★ 15
Western adventure 1986 · US · Colour · 100min

Chuck Norris here attempts to do something that he has absolutely no knack for – comedy. Neither does his co-star Louis Gossett Jr, though he at least keeps some dignity, even when he's forced to speak Pig Latin. The two stars play mercenary adventurers who are hired by Melody Anderson to find an ancient treasure south of the border, with danger, cardboard sets, and stereotypes at every turn. KB

Chuck Norris *Max Donigan* • Louis Gossett Jr *Leo Porter* • Melody Anderson *Patricia Goodwyn* • Will Sampson *Tall Eagle* • Sonny Landham *El Coyote* • John Rhys-Davies *Corky Taylor* ■ *Dir* J Lee Thompson • *Scr* Robert Gosnell, from a story by Jeffrey M Rosenbaum, Norman Aladjem, Robert Gosnell

Firewall ★★ 12
Crime thriller 2006 · US · Colour · 100min

Looking as old and exhausted as the dog-eared plot, Harrison Ford huffs and puffs his way through this flabby thriller. He plays a computer security specialist forced by psychopath Paul Bettany to hack into his own bank when his wife (a wasted Virginia Madsen) and children are kidnapped. Once past the reasonably tense set-up, disbelief and boredom set in as Richard Loncraine's direction does nothing to transcend the film's formula thrills and contrivances. AJ Violence, swearing. *DVD* 🔊

Harrison Ford *Jack Stanfield* • Paul Bettany *Bill Cox* • Virginia Madsen *Beth Stanfield* • Mary Lynn Rajskub *Janet Stone* • Robert Patrick *Gary Mitchell* • Robert Forster *Harry Romano* • Alan Arkin *Arlin Forester* ■ *Dir* Richard Loncraine • *Scr* Joe Forte

Fireworks ★★★★ 15
Psychological fantasy
1947 · US · Colour and BW Tinted · 13min

Although best known for his notorious *Hollywood Babylon* exposés, Kenneth Anger has been a fixture of American avant-garde cinema since 1947, when at 17 he filmed this remarkable short – a "psycho-dramatic trance film" which remains perhaps the peak of his oeuvre. Set against the music of Respighi, this surreal visual poem combines phallic imagery and references to Christmas, the US navy and innocent youth for an orgasmically violent gay fantasy in which Anger is punished for lusting after a hunky sailor. The film's pièta sequence – featuring a bruised Anger collapsed in the sailor's arms – and blatant sexual imagery would qualify it as an audacious and accomplished work for anyone, let alone a teenager. **DP**

Kenneth Anger *Dreamer* • Bill Seltzer *Bare-chested sailor* • Gordon Gray *Body-bearing sailor* ■ *Dir* Kenneth Anger • *Cinematographer* Kenneth Anger • *Music* Ottorino Respighi

The Firm ★★★★🄯
Thriller   1993 · US · Colour · 148min

After running rings around the US Navy in *A Few Good Men*, Tom Cruise returned to the courtroom for this big-screen adaptation of John Grisham's bestseller. The result is a lavish, star-studded legal thriller that is never less than engrossing. Cruise is a rising young lawyer who gets a dream job with a prestigious law firm only to discover that it offers more than just legal advice to one particularly sinister client. The ever excellent Gene Hackman is his jaded superior, but, as good as they are, the two stars are outshone by the seemingly never-ending parade of star supporting turns. **JF** Swearing, violence, a sex scene. **DVD BL**

Tom Cruise *Mitch McDeere* • Jeanne Tripplehorn *Abby McDeere* • Gene Hackman *Avery Tolar* • Hal Holbrook *Oliver Lambert* • Terry Kinney *Lamar Quinn* • Wilford Brimley *William Devasher* • Ed Harris *Wayne Tarrance* • Holly Hunter *Tammy Hemphill* • David Strathairn *Ray McDeere* ■ *Dir* Sydney Pollack • *Scr* David Rabe, Robert Towne, David Rayfiel, from the novel by John Grisham

The Firm ★★★🄱
Drama   2009 · UK · Colour · 86min

An East London teenager is drawn into the violent world of football hooliganism in this remake of the controversial 1988 BBC drama starring Gary Oldman as a charismatic gang leader. Here writer/director Nick Love has made the decision to shift the emphasis to tell the story from the perspective of youngster Calum MacNab. He gives a solid performance as the teenager who's attracted by the strutting machismo of the local firm, but repelled by their brutal behaviour. Given that Love's previous work has been criticised for its depiction of violence, one might have feared the worst here. But the film is clear in its disdain for the thugs' vicious excesses, as the tone is lightened by a club-hits soundtrack and an astute ear for banter-driven comedy. **TJ** Violence, swearing, sexual references, drug abuse. **DVD BL**

Paul Anderson (2) *Bex* • Calum MacNab *Dom* • Daniel Mays *Yeti* • Doug Allen *Trigger* • Joe Jackson (2) *Jay* • Richie Campbell *Snowy* ■ *Dir* Nick Love • *Scr* Nick Love, from the 1989 Screen Two film by Al Hunter [Al Ashton]

First ★★★★🄬
Sports documentary
2012 · UK · Colour · 108min

"Inspire a generation" was the slogan that defined the London Olympics, and that sentiment looms large over this portrait of the heady, euphoric days of summer 2012. Acknowledged as the official film of the Games, this lovingly crafted chronicle is more of a snapshot of the event, with the emphasis firmly on first-time Olympians from all over the world. As with most sports documentaries, the athletes experience both the agony and the ecstasy of competition, but there's also sportsmanship, mutual respect and revealing personal stories. The footage is often electrifying and accompanied by a suitably contemporary soundtrack, while the sublime David Rudisha's historic run in the 800m final makes for a rousing climax. **JA DVD BL**

Laura Trott • Missy Franklin • David Rudisha • Chad Le Clos • Katie Taylor ■ *Dir* Caroline Rowland

First a Girl ★★★🄤
Musical comedy   1935 · UK · BW · 88min

A popular hit for British screen sweetheart Jessie Matthews, this tuneful comedy plunders a German film called *Viktor und Viktoria* and was itself later reworked by director Blake Edwards as a vehicle for his wife Julie Andrews as *Victor/Victoria*.

Whichever way you look at it, this is a highly unconvincing tale of cross-dressing about a girl who impersonates a female impersonator. Matthews brings it all off charmingly, singing and dancing her merry way in a relatively lavish Michael Balcon production, directed by Victor Saville without a hint of subtext. **TS**

Jessie Matthews *Elizabeth* • Sonnie Hale *Victor* • Griffith Jones *Robert* • Anna Lee *Princess* • Alfred Drayton *McIntosh* • Constance Godridge *Darryl* • Martita Hunt *Seraphina* ■ *Dir* Victor Saville • *Scr* Marjorie Gaffney, from the play *Viktor und Viktoria* by Reinhold Schünzel

First Blood ★★★🄯
Action drama   1982 · US · Colour · 89min

Although the jingoistic sequels reduced Vietnam veteran John Rambo (Sylvester Stallone) to an indestructible cartoon figure, the film that introduced him is an involving tale of an ostracised loner pushed too far. Brian Dennehy is on fine snarling form as a bigoted small-town sheriff, the catalyst for a woodland cat-and-mouse chase in which his experienced quarry quickly assumes the feline role. The warfare is tautly assembled by director Ted Kotcheff and Stallone portrays Rambo with wounded conviction. **JC** Violence, swearing, nudity. **DVD BL**

Sylvester Stallone *John Rambo* • Richard Crenna *Colonel Trautman* • Brian Dennehy *Sheriff Will Teasle* • David Caruso *Mitch* • Jack Starrett *Galt* ■ *Dir* Ted Kotcheff • *Scr* Michael Kozoll, William Sackheim, Q Moonblood [Sylvester Stallone], from a book by David Morrell • *Music* Jerry Goldsmith

The First Born ★★★★
Silent drama   1928 · UK · BW · 101min

Miles Mander's adaptation of his own novel and play is notable for the script collaboration with Alfred Hitchcock's wife, Alma Reville, and the adult themes including adultery, illegitimacy and political hypocrisy. But while there's much to fascinate in the story of a would-be MP (Mander) who frequently cheats on his wife (Madeleine Carrol) only to doubt the parentage of their first son, what is most striking about this neglected silent melodrama is its visual virtuosity, demonstrating the sophistication of British cinema at a time when it was considered the poor relation of its transatlantic and continental counterparts. **DP**

Miles Mander *Sir Hugo Boycott* • Madeleine Carroll *Lady Madeleine Boycott* • John Loder *Lord David Harborough* • Ella Atherton *Nina de Lande* • Margot Armand *Sylvia Findlay* ■ *Dir* Miles Mander • *Scr* Miles Mander, Alma Reville, from the play and novel by Mander

First Daughter ★★
Thriller   1999 · US/Aus · Colour · 94min

Mariel Hemingway is the unlikely Secret Service agent who has been demoted to babysitting the president's daughter (Monica Keena). However, when American militia types kidnap Keena while on an adventure holiday, it's up to Hemingway and white-water rafter Doug Savant to get her back. Pretty unexceptional, but this TV movie was popular enough to spawn two sequels, *First Target* with Daryl Hannah and *First Shot*, again with Hemingway. **JF**

Mariel Hemingway *Alex McGregor* • Doug Savant *Grant Carlson* • Monica Keena *Jess Hayes* • Diamond Dallas Page *Dirk Lindman* • Gregory Harrison *President Jonathan Hayes* ■ *Dir* Armand Mastroianni • *Scr* Chad Hayes, Carey Hayes

First Daughter ★★🄿
Romantic comedy   2004 · US · Colour · 102min

Katie Holmes plays the dutiful daughter of the US president (Michael Keaton), who is looking forward to asserting her independence when she heads off to college. The Secret Service and tabloid reporters make life difficult, but things start to look up when she falls for fellow student Marc Blucas. The direction here by Forest Whitaker (who also narrates) is proficient enough, but what starts off as a fairy-tale romp gets drearily serious midway through. **JF DVD**

Katie Holmes *Samantha Mackenzie* • Marc Blucas *James Lamson* • Amerie [Amerie Rogers] *Mia* • Michael Keaton *President John Mackenzie* • Margaret Colin *Melanie Mackenzie* • Lela Rochon Fuqua [Lela Rochon] *Liz Pappas* • Michael Milhoan *Agent Bock* • Dwayne Adway *Agent Dylan* • Forest Whitaker *Narrator* ■ *Dir* Forest Whitaker • *Scr* Jessica Bendinger, Kate Kondell, from a story by Jessica Bendinger, Jerry O'Connell

The First Day of the Rest of Your Life ★★★★🄯
Drama   2007 · Fr · Colour · 112min

Rémi Bezançon's potent domestic saga is structured around five days that shape the destiny of a family living in the Paris suburbs between 1988 and 2000. The bittersweet shifts are deftly realised by some superb performances, with Zabou Breitman as the ex-hippy mother struggling to reconcile her maternal instincts with her free spirit, and Jacques Gamblin as her cabbie husband, who comes to the realisation that sanguine decency is an admirable quality in times of traumatic change. Of their children, Pio Marmaï is slightly marginalised as eldest son Albert, a medic who marries young, but the travails of genial slacker Raphaël (Grondin) and rebellious tomboy Fleur (Déborah François) are impeccably played out. The costumes and set design also contribute to the film's success. **DP** French +subtitles.

Jacques Gamblin *Robert Duval* • Zabou Breitman *Marie-Jeanne Duval* • Pio Marmaï *Albert Duval* • Déborah François *Fleur Duval* • Marc-André Grondin *Raphaël Duval* • Roger Dumas *Pierre* ■ *Dir/Scr* Rémi Bezançon

First Do No Harm ★★★🄿
Drama based on a true story
1997 · US · Colour · 90min

Only Meryl Streep could turn a standard disease-of-the-week TV movie into something special. Her mannered performance as a mother trying to get the best treatment for her epileptic son, while also struggling with marital and financial problems, is yet another of her class acts. Seth Adkins also shines as her son in this gruelling drama, which informs about epilepsy while making pertinent statements about society's attitude towards the condition. **AJ DVD**

Meryl Streep *Lori Reimuller* • Fred Ward *Dave Reimuller* • Seth Adkins *Robbie Reimuller* • Margo Martindale *Marjean* • Allison Janney *Dr Abbasac* • Oni Faida Lampley *Marisha Warren* ■ *Dir* Jim Abrahams • *Scr* Ann Beckett

First Family ★★🄯
Satirical comedy   1980 · US · Colour · 95min

This is a disappointing debut for director Buck Henry, whose screenplays for *The Graduate* and *What's Up, Doc?* showed he was adept at both satire and screwball. Here he tackles political satire but without political sting. The absurd plot concerns the kidnapping of American president Bob Newhart's daughter, Gilda Radner, by an African tribe. This witless witness to the wonders of the White House fails as entertainment. **TH**

Gilda Radner *Gloria Link* • Bob Newhart *President Manfred Link* • Madeline Kahn *Constance Link* • Richard Benjamin *Press Secretary Bunthorne* • Bob Dishy *Vice President Shockley* • Buck Henry *Father Sandstone* ■ *Dir/Scr* Buck Henry

The First Film ★★★★🄿
Documentary   2015 · UK/US/Fr · Colour · 110min

Louis Aimé Augustin Le Prince is claimed to have perfected the first practical movie camera in 1888 – seven years before the Lumiere brothers. This is a meticulously researched investigation into the achievements and mysterious disappearance of Le Prince, who vanished without trace while travelling on the Dijon-Paris express in September 1890. Working with archivist Irfan Shah, director David Nicholas Wilkinson examines the inventor's pioneering techniques and reveals how he refined the 16-lens camera he devised in the United States. Famous faces like Tom Courtenay and Joe Eszterhas chip in, but the more useful contributions come from the various experts whose insights make this compelling documentary essential for anyone with an interest in screen history. **DP**

Sarah Lancashire *Lizzie Le Prince* • Tom Courtenay • Joe Eszterhas • David Nicholas Wilkinson [David Wilkinson] *David Wilkinson* • Ronald Harwood ■ *Dir* David Nicholas Wilkinson [David Wilkinson] • *Scr* David Wilkinson, Irfan Shah

The First Grader ★★★🄬
Drama based on a true story
2010 · UK/S Afr/Fr · Colour · 98min

An 84-year-old Kenyan man demands his right to an education in this strange but true story that made headlines in 2005. When the Kenyan government launches an initiative to guarantee a primary education for everyone, former Mau Mau freedom fighter Maruge puts himself forward. He's met with resistance from the authorities, but his teacher (a soft yet steely Naomie Harris) refuses to turn him away. The fight is inspiring, as far as it goes, and the sight of an old man sitting in a classroom of six-year-olds is a potent one. But director Justin Chadwick (*The Other Boleyn Girl*) is less assured in conveying Maruge's inner turmoil, piecing together snapshots from the past and revealing the full picture too late. **SP DVD**

Naomie Harris *Jane Obinchu* • Oliver Litondo *Kimani N'gan'ga Maruge* • Tony Kgoroge *Charles Obinchu* • Vusi Kunene *Mr Kiputo* • Lwanda Jawar *Young Maruge* • Alfred Munyua *Teacher Alfred* ■ *Dir* Justin Chadwick • *Scr* Ann Peacock

The First Great Train Robbery ★★★🄬
Period crime thriller 1978 · UK · Colour · 105min

Sumptuously shot on location in Ireland by Geoffrey Unsworth, this allegedly true heist movie is a kind of "Butch Connery and the Sutherland Kid". Written and directed by Michael Crichton from his own novel, it features a pair of Victorian villains, played by Sean Connery and Donald Sutherland, who set out to steal gold destined for the army in the Crimea from a moving train. Crichton fails to sustain the tension of the robbery and too often lets the comedy run unchecked, but it's still a smashing piece of escapism. **DP DVD**

Sean Connery *Edward Pierce* • Donald Sutherland *Agar* • Lesley-Anne Down *Miriam* • Alan Webb *Edgar Trent* • Malcolm Terris *Henry Fowler* • Wayne Sleep *Clean Willy* • Michael Elphick *Burgess* ■ *Dir* Michael Crichton • *Scr* Michael Crichton, from his novel

First Kid ★★🄿
Comedy   1996 · US · Colour · 95min

This sugary family comedy was presumably designed as a vehicle for American comedy favourite Sinbad. He plays a Secret Service agent who gets the task of babysitting the US president's spoilt son (Brock Pierce). However, it's not long before the big guy warms to his charge and starts teaching him some valuable life lessons. It's predictable stuff, though the slapstick humour will delight youngsters. **JF**

Sinbad *Sam Simms* • Brock Pierce *Luke Davenport* • Blake Boyd *Dash* • Timothy Busfield *Woods* • Art LaFleur *Morton* • Lisa Eichhorn *Linda Davenport* • James Naughton *President Davenport* • Sonny Bono *Congressman Sonny Bono* ■ *Dir* David Mickey Evans • *Scr* Tim Kelleher

First Knight ★★★🄿
Adventure   1995 · US · Colour · 128min

If Kevin Costner can play Robin Hood with an American accent, then what's to stop Richard Gere giving Lancelot a Philadelphia twang? Gere is suitably dashing as the most independent knight of the Round Table, while Julia Ormond is ravishing as the constantly imperilled Guinevere. Stealing every scene, however, is Sean Connery, who, as a legend in his own lifetime, has no difficulty conveying the regal bearing of the once and future king. Very 1990s, yet

F

F

curiously and unashamedly old-fashioned. DP *DVD* *BL*

Sean Connery *King Arthur* • Richard Gere *Lancelot* • Julia Ormond *Lady Guinevere* • Ben Cross *Malagant* • Liam Cunningham *Sir Agravaine* • Christopher Villiers *Sir Kay* ■ *Dir* Jerry Zucker • *Scr* William Nicholson, from a story by William Nicholson, Lorne Cameron, David Hoselton

The First Legion ★★★ U

Drama   1951 · US · BW · 86min

Charles Boyer gives a fine performance as the former criminal attorney turned priest who investigates an apparent miracle at a Jesuit seminary. Made entirely on location at a Spanish-style inn, this is one of director Douglas Sirk's lesser-known films from the 1950s but it's skilfully directed, smoothly acted (though it takes time to accept comedian William Demarest as a Monsignor) and lighter in tone than might be expected. The ending is a mushy attempt to keep believers as well as sceptics happy. AE

Charles Boyer *Father Marc Arnoux* • William Demarest *Monsignor Michael Carey* • Lyle Bettger *Dr Peter Morrell* • Barbara Rush *Terry Gilmartin* • Leo G Carroll *Fr Paul Duquesne* ■ *Dir* Douglas Sirk • *Scr* Emmett Lavery

First Love ★★ U

Romance   1939 · US · BW · 80min

This is only significant now for Deanna Durbin receiving her first proper screen kiss, from Robert Stack in his movie debut. Hard to imagine the impact nowadays, but when singing superstar Durbin puckered up to receive her sensational smackeroo from handsome Stack, audiences were enthralled. As for the plot, it's a version of *Cinderella* with orphan Deanna hived off to an aunt and uncle. All rather charming, and Durbin sings a few choice songs. TS *DVD*

Deanna Durbin *Constance Harding* • Robert Stack *Ted Drake* • Eugene Pallette *James Clinton* • Helen Parrish *Barbara Clinton* • Lewis Howard *Walter Clinton* • Leatrice Joy *Grace Clinton* ■ *Dir* Henry Koster • *Scr* Bruce Manning, Lionel Houser

First Love ★★★★

Romance   1970 · W Ger/Swi · Colour · 92min

This is a classy adaptation of the Turgenev story about an adolescent boy who becomes infatuated with the flirtatious girl next door. She plays with him, then rejects him. John Moulder-Brown is suitably callow-looking as the boy, while Dominique Sanda is radiantly alluring. Impeccably shot by Ingmar Bergman's cameraman, Sven Nykvist, it marked the directing debut of Maximilian Schell; his style is a little academic at times, yet he assembles a fine supporting cast that includes playwright John Osborne. AT

John Moulder-Brown *Alexander* • Dominique Sanda *Sinaida* • Maximilian Schell *Father* • Valentina Cortese *Mother* • Marius Goring *Dr Lushin* • John Osborne *Maidanov* ■ *Dir* Maximilian Schell • *Scr* Maximilian Schell, John Gould, from a story by Ivan Turgenev

First Love ★★ 15

Romantic drama   1977 · US · Colour · 87min

This is a sentimental tale about a romance between college students William Katt and Susan Dey that turns sour when Katt discovers Dey is involved with a much older man. Because this was made in the 1970s, there are lots of intense discussions about sex, but Dey looks uncomfortable leaving her *Partridge Family* goody two-shoes image behind to play a woman with at least two men on the go. JB Swearing.

William Katt *Elgin Smith* • Susan Dey *Caroline* • John Heard *David* • Beverly D'Angelo *Shelley* • Robert Loggia *John March* • Tom Lacy *Professor Oxtan* • Swoosie Kurtz *Marsha* ■ *Dir* Joan Darling • *Scr* Jane Stanton Hitchcock, David Freeman, from the short story *Sentimental Education* by Harold Brodkey

First Man into Space ★★ PG

Science-fiction adventure
1958 · UK · BW · 73min

Cosmic rays mutate Earth's first astronaut into a marauding monster with a taste for blood in this briskly efficient B-movie from the golden era of British science fiction. Director Robert Day goes for both pity and scares by engendering sympathy for the one-eyed malformation while delivering uneasy shocks. Lacklustre acting from Marshall Thompson doesn't help his cause, but Marla Landi screaming every time the slime-encrusted alien appears does add an unintentional streak of light entertainment. AJ

Marshall Thompson *Commander CE Prescott* • Marla Landi *Tia Francesca* • Bill Edwards *Lt Dan Prescott* • Robert Ayres *Captain Ben Richards* • Bill Nagy *Wilson* • Carl Jaffe *Dr Paul von Essen* ■ *Dir* Robert Day • *Scr* John C Cooper, Lance Z Hargreaves, from a story by Wyott Ordung

First Men in the Moon

★★★ U

Science-fiction adventure
1964 · UK · Colour · 98min

Outstanding special effects from stop-motion magician Ray Harryhausen add further lustre to director Nathan Juran's colourfully engaging tale, adapted from the HG Wells novel, about a Victorian lunar expedition. Lionel Jeffries is splendid as the eccentric professor who uses his antigravity paint invention to achieve lift-off in this light-hearted adventure. Jeffries, Edward Judd and Martha Hyer are then captured by insectoid creatures and menaced by a Moon caterpillar in this highly enjoyable flight of sheer fantasy. AJ *DVD*

Edward Judd *Arnold Bedford* • Lionel Jeffries *Cavor* • Martha Hyer *Kate Callender* • Erik Chitty *Gibbs* • Betty McDowall *Maggie* ■ *Dir* Nathan Juran • *Scr* Nigel Kneale, Jan Read, from the novel by HG Wells

First Monday in October

★★★ 15

Comedy drama   1981 · US · Colour · 93min

There is far too much chat, even for a courtroom movie, but, if you plan your tea breaks for the segments in which the American political and legal systems are discussed, this is quite a likeable romantic comedy of sorts. Jill Clayburgh does a sterling job as the first female Supreme Court judge, whose strict principles alienate and then attract shabby liberal colleague Walter Matthau. The leads make better adversaries than possible partners and their jousting alone sustains the interest. DP Swearing.

Walter Matthau *Dan Snow* • Jill Clayburgh *Ruth Loomis* • Barnard Hughes *Chief Justice Crawford* • Jan Sterling *Christine Snow* • James Stephens *Mason Woods* • Jan Ronald Neame • *Scr* Jerome Lawrence, Robert E Lee, from their play

The First Movie ★★★

Documentary   2009 · UK/Can · Colour · 76min

In this engaging documentary, Mark Cousins arrives in the Iraqi Kurdish town of Goptapa to test his thesis on the healing power of cinema and enchants the local children by showing them such magical movies as *The Red Balloon* and *ET*. But it's the digital video footage they shoot themselves that proves the most compelling. Cousins's on-screen presence is occasionally distracting, but it's hard not to be touched by the film's sincerity and the excitement, enthusiasm and imagination of its spirited subjects. DP English, Kurdish +subtitles.

■ *Dir/Scr* Mark Cousins

First Name: Carmen ★★ 18

Drama   1983 · Fr/Swi · Colour · 80min

Ostensibly a film about a terrorist called Carmen X, this is actually a movie about the problems of making movies, interspersed with recitals of Beethoven string quartets and long sessions with director Jean-Luc Godard, sitting in a lunatic asylum and burbling on about himself, life and art.

Maybe Godard thought this could be his *8½*, and that a few explicit sex scenes would somehow attract an audience. Some of it is actually rather charming, but for most viewers this will be maddening. AT French +subtitles. *DVD*

Maruschka Detmers *Carmen X* • Jacques Bonnaffé *Joseph Bonnaffe* • Myriem Roussel *Claire* • Christophe Odent *Gang leader* • Jean-Luc Godard *Uncle Jean* • Hippolyte Girardot *Fred* ■ *Dir* Jean-Luc Godard • *Scr* Anne-Marie Miéville

First Night ★ 15

Musical romantic comedy
2010 · UK · Colour · 116min

The idea of a romantic comedy in which the characters are opera singers and the plot reflects the passions and betrayals of classic opera was reportedly one of the last projects for Rumpole creator John Mortimer. But there is no evidence of his dry wit in Christopher Menaul's finished film. The acting is broad, the script clichéd and the comedy leaden, while a trick has also been missed in Sarah Brightman's casting: instead of the prima donna part that would have eminently suited her, she's saddled with the dull role of orchestra conductor. BP Swearing, sex scenes, nudity.

Richard E Grant *Adam* • Sarah Brightman *Celia* • Mia Maestro *Nicoletta* • Julian Ovenden *Tom* • Nigel Lindsay *Martin* ■ *Dir* Christopher Menaul • *Scr* Christopher Menaul, Jeremy Sams

The First of May ★★

Drama   1999 · US · Colour · 111min

Debutant director Paul Sirmons's account of an orphan runaway's adventures with a discontented pensioner has its heart in the right place, but this suffers from the fact that it's too darn sweet for its own good. There are nice cameos from Mickey Rooney and baseball legend Joe DiMaggio, but the kitsch quotient rises unchecked and Sirmons allows young Dan Byrd to overplay almost all of his big scenes. DP

Julie Harris (2) *Carlotta* • Mickey Rooney *Boss Ed* • Robin O'Dell *Michelle* • Joe DiMaggio ■ *Dir* Paul Sirmons • *Scr* Gary Rogers

The First of the Few ★★★ U

Second World War biographical drama
1942 · UK · BW · 113min

Offered contracts and any number of enticing star roles after *Gone with the Wind*, Leslie Howard chose to leave Hollywood and return to England to make films designed to boost wartime morale. Here, he directs and stars as visionary aircraft designer RJ Mitchell, the father of the Spitfire. The fine cast includes Rosamund John as his wife and David Niven as the test pilot, while William Walton's fine score sums up an entire era of flying pictures. It was Howard's final screen performance: his plane was shot down in 1943 on a mission that immediately became shrouded in mystery - one that has never been explained. AT *DVD* *BL*

Leslie Howard *RJ Mitchell* • David Niven *Geoffrey Crisp* • Rosamund John *Diana Mitchell* • Roland Culver *Commander Bride* • Annie Firth [Anne Firth] *Miss Harper* • David Horne *Higgins* ■ *Dir* Leslie Howard • *Scr* Antone de Grunwald, Miles Malleson, from a story by Henry C James, Katherine Strueby

First Position ★★★ U

Documentary   2011 · US · Colour · 94min

Former ballet dancer Bess Kargman makes her directorial debut with this inspirational documentary about the efforts of six young people to make it to the finals of the Youth America Grand Prix, the world's premiere ballet competition held in New York. Some have overcome greater adversity than others to be there, like adopted 14-year-old Michaela - originally from Sierra Leone and orphaned when her parents were murdered in the civil war - who still battles to overcome the view held by some that black girls can't do ballet. Kargman's empathy is tangible, and behind the tales of sacrifice and pain, there is an absorbing story of focused, talented and mature young people

pursuing their dreams. TP English, Spanish, French, Hebrew +subtitles.

■ *Dir* Bess Kargman

The First Power ★★ 18

Horror thriller   1990 · US · Colour · 94min

Detective Lou Diamond Phillips catches the Pentagram Killer - so called because he carves that sign on his victims' chests - and sends him to the gas chamber. From there his demonic spirit transfers into a succession of weak bodies and continues the murderous spree. Phillips and clairvoyant Tracy Griffith (half-sister of Melanie) try to stop the carnage. A few eerie moments and a couple of excellent stunts are lost in the poor continuity, sloppy framing and senseless plot. AJ

Lou Diamond Phillips *Russell Logan* • Tracy Griffith *Tess Seaton* • Jeff Kober *Patrick Channing* • Mykel T Williamson [Mykelti Williamson] *Detective Oliver Franklin* • Elizabeth Arlen *Sister Marguerite* ■ *Dir/Scr* Robert Resnikoff

The First Rebel ★★★ U

Western   1939 · US · BW · 77min

Originally called *Allegheny Uprising* and retitled for the UK, this super little pre-American War of Independence western benefited from its casting, reteaming the leads from *Stagecoach*, John Wayne and Claire Trevor. Wayne smashes evil Brian Donlevy's illicit liquor trade as well as dealing with snarling British officer George Sanders and finding the time to romance Trevor. The film is helped immensely by the somewhat expressionistic lighting from master cinematographer Nicholas Musuraca. TS *DVD*

John Wayne *Jim Smith* • Claire Trevor *Janie* • Brian Donlevy *Callendar* • George Sanders *Capt Swanson* • Wilfrid Lawson *MacDouglas* • Robert Barrat *Duncan* ■ *Dir* William A Seiter • *Scr* PJ Wolfson

First Shot ★ 12

Action thriller   2002 · US/Can · Colour · 88min

Armand Mastroianni completes an undistinguished hat-trick with this feeble follow-up to *First Daughter* and *First Target*. Reclaiming her original role as a troubleshooting Secret Service agent from Daryl Hannah, Mariel Hemingway once again fails to convince. Here, she's on the trail of the would-be assassin who took a pot shot at the president and at the same time struggles to save her marriage to long-suffering Doug Savant. Overall it's hard to imagine a thriller with less excitement, ingenuity or credibility. DP *DVD*

Mariel Hemingway *Alex McGregor* • Doug Savant *Grant Coleman* • Jenna Leigh Green *Jess Hayes* • Wanda Cannon *Kathryn Yarnell* • Sebastian Spence *Owen Taylor* • Steve Makaj *Judd Walters* • Michelle Harrison *Courtney Robinson* ■ *Dir* Armand Mastroianni • *Scr* Carey W Hayes, Chad Hayes

First Sunday ★★ 12

Crime comedy   2008 · US · Colour · 93min

Former singer/songwriter Ice Cube and comedian Tracy Morgan (*30 Rock*) star as two bumbling, would-be crooks who plan to rob a Baltimore church to alleviate their respective financial problems, only to end up taking half the congregation hostage when the heist goes wrong. Former playwright David E Talbert mismatches his two leads nicely - Ice Cube's exasperated straight man is constantly irked by Morgan's harebrained schemer - and sticks largely to his stage roots by setting most of the action inside the church. But the redemption angle is ladled on so thick, it will test the faith of all but the most forgiving viewers. JR *DVD* *BL*

Ice Cube *Durell* • Katt Williams *Rickey* • Tracy Morgan *LeeJohn* • Loretta Devine *Sister Doris* • Michael Beach *Deacon* • Keith David *Judge B* • Bennet Galloway • Regina Hall *Omunique* • Malinda Williams *Tianna* ■ *Dir/Scr* David E Talbert

First Target ★★ 15
Action thriller　2000 · US · Colour · 88min

In this competent but colourless sequel to TV-movie thriller *First Daughter*, Daryl Hannah steps into Mariel Hemingway's shoes as Secret Service agent Alex McGregor, here trying to foil another assassination plot against the US president. Gregory Harrison reprises his role as the photogenic leader of the Free World, while Doug Savant is saddled once again with the thankless part of McGregor's boyfriend. JF

Daryl Hannah *Alex McGregor* • Gregory Harrison *President Jonathan Hayes* • Doug Savant *Grant Coleman* • Brandy Ledford *Kelsey* • Peter Flemming *Stewart McCall* ■ *Dir* Armand Mastroianni • *Scr* Carey W Hayes, Chad Hayes

The First Teacher ★★★★
Period drama　1965 · USSR · BW · 98min

Andrei Konchalovsky made his directorial debut with this scrupulous adaptation of Chingiz Aitmatov's novel of post-Revolutionary progress. Employing mostly non-professional performers and utilitising a lyrical realism, he captures the dignity of the conquered Kirghiz kulaks while contrasting their Muslim fundamentalism with the intractable steppe terrain. Bolot Beishenaliev is hugely sympathetic as the ex-Red Army recruit sent to open the region's first school, but it was Natalya Arinbasarova, as the teenager whose father refuses to let her marry an outsider, who took the acting honours at the Venice film festival. DP Russian +subtitles.

Bolot Beishenaliev *Dyuishen* • Natalya Arinbasarova *Altinai* ■ *Dir* Andrei Mikhalkov-Konchalovsky [Andrei Konchalovsky] • *Scr* Andrei Konchalovsky, Chingiz Aitmatov, Boris Dobrodeyev, from a novel by Chingiz Aytmatov

The First Texan ★★ U
Biographical western　1956 · US · Colour · 82min

Joel McCrea stars as Sam Houston, the man who avenges the fall of the Alamo and becomes the first president of the new Republic of Texas. It's a sluggish picture, more talk than action until the well-staged climactic battle of San Jacinto, but McCrea gives a sincere performance as the man who bides his time and Felicia Farr displays spirit in a humdrum romantic role. AE

Joel McCrea *Sam Houston* • Felicia Farr *Katherine* • Jeff Morrow *Jim Bowie* • Wallace Ford *Delaney* • Abraham Sofaer *Don Carlos* • Jody McCrea *Baker* ■ *Dir* Byron Haskin • *Scr* Dan Ullman [Daniel B Ullman]

The First Travelling Saleslady ★ U
Comedy western　1956 · US · Colour · 92min

You could charitably view this as an early feminist tract, but actually it's a deadly dull, badly-paced "comedy" about a corset saleswoman out West reduced to hawking barbed wire. Played by the totally miscast Ginger Rogers, interest now would come from a very young and bronzed Clint Eastwood playing Carol Channing's Cavalry boyfriend. Director Arthur Lubin, who also produced this farrago allegedly once intended for Mae West, supervises matters as though he wishes he were somewhere else. TS

Ginger Rogers *Rose Gillray* • Barry Nelson *Charles Masters* • Carol Channing *Molly Wade* • David Brian *James Carter* • James Arness *Joel Kingdom* • Clint Eastwood *Jack Rice* ■ *Dir* Arthur Lubin • *Scr* Stephen Longstreet, Devery Freeman

The First Wives Club ★★★★ PG
Comedy　1996 · US · Colour · 98min

Olivia Goldsmith's bestselling novel is turned into a hilarious film by *Police Academy* director Hugh Wilson. Hollywood divas Goldie Hawn, Bette Midler and Diane Keaton give sparkling performances as the three wealthy New Yorkers who have been deserted by their husbands in favour of much younger women (including *Sex and the City*'s Sarah Jessica Parker and *Showgirls* star Elizabeth Berkley). Instead of sitting back and taking it, the trio unites to

exact revenge and gain financial control, with Midler stealing the show from her two co-stars as the most deliciously vicious of them all. Terrific stuff. JB DVD

Goldie Hawn *Elise Elliot Atchison* • Bette Midler *Brenda Morelli Cushman* • Diane Keaton *Annie MacDuggan Paradise* • Maggie Smith *Gunilla Garson Goldberg* • Sarah Jessica Parker *Shelly Stewart* • Dan Hedaya *Morty Cushman* • Stockard Channing *Cynthia Swann Griffin* • Elizabeth Berkley *Phoebe LaVelle* ■ *Dir* Hugh Wilson • *Scr* Robert Harling, from the novel by Olivia Goldsmith

The First Year ★★★ U
Drama　1932 · US · BW · 81min

Janet Gaynor and Charles Farrell were indisputably Hollywood's sweethearts in the immediate pre-sound era, and carried on as a strictly professional perfect screen couple for a while through the early talkie years. This is a well-scripted tale of a newlywed couple's attempt to settle down and, though both Gaynor and Farrell are a shade long in the tooth for the roles, they play together superbly, with great charm and élan. TS

Janet Gaynor *Grace Livingston* • Charles Farrell (1) *Tommy Tucker* • Minna Gombell *Mrs Barstow* • Leila Bennett *Hattie* • Dudley Digges *Dr Anderson* • Robert McWade *Fred Livingston* • George Meeker *Dick Loring* ■ *Dir* William K Howard • *Scr* Lynn Starling, from a play by Frank Craven

Firstborn ★★ 15
Drama　1984 · US · Colour · 96min

In a prime example of a film that engages interest only to dramatically lose it with the dénouement, Teri Garr is a divorcee with two sons who picks up a lover that her boys realise is totally unsavoury. However by playing on her self-doubt he manages to drive a wedge between the mother and her sons. Peter Weller is excellent as the sinister suitor and Garr is convincing as the neurotic mother, but the plausible set-up is thrown away by actions more akin to *Death Wish* than domestic melodrama. FL

Teri Garr *Wendy* • Peter Weller *Sam* • Christopher Collet *Jake* • Corey Haim *Brian* • Sarah Jessica Parker *Lisa* • Richard Brandon *Dad* ■ *Dir* Michael Apted • *Scr* Ron Koslow

A Fish Called Wanda ★★★★★ 15
Comedy　1988 · UK/US · Colour · 103min

This hilarious tale of criminal incompetence and transatlantic eccentricity is easily John Cleese's finest achievement since *Fawlty Towers*. He excels as the uptight London barrister who becomes the dupe of scheming American thief Jamie Lee Curtis and her doltishly macho lover, Kevin Kline. But Cleese must share the credit for the film's international success with director Charles Crichton, who was the perfect choice for this sparkling blend of Ealing and Monty Python. Every piece of verbal or physical humour is a model of timing and restraint, and this sparkling comedy also has an underlying darkness that recalls the work of Preston Sturges and Billy Wilder. Praise doesn't come much higher than that. DP Swearing, some violence, sex scenes, nudity. DVD BD

John Cleese *Archie Leach* • Jamie Lee Curtis *Wanda* • Kevin Kline *Otto* • Michael Palin *Ken* • Maria Aitken *Wendy* • Tom Georgeson *George* • Patricia Hayes *Mrs Coady* • Geoffrey Palmer *Judge* • Cynthia Caylor [Cynthia Cleese] *Portia* ■ *Dir* Charles Crichton • *Scr* John Cleese, from a story by Charles Crichton, Cleese

Fish Tank ★★★★ 15
Social drama　2009 · UK · Colour · 117min

Director Andrea Arnold's second feature – a Jury Prize winner at Cannes – is a quietly searing drama about the directionless life of an underprivileged teenage girl on an Essex council estate. Mia (Katie Jarvis) finds escape from a claustrophobic home life with her single mother and younger sister through drink and dancing. The arrival of her mother's new boyfriend (Michael Fassbender) puts new pressures on the already unravelling family unit as Mia is drawn to the sympathetic outsider. Arnold's direction is sure-footed, creating an honest

and intelligent documentary-style drama that doesn't flinch from hard truths. Outstanding performances from every member of the cast and the beautiful cinematography make this subtle, shocking and redemptive tale a rewarding slice of cinematic reality. KK Swearing, sex scenes, nudity. DVD BD

Katie Jarvis *Mia* • Kierston Wareing *Joanne* • Michael Fassbender *Connor* • Rebecca Griffiths *Tyler* • Harry Treadaway *Billy* • Jason Maza *Liam* ■ *Dir/Scr* Andrea Arnold • *Cinematographer* Robbie Ryan

The Fisher King ★★★★★ 15
Fantasy drama　1991 · US · Colour · 131min

The Arthurian legend of a maimed warrior healed by the innocence of "a perfect fool" is given a magical update by director Terry Gilliam, tripping the light fantastic in his highly individual manner. Gilliam has an eerie knack of wringing visionary heart-tugging power from unsentimental if bizarre material, and Jeff Bridges's mythical search for redemption in the enchanted kingdom of New York fits the bill exactly. This is a magnificent perusal into what fires and feeds the soul, with super-tramp Robin Williams keeping his trademark zaniness in check until it really counts. But it's Oscar winner Mercedes Ruehl's electrifying portrayal of moral betrayal that you'll remember long after the fade-out. AJ Swearing, some violence, brief nudity. DVD

Robin Williams *Parry* • Jeff Bridges *Jack Lucas* • Amanda Plummer *Lydia* • Mercedes Ruehl *Anne Napolitano* • Michael Jeter *Homeless cabaret singer* • Adam Bryant *Radio engineer* • David Hyde Pierce *Lou Rosen* ■ *Dir* Terry Gilliam • *Scr* Richard LaGravenese

FIST ★★★ PG
Drama　1978 · US · Colour · 130min

Sylvester Stallone made a brave attempt to get away from his *Rocky* image in this unflattering portrayal of the American trade union movement. He plays Johnny Kovak, who rises to the leadership of the Federation of Interstate Truckers but finds that power corrupts. The result is not wholly one-dimensional and there are moments of real dramatic conviction. Director Norman Jewison supplies the visual punch to this drama, but Stallone is outclassed by Rod Steiger and Peter Boyle. TH Swearing. DVD

Sylvester Stallone *Johnny Kovak* • Rod Steiger *Senator Andrew Madison* • Peter Boyle *Max Graham* • Melinda Dillon *Anna Zerinkas* • David Huffman *Abe Belkin* • Kevin Conway *Vince Doyle* • Tony LoBianco *Babe Milano* ■ *Dir* Norman Jewison • *Scr* Sylvester Stallone, Joe Eszterhas, from articles by Joe Eszterhas

Fist of Fury ★★★ 18
Martial arts drama　1972 · HK · Colour · 101min

Despite a troubled shoot, this remains an essential Bruce Lee vehicle. Dating from his Hong Kong days, he plays a martial arts student who sets out to avenge the death of his beloved mentor. He uncovers a gang of smugglers who killed his boxing master when he discovered their plots. The uninitiated will cringe at the dumb script and amateurish direction, but the fight scenes, choreographed by Lee, are breathtaking and his athletic charisma will win over doubters. JF Cantonese dubbed. DVD BD

Bruce Lee *Chen Chen* • Nora Miao *Yuan Le-Erh* • James Tien *Fan Chun-Hsia* • Robert Baker (1) *Russian boxer* ■ *Dir/Scr* Lo Wei

Fist of Legend ★★★ 18
Period martial arts thriller　1994 · HK · Colour · 99min

This thriller is a virtual remake of Bruce Lee's *Fist of Fury* and more than holds its own in comparison. Set in the 1930s, Jet Li is the martial arts expert who returns to his old academy – now under the control of the Japanese – to avenge the death of his beloved tutor. The striking period settings provide a sumptuous backdrop to some superbly choreographed fight

sequences. JF Cantonese, Japanese dubbed. DVD BD

Jet Li *Chen Zhen* • Shinobu Nakayama *Mitsuko Yamada* • Chin Siu-hou *Huo Ting-en* • Ada Choi *Xian-Hong/So Lan* • Yasuaki Kurata *Fumio Funakoshi, Mitsuko's uncle* ■ *Dir* Gordon Chan • *Scr* Yip Kwong-Kim, Lan Kai-To • *Choreographer* Yuen Woo-Ping

Fist of the North Star ★★ 18
Animated science-fiction adventure　1986 · Jpn · Colour · 111min

Based on a Japanese *manga* of the same name, this animated movie gained instant cult status because of the extremely violent and gory deaths many of the grotesque characters suffer. One "hero" aims get his girlfriend back from the brute who beat him up and left him for dead, but there is not much else going on in this story about various martial arts factions and gangs at each other's throats in a post-apocalypse world. KB Japanese dubbed. DVD

John Vickery *Ken* • Melodee Spivack *Julia* • Wally Burr *Raoh* • Michael McConnohie *Shin* • Gregory Snegoff *Rei* • Tony Oliver *Bat* • Holly Sidell *Lynn* ■ *Dir* Toyoo Ashida • *Scr* Susumu Takahisa, from the graphic novels by Buronson Hara, Tetsuo Hara

Fist of the North Star ★★ 18
Science-fiction martial arts adventure　1995 · US · Colour · 88min

Martial arts star Gary Daniels is Kenshiro, the warrior on a mission to restore peace between the warring factions in his post-apocalyptic kingdom. Evil chief Lord Shin (Costas Mandylor) has other ideas. It resembles a bad spaghetti western unceremoniously placed in a science-fiction setting, and Tony Randel's direction fails to match the hyper-kinetic quality of the original popular *manga* series, despite plenty of goofy action spiced up with gore. AJ Violence, swearing. DVD

Gary Daniels *Kenshiro* • Malcolm McDowell *Ryuken* • Costas Mandylor *Lord Shin* • Dante Basco *Bat* • Nalona Herron *Lynn* • Melvin Van Peebles *Asher* • Chris Penn *Jackal* ■ *Dir* Tony Randel • *Scr* Peter Atkins, Tony Randel, from the graphic novels by Buronson Hara, Tetsuo Hara

LANDMARK FILM
Sergio Leone restyled the western, and propelled Clint Eastwood and the music of Ennio Morricone to superstardom

A Fistful of Dollars ★★★★★ 15
Classic spaghetti western　1964 · It/W Ger/Sp · Colour · 95min

Based on Akira Kurosawa's 1961 samurai classic *Yojimbo*, this was the first "spaghetti" western to find a worldwide audience. Italian director Sergio Leone's daringly brilliant use of extreme close-up and compensational depth and his unflinching depiction of violence gave the western a new lease of life. Clint Eastwood became an international superstar for his portrayal of the Man with No Name, insisting that much of his dialogue was cut to increase the drifter's air of mystery. Gian Maria Volonté lends excellent support as the snarling Ramon, and Ennio Morricone's minimalist score is a gem. What became known as Leone's *Dollars* trilogy continued with *For a Few Dollars More*. DP DVD BD

Clint Eastwood *The Man with No Name* • Marianne Koch *Marisol* • Johnny Wels [Gian Maria Volonté] *Ramon Rojo* • Pepe Calvo *Silvanito* • Wolfgang Lukschy *John Baxter* • Sieghardt Rupp *Esteban Rojo* • Antonio Prieto *Benito Rojo* • Margarita Lozano *Consuela Baxter* • Daniel Martin *Julian* • Carol Brown [Bruno Carotenuto] *Antonio Baxter* • Benito Stefanelli *Rubio* • Richard Stuyvesant [Mario Brega] *Chico* • Josef Egger *Piripero* ■ *Dir* Sergio Leone • *Scr* Sergio Leone, Duccio Tessari, Victor A Catena, G Schock, from the film *Yojimbo* by Akira Kurosawa, Ryuzo Kikushima, Hideo Oguni, from the novel *Red Harvest* by Dashiell Hammett • *Music* Dan Savio [Ennio Morricone]

A Fistful of Dynamite ★★★ 15
Spaghetti western　1971 · It · Colour · 150min

This spaghetti western from master chef Sergio Leone was originally called *Duck,*

You Sucker!, a title that is perhaps more in tune with the film's jokey intentions. Rod Steiger stars as a peasant who becomes involved with fugitive IRA explosives expert James Coburn and the Mexican Revolution. There's nothing really funny about Coburn as a walking arsenal, but Leone manages more laughs than you'd expect, thanks to his actors' gift for deadpan comedy. TH Some dialogue dubbed. Violence, swearing. **DVD**

Rod Steiger *Juan Miranda* • James Coburn *Sean Mallory* • Romolo Valli *Dr Villega* • Maria Monti *Adolita* • Rik Battaglia *Santerna* • Franco Graziosi *Governor* ■ *Dir* Sergio Leone • *Scr* Sergio Leone, Luciano Vicenzoni, Sergio Donati, from a story by Sergio Leone

A Fistful of Fingers ★★ 15
Western spoof   1995 · UK · Colour · 77min

Shot in Somerset on a minuscule budget, this spoof western from director Edgar Wright features *Monty Python* slapstick, *Airplane!*-style gags and Sergio Leone references. The Man With No Name, his face smeared in fake five o'clock shadow, pursues the outlaw Squint across the Mendips. Although most of the humour in Wright's game homage falls flat, it's hard not to enjoy the sheer gung ho ingenuity of this movie. He would go on to make *Shaun of the Dead* and *Hot Fuzz*. AJ

Graham Low *No Name/Walter Marshall* • Martin Curtis *Running Sore* • Oliver Evans *The Squint* • Quentin Green *Jimmy James* • Jeremy Beadle ■ *Dir/Scr* Edgar Wright

Fists in the Pocket
★★★★ 12
Drama   1965 · It · BW · 104min

Shot on a shoestring, Marco Bellocchio's debut feature is an aggressive, semi-autobiographical assault on family life and bourgeois parochialism. Raging at the restrictions of small-town, middle-class life, the film uses epilepsy and blindness as symbols of social malaise to which teenager Lou Castel can only respond with increasingly frenzied acts of violence when he tries to escape the family by getting married. Typified by Castel's astonishing portrayal of pent-up fury, the bruising backstreet authenticity is amazing for its time and totally convincing. DP In Italian. Violence.

Paola Pitagora *Giulia* • Lou Castel *Sandro* • Marino Mase *Augusto* • Liliana Gerace *The Mother* • Pier Luigi Troglio *Leone* • Jean MacNeil *Lucia* ■ *Dir/Scr* Marco Bellocchio

Fitzcarraldo ★★★★★ PG
Period drama   1982 · W Ger · Colour · 150min

This is German director Werner Herzog's true masterpiece, a labour of love that almost engulfed him. It's the story of a quest by the white-suited Fitzcarraldo (played by Klaus Kinski) to build an opera house in the South American jungle, funded by profits from a rubber plantation. To achieve his ambition, Kinski is required to drag a 320-ton steamship over a mountain. This, the film's central motif, Herzog actually did. There is far more to this lengthy film than a boat going up a hill, but it crowns an unforgettable piece of cinema. The making of this epic (captured in the 1982 documentary *Burden of Dreams*) sometimes threatens to eclipse the work itself, but that would be a tragedy. AC German +subtitles. **DVD**

Klaus Kinski *Fitzcarraldo* • Claudia Cardinale *Molly* • José Lewgoy *Don Aquilino* • Paul Hittscher *Paul* • Miguel Angel Fuentes *Cholo* ■ *Dir/Scr* Werner Herzog

Fitzwilly ★★ U
Comedy   1967 · US · Colour · 102min

What with Edith Evans compiling a dictionary for people who can't spell and butler Dick Van Dyke heading a crime syndicate to prevent her discovering that the family fortune has given out, this keeps threatening to turn into a gleeful screwball romp. That it fails to do so is mostly down to the killjoy direction of Delbert Mann, who doesn't seem to appreciate the comic

potential of the situations and Isobel Lennart's gag-packed script. DP

Dick Van Dyke *Fitzwilliam* • Barbara Feldon *Juliet Nowell* • Edith Evans *Victoria Woodworth* • John McGiver *Albert* • Harry Townes *Mr Nowell* • John Fiedler *Mr Dunne* • Norman Fell *Oberblatz* • Cecil Kellaway *Buckmaster* • Sam Waterston *Oliver* ■ *Dir* Delbert Mann • *Scr* Isobel Lennart, from the novel *A Garden of Cucumbers* by Poyntz Tyler

Five ★★★
Science-fiction drama   1951 · US · BW · 90min

Former radio producer-turned-exploitation merchant Arch Oboler has some interesting gimmick-laden films to his credit, most notably the first movie in 3D, the notorious *Bwana Devil*. The gimmick here is both the title and the plot, which deals with the last five survivors after the Earth has been devastated by a (then topical) A-bomb blast. It's all rather static and cheap-looking, but the dialogue is clever and the situations, though contrived, are intriguing. TS

William Phipps *Michael* • Susan Douglas *Roseanne* • James Anderson (2) *Eric* • Charles Lampkin *Charles* ■ *Dir/Scr* Arch Oboler

Five ★★★ U
Experimental documentary drama   2003 · Iran/Jpn · Colour · 125min

Subtitled *5 Long Takes Dedicated to Yasujiro Ozu*, this is an homage to those Zen-inspired "pillow shots" that the Japanese maestro used to insert between scenes. Emulating Ozu's fixed-camera perspective, Abbas Kiarostami considers, in turn, a piece of driftwood on the low tide, daytrippers strolling along a seaside promenade, some dogs romping on a beach, a paddling of indecisive ducks and an impenetrable nocturnal pond scene accompanied by a deafening chorus of frogs. Fittingly, each vignette is divided by enchanting musical interludes. This rigorous experimental exercise – filmed entirely without dialogue – won't appeal to everyone, but those who appreciate sly visual humour and cinematic poetry will find much to enjoy. DP In Iranian. **DVD**

■ *Dir/Scr* Abbas Kiarostami

Five ★★★
Comedy drama   2011 · US · Colour · 87min

Demi Moore and Jennifer Aniston are among the Hollywood heavyweights who have thrown their weight behind these short films marking International Women's Day. Each explores the painful impact of breast cancer. Moore transports us back to 1969 when the words "breast" and "cancer" are still so taboo that no one can explain to a lonely little girl why her poorly mum is off-limits, while Aniston's tale, funny, heart-rending and uplifting by turns, takes us through the stages of a woman's diagnosis. CW

■ *Dir* Jennifer Aniston, Patty Jenkins, Alicia Keys, Demi Moore, Penelope Spheeris

Five Branded Women ★★
Second World War drama   1960 · US/It/Yug · BW · 103min

A stellar cast has far too little asked of it in this uncompromising exploration of Yugoslav resistance during the Second World War. The scene in which the women have their heads shaved for dallying with Nazi officer Steve Forrest is easily the most disturbing of the picture, as the later guerrilla encounters differ little from the combat sequences seen in a dozen other war movies. DP

Van Heflin *Velko* • Silvana Mangano *Jovanka* • Vera Miles *Daniza* • Barbara Bel Geddes *Marja* • Jeanne Moreau *Ljuba* • Richard Basehart *Captain Reinhardt* • Harry Guardino *Branco* • Steve Forrest *Sergeant Keller* ■ *Dir* Martin Ritt • *Scr* Ivo Perilli, from the novel by Ugo Pirro

Five Came Back ★★★
Adventure   1939 · US · BW · 75min

Pilot Chester Morris crashes his plane in the Andes and can only take off again with the titular five. Of the 12 on board, who will escape the dreaded headhunters of the Amazon? Lucille Ball? John Carradine? C

Aubrey Smith? Wendy Barrie? This is still gripping, though showing its age now. Director John Farrow liked the plot so much he remade it in 1956 as *Back from Eternity*. TS

Chester Morris *Bill* • Lucille Ball *Peggy* • Wendy Barrie *Alice Melhorne* • John Carradine *Crimp* • Allen Jenkins *Peter* • C Aubrey Smith *Prof Henry Spengler* ■ *Dir* John Farrow • *Scr* Jerry Cady [Jerome Cady], Dalton Trumbo, Nathanael West, from a story by Richard Carroll

5 Card Stud ★★★ 12
Western   1968 · US · Colour · 98min

When a cardsharp is lynched by the five men he cheated, the men themselves start dying mysteriously. This neat little mystery is really Agatha Christie's *Ten Little Indians* transposed to the Wild West, with Dean Martin as a cardplayer turned detective and Robert Mitchum as a preacher. Made during a brief fad for poker pictures, it exists solely on the charm of its two stars. AT **DVD**

Dean Martin *Van Morgan* • Robert Mitchum *Reverend Rudd* • Roddy McDowall *Nick Evers* • Inger Stevens *Lily Langford* • Katherine Justice *Nora Evers* • John Anderson *Marshal Dana* • Yaphet Kotto *Little George* ■ *Dir* Henry Hathaway • *Scr* Marguerite Roberts, from a novel by Roy Gaulden

Five Children and It ★★ U
Period fantasy adventure   2004 · UK/Fr/US · Colour · 85min

If it wasn't for the splendid voice talent of comedian Eddie Izzard as the titular sand fairy "It", this family adventure would be a totally lacklustre affair. During the First World War, five London siblings are evacuated to their unconventional uncle Kenneth Branagh's seaside mansion. There they discover an irritable, ancient Psammead (Izzard), who possesses amazing wish-granting powers. This offers a flat script, school play-style overacting and poor special effects. SF **DVD**

Kenneth Branagh *Uncle Albert* • Zoë Wanamaker *Martha* • Eddie Izzard *It* • Freddie Highmore *Robert* • Jonathan Bailey *Cyril* • Jessica Claridge *Anthea* • Poppy Rogers *Jane* • Tara FitzGerald *Mother* • John Sessions *Peasemarsh* • Norman Wisdom *Nesbit* ■ *Dir* John Stephenson • *Scr* David Solomons, from the novel by E Nesbit

Five Corners ★★★ 15
Thriller   1987 · US · Colour · 90min

It's the cast of this virtually unreleased movie that catches the eye: Jodie Foster, Tim Robbins and John Turturro. It's set in the Bronx in 1964 where Foster has been nearly raped, Turturro emerges from jail for said crime, and Robbins is about to go south to join the civil rights movement. After much scene-setting, Turturro goes completely crazy. As a coming-of-age drama, it offers nothing new, and the film's shifts of mood from comedy to drama to horror are over-calculated, but the three young stars are always worth watching. AT Violence, swearing. **DVD**

Jodie Foster *Linda* • Tim Robbins *Harry Fitzgerald* • Todd Graff *James* • John Turturro *Heinz Sabantino* • Elizabeth Berridge *Melanie* • Rose Gregorio *Mrs Sabantino* ■ *Dir* Tony Bill • *Scr* John Patrick Shanley

5 Days of War ★★ 15
War drama based on a true story   2011 · US · Colour · 108min

Set during the swift but devastating five-day war between Russia and the Georgian Republic in 2008, this is the account of a renegade American journalist caught behind enemy lines, who is determined, not only to survive, but to persuade apathetic American TV networks to run his story. Director Renny Harlin may have fallen from his blockbuster peak, but he'll be damned if he doesn't litter a few car explosions and somersaults in his wake. The result is too lightweight, and fails to provoke any thought for a deserving subject. ReP English, Russian, Georgian +subtitles. **DVD**

Rupert Friend *Thomas Anders* • Emmanuelle Chriqui *Tatia Meddevi* • Richard Coyle *Sebastian Ganz* • Heather Graham *Miriam* ■ *Dir* Renny Harlin • *Scr* Mikko Alanne, from a screenplay (unproduced) by David Battle

Five Days One Summer
★★ PG
Drama   1982 · US · Colour · 103min

Fred Zinnemann's last film is a very personal tale, but not, alas, obvious screen material. Sean Connery goes climbing in the Swiss Alps with young Betsy Brantly, whom he introduces as his wife. Zinnemann knows how to tell a tale, and the use of Alpine scenery is striking, but the film never really builds up steam and isn't helped by the fragmentary storytelling and flashback structure. Despite the stellar presence of Connery, the chemistry simply isn't there. TS

Sean Connery *Douglas* • Betsy Brantley *Kate* • Lambert Wilson *Johann* • Jennifer Hilary *Sarah* • Isabel Dean *Kate's mother* • Gérard Buhr *Brendel* • Anna Massey *Jennifer Pierce* ■ *Dir* Fred Zinnemann • *Scr* Michael Austin, from the short story *Maiden Maiden* by Kay Boyle

Five Deadly Venoms ★★★ 18
Martial arts action adventure   1978 · HK · Colour · 97min

A moribund kung fu master sends his young protégé to spy on five former students, whom he suspects are using their skills for evil, in this atmospheric clash-of-styles classic from the Shaw Brothers' stable. Each of the five – the Scorpion, Centipede, Snake, Lizard and Toad – possesses a cache of poisonous superhero-like gimmicks, which the pupil must learn to combine if he is to stand any chance of success. The film was such a hit that its stars were reunited for a stream of subsequent productions, making this the first, and arguably the best, outing for the so-called Venom Mob. GR Mandarin +subtitles.

■ *Dir* Chang Cheh

Five Easy Pieces ★★★★★ 15
Drama   1970 · US · Colour · 98min

Jack Nicholson's in his prime in this accomplished drama. Here he's lean and hungry, fresh from *Easy Rider* and in cahoots with several of the best indie film-makers of the time: director Bob Rafelson, producer Bert Schneider and writers Carole Eastman and Robert Towne. Nicholson is simply magnetic as Bobby Dupea, emotionally repressed and unable to adjust to the two worlds he inhabits among blue-collar oil-riggers and the family home, a sort of Ibsen commune devoted to maths and Mozart. The film, superbly directed by Rafelson, shifts the late 1960s hippy drop-out genre into the Ingmar Bergman class: it's cerebral, moving and witty. AT **DVD**

Jack Nicholson *Robert Eroica Dupea* • Karen Black *Rayette Dipesto* • Susan Anspach *Catherine Van Oost* • Lois Smith *Partita Dupea* • Billy "Green" Bush [Billy Green Bush] *Elton* • Fannie Flagg *Stoney* • Ralph Waite *Carl Fidelio Dupea* ■ *Dir* Bob Rafelson • *Scr* Adrien Joyce [Carole Eastman], from a story by Bob Rafelson, Joyce Rafelson

Five Finger Exercise ★
Melodrama   1962 · US · BW · 111min

Peter Shaffer's successful stage play here becomes an embarrassing showcase for the rasping charm of Rosalind Russell, a culture vulture who's married to thick Jack Hawkins and fancies egghead German tutor Maximilian Schell, who tries to commit suicide because he feels alienated. Hopelessly stagebound. AT

Rosalind Russell *Louise Harrington* • Jack Hawkins *Stanley Harrington* • Maximilian Schell *Walter* • Richard Beymer *Philip Harrington* • Annette Gorman *Pamela Harrington* ■ *Dir* Daniel Mann • *Scr* Frances Goodrich, Albert Hackett, from the play by Peter Shaffer

5 Fingers ★★★
Spy drama   1952 · US · BW · 103min

Loosely based on fact, this stars James Mason as the Albanian valet who, while serving the British Ambassador to Turkey, comes across secret papers and peddles them to the Germans. Michael Rennie is the detective trying to plug the leak, while Danielle Darrieux is a mysterious countess.

It's a sophisticated and often witty affair dominated by Mason's suave duplicity. AT
DVD

James Mason *Cicero* • Danielle Darrieux *Anna* • Michael Rennie *George Travers* • Walter Hampden *Sir Frederic* • Oscar Karlweis *Moyzisch* • Herbert Berghof *Col von Richter* • John Wengraf *Von Papen* • *Dir* Joseph L Mankiewicz • *Scr* Michael Wilson, from the book *Operation Cicero* by LC Moyzisch

Five Golden Dragons ★★ PG
Action crime drama 1967 · UK · Colour · 100min
The most appealing thing about this unashamed slice of hokum are the villains – Christopher Lee, George Raft, Brian Donlevy and Dan Duryea as members of a secret sect in Hong Kong. The hero, Hollywood has-been Robert Cummings, washes up there and finds himself caught between the Dragons and local mafioso. An outrageously hammy Klaus Kinski also pops up in this lively affair that fleeces everything from *The World of Suzie Wong* to the *Fu Manchu* films. AT **DVD**

Robert Cummings *Bob Mitchell* • Rupert Davies *Comm Sanders* • Margaret Lee *Magda* • Klaus Kinski *Gert* • Brian Donlevy *Dragon* • Dan Duryea *Dragon* • Christopher Lee *Dragon* • George Raft *Dragon* ■ *Dir* Jeremy Summers • *Scr* Peter Welbeck [Harry Alan Towers] • *Cinematographer* John von Kotze

Five Graves to Cairo ★★★★ PG
Second World War drama
1943 · US · BW · 92min
This minor but hugely enjoyable Billy Wilder picture stars Erich von Stroheim as Field Marshal Rommel, holed up in a fly-blown hotel during the North Africa campaign. Franchot Tone is a British spy posing as a club-footed waiter, Anne Baxter is a French maid, Peter Van Eyck a Nazi sadist and Fortunio Bonanova an Italian buffoon who bursts into opera. Despite a few token shots of tanks in the desert, this is the Second World War played indoors as a game of charades, role-playing and racial stereotyping. Tense and hilarious, it's a smashing entertainment, and von Stroheim is utterly magnificent. AT **DVD**

Franchot Tone *Cpl John Bramble* • Anne Baxter *Mouche* • Akim Tamiroff *Farid* • Erich von Stroheim *Field Marshal Rommel* • Peter Van Eyck *Lt Schwegler* • Fortunio Bonanova *General Sabastiano* • Miles Mander *British colonel* ■ *Dir* Billy Wilder • *Scr* Charles Brackett, Billy Wilder, from the play *Hotel Imperial* by Lajos Bíró

The Five Heartbeats ★★★ 15
Musical drama 1991 · US · Colour · 116min
Having made a sensational debut with the blistering satire *Hollywood Shuffle*, Robert Townsend slightly missed his step with this overlong but still essentially enjoyable tribute to African-American singing groups such as the Dells (on whom this film is loosely based), who struggled in the shadow of Motown in the 1960s. The familiar round of minor gigs, auditions and disappointments is trotted out in textbook fashion, but it's lovingly done and slickly played. DP Violence, swearing.

Robert Townsend *Donald "Duck" Matthews* • Michael Wright *Eddie King Jr* • Leon Robinson [Leon] *James Thomas "JT" Matthews* • Harry Lennix *Terence "Dresser" Williams* • Tico Wells *Anthony "Choirboy" Stone* • Diahann Carroll *Eleanor Porter* ■ *Dir* Robert Townsend • *Scr* Robert Townsend, Keenen Ivory Wayans

(500) Days of Summer ★★★ 12
Romantic comedy 2009 · US · Colour · 91min
The debut of video director Marc Webb is a flouncy romantic comedy starring Joseph Gordon-Levitt (*Third Rock from the Sun*) as Tom, a wannabe architect working as a greetings card writer, who falls in and out of love with Summer (Zooey Deschanel), a beautiful if mercurial woman who starts work as his boss's secretary. The film jumps forward and back in time throughout his 500-day infatuation, and Gordon-Levitt's performance is heart-breaking to watch,

even though the action is played mostly for comedy. The idea of analysing a relationship at different points in time is fresh and interesting, but Webb cannot sustain a pace to hold the story together credibly, and the end result is rather twee. KK **DVD** **BL**

Joseph Gordon-Levitt *Tom Hansen* • Zooey Deschanel *Summer Finn* • Geoffrey Arend *McKenzie* • Chloë Grace Moretz *Rachel Hansen* • Matthew Gray Gutler *Paul* • Clark Gregg *Vance* • Rachel Boston *Alison* ■ *Dir* Marc Webb • *Scr* Scott Neustadter, Michael H Weber

Five Miles to Midnight ★★
Drama 1963 · US/Fr/It · BW · 108min
Sophia Loren slowly goes stark, staring mad. Well, she is married to Anthony Perkins who unfortunately (for her) survives a plane crash and continues to torment her and everyone else who thinks he's dead. Meanwhile, he plans to take advantage of his timely demise by defrauding the insurance company – with the help of his unwilling spouse. Fans of melodrama will enjoy this juicy item that sometimes seems Hitchcockian in tone but most of the time exists in a world of its own. AT

Sophia Loren *Lisa Macklin* • Anthony Perkins *Robert Macklin* • Gig Young *David Barnes* • Jean-Pierre Aumont *Alan Stewart* • Yolande Turner *Barbara Ford* ■ *Dir* Anatole Litvak • *Scr* Peter Viertel, Hugh Wheeler

Five Minutes of Heaven ★★★★ 15
Drama 2009 · UK/Ire · Colour · 85min
James Nesbitt reminds us here why he is one of the best actors on television. He plays the traumatised, jittery Joe, who as a boy in 1970s Northern Ireland witnessed his brother's sectarian murder by a loyalist gunman – re-created in powerful early scenes. That gunman was Alistair (Liam Neeson, also superb) and, 30 years later, the two men are to be reunited for the first time, courtesy of a TV programme about reconciliation. It's that much-touted idea that the drama, based on a true story, dismembers. There is some gentle mockery of TV flimflam, particularly the condescension of producers ("We're all going to have an important day here..." says one). DB **DVD**

Liam Neeson *Alistair Little* • James Nesbitt *Joe Griffen* • Anamaria Marinca *Vika* • Richard Dormer *Michael* • Mark Davison [Mark David] *Young Alistair* • Kevin O'Neill *Young Joe* ■ *Dir* Oliver Hirschbiegel • *Scr* Guy Hibbert

The Five Obstructions ★★★★ 15
Part-animated documentary drama
2003 · Den/Bel/Swi/Fr/Swe/Fin/UK/Nor · Colour and BW · 87min
In 1967, the Danish director Jorgen Leth made a short film called *The Perfect Human*, in which the behaviour patterns of Claus Nissen and Maiken Algren were analysed as though they were lab specimens. Over 30 years later, Lars von Trier – clearly still amused by the restrictive approach imposed by his Dogme 95 experiment – challenged his mentor to remake his film but constantly found ways of hindering its progress. This is not only a fascinating insight into the cinematic process, but also a tribute to Leth's directorial ingenuity, as he endeavours to complete three live-action and one animated variation on his intriguing theme. DP Danish, English, French, Spanish +subtitles. Some swearing, sex scenes. **DVD**

Jorgen Leth *The man* • Daniel Hernández Rodríguez *The man (Cuba)* • Jacqueline Arenal *Woman I (Cuba)* • Patrick Bauchau *M Rukov, the man (Brussels)* • Alexandra Vandernoot *The woman (Brussels)* • Claus Nissen *The man (1967)* • Maiken Algren *The woman (1967)* ■ *Dir* Jorgen Leth, Lars von Trier • *Scr* Lars von Trier, Jorgen Leth, Asger Leth, from the film *The Perfect Human* (1967) by Jorgen Leth, Ole John

The Five Pennies ★★★★ U
Musical biographical drama
1959 · US · Colour · 112min
After the success of James Stewart in *The Glenn Miller Story*, glossy bandleader biopics enjoyed a brief vogue, and this dramatic but schmaltzy Paramount music-fest was one of the best. Danny Kaye is perfectly cast as cornettist "Red" Nichols, whose life seemed like a scriptwriter's invention. When his daughter Dorothy (played as a teenager by a wonderful Tuesday Weld) contracted polio, he threw away his instrument, only to enjoy a revival as her health improved. There's a super jam session with Louis Armstrong, plus some fine new songs, including a lovely *Lullaby in Ragtime* from the film's associate producer Sylvia Fine (Mrs Danny Kaye). A 1950s studio crowd-pleaser. TS **DVD**

Danny Kaye *Loring "Red" Nichols* • Barbara Bel Geddes *Bobbie Meredith* • Louis Armstrong • Bob Crosby *Wil Paradise* • Harry Guardino *Tony Valani* • Susan Gordon *Dorothy Nichols, aged six* • Tuesday Weld *Dorothy aged 12–14* • Bob Hope ■ *Dir* Melville Shavelson • *Scr* Melville Shavelson, Jack Rose, from a story by Robert Smith

The Five Senses ★★★★ 15
Drama 1999 · Can · Colour · 104min
The danger of making a film about genetic stereotyping is that contrivance will undermine inspiration, yet Canadian director Jeremy Podeswa avoids any such pitfalls in this accomplished ensemble drama. Although it takes time to introduce us to the cake-maker with no taste, the cleaner with a nose for romance, the optician who's going deaf and the masseuse with an irresponsible teenage daughter, their stories soon interweave into a satisfying whole. With a splendid cast led by Mary-Louise Parker, this is a genuinely sensual experience which suggests people should trust their senses more and their emotions less. DP Swearing, sex scenes.

Mary-Louise Parker *Rona* • Pascale Bussières *Gail* • Richard Clarkin *Raymond* • Brendan Fletcher *Rupert* • Marco Leonardi *Roberto* • Nadia Litz *Rachel* • Molly Parker *Anna Miller* ■ *Dir/Scr* Jeremy Podeswa

Five Star Final ★★★ PG
Crime drama 1931 · US · BW · 90min
This stars Edward G Robinson as a decent editor who is ordered by his proprietor to sink the tone of the stories he prints into the gutter to raise his newspaper's circulation. Two suicides ensue when a scandal breaks on the front page. Wearing its social conscience on its rolled-up sleeve, the picture, directed by Mervyn LeRoy, remains gripping, and the excellent Robinson is well supported by HB Warner, Frances Starr and Boris Karloff as a shifty reporter. AT

Edward G Robinson *Randall* • Marian Marsh *Jenny Townsend* • HB Warner *Michael Townsend* • Anthony Bushell *Philip Weeks* • George E Stone *Ziggie Feinstein* • Frances Starr *Nancy Voorhees Townsend* • Ona Munson *Kitty Carmody* • Boris Karloff *"Reverend" Vernon Isopod* ■ *Dir* Mervyn LeRoy • *Scr* Byron Morgan, Robert Lord, from the play *Late Night Final* by Louis Weitzenkorn

The 5,000 Fingers of Dr T ★★★★★ U
Fantasy adventure 1953 · US · Colour · 88min
Criminally neglected for far too long, producer Stanley Kramer's offbeat children's nightmare, co-written by Ted Geisel (better known as Dr Seuss), is one of the best surrealistic fantasies Hollywood has ever made. Tommy Rettig hates his piano lessons so much he dreams of being forced to play the world's largest keyboard by mad musician Dr Terwilliker (the nastily marvellous Hans Conried) along with 500 other captive boys. Look for the anti-communist propaganda (symbolised by the red smoke) as the children are slave-driven to ignite an atomic bomb by their manic playing. Hugely imaginative, fun, scary and visually dazzling – the sets and backdrops are simply stunning. AJ

Peter Lind Hayes *Mr Zabladowski* • Tommy Rettig *Bart Collins* • Mary Healy *Mrs Collins* • Hans Conried *Dr Terwilliker* • John Heasley *Uncle Whitney* • Robert Heasley *Uncle Judson* • Noel Cravat *Sergeant Lunk* • Henry Kulky *Stroogo* ■ *Dir* Roy Rowland • *Scr* Ted "Dr Seuss" Geisel, Allan Scott, from a story by Ted "Dr Seuss" Geisel • *Cinematographer* Franz Planer • *Art Director* Rudolph Sternad

5x2 ★★★★ 15
Romantic drama 2004 · Fr · Colour · 90min
One of France's most prolific film-makers, director François Ozon shows no sign of a lapse in quality with this meticulously composed, astutely acted study of a marriage in crisis. Adopting a reverse chronology, Ozon tells the story of the deteriorating relationship between Valéria Bruni-Tedeschi and the womanising Stéphane Freiss, from their divorce to a seaside meeting. As Ozon expertly allows pertinent details to seep into the scenario, Bruni-Tedeschi proves anything but a helpless victim in a performance of exquisite emotional intensity. DP French +subtitles. Swearing, sex scenes. **DVD**

Valéria Bruni-Tedeschi *Marion Ferron* • Stéphane Freiss *Gilles Ferron* • Géraldine Pailhas *Valérie* • Françoise Fabian *Monique Chabart* • Michael Lonsdale [Michel Lonsdale] *Bernard Chabart* • Antoine Chappey *Christophe Ferron* • Marc Ruchmann *Mathieu* ■ *Dir/Scr* François Ozon

Five Weeks in a Balloon ★ U
Period comedy adventure
1962 · US · Colour · 101min
Pop go entertainment values in this Jules Verne adventure that is inflated beyond all probability by disaster movie maestro Irwin Allen, who here made the wrong sort of disaster. Cedric Hardwicke, singer Fabian and Red Buttons are members of a 19th-century British expedition floating over Africa, while Peter Lorre joins them for the dramatic ride. The inclusion of Fabian just shows how desperate the movie is to attract attention. TH

Red Buttons *Donald O'Shay* • Fabian *Jacques* • Barbara Eden *Susan Gale* • Cedric Hardwicke *Fergusson* • Peter Lorre *Ahmed* • Richard Haydn *Sir Henry Vining* ■ *Dir* Irwin Allen • *Scr* Charles Bennet, Irwin Allen, Albert Gail, from the novel by Jules Verne

Five Women around Utamaro ★★★★ PG
Period melodrama 1946 · Jpn · BW · 90min
Returning to the theme of female emancipation that had preoccupied him in the mid-1930s, Kenji Mizoguchi was prevented from using this film to celebrate Japan's new-found democracy and the concept of liberation through eroticism by the production guidelines issued by the US occupying force. Consequently, he found himself the subtextual subject of this exploration of the complex relationships and social injustices that inspired the 18th-century Edo printmaker, Utamaro. In depicting the twilight world of the geishas and the artist's struggle for creative freedom, screenwriter Yoshikata Yoda provides a dramatic core that enables Mizoguchi to conduct experiments reflecting Utamaro's style. DP Japanese +subtitles. **DVD** **BL**

Minosuke Bando *Utamaro* • Kotaro Bando *Seinosuke Koide* • Kinuyo Tanaka *Okita* • Kowasaki Hiroko *Oran* • Izuka Toshiko *Takasode* ■ *Dir* Kenji Mizoguchi • *Scr* Yoshikata Yoda, from the novel *Utamaro O Meguru Gonin no Onna* by Kanji Kunieda

The Five-Year Engagement ★★★★ 15
Romantic comedy 2012 · US · Colour · 119min
Jason Segel reteams with his *Forgetting Sarah Marshall* and *Get Him to the Greek* producer Judd Apatow and writer/director Nicholas Stoller in this affectionate modern romantic comedy, while Emily Blunt is the other half of a couple procrastinating over their wedding. Blunt demonstrates a refreshing lack of neuroses, an easy rapport with Segel and does a priceless impression of Cookie Monster. The laughs come easily

and the pair's quarrels ring true; one you'll enjoy. SP Swearing, sex scenes. DVD BL

Jason Segel *Tom Solomon* • Emily Blunt *Violet Barnes* • Rhys Ifans *Winton Childs* • Chris Pratt *Alex Eilhauer* • Alison Brie *Suzie Barnes-Eilhauer* ■ *Dir* Nicholas Stoller • *Scr* Nicholas Stoller, Jason Segel

Fixed Bayonets! ★★★ PG
War drama   1951 · US · BW · 88min

War may be hell, but for writer/director Samuel Fuller it's also a character workout that can temper personalities for the worse or the better. In this familiar story of a lost platoon fighting a rearguard action in Korea, it is Richard Basehart who is fused by events into purposeful command. Although the film never reaches the poetic heights of Lewis Milestone's similar *A Walk in the Sun*, there's the same understanding that men in battle are really at war within themselves. TH DVD BL

Richard Basehart *Corporal Denno* • Gene Evans *Sergeant Rock* • Michael O'Shea (1) *Sergeant Lonergan* • Richard Hylton *Wheeler* • Craig Hill *Lieutenant Gibbs* • Skip Homeier *Whitey* ■ *Dir* Samuel Fuller • *Scr* Samuel Fuller, from the novel by John Brophy

Fixing the Shadow ★★★ 18
Crime drama   1994 · US · Colour · 96min

This engrossing look at the machinations of undercover police work is uncomfortably shoe-horned into an imperfect update of the old American Indian legend of the title, about a young brave running from his shadow and then descending into the land of shadows to retrieve it. Charlie Sheen is the cop recruited by the FBI to infiltrate a biker gang who finds his life strangely mirroring the fable. This never quite achieves the depth, grit or emotional power it strives for. AJ

Charlie Sheen *Dan* • Linda Fiorentino *Renee* • Michael Madsen *Blood* • Courtney B Vance *Conroy* • Rip Torn *Prescott* • Larry Ferguson *Kelly* ■ *Dir/Scr* Larry Ferguson

Flags of Our Fathers ★★★ 15
Second World War drama
2006 · US · Colour · 126min

Joe Rosenthal's iconic photograph of US servicemen raising the Stars and Stripes above the Pacific island of Iwo Jima is the starting point for Clint Eastwood's Second World War epic. Part war movie, part deconstruction of heroism, it follows three of the group as they're sent home to bolster the fundraising effort. As they try to cope with post-traumatic stress and their reluctant status as heroes, Eastwood reveals the complex interaction of war, propaganda and real lives behind the famous image. Based on a bestselling memoir, this is a technically accomplished yet ponderously worthy film that quickly abandons its probing remit to fall back on misty-eyed platitudes. Eastwood's Oscar-nominated companion piece, *Letters from Iwo Jima*, depicts events from the Japanese perspective. JR Swearing. DVD BL

Ryan Phillippe *John "Doc" Bradley* • Jesse Bradford *Rene Gagnon* • Adam Beach *Ira Hayes* • John Benjamin Hickey *Keyes Beech* • John Slattery *Bud Gerber* • Jamie Bell *Ralph Ignatowski* • Paul Walker *Hank Hansen* • Robert Patrick *Col Chandler Johnson* • David Patrick Kelly *President Harry S Truman* ■ *Dir* Clint Eastwood • *Scr* William Broyles Jr, Paul Haggis, from the non-fiction book by James Bradley, Ron Powers • *Cinematographer* Tom Stern (2) • *Music* Clint Eastwood

Flame & Citron ★★★ 15
Fact-based Second World War drama
2008 · Cz Rep/Ger/Den/Nor/Fr/Swe/Fin · Colour · 135min

Thure Lindhardt and Mads Mikkelsen display suitable intensity as Flame and Citron, the most notorious members of the Holger Danske group that fought the Nazi occupation of Denmark during the Second World War. Set in Copenhagen in 1944, the story follows them as they stake out targets and dispatch them with ruthless efficiency. Each assassination takes its toll, and they begin to exhibit the first signs of fallibility.

Taking his cue from Jean-Pierre Melville's *Army of Shadows*, director Ole Christian Madsen generates a murky sense of paranoia and conspiracy while exploring such complex themes as resistance, collaboration and expedient levels of violence against an enemy in wartime. DP Danish, German +subtitles. DVD BL

Thure Lindhardt *Flame* • Mads Mikkelsen *Citron* • Stine Stengade *Ketty Selmer* • Peter Mygind *Aksel Winther* • Mille Hoffmeyer Lehfeldt *Bodil* • Christian Berkel *Hoffmann* • Hanns Zischler *Gilbert* ■ *Dir* Ole Christian Madsen • *Scr* Ole Christian Madsen, Lars K Andersen [Lars Andersen]

The Flame and the Arrow ★★★ U
Romantic swashbuckling adventure
1950 · US · Colour · 87min

This exuberant swashbuckler stars Burt Lancaster, playing a Robin Hood-style character from northern Italy who woos Virginia Mayo while taking on Robert Douglas's land-owning monster. Lancaster's soulmate on the swinging chandeliers is Nick Cravat (his former circus partner), who was brought into the picture to ensure that the acrobatics went smoothly. AT

Burt Lancaster *Dardo* • Virginia Mayo *Anne* • Robert Douglas *Alessandro* • Aline MacMahon *Nonna Bartoli* • Nick Cravat *Piccolo* ■ *Dir* Jacques Tourneur • *Scr* Waldo Salt, from his story *The Hawk and the Arrow*

Flame in the Streets ★★ PG
Drama   1961 · UK · Colour · 89min

Released at a time when "kitchen sink" realism was all the rage, this adaptation by Ted Willis of his own play suffers from the uncomfortable worthiness that blighted the efforts of so many British film-makers trying to tackle thorny social issues. John Mills rises above the old-fashioned liberalism to capture the confused bluster of the trade unionist who defends a black shop steward, but cannot tolerate the prospect of his daughter Sylvia Syms marrying Jamaican Johnny Sekka. DP

John Mills *Jacko Palmer* • Sylvia Syms *Kathie Palmer* • Brenda de Banzie *Nell Palmer* • Johnny Sekka *Peter Lincoln* • Earl Cameron *Gabriel Gomez* ■ *Dir* Roy Baker [Roy Ward Baker] • *Scr* Ted Willis, from his play *Hot Summer Night*

The Flame of New Orleans ★★
Comedy   1941 · US · BW · 79min

This frothy comedy from French director René Clair was his first effort on his wartime sojourn in Hollywood. Phoney countess Marlene Dietrich leaves her rich but dull new husband Roland Young at the altar and sails away with rough-trade sea captain Bruce Cabot, disguising herself in the process. However, a shadowy figure from her European past appears and threatens her plans. This twist on the old gold-digger formula offers only middling entertainment, and shows just how ordinary Dietrich could be. AT

Marlene Dietrich *Claire Ledeux* • Bruce Cabot *Robert Latour* • Roland Young *Charles Giraud* • Mischa Auer *Zolotov* • Andy Devine *First sailor* • Frank Jenks *Second sailor* ■ *Dir* René Clair • *Scr* Norman Krasna

Flame of the Barbary Coast ★★★ U
Western   1945 · US · BW · 91min

This earthquake adventure was a big picture for Republic, trumpeted as the studio's "tenth anniversary production". John Wayne excels as a cattleman, competing with slimy Joseph Schildkraut for the attentions of Ann Dvorak. The low budget is evident in the ropey old stock shots and inadequate sets, though the production received Oscar nominations for its sound and score. TS

John Wayne *Duke Fergus* • Ann Dvorak *Flaxen Tarry* • Joseph Schildkraut *Tito Morell* • William Frawley *Smooth Wylie* • Virginia Grey *Rita Dane* • Russell Hicks *Cyrus Danver* ■ *Dir* Joseph Kane • *Scr* Borden Chase

Flame Top ★★★
Biographical drama   1980 · Fin · Colour · 150min

One of the most expensive films ever made in Finland, this historical epic chronicles the life of the prolific and reclusive novelist Maiju Lassila. Forced to flee St Petersburg after the murder of a tsarist official, Lassila worked for the most part in abject poverty, enduring a tempestuous relationship with ex-actress Olga Esempio (passionately played by Rea Mauranen), before participating in the Bolshevik revolt in Helsinki. Faced with portraying such a complex character, Asko Sarkola is a touch too self-effacing. But the stately pacing lends suitable weight to unfamiliar events. DP Finnish +subtitles.

Asko Sarkola *Maiju Lassila* • Rea Mauranen *Olga Esempio* • Kari Franck *Publisher* • Esko Salminen *Stationmaster* • Ari Suonsuu *Errand boy* • Tuomo Railo *Olga's young son* ■ *Dir/Scr* Pirjo Honkasalo, Pekka Lehto

Flamenco ★★ U
Documentary   1995 · Sp · Colour · 98min

Celebrating the rich diversity and vibrant durability of the flamenco, Carlos Saura has created a handsome tribute to the various song, dance and instrumental styles that have evolved since the mid-19th century. However, in electing not to subtitle the lyrics, he deprives the uninitiated of the opportunity to enter fully into the passion and spirit of the music. The music is sublime, but Vittorio Storaro's lighting changes feel overly familiar, while Saura's approach is that of the antiquarian, not the artist. DP In Spanish. DVD

■ *Dir/Scr* Carlos Saura • *Cinematographer* Vittorio Storaro • *Art Director* Rafael Palmero

Flaming Creatures ★★★
Experimental movie   1963 · US · BW · 45min

This landmark experimental movie paved the way for the acceptance of underground culture (specifically Andy Warhol's work) and a higher profile depiction of on-screen homosexuality. An elliptical mesh of tableaux featuring drag queens in various states of orgiastic behaviour, director Jack Smith's sexual apocalypse pilfers a kitsch range of Hollywood imagery from Marilyn Monroe and Josef von Sternberg to Maria Montez and Busby Berkeley movies and shakes them up with taboo-ridden acts of wanton lust. Ground-breaking in its day for its pivotal fusion of outrageous performance art, sumptuous surfaces, twisted text and camp, it remains a fascinating shock to the system. AJ

Francis Francine • Delores Flores • Joel Markman • Shirley ■ *Dir/Scr* Jack Smith (2)

Flaming Feather ★★★ U
Western   1952 · US · Colour · 77min

Having learned his trade with silent comedies, Ray Enright had a sound sense of pace and it's readily evident in this brisk western, which was crisply photographed by multi-Oscar winner Ray Rennahan. Sterling Hayden and Forrest Tucker star as the rancher and cavalry lieutenant out to catch an outlaw and his gang of maverick American Indians who are running amok in 1870s Arizona. DP

Sterling Hayden *Tex McCloud* • Forrest Tucker *Lt Tom Blaine* • Barbara Rush *Nora Logan* • Arleen Whelan *Carolina* • Carol Thurston *Turquoise* • Edgar Buchanan *Sgt O'Rourke* • Victor Jory *Lucky Lee* • Richard Arlen *Showdown Calhoun* ■ *Dir* Ray Enright • *Scr* Gerald Drayson Adams, Frank Gruber

Flaming Star ★★★★ PG
Western   1960 · US · Colour · 88min

Originally intended as a vehicle for Marlon Brando, this immensely dignified and astoundingly violent (for its time) western became the second movie after *King Creole* to prove Elvis Presley could act. Here he plays an unhappy misfit, who must take sides when his mother's people (he is half native American) decide to go on the warpath. The tension, under the brilliant direction of Don Siegel, is beautifully sustained, and the outdoor colour and

CinemaScope photography is outstanding. This was to be the last shot Presley would get at a decent acting role with a major director; after this his film career took a major turn for the worse. TS DVD

Elvis Presley *Pacer Burton* • Steve Forrest *Clint Burton* • Barbara Eden *Roslyn Pierce* • Dolores Del Rio *Neddy Burton* • John McIntire *Sam Burton* • Rudolph Acosta [Rodolfo Acosta] *Buffalo Horn* ■ *Dir* Don Siegel • *Scr* Clair Huffaker, Nunnally Johnson, from the novel by Huffaker • *Cinematographer* Charles Clarke

The Flamingo Kid ★★★ 15
Comedy drama   1984 · US · Colour · 95min

Garry Marshall didn't stray far from his *Happy Days* sitcom roots with this slight but affectionate teenage comedy drama set in the early 1960s. Matt Dillon plays the working class kid, attempting to better himself by working at a private club, who finds himself in a paternal tug of war between rich smoothie Richard Crenna and his blue-collar dad, Hector Elizondo. The period trappings are lovingly re-created, as are the sounds of the era, and the script is a cut above the norm. JF DVD

Matt Dillon *Jeffrey Willis* • Richard Crenna *Phil Brody* • Hector Elizondo *Arthur Willis* • Jessica Walter *Phyllis Brody* • Fisher Stevens *Hawk Ganz* • Brian McNamara *Steve Dawkins* ■ *Dir* Garry Marshall • *Scr* Garry Marshall, Neal Marshall, from a story by Neal Marshall

Flamingo Road ★★★
Melodrama   1949 · US · BW · 94min

After leaving MGM under a cloud and winning her Oscar in 1945 for *Mildred Pierce* at Warner Bros, Joan Crawford played a string of *femme fatale/grande dame* roles, making mincemeat of weak leading men. Here Crawford is reunited with the brilliant director Michael Curtiz, portraying a carnival dancer stranded in deepest Florida, trapped between two men and swapping cheap philosophy with sinister sheriff Sydney Greenstreet. A torrid treat. TS

Joan Crawford *Lane Bellamy* • Zachary Scott *Fielding Carlisle* • Sydney Greenstreet *Titus Semple* • David Brian *Dan Reynolds* • Gladys George *Lute-Mae Sanders* • Virginia Huston *Annabelle Weldon* • Fred Clark *Doc Waterson* ■ *Dir* Michael Curtiz • *Scr* Robert Wilder, Edmund H North, from the play by Robert Wilder, Sally Wilder

Flanders ★★★★ 18
War drama   2005 · Fr · Colour · 91min

This troubling contemporary drama from director Bruno Dumont moves from the fields of the Great War's Western Front to the desert expanses of the War on Terror. The story begins in northern France, where the monotony of rural life is played out in the benumbed couplings of farmer Samuel Boidin and young Adelaïde Leroux. As the action moves to an unspecified war zone, Boidin and Cretel receive a terrifying lesson on the dehumanising impact of combat and humanity's latent potential for depravity. Superbly played and photographed with a sure sense of place by Yves Cape, this morally ambiguous and consciously melodramatic picture is both courageous and compelling. DP French +subtitles.

Adelaïde Leroux *Barbe* • Samuel Boidin *André Demester* • Henri Cretel *Blondel* • Jean-Marie Bruweart *Briche* • David Poulain *Leclercq* • Patrice Venant *Mordac* • David Legay *Lieutenant* • Inge Decaesteker *France* ■ *Dir/Scr* Bruno Dumont • *Cinematographer* Yves Cape

Flap ★
Comedy drama   1970 · US · Colour · 105min

You would need the world's most powerful microscope to spot any trace of the director of *The Third Man* in this utterly dismal effort. It stars Anthony Quinn as an Indian chief who starts an uprising in order to draw attention to the economic plight of all native Americans. Carol Reed's movie is pitched as a slapstick comedy and Quinn's role as a drunken lecher is far more insulting than sympathetic. AT

Anthony Quinn *Flapping Eagle* • Claude Akins *Lobo Jackson* • Tony Bill *Eleven Snowflake* • Victor Jory *Wounded Bear Mr Smith* • Don Collier *Mike Lyons* • Shelley Winters *Dorothy Bluebell* ■ *Dir* Carol Reed • *Scr* Clair Huffaker

Flash Gordon ★★★ U
Science-fiction adventure
1936 · US · BW · 205min

This is the feature-length condensation of the original 13-part *Flash Gordon* serial which inspired director George Lucas to create *Star Wars*. Breathless cliffhangers and vintage action meets cheesy special effects and hilarious overacting as charismatic hero Flash (former Olympic athlete Larry "Buster" Crabbe), along with Dale Arden (Jean Rogers) and Dr Zarkov (Frank Shannon), prevent Ming the Merciless (Charles Middleton) of the Planet Mongo conquering Earth. It's nonstop thrill-a-minute stuff (thanks to the ruthless editing) as Flash battles one adversary after another. The best of the Crabbe trilogy of Flash Gordon films, which included *Flash Gordon's Trip to Mars* and *Flash Gordon Conquers the Universe*. AJ

Larry "Buster" Crabbe *Flash Gordon* • Jean Rogers *Dale Arden* • Charles Middleton *Ming the Merciless* • Priscilla Lawson *Princess Aura* • John Lipson *King Vultan* • Richard Alexander *Prince Barin* • Frank Shannon *Dr Zarkov* ■ *Dir* Frederick Stephani • *Scr* Frederick Stephani, George Plympton, Basil Dickey, Ella O'Neill, from the comic strip by Alex Raymond

Flash Gordon ★★★ PG
Science-fiction fantasy
1980 · US · Colour · 106min

Aiming for the tongue-in-cheek frivolity of the fabulous Buster Crabbe adventures of the 1930s, Mike Hodges's big-budget fantasy is great fun, providing you ignore the plot altogether and concentrate on the corny performances and cheesy special effects. Although Ornella Muti makes a wonderfully witty Princess Aura, it's Max von Sydow who runs away with the picture as the dastardly Emperor Ming. However, the sheer badness of Sam J Jones as Flash (whose dialogue had to be dubbed by another actor) and Melody Anderson as Dale Arden also adds to the charm of this sci-fi pantomine. DP *DVD* *Blu*

Sam J Jones [Sam Jones] *Flash Gordon* • Melody Anderson *Dale Arden* • Topol *Dr Hans Zarkov* • Max von Sydow *Emperor Ming* • Ornella Muti *Princess Aura* • Timothy Dalton *Prince Barin* • John Osborne *Arborian priest* • Richard O'Brien *Fico* ■ *Dir* Mike Hodges • *Scr* Lorenzo Semple Jr, Michael Allin, from the characters by Alex Raymond • *Music* Queen, Howard Blake

Flash of Genius ★★★ 12
Biographical drama 2008 · US · Colour · 114min

In the 1960s, Robert Kearns created the world's first intermittent windscreen wiper, then watched helplessly as Detroit car giants Ford and Chrysler copied his design without giving him credit or payment. Greg Kinnear brings a quirky everyman charm to the role of the humble college professor whose only dream was to see his invention go from blueprint to dashboard, yet ended up fighting a long legal battle against Ford that almost cost him his sanity and his family. Unfortunately, this subdued drama often lacks its subject's driving passion, and is content to coast by on Kinnear's likeable central performance. JR Brief swearing. *DVD*

Greg Kinnear *Robert Kearns* • Lauren Graham *Phyllis Kearns* • Dermot Mulroney *Gil Previck* • Alan Alda *Gregory Lawson* • Jake Abel *Dennis Kearns* • Daniel Roebuck *Frank Sertin* ■ *Dir* Marc Abraham • *Scr* Philip Railsback, from the *New Yorker* magazine article by John Seabrook

A Flash of Green ★★★★
Drama 1984 · US · Colour · 131min

Ed Harris once again proves what a superb actor he is in this drama with an ecological theme, based on the John D MacDonald novel. He plays a Florida reporter who betrays more than just his profession when he agrees to help a corrupt official win backing for a controversial housing development. Victor Nunez's (*Ulee's Gold*)

film boasts both classy direction and a strong cast. Gripping stuff. JB

Ed Harris *Jimmy Wing* • Blair Brown *Kate Hubble* • Richard Jordan *Elmo Bliss* • George Coe *Brian Hass* • Joan Goodfellow *Mitchie* • Jean De Baer *Jackie Halley* • John Glover *Ross Halley* ■ *Dir* Victor Nunez • *Scr* Victor Nunez, from the novel by John D MacDonald

Flash Point ★★ 18
Martial arts crime thriller
2007 · HK · Colour · 83min

A Hong Kong cop pulls out all the stops to take down the crime empire of three Vietnamese brothers in this sloppy vehicle for martial arts star Donnie Yen. Directors John Woo and Johnnie To handle these kind of cops v gangster tales effortlessly, but in the hands of Yip Wai Shun (*Ip Man*) it never really convinces – the scene involving a bomb in a chicken being more funny than suspenseful. The decent production values and fight scenes in a lift and a street café are worthy of mention, but the all-action finale fails to thrill. JH Cantonese +subtitles. Violence. *DVD* *Blu*

Donnie Yen *Inspector Ma* • Louis Koo *Wilson* • Collin Chou *Tony* • Lui Leung Wai [Ray Lui] *Archer* ■ *Dir* Yip Wai Shun [Wilson Yip] • *Scr* Szeto Kam Yuen [Szeto Kam-yuen], Nicholl Tang [Lik-Kei Tang]

Flashback ★★★ 15
Comedy action road movie
1990 · US · Colour · 103min

This entertaining trip through flower power nostalgia stars Dennis Hopper, having a ball sending up his old screen persona. He is a 1960s activist, on the run for two decades, who is finally nabbed by the FBI but then proceeds to run rings around his fresh-faced captor, Kiefer Sutherland. The stars spark off each other nicely and there are also some neat supporting turns. The script lacks any real satirical bite, but director Franco Amurri keeps the action zipping along. JF *DVD*

Kiefer Sutherland *John Buckner* • Dennis Hopper *Huey Walker* • Carol Kane *Maggie* • Cliff De Young *Sheriff Hightower* • Michael McKean *Hal* • Richard Masur *Barry* • Paul Dooley *Donald R Stark, FBI Director* ■ *Dir* Franco Amurri • *Scr* David Loughery

Flashbacks of a Fool ★★★ 15
Drama 2008 · UK · Colour · 109min

It's plain to see why Daniel Craig wanted to make this unusual British drama. As fading, drug-addicted movie star Joe Scot, he is the very picture of quiet intensity, reflecting on tragic events in his youth that still reverberate. Viewed through the lens of writer/director Baillie Walsh, it's a polished and confident growing-pains story with all the windswept, salty atmosphere of the British seaside. However, the languid pace can be frustrating: instead of weaving past and present together, Walsh uses Craig to bookend one very long flashback. Thankfully, actor Harry Eden as the younger Scot has the charisma to keep you watching. SP *DVD*

Daniel Craig *Joe Scot* • Eve *Ophelia Franklin* • Harry Eden *Teenage Joe Scot* • Olivia Williams *Grace Scot* • Helen McCrory *Peggy Tickell* • Jodhi May *Evelyn Adams* • Miriam Karlin *Mrs Rogers* • Keeley Hawes *Adult Jessie Scot* ■ *Dir/Scr* Baillie Walsh

Flashdance ★★★ 15
Musical drama 1983 · US · Colour · 90min

Jennifer Beals stars as a welder by day and exotic dancer by night. But what she really, really wants is to join the Pittsburgh Ballet. Her dream ambition and fluffy romance with Michael Nouri look welded together from other Hollywood fairy tales of fame and fortune, yet director Adrian Lyne caught the post-disco visual mood of the time to win over even the most jaded viewer. The title song (sung by Irene Cara) won an Oscar. AJ Swearing, nudity. *DVD*

Jennifer Beals *Alex Owens* • Michael Nouri *Nick Hurley* • Lilia Skala *Hanna Long* • Sunny Johnson *Jeanie Szabo* • Kyle T Heffner *Richie* ■ *Dir* Adrian Lyne • *Scr* Joe Eszterhas, Tom Hedley, from a story by Tom Hedley

Flashpoint ★★
Political thriller 1997 · US · Colour · 84min

James Brolin made his directorial debut with this Irish political TV thriller. However, he should have paid more attention to his performance as a retired CIA agent pursuing the killers of his sister, who died in a terrorist attack on a Belfast motorcade, as it is the weak link in an otherwise effective production. There's palpable tension between Salvator Xuereb's IRA maverick and his disillusioned brother, Patrick Foy, but the best work comes from Jennie Garth as Foy's frightened girlfriend. DP Violence, swearing.

James Brolin *John Hall* • Jennie Garth *Mary* • Salvator Xuereb *Liam Fallon* • Patrick Foy *Gerry Fallon* • Cristi Conaway *Kelly Hall* • Josh Brolin *Pete* ■ *Dir* James Brolin • *Scr* Alex Simon

Flatliners ★★★ 15
Supernatural thriller 1990 · US · Colour · 109min

Is there life after death? Kiefer Sutherland, Julia Roberts and Kevin Bacon are among the medical students who are trying to find the answer by inducing their own temporary deaths in this gothic mix of old dark house and hi-tech laboratory. Director Joel Schumacher puts more flash than flesh on the story, but still delivers the expected chills with cool efficiency. Trouble is, the afterlife stuff is rather too crudely clichéd. TH Violence, swearing, a sex scene. *DVD* *Blu*

Kiefer Sutherland *Nelson Wright* • Julia Roberts *Rachel Mannus* • Kevin Bacon *David Labraccio* • William Baldwin *Joe Hurley* • Oliver Platt *Randy Steckle* • Kimberly Scott *Winnie Hicks* • Joshua Rudoy *Billy Mahoney* ■ *Dir* Joel Schumacher • *Scr* Peter Filardi • *Cinematographer* Jan De Bont

Flatliners
Supernatural horror thriller 2017 · US · Colour

This is a preview – no prints were available to review as we went to press: Medical students experience life on the other side in a supernatural chiller that, in its original 1990 incarnation, featured Julia Roberts, Kevin Bacon and Kiefer Sutherland. Now, Ellen Page, James Norton and Nina Dobrev are among those delivering the necessary belt of 2017 hip as they "flatline" themselves to a near-death state. Kiefer Sutherland turns out to link hands with the original film, while Niels Arden Oplev is at the helm, so brooding Scandinavian angst should not be in short supply. SvM

Ellen Page • Diego Luna • Nina Dobrev • James Norton • Kiersey Clemons ■ *Dir* Niels Arden Oplev • *Scr* Ben Ripley, Stephen Susco

The Flavour of Green Tea over Rice ★★★★ U
Drama 1952 · Jpn · BW · 115min

Yasujiro Ozu explores the nuances of deceit and companionship in this wry yet touching study of arranged marriage. In showing how a discontented executive (Shin Saburi) and his free-spirited wife (Michiyo Kogure) work through the crisis in their relationship, he highlights the shifting social priorities of the bourgeoisie while also evoking a fond nostalgia for the recent past. It remains an intimate Ozu offering, in spite of the diversity of locations, frequency of camera movements and rhythmic cutting. DP Japanese +subtitles. *DVD*

Shin Saburi • Michiyo Kogure • Koji Tsuruta • Keiko Tsushima • Kuniko Miyake • Chikage Awashima • Chishu Ryu ■ *Dir* Yasujiro Ozu • *Scr* Yasujiro Ozu, Kogo Noda

The Flaw ★
Crime drama 1954 · UK · BW · 60min

Director Terence Fisher, best known for his work at Hammer films, does all that can be expected with this ominously titled thriller starring John Bentley. Well-cast as a sinisterly suave racing driver, Bentley easily upstages Donald Houston, who is the

lawyer trying to thwart Bentley's plans to bump off his wealthy wife, Rona Anderson. The feeble script betrays the fact this is pure B-fodder, remade from a 1933 film. DP

John Bentley *Paul Oliveri* • Donald Houston *John Millway* • Rona Anderson *Monica Oliveri* • Doris Yorke *Mrs Bower* • Tonia Bern *Vera* ■ *Dir* Terence Fisher • *Scr* Brandon Fleming

The Flaw ★★★★
Part-animated documentary
2011 · UK · Colour · 82min

For anyone who has ever wondered how the global economy neared meltdown in 2007, David Sington's documentary is essential viewing. It focuses on four hard-working individuals who placed their trust in financiers, to illustrate the film's central thesis – that the dramatic increase in income and asset inequality was a significant cause of the economic crisis. Sington occasionally risks being wise after the event, but adeptly mixes expert analysis and animated sequences to explain the economic basics. DP

■ *Dir* David Sington

Flawless ★★ 15
Comedy drama 1999 · US · Colour · 106min

Utterly schematic, hopelessly old-fashioned and totally bogus, director Joel Schumacher's highly personal comedy drama nevertheless delivers some camp laughs along its uneven, manipulative route. After suffering a stroke, homophobic security guard Robert De Niro is rehabilitated by drag queen Philip Seymour Hoffman. Deflating the simplistic morality fable is a vicious subplot involving stolen Mob money that Hoffman may have hidden to pay for a sex-change operation. AJ *DVD*

Robert De Niro *Walt Koontz* • Philip Seymour Hoffman *Rusty Zimmerman* • Barry Miller *Leonard Wilcox* • Wilson Jermaine Heredia *Cha-Cha* • Daphne Rubin-Vega *Tia* ■ *Dir/Scr* Joel Schumacher

Flawless ★★ 12
Crime drama
2007 · UK/US/Lux · Colour · 104min

Michael Caine and Demi Moore star in this 1960s-set heist thriller from director Michael Radford, playing disgruntled employees of a London diamond brokerage. Moore plays an ambitious woman whose career is hitting the glass ceiling, and finds herself drawn into a risky scheme by Caine, the firm's caretaker, who has long plotted to bring the company to its knees. Predictably, the two distrust each other as much as they detest the firm, but find a way of working together. This is a comfortable but unspectacular thriller, elevated somewhat by its superior period detail. Unfortunately, the impressive settings and wardrobe are undermined by some dodgy ageing makeup, a few anachronisms and a distinctly hammy ending. KK *DVD*

Demi Moore *Laura Quinn* • Michael Caine *Mr Hobbs* • Lambert Wilson *Finch* • Nathaniel Parker *Ollie* • Nicholas Jones *Jameson* • Joss Ackland *Milton Kendrick Ashtoncroft* ■ *Dir* Michael Radford • *Scr* Edward A Anderson [Edward Anderson (2)]

A Flea in Her Ear ★★★
Farce 1968 · US/Fr · Colour · 94min

Doppelgangers, mistaken identity, mad chases and misunderstandings abound in this movie adaptation (by *Rumpole* creator John Mortimer) of a Feydeau farce that had scored a considerable success in London at the National Theatre. Rex Harrison stars in the double role of barrister Victor Chandebisse and hotel porter Poche, and Rosemary Harris is Gabrielle, Victor's suspicious and jealous wife. The Anglo-French cast are all on form in this classic Gallic sex comedy which was considered quite risqué in its time and was given an X certificate. DF

Rex Harrison *Victor Chandebisse/Poche* • Rosemary Harris *Gabrielle Chandebisse* • Louis Jourdan *Henri* • Rachel Roberts (1) *Suzanne* • John Williams *Dr Finache* • Grégoire Aslan *Max* •

Edward Hardwick *Pierre* ■ *Dir* Jacques Charon • *Scr* John Mortimer, from the play by John Mortimer, from the play *La Puce à l'Oreille* by Georges Feydeau

Fled ★★ 18
Action thriller   1996 · US · Colour · 93min

This far-fetched action thriller has one black and one white convict (Laurence Fishburne and Stephen Baldwin) handcuffed together as they escape from a chain gang. The exit has been organised with the knowledge of the law enforcement agencies, who have their sights set on a South American narcotics boss. Director Kevin Hooks fills in the spaces between the audience's gasps of incredulity with fist-fights. TH Swearing, violence, brief nudity.

Laurence Fishburne *Charles Piper* • Stephen Baldwin *Mark Dodge* • Will Patton *Matthew Gibson* • Robert John Burke *[Robert Burke]* *Pat Schiller* • Robert Hooks *Lieutenant Clark* • Salma Hayek *Cora* ■ *Dir* Kevin Hooks • *Scr* Preston A Whitmore II

The Fleet's In ★★★ U
Musical comedy   1942 · US · BW · 93min

This daft Paramount wartime crowd-pleaser has shy sailor William Holden taking on a bet to kiss sultry nightclub chanteuse Dorothy Lamour. Funny newcomer Betty Hutton in support became a star virtually overnight, and Jimmy Dorsey and his Orchestra feature prominently. It's all very 1940s, but alas director Victor Schertzinger died before the movie opened. Nevertheless the plot would continue to be used in Paramount pictures right up to Elvis Presley's comeback film *GI Blues* in 1960. TS

Dorothy Lamour *The Countess* • William Holden (2) *Casey Kirby* • Eddie Bracken *Barney Waters* • Betty Hutton *Bessie* • Cass Daley *Cissie* • Gil Lamb *Spike* ■ *Dir* Victor Schertzinger • *Scr* Walter DeLeon, Ralph Spence, Sid Silvers, from the play *Sailor Beware!* by Kenyon Nicholson, Charles Robinson (1), from a story by Monte Brice, J Walter Ruben

Flesh ★★★★
Drama   1932 · US · BW · 95min

This is a wonderfully melancholic study of tragic wrestler Wallace Beery and his obsessional passion for moll Karen Morley, who's emotionally involved with nasty Ricardo Cortez. This is full-blown melodrama, superbly directed by the great John Ford, someone never afraid to tackle meaty material. The insights into the world of professional wrestling are fascinating and revelatory, especially the differences in the sport between Germany (where the tale begins) and the USA, while the brilliant Beery produces another fine performance. TS

Wallace Beery *Polikai* • Karen Morley *Laura Nash* • Ricardo Cortez *Nicky* • Jean Hersholt *Mr Herman* • John Miljan *Joe Willard* • Vince Barnett *Waiter* ■ *Dir* John Ford • *Scr* Moss Hart, Leonard Praskins, Edgar Allan Woolf, from a story by Edmund Goulding

Flesh ★★★ 18
Cult sex drama   1968 · US · Colour · 85min

Set in the demimonde of male prostitutes and extroverted transvestites typical of producer Andy Warhol, director Paul Morrissey's gutter graphic sex farce was an early attempt by the pop art icon to cross over from underground cinema into the mainstream arena. With no story structure as such, Morrissey is content to focus on the fringe elements of society in a series of Manhattan vignettes, revolving around the nearly always naked Joe Dallesandro, who is either hustling gays to get money for his bad-tempered girlfriend or having sex with assorted weirdos. AJ *DVD*

Joe Dallesandro *Joe* • Geraldine Smith *Gerry* • John Christian *Young man* • Maurice Braddell *Artist* • Barry Brown *Boy on chair* • Candy Darling *Blonde on sofa* • Jackie Curtis *Redhead on sofa* • Patti D'Arbanville *Gerry's girl friend* ■ *Dir/Scr* Paul Morrissey

Flesh + Blood ★★★ 18
Period epic   1985 · US/Neth · Colour · 126min

Dutch director Paul Verhoeven's first Hollywood movie is a medieval epic which delivers the titular ingredients in proverbial buckets. It also boasts sumptuous music and splendid camerawork by Verhoeven regulars Basil Poledouris and Jan De Bont. Tough and witty, the film stars Rutger Hauer as a guerrilla warrior and Jennifer Jason Leigh as the virgin he kidnaps and rapes. It's a spectacle that anticipates Verhoeven's later films by pushing back the boundaries of sex and violence. AT *DVD*

Rutger Hauer *Martin* • Jennifer Jason Leigh *Agnes* • Tom Burlinson *Steven* • Jack Thompson *Hawkwood* • Fernando Hillbeck *Arnolfini* • Susan Tyrrell *Celine* ■ *Dir* Paul Verhoeven • *Scr* Paul Verhoeven, Gerald Soeteman, from a story by Gerald Soeteman

Flesh and Bone ★★★★ 15
Mystery drama   1993 · US · Colour · 121min

Dennis Quaid and Meg Ryan (then husband and wife) turn in two of their best performances in director Steve Kloves's unsettling modern *film noir*. James Caan plays a murderous thief who discovers his son (Quaid) is in love with a woman (Ryan) who's the sole survivor of a family he murdered many years before. But will Ryan remember his face? Combining a fascinating fatalism with uncompromising black humour, this expert thriller evokes a haunting moodiness. AJ Swearing, sex scenes. *DVD*

Dennis Quaid *Arlis Sweeney* • Meg Ryan *Kay Davies* • James Caan *Roy Sweeney* • Christopher Rydell *Reese Davies* • Gwyneth Paltrow *Ginnie* • Scott Wilson *Elliot* ■ *Dir/Scr* Steve Kloves

Flesh and Fantasy ★★★
Supernatural portmanteau   1943 · US · BW · 92min

New York wits Robert Benchley and David Hoffman link these three tales of the supernatural as they discuss dreams and elements of the supernatural. This leads into the three stories: the first is *Cinderella* with a twist, starring Betty Field and Robert Cummings; the second and best is an adaptation of Oscar Wilde's *Lord Arthur Saville's Crime* with Edward G Robinson shocked to learn from a spiritualist that he's about to become a murderer; and finally, Barbara Stanwyck's ghostly presence makes circus tightrope walker Charles Boyer lose his balance. Like all portmanteau films, a mixed blessing, but Julien Duvivier directs them all stylishly. AT

Edward G Robinson *Marshall Tyler* • Charles Boyer *Paul Gaspar* • Barbara Stanwyck *Joan Stanley* • Betty Field *Henrietta* • Robert Cummings *Michael* • Robert Benchley *Doakes* • David Hoffman *Davis* ■ *Dir* Julien Duvivier • *Scr* Ernest Pascal, Samuel Hoffenstein, Ellis St Joseph, from stories by Ellis St Joseph, Oscar Wilde (*Lord Arthur Saville's Crime*), Laslo Vadnay

Flesh and Fury ★★
Sports drama   1952 · US · BW · 82min

This was the 27-year-old Tony Curtis's 12th film and the first in which he relied on his acting ability rather than just his "pretty-boy" image. He plays a deaf-mute boxer besotted by good-time girl Jan Sterling. He's saved by honest reporter Mona Freeman, but on the way to that salvation there's time for boxing, an operation to restore his hearing and other complications. Curtis's performance gives some indication of the heights he would occasionally scale in future years. BB

Tony Curtis *Paul Callan* • Jan Sterling *Sonya Bartow* • Mona Freeman *Ann Hollis* • Wallace Ford *Jack Richardson* • Connie Gilchrist *Mrs Richardson* • Katherine Locke *Mrs Hollis* ■ *Dir* Joseph Pevney • *Scr* Bernard Gordon, from a story by William Alland

Flesh and the Devil ★★★★ U
Silent drama   1926 · US · BW · 112min

The off-screen love affair between stars Greta Garbo and John Gilbert had as much to do with this film's success as the story.

Garbo glows thanks to the lustrous camerawork of William Daniels, as she plays a temptress whose involvement with soldier Gilbert leads to the death of her husband. At the time, the love scenes were notorious, but the film as whole now seems slightly overdone. It was Garbo's third movie for MGM, and director Clarence Brown poured her more than competently into the mould that the studio most wanted: that of a *femme fatale*. TH *DVD*

John Gilbert (1) *Leo von Harden* • Greta Garbo *Felicitas von Eltz* • Lars Hanson *Ulrich von Kletzingk* • Barbara Kent *Hertha Prochvitz* • William Orlamond *Uncle Kutowski* • George Fawcett *Pastor Voss* ■ *Dir* Clarence Brown • *Scr* Benjamin F Glazer [Benjamin Glazer], from the novel *Es War; Roman in Zwei Banden* by Herman Sudermann

The Flesh and the Fiends ★★★
Horror   1959 · UK · BW · 93min

This explicitly scary and darkly atmospheric retelling of the Burke and Hare story stars Peter Cushing, exceptional as the coldly ambitious Dr Knox who scandalises the medical profession when he strikes a fatal bargain with two grave robbers to supply him with fresh corpses for experiments. The grimy poverty of 19th-century Edinburgh provides a vivid background to this unflinching shocker, which uses stark black-and-white imagery to startling effect. AJ

Peter Cushing *Dr Robert Knox* • Donald Pleasence *William Hare* • June Laverick *Martha* • George Rose *William Burke* • Dermot Walsh *Dr Geoffrey Mitchell* • Renee Houston *Helen Burke* • Billie Whitelaw *Mary Patterson* ■ *Dir* John Gilling • *Scr* John Gilling, Leon Griffiths, from a story by John Gilling

The Flesh Eaters ★★★★
Horror   1964 · US · BW · 89min

Stylishly directed, well acted and featuring some spectacular gore effects for the period, director Jack Curtis's splendidly convincing comic fantasy is long overdue for discovery as one of the most accomplished and influential shockers spearheading the nasty strain of American Gothic. Filmed in 196061 in suburban New York but not released until 1964, it features pilot Byron Sanders and two passengers, alcoholic movie star Rita Morley and her secretary Barbara Wilkin, who crash on a small island where mad Nazi scientist Martin Kosleck is creating tiny carnivorous sea creatures. AJ

Martin Kosleck *Peter Bartell* • Rita Morley *Laura Winters* • Byron Sanders *Grant Murdock* • Ray Tudor *Omar* • Barbara Wilkin *Jan Letterman* ■ *Dir* Jack Curtis (2) • *Scr* Arnold Drake

Flesh Feast ★
Horror   1970 · US · Colour · 72min

What do Hollywood glamour queens do when they retire? Play homicidal maniacs, of course. The trend started memorably with *What Ever Happened to Baby Jane?* but hit rock bottom with this tasteless and cheap mess of a movie. Lured back to the screen long after her glory days of the 1940s, Veronica Lake (in her last film) plays a scientist conducting anti-ageing experiments using live maggots that devour old skin tissue. RS

Veronica Lake *Dr Elaine Frederick* • Phil Philbin *Ed Casey* • Heather Hughes *Kristine* • Martha Mischon • Yanka Mann • Dian Wilhite • Chris Martell ■ *Dir* Brad F Grinter • *Scr* Brad F Grinter, Thomas Casey

Flesh for Frankenstein ★★★ 18
Horror   1974 · It/Fr/US · Colour · 94min

Explicit blood-letting and violence overwhelm director Paul Morrissey's shockingly funny exposé of the venal grime behind Victorian aristocracy. Udo Kier is wonderfully arrogant as the Nietzschean Baron dismembering the local townspeople to build the perfect Aryan male and his female mate. Originally shown in excellent Space-Vision 3D, a strong stomach is needed to witness the flattened down lurid gore and sickening splatter. Full of camp

quotable dialogue, this was produced by, among others, Andy Warhol and Carlo Ponti. AJ *DVD*

Joe Dallesandro *Nicholas* • Udo Kier *Frankenstein* • Monique Van Vooren *Katrin* • Arno Juerging *Otto* • Srdjan Zelenovic *Male monster* ■ *Dir* Paul Morrissey, Antonio Margheriti • *Scr* Paul Morrissey, Tonino Guerra

Flesh Gordon ★★ 18
Science-fiction sex comedy   1974 · US · Colour · 84min

This limp sex spoof of the Flash Gordon Saturday morning pictures adventure series became a theatrical, and then later, video hit. Jason Williams in the title role, Suzanne Fields, John Hoyt and a cameo from real-life porn star Candy Samples supply the talent. The Earth is being bombarded with a sex ray from the Planet Porno, and Flesh Gordon is the man to save us from our naughty selves. Not hilarious, but harmless all the same. JF *DVD*

Jason Williams *Flesh Gordon* • Suzanne Fields *Dale Ardor* • Joseph Hudgins *Dr Flexi Jerkoff* • John Hoyt *Professor Gordon* • William Hunt [William Dennis Hunt] *Emperor Wang* • Craig T Brandy *Monster* • Candy Samples ■ *Dir* Howard Ziehm, Michael Benveniste • *Scr* Michael Benveniste

Flesh Gordon Meets the Cosmic Cheerleaders ★ 18
Science-fiction sex comedy   1989 · Can · Colour · 98min

Director Howard Ziehm's sequel to his equally amateurish, but far superior, 1972 fantasy romp, resembles a bad home movie. This time all the charm, endearingly rock-bottom special effects and film buff cleverness is non-existent. Well-endowed Flesh (kick-boxer Vince Murdocco) goes to rescue his kidnapped girlfriend Robyn Kelly, but the mission is derailed by sex-starved Cosmic Cheerleaders. A dreadfully unfunny fiasco. AJ *DVD*

Vince Murdocco *Flesh Gordon* • Tony Travis *Dr Flexi Jerkoff* • Robyn Kelly *Dale Ardor* • William Hunt [William Dennis Hunt] *Emperor Wang* ■ *Dir* Howard Ziehm • *Scr* Doug Frisby, Howard Ziehm

The Flesh of the Orchid ★★★ 15
Drama   1974 · Fr/It/W Ger · Colour · 110min

This is less an exercise in hard-boiled fiction than in *Grand Guignol*. Exploiting expressionist visuals and allowing his cast to play at fever pitch, Patrice Chéreau clearly hopes to bring a sense of theatrical menace to his slow-burning tale of greed and revenge. Edwige Feuillère hits the right note of hysteria as the wicked aunt who has her niece (Charlotte Rampling) consigned to an asylum in a bid to seize her inheritance, while Bruno Cremer is charismatically sinister as the stranger who helps confound her schemes. DP French dubbed. Violence, sex scenes. *DVD*

Charlotte Rampling *Claire* • Bruno Cremer *Louis* • Edwige Feuillère *Aunt* • Simone Signoret *Lady Vamos* • Hugues Quester *Son* • Alida Valli *Woman* ■ *Dir* Patrice Chéreau • *Scr* Jean-Claude Carrière, Patrice Chéreau, from the novel by James Hadley Chase

Fletch ★★★ PG
Comedy adventure   1985 · US · Colour · 93min

Chevy Chase stars in the first of two outings as the investigative reporter with a sideline in disguises and witty repartee. Uprooted from Malibu beach (where he is disguised as a beach bum) by a millionaire who orders his own murder, Chase stumbles and bumbles through a corkscrew plot that fits his comic frame like a bespoke suit. Sleek, glossy and often very funny indeed. AT *DVD*

Chevy Chase *IM Fletcher, "Fletch"* • Joe Don Baker *Chief Karlin* • Dana Wheeler-Nicholson *Gail Stanwyk* • Tim Matheson *Alan Stanwyk* • M Emmet Walsh *Dr Dolan* • George Wendt *Fat Sam* • Geena Davis *Larry* ■ *Dir* Michael Ritchie • *Scr* Andrew Bergman, from the novel by Gregory McDonald

Fletch Lives ★★ PG

Comedy adventure 1989 · US · Colour · 90min

Chevy Chase reprises his role as the daffy investigative reporter in this adult comedy, but this time he's not blessed with a sharp enough script. Fletch is one of those characters that you either find irresistibly funny and folksy, or merely the celluloid celebration of the nightmare passenger you find yourself sitting beside in a plane. The plot, such as it is, concerns Fletch being left a plantation in Louisiana. **SH** *DVD*

Chevy Chase *Fletch* · Julianne Phillips *Becky Ann Culpepper* · Hal Holbrook *"Ham" Johnson* · R Lee Ermey *Jimmy Lee Farnsworth* · Richard Libertini *Frank Walker* · Randall "Tex" Cobb *Ben Dover* ■ Dir Michael Ritchie · Scr Leon Capetanos, from characters by Gregory McDonald

Un Flic ★★★ 12

Crime thriller 1972 · Fr · Colour · 95min

Jean-Pierre Melville wound down his incalculably influential career with this return to his favourite stomping ground, the *film noir*. This may not be his most innovative work, but the duel between cop Alain Delon and drug-smuggling bank robber Richard Crenna does contain some of his most audacious set pieces. The narrative gets a little messy in places as Melville experiments with elliptical editing and shifting time frames. Catherine Deneuve delivers a virtually silent performance as Delon's mistress. **DP** French dubbed. *DVD*

Alain Delon *Coleman* · Catherine Deneuve *Cathy* · Richard Crenna *Simon* · Riccardo Cucciolla *Paul* · Michael Conrad *Costa* · André Pousse *Albouis* · Paul Crauchet *Morand* ■ Dir/Scr Jean-Pierre Melville

Flicka ★★ U

Drama 2006 · US/UK · Colour · 90min

A contemporary take on Mary O'Hara's 1941 novel *My Friend Flicka* (that was made into a movie in 1943), this is a handsome and old-fashioned drama in which rebellious rancher's daughter Alison Lohman finds a kindred spirit in the wild mustang that she's attempting to train. Life lessons are predictably hammered home, but there's genuine honesty in the feelings on display, which gives the well-acted tale a sense of realism. Two straight to DVD sequels came out in 2010 and 2012. **SF** *DVD*

Alison Lohman *Katy McLaughlin* · Tim McGraw *Rob McLaughlin* · Maria Bello *Nell McLaughlin* · Ryan Kwanten *Howard McLaughlin* · Dallas Roberts *Gus* ■ Dir Michael Mayer (1) · Scr Mark Rosenthal, Lawrence Konner, from the novel *My Friend Flicka* by Mary O'Hara

Flight ★★

Action drama 1929 · US · BW · 116min

Jack Holt and Ralph Graves star in this Frank Capra talkie. It's a military adventure, dealing with America's invasion of Nicaragua. Because the US Navy co-operated fully with the production, loaning the unit its base and equipment in San Diego, the movie has some spectacular aerial sequences. Unfortunately the same cannot be said for the familiar love triangle storyline. **AT**

Jack Holt *Panama Williams* · Ralph Graves *Lefty Phelps* · Lila Lee *Elinor* · Alan Roscoe *Major* · Harold Goodwin (1) *Steve Roberts* ■ Dir Frank Capra · Scr Howard J Green, Frank Capra, from a story by Ralph Graves

Flight ★★★ 15

Thriller 2012 · US · Colour · 139min

The latest in cinema's long line of charismatic "functioning alcoholics" is Whip Whitaker (played by Denzel Washington), who, in this grown-up drama about addiction, seems to mix a life of booze and drugs with a spotless career as an airline pilot. The opening scene features an in-flight emergency, terrifyingly staged by director Robert Zemeckis, that sees Whitaker emerge a hero. It's quite a first act. But Whip walks away from one set of wreckage into another, when the incident is investigated by the authorities. Washington's fine, vanity-free performance

elevates *Flight* from predictable addiction-of-the-week melodrama to something much classier. **AC** Swearing, sexual references, drug abuse, nudity. *DVD* *Blu*

Denzel Washington *Whip Whitaker* · Don Cheadle *Hugh Lang* · Kelly Reilly *Nicole* · John Goodman *Harling Mays* · Bruce Greenwood *Charlie Anderson* · Melissa Leo *Ellen Block* ■ Dir Robert Zemeckis · Scr John Gatins

Flight Command ★★

Second World War drama 1940 · US · BW · 115min

MGM prepared Americans for war by sending Robert Taylor aloft as a recently qualified Naval pilot who helps design a fog landing system, saving the squadron commander in the process and making widowed Ruth Hussey all dewy-eyed. There's enough plot for a dozen movies, so emotions tend to suffer from serious air turbulence and even Red Skelton, in his second film, hasn't much time for his comedy schtick. **AT**

Robert Taylor (1) *Ensign Alan "Pensacola" Drake* · Ruth Hussey *Lorna Gary* · Walter Pidgeon *Squadron Cdr Bill Gary* · Paul Kelly (1) *Lt Cmdr "Dusty" Rhodes* · Shepperd Strudwick *Lt Jerry Banning* · Red Skelton *Lt "Mugger" Martin* ■ Dir Frank Borzage · Scr Wells Root, Cdr Harvey Haislip, from the story by Cdr Harvey Haislip, John Sutherland

Flight for Freedom ★★ U

Romantic drama 1943 · US · BW · 101min

This thinly disguised biopic is clearly based on noted aviatrix Amelia Earhart and her last mysterious journey. Though the movie was sanctioned by Earhart's widower, publisher Charles Palmer Putnam, he wouldn't let RKO use her name, and you can't blame her after seeing this melodramatic nonsense. Rosalind Russell made her debut for the studio as the plucky flier, cast opposite a happy-go-lucky Fred MacMurray. Preposterous stuff, leadenly directed. **TS**

Rosalind Russell *Tonie Carter* · Fred MacMurray *Randy Britton* · Herbert Marshall *Paul Turner* · Edward Ciannelli [Eduardo Ciannelli] *Johnny Salvini* · Walter Kingsford *Admiral Graves* ■ Dir Lothar Mendes · Scr Oliver HP Garrett, SK Lauren, Jane Murfin, from a story by Horace McCoy

Flight from Ashiya ★★

Action drama 1963 · US/Jpn · Colour · 102min

Mega-macho trio Yul Brynner, Richard Widmark, George Chakiris are engulfed by sentimentality and self-doubt as members of a US rescue mission at sea. They're trying to save the survivors of a storm-battered cargo ship off the Japanese coast but all three have psychological problems to overcome before they can get to grips with the elements. Far from being a robust action adventure, the extensive flashback sequences turn this into a glorified high-seas soap. **TH**

Yul Brynner *Sgt Mike Takashima* · Richard Widmark *Col Glenn Stevenson* · George Chakiris *Lt John Gregg* · Suzy Parker *Lucille* · Shirley Knight *Caroline* · Danièle Gaubert *Leila* ■ Dir Michael Anderson · Scr Elliott Arnold, Waldo Salt, from the novel by Elliott Arnold

Flight from Glory ★★

Action drama 1937 · US · BW · 66min

This RKO B-movie, inspired by the success of MGM's classier *Night Flight* that boasted two Barrymores and Clark Gable flying air freight across the Andes. Here it's still the Andes, but the cast only gets as high up the stellar scale as Chester Morris and Van Heflin, who have both lost their licences in America and now fly supplies to a remote mountain mining camp. When they're not in the air, romance blossoms between head honcho Morris and Whitney Bourne, Heflin's new bride. **AT**

Chester Morris *Smith* · Whitney Bourne *Lee Wilson* · Onslow Stevens *Ellis* · Van Heflin *George Wilson* · Richard Lane *Hanson* · Paul Guilfoyle (1) *Jones* ■ Dir Louis Friedlander [Lew Landers] · Scr David Silverstein, John Twist, from a story by Robert D Andrews

Flight 93 ★★ 12

Drama based on a true story 2006 · US · Colour · 85min

This well-intentioned but ultimately underwhelming 9/11 drama pales alongside the superlative, same-themed *United 93*. Turning intense tragedy into a routine disaster movie, it re-creates the events aboard the hijacked American plane that crashed into a Pennsylvania field on that devastating day in 2001. Initially, director Peter Markle takes an understated approach, respectfully reining in the schmaltz and largely sticking to the known facts. However, the closer proceedings get to the climax, the more clichés and sentimentality creep in. **SF** English, Arabic +subtitles. *DVD*

Jeffrey Nordling *Tom Burnett* · Brennan Elliott *Todd Beamer* · Kendall Cross *Deena Burnett* · Ty Olsson *Mark Bingham* · Monnae Michaell *Lisa Jefferson* · Colin Glazer *Jeremy Glick* ■ Dir Peter Markle · Scr Nevin Schreiner

Flight of Fancy ★★ PG

Drama 2000 · US · Colour · 100min

A lonely lad learns a bit about life and a lot about himself through his encounter with an intriguing stranger. Bored with his mundane island existence and unhappy with mother Talisa Soto's relationship with dull Miguel Sandoval, young Kristian de la Osa has his hopes raised when Dean Cain arrives in his bi-plane. Cain makes a suitably dashing penny-dreadful hero, but director Noel Quinones douses his dealings with the kid in queasy sentiment. **DP** *DVD*

Dean Cain *Clay* · Talisa Soto *Mercedes* · Miguel Sandoval *Frank* · Kristian de la Osa *Gabriel* ■ Dir Noel Quinones · Scr Mark Kemble, Noel Quinones, Tom Musca

Flight of Fury ★ 15

Action thriller 2007 · Rom/US/UK · Colour · 94min

This trashy, badly made mess stars Steven Seagal as a former US pilot who's shipped off to Afghanistan to stop rebels from using an experimental plane and its biological payload on US targets. The aikido master lumbers through the proceedings with little enthusiasm, and who can blame him? **JR** Violence, swearing. *DVD*

Steven Seagal *John Sands* · Steve Toussaint *Ratcher* · Angus MacInnes *General Barnes* · Mark Bazeley *Jannick* · Ciera Payton *Jessica* · Alki David *Rojar* · Tim Woodward *Admiral Pendleton* ■ Dir Michael Keusch · Scr Steven Seagal, Joe Halpin, from a story by Halpin

Flight of the Albatross ★★★

Drama 1995 · Ger/NZ · Colour · 93min

Unlike most children's dramas, this treats its audience with respect by tackling such serious subjects as conservation and the notion that cultural difference represents a challenge and not a threat. As the New Yorker who comes to the Great Kauri island in the South Pacific to visit her scientist mother, Julia Brendler is refreshingly unprecocious. The way her friendship develops with Maori Emile Taungaroa, as they tend an injured albatross, makes the issues seem alive rather than contrived. **DP**

Jack Thompson *Mike* · Taungaroa Emile *Mako* · Julia Brendler *Sarah* · Suzanne von Borsody *Claudia* · Pete Smith *Huka* · Diana Ngaromotu-Heka *Mari* ■ Dir Werner Meyer · Scr Riwia Brown, from the novel by Deborah Savage, Philippe Campbell

Flight of the Doves ★★★ U

Adventure 1971 · UK · Colour · 97min

Director Ralph Nelson followed the success of the controversial *Soldier Blue* with this charming piece of Irish whimsy that may be too self-consciously cute for adult tastes. Beautifully shot on location by ace cinematographer Harry Waxman, this blithe tale charts the trials and tribulations of a pair of Liverpudlian children who, quite unaccountably, keep running into a host of English character actors. There's a lovely performance from the marvellous Dorothy McGuire, and Roy Budd's score is great. **TS** *DVD*

Ron Moody *Hawk Dove* · Jack Wild *Finn Dove* · Dorothy McGuire *Granny O'Flaherty* · Stanley Holloway *Judge Liffy* · Helen Raye *Derval Dove* · William Rushton *Tobias Cromwell* ■ Dir Ralph Nelson · Scr Frank Gabrielson, Ralph Nelson, from a novel by Walter Macken

Flight of the Intruder ★★ 15

War drama 1991 · US · Colour · 109min

Gung-ho bombast is definitely macho director John Milius's forte. Unfortunately, it can't save this claustrophobic and endlessly talky drama, set during the winding-down stages of the Vietnam War. Milius co-wrote *Apocalypse Now*, but this moralistic study of the vainglorious US military effort isn't in the same class. The high-profile cast does what it can considering the ideological justice, but it's fighting as much of a losing battle as the one depicted. **AJ** *DVD*

Danny Glover *Commander Frank Camparelli* · Willem Dafoe *Lieutenant Commander Virgil Cole* · Brad Johnson *Lieutenant Jake* · Rosanna Arquette *Callie* ■ Dir John Milius · Scr Robert Dillon, David Shaber, from a novel by Stephen Coonts

Flight of the Navigator ★★★ U

Science-fiction adventure 1986 · US · Colour · 85min

This appealing children's adventure has just enough quirky touches to keep adults involved as well. Joey Cramer is the youngster who goes missing at the age of 12, only to turn up eight years later completely unchanged. It soon becomes apparent that his disappearance is linked to alien space travel. The scenes where Cramer attempts to get to grips with the fact that he has missed out on eight years of his life are neatly handled by director Randal Kleiser, who proves equally adept at the action sequences. **JF** *DVD* *Blu*

Joey Cramer *David Freeman* · Veronica Cartwright *Helen Freeman* · Cliff De Young *Bill Freeman* · Sarah Jessica Parker *Carolyn McAdams* · Howard Hesseman *Dr Faraday* · Paul Mall [Paul Reubens] *Max* ■ Dir Randal Kleiser · Scr Michael Burton, Matt MacManus, from a story by Mark H Baker

The Flight of the Phoenix ★★★★ PG

Adventure drama 1965 · US · Colour · 136min

James Stewart's plane crashes in the desert and when, after days in the sweltering heat, you think he might take a juicy bite out of Richard Attenborough, Peter Finch or Hardy Kruger to get some protein, a plan is hatched to build a smaller plane out of the wreckage. This survivalist epic has all the expected ingredients and more – Attenborough's nerves are shattered, Kruger is the embodiment of Germanic efficiency, Finch is stiff-upper-lipped, Stewart is Charles Lindbergh with a wing down, and all of them sweat and grow beards with élan. Director Robert Aldrich keeps things boiling for perhaps longer than is necessary but delivers a genuinely exciting climax. **AT** *DVD* *Blu*

James Stewart *Frank Towns* · Richard Attenborough *Lew Moran* · Peter Finch *Captain Harris* · Hardy Kruger *Heinrich Dorfmann* · Ernest Borgnine *Trucker Cobb* · Ian Bannen *Crow* · Ronald Fraser *Sergeant Watson* ■ Dir Robert Aldrich · Scr Lukas Heller, from the novel by Elleston Trevor

Flight of the Phoenix ★★★ 12

Action adventure 2004 · US · Colour · 108min

This remake adds little to the 1965 original, save for some superior special effects, but it's a decent enough adventure yarn. The plot remains much the same: the survivors of a plane crash in the desert seek to escape by building a second craft from the wreckage of the first. Dennis Quaid assumes the role of the pilot originally played by James Stewart, while Giovanni Ribisi steps into Hardy Kruger's shoes to play the aircraft designer who conceives the idea of a new plane to rise phoenix-like from the ashes of the old. **DA** *DVD* *Blu*

Dennis Quaid *Frank Towns* • Giovanni Ribisi *Elliott* • Tyrese Gibson *AJ* • Miranda Otto *Kelly* • Hugh Laurie *Ian* • Tony Curran *Rodney* • Kirk Jones [Sticky Fingaz] *Jeremy* • Jacob Vargas *Sammi* • Scott Michael Campbell *Liddle* • Kevork Malikyan *Rady* ■ *Dir* John Moore (3) • *Scr* Frank Scott, Edward Burns, from the film by Lukas Heller, from the novel by Elleston Trevor

The Flight of the Red Balloon ★★★★ PG
Drama   2007 · Fr/Tai · Colour · 111min

Commissioned to commemorate the 20th anniversary of the Musée d'Orsay and riffing on Albert Lamorisse's Oscar-winning 1956 short film *The Red Balloon*, this is director Hou Hsiao-Hsien's most accessible picture to date. Yet it's also a measured and visually sublime treatise on our inability to communicate in an impersonal world. Juliette Binoche excels as the mother whose chaotic existence leaves her young son in the company of a film student-cum-nanny, who challenges him to think about his situation. With the balloon symbolising freedom, rootlessness and isolation as it floats around Paris, this is a consistently beautiful picture, full of playful moments and poignant insights into strained relationships. DP French +subtitles. *DVD*

Juliette Binoche *Suzanne* • Hippolyte Girardot *Marc* • Simon Iteanu *Simon* • Fang Song *Song* ■ *Dir* Hou Hsiao-Hsien • *Scr* Hou Hsiao-Hsien, François Margolin, inspired by the short film *The Red Balloon* by Albert Lamorisse

The Flight of the White Heron ★★★ U
Documentary   1954 · UK · Colour · 95min

This little seen documentary is not just significant because it chronicles the first extensive Commonwealth tour undertaken by the Queen after her coronation, but because it was also the first time the new widescreen colour process, CinemaScope, was used in a British non-fiction film. As close-ups were still regarded as intrusive in those pre-paparazzi days, the producers scrupulously stuck to atmospheric overviews, which not only enhance the spectacle of such events as the Dunedin Highland Games, the Aboriginal corroboree and the Bondi Beach surf carnival, but also showed off Scope's unique visual potential. DP

Leslie Mitchell *Narrator* • *Producer* Jack Ramsden • *Supervising Producer* Gordon Craig • *Cinematographers* Paul Wyand, Norman Fisher, Mark McDonald

Flight to Fury ★★ 12
Crime adventure drama
1966 · US/Phil · BW · 72min

Amazingly, Jack Nicholson wrote the script for this jungle potboiler on the ship that was taking him and the crew to the Philippines where the film was to be shot. By the time they landed in Manila, Nicholson had finished his first solo screenplay. Not surprisingly he wrote the best part for himself, that of a psychopathic gem smuggler, member of a gang whose plane crashes in the jungle where they fight bandits and each other over a cache of stolen diamonds. Monte Hellman directs with gusto on a shoestring budget. RS *DVD*

Dewey Martin *Joe Gaines* • Fay Spain *Destiny Cooper* • Jack Nicholson *Jay Wickam* • Jacqueline Hellman [Jaclyn Hellman] *Gloria Walsh* ■ *Dir* Monte Hellman • *Scr* Jack Nicholson, from a story by Monte Hellman, Fred Roos

Flight to Mars ★ U
Science-fiction adventure
1951 · US · Colour · 71min

A ramshackle space opera in comic-strip style, this is about mankind's first landing on Mars and the discovery of an advanced, dying underground civilisation plotting an Earth invasion because they are running low on resources. Shot in 11 days by quickie merchants Monogram Studios, it's uninspired pulp nonsense. AJ

Marguerite Chapman *Alita* • Cameron Mitchell *Steve* • Arthur Franz *Jim* • Virginia Huston *Carol* • John Litel *Dr Lane* • Richard Gaines *Prof Jackson* ■ *Dir* Lesley Selander • *Scr* Arthur Strawn

Flight to Tangier ★ U
Action drama   1953 · US · Colour · 89min

Joan Fontaine's career was on the slide when she agreed to star in this overly complicated chase melodrama, although Jack Palance must have welcomed the chance to play a romantic lead, abdicating the villainy to Robert Douglas. It's peopled by mysterious characters behaving strangely and was originally made in 3D, which would have provided a welcome distraction. AE

Joan Fontaine *Susan* • Jack Palance *Gil Walker* • Corinne Calvet *Nicole* • Robert Douglas *Danzar* • Marcel Dalio *Gogo* ■ *Dir/Scr* Charles Marquis Warren

Flightplan ★★★ 12
Action thriller   2005 · US · Colour · 93min

German director Robert Schwentke does a neat spin on *The Lady Vanishes*. Aeronautical engineer Jodie Foster boards a plane to the US with her daughter, but when she awakes from a nap, her daughter is gone. No one remembers the little girl having been there and there's no record of her boarding the plane. With the help of an air marshal (Peter Sarsgaard), Foster tries to untangle the mystery. It's a finely acted movie, cleverly tapping into post-9/11 anxieties. These dissolve in a flurry of twists in the last act, but it still leaves an impact. LF In English, German. Violence. *DVD* SD

Jodie Foster *Kyle Pratt* • Peter Sarsgaard *Air Marshal Gene Carson* • Sean Bean *Captain Rich* • Marlene Lawston *Julia Pratt* • Erika Christensen *Fiona* • Kate Beahan *Stephanie* • Greta Scacchi *Therapist* ■ *Dir* Robert Schwentke • *Scr* Peter A Dowling, Billy Ray

The Flim-Flam Man ★★★★ U
Comedy   1967 · US · Colour · 103min

This choice comedy stars George C Scott as an elderly conman of epic proportions, who takes on Michael Sarrazin as his apprentice, until the youngster falls in love and starts to reconsider his chosen path. Written by William Rose, it's directed by Irvin Kershner with affectionate panache, helped by his second unit director and stuntman, Yakima Canutt. TH

George C Scott *Mordecai Jones* • Sue Lyon *Bonnie Lee Packard* • Harry Morgan *Sheriff Slade* • Jack Albertson *Mr Packard* • Alice Ghostley *Mrs Packard* • Albert Salmi *Deputy Meshaw* • Slim Pickens *Jarvis Bates* • Michael Sarrazin *Curley Treadaway* ■ *Dir* Irvin Kershner • *Scr* William Rose, from the story *The Ballad of the Flim Flam Man* by Guy Owen

The Flintstones ★★ U
Comedy   1994 · US · Colour · 86min

The casting is almost perfect, the re-creation of Bedrock is masterly and the special effects are clever without being overly intrusive. And yet this live-action version of the classic 1960s TV cartoon series is lacklustre. The boisterous fun that made the Hanna-Barbera original so endearing has been lost and not even John Goodman's and Elizabeth Taylor's mother-in-law can atone. DP *DVD*

John Goodman *Fred Flintstone* • Elizabeth Perkins *Wilma Flintstone* • Rick Moranis *Barney Rubble* • Rosie O'Donnell *Betty Rubble* • Kyle MacLachlan *Cliff Vandercave* • Halle Berry *Miss Stone* • Elizabeth Taylor *Pearl Slaghoople* ■ *Dir* Brian Levant • *Scr* Tom S Parker, Jim Jennewein, Steven E de Sousa, from the animated TV series by William Hanna, Joseph Barbera

The Flintstones in Viva Rock Vegas ★★★ PG
Comedy   2000 · US · Colour · 87min

It's yabba-dabba-two time as Fred and Barney first meet Wilma and Betty in a belated prequel to 1994's live-action original. The first half is cuter, with the

trademark retro gizmos, while the more plot-driven second half could tax pre-adolescent patience as Fred seeks to win Wilma's hand by striking it rich in Vegas. The casting is variable, but the girls are great, with Jane Krakowski a nicely traditional Betty, and Kristen Johnston a voluptuous Wilma. DA *DVD*

Mark Addy *Fred Flintstone* • Stephen Baldwin *Barney Rubble* • Kristen Johnston *Wilma Slaghoople* • Jane Krakowski *Betty O'Shale* • Joan Collins *Pearl Slaghoople* • Alan Cumming *The Great Gazoo/Mick Jagged* • Harvey Korman *Col Slaghoople* ■ *Dir* Brian Levant • *Scr* Harry Elfont, Deborah Kaplan, Jim Cash, Jack Epps Jr, from the animated TV series by William Hanna, Joseph Barbera

Flipper ★★★ U
Adventure   1963 · US · Colour · 86min

There can hardly be a baby boomer in Britain who didn't follow the adventures of Flipper the dolphin on TV at one time or another during the 1960s. This is the film that inspired the series. Produced by Ivan Tors, who specialised in animal adventures, it's a delight from start to finish, with Luke Halpin excelling as the small boy who befriends and tames the mischievous, scene-stealing dolphin. A sequel, *Flipper's New Adventure*, followed and it was remade in 1996. DP *DVD*

Chuck Connors *Porter Ricks* • Luke Halpin *Sandy Ricks* • Kathleen Maguire *Martha Ricks* • Connie Scott *Kim Parker* • Jane Rose *Hettie White* • Joe Higgins *LC Porett* ■ *Dir* James B Clark • *Scr* Arthur Weiss, from a story by Ricou Browning, Jack Cowden

Flipper's New Adventure ★★★ PG
Adventure   1964 · US · Colour · 94min

Following the success of the previous year's *Flipper*, cinema's most adorable dolphin returned for another adventure in the company of Luke Halpin as Sandy. Fearing they are to be separated, the duo flee to a remote island, where they encounter a British family, whose yachting holiday has been hijacked by pirates. With Pamela Franklin and Francesca Annis making early screen appearances, this exciting story makes splendid use of both its exotic locations and its aquatic superstar. TS

Luke Halpin *Sandy Ricks* • Pamela Franklin *Penny* • Tom Helmore *Sir Halsey Hopewell* • Helen Cherry *Julia* • Francesca Annis *Gwen* ■ *Dir* Leon Benson • *Scr* Art Arthur, from a story by Ivan Tors, from characters by Ricou Browning, Jack Cowden

Flipper ★★ PG
Adventure   1996 · US · Colour · 91min

Elijah Wood goes to spend the summer on an island near Florida with his fisherman uncle Paul Hogan. The island's fisherfolk turn nasty when Wood befriends a dolphin they suspect of eating all the local catch, but the tables are turned when the duo discovers a gang of hunters polluting the waters with toxic waste. Formulaic, but with idyllic locations and an upbeat soundtrack. JF *DVD* BD

Paul Hogan *Porter* • Elijah Wood *Sandy* • Jonathan Banks *Dirk Moran* • Bill Kelley *Tommy* • Chelsea Field *Cathy* • Isaac Hayes *Sheriff Buck Cowan* • Luke Halpin *Bounty fisherman* ■ *Dir* Alan Shapiro • *Scr* Alan Shapiro, from the film by Arthur Weiss, from a story by Ricou Browning, Jack Cowden

Flipping ★★★ 18
Crime drama   1996 · US · Colour · 98min

Despite the off-putting title, this is an atmospheric crime thriller, set on the seedy streets of Hollywood. David Amos is one of group of tough-guy collectors working for local crime boss Keith David. The trouble starts when the boys decide they would be better off with David out of the way. An interesting twist is Amos's unexpected relationship with cop David Proval. Sharply written and directed, this is smarter than average. DA Swearing, violence. *DVD*

Keith David *Leo Richards* • David Proval *Billy White* • David Amos *Michael Moore* • Barry Primus *Joey* • Mike Starr *CJ* • Gene Mitchell *Shot* ■ *Dir/Scr* Gene Mitchell

Flirtation Walk ★★★ U
Musical comedy   1934 · US · BW · 98min

Dedicated to the West Point Military Academy, this lively musical goes a fair way to both glamourising and glorifying that legendary institution. It also provides an ideal arena for that likeable twosome of Dick Powell and Ruby Keeler (he's a cadet, she's the general's daughter) who get to croon and stroll along a very studio-bound vision of the eponymous "walk". Director Frank Borzage makes heavy weather of the simplistic plotting, but the film was popular enough to earn a best picture Oscar nomination. TS

Dick Powell *Dick "Canary" Richard Palmer* • Grant Dorcy • Ruby Keeler *Kit Fitts* • Pat O'Brien *Scrapper Thornhill* • Ross Alexander *Oskie* • John Arledge *Spike* • John Eldredge *Lt Robert Biddle* • Henry O'Neill *Gen Jack Fitts* ■ *Dir* Frank Borzage • *Scr* Delmer Daves, from a story by Lou Edelman, Delmer Daves

Flirting ★★★★★ 15
Comedy drama   1989 · Aus · Colour · 94min

Director John Duigan began the coming-of-age story of Danny Embling in the wonderful *The Year My Voice Broke*, and continues it in this even more enjoyable and moving comedy drama. Noah Taylor reprises his role as the young boy who moves from his small Australian outback town to an all-boys boarding school. Across the lake is an all-girls school, and it is during one of the occasions where the two schools get together that he meets and falls in love with a beautiful young Ugandan pupil (Thandie Newton, making her film debut). A true gem, also notable for a brief appearance by Nicole Kidman. JB

Noah Taylor *Danny Embling* • Thandie Newton *Thandiwe Adjewa* • Nicole Kidman *Nicola Radcliffe* • Bartholomew Rose *"Gilby" Fryer* • Felix Nobis *Jock Blair* • Josh Picker *"Baka" Bourke* • Marc Gray *Christopher Laidlaw* ■ *Dir/Scr* John Duigan

Flirting with Disaster ★★★ 15
Comedy road movie   1996 · US · Colour · 88min

This madcap, country-crossing comedy makes up in eccentric characterisation what it occasionally loses in control. Ben Stiller is suitably neurotic as the orphan hoping to trace his roots before naming his new baby, as ditzy psychologist Téa Leoni leads him up endless blind alleys. Cameos by adoptive parents Mary Tyler Moore and George Segal, and ageing hippies Alan Alda and Lily Tomlin steal Stiller's thunder. DP *DVD*

Ben Stiller *Mel Coplin* • Patricia Arquette *Nancy Coplin* • Téa Leoni *Tina Kalb* • Mary Tyler Moore *Mrs Coplin* • George Segal *Mr Coplin* • Alan Alda *Richard Schlicting* • Lily Tomlin *Mary Schlicting* • Richard Jenkins *Paul* • Josh Brolin *Tony* ■ *Dir/Scr* David O Russell

Floating Skyscrapers ★★★ 18
Romantic drama   2013 · Pol · Colour · 93min

Writer/director Tomasz Wasilewski's movie was released as one of Poland's first Polish gay films. Mateusz Banasiuk plays a self-centred swimmer who craves anonymous locker room encounters to relieve the tension of living with his possessive mother (Katarzyna Herman) and manipulative girlfriend (Marta Nieradkiewicz). However, he meets fey student Bartosz Gelner and begins to fall in love. Wasilewski's kinetic direction captures the physical passion, but the movie's brutal denouement shows the reality of its social context as less politically liberating than the title suggests. DP Polish +subtitles. Violence, swearing, sex scenes, drug abuse, nudity.

Mateusz Banasiuk *Kuba* • Marta Nieradkiewicz *Sylwia* • Bartosz Gelner *Michal* • Katarzyna Herman *Ewa, Kuba's mother* • Olga Frycz *Monika* ■ *Dir/Scr* Tomasz Wasilewski

Floating Weeds ★★ PG

Drama   1959 · Jpn · Colour · 113min

Based on the same story that inspired his silent 1934 drama, *A Story of Floating Weeds*, this was among Yasujiro Ozu's weakest postwar pictures. For once his nostalgic yearnings seem to have got the better of him, as there are few contemporary resonances in this story of a travelling Kabuki player who hurts his mistress by interfering in the love life of his estranged son. Kenji Mizoguchi's regular cinematographer Kazuo Miyagawa gives the seascapes a lustre that only occasionally illuminates the rest of the production. DP Japanese +subtitles. **DVD** **Blu-ray**

Ganjiro Nakamura *Komajuro Arashi* • Haruko Sugimura *Oyoshi* • Hiroshi Kawaguchi *Kiyoshi* • Machiko Kyo *Sumiko* • Ayako Wakao *Kayo* • Chishu Ryu *Theatre owner* ■ *Dir* Yasujiro Ozu • *Scr* Yasujiro Ozu, Kogo Noda, from a story by Yasujiro Ozu, from the 1934 film *Ukigusa Monogatari [A Story of Floating Weeds]* by Tadao Ikeda

The Flock ★★ 18

Crime thriller   2007 · US · Colour · 100min

Richard Gere stars as an officer who definitely isn't a gentleman in this murky trawl through the American sexual underbelly, the first English-language film by Hong Kong director Andrew Lau (*Infernal Affairs*). A public safety officer (Gere) is employed to keep tabs on registered sex offenders – his flock – to make sure they don't re-offend. Burnt out and violent, he's about to retire when a case involving a missing girl drags him and his rookie partner (Claire Danes) deeper into the seedy underworld he abhors yet is quietly obsessed by. The film makes a vague pretence of charting Gere's inner turmoil, while layering on lashings of lurid sexual violence designed purely to titillate. It's an uncomfortable mix and the general sense that it doesn't add up probably wasn't helped by the departure of Lau during production. JR Violence, sexual references. **DVD**

Richard Gere *Agent Erroll Babbage* • Claire Danes *Allison Laurie* • Matt Schulze *Custis* • KaDee Strickland *Viola* • Avril Lavigne *Young woman* • Ray Wise *Robert Stiller* ■ *Dir* Andrew Lau • *Scr* Hans Bauer, Craig Mitchell

The Flood ★★★

Drama   1993 · Rus/Fr · Colour · 97min

This adaptation of Yevgyeni Zamyatin's novel concentrates on the emotions experienced by a childless woman when her respectable husband falls for their adopted teenage daughter. Renowned for her ability to convey psychological depth, Isabelle Huppert gives an expert reading of the transformation of humiliation and acceptance into jealousy and recrimination, as she rebels against both her situation and a discriminatory society. Director Igor Minayev's visual sense is acute, although some may find his pacing too precise. DP In French.

Isabelle Huppert *Sofia* • Boris Nevzorov *Trofim* • Masha Lipkina *Ganka* • Svetlana Kryuchkova *Pelagia* ■ *Dir* Igor Minayev • *Scr* Jacques Baynac, Igor Minayev, from a novel by Yevgyeni Zamyatin

Floods of Fear ★★ 12

Drama   1958 · UK · BW · 80min

Ealing Studios veteran Charles Crichton didn't do his reputation any favours with this sentimental melodrama. Basically an ensemble chamber piece revolving around four people trapped by floods in a gloomy house, the predictable plot barely keeps credibility afloat as an escaped convict eventually redeems himself through decisive action when tragedy looms. Typical and unremarkable 1950s British B-movie fare. AJ Swearing, violence.

Howard Keel *Donovan* • Anne Heywood *Elizabeth Matthews* • Cyril Cusack *Peebles* • Harry H Corbett *Sharkey* • John Crawford *Jack Murphy* • Eddie Byrne *Sheriff* • John Phillips (1) *Dr*

Matthews* ■ *Dir* Charles Crichton • *Scr* Vivienne Knight, Charles Crichton, from the novel by John Hawkins, Ward Hawkins

Floodtide ★★

Romantic drama   1949 · UK · BW · 89min

The grim grandeur of the Clyde shipyards provides the setting for this lacklustre melodrama which trades on the British docudramatic tradition while dealing in potboiling clichés. Having alienated his farming family by decamping to Glasgow, Gordon Jackson rises from engineer to designer at Jack Lambert's yard. But it still takes an act of reckless heroism on the eve of a prestigious launch to convince him Jackson is the right man for daughter, Rona Anderson. DP

Gordon Jackson *David Shields* • Rona Anderson *Mary Anstruther* • John Laurie *Joe Drummond* • Jack Lambert *Anstruther* • Janet Brown *Rosie* • Elizabeth Sellars *Judy* • Jimmy Logan *Tim Brogan* ■ *Dir* Frederick Wilson • *Scr* George Blake, Donald B Wilson, Frederick Wilson

The Floorwalker ★★★★ U

Silent comedy   1916 · US · BW · 24min

Chaplin makes the most of a look-alike scenario, as he discovers he's a ringer for the floorwalker in a large department store. He indulges in some of his greatest pratfalls and seriously falls for Edna Purviance. Basically a series of revue turns, with him skidding and dancing around, it is more reliant on plot than many of his early films at this time. It's a frivolity, with escapades on the escalator, but nevertheless offers some acute insights into the almost Dickensian society of the day. TH **DVD**

Charles Chaplin *Tramp* • Edna Purviance *Secretary* ■ *Dir* Charles Chaplin • *Scr* Charles Chaplin, Vincent Bryan

Florence Foster Jenkins ★★★★★ PG

Biographical comedy drama
2016 · US/UK · Colour · 110min

A heart-warming tribute to the American socialite who desperately wanted an operatic soprano career but couldn't sing a note, this fascinating biopic is a compelling rumination on the powers of self-delusion and devotion. Stephen Frears (*Philomena*) strikes just the right balance between humour and pathos, with Meryl Streep triumphant as the daydream diva. Hugh Grant also gives one of his best performances as Jenkins's complicated common-law husband, who stops at nothing to keep intrigued critics away. At the same time cringe-worthy, uplifting and sobering, this captivating look at the coloratura curiosity is hugely entertaining and masterfully moving. AJ Some swearing.

Meryl Streep *Florence Foster Jenkins* • Hugh Grant *St Clair Bayfield* • Simon Helberg *Cosme McMoon* • Rebecca Ferguson *Kathleen* • Nina Arianda *Agnes Stark* • Allan Corduner *John Totten* ■ *Dir* Stephen Frears • *Scr* Nicholas Martin • *Cinematographer* Danny Cohen

Floundering ★★

Drama   1994 · US · Colour · 97min

The psychological aftermath of the LA riots is examined in an offbeat but muddled look at the unravelling life of one resident. This doesn't pull any punches in its portrayal of crumbling social and political values, but its air of self-importance doesn't encourage identification with James LeGros, nor do his pretentious ramblings about spirituality. JC

James LeGros *John Boyz* • John Cusack *JC* • Ethan Hawke *Jimmy* • Maritza Rivera *Elle* • Steve Buscemi *Ned* • Billy Bob Thornton *Gun clerk* ■ *Dir/Scr* Peter McCarthy

Flower Drum Song ★★ U

Musical comedy   1961 · US · Colour · 125min

Interminable and grotesquely over-produced (by the king of "camp" glamour Ross Hunter) this screen version of Rodgers and Hammerstein's Broadway success about life in San Francisco's Chinatown was woefully patronising and under-directed by Henry Koster. On Broadway, the tale had charm and style but this overblown and

overlong movie just lies there and dies there. However, there's some bracing choreography and the endearing score has survived almost intact. TS **DVD**

Nancy Kwan *Linda Low* • James Shigeta *Wang Ta* • Miyoshi Umeki *Mei Li* • Juanita Hall *Auntie* • Jack Soo *Sammy Fong* • Benson Fong *Wang Chi-Wang* • Reiko Sato *Helen Chao* ■ *Dir* Henry Koster • *Scr* Joseph Fields, from the novel by CY Lee and the book of the musical by Joseph Fields • *Cinematographer* Russell Metty • *Choreographer* Hermes Pan

Flower Girl ★★

Romantic drama   2009 · US · Colour · 100min

Veteran TV director Bradford May piles on the sentiment in this pleasant though increasingly slushy drama. A by-the-numbers story of head versus heart, it sees a small-town florist (Marla Sokoloff) forced to choose between two very different suitors as she pursues her dream of a fairy-tale romance. Fortunately, there's enough genuine warmth to allow the plot's predictability to be overlooked, while a splash of humour dilutes the sugary emotion by poking gentle fun at the wedding industry. SF

Marla Sokoloff *Laurel* • Marion Ross *Rose* • Kieren Hutchison *Stephen* • Terry Maratos *Evan* ■ *Dir* Bradford May • *Scr* Marjorie Sweeney

The Flower of Evil ★★★★ 15

Mystery drama   2002 · Fr · Colour · 104min

Both Nathalie Baye and Suzanne Flon impress in this acute dissection of bourgeois mores. But while Baye's mayoral campaign in a mixed-class neighbourhood of Bordeaux makes for easy satire, the exposure of Flon's past reopens the scars inflicted by the Nazi Occupation. The sexual antics of Bernard Le Coq's philandering pharmacist and the pseudo-incestuous affair between his son, Benoît Magimel, and Baye's daughter, Mélanie Doutey, add to the sense of family strife, making Claude Chabrol's tale of domestic intrigue a morbidly fascinating experience. DP French +subtitles.

Benoît Magimel *François Vasseur* • Nathalie Baye *Anne Charpin-Vasseur* • Mélanie Doutey *Michèle Charpin-Vasseur* • Suzanne Flon *Aunt Line* • Bernard Le Coq *Gérard Vasseur* • Thomas Chabrol *Matthieu Lartigue* ■ *Dir* Claude Chabrol • *Scr* Louise L Lambrichs, Caroline Eliacheff, Claude Chabrol

The Flower of My Secret ★★★★ 15

Drama   1995 · Sp/Fr · Colour · 101min

This constitutes a marked change of pace for the cult Spanish director Pedro Almodóvar. Here he tones down his usual camp satirical sensibilities to tell the engaging story of a romance novelist (Marisa Paredes) whose work is suffering because her marriage is falling apart. And that's not all: her best friend is betraying her, her half-blind mother and her sister are driving her crazy, and her maid's son has plagiarised one of her manuscripts. Paredes gives an extraordinary performance as the writer in crisis, in a lush tragicomedy that boasts a scorching script, sharp visual contrasts and moments of truly biting humour. AJ Spanish +subtitles. Swearing. **DVD**

Marisa Paredes *Leo* • Juan Echanove *Angel* • Imanol Arias *Paco* • Carmen Elías *Betty* • Rossy de Palma *Rosa* • Chus Lampreave *Mother* • Joaquín Cortés *Antonio* • Manuela Vargas *Blanca* ■ *Dir/Scr* Pedro Almodóvar

Flowers and Trees ★★★★

Animated musical comedy
1932 · US · Colour · 8min

This classic short cartoon was not only Disney's first full colour film, it was the first film anyone had shot in Technicolor's then-new three-strip process, to which Disney had bought exclusive rights in animation for three years. The basic story, in which a romance between two trees is threatened by a covetous stump, has been so often imitated that it may now seem twee, yet the personality animation and use of colour are

so sophisticated that its beauty outweighs any contemporary qualms, turning datedness into period charm. It created a sensation among 1930s audiences and won an Oscar (the first animated film to do so). CLP

■ *Dir* Burt Gillett

Flowers for Algernon ★★

Drama   2000 · US · Colour · 120min

Cliff Robertson won an Oscar for his performance in *Charly* (1968) and it's impossible to view Matthew Modine's interpretation of the role without making unfavourable comparisons. That said, he still manages to capture something of the touching trust with which his mentally challenged character allows himself to undergo surgery in order to fulfil his ambition of becoming a genius. The scientific warnings are valid, but Modine's adoration of teacher Kelli Williams perhaps isn't the best way of making them. DP

Matthew Modine *Charlie Gordon* • Kelli Williams *Alice* • Ron Rifkin *Dr Jonah Strauss* • Bonnie Bedelia *Rose* • Richard Chevolleau *Burt* ■ *Dir* Jeff Bleckner • *Scr* John Pielmeier, from the novel by Daniel Keyes

Flowers in the Attic ★★ 15

Thriller   1987 · US · Colour · 93min

VC Andrews's twisted gothic bestseller gets a rather sanitised makeover in this big screen adaptation. Victoria Tennant is unconvincing in the villainous role of a loopy widow who keeps her own children prisoners in a creepy old mansion while she plots to rid her parents (Louise Fletcher and Nathan Davis) of their fortune. Director Jeffrey Bloom raises the odd fright, but this is silly. JF **DVD**

Clare C Peck *Narrator* • Victoria Tennant *Corinne* • Kristy Swanson *Cathy* • Jeb Stuart Adams *Chris* • Louise Fletcher *Grandmother* • Ben Ganger *Cory* • Nathan Davis *Grandfather* ■ *Dir* Jeffrey Bloom • *Scr* Jeffrey Bloom, from the novel by VC Andrews

Flowers of Shanghai ★★★★

Period drama   1998 · Tai/Jpn · Colour · 124min

This is a masterclass in studio stylisation from Taiwanese director Hou Hsiao-Hsien. His meticulous compositions and unobtrusive camera movements capture both the traditional atmosphere and the impending sense of change hanging over a Shanghai "flower house", which is more a place of education and intrigue than a brothel. In a ruthless world of exploitation and emotional blackmail, the women use everything at their disposal to retain the favour of their wealthy callers. DP In Mandarin.

Tony Chiu-Wai Leung [Tony Leung (2)] *Wang Lingsheng* • Michiko Hada *Crimson* • Michelle Reis *Emerald* • Carina Lau *Pearl* • Jack Kao *Luo* • Vicky Wei [Wei Hsiao-Hui] *Jasmin* ■ *Dir* Hou Hsiao-Hsien • *Scr* Chu Tian-Wen, from the novel *Haishang hua liezhuang (Biographies of Flowers of Shanghai)* by Han Ziyun

The Flowers of War ★★★ 15

Historical drama
2012 · Chi/HK · Colour · 136min

The infamous Rape of Nanking by the Japanese army provides the backdrop for this artfully shot and inevitably harrowing drama from Zhang Yimou (*House of Flying Daggers*). Set in 1937, the story centres around a Catholic church and the disparate groups that hide out there. Joining the resident female students are a boozy, self-serving mortician (Christian Bale), a wounded boy soldier and some local prostitutes. Bale is an engaging presence throughout, despite a credibility-stretching change in his character, and Zhang's slo-mo grenade and gunplay never overpowers the tale's themes about strength in the face of hopelessness. JH English, Mandarin, Japanese +subtitles. Violence. **DVD** **Blu-ray**

Christian Bale *John Miller* • Ni Ni *Yu Mo* • Atsuro Watabe *Col Hasegawa* • Shigeo Kobayashi *Lt Kato* • Paul Schneider (2) *Terry* ■ *Dir* Zhang Yimou • *Scr* Liu Heng, from Yan Geling's novel

Flu ★★ 15
Disaster thriller · 2013 · S Kor · Colour · 121min

Korean director Kim Sung-su's disaster thriller rather dubiously equates infestation with illegal immigrants. The rapid spread of a virulent strain of avian flu across a populous district of a major Korean city throws together rescue worker Jang Hyuk and doctor Soo Ae, who is racing to find a cure for a disease that has already infected her daughter. The restless camerawork conveys a sense of chaos and panic as the city goes into lockdown, but there is precious little tension and it's difficult to root for someone as resistible as the sniffy heroine. DP English, Korean, Indonesian +subtitles. Violence, swearing.

Soo Ae *Kim In-hae* · Jang Hyuk *Kang Ji-koo* · Andrew William Brand *Dr Bill Backman* · Park Min-ah *Kim Mi-reu* · Cha In-Pyo *President* ■ *Dir* Kim Sung-su · *Scr* Lee Young-Jong, Kim Sung-su

Flubber ★★★ U
Comedy · 1997 · US · Colour · 90min

This continues Hollywood's obsession with souping-up the hit comedies of the past – in this case *The Absent-Minded Professor* (1961) – with today's sophisticated special effects. Robin Williams plays a scientist who becomes so immersed in creating a new energy source that he once again misses his own wedding. But this time he has an excuse, because he has invented Flubber – a substance like rubber that generates its own energy, wreaking havoc everywhere it goes. Kids will love it. JF *DVD*

Robin Williams *Professor Philip Brainard* · Marcia Gay Harden *Sara Jean Reynolds* · Christopher McDonald *Wilson Croft* · Raymond J Barry *Chester Hoenicker* · Clancy Brown *Smith* · Ted Levine *Wesson* · Wil Wheaton *Bennett Hoenicker* · Edie McClurg *Martha George* ■ *Dir* Les Mayfield · *Scr* John Hughes, Bill Walsh, from the story *A Situation of Gravity* by Samuel W Taylor

The Fluffer ★★★ 18
Erotic drama · 2001 · US · Colour · 90min

The adult entertainment industry is the focus for a contemporary reworking of the traditional love triangle theme in this dark and occasionally humorous drama. This interweaves the turbulent lives of an adult movie star, his stripper girlfriend and a cameraman so enamoured with the star that he'll perform the most intimate of on-set functions for him. Though the story unfolds against a gay porn setting which may marginalise the film's appeal, the story is of equal relevance to audiences of all sexual persuasions. SF *DVD*

Scott Gurney *Michael "Mike" Rossini/Johnny Rebel* · Michael Cunio *Sean McGinnis* · Roxanne Day *Babylon* · Taylor Negron *Tony Brooks* · Deborah Harry *Marcella* ■ *Dir* Richard Glatzer, Wash West [Wash Westmoreland] · *Scr* Wash West [Wash Westmoreland]

Fluffy ★★ U
Comedy · 1965 · US · Colour · 91min

The eponymous animal is a lion who has the misfortune to be engaged in research with Professor Tony Randall who – by way of that research – falls in love with Shirley Jones. We keep watching, hoping that Randall will rise above the script, and that Jones will burst into song; a waste of the two stars – and the lion. TH

Tony Randall *Daniel Potter* · Shirley Jones *Janice Claridge* · Edward Andrews *Griswald* · Ernest Truex *Claridge* · Jim Backus *Sergeant* · Frank Faylen *Catfish* · Howard Morris *Sweeney* ■ *Dir* Earl Bellamy · *Scr* Samuel Roeca

Fluke ★★★ PG
Fantasy drama · 1995 · US · Colour · 91min

This is a well-meaning adaptation of James Herbert's fantasy about a man protecting his family from villainous intent when he's reincarnated as a dog after a fatal car crash. Directed by co-writer Carlo Carlei with razzle-dazzle visuals, what is basically a children's story becomes accessible to adults thanks to the serious issues. A charming tale that some will find slightly sappy. AJ *DVD*

Matthew Modine *Thomas Johnson/Fluke* · Nancy Travis *Carol Johnson* · Eric Stoltz *Jeff Newman* · Max Pomeranc *Brian Johnson* · Samuel L Jackson *Rumbo* ■ *Dir* Carlo Carlei · *Scr* Carlo Carlei, James Carrington, from the novel by James Herbert

Flushed Away ★★★ U
Animated comedy adventure
2006 · US/UK · Colour · 81min

The first computer-animated feature from the Aardman brigade successfully replicates their Wallace & Gromit claymation aesthetic with visually entertaining (if less charming) results. Hugh Jackman provides the voice of Roddy St James, a posh Kensington pet mouse who is flushed down the toilet into a vast rodent metropolis – a detailed mini-London constructed from rubbish. There he teams up with a streetwise rat (Kate Winslet) to foil the plans of a villainous toad (Ian McKellen) to flood the sewer city during the World Cup final. Singing slugs crooning pop hits provide hilarious comment on the action. AJ *DVD* CS

Hugh Jackman *Roddy St James* · Kate Winslet *Rita* · Ian McKellen *The Toad* · Jean Reno *Le Frog* · Bill Nighy *Whitey* · Andy Serkis *Spike* · Shane Richie *Sid* · Kathy Burke *Rita's mum* · David Suchet *Rita's dad* ■ *Dir* David Bowers, Sam Fell · *Scr* Dick Clement, Ian La Frenais, Christopher Lloyd (2), Joe Keenan, Will Davies, from a story by Sam Fell, Peter Lord, Clement, La Frenais

The Fly ★★★ PG
Horror · 1958 · US · Colour · 89min

Based on a *Playboy* short story, with a script by *Shogun* writer James Clavell, the plot has matter-transmitter experiments giving Al Hedison (later David Hedison) the head and arm of a common house fly, while Vincent Price, as Hedison's brother, has histrionics about family curses. Enjoyably unsettling once past the inconsistencies of the premise, this plush flesh-crawler includes many marvellous moments. Two sequels, *Return of the Fly* (1959) and *Curse of the Fly* (1965), followed. AJ *DVD* Blu

Al Hedison [David Hedison] *André* · Patricia Owens *Helene* · Vincent Price *François* · Herbert Marshall *Inspector Charas* · Kathleen Freeman *Emma* · Betty Lou Gerson *Nurse Andersone* · Charles Herbert *Philippe* ■ *Dir* Kurt Neumann · *Scr* James Clavell, from a short story by George Langelaan

The Fly ★★★★ 18
Horror · 1986 · US · Colour · 91min

It's easy to see why visceral visionary David Cronenberg wanted to remake the landmark 1958 chiller about scientific experiments in molecular teleportation. It plunges into the same primal territory he explored in *Shivers*, *Rabid* and *Videodrome* by regurgitating his deep-seated fears of ageing, disease, deformity and the beast within. Only Cronenberg can get away with working out his raw phobias on screen while being poignantly witty and repulsively entertaining at the same time. Jeff Goldblum's sensitive performance takes the edge off the grisly special effects, but many will find it hard to get past the gooey gore. AJ Violence, swearing, a sex scene. *DVD* Blu

Jeff Goldblum *Seth Brundle* · Geena Davis *Veronica Quaife* · John Getz *Stathis Borans* · Joy Boushel *Tawny* · Les Carlson *Dr Cheevers* · George Chuvalo *Marky* · David Cronenberg *Gynaecologist* ■ *Dir* David Cronenberg · *Scr* Charles Edward Pogue, David Cronenberg, from a short story by George Langelaan

The Fly II ★★ 18
Horror · 1989 · US · Colour · 100min

Special effects and make-up artist-turned-director Chris Walas puts too much emphasis on gore galore and pays scant attention to plot. Eric Stoltz does what he can encased in rubber, but it goes without saying that this obvious sequel has none of the sly subtlety, elegance or poignant humour David Cronenberg brought to his superior 1986 film. AJ Sex scenes, swearing, violence. *DVD*

Eric Stoltz *Martin Brundle* · Daphne Zuniga *Beth Logan* · Lee Richardson *Anton Bartok* · John Getz *Stathis Borans* · Frank Turner *Dr Shepard* ■ *Dir* Chris Walas · *Scr* Mick Garris, Jim Wheat, Frank Darabont, Ken Wheat, from a story by Mick Garris

Fly Away Home ★★★★ U
Biographical drama · 1996 · US · Colour · 102min

No one captures the inspirational beauty of nature better than director Carroll Ballard, who also made *Never Cry Wolf* and the excellent *Black Stallion*. This exhilarating picture gets off to a painful start with a fatal road accident. But the mood changes from despair to determination as Anna Paquin channels her grief into the rearing of some orphan goslings, and learning to fly a microlight plane to guide her feathered family to its winter breeding ground. With selfless support from Jeff Daniels as Paquin's inventor father and from the geese themselves (stealing every scene, whether waddling comically or flying majestically), this impeccably photographed film is an unbounded delight. DP *DVD*

Jeff Daniels *Thomas Alden* · Anna Paquin *Amy Alden* · Dana Delany *Susan Barnes* · Terry Kinney *David Alden* · Holter Graham *Barry Strickland* ■ *Dir* Carroll Ballard · *Scr* Robert Rodat, Vince McKewin, from the autobiography by Bill Lishman

Fly Me to the Moon ★★ U
Animated adventure
2007 · Bel/US · Colour · 80min

If only the right stuff used to create the amazing look of this 3D animated adventure had spilled over into its story, character and dialogue, then director Ben Stassen's zero-gravity cartoon really would have had lift-off. The predictable "follow your dreams" tale sees three young insects stow away on the 1969 Apollo 11 mission, offering a fly-on-the-wall view of man's historic Moon landing. The visual landscape is astonishingly immersive, but the saccharine narrative lacks wit and a much-needed sense of wonder. AJ *DVD*

Kelly Ripa *Nat's mom* · Christopher Lloyd *Grandpa* · Nicollette Sheridan *Nadia* · Tim Curry *Yegor* · Buzz Aldrin · Adrienne Barbeau *Scooter's mom* · Ed Begley Jr *Poopchev* · Robert Patrick *Louie* · Trevor Gagnon *Nat* · Philip Daniel Bolden *IQ* · David Gore *Scooter* ■ *Dir* Ben Stassen · *Scr* Domonic Paris

Flyboys ★★★ 12
First World War action adventure
2006 · US/UK · Colour · 132min

James Franco stars in a First World War adventure that's loosely based on the true story of the Lafayette Escadrille, a squadron made up of American men helping the French cause before the US joined the conflict. Franco plays Blaine Rawlings, who leaves Texas for France when his family lose their ranch. But the plot is merely an excuse to cram a bunch of cute kids into cockpits and send them rat-a-tat-tatting away into the wild blue yonder. On the ground, the film stalls somewhat, with clichéd characters and corny dialogue. But in the air, it soars – the dogfights some of the best ever seen on screen. *Flyboys* is great fun, and an action epic in the old-fashioned sense. DA *DVD* Blu

James Franco *Blaine Rawlings* · Martin Henderson *Reed Cassidy* · David Ellison *Eddie Beagle* · Jennifer Decker *Lucienne* · Jean Reno *Captain Thenault* · Tyler Labine *Briggs Lowry* ■ *Dir* Tony Bill · *Scr* Blake T Evans, Phil Sears, David S Ward, from a story by Evans · *Cinematographer* Henry Braham

Flying Blind ★★★ 15
Thriller · 2012 · UK · Colour · 93min

A 40-something female engineer working on an MoD aeronautics contract begins an affair with an Arab student that will have ramifications for them both in this topical, small-scale British drama. Helen McCrory gives a striking central performance and Polish director Katarzyna Klimkiewicz creates suspense and sympathy for both McCrory and Najib Oudghiri, as the security services become aware of their liaison. There is cool precision in the look of the film on what is, presumably, a modest budget and, overall, it's an intriguing and resourceful take on how the war on terror permeates even the most intimate spaces. TJ Swearing, sex scenes.

Helen McCrory *Frankie* · Najib Oudghiri *Kahil* · Kenneth Cranham *Victor* · Tristan Gemmill *Robert* · Sherif Eltayeb *Malik* ■ *Dir* Katarzyna Klimkiewicz · *Scr* Caroline Harrington, Bruce McLeod, Naomi Wallace

The Flying Deuces ★★ U
Comedy · 1939 · US · BW · 64min

Notwithstanding a script co-written by silent star Harry Langdon and direction by comedy specialist A Edward Sutherland, this is one of the weaker Laurel and Hardy pictures. Mostly pilfered from the four-reeler *Beau Hunks* and the feature *Bonnie Scotland*, the comic material is simply spread too thinly, and time hangs heavily between the Paris opening, the pair's jaunty dance on arrival at the Foreign Legion fort and the careering plane finale. DP *DVD* Blu

Stan Laurel *Stan* · Oliver Hardy *Ollie* · Jean Parker *Georgette* · Reginald Gardiner *François* · Charles Middleton *Commandant* ■ *Dir* A Edward Sutherland · *Scr* Ralph Spence, Alfred Schiller, Charles Rogers, Harry Langdon

Flying down to Rio ★★★ U
Musical · 1933 · US · BW · 89min

When it was first shown, the stars of this film were glamorous Dolores Del Rio and dashing Gene Raymond, backed by perfect Depression-era deco sets and design and imaginative choreography. But the real significance and most of the pleasure of this film today lies in the casting of two featured players who, although they knew each other in their pre-Hollywood days in New York, had never danced together until this movie. They're Fred Astaire and Ginger Rogers. TS *DVD*

Dolores Del Rio *Belinha* · Gene Raymond *Roger Bond* · Raul Roulien *Julio Rubeiro* · Ginger Rogers *Honey Hale* · Fred Astaire *Fred Ayres* · Blanche Friderici *Dona Helena de Rezende* ■ *Dir* Thornton Freeland · *Scr* Cyril Hume, HW Hanemann, Erwin Gelsey, from a play by Anne Caldwell, from a story by Lou Brock

Flying 55 ★★ U
Crime drama · 1939 · UK · BW · 68min

As with so many horse-racing melodramas, this Edgar Wallace story is pretty heavy going until we reach the course, when all the clichés and caricatures are forgotten in that frantic dash for the line. Wallace could never be accused of stinting on incident as family feuds, race fixing, blackmail and romance are all brought under starters' orders by no-nonsense director, Reginald Denham. DP *DVD*

Derrick de Marney *Bill Urquhart* · Nancy Burne *Stella Barrington* · Marius Goring *Charles Barrington* · John Warwick *Jebson* · Peter Gawthorne *Jonas Urquhart* · DA Clarke-Smith *Jacques Gregory* ■ *Dir* Reginald Denham · *Scr* Victor M Greene, Vernon Clancey, Kenneth Horne, from Edgar Wallace's novel

Flying Leathernecks ★★ PG
Second World War action drama
1951 · US · Colour · 98min

Another disappointing early work from Nicholas Ray, this is a trite reworking of many familiar themes and characters. John Wayne and Robert Ryan seem ill-at-ease in their leading roles, flying studio mock-ups of planes against Technicolor back projection and dutifully conveying a gung-ho spirit without any real enthusiasm. Acting honours are stolen by veteran Jay C Flippen, well cast as a wily sergeant; however, this is just corny, obvious and not very good. TS *DVD*

John Wayne *Major Dan Kirby* · Robert Ryan *Captain Carl Griffin* · Don Taylor *Lieutenant "Cowboy" Blithe* · William Harrigan *Curan* · Jay C Flippen *Master Sergeant Clancy* ■ *Dir* Nicholas Ray · *Scr* James Edward Grant, from a story by Kenneth Gamet

Flying Padre ★★
Documentary 1951 · US · BW · 9min

Suitably impressed by *Day of the Fight*, RKO offered 23-year-old Stanley Kubrick $1,500 to produce this item for its Pathe Screenliner series. The parsimonious budget clearly restricted Kubrick's creativity, as much of the action feels stiffly staged and he offers few insights into the routine of German-born priest Fred Stadtmuller, who needs a Piper Cub aeroplane to tend to a flock scattered 4,000 square miles across New Mexico. Kubrick clearly felt the film needed a big finale so sends the priest into the wilderness to fly a mother and her ailing child to hospital. The visuals are fine, but Kubrick later called this minor outing, "a silly thing". DP

■ *Dir* Stanley Kubrick

The Flying Scot ★ 🆄
Crime thriller 1957 · UK · BW · 66min

The most noteworthy thing about this crime programme filler is that it was scripted by Norman Hudis, who wrote six *Carry On* films. As with most British B-movies of the period, a clutch of transatlantic stars were imported to raise the profile, but they couldn't do much to distract from the mediocrity of this train robbery thriller. DP DVD

Lee Patterson *Ronnie* · Kay Callard *Jackie* · Alan Gifford *Phil* · Margaret Withers *Lady* · Mark Baker (1) *Gibbs* · Jeremy Bodkin *Charlie* ■ *Dir* Compton Bennett · *Scr* Norman Hudis, from a story by Ralph Smart, Jan Read

The Flying Scotsman ★★★ 15
Biographical sports drama
2006 · UK/Ger · Colour · 98min

The story of Scottish cycling star Graeme Obree has taken years to complete from conception to cinema release. But Jonny Lee Miller delivers possibly his best performance in a decade as the misfit who took on the establishment on a home-made bike and set a series of records. Despite its dark psychological undertones, *The Flying Scotsman* remains an old-fashioned drama of personal triumph and athletic glory against the odds, with an obsessive protagonist, a jokey sidekick (Boyd) and a long-suffering (and woefully underwritten) wife (Laura Fraser). An uplifting, feel-good tale, it belongs to a great British tradition that includes *Chariots of Fire*. BP Swearing. DVD

Jonny Lee Miller *Graeme Obree* · Laura Fraser *Anne Obree* · Billy Boyd (1) *Malky* · Brian Cox (1) *Douglas Baxter* · Morven Christie *Katie* · Steven Berkoff *Ernst Hagemann* · Sean Brown *Young Graeme Obree* ■ *Dir* Douglas Mackinnon · *Scr* John Brown (6), Simon Rose, Declan Hughes

Flying Swords of Dragon Gate ★★ 15
Period action adventure
2011 · Chi · Colour · 122min

Jet Li is reunited with *Once upon a Time in China* director Tsui Hark for this sprawling example of the *wuxia* (or swordplay) genre. Set during the Ming dynasty, it stars Li as a do-gooding thorn in the side of feuding government bureaus ruled by a pair of ruthless eunuchs. However, the Robin Hood storyline is swiftly supplanted by the search for a maid who's pregnant with the emperor's child. There are dynamic swordfights aplenty, but the action is swamped by CGI special effects and backgrounds, which creates an oppressive air of artificiality. Even Li looks bored - or is that confused? - in an adventure desperately in need of coherence. JA Mandarin +subtitles. Violence, some swearing. DVD BD

Jet Li *Zhao Huai'an* · Zhou Xun *Ling Yanqiu* · Chen Kun *Yu Huatian/Bok Chang Zhou/Wind Blade* · Li Yuchun *Gu Shaotang* · Mavis Fan *Su Huirong* ■ *Dir/Scr* Tsui Hark

Flying Tigers ★★ 🅿🅶
Second World War drama
1942 · US · BW · 97min

This very average wartime John Wayne feature sings the praises of the American Volunteer Group, the mercenaries who fought for China's freedom against superior Japanese forces in the days before Pearl Harbor. Director David Miller provides some well-staged action sequences, but Wayne and John Carroll struggle with the contrived plot. TS DVD

John Wayne *Jim Gordon* · John Carroll *Woody Jason* · Anna Lee *Brooke Elliott* · Paul Kelly (1) *Hap Davis* · Gordon Jones *Alabama Smith* · Mae Clarke *Verna Bales* ■ *Dir* David Miller (1) · *Scr* Kenneth Gamet, Barry Trivers, from a story by Kenneth Gamet

Flynn ★★★ 18
Biographical drama 1995 · Aus · Colour · 95min

Even if only half of the stories are true, dashing screen legend Errol Flynn packed enough incident into his lifetime to provide material for at least three movies. This Australian biography concentrates on his pre-Hollywood, hell-raising days, with Guy Pearce (*LA Confidential*) enjoying himself as the young Flynn, a rampant womaniser, gold prospector and possible killer. JF DVD

Guy Pearce *Errol Flynn* · Steven Berkoff *Klaus Reicher* · John Savage *Joe Stromberg* · Claudia Karvan *Penelope Watts* · Will Gluth *Professor Flynn* ■ *Dir* Frank Howson · *Scr* Frank Howson, Alister Webb

Focus ★★ 12
Period drama 2001 · US · Colour · 102min

This study of anti-Semitism in postwar America is based on the little-known novel by playwright Arthur Miller. Having each been mistaken for Jews in the past, William H Macy and wife Laura Dern are appalled to find themselves being invited to participate in Meat Loaf Aday's lynch-mob persecution of newsvendor David Paymer, after he's falsely implicated in the murder of a Puerto Rican woman in their Brooklyn neighbourhood. While his message is valid, debutant director Neal Slavin's overbearing approach debilitates the drama. DP DVD

William H Macy *Larry Newman* · Laura Dern *Gertrude Hart* · David Paymer *Finkelstein* · Meat Loaf Aday [Meat Loaf] *Fred* ■ *Dir* Neal Slavin · *Scr* Kendrew Lascelles, from the novel by Arthur Miller

Focus ★★ 15
Romantic caper 2015 · US · Colour · 100min

Will Smith plays a slick career con artist who grooms wannabe *femme fatale* Margot Robbie and then dumps her. But she pops up again a few years later in Buenos Aires where he has been offered a big-money scam. It's a tangled web indeed, but information is withheld for a grand reveal that isn't worth the trouble, and the chemistry between Smith and Robbie cannot overcome the coyness of a script that relies too heavily on cute wisecracks. The stars are likeable but they've been dealt a losing hand here. SP Violence, swearing, sex scenes. DVD BD

Will Smith *Nicky* · Margot Robbie *Jess Barrett* · Rodrigo Santoro *Garriga* · Gerald McRaney *Owens* · Adrian Martinez *Farhad* · BD Wong *Liyuan* ■ *Dir/Scr* Glenn Ficarra, John Requa

The Fog ★★★ 15
Horror 1980 · US · Colour · 86min

Director John Carpenter isn't at the peak of his form here, but this is still a reasonable enough shocker, in which spectral pirates terrorise a coastal town. Losing dramatic focus by switching between two heroines who never meet - disc jockey Adrienne Barbeau (then married to Carpenter) and Jamie Lee Curtis (starring with real-life mum Janet Leigh for the first time) - Carpenter leans hard on cheap scare tactics rather than subtle suspense. However, some sequences do turn the tension dial up quite high. AJ Violence. DVD BD

Adrienne Barbeau *Stevie Wayne* · Hal Holbrook *Father Malone* · Jamie Lee Curtis *Elizabeth Solley* · Janet Leigh *Kathy Williams* · Tom Atkins *Nick Castle* · John Houseman *Machen* ■ *Dir* John Carpenter · *Scr* John Carpenter, Debra Hill · *Cinematographer* Dean Cundey · *Music* John Carpenter

The Fog ★ 15
Horror thriller 2005 · US/Can · Colour · 98min

This inept remake of John Carpenter's 1980 ghost yarn jettisons atmosphere in favour of a cacophonous soundtrack and ineptly timed "shocks". The story remains much the same, as the seaside community of Antonio Bay is terrorised by vengeful spooks who emerge from a haunted pea-souper. AS Violence. DVD

Tom Welling *Nick Castle* · Maggie Grace *Elizabeth Williams* · Selma Blair *Stevie Wayne* · DeRay Davis *Spooner* · Kenneth Welsh *Tom Malone* · Adrian Hough *Father Malone* · Sara Botsford *Kathy Williams* · Rade Sherbedgia *Captain Blake* · Cole Heppell *Andy Wayne* ■ *Dir* Rupert Wainwright · *Scr* Cooper Layne, from the 1980 film by John Carpenter, Debra Hill

Fog Island ★
Mystery 1945 · US · BW · 69min

This uninviting tale about the search for treasure on an isolated isle has character actors George Zucco and Lionel Atwill wading through fog-shrouded dullness, not alleviated by the cumbersome direction. Zucco plays a once-rich man who invites those he thinks are responsible for his downfall to his island. AJ

George Zucco *Leo Grainger* · Lionel Atwill *Alec Ritchfield* · Jerome Cowan *Kavanaugh* · Sharon Douglas *Gail* · Veda Ann Borg *Sylvia* ■ *Dir* Terry Morse · *Scr* Pierre Gendron, from the story by Bernadine Angus

The Fog of War: Eleven Lessons from the Life of Robert S McNamara ★★★★ 🅿🅶
Documentary 2003 · US · Colour · 102min

Robert McNamara, who served Presidents Kennedy and Johnson as defence secretary, remains a vivid figure in the US, where a generation quivered in the shadow of nuclear war during the Cuban Missile Crisis and later protested when thousands were sent to die in Vietnam. Here, the 85-year-old reflects on a career of conflict, from his involvement in the firebombing of Japan during the Second World War to the Vietnam debacle. The film's title suggests that war is rarely a matter of black and white, and this is reinforced with some remarkable revelations and insights from McNamara. The overall impression - perhaps carefully constructed - is of a principled man who still believes that on the big issues he was right. Errol Morris won the best documentary Oscar for this feature. BP DVD

Robert S McNamara ■ *Dir* Errol Morris · *Music* Philip Glass

Fog over Frisco ★
Crime drama 1934 · US · BW · 69min

As a San Francisco heiress and archetypal bad girl, Bette Davis flounces and emotes with breathtaking conviction, lighting a fiery path through the inane plot and cardboard characters that surround her. It's often unintentionally funny: relish Margaret Lindsay as Bette's loyal sister, bravely dignified as she utters dialogue that beggars belief. RK

Bette Davis *Arlene Bradford* · Donald Woods *Tony* · Margaret Lindsay *Val Bradford* · Lyle Talbot *Spencer Carlton* · Arthur Byron *Everett Bradford* · Hugh Herbert *Izzy Wright* · Douglass Dumbrille *Joshua Maynard* ■ *Dir* Daniel Reed · *Scr* Robert N Lee, Eugene Solow, from the story by George Dyer

The Fold ★★ 15
Drama 2013 · UK · Colour · 89min

This small-scale British drama sees female vicar Catherine McCormack move to a new parish on the Cornish coast, where lingering guilt over the death of her daughter feeds her deepening involvement with a Bulgarian immigrant girl. Debut director John Jencks juggles more plot strands than he can handle and, although the windswept coastline provides a suitably dramatic backdrop, the storytelling's lack of focus ultimately proves the film's undoing. TJ English, Bulgarian, Polish +subtitles.

Catherine McCormack *Rebecca Ashton* · Marina Stoimenova *Radka Dimitrova* · Dakota Blue Richards *Eloise Ashton* · Owen Teale *Edward Ashton* · Oliver Dimsdale *Daniel* · Jakub Gierszal *Lukas* ■ *Dir* John Jencks · *Scr* Poppy Cogan

Folie à Deux ★★★
Documentary 2012 · UK/Hun · Colour · 101min

Film-maker Kim Hopkins's fascinating, if occasionally circuitous, profile follows mother of seven Helen Heraty as she buys the historic 72-room Gray's Court with new husband John Edwards and then vows to turn it into a boutique hotel. As the recession starts to bite, Heraty is soon in a battle with the banks that becomes something of a sideshow to her ongoing feud with her neighbours. Shot over five years, this confirms that great British eccentrics continue to thrive, but you wouldn't want to live next door to them. DP

■ *Dir* Kim Hopkins

Folies Bergère ★★★
Musical 1935 · US · BW · 84min

This super 20th Century-Fox musical revolves around one of the studio's many stock plots. Here it's the one about mistaken identity. Maurice Chevalier is in his prime as both Folies star and pompous aristocrat, getting involved with Folies co-star Ann Sothern and beautiful baroness Merle Oberon, whose scenes slow down the pace somewhat. Nevertheless, the musical numbers are elaborate, and there's a knockout (though tasteless) dance finale which won choreographer Dave Gould an Oscar. TS

Maurice Chevalier *Eugene Charlier/Baron Cassini* · Merle Oberon *Baroness Genevieve Cassini* · Ann Sothern *Mimi* · Walter Byron *Rene* · Lumsden Hare *Gustave* · Eric Blore *François* ■ *Dir* Roy Del Ruth · *Scr* Bess Meredyth, Hal Long, from the play *The Red Cat* by Hans Adler, Rudolph Lothar

Folks! ★ 15
Comedy 1992 · US · Colour · 108min

This terrible "comedy" drove a stake into the heart of Tom Selleck's career. He plays a broker whose world falls apart when he is investigated for insider trading. Senility and attempted suicide are among supposed comic effects, as Selleck wanders around wondering how he ended up in this dreadful film. JB DVD

Tom Selleck *Jon Aldrich* · Don Ameche *Harry Aldrich* · Anne Jackson *Mildred Aldrich* · Christine Ebersole *Arlene Aldrich* · Wendy Crewson *Audrey Aldrich* · Robert Pastorelli *Fred* ■ *Dir* Ted Kotcheff · *Scr* Robert Klane

Follow a Star ★★ 🆄
Comedy 1959 · UK · BW · 99min

If you can follow the plot of this Norman Wisdom comedy, you'll find faint echoes of *Singin' in the Rain*. Norman is the tailor's assistant whose voice celebrity Jerry Desmonde mimes to, without rewarding the little man's services. Norman's humour knows no restraint or timing, which makes him schmaltzily tedious, especially as he can only sing in the presence of his wheelchair-bound girlfriend June Laverick. TH DVD

Norman Wisdom *Norman Truscott* · June Laverick *Judy* · Jerry Desmonde *Vernon Carew* · Hattie Jacques *Dymphna Dobson* · Richard Wattis *Dr Chatterway* · John Le Mesurier *Birkett* · Fenella Fielding *Lady Finchington* ■ *Dir* Robert Asher · *Scr* Jack Davies, Henry Blyth, Norman Wisdom

Follow Me ★★
Detective comedy 1971 · UK · Colour · 95min

Adapted from Peter Shaffer's play *The Public Eye*, this one-hour comedy is inexcusably strung out to 95 minutes by the playwright and the director, Carol Reed.

While some of this time is justifiably taken up with photographer Christopher G Challis's loving images of London, too much is occupied with Topol's ham-fisted buffoonery. He plays a detective hired by priggish accountant Michael Jayston to spy on his free-spirited wife Mia Farrow. DP

Mia Farrow *Belinda* • Topol *Julian Cristoforou* • Michael Jayston *Charles* • Margaret Rawlings *Mrs Sidley* • Annette Crosbie *Miss Framer* ▪ *Dir* Carol Reed • *Scr* Peter Shaffer, from his play *The Public Eye*

Follow Me, Boys! ★★ U

Romantic comedy   1966 · US · Colour · 115min

In a far cry from his *film noir* tough-guy stance in the 1940s, the hit TV series *My Three Sons* gave actor Fred MacMurray a completely new avuncular image, and he spent much of his later career portraying a good guy at Disney. Here he plays a scout leader in a small-town saga of rather limited charm. The supporting cast is full of seasoned veterans, none more impressive than silent movie great Lillian Gish. The Technicolor is nice but, to be honest, it's a long slog through the corn. TS *DVD*

Fred MacMurray *Lemuel Siddons* • Vera Miles *Vida Downey* • Lillian Gish *Hetty Seibert* • Charlie Ruggles [Charles Ruggles] *John Everett Hughes* • Elliott Reid *Ralph Hastings* • Kurt Russell *Whitey* ▪ *Dir* Norman Tokar • *Scr* Louis Pelletier, from the novel *God and My Country* by MacKinley Kantor

Follow That Bird ★★★ U

Comedy   1985 · US · Colour · 84min

Fans of *Sesame Street* will be thrilled with this adventure, which features everyone's favourite resident, Big Bird. The yellow-feathered one has been evicted from the street, so he goes off on a long adventure, making new friends along the way while his friends back home desperately search for him. It's strictly for the under-fives, but adults will nonetheless be entertained by celebrity cameos from such luminaries as Sandra Bernhard, Chevy Chase and John Candy. JB

Caroll Spinney *Big Bird/Oscar* • Jim Henson *Kermit the Frog/Ernie* • Frank Oz *Cookie Monster/Bert/Grover* • Paul Bartel (1) *Grouch cook* • Sandra Bernhard *Grouch waitress* • John Candy *State trooper* • Chevy Chase *Newscaster* • Joe Flaherty *Sid Sleaze* ▪ *Dir* Ken Kwapis • *Scr* Tony Geiss, Judy Freudberg

Follow That Dream ★★★ U

Musical drama   1962 · US · Colour · 105min

This easy-going rustic drama stars Elvis Presley as a wide-eyed country boy. This was not intended as a vehicle for Elvis (the real stars are Arthur O'Connell and a troublesome homestead) but it benefits from Presley's laid-back performance as an unsophisticated hillbilly. Director Gordon Douglas seems at a loss over what to do during Elvis's (too) few songs, and directs him lying down and looking rather uncomfortable most of the time, especially during the obvious miming of the title number. TS

Elvis Presley *Toby Kwimper* • Arthur O'Connell *Pop Kwimper* • Anne Helm *Holly Jones* • Joanna Moore *Alicia Claypoole* • Jack Kruschen *Carmine* ▪ *Dir* Gordon Douglas • *Scr* Charles Lederer, from the novel *Pioneer, Go Home* by Richard Powell

Follow the Boys ★★★★ U

Musical comedy   1944 · US · BW · 105min

This wonderful nostalgic treat has now become a quintessential wartime artefact. This all-star review produced by ace packager Charles K Feldman was released by Universal as a tribute to the US forces (the "boys" of the title). It actually has a plot of sorts, with George Raft and Vera Zorina splitting up - somewhat improbably - so that Raft can organise USO shows, but, oh what shows! Here's Orson Welles famously sawing Marlene Dietrich in half, WC Fields demonstrating his great *Ziegfeld Follies* pool hall routine and Jeanette MacDonald reviving *Beyond the Blue Horizon*. Of course it's a little long, but what would you cut? TS *DVD*

George Raft *Tony West* • Vera Zorina *Gloria Vance* • Grace McDonald *Kitty West* • Charles Grapewin [Charley Grapewin] *Nick West* • George Macready *Walter Bruce* • Jeanette MacDonald • Orson Welles • Marlene Dietrich • Donald O'Connor • WC Fields • Lon Chaney Jr • Randolph Scott • Dinah Shore • Artur Rubinstein • Maria Montez • Sophie Tucker ▪ *Dir* Edward Sutherland [A Edward Sutherland] • *Scr* Lou Breslow, Gertrude Purcell

Follow the Boys ★★ U

Romantic comedy   1963 · US · Colour · 95min

This sequel of sorts to MGM's popular 1960 teenage romp *Where the Boys Are* (itself ludicrously remade in 1984) substitutes the French Riviera for Florida's Fort Lauderdale and reunites two of the female stars that made the first one so sassy - swingin' Connie Francis and kooky Paula Prentiss. It's a pleasure to look at in but frankly it smacks of desperation, with the cast too old for this would-be romp. TS

Connie Francis *Bonnie Pulaski* • Paula Prentiss *Toni Denham* • Ron Randell *Cmdr Ben Bradville* • Janis Paige *Liz Bradville* • Russ Tamblyn *Lt "Smitty" Smith* • Dany Robin *Michele* ▪ *Dir* Richard Thorpe • *Scr* David T Chantler, David Osborn, from a story by Lawrence P Bachmann

Follow the Fleet ★★★★ U

Musical comedy   1936 · US · BW · 110min

Shore-leave sailors Fred Astaire and Randolph Scott breeze into town and fall for sisters Ginger Rogers and Harriet Nelson (billed here as Harriet Hilliard). The Scott/Hilliard romance plays second fiddle to that of the swaggering Astaire and the equally sassy Rogers. The settings might not be the Art Deco delights of the couple's other pictures and not all of Irving Berlin's songs would make his greatest hits compilation, but the song-and-dance duo are as captivating as ever and *Let's Face the Music and Dance* ranks as one of their finest routines. DP *DVD*

Fred Astaire *"Bake" Baker* • Ginger Rogers *Sherry Martin* • Randolph Scott *Bilge Smith* • Harriet Hilliard [Harriet Nelson] *Connie Martin* • Astrid Allwyn *Iris Manning* • Betty Grable *Showgirl* • Harry Beresford *Captain Ezra Hickey* • Russell Hicks *Jim Nolan* • Lucille Ball *Kitty Collins* ▪ *Dir* Mark Sandrich • *Scr* Dwight Taylor, Allan Scott, from the play *Shore Leave* by Hubert Osborne, from the musical *Hit the Deck* by Herbert Fields

Follow the Sun: the Ben Hogan Story ★★ U

Sports biography   1951 · US · BW · 93min

Frederick Hazlitt Brennan adapted his own *Reader's Digest* article for this stodgy biopic that cashes in on Ben Hogan's recovery from a serious injuries received in a car crash to win the US Open in 1950. Glenn Ford's own golfing proficiency makes him a credible lead, but director Sidney Lanfield lashes on the melodrama, both during Hogan's impoverished Texan childhood and his battle for fitness alongside his devoted wife, played by Anne Baxter. DP

Glenn Ford *Ben Hogan* • Anne Baxter *Valerie Hogan* • Dennis O'Keefe *Chuck Williams* • June Havoc *Norma* • Larry Keating *Jay Dexter* • Roland Winters *Dr Graham* • Nana Bryant *Sister Beatrice* ▪ *Dir* Sidney Lanfield • *Scr* Frederick Hazlitt Brennan, from his article in *Reader's Digest*

Following ★★★ 15

Thriller   1998 · UK · BW · 70min

Shot around Soho at weekends on 16mm monochrome, Christopher Nolan's feature debut is a tortuous flashback thriller that attempts one twist too many. The opening segment is filled with sinister promise, as people-watching wannabe novelist Jeremy Theobald is played at his own game by Alex Haw, a burglar who claims to be able to define his victims' personalities by their possessions. Intriguing character study is abandoned for structural and narrative contrivance, but this is still fascinating. DP *DVD*

Jeremy Theobald *The young man* • Alex Haw *Cobb* • Lucy Russell *Blonde* • John Nolan *Policeman* • Dick Bradsell *Bald guy* • Gillian El-

Kadi *Home owner* • Jennifer Angel *Waitress* • Nicolas Carlotti *Barman* ▪ *Dir/Scr* Christopher Nolan

Folly to Be Wise ★★★ U

Comedy   1952 · UK · BW · 87min

Based on the James Bridie play that gently mocked the popular BBC radio debate programme *The Brains Trust*, this Frank Launder and Sidney Gilliat comedy seems so satisfied with its central idea that it neglects to flesh it out with wit. The various members of the splendid cast seem all too aware that they are marking time between those marvellous moments when army chaplain Alastair Sim loses control of his squabbling panellists, but they are powerless to raise the tempo. DP *DVD*

Alastair Sim *Captain Paris* • Roland Culver *George Prout* • Elizabeth Allan *Angela Prout* • Martita Hunt *Lady Dodds* • Miles Malleson *Dr Hector McAdam* • Colin Gordon *Professor James Mutch* • Edward Chapman *Joseph Byres* ▪ *Dir* Frank Launder • *Scr* Frank Launder, John Dighton, from the play *It Depends What You Mean* by James Bridie

Food Inc. ★★★ PG

Documentary   2008 · US · Colour · 93min

In this startling documentary about how big business manipulates what ultimately arrives on American consumers' tables, director Robert Kenner investigates genetically modified chickens, insect-proof soya beans and "indestructible" tomatoes. The answers are often chilling, not least when Kenner discovers that overuse of antibiotics and pesticides may well have helped boost American cases of a strain of the *E coli* virus to 70,000 a year. The heroes here are the independent organic farmers who resist legislation that demands they fall in line, although the overriding sense is that these are Davids fighting a losing battle against government-endorsed Goliaths. TeS

▪ *Dir* Robert Kenner • *Scr* Robert Kenner, Elise Pearlstein, Kim Roberts • *Cinematographer* Richard Pearce

Food of Love ★★ 15

Romantic comedy
1997 · UK/Fr · Colour · 108min

This romantic comedy set in the world of amateur dramatics subjects a willing cast to situations and dialogue worthier of a weekend playwright than someone of Stephen Poliakoff's reputation. Wearily touching on such themes as the town and country divide, middle-age regret and the continuing relevance of theatre, the action follows banker Richard E Grant's attempt to relive an idyllic summer by taking his long-disbanded thesping troupe back to a sleepy rural village for a production of *Twelfth Night*. Cringingly predictable. DP

Richard E Grant *Alex Salmon* • Nathalie Baye *Michèle* • Joe McGann *Sam* • Juliet Aubrey *Madeline* • Lorcan Cranitch *Luke* • Penny Downie *Mary* • Holly Davidson *Jessica* • Tameka Empson *Alice* • Sylvia Syms *Mrs Harvey-Brown* ▪ *Dir/Scr* Stephen Poliakoff

Food of Love ★★★ 15

Drama   2002 · Sp/Ger · Colour · 104min

Despite the occasional lapses in taste, David Leavitt's novel has been adapted with a mischievously seductive air by Catalan veteran Ventura Pons. The action centres on talented music student Kevin Bishop's tortuous liaisons with classical pianist Paul Rhys and his manager-lover, Allan Corduner. But contrasted with Bishop's discovery that he isn't concert calibre is stage mother Juliet Stevenson's realisation of her son's sexuality and the need for them to re-adjust their relationship. Pitched perfectly between vulgarity and vulnerability, Stevenson's turn is the standout in this ribald piece. DP *DVD*

Juliet Stevenson *Pamela Porterfield* • Paul Rhys *Richard Kennington* • Allan Corduner *Joseph* • Kevin Bishop *Paul Porterfield* • Geraldine McEwan *Novotna* ▪ *Dir* Ventura Pons • *Scr* Ventura Pons, from the novel *The Page Turner* by David Leavitt

The Food of the Gods ★★ 18

Science-fiction horror
1976 · US · Colour · 84min

This "revenge of nature" thriller owes much to big bug movies of the 1950s like but lacks the charm that made those schlock classics so memorable. Still, it's tough to dislike a movie that incorporates giant chickens and rats in its tale of a remote island where a mystery substance has caused the creatures to grow to an abnormal size. Director Bert I Gordon conjures up some gruesome deaths. RS

Marjoe Gortner *Morgan* • Pamela Franklin *Lorna Scott* • Ralph Meeker *Jack Bensington* • Ida Lupino *Mrs Skinner* • Jon Cypher *Brian* • Belinda Balaski *Rita* • Tom Stovall *Tom* • John McLiam *Mr Skinner* ▪ *Dir* Bert I Gordon • *Scr* Bert I Gordon, from the novel by HG Wells

Food of the Gods II ★ 18

Science-fiction horror
1989 · Can · Colour · 82min

In a completely unnecessary sequel, research scientist Paul Coufos uses a growth hormone to increase the size of lab rats and animal activists release the king-sized creatures into the streets. The rat puppets and over-sized model rodent heads are ludicrous and laughable. AJ

Paul Coufos *Prof Neil Hamilton* • Lisa Schrage *Alex Reed* • Colin Fox *Edmund Delhurst* • Frank Moore *Jacques* • Real Andrews *Mark* ▪ *Dir* Damian Lee • *Scr* Richard Bennett, E Kim Brewster, from a story by Richard Bennett

The Fool ★★★ U

Drama   1990 · UK · Colour · 140min

This is a beautifully detailed account of Victorian life in London, with Derek Jacobi as the humble clerk who leads a double life by also posing as a businessman who's accepted in high social circles - a gem of paste in a chandelier of diamonds. Director Christine Edzard needs a stronger narrative, and her superb cast can't prevent the characters from resembling the Cruikshank-illustrated cartoons of Victorian social historian Henry Mayhew. TH

Derek Jacobi *Sir John/Mr Frederick* • Cyril Cusack *The Ballad Seller* • Ruth Mitchell *The Girl* • Maria Aitken *Lady Amelia* • Irina Brook *Georgiana Shillibeer* • Paul Brooke *Lord Paramount* • Richard Caldicot *Duke* • Rosalie Crutchley *Mrs Harris* • Patricia Hayes *The Dowager* ▪ *Dir* Christine Edzard • *Scr* Christine Edzard, Olivier Stockman

Fool for Love ★★★ 15

Drama   1985 · US · Colour · 102min

Kim Basinger acts her sexual socks off in Robert Altman's adaptation of a theatrical production that works well as a piece of cinema, while still retaining its stifling atmosphere. Sam Shepard takes the starring role in his own play, about a past love that overshadows the present, and lends a special power to his role as a hick, driven by furies that would not disgrace a Greek tragedy. TH Some violence, swearing. *DVD*

Sam Shepard *Eddie* • Kim Basinger *May* • Harry Dean Stanton *Old man* • Randy Quaid *Martin* • Martha Crawford *May's mother* • Louise Egolf *Eddie's mother* • Sura Cox *Teenage May* • Jonathan Skinner *Teenage Eddie* ▪ *Dir* Robert Altman • *Scr* Sam Shepard, from his play

The Fool Killer ★★★

Period thriller   1965 · US · BW · 101min

The story of an orphan boy's adventures just after the end of the Civil War proves to be an unusual experience. Initially the boy - played by actor Eddie Albert's son, Edward - runs into a reclusive eccentric named Dirty Jim Jelliman (Henry Hull, relishing the role) who tells him yarn after yarn about the Fool Killer, a legendary slayer of idiots. The boy then encounters Anthony Perkins, a traumatised former soldier who may or may not be the eponymous axe-wielder. Surely not? AT

Anthony Perkins *Milo Bogardus* • Edward Albert *George Mellish* • Dana Elcar *Mr Dodd* • Henry Hull *Dirty Jim Jelliman* • Salome Jens *Mrs Dodd* • Charlotte Jones (1) *Mrs Ova Fanshawe* • Arnold

Moss *Rev Spotts* ■ *Dir* Servando Gonzalez • *Scr* David Friedkin, Morton Fine, from a novel by Helen Eustis

Foolin' Around ★★ PG
Romantic comedy 1980 · US · Colour · 95min

Gary Busey plays an innocent farm boy turned student who woos gorgeous Annette O'Toole. Of course, she turns out to be very rich and already engaged to another man. Busey was in his mid-30s when he played this role, but he tries his best despite this miscasting, the uneven direction and silly script. SG

Gary Busey *Wes McDaniels* • Annette O'Toole *Susan Carlson* • John Calvin *Whitley* • Eddie Albert *Daggett* • Cloris Leachman *Samantha Carlson* • Tony Randall *Peddicord* • Michael Talbott *Clay* ■ *Dir* Richard T Heffron • *Scr* Mike Kane, David Swift

Foolish Wives ★★★
Silent drama 1920 · US · BW · 107min

This legendary silent movie cost more and took longer to make than did DW Griffith's epic *Intolerance*. Originally running for five hours, it's an incredibly lavish study of corruption and sexual obsession, set largely in the casinos, hotels, cafés and boudoirs of Monte Carlo and ends, appropriately enough for a satire, in the city's sewers. A fake count seduces rich ladies, but when he tries it with an ambassador's wife he runs out of luck. Today's viewers will have problems with the pacing, the wayward plotting and the acting styles, but director Erich von Stroheim's vision of decadence still seems impressive. AT

Rudolph Christians *Andrew J Hughes* • Miss Du Pont *Helen, his wife* • Maude George *Princess Olga Petschnikoff* • Mae Busch *Princess Vera Petschnikoff* • Erich von Stroheim *Count Sergius Karamzin, Captain of Third Hussars, Imperial Russian Army* ■ *Dir* Erich von Stroheim • *Scr* Erich von Stroheim, Marian Ainslee (titles)

Foolproof ★★★ 15
Crime caper 2003 · Can · Colour · 89min

Ryan Reynolds heads the cast in this perky caper about three friends who get a kick out of planning foolproof robberies that they don't commit. But their elaborate hobby puts them in a pickle when David Suchet's gangster blackmails them into doing a $20 million bond heist for real. Good dialogue and fun performances compensate for uneven characterisation and a mass of plot holes. The central trio plays off each other well, but it's Suchet who ultimately steals the show. SF *DVD*

Ryan Reynolds *Kevin* • Kristin Booth *Sam* • Joris Jarsky *Rob* • David Suchet *Leo Gillette* ■ *Dir/Scr* William Phillips

Fools ★
Romantic drama 1970 · US · Colour · 93min

This dumb (and aptly titled) drama, set in San Francisco, is about the romance between an ageing star of horror movies and the neglected wife of a lawyer. Indifferently written, directed and acted, it's a shoddy vehicle for its two "name" stars – Jason Robards and Katharine Ross. DA

Jason Robards *Matthew Sorn* • Katharine Ross *Anais* • Scott Hylands *David Appleton* • Marc Hannibal *Dog owner* ■ *Dir* Tom Gries • *Scr* Robert Rudelson

Fools for Scandal ★★
Comedy 1938 · US · BW · 80min

Mervyn LeRoy directs Carole Lombard (sublime) and Fernand Gravet (engaging) in this mind-bendingly silly romantic comedy which starts out very well indeed in a cardboard, studio-built Paris. The action then moves to London, where penniless French aristocrat and master chef Gravet pursues famous movie star Lombard in an attempt to woo her away from her stuffy insurance man (Ralph Bellamy). The piece progressively disintegrates but there are some laughs. RK

Carole Lombard *Kay Winters* • Fernand Gravet *René* • Ralph Bellamy *Phillip Chester* • Allen Jenkins *Dewey Gibson* • Isabel Jeans *Lady Paula Malverton* • Marie Wilson *Myrtle* • Marcia Ralston *Jill* ■ *Dir* Mervyn LeRoy • *Scr* Herbert Fields,

Joseph Fields, Irving Brecher, from the play *Return Engagement* by Nancy Hamilton, James Shute, Rosemary Casey

Fool's Gold ★★ U
Western 1946 · US · BW · 63min

Silent screen matinée idol William Boyd achieved a memorable second career in the sound era as the black-clad, silver-haired gentleman cowboy with the improbable name of Hopalong Cassidy. The movies were little more than cheap programme fillers, but the character was hugely popular, and movies like this one, in which "Hoppy" tries to help when a friend's son becomes involved with outlaws, were fast-paced fun. The series would find a whole new audience on television, making William Boyd a very rich cowboy actor. TS

William Boyd (1) *Hopalong Cassidy* • Andy Clyde *California Carlson* • Rand Brooks *Lucky Jenkins* • Robert Emmett Keane *Professor Dixon* • Jane Randolph *Jessie Dixon* • Steve Barclay [Stephen Barclay] *Bruce Landy* ■ *Dir* George Archainbaud • *Scr* Doris Schroeder, from characters by Clarence E Mulford

Fool's Gold ★★ 12
Romantic action adventure 2008 · US · Colour · 107min

Co-stars Matthew McConaughey and Kate Hudson here add credence to the old adage "all that glisters is not gold". Despite being shiny, happy, good-looking blondes, they're just not enough to perk up this tired romantic comedy. The movie opens with the couple on the brink of divorce; Hudson has had enough of McConaughey's obsessive pursuit of a treasure called the Queen's Dowry and takes a job on a yacht. Through numerous contrivances, McConaughey ends up on the same vessel and manages to lure her into a seafaring treasure hunt, which just feels like an excuse to have the couple strip off and bask in the Caribbean sunshine. SP Some violence, brief swearing, nudity. *DVD* *Blu-ray*

Matthew McConaughey *Ben "Finn" Finnegan* • Kate Hudson *Tess* • Donald Sutherland *Nigel Honeycutt* • Alexis Dziena *Gemma Honeycutt* • Ewen Bremner *Alfonz* • Ray Winstone *Moe Fitch* • Kevin Hart *Bigg Bunny* • Malcolm-Jamal Warner *Cordell* ■ *Dir* Andy Tennant • *Scr* Andy Tennant, John Claflin, Daniel Zelman, from a story by Claflin, Zelman

Fools of Fortune ★★★ 15
Drama 1990 · UK · Colour · 104min

It's the 1920s in Ireland, and the wealthy Quinton family are shocked when their rural splendour is shattered by the British army of the time, the Black and Tans, who burn the house and massacre some of the family. Survivors include Julie Christie and her son, Iain Glen, whose childhood sweetheart grows into Mary Elizabeth Mastrantonio. But politics continue to play a major role in this absorbing but curiously reticent family saga. AT

Iain Glen *Willie Quinton* • Mary Elizabeth Mastrantonio *Marianne* • Julie Christie *Mrs Quinton* • Michael Kitchen *Mr Quinton* • Niamh Cusack *Josephine* • Tom Hickey *Father Kilgarriff* • John Kavanagh *Johnny Lacy* • Mick Lally *Mr Derenzy* • Niall Toibin *Lanigan* ■ *Dir* Pat O'Connor • *Scr* Michael Hirst, from the novel by William Trevor

Fools Rush In ★★
Romantic comedy 1949 · UK · BW · 81min

Kenneth Horne was one of the brightest British radio stars of the 1950s and 1960s, but the stage play that inspired this timid sitcom is a far cry from the irreverent comedy that enlivened *Beyond Our Ken* and *Round the Horne*. Sally Ann Howes postpones her wedding to reunite her caddish father, Guy Rolfe, with mother Nora Swinburne. The cast frantically over-compensates for the flimsy script. DP

Sally Ann Howes *Pamela Dickson* • Guy Rolfe *Paul Dickson* • Nora Swinburne *Angela Dickson* • Nigel Buchanan *Joe Trent* • Raymond Lovell *Sir Charles Leigh* • Thora Hird *Mrs Coot* ■ *Dir* John Paddy Carstairs • *Scr* Geoffrey Kerr, from the play by Kenneth Horne

Fools Rush In ★★★ 12
Romantic comedy 1997 · US · Colour · 104min

Ignored on its cinema release, this romantic comedy is well worth seeking out. *Friends* star Matthew Perry plays a New Yorker on business in Las Vegas who has a one-night stand with beautiful Mexican Salma Hayek, only for her to reappear three months later to tell him she's pregnant with his baby. The road to true happiness is littered with problems, with her traditional parents (and his snobby Wasp-ish ones) being the butt of many a joke along the way. Matthew's real-life dad, John Bennett Perry, plays his father. JB *DVD*

Matthew Perry *Alex* • Salma Hayek *Isabel* • Jon Tenney *Jeff* • Carlos Gomez *Chuy* • Tomas Milian *Tomas* • Siobhan Fallon *Lanie* • John Bennett Perry *Richard* ■ *Dir* Andy Tennant • *Scr* Katherine Reback, from a story by Joan Taylor, Katherine Reback

The Foot Fist Way ★★ 15
Martial arts comedy 2006 · US · Colour · 79min

There are some laugh-out-loud moments in this mock documentary from first-time director Jody Hill, but they are few and far between. Danny McBride (*Pineapple Express*, *Tropic Thunder*) is at least an amusing lead as a small-town tae kwon do teacher, who has to battle back from the double whammy of his wife's infidelity and the discovery that his idol, a martial arts movie superstar, has feet of clay. But, by and large, this low-budget nonsense is too tepid as comedy and too toothless as satire. DA *DVD*

Danny McBride (2) *Fred Simmons* • Ben Best *Chuck "The Truck" Wallace* • Mary Jane Bostic *Suzie Simmons* • Spencer Moreno *Julio Chavez* • Carlos Lopez (3) *Henry Harrison* • Jody Hill *Mike McAlister* ■ *Dir* Jody Hill • *Scr* Ben Best, Jody Hill, Danny McBride (2)

The Football Factory ★★★ 18
Drama 2004 · UK · Colour · 87min

Nick Love's unflinching look at soccer hooliganism portrays several weeks in the lives of a firm of thugs who "support" Chelsea. It is a decently acted and well-made production, but what is less evident is its moral stance; while not openly condoning the brutality it depicts, the movie doesn't condemn it either. Love's film is at its best when things are kept nice and gritty, although the crisis of conscience faced by Danny Dyer's character is less well handled. DA Drug abuse, swearing, violence. *DVD* *Blu-ray*

Danny Dyer *Tommy Johnson* • Frank Harper *Billy Bright* • Tamer Hassan *Jack* • Roland Manookian *Zeberdee* • Neil Maskell *Rod* • Dudley Sutton *Bill Farrell* • Jamie Foreman *Cabbie* ■ *Dir* Nick Love • *Scr* Nick Love, from the novel by John King

Footlight Fever ★★ U
Comedy 1941 · US · BW · 69min

Fresh from amusing in *Curtain Call* (1940), Donald MacBride and Alan Mowbray joined forces for a second time as the shady theatrical impresarios, this time needing wealthy spinster Elisabeth Risdon to back a play so that her niece, Elyse Knox, can marry impecunious actor Lee Bonnell. This has the makings of a lively farce, but the film loses momentum in the latter stages and the picture's $40,000 loss dissuaded RKO from producing further sequels. DP

Alan Mowbray *Mr Don Avery* • Donald MacBride *Mr Geoffrey "Geoff" Crandall* • Elisabeth Risdon *Aunt Hattie Drake* • Lee Bonnell *John Carter* • Elyse Knox *Eileen Drake* ■ *Dir* Irving Reis • *Scr* Ian McLellan Hunter, Bert Granet, from a story by Granet

Footlight Parade ★★★★ U
Musical 1933 · US · BW · 99min

James Cagney, hoofer extraordinaire, is better remembered for being the 1930s top gangster than as a rival to Fred Astaire. This typically fast-paced Warner Bros extravaganza is a showcase for Cagney at full pelt, playing an extrovert producer staging those now-forgotten prologues to the main feature. In this movie, Cagney has

the benefit of the genius choreography of Busby Berkeley at his peak. Witty, well cast and as brash as they come, this is a real treat. TS

James Cagney *Chester Kent* • Joan Blondell *Nan Prescott* • Dick Powell *Scotty Blair* • Ruby Keeler *Bea Thorn* • Guy Kibbee *Silas Gould* ■ *Dir* Lloyd Bacon • *Scr* Manuel Seff, James Seymour, from a story by Robert Lord, Peter Milne

Footlight Serenade ★★ U
Musical comedy 1942 · US · BW · 80min

This is an average wartime 20th Century-Fox Betty Grable vehicle, though with a little more humour than most of its ilk. The film contains some very pleasing performances, including a lightly self-mocking one from hulk Victor Mature as a Broadway-bound boxer who falls for a dancer. Phil Silvers and Jane Wyman are also impressive, but Grable is not at her best, and her leading man is the terminally bland John Payne. TS

John Payne *Bill Smith* • Betty Grable *Pat Lambert* • Victor Mature *Tommy Lundy* • Jane Wyman *Flo Laverne* • James Gleason *Bruce McKay* • Phil Silvers *Flap* • Cobina Wright Jr *Estelle Evans* • June Lang *June* • Frank Orth *Doorman* • Mantan Moreland *Dresser* ■ *Dir* Gregory Ratoff • *Scr* Robert Ellis, Helen Logan, Lynn Starling, from the story *Dynamite* by Fidel LaBarba, Kenneth Earl

Footloose ★★★ 12
Musical drama 1984 · US · Colour · 107min

Kevin Bacon stars as a free-spirited teenager fighting small-minded minister John Lithgow in a small town where rock 'n' roll and dancing are illegal. The cast performs wonders with a story that hits the drivel button and becomes overly sentimental far too frequently. Kenny Loggins's tunes aren't half bad (the title track got to number six in the UK charts), and the energy raised during the finger-snapping dance numbers is infectious. AJ Violence, swearing, brief nudity. *DVD* *Blu-ray*

Kevin Bacon *Ren MacCormack* • Lori Singer *Ariel Moore* • John Lithgow *Reverend Moore* • Dianne Wiest *Vi Moore* • Christopher Penn [Chris Penn] *Willard* • Sarah Jessica Parker *Rusty* • John Laughlin *Woody* • Elizabeth Gorcey *Wendy Jo* ■ *Dir* Herbert Ross • *Scr* Dean Pitchford • *Music* Kenny Loggins

Footloose ★★★ 12
Musical comedy drama 2011 · US · Colour · 113min

The 1984 hit teen movie may not have needed the remake treatment, but *Hustle & Flow* director Craig Brewer's update is nowhere near as bad as expected. Kenny Wormald nimbly steps into Kevin Bacon's iconic shoes as Ren MacCormack, a city boy who relocates to a southern town where dancing has been outlawed by the community leaders. MacCormack's drive to get the ban overturned sees him fall foul of the stern Reverend Moore (Dennis Quaid), while falling in love with his conflicted daughter (Julianne Hough). Fans of the original film's songs will find them spruced up here, while the eye-catching visuals and break- and country-line dancing give it all a refreshing feel. AJ *DVD* *Blu-ray*

Kenny Wormald *Ren MacCormack* • Julianne Hough *Ariel Moore* • Dennis Quaid *Reverend Shaw Moore* • Andie MacDowell *Vi Moore* • Miles Teller *Willard* • Ziah Colon *Rusty Rodriguez* ■ *Dir* Craig Brewer • *Scr* Craig Brewer, Dean Pitchford, from his 1984 film

Footrot Flats: the Dog's Tale ★★★
Animation 1986 · NZ · Colour · 71min

Down Under, Murray Ball's newspaper cartoon strip *Footrot Flats*, featuring the exploits of nice-but-dim sheep farmer Wal and his faithful canine companion, Dog, is as big as *The Gambols*. In this feature film spin-off, which became one of New Zealand's biggest releases, Wal crosses swords with the Crocopigs and Murphy's hellhounds, and still finds time to indulge his passion for rugby. JF

F

John Clarke (2) *Wal* • Peter Rowley *Dog* • Rawiri Paratene *Rangi* • Fiona Samuel *Cheeky Hobson/ Pongo* • Peter Hayden *Cooch/Irish Murphy* • Dorothy McKegg *Aunt Dolly* ■ *Dir* Murray Ball • *Scr* Murray Ball, Tom Scott

Footsteps in the Dark ★★
Comedy mystery 1941 · US · BW · 96min

This flat-footed comedy thriller features Errol Flynn looking distinctly uncomfortable in a suit and bow-tie as the investment banker who moonlights as a mystery writer called FX Pettijohn. Flynn's Holmesian character cruises the streets, discovers a murder and sets out to solve it. Warner Bros, buckling under Flynn's demands to be relieved of his swashbuckles, had in mind a *Thin Man*-style adventure and missed by yards, if not miles. AT

Errol Flynn *Francis Warren* • Brenda Marshall *Rita Warren* • Ralph Bellamy *Dr Davis* • Alan Hale *Inspector Mason* • Lee Patrick *Blondie White* • Allen Jenkins *Wilfred* • Lucile Watson *Mrs Archer* • William Frawley *Hopkins* ■ *Dir* Lloyd Bacon • *Scr* Lester Cole, John Wexley, from the play *Blondie White* by Ladislaus Fodor [Ladislas Fodor], Bernard Merivale, Jeffrey Dell

Footsteps in the Fog ★★★ U
Period thriller 1955 · UK/US · Colour · 86min

Handsome Stewart Granger and his then wife, the lovely Jean Simmons, returned to Britain at the peak of their international stardom for this suspenseful and atmospheric Victorian melodrama. In a Columbia Studios tale of lust and blackmail, the underrated Granger is particularly effective as the murderer, his unique combination of matinée idol looks and ability to appear at ease in period clothing being used to good effect. The Technicolor photography and the clever Shepperton studio interiors also complement him perfectly. TS *DVD*

Stewart Granger *Stephen Lowry* • Jean Simmons *Lily Watkins* • Bill Travers *David MacDonald* • Ronald Squire *Alfred Travers* • Finlay Currie *Inspector Peters* • Belinda Lee *Elizabeth Travers* • William Hartnell *Herbert Moresby* • Frederick Leister *Doctor Simpson* ■ *Dir* Arthur Lubin • *Scr* Dorothy Reid, Leonore Coffee, Arthur Pierson, from the novel *The Interruption* by WW Jacobs

For a Few Dollars More ★★★★★ 15
Classic spaghetti western
1965 · It/W Ger/Sp · Colour · 125min

The second instalment of Sergio Leone's *Dollars* trilogy (after *A Fistful of Dollars*) is the best and most influential of the three. Honing the stylised visuals and dark humour of the original, Leone takes this opportunity to develop such future genre staples as the uneasy alliance against a common foe and the three-way shoot-out. But, while the pursuit of bandit Gian Maria Volonté by bounty hunters Clint Eastwood (motivated by greed) and Lee Van Cleef (driven by revenge) forms the core of the action, it's the attention to everyday detail and the symbols of a passing era that give this operatic classic its distinctive aura. *The Good, the Bad and the Ugly* concluded the trilogy. DP Some dialogue dubbed. *DVD*

Clint Eastwood *Man with No Name* • Lee Van Cleef *Colonel Douglas Mortimer* • Gian Maria Volonté *Indio* • Josef Egger *Old man over railway* • Rosemary Dexter *Colonel's sister* • Mara Krup *Hotel manager's wife* • Klaus Kinski *Hunchback* ■ *Dir* Sergio Leone • *Scr* Sergio Leone, Luciano Vincenzoni, from a story by Sergio Leone, from a story by Fulvio Morsella • *Music* Ennio Morricone

For a Good Time, Call... ★★★ 18
Comedy 2012 · US · Colour · 85min

In this New York-set tale, feuding 20-somethings Lauren Anne Miller and Ari Graynor join forces to avert homelessness by setting up their own phone-sex business, with enough pink telephones, sex toys and leopard print clothes to put Katie Price to shame. Redemption comes in the form of Mimi Rogers as Miller's lookalike mother, but it's Justin Long who steals the show

with great comic timing and the snappiest lines. Co-written by Miller, this slight and slightly naff comedy with a faux lesbian-friendly twist is funny in parts. But mostly it's as up-and-down as the Manhattan skyline and like that concrete jungle, it's amusing as long as you don't mind the steaming potholes and brash attitude. KK Sexual references.

Ari Graynor *Katie Steel* • Lauren Anne Miller *Lauren Powell* • Mark Webber *Sean* • Justin Long *Jesse* • Nia Vardalos *Rachel Rodman* • Seth Rogen *Jerry* • Mimi Rogers *Adele Powell* ■ *Dir* Jamie Travis • *Scr* Lauren Anne Miller, Katie Anne Naylon

For Better and for Worse ★★
Romantic comedy 1993 · Fr/US · Colour · 89min

There's nothing worse than a low-concept comedy in which the central contrivance is matched only by the decrepitude of the dialogue. This, for example, was progressing along quite nicely as a wedding nerves romp, with some broad class divide satire thrown in for good measure. But then the groom's practical joking buddy send an invitation to the Pope, which is accepted. This is as lightweight as a handful of confetti. DP

Patrick Dempsey *Robert Faldo* • Kelly Lynch *Catherine Vernet* • Gérard Rinaldi *Touchet* • Marion Peterson *Françoise* • Catherine Alcover *Carmina Faldo* • Nicolas Vogel *Joseph Faldo* • Marianne Borgo *Nathalie Vernet* ■ *Dir* Paolo Barzman • *Scr* Tony Gilroy

For Better, for Worse ★★★ U
Romantic comedy 1954 · UK · Colour · 84min

Almost comforting in its snug predictability, this adaptation of Arthur Watkyn's stage play is now more noteworthy for its unworldly, sitcomic depiction of young bourgeois marriage than its actual entertainment value. There's a definite rapport between impoverished Dirk Bogarde and his bride, Susan Stephen, but the reliance on disapproving in-laws, nosey neighbours and dodgy tradesmen for laughs could easily have worn thin were it not for the accomplished supporting cast. DP

Dirk Bogarde *Tony Howard* • Susan Stephen *Anne Purves* • Cecil Parker *Anne's father* • Eileen Herlie *Anne's mother* • Dennis Price *Debenham* • Sidney James *Foreman* ■ *Dir* J Lee Thompson • *Scr* J Lee Thompson, from the play by Arthur Watkyn

For Better or Worse ★★★ 12
Romantic comedy 1995 · US · Colour · 85min

Also known as *Stranger Things*, this comedy marked the directorial debut of *Seinfeld* co-star Jason Alexander. While there's no shortage of kooky characters and slick wisecracks, the storyline takes some swallowing as love-scarred loser Alexander finds himself on the lam with his new sister-in-law (Lolita Davidovich) after his crooked brother (James Woods) bungles a robbery. The farce is too often encumbered by pathos, but Davidovich is pleasingly feisty, and there's a wonderful double act from Joe Mantegna and Jay Mohr as the world's dumbest gangsters. DP Violence, swearing.

Jason Alexander *Michael Makeshift* • James Woods *Reggie* • Lolita Davidovich *Valerie* • Joe Mantegna *Stone* • Jay Mohr *Dwayne* • Beatrice Arthur *Beverly* • Robert Costanzo *Landlord* • Rip Torn • Rob Reiner ■ *Dir* Jason Alexander • *Scr* Jeff Nathanson

For Colored Girls ★★ 15
Drama 2010 · US · Colour · 128min

Writer/director Tyler Perry adapts a 1974 stage play made up of poems on issues that impact women of colour, into an uneven, jerky melodrama that pivots on strong but strange moments and even stronger performances. The ground-breaking "choreo-poem" has not aged well, but the stars in Perry's cast give potent performances – among them Whoopi Goldberg and Thandie Newton as a religious zealot mother and her promiscuous daughter – that provide some thrilling

scenes within this otherwise ramshackle journey. KK Violence, swearing. *DVD*

Whoopi Goldberg *Alice/White* • Thandie Newton *Tangie/Orange* • Janet Jackson *Jo/Red* • Kerry Washington *Kelly/Blue* • Anika Noni Rose *Yasmine/Yellow* • Michael Ealy *Beau Willie* • Omari Hardwick *Carl* • Loretta Devine *Juanita/ Green* ■ *Dir* Tyler Perry • *Scr* Tyler Perry, from the play *For Colored Girls Who Have Considered Suicide When the Rainbow Is Enuf* by Ntozake Shange

For Ellen ★★★ 15
Drama 2012 · Colour · 93min

This slow burning drama from writer/ director So Yong Kim (*Treeless Mountain*) is often gently amusing and sweetly sad. Paul Dano plays the musician and immature father who arrives in upstate New York to negotiate a divorce settlement with his passive-aggressive wife (Margarita Levieva). He quickly realises the terms will deny him access to the six-year-old daughter (Shaylena Mandigo) he neglected while he was chasing rock stardom. His fraught bid to establish a relationship is beautifully played, although Dano's other encounters (with John Heder's inept lawyer and new girlfriend Jena Malone) are less well portrayed. DP Swearing.

Paul Dano *Joby Taylor* • Jon Heder *Fred Butler* • Shaylena Mandigo *Ellen Taylor* • Jena Malone *Susan* • Margarita Levieva *Claire Taylor* • Dakota Johnson *Cindy* ■ *Dir/Scr* So Yong Kim

For Freedom ★★★★ U
Second World War drama
1940 · UK · BW · 81min

British cinema excelled at docudramas during the Second World War, and Maurice Elvey and Castleton Knight's gritty account of the sinking of the German battleship *Graf Spee* established the formula. It opens as a domestic drama, as newsreel chief Will Fyffe feuds with son Anthony Hulme over a film about the Nazi invasion of Czechoslovakia. What it becomes is a compelling tribute to the heroics of HMS *Exeter* and *Ajax*. DP *DVD*

Will Fyffe *Chief* • Anthony Hulme *Steve* • EVH Emmett *Ted/Commentator* • Guy Middleton *Pierre* • Albert Lieven *Fritz* ■ *Dir* Maurice Elvey, Castleton Knight • *Scr* Leslie Arliss, Miles Malleson

For Heaven's Sake ★★★★
Silent comedy 1926 · US · BW · 58min

After several years at Pathé, Harold Lloyd made his debut for Paramount with this sprightly slapstick classic, in which he took the "comedy of thrills" to new heights in a dazzling finale featuring a double-decker bus careering through the tightest city streets. Lloyd is in characteristic go-getting mood as he sets out to woo Jobyna Ralston by supporting her father's mission. Although the scenes in the Bowery slums were intended to have some social impact, the emphasis is firmly on the comic, but none of the gags come close to the brilliance of the closing chase. DP

Harold Lloyd *J Harold Manners, the Uptown Boy* • Jobyna Ralston *Hope, the Downtown Girl* • Noah Young *Bull Brindle, the Roughneck* • James Mason [Jim Mason] *The Gangster* • Paul Weigel *Brother Paul, the Optimist* ■ *Dir* Sam Taylor • *Scr* John Grey, Ted Wilde, Clyde Bruckman

For Heaven's Sake ★★★
Fantasy comedy 1950 · US · BW · 86min

This bizarre but eminently watchable fantasy is saved from ignominy by the splendidly tongue-in-cheek acting of Clifton Webb and Edmund Gwenn as a pair of unlikely angels sent to watch over the unborn baby of Joan Bennett and Robert Cummings. What distinguishes this tale from other less successful "visitors from above" sagas is the spicy, gloriously witty script and the deft, easy direction. SH

Clifton Webb *Charles* • Joan Bennett *Lydia Bolton* • Robert Cummings *Jeff Bolton* • Edmund Gwenn *Arthur* • Joan Blondell *Daphne* • Gigi Perreau *Item* • Jack LaRue *Tony* • Harry Von Zell *Tex* • Tommy Rettig *Joe* ■ *Dir* George Seaton • *Scr* George Seaton, from the play *May We Come In?* by Harry Segall

For Hire ★★★ 15
Crime thriller 1997 · Can · Colour · 90min

In a nifty TV crime thriller with a superior plotline, Rob Lowe plays an aspiring actor who forms a friendship with shady author Joe Mantegna, only to find himself the prime suspect in a murder. Lowe is bland, but the reliable Mantegna more than compensates and director Jean Pellerin keeps you guessing right up to the end. JF Swearing, violence. *DVD*

Rob Lowe *Mitch Lawrence* • Joe Mantegna *Lou Webber* • Charles Powell *Joe Watson* • Bronwen Booth *Faye Lawrence* • Steve Adams *Tom Kellman* ■ *Dir* Jean Pellerin • *Scr* Karen Erbach, Leah M Kerr, from their story

For Keeps ★★ 15
Comedy drama 1987 · US · Colour · 94min

Molly Ringwald finds life tough as a teenage wife and mother when she gets pregnant by boyfriend Randall Batinkoff. Career and college ambitions have to be sacrificed and their relationship comes under enormous strain. This lacks depth and realism, with Ringwald portrayed as a special case rather than the archetypal girl-next-door. LH

Molly Ringwald *Darcy Elliot* • Randall Batinkoff *Stan Bobrucz* • Kenneth Mars *Mr Bobrucz* • Miriam Flynn *Mrs Elliot* • Conchata Ferrell *Mrs Bobrucz* • John Zarchen *Chris* • Sharon Brown *Lila* ■ *Dir* John G Avildsen • *Scr* Tim Kazurinsky, Denise DeClue

For Love of Ivy ★★ PG
Romantic comedy 1968 · US · Colour · 100min

Having taken Hollywood by storm with *In the Heat of the Night* and *Guess Who's Coming to Dinner*, Sidney Poitier clearly wanted to take a break from hard-hitting civil rights dramas. Daniel Mann's film is a much lighter affair, though there is still an underlying message. Poitier co-stars with Abbey Lincoln as a couple who are brought together by a liberal white family desperate to keep their treasured home-help. This worthy attempt at depicting everyday black life veers uncomfortably between the preachy and the patronising. DP *DVD*

Sidney Poitier *Jack Parks* • Abbey Lincoln *Ivy Moore* • Beau Bridges *Tim Austin* • Nan Martin *Doris Austin* • Lauri Peters *Gena Austin* • Carroll O'Connor *Frank Austin* • Leon Bibb *Billy Talbot* ■ *Dir* Daniel Mann • *Scr* Robert Alan Aurthur, from a story by Sidney Poitier

For Love of the Game ★★ 12
Sports drama 1999 · US · Colour · 132min

Kevin Costner is the legendary but ageing baseball pitcher desperate to prove there's life in the old dog yet in this glossy but overblown sports drama. A distracted Costner strives to focus long enough to pitch the perfect game, but is hampered by injuries and thoughts of partner Kelly Preston, who's wants to dump him. Long-winded and oversentimental. DA *DVD*

Kevin Costner *Billy Chapel* • Kelly Preston *Jane Aubrey* • John C Reilly *Gus Sinski* • Jena Malone *Heather* • Brian Cox (1) *Gary Wheeler* • JK Simmons *Frank Perry* • Vin Scully • Steve Lyons ■ *Dir* Sam Raimi • *Scr* Dana Stevens, from a novel by Michael Shaara

For Love or Country: the Arturo Sandoval Story ★★★ 12
Biographical drama 2000 · US · Colour · 115min

With stand-out performances from Andy Garcia as trumpeter Arturo Sandoval and Charles S Dutton as jazz legend Dizzy Gillespie, this compelling TV biopic also provides insights into the clash between political security and personal expression that dominated life in Castro's post-coup Cuba. This exposes the dilemma that made Sandoval's plight even more unbearable – his passion for his wife Mia Maestro, a committed Communist. Director Joseph Sargent avoids propagandising melodramatics. DP *DVD*

Andy Garcia *Arturo Sandoval* • Mia Maestro *Marienela* • Gloria Estefan *Emilia* • David Paymer *Embassy interviewer* • Charles S Dutton *Dizzy Gillespie* ■ *Dir* Joseph Sargent • *Scr* Timothy J Sexton

U SUITABLE FOR ALL   U SUITABLE ESPECIALLY FOR YOUNG CHILDREN (DVD ONLY)   PG PARENTAL GUIDANCE   12A UNDER 12s TO BE ACCOMPANIED (CINEMA ONLY)

For Love or Money ★★
Comedy 1963 · US · Colour · 107min

Oh dear, this is one of those would-be Swinging Sixties comedies from Universal, all gloss and glitz, but with little charm or humour. Despite the presence of a glowing Mitzi Gaynor, clever Gig Young and watchable Thelma Ritter, this attempt at levity is sunk by a desperately unfunny performance from a totally miscast Kirk Douglas, as the attorney hired by Ritter to find husbands for her three daughters. TS

Kirk Douglas *Deke Gentry* · Mitzi Gaynor *Kate Brasher* · Gig Young *"Sonny" John Dayton Smith* · Thelma Ritter *Chloe Brasher* · Julie Newmar *Bonnie Brasher* · William Bendix *Joe Fogel* · Dir Michael Gordon · Scr Michael Morris, Larry Markes

For Love or Money ★★PG
Comedy 1993 · US · Colour · 91min

Michael J Fox plays a smooth concierge who is desperate to open his own hotel, but to do that he needs the help of slimy millionaire Anthony Higgins, and Higgins's mistress (Gabrielle Anwar) happens to be the girl Fox loves. Director Barry Sonnenfeld seems strangely ill-at-ease with the material, and he is not helped by a script that swings from wild farce to slushy romance. Released on video in the UK as *The Concierge*. JF DVD

Michael J Fox *Doug Ireland* · Gabrielle Anwar *Andy Hart* · Anthony Higgins *Christian Hanover* · Michael Tucker *Mr Wegman* · Bob Balaban *Mr Drinkwater* · Isaac Mizrahi *Julian Russell* · Patrick Breen *Gary Taubin* · Udo Kier *Mr Himmelman* · Dir Barry Sonnenfeld · Scr Mark Rosenthal, Lawrence Konner

For Me and My Gal ★★★★U
Musical 1942 · US · BW · 99min

This is a fabulous star vehicle for Judy Garland, who glows with talent and basks in the best songs and production values that MGM could bestow on her. The studio also gave her a new leading man, a dancer with a neon smile who had impressed Broadway critics in *Pal Joey*. His name? Gene Kelly, here making a stunning movie debut. Director Busby Berkeley lets his leads brilliantly and, while Kelly's character is not the most endearing ever, the plot's engrossing. TS DVD

Judy Garland *Jo Hayden* · George Murphy *Jimmy K Metcalf* · Gene Kelly *Harry Palmer* · Marta Eggerth *Eve Minard* · Ben Blue *Sid Simms* · Horace McNally [Stephen McNally] *Bert Waring* · Keenan Wynn *Eddie Milton* · Richard Quine *Danny Hayden* · Dir Busby Berkeley · Scr Richard Sherman, Fred F Finklehoffe, Sid Silvers, Jack McGowan, Irving Brecher, from the story *The Big Time* by Howard Emmett Rogers · Cinematographer William Daniels (1)

For No Good Reason ★★★15
Documentary 2012 · US/UK · Colour · 85min

The satirical artist Ralph Steadman has worked alongside William S Burroughs and on *Rolling Stone* magazine, but his visceral, inky scrawls are most commonly associated with the writer Hunter S Thompson. At his studio in Kent, the artist opens up to a chain-smoking Johnny Depp about his fascinating life, inner demons and desire to change the world. Mildly marred by a soundtrack that's often too lightweight to complement the art's exquisite chaos, this is, otherwise, an intensely vibrant visual feast. GR DVD

Ralph Steadman · Johnny Depp *Johnny Depp* · Patrick Godfrey *Leonardo da Vinci* · Terry Gilliam · Bruce Robinson · Dir Charlie Paul

For One Night ★★
Drama based on a true story
2006 · US · Colour · 105min

Based on real incidents from 2002, this slight but thought-provoking drama centres on an energetic performance from Raven-Symoné, as the high-school student who challenges her county's long-held tradition of racially segregated proms. Considering the serious subject matter, director Ernest R Dickerson takes a surprisingly superficial approach, ending up with something laudable though sadly bland. SF

Raven-Symoné *Brianna McCallister* · Aisha Tyler *Desiree Howard* · Sam Jones III *Brandon Williams* · Gary Grubbs *Mr Thornton* · William Ragsdale *Earl Randall* · Dir Ernest R Dickerson · Scr Dee Harris-Lawrence

For Pete's Sake ★★PG
Comedy 1974 · US · Colour · 86min

This is one of those specially constructed star vehicles, but this time the wheels fell off with Barbra Streisand on board. It arrived with much ballyhoo and crept away shamefacedly after a major critical mauling. Streisand looks bewildered and lost as a debt-ridden wife forced to mix in unsavoury company. This smacks of shoving a famous name into a hastily put together dollar earner. Except it wasn't. SH DVD

Barbra Streisand *Henry* · Michael Sarrazin *Pete* · Estelle Parsons *Helen* · Molly Picon *Mrs Cherry* · William Redfield *Fred* · Louis Zorich *Nick* · Vivian Bonnell *Loretta* · Heywood Hall Broun *Judge Hiller* · Dir Peter Yates · Scr Stanley Shapiro, Maurice Richlin

For Queen and Country ★★★15
Thriller 1988 · UK/US · Colour · 100min

Scriptwriter Mart n Stellman made his directorial debut with this odd drama set against the gloomy backdrop of the Thatcher years of mid-1980s Britain. In an unusual bit of casting, Denzel Washington stars as the Caribbean-born Falklands war veteran who returns home to his grim South London council estate, only to be told he is no longer a British citizen. It's all rather depressing stuff, but Stellman's script captures the mood of the time and it is backed up by a nice (if unevenly accented) performance by Washington. JB DVD

Denzel Washington *Reuben* · Dorian Healy *Fish* · Amanda Redman *Stacey* · George Baker *Kilcoyne* · Bruce Payne *Colin* · Sean Chapman *Bob* · Geff Francis *Lynford* · Craig Fairbrass *Challoner* · Dir Martin Stellman · Scr Martin Stellman, Trix Worrell

For Richer or Poorer ★★12
Comedy 1997 · US · Colour · 110min

TV stars Kirstie Alley and Tim Allen star in this sitcom-style comedy about a bickering married couple who hide out in an Amish community because the Inland Revenue Service is after them for unpaid taxes. Allen and Alley don the costumes, leave their materialistic life behind and, of course, rekindle the love they lost while he was making money and she was getting manicures. JB Some swearing.

Tim Allen *Brad Sexton* · Kirstie Alley *Caroline Sexton* · Jay O Sanders *Samuel Yoder* · Michael Lerner *Phil Kleinman* · Dir Bryan Spicer · Scr Jana Howington, Steve LuKanic

For the Boys ★★★15
Drama 1991 · US · Colour · 138min

Bette Midler scooped an Oscar nomination and gave one of the best performances of her career in this otherwise overblown showbiz drama that traces the love/hate relationship of a comedy duo who only ever seem to speak to each other when America is at war. The action sags badly when Midler is off screen and, given little to do but sulk, smarm and shout, James Caan looks distinctly uncomfortable throughout. DP Violence, swearing. DVD

Bette Midler *Dixie Leonard* · James Caan *Eddie Sparks* · George Segal *Art Silver* · Patrick O'Neal (1) *Shephard* · Christopher Rydell *Danny* · Arye Gross *Jeff Brooks* · Norman Fell *Sam Schiff* · Rosemary Murphy *Luanna Trott* · Dir Mark Rydell · Scr Marshall Brickman, Neal Jimenez, Lindy Laub, from a story by Neal Jimenez, Lindy Laub

For the First Time ★★U
Musical romance
1959 · US/It/W Ger · Colour · 96min

Actually, for the last time, since this was tenor Mario Lanza's final movie. He had decided to not fulfil a concert commitment for mobster Lucky Luciano, and tragically was discovered dead in a hospital bed soon afterwards. The incidents, apparently, were not connected. This is the one where he falls for a deaf girl and belts out *Ave Maria* to her, to test whether she can actually hear. TS

Mario Lanza *Tonio "Tony" Costa* · Johanna Von Koczian *Christa Bruckner* · Zsa Zsa Gabor *Gloria de Vadnuz* · Kurt Kasznar *Ladislas Tabory* · Hans Sohnker [Hans Söhnker] *Professor Albert Bruckner* · Peter Capell *Leopold Huebner* · Renzo Cesana *Angelo* · Dir Rudolph Maté · Scr Andrew Solt

For the Love of Ada ★★PG
Comedy 1972 · UK · Colour · 84min

The 70-something romance of Ada Cresswell and Walter Bingley never made for scintillating sitcom viewing, even though the 1970 TV series was popular in its day. This movie spin-off, set on the couple's first wedding anniversary, is leisurely in the extreme, as the writers struggle to fill the extra hour. While the by-play between widow Irene Handl and Wilfred Pickles (as the gravedigger who'd buried her husband) is engaging enough, this may be too gentle for modern tastes. DP DVD

Irene Handl *Ada Bingley* · Wilfred Pickles *Walter Bingley* · Barbara Mitchell *Ruth Pollit* · Jack Smethurst *Leslie Pollit* · Arthur English *Arthur* · Andria Lawrence *Sandra* · Larry Martyn *Brian* · Dir Ronnie Baxter · Scr Harry Driver, Vince Powell

For the Love of Benji ★★U
Adventure 1977 · US · Colour · 83min

Three years after his surprise hit *Benji*, director Joe Camp finally got round to making a second film about the smart little stray. Patsy Garrett and Cynthia Smith return for this perfectly acceptable adventure, set amid the splendours of Athens, in which our canine hero escapes from the clutches of a spy ring with a secret code written on his paw. The plot could have used more imagination, but this is better than the later sequel, *Benji the Hunted* (1987). DP

Patsy Garrett *Mary* · Cynthia Smith *Cindy* · Allen Fiuzat *Paul* · Ed Nelson *Chandler Dietrich* · Art Vasil *Stelios* · Peter Bowles *Ronald* · Bridget Armstrong *Elizabeth* · Dir Joe Camp · Scr Joe Camp, from a story by Ben Vaughn, Camp

For the Love of Mary ★★U
Musical comedy 1948 · US · BW · 86min

Deanna Durbin stars as a telephonist at the White House, striking up a relationship with the president (never seen) after she suffers an attack of hiccups. He helps her to sort out her romantic problems. Directed by Frederick De Cordova, this is characteristic Durbin flimflam, allowing the star to break into song from time to time and providing fairly painless entertainment. RK DVD

Deanna Durbin *Mary Peppertree* · Edmond O'Brien *Lt Tom Farrington* · Don Taylor *David Paxton* · Jeffrey Lynn *Phillip Manning* · Ray Collins *Harvey Elwood* · Hugo Haas *Gustav Heindel* · Harry Davenport *Justice Peabody* · Dir Frederick De Cordova · Scr Oscar Brodney

For the Love of Mike ★★★
Silent romantic drama 1927 · US · BW · 75min

Having parted acrimoniously from baby-faced clown Harry Langdon, Frank Capra sought to to rebuild his career with this adaptation. It was a commercial failure, but it contains traces of the comic sentimentality that would underpin the classic "Capra-corn" formula. Set in the New York slums, the story opens with German grocer Ford Sterling, Jewish tailor George Sidney and Irish street-cleaner Hugh Cameron raising an abandoned baby. However, Ben Lyon falls from grace at Yale and endures a few trials and tribulations before returning to the straight and narrow and the arms of the debuting Claudette Colbert. DP

Claudette Colbert *Mary* · Ben Lyon *Mike* · George Sidney (1) *Abraham Katz* · Ford Sterling *Herman Schultz* · Hugh Cameron *Patrick O'Malley* · Dir Frank Capra · Scr J Clarkson Miller, from the story *Hell's Kitchen* by John Moroso

For the Moment ★★12
Second World War romantic drama
1994 · Can · Colour · 119min

This provided the first major overseas starring role for Russell Crowe and is an unassuming but nicely played drama, filmed and set in Canada. Crowe is the Australian pilot who is sent to Canada for bomber training in 1942, where he falls for local lass Christianne Hirt – the only problem being that she is already married. There are a number of other romantic subplots but, unsurprisingly, it is Crowe who catches the eye. While the material is overly familiar, this is a watchable enough affair. JF DVD

Russell Crowe *Lachlan* · Christianne Hirt *Lill* · Wanda Cannon *Betsy* · Scott Kraft *Zeek* · Peter Outerbridge *Johnny* · Dir/Scr Aaron Kim Johnston

For Their Own Good ★★★PG
Drama based on a true story
1993 · US · Colour · 91min

The thorny issue of a woman's right to have a family versus the employer's interests, is given a new twist in this TV movie. Produced by Jon Avnet (director of *Fried Green Tomatoes at the Whistle Stop Cafe*) this stars Elizabeth Perkins as a young woman who challenges her employer's ultimatum that she agree to a sterilisation or lose her job. Thought-provoking stuff. JB DVD

Elizabeth Perkins *Sally Thompson* · Charles Haid *Frank Souter* · Gary Basaraba *Roy Wheeler* · Laura San Giacomo *Jo Mandell* · CCH Pounder *Naomi Brinker* · Kelli Williams *Erma* · David Purdham *Jim Davis* · Dir Ed Kaplan · Scr Ed Kaplan, from a story by Clifford Campion, William Wages

For Those in Peril ★★★U
Second World War drama
1943 · UK · BW · 66min

Documentarist Harry Watt and future Ealing comedy scribe TEB Clarke united for this flag-waver directed by Charles Crichton, making his directorial debut. About the rivalry between David Farrar's air-sea rescue unit and a bigger patrol boat, the action sags a little as ace pilot Ralph Michael has to learn the importance of teamwork. However, the scenes in which he races against time to fish survivors out of the drink before a Nazi craft reaches them have an exciting, pseudo-newsreel feel, thanks to Douglas Slocombe's fine photography. DP

David Farrar *Murray* · Ralph Michael *Rawlings* · Robert Wyndham *Leverett* · John Slater *Wilkie* · John Batten *Wireless operator* · Robert Griffith *Griffiths* · Peter Arne *Junior officer* · James Robertson-Justice *Operations room officer* · Dir Charles Crichton · Scr Harry Watt, JOC Orton, TEB Clarke, from a story by Richard Hillary

For Those in Peril ★★★18
Drama 2013 · UK · Colour · 92min

The gritty British drama gets a twist of the surreal in this well-played but perhaps overly downbeat tale of grief and dark secrets in a remote Scottish fishing town. George McKay stars as the only survivor of a fishing accident that has apparently claimed the lives of his older brother and several local men. Ostracised by the community and blaming himself, McKay sets out on a course of self-destruction. A bold attempt to fuse mental health issues with magic realism in the last act doesn't really pan out, embodying all this offbeat film's flaws rather than its strengths. DW Violence, swearing. DVD

George MacKay *Aaron* · Kate Dickie *Cathy* · Nichola Burley *Jane* · Michael Smiley *Frank* · Dir/Scr Paul Wright (2)

For Those Who Think Young ★★U
Romantic comedy 1964 · US · Colour · 96min

Named after a Pepsi slogan (indeed, this beach movie was among the earliest Hollywood pictures to feature product placement), it's the tired old story of a group of high-school kids whose high jinks are jeopardised by a square grown-up. The

F

cast gives it a certain cachet, but United Artists would do considerably better with their other 1964 teen-market offering, *A Hard Day's Night*. DP

James Darren *Gardner "Ding" Pruitt III* • Pamela Tiffin *Sandy Palmer* • Woody Woodbury • Paul Lynde *Sid Hoyt* • Tina Louise *Topaz McQueen* • Nancy Sinatra *Karen Cross* • Bob Denver *Kelp* • Ellen McRae [Ellen Burstyn] *Dr Pauline Taylor* ▪ *Dir* Leslie H Martinson • *Scr* James O'Hanlon, George O'Hanlon, Dan Beaumont, from a story by Dan Beaumont

For Whom the Bell Tolls ★★★ U

War drama 1943 · US · Colour · 124min

Gary Cooper and Ingrid Bergman turn Ernest Hemingway's classic tale of the Spanish Civil War into a star vehicle made for two, while director Sam Wood scrubs this tale clean of political taint. Cooper plays an American member of a loyalist partisan group who falls for Bergman while on a mission to blow up a bridge. Though lacking in context, the film's focus on Cooper's love for the much-abused Bergman works well enough because of the quality of the two actors. However, it was Katina Paxinou's performance as a guerrilla fighter that won the Oscar. TH *DVD*

Ingrid Bergman *Maria* • Gary Cooper *Robert Jordan* • Akim Tamiroff *Pablo* • Katina Paxinou *Pilar* • Vladimir Sokoloff *Anselmo* • Arturo de Cordova *Agustin* • Mikhail Rasumny *Rafael* ▪ *Dir* Sam Wood • *Scr* Dudley Nichols, from the novel by Ernest Hemingway

For Your Consideration ★★★★ 12

Satirical comedy 2006 · US · Colour · 82min

Christopher Guest, the master of the mockumentary, targets the movie industry itself this time with another ensemble comedy. Guest plays Jay Berman, the director of a tacky would-be period epic starring has-been actors (Harry Shearer, Catherine O'Hara). By chance, a series of internet reports predict that this two-bit production will generate Oscar "buzz", throwing its stars and director into a tizzy, with the media predictably following suit. Unlike previous Guest films, the emphasis here is on big laughs rather than satire and in-jokes. It's a slender premise, but the combination of dry one-liners, hilarious physical comedy and the genius of Fred Willard prove irresistible. DW Brief swearing, sexual references. *DVD*

Christopher Guest *Jay Berman* • Catherine O'Hara *Marilyn Hack* • Harry Shearer *Victor Allan Miller* • Eugene Levy *Morley Orfkin* • Michael McKean *Lane Iverson* • Ricky Gervais *Martin Gibb* • Jennifer Coolidge *Whitney Taylor Brown* • Fred Willard *Chuck Porter* ▪ *Dir* Christopher Guest • *Scr* Christopher Guest, Eugene Levy

For Your Eyes Only ★★★ PG

Spy adventure 1981 · UK · Colour · 122min

Number 12 in the 007 series provides no real surprises, with the exception perhaps of Roger Moore, who gets the chance to show a little bit more grit than usual. The plot revolves around the hunt for a device from a sunken spy ship, with French star Carole Bouquet providing class as the girl who may hold the key to the puzzle. If Julian Glover is rather subdued as the number one villain, there's a colourful turn from *Fiddler on the Roof* star Topol as a rogue with shifting loyalties. Bond veteran John Glen ensures that the set pieces are spectacular enough and thankfully plays down the gadgetry. JF Violence, swearing. *DVD* *BLU*

Roger Moore *James Bond* • Carole Bouquet *Melina Havelock* • Topol *Milos Columbo* • Lynn-Holly Johnson *Bibi* • Julian Glover *Kristatos* • Cassandra Harris *Lisl* • Jill Bennett *Jacoba Brink* • Michael Gothard *Locque* • Lois Maxwell *Moneypenny* • Desmond Llewelyn *"Q"* • Charles Dance *Claus* • John Wells *Denis* • Janet Brown *Prime Minister* ▪ *Dir* John Glen • *Scr* Richard Maibaum, Michael G Wilson, from the short stories *For Your Eyes Only* and *Risico* by Ian Fleming

Forbidden ★★

Melodrama 1932 · US · BW · 87min

This undistinguished entry in the Frank Capra canon stars Barbara Stanwyck as a spinster who goes on a cruise and falls for married district attorney Adolphe Menjou. Regardless of the script, Capra could usually be relied upon to bring lightness and brisk wit to any storyline. In this case he fails – the only redeeming features being the performance of Stanwyck and the fine photography. SH

Barbara Stanwyck *Lulu Smith* • Adolphe Menjou *Bob Grover* • Ralph Bellamy *Al Holland* • Dorothy Peterson *Helen* • Thomas Jefferson *Winkinson* ▪ *Dir* Frank Capra • *Scr* Jo Swerling, from a story by Frank Capra • *Cinematographer* Joseph Walker

Forbidden ★★

Crime drama 1953 · US · BW · 84min

Tough-guy Tony Curtis is dispatched to Macao by a gang of criminals to bring back, by force if necessary, Joanne Dru, the widow of a racketeer who possesses incriminating evidence against them. Much cross and double-cross later, involving among other things Macao's chief criminal (Lyle Bettger), the plot complications are resolved and love triumphs. This sub-*noir* gangster film-cum-romance is good-looking and technically proficient, but otherwise downbeat. RK

Tony Curtis *Eddie Darrow* • Joanne Dru *Christine Lawrence* • Lyle Bettger *Justin Keit* • Marvin Miller *Cliff Chalmer* • Victor Sen Yung *Allan* • Alan Dexter *Barney* ▪ *Dir* Rudolph Maté • *Scr* William Sackheim, Gil Doud, from a story by William Sackheim

Forbidden ★★ 18

Erotic drama 2002 · US · Colour · 80min

Renee Rea stars in this soft-core thriller, which is a minor improvement on the usual erotic trash. The plot is resolutely banal, as Rea's secret encounter with Dillon Silver at his bachelor party rears its head at the most inopportune moment. But director Robert Kubilos and screenwriter Eric Mittleman succeed in creating suspenseful, as well as sexual, tension. DP Swearing, violence, sex scenes, nudity. *DVD*

Renee Rea *Nikki/Monique* • Dillon Silver *Jason* • Tracy Ryan *Lisa* • Jason Schnuit *Andy* ▪ *Dir* Robert Kubilos • *Scr* Eric Mittleman

Forbidden Cargo ★★ PG

Crime drama 1954 · UK · BW · 82min

Customs agent Nigel Patrick tries to stop drug smugglers from polluting our shores in this cosy but rather unexciting thriller. Patrick is supported by a cast of British stalwarts that includes Joyce Grenfell (as a bird-watcher named Lady Flavia Queensway), Elizabeth Sellars, Jack Warner and Terence Morgan. AT

Nigel Patrick *Michael Kenyon* • Elizabeth Sellars *Rita Compton* • Terence Morgan *Roger Compton* • Jack Warner *Alec White* • Greta Gynt *Madame Simonetta* • Theodore Bikel *Max* • Joyce Grenfell *Lady Flavia Queensway* ▪ *Dir* Harold French • *Scr* Sydney Box

The Forbidden Kingdom ★★★ 12

Martial arts action comedy 2008 · US/Chi · Colour · 99min

Kung fu superstars Jackie Chan and Jet Li team up for the first time here, playing multiple roles in a martial arts romp that merges a *Karate Kid*-style plot with assorted Chinese folk tales. Michael Angarano co-stars in this handsomely mounted tale, as an American teen who is magically whisked off to ancient China where he's enlisted to help some local martial artists free fabled warrior the Monkey King (Jet Li) and combat a despotic warlord. The proceedings may be a little too complicated for younger children, and not full-blooded enough for martial arts movie fans, but it's harmless, fight-filled entertainment with two of the best chop-socky exponents in the business. DA In English, Mandarin. *DVD* *BLU*

Jet Li *Monkey King/The Silent Monk* • Jackie Chan *Old Hop/Lu Yan* • Michael Angarano *Jason Tripitikas* • Yifei Liu *Golden Sparrow* • Collin Chou *Jade Warlord* • Bingbing Li *Ni Chang* ▪ *Dir* Rob Minkoff • *Scr* John Fusco

Forbidden Planet ★★★★★ U

Classic science-fiction adventure 1956 · US · Colour · 94min

What unknown terror roams the planet Altair-4 killing everyone apart from tormented scientist Morbius (Walter Pidgeon) and his daughter Altaira (Anne Francis)? Starship commander Leslie Nielsen finds out in one of the finest science-fiction films ever made. Loosely based on Shakespeare's *The Tempest*, which explains its overall intelligence, this is an enthralling eye-popper. The super monster effects (created by Disney animators) and outstanding technology include the unforgettable Robby the Robot, the subterranean Krell city, Morbius's futuristic home and an impressive array of space vehicles. AJ *DVD* *BLU*

Walter Pidgeon *Dr Morbius* • Anne Francis *Altaira* • Leslie Nielsen *Commander Adams* • Warren Stevens *Lieutenant "Doc" Ostrow* • Jack Kelly *Lieutenant Farman* • Richard Anderson *Chief Quinn* • Earl Holliman *Cook* • Marvin Miller *Robby the Robot* ▪ *Dir* Fred McLeod Wilcox [Fred M Wilcox] • *Scr* Cyril Hume, from a story by Irving Block, Allen Adler, from the play *The Tempest* by William Shakespeare (uncredited) • *Cinematographer* George Folsey • *Special Effects* A Arnold Gillespie, Warren Newcombe, Irving G Ries, Joshua Meador

The Forbidden Room ★★★★ 12A

Surreal romantic mystery 2015 · Can/Fr · Colour and BW · 119min

In 2012, Guy Maddin and Evan Johnson collaborated on an exhibit at the Pompidou Centre called *Seances*, which saw them shoot a short film each day in a bid to invoke the spirits of lost or forgotten films. The playful nostalgia that informed that project is very much in evidence in this amalgam of 17 mini-sagas and a slew of fragments. Once again, Maddin draws his inspiration from cinema's transition from silent and sound, but kudos should really go to the effects team that gives the digital imagery an atmospherically antiquated feel. DP Some violence, sex references *DVD* *BLU*

Roy Dupuis *Cesare* • Clara Furey *Margot* • Udo Kier *Count Yugh/The butler/The dead father/Guard/Pharmacist* • Mathieu Amalric *Thadeusz M_/Ostler* • Geraldine Chaplin *The Master Passion/Nursemaid/Aunt Chance* • Charlotte Rampling *The Ostler's Mother* ▪ *Dir* Guy Maddin, Evan Johnson • *Scr* Guy Maddin, Evan Johnson, Robert Kotyk

Forbidden Sins ★★ 18

Erotic thriller 1998 · US · Colour · 93min

Shannon Tweed is a lawyer who gets drawn into shady goings-on a strip club run by Corbin Timbrook. He has been charged with murdering one of his strippers, but things start getting complicated when Tweed falls for her client. But director Robert Angelo is more interested in getting his cast to disrobe, with Tweed and enthusiastic newcomer Amy Lindsay leading the way. JF *DVD*

Shannon Tweed *Maureen Doherty* • Corby Timbrook *David Mulholland* • Myles O'Brien *John Doherty* • Kirstine Calstrand *Virginia Hill* • Amy Lindsay *Molly Malone* ▪ *Dir* Robert Angelo • *Scr* Daryl Haney, Hel Styverson

Forbidden Territory: Stanley's Search for Livingstone ★★

Adventure based on a true story 1997 · US · Colour · 96min

Aidan Quinn is miscast as the intrepid reporter Henry Morton Stanley who transformed his fortunes with his expedition to find the missing Scottish missionary David Livingstone, who is played with suitable piety by Nigel Hawthorne. Director Simon Langton adequately exploits the African scenery and draws a showy

cameo out of Edward Fox, but this TV movie lacks drive. DP Swearing.

Aidan Quinn *Henry Morton Stanley* • Nigel Hawthorne *David Livingstone* • Edward Fox *Markham* • Fay Masterson *Alice* ▪ *Dir* Simon Langton • *Scr* John Pielmeier

Force Majeure ★★★★ 15

Drama 2014 · Swe/Den/Fr/Nor · Colour · 114min

It's a rare comedy that with just a few tweaks could easily be a heavy drama. In this subtle deadpan black comedy, a moment of panic has a husband abandon his wife and two children during an avalanche. But as the snow peters out, his cowardice weighs uncomfortably on the woman's mind. Couples, be warned: this isn't date-night material. DW Swedish, English, French, Norwegian +subtitles. *DVD* *BLU*

Johannes Bah Kuhnke [Johannes Kuhnke] *Tomas* • Lisa Loven Kongsli *Ebba* • Kristofer Hivju *Mats* • Fanni Metelius *Fanni* ▪ *Dir/Scr* Ruben Ostlund

Force of Arms ★★

Second World War drama 1951 · US · BW · 98min

William Holden and Nancy Olson star in this war movie, directed by the man who made *Casablanca*. In fact, it's a remake of Hemingway's *A Farewell to Arms*, first filmed in 1932 and updated to the Second World War. Holden's GI falls for Olson's nurse during the Italian campaign; he is then reported missing after a terrible battle. It's nothing special, despite Holden's romantic appeal. A further remake followed in 1957, reverting to Hemingway's original title. AT

William Holden (2) *Peterson* • Nancy Olson *Eleanor* • Frank Lovejoy *Maj Blackford* • Gene Evans *McFee* • Dick Wesson *Klein* • Paul Picerni *Sheridan* • Katherine Warren *Maj Waldron, WAC* • Ross Ford *Hooker* ▪ *Dir* Michael Curtiz • *Scr* Orin Jannings, from the story *Italian Story* by Richard Tregaskis

Force of Evil ★★★★ PG

Film noir 1948 · US · BW · 74min

This is a truly remarkable one-off, a quintessential *film noir* filmed on authentic New York locations by the great cinematographer George Barnes with dialogue in blank verse, co-written and directed by Abraham Polonsky. The plot revolves around corruption in the numbers racket, and holding it all together is a remarkably intense performance by John Garfield, doing some of his career best screen work here. But, be warned, this bleak and sordid philosophical allegory may not be to everyone's taste. Polonsky was blacklisted following the McCarthy witch-hunt and did not direct again until 1969. TS *DVD*

John Garfield *Joe Morse* • Beatrice Pearson *Doris Lowry* • Thomas Gomez *Leo Morse* • Howland Chamberlin *Freddy Bauer* • Roy Roberts *Ben Tucker* • Marie Windsor *Edna Tucker* • Paul McVey *Hobe Wheelock* • Tim Ryan *Johnson* ▪ *Dir* Abraham Polonsky • *Scr* Abraham Polonsky, Ira Wolfert, from the novel *Tucker's People* by Ira Wolfert

A Force of One ★★ 15

Martial arts action drama 1979 · US · Colour · 85min

Between the death of Bruce Lee and the emergence of Jackie Chan, martial arts fans had to make do with the plank of wood that was Chuck Norris, the six-times world karate champion. Displaying all his customary charm, the hairy one is characteristically cast as a Vietnam vet fighting cop-killing drug dealers in a small Californian town. This has about as much life as an opponent who's just been felled by Norris. RS *DVD*

Chuck Norris *Matt Logan* • Jennifer O'Neill *Detective Mandy Rust* • Clu Gulager *Dunne* • Ron O'Neal *Rollins* • Bill Wallace *Jerry Sparks* • Eric Laneuville *Charlie Logan* • James Whitmore Jr *Moskovitz* • Clint Ritchie *Melrose* ▪ *Dir* Paul Aaron • *Scr* Ernest Tidyman, from a story by Pat Johnson

Force 10 from Navarone ★★ 12

Second World War drama
1978 · UK · Colour · 120min

This is a totally unnecessary and belated follow-up to the massive 1961 smash hit, *The Guns of Navarone*. The cast here is no match for the original's; this time round, a tired Robert Shaw (in his penultimate picture), a pre-superstardom Harrison Ford and a mannered Edward Fox are faced not only with the enemy, but also with a cliché-ridden script. Director Guy Hamilton's uninspired movie begins with the climax of the earlier film, then spends an inordinate amount of time before reaching its own explosive finale. TS Violence, swearing, nudity. *DVD*

Robert Shaw *Mallory* · Harrison Ford *Barnsby* · Edward Fox *Miller* · Barbara Bach *Maritza* · Franco Nero *Lescovar* · Carl Weathers *Weaver* · Richard Kiel *Drazac* · Angus MacInnes *Reynolds* ■ *Dir* Guy Hamilton · *Scr* Robin Chapman, from a story by Carl Foreman, from the novel by Alistair MacLean

Forced March ★★★ 15

Drama 1989 · US/Hun · Colour · 99min

This is an ambitious film within a film about a fading US actor who travels to Hungary to star in a biography of a Hungarian-Jewish poet who died during the Holocaust. Rick King's film mixes scenes of the actor making the film with scenes from the film he's making; it also explores the cast members' varying commitment to the project. Style sometimes gets in the way of content, but this remains a powerful drama, with Chris Sarandon impressive at the head of a predominantly European cast. DA

Chris Sarandon *Kline/Miklos Radnoti* · Renée Soutendijk *Myra* · Josef Sommer *Father* · John Seitz *Hardy* ■ *Dir* Rick King · *Scr* Dick Atkins, Charles K Bardosh

Forces of Nature ★★ 12

Romantic comedy 1998 · US · Colour · 101min

Sandra Bullock and Ben Affleck fail to muster much chemistry, although he is fine as the strait-laced groom-to-be who has a *Planes, Trains and Automobiles*-style trip to his wedding. But Bullock is miscast as the quirky gal who may tempt him away from his waiting bride (Maura Tierney). Director Bronwen Hughes never brings enough farcical humour or a sense of impending catastrophe to the adventure. JB Swearing. *DVD*

Sandra Bullock *Sarah Lewis* · Ben Affleck *Ben Holmes* · Maura Tierney *Bridget* · Steve Zahn *Alan* · Blythe Danner *Virginia* · Ronny Cox *Hadley* · Michael Fairman *Richard* ■ *Dir* Bronwen Hughes · *Scr* Marc Lawrence

Forces' Sweetheart ★ U

Comedy 1953 · UK · BW · 73min

Having starred with Peter Sellers and Spike Milligan in *Down among the Dead Men* the previous year, Harry Secombe and Michael Bentine re-team for this dismally unfunny uniform debacle. Hy Hazell is the object of everyone's attention, while comic Freddie Frinton has the few good lines there are. DP

Hy Hazell *Judy James* · Harry Secombe *Private Llewellyn* · Michael Bentine *Flight Lt Robinson* · Freddie Frinton *Aloysius Dimwitty* · John Ainsworth *Lt Robinson* · Kenneth Henry *Tommy Tupp* ■ *Dir/Scr* Maclean Rogers

A Foreign Affair ★★★★ U

Romantic comedy drama 1948 · US · BW · 111min

Iowa congresswoman Jean Arthur is sent to postwar Berlin to check on things, and runs into a thriving black market, corrupt GIs and a seductive Marlene Dietrich who's having affairs with an American army captain and a former Nazi. Not for nothing is Arthur's character called Frost and the question is, will she melt? Brimming with great lines, the film's weakness is John Lund as the US soldier. But its strength is Arthur's brave performance and director Billy Wilder's take on the ruins of the city he once lived in. Only he could have toured the bomb sites and stuck *Isn't It Romantic?* on the soundtrack. AT *DVD*

Jean Arthur *Phoebe Frost* · Marlene Dietrich *Erika von Schluetow* · John Lund *Capt John Pringle* · Millard Mitchell *Col Rufus J Plummer* · Peter Von Zerneck *Hans Otto Birgel* · Stanley Prager *Mike* · Bill Murphy *Joe* ■ *Dir* Billy Wilder · *Scr* Charles Brackett, Billy Wilder, Richard Breen [Richard L Breen], Robert Harari, from a story by David Shaw, Irwin Shaw (uncredited) · *Cinematographer* Charles B Lang Jr [Charles Lang] · *Costume Designer* Edith Head

Foreign Affaires ★★ U

Comedy 1935 · UK · BW · 69min

Written by Ben Travers in the style of his Aldwych farces, this hit-and-miss affair features the accomplished team of Tom Walls and Ralph Lynn who trot out their familiar mannerisms as the artful gambler and silly-ass car dealer who find themselves being duped in a crooked Nice casino. However, it's the estimable Robertson Hare who steals the show, with his shockable pomposity and his immaculate comic timing. Walls also directs, but his theatrical expertise renders the action stiff and stagey. DP

Tom Walls *Capt Archibald Gore* · Ralph Lynn *Jefferson Darby* · Robertson Hare *Mr Hardy Hornett* · Norma Varden *Mrs Hardy Hornett* · Marie Lohr *Mrs Cope* · Diana Churchill *Sophie* ■ *Dir* Tom Walls · *Scr* Ben Travers

Foreign Body ★ 15

Comedy 1986 · UK · Colour · 106min

This is one of those comedies that manages to be both unfunny and offensive. Victor Banerjee stars as Indian immigrant Ram Das, who gets a job as a bus conductor in England until he is convinced by his cousin (Warren Mitchell, complete with blacked-up face) to pose as a private doctor. Despite an impressive cast, this is fumbled at every turn. JB

Victor Banerjee *Ram Das* · Warren Mitchell *IQ Patel* · Amanda Donohoe *Susan Partridge* · Eve Ferret *Norah Plumb* · Geraldine McEwan *Lady Ammanford* · Trevor Howard *Dr Stirrup* · Denis Quilley *Prime Minister* · Anna Massey *Miss Furze* ■ *Dir* Ronald Neame · *Scr* Celine La Freniere, from a novel by Roderick Mann

Foreign Correspondent ★★★★ PG

Spy thriller 1940 · US · BW · 115min

This immensely pleasurable spy story is set on the eve of the Second World War and ends with American reporter Joel McCrea warning of the danger to come. Director Alfred Hitchcock makes the most of some great set pieces, many of which are now acknowledged as key moments in the Hitchcock canon: an Amsterdam assassination (on a huge interior set) as umbrellas close ranks in the rain; tense moments inside a vast Dutch windmill; a plane crash where the air supply on board is slowly draining away; and a remarkable sequence in Westminster Cathedral. The plot's twists and turns are cleverly and wittily maintained, and the supporting cast is impeccably chosen. The propagandist aspects have dated the film, and it is also impaired by the lightweight casting, but this is still marvellous. TS *DVD*

Joel McCrea *Johnny Jones/Huntley Haverstock* · Laraine Day *Carol Fisher* · Herbert Marshall *Stephen Fisher* · George Sanders *Scott ffolliott* · Albert Basserman *Van Meer* · Robert Benchley *Stebbins* · Edmund Gwenn *Rowley* · Eduardo Ciannelli *Krug* ■ *Dir* Alfred Hitchcock · *Scr* Charles Bennett, Joan Harrison, James Hilton, Robert Benchley · *Cinematographer* Rudolph Maté

Foreign Intrigue ★★

Spy drama 1956 · US · Colour · 99min

Shot on location in Europe, this stars a trenchcoat-clad Robert Mitchum at his most laconic in a movie whose murky plot and even murkier colour photography leave much to be desired. This was allegedly based on the Cold War experiences of its writer/producer/director Sheldon Reynolds, whose adventures formed the basis for a TV series from which this plodding film is a spin-off. TS

Robert Mitchum *Dave Bishop* · Genevieve Page *Dominique* · Ingrid Tulean [Ingrid Thulin] *Brita* · Frederick O'Brady [Frédéric O'Brady] *Spring* · Eugene Deckers *Sandoz* · Inga Tidblad *Mrs Lindquist* ■ *Dir* Sheldon Reynolds · *Scr* Sheldon Reynolds, Harry Jack Bloom, Gene Levitt

Foreign Student ★★ 15

Period drama 1994 · US/Fr · Colour · 91min

This American co-produced melodrama was adapted from the bestselling memoirs of French film-maker Philippe Labro. Debuting director Eva Sereny capably captures the atmosphere of mid-1950s Virginia, but Robin Givens is too modern to convince as the black teacher being romanced by visiting student Marco Hofschneider. The book's fond nostalgia has been turned into mildly sensationalist sentiment, and any sense of passion or social insight is lost in the trite script. DP Swearing, nudity.

Robin Givens *April* · Marco Hofschneider *Philippe Le Clerc* · Rick Johnson (2) *Cal Cate* · Charlotte Ross *Sue Ann* · Edward Herrmann *Zach Gilmore* ■ *Dir* Eva Sereny · *Scr* Menno Meyjes, from the novel by Philippe Labro

The Foreigner ★ 15

Action adventure 2003 · US · Colour · 91min

An out-of-shape Steven Seagal demonstrates how far past his prime he really is in this appalling action adventure. Ham-fisted director Michael Oblowitz tries to disguise the film's technical incompetence with a surfeit of plot twists and badly acting villains, as freelance agent Seagal tries to transport a package from France to Germany. But the biggest crime is the action sequences, which are so poorly staged that even a thumping techno accompaniment can't inject any excitement. SF Swearing, violence. *DVD*

Steven Seagal *Jonathan Cold* · Jeffrey Pierce *Sean Cold* · Anna-Louise Plowman *Meredith von Aiken* · Harry Van Gorkum *Jerome von Aiken* · Gary Raymond *Jared Oliphant* · Max Ryan *Dunoir* · Philip Dunbar *Alexander Marquet* ■ *Dir* Michael Oblowitz · *Scr* Darren O Campbell

The Foreman Went to France ★★★ U

Second World War comedy drama 1941 · UK · BW · 81min

Charles Frend edited some of the most impressive British pictures of the 1930s, including *Goodbye, Mr Chips*. He later graduated to direction during the Second World War and shot three of the most interesting docudramas of the conflict. This engaging flag-waver was based on the true-life exploits of Melbourne Johns, who crossed the Channel to smuggle vital machine tools back to Blighty. AJ

Tommy Trinder *Tommy* · Constance Cummings *Anne* · Clifford Evans *Fred Carrick* · Robert Morley *French mayor* · Gordon Jackson *Jock* · Ernest Milton *Stationmaster* ■ *Dir* Charles Frend · *Scr* John Dighton, Angus MacPhail, Leslie Arliss, from a story by JB Priestley · *Music* William Walton

The Forest ★★ 15

Supernatural horror 2016 · US · Colour · 89min

Director Jason Zada's horror has *Game of Thrones* star Natalie Dormer in its corner and that's about it. She's in Japan looking for her twin sister who has disappeared in the Aokigahara forest, where many people go to commit suicide. There, she must face her own demons as spirits congregate to prey on those in emotional turmoil. With Dormer making one daft life-threatening decision after another, the inevitable conclusion is glaringly obvious to the genre savvy. AJ *DVD* Blu

Natalie Dormer *Sara/Jess Price* · Taylor Kinney *Aiden* · Yukiyoshi Ozawa *Michi* · Eoin Macken *Rob* ■ *Dir* Jason Zada · *Scr* Nick Antosca, Sarah Cornwall, Ben Ketai

The Forest Rangers ★★★

Romantic action drama 1942 · US · Colour · 86min

The claws are out as two of Hollywood's most glamorous and popular leading ladies of the period, Paulette Goddard and Susan Hayward, compete for the affections of he-man forest ranger Fred MacMurray. A romantic action drama, with one of the ladies getting her man to the altar but nobly rescuing her rejected rival from a spectacular forest fire, this is formulaic but fun hokum in Technicolor. The scenery helps. RK

Fred MacMurray *Don Stuart* · Paulette Goddard *Celia Huston* · Susan Hayward *Tana Mason* · Lynne Overman *Jammer Jones* · Albert Dekker *Twig Dawson* · Eugene Pallette *Mr Howard Huston* · Regis Toomey *Frank Hatfield* ■ *Dir* George Marshall · *Scr* Harold Shumate, from the short story by Thelma Strabel

Forever Amber ★★★ U

Historical melodrama 1947 · US · Colour · 132min

Otto Preminger's lavish costume drama was based on Kathleen Winsor's notorious novel about a sultry wench romping from bed to bed on her way up the social ladder in the time of Charles II. Amber is portrayed with competent efficiency by Linda Darnell, who was one of Hollywood's biggest stars of the 1940s, but, after Fox ended her studio contract, a virtual unknown by the late 1950s. The film may be short on finesse but it is long on period colour and Hollywood production values. PF

Linda Darnell *Amber St Clair* · Cornel Wilde *Bruce Carlton* · Richard Greene *Lord Harry Almsbury* · George Sanders *King Charles II* · Glen Langan [Glenn Langan] *Rex Morgan* · Richard Haydn *Earl of Radcliffe* · Jessica Tandy *Nan Britton* · Anne Revere *Mother Red Cap* ■ *Dir* Otto Preminger · *Scr* Philip Dunne, Ring Lardner Jr, Jerome Cady, from the novel by Kathleen Winsor

Forever and a Day ★★★★

Period drama 1943 · US · BW · 104min

No less than 21 writers - ranging from Christopher Isherwood to RC Sheriff - are credited with writing this all-star curio, plus seven directors and a mere four cameramen. It charts the history of a London mansion from 1804 to the Blitz, when it was converted into a residential hotel; as many stars as possible enter its impressive portals. An uneven film, obviously, and a bit rushed, but some episodes are outstanding and the whole enterprise is to be commended: everyone worked for free and profits were given to Anglo-American war charities. AT

Anna Neagle *Miriam (Susan)* · Ray Milland *Bill Trimble* · Claude Rains *Pomfret* · C Aubrey Smith *Adm Trimble* · Dame May Whitty *Mrs Trimble* · Gene Lockhart *Cobblewick* · Ray Bolger *Sentry* · Edmund Gwenn *Stubbs* · Lumsden Hare *Fitts* · Stuart Robertson *Lawyer* · Charles Coburn *Sir William* · Jessie Matthews *Mildred* · Charles Laughton *Bellamy* · Montagu Love *Sir John Bunn* · Reginald Owen *Mr Simpson* · Cedric Hardwicke *Dabb* · Buster Keaton *Dabb's assistant* · Ida Lupino *Jenny* · Merle Oberon *Marjorie* ■ *Dir* René Clair, Edmund Goulding, Cedric Hardwicke, Frank Lloyd, Victor Saville, Robert Stevenson, Herbert Wilcox · *Scr* Charles Bennett, CS Forester, Lawrence Hazard, Michael Hogan, WP Lipscomb, Alice Duer Miller, John Van Druten, Alan Campbell, Peter Godfrey, SM Herzig, Christopher Isherwood, Gene Lockhart, RC Sherriff, Claudine West, Norman Corwin, Jack Hartfield, James Hilton, Emmett Lavery, Frederick Lonsdale, Donald Ogden Stewart, Keith Winters

Forever, Darling ★★ U

Comedy 1956 · US · Colour · 90min

Lucille Ball and Desi Arnaz's second attempt to become stars of the big screen together after the popular *The Long, Long Trailer* was this unfunny lark, in which guardian angel James Mason attempts to sort out the tribulations in their screen marriage. It doesn't sound particularly funny, and it wasn't. Mason is a joy to watch, (even if he does look embarrassed about the material), but it's an unworthy vehicle for American TV's greatest stars. TS

Lucille Ball *Susan Vega* · Desi Arnaz *Lorenzo Xavier Vega* · James Mason *Guardian angel* · Louis Calhern *Charles Y Bewell* · John Emery *Edward R Winter* · John Hoyt *Bill Finlay* · Natalie Schafer *Millie Opdyke* ■ *Dir* Alexander Hall · *Scr* Helen Deutsch

F

Forever England ★★ PG
First World War drama 1935 · UK · BW · 67min

This was the first fictional film made with the full co-operation of the Royal Navy, including ships and technical advisers, and the Senior Service emerges with all colours flying. After a slow start, director Walter Forde cranks up the pace as able seaman John Mills is rescued from the wreck of HMS *Rutland* by the German battleship *Zeithen*. Crude but exciting, this was remade in 1953 as *Sailor of the King*. DP *DVD*

John Mills *Albert Brown* • Betty Balfour *Elizabeth Brown* • Barry Mackay *Lt Somerville* • Jimmy Hanley *Ginger* • Howard Marion-Crawford *Max* ■ *Dir* Walter Forde • *Scr* Michael Hogan, Gerard Fairlie, JOC Horton, from a novel by CS Forester

Forever Female ★★★
Comedy 1953 · US · BW · 93min

Adapted and updated out of all recognition from an old JM Barrie play, this comedy about the Broadway theatre is haunted by the ghost of *All about Eve* (1950), but is nonetheless bitchy, witty and romantic in its own right. A chic Ginger Rogers plays an ageing Broadway actress, married to producer Paul Douglas. Desperate to regain her former star status, Rogers competes with ambitious youngster Patricia Crowley for the lead in a new play, and falls for its author, William Holden. Polished entertainment, directed by Irving Rapper. RK

Ginger Rogers *Beatrice Page* • William Holden (2) *Stanley Krown* • Paul Douglas *E Harry Phillips* • Patricia Crowley [Pat Crowley] *Clara Mootz* • James Gleason *Eddie Woods* • Jesse White *Willie Wolfe* • Marjorie Rambeau ■ *Dir* Irving Rapper • *Scr* Julius J Epstein, Philip G Epstein, from the play *Rosalind* by JM Barrie

Forever Lulu ★ 18
Comedy adventure 1987 · US · Colour · 86min

Yikes, is this bad! Fresh-faced debutant Alec Baldwin must have wondered what sort of business he was getting into as he watched Israeli director Amos Kollek cobble together this unmitigated disaster of a movie. It was much worse for German star Hanna Schygulla because she had an international reputation on the line. Debbie Harry got it right, however - cameo, get paid and run. DP Swearing, nudity.

Hanna Schygulla *Elaine Hines* • Deborah Harry *Lulu* • Alec Baldwin *Buck* • Annie Golden *Diana* • Paul Gleason *Robert* ■ *Dir/Scr* Amos Kollek

Forever Mine ★★ 15
Romantic crime drama 1999 · UK/US · Colour · 112min

It's hard to believe that this weak, over-played picture was scripted and directed by the writer of such greats as *Taxi Driver* and *Raging Bull*. Sporting ineffective scar make-up, Joseph Fiennes stars as a financier, whose affair with married Gretchen Moll when he was a young cabana boy sparks a 16-year vendetta against her husband Ray Liotta. With his dodgy accent and clumsy dialogue, Fiennes is as unconvincing as the film. SF Swearing, sex scenes. *DVD*

Joseph Fiennes *Manuel Esquema/Alan Riply* • Ray Liotta *Mark Brice* • Gretchen Mol *Ella Brice* • Vincent Laresca *Javier* • Kevi Katsuras • Shannon Lawson • Lindsey Connell ■ *Dir/Scr* Paul Schrader • *Music* Angelo Badalamenti

Forever Young ★★★ PG
Romantic fantasy 1992 · US · Colour · 97min

Mel Gibson obviously had to dig deep to find the enthusiasm to carry off this tired role of a cryogenic Rip Van Winkle who wakes 53 years after he has been frozen and forgotten. Hollywood used to churn out this kind of fluff with practised ease and it's a pity director Steve Miner couldn't have found the same winning formula in here. That said, the reunions are touching and Jamie Lee Curtis provides charming support. DP *DVD*

Mel Gibson *Daniel McCormick* • Jamie Lee Curtis *Claire* • Elijah Wood *Nat* • Isabel Glasser *Helen* • George Wendt *Harry* • Joe Morton *Cameron* ■ *Dir* Steve Miner • *Scr* Jeffrey Abrams

Forget Me Never ★★★ PG
Drama based on a true story 1999 · US/Can · Colour · 85min

Mia Farrow gives a sensitive portrayal in this TV movie of an intelligent woman succumbing to the creeping cruelty of Alzheimer's disease. As a lawyer who hides her suspicions to protect husband Martin Sheen from the stress of her condition, she conveys an inner strength that he's unable to match when she grows increasingly dependent on a fellow sufferer for support. Sadly, director Robert Ackerman can't always distinguish between poignancy and melodrama. DP

Mia Farrow *Diane McGowin* • Martin Sheen *Jack* • Colm Feore *Albert* ■ *Dir* Robert Allan Ackerman • *Scr* Renee Longstreet, from a story by H Haden Yelin

Forget Me Not ★★★ 15
Romantic drama 2009 · UK · Colour · 91min

Singer/songwriter Tobias Menzies and bar worker Genevieve O'Reilly are thrown together for a night of conversation, reflection and revelation, which culminates in a visit to O'Reilly's beloved grandmother (Gemma Jones). What at first glance seems like a London-set *Before Sunrise* turns out to be a moving and convincingly acted study of Alzheimer's and its consequences. Menzies is entirely believable as the disaffected musician unable to commit, and O'Reilly is equally mesmerising, despite the occasional melodramatic detour in the script. Yet it's the extraordinary Jones who really touches the soul. A slow-burner, but worthy of your patience. SuR Swearing, sex scenes. *DVD*

Tobias Menzies *Will Fletcher* • Genevieve O'Reilly *Eve Fisher* • Gemma Jones *Lizzie Fisher* ■ *Dir* Alexander Holt, Lance Roehrig • *Scr* Mark Underwood, from a story by Underwood, Steve Spence, Rebecca Long

Forget Mozart ★★★
Historical detective thriller 1985 · Cz/W Ger · Colour · 93min

As anyone who has seen *Amadeus* will know, slighted court composer Antonio Salieri considered himself responsible for Mozart's death. But masons, music-hall managers and monarchs all come under investigation in this complex costume thriller, as secret policeman Armin Mueller-Stahl seeks a darker explanation that will satisfy his conspiracy theories. While it lacks the scale of Milos Forman's Oscar winner, this is still a stylish picture. DP German +subtitles.

Max Tidof *Mozart* • Armin Mueller-Stahl *Count Pergen* • Catarina Raacke *Konstanze* • Wolfgang Preiss *Swieten* • Uwe Ochsenknecht *Schikaneder* • Winfried Glatzeder *Salieri* ■ *Dir* Slavo Luther [Miloslav Luther] • *Scr* Zdenek Mahler

Forget Paris ★★★ 12
Romantic comedy 1995 · US · Colour · 97min

This cosily familiar romantic comedy begins with Billy Crystal accompanying his father's body to Paris, where a baggage handling mishap introduces him to airline employee Debra Winger. They fall in love and swiftly marry, but can they retain the romance? The film is well played - though Winger isn't really cut out for comedy - and has both wit and insight. DP

Billy Crystal *Mickey Gordon* • Debra Winger *Ellen Andrews* • Joe Mantegna *Andy* • Cynthia Stevenson *Liz* • Richard Masur *Craig* • Julie Kavner *Lucy* ■ *Dir* Billy Crystal • *Scr* Billy Crystal, Lowell Ganz, Babaloo Mandel

Forgetting Sarah Marshall ★★★ 15
Romantic comedy 2008 · US · Colour · 110min

The team responsible for *The 40 Year Old Virgin* and *Knocked Up* is behind this sometimes riotous anti-romantic comedy. After musician Peter (Jason Segel) is dumped by his TV-star girlfriend Sarah (Kristen Bell), he decides to take a trip to Hawaii to get over her. But when Peter arrives, he discovers that Sarah and her new British rock star boyfriend (Russell Brand) are staying at the same hotel. All three leads are likeable and well cast, but the film, like producer Judd Apatow's previous efforts, is somewhat overlong. As compensation, it is often laugh-out-loud funny, with a broad humour that delivers belly laughs by the barrel-load. DA *DVD*

Jason Segel *Peter Bretter* • Kristen Bell *Sarah Marshall* • Mila Kunis *Rachael* • Russell Brand *Aldous Snow* • Bill Hader *Brian* • Jonah Hill *Matthew* • Paul Rudd *Surfing instructor* • Kristen Wiig *Prahna* ■ *Dir* Nicholas Stoller • *Scr* Jason Segel

The Forgotten ★★ 12
Psychological mystery thriller 2004 · US · Colour · 87min

Joseph Ruben's psychological thriller has no real tension, relying instead on a handful of ruthlessly effective jolts to convey its air of unseen menace. Julianne Moore plays a woman grieving over the death of her eight-year-old son. Told by her psychiatrist (Gary Sinise) that the boy never existed, she's stunned to find all evidence of the child has disappeared and sets out to prove that she's not delusional. Moore's performance is undermined by a weak script and ridiculous storyline. SF Swearing, violence. *DVD*

Julianne Moore *Telly Paretta* • Dominic West *Ash Correll* • Gary Sinise *Dr Jack Munce* • Alfre Woodard *Detective Ann Pope* • Linus Roache *Friendly man* • Anthony Edwards *Jim Paretta* • Robert Wisdom *Carl Dayton* • Jessica Hecht *Eliot* ■ *Dir* Joseph Ruben • *Scr* Gerald DiPego

The Forgotten Kingdom ★★★★ 12A
Drama 2013 · Lesotho/S Afr · Colour · 100min

Taking his late father's body back for burial in his ancestral homeland prompts a young Johannesburg resident to reconnect with the land and ancient tribal ties, in this very first feature film to be shot in Lesotho. American film-maker Andrew Mudge's beautifully shot story conveys a reverence for its verdant rolling landscapes while remaining clear-eyed about the struggles of its populace. The mysteries of tribal magic are explored, but it's the country's Aids crisis that provides the crux of the plot. If the script sometimes waxes too mystical for its own good, the film's ultimately so genuine it's hard to resist. TJ In Sotho. Some violence, swearing, sexual references.

Zenzo Ngqobe *Atang* • Nozipho Nkelemba *Dineo* • Jerry Mofokeng *Katleho* • Lebohang Ntsane *Orphan boy* ■ *Dir/Scr* Andrew Mudge

Forgotten Sins ★★ 15
Drama based on a true story 1996 · US · Colour · 87min

John Shea is the father who finds his life turning into a nightmare after his grown-up daughters accuse him of abuse, following therapy to release repressed memories. Despite the well-rounded performances of Shea and William Devane, this controversial subject is treated in a trivial fashion in this TV movie. JB *DVD*

William Devane *Dr Richard Ofshe* • John Shea *Matthew Bradshaw* • Bess Armstrong *Roberta Bradshaw* • Dean Norris *Carl Messenger* • Brian Markinson *Lowell Hart* ■ *Dir* Dick Lowry • *Scr* TS Cook, from articles in *The New Yorker* by Lawrence Wright

The Formula ★★ 15
Thriller 1980 · US · Colour · 112min

This thriller about a Nazi process for synthetic fuel prompted such an acrimonious bust-up between writer Steve Shagan and director John Avildsen that the latter campaigned to remove his name from the credits. At stake was the relative emphasis to be placed on the narrative and on the theory that the oil business was exploiting the world by suppressing this ingenious formula. Marlon Brando is a mumbling tycoon, while George C Scott is as baffled as we are. DP

George C Scott *Lieutenant Barney Caine* • Marlon Brando *Adam Steiffel* • Marthe Keller *Lisa* • John Gielgud *Dr Abraham Esau* • GD Spradlin *Clements* ■ *Dir* John G Avildsen • *Scr* Steve Shagan, from his novel

Formula for Death ★★★ 15
Thriller 1995 · US · Colour · 89min

If we tell you that this TV movie is also known as *Virus* and was taken from a Robin Cook novel entitled *Outbreak*, you'll have a pretty shrewd idea what it's all about. And, although not on a par with the film of Cook's best-known book, *Coma*, this is still quite a decent TV thriller, even though the audience will probably have twigged who was responsible for the spread of a supposedly extinct plague, long before ace medical researcher Nicollette Sheridan. DP Some violence. *DVD*

Nicollette Sheridan *Dr Marissa Blumenthal* • William Devane *Dr Ralph Harbuck* • William Atherton *Dr Reginald Holloway* • Stephen Caffrey *Tad Shockley* • Dakin Matthews *Cyrill Dubcheck* • Barry Corbin *Dr Jack Clayman* ■ *Dir* Armand Mastroianni • *Scr* Roger Young, from the novel *Outbreak* by Robin Cook

Forrest Gump ★★★★ 12
Comedy drama 1994 · US · Colour · 136min

Winner of six Oscars, including best picture, actor and director, this was a box-office hit in America, though its simple-minded patriotism was greeted with a certain cynicism in Europe. Gump, played by Tom Hanks, is a chump: a semi-literate everyman who drifts through recent American history and emerges triumphant. He's an athlete, war hero and hokey southern savant, a one-man palliative for a nation's political and moral bankruptcy. Hanks's performance is truly remarkable and, this being a Robert Zemeckis film, the effects are stunning: Gump meeting people such as JFK and Nixon is amazingly believable. AT Violence, swearing, drug abuse. *DVD*

Tom Hanks *Forrest Gump* • Gary Sinise *Lieutenant Dan Taylor* • Robin Wright *Jenny Curran* • Sally Field *Mrs Gump* • Mykelti Williamson *Benjamin Buford "Bubba" Blue* • Rebecca Williams *Nurse at park bench* • Michael Conner Humphreys *Young Forrest* ■ *Dir* Robert Zemeckis • *Scr* Eric Roth, from the novel by Winston Groom

The Forsaken ★★ 18
Horror 2001 · US · Colour · 86min

A vampire yarn for the slacker generation sees hapless film editor Kerr Smith on a long-distance drive to Florida. Having picked up hitch-hiker Brendan Fehr - who just happens to be a vampire slayer - Smith then falls into the clutches of a vanload of young bloodsuckers who roam the highways and byways of America's southwest. Johnathon Schaech as the black-clad boss vamp with killer cheekbones provides some much needed charisma, but his efforts are largely wasted on material that has "straight-to-video" stamped all over it. DA *DVD*

Kerr Smith *Sean* • Brendan Fehr *Nick* • Izabella Miko *Megan* • Phina Oruche *Cym* • Simon Rex *Pen* • Carrie Snodgress *Ina* • Johnathon Schaech *Kit* ■ *Dir/Scr* JS Cardone

Forsaken ★★★
Western drama 2015 · Can/Fr/US · Colour · 90min

This traditional western follows a weary gunslinger (Kiefer Sutherland) who has turned his back on violence. Returning home for the first time in ten years, he attempts to reconnect with his estranged father (Kiefer's own father, Donald). At the same time, a ruthless land baron (Brian Cox) is taking control of the town. Even if the story unfolds exactly as expected, film fans will like seeing Kiefer share the screen with his dad for the first time. SC *DVD*

Kiefer Sutherland *John Henry Clayton* • Donald Sutherland *Reverend William Clayton* • Brian Cox (1) *James McCurdy* • Michael Wincott *Gentleman Dave Turner* • Demi Moore *Mary Alice Watson* ■ *Dir* Jon Cassar • *Scr* Brad Mirman

Forsaking All Others
★★★ PG

Comedy   1934 · US · BW · 82min

Clark Gable and Joan Crawford team up yet again for this smart MGM comedy. Gable wants to propose to childhood friend Crawford, but she's engaged to Robert Montgomery. Need you ask about the outcome? The underrated WS "Woody" Van Dyke directs adroitly, while Crawford seems to undergo more costume changes than in her entire career (and that's saying something). The ineffable Charles Butterworth offers a beautifully timed supporting performance. TS

Joan Crawford *Mary Clay* • Clark Gable *Jeff Williams* • Robert Montgomery *Dill Todd* • Charles Butterworth *Shep* • Billie Burke *Paula* • Frances Drake *Connie* • Rosalind Russell *Eleanor* ■ *Dir* WS Van Dyke • *Scr* Joseph L Mankiewicz, from a play by Edward Barry Roberts, Frank Morgan Cavett

The Forsyte Saga
★★ U

Melodrama   1949 · US · Colour · 112min

While Greer Garson looks splendid as "That Forsyte Woman" (the US title of the film), the courageously-cast Errol Flynn is by far the best thing in this stilted picture, giving a performance of considerable restraint and depth. Despite the high production values, this spiritually undernourished, leaden feature is no match for the later BBC serial. TS

Errol Flynn *Soames Forsyte* • Greer Garson *Irene Forsyte* • Walter Pidgeon *Young Jolyon Forsyte* • Robert Young (1) *Philip Bosinney* • Janet Leigh *June Forsyte* • Harry Davenport *Old Jolyon Forsyte* ■ *Dir* Compton Bennett • *Scr* Ivan Tors, James B Williams, Arthur Wimperis, from the novel *The Man of Property*, the first book in the trilogy *The Forsyte Saga* by John Galsworthy

Fort Algiers
★★ U

Adventure   1953 · US · BW · 79min

This Foreign Legion adventure showcases exotic Yvonne De Carlo (born Peggy Middleton in Vancouver) and dashing Argentinian Carlos Thompson. The stars quickly became a couple in real life, but here they pale beside big Raymond Burr, swarthy Anthony Caruso and angst-ridden Leif Erickson as the heavies. Of course, the Arabs are bad, the French are dashing, and De Carlo's a secret agent posing as a cabaret singer. TS

Yvonne De Carlo *Yvette* • Carlos Thompson *Jeff* • Raymond Burr *Amir* • Leif Erickson *Kalmani* • Anthony Caruso *Chavez* • John Dehner *Major Colle* ■ *Dir* Lesley Selander • *Scr* Theodore St John, Frederick Stephani

Fort Apache
★★★★★ U

Western   1948 · US · BW · 128min

This magnificent western – one of the highlights of American cinema - is a satisfying, finely crafted work, not least because of Ford's ability to create a tangible sense of time and place in a displaced community against the majestic surroundings of his beloved Monument Valley. Ford regular Henry Fonda is particularly outstanding, cast against type as an embittered martinet officer. Fonda breaks a peace deal with Apache leader Cochise, an agreement that was originally engineered by John Wayne, in one of his finest, most delicate portrayals. The life of the cavalry - its music, its women, its mythology - is all superbly realised. TS
DVD

John Wayne *Captain York* • Henry Fonda *Lt Col Owen Thursday* • Shirley Temple *Philadelphia Thursday* • Pedro Armendáriz *Sergeant Beaufort* • Ward Bond *Sgt Maj Michael O'Rourke* • George O'Brien *Captain Collingwood* • John Agar *Lieutenant Michael O'Rourke* • Victor McLaglen *Sergeant Festus Mulcahy* • Miguel Inclan *Chief Cochise* ■ *Dir* John Ford • *Scr* Frank S Nugent, from the story *Massacre* by James Warner Bellah • *Cinematographer* Archie Stout • *Music* Richard Hageman

Fort Apache, the Bronx
★★★★

Crime drama   1981 · US · Colour · 123min

Hard-boiled and hard-pressed cop Paul Newman tries to control crime on New York's mean streets in this tremendously exciting urban western that's laced with taut suspense and grisly shocks. Pam Grier gives an electric performance as a drug-crazed hooker – just watch for that razor blade between her teeth. It was highly controversial (the Bronx community complained about misrepresentation), but is still highly recommended. AJ Swearing, violence, sex scenes, brief nudity, drug abuse.

Paul Newman *John Murphy* • Edward Asner *Captain Dennis Connolly* • Ken Wahl *Corelli* • Danny Aiello *Morgan* • Rachel Ticotin *Isabella* • Pam Grier *Charlotte* • Kathleen Beller *Theresa* • Tito Goya *Jumper/Detective* • Miguel Pinero *Hernando* ■ *Dir* Daniel Petrie • *Scr* Heywood Gould

Fort Massacre
★★ U

Western   1958 · US · Colour · 80min

Shot in colour and CinemaScope and featuring the ever-dependable Joel McCrea (he of the laughing eyes) this is a strictly by-the-book western. McCrea is leading a troop on a mission to Indian territory, inevitably landing in constant skirmishes with those who previously owned the land. Entertaining, but unsurprising. BB

Joel McCrea *Vinson* • Forrest Tucker *McGurney* • Susan Cabot *Piute girl* • John Russell *Travis* • Anthony Caruso *Pawnee* • Denver Pyle *Collins* ■ *Dir* Joseph M Newman • *Scr* Martin Goldsmith

Fort Saganne
★★★★ 15

Historical adventure   1984 · Fr · Colour · 173min

This long and lavish desert adventure pulls out all the stops for location shooting, almost rivalling *Lawrence of Arabia*, and casts four of France's biggest stars: Gérard Depardieu, Philippe Noiret, Catherine Deneuve and Sophie Marceau. The result is an exhausting but often impressive drama in which Depardieu's legionnaire expands the French Empire from the back of a camel just prior to the First World War. Acting honours go to Noiret's choleric officer, but the star of the show is cameraman Bruno Nuytten, whose images of Mauritania will take your breath away. AT French +subtitles.

Gérard Depardieu *Charles Saganne* • Philippe Noiret *Dubreuilh* • Catherine Deneuve *Louise Tissot* • Sophie Marceau *Madeleine De Saint Ilette* • Michel Duchaussoy *Baculard* ■ *Dir* Alain Corneau • *Scr* Alain Corneau, Henri DeTurenne, Louis Gardel, from the novel by Louis Gardel

Fort Worth
★★ U

Western   1951 · US · Colour · 80min

The last film of veteran director Edwin L Marin is little more than a routine western, with a fairly innocuous plot that deals with the coming of newsprint to the west. Rugged Randolph Scott makes a most unlikely newspaper editor, and his predictable reversion to gunplay denudes the movie of any real suspense, but it's never less than watchable. TS

Randolph Scott *Ned Britt* • David Brian *Blair Lunsford* • Phyllis Thaxter *Flora Talbot* • Helena Carter *Amy Brooks* • Dick Jones [Dickie Jones] *Luther Wick* ■ *Dir* Edwin L Marin • *Scr* John Twist, from his story *Across the Panhandle*

Fortress
★★★ 18

Science-fiction action thriller   1992 · Aus/US · Colour · 91min

Christopher Lambert is sent to a maximum security prison for conceiving a second child – a crime in this imaginatively rendered totalitarian future. There he suffers hi-tech torture and intense corruption while planning a daring break out. Violent, inventive and lots of intriguing fun, Stuart Gordon makes this fantasy a suspenseful rollercoaster ride, despite its pulp limitations. AJ Violence, swearing, nudity. *DVD*

Christopher Lambert *John Brennick* • Kurtwood Smith *Prison Director Poe* • Loryn Locklin *Karen Brennick* • Lincoln Kilpatrick *Abraham* • Clifton Gonzalez Gonzalez [Clifton Collins Jr] *Nino* ■ *Dir* Stuart Gordon • *Scr* Steve Feinberg, Troy Neighbors

Fortress 2: Re-entry ★★ 15

Futuristic action thriller   1999 · US/Lux · Colour · 88min

Eight years after the moderately successful *Fortress*, Christopher Lambert is called back to reprise his role as a rebel imprisoned by an evil global corporation. Here, he's incarcerated aboard an orbiting space slammer. Escaping involves lots of running down corridors and much noisy mayhem. Less glossy and violent than the original. DA *DVD*

Christopher Lambert *John Brennick* • Patrick Malahide *Peter Teller* • Liz May Brice *Elena Rivera* • Anthony C Hall *Marcus Jackson* • Willie Garson *Stanley Nussbaum* ■ *Dir* Geoff Murphy • *Scr* John Flock, Peter Doyle, from a story and characters by Steven Feinberg, Troy Neighbors

The Fortunate Fool ★★

Comedy   1933 · UK · BW · 71min

This adaptation of Dion Titheradge's stage play merits attention because it was edited by David Lean. However, his fourth credited outing with the scissors afforded Lean few opportunities to shine, as director Norman Walker makes little attempt to open out a scenario that rather cynically cashes in on the Depression, as wealthy author Hugh Wakefield pretends to be penniless in order to gain the trust of unemployed typist Joan Wyndham. DP *DVD*

Hugh Wakefield *Jim Falconer* • Joan Wyndham *Helen* • Jack Raine *Gerald* • Elizabeth Jenns *Mildred* ■ *Dir* Norman Walker • *Scr* Dion Titheradge

The Fortune ★★ 12

Period comedy   1975 · US · Colour · 84min

Stockard Channing easily outshines Warren Beatty and Jack Nicholson in this occasionally tacky story set in the 1920s. Beatty and Nicholson play two incompetent conmen trying to extract money from an heiress. Director Mike Nichols has an impressive track-record, but here his style seems tastelessly gauche. David Shire's jazz arrangements are a major delight, however. TH *DVD*

Jack Nicholson *Oscar* • Warren Beatty *Nicky* • Stockard Channing *Freddie* • Florence Stanley *Mrs Gould* • Richard B Shull *Chief Detective* • Tom Newman *John the barber* ■ *Dir* Mike Nichols • *Scr* Adrien Joyce

Fortune and Men's Eyes ★★

Prison drama   1971 · US/Can · Colour · 102min

Homosexual activity and brutality in men's prisons were the themes of John Herbert's powerful Broadway play. However, although Herbert himself wrote the screenplay, the film version is far more exploitative, and seems to have lost the plea for prison reform along the way. Nevertheless, it still packs a punch, given its story of a young man having to submit to being sodomised regularly by his "protector". The original director Jules Schwerin was replaced by Harvey Hart, and many scenes had to be reshot. RB

Wendell Burton *Smitty* • Michael Greer *Queenie* • Zooey Hall *Rocky* • Danny Freedman *Mona* • Larry Perkins *Screwdriver* • James Barron *Holyface Peters* • Lazaro Perez *Catso* • Jon Granik *Sgt Gritt* ■ *Dir* Harvey Hart • *Scr* John Herbert, from his play

The Fortune Cookie
★★★★ U

Comedy   1966 · US · BW · 120min

Billy Wilder's first teaming of Walter Matthau and Jack Lemmon crackles throughout. Matthau is amoral lawyer "Whiplash Willie" who sees an opportunity to cash in when his brother-in-law, hapless cameraman Harry (Lemmon) is injured at a football game. Typically mining his drama from the collision between affectionate comedy and spiky cynicism, Wilder squeezes telling performances from his two stars. Matthau's lugubrious eccentricity won him an Oscar for best supporting actor, while Lemmon conveys the decency familiar from his role in *The Apartment*. AJ
DVD

Jack Lemmon *Harry Hinkle* • Walter Matthau *Willie Gingrich* • Ron Rich *Luther "Boom-Boom" Jackson* • Cliff Osmond *Mr Purkey* • Judi West *Sandy Hinkle* • Lurene Tuttle *Mother Hinkle* • Harry Holcombe *O'Brien* ■ *Dir* Billy Wilder • *Scr* Billy Wilder, IAL Diamond

Fortune Hunters ★★ U

Comedy adventure   1999 · US · Colour · 87min

The producers clearly think they're being cute in teaming Richard (*The Waltons*) Thomas and Maureen (*The Brady Bunch*) McCormick as the discontented parents of dysfunctional kids, Alison Lohman and Andrew Sandler. But the scheme backfires, as they deliver woefully stagey performances as the family is forced to pull together in order to find a misplaced lottery ticket. Woefully unfunny. DP *DVD*

Richard Thomas *Ted Hunter* • Maureen McCormick *Betsy Hunter* • C Thomas Howell *Valentino* • Corey Feldman *Charles* • Estelle Getty *Sister Rosanne* • Randy Travis *Man in jail cell* • Kaye Ballard *Mrs Crabby* • Alison Lohman *Courtney Hunter* • Adam Sandler *Shane Hunter* ■ *Dir* Neil Mandt • *Scr* Gregory Poppen, from the story *The $30,000 Bequest* by Mark Twain

Fortune Is a Woman ★★

Mystery   1956 · UK · BW · 94min

This fair-to-middling thriller by Frank Launder and Sidney Gilliat is all plot and no point. Borrowing from a thousand and one *films noirs*, it follows the misfortunes of Jack Hawkins, an insurance assessor whose investigation of a series of fires draws him into murder, marriage and blackmail with a fatalistic inevitability. Hawkins lacks vulnerability, while Arlene Dahl's *femme fatale* lacks allure. DP

Jack Hawkins *Oliver Branwell* • Arlene Dahl *Sarah Moreton* • Dennis Price *Tracey Moreton* • Violet Farebrother *Mrs Moreton* • Ian Hunter *Clive Fisher* • Christopher Lee *Charles Highbury* ■ *Dir* Sidney Gilliat • *Scr* Sidney Gilliat, Frank Launder, Val Valentine, from the novel by Winston Graham

40 Carats ★★ PG

Comedy   1973 · US · Colour · 104min

This would-be sprightly comedy suffers from severe central miscasting. Swedish import Liv Ullmann doesn't fit into the sophisticated New York whirl presented here, and no matter how hard she tries, her affair with younger Edward Albert remains unconvincing. But debonair Gene Kelly, as her ex-husband, is a joy to discover in this wisp of fluff. TS

Liv Ullmann *Ann Stanley* • Edward Albert *Peter Latham* • Gene Kelly *Billy Boylan* • Binnie Barnes *Maud Ericson* • Deborah Raffin *Trina Stanley* ■ *Dir* Milton Katselas • *Scr* Leonard Gershe, from the play by Jay Presson Allen, Pierre Barillet, Jean-Pierre Gredy

40 Days and 40 Nights
★★★ 15

Romantic comedy   2002 · US/Fr/UK/Can · Colour · 91min

Josh Hartnett casts himself into the sexual wilderness in this comedy about celibacy that is less crude than most teen-orientated offerings, and is even rather cute. Hartnett's large number of one-night stands have left him depressed and doubting the existence of his soul. To rectify his shallowness, he swears off sex for Lent, but the very next day meets the woman of his dreams. His only remaining option is to woo her the old-fashioned way. Handled with humour and charm. LH *DVD* *Blu-ray*

Josh Hartnett *Matt Sullivan* • Shannyn Sossamon *Erica Sutton* • Vinessa Shaw *Nicole* • Paulo Costanzo *Ryan* • Maggie Gyllenhaal *Sam* • Griffin Dunne *Jerry* ■ *Dir* Michael Lehmann • *Scr* Robert Perez

F

48 HRS ★★★★ 15
Action thriller 1982 · US · Colour · 99min

Trading Places apart, Eddie Murphy has never been better than in this, his exhilarating debut, still one of the best "buddy" cop thrillers to be made. Murphy is the con who is sprung from prison by racist cop Nick Nolte in an attempt to track down psychopathic duo James Remar and Sonny Landham, who have escaped from a chain gang and are now back in town. Nolte and Murphy are perfectly paired: the latter all smooth charm and wisecracks, the former the rough, gruff straight man. Murphy's taming of a redneck bar deserves its place in the cinematic history books, while director Walter Hill also delivers the goods in the action stakes with some beautifully orchestrated shoot-ups and chases. Followed by the uninspired *Another 48 HRS* in 1990. JF Swearing, violence, nudity. DVD ▶
Nick Nolte *Detective Jack Cates* • Eddie Murphy *Reggie Hammond* • Annette O'Toole *Elaine* • Frank McRae *Captain Haden* • James Remar *Albert Ganz* ■ *Dir* Walter Hill • *Scr* Roger Spottiswoode, Walter Hill, Larry Gross, Steven E de Souza

45 Years ★★★★★ 15
Drama 2015 · UK · Colour · 91min

An elegant, deeply affecting portrait of a marriage in crisis, this follows Charlotte Rampling and Tom Courtenay as a couple who are one week away from their 45th wedding anniversary. But as Swiss authorities find the body of Courtenay's previous girlfriend, who fell to her death 50 years previously, this situation gives rise to doubt and resentment. Rampling and Courtenay prove utterly convincing as two people who have been together for a long time, in an insightful, heartbreaking film that deserves to be celebrated. SC Swearing, a sex scene. DVD ▶
Charlotte Rampling *Kate Mercer* • Tom Courtenay *Geoff Mercer* • Geraldine James *Lena* • Dolly Wells *Charlotte* • David Sibley *George* ■ *Dir* Andrew Haigh • *Scr* Andrew Haigh, from a short story by David Constantine

44 Inch Chest ★★★ 18
Revenge drama 2009 · UK/US/Aus · Colour · 90min

Ray Winstone reteams with the writers of *Sexy Beast* here to play another gangster whose tough shell hides a soft centre. Colin Diamond (Winstone) is a broken man following the admission by his wife (Joanne Whalley) that she is leaving him for a young waiter. So much moping prompts his criminal pals (including John Hurt, Ian McShane and Tom Wilkinson) to kidnap "Loverboy" (Melvil Poupaud) for bloody revenge. Debuting director Malcolm Venville is careful not to overdo the gore, but there's enough foul language and vile behaviour to guarantee a wince per minute. The plot does feel sketchy and drawn-out at times, but overall, this film packs a punch. SP Violence, swearing, sexual references. DVD ▶
Ray Winstone *Colin Diamond* • Tom Wilkinson *Archie* • Ian McShane *Meredith* • John Hurt *Old Man Peanut* • Stephen Dillane *Mal* • Joanne Whalley *Liz Diamond* • Steven Berkoff *Tippi Gordon* ■ *Dir* Malcolm Venville • *Scr* Louis Mellis, David Scinto

Forty Guns ★★★ PG
Western 1957 · US · BW · 76min

Samuel Fuller was one of American cinema's true mavericks who eventually found a comfortable base at 20th Century-Fox, turning out a series of lurid melodramas that later achieved cult status, including this stylishly photographed CinemaScope western. Barbara Stanwyck plays a ruthless Arizona rancher who is a law unto herself, until marshal Barry Sullivan turns up. TS DVD ▶
Barbara Stanwyck *Jessica Drummond* • Barry Sullivan *Griff Bonnell* • Dean Jagger *Ned Logan* • John Ericson *Brockie Drummond* ■ *Dir/Scr* Samuel Fuller

40 Guns to Apache Pass ★★ PG
Western 1966 · US · Colour · 91min

Audie Murphy made his penultimate screen appearance in this low-budget western from B-movie specialist William Witney. Although it's briskly and efficiently made, it's never anything more than routine, with Murphy leading his bluecoats into brutal action against the Apache, only to discover that the tribe isn't his most pressing problem. DP
Audie Murphy *Captain Coburn* • Michael Burns *Doug* • Kenneth Tobey *Corporal Bodine* • Laraine Stephens *Ellen* • Robert Brubaker *Sergeant Walker* ■ *Dir* William Witney • *Scr* Willard Willingham, Mary Willingham

The 49th Man ★★★ U
Spy drama 1953 · US · BW · 72min

Worried about a foreign power smuggling an atomic bomb into the US, the Navy plans an elaborate hoax to test the readiness of the security services. That's one twist in the plot; the next is such a humdinger that one becomes genuinely concerned for the survival of Nevada and for the devious mind of the screenwriter Harry Essex. Designed to reassure Middle America about communist invasion and atomic terrorism, this B-movie has a sense of urgency and suitably awed acting. AT
John Ireland *John Williams* • Richard Denning *Paul Regan* • Suzanne Dalbert *Margo Wayne* • Robert Foulk *Commander Jackson* • Touch Connors [Mike Connors] *Lt Magrew* • Richard Avonde *Buzz Olin* ■ *Dir* Fred F Sears • *Scr* Harry Essex, from a story by Ivan Tors

49th Parallel ★★★★ U
Second World War drama 1941 · UK · BW · 116min

Sponsored by the Ministry of Information and 18 months in the making, this is one of the best propaganda films produced in Britain during the Second World War. With a stellar cast and a rousing score by Ralph Vaughan Williams, Michael Powell and Emeric Pressburger's gripping action drama thoroughly merited its Oscar for best original story and its nominations for best picture and screenplay. Eric Portman gives the finest performance of his career as the officer of a bombed U-boat who has to lead his surviving crew across the Canadian wilderness to neutral America. Laurence Olivier's French-Canadian accent has to be heard to be believed. DP DVD ▶
Eric Portman *Lt Ernst Hirth* • Laurence Olivier *Johnnie Barras* • Leslie Howard *Philip Armstrong Scott* • Anton Walbrook *Peter* • Raymond Massey *Andy Brock* • Glynis Johns *Anna* • Niall MacGinnis *Vogel* ■ *Dir* Michael Powell • *Scr* Rodney Ackland, Emeric Pressburger, from a story by Emeric Pressburger • *Cinematographer* Freddie Young • *Editor* David Lean

Forty Pounds of Trouble ★★★ U
Comedy 1962 · US · Colour · 105min

This is an immensely likeable reworking of the Damon Runyon tale, filmed in 1934 and 1980 as *Little Miss Marker* and in 1949 as *Sorrowful Jones*. Amiable Tony Curtis is the gambling house manager who's left holding the baby, a situation that prompts nightclub chanteuse Suzanne Pleshette to lure him away from his ex-wife. What's surprising, given its lightness of content, is that it marked the feature debut of Norman Jewison, later responsible for such worthy classics as *In the Heat of the Night*. TS
Tony Curtis *Steve McCluskey* • Phil Silvers *Bernie Friedman* • Suzanne Pleshette *Chris Lockwood* • Claire Wilcox *Penny Piper* • Larry Storch *Floyd* • Stubby Kaye *Cranston* ■ *Dir* Norman Jewison • *Scr* Marion Hargrove, from the short story *Little Miss Marker* by Damon Runyon

LANDMARK FILM
With this first significant work by choreographer Busby Berkeley, the musical comes of age

42nd Street ★★★★★ U
Musical 1933 · US · BW · 85min

One of the most important and enjoyable musicals of all time, this sizzling Warner Bros movie is also one of the best loved of the early talking pictures. The film is recognised as a masterpiece, not merely for its racy dialogue and lavish costumes, or for its now-classic "newcomer goes on instead of indisposed star" plot, but also for affording kaleidoscope choreographer Busby Berkeley a chance to show off. The production cost a then-mammoth $400,000 and it shows. This is as entertaining as it gets, with a knockout cast headed by Warner Baxter as the stressed Broadway director and Bebe Daniels as his star. Dick Powell and Ruby Keeler feature in roles that would turn them into household favourites, and a newcomer called Ginger Rogers plays Anytime Annie. TS DVD
Warner Baxter *Julian Marsh* • Bebe Daniels *Dorothy Brock* • Ruby Keeler *Peggy Sawyer* • Dick Powell *Billy Lawler* • George Brent *Pat Denning* • Una Merkel *Lolly* • Ginger Rogers *Anytime Annie* • Guy Kibbee *Abner Dillon* ■ *Dir* Lloyd Bacon • *Scr* James Seymour, Rian James, from a novel by Bradford Ropes • *Producer* Darryl F Zanuck • *Cinematographer* Sol Polito • *Music/lyrics* Harry Warren, Al Dubin

47 Ronin ★★★ 12
Period action drama 2012 · US · Colour · 113min

Set in feudal Japan, this stars Keanu Reeves as Kai, an outcast who finds himself fronting a band of masterless samurai in a bid both to avenge their dead lord and to free Kai's love from a forced marriage. Blending Japanese myth with Hollywood-style CGI, *47 Ronin* both benefits and suffers from its splendid Japanese support cast, who look great but who should not have been obliged to speak English. Handsomely staged and quite moving in its final moments, this is a decent alternative to everyday Hollywood action. DA Some violence. DVD ▶
Keanu Reeves *Kai* • Hiroyuki Sanada *Kuranosuke Oishi* • Ko Shibasaki *Mika* • Tadanobu Asano *Lord Kira* • Rinko Kikuchi *Mizuki* ■ *Dir* Carl Rinsch • *Scr* Hossein Amini, Chris Morgan, from a story by Morgan, Walter Hamada

Forty Thousand Horsemen ★★
First World War drama 1941 · Aus · BW · 80min

For 30 years, Charles Chauvel was Australia's first and possibly only major director. It was Chauvel who, in 1933, gave Errol Flynn his screen debut as Fletcher Christian in the docudrama *In the Wake of the Bounty*. This is Chauvel's big movie about the Australian Light Horse regiment's role in Palestine during the First World War. The action easily outclasses the quieter moments, involving a romance between an Aussie soldier and a beautiful French girl, which are rather awkward and poorly acted. AT
Grant Taylor *Red Gallagher* • Betty Bryant *Juliet Rouget* • Chips Rafferty *Jim* • Pat Twohill *Larry* • Harvey Adams *Von Hausen* ■ *Dir* Charles Chauvel • *Scr* Elsa Chauvel

42 ★★ 12
Biographical sports drama 2013 · US · Colour · 122min

Back in the mid-1940s, Jackie Robinson became the first African American to be plucked from the all-black Negro League and signed to an all-white Major League team, the Brooklyn Dodgers, wearing shirt number 42. Relative unknown Chadwick Boseman plays the US baseball legend, but all eyes are drawn to Harrison Ford, who chews the scenery as the grizzled Dodgers team executive who sees dollar signs at the prospect of the big black crowds he believes Robinson will bring in. It's a solid biopic, nicely acted, and with a good sense of time and place, but it may have limited impact on this side of the Pond. DA DVD
Chadwick Boseman *Jackie Robinson* • Harrison Ford *Branch Rickey* • Christopher Meloni *Leo Durocher* • Lucas Black *Pee Wee Reese* • Alan Tudyk *Ben Chapman* • John C McGinley *Red Barber* ■ *Dir/Scr* Brian Helgeland

The 40 Year Old Virgin ★★★ 15
Romantic comedy 2005 · US · Colour · 126min

This doesn't sound like much: a middle-aged stereo salesman unwittingly betrays his lack of sexual experience and his colleagues decide to help him lose his virginity. But the sharp script and comic playing transcend the mundane and raunchier aspects of the plot, with Steve Carell appealing as the hapless innocent. Sweet, superior tosh. DA DVD
Steve Carell *Andy Stitzer* • Catherine Keener *Trish* • Paul Rudd *David* • Seth Rogen *Cal* • Romany Malco *Jay* • Elizabeth Banks (2) *Beth* • Leslie Mann *Nicky* • Jane Lynch *Paula* ■ *Dir* Judd Apatow • *Scr* Judd Apatow, Steve Carell

Foul Play ★★★ PG
Comedy thriller 1978 · US · Colour · 110min

This incredibly silly but enjoyable comedy stars Goldie Hawn as a librarian who discovers a plot to kill the visiting Pope. Chevy Chase has one of his best roles as the detective who doesn't believe Hawn's life is in danger, and the cast also features Burgess Meredith and Dudley Moore having a whale of a time in between car chases and assassination attempts. JB Swearing.
Goldie Hawn *Gloria Mundy* • Chevy Chase *Tony Carlson* • Dudley Moore *Stanley Tibbets* • Burgess Meredith *Mr Hennesey* • Rachel Roberts (1) *Gerda Casswell* • Brian Dennehy *Fergie* ■ *Dir/Scr* Colin Higgins

The Founder
Biographical drama 2016 · US · Colour · 115min

This is a preview – no prints were available to review as we went to press: Both sides of capitalism are explored in *The Founder* - its dynamic creativity and its money-before-morality ethos. And it's all there in the story of Ray Kroc as he becomes a franchise agent for the McDonald brothers' small hamburger chain, before eventually going on to buy the entire operation off them in 1961. Small comfort to the McDonalds - he promises as part of the deal not to compete with them in their own neighbourhood. It's a tale of shady dealing and a fanatical zeal for the "system" that ensured Golden Arches products tasted the same no matter where you bought them. And who better to play the charming rascal himself than Michael Keaton? Who said Robert Downey Jr? SvM
Michael Keaton *Ray Kroc* • Linda Cardellini *Joan Smith* • Patrick Wilson *Rollie Smith* • Nick Offerman *Dick McDonald* • Laura Dern *Ethel Kroc* • John Carroll Lynch *Mac McDonald* ■ *Dir* John Lee Hancock • *Scr* Robert D Siegel

The Fountain ★★★★★ 12
Romantic science-fiction drama 2005 · US · Colour · 92min

You wait years for a film about ancient Mayans and then, like buses, two movies come along at once. Like Mel Gibson's *Apocalypto*, *The Fountain* is one of the most original films of recent times – though a story that features not only ancient Mayans but also a man living on a planet inside a snow globe with just a tree for company is bound to be thought pretentious as well as clever. This third feature from Darren Aronofsky (*Requiem for a Dream*) stars Hugh Jackman as a man on a 1,000-year odyssey to save his beloved (Rachel Weisz, in multiple roles). The performances and music brilliantly complement Aronofsky's philosophical musings in one of the most perplexing and visually stunning films since *2001: a Space Odyssey*. BP Some violence, brief swearing. DVD ▶
Hugh Jackman *Tomas/Tommy/Dr Tom Creo* • Rachel Weisz *Queen Isabel/Izzi Creo* • Ellen Burstyn *Dr Lillian Guzetti* • Mark Margolis *Father Avila* • Stephen McHattie *Grand Inquisitor Silecio* • Fernando Hernandez *Lord of Xibalba* • Cliff Curtis *Captain Ariel* • Donna Murphy *Betty* ■ *Dir* Darren Aronofsky • *Scr* Darren Aronofsky, from a story by Aronofsky, Ari Handel • *Music* Clint Mansell

The Fountainhead ★★★ PG
Drama   1949 · US · BW · 107min

A genuine oddity in 1940s Hollywood studio film-making, this is a deliriously entertaining adaptation by Ayn Rand of her novel inspired by the life of architect Frank Lloyd Wright. At its core is a smouldering, over-the-top love struggle between Gary Cooper and Patricia Neal as the uncompromising maverick and the cultured beauty who uneasily surrenders to him. The script is a crazed cocktail of stilted dialogue, libertarian platitudes and unhinged innuendo. The film operates on its own near-ridiculous level, heightened by striking close-ups and some superbly expressionistic interiors. DO Some violence.

Gary Cooper *Howard Roark* · Patricia Neal *Dominique Francon* · Raymond Massey *Gail Wynand* · Kent Smith *Peter Keating* · Robert Douglas *Ellsworth M Toohey* · Henry Hull *Henry Cameron* · Ray Collins *Enright* ■ *Dir* King Vidor · *Scr* Ayn Rand, from her novel · *Cinematographer* Robert Burks · *Art Directors* John Holden, Edward Carrere · *Set Decorator* William Kuehl

Four ★★★ 15
Thriller   2010 · UK · Colour · 84min

The best-laid plans of a cuckolded husband go awry in this taut thriller. Set in an abandoned warehouse, it's a character piece (the clue is in the title), in which a spurned spouse (Craig Conway) employs a brutal detective (Sean Pertwee) to abduct his wife's lover (Martin Compston) in order to scare him off. The cast is convincing, with Pertwee giving a gleefully threatening performance and Kierston Wareing's wife proving to be a terrific harridan. But ultimately it's a story that could have been done just as effectively on TV. JA Violence, swearing, sexual references. DVD Blu

Sean Pertwee *Detective* · Kierston Wareing *Wife* · Martin Compston *Lover* · Craig Conway *Husband* ■ *Dir* John Langridge · *Scr* Paul Chronnell

Four Adventures of Reinette and Mirabelle
★★★★ U
Drama   1986 · Fr · Colour · 94min

Concentrating on the contrasting attitudes of two talkative teens, this rare non-series picture from French auteur Eric Rohmer makes light of its minuscule budget and inexperienced cast to provide another richly layered and hugely satisfying drama. A sophisticated spin on the town and country mouse fable, this is a film of incidents rather than adventures, with the eccentric Joëlle Miquel landing herself in scrapes that alternately amuse and irritate her more sophisticated Parisian pal, Jessica Forde. The endless stream of chat is never less than absorbing. DP French +subtitles.

Joëlle Miquel *Reinette* · Jessica Forde *Mirabelle* · Philippe Laudenbach *Waiter* · Yasmine Haury *Kleptomaniac* · Marie Rivière *Hustler* · Béatrice Romand *Inspector* · Géraud Courant *Inspector* ■ *Dir/Scr* Eric Rohmer

Four Brothers ★★★ 15
Action drama   2005 · US · Colour · 104min

Director John Singleton's tough revenge drama remains engaging while spinning headlong into preposterousness. Mark Wahlberg, Garrett Hedlund, Tyrese Gibson and André Benjamin play the hard-nut foster brothers who precariously reunite at their foster mother's funeral to bring her murderers to justice. The spectacular action scenes are all choreographed to a golden oldie Motown soundtrack. A proficient, slick, urban western. AJ Swearing, violence. DVD Blu

Mark Wahlberg *Bobby Mercer* · Tyrese Gibson *Angel Mercer* · André Benjamin *Jeremiah Mercer* · Garrett Hedlund *Jack Mercer* · Terrence Howard *Lt Green* · Josh Charles *Detective Fowler* · Sofia Vergara *Sofi* · Chiwetel Ejiofor *Victor Sweet* · Fionnula Flanagan *Evelyn Mercer* ■ *Dir* John Singleton · *Scr* David Elliot, Paul Lovett

Four Christmases ★★ 12
Seasonal comedy   2008 · US /Ger · Colour · 84min

Vince Vaughn and Reese Witherspoon star in a lame-brained but blessedly short comedy about a happily unmarried couple who re-evaluate their relationship when forced to split their Christmas Day between all four of their divorced parents. Sissy Spacek and Robert Duvall play Vaughn's mum and dad, while Mary Steenburgen and Jon Voight are Witherspoon's. The strength of this supporting cast should guarantee some laughs, yet all four actors are criminally underused by director Seth Gordon. His emphasis on slapstick crowd-pleasing rather than quality comic interaction just about earns a few cheap ho-ho-hos. DA DVD Blu

Vince Vaughn *Brad* · Reese Witherspoon *Kate* · Robert Duvall *Howard* · Jon Favreau *Denver* · Mary Steenburgen *Marilyn* · Dwight Yoakam *Pastor Phil* · Jon Voight *Creighton* · Sissy Spacek *Paula* ■ *Dir* Seth Gordon · *Scr* Matt R Allen, Caleb Wilson, Jon Lucas, Scott Moore, from a story by Allen, Wilson

4 Clowns ★★★★★ U
Comedy compilation   1970 · US · BW · 95min

Robert Youngson's compilation of comic cuts from the early days of film comedy reveals Laurel and Hardy, Buster Keaton and the undervalued Charley Chase (in his magnificent *Limousine Love*, among others) as creatures of infinite grace and wit. You can even forgive the film's sometimes patronising commentary for showing us the dizzying standards from which so many of today's comedians have fallen. Here's a golden age which has lost none of its lustre. TH

Buster Keaton · Charley Chase · Stan Laurel · Oliver Hardy ■ *Dir* Robert Youngson

Four Corners ★★★ 15
Crime drama   2013 · S Afr · Colour · 119min

Ever since Oliver Schmitz's *Mapantsula* (1988), South African cinema has specialised in gangland sagas that expose the grim realities of township life. Here, Brendon Daniels impresses as the former member of the "28" gang who vows to go straight after wreaking vengeance on the "26" rivals who killed his father and stole his home. While cinematographer Vicci Turpin achieves a poetry in exploring the sprawling poverty of the Cape Flats shanty town, screenwriters Hofmeyr Scholtz and Terence Hammond opt for a more melodramatic approach that sees too many loose ends conveniently tied up. DP Afrikaans, English, Tsotsitaal +subtitles. Violence, swearing, drug abuse.

Brendon Daniels *Farakhan* · Jezriel Skei *Ricardo Galam* · Lindiwe Matshikiza *Dr Leila Domingo* ■ *Dir* Ian Gabriel · *Scr* Hofmeyr Scholtz, Terence Hammond, from a story by Ian Gabriel, Scholtz

Four Daughters ★★★★ U
Romantic drama   1938 · US · BW · 89min

This was a big-box office winner in its day, and deservedly so. Claude Rains is simply wonderful as the musical father watching over the lives and loves of his four disparate daughters. This is a prime example of what can be achieved with an ostensibly soapy outline: small-town life with all its foibles, but with a top-notch cast that includes John Garfield in his first role. It's a fascinating, subtle look at the complexities of parenthood and community life. So popular was the film that the cast were brought together for a follow-up (*Daughters Courageous*), two proper sequels (*Four Wives* and *Four Mothers*) and in 1955 Frank Sinatra took over Garfield's role for a remake, *Young at Heart*. SH

Claude Rains *Adam Lemp* · May Robson *Aunt Etta* · Priscilla Lane *Ann Lemp* · Lola Lane *Thea Lemp* · Rosemary Lane *Kay Lemp* · Gale Page *Emma Lemp* · Dick Foran *Ernest* ■ *Dir* Michael Curtiz · *Scr* Julius J Epstein, Lenore Coffee, from the novel *Sister Act* by Fannie Hurst

Four Days ★★ 15
Crime thriller   1999 · Can · Colour · 85min

Teenager Kevin Zegers, seeing his father William Forsythe shot during a bank robbery, grabs the money and heads north hoping his dad will follow, not knowing that another gangster, Colm Meaney, is following him on his journey. Unfortunately, despite nice performances from Zegers and Forsythe, this suffers from some rather questionable plot twists and an over the top turn from Lolita Davidovich as the local floozy. JB

Kevin Zegers *Simon* · Lolita Davidovich *Chrystal* · Colm Meaney *Fury* · William Forsythe *Milt* · Anne-Marie Cadieux *Feather* ■ *Dir* Curtis Wehrfritz · *Scr* Pinckney Benedict, from the novel by John Buell

Four Days in November
★★★★ U
Documentary   1964 · US · BW · 122min

This astonishing monochrome study of the events surrounding President John F Kennedy's assassination in November 1963 was director Mel Stuart's second film and earned him a much-deserved Oscar nomination. In a seamless blend of rare archive news footage, eyewitness reports and re-creations, the 1964 feature details every aspect of that fateful Dallas trip, culminating in the funerals of both Kennedy and his apparent killer, Lee Harvey Oswald. It's a vivid and eerie historical document that lets the material speak for itself, with little attempt to analyse proceedings. Only actor Richard Basehart's ultra-reverential narration gives the project obvious bias. SF

Richard Basehart *Narrator* ■ *Dir* Mel Stuart · *Scr* Theodore Strauss

Four Days in September
★★★★
Biographical drama   1997 · Bra · Colour · 105min

Bruno Barreto landed an Oscar nomination for this drama, based on the autobiography of revolutionary-turned-journalist Fernando Gabeira. Set in 1969, with Brazil under a military dictatorship, the film recalls the abduction of American ambassador Charles Burke Elbrick by the MR-8 movement in a bid to secure the release of 15 political prisoners and publicise its cause. Playing fair with all the participants, this is a gripping reconstruction, with the friendship between ambassador Alan Arkin and journalist Pedro Cardoso humanising a tense situation. DP Portuguese +subtitles.

Alan Arkin *Charles Burke Elbrick* · Pedro Cardoso *Fernando Gabeira/Paulo* · Fernanda Torres *Maria* · Luiz Fernando Guimaraes *Marcao* · Claudia Abreu *Renee* · Nelson Dantas *Toledo* · Matheus Nachtergaele *Jonas* · Marco Ricca *Henrique* ■ *Dir* Bruno Barreto · *Scr* Leopoldo Serran, from the novel *O Que E Isso, Companheiro?* by Fernando Gabeira

Four Days inside Guantanamo ★★★★
Documentary
2010 · Aus/Can/UK · Colour · 110min

Using film recently declassified by the Ottawa authorities, this harrowing documentary reveals the illicit tactics used in the name of freedom. The movie follows the case of Canadian Omar Khadr, who was just 15 years old when he was accused of killing a US Army sergeant in Afghanistan. Khadr endured physical and psychological torment at Guantanamo Bay before finally pleading guilty to terrorist charges. The co-directors draw upon interrogation footage, expert analysis from fellow detainees and a range of lawyers, politicians, soldiers, journalists and activists to build a damning case exposing the inhumanity of Khadr's treatment. DP English, Arabic +subtitles. DVD

■ *Dir* Luc Côté, Patricio Henríquez

The Four Days of Naples
★★★★
Second World War drama   1962 · It · BW · 119min

The raw courage of a proud people rising against the Nazi yoke is brought home with eloquence and power in this Oscar-nominated drama from director Nanni Loy. Comparisons with Roberto Rossellini's *Rome, Open City* are somewhat flattering, but what this account of the events of September 1943 shares with that neorealist masterpiece is a sense of immediacy, as the Neopolitan population rebelled against a dictate that all males between the ages of five and 50 should be dispatched to labour camps. The ensemble playing is exceptional. DP Italian +subtitles.

Lea Massari *Maria* · Jean Sorel *Livornese* · Franco Sportelli *Professor Rosati* · Charles Belmont *Sailor* · Gian Maria Volonté *Stimolo* · Frank Wolff *Salvatore* · Domenico Formato *Gennaro Capuozzo* ■ *Dir* Nanni Loy · *Scr* Pasquale Festa Campanile, Massimo Franciosa, Nanni Loy, Carlo Benari, from a story by Vasco Pratolini, Pasquale Festa Campanile, Massimo Franciosa

Four Dogs Playing Poker
★★★ 15
Crime mystery thriller
1999 · US · Colour · 92min

Four art thieves lose a stolen million-dollar object before they can deliver it to bad guy Forest Whitaker, so they take out individual life insurance policies, then secretly assign one of their number to kill one of the others so they can collect the insurance and pay their debt. The twist is that no one will know who is to be the killer and who the victim. There are some fun perfomances, but the script is quite weak. JB DVD

Olivia Williams *Audrey* · Balthazar Getty *Julian* · Stacy Edwards *Holly* · Daniel London *Kevin* · Tim Curry *Felix* · Forest Whitaker *Ellington* · George Lazenby *Carlo* ■ *Dir* Paul Rachman · *Scr* Thomas Durham, William Quist

The Four Feathers ★★★
Silent war adventure   1929 · US · BW · 81min

This spectacular version of AEW Mason's famous novel was the last major Hollywood film to be made without any spoken dialogue, carrying only music and sound effects. Richard Arlen is the young officer given white feathers for displaying cowardice by three fellow soldiers – William Powell, Clive Brook and Theodore von Eltz – and his fiancée, played by Fay Wray in an early association with the *King Kong* team of Ernest B Schoedsack and Merian C Cooper. They began their film careers making wild-life documentaries and spent a year in Africa filming dramatic sequences with hippos and baboons – scenes that are well integrated into the story of Arlen redeeming himself in action. AE

Richard Arlen *Harry Faversham* · Fay Wray *Ethne Eustace* · Clive Brook *Lt Durrance* · William Powell *Capt Trench* · Theodore von Eltz *Lt Castleton* · Noah Beery Sr [Noah Beery] *Slave trader* · Zack Williams *Idris* · Noble Johnson *Ahmed* ■ *Dir* Merian C Cooper, Ernest B Schoedsack, Lothar Mendes · *Scr* Howard Estabrook, Hope Loring, from the novel by AEW Mason · *Producer* David Selznick [David O Selznick]

The Four Feathers
★★★★★ U
Classic adventure   1939 · UK · Colour · 110min

This screen version of AEW Mason's rousing adventure is one of the finest films made by the Korda brothers – producer Alexander, director Zoltan and art director Vincent. Everything about it is spot-on: the tightly constructed script, the rich colours and evocative location work, the perfectly paced editing and the pounding score by Miklos Rozsa. And we've not even begun to extol the virtues of the performances in this classic tale of man branded a coward by his friends who sets out to redeem himself in their eyes. It's a gem! (Korda made a thinly disguised remake of his classic in 1955 as *Storm over the Nile*.) DP DVD Blu

John Clements *Harry Faversham* · Ralph Richardson *Captain John Durrance* · C Aubrey Smith *General Burroughs* · June Duprez *Ethne Burroughs* · Allan Jeayes *General Faversham* · Jack Allen *Lieutenant Willoughby* · Donald Gray *Peter Burroughs* · Frederick Culley *Dr Sutton* ■ *Dir* Zoltan Korda · *Scr* RC Sherriff, Lajos Bíró,

F

Arthur Wimperis, from the novel by AEW Mason • *Cinematographers* Georges Périnal, Jack Cardiff, Osmond Borradaile

The Four Feathers ★★U
Period adventure   1978 · US · Colour · 99min

Given that the 1939 version is one of the all-time greats of British cinema, this TV remake was on a hiding to nothing. Beau Bridges looks out of place, but gives it his best shot as the disgraced officer who redeems himself when he goes undercover as a tribesman to help his three old military chums who have accused him of cowardice. The sterling efforts of a mainly British cast, including Robert Powell and Simon Ward, can't erase memories of earlier – and better – adaptations. JF *DVD*

Beau Bridges *Harry Faversham* • Jane Seymour (2) *Ethne Eustace* • Robert Powell *Jack Durrance* • Simon Ward *William Trench* • Harry Andrews *General David Faversham* • Richard Johnson *Abou Fatma* ■ *Dir* Don Sharp • *Scr* Gerald DiPego, from the novel by AEW Mason

The Four Feathers ★★★15
Period adventure
2002 · US/UK · Colour · 125min

In visual terms, Shekhar Kapur's filming of AEW Mason's novel has the grandiose qualities to justify a new interpretation. The film's major action sequence – a desert battle between a meagre British contingent and a vast Sudanese army – certainly reaches the thrill levels of *Zulu*. Its pacing and casting, however, have significant flaws, with too many drawn-out, talky sequences. Heath Ledger has heroic appeal as the disgraced officer who adopts a secret Arabic identity to assist his battalion, but Wes Bentley and Kate Hudson are stiff and unconvincing. JC *DVD*

Heath Ledger *Harry Faversham* • Wes Bentley *Jack Durrance* • Kate Hudson *Ethne Eustace* • Djimon Hounsou *Abou Fatma* • Michael Sheen *Trench* • Alex Jennings *Colonel Hamilton* • Tim Pigott-Smith *General Feversham* • Kris Marshall *Castelton* • Rupert Penry-Jones *Willoughby* ■ *Dir* Shekhar Kapur • *Scr* Michael Schiffer, Hossein Amini, from the novel by AEW Mason

4 for Texas ★★PG
Comedy western   1963 · US · Colour · 110min

This overlong, over-indulgent comedy western is sometimes quite amusing, despite the rather tiresome antics of Frank Sinatra and Dean Martin (whose production company made the film). They play the rivals who unite to defeat baddies Victor Buono and Charles Bronson. At least Sinatra had the good sense to hire a decent director in Robert Aldrich and no film that succeeds in roping in the excesses of Martin and Bronson can be totally unwatchable. TS

Frank Sinatra *Zack Thomas* • Dean Martin *Joe Jarrett* • Anita Ekberg *Elya Carlson* • Ursula Andress *Maxine Richter* • Charles Bronson *Matson* • Victor Buono *Harvey Burden* • Edric Connor *Prince George* ■ *Dir* Robert Aldrich • *Scr* Teddi Sherman, Robert Aldrich

Four Frightened People ★★★
Adventure   1934 · US · BW · 77min

This silly but entertaining survivalist melodrama, shot partly in Hawaii, has Claudette Colbert, Herbert Marshall and others hacking through the Malayan jungle because an on-board epidemic forces them to jump from a Dutch coastal steamer. Even away from ancient Rome, Cecil B DeMille still asks Colbert to strip off and take a bath. AT

Claudette Colbert *Judy Cavendish* • Herbert Marshall *Arnold Ainger* • Mary Boland *Mrs Mardick* • William Gargan *Stewart Corder* • Leo Carrillo *Montague* ■ *Dir* Cecil B DeMille • *Scr* Bartlett Cormack, Lenore Coffee, from the novel by E Arnot Robertson

The Four Horsemen of the Apocalypse ★★★
Silent First World War drama
1921 · US · BW · 114min

So much of this film is rubbish, and the stuff about two brothers fighting on opposing sides in the First World War is extremely tedious. However, in those scenes where Latin heart-throb Rudolph Valentino dances the tango or simply glowers dangerously, one is suddenly confronted with one of the most powerful of screen legends. Director Rex Ingram handles the apocalyptic climax very well. AT

Rudolph Valentino *Julio Desnoyers* • Alice Terry *Marguerite Laurier* • Pomeroy Cannon *Madariaga, the Centaur* • Josef Swickard *Marcelo Desnoyers* • Brinsley Shaw *Celendonio* • Alan Hale *Karl von Hartrott* • Bridgetta Clark *Dona Luisa* • Mabel Van Buren *Elena* ■ *Dir* Rex Ingram (1) • *Scr* June Mathis, from the novel *Los Cuatro Jinetes del Apocalipsis* by Vicente Blasco Ibáñez

The Four Horsemen of the Apocalypse ★★★
Second World War drama
1962 · US · Colour · 153min

The story of an Argentinian family torn apart by war became famous as the silent movie in which Rudolph Valentino danced the tango and catapulted to stardom. However, despite the array of talent on display and some stunning CinemaScope photography, this would-be extravaganza remains earthbound. It's not helped by the miscasting of Glenn Ford in the Valentino role, while updating the story to the Second World War doesn't wash. TS

Glenn Ford *Julio Desnoyers* • Ingrid Thulin *Marguerite Laurier* • Charles Boyer *Marcelo Desnoyers* • Lee J Cobb *Julio Madariaga* • Paul Henreid *Etienne Laurier* ■ *Dir* Vincente Minnelli • *Scr* Robert Ardrey, John Gay, from the novel *Los Cuatro Jinetes del Apocalipsis* by Vicente Blasco Ibáñez • *Cinematographer* Milton Krasner

LANDMARK FILM
François Truffaut's cornerstone of the *nouvelle vague* achieves immortality through its dramatic – and ambiguous – freeze-frame ending

The 400 Blows ★★★★★PG
Drama   1959 · Fr · BW · 95min

Former critic François Truffaut made his feature debut with this largely autobiographical drama. Made for a mere $75,000, it has echoes of Jean Vigo's *Zéro de Conduite*, although the influence of Jean Renoir and Italian neorealism is also evident. Introducing the character of Antoine Doinel, the story paints a grimly authentic portrait of troubled adolescence, with 13-year-old Jean-Pierre Léaud conveying both mischief and vulnerability in the lead role. The film won Truffaut the best director's prize at Cannes and sent ripples around world cinema with its audacious freeze-frame finale. The character of Antoine Doinel (and, indeed, Léaud himself) was to grow and mature through four further Truffaut films: *Love at Twenty* (1962), *Stolen Kisses* (1968), *Bed and Board* (1970) and *Love on the Run* (1979). DP French +subtitles. *DVD* *Blu*

Jean-Pierre Léaud *Antoine Doinel* • Claire Maurier *Mme Doinel* • Albert Rémy *M Doinel* • Guy Decomble *Teacher* • Patrick Auffay *René Bigey* • Georges Flamant *M Bigey* ■ *Dir* François Truffaut • *Scr* François Truffaut, Marcel Moussy, from a story by François Truffaut • *Cinematographer* Henri Decaë

Four in the Morning ★★★★12
Drama   1965 · UK · BW · 90min

The title's a clever pun, since the film deals with the time of a young girl's drowning, and with the (unrelated) trials and tribulations of two unnamed couples. Acclaimed in its day as a sharp slice of British neorealism, talented director/writer Anthony Simmons has done nothing quite as good. Judi Dench won a Bafta award for her role, while Ann Lynn, Norman Rodway and Brian Phelan have seldom been better. The bleak score by John Barry is superb. TS *DVD*

Ann Lynn *Girl* • Brian Phelan *Boy* • Judi Dench *Wife* • Norman Rodway *Husband* • Joe Melia *Friend* ■ *Dir/Scr* Anthony Simmons

The Four Just Men ★★★
Drama   1939 · UK · BW · 87min

Gathering war clouds cast their shadows over this adaptation of novelist Edgar Wallace's ingenious imperial thriller. Produced by Michael Balcon at Ealing, it defiantly suggests that Britain could never fall under the sway of a dictator. But in all other respects it's a rollicking *Boys' Own* adventure, with some of the most fiendishly comic book murders you will ever see. Hugh Sinclair, Frank Lawton, Griffith Jones and Francis L Sullivan unite gallantly to prevent treacherous Basil Sydney from helping enemy agents sabotage the Suez Canal. DP

Hugh Sinclair *Humphrey Mansfield* • Griffith Jones *James Brodie* • Francis L Sullivan *Leon Poiccard* • Frank Lawton *Terry* • Anna Lee *Ann Lodge* • Alan Napier *Sir Hamar Ryman MP* ■ *Dir* Walter Forde • *Scr* Angus MacPhail, Sergei Nolbandov, Roland Pertwee, from a novel by Edgar Wallace

Four Last Songs ★★15
Romantic comedy drama
2007 · UK/Sp · Colour · 97min

Despite the gorgeous Mallorca locations, there is nothing summery about this hackneyed, overwrought comedy/drama. Stanley Tucci plays an expat American pianist eking out a living on an idyllic Mediterranean island with girlfriend and singer Jessica Stevenson. Frustrated that he is yet to achieve anything in life, he has come up with the idea of staging a concert devoted to a renowned composer who had lived on the island. However, it's not long before his dream project begins to unravel. The talented ensemble cast do their best, but they are ultimately let down by director Francesca Joseph's dreary, teary script. JF English, Spanish +subtitles.

Stanley Tucci *Larry* • Rhys Ifans *Dickie* • Hugh Bonneville *Sebastian Burrows* • Jena Malone *Frankie* • Jessica Stevenson *Miranda* • Virgile Bramly *Narciso Ortega* ■ *Dir/Scr* Francesca Joseph

Four Lions ★★★★15
Satirical black comedy
2010 · UK/Fr · Colour · 97min

Satirist extraordinaire Chris Morris (TV's *The Day Today* and *Brass Eye*) makes his directorial debut with this audacious jihad comedy, pointing out that "terrorism is about ideology, but it's also about berks". The berks in question here are a group of hapless young Muslim men from the north of England. They decide to become suicide bombers and then chaotically attempt to plan and commit a terrorist atrocity at the London Marathon. Morris's movie is very funny, occasionally emulating the faux quaintness of Ealing. Yet perhaps the most disturbing element of *Four Lions* is that the putative suicide bombers are a mostly likeable bunch. AS English, Urdu, Arabic +subtitles. *DVD* *Blu*

Riz Ahmed [Rizwan Ahmed] *Omar* • Arsher Ali *Hassan* • Nigel Lindsay *Barry* • Kayvan Novak *Waj* • Adeel Akhtar *Faisal* • Benedict Cumberbatch *Negotiator* • Julia Davis *Alice* ■ *Dir* Chris Morris [Christopher Morris (2)] • *Scr* Chris Morris, Jesse Armstrong, Sam Bain, Simon Blackwell

4 Little Girls ★★★★15
Documentary
1997 · US · BW and Colour · 102min

Spike Lee's Oscar-nominated account of the murder of four young African-Americans by white supremacist bombers is as chilling as it is compelling. Using interviews, cuttings and archive footage to establish the segregational fervour that existed in Birmingham, Alabama in 1963, Lee not only describes how Denise McNair, Cynthia Wesley, Addie Mae Collins and Carole Rosamund Robertson met their fate, but also suggests how much poorer the world has been for their loss. The arrogance of Klan killer Robert Chambliss is hard to bear, but nothing prepares you for the morgue photographs of the dead girls. Not to be ignored. DP *DVD*

■ *Dir* Spike Lee

Four Men and a Prayer ★★★12
Mystery drama   1938 · US · BW · 82min

In spite of a slow start and a humdrum romantic diversion, this is a serviceable adventure mystery from master director John Ford. The gung-ho quartet of the title are the sons of old soldier C Aubrey Smith, who come face to face with a gang of gunrunners while investigating their father's death. Although George Sanders and William Henry have some fun back in Blighty, Richard Greene and David Niven get rather bogged down feuding over Loretta Young in Buenos Aires. The Brits are solid, but it's the acting of supports Alan Hale and John Carradine that catches the eye. DP *DVD*

George Sanders *Wyatt Leigh* • David Niven *Christopher Leigh* • Richard Greene *Geoff Leigh* • William Henry *Rodney Leigh* • Loretta Young *Lynn Cherrington* • C Aubrey Smith *Colonel Loring Leigh* • J Edward Bromberg *General Torres* • Alan Hale *Furnoy* • John Carradine *General Adolfo Arturo Sebastian* ■ *Dir* John Ford • *Scr* Richard Sherman, Sonya Levien, Walter Ferris, from the novel by David Garth

Four Minutes ★★★
Sports drama based on a true story
2005 · US · Colour and BW · 90min

In these days of pampered sporting prima donnas, this account of Roger Bannister's assault on the four-minute-mile barrier makes for edifying viewing. According to Frank Deford's screenplay, Bannister (Jamie Maclachlan) was torn between his medical studies and his athletic potential, and rose to the mile challenge almost as an act of patriotism following the conquest of Everest in 1953. The romantic subplots prove something of a distraction but, once Maclachlan knuckles down to training with disabled coach Christopher Plummer, the action comes alive. DP

Jamie Maclachlan *Roger Bannister* • Christopher Plummer *Archie Mason* • Shaun Smyth *Norris McWhirter* • Amy Rutherford *Moyra Jacobsson* • Drew Carnwath *Chris Brasher* ■ *Dir* Charles Beeson • *Scr* Frank Deford, from his article *Hillary and Bannister*

Four Minutes ★★★15
Drama   2006 · Ger · Colour · 110min

Veteran actress Monica Bleibtreu plays Traude, an elderly piano teacher at a maximum security women's prison. Hannah Herzsprung is Jenny, an emotionally disturbed former child piano prodigy who has done the crime (murder) and is now doing the time. Chris Kraus's film traces the love/hate relationship that develops between these two women, who are struggling with traumatic incidents from their past. Bleibtreu is terrific as Traude, her performance an object lesson in restraint and underplaying. Herzsprung, by contrast, convincingly chews the scenery. The film's finale is perhaps a little over the top, but overall this German drama is an intense and absorbing character study. DA German +subtitles. *DVD*

Monica Bleibtreu *Traude Krüger* • Hannah Herzsprung *Jenny von Loeben* • Sven Pippig *Mütze* • Richy Müller *Kowalski* • Jasmin Tabatabai *Ayse* ■ *Dir/Scr* Chris Kraus

4 Months, 3 Weeks and 2 Days ★★★★★15
Drama
2007 · Rom/Neth/Fr/Ger · Colour · 108min

Director Cristian Mungiu's Palme d'Or winner not only explores the emotional trauma involved in an abortion, but also exposes the venality of life under the detested Ceausescu regime. Set in Bucharest in the late 1980s, the story of student Anamaria Marinca's bid to help a roommate terminate her pregnancy is full of agonising moments. Mungiu achieves a relentless control over the action that captures place, performance and psychology with devastating simplicity. DP Romanian, English +subtitles. *DVD*

Anamaria Marinca *Otilia* • Laura Vasiliu *Gabita* • Vlad Ivanov *Mr Bebe* • Alexandru Potocean *Adi Radu* • Luminita Gheorghiu *Gina Radu, Adi's* mother • Adi Carauleanu *Dr Radu, Adi's father* • *Dir/Scr* Cristian Mungiu • *Cinematographer* Oleg Mutu

Four Mothers ★★★ U

Drama 1941 · US · BW · 84min

This is the last in a trilogy about small-town family life, sparked off by the huge success of *Four Daughters* in 1938, which was followed by the less compelling *Four Wives* in 1939. The Lemp sisters, played in all three films by the Lane sisters and Gale Page, are now happily married but they are plunged into financial disaster when one of the brothers-in-law loses all their money in a failed land scheme. Cosy, comforting nostalgia. RK

Priscilla Lane *Ann Lemp Dietz* • Rosemary Lane *Kay Lemp Forrest* • Lola Lane *Thea Lemp Crowley* • Gale Page *Emma Lemp Talbot* • Claude Rains *Adam Lemp* • Jeffrey Lynn *Felix Dietz* • Eddie Albert *Clint Forrest* • May Robson *Aunt Etta* ■ *Dir* William Keighley • *Scr* Stephen Morehouse Avery, from the short story *Sister Act* by Fannie Hurst

The Four Musketeers ★★★ PG

Swashbuckling comedy adventure 1974 · Pan/Sp · Colour · 102min

This sequel was shot at the same time as its more illustrious predecessor *The Three Musketeers*, but without the knowledge of its cast, who sued producer Alexander Salkind for back-pay. The action brings Faye Dunaway to the fore, as she seeks to trap the dashing blades by imprisoning Michael York's beloved, Raquel Welch. There is a nice demonstration of screen villainy from Christopher Lee, but director Richard Lester can't resist tilting the swashbuckling into slapstick, with uneven results. Lester revisited the saga 15 years later with *The Return of the Musketeers*. DP DVD

Oliver Reed *Athos* • Faye Dunaway *Milady de Winter* • Michael York *D'Artagnan* • Raquel Welch *Constance Bonancieux* • Richard Chamberlain *Aramis* • Frank Finlay *Porthos* • Simon Ward *Duke of Buckingham* • Christopher Lee *Rochefort* • Charlton Heston *Cardinal Richelieu* • Geraldine Chaplin *Anne of Austria* ■ *Dir* Richard Lester • *Scr* George MacDonald Fraser, from the novel *The Three Musketeers* by Alexandre Dumas

Four Nights of a Dreamer ★★★

Drama 1971 · Fr/It · Colour · 82min

Having made his colour debut with *A Gentle Creature*, Robert Bresson returned to Dostoyevsky for this exploration of obsessive passion and the romantic treachery of nocturnal Paris. In relating the tale of an artist's love for the girl he dissuades from suicide, Bresson achieves an erotic realism that makes the promise of lasting love all the more tantalising and impossible. With its occasionally precious visuals and stilted dialogue, this is one of Bresson's few disappointments. DP French +subtitles.

Isabelle Weingarten *Marthe* • Guillaume Des Forêts *Jacques* • Jean-Maurice Monnoyer *The lodger* • Giorgio Maulini • Lydia Biondi [Lidia Biondi] *Marthe's mother* ■ *Dir* Robert Bresson • *Scr* Robert Bresson, from the story *White Nights* by Fyodor Dostoyevsky

The Four Poster ★★

Comedy drama 1953 · US · BW · 102min

Although they were married in real life, Rex Harrison and Lilli Palmer were not perhaps the ideal couple to star in this adaptation. Spanning 45 years of marriage, this boudoir drama requires more raw emotion than the sophisticated spouses were prepared to invest, especially in the scene of the death of their soldier son. Informative, as well as amusing, the seven animated intrascenes were created by the UPA studio duo of John Hubley and Paul Julian. DP

Rex Harrison *John* • Lilli Palmer *Abby* ■ *Dir* Irving Reis • *Scr* Allan Scott, from Jan de Hartog's play by • *Music* Dmitri Tiomkin

4: Rise of the Silver Surfer ★★★ PG

Fantasy action adventure 2007 · US · Colour · 88min

Sidestepping the fashionable angst of other comic-book adaptations, the confident *Fantastic Four* franchise delivers its second helping, with Tim Story resuming directing duties. This time, the blue-suited superhero "family" must prevent the end of the world as fabled airborne foe the Silver Surfer (voiced by Laurence Fishburne but given human shape by Doug Jones) wreaks havoc from his board. Welshman Ioan Gruffudd demonstrates an improved American accent as Mr Fantastic and *Nip/Tuck's* Julian McMahon is back to provide some belated camp vil ainy as the team's nemesis, Dr Doom. Trading in colourful spectacle, family-friendly fun and undemanding storylines, this is perfect popcorn for those who aren't looking for the teenage tantrums of Spider-Man or the sombre tone of the Dark Knight trilogy. AC DVD

Ioan Gruffudd *Reed Richards/Mr Fantastic* • Jessica Alba *Sue Storm/Invisible Woman* • Chris Evans *Johnny Storm/Human Torch* • Michael Chiklis *Ben Grimm/The Thing* • Doug Jones *Silver Surfer/Norrin Radd* • Kerry Washington *Alicia Masters* • Julian McMahon *Victor Von Doom/Dr Doom* • Laurence Fishburne *Silver Surfer* • Stan Lee *Rejected wedding guest* ■ *Dir* Tim Story • *Scr* Mark Frost, Don Payne, from a story by Mark Frost, John Turman, from characters by Stan Lee (writer), Jack Kirby (artist)

Four Rooms ★ 18

Portmanteau comedy drama 1995 · US · Colour · 93min

Here's proof that wonderkid Quentin Tarantino is fallible. He's the driving force behind this horribly botched portmanteau movie and he also directs and stars in one segment. Set in the same hotel, the four stories are loosely linked by inept bellboy Tim Roth. Allison Anders's story of a witch's coven is slight and silly; Alexandre Rockwell fares little better n a farcical yarn of a lover's tiff; while Tarantino's effort barely passes muster as an anecdote. The best of the bunch is Robert Rodriguez's, a cartoon-like tale of Roth playing babysitter to a gangster's psychopathic children. JF

Tim Roth *Ted the Bellhop* • Lawrence Bender *Long Hair Yuppy Scum* • Marisa Tomei *Margaret* • Madonna *Elspeth* • Amanda De Cadenet *Diana* • Antonio Banderas *Man* • Salma Hayek *TV dancing girl* • Quentin Tarantino *Chester* • Bruce Willis *Leo* ■ *Dir/Scr* Allison Anders, Alexandre Rockwell, Robert Rodriguez, Quentin Tarantino

The Four Seasons ★★★ 15

Comedy drama 1981 · US · Colour · 103min

Alan Alda's directorial debut is as waspishly decent-hearted as you'd expect, with its exploration of American middle-class habits. Three married couples regularly take their holidays together, but find this complacent routine faltering when one husband falls for a younger woman. A rather stodgy narrative is transcended by fine performances from Carol Burnett, Len Cariou, Sandy Dennis, Jack Weston and Alda himself. TH Swearing, brief nudity.

Alan Alda *Jack Burroughs* • Carol Burnett *Kate Burroughs* • Len Cariou *Nick Callan* • Sandy Dennis *Anne Callan* • Rita Moreno *Claudia Zimmer* • Jack Weston *Danny Zimmer* • Bess Armstrong *Ginny Newley* • Elizabeth Alda *Beth* • Beatrice Alda *Lisa* ■ *Dir/Scr* Alan Alda

Four Sided Triangle ★★ PG

Science fiction 1953 · UK · BW · 77min

When scientists Stephen Murray and John Van Eyssen fall in love with the same girl (Barbara Payton), they solve their rivalry by making a duplicate of her. One of the earliest Hammer movies made prior to their international breakthrough with *The Quatermass Xperiment* and *The Curse of Frankenstein*, this slow-moving tale is directed by Terence Fisher with little flair. AJ DVD

Barbara Payton *Lena/Helen* • Percy Marmont *Sir Walter* • James Hayter *Dr Harvey* • Stephen Murray *Bill* • John Van Eyssen *Robin* • Glynn

Dearman *Bill as a child* • Sean Barrett (1) *Robin as a child* ■ *Dir* Terence Fisher • *Scr* Terence Fisher, Paul Tabori, from the novel by William F Temple

Four Sons ★★★★

Silent First World War drama 1928 · US · BW · 100min

This heartbreaking opus from the great director John Ford, about a widow whose sons fight on opposite sides during the First World War, is a formidable piece of cinema. There are few more moving moments than those in which the postman (superbly delineated by Albert Gran) arrives bearing news of the sons, while the long-suffering Bavarian mother is brilliantly portrayed by Margaret Mann. The climactic sequence of her finally arriving at New York's Ellis Island will leave no handkerchief dry, and was amazingly influential on film-makers as diverse as Elia Kazan and Francis Ford Coppola. Fox remade the story in 1940, but the addition of sound and the efforts of director Archie Mayo could not improve on Ford's film. TS

James Hall *Joseph Bernle* • Margaret Mann *Mother Bernle* • Earle Foxe *Von Stomm* • Charles Morton *Johann Bernle* • Francis X Bushman Jr [Ralph Bushman] *Franz Bernle* • George Meeker *Andres Bernle* • Albert Gran *Letter Carrier* ■ *Dir* John Ford • *Scr* Philip Klein, HH Caldwell (titles), Katherine Hilliker (titles), from the story *Grandmother Bernle Learns Her Letters* by Ida Alexa Ross Wylie

Four Sons ★★

Second World War drama 1940 · US · BW · 88min

The remake of the 1928 silent picture is updated to cover Hitler's inexorable march into Czechoslovakia, an event which has a cataclysmic impact on a mother and her four sons. One flees to America, one becomes a Nazi, another joins the resistance and the youngest fights for the Third Reich in Poland. It probably served its propagandist purpose well enough in 1940, but it seems schematic nowadays. AT

Don Ameche *Chris* • Eugenie Leontovich *Frau Bernie* • Mary Beth Hughes *Anna* • Alan Curtis *Karl* • George Ernest *Fritz* • Robert Lowery *Joseph* • Lionel Royce *Max Sturm* ■ *Dir* Archie Mayo • *Scr* John Howard Lawson, Milton Sperling, from a story by IAR Wylie

Four Steps in the Clouds ★★★★

Comedy drama 1942 · It · BW · 96min

This charming comedy signalled a stylistic shift in Italian film-making. Its enshrinement as the herald of neorealism is perhaps a little excessive, especially as its emphasis is more firmly on serenading the national spirit and satirising the contrasting temperaments of town and country than exposing the impoverishing legacy of fascism. But the nostalgic authenticity with which Alessandro Blasetti invests his delicate tale of deception, in which henpecked Gino Cervi poses as pregnant waif Adriana Benetti's husband, gives it an irresistible slice-of-life feel. Remade in 1995 as *A Walk in the Clouds*. DP In Italian.

Gino Cervi *Paolo Bianchi* • Giuditta Rissone *Clara Bianchi* • Adriana Benetti *Maria* • Guido Celano *Pasquale, Maria's brother* • Aldo Silvani *Luca, Maria's father* ■ *Dir* Alessandro Blasetti • *Scr* Aldo De Benedetti, Giuseppe Amato, Alessandro Blasetti, Cesare Zavattini, from the story *Quattro Passi fra le Nuvole* by Cesare Zavattini, Piero Tellini

4.3.2.1 ★★ 15

Crime thriller 2010 · UK · Colour · 111min

A quartet of female pals find their lives turned upside down over a madcap weekend after unwittingly tangling with diamond thieves in this city-hopping comedy thriller from *Kidulthood* creator Noel Clarke. The multi-strand story winds backwards and forwards when required, throwing in chases, punch-ups, girl-on-girl action, and family tensions in a flurry of fast-cuts, music cues and flashy split-screen. It's about as substantial as a layer of lipstick, but the film's brazen cheek still

raises a smile. TJ Violence, swearing, sex scenes, drug abuse. DVD

Emma Roberts *Joanne "Jo"* • Noel Clarke *Tee* • Tamsin Egerton *Cassandra "Cass"* • Ophelia Lovibond *Shannon* • Shanika Warren-Markland *Kerrys* • Michelle Ryan *Kelly* • Ben Miller *Mr Phillips* • Sean Pertwee *Mr Richards* • Kevin Smith *Big Larry* ■ *Dir* Noel Clarke, Mark Davis • *Scr* Noel Clarke

Four Weddings and a Funeral ★★★★★ 15

Romantic comedy 1994 · UK · Colour · 112min

No one could have foreseen that this glorified sitcom would change the nature of British screen comedy. The tale of a foppish bachelor, his eccentric friends and their romantic escapades is extremely funny, charming, poignant and never anything less than hugely enjoyable. Neatly structured and full of genuine warmth for its characters, Richard Curtis's Oscar-nominated screenplay is superbly observed and is well served by Mike Newell's deft direction. But more important to the film's enduring appeal is the individuality of the performances. Simon Callow and Kristin Scott Thomas are outstanding alongside star Hugh Grant, who became an overnight sensation. DP Swearing. DVD

Hugh Grant *Charles* • Andie MacDowell *Carrie* • Kristin Scott Thomas *Fiona* • James Fleet *Tom* • Simon Callow *Gareth* • John Hannah *Matthew* • David Bower *David* • Charlotte Coleman *Scarlett* • Corin Redgrave *Hamish* • Rowan Atkinson *Father Gerald* • Anna Chancellor *Henrietta* • Timothy Walker *Angus* • Rosalie Crutchley *Mrs Beaumont* ■ *Dir* Mike Newell • *Scr* Richard Curtis

Four Wives ★★

Drama 1939 · US · BW · 108min

John Garfield caused a sensation in *Four Daughters* playing a brash misfit and musical genius who kills himself. This sequel keeps his memory alive as his young widow (Priscilla Lane) discovers she will be having his baby. Garfield also returns as a ghostly vision. The result is trite and overlong, but director Michael Curtiz still generates warmth between the characters and his fluid camera style keeps up the momentum. A further sequel, *Four Mothers*, followed. AE

Priscilla Lane *Ann Lemp Borden* • Rosemary Lane *Kay Lemp* • Lola Lane *Thea Lemp Crowley* • Gale Page *Emma Lemp* • Claude Rains *Adam Lemp* • John Garfield *Mickey Borden* ■ *Dir* Michael Curtiz • *Scr* Julius J Epstein, Philip G Epstein, Maurice Hanline, from the story *Sister Act* by Fannie Hurst

Four's a Crowd ★★ U

Romantic comedy 1938 · US · BW · 91min

Errol Flynn as a PR man, Rosalind Russell as an ace reporter, Patric Knowles as a playboy newspaper proprietor and Olivia de Havilland as an heiress. Blend thoroughly and hand to Michael Curtiz for careful cooking. Sadly, though, the result lacks the sparkle promised by the cast and director, and the script is merely a rehash of other, better pictures, which gives it a rather jaded air. JF

Errol Flynn *Robert "Bob" Kensington Lansford* • Olivia de Havilland *Lorri Dillingwell* • Rosalind Russell *Jean Christy* • Patric Knowles *Patterson Buckley* • Walter Connolly *John P Dillingwell* • Hugh Herbert *Silas Jenkins* ■ *Dir* Michael Curtiz • *Scr* Casey Robinson, Sid Herzig, from the novel *All Rights Reserved* by Wallace Sullivan

Fourteen Hours ★★★★

Suspense drama based on a true story 1951 · US · BW · 91min

Richard Basehart threatens to end it all from a New York skyscraper in this exciting suspense drama, gutwrenchingly directed by Henry Hathaway and based on a real-life incident. The crowd of onlookers that gathers becomes a character in itself, with stars-to-be on view including Debra Paget and Jeffrey Hunter, plus the debut of young Grace Kelly, playing an estranged wife who is prompted by Basehart's plight to take another crack at marriage. Agnes Moorehead and Robert Keith are

F

12 15 18 PASSED FOR PEOPLE OF THESE AGES AND OVER   DVD RELEASED ON DVD   RELEASED ON BLU-RAY   3D RELEASED IN 3D   CS END CREDIT SEQUENCE   **463**

particularly effective as the would-be suicide's parents. TS

Paul Douglas *Dunnigan* • Richard Basehart *Robert Cosick* • Barbara Bel Geddes *Virginia* • Debra Paget *Ruth* • Agnes Moorehead *Mrs Cosick* • Robert Keith (1) *Mr Cosick* • Howard Da Silva *Lieutenant Moksar* • Jeffrey Hunter *Danny* • Grace Kelly *Mrs Fuller* ■ *Dir* Henry Hathaway • *Scr* John Paxton, from the story *The Man on the Ledge* by Joel Sayre

1492: Conquest of Paradise ★★★★ 15

Historical drama
1992 • US/Sp/Fr/UK • Colour • 149min

Despite a rather wobbly first hour, when it's hard to understand Gérard Depardieu's accent or make out Sigourney Weaver's scheming Spanish queen in the gloomy light, Ridley Scott's film marking the 500th anniversary of the discovery of the New World gathers momentum with the voyage, captures in dazzling imagery the actual discovery, and then produces a horrific and masterly final segment as Columbus returns on a second voyage to preside over slaughter and the raising of a giant church bell. Woefully underrated by many critics, this boasts an eerily atmospheric score by Vangelis. AT Violence. *DVD*

Gérard Depardieu *Christopher Columbus* • Armand Assante *Sanchez* • Sigourney Weaver *Queen Isabel* • Loren Dean *Older Fernando* • Angela Molina *Beatrix* • Fernando Rey *Marchena* • Michael Wincott *Moxica* • Tcheky Karyo *Pinzon* • Kevin Dunn *Captain Mendez* ■ *Dir* Ridley Scott • *Scr* Roselyne Bosch

1408 ★★★ 15

Supernatural horror thriller
2007 • US • Colour • 107min

Swedish director Mikael Hafstrom bucks the current trend for gratuitous splatter horror with this simple yet effective psychological chiller. Based on a Stephen King short story, it's an old-school creep-out, in which mounting dread and twisted mind games remind us that scares don't have to come drenched with gore. In a powerfully nuanced performance, John Cusack plays a paranormal debunker who checks into the allegedly haunted suite 1408 as part of his research for a new book. Although the hotel's manager (Samuel L Jackson) warns him of his folly, the sceptical writer is determined to disprove the ghostly rumours. For the first two thirds of its running time, this is a masterclass in slow-drip fear, exploiting every sound and visual for maximum effect. It's only when Hafstrom goes CGI crazy in the final act that the film unravels. SF Violence, swearing. *DVD*

John Cusack *Mike Enslin* • Samuel L Jackson *Gerald Olin* • Mary McCormack *Lily Enslin* • Jasmine Jessica Anthony *Katie* • Tony Shalhoub *Sam Farrell* • Kim Thomson *Desk clerk* • Drew Powell *Assistant hotel manager* ■ *Dir* Mikael Hafstrom • *Scr* Matt Greenberg, Scott Alexander, Larry Karaszewski, from the short story by Stephen King

The Fourth Angel ★★ 15

Thriller
2001 • Can/UK • Colour • 91min

Originally due for an earlier US release, director John Irvin's thoughtful revenge thriller had to give way to post-11 September sensitivity. On a holiday flight to India, the family of magazine editor Jeremy Irons is involved in a hijack and killed. When the hijackers are released on a technicality, Irons turns into a gun-wielding Charles Bronson clone and starts to hunt them down. Despite moderate tension and an interesting cast, Irvin stretches credibility to breaking point. AJ *DVD*

Jeremy Irons *Jack Elgin* • Forest Whitaker *Agent Jules Bernard* • Charlotte Rampling *Kate Stockton* • Jason Priestley *Davidson* • Ian McNeice *MI5 officer* ■ *Dir* John Irvin • *Scr* Allan Scott, from the novel by Robin Hunter

The Fourth Kind ★ 15

Science-fiction mystery thriller
2009 • US • Colour • 93min

Are the unusual numbers of disappearances in an Alaskan backwater really the result of alien abduction? In this sluggish hoax UFO

thriller, psychiatrist Milla Jovovich sets out to prove that it is, by delving into the subconscious of her patients using hypnosis. Supposedly based on true events, this is a risible and boring tale containing no aliens, an off-screen abduction and unsatisfying blurred imagery. Consider it a mere close encounter of the cheating kind. AJ Violence. *DVD* *SL*

Milla Jovovich *Dr Abigail Tyler* • Elias Koteas *Dr Campos* • Will Patton *Sheriff August* • Hakeem Kae-Kazim *Alolowa* • Enzo Cilenti *Scott Stracinsky* • Mia McKenna-Bruce *Ashley* ■ *Dir* Olatunde Osunsanmi • *Scr* Olatunde Osunsanmi, from a story by Osunsanmi, Terry Lee Robbins

The Fourth Man ★★★★ 18

Black comedy thriller
1983 • Neth • Colour • 98min

This is an early nightmarish, and typically allegorical fantasy from Dutch director Paul Verhoeven and cinematographer-turned-director Jan De Bont. Homosexual writer Jeroen Krabbé suffers horrific premonitions after he meets attractive blonde Renée Soutendijk, whose last three husbands have all died in mysterious circumstances. Is he to be her fourth victim, lured into her black widow's web by her attractive bisexual lover Thom Hoffman? Obliquely eerie, explicitly erotic and perversely hilarious, this is an intricate, symbolic shocker. AJ Dutch +subtitles. *DVD*

Jeroen Krabbé *Gerard Reve* • Renée Soutendijk *Christine Halsslag* • Thom Hoffman *Herman* • Dolf de Vries *De Vries* • Geert De Jong *Ria* ■ *Dir* Paul Verhoeven • *Scr* Gerard Soeteman, from a novel by Gerard Reve • *Cinematographer* Jan De Bont

The Fourth Protocol ★★ 15

Spy thriller
1987 • UK • Colour • 113min

Before getting his big break as 007, Pierce Brosnan got to play a dastardly Russian agent out to blow up an American air base in England in this Cold War spy thriller. Michael Caine is the less-than-super agent out to stop him, and a familiar cavalcade of British actors (plus the odd visiting American) is on hand to help or hinder him. Tired and not particularly relevant. JF Swearing, violence, nudity. *DVD*

Michael Caine *John Preston* • Pierce Brosnan *Major Valeri Petrofsky* • Joanna Cassidy *Irina Vassilieva* • Ned Beatty *General Borisov* • Ray McAnally *General Karpov* ■ *Dir* John Mackenzie (1) • *Scr* Frederick Forsyth, Richard Burridge, from the novel by Frederick Forsyth

The Fourth War ★★ 15

Thriller
1990 • US • Colour • 86min

It's November 1988 and Roy Scheider is a gung-ho Vietnam veteran who embarks on a private war with Soviet hothead Jürgen Prochnow (himself an embittered casualty of Afghanistan) after he witnesses the death of a defector during one of his reckless sorties beyond the checkpoint on the Czech-West German border. This dreary piece of macho posturing is another disappointment from director John Frankenheimer. DP Violence, swearing.

Roy Scheider *Colonel Jack Knowles* • Jürgen Prochnow *Colonel NA Valachev* • Tim Reid *Lt Col Timothy Clark* • Lara Harris *Elena Novotna* • Harry Dean Stanton *General Roger Hackworth* ■ *Dir* John Frankenheimer • *Scr* Stephen Peters, Kenneth Ross, from the novel by Stephen Peters

The Fox ★★★

Drama
1967 • US • Colour • 110min

From glamour girl to drama diva, Anne Heywood made the transition in fine style, marrying producer Raymond Stross and starring in this risqué adaptation of the DH Lawrence novella. It details the long-term relationship of lesbians Heywood and Sandy Dennis that's disrupted by the arrival of handyman Keir Dullea. Dennis's twitchiness is almost laughable at times, but Heywood's portrayal of aching insecurity is memorably poignant. TH

Sandy Dennis *Jill* • Keir Dullea *Paul* • Anne Heywood *Ellen March* • Glyn Morris *Realtor* ■ *Dir* Mark Rydell • *Scr* Lewis John Carlino, Howard Koch, from the novella by DH Lawrence

Fox and His Friends ★★★★ 15

Drama
1975 • W Ger • Colour • 118min

Director Rainer Werner Fassbinder also plays the title role of an unemployed carnival worker in this penetrating melodrama. Picked up by an antique dealer after winning the lottery and introduced into an effete bourgeois homosexual milieu, he is exploited, abused and driven to despair. The working class victim was based on Armin Meier, one of Fassbinder's former lovers, a young butcher to whom the film is dedicated. Although an honest portrayal of homosexual relationships, Fassbinder's absorbing film is ultimately more concerned with class exploitation. RB German +subtitles. *SL*

Rainer Werner Fassbinder *Fox* • Peter Chatel *Eugen* • Karl-Heinz Böhm [Karlheinz Böhm] *Max* • Harry Baer *Philip* • Adrian Hoven *Father* • Ulla Jacobsson *Mother* • Christiane Maybach *Hedwig* ■ *Dir* Rainer Werner Fassbinder • *Scr* Christian Hohoff, Rainer Werner Fassbinder

The Fox and the Child ★★★ U

Wildlife drama
2007 • Fr • Colour • 90min

After *March of the Penguins*, Luc Jacquet opted for gentler, warmer climes for his follow-up feature. The mountains of Ain in his native France provide the setting for a year in the life of the relationship between a wild fox and a small girl. If *Penguins* was nature raw in beak and claw, this drama comes perilously close to a Disney true-life adventure. Wildlife movie purists may bridle at the very traditional approach of this family-friendly tale – especially the cheesily happy ending. But the photography is stunning, and the essential sweetness of the story should ensure that younger audiences at least are riveted. Kate Winslet narrates. DA French dubbed. *DVD*

Bertille Noël-Bruneau *The girl* • Isabelle Carré *The girl as an adult* • Thomas Laliberté *The boy* • Kate Winslet *Narrator* ■ *Dir* Luc Jacquet • *Scr* Luc Jacquet, Eric Rognard, from a story by Jacquet • *Cinematographer* Gérard Simon

The Fox and the Hound ★★★ U

Animated adventure
1981 • US • Colour • 79min

Disney animation was still reckoned to be in the doldrums when this charming tale of animal friendship was produced, and it probably has a lower profile than it deserves. A young hound pup is befriended by a fox cub and they become firm chums. Once grown, the hound warns his foxy friend to keep away from the hunt and his cruel master, but the fox proves his courage when he saves the hound from a marauding bear. A parable about the power of friendship. JF *DVD* *SL*

Mickey Rooney *Tod* • Kurt Russell *Copper* • Pearl Bailey *Big Mama* • Jack Albertson *Amos Slade* • Sandy Duncan *Vixey* • Jeanette Nolan *Widow Tweed* ■ *Dir* Art Stevens, Ted Berman, Richard Rich • *Scr* Larry Clemmons, Ted Berman, Peter Young, Steve Hulett, David Michener, Burny Mattinson, Earl Kress, Vance Gerry, from the novel by Daniel P Mannix

The Fox and the Hound 2 ★★ U

Animated adventure
2007 • US • Colour • 66min

This straight-to-DVD animated sequel from Disney revisits the story of Tod the fox and Copper the hound dog, but rather than picking up where the 1981 original left off, it follows the duo in their cute youth. When Copper joins visiting canine act the Singin' Strays, Tod feels left out and finds a kindred spirit in the diva-like Dixie, whose place in the act has been taken by Copper. They conspire to return things to normal and put both Tod and Copper's friendship and the band in jeopardy. The slight story is rather short on adventure, but youngsters should enjoy the slapstick chase sequences. JH

Harrison Fahn *Copper* • Jonah Bobo *Tod* • Patrick Swayze *Cash* • Reba McEntire *Dixie* • Jeff Foxworthy *Lyle* • Vicki Lawrence *Granny Rose* ■ *Dir* Jim Kammerud • *Scr* Rich Burns, Roger SH Schulman, from characters by Daniel P Mannix

Foxcatcher ★★★★★ 15

Sports drama based on a true story
2014 • US • Colour • 128min

Although the plot of *Foxcatcher* was inspired by real events widely reported at the time, it's best to learn as little about it as possible in order to fully savour this superb film's surprises and shocks. Channing Tatum and Mark Ruffalo accept an invitation to build up a top-class team for weird billionaire sponsor Steve Carell (almost unrecognisable), but is Carell just interested in the sport? Exquisitely calibrated art direction, sound design and cinematography gild the lily. LF *DVD* *SL*

Steve Carell *John du Pont* • Channing Tatum *Mark Schultz* • Mark Ruffalo *David Schultz* • Sienna Miller *Nancy Schultz* ■ *Dir* Bennett Miller • *Scr* Dan Futterman, E Max Frye

Foxes ★★★ 15

Drama
1980 • US • Colour • 101min

Ex-TV commercial director Adrian Lyne made his feature film debut with this slick movie about four teenage girls and their problems with life and men. A young Jodie Foster is the straight arrow sorting out her friends, which include podgy, unloved Marilyn Kagan, compulsive liar Kandice Stroh, and abused hooker Cherie Currie. The girls overcome the clichés. JB *DVD*

Jodie Foster *Jeanie* • Scott Baio *Brad* • Sally Kellerman *Mary* • Randy Quaid *Jay* • Marilyn Kagan *Madge* • Kandice Stroh *Deirdre* • Lois Smith *Mrs Axman* • Adam Faith *Bryan* • Cherie Currie *Annie* ■ *Dir* Adrian Lyne • *Scr* Gerald Ayres • *Producers* David Puttnam, Gerald Ayres

The Foxes of Harrow ★★

Period drama
1947 • US • BW • 117min

This overlong adaptation of Frank Yerby's popular Southern novel would have benefited from more sensible casting, Technicolor photography and a more involved director than John M Stahl at the helm. Rex Harrison is miscast as the Irish rogue who gambles his way to the top, while Maureen O'Hara plays her role with a grimness which suggests how unhappy she must have been to be subjected to her co-star's infamous on-set arrogance. The production values are undoubtably attractive, however, and the art direction was unsurprisingly nominated for an Oscar. TS

Rex Harrison *Stephen Fox* • Maureen O'Hara *Odalie D'Arceneaux* • Richard Haydn *Andre LeBlanc* • Victor McLaglen *Capt Mike Farrell* • Vanessa Brown *Aurore D'Arceneaux* • Patricia Medina *Desiree* • Gene Lockhart *The Vicomte* ■ *Dir* John M Stahl • *Scr* Wanda Tuchock, from the novel by Frank Yerby • *Art Directors* Lyle Wheeler, Maurice Ransford

Foxfire ★★★

Drama
1987 • US • Colour • 118min

This 1987 TV-movie adaptation of the Broadway play features the husband-and-wife team of Hume Cronyn (who co-wrote the stage play with Susan Cooper) and Jessica Tandy. Tandy won a Tony for the role on stage, and an Emmy for her performance here as an independent-minded widow unwilling to abandon her home in the Blue Ridge Mountains, in memory of her dead husband. It's an often moving tale, beautifully performed by Tandy and Cronyn. Country music star John Denver also features. JB

Jessica Tandy *Annie Nations* • Hume Cronyn *Hector Nations* • John Denver *Dillard Nations* • Gary Grubbs *Prince Carpenter* • Harriet Hall *Holly* • Collin Wilcox-Paxton *Madge Burton* • Joshua Bryson *Heckie* ■ *Dir* Jud Taylor • *Scr* Susan Cooper, from the play by Cooper, Hume Cronyn

Foxfire ★★★ 18

Drama
1996 • US • Colour • 97min

Four teenage girls discover their common strengths when they tire of an abusive teacher and the negligent school system that ignores him. Hedy Burress is the film's focus, with the ever-smirking Angelina Jolie as "Legs", the independent wanderer who floats into the lives of the other girls just as they need that extra push into rebellion. This probably would have had more impact if, like the book that inspired it, the film had been set in its original 1950s milieu. **ST** Swearing, violence.

Hedy Burress *Maddy Wirtz* • Angelina Jolie *Legs Sadovksy* • Jenny Lewis *Rita Faldes* • Jenny Shimizu *Goldie Goldman* • Sarah Rosenberg *Violet Kahn* ■ *Dir* Annette Haywood-Carter • *Scr* Elizabeth White, from the novel by Joyce Carol Oates

Foxfire: Confessions of a Girl Gang ★★15
Drama 2012 · Fr · Colour · 139min

This adaptation of Joyce Carol Oates's novel marks the English-language debut of French film-maker Laurent Cantet, who won the top prize at Cannes for his 2008 drama *The Class*. It's set in upstate New York in the early 1950s, where a gang of small-town high-school girls form their own gang to battle chauvinism. The characters are over-familiar, the cast merely adequate, and the pace plodding, which is disappointing from an obviously talented director. **TJ** Violence, swearing, sexual references, drug abuse. *DVD*

Raven Adamson *Legs* • Katie Coseni *Maddy* • Madeleine Bisson *Rita* • Claire Mazerolle *Goldie* • Rachael Nyhuus *Violet* • Paige Moyles *Lana* ■ *Dir* Laurent Cantet • *Scr* Laurent Cantet, from the novel *Foxfire* by Joyce Carol Oates

Foxhole in Cairo ★★
Spy drama 1960 · UK · BW · 83min

In an unremarkable wartime espionage drama, James Robertson-Justice and Adrian Hoven are British and German spies playing hide and seek with the plans for El Alamein. Fenella Fielding makes a sexy Jewish resistance fighter saved by Robertson-Justice, who prevents the Desert Fox from winning the Battle of Algiers. Albert Lieven is a convincing Rommel and if you blink you'll miss Michael Caine as a German soldier. **AT**

James Robertson-Justice *Captain Robertson DSO* • Adrian Hoven *John Eppler* • Niall MacGinnis *Radek* • Peter Van Eyck *Count Almazly* • Fenella Fielding *Yvette* • Albert Lieven *Rommel* • Michael Caine *Weber* ■ *Dir* John Moxey [John Llewellyn Moxey] • *Scr* Leonard Mosley, Donald Taylor, from the novel *The Cat and the Mice* by Leonard Mosley

Foxy Brown ★★18
Blaxploitation thriller 1974 · US · Colour · 91min

"Don't mess aroun' with Foxy Brown" read the shoutline for Pam Grier's fourth collaboration with director Jack Hill. However, far more revealing is the poster copy that sums up the slam-bam nature of one of blaxploitation's low points: "She's got drive and that ain't jive. She don't bother to bring 'em back alive!" Posing as a hooker to snare the drug dealers who killed her cop boyfriend, Grier is so preoccupied with kinky sex and violence she has to leave what little acting there is to Antonio Fargas. **DP** *DVD*

Pam Grier *Foxy Brown* • Antonio Fargas *Link Brown* • Peter Brown *Steve Elias* • Terry Carter *Michael Anderson* • Kathryn Loder *Katherine Wall* • Harry Holcombe *Judge Fenton* • Juanita Brown *Claudia* ■ *Dir/Scr* Jack Hill

Fracture ★★★15
Crime thriller 2007 · US · Colour · 108min

Gregory Hoblit's stylish crime thriller opens with Anthony Hopkins shooting his unfaithful wife (Embeth Davidtz). Hopkins decides to plead not guilty and defend himself in court, pitting his wits against Ryan Gosling's assistant DA in what will be his last case before he takes a job in the lucrative private sector. It looks like a formality (there's even a confession), but it's never that simple. Hoblit (*Primal Fear*) is an old hand at this sort of thing, and Hopkins and Gosling spark nicely off each other (just try to ignore Hopkins's inconsistent accent). Some of the plot contortions border on the preposterous, but fans of twisting courtroom thrillers will find it an entertaining diversion. **CP** Swearing. *DVD*

Anthony Hopkins *Ted Crawford* • Ryan Gosling *Willy Beachum* • David Strathairn *Joe Lobruto* • Rosamund Pike *Nikki Gardner* • Embeth Davidtz *Jennifer Crawford* • Billy Burke *Detective Rob Nunally* • Cliff Curtis *Detective Flores* • Fiona Shaw *Judge Robinson* ■ *Dir* Gregory Hoblit • *Scr* Daniel Pyne, Glenn Gers, from a story by Pyne

Fragile ★15
Supernatural horror 2005 · Sp/UK · Colour · 97min

Even by pulp horror standards, *Fragile* is dismal. It begins with a huge train crash on, of all places, the Isle of Wight. As the authorities struggle to cope with the casualties, a children's hospital is given a respite from closure. It is, of course, a terrifying gothic institution with an entire blocked-off wing where something awful once happened. Soon nurse Calista Flockhart discovers that a local urban legend has its roots in a disturbing reality. **DW** *DVD*

Calista Flockhart *Amy Nicholls* • Richard Roxburgh *Robert Marcus* • Elena Anaya *Helen Perez* • Gemma Jones *Mrs Folder* • Yasmin Murphy *Maggie* • Colin McFarlane *Roy* ■ *Dir* Jaume Balagueró • *Scr* Jaume Balagueró, Jordi Galcerán

Fragment of Fear ★★15
Thriller 1970 · UK · Colour · 91min

The poster promised "A Phantasmagoria of Fright", but director Richard C Sarafian's disappointing acaptation of John Bingham's novel delivers very little of anything. The initial premise is promising. Writer David Hemmings is investigating the murder of his aunt (Flora Robson) in Pompeii. The problem is, he's a reformed drug addict, and clues to the mystery keep being complicated by weird hallucinations. Is he going insane? A Euro-pudding cast provides some answers before the whole flimsy farrago falls apart. **AJ**

David Hemmings *Tim Brett* • Gayle Hunnicutt *Juliet Bristow* • Flora Robson *Lucy Dawson* • Wilfrid Hyde White *Mr Copsey* • Daniel Massey *Major Ricketts* • Acolfo Celi *Bardoni* ■ *Dir* Richard C Sarafian • *Scr* Paul Dehn, from the novel by John Bingham

Fragments ★★15
Drama 2008 · US · Colour · 91min

A random shooting in a diner reverberates through the lives of the traumatised survivors in this solemn, multi-stranded drama. The ensemble cast features Forest Whitaker as a cancer-riddled gambling addict, Dakota Fanning's sullen-faced born-again Christian, a peroxide-blonde waitress (Kate Beckinsale) who neglects her son as she tries to deal with events; and Guy Pearce's doctor, who decides – for reasons largely unclear – to start poisoning his wife. Handled with leaden faux gravitas, the soap opera lathers wel but heavy-handed metaphors and misty-eyed sincerity take their toll. **JR** Violence, swearing, sex scenes. *DVD*

Kate Beckinsale *Carla Davenport* • Dakota Fanning *Anne Hagen* • Guy Pearce *Dr Bruce Laraby* • Forest Whitaker *Charlie Archenault* • Embeth Davidtz *Joan* • Jackie Earle Haley *Bob* • Jennifer Hudson *Kathy* • Josh Hutcherson *Jimmy* ■ *Dir* Rowan Woods • *Scr* Roy Freirich, from his novel *Winged Creatures*

Frailty ★★★15
Horror thriller 2001 · US/Ger · Colour · 95min

The directorial debut of actor Bill Paxton is a haunting tale of a family torn apart by religious fanaticism and madness, steeped in a chilling "Southern Gothic" atmosphere. Texan Matthew McConaughey tells FBI agent Powers Boothe that the serial killer he is looking for is his brother and relates, in flashback, their horrifying family history. Using the "less is more" maxim – no gore, just powerful imagery – Paxton's assured, if morbidly bleak, creepshow is directed with artful precision. **AJ** *DVD*

Bill Paxton *Dad* • Matthew McConaughey *Fenton Meiks/Adam Meiks* • Powers Boothe *Agent Wesley J Doyle* • Matt O'Leary *Young Fenton* • Luke Askew *Sheriff Smalls* • Jeremy Sumpter

Young Adam Meiks • Derk Cheetwood *Agent Griffin Hull* • Melissa Crider [Missy Crider] *Becky* ■ *Dir* Bill Paxton • *Scr* Brent Hanley

Framed ★★
Crime drama 1947 · US · BW · 82min

Even after *Gilda*, Glenn Ford was still serving time on the treadmill of Columbia's programme fillers, this one a crime thriller in which he's an unemployed mining engineer who becomes the fall-guy for a bank robbery. He is set up by robber Janis Carter, who uses him because he looks like her accomplice Barry Sullivan. **AT**

Glenn Ford *Mike Lambert* • Janis Carter *Paula Craig* • Barry Sullivan *Stephen Price* • Edgar Buchanan *Jeff Cunningham* • Karen Morley *Mrs Price* • Jim Bannon *Jack Woodworth* ■ *Dir* Richard Wallace • *Scr* Ben Maddow, from the story by Jack Patrick

Framed ★18
Crime action 1975 · US · Colour · 100min

You've seen this a billion times before but never one more gratuitously violent. Nashville gambler Joe Don Baker is put in jail for accidentally killing a sheriff and, after being paroled, goes after the corrupt cops who set him up. This is a typical 1970s revenge saga characterised by reprehensible *Death Wish* viciousness. Unsurprising, really, as director, writer and star had previously collaborated on *Walking Tall*. **AJ**

Joe Don Baker *Ron Lewis* • Conny Van Dyke *Susan Barrett* • Gabriel Dell *Vince Greeson* • John Marley *Sal Viccarrone* ■ *Dir* Phil Karlson • *Scr* Mort Briskin, from a novel by Art Powers, Mike Misenheimer

Frances ★★★★15
Biographical drama 1982 · US · Colour · 133min

Jessica Lange is mesmerising in this uneven biopic of the spirited, politically outspoken 1930s actress Frances Farmer, who fell from grace in Hollywood and ended up institutionalised in an asylum where she later underwent a lobotomy. The film only touches on the problems in Hollywood that Frances faced, instead focusing on her hospitalisations, but this is still often riveting drama that benefits from a superb central performance from Lange (who at times looks eerily like Farmer), and solid support from Sam Shepard and Kim Stanley. **JB** *DVD*

Jessica Lange *Frances Farmer* • Sam Shepard *Harry York* • Kim Stanley *Lillian Farmer* • Bart Burns *Ernest Farmer* • Christopher Pennock *Dick Steele* • James Karen *Judge* • Gerald S O'Loughlin *Lobotomy doctor* ■ *Dir* Graeme Clifford • *Scr* Eric Bergren, Christopher DeVore, Nicholas Kazan

Frances Ha ★★★★★15
Comedy drama 2012 · US · BW · 82min

The romantic and professional travails of dancer Frances are detailed in this winning serio-comic saga. Set in Big Apple bohemia, it's filmed in black and white in a knowing tribute to Woody Allen's *Manhattan* by writer/director Noah Baumbach (*Greenberg*). His film is a triumph, combining spot-on humour and genuine insight. Much of the credit goes to leading lady and co-writer Greta Gerwig as the bumbling yet endearing Frances, in a film that's well aware of its own hipness, but never too cool to laugh and cry. **TJ** Swearing, sexual references.

Greta Gerwig *Frances* • Mickey Sumner *Sophie* • Adam Driver *Lev* • Michael Zegen *Benji* ■ *Dir* Noah Baumbach • *Scr* Noah Baumbach, Greta Gerwig

Francesca and Nunziata ★★★
Period drama 2001 · It · Colour · 125min

Lina Wertmuller renews her pivotal association with Giancarlo Giannini in this TV adaptation of a period novel. However, his indolent prince is somewhat marginalised as the focus centres on the feud between his rags-to-riches wife, Sophia Loren, and Claudia Genini, the daughter she adopted in an act of atonement for the recovery of ailing son, Raoul Bova.

Wertmuller packs her melodrama with plenty of caustic comment, but, despite Loren's bravura, it's not one of her most compelling outings. **DP** Italian +subtitles.

Sophia Loren *Francesca* • Giancarlo Giannini *Giordano* • Claudia Gerini *Nunziata* • Raoul Bova *Federico* • Carmen Femiano *Mariuccia* ■ *Dir* Lina Wertmuller • *Scr* Lina Wertmuller, Elvio Porta, from the novel *Francesca e Nunziata* by Maria Orsini Natale

Francesco ★12
Biographical religious drama 1989 · It/W Ger · Colour · 128min

In 1966, Liliana Cavani made a TV biopic about St Francis of Assisi. Years later she persuaded backers to let her try again, using Herman Hesse's book, a bigger budget and imported star Mickey Rourke. Told in flashback, it recalls his life as a group of disciples remember his conversion in prison, after which he renounced worldly possessions. The script is risible, Rourke miscast and the docudrama unconvincing. **BB** English, Italian +subtitles. *DVD*

Mickey Rourke *Francesco* • Helena Bonham Carter *Chiara* • Paolo Bonacelli *Pietro Bernardone, Francesco's father* • Andréa Ferréol *Pica, Francesco's mother* • Hanns Zischler *Pope Innocence III* • Peter Berling *Guido, Bishop of Assisi* ■ *Dir* Liliana Cavani • *Scr* Liliana Cavani, Roberta Mazzoni, from the novel *Francis of Assisi* by Herman Hesse

The Franchise Affair ★★PG
Mystery 1950 · UK · BW · 84min

The presence of postwar British cinema's golden couple, Michael Denison and Dulcie Gray, deprives this tale of superstition and recrimination of much of its suspense. As one of the women accused of kidnap and torture by the hysterical Ann Stephens, Gray fails to generate sufficient ambiguity, while lawyer Denison's decency lacks the indignation that might have injected some much-needed impetus. **DP** *DVD*

Michael Denison *Robert Blair* • Dulcie Gray *Marion Sharpe* • Anthony Nicholls *Kevin McDermott* • Marjorie Fielding *Mrs Sharpe* • Athene Seyler *Aunt Lin* • Ann Stephens *Betty Kane* • Kenneth More *Stanley Peters* ■ *Dir* Lawrence Huntington • *Scr* Robert Hall, Lawrence Huntington, from the novel by Josephine Tey

Francis ★★U
Comedy 1949 · US · BW · 90min

The adventures of Francis the talking mule (voiced by Chill Wills) proved so successful that they led to an unofficial comedy series, critically unloved but massively popular with the picture-going public. In this first entry, the pesky mule helps Donald O'Connor become a war hero. O'Connor felt that being Francis's stooge cost him true stardom, and he may not have been far wrong. The seven-strong series was used to try out new studio contractees – look out for Anthony (later Tony) Curtis in this one – while director Arthur Lubin later worked with another talking horse on TV's *Mr Ed*. **TS**

Donald O'Connor *Lt Peter Stirling* • Patricia Medina *Maureen Gelder* • ZaSu Pitts *Valerie Humpert* • Ray Collins *Colonel Hooker* • John McIntire *General Stevens* • Anthony Curtis [Tony Curtis] *Captain Jones* • Chill Wills *Francis the Talking Mule* ■ *Dir* Arthur Lubin • *Scr* David Stern, from his novel

Francis Goes to the Races ★★U
Comedy 1951 · US · BW · 87min

Following the success of *Francis*, Universal invited Donald O'Connor to reprise the role of Peter Stirling (the real name of David Stern, on whose novel the series was based), the trouble-prone everyman whose best buddy is a talking mule. Chill Wills also returned to voice the equine sage, with a brain as sharp as Bilko's, and he's soon feeding O'Connor with insider information after he lands a job at the run-down racing stable. **DP**

Donald O'Connor *Peter Stirling* • Piper Laurie *Frances Travers* • Cecil Kellaway *Colonel Travers* • Jesse White *Frank Damer* • Barry Kelley *Mallory*

F

• Chill Wills *Francis the Talking Mule* ■ *Dir* Arthur Lubin • *Scr* Oscar Brodney, from a story by Robert Arthur, from characters by David Stern

Francis Goes to West Point ★★ U

Comedy 1952 · US · BW · 81min

Donald O'Connor here makes his third appearance in Universal's talking mule comedy series. Rewarded with a scholarship for preventing a calamity at an atomic plant, O'Connor finds life at the US Army academy tough going – all the more so having invented himself a pregnant wife. However, with the help of the scheming Francis (voiced as ever by Chill Wills), he comes to the fore during a big football game versus the Navy. DP

Donald O'Connor *Peter Stirling* • Lori Nelson *Barbara Atwood* • Alice Kelley *Cynthia Daniels* • Palmer Lee [Gregg Palmer] *William Norton* • William Reynolds *Wilbur Van Allen* • Les Tremayne *Col Daniels* • Chill Wills *Francis the Talking Mule* ■ *Dir* Arthur Lubin • *Scr* Oscar Brodney, from characters by David Stern

Francis Covers the Big Town ★★ U

Comedy 1953 · US · BW · 86min

Director Arthur Lubin broke a golden rule in the fourth entry in Universal's comedy series by allowing the talking mule to speak to someone other than Donald O'Connor. Francis is called upon to give evidence in court after O'Connor – now employed as a crime reporter on a newspaper because his buddy receives tip-offs from garrulous police horses – becomes embroiled in a murder case. DP

Donald O'Connor *Peter Stirling* • Yvette Duguay [Yvette Dugay] *Maria Scola* • Gene Lockhart *Tom Henderson* • Nancy Guild *Alberta Ames* • Larry Gates *Dan Austin* • Gale Gordon *Evans* • Chill Wills *Francis the Talking Mule* ■ *Dir* Arthur Lubin • *Scr* Oscar Brodney, from characters by David Stern

Francis Joins the WACS ★★ U

Comedy 1954 · US · BW · 94min

Having been content to steal the *Francis* franchise by voicing the talking mule, Chill Wills opted to take a key supporting role in the fifth entry. He plays a general who is convinced that women should have only a token role in the US Army. However, Lynn Bari is determined to prove otherwise and receives unexpected assistance from one-time second lieutenant Donald O'Connor, who has been assigned to her unit following a bureaucratic bungle. ZaSu Pitts reprises the role she took in the series opener. DP

Donald O'Connor *Peter Stirling* • Mamie Van Doren *Col Bunky Hilstrom* • Lynn Bari *Maj Louise Simpson* • ZaSu Pitts *Lt Valerie Humpert* • Joan Shawlee *Sgt Kipp* • Chill Wills *General Kaye* • Chill Wills *Francis the Talking Mule* ■ *Dir* Arthur Lubin • *Scr* Devery Freeman, from a story by Herbert Baker, from a character created by David Stern

Francis in the Navy ★★ U

War comedy 1955 · US · BW · 80min

Tired of being upstaged by a musing mule, Donald O'Connor bade bon voyage to Universal's B series after this amiable comedy of errors, in which he plays a bosun, as well as the hapless Peter Stirling, who finds himself all at sea when he tries to prevent Francis from being sold off as army surplus. This sixth entry also ended Chill Wills's and Arthur Lubin's association with the franchise. However, it marked the second screen appearance of a young contract player named Clint Eastwood. DP

Donald O'Connor *Lt Peter Stirling/Slicker Donovan* • Martha Hyer *Betsy Donovan* • Richard Erdman *Murph* • Jim Backus *Cmdr Hutch* • Clint Eastwood *Jonesy* • David Janssen *Lt Anders* • Martin Milner *Rick* • Chill Wills *Francis the Talking Mule* ■ *Dir* Arthur Lubin • *Scr* Devery Freeman, from characters by David Stern

Francis in the Haunted House ★★ U

Comedy 1956 · US · BW · 79min

It was all change for the final entry in Universal's long-running B franchise. But despite Mickey Rooney's eager antics, Charles Lamont's bullish direction and Paul Frees's brave attempt to keep up Francis's equine quipping, what little magic this always amiable, but never remarkable series might have generated passed with the departure of their predecessors. Feeling eerily like "Abbott and Costello Meets Scooby Doo", this bland blend of knockabout and thrills is only likely to slow pulse rates. DP

Mickey Rooney *David Prescott* • Virginia Welles *Lorna MacLeod* • James Flavin *Chief Martin* • Paul Cavanagh *Neil Frazer* • Mary Ellen Kay *Lorna Ann* • David Janssen *Lt Hopkins* • Paul Frees *Francis the Talking Mule* ■ *Dir* Charles Lamont • *Scr* Herbert Margolis, William Raynor, from characters by David Stern

Francis, God's Jester ★★★★ PG

Biographical drama 1950 · It · BW · 83min

Based on the writings of St Francis of Assisi and shot with such a firm grasp of period and place that it feels like a newsreel of 13th-century Italy, this truly inspiring picture is not a saintly homage, but a neorealist study in faith and human decency. Director Roberto Rossellini draws extraordinary performances from his mainly non-professional cast, notably from Nazario Gerardi, who was himself a Franciscan friar. Ironically, the only weak link is established star Aldo Fabrizi's eye-rolling villainy. Co-authored by Italian director Federico Fellini, the script focuses on the simple joys of life rather than theology and is guaranteed to raise the spirits. DP Italian +subtitles. *DVD*

Aldo Fabrizi *Nicolaio, the Tyrant* • Arabella Lemaitre *Saint Clair* • Brother Nazario Gerardi *Saint Francis* ■ *Dir* Roberto Rossellini • *Scr* Roberto Rossellini, Federico Fellini

Francis of Assisi ★ U

Biographical drama 1961 · US · Colour · 105min

This stilted biopic of the patron saint of animals has a woefully miscast Bradford Dillman as Francis – only Pat Boone or Frankie Avalon could have been worse. Even more surprising is that Michael Curtiz should have agreed to direct it. Those expecting cuddly creatures will be disappointed, as this focuses on the life of Francis the warrior who, like El Cid before him, sorts out rival Christians and Arabs while fighting for Sicily's liberation before going into retreat. AT

Bradford Dillman *Francis Bernardone* • Dolores Hart *Clare Scefi* • Stuart Whitman *Paolo* • Pedro Armendáriz *Sultan* ■ *Dir* Michael Curtiz • *Scr* Eugene Vale, James Forsyth, Jack Thomas, from the novel *The Joyful Beggar* by Louis De Wohl

Frank ★★★★ 15

Comedy drama 2013 · UK/Ire · Colour · 91min

This strange and delightful ode to artistic expression stars Michael Fassbender – though you might not even realise it. He dons a large papier-mâché head to play the title character, who's based on the now-deceased entertainer Frank Sidebottom, the creation of musician Chris Sievey. Writer Jon Ronson draws on his own experiences as a member of Sievey's band to tell the fictional story of a keyboardist (Domhnall Gleeson, in a finely tuned performance) who falls in with a group of nutty alt-rockers, led by an artistic genius who refuses to show his face. Director Lenny Abrahamson generates plenty of laughs from the set-up and, despite his expressionless appearance, Fassbender subtly conveys the sadder elements of the story. SP Swearing, sex scenes, suicide. *DVD*

Michael Fassbender *Frank* • Domhnall Gleeson *Jon Burroughs* • Maggie Gyllenhaal *Clara* • Scoot McNairy *Don* • Carla Azar *Nana* ■ *Dir* Lenny Abrahamson • *Scr* Peter Straughan, Jon Ronson, from his newspaper article

Frank and Jesse ★★ 15

Western 1995 · US · Colour · 101min

Writer/director Robert Boris assembled a willing young cast for what he intended to be a revisionist western. But, the life and crimes of Frank and Jesse James have been re-examined so many times that there is little left to say. Boris predictably gives Rob Lowe's Jesse a conscience and suggests the James, Younger and Ford brothers were victims of a society that betrayed them after the South's defeat in the Civil War. DP Violence. *DVD*

Rob Lowe *Jesse James* • Bill Paxton *Frank James* • Randy Travis *Cole Younger* • William Atherton *Allan Pinkerton* • Todd Field *Bob Younger* • Alexis Arquette *Charlie Ford* • Dana Wheeler-Nicholson *Annie* • Maria Pitillo *Zee James* ■ *Dir/Scr* Robert Boris

Frank Lloyd Wright ★★★★

Documentary 1997 · US · Colour and BW · 146min

With exhaustive chronicles of the Civil War, the Wild West and the history of baseball already to his credit, documentarist Ken Burns here turns his attention to one of the 20th century's most influential and controversial artists. Inspired by nature in his crusade against Victorian fussiness, architect Frank Lloyd Wright may have had his personal problems and his share of criticism (particularly in his later career). But he emerges from this meticulously assembled portrait (combining archive material and expert analysis) as a visionary whose monument, the Guggenheim Museum in New York, speaks eloquently of his genius. DP

Edward Herrmann *Narrator* ■ *Dir* Ken Burns, Lynn Novick • *Scr* Godfrey C Ward

Frankenfish ★★ 15

Action horror 2004 · US · Colour · 80min

Medical examiner Tory Kittles and marine biologist China Chow face the somewhat unusual danger of being eaten by a genetically altered snakehead fish, when they're investigating some unexplained deaths in a bayou backwater. *Spawn* director Mark AZ Dippé throws all the usual clichés into an entertaining pool of action, humour and gore, that's also better written than you'd expect. The mutant mayhem is kept moving at a snappy pace and there are plenty of water level camera angles for those cheap *Jaws*-style shocks. AJ *DVD*

Tory Kittles *Sam Rivers* • KD Aubert *Eliza* • China Chow *Mary Callahan* • Tomas Arana *Jeff* • Mark Boone Junior *Joseph* • Richard Edson *Roland* ■ *Dir* Mark AZ Dippé • *Scr* Simon Barrett, Scott Clevenger • *Cinematographer* Eliot Rockett

Frankenhooker ★★★ 18

Comedy horror 1990 · US · Colour · 80min

Cult director Frank Henenlotter sews together one of his best lampoons with this madcap gore parody revealing his usual bad taste and warped sense of humour. Mad inventor James Lorinz accidentally chops up his girlfriend in a power lawnmower, saves her head and finds body parts to remake her from prostitutes addicted to the drug he's developed. Pushing cartoon violence to the limit, Henenlotter's trump card is Lorinz, who turns in a charismatic performance. AJ Swearing, drug abuse, nudity. *DVD* *Blu-ray*

James Lorinz *Jeffrey Franken* • Patty Mullen *Elizabeth* • Louise Lasser *Jeffrey's mom* • Charlotte Helmkamp *Honey* • Joseph Gonzalez *Zorro* • Shirley Stoler *Spike* • Lia Chang *Crystal* ■ *Dir* Frank Henenlotter • *Scr* Frank Henenlotter, Robert Martin

A macabre masterpiece that fixes the monstrous image of "The Creature" in the public consciousness

Frankenstein ★★★★★ PG

Classic horror 1931 · US · BW · 68min

Shocking in its day, and still a genuinely creepy experience, director James Whale's primitive yet enthralling interpretation of Mary Shelley's classic tale of man playing God is the most influential genre movie ever made. Its success kick-started the golden age of horror for Universal Studios and provided inspiration for scores of imitators and successors. Boris Karloff breathes miraculous life into his definitive monster portrayal: the most touching moment is the creature reaching up to grasp a ray of sunlight. A superb cast, imaginative set design and Whale's innovative direction using bizarre camera angles create a remarkably tense and melancholy atmosphere of gothic science gone mad. Karloff returned as the Monster in *Bride of Frankenstein* (1935). AJ *DVD* *Blu-ray*

Colin Clive *Henry Frankenstein* • Mae Clarke *Elizabeth* • John Boles *Victor Moritz* • ? [Boris Karloff] *The Monster* • Edward Van Sloan *Dr Waldman* • Frederick Kerr *Baron Frankenstein* • Dwight Frye *Fritz* • Lionel Belmore *Burgomaster* • Marilyn Harris *Little Maria* • Michael Mark *Ludwig, peasant father* ■ *Dir* James Whale • *Scr* Garrett Fort, Francis Edwards Faragoh, from the composition by John L Balderston, from the play by Peggy Webling, from the novel by Mrs Percy B [Mary] Shelley • *Cinematographer* Arthur Edeson • *Art Director* Charles D Hall • *Make-up* Jack Pierce

Frankenstein ★★ 18

Horror mystery 2004 · US · Colour · 83min

The classic mad scientist tale receives a contemporary re-invention in this atmospheric but painfully underdeveloped TV movie. Parker Posey and Adam Goldberg are the modern-day New Orleans detectives who unwittingly stumble upon the work of the still-living Dr Frankenstein (a coldly sophisticated Thomas Kretschmann) while hunting a serial killer. Director Marcus Nispel applies the same corroded, industrial look of his *Texas Chainsaw Massacre* remake to what's essentially a slow-moving police procedural with bursts of gothic weirdness. SF Violence, sex scenes. *DVD*

Parker Posey *Det Carson O'Conner* • Adam Goldberg *Det Michael Sloane* • Vincent Perez *Deucalion* • Thomas Kretschmann *Victor Helios/ Frankenstein* • Michael Madsen *Det Harker* • Ivana Milicevic *Erika* ■ *Dir* Marcus Nispel • *Scr* John Shiban, from an idea by Dean Koontz

Frankenstein ★★★ 18

Horror thriller 2015 · US/Ger · Colour · 85min

Mary Shelley's tale about man playing God gets a fascinating refit from *Candyman* director Bernard Rose. Here, married scientists (Danny Huston and Carrie-Anne Moss) give life to the perfect specimen (Xavier Samuel) but then callously abandon him when his nascent development takes a turn for the ugly. Lashings of gore evoke old Hammer movies but, significantly, Samuel's nuanced performance as a dangerously strong innocent yearning to find love and acceptance in an all-too cruel world, echoes Boris Karloff's iconic 1930s incarnation most of all. JA Violence. *DVD*

Xavier Samuel *Monster* • Carrie-Anne Moss *Marie* • Tony Todd *Eddie* • Danny Huston *Viktor Frankenstein* • Maya Erskine *Wanda* ■ *Dir* Bernard Rose • *Scr* Bernard Rose, from Mary Shelley's novel

Frankenstein and the Monster from Hell ★★★ 15

Horror 1973 · UK · Colour · 91min

The sixth Hammer *Frankenstein* (not counting 1970s aberration *The Horror of Frankenstein*) is a stylish return to their 1950s gothic roots, and is a fitting end to the series. Peter Cushing returned as the obsessed Baron Frankenstein, this time creating a new monster (Dave Prowse) from the lunatic inmates of Carlsbad's asylum for the criminally insane. Hammer protégé Shane Briant engagingly plays his willing disciple, while Madeline Smith stars as a mute girl in this efficiently horrifying exercise, packed with gruesome close-ups and laboratory black humour. AJ Violence DVD BLU

Peter Cushing *Baron Frankenstein* • Shane Briant *Dr Simon Helder* • Dave Prowse *Creature* • Madeline Smith *Sarah, the Angel* • Bernard Lee *Tarmut* • Norman Mitchell *Policeman* • Patrick Troughton *Body snatcher* ■ *Dir* Terence Fisher • *Scr* John Elder [Anthony Hinds]

Frankenstein Conquers the World ★★
Monster horror 1964 · Jpn/US · Colour · 87min

One of the more inventive re-workings of the *Frankenstein* myth collapses into a typical Toho monster battle in *Godzilla* director Inoshiro Honda's daffy spectacular. A young kid eats the Hiroshima-infected heart of the Frankenstein monster and grows into a 30-foot tall mutated caveman, who eventually saves Japan's rebuilding programme from the rampaging dinosaur Baragon. Nick Adams is the friendly American scientist in a ridiculous but still fun addition to the Japanese monster hall of fame. AJ

Nick Adams *Dr James Bowen* • Tadao Takashima *Dr Yuzo Kawaji* • Kumi Mizuno *Dr Sueko Togami* ■ *Dir* Inoshiro Honda • *Scr* Kaoru Mabuchi, from a synopsis by Jerry Sohl, from a story by Reuben Bercovitch

Frankenstein Created Woman ★★★ 15
Horror 1966 · UK · Colour · 87min

This sequel to 1964's *Evil of Frankenstein* is considered by Hammer aficionados to be the best Frankenstein made by the House of Horror. The good doctor experiments with soul transference in this offbeat entry, reanimating the corpse of young Susan Denberg. The ever-dependable Peter Cushing gives it the soul of her boyfriend, who was wrongly guillotined for murder. The chilling result is a vengeful creature luring his/her enemies to their death. Terence Fisher's neat balance of psychological horror and murky sexuality makes this a fine addition to the genre. The series continued with *Frankenstein Must Be Destroyed* (1969). AJ DVD

Peter Cushing *Baron Frankenstein* • Susan Denberg *Christina* • Thorley Walters *Dr Hertz* • Robert Morris *Hans* • Peter Blythe *Anton* • Barry Warren *Karl* • Derek Fowlds *Johann* • Alan MacNaughton *Kleve* ■ *Dir* Terence Fisher • *Scr* John Elder [Anthony Hinds]

Frankenstein Meets the Wolf Man ★★★ PG
Horror 1943 · US · BW · 73min

The fifth feature in Universal's series was the first time two celebrity monsters shared the screen. Picking up where both *The Wolf Man* (1941) and *The Ghost of Frankenstein* (1942) left off, this entertaining sequel has werewolf Lon Chaney Jr seeking out the dead Frankenstein's diary, containing the cure for his lycanthropy, and stumbling across the monster (Bela Lugosi in his only appearance as the creature) encased in ice. Not particularly horrific, this is still charming fun because of the skilled acting and trademark Universal back-lot atmosphere. AJ

Lon Chaney Jr *The Wolf Man/Lawrence Talbot* • Ilona Massey *Baroness Elsa Frankenstein* • Patric Knowles *Dr Mannering* • Lionel Atwill *Mayor* • Bela Lugosi *Monster* • Maria Ouspenskaya *Maleva* ■ *Dir* Roy William Neill • *Scr* Curt Siodmak

Frankenstein Must Be Destroyed ★★★ 18
Horror 1969 · UK · Colour · 96min

The fifth of Hammer's Frankenstein series (that began with 1957's *The Curse of Frankenstein*) is graced by an incisive performance from Peter Cushing, up to his old tricks as the Baron performing brain transplants. Freddie Jones is astonishing as the anguished victim of the transplant,

whose wife fails to recognise him and rejects him, prompting a revenge plan. The gothic gore is once more directed with spirited skill and economy by Terence Fisher (his fourth in the series). Ralph Bates took over from Cushing for 1970's disappointing *The Horror of Frankenstein*. AJ DVD

Peter Cushing *Baron Frankenstein* • Simon Ward *Dr Karl Holst* • Veronica Carlson *Anna Spengler* • Freddie Jones *Prof Richter* • Thorley Walters *Insp Frisch* ■ *Dir* Terence Fisher • *Scr* Bert Batt, from a story by Anthony Nelson Keys, Bert Batt

Frankenstein – 1970 ★
Horror 1958 · US · BW · 82min

This hugely inept plummet into gothic fakery is significant only in the fact that for the first time in his career Boris Karloff played the Baron and not the creature. Karloff is the grandson of the deceased and disfigured (courtesy of Nazi torturers) Baron Frankenstein, who finds himself so strapped for cash to buy an atomic reactor with which to resuscitate his latest creation that he allows a television crew into the family castle for a touch of *Through the Keyhole* Transylvanian-style. RS

Boris Karloff *Baron Victor von Frankenstein* • Tom Duggan *Mike Shaw* • Jana Lund *Carolyn Hayes* • Don "Red" Barry [Donald Barry] *Douglas Row* ■ *Dir* Howard W Koch • *Scr* Richard Landau, George Worthing Yates, from a story by Aubrey Schenck, Charles A Moses

Frankenstein: the True Story ★★★★ 12
Horror 1973 · US · Colour · 175min

Kenneth Branagh's 1994 version of the classic horror tale (*Mary Shelley's Frankenstein*) made much of its fidelity to the source novel, but this earlier version remains among the most faithful of the *Frankenstein* adaptations. The production is notable for the sympathy with which the monster is portrayed by Michael Sarrazin, minus the once obligatory nuts and bolts, and his relationship with his creator (Leonard Whiting) has a tragic resonance. The film is intelligently scripted by Christopher Isherwood and boasts a distinguished cast of supporting players. AJ Violence. DVD

James Mason *Dr Polidori* • Leonard Whiting *Dr Victor Frankenstein* • David McCallum (1) *Henry Clerval* • Jane Seymour (2) *Agatha/Prima* • Michael Sarrazin *The creature* • Nicola Pagett *Elizabeth Fanschawe* • Ralph Richardson *Mr Lacey* • John Gielgud *Chief Constable* • Tom Baker *Sea captain* ■ *Dir* Jack Smight • *Scr* Christopher Isherwood, Don Bachardy, from the novel by Mary Shelley

Frankenstein Unbound ★★★ 18
Science-fiction horror 1990 · US · Colour · 82min

After nearly 20 years in retirement as a director Roger Corman returned to the job with this engagingly loopy rewriting of the Frankenstein myth. Based on the novel by Brian W Aldiss, this camp confection jumbles time travel, Mary Shelley's circle of friends, her monstrous fictional creation, dream sequences and an apocalyptic future for a mind-boggling baroque soap opera. More fun and far scarier than any other recent *Frankenstein* you might care to mention. AJ Violence, swearing.

John Hurt *Dr Joseph Buchanan* • Raul Julia *Dr Victor Frankenstein* • Bridget Fonda *Mary Godwin Shelley* • Jason Patric *Lord Byron* • Michael Hutchence *Percy Shelley* • Nick Brimble *The Monster* ■ *Dir* Roger Corman • *Scr* Roger Corman, FX Feeney, from the novel by Brian W Aldiss

Frankenweenie ★★★★ PG
Animated fantasy 2012 · US · BW · 83min

Director Tim Burton's fleshed-out version of his 1984 short film brims with subtle deadpan humour and joyful, life-affirming spirit. As with *Corpse Bride* (2005), Burton uses stop-motion animation, but this time opts for a polished monochrome palette to evoke old B-movie horror flicks. The story concerns young Victor (voiced by Charlie

Tahan), who devises a formula to resurrect his dead dog, only to unleash all kinds of monster mayhem on his sleepy home town. The story wavers slightly in the middle as Victor's classmates plot to uncover his secret, but the characters nevertheless keep you transfixed, making this a genuine spine-tingling delight. SP DVD BLU 3D

Catherine O'Hara *Mrs Frankenstein/Weird girl/Gym teacher* • Martin Short *Mr Frankenstein/Nassor/Mr Bergemeister* • Martin Landau *Mr Rzykruski* • Charlie Tahan *Victor* • Winona Ryder *Elsa Van Helsing* • Atticus Shaffer *Edgar "E" Gore* ■ *Dir* Tim Burton • *Scr* John August, from a screenplay by Leonard Ripps, from an idea by Tim Burton • *Music* Danny Elfman

Frankie ★★★
Drama 2005 · Fr · Colour · 88min

In the early days of photography, some believed that the camera had the power to steal the subject's spirit. Actress-turned-director Fabienne Berthaud touches on that idea for her highly stylised debut, in which she chronicles the mental disintegration of a German-born model who's nearing the end of her all-too-brief career. Fashion business flashbacks are punctuated by painful sanatorium reveries, in which a near-catatonic Diane Kruger battles her demons against the incessant chatter of her fellow inmates. With Kruger valiantly conveying frazzled ennui, everything here smacks of authenticity. But it's never quite clear what Berthaud is trying to say about either the exploitative nature of catwalk culture or the treatment of psychiatric patients. DP Russian, English, German, French +subtitles.

Diane Kruger *Frankie* • Jeannick Gravelines *Tom* • Brigitte Catillon *Suzy the landlady* • Christian Wiggert *The photographer* • J Alexander [Jay Alexander] *Kate* • Jean-Louis Place *The psychiatrist* • Gérald Marie *Lorenzo Ferretti* • Sylvia Hoecks [Sylvia Hoeks] *Rumina* ■ *Dir/Scr* Fabienne Berthaud • *Cinematographer* Fabienne Berthaud

Frankie & Johnny ★★ U
Musical comedy drama 1966 · US · Colour · 86min

This is Elvis Presley's film version of the old jazz/folk song standard. It's gaudy and bright, but, like most of Presley's films from this period, it has an air of having just been thrown together. The Mississippi riverboat setting is undeniably attractive, but it's simply inexcusable to use repeat footage of the title number in the finale reprise. Presley and Donna Douglas pair sweetly together, and the songs pass muster, but this is merely a pleasant time-filler. TS DVD

Elvis Presley *Johnny* • Donna Douglas *Frankie* • Nancy Kovack *Nelly Bly* • Sue Ane Langdon *Mitzi* • Harry Morgan *Cully* • Audrey Christie *Peg* ■ *Dir* Frederick De Cordova • *Scr* Alex Gottlieb, from a story by Nat Perrin • *Cinematographer* Jacques Marquette

Frankie & Johnny ★★★★ 15
Romantic drama 1991 · US · Colour · 112min

In this moving and often very funny romantic drama, Al Pacino and Michelle Pfeiffer star as the short-order cook and the waitress who fall hesitantly in love. It does take a major suspension of disbelief to see this gorgeous duo as lonely hearts rejects, but they act their way out of the hole. Pfeiffer in particular shows what a fine actress she can be with a good script. What lifts this particular tale above the dross is the realistic air of vulnerability that characterises the halting affair. SH Swearing, sex scenes. DVD

Michelle Pfeiffer *Frankie* • Al Pacino *Johnny* • Hector Elizondo *Nick* • Nathan Lane *Tim* • Jane Morris *Nedda* • Greg Lewis *Tino* • Al Fann *Luther* • Kate Nelligan *Cora* ■ *Dir* Garry Marshall • *Scr* Terrence McNally, from his play *Frankie and Johnny in the Clair de Lune*

Frankie Starlight ★★★ 15
Romantic comedy 1995 · US/Ire · Colour · 96min

Is this offbeat drama, based on the reminiscences of a dwarf novelist, a charmer that slipped through the net or a

trifling whimsy? Co-scripted by Chet Raymo from his novel, the film has its moments, as wartime refugee Anne Parillaud falls for Irish customs officer Gabriel Byrne and then Texan drifter Matt Dillon. There are also two splendid performances from Alan Pentony and Corban Walker as the young and adult Frankie, the son whose love of stars and fascination with his mother's amours result in a bestseller. It's all amiable enough, but promises more than it delivers. DP Swearing, nudity.

Anne Parillaud *Bernadette De Bois* • Matt Dillon *Terry Klout* • Gabriel Byrne *Jack Kelly* • Rudi Davies *Emma Kelly* • Georgina Cates *Young Emma* • Corban Walker *Frank Bois* ■ *Dir* Michael Lindsay-Hogg • *Scr* Chet Raymo, Ronan O'Leary, from the novel *The Dork of Cork* by Chet Raymo

Franklyn ★★ 15
Fantasy thriller 2008 · UK/Cay · Colour · 94min

The fates of four troubled souls are intertwined in this overly ambitious debut feature from writer/director Gerald McMorrow. The action shifts between contemporary London and the futuristic theocracy of Meanwhile City, as the lives of jilted Sam Riley, suicidal Eva Green, devout Bernard Hill and war veteran Ryan Phillippe collide in one moment of coincidence. Or was it preordained by higher powers? McMorrow's cryptic exploration of the vagaries of destiny, romance and faith is clearly indebted to *Donnie Darko* and *Dark City*, but isn't as satisfying and, as the film piles on layer upon layer of fantasy and reality, all sense of a coherent narrative is lost. AJ DVD BLU

Eva Green *Emilia/Sally* • Ryan Phillippe *Preest/David Esser* • Sam Riley *Milo* • Bernard Hill *Peter Esser* • James Faulkner *Pastor Bone* • Stephen Walters *Wormsnakes* • Art Malik *Tarrant* • Susannah York *Margaret* ■ *Dir/Scr* Gerald McMorrow

Frantic ★★★★ 15
Thriller 1988 · US · Colour · 114min

Roman Polanski makes this account of doctor Harrison Ford looking for his missing wife in an antagonistic Paris deeply disturbing. When wife Betty Buckley disappears from their hotel suite, reality becomes nightmare and solid citizen Ford resorts to increasingly desperate measures to find her. Emmanuelle Seigner, as a punkish free spirit, is a major flaw, but as a whole the movie is taut and often funny. It's a surreal Hitchcockian idea, but Polanski embellishes it with his own baleful theme of the uneasy nature of human existence, which is given added tension by Ennio Morricone's dramatic score. TH Swearing, brief nudity, drug abuse. DVD

Harrison Ford *Dr Richard Walker* • Emmanuelle Seigner *Michelle* • Betty Buckley *Sondra Walker* • John Mahoney *Williams* • Jimmy Ray Weeks [Jimmie Ray Weeks] *Shaap* • Yorgo Voyagis *Kidnapper* • David Huddleston *Peter* • Gérard Klein *Gaillard* • Jacques Ciron *Hotel manager* ■ *Dir* Roman Polanski • *Scr* Gérard Brach, Roman Polanski • *Music* Ennio Morricone

Frantz Fanon: Black Skin White Mask ★★★ 12
Drama documentary 1996 · UK/Fr · Colour · 68min

Isaac Julien's portrait of the author of the freedom's fighter's "bible", *The Wretched of the Earth*, is a skilful combination of archive footage, contemporary interviews and dramatic reconstructions. Compelling, if erring slightly towards the hagiographic, Julien's film traces Fanon's life from his youth on Martinique, through his experience of fighting for France in the Second World War, to his gradual politicisation as a psychiatrist in Algeria during its struggle for independence. The staged elements aren't very persuasive, however, and Colin Salmon's static performance isn't helped by the pious dialogue. DP

Colin Salmon *Frantz Fanon* • Al Nedjari *Algerian patient* • John Wilson *French policeman* • Ana Ramalho *French woman* • Noirín Ní Dubhgaill *Fanon's companion* ■ *Dir* Isaac Julien • *Scr* Isaac Julien, Mark Nash

Fraternity Vacation ★ 15

Comedy 1985 · US · Colour · 89min

This cheap teen comedy features a young Tim Robbins, who today possibly wishes he was holding the negative in one hand and a flaming torch in the other. Beer, sex, beer, wet T-shirts and beer all feature fairly prominently in this slender tale of college delinquents pursuing girls. The best reason to avoid this movie are the songs by Bananarama. RS *DVD*

Stephen Geoffreys *Wendell Tvedt* • Sheree J Wilson *Ashley Taylor* • Cameron Dye *Joe Gillespie* • Leigh McCloskey *Charles "Chas" Lawlor III* • Tim Robbins *Larry "Mother" Tucker* • Britt Ekland *Evette* ■ *Dir* James Frawley • *Scr* Lindsay Harrison

Frauds ★★ 15

Black comedy thriller
1992 · Aus · Colour · 89min

This cartoonish farce gives Phil Collins a wacky, black comedy film role, but in the end it has to go down as a missed opportunity. The pop star plays a mysterious insurance broker who terrorises Hugo Weaving and Josephine Byrnes when they resort to a financial scam to get themselves out of a business mess. Collins is occasionally very creepy, but director Stephan Elliott backs off when he could have gone for the jugular. JF Violence, swearing.

Phil Collins *Roland* • Hugo Weaving *Jonathan* • Josephine Byrnes *Beth* • Peter Mochrie *Michael Allen* • Helen O'Connor *Margaret* • Andrew McMahon *Young Matthew* • Rebel Russell *Mother* • Colleen Clifford *Mrs Waterson* ■ *Dir/Scr* Stephan Elliott

Fraulein Doktor ★★

Wartime spy drama
1968 · It/Yug · Colour · 100min

This is a hopelessly melodramatic account of the exploits of a real-life double agent (previously filmed as *Mademoiselle Docteur* in 1936). Eschewing his trademark realism, Italian director Alberto Lattuada here depicts espionage as a sexily glamorous game rather than a perilous round of treachery and deceit. Suzy Kendall shines as she plots the death of Lord Kitchener and seeks the formula for a poisonous gas, but the excitement is only sporadic. DP

Suzy Kendall *Fraulein Doktor* • Kenneth More *Colonel Foreman* • James Booth *Meyer* • Capucine *Dr Saforet* • Alexander Knox *General Peronne* ■ *Dir* Alberto Lattuada • *Scr* Duilio Coletti, Stanley Mann, HAL Craig, Vittoriano Petrilli, Alberto Lattuada, from a story by Vittoriano Petrilli

Freaked ★★★ 15

Comedy horror 1993 · US · Colour · 81min

Alex Winter co-directs this idiotic "tour de farce" on warp-drive with Tom Stern, his partner on the MTV series *The Idiot Box*. Winter also plays the arrogant Hollywood celebrity and spokesperson for a toxic chemical being pawned off to the Third World as a fertiliser. On a South American promotional tour, his entourage meet crazy Freak Show owner Randy Quaid, who uses the product to turn Winter into a headlining half man/half scaly beast. Forget the insane story, just laugh out loud at the amiable absurdity, and unsubtle send-ups of everything from *The Twilight Zone* to *Hollywood Squares*. AJ *DVD*

Alex Winter *Ricky Coogin* • Megan Ward *Julie* • Michael Stoyanov *Ernie* • Keanu Reeves *The Dog Boy* (uncredited) • Randy Quaid *Elijah C Skuggs* • William Sadler *Dick Brian* • Mr T *Bearded Lady* • Brooke Shields *Skye Daley* ■ *Dir/Scr* Alex Winter, Tom Stern

Freaks ★★★★ 15

Horror 1932 · US · BW · 62min

Still banned in some countries, and suppressed in others for decades, this unique classic from Tod Browning remains one of the most nightmarish yet compassionate horror movies ever made. Browning cleverly draws the viewer into an enclosed carnival society (featuring real circus anatomical oddities essentially playing themselves) with its attendant bonds, codes and rituals, and then chillingly shows what happens when a "normal" human – conniving trapeze artist Olga Baclanova – breaks them with a swindling scam. A deserved cult masterpiece, this tale of the macabre with its blood-freezing shock ending is incredible, disturbing and, once seen, never forgotten. AJ *DVD*

Wallace Ford *Phroso* • Leila Hyams *Venus* • Olga Baclanova *Cleopatra* • Rosco Ates [Roscoe Ates] *Roscoe* • Henry Victor *Hercules* • Harry Earles *Hans* • Daisy Earles *Frieda* • Rose Dione *Madame Tetrallini* • Daisy Hilton *Siamese Twin* • Violet Hilton *Siamese Twin* ■ *Dir* Tod Browning • *Scr* Willis Goldbeck, Leon Gordon, Edgar Allan Woolf, Al Boasberg, from the book *Spurs* by Clarence Aaron "Tod" Robbins • *Cinematographer* Merritt B Gerstad • *Art Director* Cedric Gibbons

Freaky Friday ★★★ U

Comedy 1976 · US · Colour · 94min

A very early body-swap movies, this undeservedly sank without trace, although it contains an effervescent performance from Jodie Foster, who switches places with her mother for a day. It's one of those movies that starts at a brisk trot, lapses into walking pace and winds up misfiring through sheer lack of gags. However, it's well worth catching for the performances of Foster and Barbara Harris as the mum. SH *DVD*

Barbara Harris *Ellen Andrews* • Jodie Foster *Annabel Andrews* • John Astin *Bill Andrews* • Patsy Kelly *Mrs Schmauss* • Dick Van Patten *Harold Jennings* • Vicki Schreck *Virginia* • Sorrell Booke *Mr Dilk* ■ *Dir* Gary Nelson • *Scr* Mary Rodgers, from her novel

Freaky Friday ★★

Comedy 1995 · US · Colour · 120min

Shelley Long and Gaby Hoffmann have the thankless task of trying to top the double act of Barbara Harris and Jodie Foster, the stars of the 1976 version of Mary Rodgers's book. Melanie Mayron has produced a lively reworking for TV of this familiar body-swap story, in which mystical necklaces cause a mother and daughter to change places. DP

Shelley Long *Ellen Andrews* • Gaby Hoffmann *Annabelle Andrews* • Asher Metchik *Ben Andrews* • Alan Rosenberg *Bill* • Eileen Brennan *Principal Handel* • Sandra Bernhard *Frieda Debny* • Carol Kane *Miss Futterman* • Catlin Adams *Mrs Barab* ■ *Dir* Melanie Mayron • *Scr* Stu Krieger, Melanie Mayron, from the film and the book by Mary Rodgers

Freaky Friday ★★★ PG

Comedy 2003 · US · Colour · 92min

In this update of Disney's 1976 comedy, Jamie Lee Curtis and Lindsay Lohan star as a widowed psychiatrist and her teenage daughter. Curtis is about to get married again, but Lohan objects. Then a fairy-godmother figure at a Chinese restaurant puts a spell on their fortune cookies, and the transformation is made. Although the plot takes a familiar course from then on, director Mark Waters keeps up the comic momentum with skill and the two leads are excellent. TH *DVD*

Jamie Lee Curtis *Tess Coleman* • Lindsay Lohan *Anna Coleman* • Mark Harmon *Ryan* • Harold Gould *Grandpa* • Chad Michael Murray *Jake* • Stephen Tobolowsky *Mr Bates* • Christina Vidal *Maddie* • Ryan Malgarini *Harry Coleman* • Rosalind Chao *Pei-Pei* ■ *Dir* Mark Waters (1) • *Scr* Heather Hach, Leslie Dixon, from the novel by Mary Rodgers

Fred Claus ★★ PG

Seasonal comedy 2007 · US · Colour · 110min

Vince Vaughn stars as Santa Claus's ne'er-do-well brother Fred, in a comedy that comes up woefully short on festive cheer. After centuries of not talking, Fred finally calls his younger sibling St Nicholas (Paul Giamatti) to borrow some cash to start up a betting business. Nicholas agrees, but onlyon condition that Fred return to the North Pole to work off his debt. From there, the story meanders betweentedious romantic subplots, a dastardly scheme to shut down Santa's workshop and Fred's desperate attempts to prove himself. Apart from a couple of amusing cameos, the lazy plotting and second-hand jokes are an insult to a talented cast (including Rachel Weisz, Kathy Bates and Kevin Spacey). SP *DVD Blu*

Vince Vaughn *Fred Claus* • Paul Giamatti *Santa Claus* • John Michael Higgins *Willie* • Miranda Richardson *Annette Claus* • Rachel Weisz *Wanda* • Kathy Bates *Mother Claus* • Trevor Peacock *Papa Claus* • Kevin Spacey *Clyde* ■ *Dir* David Dobkin • *Scr* Dan Fogelman, from a story by Jessie Nelson

Fred: the Movie ★★ 12

Comedy 2010 · US · Colour · 79min

Fred Figglehorn, a purposely stupid and irritating character created by American actor Lucas Cruikshank, gained an enormous following on YouTube, and this movie spin-off follows the pubescent boy with a squeaky voice as he battles his teenage insecurities. The story, in which Fred spends a weekend trying to get his neighbour (played by pastel popstar Pixie Lott) to fall for him, is clichéd in the extreme, but Sioban Fallon Hogan is brilliant as Fred's slovenly mum. Kids may love this film, but adults should stand well back. KK *DVD*

Lucas Cruikshank *Fred Figglehorn* • Pixie Lott *Judy* • Jennette McCurdy *Bertha* • John Cena *Fred's dad* • Siobhan Fallon Hogan [Siobhan Fallon] *Fred's mom* ■ *Dir* Clay Weiner • *Scr* David A Goodman, from the character *Fred Figglehorn* by Lucas Cruikshank

Freddie as FRO7 ★★ U

Animated spoof adventure
1992 · UK · Colour · 90min

Technically, this ill-advised foray into full-length feature animation can't be faulted: the visuals are sumptuous and a distinguished cast of British actors provide the voices. The story, however, which revolves around a James Bond-style superagent who also happens to be a frog, is just plain daft, and there is little of the knowing humour which makes the new features from Disney so popular. JF

Ben Kingsley *Freddie the Frog* • Jenny Agutter *Daffers* • John Sessions *Scotty* • Brian Blessed *El Supremo* • Nigel Hawthorne *Brigadier G* • Michael Hordern *King* • Phyllis Logan *Nessie* • Jonathan Pryce *Trilby* • Billie Whitelaw *Messina* ■ *Dir* Jon Acevski • *Scr* Jon Acevski, David Ashton

Freddy Got Fingered ★ 18

Comedy 2001 · US · Colour · 83min

If your idea of good viewing is seeing an actor of Rip Torn's quality being deluged by elephant semen, then MTV maverick Tom Green's hideous directorial debut is what you've been waiting for. Plunging vulgarity to new depths, the humour is more bestial than lavatorial, and makes the Farrelly brothers seem like choirboys. What attempts to pass for a plot centres on Green's inability to move out from the family home after his bid to become a Hollywood animator fails. DP *DVD CS*

Tom Green (1) *Gord Brody* • Rip Torn *Jim Brody* • Marisa Coughlan *Betty* • Eddie Kaye Thomas *Freddy Brody* • Julie Hagerty *Julie Brody* • Anthony Michael Hall *Mr Davidson* • Stephen Tobolowsky *Uncle Neil* • Drew Barrymore *Mr Davidson's secretary* ■ *Dir* Tom Green (1) • *Scr* Tom Green, Derek Harvie

Freddy vs Jason ★★ 18

Horror 2003 · US · Colour · 93min

Ronny Yu's half-hearted direction comes as the only real shock worth mentioning in this pointlessly gory and daft affair that plays ludicrous havoc with the myths of both the *Elm Street* and the *Friday the 13th* horror icons. Because the Springwood folk have drugged potential Freddy (Robert Englund) victims with a dream suppressant, the razor-gloved bogeyman has been rendered impotent. Freddy then coaxes Jason Voorhees (Ken Kirzinger) into causing machete mayhem. AJ *DVD Blu*

Robert Englund *Freddy Krueger* • Ken Kirzinger *Jason Voorhees* • Monica Keena *Lori Campbell* • Jason Ritter *Will* • Kelly Rowland *Kia* • Katharine Isabelle *Gibb* • Christopher George Marquette *Linderman* • Brendan Fletcher *Mark* ■ *Dir* Ronny Yu • *Scr* Damian Shannon, Mark Swift, from characters by Wes Craven, Victor Miller

Freddy's Dead: the Final Nightmare ★★ 18

Horror 1991 · US · Colour · 85min

This gimmick-laden sixth instalment about the child-molesting dream-stalker's exploits in nightmare land is a virtual rehash of *A Nightmare on Elm Street 3: Dream Warriors*, with an astonishingly lame 3D climax tacked on. Roseanne (Barr), Johnny Depp (who starred in the original) and Alice Cooper make cameo appearances to little effect. The series concluded with *Wes Craven's New Nightmare* (1994), in which the director took his saga into another realm. AJ *DVD Blu*

Robert Englund *Freddy Krueger* • Lisa Zane *Maggie Burroughs* • Shon Greenblatt *John* • Lezlie Deane *Tracy* • Ricky Dean Logan *Carlos* • Breckin Meyer *Spencer* • Yaphet Kotto *Doc* ■ *Dir* Rachel Talalay • *Scr* Michael DeLuca, from a story by Rachel Talalay, from characters by Wes Craven

Free and Easy ★★

Comedy 1930 · US · BW · 73min

Buster Keaton's career wobbled with his first sound film and never recovered. His great days as a silent comedian in creative charge of his work were over. His grave voice suited his demeanour, but MGM put him in a musical comedy as the hick who escorts Anita Page's beauty contest winner to Hollywood. They see celebrities at a premiere and he runs through the studio, bursting in on films in production and giving glimpses of stars and directors at work. It has none of the clever construction of Keaton's earlier comedies. AE

Buster Keaton *Elmer Butts* • Anita Page *Elvira* • Trixie Friganza *Ma* • Robert Montgomery *Larry* • Fred Niblo *Director* • Edgar Dearing *Officer* • Gwen Lee • John Miljan • Lionel Barrymore • Cecil B DeMille ■ *Dir* Edward Sedgwick • *Scr* Richard Schayer, Al Boasberg, Paul Dickey

Free Birds ★★ U

Animated comedy adventure
2013 · US · Colour · 87min

Woody Harrelson and Owen Wilson provide the voices of two wily old turkeys whose desire to avoid the chop leads them to head back to the early 17th century via time machine in a bid to change the first-ever Thanksgiving menu. The film's so rooted in US customs and the country's early colonial history that some of the humour may be lost on audiences in the UK. And while there's just enough slapstick to keep younger kids mildly entertained, this is, at best, a rainy-day diversion. DA *DVD Blu Sp*

Woody Harrelson *Jake* • Owen Wilson *Reggie* • Amy Poehler *Jenny* • George Takei *S.T.E.V.E.* • Colm Meaney *Myles Standish* ■ *Dir* Jimmy Hayward • *Scr* Jimmy Hayward, Scott Mosier, from a story by David J Stern, John J Strauss

Free Enterprise ★★★ 15

Comedy 1998 · US · Colour · 109min

You can't keep a good geek down according to this slickly written indie comedy about a couple of *Star Trek* obsessives. Wannabe film-makers Eric McCormack and Rafer Weigel are inseparable. That is until McCormack meets comic book goddess Audie England and Weigel discovers his hero, William Shatner, has feet of clay. Weigel and McCormack are impressive as the slacker incarnations of Kirk and Spock, but the star is the sportingly self-mocking Shatner. DP *DVD*

Rafer Weigel *Robert* • Eric McCormack *Mark* • Audie England *Claire* • William Shatner *Bill* • Patrick Van Horn *Sean* ■ *Dir* Robert Meyer Burnett • *Scr* Mark A Altman, Robert Meyer Burnett

Free Jimmy ★★ 15

Animated comedy
2006 · UK/Nor · Colour · 81min

A drug-addicted circus elephant called Jimmy, crazed animal liberationists and a torrent of narcotics-related jokes ensure that Norway's first ever computer-animated feature is definitely not one for the kids. A bunch of thieves, voiced by Woody Harrelson, Phil Daniels and Simon Pegg

U SUITABLE FOR ALL Uc SUITABLE ESPECIALLY FOR YOUNG CHILDREN (DVD ONLY) PG PARENTAL GUIDANCE 12A UNDER 12s TO BE ACCOMPANIED (CINEMA ONLY)

(who also adapted the Norwegian screenplay), try to kidnap Jimmy in order to retrieve the drugs contraband sewn into his hide. More odd than entertaining, this rarely works as a comedy since laughs are thin on the ground and the characters are all so thoroughly unpleasant. JR Sex scenes, swearing, drug references.

Woody Harrelson *Roy Arnie* • Simon Pegg *Odd* • Phil Daniels *Gaz* • Jay Simpson *Flea* • Jim Broadbent *Igor Stromowskij* • Kyle MacLachlan *Marius* • Emilia Fox *Bettina* • Samantha Morton *Sonia* ■ *Dir* Christopher Nielsen • *Scr* Christopher Nielsen, Simon Pegg (English version)

Free Men ★★★ 12
Wartime drama 2011 · Fr · Colour · 94min

The perilous situation of the Algerian expatriate community in Nazi-occupied Paris is explored in Ismaël Ferroukhi's fact-based wartime drama. The story is actually told from the perspective of black marketeer Younes (Tahar Rahim, so good in *A Prophet*) who finds himself putting his life at risk for the Resistance cause. This is a largely untold true story, and the material's fascinating, but the idea does suffer from a lack of suspense. It's a drama that intrigues but never quite thrills, even if Rahim is never less than watchable as the small-time crook who discovers his conscience. TJ French +subtitles. Violence, swearing.

DVD *BL*

Tahar Rahim *Younes* • Michel Lonsdale *Si Kaddour Ben Ghabrit* • Mahmoud Shalaby *Salim* • Lubna Azabal *Warba Shlimane aka Leila* • Christopher Buchholz *Major von Ratibor* ■ *Dir* Ismaël Ferroukhi • *Scr* Ismaël Ferroukhi, Alain-Michel Blanc

Free Money ★ 15
Comedy 1998 · Can · Colour · 89min

This moronic comedy has Marlon Brando reaching a career-low as a religious-nut prison warden, joining a completely wasted cast. This unfunny shambles starts with the double wedding of Brando's identical twin daughters, and it's downhill from there. Attempts at quirkiness fall flat, and the nonsensical plot developments include the dumbest prison break you've ever seen. JC

DVD

Marlon Brando *Sven the Swede* • Mira Sorvino *Agent Karen Polarski* • Charlie Sheen *Bud* • Donald Sutherland *Judge Rolf Rausenberg* • Thomas Haden Church *Larry* • David Arquette ■ *Dir* Yves Simoneau • *Scr* Anthony Peck, Joseph Brutsman

A Free Soul ★★★★
Drama 1931 · US · BW · 93min

When San Francisco society girl Norma Shearer, brought up to defy convention by her adored and adoring lawyer father Lionel Barrymore, rejects perfect suitor Leslie Howard for a liaison with gangster Clark Gable, the lives of father and daughter are almost destroyed. MGM wheeled out the big guns and high style for this melodrama which, seen today, is both gripping and fascinating. Shearer picked up one of her several Oscar nominations, as did director Clarence Brown. The best actor award went to Barrymore, who makes a climactic 14-minute courtroom speech. Remade in 1953 as *The Girl Who Had Everything*, starring Elizabeth Taylor. RK

Norma Shearer *Jan Ashe* • Leslie Howard *Dwight Winthrop* • Lionel Barrymore *Stephen Ashe* • Clark Gable *Ace Wilfong* • James Gleason *Eddie* • Lucy Beaumont *Grandma Ashe* • Claire Whitney *Aunt Helen* ■ *Dir* Clarence Brown • *Scr* John Meehan, from the novel by Adela Rogers St Johns, from the play by Willard Mack

Free Willy ★★★ U
Wildlife adventure 1993 · US · Colour · 107min

This strong family picture about a boy and his whale knows exactly which strings to pull and when. Australian director Simon Wincer combines animatronic models with shots of Keiko, the real-life killer whale, with great skill. The action away from the aqua park is suffocated by political correctness, family-bonding scenes and hammed-up villainy, but it's pretty hard to resist once

Keiko and Jason James Richter are on screen together. DP *DVD*

Jason James Richter *Jesse* • Lori Petty *Rae Lindley* • Jayne Atkinson *Annie Greenwood* • August Schellenberg *Randolph Johnson* • Michael Madsen *Glen Greenwood* ■ *Dir* Simon Wincer • *Scr* Keith A Walker, Corey Blechman

Free Willy 2: the Adventure Home ★★ U
Wildlife adventure 1995 · US · Colour · 93min

After all the fuss that followed the revelation that the real Willy was being kept in less than adequate conditions, the producers of this sequel decided to take no chances and used mostly model whales. Unfortunately, they opted for a plastic replica plot, too, with Jason James Richter once more standing between the friendly orca and unscrupulous adults. DP *DVD*

Jason James Richter *Jesse* • Francis Capra *Elvis* • Mary Kate Schellhardt *Nadine* • August Schellenberg *Randolph* • Michael Madsen *Glen* • M Emmet Walsh *Wilcox* ■ *Dir* Dwight Little [Dwight H Little] • *Scr* Karen Janszen, Corey Blechman, John Mattson, from characters by Keith A Walker, Corey Blechman

Free Willy 3: the Rescue ★★★ U
Wildlife adventure 1997 · US · Colour · 81min

Jason James Richter returns for this third instalment of the eco-friendly killer whale saga. However the drama here centres on ten-year-old Vincent Berry, who's horrified to discover that his fisherman father (Patrick Kilpatrick) is an illegal whale hunter. Director Sam Pillsbury taps into America's male hunter myth, making Kilpatrick's re-evaluation a wrench from tradition. The whales are the big attraction, but this is also a subtly argued message movie. DP *DVD*

Jason James Richter *Jesse* • August Schellenberg *Randolph* • Annie Corley *Drew* • Vincent Berry *Max* • Patrick Kilpatrick *Wesley* • Tasha Simms *Mary* ■ *Dir* Sam Pillsbury • *Scr* John Mattson, from characters by Keith A Walker, Corey Blechman

Freebie and the Bean ★★★ 18
Action comedy 1974 · US · Colour · 107min

This early variation on the buddy routine is dominated by a series of spectacular car crashes as San Francisco cops James Caan and Alan Arkin pursue mobster Jack Kruschen. Hugely tasteless (racist jokes from Caan about Arkin's Mexican origins), this is a film where most of the characters are treated with contempt, but director Richard Rush puts so much energetic inventiveness into the turbulence you're almost convinced he doesn't mean it. TH Violence, swearing.

Alan Arkin *Bean* • James Caan *Freebie* • Loretta Swit *Meyers's wife* • Jack Kruschen *Red Meyers* • Mike Kellin *Lt Rosen* • Linda Marsh *Freebie's girl* • Valerie Harper *Consuelo, Bean's wife* ■ *Dir* Richard Rush • *Scr* Robert Kaufman, from a story by Floyd Mutrux

Freebird ★★ 15
Road movie comedy 2007 · UK · Colour · 89min

The Welsh valleys are invaded by Hell's Angels in this offbeat road movie comedy starring Gary Stretch and Phil Daniels. Sent to Wales to purchase a large quantity of marijuana on behalf of a dodgy gangster, dispatch rider Fred (Stretch) and his friends find themselves caught in the crossfire between two rival biker gangs. Like its slacker heroes, who spend the movie taking a smorgasbord of illegal substances, this never quite lives up to the full potential of its off-kilter styling. JR *DVD*

Geoff Bell *Tyg* • Phil Daniels *Grouch* • Gary Stretch *Fred* • Peter Bowles *The Chairman* • Laila Rouass *Lucinda* • James Puddephatt *Phil* ■ *Dir/Scr* Jon Ivay

Freedom Radio ★★ PG
Second World War drama 1940 · UK · BW · 89min

Raymond Huntley, later a fine comic stooge, is the sole reason for watching this outdated and often unintentionally funny

flag-waver. Here he plays a truly sinister Nazi, but the rest of the cast are simply dreadful as they spout platitudes in clipped accents that are totally unsuited to their middle-European characters. Clive Brook and Derek Farr are embarrassingly earnest as the heads of a pirate radio station, but even worse is Diana Wynyard's ludicrously naive collaborator. DP *DVD*

Clive Brook *Dr Karl Roder* • Diana Wynyard *Irena Roder* • Raymond Huntley *Rabenau* • Derek Farr *Hans Glaser* • Joyce Howard *Elly* • H Marion-Crawford [Howard Marion-Crawford] *Kummer* • John Penrose *Otto* ■ *Dir* Anthony Asquith • *Scr* Anatole de Grunwald, Basil Woon, Jeffrey Dell, Louis Golding, Gordon Wellesley, Bridget Boland, Roland Pertwee, from the story by Wolfgang Wilhelm, George Campbell

Freedom Road: the Vernon Johns Story ★★★
Biographical drama 1994 · US · Colour · 100min

This is a powerful and at times hard-hitting TV movie about the early days of the civil rights movement. Set in Alabama during the late 1940s and early 1950s, it's held together by a towering performance from James Earl Jones. As the preacher urging his apathetic congregation to lobby for drastic social change, Jones proves himself capable of both determined dignity and electrifying oratory. DP

James Earl Jones *Reverend Vernon Johns* • Mary Alice *Altona Johns* • Joe Seneca *Deacon Wilkes* • Cissy Houston *Rose* • Nicole Leach *Baby Dee* • Tommy Hollis *Coach Hill* ■ *Dir* Kenneth Fink • *Scr* Kevin Arkadie, from the story by Leslie Lee, Gary Steele

Freedom Song ★★★ 12
Political drama 2000 · US · Colour · 111min

Set in a small town in Mississippi in 1961, Phil Alden Robinson's fictional TV drama demonstrates that not every African-American approved of the battle against desegregation. Danny Glover gives another powerhouse performance as the father fearful that son Vicellous Reon Shannon's involvement with Vondie Curtis-Hall's suffrage campaign will cause more harm than good. Sincere. DP

Danny Glover *Will Walker* • Vondie Curtis-Hall *Daniel Wall* • Vicellous Reon Shannon *Owen Walker* • Loretta Devine *Evelyn Walker* • Michael Jai White *Coleman Vaughnes* ■ *Dir* Phil Alden Robinson • *Scr* Phil Alden Robinson, Stanley Weiser

Freedom Writers ★★★ 12
Biographical drama 2006 · US/Ger · Colour · 117min

Hollywood classroom dramas often revolve around teachers connecting with their pupils through literature or tough love. *Freedom Writers* is no exception. Hilary Swank stars as an English teacher in early 1990s Los Angeles who introduces her racially mixed class of underachievers to *The Diary of Anne Frank*. This was evidently something of a passion project for Swank (who also executive produces), and it's her likeably gauche turn as the over-eager teacher that gives this movie enough charm to coast by painlessly. However, writer/director Richard LaGravenese manages to make it implausible, which is quite a feat considering it's based on a true story. JR Violence, brief swearing. *DVD*

Hilary Swank *Erin Gruwell* • Patrick Dempsey *Scott Casey* • Scott Glenn *Steve Gruwell* • Imelda Staunton *Margaret Campbell* • April Lee Hernandez *Eva* • Mario *Andre* • Jason Finn *Marcus* ■ *Dir* Richard LaGravenese • *Scr* Richard LaGravenese, from the non-fiction book *The Freedom Writers Diary* by Erin Gruwell, Freedom Writers

Freedomland ★★ 15
Mystery thriller 2006 · US · Colour · 108min

Injured Julianne Moore stumbles into a New Jersey hospital and reports that she's been carjacked by a black man from the nearby public housing estate. Cop Samuel L Jackson is assigned to coax as many details as possible out of the disturbed, erratic woman and eventually learns that her young son was asleep in the back seat of the stolen vehicle. This movie disintegrates

into an ungainly mess and Jackson and Moore give uncharacteristically sub-par performances. LF Swearing, violence.

DVD

Samuel L Jackson *Lorenzo Council* • Julianne Moore *Brenda Martin* • Edie Falco *Karen Collucci* • Ron Eldard *Danny Martin* • William Forsythe *Boyle* • Aunjanue Ellis *Felicia* • Anthony Mackie *Billy Williams* ■ *Dir* Joe Roth • *Scr* Richard Price, from his novel

Freefall: Flight 174 ★★ PG
Drama based on a true story 1995 · US · Colour · 93min

This in-flight entertainment is one of TV moviedom's better efforts, helped by the fact that it's based on an incident that occurred in 1983. William Devane, Shelley Hack and Mariette Hartley are put through their panic-station paces as Flight 174 mysteriously runs out of fuel in midair and the tense search begins for a landing site. There's enough low-rent suspense and ham acting on offer to make this enjoyable. AJ *DVD*

William Devane *Captain Bob Pearson* • Shelley Hack *Lynn Brown* • Scott Hylands *Maurice Quintal* • Mariette Hartley *Beth Pearson* • Nicholas Turturro *Al Williams* ■ *Dir* Jorge Montesi • *Scr* Lionel Chetwynd, from the book *Freefall* by William Hoffer, Marilyn Hoffer

Freeheld ★★★ 12
Romantic drama based on a true story 2015 · US/UK · Colour · 99min

In this true-life drama, New Jersey police officer Laurel Hester (Julianne Moore) finds herself battling the local authorities when she's stricken by cancer and attempts to transfer her pension rights to same-sex partner Stacie Andree (Ellen Page). Based on a landmark US case in the legal validation of civil partnerships, it's a film filled with good intentions and fine performances (Moore is again outstanding, as is Michael Shannon playing a detective colleague), yet it proves somewhat bland in the telling. TJ Some swearing, sex references *DVD*

Julianne Moore *Laurel Hester* • Ellen Page *Stacie Andree* • Michael Shannon *Dane Wells* • Steve Carell *Steven Goldstein* • Luke Grimes *Todd Belkin* ■ *Dir* Peter Sollett • *Scr* Ron Nyswaner • *Music* Johnny Marr, Hans Zimmer

Freejack ★★ 15
Science-fiction adventure 1992 · US · Colour · 105min

Based on an imaginative and surprising novel, this opts instead for sci-fi cliché and obvious thrills as Emilio Estevez is plucked from near-death in a racing accident to house the brain of a future-age Anthony Hopkins. Mick Jagger – in his first big screen dramatic role since 1970's *Performance* and *Ned Kelly* – suitably interprets his devious mercenary as a cynical yobbo, but it's a sin not to give talent like Hopkins and Rene Russo meatier roles. JM Swearing, violence. *DVD*

Emilio Estevez *Alex Furlong* • Rene Russo *Julie Redlund* • Mick Jagger *Vacendak* • Anthony Hopkins *McCandless* • Jonathan Banks *Michelette* • David Johansen *Brad* • Amanda Plummer *Nun* • Grand L Bush *Boone* ■ *Dir* Geoff Murphy • *Scr* Steven Pressfield, Ronald Shusett, Dan Gilroy, from a story by Steven Pressfield, Ronald Shusett, from the novel *Immortality Inc* by Robert Sheckley

Freestyle ★★ 12
Romantic sports drama 2009 · UK · Colour · 112min

This London-set drama is an addition to the urban teen-movie genre in which social deprivation can be remedied by the ability to dance or plant a ball in a net. Newcomer Lucy Konadu plays Ondene, a black girl from south London with a talent for freestyle basketball, whose mother (Suzann McLean) is adamant that she focus on her Oxford entrance exams. Alas, her efforts are undermined by Ondene's new boyfriend, fancy freestyler Leon (a muscle-flexing Arinze Kene), who comes from a deprived background but has dreams of going to university. It's total fluff and nonsense, and also disingenuous and patronising when it comes to the point when Ondene must finally choose between basketball, her boyfriend and a first-class education. SP Violence. **DVD**

Lucy Konadu *Ondene* • Arinze Kene *Leon* • Suzann McLean *Hyacinth* • Alfie Allen *Gez* • *Dir* Kolton Lee • *Scr* Michael Maynard

Freeway ★★★★ 18

Satirical thriller   1996 · US · Colour · 97min

This deeply twisted version of *Little Red Riding Hood* brought the exceptionally talented Reese Witherspoon to the attention of a wider audience. She plays a feisty young teenager from a dysfunctional family who sets off to find her grandmother, falling foul of psycho Bob Wolverton (Kiefer Sutherland) en route. Witherspoon is a revelation as the foul-mouthed teenage rebel, Sutherland is great as her nemesis, and there are enjoyable cameos from Amanda Plummer, Dan Hedaya and Brooke Shields. JF **DVD**

Kiefer Sutherland *Bob Wolverton* • Reese Witherspoon *Vanessa* • Brooke Shields *Mimi Wolverton* • Wolfgang Bodison *Detective Breer* • Dan Hedaya *Detective Wallace* • Amanda Plummer *Ramona* ■ *Dir/Scr* Matthew Bright

Freeze Frame ★★★ 15

Crime thriller   2003 · UK/Ire · Colour · 95min

Funnyman Lee Evans sheds his comic skin in this satisfying slice of low-budget paranoia. He delivers a supremely creepy performance as a misfit who's so traumatised by a near murder conviction that he constantly videotapes himself in case he needs a future alibi. First-time writer/director John Simpson makes imaginative use of modern visual technology, interweaving many different formats into an absorbing and atmospheric whole. The result is disturbing and disorienting, only let down by a second-rate supporting cast. SF Violence, swearing. **DVD**

Lee Evans *Sean Veil* • Sean McGinley *Detective Inspector Emeric* • Ian McNeice *Saul Seger* • Colin Salmon *Mountjoy* • Rachael Stirling *Katie Carter* • Rachel O'Riordan *Mary Shaw* • Andrew Wilson (2) *Covert cameraman* • Andrea Grimason *Susan Jasper* • Martin McSharry *Sam Jasper* ■ *Dir/Scr* John Simpson

Freezer ★★★★ 18

Horror   2000 · Jpn · Colour · 102min

Although its cult reputation rests on the fact that a respectable woman keeps the victims of her vengeful killings in huge chest freezers in her apartment, Takashi Ishii's chiller proves much more intriguing on a psychological than a visceral level. Having attempted to rebuild her life following a rape, Harumi Inoue's pitiless dispatching of the three perpetrators is presented as an agonised struggle between her repugnance at her actions and the need to end her nightmare. Consequently, the deaths are shown in all their cruelty to reflect her pain and desperation, which makes them all the more disturbing. DP Japanese +subtitles. **DVD**

Harumi Inoue *Chihiro* • Shingo Tsurumi *Kojima* • Kazuki Kitamura *Hirokawa* • Shunsuke Matsuoka *Nogami* • Naoto Takenaka *Baba* ■ *Dir/Scr* Takashi Ishii

Freight ★★ 18

Action crime drama   2010 · UK · Colour · 86min

This vicious crime saga set in Leeds finds local businessman Billy Murray crossing swords with an East European gang of people traffickers, who force women into the sex trade while making their husbands take part in cage fights. It's a fast-paced story, if rather predictable, but the graphic violence may be too strong for some viewers. Writer/director Stuart St Paul's script also has a tendency to drift towards uncomfortable England-for-the-English racism. TeS Violence. **DVD**

Billy Murray *Gabe Taylor* • Craig Fairbrass *Jed* • Danny Midwinter *Cristi* • Sam Kennard *Stevie* • Luke Aikman *Karl* • Zsolt Nagy *Fryderyck* ■ *Dir/Scr* Stuart St Paul

French Cancan ★★★ PG

Period musical drama   1955 · Fr · Colour · 99min

Director Jean Renoir's return to France after 15 years and his reunion with fellow legend Jean Gabin was not the cinema event it promised to be. But there is still much to treasure in this exuberant tribute to the Moulin Rouge. The story – Gabin sets out to turn laundress Françoise Arnoul into a star – would not have been out of place in a glitzy Hollywood musical, but Renoir lovingly brings the glamorous world of the celebrated cancan to glorious life. JF French +subtitles. **DVD** **Blu**

Jean Gabin *Danglard* • Maria Felix *La Belle Abesse* • Françoise Arnoul *Nini* • Jean-Roger Caussimon *Baron Walter* • Gianni Esposito *Prince Alexandre* • Philippe Clay *Casimir* • Michel Piccoli *Valorgueil* ■ *Dir* Jean Renoir • *Scr* Jean Renoir, from an idea by André-Paul Antoine

The French Connection

★★★★★ 18

Crime drama   1971 · US · Colour · 99min

Based on a real-life drugs bust by New York narcotics cops, director William Friedkin's crime drama brings a fluid, documentary realism to Ernest Tidyman's adaptation that makes it one of the most influential movies of a very fertile decade for American film. Gene Hackman made his name (and won an Oscar) as wild-card detective "Popeye" Doyle, chasing down Fernando Rey's suave French drugs overlord. This is the underside of New York and a distinctly non-glamorous portrait of police life. The action, like the film's iconic car chase beneath an elevated train track, is real and dangerous. AC Violence, swearing, drug abuse, brief nudity. **DVD** **Blu**

Gene Hackman *Jimmy "Popeye" Doyle* • Fernando Rey *Alain Charnier* • Roy Scheider *Buddy Russo* • Tony LoBianco *Sal Boca* • Marcel Bozzuffi *Pierre Nicoli* • Frederic de Pasquale *Devereaux* • Bill Hickman *Mulderig* ■ *Dir* William Friedkin • *Scr* Ernest Tidyman, from the novel by Robin Moore • *Cinematographer* Owen Roizman

French Connection II

★★★★ 18

Thriller   1975 · US · Colour · 114min

John Frankenheimer's sequel to *The French Connection* may be less believable than its predecessor, but it's still a cracking thriller. Here, New York cop "Popeye" Doyle (Gene Hackman brilliantly reprising his Oscar-winning role from the original) blunders into the French operation to uncover heroin-tsar Fernando Rey's drugs ring. There's a disturbing sequence that details Hackman's withdrawal after being forcibly addicted, but after that it's revenge all the way. TH In English, French. Violence, swearing, drug abuse. **DVD** **Blu**

Gene Hackman *"Popeye" Doyle* • Fernando Rey *Alain Charnier* • Bernard Fresson *Barthélemy* • Jean-Pierre Castaldi *Raoul Diron* • Charles Millot *Miletto* • Cathleen Nesbitt *Old lady* • Pierre Collet *Old man* ■ *Dir* John Frankenheimer • *Scr* Robert Dillon, Laurie Dillon, Alexander Jacobs, from a story by Laurie Dillon, Robert Dillon

French Dressing ★★★ 12

Comedy   1964 · UK · BW · 82min

Ken Russell passed up the chance to direct the Cliff Richard musical *Summer Holiday*, choosing to break into feature films with this charming story partly inspired by Jacques Tati's *Monsieur Hulot's Holiday*. A deck-chair attendant (James Booth) at the seaside resort of Gormleigh-on-Sea (Herne Bay in disguise) aims to brighten things up by organising a film festival with a Bardot-like film star (Marisa Mell). Despite a nice cast, it was panned by critics at the time, but now seems rather cherishable. AT **DVD**

James Booth *Jim* • Roy Kinnear *Henry* • Marisa Mell *Francoise Fayol* • Alita Naughton *Judy* • Bryan Pringle *Mayor* • Robert Robinson (1) ■ *Dir* Ken Russell • *Scr* Peter Myers, Ronald Cass, Peter Brett, Johnny Speight (additional dialogue), from a story by Peter Myers, Ronald Cass

French Film ★★★ 15

Romantic comedy   2008 · UK · Colour · 84min

More "vague" than "nouvelle", this Rohmeresque wannabe is actually a quintessentially British romantic comedy from the Curtis school. Hugh Bonneville is the fogeyish critic researching for an interview with a French director (Eric Cantona) with celebrated views on *l'amour*, who comes to question whether he has ever really loved longtime partner Victoria Hamilton. Jackie Oudney's feature debut is as charmingly cine-literate as it is genially enjoyable, but the movie's surfeit of caricatures and clichés makes it just a teensy bit smug. DP Swearing. **DVD**

Anne-Marie Duff *Sophie* • Hugh Bonneville *Jed Winter* • Douglas Henshall *Marcus* • Eric Cantona *Thierry Grimandi* • Victoria Hamilton *Cheryl* • Jean Dell *Alain* • Adrian Annis *Bowler* • Henry Maynard *Waiter* ■ *Dir* Jackie Oudney • *Scr* Aschlin Ditta • *Cinematographer* Sean Van Hales

French Kiss ★★★ 15

Romantic comedy   1995 · US · Colour · 106min

It may lack the substance of *The Big Chill* director Lawrence Kasdan's previous efforts, but this amiably fluffy confection is still enjoyable. Meg Ryan, in her trademark ditzy mode, sets off for France to reclaim wandering fiancé Timothy Hutton only to find herself stuck with slobby French thief Kevin Kline. The latter's role was reported to have been created for Gérard Depardieu, but Kline acquits himself well as the Gallic rogue and the chemistry between him and Ryan is spot-on. JF Swearing. **DVD**

Meg Ryan *Kate* • Kevin Kline *Luc* • Timothy Hutton *Charlie* • Jean Reno *Jean-Paul* • François Cluzet *Bob* • Susan Anbeh *Juliette* • Renee Humphrey *Lilly* ■ *Dir* Lawrence Kasdan • *Scr* Adam Brooks

The French Lieutenant's Woman ★★★★ 12

Romantic comedy   1981 · UK · Colour · 123min

Director Karel Reisz and screenwriter Harold Pinter here take on the near-impossible filming of John Fowles's complex novel. Two stories are told in parallel, one of an affair between a disgraced Victorian governess and an English gentleman, and the other the relationship between the two film actors portraying the Victorian couple. Jeremy Irons and Meryl Streep feature in the dual roles. Victorian morality seeps hauntingly into every frame of the main story, which is decked out in convincing period detail and hangs on two scorching performances from the leads. JM Sex scenes, swearing, brief nudity. **DVD**

Meryl Streep *Sarah Woodruff/Anna* • Jeremy Irons *Charles Smithson/Mike* • Hilton McRae *Sam* • Leo McKern *Dr Grogan* • Emily Morgan *Mary* • Charlotte Mitchell *Mrs Tranter* • Lynsey Baxter *Ernestina Freeman* • Jean Faulds *Cook* ■ *Dir* Karel Reisz • *Scr* Harold Pinter, from the novel by John Fowles • *Cinematographer* Freddie Francis • *Music* Carl Davis

The French Line ★★ U

Musical comedy   1954 · US · Colour · 98min

Notorious in its day for Jane Russell's censor-provoking costume – the one with the crafty gaps in it – this was originally shot in 3D to best show off the actress's assets. It was eventually released flat, which is how this would-be comedy well and truly falls. The songs are lacklustre, the supporting cast is second rate and Russell, sadly, is past her prime. TS **Blu**

Jane Russell *Mary Carson* • Gilbert Roland *Pierre DuQueene* • Arthur Hunnicutt *"Waco" Mosby* • Mary McCarty *Annie Farrell* • Joyce MacKenzie *Myrtle Brown* ■ *Dir* Lloyd Bacon • *Scr* Mary Loos, Richard Sale, from a story by Matty Kemp, Isabel Dawn

A French Mistress ★★ PG

Comedy   1960 · UK · BW · 93min

Roy Boulting was past his comic prime by the time he made this underwhelming boys' school comedy, produced, as ever, by twin brother John, and co-scripted by longtime partner Jeffrey Dell. All those familiar faces should at least have given the action a certain cosy appeal, but they are left high and dry by a script that is little more than a bumper collection of sniggering bike-shed jokes about sex and French women. DP **DVD**

Cecil Parker *Headmaster* • James Robertson-Justice *Robert Martin* • Ian Bannen *Colin Crane* • Agnes Laurent *Madeleine Lafarge* • Raymond Huntley *Reverend Edwin Peake* • Irene Handl *Staff Sergeant Hodges* • Edith Sharpe *Matron* • Kenneth Griffith *Mr Meade* • Michael Crawford *Kent* ■ *Dir* Roy Boulting • *Scr* Roy Boulting, Jeffrey Dell, from the play by Robert Monro

French Postcards ★★ 15

Romantic comedy drama
1979 · W Ger/Fr/US · Colour · 90min

This determinedly tasteful older woman romance fails to capture the excitement of teenage initiation, despite a knowing display of exotic eccentricity from Marie-France Pisier as the tutor at the Institute of French Studies in Paris, whose unconventional methods cast a spell over impressionable all-American Miles Chapin. While the City of Light exerts its usual magic, it also exposes the banality of the American Dream. DP

Miles Chapin *Joel* • Blanche Baker *Laura* • David Marshall Grant *Alex* • Valérie Quennessen *Toni* • Debra Winger *Melanie* • Mandy Patinkin *Sayyid* • Marie-France Pisier *Mme Tessier* • Jean Rochefort *M Tessier* ■ *Dir* Willard Huyck • *Scr* Willard Huyck, Gloria Katz

French without Tears ★★★

Romantic comedy   1939 · UK/US · BW · 88min

Although director Anthony Asquith refused to "open up" plays for the screen, his understanding of the intimate relationship between camera, actors and dialogue made his films surprisingly fluent. The cast adds lustre to the simple story of young men at a French language school in the south of France, who fall for the charms of visiting flirt, Ellen Drew. This comedy is a perfect example of how a frothy, very British battle-of-the-sexes romp can work as a witty screen diversion. The editor of this entertaining bit of fluff was a young man called David Lean. BB

Ray Milland *Alan Howard* • Ellen Drew *Diana Lake* • Janine Darcey *Jacqueline Maingot* • David Tree *Chris Neilan* • Roland Culver *Commander Bill Rogers* • Guy Middleton *Brian Curtis* • Kenneth Morgan *Kenneth Lake* ■ *Dir* Anthony Asquith • *Scr* Anatole de Grunwald, Ian Dalrymple, from the play by Terence Rattigan

Frenchie ★★

Western   1950 · US · Colour · 80min

Joel McCrea and Shelley Winters, the leads in this tame reworking of *Destry Rides Again*, simply can't match the star wattage generated by their counterparts in the classic 1939 western. Winters is typically brassy as the boss of a New Orleans gambling den who heads west to find her father's killers. But while he embodies decency, McCrea has none of the vulnerability that made James Stewart's everyman so appealing. DP

Joel McCrea *Tom Banning* • Shelley Winters *Frenchie Fontaine* • Paul Kelly (1) *Pete Lambert* • Elsa Lanchester *Countess* • Marie Windsor *Diane* • John Russell *Lance Cole* • John Emery *Clyde Gorman* • Regis Toomey *Carter* ■ *Dir* Louis King • *Scr* Oscar Brodney

Frenchman's Creek ★★★

Period romantic adventure
1944 · US · Colour · 113min

Following the Oscar-winning success of *Rebecca*, Hollywood snapped up Daphne du Maurier's tale of an aristocratic woman who leaves her husband, goes to Cornwall and falls for a French pirate. Mitchell Leisen's direction typically concentrates on the colour scheme, the sets and costumes – he was once an art director – while the story rolls along by itself. Joan Fontaine is ideally cast as the imperious woman in the throes of passion but she's handicapped by the dull leading men. AT

Joan Fontaine *Lady Dona St Columb* • Arturo de Cordova *French Pirate* • Basil Rathbone *Lord Rockingham* • Nigel Bruce *Lord Godolphin* • Cecil Kellaway *William* • Ralph Forbes *Harry St*

Columb ■ *Dir* Mitchell Leisen • *Scr* Talbot Jennings, from Daphne du Maurier's novel • *Costume Designer* Raoul Pène du Bois

Frenzy ★★★★ 18
Thriller 1972 · UK · Colour · 111min

Alfred Hitchcock's penultimate film saw him return to his British roots with this thriller about a necktie murderer causing havoc in London. Jon Finch plays the chief suspect but, typically, Hitchcock is more interested in black humour than a simple whodunnit. Lots of typical Hitchcockian touches are on show – a roving, restless camera; dark shots of fleeing footsteps; a shocking corpse when least expected. *Sleuth* author Anthony Shaffer wrote the screenplay and there's plenty of other local talent on display. While some regard this as inferior fare, it remains an unsettling piece. SH
Violence, swearing. *DVD* BL

Jon Finch *Richard Blaney* • Alec McCowen *Chief Inspector Oxford* • Barry Foster *Robert Rusk* • Barbara Leigh-Hunt *Brenda Blaney* • Anna Massey *Babs Milligan* • Vivien Merchant *Mrs Oxford* • Bernard Cribbins *Felix Forsythe* • Billie Whitelaw *Hetty Porter* • Rita Webb *Mrs Rusk* • Jean Marsh *Monica Barley* ■ *Dir* Alfred Hitchcock • *Scr* Anthony Shaffer, from the novel *Goodbye Piccadilly, Farewell Leicester Square* by Arthur LaBern • *Cinematographer* Gilbert Taylor

Frequency ★★★★ 15
Fantasy thriller 2000 · US · Colour · 113min

Via an ancient ham radio set, Jim Caviezel is able to speak to his beloved fireman dad (Dennis Quaid) across 30 years of time, on the day before the latter is due to die in a warehouse blaze. Forewarned by Caviezel, Quaid escapes his fate, but his survival changes history: suddenly, Caviezel's mum (Elizabeth Mitchell) no longer exists! Paradoxes appear as the film gets increasingly complex, but Quaid and Caviezel give fine performances and director Gregory Hoblit's only serious misjudgement is a slushy finale. DA
Violence, swearing. *DVD*

Dennis Quaid *Frank Sullivan* • Jim Caviezel *John Sullivan* • André Braugher *Satch DeLeon* • Elizabeth Mitchell *Julia Sullivan* • Noah Emmerich *Gordo Hersch* • Shawn Doyle *Jack Shepard* ■ *Dir* Gregory Hoblit • *Scr* Toby Emmerich

Frequently Asked Questions about Time Travel ★ 15
Science-fiction comedy 2008 · UK/US · Colour · 79min

In this sub-par time-travel comedy, three slackers walk into their local pub and discover a hole in the space-time continuum in the gents toilet. Future babe Anna Faris materialises to mend it and advises the friends on how to avoid multiple versions of themselves in parallel universes. Resembling a leftover *Red Dwarf* sketch padded out to feature length, this is a scattershot blast at all things sci-fi and geeky, but director Gareth Carrivick and screenwriter Jamie Mathieson fail to locate the joke. Most of the budget must have gone on *Scary Movie* star Faris, who looks uncomfortable and distinctly out of place. AJ Swearing. *DVD*

Chris O'Dowd *Ray* • Dean Lennox Kelly *Pete* • Mark Wootton *Toby* • Anna Faris *Cassie* • Meredith MacNeill *Millie* ■ *Dir* Gareth Carrivick • *Scr* Jamie Mathieson

Fresh ★★★★ 18
Drama 1994 · US · Colour · 109min

The frequently explored subject of ghetto life and drugs is wonderfully enlivened here by Boaz Yakin's direction and Sean Nelson's quietly contained performance as the 12-year-old trying to extricate himself from his squalid upbringing. He is well backed up by Samuel L Jackson as the father who has failed his son in every respect but has taught him to play chess. The absence of moralising and macho posturing gives authenticity and poignancy to the film. TH
Violence, swearing, drug abuse

Sean Nelson *Fresh* • Giancarlo Esposito *Esteban* • Samuel L Jackson *Sam* • N'Bushe Wright *Nicole* • Ron Brice *Corky* • Jean LaMarre *Jake* • José Zuniga *Lt Perez* • Luis Lantigua *Chuckie* ■ *Dir/Scr* Boaz Yakin

Fresh Horses ★★ 15
Romantic drama 1988 · US · Colour · 98min

Andrew McCarthy co-stars with Molly Ringwald in this doom-laden story of ill-matched lovers. McCarthy is a university student who has a good marriage in prospect until he meets Ringwald, at which point common sense deserts him. She turns out to be an underage bride from the wrong side of the tracks, whose husband Viggo Mortensen may be a murderer. Far too superficial to work, McCarthy is very bland and Ringwald too one-dimensional to pull this off. LH

Molly Ringwald *Jewel* • Andrew McCarthy *Matt Larkin* • Patti D'Arbanville *Jean McBaine* • Ben Stiller *Tipton* • Doug Hutchinson *Sproles* ■ *Dir* David Anspaugh • *Scr* Larry Ketron, from his play

The Freshman ★★★★★ U
Silent comedy 1925 · US · BW · 69min

The bespectacled comic innocence of Harold Lloyd here takes a tumble that does him no harm at all, as the nerdish new college student who, via a series of accidents, beomes an all-star football player and so wins the hand of Jobyna Ralson. A classic of Lloyd's "Cinderfella" kind of humour – the poor boy who makes good – and there are some sly digs at the way an American educational institute values brawn instead of brain to raise funds. The final game is a knockout in more ways than one. TH

Harold Lloyd *Harold "Speedy" Lamb* • Jobyna Ralston *Peggy* • Brooks Benedict *College cad* • James Anderson (I) *Chester A "Chet" Trask* • Hazel Keener *College belle* • Joseph Harrington *College tailor* • Pat Harmon *The coach* • Charles Stevenson *Assistant coach* ■ *Dir* Fred C Newmeyer, Sam Taylor • *Scr* John Grey, Ted Wilde, Tim Whelan, Sam Taylor, Clyde Bruckman, Lex Neal, Jean Havez

The Freshman ★★★★ PG
Comedy drama 1990 · US · Colour · 98min

A mellow Marlon Brando gives perhaps his greatest comedy performance here. It's a case of self-parody, as he plays a godfather figure making film student Matthew Broderick an offer he can't refuse: a job as a delivery boy, carting around exotic animals including a giant lizard. Andrew Bergman's glorious spoof of Mafia ways spends too long satirising film-study pretension, but spins its screwball antics along at such a pace you can forgive it almost anything. TH *DVD*

Marlon Brando *Carmine Sabatini* • Matthew Broderick *Clark Kellogg* • Bruno Kirby *Victor Ray* • Penelope Ann Miller *Tina Sabatini* • Frank Whaley *Steve Bushak* • Jon Polito *Chuck Greenwald* • Paul Benedict *Arthur Fleeber* ■ *Dir/Scr* Andrew Bergman

Freud ★★★ 12
Biographical drama 1962 · US · BW · 134min

In this *noir*-ish drama, director John Huston pointedly places Freud (played with brooding intensity by Montgomery Clift) alongside Copernicus and Darwin as a revolutionary thinker, and explores his early years as he battled to convince his peers that sexuality, even in childhood, was the basis of neurosis. With its stark black-and-white photography, the movie looks like a 40s thriller, but Clift (visibly ailing from his own personal demons) is a compelling presence. JA

Montgomery Clift *Sigmund Freud* • Susannah York *Cecily Koertner* • Larry Parks *Dr Joseph Breuer* • Susan Kohner *Martha Freud* • Eric Portman *Dr Theodore Meynert* ■ *Dir* John Huston • *Scr* Charles Kaufman, Wolfgang Reinhardt, from Kaufman's story

Frida ★★★★ 15
Biographical drama 2002 · US · Colour · 117min

The extraordinary life of Mexican painter Frida Kahlo is told in fierce style by director Julie Taymor, who cleverly fuses the vivid events of Kahlo's turbulent existence with the stark images of her uncompromising self-portraits. Salma Hayek gives a career-best performance as the bisexual bohemian Marxist, whose physical suffering infused her challenging work. Charting her many affairs but mainly her stormy marriage to womanising artist Diego Rivera (Alfred Molina), Taymor's visually inventive film is riveting. AJ Swearing, nudity. *DVD* BL

Salma Hayek *Frida Kahlo* • Alfred Molina *Diego Rivera* • Geoffrey Rush *Leon Trotsky* • Ashley Judd *Tina Modotti* • Antonio Banderas *David Alfaro Siqueiros* • Edward Norton *Nelson Rockefeller* • Valeria Golino *Lupe Marin* • Saffron Burrows *Gracie* • Mia Maestro *Cristina Kahlo* • Roger Rees *Guillermo Kahlo* ■ *Dir* Julie Taymor • *Scr* Clancy Sigal, Diane Lake, Gregory Nava, Anna Thomas, from the biography *Frida: a Biography of Frida Kahlo* by Hayden Herrera

Friday ★★★ 15
Comedy 1995 · US · Colour · 87min

Rapper Ice Cube and Chris Tucker (in one of his first major roles) navigate an ordinary day in the ghetto through a haze of dope in this less preachy and more laid-back view of the "boyz" from the 'hood. Their love of the latter sees them fall foul of gun-toting gangsters, while the unemployed pair also have to endure lectures from their relatives, jealous partners and the neighbourhood bully. Director F Gary Gray (*The Negotiator*), sidesteps some of the usual clichés of the genre to deliver an affectionate, fresh portrait of inner-city life. *Next Friday* followed in 1999. JF *DVD* BL

Ice Cube *Craig* • Chris Tucker *Smokey* • Nia Long *Debbie* • Tiny "Zeus" Lister Jr [Tom "Tiny" Lister Jr] *Deebo* • John Witherspoon *Mr Jones* • Anna Maria Horsford *Mrs Jones* • Regina King *Dana* • Paula Jai Parker *Joi* ■ *Dir* F Gary Gray • *Scr* Ice Cube, DJ Pooh

Friday Foster ★★★ 18
Blaxploitation crime drama 1975 · US · Colour · 86min

Pam Grier – star of *Jackie Brown* – is here seen in an early role as a black "superwoman". She plays a fearless magazine photographer (a character taken from a comic strip) who blunders into a St Valentine's Day-style massacre involving a black millionaire. Grier is joined by a terrific black cast: Yaphet Kotto (cop), Godfrey Cambridge (fashion designer), Eartha Kitt (fashion designer), Scatman Crothers (minister). The villainous mastermind (Jim Backus) is white, though. TH

Pam Grier *Friday Foster* • Yaphet Kotto *Colt Hawkins* • Godfrey Cambridge *Ford Malotte* • Thalmus Rasulala *Blake Tarr* • Eartha Kitt *Madame Rena* • Jim Backus *Enos Griffith* • Scatman Crothers *Reverend Noble Franklin* ■ *Dir* Arthur Marks • *Scr* Orville H Hampton, Arthur Marks, from a story by Arthur Marks

Friday Night Lights ★★★★ 12
Sports drama based on a true story 2004 · US/Ger · Colour · 112min

Billy Bob Thornton delivers yet another robust but nuanced performance in this atypical American football movie that focuses not on the highs and lows of winning and losing, but on the intolerable pressure that is put on players barely old enough to shave. Based on a true story, it centres on a high-school football team from the small Texas town of Odessa, a place warped by its obsession with the game and oblivious to the human cost of this fixation. On one level, this is an intense and exciting sports drama, shot in grainy documentary style but with quick-fire editing. But, it's also intelligent and undercut with a powerful sadness. AS *DVD*

Billy Bob Thornton *Coach Gary Gaines* • Derek Luke *Boobie Miles* • Jay Hernandez *Brian Chavez* • Lucas Black *Mike Winchell* • Garrett Hedlund *Don Billingsley* • Tim McGraw *Charles Billingsley* • Connie Britton *Sharon Gaines* • Lee Thompson Young *Chris Comer* • Lee Jackson *Ivory Christian* ■ *Dir* Peter Berg • *Scr* Peter Berg, David Aaron Cohen, from the non-fiction book *Friday Night Lights: a Town, a Team and a Dream* by HG Bissinger [Buzz Bissinger]

Friday the Thirteenth ★★★★ U
Drama 1933 · UK · BW · 82min

After a bus crashes, the preceding day in the lives of six passengers unfolds, before revealing which ones survive. The formula goes at least as far back as Thornton Wilder's 1927 novel *The Bridge of San Luis Rey*, but it's an intriguing one that is given an entertaining workout here. The episodes are neatly tied together with an adroit mixture of comedy and drama, while the top-notch cast includes Jessie Matthews and co-writer Emlyn Williams as a cunningly insinuating villain. TV

Sonnie Hale *Alf, the conductor* • Cyril Smith *Fred, the driver* • Max Miller *Joe* • Alfred Drayton *Detective* • Eliot Makeham *Henry Jackson* • Ursula Jeans *Eileen Jackson* • DA Clarke-Smith *Max* • Edmund Gwenn *Wakefield* • Mary Jerrold *Flora Wakefield* • Gordon Harker *Hamilton Briggs* • Emlyn Williams *Blake* • Frank Lawton *Frank Parsons* • Belle Chrystall *Mary Summers* • Robertson Hare *Mr Lightfoot* • Martita Hunt *Agnes Lightfoot* • Jessie Matthews *Millie Adams* • Ralph Richardson *Horace, the schoolmaster* ■ *Dir* Victor Saville • *Scr* GH Moresby-White, Emlyn Williams, from a story by Sidney Gilliat, Moresby-White

Friday the 13th ★★★ 18
Horror 1980 · US · Colour · 90min

Essentially a cheap rural rip-off of John Carpenter's hugely influential *Halloween*, this mix of bloody horror and teenage terror from low-budget sleaze merchant Sean S Cunningham kick-started the stalk-and-slash vogue of the 1980s. Here the catalogue of slaughter occurs after Camp Crystal Lake reopens for business following a brutal unsolved murder. There are plenty of gory scares as numerous counsellors (including a pre-stardom Kevin Bacon) come under attack from a mystery assailant. AJ *DVD*

Betsy Palmer *Mrs Voorhees* • Adrienne King *Alice* • Harry Crosby *Bill* • Laurie Bartram *Brenda* • Mark Nelson *Ned* • Jeannine Taylor *Marcie* • Robbi Morgan *Annie* • Kevin Bacon *Jack* • Ari Lehman *Jason Voorhees* ■ *Dir* Sean S Cunningham • *Scr* Victor Miller

Friday the 13th Part 2 ★★ 18
Horror 1981 · US · Colour · 83min

The first sequel to the surprise horror hit is a virtual retread of the original, except that it introduces maniac icon Jason Voorhees (here played by Warrington Gillette) into the mayhem mix, eager to butcher another camp full of sex-starved counsellors. No real surprises, just plenty of murders, with graphic impaling being the favourite. In this mean-spirited slasher, it's the splatter that matters, not the dead-end cast. AJ *DVD*

Amy Steel *Ginny* • John Furey *Paul Holt* • Adrienne King *Alice* • Kirsten Baker *Terry* • Stuart Charno *Ted* • Warrington Gillette *Jason Voorhees* • Walt Gorney *"Crazy Ralph"* ■ *Dir* Steve Miner • *Scr* Ron Kurz, from characters by Victor Miller

Friday the 13th Part III ★★ 18
Horror 1982 · US · Colour · 91min

Jason donned his famous hockey mask for the first time in director Steve Miner's formula rehash of slasher gold. This time Jason carves his gory way through a crew of dim-witted teenagers renting a house on the shores of his beloved Camp Crystal Lake. Originally shot in 3D to disguise the creative bankruptcy, this fails to tap into the insecurities that made the original so potent. AJ *DVD* 3D

Dana Kimmell *Chris* • Paul Kratka *Rick* • Tracie Savage *Debbie* • Jeffrey Rogers *Andy* • Catherine Parks *Vera* • Richard Brooker *Jason Voorhees* ■ *Dir* Steve Miner • *Scr* Martin Kitrosser, Carol Watson, from characters by Victor Miller, Ron Kurz

F

Friday the 13th: the Final Chapter ★★18

Horror   1984 · US · Colour · 91min

The plot is as negligible as ever, the sex-obsessed teenagers interchangeable and the grisly murders all twists on the old favourites in director Joseph Zito's take on the Camp Crystal Lake blueprint. Special make-up genius Tom Savini gives the body count an extra dimension of charnel house nausea as machete-wielding Jason goes on the rampage again. AJ *DVD*

Crispin Glover *Jimmy* • Erich Anderson *Rob* • Judie Aronson *Samantha* • Peter Barton *Doug* • Kimberly Beck *Trish* • Corey Feldman *Tommy* ■ *Dir* Joseph Zito • *Scr* Barney Cohen, from a story by Bruce Hidemi Sakow, from characters by Victor Miller, Ron Kurz, Martin Kitrosser, Carol Watson

Friday the 13th: a New Beginning ★★★18

Horror   1985 · US · Colour · 87min

Has Jason returned from the dead? Or is there a copycat killer doing a good impersonation of the Camp Crystal Lake maniac? The setting for the fifth instalment is a rural rehab centre where Tommy Jarvis (John Shepherd) is still haunted by the memory of the hockey-masked murderer. Director Danny Steinmann tries hard to breathe fresh life into the hackneyed proceedings with a tongue-in-cheek script and more characterisation than the series is noted for. AJ *DVD*

Melanie Kinnaman *Pam* • John Shepherd *Tommy Jarvis* • Shavar Ross *Reggie* • Marco St John *Sheriff Cal Tucker* • Richard Young *Matt Peters* • Juliette Cummins *Robin* ■ *Dir* Danny Steinmann • *Scr* Martin Kitrosser, David Cohen, Danny Steinmann, from a story by Martin Kitrosser, David Cohen

Friday the 13th Part VI: Jason Lives ★★★15

Horror   1986 · US · Colour · 83min

A witty parody of a James Bond credits sequence immediately sets the tone for director Tom McLoughlin's slick and exuberant Jason sequel. Cleverly mining the undercurrent of humour inherent in the gory series, McLoughlin makes sure Jason's rollercoaster tracks are well-oiled and run smoothly in this vivid and creepy instalment. When Tommy Jarvis (Thom Mathews) digs up his grave to prove Jason's really dead, a bolt of lightning hits the corpse and turns it into a zombie. AJ *DVD*

Thom Mathews *Tommy Jarvis* • Jennifer Cooke *Megan Garris* • David Kagen *Sheriff Garris* • Kerry Noonan *Paula* • Renee Jones *Sissy* • Tom Fridley *Cort* • CJ Graham *Jason Voorhees* ■ *Dir* Tom McLoughlin • *Scr* Tom McLoughlin, from characters by Victor Miller

Friday the 13th Part VII: the New Blood ★18

Horror   1988 · US · Colour · 84min

Victim hears noise. Stops. Turns. Turns back. Jason appears from nowhere holding a machete/axe/spike... The Jason formula hits rock bottom with this static, boring and threadbare episode, directed by B-movie make-up man John Carl Buechler. AJ *DVD*

Lar Park-Lincoln *Tina* • Kevin Blair [Kevin Spirtas] *Nick* • Terry Kiser *Dr Crews* • Susan Jennifer Sullivan *Melissa* • Heidi Kozak *Sandra* • Kane Hodder *Jason* • William Butler *Michael* • Staci Greason *Jane* ■ *Dir* John Carl Buechler • *Scr* Daryl Haney, Manuel Fidello

Friday the 13th Part VIII: Jason Takes Manhattan ★★★18

Horror   1989 · US · Colour · 96min

Director Rob Hedden's stylish attack on the Jason franchise lifts the fear formula a cut and a slash above the average. The title is a misnomer: it takes ages for Jason to carve up the Big Apple. Having been revived by an underwater electrical cable, he stows aboard a pleasure cruiser taking Crystal Lake graduates to New York. This crisply photographed scare-fest surprisingly doesn't milk the new location for extra chills. The series continued with *Jason Goes to Hell: the Final Friday* in 1993. AJ *DVD*

Jensen Daggett *Rennie Wickham* • Scott Reeves *Sean Robertson* • Peter Mark Richman *Charles McCulloch* • Barbara Bingham *Colleen Van Deusen* • Kane Hodder *Jason* ■ *Dir* Rob Hedden • *Scr* Rob Hedden, from characters by Victor Miller

Friday the 13th ★★18

Horror   2009 · US · Colour · 101min

Horror icon Jason Voorhees is relaunched in the 12th movie to feature the unstoppable killing machine. A bullet-point compression of the original two movies establishes Jason's past and then it's on with the plot, as a lone traveller (Jared Padalecki) searches abandoned Camp Crystal Lake for his missing sister just as Jason (Derek Mears) begins to terrorise another group of randy students. While longtime fans will love the reasons behind the machete-wielding madman donning his distinctive hockey-mask disguise, the intense splatter and inventive murders are all that really matters in this mindless makeover. AJ Violence, sex scenes. *DVD* *Blu*

Jared Padalecki *Clay Miller* • Danielle Panabaker *Jenna* • Aaron Yoo *Chewie* • Amanda Righetti *Whitney Miller* • Travis Van Winkle *Trent* • Derek Mears *Jason Voorhees* ■ *Dir* Marcus Nispel • *Scr* Damian Shannon, Mark Swift, from a story by Shannon, Swift, Mark Wheaton, from characters by Victor Miller

Fried Green Tomatoes at the Whistle Stop Cafe ★★★★PG

Drama   1991 · US · Colour · 124min

Jessica Tandy received an Oscar nomination for her portrayal of a feisty old-timer in the American south, telling tales about the bigotry she encountered during her youth in the 1930s. Kathy Bates is almost as good as Tandy, playing a modern-day housewife and frump in the dumps, who visits Tandy in a nursing home and finds inspiration in her memories of the past. Essentially a story about friendship between two pairs of women, then and now, it is an intelligent woman's picture. Uplifting and gratifying. PF Some violence, swearing. *DVD* *Blu*

Mary Stuart Masterson *Idgie Threadgoode* • Mary-Louise Parker *Ruth* • Kathy Bates *Evelyn Couch* • Jessica Tandy *Ninny Threadgoode* • Gailard Sartain *Ed Couch* • Stan Shaw *Big George* • Cicely Tyson *Sipsey* • Gary Basaraba *Grady* ■ *Dir* Jon Avnet • *Scr* Fannie Flagg, Carol Sobieski, from the novel by Fannie Flagg

Frieda ★★★PG

Drama   1947 · UK · BW · 94min

Although there were plenty of tales of brave wartime resistance, few film-makers ventured into the darker territory of commitment to Nazism. Basil Dearden's bold bid to understand collaboration and the need to forgive lapses into stereotype and melodrama rather too quickly. Yet the story of RAF officer David Farrar who returns to Blighty with Mai Zetterling – the German girl who helped him when he was a prisoner of war – still touches a few raw nerves. DP

David Farrar *Robert Dawson* • Glynis Johns *Judy Dawson* • Mai Zetterling *Frieda Dawson* • Flora Robson *Nell Dawson* • Albert Lieven *Richard Mannsfeld* ■ *Dir* Basil Dearden • *Scr* Ronald Millar, Angus MacPhail, from the play by Ronald Millar

Friend Request ★★★15

Horror thriller   2016 · Ger/S Afr · Colour · 92min

Horror comes from Facebook in German director Simon Verhoeven's first horror feature, which plays hell with social media and school peer pressure. When popular student Laura (Alycia Debnam-Carey) kindly accepts the friend request from brooding emo Marina (Lisl Ahlers), her friends begin to die in mysteriously awful ways. And even when Marina kills herself, she's not quite as gone as Laura's dead friends may have wished. Debnam-Carey acquits herself well, while Ahlers's performance could serve as her audition for a remake of *The Girl with the Dragon Tattoo*. Not a great film, but quite fun. KK Violence, swearing.

Alycia Debnam-Carey *Laura* • William Moseley *Tyler* • Connor Paolo *Kobe* • Brit Morgan *Olivia* ■ *Dir* Simon Verhoeven • *Scr* Matthew Ballen, Philip Koch, Simon Verhoeven

Friendly Fire ★★★★12

Biographical military drama   1979 · US · Colour · 140min

This TV movie, chronicling the real-life efforts of Peg Mullen to compel Washington to reveal the circumstances of her son's death in Vietnam, won four Emmys, including best drama. Although both leads took acting awards, Carol Burnett's unswerving commitment is less subtly shaded than Ned Beatty's performance as her husband, torn between patriotism and the truth. This is a disturbing insight into both war and the state's ability to distort facts. DP *DVD*

Carol Burnett *Peg Mullen* • Ned Beatty *Gene Mullen* • Sam Waterston *CDB Bryan* • Dennis Erdman *Sgt Michael Mullen* • Sherry Hursey *Mary Mullen* • Timothy Hutton *John Mullen* • Fanny Spiess *Pat Mullen* ■ *Dir* David Greene • *Scr* Fay Kanin, from the novel by CDB Bryan

Friendly Persuasion ★★★★U

Period drama   1956 · US · Colour · 137min

Gary Cooper is in fine form in this marvellously humane study of an Indiana Quaker family during the American Civil War. Director William Wyler's pacing is a little slow, with the story taking time to unravel, but the film has great charm and there are impressive performances from Dorothy McGuire as Cooper's wife and a young Anthony Perkins as the son with whom he clashes. The movie also boasts a superb score from Dmitri Tiomkin, plus ravishing location colour photography from Ellsworth Fredericks. It rightly received six Oscar nominations, including one for its blacklisted screenwriter, Michael Wilson. TS

Gary Cooper *Jess Birdwell* • Dorothy McGuire *Eliza Birdwell* • Marjorie Main *Widow Hudspeth* • Anthony Perkins *Josh Birdwell* • Richard Eyer *Little Jess* • Robert Middleton *Sam Jordan* • Phyllis Love *Mattie Birdwell* ■ *Dir* William Wyler • *Scr* Michael Wilson (uncredited), from the novel by Jessamyn West

Friends ★★★15

Drama   1993 · UK/Fr · Colour · 104min

The versatile Kerry Fox stars as one of three friends who meet at university in South Africa. Fox is from a rich area of Johannesburg, while Michele Burgers is a poor Afrikaner and Dambisa Kente is a Zulu. This is one of those dramas in which important political and social issues are used as a background to the central theme of friendship. Here that friendship is severely tested when Fox's character plants a bomb as part of her anti-apartheid activities. Director Elaine Proctor's debut feature is strong on setting and politics but the characters unfortunately lack the depth of their surroundings. JB

Kerry Fox *Sophie* • Dambisa Kente *Thoko* • Michele Burgers *Aninka* • Marius Weyers *Johan* • Tertius Meintjes *Jeremy* • Dolly Rathebe *Innocentia* • Wilma Stockenstrom *Iris* ■ *Dir/Scr* Elaine Proctor

Friends and Lovers ★★

Romantic drama   1931 · US · BW · 66min

Adolphe Menjou and Laurence Olivier are British officers in India, rivals for the affections of *femme fatale* Lili Damita, whose scheming husband, Erich von Stroheim, isn't averse to a spot of blackmail. This risible melodrama has only its intriguing cast going for it. Interesting to see the 24-year-old Olivier, in one of his first Hollywood films and the always-hypnotic von Stroheim. Director Victor Schertzinger was co-credited with Max Steiner for the score. RB

Adolphe Menjou *Captain Roberts* • Lili Damita *Alva Sangrito* • Laurence Olivier *Lieutenant Nichols* • Erich von Stroheim *Victor Sangrito* • Hugh Herbert *McNellis* • Frederick Kerr *General Armstrong* ■ *Dir* Victor Schertzinger • *Scr* Wallace Smith, Jane Murfin, from the novel *Le Sphinx A Parlé* by Maurice De Kobra

Friends for Life ★★★U

Drama   1955 · It · Colour · 90min

Italian cinema has been blessed with several inspired performances by child actors, and Geronimo Meynier and Andrea Scire excel in this sensitive study of childhood friendship, although your response will very much depend on which version you see (unusually, the US ending is the more downbeat). However, Franco Rossi's deft direction ensures that Meynier's betrayal of Scire's motherless diplomat's son lingers in the mind, no matter what the dénouement at Rome airport. Charmingly scored by Nino Rota, this is touching and authentic. DP Italian +subtitles.

Geronimo Meynier *Mario* • Andrea Scire *Franco* • Luigi Tosi *Mario's father* • Vera Carmi *Mario's mother* • Carlo Tamberlani *Franco's father* • Paolo Ferrara *Professor Martenelli* • Marcella Rovena *English professor* ■ *Dir* Franco Rossi • *Scr* Ottavio Alessi, Leo Benvenuti, Piero De Bernardi, Gian-Domenico Giagni, Franco Rossi, Ugo Guerra

The Friends of Eddie Coyle ★★★★15

Crime drama   1973 · US · Colour · 101min

Robert Mitchum plays an ageing small-time gangster and cynical police informer who is relentlessly pursued by the mobsters he's betrayed. In a quality cast, Peter Boyle stands out as the hitman who's given the job of eliminating Mitchum. Peter Yates, the British director who forged his Hollywood reputation with the incredible car chase in *Bullitt*, gives this a subtle power, turning the story into a fable about urban violence TH Swearing. *DVD* *Blu*

Robert Mitchum *Eddie Coyle* • Peter Boyle *Dillon* • Richard Jordan *Dave Foley* • Steven Keats *Jackie* • Alex Rocco *Scalise* • Joe Santos *Artie Van* • Mitchell Ryan *Waters* ■ *Dir* Peter Yates • *Scr* Paul Monash, from the novel by George V Higgins

Friends with Benefits ★★★15

Romantic comedy   2011 · US · Colour · 104min

Justin Timberlake and Mila Kunis join forces to play work colleagues caught up in the hoary old conundrum as to whether friendship can survive a relationship. Plotwise, it's a well-worn furrow, last ploughed by Natalie Portman and Ashton Kutcher in *No Strings Attached*. But Timberlake and Kunis are likeable leads and they handle their banter with ease. The film perhaps tries a touch too hard to be hip, and wanders off track a little towards the end, but this is still smarter and funnier than most. DA Swearing, sex scenes. *DVD* *Blu*

Justin Timberlake *Dylan* • Mila Kunis *Jamie* • Woody Harrelson *Tommy* • Richard Jenkins *Mr Harper* • Patricia Clarkson *Lorna* • Jenna Elfman *Annie* • Emma Stone *Kayla* ■ *Dir* Will Gluck • *Scr* Will Gluck, Keith Merryman, David A Newman, from a story by Harley Peyton, Merryman, Newman

Friends with Kids ★★★15

Romantic comedy   2011 · US · Colour · 102min

Jennifer Westfeldt writes, directs and co-stars opposite Adam Scott in this story of best friends who, after watching the impact having offspring has on their friends' previously sexy, fun and exciting relationships, decide it would be better to have a child together and let love blossom elsewhere. The film reunites many of the cast from *Bridesmaids* (Jon Hamm, Kristen Wiig, Maya Rudolph and Chris O'Dowd) in supporting roles. And while it may not reach that film's comic heights, the predictable genre trappings are tempered with plenty of wit and charm. AIS Swearing, sexual references. *DVD* *Blu*

Adam Scott *Jason Fryman* • Jennifer Westfeldt *Julie Keller* • Jon Hamm *Ben* • Kristen Wiig *Missy* • Maya Rudolph *Leslie* • Chris O'Dowd *Alex* • Megan Fox *Mary Jane* ■ *Dir/Scr* Jennifer Westfeldt

Friends with Money ★★★ 15
Comedy drama   2006 · US · Colour · 87min

Jennifer Aniston stars as a maid who lacks self-esteem as well as cash. Her rich pals Frances McDormand and Catherine Keener are quick to bestow advice even while questioning their own life choices. McDormand is wickedly funny, lashing out at every impoliteness, while Keener is going stir crazy with her husband and screenwriting partner (Jason Isaacs). Together with Joan Cusack as a busybody society wife, the talented ensemble cast make the most of Nicole Holofcener's wry observations about California living. SP Swearing. *DVD*

Jennifer Aniston *Olivia* • Frances McDormand *Jane* • Joan Cusack *Franny* • Catherine Keener *Christine* • Greg Germann *Matt* • Simon McBurney *Aaron* • Jason Isaacs *David* • Scott Caan *Mike* • Ty Burrell *Aaron No 2* ■ *Dir/Scr* Nicole Holofcener

Fright ★★ 18
Thriller   1971 · UK · Colour · 83min

Employing mental illness as fodder for horror movies, however unsettling, can produce masterpieces like *Psycho* and *Repulsion*. But exploitation is all too evident in this unpleasant tale of a young babysitter terrorised by an escaped lunatic. Ian Bannen jumps through hoops in an effort to make his role convincing but the formulaic direction reduces him to just another anonymous nutter. As the terrified heroine, Susan George pouts and screams. RS

Susan George *Amanda* • Honor Blackman *Helen* • Ian Bannen *Brian* • John Gregson *Dr Cordell* • George Cole *Jim* • Dennis Waterman *Chris* • Tara Collinson *Tara* ■ *Dir* Peter Collinson • *Scr* Tudor Gates

Fright Night ★★★★ 18
Comedy horror   1985 · US · Colour · 102min

This hugely entertaining horror spoof has teenage B-movie buff William Ragsdale convinced that new neighbour Chris Sarandon is a vampire responsible for a spate of brutal killings. Only when best pal Stephen Geoffreys has become Sarandon's slave and girlfriend Amanda Bearse has also fallen under his spell, does Ragsdale succeed in enlisting the help of "fearless" TV vampire hunter Roddy McDowall to end his reign of terror. Neatly parodying Hitchcock and John Hughes movies, writer/director Tom Holland litters his rattling story with as many laughs as jolts. DP Violence, swearing. *DVD*

Chris Sarandon *Jerry Dandridge* • William Ragsdale *Charley Brewster* • Amanda Bearse *Amy Peterson* • Roddy McDowall *Peter Vincent* • Stephen Geoffreys *Evil Ed* • Jonathan Stark *Billy Cole* • Dorothy Fielding *Judy Brewster* ■ *Dir/Scr* Tom Holland (1)

Fright Night Part 2 ★★ 18
Comedy horror   1988 · US · Colour · 99min

The original *Fright Night* breathed a bit of knowing humour into the vampire genre, but this is an uninspired retread. William Ragsdale returns as student Charley Brewster, who uncovers another coven of vampires when he falls for sexy Julie Carmen. Roddy McDowall also reprises his role as the fearful vampire slayer, but he can't breathe life into the worn-out script or shapeless direction. JF

Roddy McDowall *Peter Vincent* • William Ragsdale *Charley Brewster* • Julie Carmen *Regine* • Traci Lin [Traci Lind] *Alex* • Jonathan Gries *Louie* ■ *Dir* Tommy Lee Wallace • *Scr* Tommy Lee Wallace, Tim Metcalfe, Miguel Tejada-Flores, from the characters by Tom Holland

Fright Night ★★★ 15
Comedy horror
2011 · US · Colour and BW · 101min

Colin Farrell shows a perfectly judged blend of charm, seasoned with succulent menace, in this cheerfully trashy remake of the 1985 vampire classic. He's Jerry, a beguiling stranger who moves in next door to student Charley (Anton Yelchin), an event that coincides with local kids going missing. David Tennant struggles to match up to his

forerunner, the incomparable Roddy McDowall, as ce ebrity magician and vampire expert Peter Vincent, but, like the fondly imagined original, the gags are funny without taking the edge off the scary stuff. AS Violence, swearing. *DVD* *Blu-ray* *3D*

Anton Yelchin *Charley Brewster* • Colin Farrell (2) *Jerry* • Christopher Mintz-Plasse *"Evil" Ed Thompson* • David Tennant *Peter Vincent* • Toni Collette *Jane Brewster* ■ *Dir* Craig Gillespie • *Scr* Marti Noxon, from the 1985 film

The Frightened City ★★ PG
Crime drama   1961 · UK · BW · 93min

Limping along years after Hollywood's postwar exterior-location thrillers such as *The Naked City*, this British attempt at the genre just about manages to hold the interest. The story is about London gangsters falling out over a protection racket, and features a young Sean Connery and a pre-*Pink Panther* Herbert Lom at his most seedily sinister. TH

Herbert Lom *Waldo Zhernikov* • John Gregson *Detective Inspector Sayers* • Sean Connery *Paddy Damion* • Alfred Marks *Harry Foulcher* ■ *Dir* John Lemont • *Scr* Leigh Vance, from a story by Leigh Vance, John Lemont

The Frightened Man ★★
Crime drama   1952 · UK · BW · 70min

This is a dreary little quota quickie that draws on all the stock situations one associates with British B-thrillers. Director John Gilling makes solid use of the down-at-heel locations, but he fails to inject any suspense into the story (which he wrote) of a botched jewel robbery. Given little support by the rest of the cast, Dermot Walsh tries hard as the junk dealer's son who's thrown out of university and drawn into a life of crime. DP

Dermot Walsh *Julius Roselli* • Barbara Murray *Amanda* • Charles Victor *Mr Roselli* • John Blythe *Maxie* • Michael Ward *Cornelius* • Thora Hird *Vera* ■ *Dir/Scr* John Gilling

The Frighteners ★★★★ 15
Supernatural comedy thriller
1996 · NZ/US · Colour · 105min

Peter Jackson explores the shockingly unhealthy paranormal bond between two lovers with record-breaking murder in mind. Hitting exactly the right balance between black comedy and jet-black chills, this cross between *Casper* and *The Silence of the Lambs* is another ghoulish masterpiece from the Kiwi eccentric, showcasing a dazzling array of computer-generated ghosts and blood-freezing poltergeist activity. Michael J Fox is ingeniously cast against type as a pseudo psychic dealing with all the nasty hereafter horror in a merrily menacing spectre spectacular. AJ *DVD* *Blu-ray*

Michael J Fox *Frank Bannister* • Trini Alvarado *Lucy Lynskey* • Peter Dobson *Ray Lynskey* • John Astin *The Judge* • Jeffrey Combs *Milton Dammers* • Dee Wallace Stone *Patricia Bradley* ■ *Dir* Peter Jackson • *Scr* Fran Walsh, Peter Jackson

Frightmare ★★★ 18
Horror   1974 · UK · Colour · 82min

Reviled by critics, loved by gore-hounds, British exploitation director Pete Walker's Home Counties version of *The Texas Chain Saw Massacre* is a brutally effective shocker for all its cheap nastiness and graphic blood-letting. Walker regular Sheila Keith craves human flesh and her husband, Rupert Davies, looks on impotently as she pitchforks, axes and power drills the brains out of the local farming community lured to her cannibal domain by Tarot card readings. Morally twisted in Walker's signature way, this bleak vision of the triumph of evil over good is grisly, chilling and intense. AJ Violence *DVD*

Rupert Davies *Edmund* • Sheila Keith *Dorothy* • Deborah Fairfax *Jackie* • Paul Greenwood *Graham* • Kim Butcher *Debbie* ■ *Dir* Pete Walker • *Scr* David McGillivray, from a story by Peter Walker

Frightmare ★★ 18
Horror   1981 · US · Colour · 82min

Horror movie stalwart Ferdy Mayne never quite hit the Hammer heights of Christopher Lee, but he's well cast here as an old horror movie icon, whose body is kidnapped by members of a horror film society. When his widow holds a séance the actor's re-animated corpse picks off the kids one by one in *Friday the 13th* style. This is an uneasy blend of homage, laughs and standard teens-in-jeopardy blood-letting. RS *DVD*

Ferdinand Mayne [Ferdy Mayne] *Conrad* • Luca Bercovici *Saint* • Nita Talbot *Mrs Rohmer* • Leon Askin *Wolfgang* • Jennifer Starrett *Meg* • Barbara Pilavin *Etta* • Carlene Olson *Eve* ■ *Dir/Scr* Norman Thaddeus Vane

The Fringe Dwellers ★★★ PG
Drama   1985 · Aus · Colour · 97min

Good intentions abound in this story of a teenage girl who is determined to rouse her idle father into action so that they can move into a new housing development. But the characterisations are too broad, with nearly all the whites being loathsome and the Aborigines being cheerful in their poverty. However, Kristina Nehm gives a striking performance as the ambitious Trilby, with Ernie Dingo impressive as her shiftless lover in this story of middle-class snobbery and Aboriginal exclusion. DP

Kristina Nehm *Trilby Comeaway* • Justine Saunders *Mollie Comeaway* • Bob Maza *Joe Comeaway* • Kylie Belling *Noonah Comeaway* • Denis Walker *Bartie Comeaway* ■ *Dir* Bruce Beresford • *Scr* Bruce Beresford, Rhoisin Beresford, from the novel by Nene Gare

Frisco Kid ★★
Adventure   1935 · US · BW · 77min

James Cagney sports curly hair and wing collars in this late 19th century tale of the notorious Barbary Coast in San Francisco. The story of a young sailor's rise to prominence in a corrupt world is routine, with the heroine crusading newspaper owner fighting to clean up the city. Even with the fast cutting we expect from Warner Bros, and a brief running time, the tale still flags and it's the dynamic Cagney who keeps it afloat. TV

James Cagney *Bat Morgan* • Margaret Lindsay *Jean Barrat* • Ricardo Cortez *Paul Morra* • Lili Damita *Bella Morra* • Donald Woods *Charles Ford* • Barton MacLane *Spider Burke* • George E Stone *Solly* ■ *Dir* Lloyd Bacon • *Scr* Warren Duff, Seton I Miller

The Frisco Kid ★★ PG
Comedy western   1979 · US · Colour · 113min

This comedy drama isn't as comic as it thinks it is, nor as dramatic as it should be. Gene Wilder stars as a novice rabbi sent to San Francisco and befriended by cowboy Harrison Ford on the way. There are some laughs to be had in the gaffes, but director Robert Aldrich inserts some violent action sequences into the episodic plot that jar with what should have been a much gentler affair. TH

Gene Wilder *Avram* • Harrison Ford *Tommy* • Ramon Bieri *Mr Jones* • Val Bisoglio *Chief Gray Cloud* • George DiCenzo *Darryl Diggs* • Leo Fuchs *Chief Rabbi* • Penny Peyser *Rosalie* • William Smith *Matt Diggs* ■ *Dir* Robert Aldrich • *Scr* Michael Elias, Frank Shaw

Fritz the Cat ★★★ 18
Animated erotic comedy
1972 · US · Colour · 75min

This is a radical and largely successful attempt on the part of director Ralph Bakshi to translate the underground comic character invented by Robert Crumb to the big screen. Fritz is an innocent at large at the fag end of the hippy wave. He discovers the joys of sex and student politics, before bumping painfully into various downsides of the counterculture like hard drugs and biker gangs. Quite shocking at the time, it's a fun period artefact. Followed in 1974 by *Nine Lives of Fritz the Cat*. JF *DVD*

Skip Hinnant *Fritz the Cat* • Rosetta LeNoire • John McCurry • Judy Engles ■ *Dir* Ralph Bakshi • *Scr* Ralph Bakshi, from the character created by Robert Crumb

The Frog Prince ★★★ 15
Romantic comedy   1984 · UK · Colour · 86min

This charming tale of cross-cultural courtship is set in the pre-Swinging Sixties. Cartoonist Posy Simmonds's semi-autobiographical screenplay may indulge in a little cheap caricature where both the plain-speaking and bohemian French folk are concerned, but it captures the hesitancy and naive emotionalism of first love with insight and affection. Paris is a key character here, rather than just the beautiful backdrop to mousy exchange student Jane Snowden's relationship with the dashing Alexandre Sterling. DP

Jane Snowden *Jenny* • Alexandre Sterling *Jean-Philippe* • Jacqueline Doyen *Mme Peroche* • Raoul Delfosse *Monsieur Peroche* • Jeanne Herviale *Mme Duclos* ■ *Dir* Brian Gilbert • *Scr* Posy Simmonds, Brian Gilbert, from the story by Posy Simmonds

The Frogmen ★★★ U
Second World War action drama
1951 · US · BW · 96min

Warners' veteran director Lloyd Bacon fetched up after the war at 20th Century-Fox as a sort of hack-of-all-trades. He has the benefit here of the studio's starry roster of male actors in a realistic and tense suspense drama about Pacific underwater demolition teams during the Second World War. Richard Widmark is the tough commander whose men resent him. Led by Dana Andrews, they eventually come to understand his uncompromising methods. TS

Richard Widmark *Lieutenant Commander John Lawrence* • Dana Andrews *Flannigan* • Gary Merrill *Lieutenant Commander Pete Vincent* • Jeffrey Hunter *Creighton* • Warren Stevens *Hodges* • Robert Wagner *Lieutenant Franklin* ■ *Dir* Lloyd Bacon • *Scr* John Tucker Battle, from a story by Oscar Millard

Frogs ★★ 15
Horror   1972 · US · Colour · 86min

One of the many ecologically-correct horror films of the 1970s, this is one of the silliest. Ray Milland is the wheelchair-using Southern patriarch whose birthday celebrations are disrupted by a revolt of the swamp creatures he has tried to eliminate with insecticides. The intelligent frogs also enrol snakes, bugs and snapping turtles to leap around attacking the obvious upper-class types on their private island. JF *DVD*

Ray Milland *Jason Crockett* • Sam Elliott *Pickett Smith* • Joan Van Ark *Karen Crockett* • Adam Roarke *Clint Crockett* • Judy Pace *Bella Berenson* ■ *Dir* George McCowan • *Scr* Robert Hutchison, Robert Blees, from a story by Robert Hutchison

From Beyond ★★ 18
Science-fiction horror
1986 · US · Colour · 81min

Following his gross-out hit *Re-Animator*, Stuart Gordon reunited leads Jeffrey Combs and Barbara Crampton in another HP Lovecraft-based splatter-fest. This sloppy, sometimes crude clash of horror and sci-fi elements stars Combs as a typically unhinged scientist, whose experiments with the Resonator spark off the usual orgy of murder and mutilation, turning him into a mutated creature with rubbery effect. RS

Jeffrey Combs *Crawford Tillinghast* • Barbara Crampton *Dr Katherine McMichaels* • Ken Foree *Bubba Brownlee* • Ted Sorel *Dr Edward Pretorius* ■ *Dir* Stuart Gordon • *Scr* Dennis Paoli, Stuart Gordon, Brian Yuzna, from the story by HP Lovecraft

From beyond the Grave ★★★ 15
Horror   1973 · UK · Colour · 94min

Devilish antiques dealer Peter Cushing sells evil artefacts to unsuspecting shoppers in an above average anthology from British studio Amicus, linking four R Chetwynd-

Hayes horror stories. Haunted mirrors, demonic oak doors, invisible elementals and black magic provide the shudder basics for director Kevin Connor, who complements each distinctive tale with atmospheric flourishes and eerie production values. Dotty psychic Margaret Leighton is a standout in the enthusiastic cast. AJ DVD

Peter Cushing *Proprietor* • David Warner *Edward Charlton* • Wendy Allnutt *Pamela* • Donald Pleasence *Underwood* • Ian Bannen *Christopher Lowe* • Diana Dors *Mabel Lowe* • Angela Pleasence *Emily* • Margaret Leighton *Madame Orloff* • Ian Carmichael *Reggie Warren* • Ian Ogilvy *William Seaton* • Lesley-Anne Down *Rosemary Seaton* ■ *Dir* Kevin Connor • *Scr* Raymond Christodoulou, Robin Clarke, from the short story collection *The Unbidden* by R Chetwynd-Hayes

From Dusk till Dawn ★★★★ 18

Black comedy action horror
1995 · US · Colour · 103min

Here's everything you'd expect from a splatter-fest bearing Quentin Tarantino's name (he wrote the script), as director Robert Rodriguez juggles sharp dialogue, violence, great special effects and bad taste with stylish verve. Tarantino and George Clooney play crooks heading south of the border, who take Harvey Keitel's family hostage and end up under attack from vampires, undead strippers and Hell's Angels when they hide out in a Mexican bar. Lots of energy and engaging performances keep this gore-fest firing on all its tongue-in-cheek cylinders. AJ Violence, swearing, nudity. DVD

Harvey Keitel *Jacob Fuller* • George Clooney *Seth Gecko* • Quentin Tarantino *Richard Gecko* • Juliette Lewis *Kate Fuller* • Cheech Marin [Richard "Cheech" Marin] *Border guard/Chet Pussy/Carlos* • Salma Hayek *Santanico Pandemonium* • Fred Williamson *Frost* • Danny Trejo *Razor Charlie* • Marc Lawrence (1) *Old timer* ■ *Dir* Robert Rodriguez • *Scr* Quentin Tarantino, from a story by Robert Kurtzman

From Dusk till Dawn II: Texas Blood Money ★★ 18

Action horror 1999 · US · Colour · 84min

The first of two made-for-video sequels to creator Quentin Tarantino's 1995 original is another road movie-cum-vampire shocker. Basically a reworking of the same plot, Robert Patrick and his lowlife gang plan a heist but get sidetracked by the bloodsucking undead at the Titty Twister bar, source of the carnage in the first film. AJ DVD

Robert Patrick *Buck* • Bo Hopkins *Sheriff Otis Lawson* • Duane Whitaker *Luther* • Muse Watson *CW* • Brett Harrelson *Ray Bob* • Raymond Cruz *Jesus* • Danny Trejo *Razor Eddie* • Bruce Campbell *Barry* • Tiffani-Amber Thiessen *Pam* ■ *Dir* Scott Spiegel • *Scr* Scott Spiegel, Duane Whitaker, from a story by Scott Spiegel, Boaz Yakin

From Dusk till Dawn 3: the Hangman's Daughter ★★ 18

Horror western 2000 · US · Colour · 89min

The third in the series of vampire thrillers shifts virtually the same plot as the previous two back 100 years into the Old West to ring a few, but not enough, neat changes. A gang on the run from a gun-toting posse goes to ground in an out-of-the-way Mexican bar, which turns out to be a vampire lair. AJ DVD

Marco Leonardi *Johnny Madrid* • Michael Parks *Ambrose Bierce* • Ara Celi *Esmeralda* • Danny Trejo *Razor Charlie* • Temuera Morrison *The Hangman* • Sonia Braga *Quixtla* • Rebecca Gayheart *Mary Newlie* ■ *Dir* PJ Pesce • *Scr* Alvaro Rodriguez, from a story by Alvaro Rodriguez, Robert Rodriguez

From Hell ★★★★ 18

Period horror 2001 · US · Colour · 117min

Given the intricacy of Alan Moore's graphic novel *From Hell*, it's no surprise that directors Allen and Albert Hughes have focused solely on the elements concerning Jack the Ripper. On the one hand, this is a painstakingly crafted social history that

perfectly captures the grime, grit and prejudices of Victorian times. On the other, it's a grisly and horribly believable tale of greed, revenge and lunacy with Johnny Depp as the policeman on the Ripper's trail. Both visually and intellectually engaging. SF DVD BL

Johnny Depp *Inspector Frederick "Fred" Abberline* • Heather Graham *Mary Kelly* • Ian Holm *Sir William Gull* • Robbie Coltrane *Sgt Peter Godley* • Ian Richardson *Sir Charles Warren* • Jason Flemyng *John Netley* • Katrin Cartlidge *"Dark Annie" Chapman* ■ *Dir* Albert Hughes, Allen Hughes • *Scr* Terry Hayes, Rafael Yglesias, from the graphic novel by Alan Moore, Eddie Campbell

From Hell It Came ★★

Horror 1957 · US · BW · 70min

Not a problem which pops up too often in *Gardeners' Question Time* – what do you do with a man-eating, walking tree? This is the dilemma facing Tod Andrews and Tina Carver when an island paradise becomes haunted by a sapling seeking revenge. The unknowns in the cast do their best to keep a straight face, but this really is only one for trash fans. JF

Tod Andrews *Dr William Arnold* • Tina Carver *Dr Terry Mason* • Linda Watkins *Mrs Kilgore* • John McNamara *Dr Howard Clark* • Gregg Palmer *Kimo* • Robert Swan *Witch doctor Tano* ■ *Dir* Dan Milner • *Scr* Richard Bernstein, from a story by Richard Bernstein, Jack Milner

From Hell to Texas ★★★ U

Western 1958 · US · Colour · 99min

Cowboy Don Murray accidentally kills a man and is relentlessly pursued by the victim's vengeful father (RG Armstrong). Murray's open, innocent face is perfect for this allegorical western, vividly directed by Henry Hathaway. The main interest today lies in the casting of Dennis Hopper, whose final confrontation with Murray is as taut as it is unpredictable, and Hathaway brilliantly frames the antagonists against the landscape. TS

Don Murray *Tod Lohman* • Diane Varsi *Juanita Bradley* • Chill Wills *Amos Bradley* • Dennis Hopper *Tom Boyd* • RG Armstrong *Hunter Boyd* • Jay C Flippen *Jake Leffertfinger* ■ *Dir* Henry Hathaway • *Scr* Robert Buckner, Wendell Mayes, from the book *The Hell Bent Kid* by Charles O Locke

From Hell to Victory ★★

Second World War drama
1979 · Fr/It/Sp · Colour · 102min

In Umberto Lenzi's film, a group of friends of various nationalities face separation on the eve of the Second World War. They plan an annual reunion, of course, but how many of them will survive? The battle sequences are well mounted, but the highlight is George Hamilton's laughable French accent. DP

George Peppard *Brett Rosson* • George Hamilton *Maurice* • Horst Buchholz *Jurgen Dietrich* • Jean-Pierre Cassel *Dick Sanders* • Capucine *Nicole Levine* • Sam Wanamaker *Ray MacDonald* ■ *Dir* Hank Milestone [Umberto Lenzi] • *Scr* Umberto Lenzi, Jose Luis Martinez Molls, Gianfranco Clerici

From Here to Eternity ★★★★★ PG

Second World War drama
1953 · US · BW · 118min

Director Fred Zinnemann's powerful adaptation of James Jones's bestseller won eight Oscars, upset the military and resurrected the acting career of Frank Sinatra. It's a portrait of life in and around the US Army's Schofield Barracks at Pearl Harbor in the days leading up to the Japanese attack in December 1941. Bullying, sadism and adultery eventually give way to heroism and sacrifice as the bombs fall. Amid all the brawling, Burt Lancaster and Deborah Kerr embrace in the pounding surf in what remains one of cinema's most iconic clinches. AT DVD BL

Burt Lancaster *Sergeant Milton Warden* • Deborah Kerr *Karen Holmes* • Montgomery Clift *Robert E Lee Prewitt* • Frank Sinatra *Angelo Maggio* • Donna Reed *Alma/Lorene* • Ernest Borgnine *Sergeant "Fatso" Judson* • Philip Ober

Captain Dana Holmes • Jack Warden *Corporal Buckley* • Dir Fred Zinnemann • *Scr* Daniel Taradash, from James Jones's novel • *Cinematographer* Burnett Guffey • *Editor* William Lyon

From Mao to Mozart: Isaac Stern in China ★★★★ U

Music documentary 1980 · US · Colour · 83min

Winner of the Oscar for best documentary feature, Murray Lerner's reverential, yet revealing record of Isaac Stern's 1979 goodwill tour to China is remarkable on a number of levels. Apart from the violin virtuoso's eloquent playing, it is interesting to see the enthusiasm with which he was received and the passion for western music that has been fostered under the communist system. There are sombre moments too, such as the old academic's memoir of the Cultural Revolution. But the scenes at the Peking Opera and those featuring the phenomenal child prodigies, give the film a sociological fascination to complement its sublime music. DP

■ *Dir* Murray Lerner • *Cinematographers* Nic Knowland, Nick Doob, David Bridges • *Editor* Tom Haneke

From Paris with Love ★★ 15

Action drama 2010 · Fr · Colour · 88min

John Travolta's gung-ho US undercover agent hits the French capital in this bullet-riddled action drama. Once there, he offers Jonathan Rhys Meyers's nervy US embassy functionary a lesson in devil-may-care improvisation as scores of Chinese gang members and Islamic terrorists are wasted along the way. Sadly, the one-liners aren't all that witty, the carnage lacks any genuine sense of danger, and the perfunctory plot is so vague that it's somewhat academic. TJ DVD

John Travolta *Charlie Wax* • Jonathan Rhys Meyers *James Reece* • Kasia Smutniak *Carolina* • Richard Durden *Ambassador Bennington* • Amber Rose Revah *Nichole* • Yin Bing M Wong ■ *Dir* Pierre Morel • *Scr* Adi Hasak, from a story by Luc Besson

From Russia with Love ★★★★★ PG

Spy adventure 1963 · UK · Colour · 110min

Ian Fleming received a useful boost to his sales when President Kennedy listed *From Russia with Love* as one of his ten favourite books. It is also one of the most popular Bond movies and a terrific thriller in its own right, owing much to Hitchcock and Carol Reed's *The Third Man* in its marvellous atmosphere of foreign intrigue. Superbly shot on location in Istanbul, and closely following Fleming's original story, the film has Sean Connery's spy duped into smuggling a top-secret communist decoding machine, plus blonde Russian diplomat Daniela Bianchi, from Turkey to the West via the *Orient Express*. Lotte Lenya is unforgettable as lesbian villain Rosa Klebb. AT DVD BL

Sean Connery *James Bond* • Daniela Bianchi *Tatiana Romanova* • Pedro Armendáriz *Kerim Bey* • Lotte Lenya *Rosa Klebb* • Robert Shaw *Red Grant* • Bernard Lee *"M"* • Eunice Gayson *Sylvia Trench* • Walter Gotell *Morzeny* • Lois Maxwell *Miss Moneypenny* • Francis De Wolff *Vavra* • Desmond Llewelyn *Major Boothroyd* ■ *Dir* Terence Young • *Scr* Richard Maibaum, Johanna Harwood, from the novel by Ian Fleming • *Music* John Barry (1)

From the Ashes ★★★ 12A

Sports documentary 2011 · UK · Colour · 98min

Director James Erskine's enjoyably old-fashioned sporting documentary ably places the 1981 battle for the Ashes in the context of both a summer of discontent and the turbulent career of cricketing legend Ian Botham. The great all-rounder's disastrous stint as captain came to an end amid urban riots sparked by racial tensions and the gruelling effects of Mrs Thatcher's economic policies. Combining BBC highlight clips with recollections by players and journalists, Erskine revisits the unlikely victories at Headingley, Edgbaston and Old Trafford with a restrained triumphalism

that conveys how the series win did as much to raise the nation's spirits as Prince Charles and Lady Diana's wedding. Tom Hardy's narration is occasionally over the top and things peter out before the Oval test, but few cricket lovers will complain. DP Swearing. DVD BL

Tom Hardy *Narrator* • Ian Botham • David Gower • Dickie Bird ■ *Dir/Scr* James Erskine

From the Earth to the Moon ★★ U

Science-fiction adventure
1958 · US · Colour · 99min

This clunky Jules Verne adaptation can't overcome the size of its budget, despite the cast of veterans who lurch through the material. Joseph Cotten and George Sanders star as the rival scientists with differing views on space travel. There's a certain amount of morbid enjoyment to be found in watching ageing stars such as Henry Daniell and Melville Cooper lurch through the material. TS

Joseph Cotten *Victor Barbicane* • George Sanders *Stuyvesant Nicholl* • Debra Paget *Virginia Nicholl* • Don Dubbins *Ben Sharpe* • Henry Daniell *Morgana* • Melville Cooper *Bancroft* ■ *Dir* Byron Haskin • *Scr* Robert Blees, James Leicester, from the novel by Jules Verne

From the Edge of the City ★★★ 18

Drama 1998 · Gr · Colour · 93min

This stark study of disenfranchised Russian émigrés operating on the outskirts of Athens proves that, as far as cinema is concerned, the counterculture of the streets is the same no matter where you are. In following the misfortunes of a gang of rent boys, director Constantinos Giannaris employs a technique that combines neorealistic episodes with talking head interviews and frantic time-lapse codas. While this adds immediacy, it distracts from the dramatic implications of Stathis Papadopoulos's dangerous liaison with prostitute Theodora Tzimou and her pimp Dimitris Papoulidis. DP Greek +subtitles.

Stathis Papadopoulos *Sasha* • Costas Cotsianidis *Cotsian* • Panagiotis Chartomatsidis *Panagiotis* • Dimitris Papoulidis *Giorgos* • Theodora Tzimou *Natasha* • Anestis Polychronidis *Anestis* ■ *Dir/Scr* Constantinos Giannaris

From the Hip ★ 15

Courtroom comedy drama
1987 · US · Colour · 106min

Oh dear, what has happened to Judd Nelson's career? From Brat Pack success in films such as *The Breakfast Club*, he has been reduced to making rubbish like this third-rate comedy. He's not the only one who would probably like to forget this tale of a lawyer who will do anything to clear his client of murder. JB DVD

Judd Nelson *Robin Weathers* • Elizabeth Perkins *Jo Ann* • John Hurt *Douglas Benoit* • Darren McGavin *Craig Duncan* ■ *Dir* Bob Clark • *Scr* David E Kelley, Bob Clark, from a story by David E Kelley

From the Life of the Marionettes ★★★★ 18

Drama 1980 · W Ger · BW and Colour · 99min

Ingmar Bergman's second film made during his tax exile in Germany is superior to *The Serpent's Egg* (1977). Opening with the murder of a prostitute in a blood-red room, most of the film is shot in stark monochrome with an intense whiteness in the dream sequences. Balanced between the distancing device of Brechtian titles and the use of large close-ups, Bergman creates a controlled case history in the German idiom. Many of the thoughts of the characters are delivered via speeches, most notably a monologue by an ageing gay man, a rarity in Bergman's female-dominated oeuvre. RB German +subtitles. DVD

Robert Atzorn *Peter Egermann* • Christine Buchegger *Katarina Egermann* • Martin Benrath *Mogens Jensen* • Rita Russek *Ka* • Lola Müthel

Cordelia Egermann ■ *Dir/Scr* Ingmar Bergman •
Cinematographer Sven Nykvist • *Art Director* Rolf
Zehetbauer

From the Mixed-Up Files of Mrs Basil E Frankweiler
★★★

Adventure drama 1995 · US · Colour · 92min

Adapted from the novel by EL Konigsberg,
this is a TV-movie remake of the 1973
children's film *The Hideaways*. Taking over
the title role from Ingrid Bergman, a rather
imperious Lauren Bacall has her work cut
out to prevent young Jean Marie Barnwell
and Jesse Lee from stealing the picture, as
they seek her advice in determining
whether a statue in New York's
Metropolitan Museum of Art is a genuine
Michelangelo. It's rather highbrow for
youngsters, but director Marcus Cole
cleverly turns it into an accessible detective
mystery. DP

Lauren Bacall *Mrs Basil E Frankweiler* • Jean
Marie Barnwell *Claudia* • Jesse Lee *Jamie* • M
Emmet Walsh *Morris* ■ *Dir* Marcus Cole • *Scr*
Betty Goldberg, from the novel by EL Konigsberg

From the Terrace ★★PG
Drama 1960 · US · Colour · 143min

The combination of pedestrian direction
and predictable plotting undermines Mark
Robson's adaptation of John O'Hara's
sprawling novel. Paul Newman goes
through the motions as a Wall Street
whizzkid who defies his well-heeled family
to marry Joanne Woodward, only to risk
losing her when he has a fling with Ina Balin.
Newman is upstaged by his female co-stars,
with Myrna Loy particularly effective
playing against type as a boozing matriarch.
A glitzy soap opera. DP

Paul Newman *Alfred Eaton* • Joanne Woodward
Mary St John • Myrna Loy *Martha Eaton* • Ina
Balin *Natalie* • Leon Ames *Samuel Eaton* •
Elizabeth Allen *Sage Rimmington* ■ *Dir* Mark
Robson • *Scr* Ernest Lehman, from the novel by
John O'Hara

From This Day Forward ★★★
Romantic drama 1946 · US · BW · 95min

Mark Stevens stars as an unemployed ex-
serviceman looking back to the days during
the Depression when he met and married
Joan Fontaine in this classy piece of
escapism from RKO. Stevens struggles with
his role, but his rather feeble performance
is offset by the charm of Fontaine, even if
you have to suspend disbelief to accept her
as a working-class New Yorker. Once over
that hurdle, relax and enjoy what was a box-
office hit. TS

Joan Fontaine *Susan* • Mark Stevens *Bill
Cummings* • Rosemary DeCamp *Martha* • Henry
Morgan [Harry Morgan] *Hank* • Wally Brown *Jake*
• Bobby Driscoll *Timmy* ■ *Dir* John Berry • *Scr*
Hugo Butler, Garson Kanin, Edith R Sommer,
Charles Schnee, from the novel *All Brides Are
Beautiful* by Thomas Bell

From Time to Time ★★★PG
Fantasy adventure 2009 · UK · Colour · 91min

Slipping between the 1940s and the
Napoleonic era, the tale of Mancunian
evacuee Alex Etel's encounter with a
spectral black page boy brought back from
the West Indies by his ancestor is complex
but compelling. Adapted from the children's
novel *The Chimneys of Green Knowe*, it will
probably appeal less to modern kids than
grown-ups raised on Lucy M Boston's
atmospheric stories about a magical manor
house. Nevertheless, writer/director Julian
Fellowes invests the action with plenty of
nostalgic warmth, while Maggie Smith
exudes wistful affection as Etel's
grandmother, who is never surprised by her
home's capacity for enchantment and
adventure. DP DVD Blu

Maggie Smith *Linnet* • Timothy Spall *Boggis* •
Dominic West *Caxton* • Carice van Houten *Maria* •
Eliza Hope Bennett [Eliza Bennett] *Susan* • Hugh
Bonneville *Captain Oldknow* • Alex Etel *Tolly* ■
Dir Julian Fellowes • *Scr* Julian Fellowes, from
the novel *The Chimneys of Green Knowe* by Lucy
M Boston • *Cinematographer* Alan Almond

From Up on Poppy Hill ★★U
Animated drama 2011 · Jpn · Colour · 87min

A high-school romance is the focus of this
sweet but bland Japanese animated drama
from studio Ghibli, set in 1963, a year before
the Tokyo Olympics. Sarah Bolger voices
teenage heroine Umi, who becomes
involved with student writer Shun (Anton
Yelchin) and his tumbledown academic
clubhouse that is faced with demolition. The
animation is a delight, but the scattershot
storytelling gives the colourful voice cast
(including Gillian Anderson, Bruce Dern and
Beau Bridges) no chance to shine. TJ
Japanese dubbed. DVD Blu

Sarah Bolger *Umi Matsuzaki* • Anton Yelchin
Shun Kazama • Gillian Anderson *Hana Matsuzaki*
• Christina Hendricks *Miki Hokuto* ■ *Dir* Goro
Miyazaki • *Scr* Hayao Miyazaki, Keiko Niwa, from
a story by Tetsuro Sayama, from a comic book
by Sayama, Chizuru Takahashi

The Front ★★★15
Comedy drama 1976 · US · Colour · 90min

Woody Allen is overshadowed both
physically and dramatically by his co-star
Zero Mostel in this Martin Ritt-directed
exposé of Hollywood during the witch-hunt
days of the 1950s. Allen plays a cashier who
agrees to lend his name as a cover for
blacklisted scriptwriters, and his usual
neurotic personality is kept subdued until
his character starts believing he's as good
as the authors he's helping. This is a fair
stab at wringing humour out of a grim
period. TH DVD

Woody Allen *Howard Prince* • Zero Mostel *Hecky
Brown* • Herschel Bernardi *Phil Sussman* •
Michael Murphy (1) *Alfred Miller* • Andrea
Marcovicci *Florence Barrett* ■ *Dir* Martin Ritt •
Scr Walter Bernstein

The Front Line ★★★15
Thriller 2006 · UK/Ger/Ire/Swe · Colour · 90min

In this brooding Irish crime drama, Eriq
Ebouaney plays a Congolese refugee, still
haunted by memories of war in his
homeland, who manages to secure a job as
a security guard in Dublin. Unfortunately, a
vicious mobster (James Frain) decides he's
the perfect inside man for a robbery and
kidnaps Ebouaney's family, threatening to
kill them unless he co-operates. The thriller
elements never really convince and the
heist itself is nothing special, but writer/
director David Gleeson is on surer ground
with the emotional drama and Ebouaney
brings a quiet intensity to his role as a good
man who can't escape his dark past. JF
Violence, swearing. DVD

Eriq Ebouaney *Joe Yumba* • James Frain *Eddie
Gilroy* • Gerard McScrley *Detective Inspector
Harbison* • Hakeem Kae-Kazim *Erasmus* • Fatou
N'Diaye *Kala* ■ *Dir/Scr* David Gleeson

The Front Page ★★★
Comedy drama 1931 · US · BW · 102min

Ben Hecht and Charles MacArthur's stage
success of 1928 was a natural for a movie
adaptation: set mainly in the pressroom of a
Chicago court-house, it's a gift for actors.
Adolphe Menjou plays the powerful editor,
Walter Burns, and Pat O'Brien is his ace
reporter, Hildy Johnson. Spraying smart
dialogue at the speed of Chicago's machine
guns, it carries its age with dignity. Remade
- with a sex-change operation (Hildy
becomes a woman) - as *His Girl Friday* in
1940, by Billy Wilder in 1974, and again in
Switching Channels in 1988, by this time set
in a TV newsroom. AT

Adolphe Menjou *Walter Burns* • Pat O'Brien *Hildy
Johnson* • Mary Brian *Peggy* • Edward Everett
Horton *Bensinger* • Walter Catlett *Murphy* ■
Dir Lewis Milestone • *Scr* Bartlett Cormack, Ben
Hecht (uncredited), Charles Lederer (uncredited),
from the play by Ben Hecht, Charles MacArthur

The Front Page ★★★★
Comedy drama 1974 · US · Colour · 104min

Director Billy Wilder had already made one
classic newspaper movie, *Ace in the Hole*,
before he tackled Ben Hecht and Charles
MacArthur's play, previously filmed in 1931.

Preserving the Prohibition-era setting but
rewriting nearly half the play's dialogue,
Wilder and his co-writer, IAL Diamond,
create a breathless, Faustian farce. Jack
Lemmon stars as the hotshot reporter
who's intent on getting married despite the
fact that he has clearly sold his soul to the
Devil incarnate, satanic editor Walter Burns,
played by Walter Matthau. Lemmon and
Matthau are on top form, although the
shouting, no matter how clever the
dialogue, gets a bit wearing. AT

Jack Lemmon *Hildy Johnson* • Walter Matthau
Walter Burns • Carol Burnett *Mollie Malloy* •
Susan Sarandon *Peggy Grant* • Vincent Gardenia
Sheriff • David Wayne *Bensinger* • Allen Garfield
Kruger ■ *Dir* Billy Wilder • *Scr* Billy Wilder, IAL
Diamond, from the play by Ben Hecht, Charles
MacArthur

Front Page Story ★★★PG
Drama 1953 · UK · BW · 94min

Back in the days when Rupert was only a
bear in Fleet Street and British newspapers
engaged in rivalries that were almost
gentlemanly compared with today, editor
Jack Hawkins has to choose between his
job and his marriage to Elizabeth Allan, who
sits at home and wonders where it all went
wrong. Cosily dated, but an interesting sign
of its times. TH

Jack Hawkins *John Grant* • Elizabeth Allan *Susan
Grant* • Eva Bartok *Mrs Thorpe* • Derek Farr *Teale*
• Michael Goodliffe *Kennedy* ■ *Dir* Gordon Parry
• *Scr* Jay Lewis, Jack Howells, William Fairchild,
Guy Morgan, from Robert Gaines's novel *Final
Night*

Front Page Woman ★★★
Comedy drama 1935 · US · BW · 83min

Bette Davis and George Brent co-star in this
tale about two newspaper hounds,
constantly trying to out-scoop and out-quip
each other, before deciding to settle their
professional differences in the traditional
way of romantic comedies. It wins no prizes
for realism in its depiction of newspaper life,
but at least it scores some points for
correctness ahead of its time on the
working woman issue, and there's a good
deal of enjoyment to be had en route to the
rather predictable finale. PF

Bette Davis *Ellen Garfield* • George Brent *Curt
Devlin* • Roscoe Karns *Toots* • Winifred Shaw *Inez
Cordova* • Joseph Crehan *Spike Kiley* ■
Dir Michael Curtiz • *Scr* Roy Chanslor, Lillie
Hayward, Laird Doyle, from the novel *Women
Are Bum Newspapermen* by Richard Macauley

La Frontera ★★★15
Political drama 1991 · Chil/Sp · Colour · 115min

Deftly revealing character through locale,
Ricardo Larrain's debut feature (which won
a Silver Bear at the Berlin film festival) is a
precisely paced study of the loneliness of
principle. As the Chilean maths teacher
exiled to a coastal town that was once
swept away by a tidal wave, Patricio
Contreras combines commitment and
resignation. There's amusement to be had
in the way he taunts his doltish police
guards, but the core of the film lies in his
tentative relationship with Gloria Laso, the
daughter of a fugitive from Franco's Spain,
and his uneasy friendship with a priest. DP
Spanish +subtitles.

Patricio Contreras *Ramiro Orellana* • Gloria Laso
Maite • Hector Noguera *Father Patricio* • Alonso
Venegas *Delegate* • Aldo Bernales *Diver* ■
Dir Ricardo Larrain • *Scr* Ricardo Larrain, Jorge
Goldenberg

Frontera ★★★
Drama 2014 · US · Colour

The wrong man is accused of murder in this
understated immigration drama. The man
in question is Michael Peña, a Mexican
immigrant who crosses the border with the
hope of a better life for his family, but then
a kindly woman (Amy Madigan) he
befriends is involved in a fatal accident. The
local authorities believe that Peña is
responsible, but the woman's husband (Ed
Harris) - a retired Sheriff - isn't so sure. It's
worth noting that we know exactly who the
guilty party is, and as a result *Frontera*
doesn't play out as the whodunnit that you

might be expecting. Thankfully, though,
Harris proves typically captivating, and the
film offers some genuinely affecting
moments. SC English, Spanish +subtitles.
Violence.

Ed Harris *Roy* • Michael Peña [Michael Pena]
Miguel • Eva Longoria *Paulina* • Amy Madigan
Olivia • Aden Young *Sheriff Randall Hunt* ■
Dir Michael Berry (2) • *Scr* Michael Berry (2), Luis
Moulinet III

Frontier Badmen ★★U
Western 1943 · US · BW · 77min

The bland Robert Paige is surrounded by a
highly watchable cast, notably the
tormented Diana Barrymore, alcoholic
daughter of John, as the romantic lead. In
this tale of cattlemen trying to break up a
monopoly, Lon Chaney Jr features as a
mean hired gun with a streak of sadism
unusual in a family-themed movie of this
type, and Paige's sidekick is a young Noah
Beery Jr. TS

Robert Paige *Steve* • Anne Gwynne *Chris* • Noah
Beery Jr *Jim* • Diana Barrymore *Claire* • Leo
Carrillo *Chinito* • Andy Devine *Slim* • Lon Chaney
Jr *Chango* ■ *Dir* Ford Beebe • *Scr* Gerald
Geraghty, Morgan B Cox

Frontier Blues ★★12
Comedy drama 2010 · UK/Fr · Colour · 93min

The pace of life near Iran's northern border
with Turkmenistan is unruffled, to say the
least, in this leisurely portrait of eccentric
characters coping with an isolated
existence on the margins. Babak Jalali's film
takes everything slowly, giving us plenty of
time to take in the barren landscape as we
wait in vain for anything of significance to
happen. Fans of the deadpan wit of Finnish
film-maker Aki Kaurismäki may well be
more attuned to this minimalist style than
most viewers, but even if the film is long on
wry smiles and short on outright laughter,
its gentleness and sheer peculiarity are just
about enough to sustain the interest. TJ
Farsi, Turkmen +subtitles. Swearing, sexual
references. DVD

Mahmoud Kalteh *Alam* • Khajeh Araz Dordi
Minstrel • Abolfazl Karimi *Hassan* • Behzad
Shahrivari *Uncle Kazem* ■ *Dir/Scr* Babak Jalali

Frontier Gal ★★★
Comedy western 1945 · US · Colour · 84min

This romantic western was one of the
movies that made a star out of Yvonne De
Carlo. Tight-lipped leading man Rod
Cameron is her co-star, and the splendidly
batty plot involves bandit Cameron
marrying saloon owner De Carlo and going
on the run for six years, then returning to
discover that he's now a father before
ultimately throwing the villain over a cliff.
Don't ask. De Carlo would gain icon status in
The Munsters TV series, but Cameron was
relegated to B-westerns. TS

Yvonne De Carlo *Lorena Dumont* • Rod Cameron
Johnny Hart • Andy Devine *Big Ben* • Fuzzy
Knight *Fuzzy* • Sheldon Leonard *Blackie* •
Andrew Tombes *Judge Prescott* • Clara Blandick
Abigail ■ *Dir* Charles Lamont • *Scr* Michael
Fessier, Ernest Pagano

Frontier Horizon ★★U
Western 1939 · US · BW · 54min

This was John Wayne's last appearance in
the *Three Mesquiteers* series before
Republic finally promoted him to A-
features. The dreary-as-usual plot has
Wayne, Ray Corrigan and Raymond Hatton
saving settlers from taking worthless land.
Watch for young Phyllis Isley, who would
transform herself into a major star under
the name of Jennifer Jones. AE DVD

John Wayne *Stony Brooke* • Ray "Crash"
Corrigan *Tucson Smith* • Raymond Hatton *Rusty
Joslin* • Phyllis Isley [Jennifer Jones] *Celia* ■
Dir George Sherman • *Scr* Betty Burbridge, Luci
Ward, from characters by William Colt
MacDonald

Frontier Marshal ★★★PG
Western 1939 · US · BW · 71min

Director Allan Dwan's first sound western
was this marvellously authentic-looking
version of the Wyatt Earp legend. It stars
the stone-faced Randolph Scott as the man

F

who cleaned up the West, with debonair Cesar Romero as the doom-laden Doc Holliday, renamed for some reason as Doc Halliday. It may not be historically correct, but it's entertaining, with a cracking pace and some exciting moments. **TS** *DVD*

Randolph Scott *Wyatt Earp, Sarah Allen* • Cesar Romero *Doc Halliday* • Binnie Barnes *Jerry* • John Carradine *Ben Carter* • Edward Norris *Dan Blackmore* • Lon Chaney Jr *Pringle* ■ *Dir* Allan Dwan • *Scr* Sam Hellman, from the novel *Wyatt Earp, Frontier Marshal* by Stuart N Lake

Frontier(s) ★★ 18
Horror thriller 2007 · Fr/Swi · Colour · 103min

Arguably, since the advent of "torture porn" movies like *Hostel*, French New Wave horror has become the edgiest and most brutal produced around the world. This steel-yourself shocker from writer/director Xavier Gens (*Hitman*) is a splatter spectacular about Paris thieves hiding out in a guest house near the French border that is run by degenerate neo-Nazi cannibals. The blending of caricature Nazis with a flesh-eating family straight out of *The Texas Chain Saw Massacre* is pure overkill. **AJ** French +subtitles. *DVD*

Karina Testa *Yasmine* • Samuel Le Bihan *Goëtz* • Estelle Lefébure *Gilberte* • Aurélien Wiik *Alex* • David Saracino *Tom* • Chems Dahmani *Farid* • Maud Forget *Eva* • Jean-Pierre Jorris *Von Geisler, "Father"* ■ *Dir/Scr* Xavier Gens

Frost/Nixon ★★★★ 15
Historical drama
2008 · US/UK/Fr · Colour · 116min

This dialogue-heavy but utterly compelling history lesson restages David Frost's exclusive 1977 interviews with former US President Richard Nixon, three years after he left office in disgrace over the Watergate scandal. Opening up the theatrical battle of wits with measured restraint, director Ron Howard invests everything in the strength of his practised leads, Michael Sheen and Frank Langella. And, having honed their roles in Peter Morgan's original play, the pair are quietly electrifying. A transcription of the interviews themselves would be fascinating enough, but Morgan's script gets right under the skin of the financially strapped, vanity-driven inquisitor and the morally beleaguered politician. **AC** Swearing. *DVD* *BD*

Frank Langella *Richard Nixon* • Michael Sheen *David Frost* • Kevin Bacon *Jack Brennan* • Rebecca Hall *Caroline Cushing* • Toby Jones *Swifty Lazar* • Matthew Macfadyen *John Birt* • Oliver Platt *Bob Zelnick* • Sam Rockwell *James Reston Jr* ■ *Dir* Ron Howard • *Scr* Peter Morgan (1), from his play • *Editors* Mike Hill, Dan Hanley • *Music* Hans Zimmer

Frostbite ★★ 15
Black comedy horror
2006 · Swe · Colour · 97min

An experimental drug turns the teens of a sleepy town in Lapland into fanged party animals in Sweden's first ever vampire movie. This black comedy horror makes good use of its unusual setting – with the safety of dawn a full month away in the frozen land of endless night. Despite this, and some nice *Blade*-style effects done on the cheap, it gradually runs out of steam before delivering a disappointingly abrupt open ending. Nevertheless, Banke does manage to keep the suspense buoyant, helping to disguise the film's overall failings. **AJ** Swedish, German +subtitles. Swearing, drug abuse. *DVD*

Petra Nielsen *Annika* • Grete Havneskold *Saga* • Emma T Aberg *Vega* • Jonas Karlstrom *Sebastian* • Carl-Ake Eriksson *Professor Gerhard Beckert* • Niklas Gronberg *John* ■ *Dir* Anders Banke • *Scr* Daniel Ojanlatva • *Cinematographer* Chris Maris

Frozen ★★★ 15
Thriller 2004 · UK · Colour · 86min

Shirley Henderson stars as a woman haunted by the sister who disappeared two years earlier in this tantalising thriller. Her obsession leads her to steal a security camera video and retrace her sister's movements in an atmosphere of mounting

dread. Director Juliet McKoen's debut feature plays with notions of the afterlife, and the story unfolds on a grey, cold and uninviting stretch of Morecambe Bay, helping to ground the mystery. Although the story sags a little in the middle, there's still enough going on to keep the audience's intrigued. **BP** Swearing, violence. *DVD* *BD*

Shirley Henderson *Kath Swarbrick* • Roshan Seth *Noyen Roy* • Ger Ryan *Elsie* • Richard Armitage *Steven* • Ralf Little *Eddie* • Jamie Sives *Jim* • Sean Harris *Hurricane Frank* • Shireen Shah *Vellama* ■ *Dir* Juliet McKoen • *Scr* Juliet McKoen, Jayne Steel

Frozen ★★★ 15
Thriller 2009 · US · Colour · 89min

Three snowboarders stranded on a Utah mountain chairlift are forced to make terrifying choices to stay alive in *Hatchet* director Adam Green's iced gem. Some may find the early character-building scenes a little tired, but once the premise locks tight, small actions become epic tragedies, with frostbite, hypothermia, freezer-burn and a pack of hungry wolves on the life-threatening dangers list. Green choreographs the dangling trio from a multitude of intriguing angles with a keen eye for moody menace. **AJ** Swearing. *DVD* *BD*

Shawn Ashmore *Joe Lynch* • Kevin Zegers *Dan Walker* • Emma Bell *Parker O'Neil* • Ed Ackerman *Jason* • Rileah Vanderbilt *Shannon* • Kane Hodder *Cody* ■ *Dir/Scr* Adam Green

Frozen ★★★★ PG
Animated adventure 2013 · US · Colour · 97min

Hans Christian Andersen's *The Snow Queen* gets the full revisionist Disney-princess treatment in a dazzling adventure that evokes the studio's 1990s refreshment of its animated output through an injection of Broadway talent. Tony Award-winning Idina Menzel voices Elsa, the princess whose magical frostiness is so dangerous that she is separated from younger sister Anna (Kristen Bell). After becoming queen, an angry Elsa reveals her chilling powers, causing her kingdom to suffer continuous winter. Full of vivid action and solid drama, this flawless union of sharply modern comedy and thrilling spectacle also has superb show-tune songs by Robert Lopez. **AJ** In English, Serbian. *DVD* *BD* *CS*

Kristen Bell *Anna* • Idina Menzel *Elsa* • Jonathan Groff *Kristoff* • Josh Gad *Olaf* • Santino Fontana *Hans* ■ *Dir* Chris Buck, Jennifer Lee (3) • *Scr* Jennifer Lee (3), from a story by Chris Buck, Shane Morris, Lee, from the fairy tale *The Snow Queen* by Hans Christian Andersen

The Frozen Dead ★★
Horror 1966 · UK · Colour and BW · 92min

In this clinically ghoulish low-budget British shocker, imported American star Dana Andrews is set on reviving 1,500 top Nazi officials who've been in a deep freeze since the war. Though directed with a fatal lack of gusto by Herbert J Leder, the sheer delirium of the premise takes some beating. We have a row of severed arms, all neatly mounted and awaiting use, and a woman's severed head that lives in a box and, through mental telepathy, warns others of Andrews's scheme for jackbooted world domination. **RS**

Dana Andrews *Dr Norberg* • Anna Palk *Jean Norberg* • Philip Gilbert *Dr Ted Roberts* • Kathleen Breck *Elsa Tenney* • Edward Fox *Prisoner No 3* ■ *Dir* Herbert J Leder • *Scr* Herbert J Leder, from his story

The Frozen Ghost ★★
Psychological mystery 1944 · US · BW · 61min

Lon Chaney Jr was never the most flexible of actors, but few could play innocents lured into iniquity with such lumbering geniality. In this *Inner Sanctum* instalment, he hits another streak of bad luck as a stage hypnotist whose career is ruined when a member of his audience dies during a show. However, things go from bad to worse after he lands a job at Tala Birell's wax museum and falls prey to a series of bizarre incidents designed to send him crazy. Abetted by a

practised supporting cast, director Harold Young exploits his atmospheric locations. **DP**

Lon Chaney [Lon Chaney Jr] *Alex Gregor/Gregor the Great* • Evelyn Ankers *Maura Daniel* • Milburn Stone *George Keene* • Douglass Dumbrille *Inspector Brant* • Martin Kosleck *Rudi Poldan* • Elena Verdugo *Nina Coudreau* ■ *Dir* Harold Young • *Scr* Bernard Schubert, Luci Ward, Henry Sucher, from a story by Harrison Carter, Henry Sucher

The Frozen Ground ★★★ 15
Thriller based on a true story
2013 · US · Colour · 100min

This moody fact-based thriller stars Nicolas Cage as an Alaskan state trooper on the trail of a serial killer and Vanessa Hudgens as a young prostitute who escaped his clutches. Cage must convince his bosses he's after the right man, while protecting the girl from a murderer intent on finishing the job. Cage's solid, if occasionally manic, and John Cusack is perfect as the focus of the investigation, but Hudgens impresses most, moving ever further away from the undemanding teen roles of her early career. **TeS** Swearing, drug abuse, nudity. *DVD* *BD*

Nicolas Cage *Sgt Jack Halcombe* • Vanessa Hudgens [Vanessa Anne Hudgens] *Cindy Paulson* • John Cusack *Robert Hansen* • 50 Cent [Curtis "50 Cent" Jackson] *Clate Johnson* • Radha Mitchell *Allie Halcombe* ■ *Dir/Scr* Scott Walker (4)

Frozen Land ★★★★ 18
Drama 2005 · Fin/Nor · Colour · 127min

Shades of Ingmar Bergman and Aki Kaurismäki colour this excellent ensemble treatise on the meaning of life. Opening with a Tolstoy story about a forged banknote, Finnish director Aku Louhimies shows how the most insular existence can be connected to the fate of strangers. Shiftless Niko (Jasper Paakkonen) is disowned by his unemployed father (Pertti Sveholm), alcoholic Hurskainen (Sulevi Peltola) falls off the wagon and commits a hideous crime, and teacher Antti (Petteri Summanen) comes to terms with the death of his depressed cop wife (Matleena Kuusniemi). Despite its bleak patches, this avoids being a stock exercise in Nordic miserablism thanks to some moments of dark comedy and an air of optimism. **DP** Finnish +subtitles. Sex scenes. *DVD*

Jasper Paakkonen *Niko* • Mikko Leppilampi *Tuomas* • Pamela Tola *Elina* • Petteri Summanen *Antti* • Matleena Kuusniemi *Hannele* • Sulevi Peltola *Hurskainen* • Pertti Sveholm *Smolander* ■ *Dir* Aku Louhimies • *Scr* Aku Louhimies, Jari Rantala, Paavo Westerberg, inspired by the short story *The Forged Coupon* by Leo Tolstoy

Frozen River ★★★★ 15
Drama 2008 · US · Colour · 92min

Writer/director Courtney Hunt's snowbound drama is set in the wastelands of upstate New York, where Ray Eddy (Melissa Leo) struggles to raise her kids and pay the bills. Her salvation comes in the terse, mistrusting shape of a native American from the local reservation who ropes Ray into helping her smuggle illegal immigrants from Canada over the frozen Saint Lawrence River. Crossing the river's thin ice becomes an effective metaphor for the trouble that lies ahead in this part trailer-trash domestic drama, part tense thriller, which features a fabulously sinewy performance from Leo, who's brilliant as the struggling mother suffering a lifetime of minimum-wage toil. **JR** Swearing, some violence. *DVD*

Melissa Leo *Ray Eddy* • Misty Upham *Lila Littlewolf* • Charlie McDermott *TJ* • Michael O'Keefe *Trooper Finnerty* • Mark Boone Junior *Jacques Bruno* • James Reilly *Ricky* ■ *Dir/Scr* Courtney Hunt

Fruitvale Station ★★★★ 15
Drama based on a true story
2013 · US · Colour · 81min

The film's title refers to the station in Oakland, California, where unarmed 22-year-old African-American passenger Oscar Grant was shot dead by transport police in

2009. Though one might well expect a dramatised take on the killing to be an explosive, indignant affair, this subtle, affecting movie is a surprisingly low-key character study, drenched in pathos and melancholy, with Michael B Jordan (*Chronicle*) outstanding as Grant. Tracing the last 24 hours of Grant's life, *Fruitvale Station* provides a rough sketch of a complex man whose life was at a crossroads. **DW** Violence, swearing. *DVD* *BD*

Michael B Jordan *Oscar Grant* • Melonie Diaz *Sophina* • Octavia Spencer *Wanda* • Kevin Durand *Officer Caruso* • Chad Michael Murray *Officer Ingram* ■ *Dir/Scr* Ryan Coogler

Fuck for Forest ★★★ 18
Documentary 2012 · Pol/Ger · Colour · 86min

A bizarre protest group experiences a culture shock in Michal Marczak's eye-opening if excruciating documentary. *Fuck for Forest* is a Berlin-based cabal of eco-activists that seeks to raise money for its campaigns by selling home-made erotic movies on the internet. However, the group gets a humbling reality check when they travel to a remote outpost in the Peruvian rainforest and are dismissed as patronising time-wasters by the impoverished locals. A hint of mockery occasionally informs Marczak's detached approach, but while the tactics of the group are often baffling, he also makes the serious point that charitable aid is worthless unless it meets a genuine need. **DP** English, German, Spanish, Norwegian +subtitles.

■ *Dir* Michal Marczak • *Scr* Michal Marczak, Lukasz Grudzinski

The Fugitive ★★★★ PG
Drama 1947 · US · BW · 99min

Director John Ford's mesmerising version of *The Power and the Glory* – Graham Greene's novel about a "whisky priest" – is compromised by the censorship of the time. But, even though the central relationship is no longer a sexual one and Henry Fonda's priest is not an alcoholic, it remains resolutely convincing. Pedro Armendáriz is particularly fine as the police lieutenant, and Dolores Del Rio smoulders as the woman, but the real star is the magnificent outdoor photography from Gabriel Figueroa. **TS** *DVD*

Henry Fonda *Fugitive/Priest* • Dolores Del Rio *Native woman/Maria Dolores* • Pedro Armendáriz *Police lieutenant* • J Carrol Naish *Police informer* • Leo Carrillo *Chief of police* • Ward Bond *El Gringo/James Calvert* ■ *Dir* John Ford • *Scr* Dudley Nichols, from the novel *The Power and the Glory* by Graham Greene

The Fugitive ★★★★ 15
Thriller 1993 · US · Colour and BW · 124min

The original TV series of *The Fugitive* starring David Janssen ran for 120 episodes in the 1960s and attracted a cult following. Director Andrew Davis takes the bare bones of the source material and comes up with an unstoppable juggernaut, in which the suspense never lets up and the set pieces are truly epic. Harrison Ford is fine as the innocent surgeon who is wrongfully convicted of the murder of his wife and sets off to find the real killer. But the movie is stolen from under his nose by Tommy Lee Jones, who gives an Oscar-winning performance as the marshal doggedly pursuing the wanted man. Jones reprised his role in the disappointing *US Marshals*. **JF** Violence, swearing. *DVD* *BD*

Harrison Ford *Dr Richard Kimble* • Tommy Lee Jones *Deputy Marshal Samuel Gerard* • Sela Ward *Helen Kimble* • Julianne Moore *Dr Anne Eastman* • Joe Pantoliano *Cosmo Renfro* ■ *Dir* Andrew Davis • *Scr* Jeb Stuart, David Twohy, from a story by David Twohy, from characters by Roy Huggins

The Fugitive Kind ★★ 12
Drama 1960 · US · BW · 116min

Based on an emotional play by Tennessee Williams, this stars Marlon Brando as a guitar-playing drifter who falls into the lap of Anna Magnani, a lonely woman trapped in a marriage to a dying man. There are subplots aplenty, and Joanne Woodward as well, but you get the feeling it's Williams throwing out his dirty washing and seeing how it falls. But, despite such prestige casting and Sidney Lumet as director, audiences sensed a downer and stayed away in droves. AT **DVD**

Marlon Brando *Val Xavier* • Anna Magnani *Lady Torrance* • Joanne Woodward *Carol Cutrere* • Maureen Stapleton *Vee Talbot* • Victor Jory *Jabe Torrance* ■ *Dir* Sidney Lumet • *Scr* Tennessee Williams, Meade Roberts, from the play *Orpheus Descending* by Tennessee Williams

Fugitive Pieces ★★ 15
Drama 2007 · Can/Gr · Colour · 106min

This overly talky adaptation of Anne Michaels's acclaimed novel seems more like a theatrical masterclass than a slice-of-life drama. The story flashes between young Jewish boy Jakob (Robbie Kay) – who was rescued by Greek archaeologist Athos (Rade Sherbedgia) after his family were murdered by the Nazis in Poland - and the adult Jakob (Stephen Dillane), a Holocaust historian living in Canada. The segments that portray Jakob's early life are both poignant and harrowing, but Dillane rarely conveys the torment that's supposed to be racking him, instead adopting an air of quizzical detachment that makes his plight decidedly uninvolving. DP English, Greek, Yiddish, German +subtitles. Some sex scenes.

Stephen Dillane *Jakob Beer* • Rade Sherbedgia *Athos Roussos* • Rosamund Pike *Alex* • Ayelet Zurer *Michaela* • Robbie Kay *Young Jakob* • Ed Stoppard *Ben* ■ *Dir* Jeremy Podeswa • *Scr* Jeremy Podeswa, from the novel by Anne Michaels

The Fulfillment of Mary Gray ★★
Period drama 1989 · US · Colour · 96min

Cheryl Ladd stars in this silly tale as a woman in the 1900s whose husband can't father a child. However, he has a brother who seems more capable in that department, causing all sorts of family problems. Lewis Smith and Ted Levine are the men getting their knickers (and everything else) in a twist in this so-so TV drama. JB Swearing.

Cheryl Ladd *Mary Gray* • Ted Levine *Jonathan Gray* • Lewis Smith *Aaron Gray* • Sheila Kelley (1) *Kate* ■ *Dir* Piers Haggard • *Scr* Laird Koenig, from the novel *The Fulfillment* by LaVyrle Spencer

Full Alert ★★★ 15
Crime action thriller 1997 · HK · Colour · 94min

Ringo Lam (whose *City on Fire* was a big influence on *Reservoir Dogs*) directs this gripping crime thriller. The story focuses on the cat-and-mouse games between tough cop Lau Ching Wan and Francis Ng, who is planning the ultimate robbery at a race track. As usual, the action sequences are stunningly choreographed, but Lam is equally interested in the pyschological interplay between good and evil and Ng makes for an intriguingly sympathetic villain. JF Cantonese +subtitles. **DVD**

Lau Ching Wan *Inspector Pao* • Francis Ng *Mak Kwan* • Blacky Ko [Ko Sau Leung] • Amanda Lee • Monica Chan ■ *Dir* Ringo Lam • *Scr* WK Lua, Ringo Lam, from a story by Ringo Lam

Full Circle ★★
Horror 1977 · UK/Can · Colour · 97min

Director Richard Loncraine's competent adaptation is a slow-moving, supernatural tale more concerned with atmosphere than action. Mia Farrow is an unstable mother who, feeling responsible for the choking death of their daughter, leaves her husband Keir Dullea. Moving into an eerie house haunted by the spirit of a moody child, she becomes even more guilt-stricken and obsessed. Most viewers will be three steps ahead of the catatonic Farrow. AJ

Mia Farrow *Julia Lofting* • Keir Dullea *Magnus Lofting* • Tom Conti *Mark* • Jill Bennett *Lily* • Robin Gammell *David Swift* • Cathleen Nesbitt *Mrs Rudge* • Anna Wing *Mrs Flood* ■ *Dir* Richard

Loncraine • *Scr* Dave Humphries, Harry Bromley Davenport (adaptation), from the novel *Julia* by Peter Straub

Full Contact ★★★★ 18
Action thriller 1992 · HK · Colour · 94min

Chow Yun-Fat is a Bangkok bouncer who takes violent revenge after an arms raid leads to a double-cross in this frantic "heroic bloodshed" thriller. Simon Yam, as a gay arms dealer, dominates proceedings and Anthony Wong plays Chow's duplicitous friend. This is a film of flying metal, whether in the form of speeding cars, bikes or bullets. Ringo Lam's direction is electrifying, topping the armoured car robberies with a sensational nightclub shoot-out, in which the camera takes on the perspective of the bullets. DP Cantonese +subtitles. Violence, swearing. **DVD**

Chow Yun-Fat *Jeff* • Simon Yam *Judge* • Ann Bridgewater *Mona* • Anthony Wong (1) *Sam* • Bonnie Fu *Virgin* • Frankie Chin *Deano* ■ *Dir* Ringo Lam • *Scr* Nam Yin

Full Eclipse ★★★ 18
Action horror thriller 1993 · US · Colour · 93min

This imaginative werewolf romp is given lashings of style by horror director Anthony Hickox, which compensates for the general lack of blood-spilling enforced by its TV movie status. Hard-bitten urban cop Mario Van Peebles is tricked by Patsy Kensit into joining Bruce Payne's elite corps of crime-busting lycanthropes. A simple injection turns him into a furry vigilante with an appetite for criminal-ripping frenzies, performed with Hong Kong-inspired élan. AJ **DVD**

Mario Van Peebles *Max Dire* • Patsy Kensit *Casey Spencer* • Bruce Payne *Adam Garou* • Anthony John Denison *Jim Sheldon* • Victoria Rowell *Anna Dire* • John Verea *Ramon Perez* ■ *Dir* Anthony Hickox • *Scr* Richard Christian Matheson, Michael Reaves

Full Fathom Five ★★
Action thriller 1990 · US · Colour · 82min

Roger Corman once again demonstrates his unerring ability when it comes to spotting directorial talent. Carl Franklin is now acclaimed for his thrillers *One False Move* and *Devil in a Blue Dress*, but back in 1990 he was a jobbing TV actor. This blatant cash-in on *The Hunt for Red October* features Michael Moriarty as a submarine skipper on the trail of stolen nuclear craft. Undistinguished fare. JF

Michael Moriarty *McKenzie* • Maria Rangel *Justine* • Diego Bertie *Miguel* • German Gonzales *Sebastian* ■ *Dir* Carl Franklin • *Scr* Bart Davis, from his novel

Full Frontal ★ 18
Romantic comedy drama 2002 · US · Colour · 96min

Built on Dogme 95-style foundations - with actors doing their own hair and make-up and relinquishing their traditional on-set privileges – director Steven Soderbergh's apparent attempt to get back to his grittier roots isn't nearly as clever as he thinks it is. The basic scenario is a day in the life of LA's beautiful people, and the glittering cast rambles its way through a plethora of human emotions, being neither entertaining nor interesting. It's all captured on grainy digital video for that extra touch of pretension. SF **DVD**

David Duchovny *Gus* • Nicky Katt *Hitler* • Catherine Keener *Lee* • Mary McCormack *Linda* • David Hyde Pierce *Carl* • Julia Roberts *Francesca/Catherine* • Blair Underwood *Calvin/Nicholas* • David Fincher *Film director* ■ *Dir* Steven Soderbergh • *Scr* Coleman Hough

Full Metal Jacket ★★★★★ 18
War drama 1987 · UK · Colour · 111min

Stanley Kubrick's penultimate film is a harrowing, foul-mouthed and violent Vietnam war drama. It begins with a long training camp sequence in America before moving to a bombed-out Vietnamese city. While its message is simple - innocent young Americans are taught to be machine-like killers - its technique is extraordinary. Because Kubrick refuses to travel any

distance, it was shot entirely in Britain, with palm trees uprooted from Spain and Matthew Modine and a cast of relative unknowns uprooted from Hollywood. The performances are superb, especially Lee Ermey as the drill sergeant with a colourful vocabulary, Vincent D'Onofrio as the pathetic Private Pyle and Modine as the cynical recruit named Joker. AT **DVD** **Blu**

Matthew Modine *Private Joker* • Adam Baldwin *Animal Mother* • Vincent D'Onofrio *Leonard Lawrence, Private Gomer Pyle* • Lee Ermey [R Lee Ermey] *Gunnery Sergeant Hartman* • Dorian Harewood *Eightball* • Arliss Howard *Private Cowboy* ■ *Dir* Stanley Kubrick • *Scr* Stanley Kubrick, Michael Herr, Gustav Hasford, from the novel *The Short-Timers* by Gustav Hasford • *Art Director* Anton Furst

The Full Monty ★★★★★ 15
Comedy drama 1997 · UK/US · Colour · 87min

When the going gets tough, the tough get go-going, in director Peter Cattaneo's highly engaging, genuinely poignant and hilarious full-frontal comedy drama. Robert Carlyle plays a divorced father trying to maintain joint custody of his son, who forms a strip act along with a group of other unemployed Sheffield steelworkers. Well endowed with side-splitting laughter and brilliantly performed by the superb ensemble cast, this is about men's emotional shortcomings as much as their dirty dancing techniques, and is jam-packed with many wonderful moments - the would-be Chippendales of the North absent-mindedly gyrating to the radio in a dole queue is simply inspired. AJ Swearing, nudity. **DVD** **Blu**

Robert Carlyle *Gaz* • Tom Wilkinson *Gerald* • Mark Addy *Dave* • Lesley Sharp *Jean* • Emily Woof *Mandy* • Steve Huison *Lomper* • Paul Barber *Horse* • Hugo Speer *Guy* • Deirdre Costello *Linda* • Bruce Jones *Reg* ■ *Dir* Peter Cattaneo • *Scr* Simon Beaufoy

Full Moon High ★★★ 15
Comedy horror 1982 · US · Colour · 90min

Horror specialist Larry Cohen ventures into comedy with this parody of such 1950s B-movies as *I Was a Teenage Werewolf*. But it's also a sort of *Back to the Future* with fangs, as Adam Arkin returns from Transylvania after years in a lycanthropic wilderness to discover that his old high school buddies have changed almost as drastically as he has. Playing down the special effects in order to concentrate on the social spoofing, this is a sharp and funny film. DP

Adam Arkin *Tony Walker* • Elizabeth Hartman *Miss Montgomery* • Ed McMahon *Mr Walker* • Kenneth Mars *Principal Cleveland* • Roz Kelly *Jane* • Joanne Nail *Ricky* • Pat Morita *Silversmith* • Louis Nye *Reverend* ■ *Dir/Scr* Larry Cohen

Full Moon in Blue Water ★★ 15
Comedy drama 1988 · US · Colour · 90min

Only Gene Hackman saves this from totally sinking. He plays the owner of a run-down Texas bar, who is obsessed by his long-lost wife despite the efforts of Teri Garr to grab him for herself. Full of the kind of eccentrics usually found in a Tennessee Williams play, this veers between engaging realism and overblown melodrama. TH Swearing.

Gene Hackman *Floyd* • Teri Garr *Louise* • Burgess Meredith *The General* • Elias Koteas *Jimmy* • Kevin Cooney *Charlie* • David Doty *Virgil* • Gil Glasgow *Baytch* ■ *Dir* Peter Masterson • *Scr* Bill Bozzone

Full Moon in Paris ★★★★ 15
Romantic comedy 1984 · Fr · Colour · 97min

The fourth film in Eric Rohmer's "Comedies and Proverbs" series is a sublime example of the control we land ourselves in every time we open our mouths. Surely no other film-maker has depicted with such consistency and accuracy exactly what it means to be human. In this delightful tale, Pascale Ogier's desire to spread her wings away from boyfriend Tcheky Karyo backfires when she's sucked into a new social world full of temptations and regrets. The daughter of popular star Bulle Ogier, Pascale won the best actress award at

Venice, only to die shortly afterwards at the young age of 24. DP French +subtitles. **DVD**

Pascale Ogier *Louise* • Fabrice Luchini *Octave* • Tcheky Karyo *Rémi* • Christian Vadim *Bastien* • Virginie Thévenet *Camille* • Thérèse Liotard *Marianne* • Noël Coffman *Stanislas* ■ *Dir/Scr* Eric Rohmer

Full of Life ★★★
Comedy drama 1956 · US · BW · 90min

The delightful Judy Holliday was rarely upstaged, but this warm family comedy is stolen by pudgy Salvatore Baccaloni, the Metropolitan Opera bass making his screen debut with a superb performance as her father-in-law. The film covers the final few days in Holliday's pregnancy with her first child, and the problems that arise when her husband's well-meaning but interfering Italian Catholic father comes to fix a hole in their floor. Holliday's anxieties are human and believable and the film has a beguiling charm. TV

Judy Holliday *Emily Rocco* • Richard Conte *Nick Rocco* • Salvatore Baccaloni *Papa Rocco* • Esther Minciotti *Mama Rocco* • Joe De Santis *Father Gondolfo* ■ *Dir* Richard Quine • *Scr* John Fante, from his novel

Full Tilt Boogie ★★★ 15
Documentary 1997 · US · Colour · 96min

This documentary account of the making of Robert Rodriguez's cult black comedy horror *From Dusk till Dawn* is a bit more than the marketing tool that behind-the-scenes releases have more recently become. It's authentic and entertaining - especially for fans of Rodriguez, Quentin Tarantino (the writer), or star George Clooney - and also gives a lot of its time to the unsung workers behind the camera. It may not be a great insight into film-making, but, for the most part, it's a fun glimpse into the lives of the people who get the movies made. JA **DVD**

■ *Dir* Sarah Kelly

The Full Treatment ★★
Mystery drama 1961 · UK · BW · 120min

This sees racing driver Ronald Lewis follow his marriage to Diane Cilento with a serious head injury. French psychiatrist Claude Dauphin is supposed to be helping Lewis with some serious psychological problems but he's actually more interested in pursuing Cilento. The adult theme and a few sexy scenes earned this film an X certificate on release but it looks mild now and is far too long. AT

Claude Dauphin *Dr David Prade* • Diane Cilento *Denise Colby* • Ronald Lewis *Alan Colby* • Françoise Rosay *Madame Prade* ■ *Dir* Val Guest • *Scr* Val Guest, Ronald Scott Thorn, from the novel by Ronald Scott Thorn

The Fuller Brush Girl ★★★ U
Crime comedy 1950 · US · BW · 85min

Retaining a screenplay by Frank Tashlin, this is a remake of *The Fuller Brush Man*, filmed two years earlier as a slapstick vehicle for Red Skelton (who makes a fleeting, unbilled appearance here). However, the fresh twist is gender reversal, with Lucille Ball starring as the door-to-door saleswoman who finds herself involved in a murder investigation and forced into a series of crazy situations while fleeing the cops. Co-starring Eddie Albert as her clueless boyfriend, the movie fizzes along nicely in a cocktail of comic confusion. RK

Lucille Ball *Sally Elliott* • Eddie Albert *Humphrey Briggs* • Carl Benton Reid *Christy* • Gale Robbins *Ruby Rawlings* • Jeff Donnell *Jane Bixby* • Jerome Cowan *Harvey Simpson* • Red Skelton *Red Jones* ■ *Dir* Lloyd Bacon • *Scr* Frank Tashlin

A Fuller Life ★★ 15
Documentary 2013 · US · Colour and BW · 80min

Filial pride pervades every frame of this tribute to cult film-maker Samuel Fuller, for it's directed by his daughter, Samantha (who is better known as a glass designer). Unfortunately, it's a clumsily constructed documentary that compounds its cockeyed chronology by devoting too little time to the movies on which Fuller's reputation rests. Ms Fuller relies too heavily on having such former admirers of her father's reading extracts from his 2004 autobiography, A Third Face, with varying degrees of conviction and skill. DP Violence, swearing, sexual references.

James Franco • Jennifer Beals • Bill Duke • James Toback • Kelly Ward ■ Dir Samantha Fuller • Scr From a concept by Samantha Fuller, from the autobiography A Third Face by Sam Fuller

Fulltime Killer ★★★ 18

Action thriller 2002 · HK · Colour · 100min

Consciously designed to appeal to Pan-Asian audiences, this country-hopping tale of two hitmen occasionally loses its way as it zips across the continent. However, co-directors Johnny To and Wai Ka-Fai make the most of the character contrasts and allow Andy Lau's film-mad ex-Olympian to exhibit plenty of crowd-pleasing bravura, while Takashi Sorimachi's Japanese veteran looks on with disdain. Caught in the middle of their rivalry are Taiwanese video store assistant Kelly Lin and Singaporean Interpol agent Simon Yam. The action sequences are expertly contrived, but elsewhere the editing and effects are self-indulgently flamboyant. DP Cantonese, Mandarin, Japanese, English +subtitles. DVD

Andy Lau Tok • Takashi Sorimachi O • Simon Yam Lee • Kelly Lin Chin ■ Dir Johnny To [Johnnie To], Wai Ka-Fai • Scr Joey O'Bryan, Wai Ka-Fai, from a novel by Edmond Pang

Fun ★★★ 18

Crime drama
1994 · Can/US · Colour and BW · 99min

Director Rafal Zielinski's tale of two precocious teenagers committing murder to cement their friendship makes no effort to endear the gruesome girls to the viewer. That flaw, coupled with questionable psychology and a cop-out climax, severely undermines the vérité style that the director was aiming for, despite a tightly constructed plot in black and white for the present, glorious colour for the flashbacks and compelling performances from Alicia Witt and Renee Humphrey. AJ

Renee Humphrey Hilary • Alicia Witt Bonnie • William R Moses John • Leslie Hope Jane • Ania Suli Mrs Farmer ■ Dir Rafal Zielinski • Scr James Bosley, from his play

Fun in Acapulco ★★★ U

Musical 1963 · US · Colour · 92min

Elvis Presley performs a decidedly sub-standard score in a back-projected Mexico – though Bossa Nova Baby was a minor hit. The women, though, are pretty sensational: Ursula Andress, fresh from Dr No, plus beautiful Elsa Cardenas as a sexy lady bullfighter. Director Dick Thorpe once guided the King through the untamed Jailhouse Rock, but the results are much tamer here. Paul Lukas steals the show as a batty chef. TS DVD

Elvis Presley Mike Windgren • Ursula Andress Margarita Dauphine • Elsa Cardenas Dolores Gómez • Paul Lukas Maximillian • Larry Domasin Raoul Almeido ■ Dir Richard Thorpe • Scr Allan Weiss

Fun Size ★★ 12

Comedy 2012 · US · Colour · 75min

Josh Schwartz (The OC, Gossip Girl) wreaks havoc here with his directorial debut – a gross, sprawling and barely credible teen comedy. Victoria Justice stars as a gorgeous but unpopular (why?) geek who, after getting an invitation to the Halloween party, finds herself saddled with her little brother (Jackson Nicoll) when their mother (Chelsea Handler) goes out to have a good time. Some nice performances (particularly from Nicoll) almost rescue this good-looking film, which fails miserably on all other counts. KK Swearing, sexual references. DVD

Victoria Justice Wren • Thomas Mann (2) Roosevelt • Jane Levy April • Chelsea Handler Joy • Jackson Nicoll Albert • Johnny Knoxville Jörgen ■ Dir Josh Schwartz • Scr Max Werner

Fun with Dick and Jane ★★★ PG

Comedy 1977 · US · Colour · 95min

The humour inherent in the title is lost on British audiences, since it's the name of a basic primary school book in the States. Dick (George Segal on top comic form) becomes unemployed and, with the help of his wife (Jane Fonda), decides to turn to crime. It's funny at first, but being out of work isn't much of a laugh really, and the gags become hard to sustain despite director Ted Kotcheff's pleasant handling of the situation. TS Swearing. DVD

George Segal Dick Harper • Jane Fonda Jane Harper • Ed McMahon Charlie Blanchard • Dick Gautier Dr Will • Allan Miller Loan company manager ■ Dir Ted Kotcheff • Scr David Giler, Jerry Belson, Mordecai Richler, from the story by Gerald Gaiser

Fun with Dick and Jane ★★ 12

Crime comedy 2005 · US · Colour · 86min

In this loose remake of the 1977 comedy, jobless Jim Carrey and Téa Leoni suffer the indignity of having even their lawn repossessed. The impoverished pair turn Bonnie and Clyde, only to wind up victims of director Dean Parisot's badly aimed gags as the film lurches wildly from satire to slapstick. There are a few chuckles early on, but once Carrey and Leoni resort to pulling heists, it's clear the script has hit a wall. SP Swearing. DVD

Jim Carrey Dick Harper • Téa Leoni Jane Harper • Alec Baldwin Jack McCallister • Richard Jenkins Frank Bascombe • Gloria Garayua Blanca • Carlos Jacott Oz Peterson • Angie Harmon Veronica Cleeman ■ Dir Dean Parisot • Scr Judd Apatow, Nicholas Stoller, from the 1977 film

The Fundamentals of Caring ★★★

Road movie comedy 2015 · US · Colour · 93min

Road-movie conventions are given a pleasing twist in this breezy comedy, which deals with the subject of disability without being either patronising or politically correct. Paul Rudd stars as a writer trying to deal with tragedy in his own life by starting over as a care-giver. His inexperience shows when he's given the run-around by an 18-year-old with muscular dystrophy (Submarine's Craig Roberts). Director Rob Burnett largely keeps platitudes and sermonising in check, delivering a fist-pumping pay-off that's so unexpected, it's sure to raise a smile. JH

Paul Rudd Ben Benjamin • Craig Roberts Trevor • Selena Gomez Dot • Jennifer Ehle Elsa • Megan Ferguson Peaches ■ Dir Rob Burnett • Scr Rob Burnett, from the novel The Revised Fundamentals of Caregiving by Jonathan Evison

The Funeral ★★★ 18

Crime drama 1996 · US · Colour · 95min

Probably the most conventional, formal film in Abel Ferrara's 1990s canon, this crime drama, scripted by his longtime collaborator Nicholas St John, nevertheless touches upon familiar themes of guilt and redemption. Christopher Walken, for once relatively low-key, is the head of a gangster family trying to come to grips with the death of younger brother Vincent Gallo. Walken's subtle turn is matched by fine performances from Chris Penn, Isabella Rossellini and Annabella Sciorra. A little talky at times, this remains a thoughtful slow-burner. JF Swearing, sex scenes, violence. DVD

Christopher Walken Ray Tempio • Chris Penn Chez Tempio • Vincent Gallo Johnny • Benicio Del Toro Gaspare • Annabella Sciorra Jeanette • Isabella Rossellini Clara • Gretchen Mol Helen • John Ventimiglia Sali ■ Dir Abel Ferrara • Scr Nicholas St John

Funeral in Berlin ★★★ PG

Spy thriller 1966 · UK · Colour · 97min

Following the success of The Ipcress File, Michael Caine returned as Harry Palmer in this dense thriller that is so full of ingenious plotlines that you need to have your wits about you. Caine travels behind the Iron Curtain to persuade Communist spy boss Oscar Homolka to defect, only to run into Israeli agent Eva Renzi who is tracking down Nazi war criminals. The film blends action with sardonic humour, and it's all held together by Guy Hamilton's skilful, albeit rather dour, direction. Caine returned as Palmer in the less successful Billion Dollar Brain in 1967. DP DVD

Michael Caine Harry Palmer • Eva Renzi Samantha Steel • Paul Hubschmid Johnny Vulkan • Oscar Homolka Colonel Stok • Guy Doleman Ross • Rachel Gurney Mrs Ross ■ Dir Guy Hamilton • Scr Evan Jones, from the novel by Len Deighton

The Funhouse ★★★ 15

Horror 1981 · US · Colour · 91min

Director Tobe Hooper has lots of fun pulling the rug out from under the viewer's feet in this underrated "frightmare." Four bored teenagers are challenged to spend the night in a spooky ghost train at the local carnival. Trouble is, a mutant albino wearing a Frankenstein mask knows they saw him kill a gypsy fortune teller and wants to eradicate all witnesses to his crime. It's full of clever twists, and Hooper elicits great tension from the simple cat-and-mouse concept. AJ DVD

Elizabeth Berridge Amy Harper • Cooper Huckabee Buzz • Miles Chapin Richie • Largo Woodruff Liz • Shawn Carson Joey Harper ■ Dir Tobe Hooper • Scr Larry Block

Funny about Love ★★ 15

Comedy drama 1990 · US · Colour · 97min

Despite the title, there is very little that is amusing in this lukewarm comedy about a neurotic cartoonist (Gene Wilder) and a caring caterer (Christine Lahti), who get married and want to have a baby. This project was based on a magazine article – not a good omen for director Leonard Nimoy or his stars. JB Swearing. DVD

Gene Wilder Duffy Bergman • Christine Lahti Meg Lloyd • Mary Stuart Masterson Daphne Delillo • Robert Prosky Emil T Bergman • Stephen Tobolowsky Dr Hugo Blatt ■ Dir Leonard Nimoy • Scr Norman Steinberg, David Frankel, from the article Convention of the Love Goddesses by Bob Greene

Funny Bones ★★★★ 15

Comedy drama 1994 · US/UK · Colour · 127min

This wry and caustic examination of the nature of comedy gave British stand-up comedian Lee Evans the chance to shine in his movie debut, alongside American character actor Oliver Platt. Platt plays the son of a legendary comedian (played by legendary comedian Jerry Lewis), who arrives in Blackpool to buy comedy material that he intends to pass off as his own back home in America. He discovers he has a long-lost brother in Evans, who has "funny bones" – he's effortlessly funny – whereas Platt isn't. How everything is resolved makes for eccentric viewing, with amusing highlights and quirky set pieces. AJ Swearing. DVD

Oliver Platt Tommy Fawkes • Jerry Lewis George Fawkes • Lee Evans Jack Parker • Leslie Caron Katie Parker • Richard Griffiths Jim Minty • Oliver Reed Dolly Hopkins • George Carl Thomas Parker • Freddie Davies Bruno Parker ■ Dir Peter Chelsom • Scr Peter Chelsom, Peter Flannery

Funny Dirty Little War ★★★★ 15

War black comedy 1983 · Arg · Colour · 79min

This mordantly comic film was Hector Olivera's international breakthrough, thanks to prizes at the Berlin film festival and critical acclaim. Such praise was deserved, since the Argentinian director combines robust humour with a fast-paced portrait of an imaginary war following Peron's return to power in 1974. A small town, Colonia

Vela, near the capital is occupied by a group opposed to the army and fighting breaks out, with trapped civilians suffering torture and murder. A passionate view of turbulent South American politics. BB

Federico Luppi Ignacio Fuentes • Hector Bidonde Suprino • Victor Laplace Reinaldo • Rodolfo Ranni Llanos • Miguel Angel Sola Juan • Julio DeGrazia Corporal Garcia ■ Dir Hector Olivera • Scr Roberto Cossa, from a novel by Osvaldo Soriano

Funny Face ★★★★ U

Musical comedy 1957 · US · Colour · 103min

With glowing Technicolor (photography by Ray June) and great Gershwin tunes, director Stanley Donen has created a film that looks as elegant today as it did when it first appeared. A satire on fashion magazines, the fabulous Fred Astaire stars as photographer Dick Avery (Richard Avedon was the film's consultant), who finds the face of his dreams (Audrey Hepburn) in a Greenwich Village bookstore, while Kay Thompson stands out as an imperious magazine editor. Scintillating, magical and above all romantic. TS DVD

Audrey Hepburn Jo Stockton • Fred Astaire Dick Avery • Kay Thompson Maggie Prescott • Michel Auclair Prof Emile Flostre • Robert Flemyng Paul Duval • Dovima Marion ■ Dir Stanley Donen • Scr Leonard Gershe, from his musical libretto Wedding Day

Funny Farm ★★ PG

Comedy 1988 · US · Colour · 97min

Chevy Chase plays a sports hack who finds himself wrestling with life in the country. Quite why esteemed director George Roy Hill would want to build a film around the cheesy charm of Chase is beyond understanding. However, his smart mouth, wrap-around smirk and Tinseltown teeth do join forces to provide a degree of enjoyment, even when the gags stop being funny. JM Swearing.

Chevy Chase Andy Farmer • Madolyn Smith Elizabeth Farmer • Joseph Maher Michael Sinclair • Jack Gilpin Bud Culbertson • Brad Sullivan Brock • MacIntyre Dixon Mayor Barclay ■ Dir George Roy Hill • Scr Jeffrey Boam, from the book by Jay Cronley

Funny Games ★★★ 18

Psychological horror thriller
1997 · Austria · Colour · 104min

Austrian director Michael Haneke's controversial cautionary tale is lauded in some circles for being an uncompromising study of on-screen violence and, in others, as the worst type of exploitation that panders to the same base instincts it purports to lay bare. Two young men inveigle their way into the holiday home of a middle-class family and subject them to degrading torture and sickening humiliation in a deconstruction of terror that's radical and thought-provoking, but also too clever by half. This powerful "shockumentary" is deliberately hard to watch. AJ German +subtitles. Violence, swearing. DVD

Susanne Lothar Anna • Ulrich Mühe Georg • Frank Giering Peter • Arno Frisch Paul • Stefan Clapczynski "Schorschi" • Doris Kunstmann Gerda • Christoph Bantzer Fred • Wolfgang Glück Robert ■ Dir/Scr Michael Haneke

Funny Games US ★★★ 18

Psychological horror thriller
2008 · UK/US/Fr/Austria/Ger/It · Colour · 106min

With American audiences often resistant to watching subtitled movies, Austrian director Michael Haneke (Hidden) chose to remake his controversial 1997 thriller Funny Games – in English. Michael Pitt and Brady Corbet play a pair of young men who arrive uninvited at the holiday home of an affluent American family. What follows is a line-for-line, almost shot-for-shot repeat of the original movie, as Naomi Watts, Tim Roth and their son endure a night-long ordeal of apparently motiveless torture and sadism. Haneke's stated theme – the complicity of audiences with screen violence – is challenging, if questionable. More successful is the film's darkly mischievous toying with audience expectations in what remains a shocking tale. AS Violence. **DVD** 🔵

Naomi Watts *Ann* • Tim Roth *George* • Michael Pitt *Paul* • Brady Corbet *Peter* • Siobhan Fallon Hogan [Siobhan Fallon] *Betsy* • Boyd Gaines *Fred* ■ *Dir/Scr* Michael Haneke

Funny Girl ★★★★U
Biographical musical
1968 · US · Colour · 148min

This was a spectacular switch from stage to screen for Barbra Streisand, replicating her Broadway triumph as legendary entertainer Fanny Brice. Streisand's bravura performance earned her a joint Oscar for best actress (she shared the honour with Katharine Hepburn) and the film was nominated for a further seven, including best score and best song. It traces Brice's rise from vaudeville to the Ziegfeld Follies by way of a troubled marriage to gambler Nick Arnstein, and Streisand is given fine support by the ultra-smooth Omar Sharif. The success of this marvellous film led to a sequel, *Funny Lady*, seven years later. AT **DVD**

Barbra Streisand *Fanny Brice* • Omar Sharif *Nick Arnstein* • Kay Medford *Rose Brice* • Anne Francis *Georgia James* • Walter Pidgeon *Florenz Ziegfeld* • Lee Allen *Eddie Ryan* • Mae Questel *Mrs Strakosh* ■ *Dir* William Wyler • *Scr* Isobel Lennart, from the musical by Jule Styne, Bob Merrill, Isobel Lennart

Funny Ha Ha ★★★15
Comedy drama 2002 · US · Colour · 90min

Andrew Bujalski wrote, directed, edited and stars in this low-budget comedy about Boston 20-somethings. It's held together by a quirky performance from Kate Dollenmayer as a postgraduate student attempting to engage with a world that proves consistently disappointing. The visuals are unprepossessing and the dialogue veers between quick wit and ponderous inarticulacy, making this something of an acquired taste. But the laconic humour, downbeat authenticity and improvised feel that recalls the early work of John Cassavetes, mean it's one worth acquiring. DP Swearing.

Kate Dollenmayer *Marnie* • Christian Rudder *Alex* • Andrew Bujalski *Mitchell* • Myles Paige *Dave* • Jennifer L Schaper *Rachel* • Lissa Patton Rudder *Susan* ■ *Dir/Scr* Andrew Bujalski • *Editor* Andrew Bujalski

A Funny Kind of Love ★★★18
Comedy 2014 · Aus · Colour · 96min

Other people's sexual proclivities are the subject of this multi-strand Australian first feature, which milks laughter and pathos from the complications of some unusual turn-ons. Writer/director Josh Lawson sets his stories in one ordinary patch of suburbia, and also plays the husband battling manfully to satisfy his wife's rape fantasy – a subject played for edgy comedy and just about getting away with it. The film struggles to tie all its threads together, but in essence this is a brightly performed, amusing and provocative entertainment TJ **DVD**

Josh Lawson *Paul* • Bojana Novakovic *Maeve* • Alan Dukes *Phil* • Lisa McCune *Maureen* • Kate Mulvany *Evie* ■ *Dir/Scr* Josh Lawson

Funny Lady ★★★PG
Biographical musical 1975 · US · Colour · 132min

Barbra Streisand returns to the role of Ziegfeld Follies star Fanny Brice for producer Ray Stark (the man behind *Funny Girl*). This sequel suffers a little in the hands of choreographer-turned-director Herbert Ross, who can't quite control the clichés of the plot or the rowdy performance of James Caan. Still, the musical numbers are fine, and there's some fancy footwork from Ben Vereen, plus a welcome guest appearance from *Funny Girl* co-star Omar Sharif. TS **DVD**

Barbra Streisand *Fanny Brice* • James Caan *Billy Rose* • Omar Sharif *Nick Arnstein* • Roddy McDowall *Bobby* • Ben Vereen *Bert Robbins* •

Carole Wells *Norma Butler* ■ *Dir* Herbert Ross • *Scr* Arnold Schulman, Jay Presson Allen, from a story by Arnold Schulman

The Funny Man ★★18
Horror comedy 1994 · UK · Colour · 88min

Benny Young wins a haunted house in a poker game with Christopher Lee, and then falls prey to its fourth dimensional evil spirit incarnated as a demented jester. The harlequin from hell (Tim James) then indulges in wickedly droll murders as Young's friends are systematically disembowelled and dismembered. Debut director Simon Sprackling's slapdash comic strip shows some brutal invention, but for the most part it's a childish, witless endeavour. AJ Swearing, violence. **DVD**

Tim James *The Funny Man* • Christopher Lee *Callum Chance* • Ingrid Lacey *Tina Taylor* • Matthew Devitt *Johnny Taylor* • Chris Walker *Morgan "Hard Man"* • George Morton *Alan "Crap Puppeteer"* • Rhona Cameron *Thelma Fudd* ■ *Dir/Scr* Simon Sprackling

Funny People ★★★15
Comedy drama 2009 · US · Colour · 139min

Adam Sandler built his career on dumb comedies but his best work comes when he lets the goofy mask slip to reveal a more human face. Writer/director Judd Apatow (the man behind *Knocked Up* and Sandler's real-life ex-roommate) gives him the ideal platform in this comedy drama about an A-list Hollywood funnyman confronting mortal illness. It may sound morbid, but the film is actually more funny than sad. By putting the spotlight on comedians offstage (including Seth Rogen's struggling comic), Apatow milks their social ineptitude for humour while also inspiring sympathy for Sandler's childish star. A romantic subplot tips the film way off balance late in the day, but otherwise this is a real pleasure. SP Swearing, sex scenes. **DVD** 🔵

Adam Sandler *George Simmons* • Seth Rogen *Ira Wright* • Leslie Mann *Laura* • Eric Bana *Clarke* • Jonah Hill *Leo Koenig* • Jason Schwartzman *Mark Taylor Jackson* ■ *Dir/Scr* Judd Apatow

A Funny Thing Happened on the Way to the Forum ★★★PG
Musical comedy 1966 · US/UK · Colour · 93min

This toga-clad musical farce about ancient Roman scandals was the inspiration for Frankie Howerd's popular TV series, *Up Pompeii*. Richard Lester's undisciplined direction takes its cue from the great comic line-up: Zero Mostel as the slave seeking freedom; Phil Silvers as a Bilko-like brothel keeper; Jack Gilford as Hysterium; and the great Buster Keaton, in one of his last feature films, as a man who's lost his children. Ramshackle it may be but it retains the verve and humour of its Broadway origins. TH **DVD** 🔵

Zero Mostel *Pseudolus* • Phil Silvers *Lycus* • Jack Gilford *Hysterium* • Buster Keaton *Erronius* • Michael Crawford *Hero* • Annette Andre *Philia* • Patricia Jessel *Domina* • Michael Hordern *Senex* ■ *Dir* Richard Lester • *Scr* Melvin Frank, Michael Pertwee, from the musical by Burt Shevelove, Larry Gelbart • *Cinematographer* Nicolas Roeg • *Music/lyrics* Stephen Sondheim

Fur: an Imaginary Portrait of Diane Arbus ★★★15
Fantasy biographical drama
2006 · US · Colour · 117min

With the likes of *Birth* and *Eyes Wide Shut* on her CV, it's fair to say that Nicole Kidman has been fearless in her choice of projects. It's also fair to say that this phantasmagoric biopic of US photographer Diane Arbus is definitely one of her stranger roles. Arbus, who died in 1971, was inspired by Tod Browning's cult 1932 movie *Freaks* and is best known for her photographs of people on the fringes of society. This highly fictionalised snapshot follows Arbus as she embarks on a sexually charged affair with her neighbour (Robert Downey Jr), a man with a werewolf-like abundance of hair. Kidman and Downey Jr excel as the improbable lovers, and the unusual premise

just about survives Steven Shainberg's mannered direction. JR **DVD**

Nicole Kidman *Diane Arbus* • Robert Downey Jr *Lionel Sweeney* • Ty Burrell *Allan Arbus* • Harris Yulin *David Nemerov* • Jane Alexander *Gertrude Nemerov* • Emmy Clarke *Grace Arbus* • Genevieve McCarthy *Sophie Arbus* ■ *Dir* Steven Shainberg • *Scr* Erin Cressida Wilson, inspired by the book *Diane Arbus: a Biography* by Patricia Bosworth

The Furies ★★★★
Western 1950 · US · BW · 108min

This intense, highly-charged account of power, passion, rivalry and revenge has much in common with Greek tragedy and is full of far-from-subtle Freudian elements. (Watch how Walter Huston and Barbara Stanwyck, as a father and daughter perpetually at odds, ease their faces closer until it seems they are about to kiss.) Expertly written by Charles Schnee and brilliantly directed by Anthony Mann, the film is powerfully performed. Franz Waxman's rousing score and Victor Milner's Oscar-nominated photography add to the pleasures of an overwrought but compelling piece. TV

Barbara Stanwyck *Vance Jeffords* • Walter Huston *TC Jeffords* • Wendell Corey *Rip Darrow* • Judith Anderson *Florence Burnett* • Gilbert Roland *Juan Herrera* • Thomas Gomez *El Tigre* • Beulah Bondi *Mrs Annaheim* ■ *Dir* Anthony Mann • *Scr* Charles Schnee, from the novel by Niven Busch

Furry Vengeance ★★PG
Comedy 2010 · US/UAE · Colour · 87min

The forest strikes back in this unsubtle slapstick comedy, as cold-hearted property developer Brendan Fraser incurs the wrath of woodland critters with his plans to build a plush new housing complex on an unspoiled green-belt area of Oregon. Director Roger Kumble's mix of live action and CGI pays homage to the cartoon shenanigans of Disney's rascally chipmunks Chip 'n' Dale, but the eco-friendly heart of the movie is unfortunately clumsy. Fraser's lantern-jawed mugging becomes irritating all too soon, although younger viewers may get a kick out of the ingenious antics of skunks, raccoons and grizzly bears as they get the better of numbskull humans. TeS **DVD** 🔵

Brendan Fraser *Dan Sanders* • Ken Jeong *Neal Lyman* • Brooke Shields *Tammy Sanders* • Angela Kinsey *Felder* • Skyler Samuels *Amber* • Matt Prokop *Tyler Sanders* ■ *Dir* Roger Kumble • *Scr* Michael Carnes, Josh Gilbert

Further up the Creek ★★U
Comedy 1958 · UK · BW · 86min

Made in something of a hurry by director Val Guest, as he sought to cash in on the success of *Up the Creek*, this sequel suffers from both indifferent plotting and the absence of Peter Sellers from the role of the scheming bosun. Exploiting the sale of his ship to the ruler of Algerocco by flogging tickets for a Mediterranean cruise, Frankie Howerd (not a natural before the movie camera) works every gag, as the floating con trick is called to action stations. DP **DVD**

David Tomlinson *Lt Fairweather* • Frankie Howerd *Bos'n* • Shirley Eaton *Jane* • Thora Hird *Mrs Galloway* • Lionel Jeffries *Steady Barker* ■ *Dir* Val Guest • *Scr* Val Guest, John Warren, Len Heath

Fury ★★★
Silent adventure 1923 · US · BW · 90min

This is an all-stops-out melodrama set aboard a sailing ship and at the docks of London and Glasgow. Richard Barthelmess plays the son of Tyrone Power (senior) whose wife, Dorothy Gish, has run off with another man – which proves to be upsetting for everyone. It was a big hit with 1920s audiences, who loved its heaving emotions and its vividly filmed depiction of life at sea. AT

Richard Barthelmess *Boy Leyton* • Tyrone Power *Captain Leyton* • Pat Hartigan *Morgan* • Barry Macollum *Looney Luke* • Dorothy Gish *Minnie* • Jessie Arnold *Boy's mother* ■ *Dir* Henry King • *Scr* Edmund Goulding

Fury ★★★★
Crime drama 1936 · US · BW · 92min

Austrian-born director Fritz Lang's first American movie is a searing indictment of lynch law based on a true case. The film is given tremendous intensity by the naturalistic performances of leads Spencer Tracy, as the man unjustly accused, and Sylvia Sidney as his fiancée. This is an uncomfortable film to watch, with Joseph Ruttenberg's lighting deliberately expressionistic, but the second half fails to carry the conviction of the opening scenes, and a bizarre manic thrust takes over, perhaps intended to symbolise the unchannelled fury of the mob. TS

Spencer Tracy *Joe Wilson* • Sylvia Sidney *Katherine Grant* • Walter Abel *District Attorney* • Bruce Cabot *Kirby Dawson* • Edward Ellis *Sheriff* • Walter Brennan *"Bugs" Meyers* • George Walcott *Tom* ■ *Dir* Fritz Lang • *Scr* Bartlett Cormack, Fritz Lang, from the story *Mob Rule* by Norman Krasna

The Fury ★★★★18
Psychological horror 1978 · US · Colour · 113min

Brian De Palma found himself in familiar territory with this follow-up to *Carrie* – an adaptation of John Farris's telekinetic conspiracy thriller. Adopting a broader suspense canvas than he'd utilised before (the action and slow motion sequences remain the best he's ever crafted), De Palma's gorgeous horror adventure concerns two teens with psychic powers who become pawns between spy factions. Ingeniously plotted, extravagantly staged and beautifully balanced between apocalyptic goriness and full-blooded pyrotechnic imagery, this nail-biting shocker is De Palma's most underrated movie. AJ **DVD**

Kirk Douglas *Peter Sandza* • John Cassavetes *Childress* • Carrie Snodgress *Hester* • Charles Durning *Dr Jim McKeever* • Amy Irving *Gillian Bellaver* • Fiona Lewis *Dr Susan Charles* • Andrew Stevens *Robin Sandza* • Carol Rossen *Dr Ellen Lindstrom* ■ *Dir* Brian De Palma • *Scr* John Farris, from his novel

Fury ★★18
Crime drama 2012 · Can · Colour · 89min

Nothing to do with Samuel L Jackson's Nick Fury in *Avengers Assemble*, this crime yarn features the star as Foley, a con artist fresh out of prison who's determined to go straight. But he's blackmailed into one last scam when his dead partner's son (Luke Kirby) threatens to reveal a terrible secret to Foley's new girlfriend (Ruth Negga). The performances are all fine (particularly Tom Wilkinson as the crime-boss target of the grifters) and the film is perfectly watchable. But it's just so generic that this hardly distinguishes itself from your average straight-to-DVD offering. DA Violence, sexual references. **DVD** 🔵

Samuel L Jackson *Foley* • Luke Kirby *Ethan* • Ruth Negga *Iris* • Tom Wilkinson *Xavier* • Gil Bellows *Bartender Bill* • Deborah Kara Unger *Helena* ■ *Dir* David Weaver • *Scr* David Weaver, Elan Mastai

Fury ★★★★15
Second World War drama
2014 · US · Colour · 129min

Writer/director David Ayer's heart-pounding drama follows a tank, commanded by Brad Pitt, rolling through Germany in the brutal dying days of the Second World War. Shia LaBeouf, Michael Peña and Jon Bernthal are his crew, but it's through the eyes of *Percy Jackson* star Logan Lerman's replacement driver that the reality of conflict hits home. He is the heart and soul along with Pitt, who is on towering form schooling the kid into attaining the machine-like mindset of a hardened soldier. While there are archetypes and Hollywoodisms, Ayer probes for what makes a man beneath the brutality and the bluster, resulting in a film that burns into the memory. SP Violence, swearing, sexual references. **DVD** 🔵

F

Brad Pitt *Don "Wardaddy" Collier* • Shia LaBeouf *Boyd "Bible" Swan* • Logan Lerman *Norman Ellison* • Michael Peña [Michael Pena] *Trini "Gordo" Garcia* • Jon Bernthal *Grady "Coon Ass" Travis* ■ *Dir/Scr* David Ayer

Fury at Furnace Creek ★★ U

Western   1948 · US · BW · 87min

When General Blackwell (Robert Warwick) is accused of instigating an Indian massacre, his sons Victor Mature and Glenn Langan are determined to clear his name. The solution lies in the boom town of Furnace Creek where the head of a mining syndicate, well played by Albert Dekker, is revealed as the villain. AE

Victor Mature *Cash* • Coleen Gray *Molly Baxter* • Glenn Langan *Rufe* • Reginald Gardiner *Capt Walsh* • Albert Dekker *Leverett* ■ *Dir* H Bruce Humberstone • *Scr* Charles G Booth, Winston Miller, from the novel by David Garth

Fury at Smugglers Bay ★★★ PG

Period adventure   1961 · UK · BW · 82min

Writer/director John Gilling's rumbustious tale of Cornish piracy has squire Peter Cushing and his gung-ho son John Fraser take on Bernard Lee and his band of smuggling cut-throats. This 1790s adventure is tantamount to an English western, with a saloon brawl, sword-wielding showdowns and a last-minute rescue. DP *DVD*

John Fraser *Chris Trevenyan* • Peter Cushing *Squire Trevenyan* • Bernard Lee *Black John* • June Thorburn *Jenny Trevenyan* • Michèle Mercier *Louise Lejeune* • George Coulouris *François Lejeune* • Miles Malleson *Duke of Avon* ■ *Dir/Scr* John Gilling

The Future ★★★ 12

Drama   2011 · US/Ger/Fr · Colour · 90min

Few films have been narrated by an ailing stray cat in an animal hospital. But this quirk is entirely in keeping with the offbeat insights into relationships and responsibility provided by director Miranda July's long-awaited follow-up to her splendid debut, *Me and You and Everyone We Know* (2005). July also stars as a dance teacher who, along with her partner (Hamish Linklater), decides to live life to the max in the month before they adopt the wounded feline that will take their romance to the next level. Those prepared to accept July's askew view will be amused and touched. DP Swearing, a sex scene. *DVD*

Miranda July *Sophie/Paw-Paw the cat* • Hamish Linklater *Jason* • David Warshofsky *Marshall* • Isabella Acres *Gabriella* • Joe Putterlik *Joe/The Moon* • Angela Trimbur *Dance studio receptionist* ■ *Dir/Scr* Miranda July

The Future Is Unwritten ★★★★ 15

Biographical music documentary   2006 · UK/Ire · Colour and BW · 119min

British film-maker Julien Temple made his name documenting The Sex Pistols' rise to infamy in *The Great Rock 'n' Roll Swindle* (1979) and its companion piece *The Filth and the Fury* (2000). He returns to his roots with this intimate and deeply affecting biography of Joe Strummer, frontman of that other great British punk band the Clash, who died in 2002 aged 50. Charting Strummer's turbulent life and career, from his early childhood in Turkey to his self-proclaimed role as "punk rock warlord", the film paints an affectionate, warts-and-all portrait of a musical genius with a passion for politics and a talent for reinvention. JR *DVD*

Joe Strummer • Mick Jones • Topper Headon • Bono • John Cusack • Johnny Depp • Matt Dillon ■ *Dir* Julien Temple

Future My Love ★★★ 12A

Documentary   2012 · UK/Swe · Colour and BW · 96min

Swedish director Maja Borg's intriguing but self-conscious documentary is a personal journey for the film-maker that flits between the breakdown of a romance (with Italian actress Nadya Cazan) and the collapse of the global financial system. Borg pays a visit to the home of nonagenarian social engineer and industrial designer Jacque Fresco, which is also the headquarters of the Venus Project, founded to bring about an alternative society built upon a resource-based economy. The movie is always visually striking, but the parallel themes feel more than a little unconvincing. DP Some swearing, nudity. ■ *Dir/Scr* Maja Borg

Future Shock! The Story of 2000AD ★★★★ 15

Documentary   2015 · UK · Colour and BW · 105min

Calling yourself the galaxy's greatest comic takes some front, but 2000AD has cause to back up that claim more than most, as this documentary convincingly shows. Launched in 1977, the sci-fi-skewed weekly caused an immediate sensation in the UK. Strips such as *Judge Dredd* and *Rogue Trooper* were subversive, ultraviolent and morally ambiguous, providing younger readers with the illicit thrills they craved, while giving older audiences something that was intelligent and politically engaged. Skilfully assembled and comprehensive in its research, this is a must-see for comic fans. JH *DVD*

■ *Dir* Paul Goodwin • *Interviewee* Neil Gaiman, Grant Morrison

Futuresport ★★ 15

Science-fiction action drama   1998 · US · Colour · 86min

This glossily unimaginative TV movie borrows so liberally from the far superior *Rollerball* as to appear totally redundant. Set in the future, a violent game is created in a bid to ease gang tensions, a sort of amalgam of basketball and rugby played on levitating skateboards with an electrified ball. The trio of stars – Dean Cain, Vanessa L Williams and Wesley Snipes – add much needed lustre to Ernest Dickerson's join-the-dots direction. RS Swearing, violence, nudity. *DVD*

Wesley Snipes *Obike Fixx* • Dean Cain *Tremaine "Tre" Ramzey* • Vanessa L Williams *Alex Torres* • Bill Smitrovich *Coach Douglas Freeman* • Adrian Hughes ■ *Dir* Ernest R Dickerson • *Scr* Robert Hewitt Wolfe, from a story by Steve Dejarnatt, Robert Hewitt Wolfe

Futureworld ★★★ 12

Science-fiction thriller   1976 · US · Colour · 103min

This inventive sci-fi thriller – the follow-up to the excellent *Westworld* – gives more than a nod in the direction of Don Siegel's classic *Invasion of the Body Snatchers*, with a story about the replacement of the world's ruling elite by lookalike robots. Less explosive than its predecessor, this is nevertheless an unnerving watch, and makes good use of early 3D computer animation. DP *DVD* Blu-ray

Peter Fonda *Chuck Browning* • Blythe Danner *Tracy Ballard* • Arthur Hill *Duffy* • Yul Brynner *Gunslinger* • John Ryan [John P Ryan] *Dr Schneider* • Stuart Margolin *Harry* • Jim Antonio *Ron* • Allen Ludden *Game show host* ■ *Dir* Richard T Heffron • *Scr* Mayo Simon, George Schenck

Fuzz ★★ 18

Detective comedy   1972 · US · Colour · 89min

Evan Hunter adapted this cynical cop comedy from one of the *87th Precinct* stories he wrote under his pseudonym Ed McBain. A series of vignettes involving a quartet of Boston cops is linked by ingenious bombings carried out by Yul Brynner. The stand-out scenes involve Burt Reynolds and Jack Weston posing as nuns, and Tom Skerritt and Raquel Welch trying to concentrate on a stakeout while sharing a sleeping bag. The characterisation is rounded and the station-house atmosphere well established, but the Keystone-style mayhem is slightly ham-fisted. DP

Burt Reynolds *Detective Carella* • Jack Weston *Detective Meyer* • Tom Skerritt *Detective Kling* • Yul Brynner *The Deaf Man* • Raquel Welch *Detective McHenry* • James McEachin *Detective Brown* ■ *Dir* Richard A Colla • *Scr* Evan Hunter, from the novel by Ed McBain [Evan Hunter]

The Fuzzy Pink Nightgown ★★ U

Romantic comedy   1957 · US · BW · 87min

Inspired by a true-life incident when actress Marie McDonald was purportedly kidnapped, then discovered wandering in the desert, this mild comedy tells a similar tale of a movie star (Jane Russell) kidnapped just before the release of her new film, *The Kidnapped Heiress*. Predictably, no one will believe the incident is not a publicity stunt and, just as predictably, Russell falls for handsome kidnapper Ralph Meeker. Russell took the blame for the film's commercial failure, stating that she insisted on black and white rather than colour and told director Norman Taurog to play up the romance at the expense of comedy. TV

Jane Russell *Laurel Stevens* • Ralph Meeker *Mike Valla* • Keenan Wynn *Dandy* • Adolphe Menjou *Arthur Martin* ■ *Dir* Norman Taurog • *Scr* Richard Alan Simmons, from the novel by Sylvia Tate

GBF ★★★ 15

Comedy   2013 · US · Colour · 92min

Nearly 15 years after *Jawbreaker*, director Darren Stein returns to features with another high-school comedy. It's a breezy, if hardly original, coming-out saga where clique queen bees Andrea Bowen, Xosha Roquemore and Sasha Pieterse compete to have recently outed classmate Michael J Willett accompany them to the upcoming prom. On the surface it resembles a gay reworking of a John Hughes teen flick, except the slang often rings hollow and the script too often falls back on cliché. Nevertheless, this has its moments and is perkily played by a talented ensemble. DP Sexual references.

Michael J Willett *Tanner Daniels* • Paul Iacono *Brent Van Camp* • Sasha Pieterse *Fawcett Brooks* • Andrea Bowen *'Shley Osgoode* • Xosha Roquemore *Caprice Winters* ■ *Dir* Darren Stein • *Scr* George Northy

G-Force ★★★ PG

Part-animated action adventure   2009 · US · Colour · 84min

Disney cuteness meets Jerry Bruckheimer action in this part-CGI animated tale of a guinea pig task force that's threatened with closure unless they can prove they're a worthy investment. Cue a spectacularly executed plan to breach the security of domestic appliance mogul Bill Nighy, whom they suspect of hiding an arms operation. There are lively turns from the voice cast, especially Sam Rockwell as team leader Darwin and Penélope Cruz as martial arts expert Juarez, although some of the jokes are rather adult and the action is at times almost too tense for young children. But the CGI effects are breathtaking – the problem here is getting the quality of the live action to match the animation; the solution: give Bill Nighy more to do next time. SuR *DVD* Blu-ray

Sam Rockwell *Darwin* • Penélope Cruz *Juarez* • Tracy Morgan *Blaster* • Nicolas Cage *Speckles* • Jon Favreau *Hurley* • Zach Galifianakis *Ben* • Bill Nighy *Leonard Saber* • Steve Buscemi *Bucky* ■ *Dir* Hoyt H Yeatman Jr • *Scr* The Wibberleys [Marianne & Cormac Wibberley], Ted Elliott, Terry Rossio, Tim Firth, from a story by Hoyt Yeatman, David PI James

GI Blues ★★★ U

Musical   1960 · US · Colour · 99min

Elvis Presley had been away for two years, heroically doing his military service, including a spell in Germany, and this comeback film was intended to capitalise on that. This movie substantially shifted Elvis's image – from the teenage rebel of *King Creole* to the all-American soldier boy. Sultry Juliet Prowse is the dancer he loses his heart to after he woos her for a $300 bet, and the songs are classy - a hint of Presley's best. TS *DVD*

Elvis Presley *Tulsa McCauley* • James Douglas *Rick* • Robert Ivers *Cookey* • Juliet Prowse *Lili* • Leticia Roman *Tina* • Sigrid Maier *Marla* • Arch Johnson *Sergeant McGraw* • The Jordanaires ■ *Dir* Norman Taurog • *Scr* Edmund Beloin, Henry Garson

GI Jane ★★ 15

Action drama   1997 · US/UK · Colour · 119min

Demi Moore built up her body but forgot to spend equal time on her acting skills for this high-on-testosterone, low-on-brains action film from Ridley Scott. Moore stars as the first woman to train with the macho Navy SEALs as part of a government experiment. Expect lots of lingering shots of a very buff

Demi flexing muscles, shaving her head and kicking male butt, but don't expect much in the way of great moments in acting. **JB** Swearing, violence, brief nudity. **DVD**

Demi Moore *Lt Jordan O'Neil* • Viggo Mortensen *Master Chief John Urgayle* • Anne Bancroft *Lillian DeHaven* • Jason Beghe *Royce* • Scott Wilson *CO Salem* • Lucinda Jenney *Blondell* • Morris Chestnut *McCool* • Jim Caviezel *Slovnik* • Daniel Von Bargen *Theodore Hayes* ■ *Dir* Ridley Scott • *Scr* David N Twohy [David Twohy], Danielle Alexandra, from a story by Danielle Alexandra

GI Joe: the Rise of Cobra ★★★★ 12
Action adventure 2009 · US · Colour · 113min

Action-packed to the max, and mounted on a massive scale, the big-screen transfer of Hasbro's other popular toy line (after *Transformers*) is a nonstop thrill-ride. Director Stephen Sommers delivers a terrific blend of comic-book adventure and James Bond-style spectacle, as the special-ops team of super-elite soldiers (known collectively as "GI Joe") battle the mysterious Cobra organisation. The dialogue is hilariously self-aware, the bold multi-story narrative – with smart flashbacks to the origins of key characters – doesn't flag, while the marvellous gadgetry is every action man's fantasy and is matched by the high-quality visuals. **AJ**
DVD **BL**

Channing Tatum *Duke* • Sienna Miller *The Baroness/Ana* • Dennis Quaid *General Hawk* • Joseph Gordon-Levitt *The Doctor/Rex* • Rachel Nichols *Scarlett* • Ray Park *Snake Eyes* • Christopher Eccleston *McCullen/Destro* • Marlon Wayans *Ripcord* • Jonathan Pryce *The President* • Brendan Fraser *Sergeant Stone* ■ *Dir* Stephen Sommers • *Scr* Stuart Beattie, David Elliott, Paul Lovett, from a story by Michael B Gordon, Beattie, Sommers

GI Joe: Retaliation ★★ 12
Action adventure 2013 · US · Colour · 110min

This all-action, no-plot adventure sequel sees evil organisation Cobra frame the GI Joes for crimes they didn't commit. With Dwayne Johnson leading the surviving soldiers, aided by the original GI Joe (played by Bruce Willis on sleep-walking leave from *The Expendables*), they seek to clear their names. An indigestible stew of cheesy one-liners, perfunctory military battles and bland martial arts, this lumbering movie starts off on a dud note and simply goes downhill. The best sequence is an aerial assault on a Himalayan retreat by swooping ninja assassins; otherwise, this dumb ramble isn't a patch on the original. **AJ** Some violence, swearing. **DVD** **BL**

Dwayne Johnson *Roadblock* • Bruce Willis *General Joe Colton* • Channing Tatum *Captain Duke Hauser* • Adrianne Palicki *Lady Jaye* • DJ Cotrona *Flint* • Ray Stevenson *Firefly* ■ *Dir* Jon M Chu • *Scr* Rhett Reese, Paul Wernick

GMT Greenwich Mean Time ★ 18
Drama 1998 · UK · Colour · 117min

This is unconvincing, painfully clichéd garbage about a bunch of London-based friends who are torn apart by everything from jealousy to paralysis. For two unbearable hours, the film leaps clumsily between half a dozen plot strands, as poorly defined characters spew out corny dialogue and experience a couple of traumas each. The decent drum 'n' bass soundtrack helps a little, but this is still nothing short of an ordeal. **JC**

Alec Newman *Charlie* • Melanie Gutteridge *Lucy* • Georgia MacKenzie *Rachel* • Chiwetel Ejiofor *Rix* • Steve John Shepherd *Sam* • Alicya Eyo *Bobby* • Benjamin Waters *Bean* • Anjela Lauren Smith *Sherry* ■ *Dir* John Strickland • *Scr* Simon Mirren

"G" Men ★★★
Crime drama 1935 · US · BW · 84min

This is a typically gritty Warner Bros gangster melodrama from the studio's greatest period, with James Cagney on the side of justice for once. Director William Keighley keeps the action cracking along, and there's terrific support from all those regular Warners character players, plus Ann

Dvorak as Cagney's former girlfriend. But no one else really gets a look in, as this is Cagney's movie, a vehicle to show off the abilities of one of cinema's most talented stars in one of his best roles, fast-talking, tough and terrific. **TS**

James Cagney *James "Brick" Davis* • Ann Dvorak *Jean Morgan* • Margaret Lindsay *Kay McCord* • Robert Armstrong *Jeff McCord* • Barton MacLane *Brad Collins* • Lloyd Nolan *Hugh Farrell* • William Harrigan *McKay* • Edward Pawley *Danny Leggett* ■ *Dir* William Keighley • *Scr* Seton I Miller, from the novel *Public Enemy No 1* by Gregory Rogers

G-Men from Hell ★★ 12
Action comedy fantasy 2000 · US · Colour · 94min

Inspired by Michael Allred's comic book *Grafik Muzik*, this is a brilliant premise that loses its way as Christopher Coppola strives to reproduce the twisting complexities of hard-boiled pulp. Escaping from Hell after a lifetime's iniquity, cops Tate Donovan and William Forsythe vow to go straight to avoid a reunion with the satanic Robert Goulet. However, decency becomes increasingly difficult as they investigate the murder of millionaire Barry Newman, who had hired them to keep tabs on his scheming wife, Vanessa Angel. **DP**

William Forsythe *Dean Crept* • Tate Donovan *Mike Mattress* • Bob Goldthwait [Bobcat Goldthwait] *Buster* • Barry Newman *Greydon Lake* • Vanessa Angel *Gloria Lake* • David Huddleston *Dr Boifford* • Kari Wuhrer *Marete* • Charles Fleischer *Martin/Pete* • Gregory Sporleder *Cheetah man* • Gary Busey *Lt Langdon* • Robert Goulet *Lucifer* ■ *Dir* Christopher Coppola • *Scr* Robert Cooper, Richard L Albert, Nicholas Johnson, from the comic book *Grafik Muzik* by Michael Allred

Gabbeh ★★★★ U
Fantasy documentary drama 1995 · Iran/Fr · Colour · 69min

Woven by the nomadic Ghashgai tribe of south-eastern Iran, gabbehs are intricately designed carpets, laden with symbolic figures, like the one that comes to life in Mohsen Makhmalbaf's beautifully modulated, dazzlingly composed folk tale. Relating the story of Shaghayegh Djodat's love for an unnamed horseman and the conditions set on her by her father, it shows how Djodat wins the heart of the old man washing the carpet. As past and present intermingle, their shared emotions and experiences are reflected in the brightly coloured strands. Originally intended as a documentary about the weavers, this sublime cinematic poem fulfils its director's claim to be a "song of life". **DP** Farsi +subtitles.

Shaghayegh Djodat *Gabbeh* • Abbas Sayahi *Poet/teacher* • Hossein Moharami *Old man* • Roghieh Moharami *Old woman* ■ *Dir/Scr* Mohsen Makhmalbaf

Gable and Lombard ★
Biographical romance 1976 · US · Colour · 131min

A tragic romance is presented more like a screwball comedy in this disastrous biopic that shamefully insults its subjects. James Brolin is rigidly unconvincing as Clark Gable, while Jill Clayburgh brims over with anachronistic energy as Carole Lombard, the sparky actress who stole the King of Hollywood's heart and then broke it when she was killed in a plane crash on a wartime bond rally. Director Sidney J Furie fails to capture either the atmosphere of the period or the uniqueness of the relationship. **DP**

James Brolin *Clark Gable* • Jill Clayburgh *Carole Lombard* • Allen Goorwitz [Allen Garfield] *Louis B Mayer* • Red Buttons *Ivan Cooper* • Joanne Linville *Ria Gable* • Melanie Mayron *Dixie* • Carol McGinnis *Noreen* • Noah Keen *A Broderick* ■ *Dir* Sidney J Furie • *Scr* Barry Sandler

Gabriel & Me ★★ 15
Drama 2001 · UK · Colour · 83min

Young Jimmy Spud (Sean Landless) wants to become a guardian angel and so he asks the archangel Gabriel (Billy Connolly) for some tips. But will he be able to help when his father (Iain Glen in a stand-out

performance) is diagnosed with terminal lung cancer? Lee Hall's adaptation is too faithful to his original BBC radio play and the result is a depressing kitchen sink saga. **AJ** Swearing. **DVD**

Iain Glen *Dad* • David Bradley (2) *Grandad* • Sean Landless *Jimmy Spud* • Rosie Rowell *Mam* • Billy Connolly *Gabriel* ■ *Dir* Udayan Prasad • *Scr* Lee Hall, from his radio play *I Luv You Jimmy Spud*

Gabriel over the White House ★★★
Political fantasy 1933 · US · BW · 94min

Walter Huston plays a rather corrupt US president in this witty and distinctive political satire. He survives an accident, is visited by the Archangel Gabriel and goes on to save America from the Depression and gangsters. The picture's simple-minded patriotism has to be seen to be believed, though the film went through some political cartwheels of its own during production in order to assuage MGM boss Louis B Mayer's political sympathies. **AT**

Walter Huston *Judson Hammond* • Arthur Byron *Jasper Brooks* • Karen Morley *Pendota Molloy* • Franchot Tone *Hartley Beekman* • Dickie Moore *Jimmy Vetter* • C Henry Gordon *Nick Diamond* • David Landau *John Bronson* • Samuel Hinds [Samuel S Hinds] *Dr Eastman* • William Pawley *Borell* • Jean Parker *Alice Bronson* • Claire DuBrey *Nurse* ■ *Dir* Gregory La Cava • *Scr* Carey Wilson, Bertram Bloch, from the novel *Rinehard* by TF Tweed

Gabriela ★★ 18
Romantic drama 1983 · Bra · Colour · 99min

Already the inspiration for a steamy TV soap, Jorge Amado's novel was adapted for the big screen by Bruno Barreto. Set in the 1920s, the action takes place in the scrubland village of Parati, where, despite a drought, bartender Marcello Mastroianni struggles to make a living – until he hires the shamelessly sensual Sonja Braga (reprising her role from the TV series) as his cook. Such is Barreto's fixation with Braga's body that the tone is risibly soft-core. **DP** Portuguese +subtitles.

Sonia Braga *Gabriela* • Marcello Mastroianni *Nacib* • Antonio Cantafora *Tonico Bastos* • Paulo Goulart *Colonel Joao Fulgencio* ■ *Dir* Bruno Barreto • *Scr* Bruno Barreto, Leopoldo Serran, from the novel *Gabriela, Clove and Cinnamon* by Jorge Amado

Gabrielle ★★★ 15
Period romantic drama 2005 · Fr/Ger/It · Colour · 86min

Patrice Chéreau and Anne-Louise Trividic "re-imagine" a Joseph Conrad novella for this intense Parisian domestic drama set just before the First World War. The poised and witty Isabelle Huppert's emotions and motives for betraying her manipulative husband are never quite convincing, because the co-scenarists allow Pascale Greggory's arrogant intellectual to narrate proceedings. Moreover, the dialogue is occasionally florid and the direction self-consciously theatrical. Yet the performances are always as polished as Eric Gautier's sublime period imagery. **DP** French +subtitles. **DVD**

Isabelle Huppert *Gabrielle Hervey* • Pascal Greggory *Jean Hervey* • Claudia Coli *Yvonne* • Thierry Hancisse *Editor-in-chief* • Chantal Neuwirth *Madeleine* ■ *Dir* Patrice Chéreau • *Scr* Patrice Chéreau, Anne-Louise Trividic, from the novella *The Return* by Joseph Conrad

Gaby ★★
Wartime romantic drama 1956 · US · Colour · 97min

The third screen version of the play *Waterloo Bridge*, though still hidebound by censorship, was updated to the Second World War. It stars a beguiling Leslie Caron as the ballerina forced to become a prostitute through circumstance. John Kerr is gauche as her beau, but then who could ever erase memories of Robert Taylor and Vivien Leigh in the classic 1940 version? The film does have a quaint 1950s sheen, but director Curtis Bernhardt's pacing is slow, and the overall effect is dull. **TS**

Leslie Caron *Gaby* • John Kerr *Gregory Y Wendell* • Cedric Hardwicke *Mr Carrington* • Taina Elg *Elsa* • Margalo Gillmore *Mrs Carrington* • Scott Marlowe *Jan* • Ian Wolfe *Registrar* • Joe Di Reda *Allen* • Ruta Lee *Denise* ■ *Dir* Curtis Bernhardt • *Scr* Albert Hackett, Frances Goodrich, Charles Lederer, from the play *Waterloo Bridge* by SN Behrman, Paul H Rameau, George Froeschel, from the play by Robert E Sherwood

Gaby: a True Story ★★★ 15
Biographical drama 1987 · US · Colour · 109min

Rachel Levin plays Gabriela Brimmer, the Mexico-born daughter of emigrant Austrian Jews, who used her left leg to communicate with a world that had condemned her to vegetative isolation. Argentinian actress Norma Aleandro was nominated for her supporting turn as the nanny who recognises the repressed intelligence of her charge and persuades despairing parents Liv Ullmann and Robert Loggia to further her education. Luis Mandoki melodramatises Levin's romance with fellow cerebral palsy victim Lawrence Monoson, but otherwise avoids overt sentimentality. **DP**

Liv Ullmann *Sari Brimmer* • Norma Aleandro *Florencia Morales, Gaby's Nurse* • Robert Loggia *Michel Brimmer* • Rachel Levin *Gabriela "Gaby" Brimmer* • Lawrence Monoson *Fernando* • Robert Beltran *Luis* ■ *Dir* Luis Mandoki • *Scr* Martin Salinas, Michael James Love, from a story by Luis Mandoki, from events narrated by Gabriela Brimmer

Gadjo Dilo ★★★ 15
Drama 1997 · Fr · Colour · 97min

Director Tony Gatlif completes the "Gypsy Triptych" he began with *Les Princes* (1982) and *Latcho Drom* (1993) with this striking, if sentimentalised drama. As the young Parisian seduced by culture shock, Romain Duris seems too eager to conform. But Izidor Serban is mischievously grizzled as his surrogate father, and Rona Hartner brings a fierce sense of self-worth to the role of the enticing Romanian firebrand. While it seeks to score social points, this is more a celebration of the Romany lifestyle than a plea for greater tolerance. **DP** French +subtitles. Swearing, sex scenes, sexual references.

Romain Duris *Stéphane* • Rona Hartner *Sabina* • Izidor Serban *Izidor* • Ovidiu Balan *Sami* • Angela Serban *Angela* • Aurica Ursan *Aurica* • Vasile Serban *Vasile* • Ioan Serban *Ioan* ■ *Dir/Scr* Tony Gatlif

Le Gai Savoir ★
Documentary drama 1968 · Fr · Colour · 95min

This film marked Godard's irrevocable break with narrative cinema. It's supposed to be an adaptation of Swiss philosopher Jean Jacques Rousseau's novel about education, *Emile* - at least, that's what French TV commissioned. However, it consists mainly of Jean-Pierre Léaud and Juliet Berto sitting in a black void of a TV studio beneath a transparent umbrella to protect them from atomic radiation. Their chat consists of naive slogans, Maoist ideas and general ranting about the media and capitalism. Pretentious, incredibly boring and infuriating. **AT** French +subtitles.

Juliet Berto *Patricia Lumumba* • Jean-Pierre Léaud *Emile Rousseau* ■ *Dir* Jean-Luc Godard • *Scr* Jean-Luc Godard, from the book *Emile* by Jean Jacques Rousseau

Gaiety George ★★★ U
Period musical biography 1946 · UK · BW · 93min

Richard Greene, best known to a generation as TV's Robin Hood, here portrays the father figure of Edwardian musical comedy, George Edwardes, famous for his Gaiety Girls. He's called George Howard here, renamed perhaps because Greene totally fails to evoke Edwardes's trademark flamboyance and Irish vitality. A pallid Ann Todd doesn't add much as the love interest, and the film cries out for colour. However, the period atmosphere is well re-created, ingénue Hazel Court is particularly mesmerising, and the whole is enjoyably watchable. **TS**

G

Richard Greene *George Howard* • Ann Todd *Kathryn Davis* • Peter Graves (1) *Carter* • Hazel Court *Elizabeth Brown* • Leni Lynn *Florence Stephens* • Ursula Jeans *Isobel Forbes* • Morland Graham *Morris* • Frank Pettingell *Grindley* ■ *Dir* George King, Freddie Carpenter, Leontine Sagan • *Scr* Katherine Strueby, Basil Woon, from a story by Richard Fisher, Peter Cresswell

Gaily, Gaily ★★

Period comedy 1969 · US · Colour · 106min

Released as *Chicago, Chicago* in the UK, this account of screenwriter Ben Hecht's early career should have been a stingingly satirical portrait of the Windy City at its breeziest. Instead, it's a crass comedy with the laughs writ large and the playing wildly over the top. Beau Bridges grows in confidence as the cub reporter who discovers that Melina Mercouri's "hotel" is a brothel. **DP**

Beau Bridges *Ben Harvey* • Melina Mercouri *Queen Lil* • Brian Keith *Francis X Sullivan* • George Kennedy *Axel P Johanson* • Hume Cronyn *"Honest" Tim Grogan* • Margot Kidder *Adeline* • Wilfrid Hyde White *Governor* ■ *Dir* Norman Jewison • *Scr* Abram S Ginnes, from the memoirs by Ben Hecht

Gainsbourg (Je T'Aime... Moi Non Plus) ★★★ 15

Musical biographical drama 2010 · Fr/UK · Colour and BW · 116min

First-time writer/director Joann Sfar paints a fanciful portrait of France's most unlikely sex symbol, with this look at the life and loves of Serge Gainsbourg. The fantastical elements jar when they're not confined to Gainsbourg's imagination, but more successful is the strong cast, with Eric Elmosnino an uncanny choice for the lead, and Laetitia Casta and Lucy Gordon effective as Gainsbourg's muses Brigitte Bardot and Jane Birkin. There are also plenty of fine musical moments, including the first playback of the infamous *Je T'Aime*. A little overambitious, but refreshingly free of clichés. **JH** French, Russian, English +subtitles. **DVD** **BD**

Eric Elmosnino *Serge Gainsbourg/voice of "Face"* • Lucy Gordon *Jane Birkin* • Laetitia Casta *Brigitte Bardot* • Doug Jones *"Face"* • Anna Mouglalis *Juliette Gréco* • Mylène Jampanoï *Bambou* ■ *Dir* Joann Sfar • *Scr* Joann Sfar, from her graphic novel

The Gal Who Took the West ★★ U

Comedy western 1949 · US · Colour · 84min

This B-western was photographed by William H Daniels, Garbo's favourite cameraman, and his Arizona vistas are the sole reason for enduring this unfunny attempt to parody the genre. Director Frederick De Cordova fails to invest the proceedings with any brio, hindered by a below-par screenplay that recounts the battle between cousins John Russell and Scott Brady for the affections of Yvonne De Carlo. **DP**

Yvonne De Carlo *Lillian Marlowe* • Charles Coburn *General Michael O'Hara* • Scott Brady *Lee O'Hara* • John Russell *Grant O'Hara* • Myrna Dell *Nancy* ■ *Dir* Frederick De Cordova • *Scr* William Bowers, Oscar Brodney, from their story

Galaxy Quest ★★★★★ PG

Science-fiction spoof 1999 · US · Colour · 102min

In this enormously entertaining send-up of the *Star Trek* universe, a bunch of actors from a cult sci-fi TV show are mistaken for the real thing and recruited to defend a dying alien race. It's an inspired premise, fired into orbit by a fantastic script, sublime visual effects and an absolutely perfect cast, including Tim Allen, Sigourney Weaver and Alan Rickman, hysterical as a grumpy British actor who hates his half-reptilian character. The story is so cleverly executed and the characters so nicely fleshed-out that it not only succeeds as a *Trek* spoof, a satire on the acting profession and a parody of sci-fi fans, but also as an original space saga. **JC** **DVD** **BD**

Tim Allen *Jason Nesmith/Commander Peter Quincy Taggart* • Sigourney Weaver *Gwen DeMarco/Lt Tawny Madison* • Alan Rickman *Alexander Dane/Dr Lazarus* • Tony Shalhoub *Fred Kwan/Tech Sgt Chen* • Sam Rockwell *Guy Fleegman* • Daryl Mitchell *Tommy Webber/ Laredo* • Enrico Colantoni *Mathesar* • Robin Sachs *Sarris* • Patrick Breen *Quellek* ■ *Dir* Dean Parisot • *Scr* Robert Gordon, David Howard, from a story by Howard

Galileo ★★★ PG

Historical biography 1974 · UK/Can · Colour · 138min

After fiddling on the roof for so long, Topol steps down to take on the role of the 17th-century Italian mathematician and astronomer whose heretical theories of the universe brought him into dangerous confrontation with the Roman Catholic church and the Inquisition. Adapted from the play by Bertolt Brecht and directed by Joseph Losey, this is a rather static production from the America Film Theatre. However the actors enliven the debate. **TH** **DVD**

Chaim Topol [Topol] *Galileo Galilei* • Edward Fox *Cardinal Inquisitor* • Colin Blakely *Priuli* • Georgia Brown *Ballad singer's wife* • Clive Revill *Ballad singer* • Margaret Leighton *Court lady* • John Gielgud *Old cardinal* • Michael Gough *Sagredo* • Michel Lonsdale *Cardinal Barberini (later Pope)* • Tom Conti *Andrea Sarti as a man* ■ *Dir* Joseph Losey • *Scr* Barbara Bray, Joseph Losey, Charles Laughton, from the play by Bertolt Brecht

The Gallant Hours ★★ U

Second World War biography 1960 · US · BW · 111min

James Cagney gives a sober, po-faced performance as legendary American war hero Admiral William F Halsey Jr, paying homage on bended knee to the man's formidable reputation. A strong cast, including Robert Montgomery Jr, Dennis Weaver and Ward Costello, admirably fleshes out the tale, but this all-American farrago centres firmly on Cagney, whose portrayal displays great grit but little light or shade. **SH**

James Cagney *Admiral William F Halsey Jr* • Dennis Weaver *Lt Com Andy Lowe* • Ward Costello *Captain Harry Black* • Richard Jaeckel *Lt Com Roy Webb* • Les Tremayne *Captain Frank Enright* • Robert Burton *Maj Gen Roy Geiger* • Raymond Bailey *Maj Gen Archie Vandegrift* ■ *Dir* Robert Montgomery • *Scr* Frank D Gilroy, Beirne Lay Jr

Gallant Lady ★★★

Melodrama 1934 · US · BW · 81min

Unmarried mother Ann Harding is forced to give up her baby son for adoption. Travelling abroad five years later, she meets widower Otto Kruger who is about to marry a woman whom his five-year-old son (Dickie Moore) intensely dislikes. Melodramas about self-sacrificing mother love were popular in the 1930s. Though this is not the best example of the genre, it's stylishly directed by Gregory La Cava and engages the heart thanks to Harding, one of Hollywood's most sympathetic and gifted actresses. Remade in 1938 as *Always Goodbye* with Barbara Stanwyck. **RK**

Ann Harding *Sally Wyndham* • Clive Brook *Dan Pritchard* • Otto Kruger *Philip Lawrence* • Tullio Carminati *Count Carnini* • Dickie Moore *Deedy* ■ *Dir* Gregory La Cava • *Scr* Sam Mintz, from a story by Gilbert Emery, Douglas Doty, Franc Rhodes

Gallants ★★★ 15

Martial arts comedy 2010 · HK · Colour · 94min

This quirky martial arts comedy affectionately sends up some familiar conventions of the action genre while adopting some of its fun retro stylings. The story centres on a put-upon office worker, who is ordered to sort out the lease on a tea house and former martial arts school earmarked for redevelopment. Avoiding the expected clichés, the film benefits from some quirky supporting characters, but the ostensible lead is less engaging, while some wayward pacing means the story meanders in places. **JH** Cantonese, English +subtitles. **DVD**

Wong You Nam [Wong You-nam] *Leung King Cheung* • Jia Xiao Chen *Kwai* • Teddy Robin *Master Law* • Chan Koon Tai *Dragon* • Leung Siu-lung *Tiger* ■ *Dir* Derek Kwok, Clement Cheng • *Scr* Derek Kwok, Clement Cheng, Frankie Tam

Gallipoli ★★★★ PG

First World War drama 1981 · Aus · Colour · 106min

Although its ultimate location is the Dardanelles front during the First World War, this landmark in the emergence of Australian cinema steers between overt pacifism and Anzac pride to focus on the spirit of competition and camaraderie that underpins the national character. Peter Weir refuses to shirk the issue of imperial troops fighting European battles and admirably conveys the chaos and waste of warfare by pointedly contrasting the warren-like trenches with the sunlit acres of the opening scenes. But his interest clearly lies in the specific response to the situation of zealous sprinter Mark Lee and his cynical buddy, Mel Gibson. **DP** Some swearing. **DVD**

Mel Gibson *Frank Dunne* • Mark Lee (1) *Archy Hamilton* • Bill Hunter *Major Barton* • Bill Kerr *Uncle Jack* • Robert Grubb *Billy Lewis* • Tim McKenzie *Barney Wilson* • David Argue *"Snowy"* • Ron Graham *Wallace Hamilton* • Harold Hopkins *Les McCann* ■ *Dir* Peter Weir • *Scr* David Williamson, from a story by Peter Weir, from the book *The Broken Years* by Bill Gammage and war histories by CEW Bean

Gallivant ★★★★ 15

Documentary 1996 · UK · Colour · 99min

Cruelly overlooked on its original release, this offbeat documentary has more incident and intelligence than a barrow-load of blockbusters. Compiled from over 50 hours of interviews and travelogue footage, Andrew Kötting's odyssey around the British coastline is made all the more enchanting by the frank opinions of his grandmother, Gladys, and the courage of his daughter, Eden, who makes light of Joubert's Syndrome to communicate in sign language. With its experimental use of different camera angles and speeds, the style is occasionally fussy, but the eccentric encounters are priceless and highly revealing of our diverse national characteristics. **DP** Swearing. **DVD**

■ *Dir/Scr* Andrew Kötting

The Gallows ★ 15

Horror 2015 · US · Colour · 80min

This nonsensical "found footage" shocker isn't remotely horrifying, just horrible. Twenty years after an understudy dies on stage during a high-school play, three students sabotage a tribute and find themselves inexplicably locked in the auditorium – and in grave danger. This is devoid of credibility, novelty or suspense, and populated with loathsome characters. **AJ**

Reese Mishler *Reese Houser* • Pfeifer Brown *Pfeifer Ross* • Ryan Shoos • Cassidy Gifford *Cassidy Spilker* • Travis Cluff *Mr Schwendiman* ■ *Dir/Scr* Travis Cluff, Chris Lofing

Gambit ★★★ U

Crime comedy 1966 · US · Colour · 103min

Falling into the trap of lighting up each surprise in neon well in advance, director Ronald Neame ensures that the unexpected here quickly becomes the expected and so contributes to the shallowness of the plot. However, events are regularly chirped up by Michael Caine and Shirley MacLaine, who feed their natural frivolity and nimble comic timing into the roles of a cockney crook and his Eurasian showgirl-turned-accomplice. Herbert Lom is also good fun as the hapless target of their wheeze. **JM** **DVD**

Shirley MacLaine *Nicole* • Michael Caine *Harry Deane* • Herbert Lom *Shahbandar* • Roger C Carmel *Ram* • Arnold Moss *Abdul* • John Abbott *Emile* • Richard Angarola *Colonel Salim* • Maurice Marsac *Hotel clerk* ■ *Dir* Ronald Neame • *Scr* Alvin Sargent, Jack Davies, from the short story *Who Is Mr Dean?* by Sidney Carroll

Gambit ★★ 12

Comedy caper 2012 · US · Colour · 85min

An art curator tries to get even with his bullying boss in this patchy comedy caper, based on the 1966 Michael Caine/Shirley MacLaine movie. Colin Firth makes the part of Harry Deane his own, quietly suffering humiliation at the hands of billionaire Alan Rickman. Cameron Diaz is his brassy sidekick, a Texan cowgirl who can claim a direct link to a Monet painting. Even with a script by the Coen brothers, director Michael Hoffman adds no novelty value. There are a few laughs to be had, but they are stunningly cheap. **SP** Swearing, brief nudity. **DVD** **BD**

Colin Firth *Harry Deane* • Cameron Diaz *PJ Puznowski* • Tom Courtenay *The Major* • Alan Rickman *Lionel Shahbandar* • Cloris Leachman *Grandma Merle* • Stanley Tucci *Martin Zaidenweber* ■ *Dir* Michael Hoffman • *Scr* Ethan Coen, Joel Coen, from Sidney Carroll's short story *Who Is Mr Dean?*

The Gambler ★★★★ 18

Drama 1974 · US · Colour · 106min

Quoting Dostoyevsky's gambling compulsion as an excuse for his own obsession, James Caan gives a remarkable performance as the university lecturer in hock to loan sharks for his debts. This was director Karel Reisz's most effective movie of those made during his brief stay in Hollywood. It's a film that takes its time, but the strong supporting actors give necessary substance to the movie's style. **TH** Violence, swearing.

James Caan *Axel Freed* • Lauren Hutton *Billie* • Paul Sorvino *Hips* • Morris Carnovsky *AR Lowenthal* • Jacqueline Brookes *Naomi Freed* • Burt Young *Carmine* • Carmine Caridi *Jimmy* • Vic Tayback *One* • Steven Keats *Howie* ■ *Dir* Karel Reisz • *Scr* James Toback

The Gambler ★★★ 15

Period drama 1997 · UK/Neth/Hun · Colour · 93min

A starry cast and some beautiful locations enhance this adaptation of Fyodor Dostoyevsky's autobiographical novel. Hungarian director Karoly Makk employs the unusual device of the "novel within the film" to show how the writer came to pen his intense study of gambling fever. Stylistically, however, Makk has overloaded his dice and goes for broke on far too many occasions. Rising above the wordy script and the stiff staging, Michael Gambon and Jodhi May fascinate as the author and his young muse. However, the most remarkable performance comes from dual Oscar winner Luise Rainer, appearing in her first film in 54 years. **DP** Some swearing, a sex scene.

Michael Gambon *Fyodor Dostoyevsky* • Jodhi May *Anna Snitkina* • Polly Walker *Polina* • Dominic West *Alexei* • John Wood (2) *The General* • Johan Leysen *De Grieux* • Angeline Ball *Mlle Blanche* • Tom Jansen *Stellovsky* • Luise Rainer *Grandmother* • Gijs Scholten von Asschat *Maikov* ■ *Dir* Karoly Makk • *Scr* Katharine Ogden, Charles Cohen, Nick Dear, from the novel by Fyodor Dostoyevsky

The Gambler ★★★ 15

Crime thriller 2014 · US · Colour · 110min

Mark Wahlberg is a man bent on self-destruction in director Rupert Wyatt's take on Karel Reisz's 1974 drama. Wahlberg makes a fine substitute for James Caan – wiry and blue-lipped, he's maverick literature professor splurging cash, fearlessly fraternising with underworld bosses (including a menacing John Goodman) and racing to pay off his debts. The film's self-consciously stylish visuals are sometimes out of kilter with the narrative focus on existential angst. However, the casting is perfection, even if a powerfully husky Jessica Lange and a sensitive Brie Larson are underutilised. **EAS** Swearing, nudity **DVD** **BD**

Mark Wahlberg *Jim Bennett* • Brie Larson *Amy Phillips* • John Goodman *Frank* • Jessica Lange *Roberta* • Michael Kenneth Williams *Neville* • Alvin Ing *Mister Lee* ■ *Dir* Rupert Wyatt • *Scr* William Monahan, from the 1974 film

The Gambler and the Lady ★★
Crime drama   1952 · UK · BW · 72min

What went on behind the scenes of this Hammer production is far more interesting than the on-screen action. Although Pat Jenkins has his name on the picture, a variety of sources claim that Hollywood hack Sam Newfield co-directed; others assert that horror maestro Terence Fisher also had a hand in its making. The film itself is an unremarkable crime tale about a hard-bitten American gambler (Dane Clark) who discovers the English aristocracy is a much tougher nut to crack than the underworld. DP

Dane Clark *Jim Forster* • Kathleen Byron *Pat* • Naomi Chance *Lady Susan Willens* • Meredith Edwards *Dave* • Anthony Forwood *Peter Willens* • Eric Pohlmann *Arturo Colonna* • Julian Somers *Licasi* • Anthony Ireland *Farning* • Enzo Cottichia *Angelo Colonna* ■ *Dir* Pat Jenkins, Sam Newfield • *Scr* Sam Newfield

The Gamblers ★ U
Comedy drama   1969 · US · Colour · 91min

This lacklustre caper movie is supposedly based on a Gogol play and was filmed in the spectacular Croatian seaboard city of Dubrovnik where gamblers, conmen and other dubious characters gather. As well as the usual Euro-pudding cast, creating a gaggle of accents, it features a bulging swag-bag of movie plunder. AT

Suzy Kendall *Candace* • Don Gordon *Rooney* • Pierre Olaf *Cozzier* • Kenneth Griffith *Broadfoot* • Stuart Margolin *Goldy* • Richard Woo *Koboyashi* • Faith Domergue *Signora Del Isolla* ■ *Dir* Ron Winston • *Scr* Ron Winston, from a play by Nikolai Gogol

Gambling Lady ★★★
Drama   1934 · US · BW · 66min

Here's tough and sexy Barbara Stanwyck, on her way to becoming one of Hollywood's great ladies, cast as a professional gambler born on the wrong side of the tracks who enters high society through marriage to posh Joel McCrea. This is one of those swiftly-paced, tightly-knit melodramas that leave you gasping at the end of a comparatively short running time. Pat O'Brien is the nominal co-star, but McCrea has the more important role, and looks good with Stanwyck. TS

Barbara Stanwyck *Lady Lee* • Joel McCrea *Garry Madison* • Pat O'Brien *Charlie Lang* • C Aubrey Smith *Peter Madison* • Claire Dodd *Sheila Aiken* • Philip Reed *Steve* • Philip Faversham *Don* • Robert Barrat *Mike Lee* ■ *Dir* Archie Mayo • *Scr* Ralph Block, Doris Malloy, from a story by Doris Malloy

The Game ★★★ 15
Psychological thriller
1997 · US · Colour · 123min

Michael Douglas is perfectly cast as the increasingly desperate pawn in this visually stylish thriller from *Se7en* director David Fincher. When hard-nosed businessman Douglas is given the ultimate birthday present by his brother Sean Penn – the chance to play an all-encompassing "reality game" that promises life-changing consequences – he gets swept into what he perceives as a paranoid conspiracy. Sadly, what starts off as a tense and fascinating tale soon becomes glossy and trivial. AJ Violence, swearing. *DVD* *Blu-ray*

Michael Douglas (1) *Nicholas Van Orton* • Sean Penn *Conrad Van Orton* • Deborah Kara Unger *Christine* • James Rebhorn *Jim Feingold* • Peter Donat *Samuel Sutherland* • Carroll Baker *Ilsa* • Anna Katarina *Elizabeth* • Armin Mueller-Stahl *Anson Baer* ■ *Dir* David Fincher • *Scr* John Brancato, Michael Ferris

Game Change ★★★ 15
Political drama based on a true story
2012 · US · Colour · 113min

Republican presidential candidate John McCain is struggling in the polls, so his aides recommend a running mate who will change the game at the election. Enter a little known politician from Alaska – Governor Sarah Palin. And what are the special strengths she brings to the table?

She's a woman. Sadly, however, she knows little about US political history and even less about foreign policy. Julianne Moore's portrayal of Palin is scarily accurate, while the screenwriters couldn't have been luckier - Palin's numerous well-publicised gaffs provide the best lines. SuR Swearing.

Julianne Moore *Sarah Palin* • Woody Harrelson *Steve Schmidt* • Ed Harris *John McCain* • Ron Livingston *Mark Wallace* • Peter MacNicol *Rick Davis* • Sarah Paulson *Nicolle Wallace* ■ *Dir* Jay Roach • *Scr* Danny Strong, from the non-fiction book by Mark Halperin, John Heilemann

A Game for Vultures ★ 15
Political drama   1979 · UK · Colour · 102min

Political strife in Rhodesia in the late 1970s is the backdrop for this dull and dusty home-grown epic. Richard Roundtree (*Shaft*) plays a black freedom fighter, increasingly angry at the British sanctions. Richard Harris finds it impossible to resist the charms of Joan Collins, while Ray Milland and Denholm Elliott round off a cast that's a lot better than the movie merits. A pretentious, shoddy mess. DA Violence, swearing. *DVD*

Richard Harris *David Swansey* • Richard Roundtree *Gideon Marunga* • Joan Collins *Nicolle* • Ray Milland *Colonel Brettle* • Sven-Bertil Taube *Larry Prescott* • Denholm Elliott *Raglan Thistle* • Jana Cilliers *Ruth Swansey* ■ *Dir* James Fargo • *Scr* Phillip Baird, from the novel by Michael Hartmann

The Game Is Over ★
Romantic drama   1966 · Fr/It · Colour · 98min

Jane Fonda's second film with director/husband Roger Vadim was this mildly scandalous, updated version of Zola's novel *La Curée*, in which Fonda falls passionately in love with her stepson, played by Peter McEnery. She asks her husband for a divorce, but while she is away he pressures the stepson into a marriage with the daughter of a banker. Panned at the time, it nevertheless allowed Vadim plenty of opportunities to photograph Fonda semi-naked. AT

Jane Fonda *Renée Saccard* • Peter McEnery *Maxime Saccard* • Michel Piccoli *Alexandre Saccard* • Tina Marquand [Tina Aumont] *Anne Sernet* • Jacques Monod *M Sernet* • Simone Valère *Mme Sernet* • Luong Ham Chau *Mr Chou* ■ *Dir* Roger Vadim • *Scr* Roger Vadim, Jean Cau, Bernard Frechtman, from the novel *La Curée* by Emile Zola

Game of Death ★ 18
Martial arts drama   1978 · HK · Colour · 92min

When Bruce Lee died suddenly in 1973, the industry he helped bring to a wider audience lost no time in churning out a string of shabby exploitation pieces. This is one of the best known of his posthumous releases and one of the worst. The Lee character (predominantly stand-in Kim Tai Jong) finds himself up against gangster Dean Jagger, who kidnaps his girlfriend Colleen Camp. An embarrassing mess. JF Cantonese dubbed. Swearing. *DVD* *Blu-ray*

Bruce Lee *Billy Lo* • Gig Young *Jim Marshall* • Dean Jagger *Dr Land* • Hugh O'Brian *Steiner* • Robert Wall *Carl Miller* • Colleen Camp *Ann Morris* • Kareem Abdul-Jabbar *Hakim* • Chuck Norris *Fighter* • Kim Tai Jong *Billy Lo* ■ *Dir* Robert Clouse • *Scr* Jan Spears

Game Over: Kasparov and the Machine ★★★ PG
Documentary   2003 · Can/UK · Colour · 84min

No one was surprised when grandmaster Garry Kasparov defeated IBM's chess-playing computer, Deep Blue, in 1996. But when the result was reversed in a rematch a year later, the gasps of disbelief were almost immediately drowned out by cries of "foul", as the Russian accused the American corporation of behind-the-scenes shenanigans. The fact that Vikram Jayanti's compelling documentary shows disdain for the IBM programming team and includes excerpts from Raymond Bernard's silent classic *The Chess Player* raises doubts as to its impartiality. DP *DVD*

■ *Dir* Vikram Jayanti • *Cinematographer* Maryse Alberti

The Game Plan ★★★ U
Sports comedy   2007 · US · Colour · 105min

This Disney family comedy proves once again that The Rock (aka Dwayne Johnson) is more than just a moonlighting muscleman as he throws himself into scenes of kiddie-friendly slapstick with surprising gusto. Johnson plays pro footballer Joe Kingman, a quarterback with the (fictional) Boston Rebels whose multimillion-dollar bachelor life is upended by the unexpected arrival of eight-year-old Peyton (Madison Pettis), the daughter he never knew he had. Juggling his new responsibilities delivers the usual life lessons, although the real draw lies in seeing Johnson's light comic touch put to superb use in high jinks involving water pistols, *Swan Lake* ballet recitals and a pet bulldog in a tutu. JR *DVD* *Blu-ray*

Dwayne "The Rock" Johnson [Dwayne Johnson] *Joe Kingman* • Madison Pettis *Peyton Kelly* • Kyra Sedgwick *Stella Peck* • Roselyn Sanchez *Monique Vasquez* • Morris Chestnut *Travis Sanders* • Hayes MacArthur *Kyle Cooper* • Brian White *Jamal Webber* ■ *Dir* Andy Fickman • *Scr* Nichole Millard, Kathryn Price, from a story by Millard, Price, Audrey Wells

Gamer ★ 18
Futuristic action thriller
2008 · US · Colour · 90min

This rehash of elements from *The Running Man*, *Rollerball* and *Death Race 2000* is a cynical exercise in gratuitous sex and ridiculous violence. In the near future, online gamers control death-row inmates in a shoot 'em up game called "Slayers" – their avatars are promised freedom if they complete 30 missions. Gerard Butler brings his muscular charisma to bear as the game's superstar, who is well on his way to getting out if he can overcome the evil machinations of the game's billionaire creator (Michael C Hall). Trouble is the film's hyperactive visual style, facile attempts at satire (internet users are all obese sex maniacs) and sci-fi clichés quickly turn it into an endurance test. AJ Violence, nudity, sexual references. *DVD* *Blu-ray*

Gerard Butler *Kable* • Michael C Hall *Ken Castle* • Amber Valletta *Angie* • Logan Lerman *Simon* • Alison Lohman *Trace* • John Leguizamo *Freek* • Chris "Ludacris" Bridges *Humanz Brother* • Kyra Sedgwick *Gina Parker Smith* • Milo Ventimiglia *Rick Rape* ■ *Dir/Scr* Mark Neveldine, Brian Taylor

Gamera the Invincible ★★
Monster adventure   1965 · Jpn · BW · 86min

Created by the Daiei Studio to rival Toho's *Godzilla*, Gamera is a giant prehistoric fire-breathing turtle, which is awakened by an atomic blast and spins its way to Tokyo, destroying all in its path. As with the original *Godzilla*, American stars Albert Dekker and Brian Donlevy make their appearance, in footage specially shot for the international market. Although competent in every standard Japanese monster-movie department, *Gamera* never really caught on outside its home turf despite numerous wacky sequels and a spectacular hi-tech refit in the 1990s. AJ Japanese dubbed.

Albert Dekker *Secretary of Defense* • Brian Donlevy *General Terry Arnold* • Diane Findlay *WAF A/IC Susan Embers* • John Baragrey *Miles Standish* • Dick O'Neill *General O'Neill* • Ejii Funakoshi *Dr Hidaka* • Harumi Kiritachi *Kyoke* • Yoshiro Uchida *Toshio* ■ *Dir* Noriyaki Yuasa • *Scr* Fumi Takahashi, Richard Kraft, from an idea by Yonejiro Saito

GamerZ ★★ 15
Comedy fantasy   2005 · UK · Colour · 101min

There is nothing particularly unusual in the choice of a puny, socially awkward, Scots teenager as protagonist - Bill Forsyth created the model in *Gregory's Girl* 30 years ago. But at least Gregory shared the national obsession of football; in *GamerZ*, the student hero's hobby is the role-playing game *Dungeons and Dragons*. The story is essentially lightweight and fey, though its attempts to connect to the grubbier side of reality sometimes grate. Yet it is also highly original, with the fantasy world presented

stylishly in the form of dark, animated silhouettes. But, ultimately, this still lacks the wit to propel it beyond the status of fascinating curio. BP

Ross Finbow *Ralph* • Danielle Stewart *Marlyn* • James Young (3) *Lennie* • Johnny Austin *Davy* • Ross Sutherland *Hank* • Edward Tudor-Pole *Dr Denham* ■ *Dir/Scr* Robbie Fraser

Games ★★ 15
Psychological drama   1967 · US · Colour · 96min

Despite a multiplication of psychological double-crosses, Curtis Harrington's mystery drama never really involves us in the Manhattan machinations of fortune-hunting husband James Caan and his gullible wife Katharine Ross. Simone Signoret is the amateur medium who becomes embroiled in their games, peering into a crystal ball as murky as the plot. Had Harrington been concerned more with pace and less with style, the film might have worked. TH *DVD*

Simone Signoret *Lisa* • James Caan *Paul* • Katharine Ross *Jennifer* • Don Stroud *Norman* • Kent Smith *Harry* • Estelle Winwood *Miss Beattie* • Marjorie Bennett *Nora* • Ian Wolfe *Dr Edwards* ■ *Dir* Curtis Harrington • *Scr* Gene Kearney, from a story by Curtis Harrington, George Edwards

The Games ★ PG
Sports drama   1970 · UK · Colour · 92min

What real-life athletes such as technical adviser Gordon Pirie made of this sports drama about the build-up to the marathon at the Rome Olympics is anybody's guess. It's hard to know where to look, really. At the so-obvious cardboard cutout crowds? At the mind-boggling casting of Michael Crawford as an ace marathon runner? Or at Ryan O'Neal as an American good guy, competing despite a heart condition? A sprawling mess. TS

Michael Crawford *Harry Hayes* • Stanley Baker *Bill Oliver* • Ryan O'Neal *Scott Reynolds* • Charles Aznavour *Pavel Vendek* • Jeremy Kemp *Jim Harcourt* • Elaine Taylor *Christine* • Athol Compton *Sunny Pintubi* • Fritz Wepper *Kovanda* ■ *Dir* Michael Winner • *Scr* Erich Segal, from a novel by Hugh Atkinson

Gandhi ★★★★★ PG
Epic biographical drama
1982 · UK · Colour · 183min

Richard Attenborough's stately biopic has historical scope, a sure command of thousands of extras and, most of all, the ability to focus on individual endeavour amid the spectacle. For this is one of the 20th century's most remarkable stories, that of the righteous Indian lawyer (a quietly inspirational performance by Ben Kingsley) who returned from racially segregated South Africa to drive the British out of his home country through successive acts of non-violent protest. The film begins with his assassination and flashes back to the key moments in a 30-year struggle. While Kingsley (who took one of eight Oscars) is the glue that holds this epic piece together, you must also relish the outstanding cast. AC *DVD* *Blu-ray*

Ben Kingsley *Mahatma Gandhi* • Candice Bergen *Margaret Bourke-White* • Edward Fox *General Dyer* • John Gielgud *Lord Irwin* • Trevor Howard *Judge Broomfield* • John Mills *The Viceroy* • Martin Sheen *Walker* • Rohini Hattangady [Rohini Hattangadi] *Kasturba Gandhi* • Roshan Seth *Pandit Nehru* ■ *Dir* Richard Attenborough • *Scr* John Briley • *Cinematographers* Billy Williams, Ronnie Taylor • *Editor* John Bloom • *Costume Designers* John Mollo, Bhanu Athaiya • *Production Designer* Stuart Craig

Gang in Blue ★★★
Police drama   1996 · US · Colour · 97min

Following their writing/directing collaboration on 1995's *Panther*, father and son Melvin and Mario Van Peebles went a few steps further, jointly producing, directing and starring in this police thriller. Mario plays an idealistic policeman who discovers a secret brotherhood of racists at work within his department. With a heavyweight supporting cast, this is an impassioned and intelligent film whose gloss doesn't compromise its integrity. JF Violence, swearing, sex scenes.

G

Mario Van Peebles *Michael Rhoades* • Melvin Van Peebles *Andre Speier* • Josh Brolin *Keith DeBruler* • Cynda Williams *Anita Bayard* • Stephen Lang *Moose Tavola* • JT Walsh *Sergeant William Eyler* • Zach Grenier *Beckstrom* ■ *Dir* Mario Van Peebles, Melvin Van Peebles • *Scr* Rick Natkin, David Fuller

Gang Law ★★ 18

Crime drama　　1999 · US · Colour · 92min

This is slicker than Master P's earlier work, although its dubious moral message and ultra-violence occasionally makes for uncomfortable viewing. Master P's young brother Silkk the Shocker stars as an aspiring rapper who embraces a life of crime when his girlfriend is falsely imprisoned. There's a host of cameos from other rappers, while video stars Gary Busey, C Thomas Howell and Jeff Speakman add a smidgin of marquee value. **JF** 🅓🆅🅓

Gary Busey *Tully* • Silkk the Shocker *Kool* • Jeff Speakman *Master Keaton* • Snoop Dogg *C-Dawg* • Master P *Moe* • Shireen Crutchfield *LaShawna* • C Thomas Howell *Officer Roberts* ■ *Dir/Scr* Master P

Gang Related ★★★★ 15

Crime drama　　1997 · US · Colour · 106min

Tupac Shakur's final film offers a glimpse of what a fine, subtle actor he was becoming before his tragic early death. The acclaimed rap star plays a detective who, with partner James Belushi, has established a lucrative scam ripping off and killing drug dealers and pronouncing the deaths as "gang related". However, it all goes pear-shaped when their latest victim turns out to be an undercover drugs agent and the derelict they attempt to frame (Dennis Quaid) is discovered to have a surprising past. Writer/director Jim Kouf delivers the goods thriller-wise, while mining an unexpected seam of gallows humour. **JF** Swearing, violence, nudity. 🅓🆅🅓

James Belushi *Detective Frank K Divinci* • Tupac Shakur *Detective Rodriguez* • Lela Rochon *Cynthia Webb* • Dennis Quaid *William Dane McCall/"Joe Doe"* • James Earl Jones *Arthur Baylor* • David Paymer *Elliot Goff* • Wendy Crewson *Helen Eden* • Gary Cole *Richard Simms* ■ *Dir/Scr* Jim Kouf

The Gang That Couldn't Shoot Straight ★★★ 15

Crime comedy　　1971 · US · Colour · 92min

This slapstick comedy about New York mobsters stars Jerry Orbach as the incompetent hood who makes a disastrous series of attempts to bump off a local mafioso, played by gravel-voiced Lionel Stander. Directed at breakneck pace by James Goldstone and written by Waldo Salt, with an ear for the local South Brooklyn wisecrack, it's a bit hit and miss, but it's hard to dislike a mobster movie that features a cycle race and a lion on the loose. Most eyes will be on Robert De Niro as one of the Italian cyclists who becomes an illegal immigrant and a bogus priest. **AT**

Jerry Orbach *Kid Sally* • Leigh Taylor-Young *Angela* • Jo Van Fleet *Big Momma* • Lionel Stander *Baccala* • Robert De Niro *Mario* • Irving Selbst *Big Jelly* • Herve Villechaize *Beppo* ■ *Dir* James Goldstone • *Scr* Waldo Salt, from the novel by Jimmy Breslin

Gang War ★★★

Crime drama　　1958 · US · BW · 71min

Long before the controversial *Death Wish*, Charles Bronson turned vigilante in this little-known crime thriller. Having witnessed a gangland murder, Bronson testifies in court and later finds his pregnant wife has been murdered in a revenge attack. When the police fail to arrest the killers, Bronson goes up against the Mob himself. Despite some naff scenes and a few dodgy performances, this B-movie is well worth seeking out. **AT**

Charles Bronson *Alan Avery* • Kent Taylor *Bryce Barker* • Jennifer Holden *Marie* • John Doucette *Maxie Matthews* • Gloria Henry *Edie Avery* • Gloria Grey *Marsha Brown* • Barney Phillips *Sam Johnson* • Ralph Manza *Axe Duncan* ■ *Dir* Gene Fowler Jr • *Scr* Louis Vittes, from the novel *The Hoods Take Over* by Ovid Demaris

The Gang's All Here ★★★ PG

Crime comedy　　1939 · UK · BW · 73min

This Jack Buchanan vehicle is a sequel to his earlier *Smash and Grab*, which attempted to turn Buchanan and Elsie Randolph into a British Nick and Nora Charles (*The Thin Man*). He plays John Forrest, an insurance investigator who routs an American gang in a London nightclub with Googie Withers. Jack and Googie make a very smart coupling, and this was a big hit. **TS** 🅓🆅🅓

Edward Everett Horton *Treadwell* • Otto Kruger *Mike Chadwick* • Jack Buchanan *John Forrest* • Jack LaRue *Alberni* • Googie Withers *Alice Forrest* • Syd Walker *Younce* • David Burns *Beretti* • Walter Rilla *Prince Homouska* ■ *Dir* Thornton Freeland • *Scr* Ralph Spence

The Gang's All Here ★★ U

Musical　　1943 · US · Colour · 99min

Also known as *The Girls He Left Behind*, this is a mesmerisingly awful chunk of camp kitsch, designed and filmed in garish Technicolor. Showgirl Alice Faye falls in love with soldier James Ellison just before he leaves to serve in the Pacific. This farrago proves that director Busby Berkeley left his taste behind him when he decamped to 20th Century-Fox. **TS** 🅓🆅🅓 🅱🅻

Alice Faye *Eadie Allen* • Carmen Miranda *Dorita* • Phil Baker • Eugene Pallette *Mr Mason Sr* • Charlotte Greenwood *Mrs Peyton Potter* • Edward Everett Horton *Peyton Potter* • Tony DeMarco • James Ellison *Andy Mason* ■ *Dir* Busby Berkeley • *Scr* Walter Bullock, from a story by Nancy Winter, George Root Jr, Tom Bridges

Gangs of New York ★★★ 18

Period crime drama　　2002 · US · Colour · 159min

Director Martin Scorsese's brutal, occasionally muddled, but always riveting film about Manhattan gang warfare in the 1860s begins with a gruesome street battle between the Nativists and the Dead Rabbits. The latter's leader, Liam Neeson (a brief but striking appearance), is slaughtered in front of his young son. Sixteen years later, his son (played by Leonardo DiCaprio in a disappointingly one-note performance), insinuates himself into the gang in order to avenge his father. However, his evolving relationship with Nativist boss Daniel Day-Lewis provides the young man with a dilemma. If the film never marries its complex political intrigue with the more simplistic personal stories, the epic sweep is breathtaking, the attention to detail intoxicating and Day-Lewis's turn riveting. **IF** Violence, swearing, sex scenes, nudity. 🅓🆅🅓 🅱🅻

Leonardo DiCaprio *Amsterdam Vallon* • Daniel Day-Lewis *William Cutting, "Bill the Butcher"* • Cameron Diaz *Jenny Everdeane* • Liam Neeson *Priest Vallon* • Jim Broadbent *William "Boss" Tweed* • John C Reilly *Happy Jack* • Henry Thomas *Johnny Sirocco* • Brendan Gleeson *Walter "Monk" McGinn* • Gary Lewis *Charles McGloin* • Stephen Graham *Shang* • Roger Ashton-Griffiths *PT Barnum* • David Hemmings *Mr Schermerhorn* • Barbara Bouchet *Mrs Schermerhorn* • Alec McCowen *Reverend Raleigh* • Michael Byrne *Horace Greeley* • Martin Scorsese *Wealthy homeowner* ■ *Dir* Martin Scorsese • *Scr* Jay Cocks, Steve Zaillian, Kenneth Lonergan, from the novel by Herbert Asbury

Gangs of Wasseypur ★★★★ 15

Crime drama　　2012 · Ind · Colour · 160min

Ambitious, compelling and accomplished, this Indian crime drama from director Anurag Kashyap owes a considerable debt to *The Godfather*. This first instalment of a two-part epic chronicles the first five decades of a feud between the Muslim Khan and Qureshi clans that divides the northern mining town of Wasseypur and the city of Dhanbad that eventually subsumes it. Rajeev Ravi's kinetic camerawork and Sneha Khanwalkar's homage-stuffed score are impressive, as is the performance of Manoj Bajpayee as the head of the Khan dynasty. But it's Kashyap's dynamic direction that puts this

in the top tier of sprawling gangster epics. **DP** Hindi +subtitles.

Manoj Bajpayee [Manoj Bajpai] *Sardar Khan* • Richa Chadda *Nagma Khatoon* • Reemaa Sen *Durga Khan* • Piyush Mishra *Nasir Ahmed* ■ *Dir* Anurag Kashyap • *Scr* Anurag Kashyap, Akhilesh Jaiswal, Sachin Ladia, Zeishan Quadri

Gangs of Wasseypur II ★★★★ 18

Crime drama　　2012 · Ind · Colour · 159min

Opening with the fallout from the assassination of patriarch Sardar Khan, the highly satisfying second instalment of Anurag Kashyap's period gangster epic follows Khan's reluctant warlord son (Nawazuddin Siddiqui) as he seeks vengeance. However, the dead man's jilted mistress (Reemaa Sen) and her loyal son (Zieshan Quadri) seek to play the Khan and the Qureshi clans off against each other, and have the protection of a puppet-master politician (Tigmanshu Dhulia). As in the first film, Kashyap gleefully blends Indian and American tropes, but with the plot being much less sprawling and convoluted here, there is also more time for musical interludes and comic digressions. **DP** Hindi +subtitles.

Manoj Bajpayee [Manoj Bajpai] *Sardar Khan* • Richa Chadda *Nagma Khatoon* • Nawazuddin Siddiqui *Faizal Khan* • Tigmanshu Dhulia *Ramadhir Singh* • Zeishan Quadri *Definite* • Reemaa Sen *Durga Khan* ■ *Dir* Anurag Kashyap • *Scr* Anurag Kashyap, Akhilesh Jaiswal, Sachin K Ladia, Zeishan Quadri

Gangster No 1 ★★★ 18

Crime thriller　　2000 · UK · Colour · 98min

Following in the wake of *Lock, Stock and Two Smoking Barrels*, Paul McGuigan's thriller is another tale of London gangsters, though this time without the humour. As studies of pure evil go, however, it's very convincing. Malcolm McDowell plays a crime lord who looks back on the 1960s antics of his gang. Flashbacks show him played by the impressive Paul Bettany, whose vicious behaviour leads to much blood-letting. This central section is stylistically superb, but the gratuitous violence and profanity also leave a nasty taste in the mouth. **LH** 🅓🆅🅓 🅱🅻

Malcolm McDowell *Gangster 55* • David Thewlis *Freddie Mays* • Paul Bettany *Young Gangster* • Saffron Burrows *Karen* • Kenneth Cranham *Tommy* • Jamie Foreman *Lennie Taylor* • Andrew Lincoln *Maxie King* ■ *Dir* Paul McGuigan • *Scr* Johnny Ferguson, from the play by Louis Mellis, David Scinto

Gangster Squad ★★★★ 15

Crime drama　　2012 · US · Colour · 108min

Subtlety flies out of the window, along with the baddies, in this action-heavy flick, as LA cops Ryan Gosling and Josh Brolin make a stand against Mob kingpin Mickey Cohen (Sean Penn). It may be based on a true story, but the subject of corruption at the LAPD was portrayed with much more sophistication in *LA Confidential*. Director Ruben Fleischer takes a basic, gung-ho approach but makes the most of his talent for blending violence with dark humour (*Zombieland*) and splashes the budget on a glossy re-creation of 1940s Los Angeles. Brolin's upstanding sergeant gives the film a moral backbone, though Gosling upstages him with effortless poise. Like the mission to bring down Cohen, this thriller is definitely more brawn than brains, but it sets its sights clearly from the get-go and hits the mark with relish. **SP** Violence. 🅓🆅🅓 🅱🅻

Josh Brolin *Sgt John O'Mara* • Ryan Gosling *Sgt Jerry Wooters* • Sean Penn *Mickey Cohen* • Emma Stone *Grace Faraday* • Nick Nolte *Chief Bill Parker* • Giovanni Ribisi *Officer Conwell Keeler* ■ *Dir* Ruben Fleischer • *Scr* Will Beall, from the novel *Gangster Squad: Covert Cops, the Mob, and the Battle for Los Angeles* by Paul Lieberman

Gangster Story ★★★ PG

Crime drama　　1959 · US · BW · 67min

Inside every great Hollywood actor there's a would-be director trying to get out. Clint Eastwood, Mel Gibson and Kevin Costner

are but three recent examples. Fans of Walter Matthau may be surprised to find that the untidy half of *The Odd Couple* made his directing debut as far back as 1959. He also stars in this crime drama as gangster Jack Martin, who finds himself in conflict with local hood Bruce McFarlan when he tries to muscle in on his territory. Not Oscar-winning stuff, but competent and absorbing. **TH** 🅓🆅🅓

Walter Matthau *Jack Martin* • Carol Grace *Carol* • Bruce McFarlan *Earl Dawson* • Garrett Wallberg *Adolph* • Raiken Ben Ari *Hood* ■ *Dir* Walter Matthau • *Scr* Paul Purcell, from a story by Richard Grey, VJ Rhems

Gangster's Paradise: Jerusalema ★★★★ 15

Crime drama　　2008 · S Afr · Colour · 114min

This violent crime drama, which was inspired by real events, charts the rise of Lucky Kunene (Rapulana Seiphemo) from teenage carjacker in the Soweto townships to feared head of a crime syndicate in the slums of Johannesburg. Writer/director Ralph Ziman's bold and ambitious film recalls the epic sweep of Martin Scorsese's American gangster dramas, while addressing some uncomfortable questions about underworld power struggles in post-apartheid South Africa. Seiphemo is coldly charismatic in the lead role, skilfully portraying the contradictions of a supposed man of the people operating on the fringes of the law. **TeS** Afrikaans, English +subtitles. 🅓🆅🅓 🅱🅻

Rapulana Seiphemo *Lucky Kunene* • Jeffrey Sekele *Nazareth* • Ronnie Nyakale *Zakes Mbolelo* • Shelley Meskin *Leah Freidland* • Malusi Skenjana *Tony Ngu* • Robert Hobbs *Inspector Blakkie Swart* • Jafta Mamabolo *Young Kunene* • Motlatsi Mahloko *Young Zakes* ■ *Dir/Scr* Ralph Ziman

Gangway ★★★ U

Musical comedy　　1937 · UK · BW · 86min

Try as they might, British producers of the 1930s always managed to be just out of time in their attempts to emulate the Hollywood musical. Jessie Matthews, therefore, didn't have much to beat to be hailed as the queen of the British equivalent, but her energy and charm enabled her to elevate the most mundane material and win fans on both sides of the Atlantic. Here's she plays a journalist on board a cruise ship who runs into a Scotland Yard inspector (Barry Mackay) on the trail of a jewel thief. **DP**

Jessie Matthews *Pat Wayne* • Barry Mackay *Inspector Bob Deering* • Olive Blakeney *Nedda Beaumont* • Nat Pendleton *"Smiles" Hogan* • Noel Madison *Mike Otterman* • Liane Ordeyne *Greta Brand* • Patrick Ludlow *Carl Freemason* • Alastair Sim *Taggett* ■ *Dir* Sonnie Hale • *Scr* Lesser Samuels, Sonnie Hale, from a story by Dwight Taylor

Gaolbreak ★ U

Crime drama　　1962 · UK · BW · 62min

This typically down-at-heel crime story from low-budget specialists Butcher's is spiced up by a subplot about an unwanted pregnancy. It features an early performance by Carol White, who found fame in Ken Loach's television play *Cathy Come Home* and his feature *Poor Cow*. Sadly, this tale has barely enough plot to make a TV episode, let alone keep a cinema audience happy, and seems stretched even at its one-hour running time. **DP**

Peter Reynolds *Eddie Wallis* • Avice Landone *Mrs Wallis* • David Kernan *Len Rogerson* • Carol White *Carol Marshall* • David Gregory *Ron Wallis* • John Blythe *Slim* • Robert Desmond *Page* • Geoffrey Hibbert *Dr Cambus* ■ *Dir* Francis Searle • *Scr* AR Rawlinson

Garage ★★★ 18

Drama　　2007 · Ire · Colour · 81min

Irish director Lenny Abrahamson's darkly amusing drama follows the (mis)adventures of Josie (Pat Shortt), the simpleton caretaker of a ramshackle rural petrol station. Lumbered with a young teenage assistant (Conor J Ryan), Josie finds the solitary equilibrium of his lonely existence

🆄 SUITABLE FOR ALL　🆄c SUITABLE ESPECIALLY FOR YOUNG CHILDREN (DVD ONLY)　PG PARENTAL GUIDANCE　12A UNDER 12s TO BE ACCOMPANIED (CINEMA ONLY)

G

disturbed and initially struggles to cope with an unexpected and novel friendship. Centred on a heart-rending performance from award-winning stand-up comedian Shortt, this low-key drama unfolds with gentle pathos, while also painting a believably sparse portrait of a dying rural community. Abrahamson uses the scenic locations to good effect and the supporting cast includes Anne-Marie Duff. But the film's heavy-handed symbolism does weaken the impact of later dramatic developments. JR Swearing, sexual images. **DVD**

Pat Shortt *Josie* • Anne-Marie Duff *Carmel* • Conor J Ryan [Conor Ryan] *David* • Don Wycherley *Breffni* • Andrew Bennett *Sully* • Denis Conway *Garda Michael* • Tom Hickey *Mr Skerrit* • George Costigan *Dan* ■ *Dir* Leonard Abrahamson [Lenny Abrahamson] • *Scr* Mark O'Halloran

The Garbage Pail Kids Movie ★ PG
Comedy 1987 · US · Colour · 91min

The movie spin-off from the Topps Company's bubble gum trading cards series is purposely offensive rubbish. The alien kids land on Earth in a dustbin and end up in Anthony Newley's shop. Unfortunately Newley's assistant takes the lid off the dustbin, subjecting us to a bad-taste mix of mean-spirited pranks, grotesque humour and knockabout violence. Mindless trash. AJ

Anthony Newley *Captain Manzini* • MacKenzie Astin *Dodger* • Katie Barberi *Tangerine* • Ron MacLachlan *Juice* • Kevin Thompson *Ali Gator* • Phil Fondacaro *Greaser Greg* • Robert Bell [Robert N Bell] *Foul Phil* • Larry Green *Nat Nerd* • Arturo Gil *Windy Winston* ■ *Dir* Rod Amateau • *Scr* Rod Amateau, Melinda Palmer

Garbo Talks ★★★ 15
Comedy drama 1984 · US · Colour · 100min

Director Sidney Lumet's fondness for social outsiders goes back to his first film, *12 Angry Men*, and the pattern continues with *Garbo Talks*, in which Anne Bancroft plays an affable but certifiable eccentric. The New York housewife is obsessed with the titular film star and addicted to supporting lost causes, as a result of which she is continually getting arrested. Ron Silver is suitably long-suffering as her exasperated but devoted son and Bancroft makes her character wholly credible. The result is a charming, if uneven film. TH **DVD**

Anne Bancroft *Estelle Rolfe* • Ron Silver *Gilbert Rolfe* • Carrie Fisher *Lisa Rolfe* • Catherine Hicks *Jane Mortimer* • Steven Hill *Walter Rolfe* • Howard Da Silva *Angelo Dokakis* • Dorothy Loudon *Sonya Apollinar* ■ *Dir* Sidney Lumet • *Scr* Larry Grusin

Garde à Vue ★★★★
Crime drama 1981 · Fr · Colour · 88min

By confining the bulk of the action in this tense murder investigation to a provincial police station, Claude Miller is able to control not only the steady flow of secrets and lies, but also the suspense levels, as detectives Lino Ventura and Guy Marchand seek to uncover prominent lawyer Michel Serrault's role in the rape and murder of a young girl. There are improbabilities in the plot, but such is the conviction of the exchanges that they serve only to deepen the mystery. Remade in Hollywood almost 20 years later as *Under Suspicion*. DP French +subtitles.

Lino Ventura *Inspector Antoine Gallien* • Michel Serrault *Jérôme Martinaud* • Guy Marchand *Inspector Marcel Belmont* • Romy Schneider *Chantal Martinaud* • Didier Agostini *Young policeman* • Patrick Depeyrat *1st policeman* • Pierre Maguelon *Adami* • Serge Malik *Mechanic* ■ *Dir* Claude Miller • *Scr* Claude Miller, Jean Herman, from the novel *Brainwash* by John Wainwright

The Garden ★★ 15
Experimental drama
1990 · UK · BW and Colour · 88min

Derek Jarman's uncompromising experimental work is alternately moving, annoying and boring. Christianity, the media, police brutality, advertising, Aids, old age and repression are just some of the topics that make up this angry, non-narrative view of homosexual discrimination. Using camp, weird and shocking imagery, Jarman's political treatise is a graphically dense look at gay counterculture. AJ **DVD**

Tilda Swinton *Madonna* • Johnny Mills *Lover* • Kevin Collins *Lover* • Pete Lee-Wilson *Devil* • Spencer Leigh *Mary Magdalene/Adam* • Jody Graber *Young boy* • Roger Cook *Christ* • Jessica Martin *Singer* • Michael Gough *Narrator* ■ *Dir/Scr* Derek Jarman

The Garden of Allah ★★★
Silent romance 1927 · US · BW · 82min

Directing wife Alice Terry, Rex Ingram allows the camera to caress her face without capturing the barest flicker of emotion. As the monk who abandons his vocation to run away and marry her, Ivan Petrovich at least manages to express some of the torment experienced by the Trappist lured from the right path by worldly temptation. However, it's Marcel Vibert's sinister Arab who steals this stylish but ultimately limp melodrama. DP

Alice Terry *Domini Enfilden* • Ivan Petrovich *Father Adrien/Boris Androvsky* • HH Wright *Lord Rens* ■ *Dir* Rex Ingram (1) • *Scr* Willis Goldbeck, from the novel by Robert Hichens

The Garden of Allah ★ U
Romantic melodrama 1936 · US · Colour · 75min

Directed with little sense of style or pace, and phoney beyond endurance in narrative and execution, this film is total rubbish and doesn't even appeal on the "so bad it's good" front. Marlene Dietrich and Charles Boyer look uncomfortable as they attempt to mouth unspeakable platitudes, but the early Technicolor photography is sumptuous. TS **DVD**

Marlene Dietrich *Domini Enfilden* • Charles Boyer *Boris Androvsky* • Basil Rathbone *Count Anteoni* • C Aubrey Smith *Father Roubier* • Tilly Losch *Irena* • Joseph Schildkraut *Batouch* • John Carradine *Sand diviner* ■ *Dir* Richard Boleslawski • *Scr* WP Lipscomb, Lynn Riggs, from the novel by Robert Hichens • *Cinematographer* Harold Rosson

Garden of Evil ★★ PG
Western 1954 · US · Colour · 96min

This loose rehash of *The Treasure of the Sierra Madre* squanders its cast and devotes its energies to capturing the scenery with the new CinemaScope lens. Susan Hayward convinces adventurers Gary Cooper and Richard Widmark that "there's gold in them thar hills" – as well as a husband buried in the mine they're seeking. Indian attacks impede their progress. AT **DVD**

Gary Cooper *Hooker* • Susan Hayward *Leah Fuller* • Richard Widmark *Fiske* • Cameron Mitchell *Luke Daly* • Hugh Marlowe *John Fuller* • Rita Moreno *Singer* • Victor Manuel Mendoza *Vicente Madariaga* • Fernando Wagner *Captain* ■ *Dir* Henry Hathaway • *Scr* Frank Fenton, from a story by Fred Freiberger, William Tunberg

The Garden of the Finzi-Continis ★★★★★ 12
Second World War drama
1971 · It/W Ger · Colour · 90min

Based on Giorgio Bassani's semi-autobiographical novel and the winner of the 1971 best foreign film Oscar, this sobering drama is an exquisitely played masterpiece. Eschewing both the neorealist flourishes that forged his reputation and the melodramatic excesses that marred it, Vittorio De Sica brilliantly employs flashbacks to explain the confidence of a Jewish family in their belief that Fascism will never breach the walls of their Ferrara home. Rarely has inevitability been so suspensefully presented – or faith in a doomed way of life so well portrayed – as in this genuinely moving film. DP Italian +subtitles. **DVD**

Dominique Sanda *Micol* • Lino Capolicchio *Giorgio* • Helmut Berger *Alberto* • Fabio Testi *Malnate* • Romolo Valli *Giorgio's father* • Raffaele Curi *Ernesto* • Camillo Angelini-Rota *Micol's*

---

father • Katina Viglietti *Micol's mother* • Inna Alexeieff *Micol's grandmother* ■ *Dir* Vittorio De Sica • *Scr* Cesare Zavattini, Vittorio Bonicelli, Ugo Pirro, Giorgio Bassani, from the novel by Giorgio Bassani

Garden State ★★★★ 15
Comedy drama 2003 · US · Colour · 98min

Zach Braff's engaging charm and sharp comic timing played a big part in the success of the TV comedy series *Scrubs*. Those qualities are very much to the fore here, but it's his talents behind the camera as writer and director that really impress. The story is familiar enough: an actor is forced to re-examine his rather empty, aimless life when he returns to his home town in New Jersey for the funeral of his mother. But Braff's thoughtful, mature script neatly sidesteps most of the obvious clichés, while as a director he shows a fine eye for offbeat composition. The performances are uniformly excellent, too. DA Swearing, sex scenes, drug abuse. **DVD** **BD**

Zach Braff *Andrew Largeman* • Ian Holm *Gideon Largeman* • Ron Leibman *Dr Cohen* • Method Man *Diego* • Natalie Portman *Sam* • Peter Sarsgaard *Mark* • Jean Smart *Carol* • Ann Dowd *Olivia* ■ *Dir/Scr* Zach Braff

Gardens in Autumn ★★★★ PG
Comedy 2006 · Fr/It/Rus · Colour · 121min

Michel Piccoli's cameo as the antihero's ageing mother epitomises the whimsical nature of this delicious satire on the absurdities of modern life. Having been forced to resign from the government following a scandal, Séverin Blanchet abandons the trappings of his office and returns to the working-class neighbourhood of his youth, where he spends his days catching up with old lovers, reconnecting with his family and planting trees. As in the films of Jacques Tati, the action unfolds at its own leisurely pace, with the gags building slowly and paying off with wry smiles rather than guffaws. Deftly photographed around Paris by William Lubtchansky, this is a consistently amusing minimalist masterclass. DP French +subtitles.

Séverin Blanchet *Vincent* • Michel Piccoli *Mother* • Muriel Motte *Odile* • Pascal Vincent *Théodière* • Jean Douchet *Father of bailiff* ■ *Dir/Scr* Otar Iosseliani • *Cinematographer* William Lubtchansky

Gardens of Stone ★★★ 15
War drama 1987 · US · Colour · 106min

Francis Coppola returns to the subject of the Vietnam War in this quieter, more sombre film, set on the home front. James Caan gives a powerful performance as the combat veteran whose ambivalence towards the war and the military is combined with a romantic interest in anti-war journalist Anjelica Huston. The film is marred by the tragic death of Coppola's son, Giancarlo, in a boating accident during production. PF **DVD**

James Caan *Sgt Clell Hazard* • James Earl Jones *Sgt Major "Goody" Nelson* • DB Sweeney *Private Jackie Willow* • Anjelica Huston *Samantha Davis* • Dean Stockwell *Capt Homer Thomas* • Mary Stuart Masterson *Rachel Field* • Dick Anthony Williams *Sgt Slasher Williams* ■ *Dir* Francis Coppola [Francis Ford Coppola] • *Scr* Ronald Bass, from the novel by Nicholas Proffitt

Garfield ★★ U
Part-animated comedy
2004 · US · Colour · 76min

Jim Davis's fat-cat comic strip gets the big-screen treatment here. In an inspired piece of casting, Bill Murray voices the sardonic, lasagne-loving feline, who finds his lazy lifestyle threatened when owner Jon (Breckin Meyer) decides to adopt a dog to impress beautiful vet Liz (Jennifer Love Hewitt). Aimed squarely at a younger audience, its miniscule plot barely does justice to Garfield's infamous dry wit. SF **DVD**

Breckin Meyer *Jon Arbuckle* • Jennifer Love Hewitt *Dr Liz Wilson* • Stephen Tobolowsky *Happy Chapman* • Bill Murray *Garfield* • Eve Brent *Mrs Baker* • Debra Messing *Arlene* • David Eigenberg *Nermal* ■ *Dir* Pete Hewitt [Peter Hewitt] • *Scr* Joel Cohen, Alec Sokolow, from the comic strip by Jim Davis

Garfield 2 ★★★ U
Part-animated comedy
2006 · US · Colour · 82min

What could have been a cynical retread of old ground – *Garfield 2* puts a feline spin on Mark Twain's *The Prince and the Pauper* – is actually an improvement on the first film. Garfield (again voiced by Bill Murray) stows away on a trip to London in his new owner Jon's luggage and finds himself mistaken for an upper-class English cat (Prince, voiced by Tim Curry), who has been bequeathed an estate. A number of clever sight gags (including a variation on the Groucho/Harpo mirror sequence in *Duck Soup*), some well-used locations and a strong voice cast compensate for a few too many cheap laughs. SuR **DVD**

Bill Murray *Garfield* • Breckin Meyer *Jon Arbuckle* • Jennifer Love Hewitt *Liz* • Billy Connolly *Dargis* • Ian Abercrombie *Smithee* • Roger Rees *Mr Hobbs* • Lucy Davis *Abby* • Bob Hoskins *Winston* ■ *Dir* Tim Hill • *Scr* Joel Cohen, Alec Sokolow, from characters by Jim Davis

Garfield Gets Real ★ U
Animated comedy 2007 · US · Colour · 74min

This poor, CGI spin-off from the popular comic strip makes the hit-and-miss live-action versions seem like masterpieces. Written (surprisingly) by Garfield's original creator, Jim Davis, the ill-advised adventure sees the sardonic cat and his doggie pal, Odie, escape from their cartoon universe into the just-as-fake looking "real world", and must race to return home before their strip is cancelled. Aside from the cute opening, the visuals are a particular letdown, with the characters and background animated so simply that they appear incomplete. SF **DVD**

Frank Welker *Garfield/Keith/Prop boy/Two-headed guy/Goth kid/Hardy* • Gregg Berger *Odie/Shecky/Hale* • Jason Marsden *Nermal* • Wally Wingert *Jon Arbuckle/Mike* ■ *Dir* Mark AZ Dippé, Kyung Ho Lee • *Scr* Jim Davis, from his comic strip

The Garment Jungle ★★★
Crime drama 1957 · US · BW · 87min

A good hard-hitting example of 1950s Hollywood realism, this tackles the subject of labour unions in the clothing business. It is almost a pro-union retort by Columbia to the studio's own anti-union *On the Waterfront*, three years earlier. Lee J Cobb is the heavy, a union-bashing boss involved with gangster Richard Boone. The original (uncredited) director Robert Aldrich was taken off the film towards the end of shooting and replaced by Vincent Sherman. RB

Lee J Cobb *Walter Mitchell* • Kerwin Mathews *Alan Mitchell* • Gia Scala *Theresa Renata* • Richard Boone *Artie Ravidge* • Valerie French *Lee Hackett* • Robert Loggia *Tulio Renata* • Joseph Wiseman *Kovan* • Harold J Stone *Tony* ■ *Dir* Vincent Sherman • *Scr* Harry Kleiner, from the article *Gangsters in the Dress Business* by Lester Velie

Gas, Food, Lodging ★★★★ 15
Drama 1992 · US · Colour · 101min

In this intelligent family drama, Brooke Adams stars as a single mother trying to hold down a job at a diner while coping with teenage daughters who are growing up too fast. Writer/director Allison Anders works wonders with a low budget and sketches a gritty, sympathetic portrait of lost dreams and the daily struggle of small-town American life. The cast, with Ione Skye and Fairuza Balk as the daughters, is exemplary, and there's even a decent turn from the usually wooden James Brolin. JF Swearing, sex scenes.

Brooke Adams *Nora Roberts* • Ione Skye *Trudi* • Fairuza Balk *Shade* • James Brolin *John Evans* • Robert Knepper *Dank* • David Landsbury *Hamlet*

G

Humphrey • Chris Mulkey *Raymond* • Adam Biesk *Brett* ■ *Dir* Allison Anders • *Scr* Allison Anders, from the novel *Don't Look and It Won't Hurt* by Richard Peck

Gasbags ★★★ PG

Second World War comedy
1940 · UK · BW · 73min

Intended to boost wartime morale, this is the best film ever made by the Crazy Gang, the British comedy team led by Bud Flanagan and Chesney Allen. The plot includes a flying fish-and-chip shop, while the geriatric-looking Moore Marriott – a veteran of innumerable Will Hay films – plays a prisoner of war with plans for a secret weapon tattooed on his back. No wonder the Gang have designs on him. Director Marcel Varnel has just the right surreal touch to make it work and leave audiences laughing. TH *DVD*

Bud Flanagan *Bud* • Chesney Allen *Ches* • Jimmy Nervo *Cecil* • Teddy Knox *Knoxy* • Charlie Naughton *Charlie* • Jimmy Gold *Goldy* • Moore Marriott *Jerry Jenkins* • Wally Patch *Sergeant Major* ■ *Dir* Marcel Varnel • *Scr* Val Guest, Marrott Edgar, from the story by Val Valentine, Ralph Smart

Gascoigne ★★★ 15

Documentary
2015 · UK · Colour · 86min

This film charts the rise and fall of footballer Paul Gascoigne, the maverick who hit the heights, then was brought low by a combination of bad luck, booze and, though it's not mentioned, bad company. Combining match footage with new interviews, Jane Preston's film presents a telling portrait of a likeable man who was too emotionally immature to cope with the pressures of fame and fortune. DA *DVD* ℬ

Paul Gascoigne ■ *Dir/Scr* Jane Preston

Gasland ★★★ PG

Documentary
2010 · US · Colour · 107min

Documentary-maker Josh Fox pulls few punches here as he condemns those who have laid waste to vast swathes of the United States in the search for natural gas, using a procedure called "fracking". Fox has a touch of the Michael Moores about him as he dons a gas mask and plays banjo to mock oil giant Halliburton's contention that it puts people before profit and adheres to old-fashioned American values. Although not always an easy film to watch, this trenchant treatise combines poetic images with hard-hitting evidence that is persuasively backed up by ordinary people's shocking accounts of declining water quality and associated medical problems. DP Some swearing. *DVD*

■ *Dir/Scr* Josh Fox

Gaslight ★★★ PG

Psychological drama
1940 · UK · BW · 88min

Nowadays, most viewers will probably be more familiar with George Cukor's 1944 adaptation of Patrick Hamilton's stage success than with this British original. The Hollywood version is easily the better picture, with MGM's vision of Victorian London more atmospheric than the rough-and-ready one cobbled together here by British National. Diana Wynyard is streets behind Ingrid Bergman (who won an Oscar) as the terrorised wife, but Anton Walbrook is splendidly sinister and it is a great story. MGM bought up the prints of this to ensure that its remake had the field to itself. DP
DVD ℬ

Anton Walbrook *Paul Mallen* • Diana Wynyard *Bella Mallen* • Cathleen Cordell *Nancy* • Robert Newton *Ullswater* • Frank Pettingell *Rough* • Jimmy Hanley *Cobb* • Minnie Rayner *Elizabeth* • Mary Hinton *Lady Winterbourne* ■ *Dir* Thorold Dickinson • *Scr* AR Rawlinson, Bridget Boland, from the play *Angel Street* by Patrick Hamilton

Gaslight ★★★★ PG

Period melodrama
1944 · US · BW · 108min

Ingrid Bergman won her first best actress Oscar for her performance as the socialite slowly being driven mad by suave husband Charles Boyer. This was released in Britain as *The Murder in Thornton Square*, to avoid

confusion with the equally famous 1940 British version with Anton Walbrook and Diana Wynyard. MGM actually tried to suppress the first film when they remade it as this super glossy Bergman vehicle. It's a bit dated now, but still has much to offer, notably George Cukor's intelligent direction, production designer Cedric Gibbons's terrific Victorian setting (the interior decoration won an Oscar), and the radiant Bergman. TS *DVD*

Charles Boyer *Gregory Anton* • Ingrid Bergman *Paula Alquist* • Joseph Cotten *Brian Cameron* • Dame May Whitty *Miss Thwaites* • Angela Lansbury *Nancy Oliver* • Barbara Everest *Elizabeth Tompkins* • Eustace Wyatt *Budge* ■ *Dir* George Cukor • *Scr* John Van Druten, Walter Reisch, John L Balderston, from the play *Angel Street* by Patrick Hamilton

Gas-s-s-s, or It Became Necessary to Destroy the World in Order to Save It ★★ 18

Comedy
1970 · US · Colour · 74min

A nerve gas leak in Alaska kills everyone over 25 in this hopelessly surreal comedy from cult director Roger Corman. However, the expected Utopia doesn't materialise in a freewheeling romp that features Hell's Angels, Che Guevara, Edgar Allan Poe and Martin Luther King. Corman takes aim at too many hip targets and doesn't hit any of them successfully. After the film was heavily cut by his usual distributors, he set up his own production company, New World. AJ

Robert Corff *Coel* • Elaine Giftos *Cilla* • Bud Cort *Hooper* • Talia Coppola [Talia Shire] *Coralie* • Ben Vereen *Carlos* • Cindy Williams *Marissa* • Alex Wilson *Jason* • Lou Procopio *Marshall McLuhan* • Country Joe McDonald *FM Radio* ■ *Dir* Roger Corman • *Scr* George Armitage

The Gate ★★★ 15

Horror
1987 · US/Can · Colour · 82min

Three kids (Stephen Dorff, Christa Denton and Louis Tripp) inadvertently open the gateway to hell in their back yard and unleash a horde of demonic midgets who are making way for the arrival of the Devil himself. Although full of plot holes bigger than the one in the garden, director Tibor Takacs's low-budget trip though *Gremlins* and *Poltergeist* territory has enough verve and gall to drag it above the usual level of popcorn horror fodder despite every twist being telegraphed well in advance. AJ
DVD

Stephen Dorff *Glen* • Christa Denton *Al* • Louis Tripp *Terry* • Kelly Rowan *Lori Lee* • Jennifer Irwin *Linda Lee* • Deborah Grover *Mom* • Scot Denton *Dad* • Ingrid Veninger *Paula* • Sean Fagan *Eric* ■ *Dir* Tibor Takacs • *Scr* Michael Nankin

Gate II ★ 15

Horror
1992 · Can · Colour · 88min

Director Tibor Takacs returns, along with co-star Louis Tripp, to summon up more demonic minions in a senseless sequel to their goofily ghoulish original. This time Tripp uses his computer knowledge to escape the horror fantasy adventures incurred by the ceremony that makes his wishes come true in warped ways. Dull and unimaginative. AJ

Louis Tripp *Terry* • Simon Reynolds *Moe* • James Villemaire *John* • Pamela Segall *Liz* • Neil Munro *Art* • James Kidnie *Mr Coleson* ■ *Dir* Tibor Takacs • *Scr* Michael Nankin

Gate of Flesh ★★★★ 18

Period drama
1964 · Jpn · Colour · 90min

Two years before his cult action thriller *Tokyo Drifter*, Japanese director Seijun Suzuki courted controversy with this near-the-knuckle drama, set at the end of the Second World War. Entirely business minded, a group of Tokyo prostitutes govern themselves by strict rules. These regulations have stark consequences for Yumiko Nogawa when she falls in love with a thief who hides out in the women's home. The naked beatings add a sheen of edgy exploitation, but it's the dark reality of postwar life, not the titillation, that is

Suzuki's masterstroke. SF Japanese +subtitles. Violence, swearing, sex scenes. *DVD*

Yumiko Nogawa *Maya* • Jo Shishido *Shintaro Ibuki* • Kayo Matsuo *Omino* • Misako Tominaga *Machiko* ■ *Dir* Seijun Suzuki • *Scr* Goro Tanada, from a novel by Taijiro Tamura

Gate of Hell ★★★★★ PG

Period drama
1953 · Jpn · Colour · 88min

Winner of an Oscar for best costume and an honorary statuette, as well as the Grand Prix (now Palme d'Or) at Cannes, this is one of the most sumptuously coloured films ever made. Shooting in Eastmancolor and employing the theories of "synaesthesia" learned from Sergei Eisenstein, director Teinosuke Kinugasa lovingly sculpts each image, whether it's from a battle or the doomed courtship of Machiko Kyo by heroic samurai Kazuo Hasegawa. Amid such physical beauty, it's too easy to forget the majesty of the performances, particularly Kyo's proud wife, who refuses to submit to either the lust of her suitor or the conventions of her time. DP Japanese +subtitles. *DVD* ℬ

Machiko Kyo *Lady Kesa* • Kazuo Hasegawa *Moritoh* • Isao Yamagata *Wataru* • Koreya Senda *Kiyomori* • Yataro Kurokawa *Shigemori* • Kikue Mohri *Sawa* • Kotaro Bando *Rokuroh* • Jun Tazaki *Kogenta* ■ *Dir* Teinosuke Kinugasa • *Scr* Teinosuke Kinugasa, from the play *Jigokumon* by Kan Kikuchi

The Gatekeepers ★★★★★ 15

Documentary
2012 · Is/Fr/Ger/Bel · Colour and BW · 97min

In director Dror Moreh's engrossing documentary, six former directors of Israel's internal security service, the Shin Bet, offer an inside view on the challenges of countering violent unrest within the country around the Six Day War in 1967. Because the Shin Bet works in secrecy – with only their chief's identity known to the public – this is quite a coup for Moreh, and he also makes expert use of the news archives to provide the context. It's an important and often disarming contribution to the Arab-Israeli debate that shakes up received opinion on every side of the conflict. TJ English, Hebrew +subtitles. *DVD*

■ *Dir* Dror Moreh

Gates of Paris ★★★ U

Drama
1957 · Fr/It · BW · 100min

René Clair's last film before his New Wave denunciation is unexpectedly serious and grossly underrated. Yet his return to poetic realism is only partially successful. Léon Barsacq's claustrophobic interiors are derivative to the point of cliché, while the *ménage à trois* of dipsomanic drifter Pierre Brasseur, his girlfriend Dany Carrel and fugitive killer Henri Vidal can only end in tragedy. However, there are flashes of the old inspiration, with troubadour Georges Brassens acting as a roving commentator on the action. DP French +subtitles.

Pierre Brasseur *Juju* • Georges Brassens *L'Artiste* • Henri Vidal *Pierre Barbier* • Dany Carrel *Maria* • Raymond Bussières *Alphonse* • Amédée *Paolo* ■ *Dir* René Clair • *Scr* René Clair, Jean Aurel, from the novel *La Grande Ceinture* by René Fallet

The Gathering ★★ 15

Supernatural mystery thriller
2002 · UK · Colour · 86min

Are terrifying strangers, as depicted in a recently unearthed 1st-century church mural, really following her? Or are these frightening visions just the result of a concussion received in a car crash? That's what American tourist Christina Ricci must work out in this supernatural mystery thriller. While it's initially creepy on a thought-provoking level, the chills are lacklustre and the lethargic scares very minor indeed. AJ Violence, swearing

Christina Ricci *Cassie Grant* • Ioan Gruffudd *Dan Blakeley* • Stephen Dillane *Simon Kirkman* • Kerry Fox *Marion Kirkman* • Simon Russell Beale *Luke Fraser* • Robert Hardy *The Bishop* ■ *Dir* Brian Gilbert • *Scr* Anthony Horowitz

Gator ★★★ 15

Action thriller
1976 · US · Colour · 111min

Burt Reynolds resurrected Gator McKlusky, the demon driver character he created in *White Lightning*, for this good-natured action thriller, which marked his directorial debut. The moonshining ex-con is forced by federal agents to nail an old schoolfriend who's now a corrupt politician. Surprisingly good-humoured, this features unconventional performances from Jack Weston and Jerry Reed. Reynolds employs more subtlety, both in front of and behind the camera, than one would expect from such a formula endeavour. AJ *DVD*

Burt Reynolds *Gator McKlusky* • Jack Weston *Irving Greenfield* • Lauren Hutton *Aggie Maybank* • Jerry Reed *Bama McCall* • Alice Ghostley *Emmeline Cavanaugh* • Dub Taylor *Mayor Caffrey* • Mike Douglas *Governor* ■ *Dir* Burt Reynolds • *Scr* William Norton

Gattaca ★★★★ 15

Science-fiction thriller
1997 · US · Colour · 102min

Before screenplay writer Andrew Niccol stood the science-fiction genre on its head with *The Truman Show*, he had already shaken it up with this engrossing futuristic thriller (which he also directed) built around the controversial subject of genetic engineering. In this stunningly designed tale, Ethan Hawke plays the imperfect human who attempts to join a space mission by illegally exchanging identities with Jude Law, a paraplegic with perfect DNA. Niccol mints a new genre vocabulary with his utterly absorbing, intelligent and suspenseful story, while Hawke, Law and Uma Thurman give accomplished performances. AJ Violence, swearing, sex scenes, nudity. *DVD*

Ethan Hawke *Jerome/Vincent* • Uma Thurman *Irene* • Jude Law *Eugene/Jerome* • Gore Vidal *Director Josef* • Xander Berkeley *Lamar* • Elias Koteas *Antonio* • Ernest Borgnine *Caesar* • Alan Arkin *Detective Hugo* • Loren Dean *Anton* ■ *Dir/Scr* Andrew Niccol

The Gaucho ★★★

Silent swashbuckling drama
1927 · US · BW and Colour · 96min

The last but one of Douglas Fairbanks's silent swashbucklers is a virtual rehash of his two *Zorro* films and was based on a story by Fairbanks, using his customary pseudonym of Elton Thomas. Set in South America, it gives Fairbanks the chance to demonstrate his athletic skills while saving the peasants from exploitation. Fairbanks's wife, Mary Pickford, makes a brief appearance as Our Lady of the Shrine. AT

Douglas Fairbanks *The Gaucho* • Lupe Velez *The Mountain Girl* • Geraine Greear *Girl of the Shrine* • Eve Southern *Girl of the Shrine, as a child* • Gustav von Seyffertitz *Ruiz, the Usurper* • Mary Pickford *Our Lady of the Shrine* ■ *Dir* F Richard Jones • *Scr* Lotta Woods, from a story by Douglas Fairbanks [Elton Thomas]

The Gaunt Stranger ★★★ PG

Thriller
1938 · UK · BW · 71min

Adapted by Sidney Gilliat from a thriller by Edgar Wallace, this was the first film that Michael Balcon produced at Ealing Studios. It's as much a police procedural as a whodunnit, as DI Patrick Barr, Inspector John Longden and surgeon Alexander Knox strive to protect crooked lawyer Wilfred Lawson, who has received a note warning him he has 48 hours to live. It's not too difficult to pinpoint the culprit, but this is still moodily shot and satisfyingly tense. DP *DVD*

Sonnie Hale *Samuel Cuthbert "Sam" Hackett* • Wilfrid Lawson *Maurice Meister* • Louise Henry *Cora Ann Milton* • Alexander Knox *Dr Lomond* • Patrick Barr *Det Insp Alan Wembury* ■ *Dir* Walter Forde • *Scr* Sidney Gilliat, from the play *The Ringer* by Edgar Wallace

The Gauntlet ★★★ 18

Action crime drama
1977 · US · Colour · 104min

Clint Eastwood stars in this effective action adventure as a discredited and dim cop escorting prostitute Sondra Locke to a trial in Phoenix, Arizona, with mobsters and corrupt officials trying to stop them. The shoot-outs prove less engaging than the couple's smart-talking infighting and, as director, Eastwood selflessly highlights his then-girlfriend Locke's acting range with understanding and precision. Well paced and compelling. AJ Violence, swearing, nudity. *DVD*

Clint Eastwood *Ben Shockley* • Sondra Locke *Gus Mally* • Pat Hingle *Josephson* • William Prince *Blakelock* • Bill McKinney *Constable* • Michael Cavanaugh *Feyderspiel* • Carole Cook *Waitress* ■ *Dir* Clint Eastwood • *Scr* Michael Butler, Dennis Shryack

Gawain and the Green Knight ★★ U

Fantasy 1973 · UK · Colour · 107min

With his first feature, *I, Monster*, Stephen Weeks reworked the Jekyll and Hyde story and this second effort takes on Arthurian legend. Murray Head has an appealing hero as Gawain, while the Green Knight – headless from the start – is played by the imposing Nigel Green, who died shortly after the film was completed. Weeks complained long and loud that the film was re-edited by the distributor and, in 1983, he had a second crack at the story as *Sword of the Valiant*. AT

Murray Head *Gawain* • Nigel Green *Green Knight* • Ciaran Madden *Linet* • Robert Hardy *Sir Bertilak* • David Leland *Humphrey* • Anthony Sharp *King* • Ronald Lacey *Oswald* • Murray Melvin *Seneschal* ■ *Dir* Stephen Weeks • *Scr* Stephen Weeks, Philip Breen

The Gay Adventure ★★

Portmanteau drama 1949 · UK · BW · 74min

This rather insipid portmanteau picture, made in 1949 but held up for four years, follows three men travelling from France to London. They are an "ooh-la-la" Frenchman (Jean-Pierre Aumont), an "oh I say" Englishman (Richard Murdoch) and a "gee whizz" American (Burgess Meredith). They each fantasise differently about the same blonde they see on the train. RB

Burgess Meredith *Dick* • Jean-Pierre Aumont *Andre Marchand* • Paula Valenska *Suzy/Sonia/Hedy* • Kathleen Harrison *Isobel* • Richard Murdoch *David Felton* • Julian D'Albie *Waterhouse* • Jose de Almeyda *Jones* ■ *Dir* Gordon Parry • *Scr* Paul Darcy, Sid Colin, Anatole de Grunwald

The Gay Bride ★★

Comedy crime drama 1934 · US · BW · 80min

The sublime Carole Lombard is wasted in this mishmash of crime melodrama and comedy. She marries gangster Nat Pendleton solely for his money and in anticipation of his early death. He duly gets himself killed and she moves on to another sucker. The supporting cast includes ZaSu Pitts, and the script promises much, but it runs out of steam far too soon. RK

Carole Lombard *Mary* • Chester Morris *Office boy* • ZaSu Pitts *Mirabelle* • Leo Carrillo *Mickey* • Nat Pendleton *Shoots Magiz* • Sam Hardy *Dingle* • Walter Walker *MacPherson* • Joe Twerp *Lafcadio* ■ *Dir* Jack Conway • *Scr* Bella Spewack, Sam Spewack, from the story *Repeal* by Charles Francis Coe

The Gay Caballero ★★ U

Western 1940 · US · BW · 57min

This is Cesar Romero's third outing as the ever so slightly camp cowboy the Cisco Kid, a role that suited the gay Romero perfectly. Running at less than an hour, it tells of Romero and his sidekick Chris-Pin Martin arriving in town and discovering that the Kid is presumed dead. While the plot about land rights seems hard-pressed to fill the time, this does offer B-movie thrills and a good villainess in Janet Beecher. AT

Cesar Romero *Cisco Kid* • Sheila Ryan *Susan Wetherby* • Robert Sterling *Billy Brewster* • Chris-Pin Martin *Gordito* • Janet Beecher *Kate Brewster* • Edmund MacDonald *Joe Turner* • Jacqueline Dalya *Carmelita* • Montague Shaw [C Montague Shaw] *George Wetherby* ■ *Dir* Otto Brower • *Scr* Albert Duffy, John Larkin, from a story by Walter Bullock, Albert Duffy, from characters by O Henry

The Gay Deception ★★★ U

Romantic comedy 1935 · US · BW · 77min

This gained an Academy Award nomination for best original story but it now seems routine. Francis Lederer is the prince working incognito as a bellboy in a New York hotel, and Frances Dee is the lottery winner who checks in to inject some luxury into her life. William Wyler's smooth direction, some clever comic details and spirited supporting work overcome the weak casting of the leads. AE

Francis Lederer *Sandro* • Frances Dee *Mirabel* • Benita Hume *Miss Channing* • Alan Mowbray *Lord Clewe* • Akim Tamiroff *Spellek* • Lennox Pawle *Consul General* • Adele St Maur *Lucille* • Luis Alberni *Ernest* ■ *Dir* William Wyler • *Scr* Stephen Morehouse Avery, Don Hartman

The Gay Diplomat ★★ U

Spy drama 1931 · US · BW · 66min

Aware he had a flop on his hands, RKO producer Pandro S Berman was amazed when test screening reports compared leading man Ivan Lebedeff to Rudolph Valentino. It was later discovered that the Russian had submitted some stolen preview cards. His career duly stalled and it's easy to see why, as he struggles with a thick accent and a stiff demeanour throughout this otherwise lively Great War melodrama. Sent to Bucharest to root out a female spy, Lebedeff encounters suspects Genevieve Tobin, Betty Compson and Ilka Chase at a ball held in his honour. DP

Genevieve Tobin *Countess Diana Dorchy* • Betty Compson *Baroness Alma Corri* • Ivan Lebedeff *Captain Ivan Orloff* • Ilka Chase *Madame Blinis* ■ *Dir* Richard Boleslavsky [Richard Boleslawski] • *Scr* Doris Anderson, Alfred Jackson, from a story by Benn W Levy • *Music* Max Steiner

The Gay Divorce ★★★★ U

Musical comedy 1934 · US · BW · 104min

Hollywood censorship refused to acknowledge that a divorce could possibly be gay, in the old-fashioned sense of the word, and retitled the film *The Gay Divorcee*. Here in Britain, the title reverted back to that of the original stage show. This knockout movie pairs Fred Astaire and perky Ginger Rogers in the leading roles for the first time – and how they shine. The plot's froth, but the sets (including a very deco Brighton) are ingenious, the score superb and the supporting cast witty and well chosen. A delight all round. TS *DVD*

Fred Astaire *Guy Holden* • Ginger Rogers *Mimi* • Alice Brady *Aunt Hortense* • Edward Everett Horton *Egbert* • Erik Rhodes *Rodolfo Tonetti* • Eric Blore *Waiter* • Betty Grable *Hotel guest* ■ *Dir* Mark Sandrich • *Scr* George Marion Jr, Dorothy Yost, Edward Kaufman, from the musical by Dwight Taylor, Cole Porter

The Gay Falcon ★★★

Detective mystery 1941 · US · BW · 66min

George Sanders takes on the role of writer Michael Arlen's debonair detective and ladies' man, Gay Lawrence (aka the Falcon) in this fast-moving mystery that delighted audiences and spawned 15 sequels over the next eight years, beginning with *A Date with the Falcon*. Cruising through a case involving jewel thieves and an insurance scam, Sanders revels in having Wendy Barrie and Anne Hunter squabble over him. DP *DVD*

George Sanders *Gay Lawrence/The Falcon* • Wendy Barrie *Helen Reed* • Allen Jenkins *Goldy* • Anne Hunter *Elinor* • Gladys Cooper *Maxine* • Edward Brophy *Bates* • Arthur Shields *Waldeck* • Damian O'Flynn *Weber* ■ *Dir* Irving Reis • *Scr* Lynn Root, Frank Fenton, from the character created by Michael Arlen

Gay Purr-ee ★★★ U

Animated musical adventure 1962 · US · Colour · 84min

This sophisticated and witty cartoon reunited Judy Garland with the composers from *The Wizard of Oz*, Harold Arlen and EY "Yip" Harburg. Mewsette the cat (voiced by Garland) leaves her country home seeking excitement in the big city (Paris) and soon runs into trouble. Adults will enjoy spotting the Impressionist landscapes used in some

scenes. The kids may prefer that later feline adventure, Disney's *The Aristocats*, which was probably influenced by this film's character and style. TS

Judy Garland *Mewsette* • Hermione Gingold *Mme Rubens-Chatte* • Robert Goulet *Jaune-Tom* • Red Buttons *Robespierre* • Paul Frees *Meowrice* ■ *Dir* Abe Levitow • *Scr* Chuck Jones, Dorothy Jones, Ralph Wright

The Gay Sisters ★★★

Drama 1942 · US · BW · 109min

This melodrama is from the days when gay meant, well, gay. The title is ironic as Barbara Stanwyck, Geraldine Fitzgerald and Nancy Coleman are the conniving titular trio, bent on deviously securing an inheritance through Stanwyck secretly marrying sturdy George Brent. A supporting actor called Byron Barr played a character named Gig Young in this, and subsequently changed his professional name to that of his character. TS

Barbara Stanwyck *Fiona Gaylord* • George Brent *Charles Barclay* • Geraldine Fitzgerald *Evelyn Gaylord* • Donald Crisp *Ralph Pedloch* • Byron Barr [Gig Young] *Gig Young* • Nancy Coleman *Susanna Gaylord* • Gene Lockhart *Herschell Gibbon* • Larry Simms *Austin* ■ *Dir* Irving Rapper • *Scr* Lenore Coffee, from the novel by Stephen Longstreet

The Gazebo ★★★

Black comedy 1959 · US · BW · 101min

Glenn Ford is the nervous television writer being blackmailed over compromising photographs of his wife Debbie Reynolds. And there's a small summerhouse in the grounds of a country estate under which there may or may not be a dead body. The two stars are close to their box-office prime here, and both are enchanting, but they're nearly acted off the screen by character performers John McGiver and Doro Merande. TS

Glenn Ford *Elliott Nash* • Debbie Reynolds *Nell Nash* • Carl Reiner *Harlow Edison* • John McGiver *Sam Thorpe* • Mabel Albertson *Mrs Chandler* • Martin Landau *The Duke* • Doro Merande *Matilda* • Bert Freed *Lieut Joe Jenkins* • ZaSu Pitts *Mrs MacGruder* ■ *Dir* George Marshall • *Scr* George Wells, from a play by Alec Coppel, from a story by Myra Coppel, Alec Coppel

Gazon Maudit ★★★ 18

Comedy 1995 · Fr · Colour · 102min

Josiane Balasko wrote, directed and stars in this well-meaning but uneven French sex comedy. She plays a woman whose car breaks down near the home of Victoria Abril and her philandering husband Alain Chabat. Abril invites Balasko in, and it's not long before the two women are expressing their mutual appreciation of each other, much to the anger of Chabat. All three leads play their roles with farcical verve, but they are let down by Balasko's script. Sexy and amusing this is, but hilarious and original it is not. JB French +subtitles.

Victoria Abril *Loli* • Josiane Balasko *Marijo* • Alain Chabat *Laurent* • Ticky Holgado *Antoine* • Miguel Bose *Diego* • Catherine Hiegel *Dany* • Catherine Samie *Prostitute* • Catherine Lachens *Sopha* • Michèle Bernier *Solange* ■ *Dir/Scr* Josiane Balasko

The Geisha Boy ★★★ U

Comedy 1958 · US · Colour · 88min

Jerry Lewis's frantic, jerk-around comedy style here got its most suitable director, who saw him simply as a cartoon with no connection to real life. That's because Frank Tashlin used to be a cartoonist himself, so the sight gags are often hilarious. The comedy works less well when third-rate magician Lewis joins an army tour of Japan and gets lumbered with a kid. Yet even when the twee flies thick and fast, there's some fun to be had. TH *DVD*

Jerry Lewis *Gilbert Wooley* • Marie McDonald *Lola Livingston* • Robert Kazuyoshi Hirano *Mitsuo Watanabe* • Nobu Atsumi McCarthy [Nobu McCarthy] *Kimi Sikita* • Sessue Hayakawa *Mr Sikita* • Barton MacLane *Major Ridgley* • Suzanne Pleshette *Betty Pearson* • Ryuzo Demura *Ichiyama* ■ *Dir* Frank Tashlin • *Scr* Frank Tashlin, from a story by Rudy Makoul

Gemma Bovery ★★★ 15

Drama 2014 · Fr/UK · Colour · 95min

Gemma Arterton and Jason Flemyng relocate to Normandy, where they meet a breadmaker who thinks Arterton shares a number of similarities with Madame Bovary, the heroine of his favourite novel. He starts to worry that she will suffer the same fate as her tragic counterpart. Arterton is as good as she's ever been, while Fabrice Luchini offers some terrific facial expressions as her fretful neighbour. The film itself isn't particularly funny or dramatic, but it's still engaging. SC French, English +subtitles. *DVD* *BD*

Gemma Arterton *Gemma Bovery* • Fabrice Luchini *Martin Joubert* • Jason Flemyng *Charlie Bovery* • Isabelle Candelier *Valérie* ■ *Dir* Anne Fontaine • *Scr* Anne Fontaine, Pascal Bonitzer, from Posy Simmonds's graphic novel

The Gendarme of St Tropez ★★ U

Comedy 1964 · Fr/It · Colour · 94min

This was the first of six frantic farces starring Louis De Funès as the blustering Sergeant Ludovic Cruchot. French critics detested the series – *The Gendarme in New York*, *How to Get Married*, *How to Be an Honest Cop*, *The Spacemen of St Tropez* and *The Gendarme Wore Skirts* followed – though they initially proved hugely popular with the public. There's the vaguest hint of Clouseau in this first misadventure, as De Funès launches a crusade against the local nudists. However, much of the action is taken up with the apprehension of a gang of art thieves, thanks more to Cruchot's daughter (Geneviève Grad) than the efforts of his own Keystone-style cops. DP French dubbed.

Louis De Funès *Sergeant Ludovic Cruchot* • Geneviève Grad *Nicole Cruchot* • Michel Galabru *Gerber* • Jean Lefebvre *Fougasse* • Christian Marin *Merlot* • Daniel Cauchy *Richard* • Jean-Paul Bertrand *Eddie* • Frank Vilcour *Jean-Luc* ■ *Dir* Jean Girault • *Scr* Richard Balducci, Jacques Vilfrid, Jean Girault, from the story by Richard Balducci

The Gene Krupa Story ★★★

Musical biography 1959 · US · BW · 101min

This biopic, alternatively called *Drum Crazy*, tells the story of Krupa (Sal Mineo), the greatest jazz percussionist of his time, who was convicted on a drugs charge and then found that success drained away in the aftermath of the scandal. It's a whitewash job as far as it can be, but the jazz soundtrack is more than adequate. TH

Sal Mineo *Gene Krupa* • Susan Kohner *Ethel Maguire* • James Darren *Eddie Sirota* • Susan Oliver *Dorissa Dinell* • Yvonne Craig *Gloria Corregio* • Lawrence Dobkin *Speaker Willis* • Celia Lovsky *Mother* • Red Nichols ■ *Dir* Don Weis • *Scr* Orin Jannings

Généalogies d'un Crime ★★★

Mystery thriller 1997 · Fr/Por · Colour · 113min

Exploring the essence of evil and positing predestination against conditioning, this is the ultimate cinematic riddle wrapped in a mystery inside an enigma. An intelligent film-maker with a healthy disregard for highbrow posturing, Raúl Ruiz approaches Hitchcock via Buñuel in this gnawingly complex thriller, in which flashbacks jostle with theoretical debates, as lawyer Catherine Deneuve seeks to establish whether Melvil Poupaud is a natural-born killer or was programmed by his eccentric psychologist aunt (also Deneuve) and her sinister mentor, Michel Piccoli. DP French +subtitles.

Catherine Deneuve *Jeanne/Solange* • Michel Piccoli *Georges Didier* • Melvil Poupaud *René* • Andrzej Seweryn *Christian* • Bernadette Lafont *Esther* ■ *Dir* Raoul Ruiz [Raúl Ruiz] • *Scr* Pascal Bonitzer, Raoul Ruiz

G

The General ★★★★★ U
LANDMARK FILM
Buster Keaton's inventive, flawlessly timed train chase sequence is the linchpin of his silent genius

Classic silent comedy 1927 · US · BW · 73min

Buster Keaton's greatest movie is, some would argue, the finest silent screen comedy ever made. Stone-faced engineer Buster loves his vast steam locomotive, "The General", almost as much as his girlfriend (Marion Mack). When he is rejected by the Confederate Army, Mack brands him a coward and breaks off the engagement. Later, he risks all to pursue the train with her on board when it's stolen by Yankee spies. The humour ranges from the gentle to the exhilarating, while the drama of the railtrack chase has a visual beauty that puts this comedy into the category of true classic. Keaton's genius was not just in the nuts and bolts of invention, but in the creation of character. TH *DVD*

Buster Keaton *Johnnie Gray* · Marion Mack *Annabelle Lee* · Charles Smith *Her father* · Frank Barnes (1) *Her brother* · Glen Cavender *Capt Anderson, chief spy* · Jim Farley [James Farley] *Gen Thatcher* · Frank Hagney *Recruiting officer* · Frederick Vroom *Confederate general* ■ *Dir* Buster Keaton, Clyde Bruckman · *Scr* Buster Keaton, Clyde Bruckman, Al Boasberg, Charles Smith, from the novel *The Great Locomotive Chase* by William Pittinger · *Cinematographer* J Devereaux Jennings

The General ★★★★★ 15
Biographical drama 1998 · Ire/UK · BW · 118min

Brendan Gleeson gives a towering performance here as Martin Cahill, the man dubbed "Dublin's favourite gangster". This biopic looks back at Cahill's childhood and the events that led up to his murder in 1994, and shows him to be a ruthless criminal who, nevertheless, courted popular acclaim. Living on a grim Dublin estate with his beloved wife (Maria Doyle Kennedy) and her equally beloved sister (Angeline Ball) – with whom he had an affair – Cahill managed to keep one step ahead of police inspector Ned Kenny (Jon Voight). John Boorman's film is a brilliant example of storytelling and his excellent cast rises to the occasion. TH Swearing, violence. *DVD*

Brendan Gleeson *Martin Cahill* · Adrian Dunbar *Noel Curley* · Sean McGinley *Gary* · Maria Doyle Kennedy *Frances* · Angeline Ball *Tina* · Jon Voight *Inspector Ned Kenny* · Eanna MacLiam *Jimmy* · Tom Murphy *Willie Byrne* ■ *Dir* John Boorman · *Scr* John Boorman, from the nonfiction book *The General: Godfather of Crime* by Paul Williams

General Della Rovere ★★★★ 12
Second World War drama 1959 · It/Fr · BW · 133min

The winner of the Golden Lion at Venice in 1959, this film relies totally on the astonishing performance of Vittorio De Sica. In attempting to recapture the neorealist glories of *Rome, Open City*, director Roberto Rossellini overstages the authenticity and misses the naturalism that characterised the performances in his epoch-making film. So it falls to one-time matinée idol De Sica to bring some life and truth to this sentimental tale. He's a swindler who is forced by the Nazis to impersonate a murdered resistance leader. This is moving, darkly comic and inspirational. DP Italian +subtitles. *DVD*

Vittorio De Sica *Bardone/Grimaldi* · Hannes Messemer *Colonel Mueller* · Sandra Milo *Olga* · Giovanna Ralli *Valeria* · Anne Vernon *Chiara Fassio* · Vittorio Caprioli *Banchelli* · Ivo Garrani *Fabrizio* ■ *Dir* Roberto Rossellini · *Scr* Roberto Rossellini, Sergio Amidei, Indro Montanelli, from a story by Indro Montanelli

The General Died at Dawn ★★
Adventure 1936 · US · BW · 97min

The general is a Chinese warlord (a very cheesy Akim Tamiroff) and Gary Cooper is a mercenary whose plans to assist the oppressed peasants are thwarted by Madeleine Carroll robbing him on a train. There's a lot of plot here but, rather than treat it as a thick slice of hokum, with performances to match, playwright Clifford Odets, working on his first film, and director Lewis Milestone try to say great things about the human condition. T AT

Gary Cooper *O'Hara* · Madeleine Carroll *Judy Perrie* · Akim Tamiroff *General Yang* · Dudley Digges *Mr Wu* · Porter Hall *Peter Perrie* · William Frawley *Brighton* · JM Kerrigan *Leach* · Philip Ahn *Oxford* ■ *Dir* Lewis Milestone · *Scr* Clifford Odets, from a novel by Charles G Booth · *Cinematographer* Victor Milner · *Music* Werner Janssen

The General Line ★★★★ PG
Silent political drama 1929 · USSR · BW · 100min

Shot either side of his ill-received revolutionary masterpiece, *October*, this was an effort on the part of Sergei Eisenstein to return to official favour by enthusiastically promoting the Kremlin's policy of collectivisation. However, the experiments in tonal montage, which characterise Eisenstein's last silent feature, met with disapproval and he elected to go on a prolonged sabbatical. The film recalls the rural poetry of Dovzhenko's *Earth*, while Marfa Lapkina's weatherworn face triumphantly proclaims the effectiveness of the casting principle of typage. DP

Marfa Lapkina *Marfa* · M Ivanin *Marfa's son* · Vasia Buzenkov *A komsomol, manager of dairy co* · Nejnikov *Mitrochkin, teacher* · Chukamariev *Kulak, peasant proprietor* · Kostia Vasiliev *Tractor driver* ■ *Dir/Scr* Sergei Eisenstein, Grigori V Aleksandrov

The General's Daughter ★★★ 18
Mystery thriller 1999 · US/Ger · Colour · 111min

This moderately absorbing military whodunnit is let down by the lazy hamming of star John Travolta. He plays an armed forces cop called in to investigate the horrific rape and murder of a woman officer (Leslie Stefanson), who also happens to be the daughter of heavyweight military man James Cromwell. James Woods effortlessly steals the show as one of the murder suspects. JF Violence, swearing, nudity.

John Travolta *Paul Brenner* · Madeleine Stowe *Sarah Sunhill* · James Cromwell *General Campbell* · Timothy Hutton *Colonel Kent* · Leslie Stefanson *Elisabeth Campbell* · Daniel Von Bargen *Chief Yardley* · Clarence Williams III *Colonel Fowler* · James Woods *Colonel Moore* ■ *Dir* Simon West · *Scr* Christopher Bertolini, William Goldman, from the novel by Nelson DeMille

A Generation ★★★★ 12
Second World War drama 1954 · Pol · BW · 83min

Director Andrzej Wajda made his debut with this solemn tale of love, patriotism and party unity that opened the war trilogy completed by *Kanal* and *Ashes and Diamonds*. This is a naive picture, but such is Wajda's commitment and his pictorial sense that we are carried along with the story of Tadeusz Lomnicki, the young woodworker whose passion for Urszula Modrzynska leads to his involvement with the resistance, the Warsaw ghetto and the communist agenda. Bursting with potential, the film also launched the acting careers of Roman Polanski and Zbigniew Cybulski. DP Polish +subtitles.

Tadeusz Lomnicki *Stach* · Urszula Modrzynska *Dorota* · Janusz Paluszkiewicz *Sekula* · Ryszard Kotas *Jacek* · Roman Polanski *Mundek* · Zbigniew Cybulski *Kostek* ■ *Dir* Andrzej Wajda · *Scr* Bohdan Czeszko

Generation ★★
Comedy 1969 · US · Colour · 90min

This generation-gap comedy, which betrays its Broadway origins, is not one of the high points of David Janssen's career. He plays an advertising executive, about to become a grandfather, who is horrified when his determined daughter decides to opt for a home birth. JG

David Janssen *Jim Bolton* · Kim Darby *Doris Bolton Owen* · Carl Reiner *Stan Herman* · Pete Duel *Walter Owen* · Andrew Prine *Winn Garand* · James Coco *Mr Blatto* · Sam Waterston *Desmond* · David Lewis (1) *Arlington* ■ *Dir* George Schaefer · *Scr* William Goodhart, from his play

Generation Gap ★★
Drama 2008 · US · Colour · 102min

In a gentle tale of tolerance, forgiveness and respect, Alex Black plays a troubled teen who's sent to spend a summer with his Second World War veteran grandfather (a dependable Ed Asner) after being suspended from school. Naturally, mutual antagonism follows, only to be resolved almost as quickly as it arises. But while simplistic solutions and a flimsy storyline make events frequently contrived, the universally solid performances, particularly from the older cast members, make up for even the most sugary scene. SF

Ed Asner [Edward Asner] *Bart Cahill* · Alex Black *Dylan Statlan* · Rue McClanahan *Kay* · Catherine Mary Stewart *Veronica Statlan* · Jack Conley *Johnny* · Ralph Waite *Chick* ■ *Dir* Bill L Norton · *Scr* Raymond Starmann, Sean King

Genevieve ★★★★ U
Comedy 1953 · UK · Colour · 82min

Mocking many of the character traits that supposedly made this nation great, this beloved comedy is one of the most British of British films. The good-natured round of confrontations and calamities that befall John Gregson, Dinah Sheridan, Kenneth More and Kay Kendall are familiar to generations of movie-goers and, even though each disaster is more predictable than the last, there is pleasure to be had in observing the reactions of the childish, overzealous chauvinists and their teasing, long-suffering partners. The soundtrack by harmonica maestro Larry Adler is unforgettable. DP *DVD*

Kenneth More *Ambrose Claverhouse* · John Gregson *Alan McKim* · Dinah Sheridan *Wendy McKim* · Kay Kendall *Rosalind Peters* · Geoffrey Keen *First traffic policeman* · Harold Siddons *Second traffic policeman* · Reginald Beckwith *JC Callahan* · Joyce Grenfell *Hotel proprietress* ■ *Dir* Henry Cornelius · *Scr* William Rose · *Music* Larry Adler

Genius ★★
Biographical drama 2015 · US · Colour · 104min

The stories of great writers seldom make great cinema, and *Genius* is no exception – partly since it also seeks to tell the story of one of literature's greatest editors. Played by Colin Firth, Max Perkins is a mild-mannered family man whose red pen has sharpened the prose of Ernest Hemingway and F Scott Fitzgerald. Into his orbit comes potentially the most talented of the lot: Thomas Wolfe (Jude Law). Law and Firth spark well as odd-duck buddies, and theatre director Michael Grandage brings a light touch to proceedings. DW

Guy Pearce *F Scott Fitzgerald* · Dominic West *Ernest Hemingway* · Colin Firth *Max Perkins* · Jude Law *Thomas Wolfe* · Nicole Kidman *Aline Bernstein* · Laura Linney *Louise Saunders* ■ *Dir* Michael Grandage · *Scr* John Logan, from the biography *Max Perkins: Editor of Genius* by A Scott Berg

Genius Within: the Inner Life of Glenn Gould ★★★ U
Documentary 2009 · Can/Swe/UK/Ger/US · Colour and BW · 111min

This exhaustive but only fitfully revealing profile of the maverick Canadian pianist draws on fascinating archive material and contemporary interviews to offer a valuable insight into Gould's legacy. Despite being a controlling and self-serving hypochondriac, he clearly commanded great loyalty from friends, lovers and musicologists alike. But, while the focus here falls on Gould's romantic dalliances, eccentric habits and parallel career as a radio producer, the precise nature of his genius remains elusive. So while this is informative, accessible and engaging, it's also frustratingly flawed. DP *DVD* *Blu*

■ *Dir* Michèle Hozer, Peter Raymont

Genocide ★★★★ 15
Documentary 1981 · US · Colour and BW · 83min

Everything about this Oscar-winning documentary was calculated to ensure its academic expertise was delivered with maximum emotional impact. Winston Churchill's biographer, Martin Gilbert, joined Rabbi Marvin Hier among the screenwriters, while Elmer Bernstein's evocative score played behind the authoritative, but always compassionate tones of Orson Welles and Elizabeth Taylor. Director Arnold Schwartzman's use of use of interviews, public and private papers, and archive footage is exemplary. The wealth of documentary evidence he presents in this survey of anti-Semitism and the barbaric atrocities committed by the Nazis is so overwhelmingly powerful. DP

Elizabeth Taylor *Narrator* · Orson Welles *Narrator* ■ *Dir* Arnold Schwartzman · *Scr* Arnold Schwartzman, Martin Gilbert, Marvin Hier

Genova ★★★ 15
Drama 2008 · UK/Cay · Colour · 89min

Colin Firth is in pensive mood in this drama, playing a father struggling to raise two daughters after their mother's death. Joe (Firth) hopes taking a new post in Italy will give them a fresh start, until his youngest, Mary (Perla Haney-Jardine), reports seeing and speaking to mum (Hope Davis). It sounds like the premise of a bog-standard supernatural thriller, but in the hands of British director Michael Winterbottom it's actually a down-to-earth examination of the grieving process. The fact that nothing is resolved in a conventional way might be a sticking point for some, but it's sincere and Winterbottom captures Genoa in all its eerie grandeur. SP English, Italian +subtitles. Swearing. *DVD*

Colin Firth *Joe* · Catherine Keener *Barbara* · Hope Davis *Marianne* · Willa Holland *Kelly* · Perla Haney-Jardine *Mary* ■ *Dir* Michael Winterbottom · *Scr* Michael Winterbottom, Laurence Coriat

A Gentle Creature ★★★★
Psychological drama 1969 · Fr · Colour · 88min

Based on a story by his constant inspiration, Fyodor Dostoyevsky, this is Robert Bresson's first film in colour. The purity of his vision remains intact, however, as he once more employs the blend of naturalistic acting and precise, symbolic composition that established him as one of cinema's most rigorous auteurs. Dominique Sanda makes a remarkable debut as the wife whose suicide prompts a sequence of flashbacks, as her pawnbroker husband Guy Frangin seeks clues to her despair. This is more pessimistic than Bresson's earlier works, but the essential humanism is still evident. DP French +subtitles.

Dominique Sanda *The wife* · Guy Frangin *The husband* · Jane Lobre *Anna* ■ *Dir* Robert Bresson · *Scr* Robert Bresson, from the short story *A Gentle Soul* by Fyodor Dostoyevsky

The Gentle Gunman ★★★ U
Wartime drama 1952 · UK · BW · 82min

Dirk Bogarde wrote that this "wasn't a film I particularly wanted to make". Nonetheless, playing an IRA activist who wants to step up the war against the British in 1941, he still does a good job as a man tormented by doubts. There are no doubts, though, for his brother (John Mills) who sees the war against the Nazis as more important and so is put on IRA trial for his pains. This too-balanced approach to the Irish dilemma makes this thoughtful film too glib for its own good. TH *DVD*

John Mills *Terence Sullivan* · Dirk Bogarde *Matt Sullivan* · Robert Beatty *Shinto* · Elizabeth Sellars *Maureen Fagan* · Barbara Mullen *Molly Fagan* · Eddie Byrne *Flynn* · Joseph Tomelty *Dr Brannigan* · Gilbert Harding *Henry Truethorne* · James Kenney *Johnny Fagan* ■ *Dir* Basil Dearden, Michael Relph · *Scr* Roger MacDougall, from his play

The Gentle Rain ★★
Romantic drama 1966 · US/Bra · Colour · 110min

In Rio de Janeiro, a neurotic American girl falls for a man who has lost his power of speech following a traumatic accident. What should have been a tender tale about the problems of speaking and non-speaking people relating to each other becomes a routine melodrama. Christopher George and Lynda Day do their best with less than credible material and the somewhat contrived ending. JG

Christopher George *Bill Patterson* • Lynda Day [Lynda Day George] *Judy Reynolds* • Fay Spain *Nancy Masters* • Maria Helena Dias *Gloria* • Lon Clark *Harry Masters* • Barbara Williams (1) *Girl friend* • Robert Assumpaco *Hotel manager* ■ *Dir* Burt Balaban • *Scr* Robert Cream

The Gentle Sex ★★★ U
Second World War drama
1943 · UK · BW · 88min

Viewed today, this drama seems patronising in its depiction of the contribution made to the war effort by seven socially diverse women, who volunteer for service on the same day. Yet it served its purpose both as a morale booster and as a recruitment advertisement, thanks to some astute appeals to the patriotic spirit and some spunky acting by a top-notch cast. A week after the film was released, its co-director Leslie Howard was killed when his plane was shot down while he was on a secret mission to Portugal. DP

Joan Gates *Gwen* • Jean Gillie *Good Time Dot* • Joan Greenwood *Betty* • Joyce Howard *Ann Lawrence* • Rosamund John *Maggie Fraser* • Lilli Palmer *Erna* • Barbara Waring *Joan* • John Justin *David Sheridan* ■ *Dir* Leslie Howard, Maurice Elvey • *Scr* Moie Charles, Aimee Stuart, Roland Pertwee, Phyllis Rose, from a story by Moie Charles

The Gentle Trap ★
Thriller 1960 · UK · BW · 61min

This utterly threadbare British B-movie is about an apprentice locksmith who goes on the run from the police and local gangsters. It was made by the low-budget production company Butcher's, and everyone involved made a hash of it. Only devoted fans of its leading actor Spencer Teakle and actress Felicity Young, who plays a rather feeble *femme fatale*, will bother to watch. AT

Spencer Teakle *Johnny Ryan* • Felicity Young *Jean* • Dorinda Stevens *Mary* • Martin Benson *Ricky Barnes* • Dawn Brooks *Sylvia* • Arthur Hewlett *Sam* • Alan Edwards *Al Jenkins* • Hugh Latimer *Vic Carter* ■ *Dir* Charles Saunders • *Scr* Brock Williams, Alan Osborne, from the story by Guido Coen

A Gentleman at Heart ★★ U
Comedy 1942 · US · BW · 66min

Cesar Romero is given a rare chance to play the lead and he clearly enjoys himself in this slight comedy about shady dealings in the art world. As the bookie who discovers sculptors aren't the only chisellers where fine art is concerned, Romero more than holds his own against such notorious scene-stealers as Milton Berle. J Carrol Naish is also in fine fettle as a forger dashing off old masters to order, but Carole Landis is slightly miscast as the gallery manager whom Romero romances. DP

Cesar Romero *Tony Miller* • Carole Landis *Helen Mason* • Milton Berle *Lucky Cullen* • J Carrol Naish *Gigi* • Richard Derr *Stewart Haines* • Rose Hobart *Claire Barrington* • Jerome Cowan *Finchley* • Elisha Cook Jr *Genius* ■ *Dir* Ray McCarey • *Scr* Lee Loeb, Harold Buchman, from the story *Masterpiece* by Paul Hervey

Gentleman Jim ★★★ U
Biographical drama 1942 · US · BW · 100min

Errol Flynn stars as James J Corbett, the bank clerk who went on to become the first official heavyweight champion of the world. While Flynn regarded this performance as one of his best, there is disagreement as to whether the film's portrayal of a brash extrovert is a true reflection of Corbett's personality. Despite claiming to be based on his autobiography, the movie is somewhat

fictionalised, although the actual fights are re-created with some care and it's pacily directed by action maestro Raoul Walsh. AT

Errol Flynn *James J Corbett* • Alexis Smith *Victoria Ware* • Jack Carson *Walter Lowrie* • Alan Hale *Pat Corbett* • John Loder *Clinton DeWitt* • William Frawley *Billy Delaney* • Minor Watson *Buck Ware* • Ward Bond *John L Sullivan* ■ *Dir* Raoul Walsh • *Scr* Vincent Lawrence, Horace McCoy, from the autobiography *The Roar of the Crowd* by James J Corbett

Gentleman's Agreement ★★★★ U
Drama 1947 · US · BW · 112min

An eye-opener in its day, this exposure of high-society racial prejudice still has the power to compel. The story of magazine writer Gregory Peck, passing himself off as a Jew to reveal anti-Semitism, is not violently confrontational, but is successful in showing that the subtle malaise is barely recognised as such by the people who sustain it. Writer Moss Hart pressed all the politically correct postwar buttons, and, while it's one of Peck's finest performances, other members of the cast produced work of similarly high quality – the confused liberal Dorothy McGuire, the soured poseur Celeste Holm and the cynically bitter ex-serviceman John Garfield. TH DVD

Gregory Peck *Phil Green* • Dorothy McGuire *Kathy* • John Garfield *Dave* • Celeste Holm *Anne* • Anne Revere *Mrs Green* • June Havoc *Miss Wales* • Albert Dekker *John Minify* • Jane Wyatt *Jane* ■ *Dir* Elia Kazan • *Scr* Moss Hart, from the novel by Laura Z Hobson

Gentlemen Broncos ★★★ 12
Comedy 2009 · US · Colour · 85min

In this charming oddball comedy, awkward teenage sci-fi geek Benjamin (Michael Angarano) yearns to escape his humdrum life in small-town Utah by becoming a published novelist. When his best manuscript is plagiarised by author Dr Ronald Chevalier (*Flight of the Conchords's* Jemaine Clement), Benjamin springs into action to prove the extraterrestrial yarn is his own work. *Napoleon Dynamite* director Jared Hess once again trains his camera on misfit adolescents, mocking the obsessions of sci-fi geeks with genuine affection. Angarano is winningly naturalistic as the jittery hero, but it's Clement's pompous and self-important Chevalier who steals the picture. TeS DVD

Michael Angarano *Benjamin* • Jennifer Coolidge *Judith* • Jemaine Clement *Dr Ronald Chevalier* • Mike White *Dusty* • Hector Jimenez *Lonnie Donaho* • Sam Rockwell *Bronco/Brutus* ■ *Dir* Jared Hess • *Scr* Jared Hess, Jerusha Hess

Gentlemen Marry Brunettes ★★
Musical comedy 1955 · US · Colour · 106min

Jeanne Crain and Jane Russell, showing a lot of leg and cleavage, play dual roles as brunette showgirl sisters in Paris and their blonde mother and aunt, who were the toast of Paris in the 1920s. Despite the gorgeous costumes by Travilla and Christian Dior, the Technicolor and CinemaScope, the chic Parisian settings and some good songs, this is an uninspired feeble farrago. RB

Jane Russell *Bonnie Jones/Mimi Jones* • Jeanne Crain *Connie Jones/Mitzi Jones* • Alan Young *Charlie Biddle/Mrs Biddle/Mr Biddle Sr* • Scott Brady *David Action* • Rudy Vallee • Guy Middleton *Earl of Wickenware* • Eric Pohlmann *Monsieur Ballard* • Ferdy Mayne *Monsieur Dufond* ■ *Dir* Richard Sale • *Scr* Mary Loos, Richard Sale, from the story *But Gentlemen Marry Brunettes* by Anita Loos

Gentlemen Prefer Blondes ★★★★ U
Musical comedy 1953 · US · Colour · 87min

Marilyn Monroe's star was well into the ascendant when she portrayed writer Anita Loos's gold-digging Lorelei Lee in this scintillating 20th Century-Fox musical, directed by Howard Hawks who had a clever understanding of how to exploit Monroe's star power. Monroe particularly shines in the superbly photographed (Harry

J Wild) and choreographed (Jack Cole) production numbers. The movie opens with a scene that uses the sparkling Technicolor to best effect, as Monroe and Jane Russell announce that they're just *Two Little Girls from Little Rock*, and it simply takes off from there. The men are underused and the third act is a contrived letdown, but make no mistake – this is the movie that consolidated Monroe's stardom. TS DVD ✦

Jane Russell *Dorothy Shaw* • Marilyn Monroe *Lorelei Lee* • Charles Coburn *Sir Francis Beekman* • Elliott Reid *Ernie Malone* • Tommy Noonan *Gus Esmond* • George Winslow *Henry Spofford III* • Taylor Holmes *Gus Esmond Sr* ■ *Dir* Howard Hawks • *Scr* Charles Lederer, from the play by Anita Loos, Joseph Fields, from the novel by Anita Loos

Geordie ★★★ U
Comedy drama 1955 · UK · Colour · 95min

Scripted by those bastions of postwar British cinema, Frank Launder and Sidney Gilliat, this is a pleasing picture, but it never really develops into anything substantial. The story of a Scottish gamekeeper's son who body builds his way to the Olympics was given relevance by the 1956 Melbourne games, but, shorn of its topicality, the film is too dependent on whimsy to rank among the best British comedies. Bill Travers could do with a little more charm to add to his brawn, but Alastair Sim is on hand to pep up the humour. DP

Alastair Sim *Laird* • Bill Travers *Geordie MacTaggart* • Norah Gorsen *Jean Donaldson* • Molly Urquhart *Geordie's mother* • Francis De Wolff *Henry Samson* • Jack Radcliffe *Rev McNab* ■ *Dir* Frank Launder • *Scr* Frank Launder, Sidney Gilliat, from the novel by David Walker

George A Romero's Land of the Dead ★★★ 15
Horror 2005 · Can/US/Fr · Colour · 92min

In this fourth instalment in his *Dead* series, George A Romero shows why he remains the reigning king of the zombie flick by once again balancing crowd-pleasing gore with some neat satirical jibes at modern-day America. With the planet now overrun by the undead, the living also have to deal with the new social hierarchy created by unscrupulous tycoon Dennis Hopper. To make matters worse, it seems that at least one of the zombies is starting to think for himself, setting the scene for an epic confrontation. Followed in 2007 by *Diary of the Dead*, and *George A Romero's Survival of the Dead* in 2009. JF Violence. DVD

Simon Baker (1) *Riley* • John Leguizamo *Cholo* • Asia Argento *Slack* • Robert Joy *Charlie* • Dennis Hopper *Kaufman* • Eugene Clark *Big Daddy* • Jennifer Baxter *No 9* • Boyd Banks *Butcher* • Simon Pegg *Photo booth zombie* • Edgar Wright *Photo booth zombie* ■ *Dir/Scr* George A Romero

George A Romero's Survival of the Dead ★★★ 18
Horror 2009 · US/Can · Colour · 86min

It's not only the zombies that are showing wear and tear as director George A Romero delivers the sixth instalment of his *Dead* saga. Alan Van Sprang stars as laconic antihero Sarge (briefly seen in *Diary of the Dead*), the leader of a small group of US National Guardsmen trying to survive in a world overrun with the dead. The plot does tend to meander near the end, but Romero still knows how to produce a wry, unnerving horror that has plenty to say about the times we live in, and the methods of zombie dispatch are certainly inventive enough to satisfy avid fans of the genre. JA Violence, swearing. DVD ✦

Alan Van Sprang *Sarge* • Kenneth Welsh *Patrick O'Flynn* • Kathleen Munroe *Janet/Jane* • Devon Bostick *Boy* • Richard Fitzpatrick *Seamus Muldoon* • Athena Karkanis *Tomboy* ■ *Dir/Scr* George A Romero

George and Mildred ★ 15
Comedy 1980 · UK · Colour · 89min

Brian Murphy and Yootha Joyce were consistently funny on TV as the Ropers, first in *Man about the House* and then in

their own series *George and Mildred*. But this desperate, smutty comedy of errors is no laughing matter. Made a year after the series ended, it was a sad finale for Yootha Joyce, who died before the film was released. DP DVD

Yootha Joyce *Mildred Roper* • Brian Murphy *George Roper* • Stratford Johns *Harry Pinto* • Norman Eshley *Jeffrey Fourmile* • Sheila Fearn *Ann Fourmile* • Kenneth Cope *Harvey* • David Barry *Elvis* ■ *Dir* Peter Frazer Jones • *Scr* Dick Sharples, from the characters by Brian Cooke, Johnnie Mortimer

George Balanchine's The Nutcracker ★★ U
Ballet 1993 · US · Colour · 92min

Director Emile Ardolino's version of Tchaikovsky's popular children's ballet remains stubbornly stagebound. Shooting from the stalls, Ardolino fails to capture the energy of the dancers, while the clumsily incorporated close-ups interfere with the action. Macaulay Culkin trained at the School of American Ballet, but he doesn't do much here as the prince who guides Jessica Lynn Cohen through his toyland kingdom. Kevin Kline's narration was a late addition, intended to make the story more accessible. DP

Kevin Kline *Narrator* • Macaulay Culkin *Nutcracker Prince* • Bart Robinson Cook *Herr Drosselmeier* • Jessica Lynn Cohen *Marie* • Darci Kistler *Sugarplum Fairy* • Damian Woetzel *Cavalier* • Kyra Nichols *Dewdrop* • Wendy Whelan *Coffee* • Margaret Tracey *Marzipan* ■ *Dir* Emile Ardolino • *Scr* Susan Cooper, from the story by ETA Hoffman

George Harrison: Living in the Material World ★★★★ 12
Documentary 2011 · US · Colour · 208min

George Harrison was the "quiet" Beatle. Posthumously, and very poignantly, he finds his voice in director Martin Scorsese's painstakingly assembled cinematic love letter. The surviving Beatles, Harrison's two wives and countless friends form a respectful queue in paying tribute to Harrison. And they help build the case that his talent was never truly acknowledged while he was alive. The uplifting music provides the joyous stitching in this immaculately crafted tapestry. It's long – nudging three-and-a-half hours – but its release ten years after Harrison's death is timely and fitting. TrP Swearing. DVD ✦

George Harrison • Paul McCartney • Ringo Starr • Yoko Ono • Phil Spector • George Martin (2) *George Martin* • Eric Clapton ■ *Dir* Martin Scorsese

George in Civvy Street ★ U
Comedy 1946 · UK · BW · 76min

From 1937-43 George Formby was Britain's biggest box-office draw and most of his hits had been directed by Marcel Varnel. This sad final collaboration, in which George returns from the army to run a dilapidated pub, is dispiritingly uninspired and the songs are a poor echo of Formby's earlier hits. Formby made no more films after this, and Varnel was killed the following year in a car crash. TV DVD

George Formby *George Harper* • Rosalyn Boulter *Mary Colton* • Ronald Shiner *Fingers* • Ian Fleming *Uncle Shad* • Wally Patch *Sprout* • Philippa Hiatt *Lavender* • Enid Cruickshank *Miss Gummidge* • Mike Johnson (1) *Toby* ■ *Dir* Marcel Varnel • *Scr* Peter Fraser, Ted Kavanagh, Max Kester, Gale Pedrick, from the story by Howard Irving Young

George of the Jungle ★★★ U
Comedy adventure 1997 · US · Colour · 88min

This engagingly stupid spin on *Tarzan* packs in enough dim-witted slapstick to raise a chuckle from even the most sophisticated grown-ups. Brendan Fraser is George, who has been brought up by a group of brainy gorillas led by Ape (voiced by John Cleese). Unfortunately none of their intelligence has rubbed off on George, who has an unfortunate habit of swinging into trees. The fun slows down when he gets whisked to the States by heiress Leslie Mann. Fraser didn't return for the 2003 straight-to-video sequel. JF DVD CS

Brendan Fraser *George* • Leslie Mann *Ursula Stanhope* • Thomas Haden Church *Lyle Van de Groot* • Richard Roundtree *Kwame* • Greg Cruttwell *Max* • Holland Taylor *Beatrice Stanhope* • Kelly Miller *Besty* • John Cleese *Ape* ■ *Dir* Sam Weisman • *Scr* Dana Olsen, Audrey Wells, from a story by Dana Olsen, from the characters by Jay Ward

George Washington
★★★★ 12

Drama   2000 · US · Colour · 86min

Rarely has the eccentric seemed so everyday or the desolate felt so welcoming as in this remarkable tale of social deprivation and juvenile innocence. Basking in its widescreen lyricism, the story – about a small-town black boy who refuses to allow the fragility of his skull to interfere with his superheroic ambitions – unfolds at its own gentle pace. This allows debutant director David Gordon Green to concentrate on the performances of his non-professional cast, who deliver their part-improvised lines with a delightfully unforced sense of poetry. DP DVD

Candace Evanofski *Nasia* • Donald Holden *George Richardson* • Damian Jewan Lee *Vernon* • Curtis Cotton III *Buddy* • Rachael Handy *Sonya* ■ *Dir/Scr* David Gordon Green

George Washington Slept Here
★★ U

Comedy   1942 · US · BW · 91min

Although this is one of Jack Benny's better comedies, he's still somewhat miscast as the Manhattanite whose wife purchases a surprise new home – a house in the country in which Washington reputedly stayed. Far from idyllic, their new home lacks everything from running water to walls, and Benny naturally hates it. Too calculated and predictable to be more than superficially amusing. AE

Jack Benny *Bill Fuller* • Ann Sheridan *Connie Fuller* • Charles Coburn *Uncle Stanley* • Percy Kilbride *Mr Kimber* • Hattie McDaniel *Hester* • William Tracy *Steve Eldridge* • Joyce Reynolds *Madge* • Lee Patrick *Rena Leslie* ■ *Dir* William Keighley • *Scr* Everett Freeman, from the play by George S Kaufman, Moss Hart

George White's Scandals
★★★

Musical   1934 · US · BW · 83min

George White's annual music revues had become a Broadway fixture by the early 1930s, so it seemed a good idea to put on a film version, with the impresario taking on the roles of producer, co-director and even actor. The result is merely a hackneyed backstage musical, but it gave Alice Faye a starring role in her first picture and her alluring performance won her a contract with Fox. AE

Rudy Vallee *Jimmy Martin* • Jimmy Durante *Happy McGillicuddy* • Alice Faye *Kitty Donnelly* • Adrienne Ames *Barbara Loraine* • Gregory Ratoff *Nicholas Mitwoch* • Cliff Edwards *Stew Hart* • George White ■ *Dir* George White, Thornton Freeland, Harry Lachman • *Scr* Jack Yellen, from a story by George White

George White's 1935 Scandals
★★★ U

Musical   1935 · US · BW · 84min

Ziegfeld's biggest rival, Broadway impresario George White, directs himself in this sequel to the previous year's *George White's Scandals*. Not surprisingly, he plays a Broadway impresario discovering small-town talent Alice Faye and making her into a star. The stage acts are enjoyable enough – comedian Ned Sparks, singer Cliff Edwards and tap-dancing Eleanor Powell making her debut. TH

Alice Faye *Honey Walters* • James Dunn *Eddie Taylor* • Ned Sparks *Elmer White* • Lyda Roberti *Manya* • Cliff Edwards *Dude Holloway* • Arline Judge *Midgie Malone* • Eleanor Powell *Marilyn Collins* • Emma Dunn *Aunt Jane* ■ *Dir* George White • *Scr* Jack Yellin, Patterson McNutt, from an idea by George White

George's Island
★★ PG

Adventure   1991 · Can · Colour · 86min

This Canadian family film about a modern-day search for buried treasure is a muddled mix of pirate quest and foster-home drama. Ian Bannen is a class above everyone else, as the eccentric ex-sailor whose tales of Captain Kidd unlock his grandson's imagination. But the humour is flat and often nasty, and the story – which has more than a hint of the dark fantasies of Roald Dahl – is as entertaining as a long walk off a short plank. JC DVD

Ian Bannen *Captain Waters* • Sheila McCarthy *Cloata Birdwood* • Maury Chaykin *Mr Droonfield* • Nathaniel Moreau *George Waters* • Vicki Ridler *Bonnie* • Brian Downey *Mr Beane* • Irene Hogan *Mrs Beane* • Gary Reineke *Captain Kidd* ■ *Dir* Paul Donovan • *Scr* Paul Donovan, Maura O'Connell

Georgia
★★★ 15

Mystery thriller   1988 · Aus · Colour · 89min

Australian director Ben Lewin attempts to merge Michelangelo Antonioni's *Blowup* with Akira Kurosawa's *Rashomon* in this overambitious thriller. The opening is neat and intriguing, as a series of photographs puts tax fraud investigator Judy Davis on the track of a murderer and the different witnesses give their versions of events through fragmentary flashbacks. Davis's typically solid performance just about holds things together. DP Some violence, swearing, nudity.

Judy Davis *Nina Bailey/Georgia White* • John Bach *William Karlin* • Julia Blake *Elizabeth* • Marshall Napier *Frank LeMat* • Alex Menglet *Laszlo* • Lewis Fiander *Scarlatti* • Roy Baldwin *Librarian* • Keryn Boyer *First policewoman* ■ *Dir* Ben Lewin • *Scr* Ben Lewin, Joanna Murray-Smith, Bob Weis

Georgia
★★★

Musical drama   1995 · US/Fr · Colour · 117min

Jennifer Jason Leigh and Mare Winningham compete in acting their socks off in this interesting, performance-led film from director Ulu Grosbard. Winningham is a successful folk singer with a husband and children, while Leigh is her more destructive, erratic and unpredictable sister, who sings in clubs but remains undiscovered. Written by Leigh's mother, Barbara Turner, the film has some uncomfortable moments, but it's worth persevering with for the impressive lead performances. JB

Jennifer Jason Leigh *Sadie* • Mare Winningham *Georgia* • Ted Levine *Jake* • Max Perlich *Axel* • John Doe *Bobby* • John C Reilly *Herman* • Jimmy Witherspoon *Trucker* • Jason Carter *Chasman* ■ *Dir* Ulu Grosbard • *Scr* Barbara Turner

Georgia O'Keeffe
★★

Biographical romantic drama   2009 · US · Colour

Joan Allen impresses as one of the 20th-century's most significant female artists in this classy though insufficient biopic, chronicling the painter's tempestuous, 30-year love affair with influential American photographer Alfred Stieglitz (Jeremy Irons). Capturing the bold honesty of her fascinating character, she explores the sensual woman behind the vivid pictures of flowers and landscapes. Meanwhile, director Bob Balaban compensates for Irons's customary scenery-chewing by focusing on small, intimate moments that really emphasise the intense relationship. SF

Joan Allen *Georgia O'Keeffe* • Jeremy Irons *Alfred Stieglitz* • Ed Begley Jr *Dr Lee Stieglitz* • Kathleen Chalfant *Mrs Stieglitz* ■ *Dir* Bob Balaban • *Scr* Michael Cristofer

Georgia Rule
★★★ 15

Comedy drama   2007 · US · Colour · 107min

Lindsay Lohan's off-screen antics overshadowed the production of Garry Marshall's well-acted but uneven comedy drama. Headstrong teenager Rachel (Lohan) is banished to the home of her disciplinarian grandmother Georgia (Jane Fonda), whose many "rules" have already driven away Rachel's mum (Felicity

Huffman). Marshall's quirkily amusing portrait of small-town Idaho gives way to a much darker strain of domestic drama. There's no denying the conviction of the three central performances, with Fonda bringing dignity and humour to what could have been a caricature and Huffman typically impressive as an alcoholic, uncertain whether to trust her daughter, her husband or her mother. SS DVD

Jane Fonda *Georgia* • Lindsay Lohan *Rachel* • Felicity Huffman *Lilly* • Dermot Mulroney *Simon Ward* • Cary Elwes *Arnold* • Garrett Hedlund *Harlan* ■ *Dir* Garry Marshall • *Scr* Mark Andrus

Georgy Girl
★★★★ 12

Comedy drama   1966 · UK · BW · 94min

At the time a sexual showstopper, this can now be seen as an unconscious parody of Swinging Sixties chic. It is saved from mere shock novelty by Lynn Redgrave's performance as the dowdy girl pursued by older employer James Mason, who finds her own identity looking after the illegitimate baby of flatmate Charlotte Rampling. Former TV director Silvio Narizzano piles on the tricks of cinematic trendiness, but it's the acting that stabilises the story into something memorable from a boringly self-conscious era. TH DVD

Lynn Redgrave *Georgy* • James Mason *James Leamington* • Alan Bates *Jos* • Charlotte Rampling *Meredith* • Bill Owen *Ted* • Clare Kelly *Doris* • Denise Coffey *Peg* • Rachel Kempson *Ellen* ■ *Dir* Silvio Narizzano • *Scr* Margaret Forster, Peter Nichols, from Forster's novel

Geostorm

Science-fiction action thriller
2016 · US · Colour

This is a preview – no prints were available to review as we went to press: He led the Spartan army in *300* and saved the US president (twice) from terrorists in *Olympus Has Fallen* and *London Has Fallen*; now Gerard Butler is saving the world from a massive weather event – oh, and the president for a third time. As Butler is sent into space to disable man-made, climate-controlling satellites, a plot unfolds to assassinate Potus (here, played by Andy Garcia). Supporting Brits Abbie Cornish and Jim Sturgess will be doing their best not to be upstaged by the effects. SP 3D

Gerald Butler *Jake* • Katheryn Winnick *Olivia* • Abbie Cornish *Sarah* • Jim Sturgess *Max* • Robert Sheehan *Duncan* ■ *Dir* Dean Devlin

Geppetto
★★ U

Musical fantasy   2000 · US · Colour · 84min

This Disney TV movie adopts a pantomimic tone, combining cornball sentiment, knockabout comedy and slipshod ditties in an attempt to entertain family audiences. However, Drew Carey's performance as the woodcarver whose marionette son comes to life is eminently resistible, while his picaresque pursuit of Brent Spiner's puppet show is too episodic to involve. DP DVD

Drew Carey *Geppetto* • Seth Adkins *Pinocchio* • Julia Louis-Dreyfus *Blue Fairy* • Brent Spiner *Stromboli* • René Auberjonois *Professor Buonragazzo* • Wayne Brady *Lazardo* ■ *Dir* Tom Moore • *Scr* David Stern, from the story by Carlo Collodi

The German Sisters
★★★

Political drama   1981 · W Ger · Colour · 106min

Margarethe von Trotta based this provocative drama on the true-life experiences of Christiane and Gudrun Ensslin. It's a highly politicised film, but there is also a personal emphasis, with magazine editor Jutta Lampe being shaken from her bourgeois lethargy by the state's insistence that the Stammheim prison death of her hunger-striking terrorist sister (Barbara Sukowa) was suicide. Von Trotta examines what causes individuals to depart in such radically different directions. DP In German.

Jutta Lampe *Juliane* • Barbara Sukowa *Marianne* • Rüdiger Vogler *Wolfgang* • Doris Schade *Mother* • Vérénice Rudolph *Sabine* • Luc Bondy *Werner* • Franz Rudnick *Father* • Julia Biedermann *Marianne aged 16* • Ina Robinski *Juliane aged 17* ■ *Dir/Scr* Margarethe von Trotta

Germany, Year Zero
★★★★ PG

Drama   1947 · It/W Ger/Fr · BW · 69min

The number of studio-shot scenes in the concluding part of director Roberto Rossellini's war trilogy, which also includes *Rome, Open City* and *Paisà*, shows that he was already moving away from the neorealist style. Yet the documentary footage of a decimated Berlin is still enormously powerful. The shadow of Nazism hovers over this depiction of desperation, as 12-year-old Edmund Moeschke scavenges among the ruins to feed his family and tries to alleviate the suffering of his father. DP German +subtitles.

Edmund Moeschke *Edmund* • Franz Kruger *Edmund's father* • Barbara Hintz *Eva* • Werner Pittschau *Karlheinz* ■ *Dir* Roberto Rossellini • *Scr* Roberto Rossellini, Carlo Lizzani, Max Kolpet, from a story by Roberto Rossellini

Germinal
★★★ 15

Period drama   1993 · Fr/Bel/It · Colour · 151min

Emile Zola's grimly realistic novel did much to highlight the miseries of French miners in the 1860s. In his pursuit of authenticity for this screen version of the tale, director Claude Berri broke the then budget record for a French film. The mining village is a masterpiece of period design and Yves Angelo's photography is often breathtaking, but the scale and sheen of the production in many ways count against this dour study of exploitative capitalism and stoic (rather than heroic) labour. DP French +subtitles. Violence, sex scenes, nudity. DVD

Renaud *Etienne Lantier* • Gérard Depardieu *Maheu* • Miou-Miou *Maheude* • Jean Carmet *Bonnemort* • Judith Henry *Catherine Maheu* • Jean-Roger Milo *Chaval* • Laurent Terzieff *Souvarine* • Jean-Pierre Bisson *Rasseneur* ■ *Dir* Claude Berri • *Scr* Claude Berri, Arlette Langmann, from the novel by Emile Zola

Geronimo
★★★ PG

Western   1962 · US · Colour · 98min

Today, Chuck Connors might not seem a politically correct choice to play the famous Apache leader, but back in the 1960s this was the kind of role that consolidated the star power of the former professional baseball player. Connors looks good and acquits himself well and the landscapes – shot by Mexican cinematographer Alex Phillips – are stunning. Unfortunately, the script strays from the facts of the shameful story and fails to improve upon history. TS DVD

Chuck Connors *Geronimo* • Kamala Devi *Teela* • Ross Martin *Mangus* • Pat Conway *Maynard* • Adam West *Delahay* • Lawrence Dobkin *General Crook* • Denver Pyle *Senator Conrad* ■ *Dir* Arnold Laven • *Scr* Pat Fielder, from a story by Arnold Laven, Pat Fielder

Geronimo: an American Legend
★★★★ 12

Western   1993 · US · Colour · 110min

Many critics questioned whether Walter Hill's version of the story of the Chiricahua Apache was actually about him at all. The narration presents us with the wider picture from which to draw our conclusions. The film also caused a fuss over its depiction of the native Americans. Screenwriter John Milius and Hill present the massacres perpetrated by both sides as part of the struggle for nationhood, to be seen in the context of the times. While many will find this uncomfortable to watch, there's no denying the quality of Joe Alves's painstakingly authentic design or the lovingly re-created period feel of Lloyd Ahern's cinematography. The acting is also first rate. DP Violence, swearing. DVD

Jason Patric *Lieutenant Charles Gatewood* • Gene Hackman *Brigadier General George Crook* • Robert Duvall *Al Sieber* • Wes Studi *Geronimo* • Matt Damon *Lieutenant Britton Davis* • Rodney A Grant *Mangas* • Kevin Tighe *Brigadier General Nelson Miles* • Steve Reevis *Chato* ■ *Dir* Walter Hill • *Scr* John Milius, Larry Gross, from a story by John Milius

Gerry ★★★ 15
Drama 2001 · US · Colour · 98min

Co-written by director Gus Van Sant and joint leads Matt Damon and Casey Affleck, this follows two friends – both called Gerry – who embark on a wilderness trail only to get lost without any provisions. Unwinding at a snail's pace, with a simplistic storyline and barely any dialogue, this audacious allegory is either pretentious twaddle or a poetic masterpiece, depending on personal taste. Their predicament becomes riveting, made additionally entrancing by dreamy cinematography, breathtaking landscapes and hallucinatory cloud formations. SF Swearing. *DVD*

Casey Affleck *Gerry* • Matt Damon *Gerry* ■ *Dir* Gus Van Sant • *Scr* Casey Affleck, Matt Damon, Gus Van Sant • *Cinematographer* Harris Savides

Gert and Daisy's Weekend ★★ U
Second World War comedy
1941 · UK · BW · 79min

Elsie and Doris Waters had been radio stars for some 15 years before they made this rare sortie in front of the movie camera. Starring as the cockney tittle-tattles Gert and Daisy, they escort some East End evacuees to a country house, where the kids end up as chief suspects in a jewel robbery. The sisters usually wrote their own material and took great pains to be original. Consequently, they look distinctly unhappy with the rehashed gags on offer here. DP

Elsie Waters *Gert* • Doris Waters *Daisy* • Iris Vandeleur *Ma Butler* • John Slater *Jack Densham* • Elizabeth Hunt *Maisie Butler* • Wally Patch *Charlie Peters* • Annie Esmond *Lady Plumtree* • Aubrey Mallalieu *Barnes* • Gerald Rex *George the Terror* ■ *Dir* Maclean Rogers • *Scr* Maclean Rogers, Kathleen Butler

Gertie the Dinosaur ★★★★★
Classic silent animation 1914 · US · BW · 12min

This landmark in animation was originally designed as one half of a vaudeville routine in which its creator, celebrated newspaper cartoonist Winsor McCay, appeared in person to issue instructions to a drawn dinosaur on a screen. When the act ran its course, McCay added a live-action prologue in which he accepts a bet that he can bring a dinosaur to life, then reveals the painstaking process by which he succeeded. Often cited as the first animated film due to its tremendous impact, this wasn't even McCay's first, being preceded by two others, yet such is the credibility of its "leading lady" it can be seen as the first important work of the genre. CLP

■ *Dir/Scr* Winsor McCay

Gertrud ★★★★★ PG
Drama 1964 · Den · BW · 112min

Carl Th Dreyer was a filmic genius who never shied away from controversial themes or unconventional techniques. This film is a troubling study of a married woman (played with great passion by Nina Pens Rode) who is prepared to sacrifice all in the impossible pursuit of love. In spite of the intimacy and intensity of the action, Dreyer opted to shoot in long takes with little camera movement, in order to emphasise the power of the words and performances. Much maligned on its release, this mesmerising picture was subsequently hailed as one of Dreyer's most remarkable achievements. DP Danish +subtitles. *DVD*

Nina Pens Rode *Gertrud Kanning* • Bendt Rothe *Gustav Kanning* • Ebbe Rode *Gabriel Lidman* • Baard Owe *Erland Jansson* • Axel Strobye *Axel Nygren* • Karl Gustav Ahlefeldt • Vera Gebuhr *Kanning's maid* ■ *Dir* Carl Th Dreyer • *Scr* Carl Th Dreyer, from a play by Hjalmar Soderberg

Gervaise ★★★ 12
Drama 1956 · Fr · BW · 112min

René Clément's film is a solid version of Zola's *L'Assommoir*, which dealt with the ravages of alcoholism among the working classes of 19th-century Paris. Maria Schell is an 18-year-old washerwoman who is abandoned by the father of her two children. She then marries a roofing contractor, who turns to drink after an accident leaves him incapacitated. When Schell's first lover Armand Mestral returns, further catastrophes and humiliations ensue. Schell gives a performance that won her a prize at the Venice festival but was widely criticised as an exercise in technique, lacking in conviction. AT French +subtitles. *DVD*

Maria Schell *Gervaise* • François Périer *Henri Coupeau* • Suzy Delair *Virginie* • Mathilde Casadesus *Madame Boche* • Armand Mestral *Lantier* • Jacques Harden *Goujet* ■ *Dir* René Clément • *Scr* Jean Aurenche, Pierre Bost, from the novel *L'Assommoir* by Emile Zola

Get Back ★★★ PG
Music documentary
1991 · UK · Colour and BW · 85min

Having compiled the moving scrapbook that was shown on giant screens before each concert, Richard Lester was the natural choice for this rockumentary account of Paul McCartney's 1990 world tour. Valiantly attempting to update the busy visual style he pioneered on *A Hard Day's Night*, he slightly overdoes the trickery and spends a tad too long behind the scenes. However, his coverage of the gigs is exemplary, with Macca and his superb band rattling through Beatles anthems and solo favourites with genuine pleasure. DP

Paul McCartney • Linda McCartney ■ *Dir* Richard Lester

Get Carter ★★★★ 18
Crime thriller 1971 · UK · Colour · 106min

This terrific, tough British thriller hides its story of raw revenge behind some fascinating Newcastle upon Tyne locations, courtesy of cinematographer Wolfgang Suschitzky, and its impact remains undiminished. Michael Caine is at his most impassively impressive as the London gangster who goes north after his brother is murdered and finds his teenage niece involved in a blue-film racket. Playwright John Osborne, appearing here as a North East crime boss, has a razor-slash presence, while director Mike Hodges keeps a firm hand on the proceedings. TH *DVD* *BD*

Michael Caine *Jack Carter* • John Osborne *Cyril Kinnear* • Ian Hendry *Eric Paice* • Britt Ekland *Anna Fletcher* • Bryan Mosley *Cliff Brumby* • Geraldine Moffat *Glenda* • Dorothy White *Margaret* • Alun Armstrong *Keith* ■ *Dir* Mike Hodges • *Scr* Mike Hodges, from the novel *Jack's Return Home* by Ted Lewis

Get Carter ★★ 15
Crime thriller 2000 · US · Colour · 98min

An ill-advised remake of the Newcastle classic, with a moody Sylvester Stallone taking over the vengeful Carter role and the action relocated to America. Yet, this has few similarities to the outstanding original, replacing gritty direction with flashy surface gloss, Michael Caine's unremitting viciousness with Stallone's soft-centred bruiser, and Roy Budd's haunting score with a noisy rock remix. JC *DVD*

Sylvester Stallone *Jack Carter* • Miranda Richardson *Gloria Carter* • Rachael Leigh Cook *Doreen Carter* • Mickey Rourke *Cyrus Paice* • Michael Caine *Cliff Brumby* • Alan Cumming *Jeremy Kinnear* • Rhona Mitra *Geraldine* • Gretchen Mol *Audrey* ■ *Dir* Stephen Kay • *Scr* David McKenna, from the novel *Jack's Return Home* by Ted Lewis

Get Crazy ★★★ 18
Musical comedy spoof
1983 · US · Colour · 88min

A long-time employee of the legendary music venue Fillmore East in New York, director Allan Arkush was the right man for this rock-flavoured satire. A spoof comedy, in which a New Year's Eve concert is threatened by a trio of villains (Ed Begley Jr, Bobby Sherman and Fabian), it has actors playing musicians and vice versa. Malcolm McDowell plays a Mick Jagger-like character, while Lou Reed appears as a Dylan clone. The result is cartoonish fun. FL

Malcolm McDowell *Reggie Wanker* • [Allen Garfield] *Max Wolfe* • Daniel Stern *Neil* • Gail Edwards *Willy Loman* • Miles Chapin *Sammy Fox* • Ed Begley Jr *Colin Beverly* • Lou Reed *Auden* • Bobby Sherman *Mark* • Fabian Forte [Fabian] *Marv* • Mary Woronov *Violetta* • Dick Miller *Susie's dad* ■ *Dir* Allan Arkush • *Scr* Danny Opatoshu, Henry Rosenbaum, David Taylor

Get Hard ★★★ 15
Comedy 2015 · US · Colour · 100min

Prison looms for Will Ferrell's millionaire in a broad comedy that squares up to every penitentiary stereotype going and stays standing. Kevin Hart plays his "urban" partner in crime, except that he lies about doing time in jail, profiting from the white man's prejudice to take a lucrative job training the wealthy wimp to withstand the rigours of San Quentin. For every joke that trades on the colour of Hart's skin and his perceived "hardness", Ferrell always looks the bigger fool, which is just how he likes it. The *Anchorman* star is in his comfort zone but some gags are a little too lazy – especially when it comes to the prospect of violence in the shower room. SP Swearing, sexual references. *DVD* *BD*

Will Ferrell *James King* • Kevin Hart *Darnell* • TI [Tip Harris] *Russell* • Alison Brie *Alissa* • Craig T Nelson *Martin* ■ *Dir* Etan Cohen • *Scr* Ian Roberts (2), Jay Martel, Etan Cohen, from a story by Roberts, Martel, Adam McKay

Get Him to the Greek ★★★★ 15
Comedy 2010 · US · Colour · 104min

Russell Brand reprises his role from hit comedy *Forgetting Sarah Marshall* here, only this time he's hogging the limelight as impish rock star Aldous Snow. Jonah Hill is typically hangdog as the record-company drone charged with getting Aldous to the Greek Theatre in LA for his big comeback gig. It's hardly an original premise, but there are some brilliantly funny turns from the leads. Sean Combs, as Hill's crabby boss, and Rose Byrne, as Aldous's racy rapper ex-girlfriend, also add to an increasingly delirious atmosphere. The comedy is close to the knuckle at times, but Hill and Brand counter that with an easy chemistry, while Brand even reveals his softer side. SP *DVD* *BD*

Russell Brand *Aldous Snow* • Jonah Hill *Aaron Green* • Rose Byrne *Jackie Q* • Elisabeth Moss *Daphne Binks* • Sean Combs *Sergio* • Colm Meaney *Jonathan Snow* • Kali Hawk *Kali* • Christina Aguilera • Pink • Katy Perry ■ *Dir* Nicholas Stoller • *Scr* Nicholas Stoller, from characters by Jason Segel

Get Low ★★★ PG
Period drama
2009 · US/Ger/Pol · Colour · 99min

Set in rural 1930s Tennessee, this drama has backwoods hermit Felix Bush (Robert Duvall) emerging from a self-imposed 40-year exile to plan his own funeral party. Frank Quinn (the reliably laconic Bill Murray) is the hard-up local funeral director charged with planning the bash. Former cinematographer Aaron Schneider's debut feature is beautifully shot and also benefits from charming (if extravagant) performances from the two leads, who are clearly enjoying themselves. But the plot is all rather hokey and sentimental, and frankly wouldn't disgrace an episode of *The Waltons*. AS Violence, swearing. *DVD*

Robert Duvall *Felix Bush* • Sissy Spacek *Mattie Darrow* • Bill Murray *Frank Quinn* • Lucas Black *Buddy Robinson* • Gerald McRaney *Rev Gus Horton* ■ *Dir* Aaron Schneider • *Scr* Chris Provenzano, C Gaby Mitchell, from a story by Provenzano, Scott Seeke

Get on the Bus ★★★ 15
Road movie 1996 · US · Colour · 116min

On 16 October 1995, African-American men from all over the United States converged on Washington DC for the "Million Man March". This event serves as the inspiration for another controversial look at racial politics from Spike Lee. The focus is on 12 angry men from different backgrounds who travel from Los Angeles to the rally, embarking on personal voyages of discovery. Less confrontational than Lee's usual output, the message is still hammered home. AJ

Richard Belzer *Rick* • De'Aundre Bonds *Junior* • André Braugher *Flip* • Thomas Jefferson Byrd *Evan Thomas Sr* • Gabriel Casseus *Jamal* • Albert Hall *Craig* • Hill Harper *Xavier* • Harry Lennix *Randall* • Bernie Mac *Jay* ■ *Dir* Spike Lee • *Scr* Reggie Rock Bythewood

Get on Up ★★★ 12
Musical biography 2014 · US · Colour · 138min

The life and times of music legend James Brown has the potential to make a great biopic, but for all its gloss and elaborately staged musical sequences *Get on Up* falls slightly short of the mark. Chadwick Boseman stars as the self-styled Godfather of Soul, who was born into poverty and pulled himself up by his bootstraps to become one of the most influential performers of the 20th century. TeS *DVD* *BD*

Chadwick Boseman *James Brown* • Nelsan Ellis *Bobby Byrd* • Dan Aykroyd *Ben Bart* • Viola Davis *Susie Brown* • Lennie James *Joe Brown* ■ *Dir* Tate Taylor • *Scr* Jez & John-Henry Butterworth, from a story by the Butterworths, Steven Baigelman • *Cinematographer* Stephen Goldblatt

Get Out Your Handkerchiefs ★★★ 15
Comedy 1977 · Fr/Bel · Colour · 104min

The winner of the Oscar for best foreign film, this outrageous comedy stars Gérard Depardieu and Patrick Dewaere in a savage satire on the conventionality of middle-class life and the cosiness of commercial cinema. Depardieu reins in his natural ebullience as the husband who devotes himself to finding lovers for his discontented wife, Carol Laure, thus allowing 13-year-old Riton to steal the picture as the missing piece in their bizarre *ménage à trois*. Occasionally wildly wide of the mark, this provocative picture has something to offend everyone. DP French +subtitles. *DVD*

Gérard Depardieu *Raoul* • Patrick Dewaere *Stephane* • Carole Laure *Solange* • Riton *Christian Beloeil* • Michel Serrault *Neighbor* • Eléonore Hirt *Mrs Beloeil* • Jean Rougerie *Mr Beloeil* • Sylvie Joly *Passerby* ■ *Dir/Scr* Bertrand Blier

Get over It ★★★ 12
Romantic comedy 2001 · US · Colour · 82min

Ben Foster plays a teenager who's dumped by his longtime girlfriend. He signs up to join her in the school's musical version of *A Midsummer Night's Dream* just so he can win her back. He's aided and abetted by his best friend's younger sister – as she's played by the drop-dead gorgeous Kirsten Dunst, there are no prizes for guessing that maybe young Ben is making moon-eyes in the wrong direction. This is smartly written and sassily acted, with an entertaining cameo from Martin Short as the play's campily neurotic producer. DA *DVD*

Kirsten Dunst *Kelly* • Ben Foster *Berke Landers* • Melissa Sagemiller *Allison McAllister* • Sisqo *Dennis* • Shane West *Striker* • Colin Hanks *Felix* • Swoosie Kurtz *Beverly Landers* • Ed Begley Jr *Frank Landers* • Martin Short *Dr Desmond Forrest-Oates* ■ *Dir* Tommy O'Haver • *Scr* R Lee Fleming Jr

Get Real ★★ 15
Drama 1998 · UK/S Afr · Colour · 106min

What's a 16-year-old school boy to do when he lives in Basingstoke, knows he's "dodgy" (in other words, gay) and fancies the head boy? Those are the problems facing Ben Silverstone. Director Simon Shore merely joins up the gay soap-opera dots and, despite encouraging an engaging central performance from Silverstone, does little more than indulge in a certain clichéd angst. AJ Swearing, sex scenes. *DVD*

Ben Silverstone *Steven Carter* • Brad Gorton *John Dixon* • Charlotte Brittain *Linda* • Stacy A Hart *Jessica* • Kate McEnery *Wendy* • Patrick Nielsen *Mark* • Tim Harris *Kevin* • James D White *Dave* ■ *Dir* Simon Shore • *Scr* Patrick Wilde, from his play *What's Wrong with Angry?*

G

Get Rich or Die Tryin' ★★ 15

Crime drama   2005 · US · Colour · 111min

This vehicle for hip-hop superstar Curtis "50 Cent" Jackson, partly based on his life, is virtually indistinguishable from the cliché-ridden straight-to-video gangsta thrillers that have become so popular. In an overly familiar story of a young man from the 'hood torn between becoming a rapper or a drug dealer, 50 Cent lacks the necessary charisma. JF Violence, swearing, drug abuse. **DVD**

Curtis "50 Cent" Jackson *Marcus* • Terrence Howard *Bama* • Joy Bryant *Charlene* • Bill Duke *Levar* • Adewale Akinnuoye-Agbaje *Majestic* • Omar Benson Miller *Keryl* • Viola Davis *Grandma* • Serena Reeder *Katrina* • Tory Kittles *Justice* • Marc John Jefferies *Young Marcus* ■ *Dir* Jim Sheridan • *Scr* Terence Winter

Get Santa ★★★★ U

Seasonal fantasy comedy
2014 · US/UK · Colour · 102min

Severance director Christopher Smith has created a Christmas tale that has a slightly rougher edge than usual, yet still brims with good will to all men – even hardened criminals. Rafe Spall gives a touching, dry-witted portrayal of an ex-con who's keen to spend time with his son after years behind bars. But after Santa crashes his sleigh in the boy's garage, Spall's plans for a nice day out turn into a screwball search for missing reindeer. Jim Broadbent is hilarious as the bearded one, while Smith uses light and shade to great effect, and conjures up a magical detour to Lapland and a night-time sleigh ride over London. SP **DVD** **BD**

Jim Broadbent *Santa Claus* • Rafe Spall *Steve Anderson* • Jodie Whittaker *Alison* • Kit Connor *Tom* • Warwick Davis *Sally* • Stephen Graham *Barber* ■ *Dir/Scr* Christopher Smith

Get Shorty ★★★★ 15

Crime comedy   1995 · US · Colour · 100min

This adaptation of Elmore Leonard's novel explores the murky world of Hollywood's links to organised crime. John Travolta plays a Florida gangster who arrives in Tinseltown to collect a bad debt from Gene Hackman and decides to stay, importing his strong-arm methods into movie production. The performances by the impressive cast are exquisite: the jowly Travolta has tremendous charm but also considerable menace; Danny DeVito plays a movie star to perfection; and Hackman is a sheer delight as the purveyor of schlocky monster movies. Followed by a disappointing sequel, *Be Cool* (2005). AT Violence, swearing. **DVD** **BD**

John Travolta *Chili Palmer* • Gene Hackman *Harry Zimm* • Rene Russo *Karen Flores* • Danny DeVito *Martin Weir* • Dennis Farina *Ray "Bones" Barboni* • Delroy Lindo *Bo Catlett* • James Gandolfini *Bear* • Jon Gries [Jonathan Gries] *Ronnie Wingate* • Rene Props *Nicki* ■ *Dir* Barry Sonnenfeld • *Scr* Scott Frank, from the novel by Elmore Leonard

Get Smart ★★ 12

Spy action comedy
2008 · US/Aus · Colour · 105min

Clueless spy Maxwell Smart started life in the long-running 1960s TV series, which spoofed the James Bond movies. Here Steve Carell takes over the role made famous by Don Adams, working as an analyst for spy agency CONTROL. Gorgeous Agent 99 (Anne Hathaway) remains by his side as usual, as our hapless hero travels to Russia to foil the plans of a ruthless bomb manufacturer (Terence Stamp). While many of the popular TV catchphrases and ludicrous gadgets are included here, they can't rescue this crass update. AJ Some violence, swearing. **DVD** **BD**

Steve Carell *Maxwell Smart* • Anne Hathaway *Agent 99* • Dwayne Johnson *Agent 23* • Alan Arkin *The Chief* • Terence Stamp *Siegfried* • Masi Oka *Bruce* • Bill Murray *Agent 13* ■ *Dir* Peter Segal • *Scr* Tom J Astle, Matt Ember, from characters by Mel Brooks, Buck Henry

Get to Know Your Rabbit ★★

Satirical comedy   1972 · US · Colour · 91min

Bored with corporate politics, Tom Smothers abandons his conformist job to become an itinerant tap-dancing magician, with a little help from Orson Welles. He soon finds that his change of lifestyle hasn't freed him from the exploitative, money-obsessed world he is trying to escape. Director Brian De Palma's first big-budget feature is an overlong, uninspired parable for the time, with stagey performances. This was edited against De Palma's wishes and only a few flashes of his visual talent remain. AJ

Tom Smothers *Donald Beeman* • John Astin *Mr Turnbull* • Suzanne Zenor *Paula* • Samantha Jones *Susan* • Allen Goorwitz [Allen Garfield] *Vic* • Katharine Ross *Girl* • Orson Welles *Mr Delasandro* ■ *Dir* Brian De Palma • *Scr* Jordan Crittenden

Get Well Soon ★★ 15

Romantic black comedy
2001 · US · Colour · 90min

This very offbeat satire about the cult of media personality features Vincent Gallo as a revered talk-show host suffering a nervous breakdown and Courteney Cox as his ex-wife, who still harbours feelings for him. The stars work well together and the script overflows with quirky, bittersweet twists and turns. It overdoses on its weirdness motif, however, weakened by a mental home subplot that verges on fantasy. JC **DVD**

Vincent Gallo *Bobby Bishop* • Courteney Cox *Lily* • Jeffrey Tambor *Tate Donovan* • Anne Meara *Lily's mother* ■ *Dir/Scr* Justin McCarthy

Get Yourself a College Girl ★★

Musical comedy   1964 · US · Colour · 87min

Student Mary Ann Mobley gets into trouble when she's exposed as the songwriter of some disreputable but supposedly groovy tunes. Ambitious senator Willard Waterman is around to help out, in exchange for some youth "cred" with the voters. This would-be fun teen picture is saved by the appearance of a strange melange of musicians, including early Britpoppers the Dave Clark Five and the Animals. JG

Mary Ann Mobley *Terry* • Joan O'Brien *Marge* • Chris Noel *Sue* • Nancy Sinatra *Lynne* • Chad Everett *Gary* • Fabrizio Mioni *Armand* • Willard Waterman *Senator Hubert Morrison* ■ *Dir* Sidney Miller • *Scr* Robert E Kent

The Getaway ★★★★ 18

Crime thriller   1972 · US · Colour · 117min

In this gripping, landmark thriller, ex-convict Steve McQueen and his wife Ali MacGraw head off to Mexico after a bank robbery backfires, pursued by crazed partner-in-crime Al Lettieri and the heavily armed henchmen of crime boss Ben Johnson. Directed by the master of screen violence, Sam Peckinpah, it's a modern western, a tough, disconcerting fable exploring the human soul, set in the barren landscapes of the Texan desert. The charismatic McQueen has to face the unpalatable truth about how MacGraw secured his release from jail, as their relationship – literally – comes under fire in a hail of bullets. In real life, though, the stars fell in love and subsequently married. AT Violence, swearing. **DVD** **BD**

Steve McQueen (1) *"Doc" McCoy* • Ali MacGraw *Carol McCoy* • Ben Johnson (1) *Jack Benyon* • Sally Struthers *Fran Clinton* • Al Lettieri *Rudy Butler* • Slim Pickens *Cowboy* • Richard Bright *Thief* • Jack Dodson *Harold Clinton* ■ *Dir* Sam Peckinpah • *Scr* Walter Hill, from the novel by Jim Thompson

The Getaway ★★★ 18

Crime thriller   1994 · US · Colour · 110min

This remake of Sam Peckinpah's 1972 thriller reuses much of Walter Hill's original script and stars Alec Baldwin and Kim Basinger in roles played originally by Steve McQueen and Ali MacGraw. Baldwin isn't in the same league as McQueen, but Roger Donaldson's picture has flair, and the female leads stand up to comparison. The story has a fair amount of tension, and the southwestern locations have an arid, end-of-the-line symbolism. AT Swearing, violence, sex scenes, nudity.

Alec Baldwin *Carter "Doc" McCoy* • Kim Basinger *Carol McCoy* • Michael Madsen *Rudy Travis* • James Woods *Jack Benyon* • David Morse *Jim Deer Jackson* • Jennifer Tilly *Fran Carvey* • James Stephens *Harold Carvey* • Richard Farnsworth *Slim* ■ *Dir* Roger Donaldson • *Scr* Walter Hill, Amy Jones [Amy Jones Holden], from the novel by Jim Thompson

Getaway ★★ 15

Action thriller   2013 · US/Bul · Colour · 90min

Like Blackpool through a stick of rock, this action thriller for undiscerning petrolheads has "small-screen viewing" written right through it. Ethan Hawke plays a former racing driver whose wife is kidnapped by crooks. For reasons too complicated to go into, they force him to steal an armoured sports car, and to scoot around the city causing complete and utter mayhem. There is a plot of sorts, but essentially the film exists to see how many pursuing police cars it can trash. DA **DVD** **BD**

Ethan Hawke *Brent Magna* • Selena Gomez *The Kid* • Jon Voight *The Voice* • Rebecca Budig *Leanne Magna* • Bruce Payne *Distinguished Man* ■ *Dir* Courtney Solomon • *Scr* Sean Finegan, Gregg Maxwell Parker

Gettin' Square ★★★ 15

Comedy crime drama
2003 · Aus/UK · Colour · 98min

David Wenham deservedly picked up an AFI Award (an Aussie Oscar) for his wonderful stoner turn in this sharp and likeable crime caper from Down Under. The nominal lead is Sam Worthington, who plays a reformed robber attempting to build a new career as a chef for another ex-con, expat Timothy Spall. However, their bids to go straight seem certain to be derailed by the bumbling Wenham, who has come under the scrutiny of a new crime force. JF Violence, swearing, drug abuse. **DVD**

Sam Worthington *Barry Wirth* • David Wenham *Johnny Spitieri* • Timothy Spall *Darren Barrington* • Freya Stafford *Annie Flynn* • Gary Sweet *Chicka Martin* • David Roberts (2) *Niall Toole* • David Field *Arnie DeViers* • Joe Bugner *Big Mick* ■ *Dir* Jonathan Teplitzky • *Scr* Chris Nyst

Getting Away with Murder ★ 15

Black comedy   1996 · US/Can · Colour · 87min

It's a special sort of director who takes a talented comic cast – including Dan Aykroyd, Jack Lemmon and Lily Tomlin – and still manages to turn in a completely unfunny comedy. The problem here is that the material is weird rather than wacky, as professor Aykroyd discovers that his neighbour (Lemmon) is a Nazi war criminal and decides to murder him. JB

Dan Aykroyd *Jack Lambert* • Lily Tomlin *Inga Mueller* • Jack Lemmon *Max Mueller/Karl Luger* • Bonnie Hunt *Gail Holland* • Brian Kerwin *Marty Lambert* • Jerry Adler *Judge* • Andy Romano *Psychiatrist* ■ *Dir/Scr* Harvey Miller

Getting Even with Dad ★★ PG

Comedy   1994 · US · Colour · 104min

Home Alone's Macaulay Culkin again proves more than a match for a whole bunch of adults with criminal tendencies in this inoffensive if obvious comedy. This time the victim of his machinations is his dad, crooked Ted Danson, who Culkin is trying to steer on to the straight and narrow. Most of the humiliation is saved for Danson's inept sidekicks, Saul Rubinek and Gailard Sartain. Director Howard Deutch lets sentimentality run riot. JF Swearing. **DVD** **BD**

Macaulay Culkin *Timmy* • Ted Danson *Ray* • Glenne Headly *Theresa* • Saul Rubinek *Bobby* • Gailard Sartain *Carl* • Sam McMurray *Alex* • Hector Elizondo *Lt Romayko* • Sydney Walker *Mr Wankmueller* ■ *Dir* Howard Deutch • *Scr* Tom S Parker, Jim Jennewein

Getting Gotti ★★ 15

Crime drama based on a true story
1994 · US · Colour · 89min

It was inevitable that Mafia boss John Gotti, a gangster obsessed with celebrity, would end up being the subject of a film. Anthony John Denison plays the infamous "Teflon Don", but events are seen from the perspective of the obsessed district attorney (Lorraine Bracco) who fought for years to nail the media-friendly mobster. Reasonably well played, but a little too low-key. JF

Lorraine Bracco *Diane Giacalone* • Anthony John Denison *John Gotti* • Ellen Burstyn *Jo Giacalone* • Kathleen Laskey *Cassie* • August Schellenberg *Willie Boy Johnson* • Kenneth Welsh *Bennett* • Jeremy Ratchford *Harvey Sanders* • Ron Gabriel *Gravano* ■ *Dir* Roger Young • *Scr* James S Henerson

Getting In ★★★

Black comedy thriller 1994 · US · Colour · 94min

Stephen Mailer is bound by family tradition to go to Johns Hopkins College to study medicine. A lacklustre exam performance sees him resorting to blackmail to eliminate the five people ahead of him on the reserve list. Unfortunately they're dropping down dead instead and, before he knows it, Mailer's a murder suspect. Matthew Perry and Calista Flockhart are among the strong supporting cast in Doug Liman's directorial debut. Great gags make this enjoyable. LH

Stephen Mailer *Gabriel Higgs* • Kristy Swanson *Kirby Watts* • Andrew McCarthy *Rupert Grimm* • Dave Chappelle *Rom* • Matthew Perry *Randall Burns* • Calista Flockhart *Amanda Morel* ■ *Dir* Doug Liman • *Scr* PJ Posner, Joel Posner, Jonathan Lewin

Getting It Right ★★ 15

Romantic comedy   1989 · US · Colour · 97min

A decade before her mould-breaking role in *Fight Club*, Helena Bonham Carter unsuccessfully tried to shake her period drama image in this uneven comedy. Jesse Birdsall is an inexperienced young man who finds himself pursued by three women, including Bonham Carter and Jane Horrocks. Based on Elizabeth Jane Howard's novel, this probably worked better on the page than it does on screen. JB

Jesse Birdsall *Gavin Lamb* • Helena Bonham Carter *Lady Minerva Munday* • Peter Cook *Mr Adrian* • John Gielgud *Sir Gordon Munday* • Jane Horrocks *Jenny* • Lynn Redgrave *Joan* • Shirley Anne Field *Anne* • Pauline Quirke *Muriel Sutton* ■ *Dir* Randal Kleiser • *Scr* Elizabeth Jane Howard, from her novel

The Getting of Wisdom ★★★ PG

Period drama   1977 · Aus · Colour · 97min

Film-makers during the Australian New Wave of the 1970s had a flair for giving costume movies a resounding contemporary relevance. Here Bruce Beresford provides a few choice insights into the miseries of school life and the pain of lonely adolescence. He re-creates the atmosphere of a repressive turn-of-the-century boarding school with some care, but misses the sense of danger found in the original autobiographical novel by Henry Handel Richardson that caused a scandal on its publication. DP

Susannah Fowle *Laura Tweedle Rambotham* • Barry Humphries *Reverend Strachey* • John Waters (3) *Reverend Robert Shepherd* • Sheila Helpmann *Mrs Gurley* • Patricia Kennedy *Miss Chapman* • Kerry Armstrong *Kate Horner* • Celia De Burgh *MP* • Kim Deacon *Lilith Gordon* ■ *Dir* Bruce Beresford • *Scr* Eleanor Witcombe, from the novel by Henry Handel Richardson [Ethel Florence Richardson]

Getting Straight ★★★ 15

Comedy drama   1970 · US · Colour · 119min

Made on the back of *Easy Rider* and the anti-Vietnam War campaign, this was one of several "campus movies" that enabled studio executives to look cool and save money on ties. Elliott Gould plays a Vietnam veteran who, resuming his university education, becomes embroiled in campus politics and involved with fashion victim Candice Bergen. Harrison Ford makes an early appearance in a film that is very much of its time. AT

Elliott Gould *Harry Bailey* • Candice Bergen *Jan* • Robert F Lyons *Nick* • Jeff Corey *Dr Willhunt* • Max Julien *Ellis* • Cecil Kellaway *Dr Kasper* • Jon Lormer *Vandenburg* • Leonard Stone *Lysander* • Harrison Ford *Jake* ■ *Dir* Richard Rush • *Scr* Robert Kaufman, from the novel by Ken Kolb

Getting There ★ U
Comedy drama 2002 · US · Colour · 85min

Everything that can go wrong naturally does in this tiresome Olsen twins vehicle. It sees the duo trying to reach the Winter Olympics in Utah to celebrate their 16th birthdays while enduring a catalogue of predictable mishaps and inanities. Neither the performances nor the perpetual Valley girl speak get more interesting and though die-hard Mary-Kate and Ashley fans might sing its praises, anyone else will find the film sheer torture. SF *DVD*

Mary-Kate Olsen *Kylie Hunter* • Ashley Olsen *Taylor Hunter* • Billy Aaron Brown *Danny* • Heather Lindell *Jenn* • Jeff D'Agostino *Toast* ■ *Dir* Steve Purcell • *Scr* Michael Swerdlick

Gettysburg ★★★ PG
Historical war drama
1993 · US · Colour · 259min

Ted Turner's company produced this ambitious account of the bloody battle of July 1863, which cost some 7,000 lives and secured final victory for the Union. With a running time considerably longer than *Gone with the Wind* – Turner's favourite movie – *Gettysburg* has time to consider both points of view, but it has only been going for 45 minutes before the cannons start firing. Spectacular in parts and dull in others, it makes the strategy of the battle clear but takes some liberties with the actual events. Turner makes an uncredited cameo appearance as a Confederate who gets shot when answering the call to advance. AT
DVD

Tom Berenger *Lt Gen James Longstreet (Confederate)* • Martin Sheen *General Robert E Lee (Confederate)* • Stephen Lang *Maj Gen George E Pickett (Confederate)* • Richard Jordan *Brig Gen Lewis A Armistead (Confederate)* • George Lazenby *Brig Gen J Johnston Pettigrew (Confederate)* • Jeff Daniels *Colonel Joshua Lawrence Chamberlain (Federal)* • Sam Elliott *Brigadier General John Buford (Federal)* • C Thomas Howell *Lieutenant Thomas D Chamberlain (Federal)* • Maxwell Caulfield *Colonel Strong Vincent (Federal)* ■ *Dir* Ronald F Maxwell • *Scr* Ronald F Maxwell, from the novel *The Killer Angels* by Michael Shaara

Ghidrah, the Three-Headed Monster ★★★
Science-fiction horror
1965 · Jpn · Colour · 73min

Ghidrah (or Ghidorah as Japanese movie-goers correctly know him) is a three-headed, fire-breathing dragon which lands on Earth and causes the usual global destruction. Godzilla (in his first adventure as a good monster) defends the planet, with help from Mothra and Rodan (Toho Studios's other big earners), defeating Ghidrah in a spectacular battle on Mount Fuji. With higher production values and better visual effects than normal, this engaging behemoth bash established the use of various monsters in combat combinations, which would increase in goofiness over the years. AJ Japanese dubbed.

Yosuke Natsuki *Shindo* • Yuriko Hoshi *Naoko* • Hiroshi Koizumi *Professor Murai* • Takashi Shimura *Dr Tsukamoto* ■ *Dir* Ishiro Honda [Inoshiro Honda] • *Scr* Shinichi Sekizawa

Ghost ★★★★ 15
Romantic drama 1990 · US · Colour · 121min

This romantic and glossy mix of the sentimental and the supernatural reaps higher rewards than Patrick Swayze's acting ability deserves. He's the murdered banker trying to warn girlfriend Demi Moore she's in mortal danger via psychic Whoopi Goldberg, who provides the comic moments so necessary to lighten the potentially

maudlin atmosphere. In fact, she did it so well, she won a best supporting actress Oscar. The special effects are a real treat and the love-beyond-the-grave theme is touching. TH Swearing, violence. *DVD* *Blu*

Patrick Swayze *Sam Wheat* • Demi Moore *Molly Jensen* • Whoopi Goldberg *Oda Mae Brown* • Tony Goldwyn *Carl Bruner* • Rick Aviles *Willie Lopez* • Gail Boggs *Louise* ■ *Dir* Jerry Zucker • *Scr* Bruce Joel Rubin

The Ghost ★★ 18
Action thriller 2000 · US · Colour · 82min

Chung Lai throws herself into the role of a dispassionate Tong assassin forced to seek sanctuary in the States in Douglas Jackson's impoverished action thriller. Certainly, she has the looks and some good moves, but she is no Cheng Pei Pei or Michelle Yeoh, and is further hobbled by the plodding storyline. The lack of budget is palpable, and Michael Madsen's very average performance as a bounty hunter further testifies to his post-*Reservoir Dogs* decline. DP *DVD*

Michael Madsen *Dan Olinghouse* • Cary-Hiroyuki Tagawa *Chang* • Chung Lai *Jing* • Brad Dourif *Lieutenant Garland* • Richard Hatch *Edward* ■ *Dir* Douglas Jackson • *Scr* Dave Tedder

The Ghost ★★★★ 15
Mystery thriller
2010 · Fr/Ger/UK · Colour · 122min

A hack writer charged with ghosting the memoirs of a British prime minister finds himself on dangerous ground in Roman Polanski's screen version of the Robert Harris novel. The mysterious demise of his predecessor sees Ewan McGregor's unnamed ghostwriter dispatched to the American hideaway of Pierce Brosnan, who's keen to set the record straight on a premiership clouded by contentious policies on Iraq. McGregor gives his sparkiest turn in ages, and the parallels with the Blair years are mischievously upfront. All that matters less, however, than the film's entertaining mastery of Hitchcockian unease, delivering sheer viewing pleasure from a slightly clunky plot. TJ *DVD* *Blu*

Ewan McGregor *The Ghost* • Pierce Brosnan *Adam Lang* • Kim Cattrall *Amelia Bly* • Olivia Williams *Ruth Lang* • Tom Wilkinson *Professor Paul Emmett* • Timothy Hutton *Sidney Kroll* • Eli Wallach *Old man on porch* • James Belushi *John Maddox* ■ *Dir* Roman Polanski • *Scr* Robert Harris, Roman Polanski, from Harris's novel

The Ghost and Mrs Muir ★★★★ U
Romantic fantasy 1947 · US · BW · 99min

Ethereally beautiful Gene Tierney finds herself beguiled by the ghost of bewhiskered sea captain Rex Harrison when she moves into his former home in this wonderful romantic fantasy. A marvellously lyrical Bernard Herrmann score helps underline the poignancy of this enchanting tale, and Philip Dunne's literate screenplay avoids all the pitfalls normally associated with such delicate material. Today, the settings and pace may look studio-bound, but they suit the theatricality of the subject. TS *DVD*

Gene Tierney *Lucy Muir* • Rex Harrison *Captain Daniel Gregg* • George Sanders *Miles Fairley* • Edna Best *Martha* • Vanessa Brown *Anna* • Anna Lee *Mrs Fairley* • Robert Coote *Coombe* • Natalie Wood *Young Anna* ■ *Dir* Joseph L Mankiewicz • *Scr* Philip Dunne, from the novel by RA Dick

The Ghost and the Darkness ★ 15
Period action adventure
1996 · US · Colour · 105min

Screenwriter William Goldman wanted to tell the tale of the man-eating Tsavo lions terrorising the building of a railway in East Africa in the late 19th century, but producer Michael Douglas pulled rank and decided he would also star as the enigmatic big game hunter who assists Val Kilmer's engineer. Douglas and Kilmer did not hit it off on a stressful location shoot, and this fails to convince on any level. AC Violence, swearing. *DVD*

Michael Douglas (1) *Remington* • Val Kilmer *John Patterson* • Bernard Hill *Dr Hawthorne* • John Kani *Samuel* • Tom Wilkinson *Beaumont* • Om Puri *Abdullah* • Emily Mortimer *Helena Patterson* ■ *Dir* Stephen Hopkins • *Scr* William Goldman, from the book *The Man-Eaters of Tsavo* by John Patterson

The Ghost Breakers ★★★★ PG
Horror comedy mystery 1940 · US · BW · 81min

Made to capitalise on the success the previous year of Bob Hope's comedy *The Cat and the Canary*, this lightning paced follow-up is even better than its money-spinning predecessor. Once again Hope and Paulette Goddard find themselves shacked up in a supposedly haunted house – this time it's her inherited mansion in an exotic Cuban locale. The same pleasing recipe of thrills, laughs and romance keep the potboiler simmering nicely with the added bonus of some truly spooky moments amid the fun. DF *DVD*

Bob Hope *Larry Lawrence* • Paulette Goddard *Mary Carter* • Richard Carlson *Geoff Montgomery* • Paul Lukas *Parada* • Willie Best *Alex* • Pedro De Cordoba *Havez* • Virginia Brissac *Mother zombie* • Noble Johnson *Zombie* • Anthony Quinn *Ramon Mederos/Francisco Mederos* • Lloyd Corrigan *Martin* ■ *Dir* George Marshall • *Scr* Walter DeLeon, from the play from Paul Dickey, Charles W Goddard

The Ghost Camera ★★ U
Crime mystery 1933 · UK · BW · 64min

The much-maligned "quota quickie" proved an invaluable training ground for some of Britain's most talented individuals. Director Bernard Vorhaus clearly doesn't fit into that category, but his stars Ida Lupino and John Mills certainly do. Unfortunately, much of the action is dominated by Henry Kendall as the chemist-turned-sleuth seeking to use photographic evidence to prove Mills innocent of murder. DP

Henry Kendall *John Grey* • Ida Lupino *Mary Elton* • John Mills *Ernest Elton* • S Victor Stanley *Albert Sims* • George Merritt (1) *Inspector* • Felix Aylmer *Coroner* • Davina Craig *Amelia Wilkinson* • Fred Groves *Barnaby Rudd* ■ *Dir* Bernard Vorhaus • *Scr* H Fowler Mear, from a story by J Jefferson Farjeon

The Ghost Comes Home ★★ U
Comedy drama 1940 · US · BW · 78min

Billie Burke and Frank Morgan star in this adaptation of a negligible stage play. Morgan is declared dead through a bureaucratic bungle and has to hide away in his own attic, because his family are happily living off his life insurance. The sequence in which Morgan has to don drag to foil snoopers is the highlight, while the nadir is daughter Ann Rutherford's romance with sappy John Shelton. DP

Frank Morgan *Vern Adams* • Billie Burke *Cora Adams* • Ann Rutherford *Billie Adams* • John Shelton *Lanny Shea* • Reginald Owen *Hemingway* • Donald Meek *Mortimer Hopkins Sr* ■ *Dir* William Thiele • *Scr* Richard Maibaum, Harry Ruskin, from the play *Der Mutige Seefahrer (The Courageous Seaman)* by George Kaiser [Georg Kaiser]

Ghost Dad ★ PG
Fantasy comedy 1990 · US · Colour · 80min

Bill Cosby has had a disastrous time trying to transfer his TV popularity to the big screen. After the ill-conceived spy spoof *Leonard, Part 6* came this equally daft supernatural directed by Sidney Poitier. Cosby plays a harassed businessman who is killed in a car accident and discovers he's been missing out on the joys of family life. Cosby mugs away for all he's worth, but good gags are few and far between. JF Swearing.

Bill Cosby *Elliot Hopper* • Kimberly Russell *Diane Hopper* • Denise Nicholas *Joan* • Ian Bannen *Sir Edith Moser* • Christine Ebersole *Carol* • Barry Corbin *Mr Collins* • Salim Grant *Danny Hopper* • Brooke Fontaine *Amanda Hopper* ■ *Dir* Sidney Poitier • *Scr* Chris Reese, Brent Maddock, SS Wilson, from a story by SS Wilson, Brent Maddock

Ghost Dog: the Way of the Samurai ★★★ 15
Crime drama 1999 · US/Fr · Colour · 110min

Jim Jarmusch's quirky crime drama creates a world of such deadpan solemnity that humour exists solely in the eye of the beholder. Forest Whitaker is perfectly at home here, as a bushido-obsessed hitman who communicates with his boss by pigeon and doesn't speak a word of his ice cream-selling best friend's language. The word laconic doesn't do justice to the film's tempo – though the outbursts of explosive violence tend to spoil the ambience. DP Violence. *DVD*

Forest Whitaker *Ghost Dog* • John Tormey *Louie* • Cliff Gorman *Sonny Valerio* • Henry Silva *Vargo* • Isaach de Bankole *Raymond* • Tricia Vessey *Louise Vargo* • Gene Ruffini *Old consigliere* ■ *Dir/Scr* Jim Jarmusch

The Ghost Goes West ★★★ U
Comedy 1935 · UK · BW · 78min

This is a lightweight fantasy that gets by thanks to some expert playing and the assured touch of director René Clair, who was making his English language debut after a decade of making comedies in his native France. Clair coaxes an impish performance out of Robert Donat as the ghost haunting a Scottish castle transported to Florida by vulgar millionaire Eugene Pallette. DP

Robert Donat *Murdoch/Donald Glourie* • Jean Parker *Peggy Martin* • Eugene Pallette *Joe Martin* • Elsa Lanchester *Lady Shepperton* • Ralph Bunker *Ed Bigelow* • Patricia Hilliard *Shepherdess* • Everley Gregg *Gladys Martin* ■ *Dir* René Clair • *Scr* Robert Sherwood [Robert E Sherwood], Geoffrey Kerr, René Clair, Lajos Biró, from the story *Sir Tristram Goes West* by Eric Keown

A Ghost in Monte Carlo ★★ PG
Period romantic drama
1990 · UK/US · Colour · 89min

Fans of Barbara Cartland's rich settings, English poise and tales of improbable innocents ensnared by lascivious men may well enjoy this sugary made-for-TV contrivance, which is adapted from one of her novels. Others may find it unintentionally funny, as a decent cast is forced to recite slabs of dialogue to camera in what is, sadly, an unmoving romantic drama. JM *DVD*

Lysette Anthony *Mistral* • Sarah Miles *Aunt Emilie* • Oliver Reed *Rajah* • Marcus Gilbert *Lord Robert Stanford* • Christopher Plummer *Grand Duke Ivan* • Samantha Eggar *Jeanne* • Fiona Fullerton *Lady Violet* • Jolyon Baker *Prince Nicholas* • Joanna Lumley *Lady Drayton* • Lewis Collins *Lord Drayton* • Gareth Hunt *Dulton* • Ron Moody *Alphonse* ■ *Dir* John Hough • *Scr* Terence Feely, from the novel by Barbara Cartland

The Ghost in the Invisible Bikini ★★ PG
Comedy horror 1966 · US · Colour · 79min

Exploitation movies don't come much brighter and bolder than this. Forget the plot, some aimless drivel about newly deceased Boris Karloff trying to gain entry into heaven by doing a good deed. The real fun comes from watching an eclectic cast go through its paces, including Karloff, Nancy Sinatra and Basil Rathbone who, despite his advanced years, allegedly handled his own stunts in a swordfight with teen idol Tommy Kirk. RS

Tommy Kirk *Chuck Phillips* • Deborah Walley *Lili Morton* • Aron Kincaid *Bobby* • Quinn O'Hara *Sinistra* • Jesse White *J Sinister Hulk* • Harvey Lembeck *Eric Von Zipper* • Nancy Sinatra *Vicki* • Basil Rathbone *Reginald Ripper* • Boris Karloff *Hiram Stokely, the corpse* ■ *Dir* Don Weis • *Scr* Louis M Heyward, Elwood Ullman, from a story by Heyward

G

Ghost in the Machine ★★★ 18

Science-fiction horror 1993 · US · Colour · 91min

A serial killer's death during a freak electrical storm transforms him into a computer virus. His evil spirit then murderously stalks through Cleveland's communication networks using Karen Allen's lost address book. Engaging and fast-paced, it's a very contemporary tale, laced with inventive mayhem and cool wit, sparsely augmented by well-executed special effects. AJ Swearing, violence.

Karen Allen *Terry Munroe* · Chris Mulkey *Bram* · Ted Marcoux *Karl* · Wil Horneff *Josh Munroe* · Jessica Walter *Elaine* · Brandon Quintin Adams [Brandon Adams] *Frazer* · Rick Ducommun *Phil* · Nancy Fish *Karl's landlord* ■ *Dir* Rachel Talalay · *Scr* William Davis, William Osborne

Ghost in the Noonday Sun ★ PG

Comedy adventure 1973 · UK · Colour · 88min

Peter Sellers's career was at a low ebb at the time and he hoped this desperately unfunny pirate romp about hidden treasure would revive it. He was wrong – the whole sorry mess never found its way inside cinemas. Modest laughs are to be had, especially during Spike Milligan's brief appearance, but this poor man's *Treasure Island* is for Sellers completists only. RS

Peter Sellers *Dick Scratcher* · Anthony Franciosa *Pierre* · Spike Milligan *Bombay* · Clive Revill *Bay of Algier* · Peter Boyle *Ras Mohammed* · Richard Willis *Jeremiah* · James Villiers *Parsley-Freck* ■ *Dir* Peter Medak · *Scr* Evan Jones, Spike Milligan

Ghost in the Shell ★★★★ 15

Animated science-fiction 1995 · Jpn/UK · Colour · 79min

This animated sci-fi tale is a hypnotic, animated fusion of thrilling action sequences and philosophical soul-searching. Dynamic use of traditional cel techniques and computer-aided artwork, a *Blade Runner*-esque landscape and a curvy cyborg heroine make this even more of a visual feast than the previous *manga* benchmark, *Akira*. The fluid elegance of the animation is matched by Kenji Kawai's haunting music and, although the script gets bogged down in its own artfulness, there's moody atmosphere here to match that in any Ridley Scott movie. JC Japanese dubbed. Violence, nudity. DVD BL

Mimi Woods *Kusanagi* · Richard George [Richard Epcar] *Bateau* · Abe Lasser *Puppet master* · Christopher Joyce *Togusa* · William Frederick *Aramaki* · Mike Sorich *Ishikawa* ■ *Dir* Mamoru Oshii · *Scr* Kazunori Ito, from the graphic novel *Kokaku Kidotai* by Masamune Shirow

Ghost in the Shell

Science-fiction thriller 2017 · US/UK · Colour

This is a preview – no prints were available to review as we went to press: Scarlett Johansson takes top billing in a live-action remake of the 1995 Japanese manga anime. She stars as hi-tech humanoid cop Motoko Kusanagi in somewhat controversial casting that played into the recent row over the lack of ethnic diversity in Hollywood films. She'll need to engage her brain as well as her body, though, with Kusanagi assigned to track down a mysterious hacker known as the Puppet Master. Japanese movies tend to lose something in translation, but at least you're assured a glossy spectacle. SP

Scarlett Johansson *Kusanagi* · Takeshi Kitano *Daisuke Aramaki* · Michael Pitt *Kuze, "Laughing Man"* · Pilou Asbaek *Batou* · Juliette Binoche *Dr Ouelet* ■ *Dir* Rupert Sanders · *Scr* Jamie Moss, from the graphic novel *Kokaku Kidotai* by Masamune Shirow

The Ghost of Frankenstein ★★ PG

Horror 1942 · US · BW · 67min

Technically and artistically second-rate, the fourth episode in Universal's *Frankenstein* series sees Bela Lugosi back for a second stint as the vengeful Ygor. His brain gets transplanted by mistake into Lon Chaney Jr's creature by Dr Frankensein's second son, Cedric Hardwicke. Sloppy sequel continuity means characters who died in the previous *Son of Frankenstein* suddenly appear without explanation. Creaky more than creepy. AJ

Lon Chaney Jr *Monster* · Sir Cedric Hardwicke [Cedric Hardwicke] *Frankenstein* · Ralph Bellamy *Erik* · Lionel Atwill *Dr Bohmer* · Bela Lugosi *Ygor* · Evelyn Ankers *Elsa* · Janet Ann Gallow *Cloestine* · Barton Yarborough *Dr Kettering* ■ *Dir* Erle C Kenton · *Scr* Scott Darling, from the story by Eric Taylor

The Ghost of Greville Lodge ★★ PG

Supernatural mystery 2000 · UK · Colour · 87min

In this eerie ghost story, inquisitive orphan Jon Newman is invited to his uncle's rambling country manor. When the teenager ventures through the doors of the forbidden west wing, he stumbles upon clues to the secrets of the dark old house. Newman isn't the best child actor this country has ever produced, but George Cole and Prunella Scales are always worth watching. DP DVD

George Cole *Uncle James* · Prunella Scales *Sarah* · Jon Newman *James Greville* · Billy Smith *Ben* · Rebecca Weeks *Midge* ■ *Dir* Niall Johnson · *Scr* Niall Johnson, from the novel *Down Came a Blackbird* by Nicholas Wilde

The Ghost of St Michael's ★★★★ U

Comedy thriller 1941 · UK · BW · 78min

Will Hay is back before the blackboard and on the trail of Nazi spies in this spooky comedy. Hay and his class of likely lads are evacuated to a castle on the Isle of Skye, which is haunted by a ghost whose skirling bagpipes are a portent of death. While the mystery is moderately baffling, the highlights are the classroom showdowns in which Hay's academic shortcomings are gleefully exposed by brainbox Charles Hawtrey. Hay is on fine form, and the ensemble cast is splendid. DP

Will Hay *William Lamb* · Claude Hulbert *Hilary Teasdale* · Charles Hawtrey *Percy Thorne* · Raymond Huntley *Mr Humphries* · Felix Aylmer *Dr Winter* · Elliot Mason *Mrs Wigmore* · John Laurie *Jamie* · Hay Petrie *Procurator Fiscal* · Roddy Hughes *Amberley* ■ *Dir* Marcel Varnel · *Scr* Angus MacPhail, John Dighton

Ghost Rider ★★ 15

Action fantasy horror 2007 · US · Colour · 118min

By day Johnny Blaze (Nicolas Cage) is a daredevil motorcyclist, by night he's Ghost Rider, a demonic skeletal biker working for Satan. This long-delayed adaptation of Marvel Comics' most ambivalent superhero proves that some tortured comic-book characters work better on the page. Cage gives an enjoyably idiosyncratic performance as Blaze, but he's shamefully let down by his silly-looking alter ego, a grinning skeleton topped with unconvincing CGI flames. Incredibly, writer/director Mark Steven Johnson (*Daredevil*) manages to make even the action sequences anticlimactic. *Easy Rider* star Peter Fonda provides a rare moment of wit in an otherwise charmless production. JR Violence. DVD BL

Nicolas Cage *Johnny Blaze/Ghost Rider* · Eva Mendes *Roxanne Simpson* · Peter Fonda *Mephistopheles* · Wes Bentley *Blackheart* · Sam Elliott *Caretaker* · Donal Logue *Mack* · Matt Long *Young Johnny Blaze* · Raquel Alessi *Young Roxanne* ■ *Dir* Mark Steven Johnson · *Scr* Mark Steven Johnson, from a story by Johnson, from characters created for Marvel Comics by Roy Thomas, Gary Friedrich, Mike Ploog · *Cinematographer* Russell Boyd

Ghost Rider: Spirit of Vengeance ★★ 12

Action fantasy thriller 2012 · US · Colour · 95min

This hackneyed sequel sees the flame-skulled supernatural superhero (Nicolas Cage) on the lam in Eastern Europe aiming to break the pact he made with the Devil by delivering a young boy to a cave-dwelling sect before he becomes the Antichrist on his 13th birthday. The action comes thick and slow, with part-animated inserts, split screens and a tattooed monk played by Christopher Lambert to break up the tedium. Cage indulges in his usual brand of mega-acting as the cursed stunt motorcyclist, fighting his inner demons to hilarious effect as he transforms into fire and brimstone. AJ DVD BL

Nicolas Cage *Johnny Blaze/Ghost Rider* · Violante Placido *Nadya* · Ciarán Hinds [Ciaran Hinds] *Roarke* · Idris Elba *Moreau* · Christopher Lambert *Methodius* · Johnny Whitworth *Ray Carrigan* · Fergus Riordan *Danny* · Anthony Head *Benedict* ■ *Dir* Mark Neveldine, Brian Taylor · *Scr* Scott M Gimple, Seth Hoffman, from a story by David S Goyer, from the comic book by Howard Mackie, Mike Ploog, Javier Saltares, Roy Thomas

The Ghost Ship ★★★

Psychological horror 1943 · US · BW · 69min

A successful plagiarism suit kept this film from acclaimed low-budget producer Val Lewton out of circulation for a long time. It proves to be a highly effective psychological thriller rather than just another horror picture. Under Mark Robson's direction, the normally heroic Richard Dix gives a powerful performance as the mentally unhinged ship's captain whose crew members die in mysterious circumstances. AE

Richard Dix *Captain Stone* · Russell Wade *Tom Merriman* · Edith Barrett *Ellen Roberts* · Ben Bard *Bowns* · Edmund Glover *Jacob Winslow, "Sparks"* · Skelton Knaggs *Finn* · Tom Burton *Benson* · Steve Winston *Ausman* ■ *Dir* Mark Robson · *Scr* Donald Henderson Clarke, from a story by Leo Mittler

Ghost Ship ★ U

Horror 1952 · UK · BW · 71min

Buying a vessel that's haunted, even at a bargain price, is asking for trouble, as the young couple played by Dermot Walsh and Hazel Court find out in this waterlogged British B-feature. After they discover that the previous owner killed his spouse and her lover on board, they're on their way to laying the ship's ghost. Vernon Sewell, who was able to combine film-making with a love of the sea, probably had more fun than the audience. AE

Dermot Walsh *Guy* · Hazel Court *Margaret* · Hugh Burden *Dr Fawcett* · John Robinson (1) *Dr Martineau* · Joss Ambler *Yard manager* · Joan Carol *Mrs Martineau* · Hugh Latimer *Peter* · Mignon O'Doherty *Mrs Manley* ■ *Dir* Vernon Sewell · *Scr* Vernon Sewell, Philip Thornton

Ghost Ship ★ 18

Science-fiction horror thriller 2002 · US/Aus · Colour · 86min

A hackneyed and unsophisticated morality tale, this revolves around skipper Gabriel Byrne and his salvage team who think they've struck gold when they discover a mysterious, loot-filled cruise liner that's been lost at sea since the 1960s. The ineffectual performances and threadbare plot effectively eliminate tension. Turgid nonsense. SF DVD BL

Julianna Margulies *Maureen Epps* · Ron Eldard *Dodge* · Desmond Harrington *Jack Ferriman* · Isaiah Washington *Greer* · Gabriel Byrne *Sean Murphy* · Alex Dimitriades *Santos* ■ *Dir* Steve Beck · *Scr* Mark Hanlon, John Pogue, from a story by Mark Hanlon

Ghost Story ★★ 18

Horror 1974 · UK · Colour · 87min

This is more an arty mood piece than a fully fledged horror outing by Stephen Weeks, one-time British genre hopeful and director of the equally idiosyncratic *I, Monster* and *Gawain and the Green Knight*. In England in the 1930s, a trio of friends are invited to test whether an ancestral mansion is haunted or not. One of them comes under the influence of an enigmatic doll, which relays psychic images of past events. Unexceptional special effects make this an interesting failure. AJ

Larry Dann *Talbot* · Murray Melvin *McFayden* · Vivian Mackerall *Duller* · Marianne Faithfull *Sophy* · Anthony Bate *Dr Borden* · Penelope Keith *Rennie* · Leigh Lawson *Robert* · Sally Grace *Girl* ■ *Dir* Stephen Weeks · *Scr* Rosemary Sutcliff, Stephen Weeks

Ghost Story ★★ 18

Horror 1981 · US · Colour · 105min

Peter Straub's bestselling novel about four old-timers haunted by supernatural reminders of a past dark secret makes for pretty slow going here. It's more a gothic soap opera than a horror film; in fact, most of the special effects were edited out prior to release. Yet it's worth watching for the skilled performances of veterans Fred Astaire, Melvyn Douglas, John Houseman and Douglas Fairbanks Jr (even if they're all miscast) and for the gifted Alice Krige as the central spectre. AJ

Fred Astaire *Ricky Hawthorne* · Melvyn Douglas *John Jaffrey* · Douglas Fairbanks Jr *Edward Wanderley* · John Houseman *Sears James* · Craig Wasson *Don/David* · Patricia Neal *Stella* · Alice Krige *Alma/Eva* ■ *Dir* John Irvin · *Scr* Lawrence D Cohen, from the novel by Peter Straub

Ghost Town ★★ 12

Supernatural romantic comedy 2008 · US · Colour · 98min

Ricky Gervais's deadpan humour translates uncomfortably to the big screen in David Koepp's sappy supernatural romantic comedy. In his first Hollywood starring vehicle, Gervais plays a misery-guts Manhattan dentist who dies briefly during a routine operation and wakes up with the ability to see dead people. All these ghosts are seeking closure of one sort or another, including philandering Greg Kinnear, who wants wife Téa Leoni's remarriage plans sabotaged. Expert support from Kinnear and Leoni offsets Gervais's fitfully amusing sarcasm, but no one can make this zing with the spirit it sorely needs. AJ DVD BL

Ricky Gervais *Bertram Pincus* · Téa Leoni *Gwen* · Greg Kinnear *Frank Herlihy* · Billy Campbell [Bill Campbell] *Richard* · Kristen Wiig *Surgeon* · Dana Ivey *Marjorie Pickthall* · Alan Ruck *Ghost Dad* ■ *Dir* David Koepp · *Scr* David Koepp, John Kamps

The Ghost Train ★★★ U

Comedy mystery 1931 · UK · BW · 71min

Walter Forde was clearly a big fan of this comedy chiller as, almost a decade after completing this version, he remade it as a wartime flag-waver with Arthur Askey. This story of a haunted country station may now seem short on suspense, but there are still laughs a-plenty as the husband-and-wife team of Jack Hulbert and Cicely Courtneidge take on a gang of smugglers bringing commie propaganda into England. The supporting cast is also first class. DP

Jack Hulbert *Teddy Deakin* · Cicely Courtneidge *Miss Bourne* · Ann Todd *Peggy Murdock* · Cyril Raymond *Richard Winthrop* · Allan Jeayes *Dr Sterling* · Donald Calthrop *Saul Hodgkin* · Angela Baddeley *Julia Price* · Henry Caine *Herbert Price* ■ *Dir* Walter Forde · *Scr* Angus MacPhail, Lajos Biró, Sidney Gilliat, from the play by Arnold Ridley

The Ghost Train ★★★ U

Comedy mystery 1941 · UK · BW · 81min

Arthur Askey and Richard Murdoch, the stars of the hit radio show *Band Waggon*, were reunited for this flag-waving remake of the classic play by Arnold Ridley about a haunted country station. Try as director Walter Forde might to inject some atmosphere, there's a predictability about both the proceedings and the comedy. Askey was never at his best on screen and his energetic overacting has dated badly. DP DVD

Arthur Askey *Tommy Gander* · Richard Murdoch *Teddy Deakin* · Kathleen Harrison *Miss Bourne* · Morland Graham *Dr Sterling* · Linden Travers *Julia Price* · Peter Murray Hill *Richard Winthrop* · Carole Lynn *Jackie Winthrop* · Raymond Huntley *John Price* ■ *Dir* Walter Forde · *Scr* Marriott Edgar, Val Guest, JOC Orton, Sidney Gilliat, from the play by Arnold Ridley

Ghost World ★★★ 15
Comedy drama
2001 · US/UK/Ger · Colour · 107min

A scathing yet affectionate send-up of modern American culture, this traces the attempts of teenage misfit Thora Birch and her more level-headed friend Scarlett Johansson to survive life after high school. Terry Zwigoff delivers a poignant but darkly comic overview of human behaviour as he homes in on a cast of oddballs and eccentrics pigeonholed by society's prejudices. Though hampered by occasional self-conscious kookiness, the sharp dialogue and endearing performances keep this entertaining. SF Sex scenes, swearing. *DVD* CS

Thora Birch *Enid* · Scarlett Johansson *Rebecca* · Steve Buscemi *Seymour* · Brad Renfro *Josh* · Illeana Douglas *Roberta* · Bob Balaban *Enid's dad* · Teri Garr *Maxine* ■ *Dir* Terry Zwigoff · *Scr* Daniel Clowes, Terry Zwigoff, from the graphic novel by Daniel Clowes

Ghost Busters ★★★★ PG
Supernatural comedy
1984 · US · Colour · 146min

The often dazzling, special effects-driven slapstick tends to overshadow the fact that there are some slyer, more sophisticated laughs on offer in this blockbusting family comedy. Bill Murray is terrifically deadpan and sleazy as the dubious leader of a troupe of ghostbusters (co-writers Dan Aykroyd and Harold Ramis, plus Ernie Hudson) who are called into action when ancient spirits are let loose in New York. Sigourney Weaver shows an admirably light touch as a possessed cellist, and Rick Moranis also scores in his breakthrough movie. Director Ivan Reitman stages some spectacular set pieces, including an enjoyably daft finale. The concept was so successful that the film spawned a sequel and a cartoon series. JF Brief swearing. *DVD* BD

Bill Murray *Dr Peter Venkman* · Dan Aykroyd *Dr Raymond Stantz* · Sigourney Weaver *Dana Barrett* · Harold Ramis *Dr Egon Spengler* · Rick Moranis *Louis Tully* · Annie Potts *Janine Melnitz* · Ernie Hudson *Winston Zeddemore* · William Atherton *Walter Peck* ■ *Dir* Ivan Reitman · *Scr* Dan Aykroyd, Harold Ramis

Ghostbusters II ★★★ PG
Supernatural comedy
1989 · US · Colour · 103min

Having reassembled almost the entire team behind the first blockbuster, director Ivan Reitman was not prepared to mess with a successful formula. This time the self-styled ghostbusters – Bill Murray, Dan Aykroyd, Harold Ramis and Ernie Hudson – are called back into service when evil emanating from a painting Sigourney Weaver's boss Peter MacNicol has been restoring awakens spirits around New York. The effects are bigger and more spectacular than in the original, but Ramis and Aykroyd's script fails to sparkle and there is little new here. JF *DVD* BD

Bill Murray *Dr Peter Venkman* · Dan Aykroyd *Dr Raymond Stantz* · Sigourney Weaver *Dana Barrett* · Harold Ramis *Dr Egon Spengler* · Rick Moranis *Louis Tully* · Ernie Hudson *Winston Zeddemore* · Annie Potts *Janine Melnitz* · Peter MacNicol *Janosz Poha* · Harris Yulin *Judge* ■ *Dir* Ivan Reitman · *Scr* Dan Aykroyd, Harold Ramis

Ghostbusters ★★ 12A
Supernatural comedy
2016 · US · Colour · 116min

Director Paul Feig's reboot of the beloved 1984 comedy horror is a mess of misfiring humour, noisy thrills, bloated action, chaotic CGI and zero charm. This gender-reversed update sets itself too many nostalgic hurdles and fails to clear any, as Melissa McCarthy, Kristen Wiig, Kate McKinnon and Leslie Jones become the overly zany spook exterminators who must stop a crazed janitor unleashing mayhem on Manhattan. The four comedians fail to cohere as a believable unit and barely sustain even the most obvious comic clichés. A missed opportunity in every respect. AJ CS

Melissa McCarthy *Abby Yates* · Kristen Wiig *Erin Gilbert* · Kate McKinnon *Jillian Holtzmann* · Leslie Jones *Patty Tolan* · Chris Hemsworth *Kevin* ■ *Dir* Paul Feig · *Scr* Katie Dippold

Ghosted ★★ 18
Thriller
2011 · UK · Colour · 97min

For most of its running time, this small-scale British drama seems content to dish up a diet of prison clichés, particularly Craig Parkinson's sociopathic, homosexual kingpin. But he slips into the background as the story focuses on John Lynch, who is in jail for killing a burglar and due for release, and Martin Compston, a youngster imprisoned for arson. Lynch saves Compston from Parkinson's unwanted attentions, but too late, and the final denouement manages the remarkable feat of being both implausible and predictable at the same time. BP Violence, swearing. *DVD*

John Lynch *Jack* · David Schofield *Donner* · Martin Compston *Paul* · Craig Parkinson *Clay* · Art Malik *Ahmed* ■ *Dir/Scr* Craig Viveiros

Ghosts ★★★★ 15
Drama based on a true story
2006 · UK · Colour · 95min

This sparse and incredibly moving drama is based on events that led to the deaths of 23 Chinese cockle pickers in Morecambe Bay in 2004 – a tragedy that highlighted the disquieting realities of Britain's illegal labour market. Employing hand-held cameras, non-professional actors and a screenplay that skilfully blends fact and fiction, *Ghosts* follows single mother Ai Qin (Ai Qin Li) from rural China to England's North West where she finds racism, poverty and virtual slavery. Film-maker Nick Broomfield has been a forceful presence in front of the camera in documentaries such as *Aileen: Life and Death of a Serial Killer*. But here he brings a human touch to the story behind the headlines in only his second scripted movie. JR Mandarin, English +subtitles. Swearing. *DVD*

Ai Qin Lin *Ai Qin* · Zhan Yu *Mr Lin (the gangmaster)* · Zhe Wei *Xiao Li* · Man Qin Wei *Chio* · Wen Buo *Zhai Zhai* · Devi *Zhu Bai* ■ *Dir* Nick Broomfield · *Scr* Nick Broomfield, Jez Lewis · *Cinematographer* Mark Wolf

Ghosts Can't Do It ★ 18
Erotic supernatural fantasy
1990 · US · Colour · 83min

This execrable soft-core nonsense from director John Derek and his wife Bo has Anthony Quinn committing suicide after a heart attack ruins his sex life with wife Bo Derek. The ludicrous plot then sees him return in ghostly form with a plan to kill handsome Leo Damien and take over his body so they can resume their erotic odyssey. AJ

Bo Derek *Kate* · Anthony Quinn *Scott* · Leo Damien *Fausto* · Don Murray *Winston* · Julie Newmar *Angel* ■ *Dir/Scr* John Derek

Ghosts in the Night ★★ U
Comedy drama
1943 · US · BW · 66min

Bela Lugosi's second outing with the East Side Kids was something of a comedown from his first – the more than mediocre *Spooks Run Wild*. Ignore the title, as there isn't a single ghoul occupying that old deserted house. But there are plenty of fifth columnists, operating under the fanatical eye of spymaster Lugosi. A young Ava Gardner plays Huntz Hall's sister. DP

Leo Gorcey *Mugs McGinnis* · Huntz Hall *Glimpy Williams* · Bobby Jordan *Danny* · Bela Lugosi *Emil* · Ava Gardner *Betty* · Williams Gibson · Rick Vallin *John "Jack" Gibson* · Sammy Morrison ["Sunshine Sammy" Morrison] *Scruno* · Billy Benedict *Benny* · Bobby Stone *Rocky/Dave* · Bill Bates *"Sleepy" Dave* ■ *Dir* William Beaudine · *Scr* Kenneth Higgins

Ghosts – Italian Style ★★★
Comedy
1967 · Fr/It · Colour · 92min

Every genre went "Italian style" in the 1960s and this supernatural comedy is one of the better offshoots of that craze. Sophia Loren and Vittorio Gassman are an impoverished married couple offered free accommodation in an old palace. Of course, it's haunted. Meanwhile, Loren's would-be lover, Mario Adorf, has also moved into the palace and much amusement ensues when Gassman mistakes him for a ghost. Renato Castellani's romp scores much laughter from the hereafter. AJ In Italian.

Sophia Loren *Maria* · Vittorio Gassman *Pasquale* · Mario Adorf *Alfredo* · Aldo Giuffre *Raffaele* · Margaret Lee *Sayonara* · Francesco Tensi *Professor Santanna* · Marcello Mastroianni *Headless ghost* ■ *Dir* Renato Castellani · *Scr* Renato Castellani, Adriano Baracco, Leo Benvenuti, Piero De Bernardi, Ernest Pintoff, from the play *Questi Fantasmi!* by Eduardo De Filippo

The Ghosts of Berkeley Square ★★★
Comedy
1947 · UK · BW · 100min

Robert Morley and Felix Aylmer are wonderfully mischievous as the bungling 18th-century assassins who are cursed to haunt a luxurious town house until it is visited by a reigning monarch. Amusing interludes along the way include Ernest Thesiger's attempt to prove they're a hoax and the ghosts being mistaken for First World War spies. A great opportunity to watch an accomplished cast of British character actors go through its paces, and a spirited flight of fancy that takes several sly swipes at the British cinema of the period. DP

Robert Morley *General Burlap* · Felix Aylmer *Colonel Kelsoe* · Yvonne Arnaud *Millie* · Robert Beaumont *King's equerry* · Madge Brindley *Matron* · Strelsa Brown *Rajah's Amazon attendant* · Harry Fine *1914 Colonel* · Ronald Frankau *Tex* · Ernest Thesiger *Investigator* ■ *Dir* Vernon Sewell · *Scr* James Seymour, from the novel *No Nightingales* by Caryl Brahms, SJ Simon

Ghosts of Cité Soleil ★★★★ 15
Documentary
2005 · Den/US · Colour and BW · 85min

This documentary provides a devastating insight into life in Cité Soleil, the slum area of Haiti's capital Port-au-Prince that's considered by the UN to be the most dangerous place on Earth. Danish director Asger Leth and his Serbian assistant, Milos Loncarevic, focus on events in early 2004, as the brutal Chimerès ("ghost") gangs help quell opposition to the nation's first democratically elected president, Jean-Bertrand Aristide. Haitian musician Wyclef Jean supplies some fleeting moments of human warmth, but the endless images of poverty, vandalism, voodoo and violence render this one of the most terrifying documentaries ever made. DP English, Haitian, French +subtitles.

Winson "2Pac" Jean · James "Billy" Petit Frère · Wyclef Jean *Eleonore "Lele" Senlis* · Andy Apaid · Reginald *Billy's soldier* · Franzo *2Pac's soldier* · Colin Powell ■ *Dir* Asger Leth, Milos Loncarevic · *Scr* Asger Leth · *Cinematographers* Milos Loncarevic, Frederik Jacobi, Asger Leth

Ghosts of Girlfriends Past ★★★ 12
Romantic comedy
2009 · US · Colour · 96min

This hit-and-miss take on *A Christmas Carol* stars Matthew McConaughey as a Scrooge-like bachelor whose cynical belief that love is "a magical crutch for the weak and uneducated" wreaks havoc when he attends his younger brother's wedding. As with the Charles Dickens classic, McConaughey is visited by ghosts of his past, present and future, as well as his tacky playboy role model uncle (an awkward comic turn by Michael Douglas). Their mission is to make the commitment-phobic lothario admit that he still loves his childhood sweetheart Jennifer Garner. This is undemanding but watchable fare that spells its message in big letters while throwing out a few crumbs of wisdom along the way. KK *DVD* BD

Matthew McConaughey *Connor Mead* · Jennifer Garner *Jenny Perotti* · Breckin Meyer *Paul Mead* · Lacey Chabert *Sandra Volkom* · Robert Forster *Sergeant Volkom* · Anne Archer *Vonda Volkom* · Michael Douglas (1) *Uncle Wayne* ■ *Dir* Mark Waters (1) · *Scr* Jon Lucas, Scott Moore

Ghosts of Mississippi ★★★ 15
Drama based on a true story
1996 · US · Colour · 125min

Also known as *Ghosts from the Past*, this fact-based drama stars Alec Baldwin as the lawyer who reopened the case of Medgar Evers, a black civil rights leader murdered nearly 30 years before. A white man named Byron De La Beckwith (an over-the-top James Woods) had been charged with the crime, but was released when two white juries could not unanimously find him guilty. It's a moving true story and the cast is excellent. However, Rob Reiner's uninvolving direction fails to make the story as compelling or passionate as it should be. JB Violence, swearing.

Alec Baldwin *Bobby DeLaughter* · Whoopi Goldberg *Myrlie Evers* · James Woods *Byron De La Beckwith* · Craig T Nelson *Ed Peters* · Susanna Thompson *Peggy Lloyd* · William H Macy *Charlie Crisco* ■ *Dir* Rob Reiner · *Scr* Lewis Colick

Ghosts... of the Civil Dead ★★★★ 18
Prison drama
1988 · Aus · Colour · 89min

Prison pictures don't come much tougher than this. Directed with reckless visual energy by one-time pop promo producer John Hillcoat, this drama casts an unflinching eye over the brutalities perpetrated by the staff of a state-of-the-art, maximum security prison, packed to the rafters with violent offenders. Everything from drugs and starvation to rape and self-mutilation is charted as the film, through a series of flashbacks, reveals the motives for an explosive riot that rips through the hi-tech defences. Shot with a ruthless power, made all the more chilling by the relentlessly raw realism, this is a remarkable debut. DP Violence, swearing.

Dave Field [David Field] *Wenzil* · Mike Bishop *David Yale* · Chris De Rose *Jack Grezner* · Nick Cave *Maynard* · Freddo Dierck *Robbins* · Vincent Gil *Ruben* · Bogdan Koca *Waychek* · Kevin Mackey *Glover* · Dave Mason *Lilly* ■ *Dir* John Hillcoat · *Scr* Nick Cave, Gene Conkie, Evan English, John Hillcoat, Hugo Race, John Flaus

The Ghoul ★★★★ PG
Horror
1933 · UK · BW · 80min

Following his enormous success in the US, Boris Karloff returned home to England for this highly successful clone of *The Mummy*. Under eerily effective make-up, he's a cataleptic Egyptologist rising from the dead to recover a stolen talisman. Hugely atmospheric, if slow by today's standards, the macabre mood eventually gives way to sinister slapstick, but Karloff's commanding presence elevates it to the level of seminal British *Grand Guignol*. It also marks Ralph Richardson's first screen appearance. AT *DVD*

Boris Karloff *Professor Morlant* · Cedric Hardwicke *Broughton* · Ernest Thesiger *Laing* · Dorothy Hyson *Betty Harlow* · Anthony Bushell *Ralph Morlant* · Kathleen Harrison *Kaney* · Harold Huth *Aga Ben Dragore* · DA Clarke-Smith *Mahmoud* · Ralph Richardson *Nigel Hartley* ■ *Dir* T Hayes Hunter · *Scr* Roland Pertwee, John Hastings Turner, Rupert Downing, L du Garde Peach, from the novel and play by Dr Frank King, Leonard J Hines

The Ghoul ★★ 18
Horror
1975 · UK · Colour · 89min

Shot on leftover sets from *The Great Gatsby*, Freddie Francis's flapper fright-fest (produced by his son Kevin) eschews gore in favour of more traditional terror. It's an unsavoury tale about defrocked minister Peter Cushing trying to keep his cannibal son locked in the attic. A nice feeling for the 1920s period atmosphere and a crazed performance from John Hurt give this fractured slow-mover a few kicks. AJ

Peter Cushing *Dr Lawrence* · John Hurt *Tom Rawlings* · Alexandra Bastedo *Angela* · Gwen Watford *Ayah* · Veronica Carlson *Daphne* ·

Stewart Bevan *Billy* • Ian McCulloch *Geoffrey* • Don Henderson *The Ghoul* ■ *Dir* Freddie Francis • *Scr* John Elder [Anthony Hinds]

Ghoulies ★★ 15
Comedy horror   1985 · US · Colour · 77min

Executive producer Charles Band, the self-styled B-movie king of 1980s schlock and cheap straight-to-video horror was responsible for this tacky imitation of *Gremlins*. Under the spell of his Satanist father, Peter Liapis invokes a black magic ritual in the family mansion and conjures up midget demons from another dimension who go on a teen-killing spree. Low-grade trash with a self-mocking tone. The little devils returned for three sequels. AJ *DVD*

Peter Liapis *Jonathan Graves* • Lisa Pelikan *Rebecca* • Michael Des Barres *Malcolm Graves* • Jack Nance *Wolfgang* • Peter Risch *Grizzel* • Tamara De Treaux *Greedigut* • Scott Thomson *Mike* ■ *Dir* Luca Bercovici • *Scr* Luca Bercovici, Jefery Levy

Gia ★★★ 18
Biographical drama   1998 · US · Colour · 119min

Oscar winner Angelina Jolie gives an early knockout performance in this dark and provocative TV movie. She stars as Gia Carangi, whose rise to fame as a supermodel in the 1970s brought tragedy as she became addicted to pills, cocaine and heroin. With its almost soft-core porn style, this is more an art house film then standard TV-movie fare. MC *DVD*

Angelina Jolie *Gia Carangi* • Elizabeth Mitchell *Linda* • Mercedes Ruehl *Kathleen Carangi* • Faye Dunaway *Wilhemina Cooper* • Kylie Travis *Stephanie* ■ *Dir* Michael Cristofer • *Scr* Michael Cristofer, Jay McInerney

Giant ★★★★ PG
Epic drama   1956 · US · Colour · 192min

James Dean's last film before his untimely death in a car crash reveals him for the time as more an icon than an actor – he just couldn't portray middle age in the final half of this epic drama based on writer Edna Ferber's homage to Texas. George Stevens, who won the best director Oscar (one of the film's ten nominations), manages to convey some of the swashbuckling magic of oil barons and land exploitation, and elicits strong performances from a lustrous Elizabeth Taylor and a manly Rock Hudson. Those elements, plus a tremendous scene when Dean strikes oil, make it an adventure of truly epic proportions. TH *DVD*

Elizabeth Taylor *Leslie Benedict* • Rock Hudson *Bick Benedict* • James Dean (1) *Jett Rink* • Mercedes McCambridge *Luz Benedict* • Carroll Baker *Luz Benedict II* • Dennis Hopper *Jordan Benedict III* • Sal Mineo *Angel Obregon III* • Jane Withers *Vashti Snythe* • Chill Wills *Uncle Rawley* ■ *Dir* George Stevens • *Scr* Fred Guiol, Ivan Moffat, from the novel by Edna Ferber

The Giant Gila Monster ★
Science-fiction horror   1959 · US · BW · 74min

A badly rear-projected giant lizard stomps through model Texan towns and terrorises the local teens, who always seem to be having hot-rod races or rock 'n' roll dance hall parties. Unintentionally amusing. AJ

Don Sullivan *Chace Winstead* • Lisa Simone *Lisa* • Shug Fisher *Mr Harris* • Jerry Cortwright *Bob* • Beverly Thurman *Gay* • Don Flournoy *Gordy* • Clarke Browne *Chuck* • Pat Simmons *Sherry* ■ *Dir* Ray Kellogg • *Scr* Jay Sims, Ray Kellogg, from a story by Ray Kellogg

The Giant of Marathon ★★ U
Historical adventure   1960 · It · Colour · 90min

Steve Reeves abandons the role of Hercules (for which he was most famous) to squeeze his bronzed torso into the role of the Athenian warrior Philippides, who warns his fellow Greeks of a Persian invasion. It's not the worst of its kind by a long chalk, but it's sad to see B-movie maestro Jacques Tourneur reduced to muscle-bound mediocrity like this. DP

Steve Reeves *Philippides* • Mylène Demongeot *Andromeda* • Daniela Rocca *Karis* • Ivo Garrani *Creuso* • Philippe Hersent *Callimaco* • Sergio

Fantoni *Teocrito* • Alberto Lupo *Milziade* • Daniele Varga *Dario, King of the Persians* ■ *Dir* Jacques Tourneur • *Scr* Ennio De Concini, Augusto Frassinetti, Bruno Vailati, from an idea by Raffaello Pacini, Alberto Barsanti

The Giant Spider Invasion ★ 15
Science-fiction horror   1975 · US · Colour · 79min

A rash of outsize spider sightings is traced to Wisconsin, but greedy farmer Robert Easton, thinking the radioactive spiders' eggs from another dimension are jewels, won't let the authorities investigate until it's too late. This irredeemable dreck has bottom-of-the-barrel special effects. AJ Violence *DVD*

Barbara Hale *Dr Jenny Langer* • Steve Brodie *Dr Vance* • Leslie Parrish *Ev Kester* • Alan Hale Jr *Sheriff* • Robert Easton *Kester* • Kevin Brodie *Dave Perkins* • Christiane Schmidtmer *Helga* ■ *Dir* Bill Rebane, Richard L Huff • *Scr* Richard L Huff, Robert Easton

The Giants ★★★ 15
Drama   2011 · Bel · Colour · 83min

In this altogether darker take on the type of coming-of-age drama exemplified by *Stand by Me*, three troubled teenagers – brothers Zacharie Chasseriaud and Martin Nissen, and Paul Bartel – must fend for themselves in the verdant but oppressive Ardennes forest one summer. Director Bouli Lanners (*Eldorado*) and his co-writer, Elise Ancion, in effect dump the trio in the woods with scant backstory and leave them to their own devices. Despite the film's episodic, impressionistic structure, a satisfying narrative does eventually emerge. AC French, Russian +subtitles. *DVD*

Zacharie Chasseriaud *Zak* • Martin Nissen *Seth* • Paul Bartel (2) *Dany* • Karim Leklou *Angel* • Didier Toupy *Beef* • Gwen Berrou *Martha* ■ *Dir* Bouli Lanners • *Scr* Bouli Lanners, Elise Ancion

Gideon ★★
Comedy drama   1999 · US · Colour · 100min

Christopher Lambert is surprisingly effective playing a child-man who is placed in a retirement home in rural South Carolina and slowly begins to transform the lives of its dissatisfied residents. The veteran stars in the supporting cast perform their stereotyped roles with aplomb, although Carroll O'Connor's bolshy cook, Mike Connors's ring-rusty boxer and Shirley Jones's frustrated artist are less showy than Charlton Heston's crusty philosophy professor. DP

Christopher Lambert *Gideon Dobbs* • Charlton Heston *Addison Sinclair* • Shelley Winters *Mrs Willows* • Carroll O'Connor *Leo Barnes* • Shirley Jones *Elly Morton* • Mike Connors *Harland Greer* • Barbara Bain *Sarah* • Crystal Bernard *Jean MacLemore* ■ *Dir* Claudia Hoover • *Scr* Brad Mirman

Gideon's Day ★★★★ PG
Crime drama   1958 · UK · Colour · 99min

Shown in America as *Gideon of Scotland Yard*, this cynical romp is extremely entertaining and contains a marvellous performance from Jack Hawkins as the Gideon of the title, who is followed by the camera on what must be the busiest day of his life. Hawkins was the only British actor to star for the three greatest American directors of their day: William Wyler in *Ben-Hur*, Howard Hawks in *Land of the Pharaohs* and John Ford here. TS

Jack Hawkins *Inspector George Gideon* • Dianne Foster *Joanna Delafield* • Anna Lee *Kate Gideon* • Anna Massey *Sally Gideon* • Andrew Ray *PC Simon Farnaby-Green* • Cyril Cusack *Herbert "Birdy" Sparrow* • James Hayter *Mason* • Ronald Howard *Paul Delafield* ■ *Dir* John Ford • *Scr* TEB Clarke, from the novel by JJ Marric [John Creasey]

Gideon's Trumpet ★★★★ U
Courtroom drama based on a true story   1980 · US · Colour · 103min

Henry Fonda is marvellous in this TV movie based on a true-life court case that enshrined the principle of free representation in American legal history.

Although not the obvious choice to play a semi-literate convict, Fonda manages to bring off the characterisation with a bravado that is both winning and warm. Also remarkably effective is José Ferrer as Fonda's lawyer, while John Houseman (who also executive produced) heads up a distinguished supporting cast. In a much-maligned genre, this is an example of the TV movie at its best, tackling a subject that cinema might regard as uncommercial. TS

Henry Fonda *Clarence Earl Gideon* • José Ferrer *Abe Fortas* • John Houseman *Chief Justice* • Fay Wray *Edna Curtis* • Sam Jaffe *1st Justice* • Dean Jagger *6th Justice* • Nicholas Pryor *Jacob* • William Prince *5th Justice* ■ *Dir* Robert Collins (1) • *Scr* David W Rintels, from a story by Anthony Lewis

Gidget ★★★★ U
Romantic comedy   1959 · US · Colour · 95min

A perfect period artefact, this quintessential California surf movie is actually much, much better than it should be – or was ever given credit for – largely thanks to the stylish direction by Paul Wendkos. Sandra Dee is the titular heroine and she became identified with the role, even though she didn't reprise it in the two sequels or in the two completely different TV series. Her beaus are James Darren and Cliff Robertson, and there is a very real sense of enjoyment when all three are together. And, of course, the beach looks fabulous in CinemaScope and Eastmancolor. Deborah Walley and Cindy Carol took over the role of Gidget in two 1960s sequels. TS

Sandra Dee *Francie* • James Darren *Moondoggie* • Cliff Robertson *Kahoona* • Arthur O'Connell *Russell Lawrence* • Mary LaRoche *Dorothy Lawrence* • Joby Baker *Stinky* • Tom Laughlin *Lover Boy* ■ *Dir* Paul Wendkos • *Scr* Gabrielle Upton, from the novel by Frederick Kohner

The Gift ★★★ 15
Supernatural thriller   2000 · US · Colour · 107min

Co-scripted by Billy Bob Thornton, this eerie tale sees widow Cate Blanchett blessed with ESP and roped into assisting the police find a missing woman. Her insights lead to the arrest of adulterous wife-batterer Keanu Reeves, but is he really the culprit? The strong cast rises above the rather predictable plotting and hackneyed final reel, and there are some scary moments along the way. JC Violence, swearing, sex scenes, nudity. *DVD*

Cate Blanchett *Annie Wilson* • Giovanni Ribisi *Buddy Cole* • Keanu Reeves *Donnie Barksdale* • Katie Holmes *Jessica King* • Greg Kinnear *Wayne Collins* • Hilary Swank *Valerie Barksdale* ■ *Dir* Sam Raimi • *Scr* Billy Bob Thornton, Tom Epperson

The Gift ★★★ 15
Psychological thriller   2015 · Aus/US · Colour · 108min

Relocated to Hollywood, young marrieds Jason Bateman and Rebecca Hall "accidentally" bump into one of his old school acquaintances. Soon Joel Edgerton is perpetually on their doorstep bearing gifts until it becomes clear he's after closure for something awful Bateman swears he can't remember. As director/writer, Edgerton moves his keep-you-guessing mystery along with finely crafted momentum, cleverly manipulating its genre trappings to create a real sense of creepy unease – and a couple of terrific scares – while providing undertones of serious social drama. AJ *DVD*

Jason Bateman *Simon* • Rebecca Hall *Robyn* • Joel Edgerton *Gordo* • Beau Knapp *Detective Walker* ■ *Dir/Scr* Joel Edgerton

A Gift for Heidi ★★
Adventure   1958 · US · Colour · 71min

It may be impossible to film Johanna Spyri's much loved novel without lashings of sentimentality, but never has the little Alpine orphan found herself so immersed in sticky sweetness as in this glutinous fable. The gift in question is a set of carved wooden figures depicting Faith, Hope and Charity, the true meaning of which she

comes to learn in the course of three tacky tales. Sandy Descher is just about bearable in the lead. DP

Sandy Descher *Heidi* • Douglas Fowley *Alm Uncle* • Van Dyke Parks *Peter* • Peter Capell *Doc* • Erik Jelde *Ernst* • Susan Sainio *Clara* • Oswald Ursteins *Carlo* • Clancy Cooper *Dr Roth* ■ *Dir* George Templeton • *Scr* Eugene Vale, David Dortort, from the characters by Johanna Spyri

Gift Horse ★★ PG
Second World War drama   1951 · UK · BW · 95min

Packed with stock situations, this unremarkable naval drama starts in 1940 on the broken-down tub presented to gung-ho captain Trevor Howard as part of a 50-destroyer loan made to Britain by neutral America. Director Compton Bennett stages the action with efficiency but no urgency, and Howard looks bored by the proceedings. DP *DVD*

Trevor Howard *Lieutenant Commander Hugh Fraser* • Richard Attenborough *Dripper Daniels* • Sonny Tufts *Yank Flanagan* • James Donald *Lieutenant Richard Jennings* • Joan Rice *June Mallory* • Bernard Lee *Stripey Wood* • Dora Bryan *Glad* • Hugh Williams *Captain* ■ *Dir* Compton Bennett • *Scr* William Fairchild, William Rose, Hugh Hastings, from a story by Ivan Goff, Ben Roberts

The Gift of Love ★ U
Drama   1958 · US · Colour · 105min

In 1946, Fox had a big hit with the very mushy *Sentimental Journey*, which worked because of the sincerity of Maureen O'Hara and the adroit direction of Walter Lang. This time round it's Lauren Bacall playing the dying wife who adopts a little girl to provide consolation for her husband after she's gone. Garish colour, the miscasting of Bacall and the crude direction of Jean Negulesco result in insufferable schmaltz. AE

Lauren Bacall *Julie Beck* • Robert Stack *Bill Beck* • Evelyn Rudie *Hitty* • Lorne Greene *Grant Allan* • Anne Seymour *McMasters* • Edward Platt *Dr Miller* • Joseph Kearns *Mr Rynicker* ■ *Dir* Jean Negulesco • *Scr* Luther Davis, from a story by Nelia Gardner White

Gifted Hands: the Ben Carson Story ★★★
Biographical drama   2009 · US · Colour

In this inspirational biopic from *Coach Carter* director Thomas Carter, Cuba Gooding Jr oozes integrity as the paediatric neurosurgeon renowned for his ground-breaking work separating conjoined twins. A deeply moving celebration of industriousness, faith and determination, this quality TV movie focuses largely on the educational journey of the now-retired Ben Carson, who overcame poverty, racism and serious anger issues to achieve what seemed an impossible career dream. A powerful turn from Kimberly Elise, playing Carson's troubled but supportive mother, helps drive home some of the film's most positive messages. SF

Cuba Gooding Jr *Dr Ben Carson* • Kimberly Elise *Sonya Carson* • Aunjanue Ellis *Candy* ■ *Dir* Thomas Carter • *Scr* John Pielmeier

The Gig ★★★ 15
Comedy drama   1985 · US · Colour · 87min

This wistfully funny jazz movie stars Wayne Rogers as a New York car dealer. He's been playing jazz trombone with a bunch of friends for years and books them into a swanky resort in the Catskill Mountains, the sort of place that usually hosts Jewish stand-ups and tea dances. Personally financed by its director, Frank D Gilroy, the film has a sardonic edge, a tremendous sense of place and winning performances. AT

Wayne Rogers *Marty Flynn* • Cleavon Little *Marshall Wilson* • Andrew Duncan *Jack Larmon* • Daniel Nalbach *Arthur Winslow* • Jerry Matz *Aaron Wohl* • Warren Vache *Gil Macrae* • Joe Silver *Abe Mitgang* • Jay Thomas *Rick Valentine* • Stan Lachow *George* ■ *Dir/Scr* Frank D Gilroy

Gigantic ★★ 15
Romantic comedy 2008 · US · Colour · 97min

This indie tale about the nature of love strives to be original but only ends up being self-consciously quirky and rather unsettling. Brian Weathersby (Paul Dano) sells upscale mattresses and leads a pretty boring life. Then he encounters Al Lolly (John Goodman), a larger-than-life businessman who wants the best mattress money can buy, and his wispy daughter Harriet (Zooey Deschanel) who comes to approve his purchase and promptly falls asleep in the shop. The ensuing love story judders through unlikely twists and turns, as Harriet becomes Brian's girlfriend, only to discover his obsession with adopting a Chinese orphan. Emotionally and logically disjointed, it confuses more than it entertains. KK Violence, swearing. *DVD*

Paul Dano *Brian Weathersby* • Zooey Deschanel *Harriet "Happy" Lolly* • Jane Alexander *Mrs Weathersby* • Edward Asner *Mr Weathersby* • John Goodman *Al Lolly* • Sean Dugan *Gary Wynkoop* • Brian Avers *Larry Arbogast* ■ *Dir* Matt Aselton • *Scr* Matt Aselton, Adam Nagata

Gigi ★★★★★ PG
Musical 1958 · US · Colour · 110min

Rightful winner of nine Academy Awards (including best picture), this is the last great musical from producer Arthur Freed. He coerced composers Lerner and Loewe into creating a screen original from Colette's tale following their sensational stage success with *My Fair Lady*. Superbly cast (Leslie Caron in the title role, Maurice Chevalier winning a special Oscar, Louis Jourdan), immaculately designed (for CinemaScope in Art Nouveau by Cecil Beaton) and impeccably directed by Vincente Minnelli, this is a sophisticated and entertaining musical treat. The story about the training of a young girl to become a courtesan is hardly the usual basis for a screen song-fest, but it's brilliantly and intelligently handled, with arguably the best sequences (the duet *I Remember It Well* and Gaston's soliloquy) directed by the uncredited Charles Walters, who had previously guided Caron in *Lili*. TS *DVD*

Leslie Caron *Gigi* • Maurice Chevalier *Honore Lachaille* • Louis Jourdan *Gaston Lachaille* • Hermione Gingold *Mme Alvarez* • Eva Gabor *Liane D'Exelmans* • Jacques Bergerac *Sandomir* • Isabel Jeans *Aunt Alicia* • John Abbott *Manuel* ■ *Dir* Vincente Minnelli • *Scr* Alan Jay Lerner, from the play by Anita Loos, from the novel by Colette • *Cinematographer* Joseph Ruttenberg • *Editor* Adrienne Fazan • *Art Directors* William A Horning, Preston Ames • *Costume Designer* Cecil Beaton • *Music/lyrics* Frederick Loewe • *Lyrics* Alan Jay Lerner • *Music Director* André Previn

Gigli ★ 15
Romantic crime comedy 2003 · US · Colour · 116min

There's no chemistry between Ben Affleck and Jennifer Lopez, starring as Mob operatives who kidnap the mentally disabled younger brother of a powerful federal prosecutor. Lopez is a new-age lesbian, and Affleck's Neanderthal hitman tries to prove that he's the solution to her sexual "affliction". Absolutely dreadful. SF *DVD*

Ben Affleck *Larry Gigli* • Jennifer Lopez *Ricki* • Justin Bartha *Brian* • Lainie Kazan *Larry's mother* • Missy Crider *Robin* • Lenny Venito *Louis* • Christopher Walken *Det Stanley Jacobellis* • Al Pacino *Starkman* ■ *Dir/Scr* Martin Brest

The Gigolos ★★ 12
Comedy 2006 · UK · Colour · 93min

Sacha Tarter and Trevor Sather star in this fictional portrait of male escorts doing the rounds in London's swanky West End, which they co-wrote with director Richard Bracewell. Adopting their own names here, the pair cater to the needs of mature but lonely ladies – portrayed by such luminaries of the British stage and screen as Susannah York, Anna Massey and Sian Phillips. It's a fine line between comedy and tragedy as Sacha gradually becomes more emotionally needy than his clients. The story is neither funny nor dramatic, meandering for a long time in loosely connected episodes before anything of real significance happens. SP Swearing, sexual references. *DVD*

Sacha Tarter *Sacha* • Trevor Sather *Trevor* • Susannah York *Tessa Harrington* • Anna Massey *Edwina* • Sian Philips *Baroness James* • Angela Pleasence *Joy* ■ *Dir* Richard Bracewell • *Scr* Richard Bracewell, Sacha Tarter, Trevor Sather

Gigot ★★★ U
Comedy drama 1962 · US · Colour · 104min

Director Gene Kelly embraces the inherent sentimentality in the touching tale of a Parisian mute and, aided by a magnificent performance in the title role by Jackie Gleason, achieves an almost Chaplinesque work of great poignancy. Understandably, and unfortunately, the film was re-edited by 20th Century-Fox when they realised what Kelly had delivered, and Kelly and Gleason always claimed that the original cut (no longer in existence) was far better than the one that survives. TS

Jackie Gleason *Gigot* • Katherine Kath *Colette* • Gabrielle Dorziat *Madame Brigitte* • Jean Lefebvre *Gaston* • Jacques Marin *Jean* • Albert Rémy *Alphonse* • Yvonne Constant *Lucille Duval* • Germaine Delbat *Madame Greuze* ■ *Dir* Gene Kelly • *Scr* John Patrick, from a story by Jackie Gleason

Gilda ★★★★★ PG
Classic film noir 1946 · US · BW · 105min

"There never was a woman like Gilda!" shrieked the original poster (designed by James Bond title wizard Maurice Binder). And there never was anyone to capture the imagination like Rita Hayworth, whose first appearance in this movie is a classic star introduction. Highlights include her striptease (well, she takes off a glove) and her voluptuous vamping of callow Glenn Ford, whose perverse relationship with his former boss and Gilda's husband George Macready seemed to circumvent the censors by a mile. Columbia's low-lit studio-bound Buenos Aires setting is quintessential 1940s *film noir*, and the whole is a remarkable example of Hollywood turning dross into gold. TS *DVD*

Rita Hayworth *Gilda Mundson* • Glenn Ford *Johnny Farrell* • George Macready *Ballin Mundson* • Joseph Calleia *Obregon* • Steven Geray *Uncle Pio* • Joe Sawyer *Casey* • Gerald Mohr *Captain Delgado* ■ *Dir* Charles Vidor • *Scr* Marion Parsonnet, Jo Eisinger, from a story by EA Ellington

The Gilded Cage ★★
Thriller 1954 · UK · BW · 78min

After a string of supporting roles for Universal in the early 1950s, Alex Nicol earned a dubious promotion to leading man in this British thriller, co-starring Clifford Evans. Director John Gilling tries to push this tale of art theft and murder along at a decent pace, but spotting who framed Nichol's brother is hardly taxing. DP

Alex Nicol *Steve Anderson* • Veronica Hurst *Marcia Farrell* • Clifford Evans *Ken Aimes* • Ursula Howells *Brenda Lucas* • Elwyn Brook-Jones *Bruno* • John Stuart *Harding* • Michael Alexander *Harry Anderson* • Trevor Reid *Inspector Brace* ■ *Dir* John Gilling • *Scr* Brock Williams, from a story by Paul Erickson

The Gilded Lily ★★★
Screwball comedy 1935 · US · BW · 82min

This frothy Paramount comedy rode in on the back of the phenomenal success of Columbia's *It Happened One Night*. Critics and public alike were quick to make the connection with this new vehicle for Claudette Colbert. She's delightful as a New York secretary having to make up her mind between two suitors: a charming, wealthy but caddish English aristocrat (Ray Milland) and a standard-last American newspaper reporter (Fred MacMurray). Deftly directed by Wesley Ruggles, the movie launched MacMurray to stardom. RK

Claudette Colbert *Lillian David* • Fred MacMurray *Peter Dawes* • Ray Milland *Charles Gray/Granville* • C Aubrey Smith *Lloyd Granville* • Eddie Craven *Eddie* • Luis Alberni *Nate* • Donald Meek *Hankerson* ■ *Dir* Wesley Ruggles • *Scr* Claude Binyon, from a story by Melville Baker, Jack Kirkland

Gimme Shelter ★★★★ 15
Music documentary 1970 · US · Colour · 91min

Rightly considered to be more of a 1960s watershed than Woodstock, the free concert given by the Rolling Stones at the Altamount Speedway in northern California will always be remembered for revealing the flip side of the decade of love and peace. The murder of a black spectator by a Hell's Angels bouncer during *Under My Thumb* and the violence that followed pervades this documentary, most memorably in the scene in which Mick Jagger and Charlie Watts view the incident on an editing machine. But there is also some mesmerising footage of the Stones, Jefferson Airplane and the Flying Burrito Brothers, and a slyly mocking portrait of showbiz lawyer Melvin Belli. DP *DVD*

Mick Jagger • Keith Richards (2) *Keith Richards* • Mick Taylor • Charlie Watts • Bill Wyman • Ike Turner • Tina Turner ■ *Dir* David Maysles, Albert Maysles, Charlotte Zwerin

Gimme the Loot ★★★★ 15
Crime comedy 2012 · US · Colour · 79min

Writer/director Adam Leon makes an auspicious debut with this charming Bronx tale. Graffiti artists Ty Hickson and Tashiana Washington vow to tag the giant apple at Citi Field that appears whenever the New York Mets score a home run, after the baseball-mad Woodside King Crew vandalises their wall display. But the real focus falls on the pair's hapless efforts to raise $500 – by fair means or foul – to bribe a guard at the stadium. With its living, breathing New York setting so evocatively captured by Jonathan Miller's camera, and a non-professional cast, this warm and witty study of race, class, sex and art is a far cry from the bleakly violent 'hood dramas that dominated 1990s New Black Cinema. DP Swearing, sexual references, drug abuse.

Tashiana Washington *Sofia* • Ty Hickson *Malcolm* • Meeko Gattuso *Champion* • Sam Soghor *Lenny* • Adam Metzger *Donnie* ■ *Dir/Scr* Adam Leon

Ginger & Fred ★★★★★ 15
Satirical comedy 1986 · It/Fr/W Ger · Colour · 121min

Ginger Rogers tried to sue the production company behind this masterpiece from the great Italian director Federico Fellini – a move that now seems astonishingly myopic. The film itself pays tribute to Ginger; it also meditates on urban decay (exemplified by television's down-market values) while affirming the warmth of past love. Marcello Mastroianni and Guilietta Masina (Fellini's wife) play two elderly dancers who, having discreetly modelled themselves on Astaire and Rogers, are brought out of retirement for a TV show. Fellini's attack on tacky telly is as comic as it is wounding, but Mastroianni and Masina show that human emotion can win the day. TH Italian +subtitles. Swearing. *DVD*

Giulietta Masina *Amelia Bonetti, "Ginger"* • Marcello Mastroianni *Pippo Botticella, "Fred"* • Franco Fabrizi *Show host* • Frederick von Ledenburg *Admiral* • Augusto Poderosi *Transvestite* • Martin Maria Blau *Assistant producer* • Jacques Henri Lartigue *Flying priest* ■ *Dir* Federico Fellini • *Scr* Federico Fellini, Tonino Guerra, Tullio Pinelli

Ginger & Rosa ★★★★ 12
Drama 2012 · UK/Ger/Can/Den · Colour · 86min

Elle Fanning gives an arresting performance in this bracingly original coming-of-age drama. She plays Ginger, a British teenager growing up in 1962, whose adolescent troubles are exacerbated by the looming threat of nuclear war and, more directly, by her parents (Alessandro Nivola and *Mad Men*'s Christina Hendricks). Ginger finds escape in minor adventures with best friend Rosa (Alice Englert) – until Rosa takes a romantic interest in her dad, which she reciprocates. The changing role of women is an underlying theme in this many-layered but otherwise simply told story, which is one of *Orlando* writer/director Sally Potter's more accessible offerings. SP Swearing, sexual references. *DVD* *Blu-ray*

Elle Fanning *Ginger* • Alessandro Nivola *Roland* • Christina Hendricks *Natalie* • Timothy Spall *Mark* • Oliver Platt *Mark Two* • Annette Bening *Bella* • Alice Englert *Rosa* ■ *Dir/Scr* Sally Potter

Ginger in the Morning ★★ PG
Road movie romance 1973 · US · Colour · 90min

A young Sissy Spacek plays the titular Ginger – a gangly, free-spirited teenage hitch-hiker who gets a ride from lonely travelling salesman Monte Markham. This road movie slides effortlessly into a romance, as the unlikely mutual attraction between the conservative Joe and the wild child Ginger grows apace. However, although the landscape is lovely, the action is minimal. FL

Monte Markham *Joe* • Sissy Spacek *Ginger* • Slim Pickens *Sheriff* • Mark Miller *Charlie* • Susan Oliver *Sugar* ■ *Dir* Gordon Wiles • *Scr* Mark Miller

Ginger Snaps ★★★★ 18
Horror 2000 · Can · Colour · 103min

Director John Fawcett's highly sophisticated and disturbing horror transcends the banality of the werewolf formula with verve. Teenager Katharine Isabelle is attacked by the legendary "Beast of Bailey Downs" and goes from being a death-obsessed Goth freak to a sexually charged dominatrix. Too terrified to confide in their home-loving mother (Mimi Rogers on fine form), and not wanting to go to the police when Isabelle's lust turns murderously savage, her younger sister Emily Perkins turns to enigmatic drug dealer Kris Lemche for help. Two less successful sequels followed. AJ Sex scenes, swearing. *DVD*

Emily Perkins *Brigitte* • Katharine Isabelle *Ginger* • Kris Lemche *Sam* • Mimi Rogers *Pamela* • Jesse Moss *Jason* • Danielle Hampton *Trina* ■ *Dir* John Fawcett • *Scr* Karen Walton, from a story by Karen Walton, John Fawcett

The Gingerbread Man ★★★ 15
Thriller 1997 · US · Colour · 109min

Robert Altman directs this conventional adaptation of a John Grisham story set in Savannah, Georgia. Kenneth Branagh brings a touch of bravado to the role of a successful lawyer who becomes involved with waitress Embeth Davidtz when she accuses her religious fanatic father Robert Duvall of pursuing her. Soon Branagh feels compelled to kidnap his own children to save them from danger, while the menacing atmosphere grows along with the threat of impending floods. TH Swearing. *DVD*

Kenneth Branagh *Rick Magruder* • Embeth Davidtz *Mallory Doss* • Robert Downey Jr *Clyde Pell* • Daryl Hannah *Lois Harlan* • Robert Duvall *Dixon Doss* • Tom Berenger *Pete Randle* • Famke Janssen *Leeanne* • Clyde Hayes *Carl Alden* ■ *Dir* Robert Altman • *Scr* Al Hayes, from a story by John Grisham

The Girl ★★★ 18
Erotic thriller 1986 · Swe/UK · Colour · 103min

The seduction of a leading lawyer by a 14-year-old schoolgirl is the focus of this soft-core slice of Euro erotica. Seduction leads to lust, passion and murder, though not necessarily in that order. Starring Franco Nero and Bernice Stegers, with Christopher Lee in a small supporting role, the film starts strongly in a *Lolita* vein, but then the pace slackens. Oodles of sex and nudity, though, for those who like that sort of thing. DA

Clare Powney *Pat, the girl* • Franco Nero *John Berg* • Bernice Stegers *Eva Berg* • Frank Brennan *Lindberg, reporter* • Mark Robinson *Hans, cab driver* • Clifford Rose *General Carlsson* • Rosie Jauckens *Mrs Carlsson* • Christopher Lee *Peter Storm* ■ *Dir* Arne Mattsson • *Scr* Ernest Hotch

The Girl ★★ 15
Thriller 1999 · Fr/US · Colour · 83min

With its mournful voiceover, lazy jazz score and casual shots of Paris, Sande Zeig's lesbian *noir* has all the attributes of a stylish tale of danger and deceit. But the pacing of its contrived storyline exposes the artifice of the dialogue and the limitations of the cast. Agatha de la Boulaye struggles to bring to life the American art student who risks her relationship with musician Sandra N'Kake to pursue a passion with Claire Keim. DP English, French +subtitles. *DVD*

Claire Keim *The girl* • Agatha de la Boulaye *The narrator* • Cyril Lecomte *The man* • Sandra N'Kake *Bu Save* • Ronald Guttman *Bartender* • Cyrille Hertel *Bodyguard* ■ *Dir* Sande Zeig • *Scr* Monique Wittig, Sande Zeig, from a story by Wittig

The Girl and the General ★★
First World War drama
1967 · It/Fr · Colour · 103min

Rod Steiger gives a lazy performance in this mediocre period drama. He often seems to be in a totally different movie from his co-stars, Virna Lisi and Umberto Orsini, as a peasant girl and a scheming soldier who kidnap a First World War general for a thousand lira reward. Nothing impresses about this Carlo Ponti production, not even the score by Ennio Morricone. DP Italian dubbed.

Rod Steiger *General* • Virna Lisi *Ada* • Umberto Orsini *Private Tarasconi* • Toni Gaggia *Lieutenant* ■ *Dir* Pasquale Festa Campanile • *Scr* Luigi Malerba, Pasquale Festa Campanile, from a story by Massimo Franciosa, Pasquale Festa Campanile

A Girl at My Door ★★★ 18
Drama
2014 · S Kor · Colour · 119min

A compromised small-town saga from South Korean writer/director July Jung. Arriving in a coastal backwater, a senior cop (Doona Bae) tries to impose her authority upon her subordinates. But her position is undermined by her feud with the area's principal employer (Song Sae-byuk), whose beating of his stepdaughter (Kim Sae-ron) eventually compels the cop to give the teenager sanctuary. Bae and Kim are riveting together but the provocative themes ultimately get lost in the surfeit of overwrought emotions. DP Korean +subtitles. Sex references *DVD*

Doona Bae *Young-nam* • Kim Sae-ron *Dohee* • Song Sae-byuk *Yong-ha* ■ *Dir/Scr* July Jung

The Girl Can't Help It ★★★★ U
Satirical musical comedy
1956 · US · Colour · 97min

Witty, stylish, clever and (by today's standards) extraordinarily sexist, this hilarious satire on the juke-box industry is the rock 'n' roll movie par excellence. Pneumatic Jayne Mansfield is supported by more than a dozen major music acts, including Little Richard, Eddie Cochran, Fats Domino and Gene Vincent. But director Frank Tashlin's viewpoint is pure acid, and only balladeer Julie London is filmed without cynicism. The perfect 1950s period piece. TS *DVD*

Tom Ewell *Tom Miller* • Jayne Mansfield *Jerri Jordan* • Edmond O'Brien *Murdock* • Henry Jones *Mousey* • John Emery *Wheeler* • Juanita Moore *Hilda* ■ *Dir* Frank Tashlin • *Scr* Frank Tashlin, Herbert Baker

Girl Crazy ★★★ U
Musical comedy
1943 · US · BW · 98min

A magnificent George and Ira Gershwin score and the teaming of the fabulous Judy Garland with the irrepressible Mickey Rooney make this worth seeing. Admittedly, its attitudes have dated badly and, despite Garland looking lovelier than ever, the Rooney/Garland romance really doesn't gel. This was the second version of the Gershwin musical, first filmed in 1932. It was remade in 1965 as *When the Boys Meet the Girls*. TS

Mickey Rooney *Danny Churchill Jr* • Judy Garland *Ginger Gray* • Gil Stratton *Bud Livermore* • Robert E Strickland *Henry Lathrop* • Rags Ragland *"Rags"* • June Allyson *Speciality* • Nancy Walker *Polly Williams* • Guy Kibbee *Dean Phineas Armour* ■ *Dir* Norman Taurog • *Scr* Fred F

Finklehoffe, Sid Silvers, Dorothy Kingsley, William Ludwig, from the play by George Gershwin, Ira Gershwin, Guy Bolton, Jack McGowan

The Girl from Manhattan
★★ U
Comedy drama
1948 · US · BW · 81min

A scene-stealing turn from Charles Laughton as a saintly bishop is the highlight of this amiable, but mawkish comedy. Returning to her home town to find that uncle Ernest Truex's boarding house faces demolition, New York model Dorothy Lamour locks horns with the Reverend George Montgomery, who wants to build a new church on the land. However, they soon come to join forces against crooked property developer, Howard Freeman. There's little chemistry between Lamour and Montgomery. DP

Dorothy Lamour *Carol Maynard* • George Montgomery *Rev Tom Walker* • Charles Laughton *The Bishop* • Ernest Truex *Homer Purdy* • Hugh Herbert *Aaron Goss* • Constance Collier *Mrs Brooke* • William Frawley *Mr Bernouti* • Howard Freeman *Sam Griffin* ■ *Dir* Alfred E Green • *Scr* Howard Estabrook

The Girl from Mexico ★★
Comedy
1939 · US · BW · 71min

Lupe Velez revived her Hollywood screen career with this limp slapstick comedy that exploited her tempestuous Latin image. She's hired by Donald Woods's advertising executive to sing on the radio in New York and sneaks out on the town with Leon Errol's Uncle Matt, shouting herself hoarse at a wrestling match and ruining her audition the next day. The film went down so well with American small-town audiences that it started the *Mexican Spitfire* series, which starred Lupe and Leon Errol. AE

Lupe Velez *Carmelita Fuentes* • Donald Woods *Dennis Lindsey* • Leon Errol *Uncle Matt* • Linda Hayes *Elizabeth Price* • Donald MacBride *Renner* • Edward Raquello *Tony Romano* • Elisabeth Risdon *Aunt Della* • Ward Bond *Mexican Pete* ■ *Dir* Leslie Goodwins • *Scr* Lionel Houser, Joseph A Fields, from a story by Houser

The Girl from Missouri ★★★
Romantic comedy
1934 · US · BW · 71min

Anita Loos (*Gentlemen Prefer Blondes*) co-scripted this sharp, witty comedy, which stars blonde bombshell Jean Harlow, Franchot Tone and comedian Patsy Kelly. The women play a couple of chorus-line girls on the lookout for husbands, with Harlow determined to snare a millionaire while preserving her virginity until the right man comes along. Spirited entertainment, this has an excellent supporting cast. RK

Jean Harlow *Eadie Chapman* • Lionel Barrymore *TR Paige* • Franchot Tone *T "Tom" R Paige Jr* • Lewis Stone *Frank Cousins* • Patsy Kelly *Kitty Lennihan* • Alan Mowbray *Lord Douglas* • Clara Blandick *Miss Newberry* ■ *Dir* Jack Conway • *Scr* Anita Loos, John Emerson

The Girl from Paris ★★★ 15
Comedy drama
2001 · Fr/Bel · Colour · 98min

Christian Carion's debut feature not only benefits from the striking Rhône-Alp scenery, but also the slow-burning chemistry between testy widower Michel Serrault and Mathilde Seigner, the disillusioned Parisienne who buys his run-down farm and transforms it into a thriving business. The insights into the agricultural year have undeniable charm, but there's also much to provoke in Carion's astute consideration of the need to temper tradition with change. DP French +subtitles. *DVD*

Michel Serrault *Adrien Rochas* • Mathilde Seigner *Sandrine Dumez* • Jean-Paul Roussillon *Jean Farjon* • Frédéric Pierrot *Gérard Chauvin* • Marc Berman *Stéphane* ■ *Dir* Christian Carion • *Scr* Christian Carion, Eric Assous

The Girl from Petrovka ★
Romantic comedy drama
1974 · US · Colour · 103min

Goldie Hawn and Anthony Hopkins adopt thick Russian accents for this pathetic Cold War comedy. La Hawnska grows disenchanted with life in Russia and is

romanced by American foreign correspondent Hal Holbrook. Hopkins is a black marketeer, a sort of Harry Lime figure. Subplots proliferate, but the story goes nowhere quickly. AT

Goldie Hawn *Oktyabrina* • Hal Holbrook *Joe* • Anthony Hopkins *Kostya* • Grégoire Aslan *Minister* • Anton Dolin *Ignatievitch, ballet master* • Bruno Wintzell *Alexander* • Zoran Andric *Leonid* • Hanna Hertelendy *Judge* ■ *Dir* Robert Ellis Miller • *Scr* Allan Scott, Chris Bryant, from the novel by George Feifer

The Girl from Rio ★★ 15
Cult science-fiction fantasy
1968 · UK · Colour · 93min

Goldfinger's Shirley Eaton took early screen retirement after this sexy spy movie, a follow-up to 1967's *Sumuru*. Although confusingly credited as "Sumitra" and referred to as "Sunanda", she's back playing Sumuru, the fiendish female creation of author Sax Rohmer. World domination for womankind is once more on her agenda, and to fund this she spirits away rich men to their doom in the secret city of Femina. The torture scenes are among the lamest committed to film, but fans of the spy-fi genre will appreciate the film's fab 60s stylings and gun-toting dolly birds. JH Violence, nudity. *DVD*

Shirley Eaton *Sumitra* • Richard Wyler *Jeff Sutton* • George Sanders *Masius* • Maria Rohm *Lesley* • Marta Reves *Ulla* • Jess Franco [Jesus Franco] • *Scr* Peter Welbeck [Harry Alan Towers], from a characters by Sax Rohmer

Girl from Rio ★★ 15
Comedy
2001 · UK/Sp · Colour · 98min

Writer/director Christopher Monger attempts to re-create that unique Ealing atmosphere with this tale of two cities, with the help of José Luis Alcaine's astute cinematography. But the film lapses into low farce as the location shifts from London to Rio. Hugh Laurie begins in admirably hangdog style as a cuckolded banker who finds his sole release in dance. Once he makes for Brazil, however, his character becomes a mere victim of circumstance - he's hurtled around Rio by taxi driver Santiago Segura in pursuit of the loot purloined from him by samba sensation Vanessa Nunes. Genial, but uninspired. DP *DVD*

Hugh Laurie *Raymond* • Vanessa Nunes *Orlinda* • Santiago Segura *Paulo* • Lia Williams *Cathy* • Patrick Barlow *Strothers* • Nelson Xavier *Bichero* ■ *Dir* Christopher Monger • *Scr* Christopher Monger, from a screenplay (unproduced) by Francisco Lara, Julián Ibáñez

The Girl from 10th Avenue
★★★
Drama
1935 · US · BW · 68min

Bette Davis grabs this daft melodrama between her teeth and never lets go. She's an honest working girl straightening out an alcoholic society type, while coping with the nuisance of a female nemesis who wants her man back. Bette remains unfazed, of course, and this leads to a verbal baiting, which precipitates a newspaper story causing the marriage to topple. It's great tosh, terrifically directed at a smart pace by Alfred E Green, who would later steer La Davis to her first Oscar with *Dangerous*. TS

Bette Davis *Miriam Brady* • Ian Hunter *Geoffrey Sherwood* • Colin Clive *John Marland* • Alison Skipworth *Mrs Martin* • John Eldredge *Hugh Brown* • Philip Reed *Tony Hewlett* ■ *Dir* Alfred E Green • *Scr* Charles Kenyon, from the play *Outcast* by Hubert Henry Davies

Girl Happy ★★ PG
Musical
1965 · US · Colour · 90min

This is one of Elvis Presley's weaker vehicles and a sign that worse was to come. The King plays a rock 'n' roll musician doubling up as a chaperone for mobster's daughter Shelley Fabares. Presley displays his customary charm and gives those remarkable tonsils a real work-out on generally unworthy material. TS

Elvis Presley *Rusty Wells* • Shelley Fabares *Valerie Frank* • Harold J Stone *Big Frank* • Gary Crosby *Andy* • Joby Baker *Wilbur* • Nita Talbot

Sunny Daze • Mary Ann Mobley *Deena* • Fabrizio Mioni *Romano* ■ *Dir* Boris Sagal • *Scr* Harvey Bullock, RS Allen

The Girl He Left Behind ★★★ U
Comedy
1956 · US · BW · 103min

Studio chief Jack L Warner must have had high hopes of Tab Hunter and Natalie Wood as new stars, teaming them in both the western *The Burning Hills* and this army comedy. Under the direction of veteran David Butler, Hunter is well cast as a spoiled, insufferable and unwilling draftee in the peace-time army, who itches to get back to the girl he left behind (Wood). Familiar and overlong, but Wood is vivacious. AE

Tab Hunter *Andy Sheaffer* • Natalie Wood *Susan Daniels* • Jessie Royce Landis *Madeline Sheaffer* • Jim Backus *Sergeant Hanna* • Henry Jones *Hanson* • Murray Hamilton *Sergeant Clyde* • Alan King *Maguire* • James Garner *Preston* • David Janssen *Captain Genaro* ■ *Dir* David Butler • *Scr* Guy Trosper, from the novel by Marion Hargrove

The Girl He Met Online ★★
Mystery thriller
2014 · Can · Colour · 83min

A well-cast Yvonne Zima plays a violently unstable 20-something looking for true love in another formulaic tale about the perils of internet dating. With her ultra-expressive face, Zima swings easily from mournful to psychotic; eliciting occasional sympathy for her disturbed character who's desperate to make bland Shawn Roberts "the one" after they meet online. But as the film's campy flashbacks and unsubtle dialogue keep hammering home, she's really not good at relationships, which leaves viewers watching the coincidence-heavy events merely for her inevitable meltdown. Unfortunately, when her whole world does fully unravel, dull scripting and tension-free direction render her response underwhelming, wasting Zima's larger-than-life performance and resulting in an lacklustre finale. SF

Yvonne Zima *Gillian Casey* • Shawn Roberts *Andy Collins* • Samantha Madely *Heather* • Scott Gibson *Tony* ■ *Dir* Anthony Lefresne, Curtis Crawford • *Scr* David DeCrane

The Girl Hunters ★★ 12
Mystery thriller
1963 · UK · BW · 97min

Author Mickey Spillane plays his own creation, hard-boiled private eye Mike Hammer, in this all-American B-movie that, for tax reasons, was based and financed in Britain. Little is made of a promising plot about murder and corruption in American politics, while Spillane is shown to have more ego than acting talent. British starlet Shirley Eaton plays a blonde *femme fatale* who, fatally, doesn't know one end of a shotgun from the other. AT Violence. *DVD*

Mickey Spillane *Mike Hammer* • Shirley Eaton *Laura Knapp* • Scott Peters *Pat Chambers* • Hy Gardner • Lloyd Nolan *Art Rickerby* • Guy Kingsley Poynter *Dr Larry Snyder* • James Dyrenforth *Bayliss Henry* ■ *Dir* Roy Rowland • *Scr* Roy Rowland, Robert Fellows, from the novel by Mickey Spillane

A Girl in a Million ★★
Comedy
1946 · UK · BW · 91min

An object lesson in how tastes change, this chauvinistic comedy made a star of Joan Greenwood in a role that basically dismisses women as blethering nuisances who should be seen and not heard. Having just escaped a shrewish wife, scientist Hugh Williams considers Greenwood the perfect mate, as she's been shell-shocked into silence. However, she recovers her speech once married and that's the start of the troubles. DP

Hugh Williams *Tony* • Joan Greenwood *Gay* • Basil Radford *Prendergast* • Naunton Wayne *Fotheringam* • Wylie Watson *Peabody* ■ *Dir* Francis Searle • *Scr* Sydney Box, Muriel Box

U SUITABLE FOR ALL **Uc** SUITABLE ESPECIALLY FOR YOUNG CHILDREN (DVD ONLY) **PG** PARENTAL GUIDANCE **12A** UNDER 12s TO BE ACCOMPANIED (CINEMA ONLY)

G

The Girl in Black Stockings
★★

Murder mystery   1957 · US · BW · 75min

Murder in a ritzy Utah resort hotel – with voluptuous blonde Mamie Van Doren as one of the female victims – places crippled hotel owner Ron Randell, his loving sister Marie Windsor, lawyer Lex Barker and a young Anne Bancroft under suspicion. Sheriff John Dehner investigates. Howard W Koch directs this efficient whodunnit, which has its roots in the Agatha Christie-style formula of having contrasting characters walled up in a confined location who all appear to have a motive to kill. **RK**

Lex Barker *David Hewson* • Anne Bancroft *Beth Dixon* • Mamie Van Doren *Harriet Ames* • Ron Randell *Edmund Parry* • Marie Windsor *Julia Parry* • John Dehner *Sheriff Holmes* • John Holland *Norman Grant* • Diana Vandervlis [Diana Van Der Vlis] *Louise Miles* ■ *Dir* Howard W Koch • *Scr* Richard Landau, from the story *Wanton Murder* by Peter Godfrey

A Girl in Every Port
★★

Silent comedy   1928 · US · BW · 62min

Director Howard Hawks would go on to better things, such as *Bringing Up Baby* and *To Have and Have Not*. This late silent-era vehicle for beefy Victor McLaglen is nobody's finest hour. The title tells the story: sailors McLaglen and Robert Armstrong chase women, date women and brawl over women during their travels around the four corners of the globe. Coarse-grained and only mildly amusing, the film's best episode features the always extraordinary Louise Brooks. **RK**

Victor McLaglen *Spike Madden* • Maria Casajuana *Chiquita* • Natalie Joyce *Girl in Panama* • Dorothy Mathews *Girl in Panama* • Elena Jurado *Girl in Panama* • Louise Brooks *Marie, girl in France* • Francis McDonald *Gang leader* • Phalba Morgan *Lena, girl in Holland* • Robert Armstrong *Salami* ■ *Dir* Howard Hawks • *Scr* Howard Hawks, Seton I Miller, from the story by James Kevin McGuinness

A Girl in Every Port
★ U

Comedy   1952 · US · BW · 82min

This is a dire experience for Groucho Marx enthusiasts, as he appears with a real moustache and without his brothers, scouring the horizon for non-existent laughs. The low-budget farce casts him as a fast-talking sailor, with William Bendix as his dim-witted pal. The pair try to put over a horse-race scam involving two nags, one fast and the other slow. **AE** *DVD*

Groucho Marx *Benny Linn* • Marie Wilson *Jane Sweet* • William Bendix *Tim Dunnevan* • Don DeFore *Bert Sedgwick* • Gene Lockhart *Garvey* • Dee Hartford *Millicent* • Hanley Stafford *Navy Lieutenant* • Teddy Hart *"High Life"* ■ *Dir* Chester Erskine • *Scr* Chester Erskine, from the story *They Sell Sailors Elephants* by Frederick Hazlitt Brennan

Girl in the Headlines
★★★

Crime drama   1963 · UK · BW · 93min

This sleazy whodunnit could have been compiled from a random leaf through the Sunday scandal sheets. At times it seems as if every known vice has been woven into the labyrinthine plot, which centres on the efforts of cop Ian Hendry to prise clues to the identity of a model's killer out of her friends and family. Hendry's commitment and the Watsonesque support of his sergeant (Ronald Fraser) keep you curious. **DP**

Ian Hendry *Inspector Birkett* • Ronald Fraser *Sergeant Saunders* • Margaret Johnston *Mrs Gray* • Natasha Parry *Perlita Barker* • Jeremy Brett *Jordan Barker* • Kieron Moore *Herter* • Peter Arne *Hammond Barker* • Jane Asher *Lindy Birkett* • Rosalie Crutchley *Maude Klein* ■ *Dir* Michael Truman • *Scr* Vivienne Knight, Patrick Campbell, Laurence Payne

The Girl in the News
★★★

Murder mystery   1940 · UK · BW · 78min

Carol Reed churns out this workmanlike if rather transparent murder mystery. Margaret Lockwood heads a starry British cast as a nurse, whose patients have the unfortunate habit of dying after being poisoned. It's a pretty thankless role and she adequately performs the task of looking bewildered and persecuted. **DP**

Margaret Lockwood *Anne Graham* • Barry K Barnes *Stephen Farringdon* • Emlyn Williams *Tracy* • Roger Livesey *Bill Mather* • Margaretta Scott *Judith Bentley* • Wyndham Goldie *Edward Bentley* • Irene Handl *Miss Blaker* ■ *Dir* Carol Reed • *Scr* Sidney Gilliat, from the novel by Roy Vickers

The Girl in the Park
★★★ 15

Drama   2007 · US/Ger/Sing · Colour · 110min

Award-winning playwright David Auburn makes his film-directing debut with this intriguing tale of a mother, Julia, traumatised by the disappearance of her daughter in Central Park, New York. Sixteen years later, a chance run-in with a strangely familiar young woman (Kate Bosworth) stirs her repressed maternal instincts. Auburn, who also wrote the script, then leads us into a guessing game, as Julia begins to suspect that the woman may be her daughter. Sigourney Weaver is a bold choice for Julia, bringing her innate aloofness to the role of a woman who suddenly finds an outlet for the emotions she shut down all those years ago. **SP** Swearing, sexual references. *DVD*

Sigourney Weaver *Julia Sandburg* • Kate Bosworth *Louise* • Alessandro Nivola *Chris* • Keri Russell *Celeste* • Elias Koteas *Raymond* • David Rasche *Doug* ■ *Dir/Scr* David Auburn

The Girl in the Picture
★★ U

Crime drama   1956 · UK · BW · 63min

Probably best known for his work at Disney in the 1960s, director Don Chaffey was still cutting his teeth on British B-movies when he completed this lacklustre thriller. The girl of the title is Junia Crawford, whom crime reporter Donald Houston is convinced holds the key to the murder story he's covering. As mysteries go, this is on the elementary side. **DP**

Donald Houston *John Deering* • Patrick Holt *Inspector Bliss* • Maurice Kaufmann *Rod Molloy* • Junia Crawford *Pat Dryden* • Paddy Joyce *Jack Bates* • John Miller (3) *Duncan* ■ *Dir* Don Chaffey • *Scr* Paul Rogers

The Girl in the Picture
★★★ 15

Romantic comedy   1985 · UK · Colour · 84min

John Gordon-Sinclair is the awkward wedding photographer who falls in and out of love with the beautiful Irina Brook. It never quite captures the quirky charm of Gordon-Sinclair's hit *Gregory's Girl*, but the playing in this gentle comedy is superb and it remains thoroughly enjoyable in an unassuming way. **JF**

John Gordon-Sinclair *Alan* • Irina Brook *Mary* • David McKay *Ken* • Gregor Fisher *Bill* • Caroline Guthrie *Annie* • Paul Young *Smiley* • Rikki Fulton *Minister* ■ *Dir/Scr* Cary Parker

The Girl in the Red Velvet Swing
★★ PG

Crime drama based on a true story   1955 · US · Colour · 104min

Remembered as the Hollywood debut, amid a fanfare of publicity, of Joan Collins, whose "come hither" charms are its chief focus, this is a suspect retelling of the notorious murder of the brilliant American architect Stanford White in 1906. He was shot in full view of the Manhattan crowds by Harry K Thaw, the unstable husband of White's mistress, showgirl Evelyn Nesbit. This is a superficial soap opera exercise, but Ray Milland is convincing and it's visually excellent. **RK**

Ray Milland *Stanford White* • Joan Collins *Evelyn Nesbit Thaw* • Farley Granger *Harry K Thaw* • Luther Adler *Delphin Delmas* • Cornelia Otis Skinner *Mrs Thaw* • Glenda Farrell *Mrs Nesbit* • Frances Fuller *Mrs White* ■ *Dir* Richard Fleischer • *Scr* Walter Reisch, Charles Brackett

The Girl in the Taxi
★★★ U

Musical   1937 · UK · BW · 66min

Given the Parisian setting, it's apt that André Berthomieu was hired to direct this exposé of baron Lawrence Grossmith's double life. By day, he is head of the Society for the Reward of Virtue. But once darkness falls, he becomes a notorious roué, who finds himself pursuing the same chenteuse (Frances Day) as his admiring son, Mackenzie Ward. The musical numbers are inadequate, but the farce is peppily played. **DP** *DVD*

Frances Day *Suzanne Pommarel* • Henri Garat *René Boislurette* • Jean Gillie *Jacqueline* • Mackenzie Ward *Hubert* ■ *Dir* André Berthomieu • *Scr* Fritz Gottfurcht, Austin Melford, Val Valentine

The Girl in White
★★ U

Biographical drama   1952 · US · BW · 93min

From MGM – a studio with an ongoing devotion to hospital drama – comes this biopic adapted from Dr Emily Dunning's autobiography. Recounting her experiences as the first woman to storm the male bastions of medical practice in the slums of New York at the turn of the last century, the movie's only real narrative surprise – and its major mistake – is the miscasting of sunny girl-next-door June Allyson as the tough-minded medical pioneer. **RK**

June Allyson *Dr Emily Dunning* • Arthur Kennedy *Dr Ben Barringer* • Gary Merrill *Dr Seth Pawling* • Mildred Dunnock *Dr Marie Yeomans* • Jesse White *Alec* • Marilyn Erskine *Nurse Jane Doe* ■ *Dir* John Sturges • *Scr* Philip Stevenson, Allen Vincent, Irmgard von Cube, from the non-fiction book *Bowery to Bellevue: the Story of New York's First Woman Ambulance Surgeon* by Emily Dunning Barringer

Girl, Interrupted
★★★ 15

Drama based on a true story   1999 · US · Colour · 122min

Set in a New England psychiatric institution in 1967, director/co-writer James Mangold's commendable drama has a similar agenda to Milos Forman's Oscar-winning classic *One Flew over the Cuckoo's Nest*, but never quite reaches the same peaks of poignancy. Mangold makes clever use of jarring narrative cuts to convey Winona Ryder's confused state of mind, Oscar winner Angelina Jolie is mesmerising as a troublemaker, and Whoopi Goldberg does her best work in ages as a no-nonsense nurse. **JC** Swearing, sex scenes. *DVD*

Winona Ryder *Susanna Kaysen* • Angelina Jolie *Lisa* • Brittany Murphy *Daisy* • Clea DuVall [Clea DuVall] *Georgina* • Whoopi Goldberg *Valerie* • Jeffrey Tambor *Dr Potts* • Jared Leto *Tobias Jacobs* • Vanessa Redgrave *Dr Wick* ■ *Dir* James Mangold • *Scr* Anna Hamilton Phelan, James Mangold, Susan Shilliday, Lisa Loomer, from the memoirs of Susanna Kaysen

The Girl King
★★★ 15

Historical romantic drama   2015 · Fin/Ger/Can/Swe/Fr · Colour · 105min

Sweden's 17th-century Queen Kristina was both progressive and lesbian at a time when neither was acceptable. Malin Buska plays Kristina in this handsomely mounted biopic, with Sarah Gadon (*A Royal Night Out*) as her lady-in-waiting and soulmate, and Scandi superstar Michael Nyqvist (the *Dragon Tattoo* films) as the chancellor who's caught between the rock of Swedish stolidity and the hard place of Kristina's feminism and sexuality. All are just right for this superior and hugely watchable costume drama. **DA** English, French, German +subtitles. A sex scene, nudity, some swearing.

Malin Buska *Queen Kristina* • Sarah Gadon *Countess Ebba Sparre* • Michael Nyqvist *Chancellor Axel Oxenstierna* • Lucas Bryant *Count Johan Oxenstierna* • Laura Birn *Countess Erika Erksein* ■ *Dir* Mika Kaurismäki • *Scr* Michel Marc Bouchard

A Girl like Me
★★★

Drama based on a true story   2006 · US · Colour · 103min

In 2002, 17-year-old Gwen Araujo was beaten to death in Newark, California, by a group of men. The ensuing murder trial had an unexpected twist: Gwen wasn't Gwen but Eddie, a transgender teenager. This soft-focus TV movie is worthy and sometimes woolly, skimming over the more sordid details of the case as it flashes back and forth between Gwen's life and the courtroom. But despite a heart-on-sleeve earnestness, it's brilliantly anchored by JD Pardo's winning performance. **JR**

Mercedes Ruehl *Sylvia Guerrero* • JD Pardo *Eddie/Gwen Araujo* • Rondel Reynoldson *Paediatrician* • Lupe Ontiveros *Mami* • Henry Darrow *Papi* • Corey Stoll *Joey Marino* ■ *Dir* Agnieszka Holland • *Scr* Shelley Evans

Girl Model
★★★

Documentary   2011 · US · Colour · 77min

Documentarists David Redmon and Ashley Sabin let their footage speak for itself in this harrowing exposé of the Japanese modelling market. Such is the national obsession with lithe youth that hundreds of impoverished Siberian girls place themselves in the hands of unscrupulous agents in the hope of making it big in Tokyo. It's clear from the case studies that girls are being exploited, deceived and discarded without a thought for their physical or psychological welfare. The result is intrepidly filmed, unflinchingly revelatory and deeply disconcerting. **DP** English, Russian, Japanese +subtitles. *DVD*

Ashley Arbaugh • Nadya Vall ■ *Dir* David Redmon, Ashley Sabin

The Girl Most Likely
★★★ U

Musical comedy   1957 · US · Colour · 94min

A winsome musical remake of the 1941 RKO Ginger Rogers hit *Tom, Dick and Harry*, this is a stylish, fun musical, albeit in a minor key. It's the last feature of veteran Mitchell Leisen, directed with wit and verve, and well served by some super choreography from the great Gower Champion. Jane Powell is perfect as the girl who can't choose a mate, and comedian Kaye Ballard is terrific in her first movie as Powell's best friend. The guys are lightweight but charming. **TS**

Jane Powell *Dodie* • Cliff Robertson *Pete* • Keith Andes *Neil* • Kaye Ballard *Marge* • Tommy Noonan *Buzz* • Una Merkel *Mom* • Kelly Brown *Sam* ■ *Dir* Mitchell Leisen • *Scr* Paul Jarrico (uncredited), Devery Freeman, from a story by Paul Jarrico (uncredited)

Girl Most Likely
★★ 12

Comedy   2012 · US · Colour · 98min

This comedy from *American Splendor* co-directors Shari Springer Berman and Robert Pulcini shows a lot of early promise but ultimately fails to deliver. Kristen Wiig (*Bridesmaids*) plays a struggling writer who's forced to move back home to live with her batty mum (Annette Bening) and her lover (Matt Dillon), an eccentric brother (Christopher Fitzgerald) and a lodger (Darren Criss). Wiig's character is weighed down with numerous selfish neuroses, while Bening and Dillon are wickedly funny. But these are roles they could do in their sleep. **SP** Swearing, sexual references. *DVD*

Kristen Wiig *Imogene Duncan* • Annette Bening *Zelda* • Matt Dillon *George/The Bousche* • Darren Criss *Lee* • Christopher Fitzgerald *Ralph* • June Diane Raphael *Dara* ■ *Dir* Shari Springer Berman, Robert Pulcini • *Scr* Michelle Morgan

A Girl Named Tamiko
★★

Romantic drama   1962 · US · Colour · 110min

Tough-guy director John Sturges was never really comfortable with melodrama. However, who could blame him for wanting to work in exotic Tokyo locations with lovely France Nuyen under the auspices of veteran producer Hal B Wallis? The film stars Laurence Harvey as a Russo-Chinese photographer who stops at nothing to get a US visa. It's all well made; unfortunately, it's also turgid, intractable and empty. **TS**

Laurence Harvey *Ivan Kalin* • France Nuyen *Tamiko* • Martha Hyer *Fay Wilson* • Gary Merrill *Max Wilson* • Michael Wilding *Nigel Costairs* • Miyoshi Umeki *Eiko* • Steve Brodie *James Hatten* • Lee Patrick *Mary Hatten* ■ *Dir* John Sturges • *Scr* Edward Anhalt, from a novel by Ronald Kirkbride

The Girl Next Door
★★★ U

Musical comedy   1953 · US · Colour · 91min

Dan Dailey is always a pleasure to watch, his easy-going screen persona reflecting a versatile talent and likeable personality that

G

was too often wasted in lightweight vehicles such as this. He stars as a cartoonist whose quiet life is disrupted when chanteuse June Haver moves in next door. There's nice support from crooner Dennis Day, best remembered from Jack Benny's TV and radio shows, and from the underrated Cara Williams. TS

Dan Dailey *Bill Carter* • June Haver *Jeannie* • Dennis Day *Reed Appleton* • Billy Gray *Joe Carter* • Cara Williams *Rosie* • Natalie Schafer *Evelyn* • Clinton Sundberg *Samuels* • Hayden Rorke *Fields* ■ *Dir* Richard Sale • *Scr* Isobel Lennart, from a story by L Bush-Fekete [Ladislaus Bus-Fekete], Mary Helen Fay

The Girl Next Door ★★★ 15
Comedy   2004 · US · Colour · 104min

The first half of this boisterous comedy plays like a hackneyed "boy meets girl" yarn, as nerdy high-school over-achiever Emile Hirsch falls for his gorgeous new neighbour (Elisha Cuthbert), only to discover she's a former porn star. It's cliché-ridden nonsense, but then in a welcome shift, teen fodder suddenly turns into *Risky Business*-style hilarity. With likeable performances adding to the youthful vitality, the result is an endearingly daft romp. SF Swearing. *DVD*

Emile Hirsch *Matthew Kidman* • Elisha Cuthbert *Danielle* • Timothy Olyphant *Kelly* • James Remar *Hugo Posh* • Chris Marquette [Christopher George Marquette] *Eli* • Paul Dano *Klitz* • Timothy Bottoms *Mr Kidman* • Donna Bullock *Mrs Kidman* ■ *Dir* Luke Greenfield • *Scr* Stuart Blumberg, David T Wagner, Brent Goldberg, from a story by David T Wagner, Brent Goldberg

The Girl of the Golden West ★★★ U
Musical western   1938 · US · Sepia · 120min

For its hit team of Jeanette MacDonald and Nelson Eddy, MGM bought the rights to a hoary old David Belasco stage melodrama. More than satisfactory for the duo's followers but hardly innovative in any way, this features MacDonald as the saloon proprietor in love with Eddy's dashing bandit and the object of sheriff Walter Pidgeon's affections. AE

Jeanette MacDonald *Mary Robbins* • Nelson Eddy *Ramerez/Lt Johnson* • Walter Pidgeon *Sheriff Jack Rance* • Leo Carrillo *Mosquito* • Buddy Ebsen *Alabama* • Leonard Penn *Pedro* • Priscilla Lawson *Nina Martinez* • Bob Murphy *Sonora Slim* ■ *Dir* Robert Z Leonard • *Scr* Isabel Dawn, Boyce DeGaw, from the play by David Belasco

Girl of the Night ★★
Drama   1960 · US · BW · 90min

Anne Francis makes the most of her role as a reluctant prostitute relating her seamy adventures to oh-so-earnest psychiatrist Lloyd Nolan. She hopes these sessions will help her change her life. Presented as a "medical case history", this was quite outspoken for its time, although it seems fairly tame today. The girl's tale makes for dull viewing. RB

Anne Francis *Bobbie* • Lloyd Nolan *Dr Mitchell* • Kay Medford *Rowena* • John Kerr *Larry* • Arthur Storch *Jason Franklin Jr* • James Broderick *Dan Bolton* • Lauren Gilbert *Mr Shelton* • Eileen Fulton *Lisa* ■ *Dir* Joseph Cates • *Scr* Ted Berkman, Raphael Blau, from the book *The Call Girl* by Dr Harold Greenwald

The Girl of Your Dreams ★★★ 15
Period comedy   1998 · Sp · Colour · 110min

Set in the aftermath of the Civil War, this perceptive comedy follows the misadventures of a Spanish film unit as it embarks upon a prestigious co-production at the legendary German UFA studios. Much of the attention is focused on the attempts of Spanish star Penélope Cruz to avoid the attentions of the lecherous Goebbels (Johannes Silberschneider). But director Fernando Trueba is also keen to explore the nature of propaganda and the ostensible differences between Franco and Hitler's brands of fascism. The final descent into farce is laboured, but the political observations are astute. DP Spanish, German +subtitles. *DVD*

Penélope Cruz *Macarena Granada* • Antonio Resines *Blas Fontiveras* • Neus Asensi *Lucia Gandia* • Jesús Bonilla *Bonilla* • Loles Leon *Trini Moreno* • Jorge Sanz *Julian Torralba* • Hanna Schygulla *Magda Goebbels* • Johannes Silberschneider *Goebbels* ■ *Dir* Fernando Trueba • *Scr* Rafael Azcona, David Trueba, Carlos Lopez, Manuel Angel Egea

The Girl on a Motorcycle ★★★ 15
Romantic drama   1968 · UK/Fr · Colour · 87min

This quintessential 1960s movie catches Marianne Faithfull on the cusp between beauty and seedy decline. She is required to do little more than sneer, pout and wrap her leather-encased limbs around said bike, but this image alone reduced a generation of males to pop-eyed slavering wrecks. The plot is as wafer thin but, with its gallery of cinematic icons of the day, the movie is still a delicious-looking curiosity. SH Swearing, sex scenes, nudity. *DVD*

Marianne Faithfull *Rebecca* • Alain Delon *Daniel* • Roger Mutton *Raymond* • Marius Goring *Rebecca's father* • Catherine Jourdan *Catherine* • Jean Leduc *Jean* ■ *Dir* Jack Cardiff • *Scr* Ronald Duncan, Gillian Freeman, from the novel *La Motocyclette* by Andre Pieyre de Mandiargues

Girl on Approval ★★★
Drama   1962 · UK · BW · 79min

This pithy little feature was made by Eyeline Films for the then-new British film company Bryanston. About the angst of foster parenting, this film provides excellent roles for the hitherto under-used Rachel Roberts and suave James Maxwell as the parents, and Annette Whitley as the lass up for fostering. Perhaps a little too self-consciously worthy, it is most interesting today for its view of the mores of a bygone age. TS

Rachel Roberts (1) *Anne Howland* • James Maxwell *John Howland* • Annette Whitley *Sheila* • John Dare *Stephen Howland* • Ellen McIntosh *Mary Gardner* • Michael Clarke *William Howland* ■ *Dir* Charles Frend • *Scr* Kathleen White, Kenneth Cavander, from a story by Kathleen White

The Girl on the Boat ★★ U
Comedy romance   1962 · UK · BW · 89min

Norman Wisdom tried something different from his usual slapstick with this seagoing comedy romance taken from a story by PG Wodehouse. It doesn't work for Wisdom, though it does for the less mannered professionals in support such as Richard Briers, Millicent Martin and Athene Seyler. It bombed at the box office. TH *DVD*

Norman Wisdom *Sam* • Millicent Martin *Billie Bennett* • Richard Briers *Eustace Hignett* • Sheila Hancock *Jane* • Bernard Cribbins *Peters* • Athene Seyler *Mrs Hignett* • Philip Locke *Bream Mortimer* • Noel Willman *Webster* ■ *Dir* Henry Kaplan • *Scr* Reuben Ship, from the novel by PG Wodehouse

The Girl on the Bridge ★★★ 15
Romantic drama   1999 · Fr · BW · 87min

Middle-aged knife thrower Daniel Auteuil talks the elfin Vanessa Paradis out of jumping off a bridge into the Seine, turning her desperation to his advantage by hiring her as his assistant. Their relationship deepens, and darkens, as they tour the south of France, although romance is hampered by the flings she has at every port of call. With Marianne Faithfull warbling on the soundtrack and sumptuous visuals from Jean-Marie Dreujou, this is an elegant, nostalgic treat. NS French +subtitles.

Vanessa Paradis *Adèle* • Daniel Auteuil *Gabor* • Demetre Georgalas *Takis* • Isabelle Petit-Jacques *The bride* • Frederic Pfluger *The contortionist* ■ *Dir* Patrice Leconte • *Scr* Serge Frydman

The Girl on the Train ★★★ 15
Drama   2009 · Fr · Colour · 97min

A real-life scandal is the inspiration for this ambitious but inconclusive look at identity, race and the nature of lies. Adapted from co-writer Jean-Marie Besset's play *RER*, the drama fictionalises the 2004 case in which

a young gentile woman claimed to be the victim of an anti-Semitic attack on board a Paris train. Emilie Dequenne brings a sunny naivety to the free-spirited title role, giving the early scenes a casualness that makes the subsequent, shocking revelations difficult to fathom. But the film's complex political and social themes are frustratingly simplified, reducing events to bare-bones implausibility despite the impressively subtle performances. SF In French. Violence, sex scenes *DVD*

Emilie Dequenne *Jeanne* • Michel Blanc *Samuel Bleistein* • Catherine Deneuve *Louise* • Mathieu Demy *Alex* • Ronit Elkabetz *Judith* • Nicolas Duvauchelle *Franck* ■ *Dir* André Téchiné • *Scr* Odile Barski, André Téchiné, Jean-Marie Besset, from the play *RER* by Besset

The Girl on the Train
Mystery thriller   2016 · US · Colour

This is a preview - no prints were available to review as we went to press: The audience is ready and waiting for this mystery thriller based on the hugely successful novel by British author Paula Hawkins. Emily Blunt commutes to New York City instead of London as a depressed divorcee who daydreams about a happy couple living in an apartment overlooking the train track. She then sees something she shouldn't have, propelling her into a living nightmare. Director Tate Taylor now has the daunting task of maintaining the intrigue for those who know how it ends. SP

Emily Blunt *Rachel Watson* • Rebecca Ferguson *Anna Watson* • Justin Theroux *Tom Watson* • Luke Evans *Scott Hipwell* • Edgar Ramirez *Dr Kamal Abdic* ■ *Dir* Tate Taylor • *Scr* Erin Cressida Wilson, from Paula Hawkins's novel

Girl Rush ★★
Musical comedy   1944 · US · BW · 64min

This B-movie is a real curio, so it's a shame it isn't very good. Alan Carney and Wally Brown are the two vaudevillians stranded during the gold rush days in San Francisco. A look down the cast list reveals a young Robert Mitchum in a minor role, showing little promise of the great screen career to come. The leading lady is sexy singer Frances Langford, and ditzy Vera Vague has some moments, but overall it's just daft. TS

Wally Brown *Jerry Miles* • Alan Carney *Mike Strager* • Frances Langford *Flo Daniels* • Robert Mitchum *Jimmy Smith* • Vera Vague [Barbara Jo Allen] *Suzie Banks* • Paul Hurst *Muley* • Patti Brill *Claire* • Sarah Padden *Emma* ■ *Dir* Gordon Douglas • *Scr* Robert E Kent, from a story by Laszlo Vadnay, Aladar Laszlo

The Girl Rush ★★★ U
Musical comedy   1955 · US · Colour · 84min

Rosalind Russell goes to Las Vegas to claim her inheritance in a hotel but things aren't quite what they seem. Her hotel is on the skids, thanks to the efforts of James Gleason, and Russell is labouring under the impression that she owns half of another establishment - actually owned by Fernando Lamas. This needs a brassier personality than Russell. TH

Rosalind Russell *Kim Halliday* • Fernando Lamas *Victor Monte* • Eddie Albert *Elliot Atterbury* • Gloria DeHaven *Taffy Tremaine* • Marion Lorne *Aunt Clara* • James Gleason *Ether Ferguson* ■ *Dir* Robert Pirosh • *Scr* Robert Pirosh, Jerome Davis, from a story by Henry Ephron, Phoebe Ephron

Girl Shy ★★★★★ U
Silent comedy   1924 · US · BW · 88min

The two sides of Harold Lloyd's screen persona are evident in this classic silent comedy. In the first half, Lloyd's inimitable everyman pins his hopes of advancement on his book entitled *The Secrets of Making Love*. Lloyd's timid tailor's assistant wins the heart of Jobyna Ralston, but he loses her to sleazy bigamist Carlton Griffin when his manuscript is rejected. However, when the publisher changes his mind, Lloyd shifts into fearless mode and hurtles across town using every means of transport he can comandeer to prevent Ralston's wedding. Lloyd's genius illuminates this breathtaking

chase, which is both frantic and hilarious, thanks in no small part to the precision of the editing. DP

Harold Lloyd *Harold Meadows, the Poor Boy* • Jobyna Ralston *Mary Buckingham, the Rich Girl* • Richard Daniels *Jerry Meadows, the Poor Man* • Carlton Griffith *Ronald Devore, the Rich Man* ■ *Dir* Fred C Newmeyer, Sam Taylor • *Scr* from a story by Ted Wilde, Tim Whelan, Tommy Gray, Sam Taylor

Girl 6 ★★★★ 18
Comedy drama   1996 · US · Colour · 103min

This light-hearted tale is free from the preachy philosophising often associated with film-maker Spike Lee. Theresa Randle gives the performance of her life as a struggling actress who decides to join a phone-sex agency after being asked to strip for casting director Quentin Tarantino. She becomes addicted to the buzz she gets from her conversations, as she takes on a variety of characters in order to feed the fantasies of her callers. This film lays itself wide open to every politically incorrect charge you could level at it, yet Lee comments on society's dual standards with regard to sexploitation without detracting from the humour of the piece. DP Swearing, nudity.

Theresa Randle *Girl 6* • Isaiah Washington *Shoplifter* • Spike Lee *Jimmy* • Jenifer Lewis *Boss 1, Lil* • Debi Mazar *Girl 39* • Peter Berg *Caller 1, Bob* • Michael Imperioli *Scary caller 30* • Dina Pearlman *Girl 19* • Naomi Campbell *Girl 75* • Gretchen Mol *Girl 12* • Madonna *Boss 3* • John Turturro *Murray the agent* ■ *Dir* Spike Lee • *Scr* Suzan-Lori Parks

A Girl Walks Home Alone at Night ★★★★ 15
Romantic horror thriller   2014 · US · BW · 100min

When Bela Lugosi's Dracula mentioned the "children of the night", it's doubtful he meant a chador-clad bloodsucker on a skateboard. But that's what we get here, in the first Iranian vampire film. Set in an Arab backwater, the story follows Arash Marandi's cool dude as tries to get on in spite of his drug addict dad. Meanwhile, The Girl (Sheila Vand) prowls the streets looking for a bite. But when Arash (in Dracula fancy dress, no less) encounters the ghoulish gamine, a sweet and tentative friendship begins, though you're never quite sure whether he will discover her secret in time to survive it. Dripping with hipster style, director Ana Lily Amirpour's scintillating debut is as beautiful and hypnotic as its enigmatic heroine. JA Farsi +subtitles. Violence, a sex scene, brief nudity, drug abuse. *DVD* *BL*

Sheila Vand *The Girl* • Arash Marandi *Arash* • Mozhan Marno *Atti, "The Prostitute"* • Marshall Manesh *Hossein, "The Gambler"* • Dominic Rains *Saeed, "The Pimp"* • Rome Shadanloo *Shaydah, "The Rich Girl"* ■ *Dir/Scr* Ana Lily Amirpour

The Girl Who Had Everything ★
Crime drama   1953 · US · BW · 69min

MGM squandered Elizabeth Taylor's talents in this tepid remake of its torrid 1931 hit *A Free Soul*. Taylor lacks the abandon required for the role of the spoiled daughter of a prosperous criminal lawyer who falls for his gangster client, Fernando Lamas. As the lawyer William Powell remains as suave as ever in his last role for the studio, while Lamas struggles with the part of the shady Romeo. Static. AE

Elizabeth Taylor *Jean Latimer* • Fernando Lamas *Victor Y Ramondi* • William Powell *Steve Latimer* • Gig Young *Vance Court* • James Whitmore *Charles "Chico" Menlow* • Robert Burton *John Ashmond* • William Walker *Julian* • Harry Bartell *Joe* ■ *Dir* Richard Thorpe • *Scr* Art Cohn, from the novel *A Free Soul* by Adela Rogers St Johns

The Girl Who Knew Too Much ★★ U
Spy drama   1969 · US · Colour · 96min

There's no sign of a Joker or a Riddler as the former Caped Crusader takes on the Red Menace. *Batman*'s Adam West stars in this spy film as an ex-CIA man who comes out of retirement to investigate communist infiltration of the Mob. Nancy Kwan and Buddy Greco co-star. The Cold War theme seems very dated now and this is one of many non-classics on West's CV. TH

Adam West *Johnny Cain* • Nancy Kwan *Revel Drue* • Nehemiah Persoff *Lieutenant Crawford* • Buddy Greco *Lucky Jones* • Robert Alda *Kenneth Allardice* • Patricia Smith *Tricia Grinaldi* • David Brian *Had Dixon* ■ *Dir* Francis D Lyon • *Scr* Charles Wallace

Girl with a Pearl Earring ★★★★ 12

Period drama
2003 · UK/Lux/US · Colour · 95min

British director Peter Webber makes an astonishing feature debut with this ravishing period drama. Based on the bestselling novel by Tracy Chevalier, it's an imaginary reconstruction of the story behind 17th-century Dutch master Johannes Vermeer's celebrated painting *Girl with a Pearl Earring*. Scarlett Johansson gives a heartbreakingly brilliant portrayal of Vermeer's housemaid and eventual muse. Drawn to the secretive artist (a brooding Colin Firth), she finds head and heart colliding to costly effect. The cinematography is intoxicating, transforming every detailed frame into a richly coloured *tableau vivant*, while Alexandre Desplat's beautiful score adds extra intensity. SF *DVD*

Colin Firth *Johannes Vermeer* • Scarlett Johansson *Griet* • Tom Wilkinson *Van Ruijven* • Judy Parfitt *Maria Thins* • Cillian Murphy *Pieter* • Essie Davis *Catharina Vermeer* • Joanna Scanlan *Tanneke* • Alakina Mann *Cornelia Vermeer* ■ *Dir* Peter Webber • *Scr* Olivia Hetreed, from the novel by Tracy Chevalier • *Cinematographer* Eduardo Serra

The Girl with All the Gifts ★★★★ 15

Science-fiction horror thriller
2016 · US/UK · Colour · 110min

Astutely adapted by Mike Carey from his own dystopian bestseller, this powerful cautionary tale has a fungal spore infecting the planet and turning most people into "hungries" needing human flesh. Director Colm McCarthy's film is packed with visceral action, and sports memorably haunting moments (such as London's Post Office Tower eerily covered in Triffid-like plants). These edgy scares turn it into the best zombie movie since *28 Days Later*. AJ

Gemma Arterton *Helen Justineau* • Glenn Close *Dr Caroline Caldwell* • Paddy Considine *Sgt Eddie Parks* • Dominique Tipper *Devani* ■ *Dir* Colm McCarthy • *Scr* Mike Carey, from his novel

Girl with Green Eyes ★★★★ PG

Romantic drama
1963 · UK · BW · 92min

This sensitive tale of opposites is blessed with a highly literate script and affecting performances. Rita Tushingham and Lynn Redgrave play the shopgirls who share a room but little else, until they meet shy writer Peter Finch. The decline in their relationship, as it transpires he prefers the mousey Tushingham to the blowsy Redgrave, is conveyed with great skill. Debutant director Desmond Davis captures the atmosphere of Dublin with the eye of an experienced cinematographer. DP

Peter Finch *Eugene Gaillard* • Rita Tushingham *Kate Brady* • Lynn Redgrave *Baba Brenan* • Marie Kean *Josie Hannigan* • Arthur O'Sullivan *Mr Brady* • Julian Glover *Malachi Sullivan* • TP McKenna *Priest* • Lislott Goettinger *Joanna* ■ *Dir* Desmond Davis • *Scr* Edna O'Brien, from her novel *The Lonely Girl*

The Girl with Red Hair ★★★ PG

Second World War drama
1981 · Neth · Colour · 113min

The redhead in question is Hannie Schaft, a vigilante member of the Dutch resistance whose unconventional methods often brought her into conflict with her own superiors, as well as the Nazis. Renée Soutendijk plays her as an ordinary woman whose fierce patriotism drives her to

abandon her ambitions and conquer a distaste for violence in order to become a ruthless killing machine. Debutant Ben Verbong directs with dignity and justified anger, but occasionally allows this to lapse into cliché. DP Dutch +subtitles.

Renée Soutendijk *Hannie Schaft* • Peter Tuinman *Hugo* • Ada Bouwman *Tinka* • Robert Delhez *Floor* • Johan Leysen *Frans* • Loes Luca *An* • Adrian Brine *German Officer* • Lineke Rijxman *Judith* ■ *Dir* Ben Verbong • *Scr* Ben Verbong, Pieter De Vos, from the novel by Theun De Vries

The Girl with the Dragon Tattoo ★★★★ 18

Crime thriller
2009 · Swe/Den/Ger · Colour · 152min

The film version of Stieg Larsson's bestselling mystery is full of twists and turns and stays faithful to the book's bleak atmosphere. Disgraced investigative journalist Mikael Blomkvist (Michael Nyqvist) is hired to investigate the disappearance of a young woman 40 years earlier and receives some unexpected help from misfit computer hacker Lisbeth (Noomi Rapace, the tattooed girl of the film's title) whose own past is equally mysterious and violent. Director Niels Arden Oplev builds the tension masterfully, the chilling subplots delivering shock after shock, while Rapace has an enigmatic presence that burns through the screen. TeS Swedish +subtitles. *DVD* *Blu-ray*

Michael Nyqvist *Mikael Blomkvist* • Noomi Rapace *Lisbeth Salander* • Lena Endre *Erika Berger* • Sven-Bert I Taube *Henrik Vanger* • Peter Haber *Martin Vanger* • Peter Andersson *Nils Bjurman* ■ *Dir* Niels Arden Oplev • *Scr* Nikolaj Arcel, Rasmus Heisterberg, from the novel by Stieg Larsson

The Girl Who Played with Fire ★★★ 15

Crime thriller
2009 · Swe/Den/Ger · Colour · 124min

The Girl with the Dragon Tattoo was a tough act to follow. Sadly, director Daniel Alfredson fails to replicate its striking atmosphere or mesmerising intensity in this adaptation of the second book in Stieg Larsson's trilogy. Crusading journalist Mikael Blomkvist and hacker/social misfit Lisbeth Salander spend most of the film apart as the former tries to clear the latter of a triple murder charge. Overall, it's efficient enough, but fans of the novels will thrill to it, regardless of the deficiencies. AJ Swedish +subtitles. Violence, swearing, sex scenes, nudity. *DVD* *Blu-ray*

Michael Nyqvist *Mikael Blomkvist* • Noomi Rapace *Lisbeth Salander* • Lena Endre *Erika Berger* • Peter Andersson *Nils Bjurman* • Sofia Ledarp *Malin Erikson* • Georgi Staykov *Alexander Zalachenko* ■ *Dir* Daniel Alfredson • *Scr* Jonas Frykberg, from the novel by Stieg Larsson

The Girl Who Kicked the Hornet's Nest ★★★ 15

Thriller
2009 · Swe/Den/Ger · Colour · 140min

The final film based on Stieg Larsson's bestselling thriller trilogy opens with a whimper but ends with a bang. Critically injured after the violent conclusion to *The Girl Who Played with Fire*, goth computer hacker Lisbeth Salander (Noomi Rapace) is hospitalised and awaiting a psychiatric review. Flitting between Lisbeth's woes and the investigation to clear her name led by crusading journalist Mikael Blomkvist (Michael Nyqvist), this overlong closing chapter gets bogged down with tying off loose ends. But at least, where the first two films set up Lisbeth's grievances against what Larsson called "Men Who Hate Women", this instalment allows her fearsome antiheroine to take a sweet revenge. JR Swedish +subtitles. Violence. *DVD* *Blu-ray*

Michael Nyqvist *Mikael Blomkvist* • Noomi Rapace *Lisbeth Salander* • Lena Endre *Erika Berger* • Annika Hallin *Annika Giannini* • Jacob Ericksson *Christer Malm* ■ *Dir* Daniel Alfredson • *Scr* Ulf Rydberg, from the novel by Stieg Larsson

The Girl with the Dragon Tattoo ★★★★ 18

Crime thriller
2011 · US/Swe/UK/Ger · Colour · 151min

Stieg Larsson's three novels were international bestsellers and spawned a successful Swedish film trilogy, with Noomi Rapace as computer hacker antiheroine Lisbeth Salander. Despite the familiarity of the material, director David Fincher manages to make this version feel fresh, thanks largely to Rooney Mara whose Lisbeth is an otherworldly creature. Daniel Craig gives a pleasantly restrained performance as disgraced journalist Mikael Blomkvist and Fincher really makes the story his own, concentrating on the themes of sex, sadism and power so common to his work. Steven Zaillian's screenplay is superb, capturing the essence of the book in a script as sparse as the beautifully shot frozen landscape. LB Violence, sex scenes, nudity. *DVD* *Blu-ray*

Daniel Craig *Mikael Blomkvist* • Rooney Mara *Lisbeth Salander* • Christopher Plummer *Henrik Vanger* • Stellan Skarsgård *Martin Vanger* • Steven Berkoff *Dirch Frode* • Robin Wright *Erika Berger* • Yorick van Wageningen *Nils Bjurman* • Joely Richardson *Anita Vanger* • Embeth Davidtz *Annika Blomkvist* ■ *Dir* David Fincher • *Scr* Steven Zaillian, from the novel by Stieg Larsson

Girlfight ★★★★ 15

Sports drama
2000 · US · Colour · 106min

Effortlessly linking an intense look at the lot of inner-city misfits, a fierce family drama and a sweetly engaging romance, debut director Karyn Kusama's boxing story is a lot more than a female *Rocky* set in an ultra-macho Latino landscape. Michelle Rodriguez, giving an inspiring if scary performance, enrols for fight lessons at the local male-dominated gym, and starts a tentative relationship with fellow boxer Santiago Douglas. But their burgeoning affair is put to the test when they're forced to fight in a gender-blind competition. This tense situation stays remarkably free of cliché and builds to a powerfully moving epiphany. AJ *DVD*

Michelle Rodriguez *Diana Guzman* • Jaime Tirelli *Hector* • Paul Calderon *Sandro Guzman* • Santiago Douglas *Adrian* • Ray Santiago *Tiny Guzman* ■ *Dir/Scr* Karyn Kusama

The Girlfriend Experience ★★ 15

Drama
2009 · US · Colour · 73min

Here Steven Soderbergh returns to the low-budget aesthetics and subject matter with which he first made his mark on *sex, lies, and videotape*. Sasha Grey, a real-life porn actress, plays Christine, alias Chelsea, who has to balance domestic life with her gym instructor boyfriend against her work as a high-class escort. Despite the subject matter and casting, this rather drifts along, as Chelsea listens to her clients' problems at length. It's just 77 minutes, yet seems longer – the characters blur into each other, and it's only towards the end that anything happens to upset the equilibrium of Chelsea's life, hinting at what Soderbergh might have achieved with a little more focus and a lot more plot. BP Swearing, nudity. *DVD* *Blu-ray*

Sasha Grey *Christine/"Chelsea"* • Chris Santos *Chris* • Philip Eytan *Philip* • Glenn Kenny *The erotic connisseur* • T Colby Trane *Waiter* • Peter Zizzo *Zizzo* ■ *Dir* Steven Soderbergh • *Scr* Brian Koppelman, David Levien • *Cinematographer* Peter Andrews [Steven Soderbergh]

Girlfriends ★★★★

Comedy drama
1978 · US · Colour · 87min

Claudia Weill directs what is a significant landmark in both women's film-making and American independent cinema. Smashing cosy studio stereotypes, she creates the kind of single women who might really dwell in rented apartments rather than exist solely in the hazy imagination of a Hollywood screenwriter. As wannabe photographer Susan, Melanie Mayron is fresh, honest and vulnerable, whether she's trying to break into the New York art scene

or discussing men with her soon-to-be-married flatmate, Anita Skinner. Lightly played, keenly observed and superbly understated. DP

Melanie Mayron *Susan Weinblatt* • Eli Wallach *Rabbi Gold* • Anita Skinner *Anne Munroe* • Bob Balaban *Martin* • Christopher Guest *Eric* • Gina Rogak *Julie* • Amy Wright *Ceil* • Dir Claudia Weill • *Scr* Vicki Polon, from a story by Claudia Weill, Vicki Polon

Girlhood ★★★★ 15

Drama
2014 · Fr · Colour · 108min

Director Céline Sciamma's third film explores the gang genre from a female perspective and is a stunning counterweight to the innumerable crime films about guys and their masculine angst. Newcomer Karidja Touré plays Marieme, an initially shy high-school student who's kicked out for poor grades. Marieme falls in with a trio of tough girls and soon discovers that not only does crime pay, it's a right laugh, too. Few films this year will match the girl-power positivity and sheer brio on display here, and Touré's performance is a tower of power that augurs well for her future career. LF French +subtitles. *DVD* *Blu-ray*

Karidja Touré *Marieme/Vic* • Assa Sylla *Lady* • Lindsay Karamoh *Adiatou* • Marietou Touré *Fily* ■ *Dir/Scr* Céline Sciamma

Les Girls ★★★ U

Musical
1957 · US · Colour · 109min

This late MGM musical was selected for its year's Royal Film Performance, and there was much discussion about how the Queen would relate to a sexy musical about the British upper classes in Paris. Today it's fun to watch, risqué and disarming, but not really sophisticated enough. The girls are delightful, and Gene Kelly is as watchable as ever. Director George Cukor seems uncomfortable with the material, though, and the Cole Porter score is disappointing. TS

Gene Kelly *Barry Nichols* • Mitzi Gaynor *Joy Henderson* • Kay Kendall *Lady Wren* • Taina Elg *Angele Ducros* • Jacques Bergerac *Pierre Ducros* • Leslie Phillips *Sir Gerald Wren* • Henry Daniell *Judge* • Patrick Macnee *Sir Percy* ■ *Dir* George Cukor • *Scr* John Patrick, from a story by Vera Caspary

Girls Can Play ★

Crime drama
1937 · US · BW · 59min

Rita Hayworth was several years away from her defining role in *Gilda* when she appeared in this forgettable B-movie. The plot bizarrely revolves around booze racketeer John Gallaudet and the female baseball team that represents one of his more legitimate business interests. When one of the team is murdered, dull-witted cop Guinn Williams is assigned to the case. AE

Jacqueline Wells [Julie Bishop] *Ann Casey* • Charles Quigley *Jimmy Jones* • Rita Hayworth *Sue Collins* • John Gallaudet *Foy Harris* • George McKay *Sluggy* • Patricia Farr *Peanuts* • Guinn "Big Boy" Williams *Lt Flannigan* • Joseph Crehan *Brophy* ■ *Dir* Lambert Hillyer • *Scr* Lambert Hillyer, from a story by Albert DeMond

Girls Can't Swim ★★★ 15

Drama
1999 · Fr · Colour · 97min

Subtle shifts in tone and contrasts in character are key to the success of writer/director Anne-Sophie Birot's assured feature debut. By delaying teenager Karen Alyx's arrival on the Breton coast, Birot builds up a one-sided picture of her friendship with the extrovert Isild Le Besco, who's been carried away by the temptations of post-school adolescence, while her intense, but manipulative friend mourns the death of her estranged father in Paris. Both leads impress, but there's also discreet support from Pascale Bussières and Marie Rivière as their mothers. DP French +subtitles. *DVD*

Isild Le Besco *Gwen* • Karen Alyx *Lise* • Pascale Bussières *Céline* • Pascal Elso *Alain* • Marie Rivière *Anne-Marie* • Yelda Reynaud *Solange* ■ *Dir/Scr* Anne-Sophie Birot

G

Girls! Girls! Girls! ★★★ U
Musical 1962 · US · Colour · 94min

One of Presley's more enjoyable romps, this has colourful locations, a serviceable (though silly) plot and the usual attractive co-stars, including cult sex bomb Stella Stevens, who also gets to sing. Elvis plays a tuna boat fisherman in Hawaii who shows his underlying toughness in a brief but particularly revealing scene in which he tries to seduce rich girl Laurel Goodwin. The hit song was the superb *Return to Sender* and the rest of the score is quite bearable. TS *DVD*

Elvis Presley *Ross Carpenter* · Stella Stevens *Robin Gantner* · Jeremy Slate *Wesley Johnson* · Laurel Goodwin *Laurel Dodge* · Benson Fong *Kin Yung* · Robert Strauss *Sam* · Guy Lee *Chen Yung* · Frank Puglia *Alexander Stavros* ■ *Dir* Norman Taurog · *Scr* Edward Anhalt, Allan Weiss, from a story by Allan Weiss

Girls in Uniform ★★★★
Drama 1931 · Ger · BW · 110min

This landmark in gay cinema may no longer scandalise, but it remains a touching love story, as neurotic Hertha Thiele falls under the spell of teacher Dorothea Wieck, her only source of solace in a cold Prussian boarding school. Demonstrating a sympathetic understanding of the misery of teenage isolation, director Leontine Sagan also emphasises the importance of the individual in a society still ruled by the code of militarist uniformity. This subtly subversive picture was banned by the Nazis and many of its key personnel were forced into exile. DP German +subtitles.

Emilia Unda *The Principal* · Dorothea Wieck *Fraulein von Bernburg* · Hedwig Schlichter *Fraulein von Kesten* · Hertha Thiele *Manuela von Meinhardie* · Ellen Schwannecke *Ilse von Westhagen* ■ *Dir* Leontine Sagan · *Scr* Christa Winsloe, FD Andam, from Winsloe's play *Gestern und Heute*

Girls Just Want to Have Fun ★★★ PG
Musical comedy 1985 · US · Colour · 83min

American teen flicks are never short of clichés, and this musical comedy is no exception, packing in most of the genre conventions on the way to its wildly over-the-top, all-dancing finale. However, a confident performance by Sarah Jessica Parker rescues it from obscurity. She convincingly plays a high-school student who incurs her father's wrath by entering a dance competition. JM *DVD*

Sarah Jessica Parker *Janey Glenn* · Helen Hunt *Lynne Stone* · Lee Montgomery *Jeff Malene* · Shannen Doherty *Maggie Malene* · Biff Yeager *Mr Malene* · Morgan Woodward *JP Sands* · Jonathan Silverman *Drew* ■ *Dir* Alan Metter · *Scr* Amy Spies

Girls' Night ★★★★ 15
Comedy drama 1997 · UK/US · Colour · 98min

This comedy drama enables Brenda Blethyn to give another demonstration of everywoman bravura. She stars alongside Julie Walters, who matches Blethyn in every scene. The pair play two northern girls who work in an electrics factory and have been friends since school. When Walters discovers Blethyn has cancer, she decides to take her pal to Las Vegas. There they meet cowboy Kris Kristofferson and embark on an adventure to remember. Impressive and moving. JB Sex scenes, swearing. *DVD*

Brenda Blethyn *Dawn Wilkinson* · Julie Walters *Jackie Simpson* · Sue Cleaver *Rita* · Kris Kristofferson *Cody* · Meera Syal *Carmen* · Margo Stanley *Irene* · Maggie Tagney *Anne Marie* · George Costigan *Steve Wilkinson* ■ *Dir* Nick Hurran · *Scr* Kay Mellor

Girls' Town ★
Drama 1959 · US · BW · 92min

After her questionable lifestyle involves her in the death of a young man, bad girl Mamie Van Doren is sent to a correctional institution run by nuns. Trading off Van Doren's brassy, suggestive voluptuousness, the movie brings to mind a whole lexicon of adjectives, such as sleazy, tawdry and trashy. Its only point of interest is the inclusion of such musical luminaries as Mel Tormé, Paul Anka and The Platters in the cast. RK

Mamie Van Doren *Silver Morgan* · Mel Tormé *Fred Alger* · Paul Anka *Jimmy Parlow* · Ray Anthony *Dick Culdane* · Maggie Hayes [Margaret Hayes] *Mother Veronica* · Cathy Crosby *Singer* · Gigi Perreau *Serafina Garcia* · Elinor Donahue *Mary Lee Morgan* · Harold Lloyd Jr *Chip Gardner* ■ *Dir* Charles Haas · *Scr* Robert Smith, from a story by Robert Hardy Andrews

Giro City ★★★ 15
Thriller 1982 · UK · Colour · 101min

Glenda Jackson lends her talents to this social thriller, but not to much effect. Writer/director Karl Francis's film follows two members of a British investigative documentary team as they consider the plight of a Welsh farmer facing eviction, before going on to look into the activities of the IRA. But they end up having to compromise, in a film that lacks the artistry to do its subjects justice. TH

Glenda Jackson *Sophie* · Jon Finch *O'Mally* · Kenneth Colley *Martin* · James Donnelly *James* · Emrys James *Tommy Williams* · Karen Archer *Brigitte* · Simon Jones *Henderson* · Huw Ceredig *Elwyn Davies* ■ *Dir/Scr* Karl Francis

Give a Girl a Break ★★★ U
Musical 1953 · US · Colour · 82min

This is an enjoyable diversion from MGM's stable of musical talent and offers several dazzling dance routines to compensate for the totally unmemorable score. Gower Champion plays the director of a forthcoming Broadway show from which the temperamental leading lady departs in a huff. The search for a replacement results in three possibles: mature Marge Champion (Gower's old flame and first choice); balletic Helen Woods (supported by the show's composer, Kurt Kasznar); and ingénue Debbie Reynolds, whose cause is championed by Bob Fosse. RK

Marge Champion *Madelyn Corlane* · Gower Champion *Ted Sturgis* · Debbie Reynolds *Suzy Doolittle* · Helen Wood *Joanna Moss* · Bob Fosse *Bob Dowdy* · Kurt Kasznar *Leo Belney* · Richard Anderson *Burton Bradshaw* · William Ching *Anson Pritchett* ■ *Dir* Stanley Donen · *Scr* Albert Hackett, Frances Goodrich, from a story by Vera Caspary · *Choreographers* Gower Champion, Stanley Donen

Give 'Em Hell, Harry! ★★★
Comedy drama 1975 · US · Colour · 102min

Actor James Whitmore's successful one-man show as US President Harry S Truman toured extensively in the USA and was brought to the screen by director Steve Binder. The timing seemed to be propitious. Richard Nixon was in disgrace after Watergate and Whitman's portrayal of Truman harked back to an era of cleaner, nobler politics. The 33rd US President, Truman was in office from 1945-53, ordering the bombing of Hiroshima and steering America through postwar prosperity and the first years of the Cold War. As for Whitmore, his virtuoso performance earned him an Oscar nomination. The film was recorded and edited together from two live performances in Seattle. AT

James Whitmore *Harry S Truman* ■ *Dir* Steve Binder · *Scr* Samuel Gallu

Give Me Your Hand ★★
Drama 2008 · Fr/Ger · Colour · 80min

Tensions between French twin brothers with very different personalities come to a head on a journey to their mother's funeral in Spain in this character-driven drama. Both Antoine (Alexandre Carril) and Quentin (Victor Carril) attract attention from the girls they encounter en route, but the brothers' divergent sexual orientations are to prove a source of some conflict. There's no lack of dramatic potential here, but director Pascal-Alex Vincent delivers an understated, gay-themed road movie that rarely makes that much of an impression. We get an agreeably non-touristy view of the landscapes along the way - and a dash of mild raunch - but this is otherwise a fairly forgettable encounter. TJ French, Spanish, English +subtitles.

Alexandre Carril *Antoine* · Victor Carril *Quentin* · Anaïs Demoustier *Clémentine* · Katrin Sass *Woman on train* ■ *Dir* Pascal-Alex Vincent · *Scr* Martin Drouot, Pascal-Alex Vincent, from a idea by Vincent, Olivier Nicklaus

Give My Regards to Broad Street ★★ PG
Musical 1984 · UK · Colour · 103min

Widely condemned as a worthless ego trip, Paul McCartney's musical fantasy is a great idea for a concept video that had the misfortune to be made into a feature film. The plot - about an ex-con and some missing tapes - is negligible, the references to Fellini's *8½* are laughable, and some of the musical sequences lack inspiration. However, fans will enjoy the Beatles classics and newer songs. DP

Paul McCartney *Paul* · Bryan Brown *Steve* · Ringo Starr *Ringo* · Barbara Bach *Journalist* · Linda McCartney *Linda* · Tracey Ullman *Sandra* · Ralph Richardson *Jim* · George Martin (2) *Record producer* ■ *Dir* Peter Webb · *Scr* Paul McCartney · *Music* Paul McCartney

Give My Regards to Broadway ★★★ U
Musical 1948 · US · Colour · 88min

Broadway movies with backstage emotions boiling over and the show going on regardless are a subgenre all of their own, and this is one of the most amiable, even if it lacks the usual abundance of big production numbers. Charles Winninger is the old-timer who refuses to accept that the vaudeville tradition has had its day, and devotes his energy towards putting his children on the stage. Dan Dailey, as Winninger's son, proves yet again what a versatile actor he was. TH

Dan Dailey *Bert* · Charles Winninger *Albert* · Nancy Guild *Helen* · Charlie Ruggles [Charles Ruggles] *Toby* · Fay Bainter *Fay* · Barbara Lawrence *June* · Jane Nigh *May* · Charles Russell *Arthur Waldron Jr* · Sig Rumann [Sig Ruman] *Dinkel* ■ *Dir* Lloyd Bacon · *Scr* Samuel Hoffenstein, Elizabeth Reinhardt, from a story by John Klempner

Give Us the Moon ★★★ PG
Comedy 1944 · UK · BW · 91min

Made during the Second World War but set in the postwar future, this unusual British comedy is based on a Caryl Brahms and SJ Simon novel about a Soho club founded by a group of idlers who refuse to work. The satire is slight, but co-screenwriter and director Val Guest keeps it moving along nicely, and there's terrific work from stars Margaret Lockwood, Vic Oliver and Peter Graves. There's also a wonderfully brash performance from 14-year-old Jean Simmons as Lockwood's sister, demonstrating her future star quality. TS *DVD*

Margaret Lockwood *Nina* · Vic Oliver *Sascha* · Peter Graves (1) *Peter Pyke* · Roland Culver *Ferdinand* · Max Bacon *Jacobus* · Frank Cellier *Pyke* · Jean Simmons *Heidi* · Irene Handl *Miss Haddock* ■ *Dir* Val Guest · *Scr* Val Guest, Howard Irving Young, Caryl Brahms, SJ Simon, from the novel *The Elephant Is White* by Caryl Brahms, by SJ Simon

Give Us Tomorrow ★
Thriller 1978 · UK · Colour · 94min

In trying to re-create the tension of a hostage situation following a bungled bank job, writer/director Donovan Winter shies away from portraying intimidation and human drama and instead plunges us into a risible debate on the iniquities of the class system. Derren Nesbitt's villain is far less scary than Sylvia Syms's affronted suburbanite. Hopeless. DP

Sylvia Syms *Wendy Hammond* · Derren Nesbitt *Ron* · James Kerry *Martin Hammond* · Donna Evans *Nicola Hammond* · Matthew Haslett *Jamie Hammond* · Alan Guy *Boy* · Victor Brooks *Superintendent* · Derek Anders *Inspector* ■ *Dir/Scr* Donovan Winter

The Giver ★★ 12
Science-fiction drama 2014 · US · Colour and BW · 93min

Part *Divergent*, part *Elysium* and a little bit *Logan's Run*, *The Giver* is set in yet another dully familiar dystopian future where sameness is celebrated. But rebel librarian Jeff Bridges (and, after some persuasion, his teen protégé Brenton Thwaites) is determined to put the "real" back into real life, whatever Chief Elder Meryl Streep says. The movie has its moments, but generally fails to convince the viewer of the credibility of the world it inhabits. In fact, at times, it's plain nonsensical. DA Some violence. *DVD* *Blu*

Jeff Bridges *The Giver* · Meryl Streep *Chief Elder* · Brenton Thwaites *Jonas* · Alexander Skarsgård *Father* · Katie Holmes *Mother* · Taylor Swift *Rosemary* ■ *Dir* Phillip Noyce · *Scr* Michael Mitnick, Robert B Weide, from Lois Lowry's novel

Gladiator ★★★ 15
Action drama 1992 · US · Colour · 97min

Cuba Gooding Jr plays a streetwise teenager who, along with James Marshall, is lured into the world of illegal boxing by a memorably sleazy Brian Dennehy. The plot is riddled with clichés, but this is much grittier territory than the airbrushed world of the *Rocky* films. The two leads are aided by a talented line-up of fine character actors. JF Violence, swearing, nudity. *DVD*

James Marshall *Tommy Riley* · Cuba Gooding Jr *Lincoln* · Brian Dennehy *Jimmy Horn* · Robert Loggia *Pappy Jack* · Ossie Davis *Noah* · John Heard *John Riley* · Jon Seda *Romano* ■ *Dir* Rowdy Herrington · *Scr* Lyle Kessler, Robert Mark Kamen

Gladiator ★★★★★ 15
Period epic 2000 · US · Colour · 148min

Ridley Scott and the boys from DreamWorks produced the first genuine Roman epic since 1964's *The Fall of the Roman Empire* with this virtual remake that deals with the transition of power from the sage-like Marcus Aurelius to his monstrous son, Commodus. The fictional hero, General Maximus, is Caesar's adopted heir, whom Commodus turns into an exile after killing his family. Becoming a gladiator, Maximus fights to avenge his loved ones and save the soul of Rome. The film's strengths are a fine script and excellent performances from Richard Harris and Oliver Reed, in his final film. Also superb is Joaquin Phoenix as the paranoid Commodus, while Russell Crowe is utterly convincing as the Conan/Spartacus-like hero. As always with Scott, the visuals are fabulous. AT Violence. *DVD* *Blu*

Russell Crowe *Maximus Decimus Meridius* · Joaquin Phoenix *Commodus* · Connie Nielsen *Lucilla* · Oliver Reed *Proximo* · Derek Jacobi *Gracchus* · Djimon Hounsou *Juba* · Richard Harris *Marcus Aurelius* · David Schofield *Falco* · John Shrapnel *Gaius* ■ *Dir* Ridley Scott · *Scr* David Franzoni, John Logan, William Nicholson, from a story by David Franzoni · *Cinematographer* John Mathieson

Gladiatress ★★ 15
Spoof comedy 2002 · UK · Colour · 85min

The ladies from TV's *Smack the Pony* reteam for this *Carry On*-style romp set in ancient times. Celtic princesses Worthaboutapig (Sally Phillips) and Smirgut (Fiona Allen) cross the Channel to rescue their sister (Doon Mackichan) after she's kidnapped by Romans. The production values are decent and there's some smart acting, but the jokes are as Iron Age as the setting. *Gladiatress* hits the occasional comic high, but more often plumbs excruciating comic lows, making this one best enjoyed with a bunch of rowdy pals. DA *DVD*

Sally Phillips *Worthaboutapig* · Fiona Allen *Smirgut the Fierce* · Doon Mackichan *Dwyfuc* · Ronan Vibert *Caesar* · David Hayman *General Rhinus* · Pam Ferris *Mrs Goatsplitter* · Marcia Warren *Queen Tuathfhlaifthfth* ■ *Dir* Brian Grant · *Scr* Nick Whitby

Glamour ★★
Melodrama 1934 · US · BW · 74min

Ambitious chorus girl Constance Cummings becomes a successful Broadway star and leaves her husband Paul Lukas for her younger stage partner Phillip Reed. Everything is hunky-dory until Reed, in turns, dumps her. It's a trite tale, the only redeeming feature of which is the presence of the stylish, skilful and persuasive Constance Cummings, who is always worth watching. RK

Paul Lukas *Victor Banki* · Constance Cummings *Linda Fayne* · Phillip Reed [Philip Reed] *Lorenzo Valenti* · Doris Lloyd *Nana* · Joseph Cawthorn *Carl Ibsen* ■ *Dir* William Wyler · *Scr* Doris Anderson, Gladys Unger, LG Blochman, from the short story by Edna Ferber

The Glass Bottom Boat
★★★ U
Romantic comedy 1966 · US · Colour · 105min

Doris Day shows a surprising affinity for satire in this Cold War spoof, starring as a publicist in a space laboratory who's falling in love with engineer boss Rod Taylor while writing a biography of him. Various governments are interested in Taylor's work and, as Day has a dog called Vladimir, she quickly becomes a Soviet suspect. Director Frank Tashlin was a former cartoonist and packs the film with sight gags, but Day rises above the slapstick. TH
DVD

Doris Day *Jennifer Nelson* · Rod Taylor *Bruce Templeton* · Arthur Godfrey *Axel Nordstrom* · John McGiver *Ralph Goodwin* · Paul Lynde *Homer Cripps* · Edward Andrews *General Wallace Bleecker* · Eric Fleming *Edgar Hill* · Dom DeLuise *Julius Pritter* · Robert Vaughn (1) *Napoleon Solo* ■ *Dir* Frank Tashlin · *Scr* Everett Freeman

The Glass Cage ★
Crime drama 1955 · UK · BW · 75min

John Ireland, best known for playing heavies in Hollywood B-movies, was lured to Britain for this low-budget crime drama. It's a bungled yarn about a circus performer called the "Starving Man" (Eric Pohlmann) who fasts for a living. When he is found dead in his glass cage, investigations reveal that he had witnessed the murder of a blackmailer. AT

John Ireland *Pel* · Honor Blackman *Jenny* · Geoffrey Keen *Stanton* · Eric Pohlmann *Sapolio* · Sidney James *Tony Lewis* · Liam Redmond *Lindley* · Sydney Tafler *Rorke* · Valerie Vernon *Bella* ■ *Dir* Montgomery Tully · *Scr* Richard Landau, from the novel *The Outsiders* by AE Martin

The Glass Cage ★ 18
Erotic thriller 1996 · US · Colour · 91min

This sordid tale of diamond smuggling and dirty dancing lurches from shoot-out to soft-core porn, while paying only passing attention to such trifles as character, originality and logic. As the gangster's moll condemned to gyrate at a New Orleans strip joint, Charlotte Lewis just manages to keep her dignity. The same cannot be said of Eric Roberts as a corrupt cop. DP Violence, swearing, sex scenes, drug abuse, nudity.

Charlotte Lewis *Jaqueline* · Richard Tyson *Paul Yaeger* · Eric Roberts *Detective Montrachet* · Stephen Nichols *Renzi* · Joseph Campanella *LeBeque* · Richard Moll *Ian Dexter* ■ *Dir* Michael Schroeder · *Scr* Peter Yurksaitis, David Keith Miller

The Glass House ★★★★ 15
Prison drama 1972 · US · Colour · 90min

Tom Gries had a chequered career: a one-time reporter, he produced B-pics such as *Donovan's Brain* (1953) before moving into television. He won his second Emmy for this no-nonsense, gritty prison drama. Based on a story co-written by Truman Capote, it stars Alan Alda as a college professor who falls foul of hardened lifer Vic Morrow after being jailed for manslaughter. Clu Gulager also impresses as a rookie guard. DP DVD

Vic Morrow *Hugo Slocum* · Alan Alda *Jonathan Paige* · Clu Gulager *Brain Courtland* · Billy Dee Williams *Lennox* · Kristoffer Tabori *Allan*

Campbell · Dean Jagger *Warden Auerbach* ■ *Dir* Tom Gries · *Scr* Tracy Keenan Wynn, from a story by Truman Capote, Wyatt Cooper

The Glass House ★★★ 15
Psychological thriller 2001 · US · Colour · 101min

Director Daniel Sackheim's big-screen debut is essentially an immaculately realised, join-the-dots chiller that utilises every spine-tingling trick at his disposal to elicit a powerful audience response. While there's no real innovation in this slickly enthralling tale of two orphans whose wealthy guardians are not at all what they seem, Sackheim still manages to infuse the film with a pleasing sophistication and freshness. Leelee Sobieski is a standout as the eldest child, sending hearts into mouths as she frantically battles to escape a terror no one will believe, while Stellan Skarsgård's reptilian sleaziness as her guardian is a joy to hate. SF DVD

Leelee Sobieski *Ruby Baker* · Diane Lane *Dr Erin Glass* · Stellan Skarsgård *Terry Glass* · Bruce Dern *Alvin Begleiter* · Kathy Baker *Nancy Ryan* · Trevor Morgan *Rhett Baker* · Chris Noth [Christopher Noth] *Uncle Jack* ■ *Dir* Daniel Sackheim · *Scr* Wesley Strick · *Cinematographer* Alar Kivilo

The Glass Key ★★
Crime drama 1935 · US · BW · 77min

This is a dated but still absorbing adaptation of Dashiell Hammett's novel, with George Raft as the henchman of an allegedly corrupt politician (Edward Arnold) accused of murdering a senator's son. The dialogue is pure "movie talk", sometimes hovering close to screwball comedy. There is a decent sense of intrigue, but the visual atmospherics associated with *film noir* are conspicuously absent. AT

George Raft *Ed Beaumont* · Claire Dodd *Janet Henry* · Edward Arnold *Paul Madvig* · Rosalind Keith *Opal Madvig* · Ray Milland *Taylor Henry* · Robert Gleckler *Shad O'Rory* · [Guinn "Big Boy" Williams] *Jeff* · Tammany Young *Clarkie* ■ *Dir* Frank Tuttle · *Scr* Kathryn Scola, Kubec Glasmon, Harry Ruskin, from the novel by Dashiell Hammett

The Glass Key ★★★★
Film noir 1942 · US · BW · 81min

The second, and far superior, version of Dashiell Hammett's novel, with Alan Ladd and Veronica Lake following up their first hit together, *This Gun for Hire*. Ladd plays the bodyguard to Brian Donlevy's politician, uncovering a murder plot, while Lake seesaws provocatively between them, leading to one of those legendary screen clinches. The story's focus on the bodyguard gave Akira Kurosawa the idea for his masterly 1961 samurai drama *Yojimbo* and that, in turn, was acknowledged by Sergio Leone as the inspiration for *A Fistful of Dollars*. AT DVD

Brian Donlevy *Paul Madvig* · Veronica Lake *Janet Henry* · Alan Ladd *Ed Beaumont* · Bonita Granville *Opal Madvig* · Richard Denning *Taylor Henry* · Joseph Calleia *Nick Varna* · William Bendix *Jeff* ■ *Dir* Stuart Heisler · *Scr* Jonathan Latimer, from the novel by Dashiell Hammett

The Glass Menagerie
★★★ U
Drama 1950 · US · BW · 107min

This early film version of Tennessee Williams's play relies as much on star power as the mesmeric dialogue and the involving quality of the story. Gertrude Lawrence stars as the faded southern belle mother, living in a run-down St Louis apartment with crippled, introverted daughter Jane Wyman and rebellious son Arthur Kennedy. Kirk Douglas is the gentleman caller, whose visit changes the family completely – Lawrence believes Douglas will sweep Wyman off her feet and into a wedding. Director Irving Rapper is demonstrably restrained. TH

Jane Wyman *Laura Wingfield* · Kirk Douglas *Jim O'Connor* · Gertrude Lawrence *Amanda Wingfield* · Arthur Kennedy *Tom Wingfield* · Ralph Sanford *Mendoza* · Ann Tyrrell *Clerk* · John Compton *Young man* · Gertrude Graner

Woman instructor ■ *Dir* Irving Rapper · *Scr* Tennessee Williams, Peter Berneis, from the play by Tennessee Williams

The Glass Menagerie
★★★★ PG
Drama 1987 · US · Colour · 138min

Paul Newman's reverent film version of one of Tennessee Williams's slighter fables stars his wife Joanne Woodward as a faded southern belle and dominating mother who lives with her son John Malkovich and her crippled daughter Karen Allen in a delapidated St Louis apartment. Malkovich works in a warehouse to keep the family, while Allen spends her days polishing her collection of glass animals and wistfully waiting for a "gentleman caller" to whisk her away. Woodward's iron woman is a triumph, and Malkovich is easily her match. TH

Joanne Woodward *Amanda Wingfield* · John Malkovich *Tom Wingfield* · Karen Allen *Laura Wingfield* · James Naughton *The Gentleman Caller/Jim O'Connor* ■ *Dir* Paul Newman · *Scr* from a play by Tennessee Williams

The Glass Mountain ★★
Romantic drama 1949 · UK · BW · 107min

In the second of their five screen twinnings, husband-and-wife team Michael Denison and Dulcie Gray experience a few marital difficulties after he returns from RAF duty obsessed with both an idea for an opera and Valentina Cortese, the partisan who rescued him from the mountain snow. The subject of couples forced apart because of differing wartime experiences is worthy of attention, but director Henry Cass struggles to prevent it being buried in an avalanche of sentimentality. DP

Michael Denison *Richard Wilder* · Dulcie Gray *Ann Wilder* · Valentina Cortese *Alida* · Tito Gobbi *Tito* · Sebastian Shaw *Bruce McLeod* · Antonio Centa *Gino* · Sidney King *Charles* · Elena Rizzieri *Singer* ■ *Dir* Henry Cass · *Scr* Joseph Janni, John Hunter, Emery Bonnet, John Cousins, Henry Cass

The Glass Shield ★★ 15
Police drama based on a true story
1995 · US/Fr · Colour · 105min

A worthy if over-elaborate thriller, this is based on a true story about the first black cop to be assigned to a California sheriff's department. Michael Boatman plays the eager young recruit who finds himself contending not only with the racist attitudes of his white colleagues, but also a web of corruption that leads to the highest level. There's solid support from Lori Petty and Ice Cube, but the action gets too bogged down to allow a real sense of excitement. JF

Michael Boatman *JJ Johnson* · Lori Petty *Deputy Deborah Fields* · Ice Cube *Teddy Woods* · Elliott Gould *Greenspan* · Richard Anderson *Massey* · Don Harvey *Deputy Bono* · Michael Ironside *Baker* · Michael Gregory *Roy Bush* · Bernie Casey *Locket* ■ *Dir* Charles Burnett · *Scr* Charles Burnett, from the (unproduced) screenplay *One of Us* by Ned Walsh

The Glass Slipper ★★ U
Romantic fantasy 1955 · US · Colour · 93min

This musical version of the Cinderella story, directed by Charles Walters, is solemnly narrated by Walter Pidgeon. It stars Leslie Caron and an awkwardly-cast Michael Wilding, who finds himself unsuitably involved in the ballet production numbers, choreographed by Roland Petit. These are, however, the highlights of a dull movie, in which Caron's heroine is perversely irritating, the ugly sisters even more perversely glamorous and Estelle Winwood's fairy godmother a winsome old bag. RK

Leslie Caron *Ella* · Michael Wilding *Prince Charles* · Keenan Wynn *Kovin* · Estelle Winwood *Mrs Toquet* · Elsa Lanchester *Widow Sonder* · Barry Jones *Duke* · Amanda Blake *Birdena* · Lisa Daniels *Serafina* ■ *Dir* Charles Walters · *Scr* Helen Deutsch

The Glass Wall ★★★
Drama 1953 · US · BW · 79min

One of a handful of films made by Vittorio Gassman for MGM during his marriage to Shelley Winters. The Italian heart-throb plays an illegal immigrant in the USA, who is given refuge by social outcast Gloria Grahame and jazzman Jerry Paris. The atmospherically lit, documentary-style movie has a lively jazz score, and there are brief appearances by the likes of Jack Teagarden. It was the best of Gassman's Hollywood films; his marriage to Winters proved short-lived and he returned to Italy to resume his stage and screen career. RB

Vittorio Gassman *Peter* · Gloria Grahame *Maggie* · Ann Robinson *Nancy* · Douglas Spencer *Inspector Bailey* · Robin Raymond *Tanya* · Jerry Paris *Tom* · Elizabeth Slifer *Mrs Hinckley* ■ *Dir* Maxwell Shane · *Scr* Maxwell Shane, Ivan Tors

The Glass Web ★★
Crime drama 1953 · US · BW · 81min

A TV producer is blackmailed by his former mistress: when she is murdered, the case is featured on the producer's show, *Crime of the Week*. Made when television was beginning to eat into cinema attendances, Jack Arnold's drama was originally filmed in 3D, a gimmick intended to lure audiences away from their TV sets. However, the plot is tortuous and unfolds slowly, while Edward G Robinson, playing another of the film's blackmail victims, is given little opportunity to show his talents. AT

Edward G Robinson *Henry Hayes* · John Forsythe *Don Newell* · Kathleen Hughes *Paula Ranier* · Marcia Henderson *Louise Newell* · Richard Denning *Dave Markson* · Hugh Sanders *Lieutenant Stevens* · Clark Howat *Bob Warren* · Dick Stewart *Everett* ■ *Dir* Jack Arnold · *Scr* Robert Blees, Leonard Lee, from the novel by Max Simon Ehrlich

Glassland ★★★★ 15
Drama 2014 · Ire/UK · Colour · 92min

Initially, Gerard Barrett's assured second feature appears to be a modest "issue" drama set in Dublin, but actually it's a richly nuanced character piece that should appeal to fans of down-to-earth thrillers. Jack Reynor stars as a young taxi driver who acts as carer for his alcoholic mother (Toni Collette). His best friend (Will Poulter) is a young father with dreams of leaving for foreign climes but their plans are dashed by Collette's health issues. It's a measure of *Glassland's* slow-burn intensity that nothing boils over into melodrama. Some may find the ending more cryptic than understated, but for those who embrace it, this is a haunting study of the damage done by personal demons and desperation. DW

Jack Reynor *John* · Will Poulter *Shane* · Toni Collette *Jean* · Michael Smiley *Jim* · Harry Nagle *Kit* ■ *Dir/Scr* Gerard Barrett

Glastonbury ★★★★ 15
Documentary 2006 · UK · Colour · 132min

Featuring world-famous names, lesser-known greats, thousands of extras and, inevitably, a lot of mud, this insightful documentary pays tribute to the West Country music festival that has grown from a gathering of a few hippies in organiser Michael Eavis's field into the biggest open-air, weekend-long event on the planet. Director Julien Temple combines material shot by himself and the BBC with swathes of amateur footage by festival-goers to create a thematically structured collage that reflects Glastonbury's evolution over the decades. Some might quibble with the decision not to provide subtitles explaining who anyone is, but in many ways this reflects the democratic spirit of the event. LF DVD

David Bowie · T Rex · REM · Coldplay · Oasis · Blur ■ *Dir* Julien Temple

Glastonbury Fayre ★★★ 15
Music documentary 1973 · UK · Colour · 87min

During the summer of 1971, an estimated 12,000 people packed into Worthy Farm in the Somerset countryside for the second

Glastonbury festival. Organised by Andrew Kerr and Arabella Churchill to coincide with the summer solstice, the fayre was a determined bid to hold a music festival on a non-commercial basis. It leaned heavily towards medieval mysticism, and director Peter Neal's movie captures much of the unique atmosphere. DP *DVD*

■ *Dir* Peter Neal • *Cinematographer* Nicolas Roeg

Glastonbury the Movie ★★★ 15
Music documentary 1995 · UK · Colour · 96min

What a contradiction this is – a documentary celebrating Britain's thriving counterculture that proudly proclaims itself to be the first feature completed with National Lottery funding. Employing widely differing styles and film techniques, and shot over a number of years, this tribute is more concerned with the antics of the audience than with the acts on stage. The sideshows around this site of Arthurian legend are revealing and occasionally entertaining, but the refusal to present the sights and sounds in a cohesive way deprives the footage of any anthropological value. However, fans of the bands featured won't complain. DP *DVD*

■ *Dir* Robin Mahoney, William Beaton, Matthew Salkeld, Lisa Lake, Mike Sarne [Michael Sarne]

Gleaming the Cube ★★★ 12
Action adventure 1988 · US · Colour · 100min

Despite the sometimes uneasy mix of children's caper and more adult action, this is, for the most part, an exhilarating ride. Christian Slater is the ace skateboarder who teams up with his chums and detective Steven Bauer to discover who murdered his adopted Vietnamese brother. Slater oozes charisma, and the stunning skateboarding sequences are expertly choreographed by director Graeme Clifford. JF *DVD*

Christian Slater *Brian Kelly* • Steven Bauer *Detective Al Lucero* • Ed Lauter *Mr Kelly* • Micole Mercurio *Mrs Kelly* • Art Chudabala *Vinh Kelly* • Richard Herd *Ed Lawndale* • Tuan Le *Colonel Trac* • Min Luong *Tina Trac* ■ *Dir* Graeme Clifford • *Scr* Michael Tolkin

The Gleaners and I ★★★★ U
Documentary 2000 · Fr · Colour · 78min

A profound portrait of necessity and eccentricity, Agnès Varda's documentary pays tribute to those who subsist on the margins of society. Tracing the venerable history of gleaning from medieval times, Varda travels across France to meet those who gather discarded items for survival, art and pleasure. Consciously engaging in some cinematic gleaning, she occasionally indulges herself with a charming diversion or striking image. Indeed, this is as poetic as a polemic can get. But beneath the gentle, humanist tone, there's a despair at the fact that so many people embrace a hand to mouth existence in a supposedly civilised state. DP French +subtitles. *DVD*

■ *Dir/Scr* Agnès Varda

Glee: the 3D Concert Movie ★★★ PG
Concert documentary 2011 · US · Colour · 80min

The title says it all. This is not a big-screen spin-off from the hit TV series; it's simply a film of the 2011 concert tour performed by the cast, in character, and presented in indifferent 3D. Between renditions of a bunch of hit pop songs, we are treated to some adulatory fan guff explaining how *Glee* has changed their lives, plus a few brief and contrived "backstage" bits. And that's just about it. There's fun to be had, but only if you fancy a karaoke-style singsong. DA Sexual references. *DVD* 3D

Dianna Agron *Quinn Fabray* • Chris Colfer *Kurt Hummel* • Darren Criss *Blaine Anderson* • Kevin McHale *Artie Abrams* ■ *Dir* Kevin Tancharoen

Glen or Glenda ★ 15
Drama 1953 · US · BW · 70min

The poster for Tim Burton's 1994 biopic *Ed Wood* featured a pink angora sweater – a homage to this 1950s gem. Edward D Wood Jr directs himself (billed as Daniel Davis) as Glen, the troubled transvestite who longs to share a wardrobe with his fiancée Dolores Fuller. The cross-dressing Wood aimed for a documentary realism in this plea for understanding. However, his juxtaposition of painfully earnest psychiatrist Timothy Farrell and a sneering Bela Lugosi rattling on about big green dragons quickly reduces the entire exercise to excruciating farce. So bad, it's unmissable. DP *DVD*

Bela Lugosi *The Spirit* • Lyle Talbot *Police Inspector Warren* • Timothy Farrell *Dr Alton* • Daniel Davis [Edward D Wood Jr] *Glen/Glenda* • Dolores Fuller *Barbara* • "Tommy" Haines *Alan/Ann* ■ *Dir/Scr* Edward D Wood Jr

Glengarry Glen Ross ★★★★★ 15
Drama 1992 · US · Colour · 96min

Director James Foley, working with a highly resonant screenplay by David Mamet, brings a palpable cinematic tension to what could have been a dry, theatrical piece. Rarely moving outside the real-estate office where four salesmen are under pressure to sell more or lose their jobs, the film speaks forcefully about decency being snuffed out by desire, good men taking wrong turnings despite their best efforts and the stench of the American Dream gone mad. Al Pacino, Jack Lemmon, Alan Arkin and Ed Harris all give note-perfect performances, while Alec Baldwin appears in a telling cameo and there's a major early role for Kevin Spacey. JM Swearing. *DVD* Blu

Al Pacino *Ricky Roma* • Jack Lemmon *Shelley "The Machine" Levene* • Alec Baldwin *Blake* • Ed Harris *Dave Moss* • Alan Arkin *George Aaronow* • Kevin Spacey *John Williamson* • Jonathan Pryce *James Lingk* ■ *Dir* James Foley • *Scr* David Mamet, from his play

The Glenn Miller Story ★★★★ U
Musical biographical drama 1953 · US · Colour · 107min

This biopic of the legendary trombonist and band leader will always be the most fondly remembered collaboration between director Anthony Mann and star James Stewart. Whether struggling to find the style of swing that would set him apart from his contemporaries, enjoying the brief benefits of fame or romancing June Allyson, Stewart is perfect for the role. The supporting cast is impeccable and the music, adapted by Henry Mancini, is as bewitching as ever. DP *DVD*

James Stewart *Glenn Miller* • June Allyson *Helen Burger Miller* • Charles Drake *Don Haynes* • George Tobias *Si Schribman* • Henry Morgan [Harry Morgan] *Chummy MacGregor* • Marion Ross *Polly Haynes* • Irving Bacon *Mr Miller* ■ *Dir* Anthony Mann • *Scr* Valentine Davies, Oscar Brodney

The Glimmer Man ★★ 18
Action thriller 1996 · US · Colour · 87min

Sandwiched between his eco-warrior outings *On Deadly Ground* and *Fire Down Below*, this has Steven Seagal going back to the no-brainer fare that made his name. It's a partial success, but ultimately it lacks the slick thrills of his early films. Here, new-age cop Seagal is set on the trail of a serial killer, only to discover his murky government past coming back to haunt him. JF Swearing. *DVD*

Steven Seagal *Jack Cole* • Keenen Ivory Wayans *Jim Campbell* • Bob Gunton *Frank Deverell* • Brian Cox (1) *Mr Smith* • John M Jackson *Donald* • Michelle Johnson *Jessica* • Stephen Tobolowsky *Christopher Maynard* ■ *Dir* John Gray • *Scr* Kevin Brodkin

Glitter ★ PG
Musical romantic drama 2001 · US/Can · Colour · 100min

This rags-to-riches vehicle for superstar diva Mariah Carey invites ridicule on almost every level. In her starring debut as a struggling backing singer hoisted into the big time, Carey possesses all the star quality of a pub karaoke singer but none of the memorable tunes. The gaudy 1980s setting provides a certain nostalgic amusement, though the rest of the limited entertainment on show is of the unplanned variety. JC *DVD*

Mariah Carey *Billie Frank* • Max Beesley *Julian Dice* • Da Brat *Louise* • Tia Texada *Roxanne* • Valarie Pettiford *Lillian Frank* • Ann Magnuson *Kelly* ■ *Dir* Vondie Curtis-Hall • *Scr* Kate Lanier, from a story by Cheryl L West

A Global Affair ★★ U
Comedy 1964 · US · BW · 83min

Bob Hope is a United Nations official who discovers that an abandoned baby is a good way to make yourself very popular with a bevy of international beauties. But is it Hope or the baby they're after? Not a highlight of Bob's post-*Road* career. TH

Bob Hope *Frank Larrimore* • Lilo Pulver [Liselotte Pulver] *Sonya* • Michèle Mercier *Lisette* • Elga Andersen *Yvette* • Yvonne De Carlo *Dolores* • Miiko Taka *Fumiko* • Robert Sterling *Randy* • Nehemiah Persoff *Sigura* ■ *Dir* Jack Arnold • *Scr* Arthur Marx, Bob Fisher, Charles Lederer, from a story by Eugene Vale

La Gloire de Mon Père ★★★ U
Biographical drama 1990 · Fr · Colour · 106min

Drawn from film-maker Marcel Pagnol's autobiography, this is a handsome and beautifully acted piece of French heritage cinema. The kitsch quotient may be high, but the cast is fine, with Philippe Caubère neatly capturing the arrogance of the *petit bourgeois* and Nathalie Roussel dishing out fond reproaches with true maternal gentility. Even more impressive is Julien Ciamaca as the young Marcel, struggling to deal with his father's victory at *boules* and his celebrity after he bags a brace of partridge. DP French +subtitles. *DVD*

Philippe Caubère *Joseph Pagnol* • Nathalie Roussel *Augustine Pagnol* • Thérèse Liotard *Aunt Rose* • Didier Pain *Uncle Jules* • Julien Ciamaca *Marcel aged 11* • Victorien Delamere *Paul aged 5* • Joris Molinas *Lili Des Bellons* • Paul Crauchet *Mond Des Parpaillouns* ■ *Dir* Yves Robert • *Scr* Lucette Andrei, Jérôme Tonnerre, Louis Nucera, Yves Robert, from the autobiography by Marcel Pagnol

Gloria ★★★★ 15
Thriller 1980 · US · Colour · 116min

Gena Rowlands was Oscar-nominated for her formidably engaging performance in this terrific thriller. She plays a not-so-dumb broad living in the Bronx who takes charge of a half-Puerto Rican boy (John Adames) whose parents have been killed by the Mafia. Holding an account book of gangster dealings, she and the boy go on the run from the Mob, until she turns and stands her ground. Director John Cassavetes deftly matches his trademark freewheeling camerawork to his wife Rowlands's brassy, endearing portrayal. TH Violence, swearing. *DVD*

Gena Rowlands *Gloria Swenson* • Tony Knesich *First gangster* • Gregory Cleghorne *Kid in elevator* • Buck Henry *Jack Dawn* • John Adames *Phil Dawn* • Julie Carmen *Jeri Dawn* • Jessica Castillo *Joan Dawn* • Tom Noonan *Second gangster* • Ronald Maccone *Third gangster* ■ *Dir/Scr* John Cassavetes

Gloria ★★ 15
Crime drama 1998 · US · Colour · 102min

Sharon Stone, together with a small, orphaned Hispanic boy (Jean-Luke Figueroa) and a computer disc of Mafia info, is pursued by the Mob. Stone's attempt to emulate Gena Rowlands's hard-as-nails moll in John Cassavetes's 1980 social thriller is undercut by Sidney Lumet's lacklustre direction. It's a pity for Stone's sake – she's an enterprising actress who should be admired for taking dramatic chances. Cardboard characters and cutout situations are all that are left here, without any acknowledged benefit of Cassavetes's original. TH *DVD*

Sharon Stone *Gloria* • Jean-Luke Figueroa *Nicky* • Jeremy Northam *Kevin* • Cathy Moriarty *Diane* • George C Scott *Ruby* • Mike Starr *Sean* • Barry McEvoy *Terry* • Don Billett *Raymond* • Bonnie Bedelia *Brenda* ■ *Dir* Sidney Lumet • *Scr* Steven Antin, from the film by John Cassavetes

Gloria ★★★★ 15
Romantic drama 2013 · Chil/Sp · Colour · 104min

An exceptional performance by Paulina García in the title role dominates this compelling and compassionate study of the way men and women approach a midlife crisis, which also doubles as a sly state-of-the-nation meditation on recession-hit Chile. Still devoted to her grown-up children and aware that her ex-husband has moved on, Gloria sees former naval officer Rodolfo (Sergio Hernández) as someone she could grow old with. Director Sebastián Lelio deftly prevents the film from becoming either archly comedic or mawkishly melodramatic. DP Spanish +subtitles. *DVD*

Paulina García *Gloria* • Sergio Hernández *Rodolfo* • Diego Fontecilla *Pedro* • Fabiola Zamora *Ana* • Coca Guazzini *Luz* ■ *Dir* Sebastián Lelio • *Scr* Sebastián Lelio, Gonzalo Maza

Glorious 39 ★★★★ 12
Period thriller 2009 · UK · Colour · 123min

This period thriller marks a return to the cinema for writer/director Stephen Poliakoff after a decade crafting some of the most original drama on British TV. He brings his singular vision to the story of Anne (Romola Garai), a privileged girl whose world comes crashing down when, just ahead of the Second World War, she gets wind of a sinister plot to appease Hitler that could involve members of her family. Poliakoff cleverly translates the mood of fear and uncertainty in Britain into a dark psychological maze. Garai makes a gutsy yet vulnerable heroine and Nighy is superb as her politician father. And while events become a tad too surreal in parts, it's impossible to look away. SP Swearing. *DVD*

Romola Garai *Anne Keyes* • Bill Nighy *Alexander Keyes* • Julie Christie *Aunt Elizabeth* • Eddie Redmayne *Ralph Keyes* • Juno Temple *Celia Keyes* • Jenny Agutter *Maud Keyes* • Hugh Bonneville *Gilbert* • Charlie Cox *Lawrence* • David Tennant *Hector Haldane* • Jeremy Northam *Balcombe* • Christopher Lee *Walter* ■ *Dir/Scr* Stephen Poliakoff

Glory ★★★★ 15
Historical war drama 1989 · US · Colour · 122min

This American Civil War tale is a long overdue tribute to one of the first black regiments to go into combat, the 54th Massachusetts Voluntary Infantry. The details are culled partly from the letters of the 54th's commander, Colonel Robert Gould Shaw (played by Matthew Broderick), a sensitive 25-year-old (but already a veteran) from an abolitionist family who's determined to lead his men into full battle. His racist superiors won't even allow the soldiers boots, and the troops resent the young white man's leadership, especially runaway slave Denzel Washington. While there is some stereotyping, the lasting impression is of Washington's performance and the plight of the men. Fabulously photographed by Freddie Francis, it features brilliantly staged (and shockingly violent) battle scenes. AT Violence, swearing. *DVD* Blu

Matthew Broderick *Colonel Robert Gould Shaw* • Denzel Washington *Trip* • Morgan Freeman *John Rawlins* • Cary Elwes *Cabot Forbes* • Jihmi Kennedy *Sharts* • André Braugher *Thomas Searles* • John Finn *Sergeant Mulcahy* • Donovan Leitch *Charles Morse* ■ *Dir* Edward Zwick • *Scr* Kevin Jarre, from the books *Lay This Laurel* by Lincoln Kirstein and *One Gallant Rush* by Peter Burchard, and the letters of Robert Gould Shaw

Glory Alley ★
Drama 1952 · US · BW · 79min

MGM was trying to find roles for Leslie Caron after *An American in Paris* and wanted to see if Ralph Meeker had the makings of a star. This stilted, dreary drama was no help to either of them; nor did it enhance the reputation of its director, Raoul Walsh. Meeker is the boxer accused of cowardice who goes off to become a hero in Korea. AE

Ralph Meeker *Socks Barbarosa* • Leslie Caron *Angela* • Kurt Kasznar *Judge* • Gilbert Roland *Peppi Donnato* • John McIntire *Gabe Jordan* • Louis Armstrong *Shadow Johnson* • Jack Teagarden • Larry Gates *Dr Robert Ardley* ■ *Dir* Raoul Walsh • *Scr* Art Cohn

Glory Boy ★
Drama   1971 · US · Colour · 102min

Disillusioned soldier Michael Moriarty brings two fellow Vietnam servicemen home to his father's dilapidated farm. Mitchell Ryan is the psychopathic sergeant who taunts Moriarty's patriotic father, played by veteran character actor Arthur Kennedy, and then forces himself on a young hitch-hiker, Topo Swope. Director Edwin Sherin allows a seemingly bold attempt to convey the dehumanising effect of the Vietnam War to degenerate into a sordid tale of rape and murder. AE

Michael Moriarty *Trubee Pell* • Arthur Kennedy *Walter Pell* • William Devane *Jimmy Pilgrim* • Mitchell Ryan *Sergeant Martin Flood* • Topo Swope *Helen* • Lloyd Gough *Dr Paul* ■ *Dir* Edwin Sherin • *Scr* Stanford Whitmore, from the novel *The Old Man's Place* by John Sanford

The Glory Brigade ★★★ U
War drama   1953 · US · BW · 81min

Victor Mature stars in this tale of conflict between American and Greek soldiers, fighting alongside one another during the Korean War. The film's portrayal of smart Americans and peasant Greeks seems dubious by today's standards, but director Robert D Webb specialised in action scenes and acquits himself well enough, while Lee Marvin makes a strong impression in an early starring role. The real Korean War ended only a month after this film was released. AT

Victor Mature *Lieutenant Sam Prior* • Alexander Scourby *Lieutenant Niklas* • Lee Marvin *Corporal Bowman* • Richard Egan *Sergeant Johnson* • Nick Dennis *Corporal Marakis* • Roy Roberts *Sergeant Chuck Anderson* • Alvy Moore *Private Stone* • Russell Evans *Private Taylor* ■ *Dir* Robert D Webb • *Scr* Franklin Coen

Glory Daze ★★ 15
Comedy drama   1995 · US · Colour · 95min

This pointless movie about pointless people will be of interest mainly to admirers of Ben Affleck and Matt Damon. Affleck takes the lead role as one of a gang of rich college seniors, all living in the same boarding house and fearing graduation day and the cruel realities of life beyond. There are a few laughs, but on the whole nothing much happens and a stream of bad language and scenes of boozing are supposed to make up for it. RS *DVD*

Ben Affleck *Jack* • Sam Rockwell *Rob* • French Stewart *Dennis* • Alyssa Milano *Chelsea* • Megan Ward *Joannie* • Vinnie DeRamus *Mickey* • Matthew McConaughey *Rental truck guy* • Matt Damon *Edgar Pudwhacker* • Hong Vien *Slosh* ■ *Dir/Scr* Rich Wilkes

The Glory Guys ★★★
Western   1965 · US · Colour · 119min

A large-budget and largely competent western, written by Sam Peckinpah, this focuses on a US cavalry action against the Indians and conflict within the ranks. Tom Tryon is pretty nondescript in the leading role, playing a cavalry officer loath to send his recruits into combat. Andrew Duggan does better as the general who's less fussed at the prospect of losing a few men, while a young James Caan catches the eye as a bull-headed soldier. The brutal plot takes to unfold, but builds to a rousing finale. PF

Tom Tryon *Demas Harrod* • Harve Presnell *Sol Rogers* • Senta Berger *Lou Woodard* • Andrew Duggan *General McCabe* • James Caan *Dugan* • Slim Pickens *Gregory* • Michael Anderson Jr *Martin Hale* • Peter Breck *Hodges* • Robert McQueeny [Robert McQueeney] *Marcus* ■ *Dir* Arnold Laven • *Scr* Sam Peckinpah, from the novel *The Dice of God* by Hoffman Birney

Glory Road ★★★ PG
Sports drama based on a true story   2006 · US · Colour · 113min

In 1966, basketball coach Don Haskins led his Texas Western Miners team to victory by fielding the first-ever all-black starting line-up. This watchable Disney movie follows Haskins (Josh Lucas) as he arrives at the run-down Texas college and drafts in African-American players. Slamdunk basketball action is interspersed with the players' experience of racial prejudice before the film gears up for a final showdown against bigoted coach Jon Voight's rival team. Polished ensemble playing captures the strangeness of being black in El Paso in the 60s, and a feel-good soundtrack of Motown hits keeps it all chugging along smoothly. JR *DVD*

Josh Lucas *Don Haskins* • Derek Luke *Bobby Joe Hill* • Austin Nichols *Jerry Armstrong* • Jon Voight *Adolph Rupp* • Evan Jones *Moe Iba* • Schin AS Kerr *David Lattin* • Alphonso McAuley *Orsten Artis* ■ *Dir* James Gartner • *Scr* Christopher Cleveland, Bettina Gilois

The Glory Stompers ★
Action drama   1967 · US · Colour · 85min

Violence erupts between warring bikers when Dennis Hopper's Black Souls beat up Stompers leader Jody McCrea and take his girlfriend to be sold in a Mexican white-slave market. Jock Mahoney rescues McCrea and joins his old friend on the manhunt south of the border. Risible dialogue and mindless action puts this near the bottom of the rebel riders heap. AJ

Dennis Hopper *Chino* • Jody McCrea *Darryl* • Chris Noel *Chris* • Jock Mahoney *Smiley* • Saundra Gayle *Jo Ann* • Robert Tessier *Magoo* • Astrid Warner *Doreen* • Gary Wood *Pony* ■ *Dir* Anthony M Lanza • *Scr* James Gordon White, John Lawrence

The Glove ★★
Action adventure   1978 · US · Colour · 90min

Escaped convict Roosevelt "Rosey" Grier is equipped with a custom-built steel glove that can smash through people and solid metal. Ex-cop turned bounty hunter John Saxon is offered $20,000 for his recapture. This is an odd, before-its-time combination of science-fiction, action and social issues that fails to make its mark in each area it tries to embrace. Bizarre, but entertaining by default. AJ

John Saxon *Sam Kellough* • Roosevelt Grier [Rosey Grier] *Victor Hale* • Joanna Cassidy *Sheila Michaels* • Joan Blondell *Mrs Fitzgerald* • Jack Carter *Walter Stratton* • Keenan Wynn *Bill Schwartz* • Aldo Ray *Prison guard* • Michael Pataki *Harry Iverson* ■ *Dir* Ross Hagen • *Scr* Hubert Smith, Julian Roffman

Glue ★★★ 18
Coming-of-age comedy drama   2006 · Arg/UK · Colour · 108min

The universality of adolescent angst emerges loud and clear in this engaging coming-of-age saga from director Alexis Dos Santos. Set in a small but isolated town in Patagonia, it stars Nahuel Pérez Biscayart as a typically bored teenager who fantasises about sex, experiments with drugs and dabbles in rock 'n' roll. However, a weekend of glue-sniffing and fooling around in his father's empty apartment soon changes the dynamic of his relationship with his classmates. The performances are first-rate and, though the shifts into using Super 8 film stock are self-conscious, the realism serves to reinforce the authenticity of the teenagers' lusts and frustrations. DP Spanish, English +subtitles *DVD*

Nahuel Pérez Biscayart *Lucas* • Nahuel Viale *Nacho* • Inés Efron *Andrea* • Veronica Llinas *Mecha* • Hector Diaz *Freddy* ■ *Dir/Scr* Alexis Dos Santos

The Gnome-Mobile ★★★ U
Fantasy   1967 · US · Colour · 81min

This whimsical fantasy in the Disney tradition of whiter-than-white family fun is packed with enchanting special effects and merry, if instantly forgettable, tunes. Matthew Garber and Karen Dotrice protect

gnomes living in redwood forests from mindless lumber barons. This little-known live action feature deserves better attention; kids will love it. Veteran Walter Brennan is a standout in a dual role and there's a knockout car chase finale. RS *DVD*

Walter Brennan *DJ Mulrooney/Knobby* • Tom Lowell *Jasper* • Matthew Garber *Rodney Winthrop* • Ed Wynn *Rufus* • Karen Dotrice *Elizabeth Winthrop* • Richard Deacon *Ralph Yarby* • Sean McClory *Horatio Quaxton* • Jerome Cowan *Dr Conrad Ramsey* ■ *Dir* Robert Stevenson • *Scr* Ellis Kadison, from the novel *The Gnomobile: a Gnice Gnew Gnarrative With Gnonsense, But Gnothing Gnaughty* by Upton Sinclair

Gnomeo & Juliet ★★★ U
Animated romantic fantasy   2011 · UK/US · Colour · 80min

This bright and breezy animated fantasy from *Shrek 2* director Kelly Asbury uses William Shakespeare's most famous romance for inspiration, only with gnomes and a much happier ending. This cute bit of 3D cartoonery boasts an Elton John soundtrack and a voice cast to die for. James McAvoy and Emily Blunt play the star-crossed lovers caught up in a turf war between next-door-neighbouring garden gnomes, the Reds and the Blues, but there are also the stellar talents of Michael Caine, Matt Lucas, Jason Statham and Ozzy Osbourne to listen out for. DA *DVD* *BD* *3D*

James McAvoy *Gnomeo* • Emily Blunt *Juliet* • Jason Statham *Tybalt* • Michael Caine *Lord Redbrick* • Ashley Jensen *Nanette* • Maggie Smith *Lady Blueberry* • Patrick Stewart *Bill Shakespeare* • Matt Lucas *Benny* • Julie Walters *Miss Montague* • Stephen Merchant *Paris* • Ozzy Osbourne *Fawn* • Richard Wilson *Mr Capulet* ■ *Dir* Kelly Asbury • *Scr* Mark Burton, Kevin Cecil, Andy Riley, Kelly Asbury, Steve Hamilton Shaw, John Smith, Rob Sprackling, from the play *Romeo and Juliet* by William Shakespeare • *Music* Elton John, Bernie Taupin • *Executive Producer* Elton John

Go ★★★★ 18
Comedy crime drama   1999 · US · Colour · 97min

Doug Liman's film intertwines three separate storylines to present a picture of mixed-up Los Angeles youth. It's Christmas Eve, and two supermarket checkout girls are trying to raise some rent money by rather dubious means. A colleague drives with his mates to Las Vegas, but their good-time gambling turns sour. In the meantime, two male soap stars become embroiled in a police sting. Katie Holmes, Sarah Polley, Jay Mohr and Scott Wolf are all on great form in an ensemble vision of 20-something angst that boasts a superb soundtrack. The result is original and hilarious. LH Swearing, sex scenes, drug abuse. *DVD* *BD*

Katie Holmes *Claire Montgomery* • Sarah Polley *Ronna Martin* • Desmond Askew *Simon Baines* • Scott Wolf *Adam* • Jay Mohr *Zack* • Timothy Olyphant *Todd Gaines* • Jimmy Shubert *Victor Jr* • Nathan Bexton *Mannie* ■ *Dir* Doug Liman • *Scr* John August

The Go-Between ★★★★ PG
Period drama   1971 · UK · Colour · 111min

Director Joseph Losey and writer Harold Pinter's wonderfully resonant adaptation of LP Hartley's classic Edwardian romance is a beautiful, beguiling and brilliant exposé of a repressive and manipulative class system. Julie Christie and Alan Bates excel as the upper-class girl and her farmer lover carrying on a clandestine relationship, unwittingly aided by young "postman" Dominic Guard, who delivers their letters. Gorgeously shot by Gerry Fisher on Norfolk locations, this is thought-provoking costume drama of the highest order. AJ *DVD* *BD*

Julie Christie *Marian Maudsley* • Alan Bates *Ted Burgess* • Dominic Guard *Leo Colston* • Margaret Leighton *Mrs Maudsley* • Michael Redgrave *Leo, as an old man* • Michael Gough *Mr Maudsley* • Edward Fox *Hugh Trimingham* • Richard Gibson *Marcus Maudsley* ■ *Dir* Joseph Losey • *Scr* Harold Pinter, from the novel by LP Hartley

Go Fish ★★★★ 18
Romantic drama   1994 · US · BW · 79min

Unpretentious, inoffensive and very funny, this ultra low-budget festival hit, about finding true love in the lesbian community, effortlessly cruises between queer politics and hip funkiness. It's all about the very Woody Allen-esque things that happen when terminally single Guinevere Turner goes on a blind date with the neurotic VS Brody just to please her best mates. Arty yet wholly accessible, this monochrome marvel works on numerous levels, and is a genuinely hilarious heart-warmer. AJ Swearing, nudity.

VS Brodie *Ely* • Guinevere Turner *Max* • T Wendy McMillan *Kia* • Migdalia Melendez *Evy* • Anastasia Sharp *Daria* • Mary Garvey *Student/Jury member* • Daniela Falcon *Student/Jury member* • Tracy Kimme *Student/Jury member* ■ *Dir* Rose Troche • *Scr* Rose Troche, Guinevere Turner

Go for a Take ★ U
Comedy   1972 · UK · Colour · 89min

This British comedy has minimal laughs. Reg Varney and Norman Rossington are waiters on the run from debt collectors who take refuge in a film studio, a scenario which leads to some amazingly unfunny sequences. It's enough to make the *Carry On* films seem as witty as Oscar Wilde. TH

Reg Varney *Wilfrid Stone* • Norman Rossington *Jack Foster* • Sue Lloyd *Angel Montgomery* • Dennis Price *Dracula* • Julie Ege *April* • Patrick Newell *Generous Jim* • David Lodge *Graham* • Jack Haig *Security man* ■ *Dir* Harry Booth • *Scr* Alan Hackney, from a story by Alan Hackney, Harry Booth

Go for Broke! ★★
Second World War drama   1951 · US · BW · 90min

The title was the war cry of the 442nd Regimental Combat Team, a unit made up of Japanese-Americans who fought alongside their fellow Americans against the Nazis. Van Johnson plays the lieutenant in charge of them, who overcomes his initial wariness when he sees how they fight in Italy. The cynical motivation behind this MGM effort was that, in the postwar era, Japan was becoming a major market for Hollywood movies, so a story like this was good publicity. AT

Van Johnson *Lt Michael Grayson* • Lane Nakano *Sam* • George Miki *Chick* • Akira Fukunaga *Frank* • Ken K Okamoto *Kaz* • Henry Oyasato *O'Hara* • Harry Hamada *Masami* ■ *Dir/Scr* Robert Pirosh

Go into Your Dance ★★
Musical comedy drama   1935 · US · BW · 92min

This was the only movie in which Al Jolson and his wife Ruby Keeler appeared together, and they pleasantly deliver some tuneful numbers by Harry Warren and Al Dubin (who appear briefly as themselves). The choreographer Bobby Connolly was no Busby Berkeley, but he does a reasonable job. The feeble plot attempted to combine two of Warners' specialities - the backstage musical and the gangster movie. RB

Al Jolson *Al Howard* • Ruby Keeler *Dorothy Wayne* • Glenda Farrell *Sadie Howard* • Helen Morgan (1) *Luana Bell* • Barton MacLane *The Duke* • Sharon Lynne *Blonde* • Patsy Kelly *Irma* • Benny Rubin ■ *Dir* Archie Mayo • *Scr* Earl Baldwin, from a story by Bradford Ropes

Go, Johnny, Go! ★★
Musical   1959 · US · BW · 75min

Rock legend Chuck Berry and disc jockey Alan Freed (who also produced the film) beat up the soundtrack to this otherwise dull effort. The *Pygmalion*-like storyline involves the transformation of an orphan (Jimmy Clanton) into a rock 'n' roll hero. The highlights are the songs, such as *Little Queenie*, and Ritchie Valens hitting his strident form in his only film appearance. (Valens's life was well portrayed by Lou Diamond Phillips in the film *La Bamba* 27 years later.) TH

Alan Freed • Jimmy Clanton *Johnny* • Sandy Stewart *Julie Arnold* • Chuck Berry • Herb Vigran *Bill Barnett* • Frank Wilcox *Mr Arnold* • Barbara

Woodell *Mrs Arnold* • Milton Frome *Mr Martin* • Richie Valens ■ *Dir* Paul Landres • *Scr* Gary Alexander

Go, Man, Go! ★★ U

Sports drama   1953 • US • BW • 83min

One of two films directed by James Wong Howe, the Cantonese-born cinematographer whose credits include *The Prisoner of Zenda*, *Sweet Smell of Success* and *Hud* (for which he won his second Oscar). It's the story of Abe Saperstein (played by Dane Clark), the man who founded the world famous, all-black Harlem Globetrotters basketball team. Sidney Poitier appears, along with some bona fide Globetrotters, and the message about racism retains its power. **AT**

Dane Clark *Abe Saperstein* • Pat Breslin [Patricia Breslin] *Sylvia Saperstein* • Sidney Poitier *Inman Jackson* • Ruby Dee *Irma Jackson* • The Harlem Globetrotters • Edmon Ryan *Zack Leader* ■ *Dir* James Wong Howe • *Scr* Arnold Becker (front for Alfred Palca)

Go Naked in the World ★★

Drama   1961 • US • Colour • 103min

MGM embarked on a series of lavish melodramas in the 1960s. This tosh, in which Gina Lollobrigida is taken home to meet dad Ernest Borgnine by infatuated son Anthony Franciosa, is not the best example. There's no thrill at all when we discover that Borgnine, and most of the townsfolk, already know about Lollobrigida's shady background. Given an X certificate on its original release, the film looks pretty tame today. **TS**

Gina Lollobrigida *Giulietta Cameron* • Anthony Franciosa *Nick Stratton* • Ernest Borgnine *Pete Stratton* • Luana Patten *Yvonne Stratton* • Will Kuluva *Argus Diavolos* • Philip Ober *Josh Kebner* • John Kellogg *Cobby* • Nancy R Pollock *Mary Stratton* ■ *Dir* Ranald MacDougall • *Scr* Ranald MacDougall, from the novel by Tom T Chamales

Go Now ★★ 15

Drama romance   1995 • UK • Colour • 82min

Michael Winterbottom tackles another gloomy subject in this grim drama. Robert Carlyle is in love with Juliet Aubrey, randy and raucous. His life turns sour when he discovers he has multiple sclerosis. The film chronicles his physical deterioration and how the inability to lead a normal life affects both Carlyle's morale and his relationship with Aubrey. **LH** Swearing, sex scenes.

Robert Carlyle *Nick Cameron* • Juliet Aubrey *Karen Walker* • James Nesbitt *Tony* • Sophie Okonedo *Paula* • John Brobbey *Geoff* • Darren Tighe *Dell* • Berwick Kaler *Sammy* • Sean McKenzie *George* ■ *Dir* Michael Winterbottom • *Scr* Paul Henry Powell, Jimmy McGovern

Go Tell the Spartans ★★★ 15

War drama   1977 • US • Colour • 110min

This is one of the few American movies to deal in depth with the morality of the Vietnam conflict, which officially started as "policing" action in 1964 - the year in which the film is set. It plays like a transplanted western, with veteran Burt Lancaster starring as a military adviser beset with doubts about his mission and its value. The screenplay is both clever and perceptive, and director Ted Post does what he can, but the scale is limited and the supporting cast lacks gravitas. Nevertheless, the film is surprisingly moving, peppered with witty lines spat out with relish by Lancaster. **TS** Swearing.

Burt Lancaster *Major Asa Barker* • Craig Wasson *Corporal Stephen Courcey* • Jonathan Goldsmith *Sergeant Oleonowski* • Marc Singer *Captain Al Olivetti* • Joe Unger *Lt Raymond Hamilton* • Dennis Howard *Corporal Abraham Lincoln* • David Clennon *Lt Finley Wattsberg* • Evan Kim *Cowboy* ■ *Dir* Ted Post • *Scr* Wendell Mayes, from the novel *Incident at Muc Wa* by Daniel Ford

Go to Blazes ★★ U

Comedy   1961 • UK • Colour • 79min

This substandard comedy caper is now mainly of interest for providing Maggie Smith with her second screen role. The story of some clottish crooks who train themselves up as firemen in order to use the engine they've bought as a getaway vehicle is both derivative and dull. Dave King and Daniel Massey generate few comic sparks, but there's a fun cameo from Robert Morley as an obliging arsonist. **DP** DVD

Dave King *Bernard* • Robert Morley *"Arson" Eddie* • Daniel Massey *Harry* • Dennis Price *Withers* • Coral Browne *Colette* • Norman Rossington *Alfie* • Maggie Smith *Chantal* • Miles Malleson *Salesman* • Finlay Currie *Judge* ■ *Dir* Michael Truman • *Scr* Patrick Campbell, Vivienne Knight, from a story by Peter Myers, Ronald Cass

Go West ★★★★ U

Silent comedy   1925 • US • BW • 69min

All the great comedians have headed in this direction at some time or another, and Buster Keaton may have been exceptional - but he was no exception. This is, perhaps, the only one of his silent movies which tries for a touch of Chaplin-esque sentiment: he's called Friendless and his touching way with a favourite cow - he places the milking pail beneath her hoping she will milk herself - achieves a gingerly-handled tenderness. There's a great stampede of cattle at the end which Buster tries to stop, though the cops don't believe his story. **TH**

Buster Keaton *Friendless, Homer Holiday* • Howard Truesdale *Thompson, owner of the Diamond Bar Ranch* • Kathleen Myers *Gloria, his daughter* • Ray Thompson *Foreman* • Joe Keaton *Man in barber chair* • Roscoe "Fatty" Arbuckle *Fat woman in store* • Babe London *Fat woman's daughter* • Erwin Connelly *Stockyard owner* ■ *Dir* Buster Keaton • *Scr* Raymond Cannon, from an idea by Buster Keaton

Go West ★★ U

Comedy   1940 • US • BW • 77min

The fourth film the Marx Brothers made for MGM is one of their weakest vehicles, with too much time being spent in the company of John Carroll and Diana Lewis. Sorely missing the stately presence of Margaret Dumont and saddled with a mediocre script, they are forced to plunder that Buster Keaton masterpiece *The General* for the best scene in the picture. There are a couple of other worthwhile routines, but it's all either hit and miss. **DP** DVD

Groucho Marx *S Quentin Quale* • Chico Marx *Joe Panello* • Harpo Marx *"Rusty"* • John Carroll *Terry Turner* • Diana Lewis *Eve Wilson* • Walter Woolf King *Beecher* ■ *Dir* Edward Buzzell • *Scr* Irving Brecher

Go West, Young Man ★★★

Comedy   1936 • US • BW • 79min

The lines may not be as outrageous as in her earlier films, but Mae West is as physically suggestive as ever in her own adaptation of a Lawrence Riley play. Poking fun at herself, she plays a modern-day film star on tour to promote her new picture. She perks up at the sight of handsome Randolph Scott and decides to stay on and see what develops. **AE**

Mae West *Mavis Arden* • Warren William *Morgan* • Randolph Scott *"Bud Norton"* • Alice Brady *Mrs Struthers* • Elizabeth Patterson *Aunt Kate* • Lyle Talbot *Francis X Harrigan* • Isabel Jewell *Gladys* • Margaret Perry *Joyce* ■ *Dir* Henry Hathaway • *Scr* Mae West, from the play *Personal Appearance* by Lawrence Riley

Go with Me ★★ 15

Thriller   2015 • US • Colour • 90min

Star and producer Anthony Hopkins jumps on the Scandinavian *noir* bandwagon as it's disappearing over the hill in this strangely vacant thriller set in a logging community in the US Pacific Northwest. Adapted from Castle Freeman Jr's novel, it follows forklift driver Hopkins, dim hick Alexander Ludwig and scared waitress Julia Stiles as they track down local psycho Blackway (Ray Liotta) to "persuade" him to leave the young woman alone. It's the actors who stand out, doing remarkable things with roles that must barely exist in the screenplay. **SvM** Violence, swearing.

Julia Stiles *Lillian* • Alexander Ludwig *Nate* • Anthony Hopkins *Lester* • Ray Liotta *Blackway* • Hal Holbrook *Whizzer* ■ *Dir* Daniel Alfredson • *Scr* Gregory Jacobs, Joe Gangemi, from Castle Freeman Jr's novel

Goal! ★★★ 12

Sports drama   2005 • US • Colour • 113min

Director Danny Cannon's flimsy but feel-good football drama is a fist-pumping male fantasy that bursts with heart and humour. In the first part of a planned trilogy, an insipid Kuno Becker is the talented Mexican immigrant who swaps the sunshine of LA for rainy northern England when he's given the chance to try out for Newcastle United. For all its daftness and predictability, the feature remains solidly entertaining, and Alessandro Nivola's charismatic turn as a celebrity striker makes the film. **SF** Swearing. DVD

Kuno Becker *Santiago Munez* • Stephen Dillane *Glen Foy* • Alessandro Nivola *Gavin Harris* • Anna Friel *Roz Harmison* • Marcel Iures *Erik Dornhelm* • Sean Pertwee *Barry Rankin* • Lee Ross *Bluto* ■ *Dir* Danny Cannon • *Scr* Dick Clement, Ian La Frenais

Goal II: Living the Dream ★★★ 12

Sports drama   2007 • UK/Sp • Colour • 110min

House of Wax director Jaume Collet-Serra takes over for this second instalment of the planned football trilogy. Here, soccer sensation Santiago Munez (Kuno Becker) transfers to Real Madrid and competes in the UEFA Champions League. Meanwhile, off the field, he is seduced away from his Geordie fiancée Roz (Anna Friel). As in the first film, the plot is pure Roy of the Rovers. But the football scenes are still among the best ever seen on screen, with real players seamlessly integrated with the actors. There is one small problem, though: in Santiago's world, David Beckham and Zinédine Zidane are still with Real Madrid. In the real world, of course, they're not. **DA** Violence. DVD

Kuno Becker *Santiago Munez* • Alessandro Nivola *Gavin Harris* • Anna Friel *Roz Harmison* • Stephen Dillane *Glen Foy* • Nick Cannon *TJ Harper* • Elizabeth Peña *Rosa Maria* • Leonor Varela *Jordana* • David Beckham • Zinédine Zidane ■ *Dir* Jaume Collet-Serra • *Scr* Adrian Butchart, Mike Jefferies, Terry Loane, from characters by Dick Clement, Ian La Frenais

The Goalkeeper's Fear of the Penalty Kick ★★★★ PG

Drama   1971 • Austria/W Ger • Colour • 96min

In adapting his own novel for the screen, Peter Handke retains its existential aura of Camus, Sartre and Kafka. Yet, with goalkeeper Arthur Brauss exhibiting a passion for all things American, this is recognisably a Wim Wenders movie (indeed, it was the first to bring him international recognition). With its imagery focusing on vehicles and modes of communication, and a resolute refusal to justify Brauss's motives for killing a cinema cashier, this could be described as an existential thriller. Wenders invests seemingly inconsequential objects with an almost sinister significance to reflect his antihero's mental deterioration following that fateful spot kick. **DP** German +subtitles.

Arthur Brauss *Joseph Bloch* • Kai Fischer *Hertha Gabler* • Erika Pluhar *Gloria* • Libgart Schwarz *Maid* • Marie Bardischewski *Maria* • Michael Toost *Salesman* • Bert Fortell *Customs official* • Edda Köchl *Girl in Vienna* ■ *Dir* Wim Wenders • *Scr* Wim Wenders, Peter Handke, from a novel by Peter Handke

Goat 15

Drama   2016 • US • Colour • 98min

This is a preview - no prints were available to review as we went to press: After breaking the code of silence about initiation rites in US college fraternities, Brad Land's shocking memoir was picked up by documentary maker Andrew Neel who decided to turn it into a teen drama featuring one of the Jonas brothers - Nick. However, newcomer Ben Schnetzer is the star of the show as the younger brother who must follow his hazing lead. This will have to tread a very fine line between exposing the terrible truth and revelling in it. **SP**

Ben Schnetzer *Brad Land* • James Franco *Mitch* • Nick Jonas *Brett Land* • Danny Flaherty *Will* • Virginia Gardner *Leah* ■ *Dir* Andrew Neel • *Scr* David Gordon Green, Andrew Neel, Mike Roberts, from a memoir by Brad Land

God Bless America ★★★★ 15

Black comedy   2011 • US • Colour • 100min

This tar-black, deeply funny satire from Bobcat Goldthwait stars Joel Murray as a superficially diffident cubicle worker who is fired from his job and then diagnosed with a brain tumour. With nothing to lose, he embarks on a bloody road trip and sets about eliminating the flotsam of trash culture. The film's chief pleasures are a brace of fine performances from Murray as the frustrated everyman and Tara Lynne Barr as his youthful Bonnie-ish partner in crime, as well as some pleasingly tart dialogue. **AS** Violence, swearing. DVD

Joel Murray *Frank* • Tara Lynne Barr *Roxy* • Melinda Page Hamilton *Alison* • Mackenzie Brooke Smith *Ava* • Rich McDonald *Brad* • Aris Alvarado *Steve Clark* ■ *Dir/Scr* Bobcat Goldthwait

God Bless Ozzy Osbourne ★★★★ 15

Documentary   2011 • US • Colour • 93min

Filmed over several years, during which time Ozzy Osbourne celebrated his 60th birthday, this candid portrait of the heavy metal legend chronicles his fraught journey to sobriety while also serving as a detailed no-holds-barred history of his career and wild-man past. Directors Mike Fleiss and Mike Piscitelli, with Osbourne's son Jack serving as a producer, show Ozzy as a complicated man, wracked with guilt over his previous bad behaviour - a flipside to the bumbling clown seen in the famed fly-on-the-wall MTV series. Archive footage fills in the gaps, but it's the honesty and surprising articulacy of the man that leave a lasting impression. **TeS** Swearing, drug references. DVD BD

Ozzy Osbourne • Paul McCartney • Tommy Lee ■ *Dir* Mike Fleiss, Mike Piscitelli

God Forgives... I Don't! ★★★ 15

Spaghetti western   1967 • It/Sp • Colour • 82min

This good-looking but flawed debut from Giuseppe Colizzi marked the beginning of an enduring screen partnership between Terence Hill and Bud Spencer. The people of a dustbowl town gather to welcome a train - only for it to arrive with all the passengers dead. It's an arresting opening, but Colizzi fails to maintain the dramatic tension as Hill and Spencer seek out the man responsible for the massacre to return the train's cargo of gold. The formula proved a success with Italian audiences, prompting the director and his stars to return for sequels *Ace High* (1968) and *Boot Hill* (1969). **JH** Some dialogue dubbed.

Terence Hill *Cat Stevens* • Bud Spencer *Hutch Bessy* • Frank Wolff *Bill San Antonio* • Gina Rovere *Rose* ■ *Dir* Giuseppe Colizzi • *Scr* Giuseppe Colizzi, Gumersindo Mollo

God Help the Girl ★★ 15

Musical romantic drama
2012 • UK • Colour • 107min

Indie pop band Belle and Sebastian frontman Stuart Murdoch turns writer/director for this frivolous musical offering set in Glasgow. Drawing upon songs Murdoch composed for a 2009 side project, the story follows Emily Browning's troubled 20-something heroine as she tries to move on with her life while under hospital supervision for depression. Browning is likeably vulnerable in the lead, but Murdoch's screenplay lacks the wit and polish of his songs, and his direction only comes alive during a few giddy dance numbers. **JH** Swearing, sexual references. DVD

Emily Browning *Eve* • Olly Alexander *James* • Hannah Murray *Cassie* • Pierre Boulanger *Anton* ■ *Dir/Scr* Stuart Murdoch

The Goddess ★★★

Drama   1958 · US · BW · 105min

This is an excellent rendition of the "poor, working-class girl makes it in the movies" scenario, written with depth and understanding by Paddy Chayefsky. Allegedly based on the life of Marilyn Monroe, and full of oblique references to abused childhoods and scenes of reckless pill-popping, this is nevertheless a serious attempt to explore the nature of female fame and sexual charisma. Kim Stanley turns in a fine performance as the ambitious starlet, who's part manipulative minx, part vulnerable victim, and she is ably supported by a fine cast. **SH**

Kim Stanley *Emily Ann Faulkner* • Betty Lou Holland *Mother* • Joan Copeland *Aunt* • Gerald Hiken *Uncle* • Burt Brinckerhoff *Boy* • Steven Hill *John Tower* • Gerald Petrarca *Minister* • Linda Soma *Bridesmaid* • Curt Conway *Writer* • Lloyd Bridges *Dutch Seymour* ■ *Dir* John Cromwell • *Scr* Paddy Chayefsky

Goddess ★★12

Musical comedy   2013 · Aus · Colour · 99min

A songbird mum tries to escape her domestic drudgery in this cheesy and contrived Aussie musical based on Joanna Weinberg's one-woman stage show. Basically a procession of forgettable ditties connected by minimal plotting and endless clichés, the film follows rurally isolated parent Elspeth Dickens (played by London theatre sensation Laura Michelle Kelly) as she becomes an internet star after broadcasting her woes to the world. Her energy and vocal talents hold together the uneven and increasingly forced events. **SF**

Laura Michelle Kelly *Elspeth Dickens* • Ronan Keating *James Dickens* • Magda Szubanski *Cassandra Wolfe* • Dustin Clare *Rory* ■ *Dir* Mark Lamprell • *Scr* Mark Lamprell, Joanna Weinberg (2), from Weinberg's stage show *Sink Songs*

The Godfather ★★★★★15

Classic crime drama   1972 · US · Colour · 169min

This elegiac organised-crime saga from the young Francis Ford Coppola is one of the all-time high watermarks of American cinema, rich with subtle acting and blessed with stunning cinematography from Gordon Willis. It also proves that an intelligent, sometimes slow-moving drama with impeccable artistic credentials can create queues around the block. Taken with its 1974 sequel, it defines the age in which it was made, while remaining a period piece. Beginning after the Second World War, it traces the handover of power within the Corleone family, from the old world values of Don Vito (a stately Marlon Brando) to his son, the "white sheep" Michael (Al Pacino), proving that his risky casting was inspired). The Mafia is never mentioned by name, but this is an immigrant family drama about assimilation, blood loyalty and honour. **AC** English, Italian +subtitles. Violence, swearing, sex scenes, nudity. **DVD** **Blu**

Marlon Brando *Don Vito Corleone* • Al Pacino *Michael Corleone* • James Caan *Sonny Corleone* • Richard Castellano *Clemenza* • Robert Duvall *Tom Hagen* • Sterling Hayden *McCluskey* • John Marley *Jack Woltz* • Richard Conte *Barzini* • Diane Keaton *Kay Adams* ■ *Dir* Francis Ford Coppola • *Scr* Francis Ford Coppola, Mario Puzo, from the novel by Puzo • *Cinematographer* Gordon Willis • *Production Designer* Dean Tavoularis • *Music* Nino Rota, Carmine Coppola

LANDMARK FILM
Unique in being considered not just equal to, but better than, its influential predecessor

The Godfather Part II ★★★★★15

Crime drama   1974 · US · Colour · 193min

In *The Godfather*, Don Corleone's war hero son Michael (Al Pacino) turns into a man who orders death like room service. In *Part II*, Michael is a symbol of an America born of immigrant idealism and dying of corruption. Breathtaking in scope, this sequel shows the early life of the Don, brilliantly portrayed by Robert De Niro, as he flees

Sicily and sails for New York. These sequences have the grandeur of a silent movie by DW Griffith or Erich von Stroheim; some later scenes, with Michael in Cuba, are clumsy and confusing, though the climax is as chilling as the look on Michael's face when he realises that even Family members can be rubbed out. Pacino gives a monumental performance and it was an equally monumental crime that he never won an Oscar for it. **AT** English, Italian +subtitles. Violence, swearing. **DVD** **Blu**

Al Pacino *Michael Corleone* • Robert Duvall *Tom Hagen* • Diane Keaton *Kay Corleone* • Robert De Niro *Vito Corleone* • Talia Shire *Connie* • John Cazale *Fredo Corleone* • Lee Strasberg *Hyman Roth* • Michael V Gazzo *Frank Pentangeli* ■ *Dir* Francis Ford Coppola • *Scr* Francis Ford Coppola, Mario Puzo, from characters by Mario Puzo • *Cinematographer* Gordon Willis • *Production Designer* Dean Tavoularis • *Music* Nino Rota, Carmine Coppola

The Godfather Part III ★★★15

Crime drama   1990 · US · Colour · 163min

The Godfather was a masterpiece and so, too, was its sequel. Yet this third picture is merely a distant relative and was made for purely mercenary reasons. Thanks to the badly bungled corkscrew plot, one is left with the basic theme of Michael Corleone (Al Pacino) unable to renounce crime and being slowly transformed into a martyr. Pacino has some fine moments and Andy Garcia is frequently electrifying as Sonny Corleone's bastard son Vincent Mancini, the new don on the block. However, Coppola's own daughter, Sofia, who took over at the last minute from Winona Ryder, is embarrassing as Michael's daughter Mary. **AT** English, Italian +subtitles. Violence, swearing. **DVD** **Blu**

Al Pacino *Michael Corleone* • Diane Keaton *Kay Adams* • Andy Garcia *Vincent Mancini* • Talia Shire *Connie Corleone Rizzi* • Eli Wallach *Don Altobello* • Joe Mantegna *Joey Zasa* • George Hamilton *BJ Harrison* • Bridget Fonda *Grace Hamilton* • Sofia Coppola *Mary Corleone* ■ *Dir* Francis Ford Coppola • *Scr* Francis Ford Coppola, Mario Puzo • *Cinematographer* Gordon Willis

The Godless Girl ★★★

Silent drama   1928 · US · BW · 90min

Cecil B DeMille's last silent is a plot-packed melodrama that is laced with the odd inspired image. When the female leader of a high school atheist society, Lina Basquette, and her male counterpart at the Christian club, George Duryea, come into conflict, their actions lead to a girl's death. The pair are then incarcerated in a reformatory and suffer brutal treatment at the hands of the guards. The clash is highly improbable, but it's key both to landing the pair in the reformatory and to the perennial De Millean theme of religious redemption. The encounters with sadistic warder Noah Beery are straight out of a dime dreadful. But away from the sentimental asides, De Mille makes expert use of both a subjective camera and classic visual effects. Some versions also contain primitive dialogue sequences. **DP**

Lina Basquette *Judith Craig* • Marie Prevost *Mame* • George Duryea *Bob Hathaway* • Noah Beery *Head guard* ■ *Dir* Cecil B De Mille [Cecil B DeMille] • *Scr* Jeanie Macpherson, Beulah Marie Dix (titles), from a story by Macpherson

Godmoney ★★★★18

Crime drama   1997 · US · Colour · 95min

A powerful, striking American indie film, this probably deserved better than an unheralded video release. Using a cast of unknowns, first-time director Darren Doane transforms a predictable tale of drug dealing into an arresting and chilling portrait of moral apathy in American suburbia. Newcomer Rick Rodney (a dead ringer for John Malkovich) is the New York youngster who arrives in Los Angeles, determined to put his criminal past behind him. But when he loses his job and money runs short, a tempting offer from a local drug dealer is difficult to pass up. **JF** **DVD**

Rick Rodney *Nathan* • Bobby Field *Matthew* • Christi Allen *Dana* • Stewart Teggart *Jason* • Chad Nell *John* • Sean Atkins *Jeff* ■ *Dir* Darren Doane • *Scr* Sean Atkins, Darren Doane, Sean Christopher Nelson

Gods and Generals ★★12

Historical war drama
2002 · US · Colour · 209min

The trouble with this painstakingly accurate account of the American Civil War is that most of the participants come across as walking waxworks. The second in a planned trilogy - the first being 1993's *Gettysburg* - by director Ronald F Maxwell, it sets up its lead characters with speeches that sound as if they have simply been culled from a catalogue of famous quotations. But the battlefield scenes are gorily impressive, and Robert Duvall gives real credence to his role as General Robert E Lee. **TH** **DVD**

Jeff Daniels *Lt Col Joshua Lawrence Chamberlain* • Stephen Lang *Gen Thomas "Stonewall" Jackson* • Robert Duvall *Gen Robert E Lee* • Mira Sorvino *Fanny Chamberlain* • Kevin Conway *Sgt Buster Kilrain* • C Thomas Howell *Sgt Thomas Chamberlain* • Frankie Faison *Jim Lewis* ■ *Dir* Ronald F Maxwell • *Scr* Ronald F Maxwell, from the book by Jeffrey M Shaara • *Cinematographer* Kees Von Oostrum

Gods and Monsters ★★★★★★15

Biographical drama
1998 · US/UK · Colour and BW · 105min

Ian McKellen gives a brilliant performance as 1930s director James Whale - the "Father of Frankenstein" - in this inventive biographical fantasy. Set during Whale's twilight years, when he was ostracised by Hollywood for being a box-office failure and a homosexual to boot, this focuses on his infatuation with his hunky but heterosexual gardener (Brendan Fraser). Interspersed with the unfolding relationship are half-forgotten images from Whale's shadowy past, as well as occasional drug-addled sexual hallucinations. The result is a poignant and elegant masterpiece. **AJ** Swearing, nudity, sex scene. **DVD**

Ian McKellen *James Whale* • Brendan Fraser *Clayton Boone* • Lynn Redgrave *Hanna* • Lolita Davidovich *Betty* • Kevin J O'Connor *Harry* • David Dukes *David Lewis* • Brandon Kleyla *Young James Whale* • Pamela Salem *Sarah Whale* ■ *Dir* Bill Condon • *Scr* Bill Condon, from the novel *Father of Frankenstein* by Christopher Bram

God's Country ★★★★

Documentary   1985 · US · Colour · 90min

Making his final foray into the documentary field, Louis Malle brought his trademark humanism to this study of the ultra-traditional farming community of Glencoe, Minnesota. The bulk of the action was filmed in 1979, when the aftershocks of Vietnam and Watergate could still be felt, even in this most isolated region, where patriarchy was synonymous with prejudice and a disconcerting lack of curiosity. Yet it's the closing segment, shot at the height of the Reagan era, that provides the most telling insights, as the fond-held hopes and schemes prove illusory. Touching and amusing, yet never patronising or cruel. **DP**

Louis Malle *Narrator* ■ *Dir* Louis Malle

God's Country and the Woman ★★U

Drama   1937 · US · Colour · 85min

It's hard to get excited when the woman of the title turns out to be minor Warner Bros actress Beverly Roberts, playing opposite George Brent instead of his regular co-star (and rumoured squeeze) Bette Davis. Brent plays a hunky lumberjack, and the real reason for watching is God's country itself, stunningly photographed in an early example of glorious Technicolor that almost justifies the daft plot and dialogue. **TS**

George Brent *Steve Russett* • Beverly Roberts *Jo Barton* • Barton MacLane *Bullhead* • Robert Barrat *Jefferson Russett* • Alan Hale *Bjorn Skalka* • Joseph King (1) *Red Munroe* ■ *Dir* William Keighley • *Scr* Norman Reilly Raine, from a story by Peter Milne, Charles Belden, from the novel *God's Country - and the Woman* by James Oliver Curwood • *Cinematographer* Tony Gaudio

God's Gift to Women ★

Romantic comedy   1931 · US · BW · 71min

Parisian womaniser Frank Fay is irresistible to women, as evidenced by the numbers who pursue him. He sets his determined sights on American heiress Laura La Plante, but has difficulty persuading her that he's changed his ways. *Variety* got it right in 1931 when it observed that this was "no gift to audiences". **RK**

Frank Fay *Jacques Duryea/Toto* • Laura La Plante *Diane Churchill* • Joan Blondell *Fifi* • Charles Winninger *Mr Churchill* • Alan Mowbray *Auguste* • Louise Brooks *Florine* ■ *Dir* Michael Curtiz • *Scr* Joseph Jackson, Raymond Griffith, Frederick Hazlitt Brennan, from the play *The Devil Was Sick* by Jane Hinton

God's Gun ★★18

Western   1977 · Is/It · Colour · 93min

Here's a little-seen novelty: an Italian-styled western produced in Israel and directed by that veteran of the spaghetti genre, Frank Kramer. It stars three actors old enough to know that sometimes you just take the money - Lee Van Cleef, Jack Palance and Richard Boone. Played with very little conviction, this is naff exploitation only made tolerable by its cast. **TS** Violence, sex scenes.

Lee Van Cleef *Father John/Lewis* • Jack Palance *Sam Clayton* • Richard Boone *The Sheriff* • Sybil Danning *Jenny* • Leif Garrett *Johnny* • Cody Palance *Zeke Clayton* ■ *Dir* Frank Kramer [Gianfranco Parolini] • *Scr* Gianfranco Parolini, John Fonsecan

God's Little Acre ★★★

Melodrama   1958 · US · BW · 111min

This is director Anthony Mann's version of Erskine Caldwell's steamy melodrama about a farmer in Georgia whose search for buried gold compromises his attempt to set aside an acre of his land for the Almighty. What we have here is a giant metaphor, in which everyone is possessed by gold lust and just plain ordinary lust. As the farmer, Robert Ryan delivers a performance of dignity unravelling as his family disintegrates. The picture lacks a decent female lead and is ultimately a pompous family saga. **AT**

Robert Ryan *Ty Ty Walden* • Aldo Ray *Will Thompson* • Tina Louise *Griselda* • Buddy Hackett *Pluto* • Jack Lord *Buck Walden* • Fay Spain *Darlin' Jill* • Vic Morrow *Shaw Walden* • Helen Westcott *Rosamund* ■ *Dir* Anthony Mann • *Scr* Philip Yordan (front for Ben Maddow), from the novel by Erskine Caldwell

The Gods Must Be Crazy ★★★PG

Comedy
1980 · Botswana/S Afr · Colour · 108min

There will be those who see this as inexcusably racist exploitation that mocks the traditions and expectations of the Kalahari bush tribe, whose peaceful existence is disturbed by a Coke bottle that drops from the sky. But others will applaud the barbed colonial satire that arises when N!xau ventures into civilisation to drop the contentious bottle off the edge of the world. Audiences worldwide warmed to director Jamie Uys's slapstick style, turning this latter-day Keystone comedy into a cult smash. **DP** Violence, nudity. **DVD**

Paddy O'Byrne *Narration* • N!xau *Xixo* • Marius Weyers *Andrew Steyn* • Sandra Prinsloo *Kate Thompson* • Nic De Jager *Jack Hind* • Louw Verwey *Sam Boga* • Michael Thys *Mpudi* • Fanyana Sidumo *First Card* • Joe Seakatsie *Second Card* ■ *Dir/Scr* Jamie Uys

The Gods Must Be Crazy II ★★PG

Comedy
1989 · US/Botswana/S Afr · Colour · 93min

N!xau returns as the bushman confronting civilisation, this time after his children are accidentally abducted by poachers. Jamie Uys does what he can with meagre resources for this sequel to his surprise box-offic hit, but the unsubtley of his slapstick and the dubiousness of some of his cultural observation make this every bit

G

as divisive a film as its predecessor. Frantic fun or unforgivably offensive? DP *DVD*

Nixau Xixo • Lena Ferugia *Dr Ann Taylor* • Hans Strydom *Dr Stephen Marshall* • Eiros Xiri • Nadies Xisa • Erick Bowen *Mateo* • Treasure Tshabalala *Timi* ■ *Dir/Scr* Jamie Uys

Gods of Egypt ★ 12A
Action fantasy adventure
2016 · US · Colour · 126min

This pointless action blockbuster is set in Ancient Egypt, where a mortal (Brenton Thwaites) convinces a fallen god (Nikolaj Coster-Waldau) to help him overthrow the evil god-king Set (Gerard Butler). Drenched in off-putting computer effects, the story tries to be part superhero film, part fantasy adventure, failing to meet either goal. Fresh faced Thwaites and an eye-patched Coster-Waldau are a comically bad double act, but neither compare to the scenery chewing Butler, whose performance is a mess of posturing. JL Some violence, swearing. *gp*

Nikolaj Coster-Waldau *Horus* • Brenton Thwaites *Bek* • Gerard Butler *Set* • Geoffrey Rush *Ra* ■ *Dir* Alex Proyas • *Scr* Matt Sazama, Burk Sharpless

Gods of the Plague ★★★ 18
Crime drama 1969 · W Ger · BW · 87min

Rainer Werner Fassbinder's third feature, about a man released from prison who works his way back into the underworld, is a forceful homage to Hollywood *film noir*. However, despite the trenchcoats, trilbies and cigarette smoke, it is mainly a sombre meditation on the alienated postwar German generation. Fassbinder's cast, including Hanna Schygulla and future director Margarethe von Trotta, is exemplary. RB German +subtitles.

Harry Baer *Franz* • Hanna Schygulla *Joanna* • Margarethe von Trotta *Margarethe* • Günther Kaufmann *Günther* • Carla Aulaulu *Carla* • Ingrid Caven *Magdalena Fuller* • Jan George *Cop* • Marian Seidowski *Marian* • Rainer Werner Fassbinder *Porno buyer* ■ *Dir/Scr* Rainer Werner Fassbinder

God's Pocket ★★ 15
Drama 2014 · US · Colour · 85min

Life in a 1980s blue-collar Philadelphia neighbourhood is the focus of this haphazard tale, the directorial debut of *Mad Men* star John Slattery. It features one of the last performances by Philip Seymour Hoffman, and he's the best thing about it, playing a petty criminal whose obnoxious stepson is killed on a construction site. Slattery weaves together a series of different plot strands into a fitfully amusing whole but struggles to come to any kind of meaningful conclusion. DW Violence, swearing, sex scenes. *DVD* Blu

Philip Seymour Hoffman *Mickey Scarpato* • Christina Hendricks *Jeanie Scarpato* • Richard Jenkins *Richard Shellburn* • John Turturro *Arthur "Bird" Capezio* • Caleb Landry Jones *Leon Hubbard* • Eddie Marsan *Smilin' Jack Moran* • Jack O'Connell (1) *Mole Ferrell* ■ *Dir* John Slattery • *Scr* Alex Metcalf [Alexander Metcalf], John Slattery, from Pete Dexter's novel

The Godsend ★ 15
Horror 1980 · UK · Colour · 82min

A family discovers that their adopted daughter is really a demon out to murder them one by one in this tepid, ultra-slow and raggedly acted *Omen*-style fantasy borrowing most of its plot elements from that film but doing little of note with them. This low-key item is handled like a soporific soap opera. AJ

Malcolm Stoddard *Alan Marlowe* • Cyd Hayman *Kate Marlowe* • Angela Pleasence *Stranger* • Patrick Barr *Dr Collins* • Wilhelmina Green *Bonnie* ■ *Dir* Gabrielle Beaumont • *Scr* Olaf Pooley, from the novel by Bernard Taylor • *Cinematographer* Norman Warwick

Godsend ★★ 15
Horror thriller 2003 · US/Can · Colour · 98min

Robert De Niro revives the notorious old cliché of the mad scientist in this horror thriller. When the eight-year-old son (Cameron Bright) of Greg Kinnear and Rebecca Romijn-Stamos dies, De Niro's

benign doctor offers to clone the dead boy at his Godsend Fertility Clinic. All goes well for a time, but then sinister cracks appear in the good doctor's façade, and the cloned child also begins to exhibit signs of evil. Apart from some neat shocks, the story is painfully predictable. TH Swearing, violence. *DVD*

Greg Kinnear *Paul Duncan* • Rebecca Romijn-Stamos *Jessie Duncan* • Robert De Niro *Dr Richard Wells* • Cameron Bright *Adam Duncan* • Marcia Bennett *Principal Hersch* • Zoie Palmer *Susan Pierce* • Janet Bailey *Cora Williams* • Devon Bostick *Zachary Clark Wells* ■ *Dir* Nick Hamm • *Scr* Mark Bomback

Godspell ★★★ U
Musical 1973 · US · Colour · 101min

This New York-set reworking of the Gospel according to St Matthew following a famous off-Broadway production is an uneasy enchantment that's halfway between holy foolishness and hippy indulgence. Director David Greene's musical nevertheless has moments of infectious glee, as Gospel parables are narrated by a Christ figure (Victor Garber) in a Superman sweatshirt and workman's overalls. In the UK, the role was played by David Essex among others. TH

Victor Garber *Jesus* • David Haskell *John/Judas* • Jerry Sroka *Jerry* • Lynne Thigpen *Lynne* • Katie Hanley *Katie* • Robin Lamont *Robin* • Gilmer McCormick *Gilmer* • Joanne Jonas *Joanne* • Jeffrey Mylett *Jeffrey* ■ *Dir* David Greene • *Scr* David Greene, John-Michael Tebelak, from the musical by John-Michael Tebelak, Stephen Schwartz

Godzilla ★★★★ PG
Monster horror 1954 · Jpn · BW · 92min

A gigantic dinosaur with radioactive breath is awakened by atomic testing and goes on a rampage, destroying Tokyo. The first, and best, of the long-running monster franchise from Toho Studios is sombre science fiction (in contrast to the kiddie-friendly sequels) and incorporates award-winning special effects by Eiji Tsuburaya into its nuclear-age allegory. Additional footage, directed by Terry Morse, featuring reporter Raymond Burr commenting on the manic mayhem, was spliced into a cut-down, dubbed version of the Japanese original. Director Inoshiro Honda's masterpiece is a plea for peace and no more A-bomb testing; the Americanised version doesn't. AJ Japanese +subtitles. *DVD*

Takashi Shimura *Dr Yamane* • Momoko Kochi *Emiko* • Akira Takarada *Ogata* • Akihiko Hirata *Dr Serizawa* • Sachio Sakai *Hagiwara* • Fuyuki Murakami *Dr Tabata* • Ren Yamamoto ■ *Dir* Inoshiro Honda • *Scr* Takeo Murata, Inoshiro Honda, from the story *Godzilla, King of the Monsters* by Shigeru Kayama

Godzilla ★★ PG
Monster horror 1997 · US · Colour · 132min

Japan's favourite giant lizard crawls out of radioactive waters in the South Pacific and heads for New York in this dreary American overhaul from *10,000 BC* director Roland Emmerich. The director's blockbuster behemoth replaces man-in-suit special effects with dodgy computer digitals and sub-*Jurassic Park* thrills. What it doesn't replicate is the endearing charm the celebrated fire-breather had when he stomped through cardboard skyscrapers. AJ *DVD* Blu

Matthew Broderick *Dr Niko Tatopoulos* • Jean Reno *Philippe Roaché* • Maria Pitillo *Audrey Timmonds* • Hank Azaria *Victor "Animal" Palotti* • Kevin Dunn *Colonel Hicks* • Michael Lerner *Mayor Ebert* • Harry Shearer *Charles Caiman* • Arabella Field *Lucy Palotti* ■ *Dir* Roland Emmerich • *Scr* Dean Devlin, Roland Emmerich, from a story by Ted Elliott, Terry Rossio, Dean Devlin, Roland Emmerich, from the character created by Toho Co Ltd

Godzilla ★★★ 12
Monster horror 2014 · US · Colour · 117min

In the 60th year of the movie franchise, director Gareth Edwards restores Godzilla to his rightful place as King of the Monsters with a blockbuster that makes up for in mood and spectacle what it lacks in

dramatic bite. The story begins with an emotionally devastating prologue that sees a nuclear accident in Japan tear power-plant manager Bryan Cranston's family apart. After this slow-burn opening, the real star of the show is introduced. Edwards injects proceedings with a sense of menace and the set pieces are suitably awesome but, while Edwards's Godzilla creation will go down well with fans, the human characters are less well rendered. A sequel is due in 2018, with *Godzilla vs Kong* in 2020. JH In English, Japanese. Some violence, swearing. *DVD* SD

Aaron Taylor-Johnson [Aaron Johnson] *Ford Brody* • Ken Watanabe *Ishiro Serizawa* • Elizabeth Olsen *Elle Brody* • Bryan Cranston *Joe Brody* • Juliette Binoche *Sandra Brody* • Sally Hawkins *Dr Vivienne Graham* ■ *Dir* Gareth Edwards • *Scr* Max Borenstein, from a story by David Callaham, from the character created by Toho Co Ltd

Godzilla Raids Again ★
Monster horror 1955 · Jpn/US · BW · 77min

The first *Godzilla* sequel finds the giant lizard under an assumed name – Gigantis, because Warner Bros neglected to secure the rights to the name Godzilla – as he battles Angurus before stomping towards Tokyo and trashing Osaka en route. The usual shaky backdrops and hysterical civilian panic footage make less impact this time. It was eight years before Godzilla met King Kong to triumph again. AJ A Japanese language film +both dubbed and subtitled versions.

Hiroshi Koizumi *Shoichi Tsukioka* • Setsuko Wakayama *Hedemi Yamaji* • Minoru Chiaki *Koji Kobayashi* ■ *Dir* Motoyoshi Oda • *Scr* Takeo Murata, Sigeaki Hidaka

Godzilla vs Gigan ★★★ PG
Monster horror 1972 · Jpn · Colour · 85min

More totally bonkers fantasy mayhem from Japan's Toho Studios, as Godzilla makes another appearance to save the planet from intergalactic domination. This time alien cockroaches plan to occupy the Earth and summon Ghidorah, the three-headed dragon, and Gigan, a crimson-eyed metal bird, to fight the Monster Island duo of Godzilla and Anzilla at a children's amusement park. For the first time, the monsters talk to each other, and a note of contemporary relevance is struck as shots of Tokyo depict the aliens' dying world. AJ Japanese dubbed.

Haruo Nakajima *Godzilla* • Yukietsu Omiya *Angurus* • Kanta Ina *Ghidorah* • Kengo Nakayama • Hiroshi Ichikawa • Yuriko Hishimi ■ *Dir* Jun Fukuda • *Scr* Takeshi Kimura, Shinichi Skizawa

Godzilla vs King Ghidorah ★★★ PG
Monster horror 1991 · Jpn · Colour · 102min

One of the best of the entire 22-strong Japanese *Godzilla* series, this also boasts one of the saga's most complex plots. It involves time travellers from the future intervening in the 1944 nuclear events, causing the monster lizard's birth and creating his three-headed flying nemesis Ghidorah. The time-warp elements do cause some confusion but are easy to forgive in such an imaginative story. AJ Japanese dubbed.

Anna Nakagawa *Emmy Kano* • Kosuke Toyohara *Kenichiro Terasawa* • Megumi Odaka *Miki Saegusa* • Kiwako Harada *Chiaki Moriyuma* • Shoji Kobayashi *Yuzo Tsuchiashi* ■ *Dir/Scr* Kazuki Omori

Godzilla vs Mechagodzilla ★★ PG
Monster horror 1974 · Jpn · Colour · 79min

You can't keep a good monster down, and for his 20th anniversary (and 14th film), Japan's Toho Studios created a worthy adversary for its money-making prehistoric lizard – a cyborg version of Godzilla himself! In this average entry in the variable series, Mechagodzilla is the secret weapon of ape-like aliens seeking world domination. Plenty of sparks fly in the extended cardboard battle scenes, and there are a couple of daft

new creatures, but it's pretty much comic book stuff. AJ Japanese +subtitles.

Masaaki Daimon *Keisuke Shimizu* • Kazuya Aoyama *Masahiko Shimizu* ■ *Dir* Jun Fukuda • *Scr* Hiroyasu Yamamura, Jun Fukuda

Godzilla vs Megalon ★★★ PG
Monster horror 1973 · Jpn · Colour · 78min

Megalon, a giant insect monster with drills for arms plus a death-ray head, and Gigan are teamed by the Seatopians to conquer the world in revenge for inflicting nuclear damage under the oceans. That's the cue for Godzilla to fight the monster menace and save Japan once more. Here Godzilla joins the brightly coloured Jet Jaguar robot for the barren desert battles, so part of the fun in watching cardboard model cities topple is missing. But hilariously risible dubbed dialogue, more than makes up for the lack of stupid spectacle and the plot is interspersed with a sobering anti-pollution message. AJ Japanese dubbed.

Katsuhiko Sasaki *Professor Goro Ibuki* • Hiroyuki Kawase *Rokuro Ibuki* ■ *Dir* Jun Fukuda • *Scr* Jun Fukuda, Shinichi Sekizawa, Takeshi Kimura

Godzilla vs Mothra ★★★ PG
Monster horror 1964 · Jpn · Colour · 102min

Godzilla's fourth screen appearance and Mothra's second make for an enjoyable romp through the odd conventions of Japanese monster moviedom. Mothra's giant egg is washed ashore by a hurricane and found by carnival promoters. When tiny twin guardians arrive to ask for its return to the giant moth's island home, the authorities beg for their help to get Mothra to fight Godzilla, who's once more embarking on a Tokyo attack. A funny – both intentionally and otherwise – and reasonably exciting slice of zany mayhem. AJ Japanese +subtitles.

Akira Takarada *News reporter* • Yuriko Hoshi *Girl photographer* • Hiroshi Koizumi *Scientist* • Yu Fujiki *Second reporter* • Emi Ito *One of twin girls* • Yumi Ito *One of twin girls* ■ *Dir* Inoshiro Honda • *Scr* Shinichi Sekizawa

Godzilla vs Mothra ★★★ PG
Monster horror 1992 · Jpn · Colour · 102min

Thirty years after Toho first introduced Mothra, the studio virtually remade the same story in their attempt to modernise their monster dinosaur series for a new generation. It worked and this was a huge hit in Japan. Two tiny women, known as the Cosmos, summon up the creature Mothra to fight the evil Battra, who has been sent to destroy Earth. However, Godzilla appears and a three-way battle occurs. AJ Japanese dubbed.

Tetsuya Bessho *Takuya Fujita* • Akiji Kobayashi *Ryuzo Dobashi* • Satomi Kobayashi *Masako Tezuka* • Takehiro Murata *Kenji Ando* • Megumi Odaka *Miki Saegusa* ■ *Dir* Takao Okawara • *Scr* Kazuki Omori

Godzilla's Revenge ★
Monster horror 1969 · Jpn · Colour · 70min

A bullied schoolboy realises his dream of going to Monster Island, where he meets Godzilla and his son, Minya, who teach him how to be brave. Stripped of the serious A-bomb underpinnings that made early entries in the Toho series so rich in irony, the tenth *Godzilla* movie is a very sad affair. Insult is added to injury by the inclusion of battle scenes from earlier adventures such as *Son of Godzilla* and *Ebirah, Horror of the Deep* to save money on special effects. AJ Japanese +subtitles.

Kenji Sahara *Kenkichi Miki* • Tomonori Yazaki *Ichiro Miki* • Machiko Naka *Mrs Miki* • Sachio Sakai *Senbayashi* • Chotaro Togin *Assistant detective* ■ *Dir* Ishiro Honda [Inoshiro Honda] • *Scr* Shinichi Sekizawa

Goemon ★★★ 15
Period action adventure 2009 · Jpn · Colour · 122min

A period fantasy adventure that blends eye-popping visuals with a traditional storyline, this tells the tale of Goemon – a 16th-century street thief with more than a touch of the Robin Hoods about him. He robs from the rich, he gives to the poor – and he keeps a little back for expenses. When he steals an innocuous-looking wooden box, he finds himself beset by seemingly every swordsman and ninja in Japan. Though primarily for "manga" aficionados, *Goemon's* sumptuous staging and numerous fight scenes could also appeal to fans of such romps as *The Prince of Persia*. DA Japanese +subtitles. **DVD**

Yosuke Eguchi *Goemon Ishikawa* • Takao Osawa *Saizo Kirigakure* • Ryoko Hirosue *Chacha Asai* ■ *Dir* Kazuaki Kiriya • *Scr* Kazuaki Kiriya, Tetsuo Takita, from a story by Kiriya

Gohatto ★★★★15
Historical drama   1999 · Jpn/Fr/UK · Colour · 96min

This is another variation on Herman Melville's allegorical novel *Billy Budd*, with its themes about authority, duty and homosexual repression in the military – here it's an elite samurai militia. Set in Kyoto in the mid-1860s and based on two semi-factual stories, this is ostensibly a murder mystery. But in a darkly comic and highly stylised tale, notions of loyalty and the implications of an era passing matter more than militia captain Takeshi Kitano's investigation into the sinister events that surround handsome but androgynous samurai Ryuhei Matsuda. Nagisa Oshima's film is less graphic than his celebrated sexual allegory *In the Realm of the Senses*, but it's every bit as assured. DP Japanese +subtitles. Violence, brief nudity. **DVD**

"Beat" Takeshi [Takeshi Kitano] *Captain Toshizo Hijikata* • Ryuhei Matsuda *Sozaburo Kano, young samurai* • Shinji Takeda *Lieutenant Soji Okita* • Tadanobu Asano *Hyozo Tashiro* ■ *Dir* Nagisa Oshima • *Scr* Nagisa Oshima, from the stories *Shinsengumi Keppuroku* by Ryotaro Shiba • *Music* Ryuichi Sakamoto

Goin' South ★★★PG
Western   1978 · US · Colour · 104min

After making a respectable directorial debut in 1971 with *Drive, He Said*, Jack Nicholson planned a mystical western called *Moon Trap*. But the project didn't please the studios and Nicholson eventually turned to *Goin' South*, an amiable and wayward western in which he escapes the gallows and rides away with Mary Steenburgen. Steenburgen got the part after Jane Fonda turned it down and after newcomers Jessica Lange and Meryl Streep were tested. It's easy to enjoy, even if his trademark leers are no substitute for real acting. The picture was a critical and commercial failure. AT **DVD**

Jack Nicholson *Henry Lloyd Moon* • Mary Steenburgen *Julia Tate* • Christopher Lloyd *Frank Towfield* • John Belushi *Hector* • Danny DeVito *Clyde/"Hog"* • Veronica Cartwright *Hermine* • Richard Bradford *Sheriff Andrew Kyle* • Jeff Morris *Big Abe* ■ *Dir* Jack Nicholson • *Scr* John Herman Shaner, Al Ramrus, Charles Shyer, Alan Mandel, from a story by John Herman Shaner

Goin' to Town ★★★
Musical comedy   1935 · US · BW · 74min

Mae West writes herself another juicy role as a cattle baroness who makes a fortune from the timely acquisition of an oil field. Getting her man – in this case Paul Cavanagh – doesn't prove quite so easy, so Mae sets out to improve her social standing. She has a fine time mocking the hypocrisy of high society and memorably performs a song from the opera *Samson and Delilah* by Saint-Saëns. The weak line-up of male performers leaves Mae in full command of the proceedings. AE

Mae West *Cleo Borden* • Paul Cavanagh *Edward Carrington* • Gilbert Emery *Winslow* • Marjorie Gateson *Mrs Crane Brittony* • Tito Coral *Taho* • Ivan Lebedeff *Ivan Valadov* • Fred Kohler *Buck Gonzales* • Monroe Owsley *Fletcher Colton* ■ *Dir* Alexander Hall • *Scr* Mae West, from a story by Marion Morgan, George B Dowell

Going All the Way ★15
Drama   1997 · US · Colour · 98min

A badly scripted, disappointing 1950s-set drama, this stars Jeremy Davies as the shy, nerdy photographer who makes friends with local jock Ben Affleck after they both return to their home town following service in the Korean War. Rose McGowan, Amy Locane and Rachel Weisz are the girls providing the glamour, but even this impressive young cast can't save the film from being clichéd, tediously plotted and ultimately irritating. JB Swearing, sex scenes.

Jeremy Davies *Sonny Burns* • Ben Affleck *Gunner Casselman* • Amy Locane *Buddy Porter* • Rose McGowan *Gail Thayer* • Rachel Weisz *Marty Pilcher* • John Lordan *Elwood Burns* • Bob Swan *Luke* • Jill Clayburgh *Alma Burns* • Lesley Ann Warren *Nina Casselman* ■ *Dir* Mark Pellington • *Scr* Dan Wakefield, from his novel

Going Ape! ★U
Comedy   1981 · US · Colour · 87min

The hit TV comedy series *Taxi* was still running when stars Tony Danza and Danny DeVito took time out to appear in this big-screen outing about a guy (Danza) who stands to inherit a fortune if he can successfully look after his late father's orang-utans. Writer/director Jeremy Joe Kronsberg made a name for himself with his script for *Every Which Way but Loose*, which teamed Clint Eastwood with a lovable orang-utan. Kronsberg reached the logical (but erroneous) conclusion that if one orang-utan was funny, a whole bunch must be hilarious. DF

Tony Danza *Foster* • Jessica Walter *Fiona* • Stacey Nelkin *Cynthia* • Danny DeVito *Lazlo* • Art Metrano *Joey* • Frank Sivero *Bad Habit* • Rick Hurst *Brandon* • Howard Mann *Jules Cohen* ■ *Dir/Scr* Jeremy Joe Kronsberg

Going Berserk ★★15
Comedy   1983 · US/Can · Colour · 80min

John Candy is reunited with some old chums from his Canadian TV days (Eugene Levy and Joe Flaherty) for this wildly erratic comedy. Candy plays a nice but dim driver engaged to the daughter of a politician who finds himself caught up in his prospective father-in-law's battle against a cult. Directed by David Steinberg, this is let down by a script with more misses than hits, but Candy is as effortlessly appealing as ever. JF **DVD**

John Candy *John Bourgignon* • Joe Flaherty *Chick Leff* • Eugene Levy *Sal di Pasquale* • Alley Mills *Nancy Reese* • Pat Hingle *Ed Reese* • Ann Bronston *Patti Reese* • Eve Brent Ashe [Eve Brent] *Mrs Reese* • Elizabeth Kerr *Grandmother Reese* ■ *Dir* David Steinberg • *Scr* Dana Olsen, David Steinberg

Going Clear ★★★15
Documentary   2015 · US · Colour · 120min

Considering the legal problems that beset the making and release of this documentary by Alex Gibney (*The Armstrong Lie*), it is surprisingly thin on revelations. It charts the course of the Scientology movement, the controversial "religion" founded by writer L Ron Hubbard in the 1950s. Much is made of the support given to Scientology by the likes of Tom Cruise and John Travolta, but it's a cautious exposé that morphs into a list of grievances from former employees. DW Swearing.

Paul Haggis • Jason Beghe • Marty Rathbun • Lawrence Wright ■ *Dir* Alex Gibney • *Scr* Alex Gibney, from Lawrence Wright's non-fiction book

Going Hollywood ★★U
Musical comedy   1933 · US · BW · 77min

Marion Davies and Bing Crosby co-star in this modest musical from MGM. The corny tale of a crooner, followed to Hollywood by a fan who poses as a French maid and supplants his current girlfriend and leading lady (Fifi D'Orsay), it provided Davies with an excellent showcase for her charm and her somewhat limited talents. It also disguises Crosby's lack of acting experience by letting him do what he did best – croon. RK

Bing Crosby *Bill Williams* • Marion Davies *Sylvia Bruce* • Fifi D'Orsay *Lili Yvonne* • Stuart Erwin *Ernest P Baker* • Patsy Kelly *Jill Barker* • Bobby Watson *Jack Thompson* • Three Radio Rogues *Film electricians* ■ *Dir* Raoul Walsh • *Scr* Donald Ogden Stewart, from a story by Frances Marion

Going Home ★★★
Drama   1971 · US · Colour · 97min

Having murdered his wife some years previously, Robert Mitchum comes out of jail only to be tracked down by his vengeance-seeking son (Jan-Michael Vincent). Brenda Vaccaro plays the woman caught between them in Herbert B Leonard's sombre drama, which sank without trace at the American box office and was never released in Britain. However, it's worth watching for Mitchum's brooding performance as the violent hunk and Korean War veteran who feels the pain he inflicts on others. AT

Robert Mitchum *Harry K Graham* • Brenda Vaccaro *Jenny* • Jan-Michael Vincent *Jimmy Graham* • Jason Bernard *Jimmy at six* • Sally Kirkland *Ann Graham* • Josh Mostel *Bonelli* • George DiCenzo *Sergeant* ■ *Dir* Herbert B Leonard • *Scr* Lawrence B Marcus

Going in Style ★★★PG
Comedy   1979 · US · Colour · 94min

This touching and very funny movie was part of the great second career coming of George Burns. This teams him with fellow veterans Art Carney and Lee Strasberg, father of the American Method school of acting, as three old-timers who decide to relieve their boredom by robbing a bank. This was the second feature directed by the talented Martin Brest, a film-maker whose films (including *Beverly Hills Cop*, *Midnight Run* and *Scent of a Woman*) are inexplicably better known than he is. TS Swearing.

George Burns *Joe* • Art Carney *Al* • Lee Strasberg *Willie* • Charles Hallahan *Pete* • Pamela Payton-Wright *Kathy* • Siobhan Keegan *Colleen* • Brian Neville *Kevin* • Constantine Hartofolis *Boy in park* ■ *Dir* Martin Brest • *Scr* Martin Brest, from a story by Edward Cannon

Going My Way ★★★★U
Musical drama   1944 · US · BW · 120min

Although writer/producer/director Leo McCarey bagged three Oscars for this effortless piece of Catholic whimsy, its enduring charm rests with the Oscar-winning performances of Bing Crosby and Barry Fitzgerald. The sequences in which the inner-city urchins are transformed into angelic choirboys beggar belief, but the brisk by-play between the streetwise Father Crosby and the peppery Father Fitzgerald more than compensates. Crosby reprised the role in *The Bells of St Mary's* (1945). DP **DVD**

Bing Crosby *Father "Chuck" O'Malley* • Risë Stevens *Genevieve Linden* • Barry Fitzgerald *Father Fitzgibbon* • Frank McHugh *Father Timothy O'Dowd* • James Brown (1) *Ted Haines Jr* • Gene Lockhart *Ted Haines Sr* • Jean Heather *Carol James* • Porter Hall *Mr Belknap* ■ *Dir* Leo McCarey • *Scr* Frank Butler, Frank Cavett, from a story by Leo McCarey

Going Off, Big Time ★★18
Crime comedy drama   2000 · UK · Colour · 83min

Yet another British thriller that tries to be both cool and funny but rarely succeeds. Neil Fitzmaurice, who also wrote the script, stars as a young lad who ends up in jail by accident, only to emerge as a gangster-in-the-making four years later thanks to the tutelage of old codger Bernard Hill. Most of the clichés you'd expect are here, but it's made slightly more palatable by Fitzmaurice's nice performance and snappy direction from Jim Doyle. JB Violence, swearing, drug abuse. **DVD**

Neil Fitzmaurice *Mark Clayton* • Dominic Carter *Ozzi Shepherd* • Sarah Alexander *Stacey Bannerman* • Nick Lamont [Nicholas Lamont] *Paul* • Gabbi Barr *Natasha* • Nick Moss *Charlie* • Bernard Hill *Murray* • Stan Boardman *Arthur McCann* ■ *Dir* Jim Doyle • *Scr* Neil Fitzmaurice

Going Places ★★★U
Musical comedy   1938 · US · BW · 83min

This piece of horse nonsense has Dick Powell masquerading as a famous jockey in order to drum up more business for his employers. Trouble is, he finds himself riding a temperamental horse who can only be soothed by the trumpet playing of Louis

Armstrong. His antics do, however, impress the lovely Anita Louise. Enjoy the great "Satchmo" in one of his rare featured roles. RB

Dick Powell *Peter Mason/Peter Randall* • Anita Louise *Ellen Parker* • Allen Jenkins *Droopy* • Ronald Reagan *Jack Withering* • Walter Catlett *Franklin Dexter* • Harold Huber *Maxie* • Larry Williams (1) *Frank* • Louis Armstrong *Gabe* ■ *Dir* Ray Enright • *Scr* Sig Herzig, Jerry Wald, Maurice Leo, Earl Baldwin, from the play *The Hottentot* by Victor Mapes, William Collier Sr

Going the Distance ★★★15
Romantic comedy   2010 · US · Colour · 98min

This undemanding romantic comedy sees two lovers from opposite sides of the States battling to keep the flame alive after a whirlwind romance in New York. When Erin (Drew Barrymore) is forced to leave Garrett (Justin Long) to return to college in San Francisco, it becomes a test of endurance for the pair. The story is well-observed in the way the couple tread around each other's sensibilities – even at a distance – but the gags can feel tacked-on. Clichés aside, this has a fresh, contemporary feel, and Barrymore and Long enjoy a cosy rapport. SP Swearing, sexual references, drug abuse. **DVD** **BL**

Drew Barrymore *Erin* • Justin Long *Garrett* • Christina Applegate *Corrine* • Charlie Day *Dan* • Jason Sudeikis *Box* • Ron Livingston *Will* ■ *Dir* Nanette Burstein • *Scr* Geoff LaTulippe

Going to Pieces: the Rise and Fall of the Slasher Film ★★★18
Documentary   2006 · US · Colour · 88min

Love or loathe them, slasher movies are a popular part of horror culture and here they get an in-depth dissection, examining their highs and lows. Based on Adam Rockoff's book of the same name, this documentary (also directed by the uncredited Rockoff) combines an entertaining barrage of ultra-gory clips with interviews featuring key players, past and present. John Carpenter, Wes Craven and effects maestro Tom Savini are particularly illuminating, talking extensively through everything from the slasher pic's roots and history to its conventions and marketing. There's nothing really new for long-time aficionados, but fledgling fright fans will find this a solid introduction. SF **DVD**

John Carpenter • Wes Craven • Rob Zombie • Tom Savini • Malek Akkad • Lilyan Chauvin ■ *Dir* Adam Rockoff • *Scr* Rachel Belofsky, Rudy Scalese, Michael Bohusz, J Albert Bell, from the non-fiction book by Adam Rockoff • *Cinematographer* Michael Fimognari

Going Under ★PG
Comedy   1990 · US · Colour · 77min

The best joke in this mix of lame lampoons and slapstick pratfalls is the fact that captain Bill Pullman's submarine is called *Standard*. It centres on the incompetence of Pullman's crew, purposely assembled by corrupt admiral Ned Beatty, and the craft's appearance as a whale after it is refitted. Genuinely substandard. DP

Bill Pullman *Captain Biff Banner* • Wendy Schaal *Jan Michaels* • Ned Beatty *Admiral Malice* • Robert Vaughn (1) *Wedgewood* • Roddy McDowall *The Secretary of Defense/Mr Neighbor* • Bud Cort *Randy McNally* ■ *Dir* Mark W Travis • *Scr* Darryl Zarubica, Randolph Davis

Gold ★★★12
Adventure   1974 · UK · Colour · 119min

Britain's contribution to the 1970s rash of disaster movies was shot in South Africa (to the fury of anti-apartheid groups and various trade unions). The film oversimplifies its themes of racism and exploitation, but as an action-packed adventure it delivers the goods. Seeking to prevent the sabotage that will send the price of gold soaring, Roger Moore is as wooden as a pit prop, but Bradford Dillman is a splendid villain. DP Violence, brief swearing. **DVD**

Roger Moore *Rod Slater* • Susannah York *Terry Steyner* • Ray Milland *Hurry Hirschfeld* • Bradford Dillman *Manfred Steyner* • John Gielgud *Farrell* •

G

Tony Beckley *Stephen Marais* • Simon Sabela *Big King* • Bernard Horsfall *Kowalski* ■ *Dir* Peter Hunt • *Scr* Wilbur Smith, Stanley Price, from the novel *Goldmine* by Wilbur Smith

Gold ★★ 15

Comedy drama 2014 · Ire · Colour · 88min

This Irish family drama aims to capture some of the quirky charm of 2007 indie hit *Juno*, right down to the crayon-scrawly title font, but sadly it misses its target on almost all counts. Maisie Williams is feisty enough as Abbie, whose shambolic father (David Wilmot) reappears after a ten-year absence, much to the disgust of her mother's new husband, PE teacher Frank (James Nesbitt). The other cast members wander through the featherweight screenplay on autopilot, and Niall Heery's direction is workmanlike at best. AS Swearing, a sex scene.

James Nesbitt *Frank* • David Wilmot *Ray* • Kerry Condon *Alice* • Maisie Williams *Abbie* ■ *Dir* Niall Heery • *Scr* Niall Heery, Brendan Heery

Gold

Thriller 2016 · US · Colour

This is a preview – no prints were available to review as we went to press: 2005's *Syriana*, a drama about oil-industry chicanery, was director Stephen Gaghan's last cinematic outing. Now he shifts focus to another of the world's glamour commodities in a film loosely based on real events – an outrageous fraud of the 1990s. Piling on the pounds, Michael McConaughey heads into the Indonesian jungle with geologist Edgar Ramirez in a hunt for gold. Slated for a Christmas Day release, this mix of adventure and boardroom thriller is already being tipped as an Oscar possible. A gold statuette wouldn't be inappropriate. SvM

Matthew McConaughey *Kenny Wells* • Bryce Dallas Howard *Kay* • Toby Kebbell *Jennings* • Edgar Ramirez *Michael Acosta* ■ *Dir* Stephen Gaghan • *Scr* Patrick Massett, John Zinman, Stephen Gaghan

Gold Diggers ★★ U

Musical 1983 · UK · BW · 85min

Made by an all-female crew with everyone, including star Julie Christie, receiving the same daily wage, Sally Potter's debut feature is a bold statement on behalf of the cinematic sisterhood. Her monochrome deconstruction of the Hollywood musical is less laudable, however. Although Potter neatly reproduces such genre standards as the production number and the dream sequence, the symbolism is often so dense and self-satisfied that the viewer's response is more likely to be polite admiration than wholehearted enthusiasm. DP *DVD*

Julie Christie *Ruby* • Colette Laffont *Celeste* • Hilary Westlake *Ruby's mother* • David Gale *Expert* • Tom Osborn *Expert's assistant* • Jacky Lansley *Tap dancer* • George Yiasoumi *Stage manager* ■ *Dir* Sally Potter • *Scr* Lindsay Cooper, Rose English, Sally Potter

Gold Diggers of Broadway ★★★

Musical 1929 · US · Colour · 105min

This early talkie no longer exists in its entirety. Some years ago, however, the British Film Institute found the final reel, which makes for nine minutes of fascinating viewing. Filmed in early two-strip Technicolor, it starts with a brief plot-wrapping scene between Nancy Welford and Conway Tearle. After a dazzling overhead shot of backstage activity, it launches into a climactic revue section. Lavishly staged against an impressionistic Parisian backdrop and enthusiastically performed by an array of speciality dance and acrobatic acts, even what little remains clearly indicates why the film was such a huge success on its initial release. TV

Nancy Welford *Jerry* • Conway Tearle *Stephen Lee* • Winnie Lightner *Mable* • Ann Pennington *Ann Collins* • Lilyan Tashman *Eleanor* • William Bakewell *Wally* ■ *Dir* Roy Del Ruth • *Scr* Robert Lord, from the play by Avery Hopwood • *Choreography* Larry Ceballos

Gold Diggers of 1933 ★★★★

Musical 1933 · US · BW · 97min

Some of the most powerful musical routines ever filmed are featured in this cracking Warner Bros opus, the first of the Busby Berkeley-choreographed series that followed his superb *42nd Street*. Ignore the Ruby Keeler/Dick Powell Broadway plot (though cherish the snappy dialogue) and concentrate on a real rarity, with song-and-dance direction that reflects the climate of the times. This is a movie of the Depression, mirroring the emotions of an audience tired of breadlines, Prohibition and worthless currency. It's a vital, venerable classic and Berkeley's ground-breaking kaleidoscopic is a revelation. TS

Warren William *J Lawrence Bradford* • Joan Blondell *Carol King* • Aline MacMahon *Trixie Lorraine* • Ruby Keeler *Polly Parker* • Dick Powell *Brad Roberts* • Guy Kibbee *Peabody* • Ned Sparks *Barney Hopkins* • Ginger Rogers *Fay Fortune* ■ *Dir* Mervyn LeRoy • *Scr* Erwin Gelsey, James Seymour, David Boehm, Ben Markson, from the play *Gold Diggers of Broadway* by Avery Hopwood

Gold Diggers of 1935 ★★★ U

Musical comedy 1935 · US · BW · 90min

This virtually plotless tale, one of the first to be directed by Busby Berkeley, has student Dick Powell falling for millionaire's daughter Gloria Stuart (yes, the one who appeared in James Cameron's *Titanic* 60 years later). The dance numbers live up to expectations, leading up to the memorable climax of Oscar-winning song *Lullaby of Broadway*. Powell and Stuart are colourless leads, but the real star is Berkeley's amazing choreography. TS

Dick Powell *Dick Curtis* • Gloria Stuart *Amy Prentiss* • Adolphe Menjou *Nicoleff* • Glenda Farrell *Betty Hawes* • Grant Mitchell *Louis Lawson* • Dorothy Dare *Arline Davis* • Alice Brady *Mrs Mathilda Prentiss* • Winifred Shaw *Winny* ■ *Dir* Busby Berkeley • *Scr* Manuel Seff, Peter Milne, from a story by Milne, Robert Lord

Gold Diggers of 1937 ★★★ U

Musical comedy 1936 · US · BW · 102min

The advent of film censorship placed a terrible burden on Warner Bros' potent *Gold Diggers* series. Not only was the generic title now highly suspect, but choreographer Busby Berkeley's use of semi-naked cavorting chorus girls also had to be curtailed. Consequently the production numbers in this film suffer from a lack of excitement, as well as from an obvious lack of budget. Nevertheless, the cast is likeable, even if baby-faced Dick Powell is beginning to grow tiresome in these sappy roles. This at least provides intelligent dialogue and a semi-decent plot. TS

Dick Powell *Rosmer Peek* • Joan Blondell *Norma Parry* • Glenda Farrell *Genevieve Larkin* • Victor Moore *JJ Hobart* • Lee Dixon *Boop Oglethorpe* • Osgood Perkins *Mory Wethered* • Charles D Brown *John Huge* ■ *Dir* Lloyd Bacon • *Scr* Warren Duff, from the play *Sweet Mystery of Life* by Richard Maibaum, Michael Wallace, George Haight

Gold Diggers: the Secret of Bear Mountain ★★ PG

Adventure 1995 · US · Colour · 89min

Moving from LA with her mother, Christina Ricci is lonely and lost until she befriends fellow outcast and tomboy Anna Chlumsky. The two friends determine to run away and track down legendary gold in the caves beneath Bear Mountain. This is an utterly formulaic, Disney-esque tale, with stereotypes aplenty; its only redeeming features are the touching friendship between the two girls and Ricci's inimitable charm. LH

Christina Ricci *Beth Easton* • Anna Chlumsky *Jody Salerno* • Polly Draper *Kate Easton* • Brian Kerwin *Matt Holinger* • Diana Scarwid *Lynette Salerno* • David Keith *Ray Karnisak* • Gillian Barber *Grace Briggs* ■ *Dir* Kevin James Dobson • *Scr* Barry Glasser

Gold Is Where You Find It ★★★ U

Western 1938 · US · Colour · 95min

George Brent's moustachioed gallantry graced many an action pic, but here he's starring as a mining engineer in a Technicolored slice of hokum about gold-miners and wheat farmers arguing it out in the Sacramento valley. His romantic sparring partner is farmer's daughter Olivia de Havilland, who's married to that inveterate scene-stealer, Claude Rains. AT

George Brent *Jared Whitney* • Olivia de Havilland *Serena Ferris* • Claude Rains *Col Ferris* • Margaret Lindsay *Rosanne Ferris* • John Litel *Ralph Ferris* • Tim Holt *Lanceford Ferris* • Barton MacLane *Slag Minton* ■ *Dir* Michael Curtiz • *Scr* Warren Duff, Robert Buckner, from the story by Clements Ripley

Gold of Naples ★★★★

Comedy drama 1954 · It · BW · 112min

Here are four stories for the price of one, as great Italian director (and co-writer) Vittorio De Sica illustrates scenes of working-class life in Naples. Sophia Loren makes an early appearance as a philandering wife; Silvana Mangano plays a prostitute; Toto has problems with an unwanted house guest; and De Sica finds himself upstaged by a kid in a tale about a very unsuccessful gambler. The kind of wholesome sentimentality that's good for what ails you. TH Italian +subtitles.

Toto *The husband* • Lianella Carrell *His wife* • Pasquale Cennamo *The racketeer* • Sophia Loren *Sofia, the wife* • Giacomo Furia *Rosario, the husband* • Alberto Farnese *Alfredo, the lover* • Vittorio De Sica *The Count* • Mario Passante *His valet* • Silvana Mangano *Theresa* ■ *Dir* Vittorio De Sica • *Scr* Cesare Zavattini, Vittorio De Sica, Giuseppe Marotta, from the novel by Giuseppe Marotta

LANDMARK FILM

Charlie Chaplin in his Little Tramp persona (here at his most endearing) remains the screen's most beloved clown

The Gold Rush ★★★★★ U

Classic silent comedy 1925 · US · BW · 69min

Charlie Chaplin allowed the copyright for this, the most light-hearted of his great features, to lapse in 1953 so that it passed into the public domain. As a prospector in the icebound gold fields – an outsider even in a world of outcasts – he falls for a contemptuous Georgia Hale, but finally claims the girl and the gold. The comedy dazzles (in scenes such as the dance of the bread rolls) and darkens (his starving comrade hallucinates that Charlie is a very edible chicken), but the ending is wonderfully affirmative, a fact that he couldn't help mocking. For the final embrace, shipboard photographers shout: "You've spoiled the picture!" Marvellously, he hadn't. TH *DVD* *Blu-ray*

Charles Chaplin *Lone prospector* • Mack Swain *Big Jim McKay* • Tom Murray *Black Larson* • Georgia Hale *Georgia* • Betty Morrissey *Georgia's friend* ■ *Dir/Scr* Charles Chaplin • *Cinematographer* Rollie Totheroh

The Golden Age of Buster Keaton ★★★★ U

Compilation 1975 · US · BW · 96min

The genius of the most cinematic of all the silent clowns is celebrated in this hugely entertaining compilation. Director Jay Ward deserves a pat on the back for including rarely-seen footage from the early Fatty Arbuckle shorts in which Keaton began his film career, even though they seem to be playing on fast forward. In addition to classic scenes from such shorts as *The Playhouse* and *The Electric House*, there are more sustained sequences from Keaton's features that demonstrate not only his balletic skill and mastery of props, but also his unrivalled ability to develop a gag and his immaculate comic timing. DP

Buster Keaton ■ *Dir* Jay Ward

The Golden Age of Comedy ★★★★

Compilation 1958 · US · BW · 70min

Containing material from both the Mack Sennett and Hal Roach archives, this was the first of film historian Robert Youngson's slapstick compilations and it did much to restore Laurel and Hardy's then flagging reputation. Although there are clips featuring such clowns as Harry Langdon, Ben Turpin and Charley Chase, it's the Stan and Ollie excerpts that command the most attention. Two-reelers such as *The Second Hundred Years*, *You're Darn Tootin'*, *Two Tars* and *Double Whoopee* had scarcely been seen since the silent era, but not even their hilarity could match the brilliance of the pie fight from *The Battle of the Century*. DP

Dwight Weist *Narrator* • Ward Wilson *Narrator* • *Scr* Robert Youngson • *Producer* Robert Youngson • *Music* George Steiner

Golden Balls ★★★ 18

Comedy 1993 · Sp · Colour · 88min

The middle section of director Bigas Luna's "Iberian passion" trilogy (begun by *Jamón, Jamón* and completed by *The Tit and the Moon*) continues his bawdy contemplation on greed, food and sex. In another brazen performance, Spanish heart-throb Javier Bardem is a horny young buck who wants to erect a skyscraper in honour of himself and sees everyone as potential rungs towards that goal. He's also obsessed with Julio Iglesias, Rolex watches, Salvador Dali and stealing bidets, in this fascinating study of selfishness and stubbornness. Sexually explicit and packed with unforgettable images. AJ Spanish +subtitles. *DVD*

Javier Bardem *Benito Gonzalez* • Maria de Medeiros *Marta* • Maribel Verdú *Claudia* • Elisa Touati *Rita* • Raquel Bianca *Ana the maneater* • Alessandro Gassman *Melilla's friend* • Benicio Del Toro *Bob the friend from Miami* • Francesco Ma Dominedo *Mosca* ■ *Dir* Bigas Luna • *Scr* Bigas Luna, Cuca Canals

The Golden Blade ★★ U

Adventure fantasy 1953 · US · Colour · 79min

Universal went in for camp and colourful exotic adventures, with simple good versus evil plots. Rock Hudson is Harun, the handsome and noble hero, George Macready (hiss!) is the nasty Grand Vizier, and Piper Laurie the Princess of Baghdad, the damsel in distress. More formulaic than most, it's still pleasantly escapist. RB

Rock Hudson *Harun* • Piper Laurie *Princess Khairuzan* • Gene Evans *Hadi* • Kathleen Hughes *Bakhamra* • George Macready *Jafar* • Steven Geray *Barcus* • Edgar Barrier *Caliph* ■ *Dir* Nathan Juran • *Scr* John Rich

The Golden Bowl ★★★★ 12

Period drama 2000 · UK/Fr/US · Colour · 124min

This dazzling dramatisation of Henry James's tale of love and treachery marks a return to form for the film-making team of Ismail Merchant, James Ivory and Ruth Prawer Jhabvala. Kate Beckinsale is superb as the daughter of millionaire Nick Nolte and the new wife of impoverished Italian prince Jeremy Northam. Her lack of guile is offset by manipulative Uma Thurman who, jilted by Northam, marries Nolte in an attempt to stay near him. Elegant, eloquent and imbued with turn-of-the-century opulence and social mores, the movie still has enough emotional clout to give it universal appeal. LH *DVD*

Uma Thurman *Charlotte Stant* • Kate Beckinsale *Maggie Verver* • Jeremy Northam *Prince Amerigo* • Nick Nolte *Adam Verver* • Anjelica Huston *Fanny Assingham* • James Fox *Colonel Bob Assingham* • Madeleine Potter *Lady Castledean* • Nicholas Day *Lord Castledean* ■ *Dir* James Ivory • *Scr* Ruth Prawer Jhabvala, from the novel by Henry James

Golden Boy ★★

Drama 1939 · US · BW · 99min

The story of a violinist who also boxes was once considered a daringly left wing and extremely courageous work, bringing acclaim to its author Clifford Odets. But, in this watered-down movie version, the play's sting is largely missing and the New York tenement setting is sanitised. Lee J Cobb's performance as William Holden's dad is one of the worst pieces of character overacting in movie history. The film is cliché-ridden and very dated, and the only real reasons for watching now are the leads, with Barbara Stanwyck showing the ropes to an innocent Holden. TS

Barbara Stanwyck *Lorna Moon* • William Holden (2) *Joe Bonaparte* • Adolphe Menjou *Tom Moody* • Lee J Cobb *Mr Bonaparte* • Joseph Calleia *Eddie Fuseli* • Sam Levene *Siggie* • Edward S Brophy *[Edward Brophy] Roxy Lewis* ▪ *Dir* Rouben Mamoulian • *Scr* Lewis Meltzer, Daniel Taradash, Sara Y Mason, Victor Heerman, from the play by Clifford Odets

Golden Braid ★★★★ 15
Drama   1991 · Aus · Colour · 87min

Dutch-born director Paul Cox is one of the unsung heroes of Australian cinema. His slow-moving but intense films always draw you into their core and bind you into the troubled lives of his characters. This subtly powerful drama is based on a story by Guy de Maupassant, although Cox has changed the ending to suggest that madness is not the only escape from the agony of isolation. As the clock repairer who becomes infatuated with a lock of hair, Chris Haywood manages to be both sinister and sympathetic. A truly compelling picture. DP

Chris Haywood *Bernard Simon* • Gosia Dubrowolska *Terese* • Paul Chubb *Joseph* • Norman Kaye *Psychiatrist* • Marion Heathfield *Housekeeper* • Monica Maughan *Antique-shop owner* • Robert Menzies *Ernst* • Jo Kennedy *Ernst's wife* • Paul Cox *Priest* ▪ *Dir* Paul Cox • *Scr* Paul Cox, Barry Dickins, from the story *La Chevelure* by Guy de Maupassant

The Golden Child ★★ PG
Action comedy   1986 · US · Colour · 89min

Not even Eddie Murphy can save this mediocre comedy adventure, in which he is cast rather improbably as a social worker who is asked to track down a Tibetan youngster (the "Golden Child") who holds the key to the world's survival. Murphy's quick-fire quips fizzle rather than sparkle and Michael Ritchie's direction is best described as indifferent. JF Violence, swearing. DVD

Eddie Murphy *Chandler Jarrell* • Charles Dance *Sardo Numspa* • Charlotte Lewis *Kee Nang* • Victor Wong (2) *Old man* • JL Reate *Golden Child* • Randall "Tex" Cobb *Til* • James Hong *Dr Hong* • Shakti *Kala* ▪ *Dir* Michael Ritchie • *Scr* Dennis Feldman

The Golden Coach ★★★★ U
Period drama   1953 · Fr/It · Colour · 105min

Despite a contrived storyline, this vibrant costume drama succeeds mainly because of Claude Renoir's stunning Technicolor photography. Suggesting both the untouched beauty of 18th-century Peru and the fabulous dream world of the stage, the imagery mirrors the radiance of Anna Magnani. She's the star of a touring *commedia dell'arte* troupe torn between a love for her art and the dictates of her heart. Director Jean Renoir continued to explore the contrasts between drama and life in the rest of his unofficial "theatre" trilogy, *French Cancan* and *Elena et les Hommes*. DP In English.

Anna Magnani *Camilla* • Odoardo Spadaro *Don Antonio* • Nada Fiorelli *Isabella* • Dante Rino Harlequin • Duncan Lamont *Viceroy* • George Higgins *Martinez* • Ralph Truman *Duke* ▪ *Dir* Jean Renoir • *Scr* Jean Renoir, Renzo Avanzo, Jack Kirkland, Giulio Macchi, from the play *Le Carosse du Saint-Sacrement* by Prosper Mérimée

The Golden Compass
                    ★★★ PG
Fantasy adventure
2007 · US/UK · Colour · 108min

In the first film based on Philip Pullman's *His Dark Materials* trilogy of fantasy novels, we are introduced to 12-year-old heroine Lyra (Dakota Blue Richards) who lives in a magical, neo-Victorian Oxford somewhere

in a parallel universe. It's a realm dominated by the all-powerful Magisterium (led by Derek Jacobi) and populated by daemon familiars, flying witches and evil child kidnappers. Darker and more complex than the *Harry Potter* series, this ambitious family movie occasionally feels rather muddled, but director Chris Weitz (*About a Boy*) rallies with a sprawling battle in the Arctic, an imposing CGI polar bear (voiced by Ian McKellen) and an icy turn from Nicole Kidman as evil Magisterium agent Mrs Coulter. JR DVD BD

Nicole Kidman *Marisa Coulter* • Dakota Blue Richards *Lyra Belacqua* • Sam Elliott *Lee Scoresby* • Eva Green *Serafina Pekkala* • Daniel Craig *Lord Asriel* • Tom Courtenay *Farder Corum* • Derek Jacobi *Magisterial Emmissary* • Ben Walker *Roger* • Jim Carter *John Faa* • Clare Higgins *Ma Costa* • Adam Godley *Pantalaimon* ▪ *Dir* Chris Weitz • *Scr* Chris Weitz, from the novel *His Dark Materials: Northern Lights* by Philip Pullman

The Golden Disc ★ U
Musical   1958 · UK · BW · 77min

The coffee bar was the only place to be seen in the early rock 'n' roll scene, but it is almost impossible to see how they became teen meccas from this risible British pop picture. In the very worst "it's trad, dad" manner, it shows how Lee Patterson and Mary Steele jazz up her aunt's coffee shop with a record booth and the singing talents of odd-jobman Terry Dene. DP

Lee Patterson *Harry Blair* • Mary Steele *Joan Farmer* • Terry Dene • Linda Gray (1) *Aunt Sarah* • Ronald Adam *Mr Dryden* • Peter Dyneley *Mr Washington* • David Jacobs (1) *David Jacobs* • David Williams *Recording engineer* ▪ *Dir* Don Sharp • *Scr* Don Sharp, Don Nicholl, from a story by Gee Nicholl

Golden Door ★★ PG
Period drama   2006 · It/Ger/Fr · Colour · 113min

Three generations of the Mancuso clan make their way from Sicily to the New World in the early 1900s in this epic drama from writer/director Emanuele Crialese. The film is a fractured family portrait where the leading man – widowed father Salvatore (Vincenzo Amato) – easily fades into the background, and not very much happens early on. Then, during their voyage across the Atlantic, he courts an enigmatic Englishwoman (Charlotte Gainsbourg), who quickly overtakes the film. The jumble of subplots lead nowhere and, although there are a few memorable scenes including peasants baffled by bureaucracy at Ellis Island and surreal dream sequences, they aren't enough to sustain it. SP Italian, English +subtitles. DVD

Charlotte Gainsbourg *Lucy* • Vincenzo Amato *Salvatore* • Aurora Quattrocchi *Donna Fortunata* • Francesco Casisa *Angelo* • Filippo Pucillo *Pietro* • Federica De Cola *Rita D'Agostini* • Isabella Ragonese *Rosa Napolitano* ▪ *Dir/Scr* Emanuele Crialese • *Cinematographer* Agnés Godard

The Golden Dream ★★★ 12
Drama
2013 · Guatemala/Sp/Mex/US/Ger · Colour · 108min

Spaniard Diego Quemada-Diez's movie is a shocking and compassionate drama about kids from Central America and the risks they are prepared to take to reach the United States. Shooting on Super-16 and employing non-professional leads, Quemada-Diez evokes the spirit of neo-realism as he follows teenager Brandon Load his companions northwards from Guatemala City. The performances are spirited and touching, but Quemada-Diez has a tendency to steer the principals from one set piece to the next rather than develop their characters. DP English, Spanish +subtitles. Violence, some swearing, brief nudity. DVD

Brandon López *Juan* • Rodolfo Domínguez *Chauk* • Karen Martínez *Sara* • Carlos Chajon *Samuel* ▪ *Dir* Diego Quemada-Diez • *Scr* Quemada-Diez, Gibrán Portela, Lucía Carreras, from a story by Quemada-Diez

Golden Earrings ★★ PG
Spy drama   1947 · US · BW · 91min

British intelligence agent Ray Milland, on a mission to get his hands on a secret Nazi formula for poison gas, is helped by exotic gypsy Marlene Dietrich, in whose caravan he finds sanctuary and romance. Despite stylish direction from Mitchell Leisen and the heavyweight pairing of Milland and Dietrich, the ridiculous plot manages to be both camp and humourless. RK DVD

Ray Milland *Col Ralph Denistoun* • Marlene Dietrich *Lydia* • Murvyn Vye *Zoltan* • Bruce Lester *Byrd* • Dennis Hoey *Hoff* • Quentin Reynolds • Reinhold Schünzel *Prof Krosigk* ▪ *Dir* Mitchell Leisen • *Scr* Abraham Polonsky, Frank Butler, Helen Deutsch, from the novel by Yolanda Foldes

Golden Eighties ★★★ 15
Musical drama
1986 · Fr/Bel/Swi · Colour · 96min

In the 1970s, the feminist Belgian director Chantal Akerman was known for her rather glum and static minimalist films. So it came as a surprise when Akerman turned her hand to a somewhat kitsch musical, in which the themes of love, sex and commerce are closely linked. Most of the small-scale, bittersweet film takes place in a shopping mall and revolves around a clothes boutique and a hair salon, where the characters play out their destinies to the accompaniment of an eclectic score and witty, sometimes raunchy lyrics. RB French +subtitles.

Delphine Seyrig *Jeanne Schwartz* • Myriam Boyer *Sylvie* • Fanny Cottençon *Lili* • Lio *Mado* • Pascale Salkin *Pascale* • Charles Denner *Monsieur Schwartz* • Jean-François Balmer *Monsieur Jean* ▪ *Dir* Chantal Akerman • *Scr* Chantal Akerman, Leora Barish, Henry Bean, Pascal Bonitzer, Jean Gruault

Golden Gate ★★ 15
Crime drama   1994 · US · Colour · 86min

Anyone who thinks that Matt Dillon is a one-trick actor should take a look at this moody period piece. Unfortunately, his astute performance as an eager but unguided discovering that working for the FBI doesn't automatically put him on the side of the good guys is rather wasted on such a disjointed and ultimately disappointing film. The un-American paranoia of the early 1950s is well captured, but the scenes set during the 1960s are lazily melodramatic. DP Swearing.

Matt Dillon *Kevin Walker* • Joan Chen *Marilyn Song* • Bruno Kirby *Ron Pirelli* • Teri Polo *Cynthia* • Ma Tzi *Chen Jung Song* • Stan Egi *Bradley Ichiyasu* • Jack Shearer *FBI Chief* • Peter Murnik *Byrd* • George Guidall *Meisner* ▪ *Dir* John Madden • *Scr* David Henry Hwang

Golden Girl ★★★ U
Period musical drama
1951 · US · Colour · 108min

Talented, chirpy Mitzi Gaynor adorns this typical Technicolored musical from 20th Century-Fox. Gaynor is Lotta Crabtree, a legendary and glamorous performer in the days of the Civil War, most noted for her popular song *Oh, Dem Golden Slippers*, which she sang all over the Old West before becoming the toast of New York. Dale Robertson makes a laconically attractive leading man. TS

Mitzi Gaynor *Lotta Crabtree* • Dale Robertson *Tom Richmond* • Dennis Day *Mart* • James Barton *Mr Crabtree* • Una Merkel *Mrs Crabtree* • Raymond Walburn *Cornelius* • Gene Sheldon *Sam Jordan* • Carmen D'Antonio *Lola Montez* ▪ *Dir* Lloyd Bacon • *Scr* Walter Bullock, Charles O'Neal, Gladys Lehman, from a story by Arthur Lewis, Albert Lewis, Edward Thompson

Golden Needles ★★
Martial arts action adventure
1974 · US · Colour · 92min

Soon after his ground-breaking collaboration with Bruce Lee, director Robert Clouse returned to Hong Kong for this so-so action adventure. The "golden needles" of the title make up a priceless artefact that is being hunted by a disparate group of people. Clouse stuffs the film with

plenty of martial arts mayhem, but the mix of laughs and action never gels. JF

Joe Don Baker *Dan* • Elizabeth Ashley *Felicity* • Jim Kelly *Jeff* • Burgess Meredith *Winters* • Ann Sothern *Finzie* • Roy Chiao *Lin Toa* • Frances Fong *Su Lin* ▪ *Dir* Robert Clouse • *Scr* S Lee Pogostin, Sylvia Schneble

Golden Rendezvous ★ 15
Action thriller   1977 · US · Colour · 97min

John Vernon leads a terrorist assault on a floating casino, hoping his threat to nuke the vessel and its passengers will make the president of the United States hand over a ship full of gold bullion. Richard Harris plays the officer who puts his life on the line (as the actor puts his talent on hold) to foil the plot. Amateurish. AT

Richard Harris *John Carter* • Ann Turkel *Susan Beresford* • David Janssen *Charles Conway* • Burgess Meredith *Van Heurden* • John Vernon *Luis Carreras* • Gordon Jackson *Dr Marston* • Keith Baxter *Preston* • Dorothy Malone *Elizabeth Taubman* • John Carradine *Fairweather* ▪ *Dir* Ashley Lazarus • *Scr* Stanley Price, from the novel by Alistair MacLean

Golden Salamander ★★ U
Adventure   1949 · UK · BW · 90min

Trevor Howard, usually not a dull performer, was certainly the wrong side of interesting in this utterly predictable thriller about gunrunning in the North African desert. Usually a dab hand at this sort of thing, director Ronald Neame is content to cruise in low gear. The only compensations are wily Wilfrid Hyde White and 17-year-old Anouk Aimée, who gives an assured performance. DP

Trevor Howard *David Redfern* • Anouk [Anouk Aimée] *Anna* • Herbert Lom *Rankl* • Miles Malleson *Douvet* • Walter Rilla *Serafis* • Jacques Sernas *Max* • Wilfrid Hyde White *Agno* • Peter Copley *Aribi* ▪ *Dir* Ronald Neame • *Scr* Ronald Neame, Victor Canning, Lesley Storm, from a novel by Victor Canning

The Golden Seal ★★ PG
Adventure   1983 · US · Colour · 90min

This is the kind of family-orientated outdoor adventure that seemed old-fashioned in the 1960s, yet which film-makers everywhere doggedly continue to make. Director Frank Zuniga makes the most of his rugged scenery on the Aleutian Islands, but he singularly fails to generate much suspense around the hissable Michael Beck's pursuit of the precious golden seal. DP

Steve Railsback *Jim Lee* • Penelope Milford *Tania Lee* • Michael Beck *Crawford* • Torquil Campbell *Eric* • Sandra Seacat *Gladys* • Seth Sakai *Semeyon* • Richard Narita *Alexei* ▪ *Dir* Frank Zuniga • *Scr* John Groves, from the novel *A River Ran Out of Eden* by James Vance Marshall

The Golden Thread ★★★★
Drama   1962 · Ind · BW · 132min

Produced in 1962, but withheld for three years, this complex melodrama concludes writer/director Ritwik Ghatak's trilogy on the ramifications of the partition of India that began with *The Cloud Capped Star* (1960) and *E Flat* (1961). The film's wealth of literary and cinematic references is matched by the intensity of Abhi Bhattacharya's performance as a decent man who is so tainted by his rise from a Calcutta slum that he drives sister Madhabi Mukherjee and her orphaned friend Satindra Bhattacharya to tragic fates. DP Bengali +subtitles.

Abhi Bhattacharya *Ishwar* • Madhabi Mukherjee *Sita* • Satindra Bhattacharya *Abhiram* • Bijon Bhattacharya *Harprasad* • Sriman Tarun *Young Abhiram* ▪ *Dir/Scr* Ritwik Ghatak

The Golden Voyage of Sinbad ★★★ U
Fantasy adventure   1973 · UK · Colour · 100min

John Phillip Law takes over the role of the legendary seafarer from Kerwin Mathews, who'd impressed in *The 7th Voyage of Sinbad*. However, the actors and the plot once again end up playing second fiddle to the magnificent Dynamation sequences meticulously created by the godfather of special effects, Ray Harryhausen.

Particularly memorable are the walking figurehead, the centaur and the statue that tests Sinbad's swordfighting skills. *Sinbad and the Eye of the Tiger* followed. **DP** **DVD**

John Phillip Law *Sinbad* • Caroline Munro *Margiana* • Tom Baker *Koura* • Douglas Wilmer *Vizier* • Martin Shaw *Rachid* • Grégoire Aslan *Hakim* • Kurt Christian *Haroun* • Takis Emmanuel *Achmed* ∎ *Dir* Gordon Hessler • *Scr* Brian Clemens, from a story by Brian Clemens, Ray Harryhausen

Golden Years ★★★ 12A
Comedy   2016 · UK · Colour · 96min

Silver Cinema is in something of a golden age and this Ealing-inspired caper once again demonstrates there's more to getting old than Werther's Originals and daytime TV. Fittingly, daytime presenter Nick Knowles co-wrote this spry story that relocates the premise of *Fun with Dick and Jane* to the West Country, where Bernard Hill's opportunistic OAP carries out a fortuitous raid on a security van, so furious is he with the bank for frittering away his pension. With Alun Armstrong as the copper on his trail, this is essentially a glorified sitcom – the humour is gentle and the plot increasingly improbable. **DP**

Bernard Hill *Arthur Goode* • Virginia McKenna *Martha Goode* • Una Stubbs *Shirley* • Simon Callow *Royston* • Phil Davis [Philip Davis] *Brian* • Alun Armstrong *Sid* • Sue Johnston *Nancy* ∎ *Dir* John Miller (6) • *Scr* John Miller (6), Nick Knowles, Jeremy Sheldon

GoldenEye ★★★★ 12
Spy adventure   1995 · UK/US · Colour · 124min

When "M" says to James Bond, "I think you're a sexist, misogynist dinosaur, a relic of the Cold War", who can disagree? To ram home the point, "M" is played by a woman (Judi Dench) and a key scene is set in a Russian park that is now a dumping ground for statues of redundant communist heroes. However, Pierce Brosnan, on his first mission as 007, quickly establishes himself as the best Bond since Sean Connery and makes a fetish out of the old-fashioned values of loyalty and patriotism. There are also splendid Bond girls, including Izabella Scorupco and feisty Famke Janssen, who kills by crushing her victims between her thighs. **AT** Violence. **DVD**
B⃝

Pierce Brosnan *James Bond* • Sean Bean *Alec Trevelyan* • Izabella Scorupco *Natalya Simonova* • Famke Janssen *Xenia Onatopp* • Joe Don Baker *Jack Wade* • Judi Dench *"M"* • Robbie Coltrane *Valentin Zukovsky* • Tcheky Karyo *Dimitri Mishkin* • Desmond Llewelyn *"Q"* • Samantha Bond (2) *Miss Moneypenny* ∎ *Dir* Martin Campbell • *Scr* Jeffrey Caine, Bruce Feirstein, from a story by Michael France, from characters by Ian Fleming

Goldengirl ★ 15
Drama sports   1979 · US · Colour · 100min

Susan Anton is an American athlete who is brainwashed and tortured into becoming a gold medal winner at the 1980 Moscow Olympics. Electric shock treatment and mental torture are among the methods employed by her father, Curt Jurgens, and her shrink, Leslie Caron, while her agent, James Coburn, wants to get her into bed. The film looked especially stupid in 1980 after the USA boycotted the Moscow Olympics. Poor direction and a ridiculous script don't help. **AT**

Susan Anton *Goldine Serafin* • James Coburn *Jack Dryden* • Curt Jurgens *Dr Serafin* • Leslie Caron *Dr Sammy Lee* • Robert Culp *Steve Esselton* • James A Watson Jr *Winters* ∎ *Dir* Joseph Sargent • *Scr* John Kohn, from the novel by Peter Lear

Goldfinger ★★★★★ PG
Spy adventure   1964 · UK · Colour · 105min

The third big-screen outing for Ian Fleming's suave superspy ranks among the slickest of all Bond movies. Endlessly entertaining and effortlessly performed, it's packed with classic moments. There's Shirley Eaton's legendary gold body paint; the duel with bowler-hatted sidekick Oddjob (Harold Sakata); the best name for any Bond girl in Pussy Galore (enthusiastically played by Honor Blackman); and the midair

showdown with Gert Fröbe's brilliantly bizarre villain obsessed with gold. But what makes these individual facets so memorable is the way in which they're unshowily integrated into the gripping storyline by director Guy Hamilton, who even managed to revive Sean Connery's flagging interest in 007 to coax his best performance of the entire series. **DP** **DVD** **B⃝**

Sean Connery *James Bond* • Honor Blackman *Pussy Galore* • Gert Frobe [Gert Fröbe] *Auric Goldfinger* • Shirley Eaton *Jill Masterson* • Tania Mallett *Tilly Masterson* • Harold Sakata "Tosh Togo" [Harold Sakata] *Oddjob* • Bernard Lee *"M"* • Martin Benson *Solo* • Cec Linder *Felix Leiter* • Desmond Llewelyn *"Q"* • Lois Maxwell *Miss Moneypenny* ∎ *Dir* Guy Hamilton • *Scr* Richard Maibaum, Paul Dehn, from Ian Fleming's novel • *Music* John Barry (1) • *Production Designer* Ken Adam

Goldfish Memory ★★ 15
Romantic comedy   2003 · Ire/UK · Colour · 87min

Dubliners look for love in this light-hearted romantic comedy from writer/director Liz Gill. Lecherous lecturer Sean Campion, cynical courier Keith McErlean and opportunistic bisexual Fiona O'Shaughnessy are just some of the characters who trade off partners with alarming frequency. The story is simplistic and clichéd, but this look at modern love still raises the odd smile. **KK** Swearing, sex scenes.

Sean Campion *Tom* • Flora Montgomery *Angie* • Jean Butler *Renee* • Peter Gaynor *David* • Fiona Glascott *Isolde* • Fiona O'Shaughnessy *Clara* • Keith McErlean *Red* • Justine Mitchell *Kate* ∎ *Dir/Scr* Liz Gill [Elizabeth Gill (2)]

The Goldwyn Follies ★★ U
Musical comedy   1938 · US · Colour · 110min

This might have been an unwatchable prize clunker, but for a few memorable touches. Not least of these is the fact that it contains the last song ever written by the great George Gershwin, the hypnotically beautiful *Love Walked In*. However, it's performed unmercifully by the graceless tenor Kenny Baker, whose warbling is a matter of taste. Taste does not apply to the antics of the Ritz Brothers, nor to Edgar Bergen and his dummy Charlie McCarthy. **TS**

Adolphe Menjou *Oliver Merlin* • The Ritz Brothers [Al Ritz] • The Ritz Brothers [Jimmy Ritz] • The Ritz Brothers [Harry Ritz] • Vera Zorina *Olga Samara* • Kenny Baker (1) *Danny Beecher* • Andrea Leeds *Hazel Dawes* • Edgar Bergen • Helen Jepson *Leona Jerome* • Phil Baker *Michael Day* • Alan Ladd *Auditioning singer* ∎ *Dir* George Marshall • *Scr* Ben Hecht, Sam Perrin, Arthur Phillips, from a story by Ben Hecht

The Golem ★★★★ PG
Silent horror classic   1920 · Ger · BW · 84min

This is the most eye-catching of the several versions of the ancient Jewish legend, mainly because of the Expressionist sets by Hans Poelzig, and the use of chiaroscuro to create a gothic effect. Paul Wegener, who co-directed with Carl Boese, plays the clay monster created by a rabbi to help his people fight against the Emperor's expulsion of the Jews from the ghetto in 16th-century Prague. Wegener's lumbering gait was imitated by Boris Karloff in James Whale's *Frankenstein*. **RB** **DVD**

Paul Wegener *The Golem* • Albert Steinrück *Rabbi Loew* • Lyda Salmonova *Miriam* • Ernst Deutsch *Famulus* • Hanns Sturm *Old rabbi* • Otto Gebühr *Emperor* • Lothar Müthel *Florian* • Loni Nest *Child* ∎ *Dir* Paul Wegener, Carl Boese • *Scr* Paul Wegener, Henrik Galeen, from the novel *Der Golem* by Gustav Meyrinck • *Cinematographer* Karl Freund

The Golem ★★★
Horror   1936 · Cz/Fr · BW · 83min

Julien Duvivier's sound version of this classic horror story was shot in Prague, where the Jewish folk legend was said to have originated. Harry Baur is Emperor Rudolf II, whose persecution of the Jews causes the clay monster (the Golem) to re-animate and punish the oppressors. Ironically, Baur's own Jewish wife was arrested by the Nazis during the Second World War. Despite a good French cast, this

lacks the atmosphere and narrative drive of Paul Wegener's 1920 film. **RB** French +subtitles.

Harry Baur *Emperor Rudolf II* • Roger Karl *Chancellor Lang* • Germaine Aussey *Countess Strada* • Jany Holt *Rachel* • Charles Dorat *Rabbi Jacob* • Roger Duchesne de Trignac • Aimos [Raymond Aimos] *Toussaint* • Ferdinand Hart *The Golem* ∎ *Dir* Julien Duvivier • *Scr* Julien Duvivier, André-Paul Antoine, JD Antoine, from the novel *Der Golem* by Gustav Meyrinck

Goliath and the Barbarians ★★ 15
Period adventure   1959 · It · Colour · 81min

It's AD 568 and dastardly barbarians are on the rampage, raping and pillaging in downtown Verona. But Steve Reeves stands in their way, all rippling muscles and flashing teeth, keen to play tug of war with cart horses. The English dubbing, the cardboard sets and the lack of any technical proficiency make this peculiarly endearing. **AT** Italian dubbed.

Steve Reeves *Emiliano* • Chelo Alonso *Londo* • Bruce Cabot *Alboyna* • Giulia Rubini *Sabina* • Livio Lorenzon *Igor* • Luciano Marin *Svevo* • Arturo Dominici *Delfo* • Furio Meniconi *Marco* ∎ *Dir* Carlo Campogalliani • *Scr* Carlo Campogalliani, Gino Mangini, Nino Stresa, Giuseppe Taffarel, from a story by Emimmo Salvi, Mangini

Goltzius and the Pelican Company ★★★ 18
Historical drama   2012 · UK/Neth/Fr/Cro · Colour · 112min

Like a greatest hits album, all of director Peter Greenaway's familiar trademarks are present and correct in the second of a planned Dutch Masters trilogy: the extensive nudity, richly detailed compositions, sweeping tracking shots and minimalist score. But the overall effect is less impressive than in his 80s heyday. The story has artist Hendrick Goltzius (an entertaining turn from Ramsey Nasr) enacting six sexual taboos for a nobleman (F Murray Abraham) in return for a new printing press. **AS** English, Dutch, French +subtitles. Violence, swearing, nudity. **DVD**
B⃝

F Murray Abraham *The Margrave* • Ramsey Nasr *Hendrick Goltzius* • Kate Moran *Adaela* • Giulio Berruti (2) *Thomas Boethius* • Anne Louise Hassing *Susannah* ∎ *Dir/Scr* Peter Greenaway

Gomorrah ★★★★ 15
Crime drama   2008 · It · Colour · 131min

All the usual macho clichés of gangster movies are thrown to the wind in Italian director Matteo Garrone's chilling study of the causes and effects of modern organised crime. Rooted in a run-down, hellish housing estate on the outskirts of Naples, it tells five interweaving stories that illustrate the various facets of the Camorra crime network. Both the banality and cruelty of the underworld's stranglehold is shown in the story of two *Scarface*-obsessed upstarts who try to shake the power balance. Their comeuppance is another grim footnote in a gripping catalogue of horrors. **DW** Italian +subtitles. Violence, swearing, drug abuse, nudity. **DVD** **B⃝**

Salvatore Abruzzese *Toto* • Gianfelice Imparato *Don Ciro* • Maria Nazionale *Maria* • Toni Servillo *Franco* • Carmine Paternoster *Roberto* • Salvatore Cantalupo *Pasquale* • Marco Macor *Marco* • Ciro Petrone *Ciro* ∎ *Dir* Matteo Garrone • *Scr* Maurizio Braucci, Ugo Chiti, Gianni Di Gregorio, Matteo Garrone, Massimo Gaudioso, Roberto Saviano, from the novel by Saviano

Gone ★★ 15
Thriller   2006 · Aus/UK/US/Fr · Colour · 84min

This backpacker-in-peril movie covers the same territory as *Wolf Creek*, but lacks that film's gripping suspense and visceral rawness. British tourists Sophie (Amelia Warner) and Alex (Shaun Evans) unknowingly put themselves in danger when they agree to let enigmatic American stranger Taylor (Scott Mechlowicz) show them the Australian outback. However, Taylor is a psychopath who delights in playing sadistic games with the distressed

couple. The sexy cast do a fine job of the acting, Ringan Ledwidge's direction is above average and the atmospheric desert landscapes look good. But the escalating preposterousness of the plot stretches believability. **AJ** **DVD**

Scott Mechlowicz *Taylor* • Amelia Warner *Sophie* • Shaun Evans *Alex* • Yvonne Strzechowski *Sondra* • Victoria Thaine *Lena* ∎ *Dir* Ringan Ledwidge • *Scr* Andrew Upton, James Watkins

Gone ★★ 15
Thriller   2012 · US · Colour · 90min

Amanda Seyfried stars as a young waitress driven to the edge by fear in this meandering chase thriller. When her elder sister goes missing from home, Seyfried is convinced it's the work of the same serial killer she escaped from a year earlier, although the police still believe she fabricated the abduction. After harassing potential witnesses with a gun, Seyfried herself is pursued by the authorities and desperately tries to avoid arrest before the kidnapping becomes a murder. What could have been a tense and involving story is let down by the sluggish pacing, unexplained plot turns and stilted dialogue. **TeS** Violence, some swearing, drug/sexual references. **DVD** **B⃝**

Amanda Seyfried *Jill* • Sebastian Stan *Billy* • Jennifer Carpenter *Sharon Ames* • Wes Bentley *Peter Hood* • Daniel Sunjata *Powers* ∎ *Dir* Heitor Dhalia • *Scr* Allison Burnett

Gone Are the Days ★★★
Comedy drama   1963 · US · BW · 100min

Actor Ossie Davis turns his heartfelt play *Purlie Victorious* into a screen vehicle for himself and his wife Ruby Dee. Davis plays a self-styled preacher who returns to his little Southern home town in order to start his own church. Great performances from the committed cast make the most of the somewhat dated humour, pertinently used to underscore the racist thrust of the plot. Alan Alda makes his film debut as one of the more liberal-thinking white characters. **AJ**

Ossie Davis *Purlie Victorious* • Ruby Dee *Lutiebelle* • Sorrell Booke *Capt Cotchipee* • Godfrey Cambridge *Gitlow* • Hilda Haynes *Missy* • Alan Alda *Charlie Cotchipee* • Beah Richards *Idella* • Charles Welch *Sheriff* ∎ *Dir* Nicholas Webster • *Scr* Ossie Davis, from his play *Purlie Victorious*

Gone Baby Gone ★★★★ 15
Mystery drama   2007 · US · Colour · 109min

Ben Affleck directs his little brother Casey in this absorbing adaptation of the novel by *Mystic River* author Dennis Lehane. The setting is the working-class area of South Boston, where a four-year-old girl has gone missing. Amy Ryan is brilliant as the mother who is as much hideous as heartbreaking. Casey Affleck, too, brings quiet intensity to the role of private investigator Patrick Kenzie, who obsessively follows the girl's trail at the expense of his relationship with fellow gumshoe Angie Gennaro (Michelle Monaghan). Monaghan brings the necessary mix of self-assurance and vulnerability to her role, but Affleck gets the best out of all his cast (including Ed Harris and Morgan Freeman as cops on the same case), and his sensitive handling of difficult subject matter ensures that this story leaves a lasting impression. **SP** Swearing, violence, drug abuse **DVD** **B⃝**

Casey Affleck *Patrick Kenzie* • Michelle Monaghan *Angie Gennaro* • Morgan Freeman *Captain Jack Doyle* • Ed Harris *Detective Remy Bressant* • John Ashton *Nick Poole* • Amy Ryan *Helene McCready* ∎ *Dir* Ben Affleck • *Scr* Ben Affleck, Aaron Stockard, from the novel by Dennis Lehane • *Cinematographer* John Toll

Gone Fishin' ★ PG
Comedy   1997 · US · Colour · 90min

This is a misguided and abysmal comedy vehicle for Joe Pesci and Danny Glover, who play a couple of disaster-prone chums on a fishing trip. Along the way the bumbling duo end up with a map to a missing fortune. As a result, they are pursued by a lethal conman (Nick Brimble)

and the two women on his trail (Rosanna Arquette and Lynn Whitfield). Two hours of unsuccessful fly fishing would provide more entertainment. JF *DVD*

Joe Pesci *Joe Waters* • Danny Glover *Gus Green* • Rosanna Arquette *Rita* • Lynn Whitfield *Angie* • Willie Nelson *Billy "Catch" Pooler* • Nick Brimble *Dekker Massey* • Gary Grubbs *Phil Beasly* • Carol Kane *Donna Waters* ■ *Dir* Christopher Cain • *Scr* Jill Mazursky Cody [Jill Mazursky], Jeffrey Abrams

Gone Girl ★★★★ 18
Mystery thriller 2014 · US · Colour · 142min

Whether or not you've read Gillian Flynn's bestseller, you're definitely in for a treat here. David Fincher directs this unsettling thriller, which revolves around the hunt for missing Rosamund Pike, the perfect blonde wife of perfect hunk Ben Affleck. When Pike disappears under suspicious circumstances, Affleck appears distraught but is soon the prime suspect. Oozing easy charm, Affleck's good looks mask a sense of resentment that could be lethal. The film lacks the virtuoso visuals of some of Fincher's other work, but there are a couple of shocking scenes and Pike is exceptional. LB Violence, swearing, sex scenes, nudity. *DVD*

Ben Affleck *Nick Dunne* • Rosamund Pike *Amy Dunne* • Neil Patrick Harris *Desi Collings* • Tyler Perry *Tanner Bolt* • Carrie Coon *Margo Dunne* • Kim Dickens *Det Rhonda Boney* • Missi Pyle *Ellen Abbot* ■ *Dir* David Fincher • *Scr* Gillian Flynn, from her novel

Gone in 60 Seconds ★★★ 15
Action crime drama 1974 · US · Colour · 93min

The versatile HB Halicki not only wrote, directed and starred in this grandaddy of the car-chase movie; he also supplied the vehicles, 93 of which ended up demolished. Influencing a range of films from *The Cannonball Run* to *Death Race 2000*, Halicki's story of a ring of professional car thieves culminates in the now classic 40-minute chase sequence. It was enough of a cult hit to warrant a sequel in 1989, during the filming of which Halicki was tragically killed performing a stunt. RS *DVD*

HB Halicki *Maindrian Pace* • Marion Busia *Pumpkin Chase* • Jerry Daugirda *Eugene Chase* • James McIntyre *Stanley Chase* • George Cole *Atlee Jackson* • Ronald Halicki *Corlis Pace* ■ *Dir/Scr* HB Halicki

Gone in Sixty Seconds ★★ 15
Action crime drama 2000 · US · Colour · 117min

The car's the star in this boys-and-their-toys action drama that, unfortunately, has too little action to cover for the absence of plot. Nicolas Cage is a reformed car thief who is forced to pull off an impossible job - steal 50 top-of-the-range cars in four nights - for bad guy Christopher Eccleston, in return for brother Giovanni Ribisi's life. Cage ropes in his old crew - including Angelina Jolie and Vinnie Jones - but it's over an hour before we get any stealing or crashing of any description. JB Sex scenes, swearing, violence. *DVD*

Nicolas Cage *Randall "Memphis" Raines* • Angelina Jolie *Sara "Sway" Wayland* • Giovanni Ribisi *Kip Raines* • Delroy Lindo *Det Roland Castlebeck* • Will Patton *Atley Jackson* • Christopher Eccleston *Raymond Calitri* • Chi McBride *Donny Astricky* • Robert Duvall *Otto Halliwell* ■ *Dir* Dominic Sena • *Scr* Scott Rosenberg, from the 1974 film

Gone to Earth ★★★★ PG
Period romantic drama 1950 · UK · Colour · 106min

Michael Powell and Emeric Pressburger's weirdly compelling film about a Shropshire lass who communes with nature and is at odds with the local community. Produced by Alexander Korda and David O Selznick, who saw it as a showcase for his wife, Jennifer Jones, it's a full-blooded melodrama, a piece of Celtic chemistry dominated by the unearthly beauty of Miss Jones. When Selznick saw the finished film he cut 30 minutes, retitled it *The Wild Heart* and ordered new scenes by director Rouben Mamoulian. AT *DVD*

Jennifer Jones *Hazel Woodus* • David Farrar *Jack Reddin* • Cyril Cusack *Edward Marston* • Esmond Knight *Abel Woodus* • Sybil Thorndike *Mrs Marston* • Hugh Griffith *Andrew Vessons* • Edward Chapman *Mr James* • Beatrice Varley *Aunt Prowde* • George Cole *Albert* ■ *Dir* Michael Powell, Emeric Pressburger • *Scr* Michael Powell, Emeric Pressburger, from the novel by Mary Webb

Gone Too Far! ★★ 12
Comedy 2013 · UK · Colour · 87min

A shopping trip for some okra turns into an epic odyssey for two brothers in this hollow comedy. Malachi Kirby and OC Ukeje struggle to connect after Ukeje arrives in London from Nigeria and proceeds to embarrass his brother with his thick Yoruba accent, dreadful dress sense and risible chat-up technique. There are some astute insights into the need to strike a balance between inherited and assimilated cultures, but the sketchy storyline is overly reliant on cliché, caricature and contrivance. DP *DVD*

Malachi Kirby *Yemi* • OC Ukeje *Iku* • Shanika Warren-Markland *Armani* • Adelayo Adedayo *Paris* • Tosin Cole *Razer* • Golda John *Mum* ■ *Dir* Destiny Ekaragha • *Scr* Bola Agbaje, from her play

LANDMARK FILM
The ultimate Hollywood product, this epic's box-office takings (adjusted for inflation) are second to none

Gone with the Wind
★★★★★ PG

Period romantic drama
1939 · US · Colour · 224min

At four hours and at least three directors, David O Selznick's epic American Civil War romance is less a film, more a way of life. Forever falling in and out of favour with critical consensus, it will remain an audience favourite for all time. A war movie with a beating female heart, thanks to the bestselling source novel by Margaret Mitchell, this was, in 1939, the most expensive film ever made: $4 million, and the money is up there on the screen in impressive set pieces such as the burning of Atlanta. But the key is Vivien Leigh's Scarlett O'Hara, a wilful but resourceful southern heroine, yet destined for comeuppance at the hands of Clark Gable's Rhett Butler. No mention of slavery, but this is not a history lesson, it's a love story - one of the best. AC *DVD*

Vivien Leigh *Scarlett O'Hara* • Clark Gable *Rhett Butler* • Leslie Howard *Ashley Wilkes* • Olivia de Havilland *Melanie Hamilton* • Hattie McDaniel *Mammy* • Thomas Mitchell *Gerald O'Hara* • Barbara O'Neil *Ellen O'Hara* • Laura Hope Crews *Aunt "Pittypat" Hamilton* • Ona Munson *Belle Watling* • Butterfly McQueen *Prissy* ■ *Dir* Victor Fleming • *Scr* Sidney Howard, Ben Hecht (uncredited), Jo Swerling (uncredited), Oliver HP Garrett (uncredited), from the novel by Margaret Mitchell • *Cinematographers* Ernest Haller, Lee Garmes, Ray Rennahan • *Editors* Hal C Kern, James E Newcom • *Music* Max Steiner • *Producer* David O Selznick • *Production Designer* William Cameron Menzies

Gonzo: the Life and Work of Dr Hunter S Thompson
★★★ 15

Documentary
2008 · US/UK/Jpn · Colour and BW · 119min

As the original gonzo journalist, gun nut, Nixon critic, and druggie, Hunter S Thompson scarcely needs an extra layer of myth to embellish his colourful life. This flashy but insubstantial documentary adds one anyway, in what is a bald hagiography of an unhinged American scribe whose missives from counterculture's front line - most famously *Fear and Loathing in Las Vegas* - became essential reading. Using previously unseen home movies, archive footage and interviews, combined with a narration by Johnny Depp, documentarian Alex Gibney lays bare the writer's genius and his demons. It's fascinating viewing, though the final reel thesis - that Thompson became a hostage to his own comic-book persona - seems facile. JR *DVD*

Johnny Depp *Narrator* • Sonny Barger • Tom Wolfe • Sondi Wright • Pat Buchanan • George McGovern • Ralph Steadman ■ *Dir* Alex Gibney • *Scr* Alex Gibney, from the writings of Hunter S Thompson

The Goob ★★★ 18
Drama 2014 · UK · Colour · 84min

Hard-hitting coming-of-age stories are a genre all of their own in UK cinema (*This Is England, Fish Tank, The Selfish Giant*), and *The Goob* is yet another in a long line. Newcomer Liam Walpole stars as the title character, a surly Norfolk teen who leaves school and, after inciting the wrath of his mother's psychotic lover (a somewhat overwrought Sean Harris), is put to work on a pumpkin farm, where he shyly sets his sights on immigrant worker Marama Corlett. It's far from original, but the Norfolk setting and its sincere leads keep things a touch above the usual. DW *DVD* *BD*

Liam Walpole *Goob* • Paul Popplewell *Levi* • Sienna Guillory *Janet* • Hannah Spearritt *Mary* • Joe Copsey *Rodney* • Marama Corlett *Eva* • Sean Harris *Gene Womack* ■ *Dir/Scr* Guy Myhill

Good ★★ 15
Period drama
2008 · UK/Ger/US/Hun/Cay · Colour · 91min

It's easy to say with hindsight that any one of us would have been against the Nazis had we lived in the Germany of the 1930s, but would it have been quite so clear-cut if toeing the line brought us career success? That's the nub of this period drama, which stars Viggo Mortensen as a professor who privately scorns National Socialism, but is willing to accept the benefits of a few small actions that gradually lift him up the Nazi hierarchy. It's an intriguing dilemma, or it would be if the film didn't make Mortensen such a weakly pliable individual. Moreover, the bland period re-creation does little to excite the imagination. The exception is a bristling Jason Isaacs as Mortensen's Jewish colleague, whose fierce outrage is by far the most compelling thing in the picture. TJ Swearing *DVD*

Viggo Mortensen *Professor John Halder* • Mark Strong *Bouhler* • Jason Isaacs *Maurice* • Steven Mackintosh *Freddie* • Jodie Whittaker *Anne Hartmann* • Gemma Jones *Mother* • Ruth Gemmell *Elisabeth* ■ *Dir* Vicente Amorim • *Scr* John Wrathall, from the play by CP Taylor

Good Advice ★★★ 15
Romantic comedy 2001 · US · Colour · 88min

In this good-natured romantic comedy, stockbroker Charlie Sheen disgraces himself professionally, loses his job, reputation and his girlfriend (Denise Richards), who is a less than successful agony aunt. Desperate for money, Sheen decides to keep Richards's departure a secret and ghost-writes her local newspaper column. Complications arise when the mysteriously invigorated advice page becomes a sensation. SF *DVD*

Charlie Sheen *Ryan Turner* • Angie Harmon *Paige Henson* • Denise Richards *Cindy Styne* • Barry Newman *Donald Simpson* • Estelle Harris *Iris* • Jon Lovitz *Barry Sherman* • Rosanna Arquette *Cathy Sherman* ■ *Dir* Steve Rash • *Scr* Robert Horn, Daniel Margosis

Good Boy! ★★ U
Fantasy action comedy
2003 · US · Colour · 84min

It may lack the imagination usually associated with the Jim Henson production studio, but this dogs-from-outer-space caper is affable enough. Pitching its laughs squarely at younger kids, the story centres on lonely 12-year-old Liam Aiken, who is shocked to discover his new pooch, Hubble (voiced by Matthew Broderick), is actually an alien scout from the Dog Star, Sirius. What follows is a predictable lesson in friendship and loyalty. SF *DVD*

Molly Shannon *Mrs Baker* • Liam Aiken *Owen Baker* • Kevin Nealon *Mr Baker* • Brittany Moldowan *Connie Fleming* • Hunter Elliot *Frankie* • Mikhael Speidel *Fred* • Matthew Broderick *Hubble/Canid 3942* • Delta Burke *Barbara Ann* • Vanessa Redgrave *The Greater Dane* • Carl Reiner *Shep* ■ *Dir* John Hoffman (2) • *Scr* John

Hoffman (3), from a story by John Hoffman (3), Zeke Richardson, from the story *Dogs from Outer Space* by Zeke Richardson

Good Burger ★ PG
Comedy 1997 · US · Colour · 91min

Young fans of TV channel Nickelodeon stars Kenan and Kel are about the only ones who will be remotely amused by this misjudged comedy. The duo work in a burger bar called, you guessed it, Good Burger. The pair mug at every available opportunity while trying to save their little burger bar from being taken over by corporate bad guys. Parents be warned: it does include some adult themes and occasionally cruel humour. JB

Kenan Thompson *Dexter Reed* • Kel Mitchell *Ed* • Abe Vigoda *Otis* • Sinbad *Mr Wheat* • Shar Jackson *Monique* • Dan Schneider *Mr Bailey* • Jan Schwieterman *Kurt Bozwell* • Ron Lester *Spatch* ■ *Dir* Brian Robbins • *Scr* Dan Schneider, Kevin Kopelow, Heath Siefert, from their characters

Good Bye Lenin! ★★★ 15
Comedy drama 2003 · Ger · Colour · 116min

The fall of the Berlin Wall and the reunification of Germany is less than obvious material for a comedy, but director Wolfgang Becker's smash hit illustrates the "before" and "after" from a quirky and amusing perspective. Katrin Sass plays a staunch socialist who lapses into a coma for eight months, during which time the seeds of change are planted in Berlin. When she finally wakes, doctors warn her devoted son (Daniel Brühl) that any shocks could kill her, so he sets about hiding all traces of reunification. There are some big laughs and the social comment is nicely done, but the subplots are integrated with less skill. JC German +subtitles. *DVD*

Daniel Brühl *Alex Kerner* • Katrin Sass *Christiane Kerner, Alex's mother* • Chulpan Khamatova *Lara* • Maria Simon *Ariane Kerner, Alex's sister* • Florian Lukas *Denis* • Alexander Beyer *Rainer* • Burghart Klaussner *Robert Kerner, Alex's father* ■ *Dir* Wolfgang Becker • *Scr* Bernd Lichtenberg, Wolfgang Becker

The Good Companions
★★★★ U

Musical comedy 1933 · UK · BW · 112min

Bet you didn't know this was the first talkie seen by a reigning British monarch. Adapted from the celebrated novel and play by JB Priestley, this charming musical comedy is full of surprises, not least of which is John Gielgud's facility for song and dance. Victor Saville directs with a light touch and strings together the many episodes with deceptive ease, conveying both the atmosphere of the Depression and the relief the Dinky Doos touring troupe brings to everyone. While Jessie Matthews is superb in the role that established her as an international star, Edmund Gwenn steals every scene he's in. DP

Jessie Matthews *Susie Dean* • Edmund Gwenn *Jess Oakroyd* • John Gielgud *Inigo Jolifant* • Mary Glynne *Miss Trant* • Percy Parsons *Morton Mitcham* • AW Baskcomb *Jimmy Nunn* • Dennis Hoey *Joe Brundit* ■ *Dir* Victor Saville • *Scr* WP Lipscomb, Angus MacPhail, Ian Dalrymple, from the novel and play by JB Priestley

The Good Companions
★★★ U

Musical comedy 1956 · UK · Colour · 107min

JB Priestley's 1929 novel was first filmed in 1933 with John Gielgud and Jessie Matthews. This remake has a glittering array of female talent, although the men are less showy, but this still proves how British movies of the time could cast in depth without having to offer roles to the acting knights of the realm. The story, about a concert party, has dated, and it's all a bit too polite, but the cast makes it well worth watching. AT

Eric Portman *Jess Oakroyd* • Celia Johnson *Miss Trant* • Janette Scott *Susie Dean* • John Fraser *Inigo Jolifant* • Hugh Griffith *Morton Mitcham* • Rachel Roberts (1) *Elsie Longstaff/Effie Longstaff* • Thora Hird *Mrs Oakroyd* • Alec McCowen *Albert* • Joyce Grenfell *Lady Parlitt* • Anthony Newley

G

Mulbrau ■ *Dir* J Lee Thompson • *Scr* TJ Morrison, JL Hodgson, John Whiting, from the novel and play by JB Priestley

Good Cop, Bad Cop ★★ 18

Crime thriller 1993 · US · Colour · 88min

Notable mainly for giving Pamela Anderson an early opportunity to show her ability to wear very few clothes, this is an entertaining if erratic comedy thriller. Robert Hays is the hapless executive who is forced to go on the run when he gets implicated in the murder of a powerful man's daughter. Anderson plays a prostitute who may or may not be an ally. The tone veers all over the place, but it's always watchable. JF Swearing, violence, sex scenes. *DVD*

David Keith *Mace* • Robert Hays *Mitch* • Pamela Anderson *Sarah* • Charles Napier *Mayor Stiles* • Stacy Keach *Bob Jenkins* • Leo Rossi *Detective Atkins* ■ *Dir/Scr* David A Prior

A Good Day to Die Hard ★★ 12

Action thriller 2013 · US · Colour · 93min

The rule of diminishing returns bites hard in Bruce Willis's fifth outing as resourceful wrong-place-wrong-time New York cop John McClane. Trouble follows him to Moscow where, having come to his daughter's rescue in the previous film, he teams up with his estranged CIA operative son to thwart hordes of Russian mobsters and terrorists. Director John Moore lazily stitches together a series of shootouts, car chases and explosions with a confusing plot weighed down by too many double-crosses and implausible coincidences. But worst of all, Willis's once wisecracking character seems lost without the verbal sparring partners that were such a huge part of earlier instalments. TeS Swearing, violence. *DVD* *SD*

Bruce Willis *John McClane* • Jai Courtney *Jack McClane* • Sebastian Koch *Komorov* • Cole Hauser *Collins* • Mary Elizabeth Winstead *Lucy McClane* ■ *Dir* John Moore (3) • *Scr* Skip Woods, from characters by Roderick Thorp

Good Dick ★★★ 15

Romantic drama 2008 · US · Colour · 82min

In addition to writing, directing and starring, Marianna Palka also co-produced this resolutely offbeat indie drama, in which a lonely woman with a penchant for softcore porn finds an unlikely soulmate in the geek from the local video store. There's something sinister about the way in which Jason Ritter inveigles his way into Palka's closely guarded existence, whether he's playing on her insecurities to gain her confidence, sleeping in his car outside her apartment block or spying on her through a window. But even though Ritter worms his way into her bed, Palka seems to be in control of the situation. Palka has made an accomplished debut here, but it is guaranteed to divide audiences with its unconventional attitude to women. DP Swearing, sexual references. *DVD*

Marianna Palka *Woman* • Jason Ritter *Video store clerk* • Eric Edelstein *Eric* • Martin Starr *Simon* • Mark Webber *Derek* • Tom Arnold *Dad* • Jesse García [Jesse Garcia] *José* • Elisabeth Waterston *Elisabeth* ■ *Dir/Scr* Marianna Palka

The Good Die First ★★ 15

Spaghetti western
1967 · It/W Ger · BW · 106min

It's the details that make this routine and rather anaemic spaghetti western moderate fun. Lee Van Cleef plays a bandit who undergoes a miraculous change of heart when he becomes the sheriff of a one-horse town, while Gordon Mitchell is the villain who comes up against his ex-partner when he tries to rob the local mine of its payroll. AJ Italian dubbed.

Lee Van Cleef *Cudlipp* • Gordon Mitchell (1) *Burton* • Antonio Sabato *Ben Novack* • Lionel Stander *Preacher* • Graziella Granata *Sally* • Ann Smyrner *Lola* • *Dir* Giorgio Stegani • *Scr* Warren Kiefer [Lorenzo Sabatini], Fernando Di Leo, Mino Roli, Giorgio Stegani, from a story by Kiefer [Sabatini]

The Good Die Young ★★★ PG

Crime drama 1954 · UK · BW · 93min

This well-crafted British heist thriller, atmospherically directed by Lewis Gilbert, stars Laurence Harvey as the leader of a quartet of ne'er-do-wells who team up to pull off a robbery that goes wrong. The talented cast also includes Gloria Grahame, Joan Collins, Stanley Baker, Robert Morley and Margaret Leighton. PF *DVD*

Laurence Harvey *Miles "Rave" Ravenscourt* • Gloria Grahame *Denise* • Richard Basehart *Joe* • Joan Collins *Mary* • John Ireland *Eddie* • René Ray *Angela* • Stanley Baker *Mike* • Margaret Leighton *Eve Ravenscourt* • Robert Morley *Sir Francis Ravenscourt* ■ *Dir* Lewis Gilbert • *Scr* Lewis Gilbert, Vernon Harris, from a novel by Richard Macauley

The Good Dinosaur ★★★★ PG

Animated comedy adventure
2015 · US · Colour · 89min

Pixar have gone back to basics here, with a touching children's tale about what it takes to make your mark. It's set in the prehistoric era, where young dinosaur Arlo must face his fears when he is stranded with a small cave-boy far from his family home. It may not be quite up there with the studio's finest, but the simple story is told well, with a mixture of visual gags and clever casting creating genuine emotional investment. While the storytelling is strong, the animation has to be seen to be believed. Stunning vistas turn the natural world into a larger-than-life character, providing jaw-dropping moments followed by thumping dinosaur action. JL *DVD* *SD*

Raymond Ochoa *Arlo* • Jack Bright *Spot* • Jeffrey Wright *Poppa* • Frances McDormand *Momma* • Marcus Scribner *Buck* • Steve Zahn *Thunderclap* • *Dir* Peter Sohn • *Scr* Meg LeFauve

The Good Earth ★★★

Period drama 1937 · US · Sepia · 137min

This saga about Chinese peasants won the second of two Oscars on the trot for MGM's Austrian import, Luise Rainer. It's a bit long and worthy, but is redeemed by Rainer's moving portrayal and by a cleverly filmed plague of locusts. The few location shots of China were made in 1934 for another project by director George Hill, who then committed suicide. AT

Paul Muni *Wang Lung* • Luise Rainer *O-Lan* • Walter Connolly *Uncle* • Tilly Losch *Lotus* • Charley Grapewin *Old father* • Jessie Ralph *Cuckoo* • Soo Yong *Aunt* • Keye Luke *Elder son* ■ *Dir* Sidney Franklin • *Scr* Talbot Jennings, Tess Schlesinger, Claudine West, from Pearl S Buck's novel • *Cinematographer* Karl Freund

The Good Fairy ★★★★

Comedy 1935 · US · BW · 100min

This delightful comedy stars Margaret Sullavan at her least cloying as the "good fairy" who's released from an asylum and bursts into the life of Herbert Marshall's prickly, unsuccessful Budapest lawyer, liberating him from his dreary existence. The inventive script by Preston Sturges abounds in slapstick, misunderstandings and verbal tomfoolery, while William Wyler's direction doesn't miss a trick. AE

Margaret Sullavan *Luisa "Lu" Ginglebusher* • Herbert Marshall *Dr Max Sporum* • Frank Morgan *Konrad* • Reginald Owen *Detlaff* • Alan Hale *Maurice Schlapkohl* • Beulah Bondi *Dr Schultz* • Cesar Romero *Joe* • Eric Blore *Doctor Metz* ■ *Dir* William Wyler • *Scr* Preston Sturges, from the play by Ferenc Molnar

The Good Father ★★★★ 15

Drama 1986 · UK · Colour · 86min

Oscar winner Anthony Hopkins gives another moving and impressive performance – this time as a bitter man dealing with his separation from his wife. Director Mike Newell and writer Christopher Hampton touch on a sensitive subject and handle it admirably. Hopkins's character feels he is a man with no rights – he sees his son only once a week. So he embarks on a crusade to help another wronged man (Jim Broadbent), whose ex-wife has decided to

emigrate to Australia with their child. Hopkins handles the rage and the calm of his character with precision. JB *DVD*

Anthony Hopkins *Bill Hooper* • Jim Broadbent *Roger Miles* • Harriet Walter *Emmy Hooper* • Frances Viner *Cheryl Langford* • Simon Callow *Mark Varda* • Joanne Whalley *Mary Hall* • Miriam Margolyes *Jane Powell* • Stephen Fry *Creighton* ■ *Dir* Mike Newell • *Scr* Christopher Hampton, from the novel by Peter Prince

The Good German ★★★ 15

Period romantic drama 2006 · US · BW · 103min

In *The Good German*, director Steven Soderbergh has made painstaking efforts to re-create the ambience of 1940s American studio pictures, most notably *Casablanca*. Yet, by setting himself up to be compared to the old masters, he is easily overshadowed. Even so, he has crafted a seductive thriller set against the Potsdam Conference in Berlin at the end of the Second World War. George Clooney and Cate Blanchett play erstwhile lovers divided by politics, dirty secrets and a dead body. However, a sense of carefully manipulated artifice permeates everything, and, although the intrigue is deftly handled, the romance that is so pivotal to the story isn't entirely convincing. SP English, German +subtitles. *DVD* *SD*

George Clooney *Jake Geismer* • Cate Blanchett *Lena Brandt* • Tobey Maguire *Tully* • Beau Bridges *Colonel Muller* • Tony Curran *Danny* • Leland Orser *Bernie Teitel* • Jack Thompson *Congressman Breimer* • Christian Oliver *Emil Brandt* ■ *Dir* Steven Soderbergh • *Scr* Paul Attanasio, from the novel by Joseph Kanon

The Good Girl ★★★ 15

Comedy drama 2001 · US/Ger/Neth · Colour · 89min

Small-town America comes in for another indie lashing in this patchy, pathos-packed comedy. Jennifer Aniston will surprise many as the shopgirl whose infatuation with wannabe writer Jake Gyllenhaal sends ripples through her insular Texan community. But it's the peripheral characters who bring some much-needed colour to the occasionally predictable proceedings, most notably born-again security guard Mike White and mischievous makeover clerk Zooey Deschanel. Engaging and enjoyable, but lacking edge. DP *DVD*

Jennifer Aniston *Justine Last* • Jake Gyllenhaal *Holden Worther* • John C Reilly *Phil Last* • Tim Blake Nelson *Bubba* • Zooey Deschanel *Cheryl* • Mike White *Corny* ■ *Dir* Miguel Arteta • *Scr* Mike White

The Good Guys and the Bad Guys ★★

Comedy western 1969 · US · Colour · 90min

Despite the stirring presence of Robert Mitchum and a useful support cast, director Burt Kennedy completely fails to carry off this *Ride the High Country* clone for several reasons. Co-star George Kennedy is a talented character actor but he lacks the starpower to be a convincing adversary for Mitchum. There is also an uncomfortable sense of period, as cars and horses jostle, and the comedic tone is uncertain. TS

Robert Mitchum *Marshal Flagg* • George Kennedy *Big John McKay* • Martin Balsam *Mayor Wilker* • David Carradine *Waco* • Lois Nettleton *Mary* • Tina Louise *Carmel* • John Davis Chandler *Deuce* • John Carradine *Ticker* ■ *Dir* Burt Kennedy • *Scr* Ronald M Cohen, Dennis Shryack

Good Guys Wear Black ★★ 15

Action thriller 1977 · US · Colour · 91min

Another slick, monotonously violent starring vehicle for the perpetually wooden Chuck Norris, who was a video star before the term was even invented. Inevitably, he's a Vietnam veteran, this time facing an enemy closer to home when he discovers that his old unit are being bumped off one by one and he's next on the hit list. Director Ted Post's efforts here are no more than workmanlike and the acting is all over the place. JF *DVD*

Chuck Norris *John T Booker* • Anne Archer *Margaret* • Lloyd Haynes *Murray Saunders* • James Franciscus *Conrad Morgan* • Dana Andrews *Edgar Harolds, Government man* • Jim Backus *Doorman* • Larry Casey [Lawrence P Casey] *Mike Potter* • Anthony Mannino *Gordie Jones* ■ *Dir* Ted Post • *Scr* Bruce Cohn, Mark Medoff, from a story by Joseph Fraley

Good Hair ★★★ 12

Documentary 2009 · US · Colour · 91min

Chris Rock here takes an amusing yet piquant look at the billion-dollar industry that thrives on the care and treatment of black hair. Much effort and expense is expended on achieving the prized "good hair" (here meaning long and straight – whether by extensions or chemical relaxer), and director Jeff Stilson allows Rock to run wild on the intricacies and implications of a sometimes excruciating business. For those who think that hair is not important culturally or cinematically, this is a real eye-opener. KK Swearing. *DVD*

Chris Rock • Dr Maya Angelou [Maya Angelou] *Maya Angelou* • Nia Long • Kerry Washington • Raven-Symoné • Ice-T ■ *Dir* Jeff Stilson • *Scr* Lance Crouther, Jeff Stilson, Chris Rock, Chuck Sklar

Good Kill ★★★★ 15

War drama 2014 · US · Colour · 98min

Reuniting Ethan Hawke with his *Gattaca* director Andrew Niccol, this has Hawke playing a US pilot experiencing the horrifying contradictions of modern warfare. He simmers magnificently as he's reassigned from flying combat missions to operating drone strikes from a base outside Las Vegas. Despite his comrades expressing opinions ranging from unquestioning obedience to extreme unease, it's clear that Niccol is out to make a political point about what's being done in the name of national security. TJ *DVD* *SD*

Ethan Hawke *Tom Egan* • Bruce Greenwood *Lt Col Johns* • Zoë Kravitz *Vera Suarez* • Jake Abel *Zimmer* • January Jones *Molly Egan* ■ *Dir/Scr* Andrew Niccol

The Good Lie ★★★ 12

Drama 2014 · US/Ind · Colour · 105min

Reese Witherspoon's presence as an indomitable Kansas City charity worker may be its main selling point, but the heart of this fact-based drama is the long journey taken by a group of refugees from Sudan. Teenager Arnold Oceng and some friends endure trauma and privation as they walk on foot to the safety of Kenya, only to spend 13 years in a reception camp before a US foreign aid programme flies them to Middle America. Enter Witherspoon, engaging as ever, who's there to help them adjust. Much gentle comedy ensues at the expense of their naivety, but otherwise the tone is thoroughly warm-hearted, allowing kindness and community to salve the wounds of a bitter past. TJ *DVD*

Reese Witherspoon *Carrie Davis* • Arnold Oceng *Mamere* • Ger Duany *Jeremiah* • Emmanuel Jal *Paul* ■ *Dir* Philippe Falardeau • *Scr* Margaret Nagle

Good Luck ★★★

Comedy drama 1996 · US · Colour · 95min

Paraplegic Gregory Hines teams up with bitter ex-pro football star Vincent D'Onofrio, who lost his sight in an accident, to compete in a white-water rafting race. With elements of both the buddy pic and the road movie, this comedy is all about people achieving their dreams and realising that disability needn't be a handicap to life. Some might find it a little too heavy on the schmaltz, but Richard LaBrie directs with a sure hand and he's helped by the strong rapport between the two leads, sharp dialogue and amusing doses of black comedy. RS

Gregory Hines *Bernard "Bern" Lemley* • Vincent D'Onofrio *Tony "Ole" Olezniak* • James Earl Jones *James Bing* • Max Gail *Farmer John* ■ *Dir* Richard LaBrie • *Scr* Bob Comfort

U SUITABLE FOR ALL   **Uc** SUITABLE ESPECIALLY FOR YOUNG CHILDREN (DVD ONLY)   **PG** PARENTAL GUIDANCE   **12A** UNDER 12s TO BE ACCOMPANIED (CINEMA ONLY)

Good Luck Chuck ★ 15

Romantic comedy
2007 · US/Can · Colour · 95min

In this largely laugh-free comedy, women discover that if they date and dump dentist Charlie Logan (Dane Cook), the next man that they meet will be their Mr Right. So, of course, Charlie finds himself under siege from the sorts of desperate girls who exist only in the minds of male Hollywood screenwriters. But when Charlie falls for Cam (Jessica Alba), an accident-prone penguin specialist, our hapless hero is forced to buck the trend any way he can. Owing much to the Farrelly brothers (with Alba conjuring up memories of Cameron Diaz in *There's Something about Mary*), this is nothing more than a raunchy Friday-night "lads' film". DA *DVD* SL

Dane Cook *Charlie Logan* · Jessica Alba *Cam* · Dan Fogler *Stu* · Lonny Ross *Joe* · Connor Price *Young Charlie Logan* · Sasha Pieterse *Goth girl* ■ *Dir* Mark Helfrich · *Scr* Josh Stolberg, from a short story by Steve Glenn

A Good Man ★★ 15

Action thriller   2014 · US · Colour · 98min

A bearded, bespectacled Steven Seagal ups his game in one of his better straight-to-DVD outings. Re-teaming with director Keoni Waxman, he's more energetic than usual here and actually seems to enjoy the predictable, and often preposterous, events that see his semi-retired special ops man taking on ruthless gangsters in Romania, after they target his pretty neighbour (Iulia Verdes) and her kid sister. As usual with Seagal, it's the unintentional laughs that make the movie, not least in the ludicrous final scene. SF Violence, swearing, nudity

Steven Seagal *Alexander* · Victor Webster *Sasha* · Tzi Ma *Mr Chen* · Massimo Dobrovic *Roberto* ■ *Dir* Keoni Waxman · *Scr* Keoni Waxman, Jason Rainwater

A Good Man in Africa ★★ 15

Comedy drama   1993 · US · Colour · 90min

This tale of consular shenanigans in a small African republic is a sad misfire from Bruce Beresford. William Boyd's screenplay, from his own wickedly funny novel, has casanova diplomat Colin Friels blackmailed into "persuading" doctor Sean Connery to support president elect Lou Gossett Jr's building project. Ponderous and devoid of humour, it's saved only by Connery. AJ Swearing, sex scenes, nudity. *DVD*

Colin Friels *Morgan* · Sean Connery *Dr Murray* · Joanne Whalley-Kilmer [Joanne Whalley] *Celia* · Louis Gossett Jr *Adekunle* · John Lithgow *Fanshawe* · Diana Rigg *Chloe* · Sarah-Jane Fenton *Priscilla* ■ *Dir* Bruce Beresford · *Scr* William Boyd, from his novel

Good Morning... and Goodbye ★★ 18

Satirical sex melodrama
1967 · US · Colour · 78min

This is one of exploitation maverick Russ Meyer's best sex morality fables, although devotees may be disappointed by the minimal nudity. Meyer lifts the seamy lid on rustic sexual desires, wants and shortcomings, as sexually frustrated Alaina Capri cheats on her rich farmer husband Stuart Lancaster with construction worker Patrick Wright. A forest trip to meet sorceress Haji puts the lead back in Lancaster's pencil and sorts out the muddled affairs. The film is wild and portentous in Meyer's trademark "kitsch-and-think" way. AJ *DVD*

Alaina Capri *Angel* · Stuart Lancaster *Burt* · Patrick Wright *Stone* · Haji *Sorceress* · Karen Ciral *Lana* · Don Johnson *Ray* · Tom Howland *Herb* ■ *Dir* Russ Meyer · *Scr* John E Moran [Jack Moran], from a story by Russ Meyer

Good Morning, Babylon ★★★★ 15

Period drama   1987 · It/Fr/US · Colour · 112min

A deeply affecting and beautifully shot, if rather coolly observed tale of two Italian stonemason brothers who find they can no longer make a living restoring cathedrals in their native Tuscany. Arrriving in America around the time of the First World War, they end up working for DW Griffith on his epic *Intolerance*. In their first English language film, directors Paolo and Vittorio Taviani have created a deeply symbolic story, shot through with autobiographical resonance. If this sounds a touch heavy – it is. At the same time, the film is imbued with such a lyrical love of film-making and sterling performances that you find yourself drawn into its web. SH English, Italian +subtitles.

Vincent Spano *Nicola Bonnano* · Joaquim de Almeida *Andrea Bonnano* · Greta Scacchi *Edna* · Désirée Becker *Mabel* · Omero Antonutti *Bonnano* · Charles Dance *DW Griffith* · Bérangère Bonvoisin *Mrs Griffith* ■ *Dir* Paolo Taviani, Vittorio Taviani · *Scr* Tonino Guerra, Vittorio Taviani, Paolo Taviani, from an idea by Lloyd Fonvielle

Good Morning, Boys ★★★★ U

Comedy   1937 · UK · BW · 74min

Will Hay returns to his celebrated music-hall persona of the cynically incompetent schoolmaster in the first of several films he made with French director Marcel Varnel. Having to bluff furiously to remain one step ahead of a class that contains the ever-mischievous Graham Moffat, Hay is close to his peak as he lectures to educationalists, flirts with chanteuse Lilli Palmer and helps prevent the theft of the *Mona Lisa*. DP *DVD*

Will Hay *Dr Benjamin Twist* · Martita Hunt *Lady Bagshott* · Peter Gawthorne *Col Willoughby-Gore* · Graham Moffatt *Albert* · Fewlass Llewellyn *Dean* · Mark Daly *Arty Jones* · Peter Godfrey *Cliquot* · C Denier Warren *Henri Duval* · Lilli Palmer *Yvette* ■ *Dir* Marcel Varnel · *Scr* Val Guest, Leslie Arliss, Marriott Edgar, Anthony Kimmins, from a story by Anthony Kimmins

Good Morning, Miss Dove ★★ U

Drama   1955 · US · Colour · 107min

Director Henry Koster had the biggest hit of his career with the first movie released in CinemaScope, *The Robe*, but prior to that he was better known as a purveyor of schmaltzy films. This is an ideal subject for Koster, a warm-hearted tale (told in flashback) of how a small town feels about its spinster school marm and how she affects the lives of everybody who crosses her path. Koster brings it off effectively, but star Jennifer Jones seems ill-cast as the prissy Miss Dove. TS

Jennifer Jones *Miss Dove* · Robert Stack *Tom Baker* · Kipp Hamilton *Jincey Baker* · Robert Douglas *Mr Porter* · Peggy Knudsen *Billie Jean* · Marshall Thompson *Mr Pendleton* · Chuck Connors *Bill Holloway* · Biff Elliot *Alex Burnham* · Jerry Paris *Maurice* ■ *Dir* Henry Koster · *Scr* Eleanore Griffin, from the novel by Frances Gray Patton

Good Morning, Night ★★★★ 15

Crime drama based on a true story
2003 · It · Colour · 102min

Having challenged the Roman Catholic Church in *My Mother's Smile*, director Marco Bellocchio turns his attention to Italy's turbulent political past. Set in 1978, this intense drama reconstructs the kidnap and murder of former prime minister Aldo Moro by the Red Brigade. Chiara (Maya Sansa) is part of the terrorist cell, but begins to question the motives of her hot-headed leader (Luigi Lo Cascio) and, as the crisis develops, feels more like a victim herself. Roberto Herlitzka plays Moro with a patient dignity, adding weight to what is a provocative yet deeply moving human drama. DP Italian +subtitles. *DVD*

Maya Sansa *Chiara* · Luigi Lo Cascio *Mariano* · Pier Giorgio Bellocchio [Piergiorgio Bellocchio] *Ernesto* · Giovanni Calcagno *Primo* · Paolo Briguglia *Enzo* · Roberto Herlitzka *Aldo Moro* ■ *Dir/Scr* Marco Bellocchio

Good Morning, Vietnam ★★★ 15

Biographical comedy drama
1987 · US · Colour · 116min

Robin Williams received an Oscar nomination for giving here what is essentially a stand-up comedy performance. He plays a motor-mouth disc jockey sent to Vietnam to entertain the GIs, and adds rather more salt, pepper and hot sauce to the place than the military brass would have liked. Based on the case of a real US armed forces DJ, the film is distinctive for being Hollywood's first Vietnam comedy and among the first movies to treat the Vietnamese themselves as real people. The action loses its way, however, whenever the film tries to get serious. PF Violence, swearing. *DVD*

Robin Williams *Airman Adrian Cronauer* · Forest Whitaker *Private Edward Garlick* · Tran Tung Thanh *Tuan* · Chintara Sukapatana *Trinh* · Bruno Kirby *Lieutenant Steven Hauk* · Robert Wuhl *Marty Lee Dreiwitz* · JT Walsh *Sergeant-Major Dickerson* ■ *Dir* Barry Levinson · *Scr* Mitch Markowitz

Good Neighbor Sam ★★★

Comedy   1964 · US · Colour · 130min

A very funny, though overlong, Jack Lemmon farce, this has a familiar plot that involves him pretending to be married to sexy Romy Schneider in order to help her come into a small fortune. Slight enough, but spun out with a lot of 1960s fripperies, including a high degree of risqué – for then – gags and jokes about advertising and consumerism. Underrated director David Swift directs the glossy farrago with aplomb. TS

Jack Lemmon *Sam Bissel* · Edward G Robinson *Simon Nurdlinger* · Romy Schneider *Janet Lagerlof* · Dorothy Provine *Minerva Bissel* · Michael Connors [Mike Connors] *Howard Ebbets* · Anne Seymour *Irene Krump* · Charles Lane (2) *Jack Bailey* ■ *Dir* David Swift · *Scr* James Fritzell, Everett Greenbaum, David Swift, from the novel by Jack Finney

Good News ★★★★ U

Musical comedy   1947 · US · Colour · 89min

One of the most delightful of the MGM musicals from a golden period, this college romp marked the directorial debut of *Meet Me in St Louis* choreographer Charles Walters, who would follow this movie with such greats as *Easter Parade* and *High Society*. Here, despite the presence of rather over-age students June Allyson and Peter Lawford, Walters injects real verve and genuine *joie de vivre* into such numbers as *Billion Dollar Baby* and *My Blue Heaven*. A real treat for fans of musicals. TS

June Allyson *Connie Lane* · Peter Lawford *Tommy Marlowe* · Patricia Marshall *Pat McClellan* · Joan McCracken *Babe Doolittle* · Ray McDonald *Bobby Turner* · Mel Tormé *Danny* · Robert Strickland [Robert E Strickland] *Peter Van Dyne III* · Donald MacBride *Coach Johnson* ■ *Dir* Charles Walters · *Scr* Betty Comden, Adolph Green, from the musical by Lawrence Schwab, Frank Mandel, BG De Sylva, Lew Brown, Ray Henderson

The Good Night ★★ 15

Romantic fantasy
2005 · US/UK/Ger · Colour · 93min

A faded British pop musician takes refuge in his dreams in this odd relationship fantasy from Jake Paltrow (brother of Gwyneth). Gary (Martin Freeman) is a New York-based jingle writer whose career is floundering while his smug best friend Paul (Simon Pegg) thrives, and his girlfriend (Gwyneth Paltrow) grows bored. Rather than face the realities of his life, Gary becomes obsessed with a beautiful woman (Penélope Cruz) he meets in his sleep. Paltrow's debut feature lacks spark, but it does make interesting use of its unlikely ensemble – casting Danny DeVito as a new-age guru. DW *DVD*

Penélope Cruz *Anna/Melody* · Martin Freeman *Gary* · Gwyneth Paltrow *Dora* · Simon Pegg *Paul* · Danny DeVito *Mel* · Michael Gambon *Alan Weigert* · Sonia Doubell *Shawna* ■ *Dir/Scr* Jake Paltrow · *Cinematographer* Giles Nuttgens

Good Night, and Good Luck. ★★★★ PG

Period drama based on a true story
2005 · US/Fr/UK/Jpn · BW · 89min

George Clooney's second film as director is an understated ensemble piece that charts the CBS news team's campaign against Senator Joe McCarthy during his attempts to root out "communists" in the armed forces of the mid-1950s. Clooney appears as newsroom producer Fred Friendly, but wisely retreats to the background for the most part in favour of David Strathairn. As languid anchorman Edward R Murrow (whose signature sign-off gives the film its title), Strathairn gives a magnificent performance of quiet, steadfast courage. Gorgeously shot in black and white by cinematographer Robert Elswit, this establishes Clooney's credentials as a director. AS *DVD* SL

David Strathairn *Edward R Murrow* · Patricia Clarkson *Shirley Wershba* · George Clooney *Fred Friendly* · Jeff Daniels *Sigfried "Sig" Mickelson* · Robert Downey Jr *Joe Wershba* · Frank Langella *William Paley* · Ray Wise *Don Hollenbeck* · Robert John Burke [Robert Burke] *Charlie Mack* ■ *Dir* George Clooney · *Scr* George Clooney, Grant Heslov

The Good Old Boys ★★★ PG

Western drama   1995 · US · Colour · 112min

Tommy Lee Jones makes his writing and directing debut with this period TV movie. He plays an itinerant cowboy who returns home in 1906 to his brother's struggling Texas farm, but finds it hard to settle down or be responsible. Will the call of the open range prove to be stronger than his love for Sissy Spacek? Jones proves he is not just a gifted actor but also a sensitive director, eliciting strong performances from his stellar cast. MC

Tommy Lee Jones *Hewey Calloway* · Terry Kinney *Walter Calloway* · Frances McDormand *Eve Calloway* · Sissy Spacek *Spring Renfro* · Sam Shepard *Yarnell* · Wilford Brimley *CC Tarpley* · Matt Damon ■ *Dir* Tommy Lee Jones · *Scr* Tommy Lee Jones, JT Allen, from the novel by Elmer Kelton

Good People ★★ 15

Action crime thriller
2014 · US/UK · Colour · 86min

At the start of this generic crime thriller, a large bag of dirty money is stolen by four murderous criminals. Before long, the bag falls into the hands of James Franco and Kate Hudson, a financially strapped couple who are about to be evicted. After deciding to keep the cash, their predicament gives rise to several grisly scenes, but surprises are in short supply as the story builds towards a silly *Home Alone*-style climax. The film is fitfully effective and it does possess a decent cast, but there is little inspiration to be found and the end product is serviceable at best. SC Violence, swearing.

James Franco *Tom Wright* · Kate Hudson *Anna Wright* · Tom Wilkinson *DI John Halden* · Omar Sy *Khan* · Sam Spruell *Jack Witkowski* ■ *Dir* Henrik Ruben Genz · *Scr* Kelly Masterson, from Marcus Sakey's novel

Good Sam ★★ U

Comedy drama   1948 · US · BW · 114min

Store manager Gary Cooper is such a soft touch that his marriage to Ann Sheridan suffers. After all his good deeds, the day finally arrives when Cooper needs to be bailed out of his financial troubles. But will anyone come to his rescue? This suffers from being contrived and drawn out. Coop's good Samaritan is so exasperatingly stupid at times that it's hard to feel much sympathy for him. AE

Gary Cooper *Sam Clayton* · Ann Sheridan *Lu Clayton* · Ray Collins *Rev Daniels* · Edmund Lowe *HC Borden* · Joan Lorring *Shirley Mae* · Clinton Sundberg *Nelson* · Minerva Urecal *Mrs Nelson* · Louise Beavers *Chloe* ■ *Dir* Leo McCarey · *Scr* Ken Englund, from a story by Leo McCarey, John Klorer

G

The Good Shepherd ★★★ 15
Historical spy drama
2006 · US · Colour · 160min

The second directorial outing of screen legend Robert De Niro ambitiously charts the secret history of America's Central Intelligence Agency, from the beginning of the Second World War to the Bay of Pigs invasion in 1961. There's little chance here for star Matt Damon to reprise his Jason Bourne-style superspy heroics in his role as Edward Wilson, a patriot who sacrifices everything (his marriage and perhaps even his soul) to become an automaton in this vast bureaucratic machine. Concentrating on the humdrum reality of paperwork, Eric Roth's well-researched screenplay strips the spy movie of its glamour. It's a bold narrative move that succeeds only fitfully – not least because De Niro's plodding direction robs the drama of the impact it deserves. Terrific supporting turns from William Hurt, John Turturro and Angelina Jolie add interest, though. JR Violence, swearing DVD

Matt Damon *Edward Wilson* • Angelina Jolie *Clover/Margaret Russell* • Alec Baldwin *Sam Murach* • Tammy Blanchard *Laura* • Billy Crudup *Arch Cummings* • Robert De Niro *Bill Sullivan* • Keir Dullea *Sen John Russell Sr* • Michael Gambon *Dr Fredericks* • William Hurt *Philip Allen* • Timothy Hutton *Thomas Wilson* • Joe Pesci *Joseph Palmi* • John Turturro *Ray Brocco* ■ *Dir* Robert De Niro • *Scr* Eric Roth

The Good Son ★★★ 18
Drama
1993 · US · Colour · 82min

Macaulay Culkin plays an outwardly friendly youngster who takes a murderous dislike to his cousin (Elijah Wood), who comes to stay when his mother dies and his father is away on business. Sadly, despite its controversial subject matter – the UK video release was delayed because of the tragic Jamie Bulger murder case – there's little attempt to explain Culkin's psychopathic behaviour. However, Wood is superb and director Joseph Ruben lays on some slickly scary moments. JF DVD

Macaulay Culkin *Henry Evans* • Elijah Wood *Mark Evans* • Wendy Crewson *Susan Evans* • David Morse *Jack Evans* • Daniel Hugh-Kelly *Wallace* • Jacqueline Brookes *Alice Davenport* • Quinn Culkin *Connie Evans* • Ashley Crow *Janice* ■ *Dir* Joseph Ruben • *Scr* Ian McEwan

The Good, the Bad and the Ugly ★★★★★★ 18
Classic spaghetti western
1966 · It/Sp · Colour · 174min

The concluding part of the *Dollars* trilogy (that began in 1964 with *A Fistful of Dollars*) is not only the most graphically violent of the three, but also surpasses the compassion and dark humour of its predecessors. There's nothing particularly new about a plotline involving buried treasure, but that's partly the point, as Leone is paying homage to the Hollywood western while revising its cherished traditions. He dexterously interweaves strands of communal and individual drama, which he throws into shocking relief against the bloody futility of the American Civil War. DP DVD

Clint Eastwood *"Joe"/"Blondie"* • Eli Wallach *Tuco* • Lee Van Cleef *Setenza/"Angel Eyes"* ■ *Dir* Sergio Leone • *Scr* Sergio Leone, Luciano Vincenzoni, from a story by Age-Scarpelli [Agenore Incrocci, Furio Scarpelli], Luciano Vincenzoni, Sergio Leone • *Music* Ennio Morricone • *Cinematographer* Tonino Delli Colli

The Good the Bad the Weird ★★★ 15
Period action adventure
2008 · S Kor · Colour · 124min

South Korean Kim Ji-woon (*A Bittersweet Life*) pays homage to Sergio Leone's 1966 epic in this energetic, self-dubbed "Oriental Western". Blending *The Good, the Bad and the Ugly* with *Mad Max* and a peppering of madcap humour, this supercharged action flick unfolds in 1930s Manchuria, where three outlaws clash over a stolen treasure map. Plot takes second place in the frenetic proceedings and confusing flashbacks help slow the pace midway, but they're more than compensated for by the impressive finale. SF Korean, Mandarin, Japanese +subtitles. DVD BL

Song Kang-ho *Yoon Tae-goo/The Weird* • Lee Byung-hun *Park Chang-yi/The Bad* • Jung Woo-sung *Park Do-won/The Good* ■ *Dir* Kim Ji-woon • *Scr* Kim Ji-woon, Kim Min-suk

The Good Thief ★★★ 15
Crime caper thriller
2002 · UK/Ire/Fr · Colour · 104min

Nick Nolte's American in Nice is a thief, heroin addict and professional gambler, the charming but morally dubious hero of Neil Jordan's remake of the classic French thriller *Bob Le Flambeur*. Nolte rescues a young Eastern European immigrant from a life of prostitution and then goes cold turkey in order to orchestrate a big casino heist. Unfortunately, Jordan overcomplicates proceedings with too many characters and too many rival heist plots, which detract from the towering central performance of Nolte. BP Violence, swearing, drug abuse. DVD

Nick Nolte *Bob Montagnet* • Tcheky Karyo *Roger* • Saïd Taghmaoui *Paulo* • Gérard Darmon *Raoul* • Emir Kusturica *Vladimir* • Marc Lavoine *Remi* ■ *Dir* Neil Jordan • *Scr* Neil Jordan, from the 1955 film *Bob Le Flambeur* by Jean-Pierre Melville, Auguste Le Breton

Good Times ★★ 15
Musical
1967 · US · Colour · 87min

William Friedkin, director of *The French Connection* and *The Exorcist*, made his feature debut with this silly but amusing piece of wish-fulfilment, which stars the then-married pop duo, Sonny and Cher. Although it has dated badly, this potted history of Hollywood movie styles is, in its own small way, quite a clever satire, at the expense of both Tinseltown and the audiences who'll watch any old rubbish. George Sanders puts in a rather shamefaced guest appearance. DP DVD

Sonny Bono • Cher • George Sanders *Mordicus* • Norman Alden *Warren* ■ *Dir* William Friedkin • *Scr* Tony Barrett

Good Vibrations ★★★★ 15
Biographical comedy drama
2012 · UK/Ire · Colour · 98min

The sectarian struggles of Northern Ireland in the late 1970s would seem an unlikely backdrop for a feel-good comedy drama, but this storming biopic of Belfast music promoter Terri Hooley is an exciting reminder of the prevailing power of rock. Hooley (Richard Dormer) is a small-time DJ who launches a record shop on a wing and a prayer, branching out into production when unsigned local bands start pouring through his door. None – save the Undertones – ever really dented the charts, but this unruly, charming film isn't so much bothered with Hooley's success as it is with the way he reinvigorated a city at war with itself. DW Swearing, drug abuse. DVD BL

Richard Dormer *Terri Hooley* • Jodie Whittaker *Ruth* • Michael Colgan *Dave* • Karl Johnson *George* • Liam Cunningham *Davy* • Adrian Dunbar *Andy* • Dylan Moran *Pat* ■ *Dir* Lisa Barros D'Sa, Glenn Leyburn • *Scr* Colin Carberry, Glenn Patterson, based on the true stories of Terri Hooley

The Good Wife ★★★ 15
Drama
1986 · Aus · Colour · 93min

In this moral tale of small-town lust, set in 1930s Australia, Rachel Ward yearns to break free from her dreary home life and indifferent husband Bryan Brown. After a brief tumble with her brother-in-law, the good wife goes bad and hits town looking for romance and sex. Enter Sam Neill. This erotic fandango may not exactly be *Madame Bovary*, but Ward and Neill set up a storm, while Brown demonstrates why a nice girl might consider adultery. NF Swearing. DVD

Rachel Ward *Marge Hills* • Bryan Brown *Sonny Hills* • Sam Neill *Neville Gifford* • Steven Vidler *Sugar Hills* • Jennifer Claire *Daisy* • Bruce Barry *Archie* • Clarissa Kaye-Mason [Clarissa Kaye] *Mrs Jackson* • Carole Skinner *Mrs Gibson* ■ *Dir* Ken Cameron • *Scr* Peter Kenna

Good Will Hunting ★★★★ 15
Drama
1997 · US · Colour · 121min

Matt Damon and Ben Affleck wrote and starred in this moving drama directed by Gus Van Sant. Damon plays Will, a wrong-side-of-the-tracks janitor at top college MIT, who has an exceptional mind and whose mathematical genius is discovered by professor Stellan Skarsgård. Damon, however, is an emotionally troubled young man, so psychologist Robin Williams is brought in to help him. Skilfully directed and beautifully performed by Damon, Williams, Skarsgård, Affleck and Minnie Driver (as Damon's intellectual girlfriend), this won Oscars for Damon and Affleck's screenplay as well as for Williams's subtle performance. JB Violence, swearing. DVD BL

Matt Damon *Will Hunting* • Robin Williams *Sean McGuire* • Ben Affleck *Chuckie* • Minnie Driver *Skylar* • Stellan Skarsgård *Lambeau* • John Mighton *Tom* • Rachel Majorowski *Krystyn* • Colleen McCauley *Cathy* • Casey Affleck *Morgan* ■ *Dir* Gus Van Sant • *Scr* Matt Damon, Ben Affleck

A Good Woman ★★★ PG
Period comedy drama
2004 · UK/It/Sp/US · Colour · 89min

Oscar Wilde's waspish morality tale *Lady Windermere's Fan* gets both a fresh 1930s setting and a significant US slant. Mark Umbers and a stilted Scarlett Johansson play American newlyweds, who set society tongues wagging in a resort on Italy's beautiful Amalfi coast when Umbers is spotted apparently becoming intimate with notorious New York gold-digger Helen Hunt. The intricate web of secrets and lies that emerges as the scandal spreads is a tad contrived but it's still a highly agreeable movie. SF DVD

Helen Hunt *Mrs Erlynne* • Scarlett Johansson *Meg Windermere* • Tom Wilkinson *Tuppy* • Stephen Campbell Moore *Lord Darlington* • Mark Umbers *Robert Windermere* • Milena Vukotic *Contessa Lucchino* • Diana Hardcastle *Lady Plymdale* • John Standing *Dumby* ■ *Dir* Mike Barker • *Scr* Howard Himelstein, from the play *Lady Windermere's Fan* by Oscar Wilde

A Good Year ★★★ 12
Comedy drama
2006 · US · Colour · 112min

Russell Crowe and his *Gladiator* director Ridley Scott aren't known for their comic touch, so this airy feel-good movie marks something of a departure for them both. Crowe stars as Max, a city trader who inherits a vineyard in Provence from his Uncle Henry (Albert Finney, confined to flashbacks). Max hopes to sell it on quickly but his arrival in the French countryside causes him to reassess his life, particularly after a meeting with a lovely but cynical local café owner (Marion Cotillard). Adapted from Peter Mayle's novel, this escapist fantasy proves amiably diverting and gives Crowe a rare chance to test his comic mettle. His slapstick antics and French-baiting don't always convince, but he still manages to produce a performance that's delightfully good-natured. JR DVD

Russell Crowe *Max Skinner* • Albert Finney *Uncle Henry* • Marion Cotillard *Fanny Chenal* • Abbie Cornish *Christie Roberts* • Didier Bourdon *Francis Duflot* • Tom Hollander *Charlie Willis* • Freddie Highmore *Young Max* ■ *Dir* Ridley Scott • *Scr* Marc Klein, from the novel by Peter Mayle

Goodbye Again ★★★
Romantic drama
1961 · US · BW · 119min

This is the film version of the book *Aimez-Vous Brahms* (the movie's French title) by once-fashionable, controversial novelist Françoise Sagan. It's sensitively but rather boringly directed by director Anatole Litvak. Ingrid Bergman is loved by toy boy Anthony Perkins while really harbouring a deep passion for playboy Yves Montand. Perkins picked up an acting award at Cannes and the Paris locations are attractive, but the running time stretches a very slight tale a long way. TS

Ingrid Bergman *Paula Tessier* • Yves Montand *Roger Demarest* • Anthony Perkins *Philip Van Der Besh* • Jessie Royce Landis *Mrs Van Der Besh* • Jackie Lane [Jocelyn Lane] *Maisie I* • Jean Clarke *Maisie II* • Michèle Mercier *Maisie III* • Pierre Dux *Maître Fleury* ■ *Dir* Anatole Litvak • *Scr* Samuel Taylor, from the novel *Aimez-Vous Brahms* by Françoise Sagan

Goodbye Bafana ★★ 15
Drama based on a true story
2007 · Bel/Fr/Ger/UK/S Afr/It/Lux · Colour · 113min

Joseph Fiennes stars as South African prison guard James Gregory, whose controversial memoirs detailed his unlikely relationship with the country's most notorious political prisoner, Nelson Mandela. Beginning in 1968 on Robben Island, Gregory's first period in charge of Mandela shows him as hostile towards his charge. But through their mutual knowledge of the Xhosa language, the Afrikaner's racist outlook is challenged and ultimately transformed – their bond exemplified by a bracelet originally given to the young Gregory by his black friend Bafana. Though well-intentioned, August's attempt to portray the collapse of apartheid through one man's personal epiphany feels like a missed opportunity. SP In English, Xhosa. DVD

Joseph Fiennes *James Gregory* • Dennis Haysbert *Nelson Mandela* • Diane Kruger *Gloria Gregory* • Patrick Lyster *Maj Pieter Jordaan* • Shiloh Henderson *Brent Gregory* • Megan Smith *Natasha Gregory* • Faith Ndukwana *Winnie Mandela* ■ *Dir* Bille August • *Scr* Greg Latter, Bille August, from a story by Latter, from the memoirs by James Gregory, Bob Graham

Goodbye Charlie ★★
Fantasy comedy
1964 · US · Colour · 116min

Despite stylish direction from Vincente Minnelli, the presence of Debbie Reynolds and Tony Curtis, and stalwart support from Pat Boone and Walter Matthau, this film still comes a cropper. This witless heaven-and-earth tale has Reynolds struggling manfully to portray a writer who, having been murdered by a jealous husband (Matthau), returns to Earth as a beautiful girl. Reynolds consorts with his/her best friend (Curtis) and is courted by Boone, to the discomfort of everyone – including the audience. RK

Tony Curtis *George Tracy* • Debbie Reynolds *Charlie Sorel/The Woman* • Pat Boone *Bruce Minton* • Joanna Barnes *Janie* • Ellen McRae [Ellen Burstyn] *Franny* • Laura Devon *Rusty* • Martin Gabel *Morton Craft* • Roger C Carmel *Inspector* • Walter Matthau *Sir Leopold Sartori* ■ *Dir* Vincente Minnelli • *Scr* Harry Kurnitz, from a play by George Axelrod

Goodbye Charlie Bright ★★★ 18
Drama
2000 · UK · Colour · 83min

A rite-of-passage yarn about a bunch of lifelong mates on a south London council estate and the last long, hot summer that they spend together before circumstances send them off on separate ways. The film charts their close but volatile kinship against a backdrop of the usual "laddish" behaviour. While the script and direction are erratic, the film benefits enormously from the authenticity of location filming and from credible performances by a young cast. A very bright start for writer/director Nick Love. DA DVD

Paul Nicholls *Charlie Bright* • Roland Manookian *Justin* • Phil Daniels *Eddie* • Jamie Foreman *Tony* • Danny Dyer *Francis* • Dani Behr *Blondie* • David Thewlis *Dad* ■ *Dir* Nick Love • *Scr* Nick Love, Dominic Eames, from a story by Nick Love

Goodbye Christopher Robin
Drama based on a true story
2017 · UK · Colour

This is a preview – no prints were available to review as we went to press: As every Winnie the Pooh fan knows, there really was a boy called Christopher Robin. He was author AA Milne's son and on his first birthday in 1921 he was given the teddy bear that went on to inspire a wealth of stories. But as the boy grew older, he started to resent the success of the Pooh books, feeling his childhood had been exploited. Domhnall Gleeson and Margot Robbie play Christopher Robin's parents in this dark spin on familiar material. SvM

Domhnall Gleeson *AA Milne* • Margot Robbie *Daphne Milne* ■ *Dir* Simon Curtis • *Scr* Frank Cottrell Boyce, Simon Vaughan

Goodbye, Columbus ★★★
Comedy   1969 · US · Colour · 101min

This adaptation of Philip Roth's novella stars Richard Benjamin as a librarian who woos pretty rich girl Ali MacGraw. Set in the affluent Jewish community of New York and the swanky Florida resort of Boca Raton, it's a comedy that spins on MacGraw's parents (Jack Klugman and Nan Martin) who dislike Benjamin because he's penniless. The rest of the plot revolves around MacGraw's birth control method, or lack of it. Pretty daring for 1969, it seems pretty pointless now. Even so, it's nicely acted and cleverly observed. AT Some swearing, brief nudity, sex scenes.

Richard Benjamin *Neil Klugman* • Ali MacGraw *Brenda Patimkin* • Jack Klugman *Mr Patimkin* • Nan Martin *Mrs Patimkin* • Michael Meyers *Ron* • Lori Shelle *Julie Patimkin* • Royce Wallace *Carlotta* • Sylvie Strauss *Aunt Gladys* ■ *Dir* Larry Peerce • *Scr* Arnold Schulman, from the novella by Philip Roth

Goodbye First Love
★★★★ 15
Romantic drama   2011 · Fr/Ger · Colour · 105min

Mia Hansen-Løve considerably enhanced her burgeoning reputation with a third feature that is firmly rooted in the traditions of French art cinema. It's possible to detect the influence of François Truffaut in a subtly scripted saga that turns around Lola Créton's decade-long rite of romantic passage from giddily lovesick 15-year-old to sadder, wiser 20-something. The insights into loss and healing are sentimental but sensible, while the use of Stéphane Fontaine's camerawork to convey contrasting personalities is inspired. DP French, German, Danish +subtitles. Swearing, nudity. *DVD*

Lola Créton *Camille* • Sebastian Urzendowsky *Sullivan* • Magne Havard Brekke [Magne Brekke] *Lorenz* ■ *Dir/Scr* Mia Hansen-Løve • *Cinematographer* Stéphane Fontaine

Goodbye Gemini   ★★ 15
Crime drama   1970 · UK · Colour · 85min

Set at the fag end of the Swinging Sixties, this exploitation tale stars Judy Geeson and Martin Potter as unnaturally close twins Jacki and Julian. Newly arrived in London, they soon fall in with bohemian Clive (Alexis Kanner, sporting the most miraculous sideburns) and his free-loving Chelsea set. It all turns nasty when Clive embroils Julian in a blackmail plot to get the better of gangster (albeit in a floral cravat) Mike Pratt. Despite the best efforts of Geeson and Freddie Jones as a camp antiques dealer, wooden performances and an inconsistent script make the film little more than an interesting, if rather dubious, 1960s snapshot. TP Violence. *DVD*

Judy Geeson *Jacki* • Martin Potter *Julian* • Michael Redgrave *James Harrington-Smith* • Alexis Kanner *Clive Landseer* • Mike Pratt *Rod Barstowe* • Freddie Jones *David Curry* ■ *Dir* Alan Gibson • *Scr* Edmund Ward, from the novel *Ask Agamemnon* by Jenni Hall • *Cinematographer* Geoffrey Unsworth

The Goodbye Girl ★★★★ PG
Romantic comedy   1977 · US · Colour · 105min

A Neil Simon script, Mike Nichols wielding the megaphone and Robert De Niro to star. It seemed nothing could stop *Bogart Slept Here* from becoming the movie of the year. But two weeks into production, the director and his star were at odds over everything from Method acting to comic timing. De Niro was sacked and went off to make *Taxi Driver*, leaving Nichols to shut down the picture. Two years later, Richard Dreyfuss took the lead in what was now *The Goodbye Girl*, and Neil Simon's winter of discontent was made glorious summer by this unprepossessing son of New York. Dreyfuss

is inspired, his gay Richard III the highlight of a wisecracking romantic comedy that barely pauses for breath, and he's ably matched by Marsha Mason. DP

Richard Dreyfus *Elliott Garfield* • Marsha Mason *Paula McFadden* • Quinn Cummings *Lucy McFadden* • Paul Eenedict *Mark Morgenweiss* • Barbara Rhoades *Donna Douglas* • Theresa Merritt *Mrs Crosby* ■ *Dir* Herbert Ross • *Scr* Neil Simon

Goodbye Lover   ★★ 15
Comedy crime thriller
1997 · US · Colour · 96min

Director Roland Joffé tries to make this revenge comedy amusing but fails. In the end, it's saved by the performances of Don Johnson and Ellen DeGeneres. Johnson plays the rich businessman who is pushed over a balcony by his useless brother (Dermot Mulroney) and the sister-in-law (Patricia Arquette) with whom he was having an affair. DeGeneres's cop gets the only good lines and delivers them with aplomb. JB *DVD* *CS*

Patricia Arquette *Sandra Dunmore* • Dermot Mulroney *Jake Durmore* • Ellen DeGeneres *Sgt Rita Pompano* • Mary-Louise Parker *Peggy Blaine* • Don Johnson *Ben Dunmore* • Ray McKinnon *Rollins* • Alex Rocco *Detective Crowley* ■ *Dir* Roland Joffé • *Scr* Ron Peer, Joel Cohen, Alec Sokolow

Goodbye, Mr Chips
★★★★★ U
Drama   1939 · UK/US · BW · 109min

British star Robert Donat pipped Clark Gable to the best actor Oscar in the year *Gone with the Wind* swept the awards with his marvellous portrayal of author James Hilton's crusty pedagogue. Donat ages throughout the film in a subtle and worldly-wise manner, and he's not overly reliant on movie make-up to do so. This is a warm-hearted, humanitarian work, beautifully filmed in England by MGM and is a fine example of that great studio at its peak. Immaculately directed by the underrated Sam Wood, the film introduced world audiences to Greer Garson, who replaced Norma Shearer overnight to become first lady of the MGM lot. This finely crafted tale continues to work its magic and even the most cynical viewer won't fail to be moved. TS *DVD*

Robert Donat *Charles Chipping* • Greer Garson *Katherine Ellis* • Terry Kilburn *John Colley/Peter Colley* • John Mills *Peter Colley as a young man* • Paul Henreid *Max Staefel* • Judith Furse *Flora* • Lyn Harding *Dr Wetherby* • Milton Rosmer *Charteris* ■ *Dir* Sam Wood • *Scr* RC Sherriff, Claudine West, Eric Maschwitz, Sidney Franklin, from the novella by James Hilton, serialised in *British Weekly* • *Cinematographer* FA Young [Freddie Young] • *Art Director* Alfred Junge

Goodbye, Mr Chips   ★ PG
Musical drama   1969 · US/UK · Colour · 148min

Rex Harrison and Richard Burton both had the sense to send Terence Rattigan's script back, and not even an Oscar nomination can hide the fact that this is one of Peter O'Toole's least distinguished performances. The fact that John Williams and Leslie Bricusse were also nominated for best score is preposterous, as the songs in this adaptation of James Hilton's delightful novel are shocking. DP

Peter O'Toole *Arthur "Chips" Chipping* • Petula Clark *Katherine Bridges* • Michael Redgrave *Headmaster* • George Baker *Lord Sutterwick* • Sian Phillips *Ursula Mossbank* • Michael Bryant *Max Staefel* • Patricia Hayes *Miss Honeybun* ■ *Dir* Herbert Ross • *Scr* Terence Rattigan, from the novella by James Hilton, serialised in *British Weekly*

Goodbye, My Fancy ★★★ U
Romantic drama   1951 · US · BW · 107min

This is hardly the film for which Joan Crawford will be remembered. It is, however, a fascinating example of how miscasting can ruin an otherwise engaging story. Crawford plays a congresswoman caught up in a romantic triangle while revisiting her old school to receive an honorary degree. Her presence overbalances what was a pretty flimsy

comedy in the first place. Robert Young and Frank Lovejoy are the love rivals but they can't repair the damage. DP

Joan Crawford *Agatha Reed* • Robert Young (1) *Dr James Merrill* • Frank Lovejoy *Matt Cole* • Eve Arden *Woody* • Janice Rule *Virginia Merrill* • Lurene Tuttle *Ellen Griswold* • Howard St John *Claude Griswold* • Viola Roache *Miss Shackleford* ■ *Dir* Vincent Sherman • *Scr* Ivan Goff, Ben Roberts, from Fay Kanin's play

Goodbye Pork Pie   ★★ 18
Road movie   1981 · NZ · Colour · 102min

The first New Zealand feature to recoup its costs at the domestic box office is a road movie in the good old counterculture tradition. Indeed, there's a real coming-of-age feel as unlikely buddies Tony Barry and Kelly Johnson learn about life, love and responsibility on a cross-country trek that's littered with eccentric characters and angry lawmen. It's dated in places, the sexism is unforgiveable and the episodic structure stops it building up a real head of steam, but there's plenty of action and offbeat humour. DP Swearing. *DVD*

Tony Barry *John* • Kelly Johnson *Gerry Austin* • Claire Oberman *Shirl* • Shirley Gruar *Sue* • Jackie Lowitt *Leslie Morris* • Don Selwyn *Kaitaia policeman* • Shirley Dunn *Car rental girl* • Paki Cherrington *Taxi driver* ■ *Dir* Geoff Murphy • *Scr* Geoff Murphy, Ian Mune

Goodbye Solo   ★★★★ 15
Drama   2008 · US · Colour · 91min

Writer/director Ramin Bahrani has become a champion of the outsider with his intimate studies of migrants finding their niche. Here, Senegalese cabbie Solo (Souléymane Sy Savané) becomes suspicious when a despondent elderly man (Red West) books a one-way trip to North Carolina's Blowing Rock mountain several days in advance. So he digs into the old-timer's past and sets out to restore his faith in existence. Mixing robust humour with measured melodrama, this scuffs the feel-good element with the brusque reality of life in an increasingly insular society. DP In English, French, Wolof, Spanish. Violence, swearing.

Souléymane Sy Savané *Souléymane "Solo"* • Red West *William* • Diana Franco Galindo *Alex* • Carmen Leyva *Quiera* • Lane "Roc" Williams *Roc* • Mamadou Lam *Mamadou* ■ *Dir* Ramin Bahrani • *Scr* Ramin Bahrani, Bahareh Azimi

Goodbye to Language ★ 15
Drama   2014 · Fr · Colour · 66min

French New Wave legend Jean-Luc Godard has always been something of a Marmite film-maker, but his latest seems set to polarise even those that tolerate him. Using an even more scrappy aesthetic than usual, it follows a married couple as they pontificate on life in disjointed aphorisms, while Godard gets more and more distracted by their dog (his own, it turns out). The 3D is played for novelty, as Godard intercuts two different scenes into one, creating a visual blur that becomes clearer by closing the left or right eye. Closing both might be a better option. DW In French. *DVD* *Blu-ray* *3D*

Héloïse Godet *Josette* • Kamel Abdeli *Gédéon* • Richard Chevallier *Marcus* • Zoé Bruneau *Ivitch* • Christian Gregori *Davidson* ■ *Dir/Scr* Jean-Luc Godard

GoodFellas   ★★★★★ 18
Crime drama   1990 · US · Colour · 139min

Martin Scorsese's unflinching depiction of the attraction and the brutal reality of the Mafia lifestyle is a masterwork on every artistic level. Direction, script, photography, ensemble acting (Joe Pesci won a deserved Oscar, but he's matched by Robert De Niro and Ray Liotta) and driving pop and rock soundtrack seamlessly combine to dazzling effect in this instant classic. Crackling with raw energy, Scorsese's fascinating new take on themes explored in his earlier *Mean Streets* enthrals from the first violent frames to the stunning final sequence. Be prepared to be completely bowled over by a director in full control of top-notch material at the peak of his talents. AJ Drug abuse, swearing, violence. *DVD* *Blu-ray*

Robert De Niro *James Conway* • Ray Liotta *Henry Hill* • Joe Pesci *Tommy DeVito* • Lorraine Bracco *Karen Hill* • Paul Sorvino *Paul Cicero* • Frank Sivero *Frankie Carbone* • Tony Darrow *Sonny Bunz* • Mike Starr *Frenchy* ■ *Dir* Martin Scorsese • *Scr* Nicholas Pileggi, Martin Scorsese, from the book *Wiseguy* by Nicholas Pileggi • *Cinematographer* Michael Ballhaus • *Editor* Thelma Schoonmaker

Goodnight for Justice ★★ 12
Western   2011 · US/Can · Colour · 88min

Beverly Hills, 90210 pals Luke Perry and Jason Priestley re-team for this entertaining though conventional western – the former starring, the latter directing. Based on characters conceived by Perry, it's the first of three TV movies about a Wild West circuit judge who finds his work overshadowed by his desire to avenge his parents' murder. One nice twist aside, it's contrived and clichéd, but confident direction, zesty dialogue and a mix of playfulness and gravity help to keep the story engaging. SF

Luke Perry *John Goodnight* • Lara Gilchrist *Kate Ramsey* • Ron Lea *Dan Reed* • Darla Fay *Betty* ■ *Dir* Jason Priestley • *Scr* Tippi & Neal Dobrofsky

The Goods: Live Hard Sell Hard   ★★ 15
Comedy   2009 · US · Colour · 89min

In this bustling comedy, Jeremy Piven stars as a used-car dealer with too much stock on his hands. He drafts in a team of gonzo freelance salesmen to help him, with frenetic results. The star's performance typifies what's wrong with the movie: lots of huff and puff, but the material's just not strong enough. The scene-stealer here is veteran James Brolin as the cash-strapped showroom proprietor – he demonstrates that a lighter touch can sometimes be more effective when tickling the funny bone. TJ Swearing, sexual references, nudity.

Jeremy Piven *Don "the Goods" Ready* • Ving Rhames *Jibby Newsome* • James Brolin *Ben Selleck* • David Koechner *Brent Gage* • Kathryn Hahn *Babs Merrick* • Ed Helms *Paxton Harding* • Will Ferrell *Craig McDermott* ■ *Dir* Neal Brennan • *Scr* Andy Stock, Rick Stempson

A Goofy Movie   ★★ U
Animated comedy   1995 · US · Colour · 74min

Mickey Mouse's pal Goofy gets his own movie, but fans of the original short cartoons in which he was a co-star may be shocked to discover that Goofy is now a dad, and not a cool one either, preferring to drag his son off fishing rather than let him chat up girls. The story is rather ordinary and the bland computer animation looks less interesting than anything kids can catch nowadays on TV. JB *DVD*

Bill Farmer *Goofy* • Jason Marsden *Max* • Jim Cummings *Pete* • Kellie Martin *Roxanne* • Rob Paulsen *PJ* • Wallace Shawn *Principal Mazur* • Frank Welker *Bigfoot* • Kevin Lima *Lester* • Florence Stanley *Waitress* ■ *Dir* Kevin Lima • *Scr* Jymn Magon, Chris Matheson, Brian Pimental, from a story by Jymn Magon

Goon   ★★★ 15
Comedy based on a true story
2011 · Can · Colour · 87min

In this knockabout comedy from Michael Dowse (*It's All Gone Pete Tong*), Seann William Scott plays Doug, a dim but likeable bar bouncer whose fight skills land him the job of "enforcer" with the struggling local ice-hockey team. Scott has matured both physically and as an actor since playing the sex-obsessed Stifler in the *American Pie* series and he's very likeable here. Very likeable, too, is the film itself which, despite its surface brutality, has an unexpectedly warm heart. It's no life-changer, but it is a pleasant little surprise. DA In English, French. Violence, swearing. *DVD* *Blu-ray*

Seann William Scott *Doug Glatt* • Jay Baruchel *Pat* • Alison Pill *Eva* • Liev Schreiber *Ross Rhea* • Kim Coates *Ronnie Hortense* • Eugene Levy *Dad* ■ *Dir* Michael Dowse • *Scr* Jay Baruchel, Evan Goldberg, from the novel *Goon: the True Story of an Unlikely Journey into Minor League Hockey* by Adam Frattasio, Doug Smith

The Goonies ★★★ PG
Adventure 1985 · US · Colour · 108min

Before making it big directing *Home Alone*, Chris Columbus wrote the screenplay from a story by Steven Spielberg for this good-natured romp, in which a gang of children tackles a family of crooks while searching for missing pirate treasure. The tale rattles along like a juvenile *Raiders of the Lost Ark* and the young leads are likeable enough. There's also some nice hamming from villains Anne Ramsey, Joe Pantoliano and Robert Davi. JF Some swearing, violence.
DVD **SB**

Sean Astin *Mikey* · Josh Brolin *Brand* · Jeff Cohen *Chunk* · Corey Feldman *Mouth* · Kerri Green *Andy* · Martha Plimpton *Stef* · Ke Huy Quan *Data* · John Matuszak *Sloth* · Robert Davi *Jake* · Joe Pantoliano *Francis* · Anne Ramsey *Mama Fratelli* ■ *Dir* Richard Donner · *Scr* Chris Columbus, from a story by Steven Spielberg

The Goose Steps Out ★★★★ U
Second World War comedy 1942 · UK · BW · 66min

This wonderful comedy has Will Hay sent to a Nazi academy to get hold of Frank Pettingell's plans for a gas bomb. As usual, Hay's academic shortcomings are soon exposed, this time by a class of Hitler Youth that includes Peter Ustinov, Charles Hawtrey and Barry Morse, but he still manages to insult Hitler at every turn, steal a sample bomb casing and pass on some bogus invasion plans before heading back to Blighty. The script is packed with morale-boosting jokes that still seem pretty fresh, and Hay is in prime form. DP **DVD**

Will Hay *William Potts/Muller* · Frank Pettingell *Professor Hoffman* · Julien Mitchell *General Von Glotz* · Charles Hawtrey *Max* · Peter Croft *Hans* · Anne Firth *Lena* · Leslie Harcourt *Vagel* ■ *Dir* Will Hay, Basil Dearden · *Scr* Angus MacPhail, John Dighton, from a story by Bernard Miles, Reginald Groves

The Goose Woman ★★★
Silent drama 1925 · US · BW · 75min

One of the *grand dames* of silent Hollywood, Louise Dresser, gives an impassioned performance in this emphatic adaptation of a Rex Beach story that was itself inspired by the infamous Hall-Mills or "Pig Woman" case. As the former diva who hopes to restore lost celebrity by claiming to have witnessed a killing near her humble abode, Dresser ably conveys the shabby grandeur of the faded icon, whose deception backfires when she learns her only son is implicated in the crime. This old-fangled melodrama is directed with customary gravitas by Clarence Brown. DP

Louise Dresser *Mary Holmes/Marie de Nardi* · Jack Pickford *Gerald Holmes* · Constance Bennett *Hazel Woods* · James O Barrows *Jacob Riggs* · Spottiswoode Aitken *Jacob Riggs* ■ *Dir* Clarence Brown · *Scr* Melville Brown, Dwinelle Benthall (titles), from the story by Rex Beach

Goosebumps ★★★ PG
Comedy horror adventure 2015 · US/Aus · Colour · 103min

This spooky adventure from director Rob Letterman (*Monsters vs Aliens*) takes RL Stine's popular series of children's books as its inspiration. Dylan Minnette stars as teenager Zach, whose relocation from the city to a small town brings him down, that is until his curiosity about a neighbour's mysterious bookcase of locked manuscripts gets the better of him, leading to all manner of deadly monsters being let loose on the town. None of them are particularly scary, and the film is pleasantly enjoyable throughout, combining likeable characters with knowing gags and lively set pieces. SC
DVD **SB** **UB**

Jack Black *RL Stine/"Mr Shivers"/Slappy* · Dylan Minnette *Zach Cooper* · Odeya Rush *Hannah* · Amy Ryan *Gale* ■ *Dir* Rob Letterman · *Scr* Darren Lemke, from a story by Scott Alexander, Larry Karaszewski, from the books by RL Stine · *Music* Danny Elfman

Gor ★ 15
Action fantasy 1987 · US · Colour · 90min

The sword-and-sorcery genre had well and truly run its course by the time Fritz Kiersch's lame-brained effort saw the light of day. Urbano Barberini is a nerdy professor transported to a distant planet where he sets about freeing its people from the tyrannical slavery of their overlord, played by the under-used Oliver Reed. All the staple ingredients are present, but any attempt at humour fails. Jack Palance turns up at the end to introduce himself as the villain of the sequel, *Outlaw of Gor*. RS

Urbano Barberini *Cabot* · Rebecca Ferratti *Talena* · Paul L Smith [Paul Smith] *Surbus* · Oliver Reed *Sarm* · Jack Palance *Xenos* ■ *Dir* Fritz Kiersch · *Scr* Rick Marx, Peter Welbeck [Harry Alan Towers], from the novel *Tarnsman of Gor* by John Norman

Gordon the Black Pirate ★★ U
Swashbuckling adventure 1961 · It · Colour · 82min

Like many Italian swashbucklers of the period, the action here is brisk and predictable, while the tawdry surface opulence can't disguise the cheapness of the production. (Ricardo Montalban's pirate ship was actually a fishing boat.) However, Vincent Price – who apparently only agreed to star in the picture because it allowed him to go art hunting – has a hissably good time as the governor's secretary with a nasty sideline in slavery. DP

Ricardo Montalban *Gordon, the Black Buccaneer* · Vincent Price *Romero* · Giulia Rubini *Manuela* · Liana Orfei *Luana* · Mario Feliciani *Tortuga* ■ *Dir* Mario Costa · *Scr* John Byrne, Ottavio Poggi

Gordon's War ★★
Blaxploitation crime drama 1973 · US · Colour · 89min

Vietnam veteran Paul Winfield returns home to Harlem and has to cope with his wife's death from a drug overdose. Declaring war on the ghetto underworld, he organises a strike force to rid the neighbourhood of pushers. This is a slickly packaged blaxploitation vigilante drama, shot on gritty locations and with more credible action and less comic-strip violence than most of its ilk. AJ

Paul Winfield *Gordon* · Carl Lee *Bee* · David Downing *Otis* · Tony King *Roy* · Gilbert Lewis *Spanish Harry* · Carl Gordon *Luther the Pimp* · Nathan C Heard *Big Pink* · Grace Jones *Mary* · Adam Wade *Hustler* ■ *Dir* Ossie Davis · *Scr* Howard Friedlander, Ed Spielman

The Gore-Gore Girls ★ 18
Detective horror 1972 · US · Colour · 80min

This is just as boring, amateur and stupid as splatter pioneer Herschell Gordon Lewis's previous snooze-fests. Private detective Frank Kress tries to solve a series of stripper murders at comedian Henny Youngman's club with the help of local reporter Amy Farrell. If you can stay awake long enough, the close-up mutilations may offend. One of the first movies given an American X certificate for violence. AJ
DVD

Frank Kress *Abraham Gentry* · Amy Farrell *Nancy Weston* · Hedda Lubin *Marlene* · Henny Youngman *Marzdone Mobilie* ■ *Dir* Herschell Gordon Lewis · *Scr* Alan J Dachman

Gore Vidal's Billy the Kid ★★★ 15
Western 1989 · US · Colour · 93min

In this cumbersomely monikered cable movie, Gore Vidal took another bash at the more-than-familiar story of Billy the Kid. He had already scripted the TV movie *The Death of Billy the Kid* in the 1950s, which inspired the Paul Newman vehicle *The Left-Handed Gun*. Here, again, Vidal presents Billy as a crazy, mixed-up kid who was caught up in a Wild West maelstrom from which he could only emerge feet first. Val Kilmer gives William Bonney a certain baby-faced charm, but he never hints at the complexities revealed by Newman. Though

nothing special, it's all well above usual TV-movie standards. DP

Val Kilmer *William H Bonney* · Duncan Regehr *Pat Garrett* · Julie Carmen *Celsa* · Ned Vaughn *Charlie* · Patrick Massett *Tom* · Wilford Brimley *Governor Lew Wallace* · René Auberjonois *Drunk* · Nate Esformes *Valdez* · Gore Vidal *Minister* ■ *Dir* William A Graham · *Scr* Gore Vidal

The Gorgeous Hussy ★★
Historical romantic drama 1936 · US · BW · 103min

Joan Crawford scandalises Washington society as the innkeeper's daughter who becomes President Andrew Jackson's bit-on-the-side. Crawford wanted the part because she rather resented Norma Shearer getting all the juicy historical roles MGM had to offer. Audiences were apathetic. AT

Joan Crawford *Margaret "Peggy" O'Neal Eaton* · Robert Taylor (1) *"Bow" Timberlake* · Lionel Barrymore *Andrew Jackson* · Franchot Tone *John Eaton* · Melvyn Douglas *John Randolph* · James Stewart *"Rowdy" Dow* · Alison Skipworth *Mrs Beal* · Beulah Bondi *Rachel Jackson* · Louis Calhern *Sunderland* ■ *Dir* Clarence Brown · *Scr* Ainsworth Morgan, Stephen Morehouse Avery, from the novel by Samuel Hopkins Adams

Gorgo ★★★ PG
Monster adventure 1961 · UK · Colour · 73min

This highly derivative film has borrowed from so many other monster movies that it is almost as much fun spotting the swipes as it is watching the picture itself. Special effects boffin Tom Howard's creatures are the sweetest rampaging dinosaurs you will ever see, and the model London landmarks trampled by Mrs Gorgo are risible. Bill Travers and William Sylvester keep straight faces as this enjoyable tosh unfolds. DP

Bill Travers *Joe Ryan* · William Sylvester *Sam Slade* · Vincent Winter *Sean* · Bruce Seton *Professor Flaherty* · Joseph O'Conor *Professor Hendricks* · Martin Benson *Dorkin* · Christopher Rhodes *McCartin* · Maurice Kaufmann *Radio reporter* ■ *Dir* Eugène Lourié · *Scr* John Loring [Robert L Richards], Daniel Hyatt [Daniel James], from their story

The Gorgon ★★★ 15
Horror 1964 · UK · Colour · 79min

Barbara Shelley, Hammer's best ever *femme fatale*, is possessed by the snake-tressed, stone-gazing spirit of the Greek mythological creature in director Terence Fisher's most poetic and underrated fearful fairy tale. Totally unclassifiable, it relies less on its absurd story and more on provocative imagery. But, while it may fall short of the monstrous mark, the period atmosphere is powerfully evoked and it's made headier by the peerless Peter Cushing and Christopher Lee at the height of their dramatic authority. AJ **DVD**

Peter Cushing *Namaroff* · Christopher Lee *Prof Carl Meister* · Richard Pasco *Paul Heitz* · Barbara Shelley *Carla Hoffman* · Michael Goodliffe *Professor Heitz* · Patrick Troughton *Kanof* · Jack Watson *Ratoff* · Jeremy Longhurst *Bruno Heitz* ■ *Dir* Terence Fisher · *Scr* John Gilling, from a story by J Liewellyn Devine

Gorilla at Large ★★★
Thriller 1954 · US · Colour · 81min

This above-average chiller stars Anne Bancroft, cutting a fine figure in her trapeze artist catsuit. It's a tale of bizarre killings seemingly linked to fellow amusement park employee Cameron Mitchell (resplendent in a crummy gorilla costume). Director Harmon Jones swells the story with a superb supporting cast. Originally released in 3D, so things hurtle at you for no apparent reason. RS **SB**

Cameron Mitchell *Joey Matthews* · Anne Bancroft *Laverne Miller* · Lee J Cobb *Detective Sergeant Garrison* · Raymond Burr *Cyrus Miller* · Charlotte Austin *Audrey Baxter* · Peter Whitney *Kovacs* · Lee Marvin *Shaughnessy* · Warren Stevens *Mack* ■ *Dir* Harmon Jones · *Scr* Leonard Praskins, Barney Slater

Gorillas in the Mist ★★★★ 12
Biographical drama 1988 · US · Colour · 123min

Sigourney Weaver gives a tour-de-force performance in this fascinating account of Dian Fossey's ground-breaking research into the closed world of the gorilla. She admirably paints a warts-and-all portrait of the woman who slowly gained access to a tribe of remote primates facing extinction; according to Michael Apted's biographical drama, Fossey's passion for her gorillas was offset by her coldness as a human being and a commitment to her work that bordered on obsession. Apted's direction is sympathetic and he makes the most of the stunning jungle location, while Bryan Brown is good as Weaver's lover. JF Violence, swearing. **DVD**

Sigourney Weaver *Dian Fossey* · Bryan Brown *Bob Campbell* · Julie Harris (2) *Roz Carr* · John Omirah Miluwi *Sembagare* · Iain Cuthbertson *Dr Louis Leakey* · Constantin Alexandrov *Van Vecten* · Waigwa Wachira *Mukara* · Iain Glen *Brendan* · David Lansbury *Larry* ■ *Dir* Michael Apted · *Scr* Anna Hamilton Phelan, from a story by Anna Hamilton Phelan, Tab Murphy, from the book by Dian Fossey and an article by Harold TP Hayes

Gorky Park ★★★ 15
Detective thriller 1983 · US · Colour · 123min

Moscow cop William Hurt – looking pained and acting sincere – investigates the case of three faceless corpses. Are the deaths due to Lee Marvin's business operation or are they a result of spy games? Dennis Potter's screenplay is a bit ponderous, but Michael Apted's direction makes the most of the plot convolutions and locations (with Helsinki standing in for Moscow). TH **DVD**

William Hurt *Arkady Renko* · Lee Marvin *Jack Osborne* · Brian Dennehy *William Kirwill* · Ian Bannen *Iamskoy* · Joanna Pacula *Irina Asanova* · Michael Elphick *Pasha Pavlovich* · Richard Griffiths *Anton* · Rikki Fulton *Major Pribluda* · Alexei Sayle *Golodkin* ■ *Dir* Michael Apted · *Scr* Dennis Potter, from the novel by Martin Cruz Smith

Gosford Park ★★★★ 15
Period murder mystery 2001 · US/UK · Colour · 131min

Maverick director Robert Altman takes the English country-house murder mystery and turns it on its head. A huge cast of mostly British thespians flesh out the part whodunnit, part *Upstairs, Downstairs* satire, while Altman assuredly presents the 1930s-set drama from the servants' perspective. The opening of the piece – when the guests and their maids and valets arrive at Gosford Park – is as good as anything Altman's done in 30 years: multilayered and impeccably choreographed. Meanwhile, the dramatic pace is maintained thanks to some sparkling dialogue – the Oscar-winning acidic script is by Julian Fellowes, pre-*Downton Abbey* – and fine performances. It has all the makings of a classic but then Stephen Fry's bumbling detective arrives and a surfeit of irony defuses the exquisitely constructed mood. AC Swearing, a sex scene. **DVD**

Maggie Smith *Constance, Countess of Trentham* · Michael Gambon *Sir William McCordle* · Kristin Scott Thomas *Lady Sylvia McCordle* · Emily Watson *Elsie* · Kelly Macdonald *Mary Maceachran* · Clive Owen *Robert Parks* · Helen Mirren *Mrs Wilson* · Eileen Atkins *Mrs Croft* · Alan Bates *Jennings* · Derek Jacobi *Probert* · Bob Balaban *Morris Weissman* · Jeremy Northam *Ivor Novello* · Ryan Phillippe *Henry Denton* · Richard E Grant *George* · Stephen Fry *Inspector Thompson* · Charles Dance *Raymond, Lord Stockbridge* ■ *Dir* Robert Altman · *Scr* Julian Fellowes, from an idea by Robert Altman, Bob Balaban · *Cinematographer* Andrew Dunn (1)

Gospa ★★★
Drama based on a true story 1995 · Can/Cro/US · Colour · 121min

With its title deriving from the Croat for "Our Lady", this is a reverential account of the events that followed the Marian apparition to six children in the Bosnian hill town of Medjugorje in 1981. While it's not always easy to accept Morgan Fairchild as a

G

nun, Martin Sheen gives a dignified performance as the parish priest who was prosecuted by the state for incitement to insurrection after he failed to prevent the shrine from becoming a place of pilgrimage. DP

Martin Sheen *Father Jozo Zovko* • Michael York *Milan Vikovic* • Morgan Fairchild *Sister Fafijana Zovko* • Frank Finlay *Monsignor* ■ *Dir* Jakov Sedlar • *Scr* Ivan Aralica, Paul Gronseth

The Gospel According to St Matthew ★★★★★ PG
Biblical drama 1964 · It/Fr · BW · 129min

Eschewing the crowd-pleasing grandeur of other biblical dramas, Pier Paolo Pasolini employed a neorealist approach to reaffirm the immediate social significance of Christ's teaching. This collaboration between a Marxist director and the Catholic Church (which contributed to the budget) is remarkable not only for the power of its message, but also for the gentle conviction of Enrique Irazoqui's Jesus, as he rails against injustice and works miracles with a compassion that is absent from the more reverential Hollywood testaments. With the sublime classical score underpinning the rugged beauty of Calabria, this is one of the most relevant religious films ever made. DP Italian dubbed. *DVD* *BL*

Enrique Irazoqui *Jesus Christ* • Margherita Caruso *Mary, as a girl* • Susanna Pasolini *Mary, as a woman* • Marcello Morante *Joseph* • Mario Socrate *John the Baptist* • Settimo Di Porto *Peter* • Otello Sestili *Judas* • Ferruccio Nuzzo *Matthew* ■ *Dir/Scr* Pier Paolo Pasolini • *Cinematographer* Tonino Delli Colli

Gospel of Us ★★ 12A
Religious drama 2012 · UK · Colour · 119min

Also known as *The Passion of Port Talbot*, this film captures a three-day Easter passion play that was acted out in and around the South Wales steel town, with townsfolk augmenting a core of cast and crew professionals. Michael Sheen, a local lad, is the only big name. He plays the "Christ" figure in a production that puts a modern slant on the Crucifixion story by setting it in a Port Talbot that's in thrall to a sinister corporation. There is obvious passion behind and in front of the camera, but a simpler approach by director Dave McKean would have made it a more immersive experience. DA Some violence.

Michael Sheen *The Teacher* • Matthew Aubrey *Legion* • Nigel Barrett *The Stranger/Uncle Bryn* • Jordan Bernarde *Gary/Bary* • Di Botcher *The Mother* • Darren Lawrence *Alfie* ■ *Dir* Dave McKean • *Scr* Owen Sheers

Gossip ★★ 15
Thriller 1999 · US · Colour · 90min

Three college students start a rumour about a prudish fellow student having sex at a party. It gets out of hand, leading to an accusation of rape and an innocent man's arrest. The gossip-mongers are then caught in the middle as they fight about whether to come clean. The film has striking visuals, but never fully capitalises on the dramatic potential of its premise, while the performances are shallow. ST Violence, swearing. *DVD*

James Marsden *Derrick* • Lena Headey *Cathy Jones* • Norman Reedus *Travis* • Kate Hudson *Naomi* • Joshua Jackson *Beau* • Marisa Coughlan *Sheila* • Edward James Olmos *Det Curtis* • Sharon Lawrence *Det Kelly* • Eric Bogosian *Professor Goodwin* ■ *Dir* Davis Guggenheim • *Scr* Theresa Rebeck, Gregory Poirier, from a story by Gregory Poirier

Gösta Berlings Saga ★★★★
Silent drama 1924 · Swe · BW · 183min

Widely acclaimed as Mauritz Stiller's finest film (which it isn't), this adaptation of Selma Lagerlöf's period novel is best known for bringing Greta Garbo to international attention. As the Italian countess who is delivered from the gothic nightmare of Ekeby Hall by defrocked priest Lars Hanson, she is so lovingly lit by Stiller and cameraman Julius Jaenzon that it's little wonder studio boss Louis B Mayer invited her to Hollywood. Bafflingly, the film itself,

with its multifarious melodramatic situations, was less enthusiastically received and Stiller was forced to prune several scenes to the detriment of its sprawling episodic plot. DP

Lars Hanson *Gösta Berlings* • Gerda Lundequist *Margaretha Samzelius, born Celsing* • Hilda Forsslund *Margaretha's mother* • Otto Elg-Lundberg *Major Samzelius* • Sixten Malmerfelt *Melchior Sinclaire* ■ *Dir* Mauritz Stiller • *Scr* Mauritz Stiller, Ragnar Hyltén-Cavallius, from the novel by Selma Lagerlöf

Gotcha! ★★★ 15
Comedy spy drama 1985 · US · Colour · 96min

A youthful Anthony Edwards impresses as a shy college kid who embarks upon a European vacation and gets involved with a spy ring, while Linda Fiorentino's turn as a sultry spy leaves one pondering why it took so long for her to blossom into a star. Director Jeff Kanew offers plenty of frantic scurrying about and sharp one-liners to paper over the elements of *déjà vu*, if little in the way of actual danger and suspense. RS

Anthony Edwards *Jonathan Moore* • Linda Fiorentino *Sasha Banicek/Cheryl Brewster* • Nick Corri *Manolo* • Alex Rocco *Al* • Marla Adams *Maria* • Klaus Loewitsch [Klaus Löwitsch] *Vlad* • Christopher Rydell *Bob Jensen* • Christie Claridge *Girl student* ■ *Dir* Jeff Kanew • *Scr* Dan Gordon, from a story by Paul G Hensler, Dan Gordon

Gothic ★★★ 18
Horror 1986 · UK · Colour · 83min

Ken Russell's talent to abuse past icons goes wondrously berserk here, as he resurrects the notorious 19th-century literary booze-up of Byron, Shelley, Mary Godwin and Polidori at the Villa Diodati on the shores of Lake Geneva. It's this incestuous, laudanum-quaffing occasion that led to the writing of *Frankenstein* and, while Gabriel Byrne, Julian Sands and Natasha Richardson take it seriously enough, Russell keeps undermining them with overwrought visual decadence. TH Swearing, violence, sex scenes. *DVD*

Julian Sands *Percy Bysshe Shelley* • Natasha Richardson *Mary Godwin* • Gabriel Byrne *Lord Byron* • Myriam Cyr *Claire* • Timothy Spall *Dr John Polidori* • Dexter Fletcher *Rushton* • Andreas Wisniewski *Fletcher* • Alec Mango *Murray* ■ *Dir* Ken Russell • *Scr* Stephen Volk

Gothika ★★ 15
Supernatural horror thriller 2003 · US · Colour · 94min

For this overblown horror effort, director Mathieu Kassovitz deploys every cliché in the book - and then moves on to volume two. Halle Berry plays a psychiatrist who, after a car crash, finds herself incarcerated in her own asylum accused of the murder of her husband. She has no memory of these events and, to make matters worse, is haunted by ghostly images of a young girl. Resolutely unscary. AS Violence. *DVD* *BL*

Halle Berry *Dr Miranda Grey* • Robert Downey Jr *Dr Pete Graham* • Charles S Dutton *Dr Doug Grey* • John Carroll Lynch *Sheriff Ryan* • Bernard Hill *Phil Parsons* • Penélope Cruz *Chloe Sava* • Dorian Harewood *Teddy Howard* ■ *Dir* Mathieu Kassovitz • *Scr* Sebastian Gutierrez

Goto, l'Ile d'Amour ★★★★ 15
Fantasy drama 1968 · Fr · Colour and BW · 89min

The surreal poetry that characterised Walerian Borowczyk's animation is clearly evident in his first live-action feature. Shot through with moments of extravagant colour, which lend a certain sinister enchantment to the cruel fairy-tale world of Goto, the heavily stylised visuals make the characters seem as insignificant as the array of symbolic objects (such as music boxes and phonographs) littered around the residence of Pierre Brasseur's cuckolded dictator. With its fly-catchers, duels and acts of self-sacrifice, it has an operatic feel, reinforced by the sublime Handel organ concerto and the theatricality of the

performances. DP French +subtitles. *DVD* *BL*

Pierre Brasseur *Goto III* • Ligia Branice *Glossia* • Ginette Leclerc *Gonasta* • René Dary *Gomor* • Jean-Pierre Andréani *Gono* • Michel Charrel *Grymp* ■ *Dir/Scr* Walerian Borowczyk • *Cinematographer* Paul Coteret

Le Goût des Autres ★★★★ 15
Comedy 1999 · Fr · Colour · 112min

Agnès Jaoui makes her directorial debut with this astute comedy of socio-cultural manners, which she wrote with co-star Jean-Pierre Bacri. A Woody Allenesque air pervades proceedings, as we follow the efforts of Bacri's boorish businessman to impress amateur actress Anne Alvaro. The subplots involving a drug-dealing barmaid and designer-dominated wife lack focus, but Bacri and Alvaro make a delightful odd couple and helped the film garner a best foreign film Oscar nomination and a raft of domestic awards. DP French +subtitles. Swearing, drug abuse, sex scenes. *DVD*

Anne Alvaro *Clara Davaux* • Jean-Pierre Bacri *Jean-Jacques Castella* • Brigitte Catillon *Béatrice* • Alain Chabat *Bruno Deschamps* • Agnès Jaoui *Manie* • Gérard Lanvin *Franck Moreno* ■ *Dir* Agnès Jaoui • *Scr* Agnès Jaoui, Jean-Pierre Bacri

The Governess ★★ 15
Period drama 1997 · UK/Fr · Colour · 109min

Someone laced the corsets far too tight for this rigid drama set in the mid-19th century, in which Jewish girl Minnie Driver pretends to be a Gentile so she can earn money for her family working as a governess, taking a job on a remote Scottish island. It's not long, of course, before she embarks on an affair with her stiff-upper-lipped, married employer Tom Wilkinson. There's no feeling of sensuality between the mismatched pair. JB *DVD*

Minnie Driver *Rosina DaSilva/Mary Blackchurch* • Tom Wilkinson *Mr Charles Cavendish* • Florence Hoath *Clementina Cavendish* • Jonathan Rhys Meyers *Henry Cavendish* • Harriet Walter *Mrs Cavendish* • Arlene Cockburn *Lily Milk* • Emma Bird *Rebecca* ■ *Dir/Scr* Sandra Goldbacher

Government Girl ★★★ U
Second World War comedy 1943 · US · BW · 93min

This simple but affecting tale of love among the armaments stars Sonny Tufts and Olivia de Havilland and follows the understated 1940s tradition of slipping a spot of satire in among standard wartime propaganda. The two main stars give us a lively, knockabout relationship (Tufts is a production expert and de Havilland a Washington secretary), but beneath the gloss and wisecracks is a heavier message about the stifling nature of government bureaucracy. SH

Olivia de Havilland *Smokey* • Sonny Tufts *Ed Browne* • Agnes Moorehead *Mrs Wright* • Anne Shirley *May* • Jess Barker *Dana* • James Dunn *Sergeant Joe* • Paul Stewart *Branch* • Harry Davenport *Senator MacVickers* ■ *Dir* Dudley Nichols • *Scr* Dudley Nichols, from a story by Adela Rogers St Johns

Goya in Bordeaux ★★★★ 15
Biographical drama 1999 · Sp/It · Colour · 104min

Realising a long-cherished project, Carlos Saura has impeccably captured the increasingly tormented vision of the Spanish painter, who spent his declining years in French exile. The re-creation of the sombre canvases, which reflected the impact of both Goya's Napoleonic trauma and his insulating deafness, is achieved with imaginative authenticity by Vittorio Storaro, with the tableaux sequence depicting the "Disasters of War" engravings making the most impact. As the ageing Goya, Francisco Rabal excels. However, with a mastery of sound and dance complementing the beauty, the glory belongs to Saura. DP Spanish +subtitles.

Francisco Rabal *Goya* • Maribel Verdú *Duchess of Alba* • José Coronado *Goya as a young man* • Dafne Fernandez *Rosario* • Eulalia Ramón •

Leocadia • Joaquín Climent *Moratin* • Cristina Espinosa *Pepita Tudo* • José Maria Pou *Godoy* ■ *Dir/Scr* Carlos Saura

Goya's Ghosts ★★★ 15
Historical drama 2006 · Sp/US · Colour · 109min

Anyone expecting from Milos Forman an *Amadeus*-style biopic of Spanish painter Francisco Goya is likely to feel short-changed by this ambitious historical drama. Because rather than concentrating on the artist (here portrayed with colourful irreverence by Stellan Skarsgard), the director primarily uses him as a linking device between characters. The film's focus is Goya's beautiful muse, Inés (Natalie Portman), who is imprisoned by the brutal Spanish Inquisition in 1792 following false heresy charges. While a mature Portman convinces as both an artist's inspiration and, later, a broken madwoman, Javier Bardem's mumbled performance is uncharacteristically clumsy. The story, too, lacks intensity; where the picture excels, however, is in its rich visuals, with marvellous period details breathing real life into the turbulent era. SF *DVD*

Javier Bardem *Brother Lorenzo* • Natalie Portman *Inés/Alicia* • Stellan Skarsgård *Goya* • Randy Quaid *King Carlos IV* • Michael Lonsdale [Michel Lonsdale] *Grand Inquisitor* • José Luis Gómez *Tomás Bilbatúa* • Mabel Rivera *María Isabel Bilbatúa* ■ *Dir* Milos Forman • *Scr* Milos Forman, Jean-Claude Carrière

Gozu ★★ 18
Black comedy horror 2003 · Jpn · Colour · 129min

Hideki Sone is sent to execute his fellow mobster Sho Aikawa, after their gang boss decides his violent outbursts are getting too erratic. What follows is an eccentric and largely inexplicable black comedy, laced with surreal horror as cult director Takashi Miike's bizarre imagination runs riot to sometimes questionable effect. SF Japanese +subtitles. Violence, sex scenes. *DVD*

Hideki Sone *Minami* • Sho Aikawa *Ozaki* • Kimika Yoshino *Female Ozaki* • Shohei Hino *Nose* • Keiko Tomita *Innkeeper's sister* • Harumi Sone *Kazu, autistic innkeeper* • Renji Ishibashi *Boss* ■ *Dir* Takashi Miike • *Scr* Sakichi Sato

Grabbers ★★★★ 15
Science-fiction comedy horror 2012 · UK/Ire · Colour · 90min

A lovingly crafted B-movie creature feature in the grand fun/scary tradition of *Tremors*, this has bloodthirsty alien creatures invading the quiet Irish community of Erin Island and attacking the locals. The only protection available seems to be booze: high blood-alcohol levels are fatal to the fearsome, multi-tentacled monsters. Kevin Lehane's deadpan script has plenty of knowing humour, while stars Richard Coyle and Ruth Bradley, as two very different cops, provide a persuasive romantic backdrop to the mayhem. AJ *DVD* *BL*

Richard Coyle *Garda Ciaran O'Shea* • Ruth Bradley *Garda Lisa Nolan* • Russell Tovey *Dr Adam Smith* ■ *Dir* Jon Wright • *Scr* Kevin Lehane • *Cinematographer* Trevor Forrest

Grace of Monaco ★ PG
Biographical drama 2014 · Fr/US/Bel/It · Colour · 102min

Nicole Kidman stars in this flawed portrait of Hollywood legend Grace Kelly, set in the early days of her marriage to Prince Rainier III of Monaco. Tim Roth delivers an archetypal study of the Napoleon complex as the governing head of the principality, and with supporting characters drawn in equally rough strokes (including Robert Lindsay's cigar-chomping Aristotle Onassis), it's left to Kidman to hold it together. But she's two decades too old for the part. It's all about as exciting as soggy cucumber sandwiches. SP English, French +subtitles. *DVD* *BL*

Nicole Kidman *Grace Kelly* • Tim Roth *Prince Rainier III* • Frank Langella *Father Francis Tucker* • Paz Vega *Maria Callas* • Parker Posey *Madge Tivey-Faucon* • Milo Ventimiglia *Rupert Allan* • Derek Jacobi *Count Fernando D'Aillieres* • Robert

G

Lindsay *Aristotle Onassis* • Roger Ashton-Griffiths *Alfred Hitchcock* ■ *Dir* Olivier Dahan • *Scr* Arash Amel • *Cinematographer* Eric Gautier

Grace of My Heart ★★★★ 15
Romantic musical drama
1996 · US · Colour · 111min

Smart and hip, director Allison Anders's affectionate hymn to those 1960s songwriters who made New York's Brill Building the place to be rarely misses a beat. Illeana Douglas touchingly plays a thinly disguised Carole King, anxious for fame as a singer rather than composer of girl group classics, whose string of failed relationships includes one with "surf pop" genius Matt Dillon. John Turturro's turn as a shadowy Phil Spector-like figure is absolutely brilliant, there's strong support from Bridget Fonda, and the songs written expressly for the movie by Burt Bacharach, Lesley Gore and Elvis Costello are convincing. **AJ** Swearing, sex scenes.

Illeana Douglas *Denise Waverly/Edna Buxton* • Matt Dillon *Jay Phillips* • Eric Stoltz *Howard Caszatt* • Bruce Davison *John Murray* • Patsy Kensit *Cheryl Steed* • Jennifer Leigh Warren *Doris Shelly* • John Turturro *Joel Millner* • Chris Isaak *Matthew Lewis* • Bridget Fonda *Kelly Porter* ■ *Dir/Scr* Allison Anders

Grace Quigley ★★★ 15
Black comedy 1984 · US · Colour · 87min

After seeing him murder her landlord, elderly widow Katharine Hepburn hires hitman Nick Nolte to kill aged friends and neighbours who would benefit from euthanasia. Anthony Harvey's comedy is certainly ebony-hued, but the two stars carry it off in sprightly fashion. In the end, though, it all gets rather sentimental – a result, it appears, of being mauled by distributors prior to release. The film's original title was *The Ultimate Solution of Grace Quigley*. **TH** DVD

Katharine Hepburn *Grace Quigley* • Nick Nolte *Seymour Flint* • Kit Le Fever *Muriel* • Chip Zien *Dr Herman* • William Duell *Mr Jenkins* • Elizabeth Wilson *Emily Watkins* ■ *Dir* Anthony Harvey • *Scr* A Martin Zweiback

The Gracie Allen Murder Case ★★
Detective comedy mystery
1939 · US · BW · 75min

Philo Vance creator SS Van Dine had always been a fan of George Burns and Gracie Allen. So he was as disappointed as anyone when Paramount decided to drop Burns from this tailor-made Philo Vance mystery. The ditzy Gracie concentrates on driving Warren William crazy as he attempts to clear Kent Taylor of the murder of an escaped convict. More a burlesque than a mystery, the focus is firmly on Allen, as she mangles words and muddles clues. **DP**

Gracie Allen • Warren William *Philo Vance* • Ellen Drew *Ann Wilson* • Kent Taylor *Bill Brown* • Jed Prouty *Uncle Ambrose Martin* • Jerome Cowan *Daniel Mirche* ■ *Dir* Alfred E Green • *Scr* Nat Perrin, from the story by SS Van Dine

LANDMARK FILM
Dustin Hoffman breaks the mould of the good-looking. ethnically neutral film star, and changes attitudes to film sex

The Graduate ★★★★★ 15
Satirical comedy drama
1967 · US · Colour · 101min

This landmark satire on America's bourgeoisie thrust the unknown Dustin Hoffman into the limelight and won a best director Oscar for Mike Nichols. In his first major role, Hoffman is sensational as the innocent college graduate seduced by older married woman Anne Bancroft and then falling for her daughter Katharine Ross. The humour in Calder Willingham and Buck Henry's screenplay has the bite of a dry martini, Robert Surtees's stunning, innovative camerawork contributes telling visual ironies and the Simon and Garfunkel soundtrack perfectly captures the mood of disaffected youth seething beneath the laid-back exterior of 1960s California. Nichols's Oscar launched him into the top rank of

Hollywood directors. **TH** Sex scenes, nudity. DVD Blu

Dustin Hoffman *Benjamin Braddock* • Anne Bancroft *Mrs Robinson* • Katharine Ross *Elaine Robinson* • William Daniels (2) *Mr Braddock* • Elizabeth Wilson *Mrs Braddock* • Murray Hamilton *Mr Robinson* • Brian Avery (1) *Carl Smith* • Walter Brooke *Mr Maguire* ■ *Dir* Mike Nichols • *Scr* Calder Willingham, Buck Henry, from the novel by Charles Webb • *Editor* Sam O'Steen • *Production Designer* Richard Sylbert

Graffiti Bridge ★★ 12
Musical 1990 · US · Colour · 86min

After *Purple Rain*, this is the best film from the artist who was still then known as Prince. It's a sequel of sorts, which finds him once again basically playing Prince, aka the Kid. His old adversary from *Purple Rain*, Morris Day, and his band the Times return – this time they are warring nightclub owners – and once again steal the show. But despite an impressive array of musical talent, the tunes aren't memorable, and as a film director, Prince is a brilliant musician. **JF** Some swearing.

Prince *The Kid* • Ingrid Chavez *Aura* • Morris Day • Jerome Benton *Jerome* • Michael Bland • Damon Dickson • Mavis Staples *Melody Cool* • George Clinton ■ *Dir/Scr* Prince

Gran Torino ★★★ 15
Drama 2008 · US/Ger/Aus · Colour · 111min

Clint Eastwood directs and stars in this powerful film about a war veteran who finds his patch overrun by immigrants and rival gangs. Fiercely protective of his home and beloved classic car, the Gran Torino of the title, Eastwood gradually befriends the neighbouring refugees from South East Asia. Eastwood is on top form as the curmudgeonly Walt Kowalski, although his film does occasionally falter in the way it deals with the impact and aftershocks of violence. **TeS** In English, Hmong. DVD Blu

Clint Eastwood *Walt Kowalski* • Bee Vang *Thao* • Ahney Her *Sue* • Christopher Carley *Father Janovich* • Brian Haley *Mitch Kowalski* • Geraldine Hughes *Karen Kowalski* • Brian Howe *Steve Kowalski* • Dreama Walker *Ashley Kowalski* ■ *Dir* Clint Eastwood • *Scr* Nick Schenk, from a story by Schenk, Dave Johannson

The Grand Budapest Hotel ★★★★ 15
Comedy drama 2014 · US/Ger · Colour · 95min

Who knew Ralph Fiennes could be roll-around funny? But that's exactly what he is here, as the comedy keystone in writer/director Wes Anderson's weird and wonderful crime story. M Gustave (Fiennes) is the diligent yet slightly dissolute concierge at a five-star establishment in a fictional Alpine country that is being overrun by fascists in the 1930s. When a wealthy old matriarch (Tilda Swinton) is murdered, Gustave becomes the prime suspect. Newcomer Tony Revolori plays Gustave's loyal protégé, Zero, but he is somewhat overshadowed by the rest of a starry cast that includes Edward Norton, Adrien Brody, Willem Dafoe and Bill Murray. **SP** Swearing, sexual references, brief nudity. DVD Blu

Ralph Fiennes *M Gustave* • Tony Revolori *Zero* • Edward Norton *Henckels* • Tilda Swinton *Madame D* • Adrien Brody *Dmitri* • Bill Murray *M Ivan* ■ *Dir* Wes Anderson • *Scr* Wes Anderson, from a story by Anderson, Hugo Guinness

Grand Canyon ★★★★ 15
Drama 1991 · US · Colour · 128min

After the critical mauling he received for his ill-judged black comedy *I Love You to Death*, writer/director Lawrence Kasdan returned to the ensemble territory of *The Big Chill*. However, the warm nostalgia of the latter is largely absent this time as Kasdan attempts to come to grips with the fear and violence afflicting modern-day Los Angeles. It's an ambitious task, and at times the script strays toward sentimental melodrama, but Kasdan's direction is as assured as ever. He is rewarded with excellent performances, including a scene-stealing role for Steve Martin, who plays an arrogant film producer

reportedly modelled on action master Joel Silver. **JF** DVD

Danny Glover *Simon* • Steve Martin *Davis* • Kevin Kline *Mack* • Mary McDonnell *Claire* • Mary-Louise Parker *Dee* • Alfre Woodard *Jane* • Jeremy Sisto *Roberto* • Tina Lifford *Deborah* ■ *Dir* Lawrence Kasdan • *Scr* Lawrence Kasdan, Meg Kasdan

Grand Central ★★★ 15
Romantic drama
2013 · Fr/Austria · Colour · 90min

A nuclear power station might seem an unlikely setting for an erotically charged drama but it adds further jeopardy to an already dangerous liaison. *A Prophet's* Tahar Rahim is the restless protagonist, who's befriended by an avuncular veteran before becoming passionately entangled with the man's fiancée (Léa Seydoux). Writer/director Rebecca Zlotowski takes admirable risks and Rahim makes for a complex, convincing lead, yet Seydoux remains a strutting, pouting enigma in this flawed, provocative curio. **EAS** French +subtitles. Swearing, nudity. DVD

Tahar Rahim *Gary* • Léa Seydoux *Karole* • Olivier Gourmet *Gilles* • Denis Ménochet *Toni* • Johan Libéreau *Tcherno* • Nozha Khouadra *Maria* ■ *Dir* Rebecca Zlotowski • *Scr* Rebecca Zlotowski, Gaëlle Macé

Le Grand Chemin ★★★★ 15
Drama 1987 · Fr · Colour · 106min

A sugary confection with a hard centre may not be to everyone's taste, but the crunches in this charming rites-of-passage picture make the melting moments all the more sweet. Anémone and Richard Bohringer both won Césars (the French equivalent of an Oscar) for their performances as a grief-stricken couple whose care of a nine-year-old Parisian boy results in a bitter tug of war for his affections. Young Antoine Hubert is endearingly wide-eyed throughout his introduction to the ways of grown-ups and Vanessa Guedj is quite wonderful as the knowing tomboy who acts as his guide. **DP** French +subtitles.

Anémone *Marcelle* • Richard Bohringer *Pelo* • Antoine Hubert *Louis* • Vanessa Guedj *Martine* • Christine Pascal *Claire* • Raoul Billerey *Priest* • Pascale Roberts *Yvonne* • Marie Matheron *Solange* ■ *Dir/Scr* Jean-Loup Hubert

Grand Hotel ★★★★★ U
Drama 1932 · US · BW · 107min

This star-filled melodrama became a blueprint for almost every glossy Hollywood soap opera that followed it. Greta Garbo, John and Lionel Barrymore, Joan Crawford and Wallace Beery vie for screen time as the various residents of the Berlin hotel, but it is art director Cedric Gibbons who deserves the plaudits for the luscious look of the film. One of the biggest projects in Hollywood at the time, the all-star cast caused MGM billing problems. In the end, the word "Garbo" appeared at the top of the bill to honour a clause stating she would have top billing, while the other actors were billed in alphabetical order below. **JB** DVD Blu

Greta Garbo *Grusinskaya* • John Barrymore *The Baron Felix Benvenuto Frihern Von Gaigern* • Joan Crawford *Flaemmchen* • Wallace Beery *General Director Preysing* • Lionel Barrymore *Otto Kringelein* • Jean Hersholt *Senf* ■ *Dir* Edmund Goulding • *Scr* William A Drake, from his play, from the play *Menschen im Hotel* by Vicki Baum • *Cinematographer* William Daniels (1) • *Costume Designer* Adrian

Grand National Night ★★★
Crime drama 1953 · UK · BW · 77min

Having been a hit on stage and then as a radio serial, Dorothy and Campbell Christie's play is ably brought to the screen. It's very much in the Edgar Wallace tradition, with Nigel Patrick's friends in the racing fraternity standing by him after his bitchy wife, Moira Lister, is accidentally killed during a drunken squabble. The means by which the corpse arrives in Liverpool and the final twist strain the credibility slightly. But the cat-and-mouse game involving Michael Hordern (who

excels as a dogged detective) is teased out with mischievous ingenuity. **DP**

Nigel Patrick *Gerald Coates* • Moira Lister *Babs Coates* • Beatrice Campbell *Joyce Penrose* • Betty Ann Davies *Pinkie Collins* • Michael Hordern *Inspector Ayling* • Noel Purcell *Philip Balfour* ■ *Dir* Bob McNaught • *Scr* Bob McNaught, Val Valentine, from the play by Campbell Christie, Dorothy Christie

Le Grand Pardon ★★★
Crime drama 1981 · Fr · Colour · 125min

Alexandre Arcady scored a big hit with this second feature. Inspired by actual events, it explores the tensions that exist between the Arab and Jewish gangsters who compete for influence in the Parisian underworld. There's no shortage of imposing performances, most notably from Roger Hanin, as the racketeer who takes his family and heritage as seriously as his empire, and Bernard Giraudeau, who stirs up a turf war with racial, as well as criminal implications. However, the action sequences lack invention, although the film is vastly superior to the 1992 Miami sequel, *Day of Atonement*. **DP** French, English +subtitles.

Roger Hanin *Raymond Bettoun* • Jean-Louis Trintignant *Commissionaire Duché* • Bernard Giraudeau *Pascal Villars* • Richard Berry *Maurice Bettoun* • Clio Goldsmith *Viviane* • Anny Duperey *Carole* • Richard Bohringer *The Sexton* • Robert Hossein *Manuel Carreras* ■ *Dir* Alexandre Arcady • *Scr* Alexandre Arcady, Daniel Saint-Hamont, Alain Le Henry

Grand Piano ★★★ 15
Thriller 2013 · Sp · Colour · 86min

A virtuoso pianist on the comeback trail experiences his own personal symphony of horror in this tantalising thriller. Elijah Wood returns to play a concert five years after bottling out, but this time he has death threats hanging over him. A sweeping ode to Hitchcock, this looks grand and has plenty of well-edited moments. Wood is suitably jittery, but the tension fizzles once the reasons for his torment become all-too evident. **JA** Violence, swearing. DVD Blu

Elijah Wood *Tom Selznick* • John Cusack *Clem* • Kerry Bishé *Emma Selznick* • Tamsin Egerton *Ashley* ■ *Dir* Eugenio Mira • *Scr* Damien Chazelle

Grand Prix ★★★ PG
Motor racing drama 1966 · US · Colour · 168min

One of the best motor-racing films ever made, filmed in Cinerama-SuperPanavision – the Bugatti of screen ratios. Racing fans will adore the glimpses of Graham Hill, the banking at Monza and the 1960s speed machines, which seem so flimsy compared to the cars that race today. There are spectacular stunts, of course, but the human pile-ups between the races scrape the bottom of the drama cliché barrel. **AT** DVD

James Garner *Pete Aron* • Eva Marie Saint *Louise Frederickson* • Yves Montand *Jean-Pierre Sarti* • Toshiro Mifune *Izo Yamura* • Brian Bedford *Scott Stoddard* • Jessica Walter *Pat* • Antonio Sabato *Nino Barlini* • Françoise Hardy *Lisa* ■ *Dir* John Frankenheimer • *Scr* Robert Alan Aurthur, from his story • *Editors* Fredric Steinkamp, Henry Berman, Stewart Linder, Frank Santillo

The Grand Seduction ★★ 12
Comedy 2013 · Can/US · Colour · 108min

Brendan Gleeson strays off course after putting Ireland back on the movie-making map with *The Guard* and *Calvary*. But this portrait of a Celtic community in Newfoundland is contrived in its quaintness, with Gleeson playing the loudest mouth in a fishing village where the waters have nothing left to give. There are echoes of 1983 classic *Local Hero* here, except that director Don McKellar inadvertently gives the story an unappealing, cynical edge. **SP** Sexual, drug references. DVD

Brendan Gleeson *Murray French* • Taylor Kitsch *Dr Paul Lewis* • Gordon Pinsent *Simon* • Liane Balaban *Kathleen* ■ *Dir* Don McKellar • *Scr* Michael Dowse, Ken Scott

U SUITABLE FOR ALL · Uc SUITABLE ESPECIALLY FOR YOUNG CHILDREN (DVD ONLY) · PG PARENTAL GUIDANCE · 12A UNDER 12s TO BE ACCOMPANIED (CINEMA ONLY)

Grand Slam ★★★
Crime thriller 1967 · It/Sp/W Ger · Colour · 119min

This *Rififi*-style heist movie should have been a corker. Edward G. Robinson is the brains of the operation, while Klaus Kinski and Janet Leigh co-star as a former Nazi with a hair-trigger temper and the ice-cool secretary with the key to a fabulous gem collection. There's even the added bonus of the Rio backdrop and a twist ending. Yet somehow this thriller doesn't quite come off, as Robinson and gang boss Adolfo Celi are given too little to do, Kinski over-indulges in his trademark neuroses and gigolo Robert Hoffmann's seduction of Leigh lacks wit and charm. DP

Janet Leigh *Mary Ann* • Robert Hoffmann *Jean-Paul Audry* • Edward G Robinson *Prof James Anders* • Adolfo Celi *Mark Milford* • Klaus Kinski *Erich Weiss* • Georges Rigaud *Gregg* • Riccardo Cucciolla *Agostino* ■ *Dir* Giuliano Montaldo · *Scr* Mino Roli, Marcello Fondato, Antonio de la Loma, Augusto Caminito, from a story by Roli, Caminito, Bianchini

Grand Theft Auto ★★PG
Action comedy 1977 · US · Colour · 84min

Ron Howard's full-length feature directing debut is very much a family affair. Made under the aegis of that canny judge of film talent Roger Corman, this was co-written by Howard's father Rance (who also appears) and offers a role for brother Clint. The film itself is little more than than an extended *Dukes of Hazzard* adventure. JF DVD

Ron Howard *Sam Freeman* · Nancy Morgan *Paula Powers* · Marion Ross *Vivian Hedgeworth* · Peter Isacksen *Sparky* · Barry Cahill *Digby Powers* · Hoke Howell *Preacher* · Lew Brown (2) *Jack Clepper* · Elizabeth Rogers *Priscilla Powers* ■ *Dir* Ron Howard · *Scr* Ron Howard, Rance Howard

Grand Theft Parsons ★★★★12
Black comedy based on a true story 2003 · US/UK · Colour · 84min

Jackass stunt-show star Johnny Knoxville plays his first leading role in this spirited film charting the bizarre road trip one man took in the name of friendship. Knoxville plays Phil Kaufman, the maverick road manager of cult 1970s US country singer Gram Parsons. Having made a pact with Parsons prior to the performer's untimely death, Kaufman steals the coffin to cremate the corpse according to his buddy's final wishes. Michael Shannon is hilarious as a hippy hearse-owner, while Christina Applegate adds sass as a fictional gold-digging ex of Parsons. Wittily scripted and lovingly directed. SF DVD

Johnny Knoxville *Phil Kaufman* · Christina Applegate *Barbara Mansfield* · Michael Shannon *Larry Oster-Berg* · Marley Shelton *Susie* · Robert Forster *Stanley Parsons* · Phil Kaufman *Handcuffed felon* ■ *Dir* David Caffrey · *Scr* Jeremy Drysdale

La Grande Bouffe ★★★18
Satirical comedy 1973 · Fr · Colour · 124min

Marco Ferreri's satire is like Buñuel's *The Discreet Charm of the Bourgeoisie* in reverse: where Buñuel's characters never quite get to their waiting feast, Ferreri's gather in a villa and gorge themselves on food, wine and women. This is not a picture for bulimics or the obese; nor is it as subversively funny as it might have been. Nevertheless, there are some great scenes – notably the moment when the ample buttocks of Andréa Ferréol are used to mould a vast slab of *mousse de foie gras*. AT French +subtitles. DVD

Marcello Mastroianni *Pilot* · Ugo Tognazzi *Chef* · Michel Piccoli *TV producer* · Philippe Noiret *Judge* · Andréa Ferréol *Teacher* · Monique Chaumette *Madeleine* · Florence Giorgetti *Anne* · Rita Scherrer *Anulka* ■ *Dir* Marco Ferreri · *Scr* Marco Ferreri, Rafael Arcona

La Grande Illusion ★★★★★U
Classic First World War drama 1937 · Fr · BW · 102min

Critics vie to heap superlatives on Jean Renoir's masterpiece and landmark of world cinema, but one of the film's highest accolades of all came from Nazi propaganda boss Josef Goebbels, who classified it as "Cinematographic Enemy No 1". Made on the eve of the Second World War but set in a German PoW camp during the First World War, it has also been called the ultimate ant-war film – no small claim since it does not contain a single battle scene, making its point with dialogue rather than action. Though not an easy film, it's worth the effort. PF French +subtitles. DVD BL

Jean Gabin *Maréchal* · Erich von Stroheim *Von Rauffenstein* · Pierre Fresnay *Capt De Boeldieu* · Dalio [Marcel Dalio] *Rosenthal* · Dita Parlo *Peasant woman* · Julien Carette *Actor* · Gaston Modot *Engineer* · Jean Dasté *Schoolteacher* · Georges Peclet *French soldier* · *Dir* Jean Renoir · *Scr* Charles Spaak, Jean Renoir · *Cinematographer* Christian Matras · *Art Director* Lourié [Eugène Lourié]

Les Grandes Manoeuvres ★★★★U
Romantic comedy 1955 · Fr/It · Colour · 103min

One of the pioneers of French silent and early sound cinema, René Clair's critical fortunes had dipped dramatically by the time he made his first colour feature. Yet this is one of the glories of a career studded with delights. Combining wit and grace with comic impudence, Clair concocts a frothy comedy that turns into a poignant drama, as dragoon Gérard Philipe realises that his reputation as a gadabout has thwarted his one chance of true love with Michèle Morgan whom he wagered his comrades he could seduce. DP French +subtitles. DVD

Michèle Morgan *Marie Louise Riviere* · Gérard Philipe *Lt Armand de la Verne* · Brigitte Bardot *Lucie* · Yves Robert *Felix* · Jean Desailly *Victor Duverger* · Pierre Dux *Colonel* · Jacques François *Rudolph* · Lise Delamare *Juliette* · Jacqueline Maillan *Juliette* ■ *Dir* René Clair · *Scr* René Clair, Jerome Geronimi, Jean Marsan, from a story by Courteline

Grandeur et Décadence d'un Petit Commerce de Cinéma ★★★
Drama 1986 · Fr · Colour · 90min

Ostensibly seeking to greenlight an adaptation of a James Hadley Chase novel, failed auteur Jean-Pierre Léaud and producer Jean-Pierre Mocky end up ogling the auditioning starlets, while spouting theories and dropping the names of those ensconced in the cinematic pantheon. With former New Wave icon Jean-Luc Godard interrupting these rambling discourses to denounce everything from pretentiousness to Polanski, this is a scathing exposé of the commercial considerations underpinning even the most chaste art house project. DP In French.

Jean-Pierre Léaud *Gaspar Bazin* · Jean-Pierre Mocky *Jean Almereyda* · Marie Valéra *Eurydice* ■ *Dir* Jean-Luc Godard · *Scr* Jean-Luc Godard, from a novel by James Hadley Chase

Grandma ★★★★15
Comedy drama 2015 · US · Colour · 78min

In her first leading role since 1988, Lily Tomlin triumphantly blows the doors off this calm yet controversial drama from *About a Boy* director Paul Weitz. As poet and academic Elle Reid, she must help her 18-year-old granddaughter Sage (Julia Garner) who is, in the old fashioned sense, "in trouble". Sage feels she can't ask her corporate executive mother (Marcia Gay Harden) for help and Elle thinks she knows why, beginning a process of unlocking skeletons from the family closet. It's not for the whole family, but it is one hell of a ride for anyone with a lot of miles on the biological clock. KK Swearing, drug abuse

Lily Tomlin *Elle Reid* · Julia Garner *Sage* · Marcia Gay Harden *Judy* · Judy Greer *Olivia* · Sam Elliott *Karl* · Nat Wolf[2] *Cam* ■ *Dir/Scr* Paul Weitz

Grandma's Boy ★★★★U
Silent comedy 1922 · US · BW · 61min

Harold Lloyd hit the big time with this first five-reel feature. Essentially a remake of the Douglas Fairbanks romp *The Mollycoddle* (1920), it charts Lloyd's progress from timid nobody to town hero and so anticipated the go-getter persona that would become his trademark. However, he only comes to conquer troublesome tramp Dick Sutherland and bully Charles Stevenson with the help of Grandma Anna Townsend and the talisman that supposedly got his grandfather through the Civil War. The shrunken suit and the mothballs in the candy sequences rank among the highlights. But this is a delight throughout. DP DVD

Harold Lloyd *Mildred's beau* · Mildred Davis *Mildred, the girl* · Anna Townsend *Grandmother* · Charles A Stevenson *Bully/union officer in flashback* · Noah Young *Sheriff* · Dick Sutherland *Rolling stone, tramp* ■ *Dir* Fred C Newmeyer · *Scr* Hal Roach, Sam Taylor, Jean Havez, Thomas J Crizer

A Grandpa for Christmas ★★
Seasonal comedy drama 2007 · US · Colour · 85min

Ernest Borgnine brings warmth and spirit to a simple tale of family values in this uplifting festive drama. He plays a retired musical actor who has to care for a granddaughter he didn't know existed after his estranged daughter is hospitalised. There's plenty of tugging of the heartstrings and few surprises, yet despite its saccharine predictability the feature has a wholesome charm that's hard to resist. SF

Ernest Borgnine *Bert O'Riley* · Juliette Goglia *Becca O'Riley* · Katherine Helmond *Roxie* · Richard Libertini *Karl Sugerman* · Tracy Nelson *Marie O'Riley* · Jamie Farr *Adam* ■ *Dir* Harvey Frost · *Scr* David Alexander

Grandview, USA ★★15
Drama 1984 · US · Colour · 97min

The cast may be a who's who of future stars, but the plot of this teen angst drama is right out of yesteryear. Set in the Midwest of the mid-1980s, the film follows Jamie Lee Curtis's bid to keep her father's demolition derby in business, while sidestepping the adoring advances of star driver Patrick Swayze. C Thomas Howell is also involved, but the smartest acting comes from veterans Troy Donahue and M Emmet Walsh. DP

Jamie Lee Curtis *Michelle "Mike" Cody* · C Thomas Howell *Tim Pearson* · Patrick Swayze *Ernie "Slam" Webster* · Troy Donahue *Donny Vinton* · Jennifer Jason Leigh *Candy Webster* · William Windom *Bob Cody* · Carole Cook *Betty Welles* · M Emmet Walsh *Mr Clark* ■ *Dir* Randal Kleiser · *Scr* Ken Hixon

The Grapes of Wrath ★★★★★PG
Classic period drama 1940 · US · BW · 123min

In this magnificent adaptation of John Steinbeck's Depression-era novel, Henry Fonda plays the farmer who leads his family from the dust bowl of Oklahoma to the promised land of California. The scene in which their home is bulldozed is heart-rending and their fate as migrant workers has lasting power. But the film also has some weaknesses, notably a corny religious symbolism in place of Steinbeck's raw politics. It's stupendously photographed by Gregg Toland, but the Oscars went to director John Ford and Jane Darwell, who's unforgettable. AT DVD BL

Henry Fonda *Tom Joad* · Jane Darwell *Ma Joad* · John Carradine *Casey* · Charley Grapewin *Grandpa Joad* · Dorris Bowdon *Rosaharn* · Russell Simpson *Pa Joad* · OZ Whitehead *Al* · John Qualen *Muley* · Eddie Quillan *Connie* · Zeffie Tilbury *Grandma Joad* · Frank Sully *Noah* ■ *Dir* John Ford · *Scr* Nunnally Johnson, from the novel by John Steinbeck · *Music* Alfred Newman · *Art Directors* Richard Day, Mark-Lee Kirk

Grass ★★★★15
Documentary 1999 · Can · Colour and BW · 78min

In the 1940s, New York's Mayor Fiorello La Guardia commissioned a report that discredited accepted views on the medical, psychological and social impact of marijuana. Yet its possession remains a criminal offence and documentarist Ron Mann here sets out to discover why. Although it's narrated by hemp advocate Woody Harrelson and utilises clips from famously alarmist movies such as *Reefer Madness* and *Marijuana: Assassin of Youth*, this superbly researched film isn't just a pot-head's plea for tolerance. Mann also explores the racist history of US drug laws and the way Harry J Anslinger, director of the Federal Bureau of Narcotics from 1930-67, used them to further his own career. DP DVD

Woody Harrelson *Narrator* ■ *Dir* Ron Mann · *Scr* Solomon Vesta

Grass: a Nation's Battle for Life ★★★★
Silent documentary 1925 · US · BW · 70min

Although they are best remembered for *King Kong*, Merian C Cooper and Ernest B Schoedsack were renowned travel chroniclers during the silent era. The film is full of spectacular set pieces, such as the perilous crossing of the torrential Karun river and the final barefoot ascent. But there's a troublingly civilised arrogance about the possibility that, like their mentor, Robert Flaherty, the pair manipulated the action by urging 50,000 Bakhtiari nomads to take the most treacherous (and, thus, most cinematic) route across the Zardeh Kuh mountains in search of grazing land. DP

■ *Dir* Merian Cooper [Merian C Cooper], Ernest B Schoedsack, Marguerite Harrison

The Grass Harp ★★★PG
Drama 1995 · US · Colour · 102min

Charles Matthau's film based on Truman Capote's autobiographical novel may be old-fashioned, but it also has the polish that used to make studio pictures so irresistible. The exceptional ensemble cast gives this memoir of a Deep South childhood in the late 1930s its charm. As the chalk-and-cheese sisters who raise orphan Edward Furlong, Piper Laurie and Sissy Spacek bind together the episodic narrative. They also give it a credibility that makes Jack Lemmon and Walter Matthau's more outrageous turns delightful rather than damaging. DP Some swearing. DVD

Piper Laurie *Dolly Talbo* · Sissy Spacek *Verena Talbo* · Walter Matthau *Judge Charlie Cool* · Edward Furlong *Collin Fenwick* · Nell Carter *Catherine Creek* · Jack Lemmon *Dr Morris Ritz* · Mary Steenburgen *Sister Ida* · Sean Patrick Flanery *Riley Henderson* ■ *Dir* Charles Matthau · *Scr* Stirling Silliphant, Kirk Ellis, from the novel by Truman Capote

The Grass Is Greener ★★PG
Romantic comedy 1960 · UK · Colour · 100min

Too much talk, too little action and a miscast Robert Mitchum contribute to this disappointing screen adaptation of the West End hit. The plot rests on the romantic complications that ensue when American multimillionaire Mitchum takes a tour of English earl Cary Grant's stately home and falls for his wife, played by Deborah Kerr. Director Stanley Donen, usually at home with soufflé-light comedy romance, fails to rescue this one from its all-too-evident stage origins and a leaden script. RK DVD

Cary Grant *Victor Rhyall* · Deborah Kerr *Hilary Rhyall* · Robert Mitchum *Charles Delacro* · Jean Simmons *Hattie Durrant* · Moray Watson *Sellers* ■ *Dir* Stanley Donen · *Scr* Hugh Williams, Margaret Williams, from their play

The Grasshopper ★
Drama 1970 · US · Colour · 95min

Bored with her small-town life in British Columbia, Jacqueline Bisset becomes a Las Vegas showgirl and pop star's girlfriend. Then she moves to Los Angeles, gets beaten up and learns the meaning of life. Produced and scripted by Garry Marshall and Jerry Belson, the team behind the sitcoms *Happy Days* and *Mork and Mindy*, this is a flashily directed "message movie" dressed up with lots of sex and violence. AT Swearing, violence.

G

Jacqueline Bisset *Christine Adams* • Jim Brown *Tommy Marcott* • Joseph Cotten *Richard Morgan* • Corbett Monica *Danny Raymond* • Ramon Bieri *Roosevelt Dekker* • Christopher Stone *Jay Rigney* • Roger Garrett *Buck Brown* • Stanley Adams *Buddy Miller* ■ *Dir* Jerry Paris • *Scr* Jerry Belson, Garry Marshall, from the novel *The Passing of Evil* by Mark McShane

Grassroots ★★ 15
Comedy drama based on a true story
2012 · US · Colour · 98min

After years of working in television, Stephen Gyllenhaal (father of Jake and Maggie) returns to directing movies with this quirky true-life comedy about US local politics. Jason Biggs (of *American Pie* fame) stars as an out-of-work journalist-turned-campaign manager to best friend Joel David Moore, who's determined to oust local councillor Cedric the Entertainer for failing to expand Seattle's congestion-busting monorail system. The movie is a decently made and amiably acted David-and-Goliath tale, but drifts along without really registering. DA Swearing, sexual references, drug abuse.

Jason Biggs *Phil Campbell* • Joel David Moore *Grant Cogswell* • Lauren Ambrose *Emily Bowen* • Tom Arnold *Tommy* • Cedric the Entertainer *Richard McIver* ■ *Dir* Stephen Gyllenhaal • *Scr* Stephen Gyllenhaal, Justin Rhodes, from the non-fiction book *Zioncheck for President: a True Story of Idealism and Madness in American Politics* by Phil Campbell

Grateful Dawg ★★ 12
Music documentary 2000 · US · Colour · 78min

Grateful Dead frontman guitarist Jerry Garcia and mandolin-playing musicologist David Grisman met at a concert in the mid-1960s and bonded over their shared love of bluegrass music. The pair lost touch after their short-lived band Old & In the Way split up in the late 1970s and this respectful documentary records the artistic consequences of their reunion some dozen years later. Unfortunately, director Gillian Grisman is too over-awed by her subjects to pry into the darker corners of their relationship. DP Swearing. *DVD*

■ *Dir* Gillian Grisman

Grave Encounters ★★ 15
Horror 2010 · US · Colour · 89min

This addition to the sub-genre of "found footage" shockers sees the crew of a ghost-hunting reality TV show locked inside an abandoned psychiatric hospital. As night wears on, chilling and violent apparitions of patients, doctors and nurses make their presence known, while the building itself twists and contorts to prevent its visitors from leaving. First-time directors the Vicious Brothers serve up a series of heart-racing jolts, although the majority of them are lazily signposted. Think an indoor *Blair Witch Project*, but with none of the subtlety or suspense of unseen, off-camera horrors. TeS *DVD*

Sean Rogerson *Lance Preston* • Juan Riedinger *Matt White* • Ashleigh Gryzko *Sasha Parker* • Merwin Mondesir *TC Gibson* • Mackenzie Gray *Houston Gray* ■ *Dir/Scr* The Vicious Brothers

Grave of the Fireflies ★★★★ 12
Animated Second World War drama
1988 · Jpn · Colour · 90min

Isao Takahata's film for the famous Studio Ghibli opens with the death of its narrator, 14-year-old Seita, who is looking after his young sister, Setsuko, in the days after the end of the Second World War, and it's been lauded as a pacifist statement. But, this masterpiece of Japanimation is just as much a study of the pride and selfishness that overtake ordinarily decent people in the depths of a crisis. With their mother dead and their naval father presumed killed, the siblings seek shelter with an aunt before mutual antipathy drives them on to the streets of Kobe, which has been fire-bombed by the US Air Force. The hopelessness of the children's situation makes for harrowing viewing, but the nocturnal sequence with the fireflies has an indelible melancholic beauty. DP Japanese +subtitles. Violence. *DVD*

■ *Dir* Isao Takahata • *Scr* Isao Takahata, from the novel *Hotaru No Haka* by Akiyuki Nosaka

Graves End ★★
Horror mystery 2005 · US · Colour · 90min

This convoluted but tongue-in-cheek horror mystery is set in a small American town (population 666!), where paroled criminals get a seriously unexpected welcome. Steven Williams stars as the FBI agent who uncovers dark secrets in the eponymous community while investigating a violent felon's disappearance. Despite playing like an extended soap opera episode, the film is surprisingly gruesome, while corny dialogue and exaggerated performances from the likes of Eric Roberts add to the B-movie-style fun. SF

Eric Roberts *Tarkington Alexander Graves/Tag* • Steven Williams *Paul Rickman* • Daniel Roebuck *Sheriff Hooper* • Valerie Mikita *Krissi Graves* • Fairly Tull *Maudy* • Edward Perotti *Doc* ■ *Dir* James Marlowe • *Scr* Rick Askew (2), James Marlowe, Brian Pugnetti, Anthony Santucci

Gravesend ★★★ 18
Crime drama 1995 · US · Colour · 81min

A madcap adventure for a quartet of Brooklyn buddies becomes a dead-end nightmare. This breathless "stash the stiff" opus frantically blends voiceovers, flashbacks, character profiles and graveyard humour. Salvatore Stabile's feature debut - made for just $5,000 when he was only 19 - so impressed Steven Spielberg that he offered him a contract at DreamWorks. DP Swearing, violence.

Thomas Brandise *Mikey* • Tom Malloy *Chicken* • Michael Parducci *Ray* • Tony Tucci *Zane* • Sean Quinn *Mark* • Carmel Altomare *Zane's mother* • Teresa Spinelli *Zane's grandmother* ■ *Dir/Scr* Salvatore Stabile

Graveyard Shift ★★★ 18
Supernatural horror
1986 · US/Can · Colour · 82min

This intriguing modern-dress vampire movie plays rather like *Taxi Driver* with a screenplay by Bram Stoker. Its bloodsucker hero, credibly brought to life (after death) by Silvio Oliviero, works nights as a New York cabbie - a great way to meet potential supper guests. Director Gerard Ciccoritti shows great flair for fetishist images though his rock video-style technique ultimately grates. But the urban night-time setting is neatly evoked, and it was followed by an underwhelming sequel, *The Understudy: Graveyard Shift II*. RS *DVD*

Silvio Oliviero *Stephen Tsepes* • Helen Papas *Michelle* • Cliff Stoker *Eric Hayden* • Dorin Ferber *Gilda* ■ *Dir* Gerard Ciccoritti [Jerry Ciccoritti] • *Scr* Gérard Ciccoritti

Graveyard Shift ★★ 18
Horror 1990 · US · Colour · 82min

Adapted from the Stephen King short story, this substandard chiller could just about be seen as an anti-capitalist parable. Essentially, it's an excuse to trot out all the clichés of the splatter-movie genre, with a giant man-eating rodent as the central menace. David Andrews is a bloodless hero and director Ralph S Singleton's acquiescence to racial and physical stereotypes is regrettable. DP Violence, swearing.

David Andrews (2) *John Hall* • Kelly Wolf *Jane Wisconsky* • Stephen Macht *Warwick* • Brad Dourif *Tucker Cleveland* • Andrew Divoff *Danson* ■ *Dir* Ralph S Singleton • *Scr* John Esposito, from the short story *Graveyard Shift* from the book *Night Shift* by Stephen King

Gravity ★★★★★ 12
Space thriller 2013 · US/UK · Colour · 88min

This intimate yet spectacular tale stars Sandra Bullock as a medical engineer making her first space-shuttle mission alongside experienced astronaut George Clooney. As the team carries out a service on the Hubble Space Telescope, a planned missile strike on a defunct Russian satellite sends shards of debris hurtling towards them, instantly destroying their shuttle. With limited oxygen supplies remaining, Bullock and Clooney find themselves trapped in the void, setting the clock ticking on an intense and exhilarating fight for survival. The special effects are tremendous, while Bullock's almost balletic performance imbues this fantasy with a humanity and grace that beautifully complements director Alfonso Cuarón's breathtaking vision. DW Swearing. *DVD* ▣ ▣

Sandra Bullock *Ryan Stone* • George Clooney *Matt Kowalski* • Ed Harris *Mission control* ■ *Dir* Alfonso Cuarón • *Scr* Alfonso & Jonás Cuarón • *Cinematographer* Emmanuel Lubezki • *Music* Steven Price • *Editors* Mark Sanger, Alfonso Cuarón • *Production Designer* Andy Nicholson

Gray Lady Down ★★★ PG
Disaster movie 1978 · US · Colour · 105min

A flurry of clichés almost engulfs this aquatic thriller about a Charlton Heston-commanded nuclear submarine stuck on the edge of an ocean canyon and awaiting a Stacy Keach-commanded rescue mission. Everything that can happen does happen, from ramming by a Norwegian freighter to earth slides, but David Greene's direction transcends banalities with pace and panache, while Heston's authority is the sort that could walk on water. TH *DVD*

Charlton Heston *Captain Paul Blanchard* • David Carradine *Captain Gates* • Stacy Keach *Captain Bennett* • Ned Beatty *Mickey* • Stephen McHattie *Murphy* • Ronny Cox *Commander Samuelson* • Dorian Harewood *Fowler* • Rosemary Forsyth *Vickie* ■ *Dir* David Greene • *Scr* Howard Sackler, James Whittaker, Frank P Rosenberg (adaptation), from the novel *Event 1000* by David Lavallee

Grayeagle ★★ PG
Western 1977 · US · Colour · 99min

Independent film-maker Charles B Pierce attempts a low-rent version of John Ford's classic *The Searchers*, this time telling the story from the Indians' point of view, with Ben Johnson in the lead and Natalie Wood's sister Lana as the girl kidnapped by the Cheyenne. With a cast that also includes Jack Elam, this isn't unwatchable, but its aspirations to worthiness soon become tiresome. TS

Ben Johnson (1) *John Colter* • Iron Eyes Cody *Standing Bear* • Lana Wood *Beth Colter* • Jack Elam *Trapper Willis* • Paul Fix *Running Wolf* • Alex Cord *Grayeagle* • Jacob Daniels [Jacob Jerry Daniels] *Scar* • Jimmy Clem *Abe Stoud* • Charles B Pierce *Bugler* ■ *Dir/Scr* Charles B Pierce

Gray's Anatomy ★★★
Comedy 1996 · US/UK · Colour · 80min

The writer and actor Spalding Gray is probably best known for his filmed monologue *Swimming to Cambodia*, inspired by his experiences as a minor cast member of *The Killing Fields*. This is another such monologue, this time starting from Gray's discovery of a sight defect that required some drastic surgery. Director Steven Soderbergh films Gray at a desk, circling him and presenting a strange assortment of backdrops to the diverting and wildly discursive talk. Readers are warned that the film begins with some shocking images of eye injuries. AT Swearing.

Spalding Gray ■ *Dir* Steven Soderbergh • *Scr* Spalding Gray, Renée Shafransky, from their performance piece

Grease ★★★★ PG
Musical 1978 · US · Colour · 105min

Fresh from *Saturday Night Fever*, John Travolta was the biggest movie star in the world when he teamed up with Olivia Newton-John to help turn one of Broadway's biggest hits into one of Hollywood's most successful musicals. The film aims to evoke nostalgia for a time before most of its audience would have been born - 1950s America - where Rydell High is the setting for a rather slender tale of teenage love and pre-Vietnam innocence. It succeeds in the task, thanks to some toe-tapping numbers, sprightly hoofing and slick performances. PF *DVD* ▣

John Travolta *Danny Zuko* • Olivia Newton-John *Sandy Olsson* • Stockard Channing *Betty Rizzo* • Jeff Conaway *Kenickie* • Barry Pearl *Doody* • Michael Tucci *Sonny* • Kelly Ward *Putzie* ■ *Dir* Randal Kleiser • *Scr* Bronte Woodard, Allan Carr, from the musical by Warren Casey, Jim Jacobs

Grease 2 ★★ PG
Musical 1982 · US · Colour · 109min

An unprepossessing sequel to the massive hit, this is notable for a great title song by the Four Tops and a then-unknown Michelle Pfeiffer in a clinging short skirt. This is the story of Rydell High some years on from those halcyon days of drainpipe trousers and stiff petticoats. The problem is that director and choreographer Patricia Birch tries to bring those high steppin' innocent production values to an altogether grittier era of emerging 1960s liberalism. SH *DVD*

Michelle Pfeiffer *Stephanie* • Maxwell Caulfield *Michael* • Didi Conn *Frenchy* • Eve Arden *Ms McGee* • Sid Caesar *Coach Calhoun* • Adrian Zmed *Johnny Nogerilli* • Christopher McDonald *Goose* • Peter Frechette *Lou DiMucci* • Lorna Luft *Paulette Rebchuck* ■ *Dir* Patricia Birch • *Scr* Ken Finkleman

Greased Lightning ★★ PG
Biographical comedy drama
1977 · US · Colour · 92min

Richard Pryor never really looks comfortable in this story of the America's first black stock-car racing driver, Wendell Scott, who battled prejudice to reach the top of his chosen profession. It's a fascinating story, but the main problem is that it never makes up its mind whether it is a straightforward biopic or a comedy. However, the supporting cast can't be faulted, and there's some strong racing footage. JF

Richard Pryor *Wendell Scott* • Beau Bridges *Hutch* • Pam Grier *Mary Jones* • Cleavon Little *Peewee* • Vincent Gardenia *Sheriff Cotton* • Richie Havens *Woodrow* • Julian Bond *Russell* • Earl Hindman *Beau Welles* ■ *Dir* Michael Schultz • *Scr* Kenneth Voze, Lawrence DuKore, Melvin Van Peebles, Leon Capetanos

The Great Adventure ★★★ U
Adventure 1953 · Swe · BW · 73min

This internationally acclaimed drama from film-maker Arne Sucksdorff won a prize at the Cannes film festival in 1954. Set in Sweden, it tells the simple story of two boys who secretly befriend an otter over one winter's season but then find that the animal wants to return to the wild. Visually striking, this showed nature without any hint of Disney-esque sentiment. Veteran documentary film-maker Sucksdorff not only directed the film but also wrote, produced, edited, photographed and acted in it. AE Swedish +subtitles.

Anders Norborg *Anders* • Kjell Sucksdorff *Kjell* • Arne Sucksdorff *Father* • Norman Shelley *Narrator* • Gunnar Sjöberg *Narrator* ■ *Dir/Scr* Arne Sucksdorff

The Great American Broadcast ★★★ U
Musical drama 1941 · US · BW · 91min

This is a cheerfully fictionalised account of the early days of American radio, culminating in the first coast-to-coast hook-up of stations. Jack Oakie and John Payne play the ambitious entrepreneurs and Alice Faye is their singing star, with the trio going through the usual break-ups and reconciliations. With some catchy songs (by Mack Gordon and Harry Warren) and cameos by such wireless celebrities as Jack Benny and Rudy Vallee, it's a generous measure of relaxing entertainment. AE

Alice Faye *Vicki Adams* • Jack Oakie *Chuck Hadley* • John Payne *Rix Martin* • Cesar Romero *Bruce Chadwick* • James Newill *Singer* ■ *Dir* Archie Mayo • *Scr* Don Ettlinger, Edwin Blum, Robert Ellis, Helen Logan

The Great American Cowboy ★★★
Documentary 1973 · US · Colour · 89min

This Oscar-winning documentary takes an inside look at rodeo as a professional sport. Spending months on the road with the riders travelling from one prize contest to the next, director Kieth Merrill and writer Douglas Kent Hall focus on a veteran star (Larry Mahan) and his younger rival (Phil Lyne). Subjective camerawork involves the audience in the thrills and spills of the arena, while slow-motion dissects the high-speed action. The narration is by retired cowboy star Joel McCrea. AE

Joel McCrea *Narrator* ■ *Dir* Kieth Merrill · *Scr* Douglas Kent Hall

The Great Balloon Adventure ★★
Adventure 1978 · US · Colour · 83min

Katharine Hepburn waited two years for director Richard A Colla to finance this amiable adventure, and then refused to take a penny in payment. When asked why she took on the role of a junk dealer who helps a couple of boys rebuild their grandfather's balloon and re-create his circus act, she confessed that it fulfilled a long-standing ambition to fly in a hot-air balloon. DP

Katharine Hepburn *Miss Pudd* · Kevin McKenzie *Alby* · Dennis Dimster *Chris* · Obie *Joshua* ■ *Dir* Richard A Colla · *Scr* Eugene Poinc, from a story by Maria L de Ossio, Eugene Poinc, Richard A Colla

Great Balls of Fire! ★★★ 15
Musical biography 1989 · US · Colour · 102min

There's a whole lotta shakin' goin' on in *The Big Easy* director Jim McBride's bright rock 'n' roll biography of Jerry Lee Lewis, played with style and flash by Dennis Quaid. It's an entertaining romp, following Jerry Lee's life in the 1950s up to his fall from grace in London after he married his 13-year-old cousin Myra (sweetly played by Winona Ryder). It's Quaid's on-the-edge performance and the music that makes this so much fun, plus the able support from Ryder, Alec Baldwin and Trey Wilson. JB Swearing, sex scenes. *DVD*

Dennis Quaid *Jerry Lee Lewis* · Winona Ryder *Myra Gale Lewis* · John Doe *JW Brown* · Stephen Tobolowsky *John Phillips* · Trey Wilson *Sam Phillips* · Alec Baldwin *Jimmy Swaggart* · Joe Bob Briggs *John Bloom (2)* · Dewey "Daddy-O" *Phillips* ■ *Dir* Jim McBride · *Scr* Jim McBride, Jack Baran, from the non-fiction book by Myra Lewis, Murray Silver

The Great Bank Robbery ★★ U
Comedy western 1969 · US · Colour · 97min

The idea of robbing a bank so safe that it's where the likes of Jesse James keep their loot is an amusing one, but a leaden screenplay from *The Exorcist's* William Peter Blatty and the desperately uneven direction of Hy Averback defeat the best efforts of the eclectic cast to bring the premise to life. Zero Mostel is disastrously miscast as a phoney evangelist, while "wooden" is too kind an adjective to describe the performances of Clint Walker and Kim Novak. TS

Zero Mostel *Reverend Pious Blue* · Kim Novak *Lyda Kabanov* · Clint Walker *Ben Quick* · Claude Akins *Slade* · Akim Tamiroff *Papa Pedro* · Larry Storch *Juan* · John Anderson *Kincaid* · Sam Jaffe *Brother Lilac* · Mako *Secret service agent Eliot Fong* · Elisha Cook Jr *Jeb* · Ruth Warrick *Mrs Applebee* ■ *Dir* Hy Averback · *Scr* William Peter Blatty, from the novel by Frank O'Rourke

The Great Barrier ★★ U
Historical drama 1937 · UK/US · BW · 84min

Considering the state of the British film industry in 1937, this rugged account of the building of the Canadian-Pacific railroad was ambitious in the extreme. It was shot on location in Alberta and British Columbia by former silent star Milton Rosmer, who was still a relatively inexperienced director. The safety net was Hollywood import Richard Arlen. Not even his turn as a reformed gambler who averts a strike overcomes the pioneering platitudes. DP

Richard Arlen *Hickey* · Lilli Palmer *Lou* · Antoinette Cellier *Mary Moody* · Barry Mackay *Steve* ■ *Dir* Milton Rosmer, Geoffrey Barkas · *Scr* Michael Barringer, Milton Rosmer, Ralph Spence, from the novel *The Great Divide* by Alan Sullivan

The Great Beauty ★★★★ 15
Comedy drama 2013 · It/Fr · Colour · 135min

Director Paolo Sorrentino treads bravely in the footsteps of Federico Fellini and *La Dolce Vita* with this look at the glittering social life of Rome in the company of jaded journalist Jep Gambardella (Toni Servillo). Sorrentino has an original, wryly humorous style that frequently comes to the fore during a serpentine 140 minutes during which Jep embarks on a series of reporting assignments just as some sad news reaches him that reminds him of his promising youth as a novelist. There's real richness in the episodic nature of Jep's endeavours, and his good-humoured cynicism makes him the perfect guide for a VIP tour of a secret, horribly fashionable, dangerously fascinating world. DW Italian +subtitles. Swearing, sexual references, drug abuse, nudity. *DVD* ☍

Toni Servillo *Jep Gambardella* · Carlo Verdone *Romano* · Sabrina Ferilli *Ramona* · Carlo Buccirosso *Lello Cava* · Iaia Forte *Trumeau* · Pamela Villoresi *Viola* ■ *Dir* Paolo Sorrentino · *Scr* Paolo Sorrentino, Umberto Contarello, from a story by Sorrentino

The Great Caruso ★★★★ U
Musical biography 1951 · US · Colour · 104min

This popular and sentimentalised biopic of the legendary tenor was tailor-made for MGM's own lyric tenor, Mario Lanza. The ramshackle screenplay doesn't really matter as Lanza performs such full-blooded arias as *La Donna e Mobile*, *Celeste Aida* and *Vesti la Giubba* in that remarkable golden voice, although the actual hit song from the movie was *The Loveliest Night of the Year* sung by Lanza's co-star Ann Blyth. This was Lanza's biggest success in an all-too-short career that ended with his early death at the age of 38. TS

Mario Lanza *Enrico Caruso* · Ann Blyth *Dorothy Benjamin* · Dorothy Kirsten *Louise Heggar* · Jarmila Novotna *Maria Selka* · Richard Hageman *Carlo Santi* · Carl Benton Reid *Park Benjamin* ■ *Dir* Richard Thorpe · *Scr* Sonia Levien, William Ludwig, from a story by Dorothy Caruso

Great Catherine ★ U
Historical comedy 1968 · UK · Colour · 98min

This farrago about the romantic life of the Empress of Russia is more like a *Carry On* movie transferred to St Petersburg. Peter O'Toole breezes through it all as an English Light Dragoons captain who finds himself in the Empress's bedchamber, while art house heroine Jeanne Moreau is hopelessly miscast as Catherine. The flashy, tricksy direction roots the film in the Swinging Sixties. AT

Peter O'Toole *Captain Edstaston* · Zero Mostel *Patiomkin* · Jeanne Moreau *Catherine* · Jack Hawkins *Sir George Gorse* · Akim Tamiroff *Sergeant* · Marie Lohr *Dowager Lady Gorse* · Kenneth Griffith *Naryshkin* ■ *Dir* Gordon Flemyng · *Scr* Hugh Leonard, from the play *Great Catherine Whom Glory Still Adores* by George Bernard Shaw

The Great Chase ★★★
Documentary 1961 · US · BW · 91min

The chase sequence put the movement into moving pictures and this documentary, put together by Harvey Cort, is a splendid celebration of those breakneck pursuits that proved an invaluable fall-back for dramatic and comic directors alike. The clips range from the horseback raid on a steam train in Edwin S Porter's *The Great Train Robbery* (1903) to Buster Keaton's classic railroad dash in *The General* (1927). There's also a chance to relive some of Pearl White's brushes with death in the peerless serial *The Perils of Pauline* (1914), Lillian Gish's ice floe encounter in *Way Down East* (1920) and Douglas Fairbanks's swashbuckling antics in *The Mark of Zorro* (1920). DP

Douglas Fairbanks · Mack Sennett · Lillian Gish · Buster Keaton · Pearl White ■ *Dir* Harvey Cort · *Music* Larry Adler

Great Day ★ U
Drama 1944 · UK · BW · 79min

As the village of Denley prepares to welcome First Lady Eleanor Roosevelt, alcoholic First World War veteran Eric Portman disgraces himself by stealing from a lady's purse. His daughter, Sheila Sim, dithers over whether she should marry her boss, while his wife, Flora Robson, dedicates herself to the Womens' Guild. An aberration. AT

Eric Portman *Captain Ellis* · Flora Robson *Mrs Ellis* · Sheila Sim *Margaret Ellis* · Isabel Jeans *Lady Mott* · Walter Fitzgerald *John Tyndale* · Philip Friend *Geoffrey Winthrop* · Marjorie Rhodes *Mrs Mumford* ■ *Dir* Lance Comfort · *Scr* Wolfgang Wilhelm, John Davenport, from a play by Lesley Storm

A Great Day in Harlem ★★★★★ U
Music documentary 1994 · US · BW and Colour · 59min

A famous photograph of 57 jazz musicians and a club owner outside a Harlem brownstone is the starting point for this stunningly inventive documentary. The shot covers every jazz generation up to 1958 and includes Dizzy Gillespie and Sonny Rollins. Director Jean Bach splices together voiceovers, snappy interviews, promotional films and home movies to unearth not just the spontaneity and uncertainty of jazz life, but also to home in on its passion, sensitivity and morality. Incidentally, it was *Kramer vs Kramer* director Robert Benton, then art director at *Esquire*, who commissioned the photograph. JM

Quincy Jones *Narrator* · Dizzy Gillespie · Art Blakey ■ *Dir* Jean Bach · *Scr* Jean Bach, Susan Peehl, Matthew Seig

Great Day in the Morning ★★★
Western 1956 · US · Colour · 91min

Strikingly shot by William Snyder against the jaw-dropping landscape of the Colorado Territory, this eve-of-Civil-War western features a redoubtable performance by Robert Stack as a southern maverick forced to choose between patriotism and his pocket. Competing for his attention are wealthy Virginia Mayo and saloon entertainer Ruth Roman. The dialogue in the literate script is sharp-tongued and the action is serviceably staged, but Jacques Tourneur's direction is uninspired. DP

Robert Stack *Owen Pentecost* · Virginia Mayo *Ann Merry Alaine* · Ruth Roman *Boston Grant* · Alex Nicol *Stephen Kirby* · Raymond Burr *Jumbo Means* · Leo Gordon *Zeff Masterson* ■ *Dir* Jacques Tourneur · *Scr* Lesser Samuels, from the novel by Robert Hardy Andrews · *Cinematographer* William Snyder

The Great Debaters ★★★★ 12
Drama based on a true story 2007 · US · Colour · 127min

One of Denzel Washington's occasional forays behind the camera, this is based on the true story of a mid-1930s black college debating team and was very obviously a passion project for the Oscar-winning actor and for producer Oprah Winfrey. Washington also plays the university lecturer, union organiser and poet Melvin B Tolson, who coaches the team and shapes (at least initially) their arguments. The film dramatises a forgotten chapter in the struggle against racial prejudice, and the righteous indignation of African Americans. It is perhaps too righteous at times, but ultimately it proves both emotionally involving and uplifting. BP Swearing.

Denzel Washington *Melvin B Tolson* · Forest Whitaker *Dr James Farmer Sr* · Nate Parker *Henry Lowe* · Jurnee Smollett *Samantha Booke* · Denzel Whitaker *James Farmer Jr* · John Heard *Sheriff Dozier* ■ *Dir* Denzel Washington · *Scr* Robert Eisele, from a story by Eisele, Jeffrey Porro, from an article by Tony Scherman

The Great Dictator ★★★★★ U
Satirical comedy 1940 · US · BW · 124min

Hitler didn't see the joke but he got the point. Charlie Chaplin's first dialogue feature was brilliant satire on the anti-Semitic Nazi regime, with Chaplin in the dual role of a Jewish barber and dictator Adenoid Hynkel. This features some of Chaplin's greatest comic moments - the glories of the barber shaving a customer in time to a Hungarian dance by Brahms, contrasting with Hynkel's solo ballet with a globe of the world. Bliss, even though Chaplin said that, if he had known of the Nazis' real horror, he would never have made such a burlesque, and the final speech, pleading for universal tolerance when the barber takes over from Hynkel, is passionate but mawkish. TH *DVD* ☍

Charlie Chaplin *Jewish barber/Hynkel, dictator of Tomania* · Paulette Goddard *Hannah* · Jack Oakie *Napaloni, dictator of Bacteria* · Reginald Gardiner *Schultz* · Henry Daniell *Garbitsch* · Billy Gilbert *Herring* · Grace Hayle *Madame Napaloni* · Carter DeHaven (1) *Bacterian ambassador* ■ *Dir/Scr* Charles Chaplin

The Great Ecstasy of Robert Carmichael ★★ 18
Drama 2005 · UK · Colour · 97min

Following in a limited tradition of UK-set shockers - most notably *Straw Dogs* and *A Clockwork Orange* - this extraordinary rite-of-passage drama, which takes place at the beginning of the war in Iraq, will more likely repulse audiences than provoke the discussion of the conflict hoped for by its tyro director, Thomas Clay. The setting is a bleak seaside town, where schoolboy cellist Robert is torn between practising for a recital and taking drugs with his dropout friends. In the end, drugs win the day, leading to a shockingly brutal, chemically motivated attack on a local celebrity and his wife. Although his thinking is sometimes horribly naive, this eye-opening debut shows that Clay has a visual flair that can only improve with time. DW Violence.

Dan Spencer *Robert Carmichael* · Lesley Manville *Sarah Carmichael* · Danny Dyer *Larry Haydn* · Ryan Winsley *Joe Kramer* · Charles Mnene *Ben Franklin* · Stuart Laing *Stuart Reeves* · Miranda Wilson *Monica Abbott* · Michael Howe *Jonathan Abbott* ■ *Dir* Thomas Clay · *Scr* Thomas Clay, Joseph Lang

The Great Escape ★★★★★ PG
Classic Second World War adventure 1963 · US · Colour · 165min

This is one of the all-time great war movies, a PoW adventure from director John Sturges that celebrates the indomitable spirit of the Allied forces even when their backs were to the wall. Steve McQueen, Charles Bronson and James Coburn join such British stalwarts as Richard Attenborough, Donald Pleasence, David McCallum and Gordon Jackson in an escape yarn full of collapsing tunnels, probing searchlights and courage in the face of insurmountable odds. Sturges films each intricate step leading up to the break out with a masterly attention to detail, while Elmer Bernstein's triumphant score is as enduring as this iconic movie. AC *DVD* ☍

Steve McQueen (1) *Hilts, "The Cooler King"* · James Garner *Hendley, "The Scrounger"* · Richard Attenborough *Bartlett, "Big X"* · Charles Bronson *Danny Velinski, "Tunnel King"* · Donald Pleasence *Blythe, "The Forger"* · James Donald *Ramsey, "The SBO"* · James Coburn *Sedgwick, "Manufacturer"* · John Leyton *Willie, "Tunneler"* · Gordon Jackson *MacDonald, "Intelligence"* · David McCallum (1) *Ashley-Pitt, "Dispersal"* ■ *Dir* John Sturges · *Scr* James Clavell, WR Burnett, from a book by Paul Brickhill

G

G

Great Expectations ★★★★★ PG

Classic period drama   1946 · UK · BW · 113min

David Lean's adaptation of the Charles Dickens novel is one of his early masterpieces. It's a carefully pruned version of the book that excises entire characters but retains the magical Dickens spirit as it tells the tale of orphaned Pip (played as a boy by Anthony Wager and as an adult by John Mills) who comes into an unexpected fortune. From the opening sequence on the Kentish marshes, when the young Pip encounters Finlay Currie's terrifying escaped convict, through to his love for Estella (played by Jean Simmons as a child and Valerie Hobson as an adult), this is superlative film-making from one of Britain's greatest directors. It looks magnificent and earned Oscars for cinematographer Guy Green and designers John Bryan and Wilfrid Shingleton. **AC**
DVD Blu

John Mills *Pip as an adult* • Valerie Hobson *Estella as an adult* • Bernard Miles *Joe Gargery* • Francis L Sullivan *Jaggers* • Martita Hunt *Miss Havisham* • Finlay Currie *Abel Magwitch* • Alec Guinness *Herbert Pocket* • Ivor Barnard *Wemmick* • Anthony Wager *Pip as a child* • Jean Simmons *Estella as a child* ■ *Dir* David Lean • *Scr* David Lean, Ronald Neame, Anthony Havelock-Allan, Cecil McGivern, Kay Walsh, from the novel by Charles Dickens • *Cinematographer* Guy Green • *Editor* Jack Harris • *Art Directors* John Bryan, Wilfrid Shingleton

Great Expectations ★★ U

Period drama   1974 · US/UK · Colour · 118min

Following the success of Carol Reed's *Oliver Twist*, it was only a matter of time before someone suggested another musical Dickens. Mercifully the songs were out. What's left is a retelling of Pip's progress in which the majority of scenes seem to be staged solely for the benefit of the big production number that never arrives. Only Margaret Leighton's Miss Havisham rings true. **DP** DVD

Michael York *Pip* • Sarah Miles *Estella* • Margaret Leighton *Miss Havisham* • James Mason *Magwitch* • Anthony Quayle *Jaggers* • Robert Morley *Pumblechook* • Joss Ackland *Joe Gargery* ■ *Dir* Joseph Hardy • *Scr* Sherman Yellen, from the novel by Charles Dickens

Great Expectations ★★★ 15

Romantic drama   1997 · US · Colour · 106min

After the minor miracle he worked with *A Little Princess*, Alfonso Cuarón rather lost the plot with this Dickens update. He opted for a loose retelling centred on the eerie Everglades and the New York art scene. But while he lashes on the style, he fumbles the book's underlying themes. He's also ill-served by his leads, with Ethan Hawke consumed by sensitivity and Gwyneth Paltrow too shallow to be a worthy object of obsession. So it's left to a gleefully deranged Anne Bancroft and a caringly criminal Robert De Niro to provide the substance. **DP** Swearing, some violence. DVD

Ethan Hawke *Finnegan "Finn" Bell* • Gwyneth Paltrow *Estella* • Hank Azaria *Walter Plane* • Chris Cooper *Joe* • Anne Bancroft *Nora Diggers Dinsmoor* • Robert De Niro *Lustig* • Josh Mostel *Jerry Ragno* • Kim Dickens *Maggie* ■ *Dir* Alfonso Cuarón • *Scr* Mitch Glazer, from the novel by Charles Dickens

Great Expectations ★★ 12

Period drama   2012 · UK/US · Colour · 123min

This grim and cheerless adaptation of the Charles Dickens classic is drained of colour by director Mike Newell in an attempt to affect an ominous mood. But the effect is to drain the life out of the movie. *War Horse's* Jeremy Irvine plays the grown-up orphan Pip, who is given the chance to better himself by a mysterious benefactor, But Pip's air of innocence stops the pulse of his scenes with childhood love Estella (Holliday Grainger). The high spots are provided by Ralph Fiennes (as escaped prisoner Magwitch) and Helena Bonham Carter (as bitter spinster Miss Havisham), but any raised hopes or expectations are dashed by a bungled ending. **SP** Some violence, brief swearing. DVD Blu

Jeremy Irvine *Pip* • Helena Bonham Carter *Miss Havisham* • Ralph Fiennes *Magwitch* • Robbie Coltrane *Jaggers* • Jason Flemyng *Joe Gargery* • Olly Alexander *Herbert Pocket* • Holliday Grainger *Estella* • Toby Irvine *Young Pip* ■ *Dir* Mike Newell • *Scr* David Nicholls, from Charles Dickens's novel • *Costume Designer* Beatrix Aruna Pasztor

The Great Flamarion ★★★

Film noir   1945 · US · BW · 78min

In this imaginative low-budget *film noir*, the great Erich von Stroheim (then past his peak) teamed up with talented young director Anthony Mann. Von Stroheim has the title role of the vaudeville sharpshooter who, despite an unhappy history with women, makes the mistake of falling for his alluring young assistant, played by Mary Beth Hughes. Of course this is very bad news for Hughes's husband, played by Dan Duryea. The film was made on such a shoestring that a park scene had to be faked on a soundstage with just a bench, a lamp and fog. **AE**

Erich von Stroheim *Flamarion* • Mary Beth Hughes *Connie Wallace* • Dan Duryea *Al Wallace* • Steve Barclay [Stephen Barclay] *Eddie* • Lester Allen *Tony* ■ *Dir* Anthony Mann • *Scr* Anne Wighton, Heinz Herald, Richard Weil, from the story *Big Shot* by Vicki Baum

The Great Gabbo ★★★

Musical drama   1929 · US · BW · 92min

Erich von Stroheim gives an outstanding performance as the egomaniacal ventriloquist who allows his dummy to speak the words of his heart. Based on a story by Ben Hecht and directed with no little style by James Cruze, the film slows slightly in the second half to accommodate a number of vaudeville acts (which were originally shown in somewhat blurred colour). But it's impossible to take your eyes off von Stroheim **DP**

Erich von Stroheim *Gabbo* • Betty Compson *Mary* • Don Douglas *Frank* • Margie "Babe" Kane [Marjorie Kane] *Babe* ■ *Dir* James Cruze • *Scr* Hugh Herbert, from the story *The Rival Dummy* by Ben Hecht

The Great Garrick ★★★ U

Comedy   1937 · UK · BW · 90min

Brian Aherne is the famous 18th-century actor David Garrick, who tells his London audience that he's been invited to perform at the Comédie Française and intends to give the French a lesson in acting. Hearing this, French actors hatch a plot to discredit Garrick as he spends a night in Calais. This is a bright and breezy affair, although it amounts to little more than a charade. Aherne's future sister-in-law, Olivia de Havilland, adds to the fun, plus, in her second featured role, Lana Turner. The stylish direction is by James Whale. **AT**

Brian Aherne *David Garrick* • Olivia de Havilland *Germaine De Le Corbe* • Edward Everett Horton *Tubby* • Melville Cooper *M Picard* • Luis Alberni *Basset* • Lionel Atwill *Beaumarchais* • Marie Wilson *Nicolle* • Lana Turner *Auber* ■ *Dir* James Whale • *Scr* Ernest Vadja, from his play *Ladies and Gentleman*

The Great Gatsby ★★ U

Period romantic drama   1949 · US · BW · 91min

F Scott Fitzgerald's novel provides plenty of plot for a screenwriter to work with, but his silky style simply refuses to translate to the screen. Alan Ladd's limited acting technique almost accidentally conveys some of the mystery of the millionaire who becomes the toast of Long Island society. But while he valiantly attempts to look enigmatic, Betty Field blows the whole illusion with a gauche interpretation of Daisy Buchanan. Elliott Nugent directs with some atmospheric touches, but can't counter the script's verbosity. **DP**

Alan Ladd *Jay Gatsby* • Betty Field *Daisy Buchanan* • Macdonald Carey *Nick Carraway* • Ruth Hussey *Jordan Baker* • Barry Sullivan *Tom Buchanan* • Howard Da Silva *Wilson* • Shelley Winters *Myrtle Wilson* • Henry Hull *Dan Cody* • Carole Mathews *Ella Cody* ■ *Dir* Elliott Nugent •

Scr Cyril Hume, Richard Maibaum, from the play by Owen Davis, from the novel by F Scott Fitzgerald

The Great Gatsby ★★★ PG

Period romantic drama   1974 · US · Colour · 135min

This was Paramount's third stab at bringing F Scott Fitzgerald's jazz-age classic to the screen. Robert Redford is unquestionably more handsome than Alan Ladd, but he's no more demonstrative or credible as the millionaire with a dark past. Mia Farrow, meanwhile, is better cast than Betty Field, though her Daisy Buchanan is more skittishly irresponsible than irresistibly infatuating. While Jack Clayton's direction is suitably languid, the lush imagery only reinforces the superficiality of Francis Ford Coppola's reverential script. **DP**

Robert Redford *Jay Gatsby* • Mia Farrow *Daisy Buchanan* • Bruce Dern *Tom Buchanan* • Karen Black *Myrtle Wilson* • Scott Wilson *George Wilson* • Sam Waterston *Nick Carraway* • Lois Chiles *Jordan Baker* ■ *Dir* Jack Clayton • *Scr* Francis Ford Coppola, from the novel by F Scott Fitzgerald

The Great Gatsby ★★

Period romantic drama   2000 · US/UK · Colour · 100min

Mira Sorvino and Toby Stephens star as the ill-fated couple in this made-for-TV dramatisation of F Scott Fitzgerald's romantic masterpiece. The story is told by Nick Carraway (Paul Rudd) who provides a link for mysterious millionaire Jay Gatsby (Stephens) to engineer a meeting with his old flame, Daisy Buchanan (Sorvino). On the surface, it's a handsome period piece, but beneath the gloss it's more drawing room drama than an elegy for the Jazz Age. Unfortunately, attempts to improve on Fitzgerald's deft storytelling mean it never takes flight. **GE**

Mira Sorvino *Daisy Buchanan* • Toby Stephens *Jay Gatsby* • Paul Rudd *Nick Carraway* • Martin Donovan *Tom Buchanan* ■ *Dir* Robert Markowitz • *Scr* John McLaughlin, from the novel by F Scott Fitzgerald

The Great Gatsby ★★★ 12

Romantic drama   2013 · US/Aus · Colour · 142min

Putting on a good show is paramount for Jay Gatsby, F Scott Fitzgerald's great literary creation. It's a philosophy shared by director Baz Luhrmann whose adaptation of the author's key work is full of razzmatazz. Leonardo DiCaprio plays Gatsby, the new-money millionaire who throws lavish parties in an attempt to win back his Long Island neighbour's fragile cousin, Daisy (Carey Mulligan), having lost her to playboy heir Tom Buchanan (Joel Edgerton). If the unrelenting glitz can feel counter-intuitive, Luhrmann isn't being sacrilegious. This is more an unabashed expression of love for the book that's slightly lost its way. Much like Gatsby himself. **SP** Some violence, a sex scene. DVD Blu

Leonardo DiCaprio *Jay Gatsby* • Tobey Maguire *Nick Carraway* • Carey Mulligan *Daisy Buchanan* • Joel Edgerton *Tom Buchanan* • Isla Fisher *Myrtle Wilson* • Jason Clarke (2) *George Wilson* • Callan McAuliffe *Young Jay Gatsby* ■ *Dir* Baz Luhrmann • *Scr* Baz Luhrmann, Craig Pearce, from F Scott Fitzgerald's novel • *Cinematographer* Simon Duggan

The Great Ghost Rescue ★★★ PG

Fantasy comedy   2011 · UK · Colour · 90min

After a family of ghosts is forced out of their home, this spooky tale follows their adventures as they are led by their youngest son into making their presence known to the living. A somewhat rushed opening doesn't stop the film finding its rhythm as a likeable comedy horror, while the novel (if slightly patchy) plot is garnished with light-hearted laughs and impressive special effects that never overwhelm. **JL** In English, Italian. Some swearing. DVD

Jason Isaacs *Narrator* • Toby Hall *Humphrey* • Emma Fielding *Mabel* • Kevin McKidd *Hamish* • Georgia Groome *Winifred* • Anthony Head *Prime Minister* • Steven Mackintosh *Brad/Barnabus* ■ *Dir* Yann Samuell • *Scr* Yann Samuell, David Solomons, from Eva Ibbotson's novel

Great Guns ★★ PG

Comedy   1941 · US · BW · 70min

Laurel and Hardy's first feature for 20th Century-Fox is a plodding army comedy with echoes of their own *Pack Up Your Troubles* and the Abbott and Costello hit *Buck Privates*, which had been released earlier the same year. Directed by Monty Banks, the film has sadly too little Stan and Ollie and far too much of a romance between Sheila Ryan and Dick Nelson. It's hardly vintage, so savour the laughs when they come. **DP**

Stan Laurel *Stan* • Oliver Hardy *Ollie* • Sheila Ryan *Ginger Hammond* • Dick Nelson *Dan Forrester* • Edmund MacDonald *Hippo* • Charles Trowbridge *Colonel Ridley* • Ludwig Stossel *Dr Schickel* • Kane Richmond *Captain Baker* ■ *Dir* Monty Banks • *Scr* Lou Breslow

Great Guy ★★

Crime drama   1936 · US · BW · 73min

James Cagney was in dispute with his regular employer, Warner Bros, when he appeared in this movie for minor studio, Grand National. This weak crime drama lacked the Warners gloss, but Cagney makes a point of abandoning his tough-guy image, playing an incorruptible weights-and-measures inspector who exposes a food scam to cheat customers. There is less than the usual violence, and he even allows himself to be bossed around by Mae Clarke, the actress who received his celebrated grapefruit massage in *The Public Enemy*. **AE**

James Cagney *Johnny Cave* • Mae Clarke *Janet Henry* • James Burke *Pat Haley* • Edward Brophy *Pete Reilly* • Henry Kolker *Conning* • Bernadene Hayes *Hazel Scott* ■ *Dir* John G Blystone • *Scr* Henry McCarty, Horace McCoy, Henry Johnson, Henry Ruskin, from the stories by James Edward Grant

The Great Hip Hop Hoax ★★★★ 18

Documentary   2013 · UK · Colour · 88min

Documentary film-maker Jeanie Finlay recounts the extraordinary tale of a small-town Scottish rapping duo who fooled the showbiz world into believing they were Californian skateboard kids. Arbroath-born Billy Boyd and Gavin Bain were dismissed by an indifferent music industry as a "rapping Proclaimers", so they reinvented themselves as American hip-hop act Silibil n' Brains. The film doesn't quite hit the mark as a hard-nosed exposé of a shallow, trend-led business, but it does work as a winsome study of the fickle nature of fame. Still, it's the pranksters themselves who drive it along with an undeniable charm, which partly explains how they were able to get away with it. **TeS** Swearing, sexual references.

Gavin Bain • Billy Boyd (2) *Billy Boyd* ■ *Dir* Jeanie Finlay

The Great Impostor ★★ U

Biographical comedy adventure   1960 · US · BW · 112min

By the time he made this biopic of Ferdinand Waldo Demara Jr, a notorious real-life impostor, Tony Curtis had proved that he wasn't just a pretty face. But even his considerable comic gifts were not enough to sustain this episodic, mildly amusing comedy, in which he masquerades as a professor, a Trappist monk, a navy surgeon and a prison administrator who forestalls a riot. It's a pity that in this potentially interesting case history, the character's motivations are never sufficiently explained. **RB**

Tony Curtis *Ferdinand Waldo Demara Jr* • Edmond O'Brien *Captain Glover* • Arthur O'Connell *Warden Chandler* • Gary Merrill *Pa Demara* • Joan Blackman *Catherine Lacey* • Robert Middleton *Brown* • Doodles Weaver *Farmer* ■ *Dir* Robert Mulligan • *Scr* Liam O'Brien, from the book by Robert Crichton

The Great Lie ★★★★
Romantic melodrama 1941 · US · BW · 107min

This is one of the greatest films Bette Davis made at Warner Bros. Once termed "women's pictures", they are now recognised as being among the finest products of the studio system. Here Davis is given more than a run for her money by co-star Mary Astor, who collected the best supporting actress Oscar as Davis's rival in love for handsome George Brent, allegedly Davis's lover in real life. The titular lie involves the "ownership" of Brent's child, and both female stars pull out all the stops. TS

Bette Davis *Maggie Patterson* • George Brent *Pete van Allen* • Mary Astor *Sandra Kovak* • Lucile Watson *Aunt Ada Greenfield* • Hattie McDaniel *Violet* • Grant Mitchell *Joshua Mason* • Jerome Cowan *JH "Jock" Thompson* • Charles Trowbridge *Senator Ted Greenfield* ■ *Dir* Edmund Goulding • *Scr* Lenore Coffee, from the novel *January Heights* by Polan Blanks

The Great Locomotive Chase ★★ U
Wartime action adventure
1956 · US · Colour · 71min

Davy Crockett star Fess Parker features in this folksy American Civil War action adventure. Jeffrey Hunter's Confederate railroader is up against Parker's Union spy, on a mission to destroy enemy supply lines. Hunter is tireless in pursuit of the gang that stole his train, but Parker is the hero of the piece and his audacious escape makes for a resounding finale, which partly compensates for the otherwise ponderous storytelling. DP *DVD*

Fess Parker *James J Andrews* • Jeffrey Hunter *William A Fuller* • Jeff York *William Campbell* • John Lupton *William Pittenger* • Eddie Firestone *Robert Buffum* • Kenneth Tobey *Anthony Murphy* • Slim Pickens *Pete Bracken* ■ *Dir* Francis D Lyon • *Scr* Lawrence Edward Watkin

The Great Lover ★★★ 12
Comedy 1949 · US · BW · 79min

One of Bob Hope's better vehicles casts him as a scoutmaster trying to cope with a group of dedicated "child foresters" on a transatlantic liner. The diversions include the beautiful daughter (Rhonda Fleming) of a penniless duke, and a cardsharp who is murdering passengers. The risible script makes room for a brief but splendid cameo by Jack Benny, and Richard Lyon plays one of the youths, urging the unwilling Hope to give up cigarettes and women. TV *DVD*

Bob Hope *Freddie Hunter* • Rhonda Fleming *Duchess Alexandria* • Roland Young *CJ Dabney* • Roland Culver *Grand Duke Maximillian* • Richard Lyon *Stanley* • Jim Backus *Higgins* ■ *Dir* Alexander Hall • *Scr* Edmund Beloin, Melville Shavelson, Jack Rose

The Great McGinty ★★★★ U
Comedy 1940 · US · BW · 78min

Don't be put off just because this is a comedy about American politics with no star names. Writer Preston Sturges persuaded Paramount to let him make his directing debut for a ten-dollar fee, and the result is this delicious study in comic irony. It's the story of an Irishman who rises through a corrupt party machine to become governor of a state, then is ruined in a crazy minute of honesty. Proving as brilliant a director as he was a writer, Sturges won the Oscar for best original screenplay and opened the doors for other writers such as Billy Wilder to direct their work. Brian Donlevy attacks his role with gusto, while supporting players shine in every scene. AE *DVD*

Brian Donlevy *Dan McGinty* • Muriel Angelus *Catherine McGinty* • Akim Tamiroff *Boss* • Allyn Joslyn *George* • William Demarest *Politician* • Louis Jean Heydt *Thompson* • Arthur Hoyt *Mayor Tillinghast* ■ *Dir/Scr* Preston Sturges

The Great McGonagall ★ 15
Comedy 1974 · UK · Colour · 84min

Whatever the shortcomings of the Victorian versifier – the unemployed Scot who was determined to be the Queen's laureate – he didn't deserve this snide, incoherent jeering. Comedians Spike Milligan and Peter Sellers lead with the machetes, carving fun out of a simple-minded man whose verses didn't scan and whose thoughts were banal, but it's the mutual admiration society of the principals that scores its own goal. TH

Spike Milligan *William McGonagall* • Peter Sellers *Queen Victoria* • Julia Foster *Mrs McGonagall* ■ *Dir* Joseph McGrath • *Scr* Spike Milligan, Joseph McGrath

The Great Madcap ★★★
Comedy 1949 · Mex · BW · 91min

The second film of Luis Buñuel's Mexican comeback began as a jobbing assignment, but ended up dictating the way the master surrealist would work for the remainder of his career, by teaching him the value of meticulous pre-planning. Some have sought anti-bourgeois satire in drunken patriarch Fernando Soler's revenge on the worthless family that tried to trick him into believing he had squandered his fortune. But the storyline of this gentle comedy is pure Hollywood, as hard work brings out the best in those previously content to exploit. DP Spanish +subtitles. *DVD*

Fernando Soler *Ramiro* • Rosario Granados *Virginia* • Andres Soler *Ladislao* ■ *Dir* Luis Buñuel, Fernando Soler • *Scr* Luis Alcoriza, Janet Alcoriza, from a play by Adolfo Torrado

The Great Man ★★★
Drama 1956 · US · BW · 92min

This hollow, cynical drama has a media personality's shining reputation tarnished during the preparation of a tribute. Impressing more as co-writer and director than as star, José Ferrer can do little about the predictable manner in which skeletons tumble out of various closets, but he draws wonderfully embittered performances from his expert cast. Ed Wynn is outstanding as the radio boss who discovered the "Studio King", though Julie London's abused singer, Dean Jagger's network boss and Keenan Wynn's self-seeking executive are also strong. Slick and satirical, but lacking the depth to be truly satisfying. DP

José Ferrer *Joe Harris* • Dean Jagger *Philip Carleton* • Keenan Wynn *Sid Moore* • Julie London *Carol Larson* • Joanne Gilbert *Ginny* • Ed Wynn *Paul Beaseley* • Jim Backus *Nick Cellantano* • Russ Morgan *Eddie Brand* ■ *Dir* José Ferrer • *Scr* Al Morgan, José Ferrer, from the novel by Al Morgan

The Great Man Votes ★★ U
Drama 1939 · US · BW · 71min

In a sharpish political satire, John Barrymore is a floating voter whose personal problems – widower, drunkard, two kids to raise – make him the target of spin doctors. This is a showcase for Barrymore's talent, though by this time he was several years and several bottles past his prime. AT

John Barrymore *Gregory Vance* • Peter Holden *Donald Vance* • Virginia Weidler *Joan Vance* • Katherine Alexander *Miss Billow* • Donald MacBride *Iron Hat McCarthy* • Bennie Bartlett *Dave McCarthy* • Brandon Tynan *Chester Ainslee* • Elisabeth Risdon *Phoebe Ainslee* ■ *Dir* Garson Kanin • *Scr* John Twist, from a story by Gordon Malherbe Hillman

The Great Man's Lady ★★★
Western 1942 · US · BW · 90min

This melodramatic western epic, told in flashback, features Barbara Stanwyck made-up as a 100-year-old woman. It tells the saga of how Stanwyck backed husband Joel McCrea in forging a town out of the wilderness, only to disagree about the coming of the railroad. Much of the staging is impressive despite the slow pace. TS

Barbara Stanwyck *Hannah Sempler* • Joel McCrea *Ethan Hoyt* • Brian Donlevy *Steely Edwards* • Katharine Stevens [KT Stevens] *Girl biographer* • Thurston Hall *Mr Sempler* • Lloyd Corrigan *Mr Cadwallader* • Etta McDaniel *Delilah* • Frank M Thomas *Senator Knobs* ■ *Dir* William A Wellman • *Scr* WL River, Adela Rogers St Johns, Seena Owen, from the story *The Human Side* by Vina Delmar

The Great Mr Handel ★★★ U
Biographical drama 1942 · UK · Colour · 98min

Clearly intended as a treatise on patriotism at the height of the Second World War, this handsome biopic explores how someone of German extraction could become a true Briton. Heading a capable supporting cast, Wilfrid Lawson is imposing in the title role as he atones for his squabbles with both Church and State by composing *The Messiah*. DP

Wilfrid Lawson *George Frideric Handel* • Elizabeth Allan *Mrs Cibber* • Malcolm Keen *Lord Chesterfield* • Michael Shepley *Sir Charles Marsham* • Max Kirby *Frederick, Prince of Wales* • Hay Petrie *Phineas* ■ *Dir* Norman Walter • *Scr* L DuGarde Peach, Gerald Elliott, Victor MacClure [Victor McClure]

The Great Moment ★★★★ PG
Biographical drama 1944 · US · BW · 77min

How do you make an entertaining tribute to the forgotten dentist who first discovered the anaesthetic? The great comedy writer/director Preston Sturges had the answer, but audiences didn't want to know, giving him his one flop among a string of hits. Without sacrificing scientific detail, Sturges embellishes the situations with valid slapstick humour, conveying the horror of an amputation before anaesthesia through the fainting of an unprepared onlooker. According to Sturges, the great moment in the life of the dentist, sensitively portrayed by Joel McCrea, is not his discovery, but a gesture of great humanity that ends the film on an upbeat note. AE *DVD*

Joel McCrea *WTG Morton* • Betty Field *Elizabeth Morton* • Harry Carey *Prof Warren* • William Demarest *Eben Frost* • Louis Jean Heydt *Dr Horace Wells* • Julius Tannen *Dr Jackson* • Edwin Maxwell *VP medical society* • Porter Hall *President Pierce* ■ *Dir* Preston Sturges • *Scr* Preston Sturges, from a biography by Rene Fulop-Miller

The Great Muppet Caper ★★★ U
Musical comedy 1981 · US · Colour · 93min

Although crammed full of big names, this second Muppet movie is something of a disappointment. The parodies of the Busby Berkeley-esque production numbers are artfully staged and the byplay between Charles Grodin and Miss Piggy is charged with comic eroticism. But there are too many scenes that seem to be merely passing the time until the plot is ready to resume rolling. Kermit, Fozzie and Gonzo are particularly ill-served as the reporters investigating the theft of Diana Rigg's diamond. Followed in 1984 by *The Muppets Take Manhattan*. DP *DVD*

Jim Henson *Kermit the Frog/Rowlf/Dr Teeth/Waldorf* • Frank Oz *Miss Piggy/Fozzie Bear/Animal* • Dave Goelz *Gonzo/Chester Rat/Bill the Frog/Zoot* • Diana Rigg *Lady Holiday* • Charles Grodin *Nicky Holiday* • John Cleese *Neville* • Robert Morley *British gentleman* • Peter Ustinov *Truck driver* • Jack Warden *Editor* • Peter Falk *Tramp* ■ *Dir* Jim Henson • *Scr* Tom Patchett, Jay Tarses, Jerry Juhl, Jack Rose

The Great Museum ★★★★ PG
Documentary 2014 · Austria · Colour · 94min

Opting to observe rather than analyse, this sumptuously photographed behind-the-scenes tour of the Kunsthistorisches Museum in Vienna mainly focuses on the restoration and grand re-opening of the magnificent Kunstkammer rooms. But, while they are aware of the priceless allure of Hapsburg grandeur, the museum administrators also recognise the part that marketing has to play. The sequences detailing the cleaning of a painting, the hunting of ravenous beetles and the intricate repair of a clockwork galleon are as compelling as the staff meeting exposing hierarchical snobbery and the farewell party for a long-serving curator. DP German +subtitles.

■ *Dir* Johannes Holzhausen • *Scr* From a concept by Johannes Holzhausen, Constantin Wulff

The Great Northfield Minnesota Raid ★★★
Western 1972 · US · Colour · 91min

This foray into American folk-hero territory, here the bank heist by the Jesse James gang, lacks pace but looks so purposefully authentic that you expect the brown-hued edges to curl like ancient photographs. Directed by Philip Kaufman, the film boasts Robert Duvall and Cliff Robertson in the leading roles of Jesse James and Cole Younger. Robertson's moody antiheroism is at one with the rain-soaked Northfield town in this, one of the first of the revisionist westerns. TH Violence, swearing, nudity.

Cliff Robertson *Cole Younger* • Robert Duvall *Jesse James* • Luke Askew *Jim Younger* • RG Armstrong *Clell Miller* • Dana Elcar *Allen* • Donald Moffat *Manning* • John Pearce *Frank James* ■ *Dir/Scr* Philip Kaufman

The Great O'Malley ★
Drama 1937 · US · BW · 71min

Humphrey Bogart received his first star billing for this terrible Warner Bros programmer, a grotesquely sentimentalised crime melodrama in which slum-dweller Bogart is forced into criminality because his daughter is crippled. Pat O'Brien is the Irish cop on Bogart's case. Bogart's daughter is played by a scene-stealing Sybill Jason, who also becomes a victim of O'Brien's intractability. AT

Pat O'Brien *James Aloysius O'Malley* • Humphrey Bogart *John Phillips* • Frieda Inescort *Mrs Phillips* • Henry O'Neill *Attorney for defence* • Hobart Cavanaugh *Pinky Holden* • Mary Gordon *Mrs O'Malley* • Sybill Jason *Barbara Phillips* ■ *Dir* William Dieterle • *Scr* Milton Krims, Tom Reed, from the story *The Making of O'Malley* by Gerald Beaumont

The Great Outdoors ★★ PG
Comedy 1988 · US · Colour · 86min

John Hughes's attempt to re-create the success of the previous year's adult comedy *Planes, Trains and Automobiles* backfires with this routine outing. John Candy, the obnoxious one in the aforementioned *Planes*, gets to be the nice guy this time around, finding himself stuck on vacation with his appalling brother-in-law Dan Aykroyd. Hughes's script is a mechanical retread of past glories and director Howard Deutch fails to bring much inspiration to the slapstick. Look out for a pre-stardom Annette Bening in a supporting role. JF *DVD* *CS*

Dan Aykroyd *Roman Craig* • John Candy *Chet Ripley* • Stephanie Faracy *Connie Ripley* • Annette Bening *Kate Craig* • Chris Young *Buck Ripley* • Ian Giatti *Ben Ripley* • Hilary Gordon *Cara Craig* • Rebecca Gordon *Mara Craig* ■ *Dir* Howard Deutch • *Scr* John Hughes

The Great Race ★★★★ U
Comedy 1965 · US · Colour · 153min

Jack Lemmon sports one of the most dastardly moustaches this side of a Victorian melodrama to compete against clean-cut good guy Tony Curtis in a 1908 automobile race from New York to Paris. Director Blake Edwards pays homage to the cartoon characterisation and slapstick wackiness of silent comedies in this stylised and overlong, but lavish and entertaining comedy extravaganza. Lemmon overplays to particular comic effect as the hiss-worthy villain, and the score is by Henry Mancini. PF

Tony Curtis *The Great Leslie* • Jack Lemmon *Professor Fate/Prince Hapnik* • Natalie Wood *Maggie DuBois* • Peter Falk *Max* • Keenan Wynn *Hezekiah* • Arthur O'Connell *Henry Goodbody* • Vivian Vance *Hester Goodbody* • Dorothy Provine *Lily Olay* ■ *Dir* Blake Edwards • *Scr* Arthur Ross, from a story by Arthur Ross, Blake Edwards

G

G

The Great Raid ★★ 15
Second World War drama based on a true story
2005 · US/Aus · BW and Colour · 127min

An astonishing true story is weakly told in director John Dahl's heartfelt but underwhelming account of the US Army's audacious attempt to save hundreds of PoWs from a Japanese camp in the Philippines in 1945. While Benjamin Bratt's lieutenant colonel and captain James Franco give focus to the mainly lacklustre military operation, malaria-afflicted major Joseph Fiennes emotes to little effect. However, it's the actions of the underground resistance that feel least authentic. The overall result is handsomely shot, but doesn't have the impact such important events deserve. SF In English, Tagalog, Japanese. Some violence. *DVD*

Benjamin Bratt *Lt Colonel Mucci* • James Franco *Captain Prince* • Connie Nielsen *Margaret Utinsky* • Joseph Fiennes *Major Gibson* • Marton Csokas *Captain Redding* • Scr Carlo Bernard, Doug Miro, from the non-fiction book by William B Breuer and the non-fiction book *Ghost Soldiers* by Hampton Sides

The Great Rock 'n' Roll Swindle ★★★★ 18
Drama documentary 1979 · UK · Colour · 100min

The rise and fall of the Sex Pistols is charted in director Julien Temple's docu-fiction account of the punk era in all its anarchic glory. Using backstage interviews, concert clips, newsreels, staged sequences and animation footage from their aborted vehicle *Who Killed Bambi?* (which "King Leer" Russ Meyer was set to direct), a fascinating and remarkably honest slice of rock history emerges from the swirling mass of material. All the relevant bases are touched on including *God Save the Queen*, the jaunt to Rio to visit Great Train Robber Ronnie Biggs, Nancy Spungen's manslaughter and Sid Vicious's death, with manager guru Malcolm McLaren shown as the ultimate manipulator of the masses and, fully earning the title "King Con". AJ *DVD*

Malcolm McLaren *The Embezzler* • Sid Vicious *The Gimmick* • Johnny Rotten *[John Lydon] The Collaborator* • Steve Jones *The Crook* • Paul Cook *The Tea-maker* • Ronald Biggs *The Exile* ■ Dir/Scr Julien Temple

The Great Rupert ★★ U
Comedy 1950 · US · BW · 88min

Materialism is god in this simplistic comedy curiosity about an impoverished family of New York acrobats whose fortunes are inadvertently transformed by a squirrel living in their rafters. Jimmy Durante heads the vaudeville clan, the members of which think they're receiving gifts from heaven when the titular rodent starts throwing out cash that their landlord is stashing in his nest. Stop-motion squirrel Rupert provides novelty value but the critter is so underused that neither his flashes of fun nor a sugary romantic subplot can hide the film's flimsiness. SF

Jimmy Durante *Mr Amendola* • Terry Moore *Rosalinda* • Tom Drake *Peter Dingle* • Frank Orth *Mr Dingle* • Sara Haden *Mrs Dingle* • Queenie Smith *Mrs Amendola* ■ Dir Irving Pichel • Scr Laslo Vadnay, from a story by Ted Allen

The Great St Trinian's Train Robbery ★★ U
Comedy 1966 · UK · Colour · 90min

Although Frank Launder couldn't resist the temptation of returning to his old stamping ground in 1980's *The Wildcats of St Trinian's*, this should have been the last in the film series (that began with *The Belles of St Trinian's*) based on Ronald Searle's ghoulish schoolgirls, as it had clearly run out of steam. Frankie Howerd's limitations as a film actor are all too apparent in this mix of vulgar comedy and Swinging Sixties satire. DP *DVD*

Frankie Howerd *Alphonse Askett* • Reg Varney *Gilbert* • Dora Bryan *Amber Spottiswood* • Desmond Walter-Ellis *Leonard Edwards* • Cyril Chamberlain *Maxie* • Stratford Johns *The Voice* • Richard Wattis *Bassett* • George Cole *Flash*

Harry ■ Dir Frank Launder, Sidney Gilliat • Scr Frank Launder, Ivor Herbert, from the drawings by Ronald Searle

The Great Santini ★★★ PG
Drama 1979 · US · Colour · 110min

This adaptation of Pat Conroy's novel has a title that suggests a story about an escapologist or a racing driver is in the offing. In fact, it tells of a retired fighter pilot called Bull Meechum (nicknamed "Santini"), whose drunkenness makes life a misery for his wife (Blythe Danner) and children. It's a thick slice of Deep South angst and sour mash philosophy in which drink turns dialogue into poetry, but Robert Duvall is magnificent in the lead role. AT

Robert Duvall *Bull Meechum* • Blythe Danner *Lillian Meechum* • Michael O'Keefe *Ben Meechum* • Stan Shaw *Toomer Smalls* • Lisa Jane Persky *Mary Anne Meechum* • Julie Anne Haddock *Karen Meechum* • Brian Andrews *Matthew Meechum* • Theresa Merritt *Arrabelle Smalls* ■ Dir Lewis John Carlino • Scr Lewis John Carlino, from the novel by Pat Conroy

The Great Scout & Cathouse Thursday ★★
Comedy western 1976 · US · Colour · 105min

Set in Colorado in 1908, this is a coarse, crass and calamitous misjudgement. Yet it's worth watching to witness the battle of wills between Lee Marvin and Oliver Reed, in which the former strains every sinew to stop himself lapsing into caricatured mugging, while the latter tempts him to stray with an exhibition of unabashed showboating. Caught in the middle are Robert Culp, as the politician who once gypped the feuding duo, and Kay Lenz, as the hooker who takes a fancy to Marvin. DP Violence, swearing.

Lee Marvin *Sam Longwood* • Oliver Reed *Joe Knox* • Robert Culp *Jack Colby* • Elizabeth Ashley *Nancy Sue* • Strother Martin *Billy* • Sylvia Miles *Mike* • Kay Lenz *Thursday* ■ Dir Don Taylor • Scr Richard Shapiro

The Great Silence ★★★ 15
Spaghetti western 1967 · It/Fr · Colour · 105min

What do you get when you cross an Italian director with a German villain and a French hero? The answer is a thumping good spaghetti western from director Sergio Corbucci. Klaus Kinski stars as a bounty hunter waiting to pick off the outlaws hiding in the Sierra Madre as the severe winter of 1896 drives them into the border villages. Mute gunfighter Jean-Louis Trintignant stands in his way, amid stunning shots of the snow-covered mountains. DP Italian dubbed. Violence. *DVD*

Jean-Louis Trintignant *Silenzio* • Klaus Kinski *Tigrero* • Vonetta McGee *Pauline* ■ Dir Sergio Corbucci • Scr Sergio Corbucci, Vittoriano Petrilli, Mario Amendola, Bruno Corbucci • Music Ennio Morricone

The Great Sinner ★★
Romantic drama 1949 · US · BW · 109min

Fyodor Dostoyevsky's *The Gambler* has defeated many a film-maker this side of the Russian border. In MGM's lushly upholstered version of the tale, two of the world's best-looking stars, Gregory Peck and Ava Gardner, are seemingly without a clue as to what they're supposed to be thinking or doing under the heavy hand of director Robert Siodmak. Hardly watchable. TS

Gregory Peck *Fyodor Dostoyevsky* • Ava Gardner *Pauline Ostrovski* • Melvyn Douglas *Armand Le Glasse* • Walter Huston *General Ostrovski* • Ethel Barrymore *Granny* • Frank Morgan *Aristide Pitard* • Agnes Moorehead *Emma Getzel* • Ludwig Stossel *Hotel manager* ■ Dir Robert Siodmak • Scr Ladislas Fodor, Christopher Isherwood, from a story by Ladislas Fodor, Rene Fulop-Miller, from the story *The Gambler* by Fyodor Dostoyevsky

The Great Sioux Uprising ★★ U
Western 1953 · US · Colour · 80min

This western brings a fresh perspective to a familiar horse-rustling scenario. Jeff Chandler plays a new veterinarian in town, who discovers that prominent horse trader

---

Lyle Bettger is stealing animals from the Sioux and selling them to the army. Chandler finds himself caught between the tribe and the local ranchers, while female lead Faith Domergue looks on. Don't be misled by the title: there's an attempt to rouse the Sioux, but no great uprising. AE

Jeff Chandler *Jonathan Westgate* • Faith Domergue *Joan Britton* • Lyle Bettger *Stephen Cook* • John War Eagle *Red Cloud* • Stephen Chase (1) *Major McKay* • Stacy Harris *Uriah* ■ Dir Lloyd Bacon • Scr Melvin Levy, J Robert Bren, Gladys Atwater, from a story by J Robert Bren, Gladys Atwater

LANDMARK FILM
This cornerstone western introduces continuity editing to increase tension

The Great Train Robbery ★★★
Silent crime western 1903 · US · BW · 12min

Often hailed as the cornerstone of the western genre, Edwin S Porter's 13-sequence adaptation of Scott Marble's heist thriller is also one of the most significant films in the development of screen storytelling. Among its many initiatives was the use of a screenplay, descriptive captions, panning shots and back-projected footage. But its most important contribution to film grammar was the introduction of continuity editing, in which the action cross-cuts between parallel events to increase the narrative tension. Moreover, it also culminated in the iconic shot of bandit George Barnes firing his gun directly at the camera. A pivotal picture in cinema history. DP

George Barnes *Bandit* • Gilbert M Anderson *Bandit* • Frank Hanaway *Bandit* • Tom London *Engineer* • Mary Snow *Little girl* • AC Abadie *Sheriff* • Walter Cameron *Sheriff* ■ Dir Edwin S Porter • Scr Edwin S Porter, from a story by Scott Marble

The Great Waldo Pepper ★★★ PG
Period drama 1975 · US · Colour · 102min

Scripted by William Goldman, the story of the former First World War pilot who lives on false deeds and reckless stunts should have provided biting insights into the nature of heroism and Hollywood's shameless predilection for myth-making. Instead, we get a self-pitying tale of a dreamer who has out-lived both his times and his usefulness. Robert Redford effortlessly portrays Pepper's superficial charm, but lacks the depth to convey his torment. A missed opportunity, though the aerial sequences are stunning. DP

Robert Redford *Waldo Pepper* • Bo Svenson *Axel Olsson* • Bo Brundin *Ernst Kessler* • Susan Sarandon *Mary Beth* • Geoffrey Lewis *Newton Potts* • Edward Herrmann *Ezra Stiles* ■ Dir George Roy Hill • Scr William Goldman, from a story by George Roy Hill

A Great Wall ★★★ PG
Drama 1985 · US/Chi · Colour · 95min

Peter Wang caught the eye in Wayne Wang's *Chan Is Missing*. It's hardly surprising, therefore, that his debut as actor/director should share so many of the themes of his namesake's delightful *Dim Sum*. This film focuses on the culture shock experienced by a family of first generation American Chinese during a visit to the old country. Avoiding controversial issues, it's a guided tour of Beijing with some gentle drama thrown in. DP English, Mandarin +subtitles.

Peter Wang *Leo Fang* • Sharon Iwai *Grace Fang* • Wang Xiao *Liu Yida* • Li Qinqin *Lili Chao* • Xiu Jian Yu ■ Dir Peter Wang • Scr Peter Wang, Shirley Sun

The Great Waltz ★★★★ U
Biographical drama 1938 · US · BW · 103min

In this splendid MGM retelling of the life of Johann Strauss, romantic charmer Fernand Gravet stars as Strauss, with the composer here neglecting his wife (portrayed by the regrettably forgotten double Oscar winner Luise Rainer) for an opera singer played by Miliza Korjus. Style is everything here and the cameraman Joseph Ruttenberg won the

---

Oscar for best cinematography. But who directed this opulent extravaganza? The movie is credited to Frenchman Julien Duvivier, but he left about halfway through, and others, including WS Van Dyke II and Victor Fleming, replaced him. Josef von Sternberg took charge for the sumptuous finale. TS

Luise Rainer *Poldi Vogelhuber* • Fernand Gravet *Johann Strauss* • Miliza Korjus *Carla Donner* • Hugh Herbert *Hofbauer* • Lionel Atwill *Count Hohenfried* • Curt Bois *Kienzl* • Leonid Kinskey *Dudelman* ■ Dir Julien Duvivier • Scr Samuel Hoffenstein, Walter Reisch, from a story by Gottfried Reinhardt

The Great Waltz ★★ U
Musical 1972 · US · Colour · 133min

Andrew L Stone followed up his Grieg biopic *Song of Norway* with a retread of the familiar saga of Johann Strauss. This version benefits from colour, Panavision and – predictably – some of the most beautiful waltzes this side of heaven. Horst Buchholz makes a valiant effort as young Johann, and there's a welcome on-screen appearance by Mary Costa, the singing voice of Princess Aurora in Walt Disney's animated *Sleeping Beauty*. TS

Horst Buchholz *Johann Strauss Jr* • Mary Costa *Jetty Treffz* • Rossano Brazzi *Baron Tedesco* • Nigel Patrick *Johann Strauss Sr* • Yvonne Mitchell *Anna Strauss* • James Faulkner *Josef Strauss* • Vicki Woolf *Lili Weyl* ■ Dir/Scr Andrew L Stone

The Great White Hope ★★★ 15
Sports drama based on a true story 1970 · US · Colour · 98min

This heavyweight boxing fable, based on the real-life decline and fall of turn-of-the-century black champion Jack Johnson, has a knockout performance by James Earl Jones, but it only just gets by on points as drama and is undermined by an early form of political correctness. Director Martin Ritt wears his conscience too obviously on his sleeve in showing the bigotry that destroys Jones when he falls for a white woman (Jane Alexander), but all is forgiven with Jones's endearing mix of rage and gullibility. TH

James Earl Jones *Jack Jefferson* • Jane Alexander *Eleanor* • Lou Gilbert *Goldie* • Joel Fluellen *Tick* • Chester Morris *Pop Weaver* • Robert Webber *Dixon* • Marlene Warfield *Clara* • RG Armstrong *Cap'n Dan* • Hal Holbrook *Cameron* ■ Dir Martin Ritt • Scr Howard Sackler, from his play

The Great White Hype ★★★ 15
Sports comedy drama 1996 · US · Colour · 86min

This boxing comedy – a brave attempt at satirising the unsatirisable – boasts a heavy-hitting cast that includes boisterous Damon Wayans, sinister Samuel L Jackson and a typically oddball Jeff Goldblum. Wayans is the black heavyweight champion of the world, who has beaten all there is to beat and is seeking new opponents. Step forward fair-skinned rocker Terry Conklin, who once beat Wayans as an amateur, but has since given up the fight game. Jackson persuades him to go back into training again. There are some sharp observations among the many slapstick moments. JF *DVD*

Samuel L Jackson *Reverend Fred Sultan* • Jeff Goldblum *Mitchell Kane* • Peter Berg *Terry Conklin* • Jon Lovitz *Sol* • Damon Wayans *James "the Grim Reaper" Roper* • Corbin Bernsen *Peter Prince* • Richard "Cheech" Marin *Julio Escobar* ■ Dir Reginald Hudlin • Scr Tony Hendra, Ron Shelton

The Great White Silence ★★★★ U
Silent documentary 1924 · UK · Tinted · 103min

Nobody witnessed the final days of Captain Scott and his companions after they were beaten to the South Pole by the Norwegian Roald Amundsen. However, director and cinematographer Herbert G Ponting conveys something of the hardships they endured in this compelling mix of staged and observed sequences. Released 12 years after the event, the account was compiled from footage Ponting had previously presented as an illustrated lecture. The photography is astonishing and the story indelibly tragic, making this a worthy tribute. DP **DVD** SD

Robert Falcon Scott • Lawrence Edward Grace Oates • *Dir* Herbert G Ponting • *Cinematographer* Herbert G Ponting • *Music* Simon Fisher Turner

The Great Ziegfeld ★★★★ U
Musical biography   1936 · US · BW · 168min

This sumptuously mounted MGM musical biography of Broadway's most flamboyant showman is perhaps slightly too long for today's tastes, but it thrilled cinema-goers at the time and won the best film Oscar. Luise Rainer also won the first of two successive Academy Awards as best actress for her performance here as Ziegfeld's wife, and her telephone scene is a lesson in screen acting. Suave William Powell is the Great Flo, a role he reprised eight years later in *Ziegfeld Follies*. TS **DVD**

William Powell *Florenz Ziegfeld* • Luise Rainer *Anna Held* • Myrna Loy *Billie Burke* • Frank Morgan *Billings* • Reginald Owen *Sampston* • Nat Pendleton *Sandow* • Virginia Bruce *Audrey Lane* • Ernest Cossart *Sidney* • *Dir* Robert Z Leonard • *Scr* William Anthony McGuire

The Greatest ★★★ PG
Biographical drama
1977 · US/UK · Colour · 97min

Who else but Muhammad Ali could have starred in this biopic? The charismatic boxer takes to the screen with ease, dancing through his early life as Cassius Clay before reliving the 1974 "Rumble in the Jungle" when he regained his world heavyweight title by defeating George Foreman. Ali's induction into the Nation of Islam, his controversial evasion of the Vietnam draft and his ban from the ring is also given lengthy, if not objective treatment. Rather than restaging the fights, the film sensibly uses archive footage. AT **DVD**

Muhammad Ali • Ernest Borgnine *Angelo Dundee* • John Marley *Dr Pacheco* • Lloyd Haynes *Herbert Muhammad* • Robert Duvall *Bill McDonald* • Ben Johnson (1) *Hollis* • James Earl Jones *Malcolm X* • *Dir* Tom Gries • *Scr* Ring Lardner Jr, from the book *The Greatest: My Own Story* by Muhammad Ali, Herbert Muhammad, Richard Durham

The Greatest ★★★ 15
Drama   2009 · US · Colour · 96min

Filming straight after *An Education*, Carey Mulligan offers up a touchingly vulnerable performance in this moving family drama as a young student whose boyfriend (Aaron Johnson) is killed in a car accident just after they have slept together for the first time. When Mulligan discovers that she is pregnant, she moves in with the dead boy's family, but his mother (Susan Sarandon) has still not come to terms with the tragedy. Although director Shana Feste doesn't completely avoid the usual tear-jerker clichés, the low-key direction and classy performances ensure that this weepie never gets too mawkish. JF Swearing, a sex scene, nudity. **DVD**

Carey Mulligan *Rose* • Susan Sarandon *Grace Brewer* • Pierce Brosnan *Allen Brewer* • Aaron Johnson *Bennett* • Michael Shannon *Jordan Walker* • Zoe Kravitz *Zoë Kravitz] Ashley* • Jennifer Ehle *Joan* • *Dir/Scr* Shana Feste

The Greatest Game Ever Played ★★ PG
Sports drama based on a true story
2005 · US · Colour · 115min

In 1913, a working-class youngster, Francis Ouimet (Shia LaBeouf), competed against British great Harry Vardon (Stephen Dillane) who, along with other English professionals, had dominated the game of golf for years. Although director Bill Paxton and writer Mark Frost sidestep some of the more obvious "plucky Yanks, nasty Brits" clichés, the supporting characters are little

more than caricatures and the fact that both Ouimet and Vardon were both regarded as outsiders by their respective establishments is never really explored. Depressingly bland. JF **DVD**

Shia LaBeouf *Francis Ouimet* • Stephen Dillane *Harry Vardon* • Elias Koteas *Arthur Ouimet* • Josh Flitter *Eddie Lowery* • Peyton List *Sarah Wallis* • Marnie McPhail *Mary Ouimet* • Stephen Marcus *Ted Ray* • Peter Firth *Lord Northcliffe* • *Dir* Bill Paxton • *Scr* Mark Frost, from his non-fiction book *The Greatest Game Ever Played : Vardon, Ouimet and the Birth of Modern Golf*

The Greatest Show on Earth ★★★★ U
Epic drama   1952 · US · Colour · 146min

This is, perhaps, not as great as its title would have us believe, though it did win director Cecil B DeMille an Oscar. On display is a jumbo-sized package of all the clichés that money can buy, as circus owner Charlton Heston strives to control the untamed emotions of Betty Hutton, Cornel Wilde and Gloria Grahame. James Stewart gives the most original performance, playing a clown who never takes off his make-up. As usual, DeMille megaphones his direction, but this is still marvellous entertainment. TH **DVD**

Charlton Heston *Brad*, *a clown* • James Stewart *Buttons*, *a clown* • Betty Hutton *Holly* • Dorothy Lamour *Phyllis* • Cornel Wilde *Sebastian* • Gloria Grahame *Angel* • Lyle Bettger *Klaus* • Lawrence Tierney *Henderson* • Henry Wilcoxon *Detective* • John Kellogg *Harry* • Rosemary Dvorak *Rosemary* • Bob Hope *Spectator* • Bing Crosby *Spectator* • *Dir* Cecil B DeMille • *Scr* Fredric M Frank, Barré Lyndon, Theodore St John, from a story by Theodore St John, Fredric M Frank, Frank Cavett

The Greatest Showman on Earth
Musical biographical drama   2017 · US · Colour

This is a preview - no prints were available to review prior to publication: Hollywood's first original live-action musical since 1992's *Newsies*, *The Greatest Showman on Earth* gives Hugh Jackman a chance to prove that his singing performance in *Les Misérables* was no one-off. This musical tells the story of the 19th-century American showman and genius publicist PT Barnum, and features a screenplay co-written by Bill Condon, whose CV features *Chicago* and *Dreamgirls* while the music is by Mika, writer of pop song *Grace Kelly*. Some toe-tapping should surely be in order. SvM

Hugh Jackman *PT Barnum* • *Dir* Michael Gracey • *Scr* Jenny Bicks, Bill Condon

The Greatest Story Ever Told ★★★ U
Biblical drama   1965 · US · Colour · 190min

George Stevens's epic re-telling of the life of Christ is a monumental achievement, given tremendous power by Max von Sydow's masterful portrayal of Jesus. Unfortunately, the film is fatally compromised by its cumbersome length and the casting of key players in every role. While the likes of Carroll Baker and Sidney Poitier work well, the inclusion of Pat Boone and John Wayne damages the fabric. It's a remarkable movie nonetheless, considering the fact that Stevens fell ill and the great David Lean took over. TS **DVD**

Max von Sydow *Jesus* • Dorothy McGuire *Mary* • José Ferrer *Herod Antipas* • Charlton Heston *John the Baptist* • Sidney Poitier *Simon of Cyrene* • Telly Savalas *Pontius Pilate* • John Wayne *Centurion* • Shelley Winters *Woman of no name* • Martin Landau *Caiaphas* • Claude Rains *Herod the Great* • Carroll Baker *Veronica* • David McCallum (1) *Judas Iscariot* • Robert Loggia *Joseph* • Roddy McDowall *Matthew* • Angela Lansbury *Claudia* • Donald Pleasence *Dark hermit* • Sal Mineo *Uriah* • Pat Boone *Young man at the tomb* • *Dir* George Stevens • *Scr* George Stevens, James Lee Barrett, from the book by Fulton Oursler and radio scripts by Henry Denker

Greed ★★★★★ PG
Classic silent drama   1925 · US · BW · 134min

This is the epic that ensured that director Erich von Stroheim was seen as a genius who could not be trusted. Made over two

years, this was planned to last ten hours, but MGM executives took it away from its creator and cut it down to a more commercial size. As an exercise in vicious irony, it tells the story of an unqualified dentist (Gibson Gowland), engaged to ZaSu Pitts, who becomes a lottery winner but then refuses to spend any of the money. For von Stroheim, human beings were just predatory animals and the moral squalor is never more evident than in the wedding scenes. His obsession with realistic detail reached its zenith during the final scenes in Death Valley, where the actors suffered hugely for the director's art. TH

Gibson Gowland *McTeague* • ZaSu Pitts *Trina* • Jean Hersholt *Marcus Schouler* • Chester Conklin *Mr Sieppe* • Sylvia Ashton *Mrs Sieppe* • Oscar Gottell *Sieppe Twin* • Otto Gottell *Sieppe Twin* • Frank Hayes *Old Grannis* • *Dir* Erich von Stroheim • *Scr* Erich von Stroheim, June Mathis, from the novel *McTeague* by Frank Norris • *Cinematographers* Wm H Daniels [William Daniels (1)], Ben F Reynolds

The Greed of William Hart ★★ PG
Crime melodrama   1948 · UK · BW · 71min

Tod Slaughter gives another of his outrageously over-the-top performances in this low-budget British horror picture, based on the real-life exploits of the infamous 19th-century grave robbers, Burke and Hare. Henry Oscar is equally larger-than-life as his partner in crime. The melodramatic style of the piece verges on the comical nowadays, but, taken on its own terms, the sum of the parts verges on the adequate. PF

Tod Slaughter *William Hart* • Henry Oscar *Mr Moore* • Jenny Lynn *Helen Moore* • Winifred Melville *Meg Hart* • Patrick Addison *Hugh Alston* • Arnold Bell *Doctor Cox* • *Dir* Oswald Mitchell • *Scr* John Gilling

Greedy ★★★ 12
Comedy   1994 · US · Colour · 107min

In this slightly black comedy, the money-grabbing relatives of ailing millionaire Kirk Douglas become apprehensive when the old boy hires a sexy nurse. Michael J Fox and Nancy Travis are among the vultures awaiting their inheritance, but British director Jonathan Lynn's jibes are neither heartless nor hectic enough to gain a full complement of laughs. Movie buffs will note that the family name is McTeague after Erich von Stroheim's 1925 silent classic *Greed*. TH Swearing, brief nudity. **DVD**

Michael J Fox *Daniel McTeague* • Kirk Douglas *Uncle Joe McTeague* • Nancy Travis *Robin Hunter* • Olivia D'Abo *Molly Richardson* • Phil Hartman *Frank* • Ed Begley Jr *Carl* • Jere Burns *Glen* • *Dir* Jonathan Lynn • *Scr* Lowell Ganz, Babaloo Mandel

The Greek Tycoon ★★ 15
Drama   1978 · US · Colour · 111min

Glossy tosh of a kind that the TV mini-series has made infamous, this is about the romance between a Greek shipping magnate and an American president's wife - Aristotle Onassis and Jackie Kennedy by any other name. Anthony Quinn and Jacqueline Bisset fill in the characters as best they can, but it's the lush staging that wins the day. British helmer J Lee Thompson directs this sumptuous rubbish. TH Swearing.

Anthony Quinn *Theo Tomasis* • Jacqueline Bisset *Liz Cassidy* • Raf Vallone *Spyros Tomasis* • Edward Albert *Nico Tomasis* • James Franciscus *James Cassidy* • Charles Durning *Michael Russell* • *Dir* J Lee Thompson • *Scr* Mort Fine, from a story by Mort Fine, Nico Mastorakis, Win Wells

The Green Berets ★★ PG
War drama   1968 · US · Colour · 136min

Most of the films made about the American involvement in Vietnam are highly critical and were produced long after the American withdrawal from that shameful conflict. John Wayne, however, saw Vietnam as a new Alamo, staunch Republican that he was, and both starred in and co-directed this flag-waving action adventure. There's

no denying the epic sweep of the action scenes, but even for Duke fans this is heavy-going, thick-eared nonsense. TS Violence. **DVD** SD

John Wayne *Colonel Mike Kirby* • David Janssen *George Beckworth* • Jim Hutton *Sergeant Petersen* • Aldo Ray *Sergeant Muldoon* • Raymond St Jacques *Doc McGee* • Bruce Cabot *Colonel Morgan* • George Takei *Captain Nim* • Luke Askew *Sergeant Provo* • *Dir* John Wayne, Ray Kellogg • *Scr* James Lee Barrett, from the novel by Robin Moore

The Green Butchers
★★★★ 15

Black comedy   2003 · Den · Colour · 95min

A freak accident sets off an outrageous chain of events in this jet-black Danish comedy. Mads Mikkelsen and Nikolaj Lie Kaas star as mistreated butcher's shop underlings whose decision to establish their own meat emporium seems destined for failure, until they start selling a delicious new type of "chicken". In true Sweeney Todd-style the succulent cuts have an unlikely source, posing a huge problem for the duo when eager customers demand more. The feature is brilliantly composed, skilfully mining life's cruel absurdities for maximum effect. SF Danish +subtitles. **DVD**

Mads Mikkelsen *Svend* • Nikolaj Lie Kaas *Bjarne/Eigil* • Line Kruse *Astrid* • Bodil Jorgensen *Tina* • Ole Thestrup *Holger* • Nicolas Bro *Hus Hans* • *Dir/Scr* Anders Thomas Jensen

Green Card ★★★ 15
Romantic comedy
1990 · Aus/Fr · Colour · 102min

Despite being unoriginal, improbable and not as funny as it should be, Gérard Depardieu's much-anticipated English language debut is still an easy-going comedy. Directed by Peter Weir, it has undeniable charm and features two engaging performances, with Andie MacDowell winning you over to her initially cold, calculating Manhattanite. Weir is a little heavy-handed with the comic set pieces, but he develops the romance with some care and turns the immigration inquiry into a nail-biting tear-jerker. DP Swearing. **DVD**

Gérard Depardieu *George Faure* • Andie MacDowell *Brontë Parrish* • Bebe Neuwirth *Lauren Adler* • Gregg Edelman *Phil* • Robert Prosky *Brontë's lawyer* • Jessie Keosian *Mrs Bird* • Ethan Phillips *Gorsky* • Mary Louise Wilson *Mrs Sheehan* • *Dir/Scr* Peter Weir

The Green Cockatoo ★
Crime drama   1937 · UK · BW · 63min

Sometimes even the greatest of talents don't add up to a successful movie. In this case the original story was by Graham Greene, the director was the great production designer William Cameron Menzies and the film was produced by noted director William K Howard. John Mills is miscast as a singer who sets out to avenge the murder of his brother (Robert Newton). This contrived and episodic imitation of a Hollywood gangster melodrama is set during one dark night in Soho. AE

John Mills *Jim Connor* • René Ray *Eileen* • Robert Newton *Dave Connor* • Charles Oliver *Terrell* • Bruce Seton *Madison* • Julian Vedey *Steve* • Allan Jeayes *Inspector* • Frank Atkinson *Butler* • *Dir* William Cameron Menzies • *Scr* Edward O Berkman, Arthur Wimperis, from a story by Graham Greene

Green Dolphin Street ★★
Adventure drama   1947 · US · BW · 141min

Despite its Oscar-winning earthquake, this romantic drama is a dreary and overlong tale of the dark-haired Lana Turner travelling from the Channel Islands to New Zealand to marry businessman Richard Hart, who really desires her sister, played by Donna Reed. Van Heflin is Hart's partner who secretly covets Turner. AE

Lana Turner *Marianne Patourel* • Van Heflin *Timothy Haslam* • Donna Reed *Marguerite Patourel* • Richard Hart *William Ozanne* • Frank Morgan *Dr Edmund* • Edmund Gwenn *Octavius*

G

Patourel • Dame May Whitty *Mother Superior* • Reginald Owen *Captain O'Hara* • *Dir* Victor Saville • *Scr* Samson Raphaelson, from a novel by Elizabeth Goudge

Green Fields ★★★
Comedy drama   1937 · US · BW · 105min

This adaptation of a Yiddish play proved a huge success, despite a lacklustre performance from Michael Goldstein as the scholar who abandons the synagogue in search of truth. Instead, he finds love in the form of Helen Beverly, whose family are feuding with their neighbours over the privilege of hosting a city slicker in their humble home. Noted for its broad comedy, homespun wisdom and pastoral realism, this ranks among the finer non-English-language films produced in the US. DP Yiddish +subtitles.

Michael Goldstein *Levy Yitzchok* • Helen Beverly *Tzineh* • Izidor Casher [Isidore Cashier] *David Noich* • Anna Appel *Rochel* • Max Vodnoy *Alkuneh* ■ *Dir* Edgar G Ulmer, Jacob Ben-Ami • *Scr* Peretz Hirshbein [Peretz Hirschbein], George G Moskov, from the play *Grine Felder* by Peretz Hirshbein [Peretz Hirschbein]

Green Fire ★★★ U
Romantic drama   1954 · US · Colour · 100min

This glossy MGM adventure co-stars tanned Stewart Granger and sleek Grace Kelly, who were arguably the best-looking couple in movies since Vivien Leigh and Robert Taylor in *Waterloo Bridge*. In its day, this romp was accused of wasting Kelly's talents, but she's actually well cast as the plantation owner who falls for tough emerald miner Granger, and their love scenes together sizzle. The plot's a load of old hokum about slimy Murvyn Vye trying to steal Granger's gems, but there are some fine set pieces. TS

Stewart Granger *Rian Mitchell* • Grace Kelly *Catherine Knowland* • Paul Douglas *Vic Leonard* • John Ericson *Donald Knowland* • Murvyn Vye *El Moro* • José Torvay *Manuel* • Robert Tafur *Father Ripero* ■ *Dir* Andrew Marton • *Scr* Ivan Goff, Ben Roberts

Green for Danger ★★★★ PG
Comedy thriller   1946 · UK · BW · 86min

This is the kind of brisk, bright and thoroughly engaging entertainment that the British film industry has, sadly, forgotten how to make. But, then again, there are no more Alastair Sims to transform a passage of jovial banter into a moment of nail-biting suspense simply by slowing that melancholy Scottish accent and lowering those expressive oyster eyes. Gone, too, are such expert character actors as Leo Genn, whose ability to portray heroes and villains alike deepened the mystery in whodunnits such as this one, in which a patient is murdered on the operating table. Sidney Gilliat directs with a deliciously dark wit. DP **DVD**

Alastair Sim *Inspector Cockrill* • Sally Gray *Nurse Linley* • Trevor Howard *Dr Barney Barnes* • Rosamund John *Nurse Esther Sanson* • Leo Genn *Mr Eden* • Judy Campbell *Sister Marion Bates* • Megs Jenkins *Nurse Woods* • Moore Marriott *Joe Higgins* ■ *Dir* Sidney Gilliat • *Scr* Sidney Gilliat, Claude Guerney, from a novel by Christianna Brand

Green Grass of Wyoming ★★ U
Drama   1948 · US · Colour · 84min

Winding up the Flicka trilogy, this is yet another "how to do it" horsey picture, this time offering an insider's view of the highly competitive sport of trotting. Even though cinematographer Charles Clarke was nominated for an Oscar, it is comfortably the weakest of the series, eschewing wide-eyed innocence for a *Romeo and Juliet*-style romance between Peggy Cummins and Robert Arthur, respectively niece and son of implacable trotting rivals Charles Coburn and Lloyd Nolan. DP

Peggy Cummins *Carey Greenway* • Charles Coburn *Beaver* • Robert Arthur (1) *Ken* • Lloyd Nolan *Rob McLaughlin* • Burl Ives *Gus* • Robert Adler *Joe* • Will Wright *Jake* ■ *Dir* Louis King • *Scr* Martin Berkeley, from the novel by Mary O'Hara

Green Grow the Rushes ★★ U
Comedy   1951 · UK · BW · 88min

In his last home-grown picture before joining 20th Century-Fox, Richard Burton plays the leader of a gang of brandy smugglers in a nondescript and shameless reworking of Ealing's *Whisky Galore!* Burton was never an accomplished comedian and he struggles to raise anything of his thin ration of jokes. Roger Livesey fares little better as the skipper. DP

Roger Livesey *Captain Biddle* • Honor Blackman *Meg* • Richard Burton *Hammond* • Frederick Leister *Colonel Gill* • John Salew *Finch* • Colin Gordon *Fisherwick* • Geoffrey Keen *Prudhoe* • Cyril Smith *Hewitt* • Vida Hope *Polly* • Eliot Makeham *Urquhart* ■ *Dir* Derek Twist • *Scr* Howard Clewes, Derek Twist, from a novel by Clewes

Green Hell ★
Adventure   1939 · US · BW · 84min

There's a good half hour of hilarity to be had in this famously ludicrous jungle melodrama before tedium takes over. Although capably staged in studio sets by James Whale and well enough cast, it is made unendurable by the dialogue and situations. As Vincent Price once said, "About five of the worst pictures ever made are all in this one picture." AE

Douglas Fairbanks Jr *Keith Brandon* • Joan Bennett *Stephanie Richardson* • John Howard (1) *Hal Scott* • George Sanders *Forrester* • Vincent Price *David Richardson* • Alan Hale *Dr Loren* • George Bancroft *Tex Morgan* • Ray Mala *Mala* ■ *Dir* James Whale • *Scr* Frances Marion, Harry Hervey, from a story by Frances Marion

The Green Helmet ★★ U
Motor racing drama   1960 · US · BW · 88min

Motor sport continues to be a frustratingly elusive subject for film-makers. Thus, a cameo from three-time champion Jack Brabham is the main reason for watching this undistinguished horse-power opera. The gradual disintegration of second-rate racer Bill Travers rarely gets out of low gear thanks to Michael Forlong's pedestrian direction. DP

Bill Travers *Greg Rafferty* • Ed Begley *Bartell* • Sidney James *Richie Launder* • Nancy Walters *Diane Bartell* • Ursula Jeans *Mrs Rafferty* • Megs Jenkins *Kitty Launder* • Sean Kelly *Taz Rafferty* • Jack Brabham ■ *Dir* Michael Forlong • *Scr* Jon Cleary, from his novel

The Green Horizon ★★
Drama   1981 · Jpn · Colour · 120min

Noted for introducing *cinéma vérité* realism into his fictional features, director Susumu Hani spent much of the 1970s making wildlife documentaries for Japanese television. He combines both preoccupations in this mediocre melodrama, which looks superb but makes few emotional or intellectual demands. In what proved to be his final big-screen appearance, James Stewart is wasted as the owner of an African animal sanctuary whose peaceful idyll is disrupted when pilot Philip Sayer crash-lands in the jungle and falls in love with Stewart's granddaughter. DP

James Stewart *Old Man* • Philip Sayer *Man* • Kathy *Girl* ■ *Dir* Susumu Hani, Simon Trevor • *Scr* Shintaro Tsuji, from a story by Shuji Terayama • *Cinematographer* Simon Trevor

The Green Hornet ★★ 12
Action comedy   2011 · US · Colour · 113min

Director Michel Gondry filters the masked crime-fighter's exploits through the slacker comedy idiom in this tiresome escapade. Playboy Britt Reid (Seth Rogen) inherits a media empire, teams up with tech-wizard and martial arts expert Kato (Jay Chou) and becomes the Green Hornet. The pair's attempts at heroism unwittingly threaten the underworld empire of fun villain Christoph Waltz. Unfortunately, the moronic raunchiness, off-key humour and slapstick action are irritating distractions, although Gondry does use some neat effects to add style to the light-hearted romp. AJ

Violence, swearing, sexual references. **DVD** **Blu**

Seth Rogen *Britt Reid/The Green Hornet* • Jay Chou *Kato* • Cameron Diaz *Lenore Case* • Christoph Waltz *Chudnofsky* • Edward James Olmos *Axford* • David Harbour *Scanlon* • Tom Wilkinson *James Reid* • Edward Furlong *Tupper* ■ *Dir* Michel Gondry • *Scr* Evan Goldberg, Seth Rogen, from characters by George W Trendle, Fran Striker • *Cinematographer* John Schwartzman

Green Ice ★★ 15
Crime caper   1981 · UK · Colour · 104min

One of those films that doesn't realise the offence it is causing by making comedy thrills out of a national tragedy. Ryan O'Neal and Anne Archer are fine as the couple involved in a risky heist of gems to fill rebel coffers in Colombia, and Omar Sharif is an entertaining enough villain, but the general light-heartedness of tone sits awkwardly on a story involving torture and armed struggle. TH

Ryan O'Neal *Joseph Wiley* • Anne Archer *Holbrook* • Omar Sharif *Meno Argenti* • Domingo Ambriz *Miguel* • John Larroquette *Claude* • Philip Stone *Kellerman* • Michael Sheard *Jaap* • Enrique Lucero *Lucho* ■ *Dir* Ernest Day • *Scr* Edward Anhalt, Ray Hassett, Anthony Simmons, Robert De Laurentiis, from the book by Gerald Browne

The Green Inferno ★★★ 18
Horror   2013 · US/Chil/UK · Colour · 96min

Genre guru Eli Roth returned to the director's chair after six years with this homage to 1970s Italian cannibal exploitation flicks. Lorenza Izzo stars as the student who travels to Peru to halt the annihilation of an endangered tribe. But after a brilliantly staged plane crash leaves some passengers dead, the survivors are caged by the very flesh-eaters they were trying to help. Misguided drug humour and some dodgy performances aside, Roth's beautifully photographed tract offers thrills, gore and thought-provoking horror. AJ Violence **DVD** **Blu**

Lorenza Izzo *Justine* • Ariel Levy *Alejandro* • Daryl Sabara *Lars* • Kirby Bliss Blanton *Amy* • Sky Ferreira *Kaycee* ■ *Dir* Eli Roth • *Scr* Eli Roth, Guillermo Amoedo, from a story by Roth

Green Lantern ★★ 12
Fantasy adventure   2011 · US · Colour · 113min

DC Comics' attempt to keep up with Marvel's quality superhero dramatisations falters with this disappointing origins adventure. Quick-quipping Ryan Reynolds is a good fit for the part of Hal Jordan, the cocky test pilot whose close encounter with a dying alien sees him inherit an all-powerful ring and become a member of an intergalactic peacekeeping corps. But here he's lumbered with a cliché-ridden, uninspiring script and an anodyne love interest (*Gossip Girl's* Blake Lively). There are classy turns from Mark Strong and Tim Robbins, but they just don't have enough to work with. JA **DVD** **Blu**

Ryan Reynolds *Hal Jordan/Green Lantern* • Blake Lively *Carol Ferris* • Peter Sarsgaard *Hector Hammond* • Mark Strong *Sinestro* • Temuera Morrison *Abin Sur* • Tim Robbins *Senator Hammond* ■ *Dir* Martin Campbell • *Scr* Greg Berlanti, Michael Goldenberg, Michael Green, Marc Guggenheim, from a story by Berlanti, Green, Guggenheim (all uncredited), from characters by John Broome, Gil Kane (both uncredited)

Green Light ★★
Medical drama   1937 · US · BW · 84min

This torrid tear-jerker stars Errol Flynn as a surgeon who takes the blame when a patient dies on the operating table. Flynn then finds religion, uses his own body to experiment with a new vaccine and falls in love with the dead patient's daughter. It's sanctimony all the way, and pretty daft it is, too. Made by Warner Bros to placate its restless star who was feeling trapped as an action hero, this co-stars Anita Louise and was directed by the master of cringe, Frank Borzage. AT

Errol Flynn *Dr Newell Paige* • Anita Louise *Phyllis Dexter* • Margaret Lindsay *Frances Ogilvie* • Cedric Hardwicke *Dean George Harcourt* • Walter

Abel *Dr John Stafford* • Henry O'Neill *Dr Endicott* • Spring Byington *Mrs Dexter* • Erin O'Brien-Moore *Pat Arlen* ■ *Dir* Frank Borzage • *Scr* Milton Krims, Paul Green (uncredited), from the novel by Lloyd C Douglas

The Green Man ★★★★ PG
Comedy   1956 · UK · BW · 76min

If you ever doubted that Alastair Sim was the finest British screen comedian of the sound era, then here's the proof of his immense talent. As the assassin with the mournful smile, he gives a performance of rare genius that more than makes amends for the longueurs in the script. The sequence in which he persuades three old dears to cease their recital so that his radio bomb can finish off politician Raymond Huntley is a masterclass in the lost art of farce. Huntley also excels as the pompous target, but George Cole is overly bumbling as the salesman who uncovers the plot. DP **DVD**

Alastair Sim *Hawkins* • George Cole *William Blake* • Jill Adams *Ann Vincent* • Avril Angers *Marigold* • Terry-Thomas *Boughtflower* • John Chandos *McKecknie* • Raymond Huntley *Sir Gregory Upshoot* ■ *Dir* Robert Day • *Scr* Sidney Gilliat, Frank Launder, from their play *Meet a Body*

Green Mansions ★★ PG
Romantic adventure   1959 · US · Colour · 100min

Audrey Hepburn stars a mystical "Bird Girl", communing with nature and winning the heart of Anthony Perkins in the Venezuelan jungle. Alas, the film (directed by the star's then husband, actor Mel Ferrer) is misconceived. A poor screenplay fails to capture the elusive magic of the fantasy novel from which it was adapted, and the whole thing is photographed in unattractive shades of green. However, the doe-like beauty of Hepburn, followed around by a lookalike young deer, and an equally youthful Perkins, afford some fleeting pleasure. RK **DVD**

Audrey Hepburn *Rima* • Anthony Perkins *Abel* • Lee J Cobb *Nuflo* • Sessue Hayakawa *Runi* • Henry Silva *Kua-Ko* • Nehemiah Persoff *Don Panta* • Michael Pate *Priest* ■ *Dir* Mel Ferrer • *Scr* Dorothy Kingsley, from the novel by William Henry Hudson

The Green Mile ★★★ 18
Fantasy prison drama
1999 · US · Colour · 180min

Set in a Louisiana prison in 1935, this overblown, sentimental fantasy stars Tom Hanks as a guard who forms a life-affirming relationship with a black prisoner, on death row for the murder of two little girls. Suspension of disbelief is essential if you're to enjoy Frank Darabont's reverential adaptation of Stephen King's 1996 novel. All the wardens are angels, bar one, while giant-sized newcomer Michael Clarke Duncan is too gentle to convince as a convicted child-killer. DM Violence, swearing. **DVD** **Blu**

Tom Hanks *Paul Edgecomb* • David Morse *Brutus "Brutal" Howell* • Bonnie Hunt *Jan Edgecomb* • Michael Clarke Duncan *John Coffey* • James Cromwell *Warden Hal Moores* • Michael Jeter *Eduard Delacroix* • Graham Greene (2) *Arlen Bitterbuck* • Doug Hutchison *Percy Wetmore* • Sam Rockwell *"Wild Bill" Wharton* • Harry Dean Stanton *Toot-Toot* ■ *Dir* Frank Darabont • *Scr* Frank Darabont, from the novel by Stephen King

The Green Prince ★★★ 15
Documentary
2014 · Ger/US/UK/Is · Colour · 100min

If it were proposed as fiction, the story of Mosab Hassan Yousef would beggar belief. The son of a leading light in Hamas, Yousef was persuaded to turn informer by Gonen Ben Yitzhak, a senior operative within Israel's top secret security force Shin Bet. Despite its tense, spy-movie stylings, the film stops short of a satisfying payoff, and what prompted Yousef to accept such a dangerous mission is never fully explained. But this often gripping documentary goes a long way to portraying the paranoid mindset of a man who went on to betray his closest family. DW

Mosab Hassan Yousef *Mosab Hassan Yousef* •
Gonen Ben Yitzhak *Gonen Ben Yitzhak* ■
Dir Nadav Schirman • *Scr* Nadav Schirman, from
the memoir *Son of Hamas: a Gripping Account of
Terror, Betrayal, Political Intrigue, and
Unthinkable Choices* by Mosab Hassan Yousef

The Green Ray ★★★★ PG
Comedy drama   1986 · Fr · Colour · 94min

Unlike Eric Rohmer's previous films, the
dialogue of this comedy of manners was
almost entirely improvised by the actors.
How one reacts to the film may depend on
how one reacts to the character of the
overly fastidious Delphine, played superbly
by Marie Rivière. Not knowing what to do
on her holidays, she goes to Cherbourg,
then the mountains and then Biarritz, but is
bored and depressed everywhere until she
meets the man of her dreams. The title,
taken from the Jules Verne novel, refers to
the last ray of sunset, the green of which is
supposed to make observers more aware of
the feelings of others. Rohmer's films have
much the same effect. **RB** French
+subtitles. *DVD*

Marie Rivière *Delphine* • Vincent Gauthier
Jacques • Béatrice Romand *Béatrice* • Sylvie
Richez *Sylvie* • Basile Gervaise *Grandfather* ■
Dir/Scr Eric Rohmer

The Green Room ★★★
Drama   1978 · Fr · Colour · 94min

Alfred Hitchcock's *Vertigo* haunts this film,
inspired by the works of Henry James.
Director/co-writer François Truffaut also
stars as the obituarist whose life is devoted
to the memory of his beloved wife and the
victims of the First World War. Such is the
totality of his grief that even when he
befriends Nathalie Baye, the best he can
offer her is a chance to become a fellow
mourner at his vigil. Peering through
cinematographer Nestor Almendros's
gloomy interiors, it's easy to see just how
personal a project this was, but it's harder
to share in Truffaut's obsessions. **DP** French
+subtitles.

François Truffaut *Julien Davenne* • Nathalie Baye
Cecilia Mandel • Jean Dasté *Bernard Humbert* •
Jean-Pierre Moulin *Gérard Mazet* • Antoine Vitez
Bishop's secretary • Jane Lobre *Madame
Rambaud* • Monique Dury *Editorial secretary* ■
Dir François Truffaut • *Scr* François Truffaut,
Jean Gruault, from the works of Henry James

Green Room ★★★★ 18
Thriller   2015 · US · Colour · 94min

Writer/director Jeremy Saulnier follows his
mesmerising revenge tale *Blue Ruin* with
another pulsating thriller. Here, young punk
band the Ain't Rights (led by *Star Trek*'s
Anton Yelchin) end up in the wrong place at
the wrong time when they play a gig in the
backwoods of Oregon. When they return to
the green room and find a dead body, the
quartet and local girl Amber (Imogen Poots)
are soon besieged by vicious thugs with no
qualms about eliminating the unwanted
witnesses. The contrast between the
pastoral setting and the shocking blood-
letting creates lots of breathless tension, as
the frantic five try to escape. **JA** Violence,
swearing, drug abuse

Anton Yelchin *Pat* • Imogen Poots *Amber* •
Patrick Stewart *Darcy* • Alia Shawkat *Sam* • Joe
Cole *Reece* ■ *Dir/Scr* Jeremy Saulnier

The Green Scarf ★★
Mystery   1954 · UK · BW · 88min

This murky murder mystery is set in Paris
with an oh-so-British cast as French
characters. Michael Redgrave is a lawyer
defending a blind, deaf and dumb murder
suspect (Kieron Moore) who, thinking his
wife (Ann Todd) had killed her lover,
confesses to the crime. Courtroom dramas
seldom fail to hold the attention and this is
no exception, despite the mechanical
performances, lame script and uninspiring
direction. **RB**

Michael Redgrave *Deliot* • Ann Todd *Solange* •
Leo Genn *Rodelec* • Kieron Moore *Jacques* •
Richard O'Sullivan *Jacques as a child* • Jane
Lamb *Solange as a child* • Ella Milne *Louise* •
Jane Griffiths *Danielle* ■ *Dir* George More
O'Ferrall • *Scr* Gordon Wellesley, from the novel
The Brute by Guy des Cars

Green Street ★★ 18
Drama   2004 · US/UK · Colour · 104min

Elijah Wood plays an American journalism
student who moves to London and
becomes a member of West Ham football
hooligans, the Green Street Elite. The low
production values and simplistic (not to say
nonsensical) plot do this no favours at all. It
relies on hackneyed camerawork, unsubtle
use of music and predictable character
turns. **KK** Swearing, violence. *DVD* Blu

Elijah Wood *Matt Buckner* • Charlie Hunnam *Pete
Dunham* • Claire Forlani *Shannon Dunham* • Marc
Warren (1) *Steve Dunham* • Leo Gregory *Bovver* •
Henry Goodman *Carl Buckner* • Geoff Bell
Tommy Hatcher • Rafe Spall *Swill* ■ *Dir* Lexi
Alexander • *Scr* Lexi Alexander, Dougie Brimson,
Josh Shelov

The Green Years ★★★
Drama   1946 · US · BW · 126min

MGM didn't need top stars to have a huge
box-office success with its film adaptation
of AJ Cronin's popular novel. Set in
Scotland, it's capably directed by Britain's
Victor Saville. In his first major role, nine-
year-old Dean Stockwell shines as the boy
growing up in a hostile family environment
and forging a close relationship with his
extraordinary great-grandfather. A bearded
Charles Coburn plays the alcoholic old
codger so engagingly that he received his
third Oscar nomination for best supporting
actor. **AE**

Charles Coburn *Alexander Gow* • Tom Drake
Robert Shannon • Beverly Tyler *Alison Keith* •
Hume Cronyn *Papa Leckie* • Gladys Cooper
Grandma Leckie • Dean Stockwell *Robert
Shannon as a child* • Selena Royle *Mama Leckie* •
Jessica Tandy *Kate Leckie* ■ *Dir* Victor Saville •
Scr Robert Ardrey, Sonya Levien, from the novel
by AJ Cronin

Green Zone ★★★★ 15
War action thriller
2010 · US/UK/Fr/Sp · Colour · 109min

The fruitless search for Weapons of Mass
Destruction immediately following the 2003
Iraq invasion leaves one dogged US Army
officer questioning his own side in this
blend of military action and conspiracy
thriller. This reteaming of director Paul
Greengrass and star Matt Damon delivers
plenty of high-octane *Bourne*-style
entertainment as Damon's character
barrels through a series of life-threatening
scrapes. Powerful performances from a
cast that includes Brendan Gleeson and
Greg Kinnear illustrate different sides of the
argument – even if the film ultimately
condemns the short-sightedness of the
Bush-led campaign. Exciting, believable and
thought-provoking, this is what popular
cinema is all about. **TJ** Violence, swearing.
DVD Blu

Matt Damon *Roy Miller* • Greg Kinnear *Clark
Poundstone* • Brendan Gleeson *Martin Brown* •
Amy Ryan *Lawrie Dayne* • Khalid Abdalla *Freddy*
• Jason Isaacs *Lt Briggs* ■ *Dir* Paul Greengrass •
Scr Brian Helgeland, from the non-fiction book
*Imperial Life in the Emerald City: Inside Iraq's
Green Zone* by Rajiv Chandrasekaran

Greenberg ★★★ 15
Comedy drama   2009 · US · Colour · 107min

Ben Stiller gets alarmingly morose as an
apparent no-hoper recovering from a
nervous breakdown in this comedy drama
from Noah Baumbach (*The Squid and the
Whale*). Years before, Roger Greenberg
(Stiller) ran out on a Los Angeles band that
was about to become successful. Now he's
back in LA, house-sitting for his high-flying
brother and trying to sort out his future. It
doesn't sound like a barrel of laughs, but
Stiller has a talent for comical ranting and
Rhys Ifans makes a great straight man as
his long-suffering former band-mate.
Baumbach's authentic-feeling dialogue
works best in the scenes between Roger
and his brother's personal assistant,
Florence (Greta Gerwig). Their awkward,
dysfunctional romance may not reach a
completely satisfying resolution, but this is
still rather fun. **SP** *DVD* Blu

Ben Stiller *Roger Greenberg* • Greta Gerwig
Florence Marr "Flo" • Rhys Ifans *Ivan Schrank* •
Jennifer Jason Leigh *Beth* • Brie Larson *Sara* •
Juno Temple *Muriel* • Chris Messina *Phillip
Greenberg* • Susan Traylor *Carol Greenberg* ■
Dir Noah Baumbach • *Scr* Noah Baumbach, from
a story by Jennifer Jason Leigh, Baumbach

Greenfingers ★★★ 15
Comedy drama   2000 · UK/US · Colour · 86min

Clive Owen stars as the no-hope convict
who's transferred to an open prison. An
incident with a packet of African violet
seeds means he's commanded by the
governor to create a garden. His patch
attracts the attention of gardening guru
Helen Mirren and soon Owen's team are
doing out-reach work and entering the
Hampton Court Palace show. Based on a
true story, this is desperately sweet, but
entertaining. **LH** *DVD*

Clive Owen *Colin Briggs* • Helen Mirren *Georgina
Woodhouse* • David Kelly *Fergus Wilks* • Warren
Clarke *Governor Hodge* • Danny Dyer *Tony* •
Adam Fogerty *Raw* • Paterson Joseph *Jimmy* •
Natasha Little *Primrose Woodhouse* ■
Dir/Scr Joel Hershman

The Greengage Summer ★★★ PG
Romantic drama   1961 · UK · Colour · 95min

Charmingly capturing the brilliance of youth
and the beauty of champagne country,
director Lewis Gilbert's adaptation of
Rumer Godden's novel suffers only from a
disappointingly trite ending. As the 16-year-
old forced to take charge of her siblings
when their mother falls ill, Susannah York
radiates the innocent's new-found lust for
life and, whether getting tipsy for the first
time or suffering from the initial pangs of
love, she is truly captivating. As the mystery
man who steals her heart, Kenneth More
allows her the space to mature, while also
revealing a more cynical side in his dealings
with his landlady lover, Danielle
Darrieux. **DP**

Kenneth More *Eliot* • Danielle Darrieux *Madame
Zizi* • Susannah York *Joss Grey* • Claude Nollier
Madame Corbet • Jane Asher *Hester Grey* •
Richard Williams *Willmouse Grey* ■ *Dir* Lewis
Gilbert • *Scr* Howard Koch, from the novel by
Rumer Godden

Greenmail ★★ 15
Action drama   2001 · US/Can · Colour · 92min

There's a whiff of *The Silence of the Lambs*
about this eco-thriller, as a government
agent is forced to rely on a charismatic
adversary to halt a crime spree. However,
Kelly Rowan's shaky alliance with
environmental activist Stephen Baldwin is
never in the same league, owing to
Jonathan Heap's by-the-numbers direction
of a story centring on a bombing campaign
against a controversial Seattle chemical
plant. The simmering sexual frisson
between the pair also never really rings
true. **DP** *DVD*

Stephen Baldwin *Scott Anderson* • Tom Skerritt
Tom Bradshaw • Kelly Rowan *Ashley Pryor* • DB
Sweeney *Jeremy O'Brien* ■ *Dir* Jonathan Heap •
Scr Raul Inglis, Jim Makichuk, Jonathan Walker

Greenwich Village ★★★ U
Musical   1944 · US · Colour · 78min

This jolly enjoyable Technicolor 20th
Century-Fox musical is ostensibly set in the
titular artists' quarter of New York City in
the Roaring Twenties. But, since the
speakeasy run by proprietor William Bendix
features the fabulous Carmen Miranda and
vivacious Vivian Blaine, we're clearly in the
mid-1940s, which means superb musical
arrangements and the skimpiest of plots on
which to hang them. Don Ameche is the
hick composer hired by Bendix to write a
show, but keep your eyes sharply peeled for
a glimpse of the legendary Judy
Holliday. **TS**

Carmen Miranda *Princess Querida* • Don Ameche
Kenneth Harvey • William Bendix *Danny O'Mara* •
Vivian Blaine *Bonnie Watson* • Felix Bressart
Moger • Tony De Marco • Sally De Marco • BS
Pully *Brophy* ■ *Dir* Walter Lang • *Scr* Earl
Baldwin, Walter Bullock, Michael Fessier

(adaptation), Ernest B Pagano (adaptation), from
a story by Fred Hazlitt Brennan [Frederick Hazlitt
Brennan]

Greetings ★★★ 18
Satirical comedy   1968 · US · Colour · 87min

Brian De Palma's early experimental feature
follows the efforts of two men (Robert De
Niro and Gerrit Graham) to get their best
friend out of the army draft. The slight
story is a mere springboard to attack such
political targets as Lyndon Johnson, the
Vietnam War and the Warren Commission
report on the assassination of John F
Kennedy, using *cinéma vérité*, sexual
obsession and voyeurism. Slapdash, vulgar
and smug, it was a huge youth culture hit
and spawned the sequel *Hi, Mom!*. **AJ**
Nudity, swearing. *DVD*

Jonathan Warden *Paul Shaw* • Robert De Niro
Jon Rubin • Gerrit Graham *Lloyd Clay* • Richard
Hamilton *Pop artist* • Megan McCormick *Marina* •
Alan Garfield [Allen Garfield] *Smut peddler* ■
Dir Brian De Palma • *Scr* Charles Hirsch, Brian De
Palma

Gregory's Girl ★★★★ 12
Romantic comedy   1980 · UK · Colour · 87min

This is a case of near faultless film-making
from Bill Forsyth, who latterly hasn't
fulfilled this early promise under the
auspices of Hollywood. As director, he
keeps a wry eye on the triangle linking
school goalkeeper Gordon John Sinclair
(now John Gordon), centre forward Dee
Hepburn and her pal Clare Grogan. But it is
as scriptwriter that he excels, capturing the
anxieties and insecurities of teen love and
the language of the playground with
consummate skill. He also creates a glorious
array of secondary characters, including
Robert Buchanan and William Greenlees as
Sinclair's lovelorn mates and Chic Murray as
the laconic headmaster. **DP** Swearing.
DVD Blu

Gordon John Sinclair [John Gordon-Sinclair]
Gregory • Dee Hepburn *Dorothy* • Jake D'Arcy
Phil Menzies • Clare Grogan *Susan* • Robert
Buchanan *Andy* • William Greenlees [Billy
Greenlees] *Steve* • Chic Murray *Headmaster* •
Alex Norton *Alec* ■ *Dir/Scr* Bill Forsyth

Gregory's Two Girls ★★ 15
Comedy   1999 · UK/Ger · Colour · 111min

A strong anti-American flavour laces this
sequel to Bill Forsyth's best-known film.
There's still plenty of his quirky
observational humour, though, which
provides the perfect platform for John
Gordon-Sinclair to give a genial
performance of political awareness, social
ineptitude and sexual timidity. Now a
teacher at his old school, Gregory wavers
between a crush on fifth-former Carly
McKinnon and the advances of colleague
Maria Doyle Kennedy. The plot about Third
World repression is barely credible. **DP**
DVD

John Gordon-Sinclair *Gregory Underwood* •
Dougray Scott *Fraser Rowan* • Maria Doyle
Kennedy *Bel* • Carly McKinnon *Frances* • Hugh
McCue *Douglas* • Kevin Anderson *Jon* • Fiona Bell
Maddy Underwood • Martin Schwab *Dimitri* ■
Dir/Scr Bill Forsyth

Gremlins ★★★★ 12
Black comedy horror   1984 · US · Colour · 101min

This wonderfully anarchic affair is probably
one of Hollywood's blackest mainstream
hits. Zach Galligan is the teenager who is
given a cuddly exotic pet mogwai called
Gizmo, but through carelessness
unwittingly unleashes a viciously murderous
swarm of little gremlins. There's no doubt
whose side director Joe Dante is on and he
gleefully trashes the view of small-town
America portrayed by movies such as *It's a
Wonderful Life* (which is being screened on
TV throughout the tale). Film buffs will
delight in the in-jokes and cameos. **JF**
Violence, swearing. *DVD* Blu

Zach Galligan *Billy Peltzer* • Phoebe Cates *Kate* •
Hoyt Axton *Rand Peltzer* • Frances Lee McCain
Lynn Peltzer • Polly Holliday *Mrs Deagle* • Keye
Luke *Grandfather* • John Louie *Chinese boy* •
Dick Miller *Mr Futterman* ■ *Dir* Joe Dante • *Scr*
Chris Columbus • *Executive Producer* Steven
Spielberg

Gremlins 2: the New Batch ★★★ 12

Black comedy horror
1990 · US · Colour · 102min

Joe Dante's anarchic view of life is given full rein in this chaotic but cracking sequel. The action is transplanted to a skyscraper in New York where mad scientist Christopher Lee inadvertently lets the evil gremlins loose to take over the entire building. As with the original, Dante bombards the screen with a never-ending stream of movie spoofs, slapstick violence and sly little treats for film buffs. JF Violence, swearing. *DVD* CS
Zach Galligan *Billy Peltzer* · Phoebe Cates *Kate Beringer* · John Glover *Daniel Clamp* · Robert Prosky *Grandpa Fred* · Howie Mandel *Gizmo* · Tony Randall *"Brain" Gremlin* · Robert Picardo *Forster* · Christopher Lee *Dr Catheter* · Dick Miller *Murray Futterman* ■ *Dir* Joe Dante · *Scr* Charlie Haas, from characters by Chris Columbus

Gremloids ★★★ PG

Science-fiction comedy
1990 · US · Colour · 86min

In this reasonably successful low-budget *Star Wars* spoof, a navigation mistake lands cosmic bad guy Buckethead on Earth instead of in a galaxy far, far away. He's in hot pursuit of a princess who's run off with some secret radio transmissions. Buckethead (and indeed he does have a bucket on his head!) is the Darth Vader of director Todd Durham's refreshing piece, which doesn't set its satirical sights too high and hits more targets dead on as a result. AJ
Paula Poundstone *Karen* · Chris Elliott *Hopper* · Alan Marx *Max* ■ *Dir/Scr* Todd Durham

The Grey ★★★ 15

Action drama
2012 · US/Can · Colour · 112min

Liam Neeson is magnetic as the natural leader of a group of men who survive a plane crash in the Alaskan tundra. He has to be, not only for his companions but for the sake of this thriller, which badly needs some meat on its bones. Initially Neeson's hunter is suicidal after losing the woman he loves, but he resets to survival mode when a pack of wolves begins to stalk the men across the snow. Fortunately, Neeson has the gravitas to evoke his character's inner strength but even so, this works more as a horror film than a character study. SP Swearing. *DVD* *BL* CS
Liam Neeson *Ottway* · Frank Grillo *Diaz* · Dermot Mulroney *Talget* · Dallas Roberts *Henrick* · Nonso Anozie *Burke* · James Badge Dale *Lewenden* ■ *Dir* Joe Carnahan · *Scr* Joe Carnahan, Ian Mackenzie Jeffers, from the short story *Ghost Walker* by Jeffers

The Grey Fox ★★★★ PG

Western
1982 · Can · Colour · 87min

Richard Farnsworth gives a marvellous performance in this low-budget Canadian picture. Emerging in 1901 after 33 years in jail, Farnsworth tries to pick up where he left off as one of the Old West's most notorious outlaws – but those days are long gone. Shot in pseudo-documentary style, which gives the film the flavour of old photographs, this is a real charmer in the tradition of *The Wild Bunch* and *Butch Cassidy*. AT
Richard Farnsworth *Bill Miner/George Edwards* · Jackie Burroughs *Kate Flynn* · Wayne Robson *William "Shorty" Dunn* · Timothy Webber *Sergeant Fernie* · Ken Pogue *Jack Budd* · Gary Reineke *Detective Seavey* ■ *Dir* Phillip Borsos · *Scr* John Hunter

Grey Gardens ★★★★

Documentary
1975 · US · Colour · 94min

Two years after the clean-up of the squalid 28-room Long Island mansion in which they'd incarcerated themselves for decades, 78-year-old Edith Bouvier Beale and her 56-year-old daughter Edie – aunt and first cousin of Jacqueline Onassis – were captured on film over several weeks in 1974. The mansion was still in disrepair, not unlike its resilient, spirited but rather sad and time-warped inhabitants, who in this voyeur's feast bare all and share screen time with an amusing supporting cast of cats and raccoons and occasional bemused human guests. The film casts a spell with its alternately camp, poignant and fiery scenes in which eccentric mother and daughter battle it out in the performance stakes, with endearing, flirty "Little Edie" in a category all of her own. An alien but somehow familiar world revealed. DO *DVD* *BL*
Edith Bouvier Beale · Edith B Beale Jr ■ *Dir* Ellen Hovde, Muffie Meyer, David Maysles, Albert Maysles

Grey Gardens ★★★

Biographical drama
2009 · US · Colour · 104min

Taking the above documentary as inspiration and with many scenes in common, this is a biopic of "Big" Edie (Jessica Lange) and "Little" Edie (Drew Barrymore) that depicts their lives before and after their fall from grace. The film belies its TV-movie origins, with lovingly re-created sets and fantastic costumes, while Barrymore's Golden Globe-winning performance really stands out. LB
Drew Barrymore *"Little" Edith Bouvier Beale* · Jessica Lange *"Big" Edith Bouvier Beale* · Jeanne Tripplehorn *Jacqueline Kennedy Onassis* · Daniel Baldwin *Julius Krug* · Malcolm Gets *George "Gould" Strong* · Arye Gross *Albert Maysles* · Justin Louis *David Maysles* ■ *Dir* Michael Sucsy · *Scr* Michael Sucsy, Patricia Rozema · *Cinematographer* Mike Eley

Grey Owl ★★★ PG

Biographical drama
1999 · UK/Can · Colour · 113min

Pierce Brosnan stars as the eponymous hero of this worthy biography about one of the first eco-warriors, who became a celebrated conservationist in the 1930s. As Archie Grey Owl, trapper Brosnan flutters the heart of a young Iroquois woman (Annie Galipeau). He gives up the cruelty of snares and works as a guide and naturalist before his memoirs make him famous. Director Richard Attenborough certainly conveys the magnificence of the wilderness settings, but fails to capture the essence of his potentially fascinating protagonist. TH *DVD*
Pierce Brosnan *Archibald Belaney/Grey Owl* · Annie Galipeau *Anahareo/Pony* · Renée Asherson *Carrie Belaney* · Stephanie Cole *Ada Belaney* · Nathaniel Arcand *Ned White Bear* · Stewart Bick *Cyrus Finney* · Vlasta Vrana *Harry Champlin* ■ *Dir* Richard Attenborough · *Scr* William Nicholson

The Grey Zone ★★★ 15

Second World War drama
2001 · US · Colour · 106min

David Arquette and Steve Buscemi lead the cast in this bleak Holocaust drama, adapted from writer/director Tim Blake Nelson's own stage play, which he based on the memoirs of Jewish doctor and Auschwitz survivor Miklos Nyiszli. It explores the horrific moral dilemma that faced special units of prisoners temporarily kept alive and given privileges in return for helping exterminate fellow Jews. Nelson takes a resolutely matter-of-fact approach but, despite the procedural realism, there's an unfortunate staginess that dilutes the feature's overall impact. Clipped, unnatural dialogue and healthy-looking inmates with distracting American accents compound the air of artificiality, making events neither as involving nor as powerful as they should be. SF *DVD*
David Arquette *Hoffman* · Daniel Benzali *Schlermer* · Steve Buscemi *Abramowics* · Harvey Keitel *Muhsfeldt* · Natasha Lyonne *Rosa* · Mira Sorvino *Dina* ■ *Dir* Tim Blake Nelson · *Scr* Tim Blake Nelson, from the play by Nelson, from the book *Auschwitz: a Doctor's Eyewitness Account* by Miklos Nyiszli · *Cinematographer* Russell Lee Fine

Greyfriars Bobby ★★★★ U

Period drama based on a true story
1961 · US/UK · Colour · 86min

Forget the accents and the shabby sets, this is Disney at its best. The true story of the Skye terrier who refuses to desert its master after his burial in an Edinburgh kirkyard is irresistible, and never maudlin or tacky. Laurence Naismith, Donald Crisp and Kay Walsh judge their performances to perfection and director Don Chaffey does well to restrain the enthusiasm of the youngsters. However, no one's eyes will be anywhere other than on the little dog, and don't be ashamed to cheer when he's granted the freedom of the city. DP *DVD*
Donald Crisp *John Brown* · Laurence Naismith *Mr Traill* · Alex Mackenzie *Old Jock* · Kay Walsh *Mrs Brown* · Duncan Macrae *Constable Maclean* · Andrew Cruickshank *Lord Provost* · Gordon Jackson *Farmer* · Rosalie Crutchley *Farmer's wife* · Joyce Carey *First lady* ■ *Dir* Don Chaffey · *Scr* Robert Westerby, from Eleanor Atkinson's story

Greyfriars Bobby ★★ PG

Period adventure based on a true story
2005 · UK · Colour · 100min

When his policeman master dies in 1858, Bobby the irresistibly cute white Skye terrier stays by his grave, killing rats to earn his keep at Greyfriars church. After saving urchin Oliver Golding from the workhouse, Bobby's legend grows, despite the efforts of hissable pantomime villains Sean Pertwee and Ronald Pickup. Director John Henderson's film does have a grittier, less sentimental and more Dickensian feel than the 1961 Disney classic, but the classy production design can't compensate for an unfocused screenplay. AJ
Oliver Golding *Ewan* · James Cosmo *James Brown* · Greg Wise *Minister Lee* · Gina McKee *Maureen Gray* · Ardal O'Hanlon *Coconut Tam* · Kirsty Mitchell *Ada Adams* · Christopher Lee *Sir William Chambers, the Lord Provost* · Sean Pertwee *Duncan Smithie* · Ronald Pickup *Cecil Johnson* ■ *Dir* John Henderson · *Scr* John Henderson, Richard Mathews, Neville Watchurst, from Eleanor Atkinson's story

Greystoke: the Legend of Tarzan, Lord of the Apes ★★★ PG

Adventure
1984 · UK/US · Colour · 131min

This claims to be the definitive screen version of Edgar Rice Burroughs's tale. The early scenes in the primate colony are moving and deftly handled, but once the action leaves the jungle, the film begins noticeably to sag. Christopher Lambert looks the part, but is not a skilful enough actor to carry off the complexities of Tarzan's plight in this decidedly adult version of the tale. However, Ralph Richardson injects some much-needed warmth and fun, and the film also looks glorious. Although the direction may sometimes lose its way, this still adds up to stirring entertainment. SH Brief nudity. *DVD*
Christopher Lambert *John Clayton, Tarzan* · Ralph Richardson *Earl of Greystoke* · Ian Holm *Captain Phillippe D'Arnot* · James Fox *Lord Esker* · Andie MacDowell *Jane Porter* · Cheryl Campbell *Lady Alice Clayton* · John Wells *Sir Evelyn Blount* · Nigel Davenport *Major Jack Downing* · Ian Charleson *Jefferson Brown* · Richard Griffiths *Captain Billings* ■ *Dir* Hugh Hudson · *Scr* PH Vazak [Robert Towne], Michael Austin, from the novel *Tarzan of the Apes* by Edgar Rice Burroughs · *Cinematographer* John Alcott · *Make-up* Rick Baker · *Production Designer* Stuart Craig

Gridiron Gang ★★★ 12

Sports drama
2006 · US · Colour · 120min

Fair play to him, The Rock – or Dwayne "The Rock" Johnson as he is billed here – is doing his best to avoid the usual action hero clichés. At this stage in his career, he should probably be emulating Arnold Schwarzenegger and Vin Diesel by appearing in some family-friendly action comedy. Instead, he's starring in this gritty urban drama – based on a true story – as an idealistic youth probation officer and former American football player attempting to establish a "gridiron" team made up of inmates at a maximum-security detention centre. There's an "against all odds" predictability in the way the story unfolds, but the action is skilfully directed. JF *DVD* *BL*
Dwayne "The Rock" Johnson [Dwayne Johnson] *Sean Porter* · Jade Yorker *Willie Weathers* · Xzibit *Malcolm Moore* · Leon Rippy *Paul Higa* · Kevin Dunn *Dexter* · David Thomas *Kelvin* ■ *Dir* Phil Joanou · *Scr* Jeff Maguire, from the 1993 documentary by Lee Stanley

Gridlock'd ★★★ 18

Black comedy
1996 · US/UK · Colour · 87min

In Vondie Curtis-Hall's engaging look at inner city life, Tim Roth and Tupac Shakur (who was killed while the movie was in post production) play jazz musicians trying to kick heroin. The comedy mainly springs from the bureaucratic nightmares they encounter on the rehab/welfare merry-go-round, while also trying to avoid drug dealers and suspicious cops. The angry sadness that underscores the outwardly comic playing gives this some neat twists. AJ *DVD*
Tim Roth *Stretch* · Tupac Shakur *Spoon* · Vondie Curtis-Hall *D-Reper* · Thandie Newton *Cookie* · Charles Fleischer *Mr Woodson* · Howard Hesseman *Blind man* · John Sayles *First cop* · Eric Payne *Second cop* ■ *Dir/Scr* Vondie Curtis-Hall

Il Grido ★★ 12

Drama
1957 · It/US · BW · 110min

Also known as *The Outcry*, this is a typically neorealist effort from Italian writer/director Michelangelo Antonioni. A factory worker and his child are abandoned by the mother and wander the industrialised Po Valley. Antonioni's use of a rugged-looking but bad American actor (Steve Cochran) in the lead was a mistake, though it was typical of Italian movies at the time. (They never recorded live sound or bothered about accents.) A minor work from a major director. AT
Steve Cochran *Aldo* · Alida Valli *Irma* · Betsy Blair *Elvia* · Dorian Gray *Andreina* · Lyn Shaw *Edera* · Gabriella Pallotta *Edera* ■ *Dir* Michelangelo Antonioni · *Scr* Michelangelo Antonioni, Elio Bartolini, Ennio De Concini, from a story by Michelangelo Antonioni

The Grifters ★★★★ 18

Crime drama
1990 · US · Colour · 105min

It's not quite a contradiction in terms to describe this dramatisation of Jim Thompson's novel as a highly colourful *film noir*. Director Stephen Frears neatly shifts between the audacious scams executed by a trio of con artists, sudden moments of calculated violence and the intense rivalry that develops among expert bet chiseller Anjelica Huston, her ambitious son John Cusack and his scheming girlfriend Annette Bening. Cusack gives a lightweight performance, but the powerhouse playing of his Oscar-nominated co-stars grabs the attention through every twist. DP Violence, swearing, nudity.
Anjelica Huston *Lilly Dillon* · John Cusack *Roy Dillon* · Annette Bening *Myra Langtry* · Pat Hingle *Bobo Justus* · Henry Jones *Simms* · JT Walsh *Cole* · Martin Scorsese *Narrator* ■ *Dir* Stephen Frears · *Scr* Donald E Westlake, from the novel by Jim Thompson

Grim Prairie Tales ★★★

Horror western
1990 · US · Colour · 86min

These campfire tales are told by a city traveller and a mountain man (Brad Dourif and James Earl Jones) who meet on the desolate plains one night. The stories – a mixture of horror, western and comedy – are entertainingly performed by Marc McClure, William Atherton and Scott Paulin, but the real plaudits once again belong to Jones. JB
Brad Dourif *Farley* · James Earl Jones *Morrison* · Will Hare *Lee* · Marc McClure *Tom* · William Atherton *Arthur* · Lisa Eichhorn *Maureen* · Michelle Joyner *Jenny* · Wendy Cooke *Eva* · Scott Paulin *Martin* · Bruce M Fischer *Colochez* ■ *Dir/Scr* Wayne Coe

Grimsby ★★ 15

Spy spoof
2016 · US/UK · Colour · 83min

Sacha Baron Cohen's latest comic creation is a working-class buffoon from Humberside whose reunion with his long-lost brother (Mark Strong) pitches him into the high-stakes world of international espionage. With his Liam Gallagher haircut, tattoos, England football shirt and nine children, Nobby Butcher is a grotesquely exaggerated working-class cliché, and the film seeks to combine laughter and action while placing him in a fish-out-of-water adventure with Strong's straight-faced super-spy. It's hard to know whether Baron Cohen is laughing with or at his characters when there are so few laughs at all. TJ Sex references, violence, drug abuse, swearing

DVD *BL* *CS*

Sacha Baron Cohen *Norman "Nobby" Butcher* • Mark Strong *Sebastian* • Isla Fisher *Jodie Figgis* • Rebel Wilson *Dawn Grobham* • Gabourey Sidibe *Banu the maid* • David Harewood *Black Gareth* • Johnny Vegas *Milky Pimms* • Ian McShane *MI6 boss* • Penélope Cruz *Rhonda George* ▪ *Dir* Louis Leterrier • *Scr* Sacha Baron Cohen, Phil Johnston, Peter Baynham

The Grinch ★★★★ PG
Comedy fantasy
2000 · US/Ger · Colour · 100min

Dr Seuss's cult children's favourite *How the Grinch Stole Christmas!* gets the big-budget Hollywood treatment in this seasonal spectacular from director Ron Howard. Starring an irrepressible and almost unrecognisable Jim Carrey, it's the magical and visually splendid tale of a miserable, green-furred mountain-dweller who's out to wreck the extravagant festive celebrations in the kooky town of Whoville below. A vivacious delight capable of charming the most Scrooge-like viewer, this fantasy frolic is a heart-warmer. However, parents should be warned that the often dark humour and Carrey's madcap excesses may be too much for the very young. SF *DVD* *BL*

Jim Carrey *Grinch* • Jeffrey Tambor *Mayor Augustus May Who* • Christine Baranski *Martha May Whovier* • Bill Irwin *Lou Lou Who* • Molly Shannon *Betty Lou Who* • Clint Howard *Whobris* • Taylor Momsen *Cindy Lou Who* • Anthony Hopkins *Narrator* ▪ *Dir* Ron Howard • *Scr* Jeffrey Price, Peter S Seaman, from the book by Dr Seuss • *Art Director* Michael Corenblith • *Set Designer* Merideth Boswell • *Costume Designer* Rita Ryack • *Make-up effects* Rick Baker

Grip of the Strangler ★★
Mystery horror
1958 · US · BW · 81min

Studying the 20-year-old murders of the "Haymarket Strangler", writer Boris Karloff becomes gruesomely possessed by the maniac responsible. Why? Because he *was* the maniac responsible! Karloff merely shuts one eye and bites his lower lip to become the madman in this pale Jekyll and Hyde clone. But while he shows his gift for changing personalities with the simplest shift of expression, whipping up minor scares in the process, the low budget and simplistic script fail to give him much support. AJ

Boris Karloff *James Rankin* • Jean Kent *Cora Seth* • Elizabeth Allan *Barbara Rankin* • Anthony Dawson *Detective Superintendent Burk* • Vera Day *Pearl* • Tim Turner *Kenneth McColl* ▪ *Dir* Robert Day • *Scr* Jan Read, John C Cooper, from a story by Jan Read

The Grissom Gang ★★★ 15
Crime thriller
1971 · US · Colour · 123min

This is a thoroughly brutish and violent reworking of a notorious original, directed by Robert Aldrich, a major talent with a dark imagination. Disturbingly overlong, this sombre epic remains relentlessly watchable thanks to a superb central performance from Kim Darby as the kidnapped heiress at the centre of the drama. The thugs are comic book creations, buffoonish and degenerate, and Aldrich can't decide whether the movie is a comedy, a thriller or something in between. TS Violence, swearing. *DVD*

Kim Darby *Barbara Blandish* • Tony Musante *Eddie Hagan* • Scott Wilson *Slim Grissom* • Irene Dailey *Ma Grissom* • Robert Lansing *Dave Fenner* ▪ *Dir* Robert Aldrich • *Scr* Leon Griffiths, from the novel *No Orchids for Miss Blandish* by James Hadley Chase

Grizzly ★ 15
Horror thriller
1976 · US · Colour · 87min

One of many *Jaws* rip-offs, this replaces the shark with a very angry, hungry grizzly bear who gets his kicks snacking off the visitors to a nature reserve. As the body count rises, park ranger Christopher George is joined in his pursuit by pilot Andrew Prine and naturalist Richard Jaeckel. You'll root for the bear. AT

Christopher George *Ranger* • Andrew Prine *Helicopter pilot* • Richard Jaeckel *Naturalist* • Joan McCall *Photographer* ▪ *Dir* William Girdler • *Scr* Harvey Flaxman, David Sheldon

Grizzly Falls ★★★ PG
Adventure
1999 · Can/UK · Colour · 90min

Narrated in flashback by Richard Harris, this outdoor adventure combines an acute sense of place, a sure understanding of childhood and a pronounced empathy with the animal kingdom. Bryan Brown is the nominal lead, as a hunter seeking the son kidnapped by a vengeful grizzly. Director Stewart Raffill occasionally allows the pace to slacken, but the wolf attack and the showdown with trapper Oliver Tobias add excitement to the furry feel-good. DP *DVD*

Bryan Brown *Tyrone Bankston* • Tom Jackson *Joshua* • Oliver Tobias *Genet* • Richard Harris *Old Harry* • Daniel Clark *Young Harry* ▪ *Dir* Stewart Raffill • *Scr* Richard Beattie, Stuart Margolin

Grizzly Man ★★★★★ 15
Documentary
2005 · US · Colour · 103min

Widely acclaimed by critics and industry peers as one of the best documentaries of 2005, Werner Herzog's film offers a superb study of nature – both human and animal – in all its savage beauty, cruelty and absurdity. Star of the show Timothy Treadwell was a dropout who found redemption living among grizzly bears in the Alaskan wilds for 13 summers, until one of them killed him and his girlfriend, Amie Huguenard. Herzog knits together spectacular amateur footage shot by Treadwell with original interview material, to unfold the grizzly man's story. The result provides a salutary lesson in the dangers of over-romanticising wild animals, as well as a fascinating glimpse into a well-intentioned but very troubled soul. A sparse and lovely score by Richard Thompson and some glorious images of bears round out a near-flawless package. LF Swearing. *DVD*

▪ *Dir/Scr* Werner Herzog

The Grocer's Son ★★★★ 12
Drama
2007 · Fr · Colour · 95min

Eric Guirado builds upon his experience of making documentaries about salesmen, mobile shops and the remote rural communities they serve with this assured town-and-country tale. The story of grumpy prodigal son Nicolas Cazalé's return from the big city to take over the family business after father Daniel Duval falls ill is chockful of rich detail and gentle humour. Guirado's film also invites comparisons with such bucolic charmers as Marcel Pagnol's *The Baker's Wife* (1938) – photographed with a real sense of place by Laurent Brunet, this touching tribute to a fading tradition is a humanist gem. DP French +subtitles. *DVD*

Nicolas Cazalé *Antoine Sforza* • Clotilde Hesme *Claire* • Daniel Duval *Antoine's father* • Jeanne Goupil *Antoine's mother* • Stéphan Guérin-Tillié *François Sforza* • Liliane Rovère *Lucienne* ▪ *Dir* Eric Guirado • *Scr* Eric Guirado, Florence Vignon, from an idea by Guirado • *Cinematographer* Laurent Brunet

Groove ★★★ 18
Drama
2000 · US · Colour · 80min

In this low-budget independent film, not even a police raid stops a party of San Francisco ravers from dancing 'til dawn. First-time director Greg Harrison makes things difficult for himself, setting the repetitive scenario almost entirely in a disused warehouse. But he succeeds in capturing the sweaty intensity of dance culture and maintaining our interest in the shallow characters. Hamish Linklater is utterly convincing as a strait-laced

Midwesterner whose life is transformed by his initiation into the urban dance scene. DM *DVD*

MacKenzie Firgens *Harmony Stitts* • Lola Glaudini *Leyla Heydel* • Denny Kirkwood *Colin Turner* • Hamish Linklater *David Turner* • Rachel True *Beth Anderson* • Steve Van Wormer *Ernie Townsend* ▪ *Dir/Scr* Greg Harrison

Grosse Pointe Blank ★★★★ 15
Black comedy drama
1997 · US · Colour · 102min

Named in tribute to John Boorman's cult thriller *Point Blank*, this inventive black comedy drama stars John Cusack as a hitman who returns to his home town of Grosse Pointe for a high-school reunion and another assassination. He bumps into the old flame (Minnie Driver) he jilted on prom night ten years before and discovers that conventional free-marketeers are just as ruthless as he is. Director George Armitage keeps the action smart and edgy, and there are some fine performances from a supporting cast that includes Dan Aykroyd (as a fellow hitman) and Joan Cusack. TH Swearing, violence. *DVD*

John Cusack *Martin Q Blank* • Minnie Driver *Debi Newberry* • Alan Arkin *Dr Oatman* • Dan Aykroyd *Mr Grocer* • Joan Cusack *Marcella* • Hank Azaria *Lardner* • K Todd Freeman *McCullers* • Mitchell Ryan *Mr Newberry* ▪ *Dir* George Armitage • *Scr* Tom Jankiewicz, DV DeVincentis, Steve Pink, John Cusack, from a story by Jankiewicz

The Grotesque ★ 18
Black comedy
1995 · UK · Colour · 93min

Want to know how to turn a witty and original novel into a hackneyed bore in one easy lesson? Just watch director John-Paul Davidson's lamentable black comedy based on author Patrick McGrath's wildly acerbic tale about the class struggle in 1940s England. The story of what happens when new butler Sting arrives at the house of eccentric explorer Alan Bates is stunningly conventional. AJ

Alan Bates *Sir Hugo Coal* • Sting *Fledge* • Theresa Russell *Lady Harriet Coal* • Lena Headey *Cleo Coal* • Steven Mackintosh *Sidney Giblet* • Anna Massey *Mrs Giblet* • Timothy Kightley *Harbottle* • Jim Carter *George Lecky* ▪ *Dir* John-Paul Davidson • *Scr* Patrick McGrath, from his novel

Ground Zero ★★★ 15
Thriller
1987 · Aus · Colour · 96min

Although we're used to the way governments keep us in the dark, this political thriller from Australia still manages to shock with its story, based on fact, about a man seeking reasons for his father's death during British A-bomb testing in the outback in the 1950s. Colin Friels and Jack Thompson put genuine feeling into their roles as they lift the lid on moral meltdown, but Donald Pleasence, playing the hermit-like survivor of those nuclear trials, steals every scene he's in. TH Violence, swearing.

Colin Friels *Harvey Denton* • Jack Thompson *Trebilcock* • Donald Pleasence *Prosper Gaffney* • Natalie Bate *Pat Denton* • Simon Chilvers *Commission president* • Neil Fitzpatrick *Hooking* • Bob Maza *Wallemare* ▪ *Dir* Michael Pattinson, Bruce Myles • *Scr* Jan Sardi, Mac Gudgeon

Grounded ★★ PG
Comedy
2006 · US · Colour · 86min

Think *Home Alone* in an airport, and you've pretty much got the measure of this harmless but charmless kids comedy. Young siblings Spencer and Katherine are travelling alone to spend Christmas with their estranged dad. But a blizzard shuts down the airport, stranding them in the terminal. After they're separated by an officious airport manager, Spencer is determined to be reunited with his sister to give her the picture-perfect Christmas Day she dreams of, so assembles a ragtag gang of other unaccompanied minors (including *Everybody Hates Chris*'s Tyler James Williams) and plans a great escape. Under-tens will enjoy the largely anti-adult mayhem that ensues, but adults may well wonder what they've done in a previous life to deserve this. DA *DVD*

Lewis Black *Oliver Porter* • Wilmer Valderrama *Zach Van Bourke* • Tyler James Williams *Charlie* • Dyllan Christopher *Spencer Davenport* • Brett Kelly *Timothy "Beef" Wellington* • Gina Mantegna *Grace Conrad* • Quinn Shephard *Donna Malone* • Paget Brewster *Valerie Davenport* ▪ *Dir* Paul Feig • *Scr* Jacob Meszaros, Mya Stark, Paul Feig, from the story *Babysitting* by Susan Burton

Groundhog Day ★★★★★ PG
Romantic comedy fantasy
1993 · US · Colour · 96min

Hollywood once produced three or four classic comedies each year. Nowadays we're lucky to get one a decade and this is a contender for the 1990s. Bill Murray gives one of the best performances of his career as Phil Connors, the weatherman with attitude, trapped in a day he will remember for the rest of his life because, unless he can find some answers, it *will be* the rest of his life. Director Harold Ramis uses every cinematic trick in the book to keep what is essentially a one-gag movie brimming with life and fresh ideas. Stephen Tobolowsky is superb as a nerdy insurance salesman and, as Murray's TV producer, Andie MacDowell has never been better. DP Swearing. *DVD* *BL*

Bill Murray *Phil Connors* • Andie MacDowell *Rita Hanson* • Chris Elliott *Larry* • Stephen Tobolowsky *Ned* • Brian Doyle-Murray *Buster* • Marita Geraghty *Nancy* • Angela Paton *Mrs Lancaster* • Rick Ducommun *Gus* ▪ *Dir* Harold Ramis • *Scr* Danny Rubin, Harold Ramis, from a story by Rubin

The Groundstar Conspiracy ★★
Drama
1972 · Can · Colour · 95min

This effective thriller about spies in the space programme is really one of those high-gloss flicks Universal made to show off its contract players, in this case George Peppard and Michael Sarrazin. Director Lamont Johnson handles the suspense well and, though the script could have been tighter and the leading lady (Christine Belford) more distinguished, the Vancouver locations look splendid. TS

George Peppard *Tuxan* • Michael Sarrazin *Welles* • Christine Belford *Nicole* • Cliff Potts *Mosely* • James Olson *Stanton* • Tim O'Connor *Gossage* • James McEachin *Bender* • Alan Oppenheimer *Hackett* ▪ *Dir* Lamont Johnson • *Scr* Matthew Howard, from the novel *The Alien* by LP Davies

The Group ★★★★
Drama
1966 · US · Colour · 146min

Notable as one of the first films to show the emotional development of women as individuals and not just as lost souls awaiting salvation by men, this glitzy, glossy and extremely good drama is based on the iconoclastic blockbuster by Mary McCarthy. It is beautifully played by the likes of Candice Bergen, Jessica Walter and, particularly, Joan Hackett, whose ultimate fate is skilfully drawn. SH

Candice Bergen *Elinor "Lakey" Eastlake* • Joan Hackett *Dorothy "Dottie" Renfrew* • Elizabeth Hartman *Priss Hartshorn* • Shirley Knight *Polly Andrews* • Joanna Pettet *Kay Strong* • Mary-Robin Redd *Pokey Prothero* • Jessica Walter *Libby MacAusland* • Larry Hagman *Harald Peterson* • Hal Holbrook *Gus Leroy* • Richard Mulligan *Dick Brown* ▪ *Dir* Sidney Lumet • *Scr* Sidney Buchman, from the novel by Mary McCarthy

Grow Your Own ★★★★ PG
Comedy
2007 · UK · Colour · 96min

In the noble spirit of Ealing Studios in their heyday, this apparently gentle comedy about a year in the life of a Liverpool allotment also has a serious side. Starting life as a documentary project about traumatised asylum seekers who are given plots of land to work as "therapy", this fictionalised patchwork of stories sees power-crazed allotment chairman Philip Jackson presiding over a motley community of rural gardeners. An influx of refugees from Iran, China and Zimbabwe initially brings out the worst in these Little Englanders, but eventually they unite against a common foe – a mercenary mobile phone company wanting to erect a

G

mast . With its mix of broad humour, keen social comment and moments of truly affecting emotion, there's clearly a message here about the state of race relations in Britain today. AC DVD

Benedict Wong *Kung Sang* • Philip Jackson *Big John* • Eddie Marsan *Little John* • Omid Djalili *Ali* • Diveen Henry *Miriam* • Pearce Quigley *Eddie* • Alan Williams (2) *Kenny* ■ *Dir* Richard Laxton • *Scr* Frank Cottrell Boyce, Carl Hunter

Grown Ups ★★ 12

Comedy   2010 · US · Colour · 98min

United at their childhood basketball coach's funeral, five friends and their families then spend the Fourth of July holiday at a lake house – and while some things are different after 30 years, others haven't changed at all. But Adam Sandler, a Hollywood agent, and his best friends Chris Rock, Rob Schneider, David Spade and Kevin James are all in varying degrees of midlife crisis. Director Dennis Dugan keeps the pace snappy with quick, one-off shots, but the impressive abilities of this ensemble go underused in a clichéd comedy that stalls at nice and stupid on its way to profundity. KK Some sexual references. DVD

Adam Sandler *Lenny Feder* • Chris Rock *Kurt McKenzie* • Rob Schneider *Rob Hilliard* • David Spade *Marcus Higgins* • Kevin James *Eric Lamonsoff* • Salma Hayek Pinault [Salma Hayek] *Roxanne Chase-Feder* • Maria Bello *Sally Lamonsoff* • Maya Rudolph *Deanne McKenzie* • Joyce Van Patten *Gloria* • Colin Quinn *Dickie Bailey* • Steve Buscemi *Wiley* ■ *Dir* Dennis Dugan • *Scr* Adam Sandler, Fred Wolf

Grown Ups 2 ★ 12

Comedy   2013 · US · Colour · 96min

The opening scene has a deer peeing into Adam Sandler's mouth, and that's just about as subtle as this ghastly sequel gets. But if you laughed at the first film, you'll probably laugh at this, as it's Sandler, Chris Rock, Kevin James and David Spade serving up the same old schtick: a mind-numbing mix of childish slapstick and toilet humour. Sandler's Hollywood hotshot has relocated to his hometown, and much midlife craziness ensues. When Taylor Lautner is the star cameo, you know you're in trouble. Dreadful. DA DVD

Adam Sandler *Lenny Feder* • Kevin James *Eric Lamonsoff* • Chris Rock *Kurt McKenzie* • David Spade *Marcus Higgins* • Salma Hayek Pinault [Salma Hayek] *Roxanne Chase-Feder* • Maya Rudolph *Deanne McKenzie* • Maria Bello *Sally Lamonsoff* • Taylor Lautner *Frat boy Andy* ■ *Dir* Dennis Dugan • *Scr* Fred Wolf, Adam Sandler, Tim Herlihy, from characters by Wolf, Sandler

The Grudge ★★ 15

Horror thriller   2004 · US · Colour · 87min

Takashi Shimizu directs this English-language remake of his cult horror, but adds little to the genre. Essentially a haunted-house story, it begins with student social worker Sarah Michelle Gellar making a house call and encountering some seriously spooky goings-on – the house is home to a demon and anyone who enters its walls is cursed. This chiller has installed many superfluous tricks of the horror movie trade, designed to make the film more accessible to a western audience. KK DVD

Sarah Michelle Gellar *Karen* • Jason Behr *Doug* • Clea DuVall *Jennifer Williams* • William Mapother *Matthew Williams* • KaDee Strickland *Susan Williams* • Bill Pullman *Peter* • Rosa Blasi *Maria* • Grace Zabriskie *Emma* ■ *Dir* Takashi Shimizu • *Scr* Stephen Susco, from the film *Ju-On: the Grudge* by Takashi Shimizu

The Grudge 2 ★★★ 15

Horror thriller   2006 · US · Colour · 103min

Director Takashi Shimizu has made a career out of ghost stories. Or to be precise, he's made a career out of retelling the same ghost story over and over. *The Grudge 2* is the sixth reworking of his original Japanese outing – 2000's direct-to-video *Ju-on*. It's also a direct sequel to his recent Hollywood remake starring Sarah Michelle Gellar as an American in Tokyo terrorised by ghosts. Gellar returns briefly here, but is largely supplanted by Amber Tamblyn as her sister,

who's trying to stop the supernatural beings reaching the States. Those familiar with the series will find little that's original, as Shimizu shamelessly recycles set pieces from earlier incarnations of the story. Yet his masterful ability to inject even innocuous objects with a foreboding sense of dread delivers some occasional, hair-raising chills. JR DVD

Amber Tamblyn *Aubrey Davis* • Arielle Kebbel *Allison* • Jennifer Beals *Trish* • Edison Chen *Eason* • Sarah Roemer *Lacey* • Sarah Michelle Gellar *Karen Davis* ■ *Dir* Takashi Shimizu • *Scr* Stephen Susco, from the film *Ju-On: the Grudge* and characters by Takashi Shimizu

The Grudge: Ju-On ★★ 15

Horror thriller   2003 · Jpn · Colour · 88min

This haunted house chiller lacks the eerie originality of much recent Japanese horror. This is partly due to the fact that Takashi Shimizu was remaking his own 2000 direct-to-video offering. The flashbacking story never regains the sense of foreboding that pervades careworker Megumi Okina's first visit to the abode possessed by a ghostly boy. Disconcerting, but short on terror. DP Japanese +subtitles. Violence. DVD

Megumi Okina *Rika Nishina* • Misaki Ito *Hitomi Tokunaga* • Misa Uehara (2) *Izumi Toyama* • Kanji Tsuda *Katsuya Tokunaga* • Shuri Matsuda *Kazumi Tokunaga* • Takako Fuji *Kayako* • Yuya Ozeki *Toshio* • Yui Ichikawa *Chiharu* • Kayoko Shibata *Mariko* • Yukako Kukuri *Miyuki* ■ *Dir/Scr* Takashi Shimizu

Grudge Match ★★ 12

Sports comedy   2013 · US · Colour · 113min

Boxing-movie legends Sylvester Stallone and Robert De Niro square off in director Peter Segal's lightweight, predictable "unfinished business" yarn about two over-the-hill former prizefighters coaxed out of retirement 30 years after they last faced each other in the ring. Stallone and De Niro give knowing winks towards their characters from *Rocky* and *Raging Bull*, but the surprise-free script rarely rises above an extended comedy sketch parodying past glories. TeS Violence, swearing, sexual references. DVD

Robert De Niro *Billy "The Kid" McDonnen* • Sylvester Stallone *Henry "Razor" Sharp* • Kevin Hart *Dante Slate, Jr* • Alan Arkin *Louis "Lightning" Conlon* • Kim Basinger *Sally Rose* ■ *Dir* Peter Segal • *Scr* Tim Kelleher, Rodney Rothman, from Kelleher's story • *Cinematographer* Dean Semler

The Gruesome Twosome ★★ 18

Horror   1967 · US · Colour · 71min

From its bizarre puppet-slaying opening, Herschell Gordon Lewis's schlock-fest has only one item on its agenda. The Wizard of Gore can never be accused of excessive proficiency, but he is certainly very proficient at serving up an excess of entrails and lashings of red goo. The plot involves murderous efforts of a devoted son to supply his mother's wig shop with plenty of genuine hair. Riotously third-rate, it's a textbook chunk of drive-in gothic. DP DVD

Elizabeth Davis • Chris Martell • Gretchen Welles • Rodney Bedell ■ *Dir* Herschell Gordon Lewis • *Scr* Louise Downe

Grumpy ★★

Mystery drama   1930 · US · BW · 74min

George Cukor's debut film-directing credit (albeit shared with Cyril Gardner) was this musty, dusty screen version of a long-running play, popular on both sides of the Atlantic in the 1920s. It stars veteran actor Cyril Maude, reprising his stage role of "Grumpy", a white-haired, fragile-looking retired lawyer who is both lovable and irascible. He gets to grips with solving a small mystery concerning a diamond acquired by his granddaughter's boyfriend. Cosy, and rather boring. RK

Cyril Maude *"Grumpy" Bullivant* • Phillips Holmes *Ernest Heron* • Frances Dade *Virginia* • Paul Lukas *Berci* • Halliwell Hobbes *Ruddick* ■ *Dir* George Cukor, Cyril Gardner • *Scr* Doris

Anderson, from the play *Grumpy, a Play in Four Acts* by Horace Hodges, Thomas Wigney Percyval

Grumpy Old Men ★★★ 12

Comedy drama   1993 · US · Colour · 99min

Jack Lemmon and Walter Matthau are one of the all-time great partnerships and this engaging comedy marked their seventh screen collaboration. In this high-concept tale, they are warring senior citizens whose feuding escalates as they battle for the hand of Ann-Margret. Although the script isn't quite as strong as it could be, the chemistry between the two stars is irresistible and they are matched by an equally strong supporting cast. JF Some swearing.

Jack Lemmon *John Gustafson* • Walter Matthau *Max Goldman* • Ann-Margret *Ariel Truax* • Burgess Meredith *Grandpa Gustafson* • Daryl Hannah *Melanie Gustafson* • Kevin Pollak *Jacob Goldman* • Ossie Davis *Chuck* • Buck Henry *Elliott Snyder* ■ *Dir* Donald Petrie • *Scr* Mark Steven Johnson

Grumpier Old Men ★★ 12

Comedy   1996 · US · Colour · 96min

Old stagers Walter Matthau and Jack Lemmon cruise through this unaccountably popular sequel. Ann-Margret also returns from the first film, while Sophia Loren turns up as a much married interloper who stirs up the boys' bile by buying their beloved bait shop and turning it into a restaurant. They all deserve better material. JF

Jack Lemmon *John Gustafson* • Walter Matthau *Max Goldman* • Ann-Margret *Ariel Gustafson* • Sophia Loren *Maria Ragetti* • Burgess Meredith *Grandpa Gustafson* • Daryl Hannah *Melanie Gustafson* • Kevin Pollak *Jacob Goldman* ■ *Dir* Howard Deutch • *Scr* Mark Steven Johnson, from his characters

Guadalcanal Diary ★★★★ PG

Second World War action drama
1943 · US · BW · 89min

Richard Tregaskis's novel, an "I was there" account of the struggle to recapture the South Pacific island of Guadalcanal from the Japanese during the Second World War, was difficult to film without resorting to cliché. Nevertheless, 20th Century-Fox pulls out all the stops in the authenticity stakes here, with superbly staged action sequences. Richard Jaeckel is exceptionally fine, and there's solid back-up from stars such as William Bendix, Anthony Quinn and Lloyd Nolan. Preston Foster offers some unusually unsentimental homilies as the padre and, overall, the movie contains a rare honesty. SH DVD

Preston Foster *Father Donnelly* • Lloyd Nolan *Hook Malone* • William Bendix *Taxi Potts* • Richard Conte *Captain Davis* • Anthony Quinn *Jesus "Soose" Alvarez* • Richard Jaeckel *Private Johnny Anderson* • Roy Roberts *Captain Cross* • Lionel Stander *Butch* ■ *Dir* Lewis Seiler • *Scr* Lamar Trotti, Jerry Cady [Jerome Cady], from the diary by Richard Tregaskis

Guantanamera ★★ 15

Road movie drama
1995 · Sp/Cub/Ger · Colour · 101min

This road movie – the last project completed by Tomás Gutiérrez Alea, Cuba's best-known director – has too many echoes of Alea's own *Death of a Bureaucrat* for comfort. The passing of a famous singer's funeral cortege across the island should have inspired some seething satire, but the swipes are merely passing blows at easy targets. There's simply not enough tension in the developing romance between one-time lecturer Mirtha Ibarra and her gone-to-bad student Jorge Perugorria to hold our attention. A disappointing swan song. DP

Carlos Cruz *Adolfo* • Mirtha Ibarra [Mirta Ibarra] *Georgina* • Raul Eguren *Candido* • Jorge Perugorria *Mariano* • Pedro Fernandez *Ramon* • Luis Alberto Garcia *Tony* • Conchita Brando *Yoyita* ■ *Dir* Tomás Gutiérrez Alea, Juan Carlos Tabio • *Scr* Eliseo Alberto Diego, Tomás Gutiérrez Alea, Juan Carlos Tabio

The Guard ★★★★ 15

Comedy thriller   2011 · Ire · Colour · 92min

Brendan Gleeson excels in this caustic cop/buddy drama set in the wilds of Ireland, as a foul-mouthed police sergeant who is king of all he surveys. However, the murder of his constable, a drug smuggling ring and the arrival of the FBI in the form of agent Don Cheadle disrupts his easy life. Sharply written and directed by John Michael McDonagh (and nicely photographed by Larry Smith in drizzly greys and greens), this is Gleeson's show. "I don't know if you're really smart or really stupid," the bewildered agent remarks at one point; it's an apt summary of a fascinating, darkly funny character who keeps everyone guessing to the very end. AS Violence, swearing, sexual references, drug abuse. DVD Blu

Brendan Gleeson *Sergeant Gerry Boyle* • Don Cheadle *FBI Agent Wendell Everett* • Liam Cunningham *Francis Sheehy-Skeffington* • David Wilmot *Liam O'Leary* • Mark Strong *Clive Cornell* • Fionnula Flanagan *Eileen Boyle* ■ *Dir/Scr* John Michael McDonagh • *Cinematographer* Larry Smith

The Guardian ★★★ 18

Supernatural horror   1990 · US · Colour · 88min

There's much pleasure to be had in this offering from William Friedkin, mainly from watching leading lady Jenny Seagrove in her first American starring role. The part is virtually unplayable, but, as the demonic nanny, Seagrove really makes us believe she's on nodding terms with hell. It could have been a lot more scary, but that's a minor quibble in a generally satisfying tale of the supernatural. TS Swearing, violence.

Jenny Seagrove *Camilla* • Dwier Brown *Phil* • Carey Lowell *Kate* • Brad Hall *Ned Runcie* • Miguel Ferrer *Ralph Hess* • Natalia Nogulich [Natalja Nogulich] *Molly Sheridan* ■ *Dir* William Friedkin • *Scr* Stephen Volk, William Friedkin, Dan Greenburg, from the novel *The Nanny* by Dan Greenburg

Guardian ★★ 15

Horror thriller   2000 · US · Colour · 86min

The proliferation of a dangerous new drug convinces Gulf War veteran-turned-cop Mario Van Peebles that he has to protect a "special" child from the evil spirit Telal. This demonology thriller blithely blags ideas from any number of uninspired forebears, but John Terlesky directs with brisk efficiency, though that's hardly a recommendation. DP DVD

Mario Van Peebles *John Kross* • James Remar *Carpenter* • Ice-T *Max* • Stacy Oversier *Selene* • Daniel Hugh Kelly *Agent Taylor* • Steve Zad *David Lichtmann* ■ *Dir* John Terlesky • *Scr* John Terlesky, Gary J Tunnicliffe, Jeff Yagher

The Guardian ★★★ 12

Action adventure   2006 · US · Colour · 133min

This corny but thrilling action adventure is further proof that Kevin Costner is getting better with age. He plays Ben Randall, an ace US Coast Guard Rescue swimmer who's transferred to a training facility after being involved in a tragedy at sea that left his crew dead. Among the students he's assigned is cocky Jake Fischer (Ashton Kutcher), a young hotshot who has the ability if not the attitude to take Randall's crown. If this was a western, Costner would be the old gunslinger and Kutcher the quick-draw kid who wants to take him down. Clichés aside, the film's storm-rescue sequences are outstanding and Costner demonstrates how an action hero can age gracefully. Sure, the film is a tad too long, but it's still a guilty pleasure. DA DVD Blu

Kevin Costner *Ben Randall* • Ashton Kutcher *Jake Fischer* • Melissa Sagemiller *Emily Thomas* • Bonnie Bramlett *Maggie McGlone* • Clancy Brown *Captain William "Bill" Hadley* • Sela Ward *Helen Randall* • Neal McDonough *Jack Skinner* • John Heard *Frank Larson* ■ *Dir* Andrew Davis • *Scr* Ron L Brinkerhoff

Guardians of the Galaxy ★★★★ 12

Science-fiction action adventure
2014 · US · Colour · 120min

Disney presents this child-friendly space adventure based on the Marvel comic, and, with its retro-kitsch feel, grown-ups should lap it up, too. Chris Pratt has no discernible superpower as Peter Quill, except to wisecrack his way out of sticky situations after pilfering a mystical orb coveted by power-hungry aliens Ronan (Lee Pace) and Nebula (Karen Gillan). There's plenty of action but this is, above all, a bright and breezy affair where a tough-talking raccoon (delightfully voiced by Bradley Cooper) threatens to steal the show. Pratt straddles the line between bold and brazen and remains the lynchpin in writer/director James Gunn's fun, exciting and psychedelic vision of the galaxy. A sequel is due in 2017. SP Some violence, swearing. _DVD_ ↘ 3D CS

Chris Pratt *Peter Quill/Star-Lord* · Zoe Saldana [Zoë Saldana] *Gamora* · Dave Bautista *Drax the Destroyer* · Vin Diesel *Groot* · Bradley Cooper *Rocket Raccoon* · Lee Pace *Ronan the Accuser* · Karen Gillan *Nebula* · Michael Rooker *Yondu Udonta* · Glenn Close *Nova Prime* ■ *Dir* James Gunn (2) · *Scr* Nicole Perlman, James Gunn (2), from the comic book by Dan Abnett, Andy Lanning, from characters by Gene Colan, Arnold Drake

Guardians of the Galaxy Vol 2

Science-fiction action adventure
2017 · US · Colour

This is a preview - no prints were available to review as we went to press: Few expected the 2014 film to become the highest grossing superhero movie of the year, and his winning, family friendly approach secured James Gunn his return to the director's chair for this sequel. Chris Pratt, now a bona fide star, reprises this intergalactic chancer Peter Quill and is expected to grow into his leadership role, here, while investigating the mystery surrounding his father. Zoé Saldana and the rest of the gang are also back (Bradley Cooper again voices Rocket the racoon) joined by new A-list signings Sylvester Stallone, Kurt Russell and Glenn Close. SP

Chris Pratt *Peter Quill/Star-Lord* · Vin Diesel *Groot* · Bradley Cooper *Rocket Racoon* · Zoe Saldana [Zoë Saldana] *Gamora* · Karen Gillan *Nebula* · Benicio Del Toro *The Collector* ■ *Dir* James Gunn (2) · *Scr* James Gunn (2), from the comic book by Dan Abnett, Andy Lanning

Guarding Tess ★★★ 12

Comedy drama 1994 · US · Colour · 91min

Shirley MacLaine does almost too good a job of playing cantankerous president's widow Tess Carlisle, a former First Lady from hell. MacLaine is so believable in the leading role she's almost unendurable to watch, while Nicolas Cage, as a long-suffering Secret Service minder, displays the same sure comic touch he brought to 1998's *City of Angels*. It's attractively staged by director Hugh Wilson and remains entertaining until it finally lurches into melodrama. TH Violence, swearing. _DVD_

Shirley MacLaine *Tess Carlisle* · Nicolas Cage *Doug Chesnic* · Austin Pendleton *Earl* · Edward Albert *Barry Carlisle* · James Rebhorn *Howard Shaeffer* · Richard Griffiths *Frederick* · John Roselius *Tom Bahlor* ■ *Dir* Hugh Wilson · *Scr* Hugh Wilson, Peter Torokvei

Guelwaar ★★★★

Political satire 1992 · Sen/Fr · Colour · 115min

One of the best-known of black African film-makers, Ousmane Sembene forged his reputation with the searing satire of Senegalese life, *Xala*. He is no less scathing in this supremely controlled study of the conflicts of politics, language, religion and custom that divide a state proud of its independence and yet still reliant on overseas aid. The disappearance of a political dissident's corpse exposes all manner of contradictions as Catholic priests and Muslim imams feud over the burial, while the mayor and his chief of police fight to keep the truth about his death a secret. Third World cinema close to its best. DP French +subtitles.

Omar Seck *Gora* · Ndiawar Diop *Barthelemy* · Mame Ndoumbe Diop *Nogoy Marie Thioune* · Isseu Niang *Veronique* · Myriam Niang *Helene* ■ *Dir/Scr* Ousmane Sembene

La Guerre Est Finie ★★★★ 15

Political drama 1966 · Fr/Swe · BW · 116min

Typically overlapping the present, memory and imagination, Alain Resnais here offers a troubling study of the gulf between passive commitment and direct action. Written by the exiled Spanish author Jorge Semprun, the film focuses on the three days in which middle-aged revolutionary Yves Montand comes to recognise that his unswerving allegiance to the cause of overthrowing Franco is faltering. Montand gives a performance of great solemnity, and he is well supported by Ingrid Thulin as his loyal mistress and Geneviève Bujold as the student with whom he has a brief affair. DP French +subtitles.

Yves Montand *Diego* · Ingrid Thulin *Marianne* · Geneviève Bujold *Nadine Sallanches* · Jean Dasté *Chief* · Jorge Semprun *Narrator* · Dominique Rozan *Jude* · Michel Piccoli *First customs inspector* ■ *Dir* Alain Resnais · *Scr* Jorge Semprun

Guerrilla: the Taking of Patty Hearst ★★★ 12

Documentary 2004 · US/UK · Colour · 85min

Robert Stone's meticulously researched, compelling documentary sheds new light on the 1974 kidnapping of heiress Patty Hearst by the Symbionese Liberation Army, and her apparent conversion to their cause. Director Stone uses archive footage plus interviews with surviving SLA members to investigate the events. He deliberately avoids the obvious - and possibly unanswerable - question that divided America at the time: was Hearst brainwashed or a willing collaborator with the group? Instead, the film concentrates on the equally fascinating relationship between the terrorists and the mass media that reported - and some might argue, abetted - their crimes. AS Swearing. _DVD_

■ *Dir* Robert Stone (3)

Guess Who ★★ 12

Romantic comedy 2005 · US · Colour · 101min

Bernie Mac stars as an intimidating potential father-in-law in this race-reversed comic homage to the 1967 classic *Guess Who's Coming to Dinner*. Mac is mortified when his eldest daughter (Zoë Saldana) comes home for his wedding anniversary party with white boyfriend Ashton Kutcher in tow. Mac's quick-fire delivery complements Kutcher's clownish physical comedy and though the knockabout laughs are too in-your-face, they do have a crude appeal. SF _DVD_

Bernie Mac *Percy Jones* · Ashton Kutcher *Simon Green* · Zoë Saldana *Theresa Jones* · Judith Scott *Marilyn Jones* · Hal Williams *Howard Jones* · Kellee Stewart *Keisha Jones* · Robert Curtis Brown *Dante* · RonReaco Lee *Reggie* ■ *Dir* Kevin Rodney Sullivan · *Scr* David Ronn, Jay Scherick, Peter Tolan, from a story by Ronn, Scherick

Guess Who's Coming to Dinner ★★★★ PG

Comedy drama 1967 · US · Colour · 103min

In their last movie together, Spencer Tracy and Katharine Hepburn play a rich couple whose liberal principles are tested by the proposed marriage of their daughter to a black doctor. As he is Sidney Poitier, all intellectual politesse, there's never any doubt about the outcome. The film may have a foregone conclusion, but it's worth watching as the acting is so good. Tracy and an Oscar-winning Hepburn were a deceptively rare cinema double-act, who seemed genuinely fond of each other both on and off screen. This is an outstanding swan song. TH Swearing. _DVD_

Spencer Tracy *Matthew Drayton* · Sidney Poitier *John Prentice* · Katharine Hepburn *Christina Drayton* · Katharine Houghton *Joey Drayton* · Cecil Kellaway *Monsignor Ryan* · Beah Richards *Mrs Prentice* · Roy E Glenn Sr [Roy Glenn] *Mr Prentice* · Isabell Sanford [Isabel Sanford] *Tillie* ■ *Dir* Stanley Kramer · *Scr* William Rose

The Guest ★★★★ 15

Thriller 2014 · US/UK · Colour · 95min

Downton Abbey's Dan Stevens breaks out of dowdy costume drama mode in loud and violent style with this tense throwback thriller. He plays a discharged soldier who turns up at the home of an army friend who was killed in action. The family take him in, but then the seemingly charming and humble farmboy reveals a sinister side to his nature. Stevens is a charismatic antihero and the film plays expertly with genre expectations. DW Violence, swearing, drug abuse, nudity. _DVD_ ↘

Dan Stevens *"David"* · Maika Monroe *Anna* · Brendan Meyer *Luke* · Sheila Kelley (1) *Laura* · Lance Reddick *Carver* · Tabatha Shaun *Kristen* · Chase Williamson *Zeke* · Leland Orser *Spencer Peterson* ■ *Dir* Adam Wingard · *Scr* Simon Barrett

Guest House Paradiso ★ 15

Comedy 1999 · UK · Colour · 86min

This is a big-screen version of the TV series *Bottom*, with slightly better sets and plenty of cartoon violence. Stars Rik Mayall and Adrian Edmondson have no one to blame but themselves for this puerile farce: Edmondson directs, from a script he co-wrote with Mayall. The story, for what it's worth, finds sociopaths Richie and Eddie running a revolting hotel in the shadow of a nuclear power plant. JF _DVD_

Rik Mayall *Richie Twat* · Adrian Edmondson *Eddie Elizabeth Ndingobaba* · Vincent Cassel *Gino Bolognese* · Hélène Mahieu *Gina Carbonara* · Bill Nighy *Mr Johnson* · Simon Pegg *Mr Nice* · Fenella Fielding *Mrs Foxfur* ■ *Dir* Adrian Edmondson · *Scr* Adrian Edmondson, Rik Mayall

Guest in the House ★★

Drama 1944 · US · BW · 120min

Anne Baxter stars as a mentally disturbed but beautiful young woman who falls for her doctor's brother (Ralph Bellamy). Baxter doesn't allow Bellamy's marriage or her own relationship with the doctor (Scott McKay) to stand in her way. Directed by John Brahm with lots of atmosphere and an excellent cast, this overlong drivel is all the more depressing because it compels one to keep watching. AJ

Anne Baxter *Evelyn Heath* · Ralph Bellamy *Douglas Proctor* · Aline MacMahon *Aunt Martha* · Ruth Warrick *Ann Proctor* · Scott McKay *Dan Proctor* · Jerome Cowan *Mr Hackett* · Marie McDonald *Miriam* ■ *Dir* John Brahm · *Scr* Ketti Frings, from the play *Dear Evelyn* by Hagar Wilde, Dale Eunson

Guest Wife ★★ U

Comedy 1944 · US · BW · 84min

This comedy variation on the eternal triangle theme - bachelor foreign correspondent must play married to keep his job, borrows banker friend's wife, inevitable complications ensue - is unfortunately short on intended laughs. It's an increasingly chaotic and unconvincing farce, directed with too heavy a hand by Sam Wood, in which only Claudette Colbert, at her sparkling best as the "borrowed" wife, rises above the material. RK

Claudette Colbert *Mary Price* · Don Ameche *Joe Parker* · Richard Foran [Dick Foran] *Christopher Price* · Charles Dingle *AT Worth* · Grant Mitchell *Detective* · Wilma Francis *Susy* ■ *Dir* Sam Wood · *Scr* Bruce Manning, John Klorer

A Guide for the Married Man ★★★ PG

Comedy 1967 · US · Colour · 87min

Walter Matthau, married for years, suddenly breaks one of the Ten Commandments: he covets his neighbour's wife. Fortunately, his best friend, Robert Morse, is a philanderer himself, and more than willing to teach Matthau the art of having an affair and getting away with it. This is, clearly, a variation on *The Seven Year Itch*, for which Matthau, by the way, was first choice. There's plenty to enjoy in this comedy of sexual mores, which is most notable for its glorious gallery of guest spots including Lucille Ball, Jack Benny, Jayne Mansfield, Phil Silvers and Terry-Thomas. AT

Walter Matthau *Paul Manning* · Robert Morse *Ed Stander* · Inger Stevens *Ruth Manning* · Sue Anne Langdon [Sue Ane Langdon] *Irma Johnson* · Jackie Russell *Miss Harris* · Claire Kelly *Harriet Stander* · Linda Harrison *Miss Stardust* · Elaine Devry *Jocelyn Montgomery* ■ *Dir* Gene Kelly · *Scr* Frank Tarloff, from his book

A Guide to Recognizing Your Saints ★★★ 15

Biographical drama
2006 · US/UK · Colour · 95min

Raw and powerful performances transform a low-budget coming-of-age drama into a vibrant calling card for debut writer/ director Dito Montiel. Adapted from Montiel's memoir, the ambitious biopic re-imagines his traumatic experiences growing up in the violence-soaked streets of mid-1980s New York. Robert Downey Jr is quietly reflective as the adult Dito returning to his old Queens neighbourhood after a 20-year absence, while Shia LaBeouf plays his teenage self who's struggling to balance his loyalty to friends and family with his hunger for independence. It's a familiar yet heartfelt story, boasting an emotional intensity and gritty attitude that compensate for the film's rough edges and frequently jarring visuals. SF Swearing, sexual references, drug abuse. _DVD_ CS

Robert Downey Jr *Dito Montiel* · Shia LaBeouf *Young Dito Montiel* · Chazz Palminteri *Monty Montiel* · Dianne Wiest *Flori Montiel* · Channing Tatum *Young Antonio* · Melonie Diaz *Young Laurie* · Martin Compston *Mike O'Shea* · Eric Roberts *Antonio* ■ *Dir* Dito Montiel · *Scr* Dito Montiel, from his memoirs

Guilt by Association ★★ 12

Crime drama based on a true story
2002 · US/Can · Colour · 86min

This is an unashamedly sensationalist TV movie about a single mother who finds herself charged with conspiracy when her new boyfriend is exposed as a drug dealer. Graeme Campbell directs solidly, but it's a mediocre project for Mercedes Ruehl. Yet it's to Ruehl's credit that she makes both her tribulations behind bars and her determination to protect her kids seem traumatic rather than just melodramatic. DP

Mercedes Ruehl *Susan Walker* · Alberta Watson *Angie* · Alex Carter *Russell* · Karen Glave *Roxanne* · Elisa Moolecherry *Marguerite* · Rachel McAdams *Danielle* ■ *Dir* Graeme Campbell · *Scr* Alan Hines

The Guilt of Janet Ames ★★★

Psychological drama 1947 · US · BW · 81min

Psychiatry was very much in fashion in stage and screen drama when this offbeat drama was made. Its fascinating premise also tapped into postwar guilt and paranoia, with Rosalind Russell as a woman whose husband was killed in the war when he threw himself on a grenade to save five comrades. She sets out to trace the men whose lives were spared to see if they were worthy of her husband's sacrifice. TV

Rosalind Russell *Janet Ames* · Melvyn Douglas *Smithfield Cobb* · Sid Caesar *Sammy Weaver* · Betsy Blair *Katie* · Nina Foch *Susie Pierson* · Charles Cane *Walker* · Harry Von Zell *Carter* ■ *Dir* Henry Levin · *Scr* Louella MacFarlane, Allen Rivkin, Devery Freeman, from a story by Lenore Coffee

The Guilt Trip ★★★ 12

Road movie comedy 2013 · US · Colour · 95min

In this gently humorous road movie with a twist, Seth Rogen plays an organic chemist heading out on a make-or-break journey across America to pitch a wonder cleaning product he's invented. When his domineering mother (Barbra Streisand) reveals she still harbours thoughts of her first love as a teenager, Rogen decides to

G

take her along, secretly tracking down her former beau in the hope she may find happiness in her autumn years. The tale motors by at a brisk, if predictable pace under the direction of Anne Fletcher, and the sharp-tongued sparring between the two leads pops and fizzes throughout. TeS Swearing, sexual references. **DVD**

Barbra Streisand *Joyce Brewster* • Seth Rogen *Andrew Brewster* • Adam Scott *Andrew Margolis Jr* • Colin Hanks *Rob* • Brett Cullen *Ben Graw* • Miriam Margolyes *Anita* ■ *Dir* Anne Fletcher • *Scr* Dan Fogelman

The Guilty ★★ 15
Crime thriller 2000 · Can/UK/US · Colour · 107min

Bill Pullman puts in an unusually reptilian performance as a sleazy, high-flying lawyer prepared to go to any extremes to save his career in this join-the-dots thriller. Engaging to watch and nicely shot, it's hampered by the fact that every plot twist is neon-signposted, while many characters are hammy stereotypes. Consequently what begins as a fast-paced, contemporary *film noir* soon plunges into melodrama, despite a strong turn from Gabrielle Anwar. SF Swearing, violence. **DVD**

Bill Pullman *Callum Crane* • Devon Sawa *Nathan Corrigan* • Gabrielle Anwar *Sophie Lennon* • Angela Featherstone *Tanya Duncan* • Joanne Whalley *Natalie Crane* • Darcy Belsher *Dennis* • Jaimz Woolvett *Leo* ■ *Dir* Anthony Waller • *Scr* William Davies, from the TV serial by Simon Burke

Guilty as Charged ★★★ 18
Black comedy 1991 · US · Colour · 91min

Rod Steiger revisits his homicidal persona from *No Way to Treat a Lady* in this black comedy. He's at his scenery-chewing best as mad religious tycoon Ben Kallin, dispatching criminals in his home-made electric chair. *South Park*'s Chef, Isaac Hayes, is one of Steiger's little helpers. It's all a shocker of some voltage, with Lauren Hutton looking aghast and director Sam Irvin making it stylish, if not plausible. TH **DVD**

Rod Steiger *Ben Kallin* • Lauren Hutton *Liz Stanford* • Heather Graham *Kimberly* • Lyman Ward *Mark Stanford* • Isaac Hayes *Aloysius* • Zelda Rubenstein *Edna* • Erwin Keyes *Deek* ■ *Dir* Sam Irvin • *Scr* Charles Gale

Guilty as Sin ★★★ 15
Thriller 1993 · US · Colour · 102min

Ever since his masterpiece *12 Angry Men*, director Sidney Lumet has had a taste for legal thrillers. And before it topples from high mystery to low melodrama, this film cops a plea for craftsmanship at least, with Rebecca De Mornay as the slick lawyer defending wife-killer Don Johnson, whose lethal duplicity involves the death of more than one woman. Larry Cohen's script is far more serrated than the *Jagged Edge* it resembles and so, prior to his succumbing to clichés, is Lumet's handling of some suspenseful legal scenes. TH Violence, swearing. **DVD**

Rebecca De Mornay *Jennifer Haines* • Don Johnson *David Greenhill* • Stephen Lang *Phil Garson* • Jack Warden *Moe Plimpton* • Dana Ivey *Judge Tompkins* • Ron White *Diangelo* ■ *Dir* Sidney Lumet • *Scr* Larry Cohen

Guilty by Suspicion ★★★ 15
Drama 1990 · US · Colour · 100min

The investigation of the House Un-American Activities Committee into communism in Hollywood is one of the most shameful episodes in movie history. But the film folk whose careers were destroyed by the infamous blacklist deserve a better memorial than Irwin Winkler's well-intentioned but underachieving picture. Set at the height of the 1951 witch-hunt, the action centres on film-maker Robert De Niro's dilemma - lose everything he's worked for or betray the "fellow travellers" among his friends. The film fails to generate an atmosphere of fear and suspicion. DP Swearing. **DVD**

Robert De Niro *David Merrill* • Annette Bening *Ruth Merrill* • George Wendt *Bunny Baxter* • Patricia Wettig *Dorothy Nolan* • Sam Wanamaker *Felix Graff* • Luke Edwards *Paulie Merrill* • Chris Cooper *Larry Nolan* • Ben Piazza *Darryl F Zanuck* • Martin Scorsese *Joe Lesser* ■ *Dir/Scr* Irwin Winkler

Guilty Conscience ★★★★ PG
Thriller 1985 · US · Colour · 91min

Anthony Hopkins gives a bravura performance as a lawyer who cross-examines his alter ego to concoct the perfect plan to murder his wife. But while he is scheming and dreaming of a future with his mistress, other plots are being hatched behind his back. Blythe Danner and Swoosie Kurtz match Hopkins every step of the way in a chatty but taut and clever TV movie thriller. DP **DVD**

Anthony Hopkins *Arthur Jamison* • Blythe Danner *Louise Jamison* • Swoosie Kurtz *Jackie Willis* • Wiley Harker *Older man* • Ruth Manning *Older woman* ■ *Dir* David Greene • *Scr* Richard Levinson, William Link

Guilty Hands ★★★
Crime drama 1931 · US · BW · 60min

Deliciously inventive, this crime drama stars Lionel Barrymore as the former district attorney attempting to commit the perfect murder to prevent his daughter from marrying a playboy bounder. More usually a comic snob, Alan Mowbray must have been flattered to play the scoundrel, with no less a figure than Kay Francis as his mistress. Bayard Veiller's original screenplay comes up with an unforgettable way for Mowbray to settle the score, while WS Van Dyke's direction is visually accomplished. AE

Lionel Barrymore *Richard Grant* • Kay Francis *Marjorie West* • Madge Evans *Barbara Grant* • William Bakewell *Tommy Osgood* • C Aubrey Smith *Rev Hastings* • Polly Moran *Aunt Maggie* • Alan Mowbray *Gordon Rich* • Forrester Harvey *Spencer Wilson* ■ *Dir* WS Van Dyke • *Scr* Bayard Veiller, from his story

Guilty of Romance ★★★ 18
Drama 2011 · Jpn · Colour · 113min

A gruesome crime scene in a Japanese love hotel is the starting point for the concluding film in director Sion Sono's "trilogy of hate". Megumi Kagurazaka is a revelation as Izumi, the meek housewife whose humdrum marriage to a famous romantic novelist begins to unravel after she is inadvertently drawn into the sex industry. It's a complex, graphic tale with valid things to say about female identity. It's just a shame that the eventual outcome is not as convincing as the performances of the two high-powered leads. JA Japanese +subtitles. Violence, swearing, sex scenes, nudity. **DVD** ⓑ

Megumi Kagurazaka *Izumi Kikuchi* • Makoto Togashi *Mitsuko Ozawa* • Miki Mizuno *Kazuko Yoshida* • Kanji Tsuda *Izumi's husband* • Hisako Ohkata *Mitsuko's mother* ■ *Dir/Scr* Sion Sono

The Guinea Pig ★★ U
Social drama 1948 · UK · BW · 93min

Richard Attenborough makes light of his 20-odd years to play a boy half his age in this class-barrier melodrama. Accepted by a top public school as part of an educational experiment, working-class Attenborough endures the raillery of classmates and family with practised angst as he passes from victim to insider with the help of teacher Robert Flemyng. Wallowing in the clichés of establishment privilege, director Roy Boulting makes few demands of a cast that almost sleepwalks through familiar characterisations. DP

Richard Attenborough *Jack Read* • Sheila Sim *Lynne Hartley* • Bernard Miles *Mr Read* • Cecil Trouncer *Mr Hartley, housemaster* • Robert Flemyng *Nigel Lorraine* • Edith Sharpe *Mrs Hartley* • Joan Hickson *Mrs Read* • Peter Reynolds *Grimmett* ■ *Dir* Roy Boulting • *Scr* Warren Chetham Strode, Bernard Miles, from the play by Warren Chetham Strode

Guinevere ★★★
Romantic drama 1999 · US · Colour · 104min

A knock-out performance from Sarah Polley is the main reason for seeing this insightful, if sentimental coming-of-age saga. Polley plays an affection-starved 21-year-old, who meets middle-aged photographer Stephen Rea at her sister's wedding. Attracted by his bohemian charisma, she becomes his apprentice and lover. This familiar May-December romance contains as many deft strokes as it does missteps. AJ

Stephen Rea *Connie Fitzpatrick* • Sarah Polley *Harper Sloane* • Jean Smart *Deborah Sloane* • Gina Gershon *Billie* • Jasmine Guy *Linda* • Francis Guinan *Alan Sloane* • Paul Dooley *Walter* ■ *Dir/Scr* Audrey Wells

Gulliver's Travels ★★ U
Animated fantasy 1939 · US · Colour · 76min

An age in production, this animated version of Jonathan Swift's timeless satire owes more to the imagination of the Fleischer brothers than it does to the venerable Dublin dean's. The most serious failing is the time it takes for Gulliver to embark on his Lilliputian adventures, with far too long being devoted to the pointless feud between kings Little of Lilliput and Bombo of Blefescu. Stylistic inconsistencies in the artwork also irritate. DP **DVD**

■ *Dir* Dave Fleischer • *Scr* Dan Gordon, Ted Pierce, Izzy Sparber, Edmond Seward, from a story by Edmond Seward, from the novel by Jonathan Swift • *Producer* Max Fleischer

Gulliver's Travels ★ U
Part-animated satirical fantasy 1977 · UK/Bel · Colour · 76min

This adaptation is a dismal combination of dire songs, unutterable dialogue and one of the worst mergers of animated and live-action footage ever committed to celluloid. Richard Harris looks like a man enduring a nightmare as he attempts desperately to interact with his clumsily drawn co-stars. DP

Richard Harris *Gulliver* • Catherine Schell *Girl* • Norman Shelley *Father* • Meredith Edwards *Uncle* ■ *Dir* Peter Hunt • *Scr* Don Black, from the novel by Jonathan Swift

Gulliver's Travels ★★★ PG
Comedy fantasy adventure 2010 · US · Colour · 84min

Jonathan Swift's classic 18th-century satire gets a modern-day slacker makeover here, with Jack Black as the would-be travel writer lost at sea who washes up on the shores of Lilliput. Its tiny inhabitants are at first wary of "the beast", but soon herald him as a saviour when he vanquishes their foes. Black essentially reprises his lovable-rogue character from *The School of Rock*, only this time the diminutive recipients of his pop-culture wisdom are played by a cast of British comedy stalwarts, including Billy Connolly and Catherine Tate. It's all silly, predictable fun, heavily reliant on camera trickery to grab laughs from an otherwise so-so script. TeS Brief swearing, sexual references. **DVD** ⓑ ⓑ

Jack Black *Lemuel Gulliver* • Jason Segel *Horatio* • Emily Blunt *Princess Mary* • Amanda Peet *Darcy* • Chris O'Dowd *General Edward Edwardian* • Billy Connolly *King Theodore* • Catherine Tate *Queen Isabelle* ■ *Dir* Rob Letterman • *Scr* Nicholas Stoller, from the novel by Jonathan Swift

The Gumball Rally ★★★ PG
Comedy adventure 1976 · US · Colour · 102min

A precursor to such frantic cross-country races as *The Cannonball Run* and *Smokey and the Bandit*, this is a reasonable example of the genre, unhindered by a serious plot and full of tyre-squealing action. It's directed and produced by stuntman Chuck Bail, and, though the actors are constantly upstaged by the customised autos, Michael Sarrazin and rival Tim McIntire do raise a few smiles as bungling cop Normann Burton desperately tries to stop their contest. TH

Michael Sarrazin *Michael Bannon* • Normann Burton [Norman Burton] *Roscoe* • Gary Busey Gibson • John Durren *Preston* • Norman Burton *Alice* • Harvey Jason *Lapchick* • Tim McIntire *Steve Smith* • Raul Julia *Franco* ■ *Dir* Chuck Bail • *Scr* Leon Capetanos, from a story by Leon Capetanos, Chuck Bail

Gumball 3000: the Movie ★★★ 18
Documentary 2003 · US/UK · Colour · 97min

Lasting six days and spanning 3000 miles of occasionally treacherous terrain, the Gumball Rally may seem like just another excuse for a bunch of minor celebrities, extreme sports stars and everyday opportunists to see their name in the headlines. But Steven Green's documentary reveals high levels of both competitive spirit and camaraderie, as the likes of supermodel Jodie Kidd, the *Jackass* duo Ryan Dunn and Tony Hawk, and hip-hop comics the Cuban Brothers negotiate the route from San Francisco to Miami and the various cops they encounter along it. Burt Reynolds provides the genially sardonic commentary. DP Swearing. **DVD**

Burt Reynolds *Narrator* ■ *Dir* Steven Green

Gummo ★★★★ 18
Drama 1997 · US · Colour · 85min

Abandoning any pretence of linear narrative, director Harmony Korine - writer of the highly controversial *kids* - presents an impressionistic collection of grim insights into a neighbourhood recovering from a destructive tornado. Using a variety of techniques, including hand-held camerawork, this follows two geeky adolescents, Jacob Reynolds and Nick Sutton, as they sniff glue, torture cats and gross out the locals. This extraordinary investigation into the tarnished American Dream is repulsive, shocking and definitely not for the faint-hearted. AJ Violence, swearing, sex scenes, drug abuse, nudity.

Jacob Reynolds *Solomon* • Nick Sutton *Tummler* • Jacob Sewell *Bunny Boy* • Lara Tosh *Girl in car* • Darby Dougherty *Darby* • Chloë Sevigny *Dot* • Carisa Glucksman *Helen* • Jason Guzak *Skinhead* • Casey Guzak *Skinhead* ■ *Dir/Scr* Harmony Korine

Gumshoe ★★★★ 12
Crime comedy 1971 · UK · Colour · 81min

Director Stephen Frears made his feature debut with this wonderfully understated homage to *film noir*. Albert Finney excels as the bingo caller who has dreams of writing like Dashiell Hammett and acting like Humphrey Bogart. Following the example of Woody Allen in *Play It Again, Sam*, screenwriter Neville Smith blends fond parody with an original story that has undeniable charm. But this also has an unexpectedly hard edge, thanks to its tough themes of drugs and gunrunning and Frears's astute snapshots of Liverpool. DP Swearing, violence, drug abuse. **DVD**

Albert Finney *Eddie Ginley* • Billie Whitelaw *Ellen* • Frank Finlay *William* • Janice Rule *Mrs Blankerscoon* • Carolyn Seymour *Alison Wyatt* • Fulton Mackay *John Straker* • George Innes *Bookshop proprietor* • Wendy Richard *Anne Scott* • Maureen Lipman *Naomi* ■ *Dir* Stephen Frears • *Scr* Neville Smith

Gun Crazy ★★★★ PG
Film noir 1949 · US · BW · 87min

This unsung minor masterpiece influenced everything from the work of Jean-Luc Godard to *Bonnie and Clyde* and *Natural Born Killers*. A stylish *film noir* from director Joseph H Lewis, it's about a smouldering *femme fatale* (Peggy Cummins in the role of her life) who leads the psychotic, gun-fixated John Dall astray. Originally based on a *Saturday Evening Post* short story by MacKinlay Kantor, the taut screenplay is the work of Kantor and the blacklisted Dalton Trumbo. The plot was reworked less effectively for 1992's *Guncrazy*. TS

John Dall *Bart Tare* • Peggy Cummins *Annie Laurie Starr* • Berry Kroeger *Packett* • Annabel Shaw [Anabel Shaw] *Ruby Tare* • Harry Lewis *Clyde Boston* • Morris Carnovsky *Judge Willoughby* • Stanley Praeger [Stanley Prager] *Bluey-Bluey* • Nedrick Young *Dave Allister* ■ *Dir* Joseph H Lewis • *Scr* MacKinlay Kantor, Millard Kaufman [Dalton Trumbo], from a story by MacKinlay Kantor in *The Saturday Evening Post*

Gun Duel in Durango ★★ U

Western 1957 · US · BW · 73min

Rugged George Montgomery spent most of the 1950s appearing as the hero of short and snappy minor westerns. This time he's the leader of a band of outlaws who decides it's time to change for the better. Before he can marry sweetheart Ann Robinson he has to prove himself, but his old gang have ways of persuading him to join them in another raid. Comfortably predictable, it is directed competently enough to please fans of the genre. **RB**

George Montgomery *Dan* • Ann Robinson *Judy* • Steve Brodie *Dunston* • Bobby Clark *Robbie* • Frank Ferguson *Sheriff Howard* • Donald Barry *Larry* • Denver Pyle *Ranger captain* ▪ *Dir* Sidney Salkow • *Scr* Louis Stevens

Gun for a Coward ★★ U

Western 1957 · US · Colour · 88min

This interesting western is from that period in the 1950s when juvenile delinquency was the byword and all Hollywood youths were crazy mixed-up kids. Jeffrey Hunter and Dean Stockwell are both excellent as the troubled teens coping with the death of their father, watched over by their older sibling, the reliable Fred MacMurray. Sadly, this promises more than it delivers. **TS**

Fred MacMurray *Will Keough* • Jeffrey Hunter *Bless Keough* • Janice Rule *Aud Niven* • Chill Wills *Loving* • Dean Stockwell *Hade Keough* • Josephine Hutchinson *Mrs Keough* • Betty Lynn *Claire* • Iron Eyes Cody *Chief* ▪ *Dir* Abner Biberman • *Scr* R Wright Campbell

Gun Fury ★★★ U

Western 1953 · US · Colour · 78min

Rock Hudson gives an adequate performance as a rancher whose fiancée Donna Reed is abducted. The film boasts a moody plot that pits the gauche, honest and upright Hudson against baddie Phil Carey (who's outstanding) and his gang. Originally filmed in the novelty of 3D, this exciting western was directed by Raoul Walsh, who appears to have encouraged inexperienced star Hudson to overact. **TS** 🔄

Rock Hudson *Ben Warren* • Donna Reed *Jennifer Ballard* • Phil Carey [Philip Carey] *Frank Slayton* • Roberta Haynes *Estella Morales* • Lee Marvin *Blinky* • Leo Gordon *"Jess Burgess"* • Neville Brand *Brazos* • Ray Thomas *Doc* ▪ *Dir* Raoul Walsh • *Scr* Irving Wallace, Roy Huggins, from the novel *Ten against Caesar* by Kathleen B George, Robert A Granger

Gun Glory ★★ U

Western 1957 · US · Colour · 88min

Stewart Granger, who was best as a swashbuckling hero, seems ill-at-ease as a gunfighter returning home after some years away, to find that his wife has died and his teenage son is bitter towards him. Director Roy Rowland commits the cardinal casting sin of putting his plainly inadequate son Steve in the role of Granger's son. But the plot and the lovely Rhonda Fleming make this western watchable. **RB**

Stewart Granger *Tom Early* • Rhonda Fleming *Jo* • Chill Wills *Preacher* • Steve Rowland *Young Tom Early* • James Gregory *Grimsell* • Jacques Aubuchon *Sam Winscott* • Arch Johnson *Gunn* • William Fawcett *Martin* ▪ *Dir* Roy Rowland • *Scr* William Ludwig, Philip Yordan (front for Ben Maddow), from the novel *Man of the West* by Philip Yordan

The Gun Hawk ★★

Western 1963 · US · Colour · 92min

Rory Calhoun was well past his prime when he starred in this inconsistent B-western. Again he's playing a loner gunman whose best efforts to have a quiet life are thwarted, on this occasion by cocky James Dean-lookalike Rod Lauren (his character is called Rebel just in case you missed the similarity) and determined sheriff Rod Cameron. There are some unexpected twists and turns as time seems to be running out for the notorious gunslinger, but the narrative meanders and the ropey B-movie acting belies the sombre undercurrent of the tale. **JA**

Rory Calhoun *Blaine Madden* • Rod Cameron *Sheriff Ben Corey* • Ruta Lee *Marleen* • Rod Lauren *"Reb" Roan* ▪ *Dir* Edward Ludwig • *Scr* Jo Heims, from a story by Richard Bernstein, Max Steeber

The Gun in Betty Lou's Handbag ★★★ 15

Comedy 1992 · US · Colour · 84min

Director Allan Moyle might seem curious choice for this comic slice of small-town life, considering he is best known for those celebrations of teenage angst, *Pump Up the Volume* and *Empire Records*. However, he keeps this preposterous story ticking along nicely and coaxes an engaging performance out of Penelope Ann Miller as the timid librarian who finds a murder weapon and confesses to the crime to spice up her life. DP Swearing. 📀

Penelope Ann Miller *Betty Lou Perkins* • Eric Thal *Alex Perkins* • Alfre Woodard *Ann* • Julianne Moore *Elinor* • Andy Romano *Herrick* • Ray McKinnon *Frank* • William Forsythe *Beaudeen* • Cathy Moriarty *Reba* ▪ *Dir* Allan Moyle • *Scr* Grace Cary Bickley

The Gun Runners ★★★

Crime adventure 1958 · US · Colour · 82min

This cheaply-made version of Ernest Hemingway's *To Have and Have Not* is creditably close to Howard Hawks's adaptation in 1944 and Michael Curtiz's *The Breaking Point* in 1950. Director Don Siegel draws a persuasive performance from Audie Murphy as the hard-up fishing boat captain. Patricia Owens is good as his caring wife, Everett Sloane excellent as his drunken assistant, and Eddie Albert outstanding as the treacherous gunrunner who hires his boat. **AE**

Audie Murphy *Sam Martin* • Eddie Albert *Hanagan* • Patricia Owens *Lucy Martin* • Everett Sloane *Harvey* • Richard Jaeckel *Buzurki* • Jack Elam *Arnold* ▪ *Dir* Don Siegel • *Scr* Daniel Mainwaring, Paul Monash, from the novel *To Have and Have Not* by Ernest Hemingway

Gun Shy ★ 15

Romantic crime comedy 2000 · US · Colour · 97min

Liam Neeson is woefully miscast as an undercover agent who is suffering from nerves and a very dodgy stomach, leading him to seek bowel advice from a nurse (Sandra Bullock). The movie's only saving grace is Oliver Platt as the Mafia hood Neeson is supposed to be bringing to justice. But even he can't stop this almost humour-free comedy from hurtling towards the bin marked "avoid". JB 📀

Liam Neeson *Charlie* • Oliver Platt *Fulvio Nesstra* • Sandra Bullock *Judy Tipp* • José Zuniga *Fidel Vaillar* • Richard Schiff *Elliott* • Mary McCormack *Gloria Nesstra* ▪ *Dir/Scr* Eric Blakeney

Gunbus ★ PG

First World War adventure 1986 · UK · Colour · 88min

Scott McGinnis and Jeff Osterhage try valiantly to drum up some knockabout bonhomie as Wild West outlaws enrolled in a British fighter squadron during the First World War, but everything from the stereotypical characters to the risible banter is against them. The aerial action is so inept that it only emphasises the shortcomings of this buddy movie. DP Violence.

Scott McGinnis *Barney* • Jeff Osterhage *Luke* • Ronald Lacey *Fritz* • Miles Anderson *Bannock* • Valerie Steffen *Yvette* • Ingrid Held *Mitsou* • Keith Buckley *Commander von Schlussel* • Terence Harvey *Colonel Canning* ▪ *Dir* Zoran Perisic • *Scr* Thom Keyes

Guncrazy ★★★ 15

Crime drama 1992 · US · Colour · 92min

Director Tamra Davis does a solid job with this tale of teenager Drew Barrymore who falls for an ex-con. It occasionally tries to become a 1990s version of the much more subtle *Badlands*, as the pair go on the run, firing guns aplenty, but Barrymore and co-stars James LeGros and Billy Drago keep their performances realistic rather than melodramatic. The plot is a reworking of the 1949's *Gun Crazy*. JB Violence, swearing. 📀

Drew Barrymore *Anita Minteer* • James LeGros *Howard Hickock* • Michael Ironside *Kincaid* • Ione Skye *Joy* • Billy Drago *Hank* • Joe Dallesandro *Rooney* ▪ *Dir* Tamra Davis • *Scr* Matthew Bright

A Gunfight ★★★ 15

Western 1971 · US · Colour · 89min

Kirk Douglas and Johnny Cash give excellent performances as two ageing gunfighters who have fallen on hard times. In response to speculation in the town, Douglas proposes that they should stage a gun duel and charge admission so that the survivor can make a fresh start. Tension mounts under Lamont Johnson's sharp direction of Harold Jack Bloom's screenplay, but the handling of the outcome is not wholly satisfactory. **AE**

Kirk Douglas *Will Tenneray* • Johnny Cash *Abe Cross* • Jane Alexander *Nora Tenneray* • Raf Vallone *Francisco Alvarez* • Karen Black *Jenny Simms* • Eric Douglas *Bud Tenneray* ▪ *Dir* Lamont Johnson • *Scr* Harold Jack Bloom

Gunfight at Comanche Creek ★★ U

Western 1964 · US · Colour · 90min

Audie Murphy follows in the footsteps of George Montgomery in a remake of the 1957 western *Last of the Badmen*. In this hybrid of a 1940s-style detective movie and the traditional western, detective Murphy poses as an outlaw to infiltrate a particularly ruthless gang of robbers. Their cunning plan involves using escaped convicts to commit further crimes, and then killing them so they can collect the bounty. Murphy's lightweight style undermines the suspense. **AE**

Audie Murphy *Bob Gifford* • Ben Cooper *Carter* • Colleen Miller *Abbie Stevens* • DeForest Kelley *Troop* • Jan Merlin *Nielson* • John Hubbard *Marshal Shearer* • Damian O'Flynn *Winton* • Susan Seaforth *Janie* ▪ *Dir* Frank McDonald • *Scr* Edward Bernds

The Gunfight at Dodge City ★★ U

Western 1959 · US · Colour · 80min

Joseph M Newman allows this Dodge City encounter to meander to its inevitable showdown between reformed outlaw Joel McCrea and his old gang. However, sheriff McCrea seems to have more on his mind than law and order, as both widowed saloon owner Nancy Gates and minister's daughter Julie Adams tug on his heartstrings. Snarling unconvincingly, Richard Anderson leads the assorted desperados. DP

Joel McCrea *Bat Masterson* • Julie Adams *Pauline* • John McIntire *Doc* • Nancy Gates *Lily* • Richard Anderson *Dave* • James Westerfield *Rev Howard* ▪ *Dir* Joseph M Newman • *Scr* Martin Goldsmith, Dan Ullman [Daniel B Ullman], from a story by Ullman

Gunfight at the OK Corral ★★★★ PG

Western 1957 · US · Colour · 117min

Wyatt Earp and Doc Holliday were never better portrayed on screen than here, played by movie giants Burt Lancaster and Kirk Douglas respectively. The Leon Uris screenplay may veer towards the turgid in setting up the action, but once the gunplay starts the screen positively ignites: director John Sturges's shoot-out finale is a mesmerisingly fine piece of cinema, brilliantly photographed and edited. There's also a soaring, nostalgic title ballad by Frankie Laine, and a marvellously etched supporting performance from Jo Van Fleet as Holliday's woman. TS 📀

Burt Lancaster *Wyatt Earp* • Kirk Douglas *John H "Doc" Holliday* • Rhonda Fleming *Laura Denbow* • Jo Van Fleet *Kate Fisher* • John Ireland *Johnny Ringo* • Frank Faylen *Cotton Wilson* • Earl Holliman *Charles Bassett* • Lyle Bettger *Ike Clanton* • Dennis Hopper *Billy Clanton* • DeForest Kelley *Morgan Earp* • Lee Van Cleef *Ed Bailey* ▪ *Dir* John Sturges • *Scr* Leon Uris, from the article *The Killer* by George Scullin • *Music* Dmitri Tiomkin

Gunfight in Abilene ★★

Western 1967 · US · Colour · 85min

Teen idol Bobby Darin heads a cast that includes Michael Sarrazin and a pre-*Airplane!* Leslie Nielsen in this very routine Universal western. Darin gives a capable performance as the disillusioned American Civil War veteran who's reluctantly recruited as the sheriff of Abilene by cattle baron Nielsen, but co-star Emily Banks is an unconvincing heroine and William Hale's direction is leaden. A remake of 1956's *Showdown at Abilene*. **TS**

Bobby Darin *Cal Wayne* • Emily Banks *Amy Martin* • Leslie Nielsen *Grant Evers* • Donnelly Rhodes *Joe Slade* • Don Galloway *Ward Kent* • Michael Sarrazin *Cord Decker* • Barbara Werle *Leann* ▪ *Dir* William Hale • *Scr* Berne Giler, John DF Black, from the novel *Gun Shy* by Clarence Upson Young

The Gunfighter ★★★★ U

Western 1950 · US · BW · 81min

Gregory Peck gives a performance of characteristic dignity and grit in this simmering western about the stark realities of frontier life. Having been forced to go for his gun by a bar-room braggart, gunslinger Peck rides off to a neighbouring town to visit his estranged wife and son, only to find his presence resented by the locals and his life threatened by the brothers of his latest victim. Veteran director Henry King expertly strips away the glamour of the gunfighter to reveal a man who regrets his past, but knows killing is his only future. DP 📀

Gregory Peck *Jimmy Ringo* • Helen Westcott *Peggy Walsh* • Millard Mitchell *Sheriff Mark Strett* • Jean Parker *Molly* • Karl Malden *Mac* • Skip Homeier *Hunt Bromley* • Anthony Ross *Charlie* • Verna Felton *Mrs Pennyfeather* ▪ *Dir* Henry King • *Scr* William Bowers, William Sellers, Nunnally Johnson, from a story by William Bowers, Andre De Toth

The Gunfighter's Pledge ★★ PG

Western 2008 · US · Colour · 83min

In this simple made-for-TV western, gruff sheriff Luke Perry sets out to capture the escaped convict who murdered his wife and son. But a tragic twist binds him to another broken family, and their battle against greedy land baron C Thomas Howell. Subsequent events feel like padding in preparation for the inevitable big showdown but the workmanlike script makes good use of the genre's well-trodden themes and archetypes. The only real niggle is the film's limited emotional impact – a surprising weakness given its poignant set-up and unusually large body count. SF Some violence. 📀

Luke Perry *Matt Austin* • C Thomas Howell *Horn* • Kim Coates *Tate* • Jaclyn DeSantis *Amaya* • Francesco Quinn *Sheriff* • Wyatt Smith *Billy* ▪ *Dir* Armand Mastroianni • *Scr* Jim Byrnes

Gung Ho! ★★★ PG

Second World War drama 1943 · US · BW · 82min

This drama was a huge wartime hit for Universal with its rousing fictionalised re-creation of a highly successful August 1942 attack in which a battalion of specially picked marine raiders took a Pacific island back from the Japanese. The force's motto is "gung ho", a Chinese expression for working in harmony. Randolph Scott is suitably heroic as the tough commander, and a young Robert Mitchum also appears. AE 📀

Randolph Scott *Col Thorwald* • Grace McDonald *Kathleen Corrigan* • Alan Curtis *John Harbison* • Noah Beery Jr *Kurt Richter* • J Carrol Naish *Lt Cristoforos* • Bob Mitchum [Robert Mitchum] *"Pig-Iron" Matthews* ▪ *Dir* Ray Enright • *Scr* Lucien Hubbard, from a story by Capt WS LeFrançois

Gung Ho ★★★ 15

Comedy 1986 · US · Colour · 107min

Ron Howard directs this small but often enjoyable comedy. Michael Keaton is the car factory foreman trying to create peace between the workers and the new

Japanese owners of the plant, who, of course, want their employees to be punctual, correct and up at six in the morning doing exercises in the parking lot. Keaton is a deft hand at comedy, and he is capably supported by George Wendt (*Cheers*) and Coen brothers regular John Turturro. JB ***DVD***

Michael Keaton *Hunt Stevenson* • Mimi Rogers *Audrey* • George Wendt *Buster* • Gedde Watanabe *Kazihiro* • John Turturro *Willie* • Soh Yamamura [So Yamamura] *Mr Sakamoto* ■ *Dir* Ron Howard • *Scr* Lowell Ganz, Babaloo Mandel, from a story by Edwin Blum, Lowell Ganz, Babaloo Mandel

Gunga Din ★★★★★ U
Adventure   1939 · US · BW · 112min

This absolutely spiffing action adventure, probably the best of its kind, is loosely based on the imperialist poem by Rudyard Kipling. However, it actually takes its plot premise from the Broadway classic *The Front Page*, and it's no surprise that both the play and this story were written by the same team, Ben Hecht and Charles MacArthur. Casting couldn't be bettered, as Cary Grant, Douglas Fairbanks Jr and Victor McLaglen swashbuckle their way across the 19th-century Indian frontier, only to be rescued ultimately by water boy Sam Jaffe. George Stevens makes a superb job of handling the rumbustious squaddies in his biggest budget movie. This immensely enjoyable epic is timeless. TS

Cary Grant *Cutter* • Victor McLaglen *MacChesney* • Douglas Fairbanks Jr *Ballantine* • Sam Jaffe *Gunga Din* • Joan Fontaine *Emmy* • Eduardo Ciannelli *Guru* • Montagu Love *Colonel Weed* ■ *Dir* George Stevens • *Scr* Joel Sayre, Fred Guiol, from a story by Ben Hecht, Charles MacArthur, from the poem by Rudyard Kipling

Gunhed ★★★ 12
Science-fiction action adventure
1989 · Jpn · Colour · 96min

In 2025, the super computer Kyron-5 began hostilities with mankind. By 2083, fearless techno-bounty hunters assault the computer's island HQ initiating the great Robot War. The only hope for man's future lies in fabled fighting machine Unit 507, the last of the Gunheds. Can this bio-droid penetrate the island's dizzying battle levels for victory over the machine? A smash hit in Japan, director Masato Harada's dark vision is an exciting helter-skelter action adventure, with few pauses for breath. AJ Japanese dubbed.

Landy Leyes *Gunhed* • Masahiro Takashima *Brooklyn* • Brenda Bakke *Sergeant Nim* • Yujin Harada *Steven* • Kaori Mizushima *Eleven* • Aya Enyoji *Bebe* • Mickey Curtis *Bancho* • James B Thompson *Balba* ■ *Dir* Masato Harada • *Scr* Masato Harada, James Bannon

The Gunman ★★ 15
Action thriller   2015 · Sp/UK · Colour · 110min

Sean Penn strikes all kinds of action-man poses without ever making a strong impression in this half-cocked shoot-'em-up. He plays an ex-mercenary working in Africa who is carrying the guilt of his assassination of a government official. Javier Bardem hams it up as a former cohort and love rival, but the talents of Idris Elba, Mark Rylance and Ray Winstone are largely wasted. SP Violence, swearing, a sex scene. ***DVD*** Blu

Sean Penn *Jim Terrier* • Idris Elba *Barnes* • Mark Rylance *Cox* • Jasmine Trinca *Annie* • Javier Bardem *Felix* • Ray Winstone *Stanley* ■ *Dir* Pierre Morel • *Scr* Don MacPherson, Pete Travis, from the novel *The Prone Gunman* by Jean-Patrick Manchette

Gunman's Walk ★★★
Western   1958 · US · Colour · 94min

Although he spent most of his career directing low-budget movies, Phil Karlson was one of the shrewdest of his breed. His ability to draw symbolic significance from the landscape is just one of the ways in which he hauls this pseudo-biblical western up a notch. Another is the subtle manner in which Karlson lets Tab Hunter exhibit his natural tendency to overact, making Hunter's role as the hothead son of former

gunslinger Van Heflin one of his best. Kathryn Grant also does well as the mixed-race girl who captures the heart of Heflin's clean-living younger son, James Darren. DP

Van Heflin *Lee Hackett* • Tab Hunter *Ed Hackett* • Kathryn Grant *Clee Chouard* • James Darren *Davy Hackett* • Mickey Shaughnessy *Will Motely* • Robert F Simon *Harry Brill* ■ *Dir* Phil Karlson • *Scr* Frank S Nugent, from a story by Ric Hardman

Gunmen ★★★ 18
Action adventure   1994 · US · Colour · 90min

Eclectic casting lifts what is basically a trashy and gory B-movie thriller out of the ordinary. Christopher Lambert and Mario Van Peebles play a mismatched duo forced to team up to locate a boat that holds millions of dollars stolen from drugs lord Patrick Stewart; Denis Leary and an army of swarthy bandits are also hot on their trail. The two stars spark off each other nicely and director Deran Sarafian stages some enjoyably ludicrous action set pieces. JF Violence, swearing, drug abuse, nudity.

Christopher Lambert *Dani Servigo* • Mario Van Peebles *Cole Parker* • Denis Leary *Armor O'Malley* • Patrick Stewart *Loomis* • Kadeem Hardison *Izzy* • Sally Kirkland *Bennett* ■ *Dir* Deran Sarafian • *Scr* Stephen Sommers

Gunnar Hede's Saga ★★★★
Silent drama   1922 · Swe · BW · 70min

One of the Swedish masterworks of director Mauritz Stiller, based on a novel by Selma Lagerlöf, this is the tale of an introspective young man who is cast off the family estate for befriending a young female violinist. He seeks to emulate his grandfather by bringing a vast herd of reindeer down from the snowy north but suffers a serious accident during the journey. This drive, with its stampede, puts the film in the epic class, but it is also concerned with dreams, hallucinations and the power of memory. AE

Einar Hanson *Gunnar Hede* • Pauline Brunius *Gunnar's mother* • Mary Johnson *Ingrid* • Adolf Olchansky *Mr Blomgren* • Stina Berg *Mrs Blomgren* • Hugo Björne *Gunnar's father* • Theckla Ahlander *Miss Stava* ■ *Dir* Mauritz Stiller • *Scr* Mauritz Stiller, from the novel *En Herrgårdssägen* by Selma Lagerlöf

Gunnin' for That #1 Spot ★★★ 12
Sports documentary 2008 · US · Colour · 96min

This engaging sports documentary from Beastie Boy Adam Yauch follows eight high-schoolers from across the United States as they compete in the inaugural Elite 24 basketball contest, where sponsorship deals vie with dreams of playing in the NBA. Lacking the intimacy and insight of *Hoop Dreams*, the film fails fully to indict the corporations who prey upon the wannabes and rob them of any real enjoyment, as they play to catch the eye rather than as part of a team. But the big game is archly shot and edited, prioritising the director's artistry over the athleticism of his subjects. DP ***DVD***

Jerryd Bayless • Michael Beasley • Tyreke Evans • Bobbito Garcia [Robert Garcia] *Unofficial narrator* • Donte Greene • Brandon Jennings ■ *Dir* Adam Yauch

Gunpoint ★★ PG
Western   1966 · US · Colour · 82min

A late Audie Murphy vehicle, this has the baby-faced war hero playing a sheriff trying to capture a gang of train robbers who have taken a saloon girl hostage. Murphy is always watchable and there's expert support from grizzled western veterans Denver Pyle and Edgar Buchanan, but this unoriginal movie is little better than TV fodder. Director Earl Bellamy makes good use of his locations, but the low budget is very evident. TS

Audie Murphy *Chad Lucas* • Joan Stanley *Uvalde* • Warren Stevens *Nate Harlan* • Edgar Buchanan *Bull* • Denver Pyle *Cap Hold* • Royal Dano *Ode* • Nick Dennis *Nicos* • William Bramley *Hoag* ■ *Dir* Earl Bellamy • *Scr* Willard Willingham, Mary Willingham

The Gunrunner ★★ 15
Crime drama   1984 · Can/US · Colour · 78min

Had Kevin Costner not found fame, this early outing may have remained in the obscurity it deserves. Set in the 1920s, it opens with Costner vowing to run guns for some Chinese rebels. But back in Montreal, his purpose is blunted by the fact his family has not only fallen on hard times, but has also become involved with the Mob. DP

Kevin Costner *Ted Beaubien* • Sara Botsford *Maude* • Paul Soles *Lochman* • Gerard Parkes *Wilson* • Ron Lea *George* ■ *Dir* Nardo Castillo • *Scr* Arnie Gelbart

Guns at Batasi ★★★★ PG
Drama   1964 · UK · BW · 98min

Overlooked in 1964 as a routine piece of stiff-upper-lip-manship, this film is a fascinating epitaph for the British Empire and a whole slew of movies about Imperial derring-do. Set in an Africa well brushed by what Harold Macmillan called "the wind of change", it's the story of insurrection in a newly independent state and what the resident British army does about it. Staunchly traditional, it's also subversive and satirical, with a stand-out performance by Richard Attenborough as the apoplectic RSM Lauderdale. AT

Richard Attenborough *RSM Lauderdale* • Mia Farrow *Karen Ericksson* • Jack Hawkins *Lt Col Deal* • Flora Robson *Miss Barker-Wise* • John Leyton *Pte Wilkes* • Errol John *Lt Boniface* • Earl Cameron *Capt Abraham* ■ *Dir* John Guillermin • *Scr* Robert Holles, from his novel *The Siege of Battersea*

Guns in the Heather ★★ U
Spy adventure   1969 · US · Colour · 85min

Disney decamped to Ireland for this so-so adventure, also known as *The Secret of Boyne Castle* and *Spy Busters*. Kurt Russell stars as a student who helps his brother, a CIA agent, prevent a defecting scientist from falling into the clutches of communist agents. The 18-year-old Russell gives the impression that the material is beneath him and the routine round of sanitised set pieces and narrow squeaks hardly make for gripping viewing. DP

Glenn Corbett *Tom Evans* • Alfred Burke *Kersner* • Kurt Russell *Rich Evans* • Patrick Dawson *Sean O'Connor* • Patrick Barr *Lord Boyne* • Hugh McDermott *Carleton* • Patrick Westwood *Levick* ■ *Dir* Robert Butler • *Scr* Herman Groves, Charles Frend, from a novel by Lockhart Amerman

The Guns of August ★★★
First World War documentary
1964 · US · BW · 100min

Governments on either side were slow to recognise the value of propaganda at the outbreak of the First World War. To his credit, producer/director Nathan Kroll was able to uncover a wealth of archive material, much of it previously unseen, for his adaptation of Barbara Tuchman's acclaimed, Pulitzer Prize-winning study of Europe on the precipice. Chronicling events from the funeral of Edward VII in 1910 to the armistice in 1918, the film presents an indelible image of what was meant to be the war to end all wars. DP

Fritz Weaver *Narrator* ■ *Dir* Nathan Kroll • *Scr* from the non-fiction work by Barbara W Tuchman

Guns of Darkness ★★★ 12
Drama   1962 · UK · BW · 99min

A minor film from director Anthony Asquith, this is still extremely interesting, despite the all-too-obvious overuse of Elstree interiors, doubling for a swampy South America where pacifist planter David Niven and pregnant wife Leslie Caron find themselves aiding revolutionaries. This promises more intellectually than it delivers cinematically: Niven's motivation seems unclear, and his character's boorishness makes him hard to like, let alone understand, while Caron's part is seriously underwritten. There's excellent support, though, from David Opatoshu and James Robertson-Justice. TS ***DVD***

David Niven *Tom Jordan* • Leslie Caron *Claire Jordan* • James Robertson-Justice *Hugo Bryant* • David Opatoshu *President Rivera* • Derek Godfrey *Hernandez* • Richard Pearson (1) *Bastian* • Eleanor Summerfield *Mrs Bastian* • Ian Hunter *Dr Swann* ■ *Dir* Anthony Asquith • *Scr* John Mortimer, from the novel *Act of Mercy* by Francis Clifford

Guns of Fort Petticoat ★★★
Western   1957 · US · Colour · 81min

Audie Murphy launched his own production company with this intriguing slant on the western siege theme. Branded a coward for refusing to participate in the Sand Creek massacre, Murphy heads for Texas to forge a band of seemingly defenceless women into a fighting force. It's steadily directed by George Marshall and the Indian attack on the fortified mission should keep action fans happy. But Walter Doniger's screenplay is keener to explore the unsung heroism of the frontierswoman. DP

Audie Murphy *Lieutenant Frank Hewitt* • Kathryn Grant *Ann Martin* • Hope Emerson *Hannah Lacey* • Jeff Donnell *Mary Wheeler* • Jeanette Nolan *Cora Melavan* ■ *Dir* George Marshall • *Scr* Walter Doniger, from a story by C William Harrison

Guns of Hate ★★
Western   1948 · US · BW · 61min

Tim Holt had an extraordinary career, appearing in two of the greatest westerns ever, John Ford's *Stagecoach* and *My Darling Clementine*. He chose to reject conventional Hollywood stardom to ride the movie range in a series of programme fillers and to work with the horses he loved. In this very ordinary RKO B-western he sets out to find the killers of Jason Robards. TS

Tim Holt *Bob* • Nan Leslie *Judy* • Richard Martin (1) *Chito* • Steve Brodie *Morgan* • Myrna Dell *Dixie* • Tony Barrett *Wyatt* • Jason Robards [Jason Robards Sr] *Ben Jason* ■ *Dir* Lesley Selander • *Scr* Norman Houston, Ed Earl Repp

The Guns of Navarone ★★★★ PG
Second World War adventure
1961 · UK/US · Colour · 150min

This classic wartime adventure is based on Alistair MacLean's bestselling novel about a daring commando raid on two giant German guns that are threatening British naval operations. Mountaineer Gregory Peck is handed the task of leading the mission when things begin to go wrong, and he's well supported by Anthony Quinn – on familiar territory playing a Greek. However, the acting honours are stolen by David Niven as the cynical, cowardly explosives expert. A belated follow-up, *Force 10 from Navarone*, was released 17 years later. JA ***DVD*** Blu

Gregory Peck *Capt Mallory* • David Niven *Cpl Miller* • Anthony Quinn *Andrea Stavros* • Stanley Baker *CPO Brown* • Anthony Quayle *Maj Franklin* • James Darren *Pappadimos* • Irene Papas *Maria* • Gia Scala *Anna* • James Robertson-Justice *Jensen* • Richard Harris *Barnsby* • Bryan Forbes *Cohn* ■ *Dir* J Lee Thompson • *Scr* Carl Foreman, Alistair MacLean, from the novel by Alistair MacLean

Guns of the Magnificent Seven ★★ PG
Western   1969 · US · Colour · 101min

This second sequel (after 1966's *Return of the Seven*) to a great original wisely retains the majestic Elmer Bernstein score. This time out, Yul Brynner relinquishes his role of mercenary gunman to George Kennedy, and the Mexican-set locations were actually filmed in Spain. Thankfully, this movie neither looks nor feels like a European western, despite the fact that it was made at the height of the spaghetti western's popularity. A touch of class is provided by Fernando Rey as the revolutionary leader in need of rescue by Kennedy's gang. The third and final sequel is 1972's *The Magnificent Seven Ride!* TS Violence. ***DVD***

George Kennedy *Chris* • James Whitmore *Levi Morgan* • Monte Markham *Keno* • Bernie Casey *Cassie* • Joe Don Baker *Slater* • Scott Thomas *PJ* • Fernando Rey *Quintero* ■ *Dir* Paul Wendkos • *Scr* Herman Hoffman

Guns of the Timberland ★ U

Western   1960 · US · Colour · 91min

Alan Ladd is as wooden as the scenery in this feeble logging drama produced by Aaron Spelling (*Dynasty*). Although cliché-ridden, it does raise worthwhile environmental considerations, as Ladd and his team of lumberjacks want to remove forest cover that protects the inhabitants of a valley from huge mudslides. Frankie Avalon supplies the pop music interludes and the supporting cast includes Ladd's daughter, Alana. **AE**

Alan Ladd *Jim Hadley* • Jeanne Crain *Laura Riley* • Gilbert Roland *Monty Walker* • Frankie Avalon *Bert Harvey* • Lyle Bettger *Clay Bell* • Noah Beery Jr *Blackie* • Verna Felton *Aunt Sarah* • Alana Ladd *Jane Peterson* ■ *Dir* Robert D Webb • *Scr* Aaron Spelling, Joseph Petracca, from the novel by Louis L'Amour

Gunsight Ridge ★★ U

Western   1957 · US · BW · 85min

A western starring Joel McCrea and containing a secret piano-playing villain called Velvet Clark can't be all bad, although it comes pretty close. The middle-aged McCrea is an undercover agent who rides a well-worn trail to track down the aforementioned Velvet (Mark Stevens), currently operating under the guise of a mine owner. **RB**

Joel McCrea *Mike* • Mark Stevens *Velvet Clark* • Joan Weldon *Molly* • Darlene Fields *Rosa* • Addison Richards *Sheriff Jones* • Carolyn Craig *Girl* • Robert Griffin *Babcock* • Slim Pickens *Hank Moss* ■ *Dir* Francis D Lyon • *Scr* Talbot Jennings, Elizabeth Jennings

Gunsmoke ★★ U

Western   1953 · US · Colour · 79min

This routine western stars Audie Murphy as a gunslinger who has a change of heart when he's hired by a landowner to kill a rancher. The result is nothing special, but it does offer a chance to see Susan Cabot before she became a Roger Corman cult heroine. The film has nothing to do with the TV series of the same name. **TS**

Audie Murphy *Reb Kittredge* • Susan Cabot *Rita Saxon* • Paul Kelly (1) *Dan Saxon* • Charles Drake *Johnny Lake* • Mary Castle *Cora DuFrayne* • Jack Kelly *Curly Mather* • Jesse White *Professor* • William Reynolds *Brazos* ■ *Dir* Nathan Juran • *Scr* DD Beauchamp, from the novel *Roughshod* by Norman A Fox

The Guru ★★ U

Satirical drama   1969 · US/Ind · Colour · 111min

Made shortly after the Beatles sat at the feet of the Maharishi at Rishikesh, this heavy-handed satire on colliding cultures suffers from the fact that James Ivory appears to have little sympathy for any of the characters. Michael York's pop star is portrayed as shallow, while Rita Tushingham's hippy is an opportunistic groupie. Only sitar master and spiritual mentor Utpal Dutt is permitted any depth, but the subtle blend of humility and egotism owes more to his own canny delivery than the mocking bombast of the script. **DP**

Utpal Dutt *Ustad Zafar Khan* • Michael York *Tom Pickle* • Rita Tushingham *Jenny* • Aparna Sen *Ghazala* • Madhur Jaffrey *Begum Sahiba* • Barry Foster *Chris* ■ *Dir* James Ivory • *Scr* Ruth Prawer Jhabvala, James Ivory

The Guru ★★★ 15

Romantic comedy
2002 · US/UK/Fr/Ger · Colour · 90min

This appealing romantic comedy marked the first leading role for British actor Jimi Mistry, who more than holds his own alongside Hollywood actresses Heather Graham and Marisa Tomei. Mistry plays an amiable dance instructor who moves from India to New York in search of Broadway success. His bubble quickly bursts, but he stumbles into a career as a guru to gullible socialite Tomei, dispensing second-hand sex advice gleaned from porn actress friend Graham. There's a winning sweetness to Mistry's character and the film is bright and amusing. **JC** Swearing, sex scenes. **DVD**

Heather Graham *Sharonna* • Marisa Tomei *Lexi* • Jimi Mistry *Ramu Chandra Gupta* • Christine Baranski *Chantal* • Michael McKean *Dwain* • Malachy McCourt *Father Flannagan* • Rob Morrow *Josh* • Sanjeev Bhaskar *Cook* ■ *Dir* Daisy von Scherler Mayer • *Scr* Tracey Jackson, from an idea by Shekhar Kapur

Guru ★★★★ 12

Drama   2007 · Ind · Colour · 153min

Director Mani Ratnam here crafts a gripping and convincing tale, treating crime and corruption as a quintessential part of modern Indian life. Inspired by the life of controversial entrepreneur Dhirubhai Ambani, this rags-to-riches story opens in 1951, four years after Indian independence. Abhishek Bachchan plays Gurukant Desai (aka Guru), an ambitious entrepreneur who eventually creates a vast empire by building up India's biggest polyester company - yet not always adhering to the letter of the law. But, under severe pressure from business rivals, the press and government officials, his health begins to suffer. With lavish musical interludes, and a mesmerising central performance, this is an ambitious and powerful drama. **OA** Hindi +subtitles. **DVD**

Abhishek Bachchan *Gurukant "Gurubhai" K Desai* • Aishwarya Rai *Sujata G Desai* • Mithun Chakraborty *Manikdas "Nanaji" Gupta* ■ *Dir* Mani Ratnam • *Scr* Mani Ratnam, Vijay Krishna Acharya, Anurag Kashyap, from a story by Ratnam

Guru in Seven ★★ 18

Comedy   1997 · UK · Colour · 102min

Made for a mere £33,000, this is essentially an Asian *Alfie*. Rebelling against the prejudices of his parents, artist Nitin Chandra Ganatra bets his friends that he can bed a week's worth of women following his split from the love of his life, Ernestina Quarcoo. Director Shani Grewal takes this as an excuse to savage everything from Bollywood musicals to Punjabi economic expectation, but he fails in his bid to show older subcontinentals to be every bit as suburban as the rest of Britain's bourgeoisie. **DP** Swearing. **DVD**

Saeed Jaffrey *Mr Walia* • Jacqueline Pearce *Joan* • Nitin Chandra Ganatra *Sanjay* • Lea Rochelle *Nora* • Lynne Michelle *Candy* • Elle Lewis *Holly* • Amanda Pointer *Gaynor* • Ernestina Quarcoo *Jill* ■ *Dir/Scr* Shani Grewal [Shani S Grewal]

The Guvnors ★★★ 15

Thriller   2014 · UK · Colour · 94min

Within the admittedly limited genre of cross-generational British gang thrillers, this is definitely one of the better ones. It's decently made and acted, with hip-hop star Harley Sylvester (in his debut) as the thoroughly nasty new kid on the block, complete with scar, sniff tic and attitude. When Sylvester decides to increase his standing by facing up to the old guard, humiliation, and death follow. The film flirts with corniness and contrived plot twists, but still manages to breathe life back into a well-worn genre. Watch out for a cameo from another pop star, an almost unrecognisable David Essex. **DA** Violence, swearing, drug abuse. **DVD** **Blu**

Doug Allen *Mitch* • Harley Sylvester *Adam* • David Essex *Mickey Snr* • Vas Blackwood *Bill* • Jay Simpson *Neil* • Jumayn Hunter *Woods* ■ *Dir/Scr* Gabe Turner

Guy ★★★ 18

Drama   1996 · UK /Ger · Colour · 90min

Covering the same sort of territory as *The Truman Show* and *Edtv*, Michael Lindsay-Hogg's psychological thriller steers the subject matter into much darker territory. Hope Davis is the aspiring film-maker who decides to make an ordinary stranger (Vincent D'Onofrio) the star of her new movie, provoking a complex battle of wills in which the lines between the subject and the film-maker become increasingly blurred. A small-scale but intriguing study of voyeurism. **JF**

Vincent D'Onofrio *Guy* • Hope Davis *"The Camera"* • Kimber Riddle *Veronica* • Diane Salinger *Gail* • Richard Portnow *(1)* • Valente Rodriguez *Low Rider* • Michael Massee *Mark* •

John O'Donohue *Detective* • Lucy Liu *Woman at newstand* ■ *Dir* Michael Lindsay-Hogg • *Scr* Kirby Dick

A Guy Named Joe ★★★

Wartime romantic drama
1944 · US · BW · 119min

A supernatural morale-booster for wartime, this is an MGM glossy with all that great studio's polish. Spencer Tracy stars as an air force pilot who is killed on a mission. He returns in spirit to help the living - in particular his former girlfriend Irene Dunne and her admirer, new pilot Van Johnson. Victor Fleming directed the unification of the two with splendid aplomb, and fans of the film included Steven Spielberg, who remade it as *Always* (1989). **TH**

Spencer Tracy *Pete Sandidge* • Irene Dunne *Dorinda Durston* • Van Johnson *Ted Randall* • Ward Bond *Al Yackey* • James Gleason *Col "Nails" Kilpatrick* • Lionel Barrymore *The General* • Barry Nelson *Dick Rumney* • Esther Williams *Ellen Bright* • Irving Bacon *Corporal* ■ *Dir* Victor Fleming • *Scr* Dalton Trumbo, from a story by Chandler Sprague, David Boehm, Frederick H Brennan

A Guy Thing ★★ 12

Romantic comedy   2002 · US · Colour · 97min

It appears that men can be saved from making grave marital mistakes by kooky free spirits who wake up in their beds after the bachelor party and alert them to the possibility of a new life. If you can swallow that, you may enjoy this flimsy feature. Jason Lee and Selma Blair earn their pay as groom and bride, but Julia Stiles gives a performance that deserves a better film as the spanner in the nuptial works. Energetic, but too ridiculous in places for its own good. **SuR** Some swearing. **DVD**

Jason Lee *Paul* • Julia Stiles *Becky* • Selma Blair *Karen* • James Brolin *Ken* • Shawn Hatosy *Jim* • Lochlyn Munro *Ray* • Diana Scarwid *Sandra* • David Koechner *Buck* • Julie Hagerty *Dorothy* ■ *Dir* Chris Koch • *Scr* Greg Glienna, Pete Schwaba, Matt Tarses, Bill Wrubel, from a story by Glienna

Guy X ★★ 15

Military black comedy drama
2005 · Can/Ice/UK · Colour · 96min

In this dark military satire, Jason Biggs gives a likeable performance as a hapless grunt accidentally posted to an American military base in late 1970s Greenland. There he finds that the climate, boredom and landscape have driven the majority of the soldiers loopy. Biggs soon discovers the real purpose of the base, however. At first, director Saul Metzstein invokes the atmosphere of the crazy base effectively, but the plot begins to lurch into absurdity, and this is neither funny nor satirical enough. **AS** **DVD**

Jason Biggs *Rudy Spruance* • Natascha McElhone *Sergeant Irene Teale* • Jeremy Northam *Colonel Woolwrap* • Michael Ironside *Guy X* • Sean Tucker *Lavone* • Benz Antoine *Philly* ■ *Dir* Saul Metzstein • *Scr* John Paul Chapple, Steve Attridge, from the novel *No One Thinks of Greenland* by John Griesemer

The Guys ★★★

Drama   2002 · US · BW and Colour · 100min

The sentiments are as sincere as the performances in this quiet and affecting drama in which journalist Sigourney Weaver helps New York fire captain Anthony LaPaglia write eulogies for his colleagues killed in the 11 September terrorist attacks. Co-adapted by former reporter Anne Nelson from her own autobiographical play, the slow-moving project makes little attempt to escape its stage origins. Instead, almost static camerawork concentrates the action on the two characters' dialogue. It's a respectful approach to an emotive subject, with Weaver's excessively flowery voiceover the only significant flaw. **SF** Brief swearing.

Sigourney Weaver *Joan* • Anthony LaPaglia *Nick* ■ *Dir* Jim Simpson • *Scr* Anne Nelson, Jim Simpson, from the play by Nelson

Guys and Dolls ★★★★ U

Musical comedy   1955 · US · Colour · 143min

When producer Sam Goldwyn set about filming this great Broadway musical, he went after the best dancer he could find, his ideal Sky Masterson, Gene Kelly. Louis B Mayer wouldn't release Kelly to his rival, however, so Goldwyn went for the best actor in the movies. That's how Marlon Brando became the definitive Masterson, singing the Frank Loesser songs himself, cleverly choreographed by Michael Kidd. With Salvation Army doll Jean Simmons waking up to love with *If I Were a Bell*, and Frank Sinatra and Vivian Blaine as Nathan Detroit and his ever-lovin' Miss Adelaide, what more could you want? **TS** **DVD**

Marlon Brando *Sky Masterson* • Jean Simmons *Sarah Brown* • Frank Sinatra *Nathan Detroit* • Vivian Blaine *Miss Adelaide* • Robert Keith *(1)* *Lieutenant Brannigan* • Stubby Kaye *Nicely-Nicely Johnson* • BS Pully *Big Jule* • Sheldon Leonard *Harry the Horse* • Regis Toomey *Arvide Abernathy* • Johnny Silver *(1)* *Benny Southstreet* ■ *Dir* Joseph L Mankiewicz • *Scr* Joseph L Mankiewicz, from a musical by Abe Burrows, Jo Swerling, from short stories by Damon Runyon

The Guyver ★★ 15

Science-fiction action 1991 · US · Colour · 84min

One day you're saving the universe as Luke Skywalker in *Star Wars*, the next you're playing a CIA agent who turns into a cockroach. Such is the fate of Mark Hamill in this unintentionally hilarious movie based on a popular Japanese comic book. The action is well-handled in this tale of a college student who becomes an armour-plated superhero, courtesy of the title device. Unfortunately, characterisation and dialogue play second-fiddle to a series of hilariously rubbery monsters. **RS**

Mark Hamill *Max* • Vivian Wu *Mizky* • Jack Armstrong *Sean* • David Gale *Balcus* • Michael Berryman *Lisker* • Jimmie Walker *Striker* • Spice Williams *Weber* • Peter Spellos *Ramsey* ■ *Dir* Steve Wang, Screaming Mad George [Joji Tani] • *Scr* Jon Purdy, from characters by Yoshiki Takaya

Gypo ★★★ 15

Social drama   2005 · UK · Colour · 99min

Father Ted star Pauline McLynn here delivers a gutsy performance as a woman breaking out of her domestic rut. Film-maker Jan Dunn shot this social drama in adherence to the Dogme 95 manifesto (created by Lars von Trier) and gives a bare bones documentary feel to the story of the budding friendship between McLynn's weary wife and mother and a Czech Romany refugee (Chloe Sirene). It's a poignant, if sometimes preachy, commentary on race relations in modern Britain, but Dunn's multi-threaded approach sets it apart from bog-standard kitchen sink dramas. **SP** **DVD**

Pauline McLynn *Helen* • Paul McGann *Paul* • Rula Lenska *Irina* • Chloe Sirene *Tasha* • Tamzin Dunstone *Kelly* • Tom Stuart *Darren* • Barry Latchford *Jimmy* ■ *Dir/Scr* Jan Dunn

Gypsy ★★★★ PG

Musical biography   1962 · US · Colour · 137min

Rosalind Russell stars as the fabulous Rose Hovick, the mother of real-life stripper Gypsy Rose Lee, in this marvellous presentation of the great Broadway show. Some songs are missing and Mervyn LeRoy's direction is possibly too "theatrical", but this is a bright, dazzling and above all entertaining movie. It contains a fabulous array of colourful showbiz characters and a performance by Russell that will knock your socks off. There are other great moments, too: Natalie Wood's tender, touching *Little Lamb* and her final triumphant striptease. **TS** **DVD**

Rosalind Russell *Rose* • Natalie Wood *Louise "Gypsy"* • Karl Malden *Herbie Sommers* • Paul Wallace *Tulsa* • Betty Bruce *Tessie Tura* • Parley Baer *Mr Kringelein* • Harry Shannon *Grandpa* ■ *Dir* Mervyn LeRoy • *Scr* Leonard Spigelgass, from the musical by Arthur Laurents, from the memoirs by Gypsy Rose Lee [Rose Louise Hovick] • *Music* Jule Styne • *Lyrics* Stephen Sondheim

G

Gypsy ★★★ PG
Musical biography   1993 · US · Colour · 136min

Filmed in 1962 with the splendid Rosalind Russell in the role of the most monstrous showbusiness mother of them all, this re-creation was made for US television. The score survives, and the great Jerome Robbins's choreography is faithfully duplicated by Bonnie Walker. Most things work, especially a touching performance from Cynthia Gibb as young Louise, but the whole founders on the central miscasting of Bette Midler. TS

Bette Midler *Rose Hovick* • Peter Riegert *Herbie* • Cynthia Gibb *Louise Hovick* • Jennifer Beck (1) *June Hovick* • Ed Asner [Edward Asner] *Rose's father* ■ *Dir* Emile Ardolino • *Scr* Arthur Laurents, from his musical, from the memoirs by Gypsy Rose Lee [Rose Louise Hovick] • *Music* Jule Styne • *Lyrics* Stephen Sondheim

The Gypsy and the Gentleman ★★
Period drama   1958 · UK · Colour · 107min

This is hardly the sort of potboiler you would expect from a film-maker of Joseph Losey's calibre. By attempting to re-create the look of contemporary art, however, he brings some undeserved sophistication to this otherwise garish adaptation. Melina Mercouri roars through this Regency bodice-ripper with a demented glee that totally swamps Keith Michell's brooding aristocrat. DP

Melina Mercouri *Belle* • Keith Michell *Deverill* • Patrick McGoohan *Jess* • June Laverick *Sarah* • Flora Robson *Mrs Haggard* • Lyndon Brook *John* • Clare Austin *Vanessa* • Helen Haye *Lady Ayrton* • Newton Blick *Ruddock* ■ *Dir* Joseph Losey • *Scr* Janet Green, from the novel *Darkness I Love You* by Nina Warner Hooke

The Gypsy Moths ★★★ 15
Drama   1969 · US · Colour · 102min

Steve McQueen was to have starred in this gripping, if resolutely sombre romance, but then director John Frankenheimer cast Burt Lancaster and Deborah Kerr, reuniting the stars of *From Here to Eternity*. Lancaster is one of three skydivers who arrive in Kansas to perform their death-defying stunts. Thrilling in the air and depressing on the ground, it's a study of nobodies going nowhere, with Lancaster silently morose while Kerr simmers. AT

Burt Lancaster *Mike Rettig* • Deborah Kerr *Elizabeth Brandon* • Gene Hackman *Joe Browdy* • Scott Wilson *Malcolm Webson* • William Windom *V John Brandon* • Bonnie Bedelia *Annie Burke* • Sheree North *Waitress* ■ *Dir* John Frankenheimer • *Scr* William Hanley, from the novel by James Drought

The Gypsy Warriors ★★ U
Second World War comedy drama
1978 · US · Colour · 72min

Two years before his star-making role in *Magnum PI*, Tom Selleck appeared in this Second World War comedy drama pilot, which rightly failed to become a series. It's a mediocre adventure in which Selleck and James Whitmore Jr play the square-jawed heroes who land in Occupied France to steal or destroy a lethal Nazi toxin. DP

Tom Selleck *Captain Theodore Brinkenhoff* • James Whitmore Jr *Capt Sheldon Alahern* • Lina Raymond *Leela* • Joseph Ruskin *Grenault* • Kenneth Tigar *SS Commandant Schullman* ■ *Dir* Lou Antonio • *Scr* Stephen J Cannell, Philip DeGuere

H2Oil ★★ 12A
Documentary   2009 · Can · Colour · 76min

Working on the logic that a good cause can never have too many cheerleaders, this documentary joins *Dirty Oil* and *Petropolis* in dealing with Canada's Alberta Tar Sands. Director Shannon Walsh attempts to vary the pitch with some animated sequences, but the lacklustre expert testimonies and lengthy sequences of executive intransigence in the face of community indignation fail to really grab the attention. The result is a laudable but dull exposé of a growing environmental concern. DP

■ *Dir/Scr* Shannon Walsh • *Cinematographer* Alan Kohl

HM Pulham Esq ★★★★ U
Drama   1941 · US · BW · 119min

Director King Vidor makes a memorable and moving film about a stuffy Bostonian who played safe and in old age regrets not marrying the love of his life. Robert Young showed new depths as the wistful Harry Pulham, while Hedy Lamarr demonstrated that she could be more than just a glamour figure as the advertising copywriter in New York who tries to liberate him from his stifling background of wealth and privilege. Vidor also wrote the script with his wife, Elizabeth Hill, and there's an uncredited walk-on part from Ava Gardner. AE

Hedy Lamarr *Marvin Myles* • Robert Young (1) *HM Pulham Esq* • Ruth Hussey *Kay Motford* • Charles Coburn *Pulham Sr* • Fay Holden *Mrs Pulham* • Van Heflin *Bill King* • Leif Erickson *Rodney "Bo-Jo" Brown* ■ *Dir* King Vidor • *Scr* King Vidor, Elizabeth Hill, from the novel by John P Marquand • *Art Director* Cedric Gibbons

HMS Defiant ★★★ PG
Period adventure   1962 · UK · Colour · 100min

Director Lewis Gilbert told virtually the same tale (albeit set in a different war) in *Sink the Bismarck!* as he does here in this entertaining seafaring adventure. This richly coloured romp benefits immensely from the experienced duelling of Dirk Bogarde, Alec Guinness and an underused Anthony Quayle, all of whom are clearly enjoying themselves as they swash buckles in the Napoleonic wars. It's hard to keep your eyes off the young Bogarde, who's absolutely splendid as a demented martinet. Also known as *Damn the Defiant!* TS Violence.
DVD

Alec Guinness *Captain Crawford* • Dirk Bogarde *Lieutenant Scott-Padget* • Anthony Quayle *Vizard* • Tom Bell *Evans* • Maurice Denham *Surgeon Goss* • Walter Fitzgerald *Admiral Jackson* • Victor Maddern *Dawlish* • Murray Melvin *Wagstaffe* • Nigel Stock *Senior Midshipman Kilpatrick* • Richard Carpenter *Lieutenant Ponsonby* ■ *Dir* Lewis Gilbert • *Scr* Nigel Kneale, Edmund H North, from the novel *Mutiny* by Frank Tilsley

The H-Man ★★★
Science fiction   1954 · Jpn · Colour · 78min

Taking time out from his *Godzilla/Rodan* industry, director Inoshiro Honda came up with one of his best movies. Men turn into oozing green slime after being exposed to a nuclear test zone. Rain washes some of the gelatinous residue into the Tokyo sewers where it proliferates to attack the population. Flame throwers set the city sewage system alight in a spectacular climax to an engaging fantasy chock-full of hallucinatory images and impressive visual effects. Honda's semi-sequel *The Human Vapor* (1964) failed to match the same

extraordinary weirdness. AJ Japanese dubbed.

Yumi Shirakawa *Girl* • Kenji Sahara *Detective* • Akihiko Hirata *Scientist* • Eitaro Ozawa *Inspector Tominaga* • Koreya Senda *Dr Maki* • Mitsuru Sato *Uchida* ■ *Dir* Inoshiro Honda • *Scr* Takeshi Kimura, Hideo Kaijo

Hachi: a Dog's Tale ★★★ U
Drama based on a true story
2008 · US/UK · Colour and BW · 89min

In this lovely family drama, inspired by a true story, a music professor takes a seemingly abandoned dog home and unwittingly changes both their lives. After a slightly wobbly prologue illustrating Hachi's unlikely journey from rural Japan to commuter-belt America, the film takes its time in showing how this four-legged pal becomes an essential part of the household of Richard Gere and his sceptical spouse Joan Allen. The subsequent events are moving rather than just manipulative, while the bond between man and canine is treated with a tender gravitas. TJ DVD
Blu

Richard Gere *Parker Wilson* • Joan Allen *Cate Wilson* • Sarah Roemer *Andy Wilson* • Cary-Hiroyuki Tagawa *Ken* • Jason Alexander *Carl* • Davenia McFadden *Mary Anne* • Kevin Decoste *Ronnie (11 years)* • Tora Hallström *Heather* ■ *Dir* Lasse Hallström • *Scr* Stephen P Lindsey, from the film *Hachiko Monogatari* by Kaneto Shindo

Hackers ★★★ 12
Thriller   1995 · US · Colour · 105min

Teenage hackers uncover a massive computer fraud in this adventure that's set against the intriguing backdrop of New York's cyber-culture. It's little more than a standard industrial espionage chase thriller, given a stylish patina by its digital-age atmosphere, complete with often bewildering technical data and imaginative journeys down the information super-highway. New mouse on the mat Jonny Lee Miller and tough net surfer Angelina Jolie interface well as the console-crossed lovers, each trying to prove their supremacy. AJ Swearing, brief nudity. DVD

Jonny Lee Miller *Dade Murphy* • Angelina Jolie *Kate* • Jesse Bradford *Joey* • Matthew Lillard *Cereal Killer* • Laurence Mason *Nikon* • Renoly Santiago *Phantom Phreak* • Fisher Stevens *The Plague* • Wendell Pierce *Agent Dick Gill* ■ *Dir* Iain Softley • *Scr* Rafael Moreu

Hadewijch ★★★★ 12A
Drama   2009 · Fr/Ger · Colour · 105min

Inspired by the writings of a 13th-century mystic, this stars newcomer Julie Sokolowski as Hadewijch, a young nun who is thrown out of her convent for overdoing her self-punishing devotion. Out in the real world, Hadewijch meets some Muslim boys who introduce her to a radical Islamic movement. The power of Bruno Dumont's tough yet elegant film comes from its attempts to understand terrorism through religion, drawing parallels between Catholicism and Islam that seek to explain why good, God-fearing people are so often drawn to the dark side. DW French, Arabic +subtitles.

Julie Sokolowski *Céline/Hadewijch* • Yassine Saline *Yassine Chikh* • Karl Sarafidis *Nassir Chikh* • David Dewaele *David* • Brigitte Mayeux-Clerget *Mother Superior* ■ *Dir/Scr* Bruno Dumont

Hail, Caesar! ★★★★ 12
Comedy   2016 · US · Colour · 101min

Joel and Ethan Coen's unashamed screwball comedy is a dizzy hooray to Hollywood. Josh Brolin does great, stoic work as a studio fixer in early 1950s Burbank whose headaches over a non-stop 24-hour period include the kidnapped star (George Clooney) of a costly Roman epic. Aided by cinematographer Roger Deakins, costumier Mary Zophres and composer Carter Burwell, the Coens re-create the CinemaScope age before our very eyes, with pitch-perfect movie parodies, including two flawless dance routines, one led by a cheerily homoerotic Channing Tatum in a sailor suit. It may not have a lot to say –

other than: hey, the movies are just swell – but it's all executed with true love. AC
DVD Blu

Josh Brolin *Eddie Mannix* • George Clooney *Baird Whitlock* • Tilda Swinton *Thora Thacker/Thessaly Thacker* • Ralph Fiennes *Laurence Laurentz* • Channing Tatum *Burt Gurney* • Scarlett Johansson *DeeAnna Moran* • Jonah Hill *Joe Silverman* ■ *Dir/Scr* Ethan Coen, Joel Coen • *Cinematographer* Roger Deakins • *Editors* Roderick Jaynes [Ethan Coen], Roderick Jaynes [Joel Coen]

Hail! Hail! Rock 'n' Roll! ★★★★ U
Music documentary   1987 · US · Colour · 115min

Normally pop documentaries veer from on-stage electricity and dressing-room silliness to the rambling of band members posing as philosophers. *This Is Spinal Tap* did a superb spoof on all this. Now, avoiding all the pitfalls and pratfalls of the genre, comes one of the screen's most accomplished pop biographies ever, easily on a par with *The Last Waltz*. Making no attempt to gloss over Chuck Berry's brittle personality, his arrogance and petulance, it also brings out the racism Chuck experienced in his youth and examines the nature of his unique guitar sound. Telling comments by the likes of Little Richard and Bo Diddley are joined to a big-blast concert at the Fox Theatre, St Louis, to celebrate Chuck's 60th birthday. TH

Chuck Berry • Eric Clapton • Julian Lennon • Keith Richards (2) *Keith Richards* • Linda Ronstadt • Little Richard • Jerry Lee Lewis • Roy Orbison ■ *Dir* Taylor Hackford

Hail, Hero! ★★★
Drama   1969 · US · Colour · 87min

Michael Douglas's screen debut benefits from the direction of David Miller. Something of a radical in his youth, Douglas Jr brings an authenticity to this tale about a boy who drops out of college to enlist for Vietnam, not because he believes in the war – he doesn't – but because of his hawkish parents, played by Arthur Kennedy and Teresa Wright. The pacifist message is often awkward and cringe-inducing, but one admires the film's ambition and honesty. AT

Michael Douglas (1) *Carl Dixon* • Arthur Kennedy *Albert Dixon* • Teresa Wright *Santha Dixon* • John Larch *Mr Conklin* • Charles Drake *Senator Murchiston* • Mercer Harris *Jimmy* • Peter Strauss *Frank Dixon* ■ *Dir* David Miller (1) • *Scr* David Manber, from the novel by John Weston • *Music/lyrics* Gordon Lightfoot

Hail the Conquering Hero ★★★★★ U
Second World War comedy
1944 · US · BW · 96min

This extraordinarily daring wartime comedy stars Eddie Bracken as the dejected son of a dead First World War hero, prevented by hay fever from serving in the current conflict. When some battle veterans persuade him to return home and masquerade as a valiant marine to please his dear old mother, he receives a hero's welcome from the entire town. Writer/director Preston Sturges handles the mounting complications with dazzling dexterity and draws delightful performances from his favourite character actors, most notably William Demarest as the hard-boiled sergeant and Raymond Walburn as the pompous windbag of a mayor. Ella Raines also sparkles under Sturges's encouragement. AE DVD

Eddie Bracken *Woodrow Truesmith* • Ella Raines *Libby* • Bill Edwards *Forrest Noble* • Raymond Walburn *Mayor Noble* • William Demarest *Sergeant* ■ *Dir/Scr* Preston Sturges

La Haine ★★★★ 15
Drama   1995 · Fr · BW · 93min

Responsible for causing a scandal on its domestic release, this bruising portrait of disaffected youth confirmed its writer/director Mathieu Kassovitz as the *wunderkind* of French cinema. Presenting the housing schemes on the outskirts of Paris as hotbeds of racial hatred and social unrest, the film follows three lads from different ethnic backgrounds and explores how they spend their endless spare time. Vincent Cassel is outstanding as the Jewish skinhead, but it's Kassovitz's restless camerawork and a script as funny as it is hard-hitting that make this such an impressive and important work. DP French +subtitles. Violence, swearing, drug abuse. **DVD** **BL**

Vincent Cassel *Vinz* • Hubert Kounde *Hubert* • Saïd Taghmaoui *Saïd* • Karim Belkhadra *Samir* • Edouard Montoute *Darty* • François Levantal *Astérix* • Solo Dicko *Santo* • Marc Duret *Inspector "Notre Dame"* • Héloïse Rauth *Sarah* ▪ *Dir/Scr* Mathieu Kassovitz

Hair ★★15
Musical 1979 · US · Colour · 115min

If ever a musical was caught firmly in its time, then it's *Hair*. In this film version, director Milos Forman fails to capture the enormous energy of the original stage show, which was a celebrated load of old nonsense even back in the mid-1960s. Anyone who had any pretensions to hippydom at the time will find their toes curling at the memory, and those born since will be quite bemused at all the fuss. Apart from Treat Williams's table-top dance, the leads have little to be proud of. SH Nudity. **DVD**

John Savage *Claude* • Treat Williams *Berger* • Beverly D'Angelo *Sheila* • Annie Golden *Jeannie* • Dorsey Wright *Hud* • Don Dacus *Woof* • Cheryl Barnes *Hud's fiancée* • Nicholas Ray *General* ▪ *Dir* Milos Forman • *Scr* Michael Weller, from the musical by Gerome Ragni, James Rado, Galt MacDermot

The Hairdresser's Husband ★★★★15
Drama 1990 · Fr · Colour · 78min

French director Patrice Leconte has never been a great respecter of political correctness, and this eccentric comedy sees him at his most dubious. If you can overcome his attitude to both women and Arabic culture then there are some utterly charming moments, as the wonderful Jean Rochefort delights in the delicate hands of hairdresser Anna Galiena. The scenes of a seaside childhood and the sudden tragic twist remain longest in the mind, along with Rochefort's marvellously impish performance. AJ French +subtitles. Sex scenes. **DVD**

Jean Rochefort *Antoine* • Anna Galiena *Mathilde* • Roland Bertin *Antoine's father* • Maurice Chevit *Agopian* • Philippe Clevenot *Morvoisieux* • Jacques Mathou *Monsieur Chardon* • Claude Aufaure *Customer* • Albert Delpy *Donecker* ▪ *Dir* Patrice Leconte • *Scr* Claude Klotz, Patrice Leconte

Hairspray ★★★★PG
Satirical musical comedy 1988 · US · Colour · 87min

John Waters launched Ricki Lake into stardom with this kitsch classic. Waters tones down his usual excesses, but his mischievous black sense of humour is still very much to the fore in this affectionate salute to those Z-grade teen movies. Lake is the fun-loving Tracy Turnblad, who becomes the new teen dancing queen much to the horror of wealthy snobs Debbie Harry and Sonny Bono, who want their daughter to shine. The soundtrack is a constant delight, as is the eclectic cast. JF **DVD**

Ricki Lake *Tracy Turnblad* • Divine *Edna Turnblad/Arvin Hodgepile* • Sonny Bono *Franklin von Tussle* • Ruth Brown *Motormouth Maybell* • Colleen Fitzpatrick *Amber von Tussle* • Debbie Harry [Deborah Harry] *Velma von Tussle* • Michael St Gerard *Link Larkin* • Leslie Ann Powers *Penny Pingleton* • Jerry Stiller *Wilbur Turnblad* • Pia Zadora *Beatnik girl* ▪ *Dir/Scr* John Waters (2)

Hairspray ★★★★PG
Satirical musical comedy 2007 · US · Colour · 111min

If any movie musical could threaten the standing of retro favourite *Grease*, it's this one. Set in 1962 and adapted from the hit Broadway show and John Waters's 1988 camp classic, this has the amply proportioned Tracy Turnblad (a stunning

debut by Nikki Blonsky) attempting to realise her dream of becoming a featured dancer on a local TV show. But she's confronted by the twin menaces of racial prejudice and scheming showbiz mum Velma von Tussle (Michelle Pfeiffer), who also happens to be the manager of the TV station. The cast is terrific, especially a fat-suited John Travolta as Tracy's mother, Edna. With its catchy songs, well-groomed performances and slickly teased dance routines, this tuneful toe-tapper is simply irresistible. AJ Erief swearing, sexual references. **DVD** **BL**

John Travolta *Edna Turnblad* • Michelle Pfeiffer *Velma von Tussle* • Christopher Walken *Wilbur Turnblad* • Amanda Bynes *Penny Pingleton* • James Marsden *Corny Collins* • Queen Latifah *Motormouth Maybelle* • Nikki Blonsky *Tracy Turnblad* • Brittany Snow *Amber von Tussle* • Zac Efron *Link Larkin* • Elijah Kelley *Seaweed* ▪ *Dir* Adam Shankman • *Scr* Leslie Dixon, from the musical by Mark O'Donnell, Thomas Meehan, from the 1988 film

The Hairy Ape ★★
Drama 1944 · US · BW · 91min

Many liberties are taken with Eugene O'Neill's 1920s play about dockyard politics, mainly to dilute its fairly blatant communism. The plot is further twisted into wartime flag-waver, with William Bendix as the "hairy ape", a resentful stoker on a ship that runs refugees from Lisbon to America. AT

William Bendix *Hank Smith* • Susan Hayward *Mildred Douglas* • John Loder *2nd Engineer Tony Lazar* • Dorothy Comingore *Helen Parker* • Roman Bohnen *Paddy* ▪ *Dir* Alfred Santell • *Scr* Robert D Andrews, Decla Dunning, from the play by Eugene O'Neill

Half a Sixpence ★★★★U
Musical 1967 · UK · Colour · 139min

Based on HG Wells's minor classic *Kipps*, this is one of the very few British musicals that doesn't have you squirming in your seat with embarrassment, for which we have to thank veteran Hollywood director George Sidney. Admittedly, the story drags once Tommy Steele and Julia Foster's relationship hits the rocks, but so much of what has gone on before is slickly staged and joyously played that you should forgive it this pause for breath. Rattling through David Heneker's catchy songs and hurling himself into Gillian Lynne's energetic dance routines, Steele has never been better on screen. DP

Tommy Steele *Arthur Kipps* • Julia Foster *Ann* • Cyril Ritchard *Harry Chitterlow* • Penelope Horner *Helen Walsingham* • Elaine Taylor *Kate* • Grover Dale *Pearce* • Hilton Edwards *Shalford* ▪ *Dir* George Sidney (2) • *Scr* Beverley Cross, from the novel *Kipps* by HG Wells

Half Angel ★★U
Comedy 1951 · US · Colour · 75min

Robert Riskin penned some of Frank Capra's most popular films, but he was sadly off form with this slight romantic frippery. Loretta Young lacks the frivolity to carry off the part of a starchy nurse whose true character only emerges during her frequent bouts of sleepwalking. There's little for Joseph Cotten and John Ridgely (as the suitors in love with the different aspects of her personality) to do but look on adoringly. DP

Loretta Young *Nora* • Joseph Cotten *John Raymond* • Cecil Kellaway *Mr Gilpin* • Basil Ruysdael *Dr Jackson* • Jim Backus *Michael Hogan* • Irene Ryan *Kay* • John Ridgely *Tim* • Therese Lyon *Mrs McCarey* ▪ *Dir* Richard Sale • *Scr* Robert Riskin, from a story by George Carleton Brown

Half-Baked ★18
Comedy 1998 · US · Colour · 78min

This is an unwise and utterly unfunny attempt to resurrect a genre we'd hoped had disappeared into a cultural black hole along with flared trousers: the 1970s drug comedy as typified by Cheech and Chong. Comedian Dave Chappelle stars as one of a gang of pothead pals dreaming up crazy

schemes to spring a friend from prison. RS Violence, drug abuse, nudity, swearing.

Dave Chappelle *Thurgood/Sir Smoka Lot* • Jim Breuer *Brian* • Guillermo Diaz *Scarface* • Harland Williams *Kenny* • Rachel True *Mary Jane* • Snoop Doggy Dogg [Snoop Dogg] *Scavenger Smoker* • Clarence Williams III *Samson Simpson* • Tommy Chong *Squirrel Master* • Willie Nelson *Historian Smoker* ▪ *Dir* Tamra Davis • *Scr* Dave Chappelle, Neal Brennan

The Half-Breed ★★U
Western 1952 · US · Colour · 81min

This is a very minor contribution to the cycle of films beginning with *Broken Arrow* in 1950, which challenged the usual western stereotypes favoured by Hollywood. Here the white villain wants the Apache reservation cleared of its inhabitants as there's gold for the taking. Robert Young, giving his usual polished performance as a gambler, helps Jack Buetel's eponymous hero defuse the situation, conveniently saving RKO the expense of staging a big battle scene, but disappointing fans eager for some rousing action. AE

Robert Young (1) *Dan Craig* • Janis Carter *Helen* • Jack Buetel *Charlie Wolf* • Barton MacLane *Marshal* • Reed Hadley *Crawford* • Connie Gilchrist *Ma Higgins* • Damian O'Flynn *Captain Jackson* ▪ *Dir* Stuart Gilmore • *Scr* Harold Shumate and Richard Wormser, from a story by Robert Hardy Andrews

Half Light ★★15
Supernatural thriller 2006 · UK/Ger · Colour · 105min

Demi Moore plays a successful mystery novelist who heads off to the solitude of a remote Scottish fishing village in the hope that this will help her get over her seven-year-old son's drowning. But before you can say *Don't Look Now*, the boy's ghost is giving his mother the chills, triggering events that make the stereotypical locals think she's going crazy. For all the narrative twists, this snail-paced yarn has neither atmosphere nor surprises. SF Violence. **DVD**

Demi Moore *Rachel Carlson* • Hans Matheson *Angus* • Henry Ian Cusick *Brian* • Kate Isitt *Sharon* • James Cosmo *Finley* • Therese Bradley *Morag* • Joanna Hole *Mary Murray* • Beans El Balawai *Thomas Carlson* • Mickey Wilson *Father James MacMahon* ▪ *Dir/Scr* Craig Rosenberg

Half Moon Street ★★★18
Political thriller 1986 · UK · Colour · 85min

This eagerly awaited next movie from director Bob Swaim (*La Balance*) failed miserably at the theatrical box office, but it's hard to see why. Based on Paul Theroux's novel *Doctor Slaughter*, it features ultra-sexy Sigourney Weaver as a prim Middle East scholar in the daytime and a call girl by night, while Michael Caine is Lord Bulbeck, the British diplomat who favours her favours. Adult and certainly different, there's a grim topicality about Arab wheelings and dealings in the Mayfair byway of the title, and the film's subsequent reputation will lead you to believe that it's a dog. It isn't. TS

Sigourney Weaver *Dr Lauren Slaughter* • Michael Caine *Lord Bulbeck* • Patrick Kavanagh *General Sir George Newhouse* • Faith Kent *Lady Newhouse* • Ram John Holder *Lindsay Walker* • Keith Buckley *Hugo Van Arkady* • Annie Hanson *Mrs Van Arkady* • Patrick Newman *Julian Shuttle* • Niall O'Brien *Captain Twilley* • Nadim Sawalha *Karim Hatami* ▪ *Dir* Bob Swaim • *Scr* Edward Behr, Bob Swaim, from the novel *Doctor Slaughter* by Paul Theroux

The Half Naked Truth ★★★★U
Comedy 1932 · US · BW · 76min

The now almost forgotten Lee Tracy, a wonderfully fast-talking, sour-looking, wisecracking star of the 1930s, is here at the top of his form as an unscrupulous publicity man. This delectable comedy, classily directed by Gregory La Cava, has Tracy scheming to make fiery Lupe Velez into an instant celebrity by blackmailing neurotic producer Frank Morgan. Velez, known as the "Mexican Spitfire" and soon

to marry Johnny "Tarzan" Weissmuller, committed suicide in 1944. RB

Lee Tracy *Bates* • Lupe Velez *Teresita* • Eugene Pallette *Achilles* • Frank Morgan *Farrell* • Robert McKenzie *Col Munday* • Franklin Pangborn *Hotel manager* ▪ *Dir* Gregory La Cava • *Scr* Gregory La Cava, Corey Ford, from a story by Ben Markson, HN Swanson, from the novel *Phantom Fame* by David Freedman, Bartlett Cormack

Half Nelson ★★★15
Drama 2006 · US · Colour · 102min

A troubled student helps her self-destructive teacher reclaim his wayward life in Ryan Fleck's beautifully understated drama. Titled after a wrestling hold from which it's virtually impossible to escape, this slow-burning indie feature artfully reworks the clichés of the "redemption through education" genre. An Oscar-nominated Ryan Gosling demonstrates the same quiet intensity he showcased in *The Believer*, as the charismatic educator who's an inspiration in the classroom but a disillusioned crack addict in private. While hope is the film's overriding message, what's refreshing is its refusal to offer easy answers. There's neither moralising nor contrived sentimentality, just a reflective, documentary-style honesty that's sobering and poignant. SF **DVD** **BL**

Ryan Gosling *Dan Dunne* • Shareeka Epps *Drey* • Anthony Mackie *Frank* • Monique Gabriela Curnen *Isabel* • Karen Chilton *Karen* • Tina Holmes *Rachel* • Jay O Sanders *Russ* ▪ *Dir* Ryan Fleck • *Scr* Ryan Fleck, Anna Boden

Half of a Yellow Sun ★★★15
Drama 2013 · Nig/UK · Colour · 106min

London-based writer/director Biyi Bandele unpicks Chimamanda Ngozi Adichie's non-linear novel in this harrowing but superficial drama set during a tumultuous decade of Nigerian independence. After being granted independence from Britain in 1960, the Igbo people rise up to establish the Republic of Biafra, with Thandie Newton and Anika Noni Rose as British-educated twins caught in the maelstrom, and Chiwetel Ejiofor and Joseph Mawle as their men. The tone lurches between highbrow and soap opera, but the film is elevated by committed performances and Bandele stages set pieces with cinematic flair. DP Violence, swearing, a sex scene. **DVD** **BL**

Thandie Newton *Olanna* • Chiwetel Ejiofor *Odenigbo* • Anika Noni Rose *Kainene* • Joseph Mawle *Richard* • John Boyega *Ugwu* ▪ *Dir* Biyi Bandele • *Scr* Biyi Bandele, from Chimamanda Ngozi Adichie's novel

Half Past Dead ★★12
Action crime thriller 2002 · US · Colour · 94min

Steven Seagal fails to convince here as an undercover FBI agent sent to the "New Alcatraz". Once in the hi-tech prison, Seagal finds himself at the centre of a hostage situation when a group called the "49ers" break in so they can interrogate a death-row inmate regarding the whereabouts of $200 million in gold. Writer/director Don Michael Paul overloads the film with action to compensate for the lack of style or coherence. TH Violence, swearing. **DVD** **BL**

Steven Seagal *Sascha Petrosevitch* • Morris Chestnut *Donny/49er One* • Ja Rule *Nick Frazier* • Nia Peeples *49er Six* • Tony Plana *The warden, El Fuego* • Kurupt *Twitch* • Michael "Bear" Taliferro *Little Joe* • Claudia Christian *EZ Williams* ▪ *Dir/Scr* Don Michael Paul

Half Shot at Sunrise ★★★U
Comedy 1930 · US · BW · 78min

The first to admit that their films were never on a par with their stage shows, Bert Wheeler and Robert Woolsey deserve better than the anonymity in which they now languish. Their wisecracking interchanges were littered with risqué puns and their slapstick had plenty of zip. They were top-billed for the first time in this lively comedy about a couple of First World War soldiers who keep out of the clutches of the military police to sample the delights of Paris. Some of the gags miss the mark and the musical moments are an intrusion, but it's surely sparky stuff. DP

Bert Wheeler *Tommy* • Robert Woolsey *Gilbert* • John Rutherford *MP Sergeant* • George MacFarlane *Col Marshall* • Roberta Robinson *Eileen* • Edna May Oliver *Mrs Marshall* ■ *Dir* Paul Sloane [Paul H Sloane] • *Scr* James Ashman Creelman, Anne Caldwell, Ralph Spence, from a story by Creelman

The Halfway House ★★★ PG
Portmanteau drama 1943 · UK · BW · 92min

Produced by Michael Balcon and directed by Basil Dearden, this is a halfway decent stab at the difficult art of the portmanteau picture – a selection of short stories linked by a common theme. In an admirable all-star cast, Mervyn and Glynis Johns are splendid as the ghostly hosts at a Welsh inn, where the guests are given the chance to re-evaluate their lives and make a more positive contribution to the war effort. Cowardice, black marketeering, family unity and the thorny issue of Irish neutrality are all explored in an intelligent piece of propaganda that still makes for optimistic entertainment. DP *DVD*

Françoise Rosay *Alice Meadows* • Tom Walls *Captain Harry Meadows* • Mervyn Johns *Rhys* • Glynis Johns *Gwyneth* • Alfred Drayton *Oakley* • Esmond Knight *David Davies* • Richard Bird *Sub-lieutenant Richard French* • Philippa Hiatt *Margaret* • Sally Ann Howes *Joanna French* ■ *Dir* Basil Dearden • *Scr* Angus MacPhail, Diana Morgan, from the play *The Peaceful Inn* by Denis Ogden

Hall Pass ★★ 15
Comedy 2011 · US · Colour · 100min

After turning gross-out humour into gross profit with *Dumb & Dumber* and *There's Something about Mary*, the Farrelly brothers lost the element of surprise. Here, they attempt to regain that magic touch by sending up the midlife crisis of a suburban married man. Owen Wilson's lustful imaginings ludicrously lead his other half (Jenna Fischer) to grant him a week off marriage (a marital "hall pass", if you like). Wilson's awkward charm keeps the film from being totally unbearable, but it's tough to root for him, as potentially funny insights are drowned in a constant stream of bodily fluids. SP *DVD*

Owen Wilson *Rick* • Jason Sudeikis *Fred* • Jenna Fischer *Maggie* • Christina Applegate *Grace* • Richard Jenkins *Coakley* • Stephen Merchant *Gary* ■ *Dir* Bobby Farrelly, Peter Farrelly • *Scr* Bobby Farrelly, Peter Farrelly, Kevin Barnett, Pete Jones, from a story by Jones

Hallam Foe ★★★★ 18
Psychological drama 2006 · UK · Colour · 91min

Young Adam director David Mackenzie takes another walk down the twisted path of life with this pleasingly demented yet bittersweet coming-of-age tale. Tightly scripted from the novel by Peter Jinks, it stars a superb Jamie Bell as the eponymous teen eccentric and obsessive voyeur. Convinced his mum's mysterious death was the work of his new stepmother (an icy Claire Forlani), penniless Hallam flees to Edinburgh, where he becomes sexually fixated on another woman (Sophia Myles) who bears an eerie resemblance to the late Mrs Foe. The events that unfold are intimate and unpredictable, painting a warped though charming portrait of adolescent angst. Bell and Myles are particularly electric together, but it's the rich seam of black humour that weaves the most magic here. SF *DVD*

Jamie Bell *Hallam Foe* • Sophia Myles *Kate* • Ciaran Hinds *Julius Foe* • Jamie Sives *Alasdair* • Maurice Roëves *Raymond* • Ewen Bremner *Andy* • Claire Forlani *Verity* ■ *Dir* David Mackenzie • *Scr* David Mackenzie, Ed Whitmore, from the novel by Peter Jinks • *Cinematographer* Giles Nuttgens

Hallelujah ★★ U
Drama 1929 · US · BW · 105min

Although plainly hampered by the primitive sound techniques, King Vidor received an Oscar nomination for this ground-breaking talkie. However, today it's impossible to escape the period racism in the tale of

cotton-picker Daniel L Haynes, who twice finds redemption following a crime. Although MGM made much of the all-black cast, this was more to mollify white audiences than make a social statement, and the colour prejudice is clearly evident. DP

Daniel L Haynes *Zeke* • Nina Mae McKinney *Chick* • William E Fountaine *Hot Shot* • Harry Gray *Parson* • Fannie Belle DeKnight *Mammy* • Everett McGarrity *Spunk* • Victoria Spivey *Missy Rose* ■ *Dir* King Vidor • *Scr* Wanda Tuchock, Ransom Rideout, from a story by King Vidor • *Music/lyrics* Irving Berlin

Hallelujah, I'm a Bum ★★★ U
Musical comedy 1933 · US · BW · 84min

With its rhyming dialogue and witty songs by Rodgers and Hart, this Depression-set musical doesn't quite come off, but is a brave attempt with some fine moments. Al Jolson is a hobo living in Central Park (with his sidekick played by famed silent comic Harry Langdon) who falls in love with the girlfriend of the mayor (Frank Morgan) and tries to change his ways. SN Behrman's script, based on a story by Ben Hecht, is amusing and incisive, but the title song had to be filmed twice, the word "bum" being replaced by "tramp" for British audiences. TV

Al Jolson *Bumper* • Madge Evans *June Marcher* • Frank Morgan *Mayor Hastings* • Harry Langdon *Egghead* • Chester Conklin *Sunday* • Tyler Brooke *Mayor's secretary* ■ *Dir* Lewis Milestone • *Scr* SN Behrman, from a story by Ben Hecht • *Music/lyrics* Richard Rogers, Lorenz Hart • *Music* Alfred Newman

The Hallelujah Trail ★★★ U
Comedy western 1965 · US · Colour · 139min

Beleaguered cavalry commander Burt Lancaster is under attack from a bizarre collection of pressure groups in this comedy western. Lee Remick leads a brigade of temperance women trying to stop a shipment of whiskey from reaching Denver, while local Indians are equally eager to divert the barrels. Director John Sturges is free with the wagon-trail clichés, not always to great effect, but the film's worth a look, if only for Martin Landau's performance. TH *DVD*

Burt Lancaster *Col Thadeus Gearhart* • Lee Remick *Cora Templeton Massingale* • Jim Hutton *Capt Paul Slater* • Pamela Tiffin *Louise Gearhart* • Donald Pleasence *Oracle Jones* • Brian Keith *Frank Wallingham* • Martin Landau *Chief Walks-Stooped-Over* • John Anderson *Sergeant Buell* ■ *Dir* John Sturges • *Scr* John Gay, from the novel *Hallelujah Train* by Bill Gulick

The Halliday Brand ★★
Western 1957 · US · BW · 77min

A rather dreary psychological western from cult director Joseph H Lewis, this bears all the hallmarks of a quick, cheap shoot and a poorly thought-through sub-Freudian screenplay. Having said that, Lewis fans may still find much to enjoy in this picture. In a short running time, sterling work is done by the classy lead quartet of Joseph Cotten, Ward Bond, Viveca Lindfors and Betsy Blair, but it's all very intense and brooding. TS

Joseph Cotten *Daniel* • Viveca Lindfors *Aleta* • Betsy Blair *Martha* • Ward Bond *Big Dan* • Bill Williams *Clay* • Jay C Flippen *Chad Burris* • Christopher Dark *Jivaro* • Jeanette Nolan *Nante* ■ *Dir* Joseph H Lewis • *Scr* George W George, George S Slavin

The Hallow ★★★★ 15
Horror 2015 · UK · Colour · 92min

This Irish-set creepshow is an old-fashioned reminder of the beauty of in-camera special effects. With a conscious bow to 1980s genre classic *The Evil Dead*, *The Hallow* unfolds in the dark woods, where a tree doctor (Joseph Mawle) and his wife (Bojana Novakovic) are warned by a neighbouring farmer that they have upset the spirits of the forest. First-time director Corin Hardy perfectly rations the in-jokes and suspense, building to a crescendo that

recalls the heyday of the fright-flick. DW Gory images *DVD*

Bojana Novakovic *Clare Hitchens* • Joseph Mawle *Adam Hitchens* • Michael McElhatton *Colm Donnelly* • Michael Smiley *Garda Davey* ■ *Dir* Corin Hardy • *Scr* Corin Hardy, Olga Barreneche

LANDMARK FILM
John Carpenter's low-budget movie spawned an industry of slasher franchises

Halloween ★★★★★ 18
Classic horror 1978 · US · Colour · 87min

John Carpenter practically patented the slasher genre with this simple but horribly effective low-budget suburban horror, in the process launching Jamie Lee Curtis as a new scream queen. Michael Myers is the six-year-old boy who murders his sister on Halloween and is institutionalised. Fifteen years later he escapes and returns to Haddonfield, Illinois, disguised by a white mask, to cause murderous mayhem, despite the intervention of his equally spooky psychiatrist (Donald Pleasence, in a career-reviving turn). The film is expertly plotted, building to a series of bloody crescendos as licentious babysitters and boyfriends are picked off. Its power to grip and jolt has never diminished, thanks in part to Carpenter's own pulsing score. AJ Violence, swearing, sex scenes, drug abuse, nudity. *DVD* *BLU*

Donald Pleasence *Dr Sam Loomis* • Jamie Lee Curtis *Laurie Strode* • Nancy Loomis *Annie* • PJ Soles *Lynda* • Charles Cyphers *Sheriff Leigh Brackett* • Kyle Richards *Lindsey* • Brian Andrews *Tommy* • John Michael Graham *Bob* • Nancy Stephens *Marion* • Arthur Malet *Graveyard keeper* • Mickey Yablans *Richie* • Brent Le Page *Lonnie* • Tony Moran *Michael, age 23* ■ *Dir* John Carpenter • *Scr* Debra Hill, John Carpenter

Halloween ★★★ 18
Horror 2007 · US · Colour · 116min

Rob Zombie's reboot of John Carpenter's seminal horror is better made than expected, but it's still a mixed bag. The first section details the disintegration of the young Michael Myers (Daeg Faerch) – due to a dysfunctional home life and abusive classmates – leading to blank psychosis and incarceration after murdering his family. Part two is a more brutal retread of the original's babysitting terrors, as the now grown-up Myers (Tyler Mane) searches for his adopted sister. Zombie is on firm ground in the early scenes, but he's less successful in his attempt to re-create Carpenter's landmark 1978 horror and its primal fears. As Laurie Strode, the strident Scout Taylor-Compton proves she is no Jamie Lee Curtis. AJ *DVD*

Malcolm McDowell *Dr Samuel Loomis* • Brad Dourif *Sheriff Lee Brackett* • Sheri Moon Zombie [Sheri Moon] *Deborah Myers* • Scout Taylor-Compton *Laurie Strode* • Danielle Harris *Annie Brackett* • Tyler Mane *Michael Myers* • Kristina Klebe *Lynda* • Daeg Faerch *Young Michael Myers* • Dee Wallace [Dee Wallace Stone] *Cynthia Strode* ■ *Dir* Rob Zombie • *Scr* Rob Zombie, from the 1978 film by John Carpenter, Debra Hill

Halloween II ★★ 18
Horror 1981 · US · Colour · 87min

With the exception of *H2O*, the sequels to John Carpenter's 1978 horror masterpiece have been pretty awful. However, like that film, this was the only one to feature the original star Jamie Lee Curtis, and is better for it. This takes up where the original finished, with Curtis being taken to hospital still in shock, but before long her indestructible nemesis is stalking her around the wards. Carpenter had a hand in the script, but this is a by-the-numbers retread and the direction lacks flair. JF *DVD*

Jamie Lee Curtis *Laurie Strode* • Donald Pleasence *Dr Sam Loomis* • Charles Cyphers *Sheriff Leigh Brackett* • Jeffrey Kramer *Graham* • Lance Guest *Jimmy* • Pamela Susan Shoop [Pamela Shoop] *Karen* • Hunter Von Leer *Gary Hunt* ■ *Dir* Rick Rosenthal • *Scr* John Carpenter, Debra Hill, from their characters

Halloween II ★★ 18
Horror 2009 · US · Colour and BW · 101min

Like its lumbering serial killer Michael Myers, *Halloween* is the horror franchise that just won't die. Resurrected in Rob Zombie's better-than-expected 2007 remake, the series seems cursed to repeat the same pattern of diminishing returns. This half-baked sequel starts with babysitter Laurie Strode (a permanently shell-shocked Scout Taylor-Compton) being rushed to hospital after surviving her night of terror. A long-winded subplot also sees psychiatrist Dr Loomis (Malcolm McDowell) cashing in on his former patient's reputation. Presumably it's a satirical swipe at our obsession with violence – but it seems rather rich given the film's own penchant for brutal bloodletting. JR Violence, swearing, nudity. *DVD* *BLU*

Scout Taylor-Compton *Laurie Strode* • Tyler Mane *Michael Myers* • Malcolm McDowell *Dr Samuel Loomis* • Brad Dourif *Sheriff Lee Brackett* • Sheri Moon Zombie [Sheri Moon] *Deborah Myers* • Danielle Harris *Annie Brackett* • Brea Grant *Mya Rockwell* • Howard Hesseman *Uncle Meat* ■ *Dir* Rob Zombie • *Scr* Rob Zombie, from characters by John Carpenter, Debra Hill

Halloween III: Season of the Witch ★★ 15
Science-fiction horror 1982 · US · Colour · 92min

Though fans bemoaning the absence of masked maniac Michael Myers slaughtered this second sequel to John Carpenter's 1978 masterpiece, there are still enough ghastly shocks here to give you the jitters. Tom Atkins plays the father who inadvertently stumbles across the evil plan of malevolent toymaker Dan O'Herlihy to kill the children of America with a line of lethal Halloween masks. Ultimately, it's a lack of directorial finesse and the rancid look of the piece that condemns it to the sump of 1980s horror. JA Swearing, violence. *DVD*

Tom Atkins *Dr Dan Challis* • Stacey Nelkin *Ellie* • Dan O'Herlihy *Conal* • Ralph Strait *Buddy* • Michael Currie *Rafferty* • Jadeen Barbor *Betty* • Bradley Schachter *Little Buddy* ■ *Dir/Scr* Tommy Lee Wallace

Halloween 4: the Return of Michael Myers ★★ 18
Horror 1988 · US · Colour · 88min

After the misguided, Michael Myers-less *Halloween III*, it's back-to-basics time and the result is a competent, but yawningly empty, slasher thriller. Danielle Harris steps into the Jamie Lee Curtis role, playing one of the last surviving relatives of the caged psycho, who once again escapes and heads back to his home turf for some more blood-letting. JF *DVD*

Donald Pleasence *Dr Loomis* • Ellie Cornell *Rachel Carruthers* • Danielle Harris *Jamie Lloyd* • George P Wilbur *Michael Myers* • Michael Pataki *Dr Hoffman* ■ *Dir* Dwight H Little • *Scr* Alan B McElroy, from a story by Dhani Lipsius, Larry Rattner, Benjamin Ruffner, Alan B McElroy, from the characters by Debra Hill, John Carpenter

Halloween 5: the Revenge of Michael Myers ★★ 18
Horror 1989 · US · Colour · 96min

More slashing by numbers, as Danielle Harris once again dodges nasty Uncle Michael Myers, who, surprise surprise, managed to survive this film's predecessor. Shot back to back with Part 4, the only link with John Carpenter's original is Donald Pleasence as the barking psychiatrist Dr Sam Loomis, named after a character in *Psycho*. Otherwise, it's business as usual. JF *DVD*

Donald Pleasence *Dr Loomis* • Ellie Cornell *Rachel* • Beau Starr *Meeker* • Danielle Harris *Jamie* • Wendy Kaplan *Tina* • Donald L Shanks [Don Shanks] *Michael Myers* ■ *Dir* Dominique Othenin-Girard • *Scr* Michael Jacobs, Dominique Othenin-Girard, Shem Bitterman, from the characters by Debra Hill, John Carpenter

Halloween 6: the Curse of Michael Myers ★ 18

Horror   1995 · US · Colour · 84min

The worst of the series so far. Director Joe Chappelle tries to give menace by proxy to the laughable awfulness, reviving Carpenter's original *Halloween* score as a backdrop. It doesn't work, and neither do the revelations intended to explain Michael Myers's years of murder and mayhem. Donald Pleasence gives his usual reliable performance, but sadly he died shortly after shooting. AJ Swearing, violence, nudity. *DVD*

Donald Pleasence *Dr Loomis* • Mitch Ryan [Mitchell Ryan] *Dr Wynn* • Marianne Hagan *Kara Strode* • Paul Rudd *Tommy Doyle* • Mariah O'Brien *Beth* • Kim Darby *Debra Strode* • George P Wilbur *Mike Myers* ■ *Dir* Joe Chappelle • *Scr* Daniel Farrands, from the characters by Debra Hill, John Carpenter

Halloween H2O: 20 Years Later ★★★ 18

Horror   1998 · US · Colour · 82min

John Carpenter's classic 1978 chiller gets a 1990s makeover, although in the hands of director Steve Miner the emphasis is still firmly on frights rather than in-jokes. Jamie Lee Curtis, back in the role that made her name, is now a recovering alcoholic and headteacher at an exclusive school. The problem is that the murderous Michael is keen to celebrate the 20th anniversary of his first massacre. Curtis steals the show from the teenage TV pin-ups, but Miner's direction is merely efficient and lacks Carpenter's assured touch. JF Violence, swearing. *DVD*

Jamie Lee Curtis *Laurie Strode/Keri Tate* • Michelle Williams *Molly* • Joseph Gordon-Levitt *Jimmy* • Josh Hartnett *John* • Adam Arkin *Will Brennan* • LL Cool J *Ronny* • Jodi Lyn O'Keefe *Sarah* • Adam Hann-Byrd *Charlie* • Janet Leigh *Norma* ■ *Dir* Steve Miner • *Scr* Robert Zappia, Matt Greenberg, from a story by Robert Zappia, from characters by Debra Hill, John Carpenter

Halloween: Resurrection ★ 15

Horror   2002 · US · Colour · 85min

In this seventh sequel, six students are chosen by the Dangertainment Network to spend Halloween night in the old Myers house, which has been fitted with cameras for a live internet broadcast. Given the set-up, it doesn't come as a total surprise when Michael - still not dead despite having been decapitated in *H2O* - arrives to turn things bloody for the benefit of online viewers who think it's all a charade. The stale "Big Brother" plot sinks into a morass of clichéd shocks and messy camerawork. AJ *DVD*

Busta Rhymes *Freddie Harris* • Brad Loree *Michael "The Shape" Myers* • Jamie Lee Curtis *Laurie Strode* • Bianca Kajlich *Sara Moyer* • Sean Patrick Thomas *Rudy* • Daisy McCrackin *Donna* • Katee Sackhoff *Jen* ■ *Dir* Rick Rosenthal • *Scr* Larry Brand, Sean Hood, from a story by Brand, from characters by Debra Hill, John Carpenter

The Halloween Tree ★★★★ U

Animated fantasy   1993 · US · Colour · 69min

Ray Bradbury's children's novel is superbly brought to the screen in this top-notch animation feature made for television by the Hanna-Barbera studio. Four children, who desperately want to help a sick friend, embark on a journey through the multicultural and religious history of All Hallows' Eve. Guided by Mr Moundshroud (voiced by Leonard Nimoy) they learn a 4,000-year history and moral lesson en route to a gallant sacrifice. Brilliantly adapted by Bradbury, the combination of traditional Halloween imagery with the less globally well-known ones is as inventive as *Tim Burton's The Nightmare before Christmas*. AJ

Leonard Nimoy *Mr Moundshroud* ■ *Dir* Mario Piluso • *Scr* Ray Bradbury, from his novel

Halls of Montezuma ★★★ U

Second World War action drama
1950 · US · Colour · 108min

This big-budget, ferociously patriotic 20th Century-Fox movie is directed by one of the all-time greats of the genre, Lewis Milestone. The action isn't of the highest standard, but this is enjoyable, largely thanks to an excellent cast headed by Richard Widmark, and backed up by Jack Palance, a pre-*Dragnet* Jack Webb and Robert Wagner as the youngster of the outfit. The Technicolor photography is quite outstanding, and there's no unnecessary romance. TS *DVD*

Richard Widmark *Lt Anderson* • Walter (Jack) Palance [Jack Palance] *Pigeon Lane* • Reginald Gardiner *Sgt Johnson* • Robert Wagner *Coffman* • Karl Malden *Doc* • Richard Hylton *Cpl Stuart Conroy* • Richard Boone *Lt Col Gilfilan* • Skip Homeier *Pretty Boy* • Don Hicks *Lt Butterfield* • Jack Webb *Correspondent Dickerman* ■ *Dir* Lewis Milestone • *Scr* Michael Blankfort • *Cinematographers* Winton C Hoch, Harry Jackson

Hamam: the Turkish Bath ★★★ 15

Drama   1996 · It/Tur/Sp · Colour · 93min

This atmospheric drama slowly draws you into the back streets of Istanbul and even more deeply into the lives of their inhabitants. The Turkish cast is admirable, but the focus falls firmly on Alessandro Gassman, as the Italian businessman who inherits a bath-house from an aunt and whose independent lifestyle eventually leads to tragedy. Director Ferzan Ozpetek's sunny cityscapes are striking, but it's the evocative interiors with their haunting light and architectural beauty that give this search for cultural and sexual identity its extraordinary sense of serenity and fulfilment. DP Italian, Turkish +subtitles. Swearing, nudity. *DVD*

Alessandro Gassman *Francesco* • Francesca D'Aloja *Marta* • Mehmet Gunsur *Mehmet* • Carlo Cecchi *Oscar* • Halil Ergun *Osman* ■ *Dir* Ferzan Ozpetek • *Scr* Ferzan Özpetek, Stefano Tummolini

Hambone and Hillie ★★★ PG

Comedy drama   1984 · US · Colour · 86min

Heroic canines have always been popular with movie-goers, but few tales of four-pawed adventure have been as brutal as this cross-country epic, which includes an escaped convict's horrific assault on a pregnant woman and a dog's gruesome death. Thankfully there are more wholesome episodes, such as Hambone's friendships with a lonely paraplegic. As the grandmother hoping her lost hound will find his way home, the venerable Lillian Gish is adorable. DP

Lillian Gish *Hillie Radcliffe* • Timothy Bottoms *Michael Radcliffe* • Candy Clark *Nancy Rollins* • OJ Simpson *Tucker* • Robert Walker [Robert Walker Jr] *Wanderer* • Jack Carter *Lester Burns* • Alan Hale [Alan Hale Jr] *McVickers* • Anne Lockhart *Roberta Radcliffe* ■ *Dir* Roy Watts • *Scr* Sandra K Bailey, Michael Murphey, Joel Soisson, from a story by Ken Barnett

Hamburger Hill ★★★★ 18

War drama   1987 · US · Colour · 110min

Unjustly overshadowed by Oliver Stone's *Platoon* and Stanley Kubrick's *Full Metal Jacket*, John Irvin's *Hamburger Hill* is almost their equal. The story has the classic simplicity of a past era of war movies: troops of the 101st Airborne Division attack Hill 937 in the Ashau Valley, Vietnam, and after ten days and 11 assaults, when everyone has been put through the meat grinder, the hill is renamed after America's favourite fast food. Reducing the Vietnam war to the level of symbol is an efficient means of conveying the pointless sacrifice, and Irvin does it superbly. AT Violence, swearing, brief nudity. *DVD*

Anthony Barrile *Languilli* • Michael Patrick Boatman [Michael Boatman] *Motown* • Don Cheadle *Washburn* • Michael Dolan *Murphy* • Don James *McDaniel* • Dylan McDermott *Sergeant Frantz* • MA Nickles *Galvan* ■ *Dir* John Irvin • *Scr* James Carabatsos

Hamilton ★★★

Spy thriller   1998 · Swe · Colour · 125min

Jan Guillou's Carl Hamilton is apparently the Scandinavian answer to Tom Clancy's Jack Ryan, and his bestsellers have been filmed a number of times and this is one of the most successful adaptations. *Fargo* star Peter Stormare enjoys the opportunity to be the eponymous hero who, along with sidekick Mats Langbacka, is on the trail of a Russian gang trying to unload a nuclear missile. There are also good supporting roles for Lena Olin and Mark Hamill, and award-winning commercials director Harald Zwart keeps the action racing along. JF Swedish +subtitles.

Mark Hamill *Mike Hawkins* • Lena Olin *Tessie* • Peter Stormare *Carl Hamilton* • Mats Langbacka *Ake Stalhandske* • Madeleine Elfstrand *Anna* • Thomas Hedengran *Gustavsson* • Mikael Ahlberg *Andersson* ■ *Dir* Harald Zwart • *Scr* Jonas Cornell, William Aldridge, from novels by Jan Guillou

Hamlet ★★★★★ U

Classic tragedy   1948 · UK · BW · 147min

Laurence Olivier directed himself in this astonishing Shakespeare adaptation, which won four Academy Awards. Desmond Dickinson's camerawork adds mood to the moment as Larry's blond-headed Prince Hamlet wanders around Elsinore Castle, ambiguously pursuing Ophelia (Jean Simmons), berating his mother (Eileen Herlie) and stalking his new stepfather (Basil Sydney). Olivier also played the ghost of Hamlet's father, to eerie effect. For the sake of pace, adapter Alan Dent removes the supporting characters Rosencrantz and Guildenstern, while the music adds atmospheric lustre. TH *DVD* *Blu*

Laurence Olivier *Hamlet* • Eileen Herlie *Gertrude* • Basil Sydney *Claudius* • Norman Wooland *Horatio* • Felix Aylmer *Polonius* • Terence Morgan *Laertes* • Jean Simmons *Ophelia* • Peter Cushing *Osric* • Stanley Holloway *Gravedigger* • Anthony Quayle *Marcellus* ■ *Dir* Laurence Olivier • *Scr* Alan Dent, from the play by William Shakespeare • *Music* William Walton • *Costume Designer* Roger K Furse • *Art Directors* Roger K Furse, Carmen Dillon

Hamlet ★★★★ U

Tragedy   1964 · USSR · BW · 141min

The Russian version of Shakespeare's most famous tragedy was filmed by veteran director Grigori Kozintsev to commemorate the 400th anniversary of the playwright's birth. His treatment is a study of medieval state machinations, and is set in an Elsinore whose inhabitants are contained by an impressive fortress of stone and iron. It may lack the depth of other film versions, but the images, enriched by the dramatic Shostakovich music, are bold and powerful - as is the great Russian actor Innokenti Smoktunovsky, whose Prince of Denmark is a man of action, not a brooding dreamer. RB Russian +subtitles. *DVD*

Innokenti Smoktunovsky *Hamlet* • Mikhail Nazvanov *King* • Elsa Radzin *Queen* • Yuri Tolubeyev *Polonius* • Anastasia Vertinskaya *Ophelia* • Vladimir Erenberg *Horatio* • C Olesenko *Laertes* • Vadim Medvedev *Guildenstern* • Igor Dmitriev *Rosencrantz* ■ *Dir* Grigori Kozintsev • *Scr* Grigori Kozintsev, Boris Pasternak, from the play by William Shakespeare

Hamlet ★★★

Tragedy   1964 · US · BW · 186min

When Richard Burton played the title role in John Gielgud's production of *Hamlet* on Broadway in 1964, he was the most famous young actor in the world. Fortunately his performance was captured (over two nights) using a short-lived multi-camera system, Electronovision. Dismissed at the time as poor, both picture and sound quality are in fact perfectly acceptable; indeed, the 15 cameras pick up nuances of which the theatre audience would have been unaware. The stage production, done in modern dress on crude rostra, would today be dismissed as cheap, but Burton is revealed as a technical actor in the Olivier mould, and his showy performance makes him the funniest screen Hamlet. DM

Richard Burton *Hamlet* • Hume Cronyn *Polonius* • Alfred Drake *Claudius* • Eileen Herlie *Gertrude* • William Redfield *Guildenstern* • Linda Marsh *Ophelia* • Robert Milli *Horatio* ■ *Dir* Bill Colleran, John Gielgud • *Scr* from the play by William Shakespeare

Hamlet ★★★ U

Tragedy   1969 · UK · Colour · 112min

While Kenneth Branagh shot his 1996 version of the play on lavish, expansive sets, here star Nicol Williamson and director Tony Richardson opted for extreme close-ups. While it might have made those in the back row feel part of the proceedings, Williamson's booming performance sits uncomfortably on screen. Compensations come from Roger Livesey's dual role as Lucianus and the Player King and Anthony Hopkins's Claudius. DP *DVD*

Nicol Williamson *Hamlet* • Gordon Jackson *Horatio* • Anthony Hopkins *Claudius* • Judy Parfitt *Gertrude* • Mark Dignam *Polonius* • Michael Pennington *Laertes* • Marianne Faithfull *Ophelia* • Ben Aris *Rosencrantz* • Clive Graham *Guildenstern* • Peter Gale *Osric* • Roger Livesey *Lucianus/Player King* • Michael Elphick *Captain* • Anjelica Huston *Court lady* ■ *Dir* Tony Richardson • *Scr* from the play by William Shakespeare

Hamlet ★★★★ PG

Tragedy   1990 · US · Colour · 129min

Franco Zeffirelli directs this surprisingly vigorous rendition of a play essentially about indecision and hesitancy. Mel Gibson is the screen's most muscular Prince of Denmark, but he gives a good account of himself, as does Helena Bonham Carter as Ophelia - yet it's Alan Bates who most impresses as the villainous Claudius. Not one for the purists, but a laudable attempt to introduce Shakespeare to the blockbuster generation. DP Nudity. *DVD*

Mel Gibson *Hamlet* • Glenn Close *Queen Gertrude* • Alan Bates *Claudius* • Paul Scofield *Ghost* • Ian Holm *Polonius* • Helena Bonham Carter *Ophelia* • Stephen Dillane *Horatio* • Nathaniel Parker *Laertes* • Sean Murray (1) *Guildenstern* • Michael Maloney *Rosencrantz* • Trevor Peacock *Gravedigger* • John McEnery *Osric* ■ *Dir* Franco Zeffirelli • *Scr* Franco Zeffirelli, Christopher De Vore, from the play by William Shakespeare

Hamlet ★★★★ PG

Tragedy   1996 · US · Colour · 232min

This monumental full-length, unabridged version of the play has Kenneth Branagh directing himself as the Prince. Admirable and challenging, this is a very showbizzy staging - in addition to the leading players (such as Kate Winslet as Ophelia, Julie Christie's Gertrude, Derek Jacobi as Claudius), there is a veritable galaxy of star appearances to tweak the interest. While some critics might say this is not so much a movie as a chorus-line of talents, Branagh has to be admired for the ambition of this ravishingly beautiful staging. TH *DVD* *Blu*

Kenneth Branagh *Hamlet* • Derek Jacobi *Claudius* • Julie Christie *Gertrude* • Richard Briers *Polonius* • Kate Winslet *Ophelia* • Nicholas Farrell *Horatio* • Michael Maloney *Laertes* • Brian Blessed *Ghost* • Gérard Depardieu *Reynaldo* • Jack Lemmon *Marcellus* • Charlton Heston *Player King* • Rufus Sewell *Fortinbras* • Richard Attenborough *English Ambassador* • Timothy Spall *Rosencrantz* • Reece Dinsdale *Guildenstern* • John Gielgud *Priam* • Judi Dench *Hecuba* ■ *Dir* Kenneth Branagh • *Scr* Kenneth Branagh, from the play by William Shakespeare • *Production Designer* Tim Harvey • *Art Director* Desmond Crowe

Hamlet ★★★ 12

Tragedy   2000 · US · Colour · 106min

Writer/director Michael Almereyda's distinctive new take on Shakespeare's famous tragedy retains the Bard's language but timewarps the story into a contemporary setting. Radical re-interpretations don't always come off, but Almereyda's marriage of 16th-century words and 21st-century visuals works well. So, too, does the reinvention of Elsinore as a dodgy multinational corporation, with Hamlet a paranoid pawn caught up in the struggle for its control. DA Violence. *DVD*

Ethan Hawke *Hamlet* • Kyle MacLachlan *Claudius* • Diane Venora *Gertrude* • Sam Shepard *Ghost* • Bill Murray *Polonius* • Liev Schreiber *Laertes* • Julia Stiles *Ophelia* • Karl Geary *Horatio* • Steve Zahn *Rosencrantz* • Dechen Thurman *Guildenstern* ■ *Dir* Michael Almereyda • *Scr* Michael Almereyda, from the play by William Shakespeare

Hamlet 2 ★★ 15
Comedy   2008 · US · Colour · 87min

Steve Coogan's first headlining role in a Hollywood movie is something of a disappointment. He plays a failed actor-turned-drama teacher who reaches out to a bunch of disaffected students through the medium of theatre. It's basically a spoof on movies like *Dead Poets Society* and *Dangerous Minds*, with Coogan's wannabe inspirational mentor as the hopeless case who needs his far-from-needy charges to turn his own life around. There's fun to be had in the scenes where Coogan goes off the rails, but his broad turn - pratfalls and all - lacks the subtleties of his more successful characters. JH English, Spanish +subtitles. Swearing, drug abuse. **DVD**

Steve Coogan *Dana Marschz* • Catherine Keener *Brie Marschz* • David Arquette *Gary* • Amy Poehler *Cricket Feldstein* • Elisabeth Shue • Skylar Astin *Rand* ■ *Dir* Andrew Fleming • *Scr* Andrew Fleming, Pam Brady

Hamlet Goes Business ★★★★ PG
Comedy drama   1987 · Fin · BW · 85min

Only Aki Kaurismäki could turn Shakespeare's most complex play into an offbeat drama about the rubber duck business. Transferring the action from Elsinore to a modern Finnish boardroom, the writer/director also shifts the thematic emphasis away from insanity and the inability to act and places it on cruelty and a wilful defiance of progress. Seeking revenge for the murder of his father, Pirkka-Pekka Petelius is like a character from a *film noir*, an impression reinforced by Timo Salminen's shadowy monochrome photography, while all the *dramatis personae* are wickedly reinvented. Add a stunning score, and the result is a palpable hit. DP Finnish +subtitles. **DVD**

Pirkka-Pekka Petelius *Hamlet* • Esko Salminen *Klaus* • Kati Outinen *Ophelia* • Elina Salo *Gertrud* • Esko Nikkari *Polonius* • Kari Vaananen *Lauri Polonius* • Hannu Valtonen *Simo* • Mari Rantasila *Helena* • Turo Pajala *Rosencrantz* • Aake Kalliala *Guildenstern* • Pentti Auer *Father/Ghost* ■ *Dir* Aki Kaurismäki • *Scr* Aki Kaurismäki, from the play by William Shakespeare

Hammer ★★
Crime drama   1972 · US · Colour · 92min

Tough guy Fred Williamson's breakthrough movie was this below average blaxploitation crime thriller produced by drive-in movie king Al Adamson. Williamson plays a dock worker-turned-prizefighting boxer whose Mafia manager wants him to start throwing bouts. Williamson based his character on Muhammad Ali and even copies his moves in the ring, which is the only interesting thing to cling on to as the tedium increases in this formulaic potboiler. AJ

Fred Williamson *BJ Hammer* • Bernie Hamilton *Davis* • Vonetta McGee *Lois* • William Smith *Brenner* • Charles Lampkin *Big Sid* • Elizabeth Harding *Rhoda* ■ *Dir* Bruce D Clark [Bruce Clark] • *Scr* Charles Johnson

Hammer of the Gods ★★ 18
Action drama   2013 · UK · Colour · 94min

If it's gratuitous Saxon violence you're after, then look no further. This *Game of Thrones*-meets-*Centurion* adventure sees dying Viking king James Cosmo send out his son Charlie Bewley to find his half-brother whom he believes is the only warrior who can take on the gathering Saxon armies and cement Norse rule in central Britain. An old-fashioned romp with a bit of *Lock, Stock* attitude thrown in, this is relatively fun popcorn action - at its basest level. AJ Violence, swearing, brief nudity.

Charlie Bewley *Steinar* • Clive Standen *Hagen* • James Cosmo *King Bagsecg* • Elliot Cowan *Hakan* • Glynis Barber *Astrid* • Ivan Kaye *Ivar* ■ *Dir* Farren Blackburn • *Scr* Matthew Read • *Cinematographer* Stephan Pehrsson

Hammerhead ★★
Spy adventure   1968 · UK · Colour · 99min

This late-1960s spy adventure marked the only screen appearance for James Mayo's literary creation Charles Hood, a British art connoisseur with a taste for high living, sex and violence. As played by American Vince Edwards, he's a mostly bland hero, with a greatly reduced libido, little aptitude for espionage and a regrettable taste for instant coffee and casual, short-sleeved shirts. The story takes him from London to Portugal, where he investigates the activities of the mysterious Mr Hammerhead (Richard Vaughn), and it's left to Judy Geeson to inject some pep - her outrageous double-entendre exchange with Edwards is a bawdy highlight. JH

Vince Edwards *Charles Hood* • Judy Geeson *Sue Trenton* • Peter Vaughan *Hammerhead* • Diana Dors *Kit* ■ *Dir* David Miller (1) • *Scr* William Bast, Herbert Baker, from an adaptation by John Briley of James Mayo's novel

Hammers over the Anvil ★★ 15
Period drama based on a true story   1992 · Aus · Colour · 97min

This is the dull tale of a young crippled boy (Alexander Outhred) in the Australian outback and his hero worship of the rugged Russell Crowe, who seems to spend his time either with his horses (naked and clothed) or shagging a married woman (Charlotte Rampling) who's come to town seemingly for that reason alone. Notable for Russell Crowe riding naked across a field. JB **DVD**

Russell Crowe *East Driscoll* • Charlotte Rampling *Grace McAllister* • Alexander Outhred *Alan Marshall* • Frankie J Holden *Bushman* ■ *Dir* Ann Turner • *Scr* Peter Hepworth, Ann Turner, from the journals by Alan Marshall

Hammett ★★★ 12
Crime drama   1982 · US · Colour · 93min

Wim Wenders's first Hollywood movie is a flawed but fascinating crime drama. In this fictionalised tale, Frederic Forrest plays the legendary novelist Dashiell Hammett, down on his luck and entangled in corruption and blackmail involving a Chinese prostitute. The underrated Forrest is quite superb and there are strong supporting turns from the likes of Peter Boyle and Marilu Henner. The tone is uneven, but Wenders still succeeds in summoning up an authentic *film noir* atmosphere. JF **DVD**

Frederic Forrest *Hammett* • Peter Boyle *Jimmy Ryan* • Marilu Henner *Kit Conger/Sue Alabama* • Roy Kinnear *English Eddie Hagedorn* • Elisha Cook Jr *Eli the taxi driver* • Lydia Lei *Crystal Ling* • RG Armstrong *Lieutenant O'Mara* • Richard Bradford *Detective Bradford* ■ *Dir* Wim Wenders • *Scr* Ross Thomas, Dennis O'Flaherty, Thomas Pope, from the novel by Joe Gores

Hamsun ★★★
Biographical drama   1996 · Den/Swe/Nor/Ger · Colour · 158min

Cutting a Lear-like figure as a man who has outlived his times, Max von Sydow dominates this controversial study of the Nobel laureate whose admiration for Hitler led to him being branded a traitor after the liberation of Norway. However, as Jan Troell is keen to point out, Knut Hamsun was more concerned with denouncing British imperialism and advancing the cause of Norwegian independence than bolstering the hated regime of Vidkun Quisling. This is a fascinating study and Hamsun's meeting with Hitler is riveting. DP In Swedish.

Max von Sydow *Knut Hamsun* • Ghita Norby *Marie Hamsun* • Sverre Anker Ousdal *Vidkun Quisling* • Eindride Eidsvold *Tore Hamsun* • Gard B Eidsvold *Arild Hamsun* • Anette Hoff *Ellinor Hamsun* • Åsa Söderling *Cecilia Hamsun* • Ernst Jacobi *Adolf Hitler* ■ *Dir* Jan Troell • *Scr* Per Olov Enquist, from the non-fiction book *Prosessen mot Hamsun* by Thorkild Hansen

Han Solo: a Star Wars Story
Science-fiction adventure   2018 · US · Colour

This is a preview - no prints were available to review as we went to press: Yet another film spin-off in the revitalised series finds up-and-comer Alden Ehrenreich (*Hail, Caesar!*) playing the role made iconic by Harrison Ford. It's an origin story with a script by *Star Wars* veteran Lawrence Kasdan and his son Jon that aims to show how the young outlaw came off the rails in his 20s and acquired the cynical edge that shaped Ford's portrayal. Dry humour will obviously play a key part in Ehrenreich's success. SP

Alden Ehrenreich *Han Solo* ■ *Dir* Phil Lord, Christopher Miller [Chris Miller] • *Scr* Lawrence & Jon Kasdan, from characters by George Lucas

Hana-Bi ★★★★ 18
Crime drama   1997 · Jpn · Colour · 98min

With its fragmentary structure intended to resemble the "fireworks" (the literal translation of *Hana-Bi*) of the title, this is definitely a detective film with a difference. Winner of the Golden Lion at Venice, it's a lyrical, compassionate tale as ex-cop Takeshi "Beat" Kitano (who also directs) seeks to care for both his dying wife and his partner, disabled while chasing a criminal. To counteract the grim reality of Kitano's problems back in the city, there are lengthy passages of contemplative silence and pastoral vistas, as well as symbolic paintings commenting on the action. Although there are still explosive sequences of gun-play, this is a far cry from earlier Kitano films such as *Sonatine*. DP Japanese +subtitles. Violence, swearing. **DVD**

Takeshi Kitano *Yoshitika Nishi* • Kayoko Kishimoto *Miyuki (Nishi's wife)* • Ren Osugi *Horibe* • Susumu Terajima *Detective Nakamura* • Tetsu Watanabe *Tesuka (junkyard owner)* ■ *Dir/Scr* Takeshi Kitano

Hancock ★★★ 12
Action fantasy comedy   2008 · US · Colour · 88min

Having saved the world umpteen times in many a blockbuster, Will Smith here clearly relishes the chance to muddy his nice-guy image. As scummy superhero John Hancock, he casually nails inspired gags like flying under the influence and bringing a speeding train to a crashing halt simply because he can't be bothered to lift the car in its path. Luckily, the motorist is PR expert Ray Embrey (Jason Bateman), who promises Hancock the adulation of a sceptical public if he'll only smarten up his act. Bateman (*Arrested Development*) is the perfect comic foil for Smith but, sadly, their work is undermined when Hancock falls for Ray's wife (Charlize Theron). Fortunately for director Peter Berg, Smith has enough superstar powers to rescue us all from crushing disappointment. SP **DVD** **Blu**

Will Smith *John Hancock* • Charlize Theron *Mary Embrey* • Jason Bateman *Ray Embrey* • Eddie Marsan *Red* • Johnny Galecki *Jeremy* ■ *Dir* Peter Berg • *Scr* Vince Gilligan, Vy Vincent Ngo [Vincent Ngo] • *Cinematographer* Tobias Schliessler

The Hand ★★★ 18
Horror   1981 · US · Colour and BW · 99min

Oliver Stone's second directorial effort was this fine psychological horror tale about cartoonist Michael Caine losing his hand in a freak car accident and the severed limb seeking violent revenge on all his enemies. Or is Caine committing the murders and simply hallucinating? What makes this dark fantasy more than just an angry, depressing and gory remake of the classic *The Beast with Five Fingers* is Stone's multi-dimensional and thoughtful script that explores the many facets of madness. AJ Violence, swearing, nudity.

Michael Caine *Jon Lansdale* • Andrea Marcovicci *Anne Lansdale* • Annie McEnroe *Stella Roche* • Bruce McGill *Brian Ferguson* • Viveca Lindfors *Doctor* • Rosemary Murphy *Karen Wagner* • Mara Hobel *Lizzie Lansdale* ■ *Dir* Oliver Stone • *Scr* Oliver Stone, from the novel *The Lizard's Tale* by Marc Brandel • *Cinematographer* King Baggott

Hand Gun ★★ 18
Crime thriller   1994 · US · Colour · 85min

Treat Williams plays a small-time crook who, with brother Paul Schulze, gets in over his head when his equally crooked father (Seymour Cassel) does a runner with the takings of a bank robbery. The cast features colourful character actors, but the writing lacks focus and the direction is overheated. JF Swearing, violence, sex scenes, nudity.

Treat Williams *George McCallister* • Seymour Cassel *Jack McCallister* • Paul Schulze *Michael McCallister* • Frank Vincent *Earl* • Anna Thomson [Anna Levine] *Laura* • Michael Imperioli *Benny* • Michael Rapaport *Lenny* • Star Jasper *Sally* ■ *Dir/Scr* Whitney Ransick

The Hand of Night ★ 12
Horror   1966 · UK · Colour · 86min

Hapless William Sylvester visits Morocco and is enticed into a den of vampires by beautiful Moorish princess Alizia Gur. Awkwardly combining the Dracula myth with middle-eastern mummy motifs, but bringing nothing of its own to the terror table except exotic locations, this tedious sub-Hammer horror filler is further eroded by bland performances. AJ **DVD**

William Sylvester *Paul Carver* • Diane Clare *Chantal* • Alizia Gur *Marisa* • Edward Underdown *Gunther* • Terence de Marney *Omar* • William Dexter *Leclerc* ■ *Dir* Frederic Goode • *Scr* Bruce Stewart

The Hand That Rocks the Cradle ★★★★ 15
Thriller   1992 · US · Colour · 105min

Cool, Teutonic-looking Rebecca De Mornay plays the nanny from hell, wreaking havoc on the sunny designer family life of Annabella Sciorra and Matt McCoy, in this nerve-racking psychological thriller. Director Curtis Hanson successfully plugs into every deep-seated fear of middle-class parents, with De Mornay doing a neat turn in icy malevolence wrapped up in the guise of responsible carer. This is pure hokum, of course, but extremely effective until the last 30 minutes, when the plot rapidly self-destructs. SH Violence, swearing, nudity. **DVD**

Annabella Sciorra *Claire Bartel* • Rebecca De Mornay *Mrs Mott/"Peyton Flanders"* • Matt McCoy *Michael Bartel* • Ernie Hudson *Solomon* • Julianne Moore *Marlene* • Madeline Zima *Emma Bartel* • John de Lancie *Doctor Mott* • Mitchell Laurance *Lawyer* ■ *Dir* Curtis Hanson • *Scr* Amanda Silver

A Handful of Clouds ★★★
Crime melodrama   1930 · US · BW · 78min

The chief of a bootlegging outfit decides to retire and hands over his racketeering interests to another. But he finds himself embroiled in the underworld again after his wife leaves him and his young brother is killed by his former rivals. Oscar-nominated for its story and directed with tough brio by Archie Mayo for Warner Bros, the studio that put the gangster movie on the map, the film stars clean-cut Lew Ayres as the troubled gangster and James Cagney as the man who takes over his empire. RK

Lewis Ayres [Lew Ayres] *Louis Ricarno* • Dorothy Mathews *Doris* • Leon Janney *Jackie Lamarr* • Robert Elliott *Capt O'Grady* • James Cagney *Steve Mileway* • Jerry Mandy *Joe* • Noel Madison *Rocco* ■ *Dir* Archie Mayo • *Scr* George Rosener, from the story *A Handful of Clouds* by Rowland Brown

A Handful of Dust ★★★★ PG
Period drama   1987 · UK · Colour · 113min

In this glossily depressing adaptation of Evelyn Waugh's satire on the between-wars aristocracy, James Wilby stars as the dull, duty-bound estate owner cuckolded by his wife Kristin Scott Thomas and man-about-town Rupert Graves. Directed by Charles Sturridge with the same impeccable detail he brought to his TV adaptation of *Brideshead Revisited*, the impressive performances can't lighten a cynicism which tries to persuade us that the wages of goodness are death. TH **DVD**

James Wilby *Tony Last* • Kristin Scott Thomas *Brenda Last* • Rupert Graves *John Beaver* • Anjelica Huston *Mrs Rattery* • Judi Dench *Mrs Beaver* • Alec Guinness *Mr Todd* • Richard Beale *Ben* • Jackson Kyle *John Andrew* ■ *Dir* Charles Sturridge • *Scr* Charles Sturridge, Tim Sullivan, Derek Granger, from the novel by Evelyn Waugh

Handgun ★★★★ 18
Thriller 1983 • UK/US • Colour • 95min

This is an intriguing if only partially successful attempt by British director Tony Garnett to redress the balance in favour of the female victim of male violence. Karen Young is excellent as the passive young woman whose experiences at the hands of Texan brute Clayton Day (another finely etched performance) turn her into a marauding vigilante. On the plus side, there are a great sense of menace and tension, good supporting performances and an intelligent, sensitive handling of tricky issues. The minus is Garnett's overall thesis that the way to handle violence is to strike back. SH Swearing, nudity. *DVD*

Karen Young *Kathleen Sullivan* • Clayton Day *Larry Keeler* • Suzie Humphreys *Nancy* • Helena Humann *Miss Davis* • Ben Jones *Chuck* ■ *Dir/Scr* Tony Garnett

The Handmaid's Tale ★★★ 15
Futuristic drama 1990 • US • Colour • 104min

Adapted from the Margaret Atwood bestseller, this dystopian drama has Natasha Richardson living in a born-again America run on puritanical lines in a polluted future. As one of the few fertile women around, she's ordered to bear Robert Duvall a child for wife Faye Dunaway. The republic's religious rites and oppression of women echo some of today's theocratic fanaticism, but it's a story that never gels, although Duvall is a formidable presence. TH Violence, swearing, sex scenes. *DVD*

Natasha Richardson *Kate* • Faye Dunaway *Serena Joy* • Aidan Quinn *Nick* • Elizabeth McGovern *Moira* • Victoria Tennant *Aunt Lydia* • Robert Duvall *Commander* • Blanche Baker *Ofglen* • Traci Lind *Ofwarren/Janine* ■ *Dir* Volker Schlöndorff • *Scr* Harold Pinter, from the novel by Margaret Atwood

Hands across the Table ★★★★
Screwball comedy 1935 • US • BW • 79min

A manicurist and a penniless playboy, each determined to marry money and betrothed to dull but appropriately wealthy partners, meet, fall in love, and break off their engagements. The simple plot services a superior romantic comedy: sparkling, witty and marvellously played by Carole Lombard and Fred MacMurray, both of whose progress into top stardom was hastened by the film's box-office success. Ralph Bellamy and Astrid Allwyn are the future spouses who are thrown over, and Mitchell Leisen directs with the lightness of touch you would expect from a Paramount production of the period. RK

Carole Lombard *Regi Allen* • Fred MacMurray *Theodore Drew III* • Ralph Bellamy *Allen Macklyn* • Astrid Allwyn *Vivian Snowden* • Ruth Donnelly *Laura* • Marie Prevost *Nona* • Joseph Tozer *Peter* • William Demarest *Natty* ■ *Dir* Mitchell Leisen • *Scr* Herbert Fields, Norman Krasna, Vincent Lawrence, from the story *Bracelets* by Viña Delmar [Vina Delmar]

Hands of Orlac ★★★
Silent crime horror 1924 • Austria • BW • 90min

Robert Wiene's adaptation of Maurice Renard's sensationalist novel suffers from an uncertainty of tone. For the most part, the action is staged in a realistic manner, thus making the moments of expressionist stylisation all the more incongruous. However, Conrad Veidt is mesmerising as the concert pianist living on his nerves after his shattered hands are replaced with those of a murderer. Equally compelling is Fritz Kortner's blackmailer, but not even he's prepared for the final twist. DP

Conrad Veidt *Orlac* • Fritz Kortner *Nera* • Carmen Cartellieri *Regine* • Paul Askonas *Diener* ■ *Dir* Robert Wiene • *Scr* Louis Nerz, from the novel by Maurice Renard

The Hands of Orlac ★★★★
Horror 1960 • UK/Fr • BW • 101min

Filmed twice before (most notably as *Mad Love* in 1935), this elegant version of Maurice Renard's psychological case study of murderous obsession still exerts a morbid fascination. Mel Ferrer is a little lightweight as the pianist given a convicted strangler's hands after a plane crash, but Christopher Lee is a remorseless revelation as the sadistic magician tormenting him, ensuring the chilling tension is maintained right up until the final surprise twist. AJ

Mel Ferrer *Steven Orlac* • Christopher Lee *Nero* • Dany Carrel *Li-Lang* • Felix Aylmer *Dr Cochrane* • Basil Sydney *Siedeman* • Lucile Saint-Simon *Louise Cochrane* • Donald Wolfit *Prof Volcheff* • Donald Pleasence *Coates* ■ *Dir* Edmond T Gréville • *Scr* John Baines, Donald Taylor, Edmond T Gréville, from the novel by Maurice Renard

Hands of the Ripper ★★★ 15
Horror 1971 • UK • Colour • 81min

This entertaining piece of nonsense from Hammer is about Jack the Ripper's daughter who, having watched her dad dismember mama, goes barmy whenever she gets kissed in a flickering light. Cue therapist Eric Porter, who tries to cure her but then starts covering up her murders. Porter is too serious for these proceedings, but Angharad Rees is a swell Ms Ripper. TS *DVD*

Eric Porter *Dr John Pritchard* • Angharad Rees *Anna* • Jane Merrow *Laura* • Keith Bell *Michael Pritchard* • Derek Godfrey *Dysart* • Dora Bryan *Mrs Golding* • Marjorie Rhodes *Mrs Bryant* • Lynda Baron *Long Liz* • Marjie Lawrence *Dolly* ■ *Dir* Peter Sasdy • *Scr* LW Davidson, from a story by Edward Spencer Shew

Hands over the City ★★★ U
Political drama 1963 • It • Colour • 99min

Italian director Francesco Rosi imported American actor Rod Steiger to give weighty menace to the role of a property tycoon who manipulates civic politicians to let him develop his land, despite the effect on the people living there. Steiger gives a suitably overbearing performance as the ruthless millionaire in whom fascism has not died, but the film is too angry to articulate its arguments properly. It's still great dramatic entertainment, though. TH In Italian. *DVD*

Salvo Randone *De Angeli* • Rod Steiger *Nottola* • Guido Alberti *Magliore* ■ *Dir* Francesco Rosi • *Scr* Francesco Rosi, Raffaele La Capria, Enzo Provenzale, Enzo Forcella

Hands Up! ★★★
Silent comedy 1926 • US • BW • 50min

Raymond Griffith, the debonair silent comedian who specialised in take-offs of traditional Hollywood fare, comes close to matching the best of Harold Lloyd and Buster Keaton in this delightfully brisk parody of the American Civil War. As a Confederate spy sent out west, Griffith displays considerable ingenuity in surviving firing squads and hostile tribes as he tracks down a stagecoach carrying gold to the Union side. He even finds a way of living happily ever after with both of his lady loves (Marion Nixon and Virginia Lee Corbin). AE

Raymond Griffith *Confederate spy* • Marion Nixon [Marian Nixon] *The girl he loves* • Virginia Lee Corbin *The other girl he loves* • Mack Swain *Mine owner* • Montague Love [Montagu Love] *Union general* • George Billings *Abraham Lincoln* • Noble Johnson *Sitting Bull* ■ *Dir* Clarence Badger • *Scr* Monty Brice, Lloyd Corrigan, from a story by Reginald Morris

Hang 'Em High ★★★ 18
Western 1968 • US • Colour • 110min

Clint Eastwood is once again a man of few words but many bullets in the first western he made back in America after Sergio Leone had virtually invented him – as a film star and a distinctive screen character – in the spaghetti westerns they made together. Eastwood does the strong, silent stuff with characteristic efficiency in a tale of revenge and justice for all, which is perhaps more memorable as a staging post in Eastwood's career than as a landmark in the history of the western. PF Violence, swearing. *DVD* *Blu-ray*

Clint Eastwood *Jed Cooper* • Inger Stevens *Rachel* • Ed Begley *Cap'n Wilson* • Pat Hingle *Judge Adam Fenton* • Arlene Golonka *Jennifer* • James MacArthur *Preacher* • Ruth White *Madam Peaches Sophie* • Bruce Dern *Miller* • Alan Hale Jr *Stone* • James Westerfield *Prisoner* • Dennis Hopper *Prophet* • Ben Johnson (1) *Sheriff Dave Bliss* ■ *Dir* Ted Post • *Scr* Leonard Freeman, Mel Goldberg

Hangar 18 ★ PG
Science-fiction drama 1980 • US • Colour • 96min

Two space shuttle astronauts witness a collision with a UFO that crash-lands in Texas. When the White House hides the wreck in a remote air base hangar, astronaut Gary Collins tries to uncover the conspiracy over the accident for which he is being blamed. Any resemblance to *Close Encounters* and the "Roswell incident" are purely intentional in another sluggish and slapdash slice of speculative science-fiction from the notorious Sunn Classics outfit, who exclusively made exploitation drive-in fare. AJ

Darren McGavin *Harry Forbes* • Robert Vaughn (1) *Gordon Cain* • Gary Collins *Steve Bancroft* • Joseph Campanella *Frank Lafferty* • Pamela Bellwood *Sarah Michaels* ■ *Dir* James L Conway • *Scr* Steven Thornley, James L Conway, Tom Chapman, from a novel by Robert Weverka

Hangin' with the Homeboys ★★★★ 15
Comedy drama 1991 • US • Colour • 85min

Among the last films to be released in the 'hood sequence of urban black American movies that took US cinema by storm in the early 1990s, this is the only one to focus on the interaction between black and Hispanic youths. Writer/director Joseph B Vasquez's third feature explores some overly familiar situations, but there is a real sense of life as it is lived in his depiction of a night in the lives of four friends from the Bronx. Much of this freshness is due to the fact that the young cast was encouraged to improvise. Stand-up comics Doug E Doug and Mario Joyner clearly relish the opportunity, but John Leguizamo and Nestor Serrano give the more rounded performances. DP Violence, swearing, nudity. *DVD*

Doug E Doug *Willie* • Mario Joyner *Tom* • John Leguizamo *Johnny* • Nestor Serrano *Vinny* • Kimberly Russell *Vanessa* • Mary B Ward *Luna* • Reggie Montgomery *Rasta* • Christine Claravall *Daria* • Rosemarie Jackson [Rose Jackson] *Lila* ■ *Dir/Scr* Joseph B Vasquez

The Hanging Garden ★★★ 15
Drama 1997 • Can/UK • Colour • 91min

This heavy-duty Canadian drama is about a once fat and troubled teen who returns to the family home after ten years away. He's now fit, well adjusted and happily gay, but his homecoming prompts hauntings of his past and memories of his miserable adolescence. This demanding, emotional drama is well worth persevering with. DA

Chris Leavins *Sweet William* • Troy Veinotte *Sweet William, teenager* • Kerry Fox *Rosemary* • Sarah Polley *Rosemary, teenager* • Seana McKenna *Iris* • Peter MacNeill *Whiskey Mac* ■ *Dir/Scr* Thom Fitzgerald

The Hanging Tree ★★★★ PG
Western 1959 • US • Colour • 102min

This is a superb western, set in and around a wild mining community, that climaxes in a moving demonstration of the power of love. Gary Cooper gives a magnificent performance as the spiritually wounded doctor who cares for Maria Schell's temporarily blind and abandoned Swiss immigrant. The lascivious attentions of Karl Malden add spice to the scenario and George C Scott, in his screen debut, also makes an impact as a fanatical healer. Director Delmer Daves does a wonderful job of evoking the frontier atmosphere with the able assistance of cameraman Ted McCord. AE

Gary Cooper *Doc Joe Frail* • Maria Schell *Elizabeth Mahler* • Karl Malden *Frenchy Plante* • Ben Piazza *Rune* • George C Scott *Dr George Grubb* • Karl Swenson *Mr Flaunce* • Virginia Gregg *Mrs Flaunce* • John Dierkes *Society Red* ■ *Dir* Delmer Daves • *Scr* Wendell Mayes, Halsted Welles, from the novella by Dorothy M Johnson

Hanging Up ★★ 15
Comedy melodrama 2000 • US • Colour • 90min

Delia Ephron's novel about three sisters dealing with their senile father (Walter Matthau) is translated to the screen by director Diane Keaton, who also stars as the eldest sibling. However, Keaton and her co-star Lisa Kudrow get very little screen time compared to Meg Ryan, the daughter who is usually responsible for dear old dad, so the film ends up a lifeless and clichéd tale about her relationship with Matthau. JB *DVD*

Meg Ryan *Eve* • Diane Keaton *Georgia* • Lisa Kudrow *Maddy* • Walter Matthau *Lou* • Adam Arkin *Joe* • Duke Moosekian *Omar Kunundar* • Ann Bortolotti *Ogmed Kunundar* ■ *Dir* Diane Keaton • *Scr* Delia Ephron, Nora Ephron, from the novel by Delia Ephron

The Hangman ★★ U
Western 1959 • US • BW • 86min

The writer of *Stagecoach* and one of Hollywood's most reliable directors team up for a psychological western in which Robert Taylor plays a marshal with a reputation for stringing people up. Jack Lord is Taylor's current quarry, though he's apparently gone straight and has a family. Then Taylor gets a lesson in humanity from local sheriff Fess Parker. Those looking for bursts of action and spectacular scenery should search elsewhere, but others might appreciate this low-key study of a psychotic peace officer. AT

Robert Taylor (1) *Mackenzie Bovard* • Fess Parker *Sheriff Buck Weston* • Tina Louise *Selah Jennison* • Jack Lord *Johnny Bishop* • Shirley Harmer *Kitty Bishop* • Gene Evans *Big Murph* ■ *Dir* Michael Curtiz • *Scr* Dudley Nichols, from a story by Luke Short

Hangman ★★ 18
Detective thriller 2000 • US/Can • Colour • 91min

A serial killer uses the game of Hangman to torture his victims in this low-budget thriller. Mädchen Amick is the psychiatrist who is somehow linked to each of the crimes, Lou Diamond Phillips the cop assigned to the case, and Dan Lauria gives his usual gruff performance as the police chief. Unfortunately, less attention was paid to the script than to the performances in this weak TV movie. JB *DVD*

Lou Diamond Phillips *Det Nick Roos* • Mädchen Amick *Grace* • Vincent Corazza *Joe Little* • Robert Haley *Dr Henry Mitchell* • Dan Lauria *Capt Gil Roemer* ■ *Dir* Ken Girotti • *Scr* Vladimir Nemirovsky

Hangman's House ★★
Silent melodrama 1928 • US • BW • 72min

One of John Ford's earlier essays on his beloved Ireland, this late silent production features one of the master director's favourite actors, Victor McLaglen, as the Irish patriot who kills a drunken wastrel in a duel, freeing his widow for the man she had always loved. However, the stars – June Collyer, Larry Kent, Earle Foxe – mean little and the story drags. The film's highlight these days is the glimpse of a very young John Wayne as an excited horse race spectator. AE

June Collyer *Connaught O'Brien* • Larry Kent *Dermott McDermott* • Earle Foxe *John Darcy* • Victor McLaglen *Citizen Hogan* • Hobart Bosworth *Lord Chief Justice O'Brien* • John Wayne ■ *Dir* John Ford • *Scr* Marion Orth, Philip Klein, from the novel by Brian Oswald Donn-Byrne

Hangman's Knot ★★★ PG

Western   1952 · US · Colour · 78min

Roy Huggins, legendary creator of television series including *The Fugitive* and *Maverick*, also wrote films and directed just one – this successful drama set at the end of the American Civil War. Here Randolph Scott plays an officer leading a group of Confederate soldiers who steals a Union gold shipment unaware that the war has been over for a month. Regarded as common criminals, they take refuge in a stagecoach station, where the claustrophobic action erupts. A tense chamber western that deserves reappraisal. BB **DVD**

Randolph Scott *Matt Stewart* • Donna Reed *Molly Hull* • Claude Jarman Jr *Jamie Groves* • Frank Faylen *Cass Browne* • Lee Marvin *Ralph Bainter* ■ *Dir/Scr* Roy Huggins

Hangmen Also Die! ★★★ PG

Second World War drama
1943 · US · BW · 134min

A powerful piece of wartime propaganda begins in occupied Czechoslovakia with the assassination of notorious Nazi butcher Reinhard Heydrich. This is a consummate piece of committed film-making – devised by Bertolt Brecht and the film's director, Fritz Lang – in which the Nazis are portrayed as brutal but intelligent enemies who systematically murder Czech citizens until the perpetrator is delivered to them by the underground. It may take a while to accept Hollywood actors as Czechs, but the effort is worth it. AE **DVD**

Brian Donlevy *Dr Franz Svoboda* • Walter Brennan *Prof Novotny* • Anna Lee *Mascha Novotny* • Gene Lockhart *Emil Czaka* • Dennis O'Keefe *Jan Horek* • Alexander Granach *Alois Gruber* • Margaret Wycherly *Aunt Ludmilla Novotny* ■ *Dir* Fritz Lang • *Scr* John Wexley, from a story by Fritz Lang, Bertolt Brecht

The Hangover ★★★★ 15

Comedy   2009 · US · Colour · 95min

In a surprisingly inventive comedy that doesn't rely on cheap, gross-out laughs, a stag do in Las Vegas for about-to-be-wed Doug (Justin Bartha) takes a turn for the unusual. This terrific romp from *Old School* director Todd Phillips sees Doug's three friends (Bradley Cooper, Ed Helms, Zach Galifianakis) wake up after the excessive night before with no sign of the prospective groom and no memory of the evening's events. What they do have is a wrecked hotel suite occupied by a baby and, more worryingly, a tiger. Their subsequent search for the groom is cleverly plotted and packed with believable dialogue and hilarious situations, which effectively blend the deadpan with the hysterical. KK **DVD** **BD**

Bradley Cooper *Phil Wenneck* • Heather Graham *Jade* • Justin Bartha *Doug Billings* • Zach Galifianakis *Alan Garner* • Ed Helms *Stu Price* • Jeffrey Tambor *Sid* • Sasha Barrese *Tracy Garner* • Mike Tyson ■ *Dir* Todd Phillips • *Scr* Jon Lucas, Scott Moore

The Hangover: Part II

★★★ 15

Comedy   2011 · US · Colour · 97min

Following the wildly successful 2009 comedy, this sequel takes us on another trip – to Bangkok. But the scene is otherwise the same, with Bradley Cooper, Zach Galifianakis and Ed Helms waking up minus one of their stag party – the brother of Helms's bride-to-be, whose severed finger offers the only clue to the night before. Again, the lads trawl the mean streets to find him, but the mystery is less compelling, retracing steps from the first film and refreshing old jokes. Galifianakis is just as goofy and Cooper as nonchalant, but it's the less flashy Helms who gels the team, and the trio's sheer haplessness is still funny. Part III is due in summer 2013. SP Swearing, drug abuse, nudity. **DVD** **BD**

Bradley Cooper *Phil Wenneck* • Ed Helms *Stu Price* • Zach Galifianakis *Alan Garner* • Justin Bartha *Doug Billings* • Ken Jeong *Mr Chow* • Paul Giamatti *Kingsley* • Jamie Chung *Lauren* • Mike Tyson ■ *Dir* Todd Phillips • *Scr* Scot Armstrong, Todd Phillips, Craig Mazin, from characters by Jon Lucas, Scott Moore

The Hangover Part III ★★ 15

Comedy   2013 · US · Colour · 95min

The final (one hopes) instalment of the lucrative and initially hilarious franchise ends up in Las Vegas where the whole chaotic saga began. Here, the Wolfpack of Bradley Cooper, Ed Helms and manic man-child Zach Galifianakis are forced to find nutty Ken Jeong and a cache of stolen gold because, you've guessed it, they've "lost" Justin Bartha and that's the price of his return. There's a top-notch cast, and Helms's schtick and Jeong's timing still raise a smile in a technically stunning film, but as a comedy, it's a flop. KK Swearing, sexual references, brief nudity. **DVD** **BD** **CS**

Bradley Cooper *Phil* • Ed Helms *Stu* • Zach Galifianakis *Alan* • Ken Jeong *Mr Chow* • Heather Graham *Jade* • Justin Bartha *Doug* ■ *Dir* Todd Phillips • *Scr* Todd Phillips, Craig Mazin, from characters by Jon Lucas, Scott Moore

Hangover Square ★★★

Horror   1945 · US · BW · 77min

Following his successful collaboration with director John Brahm and screenwriter Barré Lyndon on *The Lodger*, Laird Cregar again takes the role of a psychopathic killer haunting the fog-bound streets of London. Here the burly star plays a young composer who turns nasty whenever he hears harsh sounds. Linda Darnell and George Sanders (as singer and psychologist respectively) co-star in this melodrama. The score by Bernard Herrmann stands out. AE **DVD**

Laird Cregar *George Harvey Bone* • Linda Darnell *Netta Longdon* • George Sanders *Dr Allan Middleton* • Glenn Langan *Carstairs* ■ *Dir* John Brahm • *Scr* Barré Lyndon, from the novel by Patrick Hamilton

Hanky Panky ★★ 15

Comedy thriller   1982 · US · Colour · 102min

After the success of *Stir Crazy*, you could understand Gene Wilder and director Sidney Poitier wanting to reunite with Richard Pryor. When he pulled out, however, it might have been more advisable to cast an actor in the same comic mould rather than rewrite the role in a romantic vein for Gilda Radner. The script gives Wilder and Radner, who married shortly afterwards, nothing to feed off and the endless round of coincidences and bad Hitchcock parodies soon become wearisome. DP **DVD**

Gene Wilder *Michael Jordon* • Gilda Radner *Kate Hellman* • Kathleen Quinlan *Janet Dunn* • Richard Widmark *Ransom* • Robert Prosky *Hiram Calder* • Josef Sommer *Adrian Pruitt* ■ *Dir* Sidney Poitier • *Scr* Henry Rosenbaum, David Taylor

Hanna ★★★★ 12

Action thriller
2011 · US/UK/Ger · Colour · 106min

Little Red Riding Hood meets *The Bourne Identity* probably best describes this thrillingly original film from director Joe Wright. But even that doesn't really capture its unique, oddly surreal tone. Hanna (Saoirse Ronan) is a 16-year-old girl who has never left her Lapland home, where she has been tutored in the deadly skills of the assassin by her ex-CIA father (Eric Bana). When the Agency comes looking for the pair, Hanna finds herself pursued by ruthless Cate Blanchett. Wright succeeds in blending the strange, almost fairy-tale atmosphere with some expertly conceived action and unusual supporting characters, with Tom Hollander's shell-suit wearing thug a particularly exotic pleasure. AS **DVD** **BD**

Saoirse Ronan *Hanna* • Eric Bana *Erik* • Cate Blanchett *Marissa Wiegler* • Tom Hollander *Isaacs* • Olivia Williams *Rachel* • Jason Flemyng *Sebastian* ■ *Dir* Joe Wright • *Scr* David Farr, Seth Lochhead, from a story by Lochhead

Hannah and Her Sisters

★★★★★ 15

Comedy drama   1986 · US · Colour · 106min

Woody Allen returned to familiar territory and struck gold with this warm, multi-stranded, near-nepotistic family saga that contains the usual awkward dates, clandestine meetings and failed marriages. Allen's neurotic TV producer has some memorable comic scenes revolving around a cancer scare, but the maestro cedes centre stage to the siblings of the title: Mia Farrow's strait-laced Hannah, Barbara Hershey's unfaithful Lee and Dianne Wiest's kooky Holly. Scoring Max von Sydow from his beloved Ingmar Bergman's repertory company is a coup for Allen, but the surprise hit is an urbane Michael Caine as Farrow's straying husband. AC Swearing. **DVD**

Woody Allen *Mickey Sachs* • Michael Caine *Elliot* • Mia Farrow *Hannah* • Carrie Fisher *April* • Barbara Hershey *Lee* • Max von Sydow *Frederick* • Dianne Wiest *Holly* • Lloyd Nolan *Evan* • Maureen O'Sullivan *Norma* • Daniel Stern *Dusty* • Sam Waterston *David* • Tony Roberts *Mickey's ex-partner* • Julie Kavner *Gail* ■ *Dir/Scr* Woody Allen

Hannah Arendt ★★★★ 12A

Biographical drama
2012 · Ger/Lux/Fr · Colour and BW · 113min

This lucid, thoughtful drama focuses on renowned German-Jewish political theorist Hannah Arendt's attendance at the trial of Nazi chief Adolf Eichmann in Jerusalem in 1961. Arendt subsequently coined the touchstone phrase "the banality of evil", with regard to the Final Solution. But the idea that one of the architects of the Holocaust could be a bureaucrat who "only obeyed orders", as well as Arendt's assertion that some Jewish leaders were complicit in what happened, threatened to destroy her career. Sukowa is quietly impressive as the chain-smoking thinker, the period is subtly rendered and the climactic defence of her ideas before a class of students and critics is a stirring and thought-provoking coda. JA German, French, English, Hebrew, Latin +subtitles. Some swearing, sexual references.

Barbara Sukowa *Hannah Arendt* • Janet McTeer *Mary McCarthy* • Julia Jentsch *Lotte Köhler* • Axel Milberg *Heinrich Blücher* ■ *Dir* Margarethe von Trotta • *Scr* Margarethe von Trotta, Pam Katz

Hannah Montana & Miley Cyrus: Best of Both Worlds Concert ★★ U

Concert movie   2008 · US · Colour · 75min

In the phenomenally successful Disney Channel sitcom *Hannah Montana*, Miley Cyrus plays a schoolgirl by day and secret pop sensation by night. This documentary record of the 15-year-old superstar's American concert tour sees the ever-exuberant Cyrus sing her vanilla power-pop hits first in character and then as herself. Between the songs are backstage glimpses of Cyrus sharing intimate moments with real-life father and screen dad Billy Ray and footage that captures the determination of fans to secure tickets for the sold-out shows. Shot in digital 3D for an immersive on-stage experience, the movie will keep tween fans entranced and adults mystified. AJ **DVD** **3D**

Miley Cyrus [Miley Ray Cyrus] *Miley Ray Cyrus/Hannah Montana* • Joe Jonas • Kevin Jonas • Nick Jonas • Kenny Ortega • Billy Ray Cyrus ■ *Dir* Bruce Hendricks • *Scr* From the TV series *Hannah Montana* by Michael Poryes, Rich Correll [Richard Correll], Barry O'Brien

Hannah Montana: the Movie ★★★ U

Musical comedy   2009 · US · Colour · 98min

In this movie spin-off, Miley (alias pop superstar Hannah Montana) is forced to return to her home state of Tennessee to take a close look at her priorities. One of the attractions of the TV series is Miley's close relationship with best friend Lilly (Emily Osment). But here, even though

---

Osment gets second billing, she doesn't get nearly enough screen time, while Miley's prat-falling 18-year-old brother Jackson (played by diminutive 32-year-old actor Jason Earles) is also conspicuous by his near-absence. Still, the story of how Cyrus finds some perspective and a first love while warding off the attentions of the British paparazzi is clichéd yet satisfying, and the songs are irritatingly tuneful. SuR **DVD** **BD**

Miley Cyrus [Miley Ray Cyrus] *Hannah Montana/Miley Stewart* • Billy Ray Cyrus *Robby Ray Stewart* • Lucas Till *Travis Brody* • Emily Osment *Lilly Truscott* • Jason Earles *Jackson Stewart* • Peter Gunn *Oswald Granger* • Vanessa Williams [Vanessa L Williams] *Vita* • Barry Bostwick *Mr Bradley* • Margo Martindale *Ruby* ■ *Dir* Peter Chelsom • *Scr* Dan [Daniel] Berendsen, from characters by Michael Poryes, Rich [Richard] Correll, Barry O'Brien

Hannah's Law ★★

Western   2012 · US/Can · Colour · 87min

Wild West movie clichés get a female twist in this commendable but overly sanitised revenge flick from occasional *Doctor Who* director Rachel Talalay. Set in notorious, late 1800s Dodge City, the tale sees Sara Canning's moralistic bounty hunter tracking the gang that slaughtered her family 12 years previously. Strong casting, including an underused Danny Glover and Billy Zane, elevate predictable events, and it's great to have Canning's Hannah and her African-American best mate, Stagecoach Mary (Kimberly Elise), holding their own in what's generally a male domain. SF

Sara Canning *Hannah Beaumont* • John Pyper-Ferguson *Frank McMurphy* • Greyston Holt *Wyatt Earp* • Ryan Kennedy *Doc Holliday* • Billy Zane *Lockwood* ■ *Dir* Rachel Talalay • *Scr* John Fasano

Hanna's War ★★ 15

Biographical war drama
1988 · US · Colour · 143min

Menahem Golan's biopic of the Hungarian poet Hanna Senesh is undermined by a crusty script and unsubtle characterisation. Recruited by squadron leader Anthony Andrews for a vital Balkan mission, Maruschka Detmers settles for a kind of designer heroism as she battles behind the lines before suffering at the hands of Donald Pleasence's sadistic torturer. His villainy and Ellen Burstyn's cameo are the best things in this muddled melodrama. DP

Ellen Burstyn *Katalin Senesh* • Maruschka Detmers *Hanna Senesh* • Anthony Andrews *Squadron Leader McCormack* • Donald Pleasence *Rosza Gabor* • David Warner *Captain Julian Simon* ■ *Dir* Menahem Golan • *Scr* Menahem Golan, Stanley Mann, from *The Diaries of Hanna Senesh* by Hanna Senesh, from the non-fiction book *A Great Wind Cometh* by Yoel Palgi

Hannibal ★ U

Historical adventure   1959 · It · Colour · 104min

In this grotty historical epic, Victor Mature crosses the Alps to smash the Roman Empire, pausing along the way for a dalliance with Rita Gam. The pace is sluggish, the acting is wooden, the scenery looks painted on and the battles are staged with about six extras and a few circus elephants. AT Italian dubbed.

Victor Mature *Hannibal* • Rita Gam *Sylvia* • Milly Vitale *Danila* • Rik Battaglia *Hasdrubal* • Franco Silva *Maharbal* • Mario Girotti [Terence Hill] *Quintilius* • Mirko Ellis *Mago* ■ *Dir* Edgar G Ulmer • *Scr* Mortimer Braus, from an idea by Alessandro Continenza, from a story by Ottavio Poggi

Hannibal ★★★ 18

Horror thriller   2001 · US · Colour · 131min

In this long-awaited sequel to *The Silence of the Lambs*, Anthony Hopkins reprises his Oscar-winning role, this time with his tongue set firmly in his cheek. Top FBI agent Clarice Starling (creditably played by Julianne Moore) is sent to the house of one of Hopkins's former victims, Gary Oldman (an extraordinary performance), who hopes to revitilise her search for his attacker. This lacks mystery, suspense and psychological resonance, but there's plenty of gory action and black humour. The superior prequel,

Red Dragon followed in 2002. **JA** Swearing, violence, nudity. **DVD BL**

Anthony Hopkins *Hannibal Lecter* • Julianne Moore *Clarice Starling* • Gary Oldman *Mason Verger* • Ray Liotta *Paul Krendler* • Frankie R Faison [Frankie Faison] *Barney the orderly* • Giancarlo Giannini *Rinaldo Pazzi* • Francesca Neri *Allegra Pazzi* ■ *Dir* Ridley Scott • *Scr* David Mamet, Steven Zaillian, from the novel by Thomas Harris

Hannibal Brooks ★★ U
Second World War comedy drama
1968 · UK · Colour · 101min

If you were trying to escape from the Germans in the Second World War, surely the last thing you'd want is an elephant tagging along to slow things down. Yet that's what happens here, as PoW Oliver Reed tries to cross the Alps via pachyderm in Michael Winner's tepid stab at war comedy. Michael J Pollard and John Alderton join the antics, but the tale's extremely hard to swallow. **NF**

Oliver Reed *Hannibal Brooks* • Michael J Pollard *Packy* • Wolfgang Preiss *Colonel Von Haller* • Helmut Lohner *Willi* • Karin Baal *Vronia* • Peter Karsten *Kurt* • John Alderton *Bernard* ■ *Dir* Michael Winner • *Scr* Dick Clement, Ian La Frenais, from a story by Michael Winner, Tom Wright

Hannibal Rising ★★ 18
Horror thriller
2006 · Fr/UK/US/Cz Rep/It · Colour · 116min

Novelist Thomas Harris turns scriptwriter here to delve into the early influences of his most famous literary creation – cannibal sophisticate Hannibal Lecter. Beginning in Eastern Europe in the final days of the Second World War, this emotionally patchy but reasonably enjoyable prequel examines how an innocent child is transformed into a revenge-hungry monster. Despite some ludicrous dialogue and Rhys Ifans's laughable turn as Hannibal's cartoonish nemesis, visually and atmospherically the feature excels. **SF** Violence. **DVD BL**

Gaspard Ulliel *Hannibal Lecter* • Gong Li *Lady Murasaki* • Rhys Ifans *Grutas* • Kevin McKidd *Kolnas* • Dominic West *Inspector Popil* • Richard Brake *Dortlich* ■ *Dir* Peter Webber • *Scr* Thomas Harris, from his novel • *Cinematographer* Ben Davis

Hannie Caulder ★★ 15
Western
1971 · UK · Colour · 81min

It should have been a major feminist work, a mystic western about a raped and widowed frontierswoman taught to shoot by a lone bounty hunter. Trouble is, this is that rare anomaly, the British western, shot in Spain with all the associated problems of realism, not the least of which is the casting of Raquel Welch in the title role. The photography is handsome, but the pace is slack, and the violence unpleasant. **TS** **DVD**

Raquel Welch *Hannie Caulder* • Robert Culp *Thomas Luther Price* • Ernest Borgnine *Emmett Clemens* • Strother Martin *Rufus Clemens* • Jack Elam *Frank Clemens* • Christopher Lee *Bailey* • Diana Dors *Madame* ■ *Dir* Burt Kennedy • *Scr* ZX Jones [David Haft Kennedy], from a story by Peter Cooper, from characters by Ian Quicke, Bob Richards • *Cinematographer* Edward Scaife

Hanover Street ★★ PG
Romantic Second World War drama
1979 · UK/US · Colour · 104min

Director Peter Hyams is more at home with battle sequences than romantic clinches, as is his star, Harrison Ford, who often looks distinctly uncomfortable as an American pilot whose air-raid encounter with nurse Lesley-Anne Down leads to trouble with her husband, Christopher Plummer. Apart from some lovely photography, it was all done much better in 1940's *Waterloo Bridge*. **DP** Swearing, nudity. **DVD**

Harrison Ford *David Halloran* • Lesley-Anne Down *Margaret Sellinger* • Christopher Plummer *Paul Sellinger* • Alec McCowen *Major Trumbo* • Richard Masur *Lt Jerry Cimino* • Michael Sacks *Lt Martin Hyer* • Patsy Kensit *Sarah Sellinger* • Max Wall *Harry Pike* • Shane Rimmer *Col Ronald Bart* • Keith Buckley *Lt Wells* • Sherrie Hewson *Phyllis*

• John Ratzenberger *Sgt John Lucas* ■ *Dir/Scr* Peter Hyams • *Cinematographer* David Watkin

Hans Christian Andersen ★★★★ U
Musical drama
1952 · US · Colour · 107min

Danny Kaye turns in possibly his best screen performance in this sentimental Hollywood fabrication of the life of the great storyteller. Children and adults alike will enjoy the superb Frank Loesser songs, notably the charming *Inchworm*, the unforgettable *Ugly Duckling*, and the rollicking *Wonderful Copenhagen*. A big hit in its day, it's worthwhile recalling the anti-Semitism that erupted in Scandinavia back in the 1950s over the Jewish Kaye playing Denmark's treasured raconteur. **TS** **DVD**

Danny Kaye *Hans Christian Andersen* • Farley Granger *Niels* • Jeanmaire [Zizi Jeanmaire] *Doro* • Joey Walsh [Joseph Walsh] *Peter* • Philip Tonge *Otto* • Erik Bruhn *The Hussar* • Roland Petit *The Prince* • John Brown (1) *Schoolmaster* • John Qualen *Burgomaster* ■ *Dir* Charles Vidor • *Scr* Moss Hart, from a story by Myles Connolly

Hansel and Gretel ★★★ 15
Horror fantasy
2007 · S Kor · Colour · 116min

Korean horror meets the Grimm brothers in this twisted modern take on the classic fairy tale. A young man (Chun Jeong-myeoung) is plunged into an unreal world following a car accident that leaves him bewildered and lost in a forest, until he's guided to "The Home of Happy Children" by a little girl in a red cape. Increasingly puzzled, he is then unable to find his way out and back to his girlfriend. A sense of foreboding remains throughout this unnerving horror, until the disturbing truth behind the children's idyllic existence is revealed. **JA** Korean +subtitles. **DVD**

Chun Jeong-myeoung *Lee Eun-soo* • Eun Won-jae *Kim Man-bok* • Shim Eun-kyung *Kim Young-hee* ■ *Dir* Yim Phil-sung • *Scr* Kim Min-sook, Yim Phil-sung

Hansel & Gretel: Witch Hunters ★★★ 15
Action fantasy horror
2013 · Ger/US · Colour · 87min

Ever wonder what happened to Hansel and Gretel once they roasted that witch in the gingerbread house? According to this fast and furious all-action continuation of the classic fairy tale, the sibling slayers (played by a stern Jeremy Renner and a game Gemma Arterton) became bounty hunters. Their latest assignment is tracking a powerful witch bitch (Famke Janssen) who is kidnapping local children for sacrifice. *Dead Snow* director Tommy Wirkola takes an irreverent approach with jokey anachronisms including giving Hansel diabetes as a consequence of his sweet tooth. There's salty language, too, but you can't take anything too seriously in this very silly but amiable romp through Brothers Grimm land. **AJ** Violence, swearing, nudity. **DVD BL**

Jeremy Renner *Hansel* • Gemma Arterton *Gretel* • Famke Janssen *Muriel* • Pihla Viitala *Mina* • Peter Stormare *Berringer* • Zoe Bell [Zoë Bell] *Tall witch* ■ *Dir/Scr* Tommy Wirkola

Hanussen ★★★★ 15
Drama
1988 · Hun/W Ger · Colour · 111min

This film is the last and marginally least effective of the "stranger in his homeland" trilogy directed by İstván Szabó and starring Klaus Maria Brandauer. Here, the character vaunted and then victimised by a frightened regime is a war-wounded clairvoyant, whose fame is tarnished when he predicts the formation of the Third Reich. The period detail is flawless, the ensemble playing impeccable and Brandauer's performance mesmerising, but it lacks the subtle imagery and insight of its predecessors. **DP** German +subtitles. Violence, swearing, nudity.

Klaus Maria Brandauer *Klaus Schneider/"Erik-Jan Hanussen"* • Erland Josephson *Dr Bettelheim* • Ildiko Bansagi *Sister Betty* • Walter Schmidinger *Propaganda minister* • Karoly Eperjes *Captain*

Tibor Nowotny • Grazyna Szapolowska *Valery de la Meer* • Colette Pilz-Warren *Dagma* ■ *Dir* İstván Szabó • *Scr* István Szabó, Peter Dobai

The Happening ★★
Comedy
1967 · US · Colour · 91min

Very much of its hippy period, it is indicative of the quality of this film that the title song by the Supremes has survived longer in popular culture than the movie it originates from. Anthony Quinn is his usual gruff self as a kidnapped gangster, and the period cast of George Maharis, Michael Parks and Robert Walker Jr is pleasantly surprised by a young Faye Dunaway in her screen debut. It's forgettable stuff, except for a startling, unpleasant change of tone at the end. **TS** Violence, swearing, nudity.

Anthony Quinn *Roc Delmonico* • George Maharis *Taurus* • Michael Parks *Sureshot* • Robert Walker Jr *Herby* • Martha Hyer *Monica Delmonico* • Faye Dunaway *Sandy* • Milton Berle *Fred* • Oscar Homolka *Sam* ■ *Dir* Elliot Silverstein • *Scr* Frank R Pierson, James D Buchanan, Ronald Austin, from a story by Buchanan, Austin

The Happening ★★ 15
Science-fiction thriller
2008 · Ind/US · Colour · 86min

The Sixth Sense director M Night Shyamalan's follow-up to *Lady in the Water* begins intriguingly enough with American cities afflicted by a sudden and inexplicable breakdown in human behaviour, as people commit mass suicide in a variety of shocking ways. Philadelphia science teacher Mark Wahlberg and his wife Zooey Deschanel hope to avoid the chaos by heading for the country, but soon find they can't be safe if they don't know who or what is causing the attacks. There's nothing exciting about this drawn-out tale of collective paranoia among an oddball group of survivors, and it's just further evidence of the director's descent from the master of the paranormal plot twist into utter silliness. **AJ** **DVD BL**

Mark Wahlberg *Elliot Moore* • Zooey Deschanel *Alma Moore* • John Leguizamo *Julian* • Ashlyn Sanchez *Jess* • Betty Buckley *Mrs Jones* • Spencer Breslin *Josh* ■ *Dir/Scr* M Night Shyamalan • *Cinematographer* Tak Fujimoto • *Music* James Newton Howard

The Happiest Days of Your Life ★★★★ U
Comedy
1950 · UK · BW · 79min

You can almost smell the school dinners in this wonderful comedy. The bones of contention that arise when Margaret Rutherford's academy for young ladies is accidentally evacuated to a building already occupied by Alastair Sim's boys' school are beautifully observed, but the comic highlight is the precision with which the pupils scurry around the school to avoid visiting VIPs. The heads are superb and Richard Wattis, Guy Middleton and Joyce Grenfell are top class. **DP** **DVD**

Alastair Sim *Wetherby Pond* • Margaret Rutherford *Miss Whitchurch* • Joyce Grenfell *Miss Gossage* • Richard Wattis *Arnold Billings* • John Bentley *Richard Tassell* • Bernadette O'Farrell *Miss Harper* • Guy Middleton *Victor Hyde-Brown* • Edward Rigby *Rainbow* ■ *Dir* Frank Launder • *Scr* Frank Launder, John Dighton, from the play by John Dighton

The Happiest Girl in the World ★★★ 15
Satirical drama
2009 · Neth/Fr/Rom/Jpn · Colour · 103min

Romanian writer/director Radu Jude's satire is a sharp and subtle dissection of the impact two decades of free-market democracy has had on the former Eastern Bloc. Andreea Bosneag stars as Delia, the provincial teenager who travels to Bucharest to claim the luxury car she's won in a competition. Part of her prize involves shooting a commercial for the soft-drink sponsors, but her inability to deliver the lines leads to endless delays. Adding to Delia's woes are her parents, who browbeat her into selling the prize to fund the conversion of her dying grandmother's property into a guest house. Mocking

geographical and generational aspiration, Jude makes mischievous use of repetition to suggest the incompetence of the post-liberation regimes, while also denouncing the communist legacy. **DP** Romanian +subtitles.

Andreea Bosneag *Delia Fratila* • Vasile Muraru *Mr Fratila* • Violeta Haret Popa *Mrs Fratila* • Serban Pavlu *Director* • Alexandru Georgescu *The client* ■ *Dir* Radu Jude • *Scr* Radu Jude, Augustina Stanciu

The Happiest Millionaire ★★★ U
Musical
1967 · US · Colour · 158min

This film has its place in history as the last one personally produced by Walt Disney. Yet why he felt this polished but hardly glittering picture should last over two and a half hours is anyone's guess. The songs by the Sherman brothers aren't up to much, while the *Romeo and Juliet* story never catches light, in spite of the presence of Fred MacMurray, Greer Garson, Geraldine Page and Tommy Steele, making his Hollywood debut as a Buttons-like matchmaker. **DP**

Fred MacMurray *Anthony J Drexel Biddle* • Tommy Steele *John Lawless* • Greer Garson *Mrs Cordelia Biddle* • Geraldine Page *Mrs Duke* • Gladys Cooper *Aunt Mary Drexel* • Hermione Baddeley *Mrs Worth* • Lesley Ann Warren *Cordy Biddle* • John Davidson *Angie Duke* • Paul Peterson *Tony Biddle* • Eddie Hodges *Livingston Biddle* ■ *Dir* Norman Tokar • *Scr* AJ Carothers, from the play by Kyle Crichton, from the book *My Philadelphia Father* by Kyle Crichton, Cordelia Drexel Biddle

Happily N'Ever After ★★ U
Animated fantasy comedy
2006 · US/Ger · Colour · 83min

In an ironic, animated take on *Cinderella*, Sigourney Weaver voices the wicked stepmother who keeps Ella (Sarah Michelle Gellar) from marrying the preening Prince Humperdink (Patrick Warburton) by taking over the Department of Fairy Tale Land Security. There she can alter fairy-tale endings so nobody lives happily ever after. Hot on her heels is Rick (Freddie Prinze Jr), a kitchen boy at the palace and Ella's true love. Bland vocal performances and derivative jokes won't entertain youngsters used to more refined CGI fare. **JR** **DVD**

Sigourney Weaver *Frieda* • Sarah Michelle Gellar *Ella* • Freddie Prinze Jr *Rick* • Patrick Warburton *Prince Humperdink* • Andy Dick *Mambo* • Wallace Shawn *Munk* ■ *Dir* Paul J Bolger • *Scr* Doug Langdale [Douglas Langdale], Rob Moreland [Robert Moreland], from an idea by Stefan Beiten, André Sikojev, Nikolaus Weil

Happiness ★★★★★ 18
Black comedy drama
1998 · US · Colour · 133min

Todd Solondz's stunningly acted and brilliantly scripted film looks at the extraordinary lives of a group of men and women who engage in shocking antisocial behaviour, including obscene phone calls, murder and paedophilia. What's so amazing about this tragicomedy is its lack of moral judgement – the viewers are left to make up their own minds about the events – and its pungent humour that emerges from the sickest of circumstances. **JC** Violence, sex scenes, swearing, nudity. **DVD**

Jane Adams (2) *Joy Jordan* • Jon Lovitz *Andy Kornbluth* • Philip Seymour Hoffman *Allen* • Dylan Baker *Bill Maplewood* • Lara Flynn Boyle *Helen Jordan* • Louise Lasser *Mona Jordan* • Ben Gazzara *Lenny Jordan* • Jared Harris *Vlad* • Marla Maples *Ann Chambeau* • Elizabeth Ashley • Diane Freed ■ *Dir/Scr* Todd Solondz

The Happiness of the Katakuris ★★★★ 15
Musical black comedy horror
2001 · Jpn · Colour · 112min

Forget the schlock grotesqueries that have become Takeshi Miike's trademark and instead revel in the colourful kitsch of this hilarious zombie musical. The tale of a family whose dream of running a rural retreat is confounded by the guests' unfortunate habit of dying, is packed with quirky characters, macabre comedy and

H

song-and-dance routines that reveal emotion while cranking up the camp quotient. The cast is sporting to the extreme and the photography is exhilarating. DP Japanese +subtitles. **DVD**

Kenji Sawada *Masao Katakuri* • Keiko Matsuzaka *Terue Katakuri* • Shinji Takeda *Masayuki Katakuri* • Naomi Nishida *Shizue Katakuri* • Tetsuro Tanba [Tetsuro Tamba] *Nihei Katakuri* • Naoto Takenaka *Reporter/singer on TV* • Tamaki Miyazaki *Yurie Katakuri* ■ *Dir* Takashi Miike • *Scr* Kikumi Yamagishi, from the film *The Quiet Family* by Kim Ji-woon • *Cinematographer* Akio Nomura

Happy Anniversary ★★
Comedy 1959 · US · BW · 82min

Made in the days when television was a burgeoning rival to the cinema's ability to pull in mass audiences, this comedy has David Niven and Mitzi Gaynor as a happily married couple whose daughter (Patty Duke) reveals her father's past life on a children's TV show. Topical jokes for the time, but not now in these days of multi-media revolution. TH

David Niven *Chris Walters* • Mitzi Gaynor *Alice Walters* • Carl Reiner *Bud* • Loring Smith *Mr Gans* • Monique Van Vooren *Jeanette* • Phyllis Povah *Mrs Gans* • Patty Duke *Debbie Walters* ■ *Dir* David Miller (1) • *Scr* Joseph Fields, Jerome Chodorov, from the play *Anniversary Waltz* by Jerome Chodorov

Happy Birthday to Me ★★ 15
Horror 1981 · Can · Colour · 106min

No amount of high-tone style, technical expertise or lavish production values can make this outrageously contrived and overly complicated shocker any less lacklustre. Is college student Melissa Sue Anderson killing snobby sorority members during blackouts caused by a near-fatal car crash? A ludicrous bombardment of twists and turns. AJ Violence, swearing, nudity. **DVD**

Melissa Sue Anderson *Virginia* • Glenn Ford *Dr Faraday* • Lawrence Dane *Hal* • Sharon Acker *Estelle* • Frances Hyland (2) *Mrs Patterson* • Tracey Bregman [Tracy Bregman] *Ann* • Jack Blum *Alfred* • Matt Craven *Steve* ■ *Dir* J Lee Thompson • *Scr* Timothy Bond, Peter Jobin, John Saxton, John Beaird, from a story by John Saxton

Happy Endings ★★★ 15
Comedy drama 2005 · US · Colour · 127min

In Don Roos's acidic ensemble comedy drama, Lisa Kudrow plays an abortion counsellor who begins to wonder what happened to the child she gave up as a teen, the result of a coupling with her now gay step-brother (Steve Coogan). However, that is just one in a number of overlapping, loosely connected stories that explore the complex and often dysfunctional bonds between parent and child, and their impact on grown-up relationships. It's funny and touching in equal parts, although Roos's clever use of split screens and captions gives it an almost playful air at times. JF Swearing, sex scenes. **DVD**

Lisa Kudrow *Mamie* • Steve Coogan *Charley* • Jesse Bradford *Nicky* • Bobby Cannavale *Javier* • Maggie Gyllenhaal *Jude* • Jason Ritter *Otis* • Tom Arnold *Frank* • David Sutcliffe *Gil* • Sarah Clarke *Diane* • Laura Dern *Pam* ■ *Dir/Scr* Don Roos

Happy Ever After ★★ U
Comedy 1954 · UK · Colour · 84min

David Niven got so little practice at playing cads that you can almost forgive him for being so bad here, as the gruff English landlord whose new regime drives his tenants to the point of murder. This underachieving film cries out for black comedy as the locals draw lots to see who will do the dirty deed. Would-be assassins George Cole, Joseph Tomelty and Michael Shepley mug like crazy. DP

David Niven *Jasper O'Leary* • Yvonne De Carlo *Serena McGlusky* • Barry Fitzgerald *Thady O'Heggarty* • George Cole *Terence* • AE Matthews *General O'Leary* • Noelle Middleton *Kathy McGlusky* • Robert Urquhart *Dr Michael Flynn* • Michael Shepley *Major McGlusky* • Joseph Tomelty *Dooley* • Eddie Byrne *Lannigan* ■ *Dir* Mario Zampi • *Scr* Jack Davies, Michael Pertwee, LAG Strong

Happy Ever Afters ★★ 15
Comedy 2009 · Ire · Colour · 101min

Two wedding parties collide in an Irish seaside hotel in this bittersweet comedy. Stressed single mother Maura (*Happy-Go-Lucky* star Sally Hawkins) is entering into a green-card marriage with an illegal immigrant, while the occasion marks a second attempt for Freddie (Tom Riley) and Sophie (Jade Yourell) to tie the knot. Crises and confusions escalate over the course of the day, but writer/director Stephen Burke pushes the wackiness harder than credibility will really allow, and the result is a farce that soon takes leave of its senses. A shame, really, since the basic idea is an entertaining one – Hawkins does likeable ditziness to a tee and wide-eyed Sinead Maguire as her disbelieving daughter is a real find. TJ

Sally Hawkins *Maura* • Tom Riley *Freddie* • Jade Yourell *Sophie* • Ariyon Bakare *Wilson* • Sinead Maguire *Molly* • Ger Ryan *Bridie* ■ *Dir/Scr* Stephen Burke

Happy Face Murders ★★★ 18
Crime thriller based on a true story 1999 · US · Colour · 94min

Where would tele-moviedom be without stranger-than-fiction stories culled from the tabloids? Marg Helgenberger and Henry Thomas acquit themselves admirably as the cops investigating the brutal murder of a young woman. But the acting honours go to Ann-Margret, who is virtually unrecognisable as a dowdy grandmother, whose obsession with TV detective shows enables her to rig the clues to implicate her younger lover in the crime. DP

Ann-Margret *Lorraine Petrovich* • Marg Helgenberger *Jen Powell* • Henry Thomas *Dylan McCarthy* • Nicholas Campbell *Rusty Zuvic* ■ *Dir* Brian Trenchard-Smith • *Scr* John Pielmeier

The Happy Family ★★★ U
Comedy 1952 · UK · BW · 88min

One of those "they don't make 'em like this any more" comic capers, this stars Stanley Holloway and Kathleen Harrison star as a shop-keeping couple refusing to move from their humble dwelling to accommodate the 1951 Festival of Britain. It's an innocent, gentle lark, harking back to an infinitely preferable if somewhat mythically rosy era when officialdom was bumptious but owlishly benign, and the "great unwashed" behaved like a troupe of good-hearted medieval tumblers. SH

Stanley Holloway *Henry Lord* • Kathleen Harrison *Lillian Lord* • Naunton Wayne *Mr Filch* • Dandy Nichols *Ada* • John Stratton *David* • Eileen Moore *Joan* • Shirley Mitchell *Marina* • Margaret Barton *Anne* • George Cole *Cyril* ■ *Dir* Muriel Box • *Scr* Muriel Box, Sydney Box, from the play by Michael Clayton Hutton

Happy Feet ★★★★ U
Musical animated adventure 2006 · Aus · Colour · 104min

George Miller does for penguins what he did for pigs in *Babe* in this fabulous Bafta-winning family adventure. It combines jaw-dropping computer animation with contemporary and classic tunes to bring to life a simple but eloquent story of an outcast emperor penguin's struggle for acceptance. Moral and ecological messages abound as tap-dancing avian cutie Mumble (voiced by Elijah Wood) hatches without the essential ability to sing. Astonishing visuals and imaginative Busby Berkeley-style song-and-dance numbers add depth to Mumble's relentlessly paced (and occasionally scary) quest to find acceptance. The voice talent is also seriously classy, with Robin Williams a highlight in a cast that also includes Hugh Jackman and Nicole Kidman as Mumble's parents. SF **DVD** Blu

Elijah Wood *Mumble* • Robin Williams *Ramón/Lovelace* • Brittany Murphy *Gloria* • Hugh Jackman *Memphis* • Nicole Kidman *Norma Jean* • Hugo Weaving *Noah the Elder* • Anthony LaPaglia *Alpha Skua* • Miriam Margolyes *Mrs Astrakhan* • Steve Irwin *Kev* ■ *Dir* George Miller (2) • *Scr* Warren Coleman, John Collee, George Miller, Judy Morris

Happy Feet Two ★★★ U
Musical animated adventure 2011 · Aus · Colour · 95min

The dance routines and deft song mash-ups that made the Oscar-winning original so novel are surprisingly unmemorable in director George Miller's busy sequel. Tap-dancing emperor penguin Mumble (Elijah Wood), son Erik (Ava Acres) and friends must rescue the rest of their clan when an ice shelf collapses, trapping them in a gorge. The visuals are frequently spectacular and the environmental concerns are admirable, but this simply doesn't have the charm of the original. AJ **DVD** Blu 3D CS

Elijah Wood *Mumble* • Robin Williams *Ramon/Lovelace* • Hank Azaria *The Mighty Sven* • Alecia Moore [Pink] *Gloria* • Brad Pitt *Will the krill* • Matt Damon *Bill the krill* • Sofia Vergara *Carmen* • Ava Acres *Erik* ■ *Dir* George Miller (2) • *Scr* George Miller, Gary Eck, Warren Coleman, Paul Livingston, from characters by Miller, Coleman, John Collee, Judy Morris

Happy Gilmore ★★ 12
Sports comedy 1996 · US · Colour · 92min

Adam Sandler has come on a bit since he made this knockabout comedy in which he stars as a second-rate ice-hockey player whose thuggish tactics are the only thing keeping him on the team. When his slap-shot is turned into a golfer's drive, Sandler sees a way of earning enough cash on the fairway to save his granny's home from the IRS. Typical no-brainer fare. JF Swearing, violence. **DVD** Blu

Adam Sandler *Happy Gilmore* • Christopher McDonald *Shooter* • Julie Bowen *Virginia* • Frances Bay *Grandma* • Carl Weathers *Chubbs* • Alan Covert [Allen Covert] *Otto* • Robert Smigel *IRS agent* • Bob Barker • Richard Kiel *Mr Larson* • Dennis Dugan *Doug Thompson* • Lee Trevino ■ *Dir* Dennis Dugan • *Scr* Tim Herlihy, Adam Sandler

Happy Go Lovely ★★ U
Musical 1950 · UK · Colour · 93min

This lacklustre musical was shot in Britain with Hollywood journeyman Bruce Humberstone directing. Cesar Romero and Vera-Ellen were also imported to sugar the pill for American audiences, and they give polished performances as the down-at-heel producer and his protégée, although David Niven is less at home as the millionaire conned into financing their Edinburgh Festival show. DP **DVD**

David Niven *BG Bruno* • Vera-Ellen *Janet Jones* • Cesar Romero *John Frost* • Bobby Howes *Charlie* • Diane Hart *Mae* • Gordon Jackson *Paul Tracey* • John Laurie *Jonskill* ■ *Dir* Bruce Humberstone [H Bruce Humberstone] • *Scr* Val Guest, Arthur Macrae, from a story by F Dammann, H Rosenfeld

Happy Go Lucky ★★ U
Musical romantic comedy 1943 · US · Colour · 81min

New Yorker Mary Martin uses her savings for a trip to the Caribbean in search of a rich husband. She finds a suitable candidate in an eccentric millionaire (former crooner Rudy Vallee), but loses her heart to beachcomber Dick Powell. Martin and Powell are the nominal stars of this slimline escapist musical, but it's "incendiary blonde" Betty Hutton, also chasing a man (Eddie Bracken) in what passes for plot, who walks away with it. Curtis Bernhardt, taking time out from melodrama, directs. RK

Mary Martin *Marjory Stuart* • Dick Powell *Pete Hamilton* • Betty Hutton *Bubbles Hennessy* • Eddie Bracken *Wally Case* • Rudy Vallee *Alfred Monroe* • Mabel Paige *Mrs Smith* ■ *Dir* Curtis Bernhardt • *Scr* Walter DeLeon, Norman Panama, Melvin Frank, from a story by John Jacoby, Michael Uris • *Music/lyrics* Frank Loesser, Jimmy McHugh, Henry J Sayers

Happy-Go-Lucky ★★★ 15
Drama 2007 · UK/US · Colour · 113min

Writer/director Mike Leigh is his own worst enemy. After continually setting the bar so high with his searing social dramas, it somehow seems more disappointing when

one comes along that drops slightly below his usual standards. That's the case with this north London-set slice-of-life that centres on chirpy primary school teacher Sally Hawkins, who is taking driving lessons from bigoted instructor Eddie Marsan. The performances are terrific, but Hawkins's character often comes across as more irritating than she should be, and not everyone will be swept along by her journey of discovery. Even so, a lesser Leigh offering is better than none at all. AJ **DVD**

Sally Hawkins *Poppy* • Eddie Marsan *Scott* • Alexis Zegerman *Zoe* • Sylvestra Le Touzel *Heather* • Andrea Riseborough *Dawn* • Sinead Matthews *Alice* • Kate O'Flynn *Suzy* • Sarah Niles *Tash* ■ *Dir/Scr* Mike Leigh

Happy, Happy ★★★ 15
Comedy drama 2010 · Nor · Colour · 84min

This low-key charmer stars Agnes Kittelsen as Kaja, whose boundless enthusiasm for life masks an unhappiness with her inattentive husband, surly son and the prospect of an uneventful future in their rural community. When a middle-class couple rent the adjacent property, she finds a release from her frustrations with the cuckolded husband. Like its heroine, the story never dwells on the heartbreak, delivering plenty of wry smiles and surprises as the four adults are forced to confront all the glaring problems in their marriages. But the chief pleasure of Anne Sewitsky's bittersweet comedy is the believable transformation of the initially awkward Kaja into a confident and capable woman. JH Norwegian, Danish, German +subtitles. Swearing, sex scenes, nudity, drug abuse. **DVD**

Agnes Kittelsen *Kaja* • Joachim Rafaelsen *Eirik* • Maibritt Saerens *Elisabeth* • Henrik Rafaelsen *Sigve* • Oskar H Brandso [Oskar Hernaes Brandso] *Theodor* ■ *Dir* Anne Sewitsky • *Scr* Ragnhild Tronvoll

The Happy Hooker ★★ 18
Comedy 1975 · US · Colour · 93min

Liberally sprinkled with sex, satire and no little savvy, Xaviera Hollander's memoirs made her the toast of New York. However, this screen adaptation has reduced her bestselling insights to a series of cheap conquests in a battle of the sexes. Playing the Big Apple's most famous madam, Lynn Redgrave does a splendid job, but, Jean-Pierre Aumont aside, she gets little help from the rest of the cast. DP Swearing, nudity.

Lynn Redgrave *Xaviera Hollander* • Jean-Pierre Aumont *Yves St Jacques* • Lovelady Powell *Madelaine* • Nicholas Pryor *Carl Gordon* • Elizabeth Wilson *Mrs Gordon* • Tom Poston *J Arthur Conrad* • Conrad Janis *Fred* • Richard Lynch *Cop* ■ *Dir* Nicholas Sgarro • *Scr* William Richert, from the book by Xaviera Hollander, Robin Moore, Yvonne Dunleavy

The Happy Hooker Goes to Washington ★ 18
Comedy 1977 · US · Colour · 84min

The original *Happy Hooker* was a pretty tame affair, and this too suffers from a surprising prudishness. Joey Heatherton steps into Lynn Redgrave's high heels and sexy outfits as the now-famous madam, who gets involved in national politics when she is called to Capitol Hill. Few laughs, yet a further equally lamentable series entry followed in 1980. JF

Joey Heatherton *Xaviera Hollander* • George Hamilton *Ward Thompson* • Ray Walston *Senator Sturges* • Jack Carter *Senator Caruso* ■ *Dir* William A Levey • *Scr* Robert Kaufman

Happy Is the Bride ★★★ U
Comedy 1957 · UK · BW · 81min

Directed by co-scriptwriter Roy Boulting, this remake of *Quiet Wedding* hasn't the polish of Anthony Asquith's version, but what it lacks in style it almost makes up for in verve, as such practised *farceurs* as Cecil Parker, Terry-Thomas and Joyce Grenfell do their best to complicate the arrangements for Ian Carmichael and Janette Scott's nuptials. Yet the plaudits must go to Athene Seyler, who steals the show in the same role she played in the original. **DP**

Ian Carmichael *David Chaytor* • Janette Scott *Janet Royd* • Cecil Parker *Arthur Royd* • Terry-Thomas *Policeman* • Joyce Grenfell *Aunt Florence* • Eric Barker *Vicar* • Edith Sharpe *Mildred Royd* • Elvi Hale *Petula* • John Le Mesurier *Chaytor* • Nicholas Parsons *John Royd* • Athene Seyler *Aunt Harriet* ■ *Dir* Roy Boulting • *Scr* Roy Boulting, Jeffrey Dell, from the play *Quiet Wedding* by Esther McCracken

Happy Land ★★ U
Drama 1943 · US · BW · 75min

Don Ameche stars as an Iowa shopkeeper who loses his son in the Second World War and is consoled by the ghost of his own father, a veteran of the First World War. Intended to convince the bereaved that their loved ones have not died in vain, it's a fairly creepy and decidedly sudsy experience as Ameche is shown what a good life both he and his son have had. **AT**

Don Ameche *Lew Marsh* • Frances Dee *Agnes* • Harry Carey *Gramp* • Ann Rutherford *Lenore Prentiss* • Cara Williams *Gretchen Barry* • Richard Crane *Rusty* • Henry Morgan [Harry Morgan] *Tony Cavrek* ■ *Dir* Irving Pichel • *Scr* Kathryn Scola, Julien Josephson, from the novel by MacKinlay Kantor

Happy Landing ★★★ U
Comedy musical 1938 · US · BW · 101min

Norwegian Olympic Champion ice skater Sonja Henie was a petite blonde who rapidly became one of Hollywood's highest-ranking movie stars after her first two films struck gold for 20th Century-Fox. Here, the winsome Henie enjoys the company of two men and a nothing plot about a bandleader's plane landing near Henie's house in a very Hollywood Norway, hence the title. But plots don't matter when Sonja skates, Ethel Merman sings and the two guys are Don Ameche and Cesar Romero. **TS**

Sonja Henie *Trudy Erickson* • Don Ameche *Jimmy Hall* • Jean Hersholt *Herr Erickson* • Ethel Merman *Flo Kelly* • Cesar Romero *Duke Sargent* • Billy Gilbert *Counter man* • Wally Vernon *Al Mahoney* ■ *Dir* Roy Del Ruth • *Scr* Milton Sperling, Boris Ingster

Happy Mother's Day... Love, George ★★★
Mystery thriller 1973 · US · Colour · 90min

Actor Darren McGavin's directorial debut was the last movie lounge singer Bobby Darin made before his untimely death. Darin is part of a solid cast in a very strange horror soap opera about Ron Howard returning to his boyhood Nova Scotia home to discover the identity of his father. He uncovers a twisted family tree and some gruesome murders as he traces his roots in the tranquil community. Striking visuals combine with the offbeat story to unusual effect and create an unusual genre item. **AJ**

Patricia Neal *Cara* • Cloris Leachman *Ronda* • Bobby Darin *Eddie* • Tessa Dahl *Celia* • Ron Howard *Johnny* • Kathie Browne *Crystal* • Joseph Mascolo *Piccolo* • Simon Oakland *Ron Howard* ■ *Dir* Darren McGavin • *Scr* Robert Clouse • *Cinematographer* Walter Lassally

Happy New Year ★★★ 15
Comedy 1987 · US · Colour · 84min

This engaging cross between a comedy, love story, heist picture and buddy movie is an undeservedly neglected American remake of Claude Lelouch's 1974 film. It boasts winning performances by Charles Durning and Peter Falk as two old partners in crime, planning the robbery of a Palm Beach jewellery store. Lelouch himself makes a brief early appearance, but the movie ultimately belongs to Falk, who dons a series of brilliant disguises, including one as an old woman – based on his own mum. **PF**

Peter Falk *Nick* • Charles Durning *Charlie* • Wendy Hughes *Carolyn Benedict* • Tom Courtenay *Edward Sanders* • Tracy Brooks Swope *Nina* • Joan Copeland *Sunny* • Daniel Gerroll *Curator* • Bruce Malmuth *Police lieutenant* ■ *Dir* John G Avildsen • *Scr* Warren Lane [Nancy Dowd], from the 1974 film

The Happy Road ★★ U
Comedy drama 1956 · US · BW · 99min

Gene Kelly's second movie of the seven he directed solo was filmed on location in France. In it, he stars as an American widower when his children run away from their Swiss school and head for Paris. The children are not without charm, but the situations are predictable, and the view of the French is a bit too patronising. **RB**

Gene Kelly *Mike Andrews* • Barbara Laage *Suzanne Duval* • Michael Redgrave *General Medworth* • Bobby Clark *Danny Andrews* • Brigitte Fossey *Janine Duval* • Roger Treville *Dr Solaise* ■ *Dir* Gene Kelly • *Scr* Arthur Julian, Joseph Morhaim, Harry Kurnitz, from a story by Arthur Julian, Harry Kurnitz

Happy, Texas ★★★★ 12
Comedy 1999 · US · Colour · 94min

This comedy of errors is an unexpected revelation, in which Jeremy Northam stars as a convict who escapes from an overturned prison van with fellow prisoner Steve Zahn. They end up in the Texas town of Happy where they are mistaken for two homosexual carnival organisers who've been hired to help with a beauty contest for five year olds. The local (male) sheriff takes a shine to Northam, while Zahn falls for schoolteacher Illeana Douglas ("That whole gay thing is more of a hobby, really"). A small comic gem. **TH** Swearing, violence. **DVD**

Jeremy Northam *Harry Sawyer* • Steve Zahn *Wayne Wayne Wayne Jr* • Ally Walker *Josephine "Joe" McLintock* • Illeana Douglas *Ms Schaefer* • William H Macy *Sheriff Chappy Dent* • MC Gainey *Bob Maslow* • Ron Perlman *Nalhober* ■ *Dir* Mark Illsley • *Scr* Ed Stone, Mark Illsley, Phil Reeves

The Happy Thieves ★
Comedy crime drama 1962 · US · BW · 89min

Richard Condon's first novel *The Oldest Confession* was an entertaining yarn which provided the basis for this unentertaining yawn. The cause lay in the fatigued direction by George Marshall and the full-of-holes script. Nor are matters helped by the uneasy pairing of Rex Harrison and Rita Hayworth as two art thieves attempting to steal a Goya from the Prado in Madrid. The robbery, like the film, fails to come off. **RB**

Rex Harrison *Jim Bourne* • Rita Hayworth *Eve Lewis* • Joseph Wiseman *Jean Marie Calbert* • Grégoire Aslan *Dr Munoz* • Alida Valli *Duchess Blanca* • Brita Ekman [Britt Ekland] *Mrs Pickett* ■ *Dir* George Marshall • *Scr* John Gay, from the novel *The Oldest Confession* by Richard Condon

The Happy Time ★★★
Period comedy 1952 · US · BW · 93min

The screen version of a hugely successful Broadway play, set in the 1920s, concerns itself with a French-Canadian family headed by Charles Boyer and Marsha Hunt. The central focus, though, is on the growing pains and awakening sexuality of their adolescent son, Bobby Driscoll. The theme is a well-worn one now, but this is still a gentle and loving evocation of family life and teenage anxieties, as viewed in a more innocent and subtle age than our own. **RK**

Charles Boyer *Jacques Bonnard* • Louis Jourdan *Uncle Desmonde* • Marsha Hunt *Susan Bonnard* • Kurt Kaszner *Uncle Louis* • Linda Christian *Mignonette Chappuis* • Bobby Driscoll *Bibi* ■ *Dir* Richard Fleischer • *Scr* Earl Felton, from the play by Sam A Taylor, from the novel by Robert Fontaine

Happy Times ★★★ PG
Comedy 2001 · Chi · Colour · 98min

Zhang Yimou directs this charming comedy of inner-city manners. Exploring the shift in morality and reduction in privacy that have attended economic reform, this tale centres on Zhao Benshan, a middle-aged huckster, whose attempts to impress his gold-digging fiancée result in him befriending her blind, teenage stepdaughter, Dong Jie. Often shooting with hidden cameras and deftly avoiding lapses of tone and taste, Zhang concentrates on the everyday lives of these marginalised characters, while also staging some droll set pieces. DP Mandarin +subtitles. **DVD**

Zhao Benshan *Old Zhao* • Dong Jie *Wu Ying, blind girl* • Dong Lihua *Chunky mama* • Fu Biao *Little Fu* • Leng Qibin *Little fatty* • Li Xuejian *Old Li* ■ *Dir* Zhang Yimou • *Scr* Gui Zi, from the story *Shifu Yue Lai Yue Youmo* by Mo Yan

Happy Together ★★★ 15
Romantic comedy 1989 · US · Colour · 98min

A shy young writer (Patrick Dempsey) and a brash, aspiring actress (Helen Slater), owing to a mix-up, end up as roommates in an all-male college dormitory. Both leads are fine, but they don't have much to work with in what is an entertaining if made-by-numbers comedy romance. Look for Brad Pitt in an early role. **JB** Swearing, brief nudity.

Patrick Dempsey *Christopher Wooden* • Helen Slater *Alexandra "Alex" Page* • Dan Schneider *Gooseflesh* • Kevin Hardesty *Slash* • Marius Weyers *Denny Dollenbacher* • Barbara Babcock *Ruth Carpenter* • Gloria Hayes *Luisa Dellacova* • Brad Pitt *Brian* • Aaron Harnick *Wally* • Ron Sterling *Trevor* ■ *Dir* Mel Damski • *Scr* Craig J Nevius

Happy Together ★★ 15
Romantic drama 1997 · HK · Colour and BW · 92min

Director Wong Kar-Wai's reputation rests on his genius for combining audacious imagery with human stories, but this adaptation is his least coherent or convincing film. The relationship between Leslie Cheung and Tony Leung, Hong Kong lovers on holiday in Argentina, is so destructive it's hard to empathise with either character when their conversations are so accusatory and their actions so self-interested. Christopher Doyle's photography is sumptuous, but Wong's direction is over-indulgent. DP Spanish, Cantonese, Mandarin +subtitles. Swearing, sex scenes, violence. **DVD**

Leslie Kwok-Wing Cheung [Leslie Cheung] *Ho Po-Wing* • Tony Chiu-Wai Leung [Tony Leung (2)] *Lai Yiu-Fai* • Chang Chen *Chang* ■ *Dir* Wong Kar-Wai • *Scr* Wong Kar-Wai, from the novel *The Buenos Aires Affair* by Manuel Puig

Happy We ★★★
Drama 1983 · Swe · Colour · 111min

This comedy drama about the reunion of three university pals closely preceded Swedish director Lasse Hallström's breakthrough hit *My Life as a Dog*. They recall old times, re-enact the sketches they had performed in college revues and catch up on the disappointments and broken dreams of adulthood. Coaxing pleasing performances from his cast, Hallström treads the fine line between pertinence and sentiment with some skill. DP Swedish +subtitles.

Brasse Brännström *Thomas Bengtsson* • Ivan Oljelund *Erik Bengtsson* • Magnus Härenstam *Klasse Wallin* • Pia Green *Anna Wallin* • Lars Amble *Fredrik Wahlgren* ■ *Dir* Lasse Hallström • *Scr* Brasse Brännström, Lasse Hallström, Magnus Härenstam

The Happy Years ★★★ U
Period comedy 1950 · US · Colour · 109min

Set at the dawn of the 20th century, this gently humorous exercise in nostalgia stars Dean Stockwell as a precocious and trouble-prone American schoolboy in the small town of Lawrenceville. Based on the then popular magazine stories, the movie centres on the japes and scrapes of Stockwell and his young friends and the despair he causes to the stalwart schoolmaster and his long-suffering parents. Hardly life as it's lived now, but a pleasant enough movie, nicely cast and well directed. **RK**

Dean Stockwell *John Humperdink Stover* • Darryl Hickman *Tough McCarthy* • Scotty Beckett *Tennessee Shad* • Leon Ames *Samuel H Stover Sr* • Margalo Gillmore *Mrs Stover* • Leo G Carroll *The old Roman* • Robert Wagner ■ *Dir* William A Wellman • *Scr* Harry Ruskin, from Owen Johnson's stories *The Lawrenceville School*

Hara-Kiri ★★★
Silent drama 1928 · Fr · BW · 87min

Although the history books tend to concentrate on the experiments of the impressionist and surrealist avant-garde, French commercial cinema in the late silent era was also capable of producing pictures of stunning visual beauty. This Oriental melodrama from director/star Marie-Louise Iribe is a case in point. However, the story of the wife who leaves her academic husband for a shogun's son was also rather daring, especially as she elects to die by her own hand to rejoin him in the afterlife, after he is killed trying to rescue a maiden from a ravine. **DP**

Marie-Louise Iribe *Nicole Daomi* • Constant Rémy *Professor Daomi Samura* • André Berley *Police inspector* • Liao Szi-Jen *Prince Fujiwara* • Labusquière *Ambassador* • Michaud *Guide* • Wuriu *Fujiwara's brother* • Toshi Komori *Marquis Awaji* ■ *Dir* Marie-Louise Iribe • *Scr* Pierre Lestringuez

Hara-Kiri: Death of a Samurai ★★★★ 18
Period drama 2011 · Jpn/UK · Colour · 127min

Now here's an oddity: a samurai film that features precious little swordplay. Instead, Takashi Miike's faithful remake, in subtle 3D, of the 1962 original foregoes slice-and-dice in favour of things more complex and thought-provoking. A classic tale of desperation, callousness and cruelty, *Hara-Kiri* is set during a peaceful period in 17th-century Japan, when masterless and impoverished samurai, or ronin, are reduced to asking wealthy lords for permission to perform ritual suicide in their courtyards, in the hope that they'll be given money just to go away. But one such ronin (Ebizo Ichikawa) falls foul of a callous noble, who unexpectedly grants him his wish. **DA** Japanese +subtitles. Violence. **DVD** 3D

Ebizo Ichikawa *Hanshiro Tsugumo* • Koji Yakusho *Kageyu* • Eita Motome • Hikari Mitsushima *Miho* • Naoto Takenaka *Tajiri* ■ *Dir* Takashi Miike • *Scr* Kikumi Yamagishi, from the story *Ibun ronin ki* by Yasuhiko Takiguchi

Harakiri ★★★★ 15
Period drama 1962 · Jpn · BW · 132min

Masaki Kobayashi's extraordinary samurai drama is far darker than anything Akira Kurosawa made, which explains why it is not as immediately accessible. Shot in black-and-white widescreen, this epic explores and challenges the militaristic cult of the samurai who, by 1630, have been reduced to beggars and are disembowelling themselves. Since the film's premiere at Cannes in 1963, a legend grew about its violence on account of a scene where a young samurai commits ritual suicide using a bamboo sword. An unblinking and majestic piece of film-making. **AT** In Japanese. **DVD** BR

Tatsuya Nakadai *Hanshiro Tsugumo* • Shima Iwashita *Miho Tsugumo* • Akira Ishihama *Motome Chijiiwa* • Yoshio Inaba *Jinai Chijiiwa* • Rentaro Mikuni *Kageyu Saito* ■ *Dir* Masaki Kobayashi • *Scr* Shinobu Hashimoto, from the novel by Yasuhiko Takiguchi • *Cinematographer* Yoshio Miyajima

Hard-Boiled ★★★★ 18
Action crime drama 1992 · HK · Colour · 122min

Although *A Better Tomorrow* and *The Killer* caught the eye of the film buffs, this was the first film that really launched Hong Kong maestro John Woo in the UK. The plot is formulaic: mismatched cops Chow Yun-Fat and Tony Leung join forces to track down a ruthless gunrunner. However, the sensuous flair Woo brings to the many stunning action sequences remains vibrantly fresh today, while the melodramatic playing and plotting brings an odd but touching humanity to the piece. **JF** Cantonese +subtitles. Violence, swearing. **DVD**

Chow Yun-Fat *Inspector Yuen ("Tequila")* • Tony Chiu-Wai Leung [Tony Leung (2)] *Tony* • Teresa Mo *Teresa* • Philip Chan *Superintendent Pang* • Anthony Wong (1) *Johnny Wong* • Bowie Lam

Yuen's partner • Kwan Hoi-Shan *Mr Hoi* ■ *Dir* John Woo • *Scr* Barry Wong, from a story by John Woo

Hard Candy ★★ 18

Psychological thriller
2005 · US · Colour · 99min

Director David Slade makes an edgy cat-and-mouse thriller out of highly unsavoury material in his feature debut. But despite staying on the acceptable side of the controversial subject matter – Internet paedophile grooming – his use of horror conventions smacks of exploitation that many may find too intense. Fashion photographer Patrick Wilson takes 14-year-old Ellen Page back to his house after chat-room sessions, only to be bound and tortured by her. AJ Violence. DVD

Patrick Wilson *Jeff Kohlver* • Ellen Page *Hayley Stark* • Sandra Oh *Judy Tokuda* • Jennifer Holmes *Janelle Rogers* • Gilbert John *Nighthawks clerk* ■ *Dir* David Slade • *Scr* Brian Nelson

Hard Contract ★★

Crime drama
1969 · US · Colour · 105min

A philosophically soft-centred morality play has stone-faced James Coburn playing a professional killer at large in Europe, on the trail of three people he has agreed to kill for mysterious client Burgess Meredith. Coburn also has sexual hang-ups about the women (Lilli Palmer, Lee Remick) he encounters. Writer/director S Lee Pogostin takes what could have been a James Bond-style thriller and throttles it with too much chat, despite the fine cast. TH

James Coburn *John Cunningham* • Lee Remick *Sheila Metcalfe* • Lilli Palmer *Adrianne* • Burgess Meredith *Ramsey Williams* • Patrick Magee *Alexi* • Sterling Hayden *Michael Carlson* • Claude Dauphin *Maurice* • Helen Cherry *Evelyn Carlson* • Karen Black *Ellen* ■ *Dir/Scr* S Lee Pogostin

The Hard Corps ★★ 15

Action thriller
2006 · US · Colour · 105min

Hardcore kickboxing star Jean-Claude Van Damme leads a hard corps of bodyguards in this lightweight action thriller. He's a traumatised Iraq vet who's hired as chief protection officer for boxing champ Wayne Barclay (Razaaq Adoti) when a war erupts between Barclay and an ex-con rap producer (Viv Leacock). Reuniting Van Damme with director Sheldon Lettich (*Double Impact*, *AWOL*), this tries hard to extend Van Damme's appeal to young urban audiences with a hip hop soundtrack and a gangsta villain. But a dire romantic subplot and the clunky Iraq flashbacks saddle his character with bags of overwrought shell-shocked trauma. JR DVD

Jean-Claude Van Damme *Phillip Sauvage* • Vivica A Fox *Tamara Barclay* • Razaaq Adoti *Wayne Barclay* • Peter Bryant *Kendall Mullins* • Mark Griffin *Casey Bledsoe* • Ron Selmour *Simcoe* ■ *Dir* Sheldon Lettich • *Scr* Sheldon Lettich, George Saunders

Hard Country ★★

Romantic drama
1981 · US · Colour · 101min

The title of this drama could refer to the difficulties in making it in country music or it could refer to the tough life of small-town Texas. In the end, the plot revolves around Jan-Michael Vincent, who labours away at a factory by day and shakes his thing down at the saloon by night. His girlfriend Kim Basinger (in her movie debut) has to choose between settling down with Vincent or following her friend and role model (real-life country star Tanya Tucker) to the bright lights of California and a recording career. Predictable, but still watchable. FL

Jan-Michael Vincent *Kyle Richardson* • Kim Basinger *Jodie Lynn Palmer* • Michael Parks *Royce Richardson* • Gailard Sartain *Johnny Bob* • Tanya Tucker *Caroline Peters* • Daryl Hannah *Loretta Palmer* ■ *Dir* David Greene • *Scr* Michael Kane, from a story by Michael Kane, Michael Martin Murphey

A Hard Day's Night ★★★★★ U

Musical comedy
1964 · UK · BW · 84min

At a time when Elvis and Cliff were still making old-style musicals, this progenitor of the modern music video smashed the mould. Satirising the endless round of banal inquisition, petty regulation and screaming adoration to which the Fab Four were subjected, this musical odyssey enabled them to mock authority and shirk duty without allowing such anti-establishment rebelliousness to detract from the working-class respectability of their "Mop Top" image. However, Richard Lester's film is not just a homage to Buster Keaton-style slapstick and Busby Berkeley spectacle; it's also a handbook of new wave film techniques, from Fellini and the *nouvelle vague* to Free Cinema and the Czech Film Miracle. DP DVD

John Lennon *John* • Paul McCartney *Paul* • George Harrison *George* • Ringo Starr *Ringo* • Wilfrid Brambell *Grandfather* • Norman Rossington *Norm* • John Junkin *Shake* • Victor Spinetti *TV director* • Anna Quayle *Millie* • Deryck Guyler *Police inspector* • Richard Vernon *Man on train* • Eddie Malin *Hotel waiter* • Robin Ray *TV floor manager* • Lionel Blair *TV choreographer* • Kenneth Haigh *Simon* ■ *Dir* Richard Lester • *Scr* Alun Owen • *Cinematographer* Gilbert Taylor

Hard Eight ★★★ 15

Crime drama
1996 · US · Colour · 97min

The feature debut from Paul Thomas Anderson, director of *Boogie Nights*, is a minimally plotted mood piece featuring a magnetic central performance from Philip Baker Hall. He plays the sweetly bumbling elderly professional gambler who takes dim-witted John C Reilly under his wing to teach him some of the tricks of the Las Vegas casino trade. All's well until Reilly falls for hooker Gwyneth Paltrow and she takes a client hostage. Despite the somewhat lethargic pace, this is a cool, sharply observed thriller that knows its own strengths and makes the most of them. AJ DVD

Philip Baker Hall *Sydney* • John C Reilly *John* • Gwyneth Paltrow *Clementine* • Samuel L Jackson *Jimmy* • F William Parker *Hostage* • Philip Seymour Hoffman *Young craps player* ■ *Dir/Scr* Paul Thomas Anderson

Hard Evidence ★★★ 15

Thriller based on a true story
1994 · US · Colour · 90min

Since the glossy inanities of *Charlie's Angels*, Kate Jackson has carved herself a nice little niche by appearing in worthy true-life TV dramas, and this is a typically competent number. Jackson plays a single mother who takes a job with the Georgia Labor Department, only to discover that the bureaucracy is riddled with corruption. Dean Stockwell scores as Jackson's villainous boss, but Jan Egleson's direction is a touch pedestrian. JF Violence. DVD

Kate Jackson *Sandra Clayton* • John Shea *Tommy Marchant* • Dean Stockwell *Sam Caldwell* • Terry O'Quinn *Harris Wiley* • Beth Broderick *Melissa Brewer* ■ *Dir* Jan Egleson • *Scr* Richard Rashke, from his articles in the *Georgia Gazette*

Hard, Fast and Beautiful ★★ U

Drama
1951 · US · BW · 78min

This was an early Ida Lupino venture as a director for her own independent production company. Claire Trevor gives a spot-on portrayal of a frustrated woman who pins all her hopes of worldly success on the tennis-playing skills of her daughter. Sally Forrest is competent enough as the youngster propelled into becoming a champion, but the film is a little too relentless in its dramatic agenda. AE

Claire Trevor *Milly Farley* • Sally Forrest *Florence Farley* • Carleton Young *Fletcher Locke* • Robert Clarke *Gordon McKay* ■ *Dir* Ida Lupino • *Scr* Martha Wilkerson, from a novel by John R Tunis

Hard Ground ★★

Western adventure
2003 · US · Colour · 93min

A jailed bounty-hunter (Burt Reynolds) teams up with a feisty orphan (Amy Jo Johnson) and sets out to track down the ruthless leader of a gang that murdered Johnson's family. Accompanying them on the trail is Reynolds's son (Seth Peterson), who is deputy to Bruce Dern, the uncompromising sheriff who imprisoned Reynolds after he killed in self-defence. There's an explosive opening and an inevitable sharpshooting showdown, but the personal feuds don't always atone for the dull patches en route to Mexico. DP

Burt Reynolds *John McKay* • Bruce Dern *Nate Hutchinson* • Amy Jo Johnson *Elizabeth* • Seth Peterson *Joshua* • David Figlioli *Billy Bucklin* • Martin Kove *Floyd* ■ *Dir* Frank Q Dobbs • *Scr* Frank Q Dobbs, David S Cass Sr

Hard Knocks ★★★

Drama
1980 · Aus · Colour · 90min

Tracy Mann won an Australian Film Institute award as best actress for her superb performance in this affecting drama, which focuses on her attempts to leave her criminal past behind and start over again. Her subtle performance is well backed up by familiar Australian character actors Bill Hunter, Max Cullen and Tony Barry, while the believable script from director Don McLennan and Hilton Bonner (who has a supporting role) was also nominated for an award. JF

Tracy Mann *Sam* • Bill Hunter *Brady* • Max Cullen *Newman* • Tony Barry *Barry* ■ *Dir* Don McLennan • *Scr* Don McLennan, Hilton Bonner

Hard Luck ★★ 18

Crime thriller
2006 · US · Colour · 97min

Wesley Snipes is Lucky, a former con who loses his wife during Hurricane Katrina and goes on the run from corrupt cops with two briefcases of stolen cash. Uncertain whether it wants to be a gangsta movie, torture porn horror or offbeat comedy, this schizophrenic slice of straight-to-DVD exploitation from Mario Van Peebles tries in vain to wring cult potential out of the strangeness of it all. Co-star Cybill Shepherd must be down on her luck to be involved. JR Violence, swearing, sex scenes. DVD

Wesley Snipes *Lucky* • Cybill Shepherd *Cass* • Jacquelyn Quinones *Angela* • James Liao *Chang* • Aubrey Dollar *Rainn* • Kevin Thoms *Roland* • Noah Fleiss *Sol Rosenbaum* • Luis Guzmán [Luis Guzman] *Million Dollar Mendez* ■ *Dir* Mario Van Peebles • *Scr* Mario Van Peebles, Larry Brand, from a story by Brand

Hard Men ★★★ 18

Crime drama
1996 · UK/Fr · Colour and sepia · 83min

This oddly compelling and amusing journey through the greasy spoon cafés and sleazy brothels of Soho is trashy pulp fiction, boldly executed by first-time writer/director JK Amalou. It follows the fortunes of three violent gangsters who run a London numbers racket for Kray-inspired mobster Pops (played by real-life ex-con "Mad" Frankie Fraser). AJ Violence, swearing, drug abuse, nudity. DVD

Vincent Regan *Tone* • Ross Boatman *Bear* • Lee Ross *Speed* • "Mad" Frankie Fraser *Pops Den* • Ken Campbell *Mr Ross* • Mirella D'Angelo *Chantal* • Irene Ng *Suki* • Robyn Lewis *Leila* ■ *Dir/Scr* JK Amalou

Hard Promises ★★ PG

Romantic comedy
1991 · US · Colour · 91min

This forgettable comedy is made slightly less so by an experienced cast. William Petersen is Sissy Spacek's ex-husband, who is invited to her upcoming wedding and is determined to disrupt the ceremony. Petersen overpowers the rest of the cast with his relentless sliminess, which leaves you to wonder why Spacek's character married him in the first place. Populated with clichés instead of supporting characters. JB

Sissy Spacek *Chris Coalter* • William L Petersen *Joey Coalter* • Brian Kerwin *Walter Humphrey* • Mare Winningham *Dawn* • Jeff Perry *Pinky* • Olivia Burnette *Beth Coalter* • Peter MacNicol *Stuart Coalter* • Rip Torn ■ *Dir* Martin Davidson • *Scr* Jule Selbo

Hard Rain ★★★ 15

Action thriller
1997 · US/UK/Jpn/Ger/Den · Colour · 92min

Christian Slater and Minnie Driver battle the elements in this slim, waterlogged but fast-paced adventure that throws bad guys together with the forces of nature after a flood envelops a small town on the same night a daring robbery takes place. Utterly preposterous in places, this nonetheless zips along merrily and offers some impressively tongue-in-cheek performances from Morgan Freeman and Randy Quaid. JB Violence, swearing. DVD BD

Morgan Freeman *Jim* • Christian Slater *Tom* • Randy Quaid *Sheriff* • Minnie Driver *Karen* • Edward Asner *Charlie* • Richard Dysart *Henry* • Betty White *Doreen* • Michael Goorjian *Kenny* ■ *Dir* Mikael Salomon • *Scr* Graham Yost

The Hard Ride ★

Action drama
1971 · US · Colour · 92min

In a dismal *Easy Rider* rip-off, Robert Fuller is the Vietnam veteran bringing his buddy's dead body home and finding that he has inherited a motorcycle. Fuller doesn't really know one end of a bike from another but, hey man, he's soon riding the highway and getting to know native Americans, while the soundtrack offers endless songs about peace and love. AT

Robert Fuller *Phil* • Sherry Bain *Sheryl* • Tony Russel *Big Red* • William Bonner *Grady* • Marshall Reed *Father Tom* • Mikel Angel *Ralls* ■ *Dir/Scr* Burt Topper

Hard Target ★★★ 18

Action thriller
1993 · US · Colour · 91min

Cult Hong Kong director John Woo's Hollywood debut was regarded as a major disappointment by his die-hard fans, but it's a lot better than most US action fodder. It was also easily Jean-Claude Van Damme's best movie thus far. Armed with a very dodgy haircut, Van Damme plays an unemployed sailor who spoils the human hunting games of some wealthy millionaires when he fights back. The plotting is minimal, but Woo orchestrates some stunning action set pieces and a spectacular finale. JF Swearing, violence. DVD BD

Jean-Claude Van Damme *Chance Boudreaux* • Lance Henriksen *Emil Fouchon* • Yancy Butler *Natasha "Nat" Binder* • Wilford Brimley *Uncle Douvee* • Kasi Lemmons *Carmine Mitchell* • Arnold Vosloo *Pik Van Cleaf* • Bob Apisa *Mr Lopacki* • Chuck Pfarrer *Douglas Binder* ■ *Dir* John Woo • *Scr* Chuck Pfarrer

Hard Time ★★ 12

Crime drama
1998 · US · Colour · 87min

In this TV movie, Burt Reynolds (also directing) plays an unstable cop who is framed for murder when a police drugs bust goes wrong. The strong supporting cast includes old sparring partner Charles Durning, but while the handling of Reynolds the director is assured, his action-man lead performance is less convincing. Two sequels followed. JF DVD

Burt Reynolds *Logan McQueen* • Charles Durning *Duffy* • Robert Loggia *Martin* • Billy Dee Williams *Barker* • Mia Sara *Susan Myler* • Michael Buie *Higgs* ■ *Dir* Burt Reynolds • *Scr* David S Cass Sr, Steve Wesley

Hard Times ★★★★ 15

Period action drama
1975 · US · Colour · 89min

This marvellously evocative tough-as-nails Depression era drama has a sanguine James Coburn managing unsmiling brute Charles Bronson, who's well cast as a bare-knuckle fighter. Debut director Walter Hill takes an elliptical route in telling his story, which means that the overall impact is dissipated quite early on. Nevertheless, there's much to admire, particularly the combination of cinematographer Phil Lathrop's Panavision photography and editor Roger Spottiswoode's handling of the fight sequences. TS _DVD_

Charles Bronson _Chaney_ • James Coburn _Spencer "Speed" Weed_ • Jill Ireland _Lucy Simpson_ • Strother Martin _Poe_ • Maggie Blye _Gayleen Schoonover_ • Michael McGuire _Gandil_ • Robert Tessier _Jim Henry_ ■ _Dir_ Walter Hill • _Scr_ Walter Hill, Bryan Gindorff, Bruce Henstell

Hard to Be a God ★★★★ 18
Science-fiction drama 2013 · Rus · BW · 177min

For all its visual accomplishments Alexei German's final feature makes for gruelling viewing, as parallels are drawn between the Dark Ages and a century of Russian history. The impenetrable story concerns a scientist mistaken for a deity while observing the planet "Arkanar", which is in the throes of a civil war between the subversive Blacks and the authoritarian Greys (Stalin references abound). Rarely has a film focused so relentlessly on mud and bodily excretions. Exhausting, exhilarating and excessively enigmatic, this is an instant cult classic. DP In Russian +subtitles. _DVD_

Leonid Yarmolnik _Don Rumata_ • Yury Tsurilo _Baron Pampa_ ■ _Dir_ Aleksei German [Alexei German] • _Scr_ Aleksei German [Alexei German], Svetlana Karmalita, from the novel _Trudno byt bogom_ by Arkady & Boris Strugatsky

Hard to Get ★★★ U
Screwball comedy 1938 · US · BW · 78min

Yes, this is the _You Must Have Been a Beautiful Baby_ movie, with crooner Dick Powell serenading the young and lovely Olivia de Havilland in a wacky screwball comedy from Warner Bros. She's rich, he's poor, and they're supported by a great cast of hand-picked eccentrics. Penny Singleton is charming as a kooky maid, and Charles Winninger, as Olivia's rich dad, is hysterically funny. Skilled and underrated director Ray Enright keeps up the necessary pace. TS

Dick Powell _Bill Davis_ • Olivia de Havilland _Margaret Richards_ • Charles Winninger _Big Ben Richards_ • Allen Jenkins _Roscoe_ • Bonita Granville _Connie Richards_ • Penny Singleton _Hattie_ • Grady Sutton _Stanley Potter_ ■ _Dir_ Ray Enright • _Scr_ Jerry Wald, Maurice Lee, Richard Macauley, from a screen story by Wally Klein, Joseph Schrank, from the story _Classified_ by Stephen Morehouse Avery

Hard to Handle ★★★
Comedy 1933 · US · BW · 82min

The original title _A Bad Boy_ was dropped by Warner Bros, who feared audiences would expect a gangster movie. But, in this pacey Depression-era drama, James Cagney still fires on all cylinders as an entrepreneur and wittily refers back to his 1931 role in _The Public Enemy_ by promoting grapefruit rather than squashing one into the face of his girlfriend (Mary Brian). Director Mervyn LeRoy orchestrates some fine period trappings, including the sort of dance marathon later featured in _They Shoot Horses, Don't They?_. AT

James Cagney _Lefty Merrill_ • Mary Brian _Ruth Waters_ • Ruth Donnelly _Lil Waters_ • Allen Jenkins _Radio announcer_ • Claire Dodd _Marlene Reeves_ • Gavin Gordon _John Hayden_ ■ _Dir_ Mervyn LeRoy • _Scr_ Wilson Mizner, Robert Lord, from a story by Houston Branch

Hard to Kill ★★★ 18
Action thriller 1989 · US · Colour · 91min

This was the movie that set action superstar Steven Seagal on his monosyllabic road to riches. He plays a cop who is grievously wounded when a gang invades his marital bedroom and sprays it with gunfire. Seagal survives, though his wife isn't so lucky. It takes seven years to recover from the ordeal, but he emerges stronger than ever and, after the usual period of fearsome solo martial arts training, wreaks a terrible revenge on his attackers. JF _DVD_

Steven Seagal _Mason Storm_ • Kelly LeBrock _Andy Stewart_ • Bill Sadler [William Sadler] _Vernon Trent_ • Frederick Coffin _Kevin O'Malley_ • Bonnie Burroughs _Felicia Storm_ • Andrew Bloch _Captain Dan Hulland_ • Zachary Rosencrantz

Sonny Storm • Dean Norris _Detective Sergeant Goodhart_ ■ _Dir_ Bruce Malmuth • _Scr_ Steven McKay, Steven Pressfield, Ronald Shusett

The Hard Way ★★★
Melodrama 1942 · US · BW · 109min

This was Ida Lupino's chance to carry a Warner Bros melodrama, and she does the job splendidly as the tough dame from the industrial slums who ruthlessly propels talented younger sister Joan Leslie to showbiz stardom. Incisively written by Daniel Fuchs and Peter Viertel, it is visually powerful thanks to ace cameraman James Wong Howe's strong influence on director Vincent Sherman. AE

Ida Lupino _Helen Chernen_ • Joan Leslie _Katherine Chernen_ • Dennis Morgan _Paul Collins_ • Jack Carson _Albert Runkel_ • Gladys George _Lily Emery_ • Faye Emerson _Waitress_ • Paul Cavanagh _John Shagrue_ ■ _Dir_ Vincent Sherman • _Scr_ Daniel Fuchs, Peter Viertel, from a story by Jerry Wald

The Hard Way ★★★★ 15
Action comedy 1991 · US · Colour · 106min

Michael J Fox and James Woods have a wonderful time sending up their established screen personae in this cheerful comedy thriller. Fox is the pampered film star who wants to ditch his lightweight image with a grittier new role as a hard-nosed detective, and who better to teach him the ropes than real-life hard-nosed detective Woods? The two reluctant partners then get caught up in the hunt for a serial killer (an over-the-top Stephen Lang). Action specialist John Badham piles on the mayhem with explosive set pieces, but the real joy comes from the two stars, as Woods is nearly driven mad by Fox's determination to live his life. JF Swearing, violence. _DVD_

Michael J Fox _Nick Lang_ • James Woods _John Moss_ • Stephen Lang _"Party Crasher"_ • Annabella Sciorra _Susan_ • Delroy Lindo _Captain Brix_ • Luis Guzman _Pooley_ • Mary Mara _China_ • LL Cool J _Billy_ • John Capodice _Grainy_ • Christina Ricci _Bonnie_ • Penny Marshall _Angie_ ■ _Dir_ John Badham • _Scr_ Danie Pyne, Lem Dobbs, from a story by Lem Dobbs, Michael Kozoll

The Hard Word ★★★ 18
Crime comedy drama 2002 · Aus/UK · Colour · 99min

Aussie writer/director Scott Roberts's gritty debut feature is a hot-blooded crime drama that practically oozes sleazy chic. Visually stark and unsentimental, it has a brooding, muscular intensity, off-set by the darkest black comedy. Pony-tailed Guy Pearce is the leader of a trio of bank-robbing brothers who are released early from an Australian prison so they can pull off a multi-million dollar heist for their corrupt lawyer. The events that follow are scarcely original, but they're executed with precision, wit and force. SF _DVD_

Guy Pearce _Dale Twentyman_ • Rachel Griffiths _Carol Twentyman_ • Robert Taylor (4) _Frank Malone_ • Joel Edgerton _Shane Twentyman_ • Damien Richardson _Mal Twentyman_ • Rhondda Findleton _Jane Moore_ • Kate Atkinson _Pamela_ • Vince Colosimo _Det Mick Kelly_ ■ _Dir/Scr_ Scott Roberts

Hardball ★★★ 12
Sports drama 2001 · US/Ger · Colour · 101min

Keanu Reeves is a drifter who agrees to coach a Little League team of boys from a tough housing project in Chicago. In an atmosphere where guns speak louder than words, and war paint is real blood, the kids learn that what matters in life is turning up, even if you don't win. The coach is taught his own lessons of redemption, to live up to the principles of teacher Diane Lane. Despite his charm, Keanu Reeves hasn't the authority to carry it through, and his performance only underlines the clichés. TH Violence, swearing. _DVD_

Keanu Reeves _Conor O'Neill_ • Diane Lane _Elizabeth Wilkes_ • John Hawkes _Ticky Tobin_ • DB Sweeney _Matt Hyland_ • Mike McGlone _Jimmy Fleming_ • Sterling Brim _Sterling_ • Michael Jordan _Jamal_ ■ _Dir_ Brian Robbins • _Scr_ John Gatins, from the book _Hardball: a Season in the Projects_ by Daniel Coyle

Hardcore ★ 18
Sex comedy 1977 · UK · Colour · 79min

Fiona Richmond, once Britain's number one sex symbol, plays a woman called Fiona in this bizarre sex comedy. Wrapped around the flimsiest of plots (a woman arrives at a friend's villa to find someone taking away the furniture) is a catalogue of sexual adventures, which must have included every fumbling cliché writer/director James Kenelm Clarke had ever come across. DM Swearing, sex scenes, nudity.

Fiona Richmond _Fiona_ • Anthony Steel _Robert_ • Victor Spinetti _Duncan_ • Ronald Fraser _Marty_ • Graham Stark _Inspector Flaubert_ • Graham Crowden _Lord Yardarm_ ■ _Dir_ James Kenelm Clarke • _Scr_ James Kenelm Clarke, Michael Robson

Hardcore ★★★ 18
Drama 1979 · US · Colour · 103min

George C Scott stars as a Michigan Calvinist searching for his errant daughter who has become a porn actress in Los Angeles. Scott's search leads him through a warren of massage parlours, nude encounters and snuff movies, but he maintains a chilly aloofness, nursing his bigotry and heading towards that inevitable explosion of violence. Written and directed by Michigan Calvinist Paul Schrader, this flawed but generally impressive transposition of _The Searchers_ inhabits the same sleazy yet redemptive world as Schrader's script for _Taxi Driver_. AT

George C Scott _Jake Van Dorn_ • Peter Boyle _Andy Mast_ • Season Hubley _Niki_ • Dick Sargent _Wes DeJong_ • Leonard Gaines _Ramada_ ■ _Dir/Scr_ Paul Schrader

Hardcore Henry ★ 18
Science-fiction action adventure 2015 · Rus/US · Colour · 96min

Plenty of video games have been successfully transferred to cinema, but this may be the first film to want to look like a video game. Its makers (including _Wanted_ director Timur Bekmambetov, serving as producer here) shouldn't have bothered. As seen entirely through the eyes of its lead character, debuting director Ilya Naishuller (who cut his teeth on music videos) seeks to offer that immersive "first-person-shooter" thrill. But the gaming experience simply doesn't translate to the screen. DA In English, Russian. Strong violence

Sharlto Copley _Jimmy_ • Haley Bennett _Estelle_ • Danila Kozlovsky _Akan_ • Tim Roth _Henry's father_ ■ _Dir/Scr_ Ilya Naishuller

The Harder They Come ★★★ 15
Crime drama 1972 · Jam · Colour · 102min

Jamaica's first indigenous feature became something of a cult hit and made a huge star of Jimmy Cliff, whose own experiences, to a degree, inform the plot. After a hard-hitting opening, in which keenly observed documentary detail captures both the exotic and ugly sides of Kingston, this reggae reworking of the old rags-to-riches story disappointingly descends into banal blaxploitation. The struggle to make it in the music business is convincingly depicted, but director Perry Henzell loses his way when Cliff resorts to cop killing to boost his record sales. Whatever the film's shortcomings, though, the music is superb. DP +subtitles. _DVD_

Jimmy Cliff _Ivanhoe "Ivan" Martin_ • Carl Bradshaw _José_ • Basil Keane _Preacher_ • Janet Bartley _Elsa_ • Winston Stona _Police detective_ • Bobby Charlton _Record company manager_ • Ras Daniel Hartman _Pedro_ ■ _Dir_ Perry Henzell • _Scr_ Perry Henzell, Trevor Rhone [Trevor D Rhone]

The Harder They Fall ★★★ 12
Sports drama 1956 · US · BW · 104min

This riveting exposé of corruption in professional boxing is given added poignancy by the fact that the star is Humphrey Bogart in his last role, aged, mellowed and dying. He gives a terrific performance as the washed-up sports columnist forced to work for boxing

promoter Rod Steiger, and what a joy it is to revel in their contrasting acting styles: Bogie so casual and effortless, Steiger so Method and explosive. Director Mark Robson attempts rugged realism, but this is full-blooded melodrama. TS _DVD_

Humphrey Bogart _Eddie Willis_ • Rod Steiger _Nick Benko_ • Jan Sterling _Beth Willis_ • Mike Lane _Toro Moreno_ • Max Baer _Buddy Brannen_ • Jersey Joe Walcott _George_ • Edward Andrews _Jim Weyerhause_ • Harold J Stone _Art Leavitt_ • Carlos Montalban _Luis Agrandi_ ■ _Dir_ Mark Robson • _Scr_ Philip Yordan, from the novel by Budd Schulberg

Hardware ★★★★ 18
Science-fiction horror 1990 · UK · Colour · 90min

Sex, drugs and rock 'n' roll are the components greasing the splatter-punk engine of director Richard Stanley's impressive debut. Twenty-first century soldier of fortune Dylan McDermott gives his estranged sculptress girlfriend Stacey Travis a junked robot so she can weld the spare parts into surreal artwork. Neither know that the cyborg is really a scrapped prototype developed for future military warfare to kill without mercy – until it reconstructs itself and goes on the bloody rampage. A purposely trashy shock to the system, this is meant to disturb, and does so. AJ _DVD_ _Blu-ray_

Dylan McDermott _Mo_ • Stacey Travis _Jill_ • John Lynch _Shades_ • William Hootkins _Lincoln_ • Iggy Pop _Angry Bob_ • Mark Northover _Alvy_ ■ _Dir_ Richard Stanley • _Scr_ Richard Stanley, Mike Fallon, from the story _Shok!_ from the comic book _Fleetway Comics 2000 AD_ by Steve McManus, Kevin O'Neill

The Hardys Ride High ★★ U
Comedy 1939 · US · BW · 80min

The sixth in the long saga of the Hardy family. This time Mickey Rooney, Lewis Stone and company come into a $2 million inheritance and move to Detroit. The moral is that money and luxuries are no substitute for the small-town values and everyday joys of the Hardys' home town of Carvel. Rooney, now 16, starts smoking and falls for a gold-digging chorus girl. Problem is, Rooney was actually 19 at the time, but looked about nine. AT

Mickey Rooney _Andy Hardy_ • Lewis Stone _Judge James K Hardy_ • Cecilia Parker _Marian Hardy_ • Fay Holden _Mrs Emily Hardy_ • Ann Rutherford _Polly Benedict_ ■ _Dir_ George B Seitz • _Scr_ Kay Van Riper, Agnes C Johnson, William Ludwig, from characters by Aurania Rouverol

Harlan County, USA ★★★
Documentary 1976 · US · Colour · 103min

Barbara Kopple's Oscar-winning documentary, which was years in the making, is a powerful and compelling record of the strike called at the Brookside colliery in Kentucky after management refused to recognise the workers' union status. It's a shrewdly compiled piece, but in spite of the expert manipulation, what emerges is a portrait of a community bursting with initiative, intelligence, camaraderie and a real sense of justice and self-worth. Exploring every aspect of Harlan life, Kopple gives particular attention to the miners' wives as they stand by their husbands on the picket line. DP

■ _Dir/Scr_ Barbara Kopple

Harlem Nights ★★ 18
Period crime comedy 1989 · US · Colour · 110min

Eddie Murphy's directing debut and star vehicle hits engine trouble early on and conks out completely long before the home straight. The plan was to make a latter-day version of a 1930s gangster movie; the result has some nifty costumes, luscious sets and neat music, but, on almost every other count, it's a mess. PF Swearing, violence. _DVD_

Eddie Murphy _Quick_ • Richard Pryor _Sugar Ray_ • Danny Aiello _Sergeant Phil Cantone_ • Michael Lerner _Bugsy Calhoune_ • Della Reese _Vera_ • Redd Foxx _Bennie Wilson_ • Berlinda Tolbert _Annie_ • Stan Shaw _Jack Jenkins_ • Jasmine Guy _Dominique La Rue_ • Arsenio Hall _Crying man_ ■

H

Dir/Scr Eddie Murphy • *Cinematographer* Woody Omens • *Production Designer* Lawrence G Paull • *Costume Designer* Joe I Tompkins

Harlequin ★★ 15

Drama   1980 · Aus · Colour · 91min

Director Simon Wincer's second feature is an odd attempt to update the story of Rasputin to 1980s Australia. Robert Powell plays a charismatic healer who convinces senator David Hemmings and his wife that he can cure their son's leukaemia. This is typical of the kind of curio that Hemmings opted for as his once-glittering career went into a steep decline, and Wincer piles on the mystery without really developing the story. JF *DVD*

Robert Powell *Gregory Wolfe* • David Hemmings *Senator Nick Rast* • Carmen Duncan *Sandra Rast* • Broderick Crawford *Doc Wheelan* • Gus Mercurio *Mr Bergier* • Alan Cassell *Mr Porter* • Mark Spain *Alex Rast* ■ *Dir* Simon Wincer • *Scr* Everett De Roche

Harley Davidson and the Marlboro Man ★ 15

Action adventure   1991 · US · Colour · 94min

This is a blatant, dispiriting plug for leather and lung cancer, with Mickey Rourke and Don Johnson as bikers who in 1996 (for some reason this is a futuristic thing) are mistaken for drug runners instead of the slimeballs they really are. Lacking the energy and exploitation thrills of the 1960s biker movies it tries to emulate, this is more like a retread of those dreadful *Cannonball Run* movies. AT *DVD*

Mickey Rourke *Harley Davidson* • Don Johnson *Marlboro* • Chelsea Field *Virginia Slim* • Daniel Baldwin *Alexander* • Giancarlo Esposito *Jimmy Jiles* • Vanessa Williams [Vanessa L Williams] *Lulu Daniels* • Robert Ginty *Thom* • Tia Carrere *Kimiko* ■ *Dir* Simon Wincer • *Scr* Don Michael Paul

Harlow ★★

Biographical drama   1965 · US · Colour · 124min

This not altogether believable biopic of the platinum blonde bombshell views Jean Harlow as an unhappy innocent trying to become a star in 1930s Hollywood while dodging the ever-present casting couch. The film did well at the box office, and Carroll Baker, Red Buttons (as Harlow's agent) and Angela Lansbury (as Harlow's mother) rise above the limitations of the script. JG

Carroll Baker *Jean Harlow* • Martin Balsam *Everett Redman* • Red Buttons *Arthur Landau* • Mike Connors *Jack Harrison* • Angela Lansbury *Mama Jean Bello* • Peter Lawford *Paul Bern* • Leslie Nielsen *Richard Manley* ■ *Dir* Gordon Douglas • *Scr* John Michael Hayes, from the non-fiction book *An Intimate Biography* by Irving Shulman, Arthur Landau

The Harness ★★★★

Romantic drama   1971 · US · Colour · 120min

This excellent version of a heart-warming John Steinbeck story offers a leading role to underrated Lorne Greene, the Canadian actor best known as Ben Cartwright in *Bonanza*. Here he plays a farmer whose life is dominated by his sick wife until the arrival of two newcomers at his ranch. The rich photography is from one of the all-time Hollywood camera maestros, Russell Metty, and this is a TV movie of distinction from Universal, who pioneered films specifically made for the small screen. TS

Lorne Greene *Peter Randall* • Julie Sommars *Jennifer Shagaras* • Murray Hamilton *Roy Kern* • Lee H Montgomery [Lee Montgomery] *Tor Shagaras* • Louise Latham *Emma Randall* • Henry Beckman *Doc Marn* • Joan Tompkins *Millie Chappel* ■ *Dir* Boris Sagal • *Scr* Leon Tokatyan, Edward Hume, from the short story by John Steinbeck

Harold & Kumar Get the Munchies ★★★ 15

Comedy   2004 · US/Can · Colour · 84min

If the phrase "from the director of *Dude, Where's My Car?*" sends shivers down your spine, then you may be surprised by this likeable comedy from Danny Leiner. Affable young stoners John Cho and Kal Penn hit the road in search of White Castle burgers to satisfy their post-pot hunger pains. What follows is an exuberant, offbeat road movie that is a minor delight, thanks to its surprising warmth and some inspired comic riffs. IF Swearing, nudity, drug abuse. *DVD*

John Cho *Harold Lee* • Kal Penn *Kumar Patel* • Paula Garcés *Maria* • Neil Patrick Harris • David Krumholtz *Goldstein* • Eddie Kaye Thomas *Rosenberg* • Christopher Meloni *Freakshow* ■ *Dir* Danny Leiner • *Scr* Hayden Schlossberg, Jon Hurwitz

Harold & Kumar Escape from Guantanamo Bay ★★ 18

Comedy adventure   2008 · US · Colour · 96min

In this harebrained sequel to *Harold & Kumar Get the Munchies*, the dope-smoking dopes (John Cho and Kal Penn) roll up and thumb their noses at America's post-9/11 insecurities. Arrested on a flight to Amsterdam after their bong is mistaken for a terrorist bomb, the bumbling heroes are shipped off to Guantanamo Bay by an over-zealous Homeland Security chief (Rob Corddry). What follows is an irredeemably puerile procession of X-rated gags, yet the script's surprisingly barbed take on America's culture of suspicion occasionally hits the mark. JR Nudity, drug abuse, sexual references. *DVD*

John Cho *Harold* • Kal Penn *Kumar* • Rob Corddry *Ron Fox* • Jack Conley *Deputy Frye* • Roger Bart *Dr Beecher* • Neil Patrick Harris • Danneel Harris *Vanessa* ■ *Dir* Jon Hurwitz, Hayden Schlossberg • *Scr* Jon Hurwitz, Hayden Schlossberg, from characters by Hurwitz, Schlossberg

Harold and Maude ★★★★ 15

Black comedy drama   1972 · US · Colour · 87min

Rarely has such a strange love affair been presented so charmingly as the one here between morbid young Harold (Bud Cort) and 79-year-old concentration camp survivor Maude (Ruth Gordon). Depressed by life, and rejected by his wealthy mother Vivian Pickles, the death-fascinated Harold drives a hearse to funerals, meets the skittish Maude and falls in love. A cult classic, the film started life as a graduate thesis by Colin Higgins, whose landlady helped him to set it up for direction by Hal Ashby. The performances are a delightful bonus in a movie that, for all its eccentricities, likes people. TH *DVD*

Ruth Gordon *Maude* • Bud Cort *Harold* • Vivian Pickles *Mrs Chasen* • Cyril Cusack *Glaucus* • Charles Tyner *Uncle Victor* • Ellen Geer *Sunshine Dore* • Eric Christmas *Priest* • G Wood *Psychiatrist* ■ *Dir* Hal Ashby • *Scr* Colin Higgins • *Music* Cat Stevens

Harper ★★★★ 12

Detective thriller   1966 · US · Colour · 115min

Also known as *The Moving Target*, this features an early script by screenwriting guru William Goldman. Paul Newman is a Chandleresque private eye in the missing persons business, and Lauren Bacall the wealthy client who hires him to find her spouse. We know the territory: a detective, with only honour to sustain him, up against the idle rich with time on their hands and murder on their minds. Goldman's pungent script, Jack Smight's pacey direction and Newman's confident portrayal make this a classy thriller. A sequel, *The Drowning Pool*, followed nine years later. TH

Paul Newman *Lew Harper* • Lauren Bacall *Mrs Sampson* • Julie Harris (2) *Betty Fraley* • Arthur Hill *Albert Graves* • Janet Leigh *Susan Harper* • Pamela Tiffin *Miranda Sampson* • Robert Wagner *Alan Taggert* • Robert Webber *Dwight Troy* • Shelley Winters *Fay Estabrook* ■ *Dir* Jack Smight • *Scr* William Goldman, from the novel by Ross MacDonald

Harper Valley PTA ★★★

Comedy   1978 · US · Colour · 101min

Ode to Billy Joe demonstrated the potential for pop ballads to inspire movies and this spicy comedy, based on Jeannie C Riley's song about small-town hypocrisy, continued the trend. Barbara Eden takes the lead as a sexy widow whose lifestyle offends the uptight members of the local Parent-Teachers Association, but turns the tables on them by exposing their own foibles. A moderate hit theatrically, this was turned into a TV series with Eden re-creating her sassy role. DF

Barbara Eden *Stella Johnson* • Ronny Cox *Willis Newton* • Nanette Fabray *Alice Finely* • Susan Swift *Dee Johnson* • Louis Nye *Kirby Baker* • Pat Paulsen *Otis Harper Jr* ■ *Dir* Richard C Bennett • *Scr* George Edwards, Barry Schneider, from the song by Tom T Hall

The Harrad Experiment ★★ 15

Drama   1973 · US · Colour · 91min

James Whitmore and Tippi Hedren are a learned married couple who run Harrad College, a bastion of libertarian values where young people are obliged to live with each other and work out their sexual hang-ups. Doubtless Hollywood felt it was being terribly grown-up to tackle such a story, but it's relentlessly tedious and hardly likely to raise anything more than a smile, despite some rather coy nudity and dirty dialogue. AT *DVD*

James Whitmore *Philip Tenhausen* • Tippi Hedren *Margaret Tenhausen* • Don Johnson *Stanley* • B Kirby Jr [Bruno Kirby] *Harry* • Laurie Walters *Sheila* • Melanie Griffith ■ *Dir* Ted Post • *Scr* Michael Werner, Ted Cassedy, from the novel by Robert H Rimmer

The Harrad Summer ★ 15

Drama   1974 · US · Colour · 100min

Too much experience is less than a good thing, as this indifferent sequel to *The Harrad Experiment* about students at a sex-education college demonstrates. When the students return to their communities, they take their extra-curricular "homework" with them. Leads Robert Reiser and Laurie Walters don't take any acting honours with this, while director Steven Hilliard Stern's name is more distinguished than his talents. TH

Robert Reiser *Stanley Kolasukas* • Laurie Walters *Sheila Grove* • Richard Doran *Harry Schacht* • Victoria Thompson *Beth Hillyer* • Emmaline Henry *Margaret Tonhausen* • Bill Dana *Jack Schacht* ■ *Dir* Steven Hilliard Stern • *Scr* Morth Thaw, Steve Zacharias

Harriet Craig ★★★

Psychological drama   1950 · US · BW · 94min

This is a rip-roaring vehicle for Joan Crawford, who ably demonstrates on screen all those "qualities" so vividly documented in *Mommie Dearest*. Crawford, as ever, tends to chew the scenery to achieve effect, in contrast to the superb Rosalind Russell in the earlier talkie version of the play on which this was based. Nevertheless, the star breathes life into this hoary old chestnut about a woman more taken by her possessions than by her family, and makes the whole dated premise a mesmerising experience. TS

Joan Crawford *Harriet Craig* • Wendell Corey *Walter Craig* • Lucile Watson *Celia Fenwick* • Allyn Joslyn *Billy Birkmire* • William Bishop *Wes Miller* • KT Stevens *Clare Raymond* • Raymond Greenleaf *Henry Fenwick* • Ellen Corby *Lottie* ■ *Dir* Vincent Sherman • *Scr* Anne Froelick, James Gunn, from the play *Craig's Wife* by George Kelly

Harriet the Spy ★★★ PG

Comedy   1996 · US · Colour · 97min

Harriet (Michelle Trachtenberg) is the schoolgirl who spies on her friends and family, making copious observations about them in her secret notebook. It's hardly a surprise that, when the book falls into the wrong hands and Harriet's scribblings are read out, her subjects are none too pleased. While not as colourful or zippily paced as the popular children's source novel, this is a quirky film that benefits from a great group of kids and a warm adult performance from Rosie O'Donnell as Harriet's nanny. JB *DVD*

Michelle Trachtenberg *Harriet* • Gregory Smith *Sport* • Vanessa Lee Chester *Janie Gibbs* • Rosie O'Donnell *Ole Golly* • J Smith-Cameron *Mrs Welsch* • Robert Joy *Mr Welsch* • Eartha Kitt *Agatha K Plummer* ■ *Dir* Bronwen Hughes • *Scr* Douglas Petrie, Theresa Rebeck, from the novel by Louise Fitzhugh, adapted by Greg Taylor, Julie Talen

Harrigan ★★ 15

Crime drama   2013 · UK · Colour · 93min

This muddled crime drama is set in north-east England in 1974, a time of social unrest, high inflation, power cuts and the three-day week. Stephen Tompkinson is impressive as police detective Barry Harrigan, who returns to his home town after an assignment in Hong Kong. He struggles to fight opportunistic crime lords, but is hampered by superior officers all too ready to turn a blind eye to the crime spree. Director Vince Woods paints a grim portrait of an industrial city in decline, but the script, by former policeman and TV writer Arthur McKenzie (*The Bill*), is too scattergun and episodic to hang together as a cohesive narrative. TeS Violence, swearing. *DVD Blu*

Stephen Tompkinson *Detective Sergeant Barry Harrigan* • Gillian Kearney *Bridie Wheland* • Ronnie Fox *Cole* • Darren Morfitt *Swift* • Mark Stobbart *Larson* • Amy Manson *Vicky Frizell* ■ *Dir* Vince Woods • *Scr* Arthur McKenzie

Harrison's Flowers ★★ 15

War drama   2000 · Fr · Colour · 126min

The internecine slaughter in the former Yugoslavia provides little more than a heart-tugging backdrop for Elie Chouraqui's real story: worried Andie MacDowell's selfless search for missing photojournalist husband David Strathairn. Adopting a US-centric world view, this achingly sincere (and, in MacDowell's case, seriously miscast) picture seems to intimate that a calamity isn't legitimate unless it's appeared in *Newsweek*. DP *DVD*

Andie MacDowell *Sarah* • David Strathairn *Harrison* • Elias Koteas *Yeager* • Adrien Brody *Kyle* • Brendan Gleeson *Stevenson* • Alun Armstrong *Samuel Brubeck* ■ *Dir* Elie Chouraqui • *Scr* Elie Chouraqui, Isabel Ellsen, Michael Katims, Didier Le Pêcheur

Harry and Son ★★ 15

Drama   1984 · US · Colour · 111min

Paul Newman here stars, directs, co-writes and co-produces in a one-man band attempt to create a meaningful family melodrama. What we get is an awful lot of breast-beating, home truths and hysterical outbursts, but not much true understanding of why a father (Newman) and son (Robby Benson) find each other such fraught company in the first place. The members of a stellar cast stand around a lot, wringing their hands. Someone badly needed to divest Newman of one of his hats, but presumably nobody dared. SH Swearing, nudity.

Paul Newman *Harry Keach* • Robby Benson *Howard Keach* • Ellen Barkin *Katie* • Wilford Brimley *Tom* • Judith Ivey *Sally* • Ossie Davis *Raymond* • Morgan Freeman *Siemanowski* • Maury Chaykin *Lawrence* • Joanne Woodward *Lilly* ■ *Dir* Paul Newman • *Scr* Paul Newman, Ronald L Buck, from the novel *A Lost King* by Raymond DeCapite

Harry and Tonto ★★★★

Comedy   1974 · US · Colour · 115min

Art Carney strikes a blow for the older generation – and won an Oscar in the process – with this story of a widower in his 70s who, after being evicted from his New York apartment, sets off on an odyssey across America with his cat Tonto. Intending to call on his grown-up children along the way, he ends up discarding a few prejudices. Paul Mazursky directs with a keen eye for characters, including Ellen Burstyn as a daughter who finds Harry's charm a bit too much, and Larry Hagman as a son forced to confront his own failure. Hitch-hiker Melanie Mayron puts in a teenage flourish, but it's Carney's last hurrah which compels attention. TH

Art Carney *Harry* • Ellen Burstyn *Shirley* • Chief Dan George *Sam Two Feathers* • Geraldine Fitzgerald *Jessie* • Larry Hagman *Eddie* • Arthur Hunnicutt *Wade* • Melanie Mayron *Ginger* ■ *Dir* Paul Mazursky • *Scr* Paul Mazursky, Josh Greenfeld

H

Harry and Walter Go to New York ★★ U

Crime caper   1976 · US · Colour · 106min

Vaguely influenced by the success of *The Sting*, this box-office dud admittedly has an attractive cast: James Caan and Elliott Gould as song-and-dance men turned safecrackers, Michael Caine as a sort of Mabuse-like mastermind and Diane Keaton as their ditzy confederate in an elaborate bank heist. Although money has been lavished on the re-creation of the New York of 1890, the script isn't nearly as clever or funny enough. **AT**

James Caan *Harry Dighby* · Elliott Gould *Walter Hill* · Michael Caine *Adam Worth* · Diane Keaton *Lissa Chestnut* · Charles Durning *Rufus T Crisp* · Lesley Ann Warren *Gloria Fontaine* ■ *Dir* Mark Rydell · *Scr* John Byrum, Robert Kaufman, from a story by Byrum, Kaufman

Harry Black and the Tiger ★★ U

Adventure   1958 · UK · Colour · 116min

One-legged hunter (Stewart Granger) is employed to kill a man-eating Bengal tiger that is terrorising an Indian village. With him on his mission are an old flame (Barbara Rush), her son and her husband (Anthony Steel), whose wartime cowardice caused the hunter's crippling injury. Director Hugo Fregonese makes the best of the love triangle situation, but this is still weak, although the Indian locations keep things interesting to look at. **BB**

Stewart Granger *Harry Black* · Barbara Rush *Christian Tanner* · Anthony Steel *Desmond Tanner* · IS Johar *Bapu* · Martin Stephens *Michael Tanner* · Frank Olegario *Dr Chowdhury* ■ *Dir* Hugo Fregonese · *Scr* Sydney Boehm, from the novel *Harry Black* by David Walker

Harry Brown ★★★ 18

Revenge thriller   2009 · UK · Colour · 98min

Inevitably, this feature-length debut for director Daniel Barber will be labelled a *Death Wish* for the noughties, though it has as much to say about social conditions in neglected inner-city areas as it does about Michael Caine's doddery dispenser of justice. Caine plays the title character, a 70-something ex-serviceman whose life on a run-down estate ruled by gangs of feral teenagers is thrown upside down when his best friend is murdered. Determined to see justice done, Harry then hobbles into gun-toting, death-dealing action. This gritty revenge thriller is a shade melodramatic, but Caine is surprisingly convincing as the septuagenarian avenger. **DA** Violence, swearing, sex scenes, drug abuse. *DVD* *Blu-ray*

Michael Caine *Harry Brown* · Emily Mortimer *Detective Inspector Frampton* · Charlie Creed-Miles *Detective Sergeant Hicock* · Ben Drew *Noel Winters* · Liam Cunningham *Sid Rourke* · Iain Glen *Childs* · David Bradley (2) *Leonard Attwell* · Jack O'Connell (2) *Marky Hathaway* ■ *Dir* Daniel Barber · *Scr* Gary Young

Harry, He's Here to Help ★★★ 15

Black comedy   2000 · Fr · Colour · 111min

Good intentions go horribly awry in Dominik Moll's darkly comic and disturbingly ambiguous study of male malice. Laurent Lucas plays a harassed family man on holiday who encounters Sergi Lopez, a former schoolfriend made good. There's something instantly sinister about Lopez's generosity towards Lucas; it establishes a tension that is shattered with chillingly twisted logic. Turning the isolated Swiss locations to his atmospheric advantage, Moll depicts Lopez's brutally efficient crimes with restraint. **DP** French +subtitles. Violence, swearing, nudity. *DVD*

Laurent Lucas *Michel* · Sergi Lopez *Harry Balestrero* · Mathilde Seigner *Claire* · Sophie Guillemin *Prune* · Liliane Rovère *Mother* · Domnique Rozan *Father* ■ *Dir* Dominik Moll · *Scr* Dominik Moll, Gilles Marchand

The Harry Hill Movie ★★ PG

Comedy   2013 · UK · Colour · 87min

The big-collared comedian's first cinema outing revolves around a suitably silly tale about his pet hamster having only a week to live, and Harry setting off on a road trip to Blackpool with his petrol-drinking nan (Julie Walters). Distracted by the charms of a sea-dwelling siren (Sheridan Smith), Harry begins to suspect his woes are being masterminded by his separated-at-birth evil twin (Matt Lucas). Despite such dependable comedy support, the film struggles to locate its funny bone. **TeS** *DVD* *Blu-ray*

Harry Hill (2) *Harry Hill* · Julie Walters *Nan* · Matt Lucas *Otto* · Simon Bird *Vet* · Sheridan Smith *Michelle* ■ *Dir* Steve Bendelack · *Scr* James Lamont, Jon Foster (2)

Harry in Your Pocket ★★★

Crime drama   1973 · US · Colour · 102min

This is a film that boasts sleight-of-hand performing artist Tony Giorgio as its technical adviser (he also appears on-screen as a detective) and a plot concerning young Michael Sarrazin and Trish Van Devere learning how to pick a pocket or two. The stars find themselves under the tutelage of veteran pickpockets James Coburn, perfectly cast as a smoothie, and Walter Pidgeon, as a sleazy sophisticate. A heartfelt one-off. **TS** Some swearing.

James Coburn *Harry* · Michael Sarrazin *Ray Houlihan* · Trish Van Devere *Sandy Coletto* · Walter Pidgeon *Casey* · Michael C Gwynne *Fence* · Tony Giorgio *First detective* ■ *Dir* Bruce Geller · *Scr* Ron Austin, James David Buchanan

Harry Potter and the Philosopher's Stone ★★★★ PG

Fantasy adventure   2001 · US · Colour · 146min

With millions of Potter books sold around the world, this is more than just a movie adaptation – it's a cultural phenomenon. Eleven-year-old Daniel Radcliffe makes a likeable Harry – the boy who's whisked off to Hogwarts School of Witchcraft and Wizardry and is charged with finding the blood-red stone of eternal life. A scene-stealing Robbie Coltrane is among a host of familiar adult faces who breathe life into JK Rowling's charming characters. To criticise feels like an act of isolationism, yet there is a lack of emotional core – Harry's orphan status fails to move – and, at two and a half hours in length, the movie is perhaps too long for younger fidgets. However, this faithful rendition of the book demonstrated that the franchise was in safe, sensible hands. **AC** *DVD* *Blu-ray*

Daniel Radcliffe *Harry Potter* · Rupert Grint *Ron Weasley* · Emma Watson *Hermione Granger* · Robbie Coltrane *Rubeus Hagrid* · Maggie Smith *Prof Minerva McGonagall* · Alan Rickman *Prof Severus Snape* · Richard Harris *Prof Albus Dumbledore* · Ian Hart *Prof Quirrell* · Richard Griffiths *Uncle Vernon Dursley* · Fiona Shaw *Aunt Petunia Dursley* · John Cleese *Nearly Headless Nick* · Zoë Wanamaker *Madame Hooch* · John Hurt *Mr Ollivander* · Julie Walters *Mrs Molly Weasley* · David Bradley (2) *Mr Angus Filch* · Tom Felton *Draco Malfoy* · Leslie Phillips *The sorting hat (voice)* ■ *Dir* Chris Columbus · *Scr* Steve Kloves, from the novel by JK Rowling

Harry Potter and the Chamber of Secrets ★★★★ PG

Fantasy adventure   2002 · US/UK/Ger · Colour and sepia · 154min

Those who love the bestselling work of fantasy author JK Rowling will find this sequel even more to their taste, with the mood darker and more scary. Even the predatory spiders stalk Harry (an audibly older Daniel Radcliffe) through the Forbidden Forest, there's a mandrake root with an ear-splitting scream and Ron even exchanges a kiss with Hermione (Emma Watson). Director Chris Columbus has allowed some mechanical repetition to creep in, but overall this is ingenious as well as faithful. Among the adult performers, Kenneth Branagh stands out as the egotistical new teacher Gilderoy Lockhart, upstaging even the special effects. **TH** *DVD* *Blu-ray* *CS*

Daniel Radcliffe *Harry Potter* · Rupert Grint *Ron Weasley* · Emma Watson *Hermione Granger* · Richard Harris *Prof Albus Dumbledore* · Maggie Smith *Prof Minerva McGonagall* · Kenneth Branagh *Gilderoy Lockhart* · Robbie Coltrane *Rubeus Hagrid* · Alan Rickman *Prof Severus Snape* · Julie Walters *Mrs Molly Weasley* · Mark Williams *Mr Arthur Weasley* · Shirley Henderson *Moaning Myrtle* · Jason Isaacs *Lucius Malfoy* · Richard Griffiths *Uncle Vernon Dursley* · Fiona Shaw *Aunt Petunia Dursley* · Miriam Margolyes *Professor Sprout* · John Cleese *Nearly Headless Nick* ■ *Dir* Chris Columbus · *Scr* Steve Kloves, from the novel by JK Rowling

Harry Potter and the Prisoner of Azkaban ★★★★ PG

Fantasy adventure   2004 · US/UK · Colour · 135min

Mexican director Alfonso Cuarón brings a darker, edgier, scarier feel to this third instalment, which has boy wizard Harry (Daniel Radcliffe) contending not only with Gary Oldman's escaped convict, but also the difficulties involved with turning teen. But there's still plenty of fun to be had, with ghosts, ghouls and gadgets galore, the most striking gizmo being a shape-shifting triple-decker bus. David Thewlis, Emma Thompson and Timothy Spall join the list of cameoing celebrities, while the young leads are all growing into their roles. The film has the odd dull patch, but, by and large, this adventure is on a par with its predecessors. **DA** *DVD* *Blu-ray*

Daniel Radcliffe *Harry Potter* · Rupert Grint *Ron Weasley* · Emma Watson *Hermione Granger* · Michael Gambon *Prof Albus Dumbledore* · Maggie Smith *Prof Minerva McGonagall* · Robbie Coltrane *Rubeus Hagrid* · Alan Rickman *Prof Severus Snape* · David Thewlis *Prof Lupin* · Emma Thompson *Prof Sybill Trelawney* · Gary Oldman *Sirius Black* · Julie Walters *Mrs Molly Weasley* · Timothy Spall *Peter Pettigrew* ■ *Dir* Alfonso Cuarón · *Scr* Steve Kloves, from the novel by JK Rowling

Harry Potter and the Goblet of Fire ★★★★ 12

Fantasy adventure   2005 · US · Colour · 150min

As young wizard Harry Potter continues to mature, so too does this exciting fantasy franchise. This fourth instalment continues the dark atmosphere of *Prisoner of Azkaban*, offering genuine scares alongside the customary magical mayhem. Now aged 14, Daniel Radcliffe's Potter faces the ultimate challenge after being mysteriously entered into the Triwizard Tournament. The imaginative tournament scenes more than compensate for Radcliffe's anaemic performance, featuring, among other treats, a brilliant CGI dragon and creepy mermaid creatures. British director Mike Newell really stamps his mark on the movie, making Hogwarts seem like the most fabulous school ever. However, his vision is perhaps too frightening – and lengthy – for under-12s. **SF** *DVD* *Blu-ray*

Daniel Radcliffe *Harry Potter* · Rupert Grint *Ron Weasley* · Emma Watson *Hermione Granger* · Matthew Lewis *Neville Longbottom* · Robert Pattinson *Cedric Diggory* · Robbie Coltrane *Rubeus Hagrid* · Ralph Fiennes *Lord Voldemort* · Michael Gambon *Prof Albus Dumbledore* · Alan Rickman *Prof Severus Snape* · Maggie Smith *Prof Minerva McGonagall* · Frances de la Tour *Madame Maxime* · Roger Lloyd Pack *Barty Crouch* · Miranda Richardson *Rita Skeeter* · David Tennant *Barty Crouch Jr* ■ *Dir* Mike Newell · *Scr* Steve Kloves, from the novel by JK Rowling

Harry Potter and the Order of the Phoenix ★★★★ 12

Fantasy adventure   2007 · US/UK · Colour · 132min

The magic is still there but the mood remains resolutely dark in this engrossing fifth episode in the fantasy franchise. With no Quidditch matches or tournaments to divert him, the task facing Harry (Daniel Radcliffe) is to convince the wizarding community of the re-emergence of Lord Voldemort (Ralph Fiennes). His cause isn't helped when Dumbledore's position as Head of Hogwarts comes under threat. Adapting JK Rowling's bumper-size book was always going to be a challenge, and it's therefore surprising that David Yates's film is the shortest to date. Less may not necessarily be more, however, as some characters are given short shrift and subplots are sketched over. That said, Yates instils proceedings with the requisite sense of wonder, and in a spellbinding finale set in the Ministry of Magic, we finally see the forces of good and evil engaging in full-on combat, and it's well worth the wait. **JH** *DVD* *Blu-ray*

Daniel Radcliffe *Harry Potter* · Rupert Grint *Ron Weasley* · Emma Watson *Hermione Granger* · Gary Oldman *Sirius Black* · Michael Gambon *Prof Albus Dumbledore* · Ralph Fiennes *Lord Voldemort* · Imelda Staunton *Dolores Umbridge* · Alan Rickman *Prof Severus Snape* · Katie Leung *Cho Chang* · Helena Bonham Carter *Bellatrix Lestrange* · Robbie Coltrane *Rubeus Hagrid* · Maggie Smith *Prof Minerva McGonagall* · Richard Griffiths *Uncle Vernon* · Fiona Shaw *Aunt Petunia* ■ *Dir* David Yates · *Scr* Michael Goldenberg, from the novel by JK Rowling

Harry Potter and the Half-Blood Prince ★★★★ 12

Fantasy adventure   2009 · US/UK · Colour · 147min

In the outstanding sixth adaptation of JK Rowling's fantasy series, Dumbledore (Michael Gambon) lures potions professor Horace Slughorn (Jim Broadbent, in an entertainingly eccentric turn) back to Hogwarts. Harry (Daniel Radcliffe) is then charged with trying to dislodge a key clue regarding Slughorn's former pupil, the future Voldemort, from the retired teacher's resistant mind. This is a difficult book to adapt because it is mostly concerned with setting up the two-part finale, but screenwriter Steve Kloves does an admirable job of condensing the plot without losing the emotional depth of the surprisingly adult narrative. Director David Yates dazzles with an evocatively brooding style and raises the storytelling and visual-effects bar for the entire series. **AJ** *DVD* *Blu-ray*

Daniel Radcliffe *Harry Potter* · Rupert Grint *Ron Weasley* · Emma Watson *Hermione Granger* · Michael Gambon *Albus Dumbledore* · Jim Broadbent *Horace Slughorn* · Alan Rickman *Severus Snape* · Tom Felton *Draco Malfoy* · Bonnie Wright *Ginny Weasley* · Evanna Lynch *Luna Lovegood* · Helena Bonham Carter *Bellatrix Lestrange* · Jessie Cave *Lavender Brown* · Maggie Smith *Minerva McGonagall* · Robbie Coltrane *Rubeus Hagrid* · David Thewlis *Remus Lupin* ■ *Dir* David Yates · *Scr* Steve Kloves, from the novel by JK Rowling · *Cinematographer* Bruno Delbonnel

Harry Potter and the Deathly Hallows: Part 1 ★★★ 12

Fantasy adventure   2010 · UK/US · Colour · 140min

After an unbroken run of excellent family films, the Harry Potter franchise runs aground in its seventh instalment, which tackles the first half of the series's epic final volume. With Harry, Ron and Hermione on the run and the regular troupe of supporting actors reduced to the status of high-cost extras, it falls to Daniel Radcliffe, Emma Watson and Rupert Grint to carry the bulk of the action by themselves on an extended road-trip. While the production values remain impeccable, a drifting story, sluggish pacing and choppy transitions will likely frustrate all but the most devoted of fans. Ending on a skirmish rather than a climax, the film plays more like an extended prologue than a story in its own right. But some stunning set pieces and a beautiful animated segment redeem things considerably. **SM** Violence. *DVD* *Blu-ray*

Daniel Radcliffe *Harry Potter* · Rupert Grint *Ron Weasley* · Emma Watson *Hermione Granger* · Helena Bonham Carter *Bellatrix Lestrange* · Ralph Fiennes *Lord Voldemort* · Jason Isaacs *Lucius Malfoy* · Alan Rickman *Severus Snape* · John Hurt *Ollivander* · David Thewlis *Remus Lupin* · Brendan Gleeson *Alastor "Mad-Eye" Moody* · Bonnie Wright *Ginny Weasley* · Timothy

H

Spall *Wormtail* ■ *Dir* David Yates • *Scr* Steve Kloves, from the novel by JK Rowling • *Music* Alexandre Desplat • *Cinematographer* Eduardo Serra

Harry Potter and the Deathly Hallows: Part 2
★★★★★ 12

Fantasy adventure   2011 · UK/US · Colour · 125min

The fantasy franchise comes to a hugely satisfying and teary-eyed conclusion, as Voldemort and Harry clash for the last time, with a sensational revelation about the hero schoolboy's destiny, which Dumbledore had kept secret. Continuing where Part 1 left off, Harry, Hermione and Ron search for the magical horcruxes, the key to the evil lord's immortality. Every beloved character gets their moment in the spotlight as white dragons fly over London, ghouls hover eerily around Hogwarts and its plucky pupils prepare for battle. The technical wizardry on display is perfectly crafted and fires the imagination like never before, and David Yates directs with the surest of hands. AJ
DVD Blu

Daniel Radcliffe *Harry Potter* • Emma Watson *Hermione Granger* • Rupert Grint *Ron Weasley* • Ralph Fiennes *Lord Voldemort* • Helena Bonham Carter *Bellatrix Lestrange* • John Hurt *Mr Ollivander* • Bonnie Wright *Ginny Weasley* • Michael Gambon *Professor Albus Dumbledore* • Alan Rickman *Professor Severus Snape* • Evanna Lynch *Luna Lovegood* ■ *Dir* David Yates • *Scr* Steve Kloves, from the novel by JK Rowling

Harry's War
★★★

Comedy   1981 · US · Colour · 98min

Edward Herrmann here plays nicely against type as the postman who takes a stand against the Internal Revenue Service after it erroneously demands huge back taxes from his aunt, Geraldine Page. Writer/director Kieth Merrill is over-earnest in his celebration of small-town values, but this is pleasantly uplifting entertainment. DP

Edward Herrmann *Harry Johnson* • Geraldine Page *Beverly Payne* • Karen Grassle *Kathy Johnson* • David Ogden Stiers *Ernie Scelera* • Salome Jens *Wilda Crawley* • Elisha Cook Jr *Sergeant Billy* ■ *Dir/Scr* Kieth Merrill

Harsh Times
★★★ 15

Crime drama   2005 · US · Colour · 110min

David Ayer's crime drama is a powerful tale of friendship, loyalty and ambition. Christian Bale is disturbingly intense as a Gulf War veteran haunted by his combat experiences. Initially he spends his days getting wasted and joyriding with his buddy Freddy Rodriguez. However the edgy humour is soon replaced by unflinching violence and horror as Bale reaches meltdown and their misadventures become deadly. Ayer's dialogue is scorching, compensating for slightly pedestrian visuals, but his narrative lacks restraint. SF Violence, swearing, drug abuse. *DVD*

Christian Bale *Jim Davis* • Freddy Rodriguez *Mike Alvarez* • Eva Longoria *Sylvia* • Terry Crews *Darrell* • Noel Guglielmi *Flaco* • Chaka Forman *Toussant* • Blue Mesquita *Leo* • Michael Monks *Agent Hollenbeck* • JK Simmons *Agent Richards* ■ *Dir/Scr* David Ayer

Hart's War
★★★ 15

Second World War courtroom drama   2002 · US · Colour · 119min

Colin Farrell impresses as he defends a black pilot from a trumped-up murder charge in this workmanlike adaptation of John Katzenbach's novel set in a German PoW camp. Director Gregory Hoblit laudably concentrates on exposing the pernicious racism that existed within the US armed services during the Second World War, with the emphasis on courtroom drama rather than the escape subplot. Nominal star Bruce Willis is undertaxed as the senior American officer and his characterisation pales significantly beside Marcel Iures's cultured Nazi commandant. DP *DVD* Blu

Bruce Willis *Col William A McNamara* • Colin Farrell (2) *Lt Thomas W Hart* • Terrence Howard *Lt Lincoln A Scott* • Cole Hauser *Staff Sgt Vic W Bedford* • Marcel Iures *Col Werner Visser* • Linus

Roache *Capt Peter A Ross* • Rory Cochrane *Sgt Carl S Webb* ■ *Dir* Gregory Hoblit • *Scr* Billy Ray, Terry George, from the novel by John Katzenbach

Harum Scarum
★★ U

Musical comedy   1965 · US · Colour · 82min

This is another substandard entry in the screen career of Elvis Presley. Here he plays a movie star who travels to the Middle East to attend the premier of his latest film and gets caught up in a plot to assassinate a local ruler. The exotic locations add a *frisson* of interest, but this is negated by the lacklustre plot and forgettable songs. DF *DVD*

Elvis Presley *Johnny Tyronne* • Mary Ann Mobley *Princess Shalimar* • Fran Jeffries *Aishah* • Michael Ansara *Prince Dragna* • Jay Novello *Zacha* • Philip Reed *King Toranshah* • Theo Marcuse *Sinan* • Billy Barty *Baba* ■ *Dir* Gene Nelson • *Scr* Gerald Drayson Adams

The Harvest
★★ 18

Thriller   1993 · US · Colour · 93min

The illegal trade in body parts stands as a metaphor for the exploitative nature of Hollywood film-making in this flashy thriller from debut director David Marconi. Playing fast and loose with traditional narrative structures, Marconi throws in flashbacks, dream sequences and episodes that could equally be real or simply part of wannabe writer Miguel Ferrer's latest screenplay. However, too little attention is paid to either theme or characterisation. DP Violence, sex scenes, nudity, swearing. *DVD*

Miguel Ferrer *Charlie Pope* • Leilani Sarelle Ferrer [Leilani Ferrer] *Natalie Caldwell* • Henry Silva *Detective Topo* • Tim Thomerson *Steve Mobley* • Harvey Fierstein *Bob Lakin* • Anthony John Denison *Noel Guzmann* ■ *Dir/Scr* David Marconi • *Cinematographer* Emmanuel Lubezki

Harvey
★★★★★ U

Fantasy comedy   1950 · US · BW · 107min

James Stewart gives a knockout performance in this classic comedy about tipsy Elwood P Dowd and his unusual friendship with Harvey, an invisible six-foot-tall white rabbit. This is superb whimsy about the fine line between sanity and insanity, and Henry Koster directs this loving tribute to eccentricity and bar-room philosophy with a deft touch. Alongside the satiric misunderstandings, character mix-ups and revitalised clichés come poignant comments about humanity's lack of communication, which touch both the funny bone and the heart. Guaranteed to leave you with a smile on your face for ages afterwards. AJ *DVD* Blu

James Stewart *Elwood P Dowd* • Josephine Hull *Veta Louise Simmons* • Peggy Dow *Miss Kelly* • Charles Drake *Dr Sanderson* • Cecil Kellaway *Dr Chumley* • Victoria Horne *Myrtle Mae* • Jesse White *Wilson* • William Lynn *Judge Gaffney* • Wallace Ford *Lofgren* ■ *Dir* Henry Koster • *Scr* Mary Chase, Oscar Brodney, from the play by Chase • *Cinematographer* William Daniels (1)

Harvey
★★ U

Comedy   1996 · US · Colour · 87min

The original *Harvey* is one of the all-time classic comedies, providing James Stewart with one of his more memorable roles. In this bland TV-movie version, Harry Anderson does his best as cheerful drunk Elwood P Dowd, who insists that he has a giant white rabbit as a chum, and there is useful support from the likes of Swoosie Kurtz and Leslie Nielsen. But it's not a patch on the marvellous original. JF *DVD*

Harry Anderson *Elwood P Dowd* • Swoosie Kurtz *Veta* • Leslie Nielsen *Dr Chumley* • Lynda Boyd *Mrs Chumley* ■ *Dir* George Schaefer • *Scr* Joseph Dougherty, from the play by Mary Chase

The Harvey Girls
★★★ U

Musical comedy   1946 · US · Colour · 96min

Once intended as a vehicle for Lana Turner, this Technicolored musical comedy became one of Judy Garland's greatest personal triumphs. She plays a mail-order bride who joins up with waitresses sent out west by restaurateur Fred Harvey to serve the passengers on the new cross-country

railroads. The plot is as cardboard as the scenery, and John Hodiak is a lacklustre leading man, but the film belongs to Garland, and she is wonderful. TS *DVD*

Judy Garland *Susan Bradley* • John Hodiak *Ned Trent* • Ray Bolger *Chris Maule* • Preston Foster *Judge Sam Purvis* • Virginia O'Brien *Alma* • Angela Lansbury *Em* • Marjorie Main *Sonora Cassidy* • Chill Wills *HH Hartsey* • Kenny Baker (1) *Terry O'Halloran* • Cyd Charisse *Deborah* ■ *Dir* George Sidney (2) • *Scr* Edmund Beloin, Nathaniel Curtis, Harry Crane, James O'Hanlon, Samson Raphaelson, from a story by Eleanore Griffin, William Rankin, from a novel by Samuel Hopkins Adams • *Music Director* Lennie Hayton • *Choreographer* Robert Alton

Has Anybody Seen My Gal?
★★★

Musical comedy   1952 · US · Colour · 88min

Millionaire Charles Coburn decides to check whether the family of the woman he loved many years ago, but who turned down his marriage proposal, is worthy of inheriting his fortune. Masquerading as an eccentric artist and taking a job as a soda jerk, he rents a room in the family house, arranges an anonymous gift of money for them, and gleefully watches the results. Breezily directed by Douglas Sirk, with a cast that includes Rock Hudson and Piper Laurie (and with James Dean in a bit part), this beguiling comedy owes much of its appeal to Coburn's performance. RK

Charles Coburn *Samuel Fulton* • Rock Hudson *Dan Stebbins* • Piper Laurie *Millicent Blaisdell* • Gigi Perreau *Roberta Blaisdell* • Lynn Bari *Harriet Blaisdell* • Larry Gates *Charles Blaisdell* • William Reynolds *Howard Blaisdell* • Skip Homeier *Carl Pennock* • James Dean (1) *Youth* ■ *Dir* Douglas Sirk • *Scr* Joseph Hoffman, from a story by Eleanor H Porter

The Hasty Heart
★★★ U

Second World War drama   1949 · UK · BW · 102min

In transferring John Patrick's hit play to the screen, Vincent Sherman remained faithful to the text, but neglected his duty as a film director by failing to challenge the eye as well as the ear. In an overblown but Oscar-nominated performance, Richard Todd dominates the action as a self-pitying Scot who makes life unbearable for his fellow patients in a Burmese field hospital. Patricia Neal also overdoes her angel of mercy act, but there is the compensation of seeing Ronald Reagan give one of his best performances. DP *DVD*

Ronald Reagan *Yank* • Patricia Neal *Sister Margaret* • Richard Todd *Corporal Lachlan McLachlan* • Anthony Nicholls *Lt Col Dunn* • Howard Marion-Crawford *Tommy* • Ralph Michael *Kiwi* • Alfie Bass *Orderly* ■ *Dir* Vincent Sherman • *Scr* Ranald MacDougall, from the play by John Patrick

Hatari!
★★★★ U

Adventure   1962 · US · Colour · 151min

Howard Hawks's amiable safari romp, which he shot in East Africa, is ecologically sound, almost plotless and so long that you can wander in and out of it with no sense of missing anything. But if you did, you would lose out on a wonderful rollercoaster ride of fun and adventure, plus the sort of camaraderie between star John Wayne, director Hawks and writer Leigh Brackett that only long-term collaboration can produce. TS *DVD*

John Wayne *Sean Mercer* • Elsa Martinelli *Dallas* • Hardy Kruger *Kurt* • Red Buttons *Pockets* • Gérard Blain *Chip Maurey* • Michèle Girardon *Brandy* • Bruce Cabot *Indian* ■ *Dir* Howard Hawks • *Scr* Leigh Brackett, from a story by Harry Kurnitz

Hatchet
★★★ 18

Comedy horror   2006 · US · Colour · 85min

In this bloody valentine to early 1980s slasher movies, a group of tourists on a moonlit "Haunted Swamp" tour get stranded in the Louisiana bayou and discover that a horrific local legend is painfully real. The scare tactics and extreme brutality are balanced by humour and well-drawn characters, while the strong cast plays it absolutely straight. Horror icons

Robert Englund and Tony Todd add resonance to a deliberately old-school shocker. Two sequels appeared in 2010 and 2013, but didn't live up to this film's promise and went straight to DVD. AJ *DVD*

Joel David Moore *Ben* • Tamara Feldman *Marybeth* • Deon Richmond *Marcus* • Mercedes McNab *Misty* • Kane Hodder *Victor Crowley* • Robert Englund *Sampson* • Tony Todd *Clive "Rev Zombie" Washington* • Parry Shen *Shawn* ■ *Dir/Scr* Adam Green

Hatchet for the Honeymoon
★★★ 15

Horror thriller   1969 · It/Sp · Colour · 84min

Mario Bava's darkly comic and elegant shocker stars Italian 1960s staple Stephen Forsyth as a bridal gown salon owner driven to murdering his models on their wedding nights. It's when he starts wearing white veils himself to kill his wife (Laura Betti) that the real twisted trouble begins. Revealing the killer's identity from the outset is unusual for the *giallo* (Italian thriller) genre, but Bava's ironic chiller pushes rich visual delirium to both macabre and mischievous limits. AJ Italian dubbed. Violence. *DVD*

Stephen Forsyth *John Harrington* • Dagmar Lassander *Helen Wood* • Laura Betti *Mildred Harrington* • Jesus Puente *Inspector Russell* • Femi Benussi *Alice Norton* • Antonia Mas *Louise* ■ *Dir* Mario Bava • *Scr* Mario Bava, Santiago Moncado, Mario Musy, from a story by Santiago Moncado

The Hatchet Man
★★

Crime melodrama   1932 · US · BW · 74min

Edward G Robinson stars here as an Oriental gangster. Loretta Young is in Chinese make-up, too, as Robinson's ward and eventual bride, an event that causes the hatchets to come out. Sundry subplots and a trip to China, where J Carroll Naish is naturally a big cheese, fill in the screen time. The flabby romance and unusually slow direction by William A Wellman produces a disappointing result. AT

Edward G Robinson *Wong Low Get* • Loretta Young *Toya San* • Dudley Digges *Nag Hong Fah* • Leslie Fenton *Harry En Hai* • Edmund Breese *Yu Chang* • Tully Marshall *Long Sen Yat* • J Carrol Naish *Sun Yat Sen* ■ *Dir* William Wellman [William A Wellman] • *Scr* J Grubb Alexander, from the play *The Honorable Mr Wong* by Achmed Abdullah, David Belasco

The Hateful Eight
★★★★ 18

Western   2015 · US · Colour · 160min

Reservoir Dogs goes West in writer/director Quentin Tarantino's eighth feature, paying homage to the cowboy TV shows of his youth and the Sergio Corbucci back catalogue (his *Django Unchained* inspiration). In a post Civil War America still being torn apart by North/South conflicts, eight random bounty hunters, soldiers and outlaws are brought together by an epic snowstorm. Not by chance it turns out, as this allegorical vision of an immoral western frontier explodes in typical Tarantino, blood-spattered fashion. It's a bit of a slog sometimes but Tarantino's brutal wit and fine cast eventually bring it to a polished and satisfying head. AJ Violence *DVD* Blu

Samuel L Jackson *Major Marquis Warren* • Kurt Russell *John "The Hangman" Ruth* • Jennifer Jason Leigh *Daisy Domergue* • Walton Goggins *Sheriff Chris Mannix* • Michael Madsen *Joe Gage* • Bruce Dern *General Sanford Smithers* • Tim Roth *Oswaldo Mobray* • Channing Tatum *Jody Domergue* ■ *Dir/Scr* Quentin Tarantino • *Music* Ennio Morricone

A Hatful of Rain
★★★

Drama   1957 · US · BW · 108min

Don Murray stars as a Korean war veteran who keeps his heroin addiction a secret from his pregnant wife Eva Marie Saint. Described by director Fred Zinnemann as "the grimmest of all the films I ever made", this pioneering study of drug addiction remains a powerful experience, gaining enormously from the moody black-and-white CinemaScope photography of New York, its documentary detail and from Bernard Herrmann's music. AT

U SUITABLE FOR ALL   Uc SUITABLE ESPECIALLY FOR YOUNG CHILDREN (DVD ONLY)   PG PARENTAL GUIDANCE   12A UNDER 12s TO BE ACCOMPANIED (CINEMA ONLY)

Eva Marie Saint *Celia Pope* • Don Murray *Johnny Pope* • Anthony Franciosa *Polo* • Lloyd Nolan *John Pope Sr* • Henry Silva *Mother* • Gerald O'Loughlin [Gerald S O'Loughlin] *Chuck* • William Hickey *Apples* ■ *Dir* Fred Zinnemann • *Scr* Michael Vincent Gazzo, Alfred Hayes, Carl Foreman (uncredited), from the play by Gazzo • *Cinematographer* Joe MacDonald

Hatter's Castle ★★★
Period drama 1941 · UK · BW · 103min

Although certain liberties were taken with AJ Cronin's novel, this is nevertheless an enthralling melodrama that combines an oppressive Gothic atmosphere with some untethered Victorian bombast. Overshadowing such stars in the making as Deborah Kerr and James Mason, Robert Newton gnaws at the exquisitely designed scenery as the Glasgow hatter who drives his family to the verge of madness in order to line his pockets and juggle his love life. DP

Robert Newton *James Brodie* • Deborah Kerr *Mary Brodie* • Beatrice Varley *Mrs Brodie* • James Mason *Dr Renwick* • Emlyn Williams *Dennis* • Henry Oscar *Grierson* • Enid Stamp-Taylor *Nancy* ■ *Dir* Lance Comfort, James Carter • *Scr* Rodney Ackland, from the novel by AJ Cronin

Haunted ★★★ 15
Supernatural thriller 1995 · UK/US · Colour · 103min

Right from the Edwardian prologue, a palpable air of malevolence hangs over this tale of murder, madness and memory. As the sceptic whose tragic past catches up with him when he investigates the supernatural at a Sussex stately home, Aidan Quinn gives a performance of substance and subtlety that perfectly complements the quirkier cameos of his co-stars. Kate Beckinsale makes a suitably creepy coquette and Anthony Andrews revels in his eccentricity, but topping the lot is Anna Massey's deliciously Danvers-esque nanny. DP A sex scene, nudity. *DVD*

Aidan Quinn *David Ash* • Kate Beckinsale *Christina Mariell* • Anthony Andrews *Robert Mariell* • John Gielgud *Dr Doyle* • Anna Massey *Nanny Tess Webb* • Alex Lowe *Simon Mariell* • Geraldine Somerville *Kate* • Liz Smith *Old gypsy woman* ■ *Dir* Lewis Gilbert • *Scr* Tim Prager, Lewis Gilbert, Bob Kellet, from the novel by James Herbert

The Haunted Castle ★★★ PG
Silent crime drama 1921 · Ger · BW · 81min

Adapted from a serialised novel by Rudolf Stratz, FW Murnau's eighth feature is less a chiller and more a melodramatic study in moral horror. The story revolves around an aristocratic scandal and the need for the hunting party hosts at Castle Vogelöd to keep count Lotar Mehnert away from baroness Olga Tschechowa, the widow of the brother he supposedly murdered years before. Murnau tells his tale with theatrical efficiency and an element of suspense, but the dénouement is hardly surprising and Murnau had yet to devise the "unchained camera" technique that would heighten the intensity of his later work. DP *DVD* 🔵

Arnold Korff *Lora Vogelöd* • Lil Kyser-Korff *Vogelöd's wife* • Lotar Mehnert *Count Johan Oetsch* • Paul Hartmann *Count Peter Paul Oetsch* • Paul Bildt *Baron Safferstätt* ■ *Dir* FW Murnau • *Scr* Carl Mayer, from the novella by Rudolf Stratz

The Haunted Heart ★ 15
Horror 1995 · US · Colour · 91min

This dire psycho-thriller stars Diane Ladd as a doting mother who murders anyone who suggests to her son Morgan Weisser that it's time for him to leave home and make his own way in the world. Limp slaughter matches the lame script in this bust. AJ

Diane Ladd *Olivia Hendrix* • Olympia Dukakis *Mrs Jay* • Morgan Weisser *Tom* • Ele Keats *Audrey* • Matt Clark *Ben Wilson* ■ *Dir* Frank LaLoggia • *Scr* Michael Angelella

Haunted Honeymoon ★ PG
Comedy horror 1986 · US · Colour · 80min

While a funny actor, Gene Wilder is weighed down here by his own directorial incompetence. His attempt to emulate

earlier haunted-house scare movies fails because he borrows too heavily from them. Noise wins over wit in this second-rate entry in the genre, and even Dom DeLuise can't save the day. JM *DVD*

Gene Wilder *Larry Abbot* • Gilda Radner *Vickie Pearle* • Dom DeLuise *Aunt Kate* • Jonathan Pryce *Charles Abbot* • Paul L Smith [Paul Smith] *Dr Paul Abbot* • Peter Vaughan *Francis Sr* • Bryan Pringle *Pfister* • Roger Ashton-Griffiths *Francis Jr* • Jim Carter *Montego* • Eve Ferret *Sylvia* ■ *Dir* Gene Wilder • *Scr* Gene Wilder, Terence Marsh

A Haunted House ★★★ 15
Horror spoof 2013 · US · Colour · 82min

Ghostly possession films like *Paranormal Activity* are mercilessly spoofed here by co-writer/star Marlon Wayans, who had huge success with the *Scary Movie* franchise. The story sees his girlfriend (Essence Atkins) move in with baggage picked up years earlier when she made a pact with the devil for some designer shoes. Wayans relies a little too much on toilet humour, but the whole found-footage schtick is cleverly re-created and the performances (including Cedric the Entertainer as a penitentiary priest) are spot-on. DA Swearing, sexual references, drug abuse. *DVD* 🔵

Marlon Wayans *Malcolm* • Essence Atkins *Kisha* • Cedric the Entertainer *Father Williams* • Nick Swardson *Chip the psychic* • David Koechner *Dan the security man* ■ *Dir* Michael Tiddes • *Scr* Marlon Wayans, Rick Alvarez

A Haunted House 2 ★ 18
Horror spoof 2014 · US · Colour · 86min

The surprise hit horror spoof returns for a sequel, with Marlon Wayans once again plagued by scary and absurd paranormal activity after moving his family into a new house. It does raise the occasional inane chuckle, but these flickers of amusement are rare, and the cycle of gags gets tiresome early in the film's short running time. This will satisfy only the basest of humours, while simply repulsing (or offending) the rest of us. JL In English, Spanish. Swearing, sexual references, drug abuse, nudity.

Marlon Wayans *Malcolm Johnson* • Jaime Pressly *Megan* • Essence Atkins *Kisha Davis* • Gabriel Iglesias *Miguel* • Cedric the Entertainer *Father Doug Williams* • Ashley Rickards *Becky* ■ *Dir* Michael Tiddes • *Scr* Marlon Wayans, Rick Alvarez, from characters by Wayans, Alvarez

The Haunted House of Horror ★★ 15
Horror 1969 · UK · Colour · 87min

A psycho killer murders a Swinging Sixties fashion victim at a happening in a suburban London mansion. Which of the 30-something actors playing teen revellers (including Frankie Avalon on a *Beach Party* vacation) is the crazed culprit? An effective shocker in its day – partly owing to some subtle gay overtones in the whodunnit aspects of the plot – but only the trendy outfits will elicit screams of terror now. AJ *DVD*

Frankie Avalon *Chris* • Jill Haworth *Sheila* • Richard O'Sullivan *Peter* • Veronica Doran *Madge* • Julian Barnes *Richard* • Robin Stewart *Henry* • Mark Wynter *Gary* • Gina Warwick *Sylvia* • Clifford Earl *Police sergeant* ■ *Dir* Michael Armstrong • *Scr* Michael Armstrong, Peter Marcus

The Haunted Mansion ★★ PG
Comedy horror 2003 · US · Colour · 84min

Another movie based on a Disney theme-park ride, this saga can't escape the limitations of its funfair origins. Eddie Murphy plays a workaholic estate agent who interrupts the family holiday for a visit to a potential sale – a vast mansion that turns out to be haunted by a lovelorn ghost. If sumptuous photography and lavish production design were all that was needed to get by, this would qualify as an inoffensive hit, but it's just an uninspired catalogue of fright-less clichés. AJ *DVD* 🔵 CS

Eddie Murphy *Jim Evers* • Terence Stamp *Ramsley* • Nathaniel Parker *Master Edward Gracey* • Marsha Thomason *Sara Evers* • Jennifer Tilly *Madame Leota* • Wallace Shawn *Ezra* • Dina Waters *Emma* • Marc John Jefferies *Michael* • Aree Davis *Megan* ■ *Dir* Rob Minkoff • *Scr* David Berenbaum, from the Disney theme-park ride

The Haunted Palace ★★★ 15
Horror 1963 · US · Colour · 83min

Enjoy a double dose of horror from the guru of ghoul, Vincent Price, who plays two characters in Roger Corman's creepy tale of curses; although the title is borrowed from an Edgar Allan Poe story, the tale is based on an HP Lovecraft story. Price is at his deliciously evil best, wreaking terrible revenge on a local community. Horror veteran Lon Chaney Jr is also on hand to give his customary chilling support, playing Price's faithful servant. NF *DVD* 🔵

Vincent Price *Charles Dexter Ward/Joseph Curwen* • Debra Paget *Ann Ward* • Lon Chaney Jr *Simon Orne* • Frank Maxwell *Dr Marinus Willet* • Leo Gordon *Edgar Weeden* • Elisha Cook [Elisha Cook Jr] *Peter Smith* ■ *Dir* Roger Corman • *Scr* Charles Beaumont, from the story *The Case of Charles Dexter Ward* by HP Lovecraft

Haunted Summer ★★ 18
Historical romantic drama 1988 · US · Colour · 102min

This is yet another treatment of the meeting between poets Byron and Shelley, writer Mary Godwin and Dr Polidori in Italy in 1816. Despite the acting efforts of Philip Anglim, Laura Dern, Alice Krige and Eric Stoltz, this tale makes for rather unconvincing history. Director Ivan Passer seems determined to lower the drama, just as Ken Russell, with the similarly themed *Gothic*, upped it. TH

Eric Stoltz *Percy Shelley* • Philip Anglim *Lord Byron* • Alice Krige *Mary Godwin* • Laura Dern *Claire Clairmont* • Alex Winter *John Polidori* • Peter Berling *Maurice* • Don Hodson *Rushton* ■ *Dir* Ivan Passer • *Scr* Lewis John Carlino, from the novel by Anne Edwards

Haunter ★★★ 15
Supernatural horror 2013 · Can/Fr · Colour · 93min

Director Vincenzo Natali takes a break from the visceral horror he's known for to delve into the supernatural with this intriguing blend of *The Others* and *Groundhog Day*. Why is typical moody teenager Abigail Breslin seemingly living the same day over and over? Why can't the family leave their fogbound house? And who is the Pale Man? Guessing the answers won't really matter for this is an engrossing little chiller that has enough eerie twists to thicken the mystery nicely. Breslin is convincing, but it's Stephen McHattie as the smirking source of her torment who proves a magnetically malevolent presence. JA *DVD* 🔵

Abigail Breslin *Lisa* • Stephen McHattie *Pale Man* • Peter Outerbridge *Bruce* • Michelle Nolden *Carol* • Peter DaCunha *Robbie* ■ *Dir* Vincenzo Natali • *Scr* Brian King

The Haunting ★★★★★ 12
Supernatural horror 1963 · US/UK · BW · 107min

This is one of the best supernatural chillers ever made. Richard Johnson plays the psychic researcher who brings along two mediums to help him investigate a monstrously haunted mansion steeped in spectral phenomena. All the more effective for keeping its horrors unseen, director Robert Wise's masterful adaptation of Shirley Jackson's *The Haunting of Hill House* is an exercise in invisible terror; all you see are pulsating walls and all you hear are loud pounding noises. Julie Harris shines as the spinster worst affected by the poltergeist events, whose psychological state is cleverly kept in question. AJ *DVD*

Julie Harris (2) *Eleanor Vance* • Claire Bloom *Theodora* • Richard Johnson *Dr John Markway* • Russ Tamblyn *Luke Sanderson* • Fay Compton *Mrs Sanderson* • Rosalie Crutchley *Mrs Dudley* • Lois Maxwell *Grace Markway* • Valentine Dyall *Mr Dudley* • Diane Clare *Carrie Fredericks* ■ *Dir* Robert Wise • *Scr* Nelson Gidding, from the novel *The Haunting of Hill House* by Shirley Jackson

The Haunting ★★ 12
Supernatural horror 1999 · US · Colour · 107min

Director Jan De Bont's remake of Robert Wise's 1963 classic is a frightless wonder, which isn't the least bit scary, despite using computer-generated animation to show all the poltergeist activity (effectively unseen in the original, but yawningly overblown here). Hokey in the extreme, with a daft script and numerous unintentional laughs, only the beautifully designed baroque sets impress. AJ *DVD*

Liam Neeson *Dr David Marrow* • Catherine Zeta-Jones *Theo* • Owen Wilson *Luke Sanderson* • Lili Taylor *Eleanor "Nell" Vance* • Bruce Dern *Mr Dudley* • Marian Seldes *Mrs Dudley* • Virginia Madsen *Jane* ■ *Dir* Jan De Bont • *Scr* David Self, from the novel *The Haunting of Hill House* by Shirley Jackson • *Production Designer* Eugenio Zanetti

Haunting Fear ★ 18
Horror drama 1990 · US · Colour · 84min

In a Poe-faced horror romp, loosely based on Edgar Allan's *The Premature Burial*, a husband and mistress connive to drive his wife (video "scream queen" Brinke Stevens) round the twist. Jan-Michael Vincent and Karen Black star in this schlocky horror picture show from B-movie master Fred Olen Ray, and you may recognise the faces of many fright stalwarts. DA

Jan-Michael Vincent *Lt James Trent* • Karen Black *Dr Julia Harcourt* • Jay Richardson *Terry Monroe* • Michael Berryman *Mortician* • Brinke Stevens *Victoria Monroe* • Robert Quarry *Visconti* ■ *Dir* Fred Olen Ray • *Scr* Sherman Scott [Sam Newfield], from the short story *The Premature Burial* by Edgar Allan Poe

The Haunting in Connecticut ★★ 15
Horror thriller based on a true story 2009 · US · Colour · 98min

The "fact-based" story of a family dealing with supernatural forces that target their cancer-suffering teenage son in their new home, could easily have had an Amityville address. It's that predictable. Director Peter Cornwell tweaks the parade of overused scare clichés in this "true" ghostly possession tale, and Elias Koteas makes the most of his exorcist-for-hire role by piling on the gravitas. But way too many lines of dialogue come with unintentional laughs and do nothing to help maintain the purely superficial creepiness. AJ *DVD* 🔵

Virginia Madsen *Sara Campbell* • Kyle Gallner *Matt Campbell* • Amanda Crew *Wendy* • Martin Donovan (2) *Peter Campbell* • Elias Koteas *Reverend Popescu* • Sophi Knight *Mary* ■ *Dir* Peter Cornwell • *Scr* Adam Simon, Tim Metcalfe

The Haunting of Morella ★★★
Horror 1990 · US · Colour · 87min

Roger Corman recaptures the energy and essence of his own Poe series from the 1960s in this production for his New Horizons company directed by Jim Wynorski. David McCallum lends great authority to his role as a blind New England recluse whose witch wife was burned at the stake. Her spirit returns in the body of her grown-up daughter and a new reign of terror begins. Tarted up with modish gore, lesbianism and grisly violence, this entertaining neo-gothic romp is packed with cheap thrills. AJ Sex scenes, nudity.

David McCallum (1) *Gideon* • Nicole Eggert *Morella/Lenora* • Christopher Halsted *Guy* • Lana Clarkson *Coel Deveroux* • Maria Ford *Diane* • Jonathan Farwell *Doctor Gault* ■ *Dir* Jim Wynorski • *Scr* RJ Robertson, from the story by Edgar Allan Poe

Hav Plenty ★★ 15
Romantic comedy 1998 · US · Colour · 83min

Newcomer Christopher Scott Cherot writes, directs and stars in this gauche romantic comedy. Lee Plenty (Cherot) is an aspiring writer who is suffering from writer's block and living in his car until his rich friend Havilland Savage (Chenoa Maxwell) invites him to Washington DC for New Year's Eve.

H

That Hav and Plenty will make a lovely couple is a truth that seems to evade everyone except Hav's gran and, of course, the audience. FL Swearing, sex scenes.

Christopher Scott Cherot *Lee Plenty* • Chenoa Maxwell *Havilland Savage* • Hill Harper *Michael Simmons* • Tammi Katherine Jones *Caroline Gooden* • Robinne Lee *Leigh Darling* ■ *Dir/Scr* Christopher Scott Cherot

Havana ★★★ 15
Romantic thriller 1990 · US · Colour · 138min

Robert Redford's seventh collaboration with director Sydney Pollack was one of the box-office bombs of the 1990s. But this *Casablanca* clone makes for polished, if occasionally pedestrian, entertainment. As there's surprisingly little passion between Redford and his co-star Lena Olin, the main interest here lies in the excellence of the supporting cast, with Alan Arkin typically assured as a shady casino boss, Raul Julia convincing as Olin's pro-Communist husband and Tomas Milian truly unnerving as the brutal police chief. DP Swearing, violence, sex scenes. *DVD*

Robert Redford *Jack Weil* • Lena Olin *Roberta "Bobby" Duran* • Alan Arkin *Joe Volpi* • Tomas Milian *Menocal* • Daniel Davis *Marion Chigwell* • Tony Plana *Julio Ramos* • Betsy Brantley *Diane* • Lise Cutter *Patty* • Raul Julia *Arturo Duran* • Mark Rydell *Meyer Lansky* ■ *Dir* Sydney Pollack • *Scr* Judith Rascoe, David Rayfiel, from a story by Judith Rascoe

Havana Widows ★★
Comedy 1933 · US · BW · 63min

In most respects this is a *Gold Diggers* movie with Joan Blondell, but one misses the songs and those suggestive Busby Berkeley dance routines. Blondell and Glenda Farrell play unemployed chorus girls on the loose in Cuba and looking for sugardaddies after they borrow some cash from their gangster friends. Fans of this sort of movie will find it funny and charmingly raffish. AT

Joan Blondell *Mae Knight* • Glenda Farrell *Sadie Appleby* • Guy Kibbee *Deacon Jones* • Lyle Talbot *Bob Jones* • Allen Jenkins *Herman Brody* ■ *Dir* Ray Enright • *Scr* Earl Baldwin

Have Rocket, Will Travel ★★ U
Science-fiction comedy 1959 · US · BW · 76min

As their movie contract with Columbia came to an end, the Three Stooges thought their careers were over, but this juvenile romp in outer space put them back on top as firm family favourites. The trio (with new Stooge Joe De Rita) play cleaners at a rocket base who accidentally send themselves to Venus, where they encounter a talking unicorn, a brain machine, a flame-throwing giant spider and doppelgangers of themselves. This silly, aimless fun substitutes painful sight gags and weird sound effects for wit and invention. AJ

Moe Howard *Moe* • Larry Fine *Larry* • Joe De Rita *Curley Joe* • Jerome Cowan *JP Morse* • Anna-Lisa *Dr Ingrid Naarveg* • Bob Colbert *[Robert Colbert] Dr Ted Benson* ■ *Dir* David Lowell Rich • *Scr* Raphael Hayes

Having Wonderful Time ★★★
Romance 1938 · US · BW · 69min

Arthur Kober's satirical play about Jewish New Yorkers on holiday in the Catskills lost much of its nuance in this movie version – despite being adapted by Kober himself – but it certainly benefited from a sparkling RKO cast, headed by the marvellous Ginger Rogers and Lucille Ball. The film is a veritable treasure trove for fans of the period: that's Dean Jagger as Ginger's brother, plus Eve Arden and Ann Miller among the holidaymakers. Red Skelton, billed as Richard, makes an impressive feature debut, and most of the folks at Camp Kare-Free, for that matter, will seem like old buddies. TS

Ginger Rogers *Teddy Shaw* • Douglas Fairbanks Jr *Chick Kirkland* • Peggy Conklin *Fay Coleman* • Lucille Ball *Miriam* • Lee Bowman *Buzzy Armbuster* • Eve Arden *Henrietta* • Dorothea

Kent *Maxine* • Richard Skelton [Red Skelton] *Itchy Faulkner* • Dean Jagger *Charlie* ■ *Dir* Alfred Santell • *Scr* Arthur Kober, from his play

Having You ★★ 15
Comedy drama 2013 · UK · Colour · 94min

Convincing central performances and a moving finale compensate for an uneven tone in actor-turned-director Sam Hoare's contrived but heartfelt relationship drama. The convenient story sees recovering alcoholic Andrew Buchan struggle to manage his many responsibilities when an old one-night stand (Anna Friel) shows up with a seven-year-old she says is his, shortly after he's proposed to his miserably infertile girlfriend (Hoare's real-life wife Romola Garai). Unnecessary stabs at broad humour and crude sex talk jar with the predominantly sensitively handled material. SF Swearing.

Anna Friel *Anna* • Romola Garai *Camilla* • Andrew Buchan *Jack* • Philip Davis *Peter* ■ *Dir/Scr* Sam Hoare

Havoc ★★★ 18
Crime drama 2005 · US/Ger · Colour · 81min

Stephen Gaghan (writer/director of *Syriana*) won an Oscar for the screenplay of drugs drama *Traffic*. In this less expansive drama directed by Oscar-winning documentary-maker Barbara Kopple, the focus of his script is a group of affluent white teenagers in Los Angeles whose substance abuse leads them to visit the ghetto. Anne Hathaway gives a terrific performance as Allison, the rich girl from the Pacific Palisades slumming it on the mean streets of East LA. There, she meets drug dealer Hector (Freddy Rodriguez) and tries to ingratiate herself into Latino gang culture. What could have been an exploitative, tabloid tale against the dangers of drugs and crime gets an unexpected boost from Hathaway's tough yet vulnerable turn. JR Swearing, sex scenes, drug abuse.

Anne Hathaway *Allison* • Bijou Phillips *Emily* • Shiri Appleby *Amanda* • Michael Biehn *Stuart Lang* • Joseph Gordon-Levitt *Sam* • Matt O'Leary *Eric* • Freddy Rodriguez *Hector* • Laura San Giacomo *Joanna Lang* ■ *Dir* Barbara Kopple • *Scr* Stephen Gaghan, from a story by Gaghan, Jessica Kaplan

Le Havre ★★★★ PG
Comedy drama 2011 · Fin/Fr/Ger · Colour · 89min

If Marcel Carné, René Clair and Jean-Pierre Melville had ever collaborated on a film, it would probably look and feel like this enchanting modern fairy tale from Finnish auteur Aki Kaurismäki. Yet the storyline is very much of the moment, as shoeshiner André Wilms persuaded an ageing rocker (Roberto Piazza) to play a gig to raise funds to help a young African refugee (Blondin Miguel) escape the clutches of the police and join his mother in London. Kaurismäki captures the indignity and injustice endured by migrants, but this is essentially a celebration of community. DP French +subtitles. *DVD*

André Wilms *Marcel Marx* • Kati Outinen *Arletty* • Jean-Pierre Darroussin *Monet* • Blondin Miguel *Idrissa* • Jean-Pierre Léaud *Denouncer* ■ *Dir/Scr* Aki Kaurismäki

Hawa ★★★ 15
Supernatural mystery thriller 2003 · Ind · Colour · 127min

This supernatural chiller transfers the supposedly fact-based action of the 1981 sleeper *The Entity* to an Indian hill station where a divorced mother of two helps run the family antique shop. Tabu occasionally struggles to convince as the woman whose life begins to unravel after she claims to have been raped by an unseen force, but director Guddu Dhanoa sustains the sinister atmosphere to disconcerting effect. DP In Hindi. *DVD*

Tabu *Sanjana* • Shahbaaz Khan *Doctor* • Mukesh Tiwari *Psychiatrist* • Imran Khan *Sanjana's brother* • Grusha Kapoor *Pooja* ■ *Dir* Guddu Dhanoa • *Scr* Sutanu Gupta, from his story

Hawaii ★★★ PG
Period drama 1966 · US · Colour · 181min

The fact that this adaptation of James Michener's novel was nominated for seven Oscars and won none is a clue that here is a big empty movie, which middlebrow Hollywood felt had something significant to say. Packed with tempestuous love affairs, natural disasters, culture clashes and slick action sequences, the film does little more than transfer the familiar western pioneering theme to the Pacific island. This meander through 20 years of the 19th century would be intolerably dull without the towering performance of Max von Sydow, who almost makes his unyielding missionary sympathetic in spite of his monstrous views. DP

Max von Sydow *Abner Hale* • Julie Andrews *Jerusha Bromley* • Richard Harris *Rafer Hoxworth* • Carroll O'Connor *Charles Bromley* • Elizabeth Cole *Abigail Bromley* • Diane Sherry *Charity Bromley* • Heather Menzies *Mercy Bromley* • Torin Thatcher *Reverend Thorn* • Gene Hackman *John Whipple* ■ *Dir* George Roy Hill • *Scr* Dalton Trumbo, Daniel Taradash, from the novel by James Michener

The Hawaiians ★
Period drama 1970 · US · Colour · 133min

This bland family saga is unenlivened by location shooting and the reuniting of the star (Charlton Heston) and director (Tom Gries) of the classic western *Will Penny*. For its UK premier (under the title *Master of the Islands*), a huge cardboard cutout of Heston stood outside the London Pavilion. Today, that cardboard figure seems to symbolise the movie, and the publicity stunt was certainly far more entertaining than the film itself. TS

Charlton Heston *Whip Hoxworth* • Geraldine Chaplin *Purity Hoxworth* • John Phillip Law *Noel Hoxworth* • Tina Chen *Nyuk Tsin* • Alec McCowen *Micah Hale* • Mako *Mun Ki* • Don Knight *Milton Overpeck* ■ *Dir* Tom Gries • *Scr* James R Webb, from the novel *Hawaii* by James A Michener

The Hawk ★★★ 15
Thriller 1992 · UK · Colour · 83min

Rumour has it that this intriguing home-grown movie was inspired by the Yorkshire Ripper investigation of the late 1970s and early 80s. Helen Mirren stars as the housewife who begins to suspect that there's a link between a series of murders and her husband's business trips, but her fragile mental health means that no one will believe her. The quality of the performances gives this overly bleak and murky thriller some much needed depth and spark. SH Swearing, violence, nudity, drug abuse. *DVD*

Helen Mirren *Annie Marsh* • George Costigan *Stephen Marsh* • Rosemary Leach *Mrs Marsh* • Melanie Hill *Norma* • Owen Teale *Ken Marsh* • Clive Russell *Chief Inspector Daybury* • Christopher Madin *Matthew Marsh* • Marie Hamer *Jackie Marsh* • David Harewood *Sergeant Streete* • Pooky Quesnel *WPC Clarke* • Caroline Paterson *Jan* • John Duttine *John* • Nadim Sawalha *Bahnu* ■ *Dir* David Hayman • *Scr* Peter Ransley, from his novel

Hawk the Slayer ★ PG
Fantasy adventure 1980 · UK · Colour · 89min

Not so much swords and sorcery as rubber rapiers and woeful witchcraft, as good brother John Terry battles with bad brother Jack Palance for possession of a mystic blade. Gimmicky direction by Terry Marcel can't hide the low budget of this production, debased by trite ideas and a banal approach. TH *DVD*

Jack Palance *Voltan* • John Terry *Hawk* • Bernard Bresslaw *Gort* • Ray Charleson *Crow* • Peter O'Farrell *Baldin* • Morgan Sheppard *Ranulf* • Cheryl Campbell *Sister Monica* • Annette Crosbie *Abbess* • Roy Kinnear *Innkeeper* • Warren Clarke *Scar* ■ *Dir* Terry Marcel • *Scr* Harry Robertson, Terry Marcel

Hawking ★★★★★ PG
Documentary 2013 · UK · Colour · 88min

Professor Stephen Hawking is a true one-off, both in terms of his Einstein-like advances in cosmology and the cruel motor neurone disease that has immobilised him while his glittering career has progressed. Director Stephen Finnigan frames Hawking's remarkable life story with unique access to the 71-year-old's daily working life at Cambridge University, as a jet-setting superstar lecturer and as centre of last year's Paralympics opening ceremony. Hawking is surprisingly candid about his failed marriages and weakness for the limelight, while warm testimony from family and friends and subtly staged reconstruction round out a captivating study of human endeavour. AC *DVD* *BL*

Stephen Hawking • Nathan Chapple *Stephen Hawking, young adult* • Joe Lovell *Stephen Hawking, adult* ■ *Dir* Stephen Finnigan • *Scr* Ben Bowie, Stephen Finnigan, Stephen Hawking

Hawks ★★★ 15
Black comedy drama 1988 · UK · Colour · 105min

Timothy Dalton stars in this modest little black comedy set in London and the Netherlands. He's a charismatic lawyer stricken with cancer, who lifts fellow sufferer Anthony Edwards out of his gloom and whisks him away to Amsterdam for one final fling. Sentimentality is never far from the surface, but the enthusiastic playing of the two stars overcomes the more mawkish moments, and there are refreshing turns from Camille Coduri and Janet McTeer as the two English girls they meet on the continent. JF Swearing.

Timothy Dalton *Bancroft* • Anthony Edwards *Deckermensky, "Decker"* • Janet McTeer *Hazel* • Camille Coduri *Maureen* • Julie T Wallace *Ward sister* • Connie Booth *Nurse Jarvis* • Robert Lang *Walter Bancroft* • Jill Bennett *Vivian Bancroft* • Sheila Hancock *Regina* • Caroline Langrishe *Carol* ■ *Dir* Robert Ellis Miller • *Scr* Roy Clarke, from an idea by Barry Gibb, David English

Hawks and Sparrows ★★★★ PG
Fantasy 1966 · It · BW · 84min

Working for the last time in monochrome, Pier Paolo Pasolini conceived this allegorical fantasy as a showcase for the legendary comic actor, Toto, and newcomer Ninetto Davoli. In addition to playing a couple of modern-day vagabonds, they also appear in a parable related by a talking crow, in which a pair of 12th-century monks are detailed by St Francis of Assisi to convert the birds to Christianity. Their lack of success in the parable is reflected back in the present day as Pasolini parodies Fellini, Rossellini and himself, and in so doing rejects Marxism, Catholicism and neorealism as the answer to Italy's problems. With excellent music from Ennio Morricone, this is one of the controversial director's more humorous offerings. DP Italian dubbed. *DVD* *BL*

Toto *Innocenti Toto/Brother Ciccillo* • Ninetto Davoli *Innocenti Ninetto/Brother Ninetto* • Femi Benussi *Luna* • Rossana Di Rocco *Ninetto's friend* • Lena Lin Solaro *Urganda la Sconosciuta* ■ *Dir/Scr* Pier Paolo Pasolini

Häxan ★★★★ 15
Silent horror documentary 1921 · Swe · BW · 105min

Danish director Benjamin Christensen's documentary-style investigation into *Witchcraft through the Ages* (the English title) employs an array of cinematic devices, with etchings, manuscripts and re-enacted episodes (in which Christensen himself plays the Devil). Three years in the making, the film sees the witch as a harmless victim of a superstitious and repressive Church. This illuminating, frightening and amusing film was banned in some countries at the time, ostensibly because of its violence and nudity, but its anticlericalism might have weighed more heavily with the censors. RB Violence, nudity. *DVD*

Benjamin Christensen *The Devil/The fashionable doctor* • Ella La Cour *Karna, the witch* • Emmy Schönfeld *Karna's collaborator* • Kate Fabian *Lovesick maiden* ■ *Dir/Scr* Benjamin Christensen

Haywire ★★★ 15
Action thriller 2011 · US/Ire · Colour · 88min

Steven Soderbergh takes the successful caper element of his *Ocean's* films and removes all the fun to deliver this po-faced, meaningless thriller. A rogue agent (Gina Carano) trots the globe in a bid to find out which of her various employers has set her up. It doesn't really matter whether it's Ewan McGregor, Michael Douglas or Channing Tatum, as the mechanical plot is a MacGuffin - an excuse for tactile beat-'em-up set pieces that move through New York, Barcelona, New Mexico and (possibly thanks to co-funding by the Irish Film Board) a grey, wet Dublin. David Holmes's funky score seems misplaced in such a dour film, but the violence is effectively tailored around Carano's undeniable skills. AC Violence. *DVD* *SD*

Gina Carano *Mallory Kane* • Ewan McGregor *Kenneth* • Channing Tatum *Aaron* • Michael Fassbender *Paul* • Antonio Banderas *Rodrigo* • Michael Douglas (1) *Coblenz* ■ *Dir* Steven Soderbergh • *Scr* Lem Dobbs • *Cinematographer* Peter Andrews [Steven Soderbergh]

He Got Game ★★★★ 15
Sports drama 1998 · US · Colour · 130min

This superb sports drama from writer/director Spike Lee sets out to prove that basketball is not just a game, but rather an essential part of the American way of life. From the opening shots of young men at obsessive play, set to music by Aaron Copland, Lee sets the tone of a world in which Jake Shuttlesworth (a powerful portrayal by Denzel Washington) is allowed out of prison - where he's serving a term for his wife's manslaughter - to talk his son Jesus (real-life pro Ray Allen), into becoming part of the prison warden's old college basketball team, and get himself paroled into the bargain. The confrontations feel real, the games have tension and the underlying message is universally scathing - sport is no longer for kudos, but purely for the money. TH Swearing, sex scenes, violence. *DVD*

Denzel Washington *Jake Shuttlesworth* • Ray Allen *Jesus Shuttlesworth* • Milla Jovovich *Dakota Burns* • Rosario Dawson *Lala Bonilla* • Hill Harper *Coleman "Booger" Sykes* • Ned Beatty *Warden Wyatt* • Jim Brown *Spivey* • Bill Nunn *Uncle Bubba* • John Turturro *Coach Billy Sunday* • Lonette McKee *Martha Shuttlesworth* ■ *Dir/Scr* Spike Lee

He Knows You're Alone ★★ 18
Thriller 1981 · US · Colour · 89min

Recycling an idea from the Bela Lugosi shocker *The Corpse Vanishes* in 1942, this predictably heavy-handed slasher movie has a killer stalking brides-to-be, terrorising them with increasingly ugly games of cat-and-mouse. No real surprises here, unless you count the fact that the director Armand Mastroianni is the late Marcello's cousin, and a young Tom Hanks makes his film acting debut. AJ

Don Scardino *Marvin* • Caitlin O'Heaney *Amy Jensen* • Elizabeth Kemp *Nancy* • Tom Rolfing *Killer* • Lewis Arlt *Len Gamble* • Patsy Pease *Joyce* • James Rebhorn *Carl* • Tom Hanks *Elliot* • Paul Gleason *Daley* ■ *Dir* Armand Mastroianni • *Scr* Scott Parker

He Laughed Last ★★
Comedy 1956 · US · Colour · 76min

Blake Edwards's second outing as a writer/director is a satire on the gangster movie. Recording star Frankie Laine plays a nightclub owner whose employee Lucy Marlow is a dancer and hostess who inherits a mobster's fortune, much to the dismay of her policeman boyfriend. There are musical numbers, fun with gangster conventions and Marlow is a dish, but it doesn't disguise the fact that this is a dime-budget offering. AT

Frankie Laine *Gino Lupo* • Lucy Marlow *Rosemary Lebeau* • Anthony Dexter *Dominic* • Dick Long [Richard Long] *Jimmy Murphy* • Alan Reed *Big Dan Hennessy* ■ *Dir* Blake Edwards • *Scr* Blake Edwards, from a story by Blake Edwards, Richard Quine

He Loves Me... He Loves Me Not ★★★ 12
Romantic thriller 2002 · Fr · Colour · 92min

French director Laetitia Colombani's beautifully crafted debut is a romantic thriller split into interconnected halves. In the first segment, Audrey Tautou edges towards *Fatal Attraction* territory, as her apparent affair with married cardiologist Samuel Le Bihan starts to sour. However, in the second segment, the story is replayed, this time from Le Bihan's viewpoint, and previously innocuous events take on a very different and unexpected meaning. Anchored by two strong central performances, this tightly coiled, chilling treat. SF French +subtitles. *DVD*

Audrey Tautou *Angélique* • Samuel Le Bihan *Loïc* • Isabelle Carré *Rachel* • Clément Sibony *David* • Sophie Guillemin *Héloïse* • Eric Savin *Julien* • Michèle Garay *Claire Belmont* • Elodie Navarre *Anita* ■ *Dir* Laetitia Colombani • *Scr* Laetitia Colombani, Caroline Thivel

He Named Me Malala ★★★★ PG
Documentary 2015 · UAE/US · Colour · 84min

This is the story of Malala Yousafzai, the Pakistani schoolgirl who survived a Taliban ambush to become a global activist for female education and Nobel laureate. Remarkably, her father named her after a historical Afghani freedom fighter who inspired her nation to repel British colonial invaders, but on this evidence Malala's amazing courage, determination and charisma are very much her own. A communicative, accessible and ultimately inspiring picture of a young woman who is an unlikely icon of hope for our times. TJ

Malala Yousafzai • Ziauddin Yousafzai • Toor Pekai Yousafzai *Toor Pekai Yousafzai* ■ *Dir* Davis Guggenheim • *Cinematographer* Erich Roland

He Ran All the Way ★★★ PG
Crime drama 1951 · US · BW · 74min

John Garfield's final role saw him give a typically intense performance as a thug on the run after a payroll robbery. Life seems to be improving when he (briefly) finds sanctuary with Shelley Winters. Then Garfield's tendency to panic leaves Winters to choose between her father and her lover. A happy ending seems unlikely, however, as was the case with the actor, whose career suffered during the communist witch-hunts in 1950s Hollywood. JM *DVD*

John Garfield *Nick* • Shelley Winters *Peg* • Wallace Ford *Mr Dobbs* • Selena Royle *Mrs Dobbs* • Gladys George *Mrs Robey* • Norman Lloyd *Al Molin* • Bobby Hyatt *Tommy Dobbs* ■ *Dir* John Berry • *Scr* Guy Endore, Hugo Butler, from the novel by Sam Ross

He Rides Tall ★★
Western 1964 · US · BW · 83min

Tony Young was an American TV star in a violent (for its time) western series called *Gunslinger*, and Universal released two vehicles for him theatrically: this one, a stark, grim story that was X-rated in the UK, and a companion piece called *Taggart*. This is the (marginally) better of the two, but Young simply didn't have what it takes to be a movie star. TS

Tony Young *Marshal Morg Rocklin* • Dan Duryea *Bart Thorne* • Jo Morrow *Kate McCloud* • Madlyn Rhue *Ellie Daniels* • RG Armstrong *Josh McCloud* ■ *Dir* RG Springsteen • *Scr* Charles W Irwin, Robert Creighton Williams [Bob Williams], from a story by Charles W Irwin

He Said, She Said ★★★ 15
Comedy 1991 · US · Colour · 110min

Two warring TV talk-show hosts (Kevin Bacon and Elizabeth Perkins) carry on their relationship both in front of and behind the cameras. The film s split into two halves (one directed by Ken Kwapis, the other by his wife Marisa Silver) so you see the romance from each point of view. Both Bacon and Perkins are attractively amiable, but neither manages to sustain the comedy and this gets a bit tedious. JB Some swearing. *DVD*

Kevin Bacon *Dan Hanson* • Elizabeth Perkins *Lorie Bryer* • Sharon Stone *Linda* • Nathan Lane *Wally Thurman* • Anthony LaPaglia *Mark* • Stanley Anderson *Mr Weller* • Brad Pitt ■ *Dir* Ken Kwapis, Marisa Silver • *Scr* Brian Hohlfeld, from his story

He Walked by Night ★★★ PG
Thriller 1948 · US · BW · 78min

One of those economic miracles - a B-thriller made for peanuts that manages to create some vivid images and a high degree of tension. Its success is mainly owing to ace cameraman John Alton, a master of black-and-white moodiness, while Anthony Mann is thought to have given credited director Alfred Werker a hand. Richard Basehart stars as a thief who kills a cop and is tracked down by the Los Angeles police. Much emphasis is placed on detection methods and on Basehart's personality in a compelling character study that also delivers in terms of action. AT

Richard Basehart *Davis Morgan* • Scott Brady *Sergeant Marty Brennan* • Roy Roberts *Captain Breen* • James Cardwell *Chuck Jones* • Whit Bissell *Reeves* ■ *Dir* Alfred Werker • *Scr* John C Higgins, Crane Wilbur, Harry Essex, from a story by Crane Wilbur • *Cinematographer* John Alton

He Was a Quiet Man ★★★ 15
Black comedy drama 2007 · US · Colour · 91min

A downtrodden paper pusher goes from zero to hero in this surreal black comedy that's part *Falling Down*, part *Office Space*. An almost unrecognisable Christian Slater stars as bullied clerical worker Bob Maconel, who dreams of gunning down his colleagues but can't bring himself to "go postal" - until a co-worker opens fire and Bob shoots him. Slater oozes creepy desperation from every pore, while Elisha Cuthbert - as his office crush left paralysed and resentful after the incident - ensures that acid-infused tragedy infects even their sweetest intimate moments. As a satire on the frustrations of modern life, the film starts off well but then crumbles in an underdeveloped and ambiguous final act. SF *DVD*

Christian Slater *Bob Maconel* • Elisha Cuthbert *Vanessa* • William H Macy *Gene Shelby* • Sascha Knopf *Paula* • Jamison Jones *Scott Harper* ■ *Dir/Scr* Frank A Cappello [Frank Cappello]

He Was Her Man ★★★
Crime drama 1934 · US · BW · 70min

In a snappy, exuberant, Roaring Twenties thriller, James Cagney plays a safecracker who gives up a life of crime to scare off rivals who've been trying to put him inside. Joan Blondell is the wisecracker who stands by him and pulls him through, while Lloyd Bacon directs in the tradition of machine-gun macho. TH

James Cagney *Flicker Hayes* • Joan Blondell *Rose Lawrence* • Victor Jory *Nick Gardella* • Frank Craven *Pop Sims* • Harold Huber *JC Ward* • Russell Hopton *Monk* • Ralf Harolde *Red Deering* • Sarah Padden *Mrs Gardella* ■ *Dir* Lloyd Bacon • *Scr* Tom Buckingham, Niven Busch, from a story by Robert Lord

He Who Gets Slapped ★★★★★
Silent drama 1924 · US · BW · 72min

Lon Chaney Sr gives one of his best performances in the film version of Leonid Andreyev's Broadway success. The Man of a Thousand Faces plays a disillusioned scientist whose professional disappointments force him to alter his appearance and join the circus as a clown. But instead of finding happiness and freedom in a world of total make-believe, he soon discovers a different grief lies hidden beneath the greasepaint and tinsel. Beautifully told, and flawlessly directed by Victor Sjöström (making his second film in the US), this is a poetic silent masterpiece. AJ

Lon Chaney *Paul Beaumont/"He Who Gets Slapped"* • Norma Shearer *Consuelo* • John Gilbert (1) *Bezano* • Tully Marshall *Count Mancini* • Marc MacDermott *Baron Regnard* • Ford Sterling *Tricaud* ■ *Dir* Victor Seastrom [Victor Sjöström] • *Scr* Carey Wilson, Victor Seastrom [Victor Sjöström], from the play *He, the One Who Gets Slapped* by Leonid Andreyev, translated by Gregory Zilboorg

He Who Rides a Tiger ★★
Crime drama 1965 · UK · BW · 102min

This crime melodrama is a kitchen sink tale - overflowing with soap - that's as unpredictable as its cat burglar protagonist, played by Tom Bell. One moment he's soft on orphans and the eager Judi Dench; the next he's stealing jewels from stately homes and erupting into demented violence. Bell admirably combines both personality traits in his performance, but the shifts from realism to romanticism are less credible. DP

Tom Bell *Peter Rayston* • Judi Dench *Joanne* • Paul Rogers *Superintendent Taylor* • Kay Walsh *Mrs Woodley* • Ray McAnally *Orphanage superintendent* • Jeremy Spenser *The Panda* • Peter Madden *Peepers Woodley* ■ *Dir* Charles Crichton • *Scr* Trevor Peacock

Head ★★★★ PG
Musical comedy 1968 · US · Colour · 85min

Bob Rafelson had been the brains behind the Monkees, the American pop group formed in the image of the Beatles specifically for an NBC TV series. With the band's popularity on the wane, he and co-writer Jack Nicholson fashioned this psychedelic romp that beefed up the usual bubblegum slapstick with Vietnam War footage and old movie clips. It went over the heads of most fans in 1968, but it's essential viewing for anyone who knows all the words to the Monkees' theme tune. DP *DVD*

Micky Dolenz • David Jones [Davy Jones] *David Jones* • Michael Nesmith • Peter Tork • Annette Funicello *Minnie* • Timothy Carey *Lord High'n'Low* • Logan Ramsey *Officer Faye Lapid* • Abraham Sofaer *Swami* • Sonny Liston • Carol Doda *Sally Silicone* • Frank Zappa *Critic* • June Fairchild *Jumper* • Victor Mature *Big Victor* • Terry Garr [Teri Garr] *Testy True* ■ *Dir* Bob Rafelson • *Scr* Jack Nicholson, Bob Rafelson

Head above Water ★ 15
Comedy mystery thriller 1996 · US/UK · Colour · 88min

Jim Wilson, producer of Kevin Costner hits such as *The Bodyguard* and *Dances with Wolves*, came a cropper with this modest but thoroughly unfunny black comedy, a remake of a little known Norwegian film. Harvey Keitel and Cameron Diaz are the mismatched newlyweds who fast fall out when the latter's ex (Billy Zane) turns up. Wilson never gets a handle on the underwritten script, and the talented performers are reduced to unfunny mugging. JF

Harvey Keitel *George* • Cameron Diaz *Nathalie* • Craig Sheffer *Lance* • Billy Zane *Kent* • Shay Duffin *Policeman* • Mo Mo, the bird ■ *Dir* Jim Wilson (2) • *Scr* Theresa Marie, from the film *Hodet over Vannet* by Geir Eriksen, Eirik Ildahl

Head in the Clouds ★★★ 15
Period romantic drama 2004 · Can/UK/Sp/US · Colour · 116min

A glamorous *ménage à trois* is torn apart by war in this sprawling romantic drama from writer/director John Duigan. Charlize Theron is a free-spirited photographer who shares a hedonistic life in highly stylised 1930s Europe with her two similarly colourful lovers (Penélope Cruz and Theron's then real-life partner Stuart Townsend). Though neither the story nor the characters' passions feel entirely convincing, the picture remains solidly engaging. SF Sex scenes, violence. *DVD*

Charlize Theron *Gilda Bessé* • Penélope Cruz *Mia* • Stuart Townsend *Guy* • Thomas Kretschmann *Major Frans Bietrich* • Steven Berkoff *Charles Bessé* • David La Haye *Lucien* • Karine Vanasse *Lisette* • Gabriel Hogan *Julian Elsworth* • Peter Cockett *Max* • John Jorgenson *Django Reinhardt* ■ *Dir/Scr* John Duigan

Head of State ★★ 12
Comedy 2003 · US · Colour · 91min

In this political satire, Chris Rock stars as a black presidential candidate deliberately handpicked to bolster opposition votes. He also makes his directorial debut, co-writes and produces. There's no subtlety as he saturates the strength-through-adversity storyline with patronising stereotypes, repetitive sight gags and his customary quick-fire retorts. Though his concise observations on social decay are wryly amusing, the humour overall is clumsy. SF Swearing. *DVD*

Chris Rock *Mays Gilliam* • Bernie Mac *Mitch Gilliam* • Dylan Baker *Martin Geller* • Nick Searcy *Brian Lewis* • Lynn Whitfield *Debra Lassiter* • Robin Givens *Kim* • Tamala Jones *Lisa Clark* • James Rebhorn *Senator Bill Arnot* • Keith David *Bernard Cooper* ■ *Dir* Chris Rock • *Scr* Ali LeRoi, Chris Rock

Head Office ★ 15
Comedy 1986 · US · Colour · 86min

In this trite comedy, Judge Reinhold plays an inept bod, inveigled into a job in a top multinational company where he is used and abused, but still falls for his company director's daughter Lori-Nan Engler. Reinhold isn't funny enough to carry the movie and the only sparky moments are down to support characters Don Novello and Richard Masur. LH *DVD*

Eddie Albert *Helmes* • Danny DeVito *Stedman* • Lori-Nan Engler *Rachael* • Don King *Hoover* • Don Novello *Sal* • Judge Reinhold *Jack Issel* • Jane Seymour (2) *Jane* • Wallace Shawn *Hoover* • Rick Moranis *Gross* ■ *Dir/Scr* Ken Finkleman

Head On ★★★
Comedy drama 1980 · Can · Colour · 86min

Sally Kellerman and Stephen Lack star in this bizarre but sometimes intriguing drama about two drivers who are involved in a head-on crash and then become lovers. Both like playing dangerous games, sexual and otherwise, and soon the stakes begin to rise as the film flits between tension and comedy. Originally known as *Fatal Attraction*, this is an interestingly quirky movie lent weight by the lead performances and the supporting cast. JB

Sally Kellerman *Michelle Keys* • Stephen Lack *Peter Hill* • John Huston *Clarke Hill* • Lawrence Dane *Frank Keys* • John Peter Linton *Gad Bernstein* • Hadley Kay *Stanley* • Robert Silverman *Michelle's analyst* • Maxwell Moffett *Henry* ■ *Dir* Michael Grant • *Scr* James Sanderson, Paul Illidge

Head On ★★ 18
Drama 1997 · Aus · Colour · 99min

It's hard to see how writer/director Ana Kokkinos could have made her raw study of being young, gay and Greek in modern Melbourne any more abrasive. She and actor Alex Dimitriades deserve credit for making the central character so antiheroic, as he spurns cultural identity and social stability for a nihilistic diet of drugs and rough trade. DP English, Greek +subtitles. Drug abuse, sex scenes, swearing. *DVD*

Alex Dimitriades *Ari* • Paul Capsis *Johnny, "Toula"* • Julian Garner *Sean* • Elena Mandalis *Betty* • Tony Nikolakopoulos *Dimitri* • Damien Fotiou *Joe* • Eugenia Fragos *Sofia* • Dora Kaskanis *Dina* ■ *Dir* Ana Kokkinos • *Scr* Andrew Bovell, Ana Kokkinos, Mira Robertson, from the novel *Loaded* by Christos Tsiolkas

Head-On ★★★★ 18
Romantic drama 2003 · Ger/Tur · Colour · 116min

Fatih Akin's award-winning marital drama explores the extent to which Germany's Turkish population retains its national identity. Making evocative use of both Hamburg and Istanbul, Akin creates a genuine sense of community, as hard-drinking 40-something Birol Unel and parentally repressed Sibel Kekilli contract a marriage of convenience that initially suits both parties. But as Unel becomes increasingly jealous of the liberated Kekilli's string of lovers, they come to view the relationship in very different terms. The leads are excellent, with the debuting Kekilli particularly impressive. DP German, Turkish, English +subtitles. Swearing, sex scenes, drug abuse. *DVD*

Birol Unel *Cahit Tomruk* • Sibel Kekilli *Sibel Guner* • Catrin Striebeck *Maren* • Guven Kirac *Seref* • Meltem Cumbul *Selma* • Cem Akin *Yilmaz Guner* • Aysel Iscan *Birsen Guner* • Demir Gokgol *Yunus Guner* ■ *Dir/Scr* Fatih Akin

Head over Heels ★★ 12
Romantic comedy 2000 · US · Colour · 82min

Teen heart-throb Freddie Prinze Jr co-stars here with Monica Potter in a romantic comedy that starts off amusingly but sinks into mediocrity. Potter plays an unlucky-in-love art curator who moves into a luxury New York flat with four supermodels. It's not long before she then falls for neighbour Prinze Jr, that is until she sees him apparently club someone to death. Misunderstandings and nods to *Rear Window* run roughshod through what is left of the plot. LH *DVD*

Monica Potter *Amanda* • Freddie Prinze Jr *Jim Winston* • China Chow *Lisa* • Shalom Harlow *Jade* • Ivana Milicevic *Roxana* • Sarah O'Hare *Candi* ■ *Dir* Mark S Waters [Mark Waters (1)] • *Scr* Ron Burch, David Kidd, from a story by Ron Burch, David Kidd, John J Strauss, Ed Decter

Head over Heels in Love ★★★ U
Musical 1937 · UK · BW · 78min

Having made her movie name under the direction of Victor Saville, Jessie Matthews went to work for her four-time co-star and then husband Sonnie Hale, whose first outing behind the camera this was. The story centres on Jessie's inability to make up her mind between suitors Robert Flemyng and Louis Borell. Hale's inexperience shows away from the musical numbers, but Alfred Junge's sets give the film sophistication. DP

Jessie Matthews *Jeanne* • Robert Flemyng *Pierre* • Louis Borell *Marcel* • Romney Brent *Matty* • Helen Whitney Bourne *Norma* • Paul Leyssac *Max* • Eliot Makeham *Martin* ■ *Dir* Sonnie Hale • *Scr* Fred Thompson, Dwight Taylor, Marjorie Gaffney, from the play *Pierre ou Jac* by François de Crosset

Headhunters ★★★★ 15
Crime thriller 2011 · Nor/Den/Ger · Colour · 96min

Adapted from a novel by a Norwegian author best known for his crime novels, this thriller is altogether more escapist than that trademark fare. It stars Aksel Hennie as a wealthy businessman who moonlights as an art thief, but who comes unstuck when he plans to steal a work from former special forces soldier Nikolaj Coster-Waldau. The film's violence and (literally) lavatorial humour will not suit everyone, but Hennie's hangdog hero makes this a perversely entertaining ride, even at its most punishing. DW Norwegian, Danish +subtitles. Violence, swearing, sex scenes, brief nudity. *DVD* *Blu*

Aksel Hennie *Roger Brown* • Nikolaj Coster-Waldau *Clas Greve* • Synnove Macody Lund *Diana Brown* • Eivind Sander *Ove Kikerud* • Julie Olgaard *Lotte* • Reidar Sorensen *Brede Sperre* ■ *Dir* Morten Tyldum • *Scr* Lars Gudmestad, Ulf Ryberg, from the novel by Jo Nesbo

Heading South ★★★ 15
Drama 2006 · Fr/Can · Colour · 103min

Laurent Cantet's globalisation allegory - set in Haiti in the 1970s - exposes the casual arrogance of western cultural imperialism, but lacks balance because of its narrow emphasis on a pair of white, middle-aged, bourgeois women. The pivotal battle between Charlotte Rampling and Karen Young for teenager Ménothy César's attention is grounded in the women's respective frustrations back in the States. But too little is revealed of César's fraught existence away from the resort frequented by wealthy sex tourists, who pay only superficial heed to the realities of poverty and oppression all around them. DP French +subtitles. *DVD*

Charlotte Rampling *Ellen* • Karen Young *Brenda* • Louise Portal *Sue* • Ménothy César *Legba* • Lys Ambroise *Albert* • Jackenson Pierre Olmo Diaz *Eddy* ■ *Dir* Laurent Cantet • *Scr* Laurent Cantet, Robin Campillo, from three short stories by Dany Laferrière

The Headless Woman ★★★★ 12A
Mystery drama 2008 · Arg/Fr/It/Sp · Colour · 89min

When a bottle-blonde woman of a certain age (played by María Onetto) runs over something - or was it someone? - on the cross-country drive home, her life changes for ever in this teasingly enigmatic Argentinian drama. Writer/director Lucrecia Martel's character study won't appeal to those who like their storytelling cut and dried, but the film and Onetto's wide-eyed central performance are remarkable in the way they allow us to share the unsettled heroine's vision of an everyday world that no longer fits together. There's an undertow of dread here reminiscent of the work of Hitchcock and Michelangelo Antonioni, not to mention the legacy of the disappearances during Argentina's years under military rule. TJ Spanish +subtitles.

Maria Onetto *Verónica* • Claudia Cantero *Josefina* • Inés Efron *Candita* • Daniel Genoud *Juan Manuel* • César Bordón *Marcos* ■ *Dir/Scr* Lucrecia Martel

HEALTH ★★★
Satirical comedy 1980 · US · Colour · 102min

One of director Robert Altman's social comedies, this exemplifies the maxim that they shall have muesli wherever they go. It's set at a health food convention as its members try to elect a new president, though political corruption is Altman's target for satire. Among the wild and wacky women of whom Altman seems very fond are Glenda Jackson, Lauren Bacall - playing an 83-year-old virgin - and Carol Burnett. James Garner is engagingly macho in contrast. The pile-up of off-the-wall jokes does get a bit tiresome by the end, however. TH

Glenda Jackson *Isabella Garnell* • Carol Burnett *Gloria Burbank* • James Garner *Harry Wolff* • Lauren Bacall *Esther Brill* • Dick Cavett • Paul Dooley *Dr Gil Gainey* • Henry Gibson *Bobby Hammer* • Alfre Woodard *Hotel manager* ■ *Dir* Robert Altman • *Scr* Frank Barhydt, Paul Dooley, Robert Altman

Hear My Song ★★★★ 15
Comedy drama 1991 · UK · Colour · 99min

Just when you think they don't make 'em like that any more, debutant director Peter Chelsom comes along and proves that they most certainly do. This is a delicious confection, with just the right amounts of "Oirish" whimsy, scouse nous, bittersweet romance and broad comedy. Adrian Dunbar is the personification of impudent charm as the club owner seeking the tax-exiled tenor Josef Locke (played with gruff amiability by Ned Beatty). The Irish sequences get the nod over those set in Liverpool; how could a run-in with a mystery singer hope to compete with a runaway cow? A treat. DP Some violence, swearing, nudity. *DVD*

Ned Beatty *Josef Locke* • Adrian Dunbar *Micky O'Neill* • Shirley Anne Field *Cathleen Doyle* • Tara FitzGerald *Nancy Doyle* • William Hootkins *Mr X* • Harold Berens *Benny Rose* • David McCallum (1) *Jim Abbott* • John Dair *Derek* • Norman Vaughan • James Nesbitt *Fintan O'Donnell* ■ *Dir* Peter Chelsom • *Scr* Peter Chelsom, Adrian Dunbar, from a story by Peter Chelsom

Hear No Evil ★ 15
Thriller 1993 · US · Colour · 92min

This dismal stalker thriller has deaf personal trainer Marlee Matlin being pursued by cop Martin Sheen and a creepy man in black. Both of them want to get their hands on a rare coin she doesn't even know she has. It's tedious and annoying fare, packed with every cliché imaginable but little else of interest. JB Violence, swearing.

Marlee Matlin *Jillian Shanahan* • DB Sweeney *Ben Kendall* • Martin Sheen *Lieutenant Philip Brock* • John C McGinley *Mickey O'Malley* ■ *Dir* Robert Greenwald • *Scr* RM Badat [Randall Badat], Kathleen Rowell, from a story by Danny Rubin, RM Badat [Randall Badat]

Heart ★ 15
Sports drama 1987 · US · Colour · 90min

As a weary retread of one of the best boxing movies ever - Robert Wise's 1949 film *The Set-Up* - this has lost all grip. A pallid imitation of a vivid original, Brad Davis is the retired pugilist tricked into a comeback by slimy manager Steve Buscemi, while girlfriend Frances Fisher looks on aghast. As well she might: despite Buscemi's performance, this low-budget film never even begins to be a contender. TH *DVD*

Brad Davis *Eddie Brennan* • Frances Fisher *Jeannie* • Steve Buscemi *Nicky* • Robinson Frank Adu *Buddy* • Jesse Doran *Diddy* • Sam Gray *Leo* ■ *Dir* James Lemmo • *Scr* James Lemmo, Randy Jurgensen

Heart ★★★ 18
Psychological thriller 1997 · UK · Colour · 81min

This gripping and unusual psychological thriller comes from the pen of ace TV scriptwriter Jimmy McGovern. In the *Cracker* creator's first work written expressly for the big screen, a devastated Saskia Reeves allows the heart of her beloved son, killed in an accident, to be given to Christopher Eccleston. It's when Reeves strikes up an uneasy relationship with Eccleston to ensure he is a worthy recipient that the really startling aspect of the story begins to take shape. This dark passion play crackles with style, black humour and energy. AJ Swearing, violence, sex scenes.

Christopher Eccleston *Gary Ellis* • Saskia Reeves *Marie Ann McCardle* • Kate Hardie *Tess Ellis* • Rhys Ifans *Alex Madden* • Anna Chancellor *Nicola Farmer* • Bill Paterson *Mr Kreitman* • Matthew Rhys *Sean McCardle* • Jack Deam *Policeman* ■ *Dir* Charles McDougall • *Scr* Jimmy McGovern

Heart and Souls ★★★ PG
Fantasy drama 1993 · US · Colour · 99min

Four ghosts get the chance to tie up loose ends in their lives by taking over the body of uptight yuppie Robert Downey Jr, in director Ron Underwood's touching flight of comedy fantasy. Once over the far-too-elaborate set-up, this becomes a cosy whimsical fable with fewer signposted twists than initially anticipated. Endearing and sentimental, the highlight is Downey Jr's fabulously funny and versatile performance, with Tom Sizemore, Alfre Woodard, Kyra Sedgwick and Charles Grodin adding sparkling support as the spirits. AJ

Robert Downey Jr *Thomas Reilly* • Charles Grodin *Harrison Winslow* • Alfre Woodard *Penny Washington* • Kyra Sedgwick *Julia* • Tom Sizemore *Milo Peck* • David Paymer *Hal, the bus driver* • Elisabeth Shue *Anne* ■ *Dir* Ron Underwood • *Scr* Brent Maddock, SS Wilson, from a story by Brent Maddock, SS Wilson, from a screenplay (unproduced) by Eric Hansen, Gregory Hansen

Heart Beat ★★
Biographical drama 1979 · US · Colour · 108min

This is an ambitious but ultimately doomed attempt to shed light on the stars of the Beat Generation, despite some extraordinary performances from the talented cast. A loosely biographical tale, it focuses on the strange relationship between Jack Kerouac (John Heard) and the Cassadys (Nick Nolte and Sissy Spacek), but although all three have rarely been better, director John Byrum seems at a loss as to how to develop the story. JF

Nick Nolte *Neal Cassady* • Sissy Spacek *Carolyn Cassady* • John Heard *Jack Kerouac* • Ray Sharkey *Ira* • Ann Dusenberry *Stevie* • Margaret Fairchild *Mrs Kerouac* • Tony Bill *Dick* ■ *Dir* John Byrum • *Scr* John Byrum, from memoirs by Carolyn Cassady

Heart Condition ★★★ 15
Action comedy 1990 · US · Colour · 95min

Bob Hoskins and Denzel Washington star in this paranormal buddy movie as the mismatched pair - one alive, one a ghost. Hoskins, with the transplanted heart of Washington inside him, investigates the latter's death. Writer/director James D

Parriott doesn't quite pull off the invisibility gags, nor does he allow his talented stars enough space to fill their characters. Despite its flaws, it's a pleasant enough time-waster. AJ Swearing, violence.

Bob Hoskins *Jack Moony* • Denzel Washington *Napoleon Stone* • Chloe Webb *Crystal Gerrity* • Roger E Mosley *Captain Wendt* • Ja'net DuBois *Mrs Stone* • Alan Rachins *Dr Posner* • Ray Baker *Harry Zara* • Jeffrey Meek *John Graham* ■ *Dir/Scr* James D Parriott

The Heart Is a Lonely Hunter ★★★★ PG
Drama 1968 · US · Colour · 118min

Set in a small Southern town, this is a compelling version of novelist Carson McCullers's acute study of the anxieties and aspirations of a disparate group of troubled characters. Alan Arkin gives an Oscar-nominated performance as the deaf-mute who tries to bring peace and consolation to a fellow mute, an impotent café owner, an adolescent tomboy (Sondra Locke), an alcoholic Marxist and a black doctor battling against injustice. Director Robert Ellis Miller makes the novel's points without heavy-handedness and debutants Stacy Keach and Locke (also nominated for an Academy Award) hold their own in a splendid supporting cast. DP

Alan Arkin *John Singer* • Laurinda Barrett *Mrs Kelly* • Stacy Keach *Blount* • Chuck McCann *Antonapoulos* • Biff McGuire *Mr Kelly* • Sondra Locke *Mick Kelly* • Percy Rodrigues *Dr Copeland* • Cicely Tyson *Portia* • Jackie Marlowe *Bubber Kelly* • Johnny Popwell *Willie* • Wayne Smith *Harry* ■ *Dir* Robert Ellis Miller • *Scr* Thomas C Ryan, from the novel by Carson McCullers

Heart like a Wheel ★★★ PG
Biographical drama 1983 · US · Colour · 108min

Shirley Muldowney is often described as the world's first woman racing driver, though because she drives hot-rods and dragsters she isn't recognised as such in Europe. This greasy, gutsy biopic covers a span of 25 years and gives Bonnie Bedelia an acting challenge she passes with flying colours. Marriage, divorce and romance with her manager Beau Bridges are just some of the pitstops on the way to winning the world championship three times. AT

Bonnie Bedelia *Shirley Muldowney* • Beau Bridges *Connie Kalitta* • Leo Rossi *Jack Muldowney* • Hoyt Axton *Tex Roque* • Bill McKinney *Don "Big Daddy" Garlits* • Anthony Edwards *John Muldowney (age 15-23)* • Dean Paul Martin *Sonny Rigotti* ■ *Dir* Jonathan Kaplan • *Scr* Ken Friedman

Heart of a Child ★★★ 12
Drama based on a true story 1994 · US · Colour · 88min

The subject of this TV movie kept the Canadian tabloids occupied for a couple of months as two mothers-to-be on opposite sides of the country learn that the only way one of their unborn babies can survive is by receiving the heart of the other. As the women facing the agonising decision, Michele Green and Ann Jillian give solid performances, while the versatile Rip Torn does well as the doctor advising them. DP *DVD*

Ann Jillian *Alice Holc* • Michele Greene *Karen Schouten* • Terry O'Quinn *Gordon Holc* • Bruce Greenwood *Fred Schouten* • Rip Torn *Dr Leonard Bailey* • Andrew Wheeler *Dr Cramer* • Cindy Girling *Dr Cynthia Adler* • Ric Reid *Terry Waterhouse* • William B Davis *Vern* ■ *Dir* Sandor Stern • *Scr* Susan Nanus

Heart of a Dog ★★★★ PG
Documentary 2015 · Fr/US · Colour and BW · 76min

On her return to film direction for the first time since her 1986 concert film, *Home of the Brave*, versatile avant-gardist Laurie Anderson dazzles with her ingenuity and honesty in this heartfelt tribute to her mother, late husband Lou Reed and her beloved rat terrier, Lolabelle. Flitting between topics with a canine inquisitiveness, Anderson found footage, home movies, distressed found footage, animation and trick effects to connect a swooping hawk with 9/11, drone surveillance and data collection in an age of social media exhibitionism. DP
■ *Dir/Scr* Laurie Anderson

The Heart of a Man ★★ U
Musical 1959 · UK · BW · 93min

Veteran director Herbert Wilcox bowed out of films with this undistinguished and wholly unconvincing slice-of-life drama, which was produced by his actress wife Anna Neagle. Frankie Vaughan stars as the homecoming sailor who is offered £1,000 reward by an eccentric tramp if he can honestly earn £100 within a week. Following stints as a bouncer, a boxer and a commissionaire, he finally makes good as a singer and meets sultry chanteuse Anne Heywood. DP

Frankie Vaughan *Frankie* • Anne Heywood *Julie* • Tony Britton *Tony* • Peter Sinclair *Bud* • Michael Medwin *Sid* • Anthony Newley *Johnny* ■ *Dir* Herbert Wilcox • *Scr* Jack Trevor Story, Pamela Bower, from a story by Rex North

Heart of Dixie ★ 15
Drama 1989 · US · Colour · 91min

Starring Ally Sheedy, Virginia Madsen and Phoebe Cates, this is 1950s-style melodrama of the worst order. The girls are at college in the Deep South and are at odds with the racism and sexism of where they live. Romances ensue, consciousness is raised and the film improves briefly towards the end with the arrival of the first black student on campus. LH

Ally Sheedy *Maggie* • Virginia Madsen *Delia* • Phoebe Cates *Aiken* • Treat Williams *Hoyt* • Don Michael Paul *Boots* • Kyle Secor *Tuck* • Francesca Roberts *Keefi* ■ *Dir* Martin Davidson • *Scr* Tom McCown, from the novel *Heartbreak Hotel* by Ann Rivers Siddons

Heart of Glass ★★★★ PG
Period drama 1976 · W Ger · Colour · 90min

An allegorical treatise on the nature of the Germanic character, Werner Herzog's audacious tale of a 19th-century Bavarian town being cast into despondency by the death of its patron (who alone knows the secret of its trademark ruby glass) is best known for the fact its cast reportedly delivered its somnambulist performances under the influence of hypnosis. Herzog's part-mythical, part-prophetic vision of desolation and dependence (reinforced by the extraordinary blend of the Gothic and the Wagnerian in Henning von Gierke and Cornelius Siegel's stylised settings) gives this film a power that surpasses its novelty. DP German +subtitles. *DVD*

Josef Bierbichler *Has* • Stefan Güttler *Huttenbesitzer* • Clemens Scheitz *Adalbert* • Sepp Müller • Volker Prechtel ■ *Dir* Werner Herzog • *Scr* Werner Herzog, Herbert Achternbusch

The Heart of Justice ★★★★ 12
Mystery thriller 1992 · US · Colour · 87min

Director Bruno Barreto would work again with Dennis Hopper in the romantic drama *Acts of Love*, but this earlier, made-for-TV collaboration is a classier affair, with Eric Stoltz as a journalist who sets out to unravel the mysterious murder of well-known novelist Hopper. Barreto secures a clutch of superb portrayals from the likes of William H Macy, Bradford Dillman, Jennifer Connelly and Joanna Miles, and look out, too, for a delightful cameo from Vincent Price. JF Some swearing, violence, sexual references.

Jennifer Connelly *Emma Burgess* • Bradford Dillman *Mr Burgess* • Dermot Mulroney *Elliot Burgess* • Dennis Hopper *Austin Blair* • Vincent Price *Shaw* • Eric Stoltz *David Leader* • William H Macy *Booth* • Joanna Miles *Mrs Burgess* • Harris Yulin *Keneally* • Keith Reddin *Simon* ■ *Dir* Bruno Barreto • *Scr* Keith Reddin

The Heart of Me ★★★ 15
Period romantic drama 2002 · UK · Colour · 91min

Director Thaddeus O'Sullivan has given this period tale of adultery and redemption a bittersweet piquancy, while Nicholas Hooper's original score underlines its discreet romanticism. Scriptwriter Lucinda Coxon has lost some of the affecting sensibility of Rosamond Lehmann's novel about two sisters who are in love with the same man by relying too much on emotional clichés. Nevertheless, Paul Bettany, Olivia Williams and Helena Bonham Carter do make an engaging *ménage à trois*. TH *DVD*

Helena Bonham Carter *Dinah* • Olivia Williams *Madeleine* • Paul Bettany *Rickie* • Eleanor Bron *Mrs Burkett* • Luke Newberry *Anthony* • Tom Ward *Jack* • Gillian Hanna *Betty* • Andrew Havill *Charles* • Rosie Bonham Carter *Clarissa* ■ *Dir* Thaddeus O'Sullivan • *Scr* Lucinda Coxon, from the novel *The Echoing Grove* by Rosamond Lehmann

Heart of Midnight ★ 18
Horror thriller 1988 · US · Colour and BW · 106min

A sick fantasy that's neither sick nor fantastic enough, director Matthew Chapman's degrading attempt to be meaningful in a horror thriller context is a pretentiously arty bore. Jennifer Jason Leigh is the woman on the verge of a nervous breakdown who inherits a tacky LA nightclub-cum-brothel. AJ *DVD*

Jennifer Jason Leigh *Carol Rivers* • Peter Coyote *Sharpe/Larry* • Gale Mayron *Sonny* • Sam Schact *Uncle Fletcher* • Denise Dummont *Mariana* • Frank Stallone *Ledray* • Steve Buscemi *Eddy* • Brenda Vaccaro *Betty Rivers* ■ *Dir* Matthew Chapman • *Scr* Matthew Chapman, Everett DeRoche

The Heart of the Game ★★★ 12
Sports documentary 2006 · US · Colour · 93min

A tax professor coaches a basketball team of high-school girls in this documentary by Ward Serrill. The coach's off-the-wall approach and the girls' cheerful aggression puts an intriguing spin on the usual underdogs story. But Serrill later switches tactics to focus on teen prodigy Darnellia Russell, a working-class black girl drafted in to lead the mostly white Roosevelt Roughriders to victory. Through a combination of interviews and narration by rap star Chris "Ludacris" Bridges, Serrill follows Darnellia's battle off the court when unforeseen events threaten to end her career. The climactic basketball match has more drama and tension than a Hollywood screenwriter could dream up. Ultimately, this is a real-life fairy tale that aims straight at the heart, and scores. SP Swearing. *DVD*

Chris "Ludacris" Bridges [Chris Bridges] *Narrator* • Devon Crosby-Helms • Bill Resler • Maude Lepley • Darnellia Russell • Joyce Walker ■ *Dir/Scr* Ward Serrill

The Heart of the Matter ★★★
Drama 1953 · UK · BW · 105min

Graham Greene's tale of wartime infidelity and tortured conscience in Sierra Leone has, like its protagonist, not been faithful to its source. The religious and moral dilemma facing the adulterous police commissioner Scobie has been downplayed to concentrate on the human tragedy of a doomed love triangle. With the innocent intensity of her emotions clearly displayed, Maria Schell gives the best performance of the three leads, contrasting with the over-indulgent tantrums of Elizabeth Allan and the muted angst of Trevor Howard. DP

Trevor Howard *Harry Scobie* • Elizabeth Allan *Louise Scobie* • Maria Schell *Helen* • Denholm Elliott *Wilson* • Peter Finch *Father Rank* • Gérard Oury *Yusef* • George Coulouris *Portuguese captain* ■ *Dir* George More O'Ferrall • *Scr* Ian Dalrymple, Lesley Storm, from the novel by Graham Greene

Heartbeat ★★
Romantic comedy 1946 · US · BW · 101min

In 1942 Ginger Rogers, aged 30, played a 12-year-old girl for laughs in *The Major and the Minor*. Four years later, it was no laughing matter when she attempted to convince us a teenage French escapee from a reform school who becomes a pickpocket. In a film that strains for charm, only Basil Rathbone, as Ginger's mentor in the art of picking pockets, provides any. RB

Ginger Rogers *Arlette* • Jean-Pierre Aumont *Pierre* • Adolphe Menjou *Ambassador* • Basil Rathbone *Prof Aristide* • Melville Cooper *Roland Medeville* • Mikhail Rasumny *Yves Cadubert* ■ *Dir* Sam Wood • *Scr* Morrie Ryskind, Roland Leigh, from the film *Battement de Coeur* by Hans Wilhelm, Max Kolpé, Michel Duran

Heartbeat Detector ★★★★ 12
Drama 2007 · Fr · Colour · 124min

Corporate psychologist Mathieu Amalric comes to realise the danger of following orders in a compelling drama that suggests the ruthless methodology of contemporary capitalism has its roots in the authoritarian excesses of the last century. Detailed by a scheming executive to monitor the increasingly erratic behaviour of CEO Michael Lonsdale, Amalric not only discovers links between his German-owned petrochemical company and the Third Reich, but is also forced to recognise flaws in his own personality. Intensely played by a fine cast, this is a deeply disconcerting lament for the human spirit. DP French +subtitles.

Mathieu Amalric *Simon Kessler* • Michael Lonsdale [Michel Lonsdale] *Mathias Jüst* • Jean-Pierre Kalfon *Karl Rose* • Laetitia Spigarelli *Louisa* • Valérie Dréville *Lynn Sanderson* • Delphine Chuillot *Isabelle* ■ *Dir* Nicolas Klotz • *Scr* Elisabeth Perceval, from the novel *La Question Humaine* by François Emmanuel

Heartbeats ★★★ 15
Romantic comedy drama 2010 · Can/Fr · Colour · 100min

The agony and ecstasy of unrequited love are captured in this ultracool yet superficial *ménage à trois* tale from 22-year-old Canadian actor/film-maker Xavier Dolan. A pair of inseparable Montreal hipsters (Dolan himself and Monia Chokri) tear apart their friendship after both become infatuated with Niels Schneider. Dolan mixes French New Wave aesthetics with youthful pretensions and genuine technical flair to fetishise the small details of the pair's narcissistic journey. Ultimately, Dolan's image-led characters and their shallow, bitchy concerns won't appeal to everyone, but those who've experienced *l'amour fou* will find plenty to enjoy. SF French +subtitles. Swearing, sex scenes.

Monia Chokri *Marie Camille* • Niels Schneider *Nicolas* • Xavier Dolan *Francis* • Anne Dorval *Désirée* • Anthony Huneault *Antonin* ■ *Dir/Scr* Xavier Dolan

Heartbeeps ★★★ U
Science-fiction comedy 1981 · US · Colour · 74min

This underrated sci-fi comedy features a rare screen performance from cult *Taxi* star Andy Kaufman (immortalised by Jim Carrey in *Man on the Moon*) and a welcome movie outing for Broadway diva Bernadette Peters. Set in 1995, they play servant robots who meet in a factory, fall in love, run away and hide out in a junkyard where they have a robot baby. Full of charming details and honest sentiment, Stan Winston's mechanical makeovers were deservedly Oscar-nominated. AJ

Andy Kaufman *Val* • Bernadette Peters *Aqua* • Randy Quaid *Charlie* • Kenneth McMillan *Max* • Melanie Mayron *Susan* • Christopher Guest *Calvin* • Dick Miller *Watchman* ■ *Dir* Allan Arkush • *Scr* John Hill • *Music* John Williams

Heartbreak Hotel ★★ 15
Fantasy drama 1988 · US · Colour · 96min

A number of movies have sought to evoke the spirit of Elvis Presley, including films such as Jim Jarmusch's *Mystery Train* and even Tony Scott's Quentin Tarantino-scripted *True Romance*. In this whimsical fantasy, youngster Charlie Schlatter drags Elvis home to cheer up mom Tuesday Weld. Unfortunately, David Keith as Elvis neither looks nor moves remotely like the man, and the whole flimsy premise quickly collapses. TS Violence, swearing.

David Keith *Elvis Presley* • Tuesday Weld *Marie Wolfe* • Charlie Schlatter *Johnny Wolfe* • Angela Goethals *Pam Wolfe* • Jacque Lynn Colton *Rosie Pantangellio* • Chris Mulkey *Steve Ayres* ■ Dir/Scr Chris Columbus

The Heartbreak Kid ★★★ PG

Comedy   1972 · US · Colour · 101min

This marvellously witty and genuinely disturbing black comedy is given extra potency by the casting of director Elaine May's own daughter Jeannie Berlin as the Jewish wife jettisoned for a blonde "shikse" on her honeymoon. As the husband, Charles Grodin is brilliant and Cybill Shepherd is well cast as the other woman, while veteran Eddie Albert is the very antagonistic father. The acid cruelty of the first part of the film is not, alas, sustained throughout, but there's more than enough left to satisfy sophisticated audiences. TS

Charles Grodin *Lenny Cantrow* • Cybill Shepherd *Kelly Corcoran* • Jeannie Berlin *Lila Kolodny* • Eddie Albert *Mr Corcoran* • Audra Lindley *Mrs Corcoran* • William Prince *Colorado Man* • Augusta Dabney *Colorado Woman* • Mitchell Jason *Cousin Ralph* ■ Dir Elaine May • Scr Neil Simon, from the story *A Change of Plan* by Bruce Jay Friedman

The Heartbreak Kid ★★★

Romantic drama   1993 · Aus · Colour · 91min

This Australian rites-of-passage drama explores the prejudices against age-gap romances. Claudia Karvan and Alex Dimitriades give convincing performances as the middle-class teacher and the teenage student for whom she breaks her close family ties. Director Michael Jenkins makes clever use of a hand-held camera to disguise the material's stage origins and makes several telling points about Melbourne's Greek community and their place in Australian society. DP

Claudia Karvan *Christina* • Alex Dimitriades *Nick* • Nico Lathouris *George* • Steve Bastoni *Dimitri* • Doris Younane *Evdokia* • George Vidalis *Vasili* • Louis Mandylor *Eleni* • William McInnes *Southgate* ■ Dir Michael Jenkins • Scr Michael Jenkins, Richard Barrett

The Heartbreak Kid ★★★ 15

Romantic comedy   2007 · US · Colour · 110min

Ben Stiller may be older and greyer than he was in the 1998 Farrelly Brothers hit *There's Something about Mary*, but he hasn't outgrown their distinctive brand of scatological comedy. Here they deliver an outrageously crude remake of Neil Simon's 1972 tale of love and marriage, with Stiller as awkward bachelor Eddie, who marries Lila (Malin Akerman) in haste then repents at leisure during a disastrous honeymoon in Mexico. Put off by his new wife's slobbish habits, and left on his own when she's confined to her room with sunburn, Eddie falls for fellow holidaymaker Miranda (Michelle Monaghan). All sorts of comic complications ensue, often involving bodily fluids and/or functions. Surprisingly, Simon's original set-up withstands the coarseness, ensuring a sweet undertow throughout. JR Swearing, sex scenes, drug abuse, nudity. DVD

Ben Stiller *Eddie Cantrow* • Michelle Monaghan *Miranda* • Jerry Stiller *Doc* • Malin Akerman *Lila* • Rob Corddry *Mac* • Carlos Mencia *Uncle Tito* • Danny McBride (2) *Martin* • Scott Wilson *Boo* ■ Dir Bobby Farrelly, Peter Farrelly • Scr Scot Armstrong, Kevin Barnett, Leslie Dixon, Bobby Farrelly, Peter Farrelly, from the 1972 film by Neil Simon, from the story *A Change of Plan* by Bruce Jay Friedman

Heartbreak Ridge ★★★ 15

War drama   1986 · US · Colour · 124min

Clint Eastwood struts his stern stuff in this typically hard-nosed war epic, playing a grizzled gunnery sergeant training a batch of rookie soldiers. He's the main reason to watch a by-the-numbers drama, which recycles many vintage clichés of the genre. It's a movie the US Department of Defense openly condemned – "drill sergeants are not permitted by regulations to swear at recruits". AJ Violence, swearing. DVD

Clint Eastwood *Sergeant Thomas Highway* • Marsha Mason *Aggie* • Everett McGill *Major Powers* • Moses Gunn *Sergeant Webster* • Eileen Heckart *Little Mary* • Bo Svenson *Roy Jennings* • Boyd Gaines *Lieutenant Ring* • Mario Van Peebles "Stitch" *Jones* • Arlen Dean Snyder *Master Sergeant Choozoo* ■ Dir Clint Eastwood • Scr James Carabatsos

Heartbreaker ★★★★ 15

Romantic comedy   2010 · Fr/Monaco · Colour · 100min

A little Gallic charm goes a long way in this engaging romantic comedy. The set-up is a tad contrived, but star Romain Duris remains utterly sincere as double-dealing ladies' man Alex, who makes a living breaking up toxic relationships. A solemn-faced Vanessa Paradis plays his latest target, Juliette, who is engaged to an English philanthropist (Andrew Lincoln). What makes this so satisfying is that for every glamorous location and scene of wild abandon, there is a moment of real tenderness and vulnerability from the seemingly cocksure hero that is truly seductive. SP French, English +subtitles. DVD BL

Romain Duris *Alex* • Vanessa Paradis *Juliette* • Julie Ferrier *Mélanie* • François Damiens *Marc* • Helena Noguerra *Sophie* ■ Dir Pascal Chaumeil • Scr Laurent Zeitoun, Jeremy Doner, Yohan Gromb

Heartbreakers ★★★ 18

Romantic comedy   1984 · US · Colour · 94min

Although it provides in passing a snapshot of Reagan's America, this perceptive drama concentrates more on wounded individuals than prevailing social trends. It's about the corners that artist Peter Coyote and businessman Nick Mancuso have painted themselves into. However, good as they are as the self-obsessed 30-somethings who can't commit to anything that might impinge upon their precious personal freedom, it's gallery clerk Carole Laure and model Carol Wayne who hold the piece together. DP Swearing, sex scenes.

Peter Coyote *Blue* • Nick Mancuso *Eli* • Carole Laure *Liliane* • Max Gail *King* • Kathryn Harrold *Cyd* • Carol Wayne *Candy* • James Laurenson *Terry Ray* • Jamie Rose *Libby* ■ Dir/Scr Bobby Roth

Heartbreakers ★★★ 15

Comedy   2001 · US · Colour · 123min

This complex, smart-talking con-trick comedy revolves around the appeal of mother-and-daughter grifters Sigourney Weaver and Jennifer Love Hewitt. Weaver marries a man of means, while Hewitt seduces him before consummation, resulting in a nice big divorce settlement. It's well cast, with Ray Liotta as an earlier victim and Gene Hackman in fine WC Fields mode as the duo's latest patsy, a wheezing tobacco baron. Weaver and Hewitt's man-eating appeal is entirely credible but the men are funnier than the women. AC DVD

Sigourney Weaver *Angela Nardino/Max Conners/Ulga Yevanova* • Jennifer Love Hewitt *Wendy/Page Conners/Jane Helstrom* • Ray Liotta *Dean Cumanno/Vinny Staggliano* • Jason Lee *Jack Withrowe* • Anne Bancroft *Gloria Vogal/Barbara* • Jeffrey Jones *Mr Appel* • Gene Hackman *William B Tensy* • Carrie Fisher *Mrs Surpin* ■ Dir David Mirkin • Scr Robert Dunn (2), Paul Guay, Stephen Mazur

Heartburn ★★★ 15

Comedy drama   1986 · US · Colour · 104min

Based on the bestselling novel by Nora Ephron, this is an account of her tempestuous marriage to Watergate journalist Carl Bernstein. Meryl Streep is the cookery writer who marries columnist Jack Nicholson, only to discover that life isn't always happy ever after when he has an affair while she's pregnant. Nicholson gets all the best lines and does well with what is essentially a rather shallow part with few redeeming features, while Streep is somewhat at sea with the humorous side of her role and ends up as a rather unsympathetic character. JB DVD

Meryl Streep *Rachel Samstat* • Jack Nicholson *Mark Forman* • Jeff Daniels *Richard* • Maureen Stapleton *Vera* • Stockard Channing *Julie* • Richard Masur *Arthur* • Catherine O'Hara *Betty* • Steven Hill *Harry* • Milos Forman *Dmitri* • Natalie Stern *Annie* • Karen Akers *Thelma Rice* ■ Dir Mike Nichols • Scr Nora Ephron, from her autobiographical novel

Heartlands ★★★ 12

Comedy drama   2002 · UK/US · Colour · 87min

Michael Sheen is a mild-mannered, darts-playing newsagent who lives in a dull Midlands town where men still get Kevin Keegan-style perms. His unexciting little world collapses when his wife runs off to Blackpool with the captain of the darts team, so Sheen hops on his scooter in not-particularly-hot pursuit. Director Damien O'Donnell again demonstrates the knack for blending comedy and tragedy he exhibited with *East Is East*, and produces a film that's both entertaining and a wry comment on an England that other film-makers have largely ignored. BP DVD

Michael Sheen *Colin* • Mark Addy *Ron* • Jim Carter *Geoff* • Celia Imrie *Sonja* • Ruth Jones *Mandy* • Philippa Peak *Sarah* • Jane Robbins *Sandra* • Mark Strong *Ian* ■ Dir Damien O'Donnell • Scr Paul Fraser, from a story by Paul Fraser, Richard Jobson, Andrew Keyte, from an idea by Paul Fraser

Heartless ★★★★ 18

Fantasy horror   2009 · UK · Colour · 108min

Rendered desperately shy by a heart-shaped birthmark covering the left side of his face, a budding photographer wishes to escape the cruel and superficial world around him in this dark and imaginative fable from Philip Ridley. The question of just how far Jim Sturgess is prepared to go to change his life becomes the crux of this emotionally engaging yet eerie slice of urban fantasy, in which hooded demons stalk the streets of Bethnal Green. Aside from a rushed finale, Ridley keeps the bizarre events under a tight rein, conjuring up an intoxicating landscape unlike anything else seen in British cinema. TJ Violence. DVD BL

Jim Sturgess *Jamie Morgan* • Timothy Spall *George Morgan* • Clémence Poésy *Tia* • Noel Clarke *AJ* • Eddie Marsan *Weapons Man* • Luke Treadaway *Lee* • Fraser Ayres [Frazer Ayres] *Vinnie* • Joseph Mawle *Papa B* ■ Dir/Scr Philip Ridley

Hearts and Minds ★★★★ 15

War documentary   1974 · US · Colour · 111min

Failure in Vietnam remains a thorn in the hearts and minds of the American nation. Utilising archive newsreel and specially shot footage, director Peter Davis's Oscar-winning documentary tries to unravel why the United States became involved in the whole bloody business. But it's the candid interviews with those at the forefront of the conflict that made this film such a hot potato for distributors at the time of its initial release. That it can now be seen shows just how far times and politics can change, even if the lessons have yet to be learned. TH DVD

■ Dir Peter Davis

Hearts in Atlantis ★★ 12

Supernatural drama   2001 · US/Aus · Colour · 96min

Adapting two stories from the eponymous collection by Stephen King, William Goldman's uneven script spins a rose-tinted tale of coming-of-age in 1960s America that sits uneasily beside a nebulous conspiracy subplot. In a small New England town, neglected 11-year-old Anton Yelchin strikes up a meaningful friendship with mysterious neighbour Anthony Hopkins, who is soon revealed to have the power to read minds. Poorly paced and charmless. AJ Violence, swearing. DVD

Anthony Hopkins *Ted Brautigan* • Anton Yelchin *Bobby Garfield* • Hope Davis *Liz Garfield* • Mika Boorem *Carol Gerber* • David Morse *Robert Garfield* ■ Dir Scott Hicks • Scr William Goldman, from short story collection *Hearts in Atlantis* by Stephen King

Hearts of Darkness: a Film-Maker's Apocalypse ★★★★★ 15

Documentary   1991 · US · Colour · 91min

This is an enthralling documentary about the making of Francis Ford Coppola's Vietnam drama *Apocalypse Now*. Using new interviews and footage shot on location by Coppola's wife, Eleanor, this is a catalogue of madness and inspiration in the jungles of the Philippines that ranges from an overweight and unprepared Marlon Brando, the firing of Harvey Keitel, Martin Sheen's heart attack, previously unseen footage (a superb sequence in a French plantation house which Coppola foolishly cut), to crises such as typhoons and President Marcos withdrawing his helicopters to fight a real war. With contributions from Coppola, screenwriter John Milius, and a characteristically incoherent Dennis Hopper, this is an unmissable treat for fans of the movie and, indeed, for anyone interested in the cinema. AT Swearing. DVD BL

Eleanor Coppola • Dennis Hopper ■ Dir/Scr Fax Bahr, George Hickenlooper

Hearts of Fire ★ 15

Drama   1987 · US · Colour · 91min

This hilariously bad rock movie was an unfortunate swan song for the talented director Richard Marquand (*Jagged Edge*). Fiona Flanagan plays the aspiring young musician torn between a woefully miscast Rupert Everett and a monosyllabic Bob Dylan. There's no respite in the bland soundtrack. JF Swearing.

Rupert Everett *James Colt* • Bob Dylan *Billy Parker* • Fiona Flanagan *Molly McGuire* • Ian Dury *Bones* • Richie Havens *Pepper Ward* • Julian Glover *Alfred* • Suzanne Bertish *Anne Ashton* ■ Dir Richard Marquand • Scr Scott Richardson, Joe Eszterhas

Hearts of the West ★★★★ PG

Comedy drama   1975 · US · Colour · 102min

Inspired by the experiences of writer Zane Grey and shot in the style of a 1930s western series, this is a wonderfully inventive and richly nostalgic picture. Jeff Bridges stars as an unpublished writer of western stories who discovers he's being conned by gangsters. By chance he falls in with a film crew, becoming a stuntman and, briefly, a star. Bridges is excellent in the lead, but he's almost upstaged by Andy Griffith as a fellow stuntman. AT

Jeff Bridges *Lewis Tater* • Andy Griffith *Howard Pike* • Donald Pleasence *AJ Nietz* • Blythe Danner *Miss Trout* • Alan Arkin *Kessler* • Richard B Shull *Stout crook* • Herbert Edelman [Herb Edelman] *Eddie Polo* • Alex Rocco *Earl* ■ Dir Howard Zieff • Scr Rob Thompson

Hearts of the World ★★★

Silent First World War drama   1918 · US · BW · 152min

After making his epic *Intolerance*, DW Griffith wrote, produced and directed this picture as a contribution to the war effort in 1918, incorporating documentary footage and scenes shot at the Front. It stars Lillian Gish and Robert Harron as two lovers and shows the devastating effect of the war on one small French village. Griffith's feeling for his characters overcomes the contrivances of the plot and moments of sentimentality. Technical adviser Erich von Stroheim is also seen as a Prussian officer, while making his first screen appearance as the teenager with a wheelbarrow is a young Noël Coward. AE

Adolphe Lestina *Grandfather* • Josephine Crowell *Mother* • Lillian Gish *Girl* • Robert Harron *Boy* • Dorothy Gish *Little Disturber* • Erich von Stroheim *German soldier* • Noël Coward *Boy with wheelbarrow* ■ Dir DW Griffith • Scr M Gaston de Tolignac [DW Griffith], Capt Victor Marier [DW Griffith]

Heat ★★ 18
Cult drama
1972 · US · Colour · 96min

Underground icon Joe Dallesandro plays a former child actor-turned-hustler, with Sylvia Miles as a fading minor movie star. Director Paul Morrissey's *Sunset Blvd* revisited is given the usual tacky Andy Warhol spin. Andrea Feldman adds further bizarre twists and trashy turns to the "Hollyweird" parody as Miles's daughter. Sometimes hilariously camp, sometimes just very ordinary, this was the most successful of Warhol's bad taste trilogy, which also featured *Flesh* and *Trash*. AJ
DVD

Sylvia Miles *Sally* • Joe Dallesandro *Joe* • Pat Ast *Motel owner* • Andrea Feldman *Jessica* • Ray Vestal *Movie producer* • PJ Lester *Sally's former husband* ■ *Dir* Paul Morrissey • *Scr* Paul Morrissey, John Hollowell

Heat ★ 18
Crime drama
1987 · US · Colour · 96min

Once the world's biggest box office draw, poor Burt Reynolds was reduced to the status of "Burt who?" until *Boogie Nights* revived his name. His fall from grace isn't difficult to comprehend on the evidence of this drab, squalid action movie. Reynolds, relying on his trademark toughie-with-a-heart-of-gold persona, plays a freelance bodyguard who's up against Las Vegas slimeballs. Muddled, violent and humourless. RS

Burt Reynolds *Mex* • Karen Young *Holly* • Peter MacNicol *Cyrus Kinnick* • Howard Hesseman *Pinchus Zion* • Neill Barry *Danny DeMarco* • Diana Scarwid *Cassie* • Joseph Mascolo *Baby* ■ *Dir* Dick Richards • *Scr* William Goldman, from his novel

Heat ★★★★ 15
Crime thriller
1995 · US · Colour · 163min

Directed by Michael Mann, this crime thriller about a cop (Al Pacino) and a robber (Robert De Niro) is epic in scale and in length. Though punctuated by bursts of virtuoso action, including a running battle in downtown LA that ranks as one of the best action scenes ever filmed, it is the unusual emphasis on the characters that impresses most, especially De Niro as the calm, methodical loner whose life is arranged so that he can abandon everything in 30 seconds when the heat is on. Pacino, by contrast, is more of a cliché: angst-ridden and on his third marriage. AT **DVD** **Blu-ray**

Al Pacino *Vincent Hanna* • Robert De Niro *Neil McCauley* • Val Kilmer *Chris Shiherlis* • Jon Voight *Nate* • Tom Sizemore *Michael Cheritto* • Diane Venora *Justine* • Amy Brenneman *Eady* • Ashley Judd *Charlene* • Mykelti Williamson *Drucker* • Wes Studi *Casals* • Natalie Portman *Lauren* ■ *Dir/Scr* Michael Mann • *Cinematographer* Dante Spinotti

The Heat ★★★★ 15
Comedy
2013 · US/UK/Aus · Colour · 115min

Sandra Bullock and *Bridesmaids* scene-stealer Melissa McCarthy make an inspired double act in this hysterical cop comedy. It gets off to a wobbly start, but as soon as the women pool resources it becomes a fluid, fun and foul-mouthed buddy flick. The banter is cracking, and feels improvised, but the movie also trades on visual gags and clever cutting by director Paul Feig (who also made *Bridesmaids*). The plot follows a standard formula, but the simple gender twist and great casting keep things sizzling. SP Violence, swearing, sexual references. **DVD**

Sandra Bullock *Sarah Ashburn* • Melissa McCarthy *Shannon Mullins* • Demián Bechir [Demian Bichir] *Hale* • Marlon Wayans *Levy* • Michael Rapaport *Jason Mullins* • Jane Curtin *Mrs Mullins* ■ *Dir* Paul Feig • *Scr* Katie Dippold

Heat and Dust ★★★ 15
Drama
1982 · UK · Colour · 130min

Ex-BBC researcher Julie Christie travels to India to investigate her late great-aunt Olivia (Greta Scacchi) who caused a scandal in the 1920s. Adapting her own novel, Ruth Prawer Jhabvala produces a new twist on EM Forster's *A Passage to India*, using two characters and separate time zones to express similar ideas about cultural collision. It's arty and exotic, with Christie and Scacchi refusing to be upstaged by the ravishing scenery. AT **DVD**

Julie Christie *Anne* • Christopher Cazenove *Douglas* • Greta Scacchi *Olivia Rivers* • Julian Glover *Mr Crawford* • Susan Fleetwood *Mrs Crawford* • Shashi Kapoor *The Nawab* • Madhur Jaffrey *The Begum* • Nickolas Grace *Harry* • Zakir Hussain (1) *Inder Lal* • Barry Foster *Major Minnies* • Amanda Walker *Lady Mackleworth* • Patrick Godfrey *Dr Saunders* • Jennifer Kendal *Mrs Saunders* ■ *Dir* James Ivory • *Scr* Ruth Prawer Jhabvala, from her novel

Heat Wave ★★★★
Drama based on a true story
1990 · US · Colour · 92min

This Emmy Award-winning TV movie is based on actual events that occurred during the civil rights riots that turned the Watts district of Los Angeles into a battleground in the summer of 1965. As an ambitious journalist who is branded a race traitor for his coverage of the story, Blair Underwood gives a performance of dignity and integrity that invites comparisons with Sidney Poitier. Cicely Tyson and James Earl Jones are typically impressive, while director Kevin Hooks assuredly blends discussion of the social issues with explosive action. DP

Cicely Tyson *Ruthana Richardson/Motherdear* • Blair Underwood *Robert Richardson* • James Earl Jones *Junius Johnson* • Sally Kirkland *Mrs Canfield* • Margaret Avery (2) *Roxie Turpin* • Vondie Curtis-Hall *Clifford Turpin* ■ *Dir* Kevin Hooks • *Scr* Michael Lazarou

Heathers ★★★★★ 18
Black comedy
1989 · US · Colour · 98min

Michael Lehman made a stunning debut with this movie about a high-school clique terrorising fellow students. Their actions prompt Winona Ryder and Christian Slater to engineer a rash of deaths to break the clique's hold on their schoolmates. Beneath the hip, lip-glossed surface of this devastatingly witty black comedy lurks a serious satire on peer-group pretensions and other teen movies. But the message never gets in the way of the snappy dialogue or on-target jabs at the in-crowd lunacy of high-school life. AJ Violence, swearing, sex scenes. **DVD**

Winona Ryder *Veronica Sawyer* • Christian Slater *Jason "JD" Dean* • Shannen Doherty *Heather Duke* • Lisanne Falk *Heather McNamara* • Kim Walker *Heather Chandler* • Penelope Milford *Pauline Fleming* • Glenn Shadix *Father Ripper* • Lance Fenton *Kurt Kelly* • Patrick Labyorteaux *Ram Sweeney* ■ *Dir* Michael Lehman • *Scr* Daniel Waters

Heatwave ★★★ 15
Drama based on a true story
1981 · Aus · Colour · 90min

Militant liberal Judy Davis protests the crime-related gentrification of downtown Sydney, only to get caught up in political intrigue and romance with an ambitious architect (Richard Moir). Davis gives a typically fine performance, while director Phillip Noyce expertly tightens the suspense screws to produce a memorably disturbing finish. Set against a sultry Christmas backdrop, this is a jet-black thriller. AJ

Judy Davis *Kate Dean* • Richard Moir *Steven West* • Chris Haywood *Peter Hauseman* • Bill Hunter *Robert Duncan* • John Gregg *Phillip Lawson* • Anna Jem son *Victoria West* • John Meillon *Freddy Dwyer* • Dennis Miller *Mick Davies* ■ *Dir* Phillip Noyce • *Scr* Phillip Noyce, Phillip Noyce, Marc Rosenberg, Mark Stiles, Tim Gooding

Heaven ★★ 18
Documentary
1987 · US · Colour · 59min

Actress Diane Keaton's first film as director is a sweet idea gone sour. A variety of ordinary people – boxing promoter Don King being an exception – are interviewed and asked to explain their views on death and a possible afterlife. However, despite some intriguing old film clips, Keaton's patronising narration and ludicrously affected camera angles deflate the airy bubble of an idea that needed a more light-handed touch. TH

■ *Dir* Diane Keaton • *Cinematographers* Joe Kelly, Frederick Elmes

Heaven ★★
Thriller
1998 · NZ/US · Colour · 102min

The built-in bonus about films involving clairvoyants is that the director can flit between flashbacks and prophecies and bemuse the viewer into thinking something significant is going on. Scott Reynolds is partly guilty of such manipulative chicanery; however, the convoluted tale is so slickly edited that it's hard to avoid wondering how transvestite stripper Danny Edwards's visions are going to affect architect Martin Donovan in his confrontations with gambling boss Richard Schiff and embittered ex-wife Joanna Going. DP Violence, swearing, nudity.

Martin Donovan (2) *Robert Marling* • Joanna Going *Jennifer Marling* • Richard Schiff *Stanner* • Patrick Malahide *Dr Melrose* • Danny Edwards *Heaven* • Karl Urban *Sweeper* ■ *Dir* Scott Reynolds • *Scr* Scott Reynolds, from a novel by Chad Taylor

Heaven ★★★ 15
Romantic thriller
2002 · US/UK/Fr/Ger/It · Colour · 92min

German director Tom Tykwer's English-language debut falls between mainstream thriller and art house character study. There's little sense of connection between Cate Blanchett's accidental terrorist and Giovanni Ribisi's Italian cop, who helps her escape when a plan to blow up a drug-dealing tycoon backfires. Blanchett is excellent as the widowed English teacher, stripped of reason by her need for revenge, but the conclusion is unpersuasive. DP English, Italian +subtitles. Swearing, a sex scene. **DVD**

Cate Blanchett *Philippa* • Giovanni Ribisi *Filippo* • Remo Girone *Filippo's father* • Stefania Rocca *Regina* • Mattia Sbragia *Major Pini* ■ *Dir* Tom Tykwer • *Scr* Krzysztof Kieslowski, Krzysztof Piesiewicz

Heaven and Earth ★★★★ 15
War drama
1993 · US · Colour · 134min

After *Platoon* and *Born on the Fourth of July*, Oliver Stone turns his attention to the Vietnamese themselves, in particular a village girl named Le Ly (Hiep Thi Le) who endures the horrors of the war only to marry unstable American soldier (Tommy Lee Jones) who takes her to California. Unjustly slated by the critics, the picture shows all of Stone's brilliance in creating scenes of unusual vividness – it's horrifying, beautiful, ugly and moving all at the same time. It is also, at times, an unsettling black comedy about cultural and religious rituals that switches from Buddhist shrines in rice paddies to consumerist shrines in supermarkets. AT Violence, swearing. **DVD**

Tommy Lee Jones *Sergeant Steve Butler* • Joan Chen *Mama* • Haing S Ngor *Papa* • Hiep Thi Le *Le Ly* • Debbie Reynolds *Eugenia* ■ *Dir* Oliver Stone • *Scr* Oliver Stone, from the non-fiction books *When Heaven and Earth Changed Places* by Le Ly Hayslip, Jay Wurts and *Child of War, Woman of Peace* by Le Ly Hayslip, James Hayslip

Heaven Can Wait ★★★★★ U
Fantasy comedy
1943 · US · Colour · 107min

A witty satire masquerading as a family saga, this movie gets its title from the prologue in which the Devil (Laird Cregar) sits in judgement on Don Ameche's Henry Van Cleve. This is as good as Ameche gets; not only is he perfectly cast, but also brilliantly directed by the comic genius Ernst Lubitsch, working in colour for the first time. The film has great warmth, charm and honesty, and grows on you until, at the end, you're sorry to leave. Gene Tierney has never looked lovelier – and that's *really* saying something – nor *The Merry Widow* been used more emotively. Each viewing confirms this film's status as a classic. TS **DVD**

Gene Tierney *Martha* • Don Ameche *Henry Van Cleve* • Charles Coburn *Hugo Van Cleve* • Marjorie Main *Mrs Strabel* • Laird Cregar *His Excellency, the Devil* • Spring Byington *Bertha Van Cleve* • Allyn Joslyn *Albert Van Cleve* ■ *Dir* Ernst Lubitsch • *Scr* Samson Raphaelson, from the play *Birthdays* by Lazlo Bus-Fekete • *Cinematographer* Edward Cronjager

Heaven Can Wait ★★★★ PG
Fantasy comedy
1978 · US · Colour · 96min

An updated version of the 1941 film *Here Comes Mr Jordan*, this is one of the few remakes that is almost as good as the original. Warren Beatty co-directs and stars as the football player accidentally selected to die after a car accident. Realising he has been called before his time, Beatty bargains with celestial James Mason and gets the chance to live again but in someone else's body, that of a wealthy businessman whose wife is plotting to kill him. Well played, well written and well directed, this is one of the highlights of Beatty's career. JB **DVD**

Warren Beatty *Joe Pendleton* • Julie Christie *Betty Logan* • James Mason *Mr Jordan* • Jack Warden *Max Corkle* • Charles Grodin *Tony Abbott* • Dyan Cannon *Julia Farnsworth* • Buck Henry *Escort* • Vincent Gardenia *Krim* ■ *Dir* Warren Beatty, Buck Henry • *Scr* Elaine May, Warren Beatty, from the play by Harry Segall

Heaven Is for Real ★★★ PG
Drama based on a true story
2014 · US · Colour · 95min

This good-looking, earnest drama sees pastor Greg Kinnear begin a spiritual exploration when his young son (cute newcomer Connor Corum) claims to have visited Heaven while undergoing a life-saving operation. It's based on a bestselling book, and sold as a true story, so this cinematic sermon may be difficult to swallow for many, with a tendency for the saccharine that's hard to ignore, but it's a polished piece of preaching. JL **DVD**

Greg Kinnear *Todd Burpo* • Kelly Reilly *Sonja Burpo* • Thomas Haden Church *Jay Wilkins* • Connor Corum *Colton Burpo* • Lane Styles *Cassie Burpo* ■ *Dir* Randall Wallace • *Scr* Christopher Parker [Chris Parker], Randall Wallace, from the non-fiction book *Heaven Is for Real: A Little Boy's Astounding Story of His Trip to Heaven and Back* by Todd Burpo, Lynn Vincent • *Cinematographer* Dean Semler

Heaven Knows, Mr Allison ★★★★ PG
Second World War drama
1957 · US · Colour · 101min

This is a rare gem, a marvellously touching two-hander, beautifully acted by the sublime duo of Robert Mitchum and Deborah Kerr in their prime. The tale is simplicity itself: she's a nun and he's a marine, and they're stranded on a Japanese-occupied Pacific island during the Second World War. Director John Huston wisely lets the stars bring their magic touch to the clever screenplay. This is an early 20th Century-Fox CinemaScope feature, and the compositions and locations are superbly handled by the great English cameraman Ossie Morris, while Russell Lloyd's editing is dynamic, especially in Mitchum's exciting raids into enemy territory. TS **DVD**

Deborah Kerr *Sister Angela* • Robert Mitchum *Mr Allison* ■ *Dir* John Huston • *Scr* John Huston, John Lee Mahin

Heaven Only Knows ★★
Western fantasy
1947 · US · BW · 98min

An angel descends from heaven to the Wild West to attend to the soul of a villainous saloon keeper and get him married to a demure schoolteacher. The bar owner, also a ruthless killer, arrived on Earth without a soul and the angel tries to put this right. Robert Cummings makes a relatively human angel in this western fantasy, whose more mawkish elements are tempered by a vague sense of humour. AT

Robert Cummings *Mike* • Brian Donlevy *Duke* • Marjorie Reynolds *Ginger* • Jorja Cartwright *Drusilla* • Bill Goodwin *Plumber* • Stuart Erwin *Sheriff* • John Litel *Reverend* • Peter Miles *Speck*

H

O'Donnell ■ *Dir* Albert S Rogell • *Scr* Art Arthur, Ernest Haycox, Rowland Leigh, from the story by Aubrey Wisberg

Heaven Tonight ★★ 15
Musical drama   1990 · Aus · Colour · 93min

Guy Pearce makes his feature film debut in this familiar tale of a young man falling out with his family when he embarks on a musical career. The twist this time is that the biggest obstacle is his father John Waters, a 1960s rock legend who is less than enamoured by the fact that his boy is now getting all the attention. The two leads are fine, but the machinations of the music business lack realism and the songs are awful. JF

John Waters (3) *Johnny Dysart* • Rebecca Gilling *Annie Dysart* • Guy Pearce *Paul Dysart* • Kim Gyngell *Baz Schultz* ■ *Dir* Pino Amenta • *Scr* Frank Howson, Alister Webb

The Heavenly Body ★★
Romantic comedy   1943 · US · BW · 94min

The title not only refers to Hedy Lamarr, making her first attempt at light comedy, but also the heavens above in this contrived wartime comedy. William Powell exercises his perfectly honed comedy skills to little avail as the eccentric astronomer whose nocturnal gazing causes him to neglect Lamarr as his wife. After she takes up astrology, the predicted arrival of a tall, dark stranger duly occurs when James Craig comes knocking at the door. AE

William Powell *William B Whitley* • Hedy Lamarr *Vicky Whitley* • James Craig *Lloyd X Hunter* • Fay Bainter *Margaret Sibyll* • Henry O'Neill *Professor Stone* • Spring Byington *Nancy Potter* ■ *Dir* Alexander Hall • *Scr* Michael Arlen, Walter Reisch, Harry Kurnitz, from a story by Jacques Thery

Heavenly Creatures ★★★★★ 18
Biographical crime drama
1994 · NZ · Colour · 94min

This is the film that launched the career of Kate Winslet, who within three years of appearing in this fact-based New Zealand drama was starring in *Titanic*. It also transformed the fortunes of director Peter Jackson, who went from making ingenious schlock horrors to directing the *Lord of the Rings* trilogy. The real star of this masterly mix of nostalgia, innocence and menace, however, is Melanie Lynskey, who is mesmerising as the matricidal half of the teenage duo who scandalised a nation in the early 1950s. Although Winslet and Lynskey dominate the film, they are splendidly supported by Diana Kent and Clive Merrison as Winslet's parents, and by Sarah Peirse as Lynskey's ill-fated mother. DP Violence, swearing. DVD BL

Melanie Lynskey *Pauline Parker* • Kate Winslet *Juliet Hulme* • Sarah Peirse *Honora Parker* • Diana Kent *Hilda Hulme* • Clive Merrison *Henry Hulme* • Simon O'Connor *Herbert Reiper* ■ *Dir* Peter Jackson • *Scr* Peter Jackson, Frances Walsh [Fran Walsh]

The Heavenly Kid ★★ 15
Comedy fantasy   1985 · US · Colour · 87min

This dim teenage spin on *Heaven Can Wait* finds 1950s rock 'n' roll rebel Lewis Smith earning his chance to book a place in Heaven if he helps out confused 1980s teenager Jason Gedrick. Richard Mulligan fares the best in a lightweight cast, but all are let down by the lazy script. JF

Lewis Smith *Bobby* • Jason Gedrick *Lenny* • Jane Kaczmarek *Emily* • Richard Mulligan *Rafferty* • Mark Metcalf *Joe* • Beau Dremann *Bill* ■ *Dir* Cary Medoway • *Scr* Cary Medoway, Martin Copeland

Heavenly Pursuits ★★★ 15
Satirical comedy   1986 · UK · Colour · 86min

A delightful British film about miracles and religion, this is sharply written and directed by Charles Gormley. Tom Conti is the teacher at a Glasgow Catholic school who gets caught up in possible miraculous goings-on and then finds himself at the mercy of his colleagues and the media in this well-realised satire. Odd and often hilarious, this treat of a movie features

terrific performances from a cast which includes David Hayman, Helen Mirren and Ewen Bremner. JB

Tom Conti *Vic Mathews* • Helen Mirren *Ruth Chancellor* • David Hayman *Jeff Jeffries* • Brian Pettifer *Father Cobb* • Jennifer Black *Sister* • Dave Anderson *Headmaster* • Tom Busby *Monseigneur Brusse* • Ewen Bremner *Stevie Deans* ■ *Dir/Scr* Charles Gormley

Heavens Above! ★★ PG
Comedy   1963 · UK · BW · 113min

This is only a minor entry on the CVs of both Peter Sellers and the Boulting brothers. The satire at the expense of the Church of England is too gentle, the resolution is beyond contrivance and the church-goers are clumsy stereotypes. As a prison chaplain ministering to the well heeled, Sellers wallows in whimsy, leaving centre stage to the gypsy family of Irene Handl and Eric Sykes. DP DVD

Peter Sellers *Reverend John Smallwood* • Cecil Parker *Archdeacon Aspinall* • Isabel Jeans *Lady Despard* • Eric Sykes *Harry Smith* • Bernard Miles *Simpson* • Brock Peters *Matthew* • Ian Carmichael *The Other Smallwood* • Irene Handl *Rene Smith* ■ *Dir* John Boulting • *Scr* John Boulting, Frank Harvey, from an idea by Malcolm Muggeridge

Heaven's Burning ★★★★ 18
Road movie thriller
1997 · Aus/Jpn · Colour · 95min

After cracking Hollywood with his charismatic turn in *LA Confidential*, Russell Crowe headed Down Under for this stunning but criminally overlooked Australian thriller. He plays a getaway driver with a conscience who forms an odd relationship with Youki Kudoh, an unhappy Japanese woman trying to dump her possessive husband. The pair are forced to go on the run, pursued by the cops, Crowe's psychopathic ex-colleagues and Kudoh's even crazier spouse. Director Craig Lahiff makes stunning use of Australian locations and fashions a moving, melancholic romance that is peppered with shocking bursts of violence. JF Swearing, nudity.

Russell Crowe *Colin O'Brien* • Youki Kudoh *Midori Takada* • Kenji Isomura *Yukio Takada* • Ray Barrett *Cam O'Brien* • Robert Mammone *Mahood* • Petru Gheorghiu *Boorjan* ■ *Dir* Craig Lahiff • *Scr* Louis Nowra

Heaven's Gate ★★★ 15
Western   1980 · US · Colour · 217min

Michael Cimino's notorious western soared over budget and was so trashed by the New York critics that the bankrupted studio, United Artists, withdrew the film and cut it by an hour. Sadly, this is the version usually seen today. While some of the director's ambition still shines through – notably the wondrous photography, the set piece battle and the roller-skating dance – the story, about a Wyoming range war between cattlemen and persecuted immigrants, makes little sense. The full version, however, is a superb, five-star achievement. AT Violence, swearing, sex scenes, nudity. DVD BL

Kris Kristofferson *James Averill* • Christopher Walken *Nathan D Champion* • John Hurt *Billy Irvine* • Sam Waterston *Frank Canton* • Brad Dourif *Mr Eggleston* • Isabelle Huppert *Ella Watson* • Joseph Cotten *Reverend Doctor* • Jeff Bridges *John H Bridges* • Richard Masur *Cully* • Terry O'Quinn *Captain Minardi* • Mickey Rourke *Nick Ray* ■ *Dir/Scr* Michael Cimino • *Cinematographer* Vilmos Zsigmond

Heaven's Prisoners ★★★ 15
Thriller   1996 · US · Colour · 126min

Alec Baldwin stars as ex-New Orleans cop Dave Robicheaux, a man at odds with himself over his alcoholism, loss of faith and love of violence. Adapted from the second in a series of crime novels by James Lee Burke, this has Robicheaux rescuing a small girl from a lagoon air-crash and thinking he's spiritually saved, only to find he's up to his neck in drug smuggling and murder. The plot becomes a rather routine tale of vengeance, but director Phil Joanou keeps a good deal of the novel's sinister

atmosphere. TH Violence, swearing, sex scenes, nudity. DVD

Alec Baldwin *Dave Robicheaux* • Kelly Lynch *Annie Robicheaux* • Mary Stuart Masterson *Robin Gaddis* • Eric Roberts *Bubba Rocque* • Teri Hatcher *Claudette Rocque* • Vondie Curtis-Hall *Minos P Dautrieve* • Badja Djola *Batist* • Samantha Lagpacan *Alafair* • Joe Viterelli *Didi Giancano* ■ *Dir* Phil Joanou • *Scr* Harley Peyton, Scott Frank, from the novel by James Lee Burke

Heavy ★★★★ 15
Drama   1995 · US · Colour · 100min

The coming of age of an overweight, 30-something pizza chef may not seem like a very promising viewing experience, but writer/director James Mangold's marvellous feature debut has a ring of truth few real-life dramas manage. Pruitt Taylor Vince is exceptional as the withdrawn gentle giant who must cross emotional thresholds he never dared acknowledge. The drama is set in motion when Vince's imperious mother (Shelley Winters) decides to match him with new waitress Liv Tyler. Often unbearably poignant, the attention to small details pays heartfelt dividends. AJ Swearing. DVD

Pruitt Taylor Vince *Victor* • Liv Tyler *Callie* • Shelley Winters *Dolly* • Deborah Harry *Delores* • Joe Grifasi *Leo* • Evan Dando *Jeff* • David Patrick Kelly *Grey man in hospital* • Marian Quinn *Darlene* ■ *Dir/Scr* James Mangold

The Heavy ★ 18
Thriller   2009 · UK · Colour · 97min

Director Marcus Warren's thriller is one of the most inept entries in the oversubscribed canon of Brit gangster chic. Former boxer Gary Stretch plays the newly released felon forced into one last job by shady businessman Stephen Rea – to assassinate his own estranged brother, an MP who has designs on becoming prime minister. Shadowing his every move is Vinnie Jones as a rule-bending police detective. Stretch is too wooden to shoulder a lead role, while Lee Ryan (formerly of boy band Blue) is laughable as Rea's obsequious and foul-mouthed gofer. TeS DVD BL

Gary Stretch *Mitchell "Boots" Mason* • Vinnie Jones *Dunn* • Stephen Rea *Anawalt* • Lee Ryan *Rubin* • Christopher Lee *Mr Mason* ■ *Dir/Scr* Marcus Warren

Heavy Metal ★★ 15
Animated science-fiction fantasy
1981 · US · Colour · 86min

This cult favourite from the 1980s, based on an American comic book, now looks a tad dated. A mix of mythical imagery and X-rated animation, this compendium of stories was eagerly lapped up by American teens, but it pales in comparison to the amoral savagery of 1990s Japanese *anime*, while the AOR rock soundtrack is quaint rather than subversive. JF DVD

Richard Romanus *Harry Canyon* • Susan Roman *Girl/Satellite* • John Candy *Desk sergeant* • Marilyn Lightstone *Queen/Whore* • Jackie Burroughs *Katherine* • George Touliatos *Pilot* • Harold Ramis *Zeke* ■ *Dir* Gerald Potterton • *Scr* Dan Goldberg, Len Blum, from the comic magazine by Richard Corben, Angus McKie, Dan O'Bannon, Thomas Warkentin, Berni Wrightson • *Music* Elmer Bernstein

Heavyweights ★ PG
Comedy   1995 · US · Colour · 93min

This sickly teen movie from Disney is about health farm Camp Hope, where overweight kids go to diet. The camp is taken over by a maniacal fitness guru who forces the inmates to endure humiliation, starvation and abuse. Buried deep beneath the cringe-inducing sequences is a satire about commercialism, since the kids are to become part of a wider merchandising scheme. Avoid. AT DVD

Tom McGowan *Pat* • Aaron Schwartz *Gerry* • Shaun Weiss *Josh* • Tom Hodges *Lars* • Leah Lail *Julie* • Paul Feig *Tim* • Kenan Thompson *Roy* • David Bowe *Chris Donelly* ■ *Dir* Steven Brill • *Scr* Judd Apatow, Steven Brill

Hector ★★★★ 15
Drama   2015 · UK · Colour · 86min

This quietly affecting drama tells the story of Hector McAdam (Peter Mullan), an affable pensioner who has been living rough for 15 years. Every Christmas, Hector makes his way to a temporary hostel in London; this year, however, Hector's annual trip includes an important detour, as he decides to track down his brother and sister. As you might expect, Hector's cross-country odyssey is an arduous one, but the film isn't as bleak as you might expect – it's surprisingly warm and uplifting in places, while Mullan is typically impressive as the title character. SC Swearing

Peter Mullan *Hector McAdam* • Keith Allen *Jimbo* • Natalie Gavin *Hazel* • Sharon Rooney *Young mother* • Stephen Tompkinson *Derek* • Gina McKee *Lizzie* ■ *Dir/Scr* Jake Gavin

Hector and the Search for Happiness ★★ 15
Comedy drama
2014 · Ger/UK/S Af/Can · Colour · 114min

The meaning of life is pondered in piecemeal fashion in this overlong and forgettable tale, which stars Simon Pegg as a strait-laced psychiatrist disillusioned with his comfortable existence, who sets out on a global voyage of discovery. Director/co-writer Peter Chelsom peppers his narrative with fortune-cookie homilies and Pegg sleepwalks through the central role, while co-stars Rosamund Pike and Toni Collette have relatively little to do. TeS Swearing, sexual references, some violence, brief nudity. DVD BL

Simon Pegg *Hector* • Rosamund Pike *Clara* • Toni Collette *Agnes* • Stellan Skarsgård *Edward* • Jean Reno *Diego* ■ *Dir* Peter Chelsom • *Scr* Peter Chelsom, Tinker Lindsay, Maria von Heland, from François Lelord's novel *Hector's Journeys: Hector and the Search for Happiness*

Hedd Wyn ★★★ 12
Biographical drama   1992 · UK · Colour · 114min

The first film in Welsh to receive an Oscar nomination, Paul Turner's biopic has a typically British period polish. Huw Garmon gives a respectful performance as Ellis Evans, the teenage poet who wrote under the name of "Hedd Wyn" before dying in the First World War. The war scenes give the film a power and poignancy to rival that of the trench poem *Yr Arwr* (*The Hero*) which posthumously won Evans the Chair at the National Eisteddfod. DP Welsh +subtitles. Swearing.

Huw Garmon *Ellis Evans/Hedd Wyn* • Sue Roderick *Lizzie Roberts* • Judith Humphreys *Jini Owen* • Nia Dryhurst *Mary Catherine Hughes* • Grey Evans *Evan Evans* ■ *Dir* Paul Turner • *Scr* Alan Llwyd

Hedda ★★★★ PG
Drama   1975 · UK · Colour · 102min

Glenda Jackson earned her fourth and final Oscar nomination in this filmed record of her RSC triumph as Ibsen's heroine, the bored and pregnant wife of an egghead several rungs down from her on the social ladder. Jackson gives a powerful interpretation of the role, making it very much a part of the then-emerging women's movement, as does Trevor Nunn's own adaptation. Directing his first film for the cinema (he directed *Anthony and Cleopatra* for TV in 1974), Nunn commendably resists the chance to "open up" the play by keeping the action mostly within the gloomy brown walls of the Tesman drawing room. AT

Glenda Jackson *Hedda* • Peter Eyre *George Tesman* • Timothy West *Judge Brack* • Jennie Linden *Thea Elvsted* • Patrick Stewart *Ejlert Lovborg* • Constance Chapman *Julie* • Pam St Clement *Bertha* ■ *Dir* Trevor Nunn, from the play *Hedda Gabler* by Henrik Ibsen

The Hedgehog ★★★ 12A
Comedy drama   2009 · Fr/It · Colour · 99min

A charming performance by Garance Le Guillermic proves key to Mona Achache's adaptation of a popular novel by Muriel Barbery. As the 11-year-old who makes friends with concierge Josiane Balasko and retired businessman Togo Igawa to alleviate her strained relationship with her parents and sister, Le Guillermic is splendidly spirited. At times, the story feels rather like an adolescent version of *Breakfast at Tiffany's*, as Le Guillermic learns about life through classic novels and Ozu films, and influences the frumpy Balasko to achieve a touching late-life transformation. DP French +subtitles.

Garance Le Guillermic *Paloma Josse* • Josiane Balasko *Renée Michel* • Togo Igawa *Kakuro Ozu* • Anne Brochet *Solange Josse* • Ariane Ascaride *Manuela Lopez* • Wladimir Yordanoff *Paul Josse* ■ *Dir* Mona Achache • *Scr* Mona Achache, from the novel *The Elegance of the Hedgehog* by Muriel Barbery

Hedwig and the Angry Inch ★★15

Musical comedy 2001 · US · Colour · 87min

Writer/director John Cameron Mitchell adapts his successful off-Broadway rock musical and has a game try at opening up this erratic "rags to bitches" biography of a fictional German transsexual singer (played by Mitchell himself). Using surreal flashbacks, camp humour, crude animation and glam rock songs, this tells of young Hansel, living in East Germany, who has a sex-change operation to marry a GI and escape to America as Hedwig. Very much a love it or hate it experience. AJ *DVD*

John Cameron Mitchell *Hedwig/Hansel Schmidt* • Alberta Watson *Mother* • Michael Pitt *Tommy Gnosis* • Andrea Martin *Phyllis Stein* • Maurice Dean Wint *Sergeant Luther Robinson* • Miriam Shor *Yitzhak* • Stephen Trask *Skszp* ■ *Dir* John Cameron Mitchell • *Scr* John Cameron Mitchell, from the play by John Cameron Mitchell, Stephen Trask

Heidi ★★★U

Adventure 1937 · US · BW · 84min

One of Shirley Temple's most popular films, expertly directed by tough veteran Allan Dwan, on a relatively big budget that allows for expansive Christmas settings and a sleigh chase in the snow. Temple is excellent as the orphan nobody wants and, despite her awkward interpretation of a Dutch girl in one musical number, her Swiss miss is convincing. TS *DVD*

Shirley Temple *Heidi* • Jean Hersholt *Adolph Kramer* • Arthur Treacher *Andrews* • Helen Westley *Blind Anna* • Pauline Moore *Elsa* • Thomas Beck *Pastor Schultz* • Mary Nash *Fraulein Rottenmeier* • Sig Rumann [Sig Ruman] *Police captain* ■ *Dir* Allan Dwan • *Scr* Walter Ferris, Julien Josephson, from the novel by Johanna Spyri

Heidi ★★★U

Adventure drama 2005 · UK · Colour · 99min

There's nothing ground-breaking about this version of the classic story about a young Swiss girl who pines for her grandfather and alpine home when she's sent to Frankfurt. But traditional stories sometimes need a traditional telling and, within those parameters, this is decent, wholesome stuff. Emma Bolger is a cute and wide-eyed Heidi, Max von Sydow is a suitably grumpy grandpa, and there are starry support turns from Geraldine Chaplin and Diana Rigg. DA *DVD*

Max von Sydow *Uncle Alp* • Emma Bolger *Heidi* • Diana Rigg *Grandmamma* • Geraldine Chaplin *Rottenmeier* • Pauline McLynn *Aunt Detie* • Robert Bathurst *Mr Sesemann* • Jessica Claridge *Clara* • Samuel Friend *Peter* • Del Synnott *Sebastian* ■ *Dir* Paul Marcus • *Scr* Brian Finch, from the novel by Johanna Spyri

Heidi's Song ★★U

Animated musical 1982 · US · Colour · 90min

After numerous live-action versions, Johanna Spyri's much loved classic gets the cartoon treatment in this sugary, critter-strewn offering. This was a rare feature outing for the Hanna-Barbera studio. But little of the old magic is evident in this lacklustre adaptation, which is not helped by the abundance of substandard songs. DP

Lorne Greene *Grandfather* • Margery Gray *Heidi* • Sammy Davis Jr *Head Ratte* • Peter Cullen *Gruffle* • Roger DeWitt *Peter* • Richard Erdman *Herr Sessmann* • Fritz Feld *Sebastian* ■ *Dir* Robert Taylor (3) • *Scr* Joseph Barbera, Robert Taylor, Jameson Brewer, from the novel by Johanna Spyri • *Music/lyrics* Sammy Cahn, Burton Lane

Heimat ★★★★★15

Epic drama 1984 · W Ger · BW and Colour · 923min

It took over five years to shoot the 923 minutes that make up this monumental mosaic of 20th-century German history, and it was worth every second. Set in a village in the Hunsrück uplands, Edgar Reitz's masterpiece chronicles the life of the farming family into which Marita Breuer marries in 1919, paying as much attention to local detail as to the great events that shaped the nation's destiny. Wrongly dismissed in some quarters as high-class soap opera, the story not only eschews cheap melodramatics, but also meticulously develops its characters, who are played with uniform excellence by the huge cast. Also shown in 11 parts on TV, this is a stunningly photographed epic, with monochrome being tantalisingly embossed with patches of colour. DP German +subtitles. *DVD*

Michael Lesch *Paul Simon* • Marita Breuer *Maria Wiegand* • Gertrud Bredel *Katharina Simon* • Willi Burger *Mathias Simon* • Rüdiger Weigang *Eduard Simon* • Karin Kienzler *Pauline Simon* • Arno Lang *Robert Kröber* ■ *Dir* Edgar Reitz • *Scr* Edgar Reitz, Peter Steinbach • *Cinematographer* Gernat Roll

Heimat 2 ★★★★★15

Epic drama 1992 · Ger · BW and Colour · 1509min

The sequel to Edgar Reitz's magisterial 1984 film is officially the longest feature in screen history. But not one second of its 1500-plus minutes is wasted, as Reitz chronicles the social, cultural and political experiences of a group of friends at the Munich conservatoire in the 1960s. The prime focus is on country boy Henry Arnold and his passion for his elusive musical muse, Salome Kammer. But, amazingly (considering there are 71 principal characters), Reitz handles each episode with so much historical, psychological and intellectual integrity that even the most minor subplot has an affecting intimacy. A monumental masterpiece. DP *DVD*

Henry Arnold *Hermann Simon* • Eva Maria Bayerwaltes *Aunt Pauline* • Edith Behleit *Mother Lichtblau* • Johanna Bittenbinder *Erika* • Martin Maria Blau *Jean-Marie Weber* • Marinus Georg Brand *Herr Gross* • Hannes Demming *Father Aufschrey* • Veroncia Ferres *Dorli* • Salome Kammer *Clarissa Lichtblau* ■ *Dir/Scr* Edgar Reitz

Heimat 3: a Chronicle of Endings and Beginnings ★★★★★15

Epic drama 2004 · Ger/UK · Colour · 654min

Edgar Reitz concludes his remarkable history of one German family's experience of the 20th century with this compelling six-part feature. Reuniting as the Berlin Wall tumbles, composer Henry Arnold and avant-garde singer Salome Kammer agree to resume their star-crossed romance and employ workers from the former East Germany to renovate their dream house on the Rhine. As before, the accumulation of personal and period details draws us into the lives of characters whose all-too-human foibles make them all the more intriguing. Superbly directed and spiritedly played, this is a fitting finale to the most intelligent and sophisticated soap opera in cinema history. DP German +subtitles. *DVD*

Salome Kammer *Clarissa Lichtblau* • Henry Arnold *Hermann Simon* • Uwe Steimle *Gunnar* • Tom Quaas *Udo* • Peter Schneider *Tillmann* • Heiko Senst *Tobi* • Michael Kausch *Ernst Simon* • Matthias Kniesbeck *Anton* • Karen Hempel *Petra* • Peter Götz *Reinhold* • Julia Prochnow *Moni* • Antje Brauner *Jana* ■ *Dir* Edgar Reitz • *Scr* Edgar Reitz, Thomas Brussig

The Heiress ★★★★★U

Period drama 1949 · US · BW · 110min

This is an immaculately cast and brilliantly directed movie adaptation of Henry James's novel *Washington Square*. Olivia de Havilland quite rightly won her second Academy Award as the plain spinster seeking affection from fortune hunter Montgomery Clift. Clift also gives a finely controlled performance of great subtlety and, though both he and de Havilland are too good-looking for their roles, it is this quintessential Hollywood factor that keeps you riveted to the screen. As de Havilland's autocratic father, Ralph Richardson delivers arguably his finest screen work, and these flawless casting choices contribute to what is the most satisfying adaptation of James's original story. TS *DVD*

Olivia de Havilland *Catherine Sloper* • Montgomery Clift *Morris Townsend* • Ralph Richardson *Dr Austin Sloper* • Miriam Hopkins *Lavinia Penniman* • Vanessa Brown *Maria* • Mona Freeman *Marian Almond* • Selena Royle *Elizabeth Almond* • Ray Collins *Jefferson Almond* • Betty Linley *Mrs Montgomery* ■ *Dir* William Wyler • *Scr* Ruth Goetz, Augustus Goetz, from their play, from the novel *Washington Square* by Henry James • *Music* Aaron Copland • *Costume Designers* Edith Head, Gile Steele • *Art Director* John Meehan

Heist ★★★★15

Crime drama 2001 · US/Can · Colour · 104min

Writer/director David Mamet cranks up the suspense with his crack at a genre picture: the one-last-job heist. Gene Hackman is the boat-building master thief planning retirement with moll Rebecca Pidgeon. Typically, caper organiser Danny DeVito foists nervy nephew Sam Rockwell on Hackman's regular crew and the seemingly infinite double-crosses start rolling from there. As ever, Mamet's overcooked dialogue crackles, especially when delivered by Hackman, DeVito and fellow thief Delroy Lindo, and his eye for plot detail is acute. AC *DVD*

Gene Hackman *Joe Moore* • Danny DeVito *Mickey Bergman* • Delroy Lindo *Bobby Blane* • Sam Rockwell *Jimmy Silk* • Rebecca Pidgeon *Fran* • Patti LuPone *Betty Croft* ■ *Dir/Scr* David Mamet

The Heist ★★★12

Comedy caper 2009 · US · Colour · 86min

Three art gallery security guards (Christopher Walken, Morgan Freeman and William H Macy) plan an elaborate heist to steal the paintings they love before they are transferred abroad. Our three bumbling criminals are a treat to watch, which is just as well because the story unfolds without any surprises or twists. The trio's earnest attempts to pull off their scheme make for a charming experience, with the funniest moments being saved for the robbery itself. JL Swearing, brief nudity, some violence. *DVD*

Morgan Freeman *Charles Peterson* • Christopher Walken *Roger Barlow* • William H Macy *George McLendon* • Marcia Gay Harden *Rose Barlow* • Breckin Meyer *Starving artist* ■ *Dir* Peter Hewitt • *Scr* Michael LeSieur

Heist ★★15

Action thriller 2015 · US · Colour · 88min

Robert De Niro's quality control radar is now seemingly beyond repair, so it's best to accept the fact that his presence doesn't mean quality. That said, top billing here goes to Jeffrey Dean Morgan, as a croupier in desperate need of money to pay for the care of his seriously ill daughter. He reluctantly teams up with security guard Dave Bautista to relieve casino owner De Niro of the cash he's been laundering, but the robbery quickly turns pear-shaped. The pitch was probably *Speed* meets *Ocean's Eleven*, but this has neither the wit of the latter nor the tension of the former. For De Niro completists only. JF *DVD* BL

Robert De Niro *The Pope* • Jeffrey Dean Morgan *Vaughn* • Dave Bautista *Cox* • Kate Bosworth *Sydney* ■ *Dir* Scott Mann • *Scr* Stephen Cyrus Sepher, Max Adams

Hélas pour Moi ★★15

Drama 1993 · Fr/Swi · Colour · 79min

The English title is *Oh, Woe Is Me* and it's a reworking of the ancient Greek myth of Alcmene and Amphitryon. Gérard Depardieu drifts around a rainy Swiss lakeside village soliciting opinions on everything from love to the war in Bosnia. His body is then borrowed by God. This looks slapped together in a day or so, with Depardieu appearing as if in homage to Godard's earlier achievements. Wonderful music by Beethoven, Bach and Shostakovich gives the illusion of beauty. AT In French. *DVD*

Gérard Depardieu *Simon Donnadieu* • Laurence Masliah *Rachel Donnadieu* • Bernard Verley *Abraham Klimt* • Jean-Louis Loca *Max Mercure* • François Germond *Pastor* • Jean-Pierre Miquel *Other Pastor* ■ *Dir* Jean-Luc Godard • *Scr* Jean-Luc Godard, from the play *Amphitryon 38* by Jean Giraudoux

Held Up ★PG

Crime comedy 1999 · US · Colour · 85min

Jamie Foxx plays the out-of-towner who gets caught up in a convenience store robbery after being dumped by his fiancée (Nia Long) for spending their house savings on a vintage car. This crass comedy of errors a stereotyped affair from top to bottom, with Foxx's performance a long, long way behind his winning turns in *Collateral* and *Ray*. DP Some violence, swearing.

Jamie Foxx *Michael Dawson* • Nia Long *Rae* • Barry Corbin *Pembry* • John Cullum *Jack* • Jake Busey *Beaumont* • Michael Shamus Wiles *Biker* • Eduardo Yanez *Rodrigo* ■ *Dir* Steve Rash • *Scr* Erik Fleming, Jeff Eastin

Helen ★★★PG

Drama 2008 · UK/Ire · Colour · 78min

This downbeat but compelling feature follows the experiences of teenager Helen (Annie Townsend) as she becomes increasingly fixated by the missing girl whom she's asked to represent in a police reconstruction. It's not long before she adopts her yellow jacket as a uniform, dines with her parents (Sandie Malia and Dennis Jobling) and even flirts with her boyfriend (Danny Groenland). Studied and oblique, this melancholy mystery suffers from a surfeit of regional British accents. But at least Ole Birkeland's stealthy camerawork is as mesmerising as Townsend's impassive performance. DP

Annie Townsend *Helen* • Sandie Malia *Mrs Thompson* • Dennis Jobling *Mr Thompson* • Sonia Saville *Saville, police officer* • Danny Groenland *Danny* • Sheila Hamilton *Personal advisor* ■ *Dir/Scr* Joe Lawlor, Christine Molloy

The Helen Morgan Story ★★★

Musical biography 1957 · US · BW · 118min

Although Ann Blyth bears no resemblance to Helen Morgan and doesn't sing (Gogi Grant does the dubbing), she gives a sincere and effective performance as the great torch singer. This biopic plays fast and loose with the facts of Morgan's tumultuous life, but has considerable Prohibition-era atmosphere through the moody photography of Ted McCord allied to the fast-paced direction of Michael Curtiz. AE

Ann Blyth *Helen Morgan* • Paul Newman *Larry* • Richard Carlson *Wade* • Gene Evans *Whitey Krause* • Alan King *Ben* • Cara Williams *Dolly* ■ *Dir* Michael Curtiz • *Scr* Oscar Saul, Dean Reisner, Stephen Longstreet, Nelson Gidding

Helen of Troy ★★★U

Epic adventure 1955 · US/It · Colour · 115min

Filmed in Italy by Robert Wise, this excursion into Greek myth boasts a weird cast: Jack Sernas as Paris and Rossana Podesta as Helen are a lacklustre couple, while Stanley Baker's Achilles is a real heel. Janette Scott and even Brigitte Bardot add support, but it's a bit of a slog until the wooden horse lumbers into view and starts the sacking of Troy. AT *DVD*

Rossana Podesta *Helen* • Jack Sernas [Jacques Sernas] *Paris* • Cedric Hardwicke *Priam* • Stanley Baker *Achilles* • Niall MacGinnis *Menelaus* • Nora Swinburne *Hecuba* • Harry Andrews *Hector* • Brigitte Bardot *Andraste* ■ *Dir* Robert Wise • *Scr* John Twist, Hugh Gray, N Richard Nash, from the poem *The Iliad* by Homer [uncredited]

Heli ★★★ 18
Drama
2013 · Mex/Fr/Ger/Neth · Colour · 100min

Director Amat Escalante's brutal drama about a hapless family that fatally cross paths with thugs from a Mexican drug cartel was the obligatory talking point at Cannes when it premiered there in 2013. As time passes and the shock has worn off, it's easier to admire this deeply disturbing but meticulously crafted work. There are beautiful moments that sing strong and sweet, and an unflinching honesty about the hopeless pervasiveness of crime in Escalante's homeland. LF Spanish +subtitles. Violence. *DVD* *Blu-ray*

Armando Espitia *Heli* • Andrea Vergara *Estela* • Linda Gonzalez *Sabrina* • Juan Eduardo Palacios *Beto* ■ *Dir* Amat Escalante • *Scr* Amat Escalante, Gabriel Reyes

The Helicopter Spies ★★ PG
Spy adventure
1968 · US · Colour · 91min

The hilarious staccato-speak and all-action breeziness of *The Man from UNCLE* are handled with flair by David McCallum and Robert Vaughn in this feature that has been skilfully plucked from an episode of the comic book TV series. Even the ham-fisted clichés are part of the fun. Still, no amount of action can disguise the creakiness of the presentation. JM *DVD*

Robert Vaughn (1) *Napoleon Solo* • David McCallum (1) *Illya Kuryakin* • Carol Lynley *Annie* • Bradford Dillman *Luther Sebastian* • Lola Albright *Azalea* • John Dehner *Dr Kharmusi* • Leo G Carroll *Mr Waverly* ■ *Dir* Boris Sagal • *Scr* Dean Hargrove

Hell and Back Again ★★★ 15
War documentary
2011 · US/UK/Afg · Colour · 88min

The combat footage of a US Marines mission deep into Taliban territory gives this award-winning documentary the sort of urgent opening that may help to push you through its downbeat story. But the real meat of the tale comes as wounded sergeant Nathan Harris is having trouble adjusting to suburban life back in South Carolina. We see him relaxing with his wife, brandishing his automatic pistol while she sorts through a sack of his medication. The film keeps returning to Afghanistan, with footage of difficult, dangerous and even futile military activity and the result is a really effective, if unsurprising film that seems to mirror Harris's state of mind. GE *DVD*

■ *Dir* Danfung Dennis

Hell and High Water ★★★ PG
Action spy drama
1954 · US · Colour · 99min

This splendid submarine movie starring Richard Widmark makes the best of the confined surroundings to pump up the atmosphere. Twentieth Century-Fox boss Darryl F Zanuck didn't want to spend too much time on this one, so he entrusted it to jobbing director Samuel Fuller and it became yet another heady Fuller brew, full of action, espionage, romance and cardboard characterisation. The result is, of course, immensely enjoyable and a feast for Fuller fans. TS *DVD*

Richard Widmark *Adam Jones* • Bella Darvi *Denise* • Victor Francen *Professor Montel* • Cameron Mitchell *"Ski" Brodski* • Gene Evans *Chief Holter* • David Wayne *Dugboat Walker* • Stephen Bekassy *Neuman* ■ *Dir* Samuel Fuller • *Scr* Jesse L Lasky Jr [Jesse Lasky Jr], Samuel Fuller, from a story by David Hempstead

Hell below Zero ★★★ U
Adventure
1954 · UK · Colour · 86min

Alan Ladd took advantage of the tax break that helped US stars if they spent 18 months in Europe by making a series of British movies aimed at the international market, including this action adventure based on the Hammond Innes novel *The White South*. It's smoothly directed by another American, the excellent and underrated Mark Robson, and Ladd is terrific pitted against whalers in the Antarctic wastes. TS

Alan Ladd *Duncan Craig* • Joan Tetzel *Judie Nordahl* • Basil Sydney *Bland* • Stanley Baker *Erik Bland* • Joseph Tomelty *Captain McPhee* • Niall MacGinnis *Dr Howe* • Jill Bennett *Gerda Peterson* • Peter Dyneley *Miller* ■ *Dir* Mark Robson • *Scr* Alec Coppel, Max Trell, Richard Maibaum, from the novel *The White South* by Hammond Innes

Hell Bent for Leather ★★ U
Western
1960 · US · Colour · 81min

This uninspired Audie Murphy western is given a novel moral twist by the fact that evil marshal Stephen McNally keeps pursuing our baby-faced hero even though he knows he's innocent. Felicia Farr is the girl Murphy enlists to help him, and there are some mean hombres in tow. It also gains from being filmed in CinemaScope, and from the presence of old-time western hero Bob Steele. TS

Audie Murphy *Clay* • Felicia Farr *Janet* • Stephen McNally *Deckett* • Robert Middleton *Ambrose* • Rad Fulton *Moon* • Jan Merlin *Travers* • Bob Steele *Jared* ■ *Dir* George Sherman • *Scr* Christopher Knopf, from a novel by Ray Hogan

Hell Boats ★
Second World War drama
1970 · UK/US · Colour · 95min

This feeble drama was made for peanuts and features a poor cast. James Franciscus is an American lieutenant commander in the Royal Navy, who arrives in the Mediterranean to find an undisciplined rabble and a lonely wife (Elizabeth Shepherd). Things blow up (German supply dumps) and things break down (actors' accents) via wobbly back projection. AT

James Franciscus *Lt Commander Tom Jeffords* • Elizabeth Shepherd *Alison Ashurst* • Ronald Allen *Commander Roger Ashurst* • Reuven Bar Yotam *CPO Yacov* • Mark Hawkins *Lt Barlow* ■ *Dir* Paul Wendkos • *Scr* Anthony Spinner, Donald Ford, Derek Ford, from a story by SS Schweitzer

Hell Camp ★★ 18
Action drama
1986 · US · Colour · 95min

This disappointing slice of straight-to-video fodder – released in the States as *Opposing Force* – fails to deliver on an intriguing premise. Tom Skerritt and Lisa Eichhorn are among the military guinea pigs undergoing tests in the field to see how they stand up to being prisoners of war. The problem is that bonkers camp boss Anthony Zerbe starts taking the experiments a little too seriously. JF Violence, swearing, nudity.

Tom Skerritt *Major Logan* • Lisa Eichhorn *Lt Casey* • Anthony Zerbe *Becker* • Richard Roundtree *Sgt Stafford* • Robert Wightman *Gen McGowan* • John Considine *Gen MacDonald* ■ *Dir* Eric Karson • *Scr* Gil Cowan

Hell Comes to Frogtown ★ 15
Science-fiction action adventure
1988 · US · Colour · 82min

This is almost the ultimate in dumb movie plotlines. Professional wrestler "Rowdy" Roddy Piper stars as Sam Hell, the last potent man alive, who is chosen to rescue and impregnate various buxom maidens held captive by mutant frog folk. Bad enough to be beyond criticism: how can you hate a movie which includes such lines as "Eat lead, froggies!" RS

Roddy Piper *Sam Hell* • Sandahl Bergman *Spangle* • Cec Verrell *Centinella* • William Smith *Captain Devlin/Count Sodom* • Rory Calhoun *Looney Tunes* • Nicholas Worth *Bull* • Kristi Somers *Arabella* ■ *Dir* RJ Kizer, Donald G Jackson • *Scr* Randall Frakes, from a story by Donald G Jackson, Randall Frakes

Hell Divers ★★ U
Action drama
1932 · US · BW · 108min

This overlong action drama casts Clark Gable and Wallace Beery as a pair of tough officers in the US Navy. Dorothy Jordan is the woman who comes between them, though their rivalry is resolved when Beery sacrifices all to save Gable's life. The narrative mostly consists of endless flying missions that get less impressive the further the film progresses. AT

Clark Gable *Steve* • Wallace Beery *Windy* • Conrad Nagel *Duke* • Dorothy Jordan *Ann* • Marjorie Rambeau *Mame Kelsey* • Marie Prevost *Lulu* • Cliff Edwards *Baldy* • Robert Young (1) *Young officer* ■ *Dir* George Hill • *Scr* Harvey Gates, Malcolm Stuart Boylan, JK McGuinness, Ralph Graves, from a story by Lt Cdr Frank Wead [Frank Wead]

Hell Drivers ★★★★ PG
Thriller
1957 · UK · BW · 103min

This gripping British thriller is given a cutting edge of social reality by former Hollywood director Cy Endfield. Stanley Baker stars as the ex-con given the job of driving lorries at perilous speeds to meet the deadlines of a haulage company, who uncovers a racket run by his unprincipled manager. There's a splendid performance from Patrick McGoohan as a lethal rival driver and a marvellous co-starring role for Herbert Lom. Watch out, too, for a young, pre-Bond Sean Connery. TH *DVD*

Stanley Baker *Tom Yately* • Herbert Lom *Gino* • Peggy Cummins *Lucy* • Patrick McGoohan *Red* • William Hartnell *Cartley* • Wilfrid Lawson *Ed* • Sidney James *Dusty* • Jill Ireland *Jill* • Alfie Bass *Tinker* • Gordon Jackson *Scottie* • David McCallum (1) *Jimmy Yately* • Sean Connery *Johnny* ■ *Dir* C Raker Endfield [Cy Endfield] • *Scr* John Kruse, C Raker Endfield [Cy Endfield]

Hell in the Pacific ★★★★ PG
Second World War drama
1968 · US · Colour · 97min

Director John Boorman touches the primitive nerve of mankind at odds with itself and nature (anticipating his masterpiece, *Deliverance*, four years later) in this story of an American pilot and a Japanese sailor marooned on an island in wartime. The catchpenny title masks the solidly psychological nature of the action, as Lee Marvin displays a dramatic complexity rarely seen in his other works, while Toshiro Mifune exhibits honour as a sword that cuts both ways. The dynamics of the pair having to share their lives makes for compelling viewing. TH *DVD*

Lee Marvin *US marine pilot* • Toshiro Mifune *Japanese naval officer* ■ *Dir* John Boorman • *Scr* Alexander Jacobs, Eric Bercovici, from a story by Reuben Bercovitch

Hell Is a City ★★★ PG
Thriller
1959 · UK · BW · 92min

Made when Hammer wasn't just a house of horror, this brisk crime thriller was filmed on location in Manchester. Stanley Baker bristles with northern grit as the inspector out to nab the escaped convict whose crimes include murder and robbing bookie Donald Pleasence. Director Val Guest demonstrates a flair for realism and no-nonsense pacing. DP *DVD*

Stanley Baker *Inspector Martineau* • John Crawford *Don Starling* • Donald Pleasence *Gus Hawkins* • Maxine Audley *Julia Martineau* • Billie Whitelaw *Chloe Hawkins* • Joseph Tomelty *Furnisher Steele* • George A Cooper (2) *Doug Savage* ■ *Dir* Val Guest • *Scr* Val Guest, from a novel by Maurice Proctor

Hell Is for Heroes ★★★ 15
Second World War adventure
1962 · US · BW · 86min

Having already won a screenwriting Oscar for *Battleground* (1949), Robert Pirosh here came up with an even more uncompromising insight into the terrifying uncertainty of frontline life. Director Don Siegel builds steadily towards the pitiless battle sequences by allowing us to get to know the members of the small unit ordered to overpower a German pillbox, whose only hope of survival is to mislead the Germans into believing they are a much more substantial force. Steve McQueen is overly intense and Bob Newhart's comic monologue a mite ill-judged, but the rest of the cast is superb. DP *DVD*

Steve McQueen (1) *Reese* • Bobby Darin *Private Corby* • Fess Parker *Sergeant Pike* • Harry Guardino *Sergeant Larkin* • James Coburn *Corporal Henshaw* • Mike Kellin *Private Kolinsky* • Joseph Hoover *Captain Loomis* • Bill Mullikin *Private Cumberly* • LQ Jones *Sergeant Frazer* • Bob Newhart *Private Driscoll* ■ *Dir* Don Siegel • *Scr* Robert Pirosh, Richard Carr, from a story by Robert Pirosh

Hell Night ★★ 18
Horror
1981 · US · Colour · 101min

Producer Irwin Yablans's poor attempt to do for the haunted house genre what *Halloween* did for the psycho slasher, sees four teens on a fraternity initiation, locked overnight in an old dark house where a deranged madman axed his deformed family to death 12 years earlier. Former adult film-maker Tom DeSimone directs with a distinctly unpleasant edge, but Linda Blair acts as if she's in a different film from the rest of the average cast. AJ *DVD*

Linda Blair *Marti* • Vincent Van Patten *Seth* • Peter Barton *Jeff* • Kevin Brophy *Peter* • Jenny Neumann *May* • Suki Goodwin *Denise* ■ *Dir* Tom DeSimone • *Scr* Randolph Feldman

Hell on Frisco Bay ★★
Crime thriller
1955 · US · Colour · 98min

Alan Ladd stars as the former cop framed and jailed on a manslaughter charge, who is seeking revenge on the violent racketeer responsible, played by Edward G Robinson. Ladd is aided by a first-rate cast, including Joanne Dru as his wife, Fay Wray as a faded film star and Paul Stewart as her lover and Robinson's right-hand man. Jayne Mansfield has a bit in a nightclub. AE

Alan Ladd *Steve Rollins* • Edward G Robinson *Victor Amato* • Joanne Dru *Marcia Rollins* • William Demarest *Dan Bianco* • Nestor Paiva *Lou Fiaschetti* • Perry Lopez *Mario Amato* • Paul Stewart *Joe Lye* • Fay Wray *Kay Stanley* • Jayne Mansfield *Blonde* • Stanley Adams *Hammy* • Rodney Taylor [Rod Taylor] *Brodie Evans* ■ *Dir* Frank Tuttle • *Scr* Sydney Boehm, Martin Rackin, from the magazine serial *The Darkest Hour* by William P McGivern

Hell or High Water ★★★★ 15
Crime drama
2016 · · Colour · 101min

If mild-mannered British director David Mackenzie's last film – the brutal prison drama *Starred Up* – came as something of a surprise, his second US film is a revelation, mastering the style and language of the indie movie like a native. It's a rustic thriller invoking the spirit of the Coen brothers in a story of desperate men in desperate times. Set firmly in the shadow of the financial collapse of 2008, it sees two redneck brothers – ex-con Tanner (Ben Foster) and divorced father Toby (Chris Pine) – teaming up to rob a series of banks in the Texas area. DW

Ben Foster *Tanner* • Chris Pine *Toby* • Jeff Bridges *Marcus* • Katy Mixon *Jenny Ann* • Dale Dickey *Elsie* ■ *Dir* David Mackenzie • *Scr* Taylor Sheridan • *Music* Nick Cave

Hell Ship Mutiny ★ U
Adventure drama
1957 · US · BW · 66min

In the 1940s, the well built Jon Hall was a kind of male Dorothy Lamour, only instead of a sarong, he was mostly seen in a loincloth. Though still handsome here, Hall remains fully clothed, despite the South Seas setting, in this rather dire low-budget Republic adventure. He's a ship's captain helping a princess rid her island of thieves. RB

Jon Hall *Captain Knight* • John Carradine *Malone* • Peter Lorre *Lamouet* • Roberta Haynes *Mareva* • Mike Mazurki *Ross* • Charles Mauu *Tula* ■ *Dir* Lee Sholem, Elmo Williams • *Scr* DeVallon Scott, Wells Root

Hell to Eternity ★★★
Biographical Second World War drama
1960 · US · BW · 133min

Based on a true story of Second World War hero Guy Gabaldon, the film presents a slightly different angle on the war: how the Californian Japanese community was affected by the bombing of Pearl Harbor. Most of the movie, however, is the usual battle stuff, until Jeffrey Hunter, with divided loyalties due to his upbringing by Japanese foster parents, uses his adopted tongue to get an enemy battalion to surrender. RB

Jeffrey Hunter *Guy Gabaldon* • David Janssen *Bill* • Vic Damone *Pete* • Patricia Owens *Sheila* • Miiko Taka *Ester* • Sessue Hayakawa *General Matsui* • George Takei *George* ■ *Dir* Phil Karlson • *Scr* Ted Sherdeman, Walter Roeber Schmidt, from a story by Gil Doud

Hell Town ★★ U
Western 1937 · US · BW · 55min

Zane Grey's novel *Born to the West* was first filmed in 1926 and plenty of silent footage resurfaces in this Paramount remake, which was originally released under that title. But the main interest lies in the performance of a pre-fame John Wayne, as a drifter whose dalliance with Marsha Hunt incurs the wrath of his Wyoming rancher cousin, Johnny Mack Brown. Unfortunately, Wayne is easily upstaged by his co-stars, with Monte Blue taking the honours as a scheming saloon owner. DP DVD

John Wayne *Dare Rudd* • Marsha Hunt *Judy* • Johnny Mack Brown *Tom Fillmore* • Monte Blue *Bart Hammond* • Syd Saylor *Dinkey Hooley* • Alan Ladd *Inspector* ■ *Dir* Charles Barton • *Scr* Stuart Anthony, Robert Yost, from the novel *Born to the West* by Zane Grey

Hell Up in Harlem ★ 18
Crime drama 1973 · US · Colour · 90min

The weak sequel to *Black Caesar* finds Fred Williamson fighting both his father and the Mob for control of Harlem. When the Mafia kidnap his children, he leads a posse of frogmen against gangster headquarters in the Florida Keys. Plenty of double-crossing mayhem and hand-held camera action fail to enliven the usually reliable director Larry Cohen's blaxploitation caper. AJ

Fred Williamson *Tommy Gibbs* • Julius Harris *Papa Gibbs* • Gloria Hendry *Helen Bradley* • Margaret Avery (2) *Sister Jennifer* • D'Urville Martin *Reverend Rufus* • Tony King *Zach* ■ *Dir/Scr* Larry Cohen

The Hell with Heroes ★
Crime drama 1968 · US · Colour · 101min

Eminently missable, this features Rod Taylor and Peter Duel trying to make a dishonest buck after the Second World War by smuggling contraband. Harry Guardino plays Mr Big and Claudia Cardinale his mistress, a thankless role with which she looks suitably bored. TV director Joseph Sargent made his big-screen debut here. AT

Rod Taylor *Brynie MacKay* • Claudia Cardinale *Elena* • Harry Guardino *Lee Harris* • Kevin McCarthy *Colonel Wilson* • Pete Duel *Mike Brewer* • William Marshall (2) *Al Poland* • Don Knight *Pepper* ■ *Dir* Joseph Sargent • *Scr* Halsted Welles, Harold Livingston, from a story by Harold Livingston

Hellborn ★
Crime drama 1961 · US · Colour · 75min

An undercover cop in drag, a judge warning the audience of the dangers of pornography and a beauty queen cornered by a sadistic psycho killer – what else could this be but another poverty row, sexploitation quickie from Ed Wood Jr, famously acknowledged as the world's worst director? The last film directed by the cult auteur of *Plan 9 for Outer Space* has Dino Fantini going berserk watching a stag movie and turning into a sex maniac. AJ

Kenne Duncan *Lt Matt Carson* • James "Duke" Moore [Duke Moore] *Sgt Randy Stone* • Jean Fontaine *Gloria Henderson* • Carl Anthony *Johnny Ryde* • Dino Fantini *Dirk Williams* • Jeanne Willardson *Mary Smith* ■ *Dir/Scr* Edward D Wood Jr

Hellbound: Hellraiser II ★★ 18
Horror 1988 · UK · Colour · 89min

Allegory is replaced by the just plain gory in the first sequel to Clive Barker's ground-breaking macabre masochistic myth about the dark angels of hell and their Faustian bargains. Kenneth Cranham is the demented doctor anxious to meet the Cenobite messengers, while asylum inmate Ashley Laurence (still recovering from *Hellraiser* events) is forced to fight the invoked demons for her father's soul. Routinely directed by Tony Randel, some disturbing eeriness is conjured up between the blood-soaked illogicalities and outlandish inconsistencies. AJ Violence, swearing, nudity. DVD

Ashley Laurence *Kirsty Cotton* • Clare Higgins *Julia* • Kenneth Cranham *Dr Channard* • Imogen Boorman *Tiffany* • William Hope *Kyle Macrae* • Oliver Smith *Browning* • Sean Chapman *Uncle Frank* • Doug Bradley *Pinhead* ■ *Dir* Tony Randel • *Scr* Peter Atkins, from a story by Clive Barker

Hellboy ★★★ 12
Horror fantasy adventure 2004 · US · Colour · 116min

Blade II director Guillermo del Toro tackles another comic book adaptation with this faithful take on Mike Mignola's unlikely superhero, Hellboy. A visually appealing marriage of action, horror and romance, it's both intelligent and fun. In a wry and often poignant performance, Ron Perlman brings unusual depth to the titular character, a cigar-chomping demon intended by the Nazis for acts of evil, but instead raised by the Allies to be an agent of good. Though the film loses momentum towards the end, it's still a fine example of its genre. SF Violence. DVD Blu

Ron Perlman *Hellboy* • John Hurt *Professor Trevor "Broom" Bruttenholm* • Selma Blair *Liz Sherman* • Jeffrey Tambor *Tom Manning* • Karel Roden *Grigori Rasputin* • Rupert Evans (2) *John Myers* • Doug Jones *Abe Sapien* • Ladislav Beran *Kroenen* ■ *Dir* Guillermo del Toro • *Scr* Guillermo del Toro, from a story by Guillermo del Toro, Peter Briggs, from the comic book by Mike Mignola

Hellboy II: the Golden Army ★★★★ 12
Horror fantasy adventure 2008 · US/Ger · Colour · 114min

Director Guillermo del Toro's mastery of fantasy film-making and his understanding of the multi-faceted richness of the genre guides this sequel to visually imaginative and intricately detailed heights. This time our florid superhero Hellboy (Ron Perlman) must thwart the renegade elf prince Nuada (Luke Goss), who will stop at nothing (even killing his own father) to awaken the fabled indestructible Golden Army and conquer the human realm. Imbued with the ornate gothic fairy-tale style and emotional resonance of del Toro's *Pan's Labyrinth*, the film effortlessly marries dry wit and unnerving creepiness. Epic in breadth and ambition while still retaining its gentle soul, this army of golden images is another sublime example of myth-making from a master of the art. AJ DVD Blu

Ron Perlman *Hellboy* • John Hurt *Professor Broom* • Selma Blair *Liz Sherman* • Jeffrey Tambor *Tom Manning* • Doug Jones *Abe Sapien* • John Alexander *Johann Krauss* ■ *Dir* Guillermo del Toro • *Scr* Guillermo del Toro, from a story by del Toro, from the comic book by Mike Mignola

Heller in Pink Tights ★★★ PG
Western 1960 · US · Colour · 96min

George Cukor, renowned as a woman's director in Hollywood, might seem an unlikely choice to direct a western, but this is an unlikely example of the genre, dealing as it does with a group of travelling theatricals, led by stunning Sophia Loren. Anthony Quinn and Steve Forrest flex their emotions as rivals for La Loren, but the real star is Cukor's skill as a film-maker. The production design is superb, and Loren and her troupe look great in Technicolor. Good camp fun. TS DVD

Sophia Loren *Angela Rossini* • Anthony Quinn *Tom Healy* • Margaret O'Brien *Della Southby* • Steve Forrest *Clint Mabry* • Eileen Heckart *Lorna Hathaway* • Edmund Lowe *Manfred "Doc" Montague* • Ramon Novarro *De Leon* • George Mathews *Sam Pierce* ■ *Dir* George Cukor • *Scr* Dudley Nichols, Walter Bernstein, from the novel *Heller with a Gun* by Louis L'Amour • *Art Director* Hal Pereira

The Hellfire Club ★★ U
Period adventure 1961 · UK · Colour · 93min

Depravity, debauchery and devil worship? There's nothing of the sort in this would-be horror flick, in which such sins are sadly bleached of any lurid content. Keith Michell stars as the dispossessed son who returns to claim his degenerate father's estate, only to be challenged by his cousin Peter Arne, who's up to all kinds of dirty tricks by virtue of his Hellfire Club membership. TH

Keith Michell *Jason* • Adrienne Corri *Isobel* • Peter Cushing *Merryweather* • Kai Fischer *Yvonne* • Peter Arne *Thomas* • David Lodge *Timothy* • Bill Owen *Martin* • Miles Malleson *Judge* ■ *Dir* Robert S Baker, Monty Berman • *Scr* Leon Griffiths, Jimmy Sangster, from a story by Jimmy Sangster

Hellgate ★★ PG
Western 1952 · US · Colour · 87min

Hellgate is a remote prison in New Mexico where the brutal regime in the 1860s is made worse by the desert heat. Sterling Hayden plays the wrongly imprisoned veterinary surgeon, persecuted by the harsh and embittered commandant (Ward Bond), in this unremittingly grim production. AE

Sterling Hayden *Gil Hanley* • Joan Leslie *Ellen Hanley* • Ward Bond *Lt Tod Voorhees* • Jim Arness [James Arness] *George Redfield* • Marshall Bradford *Doctor Pelham* • Peter Coe *Jumper Hall* • Richard Paxton *George Nye* • John Pickard *Gundy Boyd* ■ *Dir* Charles Marquis Warren • *Scr* Charles Marquis Warren, from a story by Charles Marquis Warren, John C Champion

Hellion ★★★ 15
Social drama 2014 · US · Colour · 94min

Grief and responsibility are the two central themes in this low-key drama from promising writer/director Kat Candler. Since the death of his mother, a 13-year-old has become a bad influence on his impressionable younger brother. Making matters worse, the boys' father (*Breaking Bad*'s Aaron Paul) is so consumed by loss that he is unable to take care of them properly. This is a relatively standard indie offering, but Candler imbues it with an appealing sense of naturalism and authenticity. Paul provides an affecting display of raw emotion as the boozy, beard-sporting widower, while Wiggins is outstanding as the angry youngster. SC Violence. DVD

Josh Wiggins *Jacob Wilson* • Aaron Paul *Hollis Wilson* • Juliette Lewis *Pam Noonan* • Deke Garner *Wes Wilson* ■ *Dir/Scr* Kat Candler

Hello Again ★★★ PG
Black comedy 1987 · US · Colour · 96min

Making it to the big screen from TV's *Cheers*, Shelley Long is rather small-time in one of those supernatural plots that were popular after *Ghostbusters*. She's a plastic surgeon's plastic wife, who chokes to death and returns to a much-altered life thanks to her medium sister. Long's brittle vivacity crumples under an overload of whimsy, though Judith Ivey, as the spaced-out hippy sibling, tunes us in to the cosmos to some comical effect. TH Some swearing. DVD

Shelley Long *Lucy Chadman* • Gabriel Byrne *Kevin Scanlon* • Judith Ivey *Zelda* • Corbin Bernsen *Jason Chadman* • Sela Ward *Kim Lacey* • Austin Pendleton *Junior Lacey* ■ *Dir* Frank Perry • *Scr* Susan Isaacs

Hello Carter ★★ 15
Comedy drama 2013 · UK · Colour · 77min

Carter, a homeless Londoner, has a chance encounter with his ex-girlfriend's brother (Paul Schneider) that throws him into a night of – what is intended to be – comedy chaos. A flaky script is comprised of a series of unfortunate and increasingly unbelievable events. All this makes for a tedious watch, and Cox seems uncomfortable in the lead – only appealing in his scenes with Jodie Whittaker, thanks to their cute chemistry. JL Swearing.

Charlie Cox *Carter* • Jodie Whittaker *Jenny* • Paul Schneider (2) *Aaron* • Annabelle Wallis *Kelly* ■ *Dir/Scr* Anthony Wilcox • *Cinematographer* Andrew Dunn (1)

Hello, Dolly! ★★★★ U
Musical 1969 · US · Colour · 139min

Despite Barbra Streisand's underaged Dolly Levi, this lavish 20th Century-Fox movie version of the long-running Broadway hit is a wondrous treat under Gene Kelly's expert direction, and now looks like the virtual last gasp of the great era of costly Hollywood musicals. Among the twinkling, shining stars are Britain's own Michael Crawford and the man who had taken the title song to number one in the US charts five years earlier, Louis "Satchmo" Armstrong. The design, use of colour and, particularly, the marvellous score are quite breathtaking, and the film won three Oscars. TS DVD

Barbra Streisand *Dolly Levi* • Walter Matthau *Horace Vandergelder* • Michael Crawford *Cornelius Hackl* • Louis Armstrong *Orchestra leader* • Marianne McAndrew *Irene Molloy* • EJ Peaker *Minnie Fay* • Danny Lockin *Barnaby Tucker* • Joyce Ames *Ermengarde* ■ *Dir* Gene Kelly • *Scr* Ernest Lehman, from the musical *Hello, Dolly!* by Jerry Herman, Michael Stewart, from the play *The Matchmaker* by Thornton Wilder • *Cinematographer* Harry Stradling • *Music* Lenny Hayton, Lionel Newman • *Production Designer* John De Cuir

H

Hello Down There ★★ U
Comedy 1969 · US · Colour · 97min

This would-be comedy comes across as a sort of underwater *Swiss Family Robinson*, with Tony Randall as the designer of a submersible house who agrees to test it out on his wife and children. The plethora of generation gap jokes soon grates on the nerves, as do the bratty adolescent cast members, including a young Richard Dreyfuss, but there's no denying an ingenious premise that should dazzle the youngsters. RS

Tony Randall *Fred Miller* • Janet Leigh *Vivian Miller* • Jim Backus *TR Hollister* • Roddy McDowall *Nate Ashbury* • Merv Griffin • Ken Berry *Mel Cheever* • Kay Cole *Lorrie Miller* • Richard Dreyfuss *Harold Webster* • Harvey Lembeck *Sonarman* ■ *Dir* Jack Arnold • *Scr* Frank Telford, John McGreevey, from a story by Ivan Tors, Art Arthur

Hello, Frisco, Hello ★★ U
Period musical 1943 · US · Colour · 98min

After time off for motherhood, Alice Faye returned in another Fox period musical with her regular co-stars of the time, John Payne and Jack Oakie. The script is routine stuff about Payne's impresario making a singing star out of Faye on the turn-of-the-century Barbary Coast and how she repays the debt when he's down on his luck. To supplement the period numbers, Mack Gordon and Harry Warren wrote *You'll Never Know*, an Oscar-winning song about separated lovers with a wartime relevance that helped the film's success. AE

Alice Faye *Trudy Evans* • John Payne *Johnny Cornell* • Jack Oakie *Dan Daley* • Lynn Bari *Bernice Croft* • Laird Cregar *Sam Weaver* • June Havoc *Beulah Clancy* • Ward Bond *Sharkey* ■ *Dir* H Bruce Humberstone • *Scr* Robert Ellis, Helen Logan, Richard Macauley

Hello – Goodbye ★
Comedy 1970 · US/UK · Colour · 100min

Michael Crawford plays Harry England, a man obsessed with luxury cars, an interest which embroils him in a love affair while on a trip to France. Only later does he discover the object of his affection is actually the wife of the wealthy baron who employs him. A meandering romantic comedy, this is more like a Skoda than a Bentley. DF

Michael Crawford *Harry England* • Geneviève Gilles *Dany* • Curt Jurgens *Baron De Choisis* • Ira Fürstenberg [Ira von Fürstenberg] *Evelyne* • Lon Satton *Cole* • Peter Myers *Bentley* ■ *Dir* Jean Negulesco • *Scr* Roger Marshall

Hello, Hemingway ★★★
Drama 1990 · Cub · Colour · 88min

Set in the pre-Castro Cuba that played host to the exiled Ernest Hemingway (whose elusive presence lingers just off screen), this rites-of-passage drama draws its inspiration from the author's Pulitzer prize-winning masterpiece *The Old Man and the Sea*. However, director Fernando Perez doesn't overdo the parallels between the obsessive fisherman's battles with the elements and Elvis-besotted teenager Laura de la Uz's bid to land the scholarship in the States that will enable her to break away from her impoverished family and increasingly politicised boyfriend. DP Spanish +subtitles.

Laura de la Uz *Larita* • Raul Paz *Victor* • Herminia Sanchez *Josefa* • Caridad Hernandez *Rosenda* • Enrique Molina *Manolo* • Maria Isabel Diaz *Flora* • Micheline Calvert *Miss Amalia* • Marta Del Rio *Doctor Martinez* ■ *Dir* Fernando Perez • *Scr* Maydo Royero

Hello Sister! ★★★
Drama 1933 · US · BW · 55min

It is a sad fact that most of the nine movies directed by Erich von Stroheim were subject to a great deal of interference. He completed *Walking Down Broadway*, his first and last sound film, on time and within budget. Yet 20th Century-Fox, with some reshoots and re-editing, released it under the crass title of *Hello Sister!* Pity, because there are enough bizarre touches in this uncharacteristically simple tale of boy meets girl on Broadway, to display von Stroheim's touch. He never directed again. RB

ZaSu Pitts *Millie* • Boots Mallory *Peggy* • James Dunn *Jimmy* • Terrance Ray *Mac* • Minna Gombell *Mona* • Hattie McDaniel *Black woman in apartment house* ■ *Dir* Erich von Stroheim • *Scr* Erich von Stroheim, Leonard Spigelgass, Geraldine Nomis, Harry Ruskin, Maurine Watkins, from the play *Walking Down Broadway* by Dawn Powell • *Cinematographer* James Wong Howe

Hellraiser ★★★18
Horror 1987 · UK · Colour · 93min

Popular horror writer Clive Barker transferred his trademark perverse chills visually intact to the screen in his directorial debut. A surreal, claustrophobic and graphic shocker about the consequences of opening a Chinese puzzle box, the film allows Barker to introduce a dark new mythology to the genre, as well as the Cenobites, leather-clad, disfigured angels from hell with intriguing concepts of dimensional pleasure and pain. Despite its uneven direction and the odd Cricklewood locations, this absorbing sadomasochistic chiller really delivers the gruesome goods. A first sequel, *Hellbound: Hellraiser II*, followed in 1988. AJ Violence, swearing. DVD BD

Andrew Robinson *Larry Cotton* • Clare Higgins *Julia Cotton* • Ashley Laurence *Kirsty Swanson* • Sean Chapman *Frank Cotton* • Oliver Smith *Frank the Monster* • Doug Bradley *Lead Cenobite* ■ *Dir* Clive Barker • *Scr* Clive Barker, from his novella *The Hellbound Heart*

Hellraiser III: Hell on Earth ★★★18
Horror 1992 · US · Colour · 92min

Pinhead, the Cenobite superstar of author Clive Barker's bloody brainchild, tempts new disciples down the path of perverse pleasure in this distinct improvement on *Hellbound: Hellraiser II*. Here, director Anthony Hickox's high-energy horror comic strip is hot-wired by a keen visual sense and big dipper drive. More a supernatural sadomasochistic action thriller than the murky gothic nightmares of the previous two episodes, this is funny, original and unpredictable. AJ Swearing, sex scenes, drug abuse, nudity. DVD

Terry Farrell *Joey Summerskill* • Doug Bradley *Pinhead/Elliott Spencer* • Paula Marshall *Terri* • Kevin Bernhardt *JP Monroe* • Ken Carpenter *Doc/Camerahead* • Peter Boynton *Joey's father* • Aimee Leigh *Sandy* ■ *Dir* Anthony Hickox • *Scr* Peter Atkins, from a story by Peter Atkins, Tony Randel, from characters by Clive Barker

Hellraiser: Bloodline ★★★18
Horror 1996 · US · Colour · 81min

Showing clear signs of the studio tinkering that made director Kevin Yagher take his name off the credits, the ragged third

sequel to author Clive Barker's Cenobite saga still does the blood-drenched business. Exploring the evil origins of the lament configuration box (the key to unlocking the pleasures of Hell), genre icon Pinhead (Doug Bradley) takes sadomasochism into space in this audacious episode. Not the disaster it's made out to be. A forgettable fourth sequel, subtitled *Inferno*, followed in 2001. AJ Swearing, violence. DVD

Bruce Ramsay *Phillipe Lemarchand/John Merchant/Paul Merchant* • Valentina Vargas *Angelique* • Doug Bradley *Pinhead* ■ *Dir* Alan Smithee [Kevin Yagher] • *Scr* Peter Atkins

Hell's Angels ★★★PG
First World War drama
1930 · US · BW and Colour · 126min

Howard Hughes's legendary air epic was almost completed as a silent movie, then virtually remade as a talkie. After sacking several directors, Hughes finally directed it himself and, despite good reviews and huge queues, the film cost too much to show a profit. The First World War aerial combat scenes remain spectacular and are the reason why Hughes made the film in the first place. Jean Harlow is still sexy down the decades, but Ben Lyon and James Hall are stilted as the brothers. AT DVD

Ben Lyon *Monte Rutledge* • James Hall *Roy Rutledge* • Jean Harlow *Helen* • John Darrow *Karl Arnstedt* • Lucien Prival *Baron von Kranz* • Frank Clarke *Lt von Bruen* • Roy Wilson *Baldy* • Douglas Gilmore *Capt Redfield* ■ *Dir* Howard Hughes, Marshall Neilan, Luther Reed • *Scr* Joseph Moncure March, Harry Behn (adaptation), Howard Estabrook (adaptation), from a story by Marshall Neilan, Joseph Moncure March

Hell's Angels on Wheels ★★★18
Action drama 1967 · US · Colour · 79min

This cult biker movie, originally banned by the British censors, is full of carnage and copulation. Jack Nicholson plays a character called Poet (as characters were called in those days) who falls in with Adam Roarke's gang. Director Richard Rush uses a barrage of camera tricks, frenzied cutting and other "look at me" gimmicks to enhance the boy-meets-biker girl story. AT DVD

Jack Nicholson *Poet* • Adam Roarke *Buddy* • Sabrina Scharf *Shill* • Jana Taylor *Abigale* • John Garwood *Jock* • Richard Anders *Bull* • Mimi Machu *Pearl* • James Oliver *Gypsy* ■ *Dir* Richard Rush • *Scr* R Wright Campbell

Hell's House ★★PG
Crime 1932 · US · BW · 71min

This strictly lower-order B-picture fare concerns a youth (Junior Durkin) whose association with a racketeer (Pat O'Brien) lands him, though innocent of a crime, in a reform school run by abusive overseers. Durkin's girlfriend is played by Bette Davis in one of the many inferior roles visited on her during her Warner Bros contract. Made with no real flair, it's undemanding. RK DVD

Junior Durkin *Jimmy Mason* • Pat O'Brien *Kelly* • Bette Davis *Peggy Gardner* • Junior Coghlan *Shorty* • Charley Grapewin *Uncle Henry* • Emma Dunn *Aunt Emma* • Morgan Wallace *Frank Gebhardt* ■ *Dir* Howard Higgin • *Scr* Paul Gangelin, B Harrison Orkow, from the story by Howard Higgin

Hell's Kitchen ★★★
Crime drama 1939 · US · BW · 79min

This Dead End Kid's film was considered so provocative that later movies became less violent. A brutal depiction of life in a New York shelter school for boys, the story involves a superintendent (Grant Mitchell) imposing intolerable hardship on the youngsters, while stealing school funds. When one boy dies, after being locked in a freezer, the others hold a mock trial. BB

Billy Halop *Tony Marco* • Bobby Jordan *Joey Richards* • Leo Gorcey *Gyp Haller* • Huntz Hall *Bingo* • Gabriel Dell *Ace* • Margaret Lindsay *Beth Avery* • Ronald Reagan *Jim Donahue* • Grant Mitchell *Hiram Crispin* ■ *Dir* Lewis Seiler, EA Dupont • *Scr* Crane Wilbur, Fred Niblo Jr, from a story by Crane Wilbur

The Hellstrom Chronicle ★★★
Drama documentary 1971 · US · Colour · 89min

The microscopic action and doom-laden predictions contained in this stylised documentary reveal a sinister side to the insect antics of *Microcosmos*. Yes, the deadly purpose behind Walon Green's film is to warn us that bugs will eventually rule the planet, as they have an evolutionary durability that we can only dream of. However, it would be easier to take this unpalatable message more seriously were it not delivered by such a flagrantly bogus expert. Lawrence Pressman's performance as Nils Hellstrom is just irritatingly smug and distracts from the excellence of the photography, which clearly won this undeserving curio its Oscar. DP

Lawrence Pressman *Professor Hellstrom* ■ *Dir* Walon Green • *Scr* David Seltzer • *Music* Lalo Schifrin • *Cinematographers* Helmuth Barth, Walon Green, Vilis Lapenieks, Ken Middleham, Heinz Sielmann

Hellzapoppin' ★★★★U
Comedy 1941 · US · BW · 80min

This surreal, almost plotless film version of vaudevillians Ole Olsen and Chic Johnson's famous long-running Broadway hit is a genuine one-off. Of course, it's virtually impossible to re-create characters on screen who wreak havoc in the theatre, so a number of cinematic devices have been incorporated to hilarious effect – the actual projectionist showing the movie is turned into an on-screen character (almost). This forerunner of *The Goon Show* and Monty Python is a near masterpiece. TS

Ole Olsen *Ole* • Chic Johnson *Chic* • Martha Raye *Betty* • Hugh Herbert *Quimby* • Jane Frazee *Kitty* • Robert Paige *Jeff* • Mischa Auer *Pepi* • Richard Lane *The director* • Elisha Cook Jr *Selby* ■ *Dir* HC Potter • *Scr* Warren Wilson, Nat Perrin, Alex Gottlieb, from a story by Nat Perrin, from the play by Ole Olsen, Chic Johnson • *Music/lyrics* Sammy Fain, Charles Tobias

Help! ★★★★U
Musical comedy 1965 · UK · Colour · 91min

A disappointment after the exhilarating *A Hard Day's Night*, the second Beatles feature is still hugely enjoyable. Sweeping John, George, Paul and Ringo from Swiss ski slopes to the beaches of the Bahamas, this extremely silly story follows the attempts of an Eastern cult (led by Leo McKern and Eleanor Bron) to recover a ceremonial ring that has ended up on Ringo's finger. Pop classics (*Ticket to Ride* and the title song) abound and there are plenty of sharp one-liners. DP DVD BD

John Lennon *John* • Paul McCartney *Paul* • Ringo Starr *Ringo* • George Harrison *George* • Leo McKern *Clang* • Eleanor Bron *Ahme* • Victor Spinetti *Foot* • Roy Kinnear *Algernon* ■ *Dir* Richard Lester • *Scr* Marc Behm, Charles Wood, from a story by Marc Behm

The Help ★★★12
Drama 2011 · US/Ind/UAE · Colour · 140min

The Deep South is well-trodden territory, but this drama based on Kathryn Stockett's bestseller gives a voice to those usually cast in supporting roles. Viola Davis is the heart and guts of this adaptation as Aibileen, a black housemaid in the 1960s who dishes the dirt on her ignorant employer. Her story is co-opted by aspiring journalist Skeeter (*Easy A*'s Emma Stone), but their secret collaboration invites suspicion. Stone is an appealing heroine, pointing out the mess when others would rather sweep it under the carpet, while *Juno*'s Allison Janney provides sassy support. SP DVD BD

Emma Stone *Eugenia "Skeeter" Phelan* • Bryce Dallas Howard *Hilly Holbrook* • Viola Davis *Aibileen Clark* • Jessica Chastain *Celia Foote* • Allison Janney *Charlotte Phelan* • Sissy Spacek *Missus Walters* • Mike Vogel *Johnny Foote* ■ *Dir* Tate Taylor • *Scr* Tate Taylor, from the novel by Kathryn Stockett

Help for the Holidays ★★
Seasonal fantasy 2012 · US · Colour · 96min

A busy California family has lost their Christmas spirit and it's up to Santa's elf Summer Glau to help them regain it in this festive confection that's cute though routine. As with most seasonal fantasies, it's a patchwork of well-worn ideas and messages, yet what the TV movie lacks in originality it compensates for in sweetness. Glau is particularly nicely cast, adding both heart and playfulness to her fish-out-of-water role. SF

Summer Glau *Christine Prancer* • Eva La Rue *Sara VanCamp* • Izabela Vidovic *Ally VanCamp* • Mason Cook *Will VanCamp* ■ *Dir* Bradford May • *Scr* Abbey Cleland, Bob Saenz, from a story by Cleland

Help, I'm a Fish! ★★★U
Animated adventure
2000 · Den/Ger/Ire · Colour · 76min

Younger children will enjoy this Danish-made cartoon, voiced in its English version by, among others, Alan Rickman and Terry Jones. The easy-to-follow plot has a small child accidentally swallowing a nutty professor's fish formula, which turns her into a starfish. Her friends swallow the same potion, and follow her into the sea to give her the antidote. The animation features some neat visual touches, and the young heroes are cute, but not too cute. DA DVD

Alan Rickman *Joe* • Terry Jones *Prof HO MacKrill* • Aaron Poul *Chuck* • Jeff Pace *Fly* • Michelle Westerson *Stella* • Louise Fribo *Sasha* • David Bateson *Crab/Shark* ■ *Dir* Stefan Fjeldmark, Michael Hegner • *Scr* Stefan Fjeldmark, Karsten Kiilerich, John Stefan Olsen, from a story by Fjeldmark, Kiilerich

Hemingway's Adventures of a Young Man ★★
Adventure drama 1962 · US · Colour · 142min

Loosely assembled from ten of the autobiographical Nick Adams stories and the Italian segment of *A Farewell to Arms*, this is an ill-judged, miscast odyssey that seeks to combine the artistry of Ernest Hemingway's fiction with the macho posturing of his private life. As the titular seeker-after-experience, Richard Beymer's struggle to impose his personality on the proceedings is hampered by a script containing too many opportunities for scene-stealing cameos. DP

Richard Beymer *Nick Adams* • Diane Baker *Carolyn* • Corinne Calvet *Contessa* • Fred Clark *Mr Turner* • Dan Dailey *Billy Campbell* • James Dunn *Telegrapher* • Juano Hernandez *Bugs* • Arthur Kennedy *Dr Adams* • Ricardo Montalban *Major Padula* • Paul Newman *Ad Francis* • Susan Strasberg *Rosanna* • Jessica Tandy *Mrs Adams* • Eli Wallach *John* ■ *Dir* Martin Ritt • *Scr* AE Hotchner, from stories by Ernest Hemingway

Hemoglobin ★★★18
Horror 1997 · US/Can · Colour · 88min

Troubled Roy Dupuis and his wife visit a remote North American island in an attempt to find descendants of his twin ancestors who had lived there hundreds of years before. There they meet a clan of strange mutants with rather unsavoury eating habits. Romance, vampirism and incest are all touched on in this bizarre stomach-churner with Rutger Hauer's performance keeping a tight rein on the scare tactics. AJ

Rutger Hauer *Dr Marlowe* • Roy Dupuis *John Strauss* • Kristin Lehman *Kathleen Strauss* • Jackie Burroughs *Lexie Krongold* • Joanna Noyes *Byrde* • Felicia Shulman *Yolanda* ■ *Dir* Peter Svatek • *Scr* Charles Adair, Dan O'Bannon, Ronald Shusett

Hen in the Wind ★★★PG
Melodrama 1948 · Jpn · BW · 80min

The tale of a wife who is forced into prostitution to pay her son's hospital bills while her husband fights at the front sounds more suitable for Kenji Mizoguchi than Yasujiro Ozu. However, while this allegorical study of postwar Japan may not be thematically typical of Ozu's work, it certainly bears his stylistic imprint. Spurning reliance on symbolic close-ups, the imagery is notable for its compositional precision and the use of cutting to establish spatial relationships. DP Japanese +subtitles. *DVD*

Kinuyo Tanaka *Tokiko* • Shuji Sano *Shuichi Amamiya* • Chishu Ryu *Kazuichiro Satake* • Takeshi Sakamoto *Hikozo Sakai* • Kuniko Miyake • Chieko Murata *Akiko Ida* • Eijiro Tono • Koji Mitsuo ■ *Dir* Yasujiro Ozu • *Scr* Yasujiro Ozu, Ryosuke Saito

Henna ★★★ PG
Drama 1990 · Ind/Pak · Colour · 180min

Just before his marriage, Rishi Kapoor is swept away at sea and wakes up in Pakistan, in the care of Zeba. He finds that he has no memory of his past life. A storm on their wedding night returns Kapoor's memory and he realises he must go back to India, where he's now wanted by the police as a spy. The traditional virtues of the Indian cinema are readily apparent (songs, costumes and sparkle) and the film is put together with charm. DP Hindi, Urdu +subtitles. *DVD*

Zeba *Henna* • Rishi Kapoor *Chandra Prakash* • Ashwini Bhave *Chandni* • Saeed Jaffrey ■ *Dir* Randhir Kapoor • *Scr* Jainendra Jain, from a story by Khodzhi Ahmad Abbas, J Sathe

Hennessy ★★★★ 15
Political thriller 1975 · UK · Colour · 99min

Controversial in its time – because it showed the Royal Family under threat – this 1970s drama still has a full charge of suspense, with Rod Steiger as the embittered Belfast man intent on blowing up the state opening of Parliament to avenge the accidental slaughter of his family. Richard Johnson is working with Trevor Howard to bring down this lone terrorist on behalf of MI5, while the IRA's Eric Porter is in pursuit as well. Director Don Sharp turns in his best movie, while Steiger gives a consummate portrayal of a righteously vengeful man. TH

Rod Steiger *Hennessy* • Lee Remick *Kate Brooke* • Richard Johnson *Inspector Hollis* • Trevor Howard *Commander Rice* • Eric Porter *Tobin, IRA Leader* • Peter Egan *Williams* • Ian Hogg *Gerry* ■ *Dir* Don Sharp • *Scr* John Gay, from a story by Richard Johnson

Henri-Georges Clouzot's Inferno ★★★★★ 15
Documentary 2009 · Fr · Colour and BW · 95min

Inspired by the discovery of 185 long-forgotten cans of film, this documentary is a compelling account of the collapse of *Les Diaboliques* director Henri-Georges Clouzot's 1964 psychological thriller *L'Enfer*. The details of the location shoot are fascinating, especially as it's possible to see Italian star Serge Reggiani beginning to lose patience with his notoriously demanding director before eventually quitting the project. But it's the colour footage that Clouzot made with leading lady Romy Schneider that most seize the imagination. DP French +subtitles. Swearing, nudity. *DVD*

Romy Schneider • Serge Reggiani • Costa-Gavras ■ *Dir* Serge Bromberg, Ruxandra Medrea Annonier • *Scr* Based on an original idea by Serge Bromberg, created from the rushes of Henri-Georges Clouzot's *Inferno*, from a screenplay (unproduced) by José-André Lacour, Jean Ferry, Clouzot

Henry & June ★★★ 18
Biographical erotic drama 1990 · US · Colour · 136min

Director Philip Kaufman followed up *The Unbearable Lightness of Being* with this intellectually erotic depiction of the bizarre relationship between author Henry Miller (Fred Ward), his wife June (Uma Thurman) and the writer Anaïs Nin (Maria de Medeiros). Based on Nin's diaries, it's a rather slow and stilted film whose main interest now lies in its cast, which, as well as a young Thurman, includes Richard E Grant as Nin's bland husband and Kevin Spacey as Henry's friend. Nowhere near as sexy as the

original publicity led viewers to believe. JB *DVD*

Fred Ward *Henry Miller* • Uma Thurman *June Miller* • Maria de Medeiros *Anaïs Nin* • Richard E Grant *Hugo* • Kevin Spacey *Osborn* • Jean-Philippe Ecoffey *Eduardo* • Bruce Myers *Jack* • Jean-Louis Buñuel *Publisher/Editor* ■ *Dir* Philip Kaufman • *Scr* Philip Kaufman, Rose Kaufman, from the diaries of Anaïs Nin

Henry Fool ★★★★ 18
Comedy drama 1997 · US · Colour · 137min

Writer/director Hal Hartley is one of the quirkiest and most original of independent film-makers, and in this effort, the winner of the best screenplay at Cannes, he is on fine form. It's about a shy garbage collector and his promiscuous sister whose humdrum lives are changed for ever by the arrival of charismatic rogue Thomas Jay Ryan, who moves into the basement of their house with the apparent intention of putting the finishing touches to his memoirs. The end product is a strangely compelling and, at times, hysterically funny fable. TH Swearing, violence. *DVD*

Thomas Jay Ryan *Henry Fool* • James Urbaniak *Simon Grim* • Parker Posey *Fay* • Maria Porter *Mary* • James Saito *Mr Deng* • Kevin Corrigan *Warren* • Liam Aiken *Ned* • Camille Paglia ■ *Dir/Scr* Hal Hartley

Henry: Portrait of a Serial Killer ★★★★★ 18
Psychological horror 1986 · US · Colour · 79min

Instead of portraying a cultured, super-intelligent serial killer such as Hannibal Lecter, John McNaughton's disturbing directorial debut offers us a poor drifter(Michael Rooker) who wanders anonymously from city to city, murdering at random. No one knows he is a mass murderer until he lets flatmate and fellow ex-con Tom Towles in on his gruesome hobby. McNaughton's rough, non-judgemental direction gives the film a stylishly chilling documentary feel, while the killer's use of a camcorder asks some challengingly uncomfortable questions about voyeurism and the nature of screen violence. This is a true modern classic. JF *DVD*

Michael Rooker *Henry* • Tom Towles *Otis* • Tracy Arnold *Becky* • Mary Demas *Dead Woman/Dead Prostitute/Hooker* • Anne Bartoletti *Waitress* ■ *Dir* John McNaughton • *Scr* Richard Fire, John McNaughton

Henry: Portrait of a Serial Killer, Part II ★★ 18
Psychological horror 1996 · US · Colour · 84min

With director John McNaughton and actor Michael Rooker gone, this sequel immediately has two strikes against it, though it does end up being somewhat better than one might think. Neil Giuntoli takes over as Henry, continuing his travels around the country until he finds menial work in one location. When he finds out his boss is a professional arsonist, they start exchanging trade secrets and help each other out. KB

Neil Giuntoli *Henry* • Rich Komenich *Kai* • Kate Walsh *Cricket* • Carri Levinson *Louisa* • Daniel Allar *Rooter* • Penelope Milford *Woman in woods* ■ *Dir/Scr* Charles Parello

Henry VIII and His Six Wives ★★★ PG
Historical drama 1972 · UK · Colour · 119min

As one has the right to expect, the costumes and locations for this film version of the acclaimed BBC TV series *The Six Wives of Henry VIII* are superb. However, the story suffers from being compressed into just over two hours (the series ran for six 90-minute episodes), and, while it is understandable to focus on Anne Boleyn and the break with Rome, it overbalances the action to the detriment of the later wives. Keith Michell gives a textbook portrayal of Henry, but he is outshone by Bernard Hepton as Cranmer and Donald Pleasence as Cromwell. DP *DVD*

Keith Michell *King Henry VIII* • Frances Cuka *Catherine of Aragon* • Charlotte Rampling *Anne Boleyn* • Jane Asher *Jane Seymour* • Jenny Bos *Anne of Cleves* • Lynne Frederick *Catherine Howard* • Barbara Leigh-Hunt *Catherine Parr* • Donald Pleasence *Thomas Cromwell* • Michael Gough *Norfolk* • Brian Blessed *Suffolk* • Bernard Hepton *Archbishop Cranmer* • Michael Goodliffe *Thomas More* ■ *Dir* Waris Hussein • *Scr* Ian Thorne

Henry V ★★★★★ U
Classic historical drama 1944 · UK · Colour · 131min

Having failed to secure the services of William Wyler or Carol Reed, Laurence Olivier embarked on his directorial debut with some misgivings. David O Selznick had already refused to allow Olivier's wife Vivien Leigh to play Katharine as he didn't want his star in a bit part, and the war had necessitated the shooting of the Agincourt scenes in Ireland to find enough extras. Dislocating his ankle while filming the ambush scene, Olivier still handled the battle sequences with a skill that belied his inexperience. Released to great acclaim with victory over Hitler in sight, the film chimed in with the nation's ebullience and it remains a colourful and rousing spectacle. DP *DVD*

Laurence Olivier *King Henry V* • Robert Newton *Ancient Pistol* • Leslie Banks *Chorus* • Renee Asherson [Renée Asherson] *Princess Katharine* • Esmond Knight *Fluellen* • Leo Genn *Constable of France* • Ralph Truman *Montjoy, a French herald* • Harcourt Williams *King Charles VI of France* ■ *Dir* Laurence Olivier • *Scr* Laurence Olivier, Alan Dent, from the play by William Shakespeare • *Cinematographer* Robert Krasker • *Art Director* Paul Sheriff • *Costume Designer* Roger Furse [Roger K Furse]

Henry V ★★★★ PG
Historical drama 1989 · UK · Colour · 131min

It's hard to recall the furore that greeted this film on its original release. Almost everyone compared first-time director Kenneth Branagh with Laurence Olivier, who made his own debut behind the camera with the same play 45 years earlier. The knives were clearly out for the pretender to Olivier's throne, yet he produced a version that was as much of its time as Olivier's had been. Instead of the booming patriotism befitting the wartime flag-waver that was served up by Olivier, Branagh decided to focus on the savagery and futility of war. He thoroughly merited his best actor Oscar nomination, though his inclusion in the direction category was more than a little flattering. DP *DVD*

Kenneth Branagh *Henry V* • Derek Jacobi *Chorus* • Brian Blessed *Exeter* • Ian Holm *Captain Fluellen* • Paul Scofield *French King* • Michael Maloney *Dauphin* • Alec McCowen *Ely* • Emma Thompson *Katherine* • Richard Briers *Bardolph* • Robert Stephens *Pistol* • Robbie Coltrane *Sir John Falstaff* • Judi Dench *Mistress Quickly* ■ *Dir* Kenneth Branagh • *Scr* Kenneth Branagh, from the play by William Shakespeare

Henry's Crime ★★ 15
Crime caper 2010 · US · Colour · 103min

This light-hearted crime caper has a quality cast and a half-decent storyline, but makes rather a pig's ear of its silk purse. Keanu Reeves stars as a tollbooth attendant who is imprisoned for a robbery he didn't commit. Inspired by cell-mate James Caan, Reeves then decides he may as well commit the crime if he's already done the time. There are some decent scenes, all of them featuring the excellent Vera Farmiga (*Up in the Air*), and many of them (for reasons too complicated to go into here) involving the cute but bland Keanu pretending to be an actor. Amiably diverting it may be, but *Henry's Crime* is neither enthralling enough as a heist movie, nor amusing enough as a comedy. DA Swearing. *DVD*

Keanu Reeves *Henry* • James Caan *Max* • Vera Farmiga *Julie* • Judy Greer *Debbie* • Peter Stormare *Darek* • Bill Duke *Frank* • Fisher Stevens *Eddie* ■ *Dir* Malcolm Venville • *Scr* Sacha Gervasi, David White [David N White]

Her ★★★★ 15
Romantic drama 2013 · US · Colour · 120min

Funny, romantic, touching and thought-provoking, this terrific film from writer/director Spike Jonze inhabits pretty much the same oddball arena of his *Being John Malkovich* and *Adaptation*. In a near-future world of holographic video games and voice-activated everything, writer Joaquin Phoenix downloads a cutting-edge, intuitive piece of operational computer software (sexily voiced by Scarlett Johannson). Small wonder, then, that Phoenix is soon head-over-heels in love with "her". But can a disembodied voice truly compete in a world of physical attraction? At two hours, *Her* is a little too long, but it ably demonstrates Jonze's talent for mature and magical film-making. DA Swearing, sexual references, nudity. *DVD*

Joaquin Phoenix *Theodore Twombly* • Scarlett Johansson *Samantha* • Amy Adams *Amy* • Rooney Mara *Catherine* • Olivia Wilde *Blind date* • Chris Pratt *Paul* ■ *Dir/Scr* Spike Jonze

Her Alibi ★★ PG
Comedy thriller 1989 · US · Colour · 90min

Designed to continue Tom Selleck's rise in the movies after his success in *Three Men and a Baby*, this uneven comedy thriller is a rather ludicrous tale with a "I think my girlfriend's going to kill me" plot. This needed a decent script and better talent than actress model Paulina Porizkova in one of the lead roles. JB Swearing.

Tom Selleck *Phil Blackwood* • Paulina Porizkova *Nina Ionescu* • William Daniels (2) *Sam* • James Farentino *Frank Polito* • Hurd Hatfield *Troppa* • Patrick Wayne *Gary Blackwood* • Tess Harper *Sally Blackwood* ■ *Dir* Bruce Beresford • *Scr* Charlie Peters

Her Cardboard Lover ★ U
Romantic drama 1942 · US · Colour · 92min

Robert Taylor and Norma Shearer, under George Cukor's direction, co-star as a penniless songwriter in love with a millionairess who hires him as a secretary-cum-bodyguard to inflame the jealousy of her on-again/off-again lover, George Sanders. Despite its illustrious stars and director, this is a candidate for one of the worst films ever made. Taylor smiles a lot, Shearer – in her final film – sobs and twitters and Sanders looks uncomfortable, as well he might. To call the script witless is an understatement. RK

Norma Shearer *Consuelo Croyden* • Robert Taylor (1) *Terry Trindale* • George Sanders *Tony Barling* • Frank McHugh *Chappie Champagne* • Elizabeth Patterson *Eva* • Chill Wills *Judge* ■ *Dir* George Cukor • *Scr* John Collier, Anthony Veiller, William H Wright, Jacques Deval, from the play *Her Cardboard Lover* by Valerie Wyngate, PG Wodehouse, from the play *Dans Sa Cadeur Naïve* by Jacques Deval

Her Fatal Flaw ★★
Suspense thriller 2006 · US/Can · Colour · 96min

A Chicago lawyer's romantic nature threatens to be her undoing in this increasingly obvious yet watchable crime drama. Victoria Pratt is solidly engaging as the loved-up legal hotshot who puts her entire life on the line when she decides to defend fiancé Vincent Spano after he's accused of murder. The procedural scenes have energy, while the twisting script quickly casts doubt on Spano's innocence. Lies, corruption and conspiracy abound, but the sense of intrigue they generate is cut short thanks to visual signposting and the ease in which Pratt's character uncovers the truth. SF Some swearing, sex scenes.

Victoria Pratt *Laney Hennessy* • Vincent Spano *Robert Genaro* • Chris Kramer *Det Mark Farrow* • William B Davis *Richard O'Brien* ■ *Dir* George Mendeluk • *Scr* Hanz Wasserburger

Her Husband's Affairs ★★★
Screwball comedy 1947 · US · BW · 83min

The witty team of Ben Hecht and Charles Lederer provided better and worse screenplays than this screwball comedy with the misleading title. The "affairs" indicated are actually business ventures involving advertising man Franchot Tone, in which his wife, Lucille Ball, interferes. The comedy comes from an unlikely source – the quest to create the perfect embalming fluid – but it's Edward Everett Horton who provides most of the fun in yet another film that pokes fun at the world of advertising. **RB**

Lucille Ball *Margaret Weldon* • Franchot Tone *William Weldon* • Edward Everett Horton *JB Cruikshank* • Mikhail Rasumny *Prof Glinka* • Gene Lockhart *Peter Winterbottom* • Nana Bryant *Mrs Winterbottom* • Jonathan Hale *Governor Fox* ■ *Dir* S Sylvan Simon • *Scr* Ben Hecht, Charles Lederer

Her Majesty Love ★★★
Musical comedy   1931 · US · BW · 75min

The presence of the inimitable WC Fields (for once minus the bibulous cynicism) enlivens this lightweight musical comedy, which marked the official Hollywood debut of William Dieterle, who'd spent the previous year making German-language versions of US box-office hits. Demonstrating the juggling genius that sustained his vaudeville career, Fields upstages Broadway star Marilyn Miller, whose marriage prospects are dashed when he reveals to her beau's ennobled family that he is a barber and she's a barmaid at a Berlin cabaret. An amiable frippery. **DP**

Marilyn Miller *Lia Toerrek* • Ben Lyon *Fred von Wellingen* • WC Fields *Lia's father* • Ford Sterling *Otmar* • Leon Errol *Baron von Schwarzdorf* • Chester Conklin *Emil* • Harry Stubbs *Hanneman* • Maude Eburne *Aunt Harriette* ■ *Dir* William Dieterle • *Scr* Robert Lord, Arthur Caesar, Henry Blanke, Joseph Jackson, from a play by R Bernauer, R Oesterreicher

Her Name Is Sabine ★★★★ 12A
Documentary   2007 · Fr/Bel/Swi · Colour · 89min

French actress Sandrine Bonnaire turns film-maker with this documentary about her autistic younger sister. We see Sabine's screams, outbursts of violence and maddening repeated questions – at times, it's a fascinating exploration of how a damaged mind works, but in the main it's a pained cry of outrage at how society failed one of its more vulnerable members. Bonnaire's sharpest weapon is her home-movie footage of a happy and responsive Sabine before a series of misdiagnoses and a disastrous spell in a psychiatric hospital made her withdraw from the world. It's a deeply personal film, given added piquancy by the knowledge that while one sister tragically declined, the other became a movie star. **JkS** French +subtitles.

Sabine Bonnaire ■ *Dir* Sandrine Bonnaire • *Cinematographers* Sandrine Bonnaire, Catherine Cabrol

Her Twelve Men ★★ U
Comedy   1954 · US · BW · 91min

After several years of mediocre vehicles and with age creeping up on her, Greer Garson's swan song came with this glutinously sentimental but otherwise inoffensive film about a schoolteacher whose patience and sweet nature has the desired effect on a bunch of difficult young schoolboys. Robert Ryan and Barry Sullivan co-star with the gracious Garson under the experienced control of Robert Z Leonard, once one of the premier directors of women. **RK**

Greer Garson *Jan Stewart* • Robert Ryan *Joe Hargrave* • Barry Sullivan *Richard Y Oliver Sr* • Richard Haydn *Dr Avord Barrett* • Barbara Lawrence *Barbara Dunning* • James Arness *Ralph Munsey* • Rex Thompson *Homer Curtis* • Tim Considine *Richard Y Oliver Jr* ■ *Dir* Robert Z Leonard • *Scr* William Roberts, from the story *Miss Baker's Dozen* by Louise Baker

Her Wedding Night ★★
Comedy   1930 · US · BW · 78min

Director Frank Tuttle concocts a frenzied farce, in which Clara Bow, the original It Girl, plays a movie star whose stay in an Italian riviera town results in a ride on a romantic

merry-go-round with a composer of sentimental ditties. The pair end up mistakenly getting married while checking into what they think is a hotel. Although Bow is clearly uncomfortable with dialogue, this still has its fun moments. **DP**

Clara Bow *Norma Martin* • Ralph Forbes *Larry Charters* • Charlie Ruggles [Charles Ruggles] *Bertie Bird* • Richard "Skeets" Gallagher *Bob Talmadge* • Geneva Mitchell *Marshall* • Rosita Moreno *Lulu* • Natalie Kingston *Eva* ■ *Dir* Frank Tuttle • *Scr* Henry Myers, from the play *Little Miss Bluebeard* by Avery Hopwood

Herbie: Fully Loaded ★★★ U
Comedy   2005 · US · Colour · 96min

The Disney *Love Bug* franchise is rescued from the scrapyard and given a new lease of life. This time Lindsay Lohan takes the wheel of the star car for a jolly ride down memory lane. She and the vintage VW make a winning team, while director Angela Robinson keeps the action zipping along at a fast pace. Michael Keaton adds heart to the story playing Lohan's disapproving dad, and, as the rival speed demon, Matt Dillon is the perfect pantomime baddie. Grown-ups will find it lacking in sophisticated humour, but the spirit of mischief is hard to resist. **SP**

Lindsay Lohan *Maggie Peyton* • Michael Keaton *Ray Peyton Sr* • Matt Dillon *Trip Murphy* • Breckin Meyer *Ray Peyton Jr* • Justin Long *Kevin* • Cheryl Hines *Sally* • Jimmi Simpson *Crash* • Jill Ritchie *Charisma* ■ *Dir* Angela Robinson • *Scr* Thomas Lennon (3), Robert Ben Garant, Alfred Gough, Miles Millar, from a story by Lennon, Garant, Mark Perez, from characters by Gordon Buford

Herbie Goes Bananas ★★ U
Comedy   1980 · US · Colour · 89min

This fourth film about Herbie the Love Bug was the one that finally put the skids under the series. The novelty of having a VW Beetle with a mind of its own was already showing signs of wearing off in *Herbie Goes to Monte Carlo*, when an "exotic" location was used to cover the holes in the plot. However, the sights of South America are not enough to distract us from the flimsiness of this story, as Herbie rubs bumpers with a gang of smugglers on his way to Brazil. **DP**

Cloris Leachman *Aunt Louise* • Charles Martin Smith *Davie Johns* • John Vernon *Prindle* • Stephan W Burns *Pete Stanchek* • Elyssa Davalos *Melissa* • Joaquin Garay III *Paco* • Harvey Korman *Captain Blythe* • Richard Jaeckel *Shepard* • Alex Rocco *Quinn* ■ *Dir* Vincent McEveety • *Scr* Don Tait, from characters by Gordon Buford

Herbie Goes to Monte Carlo ★★★ U
Comedy   1977 · US · Colour · 100min

The third in Disney's series about the "Love Bug" VW Beetle with a mind of its own is rather predictable, though still entertaining. This time out, Herbie is reunited with driver Dean Jones and falls for a powder-blue Lancia (driven by Julie Sommars) during the Paris-Monte Carlo rally. Putting a headstrong intelligence under the bonnet of a car has been a winning formula, but there are only a few touches here that rise above the mechanical. **TH**

Dean Jones *Jim Douglas* • Don Knotts *Wheely Applegate* • Julie Sommars *Diane Darcy* • Jacques Marin *Inspector Bouchet* • Roy Kinnear *Quincey* ■ *Dir* Vincent McEveety • *Scr* Arthur Alsberg, Don Nelson, from characters by Gordon Buford

Herbie Rides Again ★★★ U
Comedy   1974 · US · Colour · 84min

The sequel to Disney's smash hit *The Love Bug*, this is the second of four films featuring the Volkswagen Beetle with a mind of its own. Director Robert Stevenson and scriptwriter/producer Bill Walsh return to ensure the action remains fast, furious and very funny. The original cast may have departed, but in its place are such seasoned veterans as Keenan Wynn and Helen Hayes, who are tremendous value as the tycoon determined to build an enormous

skyscraper and the dotty dear who won't leave the old homestead. DP **DVD**

Helen Hayes *Mrs Steinmetz* • Stefanie Powers *Nicole Harris* • Ken Berry *Willoughby Whitfield* • John McIntire *Mr Judson* • Keenan Wynn *Alonzo Hawk* • Huntz Hall *Judge* ■ *Dir* Robert Stevenson • *Scr* Bill Walsh, from a story by Gordon Buford

Hercules ★★★ U
Fantasy adventure   1957 · It · Colour · 98min

This film launched the immensely popular Italian film genre known as "peplum", although it is better known worldwide as the sword-and-sandal cycle. Ex-Mr Universe Steve Reeves cuts an imposing figure in the title role, though there was more to him than just bulging biceps. In lesser hands, the scenes in which he longs to become mortal might have induced giggling, and there is a definite spark between him and Sylva Koscina as his beloved, Iole. DP Italian dubbed.

Steve Reeves *Hercules* • Sylva Koscina *Iole* • Gianna Maria Canale *Antea* • Fabrizio Mioni *Jason* • Ivo Garrani *Pelias* • Arturo Dominici *Eurystheus* ■ *Dir* Pietro Francisci • *Scr* Pietro Francisci, Ennio de Concini, Gaio Frattini, from a story by Pietro Francisci

Hercules ★ PG
Fantasy adventure   1983 · US · Colour · 99min

A bizarre, misguided throwback to those dubbed monstrosities of the 1950s and 1960s, this would-be epic attempts to cash in on the brief craze for sword-and-sorcery nonsense in the early 1980s. Lou Ferrigno (*The Incredible Hulk*) gets to wear slightly more clothing than in his old TV show. Unfortunately he has more dialogue as well, while the effects are ropey. **JF**

Lou Ferrigno *Hercules* • Mirella D'Angelo *Circe* • Sybil Danning *Arianna* • Ingrid Anderson *Cassiopea* • William Berger *King Minos* • Brad Harris *King Augeas* ■ *Dir/Scr* Lewis Coates [Luigi Cozzi]

Hercules ★★★ U
Animated musical   1997 · US · Colour · 91min

In Disney's dumbed-down version of the Greek myth, Hercules, son of almighty Zeus, is brought up as a mortal, thanks to the machinations of Underworld ruler Hades, and has to pass tests to prove both his manhood and his godhood. Some of the draughtsmanship of the animation is wonderful, as are the voiceovers of James Woods and Danny DeVito, but the powerful original idea is sapped by the need to make it a teenage comic-strip cartoon. TH **DVD**

Charlton Heston *Narrator* • Tate Donovan *Hercules* • Danny DeVito *Phil* • James Woods *Hades* • Susan Egan *Meg* • Rip Torn *Zeus* • Samantha Eggar *Hera* ■ *Dir* John Musker, Ron Clements • *Scr* Ron Clements, John Musker, Donald McEnery, Bob Shaw, Irene Mecchi, from an idea by Joe Haidar • *Production Designer* Gerald Scarfe

Hercules ★★★ 12
Action adventure   2014 · US · Colour · 98min

The third Hercules movie of 2014 is by far the most successful because director Brett Ratner finds the correct balance between self-deprecating humour, heart and epic Cecil B DeMille-style action. Having completed the mythical 12 labours, and struggling to live up to his demigod reputation, Hercules (an imposing Dwayne Johnson) has turned mercenary with a five-man army of loyal followers. Ratner papers over the cracks in the narrative with incredibly exciting battle scenes that send the adrenaline racing. AJ **DVD**

Dwayne Johnson *Hercules* • Ian McShane *Amphiaraus* • Rufus Sewell *Autolycus* • Aksel Hennie *Tydeus* • Joseph Fiennes *King Eurystheus* • Rebecca Ferguson *Ergenia* ■ *Dir* Brett Ratner • *Scr* Ryan Condal, Evan Spiliotopoulos, from a comic book by Steve Moore (2) • *Cinematographer* Dante Spinotti

Hercules II ★ 15
Action fantasy   1984 · US · Colour · 88min

The second misbegotten attempt by Italian hack director Luigi Cozzi to marry *Star Wars*-style fantasy with sword-and-sandal

epic is no better than the first. Made at the same time as the original *Hercules* but released two years later, this time the task of strongman Lou Ferrigno is to find some lost thunderbolts hidden among a welter of lousy special effects. **AJ**

Lou Ferrigno *Hercules* • Milly Carlucci *Urania* • Sonia Viviani *Glaucia* • William Berger *King Minos* • Carlotta Green *Athena* • Claudio Cassinelli *Zeus* ■ *Dir* Lewis Coates [Luigi Cozzi] • *Scr* Lewis Coates [Luigi Cozzi]

Hercules in New York ★★ PG
Fantasy comedy adventure   1969 · US · Colour · 87min

Expelled from Mount Olympus by jealous dad Zeus, Hercules ends up in New York during the psychedelic 1960s. This one-joke spectacle was conceived as a pastiche of cheap sword-and-sandal epics, and would have been quickly forgotten had it not starred one Arnold Strong (real name Schwarzenegger) in his first film role. Arnie is stripped of his voice (through bad dubbing), his clothes and all dignity. DP **DVD**

Arnold Stang *Pretzie* • Arnold Strong [Arnold Schwarzenegger] *Hercules* • Deborah Loomis *Helen* • James Karen *The Professor* • Ernest Graves *Zeus* • Tanny McDonald *Juno* • Taina Elg *Nemesis* • Michael Lipton *Pluto* ■ *Dir* Arthur A Seidelman [Arthur Allan Seidelman] • *Scr* Aubrey Wisberg

Hercules Returns ★★★ 15
Comedy   1993 · Aus · Colour · 76min

A one-joke film – but a joke that's so good it just about sustains the whole running time of the film. David Argue, Bruce Spence and Mary Coustas are battling to reopen a classic cinema, much to opposition of slimy businessman Michael Carman, who plots to destroy their opening night by providing them with an Italian version of an old Hercules epic. It falls to the intrepid trio to provide all the voices themselves. The plotting is tenuous, but the redubbed beefcake epic is a constant delight. **JF**

David Argue *Brad McBain* • Michael Carman *Sir Michael Kent* • Mary Coustas *Lisa* • Bruce Spence *Sprocket* • Brendon Suhr *King* ■ *Dir* David Parker • *Scr* Des Mangan, from his live show *Double Take Meet Hercules*

The Here After ★★★ 15
Drama   2015 · Swe/Pol/Fr · Colour · 97min

A rural community is asked to forgive a shocking crime in Swedish director Magnus von Horn's quietly charged feature debut. It controversially aligns the audience with the young perpetrator (Ulrik Munther) as he returns to the care of his father after a short stretch in a secure facility, oblivious to the damaging effect his presence has on those around him. Munther turns in an unnervingly inscrutable but reliably compelling performance at the centre, but it's hard to shake the feeling that this is merely the bare bones of what could have been a much more engaging story. **EAS** Swedish +subtitles. Swearing, sexual references, some violence, brief nudity. **DVD**

Ulrik Munther *John* • Mats Blomgren *Martin* • Wieslaw Komasa *Grandfather* • Alexander Nordegren *Filip* ■ *Dir/Scr* Magnus von Horn

Here Come the Co-Eds ★★★ U
Musical comedy   1945 · US · BW · 90min

Bud Abbott and Lou Costello are two incident-prone nincompoops who get jobs as caretakers at a staid girls school. The pair create their normal slapstick mayhem and the snobbish atmosphere of the school crumbles before them. Well established by this time, they breeze through this well constructed vehicle, which is zany even by their own wacky standards. Horror star Lon Chaney Jr can also be spotted down the cast in a slightly less ghoulish role than normal. **DF**

Bud Abbott *Slats McCarthy* • Lou Costello *Oliver Quackenbush* • Peggy Ryan *Patty* • Martha O'Driscoll *Molly McCarthy* • June Vincent *Diane Kirkland* • Lon Chaney Jr *"Strangler" Johnson* •

Donald Cook *Larry Benson* ■ *Dir* Jean Yarbrough • *Scr* Arthur T Horman, John Grant, from a story by Edmund L Hartmann

Here Come the Girls ★★★

Musical comedy 1953 · US · Colour · 77min

In a terrific musical comedy, Bob Hope, "the oldest chorus boy in the business", gets his big break standing in for star crooner Tony Martin, whom one "Jack the Slasher" is threatening to kill. The central premise is not fully realised by director Claude Binyon, but the turn-of-the-century setting is attractive, the Technicolor is luscious, and there's a funny turn from Fred Clark as an irascible impresario. TS

Bob Hope *Stanley Snodgrass* • Tony Martin (1) *Allen Trent* • Arlene Dahl *Irene Bailey* • Rosemary Clooney *Daisy Crockett* • Millard Mitchell *Albert Snodgrass* • William Demarest *Dennis Logan* • Fred Clark *Harry Fraser* • Robert Strauss *Jack the Slasher* ■ *Dir* Claude Binyon • *Scr* Edmund Hartmann [Edmund L Hartmann], Hal Kanter, from a story by Edmund Hartmann [Edmund L Hartmann] • *Cinematographer* Lionel Lindon

Here Come the Huggetts ★★★

Comedy 1948 · UK · BW · 92min

Following the success of 1947's *Holiday Camp*, Jack Warner and Kathleen Harrison's Huggett clan were given a picture of their own by the Rank front office. Directed by Ken Annakin with such a keen eye for the everyday that the film almost has sociological value, this prototype soap is enlivened by the antics of Diana Dors, the blonde bombshell niece who disrupts the placid household, and the drama is liberally sprinkled with laughs. *Vote for Huggett* and *The Huggetts Abroad* followed. DP

Jack Warner *Joe Huggett* • Kathleen Harrison *Ethel Huggett* • Jane Hylton *Jane Huggett* • Susan Shaw *Susan Huggett* • Petula Clark *Pat Huggett* • Diana Dors *Diana Hopkins* • Jimmy Hanley *Jimmy* • David Tomlinson *Harold Hinchley* ■ *Dir* Ken Annakin • *Scr* Mabel Constanduros, Denis Constanduros, Peter Rogers, Muriel Box, Sydney Box, from characters by Godfrey Winn

Here Come the Waves ★★ U

Second World War musical comedy 1944 · US · BW · 99min

One among too many disposable musicals springing from the war effort, this one offers two Betty Huttons for the price of one. Bing Crosby is a crooner who joins the navy with heroic aims, but only sees action in the entertainment unit where he must handle shows put on by the navy's distaff side, including twin sisters both played by Hutton. The movie's main claim to fame is the Oscar-nominated song, *Accentuate the Positive*. RK

Bing Crosby *Johnny Cabot* • Betty Hutton *Susan Allison/Rosemary Allison* • Sonny Tufts *Windy* • Ann Doran *Ruth* • Gwen Crawford *Tex* • Noel Neill *Dorothy* • Catherine Craig *Lieutenant Townsend* ■ *Dir* Mark Sandrich • *Scr* Allan Scott, Ken Englund, Zion Myers • *Music* Harold Arlen • *Lyrics* Johnny Mercer

Here Comes Mr Jordan ★★★★ U

Screwball comedy fantasy 1941 · US · BW · 90min

This clever, charming and ingenious fantasy was a popular hit in its day. A slightly miscast but nevertheless excellent Robert Montgomery stars as a boxer who, following an air crash, is accidentally rushed to heaven before his allotted due date, and has to be found a new body until his official time is up. The preposterous plot is brilliantly constructed and charmingly performed, with James Gleason in a career-best role as the fighter's manager. Claude Rains and Edward Everett Horton keep the whimsical whole effortlessly down-to-earth. TS DVD BL

Robert Montgomery *Joe Pendleton* • Evelyn Keyes *Bette Logan* • Claude Rains *Mr Jordan* • Rita Johnson *Julia Farnsworth* • Edward Everett Horton *Messenger No 7013* • James Gleason *Max Corkle* ■ *Dir* Alexander Hall • *Scr* Sidney Buchman, Seton I Miller, from the play *Heaven Can Wait* by Harry Segall

Here Comes the Boom ★★★ 12

Action comedy 2012 · US · Colour · 100min

This hit-and-miss comedy stars Kevin James (*Zookeeper*) as a jaded biology teacher and former college wrestling champion. In order to save his school's music department and the job of timid colleague Henry Winkler, James moonlights as a mixed martial arts fighter. A series of bruising encounters brings his exploits to the attention of disapproving superiors, but will they help him win the heart of feisty school nurse Salma Hayek? James's ordinary Joe charm and quick wit help carry director Frank Coraci's film through its stuttering storyline and predictable plot twists. TeS Violence, some swearing.

Kevin James *Scott Voss* • Salma Hayek *Bella Flores* • Henry Winkler *Marty Streb* • Greg Germann *Principal Betcher* • Joe Rogan ■ *Dir* Frank Coraci • *Scr* Kevin James, Allan Loeb

Here Comes the Groom ★★ U

Comedy 1951 · US · BW · 113min

Despite a fine cast headed by Bing Crosby, Jane Wyman and Franchot Tone, this Frank Capra comedy about a newsman who imports two war orphans in order to win back a former fiancée is a disappointment. Capra's leaden approach betrays his lack of confidence in the material. TV

Bing Crosby *Pete* • Jane Wyman *Emmadel Jones* • Alexis Smith *Winifred Stanley* • Franchot Tone *Wilbur Stanley* • James Barton *Pa Jones* • Louis Armstrong • Dorothy Lamour ■ *Dir* Frank Capra • *Scr* Virginia Van Jpp, Liam O'Brien, Myles Connolly, from a story by Robert Riskin, Liam O'Brien

Here Comes the Navy ★★ U

Adventure comedy 1934 · US · BW · 88min

In effect, this is little more than a recruitment poster for the US Navy, with James Cagney pressed into heroic peacetime service by a studio worried about his image as a racketeer or sociopath. Cagney is also paired for the first time with Pat O'Brien, who steals Cagney's girl. Cagney joins the navy and woos O'Brien's sister (Gloria Stuart). There are a few songs to boot, and the whole forgettable thing is smoothly packaged. AT

James Cagney *Chesty O'Connor* • Pat O'Brien *Biff Martin* • Gloria Stuart *Dorothy Martin* • Frank McHugh *Droopy* • Dorothy Tree *Gladys* ■ *Dir* Lloyd Bacon • *Scr* Ben Markson, Earl Baldwin, from a story by Ben Markson

Here Comes the Sun ★★ U

Musical comedy 1945 · UK · BW · 83min

What makes this amiable musical comedy particularly interesting is that it marked the last screen teaming for more than a decade of those Crazy Gang stalwarts, Bud Flanagan and Chesney Allen, who dropped from the limelight the following year because of Allen's arthritis. The plot is confusing, revolving around a newspaper owner's forged will, but the stars' charming routines ably compensate. DP

Bud Flanagan *Cora a Flanagan* • Chesney Allen *Ches Allen* • Elsa Tee *Helen Blare* • Joss Ambler *Bradshaw* • Dick Francis *Governor* • John Dodsworth *Roy Lucas* ■ *Dir* John Baxter • *Scr* Geoffrey Orme, from a story by Bud Flanagan, Reginald Purdell

Here on Earth ★★ PG

Romantic drama 2000 · US · Colour · 92min

Leelee Sobieski stars in this saccharine high-school romance as a small-town girl torn between rich kid Chris Klein and farm boy Josh Hartnett. Sobieski and Klein approach their roles with dewy-eyed earnestness, while Hartnett gives the film its only solid performance. Director Mark Piznarski too often uses pop music to intensify the drama rather than trust his actors with the task. ST DVD

Leelee Sobieski *Samantha* • Chris Klein *Kelley* • Josh Hartnett *Jasper* • Michael Rooker *Malcolm Arnold* • Annie Corley *Betsy Arnold* • Bruce

Greenwood *Earl Cavanaugh* • Annette O'Toole *Jo Cavanaugh* ■ *Dir* Mark Piznarski • *Scr* Michael Seitzman

Here We Go round the Mulberry Bush ★★ 15

Comedy 1967 · UK · Colour · 94min

Originally a rather slight but charming novel by Hunter Davies about a young bloke who longs to acquire his very own dolly bird, it has been turned into an English Tourist Board commercial, extolling the delights of fab young Britain. The book's teeth have been firmly extracted and replaced instead by the soft gums of nonstop swingdom. The result is one of those curios that abound with white boots, sooty eyes, pelmet skirts and *Thunderbirds*-style dancing. SH DVD BL

Barry Evans *Jamie McGregor* • Judy Geeson *Mary Gloucester* • Angela Scoular *Caroline Beauchamp* • Sheila White *Paula* • Adrienne Posta *Linda* • Vanessa Howard *Audrey* • Diane Keen *Claire* • Denholm Elliott *Mr Beauchamp* • Christopher Timothy *Spike* ■ *Dir* Clive Donner • *Scr* Hunter Davies, Larry Kramer, from the novel *Here We Go round the Mulberry Bush* by Hunter Davies

Hereafter ★★★ 12

Psychological drama 2010 · US · Colour · 123min

In Clint Eastwood's leisurely paced but uneven meditation on mortality, TV journalist Cécile de France survives a tsunami in Indonesia and writes about her afterlife visions, medium Matt Damon struggles with his psychic gifts and an English boy is grief-stricken when his twin brother dies tragically. The lives of these lost souls eventually intersect in a tale that veers between being oddly affecting and clumsily mawkish. The screenplay from Peter Morgan (*The Queen*) doesn't shy from exploring important questions, but it offers no definite answers on life after death either. Instead, it thoughtfully reflects on how deep sorrow and melancholy can change existence, with both Damon and de France really making their performances count. Not Eastwood at his best, then, but the tsunami opening sequence remains frighteningly spectacular. AJ Swearing. DVD BL

Matt Damon *George Lonegan* • Cécile de France *Marie Lelay* • Jay Mohr *Billy* • Bryce Dallas Howard *Melanie* • Frankie McLaren *Jason/Marcus* • George McLaren *Marcus/Jason* • Thierry Neuvic *Didier* • Marthe Keller *Dr Rousseau* • Lyndsey Marshal *Jackie* ■ *Dir* Clint Eastwood • *Scr* Peter Morgan

Hero ★★★★★ 12

Martial arts fantasy 2002 · HK/Chi/US · Colour · 95min

Chinese master Zhang Yimou's first foray into *wu xia* (heroic martial arts) will inevitably invite comparisons with Ang Lee's *Crouching Tiger, Hidden Dragon*, but *Hero* could be judged as superior on a number of levels. A nameless warrior (Jet Li) has apparently risked all to slay a group of assassins intent on killing a powerful warlord, but while the story is diverting, it's the visuals that dazzle. Each sequence seemingly surpasses the last, both in inventiveness and beauty. Christopher Doyle's gorgeous, colour-saturated cinematography complements the gripping tale, though western viewers may be surprised at the film's ultimate theme: a defence of totalitarianism against the chaos and insecurity of freedom. AS Mandarin +subtitles. Violence. DVD BL

Jet Li *Nameless* • Tony Leung Chiu-Wai [Tony Leung (2)] *Broken Sword* • Maggie Cheung Man-Yuk [Maggie Cheung] *Flying Snow* • Zhang Ziyi *Moon* • Chen Dao Ming *King* • Donnie Yen *Sky* ■ *Dir* Zhang Yimou • *Scr* Zhang Yimou, Li Feng, Wang Bin, from their story

A Hero Ain't Nothin' but a Sandwich ★★

Drama 1978 · US · Colour · 107min

Ralph Nelson directs this honest, well-mounted film about the travails of a black teenage boy (Larry B Scott) drawn into drug addiction, and the effect on his caring parents (Cicely Tyson, Paul Winfield) and concerned white schoolteacher (David Groh). He produced an admirable attempt to address the social and educational problems of black urban society, which was happily devoid of sensationalism. However, the film is also talky, earnest and disappointingly dull. RK

Cicely Tyson *Sweets* • Paul Winfield *Butler* • Larry B Scott *Benjie* • Helen Martin *Mrs Bell* • Glynn Turman *Nigeria* • David Groh *Cohen* • Kevin Hooks *Tiger* ■ *Dir* Ralph Nelson • *Scr* Alice Childress, from her novel

Hero and the Terror ★ 15

Action thriller 1988 · US · Colour · 92min

Chuck Norris plays a softer hero here – a troubled cop still traumatised from his experience capturing a serial killer (Jack O'Halloran) in his past, while dealing with the upcoming birth of his girlfriend's child. The stress increases when "the Terror", as he's known, escapes and resumes his savage spree. While Norris is to be applauded for trying something different, it comes at the expense of a boring and mostly uneventful story. KB DVD

Chuck Norris *O'Brien* • Brynn Thayer *Kay* • Steve James (1) *Robinson* • Jack O'Halloran *Simon Moon* • Jeffrey Kramer *Dwight* • Ron O'Neal *Mayor* ■ *Dir* William Tannen (2) • *Scr* Dennis Shryack, Michael Blodgett, from the novel by Michael Blodgett

Hero at Large ★★★ PG

Comedy 1980 · US · Colour · 93min

This daft but occasionally funny comedy has amiable John Ritter becoming a real-life hero after foiling a crime while dressed up as superhero Captain Avenger. What is more interesting than the quick-fire action on screen is the cast, which includes a pre-stardom Anne Archer and the excellent Kevin Bacon, who found fame four years later with *Footloose*. JB

John Ritter *Steve Nichols* • Anne Archer *J Marsh* • Bert Convy *Walter Reeves* • Kevin McCarthy *Calvin Donnelly* • Harry Bellaver *Eddie* • Anita Dangler *Mrs Havacheck* • Jane Hallaren *Gloria* • Kevin Bacon *Teenager* ■ *Dir* Martin Davidson • *Scr* AJ Carothers

Hero Wanted ★★ 18

Crime drama 2008 · US · Colour · 90min

Heroism takes a battering in this low-budget action movie as Cuba Gooding Jr gets whacked, smacked and generally abused by a selection of cardboard cut-out bad guys. The plot is, at first sight at least, a standard revenge thriller with Vietnam vet-turned-garbage man Liam Case (Gooding Jr) pursuing the thugs who left an attractive bank cashier in a coma. Whether you'll care enough to piece together the chopped up continuity and elliptical editing is debatable. And even Ray Liotta's supporting role as the smart alec cop on Liam's trail is underwritten. JR DVD

Cuba Gooding Jr *Liam Case* • Ray Liotta *Detective Terry Subcott* • Norman Reedus *Swain* • Kim Coates *Skinner McGraw* • Tommy J Flanagan [Tommy Flanagan] *Derek* • Jean Smart *Melanie McQueen* ■ *Dir* Brian Smrz • *Scr* Chad & Evan Law

The Heroes ★★★

Adventure 1968 · US/Iran · Colour · 96min

The alternative title of this US-Iranian co-production, *The Invincible Six*, gives the clue to its origins. It's a rehash of *The Magnificent Seven*, with Stuart Whitman leading a band of renegade mercenaries who take pity on a village at the mercy of bandits. Veteran director Jean Negulesco puts urgency into the action and, although it's in no way the equal of the illustrious western classic, it's still tense. TH

Stuart Whitman *Tex* • Elke Sommer *Zari* • Curt Jurgens *The Baron* • Ian Ogilvy *Ronald* • Behrooz Vosugi *Jahan* • Lon Satton *Mike* • Isarco Ravaioli *Giorgio* • James Mitchum *Nazar* ■ *Dir* Jean Negulesco • *Scr* Guy Elmes, Chester Erskine, from the novel *The Heroes of Yucca* by Michael Barrett

H

Heroes and Villains ★★ 15
Romantic comedy drama
2006 · UK · Colour · 104min

This romantic comedy drama is as dreary as the skies above its London setting. It marks the feature debut of David Raymond, who wrote the script and stars as Jack, a man with little faith in love who opens an agency that puts unsuspecting flirts to the fidelity test. His jaded outlook gets in the way of a meaningful relationship with new flame Hannah (Jenna Harrison). But, in truth, the biggest hurdle for this budding romance is that both characters have the depth of rain puddles. The dialogue is lacklustre and the gags are ham-fisted, and with no real sense of anything at stake, this is one love that definitely won't last the test of time. SP

David Raymond *Jack* • James Corden *Sam* • Brendan Patricks *Nick* • Richard Sumitro *Oli* • Jenna Harrison *Hannah* • Olivia Poulet *Clare* • Jenny Agutter *June* ■ *Dir* Selwyn Roberts • *Scr* David Raymond

Heroes for Sale ★★★
Drama   1933 · US · BW · 71min

In the 1930s, Warner Bros prided itself on being the moviegoer's social conscience. But producer Hal Wallis tried to pack too many issues into this Depression melodrama, for no sooner has war veteran Richard Barthelmess conquered his morphine addiction than he's riding the rails in search of work. Even when he pals up with Robert Barrat, whose revolutionary washing machine sets him up for life, his troubles aren't over. Luckily, William Wellman concentrates on pace and people, and avoids preaching. DP

Richard Barthelmess *Tom Holmes* • Aline MacMahon *Mary Dennis* • Loretta Young *Ruth Holmes* • Gordon Westcott *Roger Winston* • Robert Barrat *Max* • Berton Churchill *Mr Winston* ■ *Dir* William A Wellman • *Scr* Robert Lord, Wilson Mizner

The Heroes of Telemark ★★★ U
Second World War thriller
1965 · UK · Colour · 124min

Reluctant scientist Kirk Douglas and fiery resistance fighter Richard Harris have to overcome their hatred of each other, as well as the Germans, to sabotage an atomic bomb project in this brawny war story set in Norway in 1942. Director Anthony Mann sustains a nail-biting tension throughout the daredevil mission. The night sequences are particularly striking, although Robert Krasker's photography throughout will have you positively pining for the fjords. DP *DVD*

Kirk Douglas *Dr Rolf Pedersen* • Richard Harris *Knut Straud* • Ulla Jacobsson *Anna* • Michael Redgrave *Uncle* • David Weston *Arne* • Anton Diffring *Major Frick* • Eric Porter *Terboven* • Mervyn Johns *Colonel Wilkinson* • Jennifer Hilary *Sigrid* ■ *Dir* Anthony Mann • *Scr* Ivan Moffat, Ben Barzman

Hero's Island ★★★
Period drama   1962 · US · Colour · 94min

This rather weird historical movie, part children's film and part symbolic drama, is set on an island off the coast of the Carolinas in the early 1700s. Two former slaves and their children go to live on the island, but the father is murdered by marauding fishermen. Castaway James Mason offers his help but because the woman is deeply religious he agrees to non-violence until there's no other alternative. Big themes bump into each other – religion, pacificism – but none are fully developed in a this flawed effort. AT

James Mason *Jacob Webber* • Kate Manx *Devon Mainwaring* • Neville Brand *Kingstree* • Rip Torn *Nicholas* • Warren Oates *Wayte* • Robert Sampson *Enoch* • Harry Dean Stanton *Dixey* ■ *Dir/Scr* Leslie Stevens (1)

Hers to Hold ★★★ U
Romance   1943 · US · BW · 90min

Having reached her 20s, Deanna Durbin was successfully relaunched as a young adult, playing a society figure in a romantic comedy that boosted the war effort with its scenes in a real aircraft factory. It's asecond sequel to *Three Smart Girls*, and Durbin sings the very popular *Say a Prayer for the Boys Over There* as well as Cole Porter's *Begin the Beguine* and a song from Bizet's *Carmen*. Joseph Cotten is her rather mature romantic interest, while Charles Winninger and Nella Walker again play her parents. AE *DVD*

Deanna Durbin *Penelope Craig* • Joseph Cotten *Bill Morley* • Charles Winninger *Judson Craig* • Evelyn Ankers *Flo Simpson* • Gus Schilling *Rosey Blake* • Nella Walker *Dorothy Craig* • Ludwig Stossel *Binns* • Samuel S Hinds *Dr Crane* ■ *Dir* Frank Ryan • *Scr* Lewis R Foster, from a story by John D Klorer

He's Just Not That into You ★★★ 12
Romantic comedy
2008 · US/Ger · Colour · 123min

An all-star cast, including Jennifer Aniston and Scarlett Johansson, talks relationships in this *Sex and the City*-inspired comedy. Oddly though, it's the less well-known Ginnifer Goodwin who stands out here as the outgoing but lonely Gigi. Her quest to discover why she never gets a second date leads to bartender Alex (Justin Long), whose blunt assessment of the situation – neatly encapsulated in the movie's title – only serves to convince her that he is "the one". Their dynamic provides the real intrigue here, although Drew Barrymore ups the kooky quotient as a hapless online dater. But there's an awful lot riding on the charms of the attractive cast. SP *DVD* Blu-ray

Ginnifer Goodwin *Gigi* • Justin Long *Alex* • Jennifer Connelly *Janine* • Scarlett Johansson *Anna* • Jennifer Aniston *Beth* • Drew Barrymore *Mary* • Kevin Connolly *Conor* • Ben Affleck *Neil* ■ *Dir* Ken Kwapis • *Scr* Abby Kohn, Marc Silverstein, from the non-fiction book by Greg Behrendt, Liz Tuccillo

He's My Girl ★★ 15
Romantic comedy   1987 · US · Colour · 99min

This cross-dressing farce should be called "Some Like It Tepid". TK Carter plays Reggie who, pretending to be his best mate David Hallyday, wins a trip to Hollywood. The problem is the winners need to be a couple. Cue Reggie becoming Regina and the two friends getting into a *Twelfth Night* set of misunderstandings on holiday. The only aspect of interest is Jennifer Tilly as a rather lovely waitress – the rest is just plain silly. LH

TK Carter *Reggie/Regina* • David Hallyday *Bryan* • David Clennon *Mason Morgan* • Misha McK *Tasha* • Jennifer Tilly *Lisa* • Warwick Sims *Simon Sledge* ■ *Dir* Gabrielle Beaumont • *Scr* Charles Bohl, Taylor Ames, from a story by Taylor Ames

Hester Street ★★★★ PG
Period drama   1975 · US · BW · 88min

This marvellously evocative study of Jewish immigrant life in turn-of-the-century New York, mainly told in delightfully subtitled Yiddish, features an outstanding lead performance from the Oscar-nominated Carol Kane. She plays the wife of Steven Keats, summoned from the old country after he has been in America for a dangerous few years. Unsurprisingly she finds him a changed man, so she sets out to make her own way in the New World. Electing to film in black-and-white, director Joan Micklin Silver creates a world so real you can smell the herrings. TS English, Yiddish +subtitles. *DVD*

Steven Keats *Jake* • Carol Kane *Gitl* • Mel Howard *Bernstein* • Dorrie Kavanaugh *Mamie* • Doris Roberts *Kavarsky* • Stephen Strimpell *Peltner* • Lauren Frost *Fanny* • Paul Freedman *Joey* ■ *Dir* Joan Micklin Silver • *Scr* Joan Micklin Silver, from the story *Yekl* by Abraham Cahan • *Cinematographer* Kenneth Van Sickle

Hexed ★★ 15
Comedy thriller   1993 · US · Colour · 88min

This early attempt to send up the *Fatal Attraction/Basic Instinct* genre is a patchy affair that's enlivened by the enthusiastic playing of the cast. Arye Gross is a compulsive liar working at a hotel whose fantasy world is interrupted when he gets mixed up with murderous *femme fatale* Claudia Christian. Director Alan Spencer struggles to bring this the brainless charm it needs. JF

Arye Gross *Matthew Welsh* • Claudia Christian *Hexina* • Adrienne Shelly *Gloria O'Connor* • Ray Baker *Victor Thummell* • R Lee Ermey *Detective Ferguson* • Michael E Knight *Simon Littlefield* ■ *Dir/Scr* Alan Spencer

Hey Arnold! the Movie ★★★ U
Animated comedy   2002 · US · Colour · 72min

Arnold is not the most attractive of cartoon heroes, with a head shaped like an elongated rugby ball and bushy hair parted like the Red Sea. However, his heart is in the right place and when he learns that a greedy land developer called Sheck is about to bulldoze his downtown neighbourhood, he determines to save it, with the help of best friend Gerald and love/hate interest Helga. Derived from the popular TV series, the film is a bit rough round the animated edges, but regular viewers will enjoy seeing their favourite characters up on the big screen. TH *DVD*

Spencer Klein *Arnold* • Francesca Marie Smith *Helga/Deep Voice* • Jamil Walker Smith *Gerald/Rasta guy* • Dan Castellaneta *Grandpa/Nick Vermicelli* • Tress MacNeille *Grandma/Mayor Dixie/Red* • Paul Sorvino *Scheck* • Jennifer Jason Leigh *Bridget* • Christopher Lloyd *Coroner* • Vincent Schiavelli *Mr Bailey* ■ *Dir* Tuck Tucker • *Scr* Craig Bartlett, Steve Viksten, from characters by Craig Bartlett

Hey Boy! Hey Girl! ★ U
Musical   1959 · US · BW · 80min

Hey Rubbish! This is one of those inane zero-budget musicals with singer Keely Smith emotionally blackmailing Louis Prima and his band, the Witnesses. She's only going to sing with them if they'll play at the church fête with which she's associated. The result is pretty lacklustre and, considering Prima and Smith were married and working together at the time, you'd expect better. TH

Louis Prima • Keely Smith *Dorothy Spencer* • James Gregory *Father Burton* • Henry Slate *Marty Moran* • Kim Charney *Buzz* • Barbara Heller *Grace Dawson* ■ *Dir* David Lowell Rich • *Scr* Raphael Hayes, James West

Hey! Hey! USA ★★ U
Comedy   1938 · UK · BW · 88min

Made without the assistance of his regular stooges, Moore Marriott and Graham Moffat, this is one of Will Hay's least memorable outings. Removed from his familiar milieu, he seems uncomfortable with the material and strives too hard for laughs. The film casts him as a stowaway on board a transatlantic liner who poses as a famous history professor to stop a kidnapping. DP *DVD*

Will Hay *Benjamin Twist* • Edgar Kennedy *Bugs Leary* • David Burns *Tony Ricardo* • Eddie Ryan *Ace Marco* • Fred Duprez *Cyrus Schultz* • Paddy Reynolds *Mrs Schultz* • Tommy Bupp *Bertie Schultz* • Arthur Goullet *Gloves Johnson* ■ *Dir* Marcel Varnel • *Scr* Marriott Edgar, Val Guest, JOC Orton

Hey, Let's Twist! ★★★ U
Musical   1961 · US · BW · 78min

Who remembers Joey Dee? When this film was made he was one of the hottest names in pop music, having introduced, with his group the Starliters, the Twist at the Peppermint Lounge in New York. An energetic, pint-sized performer, Dee made two films (the other was *Two Tickets to Paris*) which are fascinating sociological time capsules capturing the start of the Swinging Sixties. TV

Joey Dee • Teddy Randazzo *Rickey Dee* • Kay Armen *Angie* • Zohra Lampert *Sharon* • Dino Di Luca *Papa* ■ *Dir* Greg Garrison • *Scr* Hal Hackady

The Hi-Jackers ★★
Crime drama   1963 · UK · BW · 69min

This low-budget crime thriller from the Butcher's studio is set in the rough-and-ready world of trucking. However, British lorry drivers don't have the cinematic glamour of their American counterparts, so identifying the familiar British faces – Anthony Booth (Tony Blair's father-in-law), Patrick Cargill, Glynn Edwards – is the main point of interest here. JF

Anthony Booth *Terry McKinley* • Jacqueline Ellis *Shirley* • Derek Francis *Jack Carter* • Patrick Cargill *Inspector Grayson* • Glynn Edwards *Bluey* • David Gregory *Pete* • Harold Goodwin (2) *Scouse* • Anthony Wager *Smithy* • Arthur English *Bert* ■ *Dir/Scr* Jim O'Connolly

Hi-Life ★★ 15
Comedy drama   1998 · US · Colour · 81min

Sadly, despite a good cast of young American actors, this ordinary comedy-drama plays more like a soap than a serious big-screen picture. Actor Eric Stoltz owes $900 to vicious bookie Charles Durning and he borrows the money from girlfriend Moira Kelly, telling her it's to pay for sister Daryl Hannah's abortion. Kelly's brother, bartender Campbell Scott, is drawn into the whole confusing affair as the net begins to close around Stoltz's elaborate deceit. LH

Campbell Scott *Ray* • Eric Stoltz *Jimmy* • Daryl Hannah *Maggie* • Moira Kelly *Susan* • Katrin Cartlidge *April* • Charles Durning *Fatty* • Peter Riegert *Miner* ■ *Dir/Scr* Roger Hedden

The Hi-Lo Country ★★★ 15
Western drama   1998 · US · Colour · 109min

Woody Harrelson and the impressive Billy Crudup are bosom-buddy cowboys who run a ranch together in the American west after the Second World War. Their friendship becomes sorely tested when Harrelson begins an affair with the object of Crudup's desire, Patricia Arquette. This is a sumptuous, sprawling western from director Stephen Frears and producer Martin Scorsese but, while beautifully shot, there is little new here. LH Violence, sex scenes. *DVD*

Woody Harrelson *Big Boy Matson* • Billy Crudup *Pete Calder* • Patricia Arquette *Mona Birk* • Cole Hauser *Little Boy Matson* • Penélope Cruz *Josepha O'Neil* • Enrique Castillo *Levi Gomez* • Darren Burrows *Billy Harte* • Sam Elliott *Jim Ed Love* ■ *Dir* Stephen Frears • *Scr* Walon Green, from the novel by Max Evans • *Cinematographer* Oliver Stapleton

Hi, Mom! ★★★★ 18
Satirical comedy
1970 · US · BW and Colour · 86min

In director Brian De Palma's sex-fixated, counterculture satire, Robert De Niro's character from *Greetings* returns to make a semi-pornographic film about his neighbours and bomb a laudromat in the name of revolutionary politics. Meanwhile his best friend (Gerrit Graham) gets involved with a radical theatre troupe. The final reel is given over to a brilliantly extended sequence of said troupe's confrontational play, *Be Black, Baby*, where fact, fiction, theatre and film merge with stunning docudrama realism. De Niro reveals the charismatic form that would mark his later career. AJ *DVD*

Robert De Niro *Jon Rubin* • Jennifer Salt *Judy Bishop* • Lara Parker *Jeannie Mitchell* • Gerrit Graham *Gerrit Wood* • Nelson Peltz *Playboy* • Charles Durnham [Charles Durning] *Superintendent* • Allen Garfield *Joe Banner* ■ *Dir* Brian De Palma • *Scr* Brian De Palma, from a story by Charles Hirsch, Brian De Palma

Hi, Nellie! ★★★
Crime comedy   1934 · US · BW · 75min

Paul Muni takes a contemporary role for a change, as a tough newspaper editor demoted to the lonely hearts column, in a terrific example of the tough, fast-paced, beautifully-made newspaper movie that Warner Bros did so well. And who could resist a cast that boasts wisecracking Glenda Farrell (as Muni's ex) and cynical

Hideous Kinky ★★★ 12

Drama 1998 · UK/Fr · Colour · 93min

Kate Winslet followed her headline-grabbing role in the blockbuster *Titanic* with the lead in this lower-profile film, based on the book by Esther Freud. She plays Julia, who decides to uproot her two young daughters and seek adventure and possibly romance in the Morocco of 1972. While Julia's journey is quite interesting and full of colour, the tale of expatriate life in Marrakesh is often repetitive. JB *DVD*

Kate Winslet *Julia* • Saïd Taghmaoui *Bilal* • Bella Riza *Bea* • Carrie Mullan *Lucy* • Pierre Clémenti *Santoni* • Abigail Cruttenden *Charlotte* ■ *Dir* Gillies MacKinnon • *Scr* Billy MacKinnon, from the novel by Esther Freud

Hider in the House ★★ 18

Thriller 1989 · US · Colour · 103min

Until it breaks down the believability barrier, director Matthew Patrick's unusual psycho thriller is tightly constructed and grippingly written. Former mental institution inmate Gary Busey hides in the home of well-to-do Mimi Rogers and Michael McKean, obsessively spies on them and eventually intervenes in their personal affairs. Busey and Rogers raise enormous empathy before the plot degenerates into a stock shocker. AJ Violence, swearing, sex scenes, nudity.

Gary Busey *Tom Sykes* • Mimi Rogers *Julie Dryer* • Michael McKean *Phil Dryer* • Kurt Christopher Kinder *Neil Dryer* • Candy Hutson [Candace Hutson] *Holly Dryer* • Bruce Glover *Gary Hufford* ■ *Dir* Matthew Patrick • *Scr* Lem Dobbs

Hiding Out ★★ 15

Comedy thriller 1987 · US · Colour · 98min

Jon Cryer has rarely found the right vehicle for his comedic talents and, although this provides him with a rare starring role, it founders on a lame, unconvincing script. He plays a stockbroker who, finding himself on the run from the Mob, decides to hide out as a college student. Given that he looks far too young as a bearded adult, this charade works wonders, but complications ensue when a fellow student (Annabeth Gish) falls for him. Director Bob Giraldi seems unsure whether this is a teen comedy or a light-hearted thriller. JF Some violence, swearing.

Jon Cryer *Andrew Morenski* • Keith Coogan *Patrick Morenski* • Annabeth Gish *Ryan Campbell* • Gretchen Cryer *Aunt Lucy* • Oliver Cotton *Killer* • Claude Brooks *Clinton* • Lou Walker *Ezzard* ■ *Dir* Bob Giraldi • *Scr* Joe Menosky, Jeff Rothberg

Hierro ★★ 12

Psychological mystery thriller
2009 · Sp · Colour · 85min

This might come from the producers of *Pan's Labyrinth*, but Spanish director Gabe Ibáñez is no Guillermo del Toro and his bland story (that has echoes of 2006 chiller *The Orphanage*) carries little comparable emotional charge. On holiday on the remote island of El Hierro (Europe's southern most tip), Elena Anaya's young son vanishes. Although visually arresting, thanks to the use of the volcanic location and sudden surreal symbolism in key places, nothing is ever as mysterious or poetic as it should be and, while Anaya submerges herself in the scenario, the outcome is never as scary as it should be. AJ Spanish +subtitles. *DVD* ⬚

Elena Anaya *Maria* • Kaiet Rodriguez *Diego* • Hugo Arbues *Mateo* • Jon Ariño *Forense* • Miriam Correa *Julia* • Andrés Herrera *Antonio* ■ *Dir* Gabe Ibáñez • *Scr* Javier Gúllon, from a story by Jesus de la Vega

High and Low ★★★★ 12

Crime drama
1963 · Jpn · BW and Colour · 143min

Akira Kurosawa's genius for literary adaptation also included hard-boiled pulp, as he proves with this reworking of Ed McBain's *King's Ransom*. It begins on a single set, as Toshiro Mifune's corrupt tycoon debates whether to pay the ransom demanded for the chauffeur's son, who was mistakenly kidnapped instead of his own

offspring. But then the action opens out to follow the police on their desperate hunt around the seedier parts of town. Displaying a masterly control of mood and visual style, Kurosawa is more concerned with the morality of the case, but this is still riveting and tense. DP Japanese +subtitles. *DVD*

Toshiro Mifune *Kingo Gondo* • Kyoko Kagawa *Reiko, Gondo's wife* • Tatsuya Mihashi *Kawanishi* • Yutaka Sada *Aoki, the chauffeur* • Tatsuya Nakadai *Inspector Tokuro* • Takashi Shimura *Director* ■ *Dir* Akira Kurosawa • *Scr* Akira Kurosawa, Ryuzo Kikushima, Hideo Oguni, Eijiro Hisaita, from the novel *King's Ransom* by Ed McBain [Evan Hunter]

The High and the Mighty ★★ U

Disaster movie 1954 · US · Colour · 141min

As a crippled airplane flies through the sky, having passed the point of no return, it is up to washed-up pilot John Wayne to save the day. Director William A Wellman seems restrained by the CinemaScope format, and Ernest K Gann, adapting his novel to the screen, writes mundane flashbacks which dissipate the tension. Shallow characterisation doesn't help, either. A big hit in its day, this gained Oscar nominations for Wellman and supporting actresses Claire Trevor and Jan Sterling, while Dimitri Tiomkin won for his dramatic score. AE *DVD*

John Wayne *Dan Roman* • Claire Trevor *May Holst* • Laraine Day *Lydia Rice* • Robert Stack *Sullivan* • Jan Sterling *Sally McKee* • Phil Harris *Ed Joseph* • Robert Newton *Gustave Pardee* • David Brian *Ken Childs* • Paul Kelly (1) *Flaherty* ■ *Dir* William A Wellman • *Scr* Ernest K Gann, from his novel

High Anxiety ★★★ 15

Parody 1977 · US · Colour · 93min

This parody of Alfred Hitchcock's greatest hits rather sums up the strengths and weaknesses of Mel Brooks's films. By opting for the best known scenes in *Spellbound*, *Vertigo*, *North by Northwest* and *Psycho*, he settles for easy laughs and thus misses the chance to kid around with the real aficionados. Moreover, not enough thought has gone into the non-spoof scenes, many of which run out of steam. There are many funny moments, but perhaps Hitch was just too self-mocking to be spoofable. AJ Swearing. *DVD*

Mel Brooks *Richard H Thorndyke* • Madeline Kahn *Victoria Brisbane* • Cloris Leachman *Nurse Diesel* • Harvey Korman *Doctor Charles Montague* • Ron Carey *Brophy* • Howard Morris *Professor Lilloman* • Dick Van Patten *Doctor Wentworth* • Jack Riley *Desk clerk* ■ *Dir* Mel Brooks • *Scr* Mel Brooks, Ron Clark, Rudy DeLuca, Barry Levinson

High Art ★★★★ 18

Drama 1998 · US · Colour · 97min

This is an intimate, skilfully observed study of the complex relationship between two neighbours, one a previously famous photographer (Ally Sheedy), the other an assistant editor of a photography magazine (Radha Mitchell). Despite its themes of drug abuse and lesbianism, this is far from being a sensationalist drama, while the gradual deepening of the ambitious, strong-willed Mitchell's attraction to the drained, almost lifeless Sheedy is given credibility by the thoughtful script and stripped-bare performances. DP Swearing, sex scenes.

Ally Sheedy *Lucy Berliner* • Radha Mitchell *Syd* • Patricia Clarkson *Greta Krauss* • Gabriel Mann *James, Syd's boyfriend* • Bill Sage *Arnie* • Ahn Duong *Dominique, "Frame" editor* • Tammy Grimes *Vera, Lucy's mother* • David Thornton *Harry, Syd's boss* ■ *Dir/Scr* Lisa Cholodenko

High Barbaree ★★

Second World War drama
1947 · US · BW · 90min

In this Second World War yarn, Van Johnson steers his downed navy seaplane towards High Barbaree, a fabled Pacific island his uncle once told him about. Co-pilot Cameron Mitchell keeps him company while he tells his story, which leads to flashbacks re-creating Johnson's life back

home with sweetheart June Allyson. This is less a war movie than a soupy romance. AT

Van Johnson *Alec Brooke* • June Allyson *Nancy Fraser* • Thomas Mitchell *Capt Thad Vail* • Marilyn Maxwell *Diana Case* • Henry Hull *Dr Brooke* • Claude Jarman Jr *Alec, age 14* • Cameron Mitchell *Lt Moore* ■ *Dir* Jack Conway • *Scr* Anne Morrison Chapin, Whitfield Cook, Cyril Hume, from the novel by Charles Nordhoff, James Norman Hall

High Boot Benny ★★★★ 15

Thriller 1993 · Ire · Colour · 78min

In keeping with the principles of the non-sectarian school at the centre of his controversial drama, writer/director Joe Comerford tries to be even-handed, and he avoids many of the situations inherent in films about the Troubles. Frances Tomelty does well as the idealistic matron, as does Marc O'Shea as the confused teenager from Northern Ireland who seeks refuge south of the border. The tarring and feathering scene and the brutal army reprisal are chilling. DP

Marc O'Shea *Benny* • Frances Tomelty *Matron* • Alan Devlin *Manley* • Annie Farr *Dorothy* • Seamus Ball *Father Bergin* • Fiona Nicholas *Orphan* ■ *Dir/Scr* Joe Comerford

The High Bright Sun ★★ PG

Wartime drama 1965 · UK · Colour · 109min

This attempt to make emotional drama (army officer Dirk Bogarde's love for archaeology student Susan Strasberg) out of a national crisis (the Cypriot struggle against British occupation) results in one of the most stilted and wooden movies that Bogarde ever made for Rank. Director Ralph Thomas hammers away at the obvious and rapidly loses credibility, while Ian Stuart Black's dialogue is awesomely improbable. Bogarde, though, pulls the film up by its bootstraps. TH Some swearing, violence.

Dirk Bogarde *Major McGuire* • George Chakiris *Haghios* • Susan Strasberg *Juno Kozani* • Denholm Elliott *Baker* • Grégoire Aslan *Skyros* • Colin Campbell *Emile* • Joseph Furst *Dr Andros* • Katherine Kath *Mrs Andros* ■ *Scr* Ian Stuart Black, Bryan Forbes, from the novel by Ian Stuart Black

The High Cost of Loving ★★ U

Comedy 1958 · US · BW · 87min

That splendid actress Gena Rowlands, who found fame in husband John Cassavetes's powerful films, made an inauspicious screen debut in this tame domestic comedy directed by and co-starring José Ferrer. Ferrer plays a husband who thinks he is losing his office job, while his wife (Rowlands) fails to tell him she's expecting a baby. RB

José Ferrer *Jim Fry* • Gena Rowlands *Virginia Fry* • Joanne Gilbert *Syd Heyward* • Jim Backus *Paul Mason* • Bobby Troup *Steve Heyward* • Philip Ober *Herb Zorn* • Edward Platt *Eli Cave* • Charles Watts *Boylin* ■ *Dir* José Ferrer • *Scr* Rip Van Ronkel, from a story by Milo Frank Jr, Rip Van Ronkel

The High Country ★ PG

Romantic adventure 1981 · Can · Colour · 91min

After winning rave reviews for his role in *The Last Picture Show*, Timothy Bottoms was reduced to making tedious dramas such as this. He plays an escaped prisoner dragging Linda Purl through the mountains in what is an excuse for director Harvey Hart to film lots of impressive Canadian scenery in between the mediocre chase scenes. JB

Timothy Bottoms *Jim* • Linda Purl *Kathy* • George Sims *Larry* • Jim Lawrence *Casey* • Bill Berry *Carter* • Walter Mills *Clem* • Paul Jolicoeur [Paul Coeur] *Red* • Dick Butler *Herbie* ■ *Dir* Harvey Hart • *Scr* Bud Townsend

High Crimes ★★ 12

Courtroom thriller 2002 · US · Colour · 110min

Carl Franklin's military-themed legal thriller squanders its quality cast on the most formulaic of scripts. Ashley Judd plays a successful attorney whose life is thrown into chaos when her husband (Jim Caviezel)

is exposed as a former soldier accused of the murder of eight civilians during the civil war in El Salvador. Morgan Freeman is thoroughly wasted as the alcoholic lawyer who educates Judd in the peculiarities of military law. This trundles along without ever reaching the dramatic peaks one would expect. JC Violence. *DVD*

Ashley Judd *Claire Kubik* • Morgan Freeman *Charlie Grimes* • Jim Caviezel *Tom Kubik* • Amanda Peet *Jackie* • Tom Bower *Mullins* • Adam Scott *Lieutenant Embry* • Bruce Davison *Brigadier General Marks* • Juan Carlos Hernandez *Major Hernandez* ■ *Dir* Carl Franklin • *Scr* Yuri Zeltser, Cary Bickley, from the novel by Joseph Binder

High Fidelity ★★★★ 15

Comedy drama 2000 · US/UK · Colour · 109min

Stephen Frears transposes Nick Hornby's novel from north London to downtown Chicago, but this slickly scripted, knowingly played comedy stands, on its merits, as an *Alfie* for the millennial generation. As the owner of a failing vinyl emporium, John Cusack combines reluctant self-awareness with genuine delusion as he attempts to reconcile the loss of girlfriend Iben Hjejle to lusty neighbour Tim Robbins by dating singer Lisa Bonet and looking up old girlfriends. However, it's when directly addressing the viewer or compulsively compiling "top five lists" that Cusack, and the film, come alive. DP Swearing, a sex scene, brief nudity. *DVD*

John Cusack *Rob Gordon* • Iben Hjejle *Laura* • Todd Louiso *Dick* • Jack Black *Barry* • Lisa Bonet *Marie De Salle* • Catherine Zeta-Jones *Charlie* • Joan Cusack *Liz* • Tim Robbins *Ian* • Lili Taylor *Sarah* • Natasha Gregson Wagner *Caroline* ■ *Dir* Stephen Frears • *Scr* DV DeVincentis, Steve Pink, John Cusack, Scott Rosenberg, from the novel by Nick Hornby

High Heels ★★ 18

Black comedy 1991 · Sp · Colour · 109min

After a string of cult hits, it was inevitable that Pedro Almodóvar would eventually take a false step. Abandoning his trademark Euro-trash style, he attempts to tackle more serious themes in this disconcerting melodrama. He is so hell-bent on presenting a weighty treatise on families, the media and the price of fame that he allows too many scenes to become morose. The performances of Marisa Paredes and Victoria Abril just about save the day. DP Spanish +subtitles. *DVD*

Victoria Abril *Rebecca* • Marisa Paredes *Becky del Paramo* • Miguel Bose *Judge Dominguez/Femme Letal/Hugo* • Pedro Diez del Corral *Alberto* • Feodor Atkine [Féodor Atkine] *Manuel* • Ana Lizaran [Anna Lizaran] *Margarita* • Rocio Munoz *Little Rebecca* • Mairata O'Wisiedo *Judge's mother* ■ *Dir/Scr* Pedro Almodóvar

High Heels and Low Lifes ★★ 15

Crime comedy 2001 · UK · Colour · 82min

Mel Smith's noble directorial ambitions are ill-served by this lumpy comic script about a nurse and an actress (Minnie Driver and Mary McCormack) who get tangled up with London gangsters. Driver completely outacts and "out-charismas" McCormack, thus unbalancing the *Thelma & Louise* double act, and only a cameo from Michael Gambon as a camp villain truly lights up the screen. AC Swearing, violence, nudity. *DVD*

Minnie Driver *Shannon* • Michael Gambon *Kerrigan* • Mary McCormack *Frances* • Kevin McNally *Mason* • Mark Williams *Tremaine* • Danny Dyer *Danny* • Kevin Eldon *McGill* • Darren Boyd *Ray* • John Sessions *Director* ■ *Dir* Mel Smith • *Scr* Kim Fuller, from a story by Kim Fuller, from a story by Georgia Pritchett

High Hopes ★★★★ 15

Comedy drama 1988 · UK · Colour · 107min

After making *Bleak Moments*, Mike Leigh waited 17 years before directing this, his next feature. It's an amusing and affecting, if sometimes grim, look at the lives of six people in Thatcher's Britain: a working-class couple with counter-cultural pretensions, an obnoxious up-market twosome, and a pair of consumerist vulgarians. The characters may be caricatures, while the plot is slender and the film overlong, yet Leigh's unique blend of improvisation, invention and satire – what might be called misanthropy with a comic twist – combine to distinctive and telling effect. **PF** Swearing, sex scenes. *DVD* *BD*

Philip Davis *Cyril Bender* • Ruth Sheen *Shirley* • Edna Doré *Mrs Bender* • Philip Jackson *Martin Burke* • Heather Tobias *Valerie Burke* • Lesley Manville *Laetitia Boothe-Braine* • David Bamber *Rupert Boothe-Braine* • Jason Watkins *Wayne* ■ *Dir/Scr* Mike Leigh

High Lonesome ★★ U
Western   1950 · US · Colour · 81min

This is a sociologically interesting cross between a western and a juvenile problem picture, with the snarling, brooding John Barrymore Jr, son of "the Great Profile", as a teenager with a conscience. It's directed by Alan LeMay, who is, alas, no cinematic craftsman. **TS**

John Barrymore Jr [John Drew Barrymore] *Cooncat* • Chill Wills *Boatwhistle* • John Archer *Pat Farrell* • Lois Butler *Meagan Davis* • Kristine Miller *Abbey Davis* • Basil Ruysdael *Horse Davis* • Jack Elam *Smiling Man* • Dave Kashner *Roper* ■ *Dir/Scr* Alan LeMay

LANDMARK FILM
> With a gripping story that unfolds in real time, this early psychological western breaks the gun-toting mould

High Noon ★★★★★ U
Classic western   1952 · US · BW · 84min

This is the film that put director Fred Zinnemann on the Hollywood A-list, revived the career of Gary Cooper and made Grace Kelly a star. If that's not enough, this multiple Oscar winner was also one of the first psychological westerns, breaking the mould of the gun-toting tales that had dominated the genre since the early silent era. It was also a highly controversial film, being seen as an attack on those who deserted their colleagues during the communist witch-hunts that turned Hollywood into a place of fear between 1947 and 1951. **DP** *DVD*

Gary Cooper *Will Kane* • Grace Kelly *Amy Kane* • Thomas Mitchell *Jonas Henderson* • Lloyd Bridges *Harvey Pell* • Katy Jurado *Helen Ramirez* • Otto Kruger *Percy Mettrick* • Lon Chaney Jr *Martin Howe* • Henry Morgan [Harry Morgan] *William Fuller* • Lee Van Cleef *Jack Colby* • Jack Elam *Charlie* ■ *Dir* Fred Zinnemann • *Scr* Carl Foreman, from the short story *The Tin Star* by John W Cunningham • *Cinematographer* Floyd Crosby • *Music* Dmitri Tiomkin • *Editors* Elmo Williams, Harry Gerstad

High Noon ★
Western drama   2000 · US · Colour · 88min

Fred Zinnemann's 1952 masterpiece could never be improved upon. So why Rod Hardy felt compelled to try is a question that persists throughout this redundant TV remake. Confronting Will Kane with six vengeful bandits instead of four might make Tom Skerritt a better shot, but it doesn't make him Gary Cooper; with Michael Madsen in scenery-chewing support, this is downright poor. **DP**

Tom Skerritt *Will Kane* • Susanna Thompson *Amy Kane* • Reed Diamond *Harvey Pell* • Maria Conchita Alonso *Helen Ramirez* • Dennis Weaver *Mart Howe* • Michael Madsen *Frank Miller* ■ *Dir* Rod Hardy • *Scr* TS Cook, Carl Foreman, from the 1952 film by Foreman

High Plains Drifter ★★★★ 18
Western   1973 · US · Colour · 100min

Sex, sadism and the supernatural are loosely bundled in Clint Eastwood's stylishly self-conscious western: man-with-no-name satire or fable of mystic revenge, take your pick. Eastwood looms out of the desert, a mirage of retribution on a town's inhabitants who stood by while their honest sheriff was whipped to death. Eastwood seems, not altogether successfully, to be paying off debts to his former mentor, Sergio Leone – gratitude he can only express obliquely via the occult references in this distinctive variation on the spaghetti western. **TH** Violence, swearing. *DVD* *BD*

Clint Eastwood *The Stranger* • Verna Bloom *Sarah Belding* • Mariana Hill [Marianna Hill] *Callie Travers* • Mitchell Ryan *Dave Drake* • Jack Ging *Morgan Allen* • Stefan Gierasch *Mayor Jason Hobart* • Ted Hartley *Lewis Belding* ■ *Dir* Clint Eastwood • *Scr* Ernest Tidyman • *Cinematographer* Bruce Surtees

High Pressure ★★
Comedy   1932 · US · BW · 72min

William Powell stars as a racketeer who dabbles in everything, then falls for an inventor's scheme to convert sewage into artificial rubber. He sets up a corporation and sells stocks to raise some cash, romancing Evelyn Brent along the way. Powell breezes through this nonsense, which is not quite a gangster picture and not quite good enough for director Mervyn LeRoy. **AT**

William Powell *Gar Evans* • Evelyn Brent *Francine* • George Sidney (1) *Colonel Ginsburg* • Frank McHugh *Mike Donoghey* • Guy Kibbee *Clifford Gray* • Evalyn Knapp *Helen* • Ben Alexander *Geoffrey* • Harry Beresford *Dr Rudolph* ■ *Dir* Mervyn LeRoy • *Scr* Joseph Jackson, from the story *Hot Money* by SJ Peters and the play by Aben Kandell

High-Rise ★★★ 15
Science-fiction drama
2015 · UK · Colour · 113min

Based on JG Ballard's 1975 novel, this dystopian satire takes place in a swanky, towering apartment block. There, we find Dr Robert Laing (Tom Hiddleston), a well-spoken bachelor who, at the start of the film, has just moved in. While he is satisfied with life in the high-rise, many of his neighbours are unhappy, protesting that they aren't receiving the same standard of living as those on the upper floors and their frustration leads to a violent, building-wide conflict. **SC** Violence, sex, swearing *DVD* *BD*

Tom Hiddleston *Dr Robert Laing* • Jeremy Irons *Anthony Royal* • Sienna Miller *Charlotte Melville* • Luke Evans *Richard Wilder* • Elisabeth Moss *Helen Wilder* ■ *Dir* Ben Wheatley • *Scr* Amy Jump, from JG Ballard's novel

High Risk ★★
Action adventure   1981 · US · Colour · 91min

This laughable action adventure is about four chums who decide that the solution to their money woes is a quick trip to Colombia to lift a fortune from a drugs kingpin. Naturally, things don't go quite according to plan. It boasts a pretty good cast – James Coburn, James Brolin, Anthony Quinn, Lindsay Wagner – but the sheer implausibility of the tale makes it hard to feel involved or entertained. **JF**

James Brolin *Stone* • Cleavon Little *Rockney* • Bruce Davison *Dan* • Chick Vennera *Tony* • Anthony Quinn *Mariano* • Lindsay Wagner *Olivia* • James Coburn *Serrano* • Ernest Borgnine *Clint* ■ *Dir/Scr* Stewart Raffill

High Road to China ★★★ PG
Action adventure   1983 · US · Colour · 100min

Tom Selleck was offered the lead in *Raiders of the Lost Ark*, but had to refuse because he was contracted to the TV show *Magnum PI*. Instead he starred in this *Raiders* wannabe, playing a First World War flying ace who helps spoiled rich girl Bess Armstrong track down her missing father. While low on special effects, thanks to zippy direction from Brian G Hutton this romps along merrily in the style of 1940s Saturday matinées, while Selleck cuts quite a dash as the suave, wise-cracking hero. **JB** *DVD* *BD*

Tom Selleck *O'Malley* • Bess Armstrong *Eve Tozer* • Jack Weston *Struts* • Wilford Brimley *Bradley Tozer* • Robert Morley *Bentik* • Brian Blessed *Suleiman Khan* • Cassandra Gava *Alessa* ■ *Dir* Brian G Hutton • *Scr* Sandra Weintraub Roland, S Lee Pogostin, from the novel by Jon Cleary

High School ★★★
Documentary   1968 · US · BW · 75min

For over three decades, Fred Wiseman, a leading exponent of Direct Cinema or *cinéma vérité*, has entered various institutions with his hand-held camera, shot a vast amount of footage, and edited it down dispassionately, being careful not to make a subjective point. However, in his second documentary (the first, *Titicut Follies*, was set in an insane asylum), he eavesdrops on a middle-class school in Philadelphia and seems to be exposing the deadly conformity of the place. Concentrating mostly on student-teacher relationships, it has too narrow a focus, but is still fascinating. **RB**

■ *Dir/Scr* Frederick Wiseman • *Cinematographer* Richard Leiterman • *Editor* Frederick Wiseman

High School Confidential ★★★
Cult drama   1958 · US · BW · 85min

The patriotic and paternalistic Louis B Mayer would have turned in his grave had he seen this deeply subversive, hugely exploitative MGM offering about school kids getting high on marijuana. It also packs in gang warfare, hot-rod racing, alcoholism, plenty of sex and a note of seriousness when lead delinquent, Russ Tamblyn, turns out to be a narcotics agent. Jan Sterling plays an English teacher and that 1950s icon, Mamie Van Doren, turns up as Tamblyn's lascivious aunt. Rock star Jerry Lee Lewis has a cameo appearance as himself. **AT**

Russ Tamblyn *Tony Baker* • Jan Sterling *Arlene Williams* • John Drew Barrymore *JI Coleridge* • Mamie Van Doren *Gwen Dulaine* • Diane Jergens *Joan Staples* • Jerry Lee Lewis ■ *Dir* Jack Arnold • *Scr* Lewis Meltzer, Robert Blees, from a story by Robert Blees

High School High ★★ 15
Comedy   1996 · US · Colour · 81min

This misfiring spoof is chiefly aimed at the Michelle Pfeiffer hit *Dangerous Minds*, but also takes drive-by shots at all and sundry. Jon Lovitz is the idealistic teacher determined to make a difference at a school so crime-ridden the headmistress has to appeal at assembly for the return of kidnapped tutors. It's good to see perennial sidekick Lovitz in a lead role, but both the script and the supporting performances are patchy. **JF** Some violence, swearing, drug abuse, nudity. *DVD* *CS*

Jon Lovitz *Richard Clark* • Tia Carrere *Victoria Chappell* • Louise Fletcher *Mrs Doyle* • Mekhi Phifer *Griff* • Malinda Williams *Natalie* • Guillermo Diaz *Paco* • Lexie Bigham *Two Bags* • Gil Espinoza *Alonzo* ■ *Dir* Hart Bochner • *Scr* David Zucker, Robert LoCash, Pat Proft

High School Musical ★★★ U
Musical comedy drama
2006 · US · Colour · 93min

It's slight on plot and totally predictable, yet this slickly packaged musical comedy from *Dirty Dancing* choreographer Kenny Ortega certainly ticks all the right boxes for its target pre-teen audience. Not only are leads Zac Efron and Vanessa Anne Hudgens an attractive partnership, but their blossoming high-school romance is charming and full of positive life lessons. Central to these is the importance of resisting peer group pressure, as the duo encounter resistance when they audition for the school musical together. This runaway success has a cute cast and mixed bag of musical numbers, and can also be seen in special dance-along, sing-along, pop-up and ultimate edition versions. **SF** *DVD* *BD* *CS*

Zac Efron *Troy Bolton* • Vanessa Anne Hudgens *Gabriella Montez* • Ashley Tisdale *Sharpay Evans* • Lucas Grabeel *Ryan Evans* • Corbin Bleu *Chad Danforth* • Alyson Reed *Miss Darbus* ■ *Dir* Kenny Ortega • *Scr* Peter Barsocchini

High School Musical 2 ★★★ U
Musical comedy drama
2007 · US · Colour · 106min

School's out for summer in this sure-fire follow-up to the hit children's musical about student misfits who find love through song. This time around Troy (Zac Efron) and Gabriella (Vanessa Hudgens) are up against the lure of filthy lucre as the pressure of paying for college draws Troy into the clutches of the scheming Sharpay (Ashley

Tisdale). She can get him a job at her parents' country club, but will he really sing with her in the big talent show? This may not have all the innocent freshness of the original, but its sense of fun rises above the hammy script and manufactured plot. **TF** *DVD* *BD*

Zac Efron *Troy Bolton* • Vanessa Hudgens [Vanessa Anne Hudgens] *Gabriella Montez* • Ashley Tisdale *Sharpay Evans* • Lucas Grabeel *Ryan Evans* • Corbin Bleu *Chad Danforth* • Alyson Reed *Miss Darbus* ■ *Dir* Kenny Ortega • *Scr* Peter Barsocchini, from his characters

High School Musical 3: Senior Year ★★★ U
Musical comedy drama
2008 · US · Colour · 111min

In the third instalment in Disney's phenomenally popular musical franchise, Zac Efron and Vanessa Hudgens reprise their roles as sweethearts Troy and Gabriella. As high school graduation looms there are difficult decisions to make about college, sporting ambition – and love. It may seem like a rehash of the first two films, but the problems of these wholesome characters will no doubt strike a chord with enthusiastic pre-teens. And, of course, the serious moments are interspersed with cute songs and nifty dance numbers that are likely to win over even the most sceptical of older viewers. **DA** *DVD* *BD*

Zac Efron *Troy Bolton* • Vanessa Hudgens [Vanessa Anne Hudgens] *Gabriella Montez* • Ashley Tisdale *Sharpay Evans* • Corbin Bleu *Chad Danforth* • Lucas Grabeel *Ryan Evans* • Monique Coleman *Taylor McKessie* ■ *Dir* Kenny Ortega • *Scr* Peter Barsocchini, from his characters

High Season ★★ 15
Satirical drama   1987 · UK · Colour · 90min

Oddly old-fashioned, romantic fluff, this has Jacqueline Bisset as a photographer on the Greek island of Rhodes. Clare Peploe's film chronicles her encounters with all manner of people who need shooting – though not necessarily with a camera – including obnoxious tourists, spies and an egocentric ex-hubby. The main interest lies in the picture-postcard views of both the island and Bisset, and in a classy supporting cast. **DA** *DVD*

Jacqueline Bisset *Katherine* • James Fox *Patrick* • Irene Papas *Penelope* • Sebastian Shaw *Basil Sharp* • Kenneth Branagh *Rick Lamb* • Lesley Manville *Carol Lamb* • Robert Stephens *Konstantinis* ■ *Dir* Clare Peploe • *Scr* Clare Peploe, Mark Peploe

High Sierra ★★★ PG
Crime thriller   1941 · US · BW · 95min

This is the film that turned character actor Humphrey Bogart into a fully-fledged star. Bogie, in a role turned down by George Raft, plays melancholic gangster "Mad Dog" Roy Earle, making his last stand from a log cabin in the landscape of the title. The plot's actually a bit daft, and there's some risible nonsense with a disabled girl (the excellent Joan Leslie) and a dog, but this is, on the whole, a pacey melodrama. Remade in 1955 as *I Died a Thousand Times*. **TS** *DVD*

Humphrey Bogart *"Mad Dog" Roy Earle* • Ida Lupino *Marie Garson* • Alan Curtis *Babe Kozak* • Arthur Kennedy *Red Hattery* • Joan Leslie *Velma* • Henry Hull *"Doc" Banton* • Barton MacLane *Jake Kranmer* • Henry Travers *Pa* ■ *Dir* Raoul Walsh • *Scr* John Huston, WR Burnett, from the novel by WR Burnett

High Society ★★★★ U
Musical romantic comedy
1956 · US · Colour · 102min

This musical remake of the 1940 film *The Philadelphia Story* was a smash hit. It's cleverly under-directed by the brilliant Charles Walters and offers many joys, notably the teaming of crooners Crosby and Frank Sinatra for the witty Cole Porter number *Well, Did You Evah?*, and the delightful Grace Kelly in a role she plays perfectly, that of a spoiled rich brat. Sinatra and Celeste Holm make a snappy pair of journalists (and being that snap to another Porter classic, *Who Wants to Be a Millionaire?*), but Crosby seems somewhat ill at ease, and jazz great Louis Armstrong is reduced to the chorus and stooge to Crosby. TS DVD

Bing Crosby *CK Dexter-Haven* • Grace Kelly *Tracy Samantha Lord* • Frank Sinatra *Mike Connor* • Celeste Holm *Liz Imbrie* • John Lund *George Kittredge* • Louis Calhern *Uncle Willie* • Sidney Blackmer *Seth Lord* • Louis Armstrong ■ *Dir* Charles Walters • *Scr* John Patrick, from the play *The Philadelphia Story* by Philip Barry • *Music* Johnny Green (1), Saul Chaplin

High Spirits ★★★ 12

Supernatural comedy 1988 · US · Colour · 93min

Neil Jordan's boil-in-the-bag *Beetle Juice* goes for Ealing whimsy and easy laughs and, incredibly, manages both in spite of such a slender plot. Peter O'Toole hits the right note of craziness as a "haunted" castle owner whose staff of fake spectres battle real poltergeists during the American tourist season, with suitably madcap results. However, too many desperate characters veer off into so many disparate subplots that complete satisfaction is never achieved. AJ DVD

Peter O'Toole *Peter Plunkett* • Daryl Hannah *Mary Plunkett* • Steve Guttenberg *Jack* • Beverly D'Angelo *Sharon* • Liam Neeson *Martin Brogan* • Ray McAnally *Plunkett Senior* • Liz Smith *Mrs Plunkett* • Jennifer Tilly *Miranda* • Peter Gallagher *Brother Tony* • Connie Booth *Marge* ■ *Dir/Scr* Neil Jordan

High Tide ★★★ 15

Drama 1987 · Aus · Colour · 101min

This bleak tale of a woman who unexpectedly discovers her long-abandoned daughter is saved by the stirring, emotionally loaded central performance of Judy Davis, one of the most fascinating and adventurous actors working today, whose well-documented eccentricity has prevented her achieving major star status. This often thoughtful, intelligent film shows us once again what a charismatic celluloid presence she can be. SH Swearing.

Judy Davis *Lilli* • Jan Adele *Bet* • Claudia Karvan *Ally* • Colin Friels *Mick* • John Clayton *Col* • Frankie J Holden *Lester* • Monica Trapaga *Tracey* • Mark Hembrow *Mechanic* ■ *Dir* Gillian Armstrong • *Scr* Laura Jones

High Tide at Noon ★★

Drama 1957 · UK · BW · 110min

Since his graduation to features in the early 1950s, one-time documentarist Philip Leacock had mostly impressed, yet he came unstuck with this *Romeo and Juliet* story set on the Nova Scotia fishing banks. Leacock surveys the local scenery with a keen eye, but his handling of the melodramatic ructions caused by Betta St John's rejection of Patrick McGoohan and Michael Craig in favour of outsider William Sylvester is less sure. DP

Betta St John *Joanna MacKenzie* • William Sylvester *Alec Douglas* • Michael Craig *Nils* • Patrick McGoohan *Simon Breck* • Flora Robson *Donna* • Alexander Knox *Stephen* ■ *Dir* Philip Leacock • *Scr* Neil Paterson, from the novel by Elizabeth Ogilvie

High Time ★★ U

Musical comedy 1960 · US · Colour · 102min

Sammy Cahn and Jimmy Van Heusen picked up an Oscar nomination for their song *The Second Time Around*, but that's the only bright spot in Blake Edwards's twee comedy. Bing Crosby ladles on the charm as the millionaire widower who heads back to college for some long overdue education. Crosby gets to romance pouting professor Nicole Maurey, but he's clearly aware the script is ludicrously lightweight. Fabian and Tuesday Weld play his unhip fellow students. DP

Bing Crosby *Harvey Howard* • Fabian *Gil Sparrow* • Tuesday Weld *Joy Elder* • Nicole Maurey *Helene Gauthier* • Richard Beymer *Bob Bannerman* • Yvonne Craig *Randy Pruitt* • Patrick Adiarte *TJ Padmanagham* ■ *Dir* Blake Edwards • *Scr* Tom Waldman, Frank Waldman, from a story by Garson Kanin

High Velocity ★

Action drama 1977 · US · Colour · 105min

This is exploitation movie-making at its crassest. Both Ben Gazzara and Paul Winfield are utterly wasted as hard-boiled Vietnam vets hired to rescue corporate tycoon Keenan Wynn kidnapped by a guerrilla force. Amid the substandard action scenes director Remi Kramer tries to make a point about foreign businesses in Third World countries corrupting officials, but offers no genuine insight. RS

Ben Gazzara *Clifford Baumgartner* • Britt Ekland *Mrs Andersen* • Paul Winfield *Watson* • Keenan Wynn *Mr Andersen* • Alejandro Rey *Alejandro Martel* ■ *Dir* Remi Kramer • *Scr* Remi Kramer, Michael J Parsons

High Voltage ★ U

Drama 1929 · US · BW · 63min

Even if given leeway for being made in the 1920s, this terminally dull tale of a snow-bound group of bus passengers sheltering in a remote church is still unimaginatively shot with appallingly little plot development. Only future screwball comedian Carole Lombard (billed as Carol) shows any spirit, playing the smart-talking, bad girl equal to mysterious tough guy William Boyd. The action is practically static, with ludicrous dialogue doing nothing to perk up events. SF DVD

William Boyd (1) *Bill the boy* • Owen Moore *Detective Dan Egan* • Carol Lombard [Carole Lombard] *Billie Davis* • Diane Ellis *The kid* • Billy Bevan *Gus, the driver* • Phillips Smalley *Banker Henderson* ■ *Dir* Howard Higgin • *Scr* Elliott Clawson, James Gleason

High Wall ★★★

Crime drama 1947 · US · BW · 98min

A stylish, angst-ridden *film noir*, this stars Robert Taylor as the traumatised war veteran and possible wife killer who falls in love with his psychiatrist, Audrey Totter. She recommends brain surgery and truth-drugs; Taylor realises that if he has the surgery he will be judged sane and tried for murder. As the flashbacks roll past, we realise everyone has a sexual hang-up that the war just made worse. Taylor looks convincingly ravaged throughout, and Herbert Marshall makes a splendidly shady character. AT

Robert Taylor (1) *Steven Kenet* • Audrey Totter *Dr Ann Lorrison* • Herbert Marshall *Willard I Whitcombe* • Dorothy Patrick *Helen Kenet* • HB Warner *Mr Slocum* • Warner Anderson *Dr George Poward* • Moroni Olsen *Dr Phillip Dunlap* ■ *Dir* Curtis Bernhardt • *Scr* Sydney Boehm, Lester Cole, from the novel and play by Alan R Clark, Bradbury Foote

High, Wide and Handsome ★★★★ U

Musical western 1937 · US · BW · 110min

Offbeat but entertaining, this epic period musical dramatises the efforts of prospectors, led by Randolph Scott, to exploit oil under their land. Oscar Hammerstein II wrote lyrics to some wonderful songs with music by Jerome Kern, while the inventive direction comes from Rouben Mamoulian. Memorable performances are drawn from Irene Dunne as a medicine show singer and Akim Tamiroff as a wily saloon keeper, while the astonishing climax involves an entire circus and its elephants thwarting a band of saboteurs. AE

Irene Dunne *Sally Watterson* • Randolph Scott *Peter Cortlandt* • Dorothy Lamour *Molly Fuller* • Elizabeth Patterson *Grandma Cortlandt* • Raymond Walburn *Doc Watterson* • Charles Bickford *Red Scanlon* • Akim Tamiroff *Joe Varese* ■ *Dir* Rouben Mamoulian • *Scr* Oscar Hammerstein II, George O'Neil

A High Wind in Jamaica ★★★ PG

Swashbuckling adventure 1965 · UK · Colour · 102min

Alexander Mackendrick's penultimate picture is a solidly crafted adaptation of Richard Hughes's bestseller about a gnarled pirate who finds himself playing nursemaid to a group of young stowaways. Although occasionally becalmed during its more melodramatic passages, it is still marvellous entertainment. Anthony Quinn is fine in the action sequences but doesn't always convince, but James Coburn is on top form as his first mate and cinematographer Douglas Slocombe's seascapes are often very beautiful. DP DVD

Anthony Quinn *Juan Chavez* • James Coburn *Zac* • Benito Carruthers [Ben Carruthers] *Alberto* • Lila Kedrova *Rosa* • Deborah Baxter *Emily Thornton* • Viviane Ventura *Margaret Fernandez* • Martin Amis *John Thornton* • Roberta Tovey *Rachel Thornton* • Gert Frobe [Gert Fröbe] *Dutch captain* ■ *Dir* Alexander Mackendrick • *Scr* Stanley Mann, Ronald Harwood, Denis Cannan, from the novel by Richard Hughes

Higher and Higher ★★★ U

Musical 1943 · US · BW · 86min

French import Michèle Morgan was top-billed in this bright adaptation of the Broadway hit, but it's best remembered now as Frank Sinatra's first starring vehicle after becoming America's most popular teenage crooner. There's accomplished support from Jack Haley, who re-creates his Broadway role; less memorable are Mel Tormé and Victor Borge, neither of whom really cut it as movie players. Veteran director Tim Whelan doesn't get in the way. TS

Michèle Morgan *Millie* • Frank Sinatra *Frank* • Jack Haley *Mike* • Leon Errol *Drake* • Marcy McGuire *Mickey* • Victor Borge *Sir Victor Fitzroy Victor* • Mary Wickes *Sandy* • Elisabeth Risdon *Mrs Keating* • Barbara Hale *Katherine* • Mel Tormé *Marty* ■ *Dir* Tim Whelan • *Scr* Jay Dratler, Ralph Spence, William Bowers, Howard Harris, from the play by Gladys Hurlbut, Joshua Logan

Higher Learning ★★★ 15

Drama 1995 · US · Colour · 123min

In a university campus where race and peer pressure matter more than intelligence and individuality, only professor Laurence Fishburne seems capable of thinking for himself. But his idealistic beliefs seem naive alongside the eagerness with which freshmen Michael Rapaport, Omar Epps and Kristy Swanson seek to fit into their new environment. Cole Hauser is chillingly effective as a white supremacist skinhead, while Jennifer Connelly gives the most adult performance. DP Swearing, violence, drug abuse. DVD

Jennifer Connelly *Taryn* • Ice Cube *Fudge* • Laurence Fishburne *Professor Maurice Phipps* • Omar Epps *Malik Williams* • Kristy Swanson *Kristen Connor* • Michael Rapaport *Remy* • Tyra Banks *Deja* • Cole Hauser *Scott Moss* ■ *Dir/Scr* John Singleton

Highlander ★★★ 15

Action adventure fantasy 1986 · US/UK · Colour · 111min

So confused as to be hilariously watchable, director Russell Mulcahy's cult fantasy wavers between sci-fi, horror flick and music video, as 16th-century Scottish clansman Christopher Lambert is schooled in being an immortal swordsman by Sean Connery for eternal battles with the evil Clancy Brown. There are some great sword-lunging duels (the best, in fact, is in a Madison Square Garden garage at the beginning) but the plot itself is never as pointedly directed. TH Violence, swearing, nudity. DVD BL

Christopher Lambert *Connor MacLeod* • Roxanne Hart *Brenda Wyatt* • Clancy Brown *Kurgan* • Sean Connery *Ramirez* • Beatie Edney *Heather* • Alan North *Lieutenant Frank Moran* • Sheila Gish *Rachel Ellenstein* ■ *Dir* Russell Mulcahy • *Scr* Gregory Widen, Peter Bellwood, Larry Ferguson, from a story by Gregory Widen

Highlander II: the Quickening ★★ 15

Action adventure fantasy 1990 · US · Colour · 85min

Despite some absurdly silly casting (Christopher Lambert as a Scotsman?), the first *Highlander* was a worldwide smash and hoots of fun into the bargain. This time around it just doesn't click, even though both Lambert and Sean Connery return

from the original. The two leads once again exude charisma, but there's not enough flash to cover the lack of substance. JF Swearing, violence. DVD

Christopher Lambert *Connor MacLeod* • Sean Connery *Juan Villa-Lobos Ramirez* • Virginia Madsen *Louise Marcus* • Michael Ironside *General Katana* • Allan Rich *Alan Neyman* • John C McGinley *Blake* ■ *Dir* Russell Mulcahy • *Scr* Peter Bellwood, from a story by Brian Clemens, William N Panzer, from characters by Gregory Widen

Highlander III: the Sorcerer ★ 15

Action adventure fantasy 1995 · Can/Fr/UK · Colour · 93min

Just when you thought the *Highlander* saga couldn't sink any further into diluted caricature and empty rock video flash, along comes this terminally dreary second sequel. This time immortal Christopher Lambert must battle Mario Van Peebles over the fate of his adopted son in a flaccid fantasy that makes a lot of noise but not a lot of sense. AJ Sex scenes, swearing, violence. DVD

Christopher Lambert *Connor MacLeod/Russell Nash* • Mario Van Peebles *Kane* • Deborah Unger [Deborah Kara Unger] *Alex Johnson/Sarah* • Mako *Nakano* • Raoul Trujillo *1st warrior* • Jean-Pierre Pérusse *2nd warrior* • Martin Neufeld *Stenn* ■ *Dir* Andy Morahan [Andrew Morahan] • *Scr* Paul Ohl, from a story by William N Panzer, Brad Mirman, from characters by Gregory Widen

Highlander: Endgame ★ 18

Action adventure fantasy 2000 · US · Colour · 96min

The fourth instalment in the variable series is a mass of chaotic action searching for a plot among the remnants of badly directed pop promos. Christopher Lambert's Connor MacLeod character joins forces with Adrian Paul's Duncan MacLeod from the TV series to fight killer Bruce Payne. This whizzes between centuries and countries for maximum audience bewilderment. AJ DVD BL

Christopher Lambert *Connor MacLeod* • Adrian Paul *Duncan MacLeod* • Bruce Payne *Jacob Kell* • Lisa Barbuscia *Faith/Kate* • Donnie Yen *Jin Ke* • Jim Byrnes *Dawson* • Beatie Edney *Heather* • Sheila Gish *Rachel Ellenstein* ■ *Dir* Douglas Aarniokoski • *Scr* Joel Soisson, from a story by Eric Bernt, Gillian Horvath, William Panzer [William N Panzer], from characters by Gregory Widen

Highlander: the Source ★ 15

Action fantasy adventure 2007 · UK/US/Lith · Colour · 86min

An intended franchise revamp fails dismally in this fifth instalment in the ailing sci-fi saga. Set in a post-apocalypse near future, the feature sees sword-wielding immortal Duncan MacLeod (Adrian Paul, reprising his role from the *Highlander* TV spin-off) lead the last of his kind on a quest to locate the origins of their power. Washed-out visuals mirror the lacklustre plotting, as the weak cast struggles to animate risible dialogue and a script that's short on both incident and ideas. SF DVD

Adrian Paul *Duncan MacLeod* • Peter Wingfield *Methos* • Jim Byrnes *Joe Dawson* • Thekla Reuten *Anna* • Cristian Solimeno *The Guardian* ■ *Dir* Brett Leonard • *Scr* Steven Kelvin Watkins, David Abramowitz, Mark Bradley, from a story by Bradley, from characters by Gregory Widen

Highly Dangerous ★★★ U

Comedy thriller 1950 · UK · BW · 88min

Eric Ambler's playful script is the main reason for watching this lively espionage adventure, although there's also some wonderful character acting from Wilfrid Hyde White and Michael Hordern. Margaret Lockwood is particularly sprightly as an entomologist caught up in intrigue behind the Iron Curtain by reporter Dane Clark. Director Roy Ward Baker imparts a jaunty mix of thrills and comedy, but he doesn't always succeed in persuading American actor Clark (making his British screen debut) to drop the Hollywood pizzazz. DP

Margaret Lockwood *Frances Gray* • Dane Clark *Bill Casey* • Marius Goring *Anton Razinski* • Naunton Wayne *Hedgerley* • Wilfrid Hyde White

U SUITABLE FOR ALL   Uc SUITABLE ESPECIALLY FOR YOUNG CHILDREN (DVD ONLY)   PG PARENTAL GUIDANCE   12A UNDER 12s TO BE ACCOMPANIED (CINEMA ONLY)

Luke • Eugene Deckers *Alf* • Olaf Pooley *Assistant* • Michael Hordern *Rawlings* ■ *Dir* Roy Ward Baker • *Scr* Eric Ambler

Highway Patrolman ★★★ 15
Crime thriller 1991 · Mex · Colour · 100min

English director Alex Cox does his cult reputation no harm at all with this evocative Spanish-language thriller, filmed in Mexico. Well-known Latin American actor Roberto Sosa plays an idealistic cop who learns that his new job is not quite the noble career he had in mind. How disillusionment leads to corruption and worse is the prime concern of Cox's morality tale, filmed extensively with a hand-held camera using long single takes. AJ Spanish +subtitles. Sex scenes, violence, swearing. *DVD*

Roberto Sosa *Pedro Rojas* • Bruno Bichir *Anibal* • Zaide Silvia Gutierrez *Griselda* • Vanessa Bauche *Maribel* • Pedro Armendáriz Jr *Sgt Barreras* • Malena Doria *Abuela* ■ *Dir* Alex Cox • *Scr* Lorenzo O'Brien

Highway 61 ★★★
Road movie 1992 · Can · Colour · 110min

This offbeat comedy hasn't the same raw edge as the director and leads' earlier *Roadkill*, but it's dark enough, as rock 'n' roll roadie Valerie Buhagiar persuades good-natured barber Don McKellar to drive her brother's coffin across the Canadian border and down to New Orleans. Everyone along the road has "eccentric" written into their job description, but none of them is quite as weird as Earl Pastko as "Satan". Sparky, quirky and fun. DP Violence, swearing, sex scenes, drug abuse, nudity.

Valerie Buhagiar *Jackie Bangs* • Don McKellar *Pokey Jones* • Earl Pastko *Mr Skin/"Satan"* • Peter Breck *Mr Watson* • Art Bergmann *Otto* • Johnny Askwith *Claude* ■ *Dir* Bruce McDonald • *Scr* Don McKellar, from a story by McKellar, Bruce McDonald, Allan Magee

Highway to Hell ★★★ 15
Horror comedy 1992 · US · Colour · 90min

This oddball horror comedy pits the hordes of hell against a young eloping couple. An uneven contest you might think, but not when it's Chad Lowe whose fiancée is kidnapped by a cop from hell and who has just 24 hours to spring her from the underworld. Sounds daft, but director Ate De Jong delivers enough inventive visuals, including a three-headed dog and literal "hand" cuffs, to keep you decently entertained. Ben Stiller turns up dressed, bizarrely, as Attila the Hun. It's that kind of movie. RS

Patrick Bergin *Beezle* • Chad Lowe *Charlie Sykes* • Kristy Swanson *Rachel Clark* • Adam Storke *Royce* • Pamela Gidley *Clara* • Richard Farnsworth *Sam* • Jarrett Lennon *Adam* • Ben Stiller *Cook/Attila the Hun* ■ *Dir* Ate De Jong • *Scr* Brian Helgeland

Highwaymen ★★ 18
Crime thriller 2003 · US · Colour · 77min

Jim Caviezel stars as a vengeful widower stalking the killer of his wife along dusty highways. His quarry (played by Colm Feore) kills women by running over them with his customised Cadillac El Dorado, as he is too severely disabled to carry out the killings with his own hands. The story begins well enough but then just trots out all the usual serial-killer clichés. The mayhem is more bloodthirsty than chilling, while the vicious tone and tired execution of the film are a turn-off. TH *DVD*

Jim Caviezel *Rennie Cray* • Rhona Mitra *Molly Poole* • Frankie Faison *Will Macklin* • Colm Feore *James Fargo* • Andrea Roth *Alexandra Farrow* • Gordon Currie *Ray Boone* ■ *Dir* Robert Harmon • *Scr* Craig Mitchell, Hans Bauer

La Hija del Engaño ★★★
Drama 1951 · Mex · BW · 80min

Luis Buñuel virtually disowned the four features he produced in Spain for Filmofono. Indeed, he dubbed them "abominable cinema". Yet, having rejuvenated his career with *Los Olvidados*, he returned to one of this neglected quartet for a crowd-pleasing follow-up. Fernando Soler impresses as the bourgeois salesman who gives away the baby daughter he discovers is not his own, only to be reunited, years later, at his seedy nightclub. DP In Spanish.

Fernando Soler *Don Quintin* • Alicia Caro *Marta* • Ruben Rojo *Paco* • Nacho Contra *Jonron* ■ *Dir* Luis Buñuel • *Scr* Luis Alcoriza, Raquel Rojas, from the play *Don Quintin el Amargao* by Carlos Arniches

A Hijacking ★★★★ 15
Thriller 2012 · Den/Nor · Colour · 99min

In this outstanding thriller, a nightmare scenario unfolds when Somali pirates take over a Danish cargo ship in the Indian Ocean. Back in Copenhagen, the shipping company's CEO (*Borgen's* Soren Malling) is determined to stonewall the hijackers' financial demands, leaving the crew (including Pilou Asbaek, another *Borgen* alumnus) to sweat it out. While the film never quite portrays the Somalis as cartoonish bad guys, its focus is more on the fear experienced by the captives. Writer/director Tobias Lindholm calibrates every move with precision and the results are gripping. TJ Danish, English +subtitles. Swearing. *DVD* *Blu*

Pilou Asbaek *Mikkel Hartmann* • Soren Malling *Peter C Ludvigsen* • Dar Salim *Lars Vestergaard* • Roland Moller *Jan* • Gary Skjoldmose Porter *Connor Julian* ■ *Dir/Scr* Tobias Lindholm

Hijacking Hollywood ★★★
Comedy 1997 · US · Colour · 91min

This satire about movie-making has Henry Thomas as a starstruck newcomer who turns up in Hollywood to try to get work from distant relative Mark Metcalf, a major producer. However, fed up with an endless number of menial chores, mostly associated with the new blockbuster *Moby Dick 2: Ahab's Revenge*, Thomas decides to hold the production to ransom by stealing essential master footage. Constantly amusing, this is an independent comedy that deserves greater exposure. DF

Henry Thomas *Kevin Conroy* • Scott Thompson *Russell* • Mark Metcalf *Michael Lawrence* • Neil Mandt *Tad* • Nicole Gian *Sarah Lawrence* • Helen Duffy *Mother* ■ *Dir* Neil Mandt • *Scr* Neil Mandt, Jim Rossow

Hilary and Jackie ★★★★ 15
Biographical drama 1998 · UK · Colour · 117min

Emily Watson excels at portraying the often difficult, selfish and driven cellist Jaqueline du Pré in this controversial biopic of the unusual relationship between her and sister Hilary (Rachel Griffiths). The film is a fascinating, no-holds-barred account of Jackie's musical career and private life. While many column inches have been devoted to the incident when Jackie asks Hilary whether she can sleep with her husband, and then does so, the film - thanks to Watson's mesmerising performance - should be lauded for its riveting realisation of Jackie's talent and almost destructive personality. JB Swearing, sex scenes. *DVD*

Emily Watson *Jacqueline "Jackie" du Pré* • Rachel Griffiths *Hilary du Pré* • David Morrissey *Kiffer Finzi* • James Frain *Daniel Barenboim* • Charles Dance *Derek du Pré* • Celia Imrie *Iris du Pré* • Rupert Penry-Jones *Piers du Pré* • Bill Paterson *Cello teacher* ■ *Dir* Anand Tucker • *Scr* Frank Cottrell Boyce, from the non-fiction book *A Genius in the Family* by Hilary du Pré, Piers du Pré

Hilda Crane ★
Melodrama 1956 · US · Colour · 87min

Free-thinking Hilda (Jean Simmons), who escaped the suffocating clutches of her unloving, rigidly conventional family, returns from New York to her small home town two marriages and several men later. Broke and unhappy, she makes a third "respectable" marriage. This really dismal "woman's picture" is paralysed by a combination of cliché and cop-out. RK

Jean Simmons *Hilda Crane* • Guy Madison *Russell Burns* • Jean-Pierre Aumont *Jacques de Lisle* • Judith Evelyn *Mrs Crane* • Evelyn Varden *Mrs Burns* • Peggy Knudsen *Nell Bromley* • Gregg

Palmer *Dink* • Richard Garrick *Dr Francis* ■ *Dir* Philip Dunne • *Scr* Philip Dunne, from a play by Samuel Raphaelson

The Hill ★★★★★ 12
Prison drama 1965 · UK · BW · 118min

When director Sidney Lumet cast Sean Connery in *The Hill*, the former 007 cast his fake hair to the wind for the first time. It's a terse, tough, absolutely riveting picture about an army prison in North Africa where the inmates are forced to march up and down a phoney hill. It's the Greek myth of Sisyphus with a vengeance, an impudent symbol for British colonial impotence in the 1960s, though it's set during the Second World War. AT Swearing, violence.

Sean Connery *Joe Roberts* • Harry Andrews *Sergeant Major Wilson* • Ian Bannen *Harris* • Roy Kinnear *Monty Bartlett* • Ian Hendry *Staff Sergeant Williams* • Michael Redgrave *Medical officer* • Alfred Lynch *George Stevens* • Ossie Davis *Jacko King* • Jack Watson *Jock McGrath* • Norman Bird *Commandant* ■ *Dir* Sidney Lumet • *Scr* Ray Rigby, RS Allen, from their play

A Hill in Korea ★★ PG
War drama 1956 · UK · BW · 78min

A British patrol is caught behind enemy lines during the Korean War - a conflict given hardly a moment's thought by the British cinema. Badly made on Portuguese locations and containing reams of sermonising dialogue, it's nevertheless made watchable by the presence of future stars Robert Shaw and Michael Caine, who actually spent his national service in Korea and was the film's largely ignored military adviser. AT *DVD*

George Baker *Lieutenant Butler* • Harry Andrews *Sergeant Payne* • Stanley Baker *Corporal Ryker* • Harry Andrews *Private Docker* • Ronald Lewis *Private Wyatt* • Robert Shaw *Lance-Corporal Hodge* • Michael Caine *Private Lockyer* ■ *Dir* Julian Amyes • *Scr* Ian Dalrymple, Anthony Squire

Hill's Angels ★ U
Comedy 1979 · US · Colour · 95min

This slow-moving tale, released in the US as *The North Avenue Irregulars*, is typical of the poor product that Disney came up with during the 1970s. The story, in which naive young priest Edward Herrmann organises his women parishioners to combat organised crime after one of them loses the church funds at the racetrack, is a poorly realised excuse for some madcap chases. SH

Edward Herrmann *Michael Hill* • Barbara Harris *Vickie* • Susan Clark *Anne* • Karen Valentine *Jane* • Michael Constantine *Marv* • Cloris Leachman *Claire* • Patsy Kelly *Rose Rafferty* ■ *Dir* Bruce Bilson • *Scr* Don Tait, from the book *The North Avenue Irregulars* by Rev Albert Fay Hill

The Hills Have Eyes ★★★★ 18
Horror 1977 · US · Colour · 89min

Drawing inspiration from the myth of Sawney Bean and his Scottish cannibal clan, director Wes Craven crafted the best of his early low-budget horror epics. Brutal desert dwellers lay murderous siege to stranded innocent campers in the *Scream* maestro's exploration of depravity and the survival instinct. Using mirror images of two families at the opposing extremes of humanity, Craven's sharp sense of suspense and his willingness to use shock images to their limits carries a potent charge. Craven released an unworthy follow-up in 1985. AJ Violence, swearing, nudity. *DVD*

Susan Lanier *Brenda Carter* • Robert Houston *Bobby Carter* • Martin Speer *Doug Wood* • Russ Grieve *Big Bob Carter* • Dee Wallace *[Dee Wallace Stone] Lynne Wood* • Virginia Vincent *Ethel Carter* • James Whitworth *Jupiter* • Michael Berryman *Pluto* • John Steadman *Fred* • Janus Blythe *Ruby* • Lance Gordon *Mars* • Arthur King *[Peter Locke] Mercury* ■ *Dir/Scr* Wes Craven

The Hills Have Eyes ★★★★ 18
Horror 2006 · US · Colour · 103min

French director Alexandre Aja's first Hollywood feature is a ferociously effective reworking of Wes Craven's 1977 cult classic. Like the original, the tale depicts a vacationing family (headed by Ted Levine and Kathleen Quinlan) falling victim to a murderous clan after breaking down in a stretch of American desert. Here though, the savages are not simply the spawn of inbreeding, but the mutated offspring of miners affected by nuclear testing. There's no let-up, with gore precisely matched by atmospheric detail, yet, while the killers' casualness is deeply disturbing, it's the ordinary family's shocking survival tactics that give the movie its impact. SF *DVD* *Blu*

Aaron Stanford *Doug Bukowski* • Kathleen Quinlan *Ethel Carter* • Vinessa Shaw *Lynne Bukowski* • Emilie de Ravin *Brenda Carter* • Dan Byrd *Bobby Carter* • Robert Joy *Lizard* • Ted Levine *Bob Carter* • Desmond Askew *Big Brain* • Billy Drago *Jupiter* ■ *Dir* Alexandre Aja • *Scr* Alexandre Aja, Grégory Levasseur, from the 1977 film by Wes Craven

The Hills Have Eyes II ★★★ 18
Horror 2007 · US · Colour · 86min

Both Wes Craven's 1977 original and its 2006 remake were outstanding horror movies, but while the frightening viciousness on display here is never less than compelling, Martin Weisz's sequel lacks the suspense of its predecessors. A group of rookie soldiers mounts a search and rescue mission for some missing atomic scientists in the mountainous New Mexico desert. Little do they know that mutant cannibals lurk in them there hills. Series creator Craven and his son Jonathan share the screenplay credits, but their intended Iraq War allegory is hampered by macho posturing and cartoonish dialogue. However, the raw effectiveness of this brutal *Southern Comfort* retread is undeniable. AJ *DVD* *Blu*

Michael McMillian *PFC "Napoleon" Napoli* • Jessica Stroup *PFC Amber Johnson* • Jacob Vargas *PFC "Crank"* • Flex Alexander *Sergeant Jeffrey "Sarge" Millstone* • Lee Thompson Young *PFC Delmar* • Daniella Alonso *PFC Missy* • Eric Edelstein *Spitter* ■ *Dir* Martin Weisz • *Scr* Wes Craven, Jonathan Craven

The Hills of Donegal ★★
Musical romantic drama 1947 · UK · BW · 85min

A few sentimental songs enliven the opening segment of this musical romance, as Dinah Sheridan bids farewell to the stage to marry her singing partner's cousin. But no sooner have she and John Bentley settled in Donegal than he's forced to take drastic steps to prevent the tempestuous Tamara Desni from raking up an old affair. Melodramatic tarraddiddle. DP

Dinah Sheridan *Eileen Hannay* • James Etherington *Michael O'Keefe* • Moore Marriott *Old Jake* • John Bentley *Terry O'Keefe* • Irene Handl *Mrs Mactavish* • Tamara Desni *Carole Wells* ■ *Dir* John F Argyle [John Argyle] • *Scr* John Dryden

Hills of Home ★★★ U
Adventure 1948 · US · Colour · 96min

The world's most famous collie stars in a reworking of the canine classic *Greyfriars Bobby*, itself a source for the following year's *Challenge to Lassie*. Edmund Gwenn is the kindly Scottish doctor who tries to cure our heroine of her aversion to water, veteran Donald Crisp plays his friend, and Janet Leigh is simply lovely to look at. TS

Edmund Gwenn *Dr William MacLure* • Donald Crisp *Drumsheugh* • Tom Drake *Tammas Milton* • Janet Leigh *Margit Mitchell* • Rhys Williams *Mr Milton* • Reginald Owen *Hopps* ■ *Dir* Fred Wilcox [Fred M Wilcox] • *Scr* William Ludwig, from the sketches *Doctor of the Old School* by Ian MacLaren

Hills of Kentucky ★★★
Silent adventure 1927 · US · BW · 75min

One-time prop boy, director Howard Bretherton was credited with over 100 features during his career, including several B-westerns with William "Hopalong" Boyd and Buck Jones. This Rin-Tin-Tin adventure was only his second outing and his inexperience occasionally shows through. Yet the action sequences are thrilling, particularly the legendary plunge into the waterfall by the dog star to rescue Dorothy Dwan from certain death. DP

Jason Robards [Jason Robards Sr] *Steve Harley* • Dorothy Dwan *Janet* • Tom Santschi *Ben Harley* • Nanette ■ *Dir* Howard Bretherton • *Scr* Edward Clark, from the story *The Untamed Heart* by Dorothy Yost

The Hills Run Red ★★★ 12
Spaghetti western   1966 · It · Colour · 85min

It's original title *Un Fiume di Dollari* (*A River of Dollars*) may suggest a cheap Sergio Leone cash-in, but this stands up on its own merits. Hero Thomas Hunter has the look of a Clint Eastwood clone, but rather than playing strong and silent, he's an emotionally unstable mess. Double-crossed by his partner and grieving for his wife, Hunter is a man driven by revenge. The plotting is a little ragged, but the pace is lively, the action exciting and the score (Ennio Morricone under the alias Leo Nichols) rousing. JH English, Italian dubbed. Some violence. *DVD*

Thomas Hunter *Jerry Brewster* • Henry Silva *Garcia Mendez* • Dan Duryea *Getz* • Nando Gazzolo *Ken Seagull* • Nicoletta Machiavelli *Mary Ann* ■ *Dir* Lee W Beaver [Carlo Lizzani] • *Scr* Dean Craig [Piero Regnoli], from his story • *Music* Leo Nichols [Ennio Morricone]

The Hillside Strangler ★★ 18
Horror thriller based on a true story
2004 · US/UK · Colour · 93min

C Thomas Howell and Nicholas Turturro get their aspiring pimp attitudes exactly right as cousins Kenneth Bianchi and Angelo Buono who collectively became known as "The Hillside Strangler" for their series of murders in Hollywood in the late 1970s. Little else in director Chuck Parello's depressingly crude case history makes this tedious trawl through the sleazy underbelly of Tinseltown worthwhile. The murders are depicted clinically, and the viewer must decide if this is a fair factual representation or just tasteless censor baiting. AJ *DVD*

C Thomas Howell *Kenneth Bianchi* • Nicholas Turturro *Angelo Buono* • Allison Lange *Claire Shelton* • Lin Shaye *Jenny Buono* • Kent Masters-King *Gabrielle* • Cletus Young *Charlie Lloyd* • Roz Witt *Frances Bianchi* ■ *Dir* Chuck Parello [Charles Parello] • *Scr* Stephen Johnston, Chuck Parello [Charles Parello]

Himalaya ★★★ PG
Adventure drama
1999 · Nep/Swi/Fr/UK · Tinted · 104min

Travel writer Eric Valli made his feature debut with this Oscar-nominated ethnographical odyssey, which was released in the States as *Caravan*. Drawing on his own experiences, the wizened Thilen Lhondup gives a supremely naturalistic performance as the Nepalese salt trader who relies on traditional wisdom to get his yak herd to market across some of the world's most inhospitable terrain. Yet, for all Thilen's simple courage and the visual splendour of the widescreen mountainscapes, this poetic tribute to the hardy spirit of a remarkable people is short on dramatic incident. DP Tibetan +subtitles.

Thilen Lhondup *Tinlé* • Lhakpa Tsamchoe *Péma* • Gurgon Kyap *Karma* • Karma Tensing Nyima Lama *Norbou* • Karma Wangiel *Passang* ■ *Dir* Eric Valli • *Scr* Nathalie Azoulai, Olivier Dazat, Louis Gardel, Jean-Claude Guillebaud, Jacques Perrin • *Cinematographers* Eric Guichard, Jean-Paul Meurisse

Himizu ★★★★ 18
Drama   2011 · Jpn · Colour · 129min

This drama about a teenage boy trying to keep body and soul together in the wake of Japan's 2011 tsunami was shot in the devastated prefecture shortly after the event itself. Shota Sometani plays 15-year-old schoolboy Sumida who tries to make a go of the family boat-hire business, but his drunken father would rather see his son kill himself for the insurance pay-out. Writer/director Sion Sono's film delivers a broadside against the self-interest and complacency of the older generation. It's

bitter and angry fare at times, yet Sometani's committed central performance is truly touching. TJ Japanese +subtitles. Swearing.

Shota Sometani *Sumida* • Fumi Nikaido *Keiko* • Tetsu Watanabe *Shozo* • Mitsuru Fukikoshi *Keita Tamura* • Megumi Kagurazaka *Keiko Tamura* ■ *Dir* Sion Sono • *Scr* Sion Sono, from a comic book by Minoru Furuya

The Hindenburg ★★ PG
Disaster drama
1975 · US · Colour and BW · 120min

The 1970s cycle of disaster movies came crashing down amid the debris of this box-office bomb that has all the pace and substance of the famous German airship itself. In trying to combine their sabotage theory with the kind of soap-opera characterisation established in *Airport*, the scriptwriters have succeeded only in producing a bore. However, the mix of actual newsreel with new footage at the climax is well done. DP *DVD*

George C Scott *Colonel Ritter* • Anne Bancroft *The Countess* • William Atherton *Boerth* • Roy Thinnes *Martin Vogel* • Gig Young *Edward Douglas* • Burgess Meredith *Emilio Pajetta* • Charles Durning *Capt Pruss* ■ *Dir* Robert Wise • *Scr* Nelson Gidding, Richard A Levinson, William Link, from the book by Michael M Mooney

Hindle Wakes ★★★ U
Silent drama   1927 · UK · BW · 115min

Estelle Brody excels in this adaptation of the stage hit, as the mill girl seduced by a tycoon's son on the works' outing to Blackpool. With its homespun morality echoing FW Murnau's *Sunrise* and its pert heroine resembling Clara Bow in *It*, Maurice Elvey's class-conscious drama is very much in keeping with the cinematic and societal trends of 1927. It lacks the sophistication of any of the above, but it marks a major advance on silent technique and presages the docudramatic realism that would continue to characterise British movies. DP

Estelle Brody *Fanny Hawthorne* • Norman McKinnel *Nathaniel Jeffcoate* • Humberston Wright *Chris Hawthorne* • Marie Ault *Mrs Hawthorne* • John Stuart *Alan Jeffcoate* • Irene Rooke *Mrs Jeffcoate* ■ *Dir* Maurice Elvey • *Scr* Victor Saville, from the play by Stanley Houghton

Hindle Wakes ★★★ PG
Romantic drama   1931 · UK · BW · 70min

Having twice been adapted for the silent screen, Stanley Houghton's play was accorded its talkie debut in this solid, but visually conservative presentation. Making only her second picture, Belle Chrystall turns in a remarkably mature performance as the Lancashire mill lass who defies convention by refusing to marry the boss's son after a scandalous holiday romance. John Stuart ably reprises the caddish role he'd played in Maurice Elvey's 1927 version, while Sybil Thorndike and Edmund Gwenn provide practised support. DP

Belle Chrystall *Fanny Hawthorne* • Sybil Thorndike *Mrs Hawthorne* • John Stuart *Alan Jeffcoate* • Muriel Angelus *Beatrice Farrar* • Edmund Gwenn *Chris Hawthorne* • Mary Clare *Mrs Jeffcoate* • Norman McKinnel *Nat Jeffcoate* ■ *Dir* Victor Saville • *Scr* Victor Saville, Angus MacPhail, from the play *Hindle Wakes* by Stanley Houghton

Hindle Wakes ★★ PG
Romantic melodrama   1952 · UK · BW · 85min

This is a weak adaptation of Stanley Houghton's theatrical warhorse about cross-class love in the early years of the last century. The story of a Lancashire mill lass who refuses to marry the boss's son after spending her summer factory holiday with him at Blackpool is hardly likely to raise the eyebrows of the prudish or the pulse rate of the thrill-seeker. DP *DVD*

Lisa Daniely *Jenny Hawthorne* • Leslie Dwyer *Chris Hawthorne* • Brian Worth *Alan Jeffcoate* • Sandra Dorne *Mary Hollins* • Ronald Adam *Nat Jeffcoate* • Joan Hickson *Mrs Hawthorne* • Bill Travers *Bob* ■ *Dir* Arthur Crabtree • *Scr* John Baines, from the play by Stanley Houghton

Hippocrates ★★★ 15
Drama   2014 · Fr · Colour · 97min

Darkly comic, but politically gauche, medic-cum-director Thomas Lilti's second feature provides a stark insight into the demands made of junior doctors in a health system hamstrung by staff shortages and antiquated apparatus. Drawing on his own experiences, Lilti pitches intern Vincent Lacoste into a Parisian ward run by his own father (Jacques Gamblin) and opens up a series of melodramatic plot strands that help to expose the long hours and appalling living conditions endured by 20-somethings who party hard after being left to make tough calls by administrators more concerned with bottom lines than flatlines. DP French +subtitles. Swearing, sexual references. *DVD*

Vincent Lacoste *Benjamin* • Jacques Gamblin *Dr Barois* • Reda Kateb *Abdel* • Marianne Denicourt *Denormandy* • Félix Moati *Stéphane* ■ *Dir* Thomas Lilti • *Scr* Pierre Chosson, Baya Kasmi, Julien Lilti, Thomas Lilti

The Hired Gun ★★ U
Western   1957 · US · BW · 63min

It makes a bit of a change to find a western in which a female plays the key role, and Anne Francis makes the most of her opportunity as the woman, wrongly convicted of murder, who cheats the hangman by escaping across the border into Mexico. Co-star Rory Calhoun is the gunman hired to bring her back, who comes to believe in her innocence and sets about proving it. AE

Rory Calhoun *Gil McCord* • Anne Francis *Ellen Beldon* • Vince Edwards *Kell Beldon* • John Litel *Mace Beldon* • Chuck Connors *Judd Farrow* • Robert Burton *Nathan Conroy* ■ *Dir* Ray Nazarro • *Scr* David Lang, Buckley Angell

The Hired Hand ★★★★ 12
Western   1971 · US · Colour · 87min

In addition to starring here, Peter Fonda also makes a fine job of directing this cold, almost existential western about a wife (the superb Verna Bloom) torn between two drifters, her husband Fonda and the older Warren Oates. This has all the clever bleakness and sense of destiny now associated with its writer, Alan Sharp, and is richly rewarding in its portrayal of the reality of frontier life. TS Violence. *DVD*

Peter Fonda *Harry Collings* • Warren Oates *Arch Harris* • Verna Bloom *Hannah Collings* • Robert Pratt *Dan Griffin* • Severn Darden *McVey* • Ted Markland *Luke* • Owen Orr *Mace* ■ *Dir* Peter Fonda • *Scr* Alan Sharp

Hired to Kill ★ 18
Action adventure   1990 · US · Colour · 92min

Brian Thompson is cast as a soldier of fortune whose mission to overthrow a tinpot island dictator involves disguising himself as a gay fashion designer with a hit squad of female mercenaries all dressed as fashion models. Happens everyday, right? Stalwarts Oliver Reed – relishing his role as a sadistic secret police chief – and George Kennedy were somehow persuaded to appear. RS

Brian Thompson *Frank Ryan* • Oliver Reed *Michael Bartos* • José Ferrer *Rallis* • George Kennedy *Thomas* • Michelle Moffett *Ana* ■ *Dir* Nico Mastorakis, Peter Rader • *Scr* Nico Mastorakis, Kirk Ellis, Fred C Perry, from a story by Nico Mastorakis

Hired Wife ★★★
Comedy drama   1940 · US · BW · 95min

Indispensable, caring, efficient secretary Rosalind Russell proposes a marriage of convenience to her boss, Brian Aherne, so that his tax situation can benefit by putting his property in his wife's name. He's preoccupied with advertising model Virginia Bruce, but when she disappears into the arms of John Carroll, Aherne accepts Russell's offer. What follows is comfortingly predictable in this slimly plotted romantic comedy, elevated into delightful froth by Aherne's charm and Russell's splendid performance. RK

Rosalind Russell *Kendal Browning* • Brian Aherne *Stephen Dexter* • Virginia Bruce *Phyllis Walden* • Robert Benchley *Roger Van Horn* • John Carroll *Jose* ■ *Dir* William A Seiter • *Scr* Richard Connell, Gladys Lehman, from a story by George Beck

The Hireling ★★★ PG
Period drama   1973 · UK · Colour · 103min

Set in the socially divided Britain of 1923, this adaptation of an LP Hartley novel makes up in elegance and ideas for what it lacks in drama. Neurotic, upper-class Sarah Miles hires the services of chauffeur Robert Shaw, and their working relationship helps to restore some balance in her fraught existence. However, his adoration for his mistress soon adds a touch of agitation to the mix. Director Alan Bridges's period piece has a topical relevance about who is really in the driving seat, but the drama is too crass to be affecting. TH *DVD*

Robert Shaw *Leadbetter* • Sarah Miles *Lady Franklin* • Peter Egan *Captain Hugh Cantrip* • Elizabeth Sellars *Lady Franklin's mother* • Caroline Mortimer *Connie* • Patricia Lawrence *Mrs Hansen* ■ *Dir* Alan Bridges • *Scr* Wolf Mankowitz, from the novel by LP Hartley

Hiroshima, Mon Amour ★★★★ PG
Drama   1959 · Fr · BW · 86min

Alain Resnais's first feature stunned audiences in 1959, and together with Jean-Luc Godard's *A Bout de Souffle* and François Truffaut's *The 400 Blows* it heralded the French New Wave. The story tells of a French actress who has an affair in Hiroshima with a Japanese architect while recalling an earlier, wartime affair with a German soldier. Marguerite Duras's script is about collaboration as well as reconciliation, while Resnais weaves time zones, silence and sound, and juxtaposes lush images of seduction with shocking documentary footage of survivors of the atomic bomb. AT French, Japanese, English +subtitles. *DVD* *BL*

Emmanuelle Riva *Elle* • Eiji Okada *Lui* • Bernard Fresson *L'Allemand* • Stella Dassas *La Mère* • Pierre Barbaud *Le Père* ■ *Dir* Alain Resnais • *Scr* Marguerite Duras

His and Hers ★ PG
Comedy   1960 · UK · BW · 79min

Probably the main amusement for viewers of this comedy will be in spotting the familiar faces in the cast, not least Oliver Reed as a poet and Kenneth Williams as an unlikely policeman. The under-nourished screenplay has Terry-Thomas as a writer who transforms from silly ass to recognisable human being when forced to confront reality during a research trip on Bedouins in the desert. BB *DVD* *BL*

Terry-Thomas *Reggie Blake* • Janette Scott *Fran Blake* • Wilfrid Hyde White *Charles Dunton* • Nicole Maurey *Simone Rolfe* • Joan Sims *Hortense* • Kenneth Connor *Harold* • Kenneth Williams *Policeman* • Oliver Reed *Poet* ■ *Dir* Brian Desmond Hurst • *Scr* Stanley Mann, Jan Lowell, Mark Lowell

His Brother's Wife ★★★
Melodrama   1936 · US · BW · 91min

When Robert Taylor's medical scientist goes off to the jungle to find a cure for spotted fever, Barbara Stanwyck, with whom he has had a whirlwind romance, is so enraged that she takes revenge by marrying his brother. Eventually, of course, she repents and turns up in the tropics to assist her true love, whereupon the melodrama escalates into situations so absurd and dialogue so risible as to become treasurable. The stars play this hokum for all its worth. RK

Barbara Stanwyck *Rita Wilson Claybourne* • Robert Taylor (1) *Chris Claybourne* • Jean Hersholt *Professor "Pop" Fahrenheim* • Joseph Calleia *"Fish-Eye"* • John Eldredge *Tom Claybourne* • Samuel S Hinds *Dr Claybourne* ■ *Dir* WS Van Dyke • *Scr* Leon Gordon, John Meehan, from a story by George Auerbach

His Butler's Sister ★★ U
Musical comedy   1943 · US · BW · 89min

Deanna Durbin stars as a small-town girl with ambitions to be a great singer. She goes to New York to seek the help of composer Franchot Tone, only to be put to work as a maid by his butler, Pat O'Brien. Complications ensue before the inevitable resolution. The star gets to sing several numbers (including *Nessun Dorma*) in this delightful nonsense, which Frank Borzage directs in the right spirit. **RK** *DVD*

Deanna Durbin *Ann Carter* · Franchot Tone *Charles Gerard* · Pat O'Brien *Martin* · Akim Tamiroff *Popoff* · Walter Catlett *Kalb* · Elsa Janssen *Severina* ■ *Dir* Frank Borzage · *Scr* Samuel Hoffenstein, Betty Reinhardt

His Double Life ★★
Comedy drama   1933 · US · BW · 63min

Delightfully fussy character actor Roland Young is the reclusive painter who adopts the identity of his dead valet, and former silent star Lillian Gish makes an isolated comeback as the woman who weds the already-married Young under his assumed identity. However, the best version of this oft-filmed story is unquestionably *Holy Matrimony* with Monty Woolley and Gracie Fields. **AE**

Roland Young *Priam Farrel* · Lillian Gish *Alice* · Montague Love [Montagu Love] *Duncan Farrel* · Lumsden Hare *Oxford* · Lucy Beaumont *Mrs Leek* ■ *Dir* Arthur Hopkins · *Scr* Arthur Hopkins, Clara Beranger, from the play *The Great Adventure* by Arnold Bennett, from his novel *Buried Alive*

His Excellency ★★ U
Comedy   1952 · UK · BW · 80min

Robert Hamer and WP Lipscomb fired off another salvo in the Ealing assault on the bastion of privilege in this adaptation of an Adrian Alington novel that had previously been reworked for the stage by Dorothy and Campbell Christie. It's a classic Ealing scenario, as ex-docker Eric Portman is selected over blueblood Cecil Parker to become the new governor of the Mediterranean colony of Arista, but the tone of faint jingoism and patronising benevolence is decidedly off-putting. **DP** *DVD*

Eric Portman *George Harrison* · Cecil Parker *Sir James Kirkman* · Helen Cherry *Lady Kirkman* · Susan Stephen *Peggy Harrison* ■ *Dir* Robert Hamer · *Scr* Robert Hamer, WP Lipscomb, from the play *His Excellency* by Campbell & Dorothy Christie, from the novel *His Excellency* by Adrian Alington

His Girl Friday ★★★★★ U
Classic screwball comedy   1939 · US · BW · 91min

The fastest-talking comedy in the history of Hollywood, this brilliant reworking of the classic newspaper play *The Front Page* by director Howard Hawks is the perfect vehicle for Cary Grant (never better) and Rosalind Russell (never tougher) and is still achingly funny today. Limited for most of the time to two sets (the newspaper office and the pressroom at the jail), the film's great strength is the interplay between the two leads, as former spouses who are having a tough time remaining apart. It also boasts one of the blackest comedy situations ever, as a small-time loser finds himself up against city corruption and imminent execution. Clever, witty and extremely satisfying. **TS** *DVD*

Cary Grant *Walter Burns* · Rosalind Russell *Hildy Johnson* · Ralph Bellamy *Bruce Baldwin* · Gene Lockhart *Sheriff Peter B Hartwell* · Porter Hall *Murphy* · Ernest Truex *Roy B Bensinger* · Cliff Edwards *Endicott* · Clarence Kolb *Mayor* · Billy Gilbert *Joe Pettibone* ■ *Dir* Howard Hawks · *Scr* Charles Lederer, from the play *The Front Page* by Ben Hecht, Charles MacArthur

His Kind of Woman ★★★ 12
Film noir   1951 · US · BW · 114min

Made during the Howard Hughes regime at RKO, this unwieldy melodrama shows signs of the great one's tinkerings: scenes don't make sense, some exteriors were obviously filmed indoors, cast members come and go.

Robert Mitchum (looking bored) plays a gambler offered money to go to Mexico, who gets involved with chanteuse Jane Russell and actor Vincent Price (at his posturing best). Despite its flaws, the whole is still entertaining, with a fine sense of parody that has won the movie quite a cult following. **TS**

Robert Mitchum *Dan Milner* · Jane Russell *Lenore Brent* · Vincent Price *Mark Cardigan* · Tim Holt *Bill Lusk* · Charles McGraw *Thompson* · Raymond Burr *Nick Ferraro* ■ *Dir* John Farrow · *Scr* Frank Fenton, Jack Leonard, from the story *Star Sapphire* by Gerald Drayson Adams

His Lordship ★★★ U
Crime drama   1936 · UK · BW · 68min

Character star George Arliss's great days were behind him when he returned to his native England to take on a dual role in this political potboiler, which is only held together by the sheer strength of his presence. The film's stage derivation seeps through the whole enterprise, and the combination of *Boys' Own* heroics and the politics of war is as hard to take today as it probably was then. **TS**

George Arliss *Richard/Lord Dunchester* · Romilly Lunge *Bill Howard* · René Ray *Vera* · Jessie Winter *Lady Dunchester* · John Ford *Ibrahim* ■ *Dir* Herbert Mason · *Scr* Maude T Howell, L du Garde Peach, Edwin Greenwood, from the play *The Nelson Touch* by Neil Grant

His Majesty O'Keefe ★★★ U
Swashbuckling adventure
1953 · US · Colour · 89min

Burt Lancaster is in fine, devil-may-care form as a sea captain teaching islanders how to be enterprising and beat off pirates, while he himself picks up a Polynesian girl (Joan Rice) to be queen to his king. Its colonial message – naive natives ruled by intrepid white man – is dubiously patronising, but its good-natured breeziness defies serious social criticism. **TH**

Burt Lancaster *Captain David O'Keefe* · Joan Rice *Dalabo* · André Morell *Alfred Tetins* · Abraham Sofaer *Fatumak* · Archie Savage *Booguloo* · Benson Fong *Mr Chou* · Teresa Prendergast *Kakofel* ■ *Dir* Byron Haskin · *Scr* Borden Chase, James Hill, from a novel by Lawrence Klingman, Gerald Green

His New Job ★★★
Silent comedy   1915 · US · BW · 32min

In this uncharacteristic Chaplin short, his first for the Essanay studio, he disregarded the company's highly organised working methods and improvised a comedy about film-making based on what he saw around him. It shows Charlie seeking a job at a studio, quashing competition from cross-eyed Ben Turpin, and creating mayhem on the set of a costume film where Gloria Swanson (uncredited) is among the extras. This was Chaplin's first collaboration with cameraman Rollie Totheroh, with whom he worked regularly for the next 30 years. **AE**

Charles Chaplin *Film Extra* · Ben Turpin *Film Extra* · Charlotte Mineau *Actress* · Leo White · Gloria Swanson ■ *Dir/Scr* Charles Chaplin

His Woman ★★
Drama   1931 · US · BW · 76min

Gary Cooper, the unlikely captain of a tramp steamer, rescues a baby from a drifting vessel at sea and decides to keep it. Advertising for female help on the return journey to America, he gets Claudette Colbert, a girl with a shady past. The script it mediocre, as is the direction, while Cooper is at his most expressionless. Colbert, though, gives it everything, as usual. **RK**

Gary Cooper *Captain Sam Whalan* · Claudette Colbert *Sally Clark* · Averell Harris *Mate Gatson* · Richard Spiro *Sammy the baby* · Hamtree Harrington *Aloysius* · Sidney Easton *Mark* · Douglass Dumbrille *Alisandroe* · Raquel Davido *Maria Estella* ■ *Dir* Edward Sloman · *Scr* Adelaide Heilbron, Melville Baker, from the novel *The Sentimentalists* by Dale Collins

Histoire de Marie et Julien ★★★★ 15
Romantic drama   2003 · Fr/It · Colour · 144min

Jacques Rivette abandoned his *Scenes from the Parallel Life* quartet having only completed *Duelle* (1975) and *Noroît* (1976). But this reworking of the third instalment owes as much to *film noir* and classic horror as it does to its predecessors. Chronicling the romance between clock-repairer Jerzy Radziwilowicz and the mysterious Emmanuelle Béart, this is as formally and intellectually challenging as Rivette's best work. But what is most noteworthy is the intensity of the performances and the sophisticated manner in which Béart's distracted ethereality and Radziwilowicz's relationship with antique dealer Anne Brochet are established. **DP** French +subtitles *DVD*

Emmanuelle Béart *Marie* · Jerzy Radziwilowicz *Julien* · Anne Brochet *Madame X* · Bettina Kee *Adrienne* · Olivier Cruveiller *Editor* · Nicole Garcia *Friend* ■ *Dir* Jacques Rivette · *Scr* Jacques Rivette, Pascal Bonitzer, Christine Laurent · *Cinematographer* William Lubtchansky

Une Histoire Simple ★★★
Drama   1978 · Fr · Colour · 107min

Although this study of bourgeois foibles received an Oscar nomination for best foreign film, director Claude Sautet is rather guilty of revisiting old haunts without having anything particularly new to show us. However, no one depicts the suffocating ennui of a seemingly successful life with such surety, and here he's excellently served by Romy Schneider, who won a César for her portrayal of a liberated woman who aborts lover Claude Brasseur's baby only to become pregnant by ex-husband Bruno Cremer. **DP** French +subtitles

Romy Schneider *Marie* · Bruno Cremer *Georges* · Claude Brasseur *Serge* · Arlette Bonnard *Gabrielle* · Sophie Daumier *Esther* · Eva Darlan *Anna* · Francine Bergé *Francine* · Roger Pigaut *Jérôme* · Madeleine Robinson *Marie's mother* ■ *Dir* Claude Sautet · *Scr* Claude Sautet, Jean-Loup Dabadie

Histoires Extraordinaires ★★★★ 18
Portmanteau horror
1967 · Fr/It · Colour · 115min

Out of the three episodes based on the macabre tales by Edgar Allan Poe, the third – the only modern-day one, directed by Federico Fellini – is far and away the best, though it's pretty familiar Fellini territory. It stars Terence Stamp as a British actor in Rome who bets his head he can escape having an accident. Louis Malle's telling of *William Wilson*, about a man (Alain Delon) who kills his doppelganger, is handsome and straightforward; while Roger Vadim saw to it that his wife Jane Fonda wore revealing clothes and caused an incestuous *frisson* by casting her brother Peter as her lover. **RB**

Jane Fonda *Countess Frederica Metzengerstein* · Peter Fonda *Baron Wilhem* · Alain Delon *William Wilson/His double* · Brigitte Bardot *Giuseppina* · Terence Stamp *Toby Dammit* · Vincent Price *Narrator* ■ *Dir* Roger Vadim, Louis Malle, Federico Fellini · *Scr* Roger Vadim, Pascal Cousin, from the story *Metzengerstein*; Louis Malle, Daniel Boulanger, from the story *William Wilson*; Federico Fellini, Bernardino Zapponi, from the story *Never Bet the Devil Your Head*; all by Edgar Allan Poe

Historias Mínimas ★★★★ 15
Comedy drama   2002 · Arg/Sp · Colour · 87min

More than a decade after missing his step with *Eversmile, New Jersey*, Argentinian Carlos Sorin regains his sense of direction with this beguiling road movie. Making evocative use of the sprawling Patagonian landscape, he interweaves a trio of intimate narratives that force viewers to re-assess their priorities by reducing life to its essentials. Travelling salesman Javier Lombardo's bid to woo a widow with a birthday cake for her child and cash-strapped mother Javiera Bravo's game-show experience are droll and shrewd. But

the film's compassionate humanity is best exhibited in myopic octogenarian Antonio Benedictis's journey of atonement in search of his missing dog. **DP** Spanish +subtitles. *DVD*

Javier Lombardo *Roberto* · Antonio Benedictis *Don Justo* · Javiera Bravo *Mariá Flores* · Francis Sandoval *Mariá's daughter* ■ *Dir* Carlos Sorin · *Scr* Pablo Solarz

The History Boys ★★★★ 15
Drama   2006 · UK/US · Colour · 107min

Alan Bennett's hit stage play, about Sheffield grammar school boys being drilled for their Oxbridge exams, makes an efficient transition to the big screen. Director Nicholas Hytner wisely opts to change as little as possible, using the original cast and resisting the urge to open up the material cinematically. This brilliantly serves Bennett's screenplay, which is a masterpiece of wit and intellect; a perfectly balanced blend undercut with the darker subject of general studies teacher Hector's (Richard Griffiths) sexual attraction to the boys. Which leads to this film's only flaw: there's something implausible about these pupils' nonchalance towards homosexuality and their teacher's attentions to them. Still, it's not a documentary, and this niggle is more than made up for by the first-rate performances. **AS** Swearing, sexual references. *DVD*

Richard Griffiths *Hector* · Frances de la Tour *Dorothy Lintott* · Stephen Campbell Moore *Irwin* · Samuel Barnett *Posner* · Dominic Cooper *Dakin* · James Corden *Timms* · Jamie Parker *Scripps* · Russell Tovey *Rudge* · Penelope Wilton *Mrs Bibby* · Clive Merrison *Headmaster* ■ *Dir* Nicholas Hytner · *Scr* Alan Bennett, from his play

History Is Made at Night ★★★
Drama   1937 · US · BW · 97min

This bizarre piece of fluff from melodrama maestro Frank Borzage finds Charles Boyer in good form as a waiter, jewel thief and restaurateur who saves Jean Arthur from her abusive marriage to shipping magnate Colin Clive. The story moves from Paris to New York, involves kidnapping and seduction, and ends rather darkly, on a sinking ship, with a confession of murder followed by a suicide. It's a lot to fit in one movie, which might explain the various loose ends. **AT**

Charles Boyer *Paul Dumond* · Jean Arthur *Irene Vail* · Leo Carrillo *Cesare* · Colin Clive *Bruce Vail* · Ivan Lebedeff *Michael* · George Meeker *Norton* ■ *Dir* Frank Borzage · *Scr* Gene Towne, Graham Baker, from their story

History Is Made at Night ★
Spy comedy
1999 · UK/Fr/Ger/Fin · Colour · 94min

It's hard to believe that the director of *Darkness in Tallinn* could have made this dismal spy caper. Ilkka Jarvilaturi's ill-conceived comedy manages the seemingly impossible feat of making Irène Jacob look incompetent. Besides disrobing at regular intervals, she overplays every situation, although she's not helped by the usually reliable Bill Pullman, who resorts to mugging. **DP**

Bill Pullman *Harry* · Irène Jacob *Natasha* · Bruno Kirby *Max* · Glenn Plummer *Dave* · Udo Kier *Ivan* ■ *Dir* Ilkka Jarvilaturi · *Scr* Patrick Amos, from a story by Jean-Pierre Gorin, Amos

The History of Mr Polly ★★★★ U
Period drama   1948 · UK · BW · 91min

John Mills gives one of the finest performances of his career as the draper whose search for contentment involves him in an unhappy marriage and a feud at a country inn. The supporting cast is impeccable, with Betty Ann Davies neatly switching from giggling cousin to grousing wife, and Moore Marriott inch-perfect as wizened Uncle Pentstemon. The scenes with Sally Ann Howes on the wall don't quite come off, but the encounters with

Mills's ghastly family and the duel with Finlay Currie are well staged. DP **DVD**

John Mills *Alfred* Polly • Sally Ann Howes *Christabel* • Megs Jenkins *Plump woman* • Finlay Currie *Uncle Jim* • Diana Churchill *Annie* • Betty Ann Davies *Miriam* • Edward Chapman *Mr Johnson* • Shelagh Fraser *Minnie* • Moore Marriott *Uncle Pentstemon* ■ *Dir* Anthony Pelissier • *Scr* Anthony Pelissier, from the novel by HG Wells

History of the World Part 1
★★★ **15**

Comedy 1981 · US · Colour · 88min

Mel Brooks's full-frontal assault on how we got where we are today has something to offend everyone: Moses drops five of the original 15 commandments and Brooks, as a waiter at the Last Supper, asks: "Are you all together or is it separate cheques?" From a hilarious Spanish Inquisition number to a "Jews in space" routine, it's vaudeville at its most vulgar with broader strokes than Monty Python, but without the smugness. So what happened to *History of the World Part 2*? Don't ask. TH Swearing. **DVD**

Mel Brooks *Moses/Comicus/Torquemada/Jacques/King Louis XVI* • Dom DeLuise *Emperor Nero* • Madeline Kahn *Empress Nympho* • Harvey Korman *Count de Monet* • Cloris Leachman *Madame de Farge* • Ron Carey *Swiftus* • Gregory Hines *Josephus* • Pamela Stephenson *Mademoiselle Rimbaud* • Sid Caesar *Chief caveman* • Orson Welles *Narrator* ■ *Dir/Scr* Mel Brooks

A History of Violence
★★★★ **18**

Thriller 2005 · US/Ger · Colour · 91min

Although he plays it surprisingly straight for once, director David Cronenberg nevertheless brings a dry wit and a satiric edge to this dark thriller. Life is sweet for local diner owner Viggo Mortensen and his wife Maria Bello. But when Mortensen becomes a media hero after preventing a hold-up, a disfigured thug (Ed Harris) surfaces with henchmen in tow. Insisting Mortensen is his old Mob buddy, he manages to cast doubt even in Bello's mind, creating a central "is-he-or-isn't-he" mystery that's deliciously teased out. LF Swearing, violence. **DVD** **Blu**

Viggo Mortensen *Tom Stall* • Maria Bello *Edie Stall* • William Hurt *Richie Cusack* • Ashton Holmes *Jack Stall* • Stephen McHattie *Leland Jones* • Peter MacNeill *Sheriff Sam Carney* • Ed Harris *Carl Fogarty* • Heidi Hayes *Sarah Stall* • Greg Bryk *William "Billy" Orser* ■ *Dir* David Cronenberg • *Scr* Josh Olson, from the graphic novel by John Wagner, Vince Locke

Hit!
★★★ **18**

Crime drama 1973 · US · Colour · 129min

This is one of the better blaxploitation thrillers directed by the frustratingly erratic Sidney J Furie. There are shades of *French Connection II* in the plotting, which finds lawman Billy Dee Williams taking on the Gallic gangsters he blames for his daughter's death. However, this more than stands up in its own right, with Williams's compelling turn well supported by Richard Pryor. It's a touch overlong, but riveting nevertheless. JF

Billy Dee Williams *Nick Allen* • Richard Pryor *Mike Willmer* • Paul Hampton *Barry Strong* • Gwen Welles *Sherry Nielson* • Warren Kemmerling *Dutch Schiller* • Janet Brandt *Ida* ■ *Dir* Sidney J Furie • *Scr* Alan R Trustman, David M Wolf

The Hit
★★★★ **18**

Thriller 1984 · UK · Colour · 93min

Twelve years after *Gumshoe*, his directing debut, Stephen Frears made his second big-screen outing with this surreal comedy thriller – a blend of cockney gorblimey characters with a dash of Buñuel and spaghetti western. Terence Stamp plays a supergrass, exiled in Spain, where hitmen John Hurt and Tim Roth track him down and abduct him. Stamp is cool about the whole thing and seems to accept his destiny, while the hoods are as jumpy as fleas. Charismatic acting, the seemingly endless road across the Spanish plains and

the unexpected twist make for very stylish entertainment. AT

John Hurt *Braddock* • Tim Roth *Myron* • Terence Stamp *Willie Parker* • Fernando Rey *Policeman* • Laura Del Sol *Maggie* • Bill Hunter *Harry* • Lennie Peters *Mr Corrigan* ■ *Dir* Stephen Frears • *Scr* Peter Prince

Hit and Run
★★★ **PG**

Drama 1999 · US · Colour · 88min

Margaret Colin finds her life shattered when she accidentally hits a child with her car. After leaving the scene to call for help, she returns only to hear the outraged reaction from onlookers who believe it's a hit-and-run and decides to keep quiet. As her life falls apart she must wrestle with her conscience as well as the detective who suspects her. Writer Karen Stillman's thoughtful script and Colin's intense but restrained performance keep this TV tale of an innocent woman trapped by circumstance effective. MC **DVD**

Margaret Colin *Joanna Kendall* • Drew Pillsbury *Doug Kendall* • Lisa Vidal *Meredith Reed* ■ *Dir* Dan Lerner • *Scr* Karen Stillman

Hit & Run
★★ **15**

Romantic action comedy 2012 · US · Colour · 95min

A haphazardly conceived chase movie, with Dax Shepard hiding out in a small town under the witness protection programme. When Shepard's criminal past catches up with him, he and local gal Kristen Bell are forced on a violent road-trip chased by thugs from his murky past. Though the movie is given a slight lift by Tom Arnold's entertaining performance as a State Marshal with anger issues, the characterisation is underdeveloped. AS Swearing, sexual references, nudity, some violence, drug abuse. **DVD**

Kristen Bell *Annie Bean* • Dax Shepard *Yul Perrkins/"Charles Bronson"* • Tom Arnold *Randy Anderson* • Kristin Chenoweth *Debby Kreeger* • Bradley Cooper *Alex Dmitri* ■ *Dir* David Palmer, Dax Shepard • *Scr* Dax Shepard

Hit List
★★ **18**

Action thriller 1988 · US · Colour · 83min

This is the epitome of the straight-to-video movie, a ragbag of formula thrills and recycled material from better films. William Lustig peppers his tale of a professional kidnapping gone wrong with bursts of unpleasant violence and, after a tight opening, allows the script to merely become an excuse for a succession of shoot-outs and chases. Lance Henriksen scores as the psychopathic hitman, but Jan-Michael Vincent gives a marvellous impersonation of an oak desk. RS

Jan-Michael Vincent *Jack Collins* • Leo Rossi *Frank DeSalvo* • Lance Henriksen *Chris Caleek* • Charles Napier *Tom Mitchum* • Rip Torn *Vic Luca* • Jere Burns *Jared Riley* ■ *Dir* William Lustig • *Scr* John Goff, Peter Brosnan, from a story by Aubrey K Rattan

Hit Man
★★ **18**

Crime thriller 1972 · US · Colour · 86min

In this clumsy reworking of *Get Carter*, ex-pro Bernie Casey is fittingly cast as the footballer-turned-lawyer seeking revenge on the porn baron who killed the brother who was searching for his daughter's rapist. But he looks uncomfortable during his sex scenes, unlike Pam Grier whose abrasive femininity was about to make her a major star. Director George Armitage packs the picture with bloodily violent set pieces, but otherwise directs without much distinction. DP Swearing, violence, sex scenes, nudity, drug abuse.

Bernie Casey *Tyrone Tackett* • Pam Grier *Gozelda* • Lisa Moore *Laural Irvelle* • Sam Laws *Sherwood* • Candy All *Rochelle Tackett* ■ *Dir* George Armitage • *Scr* George Armitage, from the novel *Jack's Return Home* by Ted Lewis

Hit So Hard
★★★

Music documentary 2011 · US · Colour · 103min

This eye-opening but disjointed documentary charts the life and hard times of Patty Schemel, once the drummer in

Courtney Love's multi-platinum-selling band Hole, whose fall from grace and spiralling drug addictions led to homelessness and prostitution. Director P David Ebersole arguably spends too much screen time recapping the story of Love and her husband, the late Kurt Cobain, with Patty often reduced to a bystander. When the film does (eventually) focus on Schemel herself, it provides a fascinating insight into the pressures of the music business and a cautionary tale of life in the fast lane. TeS

Patty Schemel • Courtney Love • Eric Erlandson • Kurt Cobain ■ *Dir* P David Ebersole • *Scr* P David Ebersole, Todd Hughes

Hit the Deck
★★★★ **U**

Musical 1955 · US · Colour · 112min

The sailors-on-shore-leave theme may be familiar, but this version of the 1927 stage hit (with a totally new story) is immensely entertaining. Made when MGM's musical department was winding down, it still has all the studio know-how and a delightful cast. Jane Powell, Vic Damone and Tony Martin do well by the melodies, and Debbie Reynolds and Russ Tamblyn romp through an inventive routine in a fun-house, and best of all there's the irrepressible Ann Miller getting every ounce of humour from the lively script and tapping out Hermes Pan's exuberant choreography. TV

Jane Powell *Susan Smith* • Tony Martin (1) *Chief Boatswain's Mate William F Clark* • Debbie Reynolds *Carol Pace* • Walter Pidgeon *Rear Admiral Daniel Xavier Smith* • Vic Damone *Rico Ferrari* • Gene Raymond *Wendell Craig* • Ann Miller *Ginger* • Russ Tamblyn *Danny Xavier Smith* ■ *Dir* Roy Rowland • *Scr* Sonya Levien, William Ludwig, from the musical by Herbert Fields, from the play *Shore Leave* by Hubert Osborne

Hit the Ice
★★★ **U**

Musical comedy 1943 · US · BW · 79min

This was made when the comedy team of Abbott and Costello were the top money-makers for Universal Studios, which gave them good production values, amusing tailor-made scripts and sterling musical support. Bud and Lou are press photographers who get involved with gangsters at a ski resort (cue some inventive slapstick on the ice rink). The crooks include two of Hollywood's finest villains, Sheldon Leonard and Marc Lawrence. TV **DVD**

Bud Abbott *Flash Fulton* • Lou Costello *"Tubby" McCoy* • Ginny Simms *Marcia Manning* • Patric Knowles *Dr Bill Elliot* • Elyse Knox *Peggy Osborne* • Joe Sawyer *Buster* • Marc Lawrence (1) *Phil* • Sheldon Leonard *"Silky Fellowsby"* ■ *Dir* Charles Lamont • *Scr* Robert Lees, Frederic I Rinaldo, John Grant, from a story by True Boardman

Hit the Saddle
★

Western 1937 · US · BW · 61min

This B-western from the initial batch of Republic's Three Mesquiteers series has leads Ray Corrigan and Robert Livingston fighting wild horse thieves and falling out over a disreputable saloon entertainer. Max Terhune is the third Mesquiteer, supplying comic relief with his ventriloquist act. This has added interest because the beer hall floozie is Rita Hayworth, when she was still Rita Cansino. AE

Robert Livingston *Stony Brooke* • Ray "Crash" Corrigan *Tucson Smith* • Max Terhune *Lullaby Joslin* • Rita Cansino [Rita Hayworth] *Rita* • JP McGowan *Rance McGowan* • Edward Cassidy *Sheriff Miller* ■ *Dir* Mack V Wright • *Scr* Oliver Drake, from characters by William Colt MacDonald

Hitch
★★★ **12**

Romantic comedy 2005 · US · Colour · 113min

Will Smith puts his easy charm to good use in this flimsy but appealing New York-set romantic comedy. He plays a professional "date doctor" who discreetly helps ordinary guys woo the women of their dreams. When talk of his success reaches the ears of gossip columnist Eva Mendes, she decides to unmask the anonymous cupid, unaware that he's also the mishap-prone suitor trying to win her heart. Initially, the film makes up for in laughs what it lacks in

substance. Unfortunately, as the overlong tale hits its final third, it abruptly loses its spark. SF Swearing, sexual references. **DVD**

Will Smith *Alex "Hitch" Hitchens* • Eva Mendes *Sara Melas* • Kevin James *Albert Brennaman* • Amber Valletta *Allegra Cole* • Julie Ann Emery *Casey* • Michael Rapaport *Ben* • Adam Arkin *Max Trundle* ■ *Dir* Andy Tennant • *Scr* Kevin Bisch

The Hitch-Hiker
★★★★ **12**

Film noir 1953 · US · BW · 70min

Ida Lupino made history as the only woman to direct a *film noir* with this wilderness thriller, which was developed from a news story by Daniel Mainwaring (denied a credit by RKO president Howard Hughes because of his political radicalism). Making the desert seem every bit as threatening as the urban jungle, Lupino draws a performance of crackling malevolence from William Talman, as the serial killer physically and mentally scarred by his abusive childhood. Equally authentic is the impotent terror of hostages Edmond O'Brien and Frank Lovejoy. DP **DVD**

Edmond O'Brien *Roy Collins* • Frank Lovejoy *Gilbert Bowen* • William Talman *Emmett Myers* • José Torvay *Captain Alvarado* • Sam Hayes *Sam* • Wendell Niles *Wendell* ■ *Dir* Ida Lupino • *Scr* Collier Young, Ida Lupino, Robert Joseph, from a story by Daniel Mainwaring (uncredited)

Hitchcock
★★ **12**

Biographical drama 2012 · US · Colour · 94min

Released shortly after the TV drama *The Girl*, in which canonised director Alfred Hitchcock is portrayed as little more than a sadistic lech, this more agreeably comic portrayal acts as a salve, if little else. Under a mound of make-up, Anthony Hopkins gleefully plays the man as a stubborn, lugubriously wisecracking old teddy bear whose worst crimes are overeating and petty jealousy. But the film runs no deeper than that. Screenwriter John McLaughlin is surer on the making of *Psycho* than the unconvincing love triangle also involving Mrs Hitchcock, Alma Reville (a miscast Helen Mirren), and *Strangers on a Train* adapter Whitfield Cook (Danny Huston), and there's a misjudged fantasy element in which real-life serial killer Ed Gein becomes Hitchcock's ghoulish confidant. Despite amusing moments and a sprinkling of catnip for film buffs, *Hitchcock* is disappointingly inconsequential. AC Some swearing, sexual references. **DVD** **Blu**

Anthony Hopkins *Alfred Hitchcock* • Helen Mirren *Alma Reville* • Scarlett Johansson *Janet Leigh* • Toni Collette *Peggy Robertson* • Jessica Biel *Vera Miles* • James D'Arcy *Anthony Perkins* ■ *Dir* Sacha Gervasi • *Scr* John J McLaughlin, from the non-fiction book *Alfred Hitchcock and the Making of Psycho* by Stephen Rebello • *Music* Danny Elfman

Hitchcock Truffaut
★★★ **12**

Documentary 2015 · Fr/US · Colour and BW · 80min

Film historian Kent Jones tries to cover too much ground in this frustratingly brief documentary. Having traced the career arcs of Alfred Hitchcock and François Truffaut, Jones explains how they came to spend eight days chatting in a small room at Universal in 1962 and how the resulting book demonstrated what *Cahiers du Cinéma* had long declared: the Master of Suspense was a bona fide auteur. The plentiful clips from across the Hitchcock canon are slickly assembled, but there's too much awe and not enough insight. DP In English, French, Japanese. Sex references, violence **DVD**

Alfred Hitchcock • François Truffaut *François Truffaut* • Peter Bogdanovich • David Fincher • Martin Scorsese • Bob Balaban *Narrator* ■ *Dir* Kent Jones • *Scr* Kent Jones, Serge Toubiana

The Hitcher
★★★★ **18**

Thriller 1986 · US · Colour · 93min

C Thomas Howell picks up icy passenger Rutger Hauer in this feature debut from director Robert Harmon. Hauer is a serial killer who quickly embroils Howell in a

harrowing desert intrigue by implicating him in his sick crimes. Jennifer Jason Leigh, as the waitress who believes Howell's story, adds humanity along the way. Despite the film's huge lapses in logic and moments of wild self-parody, the plot twists and grim body count generate some gruesome suspense. It has become something of a cult film thanks to its surreal style and Hauer's inimitable presence. Howell returned for an inferior straight-to-video sequel in 2003. **AJ** Violence, swearing.
DVD

Rutger Hauer *John Ryder* • C Thomas Howell *Jim Halsey* • Jennifer Jason Leigh *Nash* • Jeffrey DeMunn *Captain Esteridge* ■ *Dir* Robert Harmon • *Scr* Eric Red

The Hitcher ★★18
Horror thriller 2007 · US · Colour · 80min

This remake of the 1986 cult thriller works best when it tries to emulate the intense claustrophobia of the original. Sean Bean's attempts to match Rutger Hauer's icy sneer as the menace of the highway are fairly successful. He involves innocent road trippers Sophia Bush and Zachary Knighton in his horrific murders, so the pair must elude both the pursuing redneck cops and their motiveless persecutor. But substituting the lone hero of the first movie with a bickering couple is a major misstep in a mostly enjoyable effort, as it severely diminishes the tension. And the increased scale of the action actually generates less suspense. But debut director Dave Meyers's music-video background means that the desert vistas look great, and the gory deaths deliver some well-timed shocks. **AJ**
DVD

Sean Bean *John Ryder* • Sophia Bush *Grace Andrews* • Zachary Knighton *Jim Halsey* • Neal McDonough *Lieutenant Esteridge* • Kyle Davis *Buford's store clerk* • Skip O'Brien *Harlan Bremmer Sr* • Travis Schuldt *Harlan Bremmer Jr* ■ *Dir* Dave Meyers • *Scr* Jake Wade Wall, Eric Bernt, Eric Red, from the 1986 film by Red

The Hitchhiker's Guide to the Galaxy ★★★PG
Science-fiction comedy adventure 2005 · US/UK · Colour · 104min

Douglas Adams's classic BBC radio series/ book/TV series finally made it to the big screen without sacrificing any of its late creator's jovially lugubrious vision. Martin Freeman stars as put-upon everyman Arthur Dent who, in the company of extraterrestrial friend Ford Prefect (rapper Mos Def), escapes the Earth moments before it's demolished to make way for a hyperspace bypass. Armed with Ford's copy of the eponymous guide – a PDA travelogue voiced by Stephen Fry – Arthur tries to make sense of a universe while pondering the nature of existence. A quintessentially British space odyssey. **JR** **DVD** **Blu**

Martin Freeman *Arthur Dent* • Mos Def *Ford Prefect* • Sam Rockwell *Zaphod Beeblebrox* • Zooey Deschanel *Trish McMillan/Trillian* • Bill Nighy *Slartibartfast* • Anna Chancellor *Questular* • John Malkovich *Humma Kavula* • Alan Rickman *Marvin the Paranoid Android* • Stephen Fry *The Book* • Helen Mirren *Deep Thought* ■ *Dir* Garth Jennings • *Scr* Douglas Adams, Karey Kirkpatrick from the radio series, book and TV series by Douglas Adams

Hitler ★★
Biographical drama 1962 · US · BW · 102min

According to this heavy-handed, often risible Freudian biopic of the Nazi dictator, the cause of the Second World War was Hitler's mother fixation. He is attracted to his niece and Eva Braun because of their resemblance to his mother. Richard Basehart brings a fair amount of intensity and hysteria to the title role, but most of the film is just sensationalist and phoney. **RB**

Richard Basehart *Adolf Hitler* • Cordula Trantow *Geli Raubal* • Maria Emo *Eva Braun* • Martin Kosleck *Joseph Goebbels* • John Banner *Gregor Strasser* • Martin Brandt *General Guderian* • John Wengraf *Dr Morell* • John Mitchum *Hermann Goering* ■ *Dir* Stuart Heisler • *Scr* Sam Neuman, E Charles Straus

Hitler: the Last Ten Days ★★PG
Second World War drama 1973 · UK · Colour and BW · 100min

Alec Guinness is Hitler trapped in his bunker while Berlin burns above him. It's a brave, incredibly detailed performance, but the film's Italian writer/director Ennio De Concini conspires against him, going for the obvious (cuts to black-and-white documentary footage). He also unwisely adds hindsight in Simon Ward's Hauptmann Hoffman, who not only invades the bunker armed with battalions of postwar guilt, but also plants political doubts in the mind of Eva Braun, played by German actress Doris Kunstmann. **AT**

Alec Guinness *Adolf Hitler* • Simon Ward *Hauptmann Hoffmann* • Adolfo Celi *General Krebs* • Diane Cilento *Hanna Reitsch* • Gabriele Ferzetti *Field Marshal Keitel* • Eric Porter *General Von Greim* • Doris Kunstmann *Eva Braun* • Joss Ackland *General Eurgdorf* ■ *Dir* Ennio De Concini • *Scr* Ennio De Concini, Maria Pia Lenco, Wolfgang Reinhardt, Ivan Moffat, from the non-fiction book *The Last Days of the Chancellery* by Gerhard Boldt

Hitler's Children ★★★PG
Second World War drama 1943 · US · BW · 78min

Edward Dmytryk's drama purports to show how the Nazi regime punished women for refusing to bear babies for the Third Reich. Sterilisation and public lashing are two of the penalties dished out in what is either outright exploitation or earnest education, depending on your point of view. Bonita Granville is one of the persecuted women, while Tim Holt plays her Nazi officer boyfriend who puts a stop to the floggings. This box-office goldmine is surely one of the weirdest propaganda movies ever made. **AT**
DVD

Tim Holt *Karl* • Bonita Granville *Anna* • Kent Smith *Prof Nichols* • Otto Kruger *Colonel Henkel* • HB Warner *Bishop* • Lloyd Corrigan *Franz Erhart* ■ *Dir* Edward Dmytryk • *Scr* Emmett Lavery, from the non-fiction book *Education for Death* by Gregor Ziemer

Hitler's Madman ★★★
Second World War drama 1943 · US · BW · 83min

The first Hollywood picture of melodrama king Douglas Sirk is a B-movie about the assassination of the Nazi, Reinhard Heydrich, and the savage reprisals which left the Czech village of Lidice razed to the ground. Made a short time after the actual events it depicted, the film has an urgency about it, if little of the director's later finesse. Sirk reputedly met Heydrich in Berlin in the 1920s and remembered his expressive face and Shakespearean style of declaiming – which may explain John Carradine's performance as the Nazi monster. **AT**

John Carradine *Heydrich* • Patricia Morison *Jarmila* • Alan Curtis *Karel* • Ralph Morgan *Hanka* • Howard Freeman *Himmler* • Ludwig Stossel *Mayor Bauer* • Edgar Kennedy *Nepomuk* • Ava Gardner *Katy Chotnik* ■ *Dir* Douglas Sirk • *Scr* Peretz Hirshbein, Melvin Levy, Doris Malloy, from a story by Emil Ludwig, Albrecht Joseph, from the story *Hangmen's Village* by Bart Lytton

The Hitman ★★18
Action thriller 1991 · US · Colour · 89min

This vehicle for the ageing Chuck Norris at least benefits from significantly better direction than his other movies of the period, as brother Aaron Norris gives the proceedings a sharp, atmospheric look and a harder edge to the sporadic violence. Norris, however, as a cop who goes undercover into the Mafia after nearly being killed in the line of duty, is his usual bland self. **KB**

Chuck Norris *Cliff Garret/Danny Grogan* • Michael Parks *Ronny "Del" Delaney* • Al Waxman *Marco Luganni* • Alberta Watson *Christine De Vera* • Salim Grant *Tim Murphy* • Ken Pogue *Chambers* • Marcel Sabourin *Andre Lacombe* ■ *Dir* Aaron Norris • *Scr* Don Carmody, Robert Geoffrion

Hitman ★★15
Action crime thriller 2007 · Fr/US · Colour · 90min

Like *Tomb Raider* and *Doom* before it, this cinematic adaptation of the bestselling video game series is far less entertaining than its digital source material. The hitman of the title is Agent 47 (Timothy Olyphant), a charmless, genetically engineered contract killer employed by a shadowy international organisation. After an assignment goes wrong, the bald antihero is double-crossed by his employers and pursued by an obsessed Interpol agent (Dougray Scott). Despite globetrotting through exotic locations, this fight-filled thriller rarely matches the game's cinematic flourishes and brazenly ditches the backstory for a far less inspired mythology of its own. **JR** **DVD** **Blu**

Timothy Olyphant *Agent 47* • Dougray Scott *Mike Whittier* • Olga Kurylenko *Nika Boronina* • Robert Knepper *Yuri Marklov* • Ulrich Thomsen *Mikhail Belicoff* • Michael Offei *Jenkins* ■ *Dir* Xavier Gens • *Scr* Skip Woods, from the Eidos computer game

Hitman: Agent 47 ★★15
Action crime thriller 2015 · US/Ger/Sing · Colour · 92min

The second adaptation from the hit video game series stars Rupert Friend as a genetically modified assassin who helps a young woman (Hannah Ware) take down a terrorist organisation. Lacking in subtlety or humour, the film wades through the confusing plot, with care taken only in the action scenes. Friend makes for a bland hero; Zachary Quinto, on the other hand, chases our hero with a permanently angered expression, but his equally empty performance works against the story's "Who can you trust?" theme. Better than its 2007 predecessor, but only just. **JL** Violence, swearing. **DVD** **Blu**

Rupert Friend *Agent 47* • Hannah Ware *Katia* • Zachary Quinto *John Smith* • Ciarán Hinds [Ciaran Hinds] *Litvenko* • Thomas Kretschmann *Le Clerq* ■ *Dir* Aleksander Bach • *Scr* Skip Woods, Michael Finch, from a story by Woods

Hitman's Run ★★18
Crime thriller 1999 · US · Colour · 89min

There's little spark evident in this weary action thriller. The ever-prolific Eric Roberts plays an ex-Mob assassin in the witness protection programme whose cover is blown by a teenage hacker who breaks into the FBI's security files. There is plenty of gunplay, but the direction is strictly by the numbers. **JF**

Eric Roberts *Tony Lazorka/John Dugan* • Esteban Powell *Brian Segal* • C Thomas Howell *Tom Holly* • Farrah Forke *Sarah* ■ *Dir* Mark L Lester • *Scr* Eric Barker (2)

The Hive ★
Science-fiction thriller 2007 · US · Colour · 90min

Man-eating ants rampage on a south-east Asian island in this relentlessly silly sci-fi thriller. Cue lots of repetitive scenes of people running and surprisingly little flesh-munching action, as hi-tech exterminators Team Thorax battle to save the population. The film's unintentionally hilarious blend of cod science and gung-ho military talk is delivered with straight-faced reverence by a low-level cast that includes original *Dukes of Hazzard* star Tom Wopat. **SF**

Tom Wopat *Bill* • Kal Weber *Len* • Jessica Reavis *Debs* ■ *Dir* Peter Manus • *Scr* TS Cook

The Hoax ★★★★15
Drama based on a true story 2006 · US · Colour and BW · 111min

In 1971, failing author Clifford Irving persuaded publishers McGraw-Hill that he was working on an authorised biography of eccentric recluse Howard Hughes, and thus banked a gargantuan advance. Richard Gere is well cast as the charismatic Irving and Alfred Molina is highly watchable as his nervy best friend and collaborator. This smart and playful account of one of the greatest literary scams of all time is pacey,

funny and often enjoyably tense. The real Irving was less impressed, though – cheekily objecting to the movie playing fast and loose with the facts. **AS**

Richard Gere *Clifford Irving* • Alfred Molina *Dick Suskind* • Marcia Gay Harden *Edith Irving* • Julie Delpy *Nina Van Pallandt* • Hope Davis *Andrea Tate* • Stanley Tucci *Shelton Fisher* • Eli Wallach *Noah Dietrich* ■ *Dir* Lasse Hallström • *Scr* William Wheeler, from the non-fiction book by Clifford Irving • *Cinematographer* Oliver Stapleton

The Hobbit: an Unexpected Journey ★★★12
Fantasy adventure 2012 · US/NZ · Colour · 169min

Following the hit *Lord of the Rings* trilogy, director Peter Jackson travels further back through the history of Middle-earth to tell the story of Bilbo Baggins. Martin Freeman plays the titular hobbit with curmudgeonly charm, as he reluctantly leaves home to join a band of dwarves on a quest to reclaim territory. Ian McKellen as the wizard Gandalf makes an amusing double-act with Freeman. It takes a while for the story to get going and the pace suffers, but Jackson does deliver some extraordinary set pieces, while Andy Serkis's vivid turn as Gollum is full of humour and pathos. **SP** Violence.
DVD **Blu** **3D**

Ian McKellen *Gandalf the Grey* • Martin Freeman *Bilbo Baggins* • Richard Armitage *Thorin Oakenshield* • James Nesbitt *Bofur* • Ken Stott *Balin* • Sylvester McCoy *Radagast* • Barry Humphries *Great Goblin* • Cate Blanchett *Galadriel* • Ian Holm *Old Bilbo* • Christopher Lee *Saruman* • Hugo Weaving *Lord Elrond* • Elijah Wood *Frodo* • Andy Serkis *Gollum* • Benedict Cumberbatch *Necromancer* ■ *Dir* Peter Jackson • *Scr* Peter Jackson, Fran Walsh, Guillermo del Toro, Philippa Boyens, from JRR Tolkien's novel • *Cinematographer* Andrew Lesnie • *Production Designers* Dan Hennah, Ra Vincent, Simon Bright

The Hobbit: the Desolation of Smaug ★★★12
Fantasy adventure 2013 · US/NZ · Colour · 154min

Martin Freeman as Bilbo Baggins is pushed somewhat into the background, in this second part of Peter Jackson's adaptation of the JRR Tolkien classic. Even vengeful dwarf Thorin Oakenshield (Richard Armitage), who dominated the first film, is made to look one-dimensional on this leg of the journey. The attention to detail is once again all in the visual realisation of Middle-earth and some extraordinary action scenes, including Bilbo's close encounter with the evil Dragon Smaug (boomingly voiced by Freeman's *Sherlock* co-star Benedict Cumberbatch). But the dramatic tension comes in fits and starts, and for that reason the film can be a frustrating watch, although Jackson does succeed in building anticipation for the final chapter. **SP** **DVD** **Blu** **3D**

Martin Freeman *Bilbo Baggins* • Ian McKellen *Gandalf the Grey* • Richard Armitage *Thorin Oakenshield* • Benedict Cumberbatch *Smaug/ Necromancer* • Evangeline Lilly *Tauriel* • Cate Blanchett *Galadriel* • Orlando Bloom *Legolas* • Luke Evans *Bard the Bowman* • Aidan Turner *Kili* • Stephen Fry *Master of Laketown* ■ *Dir* Peter Jackson • *Scr* Peter Jackson, Fran Walsh, Guillermo del Toro, Philippa Boyens, from JRR Tolkien's novel • *Cinematographer* Andrew Lesnie

The Hobbit: the Battle of the Five Armies ★★★★12
Fantasy adventure 2014 · US/NZ · Colour · 138min

An epic but uneven journey finally comes to an end, as Peter Jackson marshals elves, dwarves, orcs and mortal men in awesomely staged conflict, as Thorin hunkers down at Erebor to protect the glittering dunes of gold that Smaug has left behind. Despite having the title role, Martin Freeman's Bilbo (in less jovial mood) is again a supporting character – Thorin's quest is the real heart of the story. Jackson lavishes too much time on minor characters and romantic subplots, but the one-on-one battles generate much more intensity. Even if Jackson doesn't match the gravitas of

Tolkien's writing, he leaves Middle-earth on an adrenaline-pumping high. SP *DVD* *BL* *3D*
Martin Freeman *Bilbo Baggins* • Ian McKellen *Gandalf* • Richard Armitage *Thorin Oakenshield* • Evangeline Lilly *Tauriel* • Orlando Bloom *Legolas* • Cate Blanchett *Galadriel* • Benedict Cumberbatch *Smaug/Necromancer* • Luke Evans *Bard* • Christopher Lee *Saruman* • Billy Connolly *Dain* ■ *Dir* Peter Jackson • *Scr* Peter Jackson, Philippa Boyens, Guillermo del Toro, Fran Walsh, from JRR Tolkien's novel • *Cinematographer* Andrew Lesnie • *Music* Howard Shore

Hobo with a Shotgun ★★★★ 18
Revenge drama 2011 · Can/US · Colour · 82min

In this gleefully inventive bloodbath, indignant tramp Rutger Hauer turns vigilante and sets about cleaning up the mean streets of Hope City. Jason Eisener's film began life as a fake trailer that was included in the Canadian release of Quentin Tarantino and Robert Rodriguez's B-movie celebration *Grindhouse*. But unlike the similarly spawned *Machete*, this expanded release is perfectly balanced between imitation and parody. The wild overacting only adds to the winningly exuberant excess of what is a startling feature debut for the director. AJ Violence. *DVD* *BL*
Rutger Hauer *Hobo* • Gregory Smith *Slick* • Robb Wells *Logan* • Molly Dunsworth *Abby* • Brian Downey *Drake* ■ *Dir* Jason Eisener • *Scr* John Davies, from a story by Davies, Jason Eisener, Rob Cotterill

Hobson's Choice ★★★★ U
Classic comedy 1953 · UK · BW · 103min

Winner of the British Academy Award for best British film in 1954, this is a splendid adaptation of the celebrated Harold Brighouse play. The role of the Salford cobbler at war with his wilful daughter is tailor-made for Charles Laughton (who had previously enjoyed much stage success in the role of Henry Horatio Hobson), and he gives one of his very best performances. The slick by-play between the leads belies the fact that Laughton detested Brenda de Banzie as Maggie and resented John Mills for landing the son-in-law part he wanted to go to Robert Donat. Director David Lean handles cast and material with equal care, judging the moments of comedy and poignancy perfectly. DP *DVD* *BL*
Charles Laughton *Henry Horatio Hobson* • John Mills *Willie Mossop* • Brenda de Banzie *Maggie Hobson* • Daphne Anderson *Alice Hobson* • Prunella Scales *Vicky Hobson* • Richard Wattis *Albert Prosser* • Derek Blomfield *Freddy Beenstock* • Helen Haye *Mrs Hepworth* • Joseph Tomelty *Jim Heeler* ■ *Dir* David Lean • *Scr* David Lean, Norman Spencer, Wynyard Browne, from the play by Harold Brighouse

Hockney ★★★★ 15
Documentary 2014 · UK · Colour · 107min

This documentary about David Hockney draws on the artist's own family photos and home movies to provide an intimate, authoritative portrait. There's a lot to pack in, but it never feels like director Randall Wright is rushing, and the interviews with Hockney himself (now seriously hard of hearing), family and colleagues glow with warmth. The film also allows Hockney's work to speak for itself, beautifully capturing its rich colours and playful lines. Undoubtedly a splendid tribute to a genuine national treasure. TJ Swearing, brief nudity.
David Hockney ■ *Dir* Randall Wright

Hocus Pocus ★★★ PG
Black comedy 1993 · US · Colour · 92min

An unusually black comedy from Disney, this makes for patchy entertainment. Three witches – Bette Midler, Kathy Najimy and Sarah Jessica Parker – are resurrected by a group of youngsters on Halloween and proceed to cause mayhem as they plot their revenge against the community that condemned them to death three centuries earlier. The three stars are the best thing about this uneven movie, but the younger generation acquit themselves admirably. JF *DVD*
Bette Midler *Winifred Sanderson* • Sarah Jessica Parker *Sarah Sanderson* • Kathy Najimy *Mary Sanderson* • Omri Katz *Max* • Thora Birch *Dani* • Vinessa Shaw *Allison* • Amanda Shepherd *Emily* ■ *Dir* Kenny Ortega • *Scr* Neil Cuthbert, Mick Garris, from a story by Mick Garris, David Kirschner

Hoffa ★★★ 15
Biographical drama 1992 · US · Colour · 134min

Jimmy Hoffa was one of the most controversial figures in American trade union history, but Danny DeVito's portrayal seems to be a figment of screenwriter David Mamet's imagination, and too little light is shed on Hoffa's alleged involvement with the Mob. However, as a study of a man devoted to his cause, it is a powerful piece of drama, and DeVito directs with an impressive epic sweep. Jack Nicholson dominates the screen as the belligerent Teamsters' boss, and Kevin Anderson is magnificently vindictive as Robert Kennedy. DP Swearing, violence, nudity. *DVD*
Jack Nicholson *James R Hoffa* • Danny DeVito *Bobby Ciaro* • Armand Assante *Carol D'Allesandro* • JT Walsh *Frank Fitzsimmons* • John C Reilly *Pete Connelly* • Frank Whaley *Young kid* • Kevin Anderson *Robert Kennedy* ■ *Dir* Danny DeVito • *Scr* David Mamet

Hoffman ★ 15
Sex comedy 1970 · UK · Colour · 106min

Not even Peter Sellers can make this tale of middle-aged Hoffman, blackmailing Sinead Cusack to stay for a week in his apartment, anything other than tediously peculiar, if not downright perverse. Adapted by Ernest Gebler from his novel, it's a sex comedy that's neither very sexy nor very comic. TH *DVD*
Peter Sellers *Benjamin Hoffman* • Sinead Cusack *Janet Smith* • Jeremy Bulloch *Tom Mitchell* • Ruth Dunning *Mrs Mitchell* • David Lodge *Foreman* ■ *Dir* Alvin Rakoff • *Scr* Ernest Gebler, from his novel

The Holcroft Covenant ★★ 15
Spy thriller 1985 · UK · Colour · 107min

Michael Caine is chasing his father's Nazi legacy either to atone for or to rebuild Hitler's empire. It's easy to blame once-talented director John Frankenheimer (*The Manchurian Candidate*) for making this farrago unwatchable, but the more likely obstacle is the source material: Robert Ludlum's thriller is cinematically intractable. The locations look good, Lilli Palmer is graceful, and Anthony Andrews manfully struggles with his role as Caine's brother. TS
Michael Caine *Noel Holcroft* • Anthony Andrews *Johann Tennyson von Tiebolt* • Victoria Tennant *Helden Tennyson von Tiebolt* • Lilli Palmer *Althene Holcroft* • Mario Adorf *Jurgen Maas/Erich Kessler* • Michael Lonsdale [Michel Lonsdale] *Manfredi* ■ *Dir* John Frankenheimer • *Scr* George Axelrod, Edward Anhalt, John Hopkins, from the novel by Robert Ludlum

Hold Back the Dawn ★★★★
Romantic comedy drama 1941 · US · BW · 116min

A smashing comedy drama, this stars Charles Boyer as a wartime refugee who marries schoolmarm Olivia de Havilland as a means of gaining entry into the US. Paulette Goddard is his partner in the deception and his chosen companion on his wedding night. Set largely on the US-Mexican border, in one of those fly-blown hotels filled with "characters", this is a very witty but also rather dark charade, written by Charles Brackett and Billy Wilder just before Wilder became a director himself. AT
Charles Boyer *Georges Iscovescu* • Olivia de Havilland *Emmy Brown* • Paulette Goddard *Anita Dixon* • Victor Francen *Van den Luecken* • Walter Abel *Inspector Hammock* • Curt Bois *Bonbois* • Rosemary DeCamp *Berta Kurz* • Veronica Lake *Movie actress* ■ *Dir* Mitchell Leisen • *Scr* Charles Brackett, Billy Wilder, from a story by Ketti Frings

Hold Back the Night ★★★★ 15
Drama 1999 · UK/It · Colour · 99min

Strong-willed teenager (Christine Tremarco), while fleeing an abusive father, hooks up with two similarly restless souls: a grungy environmental protester (Stuart Sinclair Blyth) and a terminally ill woman (Sheila Hancock), whose dying wish is to see the sunrise at Orkney's Ring of Brodgar. Strong performances, believable characters and a script that doesn't offer easy answers combine to create an affecting journey. A brave film that favours psychological plausibility above easy audience engagement. JC Violence, swearing. *DVD*
Christine Tremarco *Charleen* • Stuart Sinclair Blyth *Declan* • Sheila Hancock *Vera* • Richard Platt *Michael* • Julie Ann Watson *Jackie* • Kenneth Colley *Bob* • Tommy Tiernan *John* ■ *Dir* Phil Davis [Philip Davis] • *Scr* Steve Chambers

Hold That Co-Ed ★★★
Musical comedy 1938 · US · BW · 80min

The "Great Profile", John Barrymore, made some six movies in 1938. Four years later he was dead, a burnt-out alcoholic once regarded as the greatest stage performer, and his finest screen portrayals were in the days of silent cinema. Here he walks away with the movie as a bluff governor who sponsors a college football team to win votes. All jolly good fun, and the old ham is a delight to watch under George Marshall's fast-paced direction. TS
John Barrymore *Governor* • George Murphy *Rusty* • Marjorie Weaver *Marjorie* • Joan Davis *Lizzie* • Jack Haley *Wilbur* • George Barbier *Breckenridge* • Ruth Terry *Edie* • Donald Meek *Dean Thatcher* ■ *Dir* George Marshall • *Scr* Karl Tunberg, Don Ettinger, Jack Yellen, from a story by Karl Tunberg, Don Ettinger

Hold That Ghost ★★★
Comedy 1941 · US · BW · 86min

This superior Abbott and Costello comedy finds the zany duo inheriting a supposedly haunted mansion, thanks to a gangster's will. The heroes intend to turn the place into a restaurant, but once on the premises they encounter all sorts of spooky phenomena. Musical relief is provided by the boys' regular collaborators, the Andrews Sisters. DF
Bud Abbott *Chuck Murray* • Lou Costello *Ferdinand Jones* • Richard Carlson *Dr Jackson* • Evelyn Ankers *Norma Lind* • Joan Davis *Camille Brewster* • Marc Lawrence (1) *Charlie Smith* ■ *Dir* Arthur Lubin • *Scr* Robert Lees, Frederic I Rinaldo, John Grant

Hold-Up ★★
Crime drama 1985 · Fr/Can · Colour · 114min

Even a tightly focused performance by Jean-Paul Belmondo can't hide the grinding predictability of a film in which a trio of bank robbers have more trouble with themselves than the law. Belmondo's natural ease and early appearance in a clown suit (in order to rob the bank) might help you stay the distance. Female lead Kim Cattrall is better than her track record suggests. The film was later remade by Bill Murray as *Quick Change*. JM French dubbed.
Jean-Paul Belmondo *Grimm* • Guy Marchand *Georges* • Kim Cattrall *Lise* • Jean-Pierre Marielle *Labrosse* • Tex Konig *Lasky* • Jacques Villeret *Cab driver* ■ *Dir* Alexandre Arcady • *Scr* Alexandre Arcady, Francis Veber, Daniel Saint-Harmont, from the novel *Quick Change* by Jay Cronley

Hold Your Man ★★★
Romantic comedy melodrama 1933 · US · BW · 88min

Clark Gable and blonde bombshell Jean Harlow co-star as a charming, womanising petty gangster and a seemingly tough young woman who, after much fencing and wisecracking, fall in love. But things go wrong when he accidentally kills a man. Sam Wood directs this bizarre and unsettling mix of comedy, romance and melodrama, which strains credibility to the limit but is still satisfying entertainment. RK
Jean Harlow *Ruby Adams* • Clark Gable *Eddie Hall* • Stuart Erwin *Al Simpson* • Dorothy Burgess *Gypsy Angikon* • Muriel Kirkland *Bertha Dillian* • Garry Owen *Slim* • Barbara Baroness *Sadie Kline* ■ *Dir* Sam Wood • *Scr* Anita Loos, Howard Emmett Rogers, from a story by Anita Loos

Holding the Man ★★★★ 15
Romantic drama based on a true story 2015 · Aus · Colour · 127min

Director Neil Armfield's first feature film since 2005's *Candy* is a quality Aussie drama based on the true story of a gay relationship – from Tim Conigrave and John Caleo's first meeting in high school, through their 15 years together, and on to the lingering impact of Aids. Saved from schmaltz by good humour, *Holding the Man* is impeccably acted by Ryan Corr and Craig Stott, and by an Aussie who's who of support stars including Guy Pearce, Anthony LaPaglia and Geoffrey Rush. DA Sex, drug abuse, swearing *DVD*
Ryan Corr *Timothy Conigrave* • Craig Stott *John Caleo* • Anthony LaPaglia *Bob Caleo* • Kerry Fox *Mary Gert Conigrave* • Guy Pearce *Dick Conigrave* • Geoffrey Rush *Barry* ■ *Dir* Neil Armfield • *Scr* Tommy Murphy, from Timothy Conigrave's memoir

The Hole ★★★
Drama 1998 · Tai/Fr · Colour · 95min

Whereas in *The River*, director Tsai Ming-liang presented water as a cause of corruption and pain, here it ebbs back towards its traditional symbolism as a source of life and a force for good. Stranded in a Taipei gripped by a mystery millennial virus, Li Kangsheng becomes obsessed with his downstairs neighbour, Yang Kuei-Mei, after a clumsy plumber leaves a hole in his floor. Interspersed with musical reveries, performed by Yang in ironic tribute to the 1950s singer Grace Chang, this is a delightfully quirky film, in which the minimalism of ennui gives way to the gentle magic of romance. DP Mandarin +subtitles.
Yang Kuei-Mei *Woman downstairs* • Li Kangsheng *Man upstairs* • Miao Tien *Salesman* • Tong Hsiang-Chu *Plumber* • Lin Hui-Chin *Neighbour* ■ *Dir* Tsai Ming-liang • *Scr* Tsai Ming-Liang, Yang Ping-Ying

The Hole ★★★ 15
Psychological thriller 2001 · UK/Fr · Colour · 98min

Director Nick Hamm's adaptation of Guy Burt's cult novel is a mixed blessing. On the one hand, this sly study in teenage angst is a harrowing thriller raising some interesting questions about love-crazed students. On the other, it's a murky muddle of unbelievable motivations and shaggy-dog daftness. Yet the slow descent into sleight-of-hand suspense strains credulity to breaking point, as posh pupil Thora Birch suddenly reappears after going missing for 18 days and police psychologist Embeth Davidtz tries to find out where she's been and what happened to her three dead companions. AJ *DVD*
Thora Birch *Elizabeth "Liz" Dunn* • Desmond Harrington *Mike* • Daniel Brocklebank *Martin* • Laurence Fox *Geoff* • Keira Knightley *Frankie* • Steven Waddington *DCS Tom Howard* • Embeth Davidtz *Dr Philipa Norwood* ■ *Dir* Nick Hamm • *Scr* Ben Court, Caroline Ip, from the novel *After the Hole* by Guy Burt

The Hole ★★★ 12
Horror thriller 2009 · US · Colour · 88min

In director Joe Dante's cute but slight teen horror, two brothers and their next-door neighbour discover a mysterious hole in the basement of their new home, boarded up and padlocked by the previous owner. Very much in the Dante family-friendly fantasy tradition of *Gremlins* and *Explorers*, this nostalgic exercise covers the baleful bases of ghosts, demons and clowns. While the film is not exactly top-notch in production, casting or originality terms, the script (by *Vacancy*'s Mark L Smith) is bright and breezy, and Dante's harder edge occasionally shines through, especially in the surreal nightmare finale. AJ *DVD* *BL*

Chris Massoglia *Dane Thompson* • Haley Bennett *Julie Campbell* • Nathan Gamble *Lucas Thompson* • Teri Polo *Susan Thompson* • Bruce Dern *Carl* ■ *Dir* Joe Dante • *Scr* Mark L Smith

A Hole in My Heart ★★18
Drama 2004 · Swe/Den · Colour · 93min

This ferocious drama from director Lukas Moodysson is a film that's not so much experienced as endured. Thorsten Flinck plays a boorish cheap hard-core flick in the front room of his shabby flat, while his reclusive son (Bjorn Almroth) hides himself away in his bedroom. Initially, corrosive humour takes the edge off the film's deeply unsettling style, but the cycle of shock becomes as monotonous as it is distasteful. SF Swedish +subtitles. Violence, sex scenes, nudity. DVD

Thorsten Flinck *Rickard* • Bjorn Almroth *Eric* • Sanna Brading *Tess* • Goran Marjanovic *Geko* ■ *Dir/Scr* Lukas Moodysson

A Hole Lot of Trouble ★★
Comedy 1969 · UK · Colour · 27min

Veteran producer/director Francis Searle ended his career with a number of comedy shorts (all about 30 minutes long) designed to accompany features in the dying days of the double bill. Such shorts took a simple idea and exploited the potential to the maximum – Eric Sykes's *The Plank* is arguably the perfect example. Here, Arthur Lowe and friends explore the comic potential surrounding a group of workman digging a hole. DF

Arthur Lowe *Whitehouse* • Bill Maynard *Bill* • Tim Barrett *Longbottom* • Victor Maddern *Percy* • Brian Weske *Digby* • Leslie Dwyer *Evangelist* • Ken Parry *Charles* • Hani Borelle *Fenella* ■ *Dir* Francis Searle • *Scr* Ian Flintoff

Holes ★★★PG
Comedy drama adventure
2003 · US · Colour · 112min

Shia LaBeouf is Stanley Yelnats, who believes that generations of his family were cursed long ago by Eartha Kitt. He's accused of theft and sentenced to a juvenile detention centre in the Texas desert. There Mr Sir (Jon Voight) makes the youngsters dig holes "to build character" and is himself in awe of the Warden (Sigourney Weaver). Flashbacks to the past introduce outlaw Kissin' Kate Barlow (Patricia Arquette). Director Andrew Davis's whimsical tone sugars the bitterness, but this is blander than it should be. TH DVD CS

Sigourney Weaver *The Warden* • Jon Voight *Mr Sir* • Patricia Arquette *Kissin' Kate Barlow* • Tim Blake Nelson *Dr Pendanski* • Dulé Hill *Sam* • Shia LaBeouf *Stanley Yelnats IV* • Henry Winkler *Stanley's father* • Nate Davis [Nathan Davis] *Stanley's grandpa* • Eartha Kitt *Madame Zeroni* • Khleo Thomas *Zero* ■ *Dir* Andrew Davis • *Scr* Louis Sachar, from his novel

Holiday ★★★
Romantic comedy 1930 · US · BW · 83min

This is a capable filming of Philip Barry's hit Broadway comedy, with Robert Ames as the young nonconformist who rescues Ann Harding from an oppressive life in high society. Mary Astor is her sister, while Monroe Owsley is her weak brother drowning in drink. Under Edward H Griffith's direction, Ann Harding gained an Oscar nomination, though this adaptation has been eclipsed by George Cukor's definitive 1938 version with Katharine Hepburn. AE

Ann Harding *Linda Seton* • Mary Astor *Julia Seton* • Edward Everett Horton *Nick Potter* • Robert Ames *Johnny Case* • Hedda Hopper *Susan Potter* • Monroe Owsley *Ned Seton* • William Holden (1) *Edward Seton* ■ *Dir* Edward H Griffith • *Scr* Horace Jackson, from the play by Philip Barry

Holiday ★★★★★U
Romantic comedy 1938 · US · BW · 91min

This absolutely magical entertainment is an expert brew of comedy, pathos and romance. Previously filmed in 1930, it's the tale of a man (Cary Grant, at his most thoughtful and charming) who falls in love with a girl (Doris Nolan). When she turns out

to be from the top drawer of mega-wealthy New York society, he finds himself enmeshed in more than he bargained for – especially after her sister (Katharine Hepburn, never more beautiful or touching) takes a shine to him. The stars sparkle amid a superb supporting cast. RK DVD

Katharine Hepburn *Linda Seton* • Cary Grant *Johnny Case* • Doris Nolan *Julia Seton* • Lew Ayres *Ned Seton* • Edward Everett Horton *Nick Potter* • Henry Kolker *Edward Seton* • Binnie Barnes *Laura Cram* • Jean Dixon *Susan Elliott Potter* • Henry Daniell *Seton Cram* ■ *Dir* George Cukor • *Scr* Donald Ogden Stewart, Sidney Buchman, from the play by Philip Barry

The Holiday ★★12
Romantic comedy 2006 · US · Colour · 130min

Cameron Diaz and Kate Winslet headline this romantic comedy for the festive season. Watching it is like unwrapping an attractively packed gift only to discover it's socks again. Writer/director Nancy Meyers should have observed the advice of her previous film, *Something's Gotta Give*, and let a few scenes go. Diaz and Jude Law make a fairly engaging couple, although the early stages of their relationship are clumsily knitted together, while Winslet and Jack Black remain an awkward pairing throughout. But the film's funny moments are as thinly scattered as the English snow, which mysteriously keeps appearing and disappearing throughout the movie. SP DVD BD

Cameron Diaz *Amanda* • Kate Winslet *Iris* • Jude Law *Graham* • Jack Black *Miles* • Eli Wallach *Arthur Abbott* • Edward Burns *Ethan* • Rufus Sewell *Jasper* • Nicholas Downs *Peter* ■ *Dir/Scr* Nancy Meyers

Holiday Affair ★★★★U
Seasonal romantic drama
1949 · US · BW · 86min

In this absolutely charming yet little-known RKO Christmas movie, Janet Leigh plays a widowed single mother torn between Robert Mitchum and Wendell Corey (that's a contest?) and, not surprisingly, drawn to the one her son prefers. There's a sweet opening sequence and a nice sense of New York at Christmas. Mitchum reveals what a subtle actor he could be and Leigh proves yet again that she was one of the most delectable of cinematic charmers. TS

Robert Mitchum *Steve* • Janet Leigh *Connie* • Wendell Corey *Carl* • Gordon Gebert *Timmy* • Griff Barnett *Mr Ennis* • Esther Dale *Mrs Ennis* • Henry O'Neill *Mr Crowley* • Henry Morgan [Harry Morgan] *Police lieutenant* ■ *Dir* Don Hartman • *Scr* Isobel Lennart, from the story *Christmas Gift* by John D Weaver

Holiday Affair ★★★U
Romantic drama 1996 · US · Colour · 85min

Get out the mistletoe, ignite the Yule log and wallow in Cynthia Gibb's romantic dilemma. In this TV remake of the 1949 film, Gibb is the widowed mother who finds herself torn between marriage to her financially secure lawyer boyfriend and a relationship with a handsome department store salesman. To add to her problems, one of her suitors is leaving town on New Year's Eve – for good. A cheerful holiday diversion. MC DVD

Cynthia Gibb *Jodie* • David James Elliott *Steve Mason* • Curtis Blanck *Timmy* • Tom Irwin *Paul Davis* • Al Waxman *Mr Crowley* ■ *Dir* Alan Myerson • *Scr* Ara Watson, Sam Blackwell, from the 1949 film

Holiday Camp ★★★U
Comedy drama 1947 · UK · BW · 93min

Directed by Ken Annakin, this compendium of interlinked stories was more notable for its scripting credits than for the quality of the writing. Ted Willis, Sydney and Muriel Box and Peter Rogers were among the contributors but, although many of the episodes are reasonably diverting, none of them gives the stars enough to chew on. What is fascinating, however, is the picture of camp life, which should keep *Hi-De-Hi!* fans entertained. Jack Warner and Kathleen Harrison steal the show as the Huggetts, who went on to feature in three more movies (beginning with *Here Come the*

Huggetts) as well as their own radio show. DP

Flora Robson *Esther Harmon* • Dennis Price *Squadron Leader Hardwicke* • Jack Warner *Joe Huggett* • Kathleen Harrison *Ethel Huggett* • Hazel Court *Joan Martin* • Peter Hammond *Harry Huggett* • Yvonne Owen *Angela Kirby* • Jimmy Hanley *Jimmy Gardner* • Esma Cannon *Elsie Dawson* ■ *Dir* Ken Annakin • *Scr* Sidney Box, Peter Rogers, Denis Constanduros, Mabel Constanduros, Ted Willis, from a story by Godfrey Winn

Holiday for Lovers ★★U
Romantic comedy 1959 · US · Colour · 102min

At a time when B-movies were overrun with delinquent juveniles, this old-fashioned family comedy had nothing more to offer than a couple of hormonally zestful bobby-soxers. Screenwriter Luther Davis and director Henry Levin do nothing to drag Ronald Alexander's play into the rock 'n' roll era, preferring instead to dabble in coy innuendo as Jill St John and Carol Lynley chase the chaps during stuffy Clifton Webb and sensible Jane Wyman's South American vacation. DP

Clifton Webb *Robert Dean* • Jane Wyman *Mary Dean* • Jill St John *Meg Dean* • Carol Lynley *Betsy Dean* • Paul Henreid *Eduardo Barroso* • Gary Crosby *Paul Gattling* • Wally Brown *Joe* ■ *Dir* Henry Levin • *Scr* Luther Davis, from the play by Ronald Alexander

Holiday in Handcuffs ★★
Seasonal romantic comedy
2007 · US · Colour · 90min

Jilted waitress Melissa Joan Hart resorts to extreme methods to impress her picky parents in this goofy seasonal romantic comedy. But from the moment she kidnaps customer Mario Lopez and demands he pose as the ideal son-in-law, you know how events will pan out. Consequently, the family Christmas that follows starts to feel like padding (and lamely scripted padding at that). SF

Melissa Joan Hart *Gertrude "Trudie" Chandler* • Mario Lopez *David Martin* • Tim Bottoms [Timothy Bottoms] *Dad Chandler* • Markie Post *Mom Chandler* • June Lockhart *Grandma* ■ *Dir* Ron Underwood • *Scr* Sara Endsley

Holiday in Mexico ★★★U
Musical 1946 · US · Colour · 127min

Made to help cement America's Good Neighbour policy, this epic MGM musical actually never left the Culver City soundstages; the clever Hanna-Barbera animated title sequence establishes the only "authentic" Mexican flavour. Nevertheless, there's much to enjoy, despite its length. It's effectively a vehicle for delightful ingénue Jane Powell, who (unbelievably) develops a crush on much older pianist José Iturbi. But there's also some knockout piano choreography, created by youngster Stanley Donen. TS

Walter Pidgeon *Jeffrey Evans* • José Iturbi • Roddy McDowall *Stanley Owen* • Ilona Massey *Toni Karpathy* • Xavier Cugat • Jane Powell *Christine Evans* • Hugo Haas *Angus* ■ *Dir* George Sidney (2) • *Scr* Isobel Lennart, from a story by William Kozlenko

Holiday Inn ★★★★U
Musical comedy 1942 · US · BW · 101min

This much loved musical paired Crosby and Astaire for the first time, playing a song-and-dance team. The ingenious but wafer-thin plot sees Crosby split from the act to run an inn which only opens on public holidays, but this is basically a vehicle for some wonderful Irving Berlin songs and some magical Astaire dance routines. Crosby's rendition of *White Christmas* really caught the public imagination, making it one of the most successful recordings of all time. DF DVD BD

Bing Crosby *Jim Hardy* • Fred Astaire *Ted Hanover* • Marjorie Reynolds *Linda Mason* • Virginia Dale *Lila Dixon* • Walter Abel *Danny Reid* • Louise Beavers *Mamie* • John Gallaudet *Parker* • James Bell *Dunbar* ■ *Dir* Mark Sandrich • *Scr* Claude Binyon, Elmer Rice, from an idea by Irving Berlin • *Choreographer* Danny Dare

Holiday on the Buses ★PG
Comedy 1973 · UK · Colour · 82min

After 1971's *On the Buses* and *Mutiny on the Buses* (1972), this third movie culled from the hit TV series is one of the worst films you'll ever see. Having been sacked from the bus depot, Stan and Jack fetch up at a Welsh holiday camp. The film's only achievement is the sheer amount of smutty sniggering it manages to cram into 85 minutes. Absolutely abysmal. DP DVD

Reg Varney *Stan Butler* • Stephen Lewis *Inspector Blake* • Bob Grant *Jack* • Doris Hare *Mrs Butler* • Michael Robbins *Arthur* • Anna Karen *Olive* • Wilfrid Brambell *Bert* • Arthur Mullard *Wally Briggs* ■ *Dir* Bryan Izzard • *Scr* Ronald Wolfe, Ronald Chesney, from their TV series *On the Buses*

Hollow ★★15
Horror thriller 2011 · UK · Colour · 91min

This barely eerie take on the found-footage horror subgenre sees two couples spend a weekend in an old cottage out in the Suffolk countryside, where the tale of an ancient "suicide tree" holds sway as a popular legend. No prizes for guessing what happens as the quartet becomes increasingly unhinged by tales of the terrifying timber's past. With its hackneyed use of shaky camerawork, clunky dialogue and exceedingly irritating characters, this is a seriously unscary experience. JA Swearing, drug abuse, brief nudity.

Emily Plumtree *Emma* • Sam Stockman *James* • Jessica Ellerby *Lynne* • Matt Stokoe *Scott* ■ *Dir* Michael Axelgaard • *Scr* Matthew Holt

Hollow Man ★★18
Science-fiction thriller
2000 · US/Ger · Colour · 107min

In this updating of the *Invisible Man* tale, arrogant scientist Kevin Bacon makes himself invisible and promptly embarks on prattish schoolboy pranks. Challenged for much of a story, the film resorts to turning Bacon's laboratory into a haunted house, from where the see-through psychopath traps his colleagues to dispose of them one by one. Unambitious. AME Violence, sex scenes, swearing, nudity. DVD BD

Elisabeth Shue *Linda McKay* • Kevin Bacon *Sebastian Caine* • Josh Brolin *Matthew Kensington* • Kim Dickens *Sarah Kennedy* • Greg Grunberg *Carter Abbey* • Joey Slotnick *Frank Chase* • Mary Randle *Janice Walton* • William Devane *Doctor Kramer* ■ *Dir* Paul Verhoeven • *Scr* Andrew W Marlowe, from a story by Gary Scott Thompson, Andrew W Marlowe

Hollow Man II ★15
Science-fiction thriller
2006 · US · Colour · 87min

In this redundant sequel to Paul Verhoeven's underwhelming original, Christian Slater plays a deranged former soldier on the trail of the scientists whose serum has rendered him invisible. It isn't being played for laughs, but you'll find plenty of unintentional ones here. SF Violence, swearing, nudity. DVD

Christian Slater *Michael Griffin* • Peter Facinelli *Detective Frank Turner* • Laura Regan *Doctor Maggie Dalton* • David McIlwraith *Doctor William Reisner* • William MacDonald *Colonel Gavin Bishop* ■ *Dir* Claudio Faeh • *Scr* Joel Soisson, from a story by Gary Scott Thompson, from characters by Thompson, Andrew W Marlowe

Hollow Point ★★18
Crime comedy 1996 · US/Can · Colour · 98min

Thomas Ian Griffith plays this "both guns blazing" adventure for laughs with the help of *Wayne's World* babe Tia Carrere. Sidney J Furie directs, but his camera trickery and Griffith's gun-toting prowess are overshadowed by the two more accomplished members of the cast, *Third Rock from the Sun*'s John Lithgow and, with his tongue very firmly in his cheek, Donald Sutherland. JB Violence, swearing, brief nudity. DVD

Tia Carrere *Diane Norwood* • Thomas Ian Griffith *Max Perish* • Donald Sutherland *Garrett Lawton* • John Lithgow *Thomas Livingston* • David

Hemblen *Oleg Krezinsky* • Carl Alacchi *Alberto Capucci* ■ *Dir* Sidney J Furie • *Scr* James H Stewart, Robert Geoffrion

Hollow Reed ★★★ 15
Drama   1995 · UK/Ger · Colour · 101min

With a subject that's usually the preserve of the TV movie, this drama gains little from being made for the cinema, but the performances make it memorable. The film is tensely moving when it concentrates on estranged gay doctor Martin Donovan, who is trying to save his son from what he believes are the attacks of ex-wife Joely Richardson's live-in lover, Jason Flemyng. However, the subsequent courtroom scenes become a gay rights manifesto during which genuine grievances over-ripen into dishonest special pleading. TH Violence, swearing, nudity.

Martin Donovan (2) *Martyn Wyatt* • Ian Hart *Tom Dixon* • Joely Richardson *Hannah Wyatt* • Sam Bould *Oliver Wyatt* • Jason Flemyng *Frank Donally* • Shaheen Khan *Dr Razmu* • Kelly Hunter *Jamie's mum* ■ *Dir* Angela Pope • *Scr* Paula Milne, from a story by Neville Bolt

Hollow Triumph ★★★ PG
Film noir   1948 · US · BW · 82min

Producer/star Paul Henreid plays a gangster on the run from gamblers he's robbed. He murders a lookalike psychiatrist and assumes his identity, even inflicting a scar on his face to complete the resemblance. The story takes some swallowing but offers ingenious twists and, in true fatalistic *film noir* fashion, shows that no matter how hard you try, you can't escape your fate. The dramatic photography is the work of John Alton, one of the masters of *film noir*, who is given full rein by director Steve Sekely. AE

Joan Bennett *Evelyn Hahn* • Paul Henreid *John Muller* • Eduard Franz *Frederick Muller* • Leslie Brooks *Virginia Taylor* • John Qualen *Swangron* ■ *Dir* Steve Sekely • *Scr* Daniel Fuchs, from the novel by Murray Forbes

The Holly and the Ivy ★★ U
Seasonal drama   1952 · UK · BW · 77min

The stage origins of this family drama are all too obvious. Vicar Ralph Richardson gathers his children around him at Christmas in his Norfolk rectory, only for the festive spirit to be dampened by a startling revelation. Celia Johnson is on hand like a thick cardigan to provide comfort, and, despite the clunky direction by George More O'Ferrall, the outcome is bleaker than you expect. TH

Ralph Richardson *Rev Martin Gregory* • Celia Johnson *Jenny Gregory* • Margaret Leighton *Margaret Gregory* • Denholm Elliott *Michael "Mick" Gregory* • John Gregson *David Patterson* • Hugh Williams *Richard Wyndham* ■ *Dir* George More O'Ferrall • *Scr* Anatole de Grunwald, from the play by Wynard Browne

Hollywood Banker ★★★ PG
Documentary   2014 · Neth/US · Colour · 81min

The name of Frans Afman may be unfamiliar to film buffs, but the same cannot be said for the blockbuster hits that this affable Dutch banker financed. Starting with *Three Days of the Condor* in 1975, Afman was able to bankroll independent movies – via a presales system that's become the industry norm – that went on to earn mega-bucks box-office income. Afman enjoyed nearly 20 years of success and a high-rolling life that allowed him to rub shoulders with producers and superstars (Schwarzenegger, Stallone, Michael Douglas). JA English, Dutch +subtitles. Some swearing. DVD

Kevin Costner • Oliver Stone • Paul Verhoeven • Yoram Globus • Menahem Golan ■ *Dir/Scr* Rozemyn Afman

Hollywood Boulevard ★★★ 18
Comedy   1976 · US · Colour · 78min

Roger Corman agreed to finance this parody of his own cash-strapped movie-making style, provided Allan Arkush and Joe Dante could complete it for less than

$90,000. Ten days later (and $10,000 under budget), they submitted this patchy but often hilarious pastiche, in which New World (Corman's production company) becomes Miracle Pictures and Corman classics are given a whole new lease of life. Candice Rialson proves a good sport , while veterans such as Paul Bartel seize the opportunity to send up the Corman canon. An inferior sequel followed in 1989. DP

Candice Rialson *Candy Wednesday* • Mary Woronov *Mary McQueen* • Rita George *Bobbi Quackenbush* • Jeffrey Kramer *Patrick Hobby* • Dick Miller *Walter Paisley* • Richard Doran *Producer* • Paul Bartel (1) *Erich Von Leppe* ■ *Dir* Joe Dante, Allan Arkush • *Scr* Patrick Hobby

Hollywood Canteen ★★★ U
Musical comedy   1944 · US · BW · 125min

This Warner Bros contribution to the war effort was the studio's top-grossing hit of 1944, thanks to the cornucopia of stars who strut their stuff or play themselves. The line-up, to mention a mere few, includes the Andrews Sisters, Jack Benny, Joan Crawford, Bette Davis, Peter Lorre, Roy Rogers and Trigger, Barbara Stanwyck and Jimmy Dorsey and his Band. The plot? Soldiers Robert Hutton and Dane Clark spend their leave at the Hollywood Canteen. Written and directed by Delmer Daves, it's a feeble excuse for what is a fascinating entertainment. RK

Robert Hutton *Slim* • Dane Clark *Sergeant* • Janis Paige *Angela* • Jonathan Hale *Mr Brodel* • Barbara Brown *Mrs Brodel* • Bette Davis • John Garfield • Joan Leslie • Jack Benny • Joan Crawford • Sydney Greenstreet • Peter Lorre • Barbara Stanwyck • Jane Wyman • Roy Rogers ■ *Dir/Scr* Delmer Daves

Hollywood Cavalcade ★★★ U
Drama   1939 · US · Colour · 88min

This amiable and colourful slice of early Hollywood life is loosely based on the story of pioneer director Mack Sennett and early comedy superstar Mabel Normand. Playing the pair, Alice Faye and Don Ameche are both coiffed and frocked shamefully out of period. Still, the re-creations of silent movie days are fun, and the great Buster Keaton appears, as indeed does the real Mack Sennett (who also supervised the direction of the silent sequences). Al Jolson himself reprises his ground-breaking role from *The Jazz Singer*, so there's a fair amount of pleasure to be had. TS

Alice Faye *Molly Adair* • Don Ameche *Michael Linnett Connors* • J Edward Bromberg *Dave Spingold* • Alan Curtis *Nicky Hayden* • Stuart Erwin *Pete Tinney* • Jed Prouty *Chief of police* ■ *Dir* Irving Cummings • *Scr* Irving Pascal, from a story by Hilary Lynn, Brown Holmes, from an idea by Lou Breslow

Hollywood Ending ★★★
Comedy drama   2002 · US · Colour · 112min

A stupendous pratfall, made all the more hilarious by its sheer unexpectedness, is the highlight of Woody Allen's gentle dig at the ethics and aesthetics of mainstream moviemaking. As ever, the ensemble is exemplary, with Téa Leoni particularly impressive as the estranged wife of Allen's washed-up director, who takes a chance on him for her Hollywood producing debut. But the central conceit that Allen is stricken psychosomatically blind just before shooting begins, yet still muddles through, strains to breaking point. DP

Woody Allen *Val Waxman* • Téa Leoni *Ellie* • George Hamilton *Ed* • Debra Messing *Lori* • Mark Rydell *Al Hack* • Tiffani Thiessen [Tiffani-Amber Thiessen] *Sharon Bates* • Treat Williams *Hal* ■ *Dir/Scr* Woody Allen

Hollywood Homicide ★★★ 12
Police comedy drama   2003 · US · Colour · 111min

In this serviceable buddy movie, Harrison Ford plays a homicide detective who's busier moonlighting with his real-estate deals than solving crimes, while partner Josh Hartnett is an affable dimwit with a yen to take to the stage. The plot makes little sense, and it all degenerates into the inevitable car chase in the final act, but

there's just enough wit in the script and chemistry between the likeable leads to offset much of the hoary genre's predictability. AS Violence, swearing. DVD

Harrison Ford *Joe Gavilan* • Josh Hartnett *KC Calden* • Lena Olin *Ruby* • Bruce Greenwood *Lt Bennie Macko* • Isaiah Washington *Antoine Sartain* • Lolita Davidovich *Cleo Ricard* • Keith David Leon • Master P *Julius Armas* • Gladys Knight *Olivia Robidoux* • Lou Diamond Phillips *Wanda* • Dwight Yoakam *Leroy Wasley* • Martin Landau *Jerry Duran* ■ *Dir* Ron Shelton • *Scr* Robert Souza, Ron Shelton

Hollywood Hot Tubs ★★ 15
Sex comedy   1984 · US · Colour · 103min

Not the worst of the teen sex comedies so popular in the 1980s, but don't take that as a recommendation. This tracks the adventures of a young teenager who gets an adolescent's dream job: fixing jacuzzis at the homes of rich Hollywood women. It's directed by prolific sex comedy maker Chuck Vincent. There's a sequel. JF DVD

Donna McDaniel *Leslie Maynard* • Michael Andrew *Jeff* • Paul Gunning *Eddie* • Katt Shea *Dee Dee* • Edy Williams *Desire* • Jewel Shepard *Crystal* ■ *Dir* Chuck Vincent • *Scr* Mark Borde, Craig McDonnell

Hollywood Hotel ★★
Musical   1937 · US · BW · 100min

Warner Bros musicals by 1937 had lost the big budgets and the vitality of such hits as *42nd Street* and *Dames*, even though Busby Berkeley was still directing and Dick Powell was still performing in them. This feeble story has Powell as a musician seeking success in Hollywood. Fortunately, it is rescued from complete mediocrity by the appearances of Benny Goodman and his orchestra and by fine Johnny Mercer-Richard Whiting songs. AE

Dick Powell *Ronnie Bowers* • Rosemary Lane *Virginia* • Lola Lane *Mona Marshall* • Hugh Herbert *Chester Marshall* • Ted Healy *Fuzzy* • Glenda Farrell *Jonesy* • Johnnie Davis *Georgia* • Benny Goodman • Susan Hayward *Starlet at table* • Ronald Reagan *Radio announcer* • Carole Landis *Hat check girl* ■ *Dir* Busby Berkeley • *Scr* Jerry Wald, Maurice Leo, Richard Macauley

The Hollywood Mom's Mystery ★★
Comedy mystery   2004 · US · Colour · 87min

Justine Bateman stars in this sprightly whodunnit as a children's illustrator whose producer-husband Andrew McCarthy is desperate to get back into the limelight. However, becoming a suspect in the murder of neighbour Angie Everhart (the trophy wife of a soap star) wasn't exactly what he had in mind, so Bateman joins up with handsome screenwriter David Gale to catch the real killer. There are a few acerbic observations on how celebrities treat their offspring, but this is undemanding entertainment, not satire. DP

Justine Bateman *Lucy Freers* • Andrew McCarthy *Kit Freers* • George Hamilton *Woody Prentice* • Angie Everhart *Julia Prentice* • David Gale *Justin Caffrey* • Elizabeth Peña *Theresa Shoe* • Martin Kove *Sandy Palumbo* ■ *Dir* David S Cass Sr • *Scr* Bruce Franklin Singer, from the novel *The Dead Hollywood Moms Society* by Lindsay Maracotta

Hollywood or Bust ★★★★ U
Comedy   1956 · US · Colour · 94min

The 17th and last film teaming Dean Martin and Jerry Lewis shows no visible signs of the rapidly approaching on-set cracks in the relationship. Brilliant comic director Frank Tashlin indulges the duo and himself in a frantically stylised, often surreal, trek across the USA, ending in the movie capital of the title. This is a remarkably lavish and well-designed comedy. Hard to believe, but this jape started life as a road movie for Humphrey Bogart and Shirley Booth called *Route 66*. TS

Dean Martin *Steve Wiley* • Jerry Lewis *Malcolm Smith* • Anita Ekberg • Pat Crowley *Terry Roberts* • Maxie Rosenbloom *"Bookie" Benny* ■ *Dir* Frank Tashlin • *Scr* Erna Lazarus, from her story *Beginner's Luck*

Hollywood Party ★★★ U
Musical comedy   1934 · US · BW and Colour · 65min

Among the most gloriously miscalculated follies of the early sound era, this MGM extravaganza was originally intended to showcase the cream of the studio's star roster. Instead, it ended up being a manic montage of cockeyed comic cuts spinning off from fading movie icon Jimmy Durante's attempt to persuade Jack Pearl to sell him some lions for his next picture. Introduced by special guest Mickey Mouse, a Technicolor musical segment, *The Hot Chocolate Soldiers*, impressed contemporary audiences, but the hilarious tit-for-tat egg smashing sequence, featuring Lupe Velez and Laurel and Hardy, is the biggest highlight today. DP

Stan Laurel *Stan* • Oliver Hardy *Ollie* • Jimmy Durante *Schnarzan the Shouting Conqueror* • Mrs Jean Durante • Lupe Velez *Lupe Velez/Jaguar Woman* • Ted Healy • Moe Howard *Moe* • Curly Howard *Curly* • Larry Fine *Larry* ■ *Dir* Richard Boleslawski, Allan Dwan, Roy Rowland • *Scr* Howard Dietz, Arthur Kober

Hollywood Revue ★★★★
Musical   1929 · US · BW · 114min

Despite some now dated and rather tedious sequences, this Oscar-nominated movie is a historical document and a "must see" for anyone with a taste for early Hollywood, musicals, MGM stars and variety programmes. It was one of the first plotless revues to showcase a studio's stars. Lavishly staged under Charles Reisner's direction, the line-up of luminaries includes Lionel Barrymore, Joan Crawford, Buster Keaton, Laurel and Hardy, Bessie Love and Jack Benny. The range of acts embraces everything from Shakespeare to a variety of musical numbers of which the highlight is a spectacular treatment of *Singin' in the Rain*, unveiled here 23 years before Gene Kelly performed it. RK

John Gilbert (1) • Norma Shearer • Joan Crawford • Bessie Love • Marion Davies • Lionel Barrymore • Ann Dvorak *Chorus girl* • Gus Edwards • Oliver Hardy • Jack Benny *Emcee* • Buster Keaton • Stan Laurel • Marie Dressler • Conrad Nagel *Emcee* ■ *Dir* Charles Reisner • *Scr* Al Boasberg, Robert E Hopkins

Hollywood Shuffle ★★★★ 15
Satire   1987 · US · Colour · 77min

Shot for just $100,000, this spot-on satire slams Uncle Tom, Rochester and Superfly types alike as it swipes at the way in which Hollywood has (and continues to) miscast and misuse its African-American talent. Forgive it for falling flat occasionally, because hilarious scenes like the "act black" training school, the "boyz from the 'hood" review show and the great roles "done black" dream sequence all more than compensate with their razor-sharp wit and insight. The man to thank for this gem is co-writer/director Robert Townsend, who also shines as a struggling actor forced to choose between a part and his principles. DP Swearing.

Robert Townsend *Bobby Taylor* • Anne-Marie Johnson *Lydia* • Starletta DuPois *Bobby's mother* • Helen Martin *Bobby's grandmother* • Craigus R Johnson *Stevie Taylor* • Ludie Washington *Tiny* • Keenen Ivory Wayans *Donald* ■ *Dir* Robert Townsend • *Scr* Keenen Ivory Wayans, Robert Townsend

Hollywoodland ★★★ 15
Mystery thriller based on a true story
2006 · US · Colour · 120min

Though it has all the hallmarks of a *film noir* – a gumshoe, a mysterious death and not one but two *femmes fatales* – *Hollywoodland* doesn't quite fit the genre bill. Instead, it's more a poignant love letter to the glory days of Tinseltown, personified by George Reeves (Ben Affleck), a struggling bit-part player who found fame in the 1950s as TV's Superman. The film takes liberties with the facts of Reeves's life, and, despite the convincingly dark, smoky atmosphere, *Hollywoodland* works better when it's evoking Reeves's heyday – a cosmetically genteel world of zoot suits and jazz bands, in which the studio system protected its investments at any price. **DW** 𝔇𝔙𝔇 Blu-ray

Adrien Brody *Louis Simo* • Diane Lane *Toni Mannix* • Ben Affleck *George Reeves* • Bob Hoskins *Edgar Mannix* • Lois Smith *Helen Bessolo* • Robin Tunney *Leonore Lemmon* • Molly Parker *Laurie Simo* ■ *Dir* Allen Coulter • *Scr* Paul Bernbaum

Holocaust 2000 ★★★
Science-fiction horror
1977 · It/UK · Colour · 101min

The coming of the Antichrist is the theme of Alberto De Martino's spaghetti horror film, in which Kirk Douglas flexes his sense of morality and does battle with the Devil. Meanwhile his cherub-faced son Simon Ward is committing obnoxious acts that are anything but angelic. Derivative of such supernatural successes as *The Omen*, this is enjoyably appalling and appallingly enjoyable. **TH**

Kirk Douglas *Robert Caine* • Agostina Belli *Sara Golan* • Simon Ward *Angel Caine* • Anthony Quayle *Professor Griffith* • Virginia McKenna *Eva Caine* • Alexander Knox *Meyer* ■ *Dir* Alberto De Martino • *Scr* Sergio Donati, Alberto De Martino, Michael Robson, from a story by Sergio Donati, Alberto De Martino

A Hologram for the King ★★ 12A
Drama
2016 · Ger/US/UK/Fr · Colour and BW · 97min

Tom Hanks wanders around Saudi Arabia in a dry adaptation of Dave Eggers's bestselling novel from writer/director Tom Tykwer (*Cloud Atlas*). He's a salesman in a midlife crisis who's pitching for a contract supplying IT systems for a new mini-city in the sand. The trouble with this fish-out-of-water story is there's little sense of place or culture, while the running jokes wear thin and there's not enough of the book's existential drama. Worse still, the depiction of Saudi Arabia is as substantial as a mirage. **SP** Some swearing, moderate sex

Tom Hanks *Alan Clay* • Sarita Choudhury *Zahra* • Sidse Babett Knudsen *Hanne* • Tom Skerritt *Ron* • Ben Whishaw *Dave* ■ *Dir* Tom Tykwer • *Scr* Tom Tykwer, from Dave Eggers's novel

Holy Man ★★ PG
Comedy drama
1998 · US · Colour · 109min

In this satire on consumerism, Eddie Murphy plays a wandering mystic who's hired by an ailing shopping channel to turn around its fortunes. As the ratings soar, Murphy also finds time to teach channel executive Jeff Goldblum and media analyst Kelly Preston the value of love. Sadly, Murphy's holy innocent begins to grate, and what was intended to be a thought-provoking comedy ends up as another wearisome effort to distance Murphy from his *48 HRS* persona. **TH** Some swearing. 𝔇𝔙𝔇

Eddie Murphy *"G"* • Jeff Goldblum *Ricky Hayman* • Kelly Preston *Kate Newell* • Robert Loggia *John McBainbridge* • Jon Cryer *Barry* • Eric McCormack *Scott Hawkes* • Morgan Fairchild • James Brown (2) *James Brown* ■ *Dir* Stephen Herek • *Scr* Tom Schulman

Holy Matrimony ★★★★ U
Comedy
1943 · US · BW · 85min

This second talkie screen adaptation of Arnold Bennett's novel *Buried Alive* is far superior to the 1933 version, *His Double Life*. Monty Woolley excels as the gruff English painter who passes himself off as his dead butler to escape the unwanted attentions of the art world. He is ably supported by Gracie Fields, in her full Hollywood debut, as the no-nonsense wife who stands by him when the truth emerges. Weepie specialist John M Stahl simply has to point the camera, as much of his work has been done for him in Nunnally Johnson's literate and smoothly developed script. **DP**

Monty Woolley *Priam Farll* • Gracie Fields *Alice Challice* • Laird Cregar *Clive Oxford* • Una O'Connor *Mrs Leek* • Alan Mowbray *Mr*

Pennington • Melville Cooper *Dr Caswell* ■ *Dir* John M Stahl • *Scr* Nunnally Johnson, from the novel *Buried Alive* by Arnold Bennett

Holy Matrimony ★ PG
Comedy
1994 · US · Colour · 89min

This dire comedy from former *Star Trek* star Leonard Nimoy suffers from a clutch of one-note performances and unlikeable characters. After Patricia Arquette and Tate Donovan rob a county fair, they hide out in the Hutterite (like the Amish, only more conservative) community where Donovan grew up. When he dies, Hutterite tradition means that Arquette has to marry his younger brother (Joseph Gordon-Levitt), even though he's just 12 years old. **JB**

Patricia Arquette *Havana* • Joseph Gordon-Levitt *Zeke* • Armin Mueller-Stahl *Uncle Wilhelm* • Tate Donovan *Peter* • John Schuck *Markowski* • Lois Smith *Orna* • Courtney B Vance *Cooper* ■ *Dir* Leonard Nimoy • *Scr* David Weisberg, Douglas S Cook

Holy Motors ★★★ 18
Drama
2012 · Fr/Ger · Colour · 111min

Controversial French director Leos Carax stays true to form here, with an eccentric rant about technology taking over humanity. Denis Lavant plays the cypher of eclectic experience, travelling by limousine between his different personas. Once more combining bouts of tedium and pretentious excess with fabulously surreal images and grandiose spasms of inspiration, this is a total mess that strains for poetic meaning. Yet it has enough hypnotic power to carry attention through even the clumsiest and obvious passages. **AJ** French, English +subtitles. Violence, swearing, nudity. 𝔇𝔙𝔇 Blu-ray

Denis Lavant *M Oscar/banker/beggar woman/ motion capture specialist/"M Merde"/father/ accordionist/killer/victim/dying man/man in foyer* • Edith Scob *Céline* • Kylie Minogue *Eva Grace/ Jean* • Eva Mendes *Kay M* • Michel Piccoli *Man with birthmark* ■ *Dir/Scr* Leos Carax

The Holy Mountain ★★★ U
Silent adventure drama
1926 · Ger · BW · 105min

Trained in modern dance, Leni Riefenstahl made her acting debut in this "mountain film" by the genre's finest exponent, Arnold Fanck. But she also picked up a few directorial tips, as the presentation of her rhythmic routine and the glorification of human athleticism would influence the visual style of her 1938 masterpiece, *Olympiad*. The story of her tangled romance with mountaineers Luis Trenker and Ernst Petersen is pure melodrama, but Fanck's use of a moving camera and time-lapse photography remains impressive. **DP** 𝔇𝔙𝔇

Leni Riefenstahl *Diotima* • Ernst Petersen *Vigo* • Luis Trenker *Vigo's friend* • Frida Richard *Diotima's mother* ■ *Dir* Arnold Fanck • *Scr* Arnold Fanck, Hans Schneeberger

The Holy Mountain ★★★★ 18
Surreal drama
1973 · US/Mex · Colour · 113min

Alexandro Jodorowsky's follow-up to his cult classic, *El Topo*, is every bit as eccentric and challenging. Memorable images abound in the opening section, in which the messianic Horacio Salinas is saved by a limbless dwarf and witnesses an amphibian reconstruction of the crimes of the Conquistadores, before the tone shifts from mystical to comic inside the chimney lair of Jodorowsky's scheming alchemist. However, the catalogue of loopy vignettes itself soon gives way to a journey to the titular mountain where the worthies who rule the world are said to reside. Don't try searching for meaning, simply surrender to the experience. **DP** 𝔇𝔙𝔇

Alexandro Jodorowsky *Alchemist* • Horacio Salinas *Christ figure* • Ramona Saunders *Written woman* ■ *Dir/Scr* Alexandro Jodorowsky

Holy Rollers ★★ 15
Crime drama
2010 · US · Colour · 88min

Director Kevin Asch's Hasidic smuggling story is not terribly dramatic, despite good

central performances from Jesse Eisenberg and Justin Bartha. Eisenberg feels undervalued in the family fabric business and by the girl he's expected to marry, and is lured into the idea of making money by transporting "medicine for rich people". Even though the movie doesn't pull its punches as the inevitable happens, the moral of the tale is a bland one: being an ecstasy mule can pay at first but not forever. **KK** Swearing, drug abuse. 𝔇𝔙𝔇 Blu-ray

Jesse Eisenberg *Sam Gold* • Justin Bartha *Yosef Zimmerman* • Danny A Abeckaser *Jackie Solomon* • Ari Graynor *Rachel* • Jason Fuchs *Leon Zimmerman* • Q-Tip *Ephraim* • Bern Cohen *Rebbe Horowitz* • Mark Ivanir *Mendel Gold* ■ *Dir* Kevin Asch • *Scr* Antonio Macia

Holy Smoke ★★★ 18
Comedy drama
1999 · US · Colour · 109min

After the class-crossing passion of *Titanic* and her emergence as a star, Kate Winslet lets her hair down (and a lot more besides) in this lampoon on Australian bigotry from Jane Campion. Winslet plays the daughter of a poor family from Sydney who becomes a disciple of an Indian guru. Fearful of his influence over her, Winslet's family hires an American "exit counsellor" and cult buster (Harvey Keitel). **TH** Swearing, sex scenes, nudity. 𝔇𝔙𝔇

Kate Winslet *Ruth Barron* • Harvey Keitel *PJ Waters* • Julie Hamilton *Miriam* • Tim Robertson *Gilbert* • Sophie Lee *Yvonne* • Dan Wyllie *Robbie* • Pam Grier *Carol* ■ *Dir* Jane Campion • *Scr* Jane Campion, from the autobiographical work *My Guru and His Disciple* by Christopher Isherwood

Holy Water ★★ 15
Comedy
2009 · UK/US · Colour · 93min

This slice of Oirish whimsy is simply too contrived and inconsequential to raise many laughs. The story follows four cash-strapped bachelors living in a remote village who try to improve their lot by stealing a consignment of Viagra and reselling it. Of course, their plans go awry, but it's thuddingly obvious what will ensue when they stash the pills in the local holy well. Stanley Townsend and Angeline Ball share the odd funny moment as the local cops amused by the antics of Linda Hamilton (of *Terminator* fame) and her American crew, as they attempt to recover the stolen shipment. But there's just no escape from the sheer volume of clichés and caricatures on show. **DP**

John Lynch *Tom "Gaffer" Gaffney* • Susan Lynch *Geraldine Gaffney* • Linda Hamilton *Cory Williams* • Cornelius Clarke *Podger Byrnes* ■ *Dir* Tom Reeve • *Scr* Michael O'Mahony, Caroline O'Meara, from a story by Tom Reeve

Homage ★★★
Psychological thriller
1995 · US · Colour · 97min

This slice of deep-fried Deep South melodrama, while it never really succeeds in throwing off its stage origins, still makes for entertainingly overheated viewing. Blythe Danner is the faded southern belle locked in a strange relationship with handyman Frank Whaley, until her actress daughter Sheryl Lee arrives to turn up the sexual tension. The three stars are superb, and Mark Medoff does his best to open up his play. **JF** Violence, sex scenes, swearing.

Blythe Danner *Katherine Samuel* • Frank Whaley *Archie Landrum* • Sheryl Lee *Lucy Samuel* • Bruce Davison *Joseph Smith* • Danny Nucci *Gilbert Tellez* ■ *Dir* Ross Kagan Marks • *Scr* Mark Medoff, from his play *The Homage That Follows*

Hombre ★★★★ PG
Western
1967 · US · Colour · 106min

Paul Newman said that his best movies all start with an "H", and this fine, grim western bears him out. This is a *Stagecoach* variation, assembling differing characters for a trek through Arizona, played by a very distinguished cast including veteran Fredric March and a gnarled Richard Boone. Only import Diane Cilento (Sean Connery's ex-wife) seems ill-at-ease in a pivotal role. The movie is beautifully shot by veteran photographer James Wong Howe, and Newman's piercing blue eyes have seldom

been more prominently featured. The plot has many valid points to make about incipient racism, and the film is deeply rewarding. **TS** Swearing.

Paul Newman *John Russell* • Fredric March *Favor* • Richard Boone *Grimes* • Diane Cilento *Jessie* • Cameron Mitchell *Braden* • Barbara Rush *Adra Favor* • Martin Balsam *Mendez* ■ *Dir* Martin Ritt • *Scr* Irving Ravetch, Harriet Frank Jr, from the novel by Elmore Leonard

Home ★★★★ 15
Drama
2008 · Swi/Fr/Bel · Colour · 97min

Swiss-French film-maker Ursula Meier describes her hypnotic, fairy-tale feature debut as "a road movie in reverse". It's a deft fable about the intrusion of the mechanical modern world, as a family living beside an abandoned, unfinished motorway discover it's about to open. As thousands of cars and lorries start to zoom past their home, Marthe (Isabelle Huppert) and her husband (Oliver Gourmet) retreat indoors and listen to traffic reports. Insanity follows slowly but surely. Capturing the mesmerising, rhythmic menace of high-speed traffic and the fractured emotions of a family under strain, this claustrophobic psychodrama leaves you gasping for fresh air. **JR** French +subtitles. Nudity, brief swearing.

Isabelle Huppert *Marthe* • Olivier Gourmet *Michel* • Adelaïde Leroux *Judith* • Madeleine Budd *Marion* • Kacey Mottet Klein *Julien* ■ *Dir* Ursula Meier • *Scr* Ursula Meier, Antoine Jaccoud, Olivier Lorelle, Gilles Taurand, Raphaelle Valbrune, Alice Winocour • *Cinematographer* Agnès Godard

Home ★★ 12A
Drama
2011 · Tur · Colour · 76min

Muzaffer Ozdemir's feature debut as writer/director reflects on the progress of modernisation in Turkey. Kanbolat Gorkem Arslan plays an Istanbul architect in a midlife crisis who returns to the rural area where he grew up, and finds that the mountain streams have been sold off to hydroelectric companies. Ozdemir, who is better known for acting in the early films of his countryman Nuri Bilge Ceylan, extracts little dramatic impetus from the situation, though the story is told with sincerity and passion. **TJ** Turkish +subtitles. Swearing.

Kanbolat Gorkem Arslan *Dogan* • Muzaffer Ozdemir • Muhammet Uzuner • Pinar Unsal ■ *Dir/Scr* Muzaffer Ozdemir

Home ★★★ U
Animated science-fiction adventure
2014 · US · Colour · 89min

ET meets *Lilo & Stitch* in this sweet, screwball culture clash comedy. The plot is over-familiar but family friendly, as alien fugitive Oh (voiced by Jim Parsons) finds an unlikely human ally in young Tip (a spirited Rihanna). Parsons is impressively dextrous, with Yoda-like dialogue, intergalactic catchphrases and persistent cuteness that might eventually grate on adults, but kids will remain entranced by the bold pop art visuals, with "bubble-power" designs and continuously amusing action. **AJ** 3D

Rihanna *Gratuity "Tip" Tucci* • Jim Parsons *Oh* • Steve Martin *Captain Smek* • Jennifer Lopez *Lucy* ■ *Dir* Tim Johnson • *Scr* Tom J Astle, Matt Ember, from the illustrated children's book *The True Meaning of Smekday* by Adam Rex

Home Alone ★★★★ PG
Comedy
1990 · US · Colour · 98min

This modest comedy became one of the highest grossing pictures of all time. Writer/producer John Hughes and director Chris Columbus tuned in to two key elements: the fantasy of Steven Spielberg's *ET*, with its children triumphing over adult adversity, and the perennial chase of Tom and Jerry cartoons. Thus Macaulay Culkin, then ten years old and already in his fifth picture, plays the youngster left stranded by his parents who fly to Paris for the holiday. He pigs out on junk food, watches videos and then copes heroically with two burglars (Joe Pesci and Daniel Stern). Surprisingly violent in a cartoon-like way, it captured every child's heart. **AT** 𝔇𝔙𝔇 Blu-ray

H

Macaulay Culkin *Kevin McCallister* • Joe Pesci *Harry* • Daniel Stern *Marv* • John Heard *Peter* • Roberts Blossom *Marley* • Catherine O'Hara *Kate* • John Candy *Gus Polinski* ■ *Dir* Chris Columbus • *Scr* John Hughes

Home Alone 2: Lost in New York ★★★ PG

Comedy　　　1992 · US · Colour · 119min

Yep, Kevin McCallister (Macaulay Culkin) has managed to ditch his family again, this time getting on the wrong plane and ending up alone in New York while they are heading for Florida. And, armed with Dad's wallet, he enjoys all of life's luxuries at the Plaza hotel until he runs into inept burglars Joe Pesci and Daniel Stern once again. What worked in the first film is not quite as entertaining here, but, as slapstick escapism goes, this is well engineered stuff. JB *DVD* *Blu-ray*

Macaulay Culkin *Kevin McCallister* • Joe Pesci *Harry Lyme* • Daniel Stern *Marvin Murchins* • Catherine O'Hara *Kate McCallister* • John Heard *Peter McCallister* • Devin Ratray *Buzz* • Hillary Wolf *Megan* • Maureen Elisabeth Shay *Linnie* ■ *Dir* Chris Columbus • *Scr* John Hughes, from his characters

Home Alone 3 ★★★ PG

Comedy　　　1997 · US · Colour · 102min

This time it's cute Alex D Linz whose befuddled parents have mistakenly left him on his own in the house, when an international espionage team come calling to steal back a top secret computer chip hidden in his new toy. Pity the hapless baddies as the plucky boy devises ingenious booby traps to foil them. Writer John Hughes's third neatly-plotted variation on the same theme is good knockabout fun. An unnecessary made-for-TV third sequel appeared in 2002. AME *DVD*

Alex D Linz *Alex Pruitt* • Olek Krupa *Beaupre* • Rya Kihlstedt *Alice* • Lenny Von Dohlen *Jernigan* • David Thornton *Unger* • Haviland Morris *Karen Pruitt* • Kevin Kilner *Jack Pruitt* ■ *Dir* Raja Gosnell • *Scr* John Hughes

Home Alone 4 ★ U

Comedy　　　2002 · US · Colour · 83min

In this vain attempt to keep the moribund franchise alive, Kevin (now played by nine-year-old Mike Weinberg) decides to escape to his dad's new girlfriend's place, which just happens to be a multi-million-dollar mansion. But old adversary Marv (French Stewart) is planning a kidnapping. And, surprise, surprise – Kevin is left to save the day. Missi Pyle (*Charlie and the Chocolate Factory*) provides a glimmer of humour as Marv's accomplice, but other than that, you have to wonder why they bothered. SuR *DVD*

Michael Weinberg [Mike Weinberg] *Kevin McCallister* • French Stewart *Marv Merchants* • Erick Avari *Prescott* • Barbara Babcock *Molly* • Jason Beghe *Peter McCallister* • Missi Pyle *Vera* ■ *Dir* Rod Daniel • *Scr* Debra Frank, Steve L Hayes, from characters by John Hughes

Home and Away ★ U

Comedy　　　1956 · UK · BW · 92min

This a non-Huggett reunion for Jack Warner and Kathleen Harrison. Written and directed by Vernon Sewell, this contrived tale of a widow trying to cheat a fortune out of the pools is meant to be whimsical and slightly wicked. However, it ends up merely frantic and unfunny, with the Warner-Harrison partnership having one of its few off days. DP

Jack Warner *George Knowles* • Kathleen Harrison *Elsie Harrison* • Lana Morris *Mary Knowles* • Charles Victor *Ted Groves* • Thora Hird *Margie Groves* • Leslie Henson *Uncle Tom* ■ *Dir* Vernon Sewell • *Scr* Vernon Sewell, RF Delderfield, from the play *Treble Trouble* by Heather McIntyre

The Home and the World ★★★★ U

Period drama　1984 · Ind · Colour · 139min

Throughout his career, Indian director Satyajit Ray turned to the works of his mentor, Rabindranath Tagore, for inspiration. Victor Banerjee loses his wife

(Swatilekha Chatterjee) after he breaks with the tradition of seclusion and introduces her to a dashing patriot (Soumitra Chatterjee) in this compelling conversation piece, based on Tagore's novel, exploring the dangers inherent in both repression and liberation. One of the few true auteurs of world cinema, Ray also wrote the script and composed the score. However, while the leads give immaculate performances and the director never used colour better, the film is not quite a masterwork. DP Bengali +subtitles. *DVD*

Soumitra Chatterjee *Sandip Mukherjee* • Victor Banerjee *Nikhilesh Choudhury* • Swatilekha Chatterjee *Bimala Choudhury* • Gopa Aich *Sister-in-law* • Jennifer Kapoor *Miss Gilby* ■ *Dir* Satyajit Ray • *Scr* Satyajit Ray, from a novel by Rabindranath Tagore

Home at Seven ★★★ U

Mystery　　　1952 · UK · BW · 81min

This was Ralph Richardson's sole venture as a film director, and a pretty fair job he makes of it, too. He also re-creates his stage role as the timid bank clerk whose dose of amnesia coincides with a murder and a robbery. The strength of the picture is that you're never quite sure whether he's bluffing or baffled, and the secret is tightly kept right to the end. It's more than a mite stagey, though, with wife Margaret Leighton and doctor Jack Hawkins particularly guilty of overseasoning the ham. DP *DVD*

Ralph Richardson *David Preston* • Margaret Leighton *Janet Preston* • Jack Hawkins *Dr Sparling* • Frederick Piper *Mr Petherbridge* • Diana Beaumont *Ellen* • Meriel Forbes *Peggy Dobson* • Michael Shepley *Major Watson* • Margaret Withers *Mrs Watson* ■ *Dir* Ralph Richardson • *Scr* Anatole de Grunwald, from the play by RC Sherriff

A Home at the End of the World ★★★ 15

Drama　　　2004 · US · Colour · 92min

Spanning three richly detailed decades from the 1960s onwards, this warm drama explores the complex bonds of love and friendship between former childhood friends, played as adults by Colin Farrell and Dallas Roberts. Reunited in early 1980s New York, the duo form an unconventional family with free-spirited older woman Robin Wright Penn. In a trio of beautifully nuanced performances, the actors breathe life into the multilayered but meandering script. SF Swearing, sex scenes, drug abuse. *DVD*

Colin Farrell (2) *Bobby Morrow* • Robin Wright Penn [Robin Wright] *Clare* • Dallas Roberts *Jonathan Glover* • Sissy Spacek *Alice Glover* • Matt Frewer *Ned Glover* • Erik Smith *Bobby (1974)* • Harris Allan *Jonathan (1974)* • Andrew Chalmers *Bobby (1967)* ■ *Dir* Michael Mayer (1) • *Scr* Michael Cunningham, from the novel by Michael Cunningham

Home before Dark ★★

Drama　　　1958 · US · BW · 136min

In this long-winded and bleak psychological drama, Jean Simmons plays a wife recovering from a mental breakdown, who returns to her unloving college professor husband (Dan O'Herlihy) and a stepsister (Rhonda Fleming) in whom her husband is more interested and a domineering stepmother (Mabel Albertson). This Mervyn LeRoy production tries to be more subtle but ends up merely dull. AE

Jean Simmons *Charlotte Bronn* • Dan O'Herlihy *Arnold Bronn* • Rhonda Fleming *Joan Carlisle* • Efrem Zimbalist Jr *Jake Diamond* • Mabel Albertson *Inez Winthrop* • Steve Dunne *Hamilton Gregory* • Joan Weldon *Frances Barrett* ■ *Dir* Mervyn LeRoy • *Scr* Robert Bassing, Eileen Bassing, from the novel *Home before Dark* by Eileen Bassing

Home for the Holidays ★★★ 15

Comedy drama　1995 · US · Colour · 98min

Jodie Foster follows up her quirky directorial debut (*Little Man Tate*) with this uneven comedy drama about a group of grown-up kids returning to the family home for a Thanksgiving that, of course, is filled

with romance, rows, misunderstandings and strange behaviour. Despite the occasional awkward switches between comedy and sentiment, this works most of the time, thanks to the impressive cast. JB Some swearing.

Holly Hunter *Claudia Larson* • Robert Downey Jr *Tommy Larson* • Anne Bancroft *Adele Larson* • Charles Durning *Henry Larson* • Dylan McDermott *Leo Fish* • Geraldine Chaplin *Aunt Glady* • Steve Guttenberg *Walter Wedman* • Claire Danes *Kitt* ■ *Dir* Jodie Foster • *Scr* WD Richter, from a short story by Chris Radant

Home Fries ★ 12

Drama　　　1998 · US · Colour · 89min

Drew Barrymore stars in this ill-conceived mix of romance, black humour and very little comedy. While her romance with Luke Wilson (she's a pregnant waitress, he's her Lamaze partner) works quite nicely, it's mixed in with a subplot (he and his brother scared their stepdad to death – literally) that doesn't work at all. Barrymore does her best, but there's little to work with. JB Swearing, violence.

Drew Barrymore *Sally* • Jake Busey *Angus* • Catherine O'Hara *Mrs Lever* • Shelley Duvall *Mrs Jackson* • Luke Wilson *Dorian* • Kim Robillard *Billy* ■ *Dir* Dean Parisot • *Scr* Vince Gilligan

Home from the Hill ★★★

Melodrama　　　1960 · US · Colour · 149min

In this splendid, engrossing MGM melodrama, Robert Mitchum delivers one of his finest performances as the Texas patriarch whose sons turn his domestic life inside out. In its day this movie was notable for the star-making performances of two Georges (Peppard and Hamilton) as Mitch's offspring, one legitimate, the other not. This is from the same period in flamboyant director Vincente Minnelli's career as *Some Came Running*, and shares with it a loving use of CinemaScope and an intense use of colour. TS

Robert Mitchum *Captain Wade Hunnicutt* • Eleanor Parker *Hannah Hunnicutt* • George Peppard *Rafe Copley* • George Hamilton *Theron Hunnicutt* • Everett Sloane *Albert Halstead* • Luana Patten *Libby Halstead* ■ *Dir* Vincente Minnelli • *Scr* Irving Ravetch, Harriet Frank Jr, from the novel by William Humphrey

Home in Indiana ★★★ U

Drama　　　1944 · US · Colour · 103min

This beguiling 20th Century-Fox horse-racing melodrama is beautifully shot by Edward Cronjager in glorious Technicolor. An unusually top-billed Walter Brennan seems to enjoy himself watching over two relative newcomers, Jeanne Crain and June Haver. Lon McCallister, who plays Brennan's young orphaned nephew, swiftly established himself as a star in this movie, but his film career only lasted another nine years. Director Henry Hathaway handles the climactic trotting race superbly, and, if it all seems familiar, Fox remade it in 1957 as *April Love*. TS

Walter Brennan *JP "Thunder" Bolt* • Lon McCallister *Sparke Thorton* • Jeanne Crain *Char* • June Haver *Cri-Cri* • Charlotte Greenwood *Penny* • Ward Bond *Jed Bruce* • Charles Dingle *Godaw Boole* • Robert Condon *Gordon Bradley* ■ *Dir* Henry Hathaway • *Scr* Winston Miller, from the novel *The Phantom Filly* by George Agnew Chamberlain

Home Movies ★★★

Comedy　　　1979 · US · Colour · 90min

Brian DePalma was teaching at New York's Sarah Lawrence College when he conceived the idea for this bold but misfiring comedy about a film-making guru who encourages his students to live as the stars of their own movies. Relishing the role of "the Maestro", Kirk Douglas turns in a devilish performance, made all the more effective by DePalma's neat tactic of shooting many of his scenes in the style of a self-aggrandising film diary. But the picture belongs to Keith Gordon as a nerd goaded into seizing editorial control of his sad existence by poaching his brother's fiancée. DP

Kirk Douglas *Dr Tuttle, "the Maestro"* • Nancy Allen *Kristina* • Keith Gordon *Denis* • Gerrit Graham *James* • Vincent Gardenia *Dr Byrd* ■ *Dir* Brian De Palma • *Scr* Robert Harders, Gloria Norris, Kim Ambler, Dana Edelman, Stephan LeMay, Charles Loventhal, from a story by Brian DePalma

A Home of Our Own ★★★ PG

Drama　　　1993 · US · Colour · 100min

Oscar winner Kathy Bates (*Misery*) gives another sterling performance, this time as a downtrodden mother determined to keep a roof over the heads of her children in this 1960s-set drama. Discovering that her eldest son Edward Furlong has turned to petty crime, she decides to uproot her brood from LA and ends up in Idaho. It's an often depressing tale, bolstered by warm performances and understated direction from Tony Bill, but it ultimately gets bogged down in its own relentlessness. JB

Kathy Bates *Frances Lacey* • Edward Furlong *Shayne Lacey* • Soon-Teck Oh *Mr Munimura* • Tony Campisi *Norman* • Amy Sakasitz *Annie Lacey* • Miles Feulner *Murray Lacey* • Clarissa Lassig *Lynn Lacey* • TJ Lowther *Craig Lacey* ■ *Dir* Tony Bill • *Scr* Patrick Duncan

Home of the Brave ★★★

Second World War drama
1949 · US · BW · 86min

Is one form of racial discrimination as bad as another? Since anti-Semitism had received a wide airing in recent movies, producer Stanley Kramer, director Mark Robson and writer Carl Foreman changed the theme of Arthur Laurents's Second World War play to attack prejudice against black people instead. In this low-budget drama, set on a South Pacific island held by the Japanese, James Edwards is excellent as the black soldier whose biggest enemy is a bigoted corporal (Steve Brodie). AE

Douglas Dick *Maj Robinson* • Steve Brodie *Corporal TJ Everett* • Jeff Corey *Doctor* • Lloyd Bridges *Finch* • Frank Lovejoy *Mingo* • James Edwards *Peter Moss* ■ *Dir* Mark Robson • *Scr* Carl Foreman, from the play by Arthur Laurents

Home of the Brave ★★★ U

Experimental concert movie
1986 · US · Colour · 91min

If you liked performance artist Laurie Andersen's 1981 Top Ten hit *O Superman*, you may find this multi-media concert film fascinating. If not, her unconventional warbling and post-hippy presentation will seem a pretentious bore. That said, Andersen's unorthodox music is mixed with a nice line in eccentric humour and accompanied by a well-staged array of colourful visuals, while cult author William S Burroughs adds to the rarefied feel. AJ

■ *Dir/Scr* Laurie Anderson

Home of the Brave ★★ 15

Drama　　　2006 · US/Mor · Colour · 104min

Four Iraq War veterans return to their Washington homes demoralised, wounded and spiritually shattered in this unsubtle, overly earnest and unconvincing melodrama. Samuel L Jackson's doctor becomes an alcoholic, Jessica Biel's teacher goes back to the classroom as an amputee, Brian Presley's infantry man mourns his killed-in-action best friend, and Curtis "50 Cent" Jackson's soldier suffers post-traumatic stress disorder. This offers very little that's new or emotionally relevant – and it's all been done far better before in such movies as *The Deer Hunter* and *Coming Home*. AJ Violence, swearing. *DVD* *Blu-ray*

Samuel L Jackson *Will Marsh* • Jessica Biel *Vanessa Price* • Brian Presley *Tommy Yates* • Curtis Jackson [Curtis "50 Cent" Jackson] *Jamal Aiken* • Christina Ricci *Sarah Schivino* ■ *Dir* Irwin Winkler • *Scr* Mark Friedman, from a story by Friedman, Irwin Winkler

Home on the Range ★★ U

Animated comedy western
2004 · US · Colour · 73min

Despite the impressive voice talent, Disney's old-fashioned, Wild West-set tale of three cows who try to save their farm from repossession is too weak and uninspiring to really charm. The animals need more depth and definition, particularly given the flimsy plotline and crudely rendered landscapes. The film has some nice moments, but this is a pedestrian affair. SF *DVD*

Roseanne Barr *Maggie* • Judi Dench *Mrs Caloway* • Jennifer Tilly *Grace* • Cuba Gooding Jr *Buck* • Randy Quaid *Alameda Slim* • Carole Cook *Pearl* • Richard Riehle *Sheriff Brown* • Charles Haid *Lucky Jack* • Steve Buscemi *Wesley* ■ *Dir* Will Finn, John Sanford (2) • *Scr* Will Finn, John Sanford (2), from a story by Will Finn, John Sanford, Michael Labash, Sam Levine, Mark Kennedy, Robert Lence

Home, Sweet Home ★★★
Silent drama　　　　1914 · US · BW · 62min

This was the film that consolidated DW Griffith's reputation and established the cinema as a mature art form and supreme entertainment experience. Slight by the standards of what was to come, this heavily sentimentalised biopic of composer John Howard Payne (writer of the song that gives the film its title) features a marvellous line-up of most of Griffith's favourite stars. Henry B Walthall is Payne and the luminous Lillian Gish his long-suffering sweetheart. It looks quaint today, but parts were risible even then, especially the hell-to-heaven "flying" finale. TS

Henry B Walthall *John Howard Payne* • Josephine Crowell *Mother* • Lillian Gish *Sweetheart* • Dorothy Gish *Sister* ■ *Dir* DW Griffith • *Scr* HE Aitken, DW Griffith, from the song by John Howard Payne

Home Sweet Homicide ★★★ U
Detective comedy drama
1946 · US · BW · 89min

This is a typically enjoyable Lloyd Bacon offering. A domestic comedy, it has siblings Peggy Ann Garner, Dean Stockwell and Connie Marshall attempting to matchmake their widowed mother, Lynn Bari, with the eligible Randolph Scott. However, there's also a mystery element by dint of the fact that she's a whodunnit writer and he's a cop investigating the same murder that the kids want to solve. Neither scenario contains a scintilla of suspense, but it's nice to be reminded of what fun family entertainment used to be. DP

Peggy Ann Garner *Dinah Carstairs* • Randolph Scott *Lt Bill Smith* • Lynn Bari *Marian Carstairs* • Dean Stockwell *Archie Carstairs* • Connie Marshall *April Carstairs* • James Gleason *Sgt Dan O'Hare* ■ *Dir* Lloyd Bacon • *Scr* F Hugh Herbert, from the novel by Craig Rice

Home Team ★ PG
Sports comedy drama
1998 · Can · Colour · 91min

Hollywood still hasn't got the hang of football (or soccer, as they insist on calling it), and this family-orientated frolic is decidedly minor league. As an ex-pro with gambling problems, Steve Guttenberg is sentenced to community service at a tough children's home, where the powers that be think that footie might be the best way to improve team spirit. DP *DVD*

Steve Guttenberg *Mr Butler* • Ryan Slater • Tyler Hynes *Chip* • Johnny Morina *Alex* ■ *Dir* Allan A Goldstein • *Scr* Pierce O'Donnell

Home to Danger ★★
Mystery　　　　　1951 · UK · BW · 67min

Rona Anderson inherits an estate when her father commits suicide and is immediately attacked by a mysterious assailant. As the corpses mount up, so do the suspects in this standard whodunnit, directed by Terence Fisher, who later hit his stride with his Hammer horrors. AT

Guy Rolfe *Robert* • Rona Anderson *Barbara* • Francis Lister *Wainwright* • Alan Wheatley *Hughes* • Bruce Belfrage *Solicitor* • Stanley Baker *Willie Dougan* ■ *Dir* Terence Fisher • *Scr* John Temple-Smith, Francis Edge

Home Town Story ★★ U
Drama　　　　　1951 · US · BW · 61min

Released during the Red Scare to reinforce confidence in corporate America, this was

distributed by MGM, but supervised by John K Ford, the head of the General Motors film unit. The scenario couldn't be much more cynically corny, as small-town editor Jeffrey Lynn abandons his paper's anti-capitalist stance after his kid sister, Melinda Plowman, is rescued in the nick of time by machinery manufactured by Donald Crisp's conglomerate. However, the picture has been delivered from its deserved obscurity by the appearance of a young Marilyn Monroe. DP *DVD*

Jeffrey Lynn *Blake Washburn* • Donald Crisp *John MacFarland* • Marjorie Reynolds *Janice Hunt* • Alan Hale Jr *Slim Haskins* • Marilyn Monroe *Iris Martin* • Barbara Brown *Mrs Washburn* • Melinda Plowman *Katie Washburn* ■ *Dir/Scr* Arthur Pierson

Homecoming ★★
Second World War medical romance
1948 · US · BW · 112min

MGM knew it would be enough to put Clark Gable together with Lana Turner for the crowds to flock in and didn't try very hard to make a worthwhile picture. Gable is the smug society doctor, married to Anne Baxter, who joins the medical corps, falls in love with Lana Turner's nurse while serving overseas and comes to dedicate himself to helping others. Anne Baxter gives the sharpest performance on view, while the glossy, long-winded direction is by Mervyn LeRoy. AE

Clark Gable *Ulysses Delby Johnson* • Lana Turner *Lt Jane "Snapshot" McCall* • Anne Baxter *Penny Johnson* • John Hociak *Dr Robert Sunday* • Ray Collins *Lt Col Avery Silver* • Gladys Cooper *Mrs Kirby* • Cameron Mitchell *Sgt Monkevickz* • Art Baker *Mr Williams* ■ *Dir* Mervyn LeRoy • *Scr* Paul Osborn, Jan Lustig, from the story *The Homecoming of Ulysses* by Sidney Kingsley

The Homecoming ★★★★ 12
Drama　　　　1973 · US/UK · Colour · 109min

One of theatrical director Peter Hall's rare forays into film, this adaptation of Harold Pinter's play is more an account of a performance than a break-out from the restraint of the stage. But it's still white hot with bitterness, resentment and rancid randiness as north London butcher Paul Rogers makes mincemeat of his family (Cyril Cusack, Ian Holm, Michael Jayston, Terence Rigby) while Vivien Merchant flaunts her high-tease power to stunning effect. Pinter's dialogue has never been so enigmatic, menacing or comic. TH *DVD*

Cyril Cusack *Sam* • Ian Holm *Lenny* • Michael Jayston *Teddy* • Vivien Merchant *Ruth* • Terence Rigby *Joey* • Paul Rogers *Max* ■ *Dir* Peter Hall • *Scr* Harold Pinter, from his play

Homecoming ★★★ U
Drama　　　　1996 · US · Colour · 100min

Distinguished actress Anne Bancroft won praise for her portrayal of a crotchety grandmother in this sentimental TV movie. When their mother abandons them in a strange city, teenager Kimberlee Peterson and her three younger siblings are forced to begin a difficult journey in search of a home. They embark on a 500-mile trek that leads them to the cantankerous grandmother they never knew. MC *DVD*

Anne Bancroft *Abigail "Ab" Tilerman* • Kimberlee Peterson *Dicey Tillerman* • Trever O'Brien *James Tillerman* • Hanna Hall *Maybeth Tillerman* • William Greenblatt *Sammy Tillerman* • Bonnie Bedelia *Eunice* • Anna Louise Richardson *Liza Tillerman* ■ *Dir* Mark Jean • *Scr* Christopher Carlson, Mark Jean, from the novel by Cynthia Voigt

Homefront ★★★ 15
Action thriller　　　2013 · US · Colour · 95min

This by-the-book thriller stars Jason Statham as Phil Broker, a federal agent who quits his job after his wife's death and moves to the Deep South to start a new life with his ten-year-old daughter. The natives are less than friendly, though, and when a local crime lord (James Franco) tries to use Broker's past to aid his meth operation, the stage is set for a fight to the end between good and evil. Sylvester Stallone's screenplay ticks all the requisite boxes for a white-knuckle clash between cultures and

consciences, while Statham displays a tender side rarely seen in his previous action work. TeS *DVD* *Blu*

Jason Statham *Phil Broker* • James Franco *Gator Bodine* • Winona Ryder *Sheryl Mott* • Kate Bosworth *Cassie Bodine* • Frank Grillo *Cyrus* ■ *Dir* Gary Fleder • *Scr* Sylvester Stallone, from Chuck Logan's novel

Homegrown ★★★ 18
Comedy drama　　1998 · US · Colour · 97min

A Cheech and Chong movie for the Tarantino generation? Not exactly, but this tale of reefer madness does have the same sharp turns from hilarity to horror, plus a starry, eclectic supporting cast who pop up with atypical characterisations. After the brutal murder of their drug dealer boss, drug harvesters Billy Bob Thornton, Hank Azaria and Ryan Phillippe decide to carry on as normal and keep the profits for themselves. The "Class A" cast and the ensuing twists and turns bring a lively buzz to proceedings. JC Swearing, drug abuse.

Billy Bob Thornton *Jack* • Hank Azaria *Carter* • Kelly Lynch *Lucy* • Ryan Phillippe *Harlan* • John Lithgow *Malcolm/Robert* • Jon Bon Jovi *Danny* • Jamie Lee Curtis *Sierra Kahan* • Judge Reinhold *Policeman* • Ted Danson *Gianni* ■ *Dir* Stephen Gyllenhaal • *Scr* Stephen Gyllenhaal, Nicholas Kazan, from a story by Stephen Gyllenhaal, Jonah Raskin

Homeless to Harvard: the Liz Murray Story ★★★
Drama based on a true story
2003 · US · Colour · 95min

Thora Birch was nominated for an Emmy for her performance in this true-story drama. Born into an impoverished Bronx family, Liz Murray spent much of her early life in squalid housing or public hostels. Her father was a drug addict, and her mother was schizophrenic, legally blind and HIV-positive. However, at the age of 15, Murray turned her life around and eventually won a scholarship to Harvard. Director Peter Levin lays on the melodrama, but Birch manages to convey Murray's spirit, while Kelly Lynch impresses as her mother. DP Drug abuse.

Thora Birch *Liz Murray* • Kelly Lynch *Jean Murray* • Michael Riley *Peter Murray* • Ellen Page *Young Lisa* • Liz Murray *Social worker* ■ *Dir* Peter Levin • *Scr* Ronni Kern

Homer and Eddie ★★ 15
Road movie　　　1989 · US · Colour · 95min

James Belushi co-stars with Whoopi Goldberg in this mediocre road movie, in which a con artist (Goldberg) takes a mentally handicapped man (Belushi) across country so he can visit his dying father. This could have been so much better, but director Andrei Konchalovsky blunders at every turn. JB

James Belushi *Homer Lanza* • Whoopi Goldberg *Eddie Cervi* • Anne Ramsey *Edna* • Karen Black *Belle* • Beah Richards *Linda Cervi* ■ *Dir* Andrei Konchalovsky • *Scr* Patrick Cirillo

The Homesman ★★★★ 15
Western　　　2014 · US/Fr · Colour · 117min

Feisty pioneer-woman Hilary Swank volunteers to transport to Iowa three other women from her town who have all been driven mad by the hard-scrabble life on the Nebraska plains. Thus begins an arduous journey in what is mostly a woman-centric story, although a problematic third-act shock changes the terms dramatically. It's a tough-minded, intelligent movie, the kind John Wayne would have probably hated, while Jones's direction is stylish and assured, and he generously gives Swank room to prove what a great actor she can be with the right material. LF In English, Danish. Violence, sex scenes, nudity. *DVD* *Blu*

Tommy Lee Jones *George Briggs* • Hilary Swank *Mary Bee Cuddy* • Meryl Streep *Altha Carter* • Grace Gummer *Arabella Sours* • Miranda Otto *Theoline Belknap* • Sonja Richter *Gro Svendsen* • William Fichtner *Vester Belknap* • John Lithgow *Reverend Dowd* ■ *Dir* Tommy Lee Jones • *Scr* Tommy Lee Jones, Kieran Fitzgerald, Wesley A Oliver, from Glendon Swarthout's novel

Homeward Bound: the Incredible Journey ★★★ U
Adventure　　1993 · US · Colour · 84min

It seemed invidious to remake the 1963 Disney true-life adventure classic *The Incredible Journey*, especially with talking animals. But while the original remains the superior picture, this is still a treat for children, thanks to the astonishing performances of its animal cast. The vocal talents of Michael J Fox, Sally Field and Don Ameche certainly help pep up the pets' personalities, although you expect more of a screenwriter like Caroline Thompson than a series of playground-level wisecracks. Nevertheless, good family fare. DP *DVD*

Michael J Fox *Chance* • Sally Field *Sassy* • Don Ameche *Shadow* • Kim Greist *Laura* • Robert Hays *Bob* • Benj Thall *Peter* • Veronica Lauren *Hope* • Kevin Chevalia *Jamie* ■ *Dir* Duwayne Dunham • *Scr* Caroline Thompson, Linda Wolverton, from the film *The Incredible Journey* by James Algar, from the novel by Sheila Burnford

Homeward Bound II: Lost in San Francisco ★★ U
Adventure　　1996 · US · Colour · 85min

This sequel opens with an airport mix-up resulting in an accidental abandonment. However, with Shadow and Sassy to help him, Chance isn't alone for long. Romance is in the air as our heroic trio are befriended by a pack of street dogs. Ralph Waite replaces the late Don Ameche as the sagacious Shadow, but not all the casting is as felicitous: the decision to have strays voiced by African-American actors has unfortunate racist overtones. DP *DVD*

Michael J Fox *Chance* • Sally Field *Sassy* • Ralph Waite *Shadow* • Robert Hays *Bob* • Kim Greist *Laura* • Veronica Lauren *Hope* ■ *Dir* David R Ellis • *Scr* Chris Hauty, from a story by Chris Hauty, Julie Hickson, from characters by Sheila Burnford

Homework ★★★★
Documentary　　1989 · Iran · Colour · 85min

This is a fascinating documentary insight into the workings of the Iranian education system from Abbas Kiarostami, who established the film department at Iran's Institute for the Intellectual Development of Children and Young Adults. There, he began a relationship with film and culture that has given rise to comparisons with Satyajit Ray and Eric Rohmer. Here, as various stressed schoolboys tell their stories, it becomes clear that Kiarostami has made an astute study into the nature of childhood, in a country where many parents are illiterate and children are forced to play their part in providing for the family. DP Farsi +subtitles.

■ *Dir* Abbas Kiarostami

Homicidal ★★★ 12
Horror　　　　1961 · US · BW · 83min

William Castle's grisly gender-switch thriller was the first and most obvious *Psycho* clone, taking transvestite terror to its illogical conclusion. A weird tale of decapitations, delirious dementia and dysfunctional drag, time has watered down Castle's sneaky surprises and tongue-in-cheek dénouement. But, while you won't need his fun 'Fright Break' – 45 seconds to leave the cinema if too nervous to cope with the climax – Castle's prowess at powerhouse panic still rustles up some scares. AJ *DVD*

Glenn Corbett *Karl* • Patricia Breslin *Miriam Webster* • Jean Arless [Joan Marshall] *Emily/Warren* • Eugenie Leontovich *Helga* • Alan Bunce *Dr Jonas* • Richard Rust *Jim Nesbitt* ■ *Dir* William Castle • *Scr* Robb White

Homicide ★★★★ 15
Crime thriller　　1991 · US · Colour · 96min

David Mamet's third outing as writer/director is a tough look at racial prejudice inside and outside the police force. Mamet's roots as a playwright are evident in some scenes, but there's no denying the power of the whole piece as Joe Mantegna's Jewish cop investigates murder and a drug cartel, and finds organised anti-Semitism and an underground Jewish resistance movement. Its conclusions are bleak, yet reaching them makes for absorbing viewing. AT Violence, swearing. **DVD**

Joe Mantegna *Bob Gold* • William H Macy *Tim Sullivan* • Natalija Nogulich *Chava* • Ving Rhames *Randolph* • Vincent Guastaferro *Lieutenant Senna* • Rebecca Pidgeon *Ms Klein* ■ *Dir/Scr* David Mamet

L'Homme de Ma Vie ★★★ 15
Drama   1992 · Fr/Can · Colour · 98min

Many viewers will only have come across the Portuguese actress Maria de Medeiros in Philip Kaufman's *Henry and June* or Quentin Tarantino's *Pulp Fiction*. However, this amusing adult comedy from Jean-Charles Tacchella affords her the chance to demonstrate the talent that had long since established her as a top European star. As the flighty 20-something searching for the rich man of her dreams, she is both kittenish and capricious, greeting each heartbreak with a shrug and a new dress. The action sags briefly, but Tacchella mostly keeps things light. DP French +subtitles. **DVD**

Maria de Medeiros *Aimée* • Thierry Fortineau *Maurice* • Jean-Pierre Bacri *Malcolm* • Anne Letourneau *Catherine* • Ginette Garcin *Arlette* ■ *Dir/Scr* Jean-Charles Tacchella

L'Homme du Train ★★★★ 12
Black comedy drama
2002 · Fr/UK/Ger/Jpn · Colour · 86min

Male bonding has been a recurring theme throughout director Patrice Leconte's career, but he's never handled the subject with such wit, sensitivity and insight as in this superb two-hander. The key to its success is the easy rapport between Jean Rochefort's retired teacher and Johnny Hallyday's taciturn thief, as they contemplate heart surgery and a bank robbery, respectively. A whiff of chauvinism pervades the subplots, but mostly the atmosphere is one of late-life regret tinged with a wistful envy for each other's lifestyle. Rochefort is typically mischievous, but the revelation is Hallyday who lowers his guard of Gallic cool to reveal genuine vulnerability. DP French +subtitles. **DVD**

Jean Rochefort *Manesquier* • Johnny Hallyday *Milan* • Jean-François Stévenin *Luigi* • Charlie Nelson *Max* • Pascal Parmentier *Sadko* • Isabelle Petit-Jacques *Viviane* ■ *Dir* Patrice Leconte • *Scr* Claude Klotz

Un Homme et une Femme
★★★★ PG
Romantic drama
1966 · Fr · BW, colour and sepia · 98min

Winner of the best foreign film Oscar and the Palme d'Or at Cannes, this teasing melodrama is one of the most famous examples of artistic triumph over adversity. The switches to sepia-tinted film stock were much applauded at the time (although they look rather flashy and trite today), but they were forced on director Claude Lelouch because he lacked the funds to shoot the picture in colour. Amid the chic cinematic trickery, Jean-Louis Trintignant and Anouk Aimée are splendid as the widowed couple teetering on the brink of romance. They would reunite in a sequel released in the UK as *A Man and a Woman: 20 Years Later*. DP French +subtitles. **DVD**

Jean-Louis Trintignant *Jean-Louis Duroc* • Anouk Aimée *Anne Gauthier* • Pierre Barouh *Pierre Gauthier* • Valérie Lagrange *Valerie Duroc* • Simone Paris *Headmistress* • Antoine Sire *Antoine Duroc* • Souad Amidou *Françoise Gauthier* • Henri Chemin *Jean-Louis's co-driver* ■ *Dir* Claude Lelouch • *Scr* Pierre Uytterhoeven, Claude Lelouch, from a story by Claude Lelouch • *Music* Francis Lai

Hondo ★★★ PG
Western   1953 · US · Colour · 80min

This fine colourful western was originally made in 3D, which explains the odd look of certain segments, notably the marvellous title sequence where John Wayne just keeps on walking off the screen and, supposedly, into the audience. Wayne, in his

prime, plays a grim, buckskin-clad cavalry scout who comes across Oscar-nominated Geraldine Page and her son Lee Aaker and eventually helps them fend off some Apache Indians. This is a mature, good-looking western. TS **DVD** **BL** **3D**

John Wayne *Hondo Lane* • Geraldine Page *Angie Lowe* • Ward Bond *Buffalo* • Michael Pate *Vittoro* • James Arness *Lennie* • Rodolfo Acosta *Silva* • Leo Gordon *Ed Lowe* • Lee Aaker *Johnny* ■ *Dir* John Farrow • *Scr* James Edward Grant, from the story *The Gift of Cochise* by Louis L'Amour

Honest ★ 18
Crime caper   2000 · UK · Colour · 105min

This crime caper is part vanity project, part nostalgic throwback to the kitsch excesses of the Swinging Sixties. Melanie Blatt and real-life siblings Natalie and Nicole Appleton play three East End sisters who support their stay-at-home dad (James Cosmo) by dressing up as fellas and robbing London's great and good. Atrociously acted, ineptly plotted and directed with little sense of pace, period or plausibility. NS **DVD**

Nicole Appleton *Gerry Chase* • Natalie Appleton *Mandy Chase* • Melanie Blatt *Jo Chase* • Peter Facinelli *Daniel Wheaton* • James Cosmo *Tommy Chase* • Jonathan Cake *Andrew Pryce-Stevens* • Corin Redgrave *Duggie Ord* ■ *Dir* David A Stewart • *Scr* David A Stewart, Dick Clement, Ian La Frenais

Honey ★★ PG
Dance drama   2003 · US · Colour · 90min

Jessica Alba stars in this spirited urban drama, the debut feature of music-video director Bille Woodruff. Alba is the aspiring choreographer who's given a big break by a sleazy video director, only to realise that her heart lies with the underprivileged kids she'd previously taught dance classes to. There's plenty for fans of hip-hop/R&B to enjoy, even if the cautionary tale is simplistic. SF **DVD** **BL**

Jessica Alba *Honey Daniels* • Mekhi Phifer *Chaz* • Joy Bryant *Gina* • Lil' Romeo *Benny* • David Moscow *Michael Ellis* • Lonette McKee *Mrs Daniels* • Zachary Isaiah Williams *Raymond* ■ *Dir* Bille Woodruff • *Scr* Alonzo Brown, Kim Watson

Honey 2 ★★ PG
Dance drama   2011 · US · Colour · 106min

This derivative teen fantasy is so watered down from the originality of *Flashdance* or even the corny power of the *Step Up* movies that its script seems to have been written by children. Katerina Graham (from TV series *The Vampire Diaries*) plays spunky, lip-biting juvenile delinquent Maria – a girl who lives to dance, and has a lot to prove. Some of the numbers at the TV "Battle Zone" competition are fun, but this film is a strictly clichéd exercise that will have you howling for all the wrong reasons. KK Swearing. **DVD** **BL**

Katerina Graham *Maria* • Randy Wayne *Brandon* • Seychelle Gabriel *Tina* • Christopher "War" Martinez *Luis* • Lonette McKee *Connie Daniels* • Gerry Bednob *Mr Kapoor* ■ *Dir* Bille Woodruff • *Scr* Alyson Fouse, Blayne Weaver, from characters by Alonzo Brown, Kim Watson

Honey, I Shrunk the Kids
★★★★ U
Comedy fantasy   1989 · US · Colour · 89min

The Absent-Minded Professor meets *The Incredible Shrinking Man* in a joyous, innocuous and thrilling Walt Disney adventure that will appeal to both young and old. Rick Moranis makes you laugh long and loud as the wacky inventor whose molecular reducer shrinks his two kids, and the children next door, to the size of Tom Thumb's thumb. How they cope with giant insects and water sprinklers in their hazardous garden-turned-jungle makes for epic chills, doubling as a neat eco-learning quest in the best Disney tradition. Two sequels and a TV series followed. AJ **DVD**

Rick Moranis *Wayne Szalinski* • Matt Frewer *Big Russ Thompson* • Marcia Strassman *Diane Szalinski* • Kristine Sutherland *Mae Thompson* • Thomas Brown [Thomas Wilson Brown] *Little Russ Thompson* • Jared Rushton *Ron*

Thompson ■ *Dir* Joe Johnston • *Scr* Ed Naha, Tom Schulman, from a story by Stuart Gordon, Brian Yuzna, Ed Naha

Honey, I Blew Up the Kid
★★★ U
Comedy fantasy   1992 · US · Colour · 85min

After nerdy scientist Rick Moranis accidentally pumps up his son into a 50ft giant, this film is reduced to a one-note romp that almost creaks to a halt. However, there is a well-sustained spirit of infectious enthusiasm, bug-eyed innocence and wild lunacy that harks back to the "creature features" of the 1950s. The central idea of a normally harmless child running amok in the adult world is strong, and Moranis is reliably goofy. JM **DVD**

Rick Moranis *Wayne Szalinski* • Marcia Strassman *Diane Szalinski* • Robert Oliveri *Nick Szalinski* • Daniel Shalikar *Adam Szalinski* • Joshua Shalikar *Adam Szalinski* • Lloyd Bridges *Clifford Sterling* • John Shea *Hendrickson* • Keri Russell *Mandy* • Amy O'Neill *Amy Szalinski* ■ *Dir* Randal Kleiser • *Scr* Thom Eberhardt, Peter Elbling, Garry Goodrow, from a story by Garry Goodrow, from characters by Stuart Gordon, Brian Yuzna, Ed Naha

Honey, We Shrunk Ourselves ★★ PG
Science-fiction comedy
1997 · US · Colour · 71min

Despite the presence of original star Rick Moranis, the concept was clearly running out of steam by the time Disney made this straight-to-video second sequel to *Honey, I Shrunk the Kids*. This time it's the adults who get downsized as Moranis, together with his wife, brother and sister-in-law, are miniaturised by his shrinking machine. The effects are fine, and director Dean Cundey keeps the action bustling, but it still feels old hat. JF **DVD**

Rick Moranis *Wayne Szalinski* • Eve Gordon *Diane Szalinski* • Robin Bartlett *Patty Szalinski* • Allison Mack *Jenny Szalinski* • Jake Richardson *Gordon Szalinski* • Bug Hall *Adam Szalinski* ■ *Dir* Dean Cundey • *Scr* Karey Kirkpatrick, Nell Scovell, Joel Hodgson, from characters by Stuart Gordon, Brian Yuzna, Ed Naha

The Honey Pot ★★★
Comedy   1967 · UK/US/It · Colour · 150min

For this amusing if laboured reworking of Ben Jonson's *Volpone*, the idea of having millionaire Rex Harrison test the loyalty of former lovers Edie Adams, Capucine and Susan Hayward by pretending to be dying is just as Jonson intended. But the intricate comedy could do without the contrived murder mystery that is unconvincingly tacked on here. Mankiewicz's dialogue has none of the original musicality and wit, yet Harrison valiantly tries to sparkle and Maggie Smith is fun as Hayward's nurse. DP

Rex Harrison *Cecil Fox* • Susan Hayward *Mrs Lone-Star Crockett Sheridan* • Cliff Robertson *William McFly* • Capucine *Princess Dominique* • Edie Adams *Merle McGill* • Maggie Smith *Sarah Watkins* • Adolfo Celi *Inspector Rizzi* ■ *Dir* Joseph L Mankiewicz • *Scr* Joseph L Mankiewicz, from the novel *The Evil of the Day* by Thomas Sterling, from the play *Mr Fox of Venice* by Frederick Knott

Honeydripper ★★★ PG
Period drama   2007 · US · Colour · 118min

This fantastical tale of the early days of rock 'n' roll is really one for fans of its leftfield writer/director John Sayles. The setting is the rural Deep South of 1950 and Danny Glover stars as Tyrone Purvis, owner of the Honeydripper Lounge, a drinks and dance joint that has seen better days. Guitarist Gary Clark Jr steals the slow but smouldering show, playing the new kid who might just be the future of music. DA **DVD**

Danny Glover *Tyrone Purvis* • Lisa Gay Hamilton *Delilah* • Yaya DaCosta *China Doll* • Charles S Dutton *Maceo* • Vondie Curtis Hall [Vondie Curtis-Hall] *Slick* • Gary Clark Jr *Sonny Blake* • Dr Mable John *Bertha Mae* • Stacy Keach *Sheriff Pugh* ■ *Dir/Scr* John Sayles

Honeymoon ★★ U
Romantic dance drama
1959 · Sp/UK · Colour · 99min

A dancer (Ludmila Tcherina) who has sacrificed her career for marriage to a possessive husband (Anthony Steel), is drawn to return to the stage while honeymooning in Spain where the great Antonio dances. The innovative film-maker Michael Powell, unable to resist Antonio's invitation to make a film with him, came unstuck with this loosely scripted co-production, which ends up as part travelogue, part dance film. Regarded as a rare disaster from the director of *The Red Shoes*, it still ravishes the eye and provides an opportunity to see Antonio perform his signature *zapateado*. RK

Anthony Steel *Kit* • Ludmilla Tcherina *Anna* • Antonio • Léonide Massine ■ *Dir* Michael Powell • *Scr* Michael Powell, Luis Escobar, Gregorio Martinez Sierra

Honeymoon ★★★ 15
Science-fiction horror
2014 · US · Colour · 83min

Leigh Janiak's first feature has more than enough taut and intimate chills to make its mark with sci-fi fans. Harry Treadaway and Rose Leslie play young newlyweds honeymooning in a remote lakeside cabin. Wandering off alone in the forest, Leslie returns disorientated and strangely forgetful of their past romantic history. The sinister thrills mainly come from the headliners' captivating performances and a script that's more concerned with showing marital relationship breakdown than anything too alien. AJ Violence, swearing, sex scenes. **DVD** **BL**

Rose Leslie *Bea* • Harry Treadaway *Paul* • Ben Huber *Will* • Hanna Brown *Annie* ■ *Dir* Leigh Janiak • *Scr* Leigh Janiak, Phil Graziadei

A Honeymoon Adventure
★★★ PG
Crime drama   1931 · UK · BW · 65min

Released stateside under its title *Footsteps in the Night*, this is a lively comic adventure from writing team Basil Dean and John Paddy Carstairs. The spirited Benita Hume shuttles between London and Scotland after her inventor husband is abducted for his secret formula during their honeymoon. Director Maurice Elvey studs his thriller with slick set pieces like the encounter in an old dark house and the train chase, and makes adept use of locations such as London's Euston Station. DP **DVD**

Benita Hume *Eve Martin* • Peter Hannen *Peter Martin* • Harold Huth *Walter Creason* • Walter Armitage *Judson* • Jack Lambert *Chauffeur* ■ *Dir* Maurice Elvey • *Scr* John Carstairs [John Paddy Carstairs], Basil Dean, Rupert Downing, from the novel *Footsteps in the Night* by Cecily Fraser

Honeymoon for One ★★
Romance   2011 · US · Colour · 95min

Love and green issues lead to a fairy-tale finale in this formulaic yet innocuous culture-clash romp, starring former *Desperate Housewives* leading lady Nicollette Sheridan. Not as slushy as the usual made-for-TV romance, it sees Sheridan's work-obsessed LA executive embark on a life-changing adventure when she ditches her unfaithful fiancé a week before the wedding and goes on their intended Irish castle honeymoon alone. There's lots of simple, visual humour in the clichéd, fish-out-of-water scenario that follows. SF Some swearing.

Nicollette Sheridan *Eve* • Greg Wise *Sean Hughes* • Patrick Baladi *Greg Young* • Jonathan Hawtrey Clark *Miles* ■ *Dir* Kevin Connor • *Scr* Rick Suvalle

Honeymoon for Three ★★
Musical   1935 · UK · BW · 80min

Not to be confused with Lloyd Bacon's 1941 Hollywood screwball, this is a typically breezy Stanley Lupino comedy that sees his impecunious playboy frog-marched to the altar by French banker Dennis Hoey. However, Lupino and Aileen Marson are not the marrying kind and plan to divorce at the earliest opportunity. Dotted with deft ditties, this amusing but dated diversion boasted Jack Cardiff as camera operator, while the director was Leo Mittler, whose *Beyond the Street* (1929) had been an important example of German studio realism before he was forced to flee the Third Reich. DP **DVD**

Stanley Lupino *Jack Denver* • Aileen Marson *Yvonne Daumery* • Jack Melford *Raymond Dirk* • Robert English *Herbert Denver* ■ *Dir* Leo Mittler • *Scr* Frank Miller, from a story by Stanley Lupino

Honeymoon Hotel ★★
Comedy 1964 · US · Colour · 88min

A bachelor (Robert Morse) is stood up at the altar and decides to go on the Caribbean honeymoon anyway. In place of the bride, he takes his pal Robert Goulet (making his movie debut as a playboy salesman) and the usual romantic complications ensue. It could have been a sophisticated sex comedy in the hands of a Billy Wilder, but this farce never manages to grow up. JG

Robert Goulet *Ross Kingsley* • Nancy Kwan *Lynn Hope* • Robert Morse *Jay Menlow* • Jill St John *Sherry* • Keenan Wynn *Mr Sampson* • Elsa Lanchester *Chambermaid* ■ *Dir* Henry Levin • *Scr* RS Allen, Harvey Bullock

Honeymoon in Vegas ★★★★15
Romantic comedy 1992 · US · Colour · 91min

Nicolas Cage is in lovably dopey form here, as he finally proposes to his long-suffering girlfriend Sarah Jessica Parker (also excellent) only to see crooked gambler James Caan win her in a poker game. Director Andrew Bergman remains a much underrated talent, and he expertly blends the classic elements of farce with a healthy dash of eccentricity to produce a delightful comedy. As Cage embarks on an epic journey to Hawaii and back to Las Vegas to reclaim his fiancée, who is gradually falling for the wealthy Caan, Bergman largely steers clear of gloopy sentimentality. JF Swearing. **DVD** **Blu**

Nicolas Cage *Jack Singer* • James Caan *Tommy Korman* • Sarah Jessica Parker *Betsy Nolan/ Donna* • Pat Morita *Mahi* • Johnny Williams *Johnny Sandwich* • John Capodice *Sally Molars* • Anne Bancroft *Bea Singer* ■ *Dir/Scr* Andrew Bergman

The Honeymoon Killers ★★★★18
Crime drama based on a true story 1969 · US · BW · 103min

A fat and lonely spinster from Alabama latches on to a Spanish-born gigolo. Posing as brother and sister, they murder elderly women for their money. Based on the real-life case of Martha Beck and Ray Fernandez, who were both executed in 1951, this cult, low-budget thriller immerses us not only in the psychology of the murderous pair, but also in the dreadful lives and trash culture of their victims. A chilling, utterly compelling picture, which François Truffaut named as one of his favourite films. AT **DVD**

Shirley Stoler *Martha Beck* • Tony LoBianco *Ray Fernandez* • Mary Jane Higby *Janet Fay* • Doris Roberts *Bunny* • Delphine Downing *Kip McArdle* ■ *Dir/Scr* Leonard Kastle

Honeymoon with Mom ★★PG
Romantic comedy 2006 · US · Colour · 86min

Shelley Long is well past her prime in this flimsy comedy. She plays a hard-nosed magazine editor who persuades her jilted-at-the-altar offspring (Virginia Williams) to use her honeymoon for a mother-daughter holiday. But, naturally, mum has ulterior motives for tagging along. Though Long's sharp tongue and brusque media ways are meant to be funny in a fish-out-of-water manner, they actually feel forced and rather ridiculous. A predictable resolution adds to the mediocrity, tying up events with the usual rash of life re-evaluations and reconciliations. SF Some swearing, sexual references. **DVD**

Shelley Long *Mom* • Jack Scalia *Nick* • Virginia Williams *Shannon Bates* • Eric Johnson (3) *Adam* ■ *Dir* Paul A Kaufman • *Scr* Duane Poole

Honeymooner ★15
Comedy drama 2010 · UK · Colour · 70min

Dumped on the eve of his marriage, Fran (Gerard Kearns) takes stock while his best mates provide a display of errant masculine behaviour in this micro-budget British comedy drama. Writer/director Col Spector's second feature promises some witty musings on the whys and wherefores of romance, but the result is both bland and underwritten, leaving us wondering why anyone would be drawn to the wet-blanket protagonist. TJ Swearing. **DVD**

Gerard Kearns *Fran* • Chris Coghill *Ben* • Al Weaver *Jon* • Lisa Faulkner *Emma* ■ *Dir/Scr* Col Spector

The Honeymooners ★★★★15
Romantic comedy 2003 · Ire/UK · Colour · 85min

The debut feature of writer/director Karl Golden, this is a charming piece of Irish whisky-soaked whimsy that was shot on digital video in just 18 days. Jonathan Byrne plays the jilted bridegroom who flees the disaster of his wedding day and meets a waitress (Alex Reid) who is also on the run, from a relationship with a married man. Holed up in a rural retreat, their relationship begins as a frosty one, but begins to thaw even as their original partners come looking for them. The delight of this small-scale piece is in the naturalistic dialogue that plays up both comedy and character, as well as the delicately nuanced performances. TH Swearing. **DVD**

Alex Reid *Claire* • Jonathan Byrne *David* • Justine Mitchell *Fiona* • Conor Mullen *Peter* • David Nolan *Ben* • Eamonn Hunt *Larry* • Briana Corrigan *Mary* ■ *Dir/Scr* Karl Golden

The Honeymooners ★PG
Comedy 2005 · US · Colour · 85min

The classic 1950s American sitcom is updated here as an African-American comedy, and the result is a desperately feeble movie. Cedric the Entertainer plays bus driver Ralph, who, along with his sewer-worker buddy Ed (Mike Epps), is constantly on the lookout for the perfect get-rich-quick scheme. The plans always come to nothing, much to exasperation of their long suffering spouses (Gabrielle Union and Regina Hall). Unimaginative, uninspiring and tedious. GM **DVD**

Cedric the Entertainer *Ralph Kramden* • Mike Epps *Ed Norton* • Gabrielle Union *Alice Kramden* • Regina Hall *Trixie Norton* • Eric Stoltz *William Davis* • Jon Polito *Kirby* • John Leguizamo *Dodge* • Carol Woods *Alice's mom* ■ *Dir* John Schultz • *Scr* Barry W Blaustein, Danny Jacobson, Don Rhymer, David Sheffield, from the TV series

Honeysuckle Rose ★★15
Drama 1980 · US · Colour · 114min

Willie Nelson, the man who wrote *Crazy* for Patsy Cline in the 1960s, became better known in later years for his battles with the IRS over back taxes. By that time he had also embarked on a film career, and this low-key entry was an early effort. In a bold piece of casting, Ne son plays a country and western star whose love for his wife (Dyan Cannon) and son is jeopardised by his career and alcoholic excesses. A crisis looms when Amy Irving, the daughter of his friend Slim Pickens, takes up with him. FL

Willie Nelson *Buck* • Dyan Cannon *Viv* • Amy Irving *Lily* • Slim Pickens *Garland* • Joey Floyd *Jamie* • Charles Levin *Sid* • Priscilla Pointer *Rosella* ■ *Dir* Jerry Schatzberg • *Scr* Carol Sobieski, William D Wittliff, John Binder, from the story *Intermezzo* by Gösta Steven, Gustaf Molander

Honeytrap ★★★18
Crime drama 2014 · UK · Colour · 97min

A teenage girl who just wants to fit in, soon finds herself running with the wrong crowd in this cautionary drama based on a tragic real-life crime committed in Croydon, in 2008. Jessica Sula stars as naive 15-year-

old Layla who has been brought up by grandparents in Trinidad, and soon faces a steep learning curve when she moves to stay with her estranged mum (Danielle Vitalis) in streetwise South London. It's familiar rites-of-passage fare, but Sula, alternating between sassy bravado and anxious vulnerability, is absolutely terrific. TJ Sex, violence, drug abuse

Jessica Sula *Layla* • Lucien Laviscount *Troy* • Ntonga Mwanza *Shaun* • Naomi Ryan *Shiree* ■ *Dir/Scr* Rebecca Johnson

The Honkers ★★★
Drama 1971 · US · Colour · 102min

James Coburn plays an ageing rodeo rider who returns to his home town after a lengthy absence to discover his long-suffering wife has taken up with another man and wants a divorce. At first, Coburn approaches the theme as cautiously as if it were a bucking bronco, but eventually he comes to terms with the role and puts in a competent performance. Actor-turned-director Steve Ihnat, who died shortly after completing the film, intended it to be a thoughtful western, but his approach lacks adventure. TH Swearing, drug abuse.

James Coburn *Lew Lathrop* • Lois Nettleton *Linda Lathrop* • Slim Pickens *Clete* • Anne Archer *Deborah Moon* • Richard Anderson *Royce* • Ted Eccles *Bobby Lathrop* • Ramon Bieri *Jack Ferguson* ■ *Dir* Steve Ihnat • *Scr* Steve Ihnat, Stephen Lodge

Honky Tonk ★★★
Romantic adventure 1941 · US · BW · 104min

There was tangible on-screen chemistry between "king of the movies" Clark Gable and up-and-coming sexpot Lana Turner, and their scenes together here sizzle. The framework is an amiable adventure with Gable as a conman and Turner the judge's daughter he falls for. There's lively support from Claire Trevor and Marjorie Main, and Chill Wills is endearing as Gable's sidekick, but it all gets far too talky around the middle, and doesn't really recover. However, as a souvenir of two great Hollywood stars in their prime and as a reminder of what MGM was capable of, this will do nicely. TS

Clark Gable *Candy Johnson* • Lana Turner *Elizabeth Cotton* • Frank Morgan *Judge Cotton* • Claire Trevor *"Gold Dust" Nelson* • Marjorie Main *Mrs Varner* • Albert Dekker *Brazos Hearn* • Chill Wills *Sniper* ■ *Dir* Jack Conway • *Scr* Pandro S Berman, John Sanford

Honky Tonk Freeway ★15
Comedy 1981 · US · Colour · 102min

This shambolic, unfunny farce concerns a small Florida town, desperately in need of trade, that goes to any lengths to ensure it's not to be bypassed by a new motorway. William Devane is the mayor orchestrating the tourist-catching antics, while Beau Bridges, Teri Garr and Jessica Tandy act like crazy as the trippers invade. Grotesque. TH

Beau Bridges *Duane Hansen* • William Devane *Mayor Calo* • Hume Cronyn *Sherm* • Beverly D'Angelo *Carmen Shelby* • Teri Garr *Ericka* • Howard Hesseman *Snapper* • Geraldine Page *Sister Mary Clarise* • Jessica Tandy *Carol* ■ *Dir* John Schlesinger • *Scr* Edward Clinton

Honkytonk Man ★★15
Drama 1982 · US · Colour · 117min

Clint Eastwood made this a family affair by featuring his son, Kyle, as the teenage nephew under the spell of an alcoholic country singer returned to rural roots. But that nepotism was as much of a mistake (Kyle's acting is not up to the demands of the role) as the idea that Eastwood himself could pass for a vocalist. A singer he's not, and this destabilises the movie. TH Swearing, a sex scene. **DVD**

Clint Eastwood *Red Stovall* • Kyle Eastwood *Whit* • John McIntire *Grandpa* • Alexa Kenin *Marlene* • Verna Bloom *Emmy* • Matt Clark *Virgil* • Barry Corbin *Derwood Arnspinger* • Jerry Hardin *Snuffy* ■ *Dir* Clint Eastwood • *Scr* Clancy Carlile, from his novel

Honolulu ★★
Musical 1939 · US · BW · 82min

A movie star (Robert Young) changes places with a plantation owner in Honolulu (also played by Young) and romances dancer Eleanor Powell whom he meets on board an ocean liner. Some great dancing from the accomplished Powell, a couple of lively numbers and the appearance of George Burns and Gracie Allen partially enliven this otherwise dead musical, with a forgettable score and pedestrian direction. RK

Eleanor Powell *Dorothy March* • Robert Young (1) *Brooks Mason/George Smith* • George Burns *Joe Duffy* • Gracie Allen *Millie de Grasse* • Clarence Kolb *Horace Grayson* • Jo Ann Sayers *Nurse* ■ *Dir* Edward Buzzell • *Scr* Herbert Fields, Frank Partos

Honor among Lovers ★★
Romantic comedy 1931 · US · BW · 75min

This trifling romantic comedy is worth seeing for its always appealing stars: Claudette Colbert as the secretary wooed by playboy exec Fredric March but marrying Monroe Owsley instead. March fires her and predicts her marriage will quickly dissolve, but changes his mind and offers them both a job. Made by Hollywood's foremost – indeed only – woman director at the time, Dorothy Arzner. AT

Claudette Colbert *Julia Traynor* • Fredric March *Jerry Stafford* • Monroe Owsley *Philip Craig* • Charles Ruggles *Monty Dunn* • Ginger Rogers *Doris Blake* • Avonne Taylor *Maybelle* • Pat O'Brien *Conroy* ■ *Dir* Dorothy Arzner • *Scr* Austin Parker, Gertrude Purcell, from the story by Austin Parker

The Honorary Consul ★★★18
Drama 1983 · UK · Colour · 99min

Michael Caine gives what was hailed at the time as the performance of his life in this Graham Greene story about an alcoholic British consul in a corrupt South American backwater, who's mistakenly kidnapped only to find that nobody wants to raise the ransom for his return. Bob Hoskins makes the most of his role as a police chief, but Richard Gere, as a doctor looking for his missing father, battles with an English accent and loses. It could have been much better without John Mackenzie's stolid direction. TH Swearing, sex scenes.

Michael Caine *Charley Fortnum* • Richard Gere *Dr Eduardo Plarr* • Bob Hoskins *Colonel Perez* • Elpidia Carrillo *Clara* • Joaquim de Almeida *Leon* • A Martinez *Aquino* • Stephanie Cotsirilos *Marta* ■ *Dir* John Mackenzie (1) • *Scr* Christopher Hampton, from the novel by Graham Greene

Honour ★★★15
Thriller 2012 · UK/US · Colour · 99min

There's a great film to be made about so-called honour killings in Britain, but this isn't that film. It tries hard, but doesn't quite succeed in an ambitious bid to be both glossy thriller and significant message movie. British Muslim Aiysha Hart falls foul of her more devout mother and older brother when she makes plans to elope with an "unsuitable" young Punjabi. Escaping a murder plot, she finds herself pursued by a professional bounty hunter (Paddy Considine). For all its flaws, this is slick and well acted, and is worth a watch if only to see how seamlessly the Glasgow where it was shot stands in for the west London where it is set. DA Violence, swearing, sexual references. **DVD**

Aiysha Hart *Mona* • Paddy Considine *Bounty* • Nikesh Patel *Tanvir* • William Ruane ■ *Dir/Scr* Shan Khan

Honour among Thieves ★★★★
Crime drama 1954 · Fr/It · BW · 87min

This brooding study of dishonour among thieves established the vogue for gangster films in 1950s France. Jean Gabin won the best actor prize at Venice for his performance as a world-weary hood on his last blag who is forced to make impossible choices when his longtime partner, René Dary, is held for ransom by ruthless rival, Lino Ventura. Director Jacques Becker stages the action efficiently enough, but his main interest lies in the dynamic that drives these luxury-loving mobsters to acts of clinical violence and guilt-free treachery. DP French +subtitles.

Jean Gabin *Max* • René Dary *Riton* • Jeanne Moreau *Josy* • Dora Doll *Lola* • Lino Ventura *Angelo* • Paul Frankeur *Pierrot* ■ *Dir* Jacques Becker • *Scr* Jacques Becker, Albert Simonin, Maurice Griffe, from a novel by Albert Simonin

Honour of the Knights
★★★★ PG

Period drama 2006 · Sp · Colour · 107min

Director Albert Serra pays homage to the pastoral idyll in this meticulously paced reverie on *Don Quixote*, which owes as much to Robert Bresson, Yasujiro Ozu and Samuel Becket as Miguel de Cervantes. Lovingly photographed in digital video by Christophe Farnarier and Eduard Grau, the film makes sublime use of the Catalan landscape and the physical attributes of the fragile Lluís Carbó and his doughty squire, Lluís Serrat. DP Catalan +subtitles. DVD

Lluís Carbó *Quixote* • Lluís Serrat *Sancho* • Jaume Badia • Glynn Bruce • Albert Pla ■ *Dir* Albert Serra • *Scr* Albert Serra, from the novel *El ingenioso hidalgo Don Quijote de la Mancha* by Miguel de Cervantes y Saavedra

Hood Rat
★★

Horror thriller 2001 · US · Colour · 87min

A horde of man-eating rats goes on the rampage in an apartment block in this entertainingly laughable horror thriller. Isaiah Washington and Ice-T share the main acting duties, the former playing a normal guy pushed over the edge by the death of his brother. But the cast suffer from Leslie Small's inadequate direction, the budget doesn't run to much more than rat-shaped shadows and the plot is too thin to cover up the movie's other deficiencies. SuR

Isaiah Washington *Max* • Ice-T *Grady* • AJ Johnson *Nina* • Tonea Stewart *Vetta Taylor* • Guy Torry *Courtney* • Tami Anderson [Tami Roman] *Judge Bankhead* ■ *Dir* Leslie Small • *Scr* Stan Foster

Hoodlum
★★ 18

Period crime drama 1997 · US · Colour · 124min

Laurence Fishburne had a supporting role in 1984's *The Cotton Club*, as a black gangster fighting Dutch Schultz's attempts to take over the Harlem numbers racket. Here the same bloody story takes centre stage, with Fishburne again refusing to bow down to Schultz, played by Tim Roth in foul-mouthed, psychopathic form. Andy Garcia is crime boss Lucky Luciano, pondering which side of the fence to sit on. Fishburne is as charismatic as ever, but the script takes some swallowing, while director Bill Duke takes an age to get the action pumping. JF Violence, some swearing. DVD

Laurence Fishburne *Ellsworth "Bumpy" Johnson* • Tim Roth *Dutch Schultz* • Vanessa L Williams *Francine Hughes* • Andy Garcia *Lucky Luciano* • Cicely Tyson *Stephanie "Queen" St Clair* • Clarence Williams III *Bub Hewlett* ■ *Dir* Bill Duke • *Scr* Chris Brancato

Hoodlum Empire
★★

Crime drama 1952 · US · BW · 97min

This nickel-and-dime gangster picture was knocked out quickly by Republic Studios following the 1950 report by the Senate Crime Investigating Committee. Chaired by Senator Este Kefauver, the report not only exposed organised crime, but also severely criticised Hollywood violence and its glamorisation of criminals. Accordingly, the film takes pains to establish its serious credentials and moral strength as Brian Donlevy digs deep into the syndicate's dark secrets. AT

Brian Donlevy *Senator Bill Stephens* • Forrest Tucker *Charley Pignatalli* • Claire Trevor *Connie Williams* • Vera Ralston *Marthe Dufour* • Luther Adler *Nick Mancani* • John Russell *Joe Gray* •

Gene Lockhart *Senator Tower* • Grant Withers *Rev Andrews* ■ *Dir* Joseph Kane • *Scr* Bruce Manning, Bob Considine

The Hoodlum Priest
★★★

Drama 1961 · US · BW · 102min

Don Murray produced and pseudonymously co-wrote this social problem picture and stars as the Jesuit priest who helps juvenile delinquents and ex-cons by establishing halfway houses for them. One of these rehabilitating hoodlums, Keir Dullea, does well until he gets trapped into robbery and murder. The blend of piety and profanity is often hard to take, though Dullea is excellent in his screen debut and Murray's commitment is obvious. AT

Don Murray *Rev Charles Dismas Clark* • Cindi Wood *Ellen Henley* • Larry Gates *Louis Rosen* • Keir Dullea *Billy Lee Jackson* • Logan Ramsey *George Hale* • Don Joslyn *Pio Gentile* • Sam Capuano *Mario Mazziotti* ■ *Dir* Irvin Kershner • *Scr* Don Deer [Don Murray], Joseph Landon

The Hoodlum Saint
★

Comedy drama 1946 · US · BW · 91min

This disjointed comedy drama with a religious angle is one of the few real duds of William Powell's long stay at MGM. He appears as a disillusioned First World War veteran who carves out a fortune for himself but disappoints the girl he loves, played by Esther Williams (who should never have left the water). Powell tells old friends in need of help to appeal to St Dismas, the "hoodlum saint", but then his own luck runs out. AE

William Powell *Terry Ellerton O'Neill* • Esther Williams *May Lorrison* • Angela Lansbury *Dusty Millard* • James Gleason *Sharp* • Lewis Stone *Father Nolan* ■ *Dir* Norman Taurog • *Scr* Frank Wead, James Hill

Hoods
★★

Crime comedy 1998 · US · Colour · 90min

A talented cast is left high and dry in this misfiring Mafia movie, which oscillates between comedy and drama. Joe Mantegna is the mob killer with a conscience who begins to question his lifestyle when he is given a contract he can't bring himself to fulfil. He is as good as always, and he's ably supported by the likes of Kevin Pollak, Joe Pantoliano and Jennifer Tilly, but Mark Malone's film wears its quirkiness too obviously on its sleeve. JF

Joe Mantegna *Angelo* • Jennifer Tilly *Mary* • Joe Pantoliano *Charlie Flynn* • Kevin Pollak *Rudy* • Vincent Berry *Carmine Dellarosa* ■ *Dir* Mark Malone • *Scr* Mark Malone, Dennis Klein

Hoodwinked
★★ U

Animated fantasy comedy 2005 · US · Colour · 77min

Little Red Riding Hood gets a low-grade *Shrek* makeover in this cheap-looking slice of CGI animation. Fitfully clever rather than funny, sluggish when it should be sassy, this uses a *Rashomon* approach to retell the classic tale from four perspectives. Despite the occasionally amusing line, the sameness of each version becomes tedious. AJ DVD CS

Anne Hathaway *Red* • Glenn Close *Granny* • Patrick Warburton *Wolf* • Jim Belushi [James Belushi] *Woodsman* • David Ogden Stiers *Nicky Flippers* • Andy Dick *Boingo* • Xzibit *Chief Grizzly* • Anthony Anderson *Detective Bill Stork* • Chazz Palminteri *Woolworth* • Cory Edwards *Twitchy* ■ *Dir* Cory Edwards, Tony Leech, Todd Edwards • *Scr* Cory Edwards, Todd Edwards, Tony Leech

The Hook
★★

War drama 1962 · US · Colour · 97min

At the end of the Korean War, three GIs rescue a North Korean from the sea and are ordered to execute him. A thought-provoking situation – the ethics involved in the difference between soldiers killing on the battlefield and face-to-face execution – is weighed down by endless debate and contrived circumstances. But the performances from Kirk Douglas, Nick Adams and Robert Walker Jr are suitably powerful. RB

Kirk Douglas *Sergeant PJ Briscoe* • Robert Walker Jr *Private OA Dennison* • Nick Adams *Private VR Hackett* • Enrique Magalona *"The gook", prisoner* • Nehemiah Persoff *Captain Van Ryn* ■ *Dir* George Seaton • *Scr* Henry Denker, from the novel *L'Hameçon* by Vahé Katcha

Hook
★★★ U

Fantasy adventure 1991 · US · Colour · 135min

In Steven Spielberg's take on *Peter Pan*, Robin Williams is the grown-up Peter, a ruthless business pirate who has no time for his family and no memory of his magical past. That changes, however, when his children are kidnapped and he gets a visit from Tinkerbell (Julia Roberts). As good as Williams is, the film is stolen by an almost unrecognisable Dustin Hoffman, whose Hook is suitably pantomimic yet oddly sympathetic. Although the sentimentality gets a little sticky at times, this remains rousing entertainment. JF DVD SB

Dustin Hoffman *Captain James Hook* • Robin Williams *Peter Banning/Peter Pan* • Julia Roberts *Tinkerbell* • Bob Hoskins *Smee* • Maggie Smith *Granny Wendy* • Caroline Goodall *Moira Banning* • Charlie Korsmo *Jack* • Phil Collins *Inspector Good* • Gwyneth Paltrow *Young Wendy* ■ *Dir* Steven Spielberg • *Scr* Jim V Hart, Malia Scotch Marmo, from a story by Jim V Hart, Nick Castle, from characters by JM Barrie • *Music* John Williams • *Art Director* Norman Garwood • *Set Designer* Garrett Lewis • *Costume Designer* Anthony Powell

The Hooligan Factory
★★★ 15

Comedy 2014 · UK · Colour · 86min

Football violence and Brit gangster movies are mercilessly parodied in this cartoonish and frequently funny comedy about the ugly side of "the beautiful game". Young wastrel Danny (Jason Maza) is taken under the wing of hard man Dex (director and co-writer Nick Nevern), recently released from prison and determined to re-establish his "firm" as the top dogs of terrace thuggery. The beating heart of this story is the ludicrous and larger-than-life Dex, who elevates the antihero to rarely seen levels of idiocy. TeS DVD SB

Jason Maza *Danny* • Nick Nevern *Dex* • Tom Burke *Bullet* • Ray Fearon *Midnight* • Steven O'Donnell [Steve O'Donnell] *Old Bill* ■ *Dir* Nick Nevern • *Scr* Nick Nevern, Michael Lindley

Hoop Dreams
★★★★★ 12

Sports documentary 1994 · US · Colour · 171min

American basketball films may not be the most riveting entertainment for the average British viewer. However, this three-hour documentary – cut down from 250 hours of footage – that follows the fortunes of two inner city Chicago kids whose only way out is through basketball, packs an enormous emotional punch. Film-maker Steve James not only displays an impassioned commitment to these central characters and their desires but also lays them bare so that our empathy is fully engaged. An often simple subject that is full of riches. JM Swearing. DVD

William Gates • Arthur Agee ■ *Dir* Steve James (2) • *Scr* Steve James, Fred Marx, Peter Gilbert • *Cinematographer* Peter Gilbert

Hooper
★★★★ PG

Action comedy 1978 · US · Colour · 95min

One of the best movies to exploit Burt Reynolds's brand of wise-guy charm, in which he's an over-the-hill stuntman determined to become a legend by completing a final outrageous feat – a record-breaking leap across a collapsed bridge in a jet-fuelled car. All this to convince young rival Jan-Michael Vincent, doubtful girlfriend Sally Field and obnoxious film-maker Robert Klein of his greatness. The director, Hal Needham, was himself a former stuntman, which may explain why there are so many chariot rides, helicopter jumps and bar-room brawls. TH Some swearing.

Burt Reynolds *Sonny Hooper* • Jan-Michael Vincent *Ski* • Sally Field *Gwen* • Brian Keith *Jocko* • John Marley *Max Berns* • Robert Klein *Roger Deal* • James Best *Cully* • Adam West *Adam* ■

Dir Hal Needham • *Scr* Thomas Rickman [Tom Rickman], Bill Kerby, from a story by Walt Green, Walter S Herndon

Hoosiers
★★★★ PG

Sports drama 1986 · US · Colour · 110min

A former army man, played with great swagger and insight by Gene Hackman, is invited by a friend and high-school principal to train the school's basketball team. And while Hackman's turning the team around, he also gets to work on the town drunk, Dennis Hopper, and fellow teacher Barbara Hershey. Set in 1951, it's a finely drawn study of postwar American mores, evocatively scored by Jerry Goldsmith and sharply directed by David Anspaugh. Also known as *Best Shot* in the UK. AT DVD

Gene Hackman *Norman Dale* • Barbara Hershey *Myra Fleener* • Dennis Hopper *Shooter* • Sheb Wooley *Cletus Summers* • Fern Persons *Opal Fleener* • Maris Valainis *Jimmy Chitwood* • Brad Boyle *Whit* • Steve Hollar *Rade* • Brad Long *Buddy* ■ *Dir* David Anspaugh • *Scr* Angelo Pizzo

Hoot
★★ PG

Adventure comedy 2006 · US · Colour · 86min

Three youngsters unite to stop a restaurant chain from building on a nesting ground for endangered owls in this well-meaning but flimsy adventure. Their subsequent attempts at sabotage are weighed down with moral and ecological messages, as they predictably run rings around the crudely drawn adults. Still, klutzy cop Luke Wilson and dumb site foreman Tim Blake Nelson seem to enjoy their cartoonish humiliation, playing up to the film's audience-pleasing concept of kid superiority, and adding to the gentle humour. Pity about the unexciting finale. SF Some violence. DVD

Luke Wilson *Officer David Delinko* • Logan Lerman *Roy Eberhardt* • Brie Larson *Beatrice Leep* • Tim Blake Nelson *Curly Branitt* • Cody Linley *Mullet Fingers* • Robert Wagner *Mayor Grandy* ■ *Dir* Wil Shriner • *Scr* Wil Shriner, from the novel by Carl Hiaasen

Hoover Street Revival
★★ 15

Documentary 2002 · UK/Fr · Colour · 99min

Sophie Fiennes barely scratches the surface in this disappointing digi-video portrait of Bishop Noel Jones, the brother of actress-singer Grace Jones, whose charismatic ministry attracts a weekly congregation of more than a thousand to the Greater Bethany Community Church in the deprived Watts district of Los Angeles. Aerial shots of the sprawling neighbourhood offer little insight into the social problems endured by its inhabitants or how Jones and his pastoral team operate among them – other than to sell videos of his grandstanding sermons. Fiennes's fragmentary approach keeps her subject and his flock at a distance. DP DVD

■ *Dir/Scr* Sophie Fiennes

Hop
★★★ U

Part-animated comedy 2011 · US · Colour · 91min

This seasonal children's yarn finds young rabbit EB (voiced by Russell Brand) reluctant to succeed his father (Hugh Laurie) as the Easter bunny. So he runs away from the family home and heads for Hollywood where he bounds into the life of a slacker human, James Marsden, and causes mayhem at every turn. Meanwhile, a mutinous chick plots to take over the family business. Director Tim Hill mines the same seam of cuteness as in his earlier *Alvin and the Chipmunks*, with Brand's manic characterisation helping to paper over the cracks of a flimsy story. It's all good fun for the very young, but the film is light on pop culture references to keep grown-ups interested. TeS DVD SB

James Marsden *Fred O'Hare* • Russell Brand *EB* • Kaley Cuoco *Sam O'Hare* • Hugh Laurie *EB's dad* • Gary Cole *Henry O'Hare* • Elizabeth Perkins *Bonnie O'Hare* • David Hasselhoff ■ *Dir* Tim Hill • *Scr* Cinco Paul, Ken Daurio, Brian Lynch, from a story by Paul, Daurio

Hope and Glory ★★★★★ 15
Second World War drama
1987 · UK · Colour · 107min

War may be hell if you're a grown-up, but it's a wheeze if you're nine years old and living in suburban London during the Blitz. Anyway, that's how it looks to the young hero of director John Boorman's whimsical, funny, nostalgic, semi-autobiographical memoir of family life in the Second World War. Sebastian Rice-Edwards gives an extraordinarily confident performance in the lead role, and he's matched by Geraldine Muir, playing his five-year-old sister. Sammi Davis as their elder sibling gives a poignant portrayal of the teenager caught between sexual awakening and the savage truths of the day. The film is on the episodic side, and Sarah Miles and Ian Bannen might both have toned down their eccentric portrayals a notch, but these are minor quibbles about a delightful movie. PF Swearing. DVD

Sebastian Rice-Edwards *Bill Rohan* · Sarah Miles *Grace Rohan* · David Hayman *Clive Rohan* · Ian Bannen *Grandfather George* · Sammi Davis *Dawn Rohan* · Susan Wooldridge *Molly* · Jean-Marc Barr *Bruce* · Geraldine Muir *Sue Rohan* ■ *Dir/Scr* John Boorman · *Cinematographer* Philippe Rousselot

Hope Floats ★★ PG
Romantic comedy drama
1998 · US · Colour · 109min

Sandra Bullock stars as Birdee, who finds out via a TV talk show that her husband has been unfaithful. So she decides to return to the small home town where she was once a beauty queen to get over the pain, with her mother (a wonderful Gena Rowlands) and young daughter at her side. There's far too much moping and sobbing, but director Forest Whitaker makes the scenes of budding romance (with Harry Connick Jr) amusing. JB Swearing. DVD BL

Sandra Bullock *Birdee Pruitt* · Harry Connick Jr *Justin Matisse* · Gena Rowlands *Ramona Calvert* · Mae Whitman *Bernice Pruitt* · Michael Paré *Bill Pruitt* · Cameron Finley *Travis* · Kathy Najimy *Toni Post* · Bill Cobbs *Nurse* · Rosanna Arquette *Connie* ■ *Dir* Forest Whitaker · *Scr* Steven Rogers

Hope Springs ★★ 12
Romantic comedy
2002 · UK/US · Colour · 88min

A by-the-numbers spark-free comedy, this stars Colin Firth as a sensitive English artist who heads to the small US town of Hope to mend his broken heart after he is betrayed by brittle fiancée Minnie Driver. There he finds more than a shoulder to cry on in the shape of free-spirited nurse Heather Graham. The film simply shambles along, hampered by limp direction. SF DVD

Colin Firth *Colin Ware* · Heather Graham *Mandy* · Minnie Driver *Vera* · Oliver Platt *Doug Reed* · Frank Collison *Fisher* · Mary Steenburgen *Joanie Fisher* · Mary Black *Mrs Peterson* · Ken Kramer *Mr Peterson* ■ *Dir* Mark Herman · *Scr* Mark Herman, from the novel *New Cardiff* by Charles Webb

Hope Springs ★★★ 12
Romantic comedy drama
2012 · US · Colour · 95min

Meryl Streep and Tommy Lee Jones are amusingly brittle as a middle-aged couple trying to recapture that old magic. Streep is the desperate housewife who finally enrols them in couples' therapy at the town of Great Hope Springs, while Steve Carell plays their counsellor, getting laughs from the brutally frank questions he delivers with a polite smile. If director David Frankel (who worked with Streep on *The Devil Wears Prada*) is after understatement and pathos, then he doesn't get to the emotional crux of the matter. But the intimate moments between the veteran twosome are refreshingly portrayed with great humour and sensitivity. SP Sexual references, some swearing. DVD BL

Meryl Streep *Kay Soames* · Tommy Lee Jones *Arnold Soames* · Steve Carell *Dr Bernard Feld* · Mimi Rogers *Carol* · Elisabeth Shue *Karen* ■ *Dir* David Frankel · *Scr* Vanessa Taylor

Hoppity Goes to Town ★★ U
Animated musical comedy
1941 · US · Colour · 77min

Partially inspired by Frank Capra's *Mr Deeds Goes to Town*, this was one of the first animated features not to be based on a classic children's fable. However, the weakness in the storyline was to prove the film's undoing. Neither Hoppity the grasshopper's battle with the villainous C Bagley Beetle for the attentions of the drippy Honey Bee nor the insect colony's need to find new lodgings are enchanting enough to hold the attention, while the voiceovers are as feeble as the songs. DP DVD

Kenny Gardner *Dick* · Gwen Williams *Mary* · Jack Mercer *Mr Bumble/Swat the Fly* · Ted Pierce *C Bagley Beetle* · Stan Freed *Hoppity* · Pauline Loth *Honey Bee* · Guinn "Big Boy" Williams *Narrator* ■ *Dir* David Fleischer [Dave Fleischer] · *Scr* David Fleischer, Dan Gordon, Isidore Sparber, William Turner, Mike Meyer, Graham Place, Bob Wickersham, Cal Howard · *Music/lyrics* Hoagy Carmichael, Frank Loesser

Hopscotch ★★★ 12
Spy comedy
1980 · US · Colour · 100min

CIA operative Walter Matthau takes revenge for being demoted to a desk job by leaking his memoirs, chapter by chapter, to other intelligence agencies. Of course, he has to be stopped, but not before leading ex-boss Ned Beatty on a merry chase around the world. There are some splendid performances – Glenda Jackson, Herbert Lom, Sam Waterston – but it's Matthau who carries it all with his brand of serene cynicism. TH DVD

Walter Matthau *Miles Kendig* · Glenda Jackson *Isobel von Schmidt* · Sam Waterston *Cutter* · Ned Beatty *Myerson* · Herbert Lom *Mikhail Yaskov* · David Matthau *Ross* ■ *Dir* Ronald Neame · *Scr* Brian Garfield, Bryan Forbes, from the novel by Brian Garfield

The Horde ★★ 18
Action horror
2009 · Fr · Colour · 92min

In this French zombie/gangster mash-up, the protagonists are trapped inside a condemned high-rise building while ghouls mass outside. Clearly, there's no way to go but up. The same could be said for the film itself, a grubby exercise in brutality with a crack-den aesthetic and a selection of disreputable heroes. Playing to the gore crowd, the film conjures up some outrageous violence (courtesy of heavy machine guns, hand grenades and machetes) but is rarely as much fun as it should be. JR French +subtitles. Violence. DVD BL

Claude Perron *Aurore* · Jean-Pierre Martins *Ouessem* · Eriq Ebouaney *Adewale* · Aurélien Recoing *Jimenez* ■ *Dir* Yannick Dahan, Benjamin Rocher · *Scr* Yannick Dahan, Benjamin Rocher, Arnaud Bordas, Stéphane Moïssakis, Nicolas Peufaillit

Horizons West ★★
Western
1952 · US · Colour · 80min

Cult director Budd Boetticher needed a much bigger budget, a far better script and another hour to do justice to this story of three brothers who become rivals after the Civil War. While Rock Hudson and James Arness are content to plough their parcels of land, Robert Ryan becomes a ruthless empire builder. Julia Adams, meanwhile, is the widow caught up in their sibling rivalry. AT

Robert Ryan *Dan Hammond* · Julia Adams [Julie Adams] *Lorna Hardin* · Rock Hudson *Neal Hammond* · John McIntire *Ira Hammond* · Judith Braun *Sally* · Raymond Burr *Cord Hardin* · James Arness *Tiny* · Dennis Weaver *Dandy Taylor* ■ *Dir* Budd Boetticher · *Scr* Louis Stevens

The Horizontal Lieutenant ★ U
Second World War romantic comedy
1962 · US · Colour · 90min

This fourth co-starring vehicle for Paula Prentiss and Jim Hutton in three years is also the weakest, largely thanks to the screenplay. Set during the Second World War and located on a Pacific Island, this so-called comedy stems from the attempt to capture a Japanese guerrilla by Hutton, who is more interested in Prentiss. BB

Jim Hutton *2d Lt Merle Wye* · Paula Prentiss *Lt Molly Blue* · Jack Carter *Lt William Monck* · Jim Backus *Cmdr Jerry Hammerslag* · Charles McGraw *Col Charles Korotny* · Miyoshi Umeki *Akiko* ■ *Dir* Richard Thorpe · *Scr* George Wells, from the novel *The Bottletop Affair* by Gordon Cotler

The Horn Blows at Midnight ★★★
Comedy
1945 · US · BW · 77min

On his subsequent radio and television shows, comedian Jack Benny got a good deal of comic mileage from mentioning this movie to its detriment. This film is by no means as bad as Benny would have you believe: it's certainly preposterous, and grossly whimsical, but its tale of a dopey trumpeter who dreams that he's an angel dispatched to Earth and able to destroy it with one blast of his horn, is not so absurd after all. Benny himself is excellent and there's fine support, particularly a cameo from camp hotel detective Franklin Pangborn. TS

Jack Benny *Athanael* · Alexis Smith *Elizabeth* · Dolores Moran *Fran* · Allyn Joslyn *Osidro* · Reginald Gardiner *Archie Dexter* · Guy Kibbee *The Chief* · John Alexander (1) *Doremus* · Franklin Pangborn *Sloan* · Margaret Dumont *Miss Rodholder* · Bobby Blake [Robert Blake] *Junior* ■ *Dir* Raoul Walsh · *Scr* Sam Hellman, James V Kern, from an idea by Aubrey Wisberg

Horns ★★★★ 15
Fantasy horror thriller
2013 · US/Can · Colour · 114min

Those who have yet to let go of Daniel Radcliffe as Harry Potter's wide-eyed boy wizard may prefer to steer clear of this ingenious, grimly funny but nevertheless dark and often bloody horror fantasy. Radcliffe stars as Ig Perrish, a smalltown DJ who, as the story begins, is accused of killing his longtime sweetheart Merrin (Juno Temple). Ig curses God, and so sprouts a set of devil horns that would seem to confirm his guilt. The black comedy is delicious, though the more violent set pieces are not for the faint of heart. DW Violence, swearing, sex scenes, nudity, drug abuse.

Daniel Radcliffe *Ig Perrish* · Joe Anderson (1) *Terry Perrish* · Juno Temple *Merrin Williams* · Kelli Garner *Glenna Shepherd* · Heather Graham *Veronica* ■ *Dir* Alexandre Aja · *Scr* Keith Bunin, from Joe Hill's novel

Horrible Bosses ★★ 15
Black comedy
2011 · US · Colour · 93min

Three exploited workers agree to kill each other's bosses in this supposedly black comedy. In practice, Jason Bateman, Jason Sudeikis and Charlie Day are just too drippy to credibly entertain such a plan, even after a boozy conference where they convince themselves they're serving the greater good. The funnier scenes happen early on when the three are subjected to various indignities in the workplace by bosses Kevin Spacey, Colin Farrell and Jennifer Aniston. A sequel is due in cinemas in late 2014. SP Swearing, sexual references, drug abuse. DVD BL

Jason Bateman *Nick Hendricks* · Charlie Day *Dale Arbus* · Jason Sudeikis *Kurt Buckman* · Jennifer Aniston *Dr Julia Harris* · Colin Farrell (2) *Bobby Pellitt* · Kevin Spacey *Dave Harken* · Donald Sutherland *Jack Pellit* · Jamie Foxx *Motherfucker Jones* ■ *Dir* Seth Gordon · *Scr* Michael Markowitz, John Francis Daley, Jonathan M Goldstein, from an unproduced screenplay by Markowitz

Horrible Bosses 2 ★★★ 15
Comedy
2014 · US · Colour · 103min

Jason Bateman, Jason Sudeikis and Charlie Day decide to be their own bosses in this workmanlike sequel. Forced into bankruptcy by greedy businessman Christoph Waltz, they then decide to kidnap his son. The laughs come off the conveyer belt at a steady rate, but they're of varying quality and work hard to be politically incorrect. If the comedy isn't as dark as the first film aspired to be, it's at least more even in tone, and the would-be kidnappers are good value. SP Swearing, some violence, a sex scene, brief nudity. DVD BL

Jason Bateman *Nick Hendricks* · Jason Sudeikis *Kurt Buckman* · Charlie Day *Dale Arbus* · Jennifer Aniston *Julia Harris* · Kevin Spacey *Dave Harken* · Jamie Foxx *Dean "MF" Jones* · Chris Pine *Rex Hanson* · Christoph Waltz *Burt Hanson* ■ *Dir* Sean Anders · *Scr* Sean Anders, John Morris, from a story by Anders, Morris, John Francis Daley, Jonathan M Goldstein, from characters by Michael Markowitz

Horrid Henry: the Movie ★ U
Comedy
2011 · UK · Colour · 88min

This charmless "naughty schoolboy" saga is aimed at primary school children, and often looks like it was made by them, although familiarity with the character may help. Theo Stevenson is OK as Henry, but the plot smacks of being made up as they went along. Henry's umpteenth failure to hand in his homework leads to the sacking of his firm-but-fair teacher (Anjelica Huston) and the threatened closure of his school. Of course, only Henry can save the day. Accompanying adults may wish they'd opted for triple detention. DA DVD BL 3D

Anjelica Huston *Miss Battle-Axe* · Richard E Grant *Vic Van Wrinkle* · Theo Stevenson *Horrid Henry* · Parminder Nagra *Miss Lovely* · Noel Fielding *Ed Banger* · Mathew Horne *Dad* · Siobhan Hayes *Mum* ■ *Dir* Nick Moore · *Scr* Lucinda Whiteley, from characters by Francesca Simon

Horror Express ★★★ 15
Horror
1972 · UK/Sp · Colour · 83min

In this rattlingly good chiller set on the Trans-Siberian railway at the turn of the last century, what is believed to be a frozen Missing Link starts to revive in the presence of classic horror movie stars Peter Cushing and Christopher Lee, here playing rival anthropologists. The suspense is kept to a maximum by the clever and beautifully timed editing of Robert Dearberg. Director Eugenio (Gene) Martin is unable to control Telly Savalas, who chews the scenery as the leader of a group of Cossacks. Shame. TS Violence DVD

Christopher Lee *Prof Alexander Saxton* · Peter Cushing *Dr Wells* · Telly Savalas *Kazan* · Silvia Tortosa *Irina* · Alberto de Mendoza *Father Pujardov* ■ *Dir* Gene Martin [Eugenio Martin] · *Scr* Armand D'Usseau, Julian Halevey [Julian Zimet], from a story by Eugenio Martin

Horror Hospital ★★ 18
Comedy horror
1973 · US · Colour · 86min

Combining audience preoccupations with medicine and terror, director Antony Balch attempts to spoof the usual horror contents by taking them so far over the edge that they self-destruct. There's a Rolls-Royce with scythes, belligerent bikers and, of course, a burns-scarred mad scientist, plus Robin Askwith as an aspiring rock musician seeking a rest cure. The result is an almost unwatchable mess, but try to stay the course: the psychological subtext is fascinating. TH Some swearing. DVD

Michael Gough *Dr Storm* · Robin Askwith *Jason Jones* · Vanessa Shaw *Judy Peters* · Ellen Pollock *Aunt Harris* · Skip Martin *Frederick* · Dennis Price *Mr Pollack* ■ *Dir* Antony Balch · *Scr* Antony Balch, Alan Watson

The Horror of Frankenstein ★★ 12
Horror
1970 · UK · Colour · 91min

Ralph Bates is no substitute for Peter Cushing in Hammer's feeble attempt to remake their classic *The Curse of Frankenstein*. He overplays the doctor as ridiculously evil in this throwaway comic variation, while David Prowse is no replacement for Christopher Lee as the Monster. There's little subtlety, and the accent is on black humour in this very lowbrow entry. Happily, Cushing reprised his role in the series finale, 1973's *Frankenstein and the Monster from Hell*. AJ DVD

Ralph Bates *Victor Frankenstein* · Kate O'Mara *Alys* · Veronica Carlson *Elizabeth* · Dennis Price *Grave robber* · David Prowse [Dave Prowse]

Monster • Bernard Archard *Elizabeth's father* • Graham James *Wilhelm* • Joan Rice *Grave robber's wife* ■ *Dir* Jimmy Sangster • *Scr* Jimmy Sangster, Jeremy Burnham, from characters by Mary Shelley

Horrors of the Black Museum ★★★ 15

Horror   1959 · UK/US · Colour · 78min

This infamously lurid horror begins with one of the most memorably vicious shocks of the 1950s fear-era – a girl unwrapping a gift of binoculars, looking through and having her eyes gouged by two spring-loaded metal spikes. Michael Gough stars as the arrogant crime book author who hypnotises his assistant into committing horrendous homicides to satisfy his readers' demands for gruesome detail. A tawdry catalogue of tortures, purple dialogue and risible acting (wooden Shirley Anne Field), this crudely effective melodrama is a British exploitation classic. AJ Violence. *DVD*

Michael Gough *Edmond Bancroft* • June Cunningham *Joan Berkley* • Graham Curnow *Rick* • Shirley Anne Field *Angela* • Geoffrey Keen *Superintendent Graham* • Gerald Andersen *Dr Ballan* • John Warwick *Inspector Lodge* • Beatrice Varley *Aggie* • Austin Trevor *Commissioner Wayne* ■ *Dir* Arthur Crabtree • *Scr* Aben Kandel, Herman Cohen

Hors la Vie ★★★★ 15

Biographical drama
1991 · Fr/It/Bel · Colour · 93min

Based on the real-life experiences of Roger Auque, this compelling drama provides a graphic insight into the plight of the political hostage, with Hippolyte Girardot magnificent in the role of the abducted French photographer. Lebanese director Maroun Bagdadi expertly conveys the claustrophobia, uncertainty and sheer terror of being at the mercy of people willing to kill for their cause. Yet he wisely avoids presenting the captors as inhuman fanatics, while also resisting the temptation to justify their actions with long tracts of rhetorical propaganda. DP French, Arabic +subtitles.

Hippolyte Girardot *Patrick Perrault* • Rafic Ali Ahmad *Walid, "Chief"* • Hussein Sbeity *Omar* • Habib Hammoud *Ali, "Philippe"* • Magdi Machmouchi *Moustap* ■ *Dir* Maroun Bagdadi • *Scr* Maroun Bagdadi, from the non-fiction book by Roger Auque, Patrick Forestier

Hors Satan ★★★★ 15

Drama   2011 · Fr/Neth · Colour · 105min

Film-maker Bruno Dumont produces further challenging work for his sixth feature. Once again making no narrative or stylistic concessions, Dumont descends on a hamlet in northern France, chronicling the unusual relationship between a mysterious guy (David Dewaele) who survives on handouts, and a goth girl (Alexandra Lemâtre) who seeks his advice in dealing with her abusive stepfather. But it remains unclear whether the man is an angel or a demon, as he commits murder, conducts an exorcism on a child and seduces a backpacker. Indeed, Dumont offers few clues to the message (if any) he is striving to convey and forces viewers to engage with the consciously sketchy characters in order to derive their own meaning. DP French +subtitles. *DVD*

David Dewaele *The Guy* • Alexandra Lemâtre *The Girl* • Christophe Bon *Guard* • Juliette Bacquet *Kid* • Aurore Broutin *Backpacker* ■ *Dir/Scr* Bruno Dumont

Horse Feathers ★★★★★ U

Comedy   1932 · US · BW · 63min

In their penultimate movie for Paramount Pictures, Groucho, Chico, Harpo and, this time around, Zeppo, display a wonderful disarray of puns, slapstick and misunderstandings as Groucho becomes head of a college that needs to win a crucial football game. Chico operates out of a speakeasy in which speech is not at all easy, while dogcatcher Harpo strums a melancholy melody. A classic which is still unmissable. TH *DVD*

Groucho Marx *Professor Wagstaff* • Harpo Marx *Pinky* • Chico Marx *Baravelli* • Zeppo Marx *Frank* • Thelma Todd *Connie Bailey* • David Landau *Jennings* • James Pierce *Mullens* • Nat Pendleton *McCarthy* ■ *Dir* Norman Z McLeod • *Scr* Bert Kalmar, Harry Ruby, SJ Perelman, Will B Johnstone, with additional dialogue by Arthur Sheekman

The Horse in the Gray Flannel Suit ★★ U

Comedy drama   1968 · US · Colour · 112min

The poster line "All's fair in love and woah" gives you some idea of the quality of this strained Disney offering. The ever-willing Dean Jones is back in harness for this silly story about an advertising executive who uses his daughter's pet nag to help sell a brand of stomach pill. Even reliable director Norman Tokar fails to get the pace above a canter. DP

Dean Jones *Fred Bolton* • Diane Baker *Suzie Clemens* • Lloyd Bochner *Archer Madison* • Fred Clark *Tom Dugan* • Ellen Janov *Helen Bolton* • Morey Amsterdam *Charlie Blake* • Kurt Russell *Ronnie Gardner* ■ *Dir* Norman Tokar • *Scr* Louis Pelletier, from the novel *The Year of the Horse* by Eric Hatch

The Horse Soldiers ★★★ PG

War drama   1959 · US · Colour · 114min

This stirring Civil War epic was not liked on its release by fans of the great western director John Ford; it's not really a western and it seemed dramatically unconvincing. Today, however, Ford's marvellous set pieces are genuinely thrilling, and there's nostalgic value in seeing two great movie stars (John Wayne and William Holden) teamed so cleverly. The film is based on a true incident (the 1863 Grierson raid deep into the South to cut supply lines to Vicksburg), and Ford tells it straight. TS *DVD*

John Wayne *Colonel John Marlowe* • William Holden (2) *Major Henry Kendall* • Constance Towers *Hannah Hunter* • Althea Gibson *Lukey* • Hoot Gibson *Brown* • Anna Lee *Mrs Buford* ■ *Dir* John Ford • *Scr* John Lee Mahin, Rackin Martin, from the novel by Harold Sinclair

Horse Thief ★★★★ PG

Drama   1986 · Chi · Colour · 86min

Tian Zhuangzhuang combines a preoccupation with cinematic technique and his reverence for the forbidding majesty of the Tibetan plains in this stunningly photographed study of life in one of China's most marginalised communities. Yet against the harsh conditions that force Rigzin Tseshang to steal horses in order to feed his family, the film tenders the consolation provided by Buddhism and its exquisitely mystical ceremonies. Employing a range of transitional and optical devices, Tian not only reveals the relevance of religion to these hardy people, but also the importance of the cultural continuity that Beijing is so determined to suppress. DP Mandarin +subtitles.

Rigzin Tseshang *Norbu* • Dan Jiji *Dolma* • Jamco Jayang *Tashi* • Gao Ba *Nowre* ■ *Dir* Tian Zhuangzhuang • *Scr* Rui Zhang

The Horse Whisperer ★★★ PG

Romantic drama   1998 · US · Colour · 162min

Robert Redford won the Hollywood bidding war over the movie rights to British author Nicholas Evans's bestseller about a Montana cowboy who cures traumatised horses. Directing himself for the first time, Redford fits the role as snugly as those faded denims, watched glowingly by Kristin Scott Thomas. She's a New Yorker with a daughter and a horse, both disabled in a road accident. So, leaving husband Sam Neill behind, they trot off to Montana to see horse shrink Redford. At nearly three hours, it's far too long, but the Montana scenery is stunning. AT *DVD*

Robert Redford *Tom Booker* • Kristin Scott Thomas *Annie MacLean* • Sam Neill *Robert MacLean* • Dianne Wiest *Diane Booker* • Scarlett Johansson *Grace MacLean* • Chris Cooper *Frank

Booker* ■ *Dir* Robert Redford • *Scr* Eric Roth, Richard LaGravenese, from the novel by Nicholas Evans

The Horseman ★★★★ 18

Revenge thriller   2008 · Aus · Colour · 94min

This low-key but powerful Australian revenge thriller recalls the mood and storylines of such movies as *Get Carter* and *The Limey*. Peter Marshall gives a magnetic central performance as the bereaved father on the trail of the lowlifes who enticed his daughter into a world of pornography, degradation and drugs. His transformation from an ordinary Aussie bloke burdened by grief to an unforgiving avenger is a revelation, though his methods of gaining information (and exacting retribution) from the perpetrators are definitely not for the squeamish. However, it's the tension of the interrogation scenes and the tender exchanges about fatherhood with a teenage hitch-hiker (Caroline Marohasy) that really stay in the memory. JA Violence, swearing. *DVD*

Peter Marshall *Christian Forteski* • Brad McMurray *Derek* • Jack Henry Finn * Christopher Sommers *Pauly* • Evert McQueen *Jim* • Steven Tandy *Devlin* • Caroline Marohasy *Alice* ■ *Dir/Scr* Steven Kastrissios

The Horseman on the Roof ★★ 15

Period drama   1995 · Fr · Colour · 130min

At the time the most expensive film ever made in France, Jean-Paul Rappeneau's drama was too burly for the costume crowd and too deep for the slam-bang brigade. This tale of 19th-century politics and plague is full of arresting set pieces, yet there is little narrative cohesion beside the predictable course of the romance between dashing revolutionary Olivier Martinez and Juliette Binoche, the loyal wife searching for her ageing husband. DP French +subtitles. Brief nudity. *DVD*

Juliette Binoche *Pauline De Théus* • Olivier Martinez *Angelo* • Laura Marioni *Carla* • Paul Chevillard *Giacomo* • Richard Sammel *Franz* • Claudio Amendola *Maggionari* • Gérard Depardieu *Police Commissioner* • Jean Yanne *Door to door salesman* ■ *Dir* Jean-Paul Rappeneau • *Scr* Jean-Paul Rappeneau, Nina Companeez, Jean-Claude Carrière, from the novel by Jean Giono • *Cinematographer* Thierry Arbogast

The Horsemen ★★ 12

Action drama   1971 · US · Colour · 102min

Buzkashi is the Afghan sport in which a headless calf's carcass is kicked about by men on horses until either someone wins (according to rules seemingly made up on the spot) or no other player is left alive. It's a natural subject for John Frankenheimer, but the lack of a story proves to be a problem. Omar Sharif and Jack Palance are the buzkashi rivals, losing leg and face respectively. AT Some violence and swearing, brief nudity *DVD*

Omar Sharif *Uraz* • Leigh Taylor-Young *Zereh* • Jack Palance *Tursen* • David De Mukhi * Peter Jeffrey *Hayatal* • Mohammed Shamsi *Osman Bey* • Saeed Jaffrey *District Chief* ■ *Dir* John Frankenheimer • *Scr* Dalton Trumbo, from a novel by Joseph Kessel

Horsemen ★★ 18

Horror thriller   2009 · US · Colour · 86min

The eponymous equestrians are the Four Horsemen of the Apocalypse who make a suitably baroque reference point in this nihilistic serial killer movie. Tracking down a quartet of vicious murderers, Dennis Quaid's widowed cop is led from one gory crime scene to the next by a trail of Biblical clues. There's no mystery surrounding the screenwriter's inspiration as complex torture devices and gratuitous gore try to outdo the horrors of *Se7en* – a film whose reputation has been tarnished by the sheer volume of immature imitators it's spawned. Some respite from the clichéd police procedure is offered by Zhang Ziyi's creepily effective turn. Other than that, Quaid can only watch as the plot unravels

into hysterical silliness. JR Violence, swearing, nudity. *DVD* *Blu*

Dennis Quaid *Aidan Breslin* • Zhang Ziyi *Kristin Spitz* • Lou Taylor Pucci *Alex Breslin* • Clifton Collins Jr *Stingray* • Patrick Fugit *Corey* • Paul Dooley *Father Whiteleather* • Peter Stormare *David Spitz* ■ *Dir* Jonas Akerlund • *Scr* David Callaham

Horses and Champions ★★ U

Sports drama   1994 · US · Colour · 90min

Timothy Bottoms stars in this run-of-the-mill melodrama. Has there ever been a movie about horses in which the rank outsider doesn't win the day? This efficient, but one-paced picture wasn't about to change the winning formula. Indeed, it even boasted of being a cross between *National Velvet* and *Cinderella* in its advertising campaign. DP

Timothy Bottoms *Ben Choice* • Christopher Boyer *Mr Smith* • Ramsay Midwood *Ferdie* • Linda L Miller *Mrs Loveridge* • Christopher Pettiet *Joe* ■ *Dir/Scr* Jonathan Tydor

The Horse's Mouth ★★★ PG

Comedy   1958 · UK · BW · 91min

Alec Guinness earned an Oscar nomination for his droll adaptation of Joyce Cary's celebrated novel. He also turns in a solid performance as Gulley Jimson, the irascible, self-obsessed artist whose decision to paint a mural arouses the curiosity of friends and foes alike. John Bratby's paintings cleverly reflect the character's temperament and they have been beautifully shot by Arthur Ibbetson, whose use of colour is painterly indeed. The problem is that the focus is so firmly on Guinness that the other characters are left on the sideline. DP *DVD*

Alec Guinness *Gulley Jimson* • Kay Walsh *Coker* • Renee Houston *Sarah* • Mike Morgan *Nosey* • Robert Coote *Sir William Beeder* ■ *Dir* Ronald Neame • *Scr* Alec Guinness, from the novel by Joyce Cary

The Hospital ★★ 15

Black comedy   1971 · US · Colour · 98min

Paddy Chayefsky won an Oscar for his script for this manic black comedy, but it's hard to see why the Academy would be taken in by its heavy-handed satire, crude characterisation and undisciplined structure. Frankly, it's a mess and a more talented director than Arthur Hiller would have been pressed to make anything of it. However, towering above all of this is a sensational performance from George C Scott as the surgeon who conquers his midlife crisis while murder, magic and madness rage around him. DP

George C Scott *Dr Herbert Bock* • Diana Rigg *Barbara Drummond* • Barnard Hughes *Drummond* • Nancy Marchand *Head Nurse Christie* • Stephen Elliott (1) *Sundstrom* • Donald Harron *Milton Mead* ■ *Dir* Arthur Hiller • *Scr* Paddy Chayefsky

The Host ★★★★ 15

Science-fiction horror
2006 · S Kor/Jpn · Colour · 119min

Chemicals dumped into South Korea's Han River create a giant mutant tadpole that unfurls under Seoul's bridges to chomp on unsuspecting citizens, in *Memories of Murder* director Bong Joon-ho's entertaining horror. A huge blockbuster in Asia, the film is a combination of *Jaws*-type shocks, character-driven suspense, and heartfelt human drama, as spunky schoolgirl Ko Ah-sung fights for survival against the kidnapping monster. The CGI effects are terrific and, although some of the quirky humour is a little tiresome, *The Host* is a thrilling and scary creature feature. AJ Korean +subtitles. Swearing. *DVD* *Blu*

Song Kang-ho *Park Gang-du* • Byun Hee-bong *Park Hee-bong* • Park Hae-il *Park Nam-il* • Bae Doo-na *Park Nam-joo* • Ko Ah-sung *Park Hyun-seo* ■ *Dir* Bong Joon-ho • *Scr* Bong Joon-ho, Ha Joon-won, Baek Chul-hyun, from a story by Bong

The Host ★★ 12
Science-fiction thriller
2013 · US · Colour · 119min

Twilight meets *Invasion of the Body Snatchers* in author Stephenie Meyer's latest soppy teen romance, swapping vampires for aliens. *Hanna* star Saoirse Ronan deserved better than this, playing a teenager whose body is implanted with an intergalactic "Soul". But as one of few humans who can fight the parasitic takeover, she uses her host to protect loved ones hidden in a cave-dwelling community. Thanks to an overly earnest approach, the minimal special effects are hokey and the story of two colliding minds couldn't be more mindless. AJ Swearing. *DVD* *BL*

Saoirse Ronan *Melanie Stryder/Wanda* • Max Irons *Jared* • Diane Kruger *Seeker/Lacey* • Jake Abel *Ian* • William Hurt *Jeb* • Frances Fisher *Maggie* ■ *Dir* Andrew Niccol • *Scr* Andrew Niccol, from Stephenie Meyer's novel

The Hostage ★★★ 12
Thriller
1966 · US · Colour · 79min

One of scores of independent features made in the 1960s, this has a dime budget, bleak locations, bags of energy, and John Carradine and Harry Dean Stanton in key roles. It's a crime story with a twist, about a six-year-old boy trapped in a removal van that contains a corpse. Shot in Iowa, it's tensely directed by Russell S Doughton and co-edited by Gary Kurtz, later the producer of *Star Wars*. AT Violence. *DVD*

Don O'Kelly *Bull* • Harry Dean Stanton *Eddie* • John Carradine *Otis Lovelace* • Danny Martins *Davey Cleaves* • Ron Hagerthy *Steve Cleaves* ■ *Dir* Russell S Doughton • *Scr* Robert Laning, from the novel by Henry Farrell

Hostage ★★★ 18
Action spy drama
1992 · UK · Colour · 96min

This British-made spy thriller about machiavellian double dealing in Whitehall too often resembles John le Carré on speed. Sam Neill stars as a disgruntled agent sent to Argentina to rescue a British subject held captive by guerrillas, only to fall in love with former 007 girl Talisa Soto. A mildly diverting and topical international morality play from acclaimed television director Robert Young is enlivened by a solid supporting cast, while James Fox camps it up gloriously as a Whitehall mandarin. RS *DVD*

Sam Neill *John Rennie* • Talisa Soto *Joanna* • James Fox *Hugo Paynter* • Art Malik *Kalim Said* • Cristina Higueras *Gabriella* • Michael Kitchen *Fredericks* ■ *Dir* Robert Young (2) • *Scr* Arthur Hopcraft, from the novel *No Place to Hide* by Ted Allbeury

Hostage ★★ 15
Crime action thriller
2004 · US/Ger · Colour · 108min

A slickly made if preposterously plotted thriller, this has Bruce Willis in dour mode as an LAPD hostage negotiator who quits his job to become a small-town police chief after an assignment ends in tragedy. Willis's past catches up with him, however, when three teenagers break into the hi-tech home of businessman Kevin Pollak, taking Pollak and his kids hostage. All this is watchable enough, but lacks the trademark twinkle and smug self-confidence that Willis brought to the *Die Hard* series. DA Swearing, violence. *DVD* *BL*

Bruce Willis *Jeff Talley* • Kevin Pollak *Walter Smith* • Jonathan Tucker *Dennis Kelly* • Ben Foster *Mars* • Marshall Allman *Kevin Kelly* • Michelle Horn *Jennifer Smith* • Jimmy Bennett *Tommy Smith* • Jimmy "Jax" Pinchak *Sean Mack* • Kim Coates *The watchman* • Serena Scott Thomas *Jane Talley* ■ *Dir* Florent Siri [Florent Emilio Siri] • *Scr* Doug Richardson, from the novel by Robert Crais

Hostages ★★★★
Documentary drama
1993 · US/UK · Colour · 90min

This is a gruelling and uncompromising account of the five-year incarceration endured by western hostages Terry Anderson, Tom Sutherland, Frank Reed, John McCarthy, Terry Waite and Brian Keenan after they were abducted in the Lebanon by a group of Hezbollah fundamentalists. Although director David Wheatley also includes actuality footage and reconstructions of the families' frustrated efforts to secure the sextet's release, it's the scenes set in the Beirut hideout that make the biggest dramatic impact. Played with conviction by a superior cast, this is a worthy tribute to the courage and determination of all involved. DP

Harry Dean Stanton *Frank Reed* • Colin Firth *John McCarthy* • Josef Sommer *Tom Sutherland* • Ciaran Hinds *Brian Keenan* • Jay O Sanders *Terry Anderson* • Conrad Asquith *Terry Waite* • Kathy Bates *Peggy Say* • Natasha Richardson *Jill Morrell* ■ *Dir* David Wheatley • *Scr* Bernard MacLaverty

Hostel ★★ 18
Horror
2005 · US · Colour · 89min

This sadistic, almost exploitative horror follows a trio of backpackers who venture into the heart of Eastern Europe on a promise of easy sex. Once there, they are lured into an abandoned factory that acts as the location for a bizarre "snuff ring" in which depraved businessmen pay for the pleasure of torturing teenagers to death. The film starts well, but writer/director Eli Roth fails to generate any real atmosphere of dread. AS Violence, sex scenes. *DVD* *BL*

Jay Hernandez *Paxton* • Derek Richardson *Josh* • Eythor Gudjonsson *Oli* • Barbara Nedeljakova *Natalya* • Jan Vlasak *Dutch Businessman* • Jana Kaderabkova *Svetlana* • Jennifer Lim *Kana* ■ *Dir/Scr* Eli Roth

Hostel: Part II ★★★ 18
Horror
2007 · US · Colour · 91min

Writer/director Eli Roth's deft sequel to his 2005 original has increased production values, better character development and a more mature style. *Hostel* featured male backpackers being tortured for sport, but the genders are switched here, as three young American girls are lured to Slovakia for a spa break. Instead, they find themselves auctioned off as victims to satisfy the sick and violent fantasies of the privileged. The hardcore theme of man's inhumanity to man is reinforced by a terrifying atmosphere, surprise narrative swerves and some well-judged gallows humour. Part III went straight to DVD in 2011. AJ Violence. *DVD* *BL*

Lauren German *Beth* • Roger Bart *Stuart* • Heather Matarazzo *Lorna* • Bijou Phillips *Whitney* • Richard Burgi *Todd* • Vera Jordanova *Axelle* ■ *Dir* Eli Roth • *Scr* Eli Roth, from characters by him • *Cinematographer* Milan Chadima

Hostile Hostages ★★★ 15
Black comedy
1994 · US · Colour · 92min

Stand-up comedian Denis Leary stars in this highly amusing attack on "relationship management", which takes effective side-swipes at the American class system. Leary plays a small-time thief holding a dysfunctional family hostage at Christmas, who ends up getting caught in the middle of their multiple feuds and neuroses. Judy Davis and Kevin Spacey's "couple from hell" give Leary solid support in director Ted Demme's bitingly dark comedy. Released on DVD under its US title, *The Ref*. AJ Swearing. *DVD*

Denis Leary *Gus* • Judy Davis *Caroline* • Kevin Spacey *Lloyd* • J Steinmiller Jr *Jesse* • Glynis Johns *Rose* • Raymond J Barry *Huff* • Christine Baranski *Connie* ■ *Dir* Ted Demme • *Scr* Richard LaGravenese, Marie Weiss, from a story by Marie Weiss

Hostile Waters ★★★ PG
Thriller based on a true story
1996 · US/UK · Colour · 91min

A heavyweight cast gives this real-life submarine disaster story a sheen of class. The setting is the Reagan era, when a Russian sub collided with an American one off the coast of Bermuda. This film traces the heroic attempts of the Soviet crew to repair their badly damaged craft, while the US worries about a potential nuclear catastrophe. Rutger Hauer, Martin Sheen and Max von Sydow head the top-notch cast in this TV movie, and director David Drury keeps the tension high. JF

Rutger Hauer *Captain Britanov* • Martin Sheen *Aurora Skipper* • Max von Sydow *Admiral Chernavin* • Rob Campbell *Sergei Preminin* • Harris Yulin *Admiral Quinn* • Regina Taylor *Lieutenant Curtis* ■ *Dir* David Drury • *Scr* Troy Kennedy Martin, from research by Tom Mangold, Peter Huchthausen, William Cran

Hostile Witness ★★ U
Courtroom drama
1968 · UK · Colour · 100min

Ray Milland directs and stars in this interesting, if disappointing tale of a barrister vowing revenge against the hit-and-run driver who killed his daughter. But he ends up questioning his own sanity when he finds himself in the dock for the murder of his neighbour. This was written for the screen by Jack Roffey from his own play, and it shows: the script reads as though it is meant for the stage and the actors emote as if they are playing to a live audience. JB

Ray Milland *Simon Crawford QC* • Sylvia Syms *Sheila Larkin* • Felix Aylmer *Mr Justice Osborne* • Raymond Huntley *John Naylor* • Geoffrey Lumsden *Major Hugh Maitland* • Norman Barrs *Charles Milburn* ■ *Dir* Ray Milland • *Scr* Jack Roffey, from his play

Hot Blood ★★★
Musical romance
1956 · US · Colour · 85min

"Be there when Jane Russell shakes her tambourines!" the posters implored, and she certainly did, flaunting the gypsy stereotype in this overly heated Romany romance. Russell and Cornel Wilde are LA gypsies forced by their families into an arranged marriage. Naturally, they fight like crazy at first, until the predictable reconciliation. However, the risible aspects are compensated for by director Nicholas Ray's dramatic use of colour and expert use of the CinemaScope screen. Ray also gets animated performances from the usually wooden leads. RB

Jane Russell *Annie Caldash* • Cornel Wilde *Stephan Torino* • Luther Adler *Marco Torino* • Joseph Calleia *Papa Theodore* • Mikhail Rasumny *Old Johnny* • Nina Koshetz *Nita Johnny* • Helen Westcott *Velma* • Jamie Russell *Xano* ■ *Dir* Nicholas Ray • *Scr* Jesse Lasky Jr, from a story by Jean Evans

The Hot Chick ★★★ 12
Comedy
2002 · US · Colour · 100min

Rob Schneider makes an enjoyable contribution to the "body-swap" subgenre with this comedy, in which an ancient earring causes small-time crook Clive and high-school princess Jessica to get under each other's skin. Schneider plays up his feminine side with disarming conviction, especially in his bonding moments with Jessica's pretty best friend Anna Faris. The humour is frequently juvenile slapstick, but executive producer Adam Sandler pops up in an amusing cameo. JC *DVD*

Rob Schneider *Clive/Jessica Spencer* • Anna Faris *April* • Matthew Lawrence *Billy* • Eric Christian Olsen *Jake* • Robert Davi *Stan* • Melora Hardin *Carol* • Alexandra Holden *Lulu* • Rachel McAdams *Jessica Spencer/Clive* • Adam Sandler *Bongo player* ■ *Dir* Tom Brady • *Scr* Tom Brady, Rob Schneider

Hot Dog – The Movie ★ 18
Comedy
1984 · US · Colour · 94min

Not a sausage or a bun in sight, yet this remains cinema's equivalent of fast food: indigestible and utterly unmemorable. This typically crude example of the 1980s party movie, distinguished by some eye-catching ski footage, stars David Naughton as one of many horny adolescents contesting the world freestyle championship. Blatantly sexist – Shannon Tweed and other similarly unclad ladies are there like so much tinsel on a Christmas tree – this plays like some tired old Hollywood executive's idea of what teens want to see. RS

David Naughton *Dan* • Patrick Houser *Harkin* • Tracy N Smith *Sunny* • John Patrick Reger *Rudi Garmisch* • Frank Koppala *Squirrel* • James Saito *Kendo* • Shannon Tweed *Sylvia Fonda* ■ *Dir* Peter Markle • *Scr* Mike Marvin

Hot Enough for June ★★★ PG
Spy satire
1964 · UK · Colour · 92min

James Bond is dead! Long live Nicolas Whistler – or at least that's what this spy spoof would have us believe. Everything here is just on the unfunny side of clever; for instance, the American title *Agent 8¾* is a reference both to Federico Fellini's *8½*, released earlier the same year, and the fact that this was the eighth collaboration between director Ralph Thomas and Dirk Bogarde. Cheerfully sending up his own Rank image as much as that of Bond, Bogarde passes muster, but the real star of the show is Robert Morley as the spymaster. DP *DVD* *BL*

Dirk Bogarde *Nicolas Whistler* • Sylva Koscina *Vlasta Simenova* • Robert Morley *Colonel Cunliffe* • Leo McKern *Simenova* • Roger Delgado *Josef* • John Le Mesurier *Allsop* • Richard Vernon *Roddinghead* ■ *Dir* Ralph Thomas • *Scr* Lukas Heller, from the novel *Night of Wenceslas* by Lionel Davidson

Hot Fuzz ★★★★ 15
Action crime comedy
2007 · UK/US/Fr · Colour · 115min

Simon Pegg and director Edgar Wright – the team behind zombie comedy *Shaun of the Dead* – return for this gleeful pastiche of American action movies. Pegg stars as an over-achieving London policeman transferred to a supposedly crime-free village in Gloucestershire. What begins as a very funny, very British murder mystery eventually mutates into an ironic action spectacular. Armed with a *Who's Who* of home-grown acting talent and a surfeit of gags, *Hot Fuzz* also showcases the continuing comic partnership of Pegg and co-star Nick Frost, here as mismatched cops who play out every buddy movie convention imaginable. More smart than silly, this is self-confident comedy that's proud to be British. JR Violence, swearing. *DVD* *BL*

Simon Pegg *Sergeant Nicholas Angel* • Nick Frost *PC Danny Butterman* • Jim Broadbent *Inspector Frank Butterman* • Kevin Eldon *Sergeant Tony Fisher* • Paddy Considine *DS Andy Wainwright* • Rafe Spall *DC Andy Cartwright* • Olivia Colman *PC Doris Thatcher* • Karl Johnson (2) *PC Bob Walker* • Timothy Dalton *Simon Skinner* • Edward Woodward *Tom Weaver* • Billie Whitelaw *Joyce Cooper* • Bill Nighy *Met Chief Inspector* ■ *Dir* Edgar Wright • *Scr* Simon Pegg, Edgar Wright

Hot Lead and Cold Feet ★★ U
Comedy western
1978 · US · Colour · 85min

Jim Dale was snapped up by Disney for this kiddie western. He plays three parts: grumpy patriarch Jasper Bloodshy and his two sons, one nerdy and feeble, the other a gunslinger. Prepare to wade through several tons of Disney treacle as Dale earns every cent of his fee. TV comic Don Knotts must have been cast to assist box-office revenue. AT

Jim Dale *Eli/Wild Billy/Jasper Bloodshy* • Karen Valentine *Jenny* • Don Knotts *Denver Kid* • Jack Elam *Rattlesnake* • John Williams *Mansfield* • Darren McGavin *Mayor Ragsdale* • Warren Vanders *Boss Snead* • Debbie Lytton *Roxanne* ■ *Dir* Robert Butler • *Scr* Joseph L McEveety, Arthur Alsberg, Don Nelson, from a story by Rod Piffath

Hot Millions ★★★ U
Comedy caper
1968 · UK · Colour · 106min

A large, disparate cast of famous faces, from Maggie Smith to Bob Newhart, pulls out some moderately funny stops in this bubbly, engaging tale of manipulative Peter Ustinov parting a large multinational from a sizeable portion of its shekels. Ustinov is thankfully given a large, containing script to curb his worst excesses, the jokes come thick and relatively fast, and there is a charming jauntiness. The enterprise tends to run dangerously low on steam towards the end, but it grabs the attention with a considerable degree of style. SH

Peter Ustinov *Marcus Pendleton/Caesar Smith* • Maggie Smith *Patty Terwilliger* • Karl Malden *Carlton J Klemper* • Bob Newhart *Willard C*

Gnatpole • Robert Morley *Caesar Smith* • Cesar Romero *Customs Officer* ■ *Dir* Eric Till • *Scr* Ira Wallach, Peter Ustinov

Hot Money ★★

Heist comedy   1979 • Can • Colour • 78min

There are only a handful of performers in cinema history whose mere presence can raise the quality of a film by at least a couple of notches. Orson Welles is one of the few, and he alone makes this tepid Canadian heist comedy worth bothering with. Sadly, we see too little of him as the sheriff to crooked deputy Michael Murphy. It's contrived, unfunny and clear to see why the film was withheld for five years – but at least there's Orson. DP

Orson Welles *Sheriff Paisley* • Michael Murphy (1) *Burt* ■ *Dir* Selig Usher [George McCowan] • *Scr* Carl DeSantis, Phyllis Camesano, Joel Cohen, Neil Cohen

The Hot Potato ★★★ PG

Crime caper based on a true story   2011 • UK • Colour • 95min

Apparently based on a true story, Tim Lewiston's film is set in 1969 and harks back to the kind of wisecracking crime caper that was then in vogue. The gleefully convoluted plot centres on a lump of uranium that lands in the lap of scrap merchant Ray Winstone after being "found" in a Ministry of Defence facility by secretary Lois Winstone's dopily dodgy boyfriend (Jack Huston). But flogging the "hot potato" proves easier said than done, as the hapless trio encounters an international roll call of villains and rogues during an eventful excursion to the continent. Slickly staged and knowingly played by a fine cast, this is always enjoyable if only fitfully amusing. DP Violence, some swearing, sexual references. *DVD*

Ray Winstone *Kenny* • Colm Meaney *Harry* • Jack Huston *Danny* • David Harewood *Harrison* • Lois Winstone *Carole* • Louise Redknapp *Irene* • John Lynch *Bill/Ben* ■ *Dir/Scr* Tim Lewiston

Hot Pursuit ★★ 15

Comedy   1987 • US • Colour • 88min

John Cusack plays a college boy in pursuit of his girlfriend who has gone on holiday with her parents; as one might expect, his journey is beset with silly disasters. It's essentially an attempt to reprise the actor's first hit – Rob Reiner's *The Sure Thing* – but, although Cusack is always engaging to watch, this film has none of the wit of that delightful comedy. JB *DVD*

John Cusack *Dan Bartlett* • Wendy Gazelle *Lori Cronenberg* • Monte Markham *Bill Cronenberg* • Shelley Fabares *Buffy Cronenberg* • Jerry Stiller *Victor Honeywell* • Ben Stiller *Chris Honeywell* • Robert Loggia *Mac MacLaren* ■ *Dir* Steven Lisberger • *Scr* Steven Lisberger, Steven Carabatsos, from Lisberger's story

Hot Pursuit ★★ 12

Action comedy   2015 • US • Colour • 87min

Reese Witherspoon stars as an uptight police officer tasked with escorting a drug dealer's wife (Sofia Vergara) across Texas in a by-the-numbers buddy chase comedy. Along the way they have to avoid corrupt cops and criminals which prompts gunfire and car chases, but mostly there's a lot of bickering as Witherspoon and Vergara insult each other for nearly 90 minutes. Everything in the film is moved aside in favour of the pair's slapstick set pieces, which become tiresome from very early on, and after the first few exchanges things go downhill very rapidly. Two very capable leads deserved better. JL In English, Spanish. *DVD*

Reese Witherspoon *Officer Rose Cooper* • Sofia Vergara *Daniella Riva* • Michael Mosley *Detective Dixon* • Robert Kazinsky *Randy* • John Carroll Lynch *Captain Emmett* ■ *Dir* Anne Fletcher • *Scr* David Feeney, John Quaintance

The Hot Rock ★★★ U

Crime caper   1972 • US • Colour • 100min

This caper movie, based on a novel by Donald E Westlake, is not without its flaws, but it boasts a sense of finesse and fun that other films in the genre sadly lack. Robert Redford and George Segal head a quartet of criminals bent on stealing a fabulous diamond from the Brooklyn Museum. Inevitably, their ineptitude at robbery is a reflection of their incompetence at living. Peter Yates, working from a William Goldman script that shouldn't have split the tale into four distinct parts, directs without momentum. TH

Robert Redford *John Dortmunder* • George Segal *Andrew Kelp* • Zero Mostel *Abe Greenberg* • Ron Leibman *Murch* • Paul Sand *Alan Greenberg* • Moses Gunn *Dr Amusa* ■ *Dir* Peter Yates • *Scr* William Goldman, from a novel by Donald E Westlake

Hot Rod ★★ 12

Action comedy   2007 • US • Colour • 84min

Rod Kimble (Andy Samberg) is the self-proclaimed Evel Knievel of suburban America, performing *Jackass*-style stunts on his moped. He's an incompetent daredevil, but when his macho stepdad Frank (Ian McShane) needs a life-saving heart operation, Rod attempts to earn $50,000 by jumping over 15 buses. Samberg, director Akiva Schaffer and Jorma Taccone (who plays Rod's stepbrother) are *Saturday Night Live* alumni who gained internet fame with a fake rap video, so it's fitting that Rod's painful, amateur stunts wouldn't look out of place on YouTube. The rest of Samberg's humour is rather more patchy – lots of mirthless interludes only occasionally enlivened by spoofs of 1980s pop videos. JR *DVD*

Andy Samberg *Rod Kimble* • Isla Fisher *Denise* • Jorma Taccone *Kevin Powell* • Bill Hader *Dave* • Danny R McBride [Danny McBride (2)] *Rico* • Sissy Spacek *Marie Powell* • Ian McShane *Frank Powell* • Chris Parnell *Barry Pasternack* ■ *Dir* Akiva Schaffer • *Scr* Pam Brady

Hot Shot ★★

Sports drama   1986 • US • Colour • 89min

This run-of-the-mill American take on soccer provides more unintentional laughs than genuine drama. Pelé, who obviously got the film bug during *Escape to Victory*, plays a football legend who is called to help a youngster embrace the greatest game. Look for early appearances by a pre-stardom Mario Van Peebles, Jimmy Smits and Billy Warlock. JF

Jim Youngs *Jimmy Kristidis* • Pelé *Santos* • David Groh *Jerry Norton* • Mario Van Peebles *Hoffman* • Billy Warlock *Vinnie Fortino* • Jimmy Smits *Stars team member* ■ *Dir* Rick King • *Scr* Rick King, Joe Sauter

Hot Shots! ★★★ 12

Spoof action   1991 • US • Colour • 81min

If ever a movie was ripe for sending up, then *Top Gun* was it, and, although this lacks the charm of classic spoofs *Airplane!* and *The Naked Gun*, there are enough good gags on show to win over those who wished Tom Cruise had gone down in flames. This time director Jim Abrahams goes solo without the Zucker brothers, but he still displays the same cheerful lack of taste and subtlety. Charlie Sheen stars as the macho fighter pilot hero, but Lloyd Bridges bags the most laughs as the untogether commanding officer. JF Swearing. *DVD* CS

Charlie Sheen *Sean "Topper" Harley/Rhett Butler/Superman* • Cary Elwes *Kent Gregory* • Valeria Golino *Ramada Thompson/Scarlett O'Hara/Lois Lane* • Lloyd Bridges *Admiral Benson* • Kevin Dunn *Lieutenant Commander Block* • William O'Leary *Pete "Dead Meat" Thompson* • Kristy Swanson *Kowalski* • Efrem Zimbalist Jr *Wilson* • Jon Cryer *Jim "Wash Out" Pfaffenbach* ■ *Dir* Jim Abrahams • *Scr* Pat Proft, Jim Abrahams

Hot Shots! Part Deux ★★ 12

Spoof action   1993 • US • Colour • 84min

The law of diminishing laughs applies to Jim Abrahams and Pat Proft's self-conscious parody of the Rambo series, with Charlie Sheen reprising his role of the superhero with zero tolerance for the enemy. Lloyd Bridges also returns, this time as the US president, but this sequel is too reminiscent of its predecessor to be terribly amusing. Still, there are some laughs to be had and

look out for a brief appearance by Rowan Atkinson. TH Swearing. *DVD* BL

Charlie Sheen *Topper Harley* • Lloyd Bridges *Tug Benson* • Valeria Golino *Ramada Rodham Hayman* • Richard Crenna *Colonel Denton Walters* • Brenda Bakke *Michelle Rodham Huddleston* • Miguel Ferrer *Harbinger* • Rowan Atkinson *Dexter Hayman* ■ *Dir* Jim Abrahams • *Scr* Jim Abrahams, Pat Proft

Hot Spell ★★★

Drama   1958 • US • BW • 88min

This rather stagey family melodrama, set in New Orleans, was the last of the five films that Shirley Booth made before returning to the stage and TV. As in her first film, *Come Back, Little Sheba* in 1952, for which she won the best actress Oscar, Booth plays a distressed housewife dreaming of better days. Her sensitive performance is contrasted with Anthony Quinn's bombastic one as her philandering husband. Shirley MacLaine, on the verge of real stardom, is touching as the couple's daughter. Sub-Tennessee Williams it may be, but it offers a certain amount of pleasure. RB

Shirley Booth *Alma Duval* • Anthony Quinn *Jack Duval* • Shirley MacLaine *Virginia Duval* • Earl Holliman *Buddy Duval* • Eileen Heckart *Fan* • Clint Kimbrough *Billy Duval* • Warren Stevens *Wyatt* • Jody Lawrance *Dora May* ■ *Dir* Daniel Mann • *Scr* James Poe, from the play *Next of Kin* by Lonnie Coleman

The Hot Spot ★★★ 18

Black comedy thriller   1990 • US • Colour • 124min

Don Johnson is the drifter, holed up in a small Texas town, who falls for bad girl Virginia Madsen and good girl Jennifer Connelly. Director Dennis Hopper turns in a faithful tribute to the *film noir* thrillers of old, but, this being the 1990s, he ups the sexual content a number of degrees. There are lots of fans, dust and people sweating, and Madsen smoulders away furiously to good effect. While not quite so convincing, Johnson is still suitably mean and brooding as the fall guy. JF Violence, swearing, sex scenes, nudity. *DVD*

Don Johnson *Harry Madox* • Virginia Madsen *Dolly Harshaw* • Jennifer Connelly *Gloria Harper* • Charles Martin Smith *Lon Gulik* • William Sadler *Frank Sutton* • Jerry Hardin *George Harshaw* • Barry Corbin *Sheriff* ■ *Dir* Dennis Hopper • *Scr* Nona Tyson, Charles Williams, from the novel *Hell Hath No Fury* by Charles Williams

Hot Target ★★ 18

Crime thriller   1985 • NZ • Colour • 91min

A rather predictable and ham-fisted attempt at a gripping thriller, this New Zealand film tries to cover its clichéd tracks with twists and turns aimed at confusing the viewer. Simone Griffeth is the wife planning to get rid of husband Bryan Marshall with the help of a lover, unaware that her accomplice is actually a thief setting her up. Are you still with us? A *film noir* that's more bland than black. JF Swearing, nudity.

Simone Griffeth *Christine Webber* • Steve Marachuk *Greg Sandford* • Bryan Marshall *Clive Webber* • Peter McCauley *Detective Inspector Nolan* ■ *Dir* Denis Lewiston • *Scr* Denis Lewiston, from a story by Gerry O'Hara

Hot to Trot ★ PG

Comedy   1988 • US • Colour • 79min

A confused and confusing comedy, this outdated tat has Bobcat Goldthwait getting tips from a talking horse (voiced by John Candy) and thinking he's on to a whinnying streak. Unsurprisingly, he's not. TH

Bobcat Goldthwait *Fred Chaney* • Dabney Coleman *Walter Sawyer* • Jim Metzler *Boyd Osborne* • Cindy Pickett *Victoria Peyton* • Virginia Madsen *Allison Rowe* • John Candy *Don* ■ *Dir* Michael Dinner • *Scr* Stephen Neigher, Hugo Gilbert, Charlie Peters, from a story by Stephen Neigher, Hugo Gilbert

The Hot Touch ★

Romantic thriller   1982 • Can/Fr • Colour • 92min

Roger Vadim was once the *enfant terrible* of French cinema. Yet, by the early 1980s, he was reduced to accepting third-rate

assignments across the Atlantic. This art-scam thriller is as bogus as the paintings churned out by Wayne Rogers for crooked dealer Patrick Macnee. Only the sinister commission from the psychopathic Lloyd Bochner – to replace a series of pictures lost in the war – has anything going for it. DP

Wayne Rogers *Danny Fairchild* • Marie-France Pisier *Dr Emillienne Simpson* • Lloyd Bochner *Severo* • Samantha Eggar *Samantha O'Brien* • Patrick Macnee *Vincent Reblack* • Melvyn Douglas *Max Reich* • Gloria Carlin *Kelly* • Allan Kolman *Lincoln Simpson* ■ *Dir* Roger Vadim • *Scr* Peter Dion, from a story by Peter Dion

Hot Tub Time Machine ★★★ 15

Science-fiction comedy   2010 • US • Colour • 94min

Disgruntled 40-something pals John Cusack, Craig Robinson and Rob Corddry attempt to rekindle the carousing days of their youth in this raucous comic fantasy. And thanks to (you guessed it) a certain "hot-tub time machine", they get the opportunity to replay the misadventures of 1986 – with the benefit of added experience. The film is loaded with 1980s nostalgia, and gleefully reproduces the crass sexism of the era's teen flicks. But the characters' midlife neuroses also bring a measure of believability to the farcical complications of the time-travel conceit. However, sustaining consistent logic to the then-and-now plotting ultimately proves too much of a challenge, and the movie falls well short of time-twisting comedy classics like *Back to the Future* and *Groundhog Day*. TJ Swearing, sex scenes, nudity, drug abuse. *DVD* BL

John Cusack *Adam* • Rob Corddry *Lou* • Craig Robinson *Nick* • Clark Duke *Jacob* • Crispin Glover *Phil* • Lizzy Caplan *April* • Lyndsy Fonseca *Jenny* • Collette Wolfe *Kelly* • Chevy Chase *Repairman* ■ *Dir* Steve Pink • *Scr* Josh Heald, Sean Anders, John Morris, from a story by Heald

Hot Tub Time Machine 2 ★ 15

Comedy   2014 • US • Colour • 93min

After their first time-travelling adventure brings Rob Corddry and Craig Robinson hindsight-assisted fame and fortune, their lives are turned upside-down, prompting them to leap once more into the magical, ski-resort jacuzzi. Nowhere to be seen, however, is the first film's major player John Cusack, which sends out its own warning about the dismal quality of this unwarranted follow-up. TJ *DVD* BL

Rob Corddry *Lou* • Craig Robinson *Nick* • Clark Duke *Jacob* • Adam Scott *Adam* • Kellee Stewart *Courtney* • Chevy Chase *Repairman* ■ *Dir* Steve Pink • *Scr* Josh Heald

Hot Water ★★★ U

Silent comedy   1924 • US • BW • 53min

Harold Lloyd's previous comedy, *Girl Shy*, was eight reels long and had theatre owners complaining about the gaps between the pratfalls. Lloyd got the message and took the scissors to *Hot Water*, cutting out the intricate plotting and concentrating on his trademark stunts. The story is simple: Lloyd is a newly married man coping with shopping, traffic and, naturally, his mother-in-law. This isn't one of Lloyd's best films, though his bespectacled character always has charm and there's a brilliant scene in a traffic jam when he's encumbered by a turkey that he's won in a raffle. AT

Harold Lloyd *Hubby* • Jobyna Ralston *Wifey* • Josephine Crowell *Mother-in-law* • Charles Stevenson *Brother-in-law* • Pat Harmon *Straphanger* • Andy DeVilla *Cop* • Mickey McBan *Brother-in-law* ■ *Dir* Sam Taylor, Fred C Newmeyer • *Scr* Thomas J Gray, Tim Whelan, John Grey, Sam Taylor

Hotel ★★★ 18

Black comedy thriller   2001 • UK/It • Colour • 111min

Director Mike Figgis confirmed his position as one of Britain's most visionary directors with this part-improvised film-making "exercise" – shot over a weekend in Venice using a cast as varied as David Schwimmer, Rhys Ifans and John Malkovich. The story, which unfolds in a decidedly obtuse and sketchy fashion, concerns the making of a movie of John Webster's *Duchess of Malfi*, against a background of murder and casual cannibalism. Salma Hayek is superbly irritating as an MTV-style documentary host, and when Burt Reynolds pops up as a financier, you know you're in weird waters. Odd, compelling and darkly funny. AC *DVD*

Rhys Ifans *Trent Stoken* • Saffron Burrows *Naomi/Duchess of Malfi* • David Schwimmer *Jonathan Danderfine* • Salma Hayek *Charlee Boux* • Burt Reynolds *Flamenco manager* • Julian Sands *O, tour guide* • Danny Huston *Hotel manager* • Lucy Liu *Kawika* • Chiara Mastroianni *Nurse* • John Malkovich *Omar Jonnson* ■ *Dir/Scr* Mike Figgis

Hotel Berlin ★★
Second World War drama
1945 · US · BW · 98min

An updated, retitled adaptation of Vicki Baum's 1943 novel *Berlin Hotel*, which, like her more famous *Grand Hotel*, observes the comings and the goings of the guests in said hotel as the Allies close in. In this case, it's mainly a Nazi packing up at war's end and preparing to leave for South America with a plan to start another world war, and a Noble prize-winning scientist whose life has been destroyed by the Nazis. Warner Bros hoped they had another *Casablanca* on their hands. They didn't. AT

Helmut Dantine *Martin Richter* • Andrea King *Lisa Dorn* • Raymond Massey *Arnim Von Dahnwitz* • Faye Emerson *Tillie Weiler* • Peter Lorre *Johannes Koenig* • Alan Hale *Hermann Plottke* • George Coulouris *Joachim Helm* ■ *Dir* Peter Godfrey • *Scr* Jo Pagano, Alvah Bessie, from the novel *Berlin Hotel* by Vicki Baum

Hotel Colonial ★★15
Adventure thriller 1987 · US/It · Colour · 101min

This beautifully shot but insubstantial melodrama is set in Latin America. John Savage plays an American out of his depth when he travels to Colombia to discover the truth behind his brother's reported death and comes up against the sinister Robert Duvall. Rachel Ward plays the love interest and all three produce capable performances, but the meandering script lacks gravitas. JF

John Savage *Marco Venieri* • Robert Duvall *Carrasco* • Rachel Ward *Irene Costa* • Massimo Troisi *Werner* ■ *Dir* Cinzia Torrini • *Scr* Enzo Monteleone, Cinzia Torrini, Ira R Barmak, Robert Katz, from a story by Enzo Monteleone • *Cinematographer* Giuseppe Rotunno

Hotel de Love ★★★15
Romantic comedy
1996 · Aus/US · Colour · 92min

This unusually well-constructed Australian romantic comedy has much of the style of *Muriel's Wedding* and features British beauty Saffron Burrows, Pippa Grandison and old stager Ray Barrett. Twin brothers (Aden Young, Simmon Bossell) fall for high school goddess Melissa (Burrows), who leads them a merry dance before heading off to college. It's a lightweight affair, but it exudes a certain charm. JF

Aden Young *Rick Dunne* • Saffron Burrows *Melissa Morrison* • Simon Bossell *Stephen Dunne* • Pippa Grandison *Alison Leigh* • Ray Barrett *Jack Dunne* • Julia Blake *Edith Dunne* • Peter O'Brien (2) *Norman* • Belinda McClory *Janet* ■ *Dir/Scr* Craig Rosenberg

Hôtel du Nord ★★★PG
Drama 1938 · Fr · BW · 96min

This brooding study may not be Marcel Carné's most accomplished film, but it's still undeniably affecting. Designer Alexandre Trauner reproduces the atmospheric settings that were essential to Carné's poetic realist style. Indeed, the tatty interiors and quaintly run-down canal landmarks are the real stars of a film that only comes fitfully to life. Doomed lovers Annabella and Jean-Pierre Aumont are just a touch too tragic, while Arletty and Louis

Jouvet are a little too unbridled in their villainy. DP French +subtitles. *DVD*

Annabella *Renée* • Arletty *Raymonde* • Louis Jouvet *M Edmond* • Jean-Pierre Aumont *Pierre* • Jeanne Marken [Jane Marken] *Louise Lecouvreur* • André Brunot *Emile Lecouvreur* • Bernard Blier *Prosper* ■ *Dir* Marcel Carné • *Scr* Marcel Carné, Henri Jeanson, Jean Aurenche (adaptation), from the novel by Eugène Dabit

Hôtel du Paradis ★★★15
Drama 1986 · UK/Fr · Colour · 113min

Jana Bokova's thoughtful study of isolation and thwarted ambition still displays a maturity rare in debutante directors. In a poignant reference to his own career, Fernando Rey plays an actor taking one last stab at legitimacy after wasting his talent in escapist entertainments. His fellow residents – among them Fabrice Luchini's frustrated film-maker and Hugues Quester's penurious thespian – are no less acquainted with disappointment. The tone is melancholic, but attention to detail makes this affecting. DP French dubbed.

Fernando Rey *Joseph* • Bérangère Bonvoisin • Hugues Quester *Maurice* • Marika Rivera *Marika* • Carola Regnier *Sarah* • Raul Gimenez *Emilio* • Michael Medwin *English producer* • Fabrice Luchini *Arthur* ■ *Dir/Scr* Jana Bokova

Hotel for Dogs ★★★U
Comedy 2008 · US/Ger · Colour · 95min

Frolicking canines and a hint of pathos combine to watchable effect in this adeptly packaged family fare. Emma Roberts and Jake T Austin take the lead roles as orphaned siblings who are assigned to yet another pair of foster parents (played entertainingly by Kevin Dillon and Lisa Kudrow), but then need to find a home for the beloved terrier they've been keeping in secret. Luckily for them, there's an abandoned hotel nearby that soon becomes a refuge not only to their furry friend but also to a whole host of doggie waifs and strays. Sure, it's all a bit too good to be true, but younger viewers will enjoy the ably choreographed four-legged mischief. TJ *DVD* *Blu*

Emma Roberts *Andi* • Jake T Austin *Bruce* • Don Cheadle *Bernie* • Kyla Pratt *Heather* • Lisa Kudrow *Lois Scudder* • Kevin Dillon *Carl Scudder* ■ *Dir* Thor Freudenthal • *Scr* Jeff Lowell, Bob Schooley, Mark McCorkle, from the novel by Lois Duncan

Hotel Imperial ★★★
Silent First World War drama
1927 · US · BW · 84min

The noted Swedish director Mauritz Stiller arrived in Hollywood in 1925 with his protégée, Greta Garbo. He could not fit in with the studio system and only completed two pictures for Paramount in two and a half years, the first being this powerful drama of wartime espionage and romance. Visually striking with its vast hotel setting and beautifully paced, it stars Pola Negri in an unusually restrained performance as the hotel chambermaid who helps an Austrian officer trapped behind Russian lines. Billy Wilder updated the story to the Second World War for *Five Graves to Cairo*. AE

Pola Negri *Anna Sedlak* • James Hall *Lieutenant Paul Almasy* • George Siegmann *General Juschkiewitsch* • Max Davidson *Elias Butterman* • Michael Vavitch *Tabakowitsch* ■ *Dir* Mauritz Stiller • *Scr* Jules Furthman, from the play by Lajos Biró • *Cinematographer* Bert Glennon

The Hotel New Hampshire ★★★15
Comedy drama
1984 · US/UK/Can · Colour · 103min

On its original release, there was anything but a critical consensus on this adaptation of John Irving's expansive novel about a dysfunctional hotel-owning family. Many blamed the book for the film's episodic structure and the sensationalist nature of the fates that befall the central characters. Others praised writer/director Tony Richardson for the fidelity of his approach. The cast does its best, although the characters are a pretty hard bunch to sympathise with. David Watkin's

photography is a bonus, however. DP Swearing, sex scenes, violence. *DVD*

Rob Lowe *John Berry* • Jodie Foster *Franny Berry* • Paul McCrane *Frank Berry* • Beau Bridges *Win Berry* • Lisa Banes *Mary Berry* • Jennie Dundas *Lilly Berry* • Seth Green *Egg Berry* • Nastassja Kinski *Susie the Bear* • Wallace Shawn *Freud* • Wilford Brimley *"Iowa Bob" Berry* • Joely Richardson *Waitress* • Matthew Modine *Sterling "Chip" Dove/Ernst* • Amanda Plummer *Fehlgeburt, "Miss Miscarriage"* ■ *Dir* Tony Richardson • *Scr* Tony Richardson, from the novel by John Irving

Hotel Paradiso ★★
Comedy 1966 · US/UK · Colour · 96min

Adapted by producer/director Peter Glenville and Jean-Claude Carrière from Georges Feydeau and Maurice Desvallières's famous stage farce *L'Hôtel du Libre Echange*, this is a classic example of how what might be hilarious in the theatre can end up being a dead duck on the screen. The action is so flatly directed that not even that great editor Anne Coates can inject any pace into the endless round of bedroom to-ing and fro-ing that should have been funnier. DP

Alec Guinness *Benedict Boniface* • Gina Lollobrigida *Marcelle Cot* • Robert Morley *Henri Cot* • Peggy Mount *Angelique Boniface* • Akim Tamiroff *Anniello* • Marie Bell *La Grande Antoinette* • Derek Fowldes [Derek Fowlds] *Maxime* ■ *Dir* Peter Glenville • *Scr* Jean-Claude Carrière, Peter Glenville, from the play *L'Hôtel du Libre Echange* by Georges Feydeau, Maurice Desvallières

Hotel Reserve ★★★U
Thriller 1944 · UK · BW · 88min

Jointly directed by Victor Hanbury, Lance Comfort and Max Greene, this subdued thriller, set just before the Second World War, is lifted by James Mason's performance as a "wronged man", in this case a refugee accused of being a spy. The plot has enough suspense and intrigue, but this movie only fitfully comes to life as Mason sets out discover the real villain. TH

James Mason *Peter Vadassy* • Lucie Mannheim *Madame Suzanne Koche* • Raymond Lovell *Monsieur Robert Duclos* • Julien Mitchell *Monsieur Beghin* • Clare Hamilton *Miss Mary Skelton* • Martin Miller *Herr Walter Vogel* • Herbert Lom *Monsieur André Roux* • Frederick Valk *Herr Emil Schimler* ■ *Dir* Victor Hanbury, Lance Comfort, Max Greene • *Scr* John Davenport, from the novel *Epitaph for a Spy* by Eric Ambler

Hotel Rwanda ★★★★12
Drama based on a true story
2004 · S Afr/US/UK/It · Colour · 116min

Don Cheadle delivers the performance of his career in this gut-wrenching drama based on events in Rwanda in the mid-1990s. It's an inspirational and shame-inducing story of one man's courage in the face of genuine horror. Cheadle plays true-life hero Paul Rusesabagina, a hotel manager who saved the lives of more than 1200 refugees – the majority of them Tutsi – by sheltering them at his workplace. Cleanly shot with an acute sense of realism, the film focuses on the emotional interaction between its characters as they struggle to survive despite appalling indifference from the West. By homing in on just one element of the Hutu campaign of genocide, Terry George gives a human face to the shocking statistics, while emphasising the chilling casualness of the violence. SF *DVD*

Don Cheadle *Paul Rusesabagina* • Sophie Okonedo *Tatiana Rusesabagina* • Nick Nolte *Colonel Oliver* • Joaquin Phoenix *Jack Daglish* • Desmond Dube *Dube* • David O'Hara *David* • Cara Seymour *Pat Archer* • Fana Mokoena *General Augustin Bizimungo* ■ *Dir* Terry George • *Scr* Terry George, Keir Pearson

Hotel Sahara ★★★U
Second World War comedy
1951 · UK · BW · 87min

A marvellous comedy idea: during the desert campaign in the Second World War, Peter Ustinov's hotel is utilised at various times by British, German, Italian and French forces. Naturally, proprietor Ustinov manages to accommodate them all, plus a

few visiting Arabs as well. Very funny, and played at a fast and furious pace by a wonderful cast. TS

Yvonne De Carlo *Yasmin Pallas* • Peter Ustinov *Emad* • David Tomlinson *Captain "Puffin" Cheynie* • Roland Culver *Major Bill Randall* • Albert Lieven *Lt Gunther Von Heilicke* • Bill Owen *Private Binns* • Sidney Tafler [Sydney Tafler] *Corporal Pullar* • Eugene Deckers *French Spahi Officer* ■ *Dir* Ken Annakin • *Scr* Patrick Kirwan, George H Brown

Hotel Sorrento ★★15
Drama 1994 · Aus · Colour · 107min

One of three sisters writes a tell-all book about life in their home town, the Australian seaside resort of Sorrento. The book purports to be fiction, but the other two siblings reckon there's more than a few grains of uncomfortable truth in it. It's nicely acted by Joan Plowright, Caroline Goodall and Tara Morice, but the material is dull and the pace is plodding. DA

Caroline Goodall *Meg Moynihan* • Caroline Gillmer *Hilary Moynihan* • Tara Morice *Pippa Moynihan* • Joan Plowright *Marge Morrisey* • John Hargreaves *Dick Bennett* • Ray Barrett *Wal Moynihan* • Ben Thomas *Troy Moynihan* • Nicholas Bell *Edwin* ■ *Dir* Richard Franklin • *Scr* Richard Franklin, Peter Fitzpatrick, from the play by Hannie Rayson

Hotel Splendide ★★15
Black comedy drama
1999 · UK/Fr · Colour · 98min

Following the death of his overbearing mother, hotel manager Stephen Tompkinson continues her policy of serving unrelievedly bland food in their remote island hostelry. But the arrival of Toni Collette drives a wedge between Tompkinson and his chef brother Daniel Craig, as she sparks a culinary revolution. While it's visually ambitious, this allegory is also dramatically wayward and symbolically gauche. DP

Toni Collette *Kath* • Daniel Craig *Ronald Blanche* • Katrin Cartlidge *Cora Blanche* • Stephen Tompkinson *Dezmond Blanche* • Hugh O'Conor *Stanley Smith* • Helen McCrory *Lorna Bull* ■ *Dir/Scr* Terence Gross

Hotel Terminus: the Life and Times of Klaus Barbie ★★★★★
Documentary
1987 · US/Fr · BW and Colour · 267min

Having been denied an Oscar for *The Sorrow and the Pity*, Marcel Ophüls finally received his due reward for this damning study of the unholy alliance of political expediency and anti-Semitic corruption that allowed former Gestapo chief Klaus Barbie (the so-called "Butcher of Lyons") to spend over 30 contented years in Bolivia, in spite of the enormity of his crimes against humanity. In the course of interviews with victims, enemies, collaborators and others, it becomes clear that Barbie had many willing accomplices – and only some wore Nazi uniforms. This epic historical documentary is also a moral indictment of timeless resonance. DP English, French, German, Spanish +subtitles.

Jeanne Moreau *Narrator* ■ *Dir* Marcel Ophüls

Hotel Transylvania ★★U
Animated comedy
2012 · US · Colour and BW · 87min

In this frenetic CGI-animated ghoul-fest, Count Dracula (voiced by Adam Sandler) has kept his daughter away from torch-bearing humans for a century by operating a castle resort for famous monsters only. But he can only watch in horror when she falls for a stray backpacker. TV-cartoon director Genndy Tartakovsky fails to add anything of note to the hackneyed overprotective-dad story, which is etched in often overbearingly exaggerated style. All the genre references are obvious, the slapstick sight gags a pale Tex Avery imitation and, despite a few witty in-jokes, it's painfully unfunny. A sequel, again with Sandler and Gomez, is due in autumn 2015. AJ *DVD* *Blu* *3D*

Adam Sandler *Dracula* • Andy Samberg *Jonathan* • Selena Gomez *Mavis Dracula* • Kevin James *Frank/Frankenstein* • Steve Buscemi *Wayne, the werewolf* • David Spade *Griffin, the invisible man* ■ *Dir* Genndy Tartakovsky • *Scr* Peter Baynham, Robert Smigel, from a story by Todd Durham, Dan & Kevin Hageman

Hotel Transylvania 2
★★★ U

Animated horror comedy
2015 · US · Colour · 85min

This sequel to the hit animated ghoul-fest re-joins Count Dracula (Adam Sandler) as he desperately tries to prove his new, half-human grandson is a vampire at heart. Aside from a vague message about parenthood, the film is an excuse for some more impressive animation and a whole lot of slapstick. The gags come so thick and fast it's inevitable that some of them hit the mark – Dracula's "alternative" lullaby and a very slow getaway prove to be dumb but delightful highlights. JL *DVD* Blu-ray 3D

Adam Sandler *Dracula* • Andy Samberg *Johnny* • Selena Gomez *Mavis* • Kevin James *Frank* • Steve Buscemi *Wayne* • Mel Brooks *Vlad* ■ *Dir* Genndy Tartakovsky • *Scr* Adam Sandler, Robert Smigel

The Hottie & the Nottie ★ 12

Romantic comedy 2008 · US · Colour · 87min

Even Paris Hilton's most loyal fans will be struggle to defend this mess of a romantic comedy. Hilton is, unsurprisingly, the titular "Hottie", the grown-up childhood sweetheart of loser Nate (Joel David Moore). Astonishingly, she is happy to hook up with him again, but not until her best pal, ugly duckling Christine Lakin (aka the Nottie), is fixed up. Hilton pretty much plays her usual (smug) self, but she is far from being the worst thing in the movie. The real problem here is Tom Putnam's sloppy direction and a script that manages to be both offensive and wimpish – even the gross-out slapstick lacks conviction. JF Sexual references. *DVD*

Paris Hilton *Cristabel Abbott* • Joel David Moore *Nate Cooper* • Christine Lakin *June Phigg* • Johann Urb *Johann Wutrich* • Adam Kulbersh *Cole Slawsen* • The Greg Wilson *Arno Blount* • Marianne Muellerleile *Mrs Blount* • Kathryn Fiore *Jane* ■ *Dir* Tom Putnam • *Scr* Heidi Ferrer

Houdini ★★★ U

Biographical drama 1953 · US · Colour · 105min

This is the first of five films real-life married couple Tony Curtis and Janet Leigh – the so-called "elite of the milkshake set" – made together. As the famous escapologist, Curtis is half-naked for most of the early scenes, a treat for his teenage fans at the time. When he finds Mrs Houdini, he pays the rent by dreaming up ever more ambitious stunts. The movie covers some 40 years, though Curtis and Leigh age no more than 40 minutes. An entertaining hagiography. AT

Tony Curtis *Houdini* • Janet Leigh *Bess* • Torin Thatcher *Otto* • Angela Clarke *Mrs Weiss* • Stefan Schnabel *Prosecuting attorney* • Ian Wolfe *Fante* • Sig Ruman *Schultz* • Michael Pate *Dooley* • Connie Gilchrist *Mrs Schultz* ■ *Dir* George Marshall • *Scr* Philip Yordan, from a biography by Harold Kellock

Hound Dog Man ★★★ U

Musical 1959 · US · Colour · 86min

Fabian was a good-looking teen idol who charmingly acknowledged that, despite carefully constructed hit records, he couldn't sing. This movie marked his screen debut, straight into a leading role in an amiable, rustic near-western. The title is deliberately redolent of Elvis Presley, but actually means what it says: Fabian hangs around the farm with some dogs. This is a beautifully filmed drama, and Fabian acquits himself remarkably well. TS

Fabian *Clint* • Carol Lynley *Dony* • Stuart Whitman *Blackie Scantling* • Arthur O'Connell *Aaron Mckinney* • Dodie Stevens *Nita Stringer* ■ *Dir* Don Siegel • *Scr* Fred Gipson, Winston Miller, from the novel by Fred Gipson

The Hound of the Baskervilles ★★★★★ PG

Classic mystery 1939 · US · BW · 76min

This must be the classiest Sherlock Holmes movie in the B-picture canon, even if Nigel Bruce's Watson is left spluttering behind Basil Rathbone's superb Holmes. The moors are scarved in fog as the intrepid sleuths follow the paw-prints of an enormous beast that's threatening the last of the Baskerville line. The supporting cast includes horror film stalwarts Lionel Atwill and John Carradine, whose presence helps to maintain the suitably macabre atmosphere. TH *DVD* Blu-ray

Richard Greene *Sir Henry Baskerville* • Basil Rathbone *Sherlock Holmes* • Wendy Barrie *Beryl Stapleton* • Nigel Bruce *Dr Watson* • Lionel Atwill *Dr James Mortimer* • John Carradine *Barryman* • Barlowe Borland *Frankland* • Beryl Mercer *Mrs Jenifer Mortimer* ■ *Dir* Sidney Lanfield • *Scr* Ernest Pascal, from the novel by Sir Arthur Conan Doyle

The Hound of the Baskervilles ★★★★★ PG

Classic mystery 1959 · UK · Colour · 83min

In this atmospheric tour de force, Hammer horror and the fabulous logic of Sir Arthur Conan Doyle prove the perfect match in what was the first Sherlock Holmes adventure after the Universal series featuring Basil Rathbone ended in 1946 with *Dressed to Kill*, and also the first in colour. Director Terence Fisher weaves a darkly romantic gothic spell around the dreaded hound from hell that stalks the foggy moors on the lookout for members of the cursed Baskerville family. Peter Cushing gives one of his finest performances as the unflappable Baker Street sleuth and he has fantastic support from André Morell and Christopher Lee. AJ *DVD* Blu-ray

Peter Cushing *Sherlock Holmes* • André Morell *Dr Watson* • Christopher Lee *Sir Henry* • Marla Landi *Cecile* • Ewen Solon *Stapleton* • Francis De Wolff *Dr Mortimer* • Miles Malleson *Bishop Frankland* • John Le Mesurier *Barryman* • David Oxley *Sir Hugo Baskerville* ■ *Dir* Terence Fisher • *Scr* Peter Bryan, from one from the novel by Sir Arthur Conan Doyle

The Hound of the Baskervilles ★★

Detective mystery 1972 · US · Colour · 90min

This poorly scripted TV pilot for a proposed Sherlock Holmes television series is appallingly directed, with no sense of atmosphere whatsoever. Yet it remains watchable thanks to the casting of the two leads: the ageing Stewart Granger shares Holmes's arrogance and humour, though physically is nothing like the gaunt detective, and Bernard Fox does well as Dr Watson. William Shatner looks hopelessly out of period, however. TS

Stewart Granger *Sherlock Holmes* • Bernard Fox *Dr Watson* • William Shatner *George Stapleton* • Anthony Zerbe *Dr John Mortimer* • Sally Ann Howes *Laura Frankland* • John Williams *Arthur Frankland* ■ *Dir* Barry Crane • *Scr* Robert E Thompson, from the novel by Sir Arthur Conan Doyle

The Hound of the Baskervilles ★ PG

Parody 1977 · UK · Colour · 81min

Paul Morrissey directed this woeful lampoon of Sir Arthur Conan Doyle's most celebrated story. Peter Cook takes on the role of Baker Street's finest, while Dudley Moore doubles up as the doggedly dim Watson and Holmes's mother. Never did the duo look so bereft of inspiration as they watch gag after gag refuse to respond to the ministrations of such comic geniuses as Spike Milligan, Kenneth Williams and Terry-Thomas. DP Some swearing. *DVD*

Peter Cook *Sherlock Holmes* • Dudley Moore *Dr Watson/Mrs Holmes/Mrs Spiggott* • Denholm Elliott *Stapleton* • Joan Greenwood *Beryl Stapleton* • Terry-Thomas *Dr Mortimer* • Max Wall *Mr Barrymore* • Irene Handl *Mrs Barrymore* • Kenneth Williams *Sir Henry Baskerville* • Roy Kinnear *Seldon* • Prunella Scales *Glynis* • Penelope Keith *Massage parlour receptionist* • Spike Milligan *Baskerville police force* ■ *Dir* Paul

Morrissey • *Scr* Peter Cook, Dudley Moore, Paul Morrissey, from the novel by Sir Arthur Conan Doyle

The Hound of the Baskervilles ★★★ 15

Detective mystery 1983 · UK · Colour · 95min

There had already been two superb versions of this classic Sherlock Holmes mystery with Basil Rathbone and Peter Cushing as Baker Street's finest. Here, director Douglas Hickox treks across Dartmoor for a further encounter with the accursed Baskervilles and their pesky pooch. Head and shoulders above a cast of familiar British faces, Ian Richardson goes for the sardonic approach as Holmes in this solid take on the tale. DP *DVD*

Ian Richardson *Sherlock Holmes* • Donald Churchill *Dr Watson* • Denholm Elliott *Dr Mortimer* • Nicholas Clay *Jack Stapleton* • Martin Shaw *Sir Henry Baskerville* • Glynis Barber *Beryl Stapleton* • Edward Judd *Mr Barrymore* • Eleanor Bron *Mrs Barrymore* • Brian Blessed *Geoffrey Lyons* • Connie Booth *Laura Lyons* • Ronald Lacey *Inspector Lestrade* ■ *Dir* Douglas Hickox • *Scr* Charles Pogue, from the novel by Sir Arthur Conan Doyle

The Hour before the Dawn ★★

Second World War spy drama
1944 · US · BW · 74min

Franchot Tone is a pacifist English lord who weds his Austrian servant, sultry Veronica Lake, not realising she is a German spy helping the Nazis plan an invasion of England. It sounds like fun, but this propaganda piece, made at the height of the Second World War, is unremittingly earnest and none too convincing. Adapted from one of Somerset Maugham's lesser works, it puts too much strain on Lake's histrionic reserves, while Tone seems bemused by the whole business. TV

Franchot Tone *Jim Hetherton* • Veronica Lake *Dora Bruckmann* • John Sutton *Roger Hetherton* • Binnie Barnes *May Hetherton* • Henry Stephenson *Gen Hetherton* • Philip Merivale *Sir Leslie Buchannan* ■ *Dir* Frank Tuttle • *Scr* Michael Hogan, Lesser Samuels, from the novel by W Somerset Maugham

Hour of the Assassin ★★★ 15

Political thriller 1987 · US · Colour · 88min

This political thriller is directed by Luis Llosa, with Peru standing in for a mythical South American country. Erik Estrada is sent there to kill a newly-elected democratic president, while Robert Vaughn is the CIA agent whose orders are to stop the assassin at any cost. No subtleties here, but the film has an exciting Costa-Gavras flavour and has quite a few surprises in its cartridge belt. TH

Erik Estrada *Martin Fierro* • Robert Vaughn (1) *Sam Merrick* • Alfredo Alvarez Calderon *Ortiz* • Orlando Sacha *Folco* • Reynaldo Arenas *Paladoro* • Lourdes Berninzon *Adriana* ■ *Dir* Luis Llosa • *Scr* Matt Leipzig

Hour of the Gun ★★★★ PG

Western 1967 · US · Colour · 97min

A superb follow-up to his own *Gunfight at the OK Corral* from director John Sturges, this film starts where the previous movie climaxed and charts the moral decline of lawman Wyatt Earp from upright marshal to relentless avenger. He's portrayed brilliantly by a grim James Garner, in a far cry from his customary jolly screen image. Doc Holliday is also perfectly played by Jason Robards, providing a marvellous contrast to Garner's Earp. With its fine use of Panavision and its memorable Jerry Goldsmith score, this prefigures the darker, anti-romantic westerns that were to come. TS *DVD*

James Garner *Wyatt Earp* • Jason Robards *Doc Holliday* • Robert Ryan *Ike Clanton* • Albert Salmi *Octavius Roy* • Charles Aidman *Horace Sullivan* • Steve Ihnat *Warshaw* • Jon Voight *Curly Bill Brocius* ■ *Dir* John Sturges • *Scr* Edward Anhalt • *Cinematographer* Lucien Ballard

The Hour of the Lynx ★★★ 15

Crime drama 2013 · Den/Swe · Colour · 88min

The Killing's Sofie Grabol and Soren Malling are reunited in a drama with a very different agenda. This time she's a Danish cleric and he's the chief warder at a unit for the criminally insane, where both are seeking to connect with a Swede whose crimes defy any rational understanding. If anything, Frederik Christian Johansen's performance as the killer outshines his distinguished Danish colleagues, though the film's clumsy flashback structure slightly hampers its overall effectiveness. A dark, haunting Nordic tale. TJ In Danish, Swedish. Violence, swearing.

Sofie Grabol *Helen* • Soren Malling *Knud* • Signe Egholm Olsen *Lisbeth* ■ *Dir* Søren Kragh-Jacobsen • *Scr* Jonas T Bengtsson, Søren Kragh-Jacobsen, from Per Olov Enquist's play

The Hour of the Pig ★★★ 15

Comedy drama 1993 · UK/Fr · Colour · 107min

Here, British director Leslie Megahey has successfully creates a distinctive other world, specifically a medieval France which is defined by upper-class corruption, peasant superstition and ecclesiastical apathy. This ludicrous mixture of dark comedy and original thrills is revealed through the story of a smart Paris lawyer (Colin Firth) who has to defend a pig on a charge of murder. Though sometimes creaking under the burden of its own ideas, the film is still intelligent and wonderfully dotty. JM

Colin Firth *Richard Courtois* • Ian Holm *Albertus* • Donald Pleasence *Pincheon* • Amina Annabi *Samira* • Nicol Williamson *Seigneur Jehan d'Auferre* • Michael Gough *Magistrate Boniface* • Harriet Walter *Jeannine* • Jim Carter *Mathieu* • Lysette Anthony *Filette d'Auferre* ■ *Dir/Scr* Leslie Megahey

Hour of the Star ★★★★ 15

Drama 1985 · Bra · Colour · 95min

Directed by a 52-year-old mother of nine, this debut stands as one of Third Cinema's most remarkable examples of magical neorealism. Suzana Amaral graphically depicts Sao Paolo's grinding poverty, while still investing her film with brave humour and touching humanity. Marcelia Cartaxo deservedly won the best actress prize at Berlin for her performance as the virginal typist, whose dreams of celebrity and romance are confounded as much by society's expectations as her own lack of self-esteem and the swaggering ignorance of her boorish boyfriend. DP Portuguese +subtitles.

Marcelia Cartaxo *Macabea* • José Dumont *Olimpico* • Tamara Taxman *Gloria* • Fernanda Montenegro *Mme Carlotta* ■ *Dir* Suzana Amaral • *Scr* Suzana Amaral, Alfredo Oroz, from a novella by Claire Lispector

The Hour of the Wolf ★★★ 15

Psychological drama 1967 · Swe · BW · 83min

This relentlessly ominous study of the price of artistic creativity comprises a series of gothic flashbacks inspired by Liv Ullmann's discovery of the diary belonging to her missing and much-tormented husband, Max von Sydow. With Sven Nykvist's camera surreally conjuring up expressionist horror, von Sydow is mocked by the ghoulish members of Erland Josephson's household and subjected to visions of demons and phantoms from his past. Nevertheless, we expect more of Bergman than eerie set pieces. DP Swedish +subtitles. Violence. *DVD*

Max von Sydow *Johan Borg* • Liv Ullmann *Alma Borg* • Erland Josephson *Baron von Merkens* • Ingrid Thulin *Veronica Vogler* ■ *Dir/Scr* Ingmar Bergman

The Hour of 13 ★★

Mystery thriller 1952 · UK · BW · 77min

The 1934 thriller, *The Mystery of Mr X*, unmasked the killer in the opening sequence, but this remake plays its cards much closer to its chest. Set in Edwardian London, this stars Peter Lawford as a Raffles-like jewel thief who becomes Inspector Roland Culver's chief suspect when a purloined pendant is found beside the body of one of ten policemen murdered in identical fashion. Lawford makes an appealing hero, but the pleasure comes from watching the accomplished supporting cast. DP

Peter Lawford *Nicholas Revel* • Dawn Addams *Jane Frensham* • Roland Culver *Connor* • Derek Bond *Sir Christopher Lenhurst* • Leslie Dwyer *Ernie Perker* • Michael Hordern *Sir Herbert Frensham* ■ *Dir* Harold French • *Scr* Leon Gordon, Howard Emmett Rogers, from the novel *X v Rex* by Philp MacDonald

The Hours ★★★★ 12
Drama 2002 · US · Colour · 110min

David Hare's magnificent screenplay is a poignant exploration of longing, desire and regret that interweaves the lives of three women from different eras. Nicole Kidman's neurosis-driven Virginia Woolf is the most developed and compelling character, but co-stars Julianne Moore and Meryl Streep are also interesting, as a stifled 1950s housewife and a present-day lesbian book editor respectively. Had Moore and Streep's scenarios been made weightier and less clichéd, the feature would have been a masterpiece. As it stands, it's a sophisticated and poetic triumph from director Stephen Daldry. SF Swearing. DVD

Meryl Streep *Clarissa Vaughan* • Julianne Moore *Laura Brown* • Nicole Kidman *Virginia Woolf* • Ed Harris *Richard Brown* • Toni Collette *Kitty* • Claire Danes *Julia Vaughan* • Jeff Daniels *Louis Waters* • Stephen Dillane *Leonard Woolf* • Allison Janney *Sally Lester* • John C Reilly *Dan Brown* • Miranda Richardson *Vanessa Bell* ■ *Dir* Stephen Daldry • *Scr* David Hare, from the novel by Michael Cunningham

Hours ★★★ 12
Thriller 2013 · US · Colour · 92min

Set against the backdrop of Hurricane Katrina, this last finished film from late *Fast & Furious* star Paul Walker is a classy battle-against-adversity thriller. Walker is a New Orleans dad whose wife dies in childbirth, leaving their newborn baby struggling for life in a hospital incubator. Left behind when the flooded hospital is abandoned and with looters on the loose, Walker battles to keep the baby's life support going. It may be the very antithesis of the big-bucks car films that made Walker a star, but this small but very decent drama is an equally fitting memorial. DA Violence, swearing.

Paul Walker *Nolan Hayes* • Genesis Rodriguez *Abigail* • Kerry Cahill *Nurse Shelly* • Yohance Myles *Dr Edmonds* ■ *Dir/Scr* Eric Heisserer

The Hours and Times ★★★★ 18
Drama 1992 · US · BW · 54min

Shortly after the birth of his son Julian, and at the end of the 1963 UK tour that saw the start of Beatlemania around the country, John Lennon accompanied the band's manager, Brian Epstein, on a short holiday to Spain. This highly plausible, carefully written and superbly played film takes its starting point from rumours of what might have occurred during the trip. Ian Hart is magnificent as the cynical Lennon, who is torn between his affection for a man to whom he owed so much and his insatiable urge to mock. David Angus also impresses as the timid, homosexual Epstein. DP Swearing, nudity. DVD

David Angus *Brian Epstein* • Ian Hart *John Lennon* • Stephanie Pack *Marianne* • Robin McDonald *Quinones* • Sergio Moreno *Miguel* ■ *Dir/Scr* Christopher Münch

The Hours of the Day ★★★ 15
Drama 2003 · Sp · Colour · 98min

With its grindingly authentic depiction of the mundane existence of a suburban Barcelona shopkeeper, Jaime Rosales's debut feature opens as a study of those trapped in the often ignored gap between poverty and comfort. But from the moment Alex Brendemühl strangles a female taxi driver on a deserted country road, the film becomes increasingly tense, as we wonder why he committed such a senseless crime and whether he will kill again. Moreover, it forces us to reconsider his relationships with his doting mother, ambitious girlfriend and loyal friend, whose hope he conspires to ruin. DP Spanish +subtitles. Swearing, violence. DVD

Alex Brendemühl *Abel* • Vicente Romero *Marcos* • María Antonia Martínez *Mother* • Agata Roca *Tere* • Pape Monsoriu *Trini* • Irene Belza *Carmen* ■ *Dir* Jaime Rosales • *Scr* Jaime Rosales, Enric Rufas

House ★★ 15
Horror comedy 1986 · US · Colour · 88min

This straightforward haunted house chiller is furnished with effective fun-fuelled scares. Blocked author William Katt (clearly playing a Stephen King clone) moves into a Gothic mansion previously owned by his nutty late aunt to work on his Vietnam memoirs. Soon strange phenomena and rubbery creatures from a sinister netherworld are roaming the floors. Director Steve Miner ably steers between broad humour and beastly visitations for tame shock value. AJ DVD

William Katt *Roger Cobb* • George Wendt *Harold Gorton* • Richard Moll *Big Ben* • Kay Lenz *Sandy* • Mary Stavin *Tanya* • Michael Ensign *Chet Parker* ■ *Dir* Steve Miner • *Scr* Ethan Wiley, from a story by Fred Dekker

House! ★★ 15
Comedy 2000 · UK · Colour · 85min

A run-down seafront bingo hall faces closure due to the twin threats of a leaking roof and competition from a new superhall. The establishment's only hope lies in a lucrative national lotto game and an usherette's psychic ability to influence the way balls fall. Kelly Macdonald and Jason Hughes give spirited performances, as do Freddie Jones and Miriam Margolyes, but they're hogtied by a weak script and ham-fisted handling that fails to generate tension. DA DVD

Kelly Macdonald *Linda* • Jason Hughes *Gavin* • Freddie Jones *Mr Anzani* • Miriam Margolyes *Beth* • Mossie Smith *Kay* • Bruce Forsyth • Keith Chegwin ■ *Dir* Julian Kemp • *Scr* Jason Sutton, from an idea by Eric Styles

House II: the Second Story ★ 15
Horror comedy 1987 · US · Colour · 84min

Director Ethan Wiley's dumb fright farce starts out as a bad John Hughes teen comedy and ends up like a demented episode of *Bonanza*. Arye Gross and Lar Park Lincoln move into their great-great-grandfather's property and dig up the legendary Old West outlaw for a crystal skull with magical properties. Zombie Gramps then leads the duo on a wild chase through endless alternate universes to battle an uninspired array of rubber creatures. AJ DVD

Arye Gross *Jesse McLaughlin* • Jonathan Stark *Charlie* • Royal Dano *Gramps* • Bill Maher *John* • John Ratzenberger *Bill Towner* • Lar Park Lincoln *Kate* • Amy Yasbeck *Lana* • Gregory Walcott *Sheriff* • Dwier Brown *Clarence* ■ *Dir/Scr* Ethan Wiley

House III: The Horror Show ★ 18
Horror 1989 · US · Colour · 91min

This grisly tale of a mass murderer sent to the electric chair who returns after death to terrorise the cop who brought him to justice bears more than a cursory resemblance to the equally turgid Wes Craven vehicle *Shocker*, released the same year. Brion James plays the killer with his tongue firmly in his cheek, while director James Isaac delivers a jumbled movie that between the bouts of predictable action is a solid bore. Yet another sequel, *House IV: Home Deadly Home*, followed in 1992. RS DVD

Lance Henriksen *Lucas McCarthy* • Brion James *Max Jenke* • Rita Taggart *Donna McCarthy* • Dedee Pfeiffer *Bonnie McCarthy* • Aron Eisenberg *Scott McCarthy* • Thom Bray *Peter Campbell* ■ *Dir* James Isaac • *Scr* Allyn Warner, Leslie Bohem, Alan Smithee

The House across the Bay ★★
Crime drama 1940 · US · BW · 87min

Joan Bennett marries likeable racketeer George Raft then shops him to the authorities for his own good. Unfortunately he gets sent to Alcatraz for longer than she anticipated, thanks to a double-cross by his lawyer Lloyd Nolan who wants Bennett all to himself. Then there's Walter Pidgeon's wealthy aviator as her third devotee. It must be the parade of jewellery and high fashion that makes her, an otherwise dull character, such an attraction. Occasional expressionistic lighting is not enough to redeem a trite and absurd story. AE

George Raft *Steve Larwitt* • Joan Bennett *Brenda Bentley* • Lloyd Nolan *Slant Kolma* • Walter Pidgeon *Tim Nolan* • Gladys George *Mary Bogale* • Peggy Shannon *Alice* ■ *Dir* Archie Mayo • *Scr* Kathryn Scola, from a story by Myles Connolly

House Arrest ★★★ PG
Comedy 1996 · US · Colour · 104min

Worried that their parents are about to get a divorce, Kyle Howard and Amy Sakasitz decide drastic action is required. So they lock them in the basement, together with their friend's bickering mum and dad. Pretty soon other pupils are queueing up for their unique marriage guidance programme. The performances of both adults and youngsters are uniformly strong and, although sentimentality isn't kept entirely at bay, this still makes for thoughtful entertainment. JF

Jamie Lee Curtis *Janet Beindorf* • Kevin Pollak *Ned Beindorf* • Kyle Howard *Grover Beindorf* • Russel Harper *TJ Krupp* • Amy Sakasitz *Stacy Beindorf* • Wallace Shawn *Vic Finley* • Jennifer Love Hewitt *Brooke Figler* • Jennifer Tilly *Cindy Figler* ■ *Dir* Harry Winer • *Scr* Michael Hitchcock

House at the End of the Street ★★ 15
Horror 2012 · US/Can · Colour · 100min

A teen chiller perfect for the *Twilight* crowd, this sees Jennifer Lawrence's new girl in town unearth deadly secrets when she falls for troubled outcast Max Thieriot, who still lives in the neighbouring house where his sister murdered their folks. Though *Hunger Games* star Lawrence is clearly slumming it, she and Thieriot deliver sympathy-inducing performances, creating characters that are surprisingly well drawn for a horror movie. But British director Mark Tonderai takes the lazy route by eschewing genuine tension in favour of sign-posted jolts and a horribly clumsy use of sound and score. SF Violence, swearing, drug abuse. DVD

Jennifer Lawrence (2) *Elissa* • Elisabeth Shue *Sarah* • Max Thieriot *Ryan* • Gil Bellows *Weaver* ■ *Dir* Mark Tonderai • *Scr* David Loucka, from a story by Jonathan Mostow

The House Bunny ★★★ 12
Comedy 2008 · US · Colour · 93min

Anna Faris sparkles as hapless man-pleaser Shelley Darlington, who's ejected from the Playboy Mansion when she hits the ripe old age of 27. Shelley then helps to transform the fortunes of a geeky girls sorority that's threatened with closure, and finds something new in herself in the process. Faris is clearly a talented and attractive actress, but she's let down here by an average script and director Fred Wolf's inability to nail the concept's true comedy potential. That said, there's nice support from Colin Hanks (son of Tom) and Rumer Willis (daughter of Demi Moore and Bruce Willis), as well as some great set and wardrobe design. Watch with low expectations and this will be pleasantly surprising. KK DVD

Anna Faris *Shelley Darlington* • Colin Hanks *Oliver* • Emma Stone *Natalie* • Kat Dennings *Mona* • Katharine McPhee *Harmony* • Rumer

Willis *Joanne* • Beverly D'Angelo *Mrs Hagstrom* • Hugh Hefner ■ *Dir* Fred Wolf • *Scr* Karen McCullah Lutz, Kirsten Smith

The House by the Cemetery ★★★ 18
Horror 1981 · It · Colour · 75min

A flesh-eating ghoul (Giovanni de Nari) inhabits the basement of a family's New England home and must continue his gruesomely bizarre surgical practices on them to remain a living dead zombie. This is Italian gore maestro Lucio Fulci's last great grisly horror movie before his work slid into the incoherent schlock gutter. Visually arresting, excessively nasty and building to a well-sustained climax of exciting gothic melodrama, this is a highly effective *Grand Guignol* shocker and a favorite among Fulci aficionados. AJ Italian dubbed. DVD BD

Katherine MacColl [Catriona MacColl] *Lucy Boyle* • Paolo Malco *Norman Boyle* • Ania Pieroni *Ann* • Silvia Collatina *Mae Freudstein* • Giovanni Frezza *Bob Boyle* • Giovanni de Nari *Dr Freudstein* ■ *Dir* Lucio Fulci • *Scr* Lucio Fulci, Giorgio Mariuzzo, from a story by Elisa Livia Briganti [Elisa Briganti]

House by the River ★★★
Film noir 1950 · US · BW · 87min

This has been described as Fritz Lang's most Teutonic American picture. However, the surfeit of atmosphere can't atone for the lack of suspense in this tired treatise on the old adage, "murder will out". The byplay between evil novelist Louis Hayward and his envious, lame brother Lee Bowman is effective, but the romance between Bowman and his prissy sister-in-law (Jane Wyatt) is less convincing. Making moody use of light and shade, Lang involves us more deeply than the plot merits. DP

Louis Hayward *Stephen Byrne* • Lee Bowman *John Byrne* • Jane Wyatt *Marjorie Byrne* • Dorothy Patrick *Emily Gaunt* • Ann Shoemaker *Mrs Ambrose* • Jody Gilbert *Flora Bantam* • Sarah Padden *Mrs Beach* ■ *Dir* Fritz Lang • *Scr* Mel Dinelli, from the novel by AP Herbert

House Calls ★★ PG
Romantic comedy 1978 · US · Colour · 93min

This hospital romance can't decide whether it wants to be a scorching screwball or a cosy sitcom. Making her Hollywood debut, Glenda Jackson is way below her *Touch of Class* form as a divorcee seeking commitment from Walter Matthau's newly footloose widower. But then, under Howard Zieff's lacklustre direction, no one emerges from this muddled comedy with much credit. DP

Walter Matthau *Dr Charley Nicholas* • Glenda Jackson *Ann Atkinson* • Art Carney *Dr Amos Willoughby* • Richard Benjamin *Dr Norman Soloman* • Candice Azzara [Candy Azzara] *Ellen Grady* • Dick O'Neill *Irwin Owett* ■ *Dir* Howard Zieff • *Scr* Julius J Epstein, Alan Mandel, Charles Shyer, Max Shulman, from a story by Max Shulman, Julius J Epstein

A House Divided ★★★ 15
Period drama based on a true story 2000 · US · Colour · 96min

This TV drama is the tale of a woman who returns to her family's plantation at the end of the Civil War, only to have to fight for her birthright when it is revealed she is mixed race, raised by her father (Sam Waterston) as white, but also the daughter of a slave he raped. Jennifer Beals gives a terrific performance as the young woman caught between her white family and the prejudices of having a black mother. JB

Sam Waterston *David Dickson* • Jennifer Beals *Amanda Dickson* • Lisa Gay Hamilton *Julia* • Tim Daly [Timothy Daly] *Charles Dubose* • Shirley Douglas *Elizabeth Dickson* • Sean McCann *Rutherford* ■ *Dir* John Kent Harrison • *Scr* Paris Qualles, from the non-fiction book *Woman of Color, Daughter of Privilege: Amanda Dickson* by Kent Anderson Leslie

The House I Live In ★★★ 15
Documentary 2012 · US · Colour · 108min

The damaging side-effects of America's so-called war on drugs come under scrutiny in this documentary from Eugene Jarecki. Constructed from reportage, expert testimony and startling statistics, it reveals a system in crisis. The film canvasses opinion from dealers, prisoners, cops and correctional officers, who all agree the present situation cannot continue. Less convincing, however, is Jarecki's somewhat self-conscious attempt to relate all this to his own family experience, resulting in a contentious – and not entirely persuasive – comparison between the war on drugs and the Holocaust. TJ *DVD*

■ *Dir/Scr* Eugene Jarecki

The House in Nightmare Park ★ PG
Comedy thriller 1973 · UK · Colour · 91min

One of the few low points in comedian Frankie Howerd's career is this failed fright farce, which invites poor comparisons with Bob Hope's horror comedy classic *The Cat and the Canary*. Howerd, who aptly plays a ham actor, is invited to perform at Ray Milland's creepy stately home and discovers he's heir to the family fortune. As the corpses pile up, so do the lame gags. DP

Frankie Howerd *Foster Twelvetrees* • Ray Milland *Stewart Henderson* • Hugh Burden *Major Reginald Henderson* • Kenneth Griffith *Ernest Henderson* • John Bennett *Patel* • Rosalie Crutchley *Jessica Henderson* • Ruth Dunning *Agnes Henderson* • Elizabeth MacLennan *Verity* ■ *Dir* Peter Sykes • *Scr* Clive Exton, Terry Nation

House in the Woods ★★★ PG
Thriller 1957 · UK · BW · 58min

This is an unexpectedly tense British B-movie from little-known director Maxwell Munden. Playing a painter who many suspect of slaughtering his spouse, Ronald Howard reveals a flair for villainy as he lurks around the country hideaway he's leased to writer Michael Gough and wife Patricia Roc. Logic is not the strong suit of the script, but the eerie exploitation of both the cottage's shadowy interiors and its isolated setting compensate. DP Some violence. *DVD*

Ronald Howard *Spencer Rowland* • Patricia Roc *Carol Carter* • Michael Gough *Geoffrey Carter* • Andrea Troubridge *Mrs Shellaby* • Bill Shine *Col Shellaby* • Norah Hammond *Mrs Bletchley* ■ *Dir* Maxwell Munden • *Scr* Maxwell Munden, from the short story *Prelude to Murder* by Walter C Brown

House of a Thousand Dolls ★★ 15
Thriller 1967 · Sp/W Ger · Colour · 91min

Vincent Price plays more of a supporting role in this tawdry and self-consciously titillating exposé of white slavery in Tangiers. As a villainous magician, he abducts young women in his famous disappearing act and passes them on to the mysterious "King of Hearts" who sets them to work in a local brothel. George Nader's investigation of the disappearances and the kingpin's real identity is the main – and boring – thrust of the story. Directed by Jeremy Summers, on typically lowbrow form, this is surprisingly exploitative for its era. AJ *DVD*

Vincent Price *Felix Manderville* • Martha Hyer *Rebecca* • George Nader *Stephen Armstrong* • Ann Smyrner *Marie Armstrong* • Wolfgang Kieling *Inspector Emil* ■ *Dir* Jeremy Summers • *Scr* Peter Welbeck [Harry Alan Towers], Carmen M Román

House of America ★★★ 15
Drama 1996 · UK/Neth · Colour and BW · 93min

By combining stylised colour with sun-tinted monochrome, first-time director Marc Evans cleverly contrasts the post-industrial Welsh wilderness with the wide-open spaces of the American neverland described by Jack Kerouac. But the film - about three kids who grow up in a run-down mining village believing their father has found the good life across the Atlantic - quickly descends into tabloid caricature. DP Swearing, sex scenes, some violence. *DVD*

Sian Phillips *Mam* • Steven Mackintosh *Sid Lewis* • Lisa Palfrey *Gwenny Lewis* • Matthew Rhys *Boyo Lewis* • Richard Harrington *Cat* ■ *Dir* Marc Evans • *Scr* Edward Thomas, from his play

House of Angels ★★★★ 15
Comedy drama 1992 · Swe · Colour · 114min

Scandinavian culture is littered with tales of respectable rural folk resisting devious city slickers. But Colin Nutley slyly inverts that scenario in this gentle satire, in which the entrenched prejudices of the countrysiders are held up to ridicule. Caricature is almost inevitable in the depiction of the locals, appalled by the fact that cabaret star Helena Bergström and her leather-clad biker buddy, Rikard Wolff, have decided to live on the farm inherited from her rich grandfather. Whimsically charming. Followed in 1994 by a disappointing sequel set in New York. DP Swedish +subtitles. Sex scenes, swearing.

Helena Bergström *Fanny Zander* • Rikard Wolff *Zac* • Per Oscarsson *Erik Zander* • Sven Wollter *Axel Flogfält* • Viveka Seldhahl *Rut Flogfält* • Reine Brynolfsson *Fleming Collmert* • Jakob Eklund *Mårten Flogfält* • Ernst Günther *Gottfried Pettersson* ■ *Dir/Scr* Colin Nutley

House of Bamboo ★★★ PG
Crime drama 1955 · US · Colour · 98min

Director Samuel Fuller was often described as a Hollywood maverick, but he functioned more than adequately as a house director of action movies at 20th Century-Fox, making tightly budgeted films look costly. This low-key crime drama is one of his better efforts, boasting good performances from three well-cast Hollywood leading men (Robert Ryan, Robert Stack, Cameron Mitchell) and some striking Tokyo photography from cameraman Joe MacDonald. TS *DVD*

Robert Ryan *Sandy Dawson* • Robert Stack *Eddie Kenner/Spanier* • Shirley Yamaguchi *Mariko* • Cameron Mitchell *Griff* • Brad Dexter *Captain Hanson* • Sessue Hayakawa *Inspector Kita* ■ *Dir* Samuel Fuller • *Scr* Harry Kleiner, Samuel Fuller

The House of Bernarda Alba ★★★ 15
Drama 1987 · Sp · Colour · 103min

While still laying the blame for Franco's tyranny on the prejudices of the bourgeoisie, Marcel Camus's adaptation of Federico Garcia Lorca's play places more emphasis on the melodramatic tensions that build up after a handsome suitor intrudes upon the solitary mourning which a widow imposes on her five daughters following their father's death. Opening out the action without diluting its intensity, Camus conjures up some evocative visuals and draws thoughtful performances from Irene Gutierrez Caba and her frustrated brood. DP In Spanish.

Irene Gutierrez Caba *Bernarda Alba* • Ana Belén *Adela* • Florinda Chico *Poncia* • Enriqueta Carballeira *Angustias* • Vicky Peña *Martirio* • Aurora Pastor *Magdalena* • Mercedes Lezcano *Amelia* • Rosario Garcia-Ortega *Maria Josefa* ■ *Dir* Mario Camus • *Scr* Mario Camus, Antonio Larreta, from the play by Federico Garcia Lorca

House of Blackmail ★★ U
Crime drama 1953 · UK · BW · 71min

Maurice Elvey was the most prolific director in British cinema history, making over 300 features after his debut in 1913. Unfortunately, this low-budget B-movie, in which a hitch-hiker finds himself in trouble after taking a lift from a woman who's being blackmailed, is not one of his best efforts. We could do with more surprises, but the pace is unrelenting and there are typically solid performances from Mary Germaine, William Sylvester and John Arnatt. DP

William Sylvester *Jimmy* • Mary Germaine *Carol Blane* • Alexander Gauge *John Markham* • John Arnatt *Peter Carter* • Dennis Shaw [Denis Shaw] *Bassett* • Ingeborg Wells *Emma* ■ *Dir* Maurice Elvey • *Scr* Allan MacKinnon

House of Cards ★★
Political thriller 1968 · US · Colour · 104min

This lacklustre political thriller is set in France, where a rich right-wing group who feel betrayed over Algerian independence are plotting to take over the country and execute De Gaulle. George Peppard is the innocent American in Paris who tumbles the plot, and Orson Welles is briefly imposing as the French publisher who is financing it. Sadly, the promising idea is rather undermined by some hammy acting. AT

George Peppard *Reno Davis* • Inger Stevens *Anne de Villemont* • Orson Welles *Charles Leschenhaut* • Keith Michell *Hubert Morillon* • Ralph Michael *Claude de Gonde* • Maxine Audley *Matilde Vosiers* • William Job *Bernard Bourdon* • Peter Bayliss *Edmond Vosier* ■ *Dir* John Guillermin • *Scr* Irving Ravetch, Harriet Frank Jr, from a novel by Stanley Ellin

House of Cards ★ 12
Drama 1993 · US · Colour · 108min

When Kathleen Turner's archaeologist husband falls to his death from a Mayan pyramid in Mexico, she packs up and returns to the States where her six-year-old daughter begins to behave very strangely. Child psychologist Tommy Lee Jones is brought in to help. At first, you think the little girl is going to take us into Stephen King territory; instead, it leads only to the usual clichéd drama. Sad to see Jones and Turner wasting their time. AT Swearing. *DVD*

Kathleen Turner *Ruth Matthews* • Tommy Lee Jones *Dr Jake Beerlander* • Asha Menina *Sally Matthews* • Shiloh Strong *Michael Matthews* • Esther Rolle *Adelle* ■ *Dir* Michael Lessac • *Scr* Michael Lessac, from a story by Michael Lessac, Robert Jay Litz

House of Dark Shadows ★★★★ 18
Horror 1970 · US · Colour · 92min

The first of two movie offshoots (along with *Night of Dark Shadows*) from the popular US daytime horror soap *Dark Shadows*, featuring a number of series regulars, is one of the best horror movies of the 1970s. Eighteenth-century vampire Barnabas Collins (Jonathan Frid) rises from his Maine grave to convert all the residents of the family mansion to his evil bloodsucking ways. Lavish production values, stunning photography, great special effects and moments of pure bone-chilling shock make this a resonant delight, exquisitely directed by series producer Dan Curtis. AJ

Jonathan Frid *Barnabas Collins* • Joan Bennett *Elizabeth Collins Stoddard* • Grayson Hall *Dr Julia Hoffman* • Kathryn Leigh Scott *Maggie Evans* • Roger Davis *Jeff Clark* • Nancy Barrett *Carolyn Stoddard* • John Karlen *Willie Loomis* • Thayer David *Prof T Eliot Stokes* • Louis Edmonds *Roger Collins* • Donald Briscoe *Todd Jennings* • David Henesy *David Collins* ■ *Dir* Dan Curtis • *Scr* Sam Hall, Gordon Russell, from the TV series created by Dan Curtis, Art Wallace • *Cinematographer* Arthur J Ornitz

House of Darkness ★★★ PG
Horror 1948 · UK · BW · 77min

Nineteen-year-old Laurence Harvey made his screen debut in this teasing Gothic chiller that confirmed the writing talent of Hammer stalwart John Gilling. Fresh from Rada, the Lithuanian-born Harvey occasionally betrays his South African upbringing, but it's his inexperience of acting to camera that undermines an otherwise pleasing melodrama. The focus falls on aspiring pianist Harvey's seething hatred for older stepbrother Alexander Archdale, whose broken violin continues to play a melancholic air long after his fratricide. Sadly, director Oswald Mitchell struggles to prevent the increasingly demented Harvey from gnawing on the scenery. DP *DVD*

Lawrence Harvey [Laurence Harvey] *Francis Merryman* • Lesley Brook *Lucy* • John Stuart Crabtree *Eric* • Lesley Osmond *Elaine Merryman* ■ *Dir* Oswald Mitchell • *Scr* John Gilling, from a story by Betty Davies

House of Dracula ★★ PG
Horror 1945 · US · BW · 64min

Not to be confused with *House of Frankenstein*, this sequel stars Glenn Strange as Frankenstein's monster, Lon Chaney Jr as the Wolf Man and, most impressively, the elegant John Carradine as Count Dracula. Needless to add, they are all splendid to watch under the famously copyrighted Universal make-up. It's the plot that's tiresome, as Onslow Stevens tries to "cure" the monsters of their evil qualities by resorting to science. Erle C Kenton's direction keeps things suitably murky, however, and that Universal house style always adds pleasure to the experience. TS

Lon Chaney Jr *Lawrence Talbot* • John Carradine *Count Dracula* • Martha O'Driscoll *Miliza Morell* • Lionel Atwill *Inspector Holtz* • Jane Adams (1) *Nina* • Onslow Stevens *Dr Edelman* • Ludwig Stossel *Ziegfried* • Glenn Strange *The Monster* ■ *Dir* Erle C Kenton • *Scr* Edward T Lowe

House of Evil ★ 15
Horror 1968 · Mex/US · Colour · 72min

Boris Karloff wanders around a castle equipped with a torture dungeon in one of the four little-seen Mexican cheapies the master of the macabre made just prior to his death in 1969. The plot is very much in the vein of *The Old Dark House* with many of the cast coming to sticky ends. All the south of the border scenes were shot by director Juan Ibanez, while Jack Hill directed the Los Angeles-based interiors with Karloff. AJ

Boris Karloff *Mathias Morthevald* • Julissa *Lucy Durand* • Andres Garcia *Carlos Bisler* • Beatriz Baz *Cordelia Rush* • Quintin Bulnes *Dr Emerich Horvath* ■ *Dir* Juan Ibanez, Jack Hill • *Scr* Jack Hill, Luis Enrique Vergara, from the story *The Fall of the House of Usher* by Edgar Allan Poe

The House of Fear ★★ U
Mystery 1944 · US · BW · 66min

Not one of the best of the Basil Rathbone-Nigel Bruce forays into Sherlock Holmes territory, which is a shame because the finale could have been wonderfully surprising if it had been treated better. The members of the "Good Comrades Club" – a group of wealthy men living in a Scottish mansion - are being killed off one by one, and the bumbling Watson himself is kidnapped when he joins Holmes to investigate. TH *DVD*

Basil Rathbone *Sherlock Holmes* • Nigel Bruce *Dr Watson* • Aubrey Mather *Alastair* • Dennis Hoey *Lestrade* • Paul Cavanagh *Simon Merrivale* • Holmes Herbert *Alan Cosgrave* ■ *Dir* Roy William Neill • *Scr* Roy Chanslor, from the story *The Adventures of the Five Orange Pips* by Sir Arthur Conan Doyle

House of Flying Daggers ★★★★ 15
Period martial arts drama 2004 · HK/Chi · Colour · 114min

In 859 AD, the declining Tang dynasty faces revolt from a secret, Robin Hood-like society, known as House of Flying Daggers. Can the blind knife-throwing showgirl Zhang Ziyi guide undercover police captain Takeshi Kaneshiro to their mysterious new leader? Visually ravishing and artfully directed, Zhang Yimou's film suffers from too many drawn-out climaxes and a tepid romantic subplot. But the director's masterful panache, poetic finesse and gravity-bending fight choreography are a continual delight, while Zhang's acrobatic *femme fatale* steals the show. AJ Mandarin +subtitles. *DVD* *Blu-ray*

Takeshi Kaneshiro *Jin* • Andy Lau *Leo* • Zhang Ziyi *Mei* • Song Dandan *Yee* ■ *Dir* Zhang Yimou • *Scr* Zhang Yimou, Li Feng, Wang Bin, from a story by Zhang Yimou, Li Feng, Wang Bin

House of Frankenstein ★★★ PG
Horror 1944 · US · BW · 67min

The sequel to *Frankenstein Meets the Wolf Man* adds John Carradine as Dracula into the engaging Universal monster mix. Mad doctor Boris Karloff escapes from prison after the building is struck by lightning and, with hunchback J Carrol Naish, seeks revenge on those who put him there. For this he enlists the help of the trio of vintage horror characters: Dracula, Frankenstein's monster and the Wolf Man. Glenn Strange plays the monster and Lon Chaney Jr the

U SUITABLE FOR ALL   Uc SUITABLE ESPECIALLY FOR YOUNG CHILDREN (DVD ONLY)   PG PARENTAL GUIDANCE   12A UNDER 12s TO BE ACCOMPANIED (CINEMA ONLY)

Wolf Man in a bundle of laughs and suspense. AJ

Boris Karloff *Dr Gustav Niemann* • Lon Chaney Jr *Lawrence Stewart Talbot* • J Carrol Naish *Daniel* • John Carradine *Count Dracula* • Anne Gwynne *Rita Hussman* • Peter Coe *Carl Hussman* • Lionel Atwill *Inspector Arnz* • Glenn Strange *The Monster* ▪ *Dir* Erle C Kenton • *Scr* Edward T Lowe, from the story *The Devil's Brood* by Curt Siodmak

House of Games ★★★★ 15

Psychological thriller 1987 • US • Colour • 97min

After several notable plays and screenplays, David Mamet became a director with this delectably clever parlour-game picture, which should delight connoisseurs of thrillers and cryptic crosswords. It's rather low on directorial flair, but high on literacy and performance values. Mamet's then-wife, Lindsay Crouse, plays a psychiatrist confronting the gambler (Joe Mantegna) who drove one of her patients to near-suicide. A card game results, with psychiatrist and gambler realising how similar their respective trades are. This deck is well and truly stacked with bluff, double-bluff and a thrilling finale. AT Violence, swearing. *DVD*

Lindsay Crouse *Margaret Ford* • Joe Mantegna *Mike* • Mike Nussbaum *Joey* • Lilia Skala *Dr Littauer* • JT Walsh *Businessman* ▪ *Dir* David Mamet • *Scr* David Mamet, from a story by David Mamet, Jonathan Katz

The House of Magic ★★★★ U

Animated adventure 2013 • Bel/Fr/UK • Colour • 81min

An utterly charming effort across the board, this action-packed fantasy attains a near perfect mix of colourful inventiveness, engaging characters and eye-popping spectacle. Abandoned cat Thunder is welcomed into the foreboding mansion of a retired magician, and must learn how to get along with the other cute animals and mysterious automated gizmos he finds there. But then the magician has an accident. With great knockout visuals and plenty of zany excitement, this is a ridiculously entertaining, bright and breezy package of wonder and laughter. AJ *DVD*

Murray Blue *Thunder/Dylan* • Kathleen Browers *Carla* • Grant George *Daniel* ▪ *Dir* Jérémie Degruson, Ben Stassen • *Scr* Ben Stassen, James Flynn (2), Dominic Paris, from a story by Stassen

The House of Mirth ★★ PG

Period romantic drama 2000 • UK/US • Colour • 140min

Edith Wharton's wonderful novel about a woman striving for financial and intellectual independence in a conservative, upper-crust society is faithfully brought to the screen by Terence Davies. Too faithfully, in fact: Davies directs at such a slow pace that much of the plot and characters seem rather lifeless. Gillian Anderson, from TV's *The X-Files*, has a good shot at playing the heroine, though in the end she lacks the power required. Despite the budget limitations, the film's look is impressive. RB *DVD*

Gillian Anderson *Lily Bart* • Eric Stoltz *Lawrence Selden* • Anthony LaPaglia *Sim Rosedale* • Laura Linney *Bertha Dorset* • Terry Kinney *George Dorset* • Dan Aykroyd *Gus Trenor* • Elizabeth McGovern *Carry Fisher* • Eleanor Bron *Mrs Peniston* • Jodhi May *Grace Stepney* ▪ *Dir* Terence Davies • *Scr* Terence Davies, from the novel by Edith Wharton

House of Mortal Sin ★★★ 15

Horror 1975 • UK • Colour • 99min

This hugely underrated shocker from cult director Pete Walker features Anthony Sharp in an extraordinary performance as a Catholic priest who sublimates his desires by violating the sanctity of the confessional and torturing his distressed victims with guilt. Anyone trying to stop his course of "divine justice" is murdered by such diverse means as incense burners and poisoned holy wafers. Walker stalwart

Sheila Keith is on hand to give this warped morality tale its clever twist. AJ *DVD*

Anthony Sharp *Father Xavier Meldrum* • Susan Penhaligon *Jenny Welch* • Stephanie Beacham *Vanessa Welch* • Norman Eshley *Father Bernard Cutler* • Sheila Keith *Miss Brabazon* • Hilda Barry *Mrs Meldrum* • Stewart Bevan *Terry* ▪ *Dir* Pete Walker • *Scr* David McGillivray

House of Mystery ★★★

Supernatural fantasy 1961 • UK • BW • 55min

This is a neat little spine-tingler from Vernon Sewell, who was a dab hand at summoning up demons from beyond. There are plenty of uneasy moments in this haunting story, in which a couple of newlyweds learn the grim secret of their dream house from the resident spook himself. DP

Jane Hylton *Stella Lemming* • Peter Dyneley *Mark Lemming* • Nanette Newman *Joan Trevor* • Maurice Kaufmann *Henry Trevor* • Colin Gordon *Burdon* • Molly Urquhart *Mrs Bucknall* ▪ *Dir* Vernon Sewell • *Scr* Vernon Sewell, from a play by Pierre Mills, C Vylars

House of 9 ★★ 18

Horror thriller 2004 • UK/Rom/Ger/Fra • Colour • 86min

An Irish priest and eight other innocents are incarcerated in an escape-proof house in this meandering horror thriller. It's heavily indebted to Agatha Christie's *And Then There Were None* but there's a soupçon of *Saw* and a dash of *Battle Royale* thrown in for good measure, as the $5 million prize offered by a disembodied voice will only go to the last person left alive. The characterisation is sketchy and there's little suspense... and even the bloodletting is tame by contemporary standards. JA In English, French. Violence, swearing. *DVD*

Dennis Hopper *Father Duffy* • Kelly Brook *Lea* • Hippolyte Girardot *Francis* • Peter Capaldi *Max Roy* ▪ *Dir* Steven R Monroe • *Scr* Philippe Vidal

House of Numbers ★★

Crime drama 1957 • US • BW • 91min

Some of this implausible but quite ingenious thriller was shot in San Quentin prison, the eponymous house of the title. Behind bars is a bad guy, who is helped in his escape by his good twin brother. As both are played by Jack Palance, fans of the ever-watchable star get a double helping particularly as he effectively differentiates the two characters. RB

Jack Palance *Bill Judlow/Arnie Judlow* • Barbara Lang *Ruth Judlow* • Harold J Stone *Henry Nova* • Edward Platt *Warden* ▪ *Dir* Russell Rouse • *Scr* Russell Rouse, Don [M] Mankiewicz, from a novel by Jack Finney

House of 1000 Corpses ★★★ 18

Horror 2001 • US • Colour • 88min

US rock star Rob Zombie is well known for his love of old horror films, so it's no surprise that his directorial debut takes a warped trip into the heart of B-movie-style terror. A homage to the so-called "grindhouse" shlockers of the 1970s, Zombie's self-penned story of two young couples falling victim to a sadistic family of inbred sickos is a low-budget nightmare with a big-budget feel. Derivative, yet darkly entertaining, the oddball feature makes up for an unfortunate lack of gore with inspired imagery, innovative cinematography and some fabulously freaky performances. A sequel, *The Devil's Rejects*, followed in 2005. SF *DVD*

Sid Haig *Captain Spaulding* • Bill Moseley *Otis* • Sheri Moon *Baby* • Karen Black *Mother Firefly* • Chris Hardwick *Jerry Goldsmith* • Erin Daniels *Denise Willis* • Jennifer Jostyn *Mary Knowles* • Rainn Wilson *Bill Hucley* ▪ *Dir/Scr* Rob Zombie

The House of Rothschild ★★★

Biographical drama 1934 • US • BW • 94min

How the Rothschild dynasty rose from German ghetto obscurity to become the foremost banking house in Europe is a fascinating study of international monetary intrigue, early 19th century-style. Set

against a lavishly mounted backdrop of the Napoleonic Wars, commanding George Arliss plays two key roles – family patriarch Mayer and his son, Nathan – while Boris Karloff eschews monster make-up in this rather entertaining history lesson. AJ

George Arliss *Mayer Rothschild/Nathan Rothschild* • Boris Karloff *Count Ledrantz* • Loretta Young *Julie Rothschild* • Robert Young (1) *Captain Fitzroy* • C Aubrey Smith *Duke of Wellington* • Arthur Byron *Baring* • Reginald Owen *Herries* ▪ *Dir* Alfred Werker • *Scr* Nunnally Johnson, from a play by George Humbert Westley

House of Sand and Fog ★★★★ 15

Drama 2003 • US/UK • Colour • 121min

Revolving around a formidable Oscar-nominated turn by Ben Kingsley, this slow-burning film tells the story of a former Iranian colonel reduced to working menial jobs in the US. Desperate to return his family to the prosperity they once knew, he spends his life's savings on the repossessed home of recovering addict Jennifer Connelly, only to come into tragic confrontation with the woman over the property. First-time director Vadim Perelman paints a vivid and moving picture of cultural alienation and desperation. If Connelly looks too well groomed for her tortured role, it certainly doesn't spoil her overall strong performance, while Shohreh Aghdashloo and Jonathan Ahdout are wonderful as Kingsley's wife and son. SF Swearing. *DVD*

Jennifer Connelly *Kathy Nicolo* • Ben Kingsley *Massoud Amir Behrani* • Ron Eldard *Lester Burdon* • Shohreh Aghdashloo *Nadi Behrani* • Jonathan Ahdout *Esmail* • Frances Fisher *Connie Walsh* • Kim Dickens *Carol* ▪ *Dir* Vadim Perelman • *Scr* Vadim Perelman, Shawn Lawrence Otto, from the novel by Andre Dubus III

House of Secrets ★★

Thriller 1956 • UK • Colour • 97min

A box-office sleeper in its day, this patchy thriller will probably seem threadbare to modern audiences, but director Guy Green uses Paris locations well and keeps the story ticking along. Groomed by Rank as the successor to Dirk Bogarde, Michael Craig never quite lived up to the hype. However, as a naval officer impersonating his counterfeiting lookalike, he holds his own. DP

Michael Craig *Larry Ellis* • Julia Arnall *Diane* • Brenda de Banzie *Madame Ballu* • Barbara Bates *Judy* • David Kossoff *Van de Heide* • Gérard Oury *Pindar* • Geoffrey Keen *Burleigh* • Anton Diffring *Lauderbache* ▪ *Dir* Guy Green • *Scr* Robert Buckner, Bryan Forbes, from the novel *Storm over Paris* by Sterling Noel

The House of Seven Corpses ★★★

Horror 1973 • US • Colour • 90min

This is an effective low-budget horror movie about making a low-budget horror movie. John Carradine is the creepy caretaker of a haunted house where a film crew is stalked by a real-life zombie while shooting an occult thriller. It's always enjoyable watching actors play actors, especially bad ones, and director Paul Harrison throws in some genuine scares and surprises to add to the cheap fun. He also sustains the tense atmosphere, until a truly horrific climax. AJ

John Ireland *Eric Hartman* • Faith Domergue *Gayle* • John Carradine *Mr Price* • Carole Wells *Anne* • Jerry Strickler *David* • Ron Foreman *Ron* ▪ *Dir/Scr* Paul Harrison

House of Strangers ★★★

Crime drama 1949 • US • BW • 100min

Famous for a prolonged wrangle over a screenwriting credit and a protest from the Bank of America, which funded most of Hollywood's studios, this crime drama features Edward G Robinson as a man who achieves the American Dream by becoming a successful banker but is then arrested for malpractice. Three of his sons take over and prevent him from resuming his responsibilities. Richard Conte's affair with Susan Hayward is a dramatic dead end and

you feel the picture would have been better as a gangster thriller about the Mafia. AT

Edward G Robinson *Gino Monetti* • Susan Hayward *Irene Bennett* • Richard Conte *Max Monetti* • Luther Adler *Joe Monetti* • Paul Valentine *Pietro Monetti* • Efrem Zimbalist Jr *Tony* ▪ *Dir* Joseph L Mankiewicz • *Scr* Philip Yordan, from the novel *I'll Never Go There Any More* by Jerome Weidman

The House of the Devil ★★★ 18

Horror thriller 2009 • US • Colour • 91min

Everything about this creepy frightener plays like a homage to the 1980s. Jocelin Donahue stars as a babysitter lured out to a spooky house for a job that just gets stranger and stranger. Her employers (Tom Noonan and Mary Woronov) are a weird couple, and the child she's supposed to watch turns out to be a bedridden mother-in-law upstairs (kept off screen, Hitchcock-style). Surprisingly, this goes light on the ketchup, instead crafting some superb moments of dread as Donahue dances around with her Walkman on, oblivious to the horror upstairs. The finale descends into predictable mayhem, but it's the build-up that'll haunt you. JR *DVD* *Blu-ray*

Jocelin Donahue *Sam* • Greta Gerwig *Megan* • Mary Woronov *Mrs Ulman* • Tom Noonan *Mr Ulman* • Dee Wallace [Dee Wallace Stone] *Landlady* ▪ *Dir/Scr* Ti West

House of the Long Shadows ★★ 15

Horror 1983 • UK • Colour • 101min

Vincent Price, Christopher Lee, Peter Cushing and John Carradine team up for the first and last time in this miscalculated update of the creaky horror classic *Seven Keys to Baldpate* from director Pete Walker. Desi Arnaz Jr is the author who bets publisher Richard Todd he can write a novel in 24 hours while holed up in an eerie Welsh mansion populated by the celebrated foursome. Tongue-in-cheek thrills and soft horror make little impact in a camp romp that wastes the talents of all involved. AJ *DVD*

Vincent Price *Lionel* • Peter Cushing *Sebastian* • Christopher Lee *Corrigan* • Desi Arnaz Jr *Kenneth Magee* • Richard Todd *Sam Allison* • John Carradine *Lord Grisbane* • Julie Peasgood *Mary Norton* ▪ *Dir* Pete Walker • *Scr* Michael Armstrong, from the novel *Seven Keys to Baldpate* by Earl Derr Biggers

The House of the Seven Gables ★★★

Period drama 1940 • US • BW • 88min

One of the pioneers of the costume drama in German silent cinema, Joe May doesn't quite catch the American idiom in this adaptation of Nathaniel Hawthorne's 19th-century classic, which is more gothic than puritan in tone. George Sanders is, however, deliciously caddish as the scheming son who exploits a curse to consign brother Vincent Price to jail in a bid to take over the family mansion. DP

George Sanders *Jaffrey Pyncheon* • Margaret Lindsay *Hepzibah Pyncheon* • Vincent Price *Clifford Pyncheon* • Dick Foran *Matthew Holgrave/Matthew Maule* • Nan Grey *Phoebe Pyncheon* • Cecil Kellaway *Philip Barton* ▪ *Dir* Joe May • *Scr* Lester Cole, Harold Greene, from the novel by Nathaniel Hawthorne

The House of the Seven Hawks ★★ U

Crime thriller 1959 • UK • BW • 91min

Workhorse director Richard Thorpe had just completed some uncredited second unit work on MGM's epic *Ben-Hur* when he was sent by the studio to Britain and Holland to direct this bland B-movie. This story of a horde of Nazi diamonds lost since the war stars Robert Taylor, also slumming as the heroic ship's skipper who rumbles the plot. Everyone apart from Taylor speaks in thick European accents, while the cast includes that legendary actor/manager, Donald Wolfit. AT

H

Robert Taylor (1) *John Nordley* • Nicole Maurey *Constanta Sluiter* • Linda Christian *Elsa* • Donald Wolfit *Van Der Stoor* • David Kossoff *Wilhelm Dekker* ■ *Dir* Richard Thorpe • *Scr* Jo Eisinger, from the novel *The House of the Seven Flies* by Victor Canning

The House of the Spaniard
★★ 🅿🅶

Crime comedy drama 1936 · UK · Colour · 66min

Fusing elements from the 1931 overthrow of the Spanish monarchy and the 1934 Asturian uprising, this has the potential to be a lively thriller. Its subject matter could not have been more topical, as Spain drifted into Civil War. But Ealing chief Michael Balcon opted to play the story for laughs by making shipping clerk Peter Haddon a buffoon who stumbles onto the fact that Spanish employee Allan Jeayes has secrets to hide. There's evocative use of locations on the Wirral, but the story lacks suspense and Haddon is nobody's idea of a hero. DP *DVD*

Brigitte Horney *Margarita de Guzman* • Peter Haddon *David Grey* • Jean Galland *Ignacio* • Allan Jeayes *Don Pedro de Guzman* • Hay Petrie *Orlando* ■ *Dir* Reginald Denham • *Scr* Basil Mason, from Arthur Behrend's novel

The House of the Spirits
★★ 🅸🅵

Drama
1993 · Por/Den/Ger/US · Colour · 140min

Isabel Allende's classic tale of dynastic rivalry and magic realism is one of those books that, for all the temptations, should have been left well alone. Danish director Bille August chose an impossibly difficult text for his first English-language film, and his own script (which takes monumental liberties with the original) is desperately pedestrian, but it's the casting that condemns this prestige project. DP Violence, swearing, nudity.

Jeremy Irons *Esteban Trueba* • Meryl Streep *Clara Del Valle* • Glenn Close *Ferula* • Winona Ryder *Blanca* • Antonio Banderas *Pedro* • Vincent Gallo *Esteban Garcia* • Vanessa Redgrave *Nivea* • Maria Conchita Alonso *Transito* • Armin Mueller-Stahl *Severo* ■ *Dir* Bille August • *Scr* Bille August, from the novel by Isabel Allende

House of Tolerance ★★★ 🅸🆅

Period drama 2011 · Fr · Colour · 125min

Director Bertrand Bonello clearly intends this study of a Parisian brothel at the beginning of the 20th century to dispel any romanticised notions about prostitution. Yet he hardly helps the cause by marrying the exquisite costumes and sublime lighting of Alain Guffroy's evocative sets with 1960s pop and soul tracks that seem more than a little self-consciously anachronistic. Bonello also disappointingly settles for stereotypes in depicting both the residents and patrons of Noémie Lvovsky's upmarket bordello. Less sentimental than Louis Malle's *Pretty Baby*, but no more incisive, this is in equal measures laudable and disingenuous. DP French +subtitles. Violence, swearing, sex scenes, nudity. *DVD*

Hafsia Herzi *Samira* • Céline Sallette *Clotilde* • Jasmine Trinca *Julie* • Illiana Zabeth *Pauline* • Noémie Lvovsky *Marie-France* • Alice Barnole *Madeleine* ■ *Dir/Scr* Bertrand Bonello

The House of Usher ★ 🅸🆅

Horror 1988 · US · Colour · 87min

This is a stupefying and sleazy modern-day redefinition of the doomed Usher family's desperate desire to continue their bloodline. Oliver Reed hams it up as the super-sensitive Roderick Usher, while Donald Pleasence doesn't leave any of the cheap scenery unchewed. A depressing mixture of rape, murder, torture and severed body parts. AJ

Oliver Reed *Roderick Usher* • Romy Windsor *Molly McNulty* • Rufus Swart *Ryan Usher* ■ Norman Coombes *Mr Derrick* • Anne Stradi *Mrs Derrick* • Carole Farquhar *Gwen* • Philip Godewa *Dr Bailey* ■ *Dir* Alan Birkinshaw • *Scr* Michael J Murray, from the story *The Fall of the House of Usher* by Edgar Allan Poe

House of Wax ★★★★ 🅿🅶

Period horror 1953 · US · Colour · 84min

Director Andre De Toth's close remake of *The Mystery of the Wax Museum* (1933) is an exciting and diverting shocker that established Vincent Price as a major horror star. Price brilliantly portrays a mad masked sculptor – his mind and body deformed in a museum blaze staged by his insurance-hungry partner – who returns to dip human corpses in boiling wax for display in his chamber of horrors. Charles Bronson plays Price's mute assistant in this atmospheric *Grand Guignol* masterpiece, one of the most effective (and profitable) movies ever to use the 3D gimmick. AJ *DVD* 🔳

Vincent Price *Professor Henry Jarrod* • Frank Lovejoy *Lieutenant Tom Brennan* • Phyllis Kirk *Sue Allen* • Carolyn Jones *Cathy Gray* • Paul Picerni *Scott Andrews* • Roy Roberts *Matthew Burke* • Charles Buchinsky [Charles Bronson] *Igor* ■ *Dir* Andre De Toth • *Scr* Crane Wilbur, from a play by Charles Belden

House of Wax ★★★ 🅸🅵

Horror 2004 · US/Aus · Colour · 108min

Except for its central premise, this "re-imagining" of the 1953 classic has little in common with the Vincent Price movie. Debuting director Jaume Collet-Serra delivers a formulaic yet surprisingly effective horror. All the genre clichés are present and correct as Elisha Cuthbert and college pals (socialite Paris Hilton among them) fall prey to a sadistic killer in a remote town dominated by a mysterious wax museum. Though convention dictates they get picked off one by one, the enjoyment is in the imaginative and ultra-gory methods of dispatch. SF Swearing, violence. *DVD* 🔵

Elisha Cuthbert *Carly Jones* • Chad Michael Murray *Nick Jones* • Brian Van Holt *Bo/Vincent* • Paris Hilton *Paige* • Jared Padalecki *Wade* • Jon Abrahams *Dalton Chapman* • Robert Ri'chard *Blake* ■ *Dir* Jaume Collet-Serra • *Scr* Carey W Hayes, Chad Hayes, from the play *The Mystery of the Wax Museum* by Charles Belden

House of Whipcord ★★ 🅸🆅

Horror 1974 · UK · Colour · 97min

Dismayed by the permissive society, a dithery old judge and his stern mistress turn their home into a house of correction where girls of loose morals (and looser costumes) are imprisoned, chastised, flogged and finally hanged. Most newspaper critics who bothered to see this exploitation movie soundly rubbished it. However, a minority saw it as an allegory about censorship and the Mary Whitehouse brigade, and a satire on Britain's right wing who wished to see the return of capital punishment. AT *DVD*

Barbara Markham *Mrs Wakehurst* • Patrick Barr *Justice Bailey* • Ray Brooks *Tony* • Ann Michelle *Julia* • Penny Irving *Ann-Marie De Vernay* • Sheila Keith *Walker* • Dorothy Gordon *Bates* • Robert Tayman *Mark Dessart* • David McGillivray *Cavan* ■ *Dir* Pete Walker • *Scr* David McGillivray, from a story by Pete Walker

The House of Yes ★★★

Comedy drama 1997 · US · Colour · 90min

This black comedy set in Washington DC stars Josh Hamilton as Parker Posey's all-American twin brother, returning to his dysfunctional family home for Thanksgiving with his fiancée Tori Spelling. Posey – who is convinced that she is Jackie Onassis and loves her brother in more than just a filial way – is not pleased and decides to re-enact the JFK assassination, with real bullets. A witty walk on the wild side with strong performances and an edgy sense of humour. LH

Parker Posey *Jackie-O* • Josh Hamilton *Marty* • Tori Spelling *Lesly* • Freddie Prinze Jr *Anthony* • Geneviève Bujold *Mrs Pascal* • Rachael Leigh Cook *Young Jackie-O* • David Love *Young Marty* ■ *Dir* Mark Waters (1) • *Scr* Mark Waters, from the play by Wendy MacLeod

House on Bare Mountain
★★

Horror 1962 · US · Colour · 61min

Nudies meet the nasties in the first topless monster flick from exploitation maestro Lee Frost (credited as RL Frost). Co-producer Bob Cresse (another sleaze icon) plays Granny Good, narrating the tale of the day her School for Good Girls was invaded by the Wolf Man, Frankenstein and Dracula. The undressed cast is clearly drunk as tepid scares punctuate the daily routine of nude art classes, bare sunbathing and naked jogging. A tacky and tawdry classic. AJ

Bob Cresse *Granny Good* • Hugh Cannon *Krakow* • Laura Eden *Prudence Bumgartner* • Warren Ames *The monster* • Jeffrey Smithers *Dracula* ■ *Dir* RL Frost [Lee Frost] • *Scr* Denver Scott

The House on Carroll Street ★★★ 🅿🅶

Thriller 1987 · US · Colour · 96min

A convincingly robust Kelly McGillis is the political activist in an slender plot about senator Mandy Patinkin smuggling Nazis into America. Hounded out of her job by the McCarthyite tendency, she takes work reading to Jessica Tandy and begins to notice strange goings-on across the way. Jeff Daniels ably plays the FBI agent she enlists to solve the mystery. Sub-Hitchcock it may be, but this is still enjoyable. TH *DVD*

Kelly McGillis *Emily Crane* • Jeff Daniels *Cochran* • Mandy Patinkin *Ray Salwen* • Jessica Tandy *Miss Venable* • Jonathan Hogan *Alan* • Remak Ramsay *Senator Byington* ■ *Dir* Peter Yates • *Scr* Walter Bernstein

House on Haunted Hill
★★★ 🄵

Horror 1958 · US · BW · 74min

In terms of sheer silly spookiness, this William Castle production has never been equalled, as Vincent Price tries to scare overnight guests to death at a creepy mansion. Originally featuring "Emergo" – a plastic skeleton flown over people's heads in the audience – the script matches that gimmick in terms of subtlety. But Castle's directorial crassness does actually supply some genuinely frightening moments, and Price performs with zest. AJ *DVD*

Vincent Price *Frederick Loren* • Carol Ohmart *Annabelle Loren* • Richard Long *Lance Schroeder* • Alan Marshal *Dr David Trent* • Carolyn Craig *Nora Manning* • Elisha Cook [Elisha Cook Jr] *Watson Pritchard* ■ *Dir* William Castle • *Scr* Robb White

House on Haunted Hill
★★★ 🅸🆅

Horror 1999 · US · Colour · 88min

Held together by stylish direction from William Malone, some genuinely nasty jolts and a keen sense of genre history, this big-budget remake of the 1958 film compares favourably with the original. The simple plot has theme park developer Geoffrey Rush (here doing a creditable Vincent Price impression) offering a group of strangers $1 million to spend the night in a supposedly spook-infested, Art Deco asylum. Malone captures the essence of the 1950s frightener while updating the shocks with computer effects and grisly gore. AJ *DVD* 🔵 🅲🆂

Geoffrey Rush *Stephen Price* • Famke Janssen *Evelyn Price* • Taye Diggs *Eddie* • Peter Gallagher *Blackburn* • Chris Kattan *Pritchett* • Ali Larter *Sara* • Bridgette Wilson *Melissa Marr* ■ *Dir* William Malone • *Scr* Dick Beebe, from a story by Robb White

The House on 92nd Street
★★★★ 🅄

Spy documentary drama
1945 · US · BW · 84min

Produced by Louis de Rochemont – co-founder/producer of the influential American newsreel *The March of Time* – this semi-documentary espionage thriller started a trend in postwar Hollywood for true-life crime dramas notable for their realism, "voice of doom" narration and understated use of authentic locations. Readily taking to the documentary style, director Henry Hathaway sets a cracking pace as double agent William Eythe keeps federal agent Lloyd Nolan informed about the activities of a Nazi spy ring operated from New York by icy blonde Signe Hasso. DP *DVD*

William Eythe *Bill Dietrich* • Lloyd Nolan *Inspector George A Briggs* • Signe Hasso *Elsa Gebhardt* • Gene Lockhart *Charles Ogden Roper* • Leo G Carroll *Colonel Hammersohn* ■ *Dir* Henry Hathaway • *Scr* Barre Lyndon, Charles G Booth, John Monks Jr, from a story by Charles G Booth

The House on Telegraph Hill
★★★★ 🅄

Thriller 1951 · US · BW · 89min

This richly layered *film noir* stars Richard Basehart as the manipulative guardian of a young heir, and the outwardly vulnerable but inwardly steely Valentina Cortese as the war refugee who enters the US on the purloined papers of the boy's dead mother. Basehart and Cortese interact splendidly, with little being said but much atmospherically hinted at, and the movie throbs with a dark subtext on human fallibility. SH *DVD*

Richard Basehart *Alan Spender* • Valentina Cortesa [Valentina Cortese] *Victoria Kowelska* • William Lundigan *Major Marc Anders* • Fay Baker *Margaret* • Gordon Gebert *Chris* ■ *Dir* Robert Wise • *Scr* Elick Moll, Frank Partos, from the novel *The Frightened Child* by Dana Lyon

The House on Trubnaya Square 🌟🌟🌟🌟🌟

Silent satirical comedy
1928 · USSR · BW · 81min

Although this was the film that launched the great Vera Maretskaya's career, co-star Vladimir Fogel died only a year later. His knowing performance as a hairdresser with ideas above his station is one of the many pleasures of this glorious silent comedy. Whether craning down the side of the titular tenement or roving Moscow's streets, Yevgeni Alexeyev's camera picks up every delicious detail of the rustic Maretskaya's rebellion against her employer's refusal to let her join a housemaid's union. Visually vibrant, satirically astute and packed with wonderfully observed characters, this is Boris Barnet's finest hour. DP

Vera Maretskaya *Parasha Pitounova* • Vladimir Fogel *Golikov* • Yelena Tyapkina *Mrs Golikova* • Vladimir Batalov *Semyen Byvalov* ■ *Dir* Boris Barnet • *Scr* Boris Zorich, Anatoly Marienhof, Vadim Shershenevich, Victor Shklovsky, Nikolai Erdman

House Party ★★★★ 🅸🅵

Comedy 1990 · US · Colour · 99min

Acting as a lighter alternative to those hard, unsettling visions of modern black America from the likes of Spike Lee, this fresh comedy makes no attempt to pander to a more mainstream audience but remains a hugely enjoyable affair. Rap duo Kid 'n' Play (Christopher Reid and Christopher Martin) take the lead roles, the former playing a grounded high school student who will stop at nothing to get to a party at his best friend's house. Directed at a frenetic pace by Reginald Hudlin, this boasts a terrific soundtrack, cameos from a host of rap stars and a scene-stealing performance from Robin Harris. JF Swearing. *DVD*

Christopher Reid *Kid* • Christopher Martin (2) *Play* • Robin Harris *Pop* • Martin Lawrence *Bilal* • Tisha Campbell *Sidney* • Adrienne-Joi Johnson *Sharane* • Paul Anthony *Stab* • Bowlegged Lou *Pee-Wee* ■ *Dir/Scr* Reginald Hudlin

House Party 2 ★★ 🅸🅵

Comedy 1991 · US · Colour · 90min

The original *House Party* was a surprise hit around the world, but this shallow sequel failed to recapture the same magic. Kid 'n' Play (Christopher Reid and Christopher Martin) return once again, but this time they're at college. To ease some financial worries, they decide to hold another massive party which is the cue for further hip-hop cameos. The duo released one further sequel in 1994, and the series limped on without them with one more (unrelated) film in 2001. JF Swearing. **DVD**

Christopher Reid *Kid* • Christopher Martin (2) *Play* • Queen Latifah *Zora* • Iman *Sheila* • Eugene Allen *Groove* • George Anthony Bell *Reverend Simms* • Martin Lawrence *Bilal* ■ *Dir* George Jackson, Doug McHenry • *Scr* Rusty Cundlieff, Daryl G Nickens, from characters by Reginald Hudlin

The House That Dripped Blood ★★★ 12

Portmanteau horror 1970 · UK · Colour · 97min

Directed with imaginative flair by Peter Duffell and featuring Christopher Lee and Peter Cushing in tailor-made roles as two of the four tenants of the menacing title abode, this is one of the best compendium films from Amicus (Hammer's main horror rival at the time). Robert Bloch's satisfying tales of terror involve possession, mysterious waxworks, voodoo and vampirism for an effective mix of creepy atmospherics and witty send-ups of the genre. AJ Violence. **DVD**

Denholm Elliott *Charles* • Joanna Dunham *Alice* • Peter Cushing *Philip* • Joss Ackland *Rogers* • Christopher Lee *Reid* • Nyree Dawn Porter *Ann* • Jon Pertwee *Paul* • Ingrid Pitt *Carla* • John Bennett *Holloway* • John Bryans *Stoker* ■ *Dir* Peter Duffell • *Scr* Robert Bloch

The House Where Evil Dwells ★ 18

Horror 1982 · US · Colour · 83min

The 19th-century ghosts of a cuckolded Japanese samurai, his unfaithful wife and her lover terrorise a young couple when they move into their Kyoto haunted house. After US diplomat and old family friend Doug McClure arrives on the scene, the three are doomed to re-enact the spiritual love triangle. The soft-core sex, low-key gore and an attack by large crabs (!) do nothing to keep the boredom at bay. AJ

Edward Albert *Ted* • Susan George *Laura* • Doug McClure *Alex* • Amy Barrett *Amy* • Mako Hattori *Otami* • Toshiyuki Sasaki *Shugoro* • Toshiya Maruyama *Masanori* • Okajima Tsuyako *Witch* • Henry Mitowa *Zen Monk* ■ *Dir* Kevin Connor • *Scr* Robert Suhosky, from the novel by James Hardiman

Houseboat ★★★★ U

Romantic comedy drama 1958 · US · Colour · 105min

This delightfully played, relatively unsophisticated comedy is based on a slim but oh-so-romantic premise. Lovely Sophia Loren takes charge of lawyer Cary Grant's three children and, eventually of course, Grant himself. Beautifully photographed by Ray June, who made a similarly fabulous job of *Funny Face*, this is an easy-on-the-eye glamfest that also contains a fabulous supporting performance from Harry Guardino as a handyman in wolf's clothing. TS **DVD**

Sophia Loren *Cinzia Zaccardi* • Cary Grant *Tom Winston* • Martha Hyer *Carolyn Gibson* • Harry Guardino *Angelo Donatello* • Eduardo Ciannelli *Arturo Zaccardi* • Murray Hamilton *Alan Wilson* ■ *Dir* Melville Shavelson • *Scr* Melville Shavelson, Jack Rose

Houseguest ★★ PG

Comedy 1995 · US · Colour · 104min

This so-so vehicle for American comedy star Sinbad went straight to video in the UK. The comedian plays a petty con artist on the run from the Mob who, passing himself off as the long-lost chum of uptight lawyer Phil Hartman, moves in with his family. Sinbad's freewheeling style raises the odd giggle, but the direction is uninspired and the result is predictable. JF **DVD**

Sinbad *Kevin Franklin* • Phil Hartman *Gary Young* • Kim Greist *Emily Young* • Chauncey Leopardi *Jason Young* • Talia Seider *Sarah Young* ■ *Dir* Randall Miller • *Scr* Lawrence Gay, Michael DiGaetano

Household Saints ★★★

Comedy drama 1993 · US · Colour · 124min

Executive produced by Jonathan Demme, this is a quirky tale of Italian-American Catholics in New York. Vincent D'Onofrio wins Tracey Ullman in a pinochle game and they marry. Though bullied by his mother (Judith Malina), she gives birth to a daughter (Lili Taylor). As Taylor grows, so do her love for Jesus and her obsession with her saintly namesake, St Teresa. Director Nancy Savoca portrays three generations of comic and tragic family life with tenderness and empathy. LH

Tracey Ullman *Catherine Falconetti* • Vincent D'Onofrio *Joseph Santangelo* • Lili Taylor *Teresa* • Judith Malina *Carmela Santangelo* • Michael Rispoli *Nicky Falconetti* • Victor Argo *Lino Falconetti* • Michael Imperioli *Leonard Villanova* • Rachael Bella *Young Teresa* ■ *Dir* Nancy Savoca • *Scr* Nancy Savoca, Richard Guay, from the novel by Francine Prose

The Householder ★★★ U

Comedy 1963 · US/Ind · BW · 96min

Adapted from her own novel by Ruth Prawer Jhabvala and produced by Ismail Merchant, James Ivory's debut feature launched one of the most successful teams in cinema history. Bearing in mind that the production nearly collapsed through lack of funds, this account of mummy's boy Shashi Kapoor's troubled early marriage to Leela Naidu is admirably authentic. Yet it took some editing assistance from Satyajit Ray to give the narrative its sense of drama and pace. Rough edges remain, but the camerawork of Ray regular Subrata Mitra is deeply sensitive and the performances are touchingly honest. DP **DVD**

Shashi Kapoor *Prem Sagar* • Leela Naidu *Indu* • Harindranath Chattopadhyay *Mr Chadda* • Durga Khote *The Mother* • Pro Sen *Sohanlal* ■ *Dir* James Ivory • *Scr* Ruth Prawer Jhabvala, from her novel

Housekeeping ★★★★ PG

Comedy drama 1987 · US · Colour · 111min

Director Bill Forsyth has been sadly underused by the American film industry, yet it all started so well with this charming and superbly controlled study of the way in which children manage to survive even the most outrageous whims of the adults entrusted with their care. Sara Walker and Andrea Burchill are splendid as the young sisters who seem to have immunised themselves against the upheavals that periodically shatter their world, while Christine Lahti has never been better as the dippy aunt who appears to be their saviour. DP Swearing.

Christine Lahti *Aunt Sylvie* • Sara Walker *Ruth* • Andrea Burchill *Lucille* • Anne Pitoniak *Lily* • Barbara Reese *Nona* • Bill Smillie *Sheriff* • Wayne Robson *Mr French* • Margot Pinvidic *Helen* ■ *Dir* Bill Forsyth • *Scr* Bill Forsyth, from the novel by Marilynne Robinson

Housemaster ★★★

Comedy drama 1938 · UK · BW · 95min

This adaptation of an Ian Hay play brought actor Otto Kruger over from America for the role of his life, as the housemaster victimised by the school's head after disciplinary measures result in a revolt of the pupils. Director Herbert Brenon demonstrates his empathy with the nuances of the English class system. TS

Otto Kruger *Charles Donkin* • Diana Churchill *Rosemary Faringdon* • Phillips Holmes *Philip de Courville* • Joyce Barbour *Barbara Fane* • René Ray *Chris Faringdon* • Cecil Parker *Sir Berkeley Nightingale* • Jimmy Hanley *Travers* ■ *Dir* Herbert Brenon • *Scr* Dudley Leslie, Elizabeth Meehan, from the play *Bachelor Born* by Ian Hay

HouseSitter ★★★ PG

Romantic comedy 1992 · US · Colour · 97min

Goldie Hawn is at her dippiest as the waitress who overturns the life of Steve Martin's staid architect in this likeable if somewhat silly movie. Martin is recovering from rejection by the love of his life (Dana Delany) when he meets Hawn, who decides to help his convalescence by moving into the dream house he has built but left empty

after getting the elbow from his dream woman. When Hawn tells the neighbourhood that she's his new wife, the comic complications pile on, to generally amusing effect. DP Swearing. **DVD**

Steve Martin *Newton Davis* • Goldie Hawn *Gwen* • Dana Delany *Becky* • Julie Harris (2) *Edna Davis* • Donald Moffat *George Davis* • Peter MacNicol *Marty* • Richard B Shull *Ralph* ■ *Dir* Frank Oz • *Scr* Mark Stein, from a story by Mark Stein, Brian Grazer

How Do I Love Thee? ★★ PG

Comedy drama 1970 · US · Colour · 108min

Jackie Gleason was perhaps not the most fortuitous choice to play an unrepentant atheist in keen debate with his philosophy professor son. Maureen O'Hara and Shelley Winters do little more than referee this talkathon, which is rarely worth listening to. DP

Jackie Gleason *Stanley Waltz* • Maureen O'Hara *Elsie Waltz* • Shelley Winters *Lena Mervin* • Rosemary Forsyth *Marion Waltz* ■ *Dir* Michael Gordon • *Scr* Everett Freeman, Karl Tunberg, from the novel *Let Me Count the Ways* by Peter DeVries

How Do You Know ★★ 12

Romantic comedy drama 2010 · US · Colour · 115min

Writer/director James L Brooks has assembled an impressive cast for his first film since *Spanglish* but sadly the tantalising line-up doesn't deliver. Reese Witherspoon plays a softball player whose career has come to an end just as she's struggling to coax confirmed bachelor Owen Wilson into a steady relationship. The third ingredient of this burgeoning love triangle is Paul Rudd, who works for his father (Jack Nicholson) and is made a scapegoat for financial irregularities at the company. Wilson does have some very funny moments as a self-aware commitment-phobe, but Nicholson is on autopilot, while Brooks makes it difficult to engage with the characters' efforts at soul-searching. SP Swearing. **DVD**

Jack Nicholson *Charles Madison* • Reese Witherspoon *Lisa Jorgenson* • Paul Rudd *George Madison* • Owen Wilson *Matty* • Kathryn Hahn *Annie* • Shelley Conn *Terry* • Mark Linn-Baker *Ron* • Tony Shalhoub *Psychiatrist* ■ *Dir/Scr* James L Brooks

How Green Was My Valley ★★★★★ U

Drama 1941 · US · BW · 117min

This magnificent Oscar-winning family saga may seem a trifle dated, with its superb but phoney studio re-creations of the valleys of South Wales. But there's no denying its power to move as well as entertain audiences, as director John Ford lovingly details life in the pits and valleys of the region. Ford rightly won the best director Oscar and the movie won best picture, but often overlooked is the sincerity of the film's hand-picked cast, notably sturdy Walter Pidgeon and fiery Ford regular Maureen O'Hara. The best supporting actor Oscar went to Donald Crisp's patriarch. TS **DVD**

Walter Pidgeon *Mr Gruffydd* • Maureen O'Hara *Angharad* • Donald Crisp *Mr Morgan* • Roddy McDowall *Huw* • Anna Lee *Bronwyn* • John Loder *Ianto* • Sara Allgood *Mrs Morgan* • Barry Fitzgerald *Cyfartha* ■ *Dir* John Ford • *Scr* Philip Dunne, from the novel by Richard Llewellyn • *Cinematographer* Arthur Miller

How I Ended This Summer ★★★ 12

Drama 2010 · Rus · Colour · 124min

Extreme isolation creates devastating paranoia and misunderstandings in this intense though occasionally obscure Russian drama set on a desolate Arctic island. Writer/director Alexei Popogrebsky's slow-paced character study concentrates on atmosphere and emotion, rather than action and motivations. But it's the complex performances that keep the narrative compelling, with Sergei Puskepalis (co-winner of the Berlin Silver Bear with Grigory Dobrygin) conveying a quiet threat that

racks up the tension during the unpredictable final third. SF Russian +subtitles. Brief swearing. **DVD**

Grigory Dobrygin *Pavel* • Sergei Puskepalis *Sergei* ■ *Dir/Scr* Alexei Popogrebsky • *Cinematographer* Pavel Kostomarov

How I Got Into College ★★★ 15

Comedy 1989 · US · Colour · 83min

This romantic teen comedy stars Corey Parker as a lovestruck, non-academic sort who plans to enrol in the same college as the girl he worships (Lara Flynn Boyle). The trouble is, he's not the college type. Luckily the college in question is about to launch a new initiative allowing some "ordinary" guys to enter their hallowed halls. Witty and likeable juvenile fare. DF

Anthony Edwards *Kip* • Corey Parker *Marlon* • Lara Flynn Boyle *Jessica* • Finn Carter *Nina* • Charles Rocket *Leo* • Christopher Rydell *Oliver* • Philip Baker Hall *Dean Patterson* ■ *Dir* Savage Steve Holland • *Scr* Terrel Seltzer

How I Live Now ★★★ 15

Futuristic drama 2013 · UK · Colour · 96min

With films such as *The Last King of Scotland* to his name, director Kevin Macdonald obviously has a flair for matching realism with adrenaline-pumping thrills. Here, his vision of England in a nuclear crisis feels even more effective because he dresses it in the conventions of a growing-pains drama. Saoirse Ronan stars as Daisy, a moody American teenager who's summering with her English cousins in a bucolic paradise when a literal bombshell drops. The mood changes drastically and Daisy is forced to embark on a perilous journey. But this is no mere tale of triumph over adversity, as it becomes increasingly clear how much modern life has distanced Daisy from the natural world. SP Violence, swearing, a sex scene. **DVD**

Saoirse Ronan *Daisy* • George MacKay *Eddie* • Tom Holland (2) *Isaac* • Harley Bird *Piper* • Danny McEvoy *Joe* • Anna Chancellor *Aunt Penn* ■ *Dir* Kevin Macdonald • *Scr* Jeremy Brock, Tony Grisoni, Penelope Skinner, from Meg Rosoff's novel

How I Spent My Summer Vacation ★★ U

Thriller 1967 · US · Colour · 89min

Made as a TV movie of the week by Universal, who pioneered such things, this confused would-be thriller was renamed *Deadly Roulette* and released in cinemas here largely because of its extremely attractive cast. A boyish Robert Wagner stars as a former soldier who seeks revenge on sophisticated, wealthy Peter Lawford following an incident when Lawford humiliated him; others aboard for the ride include Lola Albright, Jill St John and a dapper Walter Pidgeon. TS

Robert Wagner *Jack Washington* • Peter Lawford *Ned Pine* • Lola Albright *Mrs Pine* • Walter Pidgeon *Lewis Gannet* • Jill St John *Nikki Pine* • Michael Ansara *Pucci* ■ *Dir* William Hale • *Scr* Gene Kearney

How I Spent My Summer Vacation ★★★ 15

Action thriller 2012 · US · Colour · 92min

This bloody and sadistic thriller stars Mel Gibson as an unnamed criminal sentenced without trial to a tough Mexican prison compound, where inmates live with their families, and drugs and prostitution are rife. Befriending a young boy and his mother, the "gringo" plans his escape and the recovery of the millions from his last heist, stashed away by crooked guards and the jail's ruthless kingpins. The plot is intricately structured and well paced, with co-writer Gibson giving himself a generous helping of wisecracks and, as scenes of torture (including women and children) may be shocking to viewers more used to Gibson's more knockabout action fare. TeS English, Spanish +subtitles. Violence, swearing, drug abuse. **DVD**

Mel Gibson *Driver* • Daniel Giménez Cacho [Daniel Gimenez Cacho] *Javi* • Jesús Ochoa *Caracas* • Roberto Sosa *Carnal* • Dolores Heredia *Kid's mother* ■ *Dir* Adrian Grunberg • *Scr* Mel Gibson, Adrian Grunberg, Stacy Perskie

How I Won the War

★★★★ 12

Black comedy   1967 · UK · Colour · 106min

John Lennon's decision to take a break from the Beatles and accept the part of Private Gripweed was the major talking point when this film was initially released. Based on Patrick Ryan's biting attack on the follies of war and brass-hat incompetence, Richard Lester's feature broadens the satire and throws in a little surrealism and slapstick to make the subtleties of the book suitably cinematic. Getting by with a little help from his friends, Michael Crawford is admirably gung ho as the head of the special cricket pitch unit. DP Violence. *DVD*

Michael Crawford *Lt Ernest Goodbody* • John Lennon *Gripweed* • Roy Kinnear *Clapper* • Lee Montague *Sgt Transom* • Jack MacGowran *Juniper* • Michael Hordern *Grapple* • Jack Hedley *Melancholy musketeer* • Karl Michael Vogler *Odleboy* ■ *Dir* Richard Lester • *Scr* Charles Wood, from the novel by Patrick Ryan

How Much Does Your Building Weigh, Mr Foster?

★★★

Documentary   2009 · UK/Sp/Fr · Colour · 78min

This profile of architect Norman Foster often feels more like a corporate video than a critical study, with its fetishising aerial shots of his gleaming creations. And it reaches new heights of sycophancy as narrator Deyan Sudjic competes with talking heads like Alain de Botton and Bono in paying gushing tribute to the "Mozart of Modernism". However, there are revealing insights into Foster's humble origins in Manchester, his relationships with fellow architects and his approach to the aesthetics and ecology of his craft. Moreover, there's no denying the majesty of such iconic edifices as the Berlin Reichstag and London's "Gherkin". Foster is a fascinating subject, but his achievement should be scrutinised much more rigorously than this. DP *DVD*

Norman Foster ■ *Dir* Carlos Carcas, Norberto López Amado • *Scr* Deyan Sudjic

How She Move

★★ 12

Dance drama   2007 · Can · Colour · 87min

Following in the dance shoes of 2006's *Stomp the Yard*, this Canadian drama stars newcomer Rutina Wesley as Raya, a gifted ghetto teen who loses her place at an exclusive school after her sister dies of a drug overdose. Returning to the projects, she falls foul of old friends and makes a bid for financial independence by setting out to win the prestigious Step Monster competition. Though grittier than its rivals in the genre (*Step Up, You Got Served*), this follows the same tired formula of redemption through freestyle street dance, and the astounding choreography runs rings around the generic storytelling. JR Swearing, drug abuse. *DVD*

Rutina Wesley *Raya Green* • Tré Armstrong [Tracey Armstrong] *Michelle* • Clé Bennett *Garvey* • Dwain Murphy *Bishop* • Boyd Banks *Mike Evans* ■ *Dir* Ian Iqbal Rashid • *Scr* Annmarie Morais

How Stella Got Her Groove Back

★★★ 15

Romantic comedy drama
1998 · US · Colour · 119min

Based on the novel by Terry McMillan, this is a companion piece to the earlier *Waiting to Exhale*, which also starred Angela Bassett. Here she plays single mother Stella, who is encouraged by her best friend (Whoopi Goldberg) to escape her downbeat existence for a holiday in Jamaica. It's there that she meets half-her-age hunk Taye Diggs, and the audience is treated to picture-postcard shots of their romance and the island itself. Sadly, the characters are only briefly sketched. JB Some swearing, sex scenes. *DVD*

Angela Bassett *Stella* • Whoopi Goldberg *Delilah* • Regina King *Vanessa* • Taye Diggs *Winston Shakespeare* • Suzzanne Douglas *Angela* • Michael J Pagan *Quincy* • Sicily *Chantel* • Richard Lawson *Jack* ■ *Dir* Kevin Rodney Sullivan • *Scr* Ronald Bass, Terry McMillan, from the novel by Terry McMillan

How Sweet It Is!

★

Comedy   1968 · US · Colour · 97min

This is an unspeakably witless comedy about two married Americans discovering sex in Europe, hoping to bring excitement to their marriage and maturity to their teenage offspring. Debbie Reynolds canoodles with Maurice Ronet at James Garner's expense, while Paul Lynde and Terry-Thomas share the few laughs on offer. Jerry Paris directs with a total lack of sophistication. TS

James Garner *Grif Henderson* • Debbie Reynolds *Jenny Henderson* • Maurice Ronet *Philippe Maspere* • Terry-Thomas *Gilbert Tilly* • Paul Lynde *The Purser* ■ *Dir* Jerry Paris • *Scr* Garry Marshall, Jerry Belson, from the novel *The Girl in the Turquoise Bikini* by Muriel Resnik

How the Grinch Stole Christmas

Animated fantasy   2018 · US · Colour

This is a preview – no prints were available to review as we went to press: Who takes on Jim Carrey as the Grinch? Benedict Cumberbatch, that's who. But is he as versatile as he is undoubtedly brave? If Carrey could hide behind a mountain of latex in his live-action take, Cumberbatch might well be hoping that the 3D animators give him an edge when he takes to the screen as one of Dr Seuss's most famous creations. Audrey Geisel (aka Mrs Seuss) is on board as an executive producer, which should guarantee a certain level of quality. SvM Sp

Benedict Cumberbatch *The Grinch* • Kaitlyn Maher *Cindy Lou Who* ■ *Dir* Peter Candeland, Yarrow Cheney • *Scr* Michael LeSieur, from Dr Seuss's illustrated children's book

How the West Was Won

★★★★ PG

Epic western   1962 · US · Colour · 160min

This is one of only two narrative films made in three-camera Cinerama; if you look very carefully you can see the joins in its widescreen version, which are especially noticeable down the tree trunks. Of the three credited directors, Henry Hathaway shot the all-star Rivers, Plains and Outlaws sections, while George Marshall filmed that dangerous stunt-work on the railroad, and the great John Ford directed the splendid American Civil War sequence. The majestic score is by Alfred Newman, and was used again to witty comic effect in 1984's *Romancing the Stone*. TS *DVD* Blu

James Stewart *Linus Rawlings* • John Wayne *General William T Sherman* • Gregory Peck *Cleve Van Valen* • Henry Fonda *Jethro Stuart* • Carroll Baker *Eve Prescott* • Lee J Cobb *Marshal Lou Ramsey* • Carolyn Jones *Julie Rawlings* • Karl Malden *Zebulon Prescott* • George Peppard *Zeb Rawlings* • Robert Preston *Roger Morgan* • Debbie Reynolds *Lilith Prescott* • Eli Wallach *Charlie Gant* • Richard Widmark *Mike King* • Walter Brennan *Colonel Hawkins* • Raymond Massey *Abraham Lincoln* • Agnes Moorehead *Rebecca Prescott* • Thelma Ritter *Agatha Clegg* • Spencer Tracy *Narrator* ■ *Dir* John Ford, Henry Hathaway, George Marshall • *Scr* James R Webb, from articles in *Life Magazine* • *Cinematographers* William H Daniels [William Daniels (1)], Milton Krasner, Charles Lang Jr [Charles Lang], Joseph LaShelle

How to Be a Woman and Not Die in the Attempt

★★★ 15

Comedy drama   1991 · Sp · Colour · 88min

This wry and amusing comedy stars Carmen Maura as a working wife and mum who finally takes umbrage at her workaholic hubby's chauvinistic belief that she should not only bring home a wage, but also be solely responsible for bringing up their three kids. Waspishly written and beautifully acted, especially by Maura, this is proof that quality films from Spain don't have to have the name "Almodóvar" attached to them. DA Spanish +subtitles. Swearing. *DVD*

Carmen Maura *Carmen* • Antonio Resines *Antonio* ■ *Dir* Ana Belén • *Scr* Carmen Rico-Godoy, from her novel

How to Be Single

★★★ 15

Romantic comedy   2016 · US · Colour · 109min

A colourful and near-aggressively peppy crash course in the dating game and learning to love yourself. It introduces us to a newly single paralegal (Dakota Johnson), her party-girl friend (Rebel Wilson), her obstetrician sister (Leslie Mann) and a neurotic personal dating strategist (Alison Brie). It's montage-heavy and full of contradictions, yet the film's energy is undeniable and if the lessons are trite then the positivity and occasional narrative curveballs are at least appealing. It certainly knows how to have a good time. EAS Swearing, sex references

Dakota Johnson *Alice* • Rebel Wilson *Robin* • Leslie Mann *Meg* • Nicholas Braun *Josh* • Alison Brie *Lucy* ■ *Dir* Christian Ditter • *Scr* Abby Kohn, Marc Silverstein, from Liz Tuccillo's novel

How to Be Very, Very Popular

★★★ U

Musical comedy   1955 · US · Colour · 89min

This musical saw Betty Grable bring down the curtain on a career in which she had been everything the title said. But the 38-year-old star is soundly upstaged in her swan song by Sheree North, a blonde bombshell 16 years her junior in only her fourth feature. The film gave Nunnally Johnson the excuse to keep his stars in the skimpiest of costumes. Not even that old scene stealer Charles Coburn could beat that sort of competition. DP

Betty Grable *Stormy* • Sheree North *Curly* • Robert Cummings *Wedgewood* • Charles Coburn *Tweed* • Tommy Noonan *Eddie* • Orson Bean *Toby* • Fred Clark *Mr Marshall* • Charlotte Austin *Midge* ■ *Dir* Nunnally Johnson • *Scr* Nunnally Johnson, from a play by Howard Lindsay, from a novel by Edward Hope and a play by Lyford Moore, Harlan Thompson

How to Beat the High Cost of Living

★★★ 15

Crime comedy   1980 · US · Colour · 104min

Long before they got together on the small screen in the sitcom *Kate and Allie*, Susan Saint James and Jane Curtin teamed up on this appealing caper comedy. Along with Jessica Lange, they play old schoolfriends who find themselves in need of money, thanks to the incompetence of their menfolk. They hatch a plot to steal thousands from a giant plastic moneyball set up as a publicity stunt in the local shopping mall. DF

Susan Saint James *Jane* • Jane Curtin *Elaine* • Jessica Lange *Louise* • Richard Benjamin *Albert* • Eddie Albert *Max* • Cathryn Damon *Natalie* • Dabney Coleman *Jack Heintzel* ■ *Dir* Robert Scheerer • *Scr* Robert Kaufman, from a story by Leonora Thuna

How to Change the World

★★★ 15

Documentary
2015 · UK/Canada · Colour and BW · 109min

This is a frustratingly selective chronicle of the early days of the pioneering group that helped make environmentalism fashionable. Founded almost accidentally in 1969 by a bunch of Vancouver hippies, Greenpeace started to widen its sphere of activity under its reluctant leader, Bob Hunter. Director Jerry Rothwell allows himself to become distracted by feuds rather than concentrating on the landmark campaigns against whaling and seal-culling that broadened Greenpeace's appeal and demonstrated the efficacy of well-targeted activism. But this is still worth seeing, even if just for Ron Precious and Rex Weyler's field footage and photography. DP Swearing, disturbing images, nudity. *DVD*

Bob Hunter • Paul Watson (2) *Paul Watson* • Rex Weyler • Patrick Moore • Barry Pepper *Bob Hunter* ■ *Dir/Scr* Jerry Rothwell

How to Commit Marriage

★

Comedy   1969 · US · Colour · 95min

In this self-conscious, dire comedy, Bob Hope and Jane Wyman play about-to-be-divorced parents. When their daughter Joanna Cameron brings home her fiancé, they try to pretend all is well. But the boy's father (Jackie Gleason) becomes suspicious, their charade is revealed. An embarrassing attempt to cross the comedy of Hope and Gleason with the "anything goes" style of the Swinging Sixties. DF

Bob Hope *Frank Benson* • Jackie Gleason *Oliver Poe* • Jane Wyman *Elaine Benson* • Leslie Nielsen *Phil Fletcher* • Maureen Arthur *Lois Gray* • Joanna Cameron *Nancy Benson* • Tim Matheson *David Poe* ■ *Dir* Norman Panama • *Scr* Ben Starr, Michael Kanin

How to Fill a Wild Bikini

★ U

Musical comedy   1965 · US · Colour · 92min

The fifth in AIP's beach party series is the biggest washout of the lot. With Frankie Avalon away on naval reserve duty, he's limited to a cameo role as the suspicious coastguard who calls on witch doctor Buster Keaton to ensure that Annette Funicello doesn't fall into the clutches of beefcake Dwayne Hickman. Boasting some of the worst song-and-dance routines ever committed to celluloid. DP

Annette Funicello *Dee Dee* • Dwayne Hickman *Ricky* • Brian Donlevy *BD* • Harvey Lembeck *Eric Von Zipper* • Beverly Adams *Cassandra* • Buster Keaton *Bwana* • Mickey Rooney *Peachy Keane* • Frankie Avalon *Frankie* • Brian Wilson *Beach boy* • Elizabeth Montgomery *Witches' witch* ■ *Dir* William Asher • *Scr* William Asher, Leo Townsend

How to Get Ahead in Advertising

★★★ 15

Satirical comedy   1989 · UK · Colour · 90min

After the truly wonderful *Withnail & I*, this comic follow-up, which reunited Richard E Grant with writer/director Bruce Robinson, proved something of a disappointment. Grant is the troubled advertising executive who develops an evil alter ego: a boil which can not only talk but is intent on taking over his whole body. There are some neat, surreal touches, another manic performance from Grant and a solid supporting cast, but the evil side of advertising is too broad and too obvious a target. JF Swearing, some nudity. *DVD*

Richard E Grant *Dennis Bagley* • Rachel Ward *Julia Bagley* • Richard Wilson (3) *Bristol* • Jacqueline Tong *Penny Wheelstock* • John Shrapnel *Psychiatrist* • Susan Wooldridge *Monica* ■ *Dir/Scr* Bruce Robinson

How to Lose a Guy in 10 Days

★★ 12

Romantic comedy
2003 · US/Ger · Colour · 110min

Kate Hudson's journalist is assigned a magazine feature for which she must snare a guy and then make him dump her, while her target, Matthew McConaughey, is involved in a bet to make a woman fall in love with him. Both have ten days to do it in. Despite the odd mildly amusing observation on the mating rituals of New Yorkers and some pretty cinematography, the contrived plot and leaden supporting cast smother any sign of wit. AS *DVD*

Kate Hudson *Andie Anderson* • Matthew McConaughey *Benjamin Barry* • Adam Goldberg *Tony* • Michael Michele *Spears* • Shalom Harlow *Green* • Bebe Neuwirth *Lana Jong* • Robert Klein *Phillip Warren* ■ *Dir* Donald Petrie • *Scr* Kristen Buckley, Brian Regan, Burr Steers

How to Lose Friends & Alienate People

★★★ 15

Comedy based on a true story
2008 · UK/Ire · Colour · 105min

British journalist Toby Young found success when he wrote a bestselling book about his failed stint at a New York glossy. This loose adaptation stars Simon Pegg as Sidney Young, who, unlike his real-life counterpart, has a charming silly streak that keeps you grinning even as he snipes at and isolates himself from the American showbiz glitterati. It helps, too, that the stars and their PR wranglers are even bigger egomaniacs than him. Despite a tacked-on romance (with Kirsten Dunst), Pegg and director Robert B Weide (TV's *Curb Your Enthusiasm*) deliver a wickedly funny mix of social and literal slip-ups, which is bound to win over and amuse most people. SP *DVD*

Simon Pegg *Sidney Young* • Kirsten Dunst *Alison Olsen* • Danny Huston *Lawrence Maddox* • Gillian Anderson *Eleanor Johnson* • Megan Fox *Sophie Maes* • Max Minghella *Vincent Lepak* • Jeff Bridges *Clayton Harding* • Margo Stilley *Ingrid* ■ *Dir* Robert B Weide • *Scr* Peter Straughan, from the memoirs by Toby Young

How to Make a Monster
★★ PG

Horror 1958 · US · BW and Colour · 73min

When a Hollywood make-up effects man is told horror is passé, he applies special drugged cosmetics to the actors playing Frankenstein's creature and the Werewolf on his last movie so they'll think they really are monsters and murder the meddlesome moguls. Cue the reuse of old fright masks, props and veteran stars from AIP successes such as *I Was a Teenage Werewolf*, affectionately mocking the genre. AJ *DVD*

Robert H Harris *Pete Dummond* • Paul Brinegar *Rivero* • Gary Conway *Tony Mantell* • Gary Clarke (1) *Larry Drake* • Malcolm Atterbury *Richards* ■ *Dir* Herbert L Strock • *Scr* Kenneth Langtry, Herman Cohen

How to Make an American Quilt
★★★ 12

Drama 1995 · US · Colour · 111min

This low-key but enjoyable film, based on the book by Whitney Otto and directed by Jocelyn Moorhouse, features moving performances from the female-dominated cast. Winona Ryder stars as the marriage-shy young woman who listens while her older relatives recount tales of love and disappointment as they add squares to a growing and symbolic quilt. Some of the episodic tales work better than others, but all are interesting and there are splendid characterisations from the cast. JB *DVD*

Winona Ryder *Finn* • Ellen Burstyn *Hy* • Anne Bancroft *Glady Joe* • Kate Capshaw *Sally* • Dermot Mulroney *Sam* • Maya Angelou *Anna* • Alfre Woodard *Marianna* • Jean Simmons *Em* • Kate Nelligan *Constance* • Rip Torn *Arthur* • Samantha Mathis *Young Sophia* • Adam Baldwin *Finn's father* • Claire Danes *Young Glady Joe* ■ *Dir* Jocelyn Moorhouse • *Scr* Jane Anderson, from the novel by Whitney Otto • *Music* Thomas Newman

How to Make Money Selling Drugs
★★★ 18

Documentary 2012 · US · Colour · 90min

With the illegal drugs business in the US alone worth in excess of $100 billion a year, this powerful documentary lifts the lid on the people who set themselves up as outlaw entrepreneurs, and the efforts of lawmakers to shut them down. Director Matthew Cooke roles out a parade of statistics, interspersed by talking-head contributions from reformed dealers, government officials and celebrity activists such as Woody Harrelson and Susan Sarandon. Reflection on whether the war on drugs is really worth fighting could have been beneficial, however. TeS

Woody Harrelson • Susan Sarandon • Eminem ■ *Dir/Scr* Matthew Cooke

How to Marry a Millionaire
★★★★ U

Romantic comedy 1953 · US · Colour · 91min

This is a fabulously cast and witty reworking of that much-filmed 20th Century-Fox standby, the one about the three gals seeking rich husbands, smartened up and photographed in Fox's stunning new screen process, CinemaScope. Marilyn Monroe, Betty Grable, and Lauren Bacall play the girls, so who could ask for more? This film was the first shot in Scope, though released after *The Robe*, and it's preceded by an introductory orchestral sequence specially designed to show off the wonders of the then-new magnetic stereophonic sound, with Alfred Newman conducting *Street Scene*. TS *DVD* *BL*

Betty Grable *Loco* • Marilyn Monroe *Pola* • Lauren Bacall *Schatze Page* • David Wayne *Freddie Denmark* • Rory Calhoun *Eben* • Cameron Mitchell *Tom Brookman* • Alex D'Arcy *J Stewart Merrill* • Fred Clark *Waldo Brewster* • William Powell *JD Hanley* ■ *Dir* Jean Negulesco • *Scr* Nunnally Johnson, from the plays *The Greeks Had a Word for It* by Zoe Akins and *Loco* by Dale Eunson, Katherine Albert • *Music* Alfred Newman

How to Murder a Rich Uncle
★★★ U

Black comedy 1957 · UK · BW · 79min

Glorious memories of *Kind Hearts and Coronets* are occasionally stirred by this black comedy about the English aristocracy. Nigel Patrick – who also directed with an uncredited Max Varnel – stars as Sir Henry Clitterburn, down on his uppers, who plots to murder visiting Canadian uncle Charles Coburn in order to inherit a bundle. His plans go awry, of course. There's lots to enjoy here, including a lovely gallery of English eccentrics and, making his second credited screen appearance, Michael Caine. AT

Nigel Patrick *Henry* • Charles Coburn *Uncle George* • Wendy Hiller *Edith* • Katie Johnson *Alice* • Anthony Newley *Edward* • Athene Seyler *Grannie* • Noel Hood *Aunt Marjorie* • Michael Caine *Gilrony* ■ *Dir* Nigel Patrick • *Scr* John Paxton, from the play *Il Faut Tuer Julie* by Didier Daix

How to Murder Your Wife
★★★★ PG

Comedy 1965 · US · Colour · 113min

Confirmed bachelor Jack Lemmon wakes up after a night on the town married to luscious Virna Lisi, much to the dismay of his faithful butler Terry-Thomas, in director Richard Quine's brilliant, politically incorrect comedy. Thereafter, strip-cartoonist Lemmon's action-man character Bash Brannigan becomes cosily domesticated. To placate his fans, who want Brannigan restored to bachelorhood, Lemmon kills off his cartoon hero's wife; but then Lisi disappears and Lemmon finds himself accused of murder. So many scenes to cherish. TH *DVD*

Jack Lemmon *Stanley Ford* • Virna Lisi *Mrs Ford* • Terry-Thomas *Charles* • Claire Trevor *Edna* • Eddie Mayehoff *Harold Lampson* • Sidney Blackmer *Judge Blackstone* • Max Showalter *Tobey Rawlins* • Jack Albertson *Dr Bentley* • Alan Hewitt *District attorney* ■ *Dir* Richard Quine • *Scr* George Axelrod

How to Re-Establish a Vodka Empire
★★★★ 12A

Documentary 2011 · UK · Colour · 76min

First-time film-maker Daniel Edelstyn was inspired to make this documentary after chancing upon the memoirs of his remarkable Russian grandmother in the attic of his London home. He retraces her story back to a Ukrainian backwater, where he discovers that the family vodka distillery is still in operation. The movie follows Edelstyn's attempts to revive the ailing business – and to honour his ancestors who were uprooted by the Bolshevik uprising. Edelstyn has a genial on-screen presence and his mix of travelogue, dramatic reconstruction and model animation ensure this is as engrossing as it is pleasingly offbeat. DP Swearing.

Conrad Asquith *Great grandfather Ilya Zorokovich* • Anthony Styles *The evil Bolshevik Stepanovich* • Daniel Edelstyn *Daniel Edelstyn/Grandpa Max* • Hilary Powell *Hilary Powell/Granny Maroussia* ■ *Dir/Scr* Daniel Edelstyn

How to Steal a Million
★★★ U

Comedy caper 1966 · US · Colour · 118min

Audrey Hepburn hires Peter O'Toole to steal her father's fake Cellini Venus in this heist caper set in the Paris art world, which reunited Hepburn with her *Roman Holiday* director William Wyler for the third and final time. It's overlong and overwritten, and shows its age in the Swinging Sixties decor and the rather frantic mood. But there are compensations in the supporting cast, including greedy art collector Eli Wallach, the replacement for George C Scott, whom Wyler fired after only one day of shooting. AT *DVD*

Audrey Hepburn *Nicole Bonnet* • Peter O'Toole *Simon Dermott* • Eli Wallach *Davis Leland* • Hugh Griffith *Charles Bonnet* • Charles Boyer *De Solnay* • Fernand Gravey [Fernand Gravet] *Grammont* • Marcel Dalio *Senor Paravideo* • Jacques Marin *Chief guard* ■ *Dir* William Wyler • *Scr* Harry Kurnitz, from the story *Venus Rising* by George Bradshaw

How to Steal the World
★★ PG

Spy adventure 1968 · US · Colour · 86min

Stretched to feature length from a couple of TV episodes, this was the last *Man from UNCLE* picture produced by MGM, with Robert Vaughn and David McCallum looking very bored after four years of tongue-in-cheek espionage. Barry Sullivan runs through all the tricks of arch-villainy as a rogue agent, but despite guests of the calibre of Eleanor Parker and Leslie Nielsen, the series ended on a distinctly flat note. DP *DVD*

Robert Vaughn (1) *Napoleon Solo* • David McCallum (1) *Illya Kuryakin* • Barry Sullivan *Robert Kingsley* • Leslie Nielsen *Gen Harmon* • Eleanor Parker *Margitta* ■ *Dir* Sutton Roley • *Scr* Norman Hudis

How to Succeed in Business without Really Trying
★★★★ U

Musical comedy 1967 · US · Colour · 116min

This is a superb film re-creation of Frank Loesser and Abe Burrows's wonderfully acerbic stage musical, with all of Bob Fosse's original choreography preserved on film by Dale Moreda. Robert Morse repeats his Broadway role in a marvellously wicked, devastatingly funny part as a ruthless window cleaner who claws his way to the top of World Wide Wickets, the company run by, of all people, crooner Rudy Vallee. This also has to be the only musical where the hero sings the love song to himself. TS

Robert Morse *J Pierpont Finch* • Michele Lee *Rosemary Pilkington* • Rudy Vallee *JB Biggley* • Anthony Teague *Bud Frump* • Maureen Arthur *Hedy LaRue* • Murray Matheson *Benjamin Ovington* ■ *Dir* David Swift • *Scr* David Swift, from the musical by Abe Burrows, Willie Gilbert, Jack Weinstock, from the novel by Shepherd Mead • *Music/lyrics* Frank Loesser

How to Train Your Dragon
★★★★ PG

Animated comedy adventure 2010 · US · Colour · 93min

Cressida Cowell's children's book gets an exciting animated adaptation here. Teenager Hiccup (Jay Baruchel) belongs to a Viking tribe that sees dragons as their mortal enemy. But Hiccup is a secret dragon-whisperer and when he helps, rather than kills, a wounded dragon nicknamed Toothless, he sets a new course for his family and friends. The film boasts plenty of strong characters, is poignant where it counts and consistently amusing, cute, clever and touching. But where it really excels is with awesome visuals that rival *Avatar's*. The flying sequences are stunning and the battles are equally spectacular – although some younger viewers might find them rather too scary. AJ *DVD* *BL* *3D*

Jay Baruchel *Hiccup* • Gerard Butler *Stoick* • America Ferrera *Astrid* • Craig Ferguson *Gobber* • Jonah Hill *Snotlout* • Christopher Mintz-Plasse *Fishlegs* ■ *Dir* Dean DeBlois, Chris Sanders (2) [Chris Sanders (2)] • *Scr* Dean DeBlois, Christopher Sanders (2), Will Davies [William Davies], from Cressida Cowell's novel

How to Train Your Dragon 2
★★★★ PG

Animated comedy adventure 2014 · US · Colour · 97min

Picking up a few years after the first exciting adventure, this sturdy sequel finds teenage Viking Hiccup (voiced by Jay Baruchel) and his dragon pal Toothless exploring lands far from their home village, and meeting a dizzying array of friends, foes and family members, both dragon and human. It's a story crammed with set pieces that exploits the 3D format with maximum inventiveness, all aerial battles and coming-at-you swoops, and has a richness that's highly compelling. LF *DVD* *BL* *3D*

Jay Baruchel *Hiccup* • Cate Blanchett *Valka* • Gerard Butler *Stoick* • Craig Ferguson *Gobber* • Jonah Hill *Snotlout* • Kristen Wiig *Ruffnut* ■ *Dir* Dean DeBlois • *Scr* Dean DeBlois, from the *How to Train Your Dragon* series of illustrated children's books by Cressida Cowell

How We Used to Live
★★★★

Documentary 2013 · UK · Colour · 70min

Director Paul Kelly and art-pop trio St Etienne follow up their "London Trilogy" of films with this documentary, using the BFI's archive footage of London to follow the city's post-war recovery through to the dawn of Thatcherism. Creating something unique out of a much-explored subject, *How We Used to Live* is both a captivating piece of time travel and a reminder of the capital's ongoing evolution. JL

Ian McShane *Narrator* ■ *Dir* Paul Kelly (3) • *Scr* Bob Stanley, Travis Elborough

Howard, a New Breed of Hero
★ PG

Comedy fantasy 1986 · US · Colour · 104min

Marvel Comics meets George Lucas's Industrial Light and Magic, and an uneasy, bland alliance it is, too, with Howard T Duck transported to mid-1980s punkland. Howard takes to the dreadful music of the time and feisty chanteuse Lea Thompson, but fails to ignite any form of discernible plot. SH Mild swearing. *DVD*

Lea Thompson *Beverly Switzler* • Tim Robbins *Phil Blumburtt* • Jeffrey Jones *Dr Jenning* • Paul Guilfoyle (2) *Lieutenant Welker* • Liz Sagal *Ronette* • Dominique Davalos *Cal* • Holly Robinson *KC* ■ *Dir* Willard Huyck • *Scr* Willard Huyck, Gloria Katz, from a character created by Steve Gerber

Howards End
★★★★★ PG

Period drama 1992 · UK · Colour · 142min

This adaptation of EM Forster's novel – the best film made by the long-time team of director James Ivory, producer Ismail Merchant and writer Ruth Prawer Jhabvala – has an elegance that never hides grim insights into the upper middle-classes. Matriarchal Vanessa Redgrave dies after writing a letter bequeathing her country home, Howards End, to new friend Emma Thompson. But the note is destroyed by the family snobs-in-residence, whose head (Anthony Hopkins) then falls in love with Thompson. Meanwhile, the low expectations of the clerking classes are exemplified by a meek Samuel West, whose affair with Helena Bonham Carter leads to tragedy. The perfect period detail allows Hopkins and Thompson to create extraordinarily convincing portraits. TH *DVD*

Anthony Hopkins *Henry Wilcox* • Emma Thompson *Margaret Schlegel* • Helena Bonham Carter *Helen Schlegel* • Vanessa Redgrave *Ruth Wilcox* • James Wilby *Charles Wilcox* • Samuel West *Leonard Bast* • Prunella Scales *Aunt Juley* • Jemma Redgrave *Evie Wilcox* • Nicola Duffett *Jacky Bast* ■ *Dir* James Ivory • *Scr* Ruth Prawer Jhabvala, from the novel by EM Forster

The Howards of Virginia
★★★ U

Historical epic 1940 · US · BW · 110min

The clash between the forces of conservatism and the emergence of the American democratic spirit form the stuff of this historical epic. Set before and during the American Revolution, it also encompasses a love story between a progressive Virginian (Cary Grant) and the daughter (Martha Scott) of a wealthy reactionary (Cedric Hardwicke). Yet, for all its incident, political ideas and careful attention to period, it's less than compelling, and the debonair Grant is patently miscast. RK

Cary Grant *Matt Howard* • Martha Scott *Jane Peyton Howard* • Sir Cedric Hardwicke [Cedric Hardwicke] *Fleetwood Peyton* • Alan Marshal *Roger Peyton* • Richard Carlson *Thomas Jefferson* • Paul Kelly (1) *Captain Jabez Allen* • Irving Bacon *Tom Norton* • Elisabeth Risdon *Aunt Clarissa* • Alan Ladd *Neighbour* ■ *Dir* Frank Lloyd • *Scr* Sidney Buchman, from the novel *The Tree of Liberty* by Elizabeth Page

Howl ★★★ 15
Drama based on a true story
2010 · US · Colour and BW · 80min

This flawed but nevertheless interesting drama charts the early years of Beat poet Allen Ginsberg (played here by James Franco) and how his work *Howl* became the focus of an obscenity trial in 1957. Writer/directors Rob Epstein and Jeffrey Friedman interweave a sober reconstruction of the courtroom case – David Strathairn is excellent as the uptight, baffled prosecuting attorney – with a re-creation of an interview Ginsberg gave at the time, as well as a reading of the poem accompanied by animations by Eric Drooker. Franco is outstanding as the gay, insecure poet, but Drooker's sometimes laughably literal work often threatens to undercut his performance. AS Swearing, sexual references. *DVD* *SL*

James Franco *Allen Ginsberg* • David Strathairn *Ralph McIntosh* • Jon Hamm *Jake Ehrlich* • Bob Balaban *Judge Clayton Horn* • Jeff Daniels *Professor David Kirk* • Mary-Louise Parker *Gail Potter* • Treat Williams *Mark Schorer* • Alessandro Nivola *Luther Nichols* ■ *Dir/Scr* Rob Epstein, Jeffrey Friedman

Howl ★★★ 18
Horror
2015 · UK · Colour · 88min

It's "werewolves on a train" in ace make-up/effects-man-turned-director Paul Hyett's second film after *The Seasoning House*. A late night locomotive screeches to a halt in a dark forest after hitting something on the tracks. When the driver doesn't return from investigating, a disparate group work together to survive being picked off by a feral enemy. While nowhere near as brutally provocative as his first shocker, there's enough here to enjoy in the stylish set pieces even for those well-acquainted with the genre. AJ Strong violence

Ed Speleers *Joe* • Shauna Macdonald *Kate* • Rosie Day *Nina* • Sam Gittins *Billy* • Calvin Dean *Paul* ■ *Dir* Paul Hyett • *Scr* Mark Huckerby, Nick Ostler

The Howling ★★★★ 18
Horror comedy
1981 · US · Colour · 86min

Co-writer John Sayles and director Joe Dante have huge fun turning werewolf clichés on their head in this rare beast – a horror film that gore fans and film buffs can enjoy. For the former, there is Rob Bottins's amazing make-up and a witty plot in which a sceptical TV journalist (Dee Wallace) uncovers a werewolf colony. For the latter, Dante touches his cap to monster greats of the past by naming key characters after cult horror directors. JF Violence, swearing, nudity. *DVD* *CS*

Dee Wallace [Dee Wallace Stone] *Karen White* • Patrick Macnee *Dr George Waggner* • Dennis Dugan *Chris* • Christopher Stone *R William "Bill" Neill* • Belinda Balaski *Terry Fisher* • Kevin McCarthy *Fred Francis* • John Carradine *Erle Kenton* • Slim Pickens *Sam Newfield* • Elisabeth Brooks *Marsha* • Robert Picardo *Eddie* • Dick Miller *Walter Paisley* ■ *Dir* Joe Dante • *Scr* John Sayles, Terence H Winkless, from the novel by Gary Brandner

Howling II: Your Sister Is a Werewolf ★★ 18
Horror comedy
1984 · US · Colour · 86min

After the sly wit of Joe Dante's 1981 original, director Philippe Mora opts for a

very camp spin for the first of a number of sequels. The setting is Transylvania, with Reb Brown tracking down the werewolf queen (Sybil Danning). Even the presence of Christopher Lee fails to impress, though the mix of gore and clumsy parody exerts a bizarre charm. JF

Christopher Lee *Stefan Crosscoe* • Annie McEnroe *Jenny Templeton* • Reb Brown *Ben White* • Sybil Danning *Stirba* • Marsha A Hunt *Mariana* • Judd Omen *Vlad* ■ *Dir* Philippe Mora • *Scr* Robert Sarno, Gary Brandner, from the novel *The Howling* by Gary Brandner

Howl's Moving Castle ★★★ U
Animated fantasy
2004 · Jpn · Colour · 114min

The incredible imagination of *Spirited Away* director Hayao Miyazaki runs wild once again in a delightful fantasy set in a magical, war-torn land reminiscent of 19th-century Europe. This English-language version is beautifully voiced, with Christian Bale's seductive tones bringing vivid life to the vain young wizard Howl, whose romancing of 18-year-old milliner Sophie (Emily Mortimer) results in her transformation into a pensioner by a jealous witch (Lauren Bacall). The events that follow are both visually ingenious and dazzling, but the meticulous eye candy comes at the expense of plot development. SF In English, Japanese. *DVD* *SL*

Christian Bale *Howl* • Lauren Bacall *Witch of the Waste* • Emily Mortimer *Young Sophie* • Blythe Danner *Madam Suliman* • Jean Simmons *Old Sophie* • Billy Crystal *Calcifer* • Josh Hutcherson *Markl* ■ *Dir* Hayao Miyazaki • *Scr* Hayao Miyazaki, from the novel by Diana Wynne Jones

Huck and the King of Hearts ★★★
Adventure
1993 · US · Colour · 103min

In this appealing, very loose modern adaptation of the classic Mark Twain story, a cardsharp (Graham Greene) and his young pal Huck (Chauncey Leopardi) travel across America searching for Huck's grandfather. Director Michael Keusch's film gains much from its likeable cast. JB

Chauncey Leopardi *Billy "Huck" Thomas* • Graham Greene (2) *Jim* • Dee Wallace Stone *Aunt Darlene* • Joe Piscopo *Max* • Gretchen Becker *Lisa* • Ed Trotta *Ed* • John Astin *Zach* ■ *Dir* Michael Keusch • *Scr* Christopher Sturgeon, from the novel *The Adventures of Huckleberry Finn* by Mark Twain

Huckleberry Finn ★★
Adventure drama
1931 · US · BW · 79min

Jackie Coogan became a hugely popular child star after appearing with Chaplin in *The Kid* and Paramount had initial success in re-launching him in the early sound period in the title role of *Tom Sawyer* in 1930. Here he plays Tom again with Junior Durkin as Huck; together the duo save two young girls from falling into the hands of a pair of rascals. This version has some antiquated charm. AE

Jackie Coogan *Tom Sawyer* • Mitzi Green *Becky Thatcher* • Junior Durkin *Huckleberry Finn* • Jackie Searl [Jackie Searle] *Sid Sawyer* • Clarence Muse *Jim* • Clara Blandick *Aunt Polly* ■ *Dir* Norman Taurog • *Scr* Grover Jones, William Slavens McNutt, from the novel *The Adventures of Huckleberry Finn* by Mark Twain

Huckleberry Finn ★★★ U
Musical period adventure
1974 · US · Colour · 109min

Reader's Digest flirted with film production in the 1970s, and to its credit produced two very watchable Mark Twain movies, of which this is the second, continuing Jeff East's characterisation of Huckleberry Finn from 1973's *Tom Sawyer*. Both movies were shot on location and handsomely filmed in Panavision, and both had totally forgettable scores by the Sherman brothers, then coming off a roll with *Mary Poppins* and *The Jungle Book*. There's some clever casting in this one, but political correctness dilutes Paul Winfield's all-too-noble Jim. Veteran J Lee Thompson directs adequately. TS

Jeff East *Huckleberry Finn* • Paul Winfield *Jim* • Harvey Korman *King* • David Wayne *Duke* • Arthur O'Connell *Colonel Grangerford* • Gary Merrill *Pap* • Natalie Trundy *Mrs Loftus* • Lucille Benson *Widder Douglas* ■ *Dir* J Lee Thompson • *Scr* Robert B Sherman, Richard M Sherman, from the novel *The Adventures of Huckleberry Finn* by Mark Twain

The Hucksters ★★★ U
Drama
1947 · US · BW · 110min

To launch Deborah Kerr's Hollywood career, MGM surrounded her with a mighty cast of stars. The story, about the sharp practices of Madison Avenue advertising types, has dated badly; MGM wasn't in the business of criticising big business, even something as symbolically trivial as Sydney Greenstreet's bathroom soap empire. Clark Gable joins the firm and gets the job of persuading 25 society women to endorse the soap. As a star package it has still has bags of glamour and some sparkling wit. AT

Clark Gable *Victor Norman* • Deborah Kerr *Kay Dorrance* • Sydney Greenstreet *Evan Llewellyn Evans* • Adolphe Menjou *Mr Kimberly* • Ava Gardner *Jean Ogilvie* • Keenan Wynn *Buddy Hare* • Edward Arnold *Dave Lash* • Aubrey Mather *Valet* ■ *Dir* Jack Conway • *Scr* Luther Davis, Edward Chodorov, George Wells, from the novel by Frederic Wakeman

Hud ★★★★★ 12
Drama
1963 · US · BW · 107min

Paul Newman gives his finest screen performance as the heedless, sexually aggressive rancher's son whose strained relationship with his idealistic father (Melvyn Douglas) comes to a head when disease infects their cattle. Echoing his role in *Shane*, Brandon de Wilde looks on with a mixture of horror and envy as his uncle trashes towns and relationships. The film was nominated for seven Oscars, winning three – best supporting actor for Douglas, best actress for Patricia Neal (as the housekeeper) and best black-and-white cinematography for James Wong Howe. Despite his charismatic portrayal, Newman lost out to Sidney Poitier in *Lilies of the Field*. AT *DVD*

Paul Newman *Hud Bannon* • Patricia Neal *Alma Brown* • Melvyn Douglas *Homer Bannon* • Brandon de Wilde *Lon Bannon* • John Ashley *Hermy* • Whit Bissell *Burris* • Crahan Denton *Jesse* • Val Avery *Jose* ■ *Dir* Martin Ritt • *Scr* Irving Ravetch, Harriet Frank Jr, from the novel *Horseman, Pass By* by Larry McMurtry • *Music* Elmer Bernstein

Hudson Hawk ★★ 15
Action comedy
1991 · US · Colour · 95min

Bruce Willis helped write the story and the title song of this so-called action comedy, in which he stars as a retired cat burglar who is persuaded to return to his criminal activities. There are some good action scenes, especially during the heist of a Leonardo da Vinci artefact, but Willis is not a strong enough screen presence to rise above the poor material. Meanwhile, Richard E Grant and Sandra Bernhard are awful as the villains. TH Swearing, violence. *DVD*

Bruce Willis *Hudson Hawk* • Danny Aiello *Tommy Five-Tone* • Andie MacDowell *Anna Baragli* • James Coburn *George Kaplan* • Richard E Grant *Darwin Mayflower* • Sandra Bernhard *Minerva Mayflower* • David Caruso *Kit Kat* ■ *Dir* Michael Lehmann • *Scr* Steven E de Souza, Daniel Waters, from a story by Bruce Willis, Robert Kraft

Hudson's Bay ★★★
Historical adventure
1940 · US · BW · 95min

This rather spurious historical romance ended up as one of 20th Century-Fox's no-expense-spared backlot historical pageants. It features Fox's lovely contract star Gene Tierney and, on loan from Warner Bros, the distinguished and fashionable Paul Muni; they are surrounded by Fox's 1940s repertory company including Laird Cregar and Vincent Price. The trouble is that director Irving Pichel fails to bring some sense of scale to this saga of the founder of the Hudson's Bay Trading Company TS

Paul Muni *Pierre Radisson* • Gene Tierney *Barbara Hall* • Laird Cregar *Gooseberry* • John Sutton *Lord Edward Crew* • Virginia Field *Nell Gwynn* • Vincent Price *King Charles II* ■ *Dir* Irving Pichel • *Scr* Lamar Trotti

The Hudsucker Proxy ★★★★ PG
Comedy drama
1994 · US · Colour · 106min

This is a throwback to the good old days of the screwball comedy, but when Joel and Ethan Coen pay tribute to a period or a style of film-making, they never slavishly re-create. Here they marry the Art Deco designs of the 1930s with the go-get-'em attitudes of the 1950s to fashion a parable that might just have something to say about America in the 1990s. This is a classic "little man against the system" scenario, with Tim Robbins wonderfully ingenuous as the nobody who hits gold when he invents the Hula-Hoop. Paul Newman mistakes excessive for comic, unlike Jennifer Jason Leigh, whose impression of Rosalind Russell doing a Katharine Hepburn is a hoot. DP *DVD*

Tim Robbins *Norville Barnes* • Jennifer Jason Leigh *Amy Archer* • Paul Newman *Sidney J Mussburger* • Charles Durning *Waring Hudsucker* • John Mahoney *Chief* • Jim True *Buzz* • William Cobbs [Bill Cobbs] *Moses* • Bruce Campbell *Smitty* ■ *Dir* Joel Coen • *Scr* Joel Coen, Ethan Coen, Sam Raimi

Hue and Cry ★★★★ U
Comedy
1947 · UK · BW · 78min

After this early effort, director Charles Crichton went on to greater acclaim for making *The Lavender Hill Mob* and, more recently, *A Fish Called Wanda*. However there's much to enjoy in this slight but entertaining Ealing comedy caper – the first of the genre from the famous studio – as Alastair Sim and a gang of East End urchins set out to thwart some fiendish crooks. A fun frolic from a more innocent age, with some evocative location footage of postwar London. PF *DVD* *SL*

Alastair Sim *Felix H Wilkinson* • Harry Fowler *Joe Kirby* • Valerie White *Rhona* • Jack Warner *Jim Nightingale* • Frederick Piper *Mr Kirby* • Heather Delaine *Mrs Kirby* • Douglas Barr (1) *Alec* ■ *Dir* Charles Crichton • *Scr* TEB Clarke

Huge ★★ 15
Comedy drama
2009 · UK · Colour · 78min

Ben Miller's directorial debut boldly casts straight actors Noel Clarke and Johnny Harris as comics Clark and Warren, who hope to become the new Morecambe and Wise. But the almost complete absence of wit from the screenplay ensures that this study of aspiration, desperation and delusion is as unendurable as one of Warren and Clark's routines. Astute cameos abound, and Clarke and Harris work hard, but the characterisation is thin and the finale resoundingly anti-climactic. DP

Noel Clarke *Clark* • Johnny Harris *Warren* • Thandie Newton *Kris* • Michelle Ryan *Cindy* • Russell Tovey *Carl* • Tamsin Egerton *Clarisse* • Ralph Brown *Neil* • Simon Day *Noel* ■ *Dir* Ben Miller • *Scr* Simon Godley, Ben Miller, from the play by Jez Butterworth, Godley, Miller

The Huggetts Abroad ★ U
Comedy
1949 · UK · BW · 83min

Having first encountered the Huggetts in *Holiday Camp*, it's somewhat apt that we should bid them farewell at the end of another sojourn. However, it's with relief not regret that we part company with Jack Warner, Kathleen Harrison et al, as this brief series that began in 1948 with *Here Come the Huggetts* had clearly run out of steam. Warner chucks his job and hauls the family off to South Africa. Unfunny and very dull. DP *DVD*

Jack Warner *Joe Huggett* • Kathleen Harrison *Ethel Huggett* • Susan Shaw *Susan Huggett* • Petula Clark *Pet Huggett* • Dinah Sheridan *Jane Huggett* • Hugh McDermott *Bob McCoy* • Jimmy Hanley *Jimmy* ■ *Dir* Ken Annakin • *Scr* Mabel Constanduros, Denis Constanduros, Ted Willis, Gerard Bryant, from characters by Godfrey Winn

Hugo ★★★ U

Period fantasy adventure
2011 · US · Colour · 120min

In Martin Scorsese's adaptation of Brian Selznick's children's book, Asa Butterfield plays 12-year-old orphan Hugo Cabret, who lives within the walls of the Paris railway station in 1931. Chloë Grace Moretz is Isabelle, the girl he befriends in his bid to find bits and bobs for a mechanical man his late father has left him. But it's Isabelle's grandfather Georges Méliès (Ben Kingsley) who takes centre stage as the film mutates, oddly but endearingly, into a tribute to a pioneer of early cinema. It's a subject close to cinephile Scorsese's heart, though it can feel a little indulgent and heavy for kids. But, as a crazy mix of *Cinema Paradiso*, *Cronos* and *David Copperfield*, it's unusually stimulating family fare. DA DVD Blu 3D

Asa Butterfield *Hugo Cabret* • Ben Kingsley *Georges Méliès* • Sacha Baron Cohen *Station Inspector* • Chloë Moretz [Chloë Grace Moretz] *Isabelle* • Ray Winstone *Uncle Claude* • Emily Mortimer *Lisette* • Helen McCrory *Mama Jeanne* • Christopher Lee *Monsieur Labisse* • Jude Law *Hugo's father* ■ *Dir* Martin Scorsese • *Scr* John Logan, from the illustrated children's book *The Invention of Hugo Cabret* by Brian Selznick • *Cinematographer* Robert Richardson • *Music* Howard Shore • *Editor* Thelma Schoonmaker • *Costume Designer* Sandy Powell

Hukkle ★★★ 12

Crime mystery drama
2002 · Hun · Colour · 74min

Gyorgy Palfi's first feature is certainly technically accomplished. A sinister mystery lurks beneath this quirky depiction of the rhythms of rural Hungarian life and Palfi succeeds in luring us into its heart without ever quite revealing the reasons for a sudden spate of deaths. He occasionally succumbs to directorial excess, but the engaging characters and intriguing narrative make this a compelling allegory. DP Hungarian +subtitles. DVD

Jozsef Farkas *Police officer* • Ferenc Nagy *Bee-keeper* • Mihalyne Kiraly *Grandmother* • Edit Nagy *Shepherdess* • Istvan Barath *Pig owner* ■ *Dir/Scr* Gyorgy Palfi

Hulchul ★ PG

Romantic comedy 2004 · Ind · Colour · 116min

Director Priyadarshan here produces a perfect example of Bollywood comedy at its mind-numbing worst. Amrish Puri is the rigidly principled patriarch of one household, who's pitted against the clan of matriarch Lakshmi from a neighbouring village. Akshaye Khanna and Kareena Kapoor play opposing members of each family who cunningly hatch a plan to pretend to fall in love. The cast mugs and grimaces while the juvenile slapstick shows a complete lack of wit or inspiration. OA In Hindi. DVD

Akshaye Khanna *Jai* • Kareena Kapoor *Anjali* • Suniel Shetty [Sunil Shetty] *Veer* • Paresh Rawal *Kishen* • Jackie Shroff *Balram* • Arshad Warsi *Lucky* • Amrish Puri *Angaarchand* • Lakshmi *Lakshmidevi* ■ *Dir* Priyadarshan • *Scr* Neeraj Vora

Hulk ★★★ 12

Science-fiction action drama
2003 · US · Colour · 132min

Ang Lee's curate's egg of a movie is unlikely to satisfy anyone totally. The childhood trauma that feeds Bruce Banner's rage is an oddly grim subplot, while the later action scenes feel tacked on, despite their technical virtuosity. Matters aren't helped by Eric Bana's detached performance as Banner, but Nick Nolte injects a soupçon of fun as the older incarnation of his insane dad and Lee's use of editing – including split screens to suggest comic-strip frames – is quite innovative. AS Violence. DVD Blu

Eric Bana *Bruce Banner/Dr Bruce Krenzler/The Hulk* • Jennifer Connelly *Betty Ross* • Sam Elliott *General Ross* • Josh Lucas *Glenn Talbot* • Nick Nolte *David Banner* • Paul Kersey *Young David Banner* • Cara Buono *Edith Banner* • Stan Lee *Security guard* • Lou Ferrigno *Security guard* ■ *Dir* Ang Lee • *Scr* John Turman, Michael France,

James Schamus, from a story by James Schamus, from the character created by Stan Lee, Jack Kirby

Hullabaloo over Georgie and Bonnie's Pictures ★★★ PG

Comedy 1979 · UK/Ind · Colour · 33min

This Merchant Ivory production is an arch comedy of manners. Originally commissioned for television, it was shot without a completed script and occasionally loses its way. Centred around princes, palaces, *objets d'art* and those who would exploit them, this minor entry in an illustrious canon is as delicate as the miniatures that dealers Larry Pine and Peggy Ashcroft try to prize away from maharajah Victor Bannerjee and his sister, Aparna Sen. Playful, but still a worthwhile discussion of the value of art. DP

Peggy Ashcroft *Lady Gwyneth* • Victor Bannerjee [Victor Banerjee] *Georgie* • Aparna Sen *Bonnie* • Saeed Jaffrey *Sri Narain* • Jane Booker *Lynn* ■ *Dir* James Ivory • *Scr* Ruth Prawer Jhabvala

Hum ★★★ PG

Action drama 1991 · Ind · Colour · 176min

Although age was catching up with him, Amitabh Bachchan confirmed his position as a Bollywood superstar with this action drama. In the opening section, Bachchan's small-time racketeer finds himself caught up in a docklands gang war, while in the second (set several years later) he alternates between the battle against a terrorist organisation and Kimi Katkar's bid for stardom. The abrasive and suggestive nature of this film is typified by the blatant symbolism of the bar-room dance number. DP Hindi +subtitles.

Amitabh Bachchan *Tiger* • Romesh Sharma *Gonsalves* • Danny Denzongpa *Bakhtawar* • Anupam Kher *Inspector Giridhar* • Kimi Katkar ■ *Dir* Mukul S Anand • *Scr* Ravi Kapoor, Mohan Kaul

Hum Dil De Chuke Sanam ★★★ PG

Romantic musical comedy
1999 · Ind · Colour · 180min

Aishwarya Rai stars as the headstrong daughter of palace singer Vikram Gokhale, who is married off to lawyer Ajay Devgan despite her love for hedonistic musician Salman Khan. However, when her husband discovers the truth, he heads for Italy to deliver his bride to his rival. Packed with colourful ceremonials and shuttling between Europe and Rajasthan, this escapist masala is greatly enhanced by glossy photography and lively songs. DP Hindi +subtitles.

Ajay Devgan *Vanraj* • Salman Khan *Sameer* • Aishwarya Rai *Nandini* • Vikram Gokhale *Pundit Darbar* ■ *Dir* Sanjay Leela Bhansali • *Scr* Sanjay Leela Bhansali, Kenneth Phillips, from a story by Pratap Karwat

Hum Tum ★★★ PG

Romantic comedy 2004 · Ind · Colour · 142min

The Bollywood romantic comedy has never been more popular, but Kunal Kohli's globetrotting saga takes its inspiration from *When Harry Met Sally…*. Cartoonist Saif Ali Khan and Rani Mukherjee spend a decade avoiding the obvious realisation that they're made for each other. The initial encounter in Amsterdam is probably the liveliest, as subsequently Kohli struggles to find convincing reasons for keeping the couple apart. The leads are well matched, but the storyline is a tad too familiar. DP Hindi, English +subtitles. DVD

Saif Ali Khan *Karan Kapoor* • Rani Mukherjee [Rani Mukherji] *Rhea Prakash* • Rishi Kapoor • Rati Agnihotri • Kiron Kher • Jimmy Shergill • Abhishek Bachchan ■ *Dir* Kunal Kohli • *Scr* Kunal Kohli, Siddharth Raj Anand

Hum Tumhare Hain Sanam ★★★ U

Musical romantic drama
2000 · Ind · Colour · 174min

Director KS Adiyaman's remake of his own Tamil hit was finally released after a

protracted shoot spanning six years. What emerges is a typically convoluted story in which ageing Alok Nath is left to rear the orphaned children of his best friend as well as his own grandchildren. In time, his favourite grandchild Madhuri Dixit marries her devoted "stepbrother" Shah Rukh Khan. However, their happiness is short-lived. There's little in the way of subtle shading here but, with its impressive all-star cast and songs from some of India's leading composers, this is enjoyable. DP In Hindi. DVD

Shah Rukh Khan *Gopal* • Salman Khan *Suraj* • Madhuri Dixit *Radha* • Atul Agnihotri *Prashant* • Alok Nath *Devnarayan* ■ *Dir/Scr* KS Adiyaman

Human Capital ★★★★ 15

Drama 2013 · It/Fr · Colour · 110min

Italian director Paolo Virzi turns his ire on his country's elite here, relocating Stephen Amidon's novel from Connecticut to the affluent northern town of Brianza. The story's different perspectives on an accident involving a waiter cycling home after a school function offers a critique of class, hypocrisy, greed and the decline of the traditional Italian family. Matilde Gioli and Guglielmo Pinelli play the teenagers whose fathers, Fabrizio Bentivoglio and Fabrizio Gifuni, neglect their wives (Valeria Golino and Valeria Bruni Tedeschi), and what gives the unforgiving saga its edge is the low value the men set on the lives of those "beneath". Superbly played, designed and photographed, this is a worthy companion to Paolo Sorrentino's *The Great Beauty*. DP Italian +subtitles. Swearing, sex scenes, nudity.

Valeria Bruni Tedeschi [Valéria Bruni-Tedeschi] *Carla Bernaschi* • Fabrizio Bentivoglio *Dino Ossola* • Valeria Golino *Roberta Ossola* • Fabrizio Gifuni *Giovanni Bernaschi* • Luigi Lo Cascio *Donato* • Matilde Gioli *Serena Ossola* ■ *Dir* Paolo Virzi • *Scr* Francesco Bruni, Francesco Piccolo, Paolo Virzi, from Stephen Amidon's novel

Human Cargo ★★

Romantic drama 1936 · US · BW · 87min

This feeble romantic drama has Brian Donlevy and Claire Trevor as rival newshounds trying to unmask a gang smuggling aliens (the human variety) into the USA. Made by Fox, it lacks the tabloid, crusading spirit of the Warner Bros equivalents – *Five Star Final*, for instance – while the class difference between the two stars seems derived from *It Happened One Night*. Rita Hayworth, billed as Rita Cansino, makes an early appearance. AT

Claire Trevor *Bonnie Brewster* • Brian Donlevy *Packy Campbell* • Alan Dinehart *Lionel Crocker* • Ralph Morgan *District Attorney Cary* • Helen Troy *Susie* • Rita Cansino [Rita Hayworth] *Carmen Zoro* ■ *Dir* Allan Dwan • *Scr* Jefferson Parker, Doris Malloy, from the novel *I Will Be Faithful* by Kathleen Shepard

The Human Centipede (First Sequence) ★★★ 18

Horror thriller 2009 · Neth · Colour · 91min

In this controversial horror, a brilliant German surgeon (played by Dieter Laser) has the perverse dream of connecting live bodies via their gastric systems to form a "human centipede". Drugging and abducting three tourists (two American girls and one Japanese man), he sets to work in his basement operating theatre. Despite its stomach-churning premise, the film is relatively light on gore or gruesome scenes, and director Tom Six shows a deft hand when cranking up the suspense. TeS English, German, Japanese +subtitles. DVD Blu

Dieter Laser *Doctor Josef Heiter* • Ashley C Williams *Lindsay* • Ashlynn Yennie *Jenny* • Akihiro Kitamura *Katsuro* ■ *Dir/Scr* Tom Six

The Human Centipede II (Full Sequence) ★★★ 18

Horror
2011 · Neth/UK/US · BW and Colour · 84min

Director Tom Six's even more controversial sequel is everything the original wasn't – dark, graphic, gory – as it shifts effortlessly between a twisted study in obsessive

psychosis and barbed sardonic satire. Laurence R Harvey gives an astonishingly repulsive performance as a mentally disturbed security guard who becomes fixated by a DVD of the first film and decides to craft his own 12-segment creature. It's shot mostly in unsettling black-and-white and it's often unpleasant – the most extreme scenes have been extensively cut by the BBFC who initially banned this movie outright. Those of a sensitive nature should avoid. AJ Violence. DVD Blu

Laurence R Harvey *Martin* • Ashlynn Yennie *Miss Yennie, human centipede 1* • Katherine Templar *Rachel* • Maddi Black *Candy, human centipede 2* ■ *Dir/Scr* Tom Six

The Human Centipede III (Final Sequence) ★★★ 18

Horror 2015 · US · Colour · 102min

No target is safe and no shock too extreme in the mind-boggling climax to director Tom Six's contentious trilogy. At the desert George HW Bush penitentiary, a sadistic head warden (Dieter Laser, star of the original horror) and his meek accountant (Laurence R Harvey from the second part) create a human centipede of prisoners to cut costs and overcrowding. Pushing the disgust factor to unprecedented heights, it's either absolutely appalling or hilariously amusing, depending on your reaction to the series in general. AJ Violence, swearing, sex scenes. DVD Blu

Dieter Laser *Bill Boss* • Laurence R Harvey *Dwight Butler* • Bree Olsen *Daisy* • Eric Roberts *Governor Hughes* • Tommy "Tiny"/ Lister Jr [Tom "Tiny"/ Lister Jr] *Inmate 178* • Robert LaSardo *Inmate 297* • Tom Six ■ *Dir/Scr* Tom Six

The Human Comedy ★★★★ U

Second World War drama
1943 · US · BW · 116min

This beautifully realised adaptation of William Saroyan's novel looks at life in an American small town during the Second World War. Mickey Rooney gives a moving performance as the high school student turned telegraph boy around whom the everyday events revolve. Director Clarence Brown shamelessly pulls the heartstrings by leaning heavily on nostalgia, religion, family responsibility and patriotism, as he fills the screen with instantly recognisable characters everyone has met at one time or another. An emotionally engaging masterpiece of admirable simplicity. AJ

Mickey Rooney *Homer Macauley* • Frank Morgan *Willie Grogan* • James Craig *Tom Spangler* • Marsha Hunt *Diana Steed* • Fay Bainter *Mrs Macauley* • Ray Collins *Mr Macauley* • Van Johnson *Marcus Macauley* • Donna Reed *Bess Macauley* ■ *Dir* Clarence Brown • *Scr* Howard Estabrook, from the novel by William Saroyan

The Human Condition ★★★★★

Epic war drama 1958 · Jpn · BW · 579min

Adapted from Gomikawa's six-part novel, Masaki Kobayashi's epic masterpiece reflects his own experiences as a pacifist in Japan during the Second World War. Four years in the making and running for a mammoth 579 minutes, Masaki Kobayashi's heart-rending anti-war trilogy was a controversial project; the Shochiku studio was reluctant to bankroll it, but was rewarded with a work of unparalleled power and poignancy. Sent to supervise a Manchurian copper mine, Tatsuya Nakadai attempts to curb brutal overseer Eitaro Ozawa's maltreatment of the enslaved Chinese workforce, only to find himself dispatched to the front without a chance to take leave of his wife, Michiyo Aratama. This harrowing exploration of the savage horror of combat is ambitious, shocking and unforgettable. DP Japanese +subtitles. DVD Blu

Tatsuya Nakadai *Kaji* • Michiyo Aratama *Michiko* • Ineko Arima *Yang Chun Lan* • So Yamamura *Okishima* • Akira Ishihama *Chen* • Shinji Nambara *Kao* • Eitaro Ozawa *Okazaki* ■ *Dir* Masaki

Kobayashi • *Scr* Zenzo Matsuyama, Masaki Kobayashi, from the novel *Ningen No Joken* by Jumpei Gomikawa

Human Desire ★★★
Film noir 1954 · US · BW · 90min

Emile Zola's *La Bête Humaine*, about the murderous triangle that engulfs a train driver, a stationmaster and his wife, seems tailor-made for the screen. The powerful themes and images of Zola's bleak novel elude Fritz Lang in this *film noir* that was prevented from exploring the book's seamier side by the strictures of the Hollywood Production Code. Lang's preoccupation with the sights and symbolism of the railway yards too often leaves the characters stranded in the sidings. DP

Glenn Ford *Jeff Warren* • Gloria Grahame *Vicki Buckley* • Broderick Crawford *Carl Buckley* • Edgar Buchanan *Alec Simmons* • Kathleen Case *Ellen Simmons* • Peggy Maley *Jean* ■ *Dir* Fritz Lang • *Scr* Alfred Hayes, from the novel *La Bête Humaine* by Emile Zola • *Cinematographer* Burnett Guffey

The Human Factor ★★ 18
Action thriller 1975 · UK · Colour · 92min

This action film aspires to the status of political conspiracy thriller, but it's really little more than *Death Wish* with a CIA subplot. George Kennedy is the Nato bigwig based in Naples whose family is wiped out by terrorists. Kennedy plays war games for a living, so he decides to put his theories into practice and hit the vengeance trail – with messy consequences. AT *DVD*

George Kennedy *John Kinsdale* • John Mills *Mike McAllister* • Raf Vallone *Dr Lupo* • Arthur Franz *General Fuller* • Rita Tushingham *Janice Meredith* • Barry Sullivan *Edmonds* • Haydée Politoff *Pidgeon* ■ *Dir* Edward Dmytryk • *Scr* Tom Hunter, Peter Powell

The Human Factor ★★★ 15
Spy drama 1979 · UK/US · Colour · 110min

Faithfully adapted by Tom Stoppard, this espionage thriller has all the complexities of characterisation and plot one expects from a Graham Greene "entertainment". But Otto Preminger (who completed the picture with his own cash after the backers withdrew) never really comes to terms with the notions of honour, isolation and Englishness that underpin the novel. The cast sustains the suspense, with Nicol Williamson admirable as the double agent whose favour for an old friend has dire consequences. DP

Nicol Williamson *Maurice Castle* • Richard Attenborough *Colonel John Daintry* • Joop Doderer *Cornelius Muller* • John Gielgud *Brigadier Tomlinson* • Derek Jacobi *Arthur Davis* • Robert Morley *Doctor Percival* • Ann Todd *Castle's mother* • Iman *Sarah* ■ *Dir* Otto Preminger • *Scr* Tom Stoppard, from the novel by Graham Greene

Human Highway ★ 12
Fantasy musical comedy
1982 · US · Colour · 83min

What was hippy icon Neil Young thinking about when he dreamt up this abysmal anti-nuke comedy about a pair of gas station attendants (Young and Russ Tamblyn) working in the shadow of a nuclear power plant. This embarrassment includes a climactic musical number where the cast sing as they ascend toward heaven. RS

Neil Young (1) *Lionel Switch* • Russ Tamblyn *Fred Kelly* • Dean Stockwell *Otto Quartz* • Dennis Hopper *Cracker* • Charlotte Stewart *Charlotte Goodnight* • Sally Kirkland *Katherine* • Geraldine Baron *Irene* ■ *Dir* Bernard Shakey [Neil Young (1)], Dean Stockwell • *Scr* Bernard Shakey [Neil Young], Jeanne Fields, Dean Stockwell, Russ Tamblyn, James Beshears

Human Nature ★★★ 15
Comedy drama 2001 · Fr/US · Colour · 91min

Charlie Kaufman can't quite recapture the eccentric glories of *Being John Malkovich* with this gleefully lewd screenplay. However, plucky performances from Patricia Arquette and Rhys Ifans (involving much nudity) keep promo wizard Michel Gondry's makeshift feature debut from

collapsing under the weight of its percipient, but largely undeveloped ideas. The narrative involving Arquette, the lustily primitive Ifans and dullard scientist Tim Robbins exhausts its supply of laughs and logic and ends up wallowing in crass slapstick and smut. DP *DVD*

Tim Robbins *Nathan Bronfman* • Patricia Arquette *Lila Jute* • Rhys Ifans *Puff* • Miranda Otto *Gabrielle* • Robert Forster *Nathan's father* • Mary Kay Place *Nathan's mother* • Rosie Perez *Louise* ■ *Dir* Michel Gondry • *Scr* Charlie Kaufman

Human Resources ★★★ 15
Drama 1999 · Fr/UK · Colour · 99min

Class and family loyalties clash with so-called social advancement and economic expediency in Laurent Cantet's industrial drama. Cantet describes the relationship between graduate trainee Jalil Lespert (the cast's sole professional) and, playing Lespert's father, factory machinist Jean-Claude Vallod, whose uncomplaining sacrifices have helped his son progress. Yet the handling of the strike that follows Lespert's naive involvement in the debate over a shorter working week is less assured. DP French +subtitles. *DVD*

Jalil Lespert *Franck* • Jean-Claude Vallod *Father* • Chantal Barré *Mother* • Véronique de Pandelaère *Sylvie* • Michel Begnez *Olivier* • Lucien Longueville *Boss* ■ *Dir* Laurent Cantet • *Scr* Laurent Cantet, Gilles Marchand

The Human Stain ★★ 18
Romantic drama 2003 · US · Colour · 101min

Robert Benton struggles to retain the shocking power of author Philip Roth's angry meditation on race, class, sex and political correctness. Anthony Hopkins plays a university professor driven from his job after supposedly making a racial slur. Hopkins then enlists the help of a local author (Gary Sinise) to tell his story and begins a Viagra-fuelled affair with janitor Nicole Kidman. This never convinces and the opening flash-forward dissipates any suspense. AJ Swearing. *DVD*

Anthony Hopkins *Coleman Silk* • Nicole Kidman *Faunia Farley* • Ed Harris *Lester Farley* • Gary Sinise *Nathan Zuckerman* • Wentworth Miller *Young Coleman Silk* • Jacinda Barrett *Steena Paulsson* • Harry Lennix *Mr Silk* • Clark Gregg *Nelson Primus* ■ *Dir* Robert Benton • *Scr* Nicholas Meyer, from the novel by Philip Roth

Human Traffic ★★★ 18
Comedy drama 1999 · UK/Ire · Colour · 95min

Director Justin Kerrigan's debut movie is a valiant attempt to put across the atmosphere of Britain's club scene. It follows the fortunes of five friends who go out on a lost, drug- and drink-fuelled weekend in the dance halls of Cardiff. John Simm can't get it together with girls and confides in former Lorraine Pilkington as their night out turns into two days of frenzied rave-up. *Trainspotting* it isn't, but the spirited acting from the talented youngsters and the inspired visuals come out of the screen like a chemical rush. TH Swearing, drug abuse. *DVD*

John Simm *Jip* • Lorraine Pilkington *Lulu* • Shaun Parkes *Koop* • Danny Dyer *Moff* • Nicola Reynolds *Nina* • Dean Davies *Lee* • Jan Anderson *Karen Benson* • Jo Brand *Mrs Reality* • Howard Marks ■ *Dir/Scr* Justin Kerrigan • *Cinematographer* Dave Bennett

L'Humanité ★★★ 18
Crime drama 1999 · Fr · Colour · 141min

Owing to its frustrating lack of incident and pedestrian pacing, Bruno Dumont's film found little favour at Cannes, even though non-professionals Emmanuel Schotté and Severine Caneele took the main acting awards. Yet, this drawn-out investigation into the rape and murder of an 11-year-old girl exerts a macabre fascination, not least because of Schotté's eccentric turn as the thin-skinned cop whose methods are definitely unconventional. Dumont makes effective use of the Pas de Calais's soul-destroying landscape and draws a vigorously earthy performance from Caneele. DP French +subtitles.

Emmanuel Schotté *Pharaon de Winter* • Severine Caneele *Domino* • Philippe Tullier *Joseph* • Ghislain Ghesquière *Police chief* ■ *Dir/Scr* Bruno Dumont

Humanity and Paper Balloons ★★★★ PG
Period drama 1937 · Jpn · BW · 82min

Set in the run-down district of Tokyo in the 18th-century Tokugawa era, the story centres on the bungled kidnap attempt of an impoverished ronin and a desperate barber. Questioning the validity of the samurai's cherished Bushido Code, this poetic, pessimistic portrait of feudal society so enraged the authorities that Yamanaka was dispatched as a punishment to the Manchurian front, where he died at the age of 29. DP Japanese +subtitles. *DVD*

Chojuro Kawarazaki *Matajuro Unno* • Kanemon Nakamura *Shinza* • Shizue Yamagishi *Otaki* • Sukezo Sukedakaya *Landlord* ■ *Dir* Sadao Yamanaka • *Scr* Shintaro Mimura

The Humanoid ★★ PG
Science fiction 1979 · It · Colour · 95min

Mad scientist Arthur Kennedy and his girlfriend Barbara Bach want to conquer the universe but humanoid Richard Kiel prevents him with the help of dwarf guru Marco Yeh and a robot dog. Gore-maestro Aldo Lado's leaden direction fluffs any outrageous pantomime enjoyment that could have been gleaned. Ennio Morricone's avant-garde electronic score is one of the composers most unusual. AJ

Richard Kiel *Golob* • Corinne Cléry *Barbara Gibson* • Leonard Mann *Nick* • Barbara Bach *Lady Agatha* • Arthur Kennedy *Kraspin* • Marco Yeh *Tom-Tom* ■ *Dir* George B Lewis [Aldo Lado] • *Scr* Adriano Bolzoni, Aldo Lado

Hummingbird ★★ 15
Thriller 2013 · UK/US · Colour · 96min

A traumatised ex-soldier fleeing a court martial goes to ground in London in this Jason Statham vehicle from *Eastern Promises* writer Steven Knight, here making his directorial bow. Needless to say, Statham biffs a few villains en route, but he also proves he can convince as a troubled, volatile individual. Evidently, Knight's intention is to weave a modern Dickensian fable of unexpected encounters in the capital's great melting pot, but the story takes too many liberties to satisfy. TJ Violence, swearing, sexual refererences. *DVD* *Blu*

Jason Statham *Joey* • Agata Buzek *Sister Cristina* • Vicky McClure *Dawn* • Benedict Wong *Mr Choy* • David Bradley (3) *Billy* ■ *Dir/Scr* Steven Knight • *Cinematographer* Chris Menges

Humoresque ★★★★ U
Melodrama 1946 · US · BW · 119min

This wonderful Warner Bros tosh contains a fine performance from Joan Crawford as a rich, autocratic patron to intense violinist John Garfield. Based on a Fannie Hurst story, it contains some of the most riotously preposterous dialogue ever: check out Crawford's reply when asked if she likes classical music. Garfield's violin playing is dubbed by the great Isaac Stern, and lovers of melodrama will enjoy this immensely. TS *DVD*

Joan Crawford *Helen Wright* • John Garfield *Paul Boray* • Oscar Levant *Sid Jeffers* • J Carrol Naish *Rudy Boray* • Joan Chandler *Gina* • Tom D'Andrea *Phil Boray* • Peggy Knudsen *Florence* • Ruth Nelson *Esther Boray* ■ *Dir* Jean Negulesco • *Scr* Clifford Odets, Zachary Gold, from a story by Fannie Hurst

Humpday ★★★★ 15
Comedy drama 2009 · US · Colour · 90min

The pitch for writer/director Lynn Shelton's movie would seem to have something to offend everyone. Joshua Leonard plays the freewheeling singleton who turns up at married former college pal Mark Duplass's home. Both men are straight but, after a fair amount of alcohol at an arty party, they decide to try their hand at gay sex, film their efforts and enter the amateur porn contest of the title. This, they explain to

Ben's sceptical wife Anna (Alycia Delmore), will be the ultimate "art project". But Shelton's wry script, together with a troika of perfectly judged performances, transforms a set-up that has the potential to be endlessly distasteful into a deft, warm-hearted study of male friendship. And yes, it's very, very funny. AS Swearing, sex scenes, nudity, drug abuse. *DVD*

Mark Duplass *Ben* • Alycia Delmore *Anna* • Joshua Leonard *Andrew* • Lynn Shelton *Monica* • Trina Willard *Lily* ■ *Dir/Scr* Lynn Shelton

The Hunchback of Notre Dame ★★★★ PG
Classic silent drama 1923 · US · BW · 86min

The first film version of Victor Hugo's classic tale is a masterpiece of the silent era. It showcases magnificent sets and Lon Chaney's definitive take on deformed bell-ringer Quasimodo, with a secret infatuation for gypsy girl Esmeralda. From under a 72-pound rubber hump, and with his face covered by lumps of putty, the grotesque Chaney gives an eloquent performance, full of pathos and yearning, which dominates the screen despite all the other epic trappings. It's for his inimitable genius alone that this sprawling saga is now most fondly remembered. AJ *DVD*

Lon Chaney *Quasimodo* • Ernest Torrence *Clopin* • Patsy Ruth Miller *Esmeralda* • Norman Kerry *Phoebus* • Kate Lester *Mme De Gondelaurier* • Brandon Hurst *Jehan* • Raymond Hatton *Gringoire* • Tully Marshall *Louis XI* • Nigel de Brulier *Dom Claude* ■ *Dir* Wallace Worsley • *Scr* Edward T Lowe Jr, Perley Poore Sheehan, from the novel *Notre Dame de Paris* by Victor Hugo

The Hunchback of Notre Dame ★★★★★ PG
Classic gothic drama 1939 · US · BW · 111min

For many, Charles Laughton is the cinema's definitive Quasimodo, and his poignant performance reveals more subtleties with every viewing. Laughton captures the tragic soul of Notre Dame's famous bell-ringer, and both his make-up and speech patterns are truly convincing. This is a splendidly full-blooded RKO enterprise, with spectacular crowd scenes and superb supporting performances, notably from a sensual Maureen O'Hara as Esmeralda the gypsy and a callow Edmond O'Brien as the youthful romantic lead. Thomas Mitchell – best known as Scarlett O'Hara's father in *Gone with the Wind* – is marvellous, too, as the king of the beggars. Two major future directors had a big hand in this epic – Jacques Tourneur handled the crowds and Robert Wise was the film editor. TS *DVD*

Charles Laughton *Quasimodo* • Maureen O'Hara *Esmeralda* • Cedric Hardwicke *Frollo* • Thomas Mitchell *Clopin* • Edmond O'Brien *Gringoire* • Alan Marshal *Phoebus* • Walter Hampden *Claude* • Harry Davenport *Louis XI* ■ *Dir* William S Dieterle [William Dieterle] • *Scr* Sonya Levien, Bruno Frank, from the novel *Notre Dame de Paris* by Victor Hugo • *Cinematographer* Joseph August [Joseph H August] • *Art Director* Van Nest Polglase

The Hunchback of Notre Dame ★★
Gothic drama 1956 · Fr/It · Colour · 103min

This sadly misbegotten version of the Victor Hugo classic features Anthony Quinn as Quasimodo under a ton of make-up and Gina Lollobrigida, as Esmeralda, struggling beneath the weight of her own inadequacy. At least the Technicolor and widescreen presentation makes the film an interesting visual experience. Veteran Jean Delannoy directs this clumsy adaptation. TH

Gina Lollobrigida *Esmeralda* • Anthony Quinn *Quasimodo* • Jean Danet *Capt Phoebus* • Alain Cuny *Claude Frollo* • Philippe Clay *Clopin Trouillefou* • Danielle Dumont *Fleur de Lys* • Robert Hirsch *Gringoire* • Jean Tissier *Louis XI* ■ *Dir* Jean Delannoy • *Scr* Jacques Prévert, Jean Aurenche, from the novel *Notre Dame de Paris* by Victor Hugo • *Cinematographer* Michel Kelber

The Hunchback of Notre Dame ★★★★ PG
Gothic drama 1982 · US · Colour · 97min

This is one of the best adaptations, made for television, of Victor Hugo's classic tale of the misshapen Parisian bell-ringer and his ill-fated love for the gypsy girl Esmeralda. A brilliant and literate script by John Gay is seized on with relish by Anthony Hopkins and Derek Jacobi (playing Quasimodo and Dom Claude Frollo respectively) who both give their difficult characters a warmth and sympathy beyond their tragic and villainous dimensions. Wonderful period production values are the icing on the cake. AJ

Anthony Hopkins *Quasimodo* · Derek Jacobi *Dom Claude Frollo* · Lesley-Anne Down *Esmeralda* · John Gielgud *Charmolue* · Robert Powell *Phoebus* · David Suchet *Trouillefou* · Tim Pigott-Smith *Philippe* · Nigel Hawthorne *Esmeralda trial magistrate* ■ *Dir* Michael Tuchner · *Scr* John Gay, from the novel *Notre Dame de Paris* by Victor Hugo

The Hunchback of Notre Dame ★★★★ U
Animated musical drama 1996 · US · Colour · 96min

This animated version of the Victor Hugo classic is one of the better of the 1990s Disney movies. As with previous versions, it's the tale of Quasimodo, the deformed keeper of the Notre Dame bells, and his unrequited love for Esmeralda, a gypsy whose actions lead to her persecution. It's darker and more adult than previous Disney animations, but there's still room for three mischievous gargoyles. Tom Hulce, Demi Moore and Kevin Kline provide voices to match the poignancy of the drama. A typical straight-to-video sequel followed. TH

Tom Hulce *Quasimodo* · Demi Moore *Esmeralda* · Kevin Kline *Phoebus* · Jason Alexander *Hugo* · Mary Kay Bergman *Quasimodo's mother* · Corey Burton *Brutish guard* ■ *Dir* Gary Trousdale, Kirk Wise · *Scr* Irene Mecchi, Bob Tzudiker, Noni White, Jonathan Roberts, Will Finn, Tab Murphy, from a story by Tab Murphy, from the novel *Notre Dame de Paris* by Victor Hugo

The Hunchback of Notre Dame ★★ 12
Gothic drama 1997 · US · Colour · 96min

Despite lacklustre make-up, Mandy Patinkin's exceptionally sympathetic portrayal of Quasimodo is the only point of interest in this television version of Victor Hugo's tale. Although director Peter Medak is clearly more interested in bringing the man-behind-the-monster angle to the fore, he sadly understates the main thrust of the story and supplies little of the Parisian spectacle one expects to be part of any redefinition of the oft-told tale. Richard Harris is suitably menacing as Dom Frollo and Salma Hayek acquits herself nicely as the gypsy Esmeralda, but it's essentially flawed. AJ

Mandy Patinkin *Quasimodo* · Salma Hayek *Esmeralda* · Richard Harris *Dom Frollo* · Edward Atterton *Gringoire* · Benedick Blythe *Phoebus* · Nigel Terry *King Louis* · Jim Dale *Clopin* · Trevor Baxter *Chief lawyer* ■ *Dir* Peter Medak · *Scr* John Fasano, from the novel *Notre Dame de Paris* by Victor Hugo

100 Bloody Acres ★★★ 15
Comedy horror 2012 · Aus · Colour · 91min

The gags outdo the gore in this hilarious horror from Down Under. Brothers Cameron and Colin Cairnes make their directing debut with a genre staple about two brothers running a small bone fertiliser business in the outback. Guess what their secret organic ingredient is that has made them the market leader? This simple but highly effective black comedy is finely judged and balanced, while the cameo by *Wolf Creek* star John Jarratt adds extra genre credibility to the often startling and outrageous humour. AJ Violence, swearing.

Damon Herriman *Reg Morgan* · Angus Sampson *Lindsay Morgan* · Anna McGahan *Sophie* · Oliver Ackland *James* · John Jarratt *Burke* ■ *Dir/Scr* Cameron Cairnes, Colin Cairnes

The Hundred-Foot Journey ★★★ PG
Comedy drama 2014 · US · Colour · 117min

Racial divisions are viewed in soft-focus through the lens of Lasse Hallström (*Chocolat*). Helen Mirren holds her nose in the air as the snooty owner of a Michelin-starred restaurant in rural France and is very unhappy to catch a waft of curry when Om Puri and his brood open for business across the road. Puri is always good value, delivering wry laughs as he enters a game of one-upmanship with Mirren. There are few insights into what makes these characters tick and the whole thing lacks depth, but it's made with passion. SP DVD Blu-ray

Helen Mirren *Madame Mallory* · Manish Dayal *Hassan* · Om Puri *Papa* · Amit Shah *Mansur* ■ *Dir* Lasse Hallström · *Scr* Steven Knight, from the novel by Richard C Morais · *Cinematographer* Linus Sandgren

A Hungarian Fairy Tale ★★★ PG
Surreal drama 1986 · Hun · BW · 97min

This is an imaginative allegory based on the myth that a giant bird will descend on Hungary to rescue it in times of trouble. The nation appears here in the person of a small boy who is searching for the father he has never known. Beautifully shot in glowing monochrome, the film balances its precise socio-political commentary with moments of charming fantasy and black humour. DP Hungarian +subtitles.

David Vermes *Andris* · Maria Varga *Maria* · Husak Frantisek *Antal Orban* · Pal Hetenyi *Hungarian voice* · Eszter Csakanyi *Young woman* · Peter Trokan *Teacher* · Szilvia Toth *Tunde* · Judit Pogany *Tunde's mother* · Geza Balkay *Tunde's stepfather* · Gabor Reviczky *Tunde's father* ■ *Dir* Gyula Gazdag · *Scr* Gyula Gazdag, Miklos Gyorffy, Kata Tolmer

Hunger ★★★★
Drama 1966 · Den/Nor/Swe · BW · 110min

Danish director Henning Carlsen has produced a compelling character study that delves into the mind of an artist on the verge of both physical and mental collapse. Per Oscarsson won the best actor prize at Cannes for his agonisingly truthful performance as a writer in turn-of-the-century Norway, whose poverty and creative anxiety are compounded by the callous indifference of an affluent flirt (a vibrantly coquettish Gunnel Lindblom) who humiliates him just as he has reason to hope for better times. DP In Norwegian, Swedish.

Per Oscarsson *The Writer* · Gunnel Lindblom *Ylajali* · Sigrid Horne-Rasmussen *Landlady* · Osvald Helmuth *Pawnbroker* · Henki Kolstad *Editor* ■ *Dir* Henning Carlsen · *Scr* Henning Carlsen, Peter Seeberg, from the novel *Sult* by Knut Hamsun

The Hunger ★★★ 18
Horror 1983 · US · Colour · 92min

Scientist Susan Sarandon replaces ageing David Bowie in vampire Catherine Deneuve's affections in director Tony Scott's visually sumptuous adaptation of Whitley Strieber's enigmatic bestseller. Set against a generally effective backdrop of immortal decadence, embodying several centuries of glossy fashion and culture, this MTV-influenced undead tale emphasises style over content, despite an understated mix of sly humour, sexual mystery and clever make-up illusion. AJ Violence, swearing, nudity. DVD

Catherine Deneuve *Miriam* · David Bowie *John Blaylock* · Susan Sarandon *Sarah Roberts* · Cliff De Young *Tom Haver* · Beth Ehlers *Alice Cavender* · Dan Hedaya *Lieutenant Allegrezza* ■ *Dir* Tony Scott · *Scr* Ivan Davis, Michael Thomas, from the novel by Whitley Strieber

Hunger ★★★★★ 15
Drama 2008 · UK/Ire · Colour · 91min

The debut feature from Turner Prize-winning artist Steve McQueen is a harrowing, unyielding but visually poetic depiction of the protests that took place among republican prisoners in the Maze Prison, Northern Ireland, in 1981. Focusing on the hunger strike of Bobby Sands (Michael Fassbender), this often wordless film creates an unsettling atmosphere through its detailed depiction of the daily routine, be it the disinfecting of a urine-soaked corridor or the systematic beating of inmates by prison staff (led by a stoic Stuart Graham). Eschewing historical exposition beyond occasional snippets, *Hunger* forces the viewer to face up to the hardships of prison life, but avoids the soapbox. The result is a work of art from which it's impossible to avert your eyes. AC DVD

Michael Fassbender *Bobby Sands* · Liam Cunningham *Father Dominic Moran* · Stuart Graham *Raymond Lohan* · Brian Milligan *Davey Gillen* · Liam McMahon *Gerry Campbell* ■ *Dir* Steve McQueen (2) · *Scr* Steve McQueen (2), Enda Walsh

The Hunger Games ★★★★ 12
Futuristic action thriller 2012 · US · Colour · 136min

In this impressive action thriller, a failed revolution has led to the creation of 12 downtrodden districts that serve a wealthy hierarchy. As penance for the uprising, every year two young people from each district fight to the death in a combat spectacle. Although pitted against stronger rivals, resourceful heroine Jennifer Lawrence fans the flames of unrest with her iron will to survive. It's not a new idea, but director Gary Ross (*Pleasantville*) keeps the sci-fi themes relevant, the camerawork involving and the action thrilling, while Lawrence gives a magnetic performance and the dystopian design is inspired. AJ Violence. DVD Blu-ray

Jennifer Lawrence (2) *Katniss Everdeen* · Josh Hutcherson *Peeta Mellark* · Liam Hemsworth *Gale Hawthorne* · Elizabeth Banks (2) *Effie Trinket* · Stanley Tucci *Caesar Flickerman* · Woody Harrelson *Haymitch Abernathy* · Donald Sutherland *President Snow* ■ *Dir* Gary Ross · *Scr* Gary Ross, Suzanne Collins, Billy Ray, from Collins's novel · *Music* T-Bone Burnett, Danny Elfman

The Hunger Games: Catching Fire ★★★★★ 12
Futuristic action adventure 2013 · US · Colour · 140min

Expertly executed without a dull stretch, the second instalment based on the bestselling dystopian fantasy trilogy is a top-flight escapist adventure. Noble games victor Jennifer Lawrence is now a beacon of hope for rebellion so President Donald Sutherland forces her back to the arena to fight other, more experienced winners, expecting her to be crushed along with any simmering revolution. Everything is bolder, bigger and better in this enthralling segment: the spectacle channels *Ben-Hur*, the tropical combat zone is a thrilling tangle of exciting traps and plot twists, and the designer fashion is higher than before, with a terrific Lawrence as its catwalk Cleopatra. Just one warning: for those unfamiliar with the first instalment, a bit of prep will aid your enjoyment. AJ Some violence, swearing. DVD Blu-ray

Jennifer Lawrence (2) *Katniss Everdeen* · Josh Hutcherson *Peeta Mellark* · Liam Hemsworth *Gale Hawthorne* · Woody Harrelson *Haymitch Abernathy* · Donald Sutherland *President Snow* · Philip Seymour Hoffman *Plutarch Heavensbee* · Jeffrey Wright *Beetee* ■ *Dir* Francis Lawrence · *Scr* Simon Beaufoy, Michael deBruyn [Michael Arndt], from Suzanne Collins's novel · *Music* James Newton Howard · *Production Designer* Philip Messina

The Hunger Games: Mockingjay Part 1 ★★★★ 12
Action adventure 2014 · US · Colour · 117min

In the penultimate instalment of the hit franchise, there is no Hunger Games. Instead we get a society quivering on the cusp of all-out civil war, with Katniss (Jennifer Lawrence) the reluctant face of the revolution. Its predecessors worked better as individual films, with the games providing satisfying narratives within narratives. Nevertheless, Jennifer Lawrence delivers complexity and conviction, and director Francis Lawrence is a solid hand at the helm. Transitional teething problems aside, it's crammed with well-drawn characters and intelligent ideas, and remains as robust and rule-breaking as its idiosyncratic protagonist. Part 2 is due in November 2015. EAS Some violence. DVD Blu-ray

Jennifer Lawrence (2) *Katniss Everdeen* · Josh Hutcherson *Peeta Mellark* · Liam Hemsworth *Gale Hawthorne* · Woody Harrelson *Haymitch Abernathy* · Elizabeth Banks (2) *Effie Trinket* · Julianne Moore *President Alma Coin* · Philip Seymour Hoffman *Plutarch Heavensbee* · Jeffrey Wright *Beetee* · Stanley Tucci *Caesar Flickerman* · Donald Sutherland *President Snow* ■ *Dir* Francis Lawrence · *Scr* Danny Strong, Peter Craig, from the novel *Mockingjay* by Suzanne Collins

The Hunger Games: Mockingjay Part 2 ★★★★ 12
Action adventure 2015 · US · Colour · 131min

As the final instalment of the dystopian saga opens, our heroine Katniss (Jennifer Lawrence) has lost her voice. Yet you can't keep a stubborn gal down and the face of the revolution is soon ignoring orders to remain safely behind the scenes and sets off to assassinate Panem's wicked president (Donald Sutherland). Though some of the well-staged action has been edited into incoherence, gutsy Lawrence is resplendent in her resilience in a franchise-closer that's routinely stirring and occasionally gut-punching with a script that questions the morality of military tactics even in the heat of battle. It's a film of genuine integrity, performed with compelling conviction. EAS Some violence DVD Blu-ray 3D

Jennifer Lawrence (2) *Katniss Everdeen* · Josh Hutcherson *Peeta Mellark* · Liam Hemsworth *Gale Hawthorne* · Sam Claflin *Finnick Odair* · Julianne Moore *Alma Coin* · Philip Seymour Hoffman *Plutarch Heavensbee* · Woody Harrelson *Haymitch Abernathy* · Donald Sutherland *President Snow* ■ *Dir* Francis Lawrence · *Scr* Danny Strong, from the novel *Mockingjay* by Suzanne Collins

Hungry Hill ★★ PG
Period drama 1946 · UK · BW · 97min

In this adaptation of Daphne du Maurier's novel about family rivalry in 19th-century Ireland, the plot-packed, melodramatic excesses of the book seem slightly ludicrous on the screen. Margaret Lockwood admirably plays against type as the local firebrand tamed by the cruelty of the copper-mining family into which she marries. However, Brian Desmond Hurst's direction is typically florid and flabby, while the painted backdrops are just atrocious. DP

Margaret Lockwood *Fanny Ross* · Dennis Price *Greyhound John* · Cecil Parker *Copper John* · Michael Denison *Henry Brodrick* · Dermot Walsh *Wild Johnnie* · FJ McCormick *Old Tim* · Eileen Crowe *Bridget* · Jean Simmons *Jane Brodrick* ■ *Dir* Brian Desmond Hurst · *Scr* Daphne du Maurier, Terence Young, Francis Crowdy, from the novel by Daphne du Maurier · *Cinematographer* Desmond Dickinson

Hunk ★★★ PG
Comedy 1987 · US · Colour · 98min

Computer nerd Steve Levitt makes a pact with Devil's emissary Deborah Shelton so he can become a beach bum with pecs appeal in this intermittently charming comedy fantasy. A pleasant enough time-waster, with gorgeous bodies of both sexes to ogle at, and James Coco puts in a fine turn as the time-travelling Satan with a neat line in amusing historical references. AJ

John Allen Nelson *Hunk Golden* • Steve Levitt *Bradley Brinkman* • Deborah Shelton *O'Brien* • Rebeccah Bush *Sunny* • James Coco *Dr D* • Robert Morse *Garrison Gaylord* ■ *Dir/Scr* Lawrence Bassoff

Hunky Dory ★★★ 15
Comedy drama   2011 · UK · Colour · 105min

With its peculiar mix of social realism and high school musical, this Welsh-set drama plays like an episode of *Glee* directed by Ken Loach. In the scorching summer of 1976, idealistic teacher Minnie Driver rehearses a rock opera take on Shakespeare's *The Tempest*, while her Swansea secondary school class discover both themselves and each other. Director Marc Evans's coming-of-age saga is enlivened by on-the-nail performances from a caring-but-tough Driver and Aneurin Barnard as the star of the show, and pop hits from the likes of David Bowie, ELO and the Beach Boys are used to stirring effect. AJ Swearing. *DVD*

Minnie Driver *Vivienne* • Haydn Gwynne *Miss Valentine* • Robert Pugh *Headmaster* • Aneurin Barnard *Davey* • Owen Teale *Davey's dad* • Steve Speirs *Mr Cafferty* ■ *Dir* Marc Evans • *Scr* Laurence Coriat

The Hunley ★★★ 12
War drama based on a true story
1999 · US · Colour · 90min

John Gray brings history to life in this meticulous, made-for-TV reconstruction of a little-known naval engagement involving the CSS *Hunley*'s bid to break the Union's blockade of Confederacy ports. Made shortly after the submarine was raised off the coast of Charleston, the film exposes not only the bitter hatred that rent American society in the 1860s, but also the wanton barbarism this inspired. With Armand Assante heading a serviceable cast, this is both intelligent and accomplished. DP

Armand Assante *Lt George Dixon* • Donald Sutherland *Gen Pierre Beauregard* • Alex Jennings *Alexander* • Christopher Bauer [Chris Bauer] *Simkins* • Gerry Becker *Capt Pickering* ■ *Dir* John Gray • *Scr* John Gray, from a story by John Fasano, Gray

The Hunt ★★★★★
Drama   1966 · Sp · BW · 88min

Director Carlos Saura has fashioned a pitiless and scathing assault on a society and the attitudes that shaped it. His contempt scorches into the celluloid like the heat in which a trio of Civil War veterans go rabbit shooting on the arid site of a former battlefield. Equal scorn is poured on aristocratic and nouveau riche sensibilities, as a combination of vanity, snobbery, fiscal envy and politico-sexual repression drive the unrepentant Falangists to acts of savagery that leave their young companion rigid with indolent incomprehension. Deservedly, Saura's impeccable control of performance, pace and atmosphere earned him the best director prize at Berlin. DP Spanish +subtitles.

Ismael Merlo *José* • Alfredo Mayo *Paco* • José Maria Prada *Luis* • Emilio Gutiérrez Caba *Enrique* • Fernando Sanchez Polack *Juan* • Violetta Garcia *Nina* ■ *Dir* Carlos Saura • *Scr* Angelino Fons, Carlos Saura, from a story by Carlos Saura

The Hunt ★★★★ 15
Drama   2012 · Den/Swe · Colour · 115min

In this timely and intelligent reminder of the dangers of public hysteria, Mads Mikkelsen plays a kindergarten worker in a small Danish town who is accused of inappropriate sexual behaviour by one of the children. It sounds like a thriller, but the film shows early on that Mikkelsen is innocent, and instead creates drama from the ever-escalating nightmare in which he finds himself trapped. The always excellent Mikkelsen gives his best performance yet, playing a man who is far from perfect, but never once loses our sympathy. The outcome is genuinely tense, and the whole film offers a worryingly plausible reflection

of its time. DW Danish, English +subtitles. Violence, swearing, a sex scene. *DVD*

Mads Mikkelsen *Lucas* • Thomas Bo Larsen *Theo* • Lasse Fogelstrom *Marcus* • Annika Wedderkopp *Klara* • Alexandra Rapaport *Nadja* • Anne Louise Hassing *Agnes* ■ *Dir* Thomas Vinterberg • *Scr* Tobias Lindholm, Thomas Vinterberg

Hunt for Justice ★★
Political drama based on a true story
2005 · Can/Ger · Colour · 90min

The task of bringing war criminals from the former Yugoslavia to trial is explored in this thought-provoking but bitty TV docudrama. Opening in The Hague in 1996, the film keeps you watching mainly out of disbelief at the attitudes and injustices on display, as principled UN prosecutor Louise Arbour (Wendy Crewson) battles political and military opposition to indict Serbian president Slobodan Milosevic and other key figures. Sadly, the narrative isn't so impressive, oversimplifying events. SF

William Hurt *General Mortimer* • Wendy Crewson *Louise Arbour* • John Corbett *Captain John Tanner* ■ *Dir* Charles Binamé • *Scr* Ian Adams, Riley Adams, MA Lovretta

The Hunt for Red October ★★★★ PG
Thriller   1990 · US · Colour · 129min

This submarine drama marks the first screen appearance of Jack Ryan, the US agent subsequently played by Harrison Ford in *Patriot Games* and *Clear and Present Danger*, Ben Affleck in *The Sum of All Fears*, and Chris Pine in *Jack Ryan: Shadow Recruit*. Here, Alec Baldwin as Ryan plays second fiddle to Sean Connery, charismatic as ever as the Soviet commander who sparks an international crisis when he starts heading his sub straight for the USA. The no-frills direction ensures that the tension rarely slips below pressure-cooker level. JF *DVD*

Sean Connery *Captain Marko Ramius* • Alec Baldwin *Jack Ryan* • Scott Glenn *Captain Bart Mancuso* • Sam Neill *Captain Vasily Borodin* • James Earl Jones *Admiral James Greer* • Joss Ackland *Andrei Lysenko* • Richard Jordan *Jeffrey Pelt* • Peter Firth *Ivan Putin* • Tim Curry *Dr Petrov* • Courtney B Vance *Seaman Jones* • Stellan Skarsgård *Captain Tupolev* ■ *Dir* John McTiernan • *Scr* Larry Ferguson, Donald Stewart, from the novel by Tom Clancy

Hunt for the Wilderpeople ★★★★ 12A
Comedy   2016 · NZ · Colour · 101min

This charming comedy combines endearing characters with generous helpings of deadpan humour – and the result is quite wonderful. Set in New Zealand, it tells the story ofRicky Baker (Julian Dennison), a 13-year-old delinquent who ventures into the wilderness to avoid juvenile detention. Thankfully, he is tracked down by his foster uncle, Hector (Sam Neill), a grumpy, taciturn mountain man who knows how to survive in the bush. Dennison and Neill form a delightful double act, a mismatched duo who are utterly joyous to watch. SC Brief swearing.

Julian Dennison *Ricky Baker* • Sam Neill *Hector Faulkner* • Rima Te Wiata *Bella M Faulkner* • Rachel House *Paula Hall* ■ *Dir* Taika Waititi • *Scr* Taika Waititi, from Barry Crump's novel

Hunted ★★ PG
Drama   1952 · UK · BW · 81min

This cross-country adventure stop-starts too often to engross, but it benefits from the effortless rapport between Dirk Bogarde and Jon Whiteley as a pair of runaways whose friendship is forged in adversity. Fleeing after the murder of his wife's lover, Bogarde makes a credible fugitive, particularly when threatening his young companion, who thinks he's burned down his foster parents' home. Director Charles Crichton makes the most of the various locales, but there's a predictability about the round of encounters and escapes. DP *DVD*

Dirk Bogarde *Chris Lloyd* • Jon Whiteley *Robbie* • Elizabeth Sellars *Magda Lloyd* • Kay Walsh *Mrs Sykes* • Frederick Piper *Mr Sykes* • Julian Somers *Jack Lloyd* • Jane Aird *Mrs Campbell* • Jack Stewart *Mr Campbell* • Geoffrey Keen *Detective*

Inspector Deakin • Joe Linnane *Pawnbroker* ■ *Dir* Charles Crichton • *Scr* Jack Whittingham, from the story by Michael McCarthy

The Hunted ★★★ 18
Action thriller   1995 · US · Colour · 105min

In this proficient action thriller, video favourite Christopher Lambert plays a businessman based in the Far East who becomes the target of a crazed ninja gang after witnessing a murder. Help comes in the form of a modern-day samurai warrior (Yoshio Harada), who's looking to settle a centuries-old feud. Director JF Lawton ensures there's plenty of violent action, while the performances are a cut above the norm for this sort of thing. JF Nudity, a sex scene. *DVD*

Christopher Lambert *Paul Racine* • John Lone *Kinjo* • Joan Chen *Kirina* • Yoshio Harada *Takeda* • Yoko Shimada *Mieko* • Mari Natsuki *Junko* ■ *Dir/Scr* JF Lawton

The Hunted ★★ 15
Thriller   1998 · US/Can · Colour · 91min

In this instantly forgettable TV adventure, Mädchen Amick stars as an insurance investigator searching for a crashed plane carrying a stolen $12 million. Stranded in mountainous terrain after wrecking her jeep, her only ally appears to be recluse Harry Hamlin – but can he be trusted? It's adequately performed and directed, but low on surprises. JF Violence, swearing. *DVD*

Harry Hamlin *Doc Kovac* • Mädchen Amick *Samantha "Sam" Clark* • Hannes Jaenicke *Jan Kroeger* • Enuka Okuma *Tracy* • Robert Moloney *Dorse* • Peter LaCroix *Ranger McNulty* • Fulvio Cecere *Detective Cuneo* • Peter Bryant (2) *Uniformed officer* ■ *Dir* Stuart Cooper • *Scr* Bennett Cohen, David Ives

The Hunted ★★★ 15
Action thriller   2002 · US · Colour · 90min

This military thriller is far-fetched in the extreme, but luckily the action sequences have a terrific, visceral impact. A traumatised US veteran of the Kosovo conflict (Benicio Del Toro) is loose in the woods, dispatching game hunters with little more than a knife and brute strength, and the man who taught him how to kill (a typically gruff Tommy Lee Jones) is brought in to track him down. The two leads have a hard time bringing personalities to their rather clichéd characters, though both have enough natural presence to overcome this. TH Violence, swearing. *DVD*

Tommy Lee Jones *LT Bonham* • Benicio Del Toro *Aaron Hallam* • Connie Nielsen *Special Agent Abby Durrell* • Leslie Stefanson *Irene Kravitz* • John Finn *Ted Chenoweth* • José Zuniga *Moret* • Ron Canada *Van Zandt* • Mark Pellegrino *Dale Hewitt* ■ *Dir* William Friedkin • *Scr* David Griffiths, Peter Griffiths, Art Monterastelli

The Hunter ★★ 15
Action thriller based on a true story
1980 · US · Colour · 98min

Steve McQueen's final film is a badly muffed attempt to update the classic western bounty-hunter story. Known for his doggedness and unconventional methods, Ralph "Papa" Thorson brought thousands of fugitives to justice during his career, and McQueen was attracted to the all-action style and his offbeat personality. However, as directed by Buzz Kulik, the movie is not much more than a series of crash-bang pursuits. DP *DVD*

Steve McQueen (1) *Ralph "Papa" Thorson* • Eli Wallach *Ritchie Blumenthal* • Kathryn Harrold *Dotty* • Ben Johnson (1) *Sheriff Strong* • Tracey Walter *Rocco Mason* • LeVar Burton *Tommy Price* • Richard Venture *Spota* ■ *Dir* Buzz Kulik • *Scr* Ted Leighton, Peter Hyams, from the non-fiction book by Christopher Keane

The Hunter ★★★ 15
Crime drama   2010 · Iran/Ger · Colour · 88min

This sobering insight into life under Iran's Ahmadinejad regime calls to mind the violent protests that occurred during the country's 2009 elections. Distraught at the shooting of his wife and young daughter during a political demonstration, ex-con Ali (director and star Rafi Pitts) exacts revenge

on a passing police car, and becomes the victim of a relentless manhunt. The conclusion to the showdown is perhaps a touch too ironic, given the precision and restraint of the courageously critical action that precedes it. DP Farsi +subtitles. Swearing. *DVD*

Rafi Pitts *Ali Alavi* • Mitra Hajjar *Sara Alavi, Ali's wife* • Ali Nicksaulat *Officer Nazem* • Hassan Ghalenoi *Director* • Manoochehr Rahimi *Inspector* ■ *Dir/Scr* Rafi Pitts

The Hunter ★★★ 15
Adventure thriller   2011 · Aus · Colour · 97min

In his directorial debut, Australian Daniel Nettheim expertly channels the eerie nature of his homeland's glorious landscapes into a beguiling thriller, in which Willem Dafoe (at his understated best) plays a mercenary hired by a shady biotech company to find the supposedly extinct Tasmanian tiger. Posing as an academic, Dafoe finds his assignment complicated by the suspicions of local guide Sam Neill and an ongoing feud between environmentalists and loggers. Nettheim doesn't quite tie everything together, but his brooding visuals invoke a genuine sense of foreboding. JF Swearing. *DVD* *Blu*

Willem Dafoe *Martin David* • Sam Neill *Jack Mindy* • Frances O'Connor *Lucy Armstrong* • Morgana Davies *Sass Armstrong* • Finn Woodlock *Bike Armstrong* • Jacek Koman *Middleman* ■ *Dir* Daniel Nettheim • *Scr* Alice Addison, Wain Fimeri, Daniel Nettheim, from the novel by Julia Leigh

The Hunters ★★★ PG
War drama   1958 · US · Colour · 103min

Robert Mitchum plays a fighter pilot in the Korean War who falls for the wife of his colleague. The final film to be produced and directed by the actor Dick Powell, this could be dismissed as a naive piece of anti-communist propaganda, were it not for Mitchum's characteristically mesmeric presence and for some splendidly orchestrated aerial action sequences. The two-timing wife is played by May Britt, a Swedish-born beauty of dubious talent who retired in 1960 after marrying Sammy Davis Jr. AT *DVD*

Robert Mitchum *Major Cleve Saville* • Robert Wagner *Lieutenant Ed Pell* • Richard Egan *Colonel "Dutch" Imil* • May Britt *Kristina* • Lee Philips *Lieutenant Carl Abbott* • John Gabriel *Lieutenant Corona* • Stacy Harris *Colonel "Monkey" Moncavage* ■ *Dir* Dick Powell • *Scr* Wendell Mayes, from the novel by James Salter

The Hunters ★★★ 18
Crime thriller   1996 · Swe · Colour · 113min

Sibling rivalry and neighbourly envy complicate Rolf Lassgard's homecoming in this prototypical Nordic noir, which remains one of the top films in Swedish box-office history. Despite returning to Norrland under a cloud after a shooting in Stockholm, Lassgard is initially hailed as a prodigal hero by his fellow officers at the village police station. But he soon incurs the wrath of the locals when he investigates a complaint from some Lapp herders that their reindeer are being poached. Essentially a study of provincial insularity and prejudice, it's unflinchingly directed by Kjell Sundvall. DP Swedish +subtitles. Violence, swearing, nudity, scenes of animal slaughter. *DVD*

Rolf Lassgard *Erik Backstrom* • Lennart Jahkel *Leif Backstrom* • Jarmo Makinen *Tomme Harela* • Tomas Norstrom *Ove* ■ *Dir* Kjell Sundvall • *Scr* Kjell Sundvall, Bjorn Carlstrom

Hunting ★★★ 18
Drama   1992 · Aus · Colour · 93min

Atmospherically shot around Melbourne, this thriller keeps threatening to turn into something exceptional only to lapse back into mediocrity at all the wrong moments. John Savage seems to be in a different film from everyone else for the first third of the action as he arrives from the States to rescue his struggling business, but there's a spark in the love scenes he shares with secretary Kerry Armstrong. Guy Pearce is a standout. DP Violence, nudity, sex scenes. *DVD*

John Savage *Michael Bergman* • Guy Pearce *Sharp* • Kerry Armstrong *Michelle Harris* • Rebecca Rigg *Debbie McCormack* • Jeffrey Thomas *Larry Harris* • Rhys McConnochie *Bill Stockton* ■ *Dir/Scr* Frank Howson

The Hunting Party ★ 18
Western   1971 · UK · Colour · 104min

Not just tripe, but a production that is also lewd and crude. It is sad to see the great Gene Hackman slumming in this British-made, Spanish-shot western, as a vicious Texan tycoon hunting down Oliver Reed and his gang, who have kidnapped his wife, Candice Bergen. Hackman has a high-powered rifle on his side; all Reed has is a leering expression. TH Violence, nudity.

Oliver Reed *Frank Calder* • Candice Bergen *Melissa Ruger* • Gene Hackman *Brandt Ruger* • Simon Oakland *Matthew Gunn* • Mitchell Ryan *Doc Harrison* • LQ Jones *Hog Warren* • GD Spradlin *Sam Bayard* • William Watson *Loring* • Ronald Howard *Watt Nelson* ■ *Dir* Don Medford • *Scr* William Norton, Gilbert Alexander, Lou Morheim, from a story by Gilbert Alexander, Lou Morheim

The Hunting Party ★★★ 15
Comedy drama adventure
2007 · US/Cro/Bosnia · Colour and BW · 99min

"Only the most ridiculous parts of this story are true", begins this offbeat war-torn comedy. After a spectacular on-screen meltdown stalls his career, Richard Gere (a reporter on the front line during the Bosnian War) bounces back five years later with a madcap plan to secure a world exclusive interview with the Fox (Ljubomir Kerekes), a notorious Serbian war criminal. Deliberately evoking the docudrama of Michael Winterbottom's *Welcome to Sarajevo*, writer/director Richard Shepard tries to pull off a free-wheeling, irreverent approach that only half works given the grimly unfunny reality of the horrors to which the movie pays lip service. JR English, Serbo-Croat +subtitles. Violence, swearing. *DVD*

Richard Gere *Simon Hunt* • Terrence Howard *Duck* • Jesse Eisenberg *Benjamin* • Diane Kruger *Mirjana* • James Brolin *Franklin Harris* ■ *Dir* Richard Shepard • *Scr* Richard Shepard, from an *Esquire* article by Scott K Anderson

The Huntsman: Winter's War ★★★ 12A
Fantasy adventure   2016 · US · Colour · 113min

Chris Hemsworth is smooth as ever in this *Snow White and the Huntsman* spin-off. Thanks to Kristen Stewart's absence (following the scandal of her affair with previous director Rupert Sanders), it's left to Jessica Chastain and Emily Blunt to deliver as a fellow warrior and Ice Queen, respectively, while Charlize Theron also returns as the fabulously evil Ravenna. Director Cedric Nicolas-Troyan leads us on a slightly uneven ramble and needs to paper over the cracks – fortunately, he's a master of visual effects (Oscar-nominated for the first time) and again produces a cool, glittering spectacle. This is no classic, but it's still an amusing twist on the original fairy tale. SP Violence, swearing. *CS*

Chris Hemsworth *The Huntsman* • Emily Blunt *Freya* • Jessica Chastain *Sara* • Charlize Theron *Ravenna* • Nick Frost *Nion* ■ *Dir* Cedric Nicolas-Troyan • *Scr* Craig Mazin, Evan Spiliotopoulos, from characters by Evan Daugherty

Hurlyburly ★★ 18
Drama   1998 · US · Colour · 117min

David Rabe's acclaimed, hard-hitting play about moral bankruptcy in Hollywood ends up on screen 14 years later as a dated bore. An outstanding cast makes the most of Rabe's razor-sharp dialogue, which covers all offensive bases from dark misogyny to cynical drug-taking. Alas, Anthony Drazan's static direction fails to lift the stagey material, and all attempts to open out this fear and self-loathing talkfest fail miserably. AJ *DVD*

Sean Penn *Eddie* • Kevin Spacey *Mickey* • Robin Wright Penn [Robin Wright] *Darlene* • Meg Ryan *Bonnie* • Chazz Palminteri *Phil* • Garry Shandling *Artie* • Anna Paquin *Donna* ■ *Dir* Anthony Drazan • *Scr* David Rabe, from his play

The Hurricane ★★★ PG
Disaster adventure   1937 · US · BW · 99min

John Ford grudgingly took on this screen adaptation of Charles Nordhoff and James Norman Hall's South Seas yarn about a vendetta between a native sailor and the governor of Tahiti, whose problems are solved by the timely intervention of some spectacularly inclement weather. Raymond Massey, Mary Astor and Dorothy Lamour (most fetching in her trademark sarong) star, and the resulting melodrama offers solid entertainment. AT

Dorothy Lamour *Marama* • Jon Hall *Terangi* • Mary Astor *Mme Germaine DeLaage* • C Aubrey Smith *Father Paul* • Thomas Mitchell *Dr Kersaint* • Raymond Massey *Gov Eugene DeLaage* • John Carradine *Warden* ■ *Dir* John Ford • *Scr* Dudley Nichols, Oliver HP Garrett, from the novel by Charles Nordhoff, James Norman Hall as serialised in *The Saturday Evening Post*

Hurricane ★ 15
Drama   1979 · US · Colour · 114min

A dismal rehash of John Ford's 1937 movie, itself no great shakes, this has missionaries thumping their bibles while their daughters fornicate with native boys. To make this would-be epic, producer Dino De Laurentiis built the entire town of Pago Pago on the Polynesian island of Bora Bora, as well as a luxury hotel to house the cast and crew. Costing around $20 million, it was a mega-flop. AT

Jason Robards *Captain Charles Bruckner* • Mia Farrow *Charlotte Bruckner* • Max von Sydow *Dr Bascomb* • Trevor Howard *Father Malone* • Timothy Bottoms *Jack Sanford* • James Keach *Sergeant Strang* ■ *Dir* Jan Troell • *Scr* Lorenzo Semple Jr, from the novel by Charles Nordhoff, James Norman Hall

The Hurricane ★★★★ 15
Biographical drama   1999 · US · Colour · 139min

Veteran director Norman Jewison tackles bigotry and prejudice in this true story of racial injustice. Denzel Washington stars as Rubin "Hurricane" Carter, the boxer who was framed for three murders and sentenced to three life terms. Bob Dylan wrote a song about the case, and countless petitions were organised on his behalf. But it took a teenage boy named Lesra Martin (Vicellous Reon Shannon) to liberate Carter after 19 years of wrongful imprisonment. Washington's gradual progression from hate-filled loner to dignified role model is powerful. TH *DVD*

Denzel Washington *Rubin "Hurricane" Carter* • Vicellous Reon Shannon *Lesra Martin* • Deborah Kara Unger *Lisa* • Liev Schreiber *Sam* • John Hannah *Terry* • Dan Hedaya *Vincent Della Pesca* • Debbi Morgan *Mae Thelma Carter* • Clancy Brown *Lt Jimmy Williams* • Rod Steiger *Judge Sarokin* ■ *Dir* Norman Jewison • *Scr* Armyan Bernstein, Dan Gordon, Christopher Cleveland, from the autobiography *The Sixteenth Round* by Rubin "Hurricane" Carter and the biography *Lazarus and the Hurricane* by Sam Chaiton, Terry Swinton • *Cinematographer* Roger Deakins

Hurricane Smith ★★ U
Adventure   1952 · US · Colour · 90min

This treasure-seeking Paramount swashbuckler supplements its lively action with plenty of double dealing and a hint of romance. The underrated John Ireland gives a bullish performance alongside Forrest Tucker and Richard Arlen as stranded soldiers of fortune, who steal a ship and cross the South Seas to Australia in search of buried loot. DP

Yvonne De Carlo *Luana* • John Ireland *Hurricane Smith* • James Craig *Gorvahlsen* • Forrest Tucker *Dan McGuire* • Lyle Bettger *Clobb* • Richard Arlen *Brundage* • Mike Kellin *Dicer* • Murray Matheson *Dr Whitmore* ■ *Dir* Jerry Hopper • *Scr* Frank Gruber, from the story by Gordon Ray Young

Hurricane Streets ★★★ 15
Drama   1997 · US · Colour · 84min

A triple winner at the Sundance film festival (for best dramatic picture, director and cinematography), this is a gripping, gritty little drama. The impressively mature Brendan Sexton III stars as a 15-year-old petty thief with aspirations of a better life

beyond the New York gang he belongs to. He carries the weight of the film as the tough teen hampered by a poor upbringing, severe asthma and his girlfriend's overprotective father. Writer/director Morgan J Freeman has a better grasp of urban dialogue and expressive camerawork than he does focused storytelling, but it's still a creditable debut. JC Swearing, violence, drug abuse.

Brendan Sexton III *Marcus* • Shawn Elliott *Paco* • José Zuniga *Kramer* • David Roland Frank *Chip* • Carlo Alban *Benny* • Antoine McLean *Harold* • Mtume Gant *Louis* • Lynn Cohen *Lucy* • Edie Falco *Joanna* ■ *Dir/Scr* Morgan J Freeman

Hurry Sundown ★
Drama   1967 · US · Colour · 145min

Whoever would have thought that Otto Preminger could have turned out such a stinker as this? There's little pleasure in watching this overlong adaptation, which totally miscasts Michael Caine as a ruthless southerner, replete with menacing sneer and surly scowl as he tries to buy up most of Georgia. A feisty Jane Fonda's along for the ride, John Phillip Law is vacant and wan, Faye Dunaway is blowsy and tiresome, Robert Hooks is noble and dull – and they've got the more interesting roles! TS

Michael Caine *Henry Warren* • Jane Fonda *Julie Ann Warren* • John Phillip Law *Rad McDowell* • Faye Dunaway *Lou McDowell* • Robert Hooks *Reeve Scott* • Beah Richards *Rose Scott* • George Kennedy *Sheriff Coombs* • Burgess Meredith *Judge Purcell* ■ *Dir* Otto Preminger • *Scr* Thomas C Ryan, Horton Foote, from the novel by KB Gliden

The Hurt Locker ★★★★ 15
Action thriller   2008 · US · Colour · 125min

Director Kathryn Bigelow (*Point Break*) avoids both red wire/yellow wire cliché and political preaching in this 2004-set account of the lives of a US Army bomb-disposal squad in Iraq. She concentrates instead on the characters of the men who voluntarily put themselves next to deadly explosive devices, as well as re-creating the chaotic Baghdad in which they work. Covering their last 38 days in Iraq, the film follows the contrasting philosophies of a trio of soldiers, including the risk-taking Staff Sgt William James (Jeremy Renner), all of whom are aware that every job is potentially their last, in a tale that is as psychologically fascinating as it is exciting. Ralph Fiennes and Guy Pearce are among the well-known faces in smaller roles. AS Swearing. *DVD*

Jeremy Renner *Staff Sgt William James* • Anthony Mackie *Sgt JT Sanborn* • Brian Geraghty *Specialist Owen Eldridge* • Guy Pearce *Sgt Matt Thompson* • Ralph Fiennes *Contractor team leader* • David Morse *Col Reed* • Evangeline Lilly *Connie James* ■ *Dir* Kathryn Bigelow • *Scr* Mark Boal

Husbands ★ 12A
Drama   1970 · US · Colour · 131min

There are few things more tedious in cinema than flailing improvisation. This self-indulgent wallow from John Cassavetes is disappointing. Coping with the death of their buddy through booze, nostalgia and sex, New Yorkers Cassavetes, Peter Falk and Ben Gazzara cut depressing figures of suburban manhood. DP Violence, sexual references, some swearing.

Ben Gazzara *Harry* • Peter Falk *Archie* • John Cassavetes *Gus* • Jenny Runacre *Mary Tynan* • Jenny Lee Wright *Pearl Billingham* • Noelle Kao *Julie* • Leola Harlow *Leola* • Meta Shaw *Annie* ■ *Dir/Scr* John Cassavetes

Husbands and Wives ★★★★★ 15
Comedy drama   1992 · US · Colour · 103min

Throughout this excellent enterprise, Woody Allen employs a hand-held camera to convey the intensity and instability of the key relationship on screen, that between himself and Mia Farrow as a successful but troubled media couple. This dissection of two relationships (the other is between Sydney Pollack and Judy Davis) is piled high with wit and vigour as it comments on the

foibles of the artsy self-obsessed of midtown Manhattan. In a film released at the time of Woody and Mia's own troubles, rich ideas and strong performances abound. JM Swearing. *DVD*

Woody Allen *Gabe Roth* • Mia Farrow *Judy Roth* • Judy Davis *Sally* • Sydney Pollack *Jack* • Juliette Lewis *Rain* • Lysette Anthony *Sam* • Liam Neeson *Michael* • Blythe Danner *Rain's mother* ■ *Dir/Scr* Woody Allen

Hush ★ 12
Thriller   1998 · US · Colour · 91min

Don't let the classy cast (Jessica Lange, Gwyneth Paltrow) fool you: this is a truly awful film. Paltrow is the young woman who marries mummy's boy Johnathon Schaech, only to find when they visit the family home that mother (Lange) will do just about anything to keep her boy close at hand. Ludicrously serious. JB Violence, swearing. *DVD*

Jessica Lange *Martha Baring* • Gwyneth Paltrow *Helen* • Johnathon Schaech *Jackson Baring* • Nina Foch *Alice Baring* • Debi Mazar *Lisa* • Kaiulani Lee *Sister O'Shaughnessy* • David Thornton *Gavin* • Hal Holbrook *Dr Hill* ■ *Dir* Jonathan Darby • *Scr* Jonathan Darby, Jane Rusconi, from a story by Darby

Hush ★★★ 15
Thriller   2008 · UK · Colour · 87min

Former Radio 1 DJ Mark Tonderai makes his feature debut as writer and director with this gritty, low-budget road thriller. It follows the misadventures of frustrated writer Zakes Abbot (a sulky yet likeable Will Ash), who gets caught up in a night-time game of cat and mouse after his girlfriend Beth (Christine Bottomley) is kidnapped at a service station. Tonderai raises the stakes with a touch of relationship drama, but the film works best when tapping into primal fears. A scene involving a stop at a country house and the final showdown feel a little contrived, but for the most part it's a lean, efficient film that benefits from having a morally conflicted hero. SP *DVD* *Blu-ray*

Will Ash [William Ash] *Zakes Abbot* • Christine Bottomley *Beth* • Andreas Wisniewski *Tarman* • Claire Keelan *Wendy* • Stuart McQuarrie *Thorpe* • Robbie Gee *Chimponda* ■ *Dir/Scr* Mark Tonderai

Hush... Hush, Sweet Charlotte ★★★ 15
Gothic drama   1964 · US · BW · 127min

Having revived the careers of Bette Davis and Joan Crawford in the melodrama *What Ever Happened to Baby Jane?* director Robert Aldrich was anxious to recall them for *Hush... Hush, Sweet Charlotte*. While Davis readily agreed, sensing another triumph, Crawford cried off, so Aldrich cast Olivia de Havilland. The result is a delirious slice of American Gothic about two warring cousins and an inheritance. All the Deep South conventions are present – shadowy mansion, secrets in the closet – in a heady brew for fans of Hollywood's golden age. AT *DVD*

Bette Davis *Charlotte* • Olivia de Havilland *Miriam* • Joseph Cotten *Drew* • Agnes Moorehead *Velma* • Cecil Kellaway *Harry* • Victor Buono *Big Sam* • Mary Astor *Jewel Mayhew* • Wesley Addy *Sheriff* • George Kennedy *Foreman* ■ *Dir* Robert Aldrich • *Scr* Henry Farrell, Lukas Heller

Hustle ★★★★ 15
Thriller   1975 · US · Colour · 114min

Director Robert Aldrich gives this seedy story the same sense of corruption, depravity and urban alienation that made his 1955 masterpiece *Kiss Me Deadly* so memorable. Burt Reynolds stars as the world-weary detective who can barely rouse himself to mumble the sour asides contained in Steve Shagan's uncompromising script. Catherine Deneuve is less sure-footed, but Ben Johnson, Eddie Albert and Ernest Borgnine provide sinister support in this brooding thriller. DP Swearing. *DVD*

Burt Reynolds *Lt Phil Gaines* • Catherine Deneuve *Nicole Britton* • Eddie Albert *Leo Sellers* • Ben Johnson (1) *Marty Hollinger* • Eileen

H

Brennan *Paula Hollinger* • Ernest Borgnine *Santoro* • Paul Winfield *Sgt Louis Belgrave* ■ *Dir* Robert Aldrich • *Scr* Steve Shagan

Hustle & Flow ★★★ 15
Drama　　　　　　2005 · US · Colour · 111min

Terrence Howard gives a star-making turn in this urban drama as a small-time pimp who lives with three of his women in a broken-down house in Memphis. Howard dreams of trading in the life of hustling for one showing off his skills at "flow", the essence of smooth rap. Alternately unblinkingly truthful about the pimp code of conduct and as corny as cheese puffs, this works its charm by subtle degrees. **LF** Violence, swearing, drug abuse. *DVD* ⃝

Terrence Howard *DJay* • Anthony Anderson *Key* • Taryn Manning *Nola* • Taraji P Henson *Shug* • Paula Jai Parker *Lexus* • Elise Neal *Yevette* • DJ Qualls *Shelby* • Ludacris [Chris "Ludacris" Bridges] *Skinny Black* • Isaac Hayes *Arnel* ■ *Dir/Scr* Craig Brewer

The Hustler ★★★★★ 15
Classic sports drama　1961 · US · BW · 129min

This classic drama is showing its age nowadays: all that mock-poetic, soul-searching dialogue and the alcoholic heroine are firmly rooted in 1950s social realism. However, as a showcase for one of Paul Newman's best screen performances, this is still a masterpiece, with Newman, Jackie Gleason (as Minnesota Fats) and George C Scott striking sparks in the perfectly captured seedy pool-hall atmosphere. The picture is streets ahead of Martin Scorsese's flashy sequel, *The Color of Money*, for which Newman finally won his deserved Oscar. **AT** Violence. *DVD* ⃝

Paul Newman *"Fast" Eddie Felson* • Jackie Gleason *Minnesota Fats* • Piper Laurie *Sarah Packard* • George C Scott *Bert Gordon* • Myron McCormick *Charlie Burns* • Murray Hamilton *Findlay* • Michael Constantine *Big John* ■ *Dir* Robert Rossen • *Scr* Sidney Carroll, Robert Rossen, from the novel by Walter Tevis • *Cinematographer* Eugen Schüfftan

Hustler White ★★ 18
Erotic comedy drama 1996 · US · Colour · 75min

This is the closest that maverick actor/director Bruce LaBruce has come to mainstream cinema, although it is worth adding that previous works have included gay pornography, Super 8 shorts and features including *No Skin off My Ass*. Co-directed with Rick Castro, the film relates how a pretentious German film director (played by LaBruce himself) picks up a Santa Monica Boulevard hustler (Tony Ward) and is shown the underbelly of the LA gay scene. Intentionally outrageous, the film somehow remains unshocking in its depiction of perversity. **BB** *DVD*

Tony Ward (2) *Montgomery "Monti" Ward* • Bruce LaBruce *Jürgen Anger* • Kevin P Scott *Eigil Vesti* • Ivar Johnson *Piglet* • Ron Athey *Seymour Kasabian* • Miles H Wildecock II *Peter Festus* ■ *Dir/Scr* Bruce LaBruce, Rick Castro

Hybrid ★
Science-fiction horror
2007 · US · Colour · 90min

A fun B-movie concept is wasted in this abysmal sci-fi horror about a man who displays aggressive lupine behaviour after receiving a wolf's eyes in a transplant operation. Instead of a rip-roaring lycanthrope tale, the clumsy feature offers a dull and badly paced meditation on inner-acceptance, accompanied by a grating panpipe soundtrack and an overload of slow-motion shots of wolves. **SF**

Cory Monteith *Aaron* • Justine Bateman *Andrea* • Tinsel Korey *Lydia* ■ *Dir* Yelena Lanskaya • *Scr* Arne Olsen

Hyde Park on Hudson ★★★ 12
Comedy drama based on a true story
2012 · US/UK · Colour · 90min

Set shortly before the outbreak of the Second World War, director Roger Michell's film is based on the private letters and journals of Margaret Suckley, aka Daisy (Laura Linney), a distant cousin of Franklin

D Roosevelt (Bill Murray) with whom she had a close relationship. The story centres on a visit by King George VI (Samuel West) and Queen Elizabeth (Olivia Colman) to FDR's eponymous New York estate. It is as sweet and charming as it could be with a protagonist who is a serial philanderer. Murray is very mannered, which works, but the usually excellent Linney is strangely bland. It feels as if the film-makers have taken a great moment in history and, by attempting to examine the human element behind it, have lost sight of it. The result is a drama that is inoffensive and insubstantial. **BP** Swearing, a sex scene. *DVD* ⃝

Bill Murray *Franklin D Roosevelt, "FDR"* • Laura Linney *Margaret Suckley, Daisy* • Samuel West *King George VI, Bertie* • Olivia Colman *Queen Elizabeth* • Elizabeth Marvel *Marguerite LeHand, Missy* • Eleanor Bron *Mrs Woodbury Langdon, Daisy's aunt* • Olivia Williams *Eleanor Roosevelt* ■ *Dir* Roger Michell • *Scr* Richard Nelson

Hyena ★★★ 18
Crime drama　　2014 · UK · Colour · 107min

A compelling turn from Peter Ferdinando is reason enough to recommend this moody, coked-up British crime thriller. Ferdinando stars as Detective Michael Logan, a corrupt copper who leads a special task force that targets London's seediest drug traffickers. Problems arise when one of his criminal associates is butchered, while matters are further complicated by the return of an embittered former colleague (Stephen Graham) who is assigned to the case. The story that ensues is familiar and derivative, but writer/director Gerard Johnson offers a few stylish sequences and it benefits from a pulsing electronic score. **SC** *DVD*

Peter Ferdinando *Michael* • Stephen Graham *David Knight* • Neil Maskell *Martin* • Elisa Lasowski *Ariana* • MyAnna Buring *Lisa* ■ *Dir/Scr* Gerard Johnson

Hyènes ★★★
Drama　　　　1992 · Sen · Colour · 113min

Senegalese director Djibril Diop Mambety employs indigenous magic realism in this symbolic drama that focuses on the clash between progress and tradition and the blurred line between proud nationhood and post-colonial dependence. The story revolves around a returning wealthy woman who offers untold riches to her fellow villagers if they help her wreak vengeance on the former lover who once drove her into exile. It fails to deliver what it promises, but this is still challenging. **DP** French +subtitles.

Mansour Diouf *Dramaan* • Ami Diakhate *Linguere* • Mahouredia Gueye *The Mayor* • Issa Ramagelissa Samb *The Professor* ■ *Dir* Djibril Diop Mambety • *Scr* Djibril Diop Mambety, from the play *The Visit* by Friedrich Durrenmatt

The Hypnotist ★★ PG
Crime drama　　　1957 · UK · BW · 85min

Irish-born director Montgomery Tully was one of the key figures in the British B-movie industry during the 1950s and 1960s. This is one of his better efforts, as psychiatrist Roland Culver attempts to frame disturbed test pilot Paul Carpenter for the murder of his wife. Culver does a nice line in evil manipulation and Patricia Roc is typically spirited as the girlfriend standing by her man, but poor old Carpenter simply can't give a decent performance. **DP** *DVD*

Roland Culver *Dr Francis Pelham* • Patricia Roc *Mary Foster* • Paul Carpenter *Val Neal* • William Hartnell *Inspector Rose* • Kay Callard *Susie* • Ellen Pollock *Barbara Barton* ■ *Dir* Montgomery Tully • *Scr* Montgomery Tully, from a play by Falkland Cary

Hysteria ★★ 15
Mystery thriller　　1964 · UK · BW · 81min

Having presented Hammer with the sizeable hits, *Paranoiac* and *Nightmare*, Freddie Francis reteamed with screenwriter Jimmy Sangster to complete his psycho trilogy. Sadly, the bemusing experiences of amnesiac American tourist Robert Webber rarely set pulses racing, despite the menacing ministrations of nursing home

shrink Anthony Newlands and a mysterious murder. Strewn with mind-bending visuals and preposterous dialogue, this is more mediocre than macabre. **DP**

Robert Webber *Chris Smith* • Anthony Newlands *Dr Keller* • Jennifer Jayne *Gina* • Maurice Denham *Hemmings* • Lelia Goldoni *Denise* • Sue Lloyd *French girl* ■ *Dir* Freddie Francis • *Scr* Jimmy Sangster

Hysteria ★★★ 15
Period romantic comedy
2011 · US/Fr/Lux/UK · Colour · 95min

Here's a comedy that tickles parts others cannot reach – or wouldn't dare touch. It's the (mostly) true story of how Dr Mortimer Granville (Hugh Dancy) invented the vibrator, a triumph of the Victorian era that went unsung at a time of restricted female expression. Despite the subject matter, director Tanya Wexler's film has a somewhat coy tone, and elicits smirks and sniggers more than belly laughs. A romantic subplot involving Maggie Gyllenhaal helps up the stakes, but this isn't a story of historical weight as much as feather-light fun. **SP** Sexual references. *DVD*

Hugh Dancy *Mortimer Granville* • Maggie Gyllenhaal *Charlotte Dalrymple* • Jonathan Pryce *Dr Robert Dalrymple* • Felicity Jones *Emily Dalrymple* • Ashley Jensen *Fannie* • Sheridan Smith *Molly* ■ *Dir* Tanya Wexler • *Scr* Jonah Lisa Dyer, Stephen Dyer, from a story by Jonah Lisa and Stephen Dyer, Howard Gensler

Hysterical Blindness ★★ 15
Drama　　　　2002 · US · Colour · 98min

Why Mira Nair chose this as the follow-up to *Monsoon Wedding* isn't obvious. She imparts no personality whatsoever to this resolutely downbeat and utterly contrived tale of female bonding, in which New Jersey 30-something Uma Thurman and best mate Juliette Lewis (both of whom overplay to the hilt) seek solace from their humdrum existence in booze binges and unsuitable blokes. Uninspired and garishly resistible. **DP** *DVD*

Uma Thurman *Debby* • Gena Rowlands *Virginia* • Juliette Lewis *Beth* • Justin Chamber *Rick* • Ben Gazzara *Nick* ■ *Dir* Mira Nair • *Scr* Laura Cahill, from her play

I Accuse! ★★★ U
Historical drama　　1958 · UK · BW · 99min

José Ferrer directs and stars in this drama about the famous treason trial in France that saw Alfred Dreyfus framed and sentenced to life imprisonment on Devil's Island. Ferrer makes a compelling hero and he is supported by a fine cast of stalwarts. Gore Vidal's screenplay was intended, perhaps, as an allegory about the McCarthy era. The black-and-white photography is by Freddie Young, who went on to win three Oscars for his work with David Lean. **AT**

José Ferrer *Alfred Dreyfus* • Anton Walbrook *Major Esterhazy* • Viveca Lindfors *Lucie Dreyfus* • Leo Genn *Major Picquart* • Emlyn Williams *Emile Zola* • David Farrar *Mathieu Dreyfus* • Donald Wolfit *General Mercier* • Herbert Lom *Major Dupaty De Clam* ■ *Dir* José Ferrer • *Scr* Gore Vidal, from the non-fiction book *Captain Dreyfus – a Story of Mass Hysteria* by Nicholas Halasz

I Aim at the Stars ★★ U
Biographical drama　1960 · US · BW · 106min

Was it right for the Americans to employ a German scientist who had worked for Hitler on the US space programme? Was it possible for a man who invented the devastating V-2 rocket for the Nazis to have been apolitical? These are the compelling questions raised and then fudged in this tame biopic of rocket expert Wernher von Braun. Unfortunately, despite Curt Jurgens's earnest performance, we never learn much about the man's inner space. **RB**

Curt Jurgens *Wernher von Braun* • Victoria Shaw *Maria* • Herbert Lom *Anton Reger* • Gia Scala *Elizabeth Beyer* • James Daly *Major William Taggert* • Adrian Hoven *Mischke* ■ *Dir* J Lee Thompson • *Scr* Jay Dratler, from a story by George Froeschel, U Wolter, HW John

I Am a Camera ★★ 12
Comedy drama　　　1955 · UK · BW · 95min

This is a hugely disappointing film adaptation of Christopher Isherwood's stage version of Christopher Isherwood's celebrated Berlin tales. John Collier must shoulder most of the blame for his drab script that completely misses the decadence and sordid charm of the underside of pre-war German society. Laurence Harvey's lack of technique is cruelly exposed, but Julie Harris makes a spirited Sally Bowles. **DP** *DVD*

Julie Harris (2) *Sally Bowles* • Laurence Harvey *Christopher Isherwood* • Shelley Winters *Natalia Landauer* • Ron Randell *Clive* • Lea Seidl *Fraulein Schneider* • Anton Diffring *Fritz* ■ *Dir* Henry Cornelius • *Scr* John Collier, from the play *I Am a Camera* by John Van Druten, from the short story collection *The Berlin Stories* by Christopher Isherwood

I Am a Fugitive from a Chain Gang ★★★★
Classic drama　　　1932 · US · BW · 93min

The title tells all in terms of plot, but it gives no indication of the power generated by the Oscar-nominated performance of Paul Muni, as the war veteran framed for a hold-up and sentenced to work in a Georgia chain gang at the mercy of sadistic guards. One of the most forceful of Warner Bros' conscience-shaking cycle of movies in the 1930s, it exposed a pitiless regime. Director Mervyn LeRoy pushed audiences of the day to the limits of endurance. **TH**

Paul Muni *James Allen* • Glenda Farrell *Marie Woods* • Helen Vinson *Helen* • Noel Francis *Linda* • Preston Foster *Pete* • Allen Jenkins *Barney Sykes* • Berton Churchill *Judge* • Edward Ellis

Bomber Wells • David Landau *Warden* ■
Dir Mervyn LeRoy • *Scr* Howard J Green, Brown
Holmes, Sheridan Gibney, from the
autobiography *I Am a Fugitive from a Georgia
Chain Gang* by Robert E Burns

I Am Ali ★★★ PG
Documentary
2014 · US/UK · Colour and BW · 111min

Rather than examining the boxing prowess
of Muhammad Ali, this documentary
features anecdotes from those closest to
him (brother, daughters, manager, fans), so
is understandably extremely affectionate. A
fascinating glimpse into the private side of
one of history's most public
personalities. JL *DVD* BL

Jim Brown • George Foreman • Mike Tyson ■
Dir/Scr Clare Lewins

I Am Big Bird ★★★
Documentary
2014 · US · Colour · 90min

Following Constance Marks's *Being Elmo: a
Puppeteer's Journey* (2011), this is a
charming insight into the life and art of
Caroll Spinney, the puppeteer who has
played Big Bird on *Sesame Street* since it
was launched in 1969. Spinney sought
refuge in performing from paternal abuse
and school bullying, and spent some years
creating his own characters before meeting
Muppet man Jim Henson. Henson entrusted
him with Big Bird and Oscar the Grouch,
who became national treasures. Spinney
shares his unique working conditions and
methods in exhaustingly intimate detail;
nowadays, he lets protégé Matt Vogel do
much of the physically demanding stuff, but
he remains involved. DP Swearing. *DVD*

Caroll Spinney *Big Bird/Oscar* • Frank Oz ■
Dir Dave LaMattina, Chad Walker [Chad N
Walker] • *Scr* Dave LaMattina

I Am Breathing ★★★★
Documentary
2012 · UK/Den/Fin · Colour · 73min

Emma Davie and Morag McKinnon's record
of 34-year-old Neil Platt's brave fight
against motor neurone disease is an honest
and poignant chronicle of a man's final
months. Determined to savour his dwindling
time with Scottish wife Louise, toddler son
Oscar and widowed mother Lynne, the
Yorkshire-born architect also feels a duty to
share his experiences, via some hilariously
unreliable voice-recognition software, with
those similarly afflicted and their carers.
There's no soft soap or melodrama here.
This really is a matter of life and death, and
the courage shown by Neil and the devoted
and wondrously patient Louise is not only
humbling, but also genuinely moving and
quietly heroic. DP

■ *Dir* Emma Davie, Morag McKinnon

I Am Bruce Lee ★★★★ 15
Documentary 2012 · Can · Colour · 94min

Despite numerous documentaries and an
entertaining biopic (1993's *Dragon: the
Bruce Lee Story*) released since his death in
1973, this appreciation of the martial arts
icon still manages to be fresh and revealing.
This is thanks to rarely seen archive
footage (including Lee teaching superstar
pupil James Coburn in his back garden)
dovetailed with judicious footage from TV
interviews and his unforgettable film
performances. Sound bites from family,
friends and admirers add to the interest –
most poignant is Jeet Kune Do tutor Dan
Inosanto, who is lost for words when asked
about Lee's untimely passing. JA Violence,
swearing. *DVD* BL

Mickey Rourke • Manny Pacquiao • Shannon Lee
• Linda Lee Cadwell • Dan Inosanto • Gina Carano
■ *Dir* Pete McCormack

I Am Cuba ★★★★ PG
Propaganda drama
1964 · USSR/Cub · BW · 134min

Stalin's former cinema chief Mikhail
Kalazatov not only captures the vibrancy of
the people, but also the state of the nation
in this propagandist paean to the Castro
revolution, made in the aftermath of the
Cuban Missile Crisis. The four stories dwell

equally on the evils of the Batista regime
and the benefits of Communism. But what
distinguishes this from agitprop is the
stunning cinematography of Sergei
Urussevsky, whose "emotional camera"
pulls off feats of technical audacity that are
both political and artistic. DP Spanish,
Russian, English +subtitles. *DVD*

Sergio Corrieri *Alberto* • José Gallardo *Pedro* •
Raúl García *Enrique* • Luz Maria Collazo *Maria/
Betty* • Jean Bouise *Jim* ■ *Dir* Mikhail Kalatozov •
Scr Yevgeni Yevtushenko, Enrique Pineda Barnet

I Am Curious – Yellow ★★★ 15
Erotic comedy drama 1967 · Swe · BW · 116min

Although it played a key role in
undermining US censorship rules, Vilgot
Sjöman's mix of soft-core sex and political
satire is merely a curio now that its power
to shock has diminished. The vox pops that
sociologist Lena Nyman conducts on the
streets of Stockholm are quite revealing of
mid-1960s Swedish attitudes, but the
stylised couplings with boyfriend Sjöman
and car salesman Börje Ahlstedt, while
contextual, seem designed purely to titillate.
The follow-up *I Am Curious – Blue* made less
impact. DP Swedish +subtitles. Sex scenes,
nudity. *DVD*

Lena Nyman *Lena* • Börje Ahlstedt *Börje* • Vilgot
Sjöman *Director* • Peter Lindgren *Rune, Lena's
father* • Chris Wahlström *Rune's friend* ■
Dir/Scr Vilgot Sjöman

I Am Divine ★★★ 15
Documentary
2013 · US · Colour and BW · 89min

Aficionados of the films of John Waters will
need no introduction to the Pope of Trash's
muse, a 300-pound drag queen born in
conservative 1940s Baltimore. Harris Glenn
Milstead, or Divine as we now know him,
struggled with both his weight and bullies
before meeting Waters and starring in early
underground films such as *Female Trouble*
and *Pink Flamingos* (in which he notoriously
ate dog faeces). Jeffrey Schwarz interviews
friends and fans, piecing together a picture
of a gentle, perhaps surprisingly shy man
who channelled his anger at society and his
family's rejection of him into his outrageous
alter-ego. AS *DVD*

Divine • John Waters (2) *John Waters* • Ricki
Lake • Tab Hunter • Mink Stole ■ *Dir* Jeffrey
Schwarz

I Am Legend ★★★ 15
Science-fiction action horror
2007 · US · Colour · 96min

Francis Lawrence (*Constantine*) directs this
third big-screen version of Richard
Matheson's classic 1954 sci-fi tale (after *The
Last Man on Earth* in 1964 and *The Omega
Man* in 1971). Will Smith gives a virtuoso
performance as a military scientist who is
immune to a virus that turned most of
humanity into vampire-like zombies, and
effectively puts across the paranoid
loneliness of a man who could be the last
surviving human on Earth. But some
formulaic shocks, credibility-busting plot
holes and unconvincing CGI monsters shift
this apocalyptic chiller into B-movie
territory. However, there's still an eerie
charge in seeing familiar landmarks like
Times Square transformed into desolate,
overgrown wilderness. AJ Violence. *DVD*

Will Smith *Robert Neville* • Alice Braga *Anna* •
Charlie Tahan *Ethan* • Salli Richardson-Whitfield
[Salli Richardson] *Zoe* • Willow Smith *Marley* •
Dash Mihok *Alpha male* • Emma Thompson *Dr
Alice Krippen* ■ *Dir* Francis Lawrence • *Scr* Akiva
Goldsman, Mark Protosevich, from the novel by
Richard Matheson

I Am Love ★★★★ 15
Drama 2009 · It · Colour · 114min

Tilda Swinton delivers a tour-de-force lead
performance in this exquisite Italian drama.
It begins with the patriarch of the Recchi
clan handing over his textile business to his
son Tancredi (Pippo Delbono). There's
surprise, however, when the old man gives
joint control to his grandson Edo (Flavio
Parenti). It ought to be the start of an

auspicious new chapter in the Recchis'
history, but their fortunes are about to
change. Tancredi's Russian wife Emma
(Swinton) soon finds her loyalties are
compromised when she meets Edo's
handsome business partner (Edoardo
Gabbriellini). It's at this point that the film
switches from a stately ensemble piece to
an electrifying one-woman show, with
Emma embarking on an affair that has
catastrophic consequences for all. DW
Italian, Russian, English +subtitles. Sex
scenes, nudity. *DVD*

Tilda Swinton *Emma Recchi* • Flavio Parenti
Edoardo Recchi Jr • Edoardo Gabbriellini *Antonio
Biscaglia* • Alba Rohrwacher *Elisabetta Recchi* •
Pippo Delbono *Tancredi Recchi* • Maria Paiato *Ida
Marangon* • Marisa Berenson *Allegra Recchi* •
Gabriele Ferzetti *Edoardo Recchi Sr* ■ *Dir* Luca
Guadagnino • *Scr* Barbara Alberti, Ivan Cotroneo,
Walter Fasano, Luca Guadagnino, from a story
by Guadagnino

I Am Nasrine ★★★ 15
Drama 2012 · UK · Colour · 93min

Documentary-maker Tina Gharavi earned a
Bafta nomination for this sincere drama
that cannily contrasts the problems facing
young people in Tehran with those faced by
kids on Tyneside. The performances and
the contrasting vistas are impressive.
However, the film risks lapsing from social
realism into soap opera with a plot that
sees 16-year-old would-be journalist Nasrine
(Micsha Sadeghi) sent into exile by her
father after being caught on a motorbike
with a boy. Gharavi overloads the dice with
the sheer weight of the issues she tackles,
but the musings on freedom are cogent and
convincingly played out. DP In English,
Farsi. Violence, swearing, sex scenes.

Micsha Sadeghi *Nasrine* • Shiraz Haq *Ali* •
Christian Coulson *Tommy* • Steven Hooper *Leigh*
• Nichole Halls *Nichole* ■ *Dir* Tina Gharavi • *Scr*
Tina Gharavi, from her story

I Am Number Four ★★ 12
Science-fiction action thriller
2011 · US/Ind · Colour · 105min

An alien with superpowers grows up on
Earth while hiding from a deadly
intergalactic enemy, in DJ Caruso's dull
hybrid of *Twilight* and *Smallville*. Alex
Pettyfer plays Number Four, one of a
dwindling race of nine survivors from the
Planet Lorien avoiding gill-faced adversaries
the Mogadorians. Relocated to Ohio, the
boy tries to stay under the radar, but the
usual high-school dramas – romancing the
wrong girl (*Glee* star Dianna Agron) and
bullying – make that impossible. The movie
is coarsely adapted from the young adult
novel, and its uninspired number is up way
before the finale erupts in stale CGI
fireworks. AJ Some violence. *DVD* BL

Alex Pettyfer *John Smith/Number Four* •
Timothy Olyphant *Henri* • Teresa Palmer *Number
Six* • Dianna Agron *Sarah* • Callan McAuliffe *Sam*
• Kevin Durand *Mogadorian Commander* • Jake
Abel *Mark* ■ *Dir* DJ Caruso • *Scr* Alfred Gough,
Miles Millar, Marti Noxon, from a novel by
Pittacus Lore [James Frey, Jobie Hughes]

I Am Sam ★ 12
Comedy drama 2001 · US/Ger · Colour · 126min

The emotionally manipulative story of a
single parent (Sean Penn) with a mental
age of seven, this focuses on a custody
battle for his daughter, whose seventh
birthday conveniently makes him an
untenable parent. Quite apart from being
an offensive, inaccurate and unhelpful
portrait of mental illness (Penn's *Rain Man*-
influenced autism comes and goes to suit
the mawkish script), this is a blatant vanity
project for Penn and a naive piece of
schmaltz. AC *DVD*

Sean Penn *Sam Dawson* • Michelle Pfeiffer *Rita
Harrison* • Dakota Fanning *Lucy Diamond
Dawson* • Dianne Wiest *Annie* • Loretta Devine
Margaret Calgrove • Richard Schiff *Turner* •
Laura Dern *Randy Carpenter* • Mary
Steenburgen *Dr Blake* ■ *Dir* Jessie Nelson • *Scr*
Kristine Johnson, Jessie Nelson

I Am the Law ★★★ PG
Crime drama 1938 · US · BW · 79min

Edward G Robinson stars as a law professor
appointed as a special prosecutor to flush
out urban racketeers, in one of those films
where everyone who has information to
deliver is bumped off before they can
divulge it. The climax is truly weird as
Robinson shows home movies and shots of
the electric chair to his gathered suspects in
a circus tent. Interestingly, New York's
Herald Tribune found Robinson's moral
rhetoric unconvincing at the time. TS

Edward G Robinson *John Lindsay* • Barbara
O'Neil *Jerry Lindsay* • John Beal *Paul Ferguson* •
Wendy Barrie *Frankie Ballou* • Otto Kruger
Eugene Ferguson • Arthur Loft *Tom Ross* ■
Dir Alexander Hall • *Scr* Jo Swerling, from a story
by Fred Allhoff

I, Anna ★★★ 15
Psychological drama
2012 · UK/Ger/Fr · Colour · 91min

Though it bears many of the hallmarks of a
film noir, this adaptation of Elsa Lewin's
novel is, at heart, more of a brooding
character study. Charlotte Rampling gives a
fascinating performance as ageing beauty
Anna Welles, who assumes a different
identity to meet men on the speed-dating
circuit. When another lonely soul is found
dead, Anna draws the inquisitive eye of DCI
Reid (a rumpled Gabriel Byrne), but his
growing feelings for her begin to cloud his
judgement. The part is a gift for Rampling,
who imbues Anna with a startling
vulnerability and a touch of something
eerie. But by trying so hard to maintain an
air of mystery around Anna, her motives
become opaque. Like the traditional *femme
fatale*, Anna leaves you wanting to know
more. SP Swearing, sex scenes. *DVD*

Charlotte Rampling *Anna Welles* • Gabriel Byrne
DCI Bernie Reid • Eddie Marsan *DI Kevin Franks* •
Jodhi May *Janet Stone* • Ralph Brown *George
Stone* • Honor Blackman *Joan* ■ *Dir* Barnaby
Southcombe • *Scr* Barnaby Southcombe, from
Elsa Lewin's novel

I Believe in You ★★★ U
Drama 1952 · UK · BW · 94min

Michael Relph and Basil Dearden ladle on
the good intentions in this unusual drama
about the probation service, only to spoil
everything by emphasising the patronising
conceit that the proletariat will always be
ignorant ne'er-do-wells without the guiding
influence of the kindly middle classes. Cecil
Parker turns from a bumbling do-gooder
into a hard-nosed champion of the
underprivileged as he helps Harry Fowler
and Joan Collins to stumble back on to the
straight and narrow. Incapable of giving a
bad performance, Celia Johnson is sidelined
once Parker finds his feet. DP

Celia Johnson *Matty* • Cecil Parker *Henry Phipps*
• Godfrey Tearle *Mr Pyke* • Harry Fowler *Hooker* •
George Relph *Mr Dove* • Joan Collins *Norma* •
Laurence Harvey *Jordie* • Sidney James
Sergeant Brodie ■ *Dir* Michael Relph, Basil
Dearden • *Scr* Jack Whittingham, Nicholas
Phipps, Michael Relph, Basil Dearden, from the
novel *Court Circular* by Sewell Stokes

I Bought a Vampire Motorcycle ★★★ 18
Horror comedy 1989 · UK · Colour · 100min

What TV director Dirk Campbell's horror
spoof lacks in budget, finesse, genuine
scares and acting, it more than makes up
for in a wealth of clever ideas that gives a
neat spin on formula undead mythology.
After buying a possessed antique
motorbike, which uses blood for petrol and
won't kick-start during daylight hours,
sleazy rider Neil Morrissey enlists the help
of priest Anthony Daniels to exorcise the
splatter machine. Cheesy gore, a garlic-
breathed detective (Michael Elphick) and
tasteless visual gags add to the lunatic
fun. AJ *DVD*

Neil Morrissey *Nick Oddie, "Noddy"* • Amanda
Noar *Kim* • Michael Elphick *Inspector Cleaver* •
Anthony Daniels *Priest* • Andrew Powell *Roach* •
George Rossi *Chopper* • Midge Taylor *First Road*

Toad • Daniel Peacock Buzzer • Burt Kwouk Fu King owner ■ Dir Dirk Campbell • Scr Mycal Miller, John Wolskel

I Can Get It for You Wholesale ★★★ U

Drama   1951 · US · BW · 88min

A fairly tough adaptation of Jerome Weidman's colourful bestseller about the rag trade is toned down for the screen but provides a superb leading role for dynamic Susan Hayward. She's the gal who goes from seamstress to model to head of a fashion house, and still can't make up her mind whether she wants amiable Dan Dailey or suave George Sanders. This is the same tale that, in its musical incarnation on Broadway, featured a young unknown who brought the house down nightly – Barbra Streisand. TS

Susan Hayward Harriet Boyd • Dan Dailey Teddy Sherman • George Sanders Noble • Sam Jaffe Cooper • Randy Stuart Marge • Marvin Kaplan Four Eyes • Harry Von Zell Savage ■ Dir Michael Gordon • Scr Abraham Polonsky, Vera Caspary, from the novel by Jerome Weidman

I Capture the Castle ★★★★ PG

Period romantic drama
2002 · UK/S Afr · Colour · 108min

Genteel poverty has never looked so enchanting, as the Mortmain family, headed by creatively blocked writer Bill Nighy, all lead lives of bohemian chaos in a dilapidated castle. Events are recorded by the 17-year-old diarist Cassandra (Romola Garai), whose interest in the opposite sex is awakened when two American brothers (Henry Thomas and Marc Blucas) stumble across the Mortmains on their way to an inherited estate. The 1930s period trappings are laid on a little too thickly, but this is a reassuringly solid and intelligent adaptation, beautifully photographed and expertly performed. TH DVD

Henry Thomas Simon Cotton • Marc Blucas Neil Cotton • Rose Byrne Rose Mortmain • Romola Garai Cassandra Mortmain • Bill Nighy James Mortmain • Tara FitzGerald Topaz • Henry Cavill Stephen • Sinead Cusack Mrs Elspeth Cotton • David Bamber Vicar ■ Dir Tim Fywell • Scr Heidi Thomas, from the novel by Dodie Smith

I Confess ★★★★ PG

Drama   1953 · US · BW · 90min

Dismissed by the critics and shunned by the public, this is perhaps Alfred Hitchcock's most underrated film. In many ways, it shares the transference-of-guilt theme he had explored in his previous movie, Strangers on a Train. But what alienated many audiences was an unfamiliarity with the codes of Catholicism that prevent a priest from betraying the secrets of the confessional. Seen today, this is a classic Hitchcock "wrong man" story, which makes marvellous use of its Quebec setting. Montgomery Clift's haunted look is ideal, but some of his Method mannerisms jar. Talky, serious and difficult, but long overdue for reappraisal. DP DVD

Montgomery Clift Father Michael William Logan • Anne Baxter Ruth Grandfort • Karl Malden Inspector Larrue • Brian Aherne Willy Robertson • OE Hasse Otto Keller • Dolly Haas Alma Keller • Roger Dann Pierre Grandfort • Charles Andre Father Millais ■ Dir Alfred Hitchcock • Scr George Tabori, William Archibald, from the play Nos Deux Consciences by Paul Anthelme

I Could Go On Singing ★★★ U

Musical drama   1963 · UK · Colour · 95min

Judy Garland's last film, originally called The Lonely Stage, is a London-based melodrama attractively shot on location and co-starring Dirk Bogarde. Most of the movie is very average, pieced together when the star's illnesses made it necessary to finish the project in a hurry. However, what this picture does contain is arguably the finest example of improvisational screen acting ever: a single take set in a hospital where Garland and her character

merge in a shattering moment of rare movie honesty. TS

Judy Garland Jenny Bowman • Dirk Bogarde David Donne • Jack Klugman George Kogan • Aline MacMahon Ida • Gregory Phillips Matt • Pauline Jameson Miss Plimpton ■ Dir Ronald Neame • Scr Mayo Simon, from a story by Robert Dozier

I Could Read the Sky ★★★ 15

Drama   1999 · UK/Ire · Colour · 82min

Nichola Bruce's debut feature is a lyrical evocation of an Irish exile's life as he looks back from his spartan London bedsit on his youth and his itinerant struggle to find work over the water. Although Stephen Rea and Maria Doyle Kennedy contribute telling cameos, Dermot Healy, as the regret-scarred narrator, dominates proceedings. Bruce re-creates the fragmentary imperfection of memory by superimposing events into an elliptical diary of a mind. DP DVD

Dermot Healy The old man • Stephen Rea PJ • Brendan Coyle Francie • Maria Doyle Kennedy Maggie ■ Dir Nichola Bruce • Scr Timothy O'Grady, Nichola Bruce, from the novel by Steve Pyke, Timothy O'Grady

I Cover the Waterfront ★★ PG

Drama   1933 · US · BW · 60min

Journalist Ben Lyon romances Claudette Colbert as a means to expose her father (Ernest Torrence, who died before the film's release), a suspected smuggler of Chinese immigrants. Smart-aleck dialogue between Lyon and Colbert vies with various seaborne chases, and there's a surprise appearance from a shark that carries off someone's leg. AT DVD

Claudette Colbert Julie Kirk • Ben Lyon Joseph Miller • Ernest Torrence Eli Kirk • Hobart Cavanaugh McCoy • Maurice Black Ortegus • Harry Beresford Old Chris • Purnell Pratt John Phelps ■ Dir James Cruze • Scr Wells Root, Jack Jevne, from Max Miller's novel

ID ★★★★ 18

Drama   1994 · UK/Ger · Colour · 107min

This is a remarkable debut by director Philip Davis, also known as an actor in films such as Quadrophenia and High Hopes. Although some of the asides about racism in football ring a little hollow and not all of his extras resemble hardened thugs, Davis presents a highly credible picture of what anthropologist Desmond Morris has described as the soccer tribe defending its patch. Reece Dinsdale gives an eye-opening performance as the dedicated policeman who turns into a rabid hooligan, and the support from pub personnel Warren Clarke and Saskia Reeves and peaches-and-cream girlfriend Claire Skinner is also impressive. Riveting. 2016 saw a belated sequel. DP Violence, swearing, sex scenes. ◗

Reece Dinsdale John • Richard Graham (2) Trevor • Claire Skinner Marie • Sean Pertwee Martin • Saskia Reeves Lynda • Warren Clarke Bob • Philip Glenister Charlie • Perry Fenwick Eddie ■ Dir Philip Davis • Scr Vincent O'Connell, from a story by James Bannon

I, Daniel Blake ★★★★

Drama   2016 · UK/Fr · Colour

The dark-horse winner of 2016's Palme d'Or at Cannes, Ken Loach's final film is a small drama that punches above its weight. Comedian Dave Johns makes a terrific debut as a carpenter who has been signed off from work after a heart attack. Blake wants to go back to work but can't – the government says he is fit for work even though his GP doesn't, causing him to be stripped of benefits. A moving drama, this movingly gives a human face to the breadline statistics. DW

Hayley Squires Katie • Dave Johns Daniel Blake ■ Dir Ken Loach

I Declare War ★★ 15

Action comedy drama
2011 · Can · Colour · 93min

Borrowing heavily from The War of the Buttons and Lord of the Flies, this juvenile combat tale means well, but makes too many strategic errors to convince or impress. The story turns around a game of Capture the Flag being played in the woods by two armies of 13-year-olds. Periodically, the sticks and toy guns are replaced with real weapons to convey the intensity with which teenagers play, but the quality of the performances is varied and the treatment meted out to Siam Yu and the only girl (Mackenzie Munro) feels calculatingly provocative. DP Violence, swearing, sexual references.

Siam Yu Paul Kwon • Gage Munroe PK Sullivan • Michael Friend Jamie Skinner • Aidan Gouveia Quinn Wilson • Mackenzie Munro Jessica Dobrzanski ■ Dir Jason Lapeyre, Robert Wilson • Scr Jason Lapeyre

I Didn't Do It ★★ PG

Comedy thriller   1945 · UK · BW · 92min

This was George Formby's penultimate picture, and the toothy grin, gormless heroism and the cheeky songs that had seen him through 18 features were now wearing more than a little thin. This eminently forgettable comedy whodunnit did little to reverse his box-office decline. This story in which he turns detective to prove his innocence after he is accused of the murder of an acrobat is too short on gags or clues to hold the attention. DP

George Formby George Trotter • Billy Caryll Pa Tubbs • Hilda Mundy Ma Tubbs • Gaston Palmer Le Grand Gaston • Jack Daly Terry O'Rourke • Carl Jaffe Hilary Vance • Ian Fleming Inspector Twyning ■ Dir Marcel Varnel • Scr Norman Lee, Howard Irving Young, Stephen Black, Peter Fraser, Michael Vaughan

I Died a Thousand Times ★★

Crime drama   1955 · US · Colour · 109min

In this cheesy remake of High Sierra, Jack Palance steps into Humphrey Bogart's shoes as "Mad Dog" Earl, the hard-boiled gangster who wants to finish a lifetime of crime with a spectacular heist. It was a by-the-numbers story back in 1941 and it proves even more tired in this barely competent caper. Palance is certainly no Bogie, but the top-notch supporting cast is a movie buff's delight and well worth catching. AJ

Jack Palance Roy Earle • Shelley Winters Marie Gibson • Lori Nelson Velma • Lee Marvin Babe • Earl Holliman Red • Perry Lopez Louis Mendoza • Pedro Gonzalez [Pedro Gonzalez-Gonzales] Chico • Lon Chaney Jr Big Mac • Dennis Hopper Joe ■ Dir Stuart Heisler • Scr WR Burnett, from his novel High Sierra

I Do ★★★ 15

Romantic comedy   2006 · Fr · Colour · 85min

This frivolous French comedy nimbly works its way through almost every permutation of classic farce as 40-something bachelor Luis (Alain Chabat) fends off his family's demands to get married by hiring his best friend's sister, Emmanuelle (Charlotte Gainsbourg), as a fake fiancée. She's being paid to impress Luis's mother (the majestic Bernadette Lafont) before ditching him at the altar on their wedding day and leaving him forever unattached. The course of untrue love never runs smooth, and it's not long before this already ridiculous scenario spirals out of control. The odd couple pairing of Chabat and Gainsbourg reaps light comic rewards, while the breezy pacing makes this an easy watch. JR French +subtitles. DVD

Alain Chabat Luis • Charlotte Gainsbourg Emmanuelle • Bernadette Lafont Geneviève • Wladimir Yordanoff Francis Bertatoff • Grégoire Oestermann Pierre-Yves ■ Dir Eric Lartigau • Scr Laurent Zeitoun, Philippe Mechelen, Laurent Tirard, Grégoire Vigneron, Alain Chabat, from an idea by Chabat

The I Don't Care Girl ★★★ U

Biographical musical drama
1952 · US · Colour · 77min

This is an under-written but entertaining biopic of Broadway club sensation Eva Tanguay, portrayed zappily by talented 20th Century-Fox contract star Mitzi Gaynor. Mitzi's not bad at all, and she's certainly helped by some rich Technicolor and smart co-stars David Wayne and Oscar Levant. TS

Mitzi Gaynor Eva Tanguay • David Wayne Ed McCoy • Oscar Levant Bennett • Bob Graham Larry • Craig Hill Keene ■ Dir Lloyd Bacon • Scr Walter Bullock

I Don't Know How She Does It ★★ 12

Comedy   2011 · US · Colour · 85min

Sex and the City's Sarah Jessica Parker stars in this mildly diverting career-mom comedy, based on Allison Pearson's bestselling novel. Parker plays an investment fund manager with two young kids and an architect husband (Greg Kinnear), who manages to juggle her work and home lives until a career opportunity working with New York broker Pierce Brosnan plunges her life into a chaos of misdirected emails, missed school appointments and marital discord. Oh, and lice infestation. Parker rather overdoes the ditziness, while a mishmash of styles is distracting rather than endearing. DA DVD Blu

Sarah Jessica Parker Kate Reddy • Greg Kinnear Richard Reddy • Pierce Brosnan Jack Abelhammer • Olivia Munn Momo Hahn • Seth Meyers Chris Bunce • Kelsey Grammer Clark Cooper ■ Dir Douglas McGrath • Scr Aline Brosh McKenna, from Allison Pearson's novel

I Don't Want to Be Born ★★ 15

Horror   1975 · UK · Colour · 90min

Joan Collins is cursed by a dwarf and gives birth to a killer baby in this hilariously cheap British answer to Rosemary's Baby, which also goes under a number of intriguing titles, including The Devil within Her. Donald Pleasence delivers the tiny terror who begins childhood by drowning his nanny and then moves on to dunking dead mice in teacups. This is irresistible trash from sinister start to foolish finish. AJ DVD

Joan Collins Lucy Carlesi • Eileen Atkins Sister Albana • Donald Pleasence Dr Finch • Ralph Bates Gino Carlesi • Caroline Munro Mandy • Hilary Mason Mrs Hyde ■ Dir Peter Sasdy • Scr Stanley Price, from a story by Nato De Angeles

I Don't Want to Sleep Alone ★★★ 15

Drama
2006 · Tai/Fr/Austria/Chi/UK/Neth · Colour · 113min

This latter-day fairy tale draws on the spirit of The Magic Flute for its tale of exiles seeking solace in isolation. Shooting for the first time in his native Malaysia, director Tsai Ming-liang makes painterly use of locations in the run-down parts of Kuala Lumpur. They come to symbolise the Asian economic slump that has driven illegal migrants like Taiwanese waitress Chen Shiang-chyi into working for exploitative café owner Pearlly Chua, and Bangladeshi Norman Atun into taking in strays like a badly beaten Lee Kang-sheng. With Chen ministering less enthusiastically to Chua's comatose son, this near-silent melodrama has a dreamlike feel that is reinforced by recurring images of water and smog. DP Malay, Bengali, Mandarin, Taiwanese +subtitles. DVD

Lee Kang-sheng Hsiao-Kang • Chen Shiang-chyi Shiang-Chyi • Norman Atun Rawang • Pearlly Chua Coffee shop owner ■ Dir/Scr Tsai Ming-liang

I Dood It ★★ U

Musical comedy   1943 · US · BW · 102min

It's astonishing to find that Vincente Minnelli (Meet Me in St Louis, An American in Paris) directed this awkwardly contrived semi-musical from MGM. Red Skelton plays the tailor's assistant wooing actress Eleanor Powell from afar, by wearing his clients' clothes and looking a desirable fashion-plate. The title comes from Skelton's radio catch-phrase and there are some bright spots among the grey. TH

Red Skelton *Joseph Rivington Renolds* • Eleanor Powell *Constance Shaw* • Richard Ainley *Larry West* • Patricia Dane *Surelia Brenton* • Sam Levene *Ed Jackson* • Thurston Hall *Kenneth Lawlor* ■ *Dir* Vincente Minnelli • *Scr* Sig Herzig, Fred Saidy

I Dream of Murder ★★
Mystery thriller 2006 · US/Can · Colour · 89min

Dreams, infidelity and murder prove a messy combination in this underdeveloped mystery tale. Adding good looks and an average performance, *Star Trek: Enterprise's* Jolene Blalock plays a therapist who's drawn into a homicide case when one of her patients is strangled. But while trying to identify the perpetrator, she stirs up her own demons, making this flashback-heavy TV movie more about her shallow soul-searching than finding a killer. Consequently, the narrative has little drama or tension. SF

Jolene Blalock *Joanna* • Martin Cummins *Clay* • Carrie Colak *Leslie* • Judith Buchan *Dorothea* • Tom Carey *Lawyer* ■ *Dir* Neill Fearnley • *Scr* Cynthia Whitcomb

I Dream Too Much ★★
Musical comedy 1935 · US · BW · 97min

This RKO musical comedy was only Henry Fonda's third film, and he's badly miscast. He simply doesn't convince us he's the composer of Jerome Kern songs such as *I'm the Echo, The Jockey on the Carousel* and the title number. Hank's co-star is the French opera star Lily Pons, who made only two more films, yet had a town in Maryland named after her. AT

Henry Fonda *Jonathan Street* • Lily Pons *Annette Street* • Eric Blore *Roger Briggs* • Osgood Perkins *Paul Darcy* • Lucien Littlefield *Mr Dilley* • Lucille Ball *Gwendolyn Dilley* • Mischa Auer *Pianist* ■ *Dir* John Cromwell • *Scr* James Gow, Edmund North, from a story by Elsie Finn, David G Wittels

I Dreamed of Africa ★★12
Biographical drama 2000 · US · Colour · 109min

Although Kim Basinger valiantly holds her own as conservationist Kuki Gallmann, Hugh Hudson's direction sadly fails to support his efforts, never hammering home any political aspect beyond the stunning South African scenery. Basinger and husband Vincent Perez move from Italy to Kenya in the early 1970s, but end up arguing about the amount of time he spends away from home on hunting expeditions. LH *DVD*

Kim Basinger *Kuki Gallmann* • Vincent Perez *Paolo Gallmann* • Eva Marie Saint *Franca* • Daniel Craig *Declan Fielding* • Lance Reddick *Simon* • Connie Chiume *Wanjiku* ■ *Dir* Hugh Hudson • *Scr* Paula Milne, Susan Shilliday, from the memoirs by Kuki Gallmann

I Even Met Happy Gypsies ★★★★
Drama 1967 · Yug · Colour · 94min

Following his revisionist, Oscar-nominated war picture, *Three,* Aleksandar Petrovic received another best foreign film nomination for this docudramatic insight into the lifestyle of the gypsies of the Vojvodnia region, which also won the Special Jury Prize at Cannes. With a cast including non-professional performers speaking their own language (Serbo-Croat, Slovak and Romany), Petrovic illuminates the story of the feather trader who saves a girl from her abusive stepfather with a wealth of authentic detail. DP +subtitles.

Bekim Fehmiu *Bora* • Olivera Vuco *Lence* • Bata Zivojinovic *Mirta* • Gordana Jovanovic *Tisa* • Mija Aleksic *Father Pavle* • Rahela Ferari *Nun* • Severin Bijelic *Religious peasant* • Etelka Filipovski *Bora's wife* • Milorad Jovanovic *Toni* ■ *Dir/Scr* Aleksandar Petrovic

I Found Stella Parish ★★
Melodrama 1935 · US · BW · 84min

An unashamed assault on the tear ducts, this hoary melodrama rather went against the Warner Bros grain, substituting the customary hard-edged realism for a little soft-soap and glamour. Bedecked in gowns by the legendary costume designer Orry-Kelly and playing against cavernous sets, Kay Francis emotes for all she's worth as the stage diva prepared to sacrifice almost everything to prevent her daughter from learning of her misdeeds on the way to the top. DP

Kay Francis *Stella Parish* • Ian Hunter *Keith Lockridge* • Paul L∪kas *Stephen Norman* • Sybil Jason *Gloria Parish* • Jessie Ralph *Nana* • Joseph Sawyer *[Joe Sawyer] Chuck* ■ *Dir* Mervyn LeRoy • *Scr* Casey Robinson, from the story by John Monk Saunders

I, Frankenstein ★★12
Action horror 2013 · US/Aus · Colour · 88min

Members of the *Underworld* franchise regroup for this braindead re-imagining of Mary Shelley's classic character as a reluctant action hero. A game Aaron Eckhart is the monster, who has bits of other genre movies – *The Matrix, Van Helsing* – grafted on and winds up in the middle of a war between gargoyles and demons. The perfunctory story is explained in clunky exposition, and it all ends with truly horrific hints of an "I, Bride of Frankenstein" follow-up. AJ Some violence, swearing. *DVD* *Blu-ray* *3D*

Aaron Eckhart *Adam* • Bill Nighy *Naberius* • Yvonne Strahovski *Terra* • Miranda Otto *Leonore* • Jai Courtney *Gideon* • Aden Young *Victor Frankenstein* ■ *Dir* Stuart Beattie • *Scr* Stuart Beattie, Kevin Grevioux, from Grevioux's comic book

I Give It a Year ★★★15
Romantic comedy 2013 · UK/Fr/Ger/Lux · Colour · 93min

The directorial debut of comedy writer Dan Mazer (*Borat, Brüno*), this will-they-won't-they divorce romp has everything you want in a romantic comedy: sex appeal, warmth and genuine laughs. The only downside is the occasional lapse into lame sleaze. Rose Byrne and Rafe Spall star as the freshly married but hopelessly mismatched couple, and the supporting cast couldn't be better, with Simon Baker as the dishy alternative mate for Byrne, and Anna Faris as Spall's ideal partner. And who knew that Jason Flemyng and Minnie Driver had such great comic timing? Watch it, and laugh at the truth about love. KK Swearing, sexual references, sex scenes, nudity. *DVD* *Blu-ray*

Rose Byrne *Nat* • Rafe Spall *Josh* • Anna Faris *Chloe* • Simon Baker *(1) Guy* • Stephen Merchant *Danny* • Minnie Driver *Naomi* • Jason Flemyng *Hugh* ■ *Dir/Scr* Dan Mazer

I Got the Hook Up ★18
Comedy 1998 · US · Colour · 89min

This dismal comedy is rapper Master P's second feature. He teams with AJ Johnson as a couple of hustlers whose discovery of a consignment of cell phones leads them into an anarchic series of misadventures. But, despite scrapes with dissatisfied customers and the FBI, there's little to laugh at here. Michael Martin's direction is clumsy, and there are crass attitudes toward women and the disabled. Embarrassingly bad. DP

Master P *Black* • AJ Johnson *[Anthony Johnson] Blue* • Gretchen Palmer *Sweet Lorraine* • Frantz Turner *Dalton* • Tommy *"Tiny" Lister Jr [Tom "Tiny" Lister Jr] T-Lay* • Anthony Boswell *Little Brother* • Ice Cube *Gun runner* • Snoop Doggy Dogg *[Snoop Dogg] Bar patron* ■ *Dir* Michael Martin • *Scr* Master P, from a story by Master P, Leroy Douglas, Carrie Mingo

I Have Never Forgotten You: the Life and Legacy of Simon Wiesenthal ★★★★
Documentary 2007 · US · BW and Colour · 107min

The Simon Wiesenthal Centre has been responsible for a series of acclaimed documentaries (two of which were Oscar winners), but, fittingly, this is perhaps the best. Rather than revisiting the late Nazi-hunter's high-profile pursuit of such war criminals as Adolf Eichmann, film-maker Richard Trank focuses on the grief, anger and defiance that enabled Wiesenthal to turn his life into a worthy memorial for the 89 family members who perished in the Holocaust. The mix of anecdote and archive footage is perhaps a little predictable, and the contributions of narrator Nicole Kidman and interviewee Ben Kingsley seem a touch too showbiz at times. But Wiesenthal himself emerges as a man of enormous courage, infinite patience and impudent good humour. DP *DVD*

Nicole Kidman *Narrator* • Simon Wiesenthal • Ben Kingsley ■ *Dir* Richard Trank • *Scr* Rabbi Marvin Hier [Marvin Hier], Richard Trank • *Cinematographer* Jeffrey Victor

I Heard the Owl Call My Name ★★★★U
Drama 1973 · US · Colour · 74min

Adapted without condescension or overt sentimentality by director Daryl Duke, this superior TV movie makes powerful use of the British Columbian coastscape to emphasise the grinding poverty of the native Indians who dwell there and the enormity of the task facing Tom Courtenay as the inexperienced Anglican priest sent to minister to them. With humble support from Dean Jagger, as the bishop who sustains the novice's faith as isolation saps his morale, Courtenay achieves a sincerity and compassion that stands in stark contrast to his more cynical kitchen sink persona. DP

Tom Courtenay *Father Tark Brian* • Dean Jagger *Bishop* • Paul Stanley *Jim Wallace* • Marianne Jones *Keetah* • George Clutesi *George P Hudson* • Keith Pepper *Alan Spencer* ■ *Dir* Daryl Duke • *Scr* Gerald Di Pego, from the novel by Margaret Craven

I ♥ Huckabees ★★★★15
Black comedy drama 2004 · US/UK/Ger · Colour · 102min

Director David O Russell's bravely weird film is a melange of cod-existential philosophy, Gen-X angst, corporate intrigue and slapstick comedy. Jason Schwartzman is an environmental activist whose "Open Spaces Coalition" is sponsored by the Huckabees superstore chain, represented by executive Jude Law. Troubled by a series of coincidences, Schwartzman employs existential detectives (played by the brilliantly wacky Dustin Hoffman and Lily Tomlin) to investigate his life, and through them meets firefighter Mark Wahlberg. Simultaneously odd, ambitious, pretentious and optimistic, this will irritate some while delighting others. AS Swearing. *DVD*

Jason Schwartzman *Albert Markovski* • Isabelle Huppert *Caterine Vauban* • Dustin Hoffman *Bernard Jaffe* • Lily Tomlin *Vivian Jaffe* • Jude Law *Brad Stand* • Mark Wahlberg *Tommy Corn* • Naomi Watts *Dawn Campbell* • Angela Grillo *Angela Franco* ■ *Dir* David O Russell • *Scr* David O Russell, Jeff Baena

I Hired a Contract Killer ★★★15
Comedy thriller 1990 · Fin/Swe · Colour · 74min

Aki Kaurismäki made his English language debut with this doggedly downbeat slice of black comedy. The man many see as Finland's finest director transforms London into a hostile urban wilderness. It's here that discarded civil servant Jean-Pierre Léaud seeks refuge from the hitman he no longer requires, having fallen for flowerseller Margi Clarke. Kaurismäki keeps the performances edgy with short scenes and minimalist dialogue, opting for a melancholic rather than a suspenseful air. DP

Margi Clarke *Margaret* • Jean-Pierre Léaud *Henri Boulanger* • Kenneth Colley *Killer* • Trevor Bowen *Department head* • Imogen Claire *Secretary* • Nicky Tesco *Pete* • Charles Cork *Al* ■ *Dir/Scr* Aki Kaurismäki

The I Inside ★★15
Mystery thriller 2003 · UK/US · Colour · 87min

Fragments of memory become pieces of a mind-bending jigsaw puzzle in this twisting thriller. Hospitalised heir Ryan Phillippe wakes up with amnesia following a near-death experience and finds he is inexplicably able to travel in time and uses his new gift to reconstruct his terrifying lost years. This is sleekly executed and visually handsome, with some engaging performances, but it's not as clever as it believes and the too-convenient conclusion is disappointing. SF Swearing, violence. *DVD*

Ryan Phillippe *Simon Cable* • Sarah Polley *Clair* • Piper Perabo *Anna* • Stephen Rea *Dr Newman* • Stephen Lang *Mr Travitt* • Robert Sean Leonard *Peter Cable* ■ *Dir* Roland Suso Richter • *Scr* Michael Cooney, Scott Bogart *Timothy,* from the play *Point of Death* by Michael Cooney

I Killed My Mother ★★★15
Drama 2009 · Can · Colour and BW · 95min

Twenty-year-old Xavier Dolan makes an audacious start as writer, director and actor in this lively and disarmingly frank study of teenage petulance. When the adored mother of a temperamental 16-year-old Quebecois discovers he's gay, she decides to send him to a boarding school to learn some morals and manners. Although the rants become repetitive, the performances, fantasy interludes and monochrome confessional inserts are all nicely judged. DP French +subtitles. Swearing, sexual references. *DVD*

Anne Dorval *Chantale Lemming* • Xavier Dolan *Hubert Minel* • François Arnaud *Antonin Rimbaud* • Suzanne Clément *Julie Cloutier* • Patricia Tulasne *Hélène Rimbaud* ■ *Dir/Scr* Xavier Dolan

I Know What You Did Last Summer ★★★15
Horror thriller 1997 · US · Colour · 96min

Director Jim Gillespie's stalk-and-slash saga gives *Scream* writer Kevin Williamson the chance to revive his favourite psycho-killer clichés. Four high-school graduates cover up a hit-and-run accident, only to have the dark tragedy rear its head a year later when a masked fisherman starts bumping them off. The beautiful photography makes this watchable, but Gillespie's chiller trades on outdated thrills all the way through to its creak-and-shriek showdown. A sequel, *I Still Know What You Did Last Summer,* followed in 1998. AJ *DVD*

Jennifer Love Hewitt *Julie James* • Sarah Michelle Gellar *Helen Shivers* • Ryan Phillippe *Barry Cox* • Freddie Prinze Jr *Ray Bronson* • Muse Watson *Benjamin Willis* • Bridgette Wilson *Elsa Shivers* • Anne Heche *Melissa Egan* ■ *Dir* Jim Gillespie • *Scr* Kevin Williamson, from the novel by Lois Duncan

I Know Where I'm Going! ★★★★★U
Romantic comedy 1945 · UK · BW · 87min

Of all the classics produced by Michael Powell and Emeric Pressburger, this may be the most unsung but it's undoubtedly the most entrancing. As the headstrong young woman and the laird who distracts her from her stuffy fiancé, Wendy Hiller and Roger Livesey are superb, and there's knowing support from Pamela Brown, John Laurie and Finlay Currie. Erwin Hillier's photography is as beautiful as it is atmospheric, but it's the expert mix of romance and comedy, arresting use of the landscape and respectful fascination with the local culture that make this so compelling. DP *DVD*

Wendy Hiller *Joan Webster* • Roger Livesey *Torquil MacNeil* • Pamela Brown *Catriona Potts* • Nancy Price *Mrs Crozier* • John Laurie *John Campbell* • George Carney *Mr Webster* • Walter Hudd *Hunter* • Captain Duncan MacKechnie *Captain "Lochinvar"* • Petula Clark *Cheril* ■ *Dir/Scr* Michael Powell, Emeric Pressburger

I Know Who Killed Me
★★★ 18

Thriller 2007 · US · Colour · 101min

Lindsay Lohan takes on a dual role in director Chris Sivertson's twisty, perversely fascinating psycho thriller. When Grade A student Aubrey Fleming goes missing, her parents fear she's the latest victim of a serial killer with an amputee kink. But then she turns up alive and horribly maimed, insisting she's actually a pole dancer called Dakota Moss. Lohan clearly delineates the character traits of these two very different women, making a real impact as the hard-as-nails stripper. Sivertson combines elements of Alfred Hitchcock-style black comedy, Brian De Palma plot twists and Dario Argento style, as he bathes the demented narrative in a vibrant colour scheme. AJ *DVD*

Lindsay Lohan *Aubrey Fleming/Dakota Moss* • Julia Ormond *Susan Fleming* • Neal McDonough *Daniel Fleming* • Brian Geraghty *Jerrod Pointer* • Garcelle Beauvais-Nilon *Agent Julie Bascombe* • Spencer Garrett *Agent Phil Lazarus* • Gregory Itzin *Dr Greg Jameson* ■ *Dir* Chris Sivertson • *Scr* Jeffrey Hammond

I Know You Know
★★ 15

Drama 2008 · UK · Colour · 78min

Justin Kerrigan's low-budget coming-of-age story begins with Charlie (Robert Carlyle) stepping off a private jet in Cardiff. Tagging along is his 11-year-old son Jamie (Arron Fuller), who's as confused by his dad's secretive lifestyle as the audience. Is Charlie a spy? A thief? And why is his beaten-up old banger being followed by vans from a satellite TV company? Kerrigan's film hoodwinks us with a strange blend of child's-eye fantasy and thriller clichés that are by turns preposterous and heartbreaking. Never completely gelling – and relying on a late twist that's not as surprising as it ought to be – this offbeat drama intrigues but doesn't really satisfy. JR Swearing. *DVD*

Robert Carlyle *Charlie* • Arron Fuller *Jamie* • David Bradley (2) *Mr Fisher* • Valerie Lilley *Lilly* • Karl Johnson (2) *Ernie* • Aaron Lamprey *Richie* ■ *Dir/Scr* Justin Kerrigan

I Like It like That
★★★ 15

Romantic comedy 1994 · US · Colour · 102min

Written and directed by Spike Lee alumnus Darnell Martin, this is a rare look at the lives of the Latino population jostling for space in the Bronx. At the centre of this engaging film is Lauren Velez, who gets the chance to prove she's more than just a homebird when her husband is jailed and she lands a job with a record label. The racial mix is just a tad too cosy and the message that men are all the same no matter what their colour is stated too blandly. But Martin knows her patch and coaxes a lovely performance from the sassy Velez. DP Violence, swearing, sex scenes, drug abuse, nudity.

Lauren Velez *Lisette Linares* • Jon Seda *Chino Linares* • Tomas Melly *Li'l Chino Linares* • Desiree Casado *Minnie Linares* • Isaiah Garcia *Pee Wee Linares* • Jesse Borrego *Alexis* • Griffin Dunne *Stephen Price* ■ *Dir/Scr* Darnell Martin

I Live in Fear
★★★ PG

Drama 1955 · Jpn · BW · 98min

Shot at the height of the Cold War and a mere decade after the atomic assault on Japan, Akira Kurosawa's drama about life under the shadow of the bomb was originally conceived as a satire and an uncertainty of tone undermines its purpose. By having Toshiro Mifune descend into dementia, his desire to escape the holocaust by relocating his family to a Brazilian hideaway can too easily be dismissed as senile paranoia instead of prescient warning. DP Japanese +subtitles. *DVD*

Toshiro Mifune *Kiichi Nakajima* • Eiko Miyoshi *Toyo Nakajima* • Haruko Togo *Yoshi* • Takashi Shimura *Harada* ■ *Dir* Akira Kurosawa • *Scr* Akira Kurosawa, Shinobu Hashimoto, Hideo Oguni • *Music* Fumio Hayasaka

I Live in Grosvenor Square
★ U

Romance 1945 · UK · BW · 114min

This expensive, ridiculous and tedious romantic drama has Anna Neagle, a duke's granddaughter, switching her affections from Rex Harrison's army major to Dean Jagger's American sergeant. It's unbelievable that dull Jagger could oust charismatic Harrison, or that the latter would be such a generous loser – but it's typical of the way the entire production panders to the American market, where it played as *A Yank in London*. AE

Anna Neagle *Lady Patricia Fairfax* • Rex Harrison *Maj David Bruce* • Dean Jagger *Sgt John Patterson* • Robert Morley *Duke of Exmoor* • Jane Darwell *Mrs Patterson* • Nancy Price *Mrs Wilson* ■ *Dir* Herbert Wilcox • *Scr* Nicholas Phipps, William D Bayles, from a story by Maurice Cowan

I Live My Life
★★

Romantic comedy 1935 · US · BW · 85min

Animosity turns to amorousness (as you knew it would) when a rich, bored society girl and a humble archaeologist who disdains her friends and her lifestyle fall in love. Joan Crawford and Brian Aherne star in this desperately routine film, directed with a surprising lack of brio by WS Van Dyke. Designer clothes and sophisticated cocktail parties lend a fleeting and superficial gloss to the tepid screenplay. AJ

Joan Crawford *Kay* • Brian Aherne *Terry* • Frank Morgan *Bentley* • Aline MacMahon *Betty* • Eric Blore *Grove* ■ *Dir* WS Van Dyke • *Scr* Joseph L Mankiewicz, Gottfried Reinhardt, Ethel Borden, from the short story *Claustrophobia* by Abbie Carter Goodloe • *Music* Dimitri Tiomkin [Dmitri Tiomkin]

I Love a Soldier
★★

Second World War romantic drama
1944 · US · BW · 106min

Director Mark Sandrich must have longed for the good old days while handling this mediocre weepie, for while Paulette Goddard and Sonny Tufts may have looked good together, they were definitely no Fred and Ginger (whom he directed five times at RKO). The leads occasionally spark into life, as Tufts's dashing GI melts the hardened heart of Goddard's war-effort welder. DP

Paulette Goddard *Eva Morgan* • Sonny Tufts *Dan Gilgore* • Mary Treen *Cissy Grant* • Walter Sande *Stiff Banks* • Ann Doran *Jenny* • Beulah Bondi *Etta Lane* ■ *Dir* Mark Sandrich • *Scr* Allan Scott

I Love Melvin
★★★ U

Musical 1953 · US · Colour · 77min

This undervalued little musical stars Donald O'Connor and Debbie Reynolds, reunited after the success of the previous year's *Singin' in the Rain* and at the top of their form again here. O'Connor plays a photographer's assistant who cons Reynolds by telling her she's in line to be a cover girl. There are some charming duos – O'Connor's skating slides are a sight to behold – and plenty of zip. TH

Donald O'Connor *Melvin Hoover* • Debbie Reynolds *Judy LeRoy* • Una Merkel *Mom Schneider* • Richard Anderson *Harry Flack* • Allyn Joslyn *Pop Schneider* • Les Tremayne *Mr Hennenman* • Noreen Corcoran *Clarabelle* ■ *Dir* Don Weis • *Scr* George Wells, Ruth Brooks Flippen, from a story by Laslo Vadnay

I Love My... Wife
★★

Comedy 1970 · US · Colour · 95min

A credit sequence charting Elliott Gould's progress from sexual novice to hopeful bridegroom gets this adult comedy off to a lively start. However, no sooner has disillusion set in than the inspiration dries up, and what might have been an amusing insight into the sexual insecurities of the post-1960s male becomes an assault on women in general. Writer Robert Kaufman's one-liners are as smugly predictable as his coarsely satirical observations. DP

Elliott Gould *Dr Richard Burrows* • Brenda Vaccaro *Jody Borrows* • Angel Tompkins *Helene Donnelly* • Dabney Coleman *Frank Donnelly* • Joan Tompkins *Grandma Dennison* ■ *Dir* Mel Stuart • *Scr* Robert Kaufman

I Love Trouble
★★★ PG

Romantic comedy thriller
1994 · US · Colour · 117min

If you can get your head round the idea of Julia Roberts as a ruthlessly ambitious newspaper reporter, then there's plenty to enjoy in this frivolous thriller. However, it's too long and too deliberate to fulfil its ambition of re-creating the "rat-a-tat" screwball style that made the 1930s battle-of-the-sexes comedies such a delight. Nick Nolte is closer to the mark as the cynical hack tinkering with old columns to lighten the load, but neither the rivalry nor the romance between the stars is convincing. DP *DVD*

Nick Nolte *Peter Brackett* • Julia Roberts *Sabrina Peterson* • Saul Rubinek *Sam Smotherman* • James Rebhorn *The Thin Man* • Robert Loggia *Matt Greenfield* • Kelly Rutherford *Kim* • Olympia Dukakis *Jeannie* • Marsha Mason *Senator Gayle Robbins* ■ *Dir* Charles Shyer • *Scr* Nancy Meyers, Charles Shyer

I Love You Again ★★★★ PG

Screwball comedy 1940 · US · BW · 98min

Super-sophisticates William Powell and Myrna Loy take a break from their *Thin Man* series to star in this ingeniously written, absolutely hysterical MGM screwball comedy. Amnesiac Powell spends the whole movie trying to persuade his wife, Loy, not to divorce him in order to marry her 1940s version of a toyboy. It's Powell's film, as he essays pratfalls and double takes with great *élan* in this superb comedic tour de force. TS

William Powell *Larry Wilson/George Carey* • Myrna Loy *Kay Wilson* • Frank McHugh *Doc Ryan* • Edmund Lowe *Duke Sheldon* • Donald Douglas [Don Douglas] *Herbert* • Nella Walker *Kay's mother* ■ *Dir* WS Van Dyke II [WS Van Dyke] • *Scr* Charles Lederer, George Oppenheimer, Harry Kurnitz, from a story by Leon Gordon, Maurine Watkins, from a novel by Octavus Roy Cohen

I Love You, Alice B Toklas
★★ 15

Satirical comedy 1968 · US · Colour · 89min

Even when Peter Sellers could seemingly do no wrong, director Hy Averback's satirical comedy was a dubious proposition. Despite promising early scenes in which asthmatic lawyer Sellers is at odds with his pushy girlfriend (the brilliant Joyce Van Patten), it all falls apart when Sellers eats marijuana-spiked cookies and becomes a hippy dropout. Very much of its time, this provided a Hollywood breakthrough for screenwriters Paul Mazursky and Larry Tucker. TH Brief nudity. *DVD*

Peter Sellers *Harold* • Jo Van Fleet *Mother* • Leigh Taylor-Young *Nancy* • Joyce Van Patten *Joyce* • David Arkin *Herbie* • Herb Edelman *Murray* • Louis Gottlieb *Guru* ■ *Dir* Hy Averback • *Scr* Paul Mazursky, Larry Tucker

I Love You, Beth Cooper
★★ 15

Romantic comedy
2009 · US/UK/Aus · Colour · 97min

A high-school nerd's public declaration of his feelings for a cheerleader has unlikely consequences in this knockabout teen farce. Geeky Denis Cooverman (Paul Rust) delivers the title's five fateful words in his valedictory speech, little expecting that said Ms Cooper (Hayden Panettiere) will later join him and his equally dorky pal (Jack T Carpenter) as they celebrate graduation night on their own. Director Chris Columbus (*Home Alone*, *Mrs Doubtfire*) has been out of the comedy game for a while, as the clunky timing of the gags shows, but there are some amiable performances here, plus an attempt to inject some character depth into proceedings. TJ Swearing, sexual references. *DVD*

Hayden Panettiere *Beth Cooper* • Paul Rust *Denis Cooverman* • Jack T Carpenter *[Jack Carpenter]* • Rich Munsch • Lauren London *Cammy* • Lauren Storm *Treece* • Shawn Roberts *Kevin* ■ *Dir* Chris Columbus • *Scr* Larry Doyle, from his novel

I Love You, I Love You Not
★★ 15

Coming-of-age drama
1997 · US/UK · Colour · 88min

Claire Danes stars as a withdrawn teenager, falling for the school jock Jude Law at her New York school. It all goes horribly wrong when her classmates discover she said grandmother, Jeanne Moreau, is a Holocaust survivor and their anti-Semitism kicks in. Grandmother and granddaughter share their respective suffering – Danes playing Moreau in the flashback sequences in Germany. While the message is important, it's been better explored in better films. LH

Jeanne Moreau *Nana* • Claire Danes *Daisy* • Jude Law *Ethan* • Carrie Slaza *Jane* • Jerry Tanklow *Mr Gilman* • James Van Der Beek *Tony* ■ *Dir* Billy Hopkins • *Scr* Wendy Kesselman, from a play by Wendy Kesselman

I Love You, Man ★★★ 15

Comedy 2008 · US · Colour · 100min

After his stand-out performance in hit comedy *Role Models*, Paul Rudd is finally front and centre. The burden rests easy on his shoulders even though his character is a fragile fellow who relates better to women than men. It's only in the lead-up to his wedding that he decides he needs a best man and director John Hamburg treats the search like a romantic comedy. The jokes can occasionally be coarse and predictable but the awkwardness between the punch lines is where Rudd excels, timing every pause and fumbled bit of banter to optimum effect, tickling your funny bone and tugging at your heartstrings all at once. SP Swearing *DVD* ﾐ

Paul Rudd *Peter Klaven* • Jason Segel *Sydney Fife* • Rashida Jones *Zooey* • Andy Samberg *Robbie* • JK Simmons *Oz* • Jane Curtin *Joyce* • Jon Favreau *Barry* • Jaime Pressly *Denise* ■ *Dir* John Hamburg • *Scr* John Hamburg, Larry Levin, from a story by Levin

I Love You Phillip Morris
★★★ 15

Biographical comedy drama
2009 · US/Fr · Colour · 93min

Jim Carrey does his in-your-face act again here, but this true story about a conman in love isn't just another excuse for copious mugging. As Steven Russell, Carrey cuts a tragic figure when he becomes overwhelmed by his feelings for Phillip Morris (Ewan McGregor), a sensitive soul he meets in prison. The pair's tempestuous romance, though subject to coarse humour, is also tenderly portrayed by writer/directors Glenn Ficarra and John Requa (*Bad Santa*). It can feel too madcap when McGregor isn't on screen, but Carrey's performance is compelling and surprisingly poignant, and the film remains outrageously funny without resorting to cheap gags. SP Violence, swearing, sex scenes. *DVD* ﾐ

Jim Carrey *Steven Russell* • Ewan McGregor *Phillip Morris* • Leslie Mann *Debbie Russell* • Rodrigo Santoro *Jimmy Kemple* • Michael Mandel *Cleavon* • Marylouise Burke *Barbara Bascombe* ■ *Dir* Glenn Ficarra, John Requa • *Scr* Glenn Ficarra, John Requa, from the non-fiction book by Steve McVicker

I Love You to Death
★ 15

Black comedy based on a true story
1990 · US · Colour · 93min

One of those unfortunate efforts which looks a wow on paper – great plot, great director, grade-A comic cast – but which sinks like a celluloid *Titanic* under the weight of more ham than a butcher's shop. Based on a gift of a true story (woman tries desperately to kill unfaithful hubby, but he seems clottishly indestructible), yet everyone appears inexplicably hellbent on pressing the destruct button. SH Violence. *DVD*

Kevin Kline *Joey Boca* • Tracey Ullman *Rosalie Boca* • Joan Plowright *Nadja* • River Phoenix *Devo* • William Hurt *Harlan James* • Keanu Reeves *Marlon James* • Miriam Margolyes *Joey's mother* ■ *Dir* Lawrence Kasdan • *Scr* John Kostmayer

I Married a Monster from Outer Space ★★★
Science-fiction horror 1958 · US · BW · 77min

Soon-to-be-wed Tom Tryon has his body taken over by a rhubarb-faced alien in Gene Fowler Jr's smartly directed paranoia classic: substitute Gloria Talbott's UFO-duplicated husband for a red in her bed and the true anti-Communist undercurrent becomes apparent. Fowler worked as an editor for Fritz Lang, and the German expressionist influence is evident in the use of shadows and weird angles to heighten the atmospheric tension. Intelligent and well packaged. AJ

Tom Tryon *Bill Farrell* • Gloria Talbott *Marge Farrell* • Peter Baldwin *Swanson* • Robert Ivers *Harry* • Chuck Wassil *Ted* • Valerie Allen *B Girl* • Ty Hungerford *Mac* • Ken Lynch *Dr Wayne* ■ *Dir* Gene Fowler Jr • *Scr* Louis Vittes

I Married a Strange Person ★★★
Animated comedy 1997 · US · Colour · 76min

Acclaimed for the crayon-drawn *Your Face* and *One of Those Days*, Bill Plympton is revered by his fellow animators. It's easy to see why from this feature, which can be summed up in a single word – strange! Newlyweds Grant and Kerry Boyer seem blissfully happy until a pair of ducks fly into their satellite dish, transforming the TV into a malevolent machine that gives Grant the power to turn his fantasies into reality. Combining moments of mock horror (such as when a neighbour is attacked by his lawn) and surreal humour, this makes for perfect late-night escapism. DP

Charis Michaelson *Keri Boyer* • Tom Larson *Grant Boyer* • Richard Spore *Larson P Giles* • Chris Cooke *Colonel Ferguson* ■ *Dir* Bill Plympton • *Scr* Bill Plympton, PC Vey

I Married a Witch ★★★★ U
Romantic fantasy comedy 1942 · US · BW · 76min

This was one of the films French director René Clair made in Hollywood during his wartime exile. It's a comedy about a witch who is reincarnated in order to persecute the descendant of the judge who condemned her to be burned at the stake 300 years earlier. The fact that the descendant, played by Fredric March, is running for political office is curiously prescient of the McCarthy witch-hunts that occurred some five years later. Veronica Lake was usually typecast as a sultry *femme fatale*, but as the witch she shows a real flair for whimsy. AT DVD

Fredric March *Wallace Wooley/Jonathan Wooley/Nathaniel Wooley/Samuel Wooley* • Veronica Lake *Jennifer* • Robert Benchley *Dr Dudley White* • Susan Hayward *Estelle Masterson* • Cecil Kellaway *Daniel* • Elizabeth Patterson *Margaret* • Robert Warwick *JB Masterson* ■ *Dir* Rene Clair [René Clair] • *Scr* Robert Pirosh, Marc Connelly, Dalton Trumbo (uncredited), from the novel *The Passionate Witch* by Thorne Smith, as completed by Norman Matson

I Married a Woman ★★ U
Comedy 1958 · US · BW and Colour · 83min

After a decade as the blonde bombshell of British cinema, Diana Dors graces this Hollywood comedy with her considerable assets – with mixed results. She does well enough as a pouting lovely who tries to put the pep back into her marriage, but co-star George Gobel, a top TV comedian, is an eminently resistible personality whose bungling wimp routine adds considerably to the burden of watching this desperately unfunny charade. DP

Diana Dors *Janice* • George Gobel *Marshall Briggs* • Adolphe Menjou *Sutton* • Jessie Royce Landis *Mother* • Nita Talbot *Miss Anderson* • William Redfield *Eddie* • Steve Dunne *Bob* • John McGiver *Girard* • John Wayne • Angie Dickinson *Screen wife* ■ *Dir* Hal Kanter • *Scr* Goodman Ace

I Married an Angel ★ U
Fantasy musical romance 1942 · US · BW · 83min

This disastrous end to the Jeanette MacDonald/Nelson Eddy partnership is for die-hard devotees only. Mangling a hit Broadway musical by Richard Rodgers and Lorenz Hart, MGM miscast Eddy as a Budapest playboy while MacDonald fares little better, being restrained for most of the picture as an angel dreamed up by Eddy. A lighter, more satirical thrust might have improved matters, but director WS Van Dyke doesn't find much humour in the script. AE

Jeanette MacDonald *Anna Zador/Brigitta* • Nelson Eddy *Count Willie Palaffi* • Binnie Barnes *Peggy* • Edward Everett Horton *Peter* • Reginald Owen *Herman "Whiskers" Rothbart* ■ *Dir* WS Van Dyke • *Scr* An ta Loos, from the musical by Richard Rodgers, Lorenz Hart, from the play by Vaszary Janos

I Met Him in Paris ★★★
Romantic comedy 1937 · US · BW · 86min

A formula vehicle for Claudette Colbert, this comedy finds her taking a well-earned vacation from a boring fiancée in a familiar Paramount-designed Paris. There she's courted by two more men, and ends up on the Swiss ski slopes with both. Will she choose morose and cynical playwright Melvyn Douglas or charming smoothie playboy Robert Young? En route to the answer, Claude Binyon's screenplay crackles with barbed wit, delivered in best high-comedy style by the trio of attractive stars. RK

Claudette Colbert *Kay Denham* • Melvyn Douglas *George Potter* • Robert Young (1) *Gene Anders* • Lee Bowman *Berk Sutter* • Mona Barrie *Helen Anders* • George Davis *Cutter driver* ■ *Dir* Wesley Ruggles • *Scr* Claude Binyon, from the story by Helen Meinardi

I Met My Love Again ★★★
Romantic drama 1938 · US · BW · 77min

The romance of a youthful small-town couple is shattered when she is swept off her feet and elopes with a writer. Widowed ten years later, she returns home with her daughter and, to the disapproval of the over-protective townsfolk, tries to take up with her former love, now a college professor. This is basically soap opera elevated by a first-rate cast, with Henry Fonda and Joan Bennett as the lovers trying to resurrect their relationship. RK

Joan Bennett *Julie Wier Shaw* • Henry Fonda *Ives Towner* • Louise Platt *Brenda Lane* • Alan Marshal *Michael Shaw* • Dame May Whitty *Aunt William* • Alan Baxter *Tony* ■ *Dir* Arthur Ripley, Joshua Logan • *Scr* David Hertz, from the novel *Summer Lightning* by Allene Corliss • *Cinematographer* Hal Mohr

I, Monster ★★ 12
Horror 1971 · UK · Colour · 77min

Dr Jekyll and Mr Hyde become Dr Marlowe and Mr Blake in a vapid attempt to give a Freudian psychological interpretation to the oft-told tale. Christopher Lee is convincing as the doctor meddling with a dangerous formula, and the Victorian London atmosphere is well captured, but director Stephen Weeks's inexperience means that any complex themes are quickly abandoned, and the end result is flatter than you might expect. AJ DVD

Christopher Lee *Dr Marlowe/Mr Blake* • Peter Cushing *Utterson* • Mike Raven *Enfield* • Richard Hurndall *Lanyan* • George Merritt (1) *Poole* • Kenneth J Warren *Dean* • Susan Jameson *Diane* ■ *Dir* Stephen Weeks • *Scr* Milton Subotsky

I Never Promised You a Rose Garden ★★★★ 18
Drama 1977 · US · Colour · 88min

Anthony Page's adaptation of Joanne Greenberg's semi-autobiographical bestseller never explores mental illness in any real depth, but is still a highly sympathetic study of someone facing up to its consequences. This Roger Corman production is steered away from any

melodramatic pitfalls by Kathleen Quinlan's exemplary performance, as a teenage schizophrenic plagued by sexually charged fantasies and recurrent thoughts of suicide. Bibi Andersson is equally impressive as her intuitive psychiatrist. DP

Bibi Andersson *Dr Fried* • Kathleen Quinlan *Deborah Blake* • Ben Piazza *Mr Blake* • Lorraine Gary *Mrs Blake* • Darlene Craviotto *Carla* • Reni Santoni *Hobbs* • Susan Tyrrell *Lee* ■ *Dir* Anthony Page • *Scr* Lewis John Carlino, Gavin Lambert, from a novel by Hannah Green [Joanne Greenberg]

I Never Sang for My Father ★★★★ PG
Drama 1970 · US · Colour · 92min

This immensely moving screen version of Robert Anderson's sensitive play was scripted by the playwright himself, giving a superb career-best role to Melvyn Douglas as the ageing, domineering father. Gene Hackman, as the suffering adult son, and Estelle Parsons, as the daughter made an outcast because she married a Jew, are also outstanding. Gilbert Cates's direction manages to make this both depressing and uplifting at the same time, and, though resolutely theatrical, it remains compulsively watchable. TS

Melvyn Douglas *Tom Garrison* • Gene Hackman *Gene Garrison* • Dorothy Stickney *Margaret Garrison* • Estelle Parsons *Alice* • Elizabeth Hubbard *Peggy* • Lovelady Powell *Norma* ■ *Dir* Gilbert Cates • *Scr* Robert W Anderson, from his play

I Now Pronounce You Chuck & Larry ★ 12
Comedy 2007 · US · Colour · 110min

When widower Larry (Kevin James) finds he cannot name his kids as his life insurance beneficiaries, his solution to overcome the red tape is to ask buddy Chuck (Adam Sandler) to pretend to marry him. This begins the ridiculous ball of gay jokes rolling – a situation is so patently artificial that it's a wonder the city official (Steve Buscemi) investigating them needs to do any work at all. Despite a pro-gay finale, Dennis Dugan's comedy is basically a flimsy collection of homosexual gags and stereotypical performances, none worse than Rob Schneider's cameo as a Japanese wedding chapel owner. KK DVD

Adam Sandler *Chuck Levine* • Kevin James *Larry Valentine* • Jessica Biel *Alex McDonough* • Dan Aykroyd *Captain Tucker* • Ving Rhames *Duncan* • Steve Buscemi *Clint Fitzer* • Richard Chamberlain *Councilman Banks* ■ *Dir* Dennis Dugan • *Scr* Barry Fanaro, Alexander Payne, Jim Taylor • *Cinematographer* Dean Semler

I.O.U.S.A. ★★★ U
Documentary 2008 · US · Colour · 84min

Anyone baffled by complex business-news reports should find this compelling documentary a useful introduction to the workings of international trade and Wall Street, as well as the US federal budget, social security system and national debt. Taking his cue from William Bonner and Addison Wiggin's book *Empire of Debt*, director Patrick Creadon makes effective use of pie charts, timelines, graphs and talking heads to explain how wars, inflation, public works, tax cuts and presidential decisions have shaped American economics over the last 200 years. DP English, Mandarin +subtitles.

■ *Dir* Patrick Creadon • *Scr* Patrick Creadon, Christine O'Malley, Addison Wiggin

I Only Want You to Love Me ★★★ 15
Drama based on a true story 1976 · W Ger · Colour · 165min

Made for television during a creative crisis on *Satan's Brew*, this is one of Rainer Werner Fassbinder's most accessible films. This intellectually rigorous and expertly staged melodrama explores the modern tendency towards the breakdown of familial communication, and also the way in which material gestures have come to replace demonstrations of affection. Workaholic

builder Vitus Zeplichal cuts a genuinely tragic figure as his emotional inarticulacy reduces him from doting son to crazed killer. DP German +subtitles. Violence, nudity. DVD

Vitus Zeplichal *Peter* • Elke Aberle *Erika* • Alexander Allerson *Father* • Erni Mangold *Mother* • Johanna Hofer *Erika's grandmother* • Wolfgang Hess *Building superintendent* ■ *Dir/Scr* Rainer Werner Fassbinder

I Origins ★★★★ 15
Science-fiction thriller 2014 · US · Colour · 105min

Is there life after death? It sounds like grounds for a fantasy, but *I Origins* is an unusual, science-based metaphysical thriller that manages to be both provocative and romantic while maintaining a balance between both. A well-cast Michael Pitt stars as a New York biologist seeking to prove the theory of evolution, and so disprove creationism. Though a little stretched, the film's mysteries are thoughtful and even profound, with a series of twists that aren't so much played for surprise as to push at the limits of our rationality. DW Swearing, sex scenes, nudity.

Michael Pitt *Dr Ian Gray* • Brit Marling *Karen* • Astrid Bergès-Frisbey *Sofi* • Steven Yeun *Kenny* • Archie Panjabi *Priya Varma* • Cara Seymour *Dr Simmons* • William Mapother *Darryl Mackenzie* ■ *Dir/Scr* Mike Cahill

I Ought to Be in Pictures ★★★★ 15
Comedy 1982 · US · Colour · 102min

Neil Simon has adapted this all-laughing, all-crying drama from his own stage play. Playing a Hollywood-struck girl, Dinah Manoff gives a performance that avoids sentimentality, but which still involves us emotionally. She travels to Tinseltown to track down her father Walter Matthau, who's now living with girlfriend Ann-Margret. He used to be a screenwriter but these days seems more interested in drinking and gambling. Herbert Ross directs with level-headed cool, letting Simon's script do all the work. TH

Walter Matthau *Herbert Tucker* • Ann-Margret *Stephanie* • Dinah Manoff *Libby* • Lance Guest *Gordon* • Lewis Smith *Soldier* • Martin Ferrero *Monte Del Rey* ■ *Dir* Herbert Ross • *Scr* Neil Simon, from his play

IP5 ★ 15
Drama 1992 · Fr · Colour · 114min

The French cinema movement called *cinéma du look* came to a shuddering halt with this atrocious, self-referential road movie from Jean-Jacques Beineix. Sadly it was the swan song of Yves Montand, who died just days after "dying" in this film and whose gaunt expression is far more haunting than any of the director's stylised imagery. Half-baked social and ecological theories abound, as Montand joins graffiti artist Olivier Martinez and rapper Sekkou Sall in a search of the Island of Pachyderms. Painful and embarrassing. DP French +subtitles.

Yves Montand *Léon Marcel* • Olivier Martinez *Tony* • Sekkou Sall *Jockey* • Géraldine Pailhas *Gloria* • Colette Renard *Clarisse/Monique* ■ *Dir* Jean-Jacques Beineix • *Scr* Jean-Jacques Beineix, Jacques Forgeas, from a film by Forgeas

IQ ★★★★ U
Romantic comedy 1994 · US · Colour · 91min

When Meg Ryan pulls into Tim Robbins's garage, it's love at first sight for the mechanic. But this romantic tale has an added twist, for Ryan happens to be the niece of Albert Einstein (as portrayed by Walter Matthau). Since Ryan is engaged to the pompous Stephen Fry (an unlikely bit of casting), Matthau decides to use his grey cells in the matchmaking department and help Robbins win the affections of Ryan. It's immaculately set in the 1950s, and the stars are well supported by the likes of Gene Saks and Lou Jacobi. AT DVD

Meg Ryan *Catherine Boyd* • Tim Robbins *Ed Walters* • Walter Matthau *Albert Einstein* • Lou Jacobi *Kurt Godel* • Gene Saks *Boris Podolsky* • Joseph Maher *Nathan Liebknecht* • Stephen Fry

James Moreland • Tony Shalhoub *Bob Walters* ■ *Dir* Fred Schepisi • *Scr* Andy Breckman, Michael Leeson, from a story by Breckman

I Remember Mama ★★★★ U
Period drama 1948 · US · BW · 128min

Early-20th-century San Francisco is the setting for this cosy story of a family of Norwegian immigrants and their struggles for survival. Irene Dunne brings her usual class and charm to the role of the matriarch who holds everyone together and Barbara Bel Geddes plays the daughter who records day-to-day life in her diary. Directed by George Stevens with a warm heart and a diverting way with a cliché, it also has a knockout performance by Cedric Hardwicke as a run-down old actor. TH

Irene Dunne *Mama* • Barbara Bel Geddes *Katrin* • Oscar Homolka *Uncle Chris* • Philip Dorn *Papa* • Sir Cedric Hardwicke [Cedric Hardwicke] *Mr Hyde* • Edgar Bergen *Mr Thorkelson* • Rudy Vallee *Dr Johnson* • Ellen Corby *Aunt Trina* ■ *Dir* George Stevens • *Scr* DeWitt Bodeen, from a play by John Van Druten, from the novel *Mama's Bank Account* by Kathryn Forbes • *Cinematographer* Nicholas Musuraca

I, Robot ★★★★ 12
Science-fiction action thriller
2004 · US/Ger · Colour · 109min

Sci-fi writer Isaac Asimov's stories provide the inspiration for this futuristic action thriller set in Chicago in the year 2035 when robots have been fully integrated into society. When a top scientist from the US Robotics corporation turns up dead, detective Will Smith suspects the involvement of a prototype that may not be bound by the laws that govern its brethren. Smith gives a charismatic performance, and this blockbuster succeeds chiefly because of the use of CGI, blending the robots seamlessly into the human environment. Director Alex Proyas keeps the action racing along. TH Violence. DVD BL

Will Smith *Detective Del Spooner* • Bridget Moynahan *Dr Susan Calvin* • Bruce Greenwood *Lawrence Robertson* • James Cromwell *Dr Alfred Lanning* • Chi McBride *Lieutenant John Bergin* • Alan Tudyk *Sonny* • Adrian L Ricard [Adrian Ricard] *Granny* • Jerry Wasserman *Baldez* ■ *Dir* Alex Proyas • *Scr* Jeff Vintar, Akiva Goldsman, from a story by Jeff Vintar, suggested by the short story collection by Isaac Asimov

I Saw Ben Barka Get Killed
★★★★ 12A
Historical drama
2005 · Fr/Mor/Sp · Colour · 102min

The mysterious fate of Moroccan activist Mehdi Ben Barka, who was kidnapped in 1965, has already informed Yves Boisset's 1972 thriller, *The Assassination*. But Serge Le Péron is less concerned with his disappearance and the attendant world of espionage than with the Left Bank scene in mid-1960s Paris, where opportunistic ex-con Georges Figon (Charles Berling) seeks to make his name as a film producer in collaboration with screenwriter Marguerite Duras (Josiane Balasko) and director Georges Franju (Jean-Pierre Léaud). Atmosphere is everything here, as Le Péron creates political, criminal and artistic milieux that are contrastingly sinister, scurrilous and self-servingly pretentious. DP French, Arabic +subtitles.

Charles Berling *Georges Figon* • Simon Abkarian *Mehdi Ben Barka* • Jean-Pierre Léaud *Georges Franju* • Fabienne Babe *Anne-Marie Coffinet* • Mathieu Amalric *Philippe Bernier* • Azize Kabouche *Chtouki* • Josiane Balasko *Marguerite Duras* • François Hadji-Lazaro *Le Ny* ■ *Dir* Serge Le Péron • *Scr* Serge Le Péron, Frédérique Moreau, Saïd Smihi

I Saw Mommy Kissing Santa Claus ★★ PG
Seasonal romantic comedy
2001 · US/Ger · Colour · 88min

Cute young leads and a generous splash of *Home Alone*-style mischief make this festive comedy more fun than it should be. In an exaggerated case of childhood misconception, an eight-year-old wages war against Santa to protect his parents' marriage, after witnessing his mum (Connie

Sellecca) apparently smooching with the old guy. The family-friendly laughs increase along with the boy's confusion, prompting an escalation of his slapstick pranks that distracts from the film's flimsy plotting and weak adult performances. SF DVD

Connie Sellecca *Stephanie Carver* • Corbin Bernsen *David Carver* • Dylan Sprouse *Justin Carver* • Cole Sprouse *Justin Carver* • Eric Jacobs *Bobby Becker* ■ *Dir* John Shepphird • *Scr* Steve Jankowski, John Shepphird, Mike Sorrentino, Randy Vampotic

I Saw the Devil ★★★★ 18
Horror thriller 2010 · S Kor · Colour · 138min

This gruesome revenge thriller stars Lee Byung-hun as a government agent who takes the law into his own hands when his fiancée becomes the latest victim of vicious serial killer Choi Min-sik. Although director Kim Ji-woon's inventive twist on the vigilante shocker is relentlessly bloodthirsty, it never loses sight of the human fallout from violent crime, deftly weaving Lee's eye-for-an-eye actions with moments of genuine emotional grief. Choi, so powerful himself as a man obsessed with vengeance in *Oldboy*, plays the ruthless and conscience-free murderer with chilling detachment. TeS Korean +subtitles. Violence, sex scenes.

Lee Byung-hun *Soo-hyeon* • Choi Min-sik *Kyung-chul* • Jeon Gook-hwan *Captain Jang* • Oh San-ha *Ju-yeon* • Kim Yon-seo *Se-yeon* ■ *Dir* Kim Ji-woon • *Scr* Park Hoon-jung

I Saw the Light ★★ 15
Music biography
2015 · US · Colour and BW · 123min

Tom Hiddleston is the shining light in an otherwise drab portrait of country singing legend Hank Williams, who died in 1953 aged just 29. Writer/director Marc Abraham lets one scene drift into the next without punctuation, focusing primarily on the marriage between Hank and his first wife Audrey (Elizabeth Olsen) – a relationship marred by professional and personal jealousy. Hank is brought to vivid life by Hiddleston on stage (singing the title song and a memorable rendition of *Your Cheatin' Heart*), but he comes across as a passive character in his own life story, his spark of genius muted by the banality of the domestic drama. SP Swearing, drug abuse, nudity.

Tom Hiddleston *Hank Williams* • Elizabeth Olsen *Audrey Williams* • Cherry Jones *Lillie Williams* • Bradley Whitford *Fred Rose* • Maddie Hasson *Billie Jean Jones* ■ *Dir* Marc Abraham • *Scr* Marc Abraham, from the biography *Hank Williams* by Colin Escott, George Merritt and William MacEwen

I Saw What You Did ★★
Thriller 1965 · US · BW · 81min

Two teenage girls (Andi Garrett, Sarah Lane), alone one night in a large and fairly isolated house, play a prank on a number of strangers by phoning random numbers and announcing, "I saw what you did. I know who you are." When one of the calls is taken by a man who has just murdered his wife, the joke turns sour. This has its moments, as the wife-killer (John Ireland) sets out to find the perpetrator of the threatening phone call. Joan Crawford is also on hand to emote as Ireland's demanding lover. Remade as a TV movie in 1988. RK

Joan Crawford *Amy Nelson* • John Ireland *Steve Marak* • Leif Erickson *Dave Mannering* • Patricia Breslin *Ellie Mannering* • Andi Garrett *Libby* • Sarah Lane *Kit* ■ *Dir* William Castle • *Scr* William P McGivern, from the novel *Out of the Dark* by Ursula Curtiss

I See a Dark Stranger
★★★ U
Second World War drama
1946 · UK · BW · 107min

Having penned *The Lady Vanishes* for Alfred Hitchcock and *Night Train to Munich* for Carol Reed, Frank Launder and Sidney Gilliat struck out on their own for this tale of wartime treachery. Uncertain handling mars an otherwise diverting romp, in which

Deborah Kerr's Irish republican sympathies lead her, unwittingly, to spy for the Nazis. Her feisty devotion to the cause carries the film through its more implausible moments, but she struggles to get much response from a taciturn Trevor Howard. A touch too clever for its own good, but rattling entertainment all the same. DP

Deborah Kerr *Bridie Quilty* • Trevor Howard *Lieutenant David Bayne* • Raymond Huntley *Miller* • Liam Redmond *Timothy* • Michael Howard *Hawkins* ■ *Dir* Frank Launder • *Scr* Wolfgang Wilhelm, Sidney Gilliat, Frank Launder • *Producer* Sidney Gilliat

I See Ice ★★ U
Comedy 1938 · UK · BW · 78min

This typical George Formby vehicle sees the Lancashire comedian cast as a property man in an ice ballet production who, in his spare time, is an obsessive amateur photographer. Sporting a bow tie that conceals a mini-camera, George sets forth to snap candid photos and gets in all sorts of comical messes. This is fast-paced, British comedy with all the usual ingredients of the time: romance, gangsters, misunderstandings and buckets of slapstick. DF

George Formby *George Bright* • Kay Walsh *Judy Gaye* • Betty Stockfeld *Mrs Hunter* • Cyril Ritchard *Paul Martine* • Garry Marsh *Galloway* ■ *Dir* Anthony Kimmins • *Scr* Anthony Kimmins, Austin Melford

I Served the King of England ★★★★ 15
Satirical war drama
2006 · Cz Rep/Slovakia · Colour · 114min

Director Jiri Menzel's social satire combines wartime drama and erotic fantasy to charming effect. Set across several decades of turbulent social upheaval in Czechoslovakia, it's a picaresque tale about Jan Dite (Ivan Barnev) a naive but ambitious waiter (whose surname literally means "child"). Jan works his way through women and hotels until the arrival of the Nazis. Even then, he refuses to take a stand against the occupiers. Menzel has crafted a rambunctious and frisky fantasy dominated by food and sex, with a hilarious performance from Barnev that recalls the great slapstick comedians. Yet, told in flashback from the point of view of Dite's older, wiser self (played by Oldrich Kaiser), the comedy is shadowed by a serious moral fable about the dangers of political disengagement. Delightful. JR In Czech.

Ivan Barnev *Jan Dite* • Oldrich Kaiser *The older Jan* • Julia Jentsch *Liza* • Milan Lasica *Professor* • Zuzana Fialova *Marcela* • Jiri Labus *Hotel Director* ■ *Dir* Jirí Menzel • *Scr* Jirí Menzel, from the novel by Bohumil Hrabal

I Shot Andy Warhol
★★★★ 18
Biographical drama
1995 · US/UK · Colour · 99min

Valerie Solanas was famous for 15 minutes when she tried to assassinate pop art king Andy Warhol in 1968. Director Mary Harron's endlessly fascinating case history delves into the complex personality of the lesbian feminist author and finally makes sense of what tipped her over the edge into paranoid fantasy. Rarely do films capture a cultural era as precisely as this evocative saga, which does it masterfully with a sure, sophisticated style and with wit and drama to spare. AJ Swearing, sex scenes, drug abuse. DVD

Lili Taylor *Valerie Solanas* • Jared Harris *Andy Warhol* • Stephen Dorff *Candy Darling* • Martha Plimpton *Stevie* • Danny Morgenstern *Jeremiah Newton* • Lothaire Bluteau *Maurice Girodias* • Tahnee Welch *Viva* ■ *Dir* Mary Harron • *Scr* Mary Harron, Daniel Minahan • *Music* John Cale

I Shot Jesse James ★★★ U
Western 1949 · US · BW · 72min

Samuel Fuller gained his first directing opportunity with this low-budget western told in the emphatic, headline style for which he would become noted. His script takes a characteristically offbeat approach to a familiar situation – the assassination of

Jesse James – by telling it from the point of view of Bob Ford, played by John Ireland. He was the "dirty little coward" of ballad fame who took advantage of Jesse's friendship and hospitality to shoot him in the back of the head. Fuller attempts to make it the tragedy of someone who has killed a man he loved, but such a flawed character evokes little concern. AE

Preston Foster *John Kelley* • Barbara Britton *Cynthy Waters* • John Ireland *Bob Ford* • Reed Hadley *Jesse James* • J Edward Bromberg *Kane* • Victor Kilian *Soapy* ■ *Dir* Samuel Fuller • *Scr* Samuel Fuller, from articles by Homer Croy

I Spit on Your Grave ★★ 18
Horror 2010 · US · Colour · 103min

The uninspired cycle of horror remakes continues with this rehash of the infamous 1978 censor-baiter. The story is the same: a young woman (Sarah Butler) decamps to a cabin in the wilds to write a book, is brutally raped by a bunch of locals and then takes violent revenge. Aside from the total lack of originality, there's little in the way of suspense, atmosphere or characterisation. Even the eye-for-an-eye retribution Butler exacts on her tormentors is just plain nasty and par for the course when the likes of *Saw* have taken gore to another level. JA Violence, swearing, drug abuse, nudity. DVD BL

Sarah Butler *Jennifer Hills* • Jeff Branson *Johnny* • Andrew Howard *Sheriff Storch* • Daniel Franzese *Stanley* ■ *Dir* Steven R Monroe • *Scr* Stuart Morse, from the 1978 film by Meir Zarchi

I Spy ★★ 12
Spy action comedy 2002 · US · Colour · 92min

This routine reworking of the 1960s TV espionage series has US secret agent Owen Wilson going undercover as the assistant to boxing champion Eddie Murphy. Wilson uses Murphy to get close to billionaire industrialist Malcolm McDowell, who is intent on selling an invisible plane to the highest bidder. The laid-back Wilson and the motormouthed Murphy have an engaging on-screen chemistry, but the likeable twosome are sold short by witless writing and a predictable plot. IF Violence. DVD

Eddie Murphy *Kelly Robinson* • Owen Wilson *Alex Scott* • Famke Janssen *Rachel Wright* • Malcolm McDowell *Arnold Gundars* • Gary Cole *Carlos* • Phill Lewis *Jerry* • Viv Leacock *T J* • Dir Betty Thomas • *Scr* Marianne Wibberley, Cormac Wibberley, Jay Scherick, David Ronn, from a story by Marianne Wibberley, Cormac Wibberley, from characters by Morton Fine, David Friedman

I Start Counting ★★
Crime drama 1970 · UK · Colour · 107min

Director David Greene taxes the patience with this manipulative whodunit. There are so many dead ends in this adaptation that it soon becomes a matter of indifference whether Bryan Marshall is responsible for the series of sex attacks near his home. Much more intriguing, however, is the effect the slayings have on his foster sister, Jenny Agutter, whose hero worship is both disturbing and potentially deadly. DP

Jenny Agutter *Wynne* • Bryan Marshall *George* • Clare Sutcliffe *Corrine* • Simon Ward *Conductor* • Gregory Phillips *Len* • Lana Morris *Leonie* • Billy Russell *Grandad* ■ *Dir* David Greene • *Scr* Harris Richard, from a novel by Audrey Erskine Lindop

I Still Know What You Did Last Summer ★ 18
Horror 1998 · US/Ger · Colour · 96min

Noisy, flashy and deadly dull, *Judge Dredd* director Danny Cannon's sequel to *I Know What You Did Last Summer* features the return of college beauty in peril Jennifer Love Hewitt, this time fighting off the masked fisherman during hurricane season in the Bahamas. This is a plotless slab of wet T-shirt terror. A threequel, *I'll Always Know What You Did Last Summer* (2006), was this series's last gasp. AJ DVD BL

Jennifer Love Hewitt *Julie James* • Freddie Prinze Jr *Ray Bronson* • Brandy Norwood [Brandy] *Karla Wilson* • Mekhi Phifer *Tyrell* • Muse Watson *Ben Willis* • Bill Cobbs *Estes* ■ *Dir* Danny Cannon • *Scr* Trey Callaway, from characters by Lois Duncan

I Superbiker: Day of Reckoning ★★ 12A
Documentary   2013 · UK · Colour · 98min

This account of the 2012 British Superbikes season is aimed squarely at petrolheads. But once director Mark Sloper allows narrator Murray Walker to share the rules of the competition with the uninitiated, this becomes much more accessible, as connections are made between the sporting action and the six riders competing in the end of season showdown. In truth, the track highlights hardly set the adrenaline pumping, but Sloper and editor David Hughes ably convey the atmosphere of the Brands Hatch finale and the rapport between the fans and their heroes in the laudably relaxed open-paddock sessions. DP
Murray Walker Narrator ■ *Dir/Scr* Mark Sloper

I Take This Woman ★★
Romantic drama   1940 · US · BW · 97min

Intended as a vehicle for MGM's latest acquisition, Hedy Lamarr, this quickly became one of those films notorious for its troubled production history. Initial director Josef von Sternberg was replaced by Frank Borzage, before the movie was almost completely remade by the undistinguished WS Van Dyke. Lamarr is the suicidal girl who marries Spencer Tracy to forget her failed romance with Kent Taylor. The two stars are excellent but the material is trite. AE
Spencer Tracy Dr Karl Decker • *Hedy Lamarr Georgi Gragore* • *Verree Teasdale Mme Marcesca* • *Kent Taylor Phil Mayberry* • *Laraine Day Linda Rodgers* • *Mona Barrie Sandra Mayberry* • *Jack Carson Joe* • *Paul Cavanagh Bill Rodgers* • *Frances Drake Lola Estermont* • *Marjorie Main Gertie* ■ *Dir* WS Van Dyke • *Scr* James Kevin McGuinness, from the story A New York Cinderella by Charles MacArthur

I Thank a Fool ★★
Drama   1962 · UK · Colour · 99min

In this relishably hoary old melodrama, woman-with-a-past Susan Hayward becomes entangled with her old nemesis, barrister Peter Finch, and his mentally ill wife Diane Cilento. Euthanasia always provides a controversial plot point; the rest is murder mystery from another age, with ripe dialogue by Ben-Hur writer Karl Tunberg. The stellar cast do their best in one of MGM's prestige British productions, but audiences were unimpressed. DM
Susan Hayward Christine Allison • *Peter Finch Stephen Dane* • *Diane Cilento Liane Dane* • *Cyril Cusack Captain Ferris* • *Kieron Moore Roscoe* • *Athene Seyler Aunt Heather* • *Richard Wattis Ebblington* • *Peter Sallis Sleazy doctor* • *Joan Hickson Landlady* ■ *Dir* Robert Stevens • *Scr* Karl Tunberg, from a novel by Audrey Erskine Lindop

I Thank You ★★ U
Musical comedy   1941 · UK · BW · 77min

If there's one genre in which the British cinema has a tendency to fail, it's the musical comedy. Here, Marcel Varnel has an expert cast at his disposal, but not even Arthur Askey and Richard Murdoch, plus Will Hay old boys Moore Marriott and Graham Moffatt, can warm up this tepid "upstairs-downstairs" charade. DP *DVD*
Arthur Askey Arthur • *Richard Murdoch Stinker* • *Lily Morris Lady Randall* • *Moore Marriott Pop Bennett* • *Graham Moffatt Albert* • *Peter Gawthorne Dr Pope* • *Kathleen Harrison Cook* • *Felix Aylmer Henry Potter* ■ *Dir* Marcel Varnel • *Scr* Val Guest, Marriott Edgar, from a story by Howard Irving Young

I, the Jury ★
Crime thriller   1953 · US · BW · 87min

Mickey Spillane was a former trampoline artist and narcotics agent who turned to thriller writing in 1947 with I, the Jury. At the time, the novel's violence was shocking, as was the blinkered morality of its thuggish private eye Mike Hammer as he avenges his friend's murder. UA signed Spillane to a four-film deal. They may have lavished 3D on the movie but the cast is barely adequate and the novel is watered down. It

flopped, but Hammer's next cinematic exploit, Kiss Me Deadly, was a masterpiece. AT
Biff Elliot Mike Hammer • *Preston Foster Captain Pat Chambers* • *Peggie Castle Charlotte Manning* • *Margaret Sheridan Velda* • *Alan Reed George Kalecki* • *Frances Osborne Myrna* ■ *Dir* Harry Essex • *Scr* Harry Essex, from a novel by Mickey Spillane

I, the Worst of All ★★★★
Historical drama   1990 · Arg · Colour · 105min

Argentinian director Maria Luisa Bemberg is probably best known in this country for Miss Mary, a stylish period tale starring Julie Christie. This historical drama has none of the gloss of that film, yet with its stark and striking lighting designs, its symbolically lavish costumes and delicately nuanced performances, it is a deeply affecting study of Sister Juana Ines de la Cruz, one of the most important religious poets of the 17th century. A brave and beautiful film. DP Spanish +subtitles.
Assumpta Serna Sister Juana Ines de la Cruz • *Dominique Sanda Vice-Reine Maria Luisa* • *Héctor Alterio Viceroy* • *Lautaro Murua Archbishop of Mexico* • *Alberto Segado Father Miranda* ■ *Dir* Maria Luisa Bemberg • *Scr* Maria Luisa Bemberg, Antonio Larreta, from the essay The Traps of Faith by Octavio Paz, from the book Sor Juana: Her Life and Her World by Paz

I Used to Live Here ★★★
Drama   2014 · Ire · Colour · 80min

Inspired by a series of Irish Times articles on cluster suicides, Frank Berry's feature debut was workshopped with a largely non-professional cast from the Tallaght part of Dublin. Jordanne Jones impresses as 13-year-old Amy who is still struggling to get over the death of her mother when she is shaken by a classmate jumping to his death off a motorway bridge. Berry delivers an uncompromising study of a tragic trend that owes much to Andrea Arnold's brand of social realism and within that, he captures the anxieties of a dead-end adolescent existence with laudable sensitivity. DP
Jordanne Jones Amy • *Dafhyd Flynn Dylan* • *James Kelly Raymond* • *Ross Geraghty David* • *Nikita Rowley Ericka* ■ *Dir/Scr* Frank Berry

I Wake Up Screaming ★★★★ PG
Film noir   1941 · US · BW · 78min

In hindsight, this turned out to be one of 20th Century-Fox's key films noirs. It contains a quintessential plot about a beautiful murdered actress and a grab-bag of seedy unusual suspects, such as the tough sports promoter and the unseemly detective whose more-than-professional interest in the dead girl is enthralling. This is a clever, fast-moving and atmospheric thriller with a sordid undertone that leaves you wanting more. TS
Betty Grable Jill Lynn • *Victor Mature Frankie Christopher* • *Carole Landis Vicky Lynn* • *Laird Cregar Ed Cornell* • *William Gargan Jerry McDonald* • *Alan Mowbray Robin Ray* • *Elisha Cook Jr Harry Williams* ■ *Dir* H Bruce Humberstone • *Scr* Dwight Taylor, from the novel by Steve Fisher

I Walk Alone ★★★
Crime drama   1947 · US · BW · 97min

Burt Lancaster and Kirk Douglas give solid performances in this bruising film noir about ex-bootleggers who fall out over their spoils. Wendell Corey also impresses as the spineless accountant who is murdered after helping Douglas build his empire while Lancaster is doing time. The action is kept nicely on the boil by Byron Haskin, who handles the violent set pieces, the romantic interludes and the musical numbers with assurance. DP
Burt Lancaster Frankie Madison • *Kirk Douglas Noll Turner* • *Lizabeth Scott Kay Lawrence* • *Wendell Corey Dave* • *Kristine Miller Mrs Richardson* ■ *Dir* Byron Haskin • *Scr* Charles Schnee, Robert Smith, John Bright, from the play Beggars Are Coming to Town by Theodore Reeves

I Walked with a Zombie ★★★★ PG
Horror   1943 · US · BW · 65min

Is the invalid wife of a Caribbean plantation owner (Tom Conway) really the victim of a voodoo curse? In her quest to find out, nurse Frances Dee uncovers dark family secrets in cult producer Val Lewton's ingenious reworking of Jane Eyre. Jacques Tourneur's direction creates palpable fear and tension in a typically low-key nightmare from the Lewton fright factory. The lighting, shadows, exotic setting and music all contribute to the immensely disturbing atmosphere, making this stunning piece of poetic horror a classic of the genre. AJ
Tom Conway Paul Holland • *Frances Dee Betsy* • *James Ellison Wesley Rand* • *Edith Barrett Mrs Rand* • *Christine Gordon Jessica Holland* • *James Bell Dr Maxwell* • *Richard Abrams Clement* ■ *Dir* Jacques Tourneur • *Scr* Curt Siodmak, Ardel Wray, from a story by Inez Wallace • *Editor* Mark Robson

I Wanna Hold Your Hand ★★★
Comedy   1978 · US · Colour · 98min

This gentle comedy, set in 1964, focuses on four New Jersey teenagers who are obsessed with meeting the Beatles, just as the Fab Four are about to make their debut on TV's Ed Sullivan Show. You don't get the Beatles of course, but there are lots of shots of winkle-pickered shoes and the movie has bags of ingenuity and charm. Steven Spielberg acted as executive producer. AT
Nancy Allen Pam Mitchell • *Bobby DiCicco Tony Smerko* • *Marc McClure Larry Dubois* • *Susan Kendall Newman Janis Goldman* • *Theresa Saldana Grace Corrigan* • *Wendie Jo Sperber Rosie Petrofsky* ■ *Dir* Robert Zemeckis • *Scr* Robert Zemeckis, Bob Gale • *Music* The Beatles

I Want Candy ★★★ 15
Comedy   2006 · UK · Colour · 86min

Best described as a home counties American Pie, this Ealing Studios-produced comedy from director Stephen Surjik (Wayne's World 2) transcends Carry On-style crudeness thanks to film buff in-jokes and some inspired belly laughs. Joe (Tom Riley) and Baggy (Tom Burke), two naive film students from Surrey, try to get their big break by making an "adult" movie, but end up being forced to secure the services of porn megastar Candy Fiveways (Carmen Electra). The plot is as obvious as the gags, but the film's sheer eagerness to please and the efforts of a game cast make it surprisingly funny and sweet. AJ Sexual references. *DVD*
Carmen Electra Candy Fiveways • *Tom Riley Joe Clark* • *Tom Burke John "Baggy" Bagley* • *Michelle Ryan Lila Owens* • *Felicity Montagu Mum* • *Philip Jackson Dad* • *Jimmy Carr Video store manager* • *Dir* Stephen Surjik • *Scr* Pete Hewitt [Peter Hewitt], Phil Hughes, Jamie Minoprio, Jonathan M Stern

I Want to Go Home ★ 15
Satirical comedy   1989 · Fr · Colour · 101min

Written by American cartoonist and humourist Jules Feiffer, this stars Adolph Green, co-writer of On the Town, Singin' in the Rain and The Band Wagon. Despite this obvious talent, it really doesn't work at all, not even when Gérard Depardieu crops up as a university don. The involvement of Alain Resnais – one of the most deeply intellectual of French directors – is explained by his lifelong love of comics. AT *DVD*
Adolph Green Joey Wellman • *Gérard Depardieu Christian Gauthier* • *Linda Lavin Lena Apthrop* • *Micheline Presle Isabelle Gauthier* • *John Ashton Harry Dempsey* ■ *Dir* Alain Resnais • *Scr* Jules Feiffer

I Want to Live! ★★★★ 15
Biographical crime melodrama
1958 · US · BW · 116min

Four-time loser Susan Hayward finally won an Oscar for her riveting portrayal of Barbara Graham, whose wretched life saw her descend into prostitution, fraud, perjury

and drug addiction before she was finally convicted of murder. She was framed, according to the stance taken here on the notorious 1955 case, reinforcing the anti-capital punishment argument of director Robert Wise's campaigning opus. It's the depiction of Graham's brave march to her gas chamber execution that won over Academy Award voters to Hayward's side. AJ *DVD*
Susan Hayward Barbara Graham • *Simon Oakland Ed Montgomery* • *Virginia Vincent Peg* • *Theodore Bikel Carl Palmberg* • *Wesley Lau Henry Graham* ■ *Dir* Robert Wise • *Scr* Nelson Gidding, Don M Mankiewicz, from articles by Ed Montgomery, from letters by Barbara Graham

I Want to See ★★★
Documentary drama   2008 · Fr/Leb/Neth · Colour · 69min

Co-directors Joana Hadjithomas and Khalil Joreige attempt to look at their homeland of Lebanon with new eyes by arranging for French film icon Catherine Deneuve and Lebanese actor Rabih Mroué to travel by car around the country in the wake of the 2006 Israeli incursions. The pair overcome the awkward civility of their first meeting to forge a genial camaraderie, but Deneuve's real purpose is to witness first-hand the scarred landscape so familiar from decades of news bulletins. Her subsequent shock at seeing the decimated landscape is palpable and few will be unmoved by cinematographer Julien Hirsch's harrowing images of a nation laid waste by its neighbour. DP French, Arabic +subtitles.
Catherine Deneuve • *Rabih Mroué* ■ *Dir* Joana Hadjithomas, Khalil Joreige • *Cinematographer* Julien Hirsch

I Want What I Want ★
Drama   1971 · UK · Colour · 105min

Is it strange for a film producer to cast his own wife as a man who has a sex change operation? You can judge for yourself after watching this movie, in which producer Raymond Stross finds such a role for his spouse Anne Heywood – a former beauty queen whose real name was Violet Pretty. Heywood starts out as a Roy and ends up as a Wendy but nothing – not even some hideous make-up, silly clothes and a deep voice – can disguise the fact that she's a woman from start to finish. Not a very helpful contribution to a little-understood subject. AT
Anne Heywood Roy/Wendy • *Harry Andrews Father* • *Jill Bennett Margaret Stevenson* • *Paul Rogers Mr Waites* • *Michael Coles Frank* ■ *Dir* John Dexter • *Scr* Gillian Freeman, from a novel by Geoff Brown

I Want You ★★★ U
Drama   1951 · US · BW · 97min

Producer Samuel Goldwyn's attempt to follow up the critical and popular success of his seven Oscar-winning 1946 masterpiece The Best Years of Our Lives resulted in this similarly themed movie, this time portraying the effects of the Korean War on American small-town families. The screenplay by novelist Irwin Shaw is excellent, and the performances ring touching and true. This is very much a period artefact, fascinating to watch today and inspired by the induction of Goldwyn's own son. TS
Dana Andrews Martin Greer • *Dorothy McGuire Nancy Greer* • *Farley Granger Jack Greer* • *Peggy Dow Carrie Turner* • *Robert Keith (1) Thomas Greer* • *Mildred Dunnock Sarah Greer* ■ *Dir* Mark Robson • *Scr* Irwin Shaw, from stories by Edward Newhouse

I Want You ★ 18
Thriller   1998 · UK · Colour · 83min

Michael Winterbottom's turgid sexual melodrama is meant to be a deep psychological study into erotic compulsion, manipulation, bitterness and betrayal, but the director misses every target by miles. After serving nine years for murder, Alessandro Nivola heads back to his home town to pursue ex-girlfriend Rachel Weisz. Something unspeakable connects them – but what? It's not worth wading through all the empty emotions and dire dialogue to find out. AJ Swearing, sex scenes.

Labina Mitevska *Smokey* • Rachel Weisz *Helen* • Alessandro Nivola *Martin* • Luka Petrusic *Honda* • Carmen Ejogo *Amber* • Ben Daniels *DJ Bob* ■ *Dir* Michael Winterbottom • *Scr* Eoin McNamee

I Wanted Wings ★★
Action drama 1941 · US · BW · 133min

Ray Milland, William Holden and Wayne Morris join the army air corps and head for Texas for their training as fighter pilots. The script is top-heavy with plot as the three men work out their romantic entanglements, learn to fly and bond in buddy-buddy fashion. Veronica Lake (billing herself as that for the first time, having changed her professional name from Constance Keane) is the beauty. Director Mitchell Leisen apparently thought she had no talent and bullied her. AT

Ray Milland *Jeff Young* • William Holden (2) *Al Ludlow* • Wayne Morris *Tom Cassidy* • Brian Donlevy *Capt Mercer* • Constance Moore *Carolyn Bartlett* • Veronica Lake *Sally Vaughn* ■ *Dir* Mitchell Leisen • *Scr* Richard Maibaum, Beirne Lay Jr, Sig Herzig, from a story by Eleanore Griffin, Frank Wead, from the non-fiction book by Lay Jr • *Special Effects* Gordon Jennings

I Was a Communist for the FBI ★★ U
Thriller 1951 · US · BW · 81min

Although based on a *Saturday Evening Post* article given by undercover agent Matt Cvetic to journalist Pete Martin, this Red-baiting propaganda was clearly couched in fictional terms, thus making its Oscar nomination in the documentary feature category all the more puzzling. Shot as a *film noir*, it's too soused with political bile to be an effective thriller, no matter how much director Gordon Douglas cranks up the suspense. Frank Lovejoy stars as a steelworker recruited by the FBI to infiltrate his communist union. As an insight into the hysteria that gripped America in the early days of the Cold War, it's an invaluable document. DP

Frank Lovejoy *Matt Cvetic* • Dorothy Hart *Eve Merrick* • Philip Carey *Mason* • Dick Webb *Crowley* • James Millican *Jim Blandon* • Ron Hagerthy *Dick Cvetic* ■ *Dir* Gordon Douglas • *Scr* Crane Wilbur, from the article *I Posed as a Communist for the FBI* by Matt Cvetic, Pete Martin

I Was a Male War Bride ★★★★★ U
Screwball comedy 1949 · US · BW · 101min

In this hilarious comedy of errors, French army officer Cary Grant marries American WAC Ann Sheridan and attempts to get to the States using the "war bride" bill. Director Howard Hawks wrings every ounce of humour from this bizarre situation, making splendid use of European locations (with interiors filmed at Shepperton Studios), and his cast could scarcely be improved upon. This is one of Grant's cleverest, most subtle performances, but the breezy Sheridan is more than a match for him: just watch that timing in the "sleeplessness in the guest house" sequence, and the increasing sense of frustration as an uncredited Lionel Murton tells Grant again and again, "you can't sleep here" (the film's British release title). TS *DVD*

Cary Grant *Captain Henri Rochard* • Ann Sheridan *Lieutenant Catherine Gates* • William Neff *Captain Jack Rumsey* • Marion Marshall *WAC* • Randy Stuart *WAC* • Eugene Gericke *Tony Jowitt* ■ *Dir* Howard Hawks • *Scr* Charles Lederer, Leonard Spigelgass, Hagar Wilde, from the article *Male War Bride Trial to Army* in the *Baltimore Sun* by Henri Rochard

I Was a Shoplifter ★★
Crime drama 1950 · US · BW · 73min

A gang blackmails kleptomaniacs into becoming professional thieves in this moderately engaging drama. Scott Brady stars as an undercover cop, while Mona Freeman plays the judge's daughter who is recruited by the ring. The film was denounced as "a course in shoplifting" by a censor in Atlanta, who promptly banned it. Interest is added by the appearances of two future stars: Tony (here Anthony) Curtis as a lecherous killer, and Rock Hudson as a store detective. AE

Scott Brady *Jeff Andrews* • Mona Freeman *Faye Burton* • Andrea King *Ina Perdue* • Anthony Curtis [Tony Curtis] *Pepe* • Charles Drake *Herb Klaxon* • Rock Hudson *Si Swanson* ■ *Dir* Charles Lamont • *Scr* Irwin Gielgud, from his story

I Was a Spy ★★ U
Spy drama 1934 · UK · BW · 86min

Fans of vintage British cinema will enjoy this sprightly espionage yarn, set during the First World War and bearing a close resemblance to the Mata Hari legend. The lovely Madeleine Carroll plays a Belgian nurse who goes undercover with fellow spy Herbert Marshall and gets caught trying to sabotage a German munitions dump. Conrad Veidt, exiled from his homeland following the victory of the Nazis, plays a German officer. AT *DVD*

Madeleine Carroll *Martha Cnockhaert McKenna* • Conrad Veidt *Commandant Oberaertz* • Herbert Marshall *Stephan* • Gerald du Maurier *Doctor* • Edmund Gwenn *Burgomaster* • Nigel Bruce *Scotty* ■ *Dir* Victor Saville • *Scr* WP Lipscomb

I Was a Teenage Frankenstein ★★★ 15
Horror 1957 · US · BW and Colour · 73min

If *I Was a Teenage Werewolf* has one of the most famous exploitation titles of all time, this quickie sequel contains some of the best-remembered dialogue: "Answer me. You have a civil tongue in your head. I know, I sewed it in there." As the resident evil scientist, horror dependable Whit Bissell swaps lucrative lycanthropy for ugly monster-making using car-crash cadavers. Immensely idiotic, naturally, but sometimes incredibly effective (especially the lively, colour climax), this lurid hokum has an unexpectedly neat line in self-parody. AJ

Whit Bissell *Professor Frankenstein* • Phyllis Coates *Margaret* • Robert Burton *Dr Karlton* • Gary Conway *Teenage Monster* • George Lynn *Sergeant Burns* • John Cliff *Sergeant McAffee* • Marshall Bradford *Dr Randolph* ■ *Dir* Herbert L Strock • *Scr* Kenneth Langtry

I Was a Teenage Werewolf ★★ 15
Horror 1957 · US · BW · 75min

Rebel without a Cause meets *The Wolf Man* in a trend-setting cult classic, complete with rock 'n' roll, rumbles and teen traumas. Michael Landon (yes, Little Joe Cartwright from *Bonanza* himself) is the troubled student who tears his classmates to shreds after therapy administered by mad scientist Whit Bissell regresses him to his primal past. The suspense is minimal, the production values low, and the time-lapse special effects are hokey, but, even if this seminal shocker now only scrapes by on quaint nostalgia, its title will always be a part of horror history. AJ

Michael Landon *Tony* • Yvonne Lime *Arlene* • Whit Bissell *Dr Alfred Brandon* • Tony Marshall *Jimmy* • Dawn Richard *Theresa* ■ *Dir* Gene Fowler Jr • *Scr* Ralph Thornton

I Was Born, but... ★★★★★ U
Silent comedy drama 1932 · Jpn · BW · 86min

Yasujiro Ozu established himself among Japan's greatest film-makers with this exemplary *shomin-geki* or lower-middle-class domestic movie. Coaxing wondrously natural performances from Hideo Sugawara and Tokkankozo, Ozu fashions a minutely observed silent comedy, in which the brothers' disgust at their father's subservience to his boss prompts them to go on hunger strike. The opening segment is played almost entirely in dumb show, although the captions used to explain the harsh realities of the adult world are never intrusive and reinforce the film's ironic take on childhood innocence and life's little injustices. DP *DVD*

Hideo Sugawara *Older son, Ryoichi* • Tokkankozo *Younger son, Keiji* • Tatsu Saito *Father, Yoshi* • Mitsuko Yoshikawa *Mother* • Takeshi Sakamoto

I Was Happy Here ★★★
Drama 1966 · UK · BW · 90min

A bittersweet story of Irish disenchantment, this reminds us just how good Sarah Miles could be, even if she hasn't made many films of late. Here is Cass, the girl who leaves her home and boyfriend in Ireland for the bright lights of London only to find an unhappy marriage with Julian Glover. When she next returns to own country, Cass has to confront her mixed feelings about her former home. Directed by Desmond Davis from a story by Edna O'Brien, the character's winsomeness can be a bit cloying, but Miles is impressive as the wide-eyed innocent who makes us sympathise with her contrary nature. TH

Sarah Miles *Cass* • Cyril Cusack *Hogan* • Julian Glover *Dr Matthew Langdon* • Sean Caffrey *Colin Foley* • Marie Kean *Barkeeper* • Eve Belton *Kate* • Cardew Robinson *Gravedigger* ■ *Dir* Desmond Davis • *Scr* Desmond Davis, Edna O'Brien, from the short story *A Woman by the Seaside* by O'Brien

I Was Monty's Double ★★★★ U
Second World War drama 1958 · UK · BW · 96min

The Second World War as fought on the pages of popular fiction is littered with doubles planted as decoys to divert the enemy away from a vital theatre of operation. But, as is so often the case, it is the truth that provides the best stories. John Guillermin's film gains credibility not only because the title role is played by General Montgomery's double himself, ME Clifton James, but also because his autobiography has been so skilfully adapted by Bryan Forbes. Astute, unassuming and slick. DP *DVD*

John Mills *Major Harvey* • Cecil Parker *Colonel Logan* • Patrick Allen *Colonel Matthers* • ME Clifton James *ME Clifton James* • Patrick Holt *Colonel Dawson* • Leslie Phillips *Major Tennant* • Michael Hordern *Governor of Gibraltar* • Marius Goring *Neilson* • Barbara Hicks *Hester* • Sidney James *YMCA porter* • Victor Maddern *Orderly Sergeant* • Alfie Bass *Small man* • John Le Mesurier *Adjutant RAPC* ■ *Dir* John Guillermin • *Scr* Bryan Forbes, from a non-fiction book by ME Clifton James

I Went Down ★★★ 15
Crime comedy 1997 · Ire/UK/Sp · Colour · 102min

Although the absurd is never far beneath its surface, this dark crime comedy also has plenty to say about loyalty, greed and the pitfalls of macho posturing. Writer Conor McPherson asks a great deal of director Paddy Breathnach by packing so much incident into his script and the cycle of revenge, kidnaps, escapes and double-crosses prevents the action from gaining much momentum. But the exchanges between doltish hitman Brendan Gleeson and his reluctant accomplice Peter McDonald are often splutteringly funny, and there's a nice turn from Peter Caffrey as their quarry. one. DP Violence, swearing, a sex scene.

Brendan Gleeson *Bunny Kelly* • Peter McDonald *Git Hynes* • Peter Caffrey *Frank Grogan* • Antoine Byrne *Sabrina Bradley* • David Wilmot *Anto* • Michael McElhatton *Johnner Doyle* • Joe Gallagher *Steo Gannon* • Conor McPherson *Loser in nightclub* ■ *Dir* Paddy Breathnach • *Scr* Conor McPherson

I Wish ★★★★ PG
Drama 2011 · Jpn · Colour · 123min

Japanese director Hirokazu Koreeda depicts the hopes, joys and bitter disappointments of childhood with typically acute detachment in this delightful adventure. Twelve-year-old Koichi (Koki Maeda) lives with his mother in Kagoshima, which is dominated by a smouldering volcano. The boy dreams of reuniting his family, sorely missing younger brother Ryunosuke (Maeda's real-life brother, Ohshiro), who lives in the north with their musician father. Koichi persuades Ryunosuke to venture across the country to test his belief that passing bullet trains can grant wishes. The Maeda boys (an established comedy duo in their own country) excel in their roles, but it's Koreeda's control of character, locale and pace that makes this so engaging. DP Japanese +subtitles. *DVD* Blu-ray

Koki Maeda *Koichi* • Ohshiro Maeda *Ryunosuke* • Nene Ohtsuka *Nozomi, mother* • Joe Odagiri *Kenji, father* • Yui Natsukawa *Kyoko, Megumi's* ■ *Dir/Scr* Hirokazu Koreeda

I Witness ★★ 15
Thriller 2003 · US · Colour · 94min

Despite its impressive cast, this sketchy thriller fails to ignite. Jeff Daniels stars as a human-rights activist arriving in a Mexican border town to oversee union elections at a US-owned factory. When a cross-border tunnel collapses and many of the dead victims sport gunshot wounds, he realises the situation is murkier than he thought and teams up with local detective Clifton Collins Jr to investigate. SF Violence, swearing. *DVD*

Jeff Daniels *James Rhodes* • James Spader *Douglas Draper* • Portia de Rossi *Emily Thompson* • Clifton Collins Jr *Claudio Castillo* • Wade Williams *Roy Logan* • Mark Carlton *Carter* ■ *Dir* Rowdy Herrington • *Scr* Colin Greene, Robert Ozn

I Woke Up Early the Day I Died ★★
Crime comedy 1998 · US · Colour · 89min

After Tim Burton's mesmerising biopic of Edward D Wood, it probably made commercial sense to dust off one of Wood's supposedly lost screenplays and film it for a new generation. Alas, this semi-homage to the bargain basement style of film-making that was Wood's trademark fails to gel. Its slim tale of an escaped lunatic (Billy Zane) perpetrating a robbery only to lose all the cash is done in a Chaplin-esque silent movie way, heavy on the slapstick. The one point of interest is a veritable flood of cameos. RS

Billy Zane *The Thief* • Ron Perlman *Cemetary caretaker* • Tippi Hedren *Maylinda* • Andrew McCarthy *Cop* • Will Patton *Preacher* • Carel Struycken *Undertaker* ■ *Dir* Aris Iliopulos • *Scr* Edward D Wood Jr

I Wonder Who's Kissing Her Now ★★★ U
Biographical musical 1947 · US · Colour · 104min

This agreeable film biography of Joe Howard, a vaudeville singer and tunesmith in the 1890s. Mark Stevens plays Howard, while Lenore Aubert is the European star who entices him with her charms. The beauty of making a movie about a hit songwriter is that you don't have to send out for any new tunes, and Howard's own, including the title song, make easy listening. PF

Mark Stevens *Joe Howard* • June Haver *Katie* • Martha Stewart *Lulu Madison* • Reginald Gardiner *Will Hough* • Lenore Aubert *Fritzi Barrington* • William Frawley *Jim Mason* • Gene Nelson *Tommy Yale* ■ *Dir* Lloyd Bacon • *Scr* Lewis R Foster, Marion Turk

Ice Age ★★★ U
Animated comedy adventure 2002 · US · Colour · 77min

A moody mammoth, a slow-thinking sloth and a sinister sabre-toothed tiger team up during the Pleistocene era to return a lost human infant to his parents. It's wittily scripted with plenty of banter between the lead characters, voiced by Ray Romano, John Leguizamo and Denis Leary. The style of the animation is boxy, sharp-edged and with a coldness fitting the subzero setting. SF *DVD* Blu-ray

Ray Romano *Manfred* • John Leguizamo *Sid* • Denis Leary *Diego* • Goran Visnjic *Soto* • Jack Black *Zeke* • Tara Strong [Tara Charendoff] *Roshan/Start* ■ *Dir* Chris Wedge, Carlos

Saldanha • *Scr* Michael Berg, Michael J Wilson, Peter Ackerman, from a story by Michael J Wilson

Ice Age: the Meltdown
★★★ U

Animated comedy adventure
2006 · US · Colour · 87min

This second instalment sees an ease in the freeze, with global warming now well under way. That means floods and a flight for survival for our sub-zero heroes, Sid the sloth, Manny the mammoth, Diego the sabre-toothed tiger and first-film favourite Scrat, the peculiar squirrel/rat hybrid who's still after that elusive acorn. A rare sequel that's actually better than its predecessor, this is colourful, inventive and laugh-out-loud funny. SF *DVD* Blu

Ray Romano *Manny* • John Leguizamo *Sid* • Denis Leary *Diego* • Queen Latifah *Ellie* • Seann William Scott *Crash* • Josh Peck *Eddie* • Jay Leno *Fast Tony* ■ *Dir* Carlos Saldanha • *Scr* Jim Hecht, Peter Gaulke, Gerry Swallow, from a story by Gaulke, Swallow

Ice Age 3: Dawn of the Dinosaurs
★★★ U

Animated comedy adventure
2009 · US · Colour · 90min

In this entertaining second sequel, the computer-imaging techniques attain new subtleties of texture, scale and depth. Unfortunately, the story is a little thin, taking a cheeky liberty by creating a tropical lost world under the ice where dinosaurs lie in wait. Ray Romano and Denis Leary are back as the voices of mammoth Manny and sabre-toothed tiger Diego, this time attempting to rescue Sid the sloth (John Leguizamo) after he gets in trouble adopting three dinosaur eggs – a narrative decision that feels too commercially driven. Thankfully, spectacle, including a terrific computer-game-mimicking pterodactyl chase and more high-wire larks from Scrat the sabre-toothed squirrel, is never far away. Buck, the Johnny Depp-styled pirate weasel (voiced by Simon Pegg), also brings welcome comic energy. AC *DVD* Blu

Ray Romano *Manny* • John Leguizamo *Sid* • Denis Leary *Diego* • Seann William Scott *Crash* • Josh Peck *Eddie* • Queen Latifah *Ellie* • Simon Pegg *Buck* ■ *Dir* Carlos Saldanha, Michael Thurmeier [Mike Thurmeier] • *Scr* Peter Ackerman, Michael Berg, Mike Reiss, Yoni Brenner, from a story by Jason Carter Eaton

Ice Age 4: Continental Drift
★★★ U

Animated comedy adventure
2012 · US · Colour · 84min

In this fourth helping of the popular prehistoric adventure series, Manny the mammoth, Sid the sloth and Diego the sabretooth tiger embark on a distinctly *Pirates of the Caribbean*-style adventure when Scrat the squirrel-rat's obsessive pursuit of that acorn has literally earth-shattering consequences. The movie may be overly dependent on pace and spectacle, but the animation is excellent. Overall, there's enough prehysterical fun to ensure that family audiences won't be disappointed. DA *DVD* Blu 3D

Ray Romano *Manny* • John Leguizamo *Sid* • Denis Leary *Diego* • Jennifer Lopez *Shira* • Queen Latifah *Ellie* • Chris Wedge *Scrat* ■ *Dir* Steve Martino, Mike Thurmeier • *Scr* Michael Berg, Jason Fuchs, from a story by Berg, Lori Forte, from characters by Michael J Wilson

Ice Age: Collision Course
★★ U

Animated comedy
2016 · US · Colour · 94min

The *Ice Age* films have always been one of the better, more consistent family franchises. But this is a sequel too far. The plot is all over the place, and too stop/start and complex for younger kids. There are moments, but not enough of them. The plot sees Sid, Manny and Diego literally facing the fallout when prehistoric squirrel Scrat's perennial pursuit of that acorn sends a huge asteroid hurtling towards Earth. The three pals and entourage have to hatch a plan to alter the asteroid's course. DA 3D

Ray Romano *Manny* • John Leguizamo *Sid* • Denis Leary *Diego* • Queen Latifah *Ellie* • Seann William Scott *Crash* • Josh Peck *Eddie* • Simon Pegg *Buck* • Chris Wedge *Scrat* ■ *Scr* Galen T Chu, Mike Thurmeier • *Scr* Yoni Brenner, Michael J Wilson, Michael Berg, from a story by Aubrey Solomon

Ice and the Sky
★★★ U

Documentary
2015 · Fr · Colour · 89min

Fans of Luc Jacquet's Oscar-winning *March of the Penguins* (2005) may be a tad disappointed by this return to the snowy wastes, this time to recap the career of French polar explorer and glaciologist Claude Lorius. The 80-something Lorius paid his first visit to Antarctica as a 23-year-old in the 1950s when he acquired an understanding of the region's fragile eco-system. However, it was a couple of decades later that Lorius realised how imperilled the poles really were. Switching between home movies, expedition footage and glossy shots of Lorius striding across the icy wilderness, this is fascinating stuff. DP French +subtitles.

■ *Dir/Scr* Luc Jacquet

Ice Bound
★★

Drama based on a true story
2003 · Can/US · Colour · 95min

The star power of Susan Sarandon gives weight to this extraordinary true story from director Roger Spottiswoode about Dr Jerri Nielsen, who was forced to treat herself for breast cancer while marooned at a South Pole research station. It's a compelling account of individual and community heroism that's barely done justice by the budget-restricted TV format, but Sarandon is particularly affecting. SF

Susan Sarandon *Dr Jerri Nielsen* • Aidan Devine *Big John Penny* • Cynthia Mace *Claire "Fingers" Furinski* • Kathryn Zenna *Galley-Annie* ■ *Dir* Roger Spottiswoode • *Scr* Peter Pruce, Maria Nation, from the autobiography *Ice Bound: A Doctor's Incredible Battle for Survival at the South Pole* by Jerri Nielsen, Maryanne Vollers

Ice Castles
★★★ PG

Romantic sports drama
1978 · US · Colour · 104min

Lynn-Holly Johnson emotes almost as well as she skates, and Donald Wrye's sentimental melodrama exercises a curious fascination. This owes much to Colleen Dewhurst's sharp performance as the Iowa skating coach who grooms her protégée for Olympic stardom. Tom Skerritt also impresses as Johnson's farmer father, though Robby Benson is something of an irritant as the boyfriend. DP

Robby Benson *Nick Peterson* • Lynn-Holly Johnson *Alexis Winston* • Colleen Dewhurst *Beulah Smith* • Tom Skerritt *Marcus Winston* • Jennifer Warren *Deborah Macland* • David Huffman *Brian Dockett* ■ *Dir* Donald Wrye • *Scr* Donald Wrye, Gary L Baim, from a story by Baim

Ice Cold in Alex
★★★★ PG

Second World War drama
1958 · UK · BW · 124min

This is the film in which John Mills swigs the most famous glass of beer in movie history. And how well he's earned it, having steered clear of the bottle, Axis troops and a desert full of mines to bring an ambulance to safety after the fall of Tobruk in 1942. On board are second-in-command Harry Andrews, nurses Sylvia Syms and Diane Clare and Anthony Quayle's suspicious-acting South African, who bribes his way onto the ambulance with gin, threatening Mills's temper and temperance. This is a straightforward but never simplistic tale of battling the odds. Director J Lee Thompson keeps the action tense and every jolt felt in the vehicle's cabin will throw you to the edge of your armchair. DP *DVD* Blu

John Mills *Captain Anson* • Sylvia Syms *Sister Diane Murdoch* • Anthony Quayle *Captain Van der Poel* • Harry Andrews *MSM Pugh* • Diane Clare *Sister Denise Norton* • Richard Leech *Captain Crosbie* ■ *Dir* J Lee Thompson • *Scr* Christopher Landon, TJ Morrison, from the novel by Landon

Ice Dreams
★★

Romantic drama
2009 · US · Colour · 120min

A handful of heart-tugging plot strands come together in the most predictable manner in this innocuous sporting drama-cum-romance. Jessica Cauffiel stars as a former Olympic talent who's forced to face her painful past when she agrees to coach a young hopeful (Noelle Bruno). The skating scenes that consequently follow are the highlight of an otherwise skimpy and rather dull affair. Away from the rink, the simplistic dialogue only scratches the surface of the characters' problems and aspirations, making the admittedly feel-good finale appear too easily achieved. SF

Jessica Cauffiel *Amy Clayton* • Brady Smith *Tim King* • Jerry Stiller *Skipper* • Noelle Bruno *Nicky* • Kathleen Wilhoite *Debra* ■ *Dir* David Burton Morris • *Scr* James Bruner, Elizabeth Stevens

The Ice Follies of 1939
★★★

Musical
1939 · US · BW and Colour · 83min

The three-star rating is strictly for the ice-skating, some of it spectacularly executed by the dazzling International Ice Follies company, for which the rest of this movie is a thin excuse. The almost nonexistent plot has James Stewart as an ice-skater and Joan Crawford as his actress wife, suffering marital strife when she is offered a Hollywood contract. Neither the stars, nor the stalwart support of MGM character actors such as Lewis Stone can rescue the pathetic script. RK

Joan Crawford *Mary McKay* • James Stewart *Larry Hall* • Lew Ayres *Eddie Burgess* • Lewis Stone *Douglas Tolliver* • Lionel Stander *Mort Hodges* ■ *Dir* Reinhold Schünzel • *Scr* Leonard Praskins, Florence Ryerson, Edgar Allan Woolf, from a story by Praskins • *Music* Roger Edens

The Ice Harvest
★★★ 15

Comedy thriller
2005 · US · Colour · 84min

Director Harold Ramis's comic thriller follows the criminal misadventures of jaded lawyer John Cusack. He plans to skip town on Christmas Eve with a case of cash embezzled from his Mob employers. He's both helped and hindered by a sleazy Billy Bob Thornton, aiming more for menace than laughs, while Randy Quaid's crime boss sets about retrieving his stolen money. Although not that original or memorable, this still offers some dark and dry humour. SP Swearing, violence. *DVD*

John Cusack *Charlie Arglist* • Billy Bob Thornton *Vic Cavanaugh* • Connie Nielsen *Renata* • Randy Quaid *Bill Guerrard* • Oliver Platt *Pete Van Heuten* • Mike Starr *Roy* ■ *Dir* Harold Ramis • *Scr* Richard Russo, Robert Benton, from the novel by Scott Phillips

Ice Palace
★★ U

Drama
1960 · US · Colour · 143min

Edna Ferber has had many of her novels turned into films, *Giant* (1956) being perhaps the most memorable. This is a markedly less successful saga about the social development of Alaska. Filtered through the friendship-become-enmity of pioneers Richard Burton and Robert Ryan, it's a a less than enthralling plod through the early years of the 20th century. TH

Richard Burton *Zeb Kennedy* • Robert Ryan *Thor Storm* • Carolyn Jones *Bridie Ballantyne* • Martha Hyer *Dorothy Kennedy* • Jim Backus *Dave Husack* • Ray Danton *Bay Husack* • Diane McBain *Christine Storm* • Karl Swenson *Scotty Ballantyne* • George Takei *Wang* ■ *Dir* Vincent Sherman • *Scr* Harry Kleiner, from a novel by Edna Ferber

The Ice Pirates
★★★ 15

Science-fiction adventure
1984 · US · Colour · 89min

Although little more than an Errol Flynn-type intergalactic swashbuckler, this slight space opera is good inventive fun even if it does err on the crudely silly side. Space pirate Robert Urich searches the universe for the prized commodity of water, gets captured, falls in love with princess Mary Crosby and escapes with her to search for her father on a mysterious planet covered in water. Great art direction and neat special effects augment the constant stream of smart-aleck remarks and sexual innuendo. AJ

Robert Urich *Jason* • Mary Crosby *Princess Karina* • Anjelica Huston *Maida* • Michael D Roberts *Roscoe* • John Matuszak *Killjoy* • Ron Perlman *Zeno* • John Carradine *Supreme Commander* ■ *Dir* Stewart Raffill • *Scr* Stewart Raffill, Stanford Sherman

Ice Princess
★★★ U

Sports comedy drama
2005 · US · Colour · 94min

This "Cinderella on Ice" fable works like a well-oiled Zamboni. The superbly cast Michelle Trachtenberg is a geeky academic who swaps Harvard entry physics to pursue her dream of championship figure skating. Equally dynamic is frosty Kim Cattrall as her no-nonsense coach. Director Tim Fywell faultlessly avoids all the clichés, while keeping things moving efficiently and smoothly. AJ *DVD*

Joan Cusack *Joan Carlyle* • Kim Cattrall *Tina Harwood* • Michelle Trachtenberg *Casey Carlyle* • Hayden Panettiere *Gen Harwood* • Trevor Blumas *Teddy Harwood* • Kirsten Olson *Nikki* • Connie Ray *Nikki's mom* • Juliana Cannarozzo *Zoe Bloch* ■ *Dir* Tim Fywell • *Scr* Hadley Davis, from a story by Meg Cabot, Hadley Davis

Ice Station Zebra
★★★ U

Adventure
1968 · US · Colour · 145min

For a time, the action in this Cold War thriller is as frozen stiff as the title, as a far-off polar outpost becomes a magnet for Russian and American forces out to recover some satellite photographs. Then it thaws into activity when Patrick McGoohan, as a British agent, arrives on the scene to stir Rock Hudson out of his slumber. Ernest Borgnine overacts, and the then popular though now rather clichéd Alistair MacLean original is given a steady treatment by director John Sturges. TH *DVD*

Rock Hudson *Commander James Ferraday* • Ernest Borgnine *Boris Vaslov* • Patrick McGoohan *David Jones* • Jim Brown *Captain Leslie Anders* • Tony Bill *Lt Russell Walker* • Lloyd Nolan *Admiral Garvey* • Alf Kjellin *Colonel Ostrovsky* ■ *Dir* John Sturges • *Scr* Douglas Heyes, from the story by Harry Julian Fink, from the novel by Alistair MacLean

The Ice Storm
★★★★★ 15

Drama
1997 · US · Colour · 107min

Director Ang Lee's adaptation about dysfunctional families in suburban New England is an accomplished ensemble drama. Set in 1973, the film focuses on the complicated relationships between two neighbouring families, against the backdrop of Nixon's unfolding Watergate disgrace. Kevin Kline is cheating on his wife Joan Allen with bored neighbour Sigourney Weaver, while their teenage children are experimenting with their own sexual desires. Cinematographer Frederick Elmes's beautifully realised ice storm draws the drama to a cathartic climax. Outstanding performances by Allen and Weaver are matched by those of the younger cast members. JB Swearing. *DVD*

Kevin Kline *Ben Hood* • Sigourney Weaver *Janey Carver* • Joan Allen *Elena Hood* • Tobey Maguire *Paul Hood* • Christina Ricci *Wendy Hood* • Henry Czerny *George Clair* • Elijah Wood *Mikey Carver* • Adam Hann-Byrd *Sandy Carver* • Katie Holmes *Libbets Casey* ■ *Dir* Ang Lee • *Scr* James Schamus, from the novel by Rick Moody

Ice Twisters
★★

Disaster thriller
2009 · Can · Colour · 83min

You may find yourself entertained for all the wrong reasons watching this goofy, made-for-TV disaster yarn. It sees US meteorological boffin-turned-sci-fi author Mark Moses (from TV's *Desperate Housewives*) left to devise a solution when federal rain manipulation experiments start producing the sort of weather catastrophes fictionalised in his novels. Lots of cod science and enjoyably ridiculous dialogue follow, as he and the rest of the over-earnest cast respond unrealistically to the increasingly far-fetched events. SF

Mark Moses *Charlie Price* • Camille Sullivan *Joanne Dyson* • Alex Zahara *Damon* • Kaj-Erik Eriksen *Eric* ■ *Dir* Steven R Monroe • *Scr* Andrew C Erin, from a story by Paul A Birkett

Iceman ★★★★ PG
Fantasy drama   1984 • US • Colour • 96min

Two of Universal's most successful pictures are recalled in this fascinating sci-fi outing. With an opening that echoes *Frankenstein* and a plotline reminiscent of *ET*, Fred Schepisi's film couldn't have much better role models. While its subject matter is hardly new, the approach is refreshingly intelligent. John Lone gives a remarkable performance as the primitive man rescued from a 40,000-year incarceration in ice, registering fear, bewilderment, trust and curiosity with shifts of expression so subtle they cannot fail to convince. As the scientists monitoring his progress, Timothy Hutton and Lindsay Crouse also underplay to good effect. **DP** Violence, swearing.

Timothy Hutton *Dr Stanley Shephard* • Lindsay Crouse *Dr Diane Brady* • John Lone *Charlie* • Josef Sommer *Whitman* • David Strathairn *Dr Singe* • Philip Akin *Dr Vermeil* • Danny Glover *Loomis* • Amelia Hall *Mabel* ■ *Dir* Fred Schepisi • *Scr* Chip Proser, John Drimmer, from a story by Drimmer

The Iceman ★★★ 15
Crime thriller based on a true story
2012 • US • Colour • 101min

Michael Shannon's portrayal of New Jersey Mob hitman Richard Kuklinski gives this fairly average true-crime biopic a backbone of steel. Kuklinski was known as the Iceman for his modus operandi, which involved freezing the bodies of his victims to obscure the time of death. But he led a double life, hiding his sordid secret from his wife (Winona Ryder) and family right up until his arrest in 1986. Given the period setting, there are a lot of outrageous fashions to distract attention from the pedestrian storytelling. What makes it at all special is Shannon, who's terrific playing a man so psychopathic that he doesn't realise he's actually a monster. **DW** Violence, swearing, sex scenes. **DVD** 〜

Michael Shannon *Richard Kuklinski* • Winona Ryder *Deborah Pellicotti* • James Franco *Marty Freeman* • Ray Liotta *Roy Demeo* • Chris Evans *Mr Freezy* • David Schwimmer *Josh Rosenthal* • Stephen Dorff *Joey Kuklinski* ■ *Dir* Ariel Vromen • *Scr* Ariel Vromen, Morgan Land, from the non-fiction book *The Iceman: the True Story of a Cold-Blooded Killer* by Anthony Bruno and the documentary *The Iceman Tapes: Conversations with a Killer* by James Thebaut

Iceman ★★ 15
Martial arts comedy fantasy
2014 • Chi/HK • Colour • 104min

A Ming dynasty warrior finds himself transported to modern-day Hong Kong in this blockbuster remake of another martial arts fantasy, Yuen Biao's *The Iceman Cometh* (1989). Donnie Yen stars as the Imperial bodyguard who is framed as a traitor and hunted by his former compatriots, only for a freak avalanche to freeze them all in time. There's fun to be had as Yen is awoken from his cryogenic slumber 400 years later, just in time for Halloween, but the ambitious action finale leans too heavily on CGI to generate any real excitement. **JH** Cantonese, English, Hindi, Mandarin +subtitles. **DVD** 〜

Donnie Yen *He Ying* • Wang Baoqiang *Sao* • Huang Sheng-yi *May* ■ *Dir* Law Wing-cheong

Ichi the Killer ★★★ 18
Crime thriller
2001 • Jpn/HK/S Kor • Colour • 120min

Director Takashi Miike's adaptation of a *manga* serial is unrelenting, as sadomasochistic mobster Tadanobu Asano seeks to uncover the identity of a crazed leather-clad assassin who weeps openly as he dispatches his victims. Always frantic, occasionally surreal and often teetering on the brink of bad taste, the action revels in its depravity – although many will blench at the excessive gore and few will find much humour in the mean-spirited misogyny. **DP** Japanese, English +subtitles. **DVD** 〜

Tadanobu Asano *Kakihara* • Nao Omori *Ichi* • Shinya Tsukamoto *Jijii* • Alien Sun *Karen* • Susumu Terajima *Suzuki* • Sabu [Hiroyuki Tanaka] *Kaneko* ■ *Dir* Takashi Miike • *Scr* Sakichi Sato, from the *manga serial Koroshiya I* by Hideo Yamamoto

The Icicle Thief ★★★ PG
Satirical comedy
1989 • It • Colour and BW • 81min

This astute satire on the ruin of cinema by television ends up being just a tad too clever for its own good. Co-writer/director Maurizio Nichetti gives a manic performance as the director who sees his homage to the postwar classic *Bicycle Thieves* being mixed up with some commercials during a special TV screening. While the interaction of the characters from these diametrically opposed fictional worlds amuses, it's the response of the typical Italian family that gives the film its cutting edge. **DP** Italian +subtitles.

Maurizio Nichetti *Antonio Piermattei/Maurizio Nichetti* • Caterina Sylos Labini *Maria Piermattei* • Federico Rizzo *Bruno Piermattei* • Matteo Augardi *Paolo Piermattei* • Renato Scarpa *Don Italo* ■ *Dir* Maurizio Nichetti • *Scr* Maurizio Nichetti, Mauro Monti

I'd Climb the Highest Mountain ★★★ U
Drama   1951 • US • Colour • 86min

This is a clumsy and off-putting title for a charming slice of 20th Century-Fox period Americana. The slim plot in these movies seldom matters, and here a vivacious Susan Hayward narrates a series of vignettes about her marriage to a young minister (an undercast William Lundigan), all filmed in the Blue Ridge Mountains of Georgia where the original Corra Harris novel was set. The supporting cast is well chosen, with character actors Gene Lockhart, Ruth Donnelly and Alexander Knox most welcome, lending the film a spurious authenticity. **TS**

Susan Hayward *Mary Thompson/Narrator* • William Lundigan *William Thompson* • Rory Calhoun *Jack Stark* • Barbara Bates *Jenny Brock* • Gene Lockhart *Mr Brock* • Lynn Bari *Mrs Billywith* • Ruth Donnelly *Glory White* • Kathleen Lockhart *Mrs Brock* • Alexander Knox *Salter* ■ *Dir* Henry King • *Scr* Lamar Trotti, from the novel by Corra Harris

I'd Rather Be Rich ★★★ U
Romantic comedy   1964 • US • Colour • 95min

To cheer up her ailing grandfather (Maurice Chevalier), Sandra Dee agrees to introduce him to her fiancé (Andy Williams). But when he's delayed, she asks Robert Goulet to impersonate him. This is a thoroughly likeable remake of the Charles Laughton/Deanna Durbin comedy, *It Started with Eve*. **JG**

Sandra Dee *Cynthia Dulaine* • Robert Goulet *Paul Benton* • Andy Williams *Warren Palmer* • Maurice Chevalier *Philip Dulaine* • Gene Raymond *Martin Wood* • Charles Ruggles *Dr Charles Crandall* • Hermione Gingold *Miss Grimshaw* ■ *Dir* Jack Smight • *Scr* Oscar Brodney, Norman Krasna, Leo Townsend

Ida ★★★★ 12
Drama   2013 • Pol/Den • BW • 78min

British-based Polish director Pawel Pawlikowski's first movie on his home turf is a sublime monochrome drama set in Communist Poland in 1962. Agata Trzebuchowska plays Anna, an orphaned novice nun who is told by her plain-speaking aunt Wanda (Agata Kulesza) that she is in fact Jewish, her real name is Ida and her parents were killed during the Nazi occupation. This distinctly odd couple then embark on a road trip to find the graves of Ida's parents. Trzebuchowska, a non-professional making her acting debut, is a perfect fit as the sheltered teenager but Kulesza's performance is a revelation – her world-weary exterior subtly overwhelmed by a vulnerability that has unexpected consequences. Stark but beautiful, understated but hauntingly entrancing, this Oscar-winning movie confirms Pawlikowski's place among the best of

modern Polish directors. **JA** Polish +subtitles. Some swearing. **DVD** 〜

Agata Kulesza *Wanda* • Agata Trzebuchowska *Anna/Ida* • Dawid Ogrodnik *Lis* • Jerzy Trela *Szymon* ■ *Dir* Pawel Pawlikowski • *Scr* Pawel Pawlikowski, Rebecca Lenkiewicz

An Ideal Husband ★★★ U
Period comedy   1947 • UK • Colour • 92min

Oscar Wilde's clever writing is subtly interpreted here by Alexander Korda in this class production of one of his more famous drawing room comedies. A stellar list of the day's witty players (Paulette Goddard, C Aubrey Smith, Michael Wilding) lends a dash of celluloid pizzazz to the stylish tale of blackmail and politics. The downside is the rather plodding pace that seems to handcuff the insouciant players and their words. **SH** **DVD**

Paulette Goddard *Mrs Cheveley* • Michael Wilding *Viscount Goring* • Hugh Williams *Sir Robert Chiltern* • Diana Wynyard *Lady Chiltern* • C Aubrey Smith *Earl of Caversham* • Glynis Johns *Mabel Chiltern* • Constance Collier *Lady Markby* • Christine Norden *Mrs Marchmont* • Harriette Johns *Lady Basildon* • Fred Groves *Phipps* ■ *Dir* Alexander Korda • *Scr* Lajos Biró, from the play by Oscar Wilde

An Ideal Husband ★★★★ PG
Period comedy   1999 • UK/US • Colour • 93min

While it shares the wit of Alexander Korda's 1947 version, writer/director Oliver Parker's adaptation of Oscar Wilde's 1895 play has the dual advantage of impeccable casting and, in the current climate of parliamentary sleaze, topicality. This British period piece is visually spot-on, but Parker's energetic opening out of the action occasionally seems a little excessive. What matters most, however, are the performances, with Rupert Everett a standout. **DP** **DVD**

Cate Blanchett *Lady Gertrude Chiltern* • Minnie Driver *Mabel Chiltern* • Rupert Everett *Arthur Goring* • Julianne Moore *Mrs Laura Cheveley* • Jeremy Northam *Sir Robert Chiltern* • John Wood (2) *Lord Caversham* • Lindsay Duncan *Lady Markby* • Peter Vaughan *Phipps* • Jeroen Krabbé *Baron Arnheim* ■ *Dir* Oliver Parker • *Scr* Oliver Parker, from the play by Oscar Wilde

Identification of a Woman ★★★ 18
Drama   1982 • It • Colour • 122min

Throughout his career Michelangelo Antonioni has been preoccupied with transient love and urban alienation, and this was clearly a retreat into familiar territory following the lukewarm reception that his video experiment, *The Oberwald Mystery*, received. Antonioni treats the artistic and romantic problems of director Tomas Milian with a knowing irony. However, as the sequences in the fog and backwaters of Venice suggest, this is also a genuine lament for the decline in meaningful communication both between people and between the film-maker and his audience. **DP** Italian +subtitles. **DVD**

Tomas Milian *Niccolò* • Christine Boisson *Ida* • Daniela Silverio *Mavi* • Marcel Bozzuffi *Mario* • Lara Wendel *Girl at pool* • Veronica Lazar *Carla Farra* ■ *Dir* Michelangelo Antonioni • *Scr* Michelangelo Antonioni, Gérard Brach, Tonino Guerra, from a story by Antonioni

Identity ★★★ 15
Murder mystery thriller
2003 • US • Colour • 86min

A classy cast is stranded at a remote motel in the Nevada desert on the proverbial dark and stormy night. The place is suspiciously reminiscent of another roadside hostelry (proprietor: N Bates), so it's no surprise when they find themselves being picked off one by one in increasingly bloody ways. The shocks are well staged, there are flashes of wit and the performances are sly without being too tongue-in-cheek. Unfortunately, director James Mangold can't sustain the atmosphere in the face of increasingly outlandish plot twists. **AS** Violence, swearing. **DVD**

John Cusack *Ed* • Ray Liotta *Rhodes* • Amanda Peet *Paris* • John Hawkes *Larry* • Rebecca DeMornay *Caroline Suzanne* • Alfred Molina

Doctor • John C McGinley *George* • Clea DuVall *Ginny* • Jake Busey *Robert Maine* • William Lee Scott *Lou* • Leila Kenzle *Alice* • Pruitt Taylor Vince *Malcolm Rivers* • Carmen Argenziano *Defense lawyer* ■ *Dir* James Mangold • *Scr* Michael Cooney

Identity Theft: the Michelle Brown Story ★★
Drama based on a true story
2004 • Can/US • Colour • 114min

Based on the true story of banker Michelle Brown, this TV-movie drama tackles that most modern of crimes, identity fraud. Brown's nightmare began when she signed a rental form. Her bid to prove she had nothing to do with over $50,000 of goods and services charged to her name over an 18-month period makes for salutary viewing, though it's nowhere near as dramatic as the story concerning her nemesis. Consequently, while Kimberly Williams-Paisley turns in a solid performance, it pales beside that of Annabella Sciorra as the thief who is prepared to resort to plastic surgery to sustain her charade. **DP**

Kimberly Williams-Paisley [Kimberly Williams] *Michelle Brown* • Annabella Sciorra *Connie Volkos* • Jason London *Justin* • Stephen Strachan *Barry Knowland* • Claire Lapinskie [Clare Lapinskie] *Christine* • John Kapelos *Ray De Lucci* ■ *Dir* Robert Dornhelm • *Scr* Deena Goldstone

Identity Thief ★★ 15
Road movie comedy
2013 • US/Jpn • Colour • 106min

Mild-mannered accountant Jason Bateman heads to Florida to confront the woman who's been running up huge bills after stealing his identity in this raucous road movie. However, when Bateman attempts to drag loud-mouthed party girl Melissa McCarthy (*Bridesmaids*) back to face justice, the subsequent trip leads to all manner of high jinks. What results is a lopsided yarn of broad physical comedy and pithy verbal jousting between the two leads. Bateman is, to all intents and purposes, the straight man, his role similar to the exasperated character he played in TV's *Arrested Development*, but McCarthy's larger-than-life felon is often annoyingly overbearing. **TeS** **DVD** 〜

Jason Bateman *Sandy Bigelow Patterson* • Melissa McCarthy *Diana* • Jon Favreau *Harold Cornish* • Amanda Peet *Trish Patterson* • Tip "TI" Harris [Tip Harris] *Julian* ■ *Dir* Seth Gordon • *Scr* Craig Mazin, from a story by Mazin, Jerry Eeten

The Ides of March ★★★★ 15
Political drama   2011 • US • Colour • 96min

Politicians lie, which comes as no surprise in this gripping thriller directed by George Clooney. He also slips neatly into the role of a presidential candidate, but this is Ryan Gosling's film – he is enthralling as the PR man who, despite his shrewdness, is blinded by the boss's charm. As Marisa Tomei's rough-edged journo warns Gosling that his idol has feet of clay, a bombshell drops and he has to weigh up his loyalties. The acting is heavyweight, as are the moral questions about the personal cost of serving the greater good, which propel the story with unstoppable force. **SP** Swearing. **DVD** 〜

Ryan Gosling *Stephen Meyers* • George Clooney *Governor Mike Morris* • Philip Seymour Hoffman *Paul Zara* • Paul Giamatti *Tom Duffy* • Marisa Tomei *Ida Horowicz* • Jeffrey Wright *Senator Thompson* • Evan Rachel Wood *Molly Stearns* • Max Minghella *Ben Harpen* ■ *Dir* George Clooney • *Scr* George Clooney, Grant Heslov, Beau Willimon, from the play *Farragut North* by Willimon • *Cinematographer* Phedon Papamichael • *Music* Alexandre Desplat

Idiocracy ★★★ 15
Satirical science-fiction comedy
2006 • US • Colour • 83min

Writer/director Mike Judge previously turned a satirical eye on American society with the antics of animated idiots Beavis and Butt-head and cult comedy *Office Space*. Here, he takes the dumbing-down of the USA to its logical extreme. Luke Wilson plays a US Army private who is declared the "most average" soldier and cryogenically frozen in a secret experiment. Something goes wrong and he wakes up 500 years later in a world so unremittingly stupid that he's the smartest man alive. Judge's nightmarish vision of a lowest common denominator future where water has been replaced by an energy drink is hilarious, as well as depressingly believable. LB *DVD* CS

Luke Wilson *Joe Bauers* • Maya Rudolph *Rita* • Dax Shepard *Frito* • Terry Alan Crews [Terry Crews] *President Camacho* • David Herman *Secretary of State* • Earl Mann *Narrator* • Andrew Wilson • *Beef Supreme* • Thomas Haden Church ■ *Dir* Mike Judge • *Scr* Mike Judge, Etan Cohen

The Idiot ★★ PG
Drama 1951 · Jpn · BW · 166min

Famous for his versions of Shakespeare's *Macbeth* (*Throne of Blood*, 1957) and *King Lear* (*Ran*, 1985), Akira Kurosawa's attempt to adapt Dostoyevsky is far less successful. The story is updated and transposed to snowbound Okinawa where a prince and his emotionally unstable friend share a woman. Dostoyevsky's original novel was always difficult, but the Japanese version makes even stronger demands on its audience in terms of its weird performances and cultural context. AT Japanese +subtitles. *DVD*

Masayuki Mori *Kinji Kameda, the Idiot* • Toshiro Mifune *Denkichi Akama* • Setsuko Hara *Taeko Nasu* • Takashi Shimura *Ono, the father* • Yoshiko Kuga *Ayako Ono* ■ *Dir* Akira Kurosawa • *Scr* Eijiro Hisaita, Akira Kurosawa, from the novel by Feodor Mikhailovich Dostoyevsky

Idiot Box ★★★ 18
Comedy 1996 · Aus · Colour · 81min

Writer/director David Caesar's throbbing comedy adopts the abrasive approach of *Trainspotting* to debunk the contention that the media scars the impressionable. It also launches an assault on the macho cult of superiority to which the Australian male still clings. Ben Mendelsohn and Jeremy Sims are outstanding as the Aussie answer to Beavis and Butt-head, whose indiscriminate viewing prompts them to attempt a bank robbery. Often anarchically funny, the use of TV theme tunes to underscore the action is a masterstroke. DP Swearing, violence. *DVD*

Ben Mendelsohn *Kev* • Jeremy Sims *Mick* • John Polson *Jonah* • Robyn Loau *Lani* • Graeme Blundell *Detective Eric* • Deborah Kennedy *Detective Loanne* • Stephen Rae *Colin* ■ *Dir/Scr* David Caesar

The Idiots ★★★★ 18
Comedy drama 1998 · Den · Colour · 109min

The second film to emerge from the Dogme 95 collective, this utilises the group's complete rejection of film-making artifice to maximum effect and creates an unsettling experience. Lars von Trier thrusts his hand-held camera in the midst of a bunch of Danish dropouts, who test the waters of cultural acceptance by pretending to be mentally disabled in public places. Although uncomfortably comic in its portrayal of people feigning disability, the disturbing (and for a few seconds pornographic) content is balanced by mesmerising naturalistic performances and emotionally engaging situations. JC Danish +subtitles. *DVD*

Bodil Jorgensen *Karen* • Jens Albinus *Stoffer* • Anne Louise Hassing *Susanne* • Troels Lyby *Henrik* • Nikolaj Lie Kaas *Jeppe* • Louise Mieritz *Josephine* • Henrik Prip *Ped* • Luis Mesonero *Miguel* ■ *Dir/Scr* Lars von Trier • *Cinematographer* Lars von Trier

Idiot's Delight ★★★ U
Comedy 1939 · US · BW · 105min

This now somewhat dated mix of romance, comedy, and anti-war flag-waving, offers the treasurable sight of Clark Gable dancing on screen for the first and last time. He plays a hoofer who, with his all-girl dancing troupe, finds himself stranded in a European hotel as war threatens to break out. There, his old flame Norma Shearer turns up in the guise of a Russian countess,

complete with foreign accent. Impeccably directed by Garbo's favourite, Clarence Brown. RK

Norma Shearer *Irene Fellara* • Clark Gable *Harry Van* • Edward Arnold *Achille Weber* • Charles Coburn *Dr Waldersee* • Joseph Schildkraut *Capt Kirvline* • Burgess Meredith *Quillery* ■ *Dir* Clarence Brown • *Scr* Robert E Sherwood, from his play

The Idle Class ★★★ U
Silent comedy drama 1921 · US · BW · 26min

Charlie Chaplin has an early dig at the aristocracy in this sharply amusing short. He's in fine comic form playing a dual role alongside Edna Purviance. The story revolves around various opportunities for Chaplin to play extremes of character - an arrogant, drunken, wealthy husband and an endearing, sensitive but, obviously, impoverished tramp - but he still manages to deliver observations on social inequalities with intelligence. TH *DVD*

Charles Chaplin *Tramp/Husband* • Edna Purviance *Wife* • Mack Swain *Father* • Henry Bergman *Tramp/Cop* • John Rand *Tramp/Guest* • Rex Storey *Robber/Guest* ■ *Dir/Scr* Charles Chaplin

Idle Hands ★★★ 18
Horror comedy 1999 · US · Colour · 88min

The Beast with Five Fingers is given an energetic *Scream* update in a delightful slasher flick casting a winking eye on genre clichés and cannily redefining them into first class popcorn entertainment. Lazy college kid Devon Sawa can't control his supernaturally possessed hand and ends up killing his best friends without knowing it. Director Rodman Flender accurately pushes the jump-scare button on numerous remarkable occasions and always hits the funny bone dead on. AJ *DVD*

Devon Sawa *Anton* • Seth Green *Mick* • Elden Henson *Pnub* • Jessica Alba *Molly* • Christopher Hart *The Hand* • Vivica A Fox *Debi* • Jack Noseworthy *Randy* • Katie Wright *Tanya* ■ *Dir* Rodman Flender • *Scr* Terri Hughes, Ron Milbauer

Idlewild ★★★ 15
Musical drama 2006 · US · Colour · 115min

André Benjamin and Antwan A Patton - better known as André 3000 and Big Boi of urban-music duo OutKast - in this feature debut from writer/director Bryan Barber, the man behind many of their hit promos. Set in the 1930s, the action revolves around the employees of Church, the swingingest speakeasy in Georgia. Cocky Rooster (Patton) manages the joint and occasionally sings on stage, while his shy best friend Percival (Benjamin) plays the piano. As Rooster wrestles with gangsters, Percival falls for a stunning chanteuse. The dance numbers, rendered through dazzling editing, are pretty spectacular, but the acting's patchy and some viewers may bridle at the film's unabashed sexism. LF *DVD*

André Benjamin *Percival* • Antwan A Patton *Rooster* • Paula Patton *Angel* • Terrence Howard *Trumpy* • Faizon Love *"Sunshine" Ace* • Malinda Williams *Zora* • Cicely Tyson *Mother Hopkins* • Macy Gray *Taffy* ■ *Dir/Scr* Bryan Barber

The Idol ★★
Drama 1966 · UK · BW · 109min

This would-be profound psychological study centres on good-looking young American student Michael Parks who is drawn to the girlfriend of his pal John Leyton. Unfortunately, Leyton's mother (Jennifer Jones) also finds herself drawn to the young lothario. Enjoyable if you're in the right mood and John Dankworth's music is always worth listening to. JG

Jennifer Jones *Carol* • Michael Parks *Marco* • John Leyton *Timothy* • Jennifer Hilary *Sarah* • Guy Doleman *Martin Livesey* • Natasha Pyne *Rosalind* ■ *Dir* Daniel Petrie • *Scr* Millard Lampell, from a story by Ugo Liberatore

The Idolmaker ★★★★ 15
Drama 1980 · US · Colour · 113min

This exposé of the American pop music industry of the late 1950s tears the dream

to pieces mercilessly. Starring in a tale clearly inspired by the way singer Frankie Avalon was built up, only to be succeeded by Fabian, both Peter Gallagher and Paul Land are eagerly naive. They play youngsters at the mercy of Ray Sharkey, who is quite brilliant as an unscrupulous entrepreneur (based on Avalon's and Fabian's real-life manager Bob Marcucci). Director Taylor Hackford gives it a sceptical shine and makes sure the facts never obscure the bitter-pill entertainment. TH Swearing.

Ray Sharkey *Vincent Vacarri* • Tovah Feldshuh *Brenda Roberts* • Peter Gallagher *Guido, "Caesare"* • Paul Land *Tommy Dee* • Joe Pantoliano *Gino Pilato* • Maureen McCormick *Ellen Fields* • John Aprea *Paul Vacarri* • Olympia Dukakis *Mrs Vacarri* ■ *Dir* Taylor Hackford • *Scr* Edward Di Lorenzo

if... ★★★★ 15
Satirical drama 1968 · UK · BW and Colour · 106min

Clearly indebted to Jean Vigo's *Zéro de Conduite*, this striking story of schoolboy revolt was originally offered to Nicholas Ray in the hope that he would produce a British equivalent to his classic *Rebel without a Cause*. With its surrealistic elements, it was something of a departure for *This Sporting Life* director Lindsay Anderson, but he succeeds in both capturing the atmosphere and absurdities of public school life and investing the satire with plenty of venom. Malcolm McDowell gives a blistering performance in what is a key film in British cinema history. DP Violence, nudity. *DVD* *Blu-ray*

Malcolm McDowell *Mick Travers* • David Wood *Johnny* • Richard Warwick *Wallace* • Christine Noonan *The Girl* • Rupert Webster *Bobby Philips* • Robert Swann *Rowntree* • Hugh Thomas *Denson* • Peter Jeffrey *Headmaster* • Mona Washbourne *Matron* • Arthur Lowe *Mr Kemp, housemaster* • Charles Sturridge *Markland* ■ *Dir* Lindsay Anderson • *Scr* David Sherwin, from the (unproduced) screenplay *Crusaders* by Sherwin, John Howlett • *Cinematographer* Miroslav Ondricek

If a Man Answers ★★
Romantic comedy 1962 · US · Colour · 95min

After *Gidget*, Sandra Dee went on to further stardom in the *Tammy* films for producer Ross Hunter. Here Hunter teamed her with her then real-life husband, teen heart-throb Bobby Darin. Dee is a Franco/American who marries Darin and soon feels neglected. Her mother's helpful advice for saving the marriage includes treating hubby like a pet dog, and then inventing an imaginary lover to make him jealous. Too cute for its own good perhaps, but on the whole harmless fun. DF

Sandra Dee *Chantal Stacey* • Bobby Darin *Eugene Wright* • Micheline Presle *Maman Stacey* • John Lund *John Stacey* • Cesar Romero *Robert Swan/Adam Wright* • Stefanie Powers *Tina* ■ *Dir* Henry Levin • *Scr* Richard Morris, from a novel by Winifred Wolfe

If a Tree Falls: a Story of the Earth Liberation Front ★★★★
Documentary 2011 · US/UK · Colour · 85min

Marshall Curry's Oscar-nominated documentary reveals the inner politics of the Earth Liberation Front, an American activist group dubbed "eco-terrorists" after they burnt down a series of environmentally unfriendly businesses. Founded on interviews with ELF member Daniel McGowan as he awaited his 2007 trial, it's a fascinating and, ultimately, thrilling and moving tale of young idealists turning to crime and almost outfoxing the authorities, but then imploding as remorse ate them away. The film deftly paints in shades of grey and asks difficult questions of activists who object to what the wider electorate has apparently condoned, convinced they'll one day be seen as heroes. JkS

Daniel McGowen ■ *Dir* Marshall Curry, Sam Cullman

If I Had a Million ★★★ U
Comedy drama 1932 · US · BW · 80min

Paramount put its top directors, writers and stars into this episodic film built around various people's reaction to being handed a cheque for one million dollars. Charles Laughton has the most memorable response as the humble office clerk resigning his position in style, while Charlie Ruggles and WC Fields are also handed memorable comic sequences. On the more sentimental side, Wynne Gibson scores as the prostitute who knows how to indulge herself. A sensibly short running time means the idea doesn't overstay its welcome. AE *DVD*

Richard Bennett (1) *John Glidden* • Charlie Ruggles [Charles Ruggles] *Henry Peabody* • Wynne Gibson *Violet Smith* • George Raft *Edward Jackson* • WC Fields *Rollo* • Alison Skipworth *Emily La Rue* • Gene Raymond *John Wallace* • Frances Dee *Mary Wallace* • Charles Laughton *Phineas V Lambert* • Gary Cooper *Steven Gallagher* • Jack Oakie *Mulligan* • May Robson *Mary Walker* • Blanche Frederici *Mrs Garvey* ■ *Dir* Stephen Roberts, James Cruze, Norman Z McLeod, Norman Taurog, H Bruce Humberstone, Ernst Lubitsch, William A Seiter, Lothar Mendes • *Scr* Claude Binyon, Malcolm Stuart Boylan, Harvey Gates, Joseph L Mankiewicz, Oliver HP Garrett, Grover Jones, William Slavens McNutt, Whitney Bolton, Robert Sparks, Lawton Mackall, from the novel *Windfall* by Robert D Andrews

If I Stay ★★ 12
Drama 2014 · US · Colour · 106min

This corny "afterlife" romance isn't the best showcase for the talents of Chloë Grace Moretz, the young star of *Kick-Ass* and *Carrie*, though it may strike a chord with "Tweenage" girls. Moretz plays a teen cello prodigy left comatose by the car accident that kills her mum, dad and younger brother. But she is able to have out-of-body experiences, and can see her boyfriend moping around the intensive-care unit where her body lies. Does it all end happily? No prizes for guessing. DA Swearing, sex scenes. *DVD*

Chloë Grace Moretz *Mia Hall* • Jamie Blackley *Adam* • Mireille Enos *Kat* • Joshua Leonard *Denny* • Stacy Keach *Gramps* ■ *Dir* RJ Cutler • *Scr* Shauna Cross, from Gayle Forman's novel

If I Were Free ★★
Romantic drama 1933 · US · BW · 65min

London antique shop owner Irene Dunne, who has suffered an appalling marriage to Nils Asther, falls in love with lawyer Clive Brook, taking refuge in alcohol from his unhappy marriage to a wife who refuses to divorce him. This glum and plodding drama is directed by Elliott Nugent, more at home with comedy but with no room to raise a smile here. The journey to the happy ending, though slow, is mercifully short, and the stars (and supporting players) give impeccable performances. RK

Irene Dunne *Sarah Casanove* • Clive Brook *Gordon Evers* • Nils Asther *Tono Casanove* • Henry Stephenson *Hector Stribling* • Vivian Tobin *Jewel Stribling* ■ *Dir* Elliott Nugent • *Scr* Dwight Taylor, from the play *Behold, We Live!* by John Van Druten. • *Cinematographer* Edward Cronjager • *Music* Max Steiner

If I Were King ★★★★ U
Period adventure 1938 · US · BW · 100min

A sparklingly witty and polished historical romp, this gives plum roles to Ronald Colman as the romantic poet and audacious rogue François Villon and to Basil Rathbone as the wily, cackling French monarch, Louis XI, who allows Villon to save him from losing his throne. Preston Sturges's screenplay provides dialogue that is a constant delight, and no one has declaimed poetry better on screen than Colman. Frank Lloyd's direction is admirably brisk and Ellen Drew shines as the ordinary girl who loves Villon without reservation. A rare delight. AE

Ronald Colman *François Villon* • Basil Rathbone *Louis XI* • Frances Dee *Katherine de Vaucelles* • Ellen Drew *Huguette* • CV France *Father Villon* • Henry Wilcoxon *Captain of the Watch* • Heather

Thatcher *Queen* ■ *Dir* Frank Lloyd • *Scr* Preston Sturges, from the play by Justin Huntly McCarthy

If I Were You ★★★ 15

Comedy drama 2012 · Can /UK · Colour · 114min

A classy comedy of infidelity, concealed identity and amateur dramatics – and a rare film lead for *Mystic River* support star Marcia Gay Harden. She plays a woman who, through circumstance, strikes up a relationship with her husband's sexy young mistress. Prompted partly by thoughts of revenge, she agrees to a pact whereby each woman makes the big decisions in the other's love life. A smart and sassy comedy, nicely acted, and with some genuinely laugh-out-loud moments. DA Swearing.

Marcia Gay Harden *Madelyn* • Leonor Watling *Lucy* • Joseph Kell *Paul* • Aidan Quinn *Derek* • Valerie Mahaffey *Lydia* ■ *Dir/Scr* Joan Carr-Wiggin

If Lucy Fell ★★ 15

Romantic comedy 1996 · US · Colour · 88min

Writer/director/star Eric Schaeffer overstretches himself somewhat with this uneven romantic comedy. It's about two friends (Schaeffer and Sarah Jessica Parker), who have made a pact to jump off the Brooklyn Bridge together if neither finds love before Parker's 30th birthday, which is now only a month away. Their attempts at finding the ideal partner include Ben Stiller and Elle Macpherson, but you can work out who their true soulmate will be well before the end of the movie. JB Swearing. *DVD*

Sarah Jessica Parker *Lucy Ackerman* • Eric Schaeffer *Joe MacGonaughgill* • Ben Stiller *Bwick Elias* • Elle Macpherson *Jane Lindquist* • James Rebhorn *Simon Ackerman* • Robert John Burke [Robert Burke] *Handsome man* ■ *Dir* Eric Schaeffer • *Scr* Eric Schaeffer, from a story by Tony Spiridakis, Schaeffer

If Only ★★★ 15

Romantic fantasy comedy
1998 · Sp/Fr/Can/UK/Lux · Colour · 91min

In this 20-something romantic comedy Douglas Henshall stars as the "resting" actor who loses the love of his life, Lena Headey, after a stupid infidelity. Unwittingly encountering a means to turn back time, he returns to the past to try to rectify his mistake. But in spite of strong and convincing performances from Headey, Henshall and the lovely Penélope Cruz, the time travel device is a source of weakness and acts as an irritation to an otherwise entertaining movie. LH Swearing. *DVD*

Lena Headey *Sylvia Weld* • Douglas Henshall *Victor Bukowski* • Penélope Cruz *Louise* • Gustavo Salmeron *Rafael* • Mark Strong *Dave Summers* • Charlotte Coleman *Alison Hayes* • Elizabeth McGovern *Diane* ■ *Dir* Maria Ripoll • *Scr* Rafa Russo

If Only ★★ 12

Romantic drama 2004 · US/UK · Colour · 91min

A miscast Paul Nicholls and Jennifer Love Hewitt play tragic lovers in this flat and unconvincing fantasy drama about appreciating what you've got. Demonstrating zero chemistry together, they fail to add interest to their flimsy characters, as Nicholls's work-obsessed Londoner is given an opportunity to alter destiny by reliving the day his American girlfriend Hewitt was involved in a fatal accident. It's meant to be heart-tuggingly romantic, but the lack of warmth and sincerity makes it difficult to care about the pair or their predictable fates. SF *DVD*

Jennifer Love Hewitt *Samantha Andrews* • Paul Nicholls *Ian Wyndham* • Tom Wilkinson *Taxi driver* • Diana Hardcastle *Claire* ■ *Dir* Gil Junger • *Scr* Christina Welsh

If These Walls Could Talk ★★★ 15

Portmanteau drama 1996 · US · Colour · 97min

Cher and Demi Moore weigh in to the abortion debate with this surprisingly gritty compendium about the subject. The three tales in this film deal with unwanted pregnancies from the 1950s to the present.

In the first story, Moore plays a woman taking desperate measures at a time when abortion was illegal; in the second, Sissy Spacek is the 1970s mother and wife who divides her family when she contemplates abortion; and Cher takes centre stage and makes her directorial debut in the concluding story about a woman doctor facing the wrath of anti-abortionists. Although made for TV, this takes a measured, intelligent look at a controversial issue. JF *DVD*

Demi Moore *Claire Donnelly* • Shirley Knight *Mary Donnelly* • Catherine Keener *Becky* • Jason London *Kevin Donnelly* • CCH Pounder *Jenny Ford* • Sissy Spacek *Barbara Ryan Barrows* • Xander Berkeley *John Barrows* • Hedy Burress *Linda Barrows* • Janna Michaels *Sally Barrows* • Cher *Dr Beth Thompson* • Anne Heche *Christine Cullen* • Eileen Brennan *Tessie* • Jada Pinkett [Jada Pinkett Smith] *Patti* • Lindsay Crouse *Frances White* ■ *Dir* Nancy Savoca, Cher • *Scr* Nancy Savoca, from a story by Susan Nanus, Earl Wallace, from material by Stuart Kaplan (1952); Nancy Savoca, I Marlene King (1974); Nancy Savoca, Pamela Wallace, from a story by Wallace (1996)

If These Walls Could Talk 2 ★★ 15

Portmanteau drama 2000 · US · Colour · 92min

Made for TV, these three intimate but uneven portraits of the lesbian experience in America cross over three decades from the 1960s to the millennium. *1961* is the standout and features a daring performance by Vanessa Redgrave as the surviving member of a 50-year lesbian relationship. *1972* stars Chloë Sevigny in a provocative piece about a group of gay college co-eds. Last and least is *2000*, produced and directed by then couple Anne Heche and Ellen DeGeneres. Even the presence of Sharon Stone can't save this wannabe comedy about two lesbians who want a baby. MC *DVD*

Vanessa Redgrave *Edith* • Chloë Sevigny *Amy* • Sharon Stone *Fran* • Ellen DeGeneres *Kal* ■ *Dir* Jane Anderson, Martha Coolidge, Anne Heche • *Scr* Jane Anderson (1961), Sylvia Sichel, from her story (1972), Anne Heche (2000)

If Winter Comes ★★

Drama 1947 · US · BW · 96min

This is an unashamedly sentimental adaptation about an outwardly respectable publisher suspected by his neighbours of driving a pregnant girl to suicide. As the only friend of waif Janet Leigh, Walter Pidgeon's husband is caught between his demanding wife (Angela Lansbury) and his passionate mistress (Deborah Kerr). For all the suffering and stiff upper lips on show, however, this is a thoroughly resistible melodrama, while Victor Saville's direction is unshaded. DP

Walter Pidgeon *Mark Sabre* • Deborah Kerr *Nona Tybar* • Angela Lansbury *Mabel Sabre* • Binnie Barnes *Natalie Bagshaw* • Janet Leigh *Effie Bright* • Dame May Whitty *Mrs Perch* ■ *Dir* Victor Saville • *Scr* Marguerite Roberts, Arthur Wimperis, from the novel by ASM Hutchinson

If You Could Only Cook ★★★★

Comedy 1935 · US · BW · 70min

This screwball gem, directed by William A Seiter, stars Herbert Marshall and the bell-voiced Jean Arthur, posing as butler and cook in a mobster's house. The movie opened in London bearing the fraudulent legend "A Frank Capra Production" on the advertising. Bill Seiter's reaction to this ploy is unrecorded, but Capra was furious, and persuaded studio boss Harry Cohn to buy him the Broadway hit *You Can't Take It with You* in lieu of settlement. TS

Herbert Marshall *Jim Buchanan* • Jean Arthur *Joan Hawthorne* • Leo Carrillo *Mike Rossini* • Lionel Stander *Flash* • Alan Edwards *Bob Reynolds* • Frieda Inescort *Evelyn Fletcher* • Gene Morgan *Al* ■ *Dir* William A Seiter • *Scr* Howard J Green, Gertrude Purcell, from the story by F Hugh Herbert

Igby Goes Down ★★★ 15

Comedy drama 2002 · US/Ger · Colour · 93min

Writer/director Burr Steers's bittersweet comedy takes the first of many strange turns in an uncomfortable opening sequence: the asphyxiation of Susan Sarandon by sons Kieran Culkin and Ryan Philippe. Dark moments such as these permeate this offbeat coming-of-age tale, with an acid-tongued Culkin often outshining his more experienced co-stars. It may take a while to tune in to the script's coldness of heart and the savage cynicism, yet the film elicits sympathy via flashbacks to Igby's unhappy childhood. JC *DVD*

Kieran Culkin *Igby Slocumb* • Claire Danes *Sookie Sapperstein* • Jeff Goldblum *D H* • Amanda Peet *Rachel* • Ryan Phillippe *Oliver Slocumb* • Bill Pullman *Jason Slocumb* • Susan Sarandon *Mimi Slocumb* • Jared Harris *Russel* • Rory Culkin *Young Igby* • Cynthia Nixon *Mrs Piggee* ■ *Dir/Scr* Burr Steers

Igor ★★★ PG

Animated comedy
2008 · US/Fr · Colour · 83min

This dark and sometimes delicious animated comedy has more than a touch of Tim Burton's gothic charm about it. Set in the pestilential land of Malaria, the film cleverly subverts the (ab)normal by sidelining the Frankenstein-style mad scientists, and putting the spotlight instead on the "Igors" – their hunchbacked assistants. One particular Igor (voiced by John Cusack) decides he's had enough of just pushing buttons and pulling levers and devises a plan for winning the upcoming Evil Science Fair. But his creation turns out to be a sweet-natured female monster who teaches him that good is sometimes a better bet than evil. There are plenty of ghoulish gags, but Steve Buscemi steals the show as a reanimated roadkill-rabbit. DA *DVD* *Blu-ray*

John Cusack *Igor* • John Cleese *Dr Glickenstein* • Steve Buscemi *Scamper* • Sean Hayes *Brain* • Eddie Izzard *Dr Schadenfreude* • Jennifer Coolidge *Jaclyn/Heidi* • Jay Leno *King Malbert* • Molly Shannon *Eva* • *Dir* Tony Leondis [Anthony Leondis] • *Scr* Chris McKenna

Ike: Countdown to D-Day ★★★ PG

Biographical Second World War drama
2004 · US · Colour and BW · 85min

Director Robert Harmon breathes life and, more importantly, emotion into the strategic planning of the 1944 Normandy Landings in this quality Second World War drama. By focusing on the key decisions of Supreme Allied Commander Dwight D Eisenhower, he benefits from an outstanding lead performance from Tom Selleck, who delivers an in-depth portrayal of the American general that captures both his military insight and his unpretentious charm. The end result is a look behind the scenes of history that remains compelling despite its predetermined outcome. SF *DVD*

Tom Selleck *Gen Dwight D Eisenhower* • James Remar *Gen Omar Bradley* • Timothy Bottoms *Gen Walter Bedell "Beetle" Smith* • Gerald McRaney *Gen George Patton* • Ian Mune *Winston Churchill* ■ *Dir* Robert Harmon • *Scr* Lionel Chetwynd

Ikiru ★★★★★ PG

Drama 1952 · Jpn · BW · 141min

Many critics regard this contemporary drama as Akira Kurosawa's greatest achievement. The story would appear to have many pitfalls: a meek civil servant is told he has terminal cancer, so he gets drunk, confronts the emptiness of his life and finally makes amends by turning a derelict city area into a children's playground. This is almost the preserve of the American TV movie – crassly manipulative – but such is the delicacy of Kurosawa's direction, and the power of Takashi Shimura's performance, that you will be moved to tears. AT Japanese +subtitles. *DVD*

Takashi Shimura *Kanji Watanabe* • Nobuo Kaneko *Mitsuo Watanabe, Kanji's son* • Kyoko Seki *Kazue Watanabe, Mitsuo's wife* • Makoto Kobori *Kiichi Watanabe, Kanji's brother* • Kumeko Urabe *Tatsu Watanabe* ■ *Dir* Akira Kurosawa • *Scr* Akira Kurosawa, Shinobu Hashimoto, Hideo Oguni

I'll Be Home for Christmas ★★ PG

Seasonal comedy 1998 · US · Colour · 82min

A vehicle for *Home Improvement* teen actor Jonathan Taylor Thomas, this is watchable enough if you're in a festive mood. He's the smart aleck college kid who finds himself stranded in the desert, wearing a Santa suit (don't ask), and facing a bizarre journey back to his family for the holidays. While the nightmare trip home has been done better, there are some laughs to be had. JB *DVD*

Jonathan Taylor Thomas *Jake* • Jessica Biel *Allie* • Adam LaVorgna *Eddie* • Gary Cole *Jake's father* • Eve Gordon *Carolyn* • Lauren Maltby *Tracey* ■ *Dir* Arlene Sanford • *Scr* Harris Goldberg, Tom Nursall, from a story by Michael Allin

I'll Be Seeing You ★★ PG

Romantic drama 1944 · US · BW · 81min

This over-egged schmaltz from the David O Selznick stable is professionally made, as you'd expect from a major movie of its period. Ginger Rogers is impossibly cast as the girl let out of jail for Christmas, who falls for disturbed, shell-shocked soldier Joseph Cotten. The tale is basically junk, despite the valiant efforts of the two leads. The title song is a lovely and evocative wartime ballad, and deserved better than being attached to this tosh. TS *DVD*

Ginger Rogers *Mary Marshall* • Joseph Cotten *Zachary Morgan* • Shirley Temple *Barbara Marshall* • Spring Byington *Mrs Marshall* • Tom Tully *Mr Marshall* ■ *Dir* William Dieterle • *Scr* Marion Parsonnet, from the play *Double Furlough* by Charles Martin

I'll Be There ★★ 12

Romantic musical comedy
2003 · US · Colour · 100min

Young Welsh opera singer Charlotte Church tries to progress from diva to film star with this attempt at musical comedy. She shines through the story as the teenager who discovers her real father is a washed-up former pop star (Craig Ferguson). The latter finds a new direction in life when he comes across Church in Cardiff, who is the result of a brief liaison he had with her mother Jemma Redgrave. Naturally he discovers that his long-lost daughter is a singing prodigy and sets about carving out a career for her. TH *DVD*

Craig Ferguson *Paul Kerr* • Jemma Redgrave *Rebecca Edmonds* • Charlotte Church *Olivia* • Joss Ackland *Evil Edmonds* • Ralph Brown (2) *Digger McQuade* • Ian McNeice *Graham* • Steve Noonan *Gordano* • Imelda Staunton *Dr Bridget* • Phyllida Law *Mrs Williams* ■ *Dir* Craig Ferguson • *Scr* Craig Ferguson, Philip McGrade

I'll Be Your Sweetheart ★★★

Musical 1945 · UK · BW · 104min

Having cornered the market in costume dramas, Gainsborough had a tilt at period musicals with this passable imitation of glossy Fox fripperies. Unfortunately, Michael Rennie is too stolid to convince as a tunesmith stomping the streets of *fin de siècle* London to find a publisher for his ditties. More at home, however, are Garry Marsh, as an unscrupulous sheet music pirate, and Margaret Lockwood, as the blowsy music hall star who helps Rennie. Val Guest directs with brio, but the songs he's saddled with are second-rate. DP

Margaret Lockwood *Edie Storey* • Michael Rennie *Bob Fielding* • Vic Oliver *Sam Kahn* • Peter Graves (1) *Jim Knight* • Moore Marriott *George le Brunn* ■ *Dir* Val Guest • *Scr* Val Guest, Val Valentine

I'll Be Yours ★★ U

Comedy 1947 · US · BW · 89min

Deanna Durbin sings four songs in the course of persuading meat-packer Adolphe Menjou to employ struggling lawyer Tom

Drake, by pretending the young man is her jealous husband. The film is a remake of *The Good Fairy* (1935), which starred Margaret Sullavan. This time around, with the element of fantasy abandoned, the result is lacklustre, signalling the approaching end of Durbin's money-making film career. RK **DVD**

Deanna Durbin *Louise Ginglebusher* • Tom Drake *George Prescott* • William Bendix *Wechsberg* • Adolphe Menjou *J Conrad Nelson* • Walter Catlett *Mr Buckingham* • Franklin Pangborn *Barber* • *Dir* William A Seiter • *Scr* Felix Jackson, from the film *The Good Fairy* by Preston Sturges, from the play *The Good Fairy* by Ferenc Molnar, from the adaptation and translation *The Good Fairy* by Jane Hinton

I'll Cry Tomorrow ★★★★
Biographical drama   1955 · US · BW · 118min

Susan Hayward stars here in one of the two biographical roles most identified with her, the other being her Oscar-winning performance as condemned murderess Barbara Graham in *I Want to Live!* (1958). In this superior MGM biopic, Hayward plays the tormented actress and self-confessed dipsomaniac Lillian Roth – she starred with the Marx Brothers in *Animal Crackers*. Some may think that Hayward overacts the drunk scenes, but most will find her performance to be vulnerable and honest: as an actress, she was certainly a great movie star. Helen Rose's superb costume design won an Oscar. TS

Susan Hayward *Lillian Roth* • Richard Conte *Tony Bardeman* • Eddie Albert *Burt McGuire* • Jo Van Fleet *Katie Roth* • Don Taylor *Wallie* • Ray Danton *David Tredman* • Margo *Selma* ■ *Dir* Daniel Mann • *Scr* Helen Deutsch, Jay Richard Kennedy, from the book by Lillian Roth, Mike Connolly, Gerold Frank

I'll Do Anything ★★★ 12
Comedy drama   1994 · US · Colour · 111min

This swept-under-the-carpet folly was badly received, even though it's a reasonably well observed and often funny comedy about Hollywood, with Nick Nolte playing a struggling actor trying to juggle his career with single-parent duties. James L Brooks filmed the movie as a musical, but all the songs were cut out after preview audiences gave it the thumbs down. The end result holds up surprisingly well despite the obvious holes where the songs have been dropped. A real oddity that's well worth watching. AJ Swearing, nudity.

Nick Nolte *Matt Hobbs* • Whittni Wright *Jeannie Hobbs* • Albert Brooks *Burke Adler* • Julie Kavner *Nan Mulhaney* • Joely Richardson *Cathy Breslow* • Tracey Ullman *Beth Hobbs* • Ian McKellen *John Earl McAlpine* ■ *Dir/Scr* James L Brooks

Ill Manors ★★★★ 18
Drama   2012 · UK · Colour · 116min

Rapper Ben Drew, otherwise known as Plan B, turns writer/director for this shocking and gritty urban drama that focuses on the criminal underclass in east London. Riz Ahmed stars as Aaron, a young man trying to find his biological mother and escape his brutal environment, but a series of increasingly violent events threaten to keep him languishing in despair. By skilfully interweaving the experiences of several characters (drug dealers, prostitutes, gang members), and punctuating the film with songs that act as both backstories and narration, Drew delivers a bleak but thought-provoking depiction of "broken Britain"; he also shows an impressive grasp of film language and pacing in his directorial debut. TeS Violence, swearing, sex scenes, drug abuse. **DVD** 🔵

Riz Ahmed [Rizwan Ahmed] *Aaron* • Ed Skrein *Ed* • Natalie Press *Katya* • Anouska Mond *Michelle* • Lee Allen *Chris* • Jo Hartley *Carol* ■ *Dir/Scr* Ben Drew

Ill Met by Moonlight ★★★★ U
Second World War drama
1956 · UK · BW · 100min

Michael Powell and Emeric Pressburger are not best known for their war movies, but that doesn't stop this from being a satisfying example of the genre. Dirk Bogarde is on stirring form as a British officer given the task of working with the partisans in occupied Crete to kidnap the local German commander (Marius Goring), in a tale loosely based on a real operation in the Second World War. Fine acting, rugged scenery and a trenchant score all add to the film's attractions. PF **DVD**

Dirk Bogarde *Major Paddy Leigh Fermor* • Marius Goring *General Karl Kreipe* • David Oxley *Captain Billy Stanley Moss* • Cyril Cusack *Sandy* • Laurence Payne *Manoli* • Wolfe Morris *George* • Michael Gough *Andoni Zoidakis* ■ *Dir* Michael Powell, Emeric Pressburger • *Scr* Michael Powell, Emeric Pressburger, from the book by W Stanley Moss • *Music* Mikis Theodorakis

I'll Never Forget What's 'Is Name ★★★
Comedy drama   1967 · UK · Colour · 98min

After a string of Swinging Sixties satires, Michael Winner rather ran out of steam with this scathing look at the world of advertising. Substituting style for substance, the director allows the plot to ramble in places. although he redeems himself with a finale of triumphant vulgarity. Oliver Reed is moodily unconvincing as the commercials director with literary pretensions, but Orson Welles is corpulently corrupt as the man who leads him back down the path of transient achievement and empty glamour. Nearly spot-on, but frustratingly inconsequential. DP

Orson Welles *Jonathan Lute* • Oliver Reed *Andrew Quint* • Carol White *Georgina* • Harry Andrews *Gerald Slater* • Michael Hordern *Headmaster* • Wendy Craig *Louise Quint* • Marianne Faithfull *Josie* • Frank Finlay *Chaplain* • Edward Fox *Walter* ■ *Dir* Michael Winner • *Scr* Peter Draper

I'll Remember April ★★
Second World War drama
1999 · UK/US · Colour · 90min

This cynical piece of family film-making duplicitously seeks to rewrite history by soft-pedalling American treatment of its Japanese citizens during the Second World War. Set on the California coast in early 1942, it tells how a scampish quartet of ten-year-olds hide castaway sailor Yuji Okumoto in a disused factory until they can plan his escape. Trevor Morgan ostensibly has the lead, but most eyes will be on his co-star, Haley Joel Osment (*The Sixth Sense*). DP

Mark Harmon *John Cooper* • Trevor Morgan *Duke Cooper* • Pam Dawber *Barbara Cooper* • Pat Morita *Abe Tanaka* • Haley Joel Osment *Pee Wee* • Yuji Okumoto *Matsuo* ■ *Dir* Bob Clark • *Scr* Mark Sanderson

I'll See You in My Dreams ★★★ U
Musical biography   1951 · US · BW · 105min

One of Doris Day's best vehicles, this rags-to-riches biopic is based on the life of Gus Kahn, one of Tin Pan Alley's most popular songwriters. Kahn's played here by the likeable Danny Thomas, in one of his best attempts at movie stardom – he eventually found fame on American television. Day plays his wife, vying with Patrice Wymore for Thomas's charms. Michael Curtiz gives this film a warm and unpretentious style. TS

Doris Day *Grace LeBoy Kahn* • Danny Thomas *Gus Kahn* • Frank Lovejoy *Walter Donaldson* • Patrice Wymore *Gloria Knight* • James Gleason *Fred* • Mary Wickes *Anna* • Jim Backus *Sam Harris* ■ *Dir* Michael Curtiz • *Scr* Melville Shavelson, Jack Rose, from a story by Grace Kahn, Louis F Edelman

I'll See You in My Dreams ★★ 12
Comedy drama   2015 · US · Colour · 92min

Blythe Danner discovers that life really can begin at 70 in an underwhelming, geriatric comedy drama that may leave you feeling as old as the characters. Danner plays a widowed former singer who's persuaded to get back out there by gal pals June Squibb, Rhea Perlman and Mary Kay Place. The sheer calibre of the cast is what makes this coming-of-old-age tale worth watching. But it adds little to the depiction of an age group that was far more entertainingly portrayed in Lily Tomlin's *Grandma*, also released in 2015. DA Some swearing, sex references, drug abuse **DVD** 🔵

Blythe Danner *Carol Petersen* • June Squibb *Georgina* • Rhea Perlman *Sally* • Mary Kay Place *Rona* • Sam Elliott *Bill* ■ *Dir* Brett Haley • *Scr* Brett Haley, Marc Basch

I'll Sleep When I'm Dead ★★ 15
Crime drama   2003 · UK/US · Colour · 98min

Clive Owen has turned his back on crime when the suicide of his brother (Jonathan Rhys Meyers) forces him back, seeking answers and revenge. Despite the film's pedigree, an excellent cast and atmospheric camerawork, there are huge problems with the structure and woeful script. BP Swearing, violence. **DVD**

Clive Owen *Will Graham* • Charlotte Rampling *Helen* • Jonathan Rhys Meyers *Davey Graham* • Jamie Foreman *Mickser* • Ken Stott *Turner* • Sylvia Syms *Mrs Bartz* • Malcolm McDowell *Boad* ■ *Dir* Mike Hodges • *Scr* Trevor Preston

I'll Take Romance ★★★
Musical   1937 · US · BW · 85min

Billed on its original advertisements as "Her Greatest Romance!", this was the last American film and penultimate movie of the Metropolitan Opera's lyric soprano, Nashville-born Grace Moore. This is a pleasant enough trifle viewed today, one of those silly plots about a kidnapped opera star, but the story doesn't really matter, existing only as an excuse for Miss Moore to sing some arias and the particularly attractive title song. TS

Grace Moore *Elsa Terry* • Melvyn Douglas *James Guthrie* • Helen Westley *Madame Della* • Stuart Erwin *"Pancho" Brown* • Margaret Hamilton *Margot* • Walter Kingsford *William Kane* ■ *Dir* Edward H Griffith • *Scr* George Oppenheimer, Jane Murfin, from a story by Stephen Morehouse Avery

I'll Take Sweden ★★
Romantic comedy   1965 · US · Colour · 96min

Set in the 1960s, when Sweden meant "S-E-X" to a generation of film-goers, this limp comedy has an effervescing Bob Hope sadly deflated by a weak script and inept direction. Hope is Tuesday Weld's father, desperate to break up her relationship with Frankie Avalon, so he decamps to Sweden with daughter in tow. New love blossoms, to limited comic effect, but you can listen to Frankie Avalon sing. TH

Bob Hope *Bob Holcomb* • Tuesday Weld *JoJo Holcomb* • Frankie Avalon *Kenny Klinger* • Dina Merrill *Karin Grandstedt* • Jeremy Slate *Erik Carlson* ■ *Dir* Frederick De Cordova • *Scr* Nat Perrin, Bob Fisher, Arthur Marx, from a story by Nat Perrin

Illegal ★★★ U
Crime thriller   1955 · US · BW · 87min

This gripping thriller stars Edward G Robinson as the district attorney who, after sending an innocent man to the chair, changes sides and becomes a lawyer, defending a racketeer. The story has some startling twists, and with its strong performances and tightly controlled bursts of violence, this is another low-budget miracle from Lewis Allen, who also directed that marvellous assassination thriller, *Suddenly*, in 1954. AT

Edward G Robinson *Victor Scott* • Nina Foch *Ellen Miles* • Hugh Marlowe *Ray Borden* • Jayne Mansfield *Angel O'Hara* • Albert Dekker *Frank Garland* • Howard St John *EA Smith* • Ellen Corby *Miss Hinkel* • DeForest Kelley *Clary* ■ *Dir* Lewis Allen • *Scr* WR Burnett, James R Webb, from the play *The Mouthpiece* by Frank J Collins

Illegally Yours ★ PG
Romantic comedy   1988 · US · Colour · 102min

Rob Lowe revived his flagging career in the 1990s with tongue-in-cheek performances in *Wayne's World* and *Austin Powers: the Spy Who Shagged Me*, but he was still in a trough when he made this dreadful romantic comedy. Lowe finds himself serving on a jury that is trying his ex-girlfriend. Dire in the extreme. JB

Rob Lowe *Richard Dice* • Colleen Camp *Molly Gilbert* • Kenneth Mars *Hal B Keeler* • Harry Carey Jr *Wally Finnegan* ■ *Dir* Peter Bogdanovich • *Scr* MA Stewart, Max Dickens

Illicit ★★
Romantic drama   1931 · US · BW · 76min

A glum and unmemorable weepie, this recounts the love affair and marriage of Barbara Stanwyck and James Rennie. Married life, however, spells the death of romance and the onset of boredom and infidelity. The future great star of melodrama does what she can with the material, which was given a controversial makeover two years later to become *Ex-Lady*, for another up-and-coming melodrama queen, Bette Davis. RK

Barbara Stanwyck *Anne Vincent* • James Rennie *Dick Ives* • Ricardo Cortez *Price Baines* • Natalie Moorhead *Margie True* • Charles Butterworth *Georgie Evans* • Joan Blondell *Helen "Duckie" Childers* ■ *Dir* Archie Mayo • *Scr* Harvey Thew, from the play by Edith Fitzgerald, Robert Riskin

illtown ★★★
Crime drama   1996 · US · Colour · 97min

A disturbing, harrowing look at the reality of drug dealing, this excellent adaptation of the novel *The Cocaine Kids* also works as a compellingly offbeat thriller. Michael Rapaport and Lili Taylor are superb as the nice couple from the suburbs who also co-ordinate a team of teenagers who supply drugs to clubbers. However, their amoral lifestyle is threatened by the arrival of former partner Adam Trese. JF

Michael Rapaport *Dante* • Lili Taylor *Micky* • Adam Trese *Gabriel* • Tony Danza *D'Avalon* • Isaac Hayes *George* • Saul Stein *Gunther* ■ *Dir* Nick Gomez • *Scr* Nick Gomez, from the book *The Cocaine Kids* by Terry Williams

Illumination ★★★★ 15
Drama   1972 · Pol · Colour · 87min

Krzysztof Zanussi's fourth feature chronicles the academic and sentimental education of a doctorate student, whose friends are unquestioning while he spends his time searching for answers. He passes such milestones as his first affair, the death of a friend, marriage, fatherhood, military service and the discovery that he has a fatal heart disease. The insertion of documentary passages and self-conscious stylisation affects this film's accessibility, but it's still a bold attempt to say something serious about the human condition in a provocative and cinematic manner. DP Polish +subtitles. **DVD**

Stanislaw Latallo *Franciszek Retman* • Monika Denisiewicz-Olbrzychska *Agnieszka* • Malgorzata Pritulak *Malgosia* • Edward Zebrowski *Doctor* • Jan Skotnicki *Patient* ■ *Dir/Scr* Krzysztof Zanussi

The Illusionist ★★★★ PG
Period romantic mystery
2005 · US/Cz Rep · Colour · 104min

Nothing is what it seems in writer/director Neil Burger's gorgeously mounted sleight-of-hand confection set in 1900s Vienna. Edward Norton stars as Eisenheim, a magician whose growing popularity and fatal attraction to his childhood sweetheart Sophie (Jessica Biel) bring him into tragic conflict with sadistic Austro-Hungarian royal Rufus Sewell. Paul Giamatti completes a quartet of exceptional performances as the police inspector investigating Eisenheim's apparent ability to conjure the spirits of the dead. Burger keeps the guessing game going over Norton's gifts: is he just a clever trickster or does he indeed control darker sorcerous forces? And the fabulous Philip Glass score complements the sumptuous cinematography and production design. AJ Some violence. **DVD**

Edward Norton *Eisenheim* • Paul Giamatti *Chief Inspector Uhl* • Jessica Biel *Sophie* • Rufus Sewell *Crown Prince Leopold* • Edward Marsan [Eddie Marsan] *Josef Fischer* • Tom Fisher *Willigut* ■

Dir Neil Burger • *Scr* Neil Burger, from the short story *Eisenheim the Illusionist* by Steven Millhauser • *Cinematographer* Dick Pope • *Music* Philip Glass

The Illusionist ★★★★ PG
Animated drama
2010 · UK/Fr · Colour and BW · 76min

Working with an old Jacques Tati screenplay, writer/director Sylvain Chomet (*Belleville Rendez-vous*) retains a 1950s setting for this animated tale of an ageing magician, competing against pop groups for engagements. On a remote Scottish island, an innocent young woman mistakes his tricks for genuine magic and follows him to Edinburgh, where the magician takes on a series of jobs in order to keep her dreams alive. Dialogue is minimal, and the animation is old-fashioned yet distinctive, in keeping with the story. Some may think the film infuriatingly slight, but others will relish it for those very same qualities. BP English, French, Gaelic +subtitles. *DVD*
Eilidh Rankin *Alice* ■ *Dir* Sylvain Chomet • *Scr* Sylvain Chomet, from an unproduced screenplay by Jacques Tati

The Illustrated Man ★★★ 15
Science-fiction fantasy
1969 · US · Colour · 98min

Despite Rod Steiger inventing dialogue as he goes along, and the original author, Ray Bradbury, being angered by the producers' refusal to let him in on filming, this fantasy fable from director Jack Smight works surprisingly well. Steiger is in moody mode as an Everyman whose futuristic adventures are depicted in tattoos over a large part of his body. Claire Bloom, then Steiger's real-life wife, shares the drama if not the star billing, which Steiger deserved if only for the gruelling daily make-up routine. TH Violence, nudity.
Rod Steiger *Carl* • Claire Bloom *Felicia* • Robert Drivas *Willie* • Don Dubbins *Pickard* • Jason Evers *Simmons* • Tim Weldon *John* ■ *Dir* Jack Smight • *Scr* Howard B Kreitsek, from the book by Ray Bradbury

Illustrious Corpses ★★★★★
Political thriller
1976 · It · Colour · 120min

This dazzling conspiracy thriller begins with the assassination of a public prosecutor. There's a funeral, another assassination, then another before cop Lina Ventura gets on to the case, discovering that everything is rotten in the corridors of power. Inviting comparison with Hollywood movies such as *Executive Action* and *The Parallax View*, director Francesco Rosi's cynicism about Italian politics makes for a shocking and dispiriting dénouement, while his preference for staging scenes amid architectural echoes of the Roman Empire implies that history teaches us nothing. AT Italian +subtitles.
Lino Ventura *Inspector Rogas* • Alain Cuny *Judge Rasto* • Paolo Bonacelli *Dr Maxia* • Marcel Bozzuffi *Indolent man* • Tina Aumont *Prostitute* • Max von Sydow *Chief Magistrate Riches* • Fernando Rey *Minister of Justice* ■ *Dir* Francesco Rosi • *Scr* Francesco Rosi, Tonino Guerra, Lino Jannuzzi, from the novel *Il Contesto* by Leonardo Sciascia

I'm a Cyborg, but That's OK ★★★ 15
Surreal comedy drama
2006 · S Kor · Colour · 102min

Park Chan-wook wanted to follow up his brutal "vengeance" trilogy with a film that his young daughter could watch: this curious mix of fairy-tale-like fantasy and slapstick romantic comedy is the result. Events are centred around a highly stylised psychiatric hospital, where Cha Young-goon (Lim Soo-jung) chats to vending machines and tries to eat batteries, gradually getting sicker from refusing "human" food. Only kleptomaniac fellow patient Park Il-sun (played by pop star Rain) can connect with her, using his own delusions to help. The director's extraordinary imagination is evident throughout, creating a charming and vivid experience. But his wackiness sometimes undermines the narrative,

making this more a patchwork of eccentric occurrences than a coherent feature. SF Korean +subtitles. *DVD* *BL*
Lim Soo-jung *Cha Young-goon* • Rain *[Jung Ji-hoon]* *Park Il-sun* • Choi Hee-jin *Choi Seul-gi* • Oh Dahl-su *Shin Duk-cheon* • Lee Young-mi *Oh Seul-mi* • Park Jun-myun *Wang Gop-dan* ■ *Dir* Park Chan-wook • *Scr* Park Chan-wook, Chung Seo-kyung

I'm All Right Jack ★★★★★ U
Satirical comedy
1959 · UK · BW · 100min

This Boulting Brothers' sparkling comedy of industrial manners set in a factory stars Dennis Price and Richard Attenborough, knee-deep in shady dealings and in need of naive Ian Carmichael to carry them through unwittingly. Terry-Thomas also appears, playing the personnel manager driven to distraction by Carmichael's incompetence. But stealing the entire show is Peter Sellers as the union official chained to the rule book, whose faith in communism is inspired by thoughts of "all them cornfields and ballet in the evenings". DP *DVD* *BL*
Ian Carmichael *Stanley Windrush* • Peter Sellers *Fred Kite* • Terry-Thomas *Major Hitchcock* • Richard Attenborough *Sidney de Vere Cox* • Dennis Price *Bertram Tracepurcel* • Margaret Rutherford *Aunt Dolly* • Irene Handl *Mrs Kite* • Liz Fraser *Cynthia Kite* • John Le Mesurier *Waters* ■ *Dir* John Boulting • *Scr* Frank Harvey, Alan Hackney, John Boulting, from the novel *Private Life* by Hackney

I'm Dancing as Fast as I Can ★★★ 15
Drama
1982 · US · Colour · 101min

In this powerful drama, Jill Clayburgh is terrific as a pill-popping documentary film-maker who decides to go cold turkey and kick her habit. The film graphically portrays the physical and mental consequences of her gutsy decision. Unfortunately, the production is weaker than the performances – but what performances! And what a cast! In addition to Clayburgh, look out for powerhouse turns from Nicol Williamson, Daniel Stern, Dianne Wiest, Joe Pesci, John Lithgow and Geraldine Page. DA
Jill Clayburgh *Barbara Gordon* • Nicol Williamson *Derek Bauer* • Dianne Wiest *Julie Addison* • Joe Pesci *Roger* • Geraldine Page *Jean Martin* • Daniel Stern *Jim* • John Lithgow *Brunner* ■ *Dir* Jack Hofsiss • *Scr* David Rabe, from the novel by Barbara Gordon • *Cinematographer* Jan De Bont

I'm Going Home ★★★★ PG
Comedy drama
2001 · Fr/Por · Colour · 85min

Now in his 90s, Portuguese director Manoel de Oliveira again demonstrates the grace and power of cerebral film-making with this wry treatise on the threat posed to the world's literary heritage by the increasingly commercialised and dumbed-down world of "entertainment". Michel Piccoli's acclaimed thespian contemplates quitting the boards to take on his most challenging role: surrogate parent to his orphaned grandson. Thee lengthy theatrical extracts from the works of Shakespeare, Eugene Ionesco and James Joyce may frustrate some of the audience, but the film's sly wit and well-versed wisdom make reparation for such meanderings. DP French +subtitles. *DVD*
Michel Piccoli *Michel* • Antoine Chappey *George* • Leonor Baldaque *Sylvia* • Leonor Silveira *Marie* • Catherine Deneuve *Marguerite* • John Malkovich *John Crawford, the director* ■ *Dir/Scr* Manoel de Oliveira

I'm Gonna Explode ★★★ 15
Drama
2008 · Mex/US · Colour · 103min

The myopic intensity of adolescence is captured with perception and vitality here by Mexican writer/director Gerardo Naranjo. Borrowing heavily from the themes and styles of French New Wave cinema, it sees two teen misfits rallying against the adult world with predictably tragic consequences. Newcomers Juan Pablo de Santiago and María Deschamps are effortlessly convincing as the young rebels without a cause, though their naturalistic performances are held back,

after a breathless opening, by Naranjo's move into unfocused melodrama and cliché. SF Spanish +subtitles. Violence, swearing, sex scenes, nudity.
Juan Pablo de Santiago *Román* • María Deschamps *Maru* • Daniel Giménez Cacho [Daniel Gimenez Cacho] *Eugenio* • Rebecca Jones *Eva* • Martha Claudia Moreno *Helena* ■ *Dir/Scr* Gerardo Naranjo

I'm Gonna Git You Sucka ★★★ 15
Blaxploitation spoof 1988 · US · Colour · 84min

Sending up the blaxploitation movies of the 1970s is a hard thing to carry off since the originals now look pretty funny anyway. Keenen Ivory Wayans makes a fair attempt, as he writes, directs and stars in this daft tale about a man returning from the army to find his brother has overdosed on gold medallions. Of course, he must take revenge against Mr Big (John Vernon) who sold the chains to his sibling. The film features some of the best known blaxploitation stars, including Bernie Casey, Antonio Fargas and *Shaft* composer Isaac Hayes. JB Swearing, violence, sex scenes, nudity. *DVD*
Keenen Ivory Wayans *Jack Spade* • Bernie Casey *John Slade* • Antonio Fargas *Flyguy* • Steve James (1) *Kung Fu Joe* • Isaac Hayes *Hammer* • Clu Gulager *Lieutenant Baker* ■ *Dir/Scr* Keenen Ivory Wayans

I'm Losing You ★★★ 18
Drama 1998 · US · Colour · 98min

Writer/director Bruce Wagner adapts his own novel about a wealthy but misery-plagued Los Angeles family. Patriarch Frank Langella discovers he has terminal cancer but decides not to tell his family. Meanwhile son Andrew McCarthy, a "resting" actor, feuds with ex-wife Gina Gershon over their daughter. Langella's adopted daughter/niece Rosanna Arquette has just made a disturbing discovery about how her parents really died. Sharp scripting and a strong cast give this soapy film more depth than its soapy plot might suggest. LH *DVD*
Frank Langella *Perry Needham Krohn* • Amanda Donohoe *Mona Deware* • Rosanna Arquette *Rachel Krohn* • Buck Henry *Philip Dragom* • Elizabeth Perkins *Aubrey* • Andrew McCarthy *Bertie Krohn* • Gina Gershon *Lidia* • Ed Begley Jr *Zev* ■ *Dir* Bruce Wagner • *Scr* Bruce Wagner, from his novel

I'm No Angel ★★★★ U
Comedy 1933 · US · BW · 83min

This is the third, best, and most profitable of Mae West's films, in which the buxom blonde vulgarian plays Tira, a carnival entertainer determined to climb the social ladder "wrong by wrong". In the course of the action, Mae gets acquitted of murder, sings several songs, does a lion-taming act, and sues Cary Grant, the object of her affections, for breach of promise. Wesley Ruggles directs the lively proceedings, which, thanks to the Legion of Decency having not yet been formed, are generously loaded with the star's double entendres. RK *DVD*
Mae West *Tira* • Cary Grant *Jack Clayton* • Gregory Ratoff *Benny Pinkowitz* • Edward Arnold *Big Bill Barton* • Ralf Harolde *Slick Wiley* • Kent Taylor *Kirk Lawrence* • Gertrude Michael *Alicia Hatton* ■ *Dir* Wesley Ruggles • *Scr* Mae West, Harlan Thompson, from the (unproduced) screenplay *The Lady and the Lions* by Lowell Brentano

I'm Not Rappaport ★★★ 12
Comedy drama 1996 · US · Colour · 129min

A park bench provides the setting for some stimulating verbal exchanges between Walter Matthau and Ossie Davis in this pleasing demonstration of "grey power". They play octogenarian pensioners who join forces to battle against the way relatives and institutions try to pigeonhole them because of their age. Written and directed by Herb Gardner, from his Broadway play, this is a fine example of stars lifting a drama out of the realm of cliché through a mix of pratfalls and poignancy. TH

Walter Matthau *Nat Moyer* • Ossie Davis *Midge Carter* • Amy Irving *Clara Gelber* • Craig T Nelson *The Cowboy* • Boyd Gaines *Pete Danforth* • Martha Plimpton *Laurie Campbell* • Guillermo Diaz *JC* • Elina Lowensohn *Clara Lemlich* • Ron Rifkin *Feigenbaum* ■ *Dir* Herb Gardner • *Scr* Herb Gardner, from his play • *Music* Gerry Mulligan

I'm Not Scared ★★★ 15
Thriller 2003 · It/Sp/UK · Colour · 96min

Ten-year-old Giuseppe Cristiano discovers a dark secret in an underground cellar at a ruined farmhouse. It is a boy, chained up and almost blinded by the light, whom Cristiano befriends. This starts off as an offbeat horror, contrasting the beauty of the southern Italian countryside and the innocence of its protagonist with a mood of unease and foreboding. The early scenes are riveting, and the film evolves into something that is part thriller, part family drama and part rite of passage. Director Gabriele Salvatores just about holds it all together. BP Italian +subtitles. Swearing. *DVD*
Aitana Sanchez-Gijon *Anna* • Dino Abbrescia *Pino* • Giorgio Careccia *Felice* • Diego Abbatuono *Pietro* • Michele Vasca *Candela* • Antonella Stefanucci *Assunta* • Diego Abbatuono *Sergio* • Giuseppe Cristiano *Michele* • Mattia Di Pierro *Filippo* ■ *Dir* Gabriele Salvatores • *Scr* Niccolò Ammaniti, Francesca Marciano, from the novel *Io Non Ho Paura* by Niccolò Ammaniti

I'm Not There. ★★★★ 15
Music drama
2007 · US/Ger · Colour and BW · 129min

As enigmatic as the man himself, this surreal take on the life of singer/songwriter Bob Dylan breathes new life into the rock biopic. Threading together seven scenarios from his prolific career, it introduces Dylan as an eager young songsmith and ends with him as a retired outlaw living in a rural backwater. In between, we see Dylan as a rebellious poet, a protest singer, a drug-addled rock star, a matinée idol with marriage woes, and a born-again Christian. Director Todd Haynes (*Far from Heaven*) uses six different actors to portray the multi-faceted musician, including Cate Blanchett, Christian Bale and Marcus Carl Franklin, a young black boy. The music is cleverly chosen and beautifully interpreted, and while the decision to use such a variety of actors might sound pretentious, it proves to be the perfect way to portray an artist who changed his image more often than his peers changed their socks. DW *DVD* *BL*
Christian Bale *Jack Rollins/Pastor John* • Cate Blanchett *Jude Quinn* • Marcus Carl Franklin *Woody* • Richard Gere *Billy* • Heath Ledger *Robbie Clark* • Ben Whishaw *Arthur Rimbaud* • Charlotte Gainsbourg *Claire* • David Cross (2) *Allen Ginsberg* • Bruce Greenwood *Keenan Jones* • Julianne Moore *Alice Fabian* ■ *Dir* Todd Haynes • *Scr* Todd Haynes, Oren Moverman

I'm So Excited ★★★ 15
Black comedy 2013 · Sp/US · Colour · 89min

Taking its title from the hit Pointer Sisters song, this frantic black comedy from director Pedro Almodóvar sees three male air stewards try to raise morale on a stricken passenger plane as it scours Spain for a free landing strip. After a brief cameo from former Almodóvar discoveries Antonio Banderas and Penélope Cruz, the film erupts into the kind of lurid, skittish farce the director made before *Women on the Verge of a Nervous Breakdown* brought him international art house stardom, as a motley group of passengers fret over sex, love and power, while the stewards make the best of a bad thing by handing out drinks spiked with mescaline. Almodóvar fans will get a buzz of nostalgia from its amped-up silliness, but there's no escaping the fact that his more serious recent films have been much, much better. DW Spanish +subtitles. Sex scenes, drug abuse. *DVD* *BL*
Javier Cámara *Joserra* • Carlos Areces *Fajas* • Raúl Arévalo *Ulloa* • Cecilia Roth *Norma Boss* • Penélope Cruz *Jessica* • Antonio Banderas *León* • Paz Vega *Alba* ■ *Dir/Scr* Pedro Almodóvar

I'm Still Here ★★ 15
Documentary 2010 · US · Colour · 102min

This warts-and-all portrait purports to document what happened when Joaquin Phoenix – at the top of the Hollywood pile after his Oscar nomination for the Johnny Cash biopic *Walk the Line* – decided to retire from acting and pursue a hip-hop career instead. Was this a genuine creative crisis or, as some industry insiders suggested, an elaborate stunt? Actor-turned-director Casey Affleck doubtless knows the answer to that question, since he is also Phoenix's brother-in-law, but his film prefers to tease the viewer rather than end the speculation. Although there aren't enough overbearing highlights to see us through the many dull spots, the film's sheer curiosity value keeps it queasily fascinating. TJ Swearing, sex scenes, drug abuse. *DVD* *BD*

Joaquin Phoenix · Sean "P Diddy" Combs [Sean Combs] ■ *Dir* Casey Affleck

I'm with Lucy ★★★ PG
Romantic comedy
2002 · US/Fr · Colour · 86min

Monica Potter stars in this unusual but superficial romantic comedy. She plays a New York journalist who thinks she's with her dream partner until he abruptly dumps her. Potter then embarks on five blind dates that viewers learn early on result in a marriage. The fun is in guessing which one of the very different men Lucy actually chooses, as the impressively cast movie flits back and forth, gradually expanding each encounter. clichéd, but enjoyably frothy. SF *DVD*

Monica Potter *Lucy* · John Hannah *Doug* · Gael García Bernal *Gabriel* · Anthony LaPaglia *Bobby* · Henry Thomas *Barry* · David Boreanaz *Luke* · Julianne Nicholson *Jo* · Harold Ramis *Jack* · Julie Christie *Dori* · Craig Bierko *Peter* ■ *Dir* Jon Sherman · *Scr* Eric Pomerance

The Image ★★★★ 15
Drama 1990 · US · Colour · 89min

This interesting and provocative look at TV journalism has Albert Finney in fine form as the megalomaniac broadcaster who will do anything for good ratings. More hard-hitting than *Broadcast News*, and almost as impressive as *Network*, this cable-TV movie also boasts a fine cast including Kathy Baker, John Mahoney, Marsha Mason and Spalding Gray. Also watch out for a young Brad Pitt in one of his earlier (and smaller) roles. JB Swearing, nudity.

Albert Finney *Jason Cromwell* · Marsha Mason *Jean Cromwell* · John Mahoney *Irv Mickelson* · Swoosie Kurtz *Joanne Winslow-Darvish* · Kathy Baker *Marcie Guilford* · Spalding Gray *Frank Goodrich* · Brad Pitt *Steve Black* ■ *Dir* Peter Werner · *Scr* Brian Rehak

Images ★★★★
Psychological drama 1972 · Ire · Colour · 103min

Director Robert Altman is probably best known for weaving multiple plotlines round his ensemble casts in films such as *Nashville*, *Short Cuts* and *Pret-a-Porter*. This disturbing portrait of the collision between fantasy and reality in the mind of schizophrenic Susannah York isn't his most accessible work but it's worth making the effort. York and husband René Auberjonois find their country weekend is disrupted by her violent hallucinations. York won the best actress award at the 1972 Cannes film festival for her stunning performance, which is complemented by Altman's innovative direction and Vilmos Zsigmond's photography. TH

Susannah York *Cathryn* · René Auberjonois *Hugh* · Marcel Bozzuffi *Rene* · Hugh Millais *Marcel* · Cathryn Harrison *Susannah* ■ *Dir* Robert Altman · *Scr* Robert Altman, from the story *In Search of Unicorns* by Susannah York

The Imaginarium of Doctor Parnassus ★★ 12
Fantasy adventure
2009 · UK/Can/Fr · Colour · 116min

Director Terry Gilliam's fantasy touch deserts him in this confused plod through familiar themes and visuals. Recycling elements from *Time Bandits*, *Baron Munchausen* and *The Fisher King*, Gilliam's self-indulgent morality tale centres on a carnival sideshow run by once immortal Christopher Plummer, who wagers with devilish Tom Waits over the fate of daughter Lily Cole. In his last (not great) screen performance, Heath Ledger has to help win the bet. Because he died during the production, Johnny Depp, Jude Law and Colin Farrel l take over from Ledger every time he steps through the enchanted mirror. While a clever way of covering up Ledger's demise, these fantasy sequences are wilfully eccentric and totally out of synch with contemporary mores. A rambling and overbearing phantasmagoria. AJ *DVD* *BD*

Heath Ledger *Tony Shepherd* · Christopher Plummer *Doctor Parnassus* · Verne Troyer *Percy* · Andrew Garfield *Anton* · Lily Cole *Valentina* · Tom Waits *Mr Nick* · Johnny Depp *Imaginarium Tony 1* · Jude Law *Imaginarium Tony 2* · Colin Farrell (2) *Imaginarium Tony 3* ■ *Dir* Terry Gilliam · *Scr* Terry Gilliam, Charles McKeown

Imaginary Crimes ★★★ PG
Drama 1994 · US · Colour · 100min

Harvey Keitel gives one of his most nuanced performances here as a single parent trying to support his family and raise two daughters in 1960s Oregon. Always on the verge of "something big" that will make his fortune, Keitel is slowly revealed to be a self-centred conman. Fairuza Balk is also a standout as his elder daughter, an aspiring writer, who relates the tale in flashback. Great characters: shame about the soap operatics. AJ

Harvey Keitel *Ray Weiler* · Fairuza Balk *Sonya* · Kelly Lynch *Valery* · Vincent D'Onofrio *Mr Webster* · Diane Baker *Abigail Tate* · Chris Penn *Jarvis* · Amber Benson *Margaret* ■ *Dir* Anthony Drazan · *Scr* Kristine Johnson, Davia Nelson, from the novel by Sheila Ballantyne

Imaginary Friend ★★
Thriller 2012 · US · Colour · 86min

Mentally disturbed artist Lacey Chabert is revisited by the imaginary friend she invented in childhood in a seemingly average TV movie transformed by an entertaining climax. Controlling psychiatrist husband Ethan Embry says she's just delusional and wants to have her committed, revealing to savvy viewers the first – and most obvious – of the thriller's many twists. The combination of a tense score and Chabert's poker-faced reactions make the last act surprisingly enjoyable. SF

Lacey Chabert *Emma* · Ethan Embry *Brad* · Amanda Schull *Brittany* · Marc McClure *Dr McQueen* · Paul Sorvino *Jonathan* ■ *Dir* Richard Gabai · *Scr* Brian D Young, from a story by Young, Christine Gauthier

Imaginary Heroes ★★ 18
Black comedy drama
2004 · US/Ger · Colour · 106min

In this dark comedy drama, Sigourney plays the matriarch of a suburban family that falls apart when the elder son commits suicide. Weaver retreats into her hippy, pot-smoking past while hubby Jeff Daniels quits his job to spend way too much time sitting on park benches. Emile Hirsch is the neglected younger son who is left to not only cope with his own grief, but his developing sexuality as well. The movie is well made and very nicely acted, but nothing about it is particularly memorable. DA Drug abuse. *DVD*

Sigourney Weaver *Sandy Travis* · Emile Hirsch *Tim Travis* · Jeff Daniels *Ben Travis* · Michelle Williams *Penny Travis* · Kip Pardue *Matt Travis* · Deirdre O'Connell *Marge Dwyer* · Ryan Donowho *Kyle Dwyer* · Suzanne Santo *Steph Connors* ■ *Dir/Scr* Dan Harris [Daniel P Harris]

Imagine: John Lennon ★★★ 15
Documentary
1988 · US · Colour and BW · 99min

Employing a format similar to the one used in the *Anthology* series, this solidly crafted documentary traces the career of John Lennon before and after the Beatles. In addition to TV and archive footage, the film includes home-movie material from the 1970s that is far more arresting than the familiar scenes of the Fab Four in their Beatlemania heyday. Soundbites from interviews given by Lennon from the early 1960s onwards have been deftly shaped into an informative narrative. Few new facts emerge, but it is still a must for fans. TS *DVD*

John Lennon *Narrator* ■ *Dir* Andrew Solt · *Scr* Sam Egan, Andrew Solt

Imagine Me and You ★★ 12
Romantic comedy
2005 · UK/Ger/US · Colour · 89min

Mainstream lesbian romantic comedies aren't exactly common, so writer/director Ol Parker at least deserves credit for thematic innovation. Lena Headey plays the Sapphic Primrose Hill florist who falls for bride Piper Perabo while arranging the flowers at her nuptials to Matthew Goode. A platonic friendship ensues, but increasingly intense feelings begin to develop between the two women. This starts off in a frothy and cheekily humorous vein, but quickly descends into clumsy clichés. SF Swearing.

Piper Perabo *Rachel* · Lena Headey *Luce* · Matthew Goode *Heck* · Darren Boyd *Cooper* · Celia Imrie *Tessa* · Anthony Head *Ned* · Boo Jackson *H* · Sue Johnston *Ella* ■ *Dir/Scr* Ol Parker

Imagine That ★★ PG
Comedy fantasy
2009 · US/Ger · Colour · 102min

Over the Hedge director Karey Kirkpatrick's minimalist fantasy finds Eddie Murphy as a divorced workaholic businessman who only stops neglecting daughter Yara Shahidi when her imaginary playmates (three invisible princesses) start offering canny investment advice. This muddled fable about finding one's inner child through make-believe is a conceit that comes across as silly and unappealing in a movie context. However, it just manages to pull off a tearful resolution, and the best performance comes from Thomas Haden Church as a bogus native American with a neat line in phoney reservation spiritualism. AJ *DVD*

Eddie Murphy *Evan Danielson* · Thomas Haden Church *Johnny Whitefeather* · Yara Shahidi *Olivia* · Nicole Ari Parker *Trish* · Ronny Cox *Tom Stevens* · Martin Sheen *Dante D'Enzo* · DeRay Davis *John Strother* · Vanessa Williams *Lori Strother* ■ *Dir* Karey Kirkpatrick · *Scr* Ed Solomon, Chris Matheson

Imagining Argentina ★★ 15
Political drama
2003 · UK/Sp/US · Colour · 103min

Against the backdrop of Argentina's military dictatorship, Christopher Hampton explores the theme that imagination can free people trapped in horrendous circumstances but fluffs it badly. Antonio Banderas is a theatre director whose journalist wife Emma Thompson is arrested by the junta and becomes one of the "disappeared". Banderos discovers that he can psychically "see" the fates of these victims, though his wife's whereabouts remain a mystery. The dénouement is bog-standard Hollywood mush. AS Violence. *DVD*

Antonio Banderas *Carlos Rueda* · Emma Thompson *Cecilia Rueda* · Rubén Blades *Silvio Ayala* · María Canals [Maria Canals] *Esme Palomares* · Leticia Dolera *Teresa Rueda* · Kuno Becker *Gustavo Santos* · John Wood (2) *Amos Sternberg* · Claire Bloom *Sara Sternberg* ■ *Dir* Christopher Hampton · *Scr* Christopher Hampton, from the novel by Lawrence Thornton

The Imitation Game ★★★★ 12
Wartime thriller based on a true story
2014 · UK/US · Colour and BW · 109min

Benedict Cumberbatch stars as Alan Turing, the genius cryptographer who cracked the infamous Enigma code during the Second World War. The subject matter is potentially dry (particularly as much of the movie is set in a shed) but, while the script doesn't allow much exploration of Turing's homosexuality, Cumberbatch is outstanding. He also has fine sparring partners in Charles Dance (as Turing's superior), and Keira Knightley as his confidante and fiancée. Fascinating and thrilling, *The Imitation Game* keeps you gripped by always offering a reminder of what's at stake, as well as exploring the mind of a brilliant but unfairly treated war hero who should never be forgotten. JL *DVD* *BD*

Benedict Cumberbatch *Alan Turing* · Keira Knightley *Joan Clarke* · Matthew Goode *Hugh Alexander* · Rory Kinnear *Detective Robert Nock* · Allen Leech *John Cairncross* · Matthew Beard *Peter Hilton* · Charles Dance *Commander Denniston* · Mark Strong *Stewart Menzies* ■ *Dir* Morten Tyldum · *Scr* Graham Moore, from the non-fiction book *Alan Turing: the Enigma* by Andrew Hodges

Imitation of Life ★★★★★ 12
Melodrama 1934 · US · BW · 119min

Masterfully directed by John M Stahl, this is an exemplary and irresistible contribution to the vein of melodrama known as a "woman's picture", and earned an Oscar nomination for best film. The versatile and accomplished Claudette Colbert stars as the struggling widow and mother of a small daughter who joins forces with her black maid (Louise Beavers), also the mother of a small daughter, to revitalise their lives and fortunes by opening a successful pancake business. Trouble strikes on all fronts when Beavers's light-skinned daughter grows up and sets out to pass for white with devastating consequences, and Colbert's teenage daughter falls in love with her mother's beau (Warren William). A superb weepie with a moral lesson about racism. RK *DVD*

Claudette Colbert *Beatrice "Bes" Pullman* · Warren William *Stephen Archer* · Rochelle Hudson *Jessie Pullman* · Ned Sparks *Elmer Smith* · Louise Beavers *Delilah Johnson* · Fredi Washington *Peola Johnson* ■ *Dir* John M Stahl · *Scr* William Hurlbut, from the novel by Fannie Hurst

Imitation of Life ★★★★★ 12
Melodrama 1959 · US · Colour · 119min

Danish-born German émigré Douglas Sirk carved his Hollywood niche directing socially aware depictions of 1950s American bourgeois gentility, many now with camp appeal. His swan song gem is a vehicle for an unconsciously self-parodying Lana Turner, starring as an ambitious actress oblivious to various domestic troubles, including her black maid's trauma at being tragically rejected by her lighter-skinned daughter on racial grounds. This was Sirk's and producer Ross Hunter's biggest box-office collaboration. A masterfully formalised and sumptuously decorated ten-hanky weepie, it also benefits from Turner's delirious, melodramatic mood swings and a gut-wrenching funeral song performed by international gospel star Mahalia Jackson. DO *DVD*

Lana Turner *Lora Meredith* · John Gavin *Steve Archer* · Sandra Dee *Susie, age 16* · Dan O'Herlihy *David Edwards* · Susan Kohner *Sarah Jane, age 18* · Robert Alda *Allen Loomis* · Juanita Moore *Annie Johnson* ■ *Dir* Douglas Sirk · *Scr* Eleanore Griffin, Allan Scott, from the novel by Fannie Hurst · *Cinematographer* Russell Metty · *Costume Designers* Bill Thomas, Jean Louis

Immaculate Conception ★★★ 15
Drama 1991 · UK · Colour · 117min

Melissa Leo is a wife desperate to get pregnant but who only succeeds after visit to a mystic Indian fertility sect. She rates it as a miracle and embraces both baby and religion to the exclusion of all else. Hubby James Wilby feels cold-shouldered as a result and jumps to the understandable conclusion that the conception may have been rather less immaculate than his wife let on. This offbeat subject matter is handsomely mounted, with good performances from the two leads. DA English, Urdu +subtitles.

James Wilby *Alister* • Melissa Leo *Hannah* • Ronny Jhutti *Kamal* • Shabana Azmi *Samira* ■ *Dir/Scr* Jamil Dehlavi

Immediate Family ★★★ 15
Drama   1989 · US · Colour · 95min

This absorbing if schematic family drama is distinguished by an impressive cast. Glenn Close and James Woods play a wealthy childless couple who decide to adopt Mary Stuart Masterson's baby. But Masterson suddenly changes her mind, preferring to bring up the baby in near poverty with her boyfriend, Kevin Dillon. The script pushes all the expected buttons, while Jonathan Kaplan, who made *The Accused* and *Love Field*, directs. AT DVD

Glenn Close *Linda Spector* • James Woods *Michael Spector* • Mary Stuart Masterson *Lucy Moore* • Kevin Dillon *Sam* • Jane Greer *Michael's mother* • *Dir* Jonathan Kaplan • *Scr* Barbara Benedek

The Immigrant ★★★★★ U
Silent comedy drama   1917 · US · BW · 20min

One of the funniest, and bleakest, of Charlie Chaplin's early silents, with the steel of his social comment supporting the humour as he enters America, penniless and only just recovering from seasickness. Images of exclusion abound – a shot of the Statue of Liberty is followed by the immigrants being herded like cattle. Chaplin's social concerns put him closer to the writings of Charles Dickens than to the work of his fellow comedians. There's underlying bitterness here, sweetened only by his love for Edna Purviance. Profoundly affecting. TH DVD

Charles Chaplin *An immigrant* • Edna Purviance *An immigrant* • Albert Austin *Russian immigrant/a diner* • Tiny Sanford *Gambler-thief* • Eric Campbell *Head waiter* ■ *Dir/Scr* Charles Chaplin

The Immigrant ★★★★
Period romantic drama
2013 · US · Colour · 120min

Another brilliant Marion Cotillard performance illuminates a refined costume drama set in 1920s New York. She plays a Polish immigrant arriving at Ellis Island in search of the American Dream only to be manipulated into a life of prostitution by pimp Joaquin Phoenix. Her magician cousin Jeremy Renner could be her only chance of escape in a slow-developing, involving narrative that evades being both bleak and overly familiar by virtue of its refreshingly classic approach, delicate handling, terrific production values and exemplary acting. AJ

Marion Cotillard *Ewa Cybulski* • Joaquin Phoenix *Bruno Weiss* • Jeremy Renner *Orlando the Magician* • Dagmara Dominczyk *Belva* ■ *Dir* James Gray • *Scr* James Gray, Ric Menello

Immoral Mr Teas ★★ 18
Sex comedy   1959 · US · Colour · 62min

The very first nudie-cutie movie from *Playboy* photographer-turned-cult director Russ Meyer is a landmark sexploitation classic. Before this coy tale of a delivery man (Meyer's army buddy Bill Teas) with the ability to see fully-clothed women naked appeared, the soft-core sex industry consisted of either pseudo-documentaries warning of the dangers of sexual activity or nudist colony romps. Meyer's silent farce, with a leering narration, changed all that and influenced an entire generation of smut peddlers. Badly dated, but a vital history lesson in the evolution of the sex film. AJ

Bill Teas *Mr Teas* • Ann Peters • Marilyn Wesley • Michele Roberts • Dawn Danielle • Edward J Lakso *Narrator* • Peter A DeCenzie ■ *Dir/Scr* Russ Meyer

Immoral Tales ★★★ 18
Portmanteau erotic drama
1974 · Fr · Colour · 98min

Using a visual style so sumptuous it's almost tactile, this collection is as much an exercise in artistic pastiche as erotic iconography. A different sexual taboo is tackled in each episode: the loss of virginity in *The Tide*; masturbation in *Thérèse, the Philosopher*; lesbianism in *Erzsebet Bathory*; and incest in *Lucrezia Borgia*. Yet director Walerian Borowczyk seems more interested

in staging stylised tableaux than exploring the emotional make-up of his characters, and a desensitising aura of detachment pertains throughout. DP French +subtitles. DVD Blu

Lise Danvers *Julie* • Fabrice Luchini *André* • Charlotte Alexandra *Thérèse* • Paloma Picasso *Erzsebet Bathory* • Pascale Christophe *Istvan* • Florence Bellamy *Lucrezia Borgia* • Lorenzo Berinizi *Casar Borgia* ■ *Dir* Walerian Borowczyk • *Scr* Walerian Borowczyk, from the story *La Marée* by André Pieyre de Mandiargues

Immortal Bachelor ★★
Comedy   1980 · It · Colour · 90min

Often hilarious and frequently racy, this Neapolitan farce finds cleaning woman Monica Vitti on trial for murdering her philandering husband, Giancarlo Giannini. Meanwhile, jury member Claudia Cardinale fantasises about Vitti's predicament in relation to her own marriage to boring Vittorio Gassman. The quartet of fine Italian comedy stars help to move director Marcello Fondato's slight skit up a few entertainment notches. But only just... AJ Italian +subtitles.

Claudia Cardinale *Gabriella Sansoni* • Vittorio Gassman *Andrea Sansoni* • Giancarlo Giannini *Gino Benacio* • Monica Vitti *Tina Candela* ■ *Dir* Marcello Fondato • *Scr* Marcello Fondato, Francesco Scardamaglia

Immortal Beloved ★★★★ 15
Biographical romantic drama
1994 · UK/US · Colour · 115min

The director of gruesome horror flick *Candyman* might seem an unlikely biographer of Beethoven, but, in seeking to identify the "immortal beloved" addressed in the composer's will, Bernard Rose has produced a respectful and imaginative study. It's an audacious mixture of *Citizen Kane* and *Amadeus*, with some *Fantasia*-like musical sequences added. Cinema has rarely given classical music such a chance to weave its spell. Gary Oldman gives a bravura performance, although some scenes might have been played with a touch more moderato. DP Nudity. DVD

Gary Oldman *Ludwig van Beethoven* • Jeroen Krabbé *Anton Schindler* • Isabella Rossellini *Countess Anna Maria Erdödy* • Johanna Ter Steege *Joanna van Beethoven* • Valeria Golino *Julia Guicciardi* • Miriam Margolyes *Frau Strelcher* ■ *Dir/Scr* Bernard Rose

The Immortal Sergeant ★★★
Second World War drama
1943 · US · BW · 90min

Soldier Henry Fonda and other platoon members are lost in the desert wastes of Libya in this decent Second World War flag-waver. It's a story of survival in which sergeant Thomas Mitchell has the homing instincts of a pigeon, if not the stamina of a camel, enabling Fonda to become a hero by leading his people to safety. Meanwhile, assorted airborne Germans are on hand to provide bursts of action, and Maureen O'Hara appears in flashback so as not to make this an all-boy affair. AT

Henry Fonda *Colin* • Maureen O'Hara *Valentine* • Thomas Mitchell *Sergeant Kelly* • Allyn Joslyn *Cassity* • Reginald Gardiner *Benedict* • Melville Cooper *Pilcher* • Bramwell Fletcher *Symes* ■ *Dir* John M Stahl • *Scr* Lamar Trotti, from the novel by John Brophy • *Cinematographer* Arthur Miller

The Immortal Story ★★★ 15
Drama   1968 · Fr · Colour · 54min

This weird little Orson Welles movie was made for French TV. The parable-like story is by Karen Blixen (author of *Out of Africa*) and concerns a Macao trader who hires a young sailor to sleep with his "wife" – who isn't his wife at all, but a whore. Welles revels in the role of the trader, Jeanne Moreau is as good as one expects, but Norman Eshley as the sailor has an impossible task – to be pretty and plausible at the same time. It's easy to be cynical about it, but it is undeniably atmospheric, with a vivid tropical ambience. AT In French. DVD Blu

Orson Welles *Mr Clay* • Jeanne Moreau *Virginie Ducrot* • Roger Coggio *Elishama Levinsky, the Clerk* • Norman Eshley *Paul, the sailor* • Fernando Rey *Merchant in street* ■ *Dir* Orson Welles • *Scr* Orson Welles, Louise de Vilmorin, from the story by Isak Dinesen [Karen Blixen]

Immortals ★★★ 15
Action fantasy   2011 · US · Colour · 105min

Cloned from *300* and *Clash of the Titans*, this often unintentionally hilarious Greek fantasy is camper than the rows of tents housing lead villain Mickey Rourke's army. Rourke's King Hyperion is searching for a mythical bow to unleash caged immortal warriors capable of destroying the Gods. Can peasant Theseus (Henry Cavill), secretly mentored by Zeus (Luke Evans), aided by virgin oracle Phaedra (a one-note Freida Pinto), save humanity? The visuals are truly striking, but there are too many elongated battle scenes crammed with empty spectacle and mindless slow-motion splatter. Although it takes itself way too seriously, the movie will give lovers of expertly faked beefcake action their sword-and-sandal fix. AJ DVD Blu 3D

Henry Cavill *Theseus* • Mickey Rourke *King Hyperion* • Stephen Dorff *Stavros* • Luke Evans *Zeus* • Isabel Lucas *Athena* • Freida Pinto *Phaedra* • John Hurt *Old man* • Kellan Lutz *Poseidon* • Tarsem Singh • *Scr* Charley Parlapanides [Charles Parlapanides], Vlas Parlapanides • *Cinematographer* Brendan Galvin

Impact ★★★
Crime melodrama   1949 · US · BW · 111min

This is tough stuff, as Brian Donlevy's wife and lover plan on getting rid of him, but it's not quite as easy as it seems. There's a terrific supporting cast, including Charles Coburn, Anna May Wong and Mae Marsh, but you'll find yourself rooting for Donlevy, so often cast as the heavy earlier in his career. It's a clever movie that doesn't quite make it as an A-feature, but still has a good deal of class and style. TS

Brian Donlevy *Walter Williams* • Ella Raines *Marsha Peters* • Charles Coburn *Lieutenant Quincy* • Helen Walker *Irene Williams* • Anna May Wong *Su Lin* • Mae Marsh *Mrs Peters* ■ *Dir* Arthur Lubin • *Scr* Dorothy Reid, Jay Dratler

Impact ★★ U
Crime drama   1963 · UK · BW · 64min

Co-written by star Conrad Phillips and director Peter Maxwell, this was produced in a matter of days on a shoestring budget and contains no surprises as ace reporter Phillips is set up as a train robber by vengeful club boss George Pastell. Maxwell just about keeps what action there is ticking over, but he is fighting a losing battle with a cast that is substandard, even for a B-movie. DP

Conrad Phillips *Jack Moir* • George Pastell *The Duke* • Ballard Berkeley *Bill Mackenzie* • Linda Marlowe *Diana* ■ *Dir* Peter Maxwell • *Scr* Peter Maxwell, Conrad Phillips

The Impassive Footman ★★ PG
Crime drama   1932 · UK · BW · 64min

Typical of theatre director Basil Dean's non-comic output for Associated Talking Pictures in the early days of sound, this has stolid staging but the premise is quite intriguing. Tetchy hypochondriac Allan Jeayes discovers that the only man who can cure his rare spinal condition is Owen Nares, the doctor he accused of having an affair with wife Betty Stockfeld on a pleasure cruise. Nares makes a rather inert hero and Jeayes tends to play to the back row, but the wonderfully melodramatic denouement is worth the wait. DP DVD

Owen Nares *Bryan Daventry* • Betty Stockfeld *Grace Marwood* • Allan Jeayes *John Marwood* • George Curzon *Simpson* ■ *Dir* Basil Dean • *Scr* John Paddy Carstairs, Harold Dearden, John Farrow, from Herman C McNeile's play • *Cinematographer* Robert Martin (1)

The Impatient Maiden ★★★
Romantic drama   1932 · US · BW · 72min

James Whale directed just 20 features and, justifiably, his reputation stands on four

landmark horror movies. This early work blends comedy, romance and medical drama. The "maiden" of the title is 19-year-old Mae Clarke (who took over from Clara Bow), and is already suspicious of marriage – until she falls in love with doctor Lew Ayres. Whale's fluent camera, intelligent use of actors and quirky mix of pathos and humour make for a characteristically intriguing film. BB

Lew Ayres *Myron Brown* • Mae Clarke *Ruth Robbins* • Una Merkel *Betty Merrick* • Andy Devine *Clarence Howe* • John Halliday *Albert Hartman* ■ *Dir* James Whale • *Scr* Richard Schayer, Winifred Dunn, from the novel by Donald Henderson Clarke

Imperative ★★★
Drama   1982 · W Ger/Fr · BW and Colour · 96min

Coming between his key Solidarity era, *The Contract* (1980), and the Golden Lion-winning *A Year of the Quiet Sun* (1984), this is one of Krzysztof Zanussi's least-known films. It follows the trials of disillusioned academic Robert Powell, whose search for elusive truths in religion makes for absorbing if rather bleak viewing. DP

Robert Powell *Augustin* • Brigitte Fossey *Yvonne* • Sigfrit Steiner *Professor* • Matthias Habich *Theologist* • Leslie Caron *Mother* ■ *Dir/Scr* Krzysztof Zanussi

The Imperfect Lady ★
Period drama   1947 · US · BW · 97min

This lavishly mounted damp squib of a drama miscasts the essentially demure Teresa Wright as a music hall dancer of Victorian London. Ray Milland's aristocratic politician eventually persuades her to marry him but this coincides with a nasty scandal when Wright is the only alibi for accused murderer Anthony Quinn. Apparently Paulette Goddard was considered for the lead role – which might have made the picture worth watching. AE

Ray Milland *Clive Loring* • Teresa Wright *Millicent Hopkins* • Cedric Hardwicke *Lord Belmont* • Virginia Field *Rose Bridges* • Anthony Quinn *Jose Martínez* • Reginald Owen *Mr Hopkins* ■ *Dir* Lewis Allen • *Scr* Karl Tunberg, from a story by Ladislas Fodor

Imperial Venus ★★★
Historical drama   1963 · It/Fr · Colour · 140min

This sweeping costume drama was clearly a jobbing assignment for Jean Delannoy, whose prospects had suffered greatly from comparisons with the young Turks of the New Wave. There's undeniable splendour in this account of the life and loves of Napoleon's sister, Paolina, but the absence of passion renders it a stilted and stuffy affair. Like many 1960s movies from the Continent, it was made in English alongside the foreign-language version. DP

Gina Lollobrigida *Paolina* • Stephen Boyd *Jules de Canouville* • Gabriele Ferzetti *Freron* • Raymond Pellegrin *Napoleon* • Micheline Presle *Josephine* • Massimo Girotti *Leclerc* • Giulio Bosetti *Camillo Borghese* ■ *Dir* Jean Delannoy • *Scr* Jean Delannoy, Jean Aurenche, Rodolphe M Arlaud, Leonardo Benvenuti [Leo Benvenuti], Piero De Bernardi, John Michael Hayes

Imperium
Thriller based on a true story
2016 · US · Colour · 109min

This is a preview – no prints were available to review as we went to press: You have to feel for Daniel Radcliffe. How ever diverse the parts (Alan Ginsberg, Frankenstein's wingman Igor), he seems destined to be forever "former Harry Potter". He makes another stab at post-Hogwarts credibility with this fact-based tale in which he stars as a former soldier who goes undercover (buzz cut and all) for FBI handler Toni Collette to infiltrate a white supremacy group planning a terrorist attack using a dirty bomb. TP

Daniel Radcliffe *Nate Foster* • Toni Collette *Angela Zampino* • Nestor Carbonell *Tom Hernandez* • Burn Gorman *Morgan* ■ *Dir* Daniel Ragussis • *Scr* Daniel Ragussis, from a story by Michael German

The Impersonator ★★
Crime mystery 1962 · UK · BW · 63min

Signing an American star for a British movie has always been considered a sure-fire way of attracting international attention. Back in the 1960s cash-strapped UK companies had to make do with the likes of minor character actor John Crawford. To give him his due, he's the best thing in this study of insularity, playing an airman stationed near a sleepy country community who becomes the prime suspect when a number of women die in suspicious circumstances. DP

John Crawford *Jimmy Bradford* • Jane Griffiths *Ann Loring* • Patricia Burke *Mrs Lloyd* • John Salew *Harry Walker* • John Dare *Tommy Lloyd* ■ *Dir* Alfred Shaughnessy • *Scr* Alfred Shaughnessy, Kenneth Cavender

Import Export ★★★ 18
Drama 2007 · Austria/Fr · Colour · 160min

Austrian film-maker Ulrich Seidl follows up his 2001 feature debut *Dog Days* with another rigorous exploration of the dark side of human existence. Centred on labour migration between East and West, the languid, documentary-style drama examines the supposed freedoms afforded by Europe's disintegrating borders. In twin journeys of despair, a young nurse (Ekateryna Rak) swaps the Ukraine for Austria in search of a better life, while an unemployed Viennese security guard (Paul Hofmann) heads east with similar ambitions. Flawlessly natural performances from the two non-professional leads give extra edge to the bleak but compelling events, yet in striving for total realism, Seidl occasionally oversteps the mark and wallows in unpleasant details. SF German, Slovak, Russian +subtitles. DVD SD

Ekateryna Rak *Olga* • Paul Hofmann *Paul* • Michael Thomas (2) *Michael* • Maria Hofstätter *Sister Maria* • Georg Friedrich *Nurse Andi* • Erich Finsches *Erich Schlager* ■ *Dir* Ulrich Seidl • *Scr* Veronika Franz, Ulrich Seidl

The Importance of Being Earnest ★★★★ U
Period comedy 1952 · UK · Colour · 91min

Shot in sumptuous Technicolor, this respectful adaptation of Oscar Wilde's sparkling comedy of errors thankfully rarely breaks free of its theatrical origins. The steady direction of Anthony Asquith keeps Wilde's polished barbs and bons mots firmly to the fore and the film is an invaluable record of an expert cast at work. Michael Redgrave and Michael Denison are clipped and composed as the gentlemen of leisure, whose innocent deceptions imperil their romantic aspirations towards the coquettish Joan Greenwood and Dorothy Tutin. Upstaging them all is Dame Edith Evans as Lady Bracknell, whose quavering "A handbag!" is one of British cinema's great moments. DP DVD

Michael Redgrave *Jack Worthing* • Michael Denison *Algernon Moncrieff* • Edith Evans *Lady Bracknell* • Dorothy Tutin *Cecily Cardew* • Joan Greenwood *Gwendolen Fairfax* • Margaret Rutherford *Miss Prism* ■ *Dir* Anthony Asquith • *Scr* Anthony Asquith, from the play by Oscar Wilde • *Costume Designer* Beatrice Dawson

The Importance of Being Earnest ★★
Comedy drama 1992 · US · Colour · 126min

This modern take on one of Oscar Wilde's most celebrated plays is set in London, but the period is contemporary and the African-American cast make no attempt to get their tongues round British accents. The film suffers from the usual problems of trying to "open up" a stage play, and the low-budget look doesn't help. This experiment doesn't really work. JF

Brock Peters *Doctor Chausible* • CCH Pounder *Miss Prism* • Obba Babatunde *Lane* • Wren T Brown *Algernon* • Chris Calloway *Gwendolyn* • Lanei Chapman *Cecily* ■ *Dir* Kurt Baker • *Scr* Peter Andrews, Kurt Baker, from the play by Oscar Wilde

The Importance of Being Earnest ★★★ U
Period comedy drama 2002 · UK/US · Colour · 89min

This adaptation of Oscar Wilde's famously witty play benefits from superb performances from Rupert Everett, Judi Dench as Lady Bracknell and Colin Firth as Jack (who pretends to have a younger brother named Ernest, so he can escape his stuffy country home for wilder times in London). Beautifully filmed by Oliver Parker, this only falls down in the casting of Reese Witherspoon as Jack's young ward Cecily (sounding and looking too modern) and Frances O'Connor (again, looking far too contemporary) as Jack's intended Gwendolen. JB DVD

Rupert Everett *Algernon "Algy" Moncrieff* • Colin Firth *Jack Worthing/"Ernest"* • Frances O'Connor *Gwendolen Fairfax* • Reese Witherspoon *Cecily Cardew* • Judi Dench *Lady Bracknell* • Tom Wilkinson *Dr Chasuble* • Anna Massey *Miss Prism* • Edward Fox *Lane* ■ *Dir* Oliver Parker • *Scr* Oliver Parker, from the play by Oscar Wilde

The Important Man ★★★★
Drama 1961 · Mex · BW · 100min

Mexican director Ismael Rodríguez teamed with Japanese superstar Toshiro Mifune for this adaptation of the novel by Rogelio Barriga Rivas. Mifune excels as the coarse peasant, who, in spite of abusing his family and consorting with other women, has set his heart on being elected "chief for a day" in a forthcoming religious festival. Strikingly photographed by camera ace Gabriel Figueroa, this Oscar-nominated neorealist drama refuses either to sentimentalise the harsh rural conditions or excuse the boorish behaviour of its protagonist. DP In Spanish.

Toshiro Mifune *Animas Trujano* • Antonio Aguilar *Tadeo* • Columba Domínguez *Juana* • Flor Silvestre *Catalina* ■ *Dir* Ismael Rodríguez • *Scr* Ismael Rodríguez, Vincente Orona Brillas, Ricardo Garibay, from the novel *La Mayordomia* by Rogelio Barriga Rivas

The Impossible ★★★★ 12
Disaster drama based on a true story 2011 · Sp · Colour · 108min

This visceral true story follows the efforts of a family to survive the 2004 Boxing Day tsunami. Naomi Watts and Ewan McGregor give raw performances as a married couple who, along with their three boys, are caught up in the devastation in Thailand. The depiction of events is simply terrifying but director Juan Antonio Bayona doesn't rely on effects alone. The scenes of oldest son Tom Holland helping hospitalised survivors to find their loved ones are superbly handled, and the film, overall, packs a real emotional wallop. AJ In English, Thai. Brief nudity. DVD Blu

Ewan McGregor *Henry* • Naomi Watts *Maria* • Tom Holland (2) *Lucas* • Samuel Joslin *Thomas* • Oaklee Pendergast *Simon* • Geraldine Chaplin *Old woman* ■ *Dir* JA Bayona [Juan Antonio Bayona] • *Scr* Sergio G Sánchez, from a story by Maria Belon

The Imposter ★★★★ 15
Drama documentary 2012 · US/UK · Colour · 94min

If this were fiction it would stretch audiences' credulity to breaking point. But *The Imposter* is a documentary. In 1994, 13-year-old Nicholas Barclay went missing near his Texas home. Three years later a young man claimed he was the missing teenager. It is difficult to imagine how he could be less like Nicholas, yet he is readily accepted by officials and the boy's family – or at least most of them. Director Bart Layton allows the characters to tell the story with minimal reconstruction, while subtly shifting the audience's perception of events and people. In turn comic, bizarre and chilling, this plays like the outcome of a brainstorming session between the Coen Brothers, David Lynch and Alfred Hitchcock. BP DVD Blu

■ *Dir* Bart Layton

The Impostor ★★★ U
Second World War drama 1944 · US · BW · 57min

The Nazi invasion of France saves condemned murderer Jean Gabin from the guillotine when an air raid hits. He impersonates a French soldier and transforms himself into a resistance hero in North Africa, bravely launching an attack on an Italian desert base. Made by French wartime exiles in Hollywood, this is a relatively rare French flag-waver, with a charismatic performance by Gabin. AT

Jean Gabin *Clement* • Richard Whorf *Lt Varenne* • Allyn Joslyn *Bouteau* • Ellen Drew *Yvonne* • Peter Van Eyck *Hafner* • Ralph Morgan *Col De Bolvan* ■ *Dir* Julien Duvivier • *Scr* Julien Duvivier, Marc Connelly, Lynn Starling, Stephen Longstreet • *Music* Dimitri Tiomkin [Dmitri Tiomkin]

Impostor ★ 15
Science-fiction thriller 2001 · US · Colour · 91min

In 2079, is weapons expert Gary Sinise really a synthetic robot programmed by an alien enemy to assassinate a leading politician? Or is he the same human being he's convinced he's always been? Bland Sinise races against time to prove his humanity. This B-movie staggers towards an irritating ending while making numerous pit stops at "Cliché Central" along the way. AJ DVD

Gary Sinise *Spence Olham* • Madeleine Stowe *Maya Olham* • Vincent D'Onofrio *Major Hathaway* • Tony Shalhoub *Nelson Gittes* • Tim Guinee *Dr Carone* • Elizabeth Peña *Midwife* • Gary Dourdan *Captain Burke* • Lindsay Crouse *Chancellor* ■ *Dir* Gary Fleder • *Scr* Caroline Case, Ehren Kruger, David N Twohy [David Twohy], from the short story by Philip K Dick, adapted by Scott Rosenberg

The Impostors ★★★ 15
Period comedy 1998 · US · Colour · 96min

Actor Stanley Tucci followed his critically acclaimed directorial debut, *Big Night*, with this farcical comedy, in which he and the underrated Oliver Platt star as two out-of-work actors during the Depression who stow away on a luxury liner populated with eccentric passengers. A spoof on classics like *Grand Hotel*, the film features some rather old-fashioned slapstick, which often works well thanks to the timing skills of the eclectic cast. Enjoyable but uneven. JB Some swearing.

Oliver Platt *Maurice* • Stanley Tucci *Arthur* • Walker Jones *Maître d'* • Jessica Walling *Attractive woman* • David Lipman *Baker* • E Katherine Kerr *Gertrude* • George Guidall *Claudius* • William Hill *Bernardo* • Alfred Molina *Jeremy Burtom* • Lili Taylor *Lily* • Steve Buscemi *Happy Franks* • Isabella Rossellini *Queen (veiled woman)* • Billy Connolly *Sparks* • Hope Davis *Emily* • Campbell Scott *Meistrich* • Woody Allen *Audition director* ■ *Dir/Scr* Stanley Tucci

Impromptu ★★★ 15
Biographical romantic comedy 1991 · UK · Colour · 102min

Hugh Grant is Chopin, Julian Sands is Liszt, but Judy Davis is superb as notorious female novelist George Sand, who flits from love affair to duel with a wondrous disregard for the conventions of 19th-century society. There's some splendid casting in this period romance, not least Ralph Brown as Eugène Delacroix and Emma Thompson as the Duchess d'Antan. It's not exactly history, but still hugely enjoyable. DP DVD

Judy Davis *George Sand* • Hugh Grant *Frederic Chopin* • Mandy Patinkin *Alfred DeMusset* • Bernadette Peters *Marie d'Agoult* • Julian Sands *Franz Liszt* • Ralph Brown (2) *Eugene Delacroix* • Georges Corraface *Felicien Mallefille* • Anton Rodgers *Duke d'Antan* • Emma Thompson *Duchess d'Antan* • Anna Massey *George Sand's mother* ■ *Dir* James Lapine • *Scr* Sarah Kernochan

Improper Channels ★★
Comedy 1981 · Can · Colour · 91min

A comedy about child abuse? Rest assured, this Canadian screwball isn't as sinister as it sounds: five-year-old Sarah Stevens's

injuries are merely the result of a scrape in her father's camper. Officious social worker Monica Parker thinks otherwise, however, and dad Alan Arkin has to reunite with his estranged wife, Mariette Hartley, to retrieve the tot from care. Director Eric Till accentuates the ridiculousness of the situation. Unfortunately, the screenplay's attempts to put a message across not only feel preachy, but also slow down the farce. DP

Alan Arkin *Jeffrey Martley* • Mariette Hartley *Diana Martley* • Monica Parker *Gloria Washburn* • Sarah Stevens *Nancy Martley* • Danny Higham *Jack* • Richard Farrell *Fraser* ■ *Dir* Eric Till • *Scr* Ian Sutherland, Adam Arkin, Morrie Ruvinsky, from a story by Ruvinsky

Improper Conduct ★★ 18
Erotic thriller 1994 · US · Colour · 91min

Steven Bauer stars in this straight-to-video thriller, which, unconvincingly, also tries to provide a serious indictment of sexual harassment. Lee Anne Beaman plays a woman who sets out to avenge the hounding of her sister (Tahnee Welch, Raquel's daughter) who was driven out of her job after turning down the advances of the boss's son-in-law; Bauer is the lawyer friend who reluctantly helps her. JF Violence, swearing, sex scenes, nudity.

Steven Bauer *Sam* • Tahnee Welch *Ashley* • John Laughlin *Michael* • Nia Peeples *Bernadette* • Lee Anne Beaman *Kay* • Stuart Whitman *Mr Frost* ■ *Dir* Jag Mundhra • *Scr* Carl Austin, from a story by Jag Mundhra

An Impudent Girl ★★★★ 15
Drama 1985 · Fr · Colour · 92min

This is a typically insightful study of burgeoning youth from director Claude Miller. In only her third feature, Charlotte Gainsbourg is both rebellious and vulnerable as the teenager seeking an escape from her monotonous home life by hooking up with her idol, teenage pianist Clothilde Baudon. Their misadventures are more painful and revelatory than those featured in most rites-of-passage pictures, largely because the doubts and dreams the girls harbour are so normal. However, the film derives much of its honesty from the exceptional performance of Gainsbourg, whose expressions and emotions always ring true. DP French +subtitles.

Charlotte Gainsbourg *Charlotte Castang* • Bernadette Lafont *Leone* • Jean-Claude Brialy *Sam* • Raoul Billerey *Antoine* • Clothilde Baudon *Clara Bauman* ■ *Dir* Claude Miller • *Scr* Claude Miller, Luc Béraud, Bernard Stora, Annie Miller

Impulse ★★
Crime thriller 1955 · UK · BW · 80min

This is a routine British second-feature, although Arthur Kennedy is a cut above the average imported American lead. Kennedy has a fling with nightclub singer Constance Smith, who involves him in a crime. Screenwriter "Jonathan Roach" is actually Cy Endfield, taking refuge in the UK from the McCarthy witch-hunts, while Charles de Lautour took credit for Endfield as director. DM

Arthur Kennedy *Alan Curtis* • Constance Smith *Lila* • Joy Shelton *Elizabeth Curtis* • Jack Allen *Freddie* • James Carney *Jack Forrester* • Cyril Chamberlain *Gray* ■ *Dir* Charles de Lautour, Cy Endfield • *Scr* Lawrence Huntington, Jonathan Roach [Cy Endfield], John Gilling, from a story by Carl Nystrom, from a story by Robert S Baker

Impulse ★
Crime thriller 1975 · US · Colour · 89min

Film historians seeking the quintessential ham performance by William Shatner would be advised to choose this mid-1970s effort. Ruth Roman's little girl can't convince her that her new boyfriend (guess who) is really a psychotic murderer. Shatner uses his famous stop/start enunciation to ludicrous extremes. His performance alone makes this a must for bad movie fans. KB

William Shatner *Matt Stone* • Ruth Roman *Julia Marstow* • Jennifer Bishop (1) *Ann Moy* • Kim Nicholas *Tina Moy* • Harold Sakata *Karate Pete* • James Dobson *Clarence* ■ *Dir* William Grefé • *Scr* Tony Crechales

Impulse ★★★ 18
Horror   1984 · US · Colour · 86min

This sharp, underrated slice of horror manages to put a sly spin on a familiar scenario. In a typical small town, the residents are starting to behave a little oddly; there's nothing particularly outlandish in their actions, it is just that they seem to be giving in to their baser instincts. Tim Matheson is the outsider who begins to think that something is up, and he is well supported by relative newcomers Meg Tilly and Bill Paxton, plus scene-stealing veteran Hume Cronyn. JF

Tim Matheson *Stuart* • Meg Tilly *Jennifer* • Hume Cronyn *Dr Carr* • John Karlen *Bob Russell* • Bill Paxton *Eddie* • Amy Stryker *Margo* • Claude Earl Jones *Sheriff* • Robert Wightman *Howard* ■ *Dir* Graham Baker • *Scr* Bart Davis, Don Carlos Dunaway

Impulse ★★★ 18
Psychological thriller
1990 · US · Colour · 104min

Actor-turned-director Sondra Locke is probably still best known for her acrimonious split from then-partner Clint Eastwood in the late 1980s. She brings a deft hand to this rather gloomy look at LA cops and hookers, and Theresa Russell gives one of her best film performances as a hard-boiled undercover cop. There is a lot that is very ordinary about this movie, but Russell's presence ensures that it succeeds. SH Swearing, sex scenes, violence, nudity.

Theresa Russell *Lottie Mason* • Jeff Fahey *Stan Harris* • George Dzundza *Joe Morgan* • Alan Rosenberg *Charley Katz* • Nicholas Mele *Rossi* • Eli Danker *Dimarjian* ■ *Dir* Sondra Locke • *Scr* John De Marco, Leigh Chapman, from a story by De Marco

In a Better World ★★★ 15
Drama   2010 · Den/Swe · Colour · 113min

Like her best known works *After the Wedding* and *Brothers*, Susanne Bier's moving Oscar-winning drama spans two continents and explores the bonds that link family and friends. However, this time around the focus is much more on the children than the adults. Newcomer William Johnk Juels Nielsen plays troubled youngster Christian, who takes bullied student Elias (Markus Ryegaard) under his wing. But an incident with Elias's father sets in motion a tragic train of events. The superb acting - the youngsters are particularly good - and Bier's sympathetic direction help overcome the occasional lapse into melodrama. JF Danish, Swedish, English +subtitles. Violence, swearing.
DVD Blu

Mikael Persbrandt *Anton* • Trine Dyrholm *Marianne* • Ulrich Thomsen *Claus* • Markus Rygaard *Elias* • William Johnk Juels Nielsen *Christian* ■ *Dir* Susanne Bier • *Scr* Anders Thomas Jensen, from a story by Bier, Jensen

In a Lonely Place ★★★★★ PG
Classic film noir   1950 · US · BW · 89min

This dark, gripping *film noir* is one of the best dramas ever made about the movie industry. Humphrey Bogart stars as the jaded Hollywood screenwriter who becomes the prime suspect in the murder of hat-check girl Martha Stewart. In one of the roles of his career, Bogart is both sympathetic and sinister at the same time, a complex character teetering on the brink of destruction. His co-star is Gloria Grahame, then director Nicholas Ray's wife, though the part was written for Bogart's wife, Lauren Bacall, whom Warner Bros refused to loan out. AT DVD Blu

Humphrey Bogart *Dixon Steele* • Gloria Grahame *Laurel Gray* • Frank Lovejoy *Brub Nicolai* • Carl Benton Reid *Captain Lochner* • Art Smith *Mel Lippman* • Jeff Donnell *Sylvia Nicolai* • Martha Stewart *Mildred Atkinson* • Robert Warwick *Charlie Waterman* • Morris Ankrum *Lloyd Barnes* ■ *Dir* Nicholas Ray • *Scr* Andrew Solt, from the novel by Dorothy B Hughes, adapted by Edmund H North • *Cinematographer* Burnett Guffey

In a Shallow Grave ★★ 15
Romantic drama   1988 · US · Colour · 87min

This is a worthy, if sometimes melodramatic tale from the respected American Playhouse team. Michael Biehn plays a bitter war hero who becomes fascinated with a young man (Patrick Dempsey) working for him. A study in class and sexual tension, it's beautifully acted, if directed at a slack pace. JF

Michael Biehn *Garnet Montrose* • Maureen Mueller *Georgina Rance* • Michael Beach *Quintas Pearch* • Patrick Dempsey *Potter Daventry* • Thomas Boyd Mason *Edgar Doust* ■ *Dir* Kenneth Bowser • *Scr* Kenneth Bowser, from the novel by James Purdy

In a Valley of Violence
Western   2016 · UK · Colour · 104min

This is a preview - no prints were available to review prior to publication: Ti West has been threatening to make a breakout movie ever since his atmospheric *The Innkeepers* - a kind of no-budget, indie *The Shining*. Could this be the one? He's shooting on old-school 35mm and on sets built in New Mexico, and his cast is certainly eye-catching - Ethan Hawke as a drifter out for revenge, Taissa Farmiga and Karen Gillan as sisters running a hotel, and John Travolta as a marshal with a wooden leg. SvM

Karen Gillan *Ellen* • John Travolta *The marshal* • Ethan Hawke *Paul* • Taissa Farmiga *Mary Anne* ■ *Dir/Scr* Ti West

In a World... ★★★★ 15
Comedy   2013 · US · Colour · 90min

Lake Bell writes, directs and stars in this touching comedy about a woman trying to make it in the male-dominated world of voiceover artists. It sounds ripe for a spoof, but the comedy in this finely tuned film is observational rather than gag-based, while a romantic subplot involving Bell's on-screen sister adds some poignant texture. Thankfully, the movie resolves itself in true, feel-good fashion, with a number of famous guest stars adding an element of surprise whenever the story needs a lift. DW Swearing, sexual references. DVD

Lake Bell *Carol* • Fred Melamed *Sam* • Demetri Martin *Louis* • Michaela Watkins *Dani* • Rob Corddry *Moe* ■ *Dir/Scr* Lake Bell

In a Year of 13 Moons ★★★★ 18
Drama   1978 · W Ger · Colour · 119min

Inspired by the suicide of his lover, Armin Meier, this was one of Rainer Werner Fassbinder's most personal statements: as well as writer/director, he acted as cinematographer, designer and editor. The film also ranks among his most uncompromising condemnations of conformity, with transsexual Volker Spengler's desire to find emotional and social acceptance a root cause of his/her misery. Fassbinder refuses to let us identify with the characters and employs harshly lit and cluttered visuals to distract from the dialogue. Jarring, pessimistic and played with terrifying candour, this is a unique and disconcerting experience. DP German +subtitles.

Volker Spengler *Elvira Weishaupt* • Ingrid Caven *Red Zora* • Gottfried John *Anton Saitz* • Elisabeth Trissenaar *Irene* • Eva Mattes *Marie-Ann* ■ *Dir/Scr* Rainer Werner Fassbinder

In America ★★★★ 15
Drama   2003 · US/Ire/UK · Colour · 101min

Co-written by director Jim Sheridan, along with his two daughters Naomi and Kirsten, the intimate story is seen through the eyes of an 11-year-old girl, living as an illegal immigrant in a run-down New York tenement building with her younger sister and Irish parents (Samantha Morton and Paddy Considine). Though the youngsters view the US as a place of wonder, past tragedy casts a dark shadow over the family, giving the picture a profound emotional resonance. Sheridan demonstrates remarkable versatility and sensitivity, shooting on video to create an ethereal, dream-like ambience. The performances are entrancing, with real-life sisters Sarah and Emma Bolger a revelation as the screen siblings. SF DVD

Samantha Morton *Sarah* • Paddy Considine *Johnny* • Sarah Bolger *Christy* • Emma Bolger *Ariel* • Djimon Hounsou *Mateo* ■ *Dir* Jim Sheridan • *Scr* Jim Sheridan, Naomi Sheridan, Kirsten Sheridan

In & Out ★★★★ 12
Comedy   1997 · US · Colour · 86min

Kevin Kline stars as the soon-to-be-married small-town teacher who is outed by an ex-pupil-turned-Hollywood star (Matt Dillon) during his televised Oscar acceptance speech. Inspired by Tom Hanks's *Philadelphia* acceptance speech (in which he thanked his gay professor), this has some very funny moments as Kline, his wedding-obsessed mother (Debbie Reynolds) and surprised fiancée (Joan Cusack) struggle with the fact he may be gay, and there's a nice supporting turn from Tom Selleck as the openly gay reporter who comes to town to cover the story. Thanks to Kline's sharp but moving performance, what could have been a stereotypical or even camp role is actually a fleshed out and sensitive one. JB Swearing. DVD

Kevin Kline *Howard Brackett* • Joan Cusack *Emily Montgomery* • Tom Selleck *Peter Malloy* • Matt Dillon *Cameron Drake* • Debbie Reynolds *Berniece Brackett* • Glenn Close • Whoopi Goldberg • Jay Leno ■ *Dir* Frank Oz • *Scr* Paul Rudnick

In Bed with Madonna ★★★ 15
Music documentary
1991 · US · BW and Colour · 113min

Shot during the 1990 "Blond Ambition" tour and released as *Truth or Dare* in the States, this is hardly an intimate portrait of Madonna: she's so aware of the presence of the camera that it's performance all the way. The on-stage concert sequences, for all their colour and polish, are positively dull beside the monochrome backstage scenes, in which no one is spared the Ciccone wrath (even God gets His ear bent before every show). The shredding of Kevin Costner is a treat, but on the downside there's the rudeness to her childhood friend. Perhaps most revealing are the scenes with then boyfriend Warren Beatty. DP Swearing. DVD

Madonna • Sandra Bernhard • Warren Beatty • Kevin Costner ■ *Dir* Alek Keshishian

In Bruges ★★★★ 18
Black comedy drama
2008 · US/UK/Ger · Colour · 102min

Although this violent, foul-mouthed and politically incorrect black comedy drama ticks some of the usual boxes for a British gangster movie, it's both intelligent and entertaining while managing the miracle of actually being original. Professional killers Ray (Colin Farrell) and Ken (Brendan Gleeson) are laying low in the medieval city of Bruges following a horribly botched job, and their enforced sojourn in the picture-postcard location begins to have a strange effect. Gleeson is excellent, as is Farrell (more surprisingly), and it is their relationship and philosophical (as well as profane) musings that give the film its drive, resulting in a lurid but unexpectedly affecting film. DW DVD Blu

Colin Farrell (2) *Ray* • Brendan Gleeson *Ken* • Ralph Fiennes *Harry* • Clémence Poésy *Chloë* • Jérémie Rénier *Eirik* • Elizabeth Berrington *Natalie* • Zeljko Ivanek *Canadian guy* • Ciarán Hinds [Ciaran Hinds] *Catholic priest* ■ *Dir/Scr* Martin McDonagh

In Caliente ★★
Romantic musical   1935 · US · BW · 84min

"The lady in red, the fellas adore the lady in red..." and that's about all there is to adore in this lacklustre Warner Bros romantic vehicle for star Dolores Del Rio. Despite routines from ace choreographer Busby Berkeley, this musical never really gets off the backlot, and leading man Pat O'Brien lacks the requisite lightness for this type of fluff. TS

Dolores Del Rio *Rita Gomez* • Pat O'Brien *Larry MacAfrey* • Leo Carrillo *Jose Gomez* • Edward Everett Horton *Harold Brandon* • Glenda Farrell *Clara* • Phil Regan *Pat Casey* ■ *Dir* Lloyd Bacon • *Scr* Jerry Wald, Julius Epstein [Julius J Epstein], Ralph Block, Warren Duff, from the story *Caliente* by Block, Duff

In Casablanca Angels Don't Fly ★★★★ PG
Drama   2003 · Mor/It · Colour · 97min

One-time producer Mohamed Asli makes an assured directorial debut with this moving treatise on the age-old clash between town and country mores. Home is very much where the heart is for waiter Rachid El Hazmir and cook Abdelaziz Essghyr, as each man dreams of what he has left behind in an isolated village in the Atlas Mountains. But for co-worker Abdessamed Miftah El Kheir, the city offers new riches, symbolised by his passion for a pair of designer shoes. Leavening his neorealist approach with the occasional technical flourish, Asli tells each story with a fond care that is even more apparent as each man sees his cherished wish soured by cruel caprice. DP Arabic, Berber +subtitles.

Abdessamed Miftah El Kheir *Ismail* • Abderrazak El Badaoui *Restaurant owner* • Rachid El Hazmir *Said* • Leila El Ahyani *Aicha* • Abdelaziz Essghyr *Ottman* ■ *Dir* Mohamed Asli • *Scr* Siham Douguena

In Celebration ★★★
Drama   1974 · UK · Colour · 131min

Director Lindsay Anderson reunites the cast of London's Royal Court production for this screen version of David Storey's play. Three sons (Alan Bates, James Bolam, Brian Cox) return to their northern roots for the 40th wedding anniversary celebrations of parents Bill Owen and Constance Chapman. While all three have exceeded the career achievements of their miner father, their homecoming brings the usual saga of angst, buried resentments and skeletons in the closet. While its stage origins do hinder the pace of the action, this is wryly observant, and well acted. TH

Alan Bates *Andrew Shaw* • James Bolam *Colin Shaw* • Brian Cox (1) *Steven Shaw* • Constance Chapman *Mrs Shaw* • Gabrielle Daye *Mrs Burnett* • Bill Owen *Mr Shaw* ■ *Dir* Lindsay Anderson • *Scr* David Storey, from his play

In Cold Blood ★★★★ 15
Crime drama based on a true story
1967 · US · BW · 128min

Truman Capote's book about two young real-life murderers was a shocking bestseller in its day, and thought impossible to bring to the screen. Yet writer/director Richard Brooks did deliver this harrowing movie adaptation, remarkably faithful to its source and featuring two relatively unknown actors as the youngsters who wiped out a Kansas family during a robbery. The mood is properly dour and relentless, and the use of actual locations superb. The supporting cast is full of well-known Hollywood players, with the likes of John Forsythe, Will Geer and Paul Stewart ensuring that the grim subject matter remains resolutely unsensationalised. TS Violence, swearing. DVD Blu

Robert Blake *Perry Smith* • Scott Wilson *Dick Hickock* • John Forsythe *Alvin Dewey* • Paul Stewart *Reporter* • Gerald S O'Loughlin *Harold Nye* • Jeff Corey *Hickock's father* • John Gallaudet *Roy Church* • James Flavin *Clarence Duntz* • Charles McGraw *Perry's father* • Will Geer *Prosecuting attorney* ■ *Dir* Richard Brooks • *Scr* Richard Brooks, from the non-fiction book by Truman Capote • *Cinematographer* Conrad Hall

In Country ★★★ 15
Drama   1989 · US · Colour · 110min

This was Bruce Willis's first real stab at proving himself a serious actor, and he delivers a credibly moody performance as a disturbed Vietnam veteran trying to piece his life together after the conflict. Emily Lloyd also emerges with honours in one of her first American roles. However, both are let down by a meandering script that never quite gets to grips with the subject matter and uneven direction from the usually reliable Norman Jewison (director of *Moonstruck* among other hits). JF Violence.

Bruce Willis *Emmett Smith* • Emily Lloyd *Samantha Hughes* • Joan Allen *Irene* • Kevin Anderson *Lonnie Malone* • Richard Hamilton *Grampaw* • Judith Ivey *Anita Stevens* ■ *Dir* Norman Jewison • *Scr* Frank Pierson, Cynthia Cidre, from the novel by Bobbie Ann Mason

The In Crowd ★★ PG
Romantic dance drama
1988 · US · Colour · 95min

Donovan Leitch (son of Donovan and brother of Ione Skye) stars in this 1960s-set rock 'n' roll drama as the wannabe singer/dancer who becomes an overnight star. Good attention to period detail and a great R 'n' B soundtrack make this both instantly feel-good and instantly forgettable. LH

Donovan Leitch *Del Green* • Joe Pantoliano *Perry Parker* • Jennifer Runyon *Vicky* • Wendy Gazelle *Gail* • Sean Gregory Sullivan *Popeye* • Bruno Kirby *Norris* ■ *Dir* Mark Rosenthal • *Scr* Lawrence Konner, Mark Rosenthal

The In Crowd ★★ 12
Thriller
2000 · US · Colour · 101min

In an uneven career, Mary Lambert may have hit a new low with this trashy teen thriller. Swimming boldly against the postmodernist tide, she attempts to restore credence to those slasher clichés that no one can take seriously any more. Consequently, there isn't a moment's suspenseful doubt about what's really behind vixenish snob Susan Ward's interest in paroled mental patient Lori Heuring. The smug scripting and erratic performances scream "direct to video". JF Some swearing, violence. *DVD*

Susan Ward *Brittany Foster* • Lori Heuring *Adrien Williams* • Matthew Settle *Matt Curtis* • Nathan Bexton *Bobby* • Tess Harper *Dr Amanda Giles* • Ethan Erickson *Tom* ■ *Dir* Mary Lambert • *Scr* Mark Gibson, Philip Halprin

In Custody ★★ U
Drama
1993 · UK · Colour · 119min

If only Ismail Merchant had kept this adaptation of Anita Desai's novel for his second outing as a director, we might have been talking four stars here instead of two. After 30 years as producer to James Ivory, he finally seized the directorial reins on a project that was obviously close to his heart, but simply lacked the experience to bring it fully to life. The story, about an academic seeking to record the work of a dissolute Urdu poet, is thought-provoking, touching and often very amusing, but the picture lacks pace and focus. DP Urdu +subtitles. *DVD*

Shashi Kapoor *Nur* • Sameer Mitha *Manu* • Neena Gupta *Sarla* • Rupinder Kaur *Mrs Bhalla* • Om Puri *Deven* • Shahid Masood *Dhanu* • Tiblu Khan *Student* ■ *Dir* Ismail Merchant • *Scr* Anita Desai, Shahrukh Husain, from the novel by Desai

In Darkness ★★★ 15
Second World War drama based on a true story
2011 · Pol/Ger/US/It/Can · Colour · 143min

Two decades after *Europa Europa*, Agnieszka Holland returns to Nazi-occupied Poland for this Oscar-nominated true story. It focuses on the reluctant heroics of Leopold Socha, a Catholic sewer worker who overcame his ingrained anti-Semitism to shelter a group of Jewish fugitives under the streets of Lvov. Jolanta Dylewska's photography is occasionally over-murky, but the ensemble playing is admirable, with Robert Wieckiewicz standing out as Socha, the thieving opportunist whose conscience gets the better of him. A sincere, tense and deeply moving work. DP Polish, Ukrainian, Yiddish, German +subtitles. Swearing, sex scenes, brief nudity. *DVD*

Robert Wieckiewicz *Leopold Socha* • Benno Fürmann *Mundek Margulies* • Agnieszka Grochowska *Klara Keller* • Maria Schrader *Paulina Chiger* • Herbert Knaup *Ignacy Chiger* ■ *Dir* Agnieszka Holland • *Scr* David F Shamoon, from the non-fiction book *In the Sewers of Lvov* by Robert Marshall

In Dreams ★★ 18
Psychological thriller 1998 · US · Colour · 95min

Neil Jordan proves again what an inconsistent director he can be with this contrived chiller. The visuals are impressively stylised, as Jordan summons up the nightmare world in which New England resident Annette Bening becomes trapped as she finds her mind invaded by the thoughts of a serial killer. Yet his handling of the various flashbacks and reveries is haphazard, creating tension by sleight of hand rather than plot progression or sustained atmosphere. DP Violence, swearing. *DVD*

Annette Bening *Claire Cooper* • Katie Sagona *Rebecca Cooper* • Aidan Quinn *Paul Cooper* • Robert Downey Jr *Vivian Thompson* • Stephen Rea *Doctor Silverman* ■ *Scr* Bruce Robinson, Neil Jordan, from the novel *Doll's Eyes* by Bari Wood

In Enemy Country ★★
Second World War drama
1968 · US · Colour · 106min

This uninspired Second World War hokum from Universal utilised the studio's backlot when its TV series weren't in production. Still, star Tony Franciosa copes manfully, going undercover to dispose of a Nazi torpedo factory, while British interest centres on import Tom Bell and the very artificial European setting. Producer/director Harry Keller does a serviceable job, however, and scores some points for effort. TS

Tony Franciosa [Anthony Franciosa] *Colonel Charles Waslow-Carton* • Anjanette Comer *Denise Marchois* • Guy Stockwell *Lt Col Philip Braden* • Paul Hubschmid *Baron Frederick von Wittenberg* • Tom Bell *Captain Ian Peyton-Reid* ■ *Dir* Harry Keller • *Scr* Edward Anhalt, from a story by Sy Bartlett

In Fear ★★★★ 15
Psychological horror 2012 · UK · Colour · 81min

"Home invasion in a car" is director Jeremy Lovering's description of his disquieting debut feature about what happens to a young couple (Iain De Caestecker and Alice Englert) en route to an Irish music festival. It's nicely constructed, with a cloying atmosphere of ever-increasing dread as darkness and heavy rain begin to fall. And there is pulse-quickening tension enhanced by claustrophobic camerawork, with clever editing and sound that keeps the audience as off-balance as the car's occupants. Add the fantastic location (Bodmin Moor, standing in for rural Ireland) and you have a nerve-jangler that's not for the faint-hearted. JA Violence, swearing. *DVD* *Blu-ray*

Iain De Caestecker *Tom* • Alice Englert *Lucy* • Allen Leech *Max* ■ *Dir/Scr* Jeremy Lovering

In God We Trust ★ 15
Comedy
1980 · US · Colour · 92min

Marty Feldman gets it horribly wrong as writer, director and star of this dismally unfunny comedy about a naive monk who receives a crash course in worldliness when he goes to Hollywood on a fundraising mission for his monastery. Blatant in its satire and inept in its characterisation, the film misses every one of its social and religious targets. Richard Pryor does himself no favours as God in a film that's beyond salvation. DP

Marty Feldman *Brother Ambrose* • Peter Boyle *Dr Melmoth* • Louise Lasser *Mary* • Richard Pryor *God* • Andy Kaufman *Armageddon T Thunderbird* • Wilfrid Hyde White *Abbot Thelonius* • Severn Darden *Priest* ■ *Dir* Marty Feldman • *Scr* Marty Feldman, Chris Allen

In God's Hands ★★ 12
Sports adventure drama
1998 · US · Colour · 93min

Soft-core director Zalman King takes a change of pace with this saga concerning three beach bum surfers (played by three real-life champion surfers) travelling halfway around the world looking for great waves. That sentence essentially covers the entire plot of the movie, which never has a clear direction or purpose except to show

reels of surfing action. The footage is expertly photographed, but with little else going on, the movie becomes a lesser version of *The Endless Summer*. KB *DVD*

Patrick Shane Dorian *Shane* • Matt George *Mickey* • Matty Liu *Keoni* • Shaun Thompson *Wyatt* ■ *Dir* Zalman King • *Scr* Zalman King, Matt George

In Good Company ★★★ PG
Comedy drama 2004 · US · Colour · 105min

In the aftermath of a company takeover, young hotshot Topher Grace takes the job and the office of Dennis Quaid. As the displaced executive, Quaid manages to look both tough and tender – he's equally concerned for the future of his daughter Scarlett Johansson as he is for his fellow workers. These professional and personal lives collide when Grace and Johansson begin seeing each other, threatening to destroy the men's already unsteady alliance. Although there's a whiff of inevitability about it all, the fine cast still offers up plenty of surprises. KK *DVD*

Dennis Quaid *Dan Foreman* • Scarlett Johansson *Alex Foreman* • Topher Grace *Carter Duryea* • Marg Helgenberger *Ann Foreman* • David Paymer *Morty* • Philip Baker Hall *Eugene Kalb* • Clark Gregg *Steckle* • Selma Blair *Kimberly Duryea* • Frankie Faison *Corwin* ■ *Dir/Scr* Paul Weitz

In Harm's Way ★★★★ PG
Second World War action drama
1965 · US · BW · 160min

Producer/director Otto Preminger had a rough critical ride in the 1960s, not least for this marvellous Second World War epic, which begins with the Japanese attack on Pearl Harbour. The fine cast includes John Wayne and Kirk Douglas as naval officers suffering mixed fortunes during and after the attack, and they are well supported by Patricia Neal, Brandon de Wilde and Dana Andrews. The main flaw is that the special effects in the later sea battles look unconvincing (they were shot using models). Nevertheless, the film has great scale (and a great score by Jerry Goldsmith) and, unusually, the characters aren't dwarfed by the canvas. TS *DVD*

John Wayne *Captain Rockwell Torrey* • Kirk Douglas *Commander Paul Eddington* • Patricia Neal *Lieutenant Maggie Haynes* • Tom Tryon *Lieutenant William McConnel* • Paula Prentiss *Bev McConnel* • Brandon de Wilde *Ensign Jeremiah Torrey* • Jill Haworth *Ensign Annalee Dorne* • Dana Andrews *Admiral Broderick* • Stanley Holloway *Clayton Canfil* • Patrick O'Neal (1) *Commander Neal O'Wynn* • Slim Pickens *Chief Petty Officer Culpepper* • George Kennedy *Colonel Gregory* • Henry Fonda *Cincpac II* ■ *Dir* Otto Preminger • *Scr* Wendell Mayes, from the novel by James Bassett

In Hell ★★ 18
Action drama 2003 · US · Colour · 93min

Director Ringo Lam reunited with Jean-Claude Van Damme for this snarling Russian jail saga. As the desperate individual who kills the man who murdered his wife, Van Damme pouts sulkily to convey his passage through the dark night of the soul. But once he rediscovers his sense of self (with the help of cellmate Lawrence Taylor) and toughens up to beat corrupt warden Lloyd Battista's brutal system, he comes into his own in a series of prize fights. DP Swearing, violence, brief nudity. *DVD*

Jean-Claude Van Damme *Kyle LeBlanc* • Lawrence Taylor *451* • Lloyd Battista *General Hruschov* • Carlos Gomez *Tolik* • Emanuil Manolov *Ivan* • Chris Moir *Billy Cooper* • Billy Rieck *Coolhand* • Michael Bailey Smith *Valya* ■ *Dir* Ringo Lam • *Scr* Eric James Virgets, Jorge Alvarez

In Her Defense ★★ 15
Thriller 1998 · Can · Colour · 93min

Sidney J Furie just about keeps this courtroom thriller from collapsing under the weight of its clichés and contrivances. When deaf artist Marlee Matlin asks lawyer Michael Dudikoff to help her secure a divorce from her abusive millionaire husband, it's not long before they become

lovers. But then Dudikoff kills the husband in self-defence and Matlin is arrested for the crime. Watchable and proficiently done, but predictable. DP Swearing, sex scenes.

Marlee Matlin *Jane Claire* • Michael Dudikoff *Andrew Garfield* • Sophie Lorain *Debra Turner* • Steven Morgan *John Danforth* • Maurice Arsenault *Serge Richard* • David Attis *Jeffrey Fishman* • John Ball *Mark Micka* ■ *Dir* Sidney J Furie • *Scr* Marc Lynn, Jeffrey M Rosenbaum

In Her Shoes ★★★★ 12
Comedy drama
2005 · US/Ger/UK · Colour · 124min

Besides a taste for designer heels, Cameron Diaz and Toni Collette are sisters who share little in common. It's a familiar set-up, with frumpy older sis playing mum to her footloose younger sibling, yet this offers something more than your average chick flick. Director Curtis Hanson shows a surprising sensitivity, nimbly balancing drama with moments of wicked humour. Collette turns in a reliably solid performance, while Diaz brings unexpected depth and warmth to a character whose transgressions include spitefully seducing her sister's boyfriend. Even so, the film belongs to Shirley MacLaine, who plays the sisters' long-lost grandmother with grit and vulnerability. SP *DVD*

Cameron Diaz *Maggie Feller* • Toni Collette *Rose Feller* • Shirley MacLaine *Ella Hirsch* • Mark Feuerstein *Simon Stein* • Ken Howard *Michael Feller* • Candice Azzara *Sydelle Feller* • Francine Beers *Mrs Lefkowitz* • Norman Lloyd *The Professor* • Jerry Adler *Lewis Feldman* ■ *Dir* Curtis Hanson • *Scr* Susannah Grant, from the novel by Jennifer Weiner

The In-Laws ★★★ PG
Comedy
1979 · US · Colour · 98min

Arthur Hiller's frantic screwball variation on the buddy theme is never quite as funny as it thinks it is, but the laughs keep coming thanks to the inspired pairing of Alan Arkin and Peter Falk. Determined to stand by his daughter's prospective father-in-law, Arkin's New York dentist heads off to South America to help Falk's eccentric CIA agent recover some stolen Treasury plates. The fun lies in the way Falk lures Arkin into ever more ludicrous situations. DP *DVD* *Blu-ray*

Peter Falk *Vince Ricardo* • Alan Arkin *Sheldon Kornpett* • Richard Libertini *General Garcia* • Nancy Dussault *Carol Kornpett* • Penny Peyser *Barbara Kornpett* • Arlene Golonka *Jean Ricardo* • Ed Begley Jr *Barry Lutz* ■ *Dir* Arthur Hiller • *Scr* Andrew Bergman

The In-Laws ★★ 12
Comedy 2003 · US/Ger/Can · Colour · 93min

In this unnecessary reworking of the 1979 comedy, Michael Douglas and Albert Brooks take over as, respectively, a secret agent and a nervy medical professional who are united by the impending marriage of their offspring. Once Brooks has rumbled Douglas's true profession, he becomes involved in a madcap mission which involves nutty French arms dealer David Suchet. Underwritten and overplayed. TH *DVD*

Michael Douglas (1) *Steve Tobias* • Albert Brooks *Jerry Peyser* • Robin Tunney *Angela Harris* • Ryan Reynolds *Mark Tobias* • Candice Bergen *Judy Tobias* • David Suchet *Jean-Pierre Thibodoux* • Lindsay Sloane *Melissa Peyser* • Maria Ricossa *Katherine Peyser* • Russell Andrews *Agent Will Hutchins* ■ *Dir* Andrew Fleming • *Scr* Nat Mauldin, Ed Solomon, from the film by Andrew Bergman

In like Flint ★★★ PG
Spy spoof 1967 · US · Colour · 109min

James Coburn's second and final outing as super-agent Derek Flint is a leading contender for swingiest spy caper of the 1960s. This time the man from Zowie is faced with a female conspiracy to take over the world. This has more gadgets, more girls and more gags than *Our Man Flint*, while Jerry Goldsmith's playful score and some wonderfully garish sets add to the overall groove factor. JH *DVD*

James Coburn *Derek Flint* • Lee J Cobb *Cramden* • Jean Hale *Lisa* • Andrew Duggan *President Trent* • Anna Lee *Elisabeth* • Hanna Landy *Helena* • Totty Ames *Claire* ■ *Dir* Gordon Douglas • *Scr* Hal Fimberg

In Love and War ★★★

Second World War drama
1958 · US · Colour · 104min

This 20th Century-Fox film was designed to show off the studio's talented roster of contract players. It's a pleasingly clichéd wartime melodrama, offering showy roles to Robert Wagner and Jeffrey Hunter, both looking far more 1950s than 1940s, though Bradford Dillman scores highest as the thoughtful member of a trio of marines experiencing both romance and conflict. The women – the splendid Dana Wynter, Hope Lange and Sheree North – emerge with credit. **TS**

Robert Wagner *Frankie O'Neill* • Dana Wynter *Sue Trumbell* • Jeffrey Hunter *Nico Kantaylis* • Hope Lange *Andrea Lenaine* • Bradford Dillman *Alan Newcombe* • Sheree North *Lorraine* • France Nuyen *Kalai Ducanne* ■ *Dir* Philip Dunne • *Scr* Edward Anhalt, from the novel *The Big War* by Anton Myrer

In Love and War ★★★

Second World War romantic drama
2001 · US · Colour · 100min

This romantic drama is based on the wartime experiences of former *Observer* travel writer Eric Newby, who met his future wife, Wanda, while on the run from the Germans in Italy. Director John Kent Harrison details the subsequent romance of Eric and Wanda, who risked her life to hide the British soldier from the occupying forces. It's beautifully shot on location, and Callum Blue (who played Mason in US TV series *Dead like Me*) and Slovakian actress Barbora Bobulova look suitably lovestruck as the war-torn couple. **SuR**

Callum Blue *Eric Newby* • Barbora Bobulova *Wanda* • Peter Bowles *Melville* • Nick Reding *James* • John Warnaby *Feathers* • Toby Jones *Bolo* ■ *Dir* John Kent Harrison • *Scr* John Mortimer, from the autobiography *Love and War in the Apennines* by Eric Newby

In Love with Alma Cogan ★★ 12A

Comedy drama 2011 · UK · Colour · 98min

Roger Lloyd-Pack gets a rare crack at a leading role in this amiable but unremarkable comedy set in the Norfolk resort of Cromer. Forty years after meeting his singing idol, Lloyd-Pack is still the manager of the pier theatre, where he struggles to attract audiences. Much to his annoyance, councillor Gwyneth Strong insists on hiring London impresario Neil McCaul to help him ring the changes. Complete with a cameo by John Hurt as the spangly jacketed master of ceremonies and a couple of rousing Alma Cogan covers, this makes for pleasingly old-fashioned entertainment that's sadly overloaded with a surfeit of flashbacks, subplots and misfiring running gags. **DP** Some sexual references, brief swearing.

Roger Lloyd Pack *Norman* • Niamh Cusack *Sandra* • Gwyneth Strong *Laura* • Neil McCaul *Eddie* • Keith Barron *Cedric* • John Hurt *Master of Ceremonies* ■ *Dir/Scr* Tony Britten

In Memory of Myself ★★★★ U

Drama 2007 · It · Colour · 110min

Director Saverio Costanzo considers the stresses experienced by novices training for the priesthood in this austere adaptation of Furio Monicelli's 1961 novel. Gone is the gay subtext that made the source material so shocking, but it would have been an unnecessary distraction from the sense of victimisation that Christo Jivkov feels at the hands of his superiors and the relief he experiences when he discovers that Fausto Russo Alesi and Filippo Timi are also struggling with their calling. This deeply sincere film captures the sacrifices involved in the rigorous routine of prayer, self-denial and spiritual growth and, while it questions the suitability of some for the vocation, its

closing aerial image of the seminary in the Venetian lagoon remains an inspirational sight. DP Italian +subtitles. **DVD**

Christo Jivkov *Andrea* • Filippo Timi *Zanna* • Marco Baliani *Father Master* • André Hennicke [Andre Hennicke] *Father Superior* • Fausto Russo Alesi *Panella* ■ *Dir* Saverio Costanzo • *Scr* Saverio Costanzo, from the novel *Lacrime Impure: il Gesuita Perfetto* by Furio Monicelli

In My Country ★★ 15

Drama
2004 · UK/Ire/US/S Afr · Colour · 98min

Director John Boorman's well-intentioned but contrived drama takes a fictional look at the 1990s Truth and Reconciliation Commission hearings that granted amnesty to human rights abusers who publicly admitted their guilt. Seen through the eyes of two journalists – Juliette Binoche's stunned Afrikaner and Samuel L Jackson's idealistic American – events have an unrealistic feel that barely captures the deep significance and emotional intensity of these legal sessions. **SF** In English, Afrikaans. Swearing. **DVD**

Samuel L Jackson *Langston Whitfield* • Juliette Binoche *Anna Malan* • Brendan Gleeson *De Jager* • Menzi "Ngubs" Ngubane *Dumi Mkhalipi* • Sam Ngakane *Anderson* • Aletta Bezuidenhout *Elsa* • Lionel Newton *Edward Morgan* ■ *Dir* John Boorman • *Scr* Ann Peacock, from the novel *Country of My Skull* by Antjie Krog

In My Father's Den ★★★★ 15

Mystery drama
2004 · NZ/Ire/UK · Colour · 120min

The desolate landscape of New Zealand's Central Otago region reflects the emotional heft of this powerful drama. Disillusioned war photographer Matthew MacFadyen returns home for his father's funeral, then he becomes attached to sullen teen Emily Barclay, the daughter of a former lover. Making the most of an evocative soundtrack, Brad McGann skilfully updates Maurice Gee's novel of bereavement and despair without losing sight of its stark emotional pull. Enthralling, adult and moving. **JR DVD**

Matthew Macfadyen *Paul Prior* • Miranda Otto *Penny Prior* • Emily Barclay *Celia Steimer* • Colin Moy *Andrew Prior* • Jodie Rimmer *Jackie Steimer* • Jimmy Keen *Jonathan Prior* ■ *Dir* Brad McGann • *Scr* Brad McGann, from the novel by Maurice Gee

In My Skin ★★★ 18

Psychological drama 2002 · Fr · Colour · 85min

Chilling in its depiction of self-mutilation, this lacks psychological insight into why so many women feel compelled to harm their bodies. Marina de Van's use of an unflinching camera and split screens to show the wounds her seemingly successful market researcher inflicts upon herself is relentlessly assured. But her fascination with the fragility of flesh becomes all-consuming and we don't see enough of the measures she takes to explain her injuries or the impact they have on her colleagues and anxious lover, Laurent Lucas. DP French +subtitles. **DVD**

Marina de Van *Esther* • Laurent Lucas *Vincent* • Léa Drucker *Sandrine* • Thibault de Montalembert *Daniel* ■ *Dir/Scr* Marina de Van

In Name Only ★★★ U

Drama 1939 · US · BW · 90min

There's a great cast in this superior soapy drama, as unhappily married Cary Grant falls for widow Carole Lombard and tries to free himself from the clutches of his social-climbing wife, Kay Francis. Of the extraordinary crop of films made in Hollywood in 1939, this conventional melodrama is often overlooked, but, despite rather slow-moving direction from John Cromwell, it's well worth a viewing. **TS**

Carole Lombard *Julie Eden* • Cary Grant *Alec Walker* • Kay Francis *Maida Walker* • Charles Coburn *Mr Walker* • Helen Vinson *Suzanne* • Katherine Alexander *Laura* • Jonathan Hale *Dr Gateson* • Maurice Moscovich *Dr Muller* • Nella

Walker *Mrs Walker* ■ *Dir* John Cromwell • *Scr* Richard Sherman, from the novel *Memory of Love* by Bessie Brewer

In Old Arizona ★★★

Western 1929 · US · BW · 94min

This big-budget first western talkie is the best screen representation of the Cisco Kid, the colourful creation of master storyteller O Henry. In an Oscar-winning performance, Warner Baxter plays the caballero with an infectious zest, all flashing teeth and flashing spurs, stealing hearts and stagecoach strongboxes with equal abandon, while Edmund Lowe plods behind as the lawman who can never quite get his man. In the best role of her career, Dorothy Burgess makes a spirited Mexican senorita, while the ending has a sharp O Henry-ish twist. Director Raoul Walsh lost an eye during the filming which was completed by Irving Cummings. **AE**

Edmund Lowe *Sgt Mickey Dunne* • Dorothy Burgess *Tonia Maria* • Warner Baxter *The Cisco Kid* • J Farrell MacDonald *Tad* ■ *Dir* Raoul Walsh, Irving Cummings • *Scr* Tom Barry, from a story by O Henry

In Old California ★★ PG

Western 1942 · US · BW · 87min

In this very routine Republic western, John Wayne is rather oddly cast as a pharmacist who finds himself entangled in the evil schemes of a local gunman. To hold your interest, there's Binnie Barnes as a spirited saloon hostess and died-in-the-wool villain Albert Dekker. The film lacks a firm director's hand, so practised comic actors Patsy Kelly and Edgar Kennedy have plenty of opportunities to steal scenes. **TS DVD**

John Wayne *Tom Craig* • Binnie Barnes *Lacey Miller* • Albert Dekker *Britt Dawson* • Helen Parrish *Ellen Sanford* • Patsy Kelly *Helga* ■ *Dir* William McGann • *Scr* Gertrude Purcell, Frances Hyland, from a story by J Robert Bren, Gladys Atwater

In Old Chicago ★★★ U

Historical disaster drama
1937 · US · BW · 91min

Released a year after MGM's *San Francisco*, this film about the Chicago fire of 1871 is a storm in a teacup compared with MGM's stupendously filmed earthquake, and Tyrone Power is no Clark Gable. There is a lot of scene-setting and subplotting family virtues set beside political corruption before a cow kicks over a kerosene lamp and the special effects team makes the Windy City go up in smoke. Big and brash. **AT DVD**

Tyrone Power *Dion O'Leary* • Alice Faye *Belle Fawcett* • Don Ameche *Jack O'Leary* • Alice Brady *Molly O'Leary* • Andy Devine *Pickle Bixby* ■ *Dir* Henry King • *Scr* Lamar Trotti, Sonya Levien, from the story *We the O'Learys* by Niven Busch

In Old Kentucky ★★★

Comedy 1935 · US · BW · 85min

The homespun personality of Will Rogers made him one of the most popular stars of early talkies, and his amiable performance holds together this occasionally simple-minded tale of country folk and racehorse rivalries. Whether learning to tap-dance or trying to make a purchase at a fashion house, Rogers is always engaging. Sadly this was to be his last film: he was killed in a plane crash shortly after its completion. **TV**

Will Rogers (1) *Steve Tapley* • Dorothy Wilson *Nancy Martingale* • Russell Hardie *Dr Lee Andrews* • Charles Sellon *Ezra Martingale* • Bill Robinson *Wash Jackson* ■ *Dir* George Marshall • *Scr* Sam Hellman, Gladys Lehman, from the play by Charles T Dazey

In Order of Disappearance ★★★ 15

Crime comedy 2014 · Nor · Colour · 111min

A black comedy plays out in blindingly white surroundings in this askew Norwegian offering. Stellan Skarsgård stars as a modest man who ploughs the snow around his village, but when his son falls fatally foul of gangsters, this "Citizen of the Year" starts killing his way up the criminal hierarchy. A generous running time is at

odds with the slim premise, and humour comes at the expense of tension. However the casting is spot on, with Pal Sverre Hagen's exuberant villainy making an effective counterpart to Skarsgård's stone-faced everyman. **EAS** Norwegian, Swedish +subtitles. **DVD**

Stellan Skarsgård *Nils* • Bruno Ganz *Papa* • Pal Sverre Valhelm Hagen *Greven* • Jakob Oftebro *Aron Horowitz* • Birgitte Hjort Sorensen *Marit* • Kristofer Hivju *Strike* ■ *Dir* Hans Petter Moland • *Scr* Kim Fupz Aakeson

In Our Name ★★★ 18

Drama 2010 · UK · Colour · 89min

The experience of soldiers returning to civilian life is not a new subject for the movies. But the fact that the protagonist of director Brian Welsh's feature debut is a Middlesbrough mum returning from a tour of Iraq makes his low-key, well-acted drama an intriguing one. Joanne Froggatt, who's better known as a TV actress (*Coronation Street*, *Downton Abbey*), proves herself a formidable big-screen presence as Suzy, the married mother struggling to readjust to life back on a council estate with her husband (Mel Raido) and daughter (Chloe-Jayne Wilkinson). **JA** Violence, swearing, sex scenes. **DVD**

Joanne Froggatt *Suzy* • Mel Raido *Mark* • Chloe-Jayne Wilkinson *Cass* • Andrew Knott *Paul* • John Henshaw *Frank* • Janine Leigh *Marie* ■ *Dir/Scr* Brian Welsh

In Our Time ★★ U

Second World War drama
1944 · US · BW · 110min

A belated tribute to the gallant Poles who confronted the Nazis in 1939, this Warner Bros melodrama suffers from the romanticised vision of European stoicism that blighted many a Hollywood flag-waver. Initially, it's a tale of pride and prejudice, as Paul Henreid's aristocratic family disapprove of his marriage to English tourist Ida Lupino. But once their farm has been razed to the ground, intolerance is transformed into indomitability as the resistance struggle begins. **DP**

Ida Lupino *Jennifer Whittredge* • Paul Henreid *Count Stephan Orvid* • Nancy Coleman *Janina Orvid* • Mary Boland *Mrs Bromley* • Victor Francen *Count Pavel Orvid* ■ *Dir* Vincent Sherman • *Scr* Ellis St Joseph, Howard Koch

In Person ★★

Musical romantic comedy
1935 · US · BW · 87min

Ginger Rogers took a break from Fred Astaire by co-starring with the non-dancing, non-singing and, some would say, non-acting George Brent. Rogers plays a temperamental film star escaping her fans by adopting a disguise and fleeing to a mountain resort in the company of Brent. Ginger has a couple of pleasant dance routines, which only serve to remind audiences of Fred's absence. **RB**

Ginger Rogers *Carol Corliss aka Miss Colfax* • George Brent *Emory Parks* • Alan Mowbray *Jay Holmes* • Grant Mitchell *Judge Thaddeus Parks* ■ *Dir* William A Seiter • *Scr* Allan Scott, from a novel by Samuel Hopkins Adams

In Praise of Older Women ★★ 18

Drama 1978 · Can · Colour · 105min

This is soft-core smut dressed in a wispy veil of sophistication. The source material considered the socio-political situation that made the promiscuity of so many well-heeled Hungarians something more than mere lust. But Susan Strasberg's anti-Communist opinions matter less than the smouldering glances she gives Tom Berenger, whose character's sexual education began at the age of 12, when he pimped for prostitutes during the Second World War. Karen Black and Alexandra Stewart also rank among his many conquests, but they're undone by the anachronistic dialogue and the leering direction. **DP**

Tom Berenger *Andra Vayda* • Karen Black *Maya* • Susan Strasberg *Bobbie* • Helen Shaver *Ann MacDonald* • Marilyn Lightstone *Klari* • Alexandra

Stewart *Paula* • Marianne McIsaac *Julika* • Alberta Watson *Mitzi* ■ *Dir* George Kaczender • *Scr* Paul Gottlieb, from the novel by Stephen Vizinczey

In Prison My Whole Life ★★★ 15

Documentary 2008 · US/UK/It · Colour · 93min

On 9 December 1981, left-wing journalist and Black Panther member Mumia Abu-Jamal was arrested for killing Daniel Faulkner, a white Philadelphia cop. The victim was beating Abu-Jamal's brother Billy Cook at the time. John Edginton's 1997 documentary established that police intimidation and institutionalised racism ensured a guilty verdict, and Abu-Jamal remains on Death Row, despite the intercession of Amnesty International. Director Marc Evans takes a different approach, revisiting this infamous miscarriage of justice through activist William Francome's eyes, and interviews with such high-profile supporters as Alice Walker, Mos Def and Snoop Dogg help make this a well-meaning and competent examination of the American justice system. DP

Mumia Abu-Jamal • Mos Def • Steve Earle • Snoop Dogg ■ *Dir* Marc Evans • *Scr* Marc Evans, from an idea by William Francome, Katie Green

In Pursuit ★★ 15

Thriller 2000 · US · Colour · 87min

The presence of super-model Claudia Schiffer will catch the eye of laddish video renters, but even they are likely to be disappointed with this dull shadowy thriller. Daniel Baldwin is the lawyer who finds his cosy life upended when he finds himself the number one suspect in the murder of Schiffer's businessman husband. There are plenty of tortuous plot twists but none is believable and the result is another formulaic thriller. JF *DVD*

Daniel Baldwin *Rick Alvarez* • Claudia Schiffer *Catherine Wells* • Coolio *Carl Wright* • Dean Stockwell *Charles Welz* • Sarah Lassez *Abby Berkhoff* ■ *Dir* Peter Pistor • *Scr* John Penney, from a story by Peter Pistor

In Search of a Midnight Kiss ★★★★ 15

Romantic comedy 2008 · US · BW · 97min

As much a love letter to Los Angeles as Woody Allen's *Manhattan* was to New York, this is a disarming update of the classic screwball comedy. Unable to find a date for New Year's Eve, wannabe screenwriter Scoot McNairy advertises online and finds Sara Simmonds, a cursing, chain-smoking blonde who shares many of his hang-ups. However, what starts as an idyllic afternoon descends into nocturnal peril as her enraged ex-boyfriend threatens to sabotage their date. McNairy is splendidly awkward as the careworn antihero, while Simmonds excels as the tough cookie whose sharp tongue belies a forlorn fragility. But it's writer/director Alex Holdridge's quick-witted dialogue and Robert Murphy's crisp monochrome photography that make this simply irresistible. DP *DVD*

Scoot McNairy *Wilson* • Sara Simmonds *Vivian* • Brian Matthew McGuire *Jacob* • Katie Luong *Min* • Twink Caplan *Wilson's Mom* • Robert Murphy (2) *Jack* ■ *Dir/Scr* Alex Holdridge • *Cinematographer* Robert Murphy (2)

In Search of Famine ★★★★

Drama 1980 · Ind · Colour · 124min

A Calcutta film crew arrives in a remote village to document the devastating 1943 famine, but is greeted with unexpected suspicion and hostility by the poverty-stricken villagers. Unable to bridge this gap of understanding, the visitors return home empty-handed. One of Indian cinema's most insightful recorders of the country's social fabric, Mrinal Sen has created an excellent piece, which won the special jury prize at Berlin. RB In Bengali.

Dhritiman Chatterjee *Director* • Smita Patil *Actress* • Sreela Majumdar *Woman* • Gita Sen *Widow* • Dipankar Dey *Villager* ■ *Dir* Mrinal Sen • *Scr* Mrinal Sen

In Search of Gregory ★★

Psychological drama 1970 · UK/It · Colour · 89min

Having co-written such seminal pictures as *L'Avventura* and *Blowup*, it's not surprising echoes of Michelangelo Antonioni abound in this cryptic tale from Tonino Guerra. Unfortunately, director Peter Wood doesn't have the master's genius for expressing emotion through landscape, so Julie Christie's Genevan odyssey is more maddening than enigmatic. Enchanted by her father Adolfo Celi's description of a handsome house guest, Christie imagines him to be the same man whose picture she sees at the airport (Michael Sarrazin). It's an intriguing idea but it needs firmer handling than this. DP

Julie Christie *Catnerine* • Michael Sarrazin *Gregory* • John Hurt *Daniel* • Adolfo Celi *Max* • Roland Culver *Werdle* • Tony Selby *Taxi driver* • Jimmy Lynn *Air steward* ■ *Dir* Peter Wood • *Scr* Tonino Guerra, Lucile Laks

In Search of the Castaways ★★ U

Fantasy adventure 1961 · US/UK · Colour · 94min

This was Disney's second dip into the works of Jules Verne, but it can't be compared with the splendid *20,000 Leagues under the Sea*. Hayley Mills stars as a tigerish teen who ropes Maurice Chevalier and Wilfrid Hyde White into helping search for her father. But, as the action moves from South America to Australia, director Robert Stevenson subjects his cast to all manner of natural disasters. The effects have dated badly and the story rarely thrills. DP *DVD*

Maurice Chevalier *Professor Jacques Paganel* • Hayley Mills *Mary Grant* • George Sanders *Thomas Ayrton* • Wilfrid Hyde White *Lord Glenarvan* • Michael Anderson Jr *John Glenarvan* ■ *Dir* Robert Stevenson • *Scr* Lowell S Hawley, from the novel *Captain Grant's Children* by Jules Verne

In Secret ★★ 15

Period crime drama 2013 · US · Colour · 106min

This adaptation of the Emile Zola novel *Thérèse Raquin* stars Elizabeth Olsen as a sexually repressed woman in 1860s Paris who's trapped in a loveless marriage and compelled to co-habit with his stifling mother (Jessica Lange). Then up pops hubby's hunky workmate, and forbidden passions are swiftly aroused. But, this being melodrama most ripe, it all ends in deception, death and tears. A fairly fun watch for lovers of bodice rippers, this is better suited to the small screen than the big. DA Sex scenes.

Elizabeth Olsen *Thérèse Raquin* • Jessica Lange *Madame Raquin* • Oscar Isaac *Laurent LeClaire* • Tom Felton *Camille Raquin* • Shirley Henderson *Suzanne* • Matt Lucas *Olivier* • Mackenzie Crook *Grivet* ■ *Dir* Charlie Stratton • *Scr* Charlie Stratton, from the play *Thérèse Raquin* by Neal Bell, from the novel *Thérèse Raquin* by Emile Zola

In the Army Now ★ PG

Comedy 1994 · US · Colour · 88min

Pauly Shore is something of an acquired taste, but he's got no chance of raising a laugh in this marvel of military mayhem, thanks to the eight writers who toiled on the lamentable script. Comedy seems to have been the last thing on their minds when they penned this barmy story about a doltish shop assistant who finds himself in the middle of a US mission against Libya. No satire, no farce, no wit. DP *DVD*

Pauly Shore *Bones Conway* • Andy Dick *Jack Kaufman* • Lori Petty *Christine Jones* • David Alan Grier *Fred Ostroff* • Esai Morales *Sergeant Stern* ■ *Dir* Daniel Petrie Jr • *Scr* Daniel Petrie Jr, Fax Bahr, Adam Small, Ken Kaufman, Stu Krieger, from a story by Steve Zacharias, Jeff Buhai, Robbie Fox

In the Bedroom ★★★★ 15

Drama 2001 · US · Colour · 125min

This is a film about grief that touches the heart and leaves a deep and lasting impression. Tom Wilkinson and Sissy Spacek are both excellent as the parents swamped by moral and psychological trauma after the murder of their son. Trapped in a claustrophobic community, they live in close proximity to their child's killer – and the woman whose involvement with their son indirectly led to his death – and their intense grief and outrage pushes them to breaking point. The movie's measured pace and elegance of observation complement the astounding confidence of actor/director Todd Field, whose handling of the delicately balanced material makes his feature debut a rare find. LH Violence, swearing. *DVD*

Sissy Spacek *Ruth Fowler* • Tom Wilkinson *Matt Fowler* • Nick Stahl *Frank Fowler* • Marisa Tomei *Natalie Strout* • William Mapother *Richard Strout* • William Wise *Willis Grinnel* • Celia Weston *Katie Grinnel* • Karen Allen *Marla Keyes* ■ *Dir* Todd Field • *Scr* Rob Festinger, Todd Field, from the story *Killing* by Andre Dubus

In the Bleak Midwinter ★★★ 15

Comedy drama 1995 · UK · BW · 94min

After the grand-standing and faintly embarrassing excesses of *Mary Shelley's Frankenstein*, Kenneth Branagh returns to his roots for this gentle and modestly amusing dig at theatrical pretensions. With Branagh opting to remain behind the camera, the leading role goes to Michael Maloney, who plays a struggling actor attempting to stage a Christmas production of *Hamlet* with a bitchy, egocentric group of luvvies. Branagh regular Richard Briers has a ball with the material. However, the stunning black-and-white cinematography cannot disguise the slightness of the material. JF *DVD*

Michael Maloney *Joe Harper* • Richard Briers *Henry Wakefield* • Hetta Charnley *Molly* • Joan Collins *Margaretta D'Arcy* • Nicholas Farrell *Tom Newman* • Celia Imrie *Fadge* • Jennifer Saunders *Nancy Crawford* • Julia Sawalha *Nina* • John Sessions *Terry Du Bois* ■ *Dir/Scr* Kenneth Branagh

In the Blood ★★ 15

Crime drama 2014 · UK · Colour · 90min

Director Mark Abraham makes a solid debut with this low-key BritCrime entry filmed around Dunstable in Bedfordshire. Alison Steadman makes a brief cameo during the opening funeral sequence, but the focus falls firmly on 20-something Johnny (*Peaky Blinders* regular Joe Cole), who wasn't around when his grandfather (Phil Davis) passed away because he was off his head on smack. Screenwriter Andy Bloom struggles to sustain the tensions between the holed-up thugs, with much of the talented supporting cast having too little to do. But the dénouement is decent, the direction steady and the clichés are largely kept in check. DP Violence, swearing, drug abuse, nudity.

Joe Cole *Johnny* • Kenny Doughty *Jim* • Stuart Graham *Pete* • Brian McCardie *Bill* • Peter Bowles *Old Boy* ■ *Dir* Mark Abraham • *Scr* Andy Bloom

In the City of Sylvia ★★★★ PG

Drama 2007 · Sp /Fr · Colour · 85min

Director José Luis Guerín employs the city of Strasbourg as a living canvas for this mesmerising study of the impersonality of modern existence. Frequenting an outdoor café, artist Xavier Lafitte is captivated by the passing parade he sketches. However, Pilar López de Ayala proves more than a fleeting fascination and he follows her in the hope that she is the same woman he had a crush on years before. Making exceptional use of faces, locations and perspectives, Guerín has created a riveting treatise on life in an age of voyeurism and surveillance. It also works as a teasing thriller, with Lafitte's obsession becoming increasingly sinister. DP French, Spanish +subtitles.

Pilar López de Ayala [Pilar Lopez de Ayala] *Woman* • Xavier Lafitte *Man* ■ *Dir/Scr* José Luis Guerín [José Luis Guerin]

In the Company of Men ★★★★★ 18

Black comedy drama 1997 · US · Colour · 93min

Brave, hard-hitting and controversial, director Neil LaBute's pitch-black comedy detailing the complexities of office politics and male rivalry is a deliberately uncomfortable viewing experience. Aaron Eckhart and Matt Malloy are exceptional as the white-collar workers betting on who can seduce the most vulnerable girl in their office – Stacy Edwards's deaf secretary – and then dump her as an exercise in revenge against the fair sex. LaBute indulges in blatant misogyny and painful honesty to put his acerbic points across in this provocative, compelling shocker. AJ Swearing.

Aaron Eckhart *Chad* • Stacy Edwards *Christine* • Matt Malloy *Howard* • Emily Cline *Suzanne* • Jason Dixie *Keith, intern* ■ *Dir/Scr* Neil LaBute

In the Company of Spies ★★★ 15

Spy thriller 1999 · US · Colour · 100min

This CIA TV drama is written by Roger Towne, who writes a pacey actioner, and is helped by strong cast. Tom Berenger, a retired CIA agent now running a restaurant, is brought back in by his old boss Ron Silver to rescue an agent with important information who has been captured in North Korea. Well-researched and swift-moving, the script so pleased the real CIA that they allowed film-makers to use their headquarters in Langley, Virginia, as a location. JB

Tom Berenger *Kevin Jefferson* • Alice Krige *Sarah Gold* • Ron Silver *Tom Lenahan* • Clancy Brown *Dale Beckham* ■ *Dir* Tim Matheson • *Scr* Roger Towne

In the Courtyard ★★★ 15

Comedy drama 2014 · Fr · Colour · 97min

Gustave Kerven plays a depressed former musician who takes a job as a janitor, forming an unlikely bond with an equally troubled resident (Catherine Deneuve). A curious and occasionally insightful take on mental illness, the film portrays the isolation of depression from two very different perspectives, with the leads making a surprisingly appealing duo. A shame, then, that the tone should jump around a lot, with quirky comedy slowly going to a very dark place. JL French +subtitles.

Catherine Deneuve *Mathilde* • Gustave Kerven *Antoine Le Garrec* • Féodor Atkine *Serge* • Pio Marmaï *Stéphane* • Michèle Moretti *Colette* ■ *Dir* Pierre Salvadori • *Scr* David Léotard, Benoît Graffin

In the Cut ★★★ 18

Suspense thriller 2003 · US/Aus · Colour and BW · 113min

Susanna Moore's notoriously explicit novel gives director Jane Campion another opportunity to explore her favourite theme – the self-destructive elements of female desire. Meg Ryan stars as a New York teacher who falls for enigmatic detective Mark Ruffalo. He is investigating a series of murders that he himself might have committed. Campion's trademark off-kilter camerawork matches the increasingly skewed world view of her protagonist and Ryan is a revelation. Ultimately, the film works as a study of sexual longing but fails as a thriller, with a cop-out ending. StH *DVD*

Meg Ryan *Frannie Avery* • Mark Ruffalo *Det James Malloy* • Jennifer Jason Leigh *Pauline* • Nick Damici *Det Richard Rodriguez* • Sharrieff Pugh *Cornelius Webb* • Kevin Bacon *John Graham* ■ *Dir* Jane Campion • *Scr* Jane Campion, Susanna Moore, from the novel by Susanna Moore

In the Doghouse ★★ U

Comedy 1961 · UK · BW · 93min

Long before James Herriot, Alex Duncan appeared on the bestseller lists with *It's a Vet's Life*. Adapted by Michael Pertwee, the tale makes a fine vehicle for Leslie Phillips, who resorts to his trademark charm to atone for his misadventures in a new country practice. However, he also gets to reveal an unexpected action-man side as he thwarts a horse-smuggling ring run by his deadly rival (James Booth). This patchy film is perhaps most significant for bringing down the curtain on the career of Peggy Cummins. DP

Leslie Phillips *Jimmy Fox-Upton* • Peggy Cummins *Sally* • Hattie Jacques *Primrose Gudgeon* • James Booth *Bob Skeffington* • Dick Bentley *Mr Peddle* • Colin Gordon *Dean* • Joan Heal *Mrs Peddle* • Fenella Fielding *Miss Fordyce* ■ *Dir* Darcy Conyers • *Scr* Michael Pertwee, from the novel *It's a Vet's Life* by Alex Duncan

In the Electric Mist ★★15
Mystery thriller 2009 · US/Fr · Colour · 112min

Based on James Lee Burke's novel, French director Bertrand Tavernier's US debut never quite catches light. Essentially, a treatise on the past's habit of haunting the present, it centres on maverick Louisiana cop Tommy Lee Jones, who stumbles onto a link between the murder of a black man in the 1960s and the serial killing of several local girls in the wake of Hurricane Katrina. Despite the atmospheric contributions of cinematographer and composer, the film suffers from a surfeit of political and supernatural subtexts, and lacks the edge of Tavernier's fine 1981 adaptation of Jim Thompson's bayou saga *Clean Slate*. DP
Violence, swearing, nudity. DVD BL

Tommy Lee Jones *Dave Robicheaux* • Peter Sarsgaard *Elrod T Sykes* • John Goodman *Julie "Baby Feet" Balboni* • Mary Steenburgen *Bootsie* • Kelly Macdonald *Kelly* • Ned Beatty *Twinky LeMoyne* ■ *Dir* Bertrand Tavernier • *Scr Jerzy Kromolowski, Mary Olson-Kromolowski, from the novel *In the Electric Mist with Confederate Dead* by James Lee Burke • *Music* Marco Beltrami • *Cinematographer* Bruno de Keyzer

In the Fog ★★★★12A
Second World War drama
2012 · Ger/Belarus/Rus/Latvia/Neth · Colour · 128min

Russia's Sergei Loznitsa arrived on the international stage with the Palme d'Or-nominated drama *My Joy*, an ironic, freeform study of violence and corruption in the former Soviet Union. Though marginally less harsh and more linear, this follow-up nevertheless deals with similar issues of ethics and personal responsibility. It's set in a small village on the western frontier of the USSR in 1942; the Nazis are in charge and are rounding up suspected members of the resistance. One of their number, Sushenya (Vladimir Svirski), is spared, leading others in the area to believe he is a spy. This is a stark and unromantic portrait of life during wartime, depicting a desperate world in which, by the end, literally nothing is clear. DW Russian +subtitles. Some violence, swearing.

Vladimir Svirski *Sushenya* • Vlad Abashin *Burov* • Sergei Kolesov *Voitik* • Nikita Peremotovs *Grisha* • Julia Peresild *Anelya* ■ *Dir* Sergei Loznitsa • *Scr* Sergei Loznitsa, from Vasil Bykov's novel

In the French Style ★★★
Romance 1963 · US/Fr · BW · 105min

Seeing what an impact Jean Seberg made in *A Bout de Souffle*, Hollywood sent her back to Paris for this trend-chasing, slightly risqué movie based on two short stories by Irwin Shaw, who also produced here. As an American art student in Paris, Seberg has affairs with young student Philippe Forquet and journalist Stanley Baker before finally settling on someone else. Seberg is beautiful and convincing as the new independent woman, quite a contrast to a Hollywood still churning out Doris Day comedies. AT

Jean Seberg *Christina James* • Stanley Baker *Walter Beddoes* • Addison Powell *Mr James* • Jack Hedley *Bill* • Maurice Teynac *Baron* • James Leo Herlihy *Dr John Haislip* • Philippe Forquet *Guy* ■ *Dir* Robert Parrish • *Scr* Irwin Shaw, from his short stories *In the French Style* and *A Year to Learn the Language*

In the Gloaming ★★★★
Drama 1997 · US · Colour · 65min
Disabled actor Christopher Reeve made his directorial debut with this short, but

superbly realised, drama. Boasting a five-star cast, it centres on Aids patient Robert Sean Leonard's homecoming and the very different welcomes he receives from mother Glenn Close, father David Strathairn and sister Bridget Fonda. With a poignant cameo from Whoopi Goldberg as a live-in nurse, this is a painfully truthful study of a family facing tragedy and the need to express emotions before it's too late. DP

Glenn Close *Janet* • Robert Sean Leonard *Danny* • Bridget Fonda *Anne* • Whoopi Goldberg *Myrna* • David Strathairn *Martin* ■ *Dir* Christopher Reeve • *Scr* Will Scheffer, from the short story by Alice Elliott Dark

In the Good Old Summertime ★★★U
Musical comedy 1949 · US · Colour · 98min

This charming remake of the romantic classic *The Shop around the Corner* provides a showcase for the great Judy Garland (she replaced a pregnant June Allyson). Garland is touching as the enamoured pen pal who doesn't realise that colleague Van Johnson is her secret letter lover, and there are some terrific moments where the plot takes a hiatus to let Garland perform in front of an on-screen audience. The child with Garland and Johnson in the closing sequence is Garland's real-life daughter, Liza Minnelli. TS DVD

Judy Garland *Veronica Fisher* • Van Johnson *Andrew Larkin* • SZ "Cuddles" Sakall [SZ Sakall] *Otto Oberkugen* • Spring Byington *Nellie Burke* • Clinton Sundberg *Rudy Hansen* • Buster Keaton *Hickey* • Liza Minnelli ■ *Dir Robert Z Leonard • *Scr* Samson Raphaelson, Frances Goodrich, Ivan Tors, Albert Hackett, from the play *The Shop around the Corner* by Miklos Laszlo

In the Hands of the Gods ★★★★15
Documentary 2007 · UK · Colour · 101min

Regardless of his international soccer superstar status, Diego Maradona will always be remembered in England for his "hand of God" goal in the 1986 World Cup quarter final. It's ironic then that he should inspire five young British lads to travel the world to meet him, which is the premise of this incredibly uplifting documentary. The boys in question are football "freestylers", whose acrobatic skills with the ball are more likely to be found in the circus than at Wembley. They're a mixed bunch, including a troubled asylum seeker from Somalia, a likeable Liverpudlian and a quiet, thoughtful Christian. With no money and no clue, they hustle across the Americas, using their football skills to earn cash while slowly maturing. It's a road trip that's by turns hilarious, tragic and stirring, a testament to the power of dreams and football. JR DVD

Paul "Woody" Wood • Sami Hall Bassam • Jeremy Lynch • Danny Robinson • Mike "Mikey" Fisher • Diego Maradona ■ *Dir* Benjamin Turner, Gabe Turner

In the Heart of the Sea ★★12
Adventure based on a true story
2015 · US · Colour · 116min

Ron Howard's broad-brush tale of a whaleship sunk by a giant cetacean in 1820 might have been an epic on the scale of John Huston's *Moby Dick*. Instead, corporeal threat is sapped by the CGI used to create the sperm whales that draw the ship from land and the giant white that destroys it. Individuals are hard to pick out amid endless water-tank panic and eventual shipwreck, but the framing device with *Moby-Dick* author Herman Melville (Ben Whishaw) extracting testimony from haunted survivor Brendan Gleeson offers rare emotional depth. AC DVD BL

Chris Hemsworth *Owen Chase* • Benjamin Walker *George Pollard* • Cillian Murphy *Matthew Joy* • Ben Whishaw *Herman Melville* • Brendan Gleeson *Old Thomas Nickerson* ■ *Dir* Ron Howard • *Scr* Rick Jaffa, Charles Leavitt, Peter Morgan (1), from Nathaniel Philbrick's non-fiction book ■ *Cinematographer* Anthony Dod Mantle

Sidney Poitier breaks new ground as a black police inspector in the Deep South

In the Heat of the Night ★★★★★12
Crime drama 1967 · US · Colour · 108min

Winner of five Oscars, including best picture, this powerhouse drama about racial tension in the Deep South was released at the height of the civil rights movement and a year before the assassination of Martin Luther King. Sidney Poitier is the immaculately dressed Philadelphia cop who is wrongly arrested for murder while changing trains in a small town in Mississippi, ruled by Rod Steiger's rancid, bigoted police chief. The plot is a set-up, a stacked deck, yet the atmosphere is palpably unpleasant, and Poitier and Steiger have a field day. A major movie for its time, it spawned two further films featuring Poitier's character (*They Call Me Mister Tibbs!* and *The Organization*) and a television series. AT Swearing, violence. DVD

Sidney Poitier *Virgil Tibbs* • Rod Steiger *Bill Gillespie* • Warren Oates *Sam Wood* • Lee Grant *Mrs Leslie Colbert* • Quentin Dean *Dolores Purdy* • William Schallert *Webb Schubert* • James Patterson *Purdy* • Jack Teter *Philip Colbert* ■ *Dir* Norman Jewison • *Scr* Stirling Silliphant, from the novel by John Ball • *Cinematographer* Haskell Wexler • *Editor* Hal Ashby • *Music* Quincy Jones

In the House ★★★15
Comedy drama 2012 · Fr · Colour · 105min

François Ozon's darkly comic feature focuses on a teacher/student relationship that goes beyond the norm when a dour tutor (Fabrice Luchini) becomes overinvolved with his charge's creative-writing assignments. Ozon's film contemplates the difference between everyday life and fiction, and shows how messy things can get when one impinges on the other. Light, deft performances from a solid ensemble cast (which includes Kristin Scott Thomas as Luchini's wife) simply add to the enjoyment of what is a playfully disturbing tale. KK French +subtitles. Swearing, a sex scene, brief nudity.

Fabrice Luchini *Germain* • Kristin Scott Thomas *Jeanne Germain* • Emmanuelle Seigner *Esther Artole* • Denis Ménochet *Rapha Sr* ■ *Dir* François Ozon • *Scr* François Ozon, from Juan Mayorga's play *El Chico de la Ultima Fila*

In the Land of the Free... ★★★15
Documentary 2009 · US · Colour · 84min

In the late 1960s, Herman Wallace and Albert Woodfox were serving time in the Angola state penitentiary in Louisiana. They became prominent members of the Black Panther chapter that fought to improve standards, and many believe this motivated their framing for the 1972 murder of prison guard Brent Miller. The two men, along with fellow prisoner Robert King, were put in solitary confinement, becoming known as the Angola 3. They have since collectively spent over 100 years in isolation. This documentary from director Vadim Jean joins the chorus demanding justice, but – despite the earnest narration of Samuel L Jackson and the insights of the murdered guard's sceptical widow – never quite succeeds in making its case with sufficient precision and power. DP

Samuel L Jackson *Narrator* ■ *Dir/Scr* Vadim Jean • *Cinematographers* Michael Fox, Adam Stone

In the Line of Duty: Smoke Jumpers ★★PG
Action drama based on a true story
1996 · US · Colour · 87min

Despite its fascinating subject matter – the true story of daredevil parachuting firefighters – this is formulaic fare. Adam Baldwin plays the airborne fireman who is forced to re-evaluate his gung-ho career after falling for ex-firefighter and single mother Lindsay Frost. The action scenes are gripping enough, but veteran TV-movie director Dick Lowry spends too much time

exploring domestic trials and tribulations. JF DVD

Adam Baldwin *Don Mackey* • Lindsay Frost *Rene* • Timothy Carhart *Tom Classen* • Rob Youngblood *Timmerman* ■ *Dir* Dick Lowry • *Scr* Gy Waldron, Stephen Harrigan

In the Line of Fire ★★★★15
Thriller 1993 · US · Colour · 123min

Clint Eastwood in tears (not many, but they're there) is just one of the novelties in this hugely enjoyable thriller in which Eastwood is a Secret Service agent who is not only visibly ageing – a fact that he admits to his younger lover, Rene Russo – but is also shamed by his past inability to save President Kennedy from assassination. That's why he's so obsessed with John Malkovich, would-be killer of the current First Executive. Eastwood reveals the same vulnerability that made his performance in *Unforgiven* so compelling, while the Oscar-nominated Malkovich makes an admirable adversary. TH Swearing, violence, sex scenes. DVD BL

Clint Eastwood *Frank Horrigan* • John Malkovich *Mitch Leary* • Rene Russo *Lilly Raines* • Dylan McDermott *Al D'Andrea* • Gary Cole *Bill Watts* • Fred Dalton Thompson *Harry Sargent* • John Mahoney *Sam Campagna* ■ *Dir* Wolfgang Petersen • *Scr* Jeff Maguire • *Music* Ennio Morricone

In the Loop ★★★★15
Comedy 2009 · UK/Cay · Colour · 101min

The hand-held camerawork, partly improvised dialogue and inventively foul language of BBC TV's political satire *The Thick of It* goes feature length as director Armando Iannucci takes the show beyond its Westminster departmental setting. A fictionalised Anglo-American push for war in the Middle East is used to prick not just the absurdity of government spin, but also the grandstanding of Washington DC when low-ranking cabinet minister Simon Foster (Tom Hollander) accidentally precipitates a military invasion. Despite the efforts of monstrous Downing Street enforcer Malcolm Tucker (Peter Capaldi), Foster must become embroiled in shuttle diplomacy to halt the war. AC Swearing, sexual references. DVD BL

Peter Capaldi *Malcolm Tucker* • Tom Hollander *Simon Foster* • Gina McKee *Judy Molloy* • James Gandolfini *General Miller* • Chris Addison *Toby* • Anna Chlumsky *Liza Weld* • Steve Coogan *Paul Michaelson* ■ *Dir* Armando Iannucci • *Scr* Jesse Armstrong, Simon Blackwell, Armando Iannucci, Tony Roche

In the Meantime, Darling ★★
Wartime comedy 1944 · US · BW · 71min

The newlywed young wife (Jeanne Crain) of an army officer (Frank Latimore), forced by army rules to live with other wives in a hotel near the military camp, kicks against the establishment and falls into misunderstandings with her husband before he is shipped overseas and she comes to terms with reality. This potentially interesting idea is dissipated by an uninspired, indecisive script. An indifferent offering. RK

Jeanne Crain *Maggie* • Frank Latimore *Lt Daniel Ferguson* • Eugene Pallette *HB Preston* • Mary Nash *Mrs Preston* • Stanley Prager *Lt Red Pianatowski* ■ *Dir* Otto Preminger • *Scr* Arthur Kober, Michael Uris

In the Mix ★★12
Crime comedy 2005 · US · Colour · 91min

R&B star Usher does himself no favours with this clichéd and clumsy vehicle that tries to marry the worlds of hip-hop and mobsters. Playing a DJ who improbably ends up working as a bodyguard for Mafia boss Chazz Palminteri's student daughter (Emmanuelle Chriqui), his performance is reasonable - occasionally even endearing. But thanks to a terrible, throw-everything-in script and Ron Underwood's seriously amateurish direction, he's continually undermined. Atmospherically, the film's also a mess. SF DVD

Usher [Usher Raymond] *Darrell* • Chazz Palminteri *Frank* • Emmanuelle Chriqui *Dolly* • Robert Davi *Fish* • Robert Costanzo *Fat Tony* ■ *Dir* Ron Underwood • *Scr* Jacqueline Zambrano, from a story by Chanel Capra, Cara Dellaverson, Brian Rubenstein

In the Mood for Love
★★★★ PG
Romantic drama 2000 · HK/Fr · Colour · 93min

Hong Kong auteur Wong Kar-Wai returns to the more accessible narrative style of his earlier work with this ravishing romantic melodrama set in the early 1960s. Newspaper editor Tony Leung (who won the best actor prize at Cannes for his performance) moves into a noisy apartment at the same time as secretary Maggie Cheung takes possession of a flat down the hall. When they both realise their (unseen) partners are having an affair, they're drawn together by the sense of mutual humiliation and their own innocent courtship begins. This is a sumptuously shot, sensuous wade through the emotions of a repressed culture. AJ Cantonese +subtitles. DVD

Cheung Man-Yuk [Maggie Cheung] *Mrs Chan, née Su Lizhen* • Tony Leung Chiu-Wai [Tony Leung (2)] *Chow Mo-Wan* • Rebecca Pan *Mrs Suen* • Lui Chun *Mr Ho* ■ *Dir* Wong Kar-Wai • *Scr* Wong Kar-Wai, incorporating quotations from the writings of Liu Yi-Chang

In the Mouth of Madness
★★★ 18
Horror 1994 · US · Colour · 91min

Part homage to HP Lovecraft, part lampoon of Stephen King, John Carpenter's treatise on the psychological power of horror begins well, only to descend rapidly into genre cliché. The idea that a novel can turn its readers into demons might have been further developed, but screenwriter Michael De Luca is more interested in subjecting insurance fraud investigator Sam Neill to the bizarre goings-on in missing author Jürgen Prochnow's home town of Hobbs End. Many scenes are confidently handled, but bookend sequences in an asylum aren't enough to put this in the *Caligari* class. DP Swearing, violence.

Sam Neill *John Trent* • Jürgen Prochnow *Sutter Cane* • Julie Carmen *Linda Styles* • Charlton Heston *Jackson Harglow* • David Warner *Dr Wrenn* • John Glover *Saperstein* ■ *Dir* John Carpenter • *Scr* Michael De Luca

In the Name of
★★★ 15
Drama 2013 · Pol · Colour · 97min

A Polish priest struggles with his attraction to the young men in his care in this drama examining the Catholic Church's strictures on celibacy. Taking care to underline the distinction between paedophilia and the priest's homosexual desires, Malgoska Szumowska's film isn't exactly ground-breaking, but its physical candour may still make it uncomfortable viewing for some. It's arguably just a bit too low-key, yet the convincing performances (leading man Andrzej Chyra is a brooding, manly presence) and anguished understanding of all sides in this contentious arena prove engrossing and ultimately thought-provoking. TJ Polish +subtitles. Swearing, sex scenes, drug abuse, some violence. DVD

Andrzej Chyra *Father Adam* • Mateusz Kosciukiewicz *Lukasz, "Humpty"* • Maja Ostaszewska *Ewa* • Lukasz Simlat *Michal, teacher* • Tomasz Schuchardt *Adrian, "Blondie"* • Maria Maj *Lukasz's mother* ■ *Dir* Malgoska Szumowska [Malgorzata Szumowska] • *Scr* Malgoska Szumowska [Malgorzata Szumowska], Michal Englert

In the Name of Buddha
★★★ 18
Documentary drama 2002 · UK/Sri L · Colour · 146min

The UN estimates that over 60,000 Sri Lankans were killed and another 1.6 million displaced during the 20-year war between that nation's government and its Tamil population. Director Rajesh Touchriver conveys something of the scale of the tragedy in this ambitious attempt to expose the atrocities committed by both government forces and the Indian peacekeeping force. However, while his discussion of the way political leaders manipulate religious and cultural issues is calculatingly contentious, his handling of the jungle setting and the relentlessly graphic combat sequences is impressive for a first-time film-maker. DP Tamil, Hindi +subtitles.

Shiju Siva • Soniya Geetha • Jyothi Lal *Leader* • Amit Mikara ■ *Dir* Rajesh Touchriver • *Scr* Rajesh Touchriver, from a story by Sai George

In the Name of the Father
★★★★ 15
Biographical drama 1993 · Ire/UK/US · Colour · 127min

This is a stirring and exceptionally well-acted, though controversial, dramatisation of Gerry Conlon's book about the grave miscarriage of justice suffered by the Guildford Four. Daniel Day-Lewis is highly impressive as Conlon, a naive young Irishman who couldn't blow his own hat off, arrested by the police for terrorist bombings along with three equally unlikely friends. Directed by Jim Sheridan, the story packs an enormous dramatic punch. Pete Postlethwaite is brilliant as Conlon's bemused and hapless father, and the only false note is struck by Emma Thompson, hopelessly miscast (albeit Oscar-nominated) as the Four's solicitor. SH Drug abuse, violence, swearing. DVD

Daniel Day-Lewis *Gerry Conlon* • Emma Thompson *Gareth Peirce* • Pete Postlethwaite *Guiseppe Conlon* • John Lynch *Paul Hill* • Mark Sheppard *Paddy Armstrong* • Beatie Edney *Carole Richardson* • Marie Jones *Sarah Conlon* • Britta Smith *Annie Maguire* • Corin Redgrave *Robert Dixon* ■ *Dir* Jim Sheridan • *Scr* Terry George, Jim Sheridan

In the Navy
★★ U
Musical comedy 1941 · US · BW · 82min

Abbott and Costello made such an impact as bumbling army recruits in *Buck Privates* that Universal immediately repeated the formula with another service comedy. Dick Powell plays a popular crooner who, fed up with the good life, enlists in the navy (under a false name) where he encounters misfit sailors Abbott and Costello. The Andrews Sisters (a big hit in *Buck Privates*) are on hand again, enlivening the proceedings with a few songs. DF

Bud Abbott *Smokey Adams* • Lou Costello *Pomeroy Watson* • Dick Powell *Tommy Halstead* • Claire Dodd *Dorothy Roberts* • Laverne Andrews • Maxene Andrews • Patty Andrews ■ *Dir* Arthur Lubin • *Scr* Arthur T Horman, John Grant, from the story *They're in the Navy Now* by Horman

In the Realm of the Senses
★★★★ 18
Erotic drama based on a true story 1976 · Fr/Jpn · Colour · 97min

Based on a notorious murder case that scandalised Japan in the 1930s, Nagisa Oshima's tale of puissant passion is also a complex study of gender status and oppression. However, the eroticism is so hard-core it has invariably prevented a considered assessment of the writer/director's achievement. Laced with cultural and historical allusions and imagery as beautiful as it is powerful, the film follows geisha Eiko Matsuda and her lover Tatsuya Fuji as they willingly risk death in a bid to find ultimate sexual fulfilment. DP Japanese +subtitles. DVD

Tatsuya Fuji *Kichi-zo* • Eiko Matsuda *Sada* • Aoi Nakajima *Toku* • Meika Seri *Maid Matsuko* • Taiji Tonoyama *Old beggar* ■ *Dir/Scr* Nagisa Oshima

In the Shadow of the Moon
★★★ U
Documentary 2006 · UK/US · Colour and BW · 95min

The Apollo project sent nine missions to the Moon between 1968 and 1972. David Sington's involving documentary features interviews with many of the surviving astronauts – though the notoriously reclusive Neil Armstrong is notable by his absence. The film records both the incredible technical achievement of the Apollo mission itself – through previously unseen and remastered Nasa footage – as well as recording the profound spiritual, political and emotional effects on the individual astronauts. It's an impressive and often engrossing documentary, though inevitably some of the story – including opposition to the huge costs – is underplayed. But, as an account of an extraordinary technical achievement fraught with risks, it's fascinating, sometimes moving stuff. AS Some swearing. DVD BL

Buzz Aldrin • Mike Collins • Alan Bean • Jim Lovell • Edgar Mitchell • Dave Scott *Dave, Scott* • Eugene Cernan • Harrison Schmitt ■ *Dir* David Sington • *Cinematographer* Clive North

In the Soup
★★★ 15
Comedy 1992 · US · Colour · 95min

An unusual angle on the struggle to bring script to screen marks Alexandre Rockwell's larger-than-life comedy out from the many other indie films about indie films. The twist is that writer Steve Buscemi's pretentious 500-page epic is to be financed by hoodlum Seymour Cassel, who embarks on various criminal activities to raise the $250,000 budget. Good casting and some bright ideas, but the movie-making theme seems to fall by the wayside as Cassel pulls Buscemi into his unwholesome activities. As a result, the film loses its satirical edge. However, Cassel's energetic performance is a treat. JC DVD

Steve Buscemi *Aldolpho Rollo* • Seymour Cassel *Joe* • Jennifer Beals *Angelica* • Pat Moya *Dang* • Will Patton *Skippy* • Jim Jarmusch *Monty* • Carol Kane *Barbara* ■ *Dir* Alexandre Rockwell • *Scr* Alexandre Rockwell, Tim Kissell

In the Valley of Elah
★★★★ 15
Crime drama 2007 · US · Colour · 121min

Paul Haggis's directorial follow-up to his Oscar-winning *Crash* features a powerful performance from Tommy Lee Jones as the father of a missing soldier, recently returned from Iraq. When it appears as though US Army officials are orchestrating a cover-up, Hank Deerfield (the Oscar-nominated Jones) joins forces with small-town cop Emily Sanders (a world-weary Charlize Theron) to expose the truth. Inspired by a real-life story, Haggis's script expertly blends all the suspense of a traditional detective thriller with a disturbing, psychological portrait of young men trained to kill. More than anger, it is sympathy that Haggis arouses for their plight, presenting these soldiers as victims robbed of their humanity on the battlefields of Iraq. The gravity of the situation occasionally weighs too heavily and slows the pace, but it's still a compelling watch. SP Violence, swearing, nudity. DVD BL

Tommy Lee Jones *Hank Deerfield* • Charlize Theron *Det Emily Sanders* • Susan Sarandon *Joan Deerfield* • James Franco *Sgt Dan Carnelli* • Jonathan Tucker *Mike Deerfield* • Frances Fisher *Evie* • Jason Patric *Lt Kirklander* • Josh Brolin *Chief Buchwald* ■ *Dir* Paul Haggis • *Scr* Paul Haggis, from a story by Haggis, Mark Boal

In This Our Life
★★★
Melodrama 1942 · US · BW · 96min

This rip-roaring Warner Bros melodrama, directed by then newcomer John Huston, has an excellent cast including (watch closely) a cameo from his father Walter as a bartender. The scenery is chewed to bits by Bette Davis, who manages to destroy the life of her sister Olivia de Havilland and then destroys herself. There's some amazing plotting, as the wonderfully nasty Davis is involved in a hit-and-run and tries to lay the blame on the son of her black cook. This is super stuff, but should not be taken at all seriously. TS

Bette Davis *Stanley Timberlake* • Olivia de Havilland *Roy Timberlake* • George Brent *Craig Fleming* • Dennis Morgan *Peter Kingsmill* • Charles Coburn *William Fitzroy* • Hattie McDaniel *Minerva Clay* • Walter Huston *Bartender* ■

Dir John Huston • *Scr* Howard Koch, John Huston, from the novel by Ellen Glasgow • *Cinematographer* Ernie Haller [Ernest Haller] • *Music* Max Steiner

In This World
★★★★ 15
Documentary drama 2002 · UK · Colour · 86min

Director Michael Winterbottom's timely documentary-drama variation on the road movie won the Golden Bear at Berlin – as much for its humanity as its technical audacity and storyline. Shot on digital video and transferred to 35mm widescreen, this is an occasionally contrived exploration of the contentious and often overlapping issues of political asylum, economic migration and people-trafficking. En route from Afghanistan to London, the hardships of life for teenager Jamal Udin Torabi and his cousin Enayatullah, and for many of those they encounter on their journey, are arrestingly portrayed. The poverty, prejudice, exploitation, desperation and danger presented is sickeningly authentic; it's just a shame such brutal realism is compromised by a sentimental ending. DP English, Pashtu, Farsi +subtitles. DVD

Jamal Udin Torabi *Jamal* • Enayatullah *Enayat* • Wakeel Khan *Enayat's uncle* • Nabil Elouahabi *Yusif* ■ *Dir* Michael Winterbottom • *Scr* Tony Grisoni • *Cinematographer* Marcel Zyskind

In Time
★★★★ 12
Science-fiction thriller 2011 · US · Colour · 104min

This superb sci-fi thriller is set in a dystopian future where time is money – literally. The ageing process stops at 25, and the population toils to earn more hours, days, months and years or face death. But when down-at-heel Justin Timberlake unwittingly inherits an entire century, he sets off to bring down the system. Teaming up with Amanda Seyfried, the daughter of a crooked billionaire industrialist (*Mad Men's* Vincent Kartheiser), Timberlake embarks on a series of daring robberies to close the gap between the haves and the have-nots, pursued by ruthless "timekeeper" Cillian Murphy. Writer/director Andrew Niccol's elaborate premise is an intriguing starting point for a yarn full of action and moral ambiguity. TeS Some violence, brief swearing. DVD BL

Justin Timberlake *Will Salas* • Amanda Seyfried *Sylvia Weis* • Cillian Murphy *Raymond Leon* • Alex Pettyfer *Fortis* • Vincent Kartheiser *Philippe Weis* • Olivia Wilde *Rachel Salas* ■ *Dir/Scr* Andrew Niccol • *Cinematographer* Roger Deakins

In Too Deep
★★ 18
Action thriller 1999 · US · Colour · 92min

This run-of-the-mill cops-and-robbers thriller is distinguished by strong performances from Omar Epps and rapper-turned-actor LL Cool J. Epps plays a young undercover cop who gets in over his head while investigating a charismatic drugs lord. He is soon torn between duty and their budding friendship. LL Cool J plays the likeable villain, an interesting combination of kindness and malice. Beyond the acting, however, this offers no surprises, and a romance between Epps and Nia Long impedes the pace. ST DVD

Omar Epps *Jeff Cole/J Reid* • LL Cool J *Dwayne "God" Gittens* • Nia Long *Myra* • Pam Grier *Detective Angela Wilson* • Stanley Tucci *Preston D'Ambrosio* ■ *Dir* Michael Rymer • *Scr* Michael Henry Brown, Paul Aaron

In Which We Serve
★★★★★ U
Second World War drama 1942 · UK · BW · 109min

This wartime propaganda film is a thinly disguised take on the maritime exploits of Lord Mountbatten. Co-directed by the debuting David Lean and Noël Coward, it has matured to become a paean to a lost world. Told in flashback, as a group of stranded sailors await rescue after the sinking of their ship, the film is immensely moving, and contains definitive performances from Coward himself (his speech about his ship, the HMS *Torrin*, is a classic) and Celia Johnson, all beauty and stoicism in her film debut. Coward was awarded a special Oscar for his "outstanding production achievement". TS DVD

Noël Coward *Captain "D"* • John Mills *O/S "Shorty" Blake* • Bernard Miles *CPO Walter Hardy* • Celia Johnson *Alix Kinross* • Joyce Carey *Mrs Hardy* • Kay Walsh *Freda Lewis* • Derek Elphinstone *Number One* • Frederick Piper *Edgecombe* • Geoffrey Hibbert *Young stoker* • George Carney *Mr Blake* • Daniel Massey *Bobby Kinross* • Michael Wilding *"Flags"* • Richard Attenborough *Young stoker* ■ *Dir* Noël Coward, David Lean • *Scr* Noël Coward, from the experiences of Lord Louis Mountbatten

In Your Hands ★★★ 15

Crime drama   2010 · Fr · Colour · 77min

Kristin Scott Thomas continues to challenge herself in edgy Gallic art house fare, and proves a compelling presence in this story of abduction and reconciliation. She plays glacially reserved surgeon Anna, who first appears in a state of some distress after escaping from a traumatic kidnapping. Scott Thomas never tries to make Anna immediately likeable, so her journey becomes all the more involving as her altered circumstances render her unusually vulnerable. Co-star Pio Marmaï is also effective as her captor. So it's a shame the film as a whole never feels quite developed enough to convince. TJ French +subtitles. DVD BD

Kristin Scott Thomas *Anna Cooper* • Pio Marmaï *Yann* • Marie-Sohna Conde *Caroline* • Vinciane Millereau *Milène* • Jean-Louis Tribes *Michel* ■ *Dir/Scr* Lola Doillon

Inadmissible Evidence ★★★

Drama   1968 · UK · BW · 95min

Just because you're paranoid doesn't mean to say you don't have enemies. Nicol Williamson re-creates his role from John Osborne's stage play as the solicitor who fears he's being persecuted by everyone. The fact that he treats his wife (Eleanor Fazan), mistress (Jill Bennett) and colleagues with equal contempt seems to have escaped him. Williamson's tour de force of invective loses some of its impact on screen as director Anthony Page presents the speeches in fragmented form. TH

Nicol Williamson *Bill Maitland* • Eleanor Fazan *Anna Maitland* • Jill Bennett *Liz* • Peter Sallis *Hudson* • David Valla *Jones* • Eileen Atkins *Shirley* • Lindsay Anderson *Barrister* ■ *Dir* Anthony Page • *Scr* John Osborne, from his play

Inauguration of the Pleasure Dome ★★★ PG

Experimental movie   1954 · US · Colour · 36min

This is another of Kenneth Anger's medium-length ciné-poems expressing his vision of the occult. The film has gone through several incarnations – the first had a soundtrack by Harry Parch, the second uses Janacek's *Glagolithic Mass* to better effect. In 1966, Anger then added an opening reading of Coleridge's *Kubla Khan* accompanied by stills of Satanist guru Aleister Crowley and talismanic symbols, which became known as the *Sacred Mushroom Edition*. One does not have to share Anger's esoteric philosophy to relish his imagery, often outrageously camp and pretentious as it is. RB

Anaïs Nin *Astarte* • Curtis Harrington *Cesare the Somnambulist* ■ *Dir/Scr* Kenneth Anger • *Music* Leos Janacek

Inbetweeners ★★ 15

Comedy romance   2000 · UK · Colour · 90min

Anyone who's been to university will recognise most of the situations in Darren Paul Fisher's debut. But observational comedy means more than merely stringing together a few truisms in a "year-in-the-life" format: the viewer needs something more to hang on to than an endless round of naff parties, transient romances and other cynically recalled memories. Fisher is to be applauded for bringing this digital video offering in for £30,000. But some juvenile dialogue and the drama club performances

deserve censure for settling, at best, for mediocrity. DP DVD

Finlay Robertson *David Marshall* • Kate Loustau *Nicole Miles* • Lynn Edmonstone *Steph Thornhill* • Toby Walton *Jack Easterford* • Sarah Vandenbergh *Cassie Sanderson* • Johnny Ball *Lecturer* ■ *Dir/Scr* Darren Fisher

The Inbetweeners Movie ★★★ 15

Comedy   2011 · UK · Colour · 92min

Fans of E4's cult sixth-form sitcom are laser-targeted by this feature-length excursion. It simply picks up the show's much-loved suburban teens – nerdy Simon Bird, lovesick Joe Thomas, oblivious Blake Harrison and mouthy James Buckley – and plonks them into the Greek party town of Malia, where their hormonal insecurities play out against sun, sea and strobe lights. Many of the situations were covered in *Kevin & Perry Go Large*, and the gross-out is ramped up for the cinema, but a heart does beat beneath the laddish antics. AC Swearing, sexual references. DVD BD

Simon Bird *Will* • Joe Thomas (1) *Simon* • James Buckley *Jay* • Blake Harrison *Neil* • Emily Head *Carli D'Amato* • Laura Haddock *Alison* ■ *Dir* Ben Palmer • *Scr* Damon Beesley, Iain Morris

The Inbetweeners 2 ★★★ 15

Comedy   2014 · UK · Colour · 91min

This follow-up sees Simon Bird, Joe Thomas and Blake Harrison head down under to reunite with James Buckley, who boasts of his new life in Oz. A backpacking adventure then sees them flirt with disaster once again. While sticking with a familiar approach, creators Damon Beesley and Iain Morris mix in enough freshness and conflict to guarantee this is no mere retread. Unlikely to win over non-fans, but series devotees will find this more than suitable. JL DVD BD

Simon Bird *Will McKenzie* • James Buckley *Jay Cartwright* • Joe Thomas (1) *Simon Cooper* • Blake Harrison *Neil Sutherland* • Emily Berrington *Katie* • Belinda Stewart-Wilson *Polly McKenzie* • Freddie Stroma *Ben* ■ *Dir/Scr* Damon Beesley, Iain Morris

Inbred ★★★ 18

Horror   2011 · Ger/UK · Colour · 94min

British director Alex Chandon (*Cradle of Fear*) returns to feature films after a ten-year hiatus with a twisted, *Grand Guignol*-style splatterfest that mixes hardcore, townie-in-peril horror with pitch-black humour. This low-budget horror sees a sketchy quartet of southern young offenders and their care workers (including *This Is England's* Jo Hartley) fall foul of local villagers during a rehabilitation weekend in remotest Yorkshire. The largely solid cast revels in the film's crude stereotypes, clunky in-jokes, and gleefully brutal deaths, and these crowd-pleasing elements help distract from the weaknesses in pacing, plot and characterisation. SF Violence, swearing. DVD BD

Jo Hartley *Kate* • James Doherty *Jeff* • James Burrows *Tim* • Seamus O'Neill *Jim* • Terry Haywood *Zeb* ■ *Dir* Alex Chandon • *Scr* Alex Chandon, Paul Shrimpton

Incendiary ★★ 15

Drama   2008 · US/UK/Cay · Colour · 95min

Despite its title, this drama falls disappointingly flat. Michelle Williams plays a young British mother whose husband and son are killed in a terrorist attack on a London football stadium. Her grief is mixed with guilt because, at the time of the blast, she was in bed with journalist Ewan McGregor. In the aftermath of this tragedy she decides to strike up a relationship with the young son of one of the dead suicide bombers. Despite a decent performance from Williams, this adaptation of Chris Cleave's 2005 novel fails to grip or move. DA DVD

Michelle Williams *Young Mother* • Ewan McGregor *Jasper Black* • Matthew Macfadyen *Terrence Butcher* • Nicholas Greaves *Lenny* • Sidney Johnston *The Boy* • Usman Khokhar *The Bomber's Son* ■ *Dir* Sharon Maguire • *Scr* Sharon Maguire, from the novel by Chris Cleave

Incendiary Blonde ★★★

Biographical musical   1945 · US · Colour · 113min

This explosive Technicolor musical biopic gives a somewhat selective account of the colourful life of Texas Guinan, infamous nightclub queen of the Prohibition era, whose famous catchprase was "Hello suckers!" Lavishly mounted by Paramount, the movie is lively and entertaining, jam-packed with songs, including *It Had to Be You*, and lots of incident involving bootlegging gangsters, one of whom (Arturo De Cordova) is Texas's lover. Betty Hutton hurls herself at the material – both dramatic and musical – with the force of a neutron bomb. RK

Betty Hutton *Texas Guinan* • Arturo de Cordova *Bill Romero Kilgannon* • Charlie Ruggles [Charles Ruggles] *Cherokee Jim* • Albert Dekker *Joe Cadden* ■ *Dir* George Marshall • *Scr* Claude Binyon, Frank Butler, from the biography *Life of Texas Guinan* by Thomas Guinan, WD Guinan

Incendies ★★★★ 15

Drama   2010 · Can/Fr · Colour · 125min

By audacious cutting of much of the poetic dialogue from Wajdi Mouawad's acclaimed stage play, Denis Villeneuve has created a wholly cinematic drama, told in parallel and flashback, that combines twists and suspense with harrowing political insight. After the death of their mother, French-Canadian twins Jeanne (Mélissa Désormeaux-Poulin) and Simon (Maxim Gaudette) seek to carry out her last wish – to locate their lost father and a brother they didn't know existed. The action relies heavily on several outrageous contrivances, but Villeneuve's control of each revelation deepens the audience's sympathy. DP French, Arabic +subtitles. Violence. DVD BD

Lubna Azabal *Nawal Marwan* • Mélissa Désormeaux-Poulin *Jeanne Marwan* • Maxim Gaudette *Simon Marwan* • Rémy Girard *Notary Jean Lebel* ■ *Dir* Denis Villeneuve • *Scr* Denis Villeneuve, from the play by Wajdi Mouawad

Incense for the Damned ★★ 18

Horror   1970 · UK · Colour · 86min

This oddity fails to surmount its production problems. The low budget ran out in Cyprus and planned re-shoots never happened, so it was hastily patched together and then disowned by horror maestro Robert Hartford-Davis. Yet flashes of imagination shine through as Patrick Macnee helps Madeline Hinde save her fiancé Patrick Mower from some Greek Satanists. Released on video and DVD under its US title, *Bloodsuckers*. AJ Violence, sex scenes, drug abuse, nudity. DVD

Patrick Macnee *Major Derek Longbow* • Peter Cushing *Dr Goodrich* • Alex Davion [Alexander Davion] *Tony Seymour* • Johnny Sekka *Bob Kirby* • Madeline Hinde *Penelope* • Patrick Mower *Richard Fountain* • Imogen Hassall *Chriseis Constandindi* • Edward Woodward *Holmstrom* • David Lodge *Colonel* ■ *Dir* Michael Burrowes [Robert Hartford-Davis] • *Scr* Julian More, from the novel *Doctors Wear Scarlet* by Simon Raven

Inception ★★★★ 12

Science-fiction action thriller   2010 · US/UK · Colour · 141min

The subconscious mind becomes a deadly maze for Leonardo DiCaprio in this wildly inventive psychological thriller from Christopher Nolan (*The Dark Knight*). DiCaprio stars as a corporate spy who steals secrets from other people's dreams, but begins to lose his grip when tasked by business mogul Ken Watanabe with implanting a destructive idea in the mind of the heir to an energy empire (Cillian Murphy). There are some incredible, ethereal action scenes akin to *The Matrix*, and DiCaprio also has to fight projections of his wife (Marion Cotillard), giving the film a true sense of urgency. Emotional intimacy is somewhat lacking, but there's no doubt that Nolan (who also directed the equally elliptical *Memento*) knows how to craft an enthralling brainteaser. SP Some violence. DVD BD

Leonardo DiCaprio *Cobb* • Joseph Gordon-Levitt *Arthur* • Ellen Page *Ariadne* • Cillian Murphy *Robert Fischer* • Michael Caine *Miles* • Marion Cotillard *Mal* • Tom Hardy *Eames* • Ken Watanabe *Saito* • Tom Berenger *Peter Browning* • Lukas Haas *Nash* • Dileep Rao *Yusuf* • Pete Postlethwaite *Maurice Fischer* ■ *Dir/Scr* Christopher Nolan

Inchon ★

War drama   1981 · S Kor · Colour · 140min

Dollar for dollar and with adjustments for inflation, this is the biggest flop in the history of the cinema. Financed to the tune of $46 million by the Church of the Reverend Sung Myung Moon, it's a vast re-creation of a major battle in the Korean war. Laurence Olivier as Douglas MacArthur leads a peculiar cast, while ex-Bond director Terence Young juggles the explosions and romantic interludes. It opened briefly, received a critical mauling and has barely been seen again. AT

Laurence Olivier *General Douglas MacArthur* • Jacqueline Bisset *Barbara Hallsworth* • Ben Gazzara *Major Frank Hallsworth* • David Janssen *David Feld* ■ *Dir* Terence Young • *Scr* Robin Moore, Laird Koenig, from a story by Paul Savage, Moore

The Incident ★★★ 15

Drama   1967 · US · BW · 95min

This neatly compressed drama began as a live TV play called *Ride with Terror* but the planned Hollywood version, to be produced by Joseph E Levine, never came off. Tony Musante and Martin Sheen (in his screen debut) play two New York delinquents who make life a misery for the passengers on a subway train, including GI Beau Bridges, pensioner Thelma Ritter and bullied wife Jan Sterling. This structure – the 16 passengers representing a cross section of life in the big smoke – is filmed with considerable attack as the thugs taunt and expose the flaws in everyone's characters. AT DVD

Tony Musante *Joe Ferrone* • Martin Sheen *Artie Connors* • Beau Bridges *Private First Class Felix Teflinger* • Jack Gilford *Sam Beckerman* • Thelma Ritter *Bertha Beckerman* • Brock Peters *Arnold Robinson* • Ruby Dee *Joan Robinson* • Donna Mills *Alice Keenan* ■ *Dir* Larry Peerce • *Scr* Nicholas E Baehr, from his play *Ride with Terror*

The Incident ★★★ PG

Courtroom drama   1990 · US · Colour · 94min

In his TV-movie debut, Walter Matthau casts aside his usual comic persona to remind us of his oft-forgotten straight acting skills. We are so used to the rubber-faced grumpy buffoon that Matthau's stirring portrayal of a small-time war lawyer defending a German PoW is almost shocking in its disciplined precision. The finely tuned script is a big help, as is a fine supporting cast. The character was well-received, and two more TV movies followed, *Against Her Will* (1992) and *Incident in a Small Town* (1993). SH DVD

Walter Matthau *Harman Cobb* • Susan Blakely *Billie* • Robert Carradine *Prosecutor Domsczek* • Peter Firth *Wilhelm Geiger* • Barnard Hughes *"Doc" Hansen* • Harry Morgan *Judge Bell* ■ *Dir* Joseph Sargent • *Scr* Michael Norell, James Norell

Incident at Phantom Hill ★★ PG

Western   1966 · US · Colour · 83min

This dates from a period when Universal was making co-features to support its "A" product, invariably starring or trying out contract artists or television names. Here Robert Fuller (*Laramie*) stars opposite veteran baddie Dan Duryea. The tale of stolen bullion and hostile Apaches is decked out in Technicolor to very little avail. The director is former floor assistant Earl Bellamy, whose technique is strictly TV, but old-timers Duryea and *Rio Bravo's* Claude Akins keep it just about watchable. TS DVD

Robert Fuller *Matt Martin* • Jocelyn Lane *Memphis* • Dan Duryea *Joe Barlow* • Tom Simcox *Adam Long* • Linden Chiles *Dr Hanneford* •

Claude Akins *Krausman* ■ *Dir* Earl Bellamy • *Scr* Frank Nugent, Ken Pettus, from a story by Harry Tateleman

Incident in a Small Town

★★★ 15

Murder mystery 1993 · US · Colour · 86min

Walter Matthau returns in the third of his Harmon J Cobb small-screen outings – the previous two were *The Incident* and *Against Her Will* – as the wily, lawyer working courtroom miracles in postwar America. The relaxed playing of the veteran leads is the best thing about this, although director Delbert Mann also manages to inject a few surprises into the murder mystery. JF

Walter Matthau *Harmon J Cobb* • Harry Morgan *Judge Stoddard Bell* • Stephanie Zimbalist *Lily* • Nick Stahl *John* • Bernard Behrens *Judge Greeves* • Lori Hallier *Madeleine* • David Nerman *Frank* ■ *Dir* Delbert Mann • *Scr* Cindy Myers

Incognito

★ 15

Thriller 1997 · US · Colour · 103min

Director John Badham takes a good cast and a reasonably interesting concept and comes up with this deeply disappointing thriller. You can hardly blame stars like Rod Steiger, who literally phones in his brief role as the artist father of art forger Jason Patric. The plot involves Patric's decision to accept a fortune to fake a Rembrandt and the mayhem that ensues. Lovers of art and good movies should give this one a wide berth. TH Some swearing.

Jason Patric *Harry Donovan* • Irène Jacob *Marieke Van Den Broeck* • Thomas Lockyer *Alistair Davies* • Ian Richardson *Turley, prosecutor* • Rod Steiger *Milton A Donovan* ■ *Dir* John Badham • *Scr* Jordan Katz

An Inconvenient Truth

★★★ U

Documentary 2006 · US · Colour · 96min

All the alarming facts and pressing issues, both moral and political, are spelt out in this bleak documentary about the effects of global warming. Director Davis Guggenheim slickly transfers to film what is essentially former US Vice-President Al Gore's multi-media slide show, which makes crystal clear how ostrich-headed politicians remain in the face of overwhelming evidence and also exposes the lie that environmental protection policies are bad for world economies. Distilled from 30 years of research by Gore and incorporating insights from his own private life, the sobering message is relayed with caring humour and gritty determination. AJ *DVD*

Al Gore ■ *Dir* Davis Guggenheim

The Incredible Burt Wonderstone

★★★ 15

Comedy 2013 · US · Colour · 100min

The world of showbiz magic is the battleground for this watchable comedy, a rare feature outing for *30 Rock* director Don Scardino. Childhood friends Burt Wonderstone (Steve Carell) and Anton Marvelton (Steve Buscemi) are the toast of Las Vegas, until their jaded schtick and the Strip's need for younger, edgier acts bring their embittered partnership to a halt. Alone and broke, Wonderstone is forced to rekindle his love of magic. Although promising *Anchorman*-style hilarity (bad hair, even worse suits), the movie conjures few laugh-out-loud moments, relying instead on absurd set pieces, expert comic flourishes and occasional pithy quips to sustain interest. KK Swearing, sexual references. *DVD* Blu

Steve Carell *Burt Wonderstone* • Steve Buscemi *Anton Marvelton* • Jim Carrey *Steve Gray* • Olivia Wilde *Jane* • Alan Arkin *Rance Holloway* • James Gandolfini *Doug Munny* • David Copperfield ■ *Dir* Don Scardino • *Scr* John Francis Daley, Jonathan Goldstein, from a story by Daley, Goldstein, Chad Kultgen, Tyler Mitchell

The Incredible Hulk ★★★ PG

Fantasy action adventure 1977 · US · Colour · 90min

Based on the Marvel Comics cartoon, this pilot feature (released theatrically in the UK) spawned an 80-episode series. The show itself borrowed its formula from *The Fugitive*, but th s TV movie is more of a sci-fi affair, with scientist Bill Bixby channelling the grief caused by his wife's death into an exploration of the link between stress, strength and gamma radiation. Former Mr Universe Lou Ferrigno became a cult figure as Bixby's hulking green alter ego. Another TV movie, *The Return of the Incredible Hulk* was screened shortly after this launch feature. DP *DVD*

Bill Bixby *Dr David Bruce Banner* • Susan Sullivan *Dr Elaina Marks* • Jack Colvin *Jack McGee* • Lou Ferrigno *The Hulk* ■ *Dir* Kenneth Johnson • *Scr* Kenneth Johnson, Thomas E Szollosi, Richard Christian Matheson, from the comic books by Stan Lee, Jack Kirby

The Incredible Hulk Returns ★★ PG

Fantasy action adventure 1988 · US · Colour · 93min

Bursting from the pages of Marvel Comics on to our TV screens in 1978, the Incredible Hulk was, briefly, essential viewing for teenagers everywhere. But, by the time this TV movie appeared a decade later, audiences had grown out of his superheroic exploits, in much the same way that Bill Bixby grew out of his clothes (and turned into snarling Lou Ferrigno) every time he had a temper tantrum. Another Marvel regular, the mighty Thor, provides the villainy. DP Violence. *DVD*

Bill Bixby *David Banner* • Lou Ferrigno *The Incredible Hulk* • Lee Purcell *Maggie Shaw* • Tim Thomerson *Le Beau* • Eric Kramer *[Eric Allan Kramer] Thor* • Jack Colvin *Jack McGee* ■ *Dir* Nicholas Corea • *Scr* Nicholas Corea, from characters by Stan Lee, Jack Kirby

The Incredible Hulk

★★★★ 12

Science-fiction action adventure 2008 · US · Colour · 107min

Director Louis Leterrier pumps some adrenaline back into the Marvel character after the mixed reception that greeted Ang Lee's brooding *Hulk* in 2003. A typically intense Edward Norton plays Dr Bruce Banner, the scientist whose exposure to gamma rays has made him a danger to his girlfriend Betty (Liv Tyler) and a target for her dad, military honcho General Ross (a steely William Hurt). Banner is prodded into "hulking out" with satisfying frequency, bounding across the rooftops to escape his new genetically modified adversary Emil Blonsky, aka the Abomination (played by Tim Roth). But as well as delivering thumping action, the giant is sympathetic, and the romantic elements are also shrewdly handled, in a manner that's strongly redolent of *King Kong*. Unlike Lee's film, there is a real sense here that Banner and the beast inhabit the same tortured mind, making it easier to stick with him through to the earth-shaking finale. SP *DVD* Blu CS

Edward Norton *Bruce Banner/The Hulk* • Liv Tyler *Betty Ross* • William Hurt *General Thaddeus "Thunderbolt" Ross* • Tim Roth *Emil Blonsky/The Abomination* • Tim Blake Nelson *Samuel Sterns* • Christina Cabot *Majcr Kathleen "Kat" Sparr* • Ty Burrell *Dr Leonard Samson* • Robert Downey Jr *Tony Stark* ■ *Dir* Louis Leterrier • *Scr* Zak Penn, from his story, from the character created by Stan Lee, Jack Kirby

The Incredible Journey

★★★★ U

Adventure 1963 · US · Colour · 76min

Not only is this easily the best of Disney's true-life adventures, but it's also far superior to the studio's dumbed-down 1993 remake, *Homeward Bound: the Incredible Journey*. Syn (as Tao the cat), Muffey (Bodger the bull terrier) and Rink (Luath the labrador) are outstanding as the abandoned pets who make their way across the treacherous Canadian wilderness to reunite with their owners. On the way they encounter danger in the form of bears, mountain lions and a disgruntled porcupine. Subtly narrated by Rex Allen, this is only slightly spoiled by the wooden performances of the humans in the cast. Compelling family viewing. DP *DVD*

Rex Allen *Narrator* • Emile Genest *John Longridge* • John Drainie *Professor Jim Hunter* • Tommy Tweed *Hermit* • Sandra Scott *Mrs Hunter* • Syme Jago *Helvi Nurmi* • Marion Finlayson *Elizabeth Hunter* ■ *Dir* Fletcher Markle • *Scr* James Algar, from the novel by Sheila Burnford

The Incredible Melting Man

★★ 18

Horror 1977 · US · Colour · 82min

Astronaut Alex Rebar returns from Saturn a changed man. His flesh is decomposing and he finds he's developed a taste for human meat. A deliberate throwback to cheap 1950s frights, hack writer/director William Sachs's film provides little of interest, apart from showcasing Oscar winner (*An American Werewolf in London*) Rick Baker's oozing, slimy and putrefying make-up to stunning effect. AJ *DVD* Blu

Alex Rebar *Melting Man* • Burr DeBenning *Dr Ted Nelson* • Myron Healey *General Perry* • Michael Alldredge *Sheriff Blake* • Ann Sweeny *Judy Nelson* • Lisle Wilson *Dr Loring* • Jonathan Demme *Matt* ■ *Dir/Scr* William Sachs • *Make-up* Rick Baker

The Incredible Shrinking Man

★★★★★ PG

Science-fiction thriller 1957 · US · BW · 77min

A must-see classic, this is directed by the master of 1950s science fiction, Jack Arnold, and derived from the thought-provoking novel by genre luminary Richard Matheson. Grant Williams slowly shrinks after passing through a radioactive cloud and, on the way down, sees his marriage disintegrate and is terrorised by the pet cat and a basement spider. A cogent comment on the plight of the "little man", Arnold's superlative thriller still retains its irony, shock and power. Williams gives a sensitive portrayal of a man hounded by the media and consigned to a freak's world, whose descent provides a memorable climax. AJ *DVD*

Grant Williams *Scott Carey* • Randy Stuart *Louise Carey* • April Kent *Clarice* • Paul Langton *Charlie Carey* • Raymond Bailey *Dr Thomas Silver* • William Schallert *Dr Arthur Bramson* ■ *Dir* Jack Arnold • *Scr* Richard Matheson, from his novel *The Shrinking Man*

The Incredible Shrinking Woman

★★★

Science-fiction comedy 1981 · US · Colour · 88min

This is a very odd spoof on the wonderful *The Incredible Shrinking Man*, brought bang up to date with some neat special effects but lacking the shock value of the original. Lily Tomlin is very funny as the housewife accidentally sprayed with a new perfume and ending up the size of the germs she tries so hard to eradicate in her home. This is a pleasing little jaunt through highly familiar territory, directed with flair and a light touch by Joel Schumacher. SH Swearing.

Lily Tomlin *Pat Kramer/Judith Beasley* • Charles Grodin *Vance Kramer* • Ned Beatty *Dan Beame* • Henry Gibson *Dr Eugene Nortz* ■ *Dir* Joel Schumacher • *Scr* Jane Wagner, from the novel *The Shrinking Man* by Richard Matheson

The Incredibles

★★★★★ U

Animated comedy adventure 2004 · US · Colour and BW · 110min

Originally conceived as a hand-drawn project, this spectacular comic-book-style adventure is another triumph for Pixar's brand of computer-animated magic. Mr Incredible (voiced by Craig T Nelson), once one of the world's foremost superheroes, is now an insurance agent living incognito in the suburbs (thanks to a super-litigious society having turned doing good deeds into an invitation for a lawsuit). But duty eventually calls and soon he's squeezing himself back into his old costume and fighting crime on the sly. Brad Bird instils his characters with genuine personalities, emotions and values. The film's slightly overlong, but its sophistication, wit and skill more than compensate. SF *DVD* Blu

Craig T Nelson *Bob Parr/Mr Incredible* • Holly Hunter *Helen Parr/Elastigirl* • Samuel L Jackson *Lucius Best/Frozone* • Jason Lee *Buddy Pine/Syndrome* • Sarah Vowell *Violet Parr* • Spencer Fox *Dashiell "Dash" Parr* • Elizabeth Peña *Mirage* • Wallace Shawn *Gilbert Huph* • John Ratzenberger *The Underminer* • Brad Bird *Edna "E" Mode* ■ *Dir/Scr* Brad Bird

The Incredibly Strange Creatures Who Stopped Living and Became Mixed-up Zombies

★★

Horror comedy 1963 · US · Colour · 82min

This legendary turkey was billed as the "First Monster Musical" and features such awful production numbers as *The Mixed-up Zombie Stomp*, complete with tacky striptease routines. Cash Flagg (director Ray Dennis Steckler's alter ego) falls under the sinister spell of a sideshow fortune-teller who throws acid in her patron's faces and then confines them to cages where they become rabid zombies ready to break loose when the rock songs begin. A messy romp. AJ

Cash Flagg *[Ray Dennis Steckler] Jerry* • Carolyn Brandt *Marge Neilson* • Brett O'Hara *Madame Estrella* • Atlas King *Harold* ■ *Dir* Ray Dennis Steckler • *Scr* Gene Pollock, Robert Silliphant, from a story by EM Kevke

The Incredibly True Adventures of Two Girls in Love

★★★ 15

1995 · US · Colour · 91min

A likeable same-sex love story, this is the romance between two girls from differing backgrounds. One is a working-class lesbian who lives with other lesbians, including her mum. The other is from a wealthy background, hugely popular, and complete with boyfriend. Burgeoning romance arouses wrath from both sets of friends and relatives. Engaging performances and sensitive plot-handling ensure you'll be rooting for the triumph of true love. DA *DVD*

Laurel Holloman *Randy Dean* • Nicole Parker *[Nicole Ari Parker] Evie Roy* • Maggie Moore *Wendy* • Kate Stafford *Rebecca Dean* • Sabrina Artel *Vicky* • Toby Poser *Lena* ■ *Dir/Scr* Maria Maggenti

Incubus

★★★

Horror 1965 · US · BW · 78min

William Shatner speaks Esperanto and shares screen time with someone calling himself Incubus. No, it's not a "lost" episode of *Star Trek* but a rare experimental art movie that was unavailable for years until a print belatedly became available. Best described as a kind of Swedish art movie filmed in California, this finds Shatner in the land of Nomen Tuum, where he's under threat from Allyson Ames's witch and the devil's little helper, Incubus. Shatner actually handles his part and the Esperanto dialogue well, and the black-and-white photography by Conrad Hall (Oscar winner for *Butch Cassidy*) is alternately stunning and haunting. KB Esperanto +subtitles.

William Shatner *Marc* • Milos Milos *Incubus* • Allyson Ames *Kia* • Eloise Hardt *Amael* • Robert Fortier *Olin* ■ *Dir/Scr* Leslie Stevens (1)

Indecent Behavior

★★ 18

Erotic thriller 1993 · US · Colour · 94min

Shannon Tweed is the undisputed queen of the erotic thriller and this proved to be one of her most popular films. The story is completely daft: Tweed plays an extremely unlikely sex therapist, under suspicion when one of her patients dies, who becomes involved with the detective investigating the case. The plot is largely an excuse for Tweed to get up to some ludicrously stylised sex sessions set to a sub-MTV soundtrack. It's actually pretty funny, but for all the wrong reasons. Three sequels followed. JF Violence, sex scenes, swearing, nudity. *DVD*

Shannon Tweed *Rebecca Mathis* • Gary Hudson *Nick Sharkey* • Michelle Moffett *Carol Lefter* • Lawrence Hilton-Jacobs [Lawrence-Hilton Jacobs] *Lou Parsons* • Jan-Michael Vincent *Tom Mathis* ■ *Dir* Lawrence Lanoff • *Scr* Rosalind Robinson

Indecent Proposal ★★★★ 15
Drama   1993 · US · Colour · 112min

Would you pay $1 million to sleep with Demi Moore? Robert Redford thinks she's worth it, as he puts the proposal to Moore's husband Woody Harrelson, after learning they need the money. The interesting "would *you* do it?" premise of Adrian Lyne's film goes slightly awry as the moral issues are dumped in favour of all three main characters simply showing how selfish they are, and as a result this is probably best seen as a good example of the excesses and emptiness of the early 1990s. But, with a cast like this, who are we to quibble? JB Swearing, sex scenes, nudity. *DVD*

Robert Redford *John Gage* • Demi Moore *Diana Murphy* • Woody Harrelson *David Murphy* • Seymour Cassel *Mr Shackelford* • Oliver Platt *Jeremy* • Billy Connolly *Auction emcee* • Joel Brooks *Realtor* • Pierre Epstein *Van Buren* • Sheena Easton • Herbie Hancock ■ *Dir* Adrian Lyne • *Scr* Amy Holden Jones, from the novel by Jack Engelhard

Independence Day ★★★ 15
Drama   1983 · US · Colour · 109min

This perfectly realised slice of small-town life is directed by Robert Mandel, who would later gain cult credibility by directing the pilot for *The X Files*. Adapted by Alice Hoffman from her own novel, the story features Kathleen Quinlan as a bored young woman torn between making a new life for herself and her developing relationship with David Keith. Mandel's direction is unobtrusive and sympathetic. JF

Kathleen Quinlan *Mary Ann Taylor* • David Keith *Jack Parker* • Frances Sternhagen *Carla Taylor* • Cliff De Young *Les Morgan* • Dianne Wiest *Nancy Morgan* • Josef Sommer *Sam Taylor* • Richard Farnsworth *Evan* ■ *Dir* Robert Mandel • *Scr* Alice Hoffman

Independence Day ★★★★ 12
Science-fiction adventure
1996 · US · Colour · 138min

No film had presented the destruction of the Earth on such an epic scale before this preposterously successful smash-hit sci-fi adventure came along. Of course, when we say Earth, we really mean the United States. The story is simple: gigantic alien spacecraft hover above major cities and set about destroying everything below, with mind-boggling set pieces of mass destruction. Will Smith, playing the wisecracking fighter pilot, is the big winner, with his charismatic performance making him one of the biggest box-office draws in the western world. Jeff Goldblum, Hollywood's most unlikely action star, delivers a variation on his boffin role in *Jurassic Park*. But this is, after all, a special effects, not an acting, showcase, and a very entertaining one at that. A follow-up is due in 2016. JF Violence, swearing. *DVD* *BD*

Will Smith *Captain Steve Hiller* • Bill Pullman *President Thomas J Whitmore* • Jeff Goldblum *David Levinson* • Mary McDonnell *Marilyn Whitmore* • Judd Hirsch *Julius Levinson* • Robert Loggia *General William Grey* • Randy Quaid *Russell Casse* • Margaret Colin *Constance Spano* • Harvey Fierstein *Marty Gilbert* • Adam Baldwin *Major Mitchell* • Brent Spiner *Dr Brakish Okun* • Vivica A Fox *Jasmine Dubrow* ■ *Dir* Roland Emmerich • *Scr* Dean Devlin, Roland Emmerich

Independence Day: Resurgence ★★ 12A
Science-fiction adventure
2016 · US · Colour · 119min

Twenty years after the original launched Will Smith into the superstar stratosphere, director Roland Emmerich produces a belated sequel in the hope it will emulate its predecessor as one of the biggest hits of the 1990s. Set two decades after Earth's triumph over the aliens, it sees Jeff Goldblum's scientist hero nervously scanning the skies. Action heroics are provided by Liam Hemsworth, but after the

initial excitement, the story runs out of steam, leaving the final moments curiously unmemorable. AS Violence, some swearing.

Liam Hemsworth *Jake Morrison* • Jeff Goldblum *David Levinson* • Bill Pullman *Thomas J Whitmore* • Maika Monroe *Patricia Whitmore* • William Fichtner *General Adams* • Charlotte Gainsbourg *Dr Catherine Marceaux* • Judd Hirsch *Julius Levinson* • Brent Spiner *Dr Brakish Okun* • Vivica A Fox *Jasmine* ■ *Dir* Roland Emmerich • *Scr* Dean Devlin, Roland Emmerich, Nicholas Wright, James A Woods, James Vanderbilt, from a story by Devlin, Emmerich, Wright, Woods, from characters by Devlin, Emmerich

Indestructible Man ★★ PG
Science fiction   1956 · US · BW · 70min

This revenge B-movie is saved by another patented display of dolour from Lon Chaney Jr. He's transformed into a Frankensteinian lug by a jolt of electricity, this time applied to his executed cadaver by cancer specialist Robert Shayne. Thenceforth it's stalk 'n' slash 1950s-style, as Chaney seeks to prevent crooked lawyer Ross Elliott from locating loot stashed in the LA sewer system. DP *DVD*

Lon Chaney Jr *The Butcher* • Marian Carr *Eva Martin* • Robert Shayne *Prof Bradshaw* ■ *Dir* Jack Pollexfen • *Scr* Sue Bradford, Vi Russell

India Song ★★★★
Experimental fantasy drama
1975 · Fr · Colour · 118min

Marguerite Duras brings an acute sense of place to this fascinating cinematic experiment, which seeks to find audiovisual equivalents to the textual iconoclasm achieved by the *nouveau roman*. The elliptical action opens with tales of hopeless abandon that emphasise the ennui experienced by 1930s consular wife Delphine Seyrig, whose amorous adventures seem increasingly futile against the backdrop of leprosy and fading empire. Bruno Nuytten's photography is striking, but it merely serves as a counterpoint to both the audible on- and off-screen drama and Carlos D'Alessio's evocative score. DP French +subtitles.

Delphine Seyrig *Anne-Marie Stretter* • Michel Lonsdale *Vice-consul* • Mathieu Carrière *Attaché* • Claude Mann *Michael Richardson* • Vernon Dobtcheff *George Crown* • Didier Flamand *Young guest* ■ *Dir/Scr* Marguerite Duras

The Indian Fighter ★★★ PG
Western   1955 · US · Colour · 84min

Kirk Douglas stars in this underrated and beautifully made western, which was the first film to be produced by Douglas's own company, Bryna. Its classy eroticism is exemplified by the casting of Italian star Elsa Martinelli as Douglas's maid, though Diana Douglas (Kirk's ex-wife and Michael's mum) also appears as a settler with more than a passing interest in the leading man. He is in his buckskinned prime, full of virile derring-do as he leads an Oregon-bound wagon train through "Injun" territory. TS *DVD*

Kirk Douglas *Johnny Hawks* • Elsa Martinelli *Onahti* • Walter Abel *Captain Trask* • Walter Matthau *Wes Todd* • Diana Douglas *Susan Rogers* • Lon Chaney Jr *Chivington* ■ *Dir* Andre De Toth • *Scr* Frank Davis, Ben Hecht, from a story by Ben Kadish [Robert L Richards]

The Indian in the Cupboard ★★★★ PG
Fantasy adventure   1995 · US · Colour · 92min

Wrapping culture-clash comedy up with *Honey, I Shrunk the Kids*-style special effects, director Frank Oz's assured, funny version of the Lynne Reid Banks novel is a low-key fantasy. A young boy discovers that an old cupboard given to him on his birthday can animate his playthings in this enchanting family fable. Ultimately he must learn responsibility when he brings his toy Indian (well played by rap artist Litefoot) to life and starts treating him like a human

Action Man. Muppet maestro Oz and his screenwriter Melissa Mathison never get too heavy, condescending or cloying with their sweet-natured message. AJ *DVD*

Hal Scardino *Omri* • Litefoot *Little Bear* • Lindsay Crouse *Jane* • Richard Jenkins *Victor* • Rishi Bhat *Patrick* • Steve Coogan *Tommy* ■ *Dir* Frank Oz • *Scr* Melissa Mathison, from the novel by Lynne Reid Banks

The Indian Runner ★★★ 15
Drama   1991 · US · Colour · 121min

Sean Penn took everyone by surprise with this, his writing and directorial debut. It's a remarkably assured, mature drama, inspired by the Bruce Springsteen song *Highway Patrolman*, and follows the troubled relationship between David Morse and his disturbed younger brother (an electrifying Viggo Mortensen). The story is slight but Penn's commitment to his tragic characters shines through and his direction is pleasingly unflashy, aside from sudden jolts of violence. JF Swearing. *DVD*

David Morse *Joe Roberts* • Viggo Mortensen *Frank Roberts* • Valeria Golino *Maria Roberts* • Patricia Arquette *Dorothy* • Charles Bronson *Father* • Sandy Dennis *Mother* • Dennis Hopper *Caesar* • Jordan Rhodes *Randall* ■ *Dir* Sean Penn • *Scr* Sean Penn, from the song *Highway Patrolman* by Bruce Springsteen

Indian Summer ★★★★ 15
Comedy drama   1993 · US · Colour · 93min

There is a wonderful sense of place and a bittersweet atmosphere of remembrance and regret generated here by director Mike Binder, who also wrote the semi-autobiographical script. Alan Arkin is impressive as the adventure holiday camp director who invites his favourite guests to spend a final summer in the woods before he's closed down. But the quality of the ensemble acting is such that no one tries to steal a march on any other member of the cast. It's a little slow starting, but it's worth giving it time. DP Swearing, sex scenes, drug abuse. *DVD*

Alan Arkin *Uncle Lou* • Matt Craven *Jamie Ross* • Diane Lane *Beth Warden/Claire Everett* • Bill Paxton *Jack Belston* • Elizabeth Perkins *Jennifer Morton* • Kevin Pollak *Brad Berman* • Sam Raimi *Stick Coder* ■ *Dir/Scr* Mike Binder

The Indian Tomb ★★★ PG
Adventure drama
1959 · W Ger/Fr/It · Colour · 101min

The second half of Fritz Lang's two-part film (the first being *The Tiger of Eschnapur*) tells an exotic tale, evoking the world of silent serials. German architect Harald Berger and beautiful Indian dancer Seeta (unconvincingly played by Hollywood actress Debra Paget) face further perils as their romance is threatened by love rival Walter Reyer. Lang's straight-faced approach provides some unintentional laughs, but it has magical moments. RB German +subtitles.

Debra Paget *Seeta* • Walter Reyer *Chandra* • Paul Hubschmid *Harald Berger* • Claus Holm *Dr Walter Rhode* • Sabine Bethmann *Irene Rhode* • Valery Inkijinoff *Yama* ■ *Dir* Fritz Lang • *Scr* Fritz Lang, Werner Jörg Lüddecke, Thea von Harbou, from an idea by Thea von Harbou, from a novel by Richard Eichberg

Indian Uprising ★ U
Western   1951 · US · Colour · 75min

In a feeble roundup of the situations being explored in bigger and better westerns of the period, George Montgomery plays the cavalry captain who's temporarily stripped of his command while trying to keep the peace between settlers and Indians. Villains are after the gold on the Indian reservation and that stirs up Geronimo (Miguel Inclan). AE

George Montgomery *Captain Case McCloud* • Audrey Long *Norma Clemson* • Carl Benton Reid *John Clemson* • Miguel Inclan *Geronimo* • Eddy Waller *Sagebrush* ■ *Dir* Ray Nazarro • *Scr* Kenneth Gamet, Richard Schayer, from a story by Richard Schayer

Indiana Jones and the Temple of Doom ★★★★ 12
Period action adventure
1984 · US · Colour · 118min

Steven Spielberg continued his homage to the classic cliffhanger serials of his youth with this follow-up to the rousing *Raiders of the Lost Ark*. It's a trifle overblown and unsubtle, but it still has great sets, fun performances and terrific action – the standout is a wild ride through an Indian mine. Harrison Ford is engaging as Indy and goes a long way in making up for the inferior story and often gruesome gags. AJ *DVD* *BD*

Harrison Ford *Indiana Jones* • Kate Capshaw *Willie Scott* • Ke Huy Quan *Short Round* • Amrish Puri *Mola Ram* • Roshan Seth *Chatter Lal* • Philip Stone *Captain Blumburtt* • Roy Chiao *Lao Che* • David Yip *Wu Han* ■ *Dir* Steven Spielberg • *Scr* Willard Huyck, Gloria Katz, from a story by George Lucas, from characters by Lucas, Philip Kaufman

Indiana Jones and the Last Crusade ★★★★★ PG
Period action adventure
1989 · US · Colour · 126min

The Temple of Doom saw the Indiana Jones series lurch off the rails a little, but all was restored with this third movie. The masterstroke here was the introduction of Sean Connery as Indy's crotchety dad, and the snappy by-play between him and Harrison Ford adds a wonderful new twist to the adventure. The quest this time is for the Holy Grail, and finds Jones reunited with old chums, such as Denholm Elliott, and old enemies, namely the Nazis. As usual, the action is on an epic scale and delivered with breathless enthusiasm and much panache by director Steven Spielberg. There is also a neat framing sequence in the beginning with River Phoenix as the young Indy that sheds light on such things as our hero's fear of snakes. JF Swearing, violence. *DVD* *BD*

Harrison Ford *Indiana Jones* • Sean Connery *Dr Henry Jones* • Denholm Elliott *Marcus Brody* • Alison Doody *Dr Elsa Schneider* • John Rhys-Davies *Sallah* • Julian Glover *Walter Donovan* • River Phoenix *Young Indy* • Alexei Sayle *Sultan* ■ *Dir* Steven Spielberg • *Scr* Jeffrey Boam, from a story by George Lucas, Menno Meyjes, from characters by Lucas, Philip Kaufman • *Music* John Williams • *Cinematographer* Douglas Slocombe

Indiana Jones and the Kingdom of the Crystal Skull ★★★★ 12
Period action adventure
2008 · US · Colour · 117min

Almost 19 years after the release of *Indiana Jones and the Last Crusade*, director Steven Spielberg and producer George Lucas exhume their globe-trotting archaeologist for another crack of the whip. It's now 1957, and Indy (Harrison Ford) begins his latest quest via an exhilarating motorbike chase through a university campus. The sought-after prize is the fabled Crystal Skull of Akator and, this being the Cold War era, the baddies are the Soviets, led by Cate Blanchett (who clearly would have made a great Bond villain). Then it's all aboard for more of the same Saturday matinée thrills: a multi-vehicle pursuit through the Amazon jungle; giant ants; umpteen secret passageways; and even alien visitors. Though exhausting and relentless, it's hard to dislike, thanks to Ford's weary charm, his leather-clad new wingman Shia LaBeouf, and an emphasis on pleasingly "old school" stuntwork. Harrison Ford has promised a fifth instalment, due in summer 2019. AC Some violence, swearing. *DVD* *BD*

Harrison Ford *Indiana Jones* • Cate Blanchett *Irina Spalko* • Ray Winstone *George "Mac" McHale* • Shia LaBeouf *Mutt Williams* • John Hurt *Professor "Ox" Oxley* • Karen Allen *Marion Ravenwood* • Jim Broadbent *Dean Charles Stanforth* ■ *Dir* Steven Spielberg • *Scr* David Koepp, from a story by George Lucas, Jeff Nathanson, from characters by Lucas, Philip Kaufman • *Music* John Williams

Indictment: the McMartin Trial ★★★★ 18

Courtroom drama based on a true story
1995 · US · Colour · 125min

This starry made-for-TV production, executive produced by Oliver Stone, is based on a case in the US, in which a family that ran a private day care centre was accused of child abuse. James Woods is the lawyer assigned to defend one of the accused (Henry Thomas), while Mercedes Ruehl is the ruthless prosecutor. The A-list cast is uniformly superb but what distinguishes this drama is the way director Mick Jackson keeps the viewer guessing as to what actually happened to the children. JF

James Woods *Danny Davis* • Mercedes Ruehl *Lael Rubin* • Henry Thomas *Ray Buckey* • Shirley Knight *Peggy Buckey* • Sada Thompson *Virginia McMartin* • Lolita Davidovich *Kee McFarlane* • Mark Blum *Wayne Satz* • Alison Elliott (2) *Peggy Ann Buckey* • Chelsea Field *Christine Johnson* ■ *Dir* Mick Jackson • *Scr* Abby Mann, Myra Mann

Indiscreet ★★★

Romantic comedy
1931 · US · BW · 92min

One of Gloria Swanson's more successful attempts to extend her career into talkies, this comedy drama features her as the woman with a past who attempts to protect her younger sister (Barbara Kent) from the attentions of rakish Monroe Owsley. He's actually an ex-lover of Swanson's, and Kent is none too pleased when she finds out. Meanwhile Swanson has a budding romance with Ben Lyon's impulsive author. Largely scripted by the songwriting team of DeSylva, Brown and Henderson (who throw in a couple of lightweight numbers for Swanson to perform), this is a bright rehash of familiar situations, directed imaginatively by Leo McCarey. AE

Gloria Swanson *Geraldine Trent* • Ben Lyon *Tony Blake* • Monroe Owsley *Jim Woodward* • Barbara Kent *Joan Trent* • Arthur Lake *Buster Collins* • Maude Eburne *Aunt Kate* ■ *Dir* Leo McCarey • *Scr* BG DeSylva, Lew Brown, Ray Henderson, from their story *Obey That Impulse*

Indiscreet ★★★ PG

Romantic comedy
1958 · UK/US · Colour · 99min

Two of the screen's most elegant stars provide much of the pleasure in this glossy romantic comedy, adapted by Norman Krasna from his play *Kind Sir*. The action has been transplanted from New York to foggy London (it was filmed at Elstree) with Ingrid Bergman as a famous actress looking for love and Cary Grant as the diplomat who's pretending he's married when he's not. Highlights include Grant dancing a superb Highland reel and a witty supporting performance as a chauffeur in disguise from the underrated David Kossoff. It's nonsense, of course, but utterly charming. TS **DVD**

Cary Grant *Philip Adams* • Ingrid Bergman *Anna Kalman* • Cecil Parker *Alfred Munson* • Phyllis Calvert *Margaret Munson* • David Kossoff *Carl Banks* ■ *Dir* Stanley Donen • *Scr* Norman Krasna, from his play *Kind Sir*

Indiscreet ★★ PG

Romantic comedy
1988 · US/UK · Colour · 101min

What did Robert Wagner and Lesley-Anne Down hope to gain from this remake of Stanley Donen's patchy, but nonetheless hugely enjoyable, 1958 adaptation of Norman Krasna's hit play? It was surely obvious that they would be compared to the original stars, Cary Grant and Ingrid Bergman, and would be found wanting. Watch if only to remember just how good Grant and Bergman really were. DP

Robert Wagner *Philip Adams* • Lesley-Anne Down *Anna Kingston* ■ *Dir* Richard Michaels • *Scr* Walter Lockwood, Sally Robison, from the 1958 film *Indiscreet* by Norman Krasna, from his play *Kind Sir*

Indiscretion of an American Wife ★★★ U

Drama
1954 · US/It · BW · 60min

Director Vittorio De Sica's claustrophobic study of the end of a brief encounter is brilliantly filmed in stark black and white in Rome's famous Stazione Terminale. The story brings together Jennifer Jones and Montgomery Clift as lovers who can't bear to make the final break. The stars are filmed in magnificent close-ups, their anxiety almost palpable. Jones's husband, David O Selznick, recut this movie considerably, but it has a raw truth about it that is still deeply moving. TS

Jennifer Jones *Mary Forbes* • Montgomery Clift *Giovanni Doria* • Gino Cervi *Commissioner* • Dick Beymer [Richard Beymer] *Paul, Mary's nephew* ■ *Dir* Vittorio De Sica • *Scr* Cesare Zavattini, Luigi Chiarini, Giorgio Prosperi, Truman Capote, from a story by Cesare Zavattini

Indochine ★★★★ 15

Period romance
1991 · Fr · Colour · 151min

Winner of the Oscar for best foreign language film, this epic drama set in French Indochina in the 1930s also won five Césars, including best actress for the imperious Catherine Deneuve and best supporting actress for Dominique Blanc. Having hooked us on a melodramatic love triangle involving Deneuve, her teenage daughter and a handsome naval officer, the picture plunges us into a breathless adventure as the daughter encounters the brutal realities of French rule when she follows the officer to his far-flung base. DP French +subtitles. Violence, swearing, sex scenes, drug abuse. **DVD**

Catherine Deneuve *Eliane* • Vincent Perez *Jean-Baptiste* • Linh-Dan Pham *Camille* • Jean Yanne *Guy* • Dominique Blanc *Yvette* • Henri Marteau *Emile* • Carlo Brandt *Castellani* ■ *Dir* Régis Wargnier • *Scr* Régis Wargnier, Erik Orsenna, Louis Gardel, Catherine Cohen

Infamous ★★★ 15

Biographical drama
2006 · US · Colour · 113min

Coincidentally made at the same time as the Oscar-winning *Capote*, this rival project also focuses on the events surrounding the writing of *In Cold Blood* – Truman Capote's bestselling account of a shocking mass murder in a Kansas farmhouse in 1959. Where *Capote* went for understatement, however, *Infamous* turns up the volume. It boasts a terrific performance from Toby Jones in the lead (one part Deputy Dawg, two parts Oscar Wilde) and punctuates the drama with stylised talking heads from the likes of author Harper Lee (Sandra Bullock) and society maven Babe Paley (Sigourney Weaver). More bothersome, though, is the heavy-handed portrayal of Capote's relationship with killer Perry Smith (Daniel Craig) and the foregrounding of the homoerotic tension that underscores his prison visits. If *Capote* didn't exist this would be a fascinating failure, but next to it *Infamous* is somewhat superfluous. DW Violence, swearing, sex scenes. **DVD**

Toby Jones *Truman Capote* • Sandra Bullock *Nelle Harper Lee* • Daniel Craig *Perry Smith* • Jeff Daniels *Alvin Dewey* • Sigourney Weaver *Babe Paley* • Hope Davis *Slim Keith* • Peter Bogdanovich *Bennett Cerf* • Isabella Rossellini *Marella Agnelli* • Gwyneth Paltrow *Kitty Dean* • Juliet Stevenson *Diana Vreeland* ■ *Dir* Douglas McGrath • *Scr* Douglas McGrath, from the biography *Truman Capote* by George Plimpton

Infernal Affairs ★★★★ 15

Crime drama
2002 · HK · Colour · 96min

Andrew Lau directs this satisfyingly complex and simmering atmospheric crime drama. However, it's very much a team effort, with co-director Alan Mak and Felix Chong's taut screenplay bringing the best out of an impressive cast. Andy Lau plays a Hong Kong detective in the pay of Triad mobster Eric Tsang, who is being investigated by longtime undercover cop Tony Leung. The tension as both sides search for the moles betraying their plans often becomes unbearable and it's to directors Lau and Mak's credit that they refuse to allow the action to descend into clichéd showdown pyrotechnics. DP Cantonese +subtitles. Violence, drug abuse. **DVD** **Blu-ray**

Tony Leung (2) *Chan Wing Yan* • Andy Lau *Inspector Lau Kin Ming* • Anthony Wong (1) *Superintendent Wong* • Eric Tsang *Sam* • Kelly Chen *Dr Lee Sum Yee* • Sammi Cheng *Mary* • Edison Chen *Young Lau Kin Ming* • Shawn Yue *Young Chan Wing Yan* • Chapman To *Keung* ■ *Dir* Andrew Lau, Alan Mak • *Scr* Alan Mak, Felix Chong

Infernal Affairs II ★★★ 15

Crime drama
2003 · HK · Colour · 114min

Fleshing out the opening sequence of Andrew Lau and Alan Mak's original crime thriller, this is a satisfyingly complex prequel that expertly lays the ground for the entire *Infernal Affairs* trilogy. The action centres around Shawn Yue and Edison Chen, who are operating as moles in the Triads and the Hong Kong police respectively. But their positions look likely to be compromised as Francis Ng conducts a gang war against his murdered father's henchmen. DP Cantonese +subtitles. **DVD**

Edison Chen *Lau Kin Ming* • Shawn Yue *Chan Wing Yan* • Anthony Wong (1) *Superintendent Wong* • Francis Ng *Ngai Wing-Hau* • Eric Tsang *Sam* • Carina Lau *Mary* • Chapman To *Keung* • Andrew Lin *Ngai's brother* • Bey Logan *Inspector Calvin* ■ *Dir* Andrew Lau, Alan Mak • *Scr* Felix Chong, Alan Mak

Infernal Affairs 3 ★★★ 15

Crime drama
2003 · HK · Colour · 115min

The concluding part of this thrilling trilogy opens shortly after the climax of the original, with Hong Kong cop Andy Lau convinced that he's become a hero without being rumbled as a mole for Triad boss Eric Tsang. However, his cover could still be blown if newcomer Leon Lai digs too deep – that is, providing his links with mobster Chen Dao Ming aren't exposed by Tony Leung, who is working undercover in Tsang's gang. The action becomes unnecessarily intricate, but the set pieces throb with explosive panache. DP Cantonese +subtitles.

Andy Lau *Lau Kin Ming* • Tony Chiu-Wai Leung [Tony Leung (2)] *Chan Wing Yan* • Anthony Wong (1) *Superintendent Wong* • Eric Tsang *Sam* • Kelly Chen *Dr Lee Sum Yee* • Sammi Cheng *Mary* • Edison Chen *Young Lau Kin Ming* • Shawn Yue *Young Chan Wing Yan* • Leon Lai *Yeung* • Chen Dao Ming *Shen* ■ *Dir* Andrew Lau, Alan Mak • *Scr* Felix Chong, Andrew Lau

Inferno ★★★ PG

Drama
1953 · US · Colour · 83min

Sharply directed by Britain's Roy Ward Baker, this ingenious thriller rests securely on the performance of Robert Ryan as the millionaire playboy left to die in the desert with a broken leg by his wife and her lover. Most of the film covers Ryan's heroic efforts to survive the extremes of temperature, hunger and natural hazards. This was one of the most effective pictures ever made for showing in 3D, which emphasised the vastness of the desert, but the avoidance of gimmicky effects means that it works as well shown flat. AE **DVD** **Blu-ray** **3D**

Robert Ryan *Carson* • Rhonda Fleming *Geraldine Carson* • William Lundigan *Joseph Duncan* • Larry Keating *Emory* • Henry Hull *Sam Elby* • Carl Betz *Lieutenant Mark Platt* ■ *Dir* Roy Ward Baker • *Scr* Francis Cockrell • *Cinematographer* Lucien Ballard

Inferno ★★★ 18

Horror
1980 · It · Colour · 102min

Italian director Dario Argento follows up *Suspiria* with this slightly demented but compulsive shocker. Student Leigh McCloskey returns to New York from Rome following the untimely demise of his girlfriend. His sister has discovered that her apartment building has some malevolent occupants whose supernatural powers result in a number of violent deaths. Argento's technical skill creates enough striking moments to offset some inconsistencies in the plot. TH Italian dubbed. Violence. **DVD** **Blu-ray**

Leigh McCloskey *Mark Elliot* • Irene Miracle *Rose Elliot* • Eleonora Giorgi *Sara* • Daria Nicolodi *Countess Elise* ■ *Dir* Dario Argento • *Scr* Dario Argento, from a story by Dario Argento • *Music* Keith Emerson

Inferno

Mystery thriller
2016 · US · Colour

This is a preview – no prints were available to review prior to publication: After *The Da Vinci Code* and *Angels & Demons*, Sony leapfrog the third book in Dan Brown's Robert Langdon series, *The Lost Symbol*, and move director Ron Howard straight on to an adaptation of book four, the best-selling *Inferno*. This adds a touch of *Bourne Identity* intrigue to the usual Brown schematic of leavening historical esoterica with breathless chases in exotic locations, by having Tom Hanks's symbologist Robert Langdon wake up with amnesia in Italy with a US government assassin on his tail. Felicity Jones takes the role of comely assistant. SvM **3D**

Tom Hanks *Robert Langdon* • Felicity Jones *Dr Sienna Brooks* • Irrfan Khan [Irfan Khan] *Harry Sims, "The Provost"* • Omar Sy *Christoph Bruder* • Ben Foster *Bertrand Zobrist* ■ *Dir* Ron Howard • *Scr* David Koepp, from Dan Brown's novel

The Infidel ★★★ 15

Comedy
2010 · UK · Colour · 100min

Comedian David Baddiel scripts this potentially explosive fable about a London-born Pakistani man who discovers that his real parents were Jewish. The material is actually handled with great care, with Omid Djalili showing his more sensitive side when his uniquely conflicted character, Mahmud, must consider telling his family the truth. There are times when the movie is too silly, but thankfully Djalili knows how to rein himself in and director Josh Appignanesi takes a cool, candid approach that keeps the story anchored in the real world. The humour is irreverent at times, but the joke is on those who are easily offended. SP Swearing. **DVD** **Blu-ray**

Omid Djalili *Mahmud Nasir* • Richard Schiff *Lenny* • Archie Panjabi *Saamiya Nasir* • Amit Shah *Rashid Nasir* • Igal Naor *Arshad Al-Masri* • Mina Anwar *Muna* • Matt Lucas *Rabbi* • Paul Kaye *Policeman* ■ *Dir* Josh Appignanesi • *Scr* David Baddiel

The Infiltrator ★★★ 18

Political thriller
1995 · US · Colour · 88min

This intense TV thriller is based on the true story of Yaron Svoray, an Israeli-born reporter. Svoray (Oliver Platt) travels to Germany to investigate neo-Nazism and infiltrates a skinhead gang. As he gets closer to uncovering the leaders, the full horror of their violent, hate-mongering movement becomes clear. Platt's convincing performance is particularly effective in this powerful drama. MC Swearing, violence. **DVD**

Oliver Platt *Yaron Svoray* • Arliss Howard *Eaton* • Peter Riegert *Rabbi Cooper* • Alan King *Rabbi Hier* • Tony Haygarth *Gunther* • Michael Byrne *Creutz* • Julian Glover *Bielert* • Alex Kingston *Anna* ■ *Dir* John Mackenzie (1) • *Scr* Guy Andrews, from a story by Robert J Avrech, Guy Andrews, from the non-fiction book *In Hitler's Shadow: an Israeli's Amazing Journey inside Germany's Neo-Nazi Movement* by Yaron Svoray, Nick Taylor

The Infiltrator ★★★ 15

Crime drama based on a true story
2016 · US · Colour · 127min

Vicarious fans of the labyrinthine cat-and-mouse drug cartels will enjoy this taut, 80s-set thriller based on US Customs agent Bob Mazur's factual account of the same name. An undercover operation to destroy Escobar's money-laundering empire requires family man Bryan Cranston to lead a double life, posing as a flash, crooked financier with a trophy fiancée (Diane Kruger) and coming home to loyal wife Juliet Aubrey. The action moves credibly from Tampa to London and Paris, but anticlimax dogs the final act. AC

Bryan Cranston *Robert Mazur* • John Leguizamo *Emir Abreu* • Diane Kruger *Kathy Ertz* • Amy Ryan *Bonni Tischler* • Benjamin Bratt *Robert*

Alcaino • Juliet Aubrey *Evelyn Mazur* ■ *Dir* Brad Furman • *Scr* Ellen Brown Furman, from the non-fiction book *The Infiltrator: Undercover in the World of Drug Barons and Dirty Banks* by Robert Mazur

Infinite Justice ★★ 15
Drama   2006 • UK • Colour • 92min

As with Michael Winterbottom's *A Mighty Heart*, this well-meaning drama was inspired by the murder of reporter Daniel Pearl in 2002. Here, a Jewish-American journalist (Kevin Collins) travels to Karachi to uncover the financial workings of al-Qaeda, following his sister's death on 9/11. However, he soon ends up as a hostage guarded by Raza Jaffrey (Zafir in BBC TV's *Spooks*), a public-school educated British Pakistani who was radicalised by his experiences in Bosnia. Unfortunately, writer/director Jamil Dehlavi (*Jinnah*) too often reduces the debate about the so-called "war on terror" to an exchange of platitudes, which is scarcely made any more credible by the caricatured depiction of Collins's fundamentalist captors. DP *DVD*

Kevin Collins *Arnold Silverman* • Raza Jaffrey *Kamal Asad Khan* • Jennifer Calvert *Sarah Callendar* • Constantine Gregory *Abe Kautsky* • Irvine Iqbal *Waqar Islam* • Jeff Mirza *Inspector Akhtar* ■ *Dir/Scr* Jamil Dehlavi

Infinitely Polar Bear
★★★★ 15
Comedy drama   2014 • US • Colour • 84min

This likeable, light-hearted family drama begins in the late 1970s. Set in Boston, it revolves around Mark Ruffalo as a man who is suffering from bipolar disorder. His wife (Zoë Saldana) is trying to hold everything together, but she is unable to find a job that will support the family. Determined to give them a better life, she pursues an 18-month scholarship in New York, leaving Ruffalo to look after their two daughters. What follows is fairly episodic, but it is filled with joyous sequences, and it helps, of course, that Ruffalo is incredibly endearing throughout. SC *DVD*

Mark Ruffalo *Cameron* • Zoe Saldana [Zoë Saldana] *Maggie* • Keir Dullea *Murray Stuart* • Wallace Wolodarsky ■ *Dir/Scr* Maya Forbes

Infinity ★★★
Biographical romantic drama
1996 • US • Colour • 119min

Matthew Broderick both stars in and directs this feature about Nobel Prize-winning physicist Richard Feynman, who worked on the development of the atomic bomb. The opening half, where Broderick meets and romances Patricia Arquette in pre-Second World War New York, is both touching and powerful. It's an above average debut (scripted by Broderick's mother, Patricia) but viewers of a non-technical disposition might have preferred more emphasis on romance and less on science. LH

Matthew Broderick *Richard Feynman* • Patricia Arquette *Arline Greenbaum* • Peter Riegert *Mel Feynman* • Dori Brenner *Tutti Feynman* • Peter Michael Goetz *Dr Hellman* ■ *Dir* Matthew Broderick • *Scr* Patricia Broderick, from the memoirs *Surely You're Joking, Mr Feynman!* and *What Do You Care What Other People Think?* by Richard Feynman

The Informant! ★★★ 15
Biographical comedy thriller
2009 • US • Colour • 103min

Steven Soderbergh uncovers the funny side of price-fixing scams and corporate espionage in this real-life tale. There are shades of the director's earlier *Erin Brockovich* here, except that Matt Damon is overweight, insecure and endearingly naive as the whistle-blower of the piece. He plays Mark Whitacre, a biochemist and top executive at an agricultural conglomerate who buckles under the pressure of spying for the FBI. We're made privy to his added thoughts in a wry voiceover, but the tension of leading a double life doesn't come across quite as strongly in scenes at home with his trusting spouse (Melanie Lynskey). SP Swearing. *DVD* *BL*

Matt Damon *Mark Whitacre* • Scott Bakula *FBI Special Agent Brian Shepard* • Joel McHale *FBI Special Agent Bob Herndon* • Melanie Lynskey *Ginger Whitacre* • Rick Overton *Terry Wilson* • Tom Papa *Mick Andreas* • Tom Wilson [Thomas F Wilson] *Mark Cheviron* • Frank Welker *Mark Whitacre's father* ■ *Dir* Steven Soderbergh • *Scr* Scott Z Burns, from the novel *The Informant: a True Story* by Kurt Eichenwald

The Informant ★★★ 15
Crime thriller   2013 • Fr/Can • Colour • 111min

The writer and star of Jacques Audiard's *A Prophet* reunite for this lacklustre adaptation of Marc Fiévet's autobiographical book about a cash-strapped 1980s café owner who starts providing customs officials with information about smuggling across the border with Gibraltar. The sequence in which Duval bugs his premises is neatly done, but, despite establishing a solid sense of time and place, director Julien Leclercq is unable to maintain the suspense. DP In French, English. Violence, swearing, sex scenes. *DVD* *BL*

Gilles Lellouche *Marc Duval* • Tahar Rahim *Redjani Belimane* • Riccardo Scamarcio *Mario/Claudio Pasco Lanfredi* • Raphaëlle Agogué *Clara Duval* ■ *Dir* Julien Leclercq • *Scr* Abdel Raouf Dafri, from Marc Fiévet's novel *L'Aviseur*

The Informer ★★★ PG
Drama   1935 • US • BW • 91min

This screen version of Liam O'Flaherty's novel is an art film with a vengeance. Given a low budget, director John Ford had a free hand to film this grim story set in Dublin in 1922 during the Irish Civil War. Victor McLaglen, driven by poverty to inform against the IRA, is then racked by guilt as he faces inevitable retribution. Ford adopted a heavily stylised approach with overt symbolism and won an Academy Award along with leading actor McLaglen, screenwriter Dudley Nichols and composer Max Steiner. While Ford's less pretentious works are much to be preferred, this is still a powerful picture. AE *DVD*

Victor McLaglen *Gypo Nolan* • Heather Angel *Mary McPhillip* • Preston Foster *Dan Gallagher* • Margot Grahame *Katie Madden* • Wallace Ford *Frankie McPhillip* ■ *Dir* John Ford • *Scr* Dudley Nichols, from the novel by Liam O'Flaherty

The Informers ★★ 12
Crime drama   1963 • UK • BW • 100min

Nowadays British crime films of the 1950s and 1960s look rather quaint, with the dogged attempts of performers to either act tough and growl in East End argot as they plan their blags, or portray the clipped decency of the Scotland Yard flatfoot. While eminently watchable, this police procedural crime drama from director Ken Annakin is a case in point. Nigel Patrick is the archetypal inspector in a mac, while Frank Finlay is as brutal as a pantomime villain. DP *DVD*

Nigel Patrick *Chief Insp Johnnoe* • Margaret Whiting *Maisie* • Colin Blakely *Charlie Ruskin* • Derren Nesbitt *Bertie Hoyle* • Frank Finlay *Leon Sale* • Catherine Woodville *Mary Johnnoe* • Harry Andrews *Supt Bestwick* • Allan Cuthbertson *Smythe* ■ *Dir* Ken Annakin • *Scr* Alun Falconer, Paul Durst, from the novel *Death of a Snout* by Douglas Warner

The Informers ★ 15
Drama   2009 • US/Ger • Colour • 93min

This dramatisation of Bret Easton Ellis's novel is an overstuffed ensemble drama set in Los Angeles during the 1980s. The cast includes Billy Bob Thornton, Kim Basinger, Mickey Rourke and Chris Isaak, and Ellis co-wrote the script, but there's little of his satirical edge here. Instead *Buffalo Soldiers* director Gregor Jordan lingers over the bare flesh, shiny surfaces and white powder with tut-tutting seriousness, somehow under the impression that this flat, repetitive and utterly misguided film is telling us something that wasn't already old hat 20 years ago. TJ *DVD* *BL*

Billy Bob Thornton *William* • Kim Basinger *Laura* • Mickey Rourke *Peter* • Winona Ryder *Cheryl* • Jon Foster [JJ] *Graham* • Amber Heard *Christie* ■ *Dir* Gregor Jordan • *Scr* Bret Easton Ellis, Nicholas Jarecki, from the novel by Ellis

Inglorious Bastards ★★★ 15
Second World War action adventure
1978 • It • Colour • 95min

Quentin Tarantino has now remade this little-known but enjoyable wartime adventure, in which a motley group of American soldiers on their way to prison escape but still end up on a commando mission to disrupt the Nazi rocket programme. Pitched somewhere between *Kelly's Heroes* and *The Dirty Dozen*, this Italian production is no star vehicle, though Bo Svenson (*Kill Bill*), blaxploitation legend Fred Williamson (*From Dusk till Dawn*) and British actor Ian Bannen may be familiar to some. There are some fantastic locations and the Peckinpah-style action sequences are pretty spectacular, but some variable acting and dodgy dubbing prevent this from achieving classic cult status. JA English, German, French +subtitles. *DVD*

Bo Svenson *Sgt Yeager* • Peter Hooten *Tony* • Fred Williamson *Fred* • Michael Pergolani *Nick* • Jackie Basehart *Berle* • Ian Bannen *Colonel Buckner* ■ *Dir* Enzo G Castellari • *Scr* Sandro Continenza, Sergio Grieco, Franco Marotta, Romano Migliorini, Laura Toscano

Inglourious Basterds
★★★ 18
Second World War action adventure
2009 • US/Ger • Colour • 146min

Cinema saves the world in writer/director Quentin Tarantino's disjointed history-bending homage to war movies. The multi-stranded plot includes Mélanie Laurent as a Jew avoiding Gestapo capture, Brad Pitt as a lieutenant commanding a dirty dozen of Nazi hunters and Diane Kruger as a German movie star/British double agent. All of which eventually roll into the main action: to blow up the Nazi High Command at the Paris premiere of one of Goebbels's propaganda films. Delivered as a series of witty dialogue-driven vignettes containing flashes of violent action, it's a long but entertainingly showy melodrama full of cineaste jokes. Highlights include a resistance-bar rendezvous where English spy Michael Fassbender's Nazi-officer disguise is gradually penetrated, and Christoph Waltz's turn as a charmingly evil SS colonel. AJ English, German, French, Italian +subtitles. *DVD* *BL*

Brad Pitt *Lt Aldo Raine* • Mélanie Laurent *Shosanna Dreyfus* • Diane Kruger *Bridget von Hammersmark* • Eli Roth *Sergeant Donny Donowitz* • Michael Fassbender *Lt Archie Hicox* • Til Schweiger *Sgt Hugo Stiglitz* • Mike Myers *General Ed Fenech* • BJ Novak *Pfc Utivich* • Samm Levine *Pfc Hirschberg* • Samuel L Jackson *Narrator* ■ *Dir/Scr* Quentin Tarantino

Inherent Vice ★★★★ 15
Crime drama   2014 • US • Colour • 142min

Paul Thomas Anderson's gloriously rambling, dope-fogged detective yarn is set in 1970 and has Joaquin Phoenix as a Los Angeles PI – a fuzz-faced countercultural update of Elliott Gould's private dick in Robert Altman's *The Long Goodbye*. Embarking on two missing person cases, Phoenix is soon embroiled in a labyrinthine investigation involving cameoing stars like Reese Witherspoon and Owen Wilson, with Josh Brolin's cop a constant ally-cum-nemesis. Despite the pot haze, a credible plot emerges and Anderson chalks up another triumph. AC In English, Japanese. Swearing, sex scenes, drug abuse. *DVD* *BL*

Joaquin Phoenix *Larry "Doc" Sportello* • Josh Brolin *Lt Det Christian F "Bigfoot" Bjornsen* • Owen Wilson *Coy Harlingen* • Katherine Waterston *Shasta Fay Hepworth* • Reese Witherspoon *Penny Kimball* • Benicio Del Toro *Sauncho Smilax, Esq* • Martin Short *Dr Rudy Blatnoyd* • Maya Rudolph *Petunia Leeway* ■ *Dir* Paul Thomas Anderson • *Scr* Paul Thomas Anderson, from Thomas Pynchon's novel

Inherit the Wind ★★★★ U
Courtroom drama   1960 • US • BW • 123min

This is a stirring title for a gripping courtroom drama, inspired by the real-life trial in 1925 of a young Tennessee teacher charged with giving lessons on the

Darwinian theory of evolution in a state school. Very much a drama of words and ideas, the film was a critical hit but a commercial flop in its day. Yes, the plot meanders and even drags at points, but ultimately it engrosses thanks to major-league performances from Spencer Tracy and Fredric March as the opposing lawyers in what became known as the "Scopes Monkey Trial". PF *DVD*

Fredric March *Matthew Harrison Brady* • Spencer Tracy *Henry Drummond* • Gene Kelly *EK Hornbeck* • Florence Eldridge *Mrs Brady* • Dick York *Bertram T Cates* • Donna Anderson *Rachel Brown* • Harry Morgan *Judge* • Elliott Reid *Davenport* ■ *Dir* Stanley Kramer • *Scr* Nathan E Douglas [Nedrick Young], Harold Jacob Smith, from the play by Jerome Lawrence, Robert E Lee • *Cinematographer* Ernest Laszlo • *Music* Ernest Gold

Inherit the Wind ★★ PG
Courtroom drama   1988 • US • Colour • 91min

Kirk Douglas and Jason Robards are no match for Fredric March and Spencer Tracy in this only moderate TV-movie remake of the superior 1960 film of the same name, based on the real-life trial in 1925 of a teacher accused of promoting Darwin's theory of evolution. PF

Kirk Douglas *Matthew Harrison Brady* • Jason Robards Jr [Jason Robards] *Henry Drummond* • Kyle Secor *Bertram Cates* • Darren McGavin *EK Hornbeck* • Jean Simmons *Lucy Brady* • Megan Follows *Rachel Brown* • Don Hood *Mayor* • Michael Ensign *Reverend Jeremiah Brown* • John Harkins *Judge* ■ *Dir* David Greene • *Scr* John Gay, from the play by Jerome Lawrence, Robert E Lee

Inherit the Wind ★★★★
Courtroom drama   1999 • US • Colour • 127min

An all-star line-up make this drama about the famous 1925 "Scopes Monkey Trial" compelling viewing. A schoolteacher – derided for expounding Darwinian theory – is arrested and tried in a case that soon generates national interest. A stocky courtroom drama ensues and forms the bulk of what was originally a stage play of the same name. Attention to 1920s period detail and heavyweight performances make this a well-above-average, made-for-television drama. LH

Jack Lemmon *Henry Drummond* • George C Scott *Matthew Harrison Brady* • Beau Bridges *EK Hornbeck* • Piper Laurie *Sarah Brady* • Lane Smith *Reverend Jeremiah Brown* ■ *Dir* Daniel Petrie Sr [Daniel Petrie] • *Scr* Nedrick Young, Harold Jacob Smith, from the play by Jerome Lawrence, Robert E Lee

The Inheritance ★★★ 18
Drama   1976 • It • Colour • 98min

Dominique Sanda has a juicy role here as a social climber with her eyes on a fortune owned by one of Italy's grandest families. First she marries one of the sons; then she seduces his father, the lusty patriarch played by Anthony Quinn. Sadly, Quinn's life force soon runs dry as Sanda wears him out in bed. He does, though, bequeath her the entire estate, which doesn't make for harmonious family relations. Veteran director Mauro Bolognini directs this moral tale with his usual elegance and with more than a touch of the Viscontis. AT Italian dubbed.

Anthony Quinn *Gregorio Ferramonti* • Fabio Testi *Mario Ferramonti* • Dominique Sanda *Irene* • Luigi Proietti *Pippo Ferramonti* • Adriana Asti *Teta Ferramonti* ■ *Dir* Mauro Bolognini • *Scr* Ugo Pirro, Sergio Bazzini

The Inheritance ★★★ 15
Drama
2003 • Den/Nor/Swe/UK • Colour • 110min

Per Fly's film is a grittily engrossing mix of the plot machinations of a glitzy soap like *Dallas* and the grainy shooting style of Dogme 95. Ulrich Thomsen excels as the prodigal son who passes from reluctant duty to ruthless obsession as he returns from exile in Sweden to run the family firm. However, he so dominates proceedings that both Ghita Norby and Lisa Werlinder are reduced to caricatures as his scheming mother and despairing wife. The corporate

  U SUITABLE FOR ALL   **Uc** SUITABLE ESPECIALLY FOR YOUNG CHILDREN (DVD ONLY)   **PG** PARENTAL GUIDANCE   **12A** UNDER 12s TO BE ACCOMPANIED (CINEMA ONLY)

shenanigans are also a touch formulaic, but the film is still scripted and played with spirit. DP Danish, Swedish, French +subtitles. Violence. **DVD**

Ulrich Thomsen *Christoffer* • Lisa Werlinder *Maria* • Ghita Norby *Annelise* • Lars Brygmann *Ulrik* • Karina Skands *Benedikte* ■ *Dir* Per Fly • *Scr* Per Fly, Kim Leona, Mogens Rukov, Dorte Hogh

L'Inhumaine ★★★★
Silent melodrama
1923 · Fr · BW and Tinted · 130min

While not perhaps the most ambitious or accomplished experiment of the French Impressionist era, this is certainly the most artful. With a score by Darius Milhaud, exteriors designed by Robert Mallet-Stephens, a Cubist laboratory by Fernand Léger, and Georgette Leblanc's apartment given an Art Deco look by Alberto Cavalcanti, Marcel L'Herbier's silent (and in some prints tinted) melodrama has avant-garde written all over it. However, the tale of the singer who is saved from the clutches of maharajah Philippe Hériat by noble scientist Jaque Catelain is also notable for its audacious visual abstraction and the precision of its rapid cross-cutting. DP

Georgette Leblanc *Claire Lescot* • Jaque Catelain *Einar Norsen* • Marcelle Pradot *L'Innocente* • Philippe Hériat *Djorah de Manilha* • Léonid Walter de Malte *Kranine* ■ *Dir* Marcel L'Herbier • *Scr* Marcel L'Herbier, from a story by Pierre Mac Orlan [Pierre Dumarchais], Mme Georgette Leblanc-Maeterlink

Initial D – Drift Racer ★★12
Action drama   2005 · HK · Colour · 108min

This pedestrian road-racing drama isn't what you'd expect from the directors of the sophisticated *Infernal Affairs* trilogy. It's not so much fast and furious as slow and tedious. Taiwanese pop star Jay Chou plays a teen delivery boy who unwittingly earns the title of "Racing God" after perfecting the technique of drifting – putting a car into high-speed, controlled slides around bends. This dated and flat film never generates an adrenaline-rush thrill. SF Cantonese +subtitles. Swearing. **DVD**

Jay Chou *Takumi Fujiwara* • Anne Suzuki *Natsuki Mogi* • Edison Chen *Ryousuke Takahasi* • Anthony Wong (1) *Bunta Fujiwara* • Shawn Yue *Takeshi Nakazato* • Chapman To *Itsuki Tachibana* • Jordan Chan *Kyouichi Sudou* • Kenny Bee *Yuuichi Tachibana* ■ *Dir* Andrew Lau, Alan Mak • *Scr* Felix Chong, from the comic book by Shuichi Shigeno

The Initiation ★★18
Horror   1984 · US · Colour · 92min

Daphne Zuniga is the amnesiac sorority sister up to her pretty neck in bad-taste college pranks in this tacky *Nightmare on Elm Street* clone. The "Repressed Desires" costume party has to be seen to be believed, but nothing else is worth the effort in this lame stalk-and-slash item, where most of the horror takes place off screen. Vera Miles adds a touch of class to the mayhem. AJ Violence. **DVD**

Vera Miles *Frances Fairchild* • Clu Gulager *Dwight Fairchild* • Daphne Zuniga *Kelly Terry* • James Read *Peter* • Marilyn Kagan *Marcia* • Patti Heider *Nurse* • Robert Dowdell *Jason Randall* • Frances Peterson *Megan* ■ *Dir* Larry Stewart • *Scr* Charles Pratt Jr

Inkheart ★★★PG
Fantasy adventure
2007 · Ger/US · Colour · 101min

Despite flourishes of CGI, the power of the written word is what drives this fantasy adventure. But perhaps not fast enough. Based on Cornelia Funke's novel, the film stars Brendan Fraser as Mo Folchart, father to the inquisitive young Meggie (Eliza Bennett). Mo is nicknamed "Silvertongue" thanks to his ability to bring storybook characters to life. Sadly, the mythical beings he conjures (including a typically villainous Andy Serkis as the evil Capricorn) are imprisoned with his wife (Sienna Guillory) within the pages of the book, *Inkheart*. Director Iain Softley's adaptation of the bestseller is often uneven, but he does provide enough

magic and whimsy (not to mention a batty Helen Mirren) to keep the kids enchanted. SP **DVD** **BLU**

Brendan Fraser *Mo Folchart* • Paul Bettany *Dustfinger* • Helen Mirren *Elinor Loredan* • Jim Broadbent *Fenoglio* • Andy Serkis *Capricorn* • Eliza Hope Bennett [Eliza Bennett] *Meggie Folchart* ■ *Dir* Iain Softley • *Scr* David Lindsay-Abaire, from the novel by Cornelia Funke

Inland Empire ★★★★15
Mystery drama
2006 · US/Fr/Pol · Colour · 172min

Five years after *Mulholland Drive*, indie icon David Lynch returns to the big screen with his most purposely inscrutable project yet. A surreal, three-hour drama shot on digital video, it's an atmospheric enigma that's more art than entertainment. Laura Dern is astonishing as Hollywood actress Nikki Grace, who faces an escalating nightmare after winning a coveted role in a cursed studio production. Fans of the writer/director's early work, such as *Eraserhead*, will be delighted to see him revisit his experimental roots, delivering a free-flowing tale that is visually bewitching, darkly comic and frequently terrifying. Anybody else is likely to be bored and baffled, lost like Nikki herself among the melding realities, talking rabbits and other dreamlike quirks. SF English, Polish +subtitles. **DVD** **BLU**

Laura Dern *Nikki Grace/Susan Blue* • Jeremy Irons *Kingsley Stewart* • Justin Theroux *Devon Berk/Billy Side* • Harry Dean Stanton *Freddie Howard* • Terryn Westbrook *Chelsi* • Julia Ormond *Doris Side* • Diane Ladd *Marilyn Levens* • William H Macy *Announcer* ■ *Dir/Scr* David Lynch

Inn for Trouble ★★U
Comedy   1960 · UK · BW · 98min

This movie spin-off from *The Larkins*, the popular sitcom of the late 1950s, moved the family away from 66 Sycamore Street and into a country pub, and that's where the problems begin. One of the series' great strengths was its portrait of a typical urban neighbourhood, populated by familiar characters. A whole new world had to be created here, however, with only Pa and Ma (David Kossoff and Peggy Mount) and Eddie (Shaun O'Riordan) providing continuity. Even the presence of Leslie Phillips and Charles Hawtrey can't make up for the general lifelessness. DP

Peggy Mount *Ada Larkins* • David Kossoff *Alf Larkins* • Leslie Phillips *John Belcher* • Glyn Owen *Lord Bill Osborne* • Yvonne Monlaur *Yvette* • Charles Hawtrey *Sid* • AE Matthews *Sir Hector Gore-Blandish* • Shaun O'Riordan *Eddie Larkins* • Ronan O'Casey *Jeff Rogers* ■ *Dir* CM Pennington-Richards • *Scr* Fred Robinson, from his TV series *The Larkins*

The Inn of the Sixth Happiness ★★★★PG
Biographical romantic drama
1958 · UK · Colour · 151min

Ingrid Bergman's screen appeal was usually based on the vulnerability of her characters, so for her to present the tenacity and courage of Gladys Aylward, the domestic servant who set out to bring Christianity to the peasants of China, was a considerable challenge. It's a glamorised portrayal (and one with which Aylward was not completely satisfied), but it's also a gritty and completely sympathetic performance, backed by some exceptional support playing, notably from Athene Seyler. DP **DVD**

Ingrid Bergman *Gladys Aylward* • Curt Jurgens *Captain Lin Nan* • Robert Donat *Mandarin* • Ronald Squire *Sir Francis Jamison* • Noel Hood *Miss Thompson* • Athene Seyler *Mrs Lawson* • Burt Kwouk *Li* ■ *Dir* Mark Robson • *Scr* Isobel Lennart, from the novel *The Small Woman* by Alan Burgess

The Inner Circle ★★★15
Drama   1991 · It/US · Colour · 131min

While Nikita Mikhalkov remained in Russia and went on to win an Oscar for the sublime *Burnt by the Sun*, his brother Andrei Konchalovsky rather slipped into a cinematic backwater during his US exile. He

returned home to shoot this muddled but intriguing story about a nobody who allows delusions of grandeur to destroy his life after he is appointed as Stalin's projectionist. Tom Hulce gives an intelligent performance as Ivan, while Lolita Davidovich is truly touching as his wife, risking everything for the sake of a Jewish orphan. DP

Tom Hulce *Ivan Sanshin* • Lolita Davidovich *Anastasia Sanshin* • Bob Hoskins *Beria* • Aleksandr Zbruev *Stalin* • Feodor Chaliapin Jr *Professor Bartnev* ■ *Dir* Andrei Konchalovsky • *Scr* Andrei Konchalovsky, Anatoli Usov

Innerspace ★★★PG
Science-fiction comedy
1987 · US · Colour · 114min

This attempt to update *Fantastic Voyage* doesn't measure up to director Joe Dante's best work, but it's still a notch above the usual Hollywood fodder. Dennis Quaid is the hotshot military man who is miniaturised and mistakenly pumped into the body of lowly supermarket clerk Martin Short. The effects are excellent and Dante's sly humour shines through occasionally, but it lacks the anarchy the director is noted for and Short's hysterics begin to grate. JF Some swearing, violence. **DVD**

Dennis Quaid *Lt Tuck Pendelton* • Martin Short *Jack Putter* • Meg Ryan *Lydia Maxwell* • Kevin McCarthy *Victor Scrimshaw* • Fiona Lewis *Dr Margaret Canker* • Vernon Wells *Mr Igoe* ■ *Dir* Joe Dante • *Scr* Jeffrey Boam, Chip Proser, from a story by Chip Proser

The Innkeepers ★★★15
Horror thriller   2011 · US · Colour · 101min

Ti West's affectionate throwback to 1970s schlock will either appeal as an engaging character study or test the patience of anyone waiting for something to actually happen. After a century of service, the Yankee Pedlar Inn is closing down, prompting the last remaining employees to uncover proof that it is one of the USA's most haunted hotels. Once the amateur ghostbusters begin experiencing alarming events, and scares start to percolate through the panic, it becomes a weirdly effective, if rather quaint, exercise in nostalgia-brushed spookiness. With its sparkling dialogue and oddball casting (including *Top Gun's* Kelly McGillis), this is like *The Shining* but done in an indie slacker style. AJ Swearing, sexual references. **DVD** **BLU**

Sara Paxton *Claire* • Pat Healy *Luke* • Kelly McGillis *Leanne Rease-Jones* • George Riddle *Old man* • John Speredakos *Officer Mitchell* • Brenda Cooney *Madeline O'Malley* ■ *Dir/Scr* Ti West

Innocence ★★★12
Romantic drama
2000 · Aus/Bel · Colour · 95min

Paul Cox's gentle late-life romance cross-cuts between postwar Belgium and millennial Adelaide to prove that true love can never die. Julia Blake and Charles "Bud" Tingwell provide a touching insight into the depth of emotion that can still be stirred in old age, although Cox doesn't quite trust us to relate to their twilight canoodling and repeatedly flashes back to show their younger selves recklessly indulging their passion. With Terry Norris also ringing true as the husband who has long shared Blake's life, but not her bed, this is delicate without ever being patronising. DP

Julia Blake *Claire* • Charles "Bud" Tingwell [Charles Tingwell] *Andreas* • Terry Norris *John* • Robert Menzies *David* • Marta Dusseldorp *Monique* ■ *Dir/Scr* Paul Cox

Innocence ★★15
Surreal drama
2004 · Fr/Bel/UK · Colour · 114min

This dreamy film takes place in a mysterious, isolated girls' boarding school, where each new pupil arrives in a coffin and then is never permitted to leave the grounds. There's no explanation for any of the strangeness, nor is there a coherent plot. Instead, the picture offers a series of flowing, interlocking experiences, viewed

through the eyes of the latest arrival (Zoé Auclair). This exquisite feature is extremely beautiful, but for most viewers it's likely to be a case of style over baffling substance. SF French +subtitles. Nudity, sex scenes. **DVD**

Zoé Auclair *Iris* • Bérangère Haubruge *Bianca* • Léa Bridarolli *Alice* • Marion Cotillard *Mademoiselle Eva* • Hélène de Fougerolles *Mademoiselle Edith* • Ana Palomo-Diaz *Nadja* • Astrid Homme *Rose* ■ *Dir* Lucile Hadzihalilovic • *Scr* Lucile Hadzihalilovic, from the novella *Mine-Haha* by Frank Wedekind

The Innocent ★★★15
Period drama   1984 · UK · Colour · 95min

Set in the Yorkshire Dales, this coming-of-age saga takes place in the early 1930s against the backdrop of the Depression. The central character, Tim (Andrew Hawley), suffers from epilepsy, and his problems are compounded by his constantly arguing parents and the continuing affair between a family friend and a married woman. Certainly a change of pace for John MacKenzie, director of *The Long Good Friday*. His film also features early appearances from Liam Neeson and Miranda Richardson. AT

Andrew Hawley *Tim Dobson* • Kika Markham *Mrs Dobson* • Kate Foster *Win* • Liam Neeson *John Carns* • Patrick Daley *Eddie King* • Paul Askew *Stanley* • Tom Bell *Frank Dobson* • Miranda Richardson *Mary Turner* ■ *Dir* John Mackenzie (1) • *Scr* Ray Jenkins, from the novel *The Aura and the Kingfisher* by Tom Hart

The Innocent ★★15
Thriller   1993 · UK/Ger · Colour · 113min

Despite its impressive cast, this brooding, rather old-fashioned Cold War thriller never really grips. In an odd bit of casting, the always impressive American actor Campbell Scott plays an English technician in 1950s Berlin who gets caught up in a tortuous espionage plot instigated by CIA man Anthony Hopkins. While director John Schlesinger captures the grey chill of the time and place, he gets lost in the detail. JF

Anthony Hopkins *Bob Glass* • Isabella Rossellini *Maria* • Campbell Scott *Leonard Markham* • Ronald Nitschke *Otto* • Hart Bochner *Russell* • James Grant *MacNamee* • Jeremy Sinden *Captain Lofting* • Richard Durden *Black* ■ *Dir* John Schlesinger • *Scr* Ian McEwan, from his novel

Innocent Blood ★★★15
Comedy horror   1992 · US · Colour · 110min

Blood flies everywhere as the horror movie and the gangster film collide head on in this atmospheric offering from John Landis. From the moment Anne Parillaud sinks her teeth into hoodlum Robert Loggia, it's clear that this isn't going to be your average vampire chiller. The whole production drips with style as Loggia chomps his way towards fulfilling his ambition of controlling the underworld by means of the undead. Parillaud slinks through the picture, falling for Anthony LaPaglia in the process, but it's the excesses of Loggia and crooked lawyer Don Rickles that command the attention. DP Violence, swearing, sex scenes, nudity.

Anne Parillaud *Marie* • Anthony LaPaglia *Joe Gennaro* • Robert Loggia *Sal "The Shark" Macelli* • David Proval *Lenny* • Rocco Sisto *Gilly* • Don Rickles *Emmanuel Bergman* • Chazz Palminteri *Tony* • Tony Sirico *Jacko* ■ *Dir* John Landis • *Scr* Michael Wolk

Innocent Lies ★★18
Period crime mystery
1995 · UK/Fr · Colour · 84min

Supposedly inspired by the country house whodunnits of Agatha Christie, Patrick Dewolf's period curio is much darker and far less well-constructed than anything concocted by the grand old lady of crime. Indeed, this is played at such a hysterical pitch that you could be forgiven for thinking it was a parody. As the cop investigating the death of his colleague, Adrian Dunbar behaves most peculiarly, especially in the presence of the deranged Gabrielle Anwar. Only Joanna Lumley emerges with any credit as her viciously snobby mother. DP Sex scenes, violence.

Adrian Dunbar *Alan Cross* • Florence Hoath *Angela Cross* • Sophie Aubry *Solange Montfort* • Joanna Lumley *Lady Helena Graves* • Gabrielle Anwar *Celia Graves* • Alexis Denisof *Christopher Wood* • Stephen Dorff *Jeremy Graves* ■ *Dir* Patrick Dewolf • *Scr* Kerry Crabbe, Patrick Dewolf

An Innocent Man ★★★ 18
Crime thriller　　1989 · US · Colour · 108min

Tom Selleck attempted to toughen up his image with this hard-edged thriller, but it was only a partial success. He plays an airline mechanic who is framed by two bent cops and finds himself in prison, where he nurses a desire for revenge. Director Peter Yates is an old hand when it comes to this sort of thing, and he stages the action scenes with some panache. Selleck, however, isn't entirely convincing as the innocent man who is transformed from a nice middle-class chap to a hard-bitten inmate. JF Violence, swearing. *DVD*

Tom Selleck *Jimmie Rainwood* • F Murray Abraham *Virgil Cane* • Laila Robins *Kate Rainwood* • David Rasche *Mike Parnell* • Richard Young *Danny Scalise* • Badja Djola *John Fitzgerald* • Todd Graff *Robby* ■ *Dir* Peter Yates • *Scr* Larry Brothers

Innocent Moves ★★★★ PG
Biographical drama　1993 · US · Colour · 105min

Released in the US as *Searching for Bobby Fischer*, this marked the directorial debut of Steven Zaillian, who had just completed scriptwriting duties on *Schindler's List*. This true story not only reveals the unexpectedly ruthless side of competitive chess, but also explores the dangers of parents using children to fulfil their own ambitions. Conrad Hall's Oscar-nominated photography is as impressive as the acting, with young Max Pomeranc, himself a top-ranking player, upstaging the likes of Joe Mantegna and Ben Kingsley. DP *DVD*

Max Pomeranc *Josh Waitzkin* • Joe Mantegna *Fred Waitzkin* • Joan Allen *Bonnie Waitzkin* • Ben Kingsley *Bruce Pandolfini* • Laurence Fishburne *Vinnie* • Robert Stephens *Poe's teacher* • David Paymer *Kalev* ■ *Dir* Steven Zaillian • *Scr* Steven Zaillian, from the autobiographical novel by Fred Waitzkin

Innocent Sinners ★★ U
Drama　　　　1957 · UK · BW · 95min

The gentle talent of British director Philip Leacock was responsible for classic films about childhood (*The Kidnappers*) and racism (*Take a Giant Step*). This engaging film – based on a novel by Rumer Godden, another expert on youthful emotions – tells the slightly idealised story tells of a teenage girl who creates a garden in the ruins of a bombed church only to find herself in trouble with the authorities. Typically of the director, it is compassionate and nicely acted. BB

June Archer *Lovejoy Mason* • Flora Robson *Olivia Chesney* • David Kossoff *Mr Vincent* • Barbara Mullen *Mrs Vincent* • Catherine Lacey *Angela Chesney* • Susan Beaumont *Liz* ■ *Dir* Philip Leacock • *Scr* Neil Paterson, from the novel *An Episode of Sparrows* by Rumer Godden

The Innocent Sleep ★★★ 15
Mystery thriller　　1995 · UK · Colour · 95min

Rupert Graves plays a homeless man in this downbeat British thriller, set in London's Cardboard City. Graves is enjoying the five-star facilities of a warehouse underneath Tower Bridge when he realises that an assassination is in progress. He gets away but, when he goes to the police, he discovers that the detective heading the investigation was actually involved in the killing. Scott Michell's direction catches the downtrodden atmosphere of London's underworld, and he's helped by a good cast. TH

Annabella Sciorra *Billie Hayman* • Rupert Graves *Alan Terry* • Michael Gambon *Matheson* • Franco Nero *Cavani* • John Hannah *James* • Oliver Cotton *Lusano* • Tony Bluto *Thorn* • Paul Brightwell *Pelham* ■ *Dir* Scott Michell • *Scr* Ray Villis

L'Innocente ★★★★ 15
Period drama　　1976 · It · Colour · 123min

Luchino Visconti's last film is one of his best and was clearly the inspiration behind Martin Scorsese's *The Age of Innocence*. The film saw the baroque director returning to his favourite theme: the decline of turn-of-the-20th-century Italian aristocracy and its implications for today's society. Giancarlo Giannini plays the adulterous Sicilian gentleman who is mortified by his wife's own sexual misconduct, while Laura Antonelli is magnificent as the unfaithful spouse. This is a visually stunning meditation on mores and manners. AJ Italian +subtitles. *DVD*

Giancarlo Giannini *Tullio Hermil* • Laura Antonelli *Giuliana Hermil* • Jennifer O'Neill *Teresa Raffo* • Rina Morelli *Tullio's mother* • Massimo Girotti *Count Stefano Egano* • Didier Haudepin *Federico Hermil* • Marie Dubois *Princess* ■ *Dir* Luchino Visconti • *Scr* Suso Cecchi D'Amico, Enrico Medioli, Luchino Visconti, from a novel by Gabriele D'Annunzio

The Innocents ★★★★★ 12
Horror　　　　1961 · UK · BW · 95min

As this terrifying but neglected picture proves, there was much more to British cinema in the early 1960s than angry young men. Truman Capote and John Mortimer both had a hand in the script for this adaptation of Henry James's *The Turn of the Screw*, and the film bristles with menace as it draws you inexorably towards its chilling conclusion. Rarely has horror looked so beautiful, with cinematographer Freddie Francis reinforcing the eerie atmosphere. Deborah Kerr is excellent as the haunted governess, Pamela Franklin and Martin Stephens send shivers down the spine as her sinister charges, and Peter Wyngarde is evil personified as Quint. DP *DVD* *BL*

Deborah Kerr *Miss Giddens* • Michael Redgrave *Uncle* • Peter Wyngarde *Peter Quint* • Megs Jenkins *Mrs Grose* • Martin Stephens *Miles* • Pamela Franklin *Flora* • Clytie Jessop *Miss Jessel* • Isla Cameron *Anna* ■ *Dir* Jack Clayton • *Scr* William Archibald, Truman Capote, John Mortimer, from the novella *The Turn of the Screw* by Henry James

Les Innocents aux Mains Sales ★★ 15
Crime drama　1975 · Fr/It/W Ger · Colour · 120min

This is one melodrama that Rod Steiger wanted to wash his hands of. In a faintly risible plot, he's the husband whose wife (Romy Schneider) and her lover (Paolo Giusti) conspire to murder for money. Director Claude Chabrol was nearly as bored with the idea as audiences (he played poker while making the film). Nevertheless, he manages to create some genuinely creepy moments, while Steiger puts together a professional performance. TH In French. *DVD*

Rod Steiger *Louis Wormser* • Romy Schneider *Julie Wormser* • Paolo Giusti *Jeff Marle* • Jean Rochefort *Lawyer legal* • François Maistre *Inspector Lamy* • Pierre Santini *Inspector Villon* • François Perrot *Georges Thorent* • Hans Christian Blech *Judge* ■ *Dir* Claude Chabrol • *Scr* Claude Chabrol, from the novel *Damned Innocents* by Richard Neely

Innocents in Paris ★★★
Comedy　　　1953 · UK · BW · 102min

Considering the quality of the cast, this episodic British comedy could have been a great deal funnier than it is. Following a party of tourists on their weekend in Paris, Anatole de Grunwald's script has a pseudo-Ealing cosiness that prevents it from throwing caution to the wind and becoming downright comic. There are neat touches from Alastair Sim seeking to inebriate a Soviet politician and from Margaret Rutherford as an amateur artist at the Louvre, but the rest of the romance and misadventures lack a vital spark. DP *DVD*

Alastair Sim *Sir Norman Barker* • Margaret Rutherford *Gladys Inglott* • Ronald Shiner *Dicky Bird* • Claire Bloom *Susan Robbins* • Claude Dauphin *Max de Lorne* • Laurence Harvey *François* • Jimmy Edwards *Captain George*

Stilton • James Copeland *Andy MacGregor* • Gaby Bruyere *Josette* ■ *Dir* Gordon Parry • *Scr* Anatole de Grunwald

InRealLife ★★★ 15
Documentary　　2013 · UK · Colour · 89min

Director Beeban Kidron's documentary looks at the impact social media is having on human communication, but she tries to tackle so many hot-button topics that she can't do justice to any of them. As various professors and programmers lament the hijacking of the internet by commercial forces, a teenage boy concedes that porn sites have clouded his view of love and a dropout accepts that his gaming addiction cost him his place at Oxford. While Julian Assange is probably correct to assert that the net is "the greatest spying machine" ever created, more attention might have been paid to the benefits of new technologies, which are here encapsulated in the sweet online romance between gay teens Tom and Dan. DP Swearing, a sex scene.

■ *Dir* Beeban Kidron

The Insatiable Moon ★★★ 15
Drama　　　2010 · NZ · Colour · 101min

Rawiri Paratene, star of *Whale Rider*, anchors this charming New Zealand indie that's small in budget but huge in heart. He delivers an affecting performance as a mentally ill Maori man who's convinced he's God's second son. After beginning an unlikely romance with an unhappy woman, the insightful Aucklander sets about spreading more love by trying to save the threatened boarding house he shares with his richly entertaining mates. Adapted by Mike Riddell from his first novel and unevenly directed by his wife Rosemary (whose day job is being a judge), it's an original and passionate mix of spirituality and social realism that's packed with little moments of magic. SF Swearing.

Rawiri Paratene *Arthur* • Sara Wiseman *Margaret* • Ian Mune *Norm* • Greg Johnson *Bob* • Jason Hoyte *Kevin* ■ *Dir* Rosemary Riddell • *Scr* Mike Riddell, from his novel

Inseminoid ★★ 18
Science-fiction horror　1981 · UK · Colour · 88min

The basic concepts of *Alien* are taken to the sleaziest and goriest extremes in director Norman J Warren's addition to the murderous space-creature genre. Shot entirely in Chiselhurst caves, it stars Judy Geeson and Stephanie Beacham as two members of an interstellar archaeological mission. Geeson is impregnated by a nasty ET and mutates into a killer, horrifically murdering anyone who threatens her impending motherhood. The pace is fast enough to cover the film's more ridiculous aspects. AJ

Judy Geeson *Sandy* • Robin Clarke *Mark* • Jennifer Ashley *Holly* • Stephanie Beacham *Kate* • Steven Grives *Gary* • Barrie Houghton *Karl* ■ *Dir* Norman J Warren • *Scr* Nick Maley, Gloria Maley

Inserts ★★★ 18
Period drama　1975 · UK/US · Colour · 111min

This intriguing but ultimately disappointing drama looks at 1930s Hollywood, where has-been director Richard Dreyfuss is making a porno movie with a gay actor and a former silent movie queen. The decision to limit the picture to a small cast and a single interior set at a British studio may be in homage to Harold Pinter, or it may just betray a lack of finance. Even so, one sorely misses the soft light and the waving palms of Hollywood, and Bob Hoskins with an American accent doesn't help matters. Dreyfuss, though, is excellent, creating a richly complex character. AT

Richard Dreyfuss *Boy Wonder* • Jessica Harper *Cathy* • Stephen Davies *Rex* • Veronica Cartwright *Harlene* • Bob Hoskins *Big Mac* ■ *Dir/Scr* John Byrum

Inside Daisy Clover ★★ 12
Period drama　　1965 · US · Colour · 123min

Gavin Lambert's novel about the turbulent career of a precocious Hollywood musical star of the 1930s had potential to be a lot of fun. Unfortunately in the hands of director Robert Mulligan it treads an uncomfortable line between satire and drama, with disappointing results. Natalie Wood, by then a movie veteran of more than 20 years, is Daisy and Robert Redford plays her handsome husband, whose sexual orientation makes him less than an ideal spouse. The two stars reteamed soon after for *This Property Is Condemned*. TH

Natalie Wood *Daisy Clover* • Christopher Plummer *Raymond Swan* • Robert Redford *Wade Lewis* • Roddy McDowall *Walter Baines* • Ruth Gordon *The Dealer* • Katharine Bard *Melora Swan* ■ *Dir* Robert Mulligan • *Scr* Gavin Lambert, from his novel

Inside Deep Throat ★★ 18
Documentary　　2005 · US · Colour · 85min

Shot for $25,000 in 1972 by hairdresser-turned-director Gerard Damiano, *Deep Throat* became a $600-million phenomenon that brought pornography to mainstream America. The making of that notoriously amateur hard-core comedy, its acceptance as "porno-chic", the rise and fall of star Linda Lovelace and inevitable moral backlash are all brought together in this unfocused documentary. Directors Fenton Bailey and Randy Barbato ambitiously attempt to cover all bases in their efforts to put the landmark movie in historical context. Pop culturists will find it entertaining enough, if overlong and superficial in key areas. AJ Sex scenes, nudity. *DVD*

Dennis Hopper *Narrator* • Gerard Damiano • Gore Vidal • John Waters (2) *John Waters* • Hugh Hefner • Linda Lovelace ■ *Dir/Scr* Fenton Bailey, Randy Barbato

Inside I'm Dancing ★★★ 15
Comedy drama
2004 · UK/Ire/Ger · Colour · 99min

This tragicomic tale of the odd-couple friendship that develops between two severely disabled young men could have ended up as a thoroughly mawkish affair. James McAvoy is the outgoing, rebellious patient with muscular dystrophy, whose arrival at a sleepy residential care home is a tonic for diffident youth Steven Robertson (whose character has cerebral palsy). Director Damien O'Donnell has come up with a worthwhile drama that may not tread any new ground, but at least goes over old territory with skill and style. DA Swearing. *DVD*

James McAvoy *Rory O'Shea* • Steven Robertson *Michael Connolly* • Romola Garai *Siobhan* • Gerard McSorley *Fergus Connolly* • Tom Hickey *Con O'Shea* • Brenda Fricker *Eileen* ■ *Dir* Damien O'Donnell • *Scr* Jeffrey Caine, from a story by Christian O'Reilly

Inside Job ★★★★ 12
Documentary　　2010 · US · Colour · 104min

Hollywood was hit just as hard as any other industry by the global financial crisis of 2008, but while it might be a little too soon for a compelling drama about the situation, this complex documentary certainly tackles the subject head-on. Calmly narrated by Matt Damon, Charles Ferguson's powerful film explains that Wall Street's meltdown wasn't simply an unfortunate fluke but the inevitable consequence of a flawed and breathtakingly manipulated system. Worse still, Ferguson reveals how unscrupulous bankers operate with impunity, working in the knowledge that governments will always bail them out. It's a fascinating but terrifying insight into a very murky world. DW Sexual references, drug abuse. *DVD*

Matt Damon *Narrator* ■ *Dir* Charles Ferguson

Inside Llewyn Davis
★★★★★ 15

Comedy drama 2013 · US · Colour · 100min

The backbiting 1960s New York folk scene is the setting for one of the Coen brothers' most soulful films to date. It's a low-key comedy of sorts about a Greenwich Village singer and guitarist (Oscar Isaac) trying to find a balance between artistic integrity and mainstream success. Deadpan and dry-witted as ever, it hides a rich seam of sadness that comes to the fore whenever Isaac sings. The music choices alone will ensure this hauntingly beautiful film will live a long and lasting life. DW Swearing, sexual references, some violence. DVD BL

Oscar Isaac *Llewyn Davis* · Carey Mulligan *Jean Berkey* · John Goodman *Roland Turner* · Garrett Hedlund *Johnny Five* · Justin Timberlake *Jim Berkey* · F Murray Abraham *Bud Grossman* ■ *Dir/Scr* Ethan Coen, Joel Coen

The Inside Man
★★ 15

Political thriller 1984 · Swe/UK · Colour · 89min

Two years before his career-reviving performance in David Lynch's *Blue Velvet*, Dennis Hopper turned up in this Anglo-Swedish co-production as a US government agent assigned to track down a top-secret laser device stolen from a Swedish laboratory. As the nominal hero (a naive young marine caught up in the plot), Swedish actor Cory Molder chews the scenery for all he's worth, yet Gösta Ekman's policeman is nicely understated. Actor-turned-director Tom Clegg cut his teeth on such home-grown crime yarns as *McVicar*, but here the low budget and stilted dialogue ensure that he provides too little tension and even fewer thrills. SuR Some violence, swearing, nudity.

Dennis Hopper *Miller* · Hardy Kruger *Mandell* · Gösta Ekman (2) *Larsson* · Cory Molder *Kallin* · David Wilson *Baxter* · Celia Gregory *Theresa* ■ *Dir* Tom Clegg · *Scr* Alan Plater, from a story by William Aldridge, Tom Clegg, from the novel *The Fighter* by Harry Kullman

Inside Man
★★★★ 15

Crime thriller 2006 · US · Colour · 123min

Spike Lee's slick heist movie stars the sharply charismatic Denzel Washington as a police hostage negotiator called in after Clive Owen's criminal crew lays siege to a Manhattan bank. What begins as a routine scenario suddenly becomes a powder keg of corruption and intrigue, as a shady power broker (Jodie Foster) arrives to cut an independent deal with the robbers on behalf of the bank's chairman. The subsequent cat-and-mouse game has character-driven punch, plus a dynamic visual and structural style that intensifies the twisting drama. SF Violence, swearing. DVD BL

Denzel Washington *Detective Keith Frazier* · Clive Owen *Dalton Russell* · Jodie Foster *Madeleine White* · Willem Dafoe *Captain John Darius* · Chiwetel Ejiofor *Detective Bill Mitchell* · Christopher Plummer *Arthur Case* ■ *Dir* Spike Lee · *Scr* Russell Gewirtz

Inside Moves: the Guys from Max's Bar
★★★

Drama 1980 · US · Colour · 113min

This study of disability suffers from the same surfeit of sentiment that blights so many Hollywood attempts to be liberal and profound. Valerie Curtin and Barry Levinson, at the time a husband-and-wife team, have scripted several eye-opening scenes, however, while director Richard Donner brings realism to proceedings by de-glamorising his Los Angeles locations. Diana Scarwid was nominated for a best supporting actress Oscar, but it's the relationship between failed suicide John Savage and would-be basketball star David Morse that provides the dramatic core. DP

John Savage *Roary* · David Morse *Jerry Maxwell* · Diana Scarwid *Louise* · Amy Wright *Ann* · Tony Burton *Lucius Porter* · Bill Henderson *Blue Lewis* · Steve Kahan *Burt* · Jack O'Leary *Max Willatowski* ■ *Dir* Richard Donner · *Scr* Valerie Curtin, Barry Levinson, from a novel by Todd Walton

Inside Out
★★ PG

Adventure comedy 1975 · UK · Colour · 93min

Telly Savalas's popularity at the time as TV cop Kojak provided this routine caper movie with a modest audience in cinemas. It's a blatant rip-off of another Savalas picture, *The Dirty Dozen*, with several dubious types going after a stash of Nazi gold in the Cold War era. James Mason and Robert Culp bring some extra class to the proceedings. AT Some violence, swearing.

Telly Savalas *Harry Morgan* · James Mason *Ernst Furben* · Robert Culp *Sly Wells* · Aldo Ray *Sergeant Prior* · Günter Meisner *Schmidt* · Adrian Hoven *Dr Maar* · Wolfgang Lukschy *Reinhard Holtz* ■ *Dir* Peter Duffell · *Scr* Judd Bernard, Stephen Schneck

Inside Out
★★★★★ U

Animated comedy adventure 2015 · US · Colour · 90min

Another superbly rendered masterwork from Pixar, pulling off their classic trick of delivering captivating fun for kids along with wickedly smart insights. Here, the main action happens within the brain of an ice-hockey-obsessed tomboy, Riley, where emotions are comedically personified and thrown into conflict. It's the family move from Minnesota to San Francisco that causes this "head trip" when the primal instincts of Joy (voiced by comedian Amy Poehler) and Sadness (Phyllis Smith) are accidentally ejected from Memory HQ, leaving Fear (Bill Hader), Anger (Lewis Black) and Disgust (Mindy Kaling) in charge. Once more, the level of conceptual cleverness and ingenious visual design creates real magic. AJ DVD BL 3D

Amy Poehler *Joy* · Phyllis Smith *Sadness* · Bill Hader *Fear* · Lewis Black *Anger* · Mindy Kaling *Disgust* · Kaitlyn Dias *Riley* · Diane Lane *Mom* · Kyle MacLachlan *Dad* ■ *Dir* Pete Docter, Ronaldo Del Carmen · *Scr* Pete Docter, Josh Cooley, Meg LeFauve, from a story by Docter, Ronnie del Carmen

Inside Paris
★★★★ 15

Drama 2006 · Fr · Colour · 89min

Writer/director Christophe Honoré plunders the *nouvelle vague* for this ambitious bid to contrast the romance of Paris at Christmas with the memories and regrets that affect so many at this deeply personal time. Those unfamiliar with Godard, Truffaut and Rivette in their prime will doubtless revel in the audiovisual ingenuity that Honoré uses to capture the exuberance of the city, as footloose 20-something Jonathan (Louis Garrel) flits between his many lovers. But those more familiar with such bravura homages will find brother Paul (Romain Duris) and his claustrophobic battle with depression more authentic and compelling. Beautifully photographed by Jean-Louis Vialard, nimbly edited by Chantal Hymans and jazzily scored by Alex Beaupain, this is both delicate and delightful. DP French +subtitles. DVD

Romain Duris *Paul* · Louis Garrel *Jonathan* · Guy Marchand *Mirko* · Joana Preiss *Anna* · Alice Butaud *Alice* · Marie-France Pisier *Mother* ■ *Dir/Scr* Christophe Honoré · *Cinematographer* Jean-Louis Vialard · *Music* Alex Beaupain · *Editor* Chantal Hymans

The Insider
★★★★★ 15

Drama based on a true story 1999 · US · Colour · 151min

Big Tobacco comes under the spotlight in Michael Mann's virtuoso ethical drama, based on the true case of a whistle-blower whose life was ruined when he decided to tell all to *60 Minutes*. Russell Crowe plays Jeffrey Wigand, the sacked executive who went public with his firm's dark secrets, only to find his interview canned by network heads terrified of a potentially catastrophic law suit. Al Pacino sears the screen as Lowell Bergman, the producer who broke the story, while Christopher Plummer is superb as anchorman Mike Wallace. Mann has little interest in his female characters – Diane Venora is underused as Wigand's wife Liane – but this remains a dazzling exposé of money, morals and the media. NS Swearing. DVD

Al Pacino *Lowell Bergman* · Russell Crowe *Jeffrey Wigand* · Christopher Plummer *Mike Wallace* · Diane Venora *Liane Wigand* · Philip Baker Hall *Don Hewitt* · Lindsay Crouse *Sharon Tiller* · Debi Mazar *Debbie De Luca* · Stephen Tobolowsky *Eric Kluster* · Gina Gershon *Helen Caperelli* · Michael Gambon *Thomas Sandefur* · Rip Torn *John Scanlon* ■ *Dir* Michael Mann · *Scr* Eric Roth, Michael Mann, from the article *The Man Who New Too Much* by Marie Brenner

Insidious
★★★ 15

Supernatural horror thriller 2010 · US/Can · Colour · 98min

Oren Peli, writer/director of micro-budget haunted-house tale *Paranormal Activity*, is credited as a producer on this Hollywood take on his idea. Josh (Patrick Wilson) and Renai (Rose Byrne) are a normal married couple with three kids who, having moved house, find their new pad plagued by mysterious scratches, bangs and shifting furniture. For the first hour or so, the movie is basically a less restrained retread of Peli's earlier film and when this palls, director James Wan (co-creator of the *Saw* franchise) simply steals the last act of *Poltergeist*. Derivative as it is, *Insidious* is competent enough, there are a few genuine scares and the final shock twist is an effective cinematic sucker-punch. A sequel with the same main cast was released in autumn 2013. AS DVD BL

Patrick Wilson *Josh Lambert* · Rose Byrne *Renai Lambert* · Barbara Hershey *Lorraine Lambert* · Lin Shaye *Elise Rainier* · Ty Simpkins *Dalton Lambert* · Angus Sampson *Tucker* · Leigh Whannell *Specs* ■ *Dir* James Wan · *Scr* Leigh Whannell

Insidious: Chapter 2 ★★★ 15

Horror thriller 2013 · US · Colour · 101min

The original cast and crew return for another spook-house tour, rife with creaking doors, tinkling pianos and jumpy edits. Luckily, director James Wan is accomplished enough to assemble the largely generic elements into something that jangles the nerves without causing too much fearful distress. Picking up exactly where the first film ended, we find Josh Lambert (Patrick Wilson) returned from "The Further" possessed by the spirit of a serial-killer drag queen dubbed the "Bride in Black". The movie eventually descends into histrionic camp, but there's no denying Wan's gift for spectral sleight-of-hand. AJ Some violence, swearing. DVD BL

Patrick Wilson *Josh Lambert* · Rose Byrne *Renai Lambert* · Barbara Hershey *Lorraine Lambert* · Leigh Whannell *Specks* · Angus Sampson *Tucker* · Lin Shaye *Elise Rainier* ■ *Dir* James Wan · *Scr* Leigh Whannell

Insidious: Chapter 3 ★★★ 15

Horror 2015 · US/Can · Colour · 97min

Why did reclusive clairvoyant Elise Rainer step into the spooky spotlight and how did she meet that goofy ghostbusting duo? All is revealed in series writer/director Leigh Whannell's prequel taking place a few years before the Lambert haunting of 2010's original *Insidious*. Here, Elise (once more played with ghoulish gusto by Lin Shaye) comes out of terrified retirement to save a grieving teen (Stefanie Scott) from an evil entity which has attached itself after she tried to contact her dead mother. The menacing excitement and solid scares define Whannell's confident chiller, as she craftily revitalises that over-used cliché, the sudden car crash, making it a better than expected creep-fest. AJ DVD BL

Dermot Mulroney *Sean Brenner* · Stefanie Scott *Quinn Brenner* · Angus Sampson *Tucker* · Leigh Whannell *Specs* · Lin Shaye *Elise Rainier* ■ *Dir/Scr* Leigh Whannell

Insignificance
★★★★ 15

Comedy drama 1985 · UK · Colour · 103min

Director Nicolas Roeg's wild, wacky and wonderful chamber piece is an exploration of love, life and the whole damn thing. Set in a hotel room in 1954, Roeg assembles four characters who bear a striking resemblance to celebrities of that era. Theresa Russell is "Marilyn Monroe", whose interest in Michael Emil's "Einstein" extends beyond his theory of relativity. Tony Curtis is the Joe McCarthy clone, while Gary Busey is the Joe DiMaggio figure still pining for Marilyn. TH DVD

Gary Busey *Ballplayer* · Tony Curtis *Senator* · Michael Emil *Professor* · Theresa Russell *Actress* · Will Sampson *Elevator attendant* · Patrick Kilpatrick *Driver* ■ *Dir* Nicolas Roeg · *Scr* Terry Johnson, from his play

Insomnia
★★★ 15

Psychological crime thriller 1997 · Nor · Colour · 92min

Debutant director Erik Skjoldbjaerg pulls off something of a generic coup here, by staging a *film noir* in the relentless glare of the midnight sun. Set in an isolated town on the polar extremities, the action begins with a hunt for the killer of a teenage girl. But when city cop Stellan Skarsgård accidentally shoots his colleague during a bungled ambush, the emphasis shifts to his struggle to remain focused on the case while battling his suppressed sense of guilt. Dazzlingly photographed by Erling Thurmann-Andersen, this taut thriller stints on narrative complexity, but packs quite a psychological punch. DP Norwegian +subtitles. Some sex scenes. DVD

Stellan Skarsgård *Jonas Engström* · Sverre Anker Ousdal *Erik Vik* · Bjørn Floberg *Jon Holt* · Gisken Armand *Hilde Hagen* · Maria Bonnevie *Ane* · Maria Mathiesen *Tanja Lorentzen* ■ *Dir* Erik Skjoldbjaerg · *Scr* Nikolaj Frobenius, Erik Skjoldbjaerg

Insomnia
★★★★ 15

Psychological crime thriller 2002 · US · Colour · 113min

Based on the 1997 Norwegian blockbuster of the same name, Christopher Nolan's skilfully directed psychodrama proves that hit European movies can be remade successfully. Intensely gripping throughout and set in Alaska, this *noir* nightmare has hard-boiled LAPD detective Al Pacino sent to a small fishing town to investigate a brutal murder. When he mistakenly kills his partner on a fudged stakeout, the hunted killer (Robin Williams) blackmails him into pinning both deaths on someone else. And so a convoluted cat-and-mouse game begins with Pacino – terminally sleepless from the endless daylight – on dynamite form. AJ Violence, swearing, nudity. DVD

Al Pacino *Will Dormer* · Robin Williams *Walter Finch* · Hilary Swank *Ellie Burr* · Maura Tierney *Rachel Clement* · Martin Donovan (2) *Hap Eckhart* · Nicky Katt *Fred Duggar* · Jonathan Jackson *Randy Stetz* · Paul Dooley *Chief Charles Nyback* ■ *Dir* Christopher Nolan · *Scr* Hillary Seitz, from the 1997 film by Nikolaj Frobenius, Erik Skjoldbjaerg

Inspecteur Lavardin ★★★ 15

Crime mystery 1986 · Fr/Swi · Colour · 100min

In Claude Chabrol's sequel to *Cop au Vin*, Jean Poiret reprises his role as the unorthodox policeman. This time he investigates the murder of a famous Catholic writer whose naked body - with the word "pig" on a buttock - is found on a beach. Then Poiret discovers that the victim's wife, Bernadette Lafont, is an ex-girlfriend of his and the chief suspect. What follows is often quite grisly, decked out with eccentric characters. AT French +subtitles. DVD

Jean Poiret *Inspector Jean Lavardin* · Bernadette Lafont *Hélène Mons* · Jean-Claude Brialy *Claude Alvarez* · Jacques Dacqmine *Raoul Mons* · Hermine Claire *Véronique Manguin* ■ *Dir* Claude Chabrol · *Scr* Claude Chabrol, Dominique Roulet

The Inspector
★★★

Drama 1962 · UK · Colour · 111min

Having lost his Jewish fiancée to the Nazis, Dutch police inspector Stephen Boyd saves another Jewish girl (Dolores Hart) immediately after the war and attempts to smuggle her to Palestine. Bizarrely, they board a canal boat and end up in Morocco. The Americans pick them up in Tangier and ask the girl, who suffered in the death camps, to testify at the Nuremberg trials. A melodrama that doesn't quite obscure its more serious intentions, this is worth watching because of its impressive supporting cast. AT

Stephen Boyd *Peter Jongman* • Dolores Hart *Lisa Held* • Leo McKern *Brandt* • Hugh Griffith *Van der Pink* • Donald Pleasence *Sgt Wolters* • Harry Andrews *Ayoob* • Robert Stephens *Dickens* • Marius Goring *Thorens* • Finlay Currie *De Kooi* ■ *Dir* Philip Dunne • *Scr* Nelson Gidding, Jan de Hartog

An Inspector Calls ★★★★ PG
Mystery 1954 · UK · BW · 76min

It may be a gripping night out at the theatre, but JB Priestley's celebrated play loses some of its impact on screen. The revelations made by the unwelcome visitor seem so much less shocking away from the intimate confines of the stage, especially as the use of flashback to reveal the family's guilty secrets deprives us of their reactions as the truth emerges. Yet this is a highly polished production, made all the more irresistible by another superb performance from Alastair Sim. DP DVD BD

Alastair Sim *Inspector Poole* • Arthur Young (1) *Arthur Birling* • Olga Lindo *Sybil Birling* • Eileen Moore *Sheila Birling* • Bryan Forbes *Eric Birling* • Brian Worth *Gerald Croft* • Jane Wenham *Eva Smith* ■ *Dir* Guy Hamilton • *Scr* Desmond Davis, from the play by JB Priestley

Inspector Clouseau ★★★ U
Comedy 1968 · UK · Colour · 91min

Although when Peter Sellers seemed to have the character copyright on the gauche, Gallic policeman, this oddity sees Alan Arkin accenting the more positive aspects of the role as Clouseau arrives in a tediously swinging London to investigate the aftermath of the Great Train Robbery. Arkin is certainly a better straight actor than Sellers was, but he doesn't have Sellers's sense of self-importance, which is so very necessary for laughs. Worth looking at for variety's sake. TH

Alan Arkin *Inspector Jacques Clouseau* • Frank Finlay *Superintendent Weaver* • Beryl Reid *Mrs Weaver* • Delia Boccardo *Lisa Morrel* • Patrick Cargill *Sir Charles Braithwaite* • Barry Foster *Addison Steele* ■ *Dir* Bud Yorkin • *Scr* Tom Waldman, Frank Waldman, from a character created by Blake Edwards, Maurice Richlin

Inspector Gadget ★ U
Comedy action adventure
1999 · US · Colour · 75min

This screen version of the "cuddly cyborg" cartoon series is one of the most mindless Hollywood movies you're ever likely to find. Abandoning all plot after the first reel, it devotes its energies to beating us senseless with a succession of slapstick effects sequences. Matthew Broderick's performance as the computerised cop is so bland he barely exists, while the script is witless, ineptly structured and solely reliant on Gadget's extendable bits and bobs. Amazingly, there's a straight-to-video sequel. JC DVD CS

Matthew Broderick *Inspector Gadget/RoboGadget/John Brown* • Rupert Everett *Sanford Scolex* • Joely Fisher *Brenda/RoboBrenda* • Michelle Trachtenberg *Penny* • Andy Dick *Kramer* • Cheri Oteri *Mayor Wilson* • Michael G Hagerty *Sikes* • Dabney Coleman *Chief Quimby* ■ *Dir* David Kellogg • *Scr* Kerry Ehrin, Zak Penn, from a story by Dana Olsen, Kerry Ehrin, from characters by Andy Heyward, Jean Chalopin, Bruno Bianchi

The Inspector General
★★★ U

Musical comedy 1949 · US · Colour · 101min

This splendid Danny Kaye vehicle is ostensibly based on the Gogol play about a wandering buffoon mistaken for the visiting dignitary of the title. Warner Bros prepared this as a musical, importing Deanna Durbin's director Henry Koster, and giving Kaye free rein by commissioning songs from Mrs Kaye – the clever Sylvia Fine – and the brilliant Johnny Mercer. The numbers aren't particularly outstanding, but their tongue-twisting lyrics and use of romantic pathos served the star well. TS DVD

Danny Kaye *Georgi* • Walter Slezak *Yakov* • Barbara Bates *Leza* • Elsa Lanchester *Maria* • Gene Lockhart *The mayor* • Alan Hale *Kovatch* ■ *Dir* Henry Koster • *Scr* Philip Rapp, Harry Kurnitz, from the play by Nikolai Gogol

Inspiration ★★ U
Drama 1931 · US · BW · 73min

Parisian artist's model Greta Garbo and trainee diplomat Robert Montgomery fall in love, but the relationship runs into trouble when he learns of her past lovers. The only inspired element in this turgid drivel is Garbo herself, whose luminous presence and exquisite suffering almost rise above the material. Garbo and Montgomery were never teamed again after this picture. RK

Greta Garbo *Yvonne* • Robert Montgomery *Andre Martel* • Lewis Stone *Delval* • Marjorie Rambeau *Lulu* • Judith Vosselli *Odette* • Beryl Mercer *Marthe* • John Miljan *Coutant* • Edwin Maxwell *Julian Montell* • Oscar Apfel *Vignaud* ■ *Dir* Clarence Brown • *Scr* Gene Markey, from a treatment by James Forbes, from the novel *Sappho* by Alphonse Daudet

Instinct ★★ 15
Psychological drama 1999 · US · Colour · 118min

What caused anthropologist Anthony Hopkins to go on a murderous rampage while studying gorillas in Rwanda? That's what idealistic psychiatrist Cuba Gooding Jr tries to find out when Hopkins is finally arrested and placed in a mental institution in this plodding treatise on animal-versus-human instincts. The film naturally features a fine performance from Hopkins, yet this is hardly riveting because it's mainly constructed as a series of prison interviews. AJ Violence, swearing. DVD

Anthony Hopkins *Ethan Powell* • Cuba Gooding Jr *Theo Caulder* • Donald Sutherland *Ben Hillard* • Maura Tierney *Lyn Powell* • George Dzundza *Dr John Murray* • John Ashton *Guard Dacks* ■ *Dir* Jon Turteltaub • *Scr* Gerald DiPego, from his story, from the novel *Ishmael* by Daniel Quinn

Institute Benjamenta, or This Dream People Call Human Life ★★★ 12
Drama 1995 · UK · BW · 100min

The first live-action film from the talented Brothers Quay animation team both confounds and intrigues. Mark Rylance is an aspiring butler who attends a mysterious school to learn the rituals of service, but soon finds his training consists of an endless repetition of one single lesson. Alternately fascinating and banal, this hotch-potch of ideas and images is a sub-Cocteau treatise on the meaning and futility of life. Boasting good performances, atmospheric direction and evocative Hampton Court locations, this is strangely hypnotic in a tedious way. AJ DVD BD

Mark Rylance *Jakob von Gunten* • Alice Krige *Lisa Benjamenta* • Gottfried John *Johannes Benjamenta* • Daniel Smith *Kraus* • Joseph Alessi *Pepino* • Jonathan Stone *Hebling* ■ *Dir* Timothy Quay, Stephen Quay • *Scr* Alan Passes, Brothers Quay, from the novella *Jakob von Gunten* and other texts by Robert Walser

Insurgent ★★ 12
Science-fiction adventure
2015 · US · Colour · 114min

Shailene Woodley and Theo James return in this visually impressive but ultimately bland sequel to 2014 hit *Divergent*. They're now on the run from an oppressive leader (Kate Winslet), who is obsessed with hunting down the "Divergents" that threaten her regime. Despite Woodley's spirited performance, it gets bogged down by a plot that goes nowhere, with a showdown that lacks impact. JL Some violence, swearing. DVD BD 3D

Shailene Woodley *Beatrice "Tris" Prior* • Theo James *Four* • Miles Teller *Peter* • Ansel Elgort *Caleb Prior* • Kate Winslet *Jeanine Matthews* • Naomi Watts *Evelyn* ■ *Dir* Robert Schwentke • *Scr* Akiva Goldsman, Brian Duffield, Mark Bomback, from Veronica Roth's novel

Intacto ★★★ 15
Thriller 2001 · Sp · Colour · 104min

Director Juan Carlos Fresnadillo makes a solid feature debut with this study of chance, survival, identity and greed. Strewn with imposing set pieces and tellingly intimate details, it's a film that puts plot and impact above characterisation. The premise that luck can be stolen is pursued with an unrelenting logic that brings unexpected twists, as gambler Eusebio Poncela exploits the gift for good fortune of petty thief and plane-crash survivor Leonardo Sbaraglia, in order to exact his revenge on casino boss Max von Sydow. Slick and superficial, but also intriguing. DP Spanish, English +subtitles. DVD

Max von Sydow *Samuel* • Leonardo Sbaraglia *Tomas* • Eusebio Poncela *Federico* • Mónica López *Sara* • Antonio Dechent *Alejandro* ■ *Dir* Juan Carlos Fresnadillo • *Scr* Juan Carlos Fresnadillo, Andrés Koppel

The Intelligence Men ★★ U
Comedy 1965 · UK · Colour · 98min

Eric Morecambe and Ernie Wise found the transition from TV celebrities to film stars a difficult one to make. They were not helped by the fact that, for their big-screen debut, Sid Green and Dick Hills (scriptwriters of their ITV series at the time) failed to marry the familiar Eric and Ernie characteristics that kept audiences in stitches week after week with the demands of what is, in all honesty, a fitfully entertaining spy spoof. DP

Eric Morecambe *Eric* • Ernie Wise *Ernie Sage* • William Franklyn *Colonel Grant* • April Olrich *Madame Petrovna* • Richard Vernon *Sir Edward Seabrook* • Gloria Paul *Gina Carlotti* • Jacqueline Jones *Karin* • Warren Mitchell *Prozoroff* ■ *Dir* Robert Asher • *Scr* SC Green, RM Hills, from a story by Peter Blackmore

Intent to Kill ★★
Thriller 1958 · UK · BW · 88min

Cinematographer Jack Cardiff turned director with this B-thriller, set in Montreal. Critics at the time wondered why he bothered. Richard Todd plays a brain surgeon whose marital problems pale into insignificance when he's asked to operate on South American leader Herbert Lom who is the target for assassins. Forget about Lom's record on human rights – not the film's concern – and concentrate instead on the mechanics of thriller-making. AT

Richard Todd *Dr Bob McLaurin* • Betsy Drake *Nancy Ferguson* • Herbert Lom *Juan Menda* • Warren Stevens *Finch* • Carlo Justini *Francisco Flores* • Paul Carpenter *O'Brien* • Alexander Knox *Dr McNeil* • Lisa Gastoni *Carla Menda* • Peter Arne *Kral* ■ *Dir* Jack Cardiff • *Scr* Jimmy Sangster, from a novel by Michael Bryan

Intent to Kill ★ 18
Action thriller 1992 · US · Colour · 94min

If you can believe in ex-porn star Traci Lords as a nonconformist policewoman going after a drug dealer who's trying to retrieve a lost dope shipment, you'll believe the rest of this predictable action thriller. Yaphet Kotto plays Traci's captain and wins all the acting honours, but Traci gets to wear the more alluring outfits when she poses as a hooker. Otherwise this formula B-movie is notable for its high quota of graphic violence. AJ Nudity, drug abuse. DVD

Traci Lords *Vicki Stewart* • Yaphet Kotto *Captain Jackson* • Scott Patterson *Al* • Angelo Tiffe *Salvador* ■ *Dir/Scr* Charles T Kanganis

Interiors ★★★ 15
Psychological melodrama
1978 · US · Colour · 87min

Coming between Woody Allen's great comic masterpieces *Annie Hall* and *Manhattan*, this intense drama baffled fans and divided critics on its original release. The influence of Ingmar Bergman is unmistakeable, but there are also echoes of Chekhov and Eugene O'Neill in this story of a family thrown into turmoil. Allen's stylish compositions and his astute handling of the cast are impressive, but the script lacks weight and some of the more searching scenes topple over into melodrama. Oscar-nominated Geraldine Page dominates the proceedings as the mentally disturbed mother. DP DVD

Kristin Griffith *Flyn* • Mary Beth Hurt *Joey* • Richard Jordan *Frederick* • Diane Keaton *Renata* • EG Marshall *Arthur* • Geraldine Page *Eve* • Maureen Stapleton *Pearl* • Sam Waterston *Michael* ■ *Dir/Scr* Woody Allen • *Cinematographer* Gordon Willis

Interlude ★
Romantic drama 1957 · US · Colour · 88min

This virtually unwatchable drama (a remake of 1939's *When Tomorrow Comes*) features a miscast June Allyson as a woman who falls for married conductor Rossano Brazzi in Munich. Instead of having a wonderful sensual adventure, she wastes time trying to decide between Brazzi and unappealing doctor Keith Andes. Douglas Sirk provides heavy-handed and humourless direction. TS

June Allyson *Helen Banning* • Rossano Brazzi *Tonio Fischer* • Marianne Cook *Reni* • Françoise Rosay *Countess Reinhart* • Keith Andes *Dr Morley Dwyer* ■ *Dir* Douglas Sirk • *Scr* Daniel Fuchs, Franklin Coen, Inez Cocke, from the film *When Tomorrow Comes* by Dwight Taylor, from the novel *Serenade* by James M Cain

Interlude ★★★ PG
Romantic drama 1968 · US · Colour · 108min

This is a charming remake of that hoary old romance about a wide-eyed innocent abroad who falls for a sophisticated married musician, previously filmed (as *When Tomorrow Comes*) with Irene Dunne and Charles Boyer, and lugubriously with June Allyson and Rossano Brazzi. Here the casting is nearly perfect, with dashing intellectual Oskar Werner as the baton-wielder and Barbara Ferris as the reporter who becomes entranced by him. TS

Oskar Werner *Stefan Zelter* • Barbara Ferris *Sally* • Virginia Maskell *Antonia* • Donald Sutherland *Lawrence* • Nora Swinburne *Mary* • Alan Webb *Andrew* • Bernard Kay *George Selworth* • John Cleese ■ *Dir* Kevin Billington • *Scr* Lee Langley, Hugh Leonard

Intermezzo ★★★★
Romance 1936 · Swe · BW · 88min

A famous violinist employs a young pianist to give his daughter lessons, but falls in love with her, leaves his wife, and embarks on a concert tour with the girl as his accompanist. Directed by one of Sweden's foremost film-makers of the period, Gustaf Molander, and starring that country's most distinguished leading man, Gösta Ekman, this classy bittersweet romantic drama is notable for instigating the international career of Ingrid Bergman. David Selznick saw the film and, two years later, invited the relative unknown to Hollywood to star in an English-language remake. The rest, as they say, is history. RK Swedish +subtitles.

Gösta Ekman (1) *Holger Brandt* • Inga Tidblad *Margit Brandt* • Ingrid Bergman *Anita Hoffman* • Hasse Ekman *Åke Brandt* • Britt Hagman *Ann-Marie Brandt* ■ *Dir* Gustav Molander [Gustaf Molander] • *Scr* Gustav Molander, Gösta Stevens

Intermezzo ★★★★ PG
Romance 1939 · US · BW · 69min

This was producer David O Selznick's remake of the Swedish movie which also starred Ingrid Bergman. Originally only intending to purchase the story, Selznick was persuaded to also import Bergman, who here makes her American debut, and her natural beauty was the movie's initial sales gimmick. The tale of obsessive love is old hat, but is remarkably and touchingly well played by Bergman and Leslie Howard. The film was to have been directed by William Wyler, who Selznick allegedly fired in order to hire the Russian émigré Gregory Ratoff. Ratoff owed Selznick money and forfeited his director's salary to pay off his gambling debt. TS DVD

Ingrid Bergman *Anita Hoffman* • Leslie Howard *Holger Brandt* • Edna Best *Margit Brandt* • John Halliday *Thomas Stenborg* • Cecil Kellaway *Charles Moler* • Enid Bennett *Greta Stenborg* •

U SUITABLE FOR ALL   Uc SUITABLE ESPECIALLY FOR YOUNG CHILDREN (DVD ONLY)   PG PARENTAL GUIDANCE   12A UNDER 12s TO BE ACCOMPANIED (CINEMA ONLY)

Ann E. Todd *Ann Marie* • Douglas Scott *Eric Brandt* ■ *Dir* Gregory Ratoff • *Scr* George O'Neil, from the film by Gustav Molander, Gösta Stevens

interMission ★★★ 18
Crime comedy drama
2003 · Ire/UK/US · Colour · 101min

For all its crudity and violence, this edgy slice-of-life tale remains compulsively addictive. Part grimy ensemble drama, part bruise-black comedy, it follows a group of interlinking characters doing whatever it takes to stay buoyant in a crime-ridden area of Dublin. At the centre of events is Cillian Murphy, a supermarket shelf-stacker who plots revenge after ex-girlfriend Kelly Macdonald shacks up with a middle-aged bank manager. While the protagonists may not be likeable, they're certainly absorbing. SF Swearing, violence. **DVD**

Colin Farrell (2) *Lehiff* • Shirley Henderson *Sally* • Kelly Macdonald *Deirdre* • Colm Meaney *Det Jerry Lynch* • Cillian Murphy *John* • Ger Ryan *Maura* • Brian F O'Byrne *Mick* • Michael McElhatton *Sam* • Deirdre O'Kane *Noeleen* • David Wilmot *Oscar* ■ *Dir* John Crowley • *Scr* Mark O'Rowe

The Intern ★★★ 12A
Comedy
2015 · US · Colour · 121min

Robert De Niro is a senior citizen on work experience in a sprightly if rather unlikely comedy from writer/director Nancy Meyers. Anne Hathaway's young highflyer is aiming to close the generation gap, so she takes the old guy under her wing at the shopping website she's started up, before inevitably finding that she's the one who's on a learning curve. In a plot littered with dramatic shortcuts, there are wryly amusing, well-observed moments like De Niro turning up at the office in a suit, and the most important connection – between the two leads – works surprisingly well. SP Swearing, sex references

Robert De Niro *Ben Whittaker* • Anne Hathaway *Jules Ostin* • Rene Russo *Fiona* • Adam Devine *Jason* ■ *Dir/Scr* Nancy Meyers

Internal Affairs ★★★★ 18
Crime thriller
1990 · US · Colour · 109min

In this gripping thriller from *Leaving Las Vegas* director Mike Figgis, Andy Garcia stars as an Internal Affairs investigator who's determined to prove that fellow police officer Richard Gere is corrupt. Gere is especially good as the dishonest and often violent policeman, but, in the end, this film focuses more on Gere's general nastiness than the interesting vendetta between the pair that starts the movie. JB Violence, swearing, sex scenes. **DVD**

Richard Gere *Dennis Peck* • Andy Garcia *Sergeant Raymond Avilla* • Nancy Travis *Kathleen Avilla* • Laurie Metcalf *Sergeant Amy Wallace* • Richard Bradford *Lieutenant Sergeant Grieb* • William Baldwin *Van Stretch* ■ *Dir* Mike Figgis • *Scr* Henry Bean

The International ★★ 15
Thriller
2009 · US/Ger/UK · Colour · 113min

Director Tom Tykwer's thriller is hampered by a ridiculous plot and clodhopping dialogue. After an undercover colleague is murdered in front of him, Interpol agent Louis Salinger (Clive Owen) joins forces with New York district attorney Eleanor Whitman (Naomi Watts) to bring down a shady banking organisation that's funding war and terror. A host of well-shot European cities make this a stylish watch, and the fashionably bestubbled Owen delivers a gritty performance. But there's little here in the way of mystery or tension, nor any romantic spark between the leads, and a ludicrously overstaged shoot-out at New York's Guggenheim Museum obliterates what's left of the film's credibility. AS Violence, swearing. **DVD**

Clive Owen *Louis Salinger* • Naomi Watts *Eleanor Whitman* • Armin Mueller-Stahl *Wilhelm Wexler* • Ulrich Thomsen *Jonas Skarssen* • Brian F O'Byrne *The Consultant* • Patrick Baladi *Martin White* ■ *Dir* Tom Tykwer • *Scr* Eric Warren Singer [Eric Singer]

International House ★★★ U
Comedy
1933 · US · BW · 65min

In this great, if paper-thin, antique comedy, WC Fields arrives by autogyro at a hotel in China where a giant television is about to be unveiled. Many popular radio performers of the day turn up to take part in the celebrations, including Rudy Vallee, George Burns and Gracie Allen, while Cab Calloway sings *Reefer Man*. Bela Lugosi appears as a Russian general in a rollicking good show that will appeal to nostalgia lovers. AJ **DVD**

WC Fields *Professor Quail* • Bela Lugosi *General Petronovich* • Stuart Erwin *Tommy Nash* • Sari Maritza *Carol Fortescue* • George Burns *Dr Burns* • Gracie Allen *Nurse Allen* • Rudy Vallee • Cab Calloway ■ *Dir* Edward Sutherland [A Edward Sutherland] • *Scr* Frances Martin, Walter DeLeon, from a story by Lou Heifetz, Neil Brant

International Velvet ★★ PG
Drama
1978 · US/UK · Colour · 110min

More than 30 years on from the MGM classic *National Velvet*, Elizabeth Taylor has grown into Nanette Newman, lives with Christopher Plummer and has ambitions for her niece, Tatum O'Neal, to win an Olympic equestrian title. Anthony Hopkins plays Tatum's coach. Bryan Forbes considered the title "puerile" and lost his fight to change it, but this movie was probably a lost cause anyway; everything is far too sugary. AT

Tatum O'Neal *Sarah Brown* • Christopher Plummer *John Seaton* • Anthony Hopkins *Captain Johnny Johnson* • Nanette Newman *Velvet Brown* • Peter Barkworth *Pilot* • Dinsdale Landen *Mr Curtis* ■ *Dir* Bryan Forbes • *Scr* Bryan Forbes, suggested by the novel *National Velvet* by Enid Bagnold

The Internecine Project ★★★ 15
Thriller
1974 · UK · Colour · 85min

In this atmospheric thriller, James Coburn stars as the machiavellian mastermind out to hide his murky past by tricking his agents into killing each other on the same night. The execution of the scheme is the highlight, but the smart script and a marvellous mood-making score by Roy Budd (of *Get Carter* fame) add volumes to the deliciously dark intrigue. JA Violence, swearing. **DVD**

James Coburn *Robert Elliot* • Lee Grant *Jean Robertson* • Harry Andrews *Albert Parsons* • Ian Hendry *Alex Hellman* • Michael Jayston *David Baker* • Keenan Wynn *EJ Farnsworth* ■ *Dir* Ken Hughes • *Scr* Barry Levinson, Jonathan Lynn, from the novel *Internecine* by Mort W Elkind • *Cinematographer* Geoffrey Unsworth

Internes Can't Take Money ★★★
Medical drama
1937 · US · BW · 77min

A young hospital doctor helps a gangster's widow find her missing child in a modest programme filler that stars Joel McCrea as the sympathetic medic and the wonderful Barbara Stanwyck as the mother. The film was an unexpected box-office hit for Paramount, but the studio badly missed the boat: it was MGM that picked up Max Brand's Dr Kildare character, cast Lew Ayres in the role and made a series of highly successful features over a nine-year period. RK

Barbara Stanwyck *Janet Haley* • Joel McCrea *James Kildare* • Lloyd Nolan *Hanlon* • Stanley Ridges *Innes* • Gaylord Pendleton [Steve Pendleton] *Interne Jones* • Lee Bowman *Interne Weeks* • Irving Bacon *Jeff* ■ *Dir* Alfred Santell • *Scr* Rian James, Theodore Reeves, from a story by Max Brand

The Internet's Own Boy ★★★★ 12A
Documentary
2014 · US · Colour · 104min

In January 2013, Aaron Swartz hanged himself after federal prosecutors refused to plea-bargain over his conviction for computer fraud. The co-founder of the social news site Reddit faced 35 years in prison and a $1 million fine for downloading millions of documents from the JSTOR digital library. Thanks to Swartz's martyr status within the internet community, documentarist Brian Knappenberger has little trouble finding interviewees who will denounce the US Justice Department for seeking to make an example of the 26-year-old after JSTOR dropped all charges, with archive clips that reveal Swartz to have been sincere, clear-thinking and selfless. And therein lies the real tragedy of his early, hounded demise. DP Swearing.

Aaron Swartz • Tim Berners-Lee • Cory Doctorow ■ *Dir/Scr* Brian Knappenberger

The Internship ★★ 12
Comedy
2013 · US · Colour · 114min

Eight years after *Wedding Crashers*, Owen Wilson and Vince Vaughn are together again, but not as successfully, in director Shawn Levy's clunky work culture-clash comedy. They play a pair of old-school salesmen who are made redundant and decide to apply for a coveted Google internship along with a gaggle of eager young techies. Levy's film may boast a hi-tech backdrop, but it's an old banger of a comedy, with Vaughn's mile-a-minute spiel especially rusty and Wilson looking too meditative throughout. SP Swearing, sexual references. **DVD** **Blu** **CS**

Vince Vaughn *Billy McMahon* • Owen Wilson *Nick Campbell* • Rose Byrne *Dana* • Max Minghella *Graham Hawtrey* • Aasif Mandvi *Mr Chetty* • Will Ferrell *Mattress salesman* • John Goodman *Billy and Nick's boss* ■ *Dir* Shawn Levy • *Scr* Vince Vaughn, Jared Stern, from a story by Vaughn

Interpol ★
Crime thriller
1957 · UK · BW · 91min

Known as *Pickup Alley* in the US, this feeble thriller about tracking down a dope-peddling syndicate by the international police force boasted that it was filmed in London, Paris, Athens, Naples, Rome, Lisbon and New York. It looks as though they sometimes forgot to take the script with them. Trevor Howard obviously relishes acting the master villain for a change, though co-stars Victor Mature and Anita Ekberg don't try to act at all. AE

Victor Mature *Charles Sturgis* • Anita Ekberg *Gina Broger* • Trevor Howard *Frank McNally* • Bonar Colleano *Amalio* • Alec Mango *Salko* ■ *Dir* John Gilling • *Scr* John Paxton, from the novel by AJ Forrest

The Interpreter ★★★ 12
Political thriller
2005 · UK/US/Fr · Colour · 123min

This engrossing thriller has the distinction of being the first movie to film inside the United Nations headquarters in New York. Nicole Kidman plays a translator who overhears a threat to murder an African head of state (Earl Cameron) in a dialect that few can understand. Recently bereaved agent Sean Penn is then assigned to keep an eye on the imperilled interpreter, but the affair takes a sinister turn as Penn begins to suspect there is more to Kidman than meets the eye. Sydney Pollack's directing may be a little too worthy for its own good, but the performances turn this handsome and intelligent film into more than mere entertainment. KK Violence. **DVD** **Blu**

Nicole Kidman *Silvia Broome* • Sean Penn *Tobin Keller* • Catherine Keener *Dot Woods* • Jesper Christensen *Nils Lud* • Yvan Attal *Philippe* • Earl Cameron *Edmund Zuwanie* • Michael Wright *Marcus* • George Harris (2) *Kuman-Kuman* ■ *Dir* Sydney Pollack • *Scr* Charles Randolph, Scott Frank, Steven Zaillian, from a story by Martin Stellman, Brian Ward • *Cinematographer* Darius Khondji

Interrogation ★★★★ 18
Political drama
1982 · Pol · Colour · 111min

Although set in the last days of Stalinism, the parallels with the Solidarity era meant that Ryszard Bugaski's harrowing drama was immediately banned on its release in Poland. When it was eventually reissued, Krystyna Janda won the best actress prize at Cannes in 1990 for her performance as the falsely accused cabaret artist, who is pitilessly tortured on account of her sexual liaison with a major implicated in anti-government activity. Yet, in spite of the dehumanising effect of solitary confinement, and the brutality of the interrogation, she not only retains her spirit, but also tests the resolve of her captors. DP Polish +subtitles. **DVD**

Krystyna Janda *Antonia Dziwisz* • Adam Ferency *Morawsky* • Janusz Gajos *Zawada* • Agnieszka Holland *Witowska* • Olgierd Lukaszewicz ■ *Dir* Ryszard Bugajski • *Scr* Ryszard Bugajski, Janusz Dymek

The Interrupted Journey ★
Crime drama
1949 · UK · BW · 85min

This tale of the unexpected plays so many tricks on the viewer that it soon becomes impossible to identify with the plight of novelist Richard Todd, whose inability to choose between wife Valerie Hobson and mistress Christine Norden spells disaster for his fellow passengers on a speeding express. Cheap production, gimmicky script. DP

Richard Todd *John North* • Valerie Hobson *Carol North* • Christine Norden *Susan Wilding* • Tom Walls *Mr Clayton* • Dora Bryan *Waitress* • Arnold Ridley *Saunders* ■ *Dir* Daniel Birt • *Scr* Michael Pertwee

Interrupted Melody ★★★★ U
Biographical drama
1955 · US · Colour · 105min

This lush and expensive MGM biopic is about the Australian singer Marjorie Lawrence, who contracted polio at the peak of her career. It's marvellously played by underrated redhead Eleanor Parker. Glenn Ford is superb as the doctor who inspires the singer in her fight against the disease, and the supporting cast is led by Roger Moore. The writers, William Ludwig and Sonya Levien, won an Oscar for best adapted screenplay. TS

Glenn Ford *Dr Thomas King* • Eleanor Parker *Marjorie Lawrence* • Roger Moore *Cyril Lawrence* • Cecil Kellaway *Bill Lawrence* • Eileen Farrell *Singing voice* ■ *Dir* Curtis Bernhardt • *Scr* William Ludwig, Sonya Levien, from the book by Marjorie Lawrence

The Interrupters ★★★★
Documentary
2011 · US/UK/Can/Nor/Swe/Den · Colour · 127min

Director Steve James, still best known for 1994's *Hoop Dreams*, delivers another compassionate insight into troubled youth by profiling Chicago's CeaseFire organisation. Founder Gary Slutkin insists that violence is a contagious disease that can be cured, and reformed gang members draw on their own experiences to intervene in disputes and persuade antagonists that there is no need for gunfire. James occasionally allows melodrama to seep in, but it's impossible not to be moved by the small signs of hope in the midst of so much despair and degradation. DP Violence, swearing. **DVD**

■ *Dir* Steve James (2) • *Scr* Inspired by an article by Alex Kotlowitz • *Cinematographer* Steve James (2)

Intersection ★★★ 15
Drama
1994 · US · Colour · 94min

Few will remember the glossy French movie *The Things of Life*, of which this is an even glossier remake. Richard Gere is a well-groomed architect, married to Sharon Stone and having an affair with journalist Lolita Davidovich. The usual *ménage à trois*, then, with designer labels and capped teeth, all droolingly shot and written like a TV soap. The trick is to give Gere's dilemma (Sharon or Lolita?) some resonance, so a stunningly staged car smash takes centre stage and takes the decision out of his hands. AT Swearing, sex scenes, brief nudity. **DVD**

Richard Gere *Vincent Eastman* • Sharon Stone *Sally Eastman* • Lolita Davidovich *Olivia Marshak* • Martin Landau *Neal* • Jenny Morrison [Jennifer Morrison] *Meaghan Eastman* ■ *Dir* Mark Rydell • *Scr* David Rayfiel, Marshall Brickman, from the film *The Things of Life/Les Choses de la Vie* by

Paul Guimard, Jean-Loup Dabadie, Claude Sautet, from the novel *Les Choses de la Vie* by Paul Guimard

Interstellar ★★★★ 12
Science-fiction adventure
2014 · US/UK · Colour · 162min

Director Christopher Nolan goes to infinity and beyond with a cosmic epic that adds breathtaking meaning to the idea of a "race against time". When former pilot Matthew McConaughey is asked to save the world from starvation by boffin Michael Caine, he jumps at the chance. For this is no ordinary mission – it requires McConaughey to enter a wormhole to find a planet for the human race to colonise – a journey that could take years. Nolan's most ambitious film to date is a thoughtful sci-fi that echoes Kubrick's *2001*, with fine performances from Anne Hathaway and Jessica Chastain. But holding it all together is McConaughey, who guarantees this majestic film retains a human heart. JA DVD

Matthew McConaughey *Cooper* · Anne Hathaway *Amelia Brand* · Michael Caine *Professor Brand* · Jessica Chastain *Murph* · John Lithgow *Donald* · David Gyasi *Romilly* · Wes Bentley *Doyle* · Casey Affleck *Tom* · Mackenzie Foy *Young Murph* · Matt Damon *Dr Mann* · *Dir* Christopher Nolan · *Scr* Christopher Nolan, Jonathan Nolan · *Music* Hans Zimmer

Interval ★★★
Romantic drama
1973 · US/Mex · Colour · 85min

Returning to the screen after six years, a well-preserved 62-year-old Merle Oberon starred in, produced and co-edited this soapy tale of a wealthy globetrotting woman on holiday in Mexico who meets and falls in love with a painter 20 years her junior. Her final film, directed by Daniel Mann, was a case of life imitating bad art, because Oberon, then living in Mexico, fell for her young co-star, Robert Wolders, who soon became her fourth husband. RB

Merle Oberon *Serena Moore* · Robert Wolders *Chris* · Claudio Brook *Armando Vertiz* · Russ Conway *Fraser* · Charles Bateman *Husband* ■ *Dir* Daniel Mann · *Scr* Gavin Lambert

Interview ★★★ 15
Drama 2007 · US/Can/Neth · Colour · 80min

Steve Buscemi co-writes, directs and stars in this claustrophobic character study about two people with "trust" issues – a remake of the 2003 Dutch movie by the late Theo Van Gogh. Buscemi plays a jaded war journalist who is assigned an interview with a flaky soap star (Sienna Miller). He's initially unenthusiastic and struggles to get any sense out of her, but when alcohol and drugs are thrown into the mix, secrets are soon spilled. It's a stagey set-up that relies heavily on a series of contrivances, but the interplay between the actors is compelling. It's just a shame that Buscemi opts for a gimmicky twist that's easy to see coming and adds nothing to the story. SP DVD

Steve Buscemi *Pierre Peders* · Sienna Miller *Katya* · Michael Buscemi *Robert Peders* · Tara Elders *Maggie* · David Schechter *Maitre'd* · Molly Griffith *Waitress* ■ *Dir* Steve Buscemi · *Scr* Steve Buscemi, David Schechter, from the 2003 film by Theo Van Gogh,Theodor Holman

The Interview ★★★ 15
Comedy 2014 · US · Colour · 112min

The Interview's release caused a storm of controversy. But what of the film itself? Seth Rogen and James Franco play a TV producer and a sleazy celebrity presenter, who plan an interview with Kim Jong-un (Randall Park) as a ratings booster. American security forces then coerce the duo into attempting to assassinate the North Korean leader. There are some smart jabs lurking in the loose script and Rogen and Park display excellent comic timing. However, as a spoof on popular culture and politics, *The Interview* is naughty, dumb and patchily funny. KK DVD

James Franco *Dave Skylark* · Seth Rogen *Aaron Rapaport* · Lizzy Caplan *Agent Lacey* · Randall Park *Kim Jong-un* · Diana Bang *Sook* · Timothy

Simons *Malcolm* ■ *Dir* Evan Goldberg, Seth Rogen · *Scr* Dan Sterling, from a story by Evan Goldberg, Seth Rogen

Interview with the Vampire: the Vampire Chronicles ★★★ 18
Horror 1994 · US · Colour · 122min

When the highly anticipated movie version of Anne Rice's cult novel finally came to the screen, it was a decidedly anaemic affair. All sumptuously dressed up with nowhere really interesting to go, director Neil Jordan's lavish adaptation is a stylised horror tale lacking the emotional depth and jet-black darkness of the doom-laden tome. Still, Tom Cruise is fine as the vampire Lestat, whose close relationship with handsome Brad Pitt forms an erotic twist on the Dracula legend. It's Antonio Banderas who gives the most full-blooded performance as the bisexual Armand in a beautifully mounted production, low on divine decadence but high on evocative elegance. AJ Violence, swearing, nudity. DVD

Tom Cruise *Lestat de Lioncourt* · Brad Pitt *Louis Pointe du Lac* · Antonio Banderas *Armand* · Stephen Rea *Santiago* · Christian Slater *Daniel Malloy* · Kirsten Dunst *Claudia* · Domiziana Giordano *Madeleine* ■ *Dir* Neil Jordan · *Scr* Anne Rice, from her novel

Intervista ★★★★ 15
Biographical documentary drama
1987 · It · Colour · 106min

This is a breathless, brilliant insight into the vanities and inanities of the motion picture business from the inimitable Federico Fellini. A curio rather than a classic, it sweeps the viewer from the 1980s to the Cinecittà film studio of over 60 years ago, when a wide-eyed youth from Rimini came to Rome to make his name. Packed with clips from screen gems and blurring the line between past and present, studio reality and cinematic illusion, this climaxes with a wickedly staged reunion between Marcello Mastroianni and Anita Ekberg, the stars of Fellini's classic *La Dolce Vita*. DP Italian +subtitles.

Federico Fellini · Marcello Mastroianni · Anita Ekberg · Sergio Rubini *Reporter* · Maurizio Mein ■ *Dir* Federico Fellini · *Scr* Federico Fellini, Gianfranco Angelucci

Intimacy ★★★ 18
Drama 2000 · Fr/UK · Colour · 114min

This controversial first English-language film from French director Patrice Chéreau depicts the sexual act in some of the most explicit scenes ever passed by the British Board of Film Classification. Estranged love rat Mark Rylance and bored paramour Kerry Fox indulge their desperate sexual passions every Wednesday afternoon at his sleazy flat. As their casual affair grows ever more compulsive, the anonymity Rylance thought he wanted starts to drive him so crazy that he begins to follow his nameless lover. This is an intriguing exploration of the dynamics between intimate love and physical sex, but it's also theatrical and wordy. AJ Swearing, sex scenes, nudity. DVD

Mark Rylance *Jay* · Kerry Fox *Claire* · Timothy Spall *Andy* · Alastair Galbraith *Victor* · Philippe Calvario *Ian* · Marianne Faithfull *Betty* · Susannah Harker *Susan, Jay's wife* ■ *Dir* Patrice Chéreau · *Scr* Patrice Chéreau, Anne-Louise Trividic, from stories by Hanif Kureishi

Intimate Enemies ★★★ 15
War drama 2007 · Fr · Colour · 106min

Florent Emilio Siri's big-budget and sometimes spectacular film about the Algerian War has been dubbed the "French *Platoon*", and it raises many questions familiar from Hollywood's later Vietnam movies. Benoît Magimel stars as an idealistic officer who arrives in Algeria with high morals, deploring the brutality he sees around him. But the enemy he first sympathises with turns out to be just as barbaric. The result is a handsome but overly sentimental end-of-innocence story, featuring terrific set pieces and wonderful

performances from Albert Dupontel and Aurélien Recoing as Magimel's battle-hardened troops. DW French, Arabic, Kabyle +subtitles. DVD

Benoît Magimel *Lieutenant Terrien* · Albert Dupontel *Sergeant Dougnac* · Aurélien Recoing *Commandant Vesoul* · Marc Barbé *Captain Berthaut* · Eric Savin *Torturer sergeant* · Fellag [Mohamed Fellag] *Idir Danoun* · Lounès Tazairt *Saïd* · Abdelhafid Metalsi *Rachid* ■ *Dir* Florent Emilio Siri · *Scr* Florent Emilio Siri, Patrick Rotman

Intimate Relations ★★★ 15
Comedy drama based on a true story
1995 · UK/Can · Colour · 95min

This 1950s-set drama lifts the lid on the lusty bedroom antics of the supposedly staid British. Rupert Graves is the sailor who takes a room as a boarder in the home of a seemingly normal family. It's not long before Julie Walters (a great, almost sinister turn) and her teenage daughter are vying for his affections, and hapless Graves finds himself out of his depth. Writer/ director Philip Goodhew's debut feature is quirky and engrossing fare with a very dark edge. JB Violence, swearing, a sex scene.

Julie Walters *Marjorie Beasley* · Rupert Graves *Harold Guppy* · Matthew Walker *Stanley Beasley* · Laura Sadler *Joyce Beasley* · Holly Aird *Deirdre* · Les Dennis *Maurice Guppy* ■ *Dir/Scr* Philip Goodhew

The Intimate Stranger ★★
Mystery drama 1956 · UK · BW · 95min

This was the second film made in England by the blacklisted Hollywood director Joseph Losey, working under the pseudonym of Walton, which was his middle name. Blacklisted writer Howard Koch had written the script about an American film producer in London who is married to the daughter of the studio chief and is being blackmailed by a woman whose letters suggest she might be his mistress. It's a feeble effort with poor performances and cardboard sets, but the theme of the story – illusion, paranoia, guilt -- are fascinating when set beside Losey's own predicament. AT

Richard Basehart *Reggie Wilson* · Mary Murphy (1) *Evelyn Stewart* · Constance Cummings *Kay Wallace* · Roger Livesey *Ben Case* · Faith Brook *Lesley Wilson* · Mervyn Johns *Ernest Chapple* · Vernon Greeves *George Merns* · André Mikhelson *Steve Vadney* ■ *Dir* Joseph Walton [Joseph Losey] · *Scr* Peter Howard [Howard Koch], from the novel *Pay the Piper* by Paul Howard

Into Great Silence ★★★★ U
Documentary
2005 · Fr/Ger/Swi · Colour · 168min

It's difficult not to be touched by the tranquility, simplicity and beauty of the monastic lifestyle depicted in this visually arresting and spiritually uplifting documentary. Filmed over four months by Philip Gröning (who acted as a one-man crew), this is a meticulously composed insight into the daily routine of the Carthusian house of monks at the Grande Chartreuse in the French Alps. It makes moving use of stillness and silence to convey both the sanctity of the community and the truly humbling bond that inspires its members. DP French +subtitles. DVD

■ *Dir/Scr* Philip Gröning · *Cinematographer* Philip Gröning

Into the Abyss: a Tale of Death, a Tale of Life ★★★★ 12
Documentary
2011 · US/UK/Ger · Colour · 105min

German film-maker Werner Herzog (*Grizzly Man*, *Aguirre, Wrath of God*) takes another journey into the darkness of the human soul with this deeply thought-provoking documentary about an American triple murder and its consequences. Although he opposes capital punishment, Herzog remains generally unbiased, delivering a forensic and philosophical examination of the 2001 Texan case that snowballed from an intended car theft and left one of the

two teenage perpetrators, Michael Perry, sentenced to death. Via incisive, and occasionally surreal, off-camera probing, a compassionate Herzog draws profundity, candour and even humour from the most unexpected sources. SF DVD

Werner Herzog *Narrator* · *Dir/Scr* Werner Herzog

Into the Arms of Strangers: Stories of the Kindertransport ★★★ PG
Documentary
2000 · US · BW and Colour · 112min

Less penetrating than Mark Jonathan Harris's Oscar winner, *The Long Way Home*, this is, nevertheless, a moving tribute to the 10,000 Jewish children who fled Europe in the desperate months before the outbreak of the Second World War. Adhering to the testimonial format favoured by Holocaust documentaries, the film commemorates the indomitability of the survivors of the *Kindertransport* exodus. It also recalls the selfless courage of the terrified parents, who often sacrificed everything to spare their children from the coming nightmare. Yet, disappointingly, it skirts such contentious issues as the anti-Semitism in Britain and the United States at the time. DP DVD

Judi Dench *Narrator* · *Dir/Scr* Mark Jonathan Harris

Into the Blue ★★ 15
Action thriller 2005 · US · Colour · 105min

In this wishy-washy story of good-looking treasure hunters in peril, Paul Walker and Jessica Alba star as the easy-on-the-eye divers who come across a sunken stash of cocaine while on an underwater expedition. It's not long before the buff-bottomed duo are slipping into their Speedos for some slow-mo "getting away from it all" shots. However, all pretence of an interesting plot drifts to a speck on a pink-hued horizon when the owners of the drugs want their property returned. SP Violence. DVD

Paul Walker *Jared Cole* · Jessica Alba *Samantha "Sam" Nicholson* · Scott Caan *Bryce Dunn* · Josh Brolin *Derek Bates* · James Frain *Reyes* · Ashley Scott *Amanda Collins* · Dwayne Adaway *Roy* · Tyson Beckford *Primo* ■ *Dir* John Stockwell · *Scr* Matt Johnson

Into the Night ★★ 15
Comedy thriller 1985 · US · Colour · 114min

John Landis came a bit of a cropper with this lacklustre comedy caper, although it has aged better than some of his efforts. The then relatively unknown Jeff Goldblum and Michelle Pfeiffer take the lead roles: Goldblum the innocent bystander who inadvertently gets caught up with smuggler Pfeiffer and Arab terrorists. The action bustles along amusingly enough and Landis stuffs the pictures with cameos. JF DVD

Jeff Goldblum *Ed Okin* · Michelle Pfeiffer *Diana* · Stacey Pickren *Ellen Okin* · Bruce McGill *Charlie* · Kathryn Harrold *Christie* · Carl Perkins *Mr Williams* · David Bowie *Colin Morris* · Richard Farnsworth *Jack Caper* · John Landis *Savak 4* · Dan Aykroyd *Herb* · Roger Vadim *Monsieur Melville* ■ *Dir* John Landis · *Scr* Ron Koslow

Into the Storm ★★★ 12
Disaster drama 2014 · US · Colour · 89min

Fresh from the *Hobbit* trilogy, Richard Armitage has to play second fiddle to the elements in this white-knuckle adventure about tornados laying waste to a small US city. After a huge storm touches down, local teacher Armitage has to put himself in harm's way to save his kids, while a storm chaser and a meteorologist look to capture the weather on camera. Director Steven Quale ramps up the tension with jaw-dropping effects, but the subplots interrupt the mighty bluster of the action. TeS DVD

Richard Armitage *Gary* · Sarah Wayne Callies *Allison* · Matt Walsh *Pete* · Alycia Debnam-Carey *Kaitlyn* ■ *Dir* Steven Quale · *Scr* Simon Beaufoy, John Swetnam

Into the Sun ★★ 15
Action adventure 1992 · US · Colour · 96min

Anthony Michael Hall's career started slipping the minute he lost his geeky teenage looks, and this was one of his failed bids to relaunch himself as an action star. It's still worth a look, though, if only for a smarter-than-usual premise. Hall is the Hollywood star researching a new film role who is reluctantly taken under the wing of maverick air force ace Michael Paré. Soon the pair find themselves caught up in a real-life war. JF

Anthony Michael Hall *Tom Slade* · Michael Paré *Captain Paul Watkins* · Deborah Maria Moore [Deborah Moore (1)] *Major Goode* · Terry Kiser *Mitchell Burton* · Brian Haley *Lieutenant DeCarlo* ■ *Dir* Fritz Kiersch · *Scr* John Brancato, Michael Ferris, from their story

Into the West ★★★ PG
Fantasy 1992 · Ire/UK · Colour · 102min

This is a dark-hued fable about two children who run away to the wild Irish hills on a white stallion, pursued by their drunkard gypsy father (Gabriel Byrne) and Ellen Barkin. Set against some majestic scenery, this is partly a grim look at the hardships and discrimination suffered by travellers in Ireland, and partly an excursion into Gaelic myth, sensitively handled by Mike Newell. The two young leads (Ciaran Fitzgerald and Ruaidhri Conroy) are both outstanding in this poetic tale. AT *DVD*

Gabriel Byrne *Papa Riley* · Ellen Barkin *Kathleen* · Ciaran Fitzgerald *Ossie Riley* · Ruaidhri Conroy *Tito Riley* · David Kelly *Grandpa Ward* · Johnny Murphy *Tracker* ■ *Dir* Mike Newell · *Scr* Jim Sheridan, from a story by Michael Pearce

Into the Wild ★★★★ 15
Biographical adventure drama 2007 · US · Colour · 141min

In 1990, 22-year-old college graduate Christopher McCandless abandoned his middle-class family and hitch-hiked across the country. His destination: a life of solitary contemplation in the snowy wastes of Alaska. Basing his screenplay on John Krakauer's bestselling biography, writer/director Sean Penn follows McCandless (played with tragic boyishness by Emile Hirsch) on his quest to commune with nature. Penn's camera captures the grandeur of the American landscape magnificently, yet what really impresses is Hirsch's intuitive performance. His adventures on the road are offset by an intermittent voiceover from Carine McCandless (Jena Malone) detailing the impact of her brother's disappearance on the family. Celebrating McCandless's beatnik philosophy while refusing to ignore his inherent selfishness, Penn crafts an entrancing movie. JR Swearing. *DVD* *BD*

Emile Hirsch *Christopher "Chris" McCandless* · Marcia Gay Harden *Billie McCandless* · William Hurt *Walt McCandless* · Jena Malone *Carine McCandless* · Brian Dierker *Rainey* · Catherine Keener *Jan Burres* · Vince Vaughn *Wayne Westerberg* · Kristen Stewart *Tracy Tatro* · Hal Holbrook *Ron Franz* ■ *Dir* Sean Penn · *Scr* Sean Penn, from the non-fiction book by Jon Krakauer · *Cinematographer* Eric Gautier

Into the Woods ★★★ PG
Musical fantasy 2014 · US · Colour · 119min

The more poignant and darker tones of the original Broadway hit may have been Disneyfied, but Stephen Sondheim and James Lapine's magical musical still makes a potent transfer to the screen in the capable hands of director Rob Marshall (*Chicago*). Using such fairy-tale favourites as Cinderella, Rapunzel and Little Red Riding Hood to craft a new fable, the story focuses on a baker and his wife as they attempt to break a witch's curse so that they might have a child. Witch Meryl Streep, Prince Charming Chris Pine and sleazy wolf Johnny Depp give the stand-out performances in this entirely sung-through spectacle. AJ *DVD* *BD*

Meryl Streep *The witch* · Emily Blunt *The baker's wife* · James Corden *The baker* · Anna Kendrick *Cinderella* · Chris Pine *Cinderella's prince* ·

Johnny Depp *The wolf* ■ *Dir* Rob Marshall · *Scr* James Lapine, from the musical by Lapine (book), Stephen Sondheim (music & lyrics)

Intolerable Cruelty ★★★ 12
Satirical romantic comedy 2003 · US · Colour · 95min

This is by far Joel and Ethan Coen's most expensive film and also their first working from an existing script. That it turns out to be one of their weakest may not be unconnected. A slick, colourful screwball comedy, it follows the quest of ultra-successful divorce lawyer George Clooney to marry professional gold-digger Catherine Zeta-Jones using his own cast-iron "pre-nup". The film is populated with wonderful grotesque supporting characters, but these turns distract from rather than add to the central plot. AC *DVD* *BD*

George Clooney *Miles Longfellow Massey* · Catherine Zeta-Jones *Marylin Rexroth* · Geoffrey Rush *Donovan Donaly* · Cedric the Entertainer *Gus Petch* · Edward Herrmann *Rex Rexroth* · Paul Adelstein *Wrigley* · Richard Jenkins *Freddy Bender* · Billy Bob Thornton *Howard Drexler Doyle* · Julia Duffy *Sarah Batista O'Flanagan Sorkin* · Jonathan Hadary *Heinz, the Baron Krauss von Espy* ■ *Dir* Joel Coen · *Scr* Robert Ramsey, Matthew Stone, Ethan Coen, Joel Coen, from a story by Robert Ramsey, Matthew Stone, John Romano

LANDMARK FILM
Astonishing in its visual complexity, this confirms the motion picture's potential as an art form

Intolerance ★★★★★ PG
Classic silent drama 1916 · US · BW · 167min

A magnificent and deeply significant achievement of early cinema, this sprawling multilayered epic helped define storytelling in the movies, with its early use of such devices as parallel action and the dramatic close-up. Made as a riposte by genius director DW Griffith to those who accused him of racism after his ground-breaking *The Birth of a Nation*, this analyses the effects of intolerance in four tales set throughout the ages, which are interspersed with the eternal image of a mother (Lillian Gish) and baby. The Babylonian sequences are as notorious as they are astounding, with gigantic sets almost dwarfing the rampant violence and nudity, but the contemporary tale is exciting and touching, too. This is one of the most satisfying films ever made. TS *DVD* *BD*

Lillian Gish *The woman who rocks the cradle* · Mae Marsh *The Dear One* · Fred Turner *Father* · Robert Harron *Boy* · Howard Gaye *Christ* · Lillian Langdon *Mary* · Olga Grey *Mary Magdalene* · Margery Wilson *Brown Eyes* · Frank Bennett (1) *Charles IX* · Josephine Crowell *Catherine de Midici* · Constance Talmadge *Mountain girl* · Alfred Paget *Belshazzar* · Seena Owen *Attarea* ■ *Dir/Scr* DW Griffith

Intrigue ★ PG
Adventure 1947 · US · BW · 86min

In Shanghai after the Second World War, former tough-guy pilot George Raft finds himself working for a black-marketeering outfit. But when he discovers that the gang's food-price fixing is causing suffering to orphans, he sets out to remedy the situation. Edwin L Marin's direction has no discernible influence over the cliché-ridden and totally unbelievable plot, or the now ageing Raft's impassive performance. AJ

George Raft *Brad Dunham* · June Havoc *Tamara Baranoff* · Helena Carter *Linda Arnold* · Tom Tully *Marc Andrews* · Marvin Miller *Ramon* · Dan Seymour *Karidian* ■ *Dir* Edwin L Marin · *Scr* Barry Trivers, George Slavin, from a story by George Slavin

Introducing Dorothy Dandridge ★★★ 15
Biographical drama 1999 · US · Colour · 110min

Halle Berry may have won a Golden Globe for her performance, but there's a lingering feeling she was accoladed to atone for the shameful treatment meted out to the subject of Martha Coolidge's earnest, but unrevealing TV biopic. Too little is made of the institutionalised racism that blighted 1950s Tinseltown and transformed the

Oscar-nominated star of *Carmen Jones* into a marginalised, pill-popping drunk. Despite the award, Berry is too slight a talent for the part and she's easily overshadowed by Klaus Maria Brandauer's imposing Otto Preminger. Released on video and DVD as *Face of an Angel*. DP *DVD*

Halle Berry *Dorothy Dandridge* · Brent Spiner *Earl Mills* · Obba Babatunde *Harold Nicholas* · Klaus Maria Brandauer *Otto Preminger* · Loretta Devine *Ruby Dandridge* · Cynda Williams *Vivian Dandridge* ■ *Dir* Martha Coolidge · *Scr* Shonda Rhimes, Scott Abbott, from the biography *Dorothy Dandridge* by Earl Mills

The Intruder ★★★ U
Drama 1953 · UK · BW · 81min

An intriguing idea - why would a wartime hero become a peacetime thief? - is played out mechanically by director Guy Hamilton, but performed with some force by officer Jack Hawkins, who finds a former member of his regiment (Michael Medwin) burgling his home. Hamilton was still honing his craft here, but he went on to be a fine action director. TH *DVD*

Jack Hawkins *Wolf Merton* · Hugh Williams *Tim Ross* · Michael Medwin *Ginger Edwards* · George Cole *John Summers* · Dennis Price *Leonard Perry* · George Baker *Adjutant* · Richard Wattis *Schoolmaster* · Dora Bryan *Dora Bee* ■ *Dir* Guy Hamilton · *Scr* Robin Maugham, John Hunter, Anthony Squire, from the novel *Line on Ginger* by Robin Maugham

The Intruder ★★★ 15
Drama 1961 · US · BW · 82min

This is a remarkable one-off from horror producer/director Roger Corman, turning his hand to this stark tale of bigotry in the Deep South based on a controversial novel by screenwriter Charles Beaumont. William Shatner is the *agent provocateur* who incites racist riots in opposition to the then new US school integration. As Shatner's character's true motives are revealed, the film becomes particularly effective and genuinely unsettling. Not a success in its day, it has achieved a certain cult notoriety and is well worth seeking out. TS *DVD*

William Shatner *Adam Cramer* · Frank Maxwell *Tom McDaniel* · Beverly Lunsford *Ella McDaniel* · Robert Emhardt *Verne Shipman* · Jeanne Cooper *Vi Griffin* ■ *Dir* Roger Corman · *Scr* Charles Beaumont, from his novel

The Intruder ★★ 15
Drama 2004 · Fr/S Kor · Colour · 120min

In this story of a philosopher's ambivalent opinions on his heart transplant and what follows, the attention jerks back and forth between various characters doing fairly inexplicable things: elderly Michel Subor receives a new heart and sets off for the South Seas to find a son that he's never met; a dog breeder (Béatrice Dalle) refuses to look after the old man's dogs while he's away; a mysterious Russian woman shadows Subor on his numerous wanderings. It may look luscious but too much allegory can make your brain hurt. LF French, Russian, Korean, English, Tahitian +subtitles. Violence. *DVD*

Michel Subor *Louis Trebor* · Grégoire Colin *Sidney* · Katia Golubeva *Young Russian woman* · Bambou *Pharmacist* · Florence Loiret-Caille [Florence Loiret Caille] *Antoinette, customs officer* · Lolita Chammah *Little savage* · Béatrice Dalle *Queen of the Northern Hemisphere* · Alex Descas *Priest* ■ *Dir* Claire Denis · *Scr* Claire Denis, Jean-Pol Fargeau, from the novel by Jean-Luc Nancy

Intruder in the Dust ★★★
Drama 1949 · US · BW · 86min

This is a solid adaptation of William Faulkner's novel about a black man (Juano Hernandez) who faces a lynch mob after he's accused of shooting a white man. He isn't guilty, of course, but his pride and obvious contempt for the justice system harm his case. Director Clarence Brown, best known for his work with Greta Garbo, refuses to let hysteria invade the picture and he gets marvellous atmosphere from his location shooting in Oxford, Mississippi, Faulkner's home town. AT

David Brian *John Gavin Stevens* · Claude Jarman Jr *Chick Mallison* · Juano Hernandez *Lucas Beauchamp* · Porter Hall *Nub Gowrie* · Will Geer *Sheriff Hampton* ■ *Dir* Clarence Brown · *Scr* Ben Maddow, from the novel by William Faulkner

The Intruders ★★
Western 1970 · US · Colour · 100min

John Saxon plays the former resident of a Minnesota town who returns to help washed-up marshal Don Murray take on the James and Younger gangs. But it's the supporting cast, which includes Edmond O'Brien, *Forbidden Planet* star Anne Francis, Harry Dean Stanton and a fresh-faced Harrison Ford, that will keep most film buffs entertained. Credit should also go to writer Dean Riesner (a Clint Eastwood regular) for trying to introduce a psychological element into what is essentially a Saturday matinée plot. DP Some violence.

Don Murray *Sam Garrison* · Anne Francis *Leora Garrison* · Edmond O'Brien *Colonel William Bodeen* · John Saxon *Billy Pye* · Gene Evans *Cole Younger* · Stuart Margolin *Jesse James* · Harry Dean Stanton *Whit Dykstra* · Zalman King *Bob Younger* · Harrison Ford *Carl* ■ *Dir* William A Graham · *Scr* Dean Riesner, from a story by William Douglas Lansford

Intruders ★★ 15
Horror thriller 2011 · US/UK/Sp · Colour · 95min

Faceless monsters at large in children's bedrooms provide the spooky but scattergun thrills in this puzzling tale of things going bump in the night. Young Spanish boy Juan (Izán Cochero) is terrorised by a hooded figure he calls Hollowface, prompting his mother to seek the help of the clergy. The same menace also preys upon 12-year-old Mia (Ella Purnell) in London. Can her dad (Clive Owen) come to the rescue? Does Hollowface only exist in the children's heads, or is he a very real threat? Director Juan Carlos Fresnadillo (*28 Weeks Later*) delivers only brief flashes of tension, as the film's sluggish plot is bogged down by clunky dialogue and an unsatisfying resolution. TeS English, Spanish +subtitles. Swearing. *DVD* *BD*

Clive Owen *John Farrow* · Carice van Houten *Sue Farrow* · Daniel Brühl *Father Antonio* · Kerry Fox *Dr Rachel* · Pilar López de Ayala [Pilar Lopez de Ayala] *Luisa* · Ella Purnell *Mia* · Izán Corchero *Juan* ■ *Dir* Juan Carlos Fresnadillo · *Scr* Nico Casariego, Jaime Marques

Invaders from Mars ★★★★ PG
Science-fiction drama 1953 · US · Colour · 77min

William Cameron Menzies helped to design *Gone with the Wind* and directed *Things to Come*, and his Martian fairy tale has achieved cult status because of its distorted sets and abstract surrealism. Yes, you can see the zips on the aliens' suits, and, yes, the paranoia scares are strictly kids' stuff. But that's precisely why this pulp nightmare has built up a following. For it depicts perfectly, from a child's point of view, the ultimate horror of having no one to trust and nowhere to turn. AJ *DVD*

Helena Carter *Dr Pat Blake* · Arthur Franz *Dr Stuart Kelston* · Jimmy Hunt *David MacLean* · Leif Erickson *George MacLean* · Hillary Brooke *Mary MacLean* ■ *Dir* William Cameron Menzies · *Scr* William Cameron Menzies, Richard Blake, John Tucker Battle, from a story by John Tucker Battle

Invaders from Mars ★★★ PG
Science-fiction comedy 1986 · US · Colour · 94min

Director Tobe Hooper, best known for *The Texas Chain Saw Massacre*, skirts a fine line between kitsch and spoof in his big-budget remake of the 1953 B-movie. Clinging closely to the original primal paranoia story of a young boy's neighbourhood suddenly being overrun by aliens, Hooper's deadpan sci-fi comedy provides good scares, great visual design and Stan Winston's wonderfully wild Martian monster special effects. AJ

Karen Black *Linda* • Hunter Carson *David Gardner* • Timothy Bottoms *George Gardner* • Laraine Newman *Ellen Gardner* • James Karen *General Wilson* • Louise Fletcher *Mrs McKeltch* • *Dir* Tobe Hooper • *Scr* Dan O'Bannon, Don Jakoby, Richard Blake

Invasion ★★ PG

Science-fiction thriller 1965 · UK · BW · 77min

Aliens put an invisible force field around a secluded country hospital in this endearingly daffy British oddity, which must feature the cheapest alien takeover in history. Edward Judd is the scientist battling the extraterrestrial Oriental women in spacesuits, in an efficiently made and, yes, mildly exciting slice of cut-price science fiction. Director Alan Bridges imbues the Home Counties atmosphere with a peculiar ambience that's astonishingly heady at times. AJ

Edward Judd *Dr Vernon* • Yoko Tani *Lystrian leader* • Valerie Gearon *Dr Claire Harlan* • Lyndon Brook *Brian Carter* • Tsai Chin *Nurse Lim* ■ *Dir* Alan Bridges • *Scr* Roger Marshall, from a story by Robert Holmes

The Invasion ★★ 15

Science-fiction horror thriller 2007 · US/Aus · Colour · 95min

This is the third, and easily worst, remake of Don Siegel's Cold War classic *Invasion of the Body Snatchers*. Reportedly dogged by production woes (including star Nicole Kidman being injured during a car stunt), it was reshot at considerable expense by a panicky studio. It certainly shows on screen, nudging towards near-incoherence by excessive tinkering. Kidman plays a Washington psychiatrist investigating a viral epidemic from space that's turning her fellow citizens into emotionless zombies. Attempts to tap into the post-9/11 zeitgeist are largely botched, while this version's greatest asset - its subversive, anti-human subtext - is left undeveloped, lost amid the reshoots. A few taut suspense sequences aside, this update is as hollow as one of its body-snatched pod people. JR DVD

Nicole Kidman *Carol Bennell* • Daniel Craig *Dr Ben Driscoll* • Jeremy Northam *Tucker Kaufman* • Jeffrey Wright *Dr Stephen Galeano* • Veronica Cartwright *Wendy Lenk* • Josef Sommer *Dr Henryk Belicec* • Celia Weston *Ludmilla Belicec* ■ *Dir* Oliver Hirschbiegel, James McTeigue • *Scr* David [Dave] Kajganich, from the novel *The Body Snatchers* by Jack Finney • *Cinematographer* Rainer Klausmann

Invasion of the Astro-Monster ★★ U

Science-fiction adventure 1965 · Jpn · Colour · 90min

More commonly known as *Monster Zero*, this marked Godzilla's fifth film appearance and his change of status from Japan's evil enemy to much-loved national institution. The incomprehensible plot is something about Godzilla and Rodan being shipped off in space bubbles to Planet X so they can defeat three-headed Ghidrah. But don't bother trying to work out the alien double-cross, just lie back, relax and enjoy the usual cheesy special effects. AJ Japanese +subtitles.

Nick Adams *Glenn* • Akira Takarada *Fuji* • Kumi Mizuno *Namikawa* • Keiko Sawai • Akira Kubo ■ *Dir* Inoshiro Honda • *Scr* Shinichi Sekizawa • *Special Effects* Eiji Tsuburaya

Invasion of the Body Snatchers ★★★★★ PG

Classic science-fiction thriller 1956 · US · BW · 80min

Pods from outer space land in a small Californian town and start replicating the inhabitants, replacing them with unfeeling doubles, in director Don Siegel's chilling science-fiction tale. This classic of the genre (co-scripted by an uncredited Sam Peckinpah) reflects the blacklisting hysteria of the McCarthy era, as Siegel tersely piles on the nightmare with pulse-pounding briskness. Although expertly remade since (including 1993's *Body Snatchers*), the original is still the most striking, with a justly famous scalp-freezing ending. AJ DVD

Kevin McCarthy *Miles Bennell* • Dana Wynter *Becky Driscoll* • Larry Gates *Danny* • King Donovan *Jack* • Carolyn Jones *Theodora* • Jean Willes *Sally* • Ralph Dumke *Nick* • Virginia Christine *Wilma* ■ *Dir* Don Siegel • *Scr* Daniel Mainwaring, Sam Peckinpah, from the novel *The Body Snatchers* by Jack Finney

Invasion of the Body Snatchers ★★★ 15

Science-fiction thriller 1978 · US · Colour · 110min

It was always going to be hard to better Don Siegel's 1956 classic, and if director Philip Kaufman doesn't quite succeed, he does manage to summon up an equally chilling air of paranoia in this remake, set in a coldly impersonal San Francisco. Donald Sutherland stars as the health inspector who begins to worry that people are acting weirdly normal, and there is solid support from Brooke Adams and a young Jeff Goldblum, plus a creepy turn from Leonard Nimoy. JF Swearing, brief nudity. DVD Blu

Donald Sutherland *Matthew Bennell* • Brooke Adams *Elizabeth Driscoll* • Leonard Nimoy *Dr David Kibner* • Veronica Cartwright *Nancy Bellicec* • Jeff Goldblum *Jack Bellicec* • Art Hindle *Geoffrey* • Kevin McCarthy *Running man* • Robert Duvall *Priest on swing* • Don Siegel *Taxi driver* ■ *Dir* Philip Kaufman • *Scr* WD Richter, from the novel *The Body Snatchers* by Jack Finney

Invasion of the Saucer Men ★

Science-fiction comedy 1957 · US · BW · 69min

In a "so-bad-it's-almost-good" sci-fi quickie, aliens inject Hicksville teens with alcohol so they'll be arrested for drink driving. Well, it's one way to take over the world, but won't it take rather a long time? Fans of the 1960s TV series *Batman* will recognise Frank Gorshin (the Riddler) as the conman planning to keep a dead alien in his ice box. Wretched, and unintentionally funny. AJ

Steven Terrell *Johnny* • Gloria Castillo *Joan* • Frank Gorshin *Joe* • Raymond Hatton *Larkin* ■ *Dir* Edward L Cahn • *Scr* Robert J Gurney Jr, Al Martin, from a story by Paul Fairman

Invasion Quartet ★ U

Second World War comedy 1961 · UK · BW · 91min

MGM's British department showed just how far its reputation had plummeted since the glory days of the late 1930s with this woeful wartime farrago. One might have had higher hopes for a script by Jack Trevor Story and John Briley, but what they serve up here is a preposterous tale about a ragtag outfit sent into Nazi-occupied France to knock out a gun aimed at Dover. DP

Bill Travers *Major Freddie Oppenheimer* • Spike Milligan *Lt Godfrey Pringle* • Grégoire Aslan *Major Pierre Debrie* • John Le Mesurier *Colonel* • Thorley Walters *Lt Commander Cummings* • Maurice Denham *Dr Barker* • Thelma Ruby *Matron* • Millicent Martin *Sister Kay Manning* • John Wood (2) *Duty officer, War Office* • Eric Sykes *German band conductor* ■ *Dir* Jay Lewis • *Scr* Jack Trevor Story, John Briley, from a story by Norman Collins

Invasion USA ★ 18

Action adventure 1985 · US · Colour · 103min

Cold War paranoia brings out the jingoistic worst in American hardman Chuck Norris, resulting in a prime slice of hammy action. Norris plays a retired CIA man who discovers a band of marauding Russian terrorists have invaded the United States and are killing innocent people and spreading panic all across Florida. Acting completely alone, Norris massacres entire divisions of Ruskies who have no answer to his warrior-like skills. Complete trash. JF DVD

Chuck Norris *Matt Hunter* • Richard Lynch *Rostov* • Melissa Prophet *McGuire* • Alexander Zale *Nikko* • Alex Colon *Tomas* ■ *Dir* Joseph Zito • *Scr* Chuck Norris, James Bruner, from a story by Aaron Norris, James Bruner

Inventing the Abbotts ★★★ 15

Romantic drama 1997 · US · Colour · 102min

Pat O'Connor's follow-up to *Circle of Friends* isn't quite as enjoyable, but is a pleasant enough distraction. Joaquin Phoenix and Billy Crudup star as two working-class brothers in 1950s Illinois who share a fascination for the neighbouring wealthy Abbott family, and two of the daughters – Jennifer Connelly and Liv Tyler – in particular. While there is a tentative romance between Phoenix and Tyler, it's overshadowed by deception and resentment between the families, which ultimately gives the film a depressing tone. Nice performances, though. JB Swearing. DVD

Joaquin Phoenix *Doug Holt* • Billy Crudup *Jacey Holt* • Liv Tyler *Pamela Abbott* • Will Patton *Lloyd Abbott* • Kathy Baker *Helen Holt* • Jennifer Connelly *Eleanor Abbott* • Michael Sutton *Steve* • Joanna Going *Alice Abbott* ■ *Dir* Pat O'Connor • *Scr* Ken Hixon, from the story by Sue Miller

Invention of Destruction ★★★★

Part-animated fantasy 1958 · Cz · BW · 95min

Adapted from a Jules Verne novel, this ingenious fantasy (with its pirates, volcanos, submarines, underwater cycles, hidden laboratories and rocket cannon) also borrows liberally from *20,000 Leagues under the Sea* and *The Mysterious Island*. There's also a hint of Georges Méliès in Karel Zeman's audacious blend of animation, puppetry, models, glass shots and live-action, which evokes the glorious 19th-century illustrations of the novel. The story of villainous aristocrat Miroslav Holub's attempt to steal the explosive developed by professor Arnost Navratil and his intrepid assistant, Lubor Tokos, is action-packed. DP Czech +subtitles.

Arnost Navratil *Prof Roche* • Lubor Tokos *Simon Hart* • Miroslav Holub *Argitas* • Frantisek Slegr *Pirate captain* • Vaclav Kyzlink *Serke* • Hugh Downs *Narrator* ■ *Dir* Karel Zeman • *Scr* Karel Zeman, from the novel *Face au Drapeau* by Jules Verne

The Invention of Lying ★★★ 12

Comedy 2009 · US/UK · Colour · 95min

Following the lukewarm reception for *Ghost Town* in 2008, Ricky Gervais applies his low-key brand of comedy to another high-concept Hollywood movie, only this time he co-writes and co-directs for the first time. The award-winning comedian stars as mild-mannered scriptwriter Mark Bellison, whose life trundles along in a world where lying has not yet been invented. This allows for a stream of easy gags, which start to pile up until the moment when Mark's new-found ability to spin a yarn elevates him to godlike status. The story is rather convoluted, but Gervais carries the film with apt assuredness and, as co-director, he allows a great supporting cast (including Rob Lowe, Tina Fey and Jonah Hill) to shine. SP Sexual references. DVD Blu

Ricky Gervais *Mark Bellison* • Jennifer Garner *Anna McDougles* • Jonah Hill *Frank* • Rob Lowe *Brad Kessler* • Tina Fey *Shelley* • Jason Bateman *Doctor* • Christopher Guest *Nathan Goldfrappe* • Philip Seymour Hoffman *Jim the bartender* • Edward Norton *Cop* • Patrick Stewart *Narrator* ■ *Dir/Scr* Ricky Gervais, Matthew Robinson (3)

Investigation of a Citizen above Suspicion ★★★ 18

Crime drama 1970 · It · Colour · 109min

This Kafka-esque drama, which won the 1970 Oscar for best foreign film, caused a storm of protest when it was released in its native Italy. Exploring the nation's fascist legacy, director Elio Petri pulls no punches in his depiction of a police chief who murders his mistress and then taunts his underlings with a string of clues. While Gian Maria Volonté is chilling as the contemptuous cop, Petri seems as pleased with the scam as his protagonist. He overloads the symbolism and drives home his political points when a craftiness commensurate with Ennio Morricone's score would have sufficed. DP Italian +subtitles.

Gian Maria Volonté *Police Inspector* • Florinda Bolkan *Augusta Terzi* • Salvo Randone *Plumber* • Gianni Santuccio *Police commissioner* • Arturo Dominici *Mangani* ■ *Dir* Elio Petri • *Scr* Elio Petri, Ugo Pirro

Invictus ★★★★ 12

Biographical sports drama 2009 · US/S Afr · Colour · 128min

The poem *Invictus* contains the lines "I am the master of my fate: I am the captain of my soul", words that gave hope to Nelson Mandela during the darkest days of his incarceration. They also provided the inspiration for Springbok rugby captain Francois Pienaar as he led his unfancied team in the 1995 Rugby World Cup in South Africa. That event forms the basis of Clint Eastwood's heart-warming drama, which shows how newly elected President Mandela used the tournament as a catalyst to bring his divided nation together. As Mandela, Morgan Freeman is suitably statesman-like and gives a convincing performance. Less convincing is Matt Damon, whose portrayal of Pienaar is hampered by the fact that he's less imposing than the real-life player. That we can forgive such flaws is down to Eastwood's skill at blending human drama and history. CP Swearing. DVD Blu

Morgan Freeman *Nelson Mandela* • Matt Damon *Francois Pienaar* • Tony Kgoroge *Jason Tshabalala* • Julian Lewis Jones *Etienne Feyder* • Adjoa Andoh *Brenda Mazibuko* • Patrick Mofokeng *Linga Moonsamy* • Matt Stern *Hendrick Booyens* ■ *Dir* Clint Eastwood • *Scr* Anthony Peckham, from the non-fiction book *Playing the Enemy: Nelson Mandela and the Game That Made a Nation* by John Carlin • *Cinematographer* Tom Stern (2) • *Music* Kyle Eastwood, Michael Stevens

Invincible ★★ 12

Historical drama 2001 · Ger/UK/Ire/US · Colour · 132min

Werner Herzog's lumbering study of the Nazi-sympathising mesmerist Erik Jan Hanussen whose bogus accomplishments bewitched Weimar Germany never comes close to rivalling the complexity and intrigue of *Hanussen*, director István Szabó's 1988 treatment of the same story. Tim Roth delivers his lines in a near-hypnotic monotone, while the painfully uncomfortable performance of Jouko Ahola – as the Polish Jew roped in to play an Aryan strongman in Roth's act – fatally undermines the drama. DP DVD

Tim Roth *Erik Jan Hanussen* • Jouko Ahola *Zishe* • Anna Gourari *Marta Farra* • Max Raabe *Master of ceremonies* • Jacob Wein *Benjamin* • Udo Kier *Count Helldorf* ■ *Dir/Scr* Werner Herzog

Invincible ★★ PG

Sports drama based on a true story 2006 · US · Colour · 99min

Vince Papale was the Rocky-like underdog who was plucked from unemployed obscurity in the mid-1970s and offered a chance to play with the NFL Philadelphia Eagles, a publicity stunt devised to encourage locals to engage with their team. In this feel-good biography, Mark Wahlberg does a reasonable job of capturing his famous character's modest decency, but there's little else to commend this lifeless and sanitised whitewash. Nice period detailing, good soundtrack selections and strong performances – Greg Kinnear is especially magnetic as Papale's rookie coach – can't make up for the lack of sports action and clichéd inspirational message. AJ DVD

Mark Wahlberg *Vince Papale* • Greg Kinnear *Dick Vermeil* • Elizabeth Banks (2) *Janet Cantrell* • Kevin Conway *Frank Papale* • Michael Rispoli *Max Cantrell* • Kirk Acevedo *Tommy* ■ *Dir* Ericson Core • *Scr* Brad Gann

The Invisible ★★ 12

Mystery thriller 2007 · US · Colour · 98min

This crass American remake of a Swedish horror hit fails to replicate its delicate atmosphere. Director David S Goyer

U SUITABLE FOR ALL   Uc SUITABLE ESPECIALLY FOR YOUNG CHILDREN (DVD ONLY)   PG PARENTAL GUIDANCE   12A UNDER 12s TO BE ACCOMPANIED (CINEMA ONLY)

presents it as a simple teen version of *Ghost*, as opposed to a provocative parable of what it means to be invisible, literally and figuratively. In spirit form, Justin Chatwin tries to lead police to his beaten body before death can claim him, as well as communing with his would-be murderer, the poor, misunderstood Margarita Levieva. The acting is so-so and the visual trickery is reasonably accomplished. But it's saddled with a typically upbeat Hollywood ending and the heart is definitely missing. AJ Some violence, swearing. *DVD*

Justin Chatwin *Nick Powell* • Margarita Levieva *Annie Newton* • Marcia Gay Harden *Diane Powell* • Chris Marquette [Christopher George Marquette] *Pete Egan* ■ *Dir* David S Goyer • *Scr* Mick Davis, Christine Roum, from the novel *Den Osynlige* by Mats Wahl

The Invisible Agent ★★★ U
Science-fiction spy drama
1942 · US · BW · 81min

Frank Lloyd (who twice won the best director Oscar) directs this tenuously connected response to the 1933 Claude Rains classic, *The Invisible Man*. The emphasis is on flag-waving escapism, with Jon Hall inheriting the evaporating talents of grandfather Rains, this time behind enemy lines in an attempt to confound the Axis. John P Fulton's Oscar-nominated special effects steal the show, but there are also some sterling supporting performances. DP

Ilona Massey *Maria Sorenson/Maria Goodrich* • Jon Hall *Frank Raymond/Frank Griffin* • Peter Lorre *Baron Ikito* • Sir Cedric Hardwicke [Cedric Hardwicke] *Conrad Stauffer* • J Edward Bromberg *Karl Heiser* ■ *Dir* Edwin L Marin • *Scr* Curtis Siodmak [Curt Siodmak], inspired by the novel *The Invisible Man* by HG Wells

Invisible Child ★★ PG
Drama
1999 · US · Colour · 87min

This TV movie gives us a mother with an imaginary middle child. Rita Wilson's family conspires in her shared fantasy, even hiring a nanny to help with their "three" children. Things start to unravel when the nanny becomes concerned for the wellbeing of the eldest daughter and decides to alert the authorities. This uncomfortable blend of fantasy and family drama treats mental illness far too lightly, with director Joan Micklin Silver (*Crossing Delancey*) seemingly uncertain of the right tone. MC

Rita Wilson *Annie Beeman* • Victor Garber *Tim Beeman* • Mae Whitman *Rebecca "Doc" Beeman* • David Dorfman *Sam Beeman* ■ *Dir* Joan Micklin Silver • *Scr* David Field, from a story by Ron Bass, David Field

The Invisible Circus ★★ 15
Coming-of-age drama
2000 · US · Colour · 92min

This is a beautiful travelogue saddled with an inconsequential story. Jordana Brewster heads for Europe to discover why her adored sister, Cameron Diaz, committed suicide. Amsterdam, Paris and the Portuguese coastline look stunning, but the flashbacks to Diaz's transition from 1960s hippy to 1970s anarchist are totally unconvincing, as is Brewster's hesitant romance with her sister's old flame, Christopher Eccleston. Director Adam Brooks relies on dodgy fashions and bad wigs for period feel, without making us care about his characters. DP *DVD*

Cameron Diaz *Faith O'Connor* • Jordana Brewster *Phoebe O'Connor* • Christopher Eccleston *Wolf* • Blythe Danner *Gail O'Connor* • Patrick Bergin *Gene* ■ *Dir* Adam Brooks • *Scr* Adam Brooks, from the novel by Jennifer Egan

Invisible Ghost ★ PG
Psychological mystery horror
1941 · US · BW · 65min

With his old studio, Universal, pulling out of horror, Bela Lugosi signed with Poverty Row outfit Monogram. The first of several pictures he made for them, this is technically the best (director Joseph H Lewis went on to make several highly regarded *film noir* classics). But the plot, outlandish even by 1941 standards, now exhibits a naivety worthy of Ed Wood.

Doctor Lugosi thinks he's under the spell of dead wife Betty Compson, and a series of murders ensues. DM *DVD*

Bela Lugosi *Dr Charles Kessler* • Polly Ann Young *Virginia* • John McGuire *Ralph/Paul* • Clarence Muse *Evans* ■ *Dir* Joseph H Lewis • *Scr* Helen Martin, Al Martin

The Invisible Kid ★ 15
Science-fiction comedy
1988 · US · Colour · 92min

Nerd student Jay Underwood stumbles onto an invisibility formula and uses it to wander into the girls' locker rooms and cause havoc. This juvenile fantasy is laden with dumb jock gags and inane sexist humour. Karen Black, queen of the B-movie cameo, wastes her talents once more playing Underwood's air-head mother. AJ

Jay Underwood *Grover Dunn* • Karen Black *Mom* • Wally Ward *Milton McClane* • Chynna Phillips *Cindy Moore* ■ *Dir/Scr* Avery Crounse

The Invisible Man ★★★★★ PG
Classic science-fiction horror
1933 · US · BW · 68min

Claude Rains is one of the most undervalued stars of Hollywood's Golden Age. It's ironic that a familiar face that few could put a name to should have made his name in a film in which he spends most of the action swathed in bandages or invisible. In truth, the success of this superb adaptation of HG Wells's novel is down to John P Fulton and John J Mescall's pioneering special effects and the eerie atmosphere conjured up by horror maestro James Whale. When playful pranks give way to megalomania and murder, the hidden dangers of Rains's miraculous concoction begin to take effect. A classic. DP *DVD* 🔵

Claude Rains *Jack Griffin, the Invisible Man* • Gloria Stuart *Flora Cranley* • William Harrigan *Dr Kemp* • Henry Travers *Dr Cranley* • Una O'Connor *Mrs Hall* ■ *Dir* James Whale • *Scr* RC Sherriff, Philip Wylie (uncredited), from HG Wells's novel • *Cinematographer* Arthur Edeson • *Art Director* Charles D Hall

The Invisible Man ★★
Science-fiction fantasy
1975 · US · Colour · 74min

This pilot film for a short-lived TV series stars David McCallum as a scientist involved in laser research who stumbles upon the secret of invisibility. Deciding to keep it from the military, he flees with interested parties in hot pursuit. A by-the-numbers TV movie, only notable now for writer/producer Steve Bochco's involvement. He went on to become the creative force behind such landmark TV shows as *Hill Street Blues*, *NYPD Blue* and *Murder One*. AJ

David McCallum (1) *Dr Daniel Weston* • Melinda Fee *Kate Weston* • Jackie Cooper *Walter Carlson* • Henry Darrow *Dr Nick Maggio* • Alex Henteloff *Rick Steiner* ■ *Dir* Robert Michael Lewis • *Scr* Steven Bochco, from a story by Steven Bochco, Harve Bennett, from the novel by HG Wells

The Invisible Man Returns ★★★
Science-fiction thriller 1940 · US · BW · 81min

The first sequel to the Claude Rains classic, while more modestly scaled than its predecessor, still receives a first-class treatment from director Joe May and, in many instances, surpasses the visual magic of the original. Vincent Price replaces Rains and gets his first starring role as a man condemned to hang for a murder he didn't commit. He persuades the brother of the man who created the invisible serum to give him a dose so he can find the real killer. Price's rich theatrical voice assures his invisible man has a credible presence. AJ

Vincent Price *Geoffrey Radcliffe* • Sir Cedric Hardwicke [Cedric Hardwicke] *Richard Cobb* • Nan Grey *Helen Manson* • John Sutton *Dr Frank Griffin* • Cecil Kellaway *Inspector Sampson* • Alan Napier *Willie Spears* ■ *Dir* Joe May • *Scr* Kurt Siodmak [Curt Siodmak], Lester Cole, from their story • *Cinematographer* Milton Krasner • *Special Effects* John Fulton

The Invisible Man's Revenge ★★ PG
Horror 1944 · US · BW · 74min

Special effects maestro John P Fulton is (yet again) the saviour of this Universal programmer. Jon Hall (who'd headlined *The Invisible Agent* two years earlier) also returns, this time seeking retribution for his abandonment on a diamond-seeking safari by the aristocratic Lester Matthews and Gale Sondergaard. Scream queen Evelyn Ankers plays their daughter, whom Hall plans to seduce despite her romantic ties to newspaper reporter Alan Curtis. The inimitable John Carradine makes the most of his limited time as a reclusive, eccentric scientist. DP

Jon Hall *Robert Griffin/Martin Field* • Leon Errol *Herbert Higgins* • John Carradine *Dr Peter Drury* • Alan Curtis *Mark Foster* • Evelyn Ankers *Julie Herrick* • Gale Sondergaard *Lady Irene Herrick* ■ *Dir* Ford Beebe • *Scr* Bertram Millhauser, suggested by the novel *The Invisible Man* by HG Wells

The Invisible Menace ★
Murder mystery 1938 · US · BW · 54min

This dull B-feature murder mystery is set in a remote military post, in which Boris Karloff is the prime suspect who, of course, cannot possibly be the guilty one. Eddie Craven repeats his role from the stage production on which this is based. The Broadway play was a flop so the real mystery was why Warner Bros wanted to film it not once but twice – the second time as *Murder on the Waterfront* in 1943. AE

Boris Karloff *Jevries/Dolman* • Marie Wilson *Sally Pratt* • Eddie Craven *Eddie Pratt* • Regis Toomey *Lieutenant Matthews* • Henry Kolker *Colonel Hackett* ■ *Dir* John Farrow • *Scr* Crane Wilbur, from the play *Without Warning* by Ralph Spencer Zink

The Invisible Ray ★★★
Science-fiction horror 1936 · US · BW · 82min

This is the film that introduced Boris Karloff to a role he would visit throughout his career: a sympathetic scientist whose remarkable discovery makes him a threat to society. Here, he becomes contaminated by a radioactive meteor found in Africa and learns his touch means death. When he suspects Bela Lugosi of trying to take the credit for his discovery, the "Radium X" substance within the meteor causes him to go insane and seek vengeance. Innovative special effects for its era and the ever-dependable "gruesome twosome" supply the thrills. AJ

Karloff [Boris Karloff] *Dr Janos Rukh* • Bela Lugosi *Dr Felix Benet* • Frances Drake *Diane Rukh Drake* • Frank Lawton *Ronald Drake* • Violet Kemble Cooper [Violet Kemble-Cooper] *Mother Rukh* • Walter Kingsford *Sir Francis Stevens* • Beulah Bondi *Lady Arabella Stevens* ■ *Dir* Lambert Hillyer • *Scr* John Colton, from a story by Howard Higgin, Douglas Hodges • *Special Effects* John P Fulton

Invisible Stripes ★★
Crime drama 1939 · US · BW · 81min

In a routine and deeply moralistic gangster story, George Raft is determined to go straight when he comes out of prison. The great William Holden, in his second significant screen role, plays Raft's volatile younger brother, and their mother is played by, of all people, Flora Robson – who was aged 37 at the time and wears rubber wrinkles. Humphrey Bogart is in it as well, as a trigger-happy killer. Director Lloyd Bacon keeps things moving. AT

George Raft *Cliff Taylor* • Jane Bryan *Peggy* • William Holden (2) *Tim Taylor* • Humphrey Bogart *Chuck Martin* • Flora Robson *Mrs Taylor* • Paul Kelly (1) *Ed Kruger* • Lee Patrick *Molly* ■ *Dir* Lloyd Bacon • *Scr* Warren Duff, from a story by Jonathan Finn, from the novel *Invisible Stripes* by Lewis E Lawes

The Invisible Woman ★★
Science-fiction comedy 1940 · US · BW · 72min

It's hard to see how John P Fulton's special effects merited an Oscar nomination when the titular Virginia Bruce's shadow is often clearly visible, but that sums up this sloppy

lampoon. Much merriment is to be had at Bruce's encounters with her abusive boss Charles Lane and hoodlum Oscar Homolka, while Margaret Hamilton and Charles Ruggles provide amusement as a couple of scandalised domestics. But the primary reason for catching this hackneyed comedy is John Barrymore's performance as the eccentric scientist. DP

John Barrymore *Prof Gibbs* • Virginia Bruce *Kitty Carroll* • John Howard (1) *Richard Russell* • Charlie Ruggles [Charles Ruggles] *George* • Oscar Homolka *Blackie* • Edward Brophy *Bill* • Margaret Hamilton *Mrs Jackson* ■ *Dir* A Edward Sutherland • *Scr* Robert Lees, Gertrude Purcell, Fred Rinaldo [Frederic I Rinaldo], from a story by Kurt Siodmak [Curt Siodmak], Joe May

The Invisible Woman ★★★★ 12
Period biographical drama
2013 · UK · Colour · 106min

The true story of the lengthy affair between author Charles Dickens and actress Ellen Ternan, some 27 years his junior, is depicted in this adaptation of Claire Tomalin's book. Expertly played by director/star Ralph Fiennes, the Dickens we meet here is strangely unfulfilled because his wife (and mother of ten children) doesn't really understand his work. Enter actress "Nelly" Ternan, who's besotted by Dickens's literary output, and soon realises the man himself is strongly attracted to her. Abi Morgan's screenplay frames the illicit consequences within the context of Ternan's later married life and it's a dramatically effective approach. Meanwhile Fiennes's confident direction proves to be a subtle, accomplished and intelligent piece of film-making. TJ *DVD* 🔵

Ralph Fiennes *Charles Dickens* • Felicity Jones *Ellen "Nelly" Ternan* • Kristin Scott Thomas *Mrs Ternan* • Tom Hollander *Wilkie Collins* • Joanna Scanlan *Catherine Dickens* ■ *Dir* Ralph Fiennes • *Scr* Abi Morgan, from the non-fiction book *The Invisible Woman: The Story of Nelly Ternan and Charles Dickens* by Claire Tomalin

Invitation to a Gunfighter ★★★★ U
Western 1964 · US · Colour · 88min

George Segal is a Confederate soldier who returns from the war to find the Union townspeople have seized his farm and hired a gunfighter to kill him. Written and directed by Richard Wilson, an associate of Orson Welles back in the Mercury Theatre and *Citizen Kane* days, it's an allegory about political exile and conformity that spends too much time in debate at the expense of action. Nevertheless, it's lifted by a knockout performance from Yul Brynner as the Creole gunfighter. AT *DVD*

Yul Brynner *Jules Gaspard D'Estaing* • Janice Rule *Ruth Adams* • Brad Dexter *Kenarsie* • Alfred Ryder *Doc Barker* • Mike Kellin *Tom* • George Segal *Matt Weaver* • Strother Martin *Fiddler* ■ *Dir* Richard Wilson (1) • *Scr* Richard Wilson, Elizabeth Wilson, Alvin Sapinsley, from a story by Hal Goodman, Larry Klein

Invitation to Happiness ★★★
Sports drama 1939 · US · BW · 98min

A well-bred society girl and an ambitious professional boxer fall in love and marry, but the clash of their different worlds and desires leads to several difficulties. A routine romantic drama, the film is lifted by the attractive star casting of Irene Dunne and Fred MacMurray, the characteristic Paramount gloss of the production and a comedy element injected by Charles Ruggles (brother of director Wesley). Polished performances, some ringside action and a satisfactory resolution complete the package. RK

Irene Dunne *Eleanor Wayne* • Fred MacMurray *Albert "King" Cole* • Charlie Ruggles [Charles Ruggles] *Pop Hardy* • Billy Cook (1) *Albert Cole Jr* • William Collier Sr *Mr Wayne* ■ *Dir* Wesley Ruggles • *Scr* Claude Binyon, from a story by Mark Jerome

Invitation to the Dance ★★★

Dance musical   1956 · US · Colour · 93min

Gene Kelly's personal and most ambitious undertaking is a pure dance film, which he conceived, choreographed and directed. It comprises three different ballets starring Kelly and an impressive assembly of American and European dancers. Of these, *Ring around the Rosy* (music by André Previn) is the most successful and entertaining segment, concerning a bracelet which passes through many hands before coming back to its original owner. The finale, *Sinbad the Sailor*, danced to Rimsky-Korsakov's *Scheherazade*, in which Kelly dances with animated cartoon characters (and Carol Haney's Scheherazade), is the most innovative and experimental. RK

Gene Kelly *The clown/The marine/Sinbad* · Igor Youskevitch *The lover/The artist* · Claire Sombert *The loved* · David Paltenghi *The husband* · Daphne Dale *The wife* · Carol Haney *Scheherazade* · Tamara Toumanova *Streetwalker* · Tommy Rall *Boyfriend* ■ *Dir/Scr* Gene Kelly · *Choreographer* Gene Kelly

Invitation to the Wedding ★ PG

Romantic comedy   1983 · UK · Colour · 88min

A senile bishop (Ralph Richardson, indulging his real-life passion for motorbikes) mistakenly weds the daughter of an impoverished earl to a visiting American. The dull confusion is compounded by the arrival of a Texan evangelist played, astoundingly, by John Gielgud, whose self-confessed inability with accents is well demonstrated. Inept and unfunny. DM

Ralph Richardson *Bishop Willy* · John Gielgud *Clyde Ormiston* · Paul Nicholas *David Anderson* · Susan Brooks *Lady Anne* ■ *Dir* Joseph Brooks · *Scr* William Fairchild, from a story by Fairchild, Joseph Brooks, Susan Brooks

Invocation of My Demon Brother ★★★ 15

Experimental horror 1969 · US · Colour · 11min

Underground film-maker Kenneth Anger described his 11-minute short as "the shadowing forth of Our Lord Lucifer as the Powers of Darkness gather at a midnight mass". A homage to Satanist guru Aleister Crowley, it uses dynamic montage to Mick Jagger's Moog synthesiser soundtrack, rejecting narrative. Anger himself plays the Magus, while Bobby Beausoleil is Lucifer, who appears at the climax. In between are shots of a satanic ritual, a Rolling Stones concert and GIs leaping from helicopters in Vietnam. Only for those who are in tune with Anger's homoerotic sensibility and visual style. RB

Speed Hacker *Wand-bearer* · Lenore Kandel *Deaconess* · William Beutel *Deacon* · Kenneth Anger *Magus* · Anton Szandor La Vey *His Satanic Majesty* · Bobby Beausoleil *Lucifer* ■ *Dir/Scr* Kenneth Anger

Involuntary ★★★ 18

Drama   2008 · Swe/Nor/Fr · Colour · 97min

The physical and moral consequences of going along with the crowd are examined in director Ruben Ostlund's shrewd snapshot of modern Sweden. Playing like a series of observational vignettes, this semi-improvised satire moves back and forth between the experiences and dilemmas of five sets of characters. With ultra-naturalistic performances adding to the film's air of documentary-style realism, the overall effect is like eavesdropping on a stranger's most mundane moments – something you'll find either car-crash fascinating or utterly tedious. SF Swedish +subtitles. Swearing, nudity. **DVD**

Villmar Bjorkman *Villmar* · Lola Ewerlund *Lola* · Maria Lundqvist *Maria, the actress* · Henrik Vikman *Henrik, the coach driver* · Linnea Cart-Lamy *Linnea* · Sara Eriksson *Sara* ■ *Dir* Ruben Ostlund · *Scr* Erik Hemmendorff, Ruben Ostlund

Iona ★★ 15

Drama   2015 · UK · Colour · 81min

This bleak, naturalistic drama begins with a low-key getaway on a ferry, and follows a single mother (Ruth Negga) as she flees from the Scottish mainland. Accompanied by her teenage son (Ben Gallagher), she travels to a remote island in the Inner Hebrides, which is where she lived as a young girl. What has happened to them? Why are they on the run? The answer to these questions is withheld for most of the film, which is unhurried and understated to a fault. The scenery is striking, and Negga is impressive as a woman haunted by events from her past. Regrettably, though, the film itself isn't worthy of such praise. SC Swearing, sex scenes. **DVD**

Ruth Negga *Iona* · Douglas Henshall *Daniel* · Tom Brooke *Matthew* · Michelle Duncan *Elisabeth* · Ben Gallagher *Bull* ■ *Dir/Scr* Scott Graham

Ip Man ★★★ 15

Biographical martial arts drama
2008 · HK · Colour · 106min

Donnie Yen takes the lead in this first film in a recent spate dedicated to the famed kung fu master. The film introduces Ip during the 1930s boom period in his native Foshan, where a life of domestic harmony with his young family comes to an abrupt end when Japanese forces seize control. Dispossessed and hungry, Ip is forced to scratch a living, but uses his skills to resist the enemy and becomes an inspiration to his fellow citizens. Yen's performance is a bit one-dimensional, but at least he gives a good account of himself in the finely composed and inventive close-combat scenes. JH Cantonese, Japanese +subtitles. Violence. **DVD** **Blu-ray**

Donnie Yen *Ip Man* · Simon Yam *Quan* · Hiroyuki Ikeuchi *Miura* · Lam Ka Tung *Li* · Fan Sui Wong [Fan Siu-wong] *Jin* ■ *Dir* Yip Wai-shun [Wilson Yip] · *Scr* Edmond Wong

The Ipcress File ★★★★ PG

Spy thriller   1965 · UK · Colour · 102min

Len Deighton's first spy novel had everything except a name for its off-the-peg hero. Producer Harry Saltzman decided on Harry Palmer and cast the virtually unknown Michael Caine. Designed as a counterpart to the Bond movies, which Saltzman also co-produced, the story uncovers KGB operatives in the British secret service. It's cunning, calculated and still works, thanks to some droll humour, John Barry's marvellously twangy score, Sidney J Furie's energetic direction and spot-on performances. Caine reprised the role in four further films, beginning with 1966's *Funeral in Berlin*. AT Swearing. **DVD** **Blu-ray**

Michael Caine *Harry Palmer* · Nigel Green *Dalby* · Guy Doleman *Colonel Ross* · Sue Lloyd *Jean Courtney* · Gordon Jackson *Jock Carswell* · Aubrey Richards *Radcliffe* · Frank Gatliff *Bluejay/Grantby* ■ *Dir* Sidney J Furie · *Scr* Bill Canaway, James Doran, from the novel by Len Deighton · *Cinematographer* Otto Heller · *Music* John Barry (1) · *Editor* Peter Hunt · *Art Director* Ken Adam

Iphigenia ★★★

Drama   1976 · Gr · Colour · 128min

Having already made *Elektra* and *The Trojan Women*, Michael Cacoyannis completed his Euripidean trilogy with this Oscar-nominated adaptation of *Iphigenia in Aulis*. In spite of the fragmentary nature of the source, the story of the ill-fated Athenian expedition to rescue Helen of Troy still makes for compelling viewing. However, Cacoyannis's overindulgence in directorial flourishes undermines the efforts of a sterling cast. DP Greek +subtitles.

Irene Papas *Clytemnestra* · Costa Kazakos *Agamemnon* · Costa Carras Menelaus · Tatiana Papamoskou *Iphigenia* · Christos Tsangas *Ulysses* · Panos Michalopoulos *Achilles* · Angelos Yannoulis *Servant* ■ *Dir* Michael Cacoyannis · *Scr* Michael Cacoyannis, from the play *Iphigenia in Aulis* by Euripides · *Editor* Michael Cacoyannis

Iraq in Fragments ★★★ 12

Documentary   2006 · US · Colour · 89min

The word documentary doesn't adequately describe this three-part study of Iraqi life and culture after the fall of Saddam Hussein's regime. Though filmed in several key areas – the capital, Baghdad, where odd-job boy Mohammed struggles to accept the country's changes; a small village where hardline Muslims enforce Islam with menaces; and the countryside, where we see Kurdish shepherds at work – *Iraq in Fragments* doesn't offer insight so much as observation. Beautifully photographed, sometimes at astonishingly close quarters, director James Longley's film is subtle and often poetic. The impressionistic style can be distracting, though, and the film feels frustratingly incomplete at times. DW Kurdish, Arabic +subtitles. **DVD**

Mohammed Haithem · Suleiman Mahmoud Suleiman · Nadeem Hamid · Sheik Aws Al Kafaji ■ *Dir* James Longley · *Cinematographer* James Longley

Irene ★★ U

Musical comedy   1940 · US · BW and Colour · 81min

RKO threw money at this slight confection that was bought as a vehicle for the Fred Astaire and Ginger Rogers before they parted company in 1939. The studio was rewarded with its third biggest hit of the year, but there was nothing remarkable about this Cinderella story. Indeed, the songs are a pretty sorry batch. Director Herbert Wilcox coaxes a reasonably frothy performance from his wife, Anna Neagle, but Ray Milland looks distinctly uncomfortable. DP

Anna Neagle *Irene O'Dare* · Ray Milland *Don Marshall* · Billie Burke *Mrs Vincent* · Alan Marshal *Bob Vincent* · Arthur Treacher *Betherton* · Roland Young *Mr Smith* ■ *Dir* Herbert Wilcox · *Scr* Alice Duer Miller, from the musical comedy by James H Montgomery

Irina Palm ★★★ 15

Black comedy drama
2006 · Bel/Lux/UK/Ger/Fr · Colour · 99min

A desperate, middle-aged widow discovers an X-rated way of raising money in this grungy mix of pathos and dark comedy. Rock icon Marianne Faithfull plays the suburban frump who becomes a sex worker in a seedy club in London's Soho to pay for a life-saving trip for her dying grandson. Refreshingly, Faithfull's Maggie is neither degraded nor exploited. Instead she becomes empowered as she finds professional success masturbating men under the pseudonym "Irina Palm". But Faithfull, who gives an affecting performance, and co-star Miki Manojlovic (as the cynical club owner) are left to camouflage the frequent plot absurdities. SF **DVD**

Marianne Faithfull *Maggie aka Irina Palm* · Miki Manojlovic *Miki* · Kevin Bishop *Tom* · Siobhan Hewlett *Sarah* · Dorka Gryllus *Luisa* · Jenny Agutter *Jane* ■ *Dir* Sam Garbarski · *Scr* Philippe Blasband, Martin Herron, from an original script by Blasband

Iris ★★★★ 15

Biographical drama
2001 · UK/US · Colour · 86min

Richard Eyre's film succeeds on the strength of its performances alone in this biography of one of the 20th century's most talented female writers. Judi Dench *is* Iris Murdoch. Without her and the incredible support from Jim Broadbent as Murdoch's devoted husband John Bayley and Penelope Wilton as society hostess Janet Stone, this simply wouldn't have the required emotional impact. As it is, you're moved to many, many tears. Murdoch's sharp academic mind is established from the beginning but the story becomes really compelling once the parallel flashback encounters between the young Iris and John (Kate Winslet and Hugh Bonneville) run concurrently with the older writer's gradual deterioration from Alzheimer's disease. LH **DVD**

Judi Dench *Iris Murdoch* · Jim Broadbent *John Bayley* · Kate Winslet *Young Iris* · Hugh Bonneville *Young John* · Penelope Wilton *Janet Stone* · Juliet Aubrey *Young Janet Stone* · Samuel West *Young Maurice* · Timothy West *Old Maurice* · Eleanor Bron *College principal* ■ *Dir* Richard Eyre · *Scr* Richard Eyre, Charles Wood, from the books *Iris: a Memoir* and *Elegy for Iris* by John Bayley

Iris ★★★★ 12A

Documentary   2014 · US · Colour · 79min

Albert Maysles died on 5 March 2015, but the 88-year-old documentarist bowed out with this masterly portrait of New York fashionista and interior designer Iris Apfel. Although Maysles is allowed to riffle through her Park Avenue closets and accompanies her on shopping trips, this shrewdly observed tribute to an unceasingly individual style icon is also a celebration of the 93-year-old's 67-year marriage to Carl, who turned 100 during the shoot. Studded with admirers, this is less freewheelingly vérité than Maysles's best work, but it's every bit as distinctive and delightful as its subject. DP Swearing.

Iris Apfel ■ *Dir* Albert Maysles

Irish Eyes Are Smiling ★★ U

Biographical musical comedy
1944 · US · Colour · 89min

This musical comedy is based very loosely on the life of turn-of-the-century songwriter Ernest R Ball, who's played rather one-dimensionally by Dick Haymes. After its opening scenes in Cleveland, the story moves to New York as Ball searches for fame and fortune and falls in love with a burlesque entertainer (June Haver). Standard fare. SH

Monty Woolley *Edgar Brawley* · June Haver *Mary "Irish" O'Neill* · Dick Haymes *Ernest R Ball* · Anthony Quinn *Al Jackson* ■ *Dir* Gregory Ratoff · *Scr* Earl Baldwin, John Tucker Battle, from a story by EA Ellington

The Irish in Us ★★

Comedy   1935 · US · BW · 80min

Response to this comedy depends on a tolerance towards sentimental family dramas with doses of Irish blarney. Still, there's no denying the quality of the cast, especially the enchanting Olivia de Havilland, then a newcomer to the studio treadmill. The story centres around the three O'Hara brothers (James Cagney, Pat O'Brien, Frank McHugh), who live in New York, looked after by mother Mary Gordon. There's romantic rivalry between two of the brothers, family feuding and an unlikely boxing match finale. BB

James Cagney *Danny O'Hara* · Pat O'Brien *Pat O'Hara* · Olivia de Havilland *Lucille Jackson* · Frank McHugh *Mike O'Hara* · Allen Jenkins *Carbarn Hammerschlog* · Mary Gordon *Ma O'Hara* ■ *Dir* Lloyd Bacon · *Scr* Earl Baldwin, from a story idea by Frank Orsatti

The Irishman ★★★★

Period drama   1978 · Aus · Colour · 108min

British actor Michael Craig, so long under contract to Rank, had to emigrate to Australia to get a role as big and beefy as this. He's a teamster so resistant to change that he prefers his team of horses to anything mechanical. Stubborn and doomed he may be, but we're willing him to succeed through battles against progress and the sad skirmishes of a family at war with itself. Donald Crombie directs with a sharp eye for period detail (the 1920s) and Michael Craig does him proud. TH

Michael Craig *Paddy Doolan* · Robyn Nevin *Jenny Doolan* · Simon Burke *Michael Doolan* · Lou Brown *Will Doolan* · Bryan Brown *Eric Haywood* ■ *Dir* Donald Crombie · *Scr* Donald Crombie, from a novel by Elizabeth O'Conner

Irma la Douce ★★★★ 15

Comedy   1963 · US · Colour · 140min

Billy Wilder took a hit Broadway musical, cut out all the songs and still came up trumps with this near-classic comedy. Jack Lemmon plays a priggish gendarme who dons a variety of improbable but hilarious disguises to save the soul (if not the virtue)

of Shirley MacLaine's Parisian hooker. Set in and around the Les Halles food market, brilliantly re-created on a Hollywood sound stage by art director Alexander Trauner, it's a puzzle of a picture about morality and redemption, energetically performed by its two leads. Blink and you'll miss James Caan making his screen debut as one of MacLaine's clients. AT *DVD*

Jack Lemmon *Nestor* • Shirley MacLaine *Irma La Douce* • Lou Jacobi *Moustache* • Bruce Yarnell *Hippolyte* • Herschel Bernardi *Inspector LeFevre* • Hope Holliday *Lolita* • Bill Bixby *Tattooed sailor* ■ *Dir* Billy Wilder • *Scr* Billy Wilder, IAL Diamond, from the play by Alexander Breffort, from the musical by Marguerite Monnot • *Music* André Previn • *Cinematographer* Joseph LaShelle

Irma Vep ★★★★ 15
Satirical comedy 1996 · Fr · Colour · 94min

Part homage, part satire, this is a gleefully scattershot and largely improvised view of French cinema. Lured to Paris to headline in a remake of a silent classic, Hong Kong film star Maggie Cheung finds herself at the mercy of a director on the verge of a nervous breakdown, an amorous volatile crew member and a mêlée of critics without an original thought to rub together. Sportingly sending up her own superstar status, Cheung is overshadowed by Jean-Pierre Léaud, who slyly lampoons the type of tortured auteur with whom he made his name. DP English, French +subtitles. Nudity. *DVD*

Maggie Cheung • Jean-Pierre Léaud *René Vidal* • Nathalie Richard *Zoé* • Bulle Ogier *Mireille* • Lou Castel *José Murano* ■ *Dir/Scr* Olivier Assayas

The Iron Curtain ★★
Spy drama 1948 · US · BW · 86min

This early Cold War drama is a pseudo-documentary, its grave tone alerting us to imminent communist takeover if not for the efforts of Dana Andrews and Gene Tierney. It seems the Soviets are up to no good in Canada, where spies and atomic secrets lie thick on the ground. Andrews is a Soviet dissident who wants to defect with his wife Tierney. The story is based on fact, hence the low-key and, unfortunately, rather dull approach. AT

Dana Andrews *Igor Gouzenko* • Gene Tierney *Anna Gouzenko* • June Havoc *Karanova* • Berry Kroeger *Grubb* • Edna Best *Mrs Foster* • Stefan Schnabel *Ranev* • Nicholas Joy *Dr Norman* ■ *Dir* William A Wellman • *Scr* Milton Krims, from the memoirs of Igor Gouzenko

Iron Eagle ★★ 15
Action adventure 1985 · US · Colour · 111min

This is one of the better *Top Gun* cash-ins, although it hardly deserved the long-running video franchise it grew into. Jason Gedrick plays the teenage flier who goes on a secret mission to rescue his father, a hostage in an unnamed Arab country ruled by nasty David Suchet. Louis Gossett Jr is the sympathetic serviceman who breaks the rules to help him by teaching him to fly and stealing a couple of F-16s. Utter tosh, of course, but the flying sequences are quite good. JF Violence, swearing. *DVD*

Louis Gossett Jr *"Chappy" Sinclair* • Jason Gedrick *Doug Masters* • David Suchet *Minister of Defence* • Tim Thomerson *Ted Masters* ■ *Dir* Sidney J Furie • *Scr* Sidney J Furie, Kevin Elders

Iron Eagle II ★★ PG
Action adventure 1988 · Can · Colour · 95min

Despite being a sequel, this made a surprising impact at the box office. Produced in 1988, it gave a glimpse of political changes to come, with the Russians and Americans joining forces to combat a new threat from the Middle East. There's plenty of airborne gung-ho action, but the performers fail to convince and the attempts at humour fall flat. A second sequel, *Aces: Iron Eagle III* followed in 1992. JF Violence, swearing.

Louis Gossett Jr *Brig Gen Charles "Chappy" Sinclair* • Mark Humphrey *Captain Matt Cooper* • Stuart Margolin *General Stillmore* • Alan Scarfe *Colonel Vladimir Vardovsky* ■ *Dir* Sidney J Furie • *Scr* Sidney J Furie, Kevin Elders

Iron Eagle IV ★★ 12
Action adventure 1995 · Can · Colour · 91min

The *Iron Eagle* franchise struggled to number four on the back of Louis Gossett Jr's enduring popularity in the role of air-force general Chappy Sinclair (retired). He is now running an air school for young offenders and they discover the local air base is being used by criminals involved with toxic chemicals. The authorities don't believe them, so they take matters into their own hands. Only Gossett Jr is worth watching. JF *DVD*

Louis Gossett Jr *Chappy Sinclair* • Al Waxman *General Kettle* • Jason Cadieux *Doug Masters* • Joanne Vannicola *Wheeler* ■ *Dir* Sidney J Furie • *Scr* Michael Stokes, from characters by Kevin Elders, Sidney J Furie

The Iron Giant ★★★★ U
Animated science-fiction adventure 1999 · US · Colour · 82min

This version of Ted Hughes's children's fable liberally borrows images from 1950s comic book art and conventions from the era's science-fiction movies to stunning effect. To a soundtrack of *American Graffiti*-style hits, this heavy-metal *ET* tells the tale of nine-year-old Hogarth, the giant alien robot he saves from electrical overload, and the fiercely protective relationship that develops between them. But the real thrills begin when a Communist-hating FBI agent arrives who is convinced that the walking Meccano set poses a Cold War threat. With political allegory for the adults and excitement galore for the kids, this poignant fairy tale should appeal to both. AJ *DVD*

Jennifer Aniston *Annie Hughes* • Harry Connick Jr *Dean McCoppin* • Vin Diesel *The Iron Giant* • James Gammon *Marv Loach/Floyd Turbeaux* • Cloris Leachman *Mrs Tensedge* • Christopher McDonald *Kent Mansley* • John Mahoney *General Rogard* • Eli Marienthal *Hogarth Hughes* • M Emmet Walsh *Earl Stutz* ■ *Dir* Brad Bird • *Scr* Tim McCanlies, Andy Brent Forrester [Brent Forrester], from a story by Brad Bird, from the novel by Ted Hughes

The Iron Glove ★★ U
Period adventure 1954 · US · Colour · 76min

Unless you're a Robert Stack fan, there's little to recommend this period tomfoolery about a young pretender to the throne of King George I. To be fair, Stack swashes a mean buckle; he also gets to romance the lovely Ursula Theiss, who later became Robert Taylor's second wife. The Technicolor's nice, the running time is mercifully short and Alan Hale Jr is on hand to remind audiences of his father, who he so uncannily resembled. TS

Robert Stack *Charles Wogan* • Ursula Theiss *Ann Brett* • Richard Stapley *James Stuart* • Charles Irwin *James O'Toole* • Alan Hale Jr *Patrick Gaydon* • Leslie Bradley *Duke of Somerfield* ■ *Dir* William Castle • *Scr* Jesse L Lasky Jr [Jesse Lasky Jr], DeVallon Scott, Douglas Heyes, from a story by Robert E Kent, from a story by Samuel J Jacoby

The Iron Horse ★★★★★ PG
Silent epic western 1924 · US · BW · 134min

Already a veteran of more than 40 films by the tender age of 29, John Ford established himself as a major talent with this colossal tale of railroads, romance and revenge. The pioneering work on the first transcontinental railroad brings with it greed, villainy and murder as Davy Brandon's surveyor father is murdered, supposedly by Indians. The adult Davy (George O'Brien) later returns to discover the real culprit. Although brimming over with incident, it's the re-creation of the pioneering West that earns the film its place in cinema history. Twentieth Century-Fox spared no expense to give a ring of authenticity to the gaudy saloons, the dusty cattle drives and the murderous raids, but it's Ford's affinity for the period and its people that brings the scene to life. DP *DVD*

George O'Brien *Davy Brandon* • Madge Bellamy *Miriam Marsh* • Cyril Chadwick *Peter Jesson* • Fred Kohler *Bauman* • Gladys Hulette *Ruby* •

James A Marcus *Judge Haller* ■ *Dir* John Ford •
Scr Charles Kenyon, from a story by John Russell, Charles Kenyon

Iron Jawed Angels ★★★ 12
Period drama based on a true story 2004 · US · Colour · 118min

Hilary Swank joins Frances O'Connor, Julia Ormond and Anjelica Huston in this interesting made-for-TV tale about women's suffrage in early 20th-century America. Swank, O'Connor and Ormond play frontline radicals in the fight for the establishment of the female vote, while Huston portrays the disapproving voice of the movement's "old guard". The inclusion of a cheesy romantic subplot is unnecessary, but the script, if a little on the wordy side, is smart and sassy, and the performances are excellent. DA *DVD*

Hilary Swank *Alice Paul* • Frances O'Connor *Lucy Burns* • Julia Ormond *Inez Mulholland-Boissevain* • Anjelica Huston *Carrie Chapman Catt* • Molly Parker *Emily Leighton* • Patrick Dempsey *Ben Weissman* ■ *Dir* Katja von Garnier • *Scr* Sally Robinson, Eugenia Bostwick Singer [Eugenia Bostwick-Singer], Raymond Singer, Jennifer Friedes, from a story by Jennifer Friedes

The Iron Ladies ★★★ 15
Comedy based on a true story 2000 · Thai · Colour · 104min

A huge hit in its native Thailand, this comedy is a strange-but-true sports story. Had it simply been the tale of a cash-struck volleyball team which defies the odds to take the national championships by storm, it might have been entertaining. But the fact that the players are an assortment of gays, drag queens and ladyboys gives it a human diversity that ensures the triumphs over adversity aren't confined to the court. Blending sentiment, slapstick and lashings of high camp, director Yongyooth Thongkonthoon could never be accused of subtlety, but his film has honesty and zest. DP Thai +subtitles. *DVD*

Jesdaporn Pholdee *Chai* • Sashaparp Virakamin *Mon* • Aekkachai Buranaphanit *Wit* • Gokgorn Benjathikul *Pia* ■ *Dir* Yongyooth Thongkonthun • *Scr* Visuttichai Boonyakarnjana, Jira Maligool, Yongyooth Thongkonthun

The Iron Lady ★★ 12
Biographical drama 2011 · UK/Fr · Colour · 104min

Mamma Mia! director Phyllida Lloyd bravely tackles the life of Prime Minister Margaret Thatcher, told in smash-and-grab flashbacks from Lady T's amnesiac dotage. Meryl Streep, with disarming conviction and entertaining panache, plays her at various stages of adult life, and is gregariously supported by Jim Broadbent as the ghost of her late husband Denis. But, while ticking off the key historical events – the Falklands, the miners, the Brighton bombing, etc – the movie fails to find purchase on any broader motivation, beyond that of quasi-feminist megalomania. Without the award-worthy Streep, this is just high-quality historical karaoke. AC Some violence, brief nudity. *DVD*

Meryl Streep *Margaret Thatcher* • Jim Broadbent *Denis Thatcher* • Olivia Colman *Carol Thatcher* • Alexandra Roach *Young Margaret Thatcher* • Harry Lloyd *Young Denis* • Anthony Head *Geoffrey Howe* • Richard E Grant *Michael Heseltine* • Roger Allam *Gordon Reece* ■ *Dir* Phyllida Lloyd • *Scr* Abi Morgan • *Cinematographer* Elliot Davis

The Iron Maiden ★★ U
Comedy 1962 · UK · Colour · 93min

This largely misfiring British comedy attempts to marry *The Maggie* and *The Titfield Thunderbolt*, but fails to match either. Yet again we have grown men going weak at the knees over a piece of clapped-out machinery, but here it's a traction engine instead of a boat or a train and, it strains for the same level of romance. Off to a slow start, the picture fails slowly towards the middle and finishes with a traction race that's hard not to like, even if it does steal every "aren't enthusiasts funny" joke that escaped being nailed down in *Genevieve*. DP

Michael Craig *Jack Hopkins* • Anne Helm *Kathy Fisher* • Jeff Donnell *Mrs Fisher* • Alan Hale Jr
Paul Fisher • Noel Purcell *Admiral Sir Digby Trevelyan* ■ *Dir* Gerald Thomas • *Scr* Vivian A Cox, Leslie Bricusse, from a story by Harold Brooks, Kay Bannerman

Iron Maiden: Flight 666 ★★★ 15
Music documentary 2009 · US · Colour · 112min

Even those who prefer their heavy metal without tattoos can't fail to be impressed by the sheer scale of Iron Maiden's 2008 world tour: 23 concerts on five continents in just 45 days. Their tour bus is a Boeing 757, piloted by frontman Bruce Dickinson, who like the rest of the band turns out to be a polite, affable chap. We start in Mumbai where, three decades into their career, the Maiden are inspiring a new wave of hard rock. Devotees will adore the logistics; the rest of us can marvel at their ardour – like the Sao Paulo priest who proudly shows off his 162 Maiden tattoos. CW *DVD* *Blu*

Bruce Dickinson • Pat Cash • Vinny Appice • Ronnie James Dio • Janick Gers • Derrick Green ■ *Dir/Scr* Sam Dunn, Scot McFadyen

The Iron Man ★★
Sports drama 1931 · US · BW · 81min

Tod Browning directs this conventional boxing drama about a lightweight on his way to the title. Playing the boxer is Lew Ayres, who must somehow cope with the demands of his manager as well as the duplicity of his wife, played by Jean Harlow. Critics weren't entirely enthusiastic about Harlow's performance, but her move to MGM a year later saw her brief but spectacular career really take off. AT

Lew Ayres *Young Mason* • Robert Armstrong *George Regan* • Jean Harlow *Rose Mason* • John Miljan *Paul H Lewis* • Eddie Dillon [Edward Dillon] *Jeff* • Mike Donlin *McNeil* ■ *Dir* Tod Browning • *Scr* Francis Edward Faragoh, from a novel by WR Burnett

Iron Man ★★
Sports drama 1951 · US · BW · 81min

The action is clumsily choreographed in this boxing B-movie. Lumbering about the ring as though he's got a sack of coal on his back, ex-miner Jeff Chandler couldn't look any less like a potentially murderous pug. Which rather undermines the premise that he's being exploited by ruthless brother Stephen McNally, while hoping to raise the dough to open a radio shop with girlfriend Evelyn Keyes. Rockier than *Rocky V*. DP

Jeff Chandler *Coke Mason* • Evelyn Keyes *Rose Warren* • Stephen McNally *George Mason* • Rock Hudson *Tommy "Speed" O'Keefe* • Jim Backus *Max Watkins* • James Arness *Alex* ■ *Dir* Joseph Pevney • *Scr* Borden Chase, George Zuckerman, from the novel by WR Burnett

Iron Man ★★★★ 12
Fantasy action adventure 2008 · US · Colour · 120min

In this classy addition to the Marvel Comics movie canon, Robert Downey Jr stars as billionaire playboy and weapons genius Tony Stark, who's captured and held hostage during a trip to Afghanistan. His captors order him to build them a bomb, but instead he devises an armoured suit that he uses to escape. Back in America, Stark creates the crime-fighting persona of Iron Man, but his business partner (Jeff Bridges) has his own ideas about how to use the technology. Jon Favreau's direction is unfussy and controlled, and he cleverly filters the comic's 1960s origins through contemporary war on terror paranoia. In an exemplary piece of casting, Downey Jr adds depth and believability to his character as both self-indulgent waster and do-gooder superhero, while the futuristic gadgets are great fun. The only slight disappointment is an ending that isn't in keeping with the briskly told story that's gone before. A sequel is due in cinemas in summer 2010. AJ *DVD* *CS*

Robert Downey Jr *Tony Stark/Iron Man* • Terrence Howard *Jim "Rhodey" Rhodes* • Jeff Bridges *Obadiah Stane/Iron Monger* • Shaun Toub *Yinsen* • Gwyneth Paltrow *Virginia*

"Pepper" Potts • Faran Tahir *Raza* • Leslie Bibb *Christine Everhart* • Stan Lee *Man in smoking jacket* ■ *Dir* Jon Favreau • *Scr* Art Marcum [Arthur Marcum], Matt Holloway, Mark Fergus, Hawk Ostby, from characters by Stan Lee, Larry Lieber, Jack Kirby, Don Heck

Iron Man 2 ★★★ 12
Fantasy action adventure
2010 · US · Colour · 119min

There's plenty going on in returning director Jon Favreau's sequel to the smash-hit original, though it does seem to coast through overfamiliar territory. This time Tony Stark (Robert Downey Jr, good as ever) is struggling with superhero fame, shattered relationships, governmental pressure and a debilitating form of blood poisoning. Meanwhile, Russian inventor Ivan Vanko (Mickey Rourke) creates his own deadly suit and weapons manufacturer Justin Hammer (Sam Rockwell) provides him with the resources to smash Stark's vision of privatised world peace. It may lack the fresh irreverence and excitement of the first adventure, but Vanko's dramatic appearance at the Monaco Grand Prix and the final showdown at Stark Expo make for spectacular set pieces. AJ Violence. **DVD**
Blu CS
Robert Downey Jr *Tony Stark/Iron Man* • Don Cheadle *Lt Col James "Rhodey" Rhodes/War Machine* • Gwyneth Paltrow *Virginia "Pepper" Potts* • Mickey Rourke *Ivan Vanko/Whiplash* • Sam Rockwell *Justin Hammer* • Scarlett Johansson *Natasha Romanoff/Natalie Rushman* • Samuel L Jackson *Nick Fury* • Jon Favreau *Happy Hogan* • Garry Shandling *Senator Stern* • Paul Bettany *Jarvis* ■ *Dir* Jon Favreau • *Scr* Justin Theroux, from characters by Stan Lee, Larry Lieber, Jack Kirby, Don Heck

Iron Man Three ★★★★ 12
Fantasy action adventure
2013 · US · Colour · 125min

Back on track after the disappointing first sequel, this back-to-basics adventure has impressive CGI action and a substantial and involving story to match, as a soul-searching Tony Stark (Robert Downey Jr) finds himself cut adrift from everything he holds dear. When a villain known as the Mandarin (a deceptively brilliant performance from Ben Kingsley) begins a terror campaign, Stark is attacked in his Malibu home and feared dead. The man-in-the-can soon realises the Mandarin has ties to Aldrich Killian (a superbly villainous Guy Pearce), a scientist from Stark's past. Director Shane Black and his co-writer Drew Pearce fill the unpredictable plot with smart surprises, breezy black humour and an exuberant sense of fun – and there's no shortage of visual spectacle, too. AJ Some violence, swearing. **DVD Blu 3D CS**
Robert Downey Jr *Tony Stark/Iron Man* • Gwyneth Paltrow *Pepper Potts* • Don Cheadle *Lt Col James "Rhodey" Rhodes* • Guy Pearce *Aldrich Killian* • Ben Kingsley *The Mandarin* • Rebecca Hall *Dr Maya Hansen* • Jon Favreau *Happy Hogan* ■ *Dir* Shane Black • *Scr* Shane Black, Drew Pearce, from characters by Don Heck, Jack Kirby, Stan Lee, Larry Lieber • *Cinematographer* John Toll

The Iron Mask ★★
Swashbuckling adventure
1929 · US · BW · 95min

This fair swashbuckler has Douglas Fairbanks repeating his 1921 role as the noble swordsmith D'Artagnan in *The Three Musketeers*, and is done very much in the style of a silent picture. In fact, *The Iron Mask* was heavily touted as Fairbanks's first talkie, though the actor, who never really enjoyed an intimate relationship with a microphone, only spoke a brief prologue and an epilogue. Film historians have argued that Fairbanks himself had never used his own voice, citing as evidence the fact that his son, Douglas Fairbanks Jr, revoiced the film for a 1940 re-issue. AT
Douglas Fairbanks *D'Artagnan* • Belle Bennett *The Queen Mother* • Marguerite de la Motte *Constance* • Dorothy Revier *Milady De Winter* • Vera Lewis *Mme Peronee* • Rolfe Sedan *Louis XIII* ■ *Dir* Allan Dwan • *Scr* Elton Thomas, from the novels *The Three Musketeers* and *The Viscount of Bragelonne* by Alexandre Dumas

Iron Maze ★★★ 15
Mystery thriller 1991 · US/Jpn · Colour · 97min

Jeff Fahey gives one of his best performances in this moody, downbeat thriller, playing a blue-collar worker implicated in the attempted murder of a Japanese businessman bent on closing down a steelworks. The excellent JT Walsh is the sceptical cop investigating the crime, while Bridget Fonda is the interloper's American bride who may have been having an affair with Fahey. It's a little self-important for its own good, but director Hiroaki Yoshida accurately captures the bleakness of a small town dying. JF Violence, swearing, sex scenes, nudity. **DVD**
Jeff Fahey *Barry* • Bridget Fonda *Chris* • Hiroaki Murakami *Junichi Sugita* • JT Walsh *Jack Ruhle* • Gabriel Damon *Mikey* • John Randolph *Mayor Peluso* • Peter Allas *Eddie* ■ *Dir* Hiroaki Yoshida • *Scr* Tim Metcalfe, from the short story *In The Grove* by Ryunosuke Akutagawa, from a story by Hiroaki Yoshida

The Iron Mistress ★★
Biographical adventure
1952 · US · Colour · 108min

Steely-eyed Alan Ladd stars as Jim Bowie, famed inventor of the knife – the "iron mistress" – that bears his name, in this would-be rip-roaring Warner Bros adventure. Trouble is, the screenplay isn't as sharp as the knife itself, and there's a fair bit of romantic padding holding up the action, as Ladd gets rejected by Virginia Mayo only to fall for Phyllis Kirk en route to his destiny at the Alamo. There's a run-of-the-mill feeling to the tale. TS
Alan Ladd *Jim Bowie* • Virginia Mayo *Judalon de Bornay* • Joseph Calleia *Juan Moreno* • Phyllis Kirk *Ursula de Veramendi* ■ *Dir* Gordon Douglas • *Scr* James R Webb, from a story by Paul I Wellman

Iron Monkey ★★★ 12
Period martial arts adventure
1993 · HK · Colour · 86min

This assured blend of teen pic and Cantonese myth is proof positive that wire work was common in Hong Kong cinema long before dragons took to hiding. Determined to capture Yu Rong Guang, a 19th-century doctor who doubles as a masked champion of the oppressed, Qing Dynasty nasties kidnap martial arts master Donnie Yen's son to ensure his complicity, but the plan backfires. It's fun, but Yuen Woo-Ping is so preoccupied with his exhilarating stunt sequences that he does a disservice to the screenplay's sly political parallels to the present day. A sequel followed in 1996. DP Cantonese dubbed. **DVD**
Yu Rong Guang *Dr Yang/Iron Monkey* • Donnie Yen *Wong Kei Ying* • Tsang Sze-man *Young Wong Fei-hung* • Jean Wang *Miss Orchid* ■ *Dir* Yuen Woo-Ping • *Scr* Cheung Tan, Lau Tai-muk, Tang Pik-yin, Tsui Hark

The Iron Petticoat ★★★★ U
Romantic comedy 1956 · UK · Colour · 90min

There's a fabulous chemistry between Katharine Hepburn as a Russian aviatrix and Bob Hope as an American serviceman that's a sheer joy to observe in this latter-day version of *Ninotchka*, filmed in England from a clever screenplay by Hollywood veteran Ben Hecht. A wonderful supporting cast excels under the direction of underrated British great Ralph Thomas, and, with the Cold War gone, the attitudes expressed here now seem hilarious. TS **DVD**
Bob Hope *Chuck Lockwood* • Katharine Hepburn *Vinka Kovelenko* • James Robertson Justice [James Robertson-Justice] *Colonel Sklarnoff* • Robert Helpmann *Ivan Kropotkin* • David Kossoff *Dr Dubratz* • Sidney James *Paul* ■ *Dir* Ralph Thomas • *Scr* Ben Hecht, from a story by Harry Saltzman

The Iron Sheriff ★★★ U
Western 1957 · US · BW · 73min

This is another in a number of minor but competent westerns that were raised by the presence of Sterling Hayden's rugged looks. As a sheriff, Hayden sets out to prove that his son (Darryl Hickman) is innocent of robbery and murder, even though he has substantial evidence against him. What the film lacks in suspense, it makes up for in the playing and the intriguing moral dimension. RB
Sterling Hayden *Sheriff Galt* • Constance Ford *Claire* • John Dehner *Pollock* • Kent Taylor *Quincy* • Darryl Hickman *Benjie* ■ *Dir* Sidney Salkow • *Scr* Seeleg Lester

Iron Sky ★★ 15
Science-fiction action comedy
2012 · Fin/Ger/Can/Aus · Colour · 88min

In this outlandish sci-fi comedy, a group of Nazis escape Earth after the Second World War and hide out on the Moon; fast forward to 2018, and the Teutonic hordes plot their return to complete their goal of global dominance, with only American astronaut Christopher Kirby and conscientious fraulein Julia Dietze to stop them. Already a cult long before its release (it took six years to make), director Timo Vuorensola's film is a misfiring satire on modern-day right-wing politics, let down by predictable slapstick, corny dialogue and erratic acting. The special effects and set design are tremendous, but no amount of inventive CGI can compensate for the hammy human element and sluggish storyline. TeS In English, German. **DVD Blu**
Julia Dietze *Renate Richter* • Götz Otto [Gotz Otto] *Klaus Adler* • Christopher Kirby *James Washington* • Peta Sergeant *Vivian Wagner* • Stephanie Paul *President of the United States* • Udo Kier *Wolfgang Kortzfleisch* ■ *Dir* Timo Vuorensola • *Scr* Michael Kalesniko, from a story by Johanna Sinisalo, from an idea by Jarmo Puskala

The Iron Triangle ★★★ 18
War action adventure
1988 · US · Colour · 86min

This is one of a handful of American films that attempt to present all sides of the Vietnam War as fully developed characters. Political arguments are also largely ignored since this is a war between people who kill each other, take each other prisoner and sometimes find it hard to continue the killing. Beau Bridges plays an American captain who loathes the cruelty of his allies, the South Vietnamese, and is then taken prisoner; the Oscar winner from *The Killing Fields*, Haing S Ngor, plays a North Vietnamese officer. AT
Beau Bridges *Captain Keene* • Haing S Ngor *Captain Tuong* • Johnny Hallyday *Jacques* • James Ishida *Khoi* ■ *Dir* Eric Weston • *Scr* Eric Weston, John Bushelman, Larry Hilbrand

Iron Will ★★★ U
Period adventure 1994 · US · Colour · 104min

Disney drew on a true story for this cracking piece of family entertainment. Set in 1917, it stars MacKenzie Astin as the South Dakota teenager who enters the world's toughest dog-sled marathon both to prevent the loss of the family farm following the death of his dad and to pay for his education. Naturally, all manner of dangers and disasters face him on the 522-mile trek from Canada to Minnesota. With action aplenty and a neat supporting turn from Kevin Spacey as a mythologising journalist, this should keep all amused. DP **DVD**
MacKenzie Astin *Will Stoneman* • Kevin Spacey *Harry Kingsley* • David Ogden Stiers *JP Harper* • August Schellenberg *Ned Dodd* • Brian Cox (1) *Angus McTeague* ■ *Dir* Charles Haid • *Scr* John Michael Hayes, Djordje Milicevic, Jeff Arch

Ironclad ★★ 15
Period action adventure
2010 · US/UK/Ger · Colour · 115min

Historical saga meets axe-wielding action in this initially compelling but increasingly slipshod medieval adventure. Having signed Magna Carta against his will, a petulant King John (Paul Giamatti) marches against England's nobles. A troubled Knight Templar (James Purefoy) and defiant Baron Albany (Brian Cox) are determined to hold out against the king at the strategically significant Rochester Castle. Between the rip-snorting combat highlights, there's a misbegotten romance involving strong, silent Purefoy and Kate Mara's lady of the house, but Giamatti's enthusiastically ill-tempered John perks things up when he's on screen. TJ Violence. **DVD Blu**
James Purefoy *Marshall* • Brian Cox (1) *Baron Albany* • Kate Mara *Lady Isabel* • Paul Giamatti *King John* • Derek Jacobi *Reginald de Cornhill* • Charles Dance *Archbishop Langton* • Jason Flemyng *Beckett* • Mackenzie Crook *Marks* ■ *Dir* Jonathan English • *Scr* Jonathan English, Erick Kastel, from a story by English, from a screenplay (unproduced) by Stephen McDool

Ironclad 2 ★ 15
Period action adventure
2014 · UK · Colour · 107min

A brash, low budget sequel to the 2010 medieval action film, following a survivor of the siege of Rochester Castle (Tom Austen), who leads a group of mercenaries in a new battle to save his family's castle from a Celtic invasion. With all the on-screen pedigree from the first film absent and a vague re-tread of the plot, original director Jonathan English relies on vast amounts of gore and headache-inducing handheld camerawork to deliver a film that only just delivers on its title. JL Violence, sex scenes, nudity. **DVD Blu**
Tom Austen *Guy de Lusignan* • Tom Rhys Harries [Tom Harries] *Hubert De Vesci* • Roxanne McKee *Blanche* • Michelle Fairley *Joan De Vesci* • David Rintoul *Gilbert De Vesci* ■ *Dir* Jonathan English • *Scr* Jonathan English, Stephen McDool

Ironweed ★★★ 15
Period drama 1987 · US · Colour · 136min

Like a famished carnivore, Jack Nicholson sinks his teeth into this meaty role as a Depression-era alcoholic drifter. He is haunted by memories of the events that led to his current state of degradation – most tragically the accidental death of his baby son. Bag-lady Meryl Streep sees hope in his survival, but Hector Babenco's film is a grim odyssey with only the strong performances of Oscar-nominees Nicholson and Streep to sustain it. TH
Jack Nicholson *Francis Phelan* • Meryl Streep *Helen Archer* • Carroll Baker *Annie Phelan* • Michael O'Keefe *Billy Phelan* • Diane Venora *Peg Phelan* • Fred Gwynne *Oscar Reo* • Tom Waits *Rudy* ■ *Dir* Hector Babenco • *Scr* Wiliam Kennedy, from his novel

Irrational Man ★★ 12
Comedy drama 2015 · US · Colour · 90min

Joaquin Phoenix is a hard-drinking, womanising, philosophy professor who plots the perfect, random murder in a bid to give his directionless life some meaning. Phoenix is physical and terrific as the hedonist in a part that few could carry off without lapsing into parody, while Emma Stone shows once again that she has the chops for something with more bite than romantic comedy. The problem, however, is a clunky, wooden script that repeats the tropes and themes of Woody Allen's earlier, more successful efforts. DW Some swearing, sexual references. **DVD Blu**
Joaquin Phoenix *Abe* • Emma Stone *Jill* • Parker Posey *Rita* • Jamie Blackley *Roy* ■ *Dir/Scr* Woody Allen

Irreconcilable Differences ★★★★ 15
Comedy drama 1984 · US · Colour · 108min

This highly engaging comedy about the way success changes everything is written by the *Baby Boom* team of Charles Shyer (also making his directorial debut) and Nancy Meyers. Ryan O'Neal and Shelley Long star as the bright young couple who lose sight of what's important as they prosper in Tinseltown – so much so, their nine-year-old daughter sues them for divorce. Way ahead of its time and full of sharp Hollywood satire, the entire bittersweet story is told in flashback as witness-stand testimony. AJ Swearing, nudity.
Ryan O'Neal *Albert Brodsky* • Shelley Long *Lucy Van Patten Brodsky* • Drew Barrymore *Casey Brodsky* • Sam Wanamaker *David Kessler* • Allen

Garfield *Phil Hanner* • Sharon Stone *Blake Chandler* ■ *Dir* Charles Shyer • *Scr* Nancy Meyers, Charles Shyer

Irresistible ★★ 15

Psychological drama
2006 · Aus · Colour · 98min

In this muddled psychological drama, Susan Sarandon gives a dominating performance as a stressed-out book illustrator who becomes convinced that her husband's new assistant (Emily Blunt) is trying to steal her life and family. The cast do their best to animate their sketchy characters, but minimal dramatic momentum and scant interaction between the central trio turn what should have been a tense cuckoo-in-the-nest thriller into a plodding study of mental disintegration. SF Violence, swearing, sex scenes. *DVD*

Susan Sarandon *Sophie* • Sam Neill *Craig* • Emily Blunt *Mara* • Bud Tingwell [Charles Tingwell] *Sam* • William McInnes *Jimmy* • Georgie Parker *Jen* ■ *Dir/Scr* Ann Turner

Irreversible ★★★★ 18

Drama
2002 · Fr · Colour · 93min

Gaspar Noé's incendiary follow-up to *Seul contre Tous* is hard to watch and hard to forget. An intense and unflinching nightmare of rape and revenge, it is a haunting meditation on the fragility of life. Vincent Cassel and Monica Bellucci bare their souls magnificently as a middle-class couple who are plunged into a personal hell after Bellucci is raped and left for dead. Using inventive cinematography that tints every scene with acid-trip dementia, the film unfolds in reverse to embrace and deconstruct the whole spectrum of human emotion. It's distressing viewing that requires a strong stomach, yet, for all the feature's controversy, it never titillates. SF French +subtitles. *DVD*

Monica Bellucci *Alex* • Vincent Cassel *Marcus* • Albert Dupontel *Pierre* • Philippe Nahon *Philippe* • Jo Prestia *Le Ténia* ■ *Dir/Scr* Gaspar Noé

Is Anybody There? ★★★ 12

Drama
2008 · UK/US · Colour · 90min

In this 1980s-set tale, black humour and poignant drama combine when the arrival of an eccentric elderly magician (Michael Caine) puts new spark into the life of a lonely ten-year-old boy (*Son of Rambow's* Bill Milner) who lives in an old folks' home run by his parents. Considering the institution's mortality rate, it's no surprise that the boy has a morbid curiosity about the afterlife, which is piqued further by Caine's showbiz trouper whose days of pulling rabbits out of hats are coming to an end and whose mind is starting to deteriorate. Caine certainly reveals a touchingly vulnerable side, but his performance would have benefited from being in a more balanced film. TJ *DVD*
Blu-ray

Michael Caine *Clarence* • David Morrissey *Dad* • Bill Milner *Edward* • Anne-Marie Duff *Mum* • Thelma Barlow *Ena* • Rosemary Harris *Elsie* • Leslie Phillips *Reg* • Sylvia Syms *Lilian* • Peter Vaughan *Bob* ■ *Dir* John Crowley • *Scr* Peter Harness

Is Paris Burning? ★★★ PG

Second World War epic
1966 · US/Fr · BW · 165min

"Is Paris burning?" asks Adolf Hitler as the French Resistance rattles the Nazi occupiers and prepares the city for liberation. Conceived on the same lines as *The Longest Day*, this black-and-white multilingual war epic boasts an all-star cast and contains some spectacular scenes of fighting along the boulevards of the eponymous capital. Maurice Jarre's jangly music maintains the momentum, while Gore Vidal and Francis Ford Coppola were just two of the writers who laboured on the episodic script. AT In French, German, English. Violence

Jean-Paul Belmondo *Morandat* • Yves Montand *Bizien* • Orson Welles *Nordling* • Charles Boyer *Monod* • Leslie Caron *Françoise Labe* • Jean-Pierre Cassel *Henri Karcher* • Alain Delon *Jacques Chaban-Delmas* • Kirk Douglas *Patton* •

Glenn Ford *Bradley* • Robert Stack *Sibert* • Anthony Perkins *Warren* • Simone Signoret *Café proprietress* ■ *Dir* René Clément • *Scr* Francis Ford Coppola, Gore Vidal, Jean Aurenche, Pierre Bost, Claude Brule, Marcel Moussy, Beate von Molo, from the book by Larry Collins, Dominique LaPierre

Is the Man Who Is Tall Happy? ★★

Animated documentary
2013 · Fr · Colour · 88min

Left-field film-maker Michel Gondry interviews esteemed linguist and cognitive scientist Noam Chomsky on a variety of stimulating subjects – language, education, philosophy, grammar. The material can be quite dry, and the free-form, child-like doodles that fill the screen distract from the high-minded ideas being discussed. Intellectuals will find plenty to chew on, and there's a reasonable amount of mileage for fans of Gondry or Chomsky, but it's fair to say that this is a film of limited appeal. SC

■ *Dir/Scr* Michel Gondry

Is There Sex after Death? ★★★

Comedy
1971 · US · Colour · 97min

This is a series of skits, jokes and sketches, taking sex as their theme. Bawdier than Woody Allen's *Everything You Always Wanted Know about Sex*, this definitely deserved its R (Restricted) rating and would have been unmemorable if it wasn't for the wonderful performance by Buck Henry as Dr Manos, one of our guides to the weird and wonderful world of sex. This is an oddity worth seeking out for fans of vulgar and non-PC humour. DF

Buck Henry *Dr Manos* • Alan Abel *Dr Rogers* • Marshall Efron *Vince Domino* • Holly Woodlawn • Robert Downey Sr *Robert Downey* • Jim Moran *Dr Elevenike* • Rubin Carson ■ *Dir/Scr* Jeanne Abel, Alan Abel

Is Your Honeymoon Really Necessary? ★★ PG

Comedy
1953 · UK · BW · 75min

Adapted from the Vivian Tidmarsh play, this bedroom farce has been rather awkwardly converted to allow American Bonar Colleano to inherit a role originated by Ralph Lynn. However, it's a sprightly affair, with Colleano arriving in London with new wife Diana Decker, only to run into wartime bride Diana Dors, who isn't sure their divorce was entirely legal so they consult lawyer David Tomlinson. With Sidney James as Colleano's palocka pal, this may not be Maurice Elvey's finest hour, but it's fun. DP
DVD *Blu-ray*

David Tomlinson *Frank Betterton* • Diana Dors *Candy Markham* • Bonar Colleano *Commander Laurie Vining* • Diana Decker *Gillian Vining* • Sidney James *Hank Hanlon* • Audrey Freeman *Lucy* ■ *Dir* Maurice Elvey • *Scr* Talbot Rothwell, from the play by Vivian Tidmarsh

Isadora ★★★★ 12

Biographical drama 1968 · UK · Colour · 134min

Vanessa Redgrave superbly and insolently scandalises as Isadora Duncan, the improvisational and influential dancer whose life and career helped jazz up an earlier Jazz Age. She moves from James Fox to Jason Robards to Ivan Tchenko before her bizarre death – a broken neck caused by her scarf becoming entangled in the wheel of a sports car. Director Karel Reisz uses Isadora's life to celebrate a free-and-speakeasy era. Redgrave was Oscar-nominated for best actress but lost out to Barbra Streisand's *Funny Girl*. TH *DVD*
Blu-ray

Vanessa Redgrave *Isadora Duncan* • James Fox *Gordon Craig* • Jason Robards *Paris Singer* • Ivan Tchenko *Sergei Essenin* • John Fraser *Roger* • Bessie Love *Mrs Duncan* ■ *Dir* Karel Reisz • *Scr* Melvyn Bragg, Clive Exton, from the autobiography *My Life* by Isadora Duncan, from the non-fiction book *Isadora Duncan: an intimate Portrait* by Sewell Stokes

Ishqiya ★★ 15

Action drama 2010 · Ind · Colour · 110min

Naseeruddin Shah is probably best known to western audiences for his appearances in *Monsoon Wedding* and *The League of Extraordinary Gentlemen* (as a sword-wielding Captain Nemo), but much of his venerable career has been spent in Bollywood cinema. In this action drama, he brings undoubted charisma to bear as a thief who goes on the run with his nephew after a botched job. The two men then end up falling for a friend's widow (Vidya Balan), who involves them in her own machinations. It's undemanding fare but watchable, nonetheless. JA Hindi +subtitles. *DVD*

Naseeruddin Shah *Khalujaan* • Vidya Balan *Krishna* • Arshad Warsi *Babban Hussain* • Salman Shahid *Mushtaq* • Adil Hussain *Vidadhar Verma* ■ *Dir* Abhishek Chaubey • *Scr* Vishal Bhardwaj, Abhishek Chaubey, Sabrina Dhawan

Ishtar ★ 15

Comedy 1987 · US · Colour · 103min

Intended as a tribute to the Bob Hope and Bing Crosby *Road* movies, this has gone down in movie history as one of the grossest miscalculations of the blockbuster era. Even if you find it in yourself to accept the oddball casting of Warren Beatty and Dustin Hoffman as a couple of tone deaf songwriters, it's impossible to forgive the triteness and racial insensitivity of writer/director Elaine May's crass script. DP Swearing. *DVD*

Warren Beatty *Lyle Rogers* • Dustin Hoffman *Chuck Clarke* • Isabelle Adjani *Shirra Assel* • Charles Grodin *Jim Harrison* • Jack Weston *Marty Freed* • Tess Harper *Willa* • Carol Kane *Carol* ■ *Dir/Scr* Elaine May

The Island ★★★★ U

Drama 1961 · Jpn · BW · 92min

Already an established figure within Japanese cinema, Kenji Mizoguchi's protégé, Kaneto Shindo, garnered international acclaim for this austere study of the struggle for survival of a family farming a wild, isolated island. Always willing to experiment with theme and form, Shindo eliminated speech from this intense drama, as if to suggest both the couple's intuitive unity of purpose and the unjustifiable expenditure of effort when all their energies are needed to work the intractable land and fetch fresh water from the mainland. Forbiddingly photographed, there's a lingering suspicion that the rustic poetry is somewhat contrived. DP *DVD*
Blu-ray

Nobuko Otowa *Toyo* • Taiji Tonoyama *Senta* • Shinji Tanaka *Taro* • Masanori Horimoto *Jiro* ■ *Dir/Scr* Kaneto Shindo • *Cinematographer* Kiyoshi Kuroda

The Island ★★ 18

Adventure 1980 · US · Colour · 108min

This isn't so much a comedown as a plunge to the depths for Peter Benchley, the author of *Jaws*, who adapted this quite ridiculous picture from his own novel. It beggars belief that legendary composer Ennio Morricone, the usually dependable Michael Caine and more than capable director Michael Ritchie frittered away their talents on this tale of 17th-century pirates caught in the Bermuda Triangle. It's not quite bad enough to be a bona fide turkey, but it's pretty awful all the same. DP

Michael Caine *Blair Maynard* • David Warner *Jean-David Nau* • Angela Punch McGregor *Beth* • Frank Middlemass *Dr Windsor* • Don Henderson *Rollo* • Dudley Sutton *Dr Brazil* • Colin Jeavons *Hizzoner* ■ *Dir* Michael Ritchie • *Scr* Peter Benchley, from his novel

The Island ★★★ 12

Futuristic action thriller
2005 · US · Colour · 130min

This sleek, futuristic action thriller plays like a series of chase sequences dressed up with flimsy sci-fi. Yet, for all its superficiality, Michael Bay's film is relentlessly entertaining, with Ewan McGregor particularly engaging as one of the survivors of an ecological disaster that wiped out most of the planet's inhabitants. Now housed in a contained facility, he's led by curiosity to horrific discoveries about his home and the lottery draw that offers relocation to an allegedly uncontaminated paradise. Unfortunately, fellow resident Scarlett Johansson can't match McGregor's allure, and she's reduced to the role of ineffectual love interest. SF Violence, swearing. *DVD* *Blu-ray*

Ewan McGregor *Lincoln Six-Echo/Tom Lincoln* • Scarlett Johansson *Jordan Two-Delta/Sarah Jordan* • Djimon Hounsou *Albert Laurent* • Sean Bean *Merrick* • Steve Buscemi *McCord* • Michael Clarke Duncan *Starkweather* • Ethan Phillips Jones *Three-Echo* • Brian Stepanek *Gandu Three-Alpha* ■ *Dir* Michael Bay • *Scr* Caspian Tredwell-Owen, Alex Kurtzman, Roberto Orci, from a story by Tredwell-Owen

The Island ★★★ PG

Drama 2006 · Rus · Colour · 109min

This contemplative drama is set in 1976 at a tumbledown monastery on a remote island in the Russian Baltic, where a steady stream of believers seek the healing powers of the enigmatic Father Anatoly. It's hard to know what to make of this unkempt figure, who switches from haunted seer to vicious prankster in an instant. Thanks to the opening flashback, however, we soon see that memories of his traumatic Second World War experiences loom large in his psyche. Overall, the story's just a bit too neat to carry the portentous weight that director Pavel Lounguine seems to be willing into the material. Still, the mesmerising central performance from Pyotr Mamonov (a Russian rock star who retired when he found religion) makes Anatoly's every contradiction believable. TJ Russian, German +subtitles. *DVD*

Pyotr Mamonov *Father Anatoly* • Viktor Sukhorukov *Father Superior Filaret* • Dmitriy Dyuzhev *Father Iov* • Yuri Kuznetsov *Tikhon* • Viktoria Isakova *Nastya* ■ *Dir* Pavel Lounguine • *Scr* Dmitry Sobolev

Island ★★ 15

Psychological drama 2011 · UK · Colour · 96min

A young women travels to a remote Scottish island with the express intention of killing her estranged mother in this psychological drama. Natalie Press's troubled Nikki makes clear her murderous intentions in the opening voiceover, prompting mounting tension when she arrives at her destination and Janet McTeer's Phyllis doesn't recognise her. The film sets up an intriguing dramatic situation, but never quite makes the most of it thereafter. Despite the cast's best efforts, the characters seem like creations on the page rather than flesh-and-blood individuals. TJ Swearing. *DVD*

Natalie Press *Nikki Black* • Colin Morgan *Calum McLeod* • Janet McTeer *Phyllis Lovage* • Tanya Franks *Ruby* • Denise Orita *Sally* • Kate Stevens *Emma Lacey* ■ *Dir* Elizabeth Mitchell, Brek Taylor • *Scr* Elizabeth Mitchell, from the novel by Jane Rogers

The Island at the Top of the World ★★★ U

Period adventure 1974 · US · Colour · 89min

There's no question that this adventure falls below Disney's usual high standards, but it is not the unmitigated disaster that many critics considered it to be. Donald Sinden holds things together as an Edwardian explorer who sets out to rescue his son's Arctic expedition. Sinden's clash with a long lost Viking tribe stretches credibility, but the effects are pretty fair for their day, with the voyage by airship nicely done. DP *DVD*

Donald Sinden *Sir Anthony Ross* • David Hartman *Professor Ivarsson* • Jacques Marin *Captain Brieux* • Mako *Oomiak* • David Gwillim *Donald Ross* ■ *Dir* Robert Stevenson • *Scr* John Whedon, from the novel *The Lost Ones* by Ian Cameron

Island in the Sky ★★ U

Action adventure 1953 · US · BW · 105min

In one of the chilliest films ever made, John Wayne is the pilot of a transport plane that makes an emergency landing on a frozen lake. He keeps the crew in shape while they endure six days of waiting to be rescued. The realism of the photography is dissipated by the clichéd characters, but Wayne is suitably heroic. AE *DVD*

John Wayne *Captain Dooley* • Lloyd Nolan *Stutz* • Walter Abel *Colonel Fuller* • James Arness *McMullen* ■ *Dir* William A Wellman • *Scr* Ernest K Gann, from his novel

Island in the Sun ★★

Drama 1957 · US/UK · Colour · 119min

Daring and critically abused in its day, this exotic concoction was former Fox head Darryl F Zanuck's first film as an independent producer, and he spared no expense: classy cast, fabulous locations, top director Robert Rossen, major source novel but, alas, not enough thought went into the script. Author Alec Waugh's tale of interracial love deserved a more sensitive cinematic adaptation. Still, Harry Belafonte glowers at Joan Fontaine over a shared cocktail, James Mason goes suitably nuts as the crazed Maxwell Fleury, and Dorothy Dandridge and Joan Collins smoulder in the Caribbean heat. TS

James Mason *Maxwell Fleury* • Joan Fontaine *Mavis* • Joan Collins *Jocelyn* • Harry Belafonte *David Boyeur* • Dorothy Dandridge *Margot Seaton* ■ *Dir* Robert Rossen • *Scr* Alfred Hayes, from the novel by Alec Waugh

Island of Desire ★★

Second World War romantic drama 1952 · UK · Colour · 102min

After their ship is torpedoed during the Second World War, a nurse and a marine are marooned on a tropical island, where their initial hostility blossoms into love. Enter an RAF pilot, who crash-lands, and is saved by the nurse, who amputates his arm. Steamy, sensuous Linda Darnell and wooden pretty-boy Tab Hunter are the unlikely starring couple, while genuinely one-armed Englishman Donald Gray plays the airman. The Jamaican locations are eye-catching, but the rest is such inept drivel as to become hilariously enjoyable. RK

Linda Darnell *Elizabeth Smythe* • Tab Hunter *Michael J "Chicken" Dugan* • Donald Gray *William Peck* • John Laurie *Grimshaw* • Sheila Chong *Tukua* ■ *Dir* Stuart Heisler • *Scr* Stephanie Nordli, from the novel *Saturday Island* by Hugh Brooke

The Island of Dr Moreau ★★★ 15

Science-fiction horror 1977 · US · Colour · 94min

HG Wells's story about a mad scientist living on a remote island was filmed in 1932 with Charles Laughton as *Island of Lost Souls* and in 1996 with Marlon Brando. This version stars Burt Lancaster as the lunatic who thinks he's sane, conducting genetic experiments for the sake of mankind. Michael York shows up, unwisely, as does Barbara Carrera. While never trying to be a classic, it's still a ripping yarn with a moral gloss and Lancaster's taciturn evil is often frightening. AT Nudity. *DVD* *Blu-ray*

Burt Lancaster *Dr Moreau* • Michael York *Andrew Braddock* • Nigel Davenport *Montgomery* • Barbara Carrera *Maria* • Richard Basehart *Sayer of the law* • Nick Cravat *M'Ling* • John Gillespie *Tigerman* ■ *Dir* Don Taylor • *Scr* John Herman Shaner, Al Ramrus, from the novel by HG Wells

The Island of Dr Moreau
★ 12

Science-fiction horror 1996 · US · Colour · 91min

This is without a doubt the worst version of the HG Wells classic fantasy about mad Doctor Moreau (here played by Marlon Brando) genetically reshaping the animal kingdom to form a new species of man in a remote tropical paradise. Badly miscast – David Thewlis, Val Kilmer and Marlon Brando all give lousy performances – and hopelessly directed, this is a horrible miscalculation from start to finish. AJ Violence, swearing. *DVD*

Marlon Brando *Dr Moreau* • Val Kilmer *Montgomery* • David Thewlis *Edward Douglas* • Fairuza Balk *Aissa Moreau* • Ron Perlman *Sayer of the Law* • Marco Hofschneider *M'Ling* • Temuera Morrison *Azazello* • Daniel Rigney *Hyena-Swine* ■ *Dir* John Frankenheimer • *Scr* Richard Stanley, Ron Hutchinson, from the novel by HG Wells

Island of Lost Souls
★★★★★ PG

Science-fiction horror 1932 · US · BW · 70min

Banned in Britain for 21 years, the first, and best, version of HG Wells's provocative fantasy *The Island of Dr Moreau* is one of the best chillers ever made. Few horror films have as many terrifying facets or the harsh maturity of director Erle C Kenton. It's the uncompromising tale of doctor Charles Laughton grafting animals on to men in his tropical House of Pain to change evolution. Shot on beautiful sets, adding enormous atmospheric gloominess to the quite shocking and repellent imagery, Laughton turns in a memorably sadistic performance as the scarily mad scientist. Equally unforgettable is Bela Lugosi as the Sayer of the Law: "What is the law – are we not men!". AJ *DVD* *Blu-ray*

Charles Laughton *Dr Moreau* • Richard Arlen *Edward Parker* • Leila Hyams *Ruth Walker* • Bela Lugosi *Sayer of the Law* • Kathleen Burke *Lota, the panther woman* • Alan Ladd *Ape man* • Randolph Scott *Ape man* • Larry "Buster" Crabbe *Ape man* • Joe Bonomo *Ape man* ■ *Dir* Erle C Kenton • *Scr* Philip Wylie, Waldemar Young, from the novel *The Island of Dr Moreau* by HG Wells • *Cinematographer* Karl Struss

Island of Love ★★ U

Comedy 1963 · US · Colour · 100min

This smutty and unfunny comedy was a non-starter from the word go, squandering the talents of Tony Randall and Walter Matthau, and leaving Warner Bros with egg on its face. It was a limp conclusion to a three-picture deal with the studio for stage director Morton Da Costa, who had brilliantly transferred *Auntie Mame* and *The Music Man* from stage to screen. Robert Preston gave a great performance as a confidence trickster in *The Music Man*, and he's a con artist here, too, but this time he's without good material. TS

Robert Preston *Steve Blair* • Tony Randall *Paul Ferris* • Georgia Moll [Giorgia Moll] *Elena Harakas* • Walter Matthau *Tony Dallas* • Betty Bruce *Cha Cha Miller* ■ *Dir* Morton Da Costa • *Scr* David R Schwartz, from a story by Leo Katcher

Island of Terror ★★ PG

Science-fiction horror 1966 · UK · Colour · 83min

Bone marrow-sucking monsters are the by-product of cancer-cure research in this long-on-logic but high-on-hysteria cheapie, directed by Terence Fisher on a busman's holiday from Hammer Studios. Making the most of the isolated Irish setting and infusing the colourful carnage with a neat line in macabre humour, it's a reasonably tense offering, with the tentacled silicate creatures more fun than most of their B-feature sci-fi ilk. AJ Violence *DVD* *Blu-ray*

Peter Cushing *Dr Stanley* • Edward Judd *Dr David West* • Carole Gray *Toni Merrill* • Eddie Byrne *Dr Landers* • Sam Kydd *Constable Harris* ■ *Dir* Terence Fisher • *Scr* Edward Andrew Mann, Alan Ramsen

Island of the Blue Dolphins
★★★ U

Drama 1964 · US · Colour · 99min

In a Disney-style children's film, a native American girl (Celia Kaye) is forced to leave her home on an island off the California coast, after her father is murdered by white trappers. She goes back to save her brother but, when he falls prey to wild animals, she is left alone there with just a wild dog for company. Despite some weaknesses, this is well above average for its type. AT

Celia Kaye *Karana* • Larry Domasin *Ramo* • Ann Daniel *Tutok* • George Kennedy *Aleut captain* ■ *Dir* James B Clark • *Scr* Ted Sherdeman, Jane Klove, Robert B Radnitz, from the novel by Scott O'Dell

The Island on Bird Street
★★★

Second World War drama 1997 · Den/UK/Ger · Colour · 107min

This adaptation of Uri Orlev's semi-autobiographical novel earned praise at the Berlin film festival not only for director Søren Kragh-Jacobsen, but also for composer Zbigniew Preisner and newcomer Jordan Kiziuk, who excels as the 11-year-old Jew who draws on the lessons of Robinson Crusoe to survive the isolation of a Polish ghetto during the Second World War. The multinational nature of the production occasionally undermines its authenticity, but it still manages to convey the resourcefulness of a child more aware of his father's promise to return than of any Nazi threat. DP

Patrick Bergin *Stefan* • Jordan Kiziuk *Alex* • Jack Warden *Boruch* • James Bolam *Dr Studjinsky* • Simon Gregor *Henryk* • Lee Ross *Freddy* • Michael Byrne *Bolek* ■ *Dir* Søren Kragh-Jacobsen • *Scr* John Goldsmith, Tony Grisoni, from the novel by Uri Orlev

The Island President
★★★★ PG

Political documentary 2011 · US · Colour · 101min

Mohamed Nasheed had already been ousted as president of the Maldives by the time Jon Shenk completed this documentary. However, it retains its potency as a portrait of the democratically elected leader and crusading environmentalist, who sought to alert the world to the very real prospect that the 1,200 islands comprising his Indian Ocean paradise could be submerged by the rising tides of global warming. Underwater cabinet meetings and grandstanding speeches show Nasheed as a master self-publicist. But he is also tirelessly committed to his cause, which makes his patronising treatment by the industrial powers at the 2009 Climate Change Conference in Copenhagen deeply dismaying. DP *DVD*

Mohamed Nasheed ■ *Dir* Jon Shenk

Islands in the Stream
★★★ 12

Drama 1976 · US · Colour · 100min

With his grey beard, gravelly voice and perpetual squint, George C Scott is ideally cast and riveting to watch here, playing a fisherman and sculptor who prefers to sit out the Second World War in the Bahamas. Based on Ernest Hemingway's posthumously published novel, this story of a curmudgeonly father who has a troubled relationship with his wife (Claire Bloom) and three sons is rather self-important. But the scenery is pretty to look at, and Jerry Goldsmith's score is one of his best. AT Swearing. *DVD*

George C Scott *Thomas Hudson* • David Hemmings *Eddy* • Gilbert Roland *Captain Ralph* • Susan Tyrrell *Lil* • Richard Evans *Willy* • Claire Bloom *Audrey* • Julius Harris *Joseph* • Hart Bochner *Tom* ■ *Dir* Franklin J Schaffner • *Scr* Denne Bart Petitclerc, from the novel by Ernest Hemingway

The Isle ★★★ 18

Psychological drama 2000 · S Kor · Colour · 88min

Opening with a scene of lyrical tranquility, Kim Ki-Duk's fourth feature imperceptibly slides into a mêlée of pitiless cruelty and obsessive slaughter. With its latent sense of menace, the hesitant relationship between mute resort attendant Suh Jung and the suicidal Kim Yu-Seok promises much. But the use of shock tactics, particularly those involving fish hooks, deprives this visually ravishing but remorselessly sadistic melodrama of any allegorical intent it might have had. DP Korean +subtitles. Swearing, sex scenes, violence. *DVD*

Suh Jung *Hee-Jin* • Kim Yu-seok *Hyun-Shik* • Park Sung-Hee *Eun-A* • Cho Jae-Hyeon *Mang-Chee* • Jang Hang-Sun *Middle-aged man* ■ *Dir/Scr* Kim Ki-duk

Isle of Fury ★★

Adventure drama 1936 · US · BW · 60min

As an established star, Humphrey Bogart tended to gloss over his appearance in this film. Admittedly this adaptation isn't one of his image-making roles but it's not that bad either. Bogart is the fugitive who marries Margaret Lindsay and tries to start a new life on a South Seas island. Trouble arrives in the shape of detective Donald Woods who's come to track down Bogart and takes an unhealthy interest in his wife. TH

Humphrey Bogart *Val Stevens* • Margaret Lindsay *Lucille Gordon* • Donald Woods *Eric Blake* • EE Clive *Dr Hardy* • Paul Graetz *Capt Deever* ■ *Dir* Frank McDonald • *Scr* Robert Andrews, William Jacobs, from the novel *The Narrow Corner* by W Somerset Maugham

Isle of the Dead ★★★ 15

Horror 1945 · US · BW · 68min

Quarantined on a Greek island during the 1912 Balkan war, General Boris Karloff is convinced the group he's looking after will succumb to the "Vorvolaka", an ancient vitality-draining vampire. Director Mark Robson's film is creepy and claustrophobic, while at the same time intelligently raising issues about modern ideals versus pagan superstition. Karloff and Katherine Emery are both outstanding in this intense and imaginative miniature – another minor gem from cult producer Val Lewton's fright factory. AJ *DVD*

Boris Karloff *General Ferides* • Ellen Drew *Thea* • Marc Cramer *Oliver* • Katherine Emery *Mrs St Aubyn* • Jason Robards [Jason Robards Sr] *Albrecht* ■ *Dir* Mark Robson • *Scr* Ardel Wray, Josef Mischel, inspired by the painting *The Isle of the Dead* by Arnold Boecklin

Isn't It Romantic ★★ U

Period comedy drama 1948 · US · BW · 72min

Hearts are set a-flutter in the household of ex-Civil War officer Roland Culver, the father of three daughters (Veronica Lake, Mona Freeman, Mary Hatcher) when handsome smoothie Patric Knowles turns up on the doorstep, causing Lake to jilt fiancé Billy De Wolfe. The most memorable thing about this innocuous semi-musical is the durable Rodgers and Hart title song. RK

Veronica Lake *Candy* • Mona Freeman *Susie* • Mary Hatcher *Rose* • Billy De Wolfe *Horace Frazier* • Roland Culver *Major Euclid Cameron* • Patric Knowles *Richard "Rick" Brannon* ■ *Dir* Norman Z McLeod • *Scr* Josef Mischel, Richard L Breen, from the novel *Gather Ye Rosebuds* by Jeannette Covert Nolan

Isn't Life Wonderful ★★★

Silent romantic drama 1924 · US · BW · 90min

Even with a phoney happy ending, the world wasn't interested in seeing a downbeat film that portrayed the wretched hunger and poverty in Germany after the First World War. Master film-maker DW Griffith lost his independence as a result of its failure, but it is a striking picture, shot on location in Germany with many local inhabitants as extras. Carol Dempster stars as a Polish refugee and Neil Hamilton is her lover, a soldier who returns ill from the front. AE

Carol Dempster *Inga* • Neil Hamilton *Paul* • Helen Lowell *Grandmother* • Erville Alderson *Professor* • Frank Puglia *Theodor* ■ *Dir* DW Griffith • *Scr* DW Griffith, from the short story *Isn't Life Wonderful!* by Maj Geoffrey Moss

Isn't Life Wonderful! ★★ U

Comedy 1952 · UK · Colour · 83min

If your image of Donald Wolfit is all bluster and eyebrows, you won't recognise him in this whimsical comedy based on a once popular novel. There's something of the Clarence Day memoir *Life with Father* about this unremarkable period piece, as Cecil Parker presides over the antics of his underachieving kin. However, his grouchy snobbery quickly wears thin and there's precious little about his whimpering son Peter Asher, hopeless nephew Robert Urquhart or tipsy brother-in-law Wolfit to make us take their side. DP

Cecil Parker *Father* • Donald Wolfit *Uncle Willie* • Eileen Herlie *Mother* • Peter Asher *Charles* • Eleanor Summerfield *Aunt Kate* • Dianne Foster *Virginia* ■ *Dir* Harold French • *Scr* Brock Williams, from his novel *Uncle Willie and the Bicycle Shop*

Isn't She Great ★★ 15
Biographical comedy drama
1999 · US · Colour · 91min

The incredible life of Jacqueline Susann, late author of the landmark bestseller *Valley of the Dolls*, gets short shrift in a trashy biography that reduces her achievements and personal tragedies to mere rags-to-riches anecdotes. Played by Bette Midler with theatrical mugging, Susann goes from lousy actress to celebrity writer thanks to the devotion of her press agent husband, Irving Mansfield (a miscast Nathan Lane). Aside from the neat period detail and camp support from Stockard Channing, this strangely affected showbiz saga veers from vapid farce to stale banality. AJ Swearing. *DVD*

Bette Midler *Jacqueline Susann* • Nathan Lane *Irving Mansfield* • Stockard Channing *Florence Maybelle* • David Hyde Pierce *Michael Hastings* • John Cleese *Henry Marcus* • Sarah Jessica Parker *Tira Gropman* ■ *Dir* Andrew Bergman • *Scr* Paul Rudnick, from the article *Wasn't She Great* by Michael Korda • *Music* Burt Bacharach

Isolation ★★★ 15
Horror   2005 · UK/Ire · Colour · 90min

Nature bites back – literally – in this claustrophobic Irish chiller from debut feature writer/director Billy O'Brien. A farmyard-set mix of *Alien* and *The Thing*, it's a cautionary eco-fable in which "mad cow disease" takes on a horrifying new meaning. John Lynch excels as a struggling dairy farmer who faces a genetic nightmare after reluctantly allowing scientists to conduct DNA experiments on one of the last in his herd. The gory horror that follows is understated yet sustained, making effective use of the movie's low-budget resources. Like most creature features, the supporting characters are largely two-dimensional but its slow-building atmospherics and unrelenting sense of dread mark O'Brien out as a name to watch. SF Swearing. *DVD*

John Lynch *Dan* • Essie Davis *Orla* • Sean Harris *Jamie* • Marcel Iures *John* • Crispin Letts *Doctor* ■ *Dir/Scr* Billy O'Brien (2)

Istanbul ★★ U
Adventure drama   1957 · US · Colour · 84min

Not even Errol Flynn's presence can redeem this adventure drama, a remake of the Fred MacMurray/Ava Gardner movie *Singapore* (1947). Flynn plays a rover who returns to the eponymous city to recover some loot, only to find that his wife has lost both her memory and the sought-after gems. Flynn described this later as "just one of those things", though at least we get Nat King Cole singing *When I Fall in Love*. TH

Errol Flynn *Jim Brennan* • Cornell Borchers *Stephanie Bauer/Karen Fielding* • John Bentley *Inspector Nural* • Torin Thatcher *Douglas Fielding* • Leif Erickson *Charlie Boyle* • Peggy Knudsen *Marge Boyle* • Nat King Cole *Danny Rice* ■ *Dir* Joseph Pevney • *Scr* Seton I Miller, Barbara Gray, Richard Alan Simmons, from a story by Seton I Miller

LANDMARK FILM
Clara Bow is "It Girl" number one in this charming film about sex appeal

It ★★★ U
Silent comedy drama   1927 · US · BW · 76min

Clara Bow became a major star as the "It Girl" in this delightful romantic comedy of the flapper age, directed by Clarence Badger (although Josef von Sternberg filled in while Badger was ill). "It" was a quality devised by the novelist Elinor Glyn that had most to do with sex appeal, which Bow had in abundance as part of her strikingly uninhibited acting style. The story is mild: Bow's the store clerk who makes a play for her boss, Antonio Moreno, because he has "it", but there is a striking subplot when she's suspected of being an unmarried mother. Handsome newcomer Gary Cooper

can be seen in a bit role as a newspaper reporter. AE

Clara Bow *Betty Lou* • Antonio Moreno *Cyrus Waltham* • William Austin *Monty* • Jacqueline Gadsdon *Adela Van Norman* • Gary Cooper *Newspaper reporter* • Elinor Glyn ■ *Dir* Clarence Badger • *Scr* Hope Loring, Louis D Lighton, Elinor Glyn, from the story by Elinor Glyn

It! ★★
Horror   1966 · UK · Colour · 95min

Director Herbert J Leder made this dismal attempt to resurrect the legend of the Golem monster – most famously filmed in 1920 by Paul Wegener – for Swinging Sixties audiences. Roddy McDowall is an assistant museum curator, living with the mummified corpse of his mother (*Psycho* has a lot to answer for), who revives the original Golem to do his psychopathic bidding. A confused mix of black humour and horror, this lacks style, invention and (crucially) budget. RS

Roddy McDowall *Arthur Pimm* • Jill Haworth *Ellen Grove* • Paul Maxwell *Jim Perkins* • Aubrey Richards *Professor Weal* • Ernest Clark *Harold Grove* • Oliver Johnston *Trimingham* ■ *Dir/Scr* Herbert J Leder

It All Came True ★★★
Musical comedy   1940 · US · BW · 96min

Why gangster Humphrey Bogart is hiding out in a boarding house whose tenants consist totally of hand-picked eccentric character actors is neither here nor there: the following year he would hit his stardom stride with *High Sierra* and *The Maltese Falcon*, and there would be no looking back. Top-billed over Bogie, and rightly so, is the simply magnificent Ann Sheridan. She just picks up this movie, rolls it up under her arms, and walks brazenly away with it. TS

Ann Sheridan *Sarah Jane Ryan* • Humphrey Bogart *Grasselli/Chips Maguire* • Jeffrey Lynn *Tommy Taylor* • ZaSu Pitts *Miss Flint* • Una O'Connor *Maggie Ryan* • Jessie Busley *Mrs Nora Taylor* • John Litel *Mr Roberts* ■ *Dir* Lewis Seiler • *Scr* Michael Fessier, Lawrence Kimble, from the short story *Better than Life* by Louis Bromfield in *Hearst's International-Cosmopolitan*

It Always Rains on Sunday ★★★★ PG
Crime drama   1947 · UK · BW · 87min

This saga of interconnecting lives is one of Ealing's successful non-comedies. The drab city locale of Arthur La Bern's source novel is brilliantly re-created in the studio and the atmosphere is superbly captured by cameraman Douglas Slocombe. In a cast of well-known character actors, Googie Withers is outstanding as the ex-lover of convict John McCallum, while Sydney Tafler and John Slater are the embodiment of East Enders. The film marked a breakthrough in its portrayal of the English working class on screen, and much of the credit should go to director and co-writer Robert Hamer. TS *DVD* *Blu*

Googie Withers *Rose Sandigate* • Edward Chapman *George Sandigate* • Susan Shaw *Vi Sandigate* • John McCallum *Tommy Swann* • Patricia Plunkett *Doris Sandigate* • David Lines *Alfie Sandigate* • Sydney Tafler *Morry Hyams* • Betty Ann Davies *Sadie Hyams* • John Slater *Lou Hyams* • Jane Hylton *Bessie Hyams* ■ *Dir* Robert Hamer • *Scr* Angus MacPhail, Robert Hamer, Henry Cornelius, from the novel by Arthur La Bern

It Came from beneath the Sea ★★★ U
Science-fiction adventure
1955 · US · BW · 75min

Careless atomic testing spawns a giant octopus in this classic monster flick, which includes stop-motion special effects from the great Ray Harryhausen. But radiation wasn't the cause of the suction-cup horror having a shortage of titanic tentacles – the ridiculously low budget saw to that! As the killer creature rampages through San Francisco to destroy the Golden Gate bridge, B-movie star Kenneth Tobey still finds time to battle biologist Donald Curtis for vampy Faith Domergue's charms. Predictable tosh, but good 1950s fun. AJ *DVD*

Kenneth Tobey *Pete Mathews* • Faith Domergue *Lesley Joyce* • Ian Keith *Admiral Burns* • Donald Curtis *John Carter* • Dean Maddox Jr *Adam Norman* ■ *Dir* Robert Gordon • *Scr* George Worthing Yates, Hal Smith, from a story by George Worthing Yates

It Came from Outer Space ★★★★ PG
Science-fiction drama   1953 · US · BW · 76min

Based on Ray Bradbury's short story *The Meteor*, this early 3D classic was the first of many brilliant sci-fi films from director Jack Arnold. An alien spaceship lands in the Arizona desert, and its giant-eyed occupants adopt human identities while they repair their vessel. Astronomer Richard Carlson sees it happen, but no one believes him. Top heavy on eerie atmosphere and incorporating a neat plea for interracial tolerance, Arnold's tale uses stylish flourishes – including a fish-eye lens to simulate the aliens' point-of-view – resulting in a film that's as good as 1950s science fiction gets. AJ *DVD* *3D*

Richard Carlson *John Putnam* • Barbara Rush *Ellen Fields* • Charles Drake *Sheriff Matt Warren* • Russell Johnson *George* ■ *Dir* Jack Arnold • *Scr* Harry Essex, from the short story *The Meteor* by Ray Bradbury

It Conquered the World ★ PG
Science-fiction drama   1956 · US · BW · 68min

Get ready to scream with laughter as a gravitationally-challenged, fanged carrot from Venus crawls around the Los Angeles countryside like a snail on Valium. It clearly couldn't conquer the world even if It tried! Hence it prepares to turn us dumb Earthlings into zombie slaves with the aid of what are supposed to be electronic bat-mites but which more closely resemble drunken boomerangs. One of Roger Corman's all-time worst films, yet cult fans will enjoy it for exactly that reason. AT

Peter Graves (2) *Paul Nelson* • Beverly Garland *Claire Anderson* • Lee Van Cleef *Tom Anderson* • Sally Fraser *Joan Nelson* ■ *Dir* Roger Corman • *Scr* Lou Rusoff

It Could Happen to You ★★★ PG
Romantic comedy based on a true story
1994 · US · Colour · 97min

With a title and a scenario worthy of Frank Capra, this cosy little romantic comedy is, incredibly, based on a true story. Nicolas Cage (reuniting with his *Honeymoon in Vegas* director, Andrew Bergman) plays a good-hearted cop. Rosie Perez gives one of her usual performances, shrieking the place down as she discovers hubby Cage has divided his lottery winnings with waitress Bridget Fonda. Cage, Perez and Fonda are on top form and the result is both charming and disarming. DP Swearing. *DVD*

Nicolas Cage *Charlie Lang* • Bridget Fonda *Yvonne Biasi* • Rosie Perez *Muriel Lang* • Wendell Pierce *Bo Williams* • Isaac Hayes *Angel* • Red Buttons *Zakuto* ■ *Dir* Andrew Bergman • *Scr* Jane Anderson

It Follows ★★★★ 15
Horror   2014 · US · Colour · 96min

David Robert Mitchell's pleasingly creepy horror puts suburban teens at risk from a seemingly inescapable presence. Shot in decaying Detroit, it draws on influences from Japanese horror *Ring* to traditional stalk-and-slash thrillers, particularly John Carpenter's *Halloween*. Gruesome murder set pieces are not the focus here, however. Unusually sensitive to its female cast (led by the captivating Maika Monroe), *It Follows* makes explicit the usual horror movie subtext about teenage sexuality. The result is a film that's more about goosebumps than gore, with an unsettling, slow-moving, shape-changing monster that won't stop, ever, till it gets what it wants. DW *DVD* *Blu*

Maika Monroe *Jay* • Keir Gilchrist *Paul* • Daniel Zovatto *Greg* • Jake Weary *Hugh* • Olivia Luccardi *Yara* • Lili Sepe *Kelly* ■ *Dir/Scr* David Robert Mitchell

It Grows on Trees ★★ U
Fantasy comedy   1952 · US · BW · 84min

Ditzy suburban housewife Irene Dunne, married to Dean Jagger, finds that two trees she had planted in her garden are sprouting dollar bills. The Treasury Department pronounces the money legal tender, and she embarks on a massive spending spree, only to discover that the bank notes, like leaves, fade and die. A whimsical and repetitive little fable, that falls somewhere between a feel-good movie and a simplistic moral tale. It was an unworthy final film for Dunne, who went into retirement after this. RK

Irene Dunne *Polly Baxter* • Dean Jagger *Phil Baxter* • Joan Evans *Diane Baxter* • Richard Crenna *Ralph Bowen* • Edith Meiser *Mrs Pryor* • Sandy Descher *Midge Baxter* ■ *Dir* Arthur Lubin • *Scr* Leonard Praskins, Barney Slater

It Had to Be You ★★ U
Romantic comedy   1947 · US · BW · 98min

Although in characteristically sparky form, Ginger Rogers is unable to rescue this tired comedy romance with its psychological overtones. Rogers's a socialite suffering from serial desertion at the altar – she's the one who runs. Having abandoned three nearly husbands and set to try for a fourth (Ron Randell), she meets Cornel Wilde, her social inferior but her lifelong fantasy ideal made flesh. RK

Ginger Rogers *Victoria Stafford* • Cornel Wilde *"George"/Johnny Blaine* • Percy Waram *Mr Stafford* • Spring Byington *Mrs Stafford* • Ron Randell *Oliver HP Harrington* • Thurston Hall *Mr Harrington* • Charles Evans *Dr Parkinson* ■ *Dir* Don Hartman, Rudolph Maté • *Scr* Melvin Frank, Norman Panama, from a story by Allen Boretz, Don Hartman

It Had to Be You ★★
Romantic comedy   2000 · US · Colour · 90min

It's the New York locations rather than the stars that add appeal to this uneven romantic comedy. Natasha Henstridge and Michael Vartan play strangers who both check into the Plaza Hotel to plan their respective weddings – and inconveniently fall for each other. It's a predictable, undemanding time-filler, but Henstridge and Vartan play their roles with charm and vitality, and survive the clumsy, message-laden dialogue thanks to some easy chemistry. SF Swearing, sex scenes.

Natasha Henstridge *Anna Penn* • Michael Vartan *Charlie Hudson* • Michael Rispoli *Henry Taylor* • Olivia D'Abo *Tracy Meltempi* ■ *Dir/Scr* Steven Feder

It Happened at the World's Fair ★★★ PG
Musical   1962 · US · Colour · 100min

This lightweight but enjoyable Elvis film was made in the wake of *Blue Hawaii's* box-office tidal wave. Here Elvis gets involved with a Chinese child, romances nurse Joan O'Brien and gets kicked in the shins by little Kurt Russell, who would grow up to portray Elvis himself on screen in the biopic *Elvis – the Movie*. And all this against the colourful background of the Seattle World's Fair. TS

Elvis Presley *Mike Edwards* • Joan O'Brien *Diane Warren* • Gary Lockwood *Danny Burke* • Vicky Tiu *Sue-Lin* • Kurt Russell ■ *Dir* Norman Taurog • *Scr* Si Rose, Seaman Jacobs

It Happened Here ★★★★ PG
Wartime drama   1963 · UK · BW · 96min

This is a fascinating speculation on what might have happened if Hitler had successfully invaded Britain. It is also one of the most heroic films ever made, begun by teenagers Kevin Brownlow and Andrew Mollo in 1956 as a hobby. There are major flaws, naturally, mainly in the performances and the often naive writing, but forgive them. Instead, marvel at the provocative sight of the Third Reich goose-stepping down Whitehall and chill to the fascist overthrow of Little England. AT *DVD*

Pauline Murray *Pauline* • Sebastian Shaw *Dr Richard Fletcher* • Fiona Leland *Helen Fletcher* • Honor Fehrson *Honor Hutton* • Percy Binns

Immediate Action Commandant ■ *Dir* Kevin Brownlow, Andrew Mollo • *Scr* Kevin Brownlow, Andrew Mollo, from an idea by Kevin Brownlow

It Happened in Brooklyn
★★★ U

Musical　1947 · US · BW · 102min

It happened to Frank Sinatra and Kathryn Grayson, reunited after *Anchors Aweigh* in as lightweight a piece of fluff as you're ever likely to see. The great Jimmy Durante virtually stops the show in a fabulous duet with Sinatra called *The Song's Gotta Come from the Heart*. The piano work is that of a very young André Previn, and Gloria Grahame's in there, too. All that was really needed was a decent director and Technicolor, but MGM was on one of its economy drives. As it is, it's just a jolly little musical movie. TS

Frank Sinatra *Danny Webson Miller* • Kathryn Grayson *Anne Fielding* • Jimmy Durante *Nick Lombardi* • Peter Lawford *Jamie Shellgrove* • Gloria Grahame *Nurse* ■ *Dir* Richard Whorf • *Scr* Isobel Lennart, from a story by John McGowan

It Happened in Rome　★★ U

Comedy　1956 · It · Colour · 95min

Well, actually, some of it happened in Venice and Florence, as well. The trouble is, none of it is particularly interesting or original, as June Laverick, Isabelle Corey and Ingeborg Schoener city-hop in the hope of romance and adventure. The only truly significant feature of this tepid tourist advert is that it was co-written by the famous partnership of Age and Scarpelli, who penned some of the best films made by art house directors Mario Monicelli and Ettore Scola. DP

June Laverick *Margaret* • Isabelle Corey *Josette* • Ingeborg Schöner *Hilde* • Vittorio De Sica *The Count* • Isabel Jeans *Cynthia* • Massimo Girotti *Ugo Parenti* ■ *Dir* Antonio Pietrangeli • *Scr* Dario Fo, Antonio Pietrangeli, Agenore Incrocci, Furio Scarpelli

It Happened on Fifth Avenue
★

Musical comedy　1947 · US · BW · 114min

Not a lot happens, in actual fact, in this interminable and rather juvenile comedy. A glib tramp and a bevy of his friends move into an empty New York mansion in which they all decide to play toffs until they are rumbled, but there is no discernible script to speak of, and the performances range from the banal to the execrable. SH

Don DeFore *Jim Bullock* • Gale Storm *Trudy O'Connor* • Charlie Ruggles *[Charles Ruggles]* Michael O'Connor • Victor Moore *McKeever* ■ *Dir* Roy Del Ruth • *Scr* Everett Freeman, Vick Knight, from a story by Herbert Clyde Lewis, Frederick Stephani

It Happened One Night
★★★★★ U

Romantic comedy　1934 · US · BW · 100min

It started out as a minor film called *Night Bus* and MGM decided to punish its errant star Clark Gable by sending him over to Columbia to play the reporter. And what happened? As classy and charming a romantic comedy as you're ever likely to see, winning Oscars in all key departments – best film, director, stars, screenplay – thanks to whizzkid director Frank Capra and a marvellous foil to Gable in leading lady Claudette Colbert. The scene where runaway heiress Colbert hitches a lift and the infamous "Walls of Jericho" bedroom sequence have great charm, and confirm this standout movie's claims to classic status. Remade in 1956 as *You Can't Run Away from It*. TS **DVD** Blu-ray

Clark Gable *Peter Warne* • Claudette Colbert *Ellie Andrews* • Walter Connolly *Alexander Andrews* • Roscoe Karns *Oscar Shapeley* • Jameson Thomas *King Westley* • Alan Hale *Danker* • Arthur Hoyt *Zeke* • Blanche Frederici *Zeke's wife* ■ *Dir* Frank Capra • *Scr* Robert Riskin, from the story *Night Bus* by Samuel Hopkins Adams

It Happened to Jane ★★★ U

Comedy　1959 · US · Colour · 93min

This bright and breezy comedy from the quirky, witty and underrated director Richard Quine stars Doris Day as the "Jane from Maine" who becomes a national heroine when she sues Ernie Kovacs's grasping railroad boss for putting her lobster farm at risk. Jack Lemmon is on hand as Day's feckless lawyer, but the movie is stolen by Kovacs, whose performance, with hindsight, is clearly a caricature of legendary Columbia Studios head, Harry Cohn. TS **DVD**

Doris Day *Jane Osgood* • Jack Lemmon *George Denham* • Ernie Kovacs *Harry Foster Malone* • Steve Forrest *Larry Hall* • Teddy Rooney *Billy Osgood* • Russ Brown *Uncle Otis* ■ *Dir* Richard Quine • *Scr* Norman Katkov, from a story by Max Wilk, Norman Katkov

It Happened Tomorrow
★★★★

Fantasy drama　1944 · US · BW · 85min

A clever and very enjoyable fantasy with a difficult theme is handled expertly by French émigré director René Clair, who had demonstrated his understanding of American whimsy two years earlier with *I Married a Witch*. Reporter Dick Powell finds his career taking off when he's given the scoop on tomorrow's news – before it actually happens. Set in the 1890s, the strong cast includes veteran Jack Oakie as a mind-reader and Linda Darnell as Powell's girlfriend. TS

Dick Powell *Larry Stevens* • Linda Darnell *Sylvia* • Jack Oakie *Cigolini* • Edgar Kennedy *Inspector Mulrooney* • John Philliber *Pop Benson* • Edward Brophy *Jake Schomberg* ■ *Dir* René Clair • *Scr* René Clair, Dudley Nichols, Helene Fraenkel, from a story by Lord Dunsany, Hugh Wedlock, Howard Snyder, from the ideas of Lewis R Foster • *Music Director* Robert Stolz

It Happens Every Spring
★★★ U

Sports comedy　1949 · US · BW · 81min

In this original (if blinkered) little comedy, chemistry professor Ray Milland invents a substance that causes baseballs to veer away from the bats. Obviously, he then gives up the distinguished groves of academe to become a star pitcher. This daffy nonsense is endearingly played by Milland and co-stars Jean Peters and Paul Douglas. TS

Ray Milland *Vernon Simpson* • Jean Peters *Deborah Greenleaf* • Paul Douglas *Monk Lanigan* • Ed Begley *Stone* • Ted De Corsia *Dolan* ■ *Dir* Lloyd Bacon • *Scr* Valentine Davies, from a story by Valentine Davies, from the short story *The Sprightly Adventures of Instructor Simpson* by Shirley W Smith

It Lives Again ★★★ 15

Horror　1978 · US · Colour · 86min

Director Larry Cohen's sequel to his own cult classic *It's Alive* doesn't quite hit the same subversive targets as a forceful indictment of society's misuse of atomic power and drugs, but as a gory action thriller it certainly delivers. Frederic Forrest and Kathleen Lloyd are the expectant parents who get a shock when their offspring turns out to be a fanged and clawed mutant terror tot. Hardly subtle, but played with a winning conviction well above the call of duty. AJ Violence, swearing. **DVD**

Frederic Forrest *Eugene Scott* • Kathleen Lloyd *Jody Scott* • John P Ryan *Frank Davis* • John Marley *Mallory* • Andrew Duggan *Dr Perry* • Eddie Constantine *Dr Forrest* • James Dixon *Detective Perkins* ■ *Dir/Scr* Larry Cohen

It Might Get Loud ★★★

Music documentary　2008 · US · Colour · 97min

The room-shaking glory of the electric guitar is celebrated by iconic players from three generations in this documentary by *An Inconvenient Truth* director Davis Guggenheim. Led Zeppelin's Jimmy Page, U2's The Edge and the White Stripes's Jack White wax lyrical about the instrument that has made each of them their fortunes, punctuated by vintage clips of themselves and other six-string maestros. Fellow players and aspiring rock gods will thrill at the scenes of the trio jamming together, but Guggenheim's film never takes an insular "muso" view and has plenty to offer the lay person. TeS

Jimmy Page • Jack White • The Edge ■ *Dir* Davis Guggenheim

It Pays to Advertise　★★★

Comedy　1931 · US · BW · 63min

Encouraged by secretary Carole Lombard and helped by advertising pal Skeets Gallagher, Norman Foster sets himself up in competition with his wealthy soap-manufacturer father with a number of unexpected commercial and personal consequences. An innocently amusing and enjoyable romantic comedy programmer to fill a spare hour, and one to please fans of Louise Brooks who appears in a featured supporting role. RK

Norman Foster *Rodney Martin* • Carole Lombard *Mary Grayson* • Skeets Gallagher *[Richard "Skeets" Gallagher]* • Ambrose Peale • Eugene Pallette *Cyrus Martin* • Lucien Littlefield *Andrew Adams* • Louise Brooks *Thelma Temple* ■ *Dir* Frank Tuttle • *Scr* Arthur Kober, Ethel Doherty, from the play *It Pays to Advertise* by Roi Cooper Megrue, Walter Hackett

It Rains on Our Love　★★★

Romantic crime drama　1946 · Swe · BW · 95min

Following the poor reception of *Crisis*, Ingmar Bergman turned independent for this adaptation of a play by Norwegian Oskar Braaten. Shades of Vigo and the French poetic realists colour this simple story, in which ex-jailbird Birger Malmsten and actress-turned-prostitute Barbro Kollberg receive a little help from umbrella-wielding fairy godfather Gosta Cederlund in their battle against the caprices of a hypocritical, bureaucratic society. The action is never allowed to lapse into cheap melodrama and Bergman manages to end on a note of unforced optimism. DP Swedish +subtitles.

Barbro Kollberg *Maggi* • Birger Malmsten *David* • Gosta Cederlund *Gentleman with umbrella* • Julia Caesar *Mrs Ledin* • Gunnar Björnstrand ■ *Dir* Ingmar Bergman • *Scr* Herbert Grevenius, Ingmar Bergman

It Runs in the Family　★★ PG

Comedy　1994 · US · Colour · 81min

Despite the return of writer/narrator Jean Shepherd and director Bob Clark, this continuation of *A Christmas Story* (1983) is a big letdown. Though it's understandable that different actors had to be cast in the roles, the new additions have no sparkle, while Charles Grodin is grossly miscast as the Old Man. While the various vignettes were hilarious in Shepherd's books, they come across as flat and extremely rushed here. KB

Charles Grodin *Old Man* • Kieran Culkin *Ralphie Parker* • Mary Steenburgen *Mom* • Christian Culkin *Randy Parker* • Al Mancini *Zudoc* • Troy Evans *Gertz* ■ *Dir* Bob Clark • *Scr* Jean Shepherd, Leigh Brown, Bob Clark, from the novels *In God We Trust, All Others Pay Cash* and *Wanda Hickey's Night of Golden Memories and Other Disasters* by Jean Shepherd

It Runs in the Family　★★ 12

Comedy drama　2002 · US · Colour · 104min

Kirk Douglas here gives a major performance as a stroke victim, proving he is still a star of some power, overshadowing his son, Michael, and grandson, Cameron, in this sentimental comedy drama. Kirk, who has himself survived a disabling stroke, is the grand patriarch, a venerable attorney working with his son, who is married to a psychiatrist (Bernadette Peters). It's worth viewing, not particularly for the intricacies of narrative – there are none – but for seeing one of Hollywood's grandest clans in a family reunion. TH **DVD**

Michael Douglas (1) *Alex Gromberg* • Kirk Douglas *Mitchell Gromberg* • Rory Culkin *Eli Gromberg* • Cameron Douglas *Asher Gromberg* • Diana Douglas *Evelyn Gromberg* • Michelle Monaghan

Peg Maloney • Bernadette Peters *Rebecca Gromberg* • Geoffrey Arend *Malik* ■ *Dir* Fred Schepisi • *Scr* Jesse Wigutow

It Should Happen to You
★★★★ U

Romantic comedy　1954 · US · BW · 83min

Two inimitable personalities and talents, *Born Yesterday's* Judy Holliday and, making his film debut, Jack Lemmon, are paired to delightful effect in this original, satirical romantic comedy, faultlessly directed by George Cukor. Holliday is small-town girl who arrives in the crowded anonymity of the Big Apple. Longing to be a "somebody", she hires a prominent billboard on which she has her name displayed. Soon the whole town's talking, among them businessman Peter Lawford, who covets Holliday's prime advertising site. The leads are superb, the movie just short of a classic. RK **DVD**

Judy Holliday *Gladys Glover* • Peter Lawford *Evan Adams III* • Jack Lemmon *Pete Sheppard* • Michael O'Shea (1) *Brod Clinton* • Vaughn Taylor *Entrikin* • Connie Gilchrist *Mrs Riker* ■ *Dir* George Cukor • *Scr* Garson Kanin

It Shouldn't Happen to a Vet
★★★ U

Drama　1979 · UK · Colour · 88min

Neither *All Creatures Great and Small* nor this amiable sequel were as successful as James Herriott's original memoirs or the long-running BBC television series. Yet this Yorkshire comedy is, nevertheless, a pleasingly unpretentious entertainment that can be enjoyed by the whole family. The formula of pre-war country cosiness, bawdy humour, folksy characterisation and animal emergency is meticulously repeated as John Alderton capably steps into the wellies vacated by Simon Ward, while Colin Blakely hammily takes over from Anthony Hopkins, leaving Lisa Harrow alone to return from the first venture. DP

John Alderton *James Herriot* • Colin Blakely *Siegfried Farnon* • Lisa Harrow *Helen Herriot* • Bill Maynard *Hinchcliffe* • Paul Shelley *Richard Carmody* • Richard Pearson (1) *Granville* • Liz Smith *Mrs Dodds* ■ *Dir* Eric Till • *Scr* Alan Plater

It Started in Naples ★★ PG

Romantic comedy　1960 · US · Colour · 95min

Lawyer Clark Gable travels to Italy to settle his late brother's estate and runs into vengeful and hysterical Italians, Sophia Loren and lots of travelogue shots of Capri and the Amalfi coast. This is probably one of those movies where the cast and crew had more fun than the audience who watch their antics, and it's not a patch on Billy Wilder's similarly-themed *Avanti!* Loren, however, is a vivacious delight in a role that was originally written for Capri's most famous resident, Gracie Fields. AT **DVD**

Clark Gable *Mike Hamilton* • Sophia Loren *Lucia* • Marietto *Nando* • Vittorio De Sica *Mario Vitale* • Paolo Carlini *Renzo* ■ *Dir* Melville Shavelson • *Scr* Melville Shavelson, Jack Rose, Suso Cecchi D'Amico, from a story by Michael Pertwee, Jack Davies

It Started in Paradise ★★ U

Drama　1952 · UK · BW · 93min

Opening in 1938, the story starts with ambitious designer Jane Hylton persuading her inspiration-blocked boss Martita Hunt that she needs a break from their London salon. But, no sooner has Hylton risen to the top than she becomes the target of fashion school graduate, Muriel Pavlow. Only a few sparks fly in Compton Bennett's competent blend of haute couture and low cunning, but Ronald Squire enjoys himself as a caustic critic. DP

Jane Hylton *Martha Watkins* • Ian Hunter *Arthur Turner* • Martita Hunt *Mme Alice* • Muriel Pavlow *Alison* • Brian Worth *Michael* • Terence Morgan *Edouard* • Ronald Squire *"Mary Jane"* • Kay Kendall *Lady Caroline* ■ *Dir* Compton Bennett • *Scr* Hugh Hastings, Marghanita Laski, from her story

U SUITABLE FOR ALL　Uc SUITABLE ESPECIALLY FOR YOUNG CHILDREN (DVD ONLY)　PG PARENTAL GUIDANCE　12A UNDER 12s TO BE ACCOMPANIED (CINEMA ONLY)

It Started with a Kiss ★★★
Romantic comedy 1959 · US · Colour · 103min

When army sergeant Glenn Ford meets nightclub singer Debbie Reynolds, instant combustion leads to a hasty marriage. To test his affections she withholds sexual favours. Filmed on eye-catching Spanish locations, George Marshall's comedy relies on innuendo and double entendre for its laughs, with extra amusement provided by Eva Gabor as a marquesa lusting after Ford. Reynolds, pursued by a wealthy bullfighter, relishes the opportunity to escape her wholesome image in this slice of good, clean, dirty fun. RK

Glenn Ford *Sergeant Joe Fitzpatrick* • Debbie Reynolds *Maggie Putnam* • Eva Gabor *Marquesa de la Rey* • Gustavo Rojo *Antonio Soriano* • Fred Clark *General O'Connell* ■ *Dir* George Marshall • *Scr* Charles Lederer, from a story by Valentine Davies

It Started with Eve ★★★ U
Musical comedy 1941 · US · BW · 86min

Deanna Durbin, everybody's ideal teenager, was blossoming into young womanhood when she starred opposite Charles Laughton in this delightful comedy. Laughton plays a crusty millionaire whose deathbed wish is to meet his son's fiancée. Son Robert Cummings picks up hat-check girl Durbin to impersonate his bride-to-be for a day. Naturally, Laughton takes a shine to her and recovers. Remade in 1964 as *I'd Rather Be Rich* starring Sandra Dee. RB *DVD*

Deanna Durbin *Anne Terry* • Charles Laughton *Jonathon Reynolds* • Robert Cummings *J "Johnny" Reynolds Jr* • Guy Kibbee *Bishop* • Margaret Tallichet *Gloria Pennington* ■ *Dir* Henry Koster • *Scr* Norman Krasna, Leo Townsend, from the story *Almost an Angel* by Hans Kräly

It Takes Two ★★ U
Romantic comedy 1995 · US · Colour · 96min

A bland twist on *The Parent Trap*, this story has two identical-in-appearance girls from opposite sides of the tracks (US TV stars Mary-Kate and Ashley Olsen) teaming up to bring their single parents (Kirstie Alley and Steve Guttenberg) together. So cute it will make your teeth ache. Very missable, unless you happen to be a little girl aged six. JB

Kirstie Alley *Diane Barrows* • Steve Guttenberg *Roger Callaway* • Mary-Kate Olsen *Amanda Lemmon* • Ashley Olsen *Alyssa Callaway* • Philip Bosco *Vincenzo* ■ *Dir* Andy Tennant • *Scr* Deborah Dean Davis

It! The Terror from beyond Space ★★★
Science-fiction thriller 1958 · US · BW · 69min

A rocket-ship crew returning from an interplanetary mission is menaced by a blood-drinking reptilian stowaway in this low-budget classic from science fiction's golden age. If the plot sounds familiar, it's because Edward L Cahn's briskly directed shocker is frequently cited as the blueprint for Ridley Scott's *Alien*. Ray "Crash" Corrigan wears the scaly rubber suit as the Martian monster, ably menacing Marshall Thompson and his fellow astronauts in a 1950s relic that still delivers some decent scares. AJ

Marshall Thompson *Colonel Carruthers* • Shawn Smith *Ann Anderson* • Kim Spalding *Colonel Van Heusen* • Ann Doran *Mary Royce* • Dabbs Greer *Eric Royce* • Ray "Crash" Corrigan *"It"* ■ *Dir* Edward L Cahn • *Scr* Jerome Bixby

It Was an Accident ★ 18
Comedy drama 2000 · UK/Fr · Colour · 96min

First-time director Metin Hüseyin doesn't romanticise a Walthamstow trapped between its mythologised gangland past and the present, in which petty crooks are as likely to resort to murder as the big boys. But Max Beesley's manic mobster reduces the proceedings to a shambles, and Chiwetel Ejiofor is cruelly exposed by the phoney slang of Oliver Parker's dismal screenplay. Thandie Newton is given even fewer favours as the girlfriend for whom small-time crook Ejiofor is reforming. Irredeemably crude and crass. DP *DVD*

Chiwetel Ejiofor *Nicky Burkett* • Max Beesley *Mickey Cousins* • James Bolam *Fitch* • Nicola Stapleton *Kelly* • Neil Dudgeon *Holdsworth* • Hugh Quarshie *George Hurlock* • Thandie Newton *Noreen Hurlock* ■ *Dir* Metin Hüseyin • *Scr* Oliver Parker [Ol Parker], from the novel by Jeremy Cameron

The Italian ★★★ 12
Drama 2005 · Rus · Colour · 99min

Andrei Kravchuk's well-meaning exposé of the conditions in Russia's orphanages is bolstered by an impressive performance from its young lead, Kolya Spiridonov. There's something Dickensian about the opening sequences, as the six-year-old boy is pressed into service by the criminal network run by older inmates. But the neorealist influence of Vittorio De Sica takes over after Spiridonov discovers that his mother is still alive and runs away to find her before the Cruella De Vil-like Maria Kuznetsova and brutal boyfriend Nikolai Reutov can sell him to an Italian couple. Cinematographer Alexander Burov effectively contrasts the dank interiors with the romanticised vistas. DP Russian +subtitles. Violence, sexual references. *DVD*

Kolya Spiridonov *Vanya Solntsev* • Denis Moiseenko *Kolyan* • Sasha Sirotkin *Sery* • Andrei Yelizarov *Timokha* • Maria Kuznetsova *Madam* • Nikolai Reutov *Grisha* ■ *Dir* Andrei Kravchuk • *Scr* Andrei Romanov • *Cinematographer* Alexander Burov [Aleksandr Burov]

Italian for Beginners ★★★★ 15
Romantic comedy drama 2000 · Den · Colour · 107min

If it wasn't for the admirably authentic visuals - shot on digital video using natural light - it would be easy to overlook the fact this genial suburban comedy has been accorded the Dogme seal of approval. Superbly served by a great ensemble cast, writer/director Lone Scherfig allows her tale of suburban Copenhagen lonely hearts to meander towards its satisfying, if shamelessly contrived, Venetian ending. But, behind the hesitant couplings of the diverse members of an ill-attended evening class, lie some potent yet subtly expressed ideas about how difficult it's becoming to communicate, trust and have faith in the modern world. DP Danish, Italian +subtitles. *DVD*

Anders W Berthelsen *Andreas* • Anette Stovelbaek *Olympia* • Peter Gantzler *Jorgen Mortensen* • Ann Eleonora Jorgensen *Karen* • Lars Kaalund *Hal-Finn* • Sara Indrio Jensen *Giulia* ■ *Dir* Lone Scherfig • *Scr* Scherfig Lone • *Cinematographer* Jorgen Johannson

The Italian Job ★★★ PG
Comedy caper 1969 · UK/US · Colour · 95min

Smashing vehicle stunt work distinguishes this Swinging Sixties romp. Unfortunately, despite a fine cast headed by criminals Michael Caine, Noël Coward and Benny Hill, the script doesn't quite come off. If the characters had been a little better developed and the director a little less flashy, this could have been a minor classic. That said, this is a mightily popular movie, helped by Quincy Jones's soundtrack and the marvellous Coward, who masterminds the whole wheeze from his prison cell. TS Violence, swearing. *DVD* *BLU*

Michael Caine *Charlie Croker* • Noël Coward *Mr Bridger* • Benny Hill *Professor Simon Peach* • Raf Vallone *Altabani* • Tony Beckley *Freddie* • Rossano Brazzi *Beckerman* • Maggie Blye *Lorna* • Irene Handl *Miss Peach* • John Le Mesurier *Governor* ■ *Dir* Peter Collinson • *Scr* Troy Kennedy Martin • *Cinematographer* Douglas Slocombe • *Editor* John Trumper

The Italian Job ★★★ 12
Crime action thriller 2003 · US · Colour · 105min

With a revised gold bullion robbery (now set in Venice and at the beginning of the film), F Gary Gray's supercharged direction and a smart script, this caper movie is just as enjoyable a ride as the British original. Mark Wahlberg carries plenty of easy-going charm in the Michael Caine role, heading a criminal gang that's revved up for revenge after associate Edward Norton has double-crossed them and absconded to Los Angeles with the booty. Norton's talents are wasted on such a sleazy, one-dimensional villain role, but Charlize Theron is beguiling as a sassy safecracker. JC Swearing, violence. *DVD* *BLU*

Mark Wahlberg *Charlie Croker* • Charlize Theron *Stella Bridger* • Edward Norton *Steve* • Seth Green *Lyle* • Jason Statham *Handsome Rob* • Mos Def *Left Ear* • Franky G *Wrench* • Donald Sutherland *John Bridger* ■ *Dir* F Gary Gray • *Scr* Donna Powers, Wayne Powers, from the film by Troy Kennedy Martin

Italian Movie ★★★
Romantic comedy 1994 · US · Colour · 95min

Fans of *Moonstruck* and *Big Night* could do worse than check out this lively romantic comedy from director Roberto Monticello. With more shrugs and hand gestures than the entire *Godfather* trilogy, the film follows Caprice Benedetti's frantic attempts to discover why husband Michael Dellafemina's sexual prowess is on the wane. Add some financial problems, in the form of creditor James Gandolfini, and you have a spicy dish that should appeal to most tastes. DP

Michael Dellafemina *Leonardo* • Caprice Benedetti *Anna* • Janet Sarno *Nina* • James Gandolfini *Angelo* • Rita Moreno *Isabella* ■ *Dir* Roberto Monticello • *Scr* Angela Sciddurlo Rago, Eugenia Bone

An Italian Straw Hat ★★★★★★
Silent comedy 1927 · Fr · BW · 60min

The leading proponent of comic theory, Henri Bergson, considered this the near perfect film and, while others complained that its satirical assault on bourgeois sensibilities was lightweight, it's impossible not to be intoxicated by this balletic silent masterpiece. Taken at a pace to rival Mack Sennett, yet full of Chaplinesque subtlety, René Clair's adaptation bursts out on to the streets of Paris, as Albert Préjean meets with an unexpected problem en route to his wedding. His horse has eaten a lady's hat and he is now desperately seeking a replacement. The characters are pantomimic puppets, but the precision of their movement is a joy to behold. DP

Albert Préjean *Fadinard* • Olga Tchekowa *Anaïs de Beauperthuis* • Marise Maïa *The bride* • Alice Tissot *A cousin* • Jim Gérald *Beauperthuis* ■ *Dir* René Clair • *Scr* René Clair, from the play *Un Chapeau de Paille d'Italie* by Eugène Labiche, Marc Michel

Ithaca ★★
Drama 2015 · US · Colour · 96min

An old-fashioned drama set in the 1940s, *Ithaca* tells the story of a teenager (Alex Neustaedter) who loses his father (Tom Hanks, appearing briefly). To help his mother (Meg Ryan, making her directorial debut), he gets a job as a telegram messenger, which means delivering bad news from the frontlines. Sam Shepard gives a terrific supporting performance as an alcoholic telegraph operator, though the film itself is somewhat slow-paced and underwhelming despite Ryan's good intentions. SC

Alex Neustaedter *Homer Macauley* • Meg Ryan *Mrs Macauley* • Tom Hanks *Mr Macauley* • Sam Shepard *Willie Grogan* ■ *Dir* Meg Ryan • *Scr* Erik Jendresen, from the novel *The Human Comedy* by William Saroyan

It's a Big Country ★ U
Drama 1951 · US · BW · 88min

MGM's flag-waving series of eight episodes intended to illustrate the richness and diversity of American life scores straight zeroes, except for Gary Cooper's monologue about Texas, directed by Clarence Brown, which is momentarily amusing. Yawn at the mawkish or pointless material in which stars such as Fredric March and Gene Kelly appear. An obvious embarrassment before release, the picture was cut down to a standard running time. AE

Ethel Barrymore *Mrs Brian Patrick Riordan* • Keefe Brasselle *Sgt Maxie Klein* • Nancy Davis *Miss Coleman* • Van Johnson *Adam Burch* • Gene Kelly *Icarus Xenophon* • Janet Leigh *Rosa Szabo* • Fredric March *Papa Esposito* ■ *Dir* Richard Thorpe, John Sturges, Charles Vidor, Don Weis, Clarence Brown, William A Wellman, Don Hartman • *Scr* William Ludwig, Helen Deutsch, Isobel Lennart, Allen Rivkin, George Wells, Dore Schary, Dorothy Kingsley

It's a Boy/Girl Thing ★★★ 12
Romantic comedy 2006 · UK · Colour · 90min

In this likeable addition to the body-swap comedy genre, Kevin Zegers (*Transamerica*) and Samaire Armstrong (TV's *The OC*) play chalk-and-cheese neighbours and sworn enemies, who get an unexpected taste of each other's lives - the star quarterback and the bookworm - when a magical Aztec statue causes them to exchange bodies. This role-reverse romantic comedy may not be original, but it's engagingly done and there are charming performances from the two leads. Watch out, too, for the feature film debut of occasional *X Factor* judge Sharon Osbourne as Zegers's mum. DA Some swearing, sexual references. *DVD*

Kevin Zegers *Woody Deane* • Samaire Armstrong *Nell Bedworth* • Sharon Osbourne *Della Deane* • Maury Chaykin *Stan Deane* • Mpho Koaho *Harry "Horse" Horsen* • Robert Joy *Ted Bedworth* • Sherry Miller *Katherine Bedworth* ■ *Dir* Nick Hurran • *Scr* Geoff Deane, from a story by Deane, Steve Hamilton Shaw

It's a Date ★★★ U
Musical comedy 1940 · US · BW · 103min

A famous actress (Kay Francis) has to face competition when a part she was hoping to get is offered instead to her ambitious daughter (Deanna Durbin). Love intervenes in the person of millionaire Walter Pidgeon, but will he choose Durbin or her mother? Now aged 19 and making her seventh feature film, Durbin reveals a more experienced grip on the art of acting, and some maturity in her singing of the usual rag-bag of songs that embellishes her films. Remade as *Nancy Goes to Rio* in 1950. RK

Deanna Durbin *Pamela Drake* • Kay Francis *Georgia Drake* • Walter Pidgeon *John Arlen* • Eugene Pallette *Governor Allen* • Henry Stephenson *Captain Andrew* • Cecilia Loftus *Sarah Frankenstein* • Samuel S Hinds *Sidney Simpson* • SZ Sakall *Carl Ober* ■ *Dir* William A Seiter • *Scr* Norman Krasna, from a story by Jane Hall, Frederick Kohner, Ralph Block

It's a Free World... ★★★ 15
Social drama 2007 · UK/It/Ger/Sp/Pol · Colour · 91min

In director Ken Loach's typically austere drama, single mother Angie (Kierston Wareing) attempts to set up her own employment agency in an attempt to pay off her debts and provide some stability for her delinquent ten-year-old son. But the lure of cheap illegal labour becomes too tempting to resist. Subsequently, Angie's more generous actions - like helping a family of Iranian illegal immigrants - too often seem driven by the demands of an increasingly melodramatic plot. Wareing gives a fine performance, although by focusing on her story, Loach and screenwriter Paul Laverty shift the moral focus away from the exploitation of those who have risked all to come to London. DP Violence, swearing. *DVD*

Kierston Wareing *Angie* • Juliet Ellis *Rose* • Leslaw Zurek *Karol* • Joe Siffleet *Jamie* • Colin Coughlin *Geoff* ■ *Dir* Ken Loach • *Scr* Paul Laverty

It's a Gift ★★★★★ U
Classic comedy 1934 · US · BW · 65min

Shades of Bacchus! It's the inimitable WC Fields in his most perfectly formed movie. Brilliantly conceived (by Fields himself, alias Charles Bogle), and beautifully structured (by director Norman Z McLeod), this is a milestone in screen comedy, and an emphatic must-see if you've decided you don't care for Fields or have never seen him before. The lengthy two-reel sequence on the porch is one of the funniest sustained sketches in sound cinema, and the store scene with Charles Sellon as blind Mr Muckle has to be seen to be believed. Kumquats will never be the same again. TS *DVD*

WC Fields *Harold Bissonette* • Kathleen Howard *Amelia Bissonette* • Jean Rouverol *Mildred Bissonette* • Julian Madison *John Durston* • Tom Bupp [Tommy Bupp] *Norman Bissonette* • Baby LeRoy *Baby Dunk* • Charles Sellon *Mr Muckle* • Josephine Whittell *Mrs Dunk* ■ *Dir* Norman Z McLeod • *Scr* Jack Cunningham, from a story by Charles Bogle [WC Fields], from the play *The Comic Supplement (of American Life)* by JP McEvoy

It's a Grand Life ★★ U
Comedy   1953 · UK · BW · 100min

If you have an aversion to music-hall stars on celluloid, give up, for vulgar Lancashire music-hall star Frank Randle has neither the wit of George Formby nor the warmth of Gracie Fields, and by the time this army caper was made he was looking tired and rather grubby. Still, the object of his fancy here is a young Diana Dors. TS

Frank Randle *Private Randle* • Diana Dors *Corporal Paula Clements* • Dan Young *Private Young* • Michael Brennan *Sergeant Major O'Reilly* • Jennifer Jayne *Private Desmond* ■ *Dir* John E Blakeley • *Scr* HF Maltby, Frank Randle, from a story by HF Maltby

It's a Great Day ★★ U
Comedy   1955 · UK · BW · 70min

The Grove Family was one of BBC television's great popular successes, a series that today would be termed soap opera, but then was a compulsive, studio-bound rendering of the busy but uninvolving goings-on of a very average suburban family. The excellent Ruth Dunning and Edward Evans were Gladys and Bob Grove, and the acting honours, and the popularity stakes, were hijacked by formidable Nancy Roberts as Gran. This is a cheaply made feature version of the show, with the original cast, and now looks like a perfect period artefact. TS

Ruth Dunning *Gladys Grove* • Edward Evans *Bob Grove* • Sidney James *Harry Mason* • Vera Day *Blondie* • Sheila Sweet *Pat Grove* • Peter Bryant (1) *Jack Grove* • Nancy Roberts *Gran* ■ *Dir* John Warrington • *Scr* Roland Pertwee, Michael Pertwee, from their TV series *The Grove Family*

It's a Great Feeling ★★★ U
Musical comedy   1949 · US · Colour · 84min

Just about everyone who happened to have been passing through the Warners lot seems to have been roped into this ever-so-gentle Tinseltown spoof. With Jack Carson and Dennis Morgan playing themselves as a couple of likely lads, there's much fun to be had with the whole idea of on-screen persona. However, it's Doris Day who shines as the waitress they trawl round the studio as the latest singing sensation. For all the star-spotting and backslapping aside, not a lot happens to hold the attention. DP

Doris Day *Judy Adams* • Dennis Morgan • Jack Carson • Bill Goodwin *Arthur Trent* • Gary Cooper • Joan Crawford • Errol Flynn *Jeffrey Bushfinkle* • Sydney Greenstreet • Danny Kaye • Patricia Neal • Eleanor Parker • Ronald Reagan • Edward G Robinson • Jane Wyman • Raoul Walsh • Michael Curtiz • King Vidor ■ *Dir* David Butler • *Scr* Jack Rose, Melville Shavelson, from a story by IAL Diamond

It's a Lot ★★ 15
Comedy   2013 · UK · Colour · 96min

Anuvahood star Femi Oyeniran makes a disappointing debut behind the camera with this lacklustre comedy. Sadly, he is little better in front of it, playing the privately schooled son of rich parents who enrols at his cousin's inner-city state school to meet normal kids. The movie is rammed with clichés and stereotypes imported wholesale from American high-school movies, and Oyeniran and co-writer Nick Walker content themselves with slotting the pieces into place rather than giving them much UK-centricity. It's commendably played by a

spirited cast, but is short on laughs and too often soft-soaps its insights into class, colour, identity and acceptance. DP Swearing, sexual references, drug abuse.

Femi Oyeniran *Shawn* • Red Madrell *Natalie* • Jazzie Zonzolo *Kai* • Jack Doolan *James* ■ *Dir* Darwood Grace, Femi Oyeniran • *Scr* Femi Oyeniran, Nick Walker

It's a Mad Mad Mad Mad World ★★★ U
Comedy   1963 · US · Colour · 148min

Director/producer Stanley Kramer assembled the cream of Hollywood's comic talent for this monumental and mostly entertaining chase caper. The ever-versatile Spencer Tracy - in his penultimate film and clearly unwell - catches the eye as the henpecked detective at the front of the race to find a stash of stolen cash. It's rather ironic that the film was nominated for an editing Oscar, for, while the breakneck stunts undeniably have pace, the action badly needed cutting by at least 80 minutes. DP *DVD*

Spencer Tracy *Captain CG Culpeper* • Milton Berle *J Russell Finch* • Sid Caesar *Melville Crump* • Buddy Hackett *Benjy* • Ethel Merman *Mrs Marcus* • Mickey Rooney *Ding Bell* • Dick Shawn *Sylvester Marcus* • Phil Silvers *Otto Meyer* • Terry-Thomas *J Algernon Hawthorne* • Jonathan Winters *Lennie Pike* ■ *Dir* Stanley Kramer • *Scr* William Rose, Tania Rose • *Cinematographer* Ernest Laszlo • *Music* Ernest Gold

It's a Pleasure ★★
Romantic drama   1945 · US · Colour · 89min

Star ice-skating champion Sonja Henie here delivers the dazzling routines that fans had come to expect, further enhanced by an extravaganza of Technicolor. Unfortunately, whenever Henie, with her limited acting skills, leaves the ice to play out a romantic tale of woe with ice-hockey champ Michael O'Shea (also no actor), the movie collapses into a limp mess of clichés and embarrassing dialogue. The star rating is strictly for the "ice-capades". RK

Sonja Henie *Chris Linden* • Michael O'Shea (1) *Don Martin* • Marie McDonald *Gail Fletcher* • Bill Johnson (1) *Buzz Fletcher* • Gus Schilling *Bill Evans* • Iris Adrian *Wilma* ■ *Dir* William A Seiter • *Scr* Lynn Starling, Elliot Paul

It's a Very Merry Muppet Christmas Movie ★★ U
Seasonal comedy   2002 · US · Colour · 84min

When Joan Cusack threatens to close the Muppet Theatre, Kermit assumes the James Stewart role in *It's a Wonderful Life* and angel David Arquette shows him how life would have treated the likes of Fozzie and Miss Piggy had he never existed. The absence of most of the usual voice artists and the inclusion of some smutty innuendo compound this parody's mediocrity. DP *DVD*

Steve Whitmire *Kermit/Rizzo the Rat/Beaker/Bean Bunny/Mr Poodlepants* • Dave Goelz *Gonzo the Great/Dr Bunsen Honeydew/Waldorf* • Bill Barretta *Pepe the Prawn/Dr Teeth/Rowlf the Dog/Swedish Chef/Johnny Fiama/Bobo the Bear/Howard/Lew Zealand* • Eric Jacobson *Miss Piggy/Fozzie Bear/Animal/Yoda* • David Arquette *Daniel* • Joan Cusack *Rachel Bitterman* • Whoopi Goldberg *Daniel's boss* • William H Macy *Glenn* ■ *Dir* Kirk R Thatcher • *Scr* Tom Martin, Jim Lewis

It's a Wonderful Afterlife ★★ 12
Supernatural romantic comedy
2010 · UK · Colour · 96min

Though the title of this supernatural romantic comedy from director Gurinder Chadha harks back to Frank Capra's 1946 fantasy, it has little to do with that James Stewart classic. Respected Indian actress Shabana Azmi stars here as a mother who is so obsessed with marrying off her chubby daughter (Goldy Notay) that she kills anyone who stands in her way. And an unlikely plot twist sees her aided in her quest by the ghosts of her victims. The gags are brash, the plot is messy and there's an element of mild horror that feels totally random. Sadly, it leaves the central

romance buried beneath too much nonsense. SP Violence, drug abuse *DVD*

Shabana Azmi *Mrs Sethi* • Goldy Notay *Roopi* • Sendhil Ramamurthy *Detective Sergeant Murthy* • Zoë Wanamaker *Mrs Goldman* • Sanjeev Bhaskar *Curry man* • Mark Addy *Detective Inspector Smythe* ■ *Dir* Gurinder Chadha • *Scr* Gurinder Chadha, Paul Mayeda Berges

LANDMARK FILM
James Stewart stars in what is to become the ultimate Christmas movie

It's a Wonderful Life ★★★★★ U
Classic fantasy drama   1946 · US · BW · 125min

This masterpiece from Frank Capra still has a lot to say about community spirit and is a film with much more to it than feel-good sentimentality. As the suicidal man who is shown the value of his life by his guardian angel, George Bailey is Mr Deeds, John Doe and Mr Smith rolled into one, and only James Stewart could have given him the self-doubt that gnaws away at his essential decency. As with all good morality tales, the villain has to be exceptional, too, and Lionel Barrymore is at the peak of his powers as the villainous Potter. The term Capra-esque is too often misapplied: revel in the genuine article here. DP *DVD* Blu

James Stewart *George Bailey* • Donna Reed *Mary Hatch* • Lionel Barrymore *Mr Potter* • Thomas Mitchell *Uncle Billy* • Henry Travers *Clarence Oddbody* • Beulah Bondi *Mrs Bailey* • Frank Faylen *Ernie* • Ward Bond *Bert* • Gloria Grahame *Violet Bick* • HB Warner *Mr Gower* ■ *Dir* Frank Capra • *Scr* Frances Goodrich, Albert Hackett, Frank Capra, Jo Swerling, Michael Wilson, from the short story *The Greatest Gift* by Philip Van Doren Stern • *Music* Dmitri Tiomkin

It's a Wonderful World ★★★★
Screwball comedy   1939 · US · BW · 85min

This is a brilliantly funny but overlooked screwball comedy, nearly the last of its kind, in which James Stewart and wacky Claudette Colbert spend their time despising each other (until the final reel, that is). He's a private eye on the run, and she's a poet and they're looking for a killer, and... well, that's screwball enough. This is a screen original, written by the great Ben Hecht from his and Herman J Mankiewicz's story, and directed with skill and considerable pace by WS "Woody One-Take" Van Dyke II. TS

Claudette Colbert *Edwina Corday* • James Stewart *Guy Johnson* • Guy Kibbee *Captain Streeter* • Nat Pendleton *Sergeant Koretz* • Frances Drake *Vivian Tarbel* ■ *Dir* WS Van Dyke II [WS Van Dyke] • *Scr* Ben Hecht, from a story by Ben Hecht, Herman J Mankiewicz

It's a Wonderful World ★ U
Musical comedy   1956 · UK · Colour · 89min

Val Guest directs this anxious-to-please British musical comedy. Set in the era before the advent of rock 'n' roll, the film follows the fortunes of composers Terence Morgan and George Cole, who, tired of being rejected in favour of more trendy music, pin their hopes of success on re-jigging a popular song. The music is not to everyone's taste, with Mylene Nicole's performance with Ted Heath's band striking the lowest note of all. DP

Terence Morgan *Ray Thompson* • George Cole *Ken Miller* • Kathleen Harrison *Miss Gilly* • Mylene Nicole [Mylène Demongeot] *Georgie Dubois* • James Hayter *Bert Fielding* • Harold Lang *Mervyn Wade* ■ *Dir/Scr* Val Guest

It's Alive ★★★ 15
Horror   1974 · US · Colour · 87min

This breakthrough "mutant baby" movie marked the first time director Larry Cohen employed shock horror tactics to deal with serious social issues. Unsafe fertility drugs are blamed when Sharon Farrell's hideous newborn offspring, complete with claws and fangs, slaughters all the medics in the delivery room and embarks on a murder spree. Cohen's absorbing, grisly and cleverly written brainchild provides food for thought while still delivering the chilling goods. Oscar-winning make-up man Rick

Baker designs the baby, and the movie features one of Bernard Herrmann's last scores. *It Lives Again* was the first of two sequels. AJ

John Ryan [John P Ryan] *Frank Davies* • Sharon Farrell *Lenore Davies* • Andrew Duggan *Professor* • Guy Stockwell *Clayton* • James Dixon *Lieutenant Perkins* ■ *Dir/Scr* Larry Cohen

It's Alive III: Island of the Alive ★★★ 18
Horror   1987 · US · Colour · 90min

Topical issues, socially conscious humour and a great performance by Michael Moriarty (one of director Larry Cohen's rep company regulars) make this a worthy successor to the previous two killer mutant baby shockers. Moriarty plays a third-rate actor who deals with his mixed-up feelings about fathering one of the vicious tots by going to court to stop them being destroyed and getting them quarantined to a Florida island. A lively, absorbing and scary indictment crafted with Cohen's usual care and attention. AJ *DVD*

Michael Moriarty *Stephen Jarvis* • Karen Black *Ellen Jarvis* • Laurene Landon *Sally* • Gerrit Graham *Ralston* • James Dixon *Dr Perkins* • Neal Israel *Dr Brewster* ■ *Dir/Scr* Larry Cohen • *Music* Laurie Johnson, Bernard Herrmann

It's All about Love ★★★ 15
Futuristic romantic drama
2002 · Den/UK/Ger/It/Jpn/Swe/Neth/Sp/Swi/Gr/Is · Colour · 100min

Danish director Thomas Vinterberg turns his back on the stripped-down realism of Dogme 95 for his first English-language feature. The film is a lavishly created sci-fi love story in which Joaquin Phoenix and Claire Danes make handsome leads as a young married couple who decide to split after spending several years apart. But when Phoenix pays a flying visit to New York so that ice-skating superstar Danes can sign their divorce papers, he realises that his wife's celebrity lifestyle is not what it seems. Stylistically it looks gorgeous, but this cool sophistication comes at the expense of coherent plot development. Made with additional funding from Germany, Italy and Spain. SF Swearing. *DVD*

Joaquin Phoenix *John* • Claire Danes *Elena* • Douglas Henshall *Michael* • Alun Armstrong *David* • Margo Martindale *Betsy* • Mark Strong *Arthur* • Geoffrey Hutchings *Mr Morrison* • Sean Penn *Marciello* ■ *Dir* Thomas Vinterberg • *Scr* Thomas Vinterberg, Mogens Rukov

It's All Gone Pete Tong ★★ 15
Comedy drama   2004 · UK/Can · Colour · 88min

Ibiza's rave scene is a fairly easy target for a few laughs in a mock documentary, but there are too few of them in Michael Dowse's story of a DJ who reaches the top only to discover he is going deaf. Paul Kaye delivers a credible performance as the disc jockey, but his substance-abusing character is initially so loathsome that the viewer is unlikely to care about him. The movie then shifts gear and generates some interest, thanks to the performances of Kaye and Beatriz Batarda, playing the woman who teaches him to lip-read. BP Swearing, drug abuse. *DVD*

Paul Kaye *Frankie Wilde* • Beatriz Batarda *Penelope Garcia* • Kate Magowan *Sonya Slowinski* • Mike Wilmot *Max Hagger* • Dave Lawrence [David Lawrence (2)] *Horst* • Paul J Spence *Alfonse* • Pete Tong ■ *Dir/Scr* Michael Dowse

It's All Happening ★★ U
Musical   1963 · UK · Colour · 96min

Well, if it is, it's nothing to get excited about. This sentimental hokum feels like it was something Norman Wisdom rejected before being turned into a vehicle for Tommy Steele. With a cheeky grin never far from his face, Steele masterminds a talent show to raise funds for the local orphanage. The songs sound as though they were knocked out on a slow afternoon on Denmark Street, London's very own Tin Pan Alley. DP

U SUITABLE FOR ALL   Ue SUITABLE ESPECIALLY FOR YOUNG CHILDREN (DVD ONLY)   PG PARENTAL GUIDANCE   12A UNDER 12s TO BE ACCOMPANIED (CINEMA ONLY)

Tommy Steele *Billy Bowles* • Angela Douglas *Julie Singleton* • Michael Medwin *Max Catlin* • Jean Harvey (1) *Delia* • Bernard Bresslaw *Parsons* ■ *Dir* Don Sharp • *Scr* Leigh Vance

It's All True ★★★★
Political documentary drama
1993 · Fr/Bra · BW · 89min

In 1942, the day after he shot the last scene of *The Magnificent Ambersons*, Orson Welles flew to Brazil to make a semi-documentary, *It's All True*, which was to be anti-Nazi propaganda financed by the State Department. The film was never finished; meanwhile, RKO cut *Ambersons* behind Welles's back, sacking him on his return and destroying his Hollywood career. This film mixes interviews, Welles's exhilarating footage of the Rio carnival and a reconstruction of a segment in the intended documentary. It's a riveting piece of cinema archaeology, an unmissable treat for buffs and historians alike that also sheds new light on the *Ambersons* fiasco. AT

Dean Beville *Narration* • Miguel Ferrer *Narration* • Orson Welles ■ *Dir* Richard Wilson (1), Myron Meisel, Bill Krohn • *Scr* Bill Krohn, Richard Wilson, Myron Meisel, from a story by Robert J Flaherty • *Cinematographer* Gary Graver

It's Always Fair Weather ★★★★ U
Musical comedy   1955 · US · Colour · 101min

Originally intended as a follow-up to *On the Town*, this wonderfully sardonic musical failed to find much critical approval or public acclaim on its original release. Now, in these more cynical times, we can appreciate this masterwork for what it is: a genuinely clever satire on all things American. Television is the main target here, but Madison Avenue advertising and the sports world take their fair share of knocks, as wartime buddies Gene Kelly, Dan Dailey and Michael Kidd plan a reunion, only to find they've nothing in common. TS

Gene Kelly *Ted Riley* • Dan Dailey *Doug Hallerton* • Cyd Charisse *Jackie Leighton* • Dolores Gray *Madeline Bradville* • Michael Kidd *Angie Valentine* • David Burns *Tim* ■ *Dir* Gene Kelly, Stanley Donen • *Scr* Betty Comden, Adolph Green

It's Christmas, Carol! ★★
Seasonal fantasy   2012 · Can · Colour · 97min

Deceased publishing exec Carrie Fisher has one night to show her callous and money-obsessed successor (Emmanuelle Vaugier) the error of her ways in yet another take on *A Christmas Carol*. Caustic wit is the ghostly guide's main method of persuasion, as she leads the "Stalin in stilettos" on the usual life-changing, festive journey through her past, present and future. Knowing gags – including a fan-pleasing *Star Wars* quip – make the most of Fisher's enjoyably dry delivery. SF

Emmanuelle Vaugier *Carol Huffman* • Carrie Fisher *Eve* • Carson Kressley *Fred* • Olivia Cheng *Kendra* ■ *Dir* Michael M Scott [Michael Scott] • *Scr* William Penick, Christopher Sey

It's Complicated ★★★★ 15
Romantic comedy   2009 · US · Colour · 115min

Mixing elements of frisky French farce with middle-class American comedy, *It's Complicated* is a daffy and delectable spree from Nancy Meyers (*Something's Gotta Give*). Meryl Streep plays Jane, a divorced mum of three who hooks up with her remarried ex, Jake (Alec Baldwin), at their son's graduation. Adding a wrinkle to proceedings is Adam (Steve Martin), a divorced architect who woos Jane with cautious optimism. Although seemingly stuck in *Mamma Mia!* mode, Streep's polite resistance is the perfect foil for Baldwin's earnest portrayal of a horny old dog. It's a thoughtful, daring and fun film, in which Meyers, once again, has put some glamour into the sex lives of the 50-somethings. KK Swearing, sexual references, nudity, drug abuse. DVD Blu

Meryl Streep *Jane Adler* • Steve Martin *Adam* • Alec Baldwin *Jake Adler* • John Krasinski *Harley* • Lake Bell *Agness* • Rita Wilson *Trisha* ■ *Dir/Scr* Nancy Meyers

It's Great to Be Young ★★★★ U
Musical comedy   1956 · UK · Colour · 93min

This light-hearted comedy has a remarkable level of energy and a superb sense of pace. John Mills stars as trumpet-playing, jazz-loving Mr Dingle, whose enforced resignation from Angel Hill School leads to a (very minor) revolution. The kids, led by Jeremy Spenser and Dorothy Bromiley, are charming, and thanks to an excellent Ted Willis screenplay, the adults are utterly believable, as is the studio construction of the school. TS

John Mills *Dingle* • Cecil Parker *Frome* • John Salew *Routledge* • Elizabeth Kentish *Mrs Castle* • Mona Washbourne *Miss Morrow* • Mary Merrall *Miss Wyvern* • Jeremy Spenser *Nicky* • Dorothy Bromiley *Paulette* ■ *Dir* Cyril Frankel • *Scr* Ted Willis

It's in the Air ★★ U
Comedy   1938 · UK · BW · 83min

George Formby's toothy grin, innuendo-laden songs and jaunty ukelele-strumming delighted UK audiences of the 1930s and 1940s. Underdog Formby would triumph against long odds and usually walk off with the girl. Some of his most popular vehicles found him dashing about on motorbikes or in uniform, and here these elements are combined, with Formby a motorcycle enthusiast who is mistaken for an RAF pilot. DF

George Formby *George Brown* • Polly Ward *Peggy* • Garry Marsh *Commanding officer* • Julien Mitchell *Sergeant-Major* • Jack Hobbs *Corporal Craig* • C Denier Warren *Sir Philip Bargrave* ■ *Dir/Scr* Anthony Kimmins

It's in the Bag ★★ U
Comedy   1945 · US · BW · 83min

There's nothing quite like this idiosyncratic comedy, co-scripted by Alfred Hitchcock's wife, Alma Reville. It starts off with a clever Fred Allen voiceover mocking the credits and continues with various vaudeville-style sketches that are patchy fun, tending to overstay their welcome. The familiar link is a search for money hidden in one of five chairs. AE

Fred Allen (2) *Fred Floogle* • Jack Benny • William Bendix • Binnie Barnes *Eve Floogle* • Robert Benchley *Parker* • John Carradine *Pike* ■ *Dir* Richard Wallace • *Scr* Lewis R Foster, Fred Allen, Jay Dratler, Alma Reville

It's in the Water ★★★ 15
Comedy   1998 · US · Colour · 99min

There's nothing new or particularly clever about debutant Kelli Herd's queer comedy. However, it does succeed in depicting lesbians and gays as everyday people rather than a misunderstood minority. Discontented housewife Keri Jo Chapman's romance with Teresa Garrett, a divorced nurse at an Aids hospice, compensates with its feel-good geniality, which is given satirical edge by stand-out support from John Hallum and Barbara Lasater. DP DVD

Keri Jo Chapman *Alex Stratton* • Teresa Garrett *Grace Miller* • Derrick Sanders *Mark Anderson* • Timothy Vahle *Tomas* • Barbara Lasater *Lily Talbott* • Nancy Chartier *Sloan* • John Hallum *Spencer* ■ *Dir/Scr* Kelli Herd

It's Kind of a Funny Story ★★★★ 12
Comedy drama   2010 · US · Colour · 101min

If John Hughes had made *One Flew over the Cuckoo's Nest*, the result might have been something akin to this smart and darkly funny teen movie. After a failed suicide bid, angsty 16-year-old Craig (Keir Gilchrist) checks himself into a New York psychiatric hospital, anticipating some pills and a few hours peace. But the teen facility is closed, and he finds himself committed instead to the adult ward. There, he learns lessons in life and love from two fellow patients: worldly Bobby (Zach Galifianakis) and another troubled youth (Emma Roberts). The casting is pitch perfect and so is the tone – comic, but not too comic;

serious, but not too serious. DA Swearing, sexual references. DVD Blu

Keir Gilchrist *Craig* • Zach Galifianakis *Bobby* • Emma Roberts *Noelle* • Viola Davis *Dr Eden Minerva* • Lauren Graham *Lynn* • Zoë Kravitz *Nia* • Jeremy Davies *Smitty* ■ *Dir* Anna Boden, Ryan Fleck • *Scr* Anna Boden, Ryan Fleck, from the novel by Ned Vizzini

It's Love Again ★★★ U
Musical comedy   1936 · UK · BW · 80min

The ever-delightful Jessie Matthews is in fine fettle in this frothy concoction that perfectly showcases both her musical talent and her vivacious comic personality. As a showgirl posing as a big-game-hunting socialite, she runs rings round columnist Robert Young. Lacking the glamour of a Hollywood musical (in spite of some impossibly chic Art Deco sets), this is still a pleasurable romp, with Sonnie Hale (Matthews's real-life husband at the time) amusing as the rival reporter responsible for the scam and Robb Wilton hilarious as a valet. DP

Jessie Matthews *Elaine Bradford* • Robert Young (1) *Peter Carlton* • Sonnie Hale *Freddie Rathbone* • Ernest Milton *Archibald Raymond* • Robb Wilton *Boy* • Sara Allgood *Mrs Hopkins* ■ *Dir* Victor Saville • *Scr* Marion Dix, Lesser Samuels, Austin Melford

It's Love I'm After ★★★
Romantic comedy   1937 · US · BW · 90min

This funny Bette Davis/Leslie Howard vehicle crackles with sophisticated one-liners, plus much histrionic raising of eyebrows and waving of hands courtesy of a plot that revolves around a warring pair of famous Shakespearean actors. Davis shows us what an all-rounder she is, demonstrating a flair for deft comic timing, and even the normally lugubrious Howard joins in with verve and gusto. Olivia de Havilland is the perfect foil as Howard's fan. SH

Leslie Howard *Basil Underwood* • Bette Davis *Joyce Arden* • Olivia de Havilland *Marcia West* • Eric Blore *Digges* • Patric Knowles *Henry Grant* ■ *Dir* Archie Mayo • *Scr* Casey Robinson, from the story *Gentleman after Midnight* by Maurice Hanline

It's My Party ★★ 15
Comedy drama   1996 · US · Colour · 105min

Architect Eric Roberts learns he is about to lose his long battle against Aids and decides to throw a two-day pre-suicide farewell party surrounded by family and friends. But his guests are uncomfortable in the highly charged atmosphere where opinions collide and secrets spill. Unsympathetic characters clash with heavy sentiment in director Randal Kleiser's well-meaning comedy drama, which quickly wears out its celebratory welcome. AJ

Eric Roberts *Nick Stark* • George Segal *Paul Stark* • Marlee Matlin *Daphne Stark* • Roddy McDowall *Damian Knowles* • Olivia Newton-John *Lina Bingham* • Lee Grant *Amalia Stark* ■ *Dir/Scr* Randal Kleiser

It's My Turn ★★ 15
Romantic comedy   1980 · US · Colour · 86min

This is an example of the disappointing career trajectory of leading lady Jill Clayburgh, who started the 1980s with this predictable romantic drama. Clayburgh's in a relationship with Charles Grodin but then goes to a wedding and meets retired baseball player Michael Douglas. Difficult decisions lie ahead. While nicely performed, this never really gets going and ultimately offers no more depth than a TV soap. JB

Jill Clayburgh *Kate Gunzinger* • Michael Douglas (1) *Ben Lewin* • Charles Grodin *Homer* • Beverly Garland *Emma* • Steven Hill *Jacob* • Daniel Stern *Cooperman* • Dianne Wiest *Gail* ■ *Dir* Claudia Weill • *Scr* Eleanor Bergstein

It's Never Too Late ★★★ U
Comedy   1956 · UK · Colour · 92min

Phyllis Calvert stars as a materfamilias whose scriptwriting talents are discovered by a Hollywood producer, but who finds she can only write when she's surrounded by her chaotic family. This is very much of its

time, with its West End origins masked by skilful art direction, but the period cast is a British film fan's delight. Director Michael McCarthy whips up a fair old storm in this particular teacup and, although nothing really happens, there's a great deal of pleasure to be had from watching Calvert attempt to rule over her unruly household. TS DVD

Phyllis Calvert *Laura Hammond* • Patrick Barr *Charles Hammond* • Susan Stephen *Tessa Hammond* • Guy Rolfe *Stephen Hodgson* • Jean Taylor-Smith *Grannie* • Sarah Lawson *Anne* • Irene Handl • Shirley Anne Field ■ *Dir* Michael McCarthy • *Scr* Edward Dryhurst, from the play by Felicity Douglas

It's Never Too Late to Mend ★★
Melodrama   1937 · UK · BW · 95min

This is another over-ripe slice of melodrama for Tod Slaughter to sink his teeth into and, once again, he has a ball hamming things up. In this tale, he is a nasty aristocrat trying to get his evil way with sweet young thing Marjorie Taylor. To stand any chance he has to get rid of her lover, which he does by having him framed for a crime and incarcerated in a brutal prison. Don't expect any surprises and you won't be disappointed. JF

Tod Slaughter *Squire Meadows* • Marjorie Taylor *Susan Merton* • Jack Livesey *Tom Robinson* • Ian Colin *George Fielding* • Lawrence Hanray *Lawyer Crawley* • DJ Williams *Farmer Merton* • Roy Russell *Reverend Eden* • Johnny Singer *Joseph* ■ *Dir* David MacDonald • *Scr* HF Maltby, from a play by Charles Reade, Arthur Shirley

It's Not Cricket ★★★ U
Comedy   1948 · UK · BW · 70min

Basil Radford and Naunton Wayne first displayed their passion for cricket as Charters and Caldicott in Alfred Hitchcock's sparkling spy thriller *The Lady Vanishes* in 1938. Here (in one of the last of their 11 features together) they play Bright and Early, who become private detectives after they are cashiered from the army for allowing Nazi Maurice Denham to slip through their fingers. The misadventures of the bungling double act are pleasing enough, but the humour has about as much depth as the England batting order. DP DVD

Basil Radford *Major Bright* • Naunton Wayne *Captain Early* • Susan Shaw *Primrose Brown* • Maurice Denham *Otto Fisch* • Alan Wheatley *Felix* • Diana Dors *Blonde* ■ *Dir* Alfred Roome, Roy Rich • *Scr* Bernard McNab, Gerard Bryant and Lyn Lockwood

It'$ Only Money ★★★ U
Comedy   1962 · US · BW · 83min

It always proved difficult to capture the essential Jerry Lewis on film and, except in France where he is regarded as a genius, the consensus is that he was a brilliant comic who never fully translated his skills to screen. Director Frank Tashlin worked a number of times with Lewis, with mixed results, and this is one of their better collaborations. Lewis plays Lester March, a TV repair man who yearns to be a detective and persuades a real detective to let him join an investigation into a missing heir. Less slapstick than usual but still with one or two stand-out comedy routines. DF

Jerry Lewis *Lester March* • Zachary Scott *Gregory DeWitt* • Joan O'Brien *Wanda Paxton* • Mae Questel *Cecilia Albright* • Jesse White *Pete Flint* • Jack Weston *Leopold* ■ *Dir* Frank Tashlin • *Scr* John Fenton Murray

It's That Man Again ★★ U
Comedy   1942 · UK · BW · 80min

By the time Tommy Handley starred in this disappointing backstage vehicle, his radio show, *ITMA*, was attracting 40 million listeners each week, all desperate to laugh away their wartime blues. However, the comic's fast-talking style feels forced, and his weaknesses as a physical comedian restricted the type of business he was able to carry off. Thus, while casting him as the devious mayor of Foaming-at-the-Mouth seemed sound enough, the events that follow his acquisition of a bombed-out London theatre feel like so much padding. DP

Tommy Handley *Mayor Handley* • Greta Gynt *Stella Ferris* • Jack Train *Lefty/Funf* • Sidney Keith *Sam Scram* ■ *Dir* Walter Forde • *Scr* Howard Irving Young, Ted Kavanagh, from the radio series *ITMA* by Kavanagh

It's the Old Army Game
★★★

Silent farce   1926 · US · BW · 70min

Some of the best sequences from this WC Fields silent comedy were refined and reused in his great 1934 talkie *It's a Gift*, where his raspy voice and the sound effects added considerably to the impact. Still, there's much merriment to be had here as a younger-looking, dark-haired Fields (as small-town pharmacist Elmer Prettywillie) attempts to obtain a decent night's sleep, and a family excursion to a Florida estate leads to general devastation. Plus there's the considerable bonus of the luminous Louise Brooks as his assistant. AE

WC Fields *Elmer Prettywillie* • Louise Brooks *Mildred Marshall* • Blanche Ring *Tessie Overholt* • William Gaxton *George Parker* ■ *Dir* Edward Sutherland [A Edward Sutherland] • *Scr* Tom J Geraghty [Tom Geraghty], J Clarkson Miller, from the play by Joseph Patrick McEvoy [JP McEvoy], from theatrical sketches by McEvoy, WC Fields

It's Trad, Dad
★★★ U

Musical comedy   1961 · UK · BW · 73min

Richard Lester had already worked with the anarchic Goons on television and on film, and thus was no stranger to madcap mayhem. This flair was on show in this film (also known as *Ring-a-Ding Rhythm*). It's a light-hearted musical romp with the simple message that rock 'n' roll is good for you. Soulful voiced Helen Shapiro and clean-cut Craig Douglas star as the kids trying to mount a music show, despite protests from the pompous mayor. Among the acts featured are rock 'n' roller Chubby Checker and teen idol Del Shannon. DF

Helen Shapiro *Helen* • Craig Douglas *Craig* • Felix Felton *Mayor* • Arthur Mullard *Police chief* • Timothy Bateson *Coffeeshop owner* • Derek Nimmo *Head waiter* ■ *Dir* Richard Lester • *Scr* Milton Subotsky

It's Turned Out Nice Again
★★★ U

Comedy   1941 · UK · BW · 77min

George Formby's famous catchphrase was pressed into service for the title of this mischievous comedy, which proved to be his last assignment for Ealing Studios. Formby is a go-ahead ideas man at an underwear factory whose ambitious plans get his fellow knicker workers in a twist, but the action too often gets bogged down in a predictable subplot in which his smothering ma tries to break up his romance with Peggy Bryan. DP

George Formby *George Pearson* • Peggy Bryan *Lydia Pearson* • Edward Chapman *Uncle Arnold* • Elliot Mason *Mrs Pearson* • Wilfrid Hyde White *Removal man* ■ *Dir* Marcel Varnel • *Scr* Austin Melford, John Dighton, Basil Dearden, from the play *As You Were* by Hugh Mills, Wells Root

Ivan the Terrible, Part I
★★★★★ PG

Historical drama   1944 · USSR · BW · 94min

Sergei Eisenstein's consummate work, this is an intense historical portrait of the life of the 16th century tsar who clashed with the Boyars and the Church and advanced Russia's position as an empire. Conceived as a trilogy and initially championed by Stalin, the project took a controversial turn over the changed depiction of the leader in *Part II*, and *Part III* was never made. *Part I* is an iconoclastic departure from the director's polemical, montage milestones with its exaggerated, expressionistic approach derived from the stylised artifice of opera, Kabuki theatre and shadow plays. In moving beyond his trademark staccato technique, Eisenstein created an absorbing work. DO Russian +subtitles. *DVD*

Nikolai Cherkassov *Tsar Ivan IV* • Serafima Birman *The Boyarina Efrosinia Staritskaya, Tsar's Aunt* • Pavel Kadochnikov *Vladimir Andreyevich Staritsky* • Mikhail Zharov *Malyuta Skuratov* ■ *Dir/Scr* Sergei Eisenstein • *Cinematographers* Andrei Moskvin, Edouard Tissé • *Music* Sergei Prokofiev • *Art Director* Isaac Shpinel

Ivan the Terrible, Part II
★★★★★ PG

Historical drama   1946 · USSR · BW and Colour · 81min

This second part of director Sergei Eisenstein's intended trilogy was completed in early 1946, by which time Eisenstein was recuperating from a heart attack. Emphasising the personal over the public aspect of the tsar's life, the film was shown to Eisenstein's ultimate boss, Stalin, who banned it because Ivan's bodyguard and the secret service were portrayed like the "Ku Klux Klan and Ivan himself was... weak and indecisive, somewhat like Hamlet." The film remained unshown until 1958, by which time Eisenstein had been dead for ten years. Admittedly less accessible than its predecessor, *Part II* is confined almost exclusively to dark interiors and even features a startling sequence that includes the director's only colour footage. DO Russian +subtitles. *DVD*

Nikolai Cherkassov *Tsar Ivan IV* • Serafima Birman *The Boyarina Efrosinia Staritskaya, Tsar's Aunt* • Pavel Kadochnikov *Vladimir Andreyevich Staritsky* • Mikhail Zharov *Malyuta Skuratov* ■ *Dir/Scr* Sergei Eisenstein • *Music* Sergei Prokofiev

Ivanhoe
★★★★ U

Epic swashbuckling adventure   1952 · UK · Colour · 102min

A justifiable box-office smash in what was, with hindsight, one of MGM's greatest years, this rollicking Technicolor swashbuckler remains the definitive screen version of Sir Walter Scott's memorable medieval classic. The cast and the action sequences are almost perfect; though suitably handsome, American Robert Taylor is a little dull as Sir Wilfred of Ivanhoe, but Elizabeth Taylor as Rebecca is at her loveliest, Emlyn Williams is wonderfully theatrical as Wamba, and villains George Sanders, Robert Douglas and, especially, lean and mean Guy Rolfe as Prince John are superb. Interestingly, Scott's sub-theme about anti-Semitism in 1190 England is not glossed over, making this one of the few 1950s movies to deal openly with such a tricky subject. TS *DVD*

Robert Taylor (1) *Ivanhoe* • Elizabeth Taylor *Rebecca* • Joan Fontaine *Rowena* • George Sanders *De Bois-Guilbert* • Emlyn Williams *Wamba* • Robert Douglas *Sir Hugh De Bracy* ■ *Dir* Richard Thorpe • *Scr* Marguerite Roberts (uncredited), Noel Langley, from the novel by Sir Walter Scott, adapted by Aeneas MacKenzie

Ivan's Childhood
★★★★★ PG

Second World War drama   1962 · USSR · BW · 90min

Winner of the Golden Lion at Venice, Andrei Tarkovsky's debut feature – about a 12-year-old boy who becomes a spy to take revenge on the Nazis who killed his family – may surprise those familiar only with his later philosophical treatises. The film would be indistinguishable from many other examples of Soviet socialist realism, were it not for the chilling clarity of Vadim Yusov's photography and the visual flourishes that decorate the action. Even without these elements, this is still a shrewd insight into the reckless courage of youth and the grotesque poetry of combat. DP Russian +subtitles. *DVD*

Kolya Burlyaev *Ivan* • Valentin Zubkov *Capt Kholin* • E Zharikov *Lt Galtsev* • S Krylov *Cpl Katasonych* ■ *Dir* Andrei Tarkovsky • *Scr* Vladimir Bogomolov, Mikhail Papava

ivansxtc.
★★★ 18

Satirical drama   1999 · US · Colour · 92min

Illuminated by a charismatic lead performance from Danny Huston, this reworking of Leo Tolstoy's *The Death of Ivan Ilyich* charts the rapid rise and lonely downfall of a hotshot movie agent. Shot with High Definition digital cameras, Bernard Rose's arresting exposé of Hollywood dealing and hedonistic partying is more subjective than *The Player* and less cynical than *Swimming with Sharks*, though the overall emotional impact is lessened by a final section that aims for artful insight. Still, it's credible and wryly amusing. JC Swearing, sex scenes, drug abuse, nudity. *DVD*

Danny Huston *Ivan Beckman* • Peter Weller *Don West* • Lisa Enos *Charlotte White* • Adam Krentzman *Barry Oaks* • Alex Butler *Brad East* • Morgan Vukovich *Lucy Lawrence* • Tiffani-Amber Thiessen *Marie Stein* ■ *Dir* Bernard Rose • *Scr* Lisa Enos, Bernard Rose, from the novel *The Death of Ivan Ilyich* by Leo Tolstoy

I've Been Watching You
★★ 15

Horror   2000 · US · Colour · 81min

Ever since Dracula first clapped eyes on Jonathan Harker, a homoerotic undercurrent has simmered under the vampire story. Yet rarely has it been so close to the surface as in this frat boy offering from David DeCoteau. Arriving at university for his freshman year, jock Nathan Watkins is a natural for the Doma Tao Omega clique. But, what is it about president Bradley Stryker that he finds so irresistible? Elizabeth Bruderman is the nominal love interest, but she's a blood red herring. DP *DVD*

Nathan Watkins *Chris Chandler* • Josh Hammond *Dan* • Bradley Stryker *Devon* • Elizabeth Bruderman *Megan* • Forrest Cochran *Barry* • Michael Lutz *Jordan* ■ *Dir* David DeCoteau • *Scr* B Louis Levy, Matthew Jason Walsh

I've Gotta Horse
★★ U

Musical comedy   1965 · UK · Colour · 92min

Billy Fury, one of Britain's answers to Elvis back in the 1960s, deserved better than this dumb confection, which failed to do for him what similar threadbare flicks did for Cliff Richard. *Coronation Street* fans might enjoy watching Amanda Barrie in her movie heyday. However, nothing can take your mind off the terrible plot, as singer Fury misses rehearsals to watch his racehorse run in the Derby. TS

Billy Fury *Billy* • Amanda Barrie *Jo* • Michael Medwin *Hymie Campbell* • Marjorie Rhodes *Mrs Bartholemew* • Bill Fraser *Mr Bartholemew* • Peter Gilmore *Jock* • Jon Pertwee *Costumer's assistant* • Michael Cashman *Peter* ■ *Dir* Kenneth Hume • *Scr* Ronald Wolfe, Ronald Chesney, from a story by Kenneth Hume, Larry Parnes

I've Heard the Mermaids Singing
★★★ 15

Comedy drama   1987 · Can · Colour · 79min

This modest movie competently tackles the hoary theme of a young woman's self-discovery. This is a very able first-time effort from writer/director Patricia Rozema and is notable for introducing Sheila McCarthy as the scatty lead who works in a deeply chic art gallery. McCarthy drew high critical acclaim for her strong, winning performance, but this initial praise failed to translate itself into further meaty roles. The movie has an unfortunate tendency to take itself too seriously at points but, overall, this is a laudable, enjoyable and often highly original movie. SH

Sheila McCarthy *Polly Vandersma* • Paule Baillargeon *Gabrielle St Peres* • Ann-Marie MacDonald *Mary Joseph* • John Evans *Warren* • Brenda Kamino *Japanese waitress* • Richard Monette *Clive* ■ *Dir/Scr* Patricia Rozema

I've Loved You So Long
★★★ 12

Drama   2008 · Fr/Ger · Colour · 112min

French cinema is often synonymous with moody actors gazing into the middle distance, yet Kristin Scott Thomas brings so much more to this well-observed drama. She plays an ex-con who moves in with her younger sister (Elsa Zylberstein) after serving time for an offence that everyone is reluctant to talk about. The nature of her crime soon becomes clear, so the story (scripted and directed by novelist Philippe Claudel) lacks tension in that respect. Intrigue is generated by the emotional journey of repairing the bond with her sister, and, thanks to a natural chemistry between Scott Thomas and Zylberstein, this aspect of the story truly resonates. SP French, English +subtitles. *DVD* *BLU*

Kristin Scott Thomas *Juliette* • Elsa Zylberstein *Léa* • Serge Hazanavicius *Luc* • Laurent Grévill *Michel* • Frédéric Pierrot *Fauré* • Lise Ségur *P'tit Lys* ■ *Dir/Scr* Philippe Claudel

Ivy
★★

Drama   1947 · US · BW · 98min

You couldn't ask for a better mounted, more visually accomplished example of period melodrama set in Edwardian England than this account of Joan Fontaine as the determined Ivy. She poisons her husband Richard Ney and pins the blame on her lover Patric Knowles to clear the way for her conquest of Herbert Marshall's bachelor millionaire, but she reckons without Cedric Hardwicke's Scotland Yard inspector. Unfortunately, writer Charles Bennett and director Sam Wood fail to create any suspense and Ivy's ultimate fate is an irritating contrivance. AE

Joan Fontaine *Ivy Lexton* • Patric Knowles *Dr Roger Gretorex* • Herbert Marshall *Miles Rushworth* • Richard Ney *Jervis Lexton* • Sir Cedric Hardwicke [Cedric Hardwicke] *Inspector Orpington* ■ *Dir* Sam Wood • *Scr* Charles Bennett, from the novel *The Story of Ivy* by Marie Belloc-Lowndes

JCVD ★★★ 15
Comedy crime thriller
2008 · Bel/Lux/Fr · Colour · 92min

JCVD stands for Jean-Claude Van Damme, who stars as himself (more or less), in this tongue-in-cheek crime thriller. Returning to his childhood home of Brussels, JCVD's career and life are in tatters. His Hollywood standing is sliding, he's just lost custody of his daughter and his credit cards are maxed out. On visiting a local post office, he's caught up in a robbery-turned-hostage situation and is mistaken for one of the criminals. Gleefully sending himself up, Van Damme trashes his on-screen persona in an ironic and playful manner. The bleached-out visuals and the fractured narrative structure can't disguise the lack of budget, but Van Damme's witty asides make this a distinctive diversion from his usual, ultra-conservative action-movie fare. JR French, English +subtitles. *DVD* Blu

Jean-Claude Van Damme *JCVD* • François Damiens *Bruges* • Zinedine Soualem *Man in hat* • Karim Belkhadra *Nightwatchman* • Jean-Francois Wolff *Man in his 30s* • Herve Sogne *Lieutenant Smith* ■ *Dir* Mabrouk El Mechri • *Scr* Frédéric Bénudis, Mabrouk El Mechri, Christophe Turpin, from a concept by Frederic Taddei, Vincent Ravalec

J Edgar ★★★ 15
Biographical drama   2011 · US · Colour · 131min

Unrecognisable beneath his make-up, Leonardo DiCaprio gives a towering performance here as the man who headed the FBI for nearly 40 years. While presidents came and went, J Edgar Hoover maintained and expanded what became his fiefdom. His sexuality and an apparent liking for women's clothing have been the subject of much speculation (and ridicule), and director Clint Eastwood rather deftly suggests a man who is both naive and repressed, while making it clear that what really drove him was his work - and his ego. Where the film falls down is in its rather sketchy presentation of historical events, but as a portrait of Hoover the man, it's excellent. BP Violence, swearing. *DVD* Blu

Leonardo DiCaprio *J Edgar Hoover* • Naomi Watts *Helen Gandy* • Josh Lucas *Charles Lindbergh* • Judi Dench *Annie Hoover* • Armie Hammer *Clyde Tolson* • Ed Westwick *Agent Smith* • Jeffrey Donovan *Robert F Kennedy* • Lea Thompson *Lela Rogers* • Dermot Mulroney *Colonel Schwarzkopf* ■ *Dir* Clint Eastwood • *Scr* Dustin Lance Black • *Music* Clint Eastwood

JFK ★★★★★ 15
Historical thriller
1991 · US · Colour and BW · 180min

This is an overblown and factually shaky version of the events surrounding the assassination of John F Kennedy, and director Oliver Stone takes his self-appointed position as the chronicler of recent US history far too seriously to be objective or concise. Yet, decades after the event, the cover-up theory has lost none of its fascination. Whether you believe Lee Harvey Oswald acted alone on 22 November 1963 or whether you adhere to the accomplice theory, this is a compelling and persuasively staged conspiracy thriller. Stone deftly conveys a wealth of information and ensures every character makes an impact. The Oscar-winning photography and editing are superb, and the ensemble is a triumph of casting. DP Drug abuse, swearing, violence. *DVD* Blu

Kevin Costner *Jim Garrison* • Sissy Spacek *Liz Garrison* • Joe Pesci *David Ferrie* • Tommy Lee Jones *Clay Shaw* • Gary Oldman *Lee Harvey Oswald* • Jay O Sanders *Lou Ivon* • Michael Rooker *Bill Broussard* • Laurie Metcalf *Susie Cox* • Gary Grubbs *Al Oser* • John Candy *Dean Andrews* • Jack Lemmon *Jack Martin* • Walter Matthau *Senator Russell Long* • Ed Asner *[Edward Asner] Guy Bannister* • Donald Sutherland *Colonel X* • Kevin Bacon *Willie O'Keefe* • Brian Doyle-Murray *Jack Ruby* ■ *Dir* Oliver Stone • *Scr* Oliver Stone, Zachary Sklar, from the non-fiction book *On the Trail of the Assassins* by Jim Garrison, from the non-fiction book *Crossfire: the Plot That Killed Kennedy* by Jim Marrs • *Cinematographer* Robert Richardson • *Music* John Williams

JLG/JLG – Self Portrait in December ★★★
Experimental documentary
1994 · Fr/Swi · Colour · 65min

Shot around his Swiss home on Lake Léman, this documentary is a self-portrait of the *enfant terrible* who once rocked cinema on its heels, only to be marginalised (albeit partly through his own connivance) by the art form he helped transform. Discussing his diverse sources of inspiration, Jean-Luc Godard appears secure in his reputation as a film-maker who has experimented with the moving image while making heartfelt and often controversial political and artistic statements. Referencing his own output and works that continue to influence him, this is an eloquent dissertation from one of cinema's few philosopher-poets. DP French +subtitles.

■ *Dir/Scr* Jean-Luc Godard

JLS: Eyes Wide Open ★★ U
Music documentary   2011 · UK · Colour · 86min

This 3D concert film from the 2008 *X-Factor* runners-up mixes live footage filmed at London's O2 with behind-the-scenes documentary clips. It's the first film of its kind by a British act, and the 3D element brings Marvin, Aston, JB and Oritsé to life, with the performance scenes feeling like the real thing and the hits, including *Beat Again*, *The Club Is Alive* and *Everybody in Love* all present and correct. Some of the touching backstage moments feel a little over-egged for a group that has only released two albums. But if you're a fan, this is the real deal. KS 3D

Aston Merrygold • Marvin Humes • Oritsé Williams • JB Gill ■ *Dir* Andy Morahan, Ben Winston

JW Coop ★★★
Drama   1971 · US · Colour · 112min

After winning the best actor Oscar for *Charly*, Cliff Robertson used his clout to produce, direct, write and star in this story of a rodeo rider who, after spending ten years in jail, finds himself adrift in a more commercialised and cynical world. Robertson is excellent as the eponymous cowboy, but the film shows its age by confronting him with tiresome hippies. AT

Cliff Robertson *JW Coop* • Geraldine Page *Mama* • Cristina Ferrare *Bean* • RG Armstrong *Jim Sawyer* • RL Armstrong *Tooter Watson* ■ *Dir* Cliff Robertson • *Scr* Cliff Robertson, Gary Cartwright, Bud Shrake

Jabberwocky ★★ PG
Comedy fantasy   1977 · UK · Colour · 100min

Terry Gilliam's debut feature is an uneven mix of medieval tomfoolery and crude *Monty Python* humour. Fellow Python Michael Palin plays the hero who, to prove his worth and win the hand of a fair maiden, sets out to kill the fearsome "manxome foe". The production design is stunning, and the look of the Jabberwock is based on the illustrations that Sir John Tenniel created for Carroll's original book. For all that, Gilliam's grim fantasy only occasionally raises itself above the tiresome. AJ *DVD*

Michael Palin *Dennis Cooper* • Max Wall *King Bruno the Questionable* • Deborah Fallender *Princess* • John Le Mesurier *Chamberlain* • Annette Badland *Griselda Fishfinger* • Warren Mitchell *Mr Fishfinger* • Brenda Cowling *Mrs Fishfinger* • Harry H Corbett *Squire* • Rodney

Bewes *Other squire* • Bernard Bresslaw *Landlord* ■ *Dir* Terry Gilliam • *Scr* Terry Gilliam, Charles Alverson, from the poem *Jabberwocky* by Lewis Carroll

J'Accuse ★★★★
Silent war drama   1919 · Fr · BW · 150min

Intercutting newreel footage and basing his intertitles on letters from the trenches, Abel Gance's silent drama brought home to audiences, who scarcely needed reminding, the imperative to prevent the recurrence of such barbarity. The rape and pregnancy of Marise Dauvray and the fury of her enlisted husband, Severin-Mars, were powerfully depicted. But nothing compares to the finale sequence, in which deranged poet Romauld Joubé summons the dead from their graves to reinforce the futility of war. Originally shown in three feature-length chapters, the film was reduced to around 150 minutes by the director, and the discarded footage was destroyed. DP

Romuald Joubé *Jean Diaz* • Severin-Mars *François Laurin* • Marise Dauvray *Edith Laurin* • Angèle Guys *Angèle* • Maxime Desjardins *Maria Lazare* ■ *Dir/Scr* Abel Gance

J'Accuse ★★★
War drama   1938 · Fr · BW · 95min

As war loomed, Abel Gance reworked his 1919 classic to warn again of the follies of conflict. The poet is (over)played by Victor Francen, who vows to promote pacifism after surviving the slaughter of his trench patrol. However, his invention of unbreakable glass is misappropriated by the government and he is forced to summon the First World War dead from their graves to march across the country to persuade world leaders to outlaw fighting forever. Again the finale is the most moving and spectacular aspect of the picture, which is too often sidetracked by Francen's rivalry with Jean Max for Renée Devillers. DP French +subtitles.

Victor Francen *Jean Diaz* • Jean Max *Henri Chimay* • Delaître *François Laurin* • Renée Devillers *Helene* • Line Noro *Edith* ■ *Dir* Abel Gance • *Scr* Abel Gance, Steve Passeur

Jack ★★★ PG
Comedy drama   1996 · US · Colour · 108min

Robin Williams stars as a ten-year-old who looks like a 40-year-old, the result of an ageing disorder that has made his body mature at an incredible rate. Diane Lane and Brian Kerwin give subtle performances as the confused parents, and there's a sweet contribution from Jennifer Lopez as his teacher. Unfortunately, Williams goes over the top again and his exuberance is unchecked by director Francis Ford Coppola. JB Swearing. *DVD*

Robin Williams *Jack Powell* • Diane Lane *Karen Powell* • Brian Kerwin *Brian Powell* • Jennifer Lopez *Miss Marquez* • Bill Cosby *Lawrence Woodruff* • Fran Drescher *Dolores Durante* • Adam Zolotin *Louis Durante* • Michael McKean *Paulie* ■ *Dir* Francis Ford Coppola • *Scr* James DeMonaco, Gary Nadeau

Jack ★★★
Comedy drama   2004 · US · Colour · 145min

This unflinching study of teenage attitudes to sex and domestic dysfunction was adapted from her own novel by AM Homes, who also wrote *The Safety of Objects*. It turns the rite-of-passage genre on its head by forcing high-school student Anton Yelchin to come to terms not only with his parents' divorce, but also the fact that his father, Ron Silver, is gay. But it's Stockard Channing's performance as his hurt but resilient mother who holds the proceedings together. DP

Stockard Channing *Anne* • Ron Silver *Paul* • Anton Yelchin *Jack* • Erich Anderson *Steve Burka* • Brent Spiner *Vernon* • Andrew Airlie *Michael* • Wendy Crewson *Elaine Burka* ■ *Dir* Lee Rose • *Scr* AM Homes, from her novel

Jack Ahoy! ★★★
Comedy   1934 · UK · BW · 70min

This was a huge success in its day for jovial, lantern-jawed Jack Hulbert, and is one of a series of hits that still amuse today. Here,

Hulbert sings *The Hat's on the Side of My Head* and gets kidnapped by Chinese revolutionaries! There's a nice pace and an easy-going air of geniality brought to this maritime caper by skilled director Walter Forde, and its breeziness is infectious. TS

Jack Hulbert *Jack Ponsonby* • Nancy O'Neil *Patricia Fraser* • Alfred Drayton *Admiral Fraser* • Tamara Desni *Conchita* • Henry Peterson *Larios* • Sam Wilkinson *Dodger* ■ *Dir* Walter Forde • *Scr* Jack Hulbert, Leslie Arliss, Gerard Fairlie, Austin Melford, from a story by Sidney Gilliat, JOC Orton

Jack and Jill ★ PG
Comedy   2011 · US · Colour · 86min

It's hard to know what's worse in Dennis Dugan's comedy: Adam Sandler's lazy attempt to impersonate a woman or Al Pacino - playing himself - having to fall in love with the aforementioned creature. Pacino at least gets to have a bit of fun sending up his own super-serious image, but Sandler's performance has no saving graces. The ramshackle plot has Sandler as an LA advertising executive who is dreading the holiday arrival of his twin sister (Sandler again), a loud and obnoxious single woman from New Jersey. JF *DVD* Blu

Adam Sandler *Jack/Jill* • Al Pacino • Katie Holmes *Erin Sadelstein* • Elodie Tougne *Sofia Sadelstein* • Rohan Chand *Gary Sadelstein* • Eugenio Derbez *Felipe/Felipe's Grandma* ■ *Dir* Dennis Dugan • *Scr* Steve Koren, Adam Sandler, from a story by Ben Zook

Jack & Sarah ★★★ 15
Romantic comedy drama
1995 · UK · Colour · 110min

This is a refreshing spin on an ever-popular formula: men coping with babies. Richard E Grant is the lawyer who becomes a bumbling single father when his wife dies in childbirth; Samantha Mathis is the visiting American who is roped into being the child's nanny and falls for her employer. Grant and Mathis are appealing leads, but it is the classy hamming of Ian McKellen and Judi Dench that steals the show. Director Tim Sullivan just about keeps sentimentality at bay. JF Swearing, brief nudity. *DVD*

Richard E Grant *Jack* • Samantha Mathis *Amy* • Judi Dench *Margaret* • Ian McKellen *William* • Cherie Lunghi *Anna* • Eileen Atkins *Phil* • Imogen Stubbs *Sarah* • David Swift *Michael* • Laurent Grévill *Alain* • Kate Hardie *Pamela* ■ *Dir/Scr* Tim Sullivan

Jack and the Beanstalk ★★ U
Comedy   1952 · US · Colour and sepia · 82min

Director Jean Yarbrough is currently being re-assessed as one of Hollywood's unsung journeymen, but this is the least of his five collaborations with Abbott and Costello, largely because there is no enchantment (let alone comedy) in the screenplay. The dreadful songs and the garish SuperCinecolor don't help much, either, making everything look fake instead of magical. However, Buddy Baer has fun as the Giant menacing Lou. DP *DVD*

Bud Abbott *Dinklepuss* • Lou Costello *Jack* • Buddy Baer *Sergeant Riley/Giant* • Dorothy Ford *Polly* • Barbara Brown *Mother* • David Stollery *Donald* ■ *Dir* Jean Yarbrough • *Scr* Nat Curtis, from a story by Pat Costello, Felix Adler

Jack and the Beanstalk ★★ U
Comedy fantasy   2010 · US · Colour · 90min

In this charmless take on the classic fairy tale, flunking schoolboy Jack (Colin Ford) ends up on a supposedly epic mission to pass his Heroics class after swapping his Computer of Wonder (COW, geddit?) for three magic beans. Unfortunately, eye-rollingly lame humour and a dearth of excitement are likely to make the flat and flimsy quest something of an endurance test for even the youngest of viewers. Chloe Grace Moretz and, briefly, Chevy Chase are among the familiar faces trying unsuccessfully to add colour to the limply pantomimic proceedings. SF *DVD*

Colin Ford *Jack* • Chloë Grace Moretz [Chloë Grace Moretz] *Damsel in distress/Jillian* • Christopher Lloyd *Headmaster* • Adair Tishler *Rapunzel* • Billy Unger *Prince Charming* • Chevy Chase *General Antipode* • James Earl Jones *Giant* ■ *Dir* Gary J Tunnicliffe • *Scr* Flip Kobler, Cindy Marcus

Jack Be Nimble ★★★ 18

Horror thriller   1992 · NZ · Colour · 91min

This creepily gothic offering is a satisfyingly twisted affair. Alexis Arquette is Jack, a young man who embarks on a monstrous plan of revenge with the help of a hypnosis machine, after suffering years of abuse at the hands of brutal foster parents. Sarah Smuts-Kennedy plays his equally long-suffering – and now long lost – sister, while "Mr NZ Cinema" Bruno Lawrence makes one of his last appearances. It's an uneven ride but writer/director Garth Maxwell conjures up some disturbing imagery. **JF**

Alexis Arquette *Jack* • Sarah Smuts Kennedy *Dora* • Bruno Lawrence *Teddy* • Tony Barry *Clarrie* • Elizabeth Hawthorne *Clarrie's wife* • Brenda Simmons *Mrs Birch* • Gilbert Goldie *Mr Birch* • Tricia Phillips *Anne* • Paul Minifie *Kevin* ■ *Dir/Scr* Garth Maxwell

The Jack Bull ★★★★ 15

Western   1999 · US · Colour · 111min

John Badham's unheralded but outstanding TV western was written by Dick Cusack and stars his son, John, as the horse dealer whose animals are mistreated by a neighbouring rancher. When the neighbour is backed up by the courts, Cusack launches an armed insurrection on the eve of Wyoming's bid for statehood. Cusack's Myrl Redding has the tragic overtones of a Thomas Hardy hero, a man to whom dreadful things happen, even in the best of times. This is a beautifully staged, unrelentingly sombre movie with satisfying political complexity. **AT** Violence, swearing. *DVD*

John Cusack *Myrl Redding* • John Goodman *Judge Tolliver* • LQ Jones *Henry Ballard* • Miranda Otto *Cora* • John C McGinley *Woody* • John Savage *Slater* • Rodney A Grant *Billy* ■ *Dir* John Badham • *Scr* Dick Cusack, from the book *Michael Kohlhaas* by Heinrich von Kleist

Jack Frost ★★ PG

Fantasy comedy drama
1998 · US · Colour · 97min

In this charmless fantasy fable, a dead rock musician is resurrected as a snowman to watch over the son he neglected when he was alive. Michael Keaton as the sinister looking Frost-dad requires an energetic leap of imagination, and everything else is pretty unbelievable, too. If it had been played as broad farce it might have worked. Sadly, the four scriptwriters decided to aim for the emotional resonance of *Ghost*, coating this in sickly icing. **JC** *DVD*

Michael Keaton *Jack Frost* • Kelly Preston *Gabby Frost* • Joseph Cross *Charlie Frost* • Mark Addy *Mac* • Henry Rollins *Sid Gronic* • Dweezil Zappa *John Kaplan* ■ *Dir* Troy Miller • *Scr* Steve Bloom, Jonathan Roberts, Mark Steven Johnson, Jeff Cesario, from a story by Mark Steven Johnson

Jack Goes Boating ★★★ 15

Romantic comedy   2010 · US · Colour · 87min

Like Jack, the character he plays here, Philip Seymour Hoffman sometimes tries too hard with his directorial debut. Still, as Hoffman's Brooklyn limo driver embarks upon a tentative relationship with mortician's assistant Connie (Amy Ryan), there are touching insights into a life blighted by disappointment that recalls Delbert Mann's Oscar-winning *Marty*. The quaint courtship is also contrasted with the deteriorating marriage of Jack's besty friends. Hoffman has an intimate feel for the drama (based on an off-Broadway play), yet he strives to open it out for the big screen with too many lyrical montages, and this sometimes blunts the more intense exchanges. **DP** Swearing, sexual references, drug abuse. *DVD*

Philip Seymour Hoffman *Jack* • Amy Ryan *Connie* • John Ortiz (1) *Clyde* • Daphne Rubin-Vega *Lucy* • Tom McCarthy [Thomas McCarthy] *Dr Bob* ■ *Dir* Philip Seymour Hoffman • *Scr* Bob Glaudini [Robert Glaudini], from his play

Jack London ★★

Biographical drama   1944 · US · BW · 93min

This biopic of the novelist whose adventure stories have made many a movie stars Broadway actor Michael O'Shea. It's not ideal casting – you need someone like Clark Gable to pull off this globe-trotting, hard-drinking womaniser – while the film's emphasis on the Japanese-American conflict of 1904 is milked for its then contemporary relevance. Susan Hayward barely registers as London's wife and on whose memoir the film is loosely based. **AT**

Michael O'Shea (1) *Jack London* • Susan Hayward *Charmain Kittredge* • Osa Massen *Freda Maloof* • Harry Davenport *Prof Hilliard* • Frank Craven *Old Tom* • Virginia Mayo *Mamie* • Ralph Morgan *George Brett* ■ *Dir* Alfred Santell • *Scr* Ernest Pascal, from the biography *The Book of Jack London* by Charmain London

Jack of Diamonds ★★★ U

Crime drama   1967 · US/W Ger · Colour · 107min

This heist movie – appropriately enough – steals its best ideas from earlier movies, specifically *Topkapi*, while George Hamilton's role as an elegant, sophisticated cat burglar harks back to Cary Grant in Hitchcock's *To Catch a Thief*. The result is a campy, quite amusing yarn about some dazzling diamonds and a robbery that doesn't go quite according to plan. Joseph Cotten plays Hamilton's mentor and there are three glamour queens playing themselves, draped in baubles: Carroll Baker, Zsa Zsa Gabor and Lilli Palmer. **AT**

George Hamilton *Jeff Hill* • Joseph Cotten *Ace of Diamonds* • Marie Laforêt *Olga* • Maurice Evans *Nicolai* • Alexander Hegarth *Brugger* • Carroll Baker • Zsa Zsa Gabor • Lilli Palmer ■ *Dir* Don Taylor • *Scr* Jack DeWitt, Sandy Howard, Robert L Joseph

Jack Reacher ★★★ 15

Action crime thriller   2012 · US · Colour · 130min

This brash action yarn finds military cop-gone-maverick Jack Reacher (Tom Cruise) teaming up with hotshot lawyer Rosamund Pike after a sniper guns down five random victims. Writer/director Christopher McQuarrie (*The Usual Suspects* won him an Oscar) piles on the shoot-'em-up clichés and corny dialogue, which might incur the wrath of fans of source writer Lee Child's darker, more menacing Reacher novels. It's a workmanlike caper that makes for an underwhelming start to a potential franchise. **TeS** Violence, swearing. *DVD*

Tom Cruise *Jack Reacher* • Rosamund Pike *Helen Rodin* • Richard Jenkins *Alex Rodin* • David Oyelowo *Detective Emerson* • Werner Herzog *The Zec* • Robert Duvall *Cash* ■ *Dir* Christopher McQuarrie • *Scr* Christopher McQuarrie, from the novel *One Shot* by Lee Child • *Cinematographer* Caleb Deschanel

Jack Reacher: Never Go Back

Action crime thriller   2016 · US · Colour

This is a preview – no prints were available to review as we went to press: If the first Jack Reacher film gifted us the pleasure of watching Tom Cruise take on five younger assailants all at once – and win, no problem – this four-years-in-the-making follow-up is likely to see him once again rolling deep in mad action, feisty dames and cornball dialogue. Maybe Cruise hasn't quite silenced the critics, whose chief beef seemed to be that he wasn't anything like the 6ft 5in fictional hero, but director Edward Zwick knows how to weld action to subject matter with deeper themes. **SvM**

Tom Cruise *Jack Reacher* • Cobie Smulders *Susan Turner* • Patrick Heusinger *The Hunter* • Robert Knepper *General Harkness* ■ *Dir* Edward Zwick • *Scr* Edward Zwick, Marshall Herskovitz, from Lee Child's novel

Jack Reed: Badge of Honor

★★★ 15

Police drama   1993 · US · Colour · 89min

Following the success of the mini-series featuring Chicago cop Jack Reed, Brian Dennehy returned as the uncompromising lawman in this above-average TV movie. Called in on what looks like an open-and-shut case of murder, Dennehy is blocked at every turn by the FBI because his chief suspect is its star witness in a vital arms smuggling trial. It's not all crime fighting, however, as Dennehy and his screen wife (Susan Ruttan) also care for the murder victim's son. William Sadler does well as the x-ray technician with a decidedly dodgy past. But it's Dennehy who dominates proceedings – he went on to star in and direct several more feature-length Jack Reed stories, with Charles S Dutton joining the cast as Lt Silvera. **DP** *DVD*

Brian Dennehy *Jack Reed* • Susan Ruttan *Arlene Reed* • William Sadler *David Anatole* • Alice Krige *Joan Anatole* • RD Call *Lieutenant Lloyd Butler* ■ *Dir* Kevin Connor • *Scr* Andrew Laskos

Jack Ryan: Shadow Recruit

★★★ 12

Action thriller   2013 · US · Colour · 105min

This reboot for novelist Tom Clancy's CIA agent finds Chris Pine stepping into the shoes previously worn by Alec Baldwin, Harrison Ford and Ben Affleck, and presents Ryan as a fresh-faced rookie up against post-9/11 global terror threats. Dispatched to Moscow by his boss Kevin Costner, Pine's investigations into a plot to crash financial markets snowball into a series of hair-raising skirmishes that put millions of lives at risk. The thrills and spills may be strictly by the book, but Pine is good value as the government penpusher thrust into the front lines of espionage. **TeS** In English, Russian. Violence, swearing. *DVD*

Chris Pine *Jack Ryan* • Kevin Costner *William Harper* • Kenneth Branagh *Viktor Cherevin* • Keira Knightley *Cathy Muller* • Colm Feore *Rob Behringer* ■ *Dir* Kenneth Branagh • *Scr* Adam Cozad, David Koepp, from characters by Tom Clancy

Jack Said ★ 18

Crime drama
2009 · UK/Neth · Colour and BW · 100min

This low-budget British crime drama contains elements of other, better gangster flicks, but doesn't succeed in its attempt at a hard-boiled style. Adapted by Paul Tanter from his own graphic novel, it's a sort of prequel to 2008's straight-to-DVD offering *Jack Says*, with Simon Phillips as an undercover cop on the edge, who's assigned to bring down an East End crime family. His job is complicated when he falls for the sister of fellow gang member Danny Dyer, while also attracting the lustful attentions of the psycho daughter of the firm's boss, played by Ashlie Walker. It's a dour, humourless affair that could do with some cracking dialogue and a more charismatic hero. **JA** Violence, swearing, nudity. *DVD*

Simon Phillips *Jack Adleth* • Danny Dyer *Nathan* • Ashlie Walker *Natalie* • Terry Stone *The Fixer* • David O'Hara *The Boss* • Rita Ramnani *Erin* • Jimmy White *Vic Lee* ■ *Dir* Leander Basannavar, Michael Tchouboroff • *Scr* Paul Tanter, from his graphic novel, from a character by Piers Pereira

Jack the Bear ★★ 15

Drama   1993 · US · Colour · 94min

The idea that real and imaginary terrors are often indistinguishable in the mind of a child is hardly an original one and this contrived tosh draws no startling conclusions, which is all the more disappointing as it's supposed to be a chiller. Danny DeVito hurls himself into the role of the widowed father, whose job as a horror show host does little to ease the fears of his son, who is impressively played by the film's major plus factor, Robert J Steinmiller Jr. **DP**

Danny DeVito *John Leary* • Robert J Steinmiller Jr *Jack Leary* • Miko Hughes *Dylan Leary* • Gary Sinise *Norman Strick* • Art LaFleur *Mr Festinger* •

Stefan Gierasch *Grandpa Glickes* • Erica Yohn *Grandma Glickes* ■ *Dir* Marshall Herskovitz • *Scr* Steven Zaillian, from the novel *Jack the Bear* by Dan McCall

Jack the Giant Killer

★★★ PG

Fantasy   1962 · US · Colour · 95min

Having already made *Attack of the 50ft Woman*, former Oscar-winning art director Nathan "Jerry" Juran tried for the same heights, metaphorically speaking, with this charming and enjoyable children's fairy tale. Juran is reunited with Kerwin Mathews, his star in *The 7th Voyage of Sinbad*, and succeeds in creating a genuinely original romp for kids of all ages. Incidentally, on reissue the title lost its "Jack" and songs were bizarrely added to the soundtrack. **TS** *DVD*

Kerwin Mathews *Jack* • Judi Meredith *Princess Elaine* • Torin Thatcher *Pendragon* • Walter Burke *Garna* • Roger Mobley *Peter* • Don Beddoe *Imp in bottle* ■ *Dir* Nathan Juran • *Scr* Orville H Hampton, Nathan Juran, from a story by Orville H Hampton

Jack the Giant Slayer ★★ 12

Fantasy adventure   2013 · US · Colour · 113min

X-Men director Bryan Singer's fantasy flair deserts him in this flabby makeover of *Jack and the Beanstalk*. Nicholas Hoult swaps his horse for a bag of magic beans and inadvertently starts a war between humans and ogres. He then joins all the king's men to rescue the kidnapped princess (Eleanor Tomlinson). The spectacle is standard swashbuckling fare, and there's too much reliance on fake-looking CGI. But there are a few reasons to keep watching, including Stanley Tucci's hissable villain and knight Ewan McGregor being sausage-rolled up by a chef colossus. **AJ** Some violence, swearing. *DVD* Blu

Nicholas Hoult *Jack* • Ewan McGregor *Elmont* • Eleanor Tomlinson *Isabelle* • Stanley Tucci *Lord Roderick* • Ian McShane *King Brahmwell* • Bill Nighy *General Fallon* ■ *Dir* Bryan Singer • *Scr* Darren Lemke, Christopher McQuarrie, Dan Studney, from a story by Lemke, David Dobkin

Jack the Ripper ★★★

Crime drama   1958 · UK · BW · 82min

This likeable little shocker received "A" treatment on release, thus promoting "stars" Lee Patterson and Eddie Byrne to feature players, albeit very briefly. Canadian actor Patterson had quite a following in Britain during the late 1950s, thanks to a string of now forgotten programme fillers, and here his presence lends weight to the infamous tale. The film's stark title and its inevitable X certificate made it a box-office hit. The spooky atmosphere is well maintained, and the cheapness doesn't show. **TS**

Lee Patterson *Sam Lowry* • Eddie Byrne *Inspector O'Neill* • Betty McDowall *Anne Ford* • Ewen Solon *Sir David Rogers* • John Le Mesurier *Dr Tranter* • George Rose *Clarke* ■ *Dir* Robert S Baker, Monty Berman • *Scr* Jimmy Sangster, from a story by Peter Hammond, Colin Craig

The Jackal ★★★ 18

Action thriller   1997 · US · Colour · 119min

Fred Zinnemann's *The Day of the Jackal* gets the Bruce Willis treatment here. The classic thriller about an assassin at large has been relocated to America and now comes equipped with all kinds of techno-props which add nothing at all to the original's ruthless efficiency. Willis supplants Edward Fox as the killer and, surprisingly, doesn't make too bad a job of it. Willis, Richard Gere (IRA terrorist) and Diane Venora (Russian intelligence officer) compete for the "Meryl Streep Most Authentic Foreign Accent" award. **TH** Swearing, violence. *DVD* Blu

Bruce Willis *The Jackal* • Richard Gere *Declan Mulqueen* • Sidney Poitier *FBI Deputy Director Carter Preston* • Diane Venora *Major Valentina Koslova* • Mathilda May *Isabella* • JK Simmons *Witherspoon* • Richard Lineback *McMurphy* • Leslie Phillips *Woolburton* ■ *Dir* Michael Caton-Jones • *Scr* Chuck Pfarrer, from the film *The Day of the Jackal* by Kenneth Ross

Jackass: the Movie ★★★ 18
Comedy　2002 · US · Colour · 85min

Johnny Knoxville and his daredevil buddies take their eye-watering antics to new extremes in this feature-length version of the cult TV series. It builds on the group's MTV-spawned format, in which the modern-day clowns risk life and limb carrying out absurd, and often dangerous, stunts and pranks. It's far from subtle and definitely an acquired taste, but fans of the show won't be disappointed. Overall, this is spirited and darkly hilarious adults-only viewing. **SF**
DVD **CS**

Johnny Knoxville • Bam Margera • Chris Pontius • Steve-O • Dave England • Ryan Dunn • Jason "Wee Man" Acuna ■ *Dir* Jeff Tremaine • *Scr* Jeff Tremaine, Spike Jonze, Johnny Knoxville, from their TV series

jackass number two ★★★ 18
Comedy　2006 · US · Colour · 89min

Fans of the MTV-spawned *Jackass* series will be delighted to hear that actor Johnny Knoxville and his daredevil pals haven't calmed down with age. Instead, they've become even wilder since 2002's feature-length *Jackass: the Movie*, hilariously raising the stakes for bad taste stunts and pranks with this superior and more darkly imaginative sequel. The sick-puppy laughs come thick and fast as the adrenaline junkies combine agonising tests of human endurance with moments of utter grossness and juvenile stupidity. If car-crash entertainment is your idea of fun, then this strictly adults-only film is hard to beat. **SF**
DVD

Johnny Knoxville • Bam Margera • Steve-O • Chris Pontius • Ryan Dunn • Wee Man [Jason "Wee Man" Acuna] *Jason "Wee Man" Acuna* • Preston Lacy ■ *Dir* Jeff Tremaine • *Scr* Sean Cliver, Preston Lacy

Jackass 3D ★★★ 18
Comedy　2010 · US · Colour · 90min

This third big-screen spin-off from the hit TV series contains yet more stuff that you really shouldn't try at home. Johnny Knoxville and co return with another mix of stupid stunts and public pranks, many of which literally stand out, courtesy of 3D. As ever, there's an overabundance of antics involving poo and private parts, often in close proximity. But the crew's infectious good humour means that the offensiveness is actually quite minimal. Significantly, though, the best sequence involves nothing "naughty" at all – just a bar, some unsuspecting customers and lots of dwarves. Fans of the series will know what to expect, and this ably delivers it. **DA**
Violence, nudity. **DVD** **Blu** **3D**

Johnny Knoxville • Bam Margera • Steve-O • Ryan Dunn • Jason Acuna *Wee Man* • Chris Pontius ■ *Dir* Jeff Tremaine • *Scr* Preston Lacy

jackass presents: Bad Grandpa ★★★ 15
Comedy　2013 · US · Colour · 91min

Those *Jackass* jokers unleash more "don't try this at home" stuff as front man Johnny Knoxville piles on the latex as his 86-year-old screen alter ego, Irving Zisman. Set within a loose framework that sees Zisman taking his eight-year-old grandson on a cross-country road trip, the film soon reveals itself to be yet another excuse for the usual combination of stunts and staged situations, with Knoxville and kid suffering or inflicting assorted indignities on apparently unsuspecting members of the public. It's patchy and marginally less gross than previous *Jackass* films, but you are guaranteed to laugh. **DA** **DVD** **Blu**

Johnny Knoxville *Irving Zisman* • Spike Jonze *Old woman* • Jackson Nicoll *Billy* • Georgina Cates *Kimmy* ■ *Dir* Jeff Tremaine • *Scr* Spike Jonze, Johnny Knoxville, Jeff Tremaine, from a story by Knoxville, Tremaine, Fax Bahr, Adam Small

Jackboots on Whitehall ★★ 12
Animated war satire　2010 · UK · Colour · 87min

Thunderbirds meets *Braveheart* in this satirical puppet film set during an alternative Second World War. The Nazis have invaded England, and Churchill and his government have retreated to the very edge of the known world – somewhere called Scot-Land, a place inhabited by violent men, who paint their faces blue. A distinguished cast gives the characters voice and personality, with Alan Cumming's camp Hitler and Timothy Spall's bulldoggish Churchill outstanding. But their efforts are undermined by a script that is just not very funny. **BP** Violence, sexual references. **DVD**

Ewan McGregor *Chris* • Rosamund Pike *Daisy* • Timothy Spall *Churchill* • Richard E Grant *Vicar* • Tom Wilkinson *Goebbels* • Alan Cumming *Hitler* ■ *Dir* Edward McHenry • *Scr* Edward McHenry, Rory McHenry

The Jacket ★★★ 15
Psychological thriller　2005 · US/UK/Ger · Colour · 98min

Horrific sensory deprivation therapy gives Gulf War veteran Adrien Brody the ability to travel through time in this claustrophobic thriller. Brody plays a discharged marine with injury-related amnesia, who's committed to a mental institution after being tried for murder and found not guilty by reason of insanity. There, he falls into the clutches of doctor Kris Kristofferson (excellent), whose controversial treatment regimen inexplicably propels the soldier's disoriented mind into the future, where he meets a troubled young woman (Keira Knightley). This is the most accessible work to date from British director John Maybury, but, though gripping and disturbing, the overall plot has little substance. **SF** Swearing, violence. **DVD**

Adrien Brody *Jack Starks* • Keira Knightley *Jackie Price* • Kris Kristofferson *Dr Becker* • Jennifer Jason Leigh *Dr Lorenson* • Kelly Lynch *Jean* • Brad Renfro *Stranger* • Daniel Craig *Mackenzie* • Steven Mackintosh *Dr Hopkins* • Fish *Jimmy Fleisher* ■ *Dir* John Maybury • *Scr* Massy Tadjedin, from a story by Tom Bleecker, Marc Rocco

Jackie Brown ★★★★ 15
Crime thriller　1997 · US · Colour · 147min

Imaginatively dragging Elmore Leonard's bestseller *Rum Punch* into his own postmodern universe peppered with quirky dialogue and cinematic references, director Quentin Tarantino makes this re-energised crime thriller a homage to, and an updating of, 1970s pulp blaxploitation fiction. Black icon Pam Grier is great as the air hostess pressured into an entrapment scam after being arrested for cash smuggling, who uses her feminine wiles to outsmart everyone wanting to exploit or kill her. Tarantino draws maximum suspense from a superb cast and an array of visual techniques such as staging a key scene three times from three different points of view. Breathlessly exciting and cut to a fabulous array of funk classics. **AJ** Swearing, violence, drug abuse, a sex scene. **DVD** **Blu**

Pam Grier *Jackie Brown* • Samuel L Jackson *Ordell Robbie* • Robert Forster *Max Cherry* • Bridget Fonda *Melanie* • Michael Keaton *Ray Nicolette* • Robert De Niro *Louis Gara* • Michael Bowen *Mark Dargus* • Lisa Gay Hamilton *Sheronda* • Tommy "Tiny" Lister Jr [Tom "Tiny" Lister Jr] *Winston* • Hattie Winston *Simone* • Denise Crosby *Public defender* ■ *Dir* Quentin Tarantino • *Scr* Quentin Tarantino, from the novel *Rum Punch* by Elmore Leonard

Jackie Chan's First Strike ★★ 12
Action thriller　1996 · HK/US · Colour · 80min

Placing less emphasis on kung fu action and more on spectacular stunts, this Jackie Chan comedy thriller is a Bond-style romp shot on location all over the globe. A pretty idiotic plot sees Chan playing a Hong Kong cop who is hired by both the CIA and Russian intelligence to recover a stolen nuclear warhead. As ever, the storyline is a thin excuse to string together a series of breathtaking action sequences. **JF** Cantonese dubbed. Violence. **DVD**

Jackie Chan *Jackie* • Chen Chun Wu *Annie* • Jackson Lou *Tsui* • Bill Tung *Uncle Bill* • Jouri Petrov *Colonel Gregor Yegorov* ■ *Dir* Stanley Tong • *Scr* Stanley Tong, Nick Tramontane, Greg Mellot, Elliot Tong

Jackie Chan's Who Am I? ★★★★ 12
Martial arts action comedy　1998 · HK · Colour · 107min

Jackie Chan's most sensational action scenes of the 1990s, impressive production values and super-slick direction illuminate this little-known movie. Although the plot doesn't bear close scrutiny (something about a top-secret energy source, an African tribe and amnesia), the extraordinary set pieces – from a clog-assisted Rotterdam brawl, to a three-way rooftop battle – rival anything in a megabuck Hollywood blockbuster. Chan's trademark use of slapstick comedy at the height of the fighting works brilliantly, too. **JC** Violence. **DVD**

Jackie Chan *Jackie (aka Whoami)* • Michelle Ferre *Christine* • Mirai Yamamoto *Yuki* • Ron Smerczak *Morgan* • Ed Nelson *General Sherman* • Tom Pompert *CIA chairman* • Yanick Mbali *Baba* • Washington Sixolo *Village chief* ■ *Dir* Jackie Chan, Benny Chan • *Scr* Jackie Chan, Lee Reynolds, Susan Chan • *Stunt Co-ordinator* Jackie Chan

Jacknife ★★★ 15
Drama　1988 · US · Colour · 98min

Robert De Niro returns to the traumas of Vietnam in this talky, yet engrossing, drama. He plays an ex-serviceman who has come to terms with the conflict, setting out to help his old friend Ed Harris, who is still deeply disturbed by his experiences of the war. Apart from a few not entirely convincing wartime flashbacks, director David Jones concentrates on the interplay between De Niro and Harris, and they both make the most of the perceptive script. A modest, rewarding experience. **JF** Swearing. **DVD**

Robert De Niro *Joseph "Megs" Megessey* • Ed Harris *Dave* • Kathy Baker *Martha* • Charles Dutton [Charles S Dutton] *Jake* • Elizabeth Franz *Pru Buckman* • Tom Isbell *Bobby Buckman* • Loudon Wainwright III *Ferretti* • Sloane Shelton *Shirley* ■ *Dir* David Jones (3) • *Scr* Stephen Metcalfe, from his play *Strange Snow*

The Jackpot ★★★ U
Comedy　1950 · US · BW · 86min

James Stewart wins a cash bonanza on a radio quiz show and finds that his life changes in many unexpected ways. To his dismay, he discovers he has to sell the prizes to pay the taxes on them. Lightweight comedy fluff, still timely in the National Lottery era, with Stewart turning on his effortless charm to lift the innocent fun up a few likeable notches. **AJ**

James Stewart *Bill Lawrence* • Barbara Hale *Amy Lawrence* • James Gleason *Harry Summers* • Fred Clark *Mr Woodruff* • Alan Mowbray *Leslie* • Patricia Medina *Hilda Jones* • Natalie Wood *Phyllis Lawrence* • Tommy Rettig *Tommy Lawrence* ■ *Dir* Walter Lang • *Scr* Phoebe Ephron, Henry Ephron, from an article by John McNulty

Jackpot ★★★
Drama　2001 · US · Colour · 100min

From the Polish brothers, this – like its central protagonists – never quite gets going. Singer Jon Gries and manager Garrett Morris cruise the karaoke circuit hoping for fame and gain – turning in con tricks and zippy conversation. Gries has deserted his wife Daryl Hannah and child, sending home a weekly lottery ticket as child support. We've seen this all before in Bruce Paltrow's *Duets*, though this is less mainstream and more slick. **LH**

Jon Gries [Jonathan Gries] *Sunny Holiday* • Daryl Hannah *Bobbi* • Garrett Morris *Lester "Les" Irving* • Adam Baldwin *Mel James* • Peggy Lipton *Janice* • Mac Davis *Sammy Bones* ■ *Dir* Michael Polish • *Scr* Michael Polish, Mark Polish

Jackpot ★★★ 15
Crime black comedy　2011 · Nor · Colour · 85min

A massive win on the football pools turns out to be very bad news for a syndicate of Norwegian factory workers in this black comedy thriller based on a story by bestselling crime novelist Jo Nesbo. When police interview the only survivor of a bloody shoot-out at a remote sex shop, the hapless Oscar (Kyrre Hellum) certainly has a tale to tell. Although it's obviously derivative, Magnus Martens's film is also a good deal of spiky fun, crisply put together and always ready with another fiendish twist. **TJ** Norwegian +subtitles. Violence, swearing, sexual references. **DVD**

Kyrre Hellum *Oscar Svendsen* • Mads Ousdal *Thor* • Arthur Berning *Billy* • Andreas Cappelen *Dan Tresko* • Henrik Mestad *Solor* • Marie Blokhus *Gina* ■ *Dir* Magnus Martens • *Scr* Magnus Martens, from a story by Jo Nesbo

Jack's Back ★★ 18
Mystery thriller　1988 · US · Colour · 92min

James Spader enjoys himself in dual roles in this modern, nasty spin on the Jack the Ripper story. The setting is 1980s Los Angeles, where the Victorian serial killer's crimes are being visited upon a new generation. When suspicion falls on Spader, his twin brother (Spader again) sets out to prove the authorities wrong. The improbable plotting might raise some eyebrows, but director Rowdy Herrington summons up a fair amount of suspense. **JF**

James Spader *John/Rick Wesford* • Cynthia Gibb *Christine Moscari* • Rod Loomis *Dr Sidney Tannerson* • Rex Ryon *Jack Pendler* • Robert Picardo *Dr Carlos Battera* • Jim Haynie *Sergeant Gabriel* • Wendell Wright *Captain Walter Prentis* ■ *Dir/Scr* Rowdy Herrington

Jackson County Jail ★★★★
Crime drama　1976 · US · Colour · 83min

This stunning example of exploitation artfully uses the genre's stark conventions to make cogent comments on society. In one of her strongest roles, Yvette Mimieux plays an LA executive who has a disastrous encounter with southern "justice" after she is beaten up by hitch-hikers en route to New York. Michael Miller directs his gripping feminist B-movie with raw-edged grit and a clear eye for action, while co-star Tommy Lee Jones backs up Mimieux to the hilt. Upsetting, but highly recommended. **AJ** Violence, swearing.

Yvette Mimieux *Dinah Hunter* • Tommy Lee Jones *Coley Blake* • Robert Carradine *Bobby Ray* • Frederic Cook *Hobie* • Severn Darden *Sheriff Dempsey* • Nan Martin *Allison* • Mary Woronov *Pearl* • Howard Hesseman *David* ■ *Dir* Michael Miller (2) • *Scr* Donald Stewart

Jacob the Liar ★★★
Second World War comedy drama　1974 · E Ger · Colour · 95min

Czech actor Vlastimil Brodsky received the 1975 Berlin film festival Silver Bear for his mesmerising performance in the title role of this moving film. It tells of a man who survives the nightmare of a Polish ghetto, helping others to do the same. Brodsky's dilemma stems from hearing news about a Russian advance via a Nazi radio. Fearful of telling about his clandestine spying, he pretends to have a radio, slowly building stories around his scant information to create the greatest commodity available to those in captivity – hope. Remade in 1999, with Robin Williams as Jakob. **BB** German +subtitles.

Vlastimil Brodsky *Jacob* • Erwin Geschonneck *Kowalski* • Manuela Simon *Lina* • Henry Hübchen *Mischa* • Blanche Kommerell *Rosa* • Armin Mueller-Stahl *Roman Schtamm* ■ *Dir* Frank Beyer • *Scr* Jurek Becker, from his novel *Jakob der Lügner*

Jacob Two Two Meets the Hooded Fang ★★★
Fantasy　1999 · Can · Colour · 96min

It was not going to be easy to translate a children's book, written in verse, to the screen (there was a previous attempt in 1977) but this is a nice attempt, made more

J

enjoyable by an accomplished cast. Little Jacob (Max Morrow) who repeats everything twice, hence his nickname gets into trouble and is sent to the horrible children's prison island, which is ruled by the Hooded Fang (Gary Busey). It's a pantomime-style tale, and adults brought along for the ride will at least have fun spotting familiar actors in bizarre and silly roles. JB

Gary Busey *The Hooded Fang* • Miranda Richardson *Miss Fowl* • Ice-T *Justice Rough* • Mark McKinney *Mr Fish* • Max Morrow *Jacob Two Two* • Maury Chaykin *Louis Loser* ■ *Dir* George Bloomfield • *Scr* Tim Burns, from the novel *Jacob Two Two Meets the Hooded Fang* by Mordecai Richler

Jacob's Ladder ★★ 15
Horror thriller 1990 · US · Colour · 108min

What's the cause of Vietnam veteran Tim Robbins's nightmare hallucinations as he wanders New York trying to figure out their meaning? Although this assembly of horror clichés is tautly scripted by *Ghost* writer Bruce Joel Rubin, director Adrian Lyne orchestrates his satanic flashdance into a slightly pretentious mess of distorted *Platoon* images and Biblical red herrings. AJ Violence, swearing, nudity. *DVD*

Tim Robbins *Jacob Singer* • Elizabeth Peña *Jezzie* • Danny Aiello *Louis* • Matt Craven *Michael* • Pruitt Taylor Vince *Paul* • Jason Alexander *Donald Geary* • Macaulay Culkin *Gabe* • Eriq La Salle *Frank* ■ *Dir* Adrian Lyne • *Scr* Bruce Joel Rubin

Jacqueline ★★ U
Drama 1956 · UK · BW · 89min

With good intentions endlessly lapsing into self-pity, John Gregson overdoes the pathos as the shipyard worker who is plunged into the depths of despair when he loses his job as a result of vertigo. There's a similar lack of restraint about Jacqueline Ryan (whose mother, Kathleen, co-stars) as the daughter who tries to land him a farm job. Although it was based on the novel *A Grand Man*, this mawkish melodrama owes more to the films of Shirley Temple than the imagination of Catherine Cookson. DP

John Gregson *Mike McNeil* • Kathleen Ryan *Elizabeth McNeil* • Jacqueline Ryan *Jacqueline McNeil* • Noel Purcell *Mr Owen* • Cyril Cusack *Mr Flannagan* • Maureen Swanson *Maggie* • Tony Wright *Jack McBride* • Liam Redmond *Mr Lord* • Maureen Delaney *Mrs McBride* ■ *Dir* Roy Baker [Roy Ward Baker] • *Scr* Patrick Kirwan, Liam O'Flaherty, Patrick Campbell, Catherine Cookson, from the novel *A Grand Man* by Catherine Cookson

Jacquot de Nantes ★★★★★ PG
Biographical drama 1991 · Fr · Colour and BW · 113min

Agnès Varda's tribute to her late husband, Jacques Demy, was considered too cosy and sentimental in some quarters. But this is a genuinely fond and often moving portrait of the film-maker as a young man. The sequences depicting how Demy painstakingly created his earliest animated efforts are compelling and superbly convey the nascent passion for cinema that would result in such classics as *The Umbrellas of Cherbourg*. It's to Varda's credit that the film works both as biography and drama, but perhaps her finest achievement is in coaxing such a charming performance out of the inexperienced Philippe Maron. DP French +subtitles. *DVD*

Philippe Maron *Jacquot 1* • Edouard Joubeaud *Jacquot 2* • Laurent Monnier *Jacquot 3* • Brigitte De Villepoix *Marilou, Mother* • Daniel Dublet *Raymond, Father* • Clement Delaroche *Yvon 1* ■ *Dir* Agnès Varda • *Scr* Agnès Varda, from a story by Jacques Demy

Jade ★ 18
Erotic thriller 1995 · US · Colour · 91min

William Friedkin's slick direction can't hide the trashy heart of this Joe Eszterhas scripted one-dimensional psycho thriller, which *NYPD Blue* TV actor David Caruso banked on to make him a star. No such luck. He's the assistant district attorney taking on the case of old flame Linda Fiorentino, a

clinical psychologist who might be leading a double life as a murderous prostitute. Chazz Palminteri is the third part of a murky triangle. No one emerges with credit from this absurd farrago. AJ Violence, sex scenes, swearing. *DVD*

David Caruso *David Corelli* • Linda Fiorentino *Trina Gavin* • Chazz Palminteri *Matt Gavin* • Richard Crenna *Governor Edwards* • Michael Biehn *Bob Hargrove* • Donna Murphy *Karen Heller* ■ *Dir* William Friedkin • *Scr* Joe Eszterhas

The Jade Mask ★★ U
Mystery 1945 · US · BW · 63min

Having previously provided stereotypical light relief, African-American stalwart Mantan Moreland finally became Sidney Toler's official chauffeur in the fourth of Monogram's cheaply proficient Charlie Chan mysteries. Edwin Luke, younger brother of Keye Luke, takes over as son Tommy, and is on hand as the Chinese sleuth investigates the murder of a much-detested scientist, who was conducting experiments into reinforced wood. This should have been a rattling good yarn, but director Phil Rosen permits too much comic schtick to sustain the tension. DP *DVD*

Sidney Toler *Charlie Chan* • Mantan Moreland *Birmingham Brown* • Edwin Luke *Tommy* • Janet Warren *Jean* • Edith Evanson *Louise* • Hardie Albright *Meeker* • Frank Reicher *Harper* ■ *Dir* Phil Rosen • *Scr* George Callahan, from characters by Earl Derr Biggers

Jadoo ★★ 12
Comedy 2013 · UK · Colour · 80min

A minor treat for foodies, this comedy sees two sibling chefs falling out and going their separate ways to set up rival curry houses. Ten years later, Shalini (Amara Khan) tries to get her dad and uncle to stop feuding and pool their resources, with a view to providing the catering for her wedding. Set among the Anglo-Indian community in Leicester, *Jadoo* slips down easily at the start, but the mix of comedy, seriousness and sentiment soon begins to sit a little heavily. However, director Amit Gupta's loving depiction of food is something to savour. DA *DVD*

Amara Karan *Shalini* • Harish Patel *Raja* • Kulvinder Ghir *Jagi* • Tom Mison *Mark* • Madhur Jaffrey ■ *Dir/Scr* Amit Gupta

Jagarna 2: False Trail ★★★ 15
Mystery thriller 2011 · Swe · Colour · 124min

This low-key crime drama, set in the frozen wastelands of northern Sweden, sees veteran cop Erik Backstrom (Rolf Lassgard – the original incarnation of TV's *Wallander*) returning to his home town after 15 years to investigate the brutal killing of a young woman. As the case becomes more complex and the list of suspects grows, Erik has to confront his past in the shape of a nephew he barely knows and the young boy's new stepfather (Peter Stormare), who's also the obstructive chief of the local police force. Lassgard and Stormare make great adversaries, although more restless viewers may find the pace of the story just too glacial. TeS Swedish +subtitles. Violence, swearing *DVD*

Rolf Lassgard *Erik Backstrom* • Peter Stormare *Torsten* • Annika Nordin *Karin Johansson* • Kim Tjernstrom *Peter* ■ *Dir* Kjell Sundvall • *Scr* Bjorn Carlstrom, Stefan Thunberg

Jagged Edge ★★★★ 18
Thriller 1985 · US · Colour · 104min

Because writer Joe Eszterhas has continually reworked the same basic formula (hero/heroine falls for murder suspect), it's easy to forget how startling the scenario was when it was first employed in this compelling thriller. Glenn Close is the defence attorney haunted by a case from her past when the wrong man went to jail, who falls in love with her client (Jeff Bridges), a charming publisher accused of brutally murdering his wife. Director Richard Marquand never misses a beat, gleefully tossing in red herrings and keeping the viewer constantly wondering whether Bridges is innocent or guilty. It

remains an enthralling, if incredible, ride. JF Violence, swearing, brief nudity. *DVD*

Jeff Bridges *Jack Forrester* • Glenn Close *Teddy Barnes* • Peter Coyote *Thomas Krasny* • Robert Loggia *Sam Ransom* • John Dehner *Judge Carrigan* • Lance Henriksen *Frank Martin* • Leigh Taylor-Young *Virginia Howell* • Marshall Colt *Bobby Slade* ■ *Dir* Richard Marquand • *Scr* Joe Eszterhas

Jaguar Lives! ★ 12
Martial arts action adventure 1979 · US · Colour · 86min

The kung fu craze had long since expired by the time this lacklustre 007 spoof hit cinemas. Falling into the "never-heard-of-him" category is Joe Lewis as Jaguar, an agent skilled in hand-to-hand combat who sets out to smash an international drug ring, while three former Bond villains – Donald Pleasence, Christopher Lee and Joseph Wiseman – ham it up. Director Ernest Pintoff was originally a cartoonist: it should be back to the drawing board for him. RS *DVD*

Joe Lewis (1) *Jonathan Cross/Jaguar* • Christopher Lee *Adam Caine* • Donald Pleasence *General Villanova* • Barbara Bach *Anna* • Capucine *Zina Vanacore* • Joseph Wiseman *Ben Ashir* • Woody Strode *Sensei* ■ *Dir* Ernest Pintoff • *Scr* Yabo Yablonsky

Jail Bait ★★ PG
Crime 1954 · US · BW · 71min

Schlockmeister Ed Wood Jr's follow-up to his legendary *Glen or Glenda* is an unusual crime melodrama with a surprise ending. Gangster Timothy Farrell coerces the plastic surgeon father of the accomplice he's killed to alter his face so he can avoid detection. Like every Wood film, the facts behind it are more entertaining than the movie: Bela Lugosi was too ill to play the surgeon, so silent star Herbert Rawlinson took over, only to die the day after filming. AJ *DVD*

Lyle Talbot *Inspector Johns* • Dolores Fuller *Marilyn Gregor* • Steve Reeves *Lieutenant Bob Lawrence* • Herbert Rawlinson *Dr Boris Gregor* • Theodora Thurman *Loretta* • Timothy Farrell *Vic Brady* ■ *Dir* Edward D Wood Jr • *Scr* Alex Gordon, Edward D Wood Jr

Jail Bait ★★★
Drama 1972 · W Ger · Colour · 100min

Franz-Xaver Kroetz so despised this adaptation of his play that he gained an injunction forcing director Rainer Werner Fassbinder to remove two scenes he felt particularly betrayed his characters. Ultimately, Fassbinder made a show of disowning it himself, but this flawed film (which was originally made for German television) is far from a failure. Teenage lust and the chasm between the generations are the central themes, but this is also a homage to Hollywood's rebellious youth pictures of the 1950s. A boy is sent to prison for a sexual relationship with an underage girl, and continues it on his release. The violence and treachery are shocking, but perhaps the most disturbing aspect is the ease with which fascist values were still being disseminated among the lower middle-classes of Germany at the time. DP German +subtitles.

Eva Mattes *Hanni Schneider* • Harry Baer *Franz Bermeier* • Jorg von Liebenfels *Erwin Schneider, Hanni's father* • Ruth Drexel *Hilda Schneider, Hanni's mother* ■ *Dir* Rainer Werner Fassbinder • *Scr* Rainer Werner Fassbinder, from the play by Franz-Xaver Kroetz

Jailbreak ★★
Thriller 1997 · US · Colour · 89min

Executive produced by Roger Corman, this lives up to his reputation for no-nonsense, fast-moving, low-budget entertainment. It also bears the Corman hallmark by virtue of the fact that it vaguely resembles his earlier *Jackson County Jail* (1976), in which the wrongfully arrested Yvette Mimieux went on the run with suspected killer Tommy Lee Jones. Ally Sheedy and David Carradine step into the roles for director Victoria Muspratt, who keeps the action brisk and

bruising. DP Violence, swearing, a sex scene.

Ally Sheedy *Susan Reed* • David Carradine *Coley* • Charles Napier *Sheriff Dempsey* • Todd Kimsey *Hobie* ■ *Dir* Victoria Muspratt • *Scr* Victoria Muspratt, Donald Stewart II [Donald E Stewart]

Jailhouse Rock ★★★★ U
Musical drama 1957 · US · BW · 97min

This is Elvis Presley's glorious third movie, after *Love Me Tender* and *Loving You*, when the snarl and talent were for once harnessed to a suitable plot under the experienced direction of MGM veteran Richard Thorpe. Presley plays an ex-con whose subsequent Hollywood success goes to his head, causing former cellmate Mickey Shaughnessy to lay him flat with a blow to his money-spinning larynx. Elvis here reveals an acting talent on a par with that of James Dean, only previously hinted at in his first two movies. TS *DVD*

Elvis Presley *Vince Everett* • Judy Tyler *Peggy Van Alden* • Mickey Shaughnessy *Hunk Houghton* • Vaughn Taylor *Mr Shores* • Jennifer Holden *Sherry Wilson* • Dean Jones *Teddy Talbot* • Anne Neyland *Laury Jackson* • Mike Stoller *Pianist* ■ *Dir* Richard Thorpe • *Scr* Guy Trosper, from a story by Ned Young

Jakob the Liar ★★ 12
Second World War comedy drama 1999 · US · Colour · 116min

The more Robin Williams lays on the schmaltz, the fewer tears we shed in response. As Jakob, a fantasist living in a Jewish ghetto in war-torn Poland, he pulls out all the emotional stops but the result falls far short of tragic resonance. Overhearing a suggestion that all is going badly on the German front, Jakob finds he has to keep feeding his eager compatriots morsels of hope. Such fine actors as Armin Mueller-Stahl and Alan Arkin are enmeshed in a web of optimistic deceit that soon becomes as unconvincing as Williams himself. TH *DVD*

Robin Williams *Jakob Heym* • Alan Arkin *Frankfurter* • Bob Balaban *Kowalsky* • Hannah Taylor Gordon [Hannah Taylor-Gordon] *Lina* • Michael Jeter *Avron* • Armin Mueller-Stahl *Professor Kirschbaum* • Liev Schreiber *Mischa* • Nina Siemaszko *Rosa Frankfurter* ■ *Dir* Peter Kassovitz • *Scr* Peter Kassovitz, Didier Decoin, from the book *Jakob der Lügner* by Jurek Becker

Jamaica Inn ★★ PG
Period adventure 1939 · UK · BW · 94min

Alfred Hitchcock's last picture before his departure for Hollywood is the least of his three Daphne du Maurier adaptations (*Rebecca* and *The Birds* being the others). Charles Laughton's self-indulgent performance as the piratical squire goes some way to explaining the film's failure, but Hitch's lack of interest in the character's dual nature is mostly to blame. It isn't a completely lost cause, however: Maureen O'Hara is spirited yet vulnerable, while the reconstruction of Regency Cornwall brings a touch of authenticity to an otherwise lacklustre production. DP *DVD*

Charles Laughton *Sir Humphrey Pengallan* • Maureen O'Hara *Mary Yelland* • Leslie Banks *Joss Merlyn* • Emlyn Williams *Harry the Peddler* • Robert Newton *Jem Trehearne* • Wylie Watson *Salvation Watkins* ■ *Dir* Alfred Hitchcock • *Scr* Sidney Gilliat, Joan Harrison, JB Priestley, Alma Reville, from the novel *Jamaica Inn* by Daphne du Maurier • *Art Director* Tom N Moraham

Jamaica Run ★★ U
Adventure 1953 · US · Colour · 92min

Ray Milland – who never quite cut it as an action-romantic hero – skippers a schooner in the Caribbean, courting Arlene Dahl whose family live in a great mansion on Jamaica. But it seems that the provenance of the estate is in doubt and may lie at the bottom of the sea, locked in a shipwreck. Pitched as a straightforward action film, it has some good points: location shooting, a competently handled underwater fight and a splendidly gothic episode when the house erupts in flames. AT

Ray Milland *Patrick Fairlie* • Arlene Dahl *Ena Dacey* • Wendell Corey *Todd Dacey* • Patric Knowles *William Montague* • Laura Elliot *Janice Clayton* • *Dir* Lewis R Foster • *Scr* Lewis R Foster, from the novel *The Neat Little Corpse* by Max Murray

Jamboree ★★🅤
Musical drama   1957 · US · BW · 85min

Jerry Lee Lewis belting out *Great Balls of Fire* is the main reason to catch this clumsy attempt to cash in on the rock 'n' roll boom of the late 1950s. The pretence of a story a routine affair, with Kay Medford's would-be hip agent trying to break up pop hopefuls Paul Carr and Freda Holloway, as she thinks a double act would damage Carr's sex symbol prospects. The mixed-race nature of the guest list is noteworthy, with Count Basie and Fats Domino billed alongside Carl Perkins, Connie Francis and Frankie Avalon. DP

Kay Medford *Grace Shaw* • Bob Pastine *Lew Arthur* • Paul Carr *Pete Porter* • Freda Holloway *Honey Wynn* • David King-Wood *Warren Sykes* • Jean Martin *Cindy Styles* ■ *Dir* Roy Lockwood • *Scr* Leonard Kantor, Milton Subotsky • *Cinematographer* Jack Etra

James and the Giant Peach ★★★★🅤
Part-animated fantasy adventure
1996 · US · Colour · 85min

For a writer of children's stories, Roald Dahl undoubtedly had a dark imagination. Here, though, there will only be squeals of delight as James and his insect allies escape from a killer shark, skeleton pirates and a couple of awful aunts as they ride a giant peach to the city where dreams come true. It took three years to combine the live-action sequences with state-of-the-art model animation, and the latter is greatly assisted by the personality-packed voices of Susan Sarandon, Richard Dreyfuss, Simon Callow and David Thewlis. However, it's Joanna Lumley and Miriam Margolyes as the ghastly Spiker and Sponge who steal this wonderfully pantomimic show. DP *DVD* *CS*

Paul Terry *James* • Joanna Lumley *Aunt Spiker* • Miriam Margolyes *Aunt Sponge* • Pete Postlethwaite *Old Man* • Simon Callow *Grasshopper* • Richard Dreyfuss *Centipede* • Jane Leeves *Ladybug* • Susan Sarandon *Spider* • David Thewlis *Earthworm* ■ *Dir* Henry Selick • *Scr* Steven Bloom, Jonathan Roberts, from Roald Dahl's illustrated children's book

James Baldwin: the Price of the Ticket ★★★🅿🅶
Documentary   1989 · US · Colour · 86min

James Baldwin was born black, poor and homosexual, yet he became one of the most celebrated American writers and civil rights activists of his up-tight era. Combining his expressive and controversial public speeches with rare archive footage, home movies and the recollections of his close friends and family (including interviews with his brother David, and writers Maya Angelou and William Styron), director Karen Thorsen provides a powerful and moving document into his life, works and beliefs, which skilfully puts across his insightful mind and keen, irrepressible spirit. AJ

■ *Dir* Karen Thorsen

James Dean ★★★🅓
Biographical drama   2001 · US · Colour · 91min

Brad Pitt, Johnny Depp and Leonardo DiCaprio were variously linked with this TV biopic of the ultimate troubled teen. But director Mark Rydell could not have chosen better than James Franco, who follows in the tragic star's Method footsteps and truly lives the part. Whether clashing with his father (Michael Moriarty) or pushing the boundaries of screen acting with Elia Kazan (Enrico Colantoni) and Nicholas Ray (Barry Primus), Franco captures the edginess that made Dean's highly personal style unique. It's a shame that the tone becomes gossipy. DP

James Franco *James Dean/Narrator* • Michael Moriarty *Winton Dean* • Valentina Cervi *Pier Angeli* • Enrico Colantoni *Elia Kazan* • Edward

Herrmann *Raymond Massey* • Joanne Linville *Hedda Hopper* • Barry Primus *Nicholas Ray* ■ *Dir* Mark Rydell • *Scr* Israel Horovitz

The James Dean Story ★★🅿🅶
Documentary   1957 · US · BW · 79min

An early film from Robert Altman (co-directing with George W George), it relates the now familiar story of the 1950s star, who died too young after starring in only three movies. It makes use of archive material in a way that tries to inject drama into the documentary process – there's a stylised depiction of the fatal car crash – but because there's very little revelation, the overall effect is one of a boring whitewash. TH *DVD*

Martin Gabel *Narrator* ■ *Dir* George W George, Robert Altman • *Scr* Stewart Stern

James Dean – the First American Teenager ★★★🅖
Documentary   1975 · UK · Colour · 77min

Writer/director Ray Connolly, who sprayed *Stardust* with sharp pop insights, here unravels the James Dean legend with an attractive mixture of objectivity and affection. Without resorting to cheap sentimentality, this documentary successfully deals with Dean's huge social impact and endurance as an icon, while also pinning down the facts of his life, and death. Interviews with colleagues and co-stars like Natalie Wood, Dennis Hopper and Sammy Davis Jr, as well as rare screen-test footage, provide added spice. JM

Stacy Keach *Narrator* ■ *Dir/Scr* Ray Connolly

The James Gang ★★🅖
Comedy drama   1997 · UK/Can · Colour · 94min

A knowing soundtrack from Bernard Butler and gutsy performances from Helen McCrory and John Hannah are the only plus points in this willing, but otherwise sadly under-realised debut from director Mike Barker and screenwriter Stuart Hepburn. As the single mum who responds to a house fire by embarking on a hand-to-mouth crime spree, McCrory very nearly binds together the ramshackle sequence of stylised set pieces. DP Swearing, nudity, sex scenes.

John Hannah *Spendlove James* • Helen McCrory *Bernadette James* • Jason Flemyng *Frank James* • Toni Collette *Julia Armstrong* • Darren Brownlie *Spendlove Jr* • David Brownlie *Spendlove Jr* • Lauren McMurray *Geraldine James* • Lauren McCracken *Jessica James* ■ *Dir* Mike Barker • *Scr* Stuart Hepburn, from an idea by Andrew Eaton, Paul Lee

Jamón, Jamón ★★★★🅘🅘🅘
Erotic comedy drama   1992 · Sp · Colour · 90min

Director Bigas Luna represents the cutting edge of Spanish cinema with his witty exploration of flamenco love and desire. The first of a trilogy – completed by *Golden Balls* and *The Tit and the Moon* – Luna's frantic passion play rides a carnal carousel, with macho star discovery Javier Bardem posing in underwear, eating ham (*jamón*) and bullfighting in the nude. Call it paella porn or Andalucian art, it's entertaining and very hot stuff indeed. AJ Spanish +subtitles. Violence, swearing, drug abuse *DVD*

Penélope Cruz *Silvia* • Anna Galiena *Carmen* • Javier Bardem *Raul* • Stefania Sandrelli *Conchita* • Juan Diego *Manuel* • Jordi Mollà *Jose Luis* ■ *Dir* Bigas Luna • *Scr* Cuca Canals, Bigas Luna

Jane and the Lost City ★🅿🅶
Action adventure   1987 · UK · Colour · 88min

The famous comic-strip heroine searches for lost diamonds, a lost city and a lost script somewhere in darkest Africa, in a painfully cheap comedy dredging the bottom of the *Carry On* barrel for its seaside postcard puns. Watching the accident-prone Jane (Kirsten Hughes) lose her clothes in awkwardly telegraphed set-ups may keep some viewers attentive, but this is a witless fiasco. AJ

Sam Jones *"Jungle Jack" Buck* • Maud Adams *Lola Pagola* • Jasper Carrott *Heinrich* • Kirsten Hughes *Jane* • Graham Stark *Tombs* • Robin

Bailey *Colonel* • Ian Roberts (1) *Carl Donner* ■ *Dir* Terry Marcel • *Scr* Mervyn Haisman, from a story by Mervyn Haisman, Terry Marcel, Harry Robertson, from characters in the *Jane* cartoon created by Norman Pettin in the *Daily Mirror*

The Jane Austen Book Club ★★★🅓
Romantic comedy drama
2007 · US · Colour · 101min

Writer/director Robin Swicord's cosy romantic comedy follows the members of a California book group, who find their personal relationship dramas echoed in the works of Jane Austen. Maria Bello delivers the most down-to-earth turn as a character not unlike the heroine of Austen's *Emma*. Emily Blunt has the toughest task, blending comedy and pathos as a French teacher whose gothic state of mind makes her feel as if she's trapped in *Northanger Abbey*. Engaging performances and witty dialogue make up for sometimes laboured storytelling and, at times, Swicord does get beyond the quaintness of the premise to show how Austen's observations are still relevant to the romantic woes of the modern woman. SP *DVD*

Kathy Baker *Bernadette* • Maria Bello *Jocelyn* • Emily Blunt *Prudie* • Amy Brenneman *Sylvia* • Hugh Dancy *Grigg* • Maggie Grace *Allegra* • Lynn Redgrave *Sky* • Jimmy Smits *Daniel* • Marc Blucas *Dean* • Kevin Zegers *Trey* • Nancy Travis *Cat* ■ *Dir* Robin Swicord • *Scr* Robin Swicord, from the novel by Karen Joy Fowler

Jane Austen in Manhattan ★★★🅿🅶
Comedy   1980 · US/UK · Colour · 106min

When an unknown playlet by Jane Austen is auctioned in New York, it's bought by a rich foundation and two directors fight for the right to produce it on stage – as an operetta or as a trendy piece of avant-garde. Never more than an arty contrivance, this James Ivory piece celebrates acting, performance and sheer eccentricity in a series of vignettes designed to indulge his cast. In this regard it's good to see Anne Baxter get her best role since *All about Eve*, in what was her final feature film. AT *DVD*

Anne Baxter *Lilianna Zorska* • Robert Powell *Pierre* • Michael Wager *George Midash* • Tim Choate *Jamie* • John Guerrasio *Gregory* • Katrina Hodiak *Katya* • Kurt R Johnson *Victor Charlton* • Sean Young *Ariadne Charlton* ■ *Dir* James Ivory • *Scr* Ruth Prawer Jhabvala, from the libretto *Sir Charles Grandison* by Jane Austen, Samuel Richardson • *Producer* Ismail Merchant

Jane Austen's Mafia ★★🅓
Spoof   1998 · US · Colour · 83min

Jim Abrahams's Mafia spoof is in the same vein as his earlier hits *Airplane!* and *The Naked Gun*, with sadly similar jokes. That it works at all is only due to convincing performances from Olympia Dukakis, Jay Mohr, Christina Applegate and Lloyd Bridges, who plays a Don Corleone figure training his son (Mohr) to take over the family business. However, there comes a time when he's disposable, so fellow hoods send a temptress to woo Mohr away from his family and girlfriend (Applegate). LH Swearing, some violence. *DVD*

Jay Mohr *Anthony Cortino* • Billy Burke *Joey Cortino* • Christina Applegate *Diane* • Pamela Gidley *Pepper Gianini* • Olympia Dukakis *Sophia* • Lloyd Bridges *Vincenzo Cortino* ■ *Dir* Jim Abrahams • *Scr* Jim Abrahams, Greg Norberg, Michael McManus

Jane Eyre ★★★★🅿🅶
Period drama   1943 · US · BW · 96min

British director Robert Stevenson has shown an unusual talent in his warmly sympathetic treatment of films about women. This typical 20th Century-Fox period melodrama is a fine example of his work, though many will persist in attributing the film's virtues to Orson Welles, who might have made a fine job of directing it, given the chance. Welles's Edward Rochester is suitably awesome, dominating his scenes (naturally), but, unfortunately, slowing the pace whenever he appears. Joan Fontaine is fine, though wan, in the

title role. Watch for a young Elizabeth Taylor in a small but telling part early in the film. TS *DVD*

Orson Welles *Edward Rochester* • Joan Fontaine *Jane Eyre* • Margaret O'Brien *Adele* • Peggy Ann Garner *Jane, as a child* • John Sutton *Dr Rivers* • Sara Allgood *Bessie* • Henry Daniell *Brocklehurst* • Agnes Moorehead *Mrs Reed* • Elizabeth Taylor *Helen Burns* ■ *Dir* Robert Stevenson • *Scr* Aldous Huxley, Robert Stevenson, John Houseman, from the novel by Charlotte Brontë

Jane Eyre ★★★
Period romantic drama
1970 · UK/US · Colour · 110min

Charlotte Brontë's wish-fulfilling novel about the Yorkshire governess and her forbidden love for the haunted and out-of-her-class Mr Rochester, is tastefully done by director Delbert Mann. Though made for television, it boasts the heavyweight presence of George C Scott who is suitably dark and moody, while Susannah York is a plain Jane with attitude. Diverting, but it would be better to read the book. TH

George C Scott *Edward Rochester* • Susannah York *Jane Eyre* • Ian Bannen *St John Rivers* • Jack Hawkins *Mr Brocklehurst* • Nyree Dawn Porter *Blanche Ingram* ■ *Dir* Delbert Mann • *Scr* Jack Pulman, from the novel by Charlotte Brontë

Jane Eyre ★★★🅿🅶
Period romantic drama
1996 · Fr/It/UK/US · Colour · 116min

William Hurt's thoughtful, subdued interpretation of Mr Rochester makes its own gently neurotic contribution to the Brontë movie canon in Franco Zeffirelli's stylish and atmospheric take on the famous novel. Zeffirelli lays on sufficient simmering passion to make it interesting, yet at the same time brings the romantic longings of the two lead characters down to a more mundane, human level. Charlotte Gainsbourg was seen by some, however, as too fiery for the role of Jane. TH *DVD*

William Hurt *Rochester* • Charlotte Gainsbourg *Jane Eyre* • Joan Plowright *Mrs Fairfax* • Anna Paquin *Young Jane* • Geraldine Chaplin *Miss Scatcherd* • Billie Whitelaw *Grace Poole* • Maria Schneider *Mrs Rochester* • Fiona Shaw *Mrs Reed* • Elle Macpherson *Blanche Ingram* ■ *Dir* Franco Zeffirelli • *Scr* Hugh Whitemore, Franco Zeffirelli, from the novel by Charlotte Brontë

Jane Eyre ★★★🅿🅶
Period romantic drama
2011 · UK · Colour · 115min

Charlotte Brontë's gothic romance has been adapted for the screen many times, but in the title role here, Mia Wasikowska carries the burden with ease. She looks fragile as porcelain, yet stands up well against Michael Fassbender as the fiery Mr Rochester who employs her at his gloomy mansion. The emotional push and pull is carefully staged by director Cary Fukunaga but almost too carefully, with too much formality and not enough of the wild abandon that draws Jane to Rochester. It is, above all, a very respectful treatment. SP *DVD* *BD*

Michael Fassbender *Edward Rochester* • Mia Wasikowska *Jane Eyre* • Jamie Bell *St John Rivers* • Judi Dench *Mrs Fairfax* • Imogen Poots *Blanche Ingram* • Sally Hawkins *Mrs Reed* ■ *Dir* Cary Joji Fukunaga [Cary Fukunaga] • *Scr* Moira Buffini, from the novel by Charlotte Brontë • *Cinematographer* Adriano Goldman

Jane Got a Gun ★★🅓
Western   2015 · US · Colour · 98min

After a chequered production history, Gavin O'Connor's western makes it to the screen, but with a few rough edges. It sees a gang of outlaws converge on the homestead of Natalie Portman in search of her wounded husband (Noah Emmerich). Arming herself to the teeth, the feisty housewife reinvents herself as a gunslinger, enlisting the help of her embittered ex (Joel Edgerton). The film looks the part, but the meat of the story is told in frustratingly fleeting, sometimes cringingly naff flashbacks. The climactic shoot-out is, nonetheless, thrillingly staged. EAS Violence, swearing.

J

Natalie Portman *Jane Hammond* • Joel Edgerton *Dan Frost* • Ewan McGregor *John Bishop* • Rodrigo Santoro *Fitchum* • Noah Emmerich *Bill Hammond* ■ *Dir* Gavin O'Connor • *Scr* Brian Duffield, Anthony Tambakis, Joel Edgerton

Janice Beard 45 WPM ★★★★ 15

Romantic comedy 1999 · UK · Colour · 77min

Clare Kilner's highly impressive debut feature is quirky, original and touching. Scottish newcomer Eileen Walsh stars as Janice, a plain Jane whose life revolves around her attempts to get her severely agoraphobic mother out the front door. In desperation, Janice heads for London and a temp job under the not-so-kind eye of a bitchy Patsy Kensit. There she develops a relationship with postboy Rhys Ifans and becomes unwittingly embroiled in a plot to steal vital documents from her company. The retro look, innovative cinematography and spot-on script combine to make a film brimming with humour and heart. **LH** 💿
Rhys Ifans *Sean* • Patsy Kensit *Julia* • David O'Hara *O'Brien* • Eileen Walsh *Janice Beard* • Sandra Voe *Mimi* • Frances Gray *Violet* • Zita Sattar *Jane* • Amelia Curtis *June* ■ *Dir* Clare Kilner • *Scr* Clare Kilner, Ben Hopkins

Janis: Little Girl Blue ★★★★ 15

Documentary 2015 · US/UK · Colour · 103min

Janis Joplin has proved to be an elusive subject for a biopic, despite numerous attempts to bring her story to the big screen. But it is hard to imagine a Hollywood spin would be more affecting than this documentary, thanks to the blistering footage that director Amy J Berg has assembled of the singer in all her untamed glory. One of the most poignant things about Berg's film is the way it traces the arc of Joplin's growth as an artist and gives a hint of the performer she could have become, as she harnesses the innately feral talent that made her name. **WI** Swearing.
Cat Power [Chan Marshall] *Narrator* ■ *Dir/Scr* Amy J Berg [Amy Berg]

The January Man ★★★ 15

Crime thriller 1989 · US · Colour · 97min

Kevin Kline is eminently watchable in this gritty thriller as the ex-New York cop brought back on to the force to track down a serial killer. Among the heavyweight supporting cast, Susan Sarandon stands out, and this even boasts a screenplay by Oscar-winning *Moonstruck* writer John Patrick Shanley. Given the talent at his disposal, director Pat O'Connor should have turned in a much better movie, but, even though this doesn't quite live up to its promise, it's still very entertaining. **SH** 💿
Kevin Kline *Nick Starkey* • Susan Sarandon *Christine Starkey* • Mary Elizabeth Mastrantonio *Bernadette Flynn* • Harvey Keitel *Frank Starkey* • Danny Aiello *Captain Vincent Alcoa* • Rod Steiger *Mayor Eamon Flynn* • Alan Rickman *Ed* • Faye Grant *Allison Hawkins* ■ *Dir* Pat O'Connor • *Scr* John Patrick Shanley

Japanese Story ★★★★ 15

Romantic drama 2003 · Aus/UK · Colour · 101min

Sue Brooks's emotionally devastating film starts out as a relatively unpromising culture-clash romance, before becoming something unexpectedly profound. Geologist Toni Collette is saddled with an initially arrogant and cold Japanese businessman (Gotaro Tsunashima) for a research trip into the hostile Australian outback. Forced to survive a night in the freezing desert, an odd but tender relationship develops between the two. But then the drama suddenly shifts gear, forcing viewers to re-evaluate both their own basic assumptions and those of the characters. Carefully constructed, intelligent and well-acted. **AS** Swearing, sex scenes. 💿
Toni Collette *Sandy Edwards* • Gotaro Tsunashima *Tachibana Hiromitsu* • Matthew Dyktynski *Bill Baird* • Lynette Curran *Mum* •

Yumiko Tanaka *Yukiko Hiromitsu* • Kate Atkinson *Jackie* • Bill Young *Jimmy Smithers* ■ *Dir* Sue Brooks • *Scr* Alison Tilson

Japón ★★★ 18

Drama 2002 · Mex/Sp/Neth/Ger · Colour · 127min

There is much to admire in writer/director Carlos Reygadas's debut feature, from the strikingly photographed landscapes to the considered exploration of both faith and human frailty in modern Mexico and human frailty in isolation. The disparate elements don't quite coalesce into a satisfying story, but the relationship between widow Magdalena Flores and artist Alejandro Ferretis (who has ventured into the wilderness to commit suicide) is both touching and powerful in its simplicity, as she seeks to save his soul and he strives to prevent her grasping nephew from repossessing her hillside shack. **DP** Spanish +subtitles. 💿
Alejandro Ferretis *The man* • Magdalena Flores *Ascen* • Yolanda Villa *Sabina* • Martin Serrano *Juan Luis* • Rolando Hernández *The judge* • Bernabé Pérez *The singer* • Fernando Benitez *Fernando* ■ *Dir/Scr* Carlos Reygadas

Jar City ★★★ 15

Crime drama 2006 · Ice/Ger/Den · Colour · 90min

After his ill-fated excursion into American *noir* with the muddled *A Little Trip to Heaven*, Icelandic director Baltasar Kormakur (*101 Reykjavik*) is back on home turf and on surer ground with this accomplished crime drama. Ingvar E Sigurdsson stars as the grumpy detective investigating the murder of a reclusive old man, who discovers a link to a series of crimes from years earlier. Although the movie doesn't quite shake off the feeling of a small-scale TV drama – with his natty line in cardigans Sigurdsson could be a distant relative of Inspector Frost – Kormakur's economical direction and the strikingly bleak Icelandic vistas lift this out of the ordinary. **JF** Icelandic +subtitles. 💿
Ingvar E Sigurdsson *Inspector Erlendur* • Atli Rafn Sigurdson *Orn* • Erlendur Eiriksson *Security guard* • Elma Lisa Gunnarsdottir *Gunnur* • Rafnhildur Rosa Atladottir *Kola* ■ *Dir* Baltasar Kormakur • *Scr* Baltasar Kormakur, from the novel by Arnaldur Indridason

Jarhead ★★★ 15

War drama based on a true story 2005 · US/UK/Ger · Colour · 117min

Sam Mendes directs this adaptation of Anthony Swofford's memoir, in which he relates not only his experiences of the absurdly short first Gulf War but also the brutal process of being transformed into a marine. Mendes delivers some stunning imagery and he renders the everyday life of marines well, both in its tedium and occasionally unpleasant detail. He also draws good performances from his young cast, but he's hamstrung by a screenplay that delivers an inevitably anticlimactic third act. **AS** Swearing, violence. 🔵
Jake Gyllenhaal *Anthony "Swoff" Swofford* • Jamie Foxx *Staff Sergeant Sykes* • Peter Sarsgaard *Allen Troy* • Chris Cooper *Lieutenant Colonel Kazinski* • Lucas Black *Chris Kruger* • Brian Geraghty *Fergus O'Donnell* • Jacob Vargas *Cortez* • Dennis Haysbert *Major Lincoln* ■ *Dir* Sam Mendes • *Scr* William Broyles Jr, from the non-fiction book by Anthony Swofford

Jason and the Argonauts ★★★★ U

Fantasy adventure 1963 · UK · Colour · 99min

Special-effects maestro Ray Harryhausen produced his finest stop-motion magic when he turned to classic Greek myth. Todd Armstrong stars as the leader of Greece's greatest heroes whose quest for the Golden Fleece offers terrific action and a bonanza of monster mayhem, including a giant man of bronze and the (iconic) skeleton army. Sword-and-sandal cheesiness is kept at bay thanks to menacing music from Bernard Herrmann. The result is glorious entertainment. **JA** 💿
Todd Armstrong *Jason* • Nancy Kovack *Medea* • Gary Raymond *Acastus* • Laurence Naismith *Argus* • Niall MacGinnis *Zeus* • Honor Blackman

Hera • Michael Gwynn *Hermes* • Jack Gwillim *King Aeëtes* ■ *Dir* Don Chaffey • *Scr* Jan Reed, Beverly Cross

Jason Becker: Not Dead Yet ★★★★

Documentary 2012 · US/UK · Colour · 86min

Jesse Vile's documentary is an inspirational profile of the talented rock guitarist who was playing with David Lee Roth's band when he was diagnosed with Amyotrophic Lateral Sclerosis (or Lou Gehrig's disease) at the age of 19. As he began to lose mobility and the ability to communicate, his father, Gary, devised an eye alphabet that not only allowed Becker to converse, but also to keep composing. The creative process may be excruciating, but the music Becker makes is sublime, testifying to the artistry and resilience of a man who continues to beat the odds two decades after being told he had only a few years to live. **DP** Swearing. 💿
Jason Becker ■ *Dir* Jesse Vile

Jason Bourne ★★★★ 12A

Action thriller 2016 · US · Colour · 123min

Bourne is back with a vengeance as Matt Damon resumes the role that launched a game-changing franchise and influenced everything from Bond to Batman. Director Paul Greengrass brilliantly marshals the slickly edited action, as the plot – fellow runaway spy Nicky (Julia Styles) unearths a secret from his family's past – thrusts Bourne into a post-Snowden world of dodgy dealings and invasive surveillance. Thanks to breakneck action set in stunning locations, a terrific cast and the magnetic presence of Damon, it's still a case of Bourne supremacy. **JA** Violence.
Matt Damon *Jason Bourne* • Tommy Lee Jones *CIA Director Robert Dewey* • Alicia Vikander *Heather Lee* • Vincent Cassel *Asset* • Julia Stiles *Nicky* ■ *Dir* Paul Greengrass • *Scr* Paul Greengrass, Christopher Rouse, from characters by Robert Ludlum

Jason Goes to Hell: the Final Friday ★★★ 18

Horror 1993 · US · Colour · 84min

The spirit of Jason Voorhees is whisked back to Crystal Lake via a series of deadly soul transferences in director Adam Marcus's affectionate milking of *Friday the 13th* imagery, hewn from the past eight chapters and cleverly turned inside out for a new, improved joy ride. Affectionately witty, inventively shocking and shot through with a gleaming high-tone style, Marcus delivers the slasher goods and supplies edge-of-the-seat thrills on a par with the original film. A tenth instalment, *Jason X*, was released in 2002. **AJ** 💿
John D LeMay *Steven Freeman* • Kari Keegan *Jessica Kimble* • Kane Hodder *Jason Voorhees* • Steven Williams *Creighton Duke* • Steven Culp *Robert Campbell* • Erin Gray *Diana Kimble* • Rusty Schwimmer *Joey B* ■ *Dir* Adam Marcus • *Scr* Dean Lorey, Jay Huguely, from a story by Adam Marcus, Jay Huguely

Jason X ★★★ 15

Science-fiction action horror 2001 · US · Colour · 87min

In 2455, student archaeologists return to the toxic wasteland of "Old Earth" and discover a hockey-masked body frozen in a cryogenic chamber. But on the journey back to "New Earth" with their find, Jason thaws out and returns to his old stab-and-slash tricks aboard the spaceship. Director Jason Isaac's solid entry in the classic gore series is a treat for fans. **AJ** Violence, swearing. 💿
Kane Hodder *Jason* • Lexa Doig *Rowan* • Lisa Ryder *KAY-EM 14* • Chuck Campbell *Tsunaron* • Jonathan Potts *Professor Lowe* • Peter Mensah *Sgt Brodski* • Melyssa Ade *Janessa* • Melody Johnson *Kinsa* • David Cronenberg *Dr Wimmer* ■ *Dir* Jim Isaac [James Isaac] • *Scr* Todd Farmer, from the character created by Victor Miller

Jason's Lyric ★★★ 18

Drama 1994 · US · Colour · 115min

Directed by Doug McHenry, this curiously old-fashioned film attempts to put a new slant on the African-American experience. Although it revisits the familiar "going bad in the ghetto" theme, this feels more like a Hollywood problem picture of the late 1940s than an explosion of justifiable anger. This is mostly down to the fact that McHenry places as much emphasis on Allen Payne's sweet romance with Jada Pinkett as he does on his relationship with tearaway brother Bokeem Woodbine, who seems to have inherited the troubled mind of their dead father, played in flashback by Forest Whitaker. **DP** Sex scenes, violence, swearing, nudity.
Allen Payne *Jason Alexander* • Jada Pinkett [Jada Pinkett Smith] *Lyric Greer* • Forest Whitaker *Maddog* • Bokeem Woodbine *Joshua Alexander* • Suzzanne Douglas *Gloria Alexander* • Anthony "Treach" Criss *Alonzo* ■ *Dir* Doug McHenry • *Scr* Bobby Smith Jr

Jasper Penguin Explorer ★★★ U

Animated adventure 2008 · Ger/Rom/Fr · Colour · 81min

In Eckart Fingberg and co-director Kay Delventhal's lively children's CGI saga, young penguin Jasper refuses to believe the grown-ups who insist there is nothing beyond the ice caps encircling his Antarctic home. His curiosity sees him end up on board a luxury liner with his baby brother and an exotic parrot, the Kakapo. Complete with amusing secondary characters, this is an enjoyable adventure with genial heroes and atmospheric graphics. However, it might have been more effective had the finale not been quite so rushed. **DP** 💿
Rick Adams *Jasper* • Kate Rawlings *Emma* • Rob Rackstraw *Kakapo* • Steve Hudson *Dr Block/Rolf/Captain/Jasper's dad/teacher/passenger Herbert* ■ *Dir* Eckart Fingberg, Kay Delventhal • *Scr* Eckart Fingberg, Michael Madel, John Chambers

Jassy ★★★ PG

Period drama 1947 · UK · Colour · 97min

Two years after she took the nation by storm in *The Wicked Lady*, Margaret Lockwood stars here as a woman of gypsy ancestry with the gift of second sight who gets involved in the struggle to regain an inheritance. Lockwood's not all good, however, and murder is on the menu, but this time we are given hints of the heart beneath her wild exterior. This is by no means as silly as it sounds, even though the Gainsborough gang's all here, including Dennis Price hamming it up to the hilt. Great fun. **SH**
Margaret Lockwood *Jassy Woodroffe* • Patricia Roc *Dilys Helmar* • Dennis Price *Christopher Hatton* • Dermot Walsh *Barney Hatton* • Basil Sydney *Nick Helmar* • Nora Swinburne *Mrs Hatton* • John Laurie *Woodroffe* ■ *Dir* Bernard Knowles • *Scr* Dorothy Christie, Campbell Christie, Geoffrey Kerr, from the novel by Norah Lofts

Jauja ★★★★ 15

Period drama 2014 · Arg/Den/Fr/Mex/US Neth · Colour · 105min

Echoes of Lisandro Alonso's second feature, *Los Muertos* (2004), reverberate around the Argentinian auteur's first period picture (and first collaboration with a name star). But it's also possible to detect the influence of Joseph Conrad's *Heart of Darkness*, John Ford's *The Searchers* (1956) and Werner Herzog's *Aguirre, Wrath of God* (1972) in a quest saga whose metaphysical digressions and dream interludes will fascinate and frustrate in equal measure. Viggo Mortensen's bid to find 15-year-old daughter Viilbjork Malling Agger is all made immersively compelling by cinematographer Timo Salminen who uses long shots, close-ups and heightened colour to depict this mythical land of plenty. **DP** In Spanish, Danish. 💿

Viggo Mortensen *Gunnar Dinesen* • Viilbjork Malling Agger *Ingeborg* • Diego Roman *Corta* • Esteban Bigliardi *Angel Milkibar* • Ghita Norby *Woman in the cave* ■ *Dir* Lisandro Alonso • *Scr* Lisandro Alonso, Fabian Casas

Java Head ★★★ PG
Period romantic drama 1935 • UK • BW • 79min

While one of two brothers (Ralph Richardson) settles down to marriage and is given the management of the fleet by his ship-owning father (Edmund Gwenn), the other (John Loder) seeks adventure in faraway climes. He returns with a Chinese bride (Anna May Wong), but the realisation that he still loves his childhood sweetheart (Elizabeth Allan), brings tragedy. This British-made combination of adventure, romance and melodrama, set in Bristol and at sea in the mid-19th century, boasts a fine cast. RK *DVD*

Anna May Wong *Taou Yen* • Elizabeth Allan *Nettie Vollar* • John Loder *Gerrit Ammidon* • Edmund Gwenn *Jeremy Ammidon* • Ralph Richardson *William Ammidon* • Herbert Lomas *Barzil Dunsack* • George Curzon *Edward Dunsack* ■ *Dir* J Walter Ruben • *Scr* Martin Brown, Gordon Wellesley, from the novel by Joseph Hergesheimer

Jawbreaker ★★ 15
Black comedy 1999 • US • Colour • 83min

This *Heathers*-style black comedy is about a trio of high school "It" girls, whose birthday prank on their best friend goes horribly wrong. Writer/director Darren Stein has a flair for striking cartoon visuals, but the plot soon runs out and the film's tone is excessively cold and cruel. Its strongest asset is the bright young cast, headed by Rose McGowan's malicious super-bitch and Judy Greer's convincing transformation from mousy nerd to sexy bombshell. JC Swearing, sex scenes. *DVD*

Rose McGowan *Courtney Shayne* • Rebecca Gayheart *Julie Freeman* • Julie Benz *Marcie Fox* • Judy Evans Greer [Judy Greer] *Fern Mayo* • Chad Christ *Zach Tartak* • Charlotte Roldan *Liz Purr* • Pam Grier *Detective Vera Cruz* • Carol Kane *Miss Sherwood* ■ *Dir/Scr* Darren Stein

LANDMARK FILM
Don't go into the water. This first $100 million blockbuster from Spielberg sparks Hollywood's obsession with plots that can be pitched in one sentence

Jaws ★★★★★ 12
Adventure thriller 1975 • US • Colour • 118min

Peter Benchley's pulp bestseller is here turned into the scariest sea saga ever filmed, with Steven Spielberg creating maximum suspense in the first dark moments and then maintaining the momentum with brilliant sleight-of-hand direction. The tale of a great white shark terrorising a New England resort community and the modern-day Captain Ahab (Robert Shaw) employed to kill it is now a classic of the suspense thriller genre. John Williams's Oscar-winning music and the excellent performances of Roy Scheider and Richard Dreyfus add to the ingeniously mounted tension that cleverly plays on all our deepest primeval fears. AJ Violence, swearing, nudity. *DVD* *Blu*

Roy Scheider *Brody* • Robert Shaw *Quint* • Richard Dreyfuss *Hooper* • Lorraine Gary *Ellen Brody* • Murray Hamilton *Vaughn* • Carl Gottlieb *Meadows* • Jeffrey C Kramer [Jeffrey Kramer] *Hendricks* • Susan Backlinie *Chrissie* • Jonathan Filley *Cassidy* ■ *Dir* Steven Spielberg • *Scr* Peter Benchley, Carl Gottlieb, Howard Sackler, from the novel by Peter Benchley • *Music* John Williams • *Editor* Verna Fields • *Cinematographer* Bill Butler • *Production Designer* Joe Alves

Jaws 2 ★★ PG
Action adventure 1978 • US • Colour • 110min

Three years after those infamous shark attacks, another great white swims into police chief Roy Scheider's resort town to cause more havoc in this shameless sequel. Director Jeannot Szwarc tries to ape Steven Spielberg's imaginative style and visceral terror, but any suspense he attempts to build comes unglued because it floats in all-too-familiar waters. Stalwart Scheider is in full control of this follow-up

that lacks the bite of the original. DP *DVD* *Blu*

Roy Scheider *Martin Brody* • Lorraine Gary *Ellen Brody* • Murray Hamilton *Mayor Vaughan* • Joseph Mascolo *Len Peterson* • Jeffrey Kramer *Deputy Jeff Hendricks* • Collin Wilcox *Dr Lureen Elkins* • Ann Dusenberry *Tina Wilcox, Miss Amity* • Mark Gruner *Mike Brody* • Barry Coe *Andrews* ■ *Dir* Jeannot Szwarc • *Scr* Carl Gottlieb, Dorothy Tristan (uncredited), from characters by Peter Benchley

Jaws III ★★ 12
Action adventure 1983 • US • Colour • 94min

Originally called *Jaws 3-D*, once stripped of the gimmick that made it almost acceptable in theatres, this hapless opus stands as a testament to the law of diminishing returns. Director credit goes to Joe Alves, the production designer of Steven Spielberg's great original, but it's quite clear from this effort that he's no director, as a group of moderate talents act all at sea. TS *DVD* *Blu*

Dennis Quaid *Mike Brody* • Louis Gossett Jr *Calvin Bouchard* • Bess Armstrong *Kathryn Morgan* • Simon MacCorkindale *Philip FitzRoyce* • John Putch *Sean Brody* • Lea Thompson *Kelly Ann Bukowski* • PH Moriarty *Jack Tate* ■ *Dir* Joe Alves • *Scr* Richard Matheson, Carl Gottlieb, from a story by Guerdon Trueblood, from characters by Peter Benchley

Jaws the Revenge ★ 12
Action adventure 1987 • US • Colour • 86min

This is the one where the big rubber shark gets to attack an aircraft, but that's not the only silly thing about this preposterous fourth entry in the series. Michael Caine makes the most of the summer weather in the Bahamas (the setting for most of the film) and delivers a cheerfully irrelevant cameo. Laughably inept. JF Swearing, violence. *DVD* *Blu*

Lorraine Gary *Ellen Brody* • Lance Guest *Michael Brody* • Mario Van Peebles *Jake* • Karen Young *Carla Brody* • Michael Caine *Hoagie* • Judith Barsi *Thea Brody* ■ *Dir* Joseph Sargent • *Scr* Michael de Guzman, from characters by Peter Benchley

Jay and Silent Bob Strike Back ★★★ 18
Satirical road movie comedy 2001 • US • Colour • 100min

Writer/director Kevin Smith's two recurring characters – dope-smoking, jive-talking Jay (Jason Mewes) and Silent Bob (Smith himself) – now have their own vehicle: an indulgent, dim-witted odyssey from Jersey to Hollywood where the two scatological scuzzballs plan to sabotage a movie based on comic book alter egos Bluntman and Chronic. Unfortunately for an audience unfamiliar with Smith's oeuvre, the in-jokes come so fast that a detailed knowledge is required. Otherwise it's a fair-to-middling gross-out comedy elevated to high satire status by Ben Affleck, Matt Damon, Mark Hamill and many others sending themselves up. AC Violence, swearing, nudity, drug abuse. *DVD* *Blu* *CS*

Jason Mewes *Jay* • Kevin Smith (2) *Silent Bob* • Ben Affleck *Holden McNeil/Ben/Chuckie* • Matt Damon *Will Hunting/Matt Damon* • Chris Rock *Chaka* • Shannon Elizabeth *Justice the jewel thief* • Will Ferrell *Willenholly* • George Carlin *Hitchhiker* • Mark Hamill *Cock-knocker* • Carrie Fisher *Nun* • Shannen Doherty *Rene Mosier* • Seann William Scott *Brent* • Joey Lauren Adams *Alyssa Jones* • Alanis Morissette *The Woman* ■ *Dir/Scr* Kevin Smith (2)

The Jayhawkers ★★
Western 1959 • US • Colour • 103min

This western pitches Jeff Chandler, as the leader of a private army of raiders called the Jayhawkers, against Fess Parker as the former jailbird who, for reasons of personal revenge, agrees to put a stop to Chandler's empire-building ambitions. With his Napoleon complex, a dislike for all women except his mother, and a strong affection for his adversary, Jeff Chandler is far more colourful than homespun Fess Parker. Although handsomely shot by Loyal Griggs and vigorously scored by Jerome Moross, this is long-winded and muddled. AE

Jeff Chandler *Luke Darcy* • Fess Parker *Cam Bleeker* • Nicole Maurey *Jeanne Dubois* • Herbert Rudley *Governor William Clayton* • Jimmy Carter *Paul* • Leo Gordon *Jake* ■ *Dir* Melvin Frank • *Scr* Melvin Frank, Joseph Petracca, Frank Fenton, Al Bezzerides

The Jayne Mansfield Story ★ PG
Biographical drama 1980 • US • Colour • 91min

Loni Anderson, Burt Reynolds' ex-missus, plays the rather tragic figure of the 1950s sex symbol whose ample proportions helped to market her as a poor man's Marilyn Monroe. In this questionably accurate made-for-TV biopic, Mansfield is portrayed as a hard nut who will do anything for stardom. Starring opposite Anderson is Arnold Schwarzenegger as her body-builder husband Mickey Hargitay. Everybody has to start somewhere. FL

Loni Anderson *Jayne Mansfield* • Arnold Schwarzenegger *Mickey Hargitay* • Ray Buktenica *Bob Garrett* • Kathleen Lloyd *Carol Sue Peters* • GD Spradlin *Gerald Conway* ■ *Dir* Dick Lowry • *Scr* Charles Dennis, Nancy Gayle, from the book *Jayne Mansfield and the American Fifties* by Martha Saxton

Jayne Mansfield's Car ★★ 15
Drama 2012 • US/Rus • Colour • 116min

Returning to the director's chair after an 11-year absence, Billy Bob Thornton invokes the spirit of Tennessee Williams in this seething study of domestic dysfunction set in the Deep South at the height of the Vietnam War. However, the screenplay (co-written with Tom Epperson) packs in too many characters and too frequently lets the dialogue carry the expository load. The tensions between Great War veteran Robert Duvall and sons Kevin Bacon, Robert Patrick and Thornton himself never quite crackle as they are supposed to, and the dissection of American attitudes to duty, honour and death is undermined by clumsy transatlantic stereotypes and the archness of the script. DP *DVD*

Robert Duvall *Jim Caldwell* • John Hurt *Kingsley Bedford* • Billy Bob Thornton *Skip Caldwell* • Kevin Bacon *Carroll Caldwell* • Robert Patrick *Jimbo Caldwell* • Ray Stevenson *Phillip Bedford* • Frances O'Connor *Camilla Bedford* • Tippi Hedren *Naomi Caldwell* ■ *Dir* Billy Bob Thornton • *Scr* Billy Bob Thornton, Tom Epperson

Jazz on a Summer's Day ★★★
Musical documentary 1959 • US • Colour • 87min

Considering this is a record of the 1958 Newport Jazz Festival, it's telling that two of the most arresting sets come from rocker Chuck Berry and gospel singer Mahalia Jackson. However, you'll be equally enthralled by the performances of Anita O'Day and such jazz legends as Louis Armstrong, Thelonious Monk and Dinah Washington. Photographer Bert Stern's direction may be a touch self-serving, and Aram Avakian's editing takes in too many shots of the crowd and the nearby America's Cup trials, but they still capture the relaxed atmosphere of the gig and the evident enjoyment of the artists. DP *DVD*

Louis Armstrong • Thelonious Monk • Anita O'Day • Chuck Berry • Mahalia Jackson • Dinah Washington ■ *Dir* Bert Stern

LANDMARK FILM
This first feature with spoken dialogue forces cinemas to install speakers

The Jazz Singer ★★★ U
Musical drama 1927 • US • BW • 85min

In the autumn of 1927, a historic premiere took place in New York when Al Jolson spoke the prophetic words, "You ain't heard nothing yet!" in the first feature with spoken dialogue. Warner Bros had gambled everything on this "talker" that would transform cinema forever. Actually, there is very little dialogue in this crude and schmaltzy film about a cantor's son torn between a life in the theatre and the synagogue. It is Jolson's dynamic singing of *Toot, Toot, Tootsie* and *My Mammy*, recorded by the Vitaphone process on disc

and synchronised to the action, that breathes life into a film whose pioneering aspect is its main interest. There were unnecessary remakes in 1952 (with Danny Thomas) and 1980 (with Neil Diamond). RB *DVD* *Blu*

Al Jolson *Jakie Rabinowitz/Jack Robin* • May McAvoy *Mary Dale* • Warner Oland *Cantor Rabinowitz* • Eugenie Besserer *Sara Rabinowitz* • Bobby Gordon *Jakie at thirteen* • Otto Lederer *Moishe Yudelson* • Cantor Josef Rosenblatt • Richard Tucker *Harry Lee* • Myrna Loy *Chorus girl* • William Demarest *Buster Billings* ■ *Dir* Alan Crosland • *Scr* Alfred A Cohn, Jack Jarmuth, from the play *Day of Atonement* by Samson Raphaelson

The Jazz Singer ★★★ U
Musical drama 1952 • US • Colour • 106min

This is an unnecessary, though likeable, updated remake of the oft-filmed story of the cantor's son who can't choose between showbiz and Yom Kippur. The main problem is Danny Thomas, who lacks the warmth the tale needs, while Peggy Lee – in one of her two feature leads (the other was in *Pete Kelly's Blues*, for which she was Oscar-nominated) – is anodyne. Not as bad, though, as the later version with Neil Diamond. TS

Danny Thomas *Jerry Golding* • Peggy Lee *Judy Lane* • Mildred Dunnock *Mrs Golding* • Eduard Franz *Cantor Golding* • Tom Tully *McGurney* • Alex Gerry *Uncle Louie* • Allyn Joslyn *George Miller* • Harold Gordon *Rabbi Roth* ■ *Dir* Michael Curtiz • *Scr* Frank Davis, Leonard Stern, Lewis Meltzer, from the play *Day of Atonement* by Samson Raphaelson

J

The Jazz Singer ★★ PG
Musical drama 1980 • US • Colour • 110min

This is a "rocked-up" remake of the world's first talkie. *Cracklin' Rosie* man Neil Diamond updates the old Al Jolson role, playing a cantor's son who wants to make it big in the rock business. Laurence Olivier is his understandably dubious dad. Given the "rocky" nature of the film, the title now seems pretty meaningless. But, then, that description could be applied to the whole film which, though adequate, remains more a monument to the egomania of musicians than a significant contribution to world cinema. DA *DVD*

Neil Diamond *Jess Robin/Yussel Rabinovitch* • Laurence Olivier *Cantor Rabinovitch* • Lucie Arnaz *Molly Bell* • Catlin Adams *Rivka Rabinovitch* • Franklyn Ajaye *Bubba* • Paul Nicholas *Keith Lennox* • Sully Boyar *Eddie Gibbs* ■ *Dir* Richard Fleischer • *Scr* Herbert Baker, Stephen H Foreman, from the play *Day of Atonement* by Samson Raphaelson

Je T'Aime, Je T'Aime ★★★
Science-fiction fantasy drama 1968 • Fr • Colour • 94min

Returning to the subjects of lapsing time and unreliable memory that had informed all his earlier features, Alain Resnais harnessed that old sci-fi standby, the time machine, to bring an extra dimension to this intriguing study of lost happiness, despair and death. Unfortunately, as the suicide survivor dispatched to retrace his past, Claude Rich struggles to make an impact amid the fragmentary recollections of his affair with Olga Georges-Picot, for whose demise he may be responsible. DP French +subtitles.

Claude Rich *Claude Ridder* • Olga Georges-Picot *Catrine* • Anouk Ferjac *Wiana Lust* • Annie Fargue *Agnès de Smet* • Bernard Fresson *Bernard Hannecart* • Marie-Blanche Vergne [Marie-Blanche Vergnes] *Marie-Noire Demoon* ■ *Dir* Alain Resnais • *Scr* Jacques Sternberg, Alain Resnais

Je, Tu, Il, Elle ★★★★
Drama 1974 • Bel • BW • 90min

Compulsive eating and a craving for sex go hand in hand in this psychological drama from Chantal Akerman. The debuting director's decision to play the lead is not only courageous, but also reinforces her status as a symbol for universal womanhood, as she struggles to make the transition from adolescence into adulthood.

This is a powerful study of anguish and identity. **DP** French +subtitles.

Chantal Akerman *Julie* • Niels Arestrup *Truckdriver* • Claire Wauthion *Woman's lover* ■ *Dir/Scr* Chantal Akerman

Je Vous Aime ★★
Comedy   1980 · Fr · Colour · 105min

Although this involved melodrama sets up Catherine Deneuve as an icon of independent womanhood, the men in her life are so weak that ditching them seems more like common sense than an act of female empowerment. Employing a complex network of flashbacks and excruciating exchanges, director Claude Berri shows how Deneuve assembled her entourage, demonstrating admirable control of his material, but makes Deneuve seem cold and strident rather than assuredly self-contained. **DP** French +subtitles.

Catherine Deneuve *Alice* • Jean-Louis Trintignant *Julien* • Gérard Depardieu *Patrick* • Serge Gainsbourg *Simon* • Alain Souchon *Claude* • Christian Marquand *Victor* • Isabelle Lacamp *Dorothée* ■ *Dir* Claude Berri • *Scr* Claude Berri, Michel Grisolia

Je Vous Salue, Marie ★★★
Drama   1984 · Fr/Swi/UK · Colour · 86min

In this impudent updating of the immaculate conception, Myriem Roussel, the daughter of a garage owner, discovers she is pregnant even though she has never slept with her boyfriend, cab driver Thierry Rode. Jean-Luc Godard's film was predictably condemned by the Pope, while various religious groups threatened cinemas and TV stations with blasphemy suits. But the picture itself is a charming, delicate and poetic piece, set to heavenly music by Bach and Dvorak. **AT** French +subtitles.

Myriem Roussel *Marie* • Thierry Rode *Joseph* • Philippe Lacoste *Angel Gabriel* • Manon Anderson *Girl* • Juliette Binoche *Juliette* • Malachi Jara Kohan *Jesus* • Johan Leysen *Professor* • Anne Gautier *Eva* ■ *Dir/Scr* Jean-Luc Godard

The Jealous God ★★12
Romantic drama   2005 · UK · Colour · 91min

This is a well-shot tale of tested faith, love and hypocrisy. Jason Merrells plays a Catholic schoolteacher in mid-1960s Yorkshire who sets tongues wagging when he begins an affair with Protestant librarian Mairead Carty. His sister-in-law (Denise Welch) is particularly aggrieved, since she's also got designs on the shy charmer. Though the project is entirely uncinematic, it's nicely acted and there's strong attention to period detail. **SF** Swearing, sex scenes. *DVD*

Jason Merrells *Vincent* • Denise Welch *Maureen* • Mairead Carty *Laura* • Andrew Dunn (2) *Matthew* • Pamela Cundell *Mrs Rosslea* • Marcia Warren *Mrs Dungarven* • William Ilkley *Paul* • Judy Flynn *Ruth* ■ *Dir* Steven Woodcock • *Scr* Steven Woodcock, from the novel by John Braine

Jealousy ★★12
Drama   2013 · Fr · BW · 72min

Veteran French director Philippe Garrel keeps this story of tangled Parisian relationships a family affair by casting his son, Louis, in the lead. Best-known for Bertolucci's *The Dreamers*, Garrel junior, as always, exudes a tousle-headed bohemian charm, this time as a struggling actor who leaves his partner and small daughter for husky-voiced Anna Mouglalis. It's shot on 35mm black-and-white, and the atmosphere is captivating, but the drama's something of a non-event. Chic yet exasperating, it's somehow quintessentially French – just not in a good way. **TJ** In French. Swearing. *DVD*

Louis Garrel *Louis* • Anna Mouglalis *Claudia* • Olga Milshtein *Charlotte* • Rebecca Convenant *Clothilde* ■ *Dir* Philippe Garrel • *Scr* Philippe Garrel, Marc Cholodenko, Caroline Deruas-Garrel, Arlette Langmann

Jealousy, Italian Style ★★★★
Comedy drama   1970 · It · Colour · 106min

Marcello Mastroianni won the best actor prize at Cannes for his work in this scattershot satire, which takes aim at just about every aspect of Italian social and cultural life. The plot is a hybrid of high opera and low Fellini: Mastroianni's doltish communist bricklayer is a close cousin of that great clown, Toto, and Monica Vitti's flower-seller is a knowing parody of a neorealist waif. Caught between them is Giancarlo Giannini's glibly charming pizza cook. **DP** Italian dubbed.

Marcello Mastroianni *Oreste* • Monica Vitti *Adelaide* • Giancarlo Giannini *Nello* • Manolo Zarzo [Mañuel Zarzo] *Uto* • Marisa Merlini *Silvana* • Hercules Cortez *Ambleto di Meo* • Josefina Serratosa *Antonia* ■ *Dir* Ettore Scola • *Scr* Furio Scarpelli, Age [Agenore Incrocci], Ettore Scola

Jean de Florette ★★★★★ PG
Period drama   1986 · Fr/It · Colour · 115min

The first part of Claude Berri's adaptation of Marcel Pagnol's novel *L'Eau des Collines* is, quite simply, a tour de force. The screenplay (by Berri and Gérard Brach) is wholly cinematic, Bruno Nuytten's shimmering cinematography avoids mere pictorialism, while Berri's direction captures both the pace of the changing seasons and the unique atmosphere of Provence. The acting is also of the highest order. Gérard Depardieu is perhaps a little too insistent in asserting the worthiness of the hunchback, but Yves Montand and Daniel Auteuil are outstanding as the scheming Soubeyrans. The second part *Manon des Sources* continued the tale. **DP** French +subtitles. Swearing. *DVD*

Yves Montand *César Soubeyran, Le Papet* • Gérard Depardieu *Jean de Florette [Cadoret]* • Daniel Auteuil *Ugolin Soubeyran, "Galignette"* • Elisabeth Depardieu *Aimée Cadoret* • Ernestine Mazurowna *Manon Cadoret* • Marcel Champel *Pique-Bouffigue* ■ *Dir* Claude Berri • *Scr* Gérard Brach, Claude Berri, from the novel *L'Eau des Collines* by Marcel Pagnol

Jeanne Dielman, 23 Quai du Commerce, 1080 Bruxelles ★★★★
Drama   1975 · Bel/Fr · Colour · 225min

Chantal Akerman made her name with this audacious exploration of bourgeois feminism. Delphine Seyrig gives a studied display of dispassionate normalness as the widowed housewife who makes ends meet by working afternoons as a prostitute. By shooting in long takes to capture each task in minute, real-time detail, Akerman renders the act of sleeping with a client just one more chore in Seyrig's daily routine. Yet, these rhythmic repetitions make the disrupted third day, with its climactic act of violence, all the more disturbing. **DP** French +subtitles.

Delphine Seyrig *Jeanne Dielman* • Jan Decorte *Sylvain Dielman* • Henri Storck *First caller* • Jacques Doniol-Valcroze *Second caller* • Yves Bical *Third caller* • Chantal Akerman *Voice of neighbour* ■ *Dir/Scr* Chantal Akerman

Jeanne Eagels ★★
Biographical drama   1957 · US · BW · 108min

Kim Novak does a good job of bringing out the anxieties of the 1920s stage (and screen) star Jeanne Eagels in this biopic. Three top screenwriters laboured on the dreary and contrived script but director George Sidney brings considerable visual flair to dramatic highlights – like the suicide of rival actress Elsie Desmond, played by Virginia Grey. Jeff Chandler supports as the carnival operator who pops in and out of Eagels's life. **AE**

Kim Novak *Jeanne Eagels* • Jeff Chandler *Sal Satori* • Agnes Moorehead *Madame Neilson* • Charles Drake *John Donahue* • Larry Gates *Al Brooks* • Virginia Grey *Elsie Desmond* • Gene Lockhart *Equity board president* • Joe De Santis *Frank Satori* ■ *Dir* George Sidney (2) • *Scr* Daniel Fuchs, Sonya Levien, John Fante, from a story by Daniel Fuchs

Jeanne la Pucelle ★★★★★ PG
Historical biographical drama   1994 · Fr · Colour · 237min

Divided into two instalments – *Les Batailles* and *Les Prisons* – Jacques Rivette's sprawling account of Joan of Arc's rise and fall demonstrates once more his mastery of the epic form. Refusing to indulge in mere period pageantry or religious speculation, he has produced a cinematic portrait to rank alongside those of Carl Th Dreyer (*The Passion of Joan of Arc*, 1928) and Robert Bresson (*Le Procès de Jeanne d'Arc*, 1962). As the Maid of Orleans, Sandrine Bonnaire glows with the strength of her conviction, whether rallying the troops of Dauphin André Marcon or testifying to the heavenly nature of the voices that inspired her. Gaining in power throughout, this is an awesome achievement. **DP** French +subtitles.

Sandrine Bonnaire *Jeanne* • André Marcon *Charles, Dauphin of France* • Jean-Louis Richard *Le Tremoille* • Marcel Bozonnet *Regnault de Chartres* • Didier Sauvegrain *Raoul de Gaucourt* • Jean-Pierre Lorit *Jean d'Alencon* ■ *Dir* Jacques Rivette • *Scr* Pascal Bonitzer, Christine Laurent

Jeannie ★★★ U
Romantic comedy   1941 · UK · BW · 100min

Known to millions as Janet in *Dr Finlay's Casebook*, Barbara Mullen made a hugely promising (but ultimately false) start to her film career in this charming comedy. As the bonny Scottish girl at the centre of a romantic tug-of-war between sales rep Michael Redgrave and wastrel Albert Lieven, she strikes a perfect balance between worldly innocence and innate sense. Redgrave revels in the chance to display his gift for comedy, while Lieven oozes smarmy charm. **DP**

Barbara Mullen *Jeannie McLean* • Michael Redgrave *Stanley Smith* • Wilfrid Lawson *James McLean* • Albert Lieven *Count Erich Von Wittgenstein* • Gus Mcnaughton *Angus Whitelaw* • Googie Withers *Laundry girl* ■ *Dir* Harold French • *Scr* Anatole de Grunwald, Roland Pertwee, from a play by Aimee Stuart

Jeepers Creepers ★★★★ 15
Horror   2001 · US/Ger · Colour · 86min

Victor Salva cleverly revitalises the slasher scenario by including an unknown ancient evil and fashioning the best nightmare avenue since Elm Street became a dead end. A road trip home turns hellish for brother-and-sister students Justin Long and Gina Philips when they disturb a supernatural figure and its body-part-snatching business. Instantly suspenseful from the start and bolstered by believable performances, Salva's unique flight of dark imagination is a terrific variation on the "psycho from hell" formula and a memorably gruesome horror fantasy. **AJ** *DVD*

Gina Phillips [Gina Philips] *Trish Jenner* • Justin Long *Darry Jenner* • Jonathan Breck *The Creeper* • Patricia Belcher *Jezelle Gay Hartman* • Brandon Smith *Sgt Davis Tubbs* • Eileen Brennan *The Cat Lady* ■ *Dir/Scr* Victor Salva

Jeepers Creepers 2 ★★★ 15
Horror thriller   2003 · US/Neth · Colour · 99min

In Victor Salva's campy sequel to his popular horror shocker, the flying flesh eater has got one more day to gorge on human body parts before his automatic hibernation cycle begins. What unfolds is a B-movie-style monster flick, as the creature disables a school bus and then starts picking off his chosen victims from the obnoxious teens within. The bickering youngsters provide plenty of tension as they try to formulate their escape, while the isolated, largely night-time setting adds to the overall sense of vulnerability and unease. Yet, for all its gory chills, the film is tongue-in-cheek and blackly comic. **SF** Violence, swearing. *DVD*

Ray Wise *Jack Taggart* • Jonathan Breck *The Creeper* • Eric Nenninger *Scott Braddock* • Garikayi "G K" Mutambirwa [Garikayi Mutambirwa] *Deaundre "Double D" Davis* • Nicki Aycox [Nicki Lynn Aycox] *Minxie Hayes* • Drew

Tyler Bell *Jonny Young* • Billy Aaron Brown *Andy "Bucky" Buck* • Kasan Butcher *Kimball "Big K" Ward* • Travis Schiffner *Izzy Bohen* ■ *Dir* Victor Salva • *Scr* Victor Salva, from his characters

Jeff, Who Lives at Home ★★★ 15
Comedy   2011 · US · Colour · 79min

A day in the life of a 30-something slacker is laid bare in this laid-back comedy. Jason Segel plays the dopehead who lives in his mother's basement and watches *Signs*, convinced he knows the secret to life. On an errand to the hardware store, bumps into his white-collar brother (*The Hangover*'s Ed Helms) and then, his sibling's unfaithful wife (Judy Greer). The writing/directing Duplass brothers (*Cyrus*) are focused on the struggle of two mama's boys faced with grown-up choices, though, inevitably, it's Susan Sarandon's matriarch who keeps the film anchored in reality, which only seems fitting. **SP** Violence, swearing, drug abuse. *DVD* *BL*

Jason Segel *Jeff* • Ed Helms *Pat* • Judy Greer *Linda* • Susan Sarandon *Sharon* • Rae Dawn Chong *Carol* • Steve Zissis *Steve* ■ *Dir/Scr* Jay Duplass, Mark Duplass

Jefferson in Paris ★★★ 12
Biographical drama   1995 · US · Colour · 133min

Nick Nolte bursts through the polite tapestry woven by director James Ivory and producer Ismail Merchant in this study of the hypocrisy inherent in the life of US president-to-be Thomas Jefferson. He drafted the Declaration of Independence asserting that all men are created equal, yet had children by his household slave (Thandie Newton). While American ambassador to France in the late 18th century, he also had an affair with a married artist (Greta Scacchi). That Nolte makes the man at all tolerable is an indication of his acting skills, but he can't hide the fact that he is too modern a performer for this period role. **TH** *DVD*

Nick Nolte *Thomas Jefferson* • Greta Scacchi *Maria Cosway* • Jean-Pierre Aumont *D'Hancarville* • Simon Callow *Richard Cosway* • Seth Gilliam *James Hemings* • Thandie Newton *Sally Hemings* • James Earl Jones *Madison Hemings* • Michael Lonsdale [Madison Lonsdale] *Louis XVI* • Gwyneth Paltrow *Patsy Jefferson* • Estelle Eonnett *Polly Jefferson* ■ *Dir* James Ivory • *Scr* Ruth Prawer Jhabvala

Jeffrey ★★★★ 15
Romantic comedy   1995 · US · Colour · 89min

Paranoid gay man Steven Weber turns celibate due to the Aids threat, and then meets the hunk of his dreams, Michael T Weiss, who is HIV-positive. Director Christopher Ashley's poignant adaptation is not only daring and sympathetic but extremely funny: a pitch-perfect look at New York gay society facing a common enemy with suitably mordant humour. Patrick Stewart is a knockout as the flamboyant queen who advises Weber to take a chance rather than opt out of life altogether. **AJ** *DVD*

Steven Weber *Jeffrey* • Michael T Weiss *Steve* • Irma St Paule *Mother Teresa* • Patrick Stewart *Sterling* • Robert Klein *Skip Winkley* • Christine Baranski *Ann Marwood Bartle* • Bryan Batt *Darius* • Sigourney Weaver *Debra Moorhouse* • Nathan Lane *Father Dan* • Olympia Dukakis *Mrs Marcangelo* ■ *Dir* Christopher Ashley • *Scr* Paul Rudnick, from the play by Paul Rudnick

Jem and the Holograms ★ PG
Musical fantasy adventure   2015 · US · Colour · 118min

This musical drama based on a 1980s cartoon charts the rags-to-riches story of Jerrica Benton (Aubrey Peeples), a teenage girl who is catapulted to stardom after a YouTube upload goes viral. Juliette Lewis is lots of fun as a bitchy narcissistic pop mogul masterminding Jerrica's unbelievable megastardom after two pop-up concerts. A suitable counterpoint to the charming reluctant superstar. But the film is just too long and unconvincing, offering very little in terms of drama or believability. **SC** Brief swearing.

Aubrey Peeples *Jerrica/Jem* • Molly Ringwald *Aunt Bailey* • Juliette Lewis *Erica Raymond* • Ryan Guzman *Rio* ■ *Dir* Jon M Chu • *Scr* Ryan Landels

J'Embrasse Pas ★★★ 18
Drama   1991 · Fr · Colour · 110min

Although they're always technically impeccable, the films of André Téchiné are invariably rather cold and detached. Consequently, it's hard to identify here with Manuel Blanc, the country mouse who comes to Paris hoping to make it in the movies and ends up on the streets as a rent boy. Clearly Blanc is faced with an impossible task in trying to salvage scenes from the excellent Philippe Noiret, but his own acting deficiencies don't help. Emmanuelle Béart provides some soul amid the degradation and desperation. **DP** French +subtitles. Swearing.

Philippe Noiret *Romain* • Emmanuelle Béart *Ingrid* • Manuel Blanc *Pierre* • Hélène Vincent *Evelyne* • Yvan Desny [Ivan Desny] *Dimitri* • Christophe Bernard *Le Mac* ■ *Dir* André Téchiné • *Scr* André Téchiné, Jacques Nolot, Michel Grisolia, from a story by Jacques Nolot

Jennie Gerhardt ★★★
Melodrama   1933 · US · BW · 85min

Romantic melodrama weepies involving a humble maid with a past and the son of the household seldom disappoint. This one, from a novel by Theodore Dreiser, stars Sylvia Sidney, who suffered so painfully in Dreiser's *An American Tragedy* and who once famously said of her career that she was "paid by the tear". She plays a victim of poverty, who falls pregnant but loses the father to an accident before they can marry. Finding work as a maidservant, she and Donald Cook fall in love, but her past presents an obstacle. Adequate direction, excellent supporting cast. **RK**

Sylvia Sidney *Jennie Gerhardt* • Donald Cook *Lester Kane* • Mary Astor *Letty Pace* • Edward Arnold *Senator Brander* • HB Warner *William Gerhardt* • Louise Carter *Mrs Gerhardt* ■ *Dir* Marion Gering • *Scr* SK Lauren, Frank Partos, from the novel by Theodore Dreiser

Jennifer ★★
Crime drama   1953 · US · BW · 70min

The careers of married couple Ida Lupino and Howard Duff were at a low ebb when they made this slow-moving mystery in which Lupino, as a woman who has taken on the job of caretaker at a gloomy mansion, spends endless periods wandering the house in a quest to find out what happened to her predecessor, who mysteriously disappeared. The under-nourished sets, starkly lit for James Wong Howe's camera, betray the modest budget. **TV**

Ida Lupino *Agnes* • Howard Duff *Jim* • Robert Nichols *Orin* • Mary Shipp *Lorna* • Ned Glass *Grocery clerk* • Kitty McHugh *Landlady* • Russ Conway *Gardener* • Lorna Thayer *Grocery clerk* • Matt Dennis ■ *Dir* Joel Newton *Scr* Virginia Myers

Jennifer ★ 15
Horror   1978 · US · Colour · 86min

This terrible *Carrie* imitation substitutes snakes for telekinesis. Abused by her religious fanatic father Jeff Corey, withdrawn Lisa Pelikan also puts up with continual harassment from her high school classmates. It isn't long before she's using her supernatural power to call on the serpent gods to attack her tormentors. *Psycho's* John Gavin, American game show host Bert Convey and Hollywood glamour queen Nina Foch are on hand to elicit scares, but fail miserably. **AJ**

Lisa Pelikan *Jennifer Baylor* • Bert Convy *Jeff Reed* • Nina Foch *Mrs Calley* • Amy Johnston *Sandra Tremayne* ■ *Dir* Brice Mack • *Scr* Kay Cousins Johnson, from a story by Steve Krantz

Jennifer Eight ★★★ 15
Thriller   1992 · US · Colour · 119min

This thriller disappeared without trace, despite the fact that the leads are Andy

Garcia and Uma Thurman. Thurman is effective as a blind woman who hears a murder and may be in danger herself, while Garcia gives his usual charismatic turn as the cop convinced the case is linked to one he fouled up years before. Some of the twists are far-fetched, but there's still plenty to keep followers of thrillers and fans of the two stars happy. **JB** Swearing, violence, sex scenes. **DVD**

Andy Garcia *John Berlin* • Uma Thurman *Helena Robertson* • Lance Henriksen *Freddy Ross* • Kathy Baker *Margie Ross* • Graham Beckel *John Taylor* • Kevin Conway *Citrine* • John Malkovich *St Anne* • Perry Lang *Travis* ■ *Dir/Scr* Bruce Robinson

Jennifer on My Mind ★
Black comedy   1971 · US · Colour · 85min

This ghastly drugs film was one of many made as the Summer of Love crashed and burned, with Michael Brandon and Tippy Walker as a rootless drifter and a rich girl who become pot-smoking partners when they meet up in Venice, then graduate to harder stuff when they get back home. The dire script is by Erich Segal, of *Love Story* fame, and is of interest solely because of an early small role for Robert De Niro. **DA**

Michael Brandon *Marcus* • Tippy Walker *Jenny* • Lou Gilbert *Max* • Steve Vinovich *Ornstein* • Robert De Niro *Gypsy cab driver* ■ *Dir* Noel Black • *Scr* Erich Segal, from the novel *Heir* by Roger L Simon

Jennifer's Body ★★ 15
Comedy horror   2009 · US · Colour · 98min

The horror of *Carrie* and the humour of *Heathers* combine to mediocre effect in this tale of a small-town beauty who becomes possessed by a demon. Megan Fox (*Transformers*) stars as Jennifer, the high-school super bitch whose appetite for nastiness reaches scarier levels when she starts feasting on the blood of teenage boys. Writer Diablo Cody's script delves into the world of adolescent cliques and cruelty, but the teen-speak dialogue is overplayed and less whip-smart than in her Oscar-winning screenplay for *Juno*. Fox also fails to convince as the *femme fatale*, and the film ultimately ends up merely replicating the genre conventions it sets out to satirise. **TeS** Violence, swearing, sex scenes, nudity. **DVD**

Megan Fox *Jennifer Check* • Amanda Seyfried *Anita "Needy" Lesnicky* • Johnny Simmons *Chip* • Adam Brody *Nikolai* • JK Simmons *Mr Wroblewski* • Amy Sedaris *Needy's mom* ■ *Dir* Karyn Kusama • *Scr* Diablo Cody

Jenny Kissed Me ★★★ 15
Drama   1984 · Aus · Colour · 99min

Director Brian Trenchard-Smith here offers a sordid slice of Melbourne life. Ten-year-old Jenny, played by Tamsin West, has a close relationship with mother Deborra-Lee Furness's boyfriend, Ivar Kants. Although hardly creditable, the drama is just about held together by the director's uncompromising portrait of inner-city squalor and by Furness's compelling performance as she is driven into prostitution and drugs by despair. **DP**

Deborra-Lee Furness *Carol Grey* • Ivar Kants *Lindsay Fenton* • Tamsin West *Jenny Grey* • Paula Duncan *Gaynor Roberts* • Steven Grives *Mal Evans* ■ *Dir* Brian Trenchard-Smith • *Scr* Judith Colquhoun, Warwick Hind, Alan Lake

Jeopardy ★★★
Melodrama   1953 · US · BW · 68min

This suspense melodrama was one of the last films John Sturges directed before he established his reputation with *Escape from Fort Bravo*. During a camping vacation on a remote Mexican beach, husband and father Barry Sullivan is pinioned in the water by fallen timber. With just four hours before the tide comes in, wife Barbara Stanwyck drives off to find assistance. Unfortunately, she runs into fleeing killer Ralph Meeker. Despite its slender running time, credibility flies out the window about halfway through. Until then, however, this is a taut and exciting little movie, with Stanwyck gutsy and subtle. **RK**

Barbara Stanwyck *Helen Stilwin* • Barry Sullivan *Doug Stilwin* • Ralph Meeker *Lawson* • Lee Aaker *Bobby Stilwin* • Bud Wolfe *Lieutenant's driver* • Saul Gorss *Captain's driver* • Bob Castro *Machine gunner* • Paul Fierro *Mexican lieutenant* ■ *Dir* John Sturges • *Scr* Mel Dinelli, from the radio play *A Question of Time* by Maurice Zimm

Jeremiah Johnson ★★★ PG
Western adventure 1972 · US · Colour · 111min

It was a bold move for heart-throb Robert Redford to hide his features behind a full set of whiskers for his portrayal of a 19th-century mountain man. Based on a real-life trapper, Jeremiah is a disillusioned army deserter who takes to the wilds of Colorado in the 1840s in the name of self-sufficiency and solitude. Sydney Pollack's admirable film is a meditative portrait, majestically shot on location in Utah, that takes a deeper look at man versus nature. Deficient in both action and dialogue, certainly, but look at that view. **AC** **DVD**

Robert Redford *Jeremiah Johnson* • Will Geer *Bear Claw* • Stefan Gierasch *Del Gue* • Allyn Ann McLerie *Crazy woman* • Charles Tyner *Robidoux* • Josh Albee *Caleb* • Joaquin Martinez *Paints His Shirt Red* • Paul Benedict *Reverend* ■ *Dir* Sydney Pollack • *Scr* John Milius, Edward Anhalt, from the novel *Mountain Man* by Vardis Fisher, from the story *Crow Killer* by Raymond W Thorp

Jeremy ★
Romance   1973 · US · Colour · 90min

Dripping with sentimentality, this is *Love Story* without the style, and how it won writer/director Arthur Barron a prize at Cannes for best first feature is anybody's guess. Robby Benson and Glynnis O'Connor play a budding cellist and ballet student respectively whose burgeoning romance is threatened by parental intervention. What makes this so hard to watch with a straight face are the trite protestations and the achingly tasteful approach to sex. (The chess game seduction is a minor kitsch classic.) **DP**

Robby Benson *Jeremy* • Glynnis O'Connor *Susan* • Len Bari *Ralph* • Leonardo Cimino *Cello teacher* • Ned Wilson *Susan's father* • Chris Bohn *Jeremy's father* • Pat Wheel *Jeremy's mother* ■ *Dir/Scr* Arthur Barron

Jericho ★★★ U
Musical drama   1937 · UK · Colour · 71min

Anxious to atone for the failings of *Sanders of the River* (1935), Paul Robeson negotiated final cut on this study of injustice and redemption, which he always counted among his favourite films, as its positive depiction of black people stood in such stark contrast to the stereotypical portraits presented in so many movies. A disgraced Robeson jumps bail and escapes to North Africa with buddy Wallace Ford, leaving trusting captain Henry Wilcoxon to carry the can. Unfortunately, the finale sends out mixed messages, while Thornton Freeland's over-emphatic direction ensures this hardly lives up to the poster boast of being "the most spectacular adventure picture ever made". **DP** **DVD**

Paul Robeson *Cpl Jericho Jackson* • Henry Wilcoxon *Capt Mack* • Wallace Ford *Mike Clancy* • Kouka *Gara* • John Laurie *Hassan* • James Carew *Maj JR Barnes* ■ *Dir* Thornton Freeland • *Scr* Robert N Lee, Peter Ruric, George Barraud, from a story by Walter Futter

The Jericho Mile ★★★★ 12
Prison drama   1979 · US · Colour · 97min

This gripping if implausible movie – Michael Mann's debut as a director – stars Peter Strauss as a convicted murderer and loner who spends his time running around the prison perimeter fence. A warden notices his talent for running and organises a race against some Olympic hopefuls. It's a little fable about personal liberty that falls short of outright sentimentality, thanks to Strauss's ambiguous hero. **AT**

Peter Strauss *Larry "Rain" Murphy* • Richard Lawson *RC Stiles* • Roger E Mosley *"Cotton" Crown* • Brian Dennehy *"Dr D"* • Billy Green Bush *Warden Earl Gulliver* • Ed Lauter *Jerry Beloit* ■ *Dir* Michael Mann • *Scr* Patrick J Nolan, Michael Mann, from a story by Nolan

The Jerk ★★★★ 15
Comedy   1979 · US · Colour · 89min

Has Steve Martin made a funnier film? Fans of this insist he hasn't, as Martin takes on the role of simple-minded and naive Navin Johnson, who suddenly discovers that his black parents aren't his natural kith and kin. He takes his dog and leaves the plantation to make his way in a world that is as loopy as he is. There are some heavenly jokes (especially the one where he makes a fortune inventing an absurd nose support for spectacles), and Martin is in best "manic" mode. **TH** **DVD** **Blu**

Steve Martin *Navin Johnson* • Bernadette Peters *Marie Kimball* • Catlin Adams *Patty Bernstein* • Mabel King *Mother* • Richard Ward *Father* • Dick Anthony Williams *Taj* • Bill Macy *Stan Fox* • M Emmet Walsh *Madman* • Dick O'Neill *Frosty* • Carl Reiner ■ *Dir* Carl Reiner • *Scr* Steve Martin, Carl Gottlieb, Michael Elias

The Jerky Boys ★ 15
Comedy   1995 · US · Colour · 78min

From the same bad-taste school as *Wayne's World*'s comes this TV sitcom, cartoon, comic book and platinum record-selling duo. Johnny Brennan and Kamal Ahmed play the moronic pair of phone pranksters, who use crank calls to be sociable and bluff their way into Mafia high society, incurring the wrath of New York crime boss Alan Arkin. This featherlight nonsense shows a distinct lack of comic inspiration. **AJ** **DVD**

Johnny Brennan [John G Brennan] *Johnny Brennan* • Kamal Ahmed • Alan Arkin *Lazarro* • William Hickey *Uncle Freddy* • Alan North *Mickey* • Brad Sullivan *Worzic* • James Lorinz *Brett Weir* • Suzanne Shepherd *Mrs B* ■ *Dir* James Melkonian • *Scr* James Melkonian, Rich Wilkes, John G Brennan [Johnny Brennan], Kamal Ahmed

Jerry and Tom ★★★ 15
Black comedy   1998 · Can · Colour · 92min

Actor-turned-director Saul Rubinek takes a stroll into Tarantino territory for this pleasingly black and quite stylish comedy. The film opens with two hitmen – Sam Rockwell and Joe Mantegna – waiting to complete their latest assignment with the desperately wisecracking Peter Riegert. We then go back in time to see how the two became partners. Rubinek seamlessly blends the flashbacks together and still finds time to put some flesh on the bones of the duo's victims. **JF**

Joe Mantegna *Tom* • Sam Rockwell *Jerry* • Charles Durning *Vic* • Maury Chaykin *Billy* • Peter Riegert *Stanley* • William H Macy *Karl* • Ted Danson *Guy who loved Vicki* ■ *Dir* Saul Rubinek • *Scr* Rick Cleveland

Jerry Maguire ★★★★ 15
Romantic comedy   1996 · US · Colour · 133min

Writer/director Cameron Crowe here balances one of the best performances of Tom Cruise's career with a clutch of superb supporting turns. Add a witty and tear-jerking script and the result is an unusual romantic comedy drama. Cruise is Jerry Maguire, a sports agent who, guilt-ridden one night about how he and his colleagues treat sports stars as commodities, writes a mission statement which effectively costs him his job. Cruise's relationships with his sole remaining client (a marvellous, Oscar-winning turn by Cuba Gooding Jr), the woman who stands by him (Renee Zellweger) and her adorable son (Jonathan Lipnicki) bring an infectious warmth to the film, which introduced the world to the catchphrase: "Show me the money!" **JB** Swearing, a sex scene, brief nudity. **DVD** **Blu**

Tom Cruise *Jerry Maguire* • Cuba Gooding Jr *Rod Tidwell* • Renee Zellweger [Renée Zellweger] *Dorothy Boyd* • Kelly Preston *Avery Bishop* • Jerry O'Connell *Frank Cushman* • Jay Mohr *Bob Sugar* • Bonnie Hunt *Laurel Boyd* • Regina King *Marcee Tidwell* • Jonathan Lipnicki *Ray Boyd* • Todd Louiso *Chad the nanny* • Eric Stoltz *Ethan Valhere* ■ *Dir/Scr* Cameron Crowe

J

Jersey Boys ★★★ 15
Musical based on a true story
2014 · US · Colour · 128min

Clint Eastwood takes the hit musical about Frankie Valli and the Four Seasons from stage to screen, but he's not the kind of director to fall for glitz and glamour in telling their story. He's more at home on the mean streets of 1950s New Jersey, where Valli (John Lloyd Young, who played the role on Broadway) and wise-guy pal Tommy (Vincent Piazza) are caught between a life of crime and chart-topping greatness. Eastwood doesn't fully exploit his medium to flesh out the personal conflicts in the band, but his rough-and-ready style aptly reflects his young subjects, who are brimming with roguish charm. SP Swearing, sexual references, drug abuse. DVD Blu-ray

John Lloyd Young *Frankie Valli* • Erich Bergen *Bob Gaudio* • Michael Lomenda *Nick Massi* • Vincent Piazza *Tommy DeVito* • Christopher Walken *Gyp DeCarlo* • Mike Doyle *Bob Crewe* • Renée Marino *Mary* • Erica Piccininni *Lorraine* ■ *Dir* Clint Eastwood • *Scr* Rick Elice, Marshall Brickman, from their musical book

Jersey Girl ★★ 15
Romantic comedy
1992 · US · Colour · 91min

Jami Gertz stars as a girl from New Jersey who's looking for a way out of her mundane existence, and the opportunity arrives when she bumps into businessman Dylan McDermott at a Manhattan Mercedes showroom. Director David Burton Morris's bland movie falls down through lack of star power: Gertz comes across as a whining opportunist, and her scenes with McDermott lack chemistry. Some charm, but not enough to make it compelling viewing. JB

Jami Gertz *Toby Mastallone* • Dylan McDermott *Sal* • Sheryl Lee *Tara* • Joseph Bologna *Bennie Mastallone* • Joseph Mazzello *Jason* • Aida Turturro *Angie* • Molly Price *Cookie* ■ *Dir* David Burton Morris • *Scr* Gina Wendkos

Jersey Girl ★★★ 12
Comedy drama
2003 · US · Colour · 98min

This reunites Ben Affleck with his *Chasing Amy* director Kevin Smith, and sees indie icon Smith going mainstream, and tough guy Affleck going mawkish. But the result, if slushy, isn't as bad as that might sound. In fact, this is probably Affleck's best performance in recent years. He plays a tough New York PR man who is literally left holding the baby when his wife (Jennifer Lopez) dies in childbirth. The film then follows the tough time he has balancing being a single dad with his career. Liv Tyler plays the new girl in his life, while George Carlin is his sage-like father. DA Swearing. DVD

Ben Affleck *Ollie Trinke* • Raquel Castro *Gertie Trinke* • Liv Tyler *Maya* • George Carlin *Bart Trinke* • Jason Biggs *Arthur Brickman* • Jennifer Lopez *Gertrude Steiney* • Mike Starr *Block* • Stephen Root *Greenie* • Jason Lee *PR exec no 1* • Matt Damon *PR exec no 2* • Will Smith ■ *Dir/Scr* Kevin Smith (2)

Jerusalem ★★★
Period drama
1996 · Swe/Den/Fin/Nor/Ice · Colour · 168min

Bille August adapted this epic of rural discontent and religious fervour from the novel by Nobel Prize-winning author, Selma Lagerlöf, who had based her story on the actual 19th-century trek made by a group of Swedes to Jerusalem after they encountered the famed revivalist, Hellgum. Although Sven-Bertil Taube impresses as the impassioned preacher, it's the director's then wife, Pernilla August, who carries the drama as she feuds with Ulf Friberg for control of the family farm. This handsome period piece is occasionally sluggish. DP Swedish +subtitles.

Ulf Friberg *Ingmar* • Maria Bonnevie *Gertrud* • Pernilla August *Karin* • Max von Sydow *Vicar* • Olympia Dukakis *Mrs Gordon* • Reine Brynolfsson *Tim* • Lena Endre *Barbro* • Jan Mybrand *Gabriel* • Sven-Bertil Taube *Hellgum* ■ *Dir* Bille August • *Scr* Bille August, from the novel by Selma Lagerlöf

The Jerusalem File ★ PG
Political thriller
1972 · US/Is · Colour · 92min

John Flynn's second feature is a cynical slice of anti-Arab propaganda. Although it purports to steer a middle course, the script's sympathies clearly lie with the Israeli characters encountered by archaeology student Bruce Davison as he picks his way through the intricacies of the Middle Eastern situation in the aftermath of the Six Day War. Raoul Coutard's photography has an immediacy that perfectly complements the seriousness of the subject, but the sporadic outbursts of *Boys' Own* adventure sit uncomfortably with the political proselytising. DP

Bruce Davison *David* • Nicol Williamson *Lang* • Daria Halprin *Nurit* • Donald Pleasence *Samuels* • Ian Hendry *Mayers* • Koya Yair Rubin *Barak* ■ *Dir* John Flynn • *Scr* Troy Kennedy Martin • *Cinematographer* Raoul Coutard

Jesse James ★★★★ U
Classic western
1939 · US · Colour · 105min

This western virtually canonises notorious outlaw Jesse James, here sympathetically portrayed by Tyrone Power as a glamorous Robin Hood-style figure of the Old West, riding out to right wrongs alongside his brother Frank, played by Henry Fonda. The rich 20th Century-Fox Technicolor is superb, and whether the real Jesse was as dashing or handsome as Power is irrelevant: this is stirring stuff, brilliantly directed by Henry King, one of the great masters of on-screen Americana. Nunnally Johnson's screenplay ignores most of the facts, but who cares? Henry Fonda reprised his role the following year in *The Return of Frank James*. TS

Tyrone Power *Jesse James* • Henry Fonda *Frank James* • Nancy Kelly *Zee* • Randolph Scott *Will Wright* • Henry Hull *Major Rufus Cobb* • Brian Donlevy *Barshee* • John Carradine *Bob Ford* • Jane Darwell *Mrs Samuels* ■ *Dir* Henry King • *Scr* Nunnally Johnson, from historical data asembled by Rosalind Schaeffer, Jo Frances James

Jessica ★ 18
Romantic comedy drama
1962 · US/It/Fr · Colour · 104min

After her striking performance opposite John Wayne in *Rio Bravo*, Angie Dickinson deserved a major big-screen career. Instead, she ended up in films like this limp farce, playing the American midwife in a Sicilian village who prompts the jealous women into a love strike to get rid of her: no babies, no work. This was considered naughty enough in its day to be X-certificated for adults only. AE

Angie Dickinson *Jessica* • Maurice Chevalier *Father Antonio* • Noël-Noël *Old Crupi* • Gabriele Ferzetti *Edmondo Raumo* • Sylva Koscina *Nunzia Tuffi* • Agnes Moorehead *Maria Lombardo* ■ *Dir* Jean Negulesco • *Scr* Edith Sommer, from the novel *The Midwife of Pont Cléry* by Flora Sandstrom

Jesus Christ Superstar ★★ PG
Musical
1973 · US · Colour · 102min

Andrew Lloyd Webber and Tim Rice's ground-breaking musical chronicling the last seven days of Jesus Christ works better on stage than screen, judging from director Norman Jewison's worthy adaptation. The score is brilliant, and Ted Neeley, Carl Anderson and Yvonne Elliman give great performances. However, they're undermined by Jewison's attempts to give the Passion Play a mod credibility. The result is a disappointment that would look less shallow without such a wrong-headed, anachronistic approach. AJ DVD

Ted Neeley *Jesus Christ* • Carl Anderson *Judas Iscariot* • Yvonne Elliman *Mary Magdalene* • Barry Dennen *Pontius Pilate* • Bob Bingham *Caiaphas* ■ *Dir* Norman Jewison • *Scr* Melvyn Bragg, Norman Jewison, from the musical by Tim Rice, Andrew Lloyd Webber • *Cinematographer* Douglas Slocombe

Jesus of Montreal ★★★★ 18
Satirical drama
1989 · Can · Colour · 114min

Having charted *The Decline of the American Empire* in his previous picture, Québecois director Denys Arcand turned his attention to the Kingdom of God in this scathing satire. Mammon and the mores of the modern world also come in for denunciation as actor Lothaire Bluteau revives the spirit of Christ the Social Radical while revamping a long-running passion play. Touching on everything from religious hypocrisy and artistic integrity, to petty bureaucracy and the public's insatiable appetite for sensation, this compelling parable forces you to re-evaluate as you laugh. DP French +subtitles. DVD

Lothaire Bluteau *Daniel* • Catherine Wilkening *Mireille* • Johanne-Marie Tremblay *Constance* • Rémy Girard *Martin* • Robert Lepage *René* • Gilles Pelletier *Father Leclerc* • Yves Jacques *Richard Cardinal* • Denys Arcand *The Judge* ■ *Dir/Scr* Denys Arcand

Jesus' Son ★★★ 18
Road movie
1999 · US/Can · Colour · 103min

The hero of Alison Maclean's rambling but accomplished road movie is known merely as "FH". Suffice to say that this is not exactly a term of endearment - more an indication of Billy Crudup's cluelessness as he embarks on a drug-fuelled odyssey through 1970s America. Less a coherent drama than a collection of bizarre vignettes, the bitty narrative introduces a rogue's gallery of misfits whose unpredictable behaviour embroils Crudup in all manner of criminal activity. NS DVD

Billy Crudup *FH* • Samantha Morton *Michelle* • Greg Germann *Dr Shanis* • Denis Leary *Wayne* • Jack Black *Georgie* • Will Patton *John Smith* • Holly Hunter *Mira* • Dennis Hopper *Bill* ■ *Dir* Alison Maclean • *Scr* Elizabeth Cuthrell, David Urrutia, Oren Moverman, from a book of short stories by Denis Johnson

Jet Attack ★ U
War drama
1958 · US · BW · 68min

One of the six B-programme-fillers director Edward L Cahn delivered in 1958, this is interesting chiefly for its use of faded names John Agar and Audrey Totter rather than its plot about a jet scientist whose plane is shot down over Korea. A season of Cahn movies would reveal most of his films to be low-grade junk. This is no exception. TS

John Agar *Tom Arnett* • Audrey Totter *Tanya* • Gregory Walcott *Bill* • James Dobson *Sandy* • Leonard Strong *Major Wan* ■ *Dir* Edward L Cahn • *Scr* Orville H Hampton, from a story by Mark Hanna

Jet Storm ★★ PG
Drama
1959 · UK · BW · 87min

On a plane to New York, Richard Attenborough accuses a fellow passenger of killing his daughter in a hit-and-run accident. When Captain Stanley Baker investigates, it emerges that Attenborough has planted a bomb on board. Cue general hysteria. Despite the other passengers' mini-dramas - David Kossoff's Holocaust survivor, for instance - this is a star turn for Attenborough, who brings a convincing complexity to the role of bomber and bereft father. The film's moralising and eventual payoff are hard to swallow, however. AT DVD

Richard Attenborough *Ernest Tilley* • Stanley Baker *Captain Bardow* • Hermione Baddeley *Mrs Satterly* • Bernard Braden *Otis Randolf* • Diane Cilento *Angelica Como* • Barbara Kelly *Edwina Randolf* • David Kossoff *Dr Bergstein* • Virginia Maskell *Pam Leyton* • Harry Secombe *Binky Meadows* ■ *Dir* Cy Endfield • *Scr* Cy Endfield, Sigmund Miller, from a story by Sigmund Miller

La Jetée ★★★★★ PG
Classic science fiction
1962 · Fr · BW · 26min

Composed almost exclusively of still photographs, Chris Marker's classic of post-apocalyptic science fiction makes for unforgettable viewing. Beginning with the childhood memory of a woman's face, the film traces Davos Hanich's efforts to uncover the meaning of this haunting image. Exploring many of the themes found in the *ciné-romans* of Alain Resnais, Marker uses photomontage to disturbing effect, but even more devastating is the one simple but indelible live-action sequence. A unique exploration of time, memory and vision. DP French +subtitles. DVD

Hélène Chatelain *The woman* • Davos Hanich *The man* • Jacques Ledoux *The experimenter* • Jean Négroni *Narrator* ■ *Dir/Scr* Chris Marker • *Editor* Jean Ravel • *Music* Trevor Duncan

Jetsons: the Movie ★★★ U
Science-fiction animation
1990 · US · Colour · 78min

Hanna-Barbera's less successful flipside of *The Flintstones* were the Space Age equivalent. Atom-powered ovens, robot vacuum cleaners, jet-propelled cars and flying saucer-shaped houses, the Jetson family has it all. What the film doesn't have is a strong story, just a thinly disguised environmental tract about furry space creatures losing their homes due to an asteroid mining operation. The songs are instantly forgettable, the ecology issue is no substitute for the original 1960s-themed whimsy, but the animation is colourful. AJ DVD

George O'Hanlon *George Jetson* • Mel Blanc *Mr Spacely* • Penny Singleton *Jane Jetson* • Tiffany *Judy Jetson* • Patric Zimmerman *Elroy Jetson* • Don Messick *Astro* • Jean Vanderpyl *Rosie the Robot* ■ *Dir* William Hanna, Joseph Barbera • *Scr* Dennis Marks, additional dialogue Carl Sautter

Jeune & Jolie ★★★ 18
Drama
2013 · Fr · Colour · 89min

Not in the class of *Swimming Pool* or *8 Women*, this drama from François Ozon about 17-year-old Parisian Isabelle (Marine Vacth), who sees a lucrative future in prostitution, is one of the director's middling works. Despite such ostensibly dark subject matter, the film keeps a non-judgemental distance, portraying Isabelle as an otherwise sensible middle-class girl with a taste for designer clothes. The film documents her journey with a refreshing sense of realism, but, while she is undoubtedly both young and beautiful, Vacth lacks empathy as a lead and the songs on the soundtrack are disappointingly literal. DW French +subtitles. DVD Blu-ray

Marine Vacth *Isabelle* • Géraldine Pailhas *Sylvie* • Frédéric Pierrot *Patrick* • Charlotte Rampling *Alice* • Johan Leysen *Georges* ■ *Dir/Scr* François Ozon • *Cinematographer* Pascal Marti

Le Jeune Werther ★★★ 15
Drama
1992 · Fr · Colour · 90min

There isn't an adult in sight in this canny updating of Goethe's novel, *The Sorrows of Young Werther*. Determined to know why their classmate committed suicide, Ismaël Jolé-Ménébhi and Thomas Brémond soon find themselves experiencing the same pangs of unrequited love for the elusive Miren Capello. True to the Romantic spirit of the original, yet echoing the argot and attitudes of 1990s French youth, Jacques Doillon's rite-of-passage picture captures the innocence of first love while remaining refreshingly free from corny sentiment. DP French +subtitles.

Ismaël Jolé-Ménébhi *Ismael* • Marabelle Rousseau *Mirabelle* • Thomas Brémond *Theo* • Miren Capello *Miren* • Faye Anastasia *Faye* • Pierre Mezerette *Pierre* • Simon Clavière *Simon* ■ *Dir* Jacques Doillon • *Scr* Jacques Doillon, from the novel *The Sorrows of Young Werther* by JW von Goethe

Jeux Interdits ★★★★★ 12
Drama
1953 · Fr · BW · 119min

Named best foreign language film at the 1952 Oscars and awarded the Golden Lion at Venice, this is the most moving study of childhood innocence ever made. Delicately treading the line between insight and sentimentality, René Clément coaxes wondrous performances out of five-year-old Brigitte Fossey and 11-year-old Georges Poujouly (found in a camp for underprivileged kids) as the orphan and farmer's boy who cope with the traumas of the Nazi occupation by building a cemetery for martyrs, which they sanctify with totems taken from the neighbouring graveyard. Simple, poetic and painfully honest, this is one of the gems of French cinema. DP French +subtitles. DVD

Georges Poujouly *Michel Dolle* • Brigitte Fossey *Paulette* • Amédée *Francis Gouard* • Laurence Badie *Berthe Dolle* • Suzanne Courtal *Madame Dolle* • Lucien Hubert *Dolle, the father* • Jacques Marin *Georges Dolle* • André Wasley *Gouard, the father* ■ *Dir* René Clément • *Scr* René Clément, Jean Aurenche, Pierre Bost, Francois Boyer, from the novel *Les Jeux Inconnus* by Francois Boyer

Jew Süss ★★★
Period drama 1934 · UK · BW · 105min

Lion Feuchtwanger's pro-Jewish 1925 novel was adapted for this comparatively lavish British production with an obvious regard to the rise of Fascism in Germany. Set in 18th-century Württemberg, Joseph "Jew Süss" Oppenheimer has risen to a position of power and influence in the Jewish community, but how will he react to the accusation that he is not really a Jew? The great German actor Conrad Veidt, exiled in England with his Jewish wife, is splendid in the title role, and the rest of the cast, including Cedric Hardwicke and Gerald du Maurier, are good. RB

Conrad Veidt *Joseph "Jew Süss" Oppenheimer* • Benita Hume *Marie Auguste* • Frank Vosper *Duke Karl Alexander* • Cedric Hardwicke *Rabbi Gabriel* • Gerald du Maurier *Wessensee* • Pamela Ostrer *Naomi Oppenheimer* • Paul Graetz *Landauer* ■ *Dir* Lothar Mendes • *Scr* Dorothy Farnum, AR Rawlinson, from the novel *Jud Süss* by Lion Feuchtwanger

The Jewel of the Nile ★★★★PG
Action adventure 1985 · US · Colour · 105min

The sequel to *Romancing the Stone* re-teams stars Michael Douglas, Kathleen Turner and Danny DeVito, and does so without falling into too many of the usual sequel pitfalls. Turner has become bored with all the lovey-dovey stuff and jumps at the chance of hitting the exploration trail once again, at odds with Douglas but determined to get even as he chases after a gem called the Jewel of the Nile, with DeVito in hot pursuit. The action and snappy one-liners come thick and fast, making this one of those rare sequels that's not too far short of the quality of the original. TH DVD

Michael Douglas (1) *Jack Colton* • Kathleen Turner *Joan Wilder* • Danny DeVito *Ralph* • Spiros Focas *Omar* • Howard Jay Patterson *Barak* • Randall Edwin Nelson *Karak* • Samuel Ross Williams *Arak* • Timothy Daniel Furst *Sarak* • Hamid Fillali *Rachid* ■ *Dir* Lewis Teague • *Scr* Mark Rosenthal, Lawrence Konner, from characters by Diane Thomas

Jewel Robbery ★★★
Romantic comedy 1932 · US · BW · 63min

There's hardly time to catch your breath in this tight little Warner Bros movie from a period when the studio was at its height and pace was everything. Debonair Raffles-like gentleman burglar William Powell robs a jewellery store, locks up the proprietor and a smart customer, and starts making up to the latter's wife, the impossibly elegant Kay Francis who - wouldn't you guess? - longs for a little excitement in her bored life. It's not quite Lubitsch, but sophisticated and immensely enjoyable. TS

William Powell *Robber* • Kay Francis *Baroness Teri Von Horhenfels* • Hardie Albright *Paul* • André Luguet *Count André* • Henry Kolker *Baron Franz Von Horhenfels* • Spencer Charters *Johann Christian Lenz* ■ *Dir* William Dieterle • *Scr* Erwin Gelsey, from the play by Ladislaus Fodor [Ladislas Fodor]

Jezebel ★★★★U
Romantic melodrama 1938 · US · BW · 100min

This is an absolute cracker and contains, arguably, Bette Davis's best role - one which she fervently hoped would win her the part of Scarlett in the following year's *Gone with the Wind*. She had to settle for the consolation of a best actress Oscar for her role here as a beautiful but spoilt southern belle who goes completely over the top in her efforts to make her fiancé Henry Fonda jealous. This is a classic from the golden era of such overblown period blockbusters, directed by the incomparable William Wyler, with whom Davis was said to be infatuated. SR

Bette Davis *Julie Morrison* • Henry Fonda *Preston Dillard* • George Brent *Buck Cantrell* • Margaret Lindsay *Amy Bradford Dillard* • Fay Bainter *Aunt Belle Massey* • Richard Cromwell *Ted Dillard* • Donald Crisp *Dr Livingstone* • Henry O'Neill *General Theopholus Bogardus* ■ *Dir* William Wyler • *Scr* Clements Ripley, Abem Finkel, John Huston, Robert Bruckner, from the play by Owen Davis Sr [Owen Davis] • *Cinematographer* Ernest Haller • *Music* Max Steiner • *Costume Designer* Orry-Kelly

Jig ★★★PG
Dance documentary 2011 · UK · Colour · 97min

This engaging insight into the hothouse world of juvenile Irish dancing has much in common with films like *Mad Hot Ballroom* and *Only When I Dance*, which also focused on ambitious young dancers. The primary focus is not just on performers from the Emerald Isle and this allows director Sue Bourne to show a different side to the sometimes disconcerting aspects of preparing and prettifying kids for contests. However, while she captures the dedication required by youngsters, coaches and parents, Bourne struggles to convey the kitsch, competitiveness and chaos of the 2010 Irish Dancing World Championships in Glasgow and the drama only comes alive during the climactic wait for the results. DP Some swearing, drug references. DVD

■ *Dir* Sue Bourne

Jigsaw ★★
Crime drama 1949 · US · BW · 72min

Franchot Tone is a crusading DA, fighting racketeers who have bumped off a journalist and who will rack up several further corpses before the end. The group, however, is prepared for Tone and sends a female operative to seduce him. This heavy-handed blend of violence and moralising is worth watching for some unbilled cameos from Henry Fonda, John Garfield and Marlene Dietrich, who did the film as a favour to her friend Mercedes McCambridge, the wife of the film's director, Fletcher Markle. AT

Franchot Tone *Howard Malloy* • Jean Wallace *Barbara Whitfield* • Myron McCormick *Charles Riggs* • Marc Lawrence (1) *Angelo Agostini* • Winifrid Lenihan *Mrs Hartley* • Betty Harper *Caroline Riggs* • Marlene Dietrich *Nightclub patron* • Henry Fonda *Nightclub waiter* • John Garfield *Street loiterer* ■ *Dir* Fletcher Markle • *Scr* Fletcher Markle, Vincent McConnor, from the story by John Roeburt

Jigsaw ★★★PG
Mystery drama 1962 · UK · BW · 103min

This satisfying murder mystery benefits from the reassuring presence of Jack Warner as the detective on the case. Set in Brighton, director Val Guest adopts an unsensational, pseudo-documentary approach that concentrates on the often laborious details of police procedure as the identity of dead woman is ascertained and her killer is slowly unmasked. Among the cast of familiar British faces, American actress Yolande Donlan - Mrs Val Guest - is excellent as a spinster who narrowly misses being a murder victim. AT DVD

Jack Warner *Det Insp Fellows* • Ronald Lewis *Det Sgt Wilks* • Yolande Donlan *Jean Sherman* • Michael Goodliffe *Clyde Burchard* • John Le Mesurier *Mr Simpson* • Moira Redmond *Joan Simpson* ■ *Dir* Val Guest • *Scr* Val Guest, from the novel *Sleep Long, My Love* by Hillary Waugh

Jigsaw ★
Mystery drama 1968 · US · Colour · 96min

Spartacus author Howard Fast's novel *Fallen Angel* was filmed in 1965 as *Mirage*. It was an amnesia-based thriller that was hard to follow and easy to forget. This is a remake, reworked by Ranald MacDougall under the pseudonym Quentin Werty. There is one major change to the story: instead of amnesia, the hero's problem is an overdose of LSD which makes him unable to remember who was murdered, and why. AT

Harry Guardino *Arthur Belding* • Bradford Dillman *Jonathan Fields* • Hope Lange *Helen Atterbury* • Pat Hingle *Lew Haley* • Diana Hyland *Sarah* • Victor Jory *Dr Edward Arkroyd* • Paul Stewart *Dr Simon Joshua* • Susan Saint James *Ida* ■ *Dir* James Goldstone • *Scr* Quentin Werty [Ranald MacDougall], from the film *Mirage* by Peter Stone, from the novel *Fallen Angel* by Howard Fast

The Jigsaw Man ★★★15
Spy drama 1984 · UK · Colour · 89min

Another outing for Laurence Olivier and Michael Caine, but this Cold War thriller is not a fraction as effective as their *Sleuth* 12 years before. The story, about a British traitor whose face is surgically altered by the Russians so that he can be sent back on a mission, doesn't convince and, like the most irritating of jigsaws, a lot of plot-pieces seem to be missing. TH Swearing. DVD

Michael Caine *Sir Philip Kimberly* • Laurence Olivier *Admiral Sir Gerald Scaith* • Susan George *Penny* • Robert Powell *Jamie Frazer* • Charles Gray *Sir James Chorley* • Michael Medwin *Milroy* ■ *Dir* Terence Young • *Scr* Jo Eisinger, from the novel by Dorothea Bennet

Jill Rips ★★★18
Crime thriller 2000 · US · Colour · 90min

A female serial killer is choosing her prey from the sleazy world of sadomasochism. When his brother becomes her latest victim, burnt-out ex-cop Dolph Lundgren investigates. This effective psycho-chiller is directed with torrid verve and mature style by Anthony Hickox, evoking sympathy for the maniac's motives. All this, plus the sight of Lundgren in bondage being walked on by a dominatrix clad in red leather! AJ

Dolph Lundgren *Matt* • Danielle Brett *Irene* • Charlie Seixas *Jim Conway* • Richard Fitzpatrick *Eddie* • Kristi Angus *Frances* ■ *Dir* Anthony Hickox • *Scr* Kevin Bernhardt, Gareth Wardell, from Frederick Lindsay's novel

Jim Thorpe – All-American ★★U
Sports biography 1951 · US · BW · 105min

Jim Thorpe was often regarded as the finest all-round athlete America has ever produced. A native American Indian, he won a stack of Olympic gold medals in 1912, more than any other athlete had ever won, but was stripped of them because he had previously played professional baseball. He became a coach, a celebrity, a serial husband and a drunkard. As Thorpe, Burt Lancaster is ideally cast, but despite some fine support and an attempt not to sugar-coat the story, it remains conventional. AT

Burt Lancaster *Jim Thorpe* • Charles Bickford *Glenn S "Pop" Warner* • Steve Cochran *Peter Allendine* • Phyllis Thaxter *Margaret Miller* • Dick Wesson *Ed Guyac* • Jack Big Head *Little boy* ■ *Dir* Michael Curtiz • *Scr* Frank Davis, Everett Freeman, from the story *Bright Path* by Douglas Morrow, Vincent X Flaherty, from a biography by Russell J Birdwell, James Thorpe

Jimi: All Is by My Side ★★★★15
Biographical drama 2013 · UK/Ire/US · Colour · 117min

This rock 'n' roll biopic from *12 Years a Slave* writer John Ridley is a thoughtful meditation on the key year that transformed Jimi Hendrix from session guitarist to superstar. Hendrix (OutKast's André Benjamin) is a quiet, even simple man, but once in London he becomes much more complex. It never hints at the drugs that took his life at 27, and rights issues mean we never hear his most famous songs, but a thunderous rendition of *Sgt Pepper* does give a woozy approximation of his talent. DW DVD

André Benjamin *Jimi Hendrix* • Hayley Atwell *Kathy Etchingham* • Imogen Poots *Linda Keith* • Burn Gorman *Michael Jeffery* • Ashley Charles *Keith Richards* ■ *Dir/Scr* John Ridley

Jimi Hendrix ★★★★15
Documentary 1973 · US · BW and Colour · 97min

Few burned as brightly or were extinguished as quickly as Jimi Hendrix. Made just three years after his untimely death, this documentary is a crucial insight into the guitarist's roots and the tremors he sent through 1960s pop with his electrifying blend of aggression, intensity and finesse. The live sequences, some culled from Woodstock and Monterey Pop, are priceless. But the interviews are also compelling, whether with his saxophone playing father Al, longtime girlfriend Fayne Pridgeon or fellow axe hero, Pete Townshend, who seemed to both fear and revere him. But let's not forget the Experience band members, Mitch Mitchell and Noel Redding, who somehow managed to keep up with him. DP

Jimi Hendrix • Eric Clapton • Germaine Greer • Pete Townshend • Mick Jagger ■ *Dir* Joe Boyd, John Head, Gary Weis • *Scr* Joe Boyd, John Head, Gary Weis • *Cinematographer* Leon Branton

Jimmy Hollywood ★★★15
Comedy drama 1994 · US · Colour · 112min

Barry Levinson divides his time between intelligent, mainstream blockbusters such as *Sleepers* and *Rain Man*, and his more personal projects that remain best typified by *Diner*. This film falls into the latter category, a likeable enough little oddity. Joe Pesci stars as a struggling actor who becomes a vigilante when a thief snatches his car radio. Despite the farcical plot, this has a deep streak of melancholy and the film is stolen by Christian Slater, who gives a beautifully understated performance as Pesci's slow-witted chum. JF Violence, swearing.

Joe Pesci *Jimmy Alto* • Christian Slater *William* • Victoria Abril *Lorraine De La Pena* • Jason Beghe *Detective* • John Cothran Jr *Detective* • Harrison Ford ■ *Dir/Scr* Barry Levinson

Jimmy Neutron: Boy Genius ★★★U
Animated comedy adventure 2001 · US · Colour · 79min

Jimmy Neutron is a boy inventor living in the colourful community of Retroville, USA, who pilots his own rocketship and has a pet robot-dog called Goddard - after the rocket scientist Robert H Goddard - one of the cartoon's few nods to an adult audience. The communications satellite that Jimmy has fashioned out of a toaster alerts hostile aliens to the presence of his home town, and the Yookians spirit away all the grown-ups. Aimed at the very young, this lively cartoon adventure has less to keep adults amused. TH DVD

Debi Derryberry *Jimmy Neutron* • Patrick Stewart *King Goobot* • Martin Short *Ooblar* • Andrea Martin *Miss Fowl* • Megan Cavanagh *Mom/VOX* • Mark DeCarlo *Dad/Pilot/Arena guard* ■ *Dir* John A Davis • *Scr* John A Davis, Steve Oedekerk, David N Weiss, J David Stem

Jimmy the Gent ★★
Crime comedy 1934 · US · BW · 66min

James Cagney and Bette Davis star in this romantic comedy about rival teams of con-artists who track down legatees left fortunes in unclaimed wills. Davis, appalled at her employer Cagney's behaviour, leaves him for another firm. It's a profitable racket and the story always hovers on the edge of the gangster movie. Sharply performed by the two stars and lasting barely over an hour, it doesn't stop for lunch. Surprisingly, Warners didn't team Cagney and Davis together again until *The Bride Came COD* in 1941. AT

James Cagney *Jimmy Corrigan* • Bette Davis *Joan Martin* • Alice White *Mabel* • Allen Jenkins *Louie* • Arthur Hohl *Joe Rector [Monty Barton]* • Alan Dinehart *James J Wallingham* • Philip Reed *Ronnie Gatson* ■ *Dir* Michael Curtiz • *Scr* Bertram Milhauser, from the story *Heir Chaser* by Laird Doyle, Ray Nazarro

J

Jimmy's Hall ★★★★ 12

Drama   2014 · UK/Ire/Fr · Colour · 104min

Ken Loach's 1930s-set tale is more intimate, but of a piece historically, geographically and ideologically with *The Wind That Shakes the Barley* (also written by long-time collaborator Paul Laverty). Based on a true story, it stars a charismatic Barry Ward as communist agitator Jimmy Gralton, who reopens Effrinagh's Pearse-Connolly Hall as an educational social club for jazz dancing and the exchange of ideas. A little-known Irish cast (save for *Sherlock*'s Andrew Scott in a small role) lends easy authenticity to the drama which, true to Loach form, is didactic and sentimental but guided by a righteous moral compass. As much a drama about community as politics, it humanises the clash of old and new ideas, and marks Ward out as a star. **AC** Violence, swearing.
DVD Blu-ray

Barry Ward *James Gralton* • Simone Kirby *Oonagh* • Jim Norton *Father Sheridan* • Francis Magee *Mossie* ■ *Dir* Ken Loach • *Scr* Paul Laverty, from the play *Jimmy Gralton's Dancehall* by Donal O'Kelly

Jindabyne ★★★★ 15

Drama   2006 · Aus · Colour · 118min

After just three movies in 20-odd years, *Lantana* director Ray Lawrence confirms his status as one of Australia's finest film-makers. Based on a Raymond Carver short story that also inspired one of the plotlines in Robert Altman's *Short Cuts*, the film tells the tale of a group of anglers, led by Gabriel Byrne, who discover a dead Aboriginal woman floating in a river. Instead of reporting it immediately, they decide to wait until the end of the fishing trip to report their gruesome find. When word of their actions leaks out, the men find themselves ostracised by the town, the local indigenous community and, more specifically, Byrne's troubled wife Laura Linney. Lawrence elicits superb performances from the excellent ensemble cast. Although a subplot is less convincing, this is still a thoughtful, affecting study of modern-day morality. **JF** Swearing DVD

Laura Linney *Claire Kane* • Gabriel Byrne *Stewart Kane* • Deborra-Lee Furness *Jude* • John Howard *Carl* • Leah Purcell *Carmel* • Stelios Yiakmis *Rocco* • Alice Garner *Elissa* • Simon Stone *Billy* ■ *Dir* Ray Lawrence • *Scr* Beatrix Christian, from the short story *So Much Water So Close to Home* by Raymond Carver

Jingle All the Way ★★ PG

Seasonal comedy   1996 · US · Colour · 85min

Arnold Schwarzenegger is the overworked businessman who promises to buy the year's hottest toy – Turbo Man – for his neglected son. Alas, the doll sold out months previously, thus sparking a frantic hunt that sees Arnie crossing swords with an obsessed postman (Sinbad) and a crooked Santa (James Belushi). Schwarzenegger acquits himself well in the slapstick action sequences but he's a tad embarrassing during the cuddlier moments. Brian Levant's direction, meanwhile, could do with a harder edge. **JF** DVD CE

Arnold Schwarzenegger *Howard Langston* • Sinbad *Myron Larabee* • Phil Hartman *Ted Maltin* • Rita Wilson *Liz Langston* • Robert Conrad *Officer Hummell* • Martin Mull *DJ* • Jake Lloyd *Jamie Langston* • James Belushi *Mall Santa* ■ *Dir* Brian Levant • *Scr* Randy Kornfield

Jinnah ★★★

Biographical drama
1998 · Pak/UK · Colour · 110min

Christopher Lee turns in a towering performance in this sincere tribute to Mohammed Ali Jinnah, the founder of Pakistan. Director Jamil Dehlavi co-wrote the factually impeccable screenplay with Cambridge academic Akbar Ahmed. Set either side of the Partition of India, it's a necessarily episodic biopic. But the decision to use a *Christmas Carol*-like conceit to link the story (in which Lee tours key moments in his life with celestial scholar Shashi Kapoor) is a preposterous miscalculation. With James Fox stiffly uncomprehending as

Mountbatten, this is less effusive, but also less impressive than *Gandhi*. **DP**

Christopher Lee *Quaid-e-Azam Mohammed Ali Jinnah* • James Fox *Lord "Dickie" Mountbatten* • Maria Aitken *Edwina Mountbatten* • Shashi Kapoor *Narrator* ■ *Dir* Jamil Dehlavi • *Scr* Jamil Dehlavi, Akbar Ahmed

Jinxed! ★ 15

Black comedy   1982 · US · Colour · 98min

It was a disaster waiting to happen when Bette Midler, brashest of song-belters, teamed with Don Siegel, briskest of action directors. Off-screen squabbles didn't help this story of a lucky gambler's girl who ropes in Reno croupier Ken Wahl to make the game of blackjack a lethal deal for her partner. Rip Torn, as the gambler, offers a token portrait of sadistic seediness, but this goes sadly awry. **TH** Violence, swearing.

Bette Midler *Bonita Friml* • Ken Wahl *Willie Brodax* • Rip Torn *Harold Benson* • Val Avery *Milt Hawkins* • Jack Elam *Otto* ■ *Dir* Don Siegel • *Scr* David Newman, Bert Blessing, from a story by Bert Blessing

Jiro Dreams of Sushi ★★★★ U

Documentary   2011 · US · Colour · 82min

This reverential documentary chronicles one man's obsession with creating the perfect sushi. That man is 85-year-old master chef Jiro Ono, whose Tokyo restaurant was the world's first sushi establishment to be awarded three coveted Michelin stars. The inscrutable and driven Jiro may be the star attraction here, but sharing top billing are his creations, which are mouthwateringly filmed and almost guaranteed to have viewers seeking out some decent imitations immediately. A feeling of repetition makes David Gelb's picture feel longer than its modest running time suggests, but, that aside, this is a bite-sized feast for foodies everywhere. **DA** Japanese +subtitles.

■ *Dir* David Gelb

Jism ★★★ 15

Erotic thriller   2003 · Ind · Colour · 136min

Amit Saxena's smouldering Indian thriller was credited with introducing a controversially graphic element into Bollywood cinema. The story reworks that of *Double Indemnity*, although its gaudy design and synthesised soundtrack owe more to *Body Heat* than Billy Wilder's *film noir* classic. Certainly Bipasha Basu's performance is more Kathleen Turner than Barbara Stanwyck, as she seduces hapless John Abraham into murdering her husband (Gulshan Grover). The songs are slickly staged, but they too often dissipate the suspense and reduce the sensuality to kitsch. **DP** Hindi +subtitles. DVD

Bipasha Basu *Sonnia Khanna* • John Abraham *Kabir Lal* • Gulshan Grover *Rohit Khanna* • Vinay Pathak *DCP Siddharth* ■ *Dir* Amit Saxena • *Scr* Mahesh Bhatt, Niranjan Iyengar, from a story by Mahesh Bhatt

Jitterbugs ★★ U

Comedy   1943 · US · BW · 74min

Desperate for a hit after several disappointing outings, Laurel and Hardy revamped the 1933 programme filler *Arizona to Broadway*, with Ollie posing as a southern millionaire and Stan as a rich maiden aunt to help Vivian Blaine, whose mother has been swindled in a land deal. Even their most devoted fans will admit that, for the most part, this is pretty feeble stuff, with the demands of the flimsy story getting in the way of the comedy. **DP**

Stan Laurel *Stan* • Oliver Hardy *Ollie* • Vivian Blaine *Susan Cowan* • Bob Bailey *Chester Wright* • Douglas Fowley *Malcolm Bennett* ■ *Dir* Mal St Clair [Malcolm St Clair] • *Scr* Scott Darling

Jiyan ★★★ 12A

Drama   2001 · Iraq/US · Colour · 99min

In 1988, Iraqi planes bombarded the Kurdish town of Halabja with chemical and biological weapons in an assault that left 5,000 dead and a further 9,000 maimed. Bearing in mind the horror of that attack,

it's understandable that director Jano Rosebiani errs on the emotional side in relating this inspiring story of the US-based expatriate businessman who returns home to build an orphanage for the victims. Yet, there's still a touching restraint in the portrayal of Kurdo Galali's optimistic relationship with traumatised child Jiyan (Pisheng Berzinji) and her protective cousin, Choman Hawrami. The overall tone is neorealist, but a humble poetry still shines through. **DP** Kurdish +subtitles.

Kurdo Galali *Diyari Derbendikhari* • Pisheng Berzinji *Jiyan* • Choman Hawrami *Sherko* • Enwer Shexani *Salar* • Darya Qadir *Tavga* • Ehmed Sala *The Mayor* ■ *Dir/Scr* Jano Rosebiani

Jo Jo Dancer, Your Life Is Calling ★★ 18

Drama   1986 · US · Colour · 96min

Richard Pryor directs himself as comedian Jo Jo Dancer in a story that bears an uncanny resemblance to his own colourful career, both on and offstage. It tells of his early days in showbusiness and of the effects of drug use and abuse, culminating in a stay in the hospital burns unit. The results are disappointing given the dramatic possibilities offered by Pryor's life. **TH**

Richard Pryor *Jo Jo Dancer/Alter Ego* • Debbie Allen *Michelle* • Art Evans *Arturo* • Fay Hauser *Grace* ■ *Dir* Richard Pryor • *Scr* Rocco Urbisci, Paul Mooney, Richard Pryor

Joan of Arc ★★ PG

Historical epic   1948 · US · Colour · 96min

Brilliant and underrated director Victor Fleming had a serious crush on Ingrid Bergman, and this costly farrago is effectively a Technicolored love letter to Bergman, who had played the role on stage. The result brought Fleming to an early grave, a comic-strip history lesson so dull and lengthy that it was trimmed down at each screening, its original 145-minute length mercifully eventually cut to around 100 minutes. A real endurance test. **TS**

Ingrid Bergman *Jeanne d'Arc* • José Ferrer *Dauphin, Charles VII* • Francis L Sullivan *Pierre Cauchon* • J Carrol Naish *Count John of Luxembourg* • Ward Bond *La Hire* • Shepperd Strudwick *Father Jean Massieu* • Gene Lockhart *Georges La Tremouille* • Leif Erickson *Jean Dunois* ■ *Dir* Victor Fleming • *Scr* Maxwell Anderson, Andrew Solt, from the play *Joan of Lorraine* by Maxwell Anderson • *Costume Designers* Dorothy Jeakins, Karinska

Joan of Arc ★★ 15

Historical biographical drama
1999 · Fr · Colour · 151min

Kathryn Bigelow walked away from this project after refusing to cast Luc Besson's then-wife Milla Jovovich as the saint. Besson took over and cast Jovovich anyway. Sadly, she's the biggest problem in this epic story of the peasant girl who led the French to victory over the English. The prologue detailing Joan's childhood is dire, but the film does kick in after the entrance of John Malkovich as Charles VII, and there are some remarkable battle scenes before Joan's downfall. **LH** Violence, swearing. DVD

Milla Jovovich *Joan of Arc* • John Malkovich *Charles VII* • Faye Dunaway *Yolande D'Aragon* • Dustin Hoffman *The Conscience* • Tcheky Karyo *Dunois* • Pascal Greggory *Duke of Alencon* • Vincent Cassel *Gilles de Rais* • Timothy West *Cauchon* • Gina McKee *Duchess of Bedford* ■ *Dir* Luc Besson • *Scr* Andrew Birkin, Luc Besson

Joan of Paris ★★ U

Second World War drama
1942 · US · BW · 91min

Paul Henreid and Michèle Morgan made strong Hollywood debuts in this efficient slice of action, set in occupied France and briskly directed by Robert Stevenson. Morgan is the Joan of Paris, the brave barmaid who sidetracks Laird Cregar's Gestapo chief so that French pilot Paul Henreid and some downed RAF flyers can escape back to England. A pre-stardom Alan Ladd gains his first significant role as a wounded pilot nicknamed "Baby", while that worthy character actress May Robson,

well into her 80s, makes her final screen appearance. **AE**

Paul Henreid *Paul Lavallier* • Michèle Morgan *Joan* • Thomas Mitchell *Father Antoine* • Laird Cregar *Herr Funk* • May Robson *Mlle Rosay* • Alexander Granach *Gestapo agent* • Alan Ladd *Baby* ■ *Dir* Robert Stevenson • *Scr* Charles Bennett, Ellis St Joseph, from a story by Jacques Thery, Georges Kessel

Joan Rivers: a Piece of Work ★★★★

Documentary   2010 · US · Colour · 84min

Comedian Joan Rivers tells us that nobody has ever described her as beautiful. In archive footage, Johnny Carson argues that men prefer intelligence over beauty, to which Joan replies, "No man has ever put his hand up a woman's dress looking for a library card." It's a relatively mild one-liner, but one that perfectly sums up a performer able to lacerate herself far more effectively than any critic. This extraordinary documentary follows 12 months in Joan's life and reveals her to be a fretful but essentially likeable personality who spends her entire existence railing against retirement. **DvB** Swearing. DVD

Joan Rivers • Don Rickles • Melissa Rivers • Kathy Griffin ■ *Dir* Ricki Stern, Annie Sundberg

Jobman ★★★

Drama   1990 · S Afr · Colour · 97min

Something of a companion piece to the powerful Australian picture by director Fred Schepisi *The Chant of Jimmie Blacksmith*, this bold, unblinkered film shows how a decent black man is driven outside the law by the pressures of racial prejudice. One of the first films tackling bigotry and its consequences to be made and shown in apartheid South Africa, it is, sadly, deprived of pace by director Darrell Roodt. Still, Kevin Smith gives a performance of dignity and power as the deaf-and-dumb Jobman. **DP** Some swearing.

Kevin Smith (3) *Jobman* • Tertius Meintjes *Karel* • Lynn Gaines *Anna* • Marcel Van Heerden *Sergeant* • Goliath Davids *Pyp* • Josephine Liedeman *Petra* ■ *Dir* Darrell Roodt [Darrell James Roodt] • *Scr* Greg Latter, from a story by Achmat Dangor

jOBS ★★★ 15

Biographical drama   2013 · US · Colour · 121min

The nerd-to-Nasdaq rise of Apple co-founder Steve Jobs was satisfactorily dramatised in 1999 TV movie *Pirates of Silicon Valley*, with a narrative focus on his rivalry with Microsoft's Bill Gates. This bigger-budget retelling deletes Gates and pastes Jobs (Ashton Kutcher) centre stage. The film keeps a respectful distance from its subject's cancer-linked death in 2011, suggesting hagiography, but the theme is early-70s hippy idealism versus the corporate world. Yet after the barnstorming approach of similarly pitched *The Social Network*, this all feels a little conventional. **AC** Drug abuse. DVD

Ashton Kutcher *Steve Jobs* • Dermot Mulroney *Mike Markkula* • Josh Gad *Steve Wozniak* • Lukas Haas *Daniel Kottke* • Matthew Modine *John Sculley* • James Woods *Jack Dudman* ■ *Dir* Joshua Michael Stern • *Scr* Matt Whiteley

Jock of the Bushveld ★★★ PG

Period adventure   1988 · S Afr · Colour · 93min

Based on Percy Fitzpatrick's autobiographical account of life in the South African gold fields at the end of the last century, this is a stirring story that takes us from the depths of the earth to the great outdoors, via a crocodile-infested river. The hero of the title is a sort of White Fang of the velds, an ugly dog who becomes Fitzpatrick's companion and frequently his salvation. Action-packed, yet retaining a good grasp of period, this is a solid family adventure. **DP**

Jonathan Rands *Percy Fitzpatrick* • Jocelyn Broderick *Lilian Cubitt* • Olivier Ngwenya *Jim Makokel* • Gordon Mulholland *Tom Barnett* • Michael Brunner *Seedling* • Marloe Scott-Wilson *Maggie Maguire* ■ *Dir* Gray Hofmeyr • *Scr* John Cundill, from the book by Percy Fitzpatrick

Jocks ★ 15
Comedy 1986 · US · Colour · 90min

Ever wondered when Christopher Lee's career reached its lowest point? It was probably in this comedy about college athletes, in which Lee plays the school president who is obsessed with winning. The school's only chance of winning a championship lies in tennis player Scott Strader – if he can stop partying long enough to play. ST

Scott Strader *The Kid* • Perry Lang *Jeff* • Richard Roundtree *Chip Williams* • RG Armstrong *Coach Beetlebom* • Christopher Lee *President White* ■ *Dir* Steve Carver • *Scr* Michael Lanahan, David Oas

Jodhaa Akbar ★★★ 12
Epic romantic drama 2008 · Ind · Colour · 205min

If you're new to Bollywood historical epics, this is a good place to start, a torrid saga of love and politics set in the mid-16th century, which ends up as a plea for religious tolerance. Gym-honed pin-up Hrithik Roshan and Aishwarya Rai Bachchan make a glittering couple as the Muslim emperor Mohammad Akbar and his initially reluctant bride, the Hindu princess Jodhaa. The eye-wateringly sumptuous Rajasthan scenery and photography, well-composed battle scenes and a vibrant score from *Slumdog Millionaire's* AR Rahman help to make up for several convoluted subplots, and the fact that it takes so long for Akbar to convince Jodhaa that he's a good man – even after she's seen his topless training routine! GC Hindi +subtitles. DVD BD

Hrithik Roshan *Jalaluddin Mohammad Akbar* • Aishwarya Rai Bachchan [Aishwarya Rai] *Jodhaa* • Sonu Sood *Rajkumar Sujamal* • Mrs Punam S Sinha *Mallika Hamida Banu* • Kulbhushan Kharbanda *Raja Bharmal* ■ *Dir* Ashutosh Gowariker • *Scr* Haidar Ali, Ashutosh Gowariker, KP Saxena (dialogue), from a story by Ali

Joe ★★★ 18
Drama 1970 · US · Colour · 102min

Director John G Avildsen's violent "bigot-versus-counterculture" parable is very much a product of its conservative times, but its implausibility is tempered by strong performances. Peter Boyle became a star after playing the title character, a right-wing, blue-collar loud-mouth who forms a strange relationship with executive Dennis Patrick after the latter kills his wayward daughter's drug-pusher boyfriend. Shot on location in Greenwich Village with almost documentary-like precision, it's a creepy look at man's baser instincts, capped with a bloody massacre. Susan Sarandon makes her film debut as Patrick's daughter. AJ Violence, drug abuse.

Peter Boyle *Joe Curran* • Susan Sarandon *Melissa Compton* • Patrick McDermott *Frank Russo* • Dennis Patrick *Bill Compton* • Audrey Caire *Joan Compton* ■ *Dir* John G Avildsen • *Scr* Norman Wexler

Joe ★★★★ 15
Drama 2013 · US · Colour · 117min

A teenager (Tye Sheridan) finds his loyalties torn between his abusive alcoholic father (Gary Poulter, a homeless man discovered on the streets of Austin who died soon after the film was made) and hard-but-fair Joe (Nicolas Cage, making a welcome return to form) who offers the boy both employment and guidance. Director David Gordon Green built his career on coaxing astonishing performances from non-professionals, and he outdoes himself here with this raw, sucker-punch of a movie. LF Violence, swearing, sex scenes.

Nicolas Cage *Joe Ransom* • Tye Sheridan *Gary* • Ronnie Gene Blevins *Willie-Russell* • Gary Poulter *Wade aka G-Daawg* ■ *Dir* David Gordon Green • *Scr* Gary Hawkins, from Larry Brown's novel • *Cinematographer* Tim Orr

Joe and Max ★★★ 15
Biographical drama 2002 · Ger/US · Colour · 109min

Steve James, the director of the acclaimed basketball documentary *Hoop Dreams*, turns his attention to one of boxing's great rivalries in this considered biopic. When their epic 1930s bouts were hijacked by propagandists in the US and the Third Reich, Joe Louis and Max Schmeling became reluctant poster boys for, respectively, African-American pride and Aryan supremacy. Leonard Roberts and Til Schweiger impose themselves on the title roles (with Schweiger particularly impressive defending Jewish friends like manager David Paymer), as James strips away the hype to reveal the treatment these champions endured at various stages of their unlikely friendship. DP DVD

Leonard Roberts *Joe Louis* • Til Schweiger *Max Schmeling* • Peta Wilson *Anny Ondra* • David Paymer *Joe Jacobs* • Richard Roundtree *Jack Blackburn* • Bruce Weitz *Mike Jacobs* ■ *Dir* Steve James (2) • *Scr* Jason Horwitch

Joe Dirt ★ 12
Comedy 2001 · US · Colour · 87min

Is there no end to excrement jokes? Be warned, this is brimming with toilet humour and what remains is tasteless. David Spade is Joe Dirt, a trailer trash lost soul, whose cranium – split during childhood – is covered by the worst wig in cinema history. The film details Dirt's adventures since parental desertion at eight and explains his current conundrum – that he believes both a meteor and a nuclear bomb have fallen from the sky into his possession. LH Swearing, sexual references. DVD

David Spade *Joe Dirt* • Brittany Daniel *Brandy* • Dennis Miller *Zander Kelly* • Adam Beach *Kicking Wing* • Christopher Walken *Clem* • Jaime Pressly *Jill* ■ *Dir* Dennie Gordon • *Scr* David Spade, Fred Wolf

Joe Kidd ★★ 15
Western 1972 · US · Colour · 83min

The spaghetti western meets its classic American origins, but Clint Eastwood's potent "Man with No Name" persona conflicts with John Sturges's anonymous direction in this range-war saga. Eastwood's gunman is up against greedy businessman Robert Duvall's dispossessing Mexican-Americans of their land, but there's little to get excited about in this indifferent effort scripted by Elmore Leonard. The one fun highlight is when Eastwood drives a train through a saloon to mow down the villains. AJ Violence, swearing. DVD BD

Clint Eastwood *Joe Kidd* • Robert Duvall *Frank Harlan* • John Saxon *Luis Chama* • Don Stroud *Lamarr* • Stella Garcia *Helen Sanchez* • James Wainwright *Mingo* • Paul Koslo *Roy* ■ *Dir* John Sturges • *Scr* Elmore Leonard

Joe Macbeth ★★★
Crime drama 1955 · UK · BW · 92min

This interesting reworking of the "Scottish play" as a gangster movie, set in the United States but filmed in England, was directed with assurance at Shepperton by one of Britain's most talented film-makers, bohemian jazz freak and crime expert Ken Hughes. Americans Paul Douglas and Ruth Roman were imported to play the leads, and the support cast is perfect for its period, with an American-accented Sidney James as Banky, and Bonar Colleano as his revenge-seeking son Lennie. TS

Paul Douglas *Joe Macbeth* • Ruth Roman *Lily Macbeth* • Bonar Colleano *Lennie* • Grégoire Aslan *Duca* • Sidney James *Banky* • Nicholas Stuart *Duffy* • Robert Arden *Ross* • Minerva Pious *Rosie* ■ *Dir* Ken Hughes • *Scr* Phillip Yordan, from the play *Macbeth* by William Shakespeare

Joe Smith, American ★★
Second World War drama 1942 · US · BW · 63min

Based on a Paul Gallico story, this propaganda thriller was the first of a number of "important low-budget pictures" assigned by MGM to executive producer Dore Schary, who later headed the studio. It tells of how aircraft factory worker Robert Young is kidnapped by Nazis but refuses to give them information. Made to help persuade the USA to enter the Second World War, the film cannot help but be dated, though it is directed with plenty of pace by Richard Thorpe. Watch out for Ava Gardner in a bit part in one of her earliest movies. RB

Robert Young (1) *Joe Smith* • Marsha Hunt *Mary Smith* • Harvey Stephens *Freddie Dunhill* • Darryl Hickman *Johnny Smith* • Jonathan Hale *Blake McKettrick* • Ava Gardner *Girl* ■ *Dir* Richard Thorpe • *Scr* Allen Rivkin, from a story by Paul Gallico

Joe Somebody ★★ PG
Romantic comedy drama 2001 · US · Colour · 94min

There's a shrewd satirical intelligence at work in this contemporary take on the "conformity is contentment" rationale that made *Pleasantville* so effective. However, Tim Allen is too eager to please as the corporate video-maker who kicks against a system that has designated him a drone. Consequently, director John Pasquin's astutely conveyed community of spirit-sapping averageness is rapidly overturned by slapstick and schmaltz. Middlebrow mediocrity wins the day. DP DVD

Tim Allen *Joe Scheffer* • Julie Bowen *Meg Harper* • Kelly Lynch *Callie Scheffer* • Hayden Panettiere *Natalie Scheffer* • Jim Belushi [James Belushi] *Chuck Scarett* • Greg Germann *Jeremy* • Patrick Warburton *Mark McKinney* ■ *Dir* John Pasquin • *Scr* John Scott Shepherd

Joe versus the Volcano ★★★ PG
Comedy 1990 · US · Colour · 97min

For his directorial debut, Oscar-winning *Moonstruck* screenwriter John Patrick Shanley came up with this flawed but still entertaining film. Tom Hanks is the downtrodden office worker who, on discovering that he has only a short time to live, accepts the proposition of shady millionaire Lloyd Bridges who offers him anything he wants for 20 days, after which he must throw himself into an active volcano on a remote island. Meg Ryan plays three different women in Hanks's life. JF Swearing.

Tom Hanks *Joe Banks* • Meg Ryan *DeDe/Angelica/Patricia* • Lloyd Bridges *Graynamore* • Robert Stack *Dr Ellison* • Abe Vigoda *Waponis chief* • Dan Hedaya *Mr Waturi* • Amanda Plummer *Dagmar* • Ossie Davis *Marshall* ■ *Dir/Scr* John Patrick Shanley

Joe's Apartment ★★ 12
Comedy 1996 · US · Colour · 76min

This was cable channel MTV's first movie production, a bid to turn the original 1992 live action/computer-animated short into a big screen hit. Jerry O'Connell is a jobless innocent who arrives in the Big Apple and finds that life is tough. Having conned his way into a rent-controlled apartment, he finds he shares it with about 50,000 singing, dancing and (luckily) friendly cockroaches. His new-found pals come to his aid when property magnate Robert Vaughn tries to kick him out. Laughs are fairly thin on the ground. JF Swearing. DVD

Jerry O'Connell *Joe* • Megan Ward *Lily* • Billy West *Ralph Roach* • Reginald Hudlin *Rodney Roach* • Jim Turner *Walter* • Robert Vaughn (1) *Senator Dougherty* • Don Ho *Alberto Bianco* ■ *Dir/Scr* John Payson

Joey Boy ★ PG
Comedy 1965 · UK · BW · 87min

Along with longtime collaborator Sidney Gilliat, Frank Launder was one of the bastions of British cinema in the 1940s and 1950s. But his brand of comedy had passed its sell-by date by the Swinging Sixties, as this awful film demonstrates only too well. Some TV sitcom stars are left with egg on their faces, none more so than Harry H Corbett as the brains behind a gang of petty crooks who join the army to avoid prison. DP

Harry H Corbett *"Joey Boy" Thompson* • Stanley Baxter *Benny "the Kid" Lindowski* • Bill Fraser *Sergeant Dobbs* • Percy Herbert *"Mad George" Long* • Lance Percival *Clarence Doubleday* • Reg Varney *"Rabbit" Malone* ■ *Dir* Frank Launder • *Scr* Frank Launder, Mike Watts, from the novel by Eddie Chapman

Joey Breaker ★★★
Drama 1993 · US · Colour · 92min

Richard Edson is New York talent agent Joey, undergoing a *Jerry Maguire*-like crisis of conscience in this less well-known industry drama. Bob Marley's daughter Cedella plays Joey's girlfriend Cyan, who proves to be a much-needed humanising influence in his life. Writer/director Steven Starr obviously knows what he's talking about but, like our hero, we are left wondering why anyone would want to get involved in this amoral business in the first place. LH

Richard Edson *Joey Breaker* • Cedella Marley *Cyan Worthington* • Fred Fondren *Alfred Moore* • Erik King *Hip Hop Hank* • Gina Gershon *Jennie Chaser* • Philip Seymour Hoffman *Wiley McCall* ■ *Dir/Scr* Steven Starr

John and Julie ★★ U
Comedy 1955 · UK · Colour · 82min

This fantasy about the Queen's coronation arrived too late to catch the mood of national euphoria, but it's still a pleasing snapshot of 1950s Britain. Peter Sellers plays a policeman on the trail of Colin Gibson and Lesley Dudley, two little scamps who've run away from home in order to witness the pageantry. Even with such comic dependables as Wilfrid Hyde White and Sid James on hand, this is a pretty minor offering. DP

Colin Gibson (1) *John* • Lesley Dudley *Julie* • Noelle Middleton *Miss Stokes* • Moira Lister *Dora* • Wilfrid Hyde White *Sir James* • Sidney James *Mr Pritchett* • Peter Sellers *PC Diamond* • Constance Cummings *Mrs Davidson* • Mona Washbourne *Miss Rendlesham* ■ *Dir/Scr* William Fairchild

John and Mary ★★
Drama 1969 · US · Colour · 92min

A product of the Swinging Sixties, this drama of sexual mores was scripted by playwright John Mortimer and directed by Peter (*Bullitt*) Yates, but it remains conventionally stock-still in its attitudes. Icons of the time Dustin Hoffman and Mia Farrow play the eponymous couple who meet in a singles bar, make love and then spend an inordinate amount of time deciding what it all means. TH

Dustin Hoffman *John* • Mia Farrow *Mary* • Michael Tolan *James* • Sunny Griffin *Ruth* • Stanley Beck *Ernest* • Tyne Daly *Hilary* • Alix Elias *Jane* • Julie Garfield *Fran* • Olympia Dukakis *John's mother* ■ *Dir* Peter Yates • *Scr* John Mortimer, from a novel by Mervyn Jones • *Music* Quincy Jones

John Carpenter's Ghosts of Mars ★★ 15
Science-fiction action horror 2001 · US · Colour · 94min

Set in the year 2176, the plot has cop Natasha Henstridge arrive at an isolated Martian mining town to transport notorious killer Ice Cube to a high-security prison. But the colonists are being possessed by the spooks of the title, and these Martian zombies swarm to defend their planet in a siege reminiscent of Carpenter's *Assault on Precinct 13*. There are moments of tension, but no real surprises. TH Violence, swearing, drug abuse. DVD BD

Ice Cube *James "Desolation" Williams* • Natasha Henstridge *Melanie Ballard* • Jason Statham *Jericho Butler* • Clea DuVall *Bashira Kincaid* • Pam Grier *Helena Braddock* • Joanna Cassidy *Whitlock* ■ *Dir* John Carpenter • *Scr* Larry Sulkis, John Carpenter • *Music* John Carpenter

John Carpenter's The Ward ★★★ 15
Horror thriller 2010 · US · Colour · 84min

Legendary horror director John Carpenter's suspenseful, 1960s-set thriller pushes all the right shock buttons, but suffers from a lack of originality. Amber Heard stars as Kristen, a young woman committed to a mental institution after burning down a remote farmhouse, who ends up sharing a high-security ward with four equally troubled teenage girls. When patients start to disappear, seemingly at the hands of the "ghost" of another missing inmate, Kristen plans her escape. Heard makes a feisty heroine, but top marks must go to Jared Harris as the asylum's creepy chief doctor. **TeS** Violence. **DVD** **BD**

Amber Heard *Kristen* • Mamie Gummer *Emily* • Danielle Panabaker *Sarah* • Laura-Leigh *Zoey* • Lyndsy Fonseca *Iris* • Jared Harris *Dr Stringer* ■ *Dir* John Carpenter • *Scr* Michael Rasmussen, Shawn Rasmussen

John Carter ★★★ 12
Action fantasy 2012 • US • Colour • 126min

This lavish production of Edgar Rice Burroughs's space adventure *A Princess of Mars* has much to recommend it. Model-turned-actor Taylor Kitsch (*Battleship*) is muscular and cool enough as the American Civil War officer who is transported to the faraway planet Barsoom (better known as Mars), which is in the middle of its own inter-tribal conflict. Andrew Stanton (*Finding Nemo, WALL-E*) finds a good balance between intimate emotion and epic battles, aided by a heartfelt vocal performance from Samantha Morton as CGI creature Sola and Lynn Collins as a princess who's no fool with a sword. Add some eye-catching design, and you have to feel that the film's box-office failure wasn't fully deserved. **AC** Violence. **DVD** **BD** **3D**

Taylor Kitsch *John Carter* • Lynn Collins *Dejah Thoris* • Samantha Morton *Sola* • Mark Strong *Matai Shang* • Willem Dafoe *Tars Tarkas* • Thomas Haden Church *Tal Hajus* • Ciarán Hinds [Ciaran Hinds] *Tardos Mors* ■ *Dir* Andrew Stanton • *Scr* Michael Chabon, Andrew Stanton, Mark Andrews, from the novel *A Princess of Mars* by Edgar Rice Burroughs

John Dies at the End ★★ 15
Comedy fantasy horror
2012 • US • Colour and BW • 99min

Don Coscarelli's sloppy adaptation of David Wong's comic horror novel, first published as a web serial, will not emulate its online success. It's a lazily haphazard affair about two slackers taking the drug Soy Sauce, allowing them to mind read, predict the future, visit alien planets and detect the presence of monsters among humanity. Producer Paul Giamatti phones in his cameo as a black reporter some see as white, heightening the core problem in this gore-fest. Hearing other people's drug trips is a total bore, and that doesn't change when on film. **AJ** Violence, swearing. **DVD** **BD**

Chase Williamson *Dave* • Rob Mayes *John* • Paul Giamatti *Arnie* • Clancy Brown *Dr Albert Marconi* ■ *Dir* Don Coscarelli • *Scr* Don Coscarelli, from a story by David Wong

John Goldfarb, Please Come Home ★
Comedy 1964 • US • Colour • 95min

This is a lamentably unfunny satire about American colonialism. Peter Ustinov impersonates a Middle East potentate who is being courted by the US, which wants to build a military base in his country. Shirley MacLaine is a journalist doing a profile of him while Richard Crenna is Goldfarb, a spy plane pilot who is shot down and then co-opted into coaching Ustinov's football team. **AT**

Shirley MacLaine *Jenny Ericson* • Peter Ustinov *King Fawz* • Richard Crenna *John Goldfarb* • Jim Backus *Miles Whitepaper* • Scott Brady *Sakalakis* • Fred Clark *Heinous Overreach* • Wilfrid Hyde White *Guz* ■ *Dir* J Lee Thompson • *Scr* William Peter Blatty

John Grisham's The Rainmaker ★★★★ 15
Courtroom drama 1997 • US • Colour • 129min

Francis Ford Coppola's riveting courtroom drama is an exceptionally well-crafted film that's a class above every other John Grisham adaptation. Matt Damon is excellent as the inexperienced lawyer thrown into the lion's den when he takes on the case of a young man dying of leukaemia, whose insurance company refuses to honour his claim. There's also a marvellous supporting cast including Jon Voight as the slimiest lawyer imaginable

and Claire Danes as a battered wife sheltered by Damon. **JC** Swearing, violence. **DVD**

Matt Damon *Rudy Baylor* • Claire Danes *Kelly Riker* • Jon Voight *Leo F Drummond* • Mary Kay Place *Dot Black* • Mickey Rourke *Bruiser Stone* • Danny DeVito *Deck Shifflet* • Dean Stockwell *Judge Harvey Hale* • Teresa Wright *Miss Birdie* • Virginia Madsen *Jackie Lemanczyk* • Roy Scheider *Wilfred Keeley* • Danny Glover *Judge Tyrone Kippler* ■ *Dir* Francis Ford Coppola • *Scr* Francis Ford Coppola, Michael Herr, from the novel by John Grisham

John Huston & The Dubliners ★★★
Documentary 1987 • US • Colour • 60min

Having failed in the 1940s to bring *Ulysses* to the screen, John Huston finally got to adapt James Joyce in his last film, *The Dead*. Lilyan Sievernich's affectionate documentary reveals a man determined to make the most of his misfortunes – he was too ill to travel to Ireland and had to rely on Seamus Byrne's second unit to obtain the linking footage. He's seen barking orders from his wheelchair to ensure that a cast headed by his daughter, Anjelica, did justice to both the script penned by his son, Tony, and the spirit of Joyce's peerless prose. **DP**

■ *Dir* Lilyan Sievernich

John Q ★★★ 15
Action drama 2001 • US • Colour • 111min

When his young son (Daniel E Smith) collapses after a game of baseball, decent Denzil Washington is informed by smarmy surgeon James Woods that he needs a heart transplant or he'll die. But Washington can't afford the operation and his insurance won't cover it. The answer? He takes the entire hospital emergency room hostage and demands treatment for his son. Unfortunately, it is then that the clichéd characters flood in like victims of an epidemic and seriously undermine the dramatic tension. What makes this work is Washington's fiercely committed performance as a man at the end of his tether. **TH** Violence, swearing. **DVD**

Denzel Washington *John Quincy Archibald* • Robert Duvall *Lt Frank Grimes* • James Woods *Dr Raymond Turner* • Anne Heche *Rebecca Payne* • Eddie Griffin *Lester* • Kimberly Elise *Denise Archibald* • Ray Liotta *Police Chief Monroe* • Daniel E Smith *Mike Archibald* ■ *Dir* Nick Cassavetes • *Scr* James Kearns

John Tucker Must Die ★★ 12
Romantic comedy 2006 • US • Colour • 86min

Jesse Metcalfe bares his chest rather than his soul as the eponymous John Tucker in this pedestrian high-school comedy. But in a departure from his role as a lovesick gardener in TV's *Desperate Housewives*, Metcalfe shows his range by playing a calculating womaniser. Brittany Snow supplies the cute factor as the new girl who's keen to fit in but falls prey to his vengeful ex-girlfriends. Their plans to make Tucker "undateable" include tricking him into fronting an awareness campaign for a sexually transmitted disease. Despite the film's attention-grabbing title, director Betty Thomas can't supply any of the bitchy social satire that made the Lindsay Lohan vehicle *Mean Girls* so enjoyable. **SP** **DVD**

Jesse Metcalfe *John Tucker* • Brittany Snow *Kate* • Ashanti *Heather* • Sophia Bush *Beth* • Arielle Kebbel *Carrie* • Penn Badgley *Scott* • Jenny McCarthy *Lori* ■ *Dir* Betty Thomas • *Scr* Jeff Lowell

John Wick ★★★★ 15
Action thriller 2014 • US • Colour • 101min

Numerous fight sequences are staged with a great deal of skill and style in this lean, propulsive, action-packed revenge thriller. Keanu Reeves is reliably stoic as the title character, a formidable former hitman who has been out of the game for five years. He is compelled to return, however, when a trio of Russian lowlifes break into his house and kill Daisy, the adorable puppy left to him by his recently deceased wife. As John seeks retribution, the body count escalates and

the film moves from one bruising set piece to another, each of which is impressively choreographed and captured with a refreshing sense of clarity. As a film, there isn't much in the way of depth or complexity, but the constant violence is offset by some well-timed humour, adding to the entertainment value. A must-see for anyone who likes the thought of Keanu Reeves taking headshots at point-blank range. **SC** Violence, swearing. **DVD** **BD**

Keanu Reeves *John Wick* • Michael Nyqvist *Viggo Tarasov* • Alfie Allen *Iosef Tarasov* • Adrianne Palicki *Ms Perkins* • Bridget Moynahan *Helen* • Ian McShane *Winston* ■ *Dir* Chad Stahelski • *Scr* Derek Kolstad

Johnny Angel ★★★★
Crime drama 1945 • US • BW • 79min

Smoothie George Raft plays a sea captain out to find his father's killers in this tremendously entertaining melodrama, notable for a tangled flashback plot that remains wholly engrossing. The cast includes two stunning co-stars: Claire Trevor and Signe Hasso, the latter as the French girl who witnessed the murder. Hoagy Carmichael is a cab driver who rejoices in the name Celestial O'Brien, and he performs his (now classic) standard *Memphis in June*. With its tense direction from Edwin L Marin and superb, moody photography from Harry J Wild, the film deserves to be much better known. **TS**

George Raft *Johnny Angel* • Claire Trevor *Lilah* • Signe Hasso *Paulette* • Lowell Gilmore *Sam Jewell* • Hoagy Carmichael *Celestial O'Brien* • Marvin Miller *Gustafson* • Margaret Wycherly *Miss Drumm* ■ *Dir* Edwin L Marin • *Scr* Steve Fisher, Frank Gruber, from the novel *Mr Angel Comes Aboard* by Charles Gordon Booth

Johnny Apollo ★★★
Crime drama 1940 • US • BW • 94min

Handsome matinée idol Tyrone Power got a chance to prove he was more than just a pretty face in this tough melodrama about the son of crooked financier Edward Arnold going to the bad. This is a very well-acted and controlled movie, directed by talented 20th Century-Fox regular Henry Hathaway with just the right degree of understanding, and did wonders for Power's appeal at the box office. Also particularly effective is Dorothy Lamour as Ty's moll, and tough Lloyd Nolan as the rival hood. **TS**

Tyrone Power *Bob Cain/Johnny Apollo* • Dorothy Lamour *Mabel "Lucky" Dubarry* • Lloyd Nolan *Mickey Dwyer* • Edward Arnold *Robert Cain Sr* • Charley Grapewin *Judge Emmett T Brennan* • Lionel Atwill *Jim McLaughlin* • Marc Lawrence (1) *John Bates* ■ *Dir* Henry Hathaway • *Scr* Philip Dunne, Rowland Brown, from a story by Samuel G Engel, Hal Long

Johnny Be Good ★ 15
Sports comedy 1988 • US • Colour • 87min

It's tough believing that Brat Pack geekmeister Anthony Michael Hall can even kick a ball, let alone be America's hottest football prospect in this substandard teen comedy posing as a cautionary tale. Hall just can't quite decide whether to take up numerous lucrative offers from talent scouts or drop the game to attend college with his sweetheart. **RS** **DVD**

Anthony Michael Hall *Johnny Walker* • Paul Gleason *Coach Wayne Hisler* • Robert Downey Jr *Leo Wiggins* • Robert Downey Sr *NCAA Investigator* • Uma Thurman *Georgia Elkans* • Seymour Cassel *Wallace Gibson* • Steve James (1) *Coach Sanders* • Jennifer Tilly *Connie Hisler* ■ *Dir* Bud Smith • *Scr* Jeff Buhai, Steve Zacharias, David Obst

Johnny Belinda ★★★★ PG
Drama 1948 • US • BW • 102min

Jane Wyman won a well-deserved best actress Academy Award for her moving portrayal of the Nova Scotia deaf-mute rape victim in this fine Warner Bros film, in which director Jean Negulesco manages to combine outright melodrama with sensitive performances. In its day, it was a mighty popular and much parodied movie, but now the censor-circumventions make the whole thing seem as phoney as its sets, but the

strength of the acting, especially from Lew Ayres, wins through. **TS**

Jane Wyman *Belinda McDonald* • Lew Ayres *Dr Robert Richardson* • Charles Bickford *Black McDonald* • Stephen McNally *Locky McCormick* • Jan Sterling *Stella McCormick* • Agnes Moorehead *Aggie McDonald* • Holmes Herbert *Judge* • Dan Seymour *Pacquet* ■ *Dir* Jean Negulesco • *Scr* Irmgard von Cube, Allen Vincent, from the play *Johnny Belinda* by Elmer Harris • *Cinematographer* Ted McCord

Johnny Come Lately ★★★ U
Comedy drama 1943 • US • BW • 97min

A strong performance from James Cagney and a fine supporting cast lift this otherwise unexceptional newspaper picture. Cagney plays a journalist who helps a widow keep her late's husband's newspaper running, despite the local politicians and businessmen who are trying to close it down. There's civic corruption, characters with shady pasts and a little romance, but mainly it's a story about integrity. **AT**

James Cagney *Tom Richards* • Grace George *Vinnie McLeod* • Marjorie Main *Gashouse Mary* • Marjorie Lord *Jane* • Hattie McDaniel *Aida* ■ *Dir* William K Howard • *Scr* John Van Druten, from the novel *McLeod's Folly* by Louis Bromfield

Johnny Concho ★★★
Western 1956 • US • BW • 85min

Although an inexpensive western must have seemed a safe bet, it's strange that Frank Sinatra should have chosen this particular story for his producing debut. Strange because he's ideally cast as an obnoxious coward protected by his notorious gunslinger brother. After the brother is bumped off and his killers take over the town, It's predictable Sinatra should eventually summon up the courage to face them. Curiously, though, he never shakes off his odious earlier image. A very watchable drama. **AE**

Frank Sinatra *Johnny Concho* • Keenan Wynn *Barney Clark* • William Conrad *Tallman* • Phyllis Kirk *Mary Dark* • Wallace Ford *Albert Dark* • Dorothy Adams *Sarah Dark* ■ *Dir* Don McGuire • *Scr* David P Harmon, Don McGuire, from the story *The Man Who Owned the Town* by Harmon

Johnny Cool ★★★
Crime drama 1963 • US • BW • 101min

Henry Silva plays the Sicilian hitman working overtime in America in this enjoyable gangster movie. At times the picture seems to be a parody of everything mafioso; at others, the violence is quite shocking. The supporting cast is also a bizarre mix, while director William Asher (the man behind all those *Beach Party* movies) cleverly mixes and matches black comedy with *Naked City* realism. **AT**

Henry Silva *Johnny Cool/Giordano* • Elizabeth Montgomery *Dare Guiness* • Richard Anderson *Correspondent* • Jim Backus *Louis Murphy* • Joey Bishop *Used car salesman* • Brad Dexter *Lennart Crandall* • Telly Savalas *Mr Santangelo* • Sammy Davis Jr *"Educated"* ■ *Dir* William Asher • *Scr* Joseph Landon, from the novel *The Kingdom of Johnny Cool* by John McPartland

Johnny Dangerously ★★★ 15
Crime spoof 1984 • US • Colour • 86min

Before donning the black cape for Tim Burton's *Batman*, Michael Keaton played for laughs in films such as *Mr Mom, Night Shift* and this spoof of 1930s gangster movies. He stars as a good-natured gangster whose brother is a crime-busting district attorney. It's enjoyably silly stuff and zips along at a fair old pace, peppered with some great one-liners. There's fun support from a cast that includes Joe Piscopo, Peter Boyle, Dom DeLuise and Maureen Stapleton, but the film belongs to Keaton, who once again shows his comedic talents to entertaining effect. **JB** **DVD**

Michael Keaton *Johnny Dangerously* • Marilu Henner *Lil* • Joe Piscopo *Vermin* • Danny DeVito *Burr* • Maureen Stapleton *Mom* • Griffin Dunne *Tommy* • Peter Boyle *Dundee* • Richard Dimitri *Maroni* • Glynnis O'Connor *Sally* • Byron Thames *Young Johnny* • Dom DeLuise *Pope* • Ray

Walston *Vendor* ■ *Dir* Amy Heckerling • *Scr* Norman Steinberg, Bernie Kukoff, Harry Colomby, Jeff Harris

Johnny Dark ★★ U
Action drama 1954 · US · Colour · 85min

Aimed at younger audiences and showcasing Universal's new breed of stars, this lightweight drama requires acceptance of Tony Curtis as an engineering genius who can design and drive a new racing car. The director, western veteran George Sherman, knows how to keep a film on the move and ensures that the thrills and spills of the racing scenes, particularly the climactic drive from the Canadian border to Mexico, are forcefully put over. Piper Laurie makes a pleasant leading lady. **AE**

Tony Curtis *Johnny Dark* • Piper Laurie *Liz Fielding* • Don Taylor *Duke Benson* • Paul Kelly (1) *Jim Scott* • Ilka Chase *Abbie Binns* • Sidney Blackmer *James Fielding* ■ *Dir* George Sherman • *Scr* Franklin Coen

Johnny Doesn't Live Here Anymore ★★
Comedy 1944 · US · BW · 73min

The versatile Joe May was one of the directors who pulled German cinema up by its bootstraps in the aftermath of the First World War. Yet after he moved to Hollywood to escape the Nazi threat, his movies were, for the most part, routine. Simone Simon is typically charming as the career girl who suddenly finds her friend's flat being invaded by the pals to whom he's given keys. James Ellison might steal Simone's heart, but it's the laconic Robert Mitchum who steals the show in the final reel. Re-released as *And So They Were Married*. **DP**

Simone Simon *Kathie Aumont* • James Ellison *Mike O'Brien* • Robert Mitchum *CPO Jeff Daniels* • William Terry *Johnny Moore* • Minna Gombell *Mrs Collins* • Chick Chandler *Jack* ■ *Dir* Joe May • *Scr* Philip Yordan, John H Kafka, from a story by Alice Means Reeve

Johnny Eager ★★★
Crime drama 1941 · US · BW · 106min

Robert Taylor is well cast as an unscrupulous racketeer, his virtually expressionless handsome features allowing an audience to read into his character all manner of evils. His co-star is sexy Lana Turner, then 21 years old and an instantly hot on-set item with the older Taylor. Acting honours, and the Oscar, went to Van Heflin as Taylor's self-effacing alcoholic friend, whose censor-circumventing role loosely implies a homosexual bond between the two men. **TS**

Robert Taylor (1) *Johnny Eager* • Lana Turner *Lisbeth Bard* • Edward Arnold *John Benson Farrell* • Van Heflin *Jeff Hartnett* • Robert Sterling *Jimmy Lanthrop* • Patricia Dane *Garnet* • Glenda Farrell *Mae Blythe* ■ *Dir* Mervyn LeRoy • *Scr* John Lee Mahin, James Edward Grant, from a story by Grant

Johnny English ★★ PG
Spy comedy adventure 2003 · UK/US/Fr · Colour · 83min

Fans of Rowan Atkinson's rubbery-faced brand of physical comedy will know what to expect from this unassuming slice of slapstick. Based on a character portrayed by the *Mr Bean* star in a series of Barclaycard adverts, it sends up another home-grown institution – the James Bond-style superspy. Atkinson plays the titular hero, an enthusiastic but bumbling intelligence agent appointed to track down those behind the theft of the crown jewels. Director Peter Howitt forgoes subtlety for youngster-friendly sight gags. **SF DVD**
🔵 CS

Rowan Atkinson *Johnny English* • Natalie Imbruglia *Lorna Campbell* • Ben Miller *Bough* • John Malkovich *Pascal Sauvage* • Tim Pigott-Smith *Pegasus* • Kevin McNally *Prime Minister* • Oliver Ford Davies *Archbishop of Canterbury* • Greg Wise *Agent One* ■ *Dir* Peter Howitt • *Scr* Neal Purvis, Robert Wade, William Davies

Johnny English Reborn ★★★ PG
Spy comedy adventure 2011 · UK/Is/Fr/Jpn · Colour · 97min

Rowan Atkinson returns as the spy oblivious to his own incompetence in this lively sequel, which sees him lured out of retirement by his former bosses at MI7 to hunt down an international group of assassins plotting to kill the Chinese premier. Atkinson is great value as the idiot sleuth, although some of director Oliver Parker's stunts and set pieces would be more suited to the slapstick antics of Mr Bean. Straight-faced support from Gillian Anderson and Dominic West as fellow MI7 operatives adds to the fun, but it's clearly Atkinson's show from start to finish. **TeS**
DVD 🔵

Rowan Atkinson *Johnny English* • Gillian Anderson *Pamela Thornton* • Dominic West *Simon Ambrose* • Rosamund Pike *Kate Sumner* • Pierce Brosnan *???* • Ben Miller *Bough* ■ *Dir* Oliver Parker • *Scr* Hamish McColl, from a story by William Davies, from characters by Neal Purvis, Robert Wade

Johnny Frenchman ★★★ U
Drama 1945 · UK · BW · 100min

Among the few faults of the films produced at Ealing were their parochialism and their tendency to patronise in their depiction of the working classes. Screenwriter TEB Clarke's third film for the studio, this tale of the rivalry between Breton and Cornish fishing communities was intended to cement the *entente cordiale* in the latter days of the Second World War. It would have been a rather forgettable affair, but for the fact that it gave British audiences a rare chance to see the sublime French actress Françoise Rosay rising well above her capable co-stars and the level of their material. **DP** DVD

Françoise Rosay *Lanec Florrie* • Tom Walls *Nat Pomeroy* • Patricia Roc *Sue Pomeroy* • Ralph Michael *Bob Tremayne* • Paul Dupuis *Yan Kervarec* • Frederick Piper *Zacky Penrose* ■ *Dir* Charles Frend • *Scr* TEB Clarke

Johnny Got His Gun ★ 12
Drama 1971 · US · Colour and BW · 106min

Screenwriter Dalton Trumbo was imprisoned during the McCarthy witch-hunts yet won two Oscars under a pseudonym – for *Roman Holiday* and *The Brave One*. With this, Trumbo directed his own script from his own novel about a First World War soldier who has lost his arms, legs, face, sight, smell and hearing but is kept alive for medical research and experimentation. Excruciatingly awful. **AT** DVD

Jason Robards *Father* • Timothy Bottoms *Johnny/Joe Bonham* • Marsha Hunt *Mother* • Diane Varsi *Nurse* • Charles McGraw *Girl's father* ■ *Dir* Dalton Trumbo • *Scr* Dalton Trumbo, from his novel

Johnny Guitar ★★★★ PG
Cult western 1954 · US · Colour · 105min

Although Nicholas Ray's simmering western subverts this notoriously conservative genre, the real purpose of his study in mob hysteria was to condemn the Communist witch-hunt then tearing Hollywood apart. Heavy with symbolism, Philip Yordan's script also crackles with repressed sexuality, as saloon owner Joan Crawford and cattle queen Mercedes McCambridge cross swords. Providing Crawford with one of her best roles and gloriously shot in Trucolor by Harry Stradling, this baroque bonanza fascinates on so many levels that it demands to be repeatedly reviewed. **DP** DVD

Joan Crawford *Vienna* • Sterling Hayden *Johnny Guitar* • Mercedes McCambridge *Emma Small* • Scott Brady *Dancin' Kid* • Ward Bond *John McIvers* • Ben Cooper *Turkey Ralston* • John Carradine *Old Tom* • Ernest Borgnine *Bart Lonergan* ■ *Dir* Nicho as Ray • *Scr* Philip Yordan, from the novel by Ray Chanslor

Johnny Handsome ★★ 15
Crime drama 1989 · US · Colour · 89min

One of the seemingly endless series of Mickey Rourke flops, director Walter Hill's downbeat glob of calculated nastiness shoehorns numerous genres together with scant success. Rourke invests nil expression or thought into his role as a disfigured criminal who's given a new face in a prison hospital. Saved from total failure by a few energetically staged action sequences, this rancid movie also features a sleazy turn from Ellen Barkin. **AJ** Violence, swearing.
DVD

Mickey Rourke *John Sedley* • Ellen Barkin *Sunny Boyd* • Elizabeth McGovern *Donna McCarty* • Morgan Freeman *Lieutenant AZ Drones* • Forest Whitaker *Dr Steven Resher* • Lance Henriksen *Rafe Garrett* • Scott Wilson *Mikey Chalmette* ■ *Dir* Walter Hill • *Scr* Ken Friedman, from the novel *The Three Worlds of Johnny Handsome* by John Godey

Johnny Mad Dog ★★ 15
War drama 2008 · Fr/Bel/Liberia · Colour · 98min

This graphic, violent and uncomfortable exposé of the use of child soldiers in poor African countries is as harsh as its subject matter suggests. Filmed on location in Liberia with a cast of nonprofessionals, it has a suitably raw and visceral feel, revealing how children are brutally taken from their families, fed drugs, given guns and then pumped up with inflammatory revolutionary politics. Despite its finessed and shocking detail, this well-intentioned film never gives enough respite from the horror and subsequently feels like a gruelling slog. **DW** Violence, swearing, sex scenes, nudity.

Christophe Minie *Johnny Mad Dog* • Daisy Victoria Vandy *Laokolé* • Dagbeh Tweh *No Good Advice* • Barry Chernoh *Small Devil* • Mohammed Sesay *Butterfly* ■ *Dir* Jean-Stéphane Sauvaire • *Scr* Jean-Stéphane Sauvaire, from the novel by Emmanuel Dongala

Johnny Mnemonic ★ 15
Science-fiction thriller 1995 · Can/US · Colour · 92min

Director Robert Longo's turgid sci-fi thriller, based on William Gibson's cyberpunk short story, is cyber junk. Keanu Reeves sleepwalks through the title role as a 21st-century hi-tech messenger who carries top-secret information thanks to a computer chip in his brain. Empty, flashy and incredibly dull, Longo's unpleasant movie is lamely tarted up with incomprehensible surf-cowboy jargon, gratuitous violence and second-rate special effects. **AJ** Swearing, violence, nudity. DVD

Keanu Reeves *Johnny Mnemonic* • Dina Meyer *Jane* • Ice-T *J-Bone* • Takeshi [Takeshi Kitano] *Takahashi* • Denis Akiyama *Shinji* • Dolph Lundgren *Street Preacher* • Henry Rollins *Spider* ■ *Dir* Robert Longo • *Scr* William Gibson, from his short story

Johnny o'Clock ★★★
Film noir 1947 · US · BW · 95min

Robert Rossen was that rarest of film-makers, a practising communist who managed to write social criticism into his screenplays before he was blacklisted. This underrated *film noir* whodunnit marked his directorial debut, and is distinguished by superb Burnett Guffey photography – check out those expressionist angles – and a sharp and knowing screenplay, as Dick Powell's tough gambler and Lee J Cobb's policeman engage in terse exchanges over who killed the hat-check girl and the cop she fancied. **TS**

Dick Powell *Johnny O'Clock* • Evelyn Keyes *Nancy Hobbs* • Lee J Cobb *Inspector Koch* • Ellen Drew *Nelle Marchettis* • Nina Foch *Harriet Hobbs* • Thomas George *Pete Marchettis* • John Kellogg *Charlie* ■ *Dir* Robert Rossen • *Scr* Robert Rossen, from a story by Milton Holmes

Johnny Reno ★★ PG
Western 1966 · US · Colour · 79min

Dana Andrews is US marshal Johnny Reno, riding into serious trouble en route to Stone Junction. He ends up killing one would-be assassin and taking another prisoner, before coming up against Stone Junction's corrupt mayor Lyle Bettger. The story is slight, but what gives the film its modest appeal is the cast who are all much too old and experienced to have to prove anything any more. **AT** DVD

Dana Andrews *Johnny Reno* • Jane Russell *Nona Williams* • Lon Chaney Jr *Sheriff Hodges* • John Agar *Ed Tomkins* • Lyle Bettger *Jess Yates* • Tom Drake *Joe Connors* ■ *Dir* RG Springsteen • *Scr* Steve Fisher, from a story by AC Lyles, Steve Fisher, Andrew Craddock

Johnny Stecchino ★★★ 18
Comedy 1991 · It · Colour · 115min

Although it smashed box-office records at home, this anarchic comedy was little seen outside Roberto Benigni's native Italy. Miraculously pulling off slapstick gags that were stale even in the silent era, he coaxes you into siding with the naive bus driver who just happens to resemble a notorious Sicilian mobster. The comedy has a contentious edge, with some of the gags at the expense of the Mafia being daringly outspoken. With off-screen wife Nicoletta Braschi again winning the clown prince's heart, this frantic farce will either have you rolling on the carpet or scratching your head in puzzlement. **DP** Italian +subtitles.
DVD

Roberto Benigni *Dante/Johnny Stecchino* • Nicoletta Braschi *Maria* • Paolo Bonacelli *D'Agata* • Franco Volpi *Minister* • Ivano Marescotti *Dr Randazzo* • Alessandro De Santis *Lillo* ■ *Dir* Roberto Benigni • *Scr* Roberto Benigni, Vincenzo Cerami

Johnny Suede ★★★★ 15
Comedy fantasy 1991 · US · Colour · 92min

With the rave reviews from *Thelma & Louise* still ringing in his ears, Brad Pitt further demonstrated his star quality as the hero of this gentle tale, which marked the directorial debut of ex-cinematographer Tom DiCillo. Awash with pastel colours and dripping with style, this fantastical tale tells the tale of rock 'n' roll wannabe Pitt's attempts to emulate his idol, 1950s pop star Ricky Nelson. DiCillo's unerring eye for both the absurd and grim is complemented by his fine pacing and the tautness of his script. Pitt is superb and is well supported by Alison Moir and Catherine Keener. **DP**
DVD

Brad Pitt *Johnny Suede* • Richard Boes *Man in tuxedo* • Cheryl Costa *Woman in alley* • Michael Luciano *Mr Clepp* • Calvin Levels *Deke* • Nick Cave *Freak Storm* • Alison Moir *Darlette* • Catherine Keener *Yvonne* • Samuel L Jackson *B-Bop* ■ *Dir/Scr* Tom DiCillo • *Cinematographer* Joe DeSalvo

Johnny Tiger ★
Drama 1966 · US · Colour · 102min

Robert Taylor's sensitive college professor goes to Florida to teach Seminole Indians, his three children in tow. However, his noble intentions are thwarted by a dying chief who wants his grandson (Chad Everett) to renounce contact with white people. The lack of dramatic tension and some inadequate performances (notably Everett in the title role) prove to be fatal weaknesses. **AT**

Robert Taylor (1) *George Dean* • Geraldine Brooks *Dr Leslie Frost* • Chad Everett *Johnny Tiger* • Brenda Scott *Barbara Dean* • Marc Lawrence (1) *William Billie* ■ *Dir* Paul Wendkos • *Scr* Paul Crabtree, Thomas Blackburn, Philip Wylie, R John Hugh, from the story *Tiger on the Outside* by R John Hugh

Johnny Tremain ★★★ U
Historical drama 1957 · US · Colour · 80min

Covering a well-documented chapter of American history, this Disney film tells the story of Johnny, a former silversmith, who becomes committed to the revolutionary cause after being falsely accused of theft. Veteran director Robert Stevenson doesn't quite succeed in capturing the sights and sounds of the American colonial era but the kids will enjoy it. **DP**

J

Hal Stalmaster *Johnny Tremain* • Luana Patten *Cilla Lapham* • Jeff York *James Otis* • Sebastian Cabot *Jonathan Lyte* • Dick Beymer [Richard Beymer] *Rab Silsbee* • Walter Sande *Paul Revere* • Rusty Lane *Samuel Adams* • Whit Bissell *Josiah Quincy* ■ *Dir* Robert Stevenson • *Scr* Tom Blackburn, from the novel by Esther Forbes

Johnny Trouble ★★ U

Drama 1957 · US · BW · 79min

This old-fashioned, sentimental drama marked the end of the overpowering Ethel Barrymore's career. She plays an elderly widow who stubbornly refuses to leave her apartment building after it is sold, and ends up with students for neighbours. She convinces herself that young delinquent Stuart Whitman is the offspring of her own, long-absent son. Both Whitman and Carolyn Jones as his girlfriend are rather good, given the circumstances. AE

Ethel Barrymore *Mrs Chandler* • Cecil Kellaway *Tom McKay* • Carolyn Jones *Julie* • Jesse White *Parsons* • Rand Harper *Phil* • Stuart Whitman *Johnny* • Paul Wallace *Paul* • Edward Byrnes [Edd Byrnes] *Elliott* ■ *Dir* John H Auer • *Scr* Charles O'Neal, David Lord, from the story *Prodigal's Mother* by Ben Ames Williams

Johns ★★★★ 18

Drama 1995 · US · Colour · 91min

Los Angeles in all its sleazy glory is fascinatingly portrayed here by writer/director Scott Silver. David Arquette and Lukas Haas are both superb as two street hustlers determined to raise enough cash to fulfil Arquette's dream of spending Christmas Eve in a swish hotel suite. Many of the events that happen to them are based on true stories collected by Silver during his research. Very funny in places, as well as tragic and moving, this is one of those movies whose characters linger long in the memory. JB Swearing, sex scenes.

DVD

Lukas Haas *Donner* • David Arquette *John* • Arliss Howard *John Cardoza* • Keith David *Homeless John* • Christopher Gartin *Eli* • Josh Schaefer [Joshua Schaefer] *David* ■ *Dir/Scr* Scott Silver

Johnson Family Vacation ★ 12

Comedy road movie 2004 · US · Colour · 92min

This dire comedy has so few laughs it barely warrants its genre description. In an unusually flat performance, Cedric the Entertainer plays a competitive sibling who takes his estranged wife (Vanessa Williams) and three children on a cross-country road trip to compete in his family's annual reunion contest. The mishaps that follow are lame and predictable, with the limpest slapstick and sight gags replacing genuine wit. SF Swearing. *DVD*

Cedric the Entertainer *Nate Johnson/Uncle Earl* • Vanessa Williams [Vanessa L Williams] *Dorothy Johnson* • Solange Knowles *Nikki Johnson* • Bow Wow *DJ Johnson* • Gabby Soleil *Destiny Johnson* • Shannon Elizabeth *Chrishelle* • Steve Harvey *Mack Johnson* ■ *Dir* Christopher Erskin • *Scr* Todd R Jones, Earl Richey Jones

The Joke ★★★★

Drama 1968 · Cz · BW · 80min

Jaromil Jires was the most stylistically audacious director of the Czech "new wave" of the early 1960s. However, he is more restrained in this studied adaptation of Milan Kundera's scathingly satirical novel. Josef Somr gives an exceptional performance as the student who is sentenced to a spell in one of the army's brutal black units after a political joke backfires. While the themes may be a little obscure, the hardships and humiliations Somr experiences often make excruciating viewing. DP Czech +subtitles.

Josef Somr [Josef Sommer] *Ludvik* • Jana Ditetova *Helena* • Ludek Munzar *Pavel* • Evald Schorm *Kosika* • Vera Kresadlova *Brozova* ■ *Dir* Jaromil Jires • *Scr* Jaromil Jires, from the novel *The Joke* by Milan Kundera

The Joker Is Wild ★★

Biographical drama 1957 · US · BW · 128min

This workmanlike and overlong biography stars Frank Sinatra as comedian Joe E Lewis, whose vocal chords were seriously damaged by nightclub racketeers in the 1930s – which put paid to his original career as a singer. Lewis's stormy life and battle with alcoholism is not a lot of fun, though Jeanne Crain and Mitzi Gaynor add glamour as his two wives. TV

Frank Sinatra *Joe E Lewis* • Mitzi Gaynor *Martha Stewart* • Jeanne Crain *Letty Page* • Eddie Albert *Austin Mack* • Beverly Garland *Cassie Mack* • Jackie Coogan *Swifty Morgan* • Sophie Tucker ■ *Dir* Charles Vidor • *Scr* Oscar Saul, from the non-fiction book *Life of Joe E Lewis* by Art Cohn

The Jokers ★★★ U

Comedy thriller 1967 · UK · Colour · 95min

Michael Crawford and Oliver Reed are well cast as brothers who attempt to steal the Crown Jewels just for the heck of it in this light-hearted romp. It's a quintessential "Swinging London" movie, full of nice locations and ever-so-British attitudes. The Dick Clement/Ian La Frenais screenplay was virtually director-proof and was entrusted to Michael Winner, who does a decent job of it, making it seem regrettable that he ever veered away from comedy. TS

Michael Crawford *Michael Tremayne* • Oliver Reed *David Tremayne* • Harry Andrews *Inspector Marryatt* • James Donald *Colonel Gurney-Simms* • Daniel Massey *Riggs* • Michael Hordern *Sir Matthew* • Edward Fox *Lt Sprague* • Warren Mitchell *Lennie* • Frank Finlay *Harassed man* ■ *Dir* Michael Winner • *Scr* Dick Clement, Ian La Frenais, from a story by Michael Winner

Le Joli Mai ★★★★ U

Documentary 1962 · Fr · BW · 121min

Chris Marker's fascinating documentary provides an invaluable snapshot of a city in transition. With its montage sequences, newsreel footage, narrated passages and probing interviews, it recalls the "city symphonies" made in the late silent era by the likes of Dziga Vertov, with Parisians of all classes and age groups proferring their views on everything from the nature of democracy to the state of French culture. With Yves Montand making an acerbic guide (the role is performed by Simone Signoret in the English version), this is *cinéma vérité* at its wittiest and most revealing. DP In French.

Simone Signoret *Commentary* • Yves Montand *Commentary* • Chris Marker • Anna Karina ■ *Dir* Chris Marker • *Scr* Cathérine Varlin, Chris Marker

A Jolly Bad Fellow ★

Black comedy 1964 · UK · BW · 110min

This is an ill-advised attempt by co-screenwriter Robert Hamer to recapture the glories of his 1949 Ealing classic *Kind Hearts and Coronets*. Leo McKern has the misfortune to play a university professor who uses his new undetectable poison to liquidate those he feels have no right to live. Don Chaffey took on the directorial chores after Hamer's death, but he was beaten before he started with this tasteless comedy. DP

Leo McKern *Professor Bowles-Ottery* • Janet Munro *Delia Brooks* • Maxine Audley *Clarinda Bowles-Ottery* • Duncan Macrae *Dr Brass* • Dennis Price *Professor Hughes* • Miles Malleson *Dr Woolley* • Leonard Rossiter *Dr Fisher* ■ *Dir* Don Chaffey • *Scr* Robert Hamer, Donald Taylor, from the novel *Down among the Dead Men* by CE Vulliamy

The Jolson Story ★★★★★ U

Musical biography 1946 · US · Colour · 124min

One of the most popular movies ever made, this biopic stars Larry Parks as the entertainer with the big ego and the even bigger talent. In re-recording his greatest hits for this movie, Al Jolson proved to be in finer, more mellow timbre than ever. These versions are therefore the definitive ones, and Parks totally convinces as he mimes his way through such landmarks as *April Showers*, *My Mammy* and *Toot Toot Tootsie Goodbye*. Okay, so the blacking-up is

politically unfashionable these days, the lovable Jewish characters are mere caricatures, and the tale is appallingly fancified. Who cares? This is Hollywood entertainment on a grand scale, and you'll weep and cheer all the way to the uncompromising final curtain. TS *DVD*

Larry Parks *Al Jolson* • Evelyn Keyes *Julie Benson* • William Demarest *Steve Martin* • Bill Goodwin *Tom Baron* • Ludwig Donath *Cantor Yoelson* • Tamara Shayne *Mrs Yoelson* • John Alexander (1) *Lew Dockstader* ■ *Dir* Alfred E Green • *Scr* Stephen Longstreet, Harry Chandlee, Andrew Solt

Jolson Sings Again ★★ U

Musical biography 1949 · US · Colour · 91min

Made three years after the phenomenal success of *The Jolson Story*, this sequel suffers from the fact that the entertainer's later life was nowhere near as interesting as his rise to fame. Larry Parks produces another remarkable impersonation (backed by Jolson's own singing voice), particularly relishing the gag in which Parks (playing Jolson) meets Parks (playing himself) to discuss making the first film. There's too little going on to give this anything but nostalgia value. DP *DVD*

Larry Parks *Al Jolson* • Barbara Hale *Ellen Clark* • William Demarest *Steve Martin* • Ludwig Donath *Cantor Yoelson* • Bill Goodwin *Tom Baron* • Myron McCormick *Col Ralph Bryant* ■ *Dir* Henry Levin • *Scr* Sidney Buchman • *Music Director* Morris Stoloff

Jonah Hex ★ 15

Supernatural western 2010 · US · Colour · 78min

One of the lesser-known DC Comics characters is destined to remain that way thanks to this disjointed paranormal western. Disfigured bounty hunter Jonah Hex (Josh Brolin) seeks revenge on Southern general Quentin Turnbull (the hammy John Malkovich), who slaughtered his family and threatens post-American Civil War security. The film is clearly stitched together from ruthlessly edited bare bones (the running time includes extensive credits), and its *Wild Wild West* mix of gothic gun-slinging and sci-fi weaponry fails to deliver even the cheapest thrills. AJ Violence. *DVD* *BL*

Josh Brolin *Jonah Hex* • Megan Fox *Lilah* • John Malkovich *Quentin Turnbull* • Will Arnett *Lieutenant Grass* • Michael Fassbender *Burke* • Michael Shannon *Doc Cross Williams* ■ *Dir* Jimmy Hayward • *Scr* Neveldine [Mark Neveldine], Taylor [Brian Taylor], from a story by William Farmer, Neveldine, Taylor, from characters by John Albano, Tony DeZuniga

Jonah Who Will Be 25 in the Year 2000 ★★★★

Comedy 1976 · Swi/Fr · Colour and BW · 115min

Seen from the virtually apolitical vantage point of a new millennium, Alain Tanner's right-on comedy might seem a muddle of wishy-washy notions and impossible dreams. But political radicalism had only recently died when he paid this tribute to the indomitability of the May 1968 veterans, who may have failed in their intentions, but who still had the courage to act. A magnificent ensemble cast endures life's buffeting with equanimity, while Tanner and co-screenwriter John Berger intertwine the diverging destinies with a dexterity that allows for revealing monochrome reveries (both brutal and fantastical). DP French +subtitles.

Jean-Luc Bideau *Max Stigny* • Myriam Boyer *Mathilde Vernier* • Rufus *Mathieu Vernier* • Miou-Miou *Marie* • Jacques Denis *Marco Perly* • Dominique Labourier *Marguerite* • Roger Jendly *Marcel Certoux* • Myriam Mézières *Madeleine* ■ *Dir* Alain Tanner • *Scr* Alain Tanner, John Berger

Jonas Brothers: the 3D Concert Experience ★ U

Concert documentary 2009 · US · Colour · 75min

Disney Channel favourites the Jonas Brothers come to the big screen in this record of their visit to New York and concert at Madison Square Garden.

Irrespective of your views on the band, this could have been entertaining. Yet the pop-rock songs are completely forgettable, and even the brothers themselves seem bored by their music and each other. It's a blessed relief when country superstar Taylor Swift takes to the stage and puts them all in the shade. There's little here for the target audience, with lazy and unimaginative 3D effects (water bouncing off a drum kit being a notable exception), and no insight into what makes the band tick. Popular the Jonas Brothers may be, but this particular vehicle is an unabashed dud. SuR 8P

Joe Jonas • Nick Jonas • Kevin Jonas • Demi Lovato • Taylor Swift ■ *Dir* Bruce Hendricks

Jonathan Livingston Seagull ★★★ U

Fantasy 1973 · US · Colour · 94min

Despite its title, this philosophical oddity doesn't exactly soar into comprehension. Richard Bach's bestseller, very much of its time, is an "inspirational" parable about a seagull whose life parallels human existence – speed, contemplation, and finally redemption and resurrection. This intriguing existentialist idea is nearly flooded out by Neil Diamond's splashy score. TH

James Franciscus *Jonathan Livingston Seagull* • Juliet Mills *Girl* • Hal Holbrook *Elder* • Philip Ahn *Chang* • David Ladd *Fletcher* • Kelly Harmon *Kimmy* ■ *Dir* Hall Bartlett • *Scr* Hall Bartlett, Richard Bach, from the novel by Richard Bach • *Music* Neil Diamond, Lee Holdridge

The Joneses ★★★ 15

Satirical comedy drama 2009 · US · Colour · 91min

An apparently perfect family moves into an affluent American neighbourhood brandishing the latest status-symbol goods in this glossy yet subtle black comedy. Demi Moore and David Duchovny's chemistry is fluid and believable as the couple who couldn't be more beautiful and in love, while Gary Cole effectively portrays the misled neighbour whose plight brings home the consequences of their actions. Without revealing its big twist, this is a high-concept message movie that delivers its strong warning against consumer culture and personal debt in a light-handed manner. KK Swearing, nudity. *DVD*

David Duchovny *Steve* • Demi Moore *Kate* • Amber Heard *Jenn* • Ben Hollingsworth *Mick* • Gary Cole *Larry* • Glenne Headly *Summer* • Lauren Hutton *KC* ■ *Dir/Scr* Derrick Borte

Joseph Andrews ★★

Period comedy 1977 · UK · Colour · 103min

Director Tony Richardson attempted to repeat the success of his Oscar-winning *Tom Jones* with another Fielding adaptation but falls flat on his farce. The bed-and-bawdy plot sees Peter Firth as the 18th-century footman involved in romantic adventures with the likes of Ann-Margret. It certainly looks good but Richardson fails to inject the necessary verve and pacing, opting for historical stereotypes and humour which is genteel at best. TH

Ann-Margret *Lady Booby* • Peter Firth *Joseph Andrews* • Michael Hordern *Parson Adams* • Beryl Reid *Mrs Slipslop* • Jim Dale *Pedlar* • Kenneth Cranham *Wicked Squire* • John Gielgud *Doctor* • Peggy Ashcroft *Lady Tattle* ■ *Dir* Tony Richardson • *Scr* Allan Scott, Chris Bryant, Tony Richardson, from the novel by Henry Fielding

Joseph: King of Dreams ★★ U

Animated musical drama 2000 · US · Colour · 71min

DreamWorks's direct-to-video follow-up to *The Prince of Egypt* lacks the epic feel generated the first time around. The background art (some of it computer-generated) is acceptable, but the character design is not. The biggest problem is that the Biblical hero comes across here as shallow and a little smug. KB *DVD*

Ben Affleck *Joseph* • Mark Hamill *Judah* • Steven Weber *Simeon* • Jodi Benson *Asenath* • Maureen McGovern *Rachel* • Judith Light *Zuleika* ■

U SUITABLE FOR ALL Uc SUITABLE ESPECIALLY FOR YOUNG CHILDREN (DVD ONLY) PG PARENTAL GUIDANCE 12A UNDER 12s TO BE ACCOMPANIED (CINEMA ONLY)

Dir Robert C Ramirez, Rob LaDuca • Scr Eugenia Bostwick-Singer, Raymond Singer, Joe Stillman, Marshall Goldberg

Josephine and Men ★★ U

Comedy 1955 • UK • Colour • 88min

Josephine (pert, husky-voiced Glynis Johns) is one of those perverse women who is always drawn to the losers in life, her interest waning when their fortunes improve. Debonair Jack Buchanan plays her suave bachelor uncle who narrates her story in flashback. Josephine leaves her wealthy fiancé (Donald Sinden) for his friend (Peter Finch), an unsuccessful playwright – until their situations are reversed. Directed by Roy Boulting, this is pretty lightweight and not as funny as it could have been, but the cast is likeable. RB

Glynis Johns Josephine Luton • Jack Buchanan Uncle Charles Luton • Peter Finch David Hewer • Donald Sinden Alan Hartley • Ronald Squire Frederick Luton • William Hartnell Inspector Parsons ■ Dir Roy Boulting • Scr Roy Boulting, Frank Harvey, Nigel Balchin, from the story by Nigel Balchin

Josh and SAM ★ 12

Adventure 1993 • US • Colour • 93min

In this unconvincing children's adventure, brothers Jacob Tierney and Noah Fleiss are miserably shuttled between their divorced parents until Tierney steals a car to embark on a road trip with his younger sibling. Meanwhile, Tierney has convinced Fleiss that he's not a little boy but in fact a Strategically Altered Mutant. Nonsensical fare that will annoy even the youngest viewers. JB

Jacob Tierney Josh • Noah Fleiss Sam • Martha Plimpton Alison • Stephen Tobolowsky Thom Whitney • Joan Allen Caroline • Chris Penn Derek Baxter ■ Dir Billy Weber • Scr Frank Deese

Joshua ★★ 15

Psychological thriller
2007 • US • Colour • 101min

Sibling rivalry develops into something darker in this unsatisfying psychological thriller. Fragmented and relentlessly sluggish, it sees parents Sam Rockwell and Vera Farmiga driven to emotional breakdown by their nine-year-old genius son (Jacob Kogan) following the arrival of a new baby. The film's main achievement is the way it captures the boy's pain – thanks largely to Kogan's solemn performance and his often poignant dialogue. Aside from that, the narrative is too uneventful to have much impact, leaving it to the clanging soundtrack to manufacture unease. SF
DVD

Sam Rockwell Brad Cairn • Vera Farmiga Abby Cairn • Celia Weston Hazel Cairn • Dallas Roberts Ned Davidoff • Michael McKean Chester Jenkins ■ Dir George Ratliff • Scr David Gilbert, George Ratliff

Joshua Then and Now ★★

Comedy drama 1985 • Can • Colour • 118min

Just as director Ted Kotcheff's earlier film of a Mordecai Richler novel The Apprenticeship of Duddy Kravitz gave Richard Dreyfuss a juicy role, this one gives James Woods the chance to show his combustible talent. He plays the son of a stripper and a pugilist-turned-convict who marries into London society in 1950 and then sees his life and career turned upside down when he returns to Canada in 1977. So much happens to Woods that this engrossing, if sketchy, drama might have made a better mini-series to give it more time with its admittedly interesting story. AT

James Woods Joshua Shapiro • Gabrielle Lazure Pauline Shapiro • Alan Arkin Reuben Shapiro • Michael Sarrazin Kevin Hornby • Linda Sorenson Esther Shapiro • Alan Scarfe Jack Trimble ■ Dir Ted Kotcheff • Scr Mordecai Richler, from his novel

Josie and the Pussycats ★★★ PG

Comedy 2001 • US • Colour • 94min

Gleefully ridiculing fashion fads, disposable culture and product placement, writer/directors Harry Elfont and Deborah Kaplan denounce corporate greed without mocking the teenagers suckered in by pitiless exploitation. Pussycats Rachael Leigh Cook, Tara Reid and Rosario Dawson combine individuality with recognisable girlie traits, but the stars are Alan Cumming and Parker Posey, as record company executives seeking to sneak subliminal messages into the band's music. A hilariously perceptive satire on crass commercialism and public susceptibility to hype. DP DVD

Rachael Leigh Cook Josie McCoy • Tara Reid Melody Valentine • Rosario Dawson Valerie Brown • Alan Cumming Wyatt Frame • Gabriel Mann Alan M • Parker Posey Fiona ■ Dir Harry Elfont, Deborah Kaplan • Scr Harry Elfont, Deborah Kaplan, from characters in Archie Comics created by John L Goldwater, Dan DeCarlo, Richard H Goldwater

Jour de Fête ★★★★★ U

Comedy 1947 • Fr • Colour and BW • 83min

If it hadn't been for modern technology, this comic masterpiece would have been permanently lost. Jacques Tati had hoped to shoot his debut feature in pioneering colour, but the stock was underdeveloped during processing and audiences had to make do with a black-and-white back-up copy until 1997, when a fully restored colour version (with a monochrome introduction) was released. Expanded from Tati's sublime 1947 short L'Ecole des Facteurs, the action chronicles the comic misadventures of village postman François as he tries to dispose of his letters at record speed in the style of the US mail service. There's a charming melancholy about some of the humour, but the slapstick is often frantic and balletic. Sheer genius. DP French +subtitles. DVD Blu

Jacques Tati François, the postman • Guy Decomble Roger, the showman • Paul Frankeur Marcel, the showman • Maine Vallée Jeannette • Roger Rafal Barber ■ Dir Jacques Tati • Scr Jacques Tati, Henri Marquet

Le Jour Se Lève ★★★★ PG

Crime melodrama 1939 • Fr • BW • 86min

Banned as demoralising by the Vichy government following negative reviews, Marcel Carné's tale of a murderer's reminiscing is clearly symbolic of an entrapped nation awaiting its inevitable destruction. But it's also a heart-rending human story. Typically outstanding as the doomed, introspective hero, Jean Gabin is the epitome of existential despair, while Jules Berry's lecherous villain is as loathsome as Arletty's showgirl is worldly wise and Jacqueline Laurent's Françoise is innocent. Told mostly in flashback, the story perfectly illustrates Carné's mastery of poetic realism. DP French +subtitles. DVD Blu

Jean Gabin François • Jules Berry M Valentin • Jacqueline Laurent Françoise • Arletty Clara • René Génin Concierge • Mady Berry Concierge's wife • Bernard Blier Gaston • Marcel Peres Paulo ■ Dir Marcel Carné • Scr Jacques Prévert, Jacques Viot

Une Journée Tranquille ★★★ 15

Thriller 1999 • Fr • Colour • 71min

This is a methodically told shaggy-dog story with a wicked twist in the tail. Written, produced and directed by Michael Jaffer, this is a thriller that seems consciously designed to stop you getting excited. Every task undertaken by birthday boy Christian Baltauss is downbeat and deliberate, whether intimidating petty crooks, setting up a major drug deal or bumping off a pimp who deals in underage innocents. However, this dour detachment somehow lends itself to a creeping fascination with both Baltauss and his fate. DP French +subtitles.

Christian Baltauss Man • Jean-Jacques Benhamou Friend • Gilles Bellomi Associate • Georges Vaello Pimp • Alexandra Bonnet Domino ■ Dir/Scr Michael Jaffer

The Journey ★★★

Drama 1997 • US • Colour • 97min

Although it constantly runs the risk of lapsing into stereotyping and culture-clash cliché, steady direction from Harish Saluja and discerning performances give this gentle drama its charm and poignancy. As the seasoned public school teacher retiring to his doctor son's Pittsburgh home, Roshan Seth exhibits both a reverence for tradition and stubborn insensitivity as he tries to educate his neglected granddaughter against the wishes of her American mother. DP

Roshan Seth Kishan Singh • Saeed Jaffrey Ashok • Carrie Preston Laura Singh • Antony Zaki Raj Singh • Betsy Zajko Audrey • Nora Bates Jenny Singh ■ Dir Harish Saluja • Scr Harish Saluja, Lisa Kirk Puchner

Journey back to Oz ★ U

Animated fantasy 1964 • US • Colour • 85min

Liza Minnelli steps into her late mother's ruby slippers as the voice of Dorothy in this animated sequel to the much loved Judy Garland classic. Barely ringing any major changes from the evergreen original, Dorothy is transported over the rainbow again by another cyclone. There's no wizard this time (what a swizz!), just the Wicked Witch of the West's sister (voiced by Ethel Merman) to contend with. Lacklustre songs mark even more time and do little to keep boredom at bay. Made in 1964, but not released until a decade later. AJ

Liza Minnelli Dorothy • Mickey Rooney Scarecrow • Milton Berle Cowardly Lion • Danny Thomas The Tin Man • Ethel Merman Mombi, the Bad Witch ■ Dir Hal Sutherland • Scr Fred Ladd, Norm Prescott

Journey into Fear ★★★★ PG

Spy drama 1942 • US • BW • 67min

This is often identified as Orson Welles's third feature film, though he claimed to have acted only as co-writer (with star Joseph Cotten) and producer, with Norman Foster credited as sole director. Logic takes something of a back seat in this bewildering tale of arms smuggling in Turkey during the Second World War. Yet any narrative shortcomings are more than made up for by Welles's atmospheric camera angles and the gallery of disreputable characters. DP DVD

Joseph Cotten Howard Graham • Orson Welles Colonel Haki • Dolores Del Rio Josette Martel • Ruth Warrick Stephanie Graham • Agnes Moorehead Mrs Mathews • Everett Sloane Kopeikin • Jack Moss Banat • Jack Durant Gogo ■ Dir Norman Foster • Scr Joseph Cotten, Orson Welles, from a novel by Eric Ambler • Cinematographer Karl Struss

The Journey of August King ★★★ 12

Period drama 1995 • US • Colour • 88min

Jason Patric and Thandie Newton star in this period drama directed by John Duigan. Newton plays a runaway slave in 19th-century North Carolina, who finds shelter with widowed farmer August King (Patric) and enters into a relationship with him. This beautiful looking film is limited by its sluggish pace and lack of sexual tension between the leads. LH DVD

Jason Patric August King • Thandie Newton Annalees Williamsburg • Larry Drake Olaf Singletary • Sam Waterston Mooney Wright • Sara-Jane Wylde Ida Wright • Eric Mabius Hal Wright ■ Dir John Duigan • Scr John Ehle, from his novel • Cinematographer Slawomir Idziak

Journey of Hope ★★★★ PG

Drama based on a true story
1990 • Swi • Colour • 105min

Although Xavier Koller's uncompromising feature won an Oscar for best foreign film, its power derives from its basis in reality rather than the unsentimental solidity of his direction. Accompanied by his young son, Necmettin Cobanoglu travels from southern Turkey to Switzerland more in desperation than in hope, placing himself in the hands of guides who are every bit as treacherous as the forbidding mountain terrain they must cross. The physical perils are presented with a naturalism that makes them all the more terrifying, but it's the contrast between blind faith and pitiless greed that renders the action so harrowing. DP German +subtitles.

Necmettin Cobanoglu Haydar • Nur Srer Meryem • Emin Sivas Mehmet Ali • Erdinc Akbas Adana • Yaman Okay Türkmen • Yasar Gner Haci Baba ■ Dir Xavier Koller • Scr Xavier Koller, Feride Cicekoglu, Heike Hubert

The Journey of Natty Gann ★★★ PG

Period adventure 1985 • US • Colour • 96min

Meredith Salenger is so good in the role of the 14-year-old who walks 2,000 miles in search of her lumberjack father that it beggars belief that she did not go on to become a star. John Cusack impresses here as a drifter convinced the open road is no place for a girl. There's plenty of action but this Disney movie scores best for its depiction of the hardships faced by many in the 1930s. DP DVD

Meredith Salenger Natty Gann • John Cusack Harry Slade • Ray Wise Sol Gann • Lainie Kazan Connie • Scatman Crothers Sherman • Barry Miller Parker • Verna Bloom Farm woman ■ Dir Jeremy Kagan [Jeremy Paul Kagan] • Scr Jeanne Rosenberg

Journey through Rosebud ★★★

Drama 1972 • US • Colour • 91min

This is a heartfelt drama about the plight of the native American in modern society, living on reservations in conditions of Third World squalor. The message has been bottled in a rather contrived drama that seeks to draw parallels between the American Indians and the Vietnamese, with Kristoffer Tabori as the draft dodger who hides out on the Rosebud reservation in South Dakota. AT

Robert Forster Frank • Kristoffer Tabori Danny • Victoria Racimo Shirley • Eddie Little Sky Stanley Pike • Roy Jenson Park Ranger • Wright King Indian agent ■ Dir Tom Gries • Scr Albert Ruben

Journey to Italy ★★★ PG

Romantic drama 1953 • It/Fr • BW • 81min

After both Stromboli and Europa '51 had met with a less than rapturous critical reception this Rossellini/Bergman collaboration saw their careers and their marriage at a low ebb. So this film – about an English couple (George Sanders and Ingrid Bergman), whose marriage is in crisis, travelling by car to Naples – could be seen as semi-autobiographical. On its release, the film was attacked for being clumsily made and sentimental but if one accepts the narrative simplicity and that the journey is both physical and spiritual, the film offers many rewards. Both English and Italian versions were filmed. RB DVD

Ingrid Bergman Katherine Joyce • George Sanders Alexander Joyce • Maria Mauban Marie • Paul Muller Paul Dupont • Leslie Daniels Tony Burton • Dir Roberto Rossellini • Scr Vitaliano Brancati, Roberto Rossellini

Journey to Shiloh ★★

Western adventure 1967 • US • Colour • 101min

More interesting today for its cast than its content, this dates from the period when Universal reverted to producing programme westerns to show off young talent. Here, James Caan gets a crack at a leading role, seeking Confederate glory but discovering only the horrors of civil war. The episodic, rambling narrative suggests some production interference along the way, and veteran TV director William Hale soon returned to the small screen. Keep your eyes peeled for novice Harrison Ford in an early movie role. TS

James Caan Buck Burnett • Michael Sarrazin Miller Nalls • Brenda Scott Gabrielle DuPrey • Don Stroud Todo McLean • Paul Peterson JC Sutton • Michael Burns Eubie Bell • Michael Vincent [Jan-Michael Vincent] Little Bit Lucket • Harrison Ford Willie Bill Bearden ■ Dir William Hale • Scr Gene L Coon, from a novel by Will Henry [Heck Allen]

Journey to the Beginning of the World ★★★ U
Road movie 1997 · Por/Fr · Colour · 94min

Nostalgia and regret are only to be expected when an 89-year-old film-maker takes a sentimental journey around his homeland. Manoel de Oliveira's wistful odyssey is made all the more poignant, though, by the fact that it contains Marcello Mastroianni's farewell performance as the director's alter ego. However, just as the reminiscences begin to weave their spell, the emphasis shifts on to Jean-Yves Gautier trying to persuade a long-lost aunt to overcome her xenophobia and accept him as family. DP French, Portuguese +subtitles.

Marcello Mastroianni *Manoel* • Jean-Yves Gautier *Afonso* • Leonor Silveira *Judite* • Diogo Doria *Duarte* • Isabel De Castro *Maria Afonso* ■ *Dir/Scr* Manoel de Oliveira

Journey to the Center of the Earth ★★★★ U
Science-fiction adventure 1959 · US · Colour · 124min

This lavish, well crafted adaptation of Jules Verne's classic tale stars James Mason, leading an expedition into a volcano shaft and finding large mushrooms, giant lizards, an underground ocean and the lost city of Atlantis. Bernard Herrmann's fabulous music sets the mood for the spirited adventure, with the accent firmly on wholesome light-heartedness rather than vivid Verne danger. Singer Pat Boone adds his own brand of fantasy swashbuckling, which are played out against some staggeringly imaginative subterranean sets. AJ DVD

Pat Boone *Alec McEwen* • James Mason *Professor Oliver Lindenbrook* • Arlene Dahl *Carla* • Diane Baker *Jenny* • Thayer David *Count Saknussemm* • Peter Ronson *Hans* ■ *Dir* Henry Levin • *Scr* Walter Reisch, Charles Brackett, from the novel *Voyage au Centre de la Terre* by Jules Verne • *Art Directors* Lyle R Wheeler [Lyle Wheeler], Franz Bachelin, Herman A Blumenthal • *Set Designers* Walter M Scott, Joseph Kish

Journey to the Center of the Earth ★★ PG
Science-fiction adventure 1989 · US · Colour · 76min

Bearing only a passing resemblance to the Jules Verne classic, this harmless family adventure relocates the action to Hawaii where a group of teens stumbles upon an alternative world while out exploring caves. The eclectic cast includes Nicola Cowper and Kathy Ireland and, although Verne purists will be disgusted, it makes for blandly enjoyable entertainment. JF

Paul Carafotes *Richard* • Nicola Cowper *Chrystina* • Ilan Mitchell-Smith *Bryan* • Jeff Weston *Tola* • Jaclyn Bernstein *Sara* • Kathy Ireland *Wanda* ■ *Dir* Rusty Lemorande, Albert Pyun • *Scr* Rusty Lemorande, Debra Ricci, Regina Davis, Kitty Chalmers, from the novel *Voyage au Centre de la Terre* by Jules Verne

Journey to the Center of the Earth ★★ PG
Action adventure 2008 · US · Colour · 88min

The original fantasy tale by Jules Verne is merely a *Rough Guide* to surviving in the planet's bowels according to this wholesome adventure. While searching for his missing explorer brother in some Icelandic caves, scientist Brendan Fraser, his nephew Josh Hutcherson and guide Anita Briem are forced deep underground, where they discover subterranean jungles, raging oceans and prehistoric creatures. Despite insipid direction the film does boast some rollercoaster-ride thrills. But the only thing it has in common with the still-superior 1959 version is the spectacular landscapes; light-hearted banter and Disney cuteness replace any sense of wonder. AJ DVD

Brendan Fraser *Trevor Anderson* • Josh Hutcherson *Sean Anderson* • Anita Briem *Hannah Asgeirsson* ■ *Dir* Eric Brevig • *Scr* Michael Weiss [Michael D Weiss], Jennifer Flackett, Mark Levin

Journey to the Far Side of the Sun ★★★ PG
Science-fiction drama 1969 · UK · Colour · 97min

On the other side of the sun, astronaut Roy Thinnes finds a hidden planet mirroring Earth in every exact detail. Writer/producers Gerry and Sylvia Anderson, who created the cult puppet shows *Thunderbirds* and *Captain Scarlet*, as well as the live action series *UFO* and *Space 1999*, combine a clever concept with solid special effects. Add commendable direction from Robert Parrish and a memorable twist ending, and the result is a minor science-fiction gem. AJ DVD

Ian Hendry *John Kane* • Roy Thinnes *Col Glenn Ross* • Patrick Wymark *Jason Webb* • Lynn Loring *Sharon Ross* • Loni von Friedl *Lise* • Herbert Lom *Dr Hassler* ■ *Dir* Robert Parrish • *Scr* Gerry Anderson, Sylvia Anderson, Donald James

Journey 2 the Mysterious Island ★★★ PG
Action adventure 2011 · US · Colour · 90min

In this pleasant slice of family fare, teen Josh Hutcherson and stepfather Dwayne Johnson trace the actual location of author Jules Verne's supposedly fictional island. Having travelled to the South Pacific and roped in helicopter pilot Luiz Guzmán (providing stale comic relief) and his daughter Vanessa Hudgens (the teen love interest), they weather a hurricane and crash on the island. There they find Hutcherson's grandfather Michael Caine (doing his best Captain Birds Eye impression), and discover the truth about their location. It's an innocuous fantasy that pastiches Verne, *Treasure Island* and *Gulliver's Travels*. AJ DVD Blu sp

Dwayne Johnson *Hank Parsons* • Michael Caine *Alexander Anderson* • Josh Hutcherson *Sean Anderson* • Vanessa Hudgens [Vanessa Anne Hudgens] *Kailani* • Luis Guzmán [Luis Guzman] *Gabato* • Kristin Davis *Liz Anderson* ■ *Dir* Brad Peyton • *Scr* Brian and Mark Gunn, from a story by Brian and Mark Gunn, Richard Outten

Journey to the Shore ★★★ 12A
Romantic fantasy 2015 · Jpn/Fr · Colour · 128min

Director Kiyoshi Kurosawa just about succeeds in combining the supernatural and the melodramatic with his adaptation of Kazumi Yumoto's bestseller. Three years after drowning, Yusuke (Tadanobu Asano) returns to wife Mizuki (Eri Fukatsu) and persuades her to help other spirits find peace. Kurosawa seems reluctant to explore the themes of grief, loyalty and atonement, and submerges the action in a mawkish score. However, cinematographer Akiko Ashizawa's use of light should be applauded, as should Fukatsu's touching performance. DP Japanese +subtitles. Moderate sex DVD Blu

Tadanobu Asano *Yusuke* • Eri Fukatsu *Mizuki* • Masao Komatsu *Shimakage* ■ *Dir* Kiyoshi Kurosawa • *Scr* Kiyoshi Kurosawa, Takashi Ujita, from the novel *Kishibe no tabi* by Kazumi Yumoto • *Cinematographer* Akiko Ashizawa

Journey Together ★★★ PG
Second World War drama documentary 1944 · UK · BW · 91min

Richard Attenborough and Jack Watling train for Lancaster bombing missions, though their talents take them in different directions. Later the pair are shot down and bond in a life-raft in the middle of the North Sea. Designed to show the special relationship between Britain and America – Edward G Robinson waived his fee for playing a flying instructor – the film was directed for the RAF Film Unit by John Boulting. The script is based on a story written by Terence Rattigan to exorcise the shock of losing a close friend in the war. AT DVD

Richard Attenborough *David Wilton* • Jack Watling *John Aynesworth* • David Tomlinson *Smith* • Edward G Robinson *Dean McWilliams* •

Sid Rider *Fitter* • Hugh Wakefield *Acting Lieutenant* ■ *Dir* John Boulting • *Scr* John Boulting, from a story by Terence Rattigan

Journey's End ★★★
First World War drama 1930 · US/UK · BW · 130min

Gods and Monsters (1998), the excellent biopic of British-born Hollywood director James Whale, cast new light on Whale's first feature, an adaptation of RC Sherriff's First World War play. Whale, who served in the trenches, shot the picture in Hollywood because British studios were not yet fully equipped for sound. The film is a valuable record of the stage production, with the same splendidly stiff-upper-lip yet touching performances from the all-male cast and "simply topping" dialogue. Colin Clive is especially good as the captain breaking under the strain of war. RB

Colin Clive *Capt Stanhope* • Ian MacLaren *Lt Osborne* • David Manners *Second Lt Raleigh* • Billy Bevan *Second Lt Trotter* • Anthony Bushell *Second Lt Hibbert* • Robert A'Dair [Robert Adair] *Capt Hardy* ■ *Dir* James Whale • *Scr* Joseph Moncure March, from the play by RC Sherriff

Joy ★★★★ 12
Drama based on a true story 2015 · US · Colour · 118min

At the height of domestic despair, Joy Mangano happened upon an idea for a revolutionary mop and set about making it happen. Despite the quietly showy camerawork and overriding feel of the fantastical in David O Russell's fizzy feminist dramedy, *Joy* transforms the inventor's life into a gorgeous but nevertheless gritty fairy tale, as seen through the eyes of her grandmother (Diane Ladd), as Mangano (played by Russell regular Jennifer Lawrence) enters the weird world of home shopping, to amusing effect. Robert De Niro and Bradley Cooper are spot-on in support but a gutsy, understated Lawrence (playing Joy as a credible, complex character) leads by example in a role that inspires great admiration. EAS Swearing DVD Blu

Jennifer Lawrence (2) *Joy Mangano* • Robert De Niro *Rudy Mangano* • Bradley Cooper *Neil Walker* • Edgar Ramirez *Tony Miranne* • Isabella Rossellini *Trudy* • Virginia Madsen *Terry* ■ *Dir* David O Russell • *Scr* David O Russell, Annie Mumolo

Joy Division ★★ 15
Drama 2006 · UK/Hun/Ger · Colour · 100min

In this sprawling drama, Ed Stoppard (the son of playwright Tom) plays Thomas, a teenage German soldier who is captured by the Red Army during the last days of the Second World War. He is then "turned" by the Russians and sent years later as a communist spy into the Cold War Britain of the Swinging Sixties. The film is handsomely staged, and there are good performances from Stoppard and from former *EastEnders* actress Michelle Gayle, who plays the latest love of Thomas's life. But the fractured time frame is irritating, with the film flitting giddily and often confusingly between Thomas's present and his distant and more recent past. And, because it's a war film, a spy film and a love story, all at once, it has trouble satisfying any of them completely. But the film's sheer ambition merits at least some attention. DA

Ed Stoppard *Thomas (older)* • Tom Schilling *Thomas (younger)* • Bernadette Heerwagen *Melanie* • Bernard Hill *Dennis* • Michelle Gayle *Yvonne* • Lea Mornar *Astrid* ■ *Dir/Scr* Reg Traviss

Joy Division ★★★★ 15
Music documentary 2008 · UK · Colour · 95min

Hot on the heels of *Control* (Anton Corbijn's biopic of Joy Division lead singer Ian Curtis) comes this laudably frank profile of the band that launched the Manchester music scene. The focus inevitably falls on charismatic frontman Curtis, who transformed Joy Division's style in collaboration with producer Martin Hannett before taking his own life in 1980. But the surviving members (who later formed the band New Order), as well as Factory

Records boss Anthony Wilson, offer invaluable and unsentimental insights into the band's evolution and the rise of "Madchester" from the ashes of the city's post-industrial decay. With Matthew Robertson's graphics adding an impressive visual edge, this impeccably researched history is packed with rare audio clips and live footage, and fills in many of the gaps left by *Control* and Michael Winterbottom's *24 Hour Party People*. DP Swearing. DVD

Peter Hook • Bernard Sumner • Stephen Morris • Annik Honore • Tony Wilson • Martin Hannett • Malcolm Whitehead • Lindsay Reade • Peter Saville ■ *Dir* Grant Gee • *Scr* Jon Savage • *Cinematographer* Grant Gee

The Joy Luck Club ★★★★ 15
Drama 1993 · US · Colour · 133min

Faithfully adapted from Amy Tan's bestselling book, director Wayne Wang's moving yet witty melodrama mixes the stories of four Chinese-born mothers with those of their American-born daughters. Murder, suicide, betrayal and love are all captured in numerous three-hanky moments, beautifully (if sentimentally) played. Tan co-wrote the script with *Rain Man* scribe Ronald Bass and the result is a bit of a women's weepie, but it's an excellent one. JB DVD

Kieu Chinh *Suyuan* • Tsai Chin *Lindo* • France Nuyen *Ying Ying* • Lisa Lu *An Mei* • Wen Ming-Na [Ming-Na] *June* • Tamlyn Tomita *Waverly* • Lauren Tom *Lena* ■ *Dir* Wayne Wang • *Scr* Amy Tan, Ronald Bass, from a novel by Amy Tan

Joy of Living ★★★
Screwball comedy 1938 · US · BW · 90min

Irene Dunne was one of the great joys of 1930s Hollywood, both a talented singer and superb comedian. This screwball comedy with songs capitalises on those skills, and, as in Dunne's earlier musicals, the numbers were composed by Jerome Kern, including *You Couldn't Be Cuter*. She is cast as a wealthy Broadway star who escapes from her family of hangers-on and discovers a new lease of life with shipping magnate Douglas Fairbanks Jr. A fine supporting cast is somewhat wasted in this agreeable tale. AE

Irene Dunne *Margaret* • Douglas Fairbanks Jr *Dannie* • Alice Brady *Minerva* • Guy Kibbee *Dennis* • Jean Dixon *Harrison* • Eric Blore *Potter* • Lucille Ball *Salina* ■ *Dir* Tay Garnett • *Scr* Gene Towne, Graham Baker, Allan Scott, from a story by Herbert Fields, Dorothy Fields

Joy of Madness ★★★★ PG
Documentary 2003 · Iran · Colour · 70min

As those familiar with DVD extras will know, "Making of" documentaries rarely fulfil their promise. But 14-year-old Hana Makhmalbaf's record of her sister Samira's attempts to cast the acclaimed *At Five in the Afternoon* not only provides a unique insight into the pre-production process, but also reveals much about Afghan society in the wake of the Taliban. The devastation, fear and extreme poverty evident throughout Kabul are movingly conveyed. But even more telling are the contrasting attitudes of the mullah whom Samira auditions for the part of the father and Agheleh Rezaie, the teacher whose ambition is tempered by her uncertainty how far to assert women's rights in this paternalistic state. DP Farsi +subtitles. DVD

■ *Dir* Hana Makhmalbaf • *Scr* Hana Makhmalbaf

Joy of Sex ★ 15
Sex comedy 1984 · US · Colour · 89min

Using just the title of Alex Comfort's bestseller, and none of its factual content, this lame teenage sex comedy gives new meaning to the words dull, vulgar and pathetic. Michelle Meyrink mistakenly thinks she only has a few weeks left to live and embarks on a desperate, virginity-losing campaign. Distance has lent director Martha Coolidge's soporific erotic cabaret a certain campy 1980s nostalgia. AJ

Cameron Dye *Alan Holt* • Michelle Meyrink *Leslie Hindenberg* • Charles Van Eman *Max Holt* • Lisa Langlois *Melanie* • Colleen Camp *Liz Sampson* • *Dir* Martha Coolidge • *Scr* Kathleen Rowell, JJ Salter

Joy Ride 2: Dead Ahead ★★ 18
Horror thriller 2008 · US/Can · Colour · 87min

Disrespect and stupidity hurl four road-tripping youths into an escalating nightmare in this formulaic cat-and-mouse sequel. However, unlike the 2001 original (better known as *Road Kill* in the UK), this flimsy made-for-video mix of *Duel*, *The Hitcher* and *Saw* focuses on suffering rather than suspense, as Rusty Nail (played by Mark Gibbon, but without Ted Levine's vocal menace) terrorises them for borrowing his car after their vehicle breaks down en route to Las Vegas. The film does get more atmospheric, but the impact of even these scenes is undermined by the increasing lack of realism. SF Violence. *DVD*

Mark Gibbon *Rusty Nail* • Nicki Aycox *Melissa* • Nick Zano *Bobby* • Kyle Schmid *Nik* ■ *Dir* Louis Morneau • *Scr* James Robert Johnston, Bennett Yellin

Joyful Noise ★★★ PG
Comedy 2012 · US · Colour · 112min

Fancy watching something light, bright and breezy that leaves you with a cheesy smile on your face? This could be just the ticket. *Joyful Noise* stars two queens: Queen Latifah and queen of country music, Dolly Parton. They play fightin', feudin' choristers, vying for control of their small-town Georgia choir in the run-up to a major national competition. The plot is pants. The romantic subplots are pants. And the whole thing is cornier than anything made by Kellogg's. But set cynicism aside and the truth is it's heart-warming stuff. DA *DVD*

Queen Latifah *Vi Rose Hill* • Dolly Parton *GG Sparrow* • Keke Palmer *Olivia Hill* • Jeremy Jordan *Randy Garrity* • Dexter Darden *Walter Hill* ■ *Dir/Scr* Todd Graff

The Joyless Street ★★★★★
Silent drama 1925 · Ger · BW · 125min

Unique in being the only film to boast Greta Garbo and Marlene Dietrich in its cast (the latter as an uncredited extra), this silent masterpiece is also significant for its development of the technique of "seamless" editing and for pioneering the style known as "street realism". Although staged on studio sets, there's an authenticity about the Vienna depicted in this study of middle-class desperation, as both Garbo (in her last pre-Hollywood picture) and Asta Nielsen have to sell more than their souls to feed their families, while those who profiteered from the First World War indulge themselves in every vice. DP

Asta Nielsen *Maria Lechner* • Greta Garbo *Greta Rumfort* • Werner Krauss *Joseph Gieringer/The Butcher of Melchior Street* • Valeska Gert *Mrs Greifer* • Marlene Dietrich ■ *Dir* GW Pabst • *Scr* Willy Haas, from a novel by Hugo Bettauer • *Cinematographer* Guido Seeber, Curt Oertel, Walter Robert Lach • *Editor* Hans Sohnle

Joyriders ★★ 15
Road movie 1988 · UK · Colour · 92min

In spite of the arresting opening, in which a frustrated Dubliner dumps her kids as left luggage, and some glorious Irish scenery, this drama is soon trapped within the confines of its limited budget, the underdeveloped script and the overcautious approach of debut director Aisling Walsh. Some of Patricia Kerrigan's scenes with daydreaming car thief Andrew Connolly are quite touching, but the pessimism and the narrowness of approach underwhelm you. DP

Patricia Kerrigan *Mary Flynn* • Andrew Connolly *Perky Rice* • Billie Whitelaw *Tammy O'Moore* • David Kelly *Daniel Tracey* • John Kavanagh *Hotel Manager* • Deirdre Donoghue *Dolores Flynn* • Tracy Peacock *Finbar Flynn* ■ *Dir* Aisling Walsh • *Scr* Andy Smith, from a story by Andy Smith, Aisling Walsh

The Joyriders ★★
Crime drama 1999 · US · Colour · 90min

This overbearing melodrama is rendered almost unwatchable by a soundtrack strewn with purportedly inspirational songs. As the senior citizen who offers a trio of homeless delinquents a fresh start after they take him hostage with the gun he'd bought for his own suicide, Martin Landau does the job you expect of such a conscientious actor. But Bradley Battersby's feel-good direction is excruciating. DP

Martin Landau *Gordon Trout* • Kris Kristofferson *Eddie* • Heather McComb *Crystal* • Shawn Hatosy *Cam* • Elisabeth Moss *Jody* • Diane Venora *Celeste* ■ *Dir* Bradley Battersby • *Scr* Bradley Battersby, Jeff Spiegel

Ju Dou ★★★★★ 15
Period drama 1990 · Chi/Jpn · Colour · 88min

The first Chinese film to be nominated for an Oscar, this is one of the glories of recent Chinese cinema. Although superbly shot by Gu Changwei and Yang Lun, the primary credit for the film's visual splendours belongs to principal director Zhang Yimou, himself a former cinematographer, whose command of colour and camera angle complements his assured handling of this intense tale of illicit passion set in a cloth dyer's mill sometime in the 1920s. Gong Li gives a dynamic performance and this sly attack on China's elderly ruling elite is rightly considered by many to be Zhang's masterpiece. DP Mandarin +subtitles. Violence, swearing, nudity.

Li Wei *Yang Jinshan* • Gong Li *Ju Dou* • Li Baotian *Yang Tianqing* • Yi Zhang *Yang Tianbai as a child* • Jian Zheng *Yang Tianbai as a boy* ■ *Dir* Zhang Yimou, Yang Fengliang • *Scr* Liu Heng, from his story *Fuxi, Fuxi*

Ju-On: The Grudge 2 ★★★ 15
Horror thriller 2003 · Jpn · Colour · 88min

Japanese writer/director Takashi Shimizu continued to mine his *Ju-On* horror franchise with this atmospheric sequel to 2003's *The Grudge: Ju-On*. Creepier than its predecessor though never genuinely scary, the feature sees the cast and crew of a TV special fall victim to a lethal curse after filming in the original's spooky residence. While Shimizu again employs a non-linear narrative style, this time it's less confusing, thanks to more fully-fleshed characters and greater plot exposition. SF Japanese +subtitles. *DVD*

Noriko Sakai *Kyoko Harase* • Chiharu Niyama *Tomoko Miura* • Yui Ichikawa *Chiharu* • Takako Fuji *Kayako* • Yuya Ozeki *Toshio* ■ *Dir/Scr* Takashi Shimizu

Juan of the Dead ★★★ 15
Comedy horror 2011 · Sp/Cub · Colour · 92min

Despite nods to George A Romero and Lucio Fulci, Cuba's first horror movie owes greater debts to Peter Jackson and Edgar Wright as it lampoons the conventions of the zombie flick while tossing in some laudably bold socio-political satire. Juan (Alexis Dias de Villegas) and Lazaro (Jorge Molina) are ageing slackers who take advantage of a plague of the undead by charging Havana's citizens to slay and dispose of their infected loved ones. A vein of homophobia taints writer/director Alejandro Brugués's romp, yet it still manages some relishable slapstick and gory set pieces, as well as some very funny anti-American propaganda. DP Spanish +subtitles. Violence, swearing, sexual references.

Alexis Dias de Villegas *Juan* • Jorge Molina *Lazaro* • Andrea Duro *Camila* • Andros Perugorria *Vladi* • Jazz Vilá *La China* • Eliecer Ramirez *El Primo* ■ *Dir/Scr* Alejandro Brugués

Juarez ★★★ U
Historical drama 1939 · US · BW · 116min

In this epic about the French colonisation of Mexico, Paul Muni found a role that suited his stature, as Benito Pablo Juarez. This film was made in two halves, and then edited together, and it shows. Nevertheless, there is striking work on display here: Bette Davis's Empress Carlotta going mad is a highspot, and John Garfield brings an honest heartfelt intensity to the small role of Porfirio Diaz. But Brian Aherne is a stuffy Maximilian, and the plot is tortuously slow to unwind. Thank goodness for a splendid Erich Wolfgang Korngold score. TS

Paul Muni *Benito Juarez* • Bette Davis *Carlotta* • Brian Aherne *Maximilian* • Claude Rains *Napoleon III* • Gale Sondergaard *Empress Eugenie* • John Garfield *Porfirio Diaz* • Donald Crisp *Marechal Bazaine* ■ *Dir* William Dieterle • *Scr* John Huston, Wolfgang Reinhardt, Aeneas MacKenzie, from the play *Juarez & Maximillian* by Franz Werfel, from the novel *The Phantom Crown* by Bertita Harding

Jubal ★★★★ PG
Western drama 1956 · US · Colour · 97min

This adaptation of Paul I Wellman's novel *Jubal Troop* is a fine work with a magnificent, grim performance from Glenn Ford as the eponymous drifter. But look closer and you'll recognise plot themes and motivations – yup, it's *Othello* out west, with Ernest Borgnine's rancher as the Moor and Rod Steiger cast in the Iago role. Loner Ford is an almost-Cassio, and the suspense is stretched tightly as you long for Ford and Steiger to settle the score. A brutal tale, well told by Delmer Daves, and magnificently photographed by Charles Lawton Jr. TS *DVD*

Glenn Ford *Jubal Troop* • Ernest Borgnine *Shep Horgan* • Rod Steiger *Pinky* • Valerie French *Mae Horgan* • Felicia Farr *Naomi Hoktor* • Basil Ruysdael *Shem Hoktor* • Noah Beery Jr *Sam* • Charles Bronson *Reb Haislipp* ■ *Dir* Delmer Daves • *Scr* Delmer Daves, Russell S Hughes, from the novel *Jubal Troop* by Paul I Wellman

Jubilee ★★★ 18
Black comedy 1978 · UK · Colour · 100min

Queen Elizabeth I takes a trip into the future to witness "Anarchy in the UK" in Britain's first fully fledged punk movie. Director Derek Jarman, Ken Russell's former set designer, used the 1977 Silver Jubilee to comment on the disintegration of society, crafting a fiercely inventive experimental psycho-fantasy making ample use of New Wave music (Adam Ant, Chelsea, Siouxsie and the Banshees, the Slits) and the concerns of contemporary youth culture. Always more hip King's Road than hard-core street-cred, it remains an energetic and witty time capsule. AJ Violence, swearing, sex scenes, nudity.

Jenny Runacre *Bod/Queen Elizabeth I* • Little Nell *Crabs* • Toyah Willcox *Mad* • Jordan *Amyl Nitrite* • Hermine Demoriane *Chaos* • Ian Charleson *Angel* • Karl Johnson (2) *Sphinx* • Linda Spurrier *Viv* • Neil Kennedy *Max* • Orlando [Jack Birkett] *Borgia Ginz* • Wayne County *Lounge Lizard* • Richard O'Brien *John Dee* • Adam Ant *Kid* ■ *Dir/Scr* Derek Jarman

Judas Kiss ★★★ 15
Crime thriller 1998 · US · Colour · 93min

When a gang kidnaps a computer genius, a woman gets killed in the scrum. Turns out that she's the wife of a senator and then... well, that's just one twist in this strange thriller. Director Sebastian Gutierrez grafts the influence of Pedro Almodóvar onto Quentin Tarantino: the first few minutes are pornography, then it's a legit thriller, then it goes all weird again, and that's before Emma Thompson and Alan Rickman appear as New Orleans cops. She's tough and funny; he gives a creepily unreal performance. Made for cable TV, this could become a cult. AT *DVD*

Carla Gugino *Coco Chavez* • Simon Baker-Denny [Simon Baker (1)] *Junior Armstrong* • Gil Bellows *Lizard Browning* • Emma Thompson *Agent Sadie Hawkins* • Alan Rickman *Detective David Friedman* • Til Schweiger *Ruben Rubenbauer* • Greg Wise *Ben Dyson* ■ *Dir* Sebastian Gutierrez • *Scr* Sebastian Gutierrez, from a story by Deanna Fuller, Sebastian Gutierrez

Jude ★★★★ 15
Period drama 1996 · UK · Colour and BW · 117min

Co-produced by the BBC, this magnificent and appropriately distressing adaptation of Thomas Hardy's final novel did only fair business at British cinemas. As Jude, Christopher Eccleston has that haunted and naive look of a man buffeted by fate and destroyed by self-delusion, while Kate Winslet is perfect as Sue Bridehead, the fiery cousin whom Jude loves and whose vacillation drives the story along. Visually, the film is suitably gloomy and at two hours it's a brilliant distillation of a literary classic. AT Some violence, nudity, sex scenes. *DVD*

Christopher Eccleston *Jude Fawley* • Kate Winslet *Sue Bridehead* • Liam Cunningham *Phillotson* • Rachel Griffiths *Arabella* • June Whitfield *Aunt Drusilla* • Ross Colvin Turnbull *Little Jude* • James Daley *Jude as a boy* • Berwick Kaler *Farmer Troutham* ■ *Dir* Michael Winterbottom • *Scr* Hossein Amini, from the novel *Jude the Obscure* by Thomas Hardy

Judex ★★★★ PG
Mystery adventure 1963 · Fr/It · BW · 93min

A glorious evocation of a bygone era, French director Georges Franju's tribute to the pioneering silent serials of fantasy writer Louis Feuillade is a thrilling combination of subversive derring-do and lyrical symbolism. The convoluted plot centres around the attempts of Channing Pollock's clandestine crusade to protect banker's daughter, Edith Scob, from the machinations of the diabolical Francine Bergé. From the enchanting opening at a masked ball, the battle of wits between real-life conjurer Pollock and the chameleon Bergé is endlessly entertaining. But it's the stylised, often surreal, quality of the atmospheric photography that proves conclusively that pulp kitsch can, occasionally, touch poetry. DP *DVD*

Channing Pollock *Judex/Vallieres* • Francine Bergé *Diana Monti/Marie Verdier* • Edith Scob *Jacqueline Favraux* • Michel Vitold *Favraux* ■ *Dir* Georges Franju • *Scr* Francis Lacassin, Jacques Champreux, from the 1916 film • *Cinematographer* Marcel Fradetal

The Judge ★★★ 15
Drama 2014 · US · Colour · 141min

After ten years playing edgy superheroes and oddballs, Robert Downey Jr returns to the real world with the kind of slick Hollywood vehicle he was on track to make in the first place, before sobriety issues bumped him from the A-list. The good news is that Downey sparkles in the story of a smooth-talking, big-city lawyer who finds himself defending his estranged father (Robert Duvall) – the respected small-town judge of the title – on a hit-and-run charge. The bad news is that he deserves a much better showcase than this, a sentimental story that squares up to, but quickly fumbles, a potentially gripping courtroom drama. DW Swearing, sexual references. *DVD*

Robert Downey Jr *Hank Palmer* • Robert Duvall *Judge Joseph Palmer* • Vera Farmiga *Samantha* • Billy Bob Thornton *Dwight Dickham* • Vincent D'Onofrio *Glen Palmer* ■ *Dir* David Dobkin • *Scr* Bill Dubuque, Nick Schenk, from a story by Schenk, Dobkin

Judge & Jury ★★★ 18
Action horror 1995 · US · Colour · 93min

Following his execution, vicious murderer David Keith returns from the dead to take revenge on the two men he blames for his wife's death – disgraced detective Paul Koslo and over-the-hill American football player Martin Kove. A barnstorming performance from the ghostly Keith drives director John Eyres's *Shocker* retread, humorously blending chills and action for a fun, fright fix. Released on video/DVD in the UK as *From beyond the Grave*. AJ Violence, swearing. *DVD*

David Keith *Joey* • Martin Kove *Michael Silvano* • Thomas Ian Nicholas *Alex Silvano* • Laura Johnson *Grace Silvano* • Kelly Perine *Roland* • Paul Koslo *Lockhart* • Robert Miranda *Coach Wagner* • Patricia Scanlon *Mary* ■ *Dir* John Eyres • *Scr* John Eyres, Amanda Kirpaul, John Cianetti

Judge Dredd ★★★ 🔞15
Science-fiction action adventure
1995 · US · Colour · 91min

Director Danny Cannon's imaginatively over-the-top science-fiction rendering of the celebrated *2000 AD* comic-strip hero. In the future, the world has formed into densely populated Mega Cities with the Cursed Earth being the uninhabitable region lying between them. Law and order is maintained by a fleet of elite officers who are judge, jury and executioner all rolled into one, and Judge Dredd (Sylvester Stallone) is the most prolific of the brigade. Always exciting, this is an underrated fantasy, full of flash, plenty of bang and packing a considerable wallop. AJ Swearing, violence. 📀

Sylvester Stallone *Judge Dredd* • Armand Assante *Rico* • Rob Schneider *Fergie* • Jürgen Prochnow *Judge Griffin* • Max von Sydow *Judge Fargo* • Diane Lane *Judge Hershey* ■ *Dir* Danny Cannon • *Scr* William Wisher, Steven E de Souza, from a story by Wisher, Michael DeLuca, from characters by John Wagner, Carlos Ezquerra

Judge Hardy and Son ★★ 🇺
Comedy crime
1939 · US · BW · 89min

This is the eighth in the series that began in 1937 with *A Family Affair* and enshrines wholesome small-town values and smothers them in comedy. This entry has Andy (Mickey Rooney) doing some serious bonding with his dad, Judge Hardy (Lewis Stone), while also trying to win the school essay competition, as well as Ann Rutherford's pretty Polly. Then pneumonia strikes Andy's mum, and the relatives gather round her with Andy offering a prayer. This family wasn't named Hardy for nothing. AT

Lewis Stone *Judge James K Hardy* • Mickey Rooney *Andy Hardy* • Cecilia Parker *Marian Hardy* • Fay Holden *Mrs Emily Hardy* • Ann Rutherford *Polly Benedict* • Sara Haden *Aunt Milly* ■ *Dir* George B Seitz • *Scr* Carey Wilson, from characters by Aurania Rouverol

Judge Hardy's Children ★★
Comedy drama
1938 · US · BW · 78min

The third film in the series and the first to have the name "Hardy" in the title. The heavy political slant to this entry – the Hardys go to Washington DC and take part in a Supreme Court investigation into public utilities – is in direct response to Roosevelt's "New Deal". Lewis Stone, as Judge Hardy, has much to say about this but Mickey Rooney, as Andy, still gets to flirt with a succession of pretty young things, including teaching the daughter of the French ambassador how to dance. AT

Lewis Stone *Judge James K Hardy* • Mickey Rooney *Andy Hardy* • Cecilia Parker *Marian Hardy* • Fay Holden *Mrs Emily Hardy* • Ann Rutherford *Polly Benedict* • Betsy Ross Clarke [Betty Ross Clarke] *Aunt Milly* ■ *Dir* George B Seitz • *Scr* Kay Van Riper, from characters by Aurania Rouverol

Judge Priest ★★★ 🇺
Comedy drama
1934 · US · BW · 80min

In the second of three films Will Rogers made for director John Ford, the folksy humorist portrays the sensible but lonely judge in 1890 Kentucky who quietly fights prejudice to see that justice is done and talks to his dead wife at her graveside. The treatment and appearance of a black character, Stepin Fetchit, accused of stealing some chickens, may seem racially offensive these days, but his character is regarded in an affectionate, if condescending, way and reflects attitudes at the time. AE

Will Rogers (1) *Judge William Pitman Priest* • Tom Brown *Jerome Priest* • Anita Louise *Ellie May Gillespie* • Henry B Walthall *Reverend Ashby Brand* • David Landau *Bob Gillis* • Hattie McDaniel *Aunt Dilsey* • Stepin Fetchit *Jeff Poindexter* ■ *Dir* John Ford • *Scr* Dudley Nichols, Lamar Trotti, from a character created by Irvin S Cobb

The Judge Steps Out ★★★
Comedy
1949 · US · BW · 91min

Canadian-born actor Alexander Knox was an underrated figure in the cinema, despite receiving an Oscar nomination for his performance as Woodrow Wilson in *Wilson* (1944). In this movie he plays a man undergoing a midlife crisis – long before the term was fashionable. Knox also co-wrote his role as a judge who leaves the rat race, becomes a short-order cook and falls for Ann Sothern. This likeable movie wasn't a success, and Knox lapsed into supporting roles. TS

Alexander Knox *Judge Bailey* • Ann Sothern *Peggy* • George Tobias *Mike* • Sharyn Moffett *Nan* • Florence Bates *Chita* • Frieda Inescort *Evelyn Bailey* • Myrna Dell *Mrs Winthrop* ■ *Dir* Boris Ingster • *Scr* Boris Ingster, Alexander Knox, from a story by Boris Ingster

A Judgement in Stone ★ 🔞15
Thriller
1986 · Can · Colour · 100min

A role only a Bette Davis, at full twitch, could love: a woman is enmeshed in murderous hysteria because of the dyslexia which has plagued her all her life. But it's Rita Tushingham who plays the "heroine" with camp and risible results. She eventually gets a job as housemaid with a middle-class American family but goes berserk when asked to compile a shopping list. This is directed – barely – by Tushingham's husband Ousama Rawi. TH

Rita Tushingham *Eunice Parchman* • Ross Petty *George Coverdale* • Shelley Peterson *Jackie Coverdale* • Jonathan Crombie *Bobby Coverdale* • Jessica Steen *Melinda Coverdale* • Aisha Tushingham *Young Eunice* ■ *Dir* Ousama Rawi • *Scr* Elaine Waisglass, from the novel by Ruth Rendell

Judgment at Nuremberg ★★★★ 🔞PG
Historical drama
1961 · US · BW · 178min

The trial of the judges who enforced Hitler's laws allowing wartime atrocities to occur might not be obvious movie material, but in the hands of brilliant producer/director Stanley Kramer this three-hour saga is mesmerising. Kramer pulled out all the dramatic stops. As producer, he secured one of the great casts of all time, headed by Spencer Tracy as Allied judge Dan Haywood, with touching cameos by Oscar-nominated Judy Garland as Irene Hoffman and Montgomery Clift as Rudolph Petersen, both victims of Nazi tyranny. The film has great dignity, exemplified by Burt Lancaster's intellectual German Ernst Janning, and an Oscar-winning performance from Maximilian Schell. Eminently watchable. TS 📀

Spencer Tracy *Judge Dan Haywood* • Burt Lancaster *Ernst Janning* • Richard Widmark *Colonel Tad Lawson* • Marlene Dietrich *Madame Bertholt* • Maximilian Schell *Hans Rolfe* • Judy Garland *Irene Hoffman* • Montgomery Clift *Rudolph Petersen* • William Shatner *Captain Harrison Byers* ■ *Dir* Stanley Kramer • *Scr* Abby Mann

Judgment Day ★★★ 🔞18
Action thriller
1999 · US · Colour · 85min

As a giant meteor heads straight for Earth, FBI agent Suzy Amis and convict Ice-T go in search of academic Linden Ashby, who alone can prevent annihilation. Trouble is, he's been kidnapped by cult leader Mario Van Peebles, who believes the impending doom is God's will. Willing performances, sly humour and an effective (if inevitable) dénouement place this just above the direct-to-video average. DP Swearing, drug abuse, violence. 📀

Ice-T *Reese* • Suzy Amis *Tyrell* • Mario Van Peebles *Payne* • Coolio *Luther* • Linden Ashby *Corbett* • Tom "Tiny" Lister Jr *Clarence* ■ *Dir* John Terlesky • *Scr* William Carson

Judgment in Berlin ★★★ 🔞PG
Courtroom drama
1988 · US · Colour · 91min

Former Hollywood bad boy Sean Penn here proves his dramatic worth in a small part, playing the role of a key witness in the trial of two East Germans who in 1978 hijacked a Polish airliner in an attempt to escape to the west. It's an uneven but intriguing adaptation of Judge Herbert J Stern's account of the American trial of the escapees, over which he presided. Martin Sheen plays Stern with too much pomposity and Sean's father, Leo Penn, directs with cluttered symbolism. But, these flaws apart, it remains a fascinating remnant of the Cold War. TH Swearing. 📀

Martin Sheen *Herbert J Stern* • Sam Wanamaker *Bernard Hellring* • Max Gail *Judah Best* • Juergen Heinrich *Uri Andreyev* • Heinz Hoenig *Helmut Thiele* • Carl Lumbly *Edwin Palmer* • Sean Penn *Guenther X* ■ *Dir* Leo Penn • *Scr* Joshua Sinclair, Leo Penn, from the book by Herbert J Stern

Judgment Night ★★★ 🔞18
Thriller
1993 · US · Colour · 105min

Stephen Hopkins has fashioned a sleek action thriller that is thoroughly implausible, but an exciting ride all the same. Emilio Estevez, Cuba Gooding Jr, Jeremy Piven and Stephen Dorff are the pampered suburbanites lost in the ghetto, who find themselves on the run from a ruthless gang when they witness a murder. Denis Leary is marvellously over the top as the psychopathic gang leader. JF 📀

Emilio Estevez *Frank Wyatt* • Cuba Gooding Jr *Mike Peterson* • Denis Leary *Fallon* • Stephen Dorff *John Wyatt* • Jeremy Piven *Ray Cochran* • Peter Greene *Sykes* • Erik Schrody *Rhodes* ■ *Dir* Stephen Hopkins • *Scr* Lewis Colick, Jere Cunningham, Kevin Jarre, from their story

Judith ★
War drama
1966 · US · Colour · 109min

On the dockside in Palestine in 1947, a cargo ship unloads its packing cases and from one of these emerges Sophia Loren, fresh as a daisy. She rushes off to Peter Finch's kibbutz as an agent of a Jewish underground organisation to expose her former husband Hans Verner as a Nazi war criminal and a sponsor of Arab nationalism. But mostly she's there to make us crease up with laughter. Ludicrous anti-Arab propaganda. AT

Sophia Loren *Judith* • Peter Finch *Aaron Stein* • Jack Hawkins *Major Lawton* • Hans Verner *Gustav Schiller* • Zharira Charifai *Dr Rachel* • Joseph Gross *Yaneck* • Terence Alexander *Carstairs* • Zipora Peled *Hannah* ■ *Dir* Daniel Mann • *Scr* John Michael Hayes, from a story by Lawrence Durrell

Judy Berlin ★★★★ 🔞15
Comedy drama
1999 · US · BW · 93min

This surreal portrait of suburban America charts the reaction of a community to a bizarre solar eclipse. As the neighbourhood is plunged into darkness, so the inhabitants wander through their own twilight inner worlds. Aaron Harnick has returned home to his parents after a failed foray to Hollywood. Glumly pacing his childhood turf, he encounters schoolfriend Edie Falco, an aspiring and indefatigable actress, and a new-found intimacy unfolds. Eric Mendelsohn was voted best director at 1999's Sundance festival for his efforts here, and the award is well deserved. This is quirky, tender and honest. LH

Edie Falco *Judy Berlin* • Aaron Harnick *David Gold* • Bob Dishy *Arthur Gold* • Barbara Barrie *Sue Berlin* • Carlin Glynn *Maddie* • Bette Henritze *Dolores Engler* • Madeline Kahn *Alice Gold* • Julie Kavner *Marie* • Anne Meara *Bea* ■ *Dir/Scr* Eric Mendelsohn

Judy Moody and the Not Bummer Summer ★ 🔞PG
Comedy
2011 · US · Colour · 87min

There must be worse ways of spending 90-odd minutes than watching this toilet-humour fest for less-picky younger kids – it's just really hard to think of one. Irritating pre-teen Judy (Jordana Beatty) is planning a "thrilladelic" school break with her two best pals, until she finds out they are both going away for the holidays. But Judy's bummer of a summer is salvaged by the arrival of eccentric aunt Opal (Heather Graham), and by a subsequent string of not-so-jolly japes. This adaptation of the popular series of children's books is frantic rather than fun, and childish rather than charming, making this definitely one to miss. DA Brief swearing. 📀 🔵

Jordana Beatty *Judy Moody* • Heather Graham *Aunt Opal* • Parris Mosteller *Stink* • Jaleel White *Mr Todd* • Jackson "Jaxn" Odell *Zeke* • Preston Bailey *Frank Pearl* ■ *Dir* John Schultz • *Scr* Kathy Waugh, Megan McDonald, from the series of *Judy Moody* children's books by McDonald, illustrated by Peter H Reynolds

Juggernaut ★★★ 🔞PG
Thriller
1974 · UK · Colour · 105min

Director Richard Lester does his best with this solemn thriller about a luxury liner threatened by a mad bomber, but it's the superb editing that carries the day. Female lead Shirley Knight has little to do, existing simply as a romantic footnote to Omar Sharif's libido, and in the male-heavy cast, Richard Harris, David Hemmings and Anthony Hopkins provide the brains and brawn. TH 📀

Richard Harris *Fallon* • Omar Sharif *Captain Brunel* • David Hemmings *Charlie Braddock* • Anthony Hopkins *Superintendent John McCleod* • Shirley Knight *Barbara Banister* • Ian Holm *Nicholas Porter* ■ *Dir* Richard Lester • *Scr* Richard DeKoker, Alan Plater • *Editor* Anthony Gibbs

The Juggler ★
Drama
1953 · US · BW · 85min

In a film of sledgehammer subtlety, circus juggler Kirk Douglas is the Holocaust survivor who makes it to Israel where he searches for the wife he knows is dead and where, too, every Israeli soldier at the refugee camp is mistaken for a Nazi. A small boy helps him escape to Egypt where Douglas has friends he believes will help him. The film's maudlin sentimentality soars right off the scale and for Douglas, who devoted months to learning how to juggle, it's possibly the worst film of his career. AT

Kirk Douglas *Hans Muller* • Milly Vitale *Ya'El* • Paul Stewart *Detective Karni* • Joey Walsh [Joseph Walsh] *Yehoshua Bresler* • Alf Kjellin *Daniel* • Beverly Washburn *Susy* • Charles Lane (2) *Rosenberg* ■ *Dir* Edward Dmytryk • *Scr* Michael Blankfort, from his novel

Juha ★★★
Silent drama
1999 · Fin · BW · 78min

The rural idyll of an adoring couple is shattered by a city slicker in Aki Kaurismäki's bold attempt to turn back the cinematic clock to the monochromed silent era. But, while Kaurismäki's fully conversant with the silent style, he succumbs to the temptation to punctuate the action with intrusive background sounds. Similarly, the cast struggles to reproduce the expressive posturing that dominated silent screen acting, with even the usually reliable Kati Outinen seeming out of sorts. DP

Sakari Kuosmanen *Juha* • Kati Outinen *Marja* • André Wilms *Shemeikka* • Markku Peltola *Driver* ■ *Dir* Aki Kaurismäki • *Scr* Aki Kaurismaki, from a novel by Juhani Aho

Juice ★★★ 🔞15
Crime drama
1991 · US · Colour · 90min

This is a potent, if flawed, debut from Ernest R Dickerson, who earned his director's spurs after serving as cinematographer on some of Spike Lee's most incendiary works. Omar Epps plays a confused teenager who wants to be a DJ, but finds himself inexorably drawn into the world of crime when he reluctantly joins his pals on a store heist. Epps is impressive among a then largely unknown cast, although the late rapper Tupac Shakur steals the show in one of his first films. JF Violence, swearing, sex scenes. 📀

Omar Epps *Quincy ("Q")* • Tupac Shakur *Bishop* • Jermaine Hopkins *Steel* • Khalil Kain *Raheem* • Cindy Herron *Yolanda* • Vincent Laresca *Radames* • Samuel L Jackson *Trip* • George O Gore [George Gore II] *Brian* ■ *Dir* Ernest R Dickerson • *Scr* Gerard Brown, Ernest R Dickerson, from a story by Ernest R Dickerson

Juke Box Rhythm ★★ 🇺
Musical
1959 · US · BW · 82min

If the thought of Johnny Otis performing *Willie and the Hand Jive* makes you misty, this is for you. There is amiable fun in watching a very young Jack Jones near the start of his career, as a singer helping an unknown designer (Hans Conried) convince a European princess visiting New York that he should design her coronation wardrobe. All just an excuse for Otis, the Nitwits, the Treniers and the Earl Grant Trio to render the songs that were making the charts in 1959. **TV**

Jo Morrow *Princess Ann* • Jack Jones (2) *Riff Manton* • Brian Donlevy *George Manton* • George Jessel • Hans Conried *Balenko* • Karin Booth *Leslie Anders* ■ *Dir* Arthur Dreifuss • *Scr* Mary C McCall Jr, Earl Baldwin, from a story by Lou Morheim

Jules et Jim ★★★★★ PG
Drama 1962 • Fr • BW • 101min

Echoing the style of Jean Renoir while epitomising the exuberance of the *nouvelle vague*, this is a virtuoso technical performance from François Truffaut. He variously uses photographic stills, newsreel footage, freeze frames and undercranked, travelling and distorted imagery to capture both the era and the emotion described in Henri-Pierre Roché's semi-autobiographical tale. Embodying the complex contradictions of modern womanhood, Jeanne Moreau is enchanting, while, immune to her wilfulness, Oskar Werner and Henri Serre respond readily to her caprice. However, their failure to understand her motives and insecurities prevents them from detecting the incipient despair that will lead to tragedy. The masterpiece of a genius. **DP** French +subtitles. *DVD*

Jeanne Moreau *Catherine* • Oskar Werner *Jules* • Henri Serre *Jim* • Marie Dubois *Thérèse* • Vanna Urbino *Gilberte* • Sabine Haudepin *Sabine* • Boris Bassiak *Albert* ■ *Dir* François Truffaut • *Scr* Jean Gruault, François Truffaut, from a novel by Henri-Pierre Roché • *Cinematographer* Raoul Coutard • *Music* Georges Delerue

Jules Verne's Rocket to the Moon ★★ U
Science-fiction comedy
1967 • UK • Colour • 114min

No prizes for guessing where the inspiration for the alternative title to this film, *Those Fantastic Flying Fools*, came from. But beware! These not-so-magnificent men in their rocketship to the Moon provide strictly routine fantasy. A fabulous cast breathes life into an insipid concoction that has Burl Ives sending circus performers into Victorian orbit only to have them crash-land in tsarist Russia. Sadly, the comedy plummets even faster than the cheap special effects. **AJ** *DVD*

Burl Ives *Phineas T Barnum* • Troy Donahue *Gaylord Sullivan* • Gert Frobe [Gert Fröbe] *Professor von Bulow* • Hermione Gingold *Angelica* • Lionel Jeffries *Sir Charles Dillworthy* • Terry-Thomas *Captain Sir Harry Washington-Smythe* • Jimmy Clitheroe *General Tom Thumb* ■ *Dir* Don Sharp • *Scr* Dave Freeman, from a story by Peter Welbeck [Harry Alan Towers], from the writings of Jules Verne

Julia ★★★★ PG
Drama 1977 • US • Colour • 112min

Lillian Hellman's memoir provides the basis for Fred Zinnemann's sensitive movie about friendship, courage and the playwright's growing awareness of the Nazi menace during the early 1930s. Lillian (Jane Fonda) makes contact with her childhood friend Julia (Vanessa Redgrave), a committed anti-fascist. Later Lillian is persuaded to help smuggle money into Germany to aid in the fight against the Nazis. The film's strength lies not in complex plotting but in the excellent performances from Fonda, Oscar-winning Redgrave, and Jason Robards as Dashiell Hammett. Meryl Streep makes her feature debut. **TH** *DVD*

Jane Fonda *Lillian Hellman* • Vanessa Redgrave *Julia* • Jason Robards *Dashiell Hammett* • Maximilian Schell *Johann* • Hal Holbrook *Alan Campbell* • Rosemary Murphy *Dorothy Parker* • Meryl Streep *Anne Marie* ■ *Dir* Fred Zinnemann • *Scr* Alvin Sargent, from the memoirs *Pentimento* by Lillian Hellman

Julia ★★★ 15
Crime drama
2008 • Fr/US/Mex/Bel • Colour • 137min

An act of desperation spirals dramatically out of control in French writer/director Erick Zonca's twisting English-language debut. Tilda Swinton is fearlessly untamed as Julia – a man pulative, bed-hopping alcoholic whose unprincipled behaviour reaches a violent low when she is persuaded to kidnap a young boy to extort money from his rich grandfather. John Cassavetes-style realism then unexpectedly mutates into an overblown action thriller as the duo wind up in Mexico and Julia's plans crumble spectacularly. Though Julia really is a loathsome creature, Swinton infuses her with a ferocious energy that's riveting to watch and often acerbically humorous. **SF** In English, Spanish. *DVD*

Tilda Swinton *Julia Harris* • Saul Rubinek *Mitch* • Kate del Castillo *Elena* • Aidan Gould *Tom* • Jude Ciccolella *Nick* • Bruno Bichir *Diego* ■ *Dir* Erick Zonca • *Scr* Erick Zonca, Aude Py

Julia and Julia ★★ 18
Drama 1987 • It • Colour • 97min

Italian director Peter Del Monte's English debut is now primarily notable for being the first feature to be shot entirely using a high-definition video process, with the resulting footage being transferred to film for projection. However, the technique was still in its infancy and resists even master cinematographer Giuseppe Rotunno's efforts to create naturalistic visuals. The story proves equally unmalleable, as widowed travel agent Kathleen Turner seemingly enters a time warp that causes her to doubt whether Gabriel Byrne actually perished in a car smash on their honeymoon. **DP**

Kathleen Turner *Julia* • Gabriele Ferzetti *Paolo's father* • Gabriel Byrne *Paolo* • Sting *Daniel Osler* • Angela Goodwin *Paolo's mother* ■ *Dir* Peter Del Monte • *Scr* Peter Del Monte, Silvia Napolitano, Sandro Petraglia, from a story by Peter Del Monte, Silvia Napolitano

Julia Misbehaves ★★
Comedy 1948 • US • BW • 99min

With her long-lost daughter's romance about to progress to the altar, actress Julia Packett (Greer Garson) decides to go back to her conventional husband. Garson and Walter Pidgeon both flounder, especially Garson, who is called upon for some slapstick interludes in an attempt to enliven this flaccid romantic comedy. The heart-stoppingly lovely young Elizabeth Taylor plays the daughter and Peter Lawford is the man she really loves, but this is still disappointing. **RK**

Greer Garson *Julia Packett* • Walter Pidgeon *William Sylvester Packett* • Peter Lawford *Ritchie Lorgan* • Cesar Romero *Fred Gennochio* • Elizabeth Taylor *Susan Packett* • Lucile Watson *Mrs Packett* • Nigel Bruce *Col Willowbrook* ■ *Dir* Jack Conway • *Scr* William Ludwig, Harry Ruskin, Arthur Wimperis, from the novel *The Nutmeg Tree* by Margery Sharp

Julian Po ★★ 12
Comedy drama 1997 • US • Colour • 80min

Christian Slater stars in this superficial drama about a young wanderer drifting into a small-town community. Initially treating him as an unwelcome stranger, the locals change their tune when they discover he's there for the sole purpose of committing suicide. Cue neighbours knocking on his door to unburden their hearts, offer advice and convince him life is worth it. Writer/director Alan Wade handles it all with aplomb, but his characters are two-dimensional. **LH** *DVD*

Christian Slater *Julian Po* • Robin Tunney *Sarah* • Cherry Jones *Lucy* • Michael Parks *Vern* • Frankie Faison *Sheriff* • Harve Presnell *Mayor* ■ *Dir* Alan Wade • *Scr* Alan Wade, from the book *La Mort de Monsieur Golouja* by Branimir Scepanovic

Julia's Eyes ★★★ 15
Horror thriller
2010 • Sp • Colour • 112min

Director Guillem Morales's suspense-filled thriller finds a woman with a degenerate

eye disease fearing for her life after her twin sister, who suffered from the same illness, is found hanged in her basement. Convinced it was murder rather than suicide, she strives to uncover the truth before she loses her own sight. Morales delivers a series of scares and shocks that owe more than a small debt to classic Hitchcock. However, although the plot is littered with intriguing red herrings, far too many clues are given away before the explosive finale. **TeS** Spanish +subtitles. violence, swearing, nudity. *DVD* *BL*

Belén Rueda *Julia/Sara* • Lluís Homar *Isaac* • Pablo Derqui *Iván* • Francesc Orella *Inspector Dimas* ■ *Dir* Guillem Morales • *Scr* Guillem Morales, Oriol Paulo

Julie ★★★
Thriller 1956 • US • BW • 97min

Doris Day suspects her husband Louis Jourdan is trying to kill her in director Andrew L Stone's tense thriller. Stone's speciality of filming dramas in real-life situations is put to good use here, and he certainly whips up the suspense even if the plot becomes rather implausible in places. Day is radiant and Jourdan very convincing, while Barry Sullivan and Frank Lovejoy give perfectly weighted supporting performances. **TS**

Doris Day *Julie Benton* • Louis Jourdan *Lyle Benton* • Barry Sullivan *Cliff Henderson* • Frank Lovejoy *Detective Captain Pringle* • John Gallaudet *Detective Cole* • Harlan Warde *Detective Pope* ■ *Dir/Scr* Andrew L Stone

Julie & Julia ★★★★ 12
Biographical drama 2009 • US • Colour • 118min

Julia Child was America's answer to Fanny Cradock, played here with hilarious gusto by Meryl Streep. Following separate timelines, the film details Child's experiences in late 1940s Paris that led to the 1961 publication of her seminal book *Mastering the Art of French Cooking*, and the year – four decades later – that contemporary New Yorker Julie Powell (an amusingly angsty Amy Adams) spends cooking all of its 524 recipes. Though it's mostly light and frothy, Child also has a few lessons to impart on trying to balance personal and professional ambitions. The result is a warm and welcome refreshment from writer/director Nora Ephron. **SP** Brief swearing, sexual references. *DVD* *BL*

Amy Adams *Julie Powell* • Meryl Streep *Julia Child* • Jane Lynch *Dorothy McWilliams* • Vanessa Ferlito *Cassie* • Stanley Tucci *Paul Child* • Mary Lynn Rajskub *Sarah* • Chris Messina *Eric Powell* ■ *Dir* Nora Ephron • *Scr* Nora Ephron, from the autobiography *Julie & Julia* by Julie Powell and the autobiography *My Life in France* by Julia Child, Alex Prud'homme

Julie and the Cadillacs ★★ PG
Musical drama 1997 • UK • Colour • 106min

This is less a film about making it in the pop business in the early 1960s than a homage to those corny "next stop the top" movies. Nigh on every scene is geared up to slipping in one of the 17 tunes on a soundtrack that seems to have been composed exclusively of B-side pastiches and comic ensemble routines. Despite the disappointing music, director Bryan Izzard's eagerly played film is spot-on in its tell-tale details, and provides a timely reminder that pop was once about talent, not just image. **DP**

Tina Russell *Julie Carr* • Toyah Willcox *Barbara Gifford* • Victor Spinetti *Cyril Wise* • Peter Polycarpou *Phil Green* • Thora Hird *Julie's grandmother* • James Grout *Mr Watkins* • Mike Berry *Mac MacDonald* ■ *Dir* Bryan Izzard • *Scr* John Dean • *Music/Lyrics* John Dean

julien donkey-boy ★★★★ 15
Drama 1999 • US • Colour • 99min

Considering the downbeat realism of Harmony Korine's second feature *Gummo*, it wasn't a big step for the director to follow the Dogme ultra-realist style of film-making. However, there's greater narrative contrivance in this tale of the schizophrenic who finds solace from the tyranny of his abusive father by working in a school for

the blind. Visionary German director Werner Herzog startles as the perversely dysfunctional parent, while Ewen Bremner excels as the interiorised outsider. Challenging, technically astute and inventive. **DP** Swearing, sex scenes. *DVD*

Ewen Bremner *Julien* • Chloë Sevigny *Pearl* • Werner Herzog *Father* • Evan Neumann *Chris* • Joyce Korine *Grandma* • Chrissy Kobylak *Chrissy* • Brian Fisk *Pond boy* • Alvin Law *Neighbour* ■ *Dir/Scr* Harmony Korine

Juliet of the Spirits ★★★ 15
Fantasy drama
1965 • Fr/It/W Ger • Colour • 120min

Having explored his own fears and failings in 8½, Federico Fellini here tries to do the same for his wife, Giulietta Masina, in this highly stylised daydream. In his first film in colour, the director employs bold hues to suggest the fantastical world in which Masina takes refuge from the even more artificial milieu into which her pretentious, philandering husband has plunged her. Determined to break from traditional storytelling techniques, Fellini strives for visual poetry, and while he succeeds in creating some memorable imagery, his ventures into Jungian psychology, spiritualism and astrology feel too much like dilettante dabbling. **DP** Italian +subtitles. *DVD*

Giulietta Masina *Juliet* • Mario Pisu *Giorgio* • Sandra Milo *Susy/Fanny/Iris* • Caterina Boratto *Juliet's mother* • Luisa Della Noce *Adele* • Sylva Koscina *Sylva* ■ *Dir* Federico Fellini • *Scr* Federico Fellini, Tullio Pinelli, Brunello Rondi, Ennio Flaiano, from a story by Federico Fellini, Tullio Pinelli • *Cinematographer* Gianni Di Venanzo

Julieta ★★★ 15
Drama 2016 • Sp • Colour • 98min

Though it isn't vintage Pedro Almodóvar, this sumptuous saga of love, loss, grief and guilt features enough touchstones to the director's previous repertoire to please his loyal fans. Adapted from work by Nobel Prize-winning writer Alice Munro, it's another female-centric yarn where a chance encounter with her daughter's best friend sends Madrid lecturer Julieta (Emma Suarez and Adriana Ugarte at different ages) into a tailspin. The episodic structure feels scrappy, but the film can't be faulted on visual texture and the acting is classy. **AJ** In Spanish.

Adriana Ugarte *Julieta Joven* • Emma Suarez *Julieta Arcos* • Rossy de Palma *Marian* • Michelle Jenner *Beatriz* ■ *Dir/Scr* Pedro Almodóvar

Julius Caesar ★★★★★ U
Historical drama 1953 • US • BW • 116min

Marlon Brando daringly took on the role of Mark Antony (with the help of some coaching from John Gielgud), in what was to become possibly the finest cinematic version of any of Shakespeare's plays. The cast assembled by MGM is mouthwatering. Brando is magnificent, his oration at Caesar's funeral the definitive delivery, while James Mason, as Brutus – "the most noble Roman of them all" – is beautifully spoken. There's also no denying Gielgud makes a perfect "lean and hungry"-looking Cassius, Louis Calhern was clearly born to play Caesar himself, and Miklos Rozsa's majestic score is mightily impressive. Director Joseph L Mankiewicz concentrates on the drama, not the spectacle, perhaps to disguise the fact that he was forced to use up the old *Quo Vadis* sets. **TS**

James Mason *Brutus* • Marlon Brando *Mark Antony* • John Gielgud *Cassius* • Louis Calhern *Julius Caesar* • Edmond O'Brien *Casca* • Greer Garson *Calpurnia* • Deborah Kerr *Portia* • George Macready *Marullus* • Michael Pate *Flavius* • Richard Hale *Soothsayer* • Alan Napier *Cicero* ■ *Dir* Joseph L Mankiewicz • *Scr* Joseph L Mankiewicz, from the play by William Shakespeare • *Cinematographer* Joseph Ruttenberg • *Art Directors* Cedric Gibbons, Edward Carfagno

Julius Caesar ★★ PG
Historical drama 1970 • UK • Colour • 111min

This Shakespearean saga is particularly turgid, undermined by Stuart Burge's

J

pedestrian direction and a surprisingly weak Brutus from Jason Robards. John Gielgud, who was Cassius in the far superior 1953 version, now plays Caesar, while Charlton Heston takes his second (though not his last) stab at playing Mark Antony on film. AT

Charlton Heston *Mark Antony* • Jason Robards *Brutus* • John Gielgud *Julius Caesar* • Richard Johnson *Cassius* • Robert Vaughn (1) *Casca* • Richard Chamberlain *Octavius Caesar* • Diana Rigg *Portia* • Jill Bennett *Calpurnia* ■ *Dir* Stuart Burge • *Scr* Robert Furnival, from the play by William Shakespeare

Jumanji ★★★★ PG

Fantasy adventure   1995 · US · Colour · 99min

It was dismissed by many critics as a noisy, scary and worthless excuse for some ingenious computer effects, but as empty experiences go this fantasy adventure is absolutely exhilarating. Young audiences will be been held spellbound by the marauding wildlife that is unleashed when Kirsten Dunst and Bradley Pierce rescue Robin Williams from the sinister board game in which he's been trapped for 26 years. Any film where the action is determined by a roll of the dice is bound to be episodic, but this hardly detracts from the enjoyment of the spectacular set pieces. DP DVD BL

Robin Williams *Alan Parrish* • Jonathan Hyde *Van Pelt/Sam Parrish* • Kirsten Dunst *Judy* • Bradley Pierce *Peter* • Bonnie Hunt *Sarah* • Bebe Neuwirth *Nora* • David Alan Grier *Bentley* • Patricia Clarkson *Carol Parrish* ■ *Dir* Joe Johnston • *Scr* Jonathan Hensleigh, Greg Taylor, Jim Strain, from a story by Taylor, Strain, Chris Van Allsburg, from the novel by Van Allsburg

Jumbo ★★★★ U

Musical comedy   1962 · US · Colour · 122min

A wonderfully warm-hearted MGM musical about circus rivalries, this is based on showman Billy Rose's Broadway extravaganza, which actually featured an elephant on stage. Star Doris Day is, sadly, too old and wise to play the ingénue here, but she delivers the lovely Rodgers and Hart songs superbly. Unlikely co-star Stephen Boyd, still hot from *Ben-Hur*, also acquits himself surprisingly well. However, the real joys are veterans Martha Raye and Jimmy Durante, whose "What elephant?" line from this movie has rightly become classic. TS DVD

Doris Day *Kitty Wonder* • Stephen Boyd *Sam Rawlins* • Jimmy Durante *Pop Wonder* • Martha Raye *Lulu* • Dean Jagger *John Noble* • Joseph Waring *Harry* • Lynn Wood *Tina* • Charles Watts *Ellis* ■ *Dir* Charles Walters • *Scr* Sidney Sheldon, from the musical by Ben Hecht, Charles MacArthur • *Choreography* Busby Berkeley

Jump for Glory ★★

Crime drama   1937 · UK · BW · 75min

What brought renowned action director Raoul Walsh to this side of the Atlantic is an open question. The Glory of the title is the opportunist "victim" (played by the elegant Valerie Hobson) of stylish thief Douglas Fairbanks Jr, who is mortified to discover that she's engaged to his blackmailing ex-partner in crime Alan Hale. Complications follow, before the inevitable contrived ending. Known as *When Thief Meets Thief* in the US, this is amiable but overcomplicated entertainment. BB

Douglas Fairbanks Jr *Ricky Morgan* • Valerie Hobson *Glory Howard* • Alan Hale *Jim Dial/Colonel Fane* • Jack Melford *Thompson* • Anthony Ireland *Sir Timothy Haddon* ■ *Dir* Raoul Walsh • *Scr* John Meehan, Harold French, from the novel by Gordon McDonnell

Jump In! ★★ U

Comedy dance drama
2007 · US · Colour · 80min

High School Musical's Corbin Bleu gives a likeable performance here as a Brooklyn teenager torn between two vastly different worlds – amateur boxing and competitive skipping. It's far-fetched plotting for sure, though fun to watch thanks to an exuberant cast and some amazing scenes of Double Dutch rope jumping. Positive if

simplistic life lessons add to the upbeat atmosphere. SF DVD

Corbin Bleu *Izzy Daniels* • Keke Palmer *Mary Thomas* • Shanica Knowles *Shauna Lewis* • Laivan Greene *Keisha Ray* • Kylee Russell *Karin Daniels* ■ *Dir* Paul Hoen • *Scr* Doreen Spicer, Regina Hicks, Karin Gist

Jump Tomorrow ★★★★ PG

Romantic road movie
2001 · UK/US · Colour · 89min

Joel Hopkins's first feature film is a feel-good road movie with an outsider's sense of place and a sensitive insight into the workings of the human heart. Essentially telling the story of a road trip from New York to Niagara Falls, Hopkins is aided enormously by a cosmopolitan and largely unknown cast. Lead actor Tunde Adebimpe excels as the timid Nigerian pen pusher, whose life is transformed on a meandering odyssey to his wedding day in the company of eccentric Frenchman Hippolyte Girardot, ravishing Spaniard Natalia Verbeke and her snooty English fiancé James Wilby. This is a film of rare subtlety and charm. DP DVD

Tunde Adebimpe *George* • Hippolyte Girardot *Gérard* • Natalia Verbeke *Alicia* • Patricia Mauceri *Consuelo* • Isiah Whitlock Jr *George's uncle* • Kaili Vernoff *Heather Leather* • James Wilby *Nathan* ■ *Dir* Joel Hopkins • *Scr* Joel Hopkins, Nicola Usborne, Iain Tibbles

Jumper ★★★ 12

Science-fiction action thriller
2008 · US · Colour · 84min

Based on Steven Gould's sci-fi novels for teens, this big budget adventure asks: what would you do if you could "jump" anywhere in the world in the blink of an eye? Reluctant hero David (Hayden Christensen) decides to rob banks and go sightseeing. He hooks up with fellow teleporter Griffin (Jamie Bell) and begins to learn more about his extraordinary gift, as well as discovering that he's on someone's hit list – and assassin Roland (Samuel L Jackson) is on his trail. The global jumping lets the production team set up fight sequences on the Sphinx and car chases through Tokyo, but director Doug Liman (*The Bourne Identity*) disappointingly underplays ideas about the corrupting consequences of power in favour of maintaining a cool edge. JR Violence, brief swearing. DVD BL

Hayden Christensen *David Rice* • Samuel L Jackson *Roland* • Diane Lane *Mary Rice* • Jamie Bell *Griffin* • Rachel Bilson *Millie* ■ *Dir* Doug Liman • *Scr* David S Goyer, Simon Kinberg, Jim Uhls

Jumpin' at the Boneyard ★★★ 15

Drama   1991 · US · Colour · 102min

Tim Roth is mesmerising, both moving and believable as a reformed small-time crook from the Bronx. Meeting up by chance with his brother (Alexis Arquette), he uncomfortably attempts to renew family ties and ensure that his sibling won't make the same mistakes he did. Roth's turn is matched by telling performances from Arquette and a pre-fame Samuel L Jackson, even though it makes for grim viewing. JF

Tim Roth *Manny* • Alexis Arquette *Danny* • Danitra Vance *Jeanette* • Kathleen Chalfant *Mom* • Samuel L Jackson *Mr Simpson* • Luis Guzman *Taxi driver* • Elizabeth Bracco *Cathy* • Jeffrey Wright *Derek* ■ *Dir/Scr* Jeff Stanzler

Jumpin' Jack Flash ★★ 15

Comedy thriller   1986 · US · Colour · 100min

Whoopi Goldberg's first major role following her debut in *The Color Purple* is a disappointment. She stars as a computer operator who inadvertently gets involved in international espionage when a message for help from a spy appears on her screen. Penny Marshall replaced Howard Zieff in the director's chair, the script went through several writers, and this raucous comedy certainly feels as if there were too many cooks. JB Swearing. DVD

Whoopi Goldberg *Terry Doolittle* • Stephen Collins *Marty Phillips* • John Wood (2) *Jeremy Talbot* • Carol Kane *Cynthia* • Annie Potts *Liz*

Carlson • Peter Michael Goetz *Mr Page* • Jim Belushi [James Belushi] *Sperry repairman* • Tracey Ullman *Fiona* ■ *Dir* Penny Marshall • *Scr* David H Franzoni, JW Melville, Patricia Irving, Christopher Thompson, from a story by David H Franzoni

Jumping for Joy ★★ U

Comedy   1955 · UK · BW · 84min

Frankie Howerd was still best known as the headliner on radio's *Variety Bandbox* when he took his first real starring role in his third film outing. His famous nuances and grimaces were not really suited to the big screen and this tepid comedy about a racetrack dogsbody who finds himself protecting a champion greyhound from some dastardly crooks did not prove otherwise. Titter ye will not. DP

Frankie Howerd *Willie Joy* • Stanley Holloway *"Captain" Jack Montague* • AE Matthews *Lord Cranfield* • Tony Wright *Vincent* • Alfie Bass *Blagg* • Joan Hickson *Lady Cranfield* • Lionel Jeffries *Bert Benton* ■ *Dir* John Paddy Carstairs • *Scr* Jack Davies, Henry E Blyth

Jumping Jacks ★★ U

Comedy   1952 · US · BW · 95min

After impressing as comedy support in the *My Friend Irma* films, Dean Martin and Jerry Lewis were given their chance to become headliners and soon established themselves as huge box-office stars. As with much of the comedy talent of the time, the pair proved particularly popular in service comedies. In this one, they play up the slapstick as bumbling new recruits in a paratroop squad. Not as good as their earlier efforts. DF

Jerry Lewis *Hap Smith* • Dean Martin *Chick Allen* • Mona Freeman *Betty Carver* • Robert Strauss *Sgt McCluskey* ■ *Dir* Norman Taurog • *Scr* Robert Lees, Fred Rinaldo, Herbert Baker, James Allardice, Richard Weil, from a story by Brian Marlow

June Bride ★★★ U

Romantic comedy   1948 · US · BW · 96min

Anything with Bette Davis in it is worth watching, but there are also some light, fluffy, witty moments to be savoured in this tale of two very spoilt hacks on a women's magazine who fall in love again while composing a daft feature on June weddings. Robert Montgomery is Davis's able co-star and he gives her a fair old run for her money in the scene-stealing stakes. Even if this profoundly inconsequential movie gives us little more than a few wry laughs, it does so with great style and touches of flair. Debbie Reynolds makes a fleeting film debut. SR

Bette Davis *Linda Gilman* • Robert Montgomery *Carey Jackson* • Fay Bainter *Paula Winthrop* • Betty Lynn *Boo Brinker* • Tom Tully *Mr Brinker* • Barbara Bates *Jeanne Brinker* • Debbie Reynolds *Boo's girl friend* ■ *Dir* Bretaigne Windust • *Scr* Ranald MacDougall, from the play *Feature for June* by Eileen Tighe, Graeme Lorimer

June Night ★★★

Drama   1940 · Swe · BW · 86min

In the last film she made in Sweden before settling in America, Ingrid Bergman gives a performance to rival any of her early Hollywood assignments as a chemist whose affair with a sailor scandalises a quiet country town. As in so many Swedish films of the period, passions simmer beneath impassive surfaces and hypocritical citizens censure while secretly revelling in the sins of the accused. Bergman is quite captivating, and it's melodrama all the way. DP Swedish +subtitles.

Ingrid Bergman *Kerstin Nordback/Sara Nordana* • Marianne Löfgren *Asa* • Lill-Tollie Zellman *Jane Jacobs* • Marianne Aminoff *Nickan* ■ *Dir* Per Lindberg • *Scr* Ragnar Hylten-Cavallius, Per Lindberg, from a story by Tora Nordstrom-Bonnier

Junebug ★★★★ 15

Comedy drama   2004 · US · Colour · 106min

Up-market art dealer Embeth Davidtz gets more than she bargained for when she heads out to North Carolina to visit the poverty-stricken homestead of her husband

Alessandro Nivola. Willing herself to get along with his idiosyncratic family is one thing; passing up a fantastic local artist is another. Director Phil Morrison's debut feature has brilliant insight and a deft, light feel, and features a competent cast, in particular Amy Adams whose Oscar-nominated portrayal of Nivolo's naive, open-hearted and heavily pregnant sister-in-law is a joy to watch. Bittersweet and sedately paced, this is an utterly engaging experience. KK Swearing. DVD BL

Amy Adams *Ashley* • Embeth Davidtz *Madeleine* • Ben McKenzie *Johnny* • Alessandro Nivola *George* • Celia Weston *Peg* • Scott Wilson *Eugene* ■ *Dir* Phil Morrison • *Scr* Angus MacLachlan

Jungle Book ★★★ U

Adventure   1942 · US · Colour · 104min

This is a starchy affair in which animal magic, preachy parable and jungle adventure have been loosely combined, missing the wisdom, drama and humour of Kipling's classic stories. Sabu stars as Mowgli, the child raised by wolves, whose friends Baloo, Hathi and Bagheera protect him as he trails man-eating tiger Shere Khan and faces sundry human villains. Much of it seems rather stilted today, though the Technicolor jungle built in Los Angeles remains a captivating fantasy world. Heavy going for all its beauty. DP DVD

Sabu *Mowgli* • Joseph Calleia *Buldeo* • John Qualen *Barber* • Frank Puglia *Pundit* • Rosemary DeCamp *Messua* • Patricia O'Rourke *Mahala* • Ralph Byrd *Durga* • John Mather *Rao* • Faith Brook *English girl* ■ *Dir* Zoltan Korda • *Scr* Laurence Stallings, from the books by Rudyard Kipling

The Jungle Book ★★★★★ U

Animated musical adventure
1967 · US · Colour · 75min

The last animated feature made under Walt Disney's personal supervision before his death, this barnstorming classic occupies a truly rewarding perch in the studio's history, repaying repeated releases in all formats, and ageing not a jot. Based on Rudyard Kipling's stories, it drops the "Man Cub" into a jungle at first perilous, then welcoming, then perilous, and so on. As with all the best Disneys, there is a terrific voice cast and many of the songs have become standards, such as *The Bare Necessities* and *I Wanna Be Like You*. The period's feathery drawing style abounds, and an all-round warmth pervades. AC DVD BL

Phil Harris *Baloo the Bear* • Sebastian Cabot *Bagheera the Panther* • Louis Prima *King Louie of the Apes* • George Sanders *Shere Khan the Tiger* • Sterling Holloway *Kaa the Snake* • J Pat O'Malley *Colonel Hathi the Elephant/Buzzie* • Bruce Reitherman *Mowgli* • Verna Felton *Winifred the Elephant* • Clint Howard *Junior the Elephant* • Chad Stuart *Flaps the Vulture* • Lord Tim Hudson *Dizzy the Vulture* • John Abbott *Akela the Wolf* • Ben Wright (1) *Rama the Wolf* • Darleen Carr *Girl* ■ *Dir* Wolfgang Reitherman • *Scr* Larry Clemmons, Ralph Wright, Ken Anderson, Vance Gerry, from the books by Rudyard Kipling

The Jungle Book 2 ★ U

Animated adventure   2003 · US · Colour · 69min

Enticed back into the jungle by his friend Baloo the bear (voiced by John Goodman), bored man-cub Mowgli (Haley Joel Osment) battles old adversary Shere Kahn in Disney's lame assembly-line sequel to their much loved 1967 animated classic. A thinly plotted, charmless rehash, rendered in cut-rate graphics, this is unremarkable, uninspired and unsatisfying. AJ DVD

John Goodman *Baloo* • Haley Joel Osment *Mowgli* • Mae Whitman *Shanti* • Connor Funk *Ranjan* • Tony Jay *Shere Khan* • Jim Cummings *Kaa/Colonel Hathi/MC Monkey* • Bob Joles *Bagheera* • Phil Collins *Lucky* • John Rhys-Davies *Mowgli's father* ■ *Dir* Steve Trenbirth • *Scr* Karl Geurs

The Jungle Book ★★★ PG
Period adventure 1994 · US · Colour · 119min

This live-action version of the story of Mowgli, the boy brought up to adulthood by wolves, may lack the songs, but it is closer to Kipling's original tale than was the classic feature-length cartoon. Jason Scott Lee is effective battling villain Cary Elwes for the treasure buried beneath the lost city. The animal training is extraordinary, and John Cleese's regular appearances add a much-needed lightness to the tale. TH **DVD**

Jason Scott Lee *Mowgli* • Cary Elwes *Captain Boone* • Lena Headey *Kitty Brydon* • Sam Neill *Major Brydon* • John Cleese *Doctor Plumford* • Jason Flemyng *Wilkins* ■ *Dir* Stephen Sommers • *Scr* Stephen Sommers, Ronald Yanover, Mark D Geldman, from a story by Ronald Yanover, Mark D Geldman, from the books by Rudyard Kipling

The Jungle Book ★★★★ PG
Adventure 2016 · US · Colour · 101min

Not just a remake of the 1967 animated classic, *Iron Man* director Jon Favreau's jaw-dropping jungle adventure also returns to Rudyard Kipling's novel as a source to enchant a new generation of viewers. It's a tough task to follow up such a beloved Disney movie, but Favreau finds magic and wonder in the CGI-enabled action rather than song-and-dance numbers (although a couple of classic tunes remain). The animals Mowgli (Neel Sethi) encounters are staggeringly realistic and the superbly chosen voice cast puts a fresh spin on familiar scenes. Bill Murray seems born to play Baloo, while Idris Elba's Shere Khan is a more ferocious villain. Epic and a whole lot of fun, this take on *The Jungle Book* feels shiny and new. JL **DVD** **Blu-ray** **3D**

Neel Sethi *Mowgli* • Bill Murray *Baloo* • Idris Elba *Shere Khan* • Ben Kingsley *Bagheera* • Scarlett Johansson *Kaa* • Christopher Walken *King Louie* • Lupita Nyong'o *Raksha* ■ *Dir* Jon Favreau • *Scr* Justin Marks, from the *Jungle Books* short stories by Rudyard Kipling

Jungle Book: Origins
Part-animated adventure 2018 · US · Colour

This is a preview – no prints were available to review as we went to press: The world might not need another *Jungle Book* so soon after 2016's Jon Favreau hit and, if the revolving door on this one is anything to go by, film-makers agree - Ron Howard and Alejandro González Iñárritu (Oscar winners both) pulled out before Andy Serkis eventually took over directorial control. Yet the cast is top-drawer, so maybe Benedict Cumberbatch (Shere Khan), Cate Blanchett (Kaa), Tom Hollander (Tabaqui) and Andy Serkis (Baloo), know something we don't. SvM

Christian Bale *Bagheera* • Benedict Cumberbatch *Shere Khan* • Cate Blanchett *Kaa* • Naomie Harris *Nisha* • Andy Serkis *Baloo* ■ *Dir* Andy Serkis • *Scr* Callie Kloves, from the *Jungle Books* short stories by Rudyard Kipling

Jungle Cat ★★★★ U
Documentary 1959 · US · Colour · 69min

Disney's superb *True-Life Adventures* series closed with this awe-inspiring portrait of the South American jaguar. The result of over two years in the Brazilian rainforest, this is the nature documentary at its best, as a couple of jaguars meet, mate and teach their kittens about the harsh realities of life. However, it's not all encounters with crocodiles and boa constrictors, as narrator Winston Hibler guides us through a history of the cat and plenty of other Amazonian animals get their moment in the spotlight. DP

Winston Hibler *Narrator* ■ *Dir* James Algar

Jungle Fever ★★★ 18
Drama 1991 · US · Colour · 126min

Spike Lee's take on interracial romance is typically controversial, but lacks the visceral power that he brought to *Do the Right Thing*. Architect Wesley Snipes falls for his white temp Annabella Sciorra and decides to leave his wife for her. However, their relationship sees them swiftly ostracised by their family and friends. Lee's direction is

---

wonderfully fluid and, as in most of his movies, he is superbly served by the striking cinematography of Ernest Dickerson and strong lead performances. JF Swearing, sex scenes, drug abuse, nudity. **DVD**

Wesley Snipes *Flipper Purify* • Annabella Sciorra *Angie Tucci* • Spike Lee *Cyrus* • Samuel L Jackson *Gator Purify* • Ossie Davis *The Good Reverend Doctor Purify* • Ruby Dee *Lucinda Purify* • Lonette McKee *Drew* • John Turturro *Paulie Carbone* • Anthony Quinn *Lou Carbone* • Frank Vincent *Mike Tucci* • Tim Robbins *Jerry* • Halle Berry *Vivian* • Brad Dourif *Leslie* ■ *Dir/Scr* Spike Lee

Jungle Jim ★★ U
Adventure 1948 · US · BW · 72min

Retired Tarzan Johnny Weissmuller strides lumpenly through the bush protecting testy scientist Virginia Grey from hostile wildlife and ruthless treasure seeker George Reeves. So director William Berke wisely lavishes attention on JJ's pets who also distracted attention away from the cheap sets and the stock footage. Weissmuller would return as Jim for 12 sequels, plus a short-lived 1950s television series. DP

Johnny Weissmuller *Jungle Jim* • Virginia Grey *Hilary Parker* • George Reeves *Bruce Edwards* • Lita Baron *Zia* ■ *Dir* William A Berke [William Berke] • *Scr* Carroll Young, from the comic strip by Alex Raymond

Jungle 2 Jungle ★★★ PG
Comedy adventure 1997 · US · Colour · 100min

This junior version of *Crocodile Dundee* was another vehicle for *Home Improvement* star Tim Allen which failed to make much of a dent on the UK market. Allen plays a New York financier who discovers he has a teenage son (Sam Huntington) who has been brought up by an Amazonian tribe. The kid's arrival in New York is the cue for the usual "fish out of water" gags. It's an amiable but predictable affair. JF **DVD**

Tim Allen *Michael* • Martin Short *Richard* • JoBeth Williams *Patricia* • Lolita Davidovich *Charlotte* • Sam Huntington *Mimi-Siku* • Valerie Mahaffey *Jan* • Lee ee Sobieski *Karen* ■ *Dir* John Pasquin • *Scr* Bruce A Evans, Raynold Gideon, from the film *Un Indien dans la Ville* by Hervé Palud, Thierry Lhermitte, Igor Aptekman, Philippe Bruneau de la Salle

Junglee ★★★ PG
Romantic comedy 1961 · Ind · Colour · 145min

Shammi Kapoor confirmed his status as Bollywood's most dashing rebel in this charming romantic comedy. Raised to think that laughter is beneath him by his domineering mother Lalita Pawar, Kapoor is dispatched to Kashmir with sister Shashi Kala to thwart her relationship with the lowly Anoop Kumar and contract his own marriage to princess Azra. However, he quickly learns to enjoy life when he meets free spirit Saira Banoo. This lively reworking of the formulaic themes of class prejudice and domestic duty is epitomised by Kapoor's *Yahoo* song, which is a highpoint in Shankar Jaikishan's ebullient score. DP Hindi +subtitles.

Shammi Kapoor *Chandra Shekhar "Shekhar"* • Saira Banoo [Saira Banu] *Rajkumari "Raj"* • Shashi Kala [Shashikala] *Mala* • Anoop Kumar *Jeevan* • Lalita Pawar *Shekhar's mother* ■ *Dir* Subodh Mukherjee • *Scr* Subodh Mukherjee, Agha Jani Kashmiri, from a story by Mukherjee

Junior ★★★ PG
Comedy 1994 · US · Colour · 105min

Arnold Schwarzenegger reunites here with the *Twins* team of Danny DeVito and director Ivan Reitman for another comedy romp. Schwarzenegger and DeVito play struggling medical researchers working on a new fertility drug. When they lose their grant, in desperation Schwarzenegger injects himself with the experimental solution and ends up pregnant. It's pretty much a one-joke concept, but Reitman milks it for all it's worth, and only Emma Thompson as a fellow scientist and love interest looks out of place in an underwritten role. JF **DVD**

Arnold Schwarzenegger *Dr Alexander Hesse* • Danny DeVito *Dr Larry Arbogast* • Emma Thompson *Dr Diana Reddin* • Frank Langella

---

Noah Banes • Pamela Reed *Angela* • Judy Collins *Naomi* ■ *Dir* Ivan Reitman • *Scr* Kevin Wade, Chris Conrad

Junior Bonner ★★★★ PG
Drama 1972 · US · Colour · 100min

Sam Peckinpah was one of the most talented movie directors ever. He could be tough in *The Wild Bunch* and he could be tender in *The Ballad of Cable Hogue*. Peckinpah was happiest among fellow professionals, and here he tells a tale of such a pro, the rodeo rider of the title, brilliantly played by Steve McQueen. As Junior tries to ride the unrideable, we watch his life pass by in the company of the superbly cast Robert Preston and Ida Lupino as his parents, and Joe Don Baker as his venal brother. The Todd-AO widescreen compositions lose considerable impact on television, but the substance endures. TS **DVD**

Steve McQueen (1) *Junior Bonner* • Robert Preston *Ace Bonner* • Ida Lupino *Elvira Bonner* • Joe Don Baker *Curly Bonner* • Barbara Leigh *Charmagne* • Mary Murphy (1) *Ruth Bonner* • Ben Johnson (1) *Buck Roan* • Bill McKinney *Red Terwiliger* ■ *Dir* Sam Peckinpah • *Scr* Jeb Rosebrook • *Cinematographer* Lucien Ballard

The Juniper Tree ★★★
Fantasy drama 1990 · US/Ice · BW · 78min

This prize-winning film was inspired by a fairy tale by the Brothers Grimm. For most viewers, the lure will be the chance to see Icelandic pop star, Björk, in a rare acting role. But there's a genuine fascination in the way writer/director Nietzchka Keene combines the grim realism of the desolate, monochrome landscape with the enchantment of her fantastical fable, in which Bryndís Petra Bragadóttir uses the witchcraft she learned from her mother to manipulate the emotions of a widowed farmer. DP

Björk Gudmundsdóttir [Björk] *Margit* • Bryndís Petra Bragadóttir *Katla* • Valdimar Orn Flygenring *Johann* • Gudrun Gisladóttir *Mother* • Geirlaug Sunna Pormar *Jonas* ■ *Dir* Nietzchka Keene • *Scr* Nietzchka Keene, from a story by Wilhelm and Jacob Grimm

Junkhearts ★★ 15
Drama 2011 · UK · Colour · 95min

A traumatised former soldier and a homeless teenage girl form an unlikely bond in this untidy independent British drama from first-time director Tinge Krishnan. Eddie Marsan plays a one-time family man gone way off the rails whose paternal instincts are re-awakened by sparky newcomer Candese Reid's abrasive-yet-needy youngster. Hackneyed but pleasant enough in its early stages, the film goes seriously awry with the arrival of her drug-dealing boyfriend (Tom Sturridge). TJ Swearing, drug abuse, sex scenes.

Eddie Marsan *Frank* • Tom Sturridge *Danny* • Romola Garai *Christine* • Candese Reid *Lynette* • Shaun Dooley *Josh* • Bhasker Patel *Hasan* ■ *Dir* Tinge Krishnan • *Scr* Simon Frank

Juno ★★★★ 12
Comedy drama 2007 · US · Colour · 92min

US teen movies are usually replete with scenes of sexual embarrassment and excess. Refreshingly, this Oscar-winning comedy takes the genre in a more grown-up direction in dealing with the subject of teenage pregnancy. Ellen Page delivers a wonderfully convincing performance as the sassy, clever teenager who finds herself "with child" and thus in way over her head. Having decided against an abortion, she embarks on a search for the perfect adoptive couple. The film smartly reveals that, despite our heroine's quick wit, she is just as anxious and confused as any girl in that situation would be. *Superbad's* Michael Cera co-stars as geeky father-to-be Paulie, while the talented supporting cast - including Jennifer Garner, Jason Bateman and JK Simmons - ensures this is a teen comedy with class. AS Swearing. **DVD** **Blu-ray**

Ellen Page *Juno MacGuff* • Michael Cera *Paulie Bleeker* • Jennifer Garner *Vanessa Loring* • Jason Bateman *Mark Loring* • Allison Janney *Bren MacGuff* • JK Simmons *Mac MacGuff* • Olivia Thirlby *Leah* • Eileen Pedde *Gerta Rauss* ■ *Dir* Jason Reitman • *Scr* Diablo Cody

Juno and the Paycock ★★ PG
Drama 1930 · UK · BW · 90min

The constraints placed upon film-makers by the primitive nature of early sound recording equipment only partly explain Alfred Hitchcock's failure to transfer Sean O'Casey's celebrated play about the Irish Civil War successfully to the screen. Although an admirer of the material, which concerns an Irish family who think they have come into money, he found it stubbornly uncinematic and ended up staging the action in a calcified manner. However, Sara Allgood excels as Juno Boyle, thus creating the mould for every Hitchcock mother to come. DP **DVD**

Sara Allgood *Juno Boyle* • Edward Chapman *Capt John "Paycock" Boyle* • Sydney Morgan *Joxer Daly* • John Longden *Chris Bentham* • Kathleen O'Regan *Mary Boyle* • John Laurie *Johnny Boyle* ■ *Dir* Alfred Hitchcock • *Scr* Alfred Hitchcock, Alma Reville, from the play by Sean O'Casey

Junoon ★★★★ 15
Epic period drama 1978 · Ind · Colour · 121min

This visually splendid epic drama sets a personal story of love and honour across racial and religious barriers against the historical backdrop of the Indian Mutiny. As the Pathan noble who rescues Anglo-Indian widow Jennifer Kendal and her daughter Nafisa Ali from a terrorist attack, Shashi Kapoor gives a larger-than-life performance that somewhat undermines Shyam Benegal's otherwise naturalistic direction. But with Shabana Azmi outstanding as his betrayed wife, this feature is always engrossing. DP Urdu +subtitles.

Shashi Kapoor *Javed Khan* • Jennifer Kendal *Mariam Labadoor* • Nafisa Ali *Ruth Labadoor* • Shabana Azmi *Firdaus* • Naseeruddin Shah *Sarfraz Khan* • Kulbhushan Kharbanda *Ramjimal* • Tom Alter *Charles Labadoor* ■ *Dir/Scr* Shyam Benegal

Jupiter Ascending ★★ 12
Science-fiction adventure 2014 · US · Colour · 122min

Matrix masterminds the Wachowskis follow 2012's *Cloud Atlas* with another ambitious sci-fi action epic. Mila Kunis stars as a down-on-her-luck human who discovers she is intergalactic royalty and, with the help of a genetically enhanced soldier (Channing Tatum), must attempt to prevent the Earth from being "harvested" by profit-obsessed alien aristocrat Eddie Redmayne. The action jumps from the streets of Chicago to far flung planets in breathtaking fashion, but while the Wachowskis have not lost their visual flair, the disorganised plot loses your interest very early on. JL **DVD** **Blu-ray** **3D**

Mila Kunis *Jupiter Jones* • Channing Tatum *Caine Wise* • Sean Bean *Stinger Apini* • Eddie Redmayne *Balem Abrasax* • Douglas Booth *Titus Abrasax* • Tuppence Middleton *Kalique Abrasax* ■ *Dir/Scr* Andy Wachowski [Lilly Wachowski], Lana Wachowski

Jupiter's Darling ★★★ U
Musical comedy 1955 · US · Colour · 96min

This is an underrated musical comedy about Hannibal and his elephants crossing the Alps to sack Rome. Esther Williams is in her Amazonian prime here, as she lures Howard Keel's Hannibal away from the Eternal City, and the two stars are superb together. Other pleasures include George Sanders and Richard Haydn as very English patricians, and the wonderful Marge and Gower Champion, who do a terrific song-and-dance number with painted elephants. TS

Esther Williams *Amytis* • Howard Keel *Hannibal* • Marge Champion *Meta* • Gower Champion *Varius* • George Sanders *Fabius Maximus* • Richard Haydn *Horatio* • William Demarest *Mago* ■ *Dir* George Sidney (2) • *Scr* Dorothy Kingsley, from the play *Road to Rome* by Robert

J

Sherwood [Robert E Sherwood] • *Music* David Rose • *Choreographer* Hermes Pan

LANDMARK FILM
Spielberg abandons stop-motion in favour of the newly tested Computer Generated Imagery (CGI) and the industry follows

Jurassic Park ★★★★★ PG
Science-fiction adventure
1993 • US • Colour • 126min

Steven Spielberg soared to new heights with this massively successful adventure. The world's ultimate theme park, featuring genetically re-created dinosaurs, is about to open and owner Richard Attenborough decides to give a sneak preview to a select few, including scientists Sam Neill and Laura Dern. However, all is not well in this new Garden of Eden, where T-Rex and his chums are the undoubted stars of the show. Spielberg orchestrates the action with effortless verve and, although it's a little too long and full of loose ends, only the most Scrooge-like viewer will fail to be transfixed by the thrilling action and the sheer scale of the director's vision. The dinosaurs returned in *The Lost World: Jurassic Park*. JF Swearing, violence. *DVD* 🔵 📀
Sam Neill *Dr Alan Grant* • Laura Dern *Dr Ellie Sattler* • Jeff Goldblum *Ian Malcolm* • Richard Attenborough *John Hammond* • Bob Peck *Robert Muldoon* • Martin Ferrero *Donald Gennaro* • BD Wong *Dr Wu* • Joseph Mazzello *Tim* • Ariana Richards *Lex* • Samuel L Jackson *Arnold* • Wayne Knight *Nedry* ■ *Dir* Steven Spielberg • *Scr* Michael Crichton, David Koepp, from the novel by Crichton • *Cinematographer* Dean Cundey • *Visual Effects* Michael Lantieri, Dennis Muren, Phil Tippet, Stan Winston

Jurassic Park III ★★★ PG
Science-fiction adventure
2001 • US • Colour • 88min

Jumanji director Joe Johnston takes the reins in this second sequel, and he's done a creditable job with what is basically a retread of the earlier films. We're back on Isla Sorna, where genetically engineered dinosaurs run wild. Cue another band of walking packed lunches: divorcees William H Macy and Téa Leoni who are looking for their lost 14-year-old son; paleontologist Sam Neill; and his protégé Alessandro Nivola. It's familiar ground, but the set pieces and effects are excellent. AC Violence. *DVD* 🔵 📀
Sam Neill *Dr Alan Grant* • William H Macy *Paul Kirby* • Téa Leoni *Amanda Kirby* • Alessandro Nivola *Billy Brennan* • Trevor Morgan *Eric Kirby* • Michael Jeter *Udesky* • John Diehl *Cooper* • Bruce A Young *Nash* • Laura Dern *Ellie Sattler* ■ *Dir* Joe Johnston • *Scr* Peter Buchman, Alexander Payne, Jim Taylor, from characters by Michael Crichton

Jurassic World ★★★★ 12
Science-fiction adventure
2015 • US • Colour • 119min

It's hard to think of a film that comes with a greater weight of expectation than director Colin Trevorrow's *Jurassic Park* sequel/reboot, but luckily this is a roaring return to form. Full of scares, laughs and heaps of nostalgia, it's a thrilling ride throughout, ably led by dinosaur wrangler Chris Pratt and park boss Bryce Dallas Howard as they fight to protect themselves and accompanying youngsters from a genetically engineered Indominus rex. It's not quite a match for the 1993 original film, but when that theme music plays and the T rex roars, you'll be happy you visited Isla Nublar again. A sequel is due in 2018. HF Violence. *DVD* 🔵 📀
Chris Pratt *Owen* • Bryce Dallas Howard *Claire* • Irrfan Khan [Irfan Khan] *Masrani* • Vincent D'Onofrio *Hoskins* • BD Wong *Henry Wu* • Colin Trevorrow *Mr DNA* ■ *Dir* Colin Trevorrow • *Scr* Rick Jaffa, Amanda Silver, Colin Trevorrow, Derek Connolly, from a story by Jaffa, Silver, from characters by Michael Crichton

Jurassic World 2
Science-fiction adventure 2018 • US • Colour

This is a preview – no prints were available to review as we went to press: The fifth episode in the blockbusting franchise is due for release 25 years after the original *Jurassic Park*, and if the spectacle of 2015's

Jurassic World is anything to go by, we are in for a treat. The realism of the creatures expands with every sequel, thanks to the super-powered digital effects, but the confirmation of returning stars Chris Pratt and Bryce Dallas Howard gives the movie a seam of continuity that audiences love. TF
Chris Pratt *Owen* • Bryce Dallas Howard *Claire* ■ *Dir* JA Bayona [Juan Antonio Bayona] • *Scr* Derek Connolly, Colin Trevorrow, from characters by Michael Crichton

The Juror ★★ 18
Thriller 1996 • US • Colour • 113min

Demi Moore stars as the juror on a Mafia trial who is harassed, threatened and coerced by Mob henchman Alec Baldwin to bring about a hung jury. Brian Gibson's film plods along predictably, with the only spark of interest coming from implausible plot twists. Still, thanks to a hilarious performance from Baldwin, it's marginally better than the similarly themed *Trial by Jury* with Joanne Whalley-Kilmer. JB Violence, swearing, brief nudity. *DVD*
Demi Moore *Annie Laird* • Alec Baldwin *The Teacher* • Joseph Gordon-Levitt *Oliver* • Anne Heche *Juliet* • James Gandolfini *Eddie* • Lindsay Crouse *Tallow* • Tony LoBianco *Louie Boffano* • Michael Constantine *Judge Weitzel* ■ *Dir* Brian Gibson • *Scr* Ted Tally, from the novel by George Dawes Green

Jury Duty ★★ 12
Comedy 1995 • US • Colour • 84min

Pauly Shore has never enjoyed the sort of profile in the UK that he does in the US, although this enjoyably crass comedy is one his better flicks. In another variation on his lazy-slacker persona, he plays a layabout who gets himself on jury service and proceeds to create havoc at a sensational murder trial. There are good supporting turns from Stanley Tucci and Brian Doyle-Murray, and director John Fortenberry has fun sending up the courtroom-drama genre. JF
Pauly Shore *Tommy* • Tia Carrere *Monica* • Stanley Tucci *Frank* • Brian Doyle-Murray *Harry* • Abe Vigoda *Judge Powell* • Charles Napier *Jed* • Richard Edson *Skeets* ■ *Dir* John Fortenberry • *Scr* Neil Tolkin, Barbara Williams, Samantha Adams, from a story by Barbara Williams, Samantha Adams

Just a Gigolo ★★ 15
Period drama 1978 • W Ger • Colour • 88min

Neither director David Hemmings nor a dream cast can do much with this lackadaisical look at how and why a disorientated Prussian war veteran become a gigolo in post-First World War Berlin. While this expensive production captures the disillusioned flavour of the era, its fragmented structure and an awkward performance from David Bowie in the lead leave much to be desired. Marlene Dietrich appears briefly to sing the title song; it was her last screen role. AJ English, German +subtitles.
David Bowie *Paul von Przygodsky* • Sydne Rome *Cilly* • Kim Novak *Helga* • David Hemmings *Captain Hermann Kraft* • Maria Schell *Mutti* • Curd Jürgens [Curt Jurgens] *Prince* • Marlene Dietrich *Baroness von Semering* ■ *Dir* David Hemmings • *Scr* Joshua Sinclair, Ennio De Concini

Just a Kiss ★★ 15
Romantic comedy 2002 • US • Colour • 86min

Exploring how a single action, in this case an illicit kiss, can trigger off a chain of far-reaching events, this is a shallow relationship comedy laced with gallows humour. Performance-wise the film's nothing special, but it's the constant to-ing and fro-ing of timelines and the inappropriate flashes of "rotoscope" animation that are the picture's major downsides. They disturb the overall fluidity and make actor-turned-director Fisher Stevens look like he's trying way too hard to be hip and edgy. SF Swearing, sex scenes. *DVD*

Ron Eldard *Dag* • Kyra Sedgwick *Halley* • Patrick Breen *Peter* • Marisa Tomei *Paula* • Marley Shelton *Rebecca* • Taye Diggs *Andre* • Sarita Choudhury *Colleen* ■ *Dir* Fisher Stevens • *Scr* Patrick Breen

Just Another Girl on the IRT ★★★ 18
Drama 1992 • US • Colour • 93min

Terrific slice-of-life stuff, by turns funny and sad, with Ariyan Johnson excellent as an ordinary New York high-school student who's determined to better herself, but whose plans get back-burnered when she gets pregnant. Leslie Harris directs his first feature with real sensitivity. Inexplicably, he hasn't made one since. The film's title refers to the New York subway system. DA
Ariyan Johnson *Chantel* • Kevin Thigpen *Tyrone* • Ebony Jerido *Natete* • Jerard Washington *Gerard* ■ *Dir/Scr* Leslie Harris

Just Another Love Story ★★ 18
Drama 2007 • Den/Nor/Swe • Colour • 104min

The originality that Danish writer/director Ole Bornedal demonstrated in his 1994 thriller *Nightwatch* is sadly lacking from this sloppily scripted and sluggishly acted pseudo-*noir*. Married crime scene photographer Jonas (Anders W Berthelsen) becomes obsessed with Julia (Rebecka Hemse) after causing a car crash that leaves her in a coma. He manages to convince her wealthy family that he is her boyfriend and then perpetuates the charade after the amnesiac Julia wakes up. The ease with which he does this strains credibility, as does the return of her brutally vengeful lover, and the whole affair is a self-consciously stylised mish-mash of flashbacks, fears and fantasies. DP Danish +subtitles. Violence, swearing, sex scenes, nudity. *DVD*
Anders W Berthelsen *Jonas* • Rebecka Hemse *Julia Castlund* • Nikolaj Lie Kaas *Sebastian* • Charlotte Fich *Mette* • Dejan Cukic *Frank* • Karsten Jansfort *Poul* ■ *Dir/Scr* Ole Bornedal

Just around the Corner ★★ U
Musical 1938 • US • BW • 67min

Shirley Temple finds work for her architect father after befriending an eccentric old millionaire in this Depression-era fable directed by Irving Cummings. The little trouper was growing up and being given excessively mature dialogue, losing much of her bubbly charm. But she sings and dances with Bill Robinson for the fourth and last time, and that's pure magic. Joan Davis and Bert Lahr lend strong support. AE *DVD*
Shirley Temple *Penny Hale* • Charles Farrell (1) *Jeff Hale* • Joan Davis *Kitty* • Amanda Duff *Lola* • Bill Robinson *Corp Jones* • Bert Lahr *Gus* • Franklin Pangborn *Waters* • Cora Witherspoon *Aunt Julia Ramsby* • Claude Gillingwater Sr [Claude Gillingwater] *Samuel G Henshaw* ■ *Dir* Irving Cummings • *Scr* Ethel Hill, JP McEvoy, Darrell Ware, from the novel *The Lucky Penny* by Paul Gerard Smith

Just before Dawn ★★★ 18
Horror 1980 • US • Colour • 93min

This slasher movie, about a group of hikers from the city sharing the Oregon wilderness with machete-wielding mountain men, is derivative of *Deliverance* and *The Hills Have Eyes*. Director Jeff Lieberman engineers a relentless build-up of suspense, culminating in an outrageous twist near the film's end. Chris Lemmon (Jack's son) stars as one of the teenagers who ignore the warnings of forest ranger George Kennedy not to venture further. TH *DVD*
George Kennedy *Roy McLean* • Mike Kellin *Ty* • Chris Lemmon *Jonathan* • Gregg Henry *Warren* • Deborah Benson *Constance* • Ralph Seymour *Daniel* ■ *Dir* Jeff Lieberman • *Scr* Mark Arywitz, Gregg Irving, from a story by Joseph Middleton

Just between Friends ★★★ 15
Drama 1986 • US • Colour • 106min

Like that other 1960s TV sitcom star Sally Field, Mary Tyler Moore moved in more

serious circles in the 1980s and this moving drama certainly gave her a role to get her teeth into. She plays a bored California housewife, seemingly happily married to Ted Danson, whose life is turned on its head when she discovers that her husband has been cheating on her for years. Moore is good in the lead role, although the film is stolen by Christine Lahti, who is terrific as the other woman in a melodrama that packs a punch. JF Swearing.
Mary Tyler Moore *Holly Davis* • Ted Danson *Chip Davis* • Christine Lahti *Sandy Dunlap* • Sam Waterston *Harry Crandall* • Susan Rinell *Kim Davis* ■ *Dir/Scr* Allan Burns

Just Can't Get Enough ★★ 18
Drama based on a true story
2001 • US • Colour • 90min

This made-for-TV drama is based on the experiences of Dan Peterson, the business studies graduate who went to work for the legendary troupe of male strippers, the Chippendales. Jonathan Aube copes well with the descent into decadence, but he's upstaged by Shelley Malil as Steve Banerjee, the owner of Los Angeles nightclub whose business methods led to murder. Director Dave Payne catches the hedonistic 1980s air, but this never truly ignites. DP *DVD*
Jonathan Aube *Chad Patterson* • Shelley Malil *Steve Banerjee* • Paul Clark *Spencer Dabias* • John Paul Pitoc *Clayton* • Rebekah Ryan *Heather* ■ *Dir* David Payne [Dave Payne] • *Scr* Dave Payne

Just Cause ★★★ 18
Thriller 1995 • US • Colour • 97min

In this entertaining thriller, Sean Connery plays a law professor called in to help Blair Underwood, who claims he has been wrongly convicted of the murder of a young child, partly because local cop Laurence Fishburne beat a confession out of him. Connery is as charismatic as ever in a story that, though a little uneven at times, manages some pleasing twists on the usual formula. Director Arne Glimcher throws in enough red herrings to keep viewers guessing right to the end and makes good use of the Everglades locations. JF Swearing, violence. *DVD*
Sean Connery *Paul Armstrong* • Laurence Fishburne *Tanny Brown* • Kate Capshaw *Laurie Armstrong* • Blair Underwood *Bobby Earl* • Ed Harris *Blair Sullivan* • Christopher Murray *Wilcox* • Daniel J Travanti *Warden* • Ned Beatty *McNair* ■ *Dir* Arne Glimcher • *Scr* Jeb Stuart, Peter Stone, from the novel by John Katzenbach

Just Do It: a Tale of Modern-Day Outlaws ★★★ 12A
Documentary 2011 • UK • Colour • 90min

The tea-making geniality of Page 3 girl-turned-politician and environmentalist Marina Pepper epitomises this rousing insight into the tactics and logistics of 21st-century protest. As earnest activists and dour cops square off, we see the 40-something striving to keep the peace with a cuppa and a calmly made point. Director Emily James spent a year chronicling the campaigns of direct action groups such as Climate Camp and Plane Stupid. She captures the laudable commitment and quiet courage of those prepared to do more than just talk about society's ills, as they camp, march, break-in and barricade in a bid to make Britain a greener and more pleasant land. DP Some violence.
■ *Dir* Emily James

Just for the Record ★ 18
Comedy 2010 • UK • Colour • 79min

Low-budget British movies starring Danny Dyer, Craig Fairbrass and a bunch of female extras pulled out of the nearest Spearmint Rhino club usually revolve around gangsters or football hooligans, but this tries to be something smarter and funnier – and fails abysmally. It's a mockumentary about the making of a micro-budget romantic comedy – a cursed production during which everything goes wrong. Moronic and charmless, the end result is as much of a disaster as the film-within-a-film. Only Steven Berkoff's turn as the crotchety director of photography raises a rare chuckle. JR Swearing. *DVD*

Steven Berkoff *Mike Rossferry* • Phil Davis [Philip Davis] *Ed Grains* • Danny Dyer *Derek La Farge* • Craig Fairbrass *Malcolm Wickes* • Ciaran Griffiths *Danny Allgen* • Rik Mayall *Andy Wiseman* ■ *Dir* Steven Lawson • *Scr* Phillip Barron

Just for You ★★★ U
Musical comedy   1952 · US · Colour · 104min

Bing Crosby and Jane Wyman, who made such an agreeable duo in Frank Capra's *Here Comes the Groom* (1951), were teamed up again rather less successfully in this tale of Broadway producer Crosby, who ignores his teenage children (Natalie Wood, Robert Arthur) until Wyman puts him right. Ethel Barrymore is perfect as the headmistress of snooty girl's school, and Bing sings a lively Harry Warren/Leo Robin song, *Zing a Little Zong*. RB

Bing Crosby *Jordan Blake* • Jane Wyman *Carolina Hill* • Ethel Barrymore *Allida de Bronkhart* • Robert Arthur (1) *Jerry Blake* • Natalie Wood *Barbara Blake* • Cora Witherspoon *Mrs Angevine* ■ *Dir* Elliott Nugent • *Scr* Robert Carson, from the novel *Famous* by Stephen Vincent Benet

Just Friends ★★★ 12
Romantic comedy   2005 · US/Can · Colour · 90min

A snappy script breathes new life into this stereotypically idiotic tale of one man's journey to self-discovery. Obese high-school loser (Ryan Reynolds in a prosthetic fat suit) has been in love with Amy Smart for years. She loves him, too, but only like a brother. After making a success of himself in LA, he finds himself back in his New Jersey home town where he determines to win her heart – not realising that, even though he's now slim and handsome, he's not such a nice guy anymore. This has a generous helping of laughs amid the stupidity. KK *DVD*

Ryan Reynolds *Chris Brander* • Amy Smart *Jamie Palamino* • Anna Faris *Samantha James* • Chris Klein *Dusty Dinkleman* • Christopher Marquette *Michael* • Julie Haggerty [Julie Hagerty] *Chris's mum* • Stephen Root *KC* ■ *Dir* Roger Kumble • *Scr* Adam "Tex" Davis [Adam Davis]

Just Go with It ★★ 12
Romantic comedy   2011 · US · Colour · 111min

A tried-and-tested pick-up line engulfs a randy plastic surgeon in a tangled web of deceit in this hit-and-miss romantic comedy starring Adam Sandler. The ludicrously contrived series of events (based on a French farce, itself the basis for 1968 Oscar winner *Cactus Flower*) leads Sandler's assistant Jennifer Aniston to pose as his soon-to-be ex-wife on a Hawaiian holiday, designed to ease the conquest of his current infatuation, played by swimsuit model Brooklyn Decker. Broad comic turns by Nicole Kidman and Nick Swardson only exacerbate the feeling that everyone is just trying too hard for their own good. SP Swearing, sexual references. *DVD* *Blu-ray*

Adam Sandler *Dr Danny Maccabee* • Jennifer Aniston *Katherine Palmer* • Nicole Kidman *Devlin Adams* • Nick Swardson *Eddie* • Brooklyn Decker *Palmer Dodge* ■ *Dir* Dennis Dugan • *Scr* Timothy Dowling, Allan Loeb, from the film *Cactus Flower* by IAL Diamond and the play by Abe Burrows, from the play *Fleur de Cactus* by Pierre Barillet, Jean-Pierre Gredy

Just Jim ★★★ 15
Comedy   2015 · UK · Colour · 80min

This dark, peculiar comedy is a study of teenage loneliness. Set in a small Welsh village, it focuses on Craig Roberts, a socially awkward teenager who doesn't have any friends. For the first 25 minutes or so, we follow Roberts as he plays video games and walks his beloved dog. But just as things are starting to drag, Jim's world is shaken up by the arrival of Emile Hirsch, a cocksure, mysterious American who teaches him how to be cool. What follows is an unusual teen movie with a dry sense of

humour that admittedly won't be for everyone. SC Swearing, sex references *DVD*

Emile Hirsch *Dean* • Craig Roberts *Jim* • Aneirin Hughes *Dad* • Mark Lewis Jones *Donald* ■ *Dir/Scr* Craig Roberts

Just like a Woman ★★
Comedy   1966 · UK · Colour · 89min

Director Robert Fuest made his feature debut with this 1960s satire about a housewife (Wendy Craig) who rebels against her TV director husband (Francis Matthews). Craig here reveals the comic flair that enabled her to become the epitome of scatty domesticity in sitcoms such as *Not in Front of the Children* and *Butterflies*. Fuest's script strives too hard to be offbeat, however. DP

Wendy Craig *Scilla Alexander* • Francis Matthews *Lewis McKenzie* • John Wood (2) *John Martin* • Dennis Price *Bathroom salesman* • Miriam Karlin *Ellen Newman* • Peter Jones *Saul Alexander* • Clive Dunn *Graff Von Fischer* ■ *Dir/Scr* Robert Fuest

Just like a Woman ★ 15
Comedy   1992 · UK · Colour · 101min

Julie Walters is good value, but this comedy drama about transvestism is pretty worthless otherwise. Who is it aimed at? Closet cross-dressers? Ed Wood fanatics? Hard to tell, as it lurches from frilly farce to black-lace banality, with sickly sentiment piled as high as the heels. Adrian Pasdar looks uncomfortable playing Gerald/Geraldine, as will be those watching this curious frock opera that's as fake as his falsies. AJ *DVD*

Julie Walters *Monica* • Adrian Pasdar *Gerald* • Paul Freeman *Miles Millichamp* • Susan Wooldridge *Louisa* • Gordon Kennedy *CJ* ■ *Dir* Christopher Monger • *Scr* Nick Evans, from the book *Geraldine, for the Love of a Transvestite* by Monica Jay

Just like Heaven ★★★ PG
Romantic comedy   2005 · US · Colour · 90min

Reese Witherspoon stars as a workaholic emergency doctor who is involved in a serious car crash and wakes up – apparently dead – back in her own home. Not realising her predicament, she takes exception to the apartment's handsome new occupant, Mark Ruffalo, a man struggling to get over the loss of his wife. This fresh if somewhat bumpy look at the course of true love benefits from its stunning San Francisco backdrop, while Jon Heder is perfectly cast as the local bookshop psychic. KK Some swearing. *DVD*

Reese Witherspoon *Dr Elizabeth Masterson* • Mark Ruffalo *David Abbott* • Donal Logue *Jack Houriskey* • Dina Waters *Abby Brody* • Ben Shenkman *Dr Brett Rushton* • Jon Heder *Darryl* • Ivana Milicevic *Katrina* • Rosalind Chao *Fran* ■ *Dir* Mark Waters (1) • *Scr* Peter Tolan, Leslie Dixon, from the novel *If Only It Were True* by Marc Levy

Just Married ★★ 12
Romantic comedy   2003 · US · Colour · 90min

This banal offering aims for a teen twist on the romantic screwball comedy but the results are less than sparkling. Ashton Kutcher stars as the unctured new husband of rich kid Brittany Murphy, whose wealthy parents disapprove of her choice of groom. During a disastrous honeymoon – no more than a series of slapstick vignettes performed in glamorous European locations – they begin to wonder if their marriage can really work. The stars are photogenic and enthusiastic, but this is brash and charmless. JC *DVD* *Blu-ray*

Ashton Kutcher *Tom Leezak* • Brittany Murphy *Sarah McNerney* • Christian Kane *Peter Prentiss* • David Moscow *Kyle* • Monet Mazur *Lauren McNerney* • David Rasche *Mr McNerney* • Veronica Cartwright *Mrs McNerney* ■ *Dir* Shawn Levy • *Scr* Sam Harper

Just My Luck ★★ U
Comedy   1957 · UK · BW · 82min

This horse-racing comedy is not a particularly distinguished Norman Wisdom movie, but is still a pleasant time-waster. On

its original release, Rank realised the film's weaknesses and shored it up with a rock 'n' roll supporting feature. Today it's a brave viewer (or a devout fan of Wisdom) who'll watch, for the star's mawkish side is virtually given free rein as he tries to win enough money to buy a gift for Jill Dixon. TS *DVD*

Norman Wisdom *Norman* • Margaret Rutherford *Mrs Dooley* • Jill Dixon *Anne* • Leslie Phillips *Hon Richard Lumb* • Delphi Lawrence *Miss Daviot* • Edward Chapman *Mr Stoneway* • Marjorie Rhodes *Mrs Hackett* • Joan Sims *Phoebe* ■ *Dir* John Paddy Carstairs • *Scr* Alfred Shaughnessy, Peter Blackmore

Just My Luck ★★ PG
Romantic comedy   2006 · US · Colour · 98min

A lazy script takes the shine off Lindsay Lohan's role as a girl spoiled by her good fortune. After a wearisome preamble that sees her find cash on the streets, score a hot date and mistakenly get Sarah Jessica Parker's dry cleaning, Lohan kisses the hapless Chris Pine, an aspiring music promoter. Suddenly her luck runs out, but it's obvious that fate has contrived to bring them together. SP *DVD* *Blu-ray*

Lindsay Lohan *Ashley Albright* • Chris Pine *Jake Hardin* • Faizon Love *Damon Phillips* • Missi Pyle *Peggy Braden* • Bree Turner *Dana* • Samaire Armstrong *Maggie* • Tovah Feldshuh *Madame Z* • Carlos Ponce *Antonio* ■ *Dir* Donald Petrie • *Scr* Amy B Harris, I Marlene King, from a story by Jonathan Bernstein, Mark Blackwell, James Greer, King

Just Tell Me What You Want ★★★
Comedy   1980 · US · Colour · 112min

Alan King plays a spoilt and strident millionaire in this Sidney Lumet directed comedy. Married King is dallying with his long-standing mistress Ali MacGraw but failing to commit. Not surprisingly, MacGraw seeks solace with toy boy Peter Weller, prompting King to realise that he really really wants her. Adapted by Jay Presson Allen from her novel, this is a romantic comedy with an edge. King's performance has great gusto and watch out for Myrna Loy in her last and very notable performance as his long-suffering personal assistant. LH

Ali MacGraw *Bones Burton* • Alan King *Max Herschel* • Myrna Loy *Stella Liberti* • Keenan Wynn *Seymour Berger* • Tony Roberts *Mike Berger* • Peter Weller *Steven Routledge* • Sara Truslow *Cathy* ■ *Dir* Sidney Lumet • *Scr* Jay Presson Allen, from her novel

Just the Ticket ★★ 15
Romantic comedy drama
1998 · US · Colour · 110min

The combination of star Andy Garcia and a script from director Richard Wenk that was ten years in the making should guarantee an interesting film. But, sadly, this is a lacklustre affair. Can a tale of a ticket tout selling illegal entry to the Pope's New York visit in order to retire and save his relationship really work? Garcia is all Italian charm to girlfriend Andie MacDowell's southern kookiness but, acceptable performances aside, rip-roaring romantic comedy this is not. LH Swearing. *DVD*

Andy Garcia *Gary Starke* • Andie MacDowell *Linda Paliski* • Richard Bradford *Benny Moran* • Fred Asparagus *Zeus* • Elizabeth Ashley *Mrs Paliski* • André B Blake *Casino* • Ron Leibman *Barry the Book* ■ *Dir/Scr* Richard Wenk

Just Visiting ★ PG
Comedy fantasy   2001 · Fr/US · Colour · 88min

The time-travel farce *Les Visiteurs* became the highest grossing home-grown movie in French cinema history. The English-language remake from writer/director Jean-Marie Poiré relocates the action to America and increases the toilet-humour content at the expense of the original's rough charm. Tricked into poisoning his betrothed (Christina Applegate), 12th-century French nobleman Jean Reno gets wizard Malcolm McDowell to concoct a potion to send him back in time to avert the tragedy. But Reno and his idiot squire

Christian Clavier end up in modern-day Chicago. A limp re-tread, this loses something in the translation. AJ *DVD*

Jean Reno *Thibault Malfete* • Christian Clavier *André* • Malcolm McDowell *Wizard* • Christina Applegate *Julia Malfete/Princess Rosalind* • Matt Ross *Hunter* • Tara Reid *Angelique* • George Plimpton *Dr Brady* ■ *Dir* Jean-Marie Gaubert [Jean-Marie Poiré] • *Scr* Jean-Marie Poiré, Christian Clavier, John Hughes, from the film *Les Visiteurs* by Jean-Marie Poiré, Christian Clavier

Just William ★★ U
Comedy   1939 · UK · BW · 74min

Richmal Crompton's tousled terror made his screen debut in the excitable form of Dicky Lupino in this hectic adventure, co-written and directed by Graham Cutts, one of Britain's finest silent directors. Although he gets up to lots of mischief, William spends too much time on the trail of a conman and helping his father secure a seat on the council to be particularly funny. Lupino (the youngest member of that multi-talented showbiz family) hurtles around at full pelt, so it's left to Roddy McDowall to do the real acting as the hero's put-upon pal, Ginger. DP

Dicky Lupino *William Brown* • Fred Emney *Mr Brown* • Basil Radford *Mr Sidway* • Amy Veness *Mrs Bott* • Iris Hoey *Mrs Brown* • Roddy McDowall *Ginger* • Jenny Laird *Ethel Brown* • David Tree *Marmaduke Bott* ■ *Dir* Graham Cutts • *Scr* Doreen Montgomery, Ireland Wood, Graham Cutts, from the stories by Richmal Crompton

Just William's Luck ★★ U
Comedy   1947 · UK · BW · 92min

Having concluded they need bikes to emulate the heroics of the Knights of the Round Table, William and his outlaws decide to marry off their older brothers and inherit their cast-off cycles. While William Graham captures something of the scruffy boisterousness of Richmal Crompton's timeless comic creation, director Val Guest's screenplay smoothes away the rougher edges to produce a sanitised tale of childhood mayhem. DP

William Graham *William Brown* • Garry Marsh *Mr Brown* • Jane Welsh *Mrs Brown* • Hugh Cross *Robert Brown* • Kathleen Stuart *Ethel Brown* • Leslie Bradley *Boss* • AE Matthews *Tramp* • Brian Roper *Ginger* • Audrey Manning *Violet Elizabeth Bott* ■ *Dir* Val Guest • *Scr* Val Guest, from the stories by Richmal Crompton

Just Wright ★★ PG
Romantic comedy   2010 · US · Colour · 96min

Every romantic comedy needs its Mr Right, but the fact that the woman searching for him in this fluffy outing is called Ms Wright tells you a lot about just how low it sets its comic sights. It's a Cinderella fantasy set in the world of NBA basketball, with hip-hop stars Queen Latifah and Common as a plus-sized physical therapist and an injured multimillionaire player who find romance blossoming over ice packs, half-time pep talks and a shared passion for – gulp – Joni Mitchell. Over-familiar and overlong, *Just Wright* would be totally wrong if it weren't for its likeable cast. JR Some swearing. *DVD*

Queen Latifah *Leslie Wright* • Common *Scott McKnight* • Paula Patton *Morgan Alexander* • James Pickens Jr *Lloyd Wright* • Phylicia Rashad *Ella McKnight* • Pam Grier *Janice Wright* ■ *Dir* Sanaa Hamri • *Scr* Michael Elliot

Just You and Me, Kid ★ 12
Comedy   1979 · US · Colour · 94min

Not even the pleasure of seeing George Burns trading wisecracks over a game of cards with fellow old-stagers Ray Bolger and Leon Ames can enliven this crass age-gap comedy. If only he'd spent more time with them and less with Brooke Shields, the runaway he discovers naked in the boot of his car after she goes on the run from a drug dealer. There is absolutely no spark between the leads, with his knowing drawl and her eager cuteness clashing in every exchange. Even less amusing is Burl Ives's demonstration of catatonia. DP

12 15 18 PASSED FOR PEOPLE OF THESE AGES AND OVER   *DVD* RELEASED ON DVD   *Blu-ray* RELEASED ON BLU-RAY   *3D* RELEASED IN 3D   *CS* END CREDIT SEQUENCE

679

George Burns *Bill* • Brooke Shields *Kate* • Burl Ives *Max* • Lorraine Gary *Shirl* • Nicolas Coster *Harris* • Keye Luke *Dr Device* ■ *Dir* Leonard B Stern • *Scr* Oliver Hailey, from a story by Tom Lazarus, Leonard B Stern

Just Your Luck ★ 15

Comedy thriller   1996 · US · Colour · 84min

This slimly written tale begins in a café with a man dropping dead immediately after learning he's won six million dollars on the lottery. Virginia Madsen, Sean Patrick Flanery, Ernie Hudson and Jon Favreau are among the customers trying to convince the establishment's owner Jon Polito that they should cash in the ticket and keep the cash. Everyone in the group is so unlikeable that you won't care to sit through until the end to discover who ends up with the money. Witless and thin. JB Swearing, violence.

Sean Patrick Flanery *Ray* • Virginia Madsen *Kim* • Ernie Hudson *Willie* • Alanna Ubach *Angela* • Vince Vaughn *Barry* • Jon Favreau *Straker* • Jon Polito *Nick* ■ *Dir* Gary Auerbach • *Scr* Todd Alcott, Gary Auerbach, from a story by Gary Auerbach

Juste avant la Nuit ★★★★ 15

Thriller   1971 · Fr/It · Colour · 102min

Claude Chabrol follows *La Femme Infidèle* and *Le Boucher* with another masterly thriller, in which Stéphane Audran (Mrs Chabrol) refuses to believe her husband – creepy Michel Bouquet – has intentionally murdered his mistress. This little parable about guilt and bourgeois morality in the provinces amounts to as much or as little as you want to read into it. But few could resist the elegant way in which Chabrol tells the story or the immaculate acting of the cast. AT In French. *DVD*

Michel Bouquet *Charles* • Stéphane Audran *Helen* • François Périer *François* • Dominique Zardi *Prince* • Henri Attal *Cavanna* ■ *Dir* Claude Chabrol • *Scr* Claude Chabrol, from the novel *The Thin Line* by Edouard Atiyah

Justice ★★★ 15

Action thriller   2011 · US · Colour · 100min

In this tense thriller from Kiwi director Roger Donaldson, mild-mannered New Orleans schoolteacher Nicolas Cage gets involved with a shadowy group of vigilantes after his wife (January Jones) is viciously attacked and hospitalised. Then the vigilante leader (a stern-faced Guy Pearce) "requests" that the enraged husband carry out a murder in return for retribution on his wife's attacker. Cage is relatively restrained as the terror-stricken everyman of the piece, while Donaldson maintains a lively pace. But the story doesn't bear too close an examination for fear of being engulfed by its own plot holes. TeS Violence, swearing. *DVD* *BLU*

Nicolas Cage *Will Gerard* • January Jones *Laura Gerard* • Guy Pearce *Simon* • Jennifer Carpenter *Trudy* • Harold Perrineau *Jimmy* • Xander Berkeley *Lieutenant Durgan* ■ *Dir* Roger Donaldson • *Scr* Robert Tannen, Yuri Zeltser, from a story by Tannen, Todd Hickey

Justice League

Fantasy action adventure   2017 · US · Colour

This is a preview – no prints were available to review prior to publication: The DC Comics super-team equivalent to Marvel's Avengers looks set to get its own blockbuster blowout following the (hoped-for) box-office success of the Batman v Superman movie. Zack Snyder's 2016 clash-of-the-titans film looks likely to introduce other superheroes (Wonder Woman, Aquaman, Cyborg) in order for the team to face some earth-shattering threat. Looks good on paper but a decent script and cast chemistry will also be required if it's to match the uber-success of the Marvel franchise. JA

Gal Gadot *Diana Prince/Wonder Woman* • Henry Cavill *Clark Kent/Superman* • Ben Affleck *Bruce Wayne/Batman* ■ *Dir* Zack Snyder • *Scr* Chris Terrio

Justin and the Knights of Valour ★★ PG

Animated adventure   2013 · Sp · Colour · 96min

Less frantic than many recent cartoons, and none the worse for that, this endearingly old-fashioned medieval adventure perhaps isn't the most original yarn you'll ever see. But, such familiarity aside, this tale of a boy who dreams of becoming a knight in a kingdom that's banned them, but which suddenly needs them again when dark forces threaten, is decent entertainment for youngsters. The icing on the cake is the stellar British voice cast, while Antonio Banderas "presents" the film, whose CGI originated in his native Spain. DA 📀

Freddie Highmore *Justin* • Saoirse Ronan *Talia* • Julie Walters *Gran* • Antonio Banderas *Sir Clorex* • Alfred Molina *Reginald* • Mark Strong *Heraclio* ■ *Dir* Manuel Sicilia • *Scr* Manuel Sicilia, Matthew Jacobs

Justin Bieber: Never Say Never ★★★ U

Music documentary   2011 · US · Colour · 100min

Justin who? If you have to ask, you're probably neither a young girl nor into pop music. Bieber is the Canadian teen phenomenon who has gone global since his mother posted some of his performance videos on YouTube back in 2007. The bright and breezy *Never Say Never* showcases the precocious pop pup on his first pan-American tour. The film is part biopic, part concert movie and part backstage footage and, like Bieber himself, it's easy on the eye and the ear. First and foremost, of course, it is a film for fans. But accompanying adults might be surprised by how cheesily enjoyable it is. DA *DVD* *BLU* 📀

Justin Bieber • Miley Cyrus [Miley Ray Cyrus] *Miley Cyrus* • Usher [Usher Raymond] *Usher* • Jaden Smith ■ *Dir* Jon M Chu

Justine ★ 15

Drama   1969 · US · Colour · 111min

This catastrophic attempt to condense the four novels of Lawrence Durrell's celebrated *Alexandria Quartet* into a single film results in a messy farrago. Told in flashback by Justine's lover Darley (Michael York) it focuses on the influence and sexual exploits of the mysterious and beautiful Egyptian Jewess, who, with her banker husband, plans to send military aid to Palestine's Jews. RK *DVD*

Anouk Aimée *Justine* • Dirk Bogarde *Pursewarden* • Robert Forster *Narouz* • Anna Karina *Melissa* • Philippe Noiret *Pombal* • Michael York *Darley* • George Baker *Mountolive* ■ *Dir* George Cukor • *Scr* Lawrence B Marcus, from the novels *The Alexandria Quartet* by Lawrence Durrell

KM 31: Kilometro 31 ★★ 15

Horror   2005 · Mex/Sp/Bra · Colour · 100min

In this Mexican movie, Agata (Iliana Fox) is left comatose after a car crash on a haunted highway. Agata's identical twin Catalina (Fox again) discovers that her unconscious sister's soul is trapped in limbo between life and death. She then risks life and limb to free her, encountering ever more preposterous frights along the way. Although inspired by an ancient Mexican legend, the film has some all too obvious cinematic influences – ranging from *The Shining* to *The Others*, and even Japanese horror *The Ring*. Despite decent spooky effects, it never quite lives up to its early, creepy promise. DA Spanish +subtitles. *DVD*

Adrià Collado Nuño • Raúl Méndez *Omar* • Iliana Fox *Catalina/Agata* • Carlos Aragón *Ugalde* • Luisa Huertas *Old woman* • Mikel Mateos *Child* • Fernando Becerril *Doctor* • Claudette Maille *Catalina/Agata's mother* • *Dir/Scr* Rigoberto Castañeda

K-9 ★★ 15

Crime comedy   1989 · US · Colour · 97min

Hollywood, desperately looking for new variations on the mismatched-cops scenario, briefly lit upon the concept of the buddy-doggie movie. This one has James Belushi as the detective who is reluctantly partnered with a surly canine in a bid to crack a drug smuggling ring. Belushi is as affable as ever, but even he looks a little embarrassed by the affair, particularly the mawkish ending. JF Swearing, violence. *DVD*

James Belushi *Thomas Dooley* • Mel Harris *Tracy* • Kevin Tighe *Lyman* • Ed O'Neill *Lt Brannigan* • James Handy *Lt Byers* • Daniel Davis *Halstead* • Cotter Smith *Gilliam* • John Snyder *Freddie* ■ *Dir* Rod Daniel • *Scr* Steven Siegel, Scott Myers

K-911 ★★ 12

Crime comedy   1999 · US · Colour · 87min

This belated video sequel to the canine cop comedy *K-9* was, improbably, a big rental hit at the end of the 1990s. James Belushi returns for this slight tale, in which he and his canine partner are helped out by fellow cop Christine Tucci and her Doberman to track down a mysterious mugger. Belushi coasts through the slight but amiable material. A further video sequel, *K-9: P.I.*, was released in 2002. JF Swearing. *DVD*

James Belushi *Thomas Dooley* • Christine Tucci *Welles* • James Handy *Captain Byers* • Wade Andrew Williams *Devon* • JJ Johnston *Fat Tommy* ■ *Dir* Charles T Kanganis • *Scr* Gary Scott Thompson, from characters by Steven Siegel, Scott Myers

K-19: the Widowmaker ★★ 12

Action thriller based on a true story   2002 · US · Colour · 132min

This workmanlike thriller is based on the true story of a Soviet nuclear submarine that sprung a radioactive leak and almost started the Third World War in 1961. Harrison Ford plays the captain at loggerheads with his second-in-command, Liam Neeson. After about an hour of these two locking horns, the nuclear reactor leaks and the film gets interesting. The horror of the radiation effects, the race against time, the claustrophobic tension – all of this works, but it's too late. StH Violence. *DVD*

Harrison Ford *Alexei Vostrikov* • Liam Neeson *Mikhail Polenin* • Peter Sarsgaard *Vadim Radtchenko* • Joss Ackland *Marshal Zelentstov* • John Shrapnel *Admiral Bratyeev* • Donald

Sumpter *Dr Savran* • Tim Woodward *Partonov* ■ *Dir* Kathryn Bigelow • *Scr* Christopher Kyle, from a story by Louis Nowra

K-PAX ★★ 12

Science-fiction fantasy drama   2001 · US · Colour · 115min

The prospect of class acts Kevin Spacey and Jeff Bridges going head-to-head is a delicious one, especially in what is essentially a talky two-hander about a mysterious stranger (Spacey) claiming to be a visitor from the planet K-Pax and the psychologist who attempts to crack his "delusional" state. Unfortunately, the story does not match their performances. The final result is bloodless, touchy-feely schmaltz. AC Violence, swearing. *DVD* CS

Kevin Spacey *Prot* • Jeff Bridges *Dr Mark Powell* • Mary McCormack *Rachel Powell* • Alfre Woodard *Claudia Villars* • David Patrick Kelly *Howie* • Saul Williams *Ernie* ■ *Dir* Iain Softley • *Scr* Charles Leavitt, from a novel by Gene Brewer

K-Shop ★★ 18

Horror thriller   2015 · UK · Colour · 115min

A Muslim kebab shop-owner, driven to distraction by the boozy yobs who make up much of his clientele, adopts an extreme response in this dark horror fable, which plays like a modern take on *Sweeney Todd*. First-time writer/director Dan Pringle supplies plenty of proof of Britain's youth at its lagered-up worst to create a context for his initially sympathetic protagonist's journey into bloody vengeance. There's definitely more substance here than the usual penny dreadful, but sluggish pacing, a lengthy running time, and a general lack of focus work against it. TJ Violence, swearing. *DVD*

Ziad Abaza *Salah Sabir* • Scot Williams *Jason Brown* • Darren Morfitt *Steve* • Kristin Atherton *Sarah* ■ *Dir/Scr* Dan Pringle

K2 ★★★ 15

Adventure   1991 · US · Colour · 105min

In this climbing epic, Michael Biehn is perfectly cast as a brash lawyer who lives life on the edge through his passion for mountaineering. This is largely *Boys' Own* stuff, with character development taking second place to macho heroics and bonding. However, director Franc Roddam responds by staging one exhilarating cliffside set piece after another, including a breathtaking avalanche sequence. JF Swearing, nudity. *DVD*

Michael Biehn *Taylor Brooks* • Matt Craven *Harold Jamieson* • Raymond J Barry *Phillip Claiborne* • Hiroshi Fujioka *Takane Shimuzu* • Luca Bercovici *Dallas Woolf* • Patricia Charbonneau *Jacki Metcalfe* • Julia Nickson-Soul *Cindy* • Jamal Shah *Malik* • Annie Grindlay *Lisa* • Elena Stiteler *Tracey* ■ *Dir* Franc Roddam • *Scr* Patrick Meyers, Scott Roberts, from the play by Patrick Meyers

Kaagaz Ke Phool ★★★★ U

Drama   1959 · Ind · BW · 139min

Echoes of *Citizen Kane* and *A Star Is Born* ring around this Bollywood classic (the subcontinent's first in CinemaScope), which flopped on its original release. Guru Dutt excels as the director whose fortunes plummet after his star discovery, Waheeda Rehman, quits to avoid hurtful gossip. In his second role as this film's director, he also imbues the drama with a visual eloquence that conveys the "neverland" atmosphere of the movies, without losing sight of the human frailty afflicting even the most successful artists. DP Hindi +subtitles. *DVD*

Guru Dutt *Suresh Sinha* • Waheeda Rehman *Shanti* • Baby Naaz *Pummy* • Johnny Walker *Brother-in-law* • Mahesh Kaul *Father-in-law* ■ *Dir* Guru Dutt • *Scr* Abrar Alvi

Kabhi Khushi Kabhie Gham... ★★★ PG

Drama   2001 · Ind · Colour · 210min

This intense family saga is brought to life by some of Bollywood's biggest stars. Hrithik Roshan travels to London in the hope of uniting adopted sibling Shah Rukh Khan with Amitabh Bachchan, the proud father who disowned his youngest son after he married a chatty Punjabi shop owner, played by Kajol. With Jaya Bachchan piling on the piety as Amitabh's wife and Kareena Kapoor providing light relief as Kajol's mischievous sister, there are several shifts in mood and plenty of musical moments. DP Hindi +subtitles. *DVD*

Amitabh Bachchan *Yashovardhan Raichand* • Jaya Bachchan *Nandini Raichand* • Shah Rukh Khan *Rahul* • Kajol *Anjali Sharma* • Hrithik Roshan *Rohan* • Kareena Kapoor *Pooja Sharma* ■ *Dir* Karan Johar • *Scr* Karan Johar, Sheena Parekh

Kaboom ★★★ 15
Science–fiction comedy thriller
2010 · US · Colour · 82min
Mysterious Skin director Gregg Araki returns to the delicious absurdity of his 1990s "Teen Apocalypse" trilogy with this erotically charged slice of hipster film-making. Conceived as a treat for his hardcore fans, it's a flimsy but fun sci-fi comedy in which bisexual college student Smith (Thomas Dekker) and his equally hedonistic pals (including a fabulously free-spirited Juno Temple) are drawn into a convoluted end-of-days conspiracy after his ominous dreams start bleeding into reality. Araki's trademark vibrant visuals and a cool, indie soundtrack intensify the overall trippy experience. SF Swearing, sex scenes, nudity. *DVD*

Thomas Dekker *Smith* • Haley Bennett *Stella* • Chris Zylka *Thor* • Roxane Mesquida *Lorelei* • Juno Temple *London* • Andy Fischer-Price *Rex* ■ *Dir/Scr* Gregg Araki

Kadosh ★★★★ 15
Drama 1999 · Is/Fr · Colour · 116min
As if the assault on the patriarchal nature of Hassidic Judaism wasn't controversial enough, Israeli director Amos Gitai chose an Arab (Yussef Abu Warda) to play the rabbi in this compelling Jerusalem-based drama. Indeed, Gitai compounds his audacity by viewing events from the perspective of his female protagonists. He remains studiously detached in depicting how Meital Barda refuses an arranged marriage, while her childless sister (Yael Abecassis) steps aside so her husband of ten years (Yoram Hattab) can obey the rabbinical dictate that he remarry to further his line. This is intelligently scripted, powerfully played and subtle in its subversion. DP Hebrew +subtitles.

Yael Abecassis *Rivka* • Yoram Hattab *Meir* • Meital Barda *Malka* • Uri Ran Klauzner *Yossef* • Yussef Abu Warda *Rav Shimon* • Sami Hori *Yaakov* • Lea Koenig *Elisheva* • Rivka Michaeli *Gynaecologist* ■ *Dir* Amos Gitai • *Scr* Amos Gitai, Eliette Abecassis, Jacky Cukier

Kafka ★★★ 15
Psychological thriller
1991 · US/Fr · BW and Colour · 94min
Steven Soderbergh's follow-up to *sex, lies, and videotape* is a far cry from that auspicious debut. Yet, with its stylish references to German expressionism and the great Universal horror films of the 1930s, this fantasy on the life of the Czech insurance-clerk-turned-novelist is possibly even bolder and more imaginative. Jeremy Irons acquits himself admirably in the title role, Alec Guinness and Ian Holm stand out in a splendid supporting cast. DP Violence.

Jeremy Irons *Kafka* • Theresa Russell *Gabriela Rossman* • Joel Grey *Burgel* • Ian Holm *Dr Murnau* • Jeroen Krabbé *Bizzlebek* • Armin Mueller-Stahl *Inspector Grubach* • Alec Guinness *Chief clerk* • Brian Glover *Castle henchman* • Keith Allen *Assistant Ludwig* ■ *Dir* Steven Soderbergh • *Scr* Lem Dobbs • *Cinematographer* Walt Lloyd • *Art Director* Gavin Bocquet

Kagemusha ★★★★ PG
Period drama 1980 · Jpn · Colour · 152min
Returning to direction after five years, the 70-year-old Akira Kurosawa proved that his powers hadn't diminished with this sprawling tale of court intrigue. Set during the civil wars of the 16th century, this was at the time the most expensive picture ever made in Japan and won the Palme d'Or at Cannes. Admittedly, it could stand some

cutting and one or two of the set pieces smack of scale for spectacle's sake. But Tatsuya Nakadai is outstanding as the thief who becomes a puppet ruler, while Kurosawa's use of colour and his camera control are faultless. Also shown in a director's cut that restores nearly 30 minutes of footage not seen in the original western release. DP Japanese +subtitles. *DVD*

Tatsuya Nakadai *Shingen Takeda/Kagemusha* • Tsutomu Yamazaki *Nobukado Takeda* • Kenichi Hagiwara *Katsuyori Takeda* • Kota Yui *Takemaru Takeda* • Hideji Otaki *Masakage Yamagata* ■ *Dir* Akira Kurosawa • *Scr* Akira Kurosawa, Masato Ide

Kajaki. The True Story ★★★★ 15
War drama based on a true story
2014 · UK · Colour · 103min
Afghanistan in 2006, and British soldiers are about to endure a living nightmare in this fact-based drama. A foray investigating Taliban activity causes the men to stumble into an unmarked minefield left by the Russian invasion of the 1980s. Driven by a diligent commitment to reality, director Paul Katis and his expert prosthetic effects crew turn the unfolding events into a nerve-shredding experience. Indeed, the fact it's mostly a story of man v minefield gives it a universal quality that allows us to set aside questions over Britain's Afghan mission, and concentrate instead on the bravery of servicemen put in an impossible situation. TJ *DVD*

David Elliot (2) *Corporal Mark Wright* • Mark Stanley *Paul "Tug" Hartley* • Scott Kyle *Stu Pearson* • Benjamin O'Mahony *Stu Hale* • Bryan Parry *Jonesy* • Andy Gibbins *Smudge* ■ *Dir* Paul Katis • *Scr* Tom Williams

Kal Ho Naa Ho ★★★ 12
Romantic comedy 2003 · Ind · Colour · 187min
Director Nikhil Advani clearly watched plenty of Hollywood romantic comedies before embarking on his debut feature. Yet it also retains a distinctive Bollywood flavour, despite the fact that the action takes place in New York. Widow Jaya Bachchan wants to make a match between her plain daughter, Preity Zinta, and newly arrived do-gooder, Shah Rukh Khan. However, he's already agreed to help the womanising Saif Ali Khan woo Zinta. Tinkering with traditional storytelling tactics, Advani makes an impressive start, but the pace slackens. DP Hindi, English, Gujarati, Punjabi +subtitles. *DVD*

Shah Rukh Khan *Aman Mathur* • Saif Ali Khan *Rohit Patel* • Preity Zinta *Naina Catherine Kapur* • Jaya Bachchan *Jennifer Kapur* • Sonali Bendre *Doctor Priya* • Sushma Seth *Lajjo Kapur* • Dara Singh *Chaddha Uncle* ■ *Dir* Nikhil Advani • *Scr* Nikhil Advani, Karan Johar, Niranjan Iyengar

Kaleidoscope ★★★ PG
Crime comedy drama 1966 · UK · Colour · 98min
This 1960s caper is so swinging it almost comes off its hinges. Warren Beatty, not renowned at the time for his monkish lifestyle, is strangely unconvincing as the cardsharp who literally marks winning cards, while hip chick Susannah York keeps his libido on the boil. The movie defies its dated trendiness with the sheer esprit of the performances. TH *DVD*

Warren Beatty *Barney Lincoln* • Susannah York *Angel McGinnis* • Eric Porter *Harry Dominion* • Clive Revill *Inspector "Manny" McGinnis* • Murray Melvin *Aimes* • George Sewell *Billy* • Anthony Newlands *Leeds* • Jane Birkin *Exquisite Thing* ■ *Dir* Jack Smight • *Scr* Robert Carrington, Jane Howard Carrington

Kalifornia ★★ 18
Psychological thriller 1993 · US · Colour · 113min
David Duchovny plays a writer researching serial killers for a book who gets rather too close to his subject. A slow start builds to an explosive climax after Duchovny and his photographer girlfriend (Michelle Forbes) pick up two likely suspects as they travel from Kentucky to California. Brad Pitt does his mentally unbalanced act rather well, and Juliette Lewis is also good value as his

trailer-trash, childlike sweetheart. Sadly, director Dominic Sena fails to develop an interesting scenario into anything other than empty attitude and posturing. AJ Violence, swearing, sex scenes. *DVD* *Blu*

Juliette Lewis *Adele Corners* • Brad Pitt *Early Grayce* • David Duchovny *Brian Kessler* • Michelle Forbes *Carrie Laughlin* • Sierra Pecheur *Mrs Musgrave* • Gregory "Mars" Martin *Walter Livesay* • David Milford *Driver* • Marisa Raper *Little girl* • Catherine Larson *Teenage girl* ■ *Dir* Dominic Sena • *Scr* Tim Metcalfe, from the story by Stephen Levy

Kama Sutra: a Tale of Love ★★★ 18
Erotic drama
1996 · Ind/UK/Jpn/Ger · Colour · 109min
"Kama Sutra" translates as "love lessons", and that's what princess Sarita Choudhury and royal servant girl Indira Varma learn in director Mira Nair's lavish historical romance. Varma's "sexual treachery" with Choudhury's betrothed, Naveen Andrews, gets her banished from court and puts her on the road to erotic self-awareness in a complex story mixing the mystical with the psychological. Oddly affecting and beautifully filmed. AJ Violence, sex scenes, swearing, nudity. *DVD*

Naveen Andrews *Raj Singh* • Sarita Choudhury *Tara* • Ramon Tikaram *Jai Kumar* • Rekha *Rasa Devi* • Indira Varma *Maya* • Pearl Padamsee *Maham Anga* • Arundhati Rao *Annabi* ■ *Dir* Mira Nair • *Scr* Helena Kriel, Mira Nair • *Cinematographer* Declan Quinn • *Music* Mychael Danna

Kambakkht Ishq ★★ 12
Romantic action comedy
2009 · Ind · Colour · 128min
Bollywood's attempt to cross over into Hollywood continues here, with Sylvester Stallone, Brandon Routh and Denise Richards all making (and perhaps now regretting) their Indian-movie debuts in a banal tale about an Indian stuntman who takes Hollywood by storm. Akshay Kumar (who, to Bollywood fans, is more famous than Cruise, Gibson and Willis put together) plays Viraj Shergill, a philandering stuntman whose attempts to woo the seemingly unattainable Simrita Rai (Kareena Kapoor) form the crux of this poorly executed romantic action comedy. The movie gives minimal screen time to its Hollywood stars and ends up as a crass, would-be cross-cultural blockbuster. OA Hindi, English +subtitles. *DVD* *Blu*

Akshay Kumar *Viraj Shergill* • Kareena Kapoor *Simrita Rai* • Sylvester Stallone *John Rambo* • Denise Richards • Brandon Routh ■ *Dir* Sabbir Khan • *Scr* Sabbir Khan, Ishita Moitra, Anvita Dutt Guptan

Kameradschaft ★★★★★
Drama 1931 · Ger/Fr · BW · 83min
A masterpiece of studio realism and an optimistic plea for peaceful co-existence, this is one of the few social tracts of the early sound era to retain its power in this more cynical age. Based on a 1906 mining disaster (although set in the immediate aftermath of the First World War), the story of the German workers who break through national boundaries to rescue their French comrades is loaded with idealistic symbolism. But, thanks to director GW Pabst's use of light and montage, it is also full of striking images designed to highlight the fragility of humanity and the futility of conflict. DP German, French +subtitles.

Alexander Granach *Kaspar* • Fritz Kampers *Wilderer* • Daniel Mendaille *Pierre* • Ernst Busch *Kaplan* • Elisabeth Wendt *Françoise* • Gustav Püttjer *Jean* • Oskar Höcker *Emile* ■ *Dir* GW Pabst • *Scr* Ladislaus Vajda, Peter Martin Lampel, Karl Otten, Fritz Eckardt, from a story by Karl Otten • *Cinematographers* Fritz Arno Wagner, Robert Baberske

Kamikaze ★★★ 15
Satirical drama 1986 · Fr · Colour · 88min
This is a classic example of the style of French films dubbed *cinéma du look* on account of their flashy visuals and throwaway narratives. It boasts a wonderfully over-the-top central

performance from Michel Galabru as a mad scientist who invents a death ray that can zap anyone he takes a dislike to while watching TV. Great idea, but there is really only enough material in this satire on couch-potato culture for a razor-sharp sketch. DP French +subtitles.

Richard Bohringer *Detective Romain* • Michel Galabru *Albert* • Dominique Lavanant *Laure Frontenac* • Riton Leibman *Olive* • Kim Massee *Léa* • Harry Cleven *Patrick* • Romane Bohringer *Julie* ■ *Dir* Didier Grousset • *Scr* Luc Besson, Didier Grousset, Michèle Halberstadt

Kamikaze Girls: the End ★★★ 12
Fantasy comedy 2004 · Jpn · Colour · 102min
In this entertaining odd-couple odyssey, rococo-attired teenager Kyoko Fukada strikes up an unlikely friendship with Anna Tsuchiya, a biker rebel who wants Fukada to embroider a jacket for her gang leader's passing out parade. The plot is fashion fixated, but there's such chemistry between Fukada and Tsuchiya that it draws in non-aficionados. Never subtle and prone to audiovisual exhibitionism, Tetsuya Nakashima's bravura direction nevertheless consistently sustains interest. DP Japanese +subtitles. Violence, swearing. *DVD* *Blu*

Kyoko Fukada *Momoko Ryugasaki* • Anna Tsuchiya *Ichigo Shirayuri* • Hiroyuki Miyasako *Momoko's father* • Sadao Abe *Ryuuji "the Unicorn"/Doctor* • Eiko Koike *Akimi* ■ *Dir/Scr* Tetsuya Nakashima

Kamouraska ★★★
Period romantic drama
1973 · Can/Fr · Colour · 124min
This intense adaptation of Anne Hébert's novel was the most ambitious French-Canadian production to that date. It opens in a small Québecois village in 1839, as Geneviève Bujold nurses her second spouse, Marcel Cuvilier, and thinks back on her turbulent past. She recalls the brutal treatment meted out by her first husband, backwoodsman Philippe Léotard, and how she was helped to dispose of him by her lover, emigré American doctor Richard Jordan. The going is occasionally ponderous, but Bujold is outstanding. DP French, English +subtitles.

Geneviève Bujold *Elisabeth* • Richard Jordan *Nelson* • Philippe Léotard *Antoine* • Marcel Cuvelier *Jérôme* • Suzie Baillargeon *Aurélie* ■ *Dir* Claude Jutra • *Scr* Anne Hébert, Claude Jutra, from the novel *Kamouraska* by Anne Hébert

Kanal ★★★★ 12
Second World War drama
1957 · Pol · BW · 91min
The second part of Andrzej Wajda's war trilogy, which won the Special Jury prize at Cannes, is a sobering re-creation of events that occurred during the 1944 Warsaw Uprising. Echoes of *Dante's Inferno* ring through the network of sewers where a resistance unit has taken refuge from the pursuing Nazis. The symbolism is occasionally overwrought, but there's no doubting the oppressive atmosphere of the cramped tunnels, or the simple heroism of the partisans. DP Polish +subtitles. Swearing, violence.

Wienczylaw Glinski *Lt Zadra* • Tadeusz Janczar *Korab* • Teresa Izewska *Daisy* • Emil Karewicz *Madry* • Wladyslaw Sheybal *[Vladek Sheybal]* *Composer* • Tadeusz Gwiazdowski *Kula* ■ *Dir* Andrzej Wajda • *Scr* Jerzy Stefan Stawinski, from his short story

Kandahar ★★★★★ PG
Documentary drama
2001 · Iran/Fr · Colour · 81min
This piercing insight into the plight of the Afghan people – and women in particular – under the Taliban regime is a must-see experience. It's impossible not to be moved and angered by Iranian director Mohsen Makhmalbaf's hybrid of documentary and road movie (loosely based on a real-life incident), in particular the sights exiled journalist Nelofer Pazira witnesses while trying to reach her suicidal sister in Kandahar. Yet what emerges here is less a

K

condemnation of extreme patriarchy than an assertion that the spirit of sisterhood will somehow survive the monstrous repression. It's the toll of human misery caused by war that concerns Makhmalbaf, not political or religious correctness, and that's a salient lesson for us all. DP English, Farsi +subtitles. *DVD*

Nelofer Pazira *Nafas* • Hassan Tantai *Tabib Sahid* • Sadou Teymouri *Khak* • Hayatalah Hakimi *Hayat* ■ *Dir/Scr* Mohsen Makhmalbaf

Kangaroo ★★
Romantic adventure 1952 · US · Colour · 84min

Using frozen Australian earnings, 20th Century-Fox sent a full crew Down Under for this shoddy attempt to transpose a familiar western story to the outback. Australian players were relegated to minor parts, as Peter Lawford poses as the long-lost son of Finlay Currie's cattle king, who reforms after falling in love with the old man's daughter, Maureen O'Hara. Director Lewis Milestone used some of Sydney's historic landmarks to advantage, but there's little authentic local flavour to the story. AE

Maureen O'Hara *Dell McGuire* • Peter Lawford *Richard Connor* • Finlay Currie *Michael McGuire* • Richard Boone *Gamble* • Chips Rafferty *Trooper Leonard* ■ *Dir* Lewis Milestone • *Scr* Harry Kleiner, from a story by Martin Berkeley

Kangaroo ★★★🔢
Period drama 1986 · Aus · Colour · 99min

The ever-excellent Judy Davis stars with her real-life husband Colin Friels as a couple who arrive in Sydney from Cornwall, and find themselves embroiled in an incipient socialist revolution. Literary to a point, though intelligent with it, but there is a lack of real character development. Friels, who doesn't quite have genuine star power, is very effective – charming and unsettling in equal doses – while Davis is a real treat to watch. TS *DVD*

Colin Friels *Richard Somers* • Judy Davis *Harriet Somers* • John Walton *Jack Calcott* • Julie Nihill *Vicki Calcott* • Hugh Keays-Byrne *Kangaroo* • Peter Hehir *Jaz* • Peter Cummins *Struthers* ■ *Dir* Tim Burstall • *Scr* Evan Jones, from the novel by DH Lawrence

Kangaroo Jack ★★🔢
Action comedy 2003 · US · Colour · 85min

Calamity-prone friends Jerry O'Connell and Anthony Anderson are dispatched to Australia by O'Connell's mobster stepfather (Christopher Walken) to deliver $50,000 to a shady associate. When a wild kangaroo runs off with the cash, the duo set off across the outback in pursuit, assisted by wildlife conservationist Estella Warren. While too lightweight for most adults, its slapdash mixture of cheeky humour, speedily shot chase sequences and dim-witted monkey business should please youngsters. SF *DVD*

Jerry O'Connell *Charlie Carbone* • Anthony Anderson *Louis Fucci* • Estella Warren *Jessie* • Michael Shannon *Frankie the Vermin* • Christopher Walken *Sal* • Bill Hunter *Blue* • Marton Csokas *Mr Smith* • David Ngoombujarra *Mr Jimmy* ■ *Dir* David McNally • *Scr* Steve Bing, Scott Rosenberg, from a story by Steve Bing, Barry O'Brien

Kangchenjunga ★★★★
Drama 1962 · Ind · Colour · 102min

Satyajit Ray's first venture into self-scripting and colour cinematography is also his most musical work, and fittingly he composed the score as well. Manipulative holidaying patriarch Chhabi Biswas meets his match in the form of Arun Mukherjee, the proud Darjeeling local who wishes to marry his younger daughter. A true dance to the music of time, this is both sly satire and compelling drama. DP Bengali +subtitles.

Chhabi Biswas *Indranath Choudhuri* • Karuna Bannerji [Karuna Bannerjee] *Labanya* • Anil Chatterjee *Anil* • Anubha Gupta *Anima* • Subrata Sen *Shankar* • Indrani Singh *Tuklu* • Arun Mukherjee *Ashok* ■ *Dir/Scr* Satyajit Ray

Kanoon ★★★🔢
Courtroom drama 1960 · Ind · BW · 139min

In addition to using cinema to highlight the key social, political and religious issues in Indian life, director BR Chopra also tried to introduce local audiences to the film styles popular in Hollywood. Essentially a treatise on capital punishment, this is a rare example of Indian *film noir*, with Rajendra Kumar starring as an ambitious lawyer who is forced to prosecute a thief for murder, even though he's sure the culprit is his new father-in-law – who turns out to be the judge trying the case. DP Hindi +subtitles.

Ashok Kumar *Judge Badriprasad* • Nanda *Meena* • Rajendra Kumar *Public prosecutor* ■ *Dir* BR Chopra • *Scr* CJ Pavri

Kansas ★★🔢
Romantic melodrama 1988 · US · Colour · 105min

A couple of young drifters (Matt Dillon and Andrew McCarthy) meet by chance when they steal a ride on a freight car. They become partners in crime before fate makes them bitter enemies. Australian director David Stevens follows both men's fortunes as their respective paths diverge. The detailed plot meanders all over the place, but the acting is appealing; Kyra Sedgwick is especially watchable as the trailer-trash tramp who hooks up with Dillon. AJ *DVD*

Matt Dillon *Doyle Kennedy* • Andrew McCarthy *Wade Corey* • Leslie Hope *Lori Bayles* • Kyra Sedgwick *Prostitute puller* • Arlen Dean Snyder *George Bayles* • Alan Toy *Nordquist* • Harry Northup *Governor* ■ *Dir* David Stevens • *Scr* Spencer Eastman

Kansas City ★★★🔢
Period crime drama 1995 · US/Fr · Colour · 113min

Some isolated felicities – Harry Belafonte as a ruthless gangster, some terrific jazz – elevate Robert Altman's semi-autobiographical tribute to the town of his birth, but *Kansas City* is not as spot-on as the writer/director's more successful work. A thief's wife (Jennifer Jason Leigh) kidnaps a politician's drug-addicted spouse (Miranda Richardson) in an attempt to free her husband (Dermot Mulroney) from the clutches of a mob. The 1930s mood is beautifully evoked, but the film is just too confused. TH Swearing, some violence. *DVD*

Jennifer Jason Leigh *Blondie O'Hara* • Miranda Richardson *Carolyn Stilton* • Harry Belafonte *Seldom Seen* • Michael Murphy (1) *Henry Stilton* • Dermot Mulroney *Johnny O'Hara* • Steve Buscemi *Johnny Flynn* • Brooke Smith *Babe Flynn* • Jane Adams (2) *Nettie Bolt* • Gina Belafonte *Hey-Hey club hostess* ■ *Dir* Robert Altman • *Scr* Robert Altman, Frank Barhydt

Kansas City Bomber ★★★🔢
Sports drama 1972 · US · Colour · 94min

The highs, lows and pitfalls of being a roller-derby queen are put under the spotlight in the defiantly unglamorous sleeper hit that proved Raquel Welch was a lot more than a pretty face. The former Hammer sex symbol is terrific as the roller-skating champion, juggling life as a single parent with her career when she joins an unfriendly new team. Top TV movie director Jerrold Freedman gives the picture a vital documentary feel and captures some hair-raising turns in the sporting sequences. Welch's daughter is played by a young Jodie Foster. AJ

Raquel Welch *Diane "KC" Carr* • Kevin McCarthy *Burt Henry* • Helena Kallianiotes *Jackie Burdette* • Norman Alden *Horrible Hank Hopkins* • Jeanne Cooper *Vivien* • Mary Kay Pass *Lovey* • Martine Bartlett *Mrs Carr* • Jodie Foster *Rita* ■ *Dir* Jerrold Freedman • *Scr* Thomas Rickman [Tom Rickman], Calvin Clements, from a story by Barry Sandler

Kansas City Confidential ★★★🔢
Film noir 1952 · US · BW · 99min

Director Phil Karlson turned out a number of commendably gritty, modestly budgeted crime films, and this is a good example. Its ingenious story has John Payne's ex-convict become a detective to unearth an ex-policeman-turned-criminal mastermind. It features the innovative touch (taken from the 1950 Brink's hold-up) of bank robbers wearing grotesque masks to conceal their identities. AE *DVD*

John Payne *Joe Rolfe* • Coleen Gray *Helen* • Preston Foster *Timothy Foster* • Dona Drake *Teresa* • Jack Elam *Harris* • Neville Brand *Kane* • Lee Van Cleef *Tony* • Mario Siletti *Timaso* • Neville Brand *Kane* ■ *Dir* Phil Karlson • *Scr* George Bruce, Harry Essex, from a story by Harold R Greene, Rowland Brown

Kansas Raiders ★★★
Western 1950 · US · Colour · 80min

Audie Murphy is well cast as the young Jesse James, playing the outlaw as a tortured teenager who joins forces with the notorious Quantrill's Raiders. Murphy is tremendously sympathetic in the role, and he has an experienced co-star in Brian Donlevy as the demented William Quantrill. This could be seen as a western precursor to the 1950s juvenile-delinquent cycle, but the glossy Technicolor softens the impact. TS

Audie Murphy *Jesse James* • Brian Donlevy *William Quantrill* • Marguerite Chapman *Kate Clarke* • Scott Brady *Bill Anderson* • Tony Curtis *Kit Dalton* • Richard Long *Frank James* • James Best *Cole Younger* • Dewey Martin *James Younger* • Richard Egan *First lieutenant* ■ *Dir* Ray Enright • *Scr* Robert L Richards, from his story

Kaos ★★★★🔢
Period drama 1984 · It · Colour · 186min

Italian siblings Paolo and Vittorio Taviani, who write and direct all their films together, have had an up-and-down career. One of their ups is this group of four folk tales (by Luigi Pirandello about peasant life in Sicily at the turn of the 19th century – acted, in the main, by non-professionals. The misleading title is explained in the epilogue in which Pirandello is seen returning to his birthplace, the town of Kaos. Splendidly photographed landscapes (by Giuseppe Lanci) link the stories, which range from the tragic to the blackly comic, suiting the Tavianis' overcharged style. RB Italian +subtitles. *DVD*

Margarita Lozano *Mother* • Claudio Bigagli *Batà* • Ciccio Ingrassia *Don Lollò* • Franco Franchi *Zi' Diam* • Biagio Barone *Salvatore* • Salvatore Rossi *Patriarch* • Omero Antonutti *Luigi Pirandello* • Regina Bianchi *Mother* ■ *Dir* Paolo Taviani, Vittorio Taviani • *Scr* Paolo Taviani, Vittorio Taviani, Tonino Guerra, from the short story collection *Novelle per un Anno* by Luigi Pirandello

Kapo ★★★
Second World War drama 1959 · It/Fr · BW · 117min

Oscar-nominated for best foreign language film, this seeks to expose and excuse the desperate measures to which people resorted in order to survive the concentration camps. The opening episode, in which orphaned Jewish teenager Susan Strasberg is saved by a kindly doctor, is plausible enough, but the surfeit of stereotypes and clichéd situations undermines the authenticity of the Polish sequences when Strasberg's promotion to "kapo" - or prison-camp guard - induces megalomania. Strasberg's performance is as hysterical as the story is sentimental. DP English, Italian +subtitles.

Susan Strasberg *Edith/Nicole* • Laurent Terzieff *Sascha* • Emmanuelle Riva *Terese* • Didi Perego *Sofia* • Gianni Garko *German soldier* • Annabella Besi • Graziella Galvani • Mira Dinulovic ■ *Dir* Gillo Pontecorvo • *Scr* Gillo Pontecorvo, Franco Solinas

The Karate Kid ★★★🔢
Martial arts adventure 1984 · US · Colour · 121min

This became a massive worldwide success, spawning a series of sequels and probably ruining Ralph Macchio's career in the process. The actor has struggled ever since to shake off the image of the kid, the bullied youngster who is taught the secrets of karate by wise old Pat Morita and turns the tables on his tormentors. It's a shame, because here Macchio rises above the trite script to deliver a sympathetic and believable performance. Morita is equally good and look out for Elisabeth Shue in an early role. A remake, *Kung Fu Kid* with Jackie Chan and Will Smith's son Jaden, is due in cinemas in summer 2010. JF Some swearing, violence. *DVD* *BD*

Ralph Macchio *Daniel LaRusso* • Noriyuki "Pat" Morita [Pat Morita] *Miyagi* • Elisabeth Shue *Ali* • Martin Kove *Kreese* • Randee Heller *Lucille LaRusso* • William Zabka *Johnny* • Ron Thomas *Bobby* • Rob Garrison *Tommy* ■ *Dir* John G Avildsen • *Scr* Robert Mark Kamen

The Karate Kid ★★★🔢
Martial arts adventure 2010 · US/Chi · Colour · 134min

A spoilt American kid is transplanted to China in this fun remake of the 1984 children's favourite. Jaden Smith (son of Will and Jada Pinkett) moves from Detroit to Beijing with his widowed mother, only to find himself the target of bullying. Jackie Chan keeps his usual ebullience under wraps as the quiet janitor who becomes Smith's reluctant trainer. The action sequences, as expected with Chan, are amazing, while the snappy pace helps counterbalance the film's excessive running time. And sticklers will love pointing out that what Chan teaches Smith is kung fu, not karate. KK *DVD* *BD*

Jackie Chan *Mr Han* • Jaden Smith *Dre Parker* • Taraji P Henson *Sherry Parker* • Wenwen Han *Meiying* • Yu Rong Guang *Master Li* • Zhensu Wu *Meiying's dad* • Zhiheng Wang *Meiying's mom* • Zhenwei Wang *Cheng* ■ *Dir* Harald Zwart • *Scr* Christopher Murphey, from the 1984 film

The Karate Kid Part II ★★🔢
Martial arts adventure 1986 · US · · 108min

This has been a perplexingly successful film series, especially given that all the usual clichés had been exhausted well before the end of the very first film. The only interesting aspect of this dull first sequel is that the action is set largely in Japan, but that aside it is an uninspired retread of the original. JA *DVD* *BD*

Ralph Macchio *Daniel LaRusso* • Noriyuki "Pat" Morita [Pat Morita] *Miyagi* • Nobu McCarthy *Yukie* • Danny Kamekona *Sato* • Yuji Okumoto *Chozen* • Tamlyn Tomita *Kumiko* ■ *Dir* John G Avildsen • *Scr* Robert Mark Kamen, from characters by Robert Mark Kamen

The Karate Kid III ★🔢
Martial arts adventure 1989 · US · Colour · 107min

Here the "Kid" (27-year-old Ralph Macchio) has to defend his title and tackle the bad guys, initially without the help of his mentor Miyagi. The script takes leave of reality at an early stage, and it becomes increasingly daft and humourless with each scene. A third sequel, *The Next Karate Kid*, starring future Oscar winner Hilary Swank, followed in 1995. JM Swearing. *DVD*

Ralph Macchio *Daniel LaRusso* • Noriyuki "Pat" Morita [Pat Morita] *Mr Miyagi* • Robyn Lively *Jessica Andrews* • Thomas Ian Griffith *Terry Silver* • Martin L Kove [Martin Kove] *John Kreese* ■ *Dir* John G Avildsen • *Scr* Robert Mark Kamen, from characters by Robert Mark Kamen

The Karate Killers ★★🔢
Spy adventure 1967 · US · Colour · 88min

In this unfunny spy spoof, Napoleon Solo and Illya Kuryakin are dispatched to prevent the formula for turning sea water into gold from falling into the hands of a memorable, but woefully underused, rogues' gallery. *Man from UNCLE* regulars Robert Vaughn, David McCallum and Leo G Carroll cross swords with high-powered guest stars, but director Barry Shear's clumsy slapstick approach does no credit to the original TV series. DP DVD

Robert Vaughn (1) *Napoleon Solo* • David McCallum (1) *Illya Kuryakin* • Herbert Lom *Randolph* • Joan Crawford *Amanda True* • Curt Jurgens *Carl von Kesser* • Telly Savalas *Count de Franzini* • Terry-Thomas *Constable* ■ *Dir* Barry Shear • *Scr* Norman Hudis, from a story by Boris Ingster

Karin Ingmarsdotter ★★★
Silent drama 1919 · Swe · BW · 110min

Having filmed other parts of Nobel laureate Selma Lagerlöfs rural epic, Victor Sjöström presents this weighty tract on poetic justice and the evils of drink. In fact, Sjöström attempts to lighten the closing sequences, but it's hard to find the funny side as daughter Tora Teje ignores his advice and abandons the upstanding Tor Weijden on account of his father's alcoholism, only to wind up wed to a worthless boozer after all. DP

Victor Sjöström *Old Ingmar* • Tora Teje *Karin* ■ *Dir* Victor Sjöström • *Scr* Victor Sjöström, Ester Julin, from the story *Jerusalem* by Selma Lagerlöf

Katalin Varga ★★★★ 15
Revenge drama 2008 · UK/Rom · Colour · 81min

An act of violence initiates a tragic cycle of destruction in this slow-burning, Transylvania-set revenge drama. Hilda Peter is strikingly intense as the titular peasant wife who embarks on a rural road trip with her son (Norbert Tanko) after her husband discovers he is not the boy's father. She tells him they are going to visit his grandmother, but her real intention is vengeance. Shot over four years by British writer/director Peter Strickland, the foreboding feature paints an authentic and almost timeless portrait of poverty-scarred, Carpathian mountain life. Initially, events have the feeling of a simple and archaic folk tale, but it's not until the full implications of her vindictive mission hit home that the narrative reveals its true power. SF Romanian, Hungarian +subtitles. Violence, sexual references, brief nudity. DVD

Hilda Peter *Katalin Varga* • Norbert Tanko *Orban Varga* • Laszlo Matray *Zsigmond Varga* • Roberto Giacomello *Gergely* • Tibor Palffy *Antal Borlan* • Melinda Kantor *Etelka Borlan* ■ *Dir/Scr* Peter Strickland

Kate & Leopold ★★ 12
Romantic fantasy comedy 2002 · US · Colour · 113min

Romantic comedy queen Meg Ryan plays cute again in this mediocre offering that attempts to freshen the usual formula by throwing a dippy time-travelling plot into the mix. It's a rather disastrous combination. Hugh Jackman plays Leopold, an Englishman abroad in 19th-century New York who falls through a time portal to the present day where he meets and woos Ryan. LH DVD

Meg Ryan *Kate McKay* • Hugh Jackman *Leopold, Duke of Albany* • Liev Schreiber *Stuart Bessier* • Breckin Meyer *Charlie McKay* • Natasha Lyonne *Darci* • Bradley Whitford *JJ Camden* • Spalding Gray *Dr Geisler* ■ *Dir* James Mangold • *Scr* James Mangold, Steven Rogers, from a story by Steven Rogers

Katy Perry: Part of Me ★★★★ PG
Music documentary 2012 · US · Colour · 97min

A year in the life of the record-breaking pop sensation comes under the microscope in this revealing documentary. For an officially sanctioned star portrait it's surprisingly honest, with Perry speaking candidly about the failures of her early career, as ever-present cameras record the fallout of her crumbling marriage to Russell Brand. There's plenty of archive footage and intimate behind-the-scenes access to contrast with the spectacular concert sequences from Perry's gruelling *California Dreams* world tour. TeS DVD

Katy Perry ■ *Dir* Dan Cutforth, Jane Lipsitz

Katyn ★★★★ 15
Historical wartime drama 2007 · Pol · Colour · 116min

Writer/director Andrzej Wajda examines one of the Second World War's most shameful episodes in this Oscar-nominated epic. Wajda's own father perished in the Soviet massacre of over 20,000 Polish military personnel in 1940, and here he combines details from family history, contemporary documents and an acclaimed novel to assess the impact of the atrocity. Among the many stories illustrated are those of a wife, whose officer husband was caught up in the slaughter, and a survivor, whose advancement in the Communist establishment depends on his acquiescence in the lie that Katyn was actually a Nazi war crime. With its earnest complexity and impeccable period re-creation, this is a punishingly dispassionate account of tumultuous times, with the climactic depiction of the executions being particularly harrowing. DP Polish, Russian, German +subtitles. DVD BL

Artur Zmijewski *Andrzej, Captain of 8th Uhlan regiment* • Maja Cstaszewska *Anna, Captain's wife* • Andrzej Chyra *Jerzy, Lieutenant of 8th Uhlan regiment* • Danuta Stenka *General's wife* • Jan Englert *General* • Magdalena Cielecka *Agnieszka, Lieutenant pilot's sister* ■ *Dir* Andrzej Wajda • *Scr* Przemyslaw Nowakowski, Wladyslaw Pasikowski, Andrzej Wajda, from the novel *Post Mortem* by Andrzej Mularczyk • *Editors* Milenia Fiedler, Rafal Listopad • *Cinematographer* Pawel Edelman

Kazaam ★★ 12
Fantasy comedy adventure 1996 · US · Colour · 89min

An early film outing for basketball legend Shaquille O'Neal, this thinly entertaining family comedy sees the athlete playing an ancient genie who is reawakened from his boom box by bullied schoolboy Francis Capra. Problem is that his potential master doesn't believe in magic, and is reluctant to take up the three wishes offer. Actor-turned-director Paul Michael Glaser paces it nicely, but this is a kids-only affair. JF

Shaquille O'Neal *Kazaam* • Francis Capra *Max* • Ally Walker *Alice* • Marshall Manesh *Malik* • James Acheson (2) *Nick* • Fawn Reed *Asia Moon* • John Costelloe *Travis* ■ *Dir* Paul Michael Glaser • *Scr* Christian Ford, Roger Soffer, from a story by Paul Michael Glaser

Keane ★★★★ 15
Psychological drama 2004 · US · Colour · 94min

Director Lodge H Kerrigan's third feature purveys a sparse, jittery, devastatingly powerful realism. Glass-eyed Damian Lewis may be deranged by anxiety about his missing child, simply deranged, or both at once. In between his manic prowls around New York City, he befriends single mother Amy Ryan and her little girl Abigail Breslin who live in the same seedy welfare hotel as Lewis. Kerrigan plants dread seeds of anxiety and waters them with long takes, but it's Lewis's taut, entrancing performance that makes this nearly unmissable. LF Swearing, drug abuse.

Damian Lewis *William Keane* • Abigail Breslin *Kira Bedik* • Amy Ryan *Lynn Bedik* • Tina Holmes *Michelle* • Christopher Evan Welch *Motel clerk* • Liza Zayas-Colón *First ticket agent* • John Tormey *Second ticket agent* • Brenda Denmark *Commuter* ■ *Dir/Scr* Lodge Kerrigan [Lodge H Kerrigan]

Keanu ★★★ 15
Comedy 2016 · US · Colour · 99min

Nothing to do with Mr Reeves really, though he does figure, briefly and oddly. This particular Keanu is an ultra-cute kitten that escapes a drug-dealer shootout and is taken in by two ultra-middle-class black cousins. When the kitty gets kidnapped, the cousins have to infiltrate a gang to get Keanu back. *Keanu* is a first big-screen vehicle for US TV comics Keegan-Michael Key and Jordan Peele. It's a film of highs and lows, but Key and Peele are likeable and have good chemistry. They'll do well, and they'll do better. DA Violence, swearing, drug abuse, nudity

Keegan-Michael Key *Clarence/Smoke Dresden* • Jordan Peele *Rell/Oil Dresden* • Will Forte *Hulka* • Method Man *Cheddar* • Tiffany Haddish *Hi-C* • Luis Guzman *Bacon* • Keanu Reeves *Keanu* ■ *Dir* Peter Atencio • *Scr* Jordan Peele, Alex Rubens

The Keep ★★★ 18
Horror 1983 · UK · Colour · 91min

In one of the weirdest Second World War movies ever made, a bunch of German soldiers bivouac in an old Romanian castle and get gruesomely dispatched by some unseen, supernatural force. By turns chilling, stylish, portentous and just plain silly, Michael Mann's second feature was a box-office bomb that temporarily wrecked his cinema career. However, Gabriel Byrne as an SS officer with a serious haircut, and Ian McKellen as a mad professor, are worth the price of admission alone. AT

Scott Glenn *Glaeken Trismegestus* • Alberta Watson *Eva* • Jürgen Prochnow *Woermann* • Robert Prosky *Father Fonescu* • Gabriel Byrne *Raempffer* • Ian McKellen *Dr Cuza* • Morgan Sheppard *Alexandru* • Royston Tickner *Tomescu* ■ *Dir* Michael Mann • *Scr* Michael Mann, from a novel by F Paul Wilson

Keep Cool ★★★★
Comedy thriller 1997 · Chi/HK · Colour · 95min

Deprived of official funding, Zhang Yimou shot this quirky urban comedy with little formal preparation and a great deal of ingenuity. The dizzyingly mobile, hand-held technique will surprise those expecting his trademark stateliness, but the frenetic movements are totally in keeping with hip bookseller Jiang Wen's foolhardy quest to avenge himself on the club-owning mobster who steals his girl. Capturing the bustle of Beijing, as well as sustaining the breathless comic pace, Zhang still finds time to comment on the growing influence of western fads and attitudes. DP In Mandarin.

Jiang Wen *Xiao Shuai* • Li Baotian *Lao Zhang* • Qu Ying *An Hong* • Ge You *The policeman* • Zhang Yimou *The peddler* ■ *Dir* Zhang Yimou • *Scr* Ping Shu

Keep 'Em Flying ★★ U
Comedy musical 1941 · US · BW · 86min

Abbott and Costello join stunt pilot Dick Foran in the Air Corps for this feeble comedy that barely manages to taxi to the runway, let alone take off. There's plenty of plot, with Foran winning the battle for Carol Bruce's affections by helping her brother over his flying phobia. But the laughs are on wartime rations, with only Martha Raye amusing as the twin waitresses who have Costello in a spin. DP

Bud Abbott *Blackie Benson* • Lou Costello *Heathcliff* • Martha Raye *Barbara Phelps/Gloria Phelps* • Dick Foran *Jinx Roberts* • Carol Bruce *Linda Joyce* • William Gargan *Craig Morrison* ■ *Dir* Arthur Lubin • *Scr* True Boardman, Nat Perrin, John Grant, from a story by Edmund L Hartmann

Keep Fit ★★★ U
Comedy 1937 · UK · BW · 78min

It's hard now to imagine that a toothy-grinned, ukelele-strumming comic with a broad Lancashire accent could be a superstar – but George Formby certainly was. A huge box-office draw in Britain during the 1930s and 1940s, Formby's saucy wit and frantic comic style proved a great tonic to wartime audiences. This movie finds the star in fine form, belting out songs and throwing himself into comedy routines, as a weedy barber forced to compete with a more athletic rival. Add a dash of romance and the unmasking of a thief and you've got all the ingredients for a first-rate Formby film. DF DVD

George Formby *George Green* • Kay Walsh *Joan Allen* • Guy Middleton *Hector Kent* • Gus McNaughton *Publicity man* • Edmund Breon *Sir Augustus Marks* • George Benson *Ernie Gill* • Evelyn Roberts *Barker* • C Denier Warren *Editor* ■ *Dir* Anthony Kimmins • *Scr* Anthony Kimmins, Austin Melford

Keep It Up Downstairs ★ 18
Period sex comedy 1976 · UK · Colour · 90min

In the depths of its 1970s trough, British cinema relied heavily on sitcom spin-offs and smut. This dire tale of avarice, snobbery and seduction belongs firmly in the latter category. A sort of *Carry On Chatterley*, it might have been described as a costume comedy, had the cast kept its costumes on long enough. DP Sex scenes, nudity.

Diana Dors *Daisy Dureneck* • Jack Wild *Peregrine Cockshute* • William Rushton *Shuttleworth* • Aimi MacDonald *Actress* • Françoise Pascal *Mimi* • Simon Brent *Rogers* • Sue Longhurst *Lady Cockshute* ■ *Dir* Robert Young (2) • *Scr* Hazel Adair

Keep the Aspidistra Flying ★★★ PG
Period romantic comedy 1997 · UK · Colour · 96min

In director Robert Bierman's enjoyable adaptation of George Orwell's semi-autobiographical comedy, Richard E Grant is at his angst-ridden, edgy best as an advertising man who quits his job to pursue the life of a poet. Helena Bonham Carter provides a nice contrast as his very tolerant girlfriend, who loves him despite his many faults. The sharp dialogue and gently amusing tone lend appeal to a lightweight tale that's more of an appetiser than a main course. JC DVD

Richard E Grant *Gordon Comstock* • Helena Bonham Carter *Rosemary* • Julian Wadham *Ravelston* • Jim Carter *Erskine* • Harriet Walter *Julia Comstock* • Lesley Vickerage *Hermione* • Barbara Leigh-Hunt *Mrs Wisbeach* • Liz Smith *Mrs Meakin* ■ *Dir* Robert Bierman • *Scr* Alan Plater, from the novel by George Orwell

Keep the Lights On ★★★ 18
Drama 2012 · US · Colour · 102min

A gay film-maker finds himself in a turbulent romance with a literary agent in this drama set in New York. Writer/director Ira Sachs explores how a liaison initially founded on sexual need (the two connect on a gay chat line) develops into a deeper bond tested over time by drug addiction, jealousy and wandering desire. There's potential for ripe melodrama here, but Sachs prefers a subtle approach, exploring everyday moments rather than violent confrontation. The trouble is, it's just a bit too low-key and the unsympathetic couple tests our patience, so the finale isn't as emotionally charged as Sachs intends. TJ Sex scenes, drug abuse. DVD BL

Thure Lindhardt *Erik Rothman* • Zachary Booth *Paul Lucy* • Julianne Nicholson *Claire* • Souléymane Sy Savané *Alassane* ■ *Dir* Ira Sachs • *Scr* Ira Sachs, Mauricio Zacharias

Keep Your Powder Dry ★★ U
Second World War drama 1945 · US · BW · 92min

This is life in the Women's Army Corps as lived by new recruits Lana Turner, Laraine Day (locked in animosity both on screen and off) and Susan Peters, three girls from contrasting backgrounds. It's not exactly riveting, but the supporting cast boasts Agnes Moorehead. Sad footnote: Susan Peters was crippled in an accident after this and never walked again. RK

Lana Turner *Valerie Parks* • Laraine Day *Leigh Rand* • Susan Peters *Ann Darrison* • Agnes Moorehead *Lt Col Spottiswoode* • Bill Johnson (1) *Capt Bill Barclay* • Natalie Schafer *Harriet Corwin* • Lee Patrick *Gladys Hopkins* • Marta Linden *Capt Sanders* ■ *Dir* Edward Buzzell • *Scr* Mary C McCall Jr, George Bruce

Keep Your Seats, Please ★★★ U
Comedy 1936 · UK · BW · 81min

Ilya Ilf and Yevgeny Petrov's celebrated play *The Twelve Chairs* gets the George Formby treatment in this sprightly musical comedy. Taking time to intone such ukelele classics as *When I'm Cleaning Windows*, Formby exhibits a bit more nous than usual, as he and girlfriend Florence Desmond

K

12 15 18 PASSED FOR PEOPLE OF THESE AGES AND OVER DVD RELEASED ON DVD BL RELEASED ON BLU-RAY 3D RELEASED IN 3D CS END CREDIT SEQUENCE **683**

pursue a set of antique chairs, one of which contains the jewels bequeathed him by an eccentric aunt. Formby is upstaged in every scene that he shares with the lugubrious Alastair Sim, as the shady lawyer hired to track down the furniture. **DP**

George Formby *George* • Florence Desmond *Flo* • Gus McNaughton *Max* • Alastair Sim *Drayton* • Harry Tate *Auctioneer* • Hal Gordon *Sailor* ■ *Dir* Monty Banks • *Scr* Tom Geraghty, Ian Hay, Anthony Kimmins, from the play *The Twelve Chairs* by Ilya Ilf, Yevgeny Petrov

The Keeper ★★ 15
Horror   1976 · Can · Colour · 84min

In this rarely seen horror thriller from Canadian child-actor-turned-director Tom Drake, asylum head Christopher Lee plans to insure his inmates, murder their heirs with a hypnosis machine and use the money to conquer the world. Drake strives for dotty weirdness, but his psychic melodrama hits rock bottom with a thud every time detective Tell Schreiber and inspector Ross Vezarian appear on screen. Their awful acting quickly grounds any hint of style or chilling ambience. **AJ**

Christopher Lee *The Keeper* • Tell Schreiber *Dick Driver* • Sally Gray *Mae B Jones* • Ross Vezarian *Inspector Clarke* • Ian Tracey *The Kid* • Jack Leavy *Mr Big* • Leo Leavy *Mr Big* ■ *Dir* Tom Drake • *Scr* Tom Drake, from a story by David Curnick, Donald Wilson

The Keeper ★ 15
Psychological thriller
2003 · Can · Colour · 91min

Exotic dancer Asia Argento is abducted by cop Dennis Hopper, who imprisons her in a cell built in his remote ranch cellar. A deadly battle of wills between crazed captor and bewildered captive ensues. Sporting ridiculous dialogue and laughable suspense, this is a a trashy career low for both stars. **AJ** *DVD*

Dennis Hopper *Krebs* • Asia Argento *Gina* • Helen Shaver *Ruthie* • Lochlyn Munro *Sgt Burns* ■ *Dir* Paul Lynch • *Scr* Gerald Sanford

The Keeper ★ 15
Action thriller
2009 · US · Colour · 90min

Steven Seagal has never been the most expressive actor, but here he exceeds his previous efforts by delivering a performance so bland it barely registers. Not that he's helped by the lame storyline, in which he plays a medically retired cop who becomes the bodyguard of a rich old pal's adult daughter after she's nearly kidnapped. Unconvincing characters and a surprising lack of action add to the overall dullness, leaving it to the laughable dialogue to fitfully entertain. **SF** Violence, swearing, nudity, drug abuse. *DVD*

Steven Seagal *Roland Salinger* • Liezl Carstens *Nikita Wells* • Arron Shiver *Mason Silver* • Johnny Hector *Manuelo* ■ *Dir* Keoni Waxman • *Scr* Paul A Birkett, Steven Seagal

The Keeper of Lost Causes ★★ 15
Crime mystery thriller
2013 · Den/Ger/Swe · Colour · 92min

This moody tale brings to the screen the first part of Jussi Adler-Olsen's *Department Q* crime series – with *The Killing*'s Nikolaj Lie Kaas as scowling detective Carl Morck. When an error of judgement sees him relegated to the newly formed cold case department, he and his assistant revisit the disappearance of a politician (Sonja Richter). It's crisply shot, but its endless adherence to convention means an absence of surprises. Even a film that expects to become the first in a franchise needs to impress on its own. **EAS** Danish +subtitles. Violence, swearing, sex scenes, brief nudity. *DVD*

Nikolaj Lie Kaas *Carl Morck* • Fares Fares *Assad* • Sonja Richter *Merete Lynggaard* • Soren Pilmark *Marcus Jacobsen* ■ *Dir* Mikkel Norgaard • *Scr* Nikolaj Arcel, from the novel *Kvinden i buret* by Jussi Adler-Olsen

Keeper of the Flame ★★★ U
Drama   1942 · US · BW · 96min

This was the second of Katharine Hepburn and Spencer Tracy's nine films together and their first with director George Cukor. It's a protracted and rather hectoring piece of wartime propaganda, kept alive by the presence of the two stars. Hepburn is the proud widow of an American hero and journalist Tracy wants to write his biography. Tracy exudes his customary integrity and becomes a bit self-righteous as he unravels the man's secret life. Hepburn is radiant. **AT** *DVD*

Spencer Tracy *Steven O'Malley* • Katharine Hepburn *Christine Forrest* • Richard Whorf *Clive Kerndon* • Margaret Wycherly *Mrs Forrest* • Donald Meek *Mr Arbuthnot* • Stephen McNally *Freddie Ridges* • Audrey Christie *Jane Harding* • Forrest Tucker *Geoffrey Midford* ■ *Dir* George Cukor • *Scr* Donald Ogden Stewart, from the novel by IAR Wylie

Keeping Mum ★★★ 15
Black comedy   2005 · UK · Colour · 98min

This spirited black comedy boasts a delicious performance by Maggie Smith as an elderly housekeeper with a deadly way of resolving domestic unrest. Hired to look after the family of Rowan Atkinson's nerdy country vicar, she quietly sets about tackling their problems. While her *Serial Mom*-style solutions are often predictable, they're no less entertaining. Smith outshines all the cast with her immaculate comic timing, despite strong competition from Patrick Swayze as a sleazy US golf instructor. The only real downside is Atkinson, whose customary bumbling schtick feels forced and twee. **SF** Swearing, nudity. *DVD*

Rowan Atkinson *Walter Goodfellow* • Kristin Scott Thomas *Gloria Goodfellow* • Maggie Smith *"Grace Hawkins"* • Patrick Swayze *Lance* • Emilia Fox *Rosie Jones* • Liz Smith *Mrs Parker* • Tamsin Egerton *Holly Goodfellow* • James Booth *Mr Brown* • Toby Parkes *Petey Goodfellow* ■ *Dir* Niall Johnson • *Scr* Niall Johnson, Richard Russo, from a story by Russo

The Keeping Room ★★★ 15
Period drama   2014 · US · Colour · 94min

After his feature debut – the OAP vigilante movie *Harry Brown* – director Daniel Barber continues to pursue the theme of unlikely heroes. The setting is the last days of the US Civil War where the sphere of two Southern sisters (Brit Marling, Hailee Steinfeld) and their African-American maid (Muna Otaru) collides with that of two thieving Union soldiers (Sam Worthington, Kyle Soller). The tension builds slowly towards a nail-biting home-invasion finale with a refreshing feminist sting. **DW** Violence

Brit Marling *Augusta* • Hailee Steinfeld *Louise* • Sam Worthington *Moses* • Muna Otaru *Mad* ■ *Dir* Daniel Barber • *Scr* Julia Hart

Keeping Rosy ★★★ 15
Thriller   2014 · US/UK · Colour · 92min

Maxine Peake, who's known for powerful TV roles in the likes of *The Village* and *Silk*, carries this modestly scaled British thriller about a high-flying executive confronted with the rash decisions she makes on a really, really bad day. Peake is outstanding as the uptight, controlling, unravelling Charlotte, while director Steve Reeves resourcefully cranks up the tension in and around her swish apartment block. *Inbetweeners* regular Blake Harrison also shines as a cheeky-chappy security guard with his own sinister agenda. **TJ** Violence, swearing, a sex scene.

Maxine Peake *Charlotte* • Blake Harrison *Roger* • Christine Bottomley *Sarah* • Sam Hoare *Tom* • Elisa Lasowski *Mykala* ■ *Dir* Steve Reeves (2) • *Scr* Steve Reeves, Mike Oughton

Keeping the Faith ★★★ 12
Romantic comedy 2000 · US · Colour · 123min

This good-natured film has appealing actors, a few good laughs and some unpretentious insights into religion. First-time director Edward Norton also stars as a

priest, while Ben Stiller plays his best friend, a rabbi. Their friendship is tested when they both fall in love with childhood friend Jenna Elfman. Norton's movie successfully blends romance, comedy and faith into a thoughtful and entertaining mix that benefits from wonderful chemistry between the leads and a strong supporting cast, including Anne Bancroft as Stiller's mother. **ST** Swearing. *DVD*

Ben Stiller *Jake* • Edward Norton *Brian* • Jenna Elfman *Anna* • Anne Bancroft *Ruth* • Eli Wallach *Rabbi Lewis* • Ron Rifkin *Larry Friedman* • Milos Forman *Father Havel* • Holland Taylor *Bonnie Rose* • Lisa Edelstein *Ali Decker* ■ *Dir* Edward Norton • *Scr* Stuart Blumberg • *Music* Elmer Bernstein

Keeping Track ★★★ 15
Thriller   1986 · Can · Colour · 97min

This interesting, suspenseful thriller boasts a fine pair of central performances from Michael Sarrazin and Margot Kidder. They're innocent bystanders who witness a major robbery and murder and find themselves thrown full pelt into saving their own necks. What lifts this film above the mundane is its concentration on the duo's burgeoning dependence on each other and issues of trust – the crash, bang, wallop come a very ordinary second. Worth catching. **SH** Mild swearing.

Michael Sarrazin *Daniel Hawkins* • Margot Kidder *Claire Tremayne* • Alan Scarfe *Royle Wishert* • Ken Pogue *Captain McCullough* ■ *Dir* Robin Spry • *Scr* Jamie Brown, from a story by Jamie Brown, Robin Spry

Keeping Up with the Joneses
Comedy   2016 · US · Colour

This is a preview – no prints were available to review prior to publication: Any ladies out there suffering post-*Mad Men* blues can keep depression aside as Jon Hamm now concentrates on his big screen career. He stars alongside Isla Fisher and Zach Galifianakis in this comedy from director Greg Mottola about a suburban couple who get in a bit too deep after they discover their seemingly perfect new neighbours are spies. **TP**

Jon Hamm *Tim Jones* • Isla Fisher *Karen Gaffney* • Zach Galifianakis *Jeff Gaffney* • Gal Gadot *Diana Jones* ■ *Dir* Greg Mottola • *Scr* Michael LeSieur

Keeping Up with the Steins ★★★ 12
Comedy   2006 · US · Colour · 86min

One boy's bar mitzvah turns into a nightmare of one-upmanship in this good-natured comedy. Daryl Sabara (*SPYkids*) is Benjamin Fielder, whose coming of age is being ruined by his parents' need to keep up with the Joneses – or rather, the Steins, who threw their son a hugely expensive *Titanic*-themed party. Breezing along with an easy charm, this frothy farce springs few surprises, but provides likeable laughs. Director Scott Marshall (son of Garry) keeps it brisk and even ropes in his real-life dad as Benjamin's superannuated, but young-at-heart, grandfather. **JR** Swearing, nudity.

Daryl Sabara *Benjamin Fielder* • Jeremy Piven *Adam Fielder* • Jami Gertz *Joanne Fielder* • Garry Marshall *Irwin Fielder* • Larry Miller *Arnie Stein* • Cheryl Hines *Casey Nudelman* ■ *Dir* Scott Marshall • *Scr* Mark Zakarin

Keetje Tippel ★★★ 18
Period biographical drama
1975 · Neth · Colour · 99min

Paul Verhoeven's third feature is based on the memoirs of a Dutch woman who was born into poverty in the 1880s, became a prostitute, married twice and met Toulouse-Lautrec in Paris. From this material, Verhoeven creates a Dickensian view of Europe – the prostitution, workhouses, squalor and the social inequality – as Keetje (Monique van de Ven) rises up the social ladder. Rutger Hauer has a leading role, and the cameraman is Jan De Bont, later the director of *Speed* and *The Haunting*. **AT** Dutch +subtitles. *DVD*

Monique van de Ven *Keetje* • Rutger Hauer *Hugo* • Eddie Brugman *Andre* • Hannah De Leeuwe *Mina* • Andrea Domburg *Keetje's mother* • Jan Blaaser *Keetje's father* ■ *Dir* Paul Verhoeven • *Scr* Gerard Soeteman, from the books by Neel Doff

Keith Lemon: the Film ★ 18
Comedy   2012 · UK · Colour · 81min

Comedian Leigh Francis brings his alter ego to the big screen for a crass and pointless yarn that bobs about on a tidal wave of tedious toilet humour. Keith heads to London from his native Leeds to make his name as an inventor, but when his mobile phone design becomes a success he turns his back on the humble folk he once associated with. Numerous cameos by the calibre of "stars" (including David Hasselhoff, Kelly Brook and Holly Willoughby) who crop up on Lemon's TV show *Celebrity Juice* do nothing to bolster the flimsy premise. An instantly forgettable misfire. **TeS** Swearing, sexual references, brief nudity. *DVD* Blu

Leigh Francis *Keith Lemon* • Laura Aikman *Rosie* • Verne Troyer *Archimedes* • Kelly Brook • David Hasselhoff *The Hoff* • Holly Willoughby • Fearne Cotton ■ *Dir* Paul Angunawela • *Scr* Paul Angunawela, Leigh Francis

Kelly + Victor ★★★ 18
Drama   2013 · Ire/UK · Colour · 94min

Documentary-maker Kieran Evans's first feature is a striking adaptation, with Antonia Campbell-Hughes and Julian Morris as the shop assistant and scrapyard worker who embark on a dangerously intense affair. While their performances are brave, the characters' search for the ultimate erotic escape feels more like a soap opera than Nagisa Oshima's similarly themed *In the Realm of the Senses*. Where Evans and cinematographer Piers McGrail really succeed is in contrasting the confining spaces of urban Liverpool with the open vistas of the Mersey estuary and the North Wales countryside, but Evans's storytelling is never as acute as his sense of place. **DP** Violence, swearing, sex scenes, drug abuse.

Antonia Campbell-Hughes *Kelly* • Julian Morris *Victor* • William Ruane *Craig* • Shaun Mason *Dean* • Michael Ryan *Pete* • Mark Womack *Frank* ■ *Dir* Kieran Evans • *Scr* Kieran Evans, from Niall Griffiths's novel • *Cinematographer* Piers McGrail

Kelly's Heroes ★★★ PG
Second World War action adventure
1970 · US/Yug · Colour · 137min

Clint Eastwood and Telly Savalas head the cast of this enjoyable if occasionally slightly silly adventure yarn about a group of maverick GIs who decide to fill a lull in the war by knocking off a hoard of German bullion in occupied France. Savalas and the eccentric Donald Sutherland set to their assignment with gusto, while Eastwood remains as cool as ever as half of Europe is blowing up around him. Despite many flaws, it's not dull by any means. **PF** Some violence, swearing. *DVD* Blu

Clint Eastwood *Kelly* • Telly Savalas *Big Joe* • Don Rickles *Crapgame* • Donald Sutherland *Oddball* • Carroll O'Connor *General Colt* • Hal Buckley *Maitland* • Stuart Margolin *Little Joe* • Fred Pearlman *Mitchell* ■ *Dir* Brian G Hutton • *Scr* Troy Kennedy Martin

The Kennel Murder Case ★★★
Detective mystery 1933 · US · BW · 73min

William Powell plays supersleuth Philo Vance, looking into the murder of two brothers, both members of a Long Island kennel club. This doesn't faze our hero as he's also a dog fancier. Enjoyable and over in a flash – and so was Powell's four-film run as Vance, as Warner Bros replaced him with the serviceable Warren William. Powell then became Nick Charles in the *Thin Man* series. **AT**

William Powell *Philo Vance* • Mary Astor *Hilda Lake* • Eugene Pallette *Sgt Heath* • Ralph Morgan *Raymond Wrede* • Jack LaRue *Eduardo Grassi* • Helen Vinson *Doris Delafield* • Paul Cavanagh *Sir Bruce MacDonald* • Robert Barrat *Archer Coe* ■

Dir Michael Curtiz • *Scr* Robert N Lee, Peter Milne, Robert Presnell, from the novel *The Return of Philo Vance* by SS Van Dine

Kenny ★★★★ 15
Comedy 2006 · Aus · Colour · 99min

Australian comedies work best when the country's natural "larrikinism" is tempered with a touch of self-deprecation – think of *The Castle* and *"Crocodile" Dundee*. The eponymous hero of this Aussie hit (played by co-writer Shane Jacobson) is a philosophical portable loo supplier – "I don't do it for the glory" –. It's a cheerfully crude and lovably laconic spoof documentary about the unsung heroes of Splashdown, which, confusingly, is also the name of a real toilet rental company. When he's not dealing with the septic challenges of drunken festival-goers, Kenny is attempting to bond with his young son and reconnect with his grumpy old father (played by real dad, Ronald). For once, calling this toilet humour should be taken as a compliment. JF *DVD*

Shane Jacobson *Kenny Smyth* • Eve von Bibra *Jackie* • Ronald Jacobson *Father* • Jesse Jacobson *Son* • Chris Davis *Pat* • Ian Dryden *Sammy* • Morihiko Hasebe *Sushi Cowboy* ■ *Dir* Clayton Jacobson • *Scr* Clayton and Shane Jacobson

The Kentuckian ★★★ PG
Western 1955 · US · Colour · 99min

Producer/star Burt Lancaster's only film as director is this marvellously photographed outdoor adventure. The main theme is Lancaster's relationship with his young son, touchingly portrayed by Donald MacDonald. The women are weakly cast, but there are a pair of prize villains: John Carradine as a travelling quack and, in his movie debut, nasty whip-wielding baddie Walter Matthau, whose main scene was hacked to ribbons by the UK censor before the film's original release. It has happily now been restored. The marvellous score is by Bernard Herrmann. TS *DVD*

Burt Lancaster *Big Eli* • Dianne Foster *Hannah* • Diana Lynn *Susie* • John McIntire *Zack* • Una Merkel *Sophie* • Walter Matthau *Bodine* • John Carradine *Fletcher* • Donald MacDonald *Little Eli* ■ *Dir* Burt Lancaster • *Scr* AB Guthrie Jr, from the novel *The Gabriel Horn* by Felix Holt • *Cinematographer* Ernest Lazlo

Kentucky ★★★
Romantic drama 1938 · US · Colour · 95min

The main interest today in this hoary old 20th Century-Fox horse-racing saga resides in two things: the splendid richness of the Technicolor and the Oscar-winning performance of veteran Walter Brennan (his second of three supporting actor Academy Awards) – a reminder of what a fine actor he could be. Loretta Young and Richard Greene are the impossibly good-looking young leads, and the bluegrass countryside has never looked more beguiling. The plot about feuding horse-breeding families owes as much to *Romeo and Juliet* as it does to the source novel by co-screenwriter John Taintor Foote. TS

Loretta Young *Sally Goodwin* • Richard Greene *Jack Dillon* • Walter Brennan *Peter Goodwin* • Douglass Dumbrille *John Dillon* • Karen Morley *Mrs Goodwin* • Moroni Olsen *John Dillon II* • Russell Hicks *Thad Goodwin Sr* • Willard Robertson *Bob Slocum* • Charles Waldron *Thad Goodwin* ■ *Dir* David Butler • *Scr* Lamar Trotti, John Taintor Foote, from the novel *The Look of Eagles* by John Taintor Foote

The Kentucky Fried Movie ★★★ 18
Comedy 1977 · US · Colour · 83min

Director John Landis and scriptwriters Jerry Zucker, David Zucker and Jim Abrahams provide a consistently wacky collection of spoofs in a more hit-than-miss parody of TV commercials, B-movies, kung fu adventures and porno chic. A lot more vulgar than their later movies, which included *Airplane!* and *Naked Gun*, it's a breezy anthology of the sketches the trio had already presented on stage. The result is cheap and chucklesome. AJ *DVD*

Colin Male *Spokesman* • Janice Kent *Barbara Duncan* • Michael Laurence (2) *Frank Bowman* • Larry Curan *Tom Cargo* • Richard A Baker [Rick Baker] *Dino (AM Today)* • David Zucker *Man/second technician/Grunwald* • Lenka Novak *Linda Chambers* • George Lazenby *Architect* • Donald Sutherland *Clumsy waiter* ■ *Dir* John Landis • *Scr* David Zucker, Jim Abrahams, Jerry Zucker

Kentucky Moonshine ★★★
Musical comedy 1938 · US · BW · 87min

The zany comedy trio The Ritz Brothers are an acquired taste but this is probably their best film, with a funny script and a good supply of risible gags. As city slickers who, hearing that a radio show is looking for genuine hayseeds, pretend to be country bumkins, they dominate the film with their frantic mixture of slapstick, tomfoolery and musical clowning. Tony Martin is also on hand, playing it straight and singing the Lew Pollack-Sidney Mitchell songs. TV

Al Ritz *Al* • Harry Ritz *Harry* • Jimmy Ritz *Jimmy* • Tony Martin (1) *Jerry Wade* • Marjorie Weaver *Caroline* • Slim Summerville *Hank Hatfield* • John Carradine *Reef Hatfield* • Wally Vernon *Gus Bryce* ■ *Dir* David Butler • *Scr* Art Arthur, MM Musselman, from the story by MM Musselman, Jack Lait Jr

Keoma ★★★ 12
Spaghetti western 1976 · It · Colour · 96min

Originally despised, then admired for the elegance and poise of the camerawork, the spaghetti western is still one of the most watchable of all genres. This was released after the great days of the 1960s but hero Franco Nero still has plenty of the prerequisite man-alone spirit that Clint Eastwood originated. Director Enzo G Castellari attempts to fuse a popular theme – civil-rights protests – to the plot as Nero tries to clean up his town like a liberal activist. But the ruthless action is still the element of the film that works best. TH Italian dubbed. *DVD*

Franco Nero *Keoma Shannon* • Woody Strode *George* • William Berger ■ *Dir* Enzo G Castellari • *Scr* Enzo G Castellari, Mino Roli, Nico Ducci, Luigi Montefiori

Kept Husbands ★★
Drama 1931 · US · BW · 76min

Director Lloyd Bacon's creaky early talkie was promoted by RKO with the line "every inch a man - bought body and soul by his wife". This less-than-snappy slogan did nothing to drag them in off the streets at the time, and it's still not likely to set many pulses racing. However, star Joel McCrea rarely lets the side down, and he's easily the best thing in this melodrama about a steelworker who curbs the excesses of his frivolous wife Dorothy MacKaill, who just happens to be his boss's daughter. DP

Joel McCrea *Dick Brunton* • Dorothy MacKaill *Dorothy "Dot" Parker* • Robert McWade *Arthur Parker* • Florence Roberts *Mrs Henrietta Parker* • Clara Young *Mrs Post* • Mary Carr *Mrs Brunton* • Ned Sparks *Hughie* ■ *Dir* Lloyd Bacon • *Scr* Alfred Jackson, Forrest Halsey, from a story by Louis Sarecky

Kermit's Swamp Years ★★★ U
Fantasy comedy 2002 · US · Colour · 78min

This charming fantasy comedy gives an insight into Kermit the Frog's life before he joined *The Muppet Show*. The magic of Jim Henson's original creations is evident throughout and there's plenty of mischief. The storyline sees Kermit and Croaker come to the rescue of their amphibian pal Goggles after he's captured and sold to a nasty biology teacher. It's a shame there's no room for a walk-on part for Miss Piggy, but there's plenty of fun to be had from the songs and comic set pieces. DP *DVD*

Steve Whitmire *Kermit/Jack Rabbit/Chico* • Bill Barretta *Croaker/Horace D'Fly/Roy the Frog/Turtle 2* • Dave Goelz *Waldorf* • Joey Mazzarino *Goggles/Turtle 1* • John Kennedy *Blotch/Arnie the Alligator* • Cree Summer *Pilgrim/Kermit's mom/Kermit's star* ■ *Dir* David Gumpel • *Scr* Jim Lewis, Joseph Mazzarino [Joey Mazzarino], from a story by Jim Lewis

Kes ★★★★★ PG
Drama 1969 · UK · Colour · 106min

Ken Loach seems to acquire a surer mastery of his art with each picture, yet this, one of his earliest features, is still one of his best. Adapted from Barry Hines's "grim up north" novel *A Kestrel for a Knave*, it has such a ring of authenticity that you can almost smell the chips. As ever, Loach coaxes remarkable performances from his cast, with Freddie Fletcher epitomising bullying big brotherhood and Brian Glover caricaturing every games teacher who never made it. Outstanding, however, is David Bradley as the teenager who finds solace in a baby kestrel from the pain of his dysfunctional family life and torment of school. DP *DVD*

David Bradley (3) *Billy Casper* • Colin Welland *Mr Farthing* • Lynne Perrie *Mrs Casper* • Freddie Fletcher *Jud* • Brian Glover *Mr Sugden* • Bob Bowes *Mr Gryce* • Trevor Hasketh *Mr Crossley* • Eric Bolderson *Farmer* ■ *Dir* Ken Loach • *Scr* Ken Loach, Tony Garnett, Barry Hines, from the novel *A Kestrel for a Knave* by Barry Hines • *Cinematographer* Chris Menges

Kevin & Perry Go Large ★★★ 15
Comedy 2000 · UK/US · Colour · 79min

Harry Enfield takes his finest comic creations – the hormonally charged teenage boys Kevin and Perry (played by Enfield and Kathy Burke) – and successfully expands them from a sketch into a feature-length movie. Here the spotty twosome descend on an unsuspecting Ibiza, where they hope to become top DJs and, in doing so, attract loads of ladies. Ed Bye's film zips along thanks to Burke's hilarious leering and disgusting adventures that make *There's Something about Mary* look like *Mary Poppins*. JB Swearing, a sex scene. *DVD*

Harry Enfield *Kevin* • Kathy Burke *Perry* • Rhys Ifans *Eye Ball Paul* • Laura Fraser *Candice* • James Fleet *Dad* • Louisa Rix *Mum* • Paul Whitehouse *Bouncer* • Steve McFadden *Bouncer* ■ *Dir* Ed Bye • *Scr* Harry Enfield, David Cummings, from characters by Harry Enfield

The Key ★★
Political romantic drama 1934 · US · BW · 82min

The rebellion against the British in Ireland forms the background to this drama. William Powell plays a British officer and concentrates more on his amorous career than the job in hand – namely the street fighting that one glimpses whenever the script starts to flag, based around the conflict between the Black and Tans and the Irish Revolutionaries. Colin Clive makes his mark as a British officer. AT

William Powell *Capt Tennant* • Edna Best *Norah Kerr* • Colin Clive *Andrew Kerr* • Halliwell Hobbes *General* • Hobart Cavanaugh *Homer* • Henry O'Neill *Dan* • Donald Crisp *Conlan* ■ *Dir* Michael Curtiz • *Scr* Laird Doyle, from a play by R Gore Browne, JL Hardy

The Key ★★★ PG
Second World War drama 1958 · UK · BW · 114min

Playing down her usual voluptuous glamour, Sophia Loren is heartbreakingly vulnerable here as the waterfront landlady who offers her favours to naval skippers. She is both a source of solace and disquiet, as few entrusted with her key survive for long. Instead of focusing on either her torment or her affair with the gruff William Holden, Carl Foreman's script spends too much time at sea. No matter how well director Carol Reed stages the action sequences, we're soon impatient for shore leave. DP Some violence and swearing *DVD*

William Holden (2) *David Ross* • Sophia Loren *Stella* • Trevor Howard *Chris Ford* • Oscar Homolka *Captain Van Dam* • Kieron Moore *Kane* • Bernard Lee *Wadlow* • Beatrix Lehmann *Housekeeper* • Noel Purcell *Hotel porter* • Bryan Forbes *Weaver* • Michael Caine ■ *Dir* Carol Reed • *Scr* Carl Foreman, from the novel *Stella* by Jan De Hartog

The Key ★★★★
Erotic melodrama 1959 · Jpn · Colour · 107min

Kon Ichikawa's darkly comic tale of spousal obedience and sexual prowess is also a sly satire on pornography and cinematic voyeurism. Adapted from the novel by Junichiro Tanizaki, the action stems from an ageing husband's hope that his wife's infidelity with a doctor will restore his potency. However, the liaison only sparks a tragic rivalry between his liberated wife and his ultra-traditional daughter. Compromised in its content by contemporary censorship strictures, this is still a daringly subversive picture, which benefits both from the subtly coloured widescreen lensing and the exemplary performance of Machiko Kyo. DP Japanese +subtitles.

Ganjiro Nakamura *Mr Kenmochi* • Machiko Kyo *Ikuko Kenmochi* • Tatsuya Nakadai *Kimura* • Junko Kano *Toshiko Kenmochi* • Tanie Kitabayashi *Hana* ■ *Dir* Kon Ichikawa • *Scr* Natto Wada, Keiji Hasebe, Kon Ichikawa, from a novel by Junichiro Tanizaki • *Cinematographer* Kazuo Miyagawa

Key Largo ★★★ PG
Crime drama 1948 · US · BW · 96min

A great Warner Bros cast was assembled for this screen version of Maxwell Anderson's steamy play, but, despite sterling work from movie icons Humphrey Bogart and Lauren Bacall (and, best of all, Edward G Robinson as a veteran gangster), the creaky theatrical origins show through, and the climactic Florida storms are as phoney as the allegorical plot devices. Nevertheless, Claire Trevor picked up an Oscar for playing Robinson's boozy floozy, and there's a fine feeling of postwar angst evoked by director John Huston. TS *DVD*

Humphrey Bogart *Frank McCloud* • Edward G Robinson *Johnny Rocco* • Lauren Bacall *Nora Temple* • Lionel Barrymore *James Temple* • Claire Trevor *Gaye Dawn* • Thomas Gomez *Curley Hoff* • Harry Lewis *Toots Bass* • John Rodney *Deputy Clyde Sawyer* • Marc Lawrence (1) *Ziggy* ■ *Dir* John Huston • *Scr* John Huston, Richard Brooks, from the play by Maxwell Anderson • *Cinematographer* Karl Freund

Key to the City ★★
Romantic comedy 1950 · US · BW · 100min

This breezy comedy stars Clark Gable and Loretta Young, who meet at a mayoral convention. He's the ex-docker-turned-politician and she's the more classy mayor of a tiny Maine town. Set in San Francisco, where Gable has to cope with several emergencies – as well as those sorts of misunderstandings that only happen in movies – it's a demonstration of Gable's staying power. AT

Clark Gable *Steve Fisk* • Loretta Young *Clarissa Standish* • Frank Morgan *Fire chief Duggan* • Marilyn Maxwell *Sheila* • Raymond Burr *Les Taggart* • James Gleason *Sergeant Hogan* • Lewis Stone *Judge Silas Standish* • Raymond Walburn *Mayor Billy Butler* ■ *Dir* George Sidney (2) • *Scr* Robert Riley Crutcher, from a story by Albert Beich

Key Witness ★★★
Crime drama 1960 · US · BW · 81min

A group of young thugs terrorise a youth and knife him to death. Only one man – Jeffrey Hunter – is prepared to tell the police what has happened even though dozens were witnesses. The story ropes in a lot of topical social concerns – drugs, racism, bike culture – and features Dennis Hopper as the leader of the ruffians. Tautly directed by B-movie maestro Phil Karlson, this was banned by the British censor, mainly because of the frequent use of flick-knives. AT

Jeffrey Hunter *Fred Morrow* • Pat Crowley *Ann Morrow* • Dennis Hopper *"Cowboy"* • Joby Baker *"Muggles"* • Susan Harrison *Ruby* • Johnny Nash *"Apple"* • Corey Allen *"Magician"* • Frank Silvera *Detective Rafael Torno* ■ *Dir* Phil Karlson • *Scr* Alfred Brenner, Sidney Michaels, from a novel by Frank Kane

K

Keyhole ★★★ 18

Mystery horror   2011 · Can/US · BW · 89min

Canadian auteur Guy Maddin cunningly combines gangsters and ghosts for a tantalising tribute to Cinema Past. Maddin laces his old-style Hollywood melodrama with cues taken from Homer's *The Odyssey* and *The Poetics of Space*, Gaston Bachelard's 1958 treatise on the psychological impact of a house on its occupants. But, in doing so, he makes it impossible to fathom why prodigal mobster Jason Patric requires a drowning victim and her beau to help him find his ailing wife (Isabella Rossellini). The cast emotes heroically, but, for all Maddin's ingenuity and intensity, this always feels more self-indulgent than genuinely inspired. DP In English, French. *DVD*

Jason Patric *Ulysses Pick* • Isabella Rossellini *Hyacinth* • Udo Kier *Dr Lemke* • Brooke Palsson *Denny* ■ *Dir* Guy Maddin • *Scr* Guy Maddin, George Toles

The Keys of the Kingdom
★★

Drama   1944 · US · BW · 136min

Gregory Peck, in only his second picture, gained a best actor Oscar nomination playing a saintly priest who runs a mission in 19th-century China. Directed by John M Stahl from a final script by Joseph L Mankiewicz, it's a long, talkative and rather undramatic picture (only a civil war injects much action), but its success saved Peck's career after the weak showing of his first movie, *Days of Glory*. AE

Gregory Peck *Father Francis Chisholm* • Thomas Mitchell *Dr Willie Tulloch* • Vincent Price *Rev Angus Mealy* • Rose Stradner *Mother Maria Veronica* • Roddy McDowall *Francis, as a boy* • Edmund Gwenn *Rev Hamish MacNabb* • Cedric Hardwicke *Monsignor Sleeth* ■ *Dir* John M Stahl • *Scr* Joseph L Mankiewicz, Nunnally Johnson, from the novel by AJ Cronin

The Keys to the House
★★★ PG

Drama
2004 · It/Ger/Fr/UK/Nor · Colour · 106min

Deftly handling a delicate subject, this is a sensitively played and genuinely moving study of an absentee father's reconciliation with his disabled son. Italian director Gianni Amelio's life-affirming drama benefits from the joyful performance of teenager Andrea Rossi as the abandoned child. However, his naturalness at times contrasts sharply with the acting craft involved in Kim Rossi Stuart's otherwise admirable performance as the father. DP Italian +subtitles. *DVD*

Kim Rossi Stuart *Gianni* • Charlotte Rampling *Nicole* • Andrea Rossi *Paolo* • Alla Faerovich *Nadine* • Pierfrancesco Favino *Alberto* • Manuel Katzy *Taxi driver* • Michael Weiss *Andreas* ■ *Dir* Gianni Amelio • *Scr* Gianni Amelio, Sandro Petraglia, Stefano Rulli, from the autobiography *Nati Due Volte (Born Twice)* by Giuseppe Pontiggia

Keys to Tulsa ★★ 18

Crime drama   1996 · US · Colour · 109min

Don't raise your hopes about the quality of this film when you see the cool cast list – this is an interesting, if not exactly gripping, *film noir*. Eric Stoltz plays the prodigal son returning home to mum Mary Tyler Moore with the intention of straightening his life out. Lacking in tension and hindered by rather turgid direction, this is more of a well-played character piece than a taut thriller. JB *DVD*

Eric Stoltz *Richter Boudreau* • Cameron Diaz *Trudy* • Randy Graff *Louise Brinkman* • Mary Tyler Moore *Cynthia Boudreau* • James Coburn *Harmon Shaw* • Deborah Kara Unger *Vicky Michaels Stovers* • Peter Strauss *Chip Carlson* • James Spader *Ronnie Stover* ■ *Dir* Leslie Greif • *Scr* Harley Peyton, from the novel by Brian Fair Berkey

Khartoum ★★★ PG

Historical drama   1966 · UK · Colour · 130min

Charlton Heston stars in this epic about General Gordon's last stand, when Sudanese warriors, led by the Mahdi, gave

the British Empire a serious jolt. Heston's portrayal of Gordon is finely studied, suggesting a complexity that the script never quite comes to terms with. His performance contrasts with that of Laurence Olivier, whose Mahdi is all eye-rolling fanaticism. This boasts a fine supporting cast, and is often spectacular, but the direction is on the stodgy side. AT *DVD*

Charlton Heston *General Charles Gordon* • Laurence Olivier *The Mahdi* • Richard Johnson *Colonel JDH Stewart* • Ralph Richardson *Mr Gladstone* • Alexander Knox *Sir Evelyn Baring* • Johnny Sekka *Khaleel* • Nigel Green *General Wolseley* • Michael Hordern *Lord Granville* • Zia Mohyeddin *Zobeir Pasha* ■ *Dir* Basil Dearden • *Scr* Robert Ardrey

Khodorkovsky ★★★ 12

Documentary   2011 · Ger · Colour · 112min

There is little doubt where German film-maker Cyril Tuschi's sympathies lie in this admiring profile of jailed Russian oligarch Mikhail Khodorkovsky. However, he cannot resist speculating as to why one of the world's richest men decided to pick a fight with then-president Vladimir Putin in 2003, and why he opted for prison rather than exile. Tuschi reveals how a pro-communist chemistry student set up Russia's first private investment bank and, under Boris Yeltsin, acquired the privatised oil company Yukos on the cheap, transforming it into a multi-billion-dollar enterprise. Yet he offers little insight into Khodorkovsky's personality or motives. However, his assessment of the corruption, avarice and decadence that has blighted Russia since the Soviet demise is cogent, trenchant and deftly satirical. DP Russian, English, German +subtitles. *DVD*

Mikhail Khodorkovsky ■ *Dir* Cyril Tuschi

Khuda Kay Liye ★★ 15

Drama   2007 · Pak · Colour · 167min

Two Pakistani brothers (played by Fawad Khan and Shan) take very different paths in this ambitious drama. It was both controversial and well received on its release in Pakistan, but those more attuned to western dramas may find it muddled and lacking focus as it explores what it means to be a Muslim following the terrorist attacks in America on 11 September 2001. CP Urdu, English +subtitles. *DVD*

Shan [Shaan] *Mansoor* • Fawad Khan *Sarmad* • Iman Ali *Mary/Maryam* • Alex Edwards *Dave* ■ *Dir/Scr* Shoaib Mansoor

Khumba ★★★ U

Animated comedy adventure
2013 · S Afr · Colour · 81min

This animated family film about a zebra doesn't have the blockbusting production values that have made Disney, Pixar and DreamWorks leaders in the field, but its tale of being born different just about earns it its stripes. Jake T Austin voices Khumba, born with only half his stripes and blamed by his herd for the sudden drought that hits their homeland. He goes in search of a mystical water hole where, legend has it, the first zebras were granted their stripes. The movie is indebted to *The Lion King* and *Madagascar* but younger kids should enjoy the colourful safari. DA *DVD* Blu-ray

Jake T Austin *Khumba* • Liam Neeson *Phango* • Steve Buscemi *Skalk* • AnnaSophia Robb *Tombi* • Laurence Fishburne *Seko* • Richard E Grant *Bradley* • Catherine Tate *Nora* ■ *Dir* Anthony Silverston • *Scr* Anthony Silverston, Raffaella Delle Donne, Jonathan Roberts

Khyber Patrol ★★★ U

Action drama   1954 · US · Colour · 72min

Nicely paced and richly coloured shortish co-feature, following the trend set by Rock Hudson in *Bengal Brigade* and Tyrone Power in *King of the Khyber Rifles*. This time newcomer Richard Egan is offered a kickstart to stardom as he ruggedly romances lovely Dawn Addams and fights for the Empire on the Indian border, aided by pukka British actor Patric Knowles. TS

Richard Egan *Cameron* • Dawn Addams *Diana* • Raymond Burr *Ahmed* • Patric Knowles *Lieutenant Kennerly* • Paul Cavanagh *Melville* • Donald Randolph *Ishak Khan* • Philip Tonge *Colonel Rivington* • Patrick O'Moore *Brusard* ■ *Dir* Seymour Friedman • *Scr* Jack DeWitt, from a story by Richard Schayer

Kick-Ass ★★★★ 15

Action comedy drama   2009 · US/UK · Colour · 112min

Based on the graphic novel by Mark Millar (*Wanted*), director Matthew Vaughn's cutting-edge adaptation is refreshing, if somewhat controversial. It follows the exploits of high-school nerd Dave Lizewski (a perfectly cast Aaron Johnson), whose attempts to reinvent himself as real-world superhero Kick-Ass seem doomed to failure – until the boy blunder meets Big Daddy (Nicolas Cage in hilarious, Adam West as Batman mode) and his 11-year-old daughter Hit Girl (Chloë Moretz). The movie is initially unsteady, but once Hit Girl starts causing major bad-guy damage, Vaughn's witty verve, instinctive knack for bizarre counterpoint and sheer bravado speed the cartoon violence towards a manic action climax. AJ Violence, swearing, sex scenes, drug abuse. *DVD* Blu-ray

Nicolas Cage *Damon Macready/Big Daddy* • Aaron Johnson *Dave Lizewski/Kick-Ass* • Mark Strong *Frank D'Amico* • Chloë Grace Moretz *Mindy Macready/Hit Girl* • Christopher Mintz-Plasse *Chris D'Amico/Red Mist* • Clark Duke *Marty* • Xander Berkeley *Detective Gigante* • Lyndsy Fonseca *Katie Deauxma* • Michael Rispoli *Big Joe* • Omari Hardwick *Sgt Marcus Williams* • Jason Flemyng *Lobby goon* • Dexter Fletcher *Cody* ■ *Dir* Matthew Vaughn • *Scr* Matthew Vaughn, Jane Goldman, from a comic book by Mark Millar, John Romita Jr

Kick-Ass 2 ★★★ 15

Action comedy drama   2013 · US/UK · Colour · 98min

This second outing for teenage superheroes Kick-Ass and Hit Girl doesn't quite press all the buttons of its predecessor, but it still delivers a high level of action and comedy. Aaron Taylor-Johnson and Chloë Grace Moretz are trying to adjust to the growing pains of high-school life but are forced to revive their alter egos when they're targeted by the vengeful, rich brat son (Christopher Mintz-Plasse) of the crime lord they defeated in the first film. Director Jeff Wadlow brings a more pedestrian tone than in the lively and inventive original. TeS Violence, swearing, sexual references, brief nudity. *DVD* Blu-ray CS

Aaron Taylor-Johnson [Aaron Johnson] *Dave Lizewski/Kick-Ass* • Chloë Grace Moretz *Mindy Macready/Hit Girl* • Jim Carrey *Colonel Stars and Stripes/Sal Bertolini* • Christopher Mintz-Plasse *Chris D'Amico* • John Leguizamo *Javier* • Morris Chestnut *Detective Marcus Williams* ■ *Dir* Jeff Wadlow • *Scr* Jeff Wadlow, from a comic book by Mark Millar, John Romita Jr

Kickboxer ★★★ 18

Martial arts adventure   1989 · US · Colour · 97min

This is the film that first gave an indication that Jean-Claude Van Damme could escape from straight-to-video hell and into the mainstream. Van Damme is the brother of an injured kickboxing champion who enters the ring seeking revenge. However, the fight sequences are staged with such élan that it is easy to ignore the hackneyed script and the rather wooden performances. This spawned several sequels. JF Swearing, violence, nudity. *DVD*

Jean-Claude Van Damme *Kurt Sloane* • Dennis Alexio *Eric Sloane* • Dennis Chan *Xian Chow* • Tong Po • Haskell Anderson *Winston Taylor* • Rochelle Ashana *Mylee* ■ *Dir* Mark DiSalle, David Worth • *Scr* Glen Bruce, from a story by Mark DiSalle, Jean-Claude Van Damme

Kickboxer 2: the Road Back
★★ 18

Martial arts adventure   1990 · US · Colour · 90min

This explores much the same territory as its predecessor and the director is Hollywood journeyman Albert Pyun, whose name can

be found on many a straight-to-video sleeve. The film stars Sasha Mitchell as the high-kicking hero who seeks revenge on the kung fu coward who killed his brother. You probably know the rest. JF Violence, swearing.

Sasha Mitchell *David Sloan* • Peter Boyle *Justin Maciah* • Cary-Hiroyuki Tagawa *Mr Sangha* • Dennis Chan *Xian Chow* • Michel Qissi *Tong Po* • John Diehl *Morrison* ■ *Dir* Albert Pyun • *Scr* David S Goyer

Kickboxer III: the Art of War ★★ 18

Martial arts adventure   1992 · US · Colour · 87min

Tinseltown never really came knocking for Sasha Mitchell, who bravely soldiers on in the role created by Jean-Claude Van Damme. The slimmest of plots (the hunt for a kidnapped girl) helps to link the numerous biffing sequences, which are competently if unimaginatively filmed. The fourth film was originally rejected for video release in the UK. JF Violence, swearing.

Sasha Mitchell *David Sloan* • Dennis Chan *Xian Chow* • Richard Comar *Frank Lane* • Noah Verduzco *Marcos* • Ian Jacklin *Martine* ■ *Dir* Rick King • *Scr* Dennis Pratt

Kicked in the Head ★★

Black comedy thriller   1997 · US · Colour · 86min

Self-pitying lowlife Kevin Corrigan acts as a cocaine-delivery boy for his two-bit crook uncle James Woods, but things don't go as planned and he invokes the wrath of local crime boss Burt Young. Highly derivative, and populated by truly unlikeable characters, this forced black comedy thriller is neither dark nor amusing enough to perk any interest. AJ

Kevin Corrigan *Redmond* • Linda Fiorentino *Megan* • Michael Rapaport *Stretch* • James Woods *Uncle Sam* • Burt Young *Jack* • Lili Taylor *Happy* ■ *Dir* Matthew Harrison (1) • *Scr* Kevin Corrigan, Matthew Harrison

Kicking & Screaming ★★ PG

Sports comedy   2005 · US · Colour · 90min

Will Ferrell stars as the put-upon son of a macho sports fanatic in this meek comedy. He attempts to prove himself to his intimidating father (Robert Duvall) by coaching a Little League soccer team that is stuck at the bottom of the table. Full of clichéd gags and flat improvisation, this wastes the considerable talents of Robert Duvall as the bullying father. Unfocused but amiable, this raises the occasional smile. GM *DVD*

Will Ferrell *Phil Weston* • Robert Duvall *Buck Weston* • Kate Walsh *Barbara Weston* • Mike Ditka • Dylan McLaughlin *Sam Weston* • Josh Hutcherson *Bucky Weston* • Musetta Vander *Janice Weston* ■ *Dir* Jesse Dylan • *Scr* Leo Benvenuti, Steve Rudnick

Kicks ★★ 15

Drama   2009 · UK · Colour · 81min

Director Lindy Heymann and writer Leigh Campbell rather run out of ideas in this scrappy study of reckless hero worship. Distraught after learning that Liverpool's star striker Jamie Doyle is bound for Real Madrid, wannabe Wags Kerrie Hayes and Nichola Burley decide to kidnap him and hide him in a caravan until he sees sense. Capturing something of Merseyside's passion for football and the extent to which teenagers are seduced by the celebrity lifestyle, this is socially astute and eagerly played. But it's also fatally undermined by the implausibility of the situation and the banal dénouement's disappointing lack of drama. DP Swearing, sex scenes.

Kerrie Hayes *Nicole* • Nichola Burley *Jasmine* • Jamie Doyle *Lee Cassidy* • Laura Wallace *Jade* • Sarah Jane Buckley *Angie* • Nick Moss *Dave* ■ *Dir* Lindy Heymann • *Scr* Leigh Campbell, from an idea by Laurence Coriat • *Cinematographer* Eduard Grau

The Kid ★★★★ U

Silent comedy drama   1921 · US · BW · 68min

Charlie Chaplin's first feature as writer, director and star was something of a

U SUITABLE FOR ALL   Uc SUITABLE ESPECIALLY FOR YOUNG CHILDREN (DVD ONLY)   PG PARENTAL GUIDANCE   12A UNDER 12s TO BE ACCOMPANIED (CINEMA ONLY)

K

watershed in his career. After this, slapstick would slowly be replaced by more observational comedy, while an increased emphasis would be placed on both social comment and pathos. Clearly recalling his own troubled childhood in Victorian London, the film is remarkable for the chemistry between the Tramp and moppet Jackie Coogan. Chaplin may try a touch too hard for tears in places, but the scenes in which he discovers the abandoned baby and the heaven sequence show just what a gifted film-maker he was. DP *DVD* 🔵

Charlie Chaplin [Charles Chaplin] *Tramp* • Jackie Coogan *The Kid* • Edna Purviance *Mother* • Carl Miller *Artist* • Tom Wilson *Policeman* ■ *Dir/Scr* Charles Chaplin

Kid ★★ 18

Thriller　　　　1990 · US · Colour · 87min

C Thomas Howell plays the Kid, a taciturn drifter in a long coat who comes back to his home town and makes out with the prettiest girl there. However, he also goes on a killing spree aimed at those who murdered his parents years before. Apart from the obvious nod to Clint Eastwood's laconic loner, Howell seems to be going for some kind of James Dean vibe here as well, but he's out of his league and the rest of the characters are mere stereotypes. ST

C Thomas Howell *Kid* • R Lee Ermey *Luke Clanton* • Dale Dye *Garvey* • Sarah Trigger *Kate* • Michael Bowen *Harlan* • Brian Austin Green *Metal Louie* • Damon Martin *Pete* • Lenore Kasdorf *Alice* ■ *Dir* John Mark Robinson • *Scr* Leslie Bohem

The Kid ★★ 15

Drama based on a true story
2010 · UK · Colour · 106min

Actor Nick Moran (*Lock, Stock and Two Smoking Barrels*) follows up his directorial debut, pop biopic *Telstar: the Joe Meek Story*, with another London-set true story. Sadly, in relating Kevin Lewis's journey from physically and emotionally abused child to bestselling novelist, Moran displays a tendency towards melodrama that overwhelms the story. Rupert Friend gives a fine performance as the grown-up Lewis, but Natascha McElhone portrays Lewis's abusive mother like a wicked witch, and the urbane James Fox is arguably the last actor you would choose to play a south London foster dad. DA Violence, swearing. *DVD* 🔵

Rupert Friend *Kevin Lewis* • Natascha McElhone *Gloria* • Ioan Gruffudd *Colin Smith* • David O'Hara *Terry* • Bernard Hill *Uncle David* • Kate Ashfield *Madeline* • James Fox *Alan* ■ *Dir* Nick Moran • *Scr* Kevin Lewis, Nick Moran, Mark Thomas

Kid Blue ★★★

Comedy western　　1971 · US · Colour · 100min

This seriously flakey comedy western – a sort of *Easy Rider* on horseback – has Dennis Hopper as a hopeless outlaw who goes straight and is hopeless at that as well. Hopper's outsider has a wayward charm, a hippy's glazed look and a talent for slapstick humour. Less a narrative than scenes glued randomly together, it's a mess, albeit an entertaining one. Completed in 1971 under its original title *Dime Box*, it was kept on the shelf for two years. AT

Dennis Hopper *Bickford Waner* • Warren Oates *Reese Ford* • Peter Boyle *Preacher Bob* • Ben Johnson (1) *Sheriff "Mean John" Simpson* • Lee Purcell *Molly Ford* • Janice Rule *Janet Conforto* • Ralph Waite *Drummer* ■ *Dir* James Frawley • *Scr* Edwin Shrake

The Kid Brother ★★★★★ U

Silent comedy　　1927 · US · BW · 82min

The inventiveness of comedian Harold Lloyd has to be seen to be disbelieved in this comedy about the put-upon youngest of three sons and their widower father (Walter James). Ordered to close down a travelling show by his sheriff dad, Lloyd at last rebels against the constant bullying – because he's fallen in love with showgirl Jobyna Ralston – and triumphs over parental oppression. Some of the sight gags are brilliant, including the use of a butter churn as a way of wringing and hanging out

clothes. The mechanisms of laughter-making don't come much better than this, and add up to one of the comedian's best movies. TH

Harold Lloyd *Harold Hickory* • Jobyna Ralston *Mary Powers* • Walter James *Sheriff Jim Hickory* • Leo Willis *Leo Hickory* • Olin Francis *Olin Hickory* • Constantine Romanoff *Sardoni* • Eddie Boland *"Flash" Farrell* • Frank Lanning *Sam Hooper* ■ *Dir* Ted Wilde, JA Howe, Lewis Milestone • *Scr* John Grey, Tom Crizer, Lex Neal, Howard Green, Ted Wilde

A Kid for Two Farthings
★★★ U

Comedy fantasy　　1955 · UK · Colour · 86min

Influenced by the neorealist fantasies of Italian director Vittorio De Sica, this is a delightful urban fairy tale set in London's East End in the harsh days after the Second World War. The story of a small boy who finds a one-horned goat that he is convinced is a miracle-working unicorn is handled with a wonderfully light touch by director Carol Reed and beautifully played by a cast in which Celia Johnson, Diana Dors and little Jonathan Ashmore stand out. Yet, for all its charm and feel-good sentimentality, the blend of realism and fantasy is not always convincing. DP *DVD*

Celia Johnson *Joanne* • Diana Dors *Sonia* • David Kossoff *Kandinsky* • Joe Robinson *Sam* • Jonathan Ashmore *Joe* • Brenda de Banzie *"Lady" Ruby* • Vera-Day *Mimi* • Primo Carnera *Python Macklin* • Sidney James *Ince Berg* • Irene Handl *Mrs Abramowitz* • Alfie Bass *Alf, the Bird Man* ■ *Dir* Carol Reed • *Scr* Wolf Mankowitz, from his novel

The Kid from Brooklyn
★★★ U

Musical comedy　　1946 · US · Colour · 108min

Based on Harold Lloyd's 1936 comedy *The Milky Way*, this is one of Danny Kaye's best vehicles, allowing the versatile comedian to strut his stuff as the milkman who becomes a boxing champ. If you're not a Kaye fan, this may be the movie that will make you change your mind, since it's relatively free of the sentimentality that mars so much of his later work. Producer Samuel Goldwyn surrounds his star with terrific character support and some super songs. TS

Danny Kaye *Burleigh Sullivan* • Virginia Mayo *Polly Pringle* • Vera-Ellen *Susie Sullivan* • Walter Abel *Gabby Sloan* • Eve Arden *Ann Westley* • Steve Cochran *Speed Macfarlane* • Lionel Stander *Spider Schultz* • Fay Bainter *Mrs E Winthrop Lemoyne* ■ *Dir* Norman Z McLeod • *Scr* Don Hartman, Melville Shavelson, from the film *The Milky Way* by Grover Jones, Frank Butler, Richard Connell, from the play *The Milky Way* by Lynn Root, Harry Clork

The Kid from Spain
★★★★ U

Musical comedy　　1932 · US · BW · 91min

This wonderfully insane Eddie Cantor vehicle has a wacky plot of confused identities, which climaxes when Cantor, mistaken for a great bullfighter, wears down an angry bull. Famed choreographer Busby Berkeley, not quite yet in his marvellous, tasteless stride, is responsible for the production numbers. Talented Leo McCarey also directed Laurel and Hardy and the Marx Brothers, and here he's aided by the cinematography of the great Gregg Toland. TS

Eddie Cantor *Eddie Williams* • Lyda Roberti *Rosalie* • Robert Young (1) *Ricardo* • Ruth Hall *Anita Gomez* • John Miljan *Pancho* • Noah Beery *Alonzo Gomez* • J Carrol Naish *Pedro* ■ *Dir* Leo McCarey • *Scr* William Anthony McGuire, Bert Kalmar, Harry Ruby

The Kid from Texas ★★ U

Western　　　　1950 · US · Colour · 78min

This is the film that made Audie Murphy a star. Here, America's most decorated Second World War hero plays Billy the Kid and gives a performance that completely overshadows Robert Taylor's earlier romanticised portrayal of the psychopathic killer. Murphy is riveting in a film that, frankly, is just an average Universal B-feature, given weight by its perfectly cast

star and its distinguished supporting cast. TS

Audie Murphy *Billy the Kid* • Gale Storm *Irene Kain* • Albert Dekker *Alexander Kain* • Shepperd Strudwick *Jameson* • Will Geer *O'Fallon* ■ *Dir* Kurt Neumann • *Scr* Robert Hardy Andrews, Karl Kamb, from a story by Robert Hardy Andrews

Kid Galahad ★★★★ PG

Sports drama　　　1937 · US · BW · 97min

Wayne Morris features as the chivalrous hotel porter in Warner Bros' fast-paced boxing saga, impeccably directed by Michael Curtiz, and teaming Edward G Robinson, Humphrey Bogart and Bette Davis. It's the mink-clad Davis, called "Fluff", who starts the action rolling, revealing sharp insights into prizefight manners and morals. Editor George Amy does a superb job in the cutting room, keeping the film on the move, and Humphrey Bogart, as a rival fight promoter, has seldom been meaner. Terrific stuff, cleverly handled and supremely entertaining. TS

Edward G Robinson *Nick Donati* • Bette Davis *Louise "Fluff" Phillips* • Humphrey Bogart *Turkey Morgan* • Wayne Morris *"Kid Galahad"/Ward Guisenberry* • Jane Bryan *Marie Donati* • Harry Carey *Silver Jackson* ■ *Dir* Michael Curtiz • *Scr* Seton I Miller, from the novel by Francis Wallace

Kid Galahad ★★★ PG

Musical sports drama　1962 · US · Colour · 92min

First filmed in 1937 with Edward G Robinson and Bette Davis, this boxing tale was considerably re-fashioned for Elvis Presley, playing the title character, a fighter who would rather be a garage mechanic. Much of the plotting was jettisoned to make way for Presley's musical interludes, and the film lacks the brittle excitement of the original, but a strong supporting cast and solid direction by Phil Karlson make this one of the singer's better movies. TV *DVD*

Elvis Presley *Walter Gulick* • Gig Young *Willy Grogan* • Lola Albright *Dolly Fletcher* • Joan Blackman *Rose Grogan* • Charles Bronson *Lew Nyack* • Ned Glass *Lieberman* ■ *Dir* Phil Karlson • *Scr* William Fay, from the novel by Francis Wallace

Kid Glove Killer ★★★

Thriller　　　　1942 · US · BW · 73min

Director Fred Zinnemann's documentary background shines through here, as police laboratory workers Van Heflin and Marsha Hunt investigate the murder of the mayor. This was exactly the kind of movie that MGM made superbly, a B feature raised to A status with intelligent scripting, casting and direction. Heflin is impressive, but look closely at that stunning waitress with only two lines of dialogue – that's Ava Gardner. TS

Van Heflin *Gordon McKay* • Marsha Hunt *Jane Mitchell* • Lee Bowman *Gerald I Ladimer* • Samuel S Hinds *Mayor Daniels* • Cliff Clark *Captain Lynch* • Eddie Quillan *Eddie Wright* • Ava Gardner *Carhop* ■ *Dir* Fred Zinnemann • *Scr* Allen Rivkin, John C Higgins, from a story by John C Higgins

Kid Millions ★★★ U

Musical comedy
1934 · US · BW and Colour · 86min

Eddie Cantor is very much an acquired taste for modern audiences, but in his day the banjo-eyed comedian was a huge stage and screen star. The support cast is astounding: don't miss the great Nicholas Brothers dancing team, or a young Ethel Merman as a gangster's moll, or even Eve Sully as an Arab princess with a Brooklyn accent – treats indeed. The plot is one for collectors of the bizarre, as Eddie is left a fortune in Egypt. TS

Eddie Cantor *Eddie Wilson Jr* • Ann Sothern *Joan Larrabee* • Ethel Merman *Dot Clark* • George Murphy *Jerry Lane* • Jesse Block *Ben Ali* • Eve Sully *Fanya* ■ *Dir* Roy Del Ruth, Willy Pogany • *Scr* Arthur Sheekman, Nat Perrin, Nunnally Johnson

Kid Rodelo ★ U

Western adventure　1966 · US/Sp · BW · 90min

Horse opera hokum based on a Louis L'Amour tale. Ex-con Don Murray tries to

retrieve some hidden gold, while staying a jump ahead of various villains – including Broderick Crawford – and the Indians. An uneasy Spanish/US co-production, this suffers from a script crammed with clichés and fails to make the most of a good cast, which also includes Janet Leigh. JG

Don Murray *Kid Rodelo* • Janet Leigh *Nora* • Broderick Crawford *Joe Harbin* • Richard Carlson *Link* • José Nieto *Thomas Reese* ■ *Dir* Richard Carlson • *Scr* Jack Natteford, from a story by Louis L'Amour

The Kid Stays in the Picture ★★★ 15

Documentary　　　2001 · US · Colour · 89min

Brett Morgen and Nanette Burstein's documentary on Robert Evans is much like the legendary US producer's movies themselves: bold, innovatively shot and highly entertaining. However, any dips it takes into life's dark side are sanitised with a brush of old Hollywood-style whitewash, usually dispensed by the man himself. Crammed with priceless anecdotes about his cinematic achievements and bursting with juicy revelations about some of the movie industry's finest, it's scintillating viewing for anyone fascinated by the minutiae of celebrity life. Where this revelatory journey falls down is in the cleaning-up and rose-tinting of some events. SF *DVD*

Robert Evans *Narrator* ■ *Dir* Brett Morgen, Nanette Burstein • *Scr* Brett Morgen, from the autobiography by Robert Evans

Kid Vengeance ★★ 15

Western　　　　1977 · US · Colour · 86min

This repellent revenge western teams genre veterans Lee Van Cleef and Jim Brown with 1970s teenage pop star Leif Garrett in some vain hope of snaring a gullible audience. Garrett plays a kid who goes after the killer of his parents (guess who?) and teams up with Brown's prospector whose gold has been stolen by the same man. Director Joseph Manduke pastes over the paucity of plot and simplicity of dialogue with violence and a number of savage deaths. RS

Lee Van Cleef *McClain* • Jim Brown *Isaac* • John Marley *Jesus* • Glynnis O'Connor *Lisa* • Leif Garrett *Tom* • Matt Clark *Grover* ■ *Dir* Joseph Manduke • *Scr* Bud Robbins, Jay Telfer, from a story by Ken Globus

The Kid with a Bike ★★★★ 12

Drama　　　　2011 · Bel/Fr/It · Colour · 83min

An 11-year-old tearaway starts to make sense of the conflict around him in this subtle, touching drama from esteemed Belgian film-making brothers Jean-Pierre and Luc Dardenne (*The Son, L'Enfant*). Thomas Doret (a real find) plays young Cyril, languishing in care but determined to be reunited with his father. Cécile de France provides strength and hope as the kindly local hairdresser who could offer him a real home. The story moves at a cracking pace, and the Dardennes scrupulously avoid any syrupy sentiment, delivering a drama that's both emotionally wrenching and morally complex. TJ French +subtitles. Violence, swearing. *DVD* 🔵

Thomas Doret *Cyril Catoul* • Cécile de France *Samantha* • Jérémie Rénier *Guy Catoul* • Egon Di Mateo *Wes* • Fabrizio Rongione *Bookseller* ■ *Dir/Scr* Jean-Pierre Dardenne, Luc Dardenne

Kidnapped ★

Adventure　　　　1938 · US · BW · 93min

It might have seemed a good idea at the time to team David Copperfield (Freddie Bartholomew) and the Cisco Kid (Warner Baxter) in Robert Louis Stevenson's classic action tale, but 20th Century-Fox should have also included a higher production budget and a better director than Alfred Werker. Sticking to the original story might have helped, too. This is a decidedly cheap and murky adaptation, and Baxter looks, and sounds, far too unathletic and American. TS

K

Warner Baxter *Alan Breck* • Freddie Bartholomew *David Balfour* • Arleen Whelan *Jean MacDonald* • C Aubrey Smith *Duke of Argyle* • Reginald Owen *Captain Hoseason* • John Carradine *Gordon* • Nigel Bruce *Neil MacDonald* • Miles Mander *Ebenezer Balfour* • Ralph Forbes *James* • HB Warner *Angus Rankeillor* ■ *Dir* Alfred Werker • *Scr* Sonya Levien, Eleanor Harris, Ernest Pascal, Edwin Blum, from the novels *Kidnapped* and *David Balfour* by Robert Louis Stevenson

Kidnapped ★ U

Adventure 1948 · US · BW · 81min

This is another weak screen version of Robert Louis Stevenson's yarn about a boy who claims an inheritance from his uncle, but is grabbed and sold into slavery. He escapes and sets off to reclaim his prize. Made by dime-budget Monogram Pictures, it stars Roddy McDowall as the young Scot saved by adventurer Alan Breck, played here by Dan O'Herlihy. McDowall's mother plays the wife of an innkeeper, her only film role. AT

Roddy McDowall *David Balfour* • Sue England *Aileen Fairlie* • Dan O'Herlihy *Alan Breck* • Roland Winters *Captain Hoseason* • Jeff Corey *Shuan* • Housley Stevenson [Houseley Stevenson] *Ebenezer* • Winefried McDowall *Innkeeper's wife* ■ *Dir* William Beaudine • *Scr* W Scott Darling, from the novel by Robert Louis Stevenson

Kidnapped ★★★ U

Adventure 1960 · US · Colour · 90min

Robert Louis Stevenson's classic yarn is given the Walt Disney treatment, with James MacArthur playing the disinherited David Balfour and Peter Finch as the dashing Scottish loyalist who befriends him. Shot on beautiful Highland locations and with Peter O'Toole making an early screen appearance, this version of the tale is a decent enough romp. AT

Peter Finch *Alan Breck* • James MacArthur *David Balfour* • Bernard Lee *Captain Hoseason* • Niall MacGinnis *Shuan* • John Laurie *Uncle Ebenezer* • Finlay Currie *Cluny MacPherson* • Peter O'Toole *Robin Oig MacGregor* • Miles Malleson *Mr Rankeillor* ■ *Dir* Robert Stevenson • *Scr* Robert Stevenson, from the novel by Robert Louis Stevenson

Kidnapped ★★★ U

Adventure 1971 · UK · Colour · 102min

Michael Caine's witty swagger, in the role of outlaw Alan Breck, stirs some otherwise rather stiff porridge into life. Robert Louis Stevenson's stories have been filmed before, but this version is the one that is most faithful to the source, and it contains some strong performances: Trevor Howard as the Lord Advocate and Lawrence Douglas as young David keep the narrative moving along. TH *DVD*

Michael Caine *Alan Breck* • Trevor Howard *Lord Grant* • Jack Hawkins *Captain Hoseason* • Donald Pleasence *Ebenezer Balfour* • Gordon Jackson *Charles Stewart* • Vivien Heilbron *Catriona* • Lawrence Douglas *David Balfour* ■ *Dir* Delbert Mann • *Scr* Jack Pulman, from the novel by Robert Louis Stevenson,

Kidnapped ★★★ PG

Crime drama based on a true story 1995 · US · Colour · 87min

Dabney Coleman is one of the unsung heroes of Hollywood, equally at home in comedy or dramatic roles. In this gripping made-for-TV police thriller, he plays a serial abducter who begins a deadly cat-and-mouse game with frustrated FBI man Timothy Busfield. The two leads are backed up by strong supporting performances and no-nonsense direction from Bobby Roth. JF Some violence. *DVD*

Dabney Coleman *Arthur Milo* • Timothy Busfield *Agent Pete Honeycutt* • Lauren Tom *Lily Yee* • Tracey Walter *Oliver Tracy* • Barbara Williams (2) *Beth Honeycutt* ■ *Dir* Bobby Roth • *Scr* Thomas Baum

The Kidnappers ★★★★ U

Drama 1953 · UK · BW · 89min

Popular in its day and still charming, this drama tells the story of two Scottish orphans in turn-of-the-century Nova Scotia,

who steal a baby when their stern grandfather won't let them have a dog. This slight tale is perfectly performed by two child actors, Jon Whiteley and Vincent Winter, and both youngsters received special Oscars as a result. Director Philip Leacock creates a realistic, almost documentary-like atmosphere of a closed-in, isolated community, and is helped by fine performances from Duncan Macrae and Jean Anderson as the grandparents. Charlton Heston starred in a TV movie remake, *The Little Kidnappers* (1990). TS

Duncan Macrae *Granddaddy* • Jean Anderson *Grandma* • Adrienne Corri *Kirsty* • Theodore Bikel *Willem Bloem* • Jon Whiteley *Harry* • Vincent Winter *Davy* • Francis De Wolff *Jan Hooft Sr* • James Sutherland *Arron McNab* • John Rae *Andrew McCleod* ■ *Dir* Philip Leacock • *Scr* Neil Paterson

Kidnapping Freddy Heineken ★★ 15

Crime thriller based on a true story 2015 · Bel/UK/Neth · Colour · 90min

Anthony Hopkins may be the class act of this true-crime story as the famous kidnap victim who was deemed worthy of the country's largest ever ransom haul, but this really is an insipid affair. Set in Amsterdam in the early 1980s, the film follows an oddly coiffured Jim Sturgess (looking more 1970s than 80s) and the gang he assembles to snatch the titular tycoon - boss of the Heineken beer business. But, as with most best-laid plans, cracks emerge and the success of their seemingly perfect scheme is soon hanging in the balance. The characterisations are emaciated, with the exception of Sam Worthington's hothead heavy and Hopkins himself, although he's barely on screen. JA Swearing. *DVD*

Jim Sturgess *Cor Van Hout* • Sam Worthington *Willem Holleeder* • Anthony Hopkins *Freddy Heineken* • Ryan Kwanten *Jan "Cat" Boellard* • Mark van Eeuwen *Frans "Spikes" Meijer* ■ *Dir* Daniel Alfredson • *Scr* William Brookfield, from a non-fiction book by Peter R de Vries

The Kidnapping of Michel Houellebecq ★★★★ 15

Comedy drama 2014 · Fr · Colour · 96min

One of France's most famous novelists sportingly sends himself up in this comedy drama inspired by real-life events. In 2011, Michel Houellebecq vanished for several days and rumours spread that he had been kidnapped by al-Qaeda. Here writer/director Guillaume Nicloux playfully posits that Houellebecq was abducted by an inexpert trio, who chained him to a bed in the deepest Parisian suburbs while they waited for their unseen client to dictate ransom terms. Witty, pithy and surprising, the movie is consistently entertaining and provides a deceptively sharp insight into both human nature and contemporary French society. DP French +subtitles. Swearing, a sex scene, nudity.

Michel Houellebecq *Michel Houellebecq* • Luc Schwarz *Luc* • Maxime Lefrançois *Max* • Mathieu Nicourt *Mathieu* • Françoise Lebrun *Françoise* • Veran Mauberret ■ *Dir/Scr* Guillaume Nicloux

The Kidnapping of the President ★★

Thriller 1980 · Can · Colour · 113min

Terrorists kidnap President Hal Holbrook in Toronto, bundle him into a bomb-laden, booby-trapped truck and demand a hefty ransom for his release. Secret Service agent William Shatner - having beamed down from his intergalactic day job - goes to work, leaving the White House in the hands of Vice President Van Johnson and his wife Ava Gardner. AT

William Shatner *Jerry O'Connor* • Hal Holbrook *President Adam Scott* • Van Johnson *Vice President Ethan Richards* • Ava Gardner *Beth Richards* • Miguel Fernandes *Roberto Assanti* • Cindy Girling *Linda Steiner* ■ *Dir* George Mendeluk • *Scr* Richard Murphy, from a novel by Charles Templeton

kids ★★★★ 18

Drama 1995 · US · Colour · 90min

Teenager Leo Fitzpatrick plays a self-styled "virgin surgeon", who spends his days beating up street trash, getting drunk and stoned and deflowering young girls. One of his conquests (Chloë Sevigny) tries to track him down to tell him he's HIV-positive while still dazed from her own diagnosis. Acerbically scripted by Harmony Korine and directed by influential underground photographer Larry Clark, this disturbingly explicit look at Generation X "skateboard culture" poses difficult questions and offers few easy answers. Deemed offensive exploitation by some, this is in fact highly moral and thought provoking. AJ Swearing, sex scenes, drug abuse, nudity. *DVD*

Leo Fitzpatrick *Telly* • Justin Pierce *Casper* • Chloë Sevigny *Jennie* • Sarah Henderson *Girl* • Rosario Dawson *Ruby* • Harold Hunter *Harold* • Joseph Chan *Deli owner* ■ *Dir* Larry Clark • *Scr* Harmony Korine, from a story by Larry Clark, Jim Lewis

The Kids Are All Right ★★★★ 15

Comedy drama 2010 · US/Fr · Colour · 101min

A married lesbian couple have teenage children by the same anonymous sperm-donor father – Annette Bening, a doctor, is the practical, focused half of the pair, while Julianne Moore is a more scatty, creative type. Their already volatile relationship is tested further when their son seeks out his birth father (Mark Ruffalo). Pitch-perfect performances really bring out the emotion of a situation that will strike a chord with many, with Bening best of all as a woman forced to face her partner's betrayal. DW *DVD* *BD*

Julianne Moore *Jules* • Annette Bening *Nic* • Mark Ruffalo *Paul* • Mia Wasikowska *Joni* • Josh Hutcherson *Laser* • Yaya DaCosta *Tanya* • Kunal Sharma *Jai* ■ *Dir* Lisa Cholodenko • *Scr* Lisa Cholodenko, Stuart Blumberg

The Kids Are Alright ★★★ 15

Music documentary 1978 · UK · BW and Colour · 96min

The value of this "rockumentary" trip through the highs and lows of the Who's career was increased by the death of the band's extrovert drummer Keith Moon in September 1978. However, fans will probably not want to dwell on the frankly depressing final concert footage, preferring to see Moon in classic 1960s action, when his hellraising was matched by his extraordinary on-stage energy. Director Jeff Stein occasionally errs into hagiography, but there's a generous sampling of hits (and the odd miss), interviews and rare archival material. DP *DVD* *BD*

Pete Townshend • Roger Daltrey • John Entwistle *John Entwhistle* • Keith Moon • Melvin Bragg • Ringo Starr ■ *Dir/Scr* Jeff Stein

Kids in Love ★★★ 15

Drama 2016 · UK · Colour · 83min

This coming-of-age drama is a film about finding yourself. The main character is Jack (Will Poulter), a bright young man who is taking a gap year while weighing his options. One day, he meets Evelyn (Alma Jodorowsky), a beautiful French girl who introduces him to her friends. Soon, Jack is spending most of his time with a group of artsy, care-free Londoners who like to party. The film never makes it clear whether this is a good thing or a bad thing, but Poulter remains likeable and engaging throughout. SC

Will Poulter *Jack* • Alma Jodorowsky *Evelyn* • Sebastian De Souza *Milo* • Preston Thompson *Cassius* • Cara Delevingne *Viola* ■ *Dir* Chris Foggin • *Scr* Sebastian De Souza, Preston Thompson

Kids in the Hall: Brain Candy ★★ 15

Comedy 1996 · Can/US · Colour · 84min

Canada's answer to *Saturday Night Live* makes its first foray into the movies here. The all-male team's determination to play virtually every major role (as well as their penchant for dressing up in women's clothing) makes *Monty Python* a closer reference point, although they're not in the same league. However, this sketchy story of a young doctor who discovers a cure for depression has its moments. JF Swearing, brief nudity.

Dave Foley *Marv/Psychiatrist/Suicidal businessman/New guy/Raymond* • Bruce McCulloch *Grivo/Alice/Cisco/Cop/White-trash man/Cancer boy* • Kevin McDonald *Chris Cooper/Chris's dad/Doreen* • Mark McKinney *Don Roritor/Simon/German patient/Nina Bedford/Cabbie/White-trash woman* • Scott Thompson *Wally Terzinsky/Mrs Hurdicure/Baxter/Malek/Clemptor/The Queen* ■ *Dir* Kelly Makin • *Scr* Norm Hiscock, Bruce McCulloch, Kevin McDonald, Mark McKinney, Scott Thompson

Kids Return ★★★ 15

Crime comedy drama 1996 · Jpn · Colour · 103min

This was the first feature director Takeshi Kitano completed after he fractured his skull in a near-fatal scooter accident. Masanobu Ando and Ken Kaneko are two schoolboys who leave the education system with little option but to drift into boxing and crime respectively. Cross-cutting with typical energy and invention, Kitano persuades us to warm to these underachievers. DP Japanese +subtitles. *DVD*

Masanobu Ando *Shinji Takagi* • Ken Kaneko *Masaru Miyawaki* • Leo Morimoto *Teacher* • Hatsuo Yamaya *Boxing club manager* • Mitsuko Oka *Coffee shop owner, Sachiko's mother* • Ryo Ishibashi *Local yakuza chief* ■ *Dir/Scr* Takeshi Kitano

Kidulthood ★★★ 15

Social drama 2005 · UK · Colour · 91min

This is an impressive film about British teenagers on the cusp between irresponsible adolescence and responsible adulthood. The film comprises a compendium of urban clichés, encompassing everything from gun crime and school bullying to teen suicide and underage pregnancy. But the predictability of the storyline is more than offset by the dialogue, which has a genuine feel of the real about it, and by radiant performances from a young cast. Powerful and entertaining. DA Violence, swearing, drug abuse. *DVD* *BD*

Aml Ameen *Trife* • Red Madrell *Alisa* • Noel Clarke *Sam* • Jaime Winstone *Becky* • Adam Deacon *Jay* • Femi Oyeniran *Moony* • Madeleine Fairley *Claire* • Katelin Okoro *Carleen* • Rafe Spall *Lenny* ■ *Dir* Menhaj Huda • *Scr* Noel Clarke

Kika ★★ 18

Comedy 1993 · Sp · Colour · 109min

Pedro Almodóvar, famous for his absurd irony and outrageous imagination, here offers up a familiar menu of sexual deviance, rape, murder and the media. This is from his lacklustre middle period and focuses on shallow make-up artist Veronica Forqué, who makes up a dead body as a favour for a serial-killing author. But the stiff of said novelist's stepson's lesbian maid's psychologically disturbed porno-star brother suddenly comes back to life! A pointless charade. AJ Spanish +subtitles. *DVD*

Verónica Forqué *Kika* • Peter Coyote *Nicholas* • Victoria Abril *Andrea Caracortada* • Alex Casanovas *Ramón* • Rossy de Palma *Juana* • Santiago Lajusticia *Pablo* • Anabel Alonso *Amparo* • Bibi Andersen *Susana* ■ *Dir/Scr* Pedro Almodóvar

Kiki's Delivery Service ★★★ U
Animated fantasy adventure
1989/1998 · Jpn · Colour · 104min

This endearing fantasy adventure from Japanese master-animator Hayao Miyazaki is given a fresh new life in this English-language version. Kirsten Dunst lends her voice to the part of Kiki, the young witch who has to spend a year practising her craft in a new town, and she's joined by a quality cast including Phil Hartman and Janeane Garofalo. It doesn't have the blackness of Miyazaki's eco-tales, but this subtle coming-of-age story still exhibits his unmatched visuals – the detail of the flying scenes is delightful – and strong characters. TF Japanese dubbed. DVD Blu

Kirsten Dunst *Kiki* • Kath Soucie *Kiki's mother* • Debbie Reynolds *Miss Dora* • Jeff Bennett *Kiki's father* • Phil Hartman *Jiji* • Tress MacNeille *Osono* • Edie McClurg *Bertha* • Matthew Lawrence *Tombo* • Janeane Garofalo *Ursula* ■ *Dir* Hayao Miyazaki • *Scr* Hayao Miyazaki, Jack Fletcher, from a novel by Eiko Kadono

Kikujiro ★★★★★ 12
Comedy drama 1999 · Jpn · Colour · 116min

With the violence that has characterised so many of his films toned down to slapstick socko, this is Takeshi Kitano's offbeat homage to *The Wizard of Oz*. As the amoral yakuza who accompanies nine-year-old Yusuke Sekiguchi on a cross-country mission to find his mother, Kitano gives an inspired demonstration of muddle-headed, short-lived deadpan. The duo meanders from racetrack to fairground, encountering en route a paedophile, a rude hotel clerk and a couple of soft-centred bikers. There are no deep messages here, just dream sequences, unexpected revelations and several achingly funny set pieces. DP Japanese +subtitles. DVD Blu

"Beat" Takeshi [Takeshi Kitano] *Kikujiro* • Kayoko Kishimoto *Miki, Kikujiro's wife* • Yusuke Sekiguchi *Masao* • Akaji Maro *Paedophile* • Yuko Daike *Masao's mother* ■ *Dir/Scr* Takeshi Kitano

Kill! ★
Thriller 1972 · Fr/It/Sp/W Ger · Colour · 102min

Celebrated novelist Romain Gary directs this paper-thin co-production with little demonstrable understanding of the mechanics of movie-making. By allowing his tale of drug smuggling and porn peddling to quickly sprawl out of control, he sheds vital clues to the identity of the master criminal with such abandon that the solution is apparent almost from the outset. James Mason looks glum as the man from Interpol, but beside Jean Seberg as his wife he seems exhilarated. DP

James Mason *Alan* • Jean Seberg *Emily* • Stephen Boyd *Killian* • Curt Jurgens *Chief* • Daniel Emilfork *Inspector* • Henri Garcin *Lawyer* ■ *Dir/Scr* Romain Gary

Kill a Dragon ★
Martial arts action adventure
1967 · US · Colour · 97min

Rarely seen and largely unlamented, this muddled adventure with Jack Palance finds him in China to battle crime lord Fernando Lamas. The other familiar face in the cast is screen veteran Aldo Ray, but all three leads can do little with the preposterous, haphazard plotting. JF

Jack Palance *Rick* • Fernando Lamas *Patrai* • Aldo Ray *Vigo* • Alizia Gur *Tisa* • Tong Kam *Win Lim* ■ *Dir* Michael Moore (1) • *Scr* George Schenck, William Marks

Requiescant ★★★ 12
Spaghetti western
1967 · It/W Ger · Colour · 106min

In the grand tradition of *A Bullet for the General*, director Carlo Lizzani's political western finds Lou Castel's hero Requiescant helping rebel bandits in their struggle against foreign financiers who are propping up a counter-revolutionary federal government. The Italian director Pier Paolo Pasolini was so impressed with the radical script of this spaghetti western with a difference that he agreed to appear in it as a revolutionary priest. TH Italian dubbed. Violence, swearing, drug abuse. DVD Blu

Lou Castel *Requiescant* • Mark Damon *Ferguson* • Barbara Frey *Princy* • Pier Paolo Pasolini *Don Juan* • Franco Citti *Burt* ■ *Dir* Carlo Lizzani

Kill Bill Vol 1 ★★★★ 18
Part-animated martial arts drama
2003 · US · Colour and BW · 106min

Quentin Tarantino marshals a bewildering number of multi-genre references into a hypnotically entertaining whole in this violent martial arts revenge drama. Giving a searing performance, Uma Thurman plays one of the Deadly Vipers, a crack assassination squad led by the Bill of the title (David Carradine). Left for dead on her wedding day, she falls into a coma, only to awaken four years later swearing revenge on her traitorous co-workers. *Vol 1* deals with two members on her Death List Five: Vernita Green (Vivica A Fox) and O-Ren Ishii (Lucy Liu). Dripping with bloody ultra-violence and using startling flashbacks, knowingly fake dubbing and a quite brilliant *anime* section, this is both a daring experiment in sampled cinematic language and scrounged style, and a gloriously enchanting work of neo-art in itself. AJ English, Japanese +subtitles. Violence, swearing. DVD Blu

Uma Thurman *The Bride/"Black Mamba"* • David Carradine *Bill* • Lucy Liu *O-Ren Ishii/ "Cottonmouth"* • Daryl Hannah *Elle Driver/ "California Mountain Snake"* • Vivica A Fox *Vernita Green/"Copperhead"* • Michael Madsen *Budd/"Sidewinder"* • Michael Parks *Sheriff Earl McGraw* • Sonny Chiba *Hattori Hanzo* • Chiaki Kuriyama *Go Go Yubari* • Julie Dreyfus *Sofie Fatale* ■ *Dir* Quentin Tarantino • *Scr* Quentin Tarantino, from the character created by Q & U [Quentin Tarantino, Uma Thurman]

Kill Bill Vol 2 ★★★ 18
Martial arts drama
2004 · US · Colour and BW · 131min

Long-winded, overly self-indulgent and talky, director Quentin Tarantino's wrap-up of his bloody revenge saga is something of an anticlimax. Detailing how the Bride (Uma Thurman) tracks down Deadly Viper assassins Budd (Michael Madsen) and Elle Driver (Daryl Hannah), before facing Bill (David Carradine) and an unexpected "adversary", it's the same mix as before except less visually dynamic and with a lot more unnecessary exposition. Yet the borrowed style and all the usual obscure genre references still make this compressed exploitation-cinema history lesson a buff treat. AJ English, Japanese, Mandarin +subtitles. Violence. DVD Blu

Uma Thurman *Beatrix Kiddo/The Bride/"Black Mamba"/Mommy* • David Carradine *Bill/"Snake Charmer"* • Daryl Hannah *Elle Driver/"California Mountain Snake"* • Michael Madsen *Budd/ "Sidewinder"* • Michael Parks *Earl McGraw/ Esteban Vihaio* • Gordon Liu *Johnny Mo/Pai Mei* • Samuel L Jackson *Rufus* • Bo Svenson *Reverend Harmony* ■ *Dir* Quentin Tarantino • *Scr* Quentin Tarantino, from the character created by Q & U [Quentin Tarantino, Uma Thurman]

Kill Command ★★★ 15
Science-fiction action horror
2016 · UK · Colour · 99min

Set in a high-tech future, a group of human soldiers and a half-android weapons designer (Vanessa Kirby) land on a remote island for a routine training mission, only to find a deadly group of robots trying to hunt them down. Taking obvious inspiration from sci-fi staples such as *Alien* and *Predator*, the stunning special effects are the highlight of this thriller. Keeping things simple, the soulless androids make for effective villains, and questions raised as to whether we are too reliant on technology are salient and interesting. JL Swearing, violence DVD

Vanessa Kirby *Mills* • Thure Lindhardt *Captain Bukes* • David Ajala *Drifter* • Tom McKay *Cutbill* ■ *Dir/Scr* Steven Gomez

Kill List ★★★★ 18
Horror 2011 · UK · Colour · 91min

Progressing confidently from edgy soap opera to intense crime thriller to stark satanic shocker, director Ben Wheatley's down-and-dirty chiller effortlessly transforms into a uniquely terrifying experience. Bored and driving his wife crazy, an ex-soldier-turned-contract killer is talked into taking on one last job with his best mate, but their mysterious employer's peculiar hit list brings them into direct contact with the occult. Confounding expectations, Wheatley's tale of the unpredictable is darkly comic, brutally violent and a dynamo of dizzying fright stuff. AJ Violence, swearing, nudity. DVD Blu

Neil Maskell *Jay* • MyAnna Buring *Shel* • Michael Smiley *Gal* • Emma Fryer *Fiona* • Harry Simpson *Sam* ■ *Dir* Ben Wheatley • *Scr* Ben Wheatley, Amy Jump

Kill Me Again ★★★ 18
Crime thriller 1989 · US · Colour · 92min

Marking John Dahl's directorial debut, this is far from flawless, but Dahl (*The Last Seduction*) demonstrates an already instinctive touch for *femmes fatales* and flawed heroes in a typically convoluted story about private detective Val Kilmer who is persuaded by beautiful Joanne Whalley-Kilmer to help her fake her death. Notable for providing an early psycho role for *Reservoir Dogs*'s Michael Madsen, the main problem here is the two leads, who fail to convince. JF Sex scenes, violence, swearing. DVD

Joanne Whalley-Kilmer [Joanne Whalley] *Fay Forrester* • Val Kilmer *Jack Andrews* • Michael Madsen *Vince Miller* • Jonathan Gries *Alan Swayzie* • Pat Mulligan *Sammy* ■ *Dir* John Dahl • *Scr* David W Warfield, John Dahl

Kill Me If You Can ★★★★
Drama based on a true story
1977 · US · Colour · 100min

In one of his most accomplished TV-movie roles, Alan Alda is riveting in the true story of Caryl Chessman, the notorious "Red Light Bandit", who served 12 years on death row before being executed in 1960. As the erudite Chessman, Alda veers between rage and serene determination with mesmerising power, and his performance was rewarded with an Emmy nomination. TV movies rarely come this stark or involving. AJ

Alan Alda *Caryl Chessman* • Talia Shire *Rosalie Asher* • John Hillerman *George Davis* • Barnard Hughes *Judge Fricke* ■ *Dir* Buzz Kulik • *Scr* John Gay

Kill Me Later ★★★ 15
Romantic comedy drama
2001 · US · Colour · 85min

This offbeat, if patchy, comedy drama gets by on the charm of its two leads. Selma Blair is the depressed bank worker whose suicide bid is interrupted by would-be robber Max Beesley. She agrees to be his hostage on the condition that he kill her later. The sketchiness of the material occasionally shows through, and Dana Lustig's direction is also a little too tricksy for its own good. JF

Selma Blair *Shawn Holloway* • Max Beesley *Charlie Anders* • O'Neal Compton *Agent McGinley* • Lochlyn Munro *Agent Reed* • DW Moffett *Matthew Richmond* • Billy Fehr *Billy* ■ *Dir* Dana Lustig • *Scr* Annette Goliti Gutierrez, Dana Lustig

Kill Me Tomorrow ★★ U
Crime drama 1957 · UK · BW · 80min

Warner Bros rarely pushed lead roles Pat O'Brien's way. Even so, it's hard to fathom why he crossed the Atlantic for the starring role in this far-fetched B-movie. You might expect an impoverished father trying to fund his son's eye operation to resort to some pretty desperate tactics – but confessing to a murder in order to raise the money? Terence Fisher directs with little enthusiasm, but it's worth hanging in there to catch the debut of Tommy Steele. DP

Pat O'Brien *Bart Crosbie* • Lois Maxwell *Jill Brook* • George Coulouris *Heinz Webber* • Wensley Pithey *Inspector Lane* • Freddie Mills *Waxy* • Ronald Adam *Brook* • Tommy Steele ■ *Dir* Terence Fisher • *Scr* Manning O'Brine, Robert Falconer

The Kill-Off ★★★ 18
Thriller 1989 · US · Colour · 93min

The bleakness contained in Jim Thompson's hard-boiled novels has been a notoriously difficult tone to pull off in movie adaptations of his work, but director Maggie Greenwald's bitter little thriller does a better job than most. Loretta Gross stands out in the no-name ensemble cast as the vicious gossip-monger in a small American town, whose acid tongue is feared by every local resident. So they decide to do something to silence her. Not a great advert for human nature, but an engaging mood piece that's both grim and grimy. AJ Swearing, drug abuse, nudity.

Loretta Gross *Luane Devore* • Jackson Sims *Pete Pavlov* • Steve Monroe *Ralph* • Andrew Lee Barrett *Bobbie Ashton* • Cathy Haase *Danny Lee* • Jorjan Fox [Jorja Fox] *Myra Pavlov* ■ *Dir* Maggie Greenwald • *Scr* Maggie Greenwald, from a novel by Jim Thompson

Kill or Cure ★ U
Comedy mystery 1962 · UK · BW · 88min

This is the kind of comedy that could have killed off the British film industry, despite its domestic star-power and the usually reliable writing team of David Pursall and Jack Seddon. When bumbling private detective Terry-Thomas tries to investigate a murder at a posh spa, the only interest is in seeing him lock comedy horns with Eric Sykes and Lionel Jeffries. Unfortunately, it is to little effect. TH

Terry-Thomas *J Barker-Rynde* • Eric Sykes *Rumbelow* • Dennis Price *Dr Crossley* • Lionel Jeffries *Inspector Hook* • Moira Redmond *Frances Reitman* • Ronnie Barker *Burton* ■ *Dir* George Pollock • *Scr* David Pursall, Jack Seddon

Kill Switch ★ 18
Action thriller 2008 · US/Can · Colour · 92min

In this Memphis-set barrel-scraper, Steven Seagal delivers an excruciating performance as a tough detective on the hunt for two rather dull serial killers. With a weird southern accent and barely any expression, he lumbers through an unsatisfying mishmash of sub-*Se7en* crime thriller clichés, stereotypes and laughable dialogue. Jittery camerawork, excessive use of the jump cut and pointless repeat shots make the protracted fist-fights and generally unrealistic action sequences feel clumsy and tedious, while the rushed climax simply isn't worth the wait. SF In English, Russian. DVD Blu

Steven Seagal *Jacob Stillwell* • Holly Elissa Dignard *Agent Frankie Miller* • Isaac Hayes *Coroner* • Michael Filipowich *Lazerus* • Chris Thomas King *Storm* ■ *Dir* Jeff F King [Jeff King] • *Scr* Steven Seagal

Kill the Irishman ★★ 18
Crime drama based on a true story
2011 · US · Colour · 102min

Director Jonathan Hensleigh (*The Punisher*) here visits the real-life 1970s turf war between the Mafia and the Irish Mob in this underwhelming crime biopic. Ray Stevenson stars as infamous hardman Danny Greene, whose refusal to kowtow to Italian mobsters in his native Cleveland saw him elevated to hero status as a seemingly indestructible Celtic warrior, so often did he survive the myriad attempts on his life. The film is blessed with a cast of talented veterans, and even Vinnie Jones crops up as one of Greene's henchmen. But this is not on a par with gangster epics like *GoodFellas* and Hensleigh is certainly no Scorsese. JA Violence, swearing, nudity. DVD Blu

Ray Stevenson *Danny Greene* • Val Kilmer *Joe Manditski* • Christopher Walken *Shondor Birns* • Vincent D'Onofrio *John Nardi* • Vinnie Jones *Keith Ritson* ■ *Dir* Jonathan Hensleigh • *Scr* Jonathan Hensleigh, Jeremy Walters, from the non-fiction book *To Kill the Irishman* by Rick Porrello

Kill the Man ★★ 15
Comedy 1999 · US · Colour · 85min

Luke Wilson and Joshua Malina play the owners of a photocopying shop in this

K

genial but limp assault on corporate America. There's little that's original in the story of their battle against the franchise rival who muscles in on their turf. Phil LaMarr's Marxist rapper and Richard Riehle's gormless rocker supply some off-kilter sidekickery, and there's choice support from Michael McKean and Teri Garr as the bickering parents of Wilson's marriage-minded girlfriend. But it lacks the satirical edge of Frank Capra's winning "everyman against the system" formula, despite the fact that Hollywood has been trying to reproduce that magic ever since. **DP** Swearing, some sexual references, violence. **DVD**

Luke Wilson *Stanley Simon* • Joshua Malina *Bob Stein* • Paula Devicq *Vicki* • Phillip Rhys *Seth* • Phil LaMarr *Marky Marx* • Jim Fyfe *Guy* • Teri Garr *Mrs Livingston* • Michael McKean *Mr Livingston* ■ *Dir/Scr* Tom Booker, Jon Kean

Kill the Messenger ★★★ 15
Crime drama based on a true story
2014 · US · Colour · 112min

In 1996, journalist Gary Webb wrote a number of pieces implicating the CIA in a crack epidemic affecting inner-city LA and drawing a direct link between the US government and the Contras. Those reports provide the basis for this conspiracy thriller akin to *All the President's Men* in theme if not impact, with Jeremy Renner firing on all cylinders as Webb. The film's shift from the political to the personal makes for an uneven ride, though support by Andy Garcia and Ray Liotta helps. Director Michael Cuesta (TV's *Homeland*) might have done better sticking closer to Webb's investigation – still, some food for thought is better than none. **SP**

Jeremy Renner *Gary Webb* • Rosemarie DeWitt *Sue Webb* • Ray Liotta *John Cullen* • Tim Blake Nelson *Alan Fenster* • Barry Pepper *Russell Dodson* • Michael Sheen *Fred Weil* ■ *Dir* Michael Cuesta • *Scr* Peter Landesman, from Nick Schou's non-fiction book, and the non-fiction book *Dark Alliance* by Gary Webb

Kill Your Darlings ★★★ 15
Biographical drama
2013 · US · Colour · 99min

Daniel Radcliffe puts more clear water between himself and Harry Potter with a finely mature performance as Allen Ginsberg, the Beat poet, here embroiled in a real-life pre-Beat murder case that involved the stabbing in dubious circumstances of one gay man by another. Both moved in a circle of gay college camaraderie that also involved Ginsberg, William Burroughs (Ben Foster) and Jack Kerouac (Jack Huston). Less intense than *Howl* and less self-indulgent than *On the Road*, both recent films that also sought to capture pivotal moments in the Beat movement, this is a Bratpack movie, 1940s-style, that's sexy and self-aware. **DA** **DVD** ⊕

Daniel Radcliffe *Allen Ginsberg* • Dane DeHaan *Lucien Carr* • Michael C Hall *David Kammerer* • Jack Huston *Jack Kerouac* • Ben Foster *William Burroughs* • David Cross (2) *Louis Ginsberg* • Jennifer Jason Leigh *Naomi Ginsberg* • Elizabeth Olsen *Edie Parker* ■ *Dir* John Krokidas • *Scr* John Krokidas, Austin Bunn

Kill Your Friends ★★★ 18
Black comedy thriller
2015 · UK · Colour · 98min

First-time feature director Owen Harris gives this black comedy pace and lots of 1990s nostalgia with a soundtrack featuring Blur, Oasis and Radiohead. But what he doesn't do is convey the desperation that leads A&R man Steven Stelfox (Nicholas Hoult) to murder. That's despite the fact that writer John Niven adapted from his own best-selling novel based on his time in the music business. Hoult certainly inspires just the right morbid fascination as he kills his closest rival (James Corden). But the investigation is subordinate to the film's devilish sense of humour. **SP** Violence, swearing, sex scenes, drug abuse. ⊕

Nicholas Hoult *Stelfox* • Craig Roberts *Darren* • James Corden *Waters* • Joseph Mawle *Trellick* • Rosanna Arquette *Barbara* ■ *Dir* Owen Harris (2) • *Scr* John Niven, from his novel

The Killer ★★★★ 18
Action thriller
1989 · HK · Colour · 106min

This Hong Kong gangster movie is directed with such over-the-top verve by John Woo you're transfixed by its audacity, despite several stomach-churning scenes of violence. Chow Yun-Fat plays the assassin who decides to quit his profession after accidentally blinding a singer (Sally Yeh) during a hit in a nightclub. When he learns that her sight could be restored through an operation, he decides to fund it by doing just one more job. Of its amoral kind it's great bullet-dodging fun, but it's definitely not for the faint-hearted. **TH** Cantonese +subtitles. Violence, nudity. **DVD**

Chow Yun-Fat *Jeff* • Danny Lee *Inspector "Eagle" Lee* • Sally Yeh *Jennie* • Kong Chu *Sydney Fung* • Kenneth Tsang *Sergeant Randy Chung* • Chung Lam *Willie Tsang* • Shing Fui-on *Johnny Weng* ■ *Dir/Scr* John Woo

Killer ★★ 18
Crime thriller
1994 · US · Colour · 93min

Gangland hitman Anthony LaPaglia meets his match when he's assigned *femme fatale* Mimi Rogers as his last kill; the twist in director Mark Malone's contemporary *film noir* is that Rogers knows she's due to die and intends to make the heartless killer feel as guilty as possible. Is she his saviour, or his downfall? That's the central enigma of this pretentious look at the human condition. The stars deliver strong performances, but it's percolating with unfulfilled promise. **AJ** Sex scenes, swearing, violence.

Anthony LaPaglia *Mick* • Mimi Rogers *Fiona* • Matt Craven *Archie* • Peter Boyle *George* • Monika Schnarre *Laura* • Joseph Maher *Dr Alstricht* ■ *Dir* Mark Malone • *Scr* Gordon Melbourne, from a story by Mark Malone

Killer: a Journal of Murder ★★★ 18
Biographical prison drama
1995 · US · Colour and BW · 87min

This violent drama is carried along by the intensity of James Woods's performance as Carl Panzram, who, having confessed to murdering 21 people, had the dubious "honour" of being one of America's first recognised serial killers. Robert Sean Leonard plays Henry Lesser, a liberal prison guard who sees the value in Panzram writing down his story for future reference. Leonard's approach contrasts with that of Robert John Burke, who plays a hard-line warden. An absorbing, if violent, case history. **AJ** Swearing, violence.

James Woods *Carl Panzram* • Robert Sean Leonard *Henry Lesser* • Ellen Greene *Elizabeth Wyatt* • Cara Buono *Esther Lesser* • Robert John Burke [Robert Burke] *RG Greiser* • Steve Forrest *Warden Charles Casey* • Jeffrey DeMunn *Sam Lesser* ■ *Dir* Tim Metcalfe • *Scr* Tim Metcalfe, from the non-fiction book by Thomas E Gaddis, James O Long

The Killer Elite ★★★ 15
Action thriller
1975 · US · Colour · 118min

When the picture he wanted to make – *The Insurance Company* – was abruptly cancelled by the studio, Sam Peckinpah went straight on to direct this, which was already written, cast and ready to go. As a result, Peckinpah had nothing but contempt for this San Francisco-based thriller. *Godfather* co-stars James Caan and Robert Duvall are reunited in this tale of CIA spooks, car chases, martial artistry and bloody shoot-outs. The result is both quite exciting and instantly forgettable. **AT** Contains violence and swearing. **DVD**

James Caan *Mike Locken* • Robert Duvall *George Hansen* • Arthur Hill *Cap Collis* • Bo Hopkins *Jerome Miller* • Mako *Yuen Chung* • Burt Young *Mac* • Gig Young *Laurence Weyburn* • Tom Clancy *O'Leary* ■ *Dir* Sam Peckinpah • *Scr* Marc Norman, Stirling Silliphant, from the novel *Monkey in the Middle* by Robert Rostand

Killer Elite ★★ 15
Action thriller
2011 · US/Aus · Colour · 111min

This laborious 1980s-set shoot-'em-up stars Jason Statham as Danny, a retired

mercenary forced into one last job when his mentor (Robert De Niro) is held hostage by a renegade Omani sheikh. But Danny's every move is being monitored by a shadowy group of former government and military high-fliers led by Clive Owen. The permanently scowling Statham borders on caricature, while the talents of De Niro and Owen are completely wasted. **TeS** Violence, swearing. **DVD** ⊕

Jason Statham *Danny Bryce* • Clive Owen *Spike* • Robert De Niro *Hunter* • Dominic Purcell *Davies* • Aden Young *Meier* • Yvonne Strahovski *Anne* ■ *Dir* Gary McKendry • *Scr* Matt Sherring, from the novel *The Feather Men* by Ranulph Fiennes

Killer Fish ★★ 15
Adventure thriller
1978 · It/Bra · Colour · 96min

In this interestingly cast co-production, a selected handful of near-stars enjoy an exotic Brazilian location shoot while pretending to hunt for purloined jewels in a lake full of piranha. Margaux Hemingway and Marisa Berenson feature, although there's a serious warning here to models who attempt acting careers. But it's still the best cast director Antonio Margheriti, purveyor of spaghetti western and horror, ever assembled. **TS**

Lee Majors *Robert Lasky* • Karen Black *Kate Neville* • James Franciscus *Paul Diller* • Margaux Hemingway *Gabrielle* • Marisa Berenson *Ann* • Gary Collins *Tom* • Roy Brocksmith *Ollie* • Dan Pastorini *Hans* ■ *Dir* Anthony M Dawson [Antonio Margheriti] • *Scr* Michael Rogers

Killer Flood ★
Disaster movie
2003 · US · Colour · 105min

This substandard small-screen disaster movie stars Joe Lando as a disgraced architect who attempts to convince small-town residents that a dam he designed is about to rupture. Writer/director Doug Campbell tries to engage viewer empathy by throwing in a huge dollop of sentimentality, but it feels forced and empty. Still, the hammy cast seems to be having fun – especially Bruce Boxleitner as the corporate villain behind the whole mess. **SF**

Bruce Boxleitner *Mr Walker* • Michele Greene *Natalie Powell* • Joe Lando *David Powell* • Matthew Ewald *Garth Powell* ■ *Dir/Scr* Doug Campbell

Killer Force ★★
Action thriller
1975 · Swi/Ire · Colour · 98min

This thriller concerns a plot to rob a diamond mine in South Africa. Chief of security Telly Savalas teams up with Peter Fonda to foil the scheme. Director Val Guest's film features some impressive location footage; unfortunately, it also contains some tiresome philosophising. Maud Adams, as Fonda's girlfriend, seems bored rigid, while Christopher Lee appears as a disaffected British soldier. **AT**

Telly Savalas *Harry Webb* • Peter Fonda *Mike Bradley* • Christopher Lee *Chilton* • OJ Simpson *"Bopper" Alexander* • Maud Adams *Clare Chambers* • Hugh O'Brian *Lewis* ■ *Dir* Val Guest • *Scr* Val Guest, Michael Winder, Gerald Sanford

The Killer inside Me ★★ 18
Thriller
1975 · US · Colour · 91min

Adapted from a novel by Jim Thompson, a classy purveyor of cult pulp fiction, this never quite convinces as it attempts to show the disintegration of well-respected deputy sheriff Stacy Keach into uncontrollable mania. Keach is one of those risk-all actors who can do many things; one thing he can't do, though, is to stand up to the clunkingly obvious direction of Burt Kennedy. **TH**

Stacy Keach *Lou Ford* • Susan Tyrrell *Joyce Lakeland* • Tisha Sterling *Amy Stanton* • Keenan Wynn *Chester Conway* • Don Stroud *Elmer Conway* • Charles McGraw *Howard Hendricks* • John Dehner *Bob Maples* • John Carradine *Dr Smith* ■ *Dir* Burt Kennedy • *Scr* Edward Mann, Robert Chamblee, from the novel by Jim Thompson

The Killer inside Me ★★ 18
Crime thriller
2010 · US · Colour · 104min

British director Michael Winterbottom adapts the classic pulp fiction of American novelist Jim Thompson here, but something gets lost in translation. Casey Affleck wisely underplays the intensity of Lou Ford, the psychotic deputy sheriff of a sleepy Texan town, but Winterbottom indulges in repetitious close-ups of the appalling violence Ford visits upon the women in his life. They include a prostitute (Jessica Alba) and the archetypal girl next door, played by Kate Hudson. While there are hints of the turmoil inside this killer, those moments are too fleeting to create any lasting tension. **SP** Violence, sex scenes. **DVD** ⊕

Casey Affleck *Lou Ford* • Jessica Alba *Joyce Lakeland* • Kate Hudson *Amy Stanton* • Ned Beatty *Chester Conway* • Simon Baker (1) *Howard Hendricks* • Bill Pullman *Billy Boy Walker* ■ *Dir* Michael Winterbottom • *Scr* John Curran, from the novel by Jim Thompson

The Killer Is Loose ★★★
Crime drama
1956 · US · BW · 73min

A perceptive critic described Budd Boetticher's films as "small, glittering morality plays". In this neglected thriller, Wendell Corey stars as a bank clerk, involved in a robbery, whose wife is accidentally killed during the subsequent arrest. The seemingly mild-mannered clerk is sent to prison, escaping after three years. Now psychopathic and revengeful, he embarks on eye-for-an-eye retribution against the cop (Joseph Cotten) who shot his wife. This was Boetticher's first significant urban-set movie, directed with characteristic economy and building to a stunning climax. **BB**

Joseph Cotten *Sam Wagner* • Rhonda Fleming *Lila Wagner* • Wendell Corey *Leon "Foggy" Poole* • Alan Hale Jr *Denny* ■ *Dir* Budd Boetticher • *Scr* Harold Medford, from a story by John Hawkins, Ward Hawkins

Killer Joe ★★ 18
Crime thriller
2011 · US · Colour · 98min

In this southern-fried thriller, cash-strapped Emile Hirsch cooks up a plan to kill his mother and collect on the insurance, but he gets in way over his head by hiring psychopathic detective Matthew McConaughey (the Joe of the title) to do the dirty deed. The script by playwright (and Pulitzer Prize winner) Tracy Letts clearly flags itself as very black comedy, yet there seems scant justification for the carnage on display, as veteran director William Friedkin goes overboard on shock value. **TJ** Violence, swearing, drug abuse, nudity. **DVD** ⊕

Matthew McConaughey *"Killer" Joe Cooper* • Emile Hirsch *Chris Smith* • Juno Temple *Dottie Smith* • Thomas Haden Church *Ansel Smith* • Gina Gershon *Sharla Smith* ■ *Dir* William Friedkin • *Scr* Tracy Letts, from his play

Killer Klowns from Outer Space ★★★ 12
Science-fiction horror comedy
1988 · US · Colour · 82min

Combining inspired amateur brashness, delightful *Loony Tunes* design and a winningly bizarre unreality, this engagingly cheap affair from effects wizards Stephen and Charles Chiodo is an infantile and vicious delight. Alien clowns invade Earth in a spacecraft masquerading as a circus tent; they intend to cocoon the local population in candy floss and suck out their life juices, unless two teens and a cop can stop them. **AJ** Violence, swearing **DVD** ⊕

Grant Cramer *Mike* • Suzanne Snyder *Debbie* • John Allen Nelson *Officer Dave Hanson* • Royal Dano *Farmer Green* • John Vernon *Officer Mooney* ■ *Dir* Stephen Chiodo • *Scr* Stephen Chiodo, Charles Chiodo

Killer McCoy ★★
Sports drama
1947 · US · BW · 103min

In this so-called "adult drama", designed to show he wasn't just able to play Andy Hardy, Mickey Rooney is cast as the son of

U SUITABLE FOR ALL   **Uc** SUITABLE ESPECIALLY FOR YOUNG CHILDREN (DVD ONLY)   **PG** PARENTAL GUIDANCE   **12A** UNDER 12s TO BE ACCOMPANIED (CINEMA ONLY)

a drunken entertainer who accidentally kills his best friend and takes over as a lightweight boxing champion. It's as implausible as only MGM can make it, and much emphasis is put on the pain that Rooney has endured to get there and keeps enduring when being punched senseless in the ring. AT

Mickey Rooney *Tommy McCoy* • Brian Donlevy *Jim Caighn* • Ann Blyth *Sheila Carrson* • James Dunn *Brian McCoy* • Tom Tully *Cecil Y Walsh* • Sam Levene *Happy* • Walter Sande *Bill Thorne* ■ *Dir* Roy Rowland • *Scr* Frederick Hazlitt Brennan, from the 1938 film *The Crowd Roars* by Thomas Lennon (1), George Bruce, George Oppenheimer • *Music/lyrics* Stanley Donen

Killer Nun ★★★ 18
Cult horror   1978 · It · Colour · 83min

Morphine addiction, lesbianism, gore, scandal and Catholic guilt: it's all here in a gleefully demented Italian schlock cocktail that wallows in nasty sleaze while adopting an inappropriate and hilariously pious attitude. Anita Ekberg plays a paranoid nun who isn't sure if her homicidal nightmares are the real thing or not in trash merchant Giulio Berruti's bad-taste shocker, packed with sinful sex sessions and hard-edged violence. Andy Warhol icon Joe Dallesandro as a doctor and *The Third Man* beauty Alida Valli as the mother superior add extra cult value. AJ Italian +subtitles. *DVD*

Anita Ekberg *Sister Gertrud* • Joe Dallesandro *Dr Rowland* • Lou Castel *Peter* • Alida Valli *Mother Superior* ■ *Dir* Giulio Berruti (1) • *Scr* Giulio Berruti, Alberto Tarallo

Killer of Sheep ★★★★ 15
Drama   1977 · US · BW · 77min

Made in the mid-1970s, but virtually unseen until 2000, Charles Burnett's lost masterpiece is a poetic and immersive look at life for black Americans in a deprived area of Los Angeles. Downtrodden Stan (Henry Gayle Sanders) works in an abattoir, and the unremitting grind of his existence leaves him numb to the world around him, including his adoring wife (Kaycee Moore) and two children. This is an African-American art house film, and in direct opposition to the Blaxploitation movies of the era it's quiet and reflective, with snatched glimpses of life – boys playing at war, Stan and his wife dancing in their living room – that fly in the face of the inescapable poverty and hopelessness surrounding them. LB *DVD*

Henry Gayle Sanders *Stan* • Kaycee Moore *Stan's wife* • Charles Bracy *Bracy* • Angela Burnett *Stan's daughter* • Eugene Cherry *Eugene* • Jack Drummond *Stan's son* ■ *Dir/Scr* Charles Burnett

Killer Party ★★ 18
Horror   1986 · US · Colour · 87min

It's April Fool's Day in this standard dead-teens-on-campus slasher tale involving lethal fraternity high jinks and a vengeful killer wearing a diver's suit. After a promising start, involving a film-within-a-rock-video-within-a-film sucker-punch, and despite some creative modes of murder, this good-looking nonsense drifts into a repetitive groove of laughs and scares. However, the late cult director Paul Bartel is as delightful as always, playing a stuffy professor. AJ

Martin Hewitt *Blake* • Ralph Seymour *Martin* • Elaine Wilkes *Phoebe* • Paul Bartel (1) *Professor Zito* ■ *Dir* William Fruet • *Scr* Barney Cohen

The Killer Shrews ★ PG
Science-fiction horror   1959 · US · BW · 68min

For sheer nerve the makers ought to have grabbed an Oscar for attempting to demonise an animal not much bigger than a mouse. However these are not just ordinary shrews, but the rampaging and flesh-eating side effects of genetic research carried out by bonkers scientist Baruch Lumet (father of noted director Sidney Lumet). The film boasts inept special effects and bargain-basement production values, contributing to its status as a cult bad movie. RS

James Best *Thorne Sherman* • Ingrid Goude *Ann Craigis* • Baruch Lumet *Dr Craigis* • Ken Curtis *Jerry Lacer* • Gordon McLendon *Radford Baines* • Alfredo DeSoto *Mario* ■ *Dir* Ray Kellogg • *Scr* Jay Simms

The Killers ★★★★★ PG
Classic film noir   1946 · US · BW · 98min

This is one of the most powerful and influential thrillers ever made, with director Robert Siodmak's bleak and pessimistic tone virtually defining the term *film noir*. Based on a short story of remarkable power by Ernest Hemingway, the movie opens with a murder and then seeks, through flashbacks, to explain why the victim was so accepting of his fate. Burt Lancaster, all coiled anger as the fall guy, makes a stunning film debut and there's a career-defining role for Ava Gardner as the *femme fatale*. In fact, there's class all round: the Edward Hopper-influenced design is brilliantly atmospheric, Miklos Rozsa's superb score was so effective it was re-used for TV's *Dragnet* and John Huston had a hand in the taut screenplay. The Don Siegel version with Lee Marvin and Ronald Reagan is good, but don't miss this marvellous original. TS *DVD* Blu

Burt Lancaster *Ole "Swede" Anderson/Pete Lunn* • Ava Gardner *Kitty Collins* • Edmond O'Brien *Jim Reardon* • Albert Dekker *Big Jim Colfax* • Sam Levene *Lieutenant Sam Lubinsky* • Charles D Brown *Packy Robinson* • Donald MacBride *Kenyon* • Phil Brown *Nick Adams* • Charles McGraw *Al* • William Conrad *Max* • Vince Barnett *Charleston* ■ *Dir* Robert Siodmak • *Scr* Anthony Veiller, John Huston, from a short story by Ernest Hemingway • *Cinematographer* Elwood Bredell • *Set Designers* Jack Otterson, Martin Obzina • *Editor* Arthur Hilton

The Killers ★★★★ 18
Crime thriller   1964 · US · Colour · 94min

Ernest Hemingway's short story had already inspired a movie in 1946; this film was not a remake but a separate version of the tale. John Cassavetes is iced by hitmen Lee Marvin and Clu Gulager, who join forces to find out why the contract was ordered in the first place. Marvin exudes his usual power and menace in a dry run for his *Point Blank* character, and Ronald Reagan makes his last screen appearance before moving into politics. This was originally made for TV but released in cinemas because of its violent content. JA *DVD* Blu

Lee Marvin *Charlie Strom* • John Cassavetes *Johnny North* • Angie Dickinson *Sheila Farr* • Ronald Reagan *Jack Browning* • Clu Gulager *Lee* • Claude Akins *Earl Sylvester* • Norman Fell *Mickey Farmer* ■ *Dir* Donald Siegel [Don Siegel] • *Scr* Gene L Coon, from a short story by Ernest Hemingway

Killers ★ 12
Action comedy   2010 · US · Colour · 96min

Bullets fly in this dismal action comedy when suburban housewife Katherine Heigl discovers that husband Ashton Kutcher is a "retired" secret agent whose past is coming back to haunt him. Aiming for a blend of superspy capers and battle-of-the-sexes banter, this career low for *Legally Blonde* director Robert Luketic offers only underwhelming chase sequences and virtually non-existent chemistry between two stars left high and dry by a mirthless script. Only Catherine O'Hara's mugging as Heigl's boozy mum raises the vaguest suspicion of a smile. TJ Some violence, sexual references, brief swearing. *DVD* Blu

Katherine Heigl *Jen Kornfeldt* • Ashton Kutcher *Spencer Aimes* • Tom Selleck *Mr Kornfeldt* • Catherine O'Hara *Mrs Kornfeldt* • Katheryn Winnick *Vivian* • Kevin Sussman *Mac Bailey* ■ *Dir* Robert Luketic • *Scr* Bob DeRosa, TM Griffin [Ted Griffin]

Killers ★★★★ 18
Horror thriller   2014 · Indonesia/Jpn · Colour · 132min

This superior, genre-bending horror thriller is gripping from the brutally stylish start and maintains the tension throughout. Kazuki Kitamura, a self-obsessed Japanese serial killer records and posts his sick handiwork on the net. It's seen by Indonesian journalist Oka Antara, prompting him to turn vigilante. Murdering for entirely different reasons, but connected via their crimes, the two men plunge into a toxic maze of violent self-discovery and destruction. It's disturbing but this sophisticated exploration of primal psychological breakdown bristles with sly wit and exerts a wicked fascination. AJ English, Indonesian, Japanese +subtitles. *DVD* Blu

Kazuki Kitamura *Nomura* • Oka Antara *Bayu* • Luna Maya *Dina* • Rin Takanashi *Hisae* • Ray Sahetapy *Dharma* ■ *Dir* Kimo Stamboel, Timo Tjahjanto • *Scr* Timo Tjahjanto, Takuji Ushiyama, from a story by Tjahjanto, Ushiyama

Killer's Kiss ★★★ 12
Crime drama   1955 · US · BW · 64min

With films such as *Dr Strangelove*, *2001* and *A Clockwork Orange*, Stanley Kubrick became one of the world's most famous directors, but he began with low-budget thrillers. This boxing-gangland story, his second film, has the same streak of fatalism and cynicism that marks his later work. There is a terrific climax, when hero and villain have a fight surrounded by mannequins, plus a spurious ballet sequence featuring Kubrick's second wife Ruth Sobotka. It's a fascinating work, albeit weakly acted and rough at the edges. AT *DVD*

Frank Silvera *Vincent Rapallo* • Jamie Smith *Davy Gordon* • Irene Kane *Gloria Price* • Jerry Jarret *Albert* • Mike Dana *Hoodlum* • Felice Orlandi *Hoodlum* • Ralph Roberts *Hoodlum* • Phil Stevenson *Hoodlum* ■ *Dir* Stanley Kubrick • *Scr* Howard O Sackler, Stanley Kubrick, from a story by Stanley Kubrick

Killers of Kilimanjaro ★★ PG
Adventure   1960 · UK · Colour · 87min

This is a typically schlocky adventure produced by Albert Broccoli, co-written by Richard Maibaum and shot by Ted Moore before they all hit gold with the Bond movies. Robert Taylor, a pricey Hollywood import, plays an engineer who is building a railroad and looking for some missing persons who may or may not have been kidnapped. Lions and natives play the part of bad guys if this is regarded as an African western, which it is. AT

Robert Taylor (1) *Robert Adamson* • Anne Aubrey *Jane Carlton* • John Dimech *Pasha* • Grégoire Aslan *Ben Ahmed* • Anthony Newley *Hooky Hook* • Donald Pleasence *Captain* ■ *Dir* Richard Thorpe • *Scr* John Gilling, Earl Felton, Richard Maibaum, Cyril Hume, from the book *African Bush Adventures* by JA Hunter, Daniel P Mannix

The Killing ★★★★ PG
Thriller   1956 · US · BW · 80min

Stanley Kubrick's third feature is a thriller about a racetrack robbery, but he scrambles the time sequence and follows separate strands of the plot, detailing the planning, the robbery itself and the disastrous aftermath. Kubrick turns a familiar story into a masterly display of technique and a moving study of desperate characters who are in thrall to fate. Kirk Douglas was so impressed by the film that he agreed to star in Kubrick's next project, *Paths of Glory*, the success of which set the seal on Kubrick's reputation. AT *DVD* Blu

Sterling Hayden *Johnny Clay* • Coleen Gray *Fay* • Marie Windsor *Sherry Peatty* • Elisha Cook Jr *George Peatty* • Jay C Flippen *Marvin Unger* • Vince Edwards *Val Cannon* • Ted De Corsia *Randy Kennan* ■ *Dir* Stanley Kubrick • *Scr* Jim Thompson, Stanley Kubrick, from the novel *Clean Break* by Lionel White

A Killing Affair ★★★
Psychological crime thriller   1985 · US · Colour · 100min

This tale of Southern intrigue concerns the murder of Kathy Baker's fickle husband and the arrival of a mysterious stranger (Peter Weller). Is he the one responsible for the deed? Directing for the first time, David Saperstein's everyday story of backward folk in the backwoods has enough surprising twists and turns to keep you guessing. TH

Peter Weller *Baston Morris* • Kathy Baker *Maggie Gresham* • John Glover *Maggie's brother* • Bill Smitrovich *Pink Gresham* ■ *Dir* David Saperstein • *Scr* David Saperstein, from the novel *Monday, Tuesday, Wednesday* by Robert Houston

Killing Bono ★★ 15
Comedy   2010 · UK · Colour · 108min

Gore Vidal's waspish comment "Every time a friend succeeds, a little something in me dies" is the theme of this uneven adaptation of a bestselling memoir by music journalist Neil McCormick (played here by Ben Barnes). In the 1980s, he and his brother struggled to launch a music career, while their school pal Paul Hewson renamed himself Bono and proceeded to become one of pop's true megastars. Sadly, director Nick Hamm seems unable to decide what tone he's aiming for – broad knockabout comedy or bittersweet reminiscence. But there are a few laughs and warm moments to be enjoyed, as well as Pete Postlethwaite's final role as the boys' flamboyantly camp landlord. AS Swearing, sex scenes, drug abuse. *DVD*

Ben Barnes *Neil McCormick* • Robert Sheehan *Ivan McCormick* • Krysten Ritter *Gloria* • Peter Serafinowicz *Hammond* • Pete Postlethwaite *Karl* ■ *Dir* Nick Hamm • *Scr* Dick Clement, Ian La Frenais, Simon Maxwell, from the novel *I Was Bono's Doppelgänger* by Neil McCormick • *Cinematographer* Kieran McGuigan

Killing Dad ★ PG
Comedy   1989 · UK · Colour · 88min

This singularly unimpressive film from Michael Austin fails in its attempts at black comedy. Denholm Elliott plays a depressive drunk returning home to the wife (Anna Massey) and son (Richard E Grant) he deserted 23 years ago. Instead of welcoming his father back with open arms, Grant, also a hopeless case, spends the remainder of the film plotting to kill him. Embarrassing for all concerned – including Julie Walters as Elliott's tarty girlfriend – this sank without a trace of laughter. LH *DVD*

Denholm Elliott *Nathy Berg* • Julie Walters *Judith* • Richard E Grant *Alistair Berg* • Anna Massey *Edith Berg* • Laura Del Sol *Luisa* • Ann Way *Margot* • Jonathan Phillips *Terry* ■ *Dir* Michael Austin • *Scr* Michael Austin, from the novel *Berg* by Ann Quinn

The Killing Fields ★★★★★ 15
Biographical war drama
1984 · UK · Colour · 136min

Few feature films have captured a nation's agony more dramatically than Roland Joffé's *The Killing Fields*. It tells the story of Cambodia's Year Zero, when Pol Pot's Khmer Rouge entered the capital Phnom Penh, emptied it, turned the population into serfs and slaughtered nearly three million of them. To tell the story of this genocide, the picture has one conventional aspect – the perspective of American journalist Sydney Schanberg (Sam Waterston) – and one less so: the experiences of his Cambodian stringer Dith Pran (played by Haing S Ngor, a Cambodian doctor whose own suffering at the time was, if anything, even worse than that depicted in the film). The picture has scale and humanity; the evacuation of the capital is stunning, Ngor's suffering has great emotional force, while Waterston's complex mixture of shame and ambition is compelling. AT Violence, swearing. *DVD* Blu

Sam Waterston *Sydney Schanberg* • Dr Haing S Ngor [Haing S Ngor] *Dith Pran* • John Malkovich *Al Rockoff* • Julian Sands *Jon Swain* • Craig T Nelson *Military attaché* • Spalding Gray *US consul* • Bill Paterson *Dr MacEntire* • Athol Fugard *Dr Sundesval* • Graham Kennedy *Dougal* ■ *Dir* Roland Joffé • *Scr* Bruce Robinson, from the article *The Death and Life of Dith Pran* by Sydney Schanberg

The Killing Floor ★★★ PG
Historical drama
1984 · US · Colour and BW · 117min

Bill Duke makes an excellent directorial debut with this impassioned drama of union

K

and racial tension. It tells the story of a group of black workers fighting for their rights in a Chicago abattoir during the First World War. The then largely unknown cast – which includes Moses Gunn and Alfre Woodard – delivers believable performances, and Duke brings an air of gritty realism to the tale. JF Some violence, swearing.

Damien Leake *Frank Custer* • Alfre Woodard *Mattie Custer* • Clarence Felder *Bill Bremer* • Moses Gunn *Heavy Williams* • Jason Green *Frank Custer Jr* • Jamarr Johnson *Lionel Custer* • Micaeh Johnson *Sarah Custer* • Ernest Rayford *Thomas Joshua* • Stephen Henderson *James Cheeks* • Dennis Farina *Harry Brennan* ■ *Dir* Bill Duke • *Scr* Leslie Lee, from a story by Elsa Rassback, adapted by Ron Milner

Killing Kennedy ★★★
Historical drama 2013 · US · Colour · 87min

If you're a devotee of schlocky, adoring historical bio-dramas, then you'll love this, with Rob Lowe giving his all as President Jack Kennedy. It's a great impersonation, right down to JFK's Boston drawl. *Killing Kennedy* (exec produced by Ridley Scott) canters through JFK's presidency while running a parallel story on assassin Lee Harvey Oswald, who's portrayed as a pesky attention-seeker. A limpid Ginnifer Goodwin plays Jackie Kennedy as the woman history has now decided she was: a sainted drip in a pastel cardigan. AG

Rob Lowe *John F Kennedy* • Ginnifer Goodwin *Jacqueline Kennedy* • Will Rothhaar *Lee Harvey Oswald* • Michelle Trachtenberg *Marina Oswald* • Jack Noseworthy *Bobby Kennedy* • Casey Siemaszko *Jack Ruby* ■ *Dir* Nelson McCormick • *Scr* Kelly Masterson, from the non-fiction book *Killing Kennedy: The End of Camelot* by Bill O'Reilly, Martin Dugard

The Killing Kind ★★ 18
Psychological crime drama
1973 · US · Colour · 90min

In Curtis Harrington's study of disturbed mother–son relationships, John Savage returns home after a spell in prison for a rape he didn't commit and falls into the doting arms of his overbearing mother (Ann Sothern). Unfortunately, her loving care is so suffocating it drives him to take violent revenge on the lawyer (Ruth Roman) responsible for his incarceration and the girl whose evidence put him away. Good performances elevate the familiar *Psycho* shadings in a lethargically paced suspense shocker. AJ

Ann Sothern *Thelma* • John Savage *Terry* • Ruth Roman *Rhea* • Luana Anders *Librarian* • Cindy Williams *Roomer* ■ *Dir* Curtis Harrington • *Scr* Lony Crechales, George Edwards

Killing Me Softly ★ 18
Erotic thriller 2001 · US/UK · Colour · 96min

The English-language debut of acclaimed Chinese director Chen Kaige is just plain laughable. Joseph Fiennes is the stock "mysterious stranger" with whom Heather Graham falls passionately in love after a glance at a pelican crossing. Their explicit lovemaking was clearly intended as a selling point but, like the whole of this whodunnit involving dark secrets, incest and mountaineering, it's utterly fictional. One can only assume that Chen wasn't aware of how clangingly awful the dialogue was. AC

Heather Graham *Alice Loudon* • Joseph Fiennes *Adam Tallis* • Natascha McElhone *Deborah Tallis* • Ulrich Thomsen *Klaus* • Ian Hart *Daniel, senior police officer* • Jason Hughes *Jake* • Kika Markham *Mrs Blanchard* ■ *Dir* Chen Kaige • *Scr* Kara Lindstrom, from the novel *Killing Me Softly* by Nicci French [Sean French, Nicci Gerrard]

Killing Moon ★★ 15
Action thriller 1999 · US/Can · Colour · 86min

This midair TV thriller has a mystery infection sweeping through a flight from Hawaii to Los Angeles, with doctor Penelope Ann Miller racing against time to save those on board. Kim Coates and Daniel Baldwin manage to inject a measure of urgency into the proceedings. DP *DVD*

Kim Coates *Clayton Durrell* • Daniel Baldwin *Frank Conroy* • Penelope Ann Miller *Laura Chadwick* • Daniel Kash *Lt David Thatcher* • Tracey Cook *Roberta* ■ *Dir* John Bradshaw • *Scr* Tony Johnston

The Killing of a Chinese Bookie ★★★★ 15
Crime thriller 1976 · US · Colour · 128min

A powerful performance from Ben Gazzara dominates this convoluted but compelling contemporary *film noir* by John Cassavetes. Los Angeles nightclub owner Gazzara is in debt to the Mob and agrees to dispatch a troublesome bookie (Soto Joe Hugh). The overlong narrative occasionally stumbles over the improvisational techniques Cassavetes used to increase the realism of the piece, and Timothy Agoglia Carey's assassin is far too over the top. However, there is a convincing atmosphere of gangster menace. TH *DVD* 🔵

Ben Gazzara *Cosmo Vitelli* • Timothy Agoglia Carey *[Timothy Carey] Flo* • Azizi Johari *Rachel* • Meade Roberts *Mr Sophistication* • Seymour Cassel *Mort Weil* • Alice Friedland *Sherry* • Donna Gordon *Margo* • Robert Phillips *Phil* • Morgan Woodward *John the boss* • Virginia Carrington *Betty the Mother* • Soto Joe Hugh [Hugh Soto] *Chinese bookie* ■ *Dir/Scr* John Cassavetes

The Killing of John Lennon ★★★★ 15
Drama based on a true story
2006 · UK · Colour · 109min

Mark Chapman decided that John Lennon should die for failing to live by the principles espoused in his song *Imagine*, and also hoped that shooting the former Beatle would alert the world to the message in JD Salinger's novel of teenage alienation, *Catcher in the Rye*. Taking lines verbatim from Chapman's diaries and testimonies, director Andrew Piddington chillingly captures the twisted logic of the security guard who killed his hero in December 1980. Jonas Ball's compelling performance seethes with contradiction and confusion rather than mindless evil, and Roger Eaton's twitchy camerawork reinforces the torment of a dislocated mind. This powerful account of a shocking crime is made all the more disconcerting by being filmed in the actual locations where the events occurred. DP *DVD*

Jonas Ball *Mark David Chapman* • Krisha Fairchild *Mother* • Mie Omori *Gloria* • Robert C Kirk [Robert Kirk] *Detective* • Sofia Dubrawsky *Jude* • Joe Abbate *Cab driver* ■ *Dir/Scr* Andrew Piddington • *Cinematographer* Roger Eaton

The Killing of Sister George ★★★ 18
Drama 1968 · UK · Colour · 139min

An ageing actress is fired arbitrarily and her character killed off from a TV serial. She takes to the bottle as her young female friend (Susannah York) is seduced from her by a rival. Frank Marcus's touching play is not so much touched as bruised by Robert Aldrich's heavy-handed direction, which alienated the actresses during shooting and was disliked. However, this is still a fascinating if flawed look at relationships so close they're weirdly sympathetic. TH *DVD*

Beryl Reid *June Buckridge /"Sister George"* • Susannah York *Alice "Childie" McNaught* • Coral Browne *Mercy Croft* • Ronald Fraser *Leo Lockhart* • Patricia Medina *Betty Thaxter* • Hugh Paddick *Freddie* • Cyril Delevanti *Ted Baker* ■ *Dir* Robert Aldrich • *Scr* Lukas Heller, from the play by Frank Marcus

Killing Oswald ★★★
Documentary
2013 · US · Colour and BW · 102min

Released to coincide with the 50th anniversary of the assassination of John F Kennedy, director Shane O'Sullivan's documentary zeros in on the man held accountable for his killing, Lee Harvey Oswald. Whether Oswald was a "patsy" – as he himself said – or he was the killer, the expert talking heads here (historian David Kaiser, journalist Dick Russell) acknowledge enough of a conspiracy/cover-up to throw

his "lone gunman" status into serious doubt. The archive footage is engrossing, but the extensive re-enactments of Oswald's words and actions tend to create lulls and longueurs. JA

■ *Dir* Shane O'Sullivan

Killing Season ★★ 15
Action thriller 2013 · Bel/US · Colour · 87min

Robert De Niro and John Travolta play two veterans of the Serbian War – De Niro in the frontline of US special forces; Travolta a member of a Serbian death squad – in a gruelling two-hander played out in the remote Appalachian Mountains of the US. Twenty years after the war, Travolta is out to settle old scores, tracking De Niro to his remote mountain retreat. The action is repetitive and rather implausible, but watchable enough if you don't mind seeing two heavyweight stars punching well below their weight. DA *DVD* 🔵

Robert De Niro *Benjamin Ford* • John Travolta *Emil Kovac* • Milo Ventimiglia *Chris Ford* • Elizabeth Olin *Sarah Ford* ■ *Dir* Mark Steven Johnson • *Scr* Evan Daugherty

Killing Them Softly ★★★ 18
Crime thriller 2012 · US · Colour · 93min

Despite some gripping set pieces, this fails to add anything new to the already overpopulated crime genre. It begins with two petty criminals being briefed on a job that involves holding up a high-stakes poker game run by local bigshot Ray Liotta. But the victims bring in enforcer Brad Pitt, who chases down the dim-witted culprits. Pitt is terrific, and his effortlessly cool, world-weary presence makes up for the film's shortcomings, despite his relatively late entry into the proceedings. Otherwise, though, this is a talky and heavy-handed comment on post-financial crisis USA. DW *DVD* 🔵

Brad Pitt *Jackie Cogan* • Ray Liotta *Markie Trattman* • Scoot McNairy *Frankie* • Ben Mendelsohn *Russell* • Richard Jenkins *Driver* • James Gandolfini *Mickey* ■ *Dir* Andrew Dominik • *Scr* Andrew Dominik, from the novel *Cogan's Trade* by George V Higgins

The Killing Time ★ 15
Crime thriller 1987 · US · Colour · 88min

Slack morals, easy murder and brooding visuals are the very essence of classic and modern *film noir*. It's sad to see here, then, that little-known director Rick King – who was probably asked to walk west of California as a result of this effort – has made only a feeble gesture to the genre. As it is, the combination of Kiefer Sutherland, Beau Bridges, deceit and murder produces a film that comes across as too empty and confused to be of any real dramatic or entertainment value. JM Swearing, violence.

Beau Bridges *Sheriff Sam Wayburn* • Kiefer Sutherland *"Brian Mars"* • Wayne Rogers *Jake Winslow* • Joe Don Baker *Sheriff Carl Cunningham* • Michael Madsen *Stu* ■ *Dir* Rick King • *Scr* Don Bohlinger, James Nathan, Bruce Franklin Singer

Killing Time ★ 18
Thriller 1998 · UK · Colour · 85min

This is a lame attempt at transferring Quentin Tarantino-style violence to the north of England. Kendra Torgan plays a supercool Italian hit-woman, waiting for her target to arrive at a Sunderland hotel and assassinating anyone who gets in her way. Two police inspectors arrive to survey the damage. An exploitative, repetitive and pointless thriller. AJ Swearing, violence. *DVD*

Craig Fairbrass *Bryant* • Kendra Torgan *Maria – the assassin* • Peter Harding *Madison* • Neil Armstrong *John* • Ian McLaughlin *George* • Stephen D Thirkeld *Charlie* ■ *Dir* Bharat Nalluri • *Scr* Neil Marshall, Fleur Costello, Caspar Berry

Killing Zoe ★★★ 18
Crime drama 1993 · US · Colour · 91min

Roger Avary co-wrote *Pulp Fiction* with Quentin Tarantino, and his debut feature as a director deals with many of the same

themes. Eric Stoltz is a safecracker visiting his old friend Jean-Hugues Anglade in Paris; before you can say *Reservoir Dogs*, Anglade attempts to hold up a bank while high on booze and drugs. Avary gives his predictable heist tale a fresher edge than normal with some neat camerawork and a smattering of good jokes among the unflinching splatter. Julie Delpy adds a nice twist as a good-hearted prostitute. AJ *DVD* 🔵

Eric Stoltz *Zed* • Julie Delpy *Zoe* • Jean-Hugues Anglade *Eric* • Tai Thai *François* • Bruce Ramsay *Ricardo* • Kario Salem *Jean* • Salvator Xuereb *Claude* • Gary Kemp *Oliver* ■ *Dir/Scr* Roger Avary

The Killing$ of Tony Blair ★★★ 15
Documentary 2016 · UK · Colour · 90min

The career of Tony Blair is scrutinised in this comprehensive documentary, which sets out to prove the former Prime Minister abused his time in office for personal gain, and continues to do so. There's no accusation here that will be unfamiliar to Blair critics. His links with big business, conduct over the Iraq War and his conflicting interests are all covered by a number of journalists, politicians, even his sister-in-law, Lauren. What's unique is that these connections are given a flowing narrative that posits a well-researched argument. A shame, then, that host George Galloway thrusts himself centre stage at moments that don't require his presence. JL Swearing.

George Galloway • Stephen Fry • Clare Short • Will Self • Lauren Booth ■ *Dir* Greg Ward, Sanne van den Bergh

Kim ★★★ U
Adventure 1950 · US · Colour · 112min

In this colourful version of Rudyard Kipling's tale about "the little friend of all the world", Errol Flynn is splendidly tongue-in-cheek as young Kim's idol, Mahbub Ali, the swashbuckling Red Beard. A very American Dean Stockwell is the boy in question, and he does well, with Kim's "game" excellently brought to life by British director Victor Saville. Unfortunately, Saville's plodding pace and Flynn's lack of screen time don't help the heroics. Flaws apart, boys of all ages should enjoy this. TS *DVD*

Errol Flynn *Mahbub Ali, the Red Beard* • Dean Stockwell *Kim* • Paul Lukas *Lama* • Robert Douglas *Colonel Creighton* • Thomas Gomez *Emissary* • Cecil Kellaway *Hurree Chunder* • Arnold Moss *Lurgan Sahib* • Reginald Owen *Father Victor* ■ *Dir* Victor Saville • *Scr* Leon Gordon, Richard Schayer, from the novel by Rudyard Kipling

Kim ★★★ PG
Adventure 1984 · US · Colour · 135min

This is an ambitious but reasonably successful bid to adapt for TV Rudyard Kipling's classic story about a youngster used by British Intelligence in colonial India. Originally filmed in 1950 by Victor Saville, this entertaining remake features Peter O'Toole, excellent as a Buddhist monk, and there's a fine debut from Ravi Sheth as Kim. NF *DVD*

Peter O'Toole *Lama* • Bryan Brown *Mahbub Ali* • Ravi Sheth *Kim* • John Rhys-Davies *Babu* • Julian Glover *Colonel Creighton* • Alfred Burke *Lurgan Kozelski* ■ *Dir* John Davies • *Scr* James Brabazon, from the novel by Rudyard Kipling

Kin ★★ 15
Drama 2000 · S Afr/UK · Colour · 90min

While there's much to admire in Amelia Vincent's stunning widescreen photography, this blend of intimate drama and eco-crusade never escapes from its multitude of contrivances. Miranda Otto plays the game reserve worker whose bid to protect the elephants in the Namibian bush is sidetracked by the demands made by her clergyman brother, Chris Chameleon, and visiting American lawyer, Isaiah Washington. DP

Miranda Otto *Anna* • Isaiah Washington *Stone* • Chris Chameleon *Marius* • Moses Kandjoze *Naniserri* • Ndondoro Hevita *Old man* • Susan Coetzer *Katinka* ■ *Dir/Scr* Elaine Proctor

Kind Hearts and Coronets ★★★★★ U
Classic black comedy 1949 · UK · BW · 101min

Arguably the finest of the Ealing comedies, Robert Hamer's superb *comédie noire* has a deliciously witty script that slips smoothly between dastardly deaths in the guise of a self-satisfied memoir. However, the picture is elevated to greatness by the quality of its playing. Obviously, Alec Guinness, who essays the eight doomed D'Ascoynes, merits every superlative lavished on a performance of astounding versatility and virtuosity. But let's not forget Dennis Price as the ceaselessly inventive killer, and Joan Greenwood and Valerie Hobson as the vamp and the vestal in his life, who are brilliant. DP *DVD Blu*

Dennis Price *Louis Mazzini/Narrator* • Valerie Hobson *Edith D'Ascoyne* • Joan Greenwood *Sibella* • Alec Guinness *Duke/Banker/Parson/General/Admiral/Young Ascoyne D'Ascoyne/Young Henry/Lady Agatha D'Ascoyne* • Audrey Fildes *Mama* • Miles Malleson *Hangman* • Clive Morton *Prison governor* • John Penrose *Lionel* • Cecil Ramage *Crown counsel* • Hugh Griffith *Lord High Steward* ■ *Dir* Robert Hamer • *Scr* Robert Hamer, John Dighton, from the novel *Israel Rank* by Roy Horniman • *Producer* Michael Balcon

Kind Lady ★★
Period drama 1951 · US · BW · 77min

This remake of the 1935 film is here turned into an Edwardian costume drama, scripted by a trio that included Edward Chodorov, author of the original Broadway play. More glossy than its predecessor and directed by John Sturges with a keener sense of tension, it stars Ethel Barrymore as the elderly woman who is unwittingly preyed upon for her wealth. Unfortunately, classical actor Maurice Evans lacks the smooth and persuasive looks and personality of Basil Rathbone, but the movie is nonetheless moderately effective. RK

Ethel Barrymore *Mary Herries* • Maurice Evans *Henry Elcott* • Angela Lansbury *Mrs Edwards* • Keenan Wynn *Edwards* • John Williams *Mr Foster* • Doris Lloyd *Rose* • Betsy Blair *Ada Elcott* ■ *Dir* John Sturges • *Scr* Jerry Davis, Edward Chodorov, Charles Bennett, from the play by Edward Chodorov, from the story *The Silver Casket* by Hugh Walpole

A Kind of Hush ★★★ 15
Drama 1998 · UK · Colour · 91min

Theatre director Brian Stirner makes his screen debut with this uncompromising study of child abuse and its consequences. While the action deals with the revenge wrought by a bunch of teenagers on their persecutors, the story is as much about the indomitability of the human spirit as it is about justifying vengeance. The performances of the inexperienced cast bristle with anger, but it's the wiser counsel of Roy Hudd that allows them to salvage some dignity from their indignation. DP Swearing.

Harley Smith *Stu* • Marcella Plunkett *Kathleen* • Ben Roberts *Simon* • Paul Williams *Mick* • Nathan Constance *Tony* • Peter Saunders *Wivva* • Mike Fibbens *Fish* • Roy Hudd *Chef* ■ *Dir* Brian Stirner • *Scr* Brian Stirner, from the novel *Getting Even* by Richard Johnson

A Kind of Loving ★★★★ 12
Drama 1962 · UK · BW · 107min

Unlike the majority of other "grim up North" dramas that found critical favour during the social realist or kitchen sink phase of British film-making, John Schlesinger's debut feature is about making the most of life rather than carping on about the colour of the grass on the other side of the fence. Crisply adapted by Keith Waterhouse and Willis Hall, the film is like a scrapbook of typical human experience, with Schlesinger's eye for detail and his persuasive storytelling style creating characters who could have lived next door to you. Alan Bates and June Ritchie are

excellent, but Thora Hird is exceptional. DP Nudity. *DVD Blu*

Alan Bates *Vic Brown* • June Ritchie *Ingrid Rothwell* • Thora Hird *Mrs Rothwell* • Bert Palmer *Mr Brown* • Gwen Nelson *Mrs Brown* • Malcolm Patton *Jim Brown* • Pat Keen *Christine* • David Mahlowe *David* • Jack Smethurst *Conroy* • James Bolam *Jeff* • Michael Deacon *Les* ■ *Dir* John Schlesinger • *Scr* Willis Hall, Keith Waterhouse, from the novel by Stan Barstow

Kindergarten Cop ★★★ 15
Action comedy 1990 · US · Colour · 106min

This undemanding picture proves that Arnold Schwarzenegger can do comedy, providing he doesn't try too hard. As the cop forced to teach toddlers while searching for a crook's missing son, Schwarzenegger is at his best jousting with the little tykes. The romance with Penelope Ann Miller is less convincing, but not over-intrusive. Richard Tyson and Carroll Baker make almost pantomimic baddies, but this isn't really a children's film. A follow-up with Dolph Lundgren went straight to DVD in 2016. DP Violence, swearing. *DVD*

Arnold Schwarzenegger *Detective John Kimble* • Penelope Ann Miller *Joyce* • Pamela Reed *Phoebe O'Hara* • Linda Hunt *Miss Schowski* • Richard Tyson *Cullen Crisp* • Carroll Baker *Eleanor Crisp* • Cathy Moriarty *Sylvester's mother* ■ *Dir* Ivan Reitman • *Scr* Murray Salem, Herschel Weingrod, Timothy Harris, from a story by Murray Salem

The Kindred ★ 18
Science-fiction horror thriller 1986 · US · Colour · 88min

Once hailed as one of America's greatest actors, Rod Steiger suffered a career breakdown in the mid-1980s, appearing in straight-to-video horror trash, of which this is fairly typical. The man who shared screen time with Brando in *On the Waterfront* is here reduced to hamming it up as a mad scientist in a fright wig, whose experiments result in the inevitable things in the cellar. Totally uninvolving from start to finish. RS

David Allen Brooks *John Hollins* • Amanda Pays *Melissa Leftridge* • Talia Balsam *Sharon Raymond* • Kim Hunter *Amanda Hollins* • Rod Steiger *Dr Phillip Lloyd* ■ *Dir* Jeffrey Obrow, Stephen Carpenter • *Scr* Stephen Carpenter, Jeffrey Obrow, John Penney, Earl Ghaffari, Joseph Stefano

The King ★★★★ 15
Drama 2005 · US/UK · Colour · 99min

Gael García Bernal stars as a young man newly discharged from the navy who arrives in a Texas city to find William Hurt, the father he's never met. But Hurt has become a prominent churchman with a family of his own and wants nothing to do with his illegitimate son. Perhaps out of spite, perhaps out of a genuine need for love, Bernal then begins a covert affair with his half-sister (Pell James) who's unaware of his actual identity. This unsettling drama evolves into a nicely nasty slice of southern gothic. LF Sex scenes. *DVD*

Gael García Bernal *Elvis Valderez* • William Hurt *Pastor David Sandow* • Paul Dano *Paul Sandow* • Pell James *Malerie Sandow* • Laura Harring *Twyla Sandow* • Veronica Bernal *Elvis's girl* ■ *Dir* James Marsh • *Scr* James Marsh, Milo Addica

King: a Filmed Record... Montgomery to Memphis ★★★
Biographical documentary 1970 · US · BW · 177min

This fine documentary about Martin Luther King is co-directed by Hollywood heavyweights Joseph L Mankiewicz and Sidney Lumet. Using quality archive news footage, the film looks at the latter part of King's life, from his frontline civil rights activism of the mid-1950s, right through to his assassination in April 1968. The linking sequences are narrated by a host of film luminaries and admirers of King, including Paul Newman, Joanne Woodward and James Earl Jones and Sidney Poitier. There's no question who the real star is, though. DA

Paul Newman *Narrator* • Joanne Woodward *Narrator* • Ruby Dee *Narrator* • James Earl Jones *Narrator* • Clarence Williams III *Narrator* • Burt Lancaster *Narrator* • Ben Gazzara *Narrator* • Charlton Heston *Narrator* • Harry Belafonte *Narrator* • Sidney Poitier *Narrator* ■ *Dir* Sidney Lumet, Joseph L Mankiewicz

King and Country ★★★ PG
First World War drama 1964 · UK · BW · 82min

Tom Courtenay is a hapless private who has had enough of trench warfare and walks away from his post. Naturally he's caught, and Dirk Bogarde is ordered to defend him at his court martial. This moving – if sometimes pompous – tale is really an allegory about the British class system, bearing a striking resemblance to Stanley Kubrick's *Paths of Glory* (1957). AT *DVD*

Dirk Bogarde *Captain Hargreaves* • Tom Courtenay *Private Arthur Hamp* • Leo McKern *Captain O'Sullivan* • Barry Foster *Lieutenant Webb* • James Villiers *Captain Midgley* • Peter Copley *Colonel* • Barry Justice *Lieutenant Prescott* ■ *Dir* Joseph Losey • *Scr* Evan Jones, from the play *Hamp* by John Wilson, from a story by James Lansdale Hodson

The King and I ★★★★ U
Period musical 1956 · US · Colour · 127min

Yul Brynner re-created his Broadway King for posterity in this faithful adaptation of Rodgers and Hammerstein's marvellous musical success about English governess Anna Leonowens and her sexless romance with the King of Siam. Brynner is magnificent and he deservedly picked up a best actor Oscar for what is unquestionably a great performance. As Mrs Anna, Deborah Kerr is both resolute and touching, with an unbilled Marni Nixon dubbing her singing voice. Unfortunately, 20th Century-Fox's use of its own DeLuxe Color lets down the production design, and a stronger director than Walter Lang would have been beneficial. TS *DVD*

Deborah Kerr *Anna Leonowens* • Yul Brynner *The King* • Rita Moreno *Tuptim* • Martin Benson *Kralahome* • Terry Saunders *Lady Thiang* • Rex Thompson *Louis Leonowens* • Carlos Rivas *Lun Tha* • Patrick Adiarte *Prince Chulalongkorn* • Alan Mowbray *British ambassador* • Geoffrey Toone *Ramsay* ■ *Dir* Walter Lang • *Scr* Ernest Lehman, from the musical by Oscar Hammerstein II, Richard Rodgers, from the book *Anna and the King of Siam* by Margaret Landon • *Cinematographer* Leon Shamroy • *Costume Designer* Irene Sharaff

The King and I ★★ U
Animated musical 1999 · US · Colour · 85min

This breezy cartoon version of Rodgers and Hammerstein's musical may be no threat to Yul Brynner and Deborah Kerr in the original, but it introduces youngsters to some classic tunes. In an effort to make the complex plot more accessible to younger viewers, the film is rather dubiously enlivened by some new personalities – a black panther, a fire-breathing dragon and chubby Master Little. TH *DVD*

Miranda Richardson *Anna Leonowens* • Christiane Noll *Anna Leonowens (singing)* • Martin Vidnovic *King of Siam* • Ian Richardson *Kralahome* • Darrell Hammond *Master Little* • Allen D Hong *Prince Chululongkorn* • David Burnham *Prince Chululongkorn (singing)* • Armi Arabe *Tuptim* ■ *Dir* Richard Rich • *Scr* Peter Bakalian, David Seidler, Jacqueline Feather, Arthur Rankin [Arthur Rankin Jr], from the musical by Richard Rodgers, Oscar Hammerstein II

The King and Queen of Moonlight Bay ★★
Drama 2003 · US · Colour · 95min

No, this isn't a reunion for Doris Day and Gordon MacRae after their folksy 1951 musical, but Michael de Guzman's adaptation of his own novel about a teenager trying to forge a relationship with her estranged father. Set over a summer in Arizona, the largely melodramatic action centres on the optimistic Kristen Bell and her dad, handyman Tim Matheson, an alcoholic who fights shy of commitment to his long-suffering girlfriend (Sean Young). It's predictable stuff, but subplots involving platitude-spouting

academic Ed Asner and boy-next-door Bug Hall just about prevent things from becoming too syrupy. DP

Tim Matheson *Al Dodge* • Kristen Bell *Alison Dodge* • Sean Young *Sandy Bateman* • Ed Asner [Edward Asner] *Auggie* • Bug Hall *Tim Spooner* • David Correia *Ramirez* ■ *Dir* Sam Pillsbury • *Scr* Michael de Guzman, from his novel

The King and the Mockingbird ★★★★ U
Animated fairy tale 1980 · Fr · Colour · 80min

The production history of this sublime animation is almost as engrossing as the film itself, which *Spirited Away* director Hayao Miyazaki cites as a major influence on his work. Thirty years passed before French director Paul Grimault managed to complete the film, adapted, with poet Jacques Prévert, from a Hans Christian Anderson fable. It's a whimsical account of a tyrannical king who threatens to come between a beautiful shepherdess and a chimney sweep who both come to life from paintings that hang on the palace walls. Kids accustomed to the pacey, pixelated style of modern animation may find the action a tad slow, but traditionalists will relish the detail. DP French +subtitles. *DVD*

Jean Martin *The bird* • Pascal Mazzotti *The King* • Raymond Bussières *Chief of Police* • Agnès Viala *The Shepherdess* • Renaud Marx *Chimney sweep* ■ *Dir* Paul Grimault • *Scr* Paul Grimault, Jacques Prévert, from the fairy tale *The Shepherdess and the Chimney Sweep* by Hans Christian Andersen

King Arthur ★★★ 12
Period action adventure 2004 · US/Ire/UK · Colour · 120min

Antoine Fuqua's film is less a re-imagining of the Arthurian legend and more a Dark Ages-set remake of *The Magnificent Seven*. Most of the traditional elements are missing – no wizardry, no Camelot, no love triangle – and instead we get Arthur (a subdued Clive Owen) recast as a Roman captain posted to Hadrian's Wall and Guinevere (Keira Knightley) as a woad-wearing warrior. The rousing death-or-glory speeches and the obligatory love scene fall flat, and it's also a shame the mystical nature of the original myth is dismissed. But there's still much pleasure to be had in the company of the charismatic knights and from the convincingly staged battles. GM Violence, sex scenes. *DVD Blu*

Clive Owen *Arthur* • Keira Knightley *Guinevere* • Stellan Skarsgård *Cerdic* • Ray Winstone *Bors* • Ioan Gruffudd *Lancelot* • Mads Mikkelsen *Tristram* • Stephen Dillane *Merlin* • Hugh Dancy *Galahad* ■ *Dir* Antoine Fuqua • *Scr* David Franzoni

King Arthur Was a Gentleman ★★ U
Comedy 1942 · UK · BW · 94min

It was once said that the Nazis thought they would win the Second World War because Britain's most effective men of action were nitwit comedians like Will Hay and George Formby. Over 50 years on, it's not easy to see how such tepid capers could have boosted morale. Yet this is as likeable as any flag-waving comedy, with Arthur Askey as the cheery Tommy who is convinced he has found King Arthur's sword Excalibur and is invincible. This could have done with fewer songs and more gags. DP *DVD*

Arthur Askey *Arthur King* • Evelyn Dall *Susan Ashley* • Anne Shelton *Gwen Duncannon* • Max Bacon *Maxie* • Jack Train *Jack* • Peter Graves (1) *Lance* ■ *Dir* Marcel Varnel • *Scr* Val Guest, Marriott Edgar

King Boxer ★★★★ 15
Martial arts adventure 1972 · HK · Colour · 101min

This breathless Shaw Brothers movie cemented the demand for martial arts cinema among western audiences. All the genre staples are present and correct: the pure-hearted hero, a jealous rival, their exacting master, plus a fiendish baddie and his curiously haired henchmen. The sparring becomes increasingly violent as

K

the film builds to its exciting finale, with star Lo Lieh's glowing fists of fury dodging samurai slicing, crippling beatings and eye-gougings aplenty. A recommended stop off for fans of Far Eastern cinema. JH Mandarin +subtitles. Strong violence **DVD**

Lo Lieh *Chao Chih-Hao* • Tien Feng *Meng Tung-Shun* • Fang Mien *Sun Hsin-Pei* • Wang Ping *Sung Ying Ying* ▪ *Dir* Chang Chang Ho [Jeong Chang-Hwa] • *Scr* Chiang Yang

King Creole ★★★★★ PG
Musical   1958 · US · BW · 110min

This is arguably Elvis Presley's best film, and certainly his best acting performance. It's a tough New Orleans-set crime drama directed by Hollywood maestro Michael Curtiz, who invests the nightclub scenes with the kind of élan that turned the not dissimilar *Casablanca* into a classic. Elvis has tremendous support from a terrific back-up cast, notably from Walter Matthau as a reptilian villain, and from Carolyn Jones as a long-suffering moll. The songs are knockouts too, especially the Dixie-influenced title number. Don't miss. TS **DVD**

Elvis Presley *Danny Fisher* • Carolyn Jones *Ronnie* • Dolores Hart *Nellie* • Dean Jagger *Mr Fisher* • Liliane Montevecchi *"Forty" Nina* • Walter Matthau *Maxie Fields* • Jan Shepard *Mimi Fisher* • Paul Stewart *Charlie LeGrand* • Vic Morrow *Shark* ▪ *Dir* Michael Curtiz • *Scr* Herbert Baker, Michael Vincente Gazzo, from the novel *A Stone for Danny Fisher* by Harold Robbins • *Music* Walter Scharf

King David ★★ PG
Biblical epic   1985 · US · Colour · 109min

Lavish visuals and sonorous music (by Carl Davis) – both designed to match the grandeur of the subject – are badly wasted by director Bruce Beresford. In his hands, and after a promising canter through David's childhood, the spectacle quickly gets bogged down in tedious dialogue and, as the narrative begins to falter, Richard Gere (as the hero) is reduced to acting by gesture. Yet Edward Woodward, in the role of King Saul, transcends these flaws with charisma and substance. JM

Richard Gere *David* • Edward Woodward *Saul* • Alice Krige *Bathsheba* • Denis Quilley *Samuel* • Niall Buggy *Nathan* • Cherie Lunghi *Michal* • Hurd Hatfield *Ahimilech* ▪ *Dir* Bruce Beresford • *Scr* Andrew Birkin, James Costigan, from a story by James Costigan

A King in New York ★★★ U
Satirical comedy   1957 · UK · BW · 100min

An embittered Charles Chaplin all but abdicates as the king of comedy for his penultimate film, mirroring the loathing he felt for the way America had treated him in real life. As the deposed monarch of Estrovia he seeks sanctuary in the United States, where he finds himself at the mercy of both the House Un-American Activities Committee and advertising executive Dawn Addams. Made in Britain (the film's New York setting is unconvincing), there are some occasionally shrewd insights, but the scenes using a young boy to mouth Chaplin's own disgust with the USA are totally embarrassing. TH **DVD**

Charles Chaplin *King Shadhov* • Dawn Addams *Ann Kay* • Oliver Johnston *The Ambassador* • Maxine Audley *Queen Irene* • Harry Green *Lawyer Green* • Phil Brown *Headmaster* • John McLaren *Macabee Senior* • Sidney James *Mr Johnson* ▪ *Dir/Scr* Charles Chaplin

The King Is Alive ★★ 15
Drama   2000 · Den/US/Swe/Nor/Fin · Colour · 105min

Making several radical departures from the supposedly sacrosanct "vow of chastity", the fourth Dogme feature lacks the dramatic spark to match its audiovisual audacity. By working in English and outside Denmark, director Kristian Levring demonstrates a willingness to take chances. But the tale of a busload of passengers stranded in the African wilderness, who agree to enact *King Lear* while waiting for help is as predictable as a disaster movie, with each caricatured character eventually revealing their inevitable flaw. Jennifer

Leigh works the hardest to achieve the least within a committed ensemble, all of whom come to resemble specimens in a cinematic laboratory. DP **DVD**

David Bradley (2) *Henry* • Jennifer Jason Leigh *Gina* • Janet McTeer *Liz* • Miles Anderson *Jack* • Romane Bohringer *Catherine* • Bruce Davison *Ray* • Lia Williams *Amanda* ▪ *Dir* Kristian Levring • *Scr* Kristian Levring, Anders Thomas Jensen

King Jack ★★★★ 15
Coming-of-age drama   2015 · US · Colour · 80min

The anti-hero in Felix Thompson's debut feature may be an outsider – bullied by his older brother for having been their absent father's favourite – but there's nothing nerdy about 15-year-old Jack (Charlie Plummer), who is first seen spraying offensive graffiti on the home of the class bully. Sunnily photographed in the workaday Hudson Valley suburbs by Brandon Roots, this may stick close to convention, but it also offers an authentic insight into the quotidian adolescent experience. Plummer leads an admirably natural cast with an affecting blend of swagger and vulnerability. DP Swearing, violence

Charlie Plummer *Jack* • Cory Nichols *Ben* • Christian Madsen *Tom* • Danny Flaherty *Shane* • Erin Davie *Karen* ▪ *Dir/Scr* Felix Thompson • *Cinematographer* Brandon Roots

LANDMARK FILM
This mythic monster movie becomes the one by which others are measured

King Kong ★★★★★ PG
Classic fantasy adventure   1933 · US · BW · 100min

Arguably *the* monster movie of all time, this abiding take on *Beauty and the Beast* has a mythic power that belies its years. At its heart is the amazing ape (and dinosaur) animation of Willis O'Brien, his cutting-edge model work the CGI of its day, but it's the tragic story that stays etched on the memory. Robert Armstrong's Hollywood film-maker imperils starlet Fay Wray on a prehistoric island in his bid to turn a local legend into a hit on celluloid. Taking the giant gorilla Kong back to civilisation for entrepreneurial gain is bad for all concerned, not least the captive creature who ends his life atop the Empire State Building in one of cinema's greatest climaxes. This thrilling adventure offers an early eco-message. AC **DVD**

Fay Wray *Ann Darrow* • Robert Armstrong *Carl Denham* • Bruce Cabot *John Driscoll* • Frank Reicher *Capt Englehorn* • Sam Hardy *Charles Weston* • Noble Johnson *Native chief* ▪ *Dir* Merian C Cooper, Ernest B Schoedsack • *Scr* James Creelman, Ruth Rose, from an idea by Merian C Cooper, Edgar Wallace • *Cinematographers* Eddie Linden, Vernon Walker, JO Taylor • *Music* Max Steiner • *Special Effects* Willis O'Brien • *Sound Effects* Murray Spivack

King Kong ★★★ PG
Fantasy adventure   1976 · US · Colour · 129min

Rather than over-respectfully pay homage to the 1933 classic, producer Dino De Laurentiis struck box-office gold by dragging the ape-meets-girl fable into the disaster-movie age. Stop-motion effects are upgraded to a blend of man-in-a-suit and expressive full-scale face and hand models, while Jessica Lange plays the Fay Wray role with a valiant attempt at empathy. It's colourful and fun, and John Barry's score hits all the right melodramatic notes. AC **DVD**

Jessica Lange *Dwan* • Jeff Bridges *Jack Prescott* • Charles Grodin *Fred Wilson* • John Randolph *Captain Ross* • René Auberjonois *Bagley* • Ed Lauter *Carnahan* • Rick Baker *King Kong* ▪ *Dir* John Guillermin • *Scr* Lorenzo Semple Jr, from the 1933 film • *Music* John Barry (1)

King Kong Lives ★ PG
Fantasy adventure   1986 · US · Colour · 100min

As if the 1976 remake wasn't bad enough, producer Dino de Laurentiis and director John Guillermin sink to even more ludicrous depths with this awful sequel. The giant ape didn't die when he fell off the World Trade Center ten years earlier, and now Linda

Hamilton leads a surgical team attempting to revive him with a giant artificial heart. Meanwhile, back in the jungle, Brian Kerwin has discovered a female Kong. This couldn't be any worse. AJ **DVD**

Brian Kerwin *Hank Mitchell* • Linda Hamilton *Amy Franklin* • Peter Elliot *King Kong* • George Yiasoumi *Lady Kong* • John Ashton *Colonel Nevitt* ▪ *Dir* John Guillermin • *Scr* Steven Pressfield, Ronald Shusett, from characters by Merian C Cooper, Edgar Wallace

King Kong ★★★★ 12
Period fantasy adventure   2005 · NZ/US · Colour and BW · 179min

Director Peter Jackson lovingly honours the 1933 original, expertly re-creating exact sequences while embellishing them astutely to recapture its thrilling escapism for modern audiences. Set in the same year that the quintessential monster movie was made, the story sees film-maker Jack Black save Naomi Watts from the Depression breadline to star in his latest adventure that's to be shot on a mysterious island. Just as a shipboard romance is kindled between Watts and scriptwriter Adrien Brody, she is kidnapped by nasty natives who offer her to their living god, Kong. Where this remake impresses is with the poignantly fleshed out relationship that develops between Watts and her brilliantly executed CGI jungle protector. The length is extreme, but this is sensational entertainment. AJ Violence. **DVD** **Blu-ray**

Naomi Watts *Ann Darrow* • Jack Black *Carl Denham* • Adrien Brody *Jack Driscoll* • Thomas Kretschmann *Captain Englehorn* • Colin Hanks *Preston* • Jamie Bell *Jimmy* • Evan Parke *Hayes* • Andy Serkis *Kong/Lumpy the cook* • Kyle Chandler *Bruce Baxter* ▪ *Dir* Peter Jackson • *Scr* Peter Jackson, Fran Walsh, Philippa Boyens, from the 1933 film • *Music* James Newton Howard

King Kong vs Godzilla ★★★ PG
Monster horror   1962 · Jpn · Colour · 87min

Based on an early draft script by *King Kong* creator Willis O'Brien, and completely rewritten by the Japanese as a co-starring vehicle for their own monster hero Godzilla, director Inoshiro Honda's clash of the pop culture titans works more as an engagingly silly comedy more than a fully-fledged fantasy. After defeating a giant octopus threatening Japanese fishermen, Kong is drugged with narcotic berries and flown to Tokyo. Meanwhile Godzilla is woken up from frozen hibernation by an atomic sub and heads for the capital, where he battles Kong at Mount Fuji. Additional footage, starring Michael Keith and others, was directed by Thomas Montgomery for the US market. AJ In Japanese. **DVD**

Michael Keith *Eric Carter* • James Yagi *Yataka Omura* • Tadao Takashima *O Sakurai* • Mie Hama *Fumiko Sakurai* • Yu Fujiki *Kinzaburo Furue* ▪ *Dir* Inoshiro Honda • *Scr* Bruce Howard, Paul Mason, Shinichi Sekizawa, from a story by Willis O'Brien

King Lear ★★ PG
Tragedy   1970 · UK/Den · BW · 131min

If this sole attempt is anything to go by, Peter Brook's concept of filming Shakespeare was to de-emphasise the text by burying it within a phalanx of fluid camera movements and abrupt close-ups. Fortunately, Paul Scofield gives an astonishingly insightful and intense performance. Indeed, it's so good that it almost makes you forget the forbidding Danish backdrops and the directorial eccentricities. The supporting cast also strives to rescue this from the carnage. DP **DVD**

Paul Scofield *King Lear* • Irene Worth *Goneril* • Annelise Gabold *Cordelia* • Susan Engel *Regan* • Alan Webb *Duke of Gloucester* • Patrick Magee *Duke of Cornwall* • Cyril Cusack *Duke of Albany* • Jack MacGowran *The Fool* ▪ *Dir* Peter Brook • *Scr* Peter Brook, from the play by William Shakespeare

King Lear ★★★★
Tragedy   1970 · USSR · BW · 138min

Six years after his extraordinary adaptation of *Hamlet* (and, ironically, the same year that Peter Brook released his own version of the play), Grigori Kozintsev returned to Shakespeare for this dark tale of misplaced trust and filial treachery. Working from Boris Pasternak's translation (which is lost in the Bardic subtitles), Kozintsev conceived a visually arresting drama that's shot through with political folly and human suffering. To that end, he's superbly served by Juri Jarvet, who plays Lear less as a crumbling wreck than an intemperate tyrant, supported only by Oleg Dal's truly touching Fool against Elsa Radzinya and Galina Volchek's vicious termagants. DP Russian +subtitles.

Juri Jarvet *Lear* • Elsa Radzinya [Elsa Radzin] *Goneril* • Galina Volchek *Regan* • Valentina Shendrikova *Cordelia* • Karl Sebris *Earl of Gloucester* • Regimantis Adomaitis *Edmund* • Oleg Dal *Fool* ▪ *Dir* Grigori Kozintsev • *Scr* Grigori Kozintsev, from the Russian translation of William Shakespeare's play by Boris Pasternak

King Lear – Fear and Loathing ★ 15
Experimental drama   1987 · US/Fr · Colour · 90min

This isn't William Shakespeare's *King Lear*, or even Jean-Luc Godard's *King Lear*. It's just a self-indulgent mess about the idea of making a movie of *King Lear*. The project started out years before, scripted by Norman Mailer and starring Marlon Brando as a Mafia leader named Lear and Woody Allen as his Fool. Lee Marvin, Orson Welles and Dustin Hoffman were all involved at some point. By the time Godard got around to making it, he still had the clout to lure some very impressive names. AT

Burgess Meredith *Don Learo* • Peter Sellars *William Shakespeare Jr, the Fifth* • Molly Ringwald *Cordelia* • Jean-Luc Godard *Professor* • Woody Allen *Mr Alien* • Norman Mailer • Kate Mailer • Leos Carax *Edgar* ▪ *Dir* Jean-Luc Godard • *Scr* Jean-Luc Godard, from the play *King Lear* by William Shakespeare

King of Burlesque ★★★
Musical comedy   1936 · US · BW · 85min

This rousing vehicle couples two great 1930s stars at differing stages of their careers: Warner Baxter, top-billed as the titular monarch, and 20th Century-Fox's newest blonde star Alice Faye, singing her way to success with such terrific numbers as *I'm Shooting High*. The plot is familiar as Baxter marries socialite Mona Barrie and finds that burlesque, Faye and Park Avenue don't mix, but who cares when it's all done with such spit and polish? There's some really sharp dialogue and a rare appearance in features from the great Fats Waller. TS

Warner Baxter *Kerry Bolton* • Alice Faye *Pat Doran* • Jack Oakie *Joe Cooney* • Arline Judge *Connie* • Mona Barrie *Rosalind Cleve* • Fats Waller *Ben* ▪ *Dir* Sidney Lanfield • *Scr* Gene Markey, Harry Tugend, James Seymour, from a story by Vina Delmar

The King of Comedy ★★★★★ PG
Comedy drama   1983 · US · Colour · 104min

Though a box-office failure, Martin Scorsese's black comedy is now considered by many to be his unsung masterpiece. Of all the director's outings with sparring partner Robert De Niro, this is the strangest. De Niro plays an aspiring stand-up comedian and stalker-in-waiting who dreams of fronting his own TV show, rehearses for this moment of glory in his mother's basement and spends half his life waiting, symbolically, in reception. It's a powerful, complex performance, one that carries the story from farce into tragedy with ease, while Jerry Lewis is magnificent as the chilly old pro and chat-show king. AC Some swearing. **DVD** **Blu-ray**

Robert De Niro *Rupert Pupkin* • Jerry Lewis *Jerry Langford* • Diahnne Abbott *Rita* • Sandra Bernhard *Masha* • Cathy Scorsese *Dolores* • Catherine Scorsese *Mrs Pupkin* • Leslie Levinson • Roberta Posner • Martin Scorsese *TV director* •

Ed Herlihy · Liza Minnelli · Victor Borge · Tony Randall ■ *Dir* Martin Scorsese · *Scr* Paul D Zimmerman

King of Devil's Island ★★★ 12

Period drama based on a true story
2010 · Nor/Fr/Swe/Pol · Colour · 111min

The title suggests a story about French Guiana's notorious correctional facility, yet this true-life tale of a juvenile detention centre takes place on Bastoy Island, off the coast of Norway. It's set in 1915, when the arrival of two new inmates (Benjamin Helstad and Magnus Langlete, both exceptional) sets off a chain of events that tests the iron grip of prison governor Stellan Skarsgård (persuasive as ever). Marius Holst's film is certainly well made, but perhaps follows the format set by familiar clash-with-authority sagas like *Cool Hand Luke* and *Scum* rather too closely. However, the action does build slowly towards a convincingly brutal conclusion. TJ Swedish, Norwegian +subtitles. Some violence. *DVD* *BL*

Benjamin Helstad *Erling* · Trond Nilssen *Olav* · Stellan Skarsgård *Hakon* · Kristoffer Joner *Brathen* ■ *Dir* Marius Holst · *Scr* Dennis Magnusson, Eric Schmid, from a story by Mette Marit Bolstad, Lars Saabye Christensen

King of Hearts ★★★★

First World War comedy drama
1966 · Fr/It · Colour · 101min

One of the lesser luminaries of the French New Wave, Philippe de Broca scored a cult hit with this atmospheric black comedy set during the First World War. Alan Bates is superb as the Scot who comes across a small town earmarked for blanket bombing. The satirical swipes at monarchy, patriotism and war are played down in favour of whimsical comedy, as the townsfolk, each one a former asylum patient, urge Bates to become their king. The French cast is exceptional. DP English, French, German +subtitles.

Alan Bates *Private Charles Plumpick* · Pierre Brasseur *General Geranium* · Jean-Claude Brialy *The Duke aka Le Duc de Trèfle* · Geneviève Bujold *Coquelicot* · Françoise Christophe *Duchess* · Julien Guiomar *Bishop Daisy aka Monseigneur Marguerite* · Michel Serrault *Crazy barber* ■ *Dir* Philippe de Broca · *Scr* Daniel Boulanger, from an idea by Maurice Bessy

The King of Jazz ★★★

Musical revue
1930 · US · Colour · 93min

Considering the array of talent involved and the fact the film was shot in the expensive two-tone Technicolor process – including the first Technicolor animation – it's amazing that Universal entrusted this prestige project to debutant director John Murray Anderson, the only film he ever directed. However, he produces a stylish revue, showcasing the talents of songwriters Jack Yellen and Milton Ager, bandleader Paul Whiteman and first-timer Bing Crosby as a singer. It was still a spectacular flop. DP

John Boles · Laura La Plante · Jeanette Loff · Walter Brennan · Bing Crosby ■ *Dir* John Murray Anderson · *Scr* Charles MacArthur, Harry Ruskin, Edward T Lowe Jr · *Animation* Walter Lantz, Bill Nolan

The King of Kings ★★★★ PG

Silent biblical drama
1927 · US · BW and Colour · 112min

Complete with bookend sections in Technicolor (a lavish extravagance at the time), this own version of *The Ten Commandments* had a biblical story been told on such a scale as this awesome retelling of the life of Christ. HB Warner might not have had the presence of Jeffrey Hunter (who would play the role in Nicholas Ray's 1961 remake), but he looks suitably spiritual, particularly during the harrowing Crucifixion scenes. Ernest Torrence impresses as Peter and Joseph Schildkraut is equally good as Judas. Typically excessive, but truly reverential, this is a monument to the splendour of silent film. DP *DVD*

HB Warner *Jesus, the Christ* · Dorothy Cumming *Mary, the Mother* · Ernest Torrence *Peter* · Joseph Schildkraut *Judas* · James Neill *James* · Joseph Striker *John* · Robert Edeson *Matthew* · Sidney D'Albrook *Thomas* · David Imboden *Andrew* · Jacqueline Logan *Mary Magdalene* ■ *Dir* Cecil B DeMil e · *Scr* Jeanie Macpherson

King of Kings ★★★★ U

Biblical epic
1961 · US · Colour · 153min

Films that feature portrayals of Jesus Christ generally have a bad reputation. This is an exception, despite the idiotic hype that flowed when it was made. Jeffrey Hunter, who plays Jesus, was forbidden to give interviews, his chest and armpits were shaved and the film was dubbed "I Was a Teenage Jesus", because Nicholas Ray had also directed James Dean in *Rebel without a Cause*. To compensate for some weak performances and for some lapses into high camp (notably Frank Thring's pouting Herod Antipas), there is a marvellous score, Orson Welles's narration and the lavish design that one associates with producer Samuel Bronston, who also made *El Cid* and *The Fall of the Roman Empire*. AT *DVD*

Jeffrey Hunter *Jesus Christ* · Siobhan McKenna *Mary, Mother of Jesus* · Robert Ryan *John the Baptist* · Hurd Hatfield *Pontius Pilate* · Ron Randell *Lucius, the Centurion* · Viveca Lindfors *Claudia* · Rita Gam *Herodias* · Carmen Sevilla *Mary Magdalene* · Brigid Bazlen *Salome* · Harry Guardino *Barabbas* · Rip Torn *Judas* · Frank Thring *Herod Antipas* · Orson Welles *Narrator* · Gregoire Aslan [Grégoire Aslan] *King Herod* ■ *Dir* Nicholas Ray · *Scr* Philip Yordan · *Costume Designer* Georges Wakhevitch · *Music* Miklos Rozsa

The King of Kong: a Fistful of Quarters ★★★★ PG

Documentary
2007 · US · Colour · 83min

For a quarter of a century, it was assumed Billy Mitchell's high score on ape-chasing platformer Donkey Kong would never be beaten; that was until a self-effacing science teacher named Steve Wiebe claimed to have smashed the record on a machine set up in his garage. Seth Gordon's hilariously deadpan documentary captures the ensuing game of double-cross and dirty tricks, as Mitchell is gradually revealed to be a villain of Dick Dastardly proportions. With more sharp turns than a game of Pac-Man, *King of Kong* has achieved cult status as a real-life *This Is Spinal Tap* for the video game world. GR *DVD*

■ *Dir* Seth Gordon

The King of Marvin Gardens ★★★★ 15

Crime drama
1972 · US · Colour · 99min

Jack Nicholson and director Bob Rafelson's follow-up to *Five Easy Pieces* was this often pretentious yet absorbing study of two brothers. Nicholson is a radio presenter, intellectual and withdrawn; his brother, Bruce Dern, is an aspiring property developer, brash, married to Ellen Burstyn and living in a hopeless dream world. Set in a windy, charmless Atlantic City, its original title was *The Philosopher King*, and the final title derives from the American version of Monopoly. Some rate Nicholson's performance as a career best, and his wistful monologues on the radio are indeed brilliant; others may find the cerebral atmosphere easy to resist. AT Violence, swearing. *DVD*

Jack Nicholson *David Staebler* · Bruce Dern *Jason Staebler* · Ellen Burstyn *Sally* · Julia Anne Robinson *Jessica* · Benjamin "Scatman" Crothers [Scatman Crothers] *Lewis* · Charles Lavine *Grandfather* ■ *Dir* Bob Rafelson · *Scr* Jacob Brackman, from a story by Brackman, Bob Rafelson

King of New York ★★★★ 18

Crime thriller
1989 · US · Colour · 98min

A cult grew quickly around Abel Ferrara, director of those notorious "video nasties" *Driller Killer* and *Ms 45*, as well as 1992's *Bad Lieutenant* with Harvey Keitel. This is similarly sordid and blood-soaked, the tale of a New York drug trafficker, played with appalling brilliance by a reptilian Christopher Walken. Ferrara has Sergio Leone's eye for a location – his dark, brooding view of the city is impressive – but what some will regard as gripping and apocalyptic, others will find repellent. AT Drug abuse, swearing, nudity. *DVD* *BL*

Christopher Walken *Frank White* · David Caruso *Dennis Gilley* · Larry Fishburne [Laurence Fishburne] *Jimmy Jump* · Victor Argo *Lieutenant Roy Bishop* · Wesley Snipes *Thomas Flanigan* · Janet Julian *Jennifer Poe* · Joey Chin *Larry Wong* · Giancarlo Esposito *Lance* · Paul Calderon *Joey Dalesio* · Steve Buscemi *Test Tube* ■ *Dir* Abel Ferrara · *Scr* Nicholas St John

The King of Paris ★★ 12

Romantic drama
1995 · Fr/UK · Colour · 102min

A throwback to the literate films made in the 1930s, this is both sustained and undermined by its old-fashioned style. Expertly adopting the grand stage style, Philippe Noiret holds the piece together, even though his character's world is falling apart. Hungarian exile Veronika Varga exploits their romance to further her career before dumping him. Polished, yes, but also ponderous. DP French +subtitles.

Philippe Noiret *Victor Derval* · Veronika Varga *Lisa Lanska* · Jacques Roman *Romain Coste* · Manuel Blanc *Paul Derval* · Michel Aumont *Marquis de Castellac* ■ *Dir* Dominique Maillet · *Scr* Jacques Fieschi, Jérôme Tonnerre, Bernard Minoret, Dominique Maillet

The King of Pigs ★★★ 15

Animated drama
2011 · S Kor · Colour · 96min

Though it's an animation from the Far East, this brooding, adult-orientated Korean film is like little else from the region. Director Yeon Sang-ho goes for something darker and more ragged than your usual *anime*, and the violence is harsh by any standards. Having killed his wife in a moment of madness, a bankrupt businessman seeks out his childhood friend. Together they reminisce about their unhappy years at school and recall how a dropout schoolmate, the "King of Pigs", struck back on their behalf. An early shocking scene that sees a bully whipped in the face by a belt buckle sets the tone for the gritty, unflinching revelations that follow. DW Korean +subtitles. Violence, swearing. *DVD*

Yang Ik-june *Jung Jong-suk* · Oh Jeong-se *Hwang Kyung-min* · Kim Hye-na *Kim Chul* ■ *Dir/Scr* Yeon Sang-ho

King of Texas ★★ 12

Western drama
2002 · US · Colour · 91min

Transporting Shakespeare's *King Lear* to Texas in the 1840s, this hybrid, made-for-TV western lacks the finesse to avoid barnstorming in its more melodramatic showdowns. Much of the problem lies in Stephen Harrigan's unpersuasive screenplay, although Uli Edel's over-insistent direction frequently compounds matters. The casting of David Alan Grier as the slave equivalent to the Fool is laudably ambitious, but the standout is RSC alumnus Patrick Stewart. DP *DVD*

Patrick Stewart *Lear* · Marcia Gay Harden *Susannah* · Lauren Holly *Rebecca* · Roy Scheider *Westover* · David Alan Grier *Rip* · Colm Meaney *Tumlinson* · Patrick Bergin *Highsmith* · Julie Cox *Claudia* · Steven Bauer *Menchaca* ■ *Dir* Uli Edel · *Scr* Stephen Harrigan, from the play *King Lear* by William Shakespeare

King of the Ants ★★ 18

Crime horror
2003 · US · Colour · 97min

It's hard to believe that Charlie Higson from TV's *The Fast Show* wrote the script for this dark chiller based on his own novel. An intense and claustrophobic tale, it examines the cold-blooded horror that unfolds when young drifter Chris McKenna agrees to carry out a murder for corrupt building contractor Daniel Baldwin. This has its moments, making up for a shaky plot with scenes of calm and twisted brutality. SF Swearing, sex scenes, nudity, violence. *DVD*

Chris McKenna *Sean Crawley* · Kari Wuhrer *Susan Gatley* · Daniel Baldwin *Ray Mathews* · George Wendt *Duke* · Timm Sharp *George* · Ron Livingston *Eric Gatley* ■ *Dir* Stuart Gordon · *Scr* Charlie Higson, from his novel

King of the Children ★★★★

Drama
1987 · Chi · Colour · 106min

Chen Kaige explores the nature and value of education in this quietly combative inquiry into indoctrination and the unvanquishable curiosity of the individual. Set in the latter days of the Cultural Revolution, the story chronicles the conversion of Xie Yuan, a farm labourer who is ordered to supervise the local school, only for him to realise that freedom of expression and an appreciation of the world at large provide a better grounding in life than any Maoist platitude. This is a densely allegorical film, but it's also mesmerising and inspirational. DP Mandarin +subtitles.

Xie Yuan *Lao Gan* · Yang Xuewen *Wang Fu* · Chen Shaohua *Headmaster Chen* ■ *Dir* Chen Kaige · *Scr* Chen Kaige, Wan Zhi, from a short story by Ah Cheng

King of the Grizzlies ★★★ U

Adventure drama
1969 · US/Can · Colour · 89min

This family film benefits from producer Winston Hibler's extensive experience on Disney nature pictures. With Canada standing in for the Wild West, this action-packed adventure chronicles the friendship between native American John Yesno and a bear he cares for as a cub and later encounters as a hungry 10ft menace threatening Chris Wiggins's farm. Hibler's narration brings an educational angle to this beautifully photographed film. DP

John Yesno *Moki* · Chris Wiggins *Colonel Pierson* · Hugh Webster *Shorty* · Jack Van Evera *Slim* · Winston Hibler *Narrator* ■ *Dir* Ron Kelly · *Scr* Jack Spiers, Rod Peterson, Norman Wright, from the book *The Biography of a Grizzly* by Ernest Thompson Seton · *Cinematographer* Reginald Morris

King of the Gypsies ★★★

Drama
1978 · US · Colour · 111min

Sterling Hayden stars as the dying gypsy leader who disinherits his son in favour of his grandson who, in turn, rejects his birthright. Critics weren't quite sure whether to expect a musical like *Fiddler on the Roof* or a bloody dynastic saga like *The Godfather*. They were disappointed on both counts, but this does offer an impressive cast, with Eric Roberts in his debut as the heir apparent, caught between loyalty to his gypsy ancestry and the attractions of the modern world. The intimidating Hayden is like a less-mannered Anthony Quinn. AT

Sterling Hayden *King Zharko Stepanowicz* · Shelley Winters *Queen Rachel* · Susan Sarandon *Rose* · Judd Hirsch *Groffo* · Eric Roberts *Dave* · Brooke Shields *Tita* ■ *Dir* Frank Pierson · *Scr* Frank Pierson, from the book by Peter Maas

King of the Hill ★★★★ PG

Drama
1993 · US · Colour · 90min

Writer/director Steven Soderbergh's richly detailed and carefully controlled coming-of-age saga follows the adventures of a 12-year-old boy left to fend for himself in a St Louis hotel during the Depression. It's a sparkling gem, wonderfully acted by Jesse Bradford as the resourceful tyke who strides with an unsentimental confidence through every real or imagined threat to his existence. A rewarding drama from the *sex, lies, and videotape* director, full of quirky characters and deeply satisfying quiet moments. AJ Swearing.

Jesse Bradford *Aaron* · Jeroen Krabbé *Mr Kurlander* · Lisa Eichhorn *Mrs Kurlander* · Joseph Chrest *Ben* · Spalding Gray *Mr Mungo* · Elizabeth McGovern *Lydia* · Karen Allen *Miss Mathey* · Chris Samples *Billy Thompson* ■ *Dir* Steven Soderbergh · *Scr* Steven Soderbergh, from the memoirs of AE Hotchner

King of the Hill ★★★ 15
Thriller 2007 · Sp · Colour · 86min

After having casual sex at a remote motorway service station, strangers Leonardo Sbaraglia and Maria Valverde get lost in the neighbouring woods and start dodging unknown snipers. The set-up is simple and the characterisation minimal, but director Gonzalo López-Gallego never lets the suspense slack off. When the reason for the title becomes apparent and the dialogue turns increasingly chilling in its childishness, the final punch to the gut is highly effective. **AJ** Spanish +subtitles. Violence, swearing, a sex scene. *DVD*

Leonardo Sbaraglia *Quim* • Maria Valverde *Bea* ■ *Dir* Gonzalo López-Gallego • *Scr* Javier Gullón, Gonzalo López-Gallego

King of the Khyber Rifles ★★ U
Adventure 1953 · US · Colour · 99min

Twentieth Century-Fox lavished Technicolor and its biggest star, Tyrone Power, on this *Boys' Own* yarn set in the subcontinent's North-West Frontier. As a half-Indian, half-British officer who falls for the general's daughter, Power is despised by his fellow officers, but still manages to galvanise the locals against the rebels. Solid direction from Henry King and some decent heroics are let down by a weak heroine (Terry Moore) and unconvincing American locations, which stand in for Peshawar. **AT**

Tyrone Power *Captain Alan King* • Terry Moore *Susan Maitland* • Michael Rennie *Brigadier General Maitland* • Guy Rolfe *Karram Khan* • John Justin *Lieutenant Heath* ■ *Dir* Henry King • *Scr* Ivan Goff, Ben Roberts, from the novel by Talbot Mundy

King of the Roaring 20s – the Story of Arnold Rothstein ★★
Biographical drama 1961 · US · BW · 106min

Like its companion piece *The George Raft Story*, which was also directed by Joseph M Newman, this marks a fascinating return to the gangster era. David Janssen makes a seductively likeable Rothstein, the infamous 1920s gambler, and since audiences had barely heard of him, let alone remembered that he was fat and squat, Janssen gets away with it. The supporting cast is notable, featuring Diana Dors, near the end of her ill-advised stay in Hollywood. **TS**

David Janssen *Arnold Rothstein* • Dianne Foster *Carolyn Green* • Mickey Rooney *Johnny Burke* • Jack Carson *"Big Tim" O'Brien* • Diana Dors *Madge* • Dan O'Herlihy *Phil Butler* • Keenan Wynn *Tom Fowler* ■ *Dir* Joseph M Newman • *Scr* Jo Swerling, from the book *The Big Bankroll: the Life and Times of Arnold Rothstein* by Leo Katcher

King of the Underworld ★★
Crime drama 1939 · US · BW · 69min

A remake of the 1935 melodrama *Dr Socrates*, this features Kay Francis as a female doctor out for revenge. Gangster Humphrey Bogart is the object of her retribution after he killed her surgeon husband. A feeble, risible effort that only earns a second star for having the benefit of a snarling Bogart. **TH**

Humphrey Bogart *Joe Gurney* • Kay Francis *Dr Carol Nelson* • James Stephenson *Bill Stevens* • John Eldredge *Dr Niles Nelson* ■ *Dir* Lewis Seiler • *Scr* Vincent Sherman, George Bricker, from the story *Dr Socrates* by WR Burnett

King of the Wind ★★★ U
Adventure 1989 · US · Colour · 101min

This is a must-see for all keen young members of the pony set, albeit a rather dubious proposition for cynical grown-ups who regard horse racing as a short cut to bankruptcy. Despite that, this story of a legendary Arab horse and the teenage groom (Navin Chowdhry) who accompanies him from North Africa to England has some splendid photography and a remarkable cast of mainly British actors. **TH**

Frank Finlay *Edward Coke* • Jenny Agutter *Hannah Coke* • Nigel Hawthorne *Achmet* • Navin Chowdhry *Agba* • Ralph Bates *Leduc* • Neil Dickson *Earl of Godolphin* • Barry Foster *Mr Williams* • Jill Gascoine *Mrs Williams* • Joan

Hickson *Duchess of Marlborough* • Anthony Quayle *Lord Granville* • Ian Richardson *Bey of Tunis* • Peter Vaughan *Captain* • Richard Harris *King George II* • Glenda Jackson *Queen Caroline* ■ *Dir* Peter Duffell • *Scr* Phil Frey, from the novel by Marguerite Henry, adapted by Leslie Sayle • *Cinematographer* Brian Morgan

King, Queen, Knave ★★★★
Comedy 1972 · US/W Ger · Colour · 91min

This is a bold, intermittently successful attempt by Polish director Jerzy Skolimowski to bring Vladimir Nabokov's intensely literary black comedy to the screen. Gauche orphan John Moulder-Brown goes to stay with his uncle David Niven, only to be seduced by the latter's wife (Gina Lollobrigida) and asked to kill her husband. None of Nabokov's wordplay survives, but there are some startling moments of cold-hearted humour. **TH**

David Niven *Charles Dreyer* • Gina Lollobrigida *Martha Dreyer* • John Moulder-Brown *Frank* ■ *Dir* Jerzy Skolimowski • *Scr* David Seltzer, David Shaw, from a novel by Vladimir Nabokov

King Ralph ★★ PG
Comedy 1991 · US · Colour · 92min

Even the slobbish charm of John Goodman can't save this horribly misconceived caper. When the entire British royal family is wiped out in a freak photography accident, the unlikely successor turns out to be a Las Vegas entertainer (Goodman), who proceeds to bumble his way through the affairs of state with the assistance of adviser Peter O'Toole. The latter, and John Hurt as a scheming courtier, look to be having a fun time, but the talented cast is let down by the dim script. **JF** Swearing, nudity. *DVD*

John Goodman *Ralph Jones* • Peter O'Toole *Cedric Willingham* • John Hurt *Lord Graves* • Camille Coduri *Miranda* • Richard Griffiths *Phipps* • Leslie Phillips *Gordon* • James Villiers *Hale* • Joely Richardson *Princess Anna* • Julian Glover *King Gustav* ■ *Dir* David S Ward • *Scr* David S Ward, from the novel *Headlong* by Emlyn Williams

King Rat ★★★★ PG
Second World War prison drama 1965 · US · BW · 128min

Set in a Japanese PoW camp, this stars George Segal as an arch-manipulator who is the custodian of everything valuable from coffee to rats. It's a great performance - he is the alpha American amid the pukka English accents and class warfare of James Fox and Denholm Elliott. Shot in Hollywood (not that you'd notice), this gripping if overlong drama is also notable for one of John Barry's finest musical scores. **AT** *DVD*

George Segal *Corporal King* • Tom Courtenay *Lt Grey* • James Fox *Flight Lieutenant Marlowe* • Patrick O'Neal (I) *Max* • Denholm Elliott *Lt Colonel Denholm Larkin* • James Donald *Dr Kennedy* • Todd Armstrong *Tex* • John Mills *Col Smedley-Taylor* • Gerald Sim *Col Jones* • Leonard Rossiter *Major McCoy* • John Standing *Capt Daven* • Alan Webb *Col Brant* ■ *Dir* Bryan Forbes • *Scr* Bryan Forbes, from the novel by James Clavell

King Richard and the Crusaders ★★ U
Historical epic 1954 · US · Colour · 113min

Sir Walter Scott's novel *The Talisman* gets a Hollywood makeover courtesy of director David Butler. Rex Harrison blacks up to play the Muslim leader Saladin, who goes up against European powers led by Richard Lionheart (George Sanders). Laurence Harvey is the pretty juvenile lead, but it's Virginia Mayo who falls for sexy Saladin and gets the best line of dialogue: "War, war, that's all you think of, Dick Plantagenet!" **AT**

Rex Harrison *Saladin* • Virginia Mayo *Lady Edith* • George Sanders *King Richard I* • Laurence Harvey *Sir Kenneth* • Robert Douglas *Sir Giles Amaury* ■ *Dir* David Butler • *Scr* John Twist, from the novel *The Talisman* by Sir Walter Scott

King-Size Canary ★★★★★
Animated comedy 1947 · US · Colour · 8min

Tex Avery made many brilliant short cartoons during his heyday at MGM, but this is arguably the purest, with a determined,

nightmarish logic. Practically every gag is in the service of the plot in which a cat, a canary and a dog battle over a bottle of plant feed when they discover it turns them into giants. A landslide of gags is delivered at break-neck speed. **CLP**

■ *Dir* Tex Avery • *Scr* Heck Allen

King Solomon's Mines ★★★ U
Adventure 1937 · UK · BW · 76min

The first of several adaptations of H Rider Haggard's tale, with Paul Robeson as the noble African who leads a party of British treasure hunters through the jungles to the mythical diamond mine. Inevitably, Robeson breaks the journey by launching into song - great voice, pity about the loss of narrative momentum. Cedric Hardwicke plays the white hunter, while John Loder and Anna Lee embark on a gooey romance. An old-fashioned adventure spiced up with mystery. **AT** *DVD*

Paul Robeson *Umbopa* • Cedric Hardwicke *Allan Quatermain* • Roland Young *Commander Good* • John Loder *Henry Curtis* • Anna Lee *Kathy O'Brien* • Sydney Fairbrother *Gagool* ■ *Dir* Robert Stevenson • *Scr* Roland Pertwee, Michael Hogan, AR Rawlinson, Charles Bennett, (uncredited) Ralph Spence, from the novel *King Solomon's Mines* by H Rider Haggard

King Solomon's Mines ★★★ PG
Adventure 1950 · US · Colour · 98min

Stewart Granger and Deborah Kerr star in this stirring adaptation of Sir Henry Rider Haggard's 1885 novel about the search for a lost city, the resting place of Solomon's royal booty. It's full of animal action, frenzied natives and sentimental love scenes, with Compton Bennett directing the static bits and Andrew Marton handling the exteriors. The novel was an immediate success, but, curiously, it was not filmed until 1937. This remake won Oscars for its photography and editing. **AT**

Deborah Kerr *Elizabeth Curtis* • Stewart Granger *Allan Quatermain* • Richard Carlson *John Goode* • Hugo Haas *Van Brun* ■ *Dir* Compton Bennett, Andrew Marton • *Scr* Helen Deutsch, from the novel by H Rider Haggard • *Cinematographer* Robert Surtees • *Editors* Ralph E Winters, Conrad A Nervig

King Solomon's Mines ★★ PG
Adventure 1985 · US · Colour · 95min

Richard Chamberlain and Sharon Stone head off into the crocodile- and snake-infested jungle in search of buried treasure. Any similarity between their adventures and H Rider Haggard's source novel is probably accidental, but there's an old-fashioned charm to the enterprise that makes us overlook its faults. This was Sharon Stone's first starring role and it's obvious she was going places. A sequel, *Allan Quartermain and the Lost City of Gold*, followed in 1987. **AT** *DVD*

Richard Chamberlain *Allan Quatermain* • Sharon Stone *Jessie Huston* • Herbert Lom *Colonel Bockner* • John Rhys-Davies *Dogati* • Ken Gampu *Umbopa* ■ *Dir* J Lee Thompson • *Scr* Gene Quintano, James R Silke, from the novel by H Rider Haggard

The King Steps Out ★★★
Romantic musical 1936 · US · BW · 85min

Opera soprano Grace Moore shines in this adaptation of an operetta by the Marischka brothers, expertly transferred to the screen by the great director Josef von Sternberg. The plot's slight, but Moore and co-star Franchot Tone are both charming in their roles of princess and emperor. Moore was to make only three more features, her weight problem - glimpsed here but kept at bay - interfering with her casting, and she died in an air crash in 1947. **TS**

Miss Grace Moore [Grace Moore] *Elizabeth/ "Cissy"* • Franchot Tone *Emperor Franz Josef* • Walter Connolly *Maximilian, Duke of Bavaria* • Raymond Walburn *Von Kempen* • Elisabeth Risdon *Sofia* • Nana Bryant *Louise* ■ *Dir* Josef von Sternberg • *Scr* Sidney Buchman, from the operetta *Sissy* by Hubert Marischka, Ernst Marischka, from the play *Sissy's Brautfahrt* by Ernst Decsay, Gustav Hohn

The Kingdom ★★★★ 18
Black comedy horror thriller 1994 · Den/Swe/Ger · Colour · 239min

This lengthy but eerily engrossing movie comprises the first four episodes of Lars von Trier's 13-part Danish TV series, a supernatural soap about the bizarre doctors, nurses, patients and restless spirits in a Copenhagen hospital. Shot with a visual style that mirrors the colour of bodily fluids, and filled with an incredible gallery of eccentric characters, von Trier's opus is darkly humorous and extremely creepy. After nearly four hours, though, those seeking a neat resolution might be a bit miffed. **JC** Danish, Swedish +subtitles. Some violence. *DVD*

Ernst-Hugo Jaregard *Stig Helmer* • Kirsten Rolffes *Mrs Drusse* • Ghita Norby *Rigmor* • Soren Pilmark *Krogen* • Holger Juul Hansen *Dr Moesgaard* • Annevig Schelde Ebbe *Mary* ■ *Dir* Lars von Trier • *Scr* Tomas Gislason, Lars von Trier, from a story by von Trier, Niels Vorsel

The Kingdom ★★★ 15
Action thriller 2007 · US · Colour · 105min

With a set-up revolving around the devastating bombing of an American facility in Saudi Arabia, *The Kingdom* undoubtedly has currency. Jamie Foxx stars as Ronald Fleury, the leader of an American team of counter-terrorism experts whose attempt to pursue a secret investigation is hampered by the Saudi authorities. After a promising start, the film soon settles down into the routine clichés of a Hollywood action movie - there are few attempts here to address the complexity of the situation in the Middle East. If you can overlook the crassness of the screenplay, Peter Berg's high-energy direction does deliver some genuinely exciting sequences, and he's well served by a cast that also includes Jennifer Garner, Chris Cooper and Jason Bateman. **AS** *DVD* Blu

Jamie Foxx *Ronald Fleury* • Chris Cooper *Grant Sykes* • Jennifer Garner *Janet Mayes* • Jason Bateman *Adam Leavitt* • Ashraf Barhom *Colonel Faris Al Ghazi* • Ali Suliman *Sgt Haytham* • Jeremy Piven *Damon Schmidt* ■ *Dir* Peter Berg • *Scr* Matthew Michael Carnahan

The Kingdom of Dreams and Madness ★★★ PG
Documentary 2013 · Jpn · Colour · 113min

Mami Sunada's profile of Hayao Miyazaki and Isao Takahata is less a eulogy for the septuagenarian master animators than a behind-the-scenes peek at the making of *The Wind Rises* and *The Tale of Princess Kaguya*. Takahata proves somewhat elusive, but the avuncular Miyazaki chats genially about his inspirations, methods, and colleagues at the fabled Studio Ghibli. It feels at times like a corporate promo, but Sunada's perceptive insights help explain how Ghibli transformed anime. **DP** Japanese +subtitles.

Hayao Miyazaki • Toshio Suzuki • Isao Takahata ■ *Dir* Mami Sunada

Kingdom of Heaven ★★★★ 15
Epic period drama 2005 · US/UK/Sp/Ger · Colour · 138min

Ridley Scott directs this exciting mix of action, adventure and history lesson. At the outset, Orlando Bloom is just a 12th-century French blacksmith, but within minutes he has lost his family and been invited to the Holy Land by a Crusader father (Liam Neeson) previously unknown to him. The uneasy peace in Jerusalem between the Christians, under King Baldwin IV (Edward Norton), and the neighbouring Muslim forces of Saladin (a wonderful Ghassan Massoud) is threatened by fanatics, prompting Bloom to defend the city against overwhelming odds. Bloom is rather unconvincing as a leader of men, but the siege is breathtaking, the characters

colourful and the dialogue intelligent. BP
English, Arabic +subtitles. **DVD BL**

Orlando Bloom *Balian* • Eva Green *Princess Sibylla* • Jeremy Irons *Tiberias* • David Thewlis *Hospitaler* • Brendan Gleeson *Reynald of Chatillon* • Marton Csokas *Guy de Lusignan* • Liam Neeson *Godfrey of Ibelin* • Ghassan Massoud *Saladin* • Edward Norton *King Baldwin* • Alexander Siddig *Nasir* • Michael Sheen *Priest* • Kevin McKidd *English Sergeant* • Jon Finch *Patriarch of Jerusalem* • Iain Glen *Richard Coeur de Lion* ■ *Dir* Ridley Scott • *Scr* William Monahan

Kingdom of the Spiders ★★★ PG

Horror 1977 · US · Colour · 90min

Angered by pesticides, swarms of tarantulas attack an Arizona town in this neat low-budget chiller, directed by dependable B-movie veteran John "Bud" Cardos. William Shatner, in one of his better non-*Star Trek* roles, plays a veterinarian who joins forces with insect expert Tiffany Bolling to ascertain why nature has run amok. The creepiness is made more credible by an above-average script and some admirable staging. AJ

William Shatner *Rack Hansen* • Tiffany Bolling *Diane Ashley* • Woody Strode *Walter Colby* • Lieux Dressler *Emma Washburn* • David McLean *Sheriff Gene Smith* • Altovise Davis *Birch Colby* ■ *Dir* John "Bud" Cardos • *Scr* Richard Robinson, Alan Caillou, from a story by Jeffrey M Sneller, Stephen Lodge

Kingfish: a Story of Huey P Long ★★ 15

Biographical drama 1995 · US · Colour · 93min

A fine slice of American history is served up in John Goodman's dynamic portrayal of Huey P Long, the barnstorming Louisiana politician (1893-1935) who became governor and senator with his legendary persuasive powers and his zealous devotion to helping the poor and antagonising the rich. Although Goodman plays his role with gusto, this TV movie races through Long's career at such a chaotic pace that viewers are left dazed. If you want better, the same subject can be visited in the 1949 multi-Oscar winning film *All the King's Men*. MC

John Goodman *Huey P Long Jr* • Matt Craven *Seymour Weiss* • Anne Heche *Aileen Dumont* • Ann Dowd *Rose Long* • Jeff Perry *Earl Long* • Bob Gunton *Franklin D Roosevelt* ■ *Dir* Thomas Schlamme • *Scr* Paul Monash

Kingpin ★★ 12

Sports comedy 1996 · US · Colour · 108min

This typically vulgar tale from the Farrelly brothers lacks the soft centre that sweetened the taste of their later hit *There's Something about Mary*. Humour-wise, it's a very mixed bag, populated by the most irredeemably unpleasant characters. Ex-bowling prodigy Woody Harrelson's detachable rubber hand is overused to the point of annoyance, but there are some very funny moments involving Randy Quaid's *Forrest Gump*-like naivety, while Bill Murray's flamboyant villain gains the most laughs. JC Violence, swearing. **DVD**

Woody Harrelson *Roy Munson* • Randy Quaid *Ishmael Boorg* • Vanessa Angel *Claudia* • Bill Murray *Ernie McCracken* • Chris Elliott *The gambler* • William Jordan *Mr Boorg* • Richard Tyson *Owner of Stiffy's* ■ *Dir* Peter Farrelly, Bobby Farrelly • *Scr* Barry Fanaro, Mort Nathan

Kings and Desperate Men ★ 15

Drama 1981 · Can · Colour · 112min

The presence of Margaret Trudeau is the only noteworthy aspect of this sloppy kidnap drama. But the former Canadian prime minister's ex-wife takes a back seat as her husband (Patrick McGoohan) is held hostage on his talk radio show by a gang of rookie terrorists. Fleetingly, at the start of the siege, this threatens to become gripping. Then McGoohan begins chomping on the scenery, and the dual ineptitude of Alexis Kanner's acting and direction becomes clear. DP

Patrick McGoohan *John Kingsley* • Alexis Kanner *Lucas Miller* • Andrea Marcovicci *Girl* • Margaret Trudeau *Elizabeth Kingsley* • August Schellenberg *Aloini* ■ *Dir* Alexis Kanner • *Scr* Edmund Ward, Alexis Kanner

Kings & Queen ★★★★ 15

Comedy drama 2004 · Fr · Colour · 146min

Mathieu Amalric won a César for his performance as a neurotic viola player in Arnaud Desplechin's astute study of emotional self-delusion. Emmanuelle Devos is perhaps even more impressive as his obsessional ex-wife, who asks him to adopt the child of her first marriage to facilitate the success of her impending third. Desplechin employs an array of flashbacks, reveries and confessions to chronicle this bizarre relationship. Equally effective are the intimate encounters between Amalric and ten-year-old Valentin Lelong, and Devos and her novelist father (Maurice Garrel). DP French, English, German +subtitles. Swearing. **DVD**

Emmanuelle Devos *Nora* • Mathieu Amalric *Ismaël* • Catherine Deneuve *Madame Vasset* • Maurice Garrel *Louis Jenssens* • Nathalie Boutefeu *Chloé Jenssens* • Jean-Paul Roussillon *Abel Vuillard* • Magali Woch *Arielle* • Hippolyte Girardot *Mr Mamanne* • Valentin Lelong *Elias* ■ *Dir* Arnaud Desplechin • *Scr* Roger Bohbot, Arnaud Desplechin

King's Game ★★★ 12

Political thriller 2004 · Den/Swe/Nor · Colour · 102min

This consistently engaging and well-written political thriller recalls those solid, slightly cynical journalist-as-hero movies of the 1970s. Here, young reporter Anders W Berthelsen can't believe his luck when a major scoop about the private life of female political candidate Nastja Arcel falls into his lap. Of course, once the story has broken, Berthelsen realises that candidate's enemies – shadowy spin doctors with secrets of their own – are manipulating him for their own ends. Nikolaj Arcel's direction is taut and the crisp dialogue works even in the subtitles. LF Danish +subtitles. **DVD**

Anders W Berthelsen *Ulrik Torp* • Soren Pilmark *Erik Dreier Jensen* • Nastja Arcel *Lone Kjeldsen* • Nicolas Bro *Henrik Moll* • Lars Mikkelsen *Peter Schou* • Ulf Pilgaard *Gunnar Torp* • Charlotte Munck *Mette Torp* • Lars Brygmann *Mads Kjeldsen* • Helle Fagralid *Signe Jonsen* ■ *Dir* Nikolaj Arcel • *Scr* Nikolaj Arcel, Rasmus Heisterberg, from the novel by Niels Krause-Kjaer

The Kings of Summer ★★★ 15

Coming-of-age comedy drama 2013 · US · Colour · 91min

This coming-of-age flick is a slightly ragged affair that owes more than a little to Rob Reiner's *Stand by Me*. Joe and Patrick are a couple of pals who, tiring of what they see as parental oppression, run away to the woods to fend for themselves. The boys' attempts at self-sufficiency are as shambolic as their accommodation, with most of the food coming from a store across the street. The later intrusion of girls destabilises their relationship with each other – the film's main strength – as well as the rhythm of the screenplay. But these latter-day "Swallows and Amazons" have enough charm to withstand a few bumps and the performances are likeable. AS Swearing. **DVD BL**

Nick Robinson *Joe* • Gabriel Basso *Patrick* • Moises Arias *Biaggio* • Nick Offerman *Frank* • Megan Mullally *Mrs Keenan* • Marc Evan Jackson *Mr Keenan* ■ *Dir* Jordan Vogt-Roberts • *Scr* Chris Galletta

Kings of the Road ★★★★ 18

Road movie 1976 · W Ger · BW · 168min

This is an elegiac epic as much about American cultural imperialism as the forgotten border country between East and West Germany. Making evocative use of rock music and touching on topics as diverse as exile, communication and the decline of the national film industry, the action is void of contrived incident and conventional characterisation. They are

barely missed, however, as Wenders demonstrates his mastery of the long take and the visual metaphor, exploiting Robbie Müller's stylish monochrome photography to locate the poetry in a desolate landscape. DP German +subtitles. **DVD**

Rüdiger Vogler *Bruno Winter* • Hanns Zischler *Robert Lander* • Lisa Kreuzer *Cashier* • Rudolf Schündier *Robert's father* • Marquard Bohm *Man who has lost his wife* ■ *Dir/Scr* Wim Wenders

Kings of the Sun ★★★ PG

Adventure 1963 · US · Colour · 103min

This is one of Hollywood's rare excursions into Meso-American history, with George Chakiris (*West Side Story*) looking convincingly Mayan and virile even when addressing characters with names like Ixzubin and Ah Zok. It's all faintly ridiculous, but there are some spectacular scenes in authentic Mayan sites like Chichen Itza. According to this story, the Mayans built the first permanent settlement in Texas. AT **DVD**

Yul Brynner *Black Eagle* • George Chakiris *Balam* • Shirley Anne Field *Ixchel* • Brad Dexter *Ah Haleb* • Barry Morse *Ah Zok* • Armando Silvestre *Isatai* • Leo Gordon *Hunac Ceel* • Victoria Vetri *Ixzubin* ■ *Dir* J Lee Thompson • *Scr* Elliott Arnold, James R Webb, from a story by Elliott Arnold • *Music* Elmer Bernstein

The King's Pirate ★★ U

Swashbuckling adventure 1967 · US · Colour · 99min

Just what the movie world didn't need in the Swinging Sixties: a low-budget remake of the Errol Flynn/Maureen O'Hara swashbuckler *Against All Flags*, with TV star Doug McClure gauche and inadequate in the Flynn role. However, McClure's co-stars Jill St John and Guy Stockwell (Dean's brother), who both have some style and look comfortable in period costume, make amends. If you look closely you'll see an awful lot of the original film on display, with the new material cleverly shot around the footage by talented director Don Weis. TS

Doug McClure *Lt Brian Fleming* • Jill St John *Jessica Stephens* • Guy Stockwell *John Avery* • Mary Ann Mobley *Princess Patma* • Kurt Kasznar *Zucco* ■ *Dir* Don Weis • *Scr* Paul Wayne, Aeneas MacKenzie, Joseph Hoffman, from a story by Aeneas MacKenzie

King's Rhapsody ★★ U

Romantic drama 1955 · UK · Colour · 92min

It was a sad sight to watch the great swashbuckler Errol Flynn in his two British movies for Herbert Wilcox. Clearly paunchy and slightly raddled, he managed to retain that twinkle in the eye but conveyed a general sense of slumming as he played opposite Mrs Wilcox, Anna Neagle. This is a sorry, tawdry affair, a Ruritanian romance that was past its sell-by date even as a play on the London stage. Flynn looks clearly the worse for drink in the many sequences where dialogue is played off him. Of course, that in itself is a reason for watching and enjoying this antiquated romp. TS

Anna Neagle *Marta Karillos* • Errol Flynn *King Richard of Laurentia* • Patrice Wymore *Princess Christiane* • Martita Hunt *Queen Mother* • Finlay Currie *King Paul* • Francis De Wolff *Prime Minister* • Joan Benham *Countess Astrid* ■ *Dir* Herbert Wilcox • *Scr* Pamela Bower, Christopher Hassall, AP Herbert, from the play by Ivor Novello

Kings Row ★★★★

Melodrama 1942 · US · BW · 126min

Henry Bellamann's bestseller was the *Peyton Place* of its day, a steamy study of small-town mentality. Warner Bros did it full justice on the screen, subtly circumventing the censor and delivering a complex adult movie, with notable scenes and impeccable performances, offering career best opportunities to future US president Ronald Reagan ("Where's the rest of me?" he shrieks after a wanton and unnerving amputation) and Ann Sheridan, the girl from the wrong side of the tracks. Only weak lead Robert Cummings is uncomfortably cast. Strong, intelligent entertainment. TS

Ann Sheridan *Randy Monaghan* • Robert Cummings *Parris Mitchell* • Ronald Reagan *Drake McHugh* • Betty Field *Cassandra Tower* • Charles Coburn *Dr Henry Gordon* • Claude Rains *Dr Alexander Tower* • Judith Anderson *Mrs Harriet Gordon* • Nancy Coleman *Louise Gordon* ■ *Dir* Sam Wood • *Scr* Casey Robinson, from a novel by Henry Bellamann • *Music* Erich Wolfgang Korngold

The King's Speech ★★★★ 12

Historical drama 2010 · UK/Aus/US · Colour · 113min

In this marvellously moving tale, Colin Firth gives an Oscar-winning performance as King George VI, the British monarch who suffered from a terrible nervous stammer. From the outset, when he freezes on national radio, the tension of striving to uphold his image is palpable. His wife Elizabeth (the future Queen Mother, played by a Helena Bonham Carter) engages the services of speech therapist Lionel Logue (Geoffrey Rush), and it's the men's relationship that then takes centre stage. This is the type of thing the British film industry does so well – a bit of history, a bit of social comedy, a few liberties with the truth and a flag-waving finale. SP Swearing. **DVD BL**

Colin Firth *"Albert", King George VI* • Helena Bonham Carter *Queen Elizabeth* • Geoffrey Rush *Lionel Logue* • Guy Pearce *"David", Edward VIII* • Michael Gambon *King George V* • Timothy Spall *Winston Churchill* • Jennifer Ehle *Myrtle Logue* • Derek Jacobi *Archbishop Cosmo Lang* • Claire Bloom *Queen Mary* • Anthony Andrews *Stanley Baldwin* ■ *Dir* Tom Hooper • *Scr* David Seidler

The King's Thief ★ U

Period adventure 1955 · US · Colour · 78min

David Niven is cast against type in this frightful Restoration melodrama as the villainous first minister of George Sanders (shamelessly overacting in his second turn as Charles II), intent on bumping off enemies. But plucky Ann Blyth, who enlists the help of highwayman Edmund Purdom, helps expose the nasty Niven. The "swashbuckless" plot limps along, with drab colour, indifferent performances and slack direction. DP

David Niven *Duke of Brampton* • Ann Blyth *Lady Mary* • Edmund Purdom *Michael Dermott* • George Sanders *Charles II* • Roger Moore *Jack* • John Dehner *Captain Herrick* • Sean McClory *Sheldon* • Tudor Owen *Simon* • Melville Cooper *Henry Wynch* ■ *Dir* Robert Z Leonard • *Scr* Christopher Knopf, from a story by Robert Hardy Andrews

The King's Whore ★★★ 15

Historical romantic drama 1990 · Fr/UK/Austria/It · Colour · 89min

Timothy Dalton's theatrical background serves him well in the role of an Italian king who takes a shine to the wife of a French count. She doesn't fancy him, however, and the king's passion leads him to declare war on France. Director Axel Corti evidently admires *Barry Lyndon* and has a clear view of what the 17th century looked, sounded and smelt like. It's a lavish movie, though there are the usual Euro-pudding lumps: a mishmash of a cast and an uneven script written by many hands. AT

Timothy Dalton *King Vittorio Amadeo* • Valeria Golino *Jeanne de Luynes* • Robin Renucci *Charles de Luynes* • Stéphane Freiss *Count di Verua* • Feodor Chaliapin [Feodor Chaliapin Jr] *Scaglia* • Paul Crauchet *Duke of Luynes* • Margaret Tyzack *Dowager Countess* ■ *Dir* Axel Corti • *Scr* Axel Corti, Frederic Raphael, Daniel Vigne, from the novel *Jeanne de Luynes, comtesse de Verue* by Jacques Tournier • *Cinematographer* Gernot Roll

Kingsman: The Secret Service ★★★★ 15

Spy action adventure 2015 · US/UK · Colour · 123min

Cult TV show *The Avengers* meets Bond in Matthew Vaughn's vibrant caper. Colin Firth stars as a John Steed-like agent in the Kingsman organisation, whose operatives are codenamed after Round Table knights of lore – Firth is Galahad, Michael Caine is Arthur, Mark Strong is Merlin. Firth recruits a dead colleague's tearaway son (Taron Egerton) and puts him through his secret-

K

service paces. Lying in wait for them, however, is billionaire villain Samuel L Jackson. Vaughn injects some much-needed fun into an increasingly grim genre, with Firth a quite excellent action hero. JA Violence, swearing, nudity. **DVD** **BL**
Colin Firth *Harry Hart/Galahad* • Michael Caine *Arthur* • Samuel L Jackson *Valentine* • Taron Egerton *Gary "Eggsy" Unwin* • Jack Davenport *Lancelot* • Mark Hamill *James Arnold* • Mark Strong *Merlin* • Sofia Boutella *Gazelle* ■ *Dir* Matthew Vaughn • *Scr* Matthew Vaughn, Jane Goldman, from the comic book *The Secret Service* by Mark Millar (writer), Dave Gibbons (artist)

Kingsman: The Golden Circle

Spy action adventure   2017 • UK/US • Colour

This is a preview – no prints were available to review as we went to press: *The Kingsman* series has a mix-and-match approach to casting – if they're available, we can use them. This sequel to 2014's spy-from-the-streets caper is a no-show for Michael Caine, Mark Hamill and Samuel L Jackson. But alongside returning stars Taron Egerton, Colin Firth and Mark Strong, those absences are balanced by Channing Tatum, Julianne Moore, Jeff Bridges and Halle Berry, among others. Elton John even pops up in a cameo, as the Kingsman HQ is attacked. SvM
Taron Egerton *Gary "Eggsy" Unwin* • Julianne Moore *Poppy* • Halle Berry *Ginger* • Mark Strong *Merlin* • Pedro Pascal *Jack Daniels* • Elton John • Colin Firth *Harry Hart* ■ *Dir* Matthew Vaughn • *Scr* Jane Goldman, Matthew Vaughn, from characters by Dave Gibbons, Mark Millar

K Kini and Adams ★★★

Drama   1997 • UK/Fr/Zim • Colour • 93min

Burkina Faso's best-known director, Idrissa Ouedraogo, made his English-language debut with this investigation into the impact of industrialisation on rural Africa. Vusi Kunene and David Mohloki impress as the longtime buddies who fall out over the former's relationship with quarry foreman John Kani and gold-digging prostitute Netsayi Chigwendere. Although slightly muddled, this drama is still revealing in its discussion of women and their place in what is still, primarily, a patriarchal society. Made with additional backing from Switzerland and Ouedrago's home country. DP
Vusi Kunene *Kini* • David Mohloki *Adams* • John Kani *Ben* • Nthati Moshesh *Aida* • Netsayi Chigwendere *Binja* ■ *Dir* Idrissa Ouedraogo • *Scr* Idrissa Ouedraogo, Olivier Lorelle, Santiago Amigorena

Kinjite: Forbidden Subjects

★ **18**
Action crime thriller   1989 • US • Colour • 93min

You'll need a cast-iron gut to endure this Charles Bronson vehicle, in which the vigilante's friend plays an LA vice cop who teams up with a Japanese businessman whose daughter has been kidnapped by a gang who enslave children in the sex trade. This utterly repellent premise is handled by director J Lee Thompson as if it were an episode of *Kojak*. RS **DVD**
Charles Bronson *Lieutenant Crowe* • Perry Lopez *Eddie Rios* • Juan Fernandez *Duke* • Sy Richardson *Lavonne* • Peggy Lipton *Kathleen Crowe* • Nicole Eggert *DeeDee* • Bill McKinney *Father Burke* • James Pax *Hiroshi Hada* ■ *Dir* J Lee Thompson • *Scr* Harold Nebenzal

Kinky Boots ★★★ **12**

Comedy drama based on a true story
2005 • US/UK • Colour • 102min

Mild-mannered Charlie Price (played by Australian Joel Edgerton) inherits an ailing shoe factory and, after a chance meeting with Soho drag queen Lola (Chiwetel Ejiofor), embarks on a bold new business plan. Despite opposition from his fiancée and the prejudices of his workforce, Edgerton moves into reinforced heels for the "specialist" male market. While the outcome – at a make-or-break fashion show in Milan – is as predictable as the romance with worker Sarah-Jane Potts, this is big-hearted stuff that should be applauded for eschewing star names. AC Swearing. **DVD**
Joel Edgerton *Charlie Price* • Chiwetel Ejiofor *Lola* • Sarah-Jane Potts [Sarah Jane Potts] *Lauren* • Jemima Rooper *Nicola* • Linda Bassett *Melanie* • Nick Frost *Don* • Ewan Hooper *George* • Robert Pugh *Harold Price* ■ *Dir* Julian Jarrold • *Scr* Geoff Deane, Tim Firth

Kinsey ★★★★ **15**

Biographical drama
2004 • US • Colour and BW • 113min

Most people will find it difficult to imagine the level of sexual ignorance prevalent in 1948 when Alfred Kinsey published his ground-breaking book *Sexual Behaviour in the Human Male*. Director Bill Condon's excellent biopic charts the life of the academic (Liam Neeson) from his repressive religious childhood, when he is bullied by his moralistic father (John Lithgow), through his unsatisfactory first attempt at lovemaking with his wife (Laura Linney), which provokes his desire to research – and educate others about – human sexuality. Neeson has never been better, and there's also a fantastic performance from Peter Sarsgaard as a researcher and sexual adventurist. AS **DVD**
Liam Neeson *Alfred Charles Kinsey* • Laura Linney *Clara Bracken McMillen* • Chris O'Donnell *Wardell Pomeroy* • Peter Sarsgaard *Clyde Martin* • Timothy Hutton *Paul Gebhard* • John Lithgow *Alfred Seguine Kinsey* • Tim Curry *Thurman Rice* • Oliver Platt *Herman Wells* • Dylan Baker *Alan Gregg* • Julianne Nicholson *Alice Martin* ■ *Dir/Scr* Bill Condon

Kipps ★★★ **U**

Comedy   1941 • UK • BW • 112min

Critics were divided on the release of Carol Reed's adaptation of HG Wells's novel about the draper's clerk who discovers that, when it comes to social climbing, he has no head for heights. Some detected a certain detachment in Reed's direction, allowing Frank Launder and Sidney Gilliat's script to meander and supporting players to overact. But others claimed the film was stuffed with sly Wellsian satire, expertly staged set pieces and top-class acting from Michael Redgrave in the title role. While there is much to enjoy here, there are some interminable stretches. DP
Michael Redgrave *Arthur Kipps* • Phyllis Calvert *Ann Pornick* • Diana Wynyard *Helen Walshingham* • Phillip Frost *Arthur as a boy* • Diana Calderwood *Ann as a girl* • Arthur Riscoe *Chitterlow* • Max Adrian *Chester Coote* • Helen Haye *Mrs Walshingham* • Michael Wilding *Ronnie Walshingham* ■ *Dir* Carol Reed • *Scr* Frank Launder, Sidney Gilliat, from the novel by HG Wells

Kippur ★★★ **15**

War drama based on a true story
2000 • Fr/It/Is • Colour • 115min

This is a semi-autobiographical account of the ordeal experienced by seven members of a helicopter rescue unit, following the 1973 Day of Atonement attack on Israel by Syrian and Egyptian troops. Doubts have been raised about both the slowness of the opening scenes, as reservists Liron Levo and Tomer Ruso are diverted from the Golan Heights to the field hospital at Ramat David, and the repetitive nature of the various recovery missions. But Amos Gitai is seeking to show how the incessant carnage affects the morale of these hardly committed men, while also emphasising the human toll of this intractable struggle. DP Hebrew +subtitles. **DVD**
Liron Levo *Weinraub* • Tomer Ruso *Ruso* • Uri Ran Klauzner *Dr Klauzner* • Yoram Hattab *Pilot* • Juliano Merr *Captain* ■ *Dir* Amos Gitai • *Scr* Amos Gitai, Marie-Jose Sanselme

Kirikou and the Sorceress

★★★★ **U**
Animated fantasy adventure
1998 • Fr/Bel/Lux • Colour • 70min

With a story inspired by a West African fable, graphics gleaned from indigenous art and a score by Senegalese star Youssou N'Dour, this is a glorious escape from the bland correctness and commercial cynicism of mainstream animation. Michel Ocelet's film challenges youngsters both to question social hierarchies and respect traditional values. But the infant Kirikou's quest to discover who Karaba eats the local menfolk and surrounds herself with mischievous fetishes will also seize their imagination. DP French dubbed. **DVD**
Doudou Gueye Thiaw *Kirikou* • Maimouna Ndiaye *Kirikou's mother* • Awa Sene Sarr *Karaba the sorceress* • Robert Lionsol *Wise man of the mountain* • William Nadylam-Yotnda Sébastien Hébrant *Kirikou as a young man* • Tshilombo Lubambu *Kirikou's uncle* ■ *Dir* Michel Ocelot • *Scr* Michel Ocelot, Raymond Burlet

Kismet ★★★ **U**

Fantasy adventure   1944 • US • Colour • 99min

Arabian Nights-style tales were seldom the stuff of A-features, least of all at opulent MGM, but this adaptation of Edward Knoblock's play about the beggar-magician who aspires to royalty gets the full gloss treatment, with top stars Ronald Colman and Marlene Dietrich looking glamorous but ill at ease in this version of an oft-told hokey tale. The real value of this is by way of comparison to the 1955 musical version. And, of course, Dietrich. TS
Ronald Colman *Hafiz* • Marlene Dietrich *Jamilla* • James Craig *Caliph* • Edward Arnold *Mansur the Grand Vizier* • Hugh Herbert *Feisal* • Joy Ann Page [Joy Page] *Marsinah* • Florence Bates *Karsha* • Harry Davenport *Agha* ■ *Dir* William Dieterle • *Scr* John Meehan, from the play by Edward Knoblock • *Music* Herbert Stothart

Kismet ★★★ **U**

Fantasy musical   1955 • US • Colour • 108min

Panned in its day, this *Arabian Nights* farrago does have elements to recommend it now, notably muscular baritone Howard Keel having the time of his life. He plays Haaj – the beggar whose daughter has fallen for a caliph – with enormous energy, filling the screen with his unfairly maligned performance. The rest of the cast also works hard, particularly the raunchy Dolores Gray, and Ann Blyth and Vic Damone make a perfectly acceptable pair of lovebirds and get all the best songs, especially the hit *Stranger in Paradise*. TS
Howard Keel *Haaj, the Poet* • Ann Blyth *Marsinah* • Dolores Gray *Lalume* • Vic Damone *Caliph* • Monty Woolley *Omar* • Sebastian Cabot *Wazir* • Jay C Flippen *Jawan* • Mike Mazurki *Chief policeman* • Jack Elam *Hassan-Ben* ■ *Dir* Vincente Minnelli • *Scr* Charles Lederer, Luther Davis, from the play by Edward Knoblock • *Music/lyrics* George Forrest, Robert Wright

Kisna – the Warrior Poet

★★★ **PG**
Romantic adventure
2004 • Ind • Colour • 162min

Cinematography and music combine to stirring effect in director Subhash Ghai's entertaining adventure. Vivek Oberoi stars as Kisna, the son of a stable boy, who gets caught between two cultures when he falls for Katherine (Antonia Bernath), a British deputy commissioner's daughter. Set in pre-independence India, Ghai's epic melodrama contains moments of triumph and tragedy as the lovers struggle to stay together. Oberoi brings a wealth of melancholy to the role of Kisna, but surrenders centre stage to Bernath, who gives a very impressive performance. OA Hindi, English +subtitles. **DVD**
Vivek Oberoi *Kisna* • Isha Sharwani *Laxmi* • Antonia Bernath *Katherine Beckett* • Polly Adams *Lady Katherine* • Rajat Kapoor *Prince Raghuraj* • Caroline Langrishe *Jennifer Beckett* • Michael Maloney *Peter Beckett* • Amrish Puri *Bhairo Singh* • Om Puri *Jumman Kisti* ■ *Dir* Subhash Ghai • *Scr* Sachin Bhowmick, Farrukh Dhondy, Subhash Ghai, Margaret Glover

The Kiss ★★★

Silent drama   1929 • US • Colour • 64min

In provincial France, Greta Garbo is tried for the murder of her husband Anders Randolf who, in a jealous fit, tried to kill the handsome Lew Ayres, who is infatuated with her. Defence lawyer Conrad Nagel is her own former lover. This thin melodrama is elevated by the silent but eloquent presence of Garbo, starring in a silent movie for the last time. Directed by France's Jacques Feyder, imported for the occasion, it was also MGM's final silent production, and marked the impressive debut of Ayres, soon to be a star of the talkies. RK
Greta Garbo *Irene* • Conrad Nagel *André* • Anders Randolf *Guarry* • Holmes Herbert *Lassalle* • Lew Ayres *Pierre* • George Davis *Durant* ■ *Dir* Jacques Feyder • *Scr* Hans Kräly, from a story by George M Saville

The Kiss ★★ **18**

Erotic horror   1988 • US/Can • Colour • 93min

Zombie cats, mutilation by escalator, supernatural mumbo jumbo and African demons are all to be found in this ludicrous chiller about an ancient witch (Joanna Pacula) who wants to pass on the secret of eternal youth via a kiss to her young niece (Meredith Salenger). Inane trash would be the best way to describe the directing debut of Pen Densham. Yet for all its faults, this stilted shocker is packed with enough gratuitous incident to rivet the viewer. AJ
Joanna Pacula *Felice* • Meredith Salenger *Amy* • Mimi Kuzyk *Brenda* • Nicholas Kilbertus *Jack* • Jan Rubes *Tobin* ■ *Dir* Pen Densham • *Scr* Stephen Volk, Tom Ropelewski, from a story by Stephen Volk

Kiss and Make-Up ★★

Romantic comedy   1934 • US • BW • 70min

Cary Grant stars here as a top Parisian beauty consultant who falls for his client Genevieve Tobin. He soon discovers her charms are only skin deep and it's really his secretary Helen Mack he loves, but she's about to marry the flighty Tobin's ex-husband... Thin as lip gloss, but a sprinkling of witty cracks, the always expert Tobin and the incomparably polished Grant make this a watchable diversion. RK
Cary Grant *Dr Maurice Lamar* • Genevieve Tobin *Eve Caron* • Helen Mack *Annie* • Edward Everett Horton *Marcel Caron* • Lucien Littlefield *Max Pascal* • Mona Maris *Countess Rita* • Clara Lou Sheridan [Ann Sheridan] *Beauty operator* ■ *Dir* Harlan Thompson • *Scr* George Marion Jr, Harlan Thompson, from the play *Kozmetika* by Istvan Bekeffi, adapted by Jane Hinton

Kiss and Tell ★★★

Romantic comedy   1945 • US • BW • 90min

Once the world's biggest and smallest star, Shirley Temple was just another pretty teenage actress in the 1940s. This is one of her better later vehicles, thought quite shocking at the time. The mildly amusing comedy had the 17-year-old Temple pretending to be pregnant in order to divert attention from her brother's secret marriage. The film produced a sequel, *A Kiss for Corliss* in 1949, the year Temple retired from the movies. RB
Shirley Temple *Corliss Archer* • Jerome Courtland *Dexter Franklin* • Walter Abel *Mr Archer* • Katharine Alexander [Katherine Alexander] *Mrs Archer* • Robert Benchley *Uncle George Archer* • Porter Hall *Mr Franklin* • Virginia Welles *Mildred Pringle* • Tom Tully *Mr Pringle* • Darryl Hickman *Raymond Pringle* ■ *Dir* Richard Wallace • *Scr* F Hugh Herbert, from his play

A Kiss at Midnight ★★

Romantic drama   2008 • US • Colour • 97min

Professional matchmakers get a taste of their own medicine in this undemanding romantic drama. Faith Ford and Cameron Daddo play the unaware business rivals, brought together when the latter's precocious young daughters decide to secretly use his online dating service to find him a potential wife. Fortunately, a cute cast and fun performances help compensate for all the clichés, while veteran TV director Bradford May manages to rein in the sentimentality until the emotionally manipulative climax. SF
Faith Ford *Susan Flowers* • Cameron Daddo *Josh Sherman* • Dyan Cannon *Kay Flowers* • Kim Rhodes *Maureen O'Connor* • Abigail Mavity *Jennifer Sherman* ■ *Dir* Bradford May • *Scr* Anna Sandor

U SUITABLE FOR ALL   **Uc** SUITABLE ESPECIALLY FOR YOUNG CHILDREN (DVD ONLY)   **PG** PARENTAL GUIDANCE   **12A** UNDER 12s TO BE ACCOMPANIED (CINEMA ONLY)

A Kiss before Dying ★★★ 12
Crime drama 1956 · US · Colour · 93min

This is a fine adaptation of author Ira Levin's dark tale about a social climber who kills his wealthy girlfriend when her pregnancy threatens her inheritance. It stars a cast-against-type Robert Wagner, cleverly made-up as a villain and relishing the kind of role he seldom played again. This *film noir* is actually shot in bright daylight colours by cinematographer Lucien Ballard, who makes excellent use of locations. A young Joanne Woodward plays the victim and a superb Mary Astor is Wagner's mother. AT *DVD*

Robert Wagner *Bud Corliss* · Jeffrey Hunter *Gordon Grant* · Virginia Leith *Ellen Kingship* · Joanne Woodward *Dorothy Kingship* · Mary Astor *Mrs Corliss* · George Macready *Leo Kingship* ■ Dir Gerd Oswald · Scr Lawrence Roman, from the novel by Ira Levin

A Kiss before Dying ★★ 18
Thriller 1991 · US · Colour · 89min

Despite a chilling performance from Matt Dillon, this attempt to update Ira Levin's novel for the 1990s doesn't quite get there. Dillon makes for a charming psychopath, killing his way to the top of the corporate ladder by romancing twin wealthy heiresses, both played unconvincingly by Sean Young, and director James Dearden stages some effective, if derivative, set pieces. JF Violence, swearing, nudity.

Matt Dillon *Jonathan Corliss* · Sean Young *Ellen/Dorothy Carlsson* · Max von Sydow *Thor Carlsson* · Jim Fyfe *Terry Dieter* · Ben Browder *Tommy Roussell* · Diane Ladd *Mrs Corliss* · Martha Gehman *Patricia Farren* · Shane Rimmer *Commissioner Mallet* · James Russo *Dan Corelli* ■ Dir James Dearden · Scr James Dearden, from the novel by Ira Levin

The Kiss before the Mirror ★★★
Crime drama 1933 · US · BW · 67min

James Whale directed this atmospheric adaptation of Ladislas Fodor's stage play, and also the 1938 remake, *Wives under Suspicion*. However, the enforcement of the Production Code in 1934 ensured that this is a much racier version that wallows in the lurid details of adultery and criminal passion. Paul Lukas turns in a solid performance, as a Viennese lawyer who admits to murdering his cheating wife. But he's well matched by Frank Morgan, as the defending attorney who comes to suspect spouse Nancy Carroll of deception as the case preys on his mind. DP

Nancy Carroll *Maria Held* · Frank Morgan *Dr Paul Held* · Paul Lukas *Dr Walter Bernsdorf* · Gloria Stuart *Frau Lucie Bernsdorf* · Jean Dixon *Hilda Frey* · Walter Pidgeon *Bachelor* · Charley Grapewin *Mr Schultz* · Donald Cook *Maria's lover* ■ Dir James Whale · Scr William Anthony McGuire, from the play by Ladislas Fodor

Kiss Daddy Good Night ★★★ 15
Psychological crime thriller
1987 · US · Colour · 78min

The intriguing debut of Uma Thurman is an oddball affair. Playing a precocious young vamp, she picks up wealthy men in order to rob them. Unfortunately for the young "Poison Ivy", someone then begins to stalk her. It's untidily made, but Thurman has real presence and Steve Buscemi pops up in an early role. TH Swearing, violence. *DVD*

Uma Thurman *Laura* · Paul Dillon *Sid* · Paul Richards (2) *William B Tilden* · Steve Buscemi *Johnny* · Annabelle Gurwitch *Sue* · David Brisbin *Nelson Blitz* ■ Dir Peter Ily Huemer · Scr Peter Ily Huemer, Michael Gabrieli, from a story by Peter Ily Huemer

A Kiss for Corliss ★ U
Comedy 1949 · US · BW · 88min

No displays of affection were shown for this limp comedy, a sad end to the phenomenal career of Shirley Temple. Four years earlier she had starred as irrepressible teenager Corliss Archer in *Kiss and Tell*. In this sequel – in which Corliss is suspected of having spent the night with a playboy (David

Niven) – the same director (Richard Wallace) guided her, sometimes ill-advisedly. As the plot's implausibilities increase, even the usually reliable Niven resorts to desperate mugging. TV

Shirley Temple *Corliss Archer* · David Niven *Kenneth Marquis* · Tom Tully *Harry Archer* · Virginia Welles *Mildred Pringle* · Darryl Hickman *Dexter Franklin* ■ Dir Richard Wallace · Scr Howard Dimsdale, from a story by Dimsdale, from characters by F Hugh Herbert

A Kiss in the Dark ★★ U
Romantic comedy 1949 · US · BW · 87min

Concert pianist David Niven inherits an apartment block and becomes involved with his disparate collection of tenants, including photographic model Jane Wyman, with whom he falls in love. Niven's flair for comedy and the confident presence of Wyman only just keep this afloat. Director Delmer Daves does his best, but the script is under-stocked with laughs. RK

David Niven *Eric Phillips* · Jane Wyman *Polly Haines* · Victor Moore *Horace Willoughby* · Wayne Morris *Bruce Arnold* · Broderick Crawford *Mr Botts* · Joseph Buloff *Peter Danilo* · Maria Ouspenskaya *Madame Karina* ■ Dir Delmer Daves · Scr Harry Kurnitz, from a story by Everett Freeman, Devery Freeman

Kiss Kiss (Bang Bang) ★★
Comedy thriller 2001 · UK · Colour · 97min

The "hitman-with-a-heart" has become something of a cliché these days and while Stewart Suggs does come up with a few unexpected variations on the formula, it's still a predictable Tarantino-esque ride. Stellan Skarsgård plays an assassin who wants out of the game but, needing cash, becomes a reluctant nursemaid to the physically disabled Chris Penn. JF

Stellan Skarsgård *Felix* · Chris Penn *Bubba* · Paul Bettany *Jimmy* · Sienna Guillory *Kat* · Allan Corduner *Big Bob* · Ashley Artus *Mick Foot* · Martine McCutcheon *Mia* · Jacqueline McKenzie *Sherry* · Peter Vaughan *Daddy Zoo* ■ Dir/Scr Stewart Sugg

Kiss Kiss Bang Bang
Action comedy thriller
★★★★ 15
2005 · US · Colour · 98min

Shane Black's crime comedy is a hilarious game of nudge-nudge, wink-wink, with the compelling Robert Downey Jr as a petty thief who winds up playing gumshoe. He guides us through a tangled murder case with his playful voiceover assuring: "Don't worry. I saw *Lord of the Rings* - I'm not going to end this 17 times." Val Kilmer helps him navigate the twists and turns as a top private eye who's armed with a brilliant battery of one-liners of his own: "This isn't good cop, bad cop. This is fag and New Yorker." It may just be a fly-by-night fancy, but this quirky *noir* still packs more heat than your average 1980s action hero. SP Swearing. *DVD*

Robert Downey Jr *Harry Lockhart* · Val Kilmer *"Gay" Perry* · Michelle Monaghan *Harmony Faith Lane* · Corbin Bernsen *Harlan Dexter* · Dash Mihok *Mr Frying Pan* · Larry Miller *Dabney Shaw* · Rockmond Dunbar *Mr Fire* · Shannyn Sossamon *Pink hair girl* ■ Dir Shane Black · Scr Shane Black, from his story, from the novel *Bodies Are Where You Find Them* by Brett Halliday

Kiss Me Again ★★★
Silent comedy 1925 · US · BW · 75min

This sophisticated romantic comedy was made by director Ernst Lubitsch during his Warner Bros days, and concerns a classic love triangle featuring a bored wife (Marie Prevost), her husband (Monte Blue), and her lover (John Roche). As handled by the masterly Lubitsch, displaying the "touch" and high style for which he would become famous at Paramount during the 1930s, the simple plot is transformed into an exercise in wit, depth and intelligence. The "It" Girl, Clara Bow, features in support. RK

Marie Prevost *Loulou Fleury* · Monte Blue *Gaston Fleury* · John Roche *Maurice Ferriere* · Clara Bow *Grizette, Dubois's secretary* · Willard Louis

Avocat Dubois ■ Dir Ernst Lubitsch · Scr Hans Kräly, from the play *Divorçons* by Victorien Sardou, Emile de Najac

Kiss Me Deadly ★★★★★ 12
Classic film noir 1955 · US · BW · 103min

One of the greatest examples of *film noir*, this early feature by director Robert Aldrich made him a name in arty circles (the critics of the French magazine *Cahiers du Cinéma* loved him and the film) and a formidable presence in cinema. He took a piece of Mickey Spillane pulp fiction and turned it into an astonishing fable, with Pandora's Box transformed into a nuclear furnace. The look is stylish and the tension builds to a climax that is near-apocalyptic. Spillane's detective Mike Hammer (Ralph Meeker) is a flawed antihero who, after picking up a girl on the run, finds himself in over his head in events beyond his control. Albert Dekker is a classily obnoxious villain, but it's the women you have to watch. As the title suggests, their embrace is lethal. TH *DVD*

Ralph Meeker *Mike Hammer* · Albert Dekker *Dr Soberin* · Paul Stewart *Carl Evello* · Maxine Cooper *Velda* · Gaby Rodgers *Gabrielle/Lily Carver* · Wesley Addy *Pat Chambers* · Juano Hernandez *Eddie Yeager* · Nick Dennis *Nick* · Cloris Leachman *Christina Bailey/Berga Torn* ■ Dir Robert Aldrich · Scr Al Bezzerides, from the novel by Mickey Spillane · Cinematographer Ernest Laszlo

Kiss Me Goodbye ★★★ PG
Romantic comedy 1982 · US · Colour · 101min

Sally Field stars in this nicely played romantic fantasy as the widow rebuilding her life with hunky fiancé Jeff Bridges, only for her happy new existence to be complicated by the ghostly arrival of her late husband (James Caan), who is intent on stopping the wedding. Caan, exhibiting a deft comic touch, is deliciously enjoyable as the apparition, while Field and Bridges have fun with their romantic roles. JB

Sally Field *Kay Villano* · James Caan *Jolly Villano* · Jeff Bridges *Rupert Baines* · Paul Dooley *Kendall* · Claire Trevor *Charlotte Banning* · Mildred Natwick *Mrs Reilly* · Dorothy Fielding *Emily* · William Prince *Reverend Hollis* ■ Dir Robert Mulligan · Scr Charlie Peters, from the film *Dona Flor and Her Two Husbands* by Bruno Barreto, from the novel *Dona Flor and Her Two Husbands* by Jorge Amado

Kiss Me, Guido ★★ 15
Comedy 1997 · US/UK · Colour · 85min

Heterosexual pizza chef Nick Scotti misunderstands a Manhattan apartment advertisement and moves in with gay choreographer Anthony Barrile, with the expected culture-clash fall-out. When wannabe actor Scotti takes over Barrile's camp role in an off-Broadway play, things get even more farcical. Tony Vitale's first feature borders on the amateurish and indulges in strained humour as Italian-American stereotypes get pitted against gay ones. Luckily, the likeable performances and classic disco soundtrack paper over the not-so-wisecracks. AJ Swearing, violence, a sex scene, nudity.

Nick Scotti *Frankie* · Anthony Barrile *Warren* · Anthony DeSando *Pino* · Molly Price *Meryl* · Craig Chester *Terry* · Christopher Lawford *Dakota* ■ Dir/Scr Tony Vitale

Kiss Me Kate ★★★★ U
Musical comedy 1953 · US · Colour · 105min

This splendid MGM version of Cole Porter's smash-hit Broadway show was originally filmed in 3D, hence all those shots where Ann Miller and Howard Keel chuck things about. Director George Sidney utilises fabulous, cleverly disguised long takes in his filming of Keel, never better than as Fred Graham-cum-Petruchio, and Kathryn Grayson, playing difficult diva Lilli Vanessi, alias Shakespeare's tamed shrew Kate. Miller nearly steals the show with *Too Darn Hot*, and straight men Keenan Wynn and James Whitmore are wonderful in *Brush Up Your Shakespeare*. TS *DVD*

Kathryn Grayson *Lilli Vanessi, "Katherine"* · Howard Keel *Fred Graham, "Petruchio"* · Ann Miller *Lois Lane, "Bianca"* · Keenan Wynn *Lippy* · Bobby Van *"Gremio"* · Tommy Rall *Bill Calhoun,*

"Lucentio" · James Whitmore *Slug* · Kurt Kasznar *"Baptista"* · Bob Fosse *"Hortensio"* · Ron Randell *Cole Porter* ■ Dir George Sidney (2) · Scr Dorothy Kingsley, from the play by Cole Porter, Samuel Spewack, Bella Spewack, from the play *The Taming of the Shrew* by William Shakespeare

Kiss Me, Stupid ★★★ PG
Comedy 1964 · US · BW · 121min

Dean Martin is certainly an acquired taste: if you're a fan, then Billy Wilder's rather obvious satire on personal ambition and sexual manipulation sees the court jester of the Rat Pack on full throttle. He plays a sex-obsessed bar-room warbler, with Kim Novak as a hooker and Ray Walston as the amateur songwriter desperate to keep Martin's greasy paws off his wife. It's Wilder, so almost by definition it's smart and sharp, but also amazingly sexist. SH *DVD*

Dean Martin *Dino* · Kim Novak *Polly the Pistol* · Ray Walston *Orville J Spooner* · Felicia Farr *Zelda Spooner* · Cliff Osmond *Barney Millsap* · Barbara Pepper *Big Bertha* ■ Dir Billy Wilder · Scr Billy Wilder, IAL Diamond, from the play *L'Ora della Fantasia* by Anna Bonacci

Kiss of Death ★★★★ 12
Film noir 1947 · US · BW · 94min

Nothing in today's cinema of violence is as menacing as Richard Widmark's demented chuckle in this super-tough *film noir* thriller from ace director Henry Hathaway. Widmark's screen debut has passed into screen legend, most notably for the scene in which he shoves an elderly lady in a wheelchair down a flight of stairs in a fit of pique. The scene was thought too horrific for British audiences and was cut on UK release by a squeamish British censor. Shot in gritty style on authentic New York locations, the film features a surprisingly fine and sympathetic leading performance from the usually derided Victor Mature. An adult and involving crime drama with a truly tragic dimension. TS *DVD* *Blu*

Victor Mature *Nick Bianco* · Brian Donlevy *D'Angelo* · Coleen Gray *Nettie* · Richard Widmark *Tom Udo* · Karl Malden *Sergeant William Cullen* · Taylor Holmes *Earl Howser* · Howard Smith *Warden* · Anthony Ross *Williams* ■ Dir Henry Hathaway · Scr Ben Hecht, Charles Lederer, Philip Dunne [uncredited],from a story by Eleazar Lipsky

Kiss of Death ★★★ 18
Crime thriller 1994 · US · Colour · 96min

Few screen debuts were as chilling as Richard Widmark's in the 1947 original, though in this remake Nicolas Cage is agreeably nasty, with a goatee beard and bulging biceps to complement a serious streak of social irresponsibility. The plot has been thoroughly made over, though it's still about an ex-con (David Caruso) who is determined to go straight, but is forced into becoming an informer for nasty cop Samuel L Jackson. A gripping effort, laced with black humour and directed with a sharp eye for the hell-holes of New York. AT Swearing, violence, brief nudity. *DVD*

David Caruso *Jimmy Kilmartin* · Samuel L Jackson *Calvin* · Nicolas Cage *Little Junior* · Helen Hunt *Bev* · Kathryn Erbe *Rosie* · Stanley Tucci *Frank Zioli* · Michael Rapaport *Ronnie* · Ving Rhames *Omar* · Philip Baker Hall *Big Junior* ■ Dir Barbet Schroeder · Scr Richard Price, from a story by Eleazar Lipsky, from the 1947 film

Kiss of Fire ★★ U
Period romantic drama
1955 · US · Colour · 87min

This minor costume drama, set in the 18th century, has pretty Barbara Rush as a pretender to the Spanish throne, who makes a hazardous journey from Santa Fe to Monterey, in order to get a ship to Spain. A little excitement is engendered by a few villains, Indians on the warpath, and a bit of swashbuckling, but the direction and dialogue are rather soggy. RB

Jack Palance *El Tigre* · Barbara Rush *Princess Lucia* · Rex Reason *Duke of Montera* · Martha Hyer *Felicia* · Alan Reed *Diego* · Leslie Bradley

K

Vega • *Dir* Joseph M Newman • *Scr* Franklin Coen, Richard Collins, from the novel *The Rose and the Flame* by Jonreed Lauritzen

Kiss of Life ★★ 12
Fantasy drama
2003 · UK/Fr/Can · Colour · 83min

British debutante director Emily Young's training in Poland is evident throughout this meditation on love and loss, in which the spirit of an accident victim returns to her London home and is confused to find that her children can't see her. Ingeborga Dapkunaite lacks the emotional resources to convey the feelings and frustrations that family life gives rise to. And as the husband (an overseas aid worker played by Peter Mullan) tries to get home for her birthday, his homeward trek through Eastern European squalor features encounters that are either too slight or too consciously symbolic to be of interest. DP In English, Serb-Croat. **DVD**

Ingeborga Dapkunaite *Helen* • Peter Mullan *John* • David Warner *Pap* • Millie Findlay *Kate* • James E Martin *Telly* • Ivan Bijuk *Old man* ■ *Dir/Scr* Emily Young

Kiss of the Dragon ★★★★ 18
Martial arts action thriller
2001 · Fr/US · Colour · 94min

This furiously kinetic film combines the fighting talents of Asian superstar Jet Li with the canny genre production and scripting know-how of French auteur Luc Besson. Outrageously violent, hard-edged and constantly exciting, the film has Li as a Chinese intelligence officer sent to Paris on an undercover assignment, who becomes embroiled in a drug cartel conspiracy. Helped by hooker Bridget Fonda and hindered by super-nasty corrupt cop Tcheky Karyo, Li must use his amazing skills to see justice done. The breathtaking array of dazzling martial arts sequences is superb. AJ Violence, sex scenes, swearing, drug abuse. **DVD** **BD**

Jet Li *Liu Jiuan* • Bridget Fonda *Jessica* • Tcheky Karyo *Jean-Pierre Richard* • Ric Young *Mr Big* • Burt Kwouk *Uncle Tai* • Laurence Ashley *Aja* ■ *Dir* Chris Nahon • *Scr* Luc Besson, Robert Mark Kamen, from a story by Jet Li

Kiss of the Spider Woman ★★★★ 15
Drama
1985 · US/Bra · BW and Colour · 115min

This is an unusual, intimate tale of two very different prisoners – a flamboyant gay man (William Hurt) and a reactionary political prisoner (Raul Julia) – who share a cell in a South American jail. The *Spider Woman* of the title refers to an old movie plot Hurt lovingly recounts to Julia. Hector Babenco's film hinges on the believability of their relationship and the way the vast gap between their opposing beliefs and attitudes slowly begins to narrow. The leads are top-notch, and the juxtaposition of dream-like monochrome fantasy with harsh, squalid reality is wonderfully conceived. JC **DVD**

William Hurt *Molina* • Raul Julia *Valentin* • Sonia Braga *Leni Lamaison/Marta/Spider Woman* • José Lewgoy *Warden* • Nuno Leal Maia *Gabriel* • Antonio Petrim *Clubfoot* ■ *Dir* Hector Babenco • *Scr* Leonard Schrader, from a novel by Manuel Puig

Kiss of the Vampire ★★ 12
Horror
1962 · UK · Colour · 84min

Newlyweds honeymooning in Bavaria find themselves up to their necks in vampires in this lesser-known Hammer horror from director Don Sharp. Studio stalwarts Peter Cushing and Christopher Lee are absent here, so it's Clifford Evans (*The Curse of the Werewolf*) who takes on the mantle of the vampire killer determined to put an end to the evil reign of chief bloodsucker Noel Willman. It's pretty formulaic stuff, but the camerawork (by veteran British cinematographer Alan Hume) at least makes the tale a vivid experience. JA **DVD** **BD**

Clifford Evans *Prof Zimmer* • Noel Willman *Dr Ravna* • Edward De Souza *Gerald Harcourt* • Jennifer Daniel *Marianne Harcourt* • Barry

Warren *Carl Ravna* ■ *Dir* Don Sharp • *Scr* John Elder [Anthony Hinds] • *Cinematographer* Alan Hume

Kiss the Boys Goodbye ★★★ U
Musical comedy
1941 · US · BW · 84min

Claire Boothe's Broadway satire on Hollywood's search for an actress to play Scarlett O'Hara loses its caustic edge in the transformation into a musical comedy film. The hunt is on for a southern belle to star in a New York show, and Mary Martin heads south and ropes in her aunt and uncle to help her gain an audition and become the discovery of Don Ameche's director and Oscar Levant's composer. Not as sharp or topical as the play, but still a lot of fun. AE

Mary Martin *Cindy Lou Bethany* • Don Ameche *Lloyd Lloyd* • Oscar Levant *Dick Rayburn* • Virginia Dale *Gwen Abbott* • Barbara Jo Allen *Myra Stanhope* • Raymond Walburn *Top Rumson* • Elizabeth Patterson *Aunt Lilly Lou* • Jerome Cowan *Bert Fisher* ■ *Dir* Victor Schertzinger • *Scr* Harry Tugend, Dwight Taylor, from a play by Clare Boothe [Luce] • *Music Director* Victor Young

Kiss the Girls ★★★ 18
Detective thriller
1997 · US · Colour · 110min

All surface gloss with little real substance, this gets by thanks to the atmospheric photography and great performances from Morgan Freeman and Ashley Judd. Freeman is a forensic psychologist whose niece has been abducted by a serial kidnapper known as "Casanova"; Judd is the only woman to have escaped from the villain's secret lair. Can Judd guide Freeman to the culprit? If all logic and credibility completely disappear as the conclusion nears, it's still a compelling enough thriller. AJ Swearing, violence. **DVD**

Morgan Freeman *Alex Cross* • Ashley Judd *Kate McTiernan* • Cary Elwes *Nick Ruskin* • Alex McArthur *Sikes* • Tony Goldwyn *Will Rudolph* • Jay O Sanders *Kyle Craig* • Bill Nunn *Sampson* • Brian Cox (1) *Chief Hatfield* ■ *Dir* Gary Fleder • *Scr* David Klass, from the novel by James Patterson • *Cinematographer* Aaron Schneider

Kiss the Girls and Make Them Die ★★★
Spy caper
1966 · It · Colour · 106min

This breezy Bondian caper stars Mike Connors (of *Mannix* fame) as an American agent in Brazil investigating the activities of industrialist Raf Vallone, whose charming playboy demeanour masks a more sinister side. Along for the ride are Dorothy Provine and Terry-Thomas, who make for an amusing Lady Penelope and Parker double-act with their gadget-stuffed Rolls Royce (tea on tap!). The plot doesn't hold up to scrutiny (and the prologue hints at another film altogether), but the wry spy shenanigans build to a suitably barmy finale. JH

Mike Connors *Michael Connors* • Dorothy Provine *Susan Fleming* • Raf Vallone *Mr Ardonian* • Terry-Thomas *Lord Aldric/James* • Margaret Lee *Grace* ■ *Dir* Henry Levin, Arduino Maiuri [Dino Maiuri] • *Scr* Dino Maiuri, Jack Pulman

Kiss Them for Me ★★ U
Wartime comedy drama
1957 · US · Colour · 98min

Oh dear. The combined talents of star Cary Grant and director Stanley Donen, so successful in both *Indiscreet* and *Charade*, fail miserably here, in a remake of that old perennial "three sailors on the town" plot (a veritable Donen classic), this time set in San Francisco during the Second World War and based loosely on the novel *Shore Leave*. The movie never really catches fire, and is worth viewing now only as a 1950s period piece. TS **DVD**

Cary Grant *Crewson* • Jayne Mansfield *Alice* • Suzy Parker *Gwenneth* • Leif Erickson *Eddie Turnbill* • Ray Walston *Lieutenant "Mac" McCann* • Larry Blyden *Mississip* • Nathaniel Frey *Chief Petty Officer Ruddle* • Werner Klemperer *Commander Wallace* ■ *Dir* Stanley Donen • *Scr* Julius Epstein, from the play by Luther Davis, from the novel *Shore Leave* by Frederic Wakeman

Kiss Tomorrow Goodbye ★★★★ PG
Crime drama
1950 · US · BW · 102min

James Cagney is in *White Heat* mode playing tough and mean in this cracking Warner Bros crime drama. The pace never lets up, and there's not a key character on show who displays any kind of morals or ethics whatsoever – even the cops are bent. Especially notable are Luther Adler as a phoney lawyer with a cheap line in philosophy and producer William Cagney as – surprise! – Cagney's screen brother. Underrated when it first appeared, this movie's sheer constant venality gives it a very contemporary sheen. TS **DVD**

James Cagney *Ralph Cotter* • Barbara Payton *Holiday Carleton* • Helena Carter *Margaret Dobson* • Ward Bond *Inspector Weber* • Luther Adler *Cherokee Mandon* • William Cagney *Ralph's brother* ■ *Dir* Gordon Douglas • *Scr* Harry Brown, from the novel by Horace McCoy

Kissed ★★★ 18
Romantic drama
1996 · Can · Colour · 75min

Director Lynne Stopkewich's exploration of the taboo of necrophilia will divide opinion. Molly Parker plays a young woman so fascinated by death she goes to work as a mortician in a funeral parlour. There she indulges her sexual fantasies with the deceased until a living, breathing boyfriend appears. But can he measure up to the safe embraces of her former lovers? It sounds completely nauseating, but, although the script is insultingly naive in places, the subject is tackled with discretion and the film makes its mark, thanks to Parker's sensitive central performance. AJ Swearing, sex scenes. **DVD**

Molly Parker *Sandra Larson* • Peter Outerbridge *Matt* • Jay Brazeau *Mr Wallis* • Natasha Morley *Young Sandra* • Jessie Winter Mudie *Carol* • James Timmons *Jan* • Joe Maffei *Biology teacher* • Robert Thurston *Detective* ■ *Dir* Lynne Stopkewich • *Scr* Lynne Stopkewich, Angus Fraser, from the story *We So Seldom Look on Love* by Barbara Gowdy

Kisses ★★★★ 15
Drama
2008 · Ire/Swe · Colour and BW · 75min

On the run from their troubled cash-strapped families on the outskirts of Dublin, two youngsters seek refuge in the city centre at night in this gritty low-budget Irish drama. The accents are so authentic it's hard to pick out every word, but the emotional contours of writer/director Lance Daly's compact feature are in sharp relief, a palpable compassion for a boy and girl too naive to understand what sort of danger they're in. Moving purposefully from black-and-white (grim suburbia) to colour (the bright lights), the film comes across as slightly contrived at times – especially with the number of references to Bob Dylan that Daly squeezes in – yet the sheer truthfulness of the central performances proves almost heart-breaking. TJ

Kelly O'Neill *Kylie* • Shane Curry *Dylan* • Paul Roe *Dylan's Da* • Neili Conroy *Dylan's Ma* • David Bendito *Dredger captain* • Elizabeth Fuh *Gardiner street girl* • Cathy Malone *Kylie's Ma* • Stephen Rea *Down Under Dylan* ■ *Dir/Scr* Lance Daly

Kisses for My President ★★ U
Comedy
1964 · US · BW · 113min

Polly Bergen stars as the first woman president of the United States in this thunderingly mawkish pre-feminist tract. A lot of talent that should have known better appears alongside Bergen, including the Fred MacMurray (as the protocol-cursed "First Man"), but everyone seems to be struggling with the material. Director Curtis Bernhardt fails to find the right screwball tone, and the result is surprisingly witless and cloying. The sets look cheap, too. TS

Fred MacMurray *Thad McCloud* • Polly Bergen *Leslie McCloud* • Arlene Dahl *Doris Reid* • Edward Andrews *Senator Walsh* • Eli Wallach *Valdez* • Donald May *John O'Connor* • Harry Holcombe *Bill Richards* • Anna Capri [Ahna Capri] *Gloria McCloud* ■ *Dir* Curtis Bernhardt • *Scr* Claude Binyon, Robert G Kane

Kissin' Cousins ★★ U
Musical
1964 · US · Colour · 87min

Most of Elvis Presley's movie vehicles arouse the suspicion that their makers thought cheapness and speed more important than quality, but this double-trouble romantic comedy is a pleasant way to pass the time. Elvis plays the two leads: a (blond!) hillbilly, resisting the US Air Force's plan to build a base on his family's land, as well as the lieutenant cousin whose job it is to persuade them. JG

Elvis Presley *Josh Morgan/Jodie Tatum* • Arthur O'Connell *Pappy Tatum* • Glenda Farrell *Ma Tatum* • Jack Albertson *Capt Robert Salbo* • Pam Austin [Pamela Austin] *Selena Tatum* • Cynthia Pepper *Midge* • Yvonne Craig *Azalea Tatum* ■ *Dir* Gene Nelson • *Scr* Gerald Drayson Adams, Gene Nelson, from a story by Gerald Drayson Adams, Gene Nelson

Kissing a Fool ★★ 15
Romantic comedy
1998 · US · Colour · 89min

David Schwimmer tries to shrug off his nice-guy image to play a self-centred sports journalist, who tests his girlfriend's fidelity by asking his best friend Jason Lee to seduce her. Told in flashback at the girlfriend's wedding to one of the men (but which one?), this has good performances from Lee and Mili Avital, but a miscast Schwimmer struggles to convince as the sleazy rogue in this only moderately enjoyable effort. JC Swearing, sexual references.

David Schwimmer *Max Abbitt* • Jason Lee *Jay Murphy* • Mili Avital *Samantha Andrews* • Bonnie Hunt *Linda* • Vanessa Angel *Natasha* • Kari Wuhrer *Dara* ■ *Dir* Doug Ellin • *Scr* Doug Ellin, James Frey, from a story by James Frey

The Kissing Bandit ★★ U
Musical comedy
1949 · US · Colour · 100min

A major flop on its first release, this film became famous because its star, Frank Sinatra, would constantly joke about it being the low point of his career. The idea of casting the then-puny actor as the son of a desperado noted for his female conquests probably seemed amusing at the time, but the star is uneasy, the direction by Laslo Benedek (his first film) too stolid and the score mundane. TV

Frank Sinatra *Ricardo* • Kathryn Grayson *Teresa* • J Carrol Naish *Chico* • Mildred Natwick *Isabella* • Ricardo Montalban *Fiesta dancer* • Ann Miller *Fiesta dancer* • Cyd Charisse *Fiesta dancer* ■ *Dir* Laslo Benedek • *Scr* Isobel Lennart, John Briard Harding

Kissing Jessica Stein ★★★ 15
Romantic comedy
2001 · US · Colour · 92min

Two unknowns, Jennifer Westfeldt and Heather Juergensen, wrote an off-Broadway play about female sexuality and two women who attempt a lesbian affair. A few years later and they're both starring in the spin-off film – a witty, quirky, original New York story about a straight Jewish journalist (Westfeldt) who responds to a singles ad and ends up on a date with the also straight "but willing to experiment" Juergensen. As the women walk the Sapphic way, they have to deal with the shock waves this sends through family and friends. A sparklingly funny gem. LH Swearing, sex scenes. **DVD**

Jennifer Westfeldt *Jessica Stein* • Heather Juergensen *Helen Cooper* • Scott Cohen *Josh Meyers* • Tovah Feldshuh *Judy Stein* • Jackie Hoffman *Joan* • Michael Mastro *Martin* ■ *Dir* Charles Herman-Wurmfeld • *Scr* Heather Juergensen, Jennifer Westfeldt, from their play *Lipschtick*

Kissinger and Nixon ★★★
Historical drama
1995 · US · Colour

Riveting performances by Beau Bridges as the paranoid and prickly Nixon and Ron Silver as the ambitious Kissinger make this intense TV movie well worth watching. It recounts the 1972-3 Vietnam peace negotiations in which President Richard Nixon and his national security adviser, Henry Kissinger, were often at odds.

U SUITABLE FOR ALL   Uc SUITABLE ESPECIALLY FOR YOUNG CHILDREN (DVD ONLY)   PG PARENTAL GUIDANCE   12A UNDER 12s TO BE ACCOMPANIED (CINEMA ONLY)

Veteran director Daniel Petrie keeps Lionel Chetwynd's intelligent script moving briskly and produces a fascinating behind-the-scenes look at politics and power in action. MC

Ron Silver *Henry Kissinger* • Beau Bridges *Richard Nixon* • Matt Frewer *Alexander Haig* • Ron White *HR "Bob" Haldeman* • George Takei *Le Duc Tho* • Kenneth Welsh *James "Scotty" Reston* • Tony Rosato *Charles Colson* ■ *Dir* Daniel Petrie • *Scr* Lionel Chetwynd, from the biography *Kissinger: a Biography* by Walter Isaacson

Kit Carson ★★★ U
Western 1940 · US · BW · 96min

There was a time when Kit Carson and Buffalo Bill were the heroes of schoolboys everywhere, with their (largely fictional) achievements celebrated in comics. This is the definitive biopic of frontier scout Carson's adventurous life. Jon Hall makes a solid enough Carson as he tangles with expedition leader Dana Andrews for the love of Lynn Bari, but the script doesn't allow for much character depth. Since much of Carson's life was fictionalised in his own lifetime via dime novels, who could blame Hollywood for turning history into a rattling adventure? TS

Jon Hall *Kit Carson* • Lynn Bari *Dolores Murphy* • Dana Andrews *Captain John C Fremont* • Harold Huber *Lopez* • Ward Bond *Ape* • Renie Riano *Miss Genevieve Pilchard* ■ *Dir* George B Seitz • *Scr* George Bruce

The Kitchen ★★★ PG
Drama 1961 · UK · BW · 70min

Dramatist Arnold Wesker drew on his experience as a pastry chef when he wrote his play, *The Kitchen*, here filmed with some of the cast from the original London stage production. Virtually plotless, the action records one day of hard work and thwarted ambition in a restaurant kitchen. The long, philosophical conversations do not adapt well to the screen, but the sequences showing food being churned out factory-style to the detriment of the workers' mental and physical health have a manic intensity. In its day, the play was regarded as an allegory of life's struggle. DM

Carl Mohner *Peter* • Mary Yeomans *Monica* • Brian Phelan *Kevin* • Tom Bell *Paul* • Howard Greene *Raymond* • Eric Pohlmann *Mr Marango* • James Bolam *Michael* ■ *Dir* James Hill • *Scr* Sidney Cole

Kitchen ★★★ 15
Romantic drama
1997 · HK/Jpn · Colour · 120min

Employing various distancing devices, director Ho Yim studiously chronicles the relationship between the timid Yasuko Tomita and hairdresser Jordan Chan and the impact it has on his transsexual mother, Law Kar-Ying. While this strategy occasionally makes it difficult to identify with the characters, the tone shifts deftly between tenderness and eroticism, and there is a pleasing hesitancy about the romance. Admirable, if not always engrossing. DP Cantonese +subtitles. Violence, swearing, nudity.

Jordan Chan *Louie* • Yasuko Tomita *Aggie* • Law Kar-Ying *Emma* • Karen Mok *Jenny* • Lau Siu-Ming *Mr Chiu* • Lo Koon-Lan *Chika* ■ *Dir* Ho Yim • *Scr* Ho Yim, from the novella by Banana Yoshimoto

Kitchen Stories ★★★★ PG
Period comedy 2003 · Nor/Swe · Colour · 90min

In this charming 1950s-set comedy, Bent Hamer concentrates on the slow-burning relationship between curmudgeonly Norwegian farmer Joachim Calmeyer and Tomas Norstrom, the jobsworthy representative of a Swedish furnishing institute detailed to record Calmeyer's kitchen habits. The initial series of near-wordless encounters is paced to perfection, but the humour becomes more personal and affecting once the bachelors break the rules of the exercise and begin communicating. The performances are a joy, especially once the duo begin to revel in their minor acts of rebellion. DP Norwegian +subtitles. *DVD*

Joachim Calmeyer *Isak Bjorvik* • Tomas Norstrom *Folke Nilsson* • Reine Brynolfsson *Malmberg* • Bjørn Floberg *Grant* ■ *Dir* Bent Hamer • *Scr* Bent Hamer, Jorgen Bergmark

The Kitchen Toto ★★ 15
Drama 1987 · UK · Colour · 91min

Bob Peck gives one of his all too rare film performances as the British Chief of Police handling unrest in Kenya during the 1950s. The tale is told through the eyes of Edwin Mahinda, a young Kikuyu boy whose loyalties are torn between the Mau Mau, his tribe's rebel group (the killers of his minister father) and the British whose service he is in. Director Harry Hook as a native Kenyan obviously understands the issues here, but does a poor job in making them comprehensible to your average viewer. LH

Edwin Mahinda *Mwangi* • Bob Peck *John Graham* • Phyllis Logan *Janet Graham* • Nicholas Charles Mugo • Ronald Pirie *Edward Graham* • Robert Urquhart *DC McKinnon* • Kirsten Hughes *Mary McKinnon* • Edward Judd *Dick Luis* ■ *Dir/Scr* Harry Hook

The Kite Runner ★★★ 12
Drama 2007 · US · Colour · 122min

For the most part, this adaptation of Khaled Hosseini's bestselling novel coasts on the charm of its two young leads. In 1978, wealthy Amir (Zekiria Ebrahimi) finds his friendship with Hassan (Ahmad Khan Mahmoodzada), the son of a servant, severely tested after a horrifying attack on Hassan that Amir fails to prevent. The adult Amir (Khalid Abdalla) seeks redemption, returning to Taliban-ruled Afghanistan after 20 years living in America. Director Marc Forster (*Finding Neverland*) achieves a surface feeling of authenticity, yet fails to portray any shades of grey in the changing political landscape of Afghanistan. This is a simple tale of good versus evil, but its harsh nature – innocence not so much lost as wrenched away – means that it can't fail to tug the heartstrings. SP Dari, English +subtitles. Violence, some swearing. *DVD*

Khalid Abdalla *Amir* • Homayoun Ershadi *Baba* • Zekiria Ebrahimi *Young Amir* • Ahmad Khan Mahmoodzada *Young Hassan* • Shaun Toub *Rahim Khan* • Nabi Tanha *Ali* • Ali Danish Bakhtyari *Sohrab* • Saïd Taghmaoui *Farid* ■ *Dir* Marc Forster • *Scr* David Benioff, from the novel by Khaled Hosseini

Kitne Door... Kitne Paas ★★★ PG
Romantic road movie
2001 · Ind · Colour · 146min

Director Mehul Kumar makes a tidy job of this romantic road movie, which comes across as a Bollywood blend of *It Happened One Night* and *Planes, Trains and Automobiles*. Fardeen Khan and Amrita Arora star as two young Gujuratis who return to India for their respective arranged marriages after working in the United States, only to fall in love on the nightmare journey home. Glossing over the realities of life in the Indian countryside, this is escapism pure and simple, with the emphasis being on the lover's decreasingly tempestuous relationship rather than the clash between tradition and progress. DP Hindi +subtitles. *DVD*

Fardeen Khan *Jatin* • Amrita Arora *Karishma* • Govind Namdev *Karishma's father* • Shama Deshpande *Karishma's mother* • Beena *Jatin's mother* ■ *Dir* Mehul Kumar • *Scr* Imtiaz Patel, Yunus Sejawal, Mehul Kumar, from a story by Mehul Kumar

Kitty ★
Wartime melodrama 1928 · UK · BW · 92min

This silent melodrama had some spoken dialogue later tacked on to some sequences, making it officially Britain's first sound film. However, these awkward and pointless scenes only make worse what comes before in the tale of a possessive mother (Dorothy Cumming), whose vicious bad-mouthing of her RAF pilot son's fiancée causes him to crash and become paralysed. How the lovers, John Stuart and Estelle Brody, overcome Cumming's efforts to keep them apart, constitutes the plot of this ludicrously unconvincing tear-jerker. RK

Estelle Brody *Kitty Greenwood* • John Stuart *Alex St George* • Marie Ault *Sarah Greenwood* • Dorothy Cumming *Mrs St George* • Winter Hall *John Furnival* • Olaf Hytten *Leaper* ■ *Dir* Victor Saville • *Scr* Violet E Powell, Benn W Levy, from the novel by Warwick Deeping

Kitty ★★★★
Period drama 1945 · US · BW · 103min

Paulette Goddard is the cockney waif plucked from the streets of 18th-century London to be tutored for marriage into high society in this sumptuously mounted drama. Beautifully acted, well photographed and brilliantly directed, this is a harsh variation of *Pygmalion* with Goddard being forced into two unsuitable marriages. Ray Milland is his dependable self as the nobleman pulling the strings, Constance Collier is a dissipated aunt and Sara Allgood a Hogarthian wreck, but the real scene-stealing is done by Reginald Owen as a lecherous old duke. AE

Paulette Goddard *Kitty* • Ray Milland *Sir Hugh Marcy* • Patric Knowles *Brett Hardwood, the Earl of Carstairs* • Reginald Owen *Duke of Malmunster* • Cecil Kellaway *Thomas Gainsborough* • Constance Collier *Lady Susan Dewitt* • Dennis Hoey *Jonathan Selby* • Sara Allgood *Old Meg* ■ *Dir* Mitchell Leisen • *Scr* Darrell Ware, Karl Tunberg, from a novel by Rosamund Marshall • *Cinematographer* Daniel L Fapp • *Music* Victor Young • *Art Directors* Hans Dreier, Walter Tyler

Kitty Foyle ★★★
Drama 1940 · US · BW · 106min

Ginger Rogers won her best actress Oscar for this melodrama, which proved that she had a career outside her partnership with Fred Astaire. What Rogers was particularly good at was portraying the common, not to say vulgar, shop girl, and that is what Kitty Foyle is: a shop girl who can't make up her mind which man to choose – doctor James Craig or playboy Dennis Morgan? TS

Ginger Rogers *Kitty Foyle* • Dennis Morgan *Wyn Strafford* • James Craig *Mark* • Eduardo Ciannelli *Giono* • Ernest Cossart *Pop* • Gladys Cooper *Mrs Strafford* ■ *Dir* Sam Wood • *Scr* Dalton Trumbo, Donald Ogden Stewart, from the novel by Christopher Morley

Klimt ★★★ 15
Biographical drama
2006 · Austria/Ger/UK/Fr · Colour · 126min

Director Raúl Ruiz dispenses with the conventional chronology of the biopic here, to re-create the world that shaped an artist's mind. Ruiz presents the life of Art Deco master Gustav Klimt as a dream world revisited from his deathbed in Vienna in 1918. Consequently, incidents whirl like the dizzying images passing through John Malkovich's subconscious, as he recalls the women, patrons and intellectuals who fêted and frustrated him. It's a demanding portrait, but always a compelling one. The period trappings couldn't be more exquisite and Ricardo Aronovich's photography has a gallery quality. But Gilbert Adair's dialogue is occasionally awkward and Ruiz's staging and structuring often feel self-conscious. DP English, German, French +subtitles. *DVD*

John Malkovich *Gustav Klimt* • Veronica Ferres *Emilie Flöge* • Saffron Burrows *Lea de Castro* • Stephen Dillane *Secretary* • Sandra Ceccarelli *Serena Lederer* • Nikolai Kinski *Egon Schiele* • Aglaia Szyszkowitz *Mizzi* ■ *Dir* Raúl Ruiz • *Scr* Raúl Ruiz, Gilbert Adair, from an idea by Dieter Pochlatko, Herbert Vesely

Klitschko ★★★ 12
Sports documentary 2011 · Ger · Colour · 117min

A fascinating documentary about two fascinating men, Wladimir and Vitali Klitschko, the Ukrainian-born boxing brothers who both rose to become world champions but have always refused to fight each other. Ample access to the brothers, their families and entourage allows a rounded portrait of the pair, who are multilingual, self-deprecating and educated (each has a PhD). It's a touch long for non-fans, but it's entertaining and informative, offering something to even the die-hard anti-pugilist. SvM Russian, German, English +subtitles.

Wladimir Klitschko • Vitali Klitschko • Natalia Klitschko • Don King • Lennox Lewis ■ *Dir* Sebastian Dehnhardt

Klondike Annie ★★★ U
Musical comedy drama 1936 · US · BW · 73min

Even in her later pictures, Mae West refused to be tamed, provoking the usual fierce attacks from the forces of righteousness. In this picture, they objected to her being the mistress of an Oriental, a murderess who then masquerades as a missionary, and a performer of songs such as *I'm an Occidental Woman in an Oriental Mood for Love*. Mae wrote the script and typically cast as the men in her life lumpish actors who wouldn't steal any of her limelight. Audiences loved it then, and it's still good fun. AE *DVD*

Mae West *"The Frisco Doll"*, Rose Carlton • Victor McLaglen *Capt Bull Brackett* • Philip Reed *Inspector Jack Forrest* • Helen Jerome Eddy *Sister Annie Alden* • Harry Beresford *Brother Bowser* • Harold Huber *Chan Lo* ■ *Dir* Raoul Walsh • *Scr* Mae West

Klown ★★ 18
Comedy 2010 · Den · Colour · 87min

This spin-off from a cult Danish TV show owes much to *Curb Your Enthusiasm* and is a far from subtle romp whose brand of gross-out humour is likely to appeal to fans of *The Hangover*. Needing to prove he has the potential to be a good dad to his pregnant girlfriend, middle-aged klutz Frank (Frank Hvam) invites a teenager on the trip of a lifetime. However, the expedition to a music festival also includes a visit to an upmarket brothel, although this is almost incidental alongside the chaos that occurs at a campsite and the outdoor festival itself. Clearly comfortable in familiar roles, the leads handle the pratfalls and un-PC misunderstandings with some aplomb. But the endless contrivances have long ceased to amuse before they eventually overwhelm. DP Danish +subtitles.

Frank Hvam *Frank* • Casper Christensen *Casper* • Marcuz Jess Petersen *Bo* • Mia Lyhne *Mia* ■ *Dir* Mikkel Norgaard • *Scr* Casper Christensen, Frank Hvam, from a story by Christensen, Hvam, Mikkel Norgaard

Klute ★★★★★ 18
Thriller 1971 · US · Colour · 107min

This is a quite exceptional adult thriller, given a striking immediacy by Alan J Pakula's highly atmospheric direction and laced with genuinely nail-biting suspense. Jane Fonda deservedly won the best actress Oscar for her remarkably cool walk on the wild side as a call girl stalked by a homicidal maniac. But Donald Sutherland is on top form, too, playing the gentle small-town detective who teaches her the difference between love and sex as he closes in on the killer. AJ Violence, swearing, sex scenes, nudity.

Jane Fonda *Bree Daniels* • Donald Sutherland *John Klute* • Charles Cioffi *Peter Cable* • Nathan George *Lieutenant Trask* • Roy R Scheider [Roy Scheider] *Frank Ligourin* • Dorothy Tristan *Arlyn Page* • Rita Gam *Trina* • Vivian Nathan *Psychiatrist* ■ *Dir* Alan J Pakula • *Scr* Andy Lewis, Dave Lewis • *Cinematographer* Gordon Willis

The Knack... and How to Get It ★★★ 15
Comedy 1965 · UK · BW · 85min

This Palme d'Or-winning comedy is an energetic example of Richard Lester's fascination with the more manic methods of the French New Wave. In opening out Ann Jellicoe's stage play, he makes dizzying use of swinging London, as timid teacher Michael Crawford wheels home the brass bed that his womanising tenant Ray Brooks has assured him will transform his romantic fortunes. Although perfectly in tune with its time, the film is now hard to watch without wincing at the incessant stream of sexist witticisms and the painfully eager

K

performances of Crawford and Brooks. **DP** *DVD*

Rita Tushingham *Nancy Jones* • Ray Brooks *Tolen* • Michael Crawford *Colin* • Donal Donnelly *Tom* • John Bluthal *Angry father* • Wensley Pithey *Teacher* • William Dexter *Dress shop owner* • Peter Copley *Picture owner* ■ *Dir* Richard Lester • *Scr* Charles Wood, from the play by Ann Jellicoe

Knave of Hearts ★★★★
Romantic drama 1954 · Fr/UK · BW · 109min

Gallic heart-throb Gérard Philipe was destined for a tragically early death but he made a charming philanderer in this ironic romantic drama. In the episodic story, set and shot on location in London, Philipe, though married to Valerie Hobson, still finds himself attracted to Natasha Parry. Directed and co-written by René Clément, the film offers a refreshing view of England and English women as seen through French eyes. **RB**

Gérard Philipe *Andre Ripois* • Valerie Hobson *Catherine* • Joan Greenwood *Norah* • Margaret Johnston *Anne* • Natasha Parry *Patricia* • Germaine Montero *Marcelle* • Diana Decker *Diana* • Percy Marmont *Catherine's father* ■ *Dir* René Clément • *Scr* Hugh Mills, René Clément, Hugh Queneau, from the novel *Lovers, Happy Lovers!* by Louis Hemon

Knickerbocker Holiday ★★ U
Musical comedy drama 1944 · US · BW · 85min

Originally a heavyweight and unappealingly heavy-handed musical, this makes for a lightweight, and equally unappealing, film. Stripped of most of Kurt Weill's songs (and with its politics watered down) what is left is a tedious period piece, set in New York during the Pieter Stuyvesant era, about a romance between a subversive journalist (Nelson Eddy) and the daughter (Constance Dowling) of a Dutch councillor. **RK**

Nelson Eddy *Brom Broeck* • Charles Coburn *Pieter Stuyvesant* • Constance Dowling *Tina Tienhoven* • Ernest Cossart *Tienhoven* • Johnnie "Scat" Davis [Johnnie Davis] *Ten Pin* • Richard Hale *Tammany* • Shelley Winters *Ulda Tienhoven* • Glenn Strange *Big Muscle* ■ *Dir* Harry Joe Brown • *Scr* David Boehm, Roland Leigh, Harold Goldman, Thomas Lennon (1), from the musical by Kurt Weill, Maxwell Anderson

Knife in the Head ★★★★
Political thriller 1978 · W Ger · Colour · 112min

Chillingly suggesting that the West Germany of the 1970s was on the brink of a new form of totalitarianism, this multilayered film is at once a socialist tract, an uncompromising thriller and a downbeat human drama. Severely wounded after he is unwittingly caught up in a police raid, scientist Bruno Ganz (giving a quietly heroic performance) has to rebuild his life from scratch, inadvertently becoming a political pawn in the process. Shot with calculated detachment by director Reinhard Hauff. **DP** In German.

Bruno Ganz *Dr Berthold Hoffmann* • Angela Winkler *Ann Hoffmann* • Hans Christian Blech *Scholz* • Udo Samel *Schurig* • Eike Gallwitz *Dr Groeske* • Carla Egerer *Nurse Angelika Mueller* ■ *Dir* Reinhard Hauff • *Scr* Peter Schneider

Knife in the Water ★★★★ PG
Psychological drama 1962 · Pol · BW · 94min

Nominated for the best foreign language film Oscar, the only feature completed by Roman Polanski in his native Poland is a lean, calculated study of male posturing and the hostilities that reinforce the generation gap. Shot in a steely black and white that intensifies both the film's chilling atmosphere and the crackling charge of sexual electricity that courses between the protagonists, the action is given an unbearable tension by its claustrophobic setting on board a yacht during a weekend cruise. The cast is superb, with the non-professional Zygmunt Malanowicz judging his swaggering brio to perfection. **DP** Polish +subtitles. *DVD*

Leon Niemczyk *Andrzej* • Jolanta Umecka *Christine* • Zygmunt Malanowicz *Young man* ■ *Dir* Roman Polanski • *Scr* Jerzy Skolimowski, Jakub Goldberg, Roman Polanski • *Cinematographer* Jerzy Lipman

Knight and Day ★★★ 12
Action adventure 2010 · US · Colour · 104min

A flop in the US, *Knight and Day* is at best a perfectly serviceable confection, a caper movie in the *North by Northwest* mould except pumped up with state-of-the-art effects. Tom Cruise is the mysterious "rogue agent" who embroils ditzy mechanic Cameron Diaz in a jet-setting espionage adventure. Despite big set pieces - mainly chases, by road, air and rail - ably handled by director James Mangold and fabulous locations, the film sort of goes in one side of the brain and out the other, leaving little trace, while the expected chemistry between the two leads never comes alight. Unlike all the vehicles exploding around them. **AC** Violence, brief swearing. *DVD* *Blu-ray*

Tom Cruise *Roy Miller* • Cameron Diaz *June Havens* • Peter Sarsgaard *Fitzgerald* • Maggie Grace *April Havens* • Paul Dano *Simon Feck* ■ *Dir* James Mangold • *Scr* Patrick O'Neill

A Knight in Camelot ★★ PG
Fantasy comedy adventure 1998 · US · Colour · 84min

Whoopi Goldberg brings her wacky comic sensibilities to this updated TV-movie version of Mark Twain's *A Connecticut Yankee in King Arthur's Court*. A computer researcher accidentally transports herself back to medieval times. Taken for a witch, Goldberg is thrown into a dungeon, but her laptop computer gets her out of trouble when she's able to predict a solar eclipse - proving to King Arthur (Michael York) and the jealous wizard Merlin (Ian Richardson) that she has magical powers. Preachy. **MC** *DVD*

Whoopi Goldberg *Vivien Morgan* • Michael York *King Arthur* • Amanda Donohoe *Queen Guinevere* • Ian Richardson *Merlin* • James Coombes *Sir Lancelot* • Robert Addie *Sir Sagramour* ■ *Dir* Roger Young • *Scr* Joe Wiesenfeld, from the novel *A Connecticut Yankee in King Arthur's Court* by Mark Twain

Knight Moves ★★★ 18
Thriller 1992 · US/Ger · Colour · 111min

This is a lively thriller starring Christopher Lambert as a chess master whose bid to win a major tournament takes an unexpected turn when his lover ends up murdered. As corpses start piling up like captured pieces, cop Tom Skerritt and psychologist Diane Lane start whittling away at Lambert's defence. Solid performances and some decent plot twists keep the picture on the boil. **AT** Swearing, violence. *DVD*

Christopher Lambert *Peter Sanderson* • Diane Lane *Kathy Sheppard* • Tom Skerritt *Frank Sedman* • Daniel Baldwin *Andy Wagner* • Charles Bailey-Gates *David Willerman* • Arthur Brauss *Viktor Yurilivich* • Katherine Isobel [Katharine Isabelle] *Erica Sanderson* • Ferdinand Mayne [Ferdy Mayne] *Jeremy Edmonds* • Don Thompson *Father* ■ *Dir* Carl Schenkel • *Scr* Brad Mirman

Knight of Cups ★★ 15
Romantic drama 2015 · US · Colour · 117min

Terrence Malick, one of American cinema's true artists (*Badlands*, *The Thin Red Line*), has been somewhat churning them out recently, this being the third of three expressionistic canvases (together with *The Tree of Life* and *To the Wonder*) in just over five years. Christian Bale convinces as the restless, shallow Hollywood screenwriter, measuring out his life in glamorous parties and past relationships, but Malick's surface poetry has a narrow palette that soon leads to tedium. **AC** Swearing, sexual references, nudity.

Christian Bale *Rick* • Cate Blanchett *Nancy* • Natalie Portman *Elizabeth* • Brian Dennehy *Joseph* • Antonio Banderas *Tonio* • Freida Pinto *Helen* ■ *Dir/Scr* Terrence Malick

Knight of the Plains ★★ U
Western 1939 · US · BW · 62min

Probably the most interesting fact about this B-western for viewers today is that it was co-produced by the great comedian Stan Laurel. It's a very average tale, featuring former opera singer-turned-singing cowboy Fred Scott, who's aided in his battle against villain John Merton by comic sidekick Al St John. Laurel's involvement seems to have been purely financial, and this is no different from other Scott star vehicles: mercifully short with a sort of period charm. **TS**

Fred Scott *Fred "Melody" Brent* • Al St John *"Fuzzy"* • Marion Weldon *Gail Rand* • Richard Cramer *Clem Peterson* • John Merton *Dan Carson/Pedro De Cordova* • Frank Larue *JC Rand* ■ *Dir* Sam Newfield • *Scr* Fred Myton

Knight without Armour ★★★ U
First World War spy romance 1937 · UK · BW · 103min

In 1937 Marlene Dietrich, the highest paid actress in Hollywood, accepted a modest $350,000 to star in this lavish, British-made Alexander Korda production. This story of the First World War, Russian Revolution, rebelling peasantry and espionage, became a critical and commercial hit. Dietrich is radiant throughout, while love interest appears in the shape of spy Robert Donat, who wears heroism on his sleeve and what looks like a dead yak on his head. The script is pure drivel, but Jacques Feyder's direction has a real sheen. **AT**

Marlene Dietrich *Alexandra Adraxine, nee Vladinoff* • Robert Donat *AJ Fothergill/Peter Ouranoff* • Irene Vanbrugh *Duchess of Zorin* • Herbert Lomas *General Gregor Vladinoff* • Austin Trevor *Colonel Adraxine* • Basil Gill *Axelstein* • David Tree *Maronin* ■ *Dir* Jacques Feyder • *Scr* Lajos Bíró, Arthur Wimperis, Frances Marion, from the novel *Without Armour* by James Hilton

Knightriders ★★★ 15
Cult drama 1981 · US · Colour · 140min

A travelling commune of motorcyclists try to live their lives according to the doctrine of King Arthur and the knights of the round table by organising medieval-style fairs, complete with jousting competitions. But self-styled monarch Ed Harris finds his Hell's Angels Camelot and his efforts to uphold a chivalrous code under threat from bickering and money problems. This unusual fable is a captivating departure from zombie horror king George Romero. **AJ** *DVD* *Blu-ray*

Ed Harris *Billy* • Tom Savini *Morgan* • Gary Lahti *Alan* • Amy Ingersoll *Linet* • Patricia Tallman *Julie* • Christine Forrest *Angie* • Warner Shook *Pippin* • Stephen King ■ *Dir/Scr* George A Romero

Knights of the Round Table ★★★ PG
Period adventure 1953 · US · Colour · 111min

This 1950s Hollywood retelling of the Arthurian legend finds Lancelot being given his marching orders by Arthur for his, shall we say, inappropriate affection for Guinevere, but galloping back to rescue the day by overcoming the wicked Mordred. Shot in Britain, as MGM's first CinemaScope movie, it stars the good-looking but passionless Robert Taylor and Ava Gardner as the doomed lovers. The finished product is long on pomp and pageantry, though sadly not as stirring as it sounds or should be. **PF**

Robert Taylor (1) *Sir Lancelot* • Ava Gardner *Queen Guinevere* • Mel Ferrer *King Arthur* • Stanley Baker *Sir Modred* • Anne Crawford *Morgan Le Fay* • Felix Aylmer *Merlin* • Maureen Swanson *Elaine* • Robert Urquhart *Sir Gawaine* ■ *Dir* Richard Thorpe • *Scr* Talbot Jennings, Jan Lustig, Noel Langley, from the prose romance *Le Mort d'Arthur* by Sir Thomas Malory

Knights of the Round Table: King Arthur
Period action fantasy 2016 · US · Colour

This is a preview - no prints were available to review as we went to press: Apparently the first in a series of six films set in the

Arthurian universe, if all goes well, this return to very familiar territory has a few things going for it. Guy Ritchie's blokey, playful direction for one, a script by Joby Harold, whose *Awake* skilfully, grippingly and swiftly told the story of a heart-transplant patient anaesthetised but still aware of what's going on around him as the surgeons dive in. And there's Charlie Hunnam as a ducking, diving, geezerish Arthur. **SvM**

Charlie Hunnam *King Arthur* • Jude Law *Vortigern* • Eric Bana *Uther Pendragon* • Djimon Hounsou *Sir Bedivere* • Astrid Bergès-Frisbey *Guinevere* ■ *Dir* Guy Ritchie • *Scr* Joby Harold • *Cinematographer* John Mathieson

Knights of the South Bronx ★★★
Drama based on a true story 2005 · US · Colour · 89min

Learning chess gives new meaning to the lives of disadvantaged inner-city kids in this uplifting melodrama from Allen Hughes, who's better known as a co-director with brother Albert (*From Hell*). Based on real events, it stars Ted Danson as a businessman-turned-substitute teacher who uses the game as a way of connecting with his pupils in a tough Bronx school. Although the well-trodden "tutor as inspiration" plotline ultimately holds no surprises, Hughes wisely adds some of his trademark urban grit to temper the inevitable schmaltz. **SF**

Ted Danson *Richard Mason* • Malcolm David Kelley *Jimmy* • Keke Palmer *Kenya Russell* • Clifton Powell *Cokey* • Devon Bostick *Darren* ■ *Dir* Allen Hughes • *Scr* Jamal Joseph, Dianne Houston, from a story by Joseph

A Knight's Tale ★★★★ PG
Romantic period adventure 2001 · US · Colour · 126min

This irreverent medieval caper sets out its stall right at the start, when Queen's anthem *We Will Rock You* thuds on to the soundtrack at a joust. So far, so anachronistic. But the real twist is that the 14th-century spectators join in and clap in time. It's that kind of film, full of such cheeky flourishes - jousting fans sing rock songs, emcees talk up contestants like it's WWF wrestling, and dancers at a royal banquet groove to David Bowie's *Golden Years*. Heart-throb-in-waiting Heath Ledger dreams of being a knight, and so impersonates one with the help of sidekicks Mark Addy, Alan Tudyk and Paul Bettany (who casually steals the film with his portrayal of writer Geoffrey Chaucer). Tremendous, infectious fun. **AC** Violence, nudity. *DVD* *Blu-ray* *CS*

Heath Ledger *William Thatcher/Sir Ulric of Liechtenstein* • Rufus Sewell *Count Adhemar* • Mark Addy *Roland* • Paul Bettany *Geoffrey Chaucer* • Shannyn Sossamon *Lady Jocelyn* • Alan Tudyk *Wat* • Laura Fraser *Kate* • Christopher Cazenove *John Thatcher* ■ *Dir/Scr* Brian Helgeland

Knock Knock ★★ 18
Horror thriller 2015 · US · Colour · 95min

Hostel director Eli Roth comes unstuck with this silly, unconvincing and repetitive home-invasion shocker. Married architect Keanu Reeves takes pity on the two lost partygoers (Lorenza Izzo and Ana de Armas) who appear on his doorstep. Once invited inside they seduce him, trash the place, tie him up and begin their mission of his total degradation. The twisted humour is overdone, and Reeves's sloppily written trades in dumb clichés. **AJ** Violence, swearing, sex scenes, nudity.

Keanu Reeves *Evan Webber* • Ana de Armas *Bel* • Lorenza Izzo *Genesis* • Ignacia Allamand *Karen Alvarado* ■ *Dir* Eli Roth • *Scr* Eli Roth, Nicolás López, Guillermo Amoedo

Knock Off ★★ 18
Action thriller 1998 · HK/US · Colour · 87min

This Jean-Claude Van Damme vehicle is another superficially authentic but ultimately fake Hong Kong thriller. True, director Tsui Hark has all the right credentials but, as with their previous project *Double Team*, this just isn't the real thing. Played more for laughs than that collaboration, this tale finds reformed counterfeiter Van Damme and partner Rob Schneider caught up in a plot to send miniature bombs all over the world. JF Swearing, violence. *DVD*

Jean-Claude Van Damme *Marcus Ray* • Rob Schneider *Tommy Hendricks* • Lela Rochon *Karen* • Paul Sorvino *Johansson* • Carmen Lee *Ling Ho* • Wyman Wong *Eddie* • Glen Chin *Skinny* • Michael Miller (3) *Tickler* • Steve Brettingham *Hawkeye* • Mark Haughton *Bear* ■ *Dir* Tsui Hark • *Scr* Steven E de Souza

Knock on Any Door ★★★ PG
Crime drama   1949 · US · BW · 99min

Nicholas Ray's sympathy for the disadvantaged young - he would direct *Rebel without a Cause* six years later - is well to the fore in this sincerely meant but now very dated drama. John Derek stars as a slum youth who turns to crime and is charged with murder, while Humphrey Bogart plays his understanding, albeit powerless, attorney. A belated sequel, *Let No Man Write My Epitaph*, followed in 1960. TH *DVD*

Humphrey Bogart *Andrew Morton* • John Derek *Nick Romano* • George Macready *District Attorney Kerman* • Allene Roberts *Emma* • Mickey Knox *Vito* • Barry Kelley *Judge Drake* • Cara Williams *Nelly* • Jimmy Conlin *Kid Fingers* ■ *Dir* Nicholas Ray • *Scr* Daniel Taradash, John Monks Jr, from a novel by Willard Motley

Knock on Wood ★★★ U
Musical comedy   1954 · US · Colour · 103min

Comedy writers/directors Melvin Frank and Norman Panama earned themselves a best story and screenplay Oscar nomination for this crack-a-minute showcase for the talents of Danny Kaye. The breathless delivery, facial contortions and crowded gallery of eccentric characterisations that made him one of the finest cabaret performers of his generation never fitted entirely comfortably into a film narrative, with the action too often stalling to enable him to rattle through yet another of his patter routines. DP

Danny Kaye *Jerry Morgan* • Mai Zetterling *Ilse Nordstrom* • Torin Thatcher *Godfrey Langston* • David Burns *Marty Brown* • Leon Askin *Gromek* • Abner Biberman *Papinek* ■ *Dir/Scr* Norman Panama, Melvin Frank

Knockaround Guys ★★ 15
Crime comedy   2001 · US · Colour · 87min

The retrieval of a stolen bag of Mob money sees low-level gangsters Barry Pepper, Vin Diesel and a couple of less intimidating associates exerting their muscle on a corrupt small-town sheriff. This downbeat, plodding drama gets some mileage out of its superior cast, but film-makers Brian Koppelman and David Levien are undeserving of this line-up, since their dialogue is mechanical and co-direction lifeless. Clint Mansell's moody score does enhance the atmosphere, but it's a dreary journey to reach the climactic shoot-out. JC *DVD*

Barry Pepper *Matty Demaret* • Vin Diesel *Taylor Reese* • Seth Green *Johnny Marbles* • Dennis Hopper *Benny "Chains" Demaret* • John Malkovich *Teddy Deserve* • Andrew Davoli *Chris Scarpa* • Tom Noonan *Sheriff* ■ *Dir/Scr* Brian Koppelman, David Levien

Knocked Up ★★★★ 15
Romantic comedy   2007 · US · Colour · 127min

Writer/director Judd Apatow follows up his hit comedy *The 40 Year Old Virgin* with another refreshingly bold entry in a genre formerly mired in facile, post-Farrelly brothers gross-out. Pudgy, curly-haired Seth Rogen plays a harmless pothead who impregnates Katherine Heigl's media career girl during a drunken one-night stand. Prompted by the impending birth to give the relationship a go, our odd couple learns lessons about responsibility and life in general, but to hilarious rather than schmaltzy effect. Married-with-kids Paul Rudd and Leslie Mann (also *Virgin* alumni) are the foils for the younger pair, and

Rogen's buddies, led by Jonah Hill, the geek chorus. Thanks to quality, near-the-knuckle repartee and believable chemistry between the leads, *Knocked Up* proves that hit comedy doesn't have to dumb down. AC *DVD* *Blu-ray*

Seth Rogen *Ben Stone* • Katherine Heigl *Alison Scott* • Paul Rudd *Pete* • Leslie Mann *Debbie* • Jay Baruchel *Jay* • Jonah Hill *Jonah* • Jason Segel *Jason* • Alan Tudyk *Jack* • Loudon Wainwright [Loudon Wainwright III] *Dr Howard* ■ *Dir/Scr* Judd Apatow • *Cinematographer* Eric Edwards [Eric Alan Edwards]

The Knot ★★ 15
Romantic comedy   2012 · UK · Colour · 91min

This British romantic comedy is one part *Bridesmaids*, one part *A Few Best Men* and one part *The Wedding Video*. Talulah Riley and Matthew McNulty play the happy couple whose preparations are going anything but smoothly, and the decent production values and a likeable cast (led by Noel Clarke, who co-wrote the script, and Mena Suvari) make for diverting enough entertainment. But the ill-judged slapstick and daft plot developments are hard to ignore, and don't give enough lift to the unoriginal story. DA Swearing, a sex scene, drug abuse, nudity.

Noel Clarke *Peter* • Mena Suvari *Sarah* • Matthew McNulty *Jeremy* • Talulah Riley *Alexandra* • Jason Maza *Ralphus* ■ *Dir* Jesse Lawrence • *Scr* Noel Clarke, Geoff Carino, Davie Fairbanks

Knowing ★★★ 15
Disaster thriller   2009 · Aus/US/UK · Colour · 116min

Nicolas Cage stars in this thriller from *I, Robot* director Alex Proyas that serves up a heady mix of allegory and melodrama in a modern twist on the paranoia of vintage sci-fi movies. When h s son gets a document from a time capsule buried at his school 50 years earlier, widowed scientist Cage discovers the listed numbers predicted every major global disaster - with more prophesied to come. Po-faced and absurdly portentous this may be, yet the propulsive narrative blends politically anxious ideas and new-age spirituality together with superb special effects in a gleefully eccentric catastrophe thriller. AJ Brief swearing. *DVD* *Blu-ray*

Nicolas Cage *John Koestler* • Rose Byrne *Diana Wayland* • Chandler Canterbury *Caleb Koestler* • Lara Robinson *Abby Wayland/Lucinda* • Ben Mendelsohn *Phil Beckman* • Nadia Townsend *Grace* ■ *Dir* Alex Proyas • *Scr* Ryne Douglas Pearson, Juliet Snowden, Stiles White • *Music* Marco Beltrami

Knuckle ★★★ 15
Sports documentary   2011 · UK/Ire · Colour · 92min

More "My Big Fat Gypsy Punch-Up" than *Raging Bull*, this engrossing documentary nonetheless gives an insight into Irish Traveller culture and the secret world of bare-knuckle boxing. Director Ian Palmer was first asked to record a single fight for a bit of extra cash, but ended up filming on-and-off for 12 years. It's all a little rough and ready, and by its nature rather repetitive, but as a look inside a normally hidden part of an already insular culture, *Knuckle* packs a genuine punch. LB Violence, swearing. *DVD*

■ *Dir* Ian Palmer • *Cinematographers* Ian Palmer, Michael Doyle

Knute Rockne – All American ★★ U
Biographical drama   1940 · US · BW · 97min

In this biopic of the Norwegian-born American football coach - a national hero who died prematurely in a plane crash - Rockne is played by Pat O'Brien, who performs to the gallery and still seems to be wearing the dog collar from all those Cagney gangster pictures. But the movie is now more famous for Ronald Reagan in his favourite role as "The Gipper", Rockne's star player George Gipp, who died young of pneumonia. "Win one for the Gipper" is the well-known line which Reagan reprised on his presidential campaign trail, recalling not

only his film role but also an age of patriotic achievement. AT

Pat O'Brien *Knute Rockne* • Ronald Reagan *George Gipp* • Gale Page *Bonnie Skilles Rockne* • Donald Crisp *Father Callahan* • Albert Basserman *Father Julius Nieuwland* ■ *Dir* Lloyd Bacon • *Scr* Robert Buckner, from the private papers of Mrs Knute Rockne

Koi... Mil Gaya ★★★ 12
Science-fiction romantic drama   2003 · Ind · Colour · 156min

Director Rakesh Roshan has wisely entrusted the special effects for this sci-fi film to James Colmer, who worked on the likes of *Independence Day*. But while the technology is cutting edge, the narrative owes more to the Cold War allegories of the 1950s when extraterrestrials came to Earth to urge us to get along despite our differences. Mentally disabled Hrithik Roshan accidentally makes contact with a spaceship using his inventor father's equipment. It's slick, sentimental entertainment, although the songs will probably alienate sci-fi aficionados. DP Hindi +subtitles. *DVD*

Rekha *Sonia Mehra* • Hrithik Roshan *Rohit Mehra* • Preity Zinta *Nisha* • Prem Chopra *Harbans Saxena* • Rajat Bedi *Raj Saxena* • Johnny Lever *Chelaram Sukhwani* ■ *Dir* Rakesh Roshan • *Scr* Sachin Bhowmick, Honey Irani, Robin Bhatt, Rakesh Roshan, Javed Siddiqui

Kolobos ★ 18
Horror   1999 · US · Colour · 82min

Five people sign up for a free holiday in return for participating in an experimental film. The catch? Once they are all locked in a deserted house and the video cameras are switched on, they are successively killed in increasingly violent ways. The characters are laughably stock, the dialogue inane and the effects are rendered so cheaply even rabid gore-hounds will feel cheated. AJ *DVD*

Amy Weber *Kyra* • Donny Terranova *Tom* • Nichole Pelerine *Erica* • John Fairlie *Gary* • Promise LaMarco *Tina* ■ *Dir* Daniel Liatowitsch, David Todd Ocvirk • *Scr* Nne Ebong, Daniel Liatowitsch, David Todd Ocvirk

Kolya ★★★★ 12
Comedy drama   1996 · Cz Rep/UK/Fr · Colour · 100min

The winner of the Oscar for best foreign film, this is a delightful odd-couple story set in Prague during the last days of Communism. The director's father, Zdenek Sverak (who also scripted), is superb as the former Philharmonic cellist who takes custody of five-year-old Andrej Chalimon after his mother (a Russian interpreter with whom the impoverished musician had contracted a marriage of convenience) flits to the west. With no political axe to grind, Jan Sverak goes for the human interest angle and produces a joyous film, which provokes more than its fair share of smiles and surreptitious dabs of the eyes. DP Czech +subtitles. Some swearing. *DVD*

Zdenek Sverak *Frantisek Louka* • Andrej Chalimon *Kolya* • Libuse Safrankova *Klara* • Ondrej Vetchy *Mr Broz* • Stella Zazvorkova *Mother* • Ladislav Smoljak *Mr Houdek* • Irena Livanova *Nadezda* • Lilian Malkina *Aunt Tamara* ■ *Dir* Jan Sverak • *Scr* Zdenek Sverak, from a story by Pavel Taussig

Komodo ★★ 12
Fantasy thriller   1999 · US · Colour · 85min

In this undernourished eco-horror, a teenager is taken back to the island off the coast of the US where his parents were eaten by Komodo dragons, because his psychiatrist Jill Hennessey thinks it will cure his traumatic amnesia. Other potential victims for the ravenous lizards include evil hunters hired by an oil company to eradicate the slithering menace so they can drill the place dry. The ridiculous premise is given routine direction by special-effects artist Michael Lantieri. AJ *DVD*

Jill Hennessy *Victoria* • Billy Burke *Oates* • Kevin Zegers *Patrick Connelly* • Paul Gleeson *Denby* • Nina Landis *Annie* ■ *Dir* Michael Lantieri • *Scr* Hans Bauer, Craig Mitchell

Kon-Tiki ★★★★ 15
Action adventure based on a true story   2012 · UK/Nor/Den/Swe/Ger/Malta · Colour and BW · 118min

Filmed on the open sea, this handsome adventure story feels both authentic and modern while delivering the reassuring throwback thrills of the classic 1950s matinee feature. Pal Sverre Hagen stars as Thor Heyerdahl, the ethnographer who took his life in his hands when, in 1947, he set out to prove his theories of migration by setting sail from Peru to Polynesia on a primitive raft made of balsa wood logs. As Heyerdahl, Hagen has the right amount of daring and gravitas, though his recklessness - hinted at in scenes of marital discord - is somewhat soft-pedalled in favour of the bigger picture: a man who put his ideas to the test by playing the highest stakes imaginable. DW Norwegian +subtitles. *DVD*

Pal Sverre Hagen [Pal Sverre Valheim Hagen] *Thor Heyerdahl* • Anders Baasmo Christiansen *Herman Watzinger* • Tobias Santelmann *Knut Haugland* • Gustaf Skarsgard *Bengt Danielsson* • Odd Magnus Williamson *Erik Hesselberg* • Jakob Oftebro *Torstein Raaby* • Agnes Kittelsen *Liv Heyerdahl* ■ *Dir* Joachim Ronning, Espen Sandberg • *Scr* Petter Skavlan

Kong: Skull Island
Fantasy action adventure   2017 · US · Colour

This is a preview - no prints were available to review as we went to press: Since first stomping onto the big screen in 1933, King Kong has endured through the years in countless films. Here, recent Oscar winner Brie Larson (*Room*) and Tom Hiddleston will try not to be upstaged in a story that aims to explain how the big ape came to be worshipped like a god on Skull Island. You can expect Larson to make the oversized primate weak at the knees between big-budget action scenes directed by Jordan Vogt-Roberts. SP

Brie Larson *Weaver* • Samuel L Jackson • Tom Hiddleston *Captain James Conrad* • John Goodman *Randa* • Tom Wilkinson ■ *Dir* Jordan Vogt-Roberts • *Scr* Max Borenstein, Derek Connolly, John Gatins, Dan Gilroy

Konga ★★ PG
Science-fiction horror   1960 · UK · Colour · 85min

Michael Gough as a botanist inventing a growth serum, a ratty zip-up gorilla suit, Margo Johns as a comely housekeeper, a miniature cardboard Big Ben and pop star Jess Conrad - what more could you want in a cheap and cheerful British *King Kong* imitation originally titled *I Was a Teenage Gorilla*? With its crude horror always verging on the farcical, the entertainment value stems from the sheer incompetence on full view. Filmed on location in Croydon High Street. AJ *DVD*

Michael Gough *Dr Charles Decker* • Margo Johns *Margaret* • Jess Conrad *Bob Kenton* • Claire Gordon *Sandra Banks* • Austin Trevor *Dean Foster* • Jack Watson *Superintendent Brown* ■ *Dir* John Lemont • *Scr* Herman Cohen, Aben Kandel

Königsmark ★★★
Romantic drama   1935 · Fr · BW · 114min

Silent master Maurice Tourneur directs this Ruritanian melodrama with all the visual majesty you would expect of someone who once worked as an assistant to the sculptor Auguste Rodin. It's a tantalising tale of romance and revenge, as princess Elissa Landi teams with Pierre Fresnay to avenge the murder of her husband. Amid the lavish trappings and grand posturings, Landi gives a splendid performance, echoing the tragedy of *Hamlet* (the clear inspiration for Pierre Benoît's source novel) after she guns down a spying maid. DP In French.

Elissa Landi *Princess Aurore* • Pierre Fresnay *Raoul Vignerte* • John Lodge *Grand Duke Frederick* • Frank Vosper *Major Baron de Boise* • Marcelle Rogez *Countess Melusine* • Allan Jeayes *Grand Duke Rodolphe* • Romilly Lunge *Lieutenant de Hagen* • Cecil Humphreys de Marçais ■ *Dir* Maurice Tourneur • *Scr* from the novel by Pierre Benoît

K

Kontroll ★★★ 15

Thriller 2003 · Hun · Colour · 106min

Nimrod Antal's directorial debut is both a simmering study of despised outcasts and an understated murder mystery that makes atmospheric use of its Budapest Metro setting. As the leader of a crew of apathetic ticket inspectors, Sandor Csanyi is impressively intense, contemplating unexplained anxieties that are only relieved by his crush on kooky Eszter Balla. However, Antal wisely lightens the mood with some bleakly comic encounters with fare-dodging passengers that allow the bullish supporting cast to shine. DP Hungarian +subtitles. Swearing, violence.
DVD

Sandor Csanyi *Bulcsu* • Zoltan Mucsi *Professor* • Csaba Pindroch *Muki* • Sandor Badar *Lecso* • Zsolt Nagy *Tibi* • Bence Matyassy *Bootsie* • Eszter Balla *Sofie* ■ *Dir* Nimrod Antal • *Scr* Jim Adler, Antal Nimrod

Korczak ★★★ PG

Historical drama
1990 · Pol/W Ger/Fr/UK · BW · 117min

Scripted by Agnieszka Holland and shot in sombre monochrome by Robby Müller, this is an earnest attempt to portray the atrocities of the Holocaust without undue sentiment or sensationalism. Indeed, this is such a determinedly sensitive study that it's often hard to recognise it as the work of Andrzej Wajda, whose "war trilogy" was so full of anger at the loss of a generation. Tracing real-life events from 1936 to 1942, the film benefits from a dignified performance from Wojtek Pszoniak as Janusz Korczak, the doctor who ministered to the children of the Warsaw ghetto. DP Polish +subtitles.

Wojtek Pszoniak [Wojciech Pszoniak] *Dr Janusz Korczak* • Ewa Dalkowska *Stefa* • Piotr Kozlowski *Heniek* ■ *Dir* Andrzej Wajda • *Scr* Agnieszka Holland

Kotch ★★★ PG

Comedy drama 1971 · US · Colour · 109min

We always knew that Walter Matthau and Jack Lemmon had their communal heart in the right place. But here it's worn a bit too strenuously on the frayed sleeve of Matthau, as an unwanted old man who walks out on his impatient son and daughter-in-law, and befriends a pregnant teenager. Lemmon, as debut director, accords his friend a leisurely pace and some great close-ups. The film's sentimentality veers into schmaltz, but what do you expect from this wonderfully odd couple? TH
DVD

Walter Matthau *Joseph P Kotcher* • Deborah Winters *Erica Herzenstiel* • Felicia Farr *Wilma Kotcher* • Charles Aidman *Gerald Kotcher* • Ellen Geer *Vera Kotcher* • Darrell Larson *Vincent Perrin* ■ *Dir* Jack Lemmon • *Scr* John Paxton, from the novel by Katherine Topkins

The Kovak Box ★★ 15

Science-fiction mystery thriller
2006 · Sp/UK · Colour · 105min

The melancholy tones of Billie Holiday's *Gloomy Sunday* are the trigger for a suspicious spate of suicides in this intriguing though underdeveloped mystery thriller. A restrained Timothy Hutton plays the uninspired sci-fi writer who finds real life imitating his first novel, when his fiancée unexpectedly adds to the death toll in a Mallorcan resort. Initially, slick production values and smart plot details keep this concept-heavy feature tripping along, while an enjoyable splash of Hitchcock-style suspense helps distract from the often unconvincing dialogue. But it's David Kelly's gleeful malevolence as the apparent mastermind of events that compensates for an underwhelming climax. SF English, Spanish +subtitles. **DVD**

Timothy Hutton *David Norton* • Lucía Jiménez *Silvia Melero* • David Kelly *Frank Kovak* • Georgia MacKenzie [Georgia Mackenzie] *Jane Graham* ■ *Dir* Daniel Monzón • *Scr* Jorge Guerricaechevarría, Daniel Monzón

Koyaanisqatsi ★★★ U

Experimental documentary
1982 · US · Colour · 84min

This offbeat documentary-cum-meditation about the decline of western civilisation uses the difference between the untamed American wilderness and hysterical, rush-hour Manhattan as its crux. Director Godfrey Reggio shuns narration in favour of powerful, repetitive music by minimalist composer Philip Glass to match his striking visuals. Made in the early 1980s when ecological warnings were starting to take hold, it was, for all its vacuity, a surprising success. The title is a Hopi Indian word meaning "life out of balance". Followed in 1988 by *Powaqqatsi*. TH **DVD Blu-ray**

■ *Dir* Godfrey Reggio • *Scr* Ron Fricke, Michael Hoenig, Alton Walpole, Godfrey Reggio • *Producers* Godfrey Reggio, Francis Coppola [Francis Ford Coppola] • *Cinematographer* Ron Fricke • *Music Director* Michael Hoenig

Kramer vs Kramer ★★★★ PG

Drama 1979 · US · Colour · 100min

This runaway success won the Oscar for best picture and scooped best actor and supporting actress statuettes for Dustin Hoffman and Meryl Streep. It now looks a little overwrought in places, but remains an involving, moving and discerning study of the suffering endured by all embroiled in a divorce. You could cut the tension in the courtroom sequences with a knife, but writer/director Robert Benton deserves greatest credit for the scenes in which Hoffman tries to win over his six-year-old son, Justin Henry. What could so easily have become something false and nasty is handled with truth and restraint. DP **DVD Blu-ray**

Dustin Hoffman *Ted Kramer* • Meryl Streep *Joanna Kramer* • Jane Alexander *Margaret Phelps* • Justin Henry *Billy Kramer* • Howard Duff *John Shaunessy* • George Coe *Jim O'Connor* • JoBeth Williams *Phyllis Bernard* • Bill Moor *Gressen* • Howland Chamberlain [Howland Chamberlin] *Judge Atkins* ■ *Dir* Robert Benton • *Scr* Robert Benton, from the novel by Avery Corman

Krampus ★★★ 15

Seasonal comedy horror
2015 · US · Colour · 93min

When a young boy (Emjay Anthony) loses belief and bah-humbugs Christmas, mum Toni Collette, dad Adam Scott and obnoxious extended family find their home besieged by Krampus – Santa's horned, hooved evil twin – and his army of elves, demonic toys and killer gingerbread men. A cop-out ending detracts from the path that the film has been hurtling down. Still, this mix of horror and humour is perfect if you're sick to the stomach of traditional Christmas slush. DA **DVD Blu-ray**

Adam Scott *Tommy* • Toni Collette *Sarah* • David Koechner *Howard* • Allison Tolman *Linda* • Conchata Ferrell *Aunt Dorothy* ■ *Dir* Michael Dougherty • *Scr* Todd Casey, Michael Dougherty, Zach Shields

The Krays ★★★★ 18

Biographical crime drama
1990 · UK · Colour · 114min

This is an intelligent biopic of Britain's most famous gangsters, the twins who made life safe for East Enders when they weren't running protection rackets or inflicting gangland punishments on rival mobsters. To be fair, writer Philip Ridley and director Peter Medak largely avoid glamorising the violent world of Reggie and Ronnie, and are more interested in unravelling their complex personalities. They are helped by surprisingly convincing lead performances from Martin and Gary Kemp, although Billie Whitelaw effortlessly rises above everybody else as the boys' best friend, their mum. JF Swearing, violence, nudity. **DVD**

Gary Kemp *Ronnie Kray* • Martin Kemp *Reggie Kray* • Billie Whitelaw *Violet Kray* • Tom Bell *Jack "The Hat"* • Charlotte Cornwell *May* • Kate Hardie *Frances* • Avis Bunnage *Helen* • Gary Love *Steve* • Steven Berkoff *George Cornell* • Jimmy Jewel

---

"Cannonball" Lee • Barbara Ferris *Mrs Lawson* • Victor Spinetti *Mr Lawson* ■ *Dir* Peter Medak • *Scr* Philip Ridley

The Kreutzer Sonata ★★★★★ 15

Drama 1987 · USSR · Colour · 135min

This is one of the truly great Russian films of the 1980s and a "must see" on all counts. Tolstoy's stifling, gripping tale of a dramatic, violent relationship between a man and his virtuoso musician wife is done great service by deep, multilayered direction and the searing performance of Oleg Yankovsky, who tells his story in flashback. Yankovsky's portrayal of jealousy erupting into hate is a cinematic triumph; the movie never lets its vice-like grip on the audience's emotions slacken. SH Russian +subtitles.

Oleg Yankovsky *Vasili Pozdnyshev* • Aleksandr Trofimov *Pozdnyshev's fellow traveller* • Irina Seleznyova *Lisa Pozdnyshev* • Dmitri Pokrovsky *Trukhachevsky* ■ *Dir* Mikhail Schweitzer, Sofia Milkina • *Scr* Mikhail Schweitzer, from the novel by Leo Tolstoy

The Kreutzer Sonata ★★★ 18

Drama 2008 · US/UK · Colour · 99min

This intense, if inconsistent, variation on Tolstoy's much-filmed tale stars Danny Huston as a jealous Californian philanthropist who succumbs to murderous rage after becoming convinced that his younger pianist wife (Elisabeth Röhm) is having an affair with the violinist (Matthew Yang King) she accompanies in a charity performance of the Beethoven sonata of the title. There's certainly plenty of passion in the opening sequences, but while Rose ably demonstrates how quickly ardour cools once routine sets in, he fails to sustain the necessary atmosphere as Huston seeks to catch his spouse *in flagrante*. DP Violence, swearing, sex scenes, nudity, drug abuse.

Danny Huston *Edgar* • Elisabeth Röhm *Abigail* • Matthew Yang King *Aiden* • Anjelica Huston *Elinore* • Stella Huston *Lexi* • Annie Morgan *Ginger* • Jamie Harris *Charles* • Devon Sorvari *Cynthia* ■ *Dir* Bernard Rose • *Scr* Lisa Enos, Bernard Rose, from the novella by Leo Tolstoy

Krippendorf's Tribe ★★ 12

Comedy 1998 · US · Colour · 90min

Richard Dreyfuss plays an anthropologist whose tribe-seeking mission in New Guinea was a failure, forcing him to fabricate footage of a new tribe concocted from the names of his three kids. Not exactly a great comedy premise in the first place and it runs out of ideas (and laughs) well before the halfway mark. On this occasion, Dreyfuss's screen spark seems to have been "shorted", although Jenna Elfman has an appealingly kooky comic flair. Hardly worth seeking out. JC

Richard Dreyfuss *James Krippendorf* • Jenna Elfman *Veronica Micelli* • Natasha Lyonne *Shelly* • Lily Tomlin *Ruth Allen* • Gregory Smith *Mickey* • Carl Michael Lindner *Edmund* • David Ogden Stiers *Henry Spivey* ■ *Dir* Todd Holland • *Scr* Charlie Peters, from the novel by Frank Parkin

Kristin Lavransdatter ★★★

Period drama
1995 · Ger/Nor/Swe · Colour · 180min

Adapted from Sigrid Undset's Pulitzer Prize-winning novel, Liv Ullmann's film possesses all the beauty of a medieval tapestry, yet its length and inertia often make this epic seem more like a book of hours. Elizabeth Matheson's statuesque performance makes it difficult to sympathise with the landowner's daughter caught between duty and passion. However, neither she nor her less-than-gallant lover, Björn Skagestad, is given much assistance from either Ullmann's hoary script or her hesitant pacing. Fortunately, Sven Nykvist's photography is a delight. DP In Norwegian.

Lena Endre *Eline Ormsdatter* • Erland Josephson *Broder Edvin* • Elisabeth Matheson *Kristin Lavransdatter* • Sverre Anker Ousdal *Lavrans* • Björn Skagestad *Erlend* ■ *Dir* Liv Ullmann • *Scr* Liv Ullmann, from the novel by Sigrid Undset

---

Kronk's New Groove ★★ U

Animated comedy 2005 · US · Colour · 71min

The muscle-bound sidekick of the evil Yzma from *The Emperor's New Groove* has seemingly turned over a new leaf in this sequel, but can Kronk keep on the straight and narrow? If you enjoyed its predecessor, you'll warm to this second helping of goofy mayhem from Disney, even if you can't escape the feeling that the idea has been stretched to breaking point. SuR

Patrick Warburton *Kronk* • Tracey Ullman *Miss Birdwell* • Eartha Kitt *Yzma* • David Spade *Kuzco* • John Goodman *Pacha* • John Mahoney *Papi* ■ *Dir* Saul Andrew Blinkoff, Elliot M Bour • *Scr* Tom Rogers, from a story by Michael LaBash, Anthony Leondis, Rogers

Kronos ★★★

Science-fiction thriller 1957 · US · BW · 78min

An enormous alien robot lands off the California coast and tramples on everything in sight as it advances towards Los Angeles on an energy-sucking spree. Despite its reliance on stock footage, cost-cutting special effects (mainly large-size props) and average direction, this unusually slanted invasion thriller is a perfect example of engagingly deranged 1950s B-movie-making. A minor classic. AJ

Jeff Morrow *Dr Leslie Gaskell* • Barbara Lawrence *Vera Hunter* • John Emery *Dr Eliot* • George O'Hanlon *Dr Arnie Culver* • Morris Ankrum *Dr Albert R Stern* • Kenneth Alton McCrary ■ *Dir* Kurt Neumann • *Scr* Lawrence Louis Goldman, from a story by Irving Block

Krull ★★★ PG

Fantasy adventure
1983 · UK/US · Colour · 115min

Engaging without ever being enthralling, this fantasy performed badly at the box office and Columbia saw little return on its $27 million investment. Yet this maligned movie has many moments to enjoy, as Ken Marshall's prince seeks to release princess Lysette Anthony from the clutches of the Beast. The special effects may fall far short of spectacular, but they help to create a charming neverland and add considerably to the excitement of the quest. The acting honours go to Bernard Bresslaw as a cyclops and Freddie Jones as a seer. DP **DVD**

Ken Marshall *Prince Colwyn* • Lysette Anthony *Princess Lyssa* • Freddie Jones *Ynyr* • Francesca Annis *Widow of the Web* • Alun Armstrong *Torquil* • David Battley *Ergo* • Bernard Bresslaw *Cyclops* • Liam Neeson *Kegan* • Todd Carty *Oswyn* • Robbie Coltrane *Rhun* • John Welsh *Seer* ■ *Dir* Peter Yates • *Scr* Stanford Sherman

Kubo and the Two Strings

Animated fantasy drama 2016 · US · Colour

This is a preview – no prints were available to review as we went to press: Animation house Laika (*Coraline*, *ParaNorman*) pays homage to the likes of Akira Kurosawa and Hayao Miyazaki. Set in feudal Japan, the action revolves around a one-eyed boy, Kubo (voiced by Art Parkinson of *Game of Thrones*), who accidentally conjures a restless spirit from his past. With the help of a monkey (Charlize Theron) and a wisecracking samurai beetle (Matthew McConaughey) Kubo aims to put old ghosts to rest. SP

Rooney Mara *The sisters* • Charlize Theron *Monkey* • Matthew McConaughey *Beetle* • George Takei *Hosato* • Ralph Fiennes *Moon king/Raiden* ■ *Dir* Travis Knight • *Scr* Marc Haimes, Chris Butler, from a story by Haimes, Butler, Shannon Tindle

Kuch Naa Kaho ★★★ U

Musical romantic comedy
2003 · Ind · Colour · 168min

Veteran director Ramesh Sippy acts as producer on his son Rohan's debut feature, which piles one romantic comedy cliché upon another yet still manages to amuse. Abhishek Bachchan (himself the son of a Bollywood legend) stars as an Indian-American who returns to Mumbai for a family wedding only to find himself ensnared in his mother Suhasini Mulay's plot to find him a bride. However, he inevitably falls for the one woman who isn't interested in him, matchmaker Aishwarya Rai. DP Hindi +subtitles. *DVD*

Aishwarya Rai *Namrata* • Abhishek Bachchan *Raj* • Satish Shah *Rakesh* • Suhasini Mulay *Dr Malhotra* ■ *Dir* Rohan Sippy • *Scr* Neeraj Vora, Naushil Mehta, Nidhi Tuli, from a story by Rohena Gera

Kuffs ★★ 15
Comedy thriller 1991 · US · Colour · 97min

Only Christian Slater devotees will warm to this odd mix of comedy and action. He plays the dropout whose brother – the owner of a privately funded San Francisco police franchise – is murdered in front of him. Slater is forced to shape up when he takes over the franchise in an attempt to find the killer. With Slater's smug smart-aleck asides to the camera and with silly sound effects throughout, this is pure trash with just enough flash to make it mildly watchable. AJ Violence, swearing.

Christian Slater *George Kuffs* • Milla Jovovich *Maya Carlton* • Tony Goldwyn *Ted Bukovsky* • Bruce Boxleitner *Brad Kuffs* • Troy Evans *Captain Morino* • George De La Pena *Sam Jones* • Craig Benton *Paint store owner* • Ashley Judd *Paint store owner's wife* ■ *Dir* Bruce A Evans • *Scr* Bruce A Evans, Raynold Gideon

Kühle Wampe ★★★★ PG
Drama 1931 · Ger · BW · 68min

Evicted from a Berlin tenement, Hertha Thiele's family makes the most of life in a camp for the dispossessed, despite the suicide of her son. Condemning big business and positing all sorts of social alternatives, Bertolt Brecht's Marxist manifesto may not sound the stuff of entertainment but the only film he didn't disown is anything but a dry political tract. It is often riotously funny, but the over-riding impression it leaves is of a lost age of innocence and a tragically missed opportunity to create a fairer world. DP German +subtitles.

Hertha Thiele *Annie Bönike* • Ernst Busch *Fritz* • Martha Wolter ■ *Dir* Slatan Dudow • *Scr* Bertolt Brecht, Ernst Ottwald

Kull the Conqueror ★★ 12
Fantasy action adventure 1997 · US · Colour · 91min

Hercules star Kevin Sorbo made the switch from television to the big screen with this sword-and-sorcery epic, based on characters created by Robert E Howard of *Conan* fame. Sorbo becomes King of Valusia, but his attempts to free his people put him up against shape-shifting sorceress Tia Carrere. The disjointed proceedings deal with the clichéd good-versus-evil conventions of the genre, but with a darker hue and edgier atmosphere than normal. AJ

Kevin Sorbo *Kull* • Tia Carrere *Akivasha* • Thomas Ian Griffith *Taligaro* • Litefoot *Ascalante* • Roy Brocksmith *Tu* • Harvey Fierstein *Juba* • Karina Lombard *Zareta* • Edward Tudor-Pole *Enaros* • Douglas Henshall *Ducalon* ■ *Dir* John Nicolella • *Scr* Charles Edward Pogue, from the Marvel Comics character created by Robert E Howard

Kumiko, the Treasure Hunter ★★★★ 12
Drama 2014 · US · Colour · 100min

An unlikely mix of true-life tragedy and urban myth inspired this sweet, melancholy comedy, in which the title character, a bored and lonely Japanese office girl (Rinko Kikuchi), becomes obsessed with her VHS copy of the 1996 Coen brothers film *Fargo*, in particular its final scene. Believing a suitcase full of cash is hidden in the snowy wastes of North Dakota, she sets off for the USA. Her sad but compelling presence brings much-needed pathos to the film's final stretch, a surreal, quirky road trip in which Kikuchi seems to be at cross-purposes with everyone she meets. DW In English, Japanese. *DVD* ◐

Rinko Kikuchi *Kumiko* • Nobuyuki Katsube *Sakagami* • Kanako Higashi *Michi* • Ayaka Ohnishi *Chieko* ■ *Dir* David Zellner • *Scr* David & Nathan Zellner

Kundun ★★★ 12
Religious biographical drama 1997 · US · Colour · 128min

Emerging from his usual gangster-ridden mean streets, director Martin Scorsese sets his sights higher to the wide-open Himalayan spaces for this biography of the Dalai Lama. Scorsese's epic follows the Tibetan leader from his supposed reincarnation as the son of a humble family, through his investiture and his attempts to build a working relationship with – and eventual rejection of – Chinese socialism to his exile. Trouble is, the screenplay (by Melissa Mathison, who also wrote the script for *ET*) paints too rosy a picture of Buddhism, never questioning a country in which priests and poor are set so far apart. Roger Deakin's photography, though, is as luminous as a halo. TH *DVD*

Tenzin Tsarong Truthob *Dalai Lama as an adult* • Tencho Gyalpo *Dalai Lama's mother* • Tsewang Migyur Khangsar *Dalai Lama's father* ■ *Dir* Martin Scorsese • *Scr* Melissa Mathison

Kung Fu Hustle ★★★★ 15
Period martial arts comedy 2004 · HK/Chi · Colour · 95min

As in his previous film *Shaolin Soccer*, writer/director/star Stephen Chow casts himself as the hapless, idiotic hero – here, a poor, weedy guy who wants to be a member of the infamous Axe Gang that terrorises 1940s Shanghai. In the middle of a homage to Scorsese's *Gangs of New York*, a hilariously impressive martial arts battle begins, with the exemplary fight scenes. Featuring more action than most action films, more comedy than most comedies and certainly more "nonsense" than most films in general, this is a dazzling and outrageous movie. KK Cantonese, Mandarin +subtitles. *DVD* ◐

Stephen Chow *Sing* • Yuen Wah *Landlord* • Leung Siu-lung *The Beast* • Dong Zhi-hua *Donut* • Chiu Chi-ling *Tailor* • Xing Yu *Coolie* • Chan Kwok Kwan *Brother Sum* • Lam Tze-chung *Sing's sidekick* ■ *Dir* Stephen Chow • *Scr* Stephen Chow, Tsang Kan-cheong [Tsang Kan-Cheung], Lola Huo, Chan Man-keung

Kung Fu Killer ★★★ 15
Action thriller 2014 · Chi/HK · Colour · 95min

There's a serial killer on the loose targeting martial arts masters in this efficient thriller that's sure to tick all the boxes for fans of Asian action movies. Donnie Yen plays it moody as the jailed kung fu instructor freed by the cops to help track down a murderer who is despatching his victims using their own specialist styles. The cat-and-mouse plotting throws up some nice twists, while Yen demonstrates his virtuoso action choreography in a series of vigorous set pieces. JH Cantonese, Mandarin +subtitles. *DVD* ◐

Donnie Yen *Hahou Mo* • Wang Baoqiang *Fung Yu-Sau* • Charlie Yeung *Detective Luk Yuen-Sum* • Alex Fong *Chief Inspector Lam* ■ *Dir* Teddy Chen • *Scr* Mak Tin Shu, Lau Ho Leung, from a story by Teddy Chen, Lau Ho Leung

Kung-Fu Master ★★★
Romantic drama 1987 · Fr · Colour · 80min

Agnès Varda was taking a risk in producing this potentially scandalous love story involving a 40-something woman and a 15-year-old boy. But this is not a film about physical desire. It's a considered study of the continued existence of the poetic values of courtly love (ingeniously symbolised by the arcade kung fu game that encapsulates chivalric heroism) and whether any idealised emotions can endure in the face of everyday reality. It's not always credible, but that it works at all is down to the sensitivity of Jane Birkin and the director's own son, Mathieu Demy. DP French, English +subtitles.

Jane Birkin *Mary-Jane* • Mathieu Demy *Julien* • Charlotte Gainsbourg *Lucy* ■ *Dir* Agnès Varda • *Scr* Agnès Varda, from an idea by Jane Birkin

Kung Fu Panda ★★★ PG
Animated comedy adventure 2008 · US · Colour · 88min

Clumsy noodle seller Po the Panda (voiced by Jack Black) becomes the martial arts master Dragon Warrior of ancient legend in this visually arresting CGI animated adventure from DreamWorks. Taking a typical fists-of-fury plot, making the leads adorable animals and using Hong Kong action clichés to good effect, the film-makers were right to put most of their energies into the fight scenes, which are swiftly paced and great fun to watch. Quite the most intricately choreographed sequence is Master Shifu (Dustin Hoffman) realising the way to get Po to train is by using food as inspirational bait – cue a dazzling dim-sum battle. The main drawback is an overly familiar "believe in yourself" message. But Black's boundless enthusiasm gives Po a lovably goofball spark, and overall this is a beautifully designed cherry blossom-hued cartoon that's brighter, breezier and bouncier than most. AJ *DVD* ◐ CS

Jack Black *Po* • Dustin Hoffman *Master Shifu* • Angelina Jolie *Tigress* • Ian McShane *Tai Lung* • Jackie Chan *Monkey* • Seth Rogen *Mantis* • Lucy Liu *Viper* • David Cross (2) *Crane* ■ *Dir* Mark Osborne, John Stevenson • *Scr* Jonathan Aibel, Glenn Berger

Kung Fu Panda 2 ★★★ PG
Animated comedy adventure 2011 · US · Colour · 90min

The kung fu-fighting animal novelty has slightly worn off with this follow-up. In the still gorgeously designed China, Dragon Warrior Po (voiced by Jack Black) must find his "inner peace" and learn the truth about his childhood. Only then can he defeat evil peacock Lord Shen (a deliciously malevolent Gary Oldman) and his plan to stop kung fu with a new weapon. The movie is as busy and crisply detailed as ever, and the action sequences score high. But the plot is all rather familiar and the dry humour feels forced, with the best scenes belonging to Shen's fast-feather dexterity. A further sequel is due in March 2016. AJ *DVD* ◐ 3D

Jack Black *Po* • Angelina Jolie *Tigress* • Dustin Hoffman *Master Shifu* • Gary Oldman *Lord Shen* • Jackie Chan *Monkey* • Seth Rogen *Mantis* • Lucy Liu *Viper* • David Cross (2) *Crane* ■ *Dir* Jennifer Yuh Nelson [Jennifer Yuh] • *Scr* Jonathan Aibel, Glenn Berger

Kung Fu Panda 3 ★★★ PG
Animated comedy adventure 2016 · Chi/US · Colour · 94min

The tonal mix of life-lessons, energetic action, sharp repartee and zany humour are right on the money in this latest chapter in the affable animation saga. Some favourite characters are sidelined and past themes reproduced, but the inventive visual side is stirring, dazzling and vibrant as Po (voiced by Jack Black) is reunited with his long-lost father (Bryan Cranston) and pitted against a supernatural warrior (JK Simmons) who is collecting the chi energy of China's greatest martial artists to extend his powers. AJ *DVD* ◐ 3D

Jack Black *Po* • Angelina Jolie *Tigress* • Dustin Hoffman *Shifu* • JK Simmons *Kai* • Lucy Liu *Viper* • Jackie Chan *Monkey* • Bryan Cranston *Li* • Kate Hudson *Mei Mei* ■ *Dir* Alessandro Carloni, Jennifer Yuh • *Scr* Jonathan Aibel, Glenn Berger

Kung Phooey! ★★ 12
Martial arts spoof 2003 · US · Colour · 87min

Darryl Fong seeks to explode a few myths with this martial arts spoof. But the staleness of the plot and the lameness of the gags means that this coarse satire doesn't succeed. Michael Chow stars as a monk who arrives stateside to help uncle Wallace Choy recover an enchanted peach from monosodium glutamate smuggler Joyce Thi Brew. But Chow's ineptitude and Brew's pantomimic villainy become tiresome as the screenplay runs out of steam. DP *DVD*

Michael Chow *Art Chew* • Joyce Thi Brew *Helen Hu* • Colman Domingo *Roy Lee* • Darryl Fong *Waymon* • Karena Davis *Sue Shee* • Wallace Choy *Uncle Wong* ■ *Dir/Scr* Darryl Fong

Kurosawa ★★★
Documentary 2001 · US/UK/Jpn · Colour · 115min

Frequently hailed as the most western of all Japanese directors, Akira Kurosawa was certainly responsible for introducing his country's rich cinematic heritage to the rest of the world. This reverential, but informed documentary traces his life from his traumatic early years, through his wartime apprenticeship and rise to international eminence with *Rashomon* and *Seven Samurai*, to his later masterpieces, which offered a judicious blend of the literary and the original, the historical and the contemporary, the epic and the intimate. Punctuated with apposite clips and revealing interviews, it's a worthy tribute a master of the art. DP English, Japanese +subtitles.

Sam Shepard *Narrator* • Paul Scofield *Reader* ■ *Dir/Scr* Adam Low

Kursk: a Submarine in Troubled Waters ★★★
Documentary 2004 · Fr · Colour · 72min

A disturbing web of secrets and lies is uncovered in this eye-opening documentary investigating the sinking of Russian nuclear submarine the *Kursk* in August 2000. Combining expert and eyewitness analysis, alongside extensive media coverage of the incident and its aftermath, the film painstakingly challenges the notion of a tragic accident. Yet in doing so, it raises many new questions that are frustratingly left unanswered, ultimately undermining the power of an otherwise solid project. SF

Peter Coyote *Narrator* ■ *Dir/Scr* Jean-Michel Carré

Kurt & Courtney ★★★ 15
Documentary 1997 · UK · Colour · 92min

Documentarist Nick Broomfield has always employed a blend of charm and innocence to expose the frailties of his subjects. But here that tactic somewhat backfires because the people he meets in seeking to establish the facts about the death of grunge rock star Kurt Cobain have much darker agendas than his own idle curiosity. Cobain's widow Courtney Love certainly comes across as a difficult character (an impression compounded by her campaign to block the film's screening at the Sundance festival), but at least she is devoid of the bile and envy that motivates most of the others in the film. DP Swearing. *DVD*

Kurt Cobain • Courtney Love ■ *Dir* Nick Broomfield • *Editor* Mark Atkins (1) • *Cinematographers* Joan Churchill, Alex Vendler

Kwaidan ★★★ PG
Portmanteau fantasy 1964 · Jpn · Colour · 182min

This portmanteau film of four ghost stories is perhaps best viewed as separate films – one episode was originally cut to shorten the running time. One story concerns a samurai haunted by the beauty of his first wife; another is an ingenious tale about a man who drinks not only a cup of tea but also the man reflected on the surface of the drink. Viewers expecting a compendium of horror will be disappointed, for these tales are gentle, ironic and sad. All are stunningly photographed and exquisitely designed. AT Japanese +subtitles. *DVD*

Rentaro Mikuni *Samurai* • Michiyo Aratama *1st wife* • Misako Watanabe *2nd wife* • Keiko Kishi *The woman* • Tatsuya Nakadai *Minokichi* • Katsuo Nakamura *Hoichi* • Rentaro Mikuni *Samurai* ■ *Dir* Masaki Kobayashi • *Scr* Yoko Mizuki, from stories by Lafcadio Hearn

LA Confidential ★★★★★ 18

Crime drama 1997 · US · Colour · 132min

Curtis Hanson's superlative filming of James Ellroy's complex 1950s detective story fuses period authenticity, fluid direction and searing, full-blooded performances. From the apparently open-and-shut case of a diner bloodbath, the sleazy scenario takes a trio of cops – ambitious rookie Guy Pearce, smooth TV adviser Kevin Spacey and hardman Russell Crowe – down a corpse-strewn path of crime, corruption and celebrity lookalikes. The roles fit the actors like tightly stitched gloves, and the film's brutality is amplified by the absence of clear-cut heroes, with the police as morally dubious as the villains. The excellent script won an Oscar, as did Kim Basinger for her hard-edged vamp, but the picture really deserved a hatful. JC
Swearing, violence, sex scenes. DVD 🅱️ CS

Kevin Spacey *Jack Vincennes* • Russell Crowe *Bud White* • Guy Pearce *Edmund "Ed" Exley* • James Cromwell *Captain Dudley Smith* • Kim Basinger *Lynn Bracken* • Danny DeVito *Sid Hudgens* • David Strathairn *Pierce Patchett* • Ron Rifkin *District Attorney Ellis Loew* • Matt McCoy *"Badge of Honor" star Brett Chase* • Paul Guilfoyle (2) *Mickey Cohen* ■ *Dir* Curtis Hanson • *Scr* Curtis Hanson, Brian Helgeland, from the novel by James Ellroy • *Cinematographer* Dante Spinotti • *Music* Jerry Goldsmith

LA Story ★★★★ 15

Romantic comedy 1991 · US · Colour · 90min

This warm-hearted salute to Los Angeles pretensions is a romantic comedy that boasts just enough quirkiness to satify the fans of Steve Martin who were worried that he might be selling out and abandoning his "wild and crazy" persona. He plays a weatherman, who falls for visiting British journalist Victoria Tennant while undergoing a mild midlife crisis. Martin as writer has fun sending up some of the crazier aspects of LA life and stages some lovely comic set pieces; if anything, a sniff of sentimentality is the film's failing. JF
Swearing, nudity. DVD

Steve Martin *Harris K Telemacher* • Victoria Tennant *Sara McDowel* • Richard E Grant *Roland* • Marilu Henner *Trudi* • Sarah Jessica Parker *SanDeE** • Susan Forristal *Ariel* • Kevin Pollak *Frank Swan* • Sam McMurray *Morris Frost* • Patrick Stewart *Maître d' at L'Idiot* ■ *Dir* Mick Jackson • *Scr* Steve Martin

LA without a Map ★★★ 15

Romantic comedy
1998 · UK/Fr/Fin/Lux · Colour · 102min

Mika Kaurismäki's film is a sharp comedy stab at Los Angeles, in which David Tennant plays the Englishman abroad – a Bradford undertaker who leaves his rain-swept, gloomy existence to track down beautiful American Vinessa Shaw in sunny Hollywood after spotting her in his local graveyard. Of course, everything which can go wrong once he gets there invariably does, but it's fun, unpredictable stuff, peppered with some fantastic supporting turns from Julie Delpy, Vincent Gallo and, playing himself in a deliciously tongue-in-cheek manner, Johnny Depp. JB DVD

David Tennant *Richard Tennant* • Vinessa Shaw *Barbara* • Julie Delpy *Julie* • Vincent Gallo *Moss* • Cameron Bancroft *Patterson* • Joe Dallesandro *Michael* • Anouk Aimée • Saskia Reeves *Joy* • Johnny Depp ■ *Dir* Mika Kaurismäki • *Scr* Richard Rayner, Mika Kaurismäki, from the novel by Richard Rayner

LIE ★★★★ 18

Drama 2001 · US · Colour · 97min

Paedophilia is given a chillingly benevolent face in director Michael Cuesta's emotive debut. The film lays bare the cycle of abuse that tarnishes the lives of a group of delinquent boys from Long Island, New York. Standing out among them is Howie (Paul Franklin Dano), a 15-year-old struggling to cope with his mother's death, whose innocence attracts the local paedophile, Big John (Brian Cox). Though the film controversially questions the nature of all adult/child relationships, it's not explicit and doesn't resort to shock tactics. Instead, Cuesta combines intelligence with restraint, leaving the astonishingly moving performances of his cast to speak for themselves. SF DVD

Brian Cox (1) *Big John Harrigan* • Paul Franklin Dano [Paul Dano] *Howie Blitzer* • Billy Kay *Gary Terrio* • Bruce Altman *Marty Blitzer* • James Costa *Kevin Cole* • Tony Donnelly *Brian* • Walter Masterson *Scott* ■ *Dir* Michael Cuesta • *Scr* Stephen M Ryder, Michael Cuesta, Gerald Cuesta

LOL ★★ 12

Comedy 2011 · US · Colour · 96min

Director Lisa Azuelos's US remake of her 2008 hit stars Miley Cyrus and Demi Moore, but neither can save the film from sitcom-style tedium. Cyrus, in fact, tries far too hard as Lola, a high-school student trying to figure out her relationship with her best friend (Douglas Booth), when she isn't clashing with her mother (Demi Moore). Mum, meanwhile has her own romantic entanglements and also has to deal with *her* mother (Marlo Thomas), who is hardly a model parent. An "accidentally" read diary lends a tinge of melodrama to the predictable plot, but there's little meaning or purpose here, and even less entertainment. KK Some swearing, sexual references, drug abuse. DVD

Miley Cyrus [Miley Ray Cyrus] *Lola* • Demi Moore *Anne* • Ashley Greene *Ashley* • Douglas Booth *Kyle* • Adam G Sevani *Wen* • Thomas Jane *Alllen* • Jay Hernandez *James* • Marlo Thomas *Gran* ■ *Dir* Lisa Azuelos • *Scr* Lisa Azuelos, Kamir Aïnouz

The L-Shaped Room ★★★★ 15

Drama 1962 · UK · BW · 120min

This was an angry young film in its day, which comes to life under the sensitive direction of Bryan Forbes. Set in shabby bedsit land, it features Leslie Caron in an Oscar-nominated role as the unmarried, pregnant girl with a decision to make. Wonderful performances – by Tom Bell, Brock Peters, Bernard Lee and music-hall veteran Cicely Courtneidge – make the tenement in which the L-shaped abode is situated a place of vitality, concern and eventual affirmation. TH DVD

Leslie Caron *Jane Fosset* • Tom Bell *Toby* • Brock Peters *Johnny* • Cicely Courtneidge *Mavis* • Bernard Lee *Charlie* • Avis Bunnage *Doris* • Patricia Phoenix *Sonia* • Emlyn Williams *Dr Weaver* • Anthony Booth *Youth in street* ■ *Dir* Bryan Forbes • *Scr* Bryan Forbes, from the novel by Lynne Reid Banks

L.627 ★★★★ 15

Crime drama 1992 · Fr · Colour · 140min

This ultra-realistic police drama is one of versatile director Bertrand Tavernier's finest achievements. Written by ex-policeman Michel Alexandre, it follows Didier Bezace's narcotics unit as it pursues a gang of drug traffickers in Paris. Whether exploring the links between drugs and racism or revealing the prejudices and inadequacies of the force, Tavernier retains an admirable objectivity, which actually adds to the steel of the picture rather than tempering it. DP French +subtitles. Violence, swearing, drug abuse, nudity. DVD

Didier Bezace *Lucien "Lulu" Marguet* • Charlotte Kady *Marie* • Philippe Torreton *Antoine* • Nils Tavernier *Vincent* • Jean-Paul Comart *Dominique "Dodo" Cantoni* • Jean-Roger Milo *Manuel* • Lara Guirao *Cécile* ■ *Dir* Bertrand Tavernier • *Scr* Michel Alexandre

La La Land

Romantic comedy drama 2016 · US · Colour

This is a preview – no prints were available to review prior to publication: "Write what you know," Mark Twain famously instructed would-be authors. And for his debut feature, writer/director Damien Chazelle turned his time as a jazz drummer getting lessons in tough love from a steely tutor into *Whiplash*, the "from nowhere" critical and audience hit of 2014. But how to follow up? By writing/directing a film about Hollywood, of course, though Chazelle keeps one foot on really familiar ground by making this a story about a jazzer and an actress. As a mark of how hot Chazelle is right now, Ryan Gosling and Emma Stone are his leads. SvM

Ryan Gosling *Sebastian* • Emma Stone *Mia* • JK Simmons *Boss* ■ *Dir/Scr* Damien Chazelle

Labor Day ★★★★ 12

Drama 2013 · US · Colour · 111min

In this romantic drama from writer/director Jason Reitman (*Up in the Air*), Josh Brolin plays escaped convict Frank Chambers, who forces Kate Winslet's lonely, fragile single mother Adele and her adolescent son Henry (Gattlin Griffith) to give him shelter. Before you can say "howdy" they are in love – all three of them. The speed of the emotional developments stretches credibility, while more time is devoted to baking a pie than might be allocated on a Jamie Oliver cookery programme. However, the pacing actually works in terms of building atmosphere and tension, and the whole thing hangs together remarkably well because Winslet and Brolin have time to flesh out their characters. BP DVD BLU

Kate Winslet *Adele* • Josh Brolin *Frank Chambers* • Gattlin Griffith *Henry Wheeler* • Clark Gregg *Gerald* • JK Simmons *Mr Jervis* • Tobey Maguire *Adult Henry* ■ *Dir* Jason Reitman • *Scr* Jason Reitman, from Joyce Maynard's novel

Labyrinth ★★★ U

Fantasy adventure 1986 · US · Colour · 96min

The Muppet team goes into *Alice in Wonderland* territory as babysitter Jennifer Connelly wishes her younger brother into the Goblin King's clutches and has only hours to rescue him from a castle maze. With plenty of fuzzball gremlins, cute sugar plum fairies and clumsy Hoggle the dwarf to keep the children amused (adults will laugh at David Bowie's Tina Turner wig for entirely different reasons), Jim Henson's panto *Monty Python* (written by clan member Terry Jones) is weak on suspense and thrills, but is still firm fantasy fun. AJ DVD BLU

David Bowie *Jareth, King of the Goblins* • Jennifer Connelly *Sarah* • Toby Froud *Toby* • Shelley Thompson *Stepmother* • Christopher Malcolm *Father* • Natalie Finland *Fairy* • Brian Henson *Hoggle* • Michael Hordern *Wiseman* ■ *Dir* Jim Henson • *Scr* Terry Jones, from a story by Dennis Less, Jim Henson

Labyrinth ★★★

Drama documentary
1991 · Ger · Colour and BW · 86min

A leading member of the Czech New Wave, Jaromil Jires has garnered little international attention since his 1968 adaptation of Milan Kundera's *The Joke*. This was his first feature to gain foreign distribution after the Velvet Revolution, and its blend of dramatic re-creation and archival footage reveals his powers to be undiminished. Maximilian Schell stars as a director whose research for a film on Franz Kafka is sidetracked by a sudden obsession with the historical persecution of the Jews. With Charlie Chaplin's son, Christopher, cameoing as Kafka, this is both stylish and provocative. DP German +subtitles.

Maximilian Schell *The Director* • Christopher Chaplin *Franz Kafka* • Milos Kopecky *Rabbi Low* • Otto Sevcik *SS Gunther* ■ *Dir* Jaromil Jires • *Scr* Jaromil Jires, Alex Koenigsmark, Hans-Jorg Weyhmuller

Labyrinth of Lies ★★★★

Historical drama 2014 · Ger · Colour · 121min

A complex drama set in 1950s West Germany, where an idealistic young prosecutor tries to bring former Nazi officers to justice, only to be met with obstruction from a society unwilling to face the crimes of its past. Seen through the eyes of Alexander Fehling's earnest lead character, the much-explored issue of Nazi war crimes here is seen from a German viewpoint. Though the horrific events in the background have been softened, this nevertheless remains compelling thanks to a well-written romantic subplot that adds a human element to a complicated moral issue. JL In German.

Alexander Fehling *Johann Radmann* • André Szymanski *Thomas Gnielka* • Friederike Becht *Marlene Wondrak* • Johannes Krisch *Simon Kirsch* ■ *Dir* Giulio Ricciarelli • *Scr* Elisabeth Bartel, Giulio Ricciarelli, from Bartel's story

Labyrinth of Passion ★★★ 18

Comedy 1982 · Sp · Colour · 94min

This was the second full-length internationally-released feature from Spanish cult director Pedro Almodóvar, and it marked the first appearance of future Hollywood superstar Antonio Banderas. A freewheeling, pop culture screwball comedy, the frenetic action revolves around numerous love affairs between nymphomaniacs, analysts, visiting royalty and Islamic extremists in Madrid. It's much the same uneven gay/bisexual mix Almódovar camp followers expect and adore. AJ Spanish +subtitles. DVD

Cecilia Roth *Sexilia* • Imanol Arias *Riza Niro* • Helga Liné *Toraya* • Marta Fernandez-Muro *Queti* ■ *Dir/Scr* Pedro Almodóvar

The Lacemaker ★★★★ 15

Romantic drama 1977 · Fr · Colour · 102min

This is an agonisingly acute study of incompatability from Swiss director Claude Goretta. Isabelle Huppert gives one of her finest performances as the shy hairdresser whose life falls apart when her romance with student Yves Beneyton brings on an inferiority complex. By giving the couple's early scenes a joyous feel, tinged with a sense of innocent excitement, Goretta makes the struggle to preserve their relationship all the more unbearable, although the Parisian segment strives too deliberately to achieve its effect. The final shot is one of the most gut-wrenching ever filmed. DP French +subtitles.

Isabelle Huppert *Béatrice (Pomme)* • Yves Beneyton *François Beligne* • Florence Giorgetti *Marylène Thorent* • Anne-Marie Düringer [Annemarie Düringer] *Pomme's mother* ■ *Dir* Claude Goretta • *Scr* Pascal Lainé, Claude Goretta, from a novel by Pascal Lainé

Lackawanna Blues ★★★ 12

Music drama 2005 · US · Colour · 94min

Theatrical titan George C Wolfe makes an auspicious screen debut with this spirited adaptation by Ruben Santiago-Hudson of his award-winning stage memoir. Despite radically reshaping what had been a one-man show, Wolfe retains both the insight into character and the penchant for storytelling that had made the play so memorable. This is essentially a rite-of-passage piece, as young Marcus Carl Franklin is entrusted to S Epatha Merkerson, who runs a Lackawanna boarding house that attracts the damaged and the discarded. But the script also revels in its early 60s ghetto atmosphere, with the anecdotes and nightclub sequences providing compelling distractions from the excellent ensemble's daily reality. DP DVD

S Epatha Merkerson *Rachel "Nanny" Crosby* • Marcus Franklin [Marcus Carl Franklin] *Ruben Santiago Jr, as a boy* • Mos Def *The Bandleader* • Carmen Ejogo *Alean* • Julie Benz *Laura* • Robert A Bradley *Otis McClanahan* ■ *Dir* George C Wolfe • *Scr* Ruben Santiago-Hudson, from his play

Lacombe Lucien ★★★★ 12
Second World War drama
1974 · Fr · Colour · 132min

Louis Malle's absorbing and provocative film about the Nazi occupation of France features Pierre Blaise as the loutish young peasant who, shunned by the Resistance, joins the Gestapo and terrorises the Jewish family he moves in with. It's a moral quagmire of a movie, charting a peasant's road to fascism and redemption; Malle's clinical depiction of torture and other crimes, and his refusal to condemn his "hero" caused the film to be vilified by some in France. Beautifully made and disturbingly acted by the non-professional Blaise, it remains one of the few major films about the issue of collaboration. AT French +subtitles. *DVD*

Pierre Blaise *Lucien* · Aurore Clément *France* · Holger Lowenadler *Albert Horn* · Thérèse Giehse *Bella Horn* · Stéphane Bouy *Jean Bernard* · Loumi Iacobesco *Betty Beaulieu* · René Bouloc *Faure* ■ *Dir* Louis Malle · *Scr* Louis Malle, Patrick Modiano · *Cinematographer* Tonino Delli Colli

The Lad ★★
Thriller
1935 · UK · BW · 72min

Gordon Harker was such a favourite of crime writer Edgar Wallace that he frequently had material especially tailored for him. It's hardly surprising, therefore, that the actor is totally at home in this serviceable adaptation of one of Wallace's most popular thrillers. Posing as a detective to gain entrance to a country house, Harker soon realises he's not alone in having designs on a fabled family necklace. The action is brisk, but the performances are stiff. DP

Gordon Harker *Bill Shane* · Betty Stockfeld *Lady Fandon* · Jane Carr (1) *Pauline* · Gerald Barry *Lord Fandon* · Geraldine Fitzgerald *Joan* · Barbara Everest *Mrs Lorraine* · John Turnbull *Inspector Martin* ■ *Dir* Henry Edwards · *Scr* Gerard Fairlie, from the novel by Edgar Wallace

Ladder 49 ★★ 12
Action drama
2004 · US · Colour · 110min

In this intended tribute to American firefighters, Joaquin Phoenix plays the raw recruit who earns his stripes under the auspices of father figure John Travolta and goes on to become a firehouse legend. His progress through life is recounted in flashback as he lies trapped in a burning building. This predictable story doesn't shy away from emotion – in fact it heads straight for it as if answering an alarm. Though stirring at times, this melodrama fails to live up to its intention. KK Swearing. *DVD* *Blu-ray*

Joaquin Phoenix *Jack Morrison* · John Travolta *Mike Kennedy* · Jacinda Barrett *Linda Morrison* · Robert Patrick *Lenny Richter* · Morris Chestnut *Tommy Drake* · Billy Burke *Dennis Gauquin* · Balthazar Getty *Ray Gauquin* · Tim Guinee *Tony Corrigan* ■ *Dir* Jay Russell · *Scr* Lewis Colick

Ladies and Gentlemen, the Fabulous Stains ★★
Musical comedy drama
1981 · US · Colour · 87min

Director Lou Adler produced *The Rocky Horror Picture Show* and clearly thought he was crafting another cult item with this determinedly offbeat tale of the rise and fall, and rise again, of an all-girl punk band named the Fabulous Stains. Instead it languished on the shelf for years. What makes it worth watching is the cast: the Tubes' Fee Waybill (in a great cameo), Ray Winstone, Sex Pistols' Steve Jones and Paul Cook, and the Clash's Paul Simonon. Supposedly a music business satire, the whole concept rings hollow and wears out its initial welcome pretty quickly. AJ

Diane Lane *Corinne Burns* · Ray Winstone *Billy* · Peter Donat *Harley Dennis* · David Clennon *Dave Robell, the agent* · John Lehne *Stu McGrath* · Cynthia Sikes *Alicia Meeker* · Laura Dern *Jessica McNeil* · Marin Kanter *Tracy Burns* · Paul Cook *Danny* · Steve Jones *Steve* · Paul Simonon *Johnny* · John "Fee" Waybill *Lou Corpse* · Christine Lahti *Aunt Linda* ■ *Dir* Lou Adler · *Scr* Rob Morton

Ladies in Lavender ★★★ 12
Period drama
2004 · UK · Colour · 99min

The almost idyllic daily existence of two elderly sisters (played by the excellent Judi Dench and Maggie Smith) in mid-1930s Cornwall is thrown into upheaval when a handsome young man (Daniel Brühl) who can't speak English washes up on a nearby beach. Charles Dance, in his directorial debut, steers the story into unexpectedly subtle emotional regions that rely on character evolution and deft performances from the fine cast. This is a lively tale brimming with insight and a plot twist or two. KK In English, German. *DVD*

Judi Dench *Ursula Widdington* · Maggie Smith *Janet Widdington* · Daniel Brühl *Andrea Marowski* · Miriam Margolyes *Dorcas* · Natascha McElhone *Olga Danilof* · David Warner *Dr Francis Mead* · Freddie Jones *Jan Pendered* · Clive Russell *Adam Penruddocke* ■ *Dir* Charles Dance · *Scr* Charles Dance, from a short story by William J Locke

Ladies in Love ★★★
Romantic comedy
1936 · US · BW · 97min

Three young lovelies (including Janet Gaynor and Loretta Young) rent a luxury apartment in Budapest in the hope of attracting their dream husbands. One of their beaus is played by Tyrone Power in a very early role that hints at his charismatic screen presence. There is no deep subtext involved – what you see is a huge chunk of good old-fashioned entertainment. Who cares if it all seems rather chauvinistic and fey for our modern palate? It works. SH

Janet Gaynor *Martha Kerenye* · Loretta Young *Susie Schmidt* · Constance Bennett *Yoli Haydn* · Simone Simon *Marie Armand* · Don Ameche *Dr Rudi Imre* · Paul Lukas *John Barta* · Tyrone Power Jr [Tyrone Power] *Karl Lanyi* ■ *Dir* Edward H Griffith · *Scr* Melville Baker, from a play by Ladislaus Bus-Fekete

Ladies in Retirement ★★★
Crime melodrama
1941 · US · BW · 91min

Ida Lupino is at her most dramatically wild-eyed as the housekeeper to a retired actress (Isobel Elsom) who hatches a plot to help her two sisters (Elsa Lanchester and Edith Barrett). With Louis Hayward as the suspicious relative who uncovers the crime, there's an artificial symmetry that betrays the film's stage origins. It transfixes you with a purposeful expertise, though, mainly because Lupino can gain your sympathy while doing the most dastardly things. She can also imbue the act of washing-up with a menace you wouldn't believe. Remade in 1969 as *The Mad Room* with Stella Stevens. TH

Ida Lupino *Ellen Creed* · Louis Hayward *Albert Feather* · Evelyn Keyes *Lucy* · Elsa Lanchester *Emily Creed* · Edith Barrett *Louisa Creed* · Isobel Elsom *Leonora Fiske* · Emma Dunn *Sister Theresa* ■ *Dir* Charles Vidor · *Scr* Garrett Fort, Reginald Denham, from the play by Reginald Denham, Edward Percy

Ladies' Man ★★★ U
Comedy drama
1931 · US · BW · 76min

Smoothly amoral high-society man-about-town William Powell is loved by Kay Francis and lusted after by several society matrons whom he is happy to "escort" in return for their lavish tokens of gratitude. When, however, Carole Lombard, daughter of one of his ladies, falls for him, disaster strikes. A highly sophisticated and brittle comedy of Park Avenue manners, the film boasts a sharp script by Herman J Mankiewicz that manages to combine wit with a penetrating exposé of the milieu in which it is set. RK

William Powell *Jamie Darricott* · Kay Francis *Norma Page* · Carole Lombard *Rachel Fendley* · Gilbert Emery *Horace Fendley* · Olive Tell *Mrs Fendley* · Martin Burton *Anthony Fendley* · John Holland *Peyton Waldon* · Frank Atkinson *Valet* ■ *Dir* Lothar Mendes · *Scr* Herman J Mankiewicz, from a story by Rupert Hughes

The Ladies' Man ★★★★ U
Comedy
1961 · US · Colour · 91min

This is perhaps the most inventive and wittiest movie written, starring and directed by Jerry Lewis, one of the great clowns in the history of cinema. Playing a bitter, jilted man in a house full of women, Lewis proves himself a master of comic cinema, playing with the medium itself in a series of spirited gags in a marvellously constructed and elaborate set. Handyman Jerry is handsomely supported by viragos Helen Traubel and Kathleen Freeman, and there is a cameo from George Raft. TS *DVD*

Jerry Lewis *Herbert H Heebert* · Helen Traubel *Helen Welenmelon* · Pat Stanley *Fay* · Kathleen Freeman *Katie* · George Raft ■ *Dir* Jerry Lewis · *Scr* Jerry Lewis, Bill Richmond

The Ladies Man ★★ 15
Comedy
2000 · US · Colour · 80min

Tim Meadows stars as a randy radio "love doctor" who talks twaddle to the lovelorn but is inexplicably a turn-on to the tuned-in. Derived from Meadows's regular slot on cult American comedy show *Saturday Night Live*, this big-screen treatment has him facing the twin problems of finding a wealthy but anonymous former flame while avoiding an angry posse of hubbies whose wives he's bedded. If this daft dollop of double entendres could do with the occasional dose of Viagra, at least Meadows's endearingly awful alter ego maintains a level of fun. DA *DVD*

Tim Meadows *Leon Phelps* · Karyn Parsons *Julie Simmons* · Billy Dee Williams *Lester* · Tiffani Thiessen [Tiffani-Amber Thiessen] *Honey DeLune* · Lee Evans *Barney* · Will Ferrell *Lance DeLune* ■ *Dir* Reginald Hudlin · *Scr* Tim Meadows, Dennis McNicholas

Ladies of Leisure ★★★
Romantic drama
1930 · US · BW · 98min

The glorious combination of director Frank Capra and leading lady Barbara Stanwyck makes this whiskered plot worth watching. Stanwyck stars as a reformed gold-digger who falls for would-be artist Ralph Graves, but nobody believes her capable of true lurv. Well, would you? Capra's delicate soufflé touch gives the script the bounce and pace it needs and, of course, Stanwyck is stunning. SH

Barbara Stanwyck *Kay Arnold* · Ralph Graves *Jerry Strange* · Lowell Sherman *Bill Standish* · Marie Prevost *Dot Lamar* · Nance O'Neil *Mrs Strange* · George Fawcett *Mr Strange* ■ *Dir* Frank Capra · *Scr* Jo Swerling, from the play *Ladies of the Evening* by Milton Herbert Gropper

Ladies of the Chorus ★ U
Romantic musical
1949 · US · BW · 57min

A chorus girl in burlesque on Broadway steps out of her class, as did her mother before her, and falls in love with a smooth socialite. Directed by Phil Karlson from a monumentally feeble script, this dire but mercifully short musical programme filler marks the less than notable first leading role for Marilyn Monroe. She is adequate to the undemanding task without giving any hint of the screen goddess she would become. RK

Marilyn Monroe *Peggy Martin* · Adele Jergens *May Martin* · Rand Brooks *Randy Carroll* · Nana Bryant *Mrs Adele Carroll* · Eddie Carr *Billy Mackay* ■ *Dir* Phil Karlson · *Scr* Harry Sauber, Joseph Carol, from the story by Harry Sauber

Ladies of the House ★★
Drama
2008 · US · Colour · 102min

Pam Grier, Lance Henriksen and one-time *Brady Bunch* star Florence Henderson are among the well-known faces in this warm though implausible tale in which three mature women renovate a run-down house to raise funds for their local church. With the neglected building serving as a metaphor for the ladies' problematic personal lives, sentimentality and seriousness quickly creep into the mix. Consequently, what begins as undemanding fluff soon hijacks the heartstrings, manipulating viewers right up to the film's predictable, feel-good finale. SF

Florence Henderson *Rose* · Lance Henriksen *Frank* · Donna Mills *Elizabeth* · Gordon Thomson *Richard* · Pam Grier *Birdie* · Richard Roundtree *Stan* ■ *Dir* James A Contner · *Scr* Karen Struck

Ladies' Room ★★ 12
Fantasy drama
2000 · UK/Can · Colour · 84min

Purgatory is envisaged as a rest-room in this undistinguished fantasy from Gabriella Christiani. Thanks to some portentous scripting and bombastic acting, the mix of heavy melodrama and dark farce never gels, and the movie ends up resembling the stagiest of plays. Molly Parker and Lorraine Bracco put on brave faces, but John Malkovich (complete with comic Italian accent) is particularly poor. DP *DVD*

Molly Parker *Julia* · Veronica Ferres *Lauren* · Lorraine Bracco *Gemma* · Greta Scacchi *Lucia* · John Malkovich *Roberto* · Allan Fawcett [Alan Fawcett] *Bill* · Dorothée Berryman *Bag Lady* ■ *Dir* Gabriella Christiani · *Scr* Adrianna Plitz, Matalina Di Leandro, Amanda Roberts, Charlotte Pitts

Ladies Should Listen ★★
Romantic comedy
1934 · US · BW · 62min

Cary Grant stars in this romantic comedy about a man-about-town whose switchboard operator Frances Drake is secretly in love with him. She involves herself in his affairs, business and otherwise, leading to inevitable complications. It's not surprising that this title hardly springs to mind when considering the films of the incomparable Grant. Directed by Frank Tuttle, and with a reliable supporting cast of character players, it's no more than a passing entertainment, with a lazily superficial script. RK

Cary Grant *Julian de Lussac* · Frances Drake *Anna Mirelle* · Edward Everett Horton *Paul Vernet* · Nydia Westman *Susi Flamberg* · Clara Lou Sheridan [Ann Sheridan] *Adele* ■ *Dir* Frank Tuttle · *Scr* Guy Bolton, Claude Binyon, Frank Butler, from the play by Guy Bolton, from the play *La Demoiselle de Passy* by Alfred Savoir

Ladies They Talk About ★★★
Prison drama
1933 · US · BW · 64min

Gang moll Barbara Stanwyck is sent to San Quentin through the efforts of powerful crime-fighting evangelist Preston Foster, who puts principle before love. Five years and several dramatic incidents later they are reunited. An entertaining crime melodrama, making a sincere attempt to portray life in a women's prison, this sometimes resembles a social gathering. The highly unlikely plot is much enlivened by acid comedy (despite some Hays Office objections), and Stanwyck's cool performance. RK

Barbara Stanwyck *Nan Taylor* · Preston S Foster [Preston Foster] *David Slade* · Lyle Talbot *Don* · Dorothy Burgess *Susie* · Lillian Roth *Linda* · Maude Eburne *Aunt Maggie* ■ *Dir* Howard Bretherton, William Keighley · *Scr* Brown Holmes, William McGrath, Sidney Sutherland, from the play by Dorothy Mackaye, Carlton Miles

Ladies Who Do ★★ U
Comedy
1963 · UK · BW · 81min

A firm favourite in such TV series as *The Larkins* and *George and the Dragon*, Peggy Mount found films harder to come by. In the sixth of her ten pictures, she's joined by those other sitcom stalwarts Miriam Karlin and Dandy Nichols, as a trio of charladies who make a killing on the stock market through the tips they find among the office rubbish. With Harry H Corbett in support, this should have been quite amusing, but the ponderous script and the flat direction make it a one-joke bore. DP *DVD*

Peggy Mount *Mrs Cragg* · Robert Morley *Colonel Whitforth* · Harry H Corbett *James Ryder* · Miriam Karlin *Mrs Higgins* · Avril Elgar *Emily Parish* · Dandy Nichols *Mrs Merryweather* · Jon Pertwee *Mr Tait* · Nigel Davenport *Mr Strang* · Graham Stark *Foreman* · Ron Moody *Inspector* ■ *Dir* CM Pennington-Richards · *Scr* Michael Pertwee, from an idea by John Bignell

The Lady ★ 12
Biographical drama
2011 · Fr/UK · Colour · 126min

Quite where this inert biopic of Burmese opposition leader Aung San Suu Kyi went wrong is hard to fathom. It has a talented cast (led by Michelle Yeoh and David Thewlis), high-end production values and, in French director Luc Besson, a great potential for visual style and epic action. But this story of triumph against bullying and repression is simply worthy and dull, revealing little about Suu Kyi's mettle and true feelings or indeed any wider truths about her undeniable impact on the world stage. **DW** Some violence. **DVD BL**

Michelle Yeoh *Aung San Suu Kyi* • David Thewlis *Michael Aris/Anthony Aris* • Jonathan Raggett *Kim Aris* • Jonathan Woodhouse *Alexander Aris* ■ *Dir* Luc Besson • *Scr* Rebecca Frayn

The Lady & the Duke
★★★★ **PG**

Historical drama 2001 · Fr/Ger · Colour · 123min

Eric Rohmer here creates a compelling study of quiet courage in the face of ever-present danger during the French Revolution. The story of royalist Scot Grace Elliott's (Lucy Russell) friendship with a radical sympathiser, the Duke of Orléans (Jean-Claude Dreyfus), is played out against Jean-Baptiste Marot's stunning canvasses, based on paintings and street maps of the period and brought to vivid life through the selective use of computer animation. The tender relationship between the ex-lovers is elegantly expressed through the literate dialogue, yet Rohmer imparts plenty of suspense into the proceedings as well. **DP** French +subtitles. Violence. **DVD**

Lucy Russell *Grace Elliott* • Jean-Claude Dreyfus *Le Duc d'Orléans* • François Marthouret *Dumouriez* • Léonard Cobiant *Marquis de Champcenetz* • Caroline Morin *Nanon* • Alain Libolt *Duc de Biron* ■ *Dir* Eric Rohmer • *Scr* Eric Rohmer, from the memoir *Journal of My Life during the French Revolution* by Grace Elliott

The Lady and the Monster

Science-fiction horror 1944 · US · BW · 86min ★★

The first of several adaptations of Curt Siodmak's cult novel *Donovan's Brain* was brought to the screen by Republic boss Herbert Yates as a change of pace for Vera Hruba Ralston, the Czech figure skater he would eventually marry. However, the only memorable thing about this laboured romp are the disconcerting expressionist images and Erich von Stroheim's gleefully deranged showboating. Sadly, Ralston's approximation of terror, as her lover Richard Arlen is possessed by the brain's malignant spirit and goes on a killing spree, is remembered only for its ineptitude. Re-edited and re-released in 1949 as *The Tiger Man*. **DP**

Vera Hruba Ralston [Vera Ralston] *Janice Farrell* • Richard Arlen *Patrick Cory* • Erich von Stroheim *Prof Franz Mueller* • Helen Vinson *Chloe Donovan* • Mary Nash *Mrs Fame* • Sidney Blackmer *Eugene Fulton* ■ *Dir* George Sherman • *Scr* Frederick Kohner, Dane Lussier, from the novel *Donovan's Brain* by Curt Siodmak

Lady and the Tramp
★★★★★ **U**

Animated musical adventure
1955 · US · Colour · 72min

The Disney studio's first venture into CinemaScope remains one of its most enduring favourites. Ending a sequence of fairy-tale adaptations, it returned to the animal world of *Dumbo* and *Bambi* to create a cast of charming creatures, headed by a pampered cocker spaniel called Lady and a spaghetti-munching mongrel called Tramp. In addition to voicing Lady's mistress and Siamese cats Si and Am, Peggy Lee also co-composed the unforgettable songs (with Sonny Burke). A joy for children and romantics alike. **DP** **DVD BL**

Peggy Lee *Darling/Peg/Si/Am* • Barbara Luddy *Lady* • Larry Roberts *Tramp* • Bill Thompson *Jock/Bull/Dachsie* • Bill Baucon *Trusty* • Stan Freberg *Beaver* • Verna Felton *Aunt Sarah* ■ *Dir* Hamilton Luske, Clyde Geronimi, Wilfred Jackson • *Scr* Erdman Penner, Joe Rinaldi, Ralph Wright, Don DaGradi, from the novel *Lady* by Ward Greene

Lady and the Tramp II: Scamp's Adventure
★★ **U**

Animated musical adventure
2000 · US/Aus · Colour · 66min

One of the longest delayed sequels in screen history will disappoint those with fond memories of the 1955 original. The highly conformist message will jar with those who remember Tramp as a kind of canine James Dean. Scott Wolf voices Scamp with puppyish enthusiasm, lending excitement to his adventures and vulnerability to his clash with Chazz Palminteri's junkyard bruiser. There's even a little canoodling over the pasta with a pooch named Angel (Alyssa Milano). Fun, but not a patch on its predecessor. **DP** **DVD BL**

Scott Wolf *Scamp* • Alyssa Milano *Angel* • Chazz Palminteri *Buster* • Jeff Bennett *Tramp/Jock/Dogcatcher* • Jodi Benson *Lady* • Bill Fagerbakke *Mooch* ■ *Dir* Darrell Rooney • *Scr* Jeannine Roussel, Bill Motz, Bob Roth, from characters created in the 1955 film

Lady Be Good
★★ **U**

Musical 1941 · US · BW · 111min

This is a musical of two halves: a weak, badly-written and boring plot (the several acrimonious partings and tearful reconciliations of songwriting duo Robert Young and Ann Sothern), and a series of good songs, dazzling tap dancing from Eleanor Powell and a fabulous finale staged by Busby Berkeley. The stand-out song is Jerome Kern's Oscar winner, *The Last Time I Saw Paris*, sung by Ann Sothern. **RK**

Eleanor Powell *Marilyn Marsh* • Ann Sothern *Dixie Donegan* • Robert Young (1) *Eddie Crane* • Lionel Barrymore *Judge Murdock* • John Carroll *Buddy Crawford* • Red Skelton *Joe "Red" Willet* • Virginia O'Brien *Lull* • Tom Conway *Mr Blanton* • Dan Dailey Jr [Dan Dailey] *Bill Pattison* • Phil Silvers *MC* ■ *Dir* Norman Z McLeod • *Scr* Jack McGowan, Kay Van Riper, John McClain, from a story by Jack McGowan • *Costume Designer* Adrian

Lady Beware
★★ **18**

Thriller 1987 · US · Colour · 103min

The story is familiar enough, but this slick straight-to-video thriller is still worth a look. Diane Lane gives one of her best performances as a department store window dresser whose mannequin displays attract the unwelcome attentions of a disturbed secret admirer (Michael Woods, brother of James). Director Karen Arthur succeeds in generating a creepy sense of menace. **JF**

Diane Lane *Katya Yarno* • Michael Woods *Jack Price* • Cotter Smith *Mac Odell* • Tyra Ferrell *Nan* • Peter Nevargic *Lionel* • Edward Penn *Thayer* ■ *Dir* Karen Arthur • *Scr* Susan Miller, Charles Zev Cohen

Lady by Choice
★★★

Comedy 1934 · US · BW · 74min

This entertaining, if duller-edged, follow-up to Frank Capra's wonderful *Lady for a Day* is directed by David Burton with a rather more plodding hand. May Robson reprises a role similar to that of her scruffy fruit vendor Apple Annie (with a faint hint of ennui), this time given a major wash and brush-up à la *Pygmalion* by hoofer Carole Lombard. The latter, whose career was so tragically cut short, is always a joy to watch and this big-hearted movie shows her gift for bons mots to good advantage. But overall, this is short on pizzazz. **SH**

Carole Lombard *"Alabam" Georgia Lee* • May Robson *Patsy Patterson* • Roger Pryor *John Mills* • Walter Connolly *Judge Daly* • Arthur Hohl *Charlie Kendall* • Raymond Walburn *Front O'Malley* ■ *Dir* David Burton (1) • *Scr* Jo Swerling, from a story by Dwight Taylor

Lady Caroline Lamb
★★★ **15**

Historical drama 1972 · UK/It · Colour · 117min

Robert Bolt turned writer/director and wrote this historical drama for his wife, Sarah Miles. Lady Caroline Lamb was married to a future Prime Minister, had a celebrated affair with Lord Byron and generally scandalised Regency society. Miles plays the part to the hilt, appearing in some bizarre costumes and exploiting her own natural talent and extrovert character to advantage, being by turns ravishing, captivating, infuriating and pathetic. Laurence Olivier plays a camp Wellington with a false nose, Jon Finch is quietly authoritative as William Lamb/Lord Melbourne and Richard Chamberlain is perfectly pompous as Byron. Done in the rather flat style of a 1950s costume drama. **AT**

Sarah Miles *Lady Caroline Lamb* • Jon Finch *William Lamb* • Richard Chamberlain *Lord Byron* • John Mills *Canning* • Margaret Leighton *Lady Melbourne* • Pamela Brown *Lady Bessborough* • Ralph Richardson *The King* • Laurence Olivier *Duke of Wellington* ■ *Dir/Scr* Robert Bolt

Lady Chatterley
★★★★ **18**

Period romantic drama 2006 · Fr/Bel · Colour · 161min

DH Lawrence's notorious novel has been filmed several times, but French director Pascale Ferran is the first woman to tackle this tale of illicit love in 1920s England. Drawing on Lawrence's second version of the text, *John Thomas and Lady Jane*, Ferran eschews brusque softcore in depicting the passion that erupts between a naive young aristocrat and a gruffly sensitive gamekeeper. There's plenty of nudity and physicality, but the sex is never bestial or lewd, as Ferran equates their passion with the natural world that offers her an escape from the stuffiness of an ancestral hall and him an opportunity to forget the perils of the mines. **DP** French +subtitles. Sex scenes, nudity. **DVD**

Marina Hands *Constance Chatterley* • Jean-Louis Coulloc'h *Parkin* • Hippolyte Girardot *Sir Clifford Chatterley* • John Alexandridis *Mrs Bolton* • Hélène Fillières *Hilda* • Bernard Verley *Sir Malcolm, Constance's father* • Siane Lemoine *Charlotte Parkin* ■ *Dir* Pascale Ferran • *Scr* Pascale Ferran, Roger Bohbot, Pierre Trividic, from the novel *John Thomas and Lady Jane* by DH Lawrence • *Cinematographer* Julien Hirsch

Lady Chatterley's Lover
★ **18**

Erotic drama 1981 · Fr/UK · Colour · 100min

Sylvia Kristel's acting deficiencies were barely noticeable in the *Emmanuelle* pictures that made her name. Here, though, she is required to do more, and she is found severely wanting. Not that Nicholas Clay has anything to be proud of in his performance as the gamekeeper. There are lots of period trappings, and Robert Fraisse's photography manages to be both nostalgic and pornographic. But poor DH Lawrence scarcely gets a look-in. **DP** **DVD**

Sylvia Kristel *Lady Constance Chatterley* • Nicholas Clay *Oliver Mellors* • Shane Briant *Sir Clifford Chatterley* • Ann Mitchell *Mrs Bolton* • Elizabeth Spriggs *Lady Eva* • Pascale Rivault *Hilda* • Anthony Head *Anton* • Bessie Love *Flora* ■ *Dir* Just Jaeckin • *Scr* Christopher Wicking, Just Jaeckin, from the novel *Lady Chatterley's Lover* by DH Lawrence

The Lady Cop
★★★

Detective drama 1979 · Fr · Colour · 103min

Director Yves Boisset lifts the lid on provincial life in this simmering study of injustice and iniquitous influence. Demoted for linking the mayor to a gay scandal, Parisian detective Miou-Miou discovers that the drama group in a small northern town is behind the staging of some less than innocent entertainments. Miou-Miou is gutsily efficient, but the standout here is comedian Jean-Marc Thibault, who reveals a darker side as her boss. **DP** French dubbed.

Miou-Miou *Inspecteur Corinne Levasseur* • Jean-Marc Thibault *Commissaire Porel* • Leny Escudero *Diego Cortez* • Jean-Pierre Kalfon *Backmann* ■ *Dir* Yves Boisset • *Scr* Yves Boisset, Claude Veillot

The Lady Eve
★★★★★ **U**

Classic screwball comedy
1941 · US · BW · 89min

This wonderfully witty masterpiece, written and directed by the inimitable Preston Sturges, gives a couple of near career-best roles to two of Hollywood's finest players, who are perfectly cast here. Henry Fonda, a wealthy young man obsessed by snakes, lays himself wide open to the schemes of professional con artist Charles Coburn and his daughter, Barbara Stanwyck. Fonda's buddy William Demarest intervenes, but Stanwyck, undeterred, later reappears in disguise at his palatial manse. A sparkling combination of romance and screwball comedy. **TS** **DVD**

Barbara Stanwyck *Jean Harrington/Lady Eve Sidwich* • Henry Fonda *Charles Poncefort Pike* • Charles Coburn *"Colonel" Harrington* • Eugene Pallette *Mr Pike* • William Demarest *Muggsy* • Eric Blore *Sir Alfred McGlennan Keith/"Pearlie"* • Melville Cooper *Gerald* • Martha O'Driscoll *Martha* • Janet Beecher *Mrs Pike* • Robert Greig *Burrows* • Wilson Benge *Butler* ■ *Dir* Preston Sturges • *Scr* Preston Sturges, from the story *The Faithful Heart* by Monckton Hoffe

Lady for a Day
★★★★ **U**

Comedy 1933 · US · BW · 95min

This is a wonderful screen version of Damon Runyon's tale of Apple Annie, the Times Square fruit seller who brings so much luck to Dave the Dude that, when her daughter arrives from Europe with an aristocratic fiancé, he puts her up in a hotel and turns her into the titular lady. A fabulous cast incarnates Runyon's street characters, but none is more impressive than Australian-born May Robson in the leading role, the performance of a lifetime which rightly won her an Oscar nomination. Columbia's whizzkid Frank Capra - he also directed the 1961 remake *Pocketful of Miracles* - also secured Academy nominations for best picture and best director. **TS** **DVD**

Warren William *Dave the Dude* • May Robson *Apple Annie* • Guy Kibbee *Judge Blake* • Glenda Farrell *Missouri Martin* • Ned Sparks *Happy McGuire* • Walter Connolly *Count Romero* • Jean Parker *Louise* • Nat Pendleton *Shakespeare* • Barry Norton *Carlos* ■ *Dir* Frank Capra • *Scr* Robert Riskin, from the story *Madame la Gimp* by Damon Runyon

Lady for a Night
★★ **U**

Period melodrama 1942 · US · BW · 87min

Great idea from Republic, shame about the execution. At one of the big studios, this riverboat romantic drama could have been done properly with a decent budget and possibly colour. As it is, John Wayne is awkwardly cast alongside top-billed Joan Blondell in a murder-driven plot. Director Leigh Jason wasn't the right choice to make all this back projection work, and the result is very average indeed. **TS**

Joan Blondell *Jenny Blake* • John Wayne *Jack Morgan* • Philip Merivale *Stephen Alderson* • Blanche Yurka *Julia Alderson* • Ray Middleton *Alan Alderson* • Edith Barrett *Katherine Alderson* • Leonid Kinskey *Boris* ■ *Dir* Leigh Jason • *Scr* Isabel Dawn, Boyce DeGaw, from a story by Garrett Fort

Lady from Louisiana
★★ **PG**

Drama 1941 · US · BW · 82min

John Wayne considered himself too big a star to be landed with the part of a young lawyer in this bog-standard Republic programmer. Certainly, there's nothing remarkable about this tale of a crooked lottery in New Orleans. Ona Munson could be forgiven for sharing her co-star's disappointment, as her own career had failed to take off in spite of a splendid performance in *Gone with the Wind*. There is little chemistry between the pair and the spectacular storm finale is all too long in coming. **DP**

John Wayne *John Reynolds* • Ona Munson *Julie Mirbeau* • Ray Middleton *Blackie Williams* • Henry Stephenson *General Mirbeau* • Helen Westley *Mrs Brunot* • Jack Pennick *Cuffy* • Dorothy Dandridge *Felice* ■ *Dir* Bernard Vorhaus • *Scr* Vera Caspary, Michael Hogan, Guy Endore, from a story by Edward James, Francis Faragoh

The Lady from Shanghai
★★★★ **PG**

Romantic crime drama 1948 · US · BW · 83min

This is a marvellous murky film with *noir* touches from arguably the American cinema's greatest director, Orson Welles (though cutting his beloved Rita Hayworth's

L

hair short and dyeing it platinum for her role here was perhaps not one of his better ideas). Even stranger was his decision to play his own part with a bizarre Irish accent. Nevertheless, Everett Sloane as Hayworth's disabled husband is even better than he was in *Citizen Kane*, and the climactic hall of mirrors sequence is magnificently shot and justly famed. **TS** *DVD*

Rita Hayworth *Elsa Bannister* • Orson Welles *Michael O'Hara* • Everett Sloane *Arthur Bannister* • Glenn Anders *George Grisby* • Ted De Corsia *Sidney Broome* • Erskine Sanford *Judge* • Gus Schilling *Goldie* • Carl Frank *District Attorney* • Louis Merrill *Jake* • Evelyn Ellis *Bessie* ■ *Dir* Orson Welles • *Scr* Orson Welles, from the novel *If I Die Before I Wake* by Sherwood King

The Lady Gambles ★★★
Melodrama 1949 · US · BW · 98min

A happily married couple (Barbara Stanwyck, Robert Preston) take a trip to Las Vegas where the warm, wonderful, well-balanced wife develops a gambling addiction that drives her husband away and propels her into the most desperate of conditions. Directed by Michael Gordon, this is melodrama in capitals and italics, played for all its worth by the great Stanwyck. In her harrowing descent to the gutter she suffers with such conviction that fans both of the star and of soap opera can easily overlook the fact that this is perfunctorily written hokum. **AT**

Barbara Stanwyck *Joan Boothe* • Robert Preston *David Boothe* • Stephen McNally *Corrigan* • Edith Barrett *Ruth Phillips* • Elliott Sullivan *Barky* • Houseley Stevenson *Pawnbroker* • Peter Leeds *Hotel clerk* • Don Beddoe *Mr Sutherland* • Anthony Curtis [Tony Curtis] *Bellboy* ■ *Dir* Michael Gordon • *Scr* Roy Huggins, Halsted Welles, from a story by Lewis Meltzer, Oscar Saul

Lady Godiva ★ U
Historical drama 1955 · US · Colour · 89min

Maureen O'Hara, wrapped in yards of red hair to hide her nakedness, rides through 11th-century Coventry in this tedious, cardboard piece, obviously filmed on the Universal backlot. She is the Saxon bride of Saxon nobleman George Nader, determined to thwart plans for an alliance with the Normans. Cast as the First Saxon is 25-year-old Clint Eastwood. **RB**

Maureen O'Hara *Lady Godiva* • George Nader *Lord Leofric* • Eduard Franz *King Edward* • Leslie Bradley *Count Eustace* • Victor McLaglen *Grimald* • Torin Thatcher *Lord Godwin* • Clint Eastwood *1st Saxon* ■ *Dir* Arthur Lubin • *Scr* Oscar Brodney, Harry Ruskin, from a story by Oscar Brodney

Lady Godiva ★★ 12
Romantic drama 2007 · UK · Colour · 89min

Vicky Jewson's film opens in medieval times with Lady Godiva's infamous ride through Coventry, before shifting to modern-day Oxford, where Phoebe Thomas is struggling to relaunch her late brother's community art project. The two stories connect when Thomas is offered the necessary funds by her new celebrity boyfriend (Matthew Chambers), on condition that she ride naked through the city on horseback. Veering between romantic comedy and soap, the story isn't always original or convincing, but Jewson coaxes committed performances out of Chambers and the Pre-Raphaelite-looking Thomas. **DP** Brief swearing, nudity. *DVD*

Phoebe Thomas *Jemima Honey/Lady Godiva* • Matthew Chambers *Michael Bartle* • James Wilby *Leofric, Earl of Mercia* • Isabelle Amyes *Mrs Bartle* • Julia Verdin *Veronica* • Matthew Turpin *Prince William* • Nicholas Parsons ■ *Dir/Scr* Vicky Jewson

Lady Godiva Rides Again ★★ PG
Comedy 1951 · UK · BW · 93min

Apart from a wonderful speech by Alastair Sim's world-weary producer about the errant ways of the British film industry, this is a hugely disappointing satire from the usually reliable pairing of Frank Launder and Sidney Gilliat. It was cruelly ironic that Pauline Stroud's real-life flirtation with

movie fame should turn out to be as brief as that of the pageant queen she plays here, but she's not helped by a script so thin it wouldn't hide Godiva's blushes. Although the supporting cast reads like a who's who of 1950s comedy, no one is around long enough to make much of an impact. **DP** *DVD*

Dennis Price *Simon Abbott* • John McCallum *Larry Burns* • Stanley Holloway *Mr Clark* • Pauline Stroud *Marjorie Clark* • Gladys Henson *Mrs Clark* • Bernadette O'Farrell *Janie* • George Cole *Johnny* • Diana Dors *Dolores August* • Eddie Byrne *Eddie Mooney* • Kay Kendall *Sylvie* • Renee Houston *Beattie* • Dora Bryan *Publicity woman* • Sidney James *Lew Beeson* • Joan Collins *Beauty contestant* ■ *Dir* Frank Launder • *Scr* Frank Lauder, Val Valentine

Lady in a Cage ★★★ 18
Drama 1964 · US · BW · 94min

This exercise in sadism and mental torture was banned outright in Britain and the fact that it stars Olivia de Havilland and is from the director of *633 Squadron* makes all the more surprising. De Havilland plays a rich invalid who is trapped in her mechanical lift – the cage of the title – and is then systematically terrorised by a drunk, a prostitute and three thugs, one of whom is played by James Caan. It's an allegory about the beast in man and woman and has a surprise twist regarding de Havilland's past life. **AT** *DVD*

Olivia de Havilland *Mrs Hilyard* • Ann Sothern *Sade* • Jeff Corey *Nino* • James Caan *Randall* • Jennifer Billingsley *Elaine* • Rafael Campos *Essie* • William Swan *Malcolm Hilyard* ■ *Dir* Walter Grauman • *Scr* Luther Davis

Lady in a Jam ★★
Comedy 1942 · US · BW · 78min

Irene Dunne is the eponymous character, a harebrained heiress who loses all her money while indulging her obsession for numerology, and whose behaviour has her kept under observation by psychiatrist Patric Knowles, posing as a chauffeur. A feeble romantic comedy that dredges the bottom of the barrel for its sprinkling of laughs, it squanders the star's superior gifts and the talent of director Gregory La Cava. **RK**

Irene Dunne *Jane Palmer* • Patric Knowles *Dr Enright* • Ralph Bellamy *Stanley Gardner* • Eugene Pallette *Billingsley* • Samuel S Hinds *Dr Brewster* • Queenie Vassar *Cactus Kate Palmer* ■ *Dir* Gregory La Cava • *Scr* Eugene Thackrey, Frank Cockrell, Otho Lovering • *Cinematographer* Hal Mohr

Lady in Cement ★★ 15
Crime drama 1968 · US · Colour · 89min

This is a great title for the second of two movies starring Frank Sinatra as a world-weary private detective. However, the film itself is not quite as effective as the first one (*Tony Rome*). Both Sinatra and skilled director Gordon Douglas seem merely to be going through the paces, but there is excellent support from Dan Blocker and comedian Joe E Lewis. Thick-eared and not as tough as it thinks it is, this does at least give us Raquel Welch in her heyday. **TS** Violence, brief nudity. *DVD*

Frank Sinatra *Tony Rome* • Raquel Welch *Kit Forrest* • Richard Conte *Lieutenant Santini* • Martin Gabel *Al Mungar* • Lainie Kazan *Maria Baretto* • Pat Henry *Rubin* • Steve Peck *Paul Mungar* • Dan Blocker *Gronsky* ■ *Dir* Gordon Douglas • *Scr* Marvin H Albert, Jack Guss, from the novel by Marvin H Albert

The Lady in Question ★★★
Melodrama 1940 · US · BW · 79min

Six years before their sensational pairing in Charles Vidor's erotically charged *Gilda* brought them stardom, a still youthful Rita Hayworth and Glenn Ford appeared in this reworking of the French classic, *Gribouille*. Brian Aherne stars as a kind-hearted French family man who, called to jury duty, takes pity on the accused (Hayworth). He gives her a job and lodging in his home, causing numerous upheavals and complications involving his wife (Irene Rich) and son (Ford). A curious, occasionally irritating, but entertaining mix of bluff domestic comedy

and near tragedy, with Hayworth ravishingly lovely and quite touching. **RK**

Brian Aherne *André Morestan* • Rita Hayworth *Natalie Roguin* • Glenn Ford *Pierre Morestan* • Irene Rich *Michèle Morestan* • George Coulouris *Defense attorney* • Lloyd Corrigan *Prosecuting attorney* • Evelyn Keyes *Françoise Morestan* ■ *Dir* Charles Vidor • *Scr* Lewis Meltzer, from the film *Gribouille* by HG Lustig, Marcel Archard

The Lady in Question ★★★
Period murder mystery 1999 · US · Colour · 100min

Having received favourable reviews for *Murder in a Small Town*, Gene Wilder reprises the role of theatre impresario-turned-detective Larry "Cash" Carter in this satisfying murder mystery TV sequel. Again set in Stamford, Connecticut, in the late 1930s, the tale hinges on the murder of Claire Bloom's anti-Nazi activist. Having established the period charm, director Joyce Chopra is largely content to let Wilder (who also co-scripted) take over. Overall, this is knotty, nostalgic and nicely judged. **DP**

Gene Wilder *Larry "Cash" Carter* • Mike Starr *Tony Rossini* • Cherry Jones *Mimi Barnes* • Michael Cumpsty *Klaus Gruber* • Claire Bloom *Emma Sachs* • Barbara Sukowa *Rachel Singer* ■ *Dir* Joyce Chopra • *Scr* Gene Wilder, Gilbert Pearlman

The Lady in Red ★★★★ 18
Period crime drama 1979 · US · Colour · 83min

Produced on a slimline budget by Roger Corman's studio, this splendid retro gangster movie was shot in about a month by Lewis Teague from a script by John Sayles. Pamela Sue Martin plays a star-struck country girl who hopes to be a Hollywood star but gets caught up in Chicago's vice rings, working for madam Louise Fletcher and spending time in prison. On release she falls in love with gangster John Dillinger (Robert Conrad). Sayles's script does an impressive sweep of Chicago's underworld, social strata and economy in the 1930s. As it's a Corman picture, there's a lot of sex and bullets, too. **AT**

Pamela Sue Martin *Polly Franklin* • Robert Conrad *John Dillinger* • Louise Fletcher *Anna Sage* • Robert Hogan *Jake Lingle* • Laurie Heineman *Rose Shimkus* • Glenn Withrow *Eddie* • Rod Gist *Pinetop* • Peter Hobbs *Pops Geissler* • Christopher Lloyd *Frognose* ■ *Dir* Lewis Teague • *Scr* John Sayles

Lady in the Dark ★★★ U
Musical 1944 · US · Colour · 99min

Fashion magazine editor Ginger Rogers, fearing for her mental health because of conflicts with three men in her life (Ray Milland, Warner Baxter, Jon Hall), consults psychiatrist Barry Sullivan, to whom she relates her dreams. These provide the basis for the film's production numbers, lavishly staged and extravagantly dressed. A major Broadway musical hit three years earlier, Paramount spared no expense in bringing it to the screen with a gold-plated design and production team and Mitchell Leisen directing. The public loved it, but it lost Danny Kaye (replaced by Mischa Auer) and much of its brilliant original score in the transfer and got a critical thumbs-down. **RK**

Ginger Rogers *Liza Elliott* • Ray Milland *Charley Johnson* • Jon Hall *Randy Curtis* • Warner Baxter *Kendall Nesbitt* • Barry Sullivan *Dr Brooks* • Mischa Auer *Russell Paxton* ■ *Dir* Mitchell Leisen • *Scr* Frances Goodrich, Albert Hackett, from the musical by Moss Hart, Kurt Weill, Ira Gershwin • *Costume Designers* Raoul Pene du Bois, Edith Head

Lady in the Lake ★★★★
Film noir 1947 · US · BW · 102min

Robert Montgomery stars and directs himself as Philip Marlowe. Made only a year after Humphrey Bogart played Marlowe in *The Big Sleep*, Montgomery was looking for an offbeat approach that would surprise audiences and lessen the problems of directing himself while increasing the pressure on his co-stars. Just as Raymond Chandler's novels are written in the first person, so *Lady in the Lake* is a film in the

first person: the camera is Marlowe and we only see what he would see, glimpsing Montgomery's face only in brief opening and closing sequences and when Marlowe looks in the mirror. Meanwhile, the camera smokes, gets kissed (by Audrey Totter) and punched (by various heavies). A gimmick, but it works. **AT**

Robert Montgomery *Philip Marlowe* • Lloyd Nolan *Lieutenant DeGarmot* • Audrey Totter *Adrienne Fromsett* • Tom Tully *Captain Kane* • Leon Ames *Derace Kingsby* • Jayne Meadows *Mildred Havelend* • Morris Ankrum *Eugene Grayson* • Lila Leeds *Receptionist* • Richard Simmons [Dick Simmons] *Chris Lavery* ■ *Dir* Robert Montgomery • *Scr* Steve Fisher, Raymond Chandler (uncredited), from the novel by Raymond Chandler

The Lady in the Van ★★★ 12
Comedy drama based on a true story 2015 · UK · Colour · 104min

Maggie Smith lets her hair down in the role of a real-life bumptious bag lady who lived in a van and found a permanent parking spot outside the home of writer Alan Bennett. Naturally, he put pen to paper to turn this quintessentially British story of human connection into a book, then a play and now a film directed by Nicholas Hytner. Alex Jennings, as the cardi-clad Bennett, berates himself in dual roles – as the Bennett who lives life and the Bennett who writes – looking on with contempt and scathing witticisms. But this is clearly Smith's show. She is funny without tipping into caricature, yet openly vulnerable, too, and the friendship that develops between the two defies Hollywood conventions. **SP** Some swearing. *DVD* *Blu*

Maggie Smith *Miss Shepherd* • Alex Jennings *Alan Bennett* • Jim Broadbent *Underwood* • Frances de la Tour *Ursula Vaughan Williams* • Roger Allam *Rufus* • Dominic Cooper *Theatre actor* ■ *Dir* Nicholas Hytner • *Scr* From a memoir by Alan Bennett, from Bennett's play

Lady in the Water ★★ PG
Fantasy mystery thriller 2006 · US · Colour · 105min

Inspired by a bedtime story that director M Night Shyamalan created for his children, this muddled fantasy mystery shows every sign of having been made up as it goes along. Paul Giamatti plays the superintendent of an apartment block who discovers a sea nymph of Asian legend (Bryce Dallas Howard) has become stranded in the communal swimming pool. He aids her return to the Blue World, encountering a daft array of "mythological" creatures along the way. Giamatti does his best to hold this self-indulgent nonsense together and fans of the director's previous work may find some entertainment in this deeply silly, artificial and hopelessly naive tale. **AJ** *DVD* *Blu*

Paul Giamatti *Cleveland Heep* • Bryce Dallas Howard *Story* • Jeffrey Wright *Mr Dury* • Bob Balaban *Harry Farber* • Sarita Choudhury *Anna Ran* • Cindy Cheung *Young-Soon Choi* • M Night Shyamalan *Vick Ran* ■ *Dir/Scr* M Night Shyamalan

Lady in White ★★★★ 15
Supernatural thriller 1988 · US · Colour · 108min

Frank LaLoggia's ghost story brings a wonderful sense of magical euphoria back to the genre. This highly romanticised, sentimental chiller puts Stephen King's brand of dark and violent suspense and Frank Capra's emotional fantasy into a Norman Rockwell setting with enthralling results. Lukas Haas is fantastic as the key holder to a past Halloween tragedy still haunting his sleepy community, in this evocative mini-masterpiece, jam-packed with dreamy atmosphere and incandescent supernatural enchantment. **AJ** Violence, swearing. *DVD*

Lukas Haas *Frankie Scarlatti* • Len Cariou *Phil* • Alex Rocco *Angelo Scarlatti* • Katherine Helmond *Amanda Harper* • Jason Presson *Gino Scarlatti* • Renata Vanni *Mama Assunta* • Angelo Bertolini *Papa Charlie* • Jared Rushton *Donald* ■ *Dir/Scr* Frank LaLoggia

L

The Lady Is Willing ★

Comedy   1942 · US · BW · 90min

A glamorous stage star (Marlene Dietrich) finds an abandoned toddler in Manhattan and, in order to adopt him, undertakes a marriage of convenience with paediatrician Fred MacMurray. This leaden nonsense has nothing to recommend it other than the bizarre fascination of watching its *femme fatale* star attempting to play maternal in an uneasy mix of soap opera and romantic comedy. RK

Marlene Dietrich *Elizabeth Madden* • Fred MacMurray *Dr Corey McBain* • Aline MacMahon *Buddy* • Stanley Ridges *Kenneth Hanline* • Arline Judge *Frances* • Roger Clark *Victor* ■ *Dir* Mitchell Leisen • *Scr* James Edward Grant, Albert McCleery, from a story by James Edward Grant

Lady Jane ★★★ PG

Historical drama   1985 · UK · Colour · 135min

Historical biopics are notoriously difficult to do well. It's easy enough to establish the correct period look, but the action is invariably hamstrung by the need to provide background information on each character and episode. Trevor Nunn's account of the events that culminated in the brief reign of Lady Jane Grey falls into the familiar traps, with the romance between Jane and the dissolute Guildford Dudley being couched in terms more befitting a Brat Pack movie. However Helena Bonham Carter plays Jane with admirable earnestness and she is well supported by Patrick Stewart as her father. DP DVD

Helena Bonham Carter *Lady Jane Grey* • Cary Elwes *Guilford Dudley* • John Wood (2) *John Dudley, Duke of Northumberland* • Michael Hordern *Dr Feckenham* • Jill Bennett *Mrs Ellen* • Jane Lapotaire *Princess Mary* • Sara Kestelman *Frances Grey, Duchess of Suffolk* • Patrick Stewart *Henry Grey, Duke of Suffolk* • Warren Saire *King Edward VI* • Joss Ackland *Sir John Bridges* • Ian Hogg *Sir John Gates* ■ *Dir* Trevor Nunn • *Scr* David Edgar, from a story by Chris Bryant

Lady Killer ★★★★

Comedy thriller   1933 · US · BW · 76min

James Cagney's rat-a-tat delivery and the film's pell-mell propulsion make this a joyous Warner Bros sideswipe at Hollywood itself. Cagney is the cinema usher who graduates to gangsterdom, ending up as a film star writing fan letters to himself. He co-stars again with Mae Clarke from *Public Enemy*, only this time he pulls her out of bed by her hair instead of filling her face with grapefruit. The legend is that it's based on the rise and fall of George Raft, but who cares? The fast-paced action and Cagney's mesmeric energy make this so worthwhile. TH

James Cagney *Dan Quigley* • Leslie Fenton *Duke* • Margaret Lindsay *Lois Underwood* • Henry O'Neill *Ramick* • Willard Robertson *Conroy* • Douglas Cosgrove *Jones* • Raymond Hatton *Pete* • Russell Hopton *Smiley* ■ *Dir* Roy Del Ruth • *Scr* Ben Markson, Lillie Hayward, from the story *The Finger Man* by Rosalind Keating Shaffer

Lady L ★★★★

Period comedy   1965 · Fr/It · Colour · 123min

Like its writer and director, Peter Ustinov, this is an immense charmer. It's set at the turn of the last century, about laundress Sophia Loren whose amorous adventures, told in flashback, take her downstairs and then upstairs in the class system. Though involved with anarchist Paul Newman, she still marries eccentric aristocrat David Niven. The elegant dazzle and elaborate sets may be there to blind us to the lack of real substance but with an impressive cast, who cares? A stylish diversion. TH

Sophia Loren *Lady L* • Paul Newman *Armand* • David Niven *Lord Lendale* • Claude Dauphin *Inspector Mercier* • Philippe Noiret *Gérôme* • Michel Piccoli *Lecoeur* • Cecil Parker *Sir Percy* • Jean Wiener *Krajewski* • Daniel Emilfork *Kobeleff* • Peter Ustinov *Prince Otto* ■ *Dir* Peter Ustinov • *Scr* Peter Ustinov, from the novel by Romain Gary

Lady Liberty ★★

Comedy   1971 · It/Fr · Colour · 95min

The original Italian title of this frolic is *La Mortadella* – the name of Italy's fattest sausage. The plot has Sophia Loren arriving in New York clutching this huge sausage, which sends the US customs officials first into a dither, and then into lip-smacking mode. Like the sausage itself, this comedy was made for the Italian market and racked up few export sales. The English version was written by Ring Lardner Jr, a blacklisted screenwriter who won an Oscar for *MASH*. AT

Sophia Loren *Maddalena Ciarrapico* • William Devane *Jock Fenner* • Luigi Proietti *Michele Bruni* • Beeson Carroll *Dominic* • Bill Deprato *Pasquale* • Danny DeVito *Mancuso* • Susan Sarandon *Sally* ■ *Dir* Mario Monicelli • *Scr* Leonard Melfi, Suso Cecchi D'Amico, Don Carlos Dunaway, RW Spera, Mario Monicelli, Ring Lardner Jr, from a story by Leonard Melfi, from an idea by RW Spera

Lady Luck ★★

Comedy   1946 · US · BW · 97min

Robert Young plays a gambler whom Barbara Hale won't marry until he breaks his habit, because her dad – lovable Frank Morgan – comes from a long line of inveterate gamblers. Films like this are pleasant enough time-wasters, but they didn't give Young box-office clout. He eventually achieved international popularity in two television series, *Father Knows Best* (1954-60) and *Marcus Welby, MD* (1969-76). TS

Robert Young (1) *Larry Scott* • Barbara Hale *Mary Audrey* • Frank Morgan *William Audrey* • James Gleason *Sacramento Sam* • Don Rice *Eddie* • Harry Davenport *Judge Martin* ■ *Dir* Edwin L Marin • *Scr* Lynn Root, Frank Fenton, from the story by Herbert Clyde Lewis

Lady of Burlesque ★★★ PG

Comedy mystery   1943 · US · BW · 89min

When a chorus girl is strangled with a G-string, the show's star, Barbara Stanwyck, teams up with Michael O'Shea, the comic whose advances she has been spurning, to find the killer. Based on a novel written by America's most famous stripper, Gypsy Rose Lee, the movie has the perfect leading lady in Stanwyck. Directed by William A Wellman and Oscar-nominated for its music (by Arthur Lange), it's a cracking little drama (released as *Striptease Lady* in the UK) that combines suspense and comedy with the smell of the greasepaint. RK DVD

Barbara Stanwyck *Dixie Daisy* • Michael O'Shea (1) *Biff Brannigan* • J Edward Bromberg *SB Foss* • Iris Adrian *Gee Gee Graham* • Gloria Dickson *Dolly Baxter* • Charles Dingle *Inspector Harrigan* ■ *Dir* William A Wellman • *Scr* James Gunn, from the novel *The G-String Murders* by Gypsy Rose Lee • *Music* Arthur Lange

Lady of Deceit ★★★

Film noir   1947 · US · BW · 92min

This is a smashing hard-bitten *film noir* from that great postwar period when weak men fell headlong for tough *femmes fatales*, and destiny took no prisoners. Lawrence Tierney – better-known today for masterminding those pesky *Reservoir Dogs* – is married to pretty Audrey Long but is head-over-heels in love with her divorced sister, sultry Claire Trevor; you just know no good can come of this. TS

Lawrence Tierney *Sam Wild* • Claire Trevor *Helen Trent* • Walter Slezak *Arnett* • Phillip Terry *Fred* • Audrey Long *Georgia Staples* • Elisha Cook Jr *Marty* • Isabel Jewell *Laury Palmer* • Esther Howard *Mrs Kraft* ■ *Dir* Robert Wise • *Scr* Richard Macauley, Eve Green, from the novel *Deadlier Than the Male* by James Gunn

The Lady of Musashino ★★★ PG

Drama   1951 · Jpn · BW · 84min

Following the critical and commercial disappointment of *Miss Oyu*, Kenji Mizoguchi similarly failed to catch the national mood with this downbeat assessment of postwar society. The story centres on a suburban housewife whose despair at the spread of progressive attitudes and her husband's philanderings drives her to dependence on a like-minded neighbour, who eventually betrays her trust. Kinuyo Tanaka excels in the lead role and her contrast with cousin-in-law Yukiko Todoroki is as striking as that between the Musashino Plain and downtown Tokyo. DP Japanese +subtitles. DVD

Kinuyo Tanaka *Michiko* • Masayuki Mori *Tadao* • So Yamamura *Eiji* • Yukiko Todoroki *Tomiko* • Minako Nakamura *Yukiko Ono* ■ *Dir* Kenji Mizoguchi • *Scr* Yoshikata Yoda, from the novel *Musashino Fujin* by Shohei Ooka

Lady of the Tropics ★★★

Melodrama   1939 · US · BW · 91min

An aimless, penniless New Yorker (Robert Taylor), cruising the Far East with his intended fiancée's wealthy family, falls in love with a girl of mixed race (Hedy Lamarr) in Saigon. He abandons everything to marry her, but with tragic consequences. The film, directed by Jack Conway, does full justice to Lamarr's fabled beauty, which, together with a superbly polished and sinister performance from Joseph Schildkraut as the villain of the piece, makes this nonsensical melodrama very watchable. RK

Robert Taylor (1) *Bill Carey* • Hedy Lamarr *Manon De Vargnes* • Joseph Schildkraut *Pierre Delaroch* • Gloria Franklin *Nina* • Ernest Cossart *Father Antoine* • Natalie Moorhead *Mrs Hazlitt* ■ *Dir* Jack Conway • *Scr* Ben Hecht

Lady on a Train ★★★ U

Crime comedy   1945 · US · BW · 90min

With a licence to trill, opera singer Deanna Durbin's cinematic singing career was one of the most remarkable success stories of the 1930s and 1940s. This movie backed up her vocal talents with a better story than usual when, in the style of Agatha Christie, she sees a murder being committed on a passing train – and then has to try to convince the police. Her singing of *Night and Day* is the high-note. TH DVD

Deanna Durbin *Nikki Collins* • Ralph Bellamy *Jonathan* • Edward Everett Horton *Mr Haskell* • George Coulouris *Mr Wyman* • Allen Jenkins *Danny* • Dan Duryea *Arnold* ■ *Dir* Charles David • *Scr* Edmund Beloin, Robert O'Brien, from a story by Leslie Charteris • *Music* Miklos Rozsa

The Lady Pays Off ★ U

Comedy drama   1951 · US · BW · 79min

"Teacher of the Year" Linda Darnell faces something of an image crisis after she runs up gambling debts of $7,000 in Stephen McNally's Reno casino. McNally gives her an ultimatum: she has to coach his daughter or face exposure. That's quite a clever premise for a plot, but then things get unbelievably tacky, with Darnell faking romantic interest in McNally, only to be redeemed by the awfully cute little girl. AT

Linda Darnell *Evelyn Warren* • Stephen McNally *Matt Braddock* • Gigi Perreau *Diana Braddock* • Virginia Field *Kay Stoddard* ■ *Dir* Douglas Sirk • *Scr* Frank Gill Jr, Albert J Cohen

Lady Sings the Blues ★★★★

Musical biography   1972 · US · Colour · 143min

This biopic of jazz legend Billie Holliday, solely financed by Berry Gordy's Tamla Motown record label, stars Diana Ross in her screen debut. Like all Hollywood biopics, it's a typical rollercoaster ride, with Holliday suffering highs, lows, marriage, divorce, drug addiction, adulation and an early death. Ross is required to age some 20 years and gives a rich, compelling performance that only occasionally shouts "Gimme an Oscar". (She got a nomination, but lost out to Liza Minnelli in *Cabaret*). The 1930s ambience, nightclubs and drug culture are superbly evoked. AT

Diana Ross *Billie Holiday* • Billy Dee Williams *Louis McKay* • Richard Pryor *"Piano Man"* • James Callahan *Reg Hanley* • Paul Hampton *Harry* • Sid Melton *Jerry* • Virginia Capers *Mama Holiday* ■ *Dir* Sidney J Furie • *Scr* Terence McCloy, Chris Clark, Suzanne DePasse, from the autobiography by Billie Holiday, William Dufty

Lady Snowblood ★★★ 18

Period martial arts drama   1973 · Jpn · Colour · 97min

Already a cult figure, Meiko Kaji acquired star status in this blood-geysering Meiji period action drama. Much of the opening segment focuses on her mother's desperate bid to have a child to avenge the murder of her husband. But once Kaji begins training for her mission, the emphasis shifts to the barbaric. The film gains kudos by the co-starring turn of Akira Kurosawa's son, Toshio. A sequel followed in 1974. DP Japanese +subtitles. DVD

Meiko Kaji *Yuki* • Toshio Kurosawa ■ *Dir* Toshiya Fujita • *Scr* Kazuo Uemura, Kazuo Koike, from a comic book by Kazuo Koike

A Lady Takes a Chance ★★★ U

Romantic comedy   1943 · US · BW · 82min

A nicely packaged star vehicle for Jean Arthur, successfully paired with John Wayne in a romantic comedy about a rodeo star and a city gal. Arthur's second husband, the former singer Frank Ross, was the producer and surrounded her with talent: especially watchable is funny Phil Silvers as a tour guide. In this slight but engaging comedy, William A Seiter cleverly keeps the romance bubbling. TS DVD

Jean Arthur *Mollie Truesdale* • John Wayne *Duke Hudkins* • Phil Silvers *Smiley Lambert* • Mary Field *Florrie Bendix* • Don Costello (1) *Drunk* • Grady Sutton *Malcolm* • Grant Withers *Bob* • Hans Conried *Gregg* ■ *Dir* William A Seiter • *Scr* Robert Ardrey, Garson Kanin (uncredited), from a story by Jo Swerling

The Lady Takes a Flyer ★★

Drama   1958 · US · Colour · 94min

Jack Arnold, who made his name directing some of the best sci-fi pictures of the 1950s, such as *It Came from Outer Space* and *The Incredible Shrinking Man*, subsequently had an incredibly shrinking career. This predictable confection starred blonde Lana Turner and white-haired Jeff Chandler as a squabbling married couple – both are pilots – each with rivals for their affections. RB

Lana Turner *Maggie Colby* • Jeff Chandler *Mike Dandridge* • Richard Denning *Al Reynolds* • Andra Martin *Nikki Reynolds* • Chuck Connors *Phil Donahue* • Reta Shaw *Nurse Kennedy* ■ *Dir* Jack Arnold • *Scr* Danny Arnold, from the story by Edmund H North

The Lady Vanishes ★★★★★ U

Classic thriller   1938 · UK · BW · 92min

A close second behind *The 39 Steps* as the best film of Alfred Hitchcock's British period, this sublime comedy thriller was co-scripted by Alma Reville (Mrs Hitchcock) with Frank Launder and Sidney Gilliat. There isn't a wasted frame, as Michael Redgrave and Margaret Lockwood search a Balkan express for dotty Dame May Whitty. Basil Radford and Naunton Wayne drew all the plaudits as the cricket-mad Charters and Caldicott, but the support playing of Paul Lukas, Mary Clare and Cecil Parker is also first class. Hitchcock cameo fans should keep their eyes peeled during the London station scene. DP DVD

Margaret Lockwood *Iris Henderson* • Michael Redgrave *Gilbert* • Paul Lukas *Dr Hartz* • Dame May Whitty *Miss Froy* • Cecil Parker *Mr Todhunter* • Linden Travers *"Mrs" Todhunter* • Naunton Wayne *Caldicott* • Basil Radford *Charters* • Mary Clare *Baroness* • Googie Withers *Blanche* ■ *Dir* Alfred Hitchcock • *Scr* Sidney Gilliat, Frank Launder, Alma Reville, from Ethel Lina White's novel *The Wheel Spins*

The Lady Vanishes ★★★ PG

Thriller   1979 · UK · Colour · 95min

This is a watchable remake of the much-loved 1938 Hitchcock classic. It's slicker than the original – gone are the amateur model shots – and though it lacks the charm and atmosphere of impending war that gave the original so much power, there are other fringe benefits. Miss Froy (Angela Lansbury in high camp mode) still goes missing on a train, leaving Elliott Gould and

Cybill Shepherd to flit from one compartment to the next, revelling in some brash and breezy chemistry as they go. AT
DVD

Elliott Gould *Robert Condon* • Cybill Shepherd *Amanda Kelly* • Angela Lansbury *Miss Froy* • Herbert Lom *Dr Hartz* • Arthur Lowe *Charters* • Ian Carmichael *Caldicott* • Gerald Harper *Mr Todhunter* • Jean Anderson *Baroness Kisling* ■ *Dir* Anthony Page • *Scr* George Axelrod, from the 1938 film

The Lady Wants Mink ★★ U

Comedy 1953 · US · Colour · 92min

You must leave your contemporary prejudices aside to enjoy this teaming of two of the most acerbic women in Hollywood history: Ruth Hussey and the redoubtable Eve Arden, who could make any line sound witty. Hussey stars as the wife breeding minks so she can own a fur coat. Husband Dennis O'Keefe has no chance of competing with Hussey, let alone Arden, but veterans William Demarest and Gene Lockhart do what they can with the feeble material. TS

Dennis O'Keefe *Jim Connors* • Ruth Hussey *Nora Connors* • Eve Arden *Gladys Jones* • William Demarest *Harvey Jones* • Gene Lockhart *Mr Heggie* • Hope Emerson *Mrs Hoxie* ■ *Dir* William A Seiter • *Scr* Dane Lussier, Richard Alan Simmons, from a story by Leonard Neubauer, Lou Schor

Lady Windermere's Fan ★★★

Silent drama 1916 · UK · BW · 65min

Fred Paul's 1916 adaptation of Oscar Wilde's play is a rare surviving example of British *film d'art*. There's nothing particularly cinematic about the fixed-camera staging. But the sets are lovingly decorated and the playing is much less gesticulatory than the period norm. However, what will interest Wilde scholars is the way screenwriter Benedict James shifts the emphasis of the play by revealing at the outset the true identity of Mrs Erlynne. Thus, instead of being a jezebel, she is portrayed as a woman wronged by snobbery who is prepared to risk her newly regained reputation to save her daughter's honour. DP

Milton Rosmer *Lord Windermere* • Netta Westcott *Lady Windermere* • Nigel Playfair *Lord Augustus Lorton* • Irene Rooke *Mrs Erlynne* • Arthur Wontner *Lord Darlington* ■ *Dir* Fred Paul • *Scr* Benedict James, from the play by Oscar Wilde

Lady Windermere's Fan ★★★★

Silent drama 1925 · US · BW · 94min

The Lubitsch "touch" – the ironic, risqué style of director Ernst Lubitsch – was never more blatant in the way he lightens up one of Oscar Wilde's most judgemental plays, when adventuress Mrs Erlynne intrudes on the great and the good and threatens scandal. Ronald Colman, May McAvoy and Irene Rich look aghast in one of the director's best silent movies. TH

Ronald Colman *Lord Darlington* • Irene Rich *Mrs Erlynne* • May McAvoy *Lady Windermere* • Bert Lytell *Lord Windermere* • Edward Martindel *Lord Augustus* ■ *Dir* Ernst Lubitsch • *Scr* Julien Josephson, from the play by Oscar Wilde

Lady with a Past ★★★★

Romantic comedy 1932 · US · BW · 70min

The delightful Constance Bennett (older sister of Joan), briefly the highest paid female star in Hollywood in the 1930s, was seen at her best in sophisticated, slightly risqué comedies. Here she is a good little rich girl, who discovers that she is much more popular with men if they think she's bad. Naturally, it all takes place in a chic and naughty Paris. Ben Lyon wittily plays Bennett's paid escort. David Manners is perfect as the man who falls for her new self. RB

Constance Bennett *Venice Muir* • Ben Lyon *Guy Bryson* • David Manners *Donnie Wainwright* • Don Alvarado *The Argentine* • Albert Conti *René* •

Merna Kennedy *Ann Duryea* ■ *Dir* Edward H Griffith • *Scr* Horace Jackson, from the story by Harriet Henry

The Lady with Red Boots ★★★

Fantasy drama 1974 · Fr/It/Sp · Colour · 92min

Juan Buñuel, son of the legendary Spanish director, called on two of his father's best known stars, Catherine Deneuve and Fernando Rey, for this psychological thriller in which the cruel tricks played by writer Deneuve on manipulative millionaire Rey end in tragedy. Exploring the relationship between life and art, this highly stylised picture has all the hallmarks of a Buñuel film. However Juan lacks the control that characterised his father's use of satire and realism, and the outcome is confusing. DP French +subtitles.

Catherine Deneuve *Françoise* • Fernando Rey *Perrot* • Adalberto Maria Merli *Man* • Jacques Weber *Painter* ■ *Dir* Juan Buñuel • *Scr* Juan Buñuel, Roberto Bodegas (dialogue)

The Lady with the Lamp ★★ U

Biographical drama 1951 · UK · BW · 99min

Anna Neagle dons a simple cloth cap in this reverential biopic of Florence Nightingale. Once again under the tutelage of husband Herbert Wilcox, she gives an imperious performance as the daughter of a Hampshire landowner who reformed nursing and became a national icon during the Crimean War. To placate movie audiences, a disproportionate amount of time is devoted to the romance with Michael Wilding. DP

Anna Neagle *Florence Nightingale* • Michael Wilding *Sidney Herbert* • Gladys Young *Mrs Bracebridge* • Felix Aylmer *Lord Palmerston* • Julian D'Albie *Mr Bracebridge* • Arthur Young (1) *WE Gladstone* • Edwin Styles *Mr Nightingale* • Helen Shingler *Parthenope Nightingale* • Helena Pickard *Queen Victoria* ■ *Dir* Herbert Wilcox • *Scr* Warren Chetham Strode, from the play by Reginald Berkeley

The Lady with the Little Dog ★★★★

Drama 1960 · USSR · BW · 88min

This remains one of the most admired film adaptations of Anton Chekhov. The sensitive direction subtly evokes the prose of Chekhov's short love story, reflecting the lovers' psychology. The contrast between the seaside resort of Yalta in summer, where the two unhappily married people meet and fall in love, and Moscow in winter, is vividly portrayed. Iya Savvina gives a beautiful performance in the title role. RB Russian +subtitles.

Iya Savvina *Anna Sergeyevna* • Alexei Batalov *Dmitri Gurov* • Nina Alisova *Madame Gurov* ■ *Dir* Josef Heifitz • *Scr* Josef Heifitz, from the story *Dama s Sobachkoy* by Anton Chekhov

A Lady without Passport ★★★

Crime drama 1950 · US · BW · 73min

Director Joseph H Lewis was acknowledged as the great stylist of the Hollywood B-picture, but his touch was not noticeable in this *film noir* thriller about illegal aliens – which include glamorous Hedy Lamarr – trying to enter the United States. The focus of attention is so ambiguous it comes across as confused, without any of the expected thrills. TH

Hedy Lamarr *Marianne Lorress* • John Hodiak *Pete Karczag* • James Craig *Frank Westlake* • George Macready *Palinov* • Steven Geray *Frenchman* • Bruce Cowling *Archer Delby James* ■ *Dir* Joseph H Lewis • *Scr* Howard Dimsdale, Cyril Hume, from a story by Lawrence Taylor

Ladybird Ladybird ★★★★ 18

Drama 1994 · UK · Colour · 97min

Stand-up comic Crissy Rock won a Silver Bear at the Berlin film festival for her gutsy, warts-and-all performance in this harrowing drama from Ken Loach that will leave you emotionally exhausted. She hurls herself into the part of a mouthy Merseysider,

whose string of abusive relationships results in her children being taken by the social services, and is simply but effectively supported by Vladimir Vega as a Paraguayan refugee who becomes her lover. Loach expertly prevents the endless crises from slipping into hysterical melodrama. DP Violence, swearing, nudity.
DVD

Crissy Rock *Maggie* • Vladimir Vega *Jorge* • Sandie Lavelle *Mairead* • Mauricio Venegas *Adrian* • Ray Winstone *Simon* • Clare Perkins *Jill* • Jason Stracey *Sean* ■ *Dir* Ken Loach • *Scr* Rona Munro

Ladybug, Ladybug ★★★

Drama 1963 · US · BW · 81min

This is one of the American film industry's odder responses to the Cold War and the possibility of nuclear oblivion. Made for $350,000 by the husband and wife team of Frank and Eleanor Perry, it's set in an ordinary school in Ordinaryville, USA, and shows what happens when the head teacher has to prepare the school and its pupils for a nuclear blast. Vaguely resembling Peter Watkins's banned BBC film *The War Game*, the Perrys' weird blend is part public information, part corny melodrama, mixed in with *Lord of the Flies*. A very arty relic. AT

June Connell *Mrs Maxton* • William Daniels (2) *Mr Calkins* • James Frawley *Truck driver* • Richard Hamilton *JoAnn's father* • Kathryn Hays *Mrs Forbes* • Jane Hoffman *Mrs Hayworth* ■ *Dir* Frank Perry • *Scr* Eleanor Perry, from an article by Lois Dickert

Ladybugs ★★ PG

Comedy 1992 · US · Colour · 84min

In this raucous Rodney Dangerfield comedy, the burly comic, whose abrasive style has never really found a niche in film, blusters in typical fashion as a salesman whose only chance of promotion lies in turning the company's girls' soccer team into champions. Naturally, it requires a lad in drag to act as playmaker and there is a record attempt at cramming the most locker-room gags into a single picture. Sadly the laughs are in short supply – until, that is, you see Hollywood's idea of a football match. DP Some swearing.

Rodney Dangerfield *Chester Lee* • Jackée *Julie Benson* • Jonathan Brandis *Matthew/Martha* • Ilene Graff *Bess* • Vinessa Shaw *Kimberly Mullen* • Tom Parks *Dave Mullen* • Jeannetta Arnette [Jeanetta Arnette] *Glynnis Mullen* ■ *Dir* Sidney J Furie • *Scr* Curtis Burch

Ladyhawke ★★★★ PG

Fantasy adventure 1985 · US · Colour · 115min

Michelle Pfeiffer as the title's pretty predator and Rutger Hauer as a legendary lycanthrope give human poignancy to this medieval fairy tale of lovers cursed to shape-change into animals. Richard Donner proves to have an elegant eye for ancient as well as everyday fables, and it's all ravishingly filmed in Italy. Leo McKern dispels the dark from the Dark Ages with a comic turn as a Friar Tuck-ish priest, and Matthew Broderick makes an appealing young hero. TH Some violence. DVD

Matthew Broderick *Phillipe Gaston* • Rutger Hauer *Etienne of Navarre* • Michelle Pfeiffer *Isabeau of Anjou* • Leo McKern *Father Imperius* • John Wood (2) *Bishop* • Ken Hutchison *Captain Marquet* • Alfred Molina *Cezar* ■ *Dir* Richard Donner • *Scr* Edward Khmara, Michael Thomas, Tom Mankiewicz, from a story by Edward Khmara • *Cinematographer* Vittorio Storaro

The Ladykillers ★★★★★ U

Classic black comedy 1955 · UK · Colour · 86min

A supreme blend of the seedy and the sinister, this was Ealing's last post on the comedy front. Directed with a mischievous glint by Alexander Mackendrick, the picture loses its way momentarily in the middle, when the stock scenario of a gang of ruthless thugs being stymied by a dotty innocent (the marvellous Katie Johnson as their landlady) wears a little thin. Nevertheless, this is British comedy at its best, with eccentric characters never for a second seeming out of place in the most

everyday locations. Alec Guinness and his minions, among them Herbert Lom and Peter Sellers, are a marvellous collection of misfits, but they lose every scene to the Bafta-winning Johnson. DP DVD ⊘

Alec Guinness *Professor Marcus* • Cecil Parker *Major Courtney* • Herbert Lom *Louis* • Peter Sellers *Harry* • Danny Green *One-Round* • Katie Johnson *Mrs Wilberforce* • Jack Warner *Police superintendent* • Philip Stainton *Police sergeant* • Frankie Howerd *Barrow boy* • Kenneth Connor *Cab driver* • Edie Martin *Lettice* ■ *Dir* Alexander Mackendrick • *Scr* William Rose, from his story

The Ladykillers ★★★ 15

Black comedy 2004 · US · Colour · 99min

The Coen brothers (with Ethan gaining his first credit as co-director) have audaciously transplanted the premise of the delightful Ealing original (widow innocently lets rooms to a motley gang of criminals) from a dank north London suburb to the Deep South Bible Belt. Tom Hanks takes on the Guinness part of criminal mastermind, with Irma P Hall playing an anti-smoking Baptist who's not averse to face-slapping when she hears bad language. Hanks performs admirably as the eccentric professor, whose every utterance reeks of pompous southern verbosity. But the siblings' renowned quirkiness somehow seems at odds with the original offbeat masterpiece. TH Swearing.
DVD

Tom Hanks *Prof Goldthwait Higginson Dorr III* • Irma P Hall *Mrs Marva Munson* • Marlon Wayans *Gawain MacSam* • JK Simmons *Garth Pancake* • Ma Tzi *The General* • Ryan Hurst *Lump* ■ *Dir* Joel Coen, Ethan Coen • *Scr* Joel Coen, Ethan Coen, from the film by William Rose

A Lady's Morals ★★★

Musical romance 1930 · US · BW · 86min

This is the first of eight films made by talented Metropolitan Opera soprano Grace Moore before she was tragically killed in a plane crash in 1947. Moore stars as the famous opera singer Jenny Lind, the "Swedish Nightingale", in this highly fanciful treatment of what purports to be a complicated romantic relationship in Lind's life. An awesome hotch-potch of styles – it begins like a comic operetta and progresses to tragic romantic melodrama – it is nonetheless very charming. RK

Grace Moore *Jenny Lind* • Reginald Denny *Paul Brandt* • Wallace Beery *Barnum* • Gus Shy *Olaf* • Gilbert Emery *Broughm* ■ *Dir* Sidney Franklin • *Scr* Hans Kräly, Claudine West, John Meehan, Arthur Richman, from a story by Dorothy Farnum

Lagaan: Once upon a Time in India ★★★ PG

Romantic musical drama 2001 · Ind · Colour · 215min

This sprawling historical masala is the most expensive picture ever produced in Bollywood. Set in the 1890s, its main thrust concerns the resistance mounted by peasants of the arid Bhuj region to an unjust agricultural tax. But the focus ultimately falls on the love triangle that forms between Gracy Singh, protest leader Aamir Khan and Rachel Shelley, the Raj rose who offers to teach the locals to beat a British XI at cricket and thus halve the levy. With broad comedy, glossy dance routines and romantic tension, it's epic entertainment. DP Hindi, Bhojpuri, English +subtitles. DVD

Aamir Khan *Bhuvan* • Gracy Singh *Guari* • Rachel Shelley *Elizabeth Russell* • Paul Blackthorne *Captain Andrew Russell* • AK Hangal *Shambukaka* • Suhasini Mulay *Yashodamai* • Kulbhushan Kharbanda *Rajah Puran Singh* • Raghuveer Yadav [Raghuvir Yadav] *Bhura* ■ *Dir* Ashutosh Gowariker • *Scr* Ashutosh Gowariker, Kumar Dave, Sanjay Dayma, from a story by Ashutosh Gowariker

Lagerfeld Confidentiel ★★ 12

Documentary 2007 · Fr · Colour · 85min

Director Rodolphe Marconi supposedly amassed over 200 hours of digital and Super 8 footage over the two years that he tailed Karl Lagerfeld. However, he clearly

L

couldn't summon the courage to ask the über-designer a meaningful or even direct question and, consequently, this obsequious portrait only allows us to see what the Chanel supremo is willing to exhibit. Whether fussing over rings in his apartment, sketching designs, supervising runway shows or photographing models and celebs like Nicole Kidman, Lagerfeld insists on being the centre of attention and Marconi is happy to indulge his self-obsession. It's a pity, as occasionally in the spotlight interviews, Lagerfeld hints that he might have been more forthcoming on topics such as his mother, his art and his sex life if he'd been pressed just a little harder. DP French, English +subtitles. *DVD*

Karl Lagerfeld • Nicole Kidman • Princess Caroline of Monaco ◾ *Dir/Scr* Rodolphe Marconi

The Lair of the White Worm ★★★ 18
Horror   1988 · UK · Colour · 89min

Nude nuns, lesbian catfights and snake-cult rituals; what else could this be but a Ken Russell fantasy sextravaganza? Based on Bram Stoker's least famous novel, and starring a then unknown Hugh Grant, this Christianity versus Paganism tract is a delirious hoot from start to finish, so serious horror fans had better look elsewhere. Those in the mood for side-splitting nonsense – the kind that has reptilian Amanda Donohoe nakedly writhing through her country mansion to snake-charming music – are on the right track. AJ Violence, swearing, sex scenes.

Amanda Donohoe *Lady Sylvia Marsh* • Hugh Grant *Lord James D'Ampton* • Catherine Oxenberg *Eve Trent* • Peter Capaldi *Angus Flint* • Sammi Davis *Mary Trent* • Stratford Johns *Peters* • Paul Brooke *PC Erny* • Imogen Claire *Dorothy Trent* • Chris Pitt *Kevin* • Gina McKee *Nurse Gladwell* ◾ *Dir* Ken Russell • *Scr* Ken Russell, from the novel by Bram Stoker

Laissez-passer ★★★ 12
War drama based on a true story
2001 · Fr/Ger/Sp · Colour · 163min

Bertrand Tavernier's memoir of French film-making during the German Occupation caused a predictable storm in a country still scarred by its unresolved past. However, those unfamiliar with the Nazi-controlled Continental Films and the struggle for free artistic expression may decide that too much specialised knowledge is required to appreciate fully this sprawling account of the parallel careers of assistant director Jean Devaivre (Jacques Gamblin) and screenwriter Jean Aurenche (Denis Podalydès). The insight into studio politics is fascinating, but the domestic and espionage strands are less convincing. DP French +subtitles. *DVD*

Jacques Gamblin *Jean Devaivre* • Denis Podalydès *Jean Aurenche* • Marie Gillain *Olga* • Charlotte Kady *Suzanne Raymond* • Marie Desgranges *Simone Devaivre* • Maria Pitarresi *Reine Sorignal* • Ged Marlon *Jean-Paul Le Chanois* • Philippe Morier-Genoud *Maurice Tourneur* ◾ *Dir* Bertrand Tavernier • *Scr* Jean Cosmos, Bertrand Tavernier, from the remembrances of Jean Aurenche, Jean Devaivre

Lake Consequence ★★ 18
Erotic melodrama   1992 · US · Colour · 86min

Joan Severance plays a repressed housewife with a loving husband and son, whose temperature is raised by free-spirited gardener Billy Zane. Rope in the latter's girlfriend (May Karasun), a diabolical script and a hot-tub built for three, and you have a top-shelf title of little distinction. JC

Joan Severance *Irene* • Billy Zane *Billy* • Whip Hubley *Jim* • May Karasun *Grace* • Courtland Mead *Christopher* ◾ *Dir* Rafael Eisenman • *Scr* Zalman King, Melanie Finn, Henry Cobbold, from a story by MacGregor Douglas

The Lake House ★★★ PG
Romantic fantasy drama
2006 · US · Colour · 94min

More than a decade after *Speed*, Keanu Reeves and Sandra Bullock reteam as star-crossed lovers sharing the same house in different time zones, with their sole means

of communication a magic mailbox. This is the sort of film they just don't make any more, because perhaps movie-makers think audiences are too cynical to accept its absurdities. But there's a surprising chemistry between the stars, especially in circumstances that mean they rarely share the screen. Unfashionable it may be, but this is an entertaining tale. DA *DVD* *Blu*

Keanu Reeves *Alex Burnham* • Sandra Bullock *Kate Forster* • Dylan Walsh *Morgan* • Shohreh Aghdashloo *Dr Anna Klyczynski* • Christopher Plummer *Simon Wyler* • Ebon Moss-Bachrach *Henry Wyler* • Willeke van Ammelrooy *Kate's mother* • Lynn Collins *Mona* ◾ *Dir* Alejandro Agresti • *Scr* David Auburn, from the film *Siworae* (2000) by Kim Eun-jeong, Yeo Ji-na

Lake Placid ★★★ 15
Adventure thriller   1999 · US · Colour · 78min

Writer/producer David E Kelley here turns his hand to a daft creature feature that will tickle fans of *Tremors*. There's something under the surface of Black Lake that's making monster munchies out of visitors, so warden Bill Pullman, paleontologist Bridget Fonda and nutty millionaire Oliver Platt decide to hunt down the critter before any other bits of semi-digested locals pop to the surface. Fonda and Pullman play it for laughs, but the show is stolen by Platt. Two straight-to-DVD spin-offs were made in 2007 and 2010. JB *DVD*

Bill Pullman *Jack Wells* • Bridget Fonda *Kelly Scott* • Oliver Platt *Hector Cyr* • Brendan Gleeson *Sheriff Hank Keough* • Betty White *Mrs Delores Bickerman* ◾ *Dir* Steve Miner • *Scr* David E Kelley

Lake Tahoe ★★★ 12
Comedy drama
2008 · Mex/Jpn /US · Colour · 77min

There are shades of early Jim Jarmusch in Fernando Eimbcke's offbeat and deceptively simple second feature. A sweet and tender slice-of-life tale, it's action-light but richly atmospheric, as melancholy teen Diego Cataño accidentally crashes the family car then trudges around a sleepy Mexican town looking for help. Natural performances and beautifully coloured, mostly wide-angle visuals add to the languid film's low-key charms, tempering some of Eimbcke's more jarring stylistic flourishes – particularly his lengthy blocks of black screen. SF Spanish, English +subtitles. *DVD*

Diego Cataño *Juan* • Héctor Herrera *Don Heber* • Daniela Valentine *Lucia* • Juan Carlos Lara II *David* • Yemil Sefani *Joaquin* ◾ *Dir* Fernando Eimbcke • *Scr* Fernando Eimbcke, Paula Markovitch

Lakeview Terrace ★★★ 15
Thriller   2008 · US · Colour · 105min

This powerful thriller from writer/director Neil LaBute provides Samuel L Jackson with a really decent leading role. The *In the Company of Men* director is once more focused on the ugly side of human nature with the tale of a racist cop tormenting his new mixed-race neighbours. Jackson plays Abel Turner, a stressed single father and veteran LA cop who is self-appointed law in his suburban enclave. Turner's racist feathers are ruffled when Chris and Lisa Mattson (Patrick Wilson and Kerry Washington) move in next door. Sadly, the movie's promising build-up slips into audience-pleasing melodrama in its dying moments. Until then, LaBute almost makes amends for his ghastly remake of *The Wicker Man*. DA Violence, swearing. *DVD* *Blu*

Samuel L Jackson *Abel Turner* • Patrick Wilson *Chris Mattson* • Kerry Washington *Lisa Mattson* • Jay Hernandez *Javier Villareal* • Regine Nehy *Celia Turner* • Jaishon Fisher *Marcus Turner* ◾ *Dir* Neil LaBute • *Scr* David Loughery, Howard Korder, from a story by Loughery

Lakshya ★★★ 12
War drama   2004 · Ind · Colour · 288min

Director Farhan Akhtar brought his famous father, Javed Akhtar, out of semi-retirement to script this epic tale of a spoilt brat's discovery of his true self on the field

of combat. Wastrel Hrithik Roshan is persuaded by journalist girlfriend Preity Zinta to seek a purpose in life and enrol as an army cadet under colonel Amitabh Bachchan. A full-throttled adventure that makes spectacular use of the mountain scenery around Ladakh. DP Hindi +subtitles. *DVD*

Hrithik Roshan *Karan Shergill* • Amitabh Bachchan *Col Sunil Damle* • Preity Zinta *Romila Dutta* • Om Puri *Major Pritam Singh* • Sushant Singh *Captain Jalal Akbar* • Sharad Kapoor *Major Binod Sengupta* ◾ *Dir* Farhan Akhtar • *Scr* Javed Akhtar

Lamb ★★★★ 15
Drama   1985 · UK · Colour · 105min

Although the central characters are a Christian Brother and one of his unruly students, this is one of the most sensitive "father and son" studies since *Bicycle Thieves*. Liam Neeson gives a dedicated performance as the religious teacher who finds a new vocation when he "kidnaps" epileptic Hugh O'Conor to spare him from the vindictive violence of headmaster Ian Bannen. Bernard MacLaverty adapts his own novel with care and genuine concern for his characters, without letting the action get bogged down in either spirituality or sentimentality. Director Colin Gregg makes London look disturbingly unwelcoming and handles the tragic conclusion with delicacy and truth. DP *DVD*

Liam Neeson *Brother Sebastian, Michael Lamb* • Harry Towb *Priest* • Hugh O'Conor *Owen Kane* • Frances Tomelty *Mrs Kane* • Ian Bannen *Brother Benedict* • Ronan Wilmot *Brother Fintan* • Denis Carey *Mr Lamb* ◾ *Dir* Colin Gregg • *Scr* Bernard MacLaverty, from his novel

Lambada ★★ 15
Drama   1990 · US · Colour · 100min

Remember the lambada, that dance fad that lasted about as long as an episode of *Come Dancing*? Well, this is the movie-of-the-dance as directed by Joel Silberg, who did a similar service to break-dancing in *Breakin'*. The plot is extremely unlikely (J Eddie Peck, maths teacher by day, dancer by night, teaches dropouts in the backroom of the dance club) and the dancing scenes are filmed as if they were soft porn, but Peck and his co-stars do their best with what's left. JB *DVD*

J Eddie Peck *Kevin Laird* • Melora Hardin *Sandy* • Shabba-Doo *Raone* • Ricky Paull Goldin *Dean* • Basil Hoffman *Superintendent Leland* • Dennis Burkley *Uncle Big* • Keene Curtis *Principal Singleton* ◾ *Dir* Joel Silberg • *Scr* Sheldon Renan, Joel Silberg, from a story by Joel Silberg

Lambada! The Forbidden Dance ★ 15
Drama   1990 · US · Colour · 93min

One of two Lambada movies released at the same time to cash in on the dance craze. Here, the hip-swivelling Latin dance is merely a subplot to spice up the dire tale of a Brazilian princess who goes to America to campaign on behalf of the rainforest and ends up strutting her funky stuff on TV. A ludicrous premise if ever there was one. JB

Laura Herring [Laura Harring] *Nisa* • Jeff James *Jason* • Sid Haig *Joa* • Richard Lynch *Benjamin Maxwell* • Barbra Brighton *Ashley* • Angela Moya *Carmen* ◾ *Dir* Greydon Clark • *Scr* Roy Langsdon, John Platt

Lambert & Stamp ★★★ 15
Documentary
2014 · US · Colour and BW · 117min

Kit Lambert and Chris Stamp were to the Who what Brian Epstein and Andrew Loog Oldham were, respectively, to the Beatles and Stones: managers, image-shapers and Svengali figures. This energetic documentary charts the unlikely relationship between the Oxbridge-educated Lambert, the rough-around-the-edges East End boy Stamp and the band they took on, initially at least, to fulfil their dreams of being film-makers. The film begins with a bang but falters towards the end, though for the most part this offers an often fascinating insider's view of an iconic

band. JH English, German, French +subtitles. Swearing, brief nudity.

Chris Stamp • Pete Townshend • Roger Daltrey ◾ *Dir* James D Cooper

The Lamp Still Burns ★★
Drama   1943 · UK · BW · 90min

Few actresses could suffer with the style and dignity of Rosamund John. In the third and last of the films she made for Leslie Howard (here producing his final picture), she plays a trainee nurse learning that gentility gets you nowhere in a crisis. Every hospital cliché has been scrubbed down and pressed into service – the cold efficient matron, the cantankerous patient and the handsome young doctor – and the wartime references give the film a home-front heroism that now makes the whole thing seem as stiff as a starched uniform. DP

Rosamund John *Hilary Clarke* • Stewart Granger *Larry Rains* • Godfrey Tearle *Sir Marshall Frayne* • Sophie Stewart *Christine Morris* • John Laurie *Mr Hervey* • Margaret Vyner *Pamela Siddell* • Cathleen Nesbitt *Matron* • Eric Micklewood *Dr Trevor* • Joyce Grenfell *Dr Barratt* ◾ *Dir* Maurice Elvey • *Scr* Elizabeth Baron, Roland Pertwee, Major Neilson, from the novel *One Pair of Feet* by Monica Dickens

Lancelot and Guinevere ★★
Adventure drama   1963 · UK · Colour · 116min

Real-life married couple Cornel Wilde and Jean Wallace play Lancelot and Guinevere, whose lingering love for each other almost destroys King Arthur's Camelot. The supporting cast is second-string British; the interiors were shot at Pinewood; Yugoslavia's army gets to dress up in medieval armour and run all over Ye Olde England. In other words, it's a cheapo that manages to look reasonably well-nourished. Wilde directs with dash and sometimes startling style. Sometimes the film shows signs of heavy cutting; the original plan was for a three-hour epic with an intermission. AT

Cornel Wilde *Sir Lancelot* • Jean Wallace *Queen Guinevere* • Brian Aherne *King Arthur* • George Baker *Sir Gawaine* • Archie Duncan *Sir Lamorak* ◾ *Dir* Cornel Wilde • *Scr* Richard Schayer, Jefferson Pascal, from the prose romance *La Morte d'Arthur* by Sir Thomas Malory

Lancelot du Lac ★★★ PG
Period drama   1974 · Fr/It · Colour · 79min

In his most expensive movie, director Robert Bresson manages to re-create the rich tapestry that is the timeworn world of King Arthur, his Knights and the Round Table code. Lancelot (Luc Simon) returns with fellow knights after a fruitless attempt to unearth the Holy Grail. All are suffering from a tremendous loss of faith, which drives Lancelot straight back into the arms of Arthur's Guenièvre (Laura Duke Condominas). Instead of a straightforward moody swashbuckler, Bresson's skill lies in his ability here to make the film about crisis of belief and it is a fascinating study. LH French +subtitles. *DVD*

Luc Simon *Lancelot du Lac* • Laura Duke Condominas *Guenièvre* • Humbert Balsan *Gawain* • Vladimir Antolek-Oresek *Artus* • Patrick Bernard *Mordred* • Arthur De Montalembert *Lionel* ◾ *Dir/Scr* Robert Bresson • *Cinematographer* Pasqualino De Santis

Lancer Spy ★★★
Spy drama   1937 · US · BW · 84min

In this atypical 20th Century-Fox 1930s melodrama, the urbane George Sanders has a rare meaty double role, starring as both a Prussian baron and the British officer sent out to replace him, only to find himself enmeshed in the caresses of cabaret singer Dolores Del Rio. The first half is very exciting, with a cast full of wonderfully sinister faces, including Peter Lorre and Lionel Atwill. But director Gregory Ratoff seems to tire of the romp, and the film grows lacklustre. Not as swashbuckling as it ought to have been. TS

Dolores Del Rio *Dolores Daria* • George Sanders *Lieutenant Bruce/Baron Von Rohback* • Peter Lorre *Major Sigfried Gruning* • Virginia Field *Joan*

Bruce • Sig Rumann [Sig Ruman] *Lt Col Gottfried Hollen* • Joseph Schildkraut *Prince Ferdi Zu Schwarzwald* • Maurice Moscovich *General Von Meinhardt* • Lionel Atwill *Colonel Fenwick* ■ *Dir* Gregory Ratoff • *Scr* Philip Dunne, from the story by Marthe McKenna

Land and Freedom ★★★★ 15
Wartime drama
1995 · UK/Sp/Ger · Colour · 104min

While the Spanish Civil War seemed an obvious choice of subject for Ken Loach, it was also quite a stretch in terms of action and scale after such domestic dramas as *Family Life* and *Raining Stones*. That he handles the combat scenes and period detail with such confidence adds to his reputation as one of Britain's most vital film-makers. Ian Hart's fallible unemployed Liverpudlian is our "guide" to the conflict as he signs up to fight against Franco. Some have criticised the film for speechmaking and didacticism, but this is all part of Loach's bid to open up the politics of the time. Its full-bodied performances and courage to question make it rich and thought provoking. AC English, Spanish, Catalan +subtitles. DVD

Ian Hart *David Carne* • Rosana Pastor *Blanca* • Iciar Bollain *Maite* • Tom Gilroy *Gene Lawrence* • Marc Martinez *Vidal* • Frédéric Pierrot *Bernard* • Suzanne Maddock *Kim* • Mandy Walsh *Dot* • Angela Clarke *Kitty* ■ *Dir* Ken Loach • *Scr* Jim Allen

The Land before Time
★★★★ U
Animated adventure 1988 · US · Colour · 65min

If your little dinosaur lovers are still a bit young for *Jurassic Park*, then this charming cartoon should have them in raptures. Directed by Don Bluth, it's a prehistoric reworking of his own *An American Tail*, with a displaced young apatosaurus called Littlefoot and his four dino-tot companions setting out across a strange and dangerous land in search of their families. Their adventures are pretty hair-raising as they encounter not only deadly predators, but also all manner of environmental hazards. Youngsters will love the adorable critters in this and its sequels (12 so far). DP DVD

Fred Gwynne *Narrator* • Gabriel Damon *Littlefoot* • Helen Shaver *Littlefoot's mother* • Bill Erwin *Grandfather* • Candice Houston *Cera* • Pat Hingle *Rooter* ■ *Dir* Don Bluth • *Scr* Stu Krieger, from a story by Judy Freudberg, Tony Geiss

The Land Girls ★★ 12
Period drama 1997 · UK/Fr · Colour · 110min

Life on the home front is given a distinctly rosy glow in this naffly nostalgic adaptation of Angela Huth's novel. Anna Friel's randy northerner, Rachel Weisz's sheltered blue-stocking and Catherine McCormack's bourgeois prude are surely the most stereotypical volunteers in the history of the Women's Land Army. Consequently, from the moment these urban interlopers arrive at Tom Georgeson's Dorset farm, there isn't a single scene that ends unexpectedly. DP DVD

Catherine McCormack *Stella* • Rachel Weisz *Ag* • Anna Friel *Prue* • Steven Mackintosh *Joe Lawrence* • Tom Georgeson *Mr Lawrence* • Maureen O'Brien *Mrs Lawrence* ■ *Dir* David Leland • *Scr* David Leland, Keith Dewhurst, from the novel by Angela Huth

Land of Silence and Darkness ★★★★ U
Documentary 1971 · W Ger · Colour · 81min

Film-maker Werner Herzog tries to explain the unfathomable in this ambitious study of what it must be like to be deaf and blind. His aim is to suggest something of the isolation that separates such people from the world the rest of us take for granted. Robbed of her sight and hearing after a childhood fall, Fini Straubinger is an erudite, 50-something German woman who accepts new experiences like flying in a plane, while also visiting those born with her disability and trying to make empathetic contact with them through touch. As the final sequence depicting Heinrich Fleischmann (who was also neglected by his parents) hugging a

tree affirms, this is more a celebration of sensorial courage and inquisitiveness than a plea for pity. DP German +subtitles.
Fini Straubinger ■ *Dir/Scr* Werner Herzog

Land of the Blind ★ 15
Drama 2006 · UK · Colour and BW · 97min

Indiscriminately appropriating literary, artistic and factual allusions, Robert Edwards turns a supposedly earnest political morality tale into an unintentional farce in this dystopic travesty. Set in Year Minus 5, the action centres on prison guard Ralph Fiennes, who facilitates poet-terrorist Donald Sutherland's coup against corrupt dictator Tom Hollander, only to find himself incarcerated when his hero's regime proves to be even more repressive and eccentric. The sequences of Hollander indulging in decadence with pitiless wife Lara Flynn Boyle are utterly risible. But no one emerges from this Orwellian farrago with any credit, particularly one-time soldier Edwards, who cut his teeth making documentaries. DP Violence, brief swearing, sexual references. DVD

Ralph Fiennes *Joe* • Donald Sutherland *Thorne* • Tom Hollander *President Maximilian II* • Mark Warren *Pool* • Lara Flynn Boyle *First Lady Josephine* • Laura Fraser *Madeleine* • Jonathan Hyde *Smith* ■ *Dir/Scr* Robert Edwards

Land of the Lost ★★ 12
Science-fiction comedy adventure
2009 · US/Jpn · Colour · 97min

In a parallel universe where oddness is the norm, Will Ferrell should feel right at home. Instead, he's swamped by big-budget effects in this comedy – based on an old TV show – in which he's a disgraced scientist who enters a wilderness inhabited by dinosaurs and lizard-men through a hole in the space-time continuum. Anna Friel is the research assistant who accompanies him, along with Danny McBride as the requisite foul-mouthed sloo whose coarse humour doesn't make for ideal family entertainment. Ferrell manages to enliven a few moments with his trademark silliness, but too often it feels like he's just marking time. SP Brief swearing, sexual references. DVD ⓑ

Will Ferrell *Dr Rick Marshall* • Danny McBride (2) *Will Stanton* • Anna Friel *Holly Cantrell* • Jorma Taccone *Chaka* • John Boylan (2) *Enik* • Matt Lauer • Leonard Nimoy *The Zarn* ■ *Dir* Brad Silberling • *Scr* Chris Henchy, Dennis McNicholas, from the TV series by Marty & Sid Krofft

Land of the Pharaohs
★★★ U
Historical epic 1955 · US · Colour · 103min

The stiff dialogue in parts of this Hollywood epic about pyramid building and palace intrigue in ancient Egypt prompts the conclusion that co-writer William Faulkner would have been better off sticking to novels. But director Howard Hawks, the master storyteller, found it hard to make a bad movie and, all in all, this is a handsome and very serviceable historical melodrama, conceived and realised on the grand scale. Joan Collins is deliciously villainous as Princess Nellifer. FF

Jack Hawkins *Pharaoh* • Joan Collins *Princess Nellifer* • Dewey Martin *Senta* • Alexis Minotis *Hamar* • James Robertson-Justice *Vashtar* • Luisa Boni *Kyra* • Sydney Chaplin *Treneh* • James Hayter *Vashtar's servant* ■ *Dir* Howard Hawks • *Scr* William Faulkner, Harry Kurnitz, Harold Jack Bloom

Land Raiders ★★
Western 1969 · US · Colour · 101min

This undistinguished western has a truly motley cast that makes this worth watching. Telly Savalas and *Route 66's* George Maharis are surely the most unlikely brothers, but not quite as unlikely as the latter's Mexican accent. Also along for the bleak and dusty ride are stunning redhead Arlene Dahl and Janet Landgard. Connoisseurs of the ludicrous will also enjoy finding Guy Rolfe and George Coulouris among the dross. It's sadistic, too. TS

Telly Savalas *Vince Carden* • George Maharis *Paul Cardenas* • Arlene Dahl *Martha Carden* • Janet Landgard *Kate Mayfield* • Jocelyn Lane *Luisa Rojas* • George Coulouris *Cardenas* ■ *Dir* Nathan H Juran [Nathan Juran] • *Scr* Ken Pettus, from a story by Ken Pettus, Jesse Lasky Jr, Pat Silver

The Land That Time Forgot
★★ PG
Fantasy adventure 1974 · UK · Colour · 86min

The first, and worst, of the trilogy of Edgar Rice Burroughs lost world adventures produced by Amicus, despite the fact that it was co-scripted by sci-fi giant Michael Moorcock. In director Kevin Connor's excessively fake and slipshod saga, a First World War submarine discovers an uncharted haven for dinosaurs, cavemen and volcanoes. Doug McClure is out of his depth and the puppet monsters are just as weak. *At the Earth's Core* (1976) and *The People That Time Forgot* (1977) followed. AJ DVD

Doug McClure *Bowen Tyler* • John McEnery *Captain Von Schoenvorts* • Susan Penhaligon *Lisa Clayton* • Keith Barron *Bradley* • Anthony Ainley *Dietz* • Godfrey James *Borg* • Bobby Farr *Ahm* • Declan Mulholland *Olson* ■ *Dir* Kevin Connor • *Scr* James Cawthorn, Michael Moorcock, from the novel by Edgar Rice Burroughs

Land without Bread ★★★★★
Documentary 1933 · Sp · BW · 29min

This is an extraordinary documentary by the surrealist director, Luis Buñuel, about a poverty-blighted region of north Spain, hemmed in by mountains. In-breeding between inhabitants has resulted in a race of grotesque dwarfs, and the final scene of contrast is the interior of a gold-encrusted Catholic church opposed to the dreadful misery of its context. One of Buñuel's most formidable anti-clerical swipes, it's still as angry as when it was made. Its images may be hideous, but they are true. TH In Spanish.

Abel Jacquin *Narrator* ■ *Dir/Scr* Luis Buñuel

Land without Music ★★ U
Musical 1936 · UK · BW · 85min

Walter Forde was a highly versatile director, but, on the evidence of this frippery, light opera was definitely not his forte. The story is paper-thin, as famous tenor Richard Tauber returns to his homeland to lead a melodic revolution against princess Diana Napier (Tauber's real-life wife), who has outlawed music. There are few memorable moments, and most of them are provided by the watchable Jimmy Durante, playing a journalist with a song in his heart. DP

Richard Tauber *Mario Carlini* • Jimmy Durante *Jonah J Whistler* • Diana Napier *Princess Regent* • June Clyde *Sadie Whistler* • Derrick de Marney *Rudolpho Strozzi* • Esme Percy *Austrian Ambassador* • George "Gabby" Hayes *Captain Strozzi* • John Hepworth *Pedro* ■ *Dir* Walter Forde • *Scr* Rudolph Bernauer, Marian Dix, L DuGarde Peach, from a story by Fritz Koselka, Armin Robinson

Landfall ★★ U
Second World War drama
1949 · UK · BW · 84min

Fighter pilot Michael Denison, poor chap, thinks he has sunk a British submarine while patrolling the skies over the English Channel. The court thinks so, too, and he gets transferred to desk duties and unburdens his guilt to barmaid Patricia Plunkett who decides to prove he actually sunk a German sub. Laurence Harvey can also be glimpsed in this dainty item from a vanished era of British war movies. AT DVD

Michael Denison *Rick* • Patricia Plunkett *Mona* • Edith Sharpe *Rick's mother* • Sebastian Shaw *Wing-Cdr Dickens* • Maurice Denham *Wing-Cdr Hewitt* • Laurence Harvey *P/O Weaver* ■ *Dir* Ken Annakin • *Scr* Talbot Jennings, Gilbert Gunn, Anne Burnaby, from the novel by Nevil Shute

The Landlord ★★★★ 12
Comedy drama 1970 · US · Colour · 105min

Former editor turned director Hal Ashby made a terrific debut as director with this comedy drama, featuring a superb Beau Bridges as the wealthy scion who learns about humanity and the African-American experience in New York from his tenants. Pearl Bailey and Diana Sands shine, and there's good work too from Robert Klein and Lee Grant. Fans of Ashby's subsequent cult classic *Harold and Maude* should check this enjoyable movie out. TS Brief swearing, drug abuse. DVD

Beau Bridges *Elgar Enders* • Pearl Bailey *Marge* • Marki Bey *Lanie* • Diana Sands *Fanny* • Louis Gossett [Louis Gossett Jr] *Copee* • Douglas Grant *Walter Gee* • Melvin Stewart *Professor Duboise* • Lee Grant *Mrs Enders* • Robert Klein *Peter* ■ *Dir* Hal Ashby • *Scr* William Gunn [Bill Gunn], from the novel by Kristin Hunter

Landscape after Battle
★★★★ 12
Second World War drama
1970 · Pol · Colour · 104min

As much a treatise on Polish anti-Semitism as a denunciation of the Nazis, Andrzej Wajda's grimly stylised picture is based on the writings of Tadeusz Borowski, a Holocaust survivor who committed suicide in 1959 at the age of 29. Wajda sends his restless camera in search of the grotesque ironies of life in a camp for displaced persons. Yet he also employs a lyrical expressionism to chronicle the romance between Daniel Olbrychski's writer and Stanisława Celinska's terrified refugee. Both visually and intellectually disconcerting, this is a film of brutal poetic power. DP In Polish.

Daniel Olbrychski *Tadeusz* • Stanisława Celinska *Nina* • Aleksander Bardini *Professor* ■ *Dir* Andrzej Wajda • *Scr* Andrzej Brzozowski, Andrzej Wajda, from the short stories by Tadeusz Borowski

Landscape in the Mist
★★★ 15
Road movie drama
1988 · Gr/Fr/It · Colour · 124min

Convinced that their father resides in Germany, Greek children Tania Palaiologou and Michalis Zeke set out to find him on an odyssey that is littered with symbolic incidents and totemic characters. Despite Giorgos Arvanitis's moody photography, it's a gruelling experience, with only circus performer Stratos Tzortzoglou sympathising with their plight. But while the human story is relentlessly bleak, Theo Angelopoulos succeeds in depicting a nation obsessed with its past, by combining contemporary settings with countless allusions to ancient history and mythology. DP Greek +subtitles.

Michalis Zeke *Alexander* • Tania Palaiologou *Voula* • Stratos Tzortzoglou *Orestes* ■ *Dir* Theo Angelopoulos • *Scr* Theo Angelopoulos, Tonino Guerra, Thanassis Valtinos

Lansky ★★ 15
Biographical crime drama
1999 · US · Colour · 111min

A mumbling, whiny performance from Richard Dreyfuss undermines this cradle-to-grave TV biopic of gangster Meyer Lansky, associate of the equally notorious Bugsy Siegel. A Jewish immigrant, Lansky rises from the impoverished streets of New York's Lower East Side at the turn of the century and embarks on a life of crime. Lansky's life is unfortunately dramatised in cool, detached strokes by distinguished playwright David Mamet. MC DVD

Richard Dreyfuss *Meyer Lansky* • Eric Roberts *Ben "Bugsy" Siegel* • Anthony LaPaglia *Charles "Lucky" Luciano* • Beverly D'Angelo *Teddy Lansky* • Illeana Douglas *Anna Lansky* ■ *Dir* John McNaughton • *Scr* David Mamet, from the biography *Meyer Lansky: Mogul of the Mob* by Uri Dan, Dennis Eisenberg, Eli Landau

Lantana ★★★★ 15
Thriller 2001 · Aus/Ger · Colour · 115min

Ray Lawrence belies his roots in commercials with this engrossing adaptation of Andrew Bovell's play. It's a supremely controlled ensemble piece, in which chance and coincidence increase the tension of what is, ostensibly, a suburban thriller. But, as the mesh of interweaving relationships becomes increasingly complex, the identity and fate of a missing woman become less important than the resolution of the domestic crises involving psychiatrist Barbara Hershey and husband Geoffrey Rush, world-weary cop Anthony LaPaglia and the unhappy souls who inhabit the fringes of their lives. DP *DVD*

Anthony LaPaglia *Leon Zat* • Geoffrey Rush *John Knox* • Barbara Hershey *Dr Valerie Somers* • Kerry Armstrong *Sonja Zat* • Rachael Blake *Jane O'May* • Glenn Robbins *Pete O'May* • Vince Colosimo *Nik Daniels* • Daniela Farinacci *Paula Daniels* ■ *Dir* Ray Lawrence • *Scr* Andrew Bovell, from his play *Speaking in Tongues*

Lapse of Memory ★★PG

Thriller   1992 · Can/Fr · Colour · 81min

Originally made in 1983 as the little seen *I Am the Cheese*, this is one of those repressed memory thrillers in which a sudden recollection spells danger for a previously contented amnesiac. Teenager Mathew Mackay struggles valiantly with the realisation that adoptive parents John Hurt and Marthe Keller are on the run from the Mob, but there's nothing that hasn't been done better in several similar scenarios. DP

John Hurt *Conrad Farmer* • Marthe Keller *Linda Farmer* • Mathew Mackay *Bruce Farmer* • Kathleen Robertson *"Patrick"* • Marion Peterson *Dr Lauren Brint* ■ *Dir* Patrick Dewolf • *Scr* Patrick Dewolf, Philippe Le Guay, from the novel *I Am the Cheese* by Robert Cormier

Laputa: Castle in the Sky
★★★PG

Animated fantasy adventure   2003 · Jpn · Colour · 124min

Anna Paquin supplies the voice of young heroine Sheeta in this inventive fast-paced animation from *Spirited Away* director Hayao Miyazaki. Taking its inspiration from *Gulliver's Travels*, it follows Sheeta's journey to find the flying city of Laputa and her battles with villains along the way. SF Japanese dubbed. *DVD* BL

Anna Paquin *Sheeta* • James Van Der Beek *Pazu* • Cloris Leachman *Dola* • Mark Hamill *Col Muska* • Richard Dysart *Uncle Pomme* ■ *Dir* Hayao Miyazaki • *Scr* Hayao Miyazaki, John Semper (English version), from the comic book *Tenku no shiro Rapyuta* by Hayao Miyazaki

Lara Croft: Tomb Raider
★★12

Action adventure   2001 · US/Ger/UK/Jpn · Colour · 96min

Angelina Jolie makes a credible enough Lara - athletic, somewhat top-heavy and with an English accent borrowed from Liz Hurley (rumoured to be an early contender for the role). The story is unsatisfying - a two-act yarn about finding two halves of an artefact in Cambodia and Siberia - and Simon West's direction does little to whip up any momentum as Lara performs endless leaps in the dark. A passable action caper only. AC Nudity, violence. *DVD* BL

Angelina Jolie *Lara Croft* • Jon Voight *Lord Croft* • Noah Taylor *Bryce* • Iain Glen *Manfried Powell* • Daniel Craig *Alex West* • Christopher Barrie [Chris Barrie] *Hillary* • Leslie Phillips *Wilson* ■ *Dir* Simon West • *Scr* Patrick Massett, John Zinman, Simon West, from a story by Sara B Cooper, Mike Werb, Michael Colleary, from the computer game *Tomb Raider* by Core Design

Lara Croft, Tomb Raider: the Cradle of Life ★12

Action adventure   2003 · US/UK/Ger/Jpn · Colour · 112min

Director Jan De Bont does nothing in this sequel to refresh the action franchise, nor untangle it from panic-led editing. This is unconvincing, witless, pancake-flat stuff. Teamed with disgraced former agent Gerard Butler, Angelina Jolie searches for the fabled Pandora's Box. Ciaran Hinds gives it his pantomime-all as the evil scientist, but the plot makes little sense and

the set pieces are ho-hum. AC Violence, swearing *DVD* BL

Angelina Jolie *Lara Croft* • Gerard Butler *Terry Sheridan* • Ciaran Hinds *Jonathan Reiss* • Christopher Barrie [Chris Barrie] *Hillary* • Noah Taylor *Bryce* • Djimon Hounsou *Kosa* ■ *Dir* Jan De Bont • *Scr* Dean Georgaris, from a story by Steven E de Souza, James V Hart, from the computer game *Tomb Raider* by Core Design

The Laramie Project
★★★15

Drama based on a true story   2002 · US · Colour · 91min

Adapted by director Moises Kaufman from his own play, which was itself based on testimony from the citizens of Laramie, Wyoming, this is a sobering account of the savage murder of HIV-positive student Matthew Shepard in 1998. However, Kaufman dissipates the impact of his exposure of homophobia in small-town America by studding the flashbacking action with cameos from well-meaning stars. Worthy, but flawed. DP *DVD*

Christina Ricci *Romaine Patterson* • Steve Buscemi *Doc O'Conner* • Laura Linney *Sherry Johnson* • Summer Phoenix *Jen Malskog* • Clea DuVall *Amanda Gronich* • Peter Fonda *Dr Cantway* • Janeane Garofalo *Catherine Connolly* ■ *Dir* Moises Kaufman • *Scr* Moises Kaufman, from the play by Moises Kaufman and members of the Tectonic Theater Project

Larceny, Inc ★★

Crime comedy   1942 · US · BW · 95min

Under cover of a smart luggage store, a gang of crooks plan to tunnel their way into the bank vault next door. However, the shop is so successful their plot is thwarted. Based on a Broadway show by husband and wife team SJ and Laura Perelman, this comedy boasts an enticing cast led by Edward G Robinson and featuring Anthony Quinn as one of the mobsters. Unfortunately, there aren't many laughs. Perhaps Warner Bros should have cast comedians as heavies rather than the other way around. AT

Edward G Robinson *J Chalmers "Pressure" Maxwell* • Jane Wyman *Denny Costello* • Broderick Crawford *Jug Martin* • Jack Carson *Jeff Randolph* • Anthony Quinn *Leo Dexter* • Edward S Brophy [Edward Brophy] *Weepy Davis* • Jackie Gleason *Hobart* ■ *Dir* Lloyd Bacon • *Scr* Everett Freeman, Edwin Gilbert, from the play *The Night Before Christmas* by Laura Perelman, SJ Perelman

Large ★15

Comedy   2000 · UK · Colour · 78min

The Birmingham-set plot revolves around teenage slacker Luke de Woolfson who must turn over a new leaf before his 18th birthday so he can inherit the fortune of his dead rock star father. However, his mates and a grasping stepmother have other ideas. Debuting writer/director Justin Edgar throws in taste-free comic clichés and a bunch of relatively unknown actors cast as one-dimensional grotesques, and the result is appalling and amateurish. JC *DVD*

Luke de Woolfson *Jason Mouseley* • Melanie Gutteridge *Sophie* • Simon Lowe *Rob* • Lee Oakes *Ian* • Mirren Delaney *Lisa Gates* • Emma Catherwood *Rachel "Measley" Beasley* • Les Dennis *Steve* ■ *Dir* Justin Edgar • *Scr* Justin Edgar, Michael Dent

Larger than Life ★★PG

Comedy   1996 · US · Colour · 89min

Bill Murray fans will have their allegiance tested by this extremely lightweight comedy about a motivational speaker who inherits an elephant from his estranged circus clown dad. Their cross-country journey to the animal's California destination is filled with calamitous incidents, but the laughs are spread thinly and this only just about gets by on the star's cynical charm. JC *DVD*

Bill Murray *Jack Corcoran* • Janeane Garofalo *Mo* • Matthew McConaughey *Tip Tucker* • Linda Fiorentino *Terry* • Anita Gillette *Mom* ■ *Dir* Howard Franklin • *Scr* Roy Blount Jr, from the story by Pen Densham, Garry Williams

Largo Winch ★★★15

Adventure   2008 · Fr/Bel · Colour · 104min

Largo Winch - hero of a popular Belgian comic book - had already been the subject of a 2001 TV series prior to this good-looking adventure. Determined to find the killer of his adoptive industrialist father and hold on to his inheritance, Largo (French comedian Tomer Sisley) is soon dashing around the world with various villains on his tail. He's more Bruce Wayne than James Bond, but there are plenty of nods to 007 with chases, fights, sun-kissed locations and sassy ladies. There's even a secret island hide-out and a decidedly John Barry-like score from composer Alexandre Desplat. But Winch is ultimately his own (very laid-back) man and would return for a sequel in 2011. JA French, English, Serbian, Portuguese +subtitles. Violence, a sex scene, nudity. *DVD*

Tomer Sisley *Largo Winch* • Kristin Scott Thomas *Ann Ferguson* • Miki Manojlovic *Nerio Winch* • Mélanie Thierry *Léa/Naomi* • Gilbert Melki *Freddy* ■ *Dir* Jérôme Salle • *Scr* Julien Rappeneau, Jérôme Salle, from a comic book by Van Hamme [Jean Van Hamme], Francq • *Music* Alexandre Desplat

Larks on a String ★★★★15

Satire   1969 · Cz · Colour · 90min

Made towards the end of the period of creativity known as the "Czech Film Miracle", this caustic comedy was banned "for ever" by the authorities and director Jirí Menzel - co-writer/director of the Oscar-winning *Closely Observed Trains* - was prevented from filming for several years. Finally reaching cinema screens in 1990, after the Velvet Revolution, it justly shared the Golden Bear at the Berlin film festival that year. Set in a scrap-metal yard populated with discarded intellectuals and waiters, it is a sniping, eminently watchable romantic satire which, in keeping with many films of the time, sought to show how the Communist Party had failed the Czech working classes. DP Czech +subtitles. *DVD*

Jitka Zelenohorska *Jitka* • Vaclav Neckar *Pavel* • Leos Sucharipa *Public prosecutor* • Jaroslav Satoransky *Angel* ■ *Dir* Jirí Menzel • *Scr* Jirí Menzel, from a novel by Bohumil Hrabal

Larry Crowne ★★12

Romantic comedy drama   2011 · US · Colour · 94min

The megawatt pairing of Tom Hanks and Julia Roberts brings precious little sparkle to this romantic comedy. Hanks's affable everyman enrols in glass-half-empty Roberts's public speaking class, and woos her with optimism. Actually, the stars share little quality time. Instead, there are dull scenes of her marital discontent, alongside more slapstick moments as he relives his youth. Maybe Hanks, also producer, director and co-writer, should have taken a leaf out of his character's book and taken the time to develop his ideas. SP Some swearing. *DVD* BL

Tom Hanks *Larry Crowne* • Julia Roberts *Mercedes Tainot* • Bryan Cranston *Dean* • Wilmer Valderrama *Dell Gordo* • Pam Grier *Frances* • Nia Vardalos ■ *Dir* Tom Hanks • *Scr* Tom Hanks, Nia Vardalos

Lars and the Real Girl
★★★12

Comedy drama   2007 · US · Colour · 102min

Remember when Cliff Richard got himself a crying, talking, sleeping, walking, living doll? Midwestern weirdo Lars (Ryan Gosling) doesn't go quite that far; instead, bereft of human companionship, he sends off for a Real Doll life-size mannequin, and presents her as Bianca, his new-found internet friend. Conscious of Lars's fragile mental state, close-knit family, friends and townsfolk indulge him in his delusion, and treat Bianca as real, too. And, gradually, the custom-made cutie does assume sort-of-real status, becoming a pillar of local society. Its whimsy won't be to everyone's taste, but this is an endearing fable that's nicely acted by a cast that also includes Emily Mortimer

and Patricia Clarkson. DA Sexual references. *DVD*

Ryan Gosling *Lars* • Emily Mortimer *Karin* • Paul Schneider (2) *Gus* • Kelli Garner *Margo* • Nancy Beatty *Mrs Gruner* • Karen Robinson *Cindy* • Patricia Clarkson *Dagmar* • RD Reid *Reverend Bock* ■ *Dir* Craig Gillespie • *Scr* Nancy Oliver

Las Vegas Roundabout ★★

Crime drama   1975 · US · Colour · 90min

In this pilot for the popular crime series *Switch* that ran for three years in the mid-1970s, Robert Wagner plays the reformed con and Eddie Albert the retired cop who team up to trick unsuspecting crooks into returning their ill-gotten gains. This feature-length outing sees Wagner and Albert helping out Charles Durning's notorious safecracker, who's been framed for a diamond robbery. DP

Robert Wagner *Peterson T "Pete" Ryan* • Eddie Albert *Frank McBride* • Charles Durning *Phil Beckman* • Sharon Gless *Maggie* • Ken Swofford *Captain Griffin* • Jaclyn Smith *Alice* ■ *Dir* Robert Day • *Scr* Alan Godfrey, Glen A Larson

The Las Vegas Story ★★

Crime drama   1952 · US · BW · 88min

There's no real chemistry between Jane Russell and former flame Victor Mature in this routine RKO drama, which involves a phoney murder plot set in a patently studio-bound Las Vegas. Russell performs as though there's no tomorrow, while troupers Vincent Price and Hoagy Carmichael provide professional support, but there's no denying that this film is far from their best. Director Robert Stevenson does what he can with the resolutely substandard screenplay. TS

Jane Russell *Linda Rollins* • Victor Mature *Dave Andrews* • Vincent Price *Lloyd Rollins* • Hoagy Carmichael *Happy* • Brad Dexter *Thomas Hubler* • Gordon Oliver *Drucker* • Jay C Flippen *Harris* ■ *Dir* Robert Stevenson • *Scr* Earl Felton, Harry Essex, Paul Jarrico (uncredited), from a story by Jay Dratler

Lassie ★★★★PG

Period adventure   2005 · Ire/UK/Fr/US · Colour · 95min

Based on the same novel as 1943 classic *Lassie Come Home*, this solidly entertaining film explores the bond between the collie and a poor miner's son in 1930s Yorkshire. Jonathan Mason conveys just the right amount of pathos as the lad left brokenhearted when his destitute parents sell the pet to Peter O'Toole's local aristocrat. However, not even the duke taking the dog away to Scotland can sever their ties, prompting an adventure-packed escape as she struggles to return home. Thanks to handsome cinematography and well-fleshed characters played by an impressive cast, this delightful film quickly transcends the predictable storyline. SF *DVD*

Peter O'Toole *The Duke* • Samantha Morton *Sarah Carraclough* • John Lynch *Sam Carraclough* • Jonathan Mason *Joe* • Peter Dinklage *Rowlie* • Hester Odgers *Cilla* • Steve Pemberton *Hynes* • Jemma Redgrave *Daisy* • Gregor Fisher *Mapes* • Edward Fox *Hulton* • Robert Hardy *Mr Justice Murray* • Nicholas Lyndhurst *Buckles* ■ *Dir* Charles Sturridge • *Scr* Charles Sturridge, from the novel *Lassie Come Home* by Eric Knight

Lassie: a New Generation
★★U

Adventure   1994 · US · Colour · 91min

This is an awesomely sentimental updating of the classic film about the world's most intelligent canine. Here, Jon Tenney and Helen Slater are the city folk finding their feet in the country who are lucky enough to fall under the protective paw of the lovable collie. JF *DVD*

Jon Tenney *Steve Turner* • Helen Slater *Laura Turner* • Brittany Boyd *Jennifer Turner* • Frederic Forrest *Sam Garland* ■ *Dir* Daniel Petrie • *Scr* Matthew Jacobs, Gary Ross, Elizabeth Anderson

Lassie Come Home
★★★★★ U

Adventure 1943 · US · Colour · 85min

This is the first and best of the canine capers featuring the lovable collie, whose popularity never waned even though she was actually played by a male dog called Pal. Here, Roddy McDowall is heartbroken when his pet is sold to the local squire, who then moves to Scotland with his granddaughter Elizabeth Taylor. But Lassie takes the high road back to her young master, while everyone dissolves into tears of happiness. Taylor never looked lovelier and Britain glows through MGM-tinted eyes. An absolute delight. TH **DVD**

Roddy McDowall *Joe Carraclough* · Donald Crisp *Sam Carraclough* · Edmund Gwenn *Rowlie* · Dame May Whitty *Dolly* · Nigel Bruce *Duke of Rudling* · Elsa Lanchester *Mrs Carraclough* · Elizabeth Taylor *Priscilla* ■ *Dir* Fred M Wilcox · *Scr* Hugo Butler, from the novel by Eric Knight

Lassie's Great Adventure
★★★ U

Adventure 1963 · US · Colour · 100min

The intrepid collie finds herself adrift in a balloon with Jon Provost in this outdoor survival story. Lassie and her master trek across the wilds, ward off a ferocious boar, negotiate racing rapids and befriend a native American trapper – all while Provost's parents await news from mountain rescue teams and Mountie patrols. The youngster's ingenuity is unbelievable, but the scenery is fabulous and the dog magnificent. DP **DVD**

June Lockhart *Ruth Martin* · Hugh Reilly *Paul Martin* · Jon Provost *Timmy* · Robert Howard *Sgt Sprague* · Will C White *Constable MacDonald* · Richard Kiel *Chinook Pete* · Walter Stocker *John Stanley* ■ *Dir* William Beaudine · *Scr* Monroe Manning, Charles O'Neal, from a story by Sumner Arthur Long

Lassiter
★★ 18

Period action adventure
1984 · US · Colour · 95min

The modestly amiable Tom Selleck never fully recovered from the career blow of losing out on the Indiana Jones role, and this poorly conceived star vehicle did him no favours either. Set in 1934 he plays a London-based American jewel thief blackmailed by Bob Hoskins of the Yard into nabbing a cache of diamonds held in the German embassy. This is let down by an erratic script that doesn't know when to quit with the double-crosses, shaky period atmosphere and uninspired direction. RS

Tom Selleck *Lassiter* · Jane Seymour (2) *Sara* · Lauren Hutton *Kari* · Bob Hoskins *Becker* · Joe Regalbuto *Breeze* · Ed Lauter *Smoke* · Warren Clarke *Max Hofer* ■ *Dir* Roger Young · *Scr* David Taylor

Last Action Hero
★★★★ 15

Comedy action adventure
1993 · US · Colour · 125min

This is a smart, funny blockbuster that gave director John McTiernan the opportunity to send up not only Arnold Schwarzenegger's heroic image, but also the action genre itself. The story centres around youngster Austin O'Brien, who finds himself sucked into the celluloid world of his biggest hero (Schwarzenegger), as he tracks bad guys Charles Dance and Anthony Quinn in his new film. Things become complicated when the fictional characters take the chance to escape into the real world. Schwarzenegger has rarely been better, and although McTiernan has fun spoofing the conventions of the action genre, he still manages to slip in some spectacular set pieces. JF Swearing, violence. **DVD**

Arnold Schwarzenegger *Jack Slater* · F Murray Abraham *John Practice* · Art Carney *Frank* · Charles Dance *Benedict* · Frank McRae *Dekker* · Tom Noonan *Ripper* · Robert Prosky *Nick* · Anthony Quinn *Vivaldi* · Mercedes Ruehl *Mom* · Austin O'Brien *Danny Madigan* · Ian McKellen *Death* ■ *Dir* John McTiernan · *Scr* Shane Black, David Arnott, from a story by Zak Penn, Adam Leff

The Last Adventurers
★★

Romantic melodrama 1937 · UK · BW · 77min

It's a pity there's not much entertainment value to be had from this wonderful curio about a twice-shipwrecked castaway saved by a sea captain whose daughter he then falls in love with, much to the old tar's displeasure. What is fascinating about Roy Kellino's adventure is that it was edited, with greater tautness than it deserves, by director-in-waiting David Lean. The casting is also noteworthy, including future *Carry On* star Esma Cannon in a rare glamour role. DP

Niall MacGinnis *Jeremy Bowker* · Roy Emerton *John Arkell* · Linden Travers *Ann Arkell* · Peter Gawthorne *Fergus Arkell* · Katie Johnson *Susan Arkell* · Kay Walsh *Margaret Arkell* · Johnnie Schofield *Stalky* · Norah Howard *Mary Allen* · Ballard Berkeley *Fred Delvin* · Esma Cannon *Polly Shepherd* · Tony Wylde *Glory Be* ■ *Dir* Roy Kellino · *Scr* Denison Clift

The Last Airbender
★★ PG

Fantasy adventure 2010 · US · Colour · 98min

M Night Shyamalan's once glorious reputation tarnishes further with this tediously juvenile fantasy adventure in which the Fire Nation wants to rule Air, Water and Earth. But will young avatar Aang (Noah Ringer) fulfil his destiny as controller of all four elements and impose harmony back on the universe? Based on a popular US anime series, this often incomprehensible film is so overloaded with CGI animation, the conversion almost feels redundant. A few epic vistas and spectacular images are visually striking – the tsunami wall of water holding the Fire Nation's ships at bay – but most of this is lacking in excitement. AJ **DVD**

Noah Ringer *Aang* · Jackson Rathbone *Sokka* · Dev Patel *Prince Zuko* · Nicola Peltz *Katara* · Cliff Curtis *Fire Lord Ozai* · Jessica Andres *Suki* ■ *Dir* M Night Shyamalan · *Scr* M Night Shyamalan, from the animated TV series by Bryan Konietzko, Michael Dante DiMartino

The Last American Hero
★★★★ PG

Biographical drama 1973 · US · Colour · 90min

While everyone writes about the American cinema in the early 1970s in terms of hotshot talents such as Coppola, Scorsese, Bogdanovich and Friedkin, a lot of other fine movies were being made, lower-key affairs such as this immensely likeable picture directed by Lamont Johnson. The excellent Jeff Bridges stars as a moonshiner's son, who begins a career in stock car racing in order to pay the legal fees of his imprisoned father. By no means an action movie or demolition derby, this is a funky character piece, written with insight and celebrating the survival of the pioneer spirit in modern America. AT **DVD**

Jeff Bridges *Junior Jackson* · Valerie Perrine *Marge* · Geraldine Fitzgerald *Mrs Jackson* · Ned Beatty *Hackel* · Art Lund *Elroy Jackson Sr* · Gary Busey *Wayne Jackson* · William Smith II [William Smith] *Kyle Kingman* · Ed Lauter *Burton Colt* ■ *Dir* Lamont Johnson · *Scr* William Roberts, from articles by Tom Wolfe

The Last Angry Man
★★★ U

Drama 1959 · US · BW · 99min

Paul Muni's last Hollywood film (and his first in over a decade) gave him the kind of worthy character he relished portraying: a dedicated doctor working among the Brooklyn poor who has to choose between appearing in a live television tribute and helping a patient in trouble with the police. Muni retained the knack of letting you know you were seeing great acting, and he duly picked up his fifth Oscar nomination as best actor. The character could have been done with a few faults, but Muni still wins you over and his death scene is very moving. AE

Paul Muni *Dr Sam Abelman* · David Wayne *Woodrow Wilson Thrasher* · Betsy Palmer *Anne Thrasher* · Luther Adler *Dr Max Vogel* · Joby Baker *Myron Malkin* · Joanna Moore *Alice Taggert* · Nancy K Pollock *Sarah Abelman* · Billy Dee Williams *Josh Quincy* ■ *Dir* Daniel Mann · *Scr* Gerald Green, Richard Murphy, from the novel by Gerald Green

The Last Battle
★★★★ 15

Science fiction 1983 · Fr · BW · 88min

With his first feature – an arresting poetic vision of post-apocalyptic Paris after an unspecified cataclysm has reduced the Earth to a desolate wasteland – director Luc Besson laid the groundwork for *The Fifth Element* and began his long relationship with actor Jean Reno. Four survivors battle for the future of mankind in this stark alternative to *Mad Max*, which conveys its raw emotions in carefully orchestrated visuals without any dialogue (poisonous gases having rendered the characters' vocal chords useless). It's a remarkable achievement that deals with hackneyed holocaust clichés on a compelling, humanistic plane. AJ **DVD**

Pierre Jolivet *Young man* · Jean Bouise *Old doctor* · Fritz Wepper *Gang leader* · Jean Reno *Swordsman* ■ *Dir* Luc Besson · *Scr* Luc Besson, Pierre Jolivet

The Last Blitzkrieg
★

Second World War drama
1958 · US · BW · 84min

Looking around for a Hollywood actor to play the English-speaking son of a top Nazi general, producer Sam Katzman should never have settled for Van Johnson, whose lightweight presence destroys the picture. Although this was filmed in Holland and uses some local players and crew, the obvious reliance on stock battle footage undermines credibility. AE

Van Johnson *Sgt Von Kroner/Sgt Richardson* · Kerwin Mathews *Wilitz* · Dick York *Sergeant Ludwig* · Larry Storch *Ennis* · Lise Bourdin *Monique* ■ *Dir* Arthur Dreifuss · *Scr* Lou Morheim

The Last Boy Scout
★★★ 18

Action thriller 1991 · US · Colour · 105min

The mismatched buddy movie reaches an apotheosis of sorts here in director Tony Scott's flashy, foul-mouthed and formula no-brainer, which forsakes plot for overblown shoot-outs and endless car chases. Lifting it marginally above the thick-ear realm is the engaging chemistry between seedy gumshoe Bruce Willis and ex-footballer Damon Wayans. Both actors let humour spring effortlessly from their own personalities as well as from their screen characters, and the snappy put-downs make the epic mindlessness bearable. AJ Violence, drug abuse, swearing, nudity. **DVD**

Bruce Willis *Joe Hallenbeck* · Damon Wayans *Jimmy Dix* · Chelsea Field *Sarah Hallenbeck* · Noble Willingham *Sheldon "Shelley" Marcone* · Taylor Negron *Milo* · Danielle Harris *Darian Hallenbeck* · Halle Berry *Cory* · Bruce McGill *Mike Matthews* · Chelcie Ross *Senator Baynard* ■ *Dir* Tony Scott · *Scr* Shane Black, from a story by Shane Black, Greg Hicks

The Last Broadcast
★★★ 18

Horror 1998 · US · Colour · 86min

A documentary crew disappears after going into the woods to make a film about a local legend. Sounds familiar? This shoestring documentary-style horror movie was actually made before *The Blair Witch Project*, though it didn't have the same impact. More formally structured than *Blair Witch*, this is about as scary (in other words, not very) and offers further proof of how easy it is for film-makers to manipulate fiction into a convincing form of "fact". DA **DVD**

David Beard *David Leigh, the film-maker* · James Seward *Jim Suerd, the accused* · Stefan Avalos *Steven Avkast, "Fact or Fiction" host* · Lance Weiler *Locus Wheeler, "Fact or Fiction" host* ■ *Dir/Scr* Stefan Avalos, Lance Weiler

The Last Bus Home
★★ 15

Musical comedy drama
1997 · Ire · Colour · 90min

Rather optimistically pitched as the punk version of *The Commitments*, this low-budget Irish effort remains an entertainingly rough-and-ready tale of the music business. Set at the end of the 1970s, it features Annie Ryan and Brian F O'Byrne as idealistic punks determined to take the music world by storm with their band Dead Patriots. Slick it ain't, but maybe that was the point, and old New Wavers and punks will love the attitude and the vintage soundtrack. JF **DVD**

Annie Ryan *Reena* · Brian F O'Byrne *Jessop* · John Cronin *Petie* · Barry Comerford *Joe* · Anthony Brophy *Billy* · Gemma Craven *Reena's mother* · Donal O'Kelly *Richie* · Brendan Coyle *Steve Burkett* ■ *Dir/Scr* Johnny Gogan

The Last Butterfly
★★

Second World War drama
1990 · Fr/Cz/UK · Colour · 110min

This obscure entry into the Holocaust genre, shot in Czechoslovakia, stars Tom Courtenay as a French mime artist who is duped by the Nazis into performing at a town set aside for Jews. Only when Courtenay arrives does he tumble the fact that his act is purely to impress visiting Red Cross officials; when they are gone the Jews will be shipped to the death camps. Courtenay's mime act, a version of *Hansel and Gretel*, is the highlight in a worthy effort that never quite delivers its promised impact. AT

Tom Courtenay *Antoine Moreau* · Brigitte Fossey *Vera* · Ingrid Held *Michele* · Freddie Jones *Rheinberg* · Milan Knazko *Gruber* ■ *Dir* Karel Kachyna · *Scr* Karel Kachyna, Ota Hofman, from the novel *Les Enfants de Terezin* by Michael Jacot, Alex North

The Last Castle
★★★ 15

Prison thriller 2001 · US · Colour · 125min

Robert Redford plays a court-martialled three-star general who's sent to a military jail, where he becomes embroiled in an acrimonious battle of wills with martinet warden James Gandolfini (of *Sopranos* fame). However, despite trying to produce a character study rather than an action melodrama, director Rod Lurie offers up a fairly generic prison flick. The pedestrian approach aside, though, it's still entertaining. TH Violence, swearing. **DVD**

Robert Redford *Lieutenant General Eugene R Irwin* · James Gandolfini *Colonel Winter* · Mark Ruffalo *Clifford Yates* · Clifton Collins Jr *Corporal Ramon Aguilar* · Delroy Lindo *General James "Jim" Wheeler* · Steve Burton *Captain Peretz* ■ *Dir* Rod Lurie · *Scr* David Scarpa, Graham Yost, from a story by David Scarpa

The Last Challenge
★★★

Western 1967 · US · Colour · 95min

Here's a western which satisfyingly refreshes some stock characters and situations. It also has assured performances from Glenn Ford as the gunfighter turned lawman, Angie Dickinson as the saloon keeper who loves him, and Chad Everett as the young gunslinger who wants to kill him to build a reputation. On the strength of performances like the one he gives here, Everett deserved to become a big star; elsewhere, Jack Elam has a straight role as a hired gun. Richard Thorpe's slack direction lets the strong script (by John Sherry and Robert Emmett Ginna) carry the picture. AE

Glenn Ford *Marshal Dan Blaine* · Angie Dickinson *Lisa Denton* · Chad Everett *Lot McGuire* · Gary Merrill *Squint Calloway* · Jack Elam *Ernest Scarnes* · Delphi Lawrence *Marie Webster* ■ *Dir* Richard Thorpe · *Scr* John Sherry, Robert Emmett Ginna, from the novel *Pistolero's Progress* by John Sherry

The Last Chance
★★

Drama 2003 · US · Colour · 100min

A grumpy Texas rancher and his estranged daughter re-learn the importance of family in this old-fashioned drama that's flimsy but full of heart. Lance Henriksen delivers a convincing mix of stubbornness, decency and desperation as the proud cattleman whose struggles to stay financially afloat are complicated by the return of his headstrong offspring (Jennie Garth). The touching though rushed lesson about love, traditional values and embracing change also features show-stealing support from MC Gainey as a wise old ranch hand. SF

L

Jennie Garth *Jacqueline "Jake" Cooper* • Lance Henriksen *John William Cooper* • MC Gainey *Amos Russell* • Bradley Cooper *Morgan Murphy* • Dylan Wagner *Billy* ■ *Dir* Joyce Chopra • *Scr* JP Martin

Last Chance Harvey ★★12
Romantic comedy   2008 · US · Colour · 89min

Dustin Hoffman and Emma Thompson lend some weight to this otherwise unchallenging romantic comedy about an awkward midlife attraction. When New Yorker Harvey Shine (Hoffman) heads to London to attend the wedding of his estranged daughter, he strikes up an unexpected friendship with Kate Walker (Thompson), a cautious spinster burdened with a highly strung mother (Eileen Atkins). The misfortunes each has endured in their lives may carry too many pity points, but their encounter still manages to charm. This is a traditional, sweet and polite comedy meant for hopeless romantics – and that's not necessarily a bad thing. KK DVD Blu

Dustin Hoffman *Harvey Shine* • Emma Thompson *Kate Walker* • Eileen Atkins *Maggie* • Liane Balaban *Susan* • James Brolin *Brian* • Kathy Baker *Jean* • Richard Schiff *Marvin* ■ *Dir/Scr* Joel Hopkins

The Last Command ★★★★★PG
Silent drama   1928 · US · BW · 88min

The love/hate relationship between moody actor Emil Jannings and archetypal tyrant-director Josef von Sternberg created this masterpiece with its story of a tsarist general (Jannings) working for peanuts as a bit-player in Hollywood. The extended flashback takes in his life in revolutionary Russia – including his seduction of a communist actress (Evelyn Brent) – and his feud with a radical theatrical director who becomes his grudging benefactor in Tinseltown. Jannings is satisfyingly arrogant to the point of dementia, while von Sternberg's visuals have a poetic lyricism to offset the sour nature of the story. TH DVD Blu

Emil Jannings *Gen Dolgorucki/Grand Duke Sergius Alexander* • Evelyn Brent *Natascha Dobrowa* • William Powell *Leo Andreiev* • Nicholas Soussanin *Adjutant* ■ *Dir* Josef von Sternberg • *Scr* John F Goodrich, Herman J mankiewicz (titles), from the story by Lajos Biró • *Cinematographer* Bert Glennon

The Last Command ★★★PG
Historical western   1955 · US · Colour · 105min

This recounting of the story of the Alamo is directed by veteran Frank Lloyd on what must have been Republic Studios' highest-ever budget. The tale is well told, with star Sterling Hayden making a most impressive Jim Bowie and veteran character actor Arthur Hunnicutt portraying a grizzled and probably accurate Davy Crockett. There's a healthy air of historical accuracy and it's enjoyable, although lacking in stature. TS

Sterling Hayden *James Bowie* • Anna Maria Alberghetti *Consuela* • Richard Carlson *William Travis* • Arthur Hunnicutt *Davy Crockett* • Ernest Borgnine *Mike Radin* • J Carrol Naish *Santa Anna* ■ *Dir* Frank Lloyd • *Scr* Warren Duff, from a story by Sy Bartlett

Last Dance ★★★18
Crime drama   1996 · US · Colour · 98min

This prison drama has Sharon Stone languishing on death row for a dozen years, condemned to die for murdering two teenagers. Rob Morrow and Randy Quaid are the parole officers who oppose capital punishment, while flashbacks gradually reveal the true nature of Stone's crime. Stone's performance as the teenage social outcast now grown up is generally impressive and Bruce Beresford's direction is typically elegant and controlled, though the ending is a bit of a cop-out. AT Swearing, violence. DVD

Sharon Stone *Cindy Liggett* • Rob Morrow *Rick Hayes* • Randy Quaid *Sam Burns* • Peter Gallagher *John Hayes* • Jack Thompson *The Governor* • Jayne Brook *Jill* • Pamela Tyson *Legal aid attorney* • Skeet Ulrich *Billy* ■ *Dir* Bruce Beresford • *Scr* Ron Koslow, from a story by Ron Koslow, Steven Haft

The Last Dance ★★
Drama   2000 · US · Colour · 96min

Maureen O'Hara has aged gracefully and chosen her twilight movies with considerable care. In this TV movie she plays a retired schoolteacher who transforms the lives of male nurse Eric Stoltz and his teacher wife, Trini Alvarado, who runs a catering business on the side to provide for their two kids. Kevin Dowling's restrained direction and the warmth of the performances ensure that this TV movie remains on the right side of sentimental. DP

Maureen O'Hara *Helen Parker* • Eric Stoltz *Todd Cope* • Trini Alvarado *Denise Cope* ■ *Dir* Kevin Dowling • *Scr* Dalene Young, from a story by Beth Polson, from the short story *The Shift* by Todd F Cope

The Last Days ★★★★PG
Documentary   1998 · US · Colour and BW · 87min

Steven Spielberg's obsession with the Holocaust continues with this remarkable documentary, in which five elderly survivors of the concentration camps return to compare then with now. The *Schindler's List* director executive-produced the film with the Shoah Foundation. Such was the Nazis' hatred for the Jews that, even though they knew they were defeated, they still set out to destroy them in Hungary during the "last days" of the Second World War. James Moll has assembled some poignant archive material which, combined with the survivors' testimony, makes piteously compelling viewing. However, the conclusion manages to be uplifting by showing the children and grandchildren who surround the survivors in their personal last days. TH

■ *Dir/Scr* James Moll

Last Days ★★★15
Drama   2004 · US · Colour · 92min

Gus Van Sant uses the 1994 suicide of Nirvana frontman Kurt Cobain to explore death and loneliness. Michael Pitt, a rangy Cobain lookalike, portrays rocker-in-exile Blake as muttering and paranoid, stumbling around an unheated mansion and the adjacent woods in search of a release from his demons. For the most part we must accept the "genius" that attracts parasitic hangers-on, but through two songs, written and played by Pitt, we finally see the incoherent Blake communicating. Van Sant's use of long Steadicam shots, jarring sound design and disjointed, impressionistic style will irritate some, but haunt others. AC Swearing. DVD

Michael Pitt *Blake* • Lukas Haas *Luke* • Asia Argento *Asia* • Scott Green *Scott* • Nicole Vicius *Nicole* • Ricky Jay *Detective* • Ryan Orion Donovan • Harmony Korine *Guy in club* ■ *Dir/Scr* Gus Van Sant

Last Days in Vietnam ★★★★
War documentary   2014 · US · Colour and BW · 98min

This Oscar-nominated film documents events from the closing stages of the Vietnam War, when American soldiers stationed in the south tried to evacuate Vietnamese citizens fleeing the advancing Communist forces. With testimony from everyone from Henry Kissinger to a local Saigon student, this has a moving story to tell. Amid the American perspectives on the war as a whole, the film also explores the plight of ordinary Vietnamese civilians going to great lengths to survive. JL English, Vietnamese +subtitles.

Henry Kissinger ■ *Dir* Rory Kennedy

The Last Days of Chez Nous ★★★15
Drama   1992 · Aus · Colour · 92min

Although she is becoming increasingly known for her costume dramas, Australian director Gillian Armstrong's documentary experience of capturing the rhythms of everyday speech and making the most of confined spaces serves her well in this chatty character study, in which novelist Lisa Harrow reassesses her relationships with her husband Bruno Ganz and every member of her less-than-predictable family. Unfortunately, Harrow is the weakest link in a strong cast, with Kerry Fox typically arresting as the sister who makes a move on Ganz, and Bill Hunter excellent as their bluff father. DP

Lisa Harrow *Beth* • Bruno Ganz *JP* • Kerry Fox *Vicki* • Miranda Otto *Annie* • Kiri Paramore *Tim* • Bill Hunter *Beth's father* • Lex Marinos *Angelo* • Mickey Camilleri *Sally* ■ *Dir* Gillian Armstrong • *Scr* Helen Garner

The Last Days of Disco ★★★15
Comedy drama   1998 · US · Colour · 108min

Writer/director Whit Stillman captures – not completely successfully – the lives of the bright young things in the early 1980s who work by day and boogie on down at night before the death knell sounded for disco. Kate Beckinsale and Chloë Sevigny are overly mannered as the two girls who use an exclusive disco to meet rich kids, while Matt Keeslar and Robert Sean Leonard are among the male yuppie types who hook up with them. None of the characters in Stillman's sharply scripted world are remotely engaging, so just enjoy the disco music. JB Violence, swearing, drug abuse, nudity.

Chloë Sevigny *Alice* • Kate Beckinsale *Charlotte* • Chris Eigeman *Des* • MacKenzie Astin *Jimmy* • Matt Keeslar *Josh* • Robert Sean Leonard *Tom* • Jennifer Beals *Nina* ■ *Dir/Scr* Whit Stillman

The Last Days of Dolwyn ★★PG
Drama   1949 · UK · BW · 91min

Freely adapted from a historical incident, this is a classic example of how to squeeze all the life out of an intriguing situation by coating it with a thick layer of significance. The flooding of a Welsh valley, the refusal of an old woman to leave her home and the attempts of a murderer to conceal his crime should add up to a compelling drama. But Emlyn Williams spoils everything with a stagey approach, which sees everyone speaking in deliberate tones that owe nothing to real life. Richard Burton impresses in his debut, but the film belongs squarely to Dame Edith Evans. DP DVD

Dame Edith Evans [Edith Evans] *Merri* • Emlyn Williams *Rob* • Richard Burton *Gareth* • Anthony James *Dafydd* • Barbara Couper *Lady Dolwyn* • Alan Aynesworth *Lord Lancashire* • Andrea Lea *Margaret* • Hugh Griffith *Minister* ■ *Dir/Scr* Emlyn Williams

The Last Days of Frankie the Fly ★★18
Black comedy drama   1996 · US · Colour · 91min

Quentin Tarantino has a lot to answer for. If he hadn't cast Michael Madsen as the sadistic Mr Blonde in *Reservoir Dogs*, we might never have been able to enjoy his performance as a Mob boss in this black comedy drama. Dennis Hopper is Madsen's luckless henchman who gets bitten by the movie-making bug and an insane desire to showcase the acting talents of Daryl Hannah. A game cast try to add punchy humour to the movie satire but fails. AJ Swearing, violence. DVD

Dennis Hopper *Frankie* • Daryl Hannah *Margaret* • Kiefer Sutherland *Joey* • Michael Madsen *Sal* • Dayton Callie *Vic* ■ *Dir* Peter Markle • *Scr* Dayton Callie

The Last Days of Mussolini ★★★★12
Second World War drama   1974 · It · Colour · 124min

Rod Steiger contributes his own personal portrayal of the Fascist tyrant in an Italian film that allows the man to have a certain amount of vulnerability. Carlo Lizzani's drama shows him on the run – with mistress Lisa Gastoni – in the days before his own people caught him and strung him upside down from a lamp post. Steiger is tremendous as Mussolini, whom he would play again seven years later in *Lion of the Desert*. TH DVD

Rod Steiger *Benito Mussolini* • Lisa Gastoni *Clara Petacci* • Henry Fonda *Cardinal Schuster* • Franco Nero *Col Valerio* • Lino Capolicchio *Pedro* ■ *Dir* Carlo Lizzani • *Scr* Carlo Lizzani, Fabio Pittorru • *Music* Ennio Morricone

The Last Days of Pompeii ★★★PG
Period drama   1935 · US · BW · 95min

After trashing much of Manhattan in *King Kong*, producer Merian C Cooper and director Ernest B Schoedsack turned their attention to ancient Rome's most famous natural disaster. Basil Rathbone gives a fine performance as Pontius Pilate and Preston Foster is adequate in the lead role as a young blacksmith who becomes an amoral gladiator. If you can ignore the piety, this is a rousing yarn, with some good arena scenes and the best special effects money could buy at the time. AT DVD

Preston Foster *Marcus* • Basil Rathbone *Pontius Pilate* • Alan Hale *Burbix* • John Wood (1) *Flavius (as a man)* • Louis Calhern *Prefect* ■ *Dir* Ernest B Schoedsack • *Scr* Ruth Rose, Boris Ingster, from a story by James Ashmore Creelman, Melville Baker

The Last Days of Pompeii ★★
Period adventure   1960 · It · Colour · 94min

Steve Reeves, the uncrowned king of the muscleman epic, is gladiator Glaucus, searching downtown Pompeii for the people who murdered his father. At first it looks like the Christians but then an insurrectionist plot is traced back to the temple priests and an Egyptian princess. Just when things seems to get sorted, Vesuvius blows its top! AT Italian dubbed.

Steve Reeves *Glaucus* • Christine Kaufmann *Ione* • Barbara Carroll *Nydia* • Anne-Marie Baumann *Julia* • Mimmo Palmara *Gallinus* • Fernando Rey *High priest* ■ *Dir* Mario Bonnard • *Scr* Ennio De Concini, Sergio Leone, Duccio Tessari, Sergio Corbucci

The Last Days on Mars ★★★15
Science-fiction horror   2013 · UK/Ire · Colour · 94min

In this solid but derivative space horror, a group of scientists are preparing to leave the red planet when one of their number goes missing. A rescue party led by captain Elias Koteas and senior engineer Liev Schreiber heads out to search for their colleague, but they discover more than they bargained for. First-time director Ruairi Robinson brazenly wears his sci-fi influences (*Alien*, *The Thing*) on his sleeve, but he tends to telegraph the shocks too far in advance. The cast is dependable, even if most of the roles are familiar archetypes. TeS Violence, swearing. DVD Blu

Liev Schreiber *Vincent Campbell* • Romola Garai *Rebecca Lane* • Elias Koteas *Charles Brunel* • Olivia Williams *Kim Aldrich* • Johnny Harris *Robert Irwin* • Goran Kostic *Marko Petrovic* ■ *Dir* Ruairi Robinson • *Scr* Clive Dawson, from the short story *The Animators* by Sydney J Bounds

The Last Debate ★★★15
Drama   2000 · US · Colour · 95min

Director John Badham is best known for his no-nonsense action thrillers but he acquits himself pretty well with this absorbing TV movie about political skulduggery and media ethics. It focuses on a televised political debate in which journalists roast a candidate over a supposed scandal in his past. However, the interviewers find themselves in the firing line when another reporter (Peter Gallagher) questions the motives of those posing the questions. Venerable James Garner steals the show as the veteran panel moderator. JF

James Garner *Mike Howley* • Peter Gallagher *Tom Chapman* • Audra McDonald *Barbara Manning* • Donna Murphy *Joan Naylor* ■ *Dir* John Badham • *Scr* Jon Maas, from the novel by Jim Lehrer

U SUITABLE FOR ALL   Uc SUITABLE ESPECIALLY FOR YOUNG CHILDREN (DVD ONLY)   PG PARENTAL GUIDANCE   12A UNDER 12s TO BE ACCOMPANIED (CINEMA ONLY)

The Last Detail ★★★★ 18
Drama 1973 · US · Colour · 99min

Back in the early 1970s, star Jack Nicholson, writer Robert Towne and director Hal Ashby were the hippest team in Hollywood. Nicholson and Towne went on to *Chinatown* and Ashby and Towne to *Shampoo*; they could do no wrong. This collaboration has a combustible power as it follows the fortunes of two naval petty officers (Nicholson and Otis Young) and the pathetic young criminal (Randy Quaid) they have to escort to jail. Towne's script consists almost entirely of profanities and justifiably so, considering the characters aren't choirboys. TH Violence, sex scenes, nudity. *DVD*

Jack Nicholson *Billy "Bad Ass" Buddusky* · Otis Young *"Mule" Mulhall* · Randy Quaid *Larry Meadows* · Clifton James *Chief master-at-arms* · Michael Moriarty *Marine duty officer* · Carol Kane *Young whore* ■ *Dir* Hal Ashby · *Scr* Robert Towne, from the novel by Darryl Ponicsan

The Last Diamond ★★★ 15
Heist thriller 2014 · Fr/Lux/Bel · Colour · 106min

The Serpent director Eric Barbier and star Yvan Attal reunite for this caper harking back to the French heist movie's glory days. Attal plays the safecracker linking up with accomplice Jean-François Stévenin and unreliable go-between Antoine Basler to steal a diamond being auctioned by jewellery expert Bérénice Bejo. The heist itself is meticulously staged, and the pace really picks up after the robbery when Bejo realises she's been duped. DP In French. Violence, swearing.

Yvan Attal *Simon* · Bérénice Bejo *Julia* · Jean-François Stévenin *Albert* · Antoine Basler *Scylla* ■ *Dir* Eric Barbier · *Scr* Eric Barbier, Marie Eynard, Tran-Minh Nam

Last Embrace ★★★★ 18
Thriller 1979 · US · Colour · 97min

Jonathan Demme's early work shows some debt to Hitchcock. As Roy Scheider convincingly plays an agent being used for target practice with a riveting mix of bleakness, determination and paranoia, Demme never loses his grip, piling on the unsettling Hitch-style claustrophobia. The suspense is aided enormously by Tak Fujimoto's atmospheric camerawork and Miklos Rozsa's thoughtful, vibrant score. JM Swearing, a sex scene, nudity. *Blu-ray*

Roy Scheider *Harry Hannan* · Janet Margolin *Ellie Fabian* · John Glover *Richard Peabody* · Sam Levene *Sam Urdell* · Charles Napier *Dave Quittle* · Christopher Walken *Eckart* · Jacqueline Brookes *Dr Coopersmith* · Mandy Patinkin *Commuter* ■ *Dir* Jonathan Demme · *Scr* David Shaber, from the novel *The Thirteenth Man* by Murray Teigh Bloom

The Last Emperor ★★★★ 15
Epic biographical drama 1987 · It/UK/Chi · Colour · 209min

The first western production to be allowed to film inside Beijing's Forbidden City and the winner of nine Oscars, Bernardo Bertolucci's majestic epic is one of the most visually arresting pictures of its time. The design beautifully juxtaposes the pre- and post-revolutionary Chinese worlds, and the red and yellow trappings of the simple uniforms of Mao's republic are stunningly displayed. However, the glorious images distance the viewer from the momentous events that overtook 20th-century China and, in spite of a multifaceted performance from John Lone, Emperor Pu Yi remains a stranger, even at the end of the film. DP Swearing, brief nudity. *DVD*

John Lone *Aisin-Gioro "Henry" Pu Yi, as an adult* · Joan Chen *Elizabeth* · Peter O'Toole *Reginald Johnston, "RJ"* · Ying Ruocheng *Governor* · Victor Wong (2) *Chen Pao Shen* · Dennis Dun *Big Li* · Ryuichi Sakamoto *Masahiko Amakasu* · Maggie Han *Eastern Jewel* · Ric Young *Interrogator* ■ *Dir* Bernardo Bertolucci · *Scr* Bernardo Bertolucci, Mark Peploe, Enzo Ungari · *Cinematographer* Vittorio Storaro

The Last Escape ★★ U
Second World War drama 1970 · US · Colour · 90min

United Artists had a pair of big hits in the 1960s with two war movies – *The Great Escape* and *633 Squadron*, both terrific action movies with knockout music scores. Having securec an audience for this type of subject, UA then worked the subject of the Second World War into the ground with films such as this one. It isn't any good, and smells of catchpenny picture-making, but Margit Saad looks nice and Stuart Whitman is amiable. TS

Stuart Whitman *Captain Lee Mitchell* · John Collin *Sgt Henry McBee* · Pinkas Braun *Von Heinken* · Martin Jarvis *Lt Donald Wilcox* · Günther Neutze *Major Hessel* · Margit Saad *Karen Gerhardt* · Patrick Jordan *Major Griggs* · Johnny Briggs *Corporal O'Connell* ■ *Dir* Walter E Grauman [Walter Grauman] · *Scr* Herman Hoffman, from a story by John C Champion, Barry Trivers

Last Exit to Brooklyn ★★★ 18
Drama 1989 · W Ger · Colour · 98min

Director Uli Edel's hard-hitting adaptation is as depressing a film as you'll ever see. That's not to say it isn't an accomplished movie, but its brutal early-1950s Brooklyn backdrop, plus the gallery of abusive lowlifes, make fcr very uncomfortable viewing, especia ly during the climactic drunken gang bang involving prostitute Jennifer Jason Leigh. Artistically shot and lit by cinematographer Stefan Czapsky, the film also benefits from some strong acting and a moody score from Mark Knopfler. JC Swearing, sex scenes, violence, nudity, drug abuse. *DVD*

Stephen Lang *Harry Black* · Jennifer Jason Leigh *Tralala* · Burt Young *Big Joe* · Peter Dobson *Vinnie* · Jerry Orbach *Boyce* · Stephen Baldwin *Sal* · Jason Andrews *Tony* · Ricki Lake *Donna* · Hubert Selby Jr *Cab driver* ■ *Dir* Ulrich Edel [Uli Edel] · *Scr* Desmond Nakano, from the short story collection by Hubert Selby Jr

The Last Exorcism ★★★ 15
Horror thriller 2010 · Fr/US · Colour · 83min

There's not much particularly original about this demon-themed shocker, but the direction and performances are solid enough. Cotton Marcus (the excellent Patrick Fabian) is a disillusioned evangelical pastor who grants a documentary crew permission to film him faking an exorcism. All goes to plan a: the conveniently isolated farmhouse location, until the possessed child (the extraordinarily flexible Ashley Bell) turns out to be more demonically afflicted than anyone had prepared for. It's all moderately spooky for the first hour or so, but things take a turn for the overwrought in the final reel. AS Violence. *DVD* *Blu-ray*

Patrick Fabian *Cotton Marcus* · Ashley Bell *Nell Sweetzer* · Iris Bahr *Iris Reisen* · Louis Herthum *Louis Sweetzer* · Ca eb Landry Jones *Caleb Sweetzer* · Tony Bentley *Pastor Manley* · John Wright Jr *John Marcus* · Shanna Forrestall *Shanna Marcus* ■ *Dir* Daniel Stamm · *Scr* Huck Botko, Andrew Gurland

The Last Exorcism Part II ★★ 15
Horror thriller 2013 · US · Colour · 85min

This tedious sequel drops the found-footage format for a visually straightforward narrative that barely rises above the conventional. Afte: gaining internet fame as "Crazy possessed girl in woods", Ashley Bell attempts to recover from her ordeal in a New Orleans halfway house. She receives ghostly warnings from her deceased dad, and it seems that the demon Abalam is still determined to seduce her to the dark side. Director Ed Gass-Donnelly slowly builds the menace with false frights and sudden sounds, but unfortunately the audience is ahead of him every step of the way. AJ violence, swearing, sex scenes. *DVD* *Blu-ray*

Ashley Bell *Nell Sweetzer* · Julia Garner *Gwen* · Spencer Treat Clark *Chris* · Louis Herthum *Louis Sweetzer* · David Jensen *Calder* ■ *Dir* Ed Gass-Donnelly · *Scr* Ed Gass-Donnelly, Damien Chazelle, from a story by Chazelle, from characters by Huck Botko, Andrew Gurland

The Last 5 Years ★★★ 12
Romantic musical 2014 · US · Colour · 90min

Based on an off-Broadway musical, this three-tissue tearjerker traces the rise and fall of the relationship between a struggling actress (Anna Kendrick) and her novelist lover (Jeremy Jordan, who made a name for himself in musical theatre). What distinguishes the film, apart from the perky performances of its two leads, is that it's almost entirely dialogue-free. The tangled timeframes cause some confusion, as to who's doing what, when. But, even if this doesn't go down in cinema history as a great musical, it's certainly well worth a watch and a listen. DA *DVD*

Anna Kendrick *Cathy Hyatt* · Jeremy Jordan *Jamie Wellerstein* · Natalie Knepp *Alise Michaels* · Tamara Mintz *Danica Schwartz* ■ *Dir/Scr* Richard LaGravenese · *Cinematographer* Steven Meizler

The Last Flight ★★★
Drama 1931 · US · BW · 80min

This fascinating early talkie is one of the few key films to deal with the legendary "lost generation", those American expatriates who found themselves in Paris or Madrid in the 1920s, characters beloved by authors F Scott Fitzgerald (who coined the phrase) and Ernest Hemingway. Former silent screen matinée idol Richard Barthelmess plays a flying ace and today's audiences may find his performance a little mannered, though his face remains tenderly expressive. The film marks the Hollywood debut of German émigré director Wilhelm (later William) Dieterle. TS

Richard Barthelmess *Cary Lockwood* · John Mack Brown [Johnny Mack Brown] *Bill Talbot* · Helen Chandler *Nikki* · David Manners *Shep Lambert* · Elliott Nugent *Francis* · Walter Byron *Frink* ■ *Dir* Wilhelm Dieterle [William Dieterle] · *Scr* John Monk Saunders, from the novel *Single Lady* by John Monk Saunders

The Last Flight of Noah's Ark ★ U
Adventure 1980 · US · Colour · 93min

Quite what Disney hoped to achieve with this anaemic adventure is anyone's guess. Director Charles Jarrott seemed to think he could thrill youngsters with a plane crash, a storm at sea, a pair of young stowaways and some scene-stealing animals, while amusing the grown-ups with the *African Queen*-like banter between pilot Elliott Gould and missionary Geneviève Bujold. Wrong. DP

Elliott Gould *Noah Dugan* · Geneviève Bujold *Bernadette Lafleur* · Ricky Schroder [Rick Schroder] *Bobby* · Tammy Lauren *Julie* · Vincent Gardenia *Stoney* · John Fujioka *Cleveland* · Yuki Shimoda *Hiro* ■ *Dir* Charles Jarrott · *Scr* Steven W Carabatsos, Sandy Glass, George Arthur Bloom, from the story by Ernest K Gann

The Last Frontier ★★★
Western 1955 · US · Colour · 98min

This is a majestic and brooding western from director Anthony Mann, set mostly at night. In the story of three fur trappers who take jobs as cavalry scouts after losing their pelts to Indians, Mann's use of early CinemaScope is exemplary, with splendid tracking and panning shots, and there's some fascinating political commentary about the civilising of noble savage Victor Mature. Robert Preston is excellent as a single-minded military martinet, while young Anne Bancroft shows early promise. TS

Victor Mature *Jed* · Guy Madison *Captain Riordan* · Robert Preston *Colonel Frank Marston* · James Whitmore *Gus* · Anne Bancroft *Corinna Marston* · Russell Collins *Captain Clark* · Peter Whitney *Sergeant Major Decker* · Pat Hogan *Mungo* ■ *Dir* Anthony Mann · *Scr* Philip Yordan, Russell S Hughes, from the novel *The Gilded Rooster* by Richard Emery Roberts

The Last Gangster ★★★
Crime drama 1937 · US · BW · 81min

Edward G Robinson turns on the menace in the title role of what was among the last products of the golden age of 1930s gangster movies. Some critics rated his portrayal of a pathological hood out for revenge as highly as his famed performance seven years earlier in *Little Caesar*. Taut direction, snappy writing and a talented supporting cast, including James Stewart, add to the value of an engrossing melodrama, only let down by a soppy ending. PF

Edward G Robinson *Joe Krozac* · James Stewart *Paul North* · Rose Stradner *Talva Krozac* · Lionel Stander *Curly* · Douglas Scott *Paul North Jr* · John Carradine *Casper* · Sidney Blackmer *San Francisco editor* · Edward Brophy *"Fats" Garvey* ■ *Dir* Edward Ludwig · *Scr* John Lee Mahin, from a story by William A Wellman, Robert Carson

Last Gasp ★★ 18
Thriller 1995 · US · Colour · 88min

Ruthless real estate developer Robert Patrick slaughters a tribe of Mexican Indians for their land, only to become possessed by one of their spirits. Turning into a homicidal maniac with a painted face, he will stop at nothing to guard the ancient territory. Joanna Pacula is the concerned wife of one of his victims who tries to uncover the secret behind her husband's disappearance. More depressing than creepy. AJ *DVD*

Robert Patrick *Leslie Chase* · Joanna Pacula *Nora Weeks* · Vyto Ruginis *Ray Tattinger* · Mimi Craven *Goldie* · Alexander Enberg *Duane* ■ *Dir* Scott McGinnis · *Scr* Pierce Milestone, Stanley Isaacs, David N Twohy [David Twohy]

The Last Great Wilderness ★★★ 18
Road movie comedy thriller 2002 · UK/Den · Colour · 92min

Alastair Mackenzie stars in this offbeat drama directed by his brother David. Mackenzie plays Charlie, who's on his way to Skye to burn down the house of the pop star who ran off with his wife. On the road he meets Vincente (Jonny Phillips), who's on the run from thugs employed by a cuckolded husband, and they stumble across an isolated retreat, where the residents include a sex addict and a paedophile. Though hampered by budgetary restrictions, this is nevertheless a brave venture that taps into the spirit of *The Wicker Man*, but ultimately defies categorisation. BP *DVD*

Alastair Mackenzie (2) *Charlie* · Jonny Phillips *Vincente* · Ewan Stewart *Magnus* · David Hayman *Ruaridh* · Victoria Smurfit *Claire* · Louise Irwin *Morag* · Jane Stenson *Flora* · John Comerford *Paul* ■ *Dir* David Mackenzie · *Scr* Michael Tait, Alastair Mackenzie, Gillian Berrie, David Mackenzie

The Last Grenade ★★
Action drama 1970 · UK · Colour · 93min

Stanley Baker never quite attained the heady heights his obvious talents deserved and by the 1970s was the forgotten star of British cinema. Films like this only accelerated his decline, a predictable revenge drama with plenty of explosions and fights but little cranial activity. Baker plays a tough mercenary who vows retribution against a traitorous ex-colleague. Along the way he falls for the charms of Honor Blackman in a subplot riddled with the kind of dialogue even soap operas would reject. RS

Stanley Baker *Major Harry Grigsby* · Alex Cord *Kip Thompson* · Honor Blackman *Mrs Katherine Whiteley* · Richard Attenborough *General Charles Whiteley* · Rafer Johnson *Joe Jackson* · Andrew Keir *Gordon Mackenzie* · Ray Brooks *Lieutenant David Coulson* · Julian Glover *Andy Royal* · John Thaw *Terry Mitchell* ■ *Dir* Gordon Flemyng · *Scr* Kenneth Ware, John Sherlock, James Mitchell, from the novel *The Ordeal of Major Grigsby* by John Sherlock

L

The Last Hard Men ★
Western   1976 · US · Colour · 97min

You expect a lot better than this violent, sadistic revenge western from a picture starring Charlton Heston and James Coburn. The latter is the villain whose plan for getting back at former lawman Heston includes kidnapping his virginal daughter (played by Barbara Hershey) and having her raped within his sight. Director Andrew V McLaglen copies Sam Peckinpah's use of slow motion for key moments but misses the relentless intensity. Nasty. AE

Charlton Heston *Sam Burgade* · James Coburn *Zach Provo* · Barbara Hershey *Susan Burgade* · Jorge Rivero *Cesar Menendez* · Michael Parks *Sheriff Noel Nye* · Larry Wilcox *Mike Shelby* ■ *Dir* Andrew V McLaglen · *Scr* Guerdon Trueblood, from the novel *Gun Down* by Brian Garfield

Last Holiday ★★★ U
Comedy drama   1950 · UK · BW · 88min

Alec Guinness holds centre stage in this amiable ensemble affair, playing a stuffed shirt who, having been diagnosed with a fatal illness, discovers too late that he's been missing out on the finer things in life. It's the supporting cast, however, that gives the film the animated gentility that is so achingly British. Kay Walsh, Wilfrid Hyde White, Sid James and Ernest Thesiger stand out among the eccentrics and everyday folk who populate JB Priestley's heart-warming script. Corny, perhaps, but nice. DP

Alec Guinness *George Bird* · Beatrice Campbell *Sheila Rockingham* · Kay Walsh *Mrs Poole* · Bernard Lee *Inspector Wilton* · Wilfrid Hyde White *Chalfont* · Muriel George *Lady Oswington* · Sidney James *Joe Clarence* ■ *Dir* Henry Cass · *Scr* JB Priestley

Last Holiday ★★★ 12
Comedy   2006 · US · Colour · 106min

After being informed that she has just weeks to live, New Orleans sales assistant Queen Latifah jets off to snowy Europe to meet her hero, chef Gérard Depardieu, and make the luxurious most of her supposed time left in the glamorous Grand Hotel Pupp. Without Latifah's hugely likeable performance, director Wayne Wang's cute and glossy Hollywood version of the 1950 British satire would be a drab wish-fulfilment fantasy. Instead, the gentle comedy shines through the frothy predictability with an unforced lightness of touch. AJ Swearing. DVD

Queen Latifah *Georgia Byrd* · LL Cool J *Sean Matthews* · Timothy Hutton *Matthew Kragen* · Giancarlo Esposito *Senator Dillings* · Alicia Witt *Ms Burns* · Gérard Depardieu *Chef Didier* · Michael Nouri *Congressman Stewart* · Jane Adams (2) *Rochelle* ■ *Dir* Wayne Wang · *Scr* Jeffrey Price, Peter S Seaman, from the 1950 film by JB Priestley

The Last Horror Movie ★★ 18
Horror thriller   2003 · UK · Colour · 75min

This thriller is no doubt meant to be provocative and controversial, but it just tries too hard. The film follows the "exploits" of serial killer Kevin Howarth, who interrupts *vérité* video footage of his appallingly brutal crimes with speeches delivered to camera, attempting to explain his nihilist motives while challenging the audience for continuing to watch. Its pseudo-intellectual overtones sit uneasily with its more avowed exploitation elements and the extreme violence will be too much for some audiences. AS DVD

Kevin Howarth *Max Parry* · Mark Stevenson *Assistant* · Antonia Beamish *Petra* · Christabel Muir *Sam* · Jonathan Coote *John* · Rita Davies *Grandma* · John Berlyne *Phil* · Jim Bywater *Bill* ■ *Dir* Julian Richards · *Scr* James Handel, from an idea by Julian Richards

Last House on the Left ★★★ 18
Horror   1972 · US · Colour · 81min

This was the legendary graphic shocker which put director Wes Craven on the road to horror fame. Inspired by Ingmar Bergman's *The Virgin Spring*, and infused by a repellent Vietnam sensibility, two girls are kidnapped on the way to a rock concert by four sadistic convicts and are subjected to humiliating rape, torture and death. Their parents then mete out an equally horrific revenge when the foursome conveniently turn up on their doorstep. This hard-to-watch and highly controversial cult film gains enormous power from its low-budget trappings and *cinéma vérité* approach. A benchmark in the annals of cinematic offensiveness. AJ DVD

David A Hess [David Hess] *Krug* · Lucy Grantham *Phyllis* · Sandra Cassel *Mari Collingwood* · Marc Sheffler *Junior* ■ *Dir/Scr* Wes Craven

The Last House on the Left ★★ 18
Horror   2008 · US/S Afr · Colour · 105min

This remake of Wes Craven's 1972 notorious shocker – in which two girls are subjected to a horrific ordeal by a bunch of lowlifes – replaces low-budget coarseness and sick imagery with a refined visual sophistication. The result is that a once powerfully intense political statement on how ordinary people are driven to acts of inhuman violence is blunted by director Dennis Iliadis into a predictable splatter-laden revenge saga. AJ Violence, swearing, drug abuse, nudity. DVD

Tony Goldwyn *John Collingwood* · Monica Potter *Emma Collingwood* · Garret Dillahunt *Krug* · Aaron Paul *Francis* · Spencer Treat Clark *Justin* · Riki Lindhome *Sadie* · Martha MacIsaac *Paige* · Sara Paxton *Mari Collingwood* ■ *Dir* Dennis Iliadis · *Scr* Adam Alleca, Carl Ellsworth, from the 1972 film

The Last Hunt ★★★★
Western   1956 · US · Colour · 108min

Robert Taylor plays against his heroic, matinée idol image as a crazed, racist buffalo hunter who slaughters animals, tribesmen and anything else that comes close in an early "anti-western". Stewart Granger is another hunter, not quite in Taylor's league, who finally becomes disillusioned and steals pretty native American woman Debra Paget away from his partner. Director Richard Brooks achieves much authenticity by staging the action in Custer State Park, South Dakota, during the annual cull of the buffalo herd. AT

Robert Taylor (1) *Charles Gilson* · Stewart Granger *Sandy McKenzie* · Lloyd Nolan *Woodfoot* · Debra Paget *Indian girl* · Russ Tamblyn *Jimmy* · Constance Ford *Peg* ■ *Dir* Richard Brooks · *Scr* Richard Brooks, from the novel by Milton Lott

The Last Hurrah ★★★ U
Political drama   1958 · US · BW · 120min

Spencer Tracy stars as an old-time political operator standing for mayor one last time and observed with wide-eyed approval by his nephew, Jeffrey Hunter. This is a great part for Tracy and he runs and runs with it, turning on the Irish-American blarney when it suits him, showing expediency and iron-hard calculation when he thinks no one is looking. As so often with John Ford's films, there's also a flabby sentimentality even when he's dealing with the cut-throat electoral process, but the film's optimism anticipated the defeat of Nixon and the triumph of Kennedy in 1961. AT

Spencer Tracy *Frank Skeffington* · Jeffrey Hunter *Adam Caulfield* · Dianne Foster *Maeve Caulfield* · Pat O'Brien *John Gorman* · Basil Rathbone *Norman Cass Sr* · Donald Crisp *The Cardinal* · James Gleason *Cuke Gillen* · Edward Brophy *Ditto Boland* ■ *Dir* John Ford · *Scr* Frank Nugent, from the novel by Edwin O'Conner

Last Images of the Shipwreck ★★★ 15
Drama   1989 · Arg/Sp · Colour · 122min

Although it provides an unflinching glimpse of Buenos Aires low life, Eliseo Subiela's second feature is primarily concerned with the relationship between life and art. Trapped in both his marriage and his job, insurance salesman Lorenzo Quinteros becomes convinced that he has found the subject for his novel after he meets prostitute Noemi Frenkel and her three bizarre brothers. The pacing is occasionally ponderous and the fantasy elements incongruous, but the performances are first-rate. DP Spanish +subtitles.

Lorenzo Quinteros *Roberto* · Noemi Frenkel *Estela* · Hugo Soto *Claudio* · Pablo Brichta *Jose* · Sara Benitez *Mother* · Andres Tiengo *Mario* ■ *Dir/Scr* Eliseo Subiela

The Last Impresario ★★★ 15
Documentary   2013 · Aus · Colour · 92min

Described by actress Greta Scacchi as "the most famous person you've never heard of", Glasgow-born impresario Michael White has been pushing theatrical and artistic boundaries since the early 1960s. He famously brought *Oh! Calcutta!* and *The Rocky Horror Show* to the stage, and had an unrivalled genius for partying with beautiful people. Australian actress-turned-director Gracie Otto chronicles his triumphs over adversity with a decent appreciation of how his collaborations with the likes of Yoko Ono, Merce Cunningham and the *Beyond the Fringe* satirists helped define the British arts scene of the 1960s. DP Swearing, sexual references, nudity.

■ *Dir/Scr* Gracie Otto

The Last Island ★★★★
Drama   1990 · Neth · Colour · 115min

A superior screenplay, telling characterisation and strong ensemble acting are the qualities that make this tale about the survivors of an airline crash marooned on a desert island into an engrossing and distinctive drama. Sharp direction by noted film-maker Marleen Gorris also helps expose the brutish realities that lie beneath the biscuit-thin veneer of what we like to think of as civilisation. Almost an adult version of *Lord of the Flies*. PF English, Dutch +subtitles. Swearing.

Patricia Hayes *Mrs Godame* · Paul Freeman *Sean* · Shelagh McLeod *Joanna* · Ian Tracey *Jack* · Marc Berman *Pierre* · Kenneth Colley *Nick* · Mark Hembrow *Frank* ■ *Dir/Scr* Marleen Gorris

The Last Journey ★★★ U
Thriller   1936 · UK · BW · 62min

By turns thrilling, ludicrous, tense and just plain naff, this British B-movie is well worth seeking out. Julian Mitchell plays a train driver who is forced into retirement and is so consumed by jealousy over his fireman's dalliance with his wife that he decides his last journey will end in disaster. After he forces the fireman to stoke the engine up to dangerously high speed, passenger and brain specialist Godfrey Tearle starts his heroic clamber along the speeding train to do his "there there, old chap, let's all have a nice cup of tea" speech. AT

Godfrey Tearle *Sir Wilfred Rhodes* · Hugh Williams *Gerald Winter* · Judy Gunn *Diana Gregory* · Mickey Brantford *Tom* · Julien Mitchell *Bob Holt* · Olga Lindo *Emily Holt* · Michael Hogan (1) *Charlie* ■ *Dir* Bernard Vorhaus · *Scr* John Soutar, H Fowler Mear, from the story *The Last Journey* by J Jefferson Farjeon

The Last King ★★★ 15
Historical adventure   2016 · Nor · Colour · 99min

The dynastic travails of 13th-century Norway provide the backdrop for this rollicking adventure, evidently targeted at *Game of Thrones* fans. The story of loyal retainers safeguarding the infant heir to the throne is largely a true one, however, and familiar to native viewers… which leaves English audiences with a bit of catching up to do. Director Nils Gaup does a sterling job with the action, however, and, though the resolution is predictable enough, the movie's solidly satisfying overall, with grizzled Nikolaj Lie Kaas making a very hissable villain. TJ In Norwegian. Violence.

Jakob Oftebro *Happens Valdemon* · Kristofer Hivju *Torstein* · Pal Sverre Valheim Hagen *Gisle* · Benjamin Helstad *King* ■ *Dir* Nils Gaup · *Scr* Ravn Lanesskog

The Last King of Scotland ★★★★ 15
Historical thriller   2006 · UK/US · Colour · 117min

Forest Whitaker won an Oscar for his electrifying performance as 1970s Ugandan dictator Idi Amin in this powerful thriller. Based on Giles Foden's novel, the movie portrays the relationship between one of the 20th century's most notorious despots and a fictional Scottish doctor (James McAvoy). Switching effortlessly from eccentric charmer to brutal megalomaniac, Amin plunges his young protégé into an escalating nightmare. It's a morally ambiguous turn that gives a daringly human face to Amin. Yet *Touching the Void* director Kevin Macdonald (brother of *Trainspotting* producer Andrew, executive producer here) also draws on his documentary-making past to raise disturbing questions about ethics and the corruption of the soul. SF Violence, swearing, sex scenes. DVD

Forest Whitaker *Idi Amin* · James McAvoy *Nicholas Garrigan* · Kerry Washington *Kay Amin* · Gillian Anderson *Sarah Merrit* · Simon McBurney *Nigel Stone* · David Oyelowo *Dr Junju* · Giles Foden *British journalist* ■ *Dir* Kevin Macdonald · *Scr* Jeremy Brock, Peter Morgan (1), from the novel by Giles Foden

The Last Kiss ★★★ 15
Romantic comedy drama   2006 · US · Colour · 99min

As American remakes of European films go, this one isn't too bad, but then again Gabriele Muccino's original 2001 Italian version was no great masterpiece, either. The story revolves around a group of friends approaching their 30th birthdays and their families, all of them struggling with the nature of commitment and the demands of monogamy. Out of the ensemble cast, Zach Braff (*Garden State*) gets the most screen time as architect Michael who's expecting a baby with his girlfriend (Jacinda Barrett), but is tempted by one last fling. Meanwhile, Blythe Danner and Tom Wilkinson play Michael's prospective parents-in-law, a generation older but still struggling with the same sort of problems. Director Tony Goldwyn's use of effectively comedy punctuates the drama, while *Crash* writer Paul Haggis deftly weaves together the multi-stranded elements of this cautionary tale. LF DVD

Zach Braff *Michael* · Jacinda Barrett *Jenna* · Casey Affleck *Chris* · Rachel Bilson *Kim* · Michael Weston *Izzy* · Blythe Danner *Anna* · Tom Wilkinson *Stephen* ■ *Dir* Tony Goldwyn · *Scr* Paul Haggis, from the film *L'Ultimo Bacio* by Gabriele Muccino

The Last Knights ★★ 15
Period action adventure
2015 · S Kor/Cz Rep · Colour · 112min

Clive Owen stars in this medieval adventure, playing a loyal knight out for revenge when his master, played by Morgan Freeman, is murdered by a powerful and corrupt nobleman. Told at an agonisingly slow pace, there is a lot of talking but precious little action, with the monotony made even duller thanks to grey cinematography, draining the life out of the lavish castles and gorgeous landscapes. The cast is a saving grace, rallying valiantly against the listless material they have to work with. JL DVD

Clive Owen *Raiden* · Morgan Freeman *Bartok* · Aksel Hennie *Gezza mott* · Daniel Adegboyega *Rodrigo* · Shohreh Aghdashloo *Maria* ■ *Dir* Kazuaki Kiriya

The Last Laugh ★★★★★ U
Classic silent drama   1924 · Ger · BW · 90min

FW Murnau, who had made an impact with his expressionist masterpiece, *Nosferatu, a Symphony of Horrors* (1922), here moved closer to the *Kammerspielfilm* (chamber film), which dealt with ordinary people and events with an element of social criticism. The imposing Emil Jannings plays an elderly doorman at a luxury hotel, proud of his work and uniform, who is reduced to becoming a lavatory attendant. Murnau's *mise en scène* and the brilliant camerawork

L

allow the story to be told without the use of intertitles, except for one that introduces the epilogue. The happy ending, tacked on at the insistence of the producer, can also be accepted as the man's dream. RB DVD Blu

Emil Jannings *Doorman* • Maly Delschaft *His daughter* • Max Hiller *Her fiancé* • Emilie Kurz *His aunt* • Hans Unterkircher *Hotel manager* ■ *Dir* FW Murnau • *Scr* Carl Mayer • *Cinematographer* Karl Freund

The Last Legion ★★★★ 12
Period action adventure
2006 · US/UK/Fr · Colour · 97min

Despite a starry cast, *The Last Legion* sat on the shelf for quite a while before receiving a muted US release. Nevertheless, this is a surprisingly entertaining, fast-moving and unashamedly old-fashioned sword-and-sandal epic that mixes Roman history with Celtic myth. It's AD 476, Rome has been overrun by Goths and the boy emperor Romulus Augustus is imprisoned on the island of Capri. He is rescued by loyal general Aurelius (Colin Firth), and the pair set off for Britannia, pursued by Wulfilla (Kevin McKidd) and his hairy hordes. The film manages to blend imaginative plotting with splendid action, including unlikely hand-to-hand combat between Bollywood superstar Aishwarya Rai, as a nimble Byzantine warrior, and craggy Scots character actor James Cosmo, playing a Goth axeman. BP DVD

Colin Firth *Aurelius* • Ben Kingsley *Ambrosinus* • Aishwarya Rai *Mira* • Peter Mullan *Odoacer* • Kevin McKidd *Wulfilla* • John Hannah *Nestor* • Thomas Sangster [Thomas Brodie-Sangster] *Romulus* • Iain Glen *Orestes* ■ *Dir* Doug Lefler • *Scr* Jez Butterworth, Tom Butterworth, from a story by Carlo Carlei, Peter Rader, Valerio Manfredi, from the novel by Manfredi • *Cinematographer* Marco Pontecorvo

Last Life in the Universe ★★★★ 15
Romantic comedy drama
2003 · Thai/Neth/HK/UK · Colour · 103min

Beautifully photographed by Christopher Doyle, Pen-ek Ratanaruang's enigmatic character study owes less to traditional Thai melodrama than the steely stylisation of the new wave of Japanese film-makers. The main focus falls on the unlikely relationship between meticulous librarian Tadanobu Asano and slapdash bar-girl Sinitta Boonyasak, whose sister's traffic death postponed one of Asano's frequent attempted suicides. Drily witty and occasionally truly magical, this is a slow-burning and deeply seductive story. DP Thai, Japanese, English +subtitles. Sex scenes, swearing, violence. DVD

Tadanobu Asano *Kenji* • Sinitta Boonyasak *Noi* • Laila Boonyasak *Nid* • Yutaka Matsushige *Yukio* • Takashi Miike *Yakuza* ■ *Dir* Pen-ek Ratanaruang • *Scr* Prabda Yoon, Pen-ek Ratanaruang

Last Light ★★★ 18
Prison drama
1993 · US · Colour · 100min

Kiefer Sutherland made an impressive debut behind the camera with this bleak prison TV drama. He also takes the starring role as the brutalised prisoner on death row who forms a cautious and unlikely friendship with sensitive guard Forest Whitaker. Sutherland puts in one of his best performances, and he is matched by Whitaker, while there are also fine supporting turns from Amanda Plummer and Kathleen Quinlan. Despite its grim subject matter, this is gripping. JF DVD

Kiefer Sutherland *Denver Bayliss* • Forest Whitaker *Fred Whitmore* • Amanda Plummer *Lillian Burke* • Kathleen Quinlan *Kathy Rubicek* • Lynne Moody *Hope Whitmore* • Clancy Brown *Lionel McMannis* ■ *Dir* Kiefer Sutherland • *Scr* Robert Eisele

The Last Man on Earth ★★★
Horror
1964 · It/US · BW · 85min

Based on Richard Matheson's classic horror novel *I Am Legend* (as was *The Omega Man* in 1971), directors Ubaldo Ragona (Italian version) and Sidney Salkow's (US version)

atmospheric shocker pits Vincent Price against people infected with a mysterious plague that has turned them into vampires. Shot on stark Rome locations (standing in for Los Angeles), Price delivers a restrained performance in this engrossing slice of futuristic horror. AJ

Vincent Price *Robert Morgan* • Franca Bettoja *Ruth* • Emma Danieli *Virginia* • Giacomo Rossi-Stuart [Giacomo Rossi Stuart] *Ben Cortman* ■ *Dir* Ubaldo Ragona, Sidney Salkow • *Scr* William P Leicester, Logan Swanson, from the novel *I Am Legend* by Richard Matheson

The Last Man on the Moon ★★★★ PG
Documentary
2015 · UK · Colour · 95min

Everyone knows of Neil Armstrong and his first walk on the Moon, but the achievements of astronaut Eugene Cernan are less well documented. Cernan was the final *Apollo* astronaut to leave the lunar surface in 1972, but, as the fabulous – and often previously unseen – footage here shows, he was a constant, Zelig-like presence throughout the space race. As he ruminates on his journeys to the stars, Mark Craig's film is all the more affecting for weaving achingly personal testimony into the absorbing story. JH

Eugene Cernan • Alan Bean • Charlie Duke • Gene Kranz ■ *Dir/Scr* Mark Craig

Last Man Standing ★ 18
Period crime drama 1996 · US · Colour · 96min

Gun-for-hire Bruce Willis arrives in a small Texas town and gets involved in a gang war over bootleg alcohol in director Walter Hill's weak Prohibition-era remake of the Japanese classic *Yojimbo*. Every cliché in the Sergio Leone catalogue is dragged out and used to minor effect in this ham-fisted action thriller that's given an unattractive dusty look with uniformly weak performances to match. AJ Violence, swearing, sex scenes, nudity. DVD

Bruce Willis *John Smith* • Christopher Walken *Hickey* • Alexandra Powers *Lucy Kalinski* • David Patrick Kelly *Doyle* • William Sanderson *Joe Monday* • Karina Lombard *Felina* • Ned Eisenberg *Fredo Strozzi* • Michael Imperioli *Giorgio Carmonte* ■ *Dir* Walter Hill • *Scr* Walter Hill, from the film *Yojimbo* by Akira Kurosawa, Ryuzo Kikushima, Hideo Oguni, from the novel *Red Harvest* by Dashiel Hammett

The Last Married Couple in America ★★
Comedy 1980 · US · Colour · 102min

This last gasp of the 1970s fashion for marital comedies dealing with the sexual "liberation" of middle-class couples stars Natalie Wood and George Segal. They're a husband and wife who endeavour to deal with a surfeit of divorces among their friends. Despite the more than usual utterance of expletives, the competent direction of Gilbert Cates, a bunch of "swinging" couples paying for the wages of sin, and Richard Benjamin in neurotic mode, it is always superficial. RK

George Segal *Jeff Thomson* • Natalie Wood *Mari Thomson* • Richard Benjamin *Marv Cooper* • Arlene Golonka *Sally Cooper* • Allan Arbus *Al Squib* • Marilyn Sokol *Alice Squib* • Dom DeLuise *Walter Holmes* • Valerie Harper *Barbara* ■ *Dir* Gilbert Cates • *Scr* John Herman Shaner

The Last Marshal ★ 18
Action thriller 1999 · US · Colour · 97min

Stuntman Mike Kirton made his directorial debut with this bruising cop flick. So it's no surprise that a couple of the action sequences, notably the chase involving a speedboat and a motorbike, are slickly accomplished. But the remainder is strewn with racist and misogynist slurs that are spewed out by Scott Glenn with all the meat-headed macho he can muster. As the Texas lawman in Miami, Glen pursues a gang of drug smugglers with pitiless violence. DP Swearing, violence, nudity. DVD

Scott Glenn *Cole McClary* • Constance Marie *Rosa* • Randall Batinkoff *Jamie* • Vincent Castellanos *Toeres* ■ *Dir* Mike Kirton • *Scr* Scott Wiper, Mike Kirton

The Last Metro ★★★ PG
Wartime drama 1980 · Fr · Colour · 126min

Considering he'd always wanted to make a film about the Occupation, François Truffaut largely ignores its hideous realities in this nostalgic tribute to the theatre. The dynamic between the members of Jewish manager Heinz Bennent's company is well sustained, as is the mystery of whether Bennent's wife Catherine Deneuve prefers him to actor/Resistance fighter Gérard Depardieu. But the life of this enclosed ensemble is too divorced from history to make the movie anything more than just a handsomely mounted, meticulously performed fantasy. DP French +subtitles. DVD Blu

Catherine Deneuve *Marion Steiner* • Gérard Depardieu *Bernard Granger* • Jean Poiret *Jean-Loup Cottins* • Heinz Bennent *Lucas Steiner* • Andréa Ferréol *Arlette Guillaume* • Paulette Dubost *Germaine Fabre* • Sabine Haudepin *Nadine Marsac* • Jean-Louis Richard *Daxiat* ■ *Dir* François Truffaut • *Scr* François Truffaut, Suzanne Schiffman, Jean-Claude Grumberg, from a story by François Truffaut, Suzanne Schiffman

The Last Mile ★★
Crime drama 1959 · US · BW · 82min

The title is the term given to the walk from a death row cell to the electric chair, and is also the title of the play through which Spencer Tracy and Clark Gable won Hollywood contracts. In contrast, Mickey Rooney's reputation had long been established when he took the part of a vicious convict who organises a prison riot. The claim in the prologue that such things no longer happen in US prisons is as unconvincing as much of this clichéd but lively film. RB

Mickey Rooney *"Killer" John Mears* • Alan Bunce *Warden* • Frank Conroy *O'Flaherty (Guard)* • Leon Janney *Callahan (Guard)* • Frank Overton *Father O'Connors* • Clifford David *Convict Richard Walters* • Harry Millard *Convict Fred Mayor* • Ford Rainey *Convict "Red" Kirby* ■ *Dir* Howard W Koch • *Scr* Milton Subotsky, Seton I Miller, from the play by John Wexley

The Last Mimzy ★★★★ PG
Science-fiction fantasy adventure
2007 · US · Colour · 92min

With its willingness to deal with big issues in a non-patronising manner, this is probably the most intelligent kids movie since *ET*. Ten-year-old Noah (Chris O'Neil) and his five-year-old sister Emma (Rhiannon Leigh Wryn) discover a strange box of tricks washed up on the beach. After they unpack the mysterious contents, the children begin to develop amazing new abilities, but their parents (Joely Richardson and Timothy Hutton) are too preoccupied with their own lives to pay much attention. The special effects are decent, the story is highly involving, and the slightly new-age message is refreshing. However, its the superb performances of the two young leads that really steal the film. DA DVD

Timothy Hutton *David Wilder* • Joely Richardson *Jo Wilder* • Rainn Wilson *Larry White* • Rhiannon Leigh Wryn *Emma Wilder* • Chris O'Neil *Noah Wilder* • Kathryn Hahn *Naomi Shwartz* • Michael Clarke Duncan *Nathanial Boardman* ■ *Dir* Bob Shaye [Robert Shaye] • *Scr* Bruce Joel Rubin, Toby Emmerich, from the short story *Mimsy Were the Borogoves* by Lewis Padgett

The Last Mistress ★★ 15
Period romantic drama
2007 · Fr/It · Colour · 109min

Controversial French director Catherine Breillat (*A Ma Soeur!*, *Romance*) dispenses with her usual taboo-breaking tactics for this 19th-century-set drama. Asia Argento plays the tempestuous mistress of the title, whose long-term affair with dissolute young aristocrat Ryno de Marigny (newcomer Fu'ad Aït Aattou) is due to be severed by his forthcoming marriage. For a story so steeped in passion, this lethargic feature is surprisingly dry and stilted. Argento's

performance verges on caricature, while Aattou is beautiful yet bland. Everything looks suitably ravishing, but beneath the surface there's no vitality, ensuring that even the supposedly intense sex scenes are tedious and unconvincing. SF French +subtitles. Sex scenes, nudity. DVD

Asia Argento *Vellini* • Fu'ad Aït Aattou *Ryno de Marigny* • Roxane Mesquida *Hermangarde* • Claude Sarraute *Marquise de Flers* • Yolande Moreau *Comtesse d'Artelles* • Michael Lonsdale [Michel Lonsdale] *Vicomte de Prony* • Anne Parillaud *Mme de Solcy* ■ *Dir* Catherine Breillat • *Scr* Catherine Breillat, from the novel *Une Vieille Maîtresse* by Jules Barbey d'Aurevilly

The Last Mitterrand ★★★ PG
Biographical drama 2005 · Fr · Colour · 111min

As President François Mitterrand (Michel Bouquet) engages in his final battle with cancer, a journalist (Jalil Lespert) endeavours to extract his memoirs and life lessons for a biography. Director Robert Guédiguian's semi-fictional look at Mitterrand's career attempts to contrast his socialist dream alternative with global capitalism to raise pertinent questions about both. A more than passing knowledge of French politics and Mitterrand's personal history is vital to glean maximum enjoyment from this conversation-based relationship between a writer searching for certainties and a statesman unsure of his legacy. AJ French +subtitles. DVD

Michel Bouquet *The President* • Jalil Lespert *Antoine Moreau* • Philippe Fretun *Dr Jeantot* • Anne Cantineau *Jeanne* • Sarah Grappin *Judith* • Catherine Salviat *Mado* • Jean-Claude Frissung *René* • Philippe Lemercier *Fleury, the bodyguard* ■ *Dir* Robert Guédiguian • *Scr* Georges-Marc Benamou, Gilles Taurand, from the book *Le Dernier Mitterrand* by Georges-Marc Benamou

The Last Movie ★
Experimental drama 1971 · US · Colour · 107min

After the huge success of *Easy Rider* (1969), director Dennis Hopper could have made any movie he wanted. Sadly he did just that, and the resulting fiasco is one of the all-time classics of pretentiously incomprehensible cinema. Outlining the hippy antics of a film crew in South America aiming to shoot a western, Hopper uses movie-making as a metaphor for imperialism in this mess of over-indulgent allegory and mind-numbing ranting. AJ

Dennis Hopper *Kansas* • Stella Garcia *Maria* • Samuel Fuller *Director* • Daniel Ades *Thomas Mercado* • Tomas Milian *Priest* • Don Gordon *Neville* • Julie Adams *Mrs Anderson* • Peter Fonda *Sheriff* • Kris Kristofferson *Minstrel Wrangler* • Henry Jaglom *Minister's son* • Michelle Phillips *Banker's daughter* • Dean Stockwell *Billy the Kid* • Russ Tamblyn *Member of Billy's gang* ■ *Dir* Dennis Hopper • *Scr* Stewart Stern, from a story by Stewart Stern, Dennis Hopper

Last Night ★★★★ 15
Drama 1998 · Can/Fr · Colour · 91min

"A small film that is really a big film" is how David Cronenberg, best known as a director but acting here, describes director Don McKellar's deeply moving tale. Set against the countdown to an unexplained Armageddon, this captivating ensemble piece makes imminent oblivion seem life-affirming. As McKellar reneges on a nostalgic family Christmas, old school pal Callum Keith Rennie completes his sexual wish-list, teacher Geneviève Bujold revisits her favourite students and Sandra Oh attempts to cross town to fulfil her suicide pact with husband Cronenberg. Poignant, provocative and visually striking. DP Sex scenes, swearing, violence. DVD

Don McKellar *Patrick Wheeler* • Sandra Oh *Sandra* • Callum Keith Rennie *Craig Zwiller* • Sarah Polley *Jennifer Wheeler* • David Cronenberg *Duncan* • Robin Gammell *Mr Wheeler* • Roberta Maxwell *Mrs Wheeler* • Tracy Wright *Donna* • Geneviève Bujold *Mrs Carlton* ■ *Dir/Scr* Don McKellar • *Cinematographer* Douglas Koch

Last Night ★★★ 12

Romantic drama 2009 · US/Fr · Colour · 88min

A young couple find their fidelity tested in this intimate drama. Keira Knightley delivers a mature performance as a writer who begins to suspect her husband, Sam Worthington, is getting a bit too cosy with sultry colleague Eva Mendes. As he heads off on business, the film cuts back and forth to track events at home and away, while an unexpected encounter with old flame Guillaume Canet (Gallic and smug, in that order) puts Knightley's own integrity on the spot. All in all, this is a low-key affair, but its strength is in the keen observation of how relationships develop. The storytelling gets a bit predictable, yet Knightley brings her side of the tale alive, and an ever-present rippling piano score from Clint Mansell adds a touch of class. **TJ** Brief swearing, sex scenes. **DVD BL**

Keira Knightley *Joanna Reed* • Sam Worthington *Michael Reed* • Guillaume Canet *Alex* • Eva Mendes *Laura* • Griffin Dunne *Truman* ■ *Dir/Scr* Massy Tadjedin • *Music* Clint Mansell

The Last of England ★ 18

Drama 1987 · UK · Colour and BW · 87min

Director Derek Jarman's angry polemic on the state of Britain in the mid-1980s is one for his die-hard fans only. Scattershot images of inner-city decay and violent paramilitaries collide with clips from Jarman's own home movies as actor Nigel Terry gives voice to concerns about the urban plight invading the collective unconsciousness. Jarman experiments with technique in a boring melange of images jazzed up with deliberately confrontational material. Redundant and old-fashioned. **AJ** **DVD**

Spring • Gerrard McArthur • Tilda Swinton • Nigel Terry ■ *Dir/Scr* Derek Jarman • *Music* Simon Fisher Turner

The Last of Mrs Cheyney ★★★

Comedy 1929 · US · BW · 94min

MGM's favourite actress – after she married studio boss Irving Thalberg – Norma Shearer gives gloss, but not much conviction to the role of the eponymous Mrs Cheyney. Playing an adventuress let loose in English high society, she wreaks moral havoc with Basil Rathbone and Hedda Hopper (who went on to be a feared gossip columnist). Adapted from an oft-filmed stage play by Frederick Lonsdale it already seemed dated at the time it was released, but its social nuances are still fascinating. **TH**

Norma Shearer *Mrs Cheyney* • Basil Rathbone *Lord Arthur Dilling* • George Barraud *Charles* • Herbert Bunston *Lord Elton* • Hedda Hopper *Lady Maria* • Moon Carroll *Joan* • Madeleine Seymour *Mrs Wynton* • Cyril Chadwick *Willie Wynton* ■ *Dir* Sidney Franklin • *Scr* Hans Kräly, Claudine West, from the play by Frederick Lonsdale • *Art Director* Cedric Gibbons

The Last of Mrs Cheyney ★★★

Comedy drama 1937 · US · BW · 98min

This Frederick Lonsdale theatrical chestnut has always attracted great female stars to its showy, creaky title role. The 1929 Norma Shearer version is rarely shown, but movie fans have the consolation of the 1951 remake called *The Law and the Lady* with a Cecil Beaton-dressed Greer Garson, and this rather slow, dated but still glossy and engaging Joan Crawford version from MGM's golden age. **TS**

Joan Crawford *Fay Cheyney* • William Powell *Charles* • Robert Montgomery *Lord Arthur Dilling* • Frank Morgan *Lord Kelton* • Jessie Ralph *Duchess* • Nigel Bruce *Sir William* • Benita Hume *Kitty* • Colleen Clare *Joan* • Ralph Forbes *Cousin John* ■ *Dir* Richard Boleslawski • *Scr* Leon Gordon, Samson Raphaelson, Monckton Hoffe, from the play by Frederick Lonsdale

The Last of Sheila ★★★

Murder mystery 1973 · US · Colour · 123min

Sharing a liking for whodunnits and word games, composer Stephen Sondheim and actor Anthony Perkins joined forces to write this murder mystery movie. Aboard a luxury yacht, widowed Hollywood producer James Coburn gets his friends and colleagues to play a Cluedo-like game, the result of which will reveal the killer of Coburn's wife. A conceit from start to finish, it should delight connoisseurs of camp, though few critics at the time appreciated the joke. **AT**

James Coburn *Clinton* • James Mason *Philip* • Raquel Welch *Alice* • Richard Benjamin *Tom* • Joan Hackett *Lee* • Ian McShane *Anthony* • Dyan Cannon *Christine* ■ *Scr* Anthony Perkins, Stephen Sondheim • *Production Designer* Ken Adam

Last of the Badmen ★★

Western 1957 · US · Colour · 79min

This western has a cracking premise: a gang springs outlaws from jail, uses them for hold-ups until the price on their head increases, then turns in their corpses and collects the reward. Unfortunately, George Montgomery is wooden as the detective who goes undercover to investigate the racket, and the intriguing plotline is inadequately realised thanks to the paucity of the budget. The story was used again in 1964 for *Gunfight at Comanche Creek*. **TS**

George Montgomery *Dan Barton* • James Best *Ted Hamilton* • Meg Randall *Lila* • Douglas Kennedy *Hawkins* • Michael Ansara *Kramer* • Keith Larsen *Roberts* • Robert Foulk *Taylor* • Willis Bouchey *Marshal Parker* ■ *Dir* Paul Landres • *Scr* Daniel B Ullman, David Chantler, from the story by Ullman

Last of the Comanches ★★

Western 1952 · US · Colour · 85min

Broderick Crawford is not the most charismatic of western stars but he's effectively cast as the burly cavalry sergeant fleeing across the desert from an Indian massacre with a handful of fellow soldiers. They pick up others en route and keep the Comanches at bay from an abandoned mission. The long siege is moderately suspenseful under director Andre De Toth's handling, while the excellent photography and score deserve a better picture. **AE**

Broderick Crawford *Sgt Matt Trainor* • Barbara Hale *Julia Lanning* • Johnny Stewart *Little Knife* • Lloyd Bridges *Jim Starbuck* • Mickey Shaughnessy *Rusty Potter* • George Mathews *Romany O'Rattigan* ■ *Dir* Andre De Toth • *Scr* Kenneth Gamet • *Cinematographers* Ray Cory, Charles Lawton Jr • *Music* George Duning

Last of the Dogmen ★★ PG

Romantic western adventure 1995 · US · Colour · 112min

In this dumb modern western, a bounty hunter (Tom Berenger) on the trail of escaped convicts discovers a tribe of Cheyenne Indians living undisturbed in the Rocky Mountains. It's a pedestrian copy of *Dances with Wolves*, with native bonding and a spiky relationship between Berenger and a professor of Indian anthropology who's conveniently both female and attractive (Barbara Hershey). The script isn't sharp enough to overcome the implausible premise. **JC** **DVD**

Tom Berenger *Lewis Gates* • Barbara Hershey *Professor Lillian Sloan* • Kurtwood Smith *Sheriff Deegan* • Andrew Miller *Briggs* • Steve Reevis *Yellow Wolf* • Wilford Brimley *Narrator* ■ *Dir/Scr* Tab Murphy

The Last of the Fast Guns ★★★ U

Western 1958 · US · Colour · 81min

Veteran director George Sherman brings his eye for environment and sureness of touch to this lively western. Hired by Carl Benton Reid to find his missing brother Eduard Franz, Jock Mahoney struts through northern Mexico with admirable purpose, countering the threat posed by Reid's grasping partner, Gilbert Roland (who stands to assume sole control of their business if Mahoney fails), with square-jawed efficiency. **DP**

Jock Mahoney *Brad Ellison* • Gilbert Roland *Miles Lang* • Linda Cristal *Maria O'Reilly* • Eduard Franz *Padre Jose* • Lorne Greene *Michael O'Reilly* • Carl Benton Reid *John Forbes* ■ *Dir* George Sherman • *Scr* David P Harmon

The Last of the Good Old Days ★★★★

Comedy 1989 · Cz · Colour · 97min

With a blend of bedroom farce and socio-political allegory that recalls Jean Renoir's *La Règle du Jeu*, this is a deliciously barbed satire on the Czech ruling elite. With aristocrats and their domestics siding against the bourgeoisie and the bureaucrats, this inter-war country house comedy bristles with class conflict as self-made slob Marian Labuda tries to keep his innocent daughter away from indolent duke Josef Abrham. Wittily scripted by Jirí Blazek and shot in autumnal hues to suggest the passage of an era, this superbly acted period piece is hugely enjoyable. **DP** In Czech.

Josef Abrham *Duke Alexei* • Marian Labuda *Josef Stoklasa* • Jaromir Hanzlik *Bernard Spera, the Librarian* • Rudolf Hrusinsky *Jakub Lhota* ■ *Dir* Jirí Menzel • *Scr* Jiri Blazek, from a novel by Vladislav Vancura

Last of the High Kings ★★ 15

Comedy drama 1996 · Ire/UK/Den · Colour · 100min

This pleasant, if unremarkable, rites-of-passage drama revolves around the growing pains of Dublin lad Jared Leto as he tries to cope with being a descendant of Celtic Kings. His wacky family includes an overly mothering mother and a virtually unseen father (Gabriel Byrne) who communicates from America in Shakespearean couplets. When Christina Ricci arrives for the summer holidays, virginity-loss becomes a top agenda item. Set in the 1970s, the film is stolen by Stephen Rea in a small cameo as a know-it-all taxi driver, while Leto rather overdoes the cute confusion. **AJ** Some swearing, a sex scene.

Catherine O'Hara *Cathleen* • Jared Leto *Frankie Griffin* • Christina Ricci *Erin* • Gabriel Byrne *Jack Griffin* • Stephen Rea *Cab driver* • Colm Meaney *Jim Davern* • Lorraine Pilkington *Jayne Wayne* • Emily Mortimer *Romy* ■ *Dir* David Keating • *Scr* David Keating, Gabriel Byrne, from the novel by Ferdia MacAnna

Last of the Mobile Hot-Shots ★★

Drama 1970 · US · Colour · 107min

One of Sidney Lumet's lesser-known works, this trip into Tennessee Williams territory ultimately fails to live up to its promise. However, it is still worth a look for the talent alone. The script, based on Williams's play *The Seven Descents of Myrtle*, was co-written by Gore Vidal, while the interesting cast is headed up by James Coburn and Lynn Redgrave. (Released in the UK as *Blood Kin*.) **JF**

Lynn Redgrave *Myrtle* • Robert Hooks *Chicken* • Perry Hayes *George* • Reggie King *Rube* • James Coburn *Jeb* ■ *Dir* Sidney Lumet • *Scr* Gore Vidal, Mark Valenti, from the play *The Seven Descents of Myrtle* by Tennessee Williams

The Last of the Mohicans ★★★★★

Silent period adventure 1920 · US · BW · 74min

This silent adaptation of James Fenimore Cooper's famous story was the masterpiece of Maurice Tourneur, the French-born director and father of Jacques. It has visuals to die for and some of the most ferocious massacre scenes ever filmed. Yet human values are never sacrificed in this story of an Indian scout, the last survivor of the Mohican tribe, escorting two girls through perilous territory. The picture has a ruggedness to make pulses beat faster and a poignancy that touches the heart, while the ending is starkly tragic. Tourneur makes this special – despite being forced by an accident to share directorial duties with Clarence Brown. Watch for Boris Karloff in an early role. **TH**

Wallace Beery *Magua* • Barbara Bedford *Cora Munro* • Albert Roscoe *Uncas* • Lillian Hall *Alice Munro* • Harry Lorraine *Hawkeye, a scout* • Theodore Lerch *Chingachgook* • Henry Woodward *Major Heyward* • James Gordon *Colonel Munro* • George Hackathorne *Captain Randolph* • Nelson McDowell *David Gamut* • Boris Karloff *Marauding Indian* ■ *Dir* Maurice Tourneur, Clarence Brown • *Scr* Robert A Dillon, from the novel by James Fenimore Copper

The Last of the Mohicans ★★★

Period adventure 1936 · US · BW · 91min

Though not a patch on the 1920 or 1992 versions, this is an honest attempt at filming the James Fenimore Cooper classic. Randolph Scott makes a strapping Hawkeye, but Robert Barrat is ill-cast as Chingachgook, the native American of the title. The action sequences are remarkably well-staged by director George B Seitz. **TS**

Randolph Scott *Hawkeye* • Binnie Barnes *Alice Munro* • Heather Angel *Cora Munro* • Hugh Buckler *Colonel Munro* • Henry Wilcoxon *Major Duncan Heyward* • Robert Barrat *Chingachgook* ■ *Dir* George B Seitz • *Scr* Philip Dunne, John Balderston, Paul Perez, Daniel Moore, from the novel by James Fenimore Cooper

The Last of the Mohicans ★★★★ 15

Period adventure 1992 · US · Colour · 107min

In an exciting mix of high adventure, romance and history lesson, Daniel Day-Lewis stars as Hawkeye, the frontiersman raised by Mohicans who gets caught between cultures when he falls for Madeleine Stowe. In the ensuing bloody battles, he refuses to give up his tribe's cause, or his love. Directed by Michael Mann, the well-staged action sequences and his grandiose sense of scale combine to produce an epic that harks back to the good old-fashioned adventure films of Hollywood's heyday. **AJ** **DVD BL**

Daniel Day-Lewis *Hawkeye* • Madeleine Stowe *Cora Munro* • Russell Means *Chingachgook* • Eric Schweig *Uncas* • Jodhi May *Alice Munro* • Steven Waddington *Major Duncan Heyward* • Wes Studi *Magua* • Maurice Roëves *Colonel Edmund Munro* • Patrice Chéreau *General Montcalm* • Mark A Baker *Colonial man* ■ *Dir* Michael Mann • *Scr* Michael Mann, Christopher Crowe, from the 1936 film, from the novel by James Fenimore Cooper • *Cinematographer* Dante Spinotti

The Last of the Unjust ★★★★

Documentary 2013 · Fr/Austria · Colour · 220min

Returning to the Holocaust for the fourth time since his monumental 1985 documentary *Shoah*, 87-year-old Claude Lanzmann draws on unused footage of a 1975 interview in Rome with Viennese rabbi Benjamin Murmelstein to assess his role as the sole surviving member of the Jewish Council installed by the Nazis to help run the Theresienstadt ghetto camp. Having been acquitted of collaboration by a Prague court, Murmelstein knows he is a divisive figure and Lanzmann presses him hard about his relationship with Adolf Eichmann, the architect of the Final Solution. **DP** German, French, English +subtitles.

Benjamin Murmelstein • Claude Lanzmann *Interviewer* ■ *Dir* Claude Lanzmann

Last Orders ★★★★ 15

Drama 2001 · UK/Ger · Colour · 105min

A meditative Booker Prize-winning novel (by Graham Swift) told through multiple interior monologues should have been a tough one to adapt for the screen. But Australian writer/director Fred Schepisi has done a sterling job, assembling a dream cast to flesh out this deceptively simple, 1980s-set tale of four friends – Bob Hoskins, Ray Winstone, Tom Courtenay, David Hemmings, all on peak form – heading from London to Margate to scatter the ashes of a fifth (Michael Caine, seen in intelligently interwoven flashback). Not only is *Last*

L

Orders a touching and perceptive drama about the war generation, it's also a moving and funny road movie about friendship, deceit and loss. AC Swearing. *DVD*

Michael Caine *Jack Dodds* • Bob Hoskins *Ray "Lucky" Johnson* • Tom Courtenay *Vic Tucker* • David Hemmings *Lenny Tate* • Ray Winstone *Vince Dodds* • Helen Mirren *Amy* ■ *Dir* Fred Schepisi • *Scr* Fred Schepisi, from the novel by Graham Swift

The Last Outlaw ★★★
Western 1936 · US · BW · 72min

The great John Ford directed a short, silent version of this story in 1919 and his screenplay forms the basis of director Christy Cabanne's lively comedy western. Ford's influence further pervades the work as it stars his favourite actor, Harry Carey, as the eponymous bank robber. He plays an old-time outlaw who's been in prison for 25 years and, unsurprisingly, has trouble in adjusting to the modern West when he returns home to see a daughter he's never met. BB

Harry Carey *Dean Payton* • Hoot Gibson *Chuck Wilson* • Tom Tyler *Al Goss* • Henry B Walthall *Under Sheriff Calvin Yates* • Margaret Callahan *Sally Mason* ■ *Dir* Christy Cabanne • *Scr* John Twist, Jack Townley, from a story by John Ford, E Murray Campbell

The Last Outlaw ★★15
Western 1993 · US · Colour · 89min

Kiwi director Geoff Murphy followed up the success of *Young Guns II* with another stab at the western genre. A ridiculously coiffeured Mickey Rourke is left for dead by his gang of outlaws, so he hooks up with the local sheriff to gain his revenge. Rourke's performance is as outlandish as his hair, but the rest of the cast is a tad more convincing, while Murphy's no-nonsense direction keeps things at a rollicking pace. JF *DVD*

Mickey Rourke *Graff* • Dermot Mulroney *Eustis* • Ted Levine *Potts* • John C McGinley *Wills* • Steve Buscemi *Philo* • Keith David *Lovecraft* ■ *Dir* Geoff Murphy • *Scr* Eric Red

The Last Outpost ★★
First World War drama 1935 · US · BW · 70min

This teaming of Cary Grant and Claude Rains is a far cry from their later brilliance in Hitchcock's *Notorious*, although in both films Grant is in love with Rains's wife. Set in Africa during the First World War, this earlier movie combines action scenes with amorous rivalry that drives Rains to plot Grant's murder. Gertrude Michael plays the woman in the triangle. Originally directed by Louis Gasnier, then largely reshot by Charles Barton. AE

Cary Grant *Michael Andrews* • Gertrude Michael *Rosemary Haydon* • Claude Rains *John Stevenson* • Margaret Swope *Nurse Rowland* • Jameson Thomas *Cullen* • Colin Tapley *Lieutenant Prescott* • Akim Tamiroff *Mirov* ■ *Dir* Louis Gasnier, Charles Barton • *Scr* Philip MacDonald, from the short story *The Drum* by F Britten Austen, adapted by Frank Partos, Charles Brackett

The Last Party ★★★
Documentary 1993 · US · Colour · 96min

Most definitely not your typical Robert Downey Jr film. Downey is the host for a heavily satirical documentary that takes a tongue-in-cheek look at the 1992 race for the US Presidency. And one suspects he may have used his heavy-duty Hollywood clout to rope in the famous names and faces who help him trawl his non-comprehending way through the complex workings of the Republican and Democratic conventions. Unrated and little seen, probably because America is a little sensitive to its politicians being slyly sent up like this. A follow-up, *Last Party 2000*, appeared in 2001. DA

Robert Downey Jr *Host* ■ *Dir* Mark Benjamin, Marc Levin • *Scr* Marc Levin, Josh Richman, Donovan Leitch, Mark Benjamin

Last Passenger ★★★15
Action thriller 2013 · UK · Colour · 96min

Director Omid Nooshin handles this commuter-train variation on *Runaway Train* with admirable aplomb. Heading towards a yuletide night shift, widowed doctor Dougray Scott notices that all is not well aboard his train and, on discovering that it is hurtling towards its doom at Hastings, he enlists the help of his fellow travellers to try and avert a disaster. Less interested in the motives of the madman behind the mayhem than the mechanics of the survival schemes, Nooshin capably combines character insight with high-speed set pieces. But, while the performances are game, this lacks genuine spectacle and a palpable sense of dread. DP Swearing.

Dougray Scott *Lewis Shaler* • Kara Tointon *Sarah Barwell* • Iddo Goldberg *Jan Klimowski* • David Schofield *Peter Carmichael* • Lindsay Duncan *Elaine Middleton* • Joshua Kaynama *Max Shaler* ■ *Dir* Omid Nooshin • *Scr* Omid Nooshin, Andy Love

The Last Picture Show
★★★★★15
Classic drama 1971 · US · BW · 114min

Beautifully adapted by director Peter Bogdanovich and Larry McMurtry (from the latter's novel), this is a masterclass in how to create fully rounded characters and then give them real lives to lead. While the nostalgic elements of this memoir of small-town Texas in the 1950s are lovingly realised (a miraculous blend of John Ford and Howard Hawks), it's the re-creation of that long-lost sense of community, in which everyone knew and respected one another, that makes this such a rewarding experience. Jeff Bridges and Cybill Shepherd excel, but it's the playing of Timothy Bottoms, Ben Johnson and Cloris Leachman that gives the film its authenticity. A sequel, *Texasville*, eventually followed in 1990 and a director's cut was released in 2000 with an extra six minutes of footage. DP Violence, swearing, brief nudity. *DVD*

Timothy Bottoms *Sonny Crawford* • Jeff Bridges *Duane Jackson* • Cybill Shepherd *Jacy Farrow* • Ben Johnson (1) *Sam the Lion* • Cloris Leachman *Ruth Popper* • Ellen Burstyn *Lois Farrow* • Eileen Brennan *Genevieve* • Clu Gulager *Abilene* • Sam Bottoms *Billy* • Randy Quaid *Lester Marlow* ■ *Dir* Peter Bogdanovich • *Scr* Larry McMurtry, Peter Bogdanovich, from the novel by McMurtry

The Last Producer ★★15
Drama 2000 · US · Colour · 85min

Burt Reynolds mugs his way through this Tinseltown tat. A poor relation of *Get Shorty*, the story revolves around Reynolds's has-been producer, who lands himself in hot water with loan sharks and insurance crooks in a bid to secure the rights to a screenplay he's confidant will put him back on top. Yet it's the supporting cast that catches the eye. DP *DVD*

Burt Reynolds *Sonny Wexler* • Ann-Margret *Mira Wexler* • Benjamin Bratt *Damon Black* • Charles Durning *Syd Wolf* • Greg Germann *Reuben Tallridge* • Rod Steiger *Sherri Ganse* • Lauren Holly *Frances Chadway* • Sean Astin *Bo Pomerants* ■ *Dir* Burt Reynolds • *Scr* Clyde Hayes

The Last Remake of Beau Geste ★★★PG
Comedy 1977 · US · Colour · 80min

This scrappy but good-natured send-up of the oft-filmed desert yarn is directed by and stars the goggle-eyed surrealist comedian Marty Feldman. As a director, Feldman is ramshackle, and there are certain Python elements in the spoof that casts him with Michael York as brothers who search the Sahara for Ann-Margret and a missing diamond. Some of it works and a lot of it doesn't, but it's worth seeing for the virtual who's who of British comedy. Film buffs will like the sudden appearance of Feldman in the 1939 version with Gary Cooper. AT *DVD*

Ann-Margret *Flavia Geste* • Marty Feldman *Digby Geste* • Michael York *Beau Geste* • Peter Ustinov *Sergeant Markov* • James Earl Jones *Sheikh Abdul* • Trevor Howard *Sir Hector Geste* • Henry Gibson *General Pecheur* • Roy Kinnear *Corporal Boldini* • Spike Milligan *Crumble* • Terry-Thomas *Prison governor* • Irene Handl *Miss Wormwood* • Sinead Cusack *Isabel Geste* ■ *Dir* Marty Feldman • *Scr* Marty Feldman, Chris Allen, from a story by Sam Bobrick, from the novel by PC Wren

Last Resort ★★★★15
Drama 2000 · UK · Colour · 73min

Documentarist Pawel Pawlikowski thoroughly merited his Bafta for this second foray into fictional film. It's the gnawing sense of realism here that makes Russian emigrant Dina Korzun's plight all the more distressing. Arriving in the UK, she's detained in a holding centre, after being disowned by her fiancé. Korzun is equally misused by bureaucrats and internet pornographers as she tries to build a new life for herself and son, Artiom Strelnikov. With amusement arcade attendant Paddy Considine providing humour and humanity, this is a powerful indictment of political hypocrisy and everyday indifference. DP *DVD*

Dina Korzun *Tanya* • Paddy Considine *Alfie* • Artiom Strelnikov *Artiom* • Lindsay Honey *Les* • Perry Benson *Immigration officer* • Katie Drinkwater *Katie* ■ *Dir* Pawel Pawlikowski • *Scr* Pawel Pawlikowski, Rowan Joffe • *Cinematographer* Ryszard Lenczewski

The Last Ride ★★12
Action drama 2004 · US · Colour · 81min

The cars take centre stage in this slick and energetic action drama, made from a story co-written by *The Fast and The Furious* director Rob Cohen. It plays like an extended commercial for Pontiac GTOs, interrupted by a predictable revenge scenario involving ex-con Dennis Hopper's obsession with getting even with the cop who nailed him (Fred Ward). Nonetheless, Hopper shines in his customarily outlandish way and brings surprising emotional depth amid the tyre-screeching chase sequences. SF *DVD*

Dennis Hopper *Ronnie Purnell* • Will Patton *Aaron Purnell* • Fred Ward *Darryl Kurtz* • Nadine Velazquez *JJ Cruz* • Chris Carmack *Matthew* • Deena Dill *Kate Purnell* ■ *Dir* Guy Norman Bee • *Scr* Ron McGee, from a story by McGee, Rob Cohen

Last Rites ★18
Thriller 1988 · US · Colour · 103min

This misfiring thriller marks one of the lowest points in Tom Berenger's career. He stars as a Catholic priest caught up in a totally bewildering plot revolving around murder and the Mafia. Poor writing, direction and acting must have left Berenger (Oscar-nominated for his role in Oliver Stone's *Platoon* two years earlier) wondering how he got talked into this one. NF Violence, swearing.

Tom Berenger *Father Michael Pace* • Daphne Zuniga *Angela* • Chick Vennera *Nuzo* • Anne Twomey *Zena Pace* • Dane Clark *Carlo Pace* • Paul Dooley *Father Freddie* ■ *Dir/Scr* Donald P Bellisario

Last Rites ★★★15
Psychological thriller 1998 · US · Colour · 83min

Randy Quaid turns on the chilling charm in this smart made-for-TV thriller. He plays a killer on death row who survives his date with death, thanks to a timely bolt of lightning striking the prison. Awaking the next morning, he has no memory of his murderous past and it is up to shrink Embeth Davidtz to work out whether he is telling the truth and whether his newly-acquired "psychic" powers are genuine. Director Kevin Dowling has fun spinning out the mind games and the result is gripping. JF

Randy Quaid *Jeremy Dillon* • Embeth Davidtz *Dr Lauren Riggs* • A Martinez *Matt* • Clarence Williams III *Warden Pierce* • Paul Benjamin *Fez* • Jack Coleman *Gary Blake* ■ *Dir* Kevin Dowling • *Scr* Tim Frost, from a story by Richard Outten

The Last Run ★★★★18
Crime drama 1971 · US · Colour · 91min

John Huston started this thriller but quit after three weeks; a natural enmity between him and George C Scott and an awful lot of booze led to him being replaced by Richard Fleischer. The result, though, is marvellous, with Scott playing a lonely, burned-out gangster who agrees to do one last job – driving Spain's most wanted man and his girlfriend to the border, with the Mob and the police in pursuit. It's a riveting story, with Scott playing to perfection a man staring fate straight between the eyes. The Spanish landscape is superbly captured, and the score is particularly haunting. AT

George C Scott *Harry Garmes* • Tony Musante *Paul Ricard* • Colleen Dewhurst *Monique* ■ *Dir* Richard Fleischer • *Scr* Alan Sharp • *Cinematographer* Sven Nykvist • *Music* Jerry Goldsmith

The Last Safari ★★
Action adventure 1967 · UK · Colour · 110min

Stewart Granger, recalling his heyday in *King Solomon's Mines*, is a former white hunter who loathes the tourists he shows around the bush. One such tourist is top-billed Kaz Garas (plucked from American TV) and his mistress, Gabriella Licudi, who discover that Stewart is haunted by the death of his best pal under the feet of an elephant. Shot in Kenya and full of travelogue sequences, it squanders any drama in the story, while the location photography is undermined by some eye-jarring process shots. AT

Kaz Garas *Casey* • Stewart Granger *Miles Gilchrist* • Gabriella Licudi *Grant* • Johnny Sekka *Jama* • Liam Redmond *Alec Beaumont* ■ *Dir* Henry Hathaway • *Scr* John Gay, from the novel *Gilligan's Last Elephant* by Gerald Hanley

The Last Samurai ★★★★15
Period action drama 2003 · US · Colour · 147min

Edward Zwick's sweeping action drama set in the 19th century charts a poignant personal odyssey prompted by the clash of old and new cultures. Tom Cruise plays a disillusioned US captain hired by the young Japanese emperor to train the country's first modern, conscript army. After leading an inadequate campaign against the samurai warriors, the military man is captured by these alleged national enemies who teach him to reassess his beliefs and values. An epic movie in every way, the beautifully shot tale features a strong storyline, robust performances and spine-tingling, violent battle sequences. It suffers only from being overly idealistic and occasionally stereotypical. SF English, Japanese +subtitles. Violence. *DVD* *Blu-ray*

Tom Cruise *Captain Nathan Algren* • Timothy Spall *Simon Graham* • Billy Connolly *Sergeant Zebulon Gant* • Tony Goldwyn *Colonel Benjamin Bagley* • Ken Watanabe *Katsumoto* • Hiroyuki Sanada *Ujio* • Koyuki *Taka* • Shichinosuke Nakamura *Emperor Meiji* ■ *Dir* Edward Zwick • *Scr* John Logan, Marshall Herskovitz, Edward Zwick, from the story by John Logan

The Last Seduction
★★★★18
Thriller 1993 · US · Colour · 105min

John Dahl secured his reputation as one of the hottest directors of the 1990s with this bitter and twisted excursion into neon-shaded contemporary *film noir*. At its commanding centre is sizzling and smouldering Linda Fiorentino in a star-making role as the man-eating *femme fatale* from hell. A gorgeous go-getter, she swaps dirty talk for dirty deeds when she cons husband Bill Pullman into doing a big drugs deal, only to run off with the money. Hiding out in a small town, the manipulative mantrap seduces besotted insurance agent Peter Berg into carrying out her every whim. Pulp fiction rarely comes as well appointed or as absorbingly clever. AJ Violence, swearing, sex scenes, nudity. *DVD* *Blu-ray*

L

The Last Seduction 2 ★★ 18
Romantic crime thriller
1998 · UK/US · Colour · 94min

This dull, irrelevant sequel follows one of the hippest, sexiest *films noirs* of the last three decades. Joan Severance steps into Linda Fiorentino's stilettos as the murderous ice maiden, who, finding the US too hot for her, heads for Barcelona and sets her sights on violent Irish crook Con O'Neill. However, on her tail is private eye Beth Goddard, who is not above using her own feminine wiles to nab her prey. JF Swearing, sex scenes, violence. **DVD**

Joan Severance *Bridget Gregory* • Beth Goddard *Murphy* • Con O'Neill *Troy Fenton* • Rocky Taylor *Gabriel* • Dean Williamson *Earl McLaughlin* ■ *Dir* Terry Marcel • *Scr* Dave Cummings

The Last September
★★★ 15
Period drama   1999 · UK/Ire/Fr · Colour · 98min

Theatre director Deborah Warner has rounded up a company of stellar British talent for this stylised depiction of the decline of English power in Ireland after the 1916 Easter rising. Maggie Smith and Michael Gambon are superlatively arch as aristocrats hosting relentless house parties and family gatherings despite the unrest, while Keeley Hawes plays the wayward niece whose rejection of an English soldier in favour of an Irish anarchist ultimately leads to tragedy. Slow and studied, Warner's film debut shows flashes of inspiration despite an innate theatricality that at times appears ridiculous and unreal. LH

Maggie Smith *Lady Myra* • Michael Gambon *Sir Richard Naylor* • Jane Birkin *Francie Montmorency* • Fiona Shaw *Marda Norton* • Lambert Wilson *Hugo Montmorency* • David Tennant *Captain Gerald Colthurst* • Richard Roxburgh *Daventry* • Keeley Hawes *Lois Farquar* ■ *Dir* Deborah Warner • *Scr* John Banville, from a novel by Elizabeth Bowen

The Last Seven
★ 18
Mystery thriller 2010 · UK · Colour · 83min

A man wakes up in a deserted London and joins a motley bunch of individuals in trying to figure out just what's going on in this low-budget British puzzler. The slow build-up really drags, with sundry less-than-gifted actors (among them leading man Simon Phillips) trudging around London's financial district and delivering clunky dialogue. Hard man Tamer Hassan is on uncharacteristically subdued form as a soldier, while his frequent co-star Danny Dyer contributes little except supposed marquee value with a sinister cameo. TJ Violence. **DVD**

Tamer Hassan *Jack Mason* • Simon Phillips *William Blake* • Danny Dyer *Angel of Death* • Sebastian Street *Robert Kendrick* • Daisy Head *Chloe* • Ronan Vibert *Isaac* ■ *Dir* Imran Naqvi • *Scr* John Stanley

The Last Shot
★★★ 15
Comedy crime caper 2004 · US · Colour · 93min

Catch Me If You Can screenwriter Jeff Nathanson made his directorial debut with this slight but frothy crime caper. "Inspired" by a true story, the self-penned comedy sees FBI man Alec Baldwin posing as a movie producer as part of a sting to bring down gangster Tony Shalhoub. What follows is an amusing though underdeveloped satire of the Hollywood system, as Baldwin agrees to bankroll the latest project of struggling scriptwriter Matthew Broderick. The duo's easy-going chemistry keeps the quirky feature buoyant, even during occasional plot lulls, while fun support from the likes of Ray Liotta as Baldwin's brother and Toni Collette as a diva adds extra bite and vibrancy. SF Violence, swearing, brief nudity. **DVD**

Matthew Broderick *Steven Schats* • Alec Baldwin *Joe Devine* • Toni Collette *Emily French* • Tony Shalhoub *Tommy Sanz* • Calista Flockhart *Valerie Weston* • Tim Blake Nelson *Marshal Paris* • Ray Liotta *Jack Devine* • Joan Cusack *Fanny Nash* ■ *Dir* Jeff Nathanson • *Scr* Jeff Nathanson, from an article by Steve Fishman

The Last Song
★★★ PG
Drama   2010 · US · Colour · 103min

Summer at her father's beach house proves something of a learning experience for a restless teenage girl in this coming-of-age tale, which sees *Hannah Montana* star Miley Cyrus take on more of an adult role. Nicholas Sparks's adaptation of his bestselling novel certainly keeps her on her toes, what with repairing broken relations with estranged dad Greg Kinnear (impeccable, as ever), saving nesting turtles and embarking on a turbulent romance with wealthy hunk Liam Hemsworth. Ms Cyrus is evidently more comfortable playing the pouty adolescent than responding to the full-on melodrama thrown at her by the story, but the film can't be faulted for trying to take its star and her junior female fanbase out of their comfort zone. TJ **DVD** Blu

Miley Cyrus [Miley Ray Cyrus] *Veronica "Ronnie" Miller* • Greg Kinnear *Steve Miller* • Bobby Coleman *Jonah Miller* • Liam Hemsworth *Will Blakelee* • Hallock Beals *Scott* • Kelly Preston *Kim Miller* ■ *Dir* Julie Anne Robinson • *Scr* Nicholas Sparks, Jeff Van Wie, from Sparks's novel

The Last Stage
★★★★
War drama based on a true story
1947 · Pol · BW · 105min

One of the first postwar films made about the Holocaust, Wanda Jakubowska's masterpiece is all the more arresting because of its studied naturalism. As both the director and her co-scenarist, Gerda Schneider, had survived the horrors of Auschwitz, there's a dreadful authenticity to this memoir of a hospital interpreter who ministered to so many women during the final hours of their lives. This is a film devoid of easy emotion and cheap correctness. Instead, events are presented with a chilling normality that suggests the sort of detachment that enabled prisoners to bear the enormity of living with genocide. DP Polish +subtitles.

Barbara Drapinska *Marthe* • Wanda Bartowna *Helene* • Tatiana Gorecka *Eugenie* • Antonina Gorecka *Anna* • Huguette Faget *Michele* • Alina Janowska *Dessa* ■ *Dir* Wanda Jakubowska • *Scr* Wanda Jakubowska, Gerda Schneider

The Last Stand
★★★ 15
Action thriller   2013 · US · Colour · 102min

Arnold Schwarzenegger takes on his first lead role for ten years here, having retired as governor of California. He stars as former LA narcotics squad detective Ray Owens, who's coasting towards retirement as the sheriff of a sleepy town near the border with Mexico. Until the boss of a drugs cartel (Eduardo Noriega) escapes from FBI custody and heads his way. Director Kim Jee-woon ticks just about every box long-term Arnie fans will want ticked, while Schwarzenegger gamely mocks his own action-hero persona. Johnny Knoxville provides abundant comic relief as the misfit owner of an artillery museum who's drafted in to help save the day. TeS Violence, swearing. **DVD** Blu

Arnold Schwarzenegger *Sheriff Ray Owens* • Forest Whitaker *Agent John Bannister* • Johnny Knoxville *Lewis Dinkum* • Rodrigo Santoro *Frank Martinez* • Jaimie Alexander *Sarah Torrance* • Luis Guzmán [Luis Guzman] *Mike Figueroa* • Eduardo Noriega *Gabriel Cortez* • Peter Stormare *Burrell* • Harry Dean Stanton *Mr Parsons* ■ *Dir* Kim Jee-woon [Kim Ji-woon] • *Scr* Andrew Knauer

The Last Starfighter
★★★ PG
Science-fiction adventure
1984 · US · Colour · 96min

Lance Guest's prowess at video games is monitored by emissaries from the Star League of the future, who recruit him to defend the universe from evil invaders in this glossy, space-age fairy tale. While highly derivative *Star Trek*-like aliens mix with *Star Wars*-inspired dog-fights against a computer-graphic backdrop, the sensitive love story between Guest and Catherine Mary Stewart cuts through the cuteness and gives the adventures a boost. AJ Violence, swearing.

Lance Guest *Alex Rogan* • Dan O'Herlihy *Grig* • Catherine Mary Stewart *Maggie Gordon* • Barbara Bosson *Jane Rogan* • Norman Snow *Xur* • Robert Preston *Centauri* • Kay E Kuter *Enduran* • Chris Hebert *Louis Rogan* ■ *Dir* Nick Castle • *Scr* Jonathan Betuel

The Last Station
★★ 15
Biographical drama
2009 · Ger/Rus/UK · Colour · 107min

This true-story drama about Leo Tolstoy's final days boasts a fascinating premise and a fine cast, but ends up delivering less than the sum of its parts. Christopher Plummer looks great as the Russian writer, complete with peasant's garb and flowing, white beard. The sparks fly between him and Helen Mirren as Countess Sofya Tolstoy as they argue violently over the posthumous rights to his works. Their scenes have the energy of a Russian *Who's Afraid of Virginia Woolf?*, but Michael Hoffman's direction lacks the inspiration his stars and his subject clearly have in spades. BP Swearing, sex scenes, nudity. **DVD** Blu

Helen Mirren *Sofya Tolstoy* • Christopher Plummer *Leo Tolstoy* • James McAvoy *Valentin Bulgakov* • Paul Giamatti *Vladimir Chertkov* • Anne-Marie Duff *Sasha Tolstoy* • Kerry Condon *Masha* ■ *Dir* Michael Hoffman • *Scr* Michael Hoffman, from the novel by Jay Parini

Last Summer
★★★★
Psychological drama 1969 · US · Colour · 96min

Talented Frank Perry directs this unnerving teenage odyssey, which contains some of the finest youth performances in American film. Barbara Hershey excels as the sadistic young tease, responsible for creating a jealousy with brutal and tragic consequences, and the performances Perry elicited from the boys Richard Thomas and Bruce Davison helped them to sterling careers after this movie. Oscar-nominated Catherine Burns proved harder to cast later on, but her brilliant acting illuminates this film. A brave, unsentimental, ultimately callous rites-of-passage movie. TS

Barbara Hershey *Sandy* • Richard Thomas *Peter* • Bruce Davison *Dan* • Cathy Burns [Catherine Burns] *Rhoda* • Ernesto Gonzalez *Anibal* • Ralph Waite *Peter's father* • Peter Turgeon *Mr Caudell* ■ *Dir* Frank Perry • *Scr* Eleanor Perry, from the novel by Evan Hunter

Last Summer in the Hamptons
★★★ 15
Comedy drama   1995 · US · Colour · 107min

In this bittersweet comedy, a matriarch gathers together her theatrical family for a swan song retreat at their doomed Long Island summer house. Independent writer/director Henry Jaglom's talkfest indulges three generations of thespian intellectuals motivated by an undiluted need to articulate neurosis, self-doubt and desire, and the result is very entertaining. While Jaglom lacks the visual wit and cheeky detachment of Woody Allen, he still concocts a steady stream of tickling episodes. DO Swearing.

Victoria Foyt *Oona Hart* • Viveca Lindfors *Helena Mora* • Jon Robin Baitz *Jake Axelrod* • Melissa Leo *Trish Axelrod* • Martha Plimpton *Chloe Garfield* • Holland Taylor *Davis Mora Axelrod* • Ron Rifkin *Eli Garfield* • Roddy McDowall *Thomas* • Roscoe Lee Browne *Freddy* • André Gregory [Andre Gregory] *Ivan Axelrod* • Henry Jaglom *Max Berger* ■ *Dir* Henry Jaglom • *Scr* Henry Jaglom, Victoria Foyt

The Last Sunset
★★★ 12
Western   1961 · US · Colour · 107min

Multilayered and superbly cast, this incorporates themes not usually found in westerns, or in many other American movies of the period, notably incest and suicide. Under the heavy hand of *Dirty Dozen* director Robert Aldrich, this Freud-on-the-range saga doesn't quite come off, but the magnificent cast ensures that the film is not just for fans of the genre – Rock Hudson and Kirk Douglas are at ease in the saddle and a joy to watch. Carol Lynley is excellent as a gal brought up on a savage frontier. TS **DVD**

Rock Hudson *Dana Stribling* • Kirk Douglas *Brendan O'Malley* • Dorothy Malone *Belle Breckenridge* • Joseph Cotten *John Breckenridge* • Carol Lynley *Missy Breckenridge* • Neville Brand *Frank Hobbs* • Regis Toomey *Milton Wing* • Rad Fulton *Julesburg Kid* ■ *Dir* Robert Aldrich • *Scr* Dalton Trumbo, from the novel *Sundown at Crazy Horse* by Howard Rigsby

The Last Supper
★★★
Religious drama   1976 · Cub · Colour · 112min

This allegory of "Christian liberalism", as the Cuban director Tomás Gutiérrez Alea describes it, has much in common with Luis Buñuel's *Viridiana* in its context and caustic wit. A plantation owner decides to re-create the Last Supper, casting 12 of his slaves as the Apostles, but the situation turns nasty. Filmed in muted colours with a powerful black cast, the picture belabours its message. RB Spanish +subtitles.

Nelson Villagra *Count* • Silvano Rey *Chaplain* • Luis Alberto Garcia *Don Manuel* • José Antonio Rodriguez *Don Gaspar* • Samuel Claxton *Sebastian* • Mario Balmaseda *Martin Sanchez* ■ *Dir* Tomás Gutiérrez Alea • *Scr* Tomás Gutiérrez Alea, Tomás Gonzalez, Maria Eugenia Haya

The Last Supper
★★★ 15
Black comedy   1995 · US · Colour · 87min

Five liberal students serve poisoned alcohol to a collection of bigoted extremists in this entertaining but insubstantial black comedy. It could be an intriguing, double-edged premise – are Cameron Diaz, Ron Eldard and the rest any less twisted than their victims? – but Dan Rosen's script presents the culinary vigilantes in purely one-dimensional terms. By far the movie's strongest features are its various dinner guests, particularly racist trucker Bill Paxton (the first victim), male chauvinist Mark Harmon and homophobic priest Charles Durning. JC Violence, swearing, sex scenes. **DVD**

Cameron Diaz *Jude* • Ron Eldard *Pete* • Annabeth Gish *Paulie* • Jonathan Penner *Marc* • Courtney B Vance *Luke* • Jason Alexander *Anti-environmentalist* • Nora Dunn *Sheriff Stanley* • Charles Durning *Reverend Gerald Hutchens* • Mark Harmon *Dominant Male* • Bill Paxton *Zack* ■ *Dir* Stacy Title • *Scr* Dan Rosen

Last Tango in Paris
★★★★★ 18
Drama   1972 · It/Fr · Colour · 123min

Bernardo Bertolucci's still controversial psychodrama blazed new cinematic frontiers in the way sex was treated on screen. Artfully shot, it's the steamy and thought-provoking tale of the intense love affair that ignites between two strangers. Marlon Brando is trying to get over his wife's suicide, Maria Schneider is about to marry, and both cling to their anonymous liaisons in order to separate their sexual desires from their oppressive daily realities. More existential than erotic, this brilliant study of a broken, tortured man allows Brando to deliver a devastating performance. Gato Barbieri's marvellous jazz score creates a delirious atmosphere, conducive to the breaking of taboos. AJ English, French +subtitles. Swearing, sex scenes, nudity. **DVD** Blu

Marlon Brando *Paul* • Maria Schneider *Jeanne* • Jean-Pierre Léaud *Tom* • Catherine Allégret *Catherine* ■ *Dir* Bernardo Bertolucci • *Scr* Bernardo Bertolucci, Franco Arcalli • *Cinematographer* Vittorio Storaro

The Last Temptation of Christ
★★★★ 18
Religious drama   1988 · US · Colour · 156min

Ignore all the controversy and see Martin Scorsese's moving adaptation of Nikos Kazantzakis's novel for what it is – a challenging essay on the life of Jesus had he ignored his divine destiny and chosen to pursue human aims instead. Certainly

U SUITABLE FOR ALL   **Uc** SUITABLE ESPECIALLY FOR YOUNG CHILDREN (DVD ONLY)   **PG** PARENTAL GUIDANCE   **12A** UNDER 12s TO BE ACCOMPANIED (CINEMA ONLY)

neither blasphemous nor offensive, Scorsese's re-creation of the biblical milieu is highly evocative and the all-star performances are welcome modern reinterpretations of scripture stereotypes. It's slightly too long, and Scorsese does pull some punches in deference to the subject matter, but these are minor criticisms of what is a contentious but sincere work that merits reappraisal. AJ *DVD* *BD*

Willem Dafoe *Jesus Christ* • Harvey Keitel *Judas Iscariot* • Barbara Hershey *Mary Magdalene* • Harry Dean Stanton *Saul/Paul* • David Bowie *Pontius Pilate* • Verna Bloom *Mary, mother of Jesus* • Andre Gregory *John the Baptist* • Juliette Caton *Girl angel* • Roberts Blossom *Aged master* • Irvin Kershner *Zebedee* ■ *Dir* Martin Scorsese • *Scr* Paul Schrader, from the novel *The Last Temptation* by Nikos Kazantzakis

The Last Thakur ★★★ 15

Drama   2008 · UK/Ban/Swi · Colour · 79min

Atmosphere rather than narrative is the driving force behind this brooding Bangladeshi "western". A low-budget tale of corruption, rivalry and revenge, it unfolds in a contemporary rural town where two local grandees – Tariq Anam Khan's titular Hindu landlord and the venal Muslim chairman (Ahmed Rubel) – are bitterly feuding over territory. Enter an archetypically laconic gunman (Tanveer Hassan) with his own score to settle, and simmering tensions start coming to the boil. Director Sadik Ahmed proves impressively adept at mood, delivering an ambitious calling card with his observational approach and handsome, widescreen visuals. SF Bengali +subtitles. Violence, swearing. *DVD*

Tariq Anam Khan *Thakur* • Ahmed Rubel *Chairman* • Tanveer Hassan *Kala* • Anisur Rahman Milon *Tanju* ■ *Dir* Sadik Ahmed • *Scr* Sadik Ahmed, Heather Taylor

The Last Time I Committed Suicide ★★★ 15

Biographical drama   1996 · US · Colour · 93min

Beat Generation figure Neal Cassady was a restless spirit who provided friendship and inspiration to cultural icons Jack Kerouac and Ken Kesey. Thomas Jane captures Cassady's cool edginess and his sharp, self-aware narration adds much spirit to the rather laid-back, low-key story. This film's sticking point is the miscasting of Keanu Reeves, who is unconvincing as his irresponsible best friend. That said, director Stephen Kay's evocative, dimly-lit ambience and the jazzy soundtrack give the film a stylish vibe. JC Swearing. *DVD*

Thomas Jane *Neal Cassady* • Keanu Reeves *Harry* • Pat McNamara *Father Fletcher* • Kate Williamson *Nurse Waring* • Claire Forlani *Joan* • Gretchen Mol *Cherry Mary* ■ *Dir/Scr* Stephen Kay

The Last Time I Saw Paris ★★★ U

Romantic drama   1954 · US · Colour · 115min

In the hands of talented writer/director Richard Brooks this version of F Scott Fitzgerald's *Babylon Revisited* is remarkably faithful to the original's style and tone. It's also beautifully cast, with Elizabeth Taylor in her sublime prime as the tragic love of alcoholic writer Van Johnson. MGM lavished the best available talent on her and Fitzgerald's vision of Paris's "lost generation" is well captured. The second half reveals the weaknesses of the original, but this is still intelligent and glossy film-making. TS *DVD*

Elizabeth Taylor *Helen Ellsworth* • Van Johnson *Charles Wills* • Walter Pidgeon *James Ellsworth* • Donna Reed *Marion Ellsworth* • Eva Gabor *Lorraine Quarl* • Kurt Kasznar *Maurice* • Roger Moore *Paul* ■ *Dir* Richard Brooks • *Scr* Philip G Epstein, Julius J Epstein, Richard Brooks, from the story *Babylon Revisited* by F Scott Fitzgerald • *Cinematographer* Joseph Ruttenberg • *Costume Designer* Helen Rose • *Music* Conrad Salinger

The Last Train ★★

Drama   1972 · Fr · Colour · 95min

This drama is set during the Nazi invasion of France, with Jean-Louis Trintignant mislaying his wife in the rush to get the last train from Paris and then helping Romy Schneider by posing as her husband. They fall in love, and then Trintignant's real wife shows up with their child. This is a solidly made story, based on a Georges Simenon novel, that traces heavily on the then commercial appeal of its two glamorous stars. AT

Romy Schneider *Anna* • Jean-Louis Trintignant *Julien* • Maurice Biraud *Deserter* • Régine *Large woman* • Serge Marquand *Man* ■ *Dir* Pierre Granier-Deferre • *Scr* Pascal Jardin, from a novel by Georges Simenon

Last Train from Gun Hill ★★★★ 15

Western   1959 · US · Colour · 90min

This very fine adult western is made by the same team (including director John Sturges and producer Hal Wallis) that worked on *Gunfight at the OK Corral*, with Kirk Douglas again in a starring role. Here, Douglas is at his most intense as a man seeking revenge following the rape and murder of his wife. Anthony Quinn makes a tough adversary, and the rich Technicolor and VistaVision photography is exemplary. Intelligent, finely wrought and well cast. TS *DVD*

Kirk Douglas *Matt Morgan* • Anthony Quinn *Craig Belden* • Carolyn Jones *Linda* • Earl Holliman *Rick Belden* • Ziva Rodann *Catherine Morgan* • Brad Dexter *Beero* • Brian Hutton [Brian G Hutton] *Lee* ■ *Dir* John Sturges • *Scr* James Poe, from the story *Showdown* by Les Crutchfield

The Last Train from Madrid ★★★

Period war drama   1937 · US · BW · 85min

One of the first Hollywood movies to use the Spanish Civil War as background, this avoided taking sides, and was really an excuse to get a number of Paramount contract players together to tell various, rather feeble, stories. But for those who like train movies, an almost vanished genre, there is much to enjoy. Dorothy Lamour, in one of her few dramatic roles, heads a good cast including Lew Ayres, who was to become a conscientious objector during the war, an action which ruined his career. RB

Dorothy Lamour *Carmelita Castillo* • Lew Ayres *Bill Dexter* • Gilbert Roland *Eduardo De Soto* • Karen Morley *Helene Rafitte* • Lionel Atwill *Colonel Vigo* • Helen Mack *Lola* • Robert Cummings *Juan Ramos* ■ *Dir* James Hogan • *Scr* Louis Stevens, Robert Wyler, from a story by Paul Harvey Fox, Elsie Fox

The Last Tycoon ★★★★ 12

Period romantic drama   1976 · US · Colour · 117min

F Scott Fitzgerald's unfinished novel about Hollywood shows a studio boss, Monroe Stahr, in love with a young actress he spots on a film set. Stahr was based on MGM's Irving Thalberg and Robert De Niro plays him with all the personality of a paper cup, only coming alive when he's talking pictures, while the girl, Ingrid Boulting, is catatonic throughout. Yet this is all deliberate, allowing director Elia Kazan and scriptwriter Harold Pinter to explore the schism between the fantasy on the screen and the void in our lives. This approach led the film to critical and box-office doom. A pity, as it's a class act, with the strong cast bringing the edges of the story to vivid life. AT Swearing. *DVD*

Robert De Niro *Monroe Stahr* • Tony Curtis *Rodriguez* • Robert Mitchum *Pat Brady* • Jeanne Moreau *Didi* • Jack Nicholson *Brimmer* • Donald Pleasence *Boxley* • Ingrid Boulting *Kathleen Moore* • Ray Milland *Fleishacker* • Dana Andrews *Red Ridingwood* • Theresa Russell *Cecilia Brady* • Peter Strauss *Wylie* • John Carradine *Guide* • Anjelica Huston *Edna* ■ *Dir* Elia Kazan • *Scr* Harold Pinter, from the novel by F Scott Fitzgerald

The Last Unicorn ★★ U

Animated adventure   1980 · US · Colour · 88min

If it weren't for the lacklustre artwork, this animated fantasy might have been quite enchanting. The voices are top-notch and there's little wrong with Peter S Beagle's story, in which a brainy butterfly, a pirate cat, an apprentice wizard and a handsome prince join with a unicorn to help rescue her species. Younger viewers will probably forgive the flat animation, but the grown-ups are going to hate the tacky songs. DP *DVD*

Alan Arkin *Schmendrick the Magician* • Jeff Bridges *Prince Lir* • Mia Farrow *The Last Unicorn/Lady Amalthea* • Tammy Grimes *Molly Grue* • Robert Klein *The Butterfly* • Angela Lansbury *Mommy Fortuna* • Christopher Lee *King Haggard* • Keenan Wynn *Captain Cully* ■ *Dir* Arthur Rankin Jr, Jules Bass • *Scr* Peter S Beagle, from his novel

The Last Valley ★★★★ 15

Period drama   1971 · UK · Colour · 119min

This strange, ambitious and fascinating historical epic features mercenary soldier Michael Caine and scholar Omar Sharif, who discover a peaceful, hidden valley that's managed to avoid being ensnared in the Thirty Years War. What ensues in this Shangri-la is a debate about war, religion, the nature of the soul and the value of society – until something snaps when the swords come out to play and the stake is readied for a burning. Beautifully shot in Austria in 70mm, it contains one of Caine's very finest performances, a script that sidesteps pomposity and a marvellous score by John Barry. AT *DVD*

Michael Caine *The Captain* • Omar Sharif *Vogel* • Florinda Bolkan *Erica* • Nigel Davenport *Gruber* • Per Oscarsson *Father Sabastian* • Arthur O'Connell *Hoffman* • Madeline Hinde *Inge* • Yorgo Voyagis *Pirelli* • Christian Roberts *Andreas* ■ *Dir* James Clavell • *Scr* James Clavell, from the novel by JB Pick • *Cinematographer* John Wilcox

Last Vegas ★★★ 12

Comedy   2013 · US · Colour · 100min

Robert De Niro, Michael Douglas, Morgan Freeman and Kevin Kline form an attention-grabbing line-up in director Jon Turteltaub's geriatric take on *The Hangover*. It's just as well they have presence because that's all there is to sustain this flimsy story, in which Douglas's pensionable lothario finally decides to settle down – with a woman who could be his granddaughter. A few spats thicken the plot, and overall it's clear to see the guys are having a great time. So for all its laziness, it's impossible to hate this movie. SP *DVD* *BD*

Michael Douglas (1) *Billy* • Robert De Niro *Paddy* • Morgan Freeman *Archie* • Kevin Kline *Sam* • Mary Steenburgen *Diana* ■ *Dir* Jon Turteltaub • *Scr* Dan Fogelman

The Last Voyage ★★★

Disaster drama   1960 · US · Colour · 91min

Writer/director Andrew L Stone's speciality was filming on location; for this exciting melodrama, he purchased the liner *Ile de France* and put his stellar cast through its paces on her partially scuppered decks. It's exciting and well shot, with no visible studio footage at all. Robert Stack and Dorothy Malone head the cast, while George Sanders is excellent as the troubled captain. TS

Robert Stack *Cliff Henderson* • Dorothy Malone *Laurie Henderson* • George Sanders *Captain Robert Adams* • Edmond O'Brien *Second Engineer Walsh* • Woody Strode *Hank Lawson* • Jack Kruschen *Chief Engineer Pringle* • Tammy Marihugh *Jill Henderson* ■ *Dir/Scr* Andrew L Stone

The Last Wagon ★★★★ 12

Western   1956 · US · Colour · 95min

This smashing CinemaScope western deserves to be better known, directed by one of the relatively unsung masters of the genre, Delmer Daves. The ever-excellent Richard Widmark plays trapper Todd, a renegade forced to help wagon train survivors through hostile Apache territory, and he hardly speaks a word for the first half-hour of the movie. Daves's use of landscape is exemplary, with opening sequence crane shots that deserve to be ranked among the cinema's finest. TS *DVD*

Richard Widmark *Comanche Todd* • Felicia Farr *Jenny* • Susan Kohner *Jolie* • Tommy Rettig *Billy* • Stephanie Griffin *Valinda* • Ray Stricklyn *Clint* • Nick Adams *Ridge* • Carl Benton Reid *General Howard* ■ *Dir* Delmer Daves • *Scr* James Edward Grant, Delmer Daves, Gwen Bagni Gielgud, from a story by Gwen Bagni Gielgud

The Last Waltz ★★★★★ U

Music documentary   1978 · US · Colour · 112min

As one of the supervising editors of the remarkable rockumentary *Woodstock*, Martin Scorsese was the perfect choice of director for this stunning movie of The Band's farewell gig on Thanksgiving Day, 1976. Taking a break from shooting *New York, New York*, he nevertheless planned this film to the last detail during rehearsals and was well served by seven cameramen, including Michael Chapman, Vilmos Zsigmond and Laszlo Kovacs, whose pinpoint shots allow you to concentrate on the performances and the brilliant music. The guests are a *Who's Who* of electric folk and R&B, making this an unmissable slice of nostalgia and a masterpiece of pop cinema. DP *DVD*

■ *Dir* Martin Scorsese

The Last Warning ★★★

Silent mystery melodrama   1928 · US · BW · 87min

This part-talkie lacks the eerie atmosphere of Paul Leni's earlier hit *The Cat and the Canary*. Using a theatre set originally designed for Rupert Julian's 1925 version of *The Phantom of the Opera*, it relieves the occasionally histrionic acting with some shadowy photography and a couple of quaint effects. Leading lady Laura La Plante, understudy John Boles and producer Roy D'Arcy are the prime suspects among a troupe reuniting to perform a play, which, five years earlier, witnessed the death of the production's star. DP

Laura La Plante *Doris* • Montague Love [Montagu Love] *McHugh* • Roy D'Arcy *Carlton* • Margaret Livingston *Evalinda* • John Boles *Qualie* • Burr McIntosh *Josiah* ■ *Dir* Paul Leni • *Scr* Alfred A Cohn, Robert F Hill, JG Hawks, Tom Reed (titles), from the story *House of Fear* by Wadsworth Camp, from the play *The Last Warning; a Melodrama in Three Acts* by Thomas F Fallon

The Last Wave ★★★★

Supernatural drama   1977 · Aus · Colour · 105min

Peter Weir was inspired to make this film after he found a piece of broken statue on a Tunisian beach. Although Richard Chamberlain is clearly out of his depth in the lead, this is a mesmerising supernatural drama, in which a dramatic change in the weather and a series of troubling dreams prompt a Sydney lawyer to venture into the city's aboriginal underworld. Aboriginal pressure groups felt Weir had debased their mythology, but David Gulpilil and the other indigenous cast members obviously felt otherwise. DP

Richard Chamberlain *David Burton* • Olivia Hamnett *Annie Burton* • Gulpilil [David Gulpilil] *Chris Lee* • Frederick Parslow *Reverend Burton* • Vivean Gray *Dr Whitburn* ■ *Dir* Peter Weir • *Scr* Peter Weir, Tony Morphett, Petru Popescu

The Last Witch Hunter ★★★ 15

Fantasy action adventure   2015 · US · Colour · 102min

Cut from the same action fantasy material as *Highlander*, this entertaining romp finds witch hunter Vin Diesel – cursed with immortality – trying to stop the rebirth in modern Manhattan of a Witch Queen. Stemming from the brawny superstar's love of the *Dungeons and Dragons* game, and offering an impressively textured universe considering it's not based on an established property, this family-friendly horror hokum always remains intriguing and imaginative. Michael Caine adds a welcome touch of class. AJ Some violence, swearing. *DVD* *BD*

Vin Diesel *Kaulder* • Rose Leslie *Chloe* • Elijah Wood *Dolan 37th* • Michael Caine *Dolan 36th* • Julie Engelbrecht *Witch Queen* • Rena Owen *Glaeser* ■ *Dir* Breck Eisner • *Scr* Matt Sazama, Cory Goodman, Burk Sharpless

The Last Woman on Earth ★☆ 12

Science fiction   1960 · US · Colour · 64min

Crooks Anthony Carbone and Ed Wain fight over Betsy Jones-Moreland when they turn out to be the only survivors of a nuclear war in Puerto Rico. Not one of cult director Roger Corman's best efforts, this sci-fi *ménage à trois* tale is cheap, dull and unappealing. "Ed Wain" is the pseudonym of future Oscar-winning screenwriter Robert Towne, who hadn't finished the script in time and was brought along to complete it on location. Ever the cost-cutter, Corman then had Towne play the second lead, even though he'd never acted before. AJ *DVD*

Antony Carbone *Harold* • Betsy Jones-Moreland *Evelyn* • Edward Wain [Robert Towne] *Martin* ■ *Dir* Roger Corman • *Scr* Edward Wain [Robert Towne]

Last Year at Marienbad ★★★★★ U

Drama   1961 · Fr/It · BW · 90min

Written by modernist novelist Alain Robbe-Grillet, this is a complex cinematic riddle without an answer. Are Delphine Seyrig and Giorgio Albertazzi really reuniting a year after their first meeting? Or was she killed by her jealous husband, Sacha Pitoeff? Does the film take place in Albertazzi's memory, or is it simply an erotic fantasy on Seyrig's part? The winner of the Golden Lion at the Venice film festival, Alain Resnais' film is a triumph of camera movement, symbolic decor, abstract structure and stylised playing. A masterpiece, but beware: it is as likely to irritate as it is to mesmerise. DP French +subtitles. *DVD*

Delphine Seyrig *A/Woman* • Giorgio Albertazzi *X/Stranger* • Sacha Pitoeff *M/Man/Husband or Lover* ■ *Dir* Alain Resnais • *Cinematographer* Sacha Vierny

The Last Yellow ★★ 15

Comedy drama   1999 · UK/Ger · Colour · 89min

A promising cast can't disguise the stage origins of Julian Farino's dark comedy. The setting is Leicester, where bespectacled nerd Charlie Creed-Miles hires lodger Mark Addy to wreak revenge on the thug who gave his brother brain damage. The relationship between the two hapless avengers is well-drawn, but the intriguing preamble gives way to a disappointingly theatrical three-hander between the duo and their intended victim's trashy girlfriend (Samantha Morton). NS Violence, swearing. *DVD*

Mark Addy *Frank* • Charlie Creed-Miles *Kenny* • Samantha Morton *Jackie* • Kenneth Cranham *Len* • Alan Atherall *Donut* ■ *Dir* Julian Farino • *Scr* Paul Tucker, from his play

Latcho Drom ★★★★

Music documentary   1993 · Fr · Colour · 103min

This is the second of Tony Gatlif's trilogy, which includes *Les Princes* (1982) and *Gadjo Dilo* (1997). Following the Romanies from their homelands in northern India across Africa and middle Europe to Spain, Gatlif's abstract odyssey is more a celebration of human indomitability and cultural vivacity than a protest against centuries of prejudice and injustice. What is so fascinating about this graceful musical tribute is not just how the lyrics become increasingly bitter in countries where the persecution of the Romany peoples has been most vicious, but also how the music has both influenced and embraced the indigenous folk sound. DP In French, Romany.

■ *Dir/Scr* Tony Gatlif

Late August, Early September ★★ 15

Drama   1998 · Fr · Colour · 106min

Although the circle of friends around novelist François Cluzet chatter endlessly, they fail to interest us in either their personalities or their problems. Only Jeanne Balibar's intense misery at losing noncommittal literary editor Mathieu Amalric to designer Virginie Ledoyen strikes a chord. Employing tired New Wave techniques to achieve its multi-perspective structure, Olivier Assayas's trite picture is also guilty of some regrettable gender stereotyping. DP French +subtitles. Swearing, sex scenes.

Virginie Ledoyen *Anne Rosenwald* • Mathieu Amalric *Gabriel Deshays* • François Cluzet *Adrien Willer* • Jeanne Balibar *Jenny* • Alex Decas *Jérémie* ■ *Dir/Scr* Olivier Assayas

Late Autumn ★★★★ PG

Drama   1960 · Jpn · Colour · 125min

Coming towards the end of his illustrious 35-year career, Yasujiro Ozu (*Tokyo Story*) had a little fun at his own expense in this gently comic, petit bourgeois drama. Confounding stylistic expectations, he experiments with a variety of transitional devices while structuring the narrative around blocks of linked scenes. His third film on the subject of arranged marriage is also one of his most slyly satirical, with the triumvirate of businessmen trying to find partners for widow Setsuko Hara and her independent daughter, Yoko Tsukasa, being ridiculed both for their insufferable interference and their smug acquiescence in postwar Japan's sociopolitical status quo. DP Japanese +subtitles. *DVD*

Setsuko Hara *Akiko Miwa* • Yoko Tsukasa *Ayako* • Mariko Okada *Yuriko Sasaki* • Keiji Sada *Shotaro Goto* • Chishu Ryu *Shukichi Miwa* ■ *Dir* Yasujiro Ozu • *Scr* Yasujiro Ozu, Kogo Noda

Late Bloomers ★★★ 15

Comedy drama   1995 · US · Colour · 107min

This engaging lesbian comedy drama explores an extraordinary situation through the eyes of everyday people. Neither basketball coach Connie Nelson nor school secretary and mother of two Dee Hennigan expect to fall in love. So there's something charming about the way in which they see each other through the inevitable merry-go-round of confusion and derision that attends their romance. The homophobic reaction of their conservative neighbours is a touch formulaic, but this is offset by the nicely handled relationship with incomprehending teenage daughter Lisa Peterson. DP

Connie Nelson *Dinah Groshardt* • Dee Hennigan *Carly Lumpkin* • Gary Carter *Rom Lumpkin* • Lisa Peterson *Val Lumpkin* • Esteban Powell *Jamie Hooper* • Joe Nemmers *Rick Musso* ■ *Dir* Julia Dyer • *Scr* Gretchen Dyer

The Late Edwina Black ★

Crime mystery   1951 · UK · BW · 82min

Apart from questioning how closely they read the script when they were offered their parts, the first duty here is to exonerate the actors of any responsibility for this feeble Victorian whodunnit. You could give director Maurice Elvey a ticking off for not trying a little harder to find ways of keeping the killer's identity a secret, but then what can he do with a story that was intent on giving the game away almost before it started? DP

David Farrar *Gregory Black* • Geraldine Fitzgerald *Elizabeth* • Roland Culver *Inspector* • Jean Cadell *Ellen the housekeeper* • Mary Merrall *Lady Southdale* • Harcourt Williams *Doctor Prendergast* ■ *Dir* Maurice Elvey • *Scr* Charles Frank, David Evans, from the play by William Dinner, William Morum

Late for Dinner ★★ PG

Comedy   1991 · US · Colour · 88min

Brian Wimmer and Peter Berg show why they are fully paid-up members of the straight-to-video club as two fugitives who emerge from a 29-year suspended animation experiment to find that (you'll

never guess it) the world has moved on since 1962 and they are slightly out of place. DP

Brian Wimmer *Willie Husband* • Peter Berg *Frank Lovegren* • Marcia Gay Harden *Joy Husband* • Colleen Flynn *Jessica Husband* • Kyle Secor *Leland Shakes* • Michael Beach *Dr David Arrington* • Bo Brundin *Dr Dan Chilblains* • Peter Gallagher *Bob Freeman* ■ *Dir* WD Richter • *Scr* Mark Andrus

The Late George Apley ★★★

Satirical comedy   1947 · US · BW · 98min

John P Marquand's novel in diary form about the rigidities of Boston patrician existence at the turn of the century was brought to the screen by director Joseph L Mankiewicz and contains exemplary performances from British actors Ronald Colman and Peggy Cummins. Although lacking the barbs of the book, and minus the epilogue that gives the work its title, the movie is witty and stylish. TS

Ronald Colman *George Apley* • Peggy Cummins *Eleanor Apley* • Vanessa Brown *Agnes* • Richard Haydn *Horatio Willing* • Charles Russell *Howard Boulder* • Richard Ney *John Apley* • Percy Waram *Roger Newcombe* • Mildred Natwick *Amelia Newcombe* ■ *Dir* Joseph L Mankiewicz • *Scr* Philip Dunne, from the play by John P Marquand, George S Kaufman, from the novel by John P Marquand

Late Night Shopping ★★★ 15

Comedy   2001 · UK/Ger · Colour · 87min

Regardless of the quality of this spirited sub-slacker comedy, debutant director Saul Metzstein is to be applauded for his casting and choice of cinematographer. Brian Tufano brings the same exemplary sense of place that elevated *Trainspotting*, *East Is East* and *Billy Elliot* to this tangled tale of four flailing friends. Occasional episodes sit uneasily, but such is the pace and perception of Jack Lothian's script and the unforced affability of Metzstein's direction that the *Friends* clichés and easy resolutions can be forgiven. DP *DVD*

Luke de Woolfson *Sean* • James Lance *Vincent* • Kate Ashfield *Jody* • Enzo Cilenti *Lenny* • Heike Makatsch *Madeline* • Shauna Macdonald *Gail* • Sienna Guillory *Susie* ■ *Dir* Saul Metzstein • *Scr* Jack Lothian

A Late Quartet ★★★ 15

Drama   2012 · US · Colour · 105min

Documentarist Yaron Zilberman makes a steady move to fiction with this subtly observed drama about a string quartet experiencing discord after 25 years of harmony. Christopher Walken plays the cellist whose discovery that he has Parkinson's disease sparks the unrest. This prompts second violinist Philip Seymour Hoffman to jostle for position with first violinist Mark Ivanir who also has his eye on Hoffman's daughter (Imogen Poots). Essentially, this is a highbrow soap opera, but it's impeccably acted, and filled with glorious music, shrewd contrasts and engaging insights. DP Swearing, a sex scene, nudity. *DVD*

Philip Seymour Hoffman *Robert Gelbart* • Mark Ivanir *Daniel Lerner* • Christopher Walken *Peter Mitchell* • Catherine Keener *Juliette Gelbart* • Imogen Poots *Alexandra Gelbart* ■ *Dir* Yaron Zilberman • *Scr* Yaron Zilberman, Seth Grossman • *Music* Angelo Badalamenti

The Late Shift ★★★★

Comedy drama based on a true story   1996 · US · Colour · 96min

British TV fans may not recognise the protagonists in this true-life drama about the battle of the talk-show hosts, but it's still interesting to see the behind-the-scenes intrigue of American TV, *Larry Sanders* style. When Johnny Carson, king of the late night talkshow, announced his retirement from the *Tonight Show*, a battle began for his coveted job, with David Letterman and Jay Leno (played here by dead-ringers John Michael Higgins and Daniel Roebuck) the two main contenders. It was Leno's tough-as-nails manager Helen Kushnick

(Kathy Bates) who was credited with getting Leno the job, but this TV movie delves into all the political manoeuvres on both sides. Director Betty Thomas injects the fascinating story – a riveting battle of egos – with nice touches of humour. JB

Kathy Bates *Helen Kushnick* • John Michael Higgins *David Letterman* • Daniel Roebuck *Jay Leno* • Bob Balaban *Warren Littlefield* • Ed Begley Jr *Rod Perth* ■ *Dir* Betty Thomas • *Scr* George Armitage, from the non-fiction bestseller by Bob Carter

The Late Show ★★★ 15

Comedy   1977 · US · Colour · 89min

This is a patchy Robert Benton-directed homage to those old homburg-and-raincoat private eye movies which flourished in the 1940s. Art Carney and Lily Tomlin overact wildly as the curmudgeonly old PI and the neurotic object of his attentions, and the ensuing plot convolutions are so tangled as to be incomprehensible. Benton's crisp direction and a neat suburban atmosphere save the day, but this fails to hit the target. SH

Art Carney *Ira Wells* • Lily Tomlin *Margo* • Bill Macy *Charlie Hatter* • Eugene Roche *Ron Birdwell* • Joanna Cassidy *Laura Birdwell* ■ *Dir/Scr* Robert Benton

Late Spring ★★★★ U

Drama   1949 · Jpn · BW · 107min

Yasujiro Ozu began to exhibit here the stylistic and thematic tropes that would sustain him for the remainder of his career: the "pillow shots" between scenes offering poetic digressions from the main action; the low-angle, almost static camerawork; and the preoccupation with lower-middle-class attitudes and the need to progress. Often ranked alongside *Tokyo Story*, the tale of professor Chishu Ryu's attempts to marry off Setsuko Hara, the daughter on whom he depends, remained one of the director's favourites. With its harmony of composition, tone and performance, it's easy to see why. DP Japanese +subtitles. *DVD*

Chishu Ryu *Professor Shukichi Somiya* • Setsuko Hara *Noriko, Somiya's daughter* • Yumeji Tsukioka *Aya Kitagawa* • Haruko Sugimura *Masa Taguchi, Noriko's aunt* • Hohi Aoki *Katsuyochi Taguchi* ■ *Dir* Yasujiro Ozu • *Scr* Kogo Noda, from the novel *Chichi to Musume* (*Father and Daughter*) by Kazuo Hirotsu • *Cinematographer* Yuharu Atsuta [Yushun Atsuta]

The Lathe of Heaven ★★★

Science-fiction drama
1979 · US · Colour · 105min

Bruce Davison's dreams have the power to change reality in a classy adaptation of Ursula K LeGuin's popular novel. Can psychologist Kevin Conway manipulate him into dreaming a better world? Taking on lofty Kafka-esque subtexts, and using Texas landscapes to suggest the future, this subtle fantasy raises pertinent questions about individualism and the march of progress. A disappointing TV movie remake starring James Caan appeared in 2002. AJ

Bruce Davison *George Orr* • Kevin Conway *Dr William Haber* • Margaret Avery (2) *Heather LeLache* • Peyton Park *Mannie Ahrens* • Niki Flacks *Penny Crouch* • Vandi Clark *Aunth Ethel* ■ *Dir* David Loxton, Fred Barzyk • *Scr* Roger E Swaybill, Diane English, from the novel by Ursula K Le Guin

Latin Lovers ★★ U

Musical comedy   1953 · US · Colour · 104min

Multi-millionairess Lana Turner, on vacation in Rio and hungry to be loved for herself rather than her money, has problems deciding whether to choose rich John Lund or less rich but glamorous "Latin Lover" Ricardo Montalban. This is hoary old romantic drivel, written by Isobel Lennart with an attempt at wit which occasionally succeeds, and directed on automatic pilot by Mervyn LeRoy. Leaden, but periodically enlivened by a song. RK

Lana Turner *Nora Taylor* • Ricardo Montalban *Roberto Santos* • John Lund *Paul Chevron* • Louis Calhern *Grandfather Santos* • Jean Hagen

Anne Kellwood • Eduard Franz *Dr Lionel Y Newman* • Beulah Bondi *Analyst* ■ *Dir* Mervyn LeRoy • *Scr* Isobel Lennart

Latitude Zero ★★★

Science-fiction adventure
1969 · Jpn/US · Colour · 104min

The *Godzilla* team of director Inoshiro Honda and special effects genius Eiji Tsuburaya inhabit Jules Verne territory in this absurdly enjoyable underwater fantasy mixing monsters and morality. Submarine commander Joseph Cotten ferries scientists to the underwater city of Latitude Zero, where radiation-immunisation research is being carried out. Cesar Romero is the evil genius who experiments with human brain transplants in animals and whose mission it is to destroy the undersea complex because of its good works. Delightfully campy. AJ

Joseph Cotten *Capt Craig McKenzie* • Cesar Romero *Malic* • Richard Jaeckel *Perry Lawton* • Patricia Medina *Lucretia* • Linda Haynes *Dr Anne Barton* • Akira Takarada *Dr Ken Tashiro* • Mari Nakayama *"Tsuroko" Okada* ■ *Dir* Ishiro Honda [Inoshiro Honda] • *Scr* Shinichi Sekizawa, Ted Sherdeman, from stories by Ted Sherdeman

Lauda: the Untold Story
★★★ PG

Documentary
2014 · Austria/UK · Colour · 89min

Often portrayed as a bit of a nerdy dullard – not least in 2013's racing drama *Rush* – Formula One legend Niki Lauda comes across as an admirably cool, open and fascinating customer in this documentary about his career and his efforts to make racing safer. The access is first-rate – with drivers including Jackie Stewart, Jochen Mass and Lewis Hamilton lining up to praise Lauda as a driver and an activist – and the archive footage is well researched and utilised. There's even plenty here for those who view televised Grand Prix races as an invitation to snooze. SvM

Niki Lauda • Mark Weber • Jochen Mass • Jackie Stewart (I) *Jackie Stewart* ■ *Dir* Hannes Michael Schalle, Guenther Mitterhuber, Alistair Audsley

Laugh, Clown, Laugh ★★★

Silent romantic drama 1928 · US · BW · 65min

Lon Chaney does the noble thing by Loretta Young in Herbert Brenon's silent take on David Belasco and Tom Cushing's stage play. As the clown who persuades his partner Bernard Siegel to care for an abandoned waif, Chaney is both avuncular and vulnerable, as he realises that Young's heart belongs to dashing nobleman, Nils Asther. In her first starring role, the 15-year-old Young is enchantingly natural, but it's Chaney's command of mime that makes this moving. DP

Lon Chaney *Tito* • Bernard Siegel *Simon* • Loretta Young *Simonette* • Cissy Fitz-Gerald *Giacinta* • Nils Asther *Luigi* • Gwen Lee *Lucretia* ■ *Dir* Herbert Brenon • *Scr* Joseph Farnham (titles), Elizabeth Meehan (adaptation), from a play by David Belasco, Tom Cushing

Laughing at Life ★★

Drama 1933 · US · BW · 72min

Made for a pittance and looking cheaper, this drama marks director Ford Beebe's second feature. Yet, already, the brisk, no-nonsense style that would characterise his work is clearly evident, as Victor McLaglen's mercenary departs for Latin America and runs into his long-lost son while mixed up with a gunrunning racket. DP

Victor McLaglen *Dennis P McHale* • Conchita Montenegro *Panchita* • William "Stage" Boyd *Mason* • Lois Wilson *Mrs McHale* • Henry B Walthall *Regent Valenzuela* • Regis Toomey *Pat Collins* ■ *Dir* Ford Beebe • *Scr* Prescott Chaplin, Thomas Dugan, from a story by Ford Beebe

Laughing Sinners ★★

Melodrama 1931 · US · BW · 72min

The Joan Crawford-Clark Gable duo would have better outings than this one in which Salvation Army officer Gable saves unhappy nightclub entertainer Crawford

from herself after she's dumped by the slick cad (Neil Hamilton) she worships. Nonetheless, it starts well enough, and is a must for Crawford fans, who will enjoy being reminded that she was once very pretty, a good dancer, and is more talented than many of her later scenery-chewing roles allowed. RK

Joan Crawford *Ivy Stevens* • Neil Hamilton *Howard Palmer* • Clark Gable *Carl Loomis* • Marjorie Rambeau *Ruby* • Guy Kibbee *Cass Wheeler* • Cliff Edwards *Mike* ■ *Dir* Harry Beaumont • *Scr* Bess Meredyth, Martin Flavin, Edith Fitzgerald, from the play *Torch Song* by Kenyon Nicholson

Laughter ★★★

Comedy drama 1930 · US · BW · 85min

This lively precursor of screwball comedy boasts ingratiating performances from Fredric March as an uninhibited composer and Nancy Carroll as his old girlfriend, who marries Frank Morgan for his money. Their conduct is shameless but great fun, as Carroll soon finds her new life empty and can't resist March's charms. Only Glenn Anders – overacting as a sourpuss romantic rival – spoils the atmosphere of sparkling jollity set up by director Harry d'Abbadie D'Arrast. AE

Fredric March *Paul Lockridge* • Nancy Carroll *Peggy Gibson* • Frank Morgan *C Mortimer Gibson* • Glenn Anders *Ralph Le Saint* • Diane Ellis *Marjorie Gibson* • Leonard Carey *Benham* • Ollie Burgoyne *Pearl* ■ *Dir* Harry d'Abbadie D'Arrast • *Scr* Donald Ogden Stewart, from a story by Harry D'Abbadie D'Arrast, Douglas Doty

Laughter in Paradise
★★★★ U

Comedy 1951 · UK · BW · 92min

Films made up of interwoven stories are notoriously difficult to do well, as it's all too easy either to lose the thread of the difficult episodes or to become impatient with the less substantial ones. That director Mario Zampi nearly brings off the trick here is down almost entirely to the fantastic performance of Alastair Sim as the henpecked thriller writer whose inheritance depends on him receiving a 28-day jail sentence. The scene in which he tries to shoplift is one of the funniest in a career overladen with choice comic moments. DP

Alastair Sim *Deniston Russell* • Fay Compton *Agnes Russell* • Beatrice Campbell *Lucille Grayson* • Veronica Hurst *Joan Webb* • Guy Middleton *Simon Russell* • George Cole *Herbert Russell* • AE Matthews *Sir Charles Robson* • Joyce Grenfell *Elizabeth Robson* • Anthony Steel *Roger Godfrey* • John Laurie *Gordon Webb* • Michael Pertwee *Stuart* • Audrey Hepburn *Cigarette girl* ■ *Dir* Mario Zampi • *Scr* Michael Pertwee, Jack Davies

Laughter in the Dark ★★★

Drama 1969 · UK · Colour · 106min

Vladimir Nabokov's novel, set in 1930s Germany, is a study in sexual psychopathy and sadism. It's about an art dealer who is blinded in a car crash and whose wife, an usherette at a cinema, gets her lover to move in with them, taunting the disabled husband until he can take no more humiliation. Updated to the London art world in the 1960s, with further scenes set in Majorca, this is a gripping drama that's flawed only because everyone in it – even the blind husband – is unpleasant. Anna Karina is the wife-usherette, but everyone is eclipsed by the powerhouse Nicol Williamson. AT

Nicol Williamson *Sir Edward More* • Anna Karina *Margot* • Jean-Claude Drouot *Herve Tourace* • Peter Bowles *Paul* • Sian Phillips *Lady Elizabeth More* • Sebastian Breaks *Brian* • Kate O'Toole *Amelia More* ■ *Dir* Tony Richardson • *Scr* Edward Bond, from the novel by Vladimir Nabokov

Laughter on the 23rd Floor
★★★ 15

Comedy 2000 · US · Colour · 98min

Mark Linn-Baker plays a comedy writer in this made-for-cable Neil Simon memoir of his own days on the legendary weekly programme, *Your Show of Shows* with Sid

Caesar. Richard Benjamin directs this adaptation, where quips fly faster than arrows (and do more damage) and everyone is so wrapped up in hitting deadlines that no one notices that frontman Nathan Lane is slowly going down the pan. Slick, smart and poignantly witty. DP

Nathan Lane *Max Prince* • Mark Linn-Baker *Val* • Victor Garber *Kenny* • Saul Rubinek *Ira* • Peri Gilpin *Carol* • Dan Castellaneta *Milt* • Richard Portnow *Harry* ■ *Dir* Richard Benjamin • *Scr* Neil Simon, from his play

Laura ★★★★★ PG

Classic film noir 1944 · US · BW · 83min

"I shall never forget the night Laura died..." begins the narrator, and neither will you. This taut, romantic mystery, in which New York detective Dana Andrews falls in love with an image, encapsulates what *film noir* is all about. Otto Preminger's moody, stark direction is greatly helped by the casting of beautiful Gene Tierney in the title role, a southern-accented Vincent Price as a smarmy gigolo and the incomparable Clifton Webb as a columnist. The David Raksin score is, quite simply, matchless. This classic is a rattling good thriller that bears repeated viewing. TS **DVD**

Gene Tierney *Laura Hunt* • Dana Andrews *Det Mark McPherson* • Clifton Webb *Waldo Lydecker* • Vincent Price *Shelby Carpenter* • Judith Anderson *Ann Treadwell* • Dorothy Adams *Bessie Clary* • James Flavin *McAvity* • Clyde Fillmore *Bullitt* • Ralph Dunn *Fred Callahan* • Grant Mitchell *Corey* • Kathleen Howard *Louise* • Lee Tung Foo *Servant* • Cy Kendall *Inspector* ■ *Dir* Otto Preminger • *Scr* Jay Dratler, Samuel Hoffenstein, Betty Reinhardt, Jerome Cady, from the novel by Vera Caspary • *Cinematographers* Joseph LaShelle, Lucien Ballard

Laura's Star ★★ U

Animated fantasy
2004 · Ger/Hun · Colour · 80min

A little girl befriends a fallen star in this animated tale based on the children's book by Klaus Baumgart. The film takes what would be a decent premise for a short and drags it out to feature length. As sweet as it often is, there's not much to excite the imagination, as seven-year-old Laura struggles to settle into her new home in the city after moving from the country. SF German dubbed.

Clemmie Hooton *Laura* • Anthony Da Silva *Tommy* • Matthew Thomas-Davis *Max* • Rebecca Vere *Mother/Sun* • Nick Saich *Father/Moon* • Mirko Nontschew *Robot cat/Bear* ■ *Dir* Piet de Rycker, Thilo Graf Rothkirch • *Scr* Piet de Rycker, from the illustrated book by Klaus Baumgart

Laurel and Hardy's
Laughing 20s ★★★★ U

Comedy compilation 1965 · US · BW · 86min

Robert Youngson's Laurel and Hardy compilation was advertised with a sworn statement from a research company that promised 253 laughs, "the record for laugh content of any comedy we have measured in our 30 years of experience". This collection lives up to that hype and is a treat for enthusiasts. The majority of the scenes are taken from Stan and Ollie's silent shorts, among them *Putting Pants on Philip*, *From Soup to Nuts*, *Wrong Again*, *The Finishing Touch* and *Liberty*. However, there is also a rare opportunity to see some of the other comics in the Hal Roach stable in action, among them the dapper Charley Chase and the scowling Edgar Kennedy. DP

Stan Laurel *Stan* • Oliver Hardy *Ollie* • Charley Chase • Edgar Kennedy • James Finlayson • Jay Jackson *Narrator* ■ *Dir/Scr* Robert Youngson

Laurel Canyon ★★★ 18

Drama 2002 · US · Colour · 98min

This is an engaging and skilfully observed drama, depicting the moth-to-a-flame effect of radically divergent personalities. Conservative couple Christian Bale and Kate Beckinsale find their relationship threatened by 1960s-style bohemianism, when they move in with his LA music-biz mother, Frances McDormand. McDormand delivers a strong performance, but disappointingly writer/director Lisa

Cholodenko only scratches the surface of her libertine lifestyle, failing to explain Bale and Beckinsale's extreme reactions. SF Swearing, drug abuse, nudity. **DVD**

Frances McDormand *Jane* • Christian Bale *Sam* • Kate Beckinsale *Alex* • Natascha McElhone *Sara* • Alessandro Nivola *Ian* • Louis Knox Barlow *Fripp* • Russell Pollard *Rowan* • Imaad Wasif *Dean* ■ *Dir/Scr* Lisa Cholodenko

Laurence Anyways ★★★ 15

Romantic drama 2012 · Can/Fr · Colour · 161min

"L'amour fou" continues to preoccupy *Heartbeats* writer/director Xavier Dolan in his wildly ambitious third feature. A beautiful and typically self-indulgent melodrama, this Cannes prize winner explores the obsessive relationship between a Montreal teacher (Melvil Poupaud) and his volatile girlfriend (Suzanne Clément), after he announces he wants to live as a woman. Poupaud and especially Clément's unaffected performances anchor the overlong film, their intimacy emphasising the simplistic central point that it's the person inside, not outside, that counts. But you only feel the raw emotion of the lovers' turbulent, decade-spanning journey in a few, admittedly exceptional, scenes. SF French +subtitles. **DVD**

Melvil Poupaud *Laurence James Emmanuel Alia* • Suzanne Clément *Frédérique Bellair, "Fred"* • Nathalie Baye *Julienne Alia* • Monia Chokri *Stéfanie Bellair* ■ *Dir/Scr* Xavier Dolan

Lava ★★ 18

Black comedy crime thriller
2000 · UK · Colour · 95min

Prompted by the true-life event that he witnessed that also inspired his brother Paul's screenplay for *The Last Yellow*, writer/director Joe Tucker's film is a tale of spiralling violence within the confines of a Notting Hill flat. Tucker also takes the lead role as a militaristic headcase who offers to avenge an assault that left his friend's (James Holmes) brother in a near-vegetative state. But as the body count increases, the film becomes more reliant on the bleak comedy generated by Tucker's macho posturing and Holmes's nerdy timidity. Nicola Stapleton fizzes as a thug's foul-mouthed girlfriend. DP **DVD**

Joe Tucker *Smiggy* • Nicola Stapleton *Julie* • James Holmes *Phillip* • Grahame Fox *Darrel* • Mark Leadbetter *Neville* • Tameke Empson *Maxine* • Leslie Grantham *Mr Aladdin* • Tom Bell *Eric* ■ *Dir/Scr* Joe Tucker

The Lavender Hill Mob
★★★★★ U

Classic crime comedy 1951 · UK · BW · 77min

In this superb and subtle crime film spoof, the inimitable Alec Guinness stars as the mild-mannered bank agent who discovers he has a devious criminal mind, and decides to steal a million in gold bullion. Guinness is well supported by the impressive Stanley Holloway, Alfie Bass and Sid James as members of the gang he recruits. Watch out too for a couple of blink-and-miss-them walk-ons from James (billed as William) Fox and Audrey Hepburn. TEB Clarke deservedly won an Oscar for his beautifully constructed story and screenplay. Guinness lost out to Gary Cooper in *High Noon* in the best actor category. DP **DVD** **Blu**

Alec Guinness *Henry Holland* • Stanley Holloway *Pendlebury* • Sidney James *Lackery* • Alfie Bass *Shorty* • Marjorie Fielding *Mrs Chalk* • John Gregson *Farrow* • Edie Martin *Miss Evesham* • Clive Morton *Station sergeant* • John Salew *Parkin* • Ronald Adam *Turner* • Arthur Hambling *Wallis* • Gibb McLaughlin *Godwin* • Audrey Hepburn *Chiquita* • William Fox [James Fox] *Gregory* ■ *Dir* Charles Crichton • *Scr* TEB Clarke

LaVyrle Spencer's Home
Song ★★

Drama 1996 · US · Colour · 96min

The story for this TV movie is rich in melodramatic potential but, sadly, the rather wooden cast fails to make the most of it. Lee Horsley plays a school headmaster whose life is turned on its head when a son he didn't know he had suddenly appears on the scene, stirring up family tension. The

L

soapy storyline exerts some pull, but the direction is strictly by the book. **JF**

Lee Horsley *Tom Gardner* • Polly Draper *Claire Gardner* • Deborah Raffin *Monica Arins* • Ari Meyers *Chelsea Gardner* • Christopher Cazenove *Grandpa Gardner* ■ *Dir* Nancy Malone • *Scr* Patricia K Meyer, from the novel by Spencer

Law Abiding Citizen ★★★ 18

Crime thriller　2009 · US /UK · Colour · 104min

300 star Gerard Butler turns vigilante here, as Philadelphia family man Clyde Shelton, who's enraged when hotshot prosecutor Nick Rice (Jamie Foxx) strikes a deal with one of the men responsible for the brutal murder of his wife and daughter. Director F Gary Gray (*The Negotiator*) offers an intriguing spin on the revenge thriller while throwing a spotlight on the loopholes and inadequacies of the justice system, although the plot's quick-fix resolution may disappoint some viewers. Foxx is perfectly cast as the moral compass of the film, but it's Butler's edgy portrayal that leaves a lasting impression. **TeS** Violence, swearing. *DVD* *Blu*

Jamie Foxx *Nick Rice* • Gerard Butler *Clyde Shelton* • Leslie Bibb *Sarah Lowell* • Bruce McGill *Jonas Cantrell* • Colm Meaney *Detective Dunnigan* • Viola Davis *Mayor April Henry* • Michael Irby *Detective Sean Garza* • Regina Hall *Kelly Rice* ■ *Dir* F Gary Gray • *Scr* Kurt Wimmer

Law and Disorder ★★★ U

Comedy　1958 · UK · BW · 72min

This is a smashing little comedy from the *Lavender Hill Mob* pairing of director Charles Crichton and co-writer TEB Clarke. Michael Redgrave is on sparkling form as a minor league crook whose detentions at Her Majesty's pleasure are explained away to his son as missionary excursions to Africa. The plot slows slightly after the son becomes judge Robert Morley's assistant and Redgrave slips into retirement. **DP**

Michael Redgrave *Percy Brand* • Robert Morley *Judge Crichton* • Ronald Squire *Colonel Masters* • Elizabeth Sellars *Gina Lasalle* • Joan Hickson *Aunt Florence* • Lionel Jeffries *Major Proudfoot* • Jeremy Burnham *Colin Brand* • Brenda Bruce *Mary Cooper* • George Coulouris *Bennie* • John Le Mesurier *Sir Humphrey Pomfret* ■ *Dir* Charles Crichton • *Scr* TEB Clarke, Patrick Campbell, Vivienne Knight, from the novel *Smuggler's Circuit* by Denys Roberts

Law and Disorder ★★★ 18

Comedy drama　1974 · US · Colour · 97min

Exiled Czech director Ivan Passer's second American film was this uneven satire on the decline of neighbourhood life. When Carroll O'Connor and Ernest Borgnine set about organising a vigilante force to combat the rising tide of crime, the film is both insightful and amusing, but it never recovers from the sudden change in tone once they realise the enormity of their undertaking. Karen Black is superb as a chirpy hairdresser, while the leads have an unexpected chemistry. **DP**

Carroll O'Connor *Willie* • Ernest Borgnine *Cy* • Ann Wedgeworth *Sally* • Anita Dangler *Irene* • Leslie Ackerman *Karen* • Karen Black *Gloria* • Jack Kehoe *Elliott* • David Spielberg *Bobby* ■ *Dir* Ivan Passer • *Scr* Ivan Passer, William Richert, Kenneth Harris Fishman

The Law and Jake Wade ★★★★ U

Western　1958 · US · Colour · 86min

Robert Taylor and Richard Widmark star as adversaries in this handsomely mounted western directed by that master of the genre, John Sturges. It's the tale of two outlaws who once rode together, but now the evil Widmark is back and trying to coerce a reformed Taylor into revealing where their ill-gotten loot is buried. Robert Surtees's photography is often breathtaking, while the clever, laconic screenplay tends to be underrated, as was this fine, tense western. **TS**

Robert Taylor (1) *Jake Wade* • Richard Widmark *Clint Hollister* • Patricia Owens *Peggy Carter* • Robert Middleton *Ortero* • Henry Silva *Rennie* • DeForest Kelley *Wexler* • Burt Douglas

---

Lieutenant • Eddie Firestone *Burke* ■ *Dir* John Sturges • *Scr* William Bowers, from the novel by Marvin H Albert

Law and Order ★★★★

Western　1932 · US · BW · 70min

Terrific version of the Wyatt Earp legend, with the names changed since some of the participants in the tale were still alive at the time of this movie. (Earp himself had only been dead four years.) Co-scripter Huston's father Walter is superb as the town-taming marshal, and the great western star Harry Carey is cleverly cast as his tortured crony. The tone is rightly sombre, and the infamous shoot-out at the OK Corral is quite brilliantly directed, surprising since this is the A-feature debut of Edward L Cahn, whose career plummeted thereafter. **TS**

Walter Huston *Frame Johnson* • Harry Carey *Ed Brant* • Raymond Hatton *Deadwood* • Russell Simpson *Judge Williams* • Russell Hopton *Luther Johnson* • Ralph Ince *Poe Northrup* • Harry Woods *Walt Northrup* • Richard Alexander *Kurt Northrup* • Walter Brennan *Lanky Smith* ■ *Dir* Edward L Cahn • *Scr* John Huston, Tom Reed, from the story *Saint Johnson* by WR Burnett

Law and Order ★★★

Western　1936 · US · BW · 59min

This low-budget western was released, somewhat aptly, by a production company named Reliable, because it contains just about everything you could possibly want from a Wild West matinée. Tom Tyler and Rex Lease play the Texas Rangers who romance Margaret Nearing while tackling Alan Bridge and his band of smugglers. The plot has several nice touches and the camerawork is above average. **DP**

Tom Tyler *Tom* • Rex Lease *Jimmy* • Margaret Nearing *Joan* • Alan Bridge [Al Bridge] *Travis* • Bill Gould *Drummond* ■ *Dir* Henri Samuels [Harry S Webb] • *Scr* Jay J Bryan, Rose Gordon, Carl Krusada

Law and Order ★★ U

Western　1953 · US · Colour · 79min

Town marshal Ronald Reagan plans to retire when he gets married, but, almost inevitably, is called on to fight one more battle against the bad guys. The theme recalls *High Noon*, and, like Gary Cooper, Reagan is the silent, brooding type. However, that's where the comparisons end in this remake of the superior 1932 original starring Walter Huston. **AT**

Ronald Reagan *Frame Johnson* • Dorothy Malone *Jeannie Bristow* • Alex Nicol *Lute Johnson* • Preston Foster *Kurt Durling* • Russell Johnson *Jimmy Johnson* • Barry Kelley *Fin Elder* • Ruth Hampton *Maria* • Chubby Johnson *Denver Cahoon* • Dennis Weaver *Frank Durling* • Jack Kelly *Jed* ■ *Dir* Nathan Juran • *Scr* John Bagni, Gwen Bagni, DD Beauchamp, from the novel *Saint Johnson* by WR Burnett

The Law and the Lady ★★

Period crime comedy　1951 · US · BW · 104min

The Last of Mrs Cheyney, a slick, sophisticated and successful 1920s play by Frederick Lonsdale, had been twice filmed with Norma Shearer in 1929 and Joan Crawford in 1937. This third version, set at the turn of the 19th century and offering the odd amusing moment and an occasional burst of sharp repartee, is an otherwise pointless and inferior remake. A miscast Greer Garson and an unimpressive Michael Wilding play the sacked housemaid and the ne-er-do-well who team up to con wealthy high society. Overlong and erratic. **RK**

Greer Garson *Jane Hoskins* • Michael Wilding *Nigel Duxbury/Lord Minden* • Fernando Lamas *Juan Dinas* • Marjorie Main *Mrs Wortin* • Hayden Rorke *Tracy* ■ *Dir* Edwin H Knopf • *Scr* Leonard Spigelgass, Karl Tunberg, from the play *The Last of Mrs Cheyney* by Frederick Lonsdale

The Law of Desire ★★★ 18

Black comedy drama　1987 · Sp · Colour · 97min

Released the year before *Women on the Verge of a Nervous Breakdown* catapulted Pedro Almódovar to international fame, this is a typically tangled, relationship comedy drama centring on a homosexual love

---

triangle between a film director and his two lovers and the film-maker's really strange family. Items that can be ticked-off on the Almodóvar checklist include early regulars Antonio Banderas and Carmen Maura (delivering a knockout performance), an off-kilter representation of romance, explicit sex, the murder of one of the central characters and outrageous plot twists. Not one of his very best, but still funny and touching. **JC** Spanish +subtitles. *DVD*

Eusebio Poncela *Pablo Quintero* • Carmen Maura *Tina Quintero* • Antonio Banderas *Antonio Benítez* • Miguel Molina *Juan Bermudez* ■ *Dir/Scr* Pedro Almódovar

The Law West of Tombstone ★★

Comedy western　1938 · US · BW · 72min

Here's a programme filler that manages to cram into one short movie three key western plot figures, thinly-disguised caricatures of no less than Billy the Kid, Judge Roy Bean and the boys. In his last RKO western, Harry Carey plays the Judge, while youngster Tim Holt (son of cowboy veteran Jack Holt) makes his RKO debut. **TS**

Harry Carey *Bill Parker* • Tim Holt *The Tonto Kid* • Evelyn Brent *Clara Martinez* • Jean Rouverol *Nitta Moseby* • Clarence Kolb *Sam Kent* • Allan Lane *Danny* • Esther Muir *Mme Mustache* • Bradley Page *Doc Howard* • Kermit Maynard ■ *Dir* Glenn Tryon • *Scr* John Twist, Clarence Upson Young, from the story by Clarence Upson Young

The Lawless ★★★

Drama　1950 · US · BW · 79min

This pungent low-budget drama was one of the best films that Joseph Losey directed in Hollywood. Gaining a sense of realism from being largely filmed on location with locals as extras, it focuses on the prejudice suffered by Mexican "fruit tramps", itinerant workers who harvested crops in California. The scenes of a manhunt and mob violence have considerable force. This kind of film-making, presenting a bad image of American society, contributed to Losey's blacklisting and flight to Europe. **AE**

Macdonald Carey *Larry Wilder* • Gail Russell *Sunny Garcia* • John Sands [Johnny Sands] *Joe Ferguson* • Lee Patrick *Jan Dawson* • John Hoyt *Ed Ferguson* • Lalo Rios *Paul Rodriguez* ■ *Dir* Joseph Losey • *Scr* Geoffrey Homes [Daniel Mainwaring], from his novel *The Voice of Stephen Wilder*

Lawless ★★★ 18

Period crime drama　2012 · US · Colour · 110min

Prohibition-era Virginia is the setting for this crime drama that pits a determined family of rural bootleggers, led by an imposing Tom Hardy, against the combined might of country sheriffs, including Guy Pearce's ruthless special deputy. Convincing in its period detail, beautifully photographed and blessed with a swampy, rootsy score by screenwriter Nick Cave, John Hillcoat's film gets so much right it's a shame the central storyline is a muddled affair, extracting only moderate dramatic impact from its escalating mayhem. **TJ** Violence, swearing, a sex scene, nudity. *DVD* *Blu*

Shia LaBeouf *Jack Bondurant* • Tom Hardy *Forrest Bondurant* • Guy Pearce *Charley Rakes* • Jessica Chastain *Maggie Beauford* • Mia Wasikowska *Bertha Minnix* • Gary Oldman *Floyd Banner* ■ *Dir* John Hillcoat • *Scr* Nick Cave, from the novel *The Wettest County in the World* by Matt Bondurant • *Music* Nick Cave, Warren Ellis (1)

The Lawless Breed ★★★

Biographical western　1952 · US · Colour · 82min

In this splendidly titled biopic, notorious western outlaw John Wesley Hardin is sensitively portrayed by Rock Hudson in a star-making role that was to lift him out of the "beefcake" stakes for ever. It's directed by the veteran who first cast Hudson in a movie, the great Raoul Walsh. Hudson excels here, eliciting sympathy for a character who was clearly no good, and the flashback structure allows for an almost Thomas Hardy-like sense of life controlled

---

by destiny. Better than the average B-feature. **TS**

Rock Hudson *John Wesley Hardin* • Julia Adams [Julie Adams] *Rosie* • Mary Castle *Jane Brown* • John McIntire *JG Hardin/John Clements* • Hugh O'Brian *Ike Hanley* • Dennis Weaver *Jim Clements* • Lee Van Cleef *Dirk Hanley* ■ *Dir* Raoul Walsh • *Scr* Bernard Gordon, from a story by William Alland

The Lawless Frontier ★★ U

Western　1935 · US · BW · 50min

This is another mediocre John Wayne programme filler from that period before his rescue from B-movies by director John Ford with the role of the "Ringo Kid" in 1939's *Stagecoach*. This has one of the most standard of all plots: Wayne is avenging the murder of his parents in under an hour's running time. As ever in these Lone Star westerns, the Yakima Canutt stunts help the film, and Canutt himself is on hand as a baddie. **TS** *DVD*

John Wayne *John Tobin* • Sheila Terry *Ruby* • George Hayes [George "Gabby" Hayes] *Dusty* • Earl Dwire *Zanti* • Yakima Canutt *Joe* ■ *Dir/Scr* Robert N Bradbury

The Lawless Heart ★★★ 15

Comedy drama　2001 · UK/US · Colour · 95min

Gentle, wry humour illuminates the subtleties of modern relationships in this unassuming but poignant British comedy. The film examines how the sudden death of a mutual friend forces a trio of men to reassess their own lives and desires. Told from three different perspectives, each intricately crafted segment adds essential pieces to an emotional jigsaw of love, lust and questioned loyalties. Douglas Henshall is the least convincing, but Bill Nighy and Tom Hollander's understated performances bring quiet dignity to a sharply observant tale. **SF** *DVD*

Bill Nighy *Dan* • Douglas Henshall *Tim Marsh* • Tom Hollander *Nick* • Clémentine Célarié *Corinne* • Josephine Butler *Leah* ■ *Dir/Scr* Neil Hunter, Tom Hunsinger

A Lawless Street ★★ U

Western　1955 · US · Colour · 78min

This routine Randolph Scott western is uninspiringly directed by Joseph H Lewis who fails to secure a satisfactory conclusion to the tale. Co-star Angela Lansbury was on her way up, between an MGM contract and Broadway revivalism, and a darn fine western heroine she makes, playing lawman Scott's wife. She leaves him and refuses to return until he gives up his badge. **TS**

Randolph Scott *Calem Ware* • Angela Lansbury *Tally Dickinson* • Warner Anderson *Hamer Thorne* • Jean Parker *Cora Dean* • Wallace Ford *Dr Amos Wynn* • John Emery *Cody Clark* • James Bell *Asaph Dean* • Ruth Donnelly *Molly Higgins* ■ *Dir* Joseph H Lewis • *Scr* Kenneth Gamet, from the novel *Marshal of Medicine Bend* by Brad Ward

Lawman ★★ 15

Western　1971 · US · Colour · 94min

As a producer, Michael Winner is capable of assembling major players in promising material, but as a director he's no great shakes, sabotaging his own films by doing his own editing and by relying too much on the zoom lens. This is an authentic-looking, tough western, filmed in situ in Durango, with a distinguished cast and a fine screenplay by Gerald Wilson, but it is totally destroyed by inept timing and a clumsy, ugly visual style. **TS** *DVD*

Burt Lancaster *Jered Maddox* • Robert Ryan *Cotton Ryan* • Lee J Cobb *Vincent Bronson* • Sheree North *Laura Shelby* • Joseph Wiseman *Lucas* • Robert Duvall *Vernon Adams* • Albert Salmi *Harvey Stenbaugh* ■ *Dir* Michael Winner • *Scr* Gerald Wilson

Lawn Dogs ★★★★ 15

Drama　1997 · UK · Colour · 96min

Fairy-tale themes embellish a starkly contemporary story in director John Duigan's masterful tale of helpless innocence abroad. Sam Rockwell is a lawnmower man for the exclusive Kentucky suburb Camelot Gardens, who strikes up a

---

friendship with Mischa Barton, a new kid on the block recovering from a heart operation. How people misconstrue the relationship between the "lawn dog" and the vibrantly imaginative youngster makes for a witty and warm film. Duigan's visual trump card is his clever coupling of the deformed American Dream with the potent power of Eastern European fable, and his magical mystery tour through the childhood psyche is a quality diversion oozing with taste and class. AJ Violence, swearing, a sex scene, brief nudity. DVD

Mischa Barton *Devon* • Sam Rockwell *Trent* • Kathleen Quinlan *Clare* • Christopher McDonald *Morton* • Bruce McGill *Nash* • Eric Mabius *Sean* • David Barry Gray *Brett* ■ *Dir* John Duigan • *Scr* Naomi Wallace

The Lawnmower Man ★★★ 15

Science-fiction thriller
1992 · UK/US · Colour · 108min

Once eye-popping special effects are the attraction of this science-fiction tale, vaguely based on a Stephen King short story, but otherwise notable only for crossing a variation on the Frankenstein theme with the cinematic opportunities offered by "virtual reality". Pierce Brosnan plays a misguided scientist who selects his simple-minded gardener (Jeff Fahey) as a guinea pig for his experiments with hi-tech teaching aids and intelligence-boosting drugs. The film boasts cinema's first known cybersex scene. PF Violence, nudity, swearing. DVD

Jeff Fahey *Jobe Smith* • Pierce Brosnan *Dr Lawrence Angelo* • Jenny Wright *Marnie Burke* • Mark Bringleson *Sebastian Timms* • Geoffrey Lewis *Terry McKeen* • Jeremy Slate *Father McKeen* • Dean Norris *Director* • Colleen Coffey *Caroline Angelo* ■ *Dir* Brett Leonard • *Scr* Brett Leonard, Gimel Everett, from the short story by Stephen King

Lawnmower Man 2: Beyond Cyberspace ★ 12

Science fiction 1995 · US · Colour · 89min

Stephen King's name is nowhere to be seen, nor are any of his clever plot concepts, in this thin sequel to the surprise hit. What remains is a tedious slice of confusing science fiction, as Matt Frewer attempts to take over the world through cyberspace. Scientist Patrick Bergin must stop him, aided by three computer whizzkids, with only a barrage of special effects to call on for help in director Farhad Mann's virtual unreality jumble. AJ Violence, swearing. DVD

Patrick Bergin *Dr Benjamin Trace* • Matt Frewer *Jobe* • Austin O'Brien *Peter* • Ely Pouget *Dr Cori Platt* • Kevin Conway *Walker* • Trever O'Brien *Young Peter* • Camille Cooper *Jennifer* ■ *Dir* Farhad Mann • *Scr* Farhad Mann, from a story by Michael Miner, Farhad Mann, from the film *The Lawnmower Man* by Brett Leonard, Gimel Envett

Lawrence of Arabia ★★★★★ PG

Epic historical adventure
1962 · UK · Colour · 217min

This is director David Lean's magisterial portrayal of one of Britain's most enigmatic yet charismatic heroes, TE Lawrence, whose precise role in the Arab revolt against the Turks during the First World War still perplexes military historians. Peter O'Toole's flamboyant performance hints at every aspect of Lawrence's complex character (including his masochism), while Robert Bolt and Michael Wilson's script develops into a withering satire on the ball-and-socket mentality of Lawrence's superiors. Taking 15 months to shoot in Saudi Arabia, Morocco, Spain and England, Lean's obsession with the desert mirrors Lawrence's own, via some awesomely beautiful images, notably the mirage that introduced the world to a new star, Omar Sharif. Winner of seven Oscars and restored to its original glory in 1989, this is movie-making on the grandest scale. AT Violence. DVD Blu

Peter O'Toole *TE Lawrence* • Alec Guinness *Prince Feisal* • Anthony Quinn *Auda Abu Tayi* • Jack Hawkins *General Allenby* • José Ferrer *Turkish Bey* • Anthony Quayle *Colonel Harry Brighton* • Claude Rains *Mr Dryden* • Arthur Kennedy *Jackson Bentley* • Donald Wolfit *General Murray* • Omar Sharif *Sherif Ali Ibn El Kharish* ■ *Dir* David Lean • *Scr* Robert Bolt, Michael Wilson (uncredited), from the book *The Seven Pillars of Wisdom* by TE Lawrence • *Cinematographer* Freddie Young • *Music* Maurice Jarre • *Art Director* John Box

Laws of Attraction ★★ 12

Romantic comedy
2003 · UK/Ire/Ger · Colour · 90min

Pierce Brosnan and Julianne Moore star here as rival divorce lawyers who fall in love after they get married. The leads do their best, but unfortunately lack any real chemistry or the effortless ease that Spencer Tracy and Katharine Hepburn would have brought to the roles. Overall, the film is neither as sharp nor as funny as it should be, and the best lines go to Frances Fisher, as Moore's mum. Watchable in an undemanding way. DA DVD

Pierce Brosnan *Daniel Rafferty* • Julianne Moore *Audrey Woods* • Parker Posey *Serena* • Michael Sheen *Thorne Jamison* • Frances Fisher *Sara Miller* • Nora Dunn *Judge Abramovitz* ■ *Dir* Peter Howitt • *Scr* Aline Brosh McKenna, Robert Harling, from a story by Aline Brosh McKenna

Laws of Gravity ★★★★ 18

Crime drama 1992 · US · Colour · 94min

One of the most impressive directorial debuts of the decade, this sassily-scripted drama cost 29-year-old Nick Gomez a mere $38,000. Shot with twitchy hand-held energy by documentary veteran Jean de Segonzac, the action so reeks of those familiar Brooklyn streets that, while comparisons with Martin Scorsese's *Mean Streets* are inevitable, the is in no way unflattering. Adam Trese gives a hair-trigger performance as the small-time hood whose misdemeanours bring Peter Greene's gang into dispute with gun dealer Paul Schulze. But every bit as impressive is Edie Falco as Greene's feisty girlfriend. DP Swearing, violence.

Peter Greene *Jimmy* • Edie Falco *Denise* • Paul Schulze *Frankie* • Tony Fernandez *Tommy* • James McCauley *Kenny* • Anibal Lierras *Ray* • Miguel Sierra *Vasquez* • Adam Trese *Jon* ■ *Dir/Scr* Nick Gomez

The Lawyer ★★★

Courtroom drama 1969 · US · Colour · 119min

Sidney J Furie's moderate courtroom drama was loosely based on the true story of Dr Sam Sheppard, whose arrest in 1954 for the alleged murder of his wife attracted the kind of media storm that gathered over the OJ Simpson affair. Barry Newman plays the lawyer defending a client who refuses to co-operate, whose family doubts his innocence and whose notoriety may prejudice a fair hearing. Too much time is spent in the company of Newman and his wife Diana Muldaur, but the formula worked well enough to resurface in the TV series *Petrocelli*. DP

Barry Newman *Tony Petrocelli* • Harold Gould *Eric P Scott* • Diana Muldaur *Ruth Petrocelli* • Robert Colbert *Jack Harrison* • Kathleen Crowley *Alice Fiske* • Warren Kemmerling *Sergeant Moran* • Booth Colman *Judge Crawford* ■ *Dir* Sidney J Furie • *Scr* Sidney J Furie, Harold Buchman

Lawyer Man ★★★

Drama 1932 · US · BW · 72min

William Powell stars as the lawyer of the title, a socially conscious do-gooder with a shabby office on the Lower East Side of New York, an eye for the ladies, and a devoted, wisecracking secretary (Joan Blondell). Things come unstuck when he is seduced into partnership with a smart uptown lawyer and overreaches himself. This cynical look at legal ethics and political corruption, decently played and directed, holds the attention, as does Powell, despite the loss of plot credibility about two-thirds of the way through. RK

William Powell *Anton Adam* • Joan Blondell *Olga Michaels* • Helen Vinson *Barbara Bentley* • Alan Dinehart *Granville Bentley* • Allen Jenkins *Issy Levine* • David Landau *John Gilmurry* • Claire Dodd *Virginia St Johns* • Sheila Terry *Flo* • Kenneth Thomson *Dr Frank Gresham* ■ *Dir* William Dieterle • *Scr* Rian James, James Seymour, from the novel by Max Trell

Laxdale Hall ★★ U

Comedy 1953 · UK · BW · 73min

The huge success of director Alexander Mackendrick's *Whisky Galore!* meant it was inevitable that film-makers would cast around for more stories of wily Scots running rings around the stiff-necked English. However, lightning didn't strike twice and this tale of the battle between Whitehall and a tiny Hebridean island, whose inhabitants won't pay a road tax, lacks the magic sparkle of Mackendrick's classic. JF DVD

Ronald Squire *General Matheson* • Kathleen Ryan *Catriona Matheson* • Raymond Huntley *Samuel Pettigrew MP* • Sebastian Shaw *Hugh Marvell MP* • Fulton Mackay *Andrew Flett* • Jean Colin *Lucy Pettigrew* • Jameson Clark *Roderick McLeod* • Prunella Scales *Morag McLeod* ■ *Dir* John Eldridge • *Scr* Alfred Shaughnessy, John Eldridge, from the novel by Eric Linklater

Lay the Favorite ★★★ 15

Comedy 2012 · US · Colour · 89min

Following her sobering role as a debunker of spiritualism in *The Awakening*, Rebecca Hall shows off her comic credentials in this giddy fact-based romp set in the world of high-stakes professional betting. She plays a ditzy former private dancer with a gift for numbers who goes to Las Vegas to become a cocktail waitress and ends up acting as the good-luck charm for a fretful, old-school gambler (Bruce Willis). Despite some uneven storytelling, director Stephen Frears's comedic touch is fantastically feel-good, adorning even the scarier twists and turns with a glossy and uplifting hopefulness. KK Swearing, sexual references, drug abuse. DVD

Rebecca Hall *Beth Raymer* • Bruce Willis *Dink Heimowitz* • Catherine Zeta-Jones *Tulip Heimowitz* • Joshua Jackson *Jeremy* • Vince Vaughn *Rosie* • Laura Prepon *Holly* ■ *Dir* Stephen Frears • *Scr* DV DeVincentis, from a memoir *Lay the Favourite: a Memoir of Gambling* by Beth Raymer

Layer Cake ★★★ 15

Crime thriller 2004 · UK/US · Colour · 101min

Daniel Craig plays a rising young drug dealer whose ambition is to make some quick money and then retire early to enjoy it. His plans – involving a massive shipment of ecstasy – are complicated by drugs lord Kenneth Cranham, who asks him to find the missing wayward daughter of an associate (dodgy businessman Michael Gambon). The performances are good, and Matthew Vaughn directs with assuredness and aplomb, but there's an overfamiliarity about the subject matter. DA DVD Blu

Daniel Craig *XXXX* • Colm Meaney *Gene* (2) *Morty* • Jamie Foreman *JD, "The Duke"* • Michael Gambon *Eddie Temple* • Marcel lures *Slavo* • Tom Hardy *Clarkie* • Ben Whishaw *Sidney* • Sienna Miller *Tammy* ■ *Dir* Matthew Vaughn • *Scr* JJ Connolly, from his novel

The Lazarus Project ★★ 12

Mystery thriller
2008 · US/Can/UK · Colour · 95min

A family man and reluctant criminal (played by *Fast & Furious* regular Paul Walker) gets a second chance at life in *Eagle Eye* scribe John Patrick Glenn's intriguing if slow-paced directorial debut. Inexplicably finding himself the groundskeeper at a psychiatric hospital, Walker experiences increasingly strange events that leave him questioning his situation. Suspenseful scoring and gloomy visuals heighten the initially strong sense of mystery and unease, before a plainly bogus twist sends the hole-filled tale into the realms of total ridiculousness. SF DVD Blu

Paul Walker *Ben Garvey* • Piper Perabo *Lisa Garvey* • Brooklyn Proulx [Brooklynn Proulx] *Katie Garvey* • Bob Gunton *Father Ezra* • Lambert Wilson *Avery* ■ *Dir/Scr* John Patrick Glenn [John Glenn]

Lazybones ★★

Romantic comedy 1935 · UK · BW · 65min

This early studio-based, Michael Powell-directed romantic comedy casts Ian Hunter as an extremely idle baronet who is also completely penniless. Seeking a solution to his lack of solvency, Hunter pursues American heiress Claire Luce, only to discover that she's been swindled by her advisers and is overdrawn as well. The plot is predictable, but the film nevertheless displays the first hints of Powell's inimitable style. LH

Claire Luce *Kitty McCarthy* • Ian Hunter *Sir Reginald Ford* • Sara Allgood *Bridget* • Bernard Nedell *Mike McCarthy* • Michael Shepley *Hildebrand Pope* • Bobbie Comber *Kemp* • Denys Blakelock *Hugh Ford* ■ *Dir* Michael Powell • *Scr* Gerard Fairlie, from a play by Ernest Denny

Le Mans ★★★ PG

Sports drama 1971 · US · Colour · 104min

Steve McQueen's pet project about France's 24-hour car race was started by director John Sturges, who soon clashed with the star and was replaced by up-and-coming TV director Lee H Katzin. Unlike John Frankenheimer's similar *Grand Prix* (1966), there's a minimum of detail concerning the emotional lives of the drivers. Instead there's the star looking charismatic and some of the most beautiful racing footage ever filmed. For fans of McQueen and auto racing, that's probably sufficient. AT DVD Blu

Steve McQueen (1) *Michael Delaney* • Siegfried Rauch *Erich Stahler* • Elga Andersen *Lisa Belgetti* • Ronald Leigh-Hunt *David Townsend* • Fred Haltiner *Johann Ritter* • Luc Merenda *Claude Aurac* • Christopher Waite *Larry Wilson* • Louise Edlind *Anna Ritter* ■ *Dir* Lee H Katzin • *Scr* Harry Kleiner

Leadbelly ★★★

Musical biography 1976 · US · Colour · 126min

Roger E Mosley stars as the famous rough 'n' tough American folk singer Huddie Ledbetter, known as Leadbelly, the traumas of whose eventful life included serving time on a chain gang. Made by Gordon Parks, the first black director of major Hollywood features (including *Shaft*), this is a technically proficient biopic, boasting stylish cinematography from Bruce Surtees, as well as all-round excellent performances. RK

Roger E Mosley *Huddie "Leadbelly" Ledbetter* • Paul Benjamin *Wes Ledbetter* • Madge Sinclair *Miss Eula* • Alan Manson *Chief Prison Guard* • Albert P Hall [Albert Hall] *Dicklicker* • Art Evans *Blind Lemon Jefferson* ■ *Dir* Gordon Parks • *Scr* Ernest Kinoy

The Leading Man ★★★ 15

Romantic comedy drama
1996 · UK · Colour · 95min

Set in theatrical London, this perceptive adult comedy drama from director John Duigan involves the amorous encounters of a writer, his actress-mistress, his wife and a famous Hollywood hunk who's decided to tread the boards and is happy to provide a "distraction" to the playwright's extramarital activities. Although the thespian backdrop and central characters are a little underdeveloped, the bright, eclectic cast makes the romantic complications ring true. JC DVD

Jon Bon Jovi *Robin Grange* • Lambert Wilson *Felix Webb* • Anna Galiena *Elena Webb* • Thandie Newton *Hilary Rule* • Barry Humphries *Humphrey Beal* • David Warner *Tod* • Patricia Hodge *Delvene* • Diana Quick *Susan* ■ *Dir* John Duigan • *Scr* Virginia Duigan

L

The League of Extraordinary Gentlemen ★★ 12

Period fantasy adventure
2003 · US/Ger · Colour · 105min

Blade director Stephen Norrington tackles another comic book adaptation with this ambitious take on Alan Moore's Victorian superhero fantasy. It springs from a fabulous concept, in which fictional adventurer Allan Quatermain (a charismatic Sean Connery) is teamed up with fellow 19th-century literary icons to save the world from a megalomaniac madman, The Fantom. Although the special effects can be extremely ropey at times, the fast pace, quick-witted dialogue and overall spectacle help compensate for such shortcomings. SF Some violence. *DVD* *SD*

Sean Connery *Allan Quatermain* • Shane West *Agent Tom Sawyer* • Stuart Townsend *Dorian Gray* • Peta Wilson *Mina Harker* • Jason Flemyng *Dr Henry Jekyll/Mr Edward Hyde* • Naseeruddin Shah *Captain Nemo* • Tony Curran *Rodney Skinner, the invisible man* • David Hemmings *Nigel* ■ *Dir* Stephen Norrington • *Scr* James Dale Robinson [James Robinson], from the graphic novel by Alan Moore, Kevin O'Neill

The League of Frightened Men ★★

Murder mystery 1937 · US · BW · 71min

A group of Harvard graduates hires detective Nero Wolfe to find out how and why three of their number have died in mysterious circumstances. Having brought Rex Stout's famously sedentary and epicurean detective to the screen the previous year (in *Meet Nero Wolf*), with a very well-cast Edward Arnold, Columbia seemed poised for series. However, this serviceable but static second outing, with Walter Connolly taking over the role of Wolfe, proved the last, probably because an armchair-bound hero limited the possibilities for action. RK

Walter Connolly *Nero Wolfe* • Lionel Stander *Archie Goodwin* • Eduardo Ciannelli *Paul Chapin* • Irene Hervey *Evelyn Hibbard* • Victor Killian [Victor Kilian] *Pitney Scott* • Nana Bryant *Agnes Burton* ■ *Dir* Alfred E. Green • *Scr* Eugene Solow, Guy Endore, from the novel by Rex Stout

The League of Gentlemen ★★★★ PG

Crime caper 1960 · UK · BW · 108min

This was the first feature from the Allied Film Makers company, with most of its founder members – producer Michael Relph, director Basil Dearden, screenwriter Bryan Forbes and actors Jack Hawkins and Richard Attenborough – making solid contributions to this rousing crime caper. Dating from a time when every third word a crook said didn't begin with an "f", this distant ancestor of such bungled heist pics as *Reservoir Dogs* gets off to a rather stodgy start, but, once Hawkins has assembled his far from magnificent seven and his intricate plan begins to unravel, the action really hots up. DP *DVD*

Jack Hawkins *Lt Col Hyde* • Nigel Patrick *Peter Graham Race* • Roger Livesey *Mycroft* • Richard Attenborough *Edward Lexy* • Bryan Forbes *Martin Porthill* • Kieron Moore *Stevens* • Robert Coote *Bunny Warren* • Terence Alexander *Rupert Rutland-Smith* ■ *Dir* Basil Dearden • *Scr* Bryan Forbes, from a novel by John Boland

The League of Gentlemen's Apocalypse ★★★ 15

Black comedy 2005 · UK/Ire · Colour · 87min

This is a feature-length spin-off from the cult TV series about the twisted world of Royston Vasey. The sketch-show style of the programme means that the screenplay can concentrate on gags rather than character development. The plot itself is all but impossible to describe – suffice to say a trio of (fictional) characters break through into the real world to confront the show's writers. It's unlikely to win over any new converts, but fans will no doubt revel in its gleeful weirdness. AS Swearing, sexual references, violence. *DVD*

Mark Gatiss *Matthew Chinnery/Hilary Briss/ Mickey/Mark Gatiss/Sir Nicholas Sheet-Lightning* • Steve Pemberton *Tubbs Tattsyrup/Pauline/ Herr Lipp/Steve Pemberton/Lemuel Blizzard* • Reece Shearsmith *Edward Tattsyrup/Papa Lazarou/Geoff Tipps/The Rev Bernice Woodall/ Reece Shearsmith/Father Halfhearte/Red Devil* • Michael Sheen *Jeremy Dyson* • David Warner *Dr Erasmus Pea* • Victoria Wood *Queen Mary II* • Bernard Hill *King William III* ■ *Dir* Steve Bendelack • *Scr* Jeremy Dyson, Mark Gatiss, Steve Pemberton, Reece Shearsmith

A League of Their Own ★★★ PG

Period sports comedy drama 1992 · US · Colour · 122min

Before he won a couple of Oscars for more serious fare, Tom Hanks provided the laughs as the alcoholic ex-professional hired to coach a women's baseball team during the Second World War. The assembled players include Geena Davis and Lori Petty as sisters, Madonna as the team floozy and comedian Rosie O'Donnell as her best friend. Penny Marshall, who also directed Hanks in *Big*, has put together a somewhat uneven film, but any roughness is smoothed over by the talented cast and a great deal of affection for the era. JB *DVD*

Tom Hanks *Jimmy Dugan* • Geena Davis *Dottie Hinson* • Lori Petty *Kit Keller* • Madonna *Mae Mordabito* • Rosie O'Donnell *Doris Murphy* • Megan Cavanagh *Marla Hooch* • Tracy Reiner *Betty Horn* • Bitty Schram *Evelyn Gardner* • Ann Cusack *Shirley Baker* ■ *Dir* Penny Marshall • *Scr* Lowell Ganz, Babaloo Mandel, from a story by Kim Wilson, Kelly Candaele

Lean on Me ★★★ 15

Drama based on a true story 1989 · US · Colour · 103min

Morgan Freeman takes over as principal of a problem New Jersey high school and eventually wins the hearts of his students after a rigorous clean-up campaign. The tough-love formula works like a charm thanks to Freeman's engaging central performance, and energetic direction by John G Avildsen. AJ

Morgan Freeman *Joe Clark* • Robert Guillaume *Dr Frank Napier* • Beverly Todd *Ms Levias* • Lynne Thigpen *Leona Barrett* • Jermaine Hopkins *Thomas Sams* • Karen Malina White *Keneesha Carter* • Alan North *Mayor Don Bottman* • Ethan Phillips *Mr Rosenberg* ■ *Dir* John G Avildsen • *Scr* Michael Schiffer

Leap of Faith ★★★ PG

Satirical drama 1992 · US · Colour · 103min

Steve Martin takes on the role of a cynical bogus evangelist who runs a travelling gospel show in a film that can't make up its mind whether it wants to be a comedy or a straight drama. When Martin and his team arrive at a poor Kansas town to fleece the residents, they find their consciences pricked as they get to know the townspeople. The interesting cast performs well, but the film loses its way as the plot becomes tangled with saccharine twists. JB *DVD*

Steve Martin *Jonas Nightengale* • Debra Winger *Jane* • Liam Neeson *Will* • Lolita Davidovich *Marva* • Lukas Haas *Boyd* • Meat Loaf *Hoover* • Philip Seymour Hoffman *Matt* • MC Gainey *Tiny* ■ *Dir* Richard Pearce • *Scr* Janus Cercone

Leap Year ★★★ PG

Romantic comedy 2010 · US/Jpn · Colour · 96min

Over-organised Anna (Amy Adams) rushes from Boston to Ireland to propose to her beau (Adam Scott) on 29 February, only to be confounded by the one thing she can't control – the weather. Miles off course, in the wilds of Dingle, she enlists the help of handsome minicab driver-cum-publican Declan (Matthew Goode). This frothy romance has just enough blarney to charm the susceptible, Adams is enchanting, and Goode just manages to hang on to an often strained Irish accent. KK *DVD* *SD*

Amy Adams *Anna Brady* • Matthew Goode *Declan* • John Lithgow *Jack* • Adam Scott *Jeremy* ■ *Dir* Anand Tucker • *Scr* Deborah Kaplan, Harry Elfont

Leap Year ★★ 18

Drama 2010 · Mex · Colour · 88min

An award winner at Cannes in 2010, Australian director Michael Rowe's first film is an uncomfortable treatise on sex, grief, fear and death. Set in Mexico City, it centres on young freelance journalist Laura (Mónica del Carmen) who lives alone in her city apartment and seeks solace with a string of one-night stands. That is until violent, dangerous Arturo (Gustavo Sánchez Parra) comes into her life – and is invited to a fatal tryst. Is this claustrophobic story depressing or riveting? Against women or for their sexual liberation? The film stays neutral on these points, which may not be to everyone's satisfaction. KK Spanish +subtitles. Violence, sex scenes. *DVD*

Mónica del Carmen *Laura* • Gustavo Sánchez Parra *Arturo* • Marco Zapata *Raúl* • Armando Hernández *Man 3* ■ *Dir* Michael Rowe (1) • *Scr* Michael Rowe, Lucía Carreras

Learning to Drive ★★ 15

Romantic comedy 2014 · UK/US · Colour · 89min

Spanish director Isabel Coixet struggles to find anything new or insightful to say about the human condition in this prosaic reworking of Katha Pollitt's New Yorker essay. Ben Kingsley and Patricia Clarkson do what they can, but neither Clarkson's divorcing Manhattan literary critic nor Kingsley's Sikh driving instructor-cum-cabby rings entirely true. Thelma Schoonmaker edits proficiently and there's a pleasing Indian-inspired score, but the film strains so hard to be equitable that it fails to engage. DP Swearing, sexual references.

Patricia Clarkson *Wendy* • Ben Kingsley *Darwan* • Jake Weber *Ted* • Sarita Choudhury *Jasleen* • Grace Gummer *Tasha* • Avi Nash *Preet* ■ *Dir* Isabel Coixet • *Scr* Sarah Kernochan

The Learning Tree ★★★

Period drama 1969 · US · Colour · 106min

Best known for his film about the black private eye *Shaft*, novelist, photographer, poet, composer and film-maker Gordon Parks was a one-man cultural phenomenon. One of the godfathers of independent African-American cinema, he based his feature debut on his autobiographical novel about a young man coming of age in 1920s Kansas. While he and cinematographer Burnett Guffey lovingly re-create the look and feel of the period, Parks struggles to animate the inexperienced cast. Historically important, but overly determined to be both authentic and significant. DP Violence, swearing, nudity.

Kyle Johnson *Newt Winger* • Alex Clarke *Marcus Savage* • Estelle Evans *Sarah Winger* • Dana Elcar *Sheriff Kirky* • Mira Waters *Arcella Jefferson* • Joel Fluellen *Uncle Rob* • Malcolm Atterbury *Silas Newhall* • Richard Ward *Booker Savage* ■ *Dir* Gordon Parks • *Scr* Gordon Parks, from his novel

Lease of Life ★★★ U

Drama 1954 · UK · Colour · 90min

Robert Donat is always unfairly overlooked in discussions of great British screen actors. An Oscar winner for *Goodbye, Mr Chips*, he fought chronic asthma throughout his life to give several moving and convincing performances, which usually belied the quality of the material. This tale of a Yorkshire vicar with only a year to live is a case in point. Thriller specialist Eric Ambler makes a mawkish mess of what is essentially a domestic drama but, through the gentle fidelity of his performance, Donat creates a decent and dignified character. DP

Robert Donat *William Thorne* • Kay Walsh *Vera Thorne* • Adrienne Corri *Susan Thorne* • Denholm Elliott *Martin Blake* • Walter Fitzgerald *Dean* • Cyril Raymond *Headmaster* • Reginald Beckwith *Foley* ■ *Dir* Charles Frend • *Scr* Eric Ambler, from a story by Frank Baker (2), Patrick Jenkins

The Leather Boys ★★★ 15

Drama 1963 · UK · BW · 106min

Nearly 50 years on, it's almost impossible to see why this was once regarded as an unacceptably frank insight into the gay lifestyle. Colin Campbell is so hopelessly out of his depth as the young newlywed wrestling with his sexual identity that not even the excellence of Rita Tushingham and Dudley Sutton can salvage what were intended to be powerful scenes. Sidney J Furie's film is now something of a quaint period piece, full of techniques borrowed from the French New Wave. The end result is fussy and flash, but the wedding and the Butlin's sequences are priceless relics of 1960s life. DP *DVD*

Rita Tushingham *Dot* • Colin Campbell *Reggie* • Dudley Sutton *Pete* • Gladys Henson *Gran* • Avice Landone *Reggie's mother* • Lockwood West *Reggie's father* • Betty Marsden *Dot's mother* ■ *Dir* Sidney J Furie • *Scr* Gillian Freeman, from the novel by Eliot George [GillianFreeman]

Leather Jackets ★★★ 18

Crime drama 1991 · US · Colour · 90min

English actor Cary Elwes is almost unrecognisable in this brooding, underrated crime drama, which also provided an early starring role for Bridget Fonda. The story focuses on the complicated relationships between reformed crook DB Sweeney, his fiancée (Fonda) and his best friend (Elwes), who is on the run from Asian mobsters. Director Lee Drysdale captures the bleakness of small-town life and is rewarded with fine performances. JF

DB Sweeney *Mickey* • Bridget Fonda *Claudi* • Cary Elwes *Dobbs* • Christopher Penn *Chris Penn* *Big Steve* • Jon Polito *Fat Jack* • Craig Ng *Tron* • Marshall Bell *Stranger* • James LeGros *Carl* • Ginger Lynn Allen *Bree* ■ *Dir/Scr* Lee Drysdale

Leatherface: the Texas Chainsaw Massacre III ★★★ 18

Horror 1990 · US · Colour · 85min

Gory, graphic and gruesome, director Jeff Burr's second sequel to Tobe Hooper's classic gut-wrencher combines the suffocating atmosphere of the original with the razor-sharp black comedy of Hooper's second reworking. Kate Hodge and William Butler are the ingenuous tourists who this time take a backwoods detour and end up being prospective sausage filler thanks to Leatherface and his splatter happy family of cannibals. More provocative and taboo-busting than the first two entries in the censor-upsetting series. The final sequel was *Texas Chainsaw Massacre: the Next Generation*. AJ *DVD*

Kate Hodge *Michelle* • William Butler *Ryan* • Viggo Mortensen *Tex* • Ken Foree *Benny* • Joe Unger *Tinker* • Tom Everett *Alfredo* • Toni Hudson *Sara* • Miriam Byrd-Nethery *Mama* • RA Mihailoff *Leatherface* ■ *Dir* Jeff Burr • *Scr* David J Schow, from characters by Kim Henkel, Tobe Hooper

Leatherheads ★★ PG

Period romantic comedy 2007 · US · Colour · 108min

With this misty-eyed, 1920s-set romantic comedy, director/star George Clooney clumsily attempts to recapture the zip and zing of the screwball classics. Playing an ageing American football player, he is coolly charismatic, but Renée Zellweger is miscast as the sharp-tongued reporter he tries to "huddle up" with. In the disorienting plot, Clooney gets creamed on the field, experiences a midlife crisis, then recruits a college star (John Krasinski) to help his team make the headlines. Complications naturally ensue and Zellweger gets pulled back and forth between the men. On the whole, however, there is a total lack of forward motion. SP Brief swearing. *DVD* *SD*

George Clooney *Dodge Connelly* • John Krasinski *Carter Rutherford* • Renée Zellweger *Lexie Littleton* • Stephen Root *Suds* • Wayne Duvall *Coach Ferguson* • Jonathan Pryce *CC Frazier* ■ *Dir* George Clooney • *Scr* Duncan Brantley, Rick Reilly

The Leatherneck ★★
Drama 1929 · US · BW · 76min

William Boyd is defending himself against charges of murder and desertion in the aftermath of the First World War. This undernourished drama with moments of romance is notable only for what became of its stars – William Boyd turned cowboy and carved out a lucrative career as Hopalong Cassidy, while Alan Hale picked up a contract with Warner Bros and became a character stalwart. TH

William Boyd (1) *Joseph Hanlon* • Alan Hale *Otto Schmidt* • Robert Armstrong *William Calhoun* • Fred Kohler *Heckla* ■ *Dir* Howard Higgin • *Scr* Elliott Clawson, John W Krafft

Leave All Fair ★★★
Biographical drama 1985 · NZ · Colour · 88min

This is a subtle, elegantly told story about the New Zealand writer Katherine Mansfield who died in 1923 and is recalled decades later by her husband (the literary critic John Middleton Murry) while visiting a publisher in Paris. Financed in New Zealand but shot entirely in France, the film's chief virtues are the superb performances by John Gielgud as the husband and Jane Birkin (an unusual casting choice) in a dual role as Mansfield and a woman who resembles the writer. Birkin adds layers of nuance to an otherwise conventional storyline. AT

John Gielgud *John Middleton Murry* • Jane Birkin *Marie Taylor/Katherine Mansfield* • Féodor Atkine *André de Sarry* • Simon Ward *Young John* ■ *Dir* John Reid • *Scr* Stanley Harper, Maurice Pons, John Reid

Leave 'Em Laughing ★★★★
Biographical drama 1981 · US · Colour · 103min

Mickey Rooney turns in a stand-out performance as the real-life New York comedian Jack Thum who, with wife Anne Jackson, cared for dozens of homeless youngsters, despite the rigours of the comedy circuit and cancer. A TV movie that plucks hard on the heartstrings, it's redeemed by Rooney's brisk, no-nonsense take on the situation, helped by similar direction from Jackie Cooper, whose own childhood was spent in the *Our Gang* children's movies. TH

Mickey Rooney *Jack Thum* • Anne Jackson *Shirlee Thum* • [Allen Garfield] *Dr Arthur Abrams* • Elisha Cook [Elisha Cook Jr] *Jetter* • Michael LeClair *Tom* • William Windom *Smiley Jenkins* • Red Buttons *Roland Green* ■ *Dir* Jackie Cooper • *Scr* Cynthia W Mandelberg [Cynthia Whitcomb], from a story by Peggy Chantler-Dick

Leave Her to Heaven ★★★★ⓤ
Crime melodrama 1945 · US · Colour · 105min

Here's a wonderful chunk of 20th Century-Fox tosh in the most glowing Oscar-winning Technicolor you're ever likely to see. The sublimely beautiful Gene Tierney drops overacting Vincent Price to go off with dull but handsome author Cornel Wilde, and lets her pretty foster sister Jeanne Crain and Wilde take the blame for murder. This is glorious melodrama that knows no bounds. TS *DVD*

Gene Tierney *Ellen Berent* • Cornel Wilde *Richard Harland* • Jeanne Crain *Ruth Berent* • Vincent Price *Russell Quinton* • Mary Phillips [Mary Philips] *Mrs Berent* • Ray Collins *Glen Robie* • Gene Lockhart *Dr Saunders* ■ *Dir* John M Stahl • *Scr* Jo Swerling, from the novel *Leave Her to Heaven* by Ben Ames Williams • *Cinematographer* Leon Shamroy

Leave It to Beaver ★★ⓅⒼ
Comedy 1997 · US · Colour · 84min

The popular 1950s sitcom gets a modern big-screen update, but this forgettable family movie is only really of interest to fans or the easily amused. Unlike the enjoyably daft *Brady Bunch* movies, little or no concession has been made for contemporary audiences, aside from mild swearing and the occasional satirical moment. Saddled with a pedestrian script, stars Janine Turner and Christopher McDonald look far from comfy in their parental roles, although young Cameron Finley has a certain cute appeal. JC

Christopher McDonald *Ward Cleaver* • Janine Turner *June Cleaver* • Cameron Finley *Theodore "Beaver" Cleaver* • Erik Von Detten *Wally Cleaver* • Adam Zolotin *Eddie Haskell* • Barbara Billingsley *Aunt Martha* • Ken Osmond *Eddie Sr* ■ *Dir* Andy Cadiff • *Scr* Brian Levant, Lon Diamond, from the TV series by Bob Mosher, Joe Connelly

Leave of Absence ★★★⑫
Drama 1994 · US · Colour · 87min

The ever-reliable Brian Dennehy delivers one of his most subtle and touching performances in this thoughtful drama. He plays a successful career man who falls for Jacqueline Bisset while married to Blythe Danner, then pushes his marriage to the edge by caring for Bisset when she falls victim to a terminal disease. It's made for TV, but it's in a different league from the usual small-screen fodder. JF *DVD*

Brian Dennehy *Sam Mercer* • Jacqueline Bisset *Nell Bergen* • Blythe Danner *Eliza Mercer* • Jessica Walter *Bess Kaufman* • Noelle Parker *Zoey Mercer* • Polly Bergen *Janet* • Grayce Spence *Phyllis* • Tonea Stewart *Cora Winsor* ■ *Dir* Tom McLoughlin • *Scr* Betty Goldberg, from a story by Polly Bergen

Leave to Remain ★★★⑮
Drama 2013 · UK · Colour · 89min

A laudable concept falls some way short of convincing in writer/director Bruce Goodison's feature debut. Toby Jones stars as a care worker at a hostel for young refugees, who not only arranges cultural activities, but is also prepared to lie to help his favourites. Goodison and co-writer Charlotte Colbert worked with real asylum seekers over a number of years, so authenticity permeates proceedings. But the imposition of an emotive narrative means the material lacks objectivity. The performances by the non-professional actors are excellent, but the social realism is ultimately overly tinged with melodrama. DP Swearing, sexual references, drug abuse.

Noof Ousellam *Omar* • Masieh Zarrien *Abdul* • Yasmin Mwanza *Ziz'di* • Toby Jones *Nigel Hapgood* • Melanie Wilder *Chloe* ■ *Dir* Bruce Goodison • *Scr* Charlotte Colbert, Bruce Goodison

Leaves from Satan's Book ★★★
Silent religious drama 1919 · Den · BW · 110min

This chronicle of evil through the ages was Carl Th Dreyer's second feature and gives notice of the thematic preoccupations that would concern him throughout his career. The satanic Helge Nissen poses as a New Testament Pharisee, a Spanish Inquisitor, a French revolutionary spy and a monk caught up in the 1918 Russo-Finnish War. But Dreyer is less interested in sin per se than in exploring the strength of faith exhibited by those facing temptation. The finale is easily the most accomplished cinematically, with Clara Pontoppidan's suicide being a moving montage of meticulously matched close-ups. DP

Helge Nissen *Satan* • Halvard Hoff *Jesus* • Jacob Texiere *Judas* • Erling Hansson *John* • Hallander Hellermann *Don Gomez* • Ebon Strandin *Isabella, his daughter* • Tenna Kraft *Marie Antoinette* • Emma Wiehe *Contesse de Chambord* • Carlo Wieth *Paavo Ralya* • Clara Pontoppidan *Siri* ■ *Dir* Carl Th Dreyer • *Scr* Carl Th Dreyer, Edgar Höyer, from the novel *Satans Sorger* by Marie Corelli

Leaving ★★★⑮
Romantic drama 2008 · Fr · Colour · 82min

After a tragic prologue, writer/director Catherine Corsini's histrionic romance flashes back to reveal a saga of marital malevolence. Kristin Scott Thomas gives another magnetic performance as the bored housewife who risks everything to leave her doctor-husband Yvan Attal after meeting Spanish handyman Sergi López. And Agnès Godard's intrusive handheld camerawork and the inspired use of music originally composed for Truffaut's films gives the affair a touch of class. DP French, English, Catalan +subtitles. Swearing, sex scenes. *DVD*

Kristin Scott Thomas *Suzanne* • Sergi López [Sergi Lopez] *Ivan* • Yvan Attal *Samuel* • Bernard Blancan *Rémi* • Aladin Reibel *Dubreuil* • Alexandre Vidal *David* ■ *Dir* Catherine Corsini • *Scr* Catherine Corsini, Gaëlle Macé • *Cinematographer* Agnès Godard

Leaving Las Vegas ★★★★⑱
Drama 1995 · US · Colour · 107min

Mike Figgis's agonising study of alcoholic self-destruction impresses with its uncompromising honesty and exceptional performances. Nicolas Cage won a well-deserved Oscar for his portrayal of a failed Hollywood screenwriter who goes to Vegas to drink himself to death. Just as memorable is Oscar-nominated Elisabeth Shue as the prostitute who befriends him. Shooting in Super 16mm, Figgis strips away the gaudy glamour of Nevada's temptation capital, revealing it to be a tawdry, neon-lit tourist trap. This is downbeat all the way, but the sensitivity of the direction and the authenticity of the acting also give it a redemptive feel. DP Violence, swearing, nudity, drug abuse. *DVD*

Nicolas Cage *Ben Sanderson* • Elisabeth Shue *Sera* • Julian Sands *Yuri* • Richard Lewis *Peter* • Valeria Golino *Terri* • Steven Weber *Marc Nussbaum* • Kim Adams *Sheila* • Laurie Metcalf *Landlady* • Julian Lennon *Bartender in biker bar* ■ *Dir* Mike Figgis • *Scr* Mike Figgis, from the novel by John O'Brien

Leaving Lenin ★★★⑫
Comedy drama 1993 · UK · Colour · 89min

A far cry from the wild things in *Twin Town*, the teens on this school trip have a comfortable life and much to look forward to. But they still have plenty to find out about themselves, and St Petersburg in the post-Communist era turns out to be the perfect scene for self-discovery. Shooting with an enthusiastic eye for the sights of the city and the naturalism of his young cast, director Endaf Emlyn makes the most of a rather contrived situation. DP Welsh +subtitles.

Sharon Morgan *Eileen* • Wyn Bowen Harries *Mostyn* • Ifan Huw Dafydd *Mervyn* • Steffan Trevor *Spike* • Catrin Mai *Rhian* • Ivan Shvedov *Sasha* • Richard Harrington *Charlie* • Shelley Rees *Sharon* ■ *Dir* Endaf Emlyn • *Scr* Endaf Emlyn, Sion Eiri

Leaving Normal ★★★⑮
Comedy drama 1992 · US · Colour · 105min

A kind of sub-*Thelma & Louise*, this stars Meg Tilly as a bored housewife departing her second failed marriage and Christine Lahti as a world-weary waitress. The two meet at a bus stop in the town of Normal, Wyoming, and decide to head for the wilds of Alaska, where Lahti has inherited a house. Sentimental stuff from director Edward Zwick that owes much to his previous TV work on the acclaimed *thirtysomething*. JB Swearing, nudity.

Christine Lahti *Darly* • Meg Tilly *Marianne* • Patrika Darbo *66* • Lenny Von Dohlen *Harry* • Maury Chaykin *Leon* • Brett Cullen *Kurt* • James Gammon *Walt* • Eve Gordon *Emily* ■ *Dir* Edward Zwick • *Scr* Edward Solomon

Lebanon ★★★★⑮
War drama 2009 · Ger/Is/Fr · Colour · 89min

Put simply, this is submarine drama *Das Boot*, but set in a tank in the Middle East. It follows 24 hours in the lives of a four-man crew of Israeli conscripts at the start of Israel's first war with Lebanon, in 1982. The action takes place almost entirely within the confines of the tank's interior as the soldiers search a hostile town for signs of the enemy, and brilliantly conveys the claustrophobia of tank warfare. Writer/director Samuel Maoz fought in the Lebanon conflict and his first-hand experience of combat shows – the sheer terror of the hapless young men who inhabit the tin-can killing machine is palpable. DA Hebrew, Arabic, French, English +subtitles. *DVD*

Yoav Donat *Shmulik* • Itay Tiran *Assi* • Oshri Cohen *Hertzel* • Michael Moshonov *Yigal* • Zohar Strauss *Jamil* • Dudu Tassa *Syrian captive* ■ *Dir/Scr* Samuel Maoz

La Lectrice ★★★★⑱
Erotic comedy 1988 · Fr · Colour · 94min

Miou-Miou gives a beautifully judged performance as a professional reader in this wry erotic comedy from Michel Deville. This is the sort of French film that Hollywood thinks it can remake, but there's no one on the current A-list capable of reproducing Miou-Miou's subtle shifts from intellectual to companion, revolutionary to temptress, to suit the needs of her clients. Co-written by the director and his wife, Rosalinde, the script is a wonderful advertisement for books and the pleasures of reading. DP French +subtitles. Nudity. *DVD*

Miou-Miou *Constance/Marie* • Régis Royer *Eric* • Christian Ruché *Jean/Philippe* • Charlotte Farran *Coralie* • Brigitte Catillon *Eric's mother/Jocelyne* ■ *Dir* Michel Deville • *Scr* Rosalinde Deville, Michel Deville, from the novel and short story by Raymond Jean

Left Behind ★⑮
Action thriller 2014 · US/Can · Colour · 104min

This biblical disaster movie presents a bizarre, apocalyptic phenomenon to the passengers of a commercial airplane. Without warning, a number of them vanish into thin air, leaving nothing behind but their clothing and personal effects. As the remaining passengers try to make sense of this, the captain (Nicolas Cage) learns that the same thing has happened to millions of people around the world. The sad truth is that *Left Behind* is lacking in both drama and intensity, while Cage is frustratingly restrained in the lead role. SC *DVD* 🔵

Nicolas Cage *Rayford Steele* • Chad Michael Murray *Cameron "Buck" Williams* • Cassi Thomson *Chloe Steele* • Nicky Whelan *Hattie Durham* • Jordin Sparks *Shasta Carvell* • Lea Thompson *Irene Steele* ■ *Dir* Vic Armstrong • *Scr* Paul Lalonde, John Patus, from the novel *Left Behind: A Novel of the Earth's Last Days* by Jerry B Jenkins, Tim LaHaye

The Left Hand of God ★★
Romantic wartime adventure 1955 · US · Colour · 87min

This 20th Century-Fox film, made in CinemaScope, has a miscast and extremely uncomfortable-looking (he was ill at the time) Humphrey Bogart posing as a priest in China in 1947, dallying with the lovely Gene Tierney and coping with warlord Lee J Cobb, complete with Hollywood oriental make-up. William E Barrett's original novel offered some provocative views on how a priest's mantle affects the man who wears it, but Bogart fails to convince as a tortured soul. TS

Humphrey Bogart *Jim Carmody* • Gene Tierney *Ann Scott* • Lee J Cobb *Mieh Yang* • Agnes Moorehead *Beryl Sigman* • EG Marshall *Dr Sigman* • Jean Porter *Mary Yin* ■ *Dir* Edward Dmytryk • *Scr* Alfred Hayes, from the novel by William E Barrett

The Left Handed Gun ★★★★ⓅⒼ
Western 1958 · US · BW · 98min

Paul Newman stepped into the role earmarked for James Dean and delivers a brilliant, Brando-esque screen portrayal of outlaw Billy the Kid as envisaged by writer Gore Vidal. In this terrific movie debut from director Arthur Penn, character actor John Dehner got the break of his life co-starring as Pat Garrett, while casting Hurd Hatfield as a nervous chronicler of the times was a clever touch. The film was heavily truncated on its UK cinema release. TS *DVD*

Paul Newman *Billy Bonney* • Lita Milan *Celsa* • John Dehner *Pat Garrett* • Hurd Hatfield *Moultrie* • James Congdon *Charlie Boudre* • James Best *Tom Folliard* ■ *Dir* Arthur Penn • *Scr* Leslie Stevens, from the teleplay *The Death of Billy the Kid* by Gore Vidal • *Editor* Folmar Blangsted

L

Left Luggage ★★ PG

Drama 1997 · Neth/Bel/US · Colour · 96min

Set in 1970s Antwerp, Jeroen Krabbé's first feature as director settles for cheap sentiment when it might have more profitably explored the challenges faced by a strict, patriarchal culture confronted with a changing world. All the characters – from David Bradley's bigoted concierge to Isabella Rossellini's dutiful Hasidic wife – are one-dimensional, with even Laura Fraser's questioning student-cum-nanny governed more by her emotions than her reason. DP Swearing. *DVD*

Isabella Rossellini *Mrs Kalman* • Maximilian Schell *Chaja's father* • Marianne Sägebrecht *Chaja's mother* • Chaim Topol [Topol] *Mr Apfelshnitt* • Laura Fraser *Chaja* • Jeroen Krabbé *Mr Kalman* • Adam Monty *Simcha Kalman* • David Bradley (2) *Concierge* ■ *Dir* Jeroen Krabbé • *Scr* Jeroen Krabbé, Edwin de Vries, from the novel *The Shovel and the Loom* by Carl Friedman

Left, Right and Centre ★★ U

Political comedy 1959 · UK · BW · 88min

Playing another in a long line of silly asses, Ian Carmichael is spot-on as the TV pundit who runs for the Conservatives in a local election. It's hardly a searing satire, but director and co-writer Sidney Gilliat scores a few points at the expense of both the media and the establishment. Stealing everyone's thunder, however, is Alastair Sim as Carmichael's impoverished uncle seeking ways to maintain his stately pile. DP

Ian Carmichael *Robert Wilcot* • Patricia Bredin *Stella Stoker* • Alastair Sim *Lord Wilcot* • Eric Barker *Bert Glimmer* • Richard Wattis *Harding-Pratt* • Gordon Harker *Hardy* • Jack Hedley *Bill Hemingway* • Leslie Dwyer *Alf Stoker* ■ *Dir* Sidney Gilliat • *Scr* Sidney Gilliat, from the story by Sidney Gilliat, Val Valentine

Left to Die: the Sandra and Tammi Chase Story ★★

Drama based on a true story 2012 · US · Colour

Barbara Hershey gives a strong performance here, as an American mum arrested for allegedly drug trafficking in Ecuador in this biased but unsettling true-life drama. A real tourist's worst nightmare tale, the unsubtle TV movie does all it can to stir up viewer indignation, as Hershey's ailing Sandra Chase is thrown into a seriously hellish prison for 22 months without trial, while daughter Tammi (an unconvincing Rachael Leigh Cook) fights for her release. Ecuador's legal system comes in for some severe vilification, but despite this events often lack the emotional punch they deserve. SF

Barbara Hershey *Sandra Chase* • Rachael Leigh Cook *Tammi Chase* • Vincent Irizarry *Nick Sakeris* • Nicholas Gonzalez *Alex* ■ *Dir* Leon Ichaso • *Scr* Suzette Couture, Agatha Dominik

The Legacy ★★ 18

Horror 1978 · UK · Colour · 97min

This modern variation on *The Old Dark House* formula finds Californians Katharine Ross and Sam Elliott stranded with a group of strangers – the Who's Roger Daltrey among them – in an English country mansion. As the guests are bumped off one by one, a Satanism subplot is introduced into the already unfocused proceedings to add extra suspense – it doesn't. This botched supernatural thriller has only some fiendishly clever death scenes to commend it. AJ *DVD*

Katharine Ross *Maggie Walsh* • Sam Elliott *Pete Danner* • John Standing *Jason Mountolive* • Ian Hogg *Harry* • Margaret Tyzack *Nurse Adams* • Charles Gray *Karl Liebknecht* • Lee Montague *Jacques Grandier* • Hildegard Neil *Barbara Kirstenburg* • Roger Daltrey *Clive Jackson* ■ *Dir* Richard Marquand • *Scr* Jimmy Sangster, Patrick Tilley, Paul Wheeler, from the story by Jimmy Sangster

Legacy ★★★ PG

Drama 2007 · Fr · Colour · 72min

Film-maker Gela Babluani follows up his startling debut *13* (*Tzameti*) with another offbeat curio, this time set in his Georgian homeland. Co-directed by his father

Temour, it's a slow-burning account of long-running blood feuds and warped codes of honour. A deadpan Pascal Bongard is the dishevelled Tbilissi interpreter who agrees to accompany three French friends on a two-day bus trip to claim a castle one of them has inherited. En route they're diverted from their mission when they meet an old man and his coffin-carrying grandson (*Tzameti*'s Georges Babluani), who are preparing for a fatal ritual to end hostilities with a rival clan. The picture is beautifully shot and rich with regional colour, but it's missing the bite and suspense of its superior predecessor. SF French, Georgian +subtitles. *DVD*

Sylvie Testud *Patricia ("Pat")* • Stanislas Merhar *Jean* • Olga Legrand *Céline* • Pascal Bongard *Nikolaï* • Georges Babluani *Young man* • Leo Gaparidze *Grandfather* ■ *Dir* Gela Babluani, Temour Babluani • *Scr* Temour Babluani, Gela Babluani, Jacques Dubuisson

Legacy: Black Ops ★★★ 15

Psychological thriller 2010 · Nig/UK · Colour · 88min

Idris Elba (star of TV crime dramas *The Wire* and *Luther*) delves deep here in portraying the mental deterioration of traumatised soldier/assassin Malcolm Gray, recently returned from a botched mission in Eastern Europe. Now holed up in a shabby New York motel, Elba's battle-scarred warrior proceeds to hallucinate about gaining revenge on his brother (Eamonn Walker), a rising US politician that Gray believes betrayed him. The film is a little overcooked, and maybe a touch too convoluted. But Elba is twitchily terrific as the paranoid Gray, who no longer knows what's real and what isn't. DA Violence, swearing. *DVD*

Idris Elba *Malcolm Gray* • Eamonn Walker *Darnell Gray Jr* • Monique Gabriela Curnen *Valentina Gray* • Clarke Peters *Ola Adenuga* • Julian Wadham *Gregor Salenko* ■ *Dir/Scr* Thomas Ikimi

Legal Eagles ★★★ PG

Comedy thriller 1986 · US · Colour · 110min

This high-gloss courtroom comedy thriller was director Ivan Reitman's next movie after his mega-hit *Ghost Busters*. Robert Redford and Debra Winger star as attorneys involved in the unusual case of an artist (Daryl Hannah) accused of stealing a painting by her late father. It's not long before district attorney Redford has hopped over the fence to help defence lawyer Winger get to the bottom of the conspiracy behind the case. There's plenty of star appeal and sexual chemistry, but the script tends towards flabbiness. PF *DVD*

Robert Redford *Tom Logan* • Debra Winger *Laura Kelly* • Daryl Hannah *Chelsea Deardon* • Brian Dennehy *Cavanaugh* • Terence Stamp *Victor Taft* • Steven Hill *Bower* • David Clennon *Blanchard* • John McMartin *Forrester* ■ *Dir* Ivan Reitman • *Scr* Jim Cash, Jack Epps Jr, from a story by Jim Cash, Ivan Reitman

Legalese ★★★

Satirical courtroom drama 1998 · US · Colour · 92min

Veteran James Garner lends his unique charm to this satirical TV drama that once again exposes the failings of the legal profession. Sleazy lawyer Garner takes on the case of actress Gina Gershon, who is charged with murder. There's nothing new or shocking here, but it's fun to watch old pro Garner at work, and there's good support from Kathleen Turner as a talk-show host. MC

James Garner *Norman Keane* • Kathleen Turner *Brenda Whitlass* • Gina Gershon *Angela Beale* • Mary-Louise Parker *Rita Martin* • Edward Kerr *Roy Guyton* • Brian Doyle-Murray *Harley Guyton* ■ *Dir* Glenn Jordan • *Scr* Billy Ray

Legally Blonde ★★★★ 12

Comedy 2001 · US · Colour · 92min

Reese Witherspoon stars as a sorority queen who's dumped by her rich boyfriend Matthew Davis before he goes to Harvard Law School, as he thinks she's not smart enough to be his wife. The Valley Girl follows him there to prove him wrong and

get him back. It's all desperately silly but wildly entertaining; the sight of a pink-clad Witherspoon tottering on stilettos through Harvard's revered halls is hilarious, and the star is perfect as the girl whose specialist subjects are *Cosmopolitan* and manicures. JB *DVD* *SB*

Reese Witherspoon *Elle Woods* • Luke Wilson *Emmett Richmond* • Selma Blair *Vivian Kensington* • Matthew Davis *Warner Huntington* • Victor Garber *Professor Callahan* • Jennifer Coolidge *Paulette* • Holland Taylor *Professor Stromwell* • Ali Larter *Brooke Taylor-Windham* • Raquel Welch *Mrs Windham Vandermark* ■ *Dir* Robert Luketic • *Scr* Karen McCullah Lutz, Kirsten Smith, from a novel by Amanda Brown

Legally Blonde 2: Red, White & Blonde ★★ PG

Comedy 2003 · US · Colour · 90min

Reese Witherspoon returns as ditzy blonde socialite Elle Woods in this frothy but dumb sequel to the 2001 hit comedy. Having graduated from Harvard, the pink-clad cutie is now a rising young lawyer, intent on legally ending the animal experimentation that's keeping her beloved dog's mother locked up in a cosmetics lab. Without Witherspoon, however, the film would be a mess – some of the scenes are toe-curlingly embarrassing, while the plotline is beyond preposterous. A belated third film, *Legally Blondes* featuring Elle Woods's pink obsessed British cousins, vanished without trace in 2008. SF *DVD*

Reese Witherspoon *Elle Woods* • Sally Field *Congresswoman Rudd* • Regina King *Grace Rossiter* • Jennifer Coolidge *Paulette Parcelle* • Bruce McGill *Stanford Marks* • Dana Ivey *Libby Hauser* • Bob Newhart *Sid Post* • Luke Wilson *Emmett Richmond* ■ *Dir* Charles Herman-Wurmfeld • *Scr* Kate Kondell, from a story by Eve Ahlert, Dennis Drake, Kate Kondell, characters by Amanda Brown

Legally Blondes ★ PG

Comedy 2008 · US · Colour · 82min

Two pink-obsessed, British teens make charmless heroines in this spin-off from the Reese Witherspoon comedies. English twins Milly and Becky Rosso fall as flat as the film's jokes when their characters (cousins of Elle Woods) move to LA and are targeted by the school's resident mean girl. Tweens are the target of the shallow messages hammered home in a stream of boring montage scenes, while recycled ideas from the original *Legally Blonde* reinforce the staleness of the project. SF Some swearing. *CS*

Milly Rosso *Annie Woods* • Becky Rosso *Izzy Woods* • Lisa Banes *Headmistress Higgins* • Christopher Cousins *Richard Woods* • Curtis Armstrong *Mr Golden* • Dana Gooray *Steve Holland* ■ *Scr* Chad Gomez Creasey, Dara Resnik Creasey, from a character by Amanda Brown

Legend ★★ PG

Fantasy adventure 1985 · US · Colour · 89min

This is probably one of the few films on director Ridley Scott's CV he would prefer to forget. It's a daft fairy tale filled with all manner of goblins, elves and pixies, as well as Tom Cruise as a young peasant who falls in love with princess Mia Sara. He takes her to see the last surviving unicorns, little knowing that the Lord of Darkness (Tim Curry) has his own evil plan for the mythical creatures. Curry is certainly the best thing in the film, which surprisingly did nothing to dim Cruise's rising star. JB *DVD* *Blu*

Tom Cruise *Jack* • Tim Curry *Darkness* • Mia Sara *Lili* • David Bennent *Gump* • Alice Playten *Blix* • Billy Barty *Screwball* • Cork Hubbert *Brown Tom* • Peter O'Farrell *Pox* • Robert Picardo *Meg Mucklebones* ■ *Dir* Ridley Scott • *Scr* William Hjortsberg

The Legend ★★★ 15

Martial arts comedy adventure 1993 · HK · Colour · 91min

After several outings as Wong Fei-Hong, the exciting Jet Li plays another character from Chinese legend in this hugely entertaining adventure that recalls the kind of knockabout costume dramas on which the Hong Kong film industry was founded. The

lively blend of action and comedy is typified by the pantomime contest to reach the top of a wooden tower defended by the athletic Sibelle Hu. This is also an excellent vehicle for one of Hong Kong's top female stars, Josephine Siao. DP Cantonese +subtitles. *DVD*

Jet Li *Fong Sai-Yuk* • Li Jai-Xing *Ting Ting* • Josephine Siao *Mother Fong* • Chu Kong *Father Fong* • Chan Sung-Yun *"Tiger" Lei* • Sibelle Hu *Lei Siu-Huan* ■ *Dir* Yuen Kwai [Corey Yuen] • *Scr* Chai Kung-Yung, Chang Jiang-Chung, Ji Ang

Legend ★★★ 18

Biographical drama 2015 · UK · Colour · 125min

With a title denoting the pedestal on which it places its subjects, this stars Tom Hardy as East End gangster twins Ronnie and Reggie Kray. Brian Helgeland fashions their reign of terror into a battle for Reggie's soul between the wife that wants him clean and the unstable brother loathe to lose his partner in crime. Unfortunately, the upbeat handling seems off, with Helgeland withholding the impact of the violence until the final act, while the insight-free screenplay flirts with Martina Cole-esque crime clichés. Still, Hardy creates two distinct, compelling characters, although the relationship between them is somewhat lost in trickery. EAS *DVD* *Blu*

Tom Hardy *Ronald Kray/Reginald Kray* • Emily Browning *Frances Shea* • Christopher Eccleston *Nipper Read* • David Thewlis *Leslie Payne* • Chazz Palminteri *Angelo Bruno* • Tara FitzGerald *Mrs Shea* ■ *Dir/Scr* Brian Helgeland • *Cinematographer* Dick Pope

The Legend II ★★ 15

Martial arts comedy adventure 1993 · HK · Colour · 96min

You'll remember from the first movie that, after completing his tower-climbing exertions, Fong Sai-Yuk (Jet Li) sided with the Red Flower Society in its battle against the corrupt ruling dynasty. Well, this sequel concentrates on that rebellion, while providing only the briefest of history lessons to help us get by. This has all the hallmarks of a hurried cash-in, with Li allowing his temper to land him in unlikely situations. DP Cantonese dubbed. *DVD*

Jet Li *Fong Sai-Yuk* • Josephine Siao *Mother Fong* • Li Jai-Xing *Ting Ting* • Adam Cheng *Mr Chen* ■ *Dir* Yuen Kwai [Corey Yuen] • *Scr* Chan Kin Chung, Jay On

The Legend of Bagger Vance ★★★ PG

Period sports drama 2000 · US · Colour · 121min

Will Smith transcends his blockbuster image with a performance of real tenderness and integrity as a golfing guru in director Robert Redford's 1930s-set drama. With her late father's resort facing ruin, Charlize Theron launches a big-name golf tournament in Savannah. Lining up against golfing legends is local boy Matt Damon, an emotionally scarred First World War veteran. Damon has taken to the bottle, until caddy Bagger Vance (Smith) provides the healing touch. As an old-fashioned tale of love and redemption, it rings true. TH *DVD*

Will Smith *Bagger Vance* • Matt Damon *Rannulph Junuh* • Charlize Theron *Adele Invergordon* • Bruce McGill *Walter Hagen* • Joel Gretsch *Bobby Jones* • J Michael Moncrief *Hardy Greaves* ■ *Dir* Robert Redford • *Scr* Jeremy Leven, from the novel by Steven Pressfield

The Legend of Barney Thomson ★★ 15

Comedy thriller 2015 · Can/UK · Colour · 96min

This jet-black comedy is the sort where complications arise because every character is incompetent. Set in Glasgow, it follows Robert Carlyle as the dour, middle-aged barber of the title who leads a boring life with his abrasive, bingo-loving mother (Emma Thompson). One night, Barney is told that his services are no longer required, and he accidentally kills his boss during a brief scuffle. As the bodies pile up in macabre fashion, the popular Scottish actor also serves as director, making great use of locations in his home city, and at least ensuring that his homicidal sad-sack remains sympathetic. **SC**

Robert Carlyle *Barney Thomson* • Emma Thompson *Cemolina* • Ray Winstone *Detective Inspector Holdall* • James Cosmo *James Henderson* • Ashley Jensen *Detective Inspector June Robertson* ■ *Dir* Robert Carlyle • *Scr* Richard Cowan, Colin McLaren

The Legend of Billie Jean
★★ 15

Drama 1985 · US · Colour · 91min

After making her name a year earlier with *Supergirl*, Helen Slater opted for a more modest heroic role with this well-meaning if muddled teen thriller. She plays a young girl who, along with her brother and some friends, inadvertently become an 1980s version of Bonnie and Clyde's gang. There's no faulting the feisty performances from the youngsters or the grown-ups, but the "kids good, adults bad" message is trite and clumsily handled. **JF**

Helen Slater *Billie Jean* • Christian Slater *Binx* • Keith Gordon *Lloyd* • Richard Bradford *Pyatt* • Martha Gehman *Ophelia* • Yeardley Smith *Putter* • Barry Tubb *Hubie* • Dean Stockwell *Muldaur* • Peter Coyote *Ringwald* ■ *Dir* Matthew Robbins • *Scr* Mark Rosenthal, Lawrence Konner

The Legend of Boggy Creek
★★

Horror documentary drama
1972 · US · Colour · 90min

Long before *The Blair Witch Project* put Burkittsville on the map, this horror docudrama featured encounters with a hairy Bigfoot-type monster supposedly prowling the environs of Fouke, Arkansas. Producer/director Charles B Pierce captures a quality of folk legend and the panic, fear and terror the fabled creature has created in the small town thanks to candid interviews with local residents who claim to have seen the mysterious beast. The obtrusive pop songs are a mistake, and so are the mocked-up monster shots. **AJ**

Vern Stearman *Narration* ■ *Dir* Charles B Pierce • *Scr* Earl E Smith

The Legend of Hell House
★★★ 15

Horror 1973 · UK · Colour · 93min

Richard Matheson's adaptation of his own novel is long on theory and short on terror. Dying millionaire Roland Culver offers a handsome reward to scientist Clive Revill and psychics Pamela Franklin and Roddy McDowall if they can discover the secret of the afterlife in a house with a history of violent hauntings. Although director John Hough makes atmospheric use of the eerie sets, he is too content to send shivers rather than shock, and thus dilutes the efforts of a cast that has valiantly entered into the spirit of the thing. **DP** A sex scene, swearing, nudity. *DVD*

Pamela Franklin *Florence Tanner* • Roddy McDowall *Ben Fischer* • Clive Revill *Dr Chris Barrett* • Gayle Hunnicutt *Ann Barrett* • Roland Culver *Rudolph Deutsch* • Peter Bowles *Hanley* • Michael Gough *Corpse* ■ *Dir* John Hough • *Scr* Richard Matheson, from his novel *Hell House*

The Legend of Hercules ★ 12

Fantasy action adventure
2014 · US · Colour · 98min

Cloned from the same visual aesthetic textbook as *300*, this is a low-rent trudge through Greek mythology from director Renny Harlin (whose *Cliffhanger* glory days are clearly far behind him). *Twilight* hunk Kellan Lutz gets top billing here as the son of Zeus, who's betrayed into gladiatorial slavery but fights his way back home. What little spectacle is on offer is further debased by murky CGI and dodgy special effects. **AJ** Some violence. *DVD*

Kellan Lutz *Hercules* • Scott Adkins *King Amphitryon* • Liam McIntyre *Sotiris* • Liam Garrigan *Iphicles* ■ *Dir* Renny Harlin • *Scr* Sean Hood, Daniel Giat

The Legend of Lylah Clare
★★★

Drama 1968 · US · Colour · 129min

This overlong melodrama is notoriously fascinating for movie cultists, dealing as it does with a sublimely silly plot involving a long-dead movie star about to have her life story filmed by her husband. Kim Novak incarnates Lylah and her lookalike, and Peter Finch is the demonic director. Both pull out all the stops (well, Kim pulls out her one) and the film topples over into absurdity. The mixture of tormented sexuality and outright sadism makes this a very peculiar experience. **TS**

Kim Novak *Lylah Clare/Elsa Brinkmann* • Peter Finch *Lewis Zarkan* • Ernest Borgnine *Barney Sheean* • Milton Selzer *Bart Langner* • Rossella Falk *Rossella* • Gabriele Tinti *Paolo* • Valentina Cortese *Countess Bozo Bedoni* • Jean Carroll *Becky Langner* ■ *Dir* Robert Aldrich • *Scr* Hugo Butler, Jean Rouverol, from the screenplay (unproduced) by Robert Thom, Edward DeBlasio

The Legend of 1900
★★★★ 15

Epic period drama 1999 · It · Colour · 119min

Every bit as lush, nostalgic and romantic as his *Cinema Paradiso*, director Giuseppe Tornatore's English language debut is a dreamy cross between *Life Is Beautiful* and *Titanic*. While about as plausible as the former and slightly less spectacular than the latter, this epic rumination on the human condition is still an engaging fable, delicately shot through with keen emotions and stunning visuals. It tells the strange tale of orphan Tim Roth, born on a cruise liner at the beginning of the 20th century, who becomes a star piano prodigy during the Roaring Twenties. Told in melancholy flashback by trumpet player Pruitt Taylor Vince, this bittersweet mood piece is packed with stunning images. **AJ** *DVD*

Tim Roth *Danny Boodman TD Lemon Novecento* • Pruitt Taylor Vince *Max Tooney* • Mélanie Thierry *The girl* • Bill Nunn *Danny Boodman* • Peter Vaughan *Music shop owner* • Niall O'Brien *Plymouth harbour master* • Gabriele Lavia *Farmer* • Alberto Vásquez *Mexican stoker* ■ *Dir* Giuseppe Tornatore • *Scr* Giuseppe Tornatore, from the stage monologue *Novecento* by Alessandro Baricco • *Music* Ennio Morricone • *Cinematographer* Lajos Koltai

The Legend of Tarzan
★★ 12A

Action adventure 2016 · US · Colour · 109min

If there was a good reason to revive the legend of Tarzan, director David Yates doesn't find it. He introduces our hero as a member of the House of Lords (Alexander Skarsgård), musing on the plight of the Congolese whose country, in 1884, is being carved up between Britain and Belgium. By the time Tarzan returns to the jungle (to confront slave traders) and does his trademark yodel, the excitement is gone. The script is too uncertain, treading softly-softly to make the character seem less of a relic. Tarzan just never finds his feet. **SP** Some violence, swearing. ■

Alexander Skarsgård *John Clayton/Tarzan* • Samuel L Jackson *George Washington Williams* • Margot Robbie *Jane Clayton* • Djimon Hounsou *Chief Mbonga* • Christoph Waltz *Leon Rom* • John Hurt *Professor Archimedes Q Porter* ■ *Dir* David Yates • *Scr* Stuart Beattie, Craig Brewer, Adam Cozad, from Edgar Rice Burroughs's novel *Tarzan of the Apes*

Legend of the Fist: the Return of Chen Zhen ★ 18

Period martial arts thriller
2010 · HK/Chi · Colour · 102min

As the Japanese military seek to extend their influence in Shanghai in 1925, a mysterious Chinese playboy becomes the figurehead of the underground resistance movement. This lavish vehicle for martial arts stalwart Donnie Yen sees the star trying to emulate illustrious forebears Bruce Lee (*Fist of Fury*) and Jet Li (*Fist of Legend*), who played Chen Zhen at the top of their game. Sadly, Yen falls far short of their efforts, partly due to lacklustre close combat scenes, but mainly because poor storytelling renders the

myriad intrigues between rival Chinese and Japanese forces both turgid and incoherent. **TJ** Cantonese, Japanese +subtitles. Violence. *DVD* *BL*

Donnie Yen *Chen Zhen* • Shu Qi *Kiki* • Anthony Wong (1) *Liu Yutian* • Huang Bo *Huang* • Zhou Yang *Qi Zhishan* • Huo Si Yan *Weiwei* ■ *Dir* Andrew Lau • *Scr* Gordon Chan, Cheung Chi Sing

Legend of the Guardians: the Owls of Ga'Hoole
★★★ PG

Animated fantasy adventure
2010 · US/Aus · Colour · 92min

Director Zack Snyder (*300*, *Watchmen*) makes his animation debut with this film based on the first three novels of Kathryn Lasky's 15-book series for older children, which follows a brace of owl brothers who are kidnapped by an evil owl army. There's a lot of death, slavery and brainwashing, and the sight of warring owls sporting gladiator helmets and speaking profoundly about gizzards verges on the ridiculous. But Snyder stays serious, helped by an accomplished Anglo/Australian voice cast led by Helen Mirren and Geoffrey Rush, and delivers a breathtakingly beautiful film for courageous kids who aren't afraid of heights. **KK** Some violence. *DVD* *BL* *3D*

Jim Sturgess *Soren* • Ryan Kwanten *Kludd* • Adrienne DeFaria *Eglantine* • Helen Mirren *Nyra* • Geoffrey Rush *Ezylryb* • Emily Barclay *Gylfie* • David Wenham *Digger* • Anthony LaPaglia *Twilight* ■ *Dir* Zack Snyder • *Scr* Emil Stern, John Orloff, from the *Guardians of Ga'Hoole* series of books by Kathryn Lasky

The Legend of the Holy Drinker
★★★★ PG

Drama 1988 · It/Fr · Colour · 122min

This magical, generous-of-spirit film has Rutger Hauer turning in one of his finest performances, as a tramp in Paris who is given a life-saving donation by a stranger on condition that he repay it to a shrine of St Theresa. But the new life the money helps him attain diverts him from his quest to pay off the debt. Italian director Ermanno Olmi has created a film that, while not pressing the religious nerve too painfully, still tackles the idea of "legend" with lyricism, evoking a magnificent Paris in the process. **TS**

Rutger Hauer *Andreas Kartak* • Anthony Quayle *Distinguished gentleman* • Sandrine Dumas *Gabby* • Dominique Pinon *Woitech* • Sophie Segalen *Karoline* ■ *Dir* Ermanno Olmi • *Scr* Tullio Kezich, Ermanno Olmi, from the novella *Die Legende des beiligen Trinkers* by Joseph Roth

The Legend of the Lone Ranger
★★★ 12

Western 1981 · US · Colour · 93min

This self-conscious attempt to bring back to the big screen the noble masked western avenger must be counted a failure, largely owing to undercasting. Yet this Panavisioned retelling of the origins of the blue-clad hero and his Indian sidekick Tonto is not without grandeur, and director and erstwhile cinematographer William A Fraker creates some dazzling imagery and scenic splendour, though he is terribly hampered by the plot provided. **TS** *DVD* *BL*

Klinton Spilsbury *John Reid (the Lone Ranger)* • Michael Horse *Tonto* • Christopher Lloyd *Cavendish* • Jason Robards *President Grant* • Matt Clark *Sheriff Wiatt* • Juanin Clay *Amy Striker* • John Hart *Lucas Striker* • Richard Farnsworth *Wild Bill Hickok* • Ted Flicker [Theodore J Flicker] *Buffalo Bill Cody* ■ *Dir* William A Fraker • *Scr* Ivan Goff, Ben Roberts, Michael Kane, William Roberts, Jerry Berloshan, from characters by Fran Striker, George W Trendle

Legend of the Lost
★★ U

Adventure 1957 · US · Colour · 104min

Big John Wayne stars as hard-drinking Joe January, not out west this time, but engaged as a guide by explorer Rossano Brazzi to search for Saharan treasure. Sophia Loren provides the love interest as a street girl looking for adventure. Unfortunately, what should have been a

romp is taken far too seriously, and the Libyan locations are the main reasons for watching this languid travelogue. **TS** *DVD*

John Wayne *Joe January* • Sophia Loren *Dita* • Rossano Brazzi *Paul Bonnard* • Kurt Kasznar *Prefct Dukas* • Sonia Moser *Girl* • Angela Portaluri *Girl* • Ibrahim El Hadish *Galli Galli* ■ *Dir* Henry Hathaway • *Scr* Robert Presnell Jr, Ben Hecht • *Cinematographer* Jack Cardiff

The Legend of the 7 Golden Vampires
★★★ 15

Martial arts horror
1974 · UK/HK · Colour · 85min

In its waning years, Hammer tried to make imaginative changes to the old favourites and this east-meets-west tale was one of the studio's better attempts to update the vampire formula. Peter Cushing's Van Helsing treks to China to take on Dracula with the help of a martial arts clan in this highly entertaining and surprisingly thoughtful kung fu horror movie. It sounds ludicrous, but it works. **AJ** *DVD*

Peter Cushing *Professor Lawrence Van Helsing* • David Chiang *Hsi Ching* • Julie Ege *Vanessa Buren* • Robin Stewart *Leyland Van Helsing* • Szu Shih *Mai Kwei* • John Forbes-Robertson *Dracula* • Robert Hanna *British consul* ■ *Dir* Roy Ward Baker • *Scr* Don Houghton

The Legend of the Suram Fortress
★★★ PG

Fantasy drama 1984 · USSR · Colour · 82min

After a 15-year hiatus, during which time he was twice jailed by the Soviet authorities, Sergei Paradjanov returned to directing with this beguiling allegory on the malingering disintegration of the USSR. The narrative concerns the revenge of a fortune-teller, who convinces a young man that he must be walled up inside a medieval Georgian fortress to save it from collapse. But such is the density of the symbolic and cultural references that western audiences would be advised simply to surrender themselves to the glorious visuals, composed with a uniquely painterly eye by Paradjanov and his star and co-director, Dodo Abashidze. **DP** Georgian +subtitles. Some violence. *DVD*

Venerik'o Andzhaparidze • Dodo Abashidze ■ *Dir* Dodo Abashidze, Sergei Paradjanov • *Scr* Vazha Ghigashvili

Legend of the Werewolf
★★ 18

Horror 1974 · UK · Colour · 86min

David Rintoul plays a lycanthropic zoo keeper in a Paris-based slice of cod Hammer horror directed by Freddie Francis for Tyburn, his son Kevin's company. Although he offers little in the way of new ideas or situations, Francis does summon up a gothic moodiness between the few scares. Loyal Peter Cushing fans will want to check out his usual top-notch performance as the coroner pursuing the snarling Rintoul. **AJ**

Peter Cushing *Paul Cataflanque* • Ron Moody *Zoo keeper* • Hugh Griffith *Maestro Pamponi* • David Rintoul *Etoile* • Stefan Gryff *Max Gerard* • Lynn Dalby *Christine* • Renee Houston *Chou-Chou* • Marjorie Yates *Madame Tellier* • Roy Castle *Photographer* • Michael Ripper *Sewerman* ■ *Dir* Freddie Francis • *Scr* John Elder [Anthony Hinds]

Legend of the White Horse
★ PG

Fantasy adventure
1985 · US/Pol · Colour · 87min

Billed as a family film, this preposterous fantasy could be a scary outing for the under-12s. Geologist father Christopher Lloyd goes to a fictitious country on an environmental "dig" and finds his plans interrupted, not to say stopped, by a white horse which turns into a dragon and several other menaces. A Polish-American production, this is a farrago hardly worth retrieving. **TH**

Christopher Lloyd *Jim Martin* • Dee Wallace Stone *Alta* • Allison Balson *Jewel* ■ *Dir* Jerzy Domaradzki, Janusz Morgenstern • *Scr* Robert C Fleet

The Legend of Tom Dooley
★★★ U

Western 1959 · US · BW · 79min

Inspired by folk group the Kingston Trio's hit song (which they perform on the soundtrack here) this Civil War western follows the lyrics all the way to their downbeat conclusion and turns out to be an unexpectedly resonant little picture. Michael Landon and Richard Rust are excellent as two of the Confederate soldiers who, not realising that the war is over, rob a Union stage and have to go on the run. Jo Morrow is good as the northern girl with whom Landon attempts to elope. Writer/producer Stan Shpetner deserves credit for an intelligent script, and director Ted Post handles his young cast well. AE

Michael Landon *Tom Dooley* • Jo Morrow *Laura* • Jack Hogan *Charlie Grayson* • Richard Rust *Country Boy* • Dee Pollock *Abel* • Ken Lynch *Father* • Howard Wright *Sheriff* • Ralph Moody *Doc Henry* ■ *Dir* Ted Post • *Scr* Stanley Shpetner

The Legend of Young Dick Turpin
★ U

Action adventure 1965 · US · Colour · 89min

One of England's most famous, home-grown outlaws, Dick Turpin didn't have the headline notoriety of Jesse James, but his country-long ride still has a substantial interest. Unfortunately this movie, with David Weston and George Cole, is lumpen and packed with all the usual clichés. TH

David Weston *Dick Turpin* • George Cole *Mr Evans* • Bernard Lee *Jeremiah* • Maurice Denham *Mr Fielding* ■ *Dir* James Neilson • *Scr* Robert Westerby

The Legend of Zorro
★★★ PG

Swashbuckling action adventure
2005 · US · Colour · 125min

Antonio Banderas and Catherine Zeta-Jones return for this colourful and entertaining sequel to 1998's *The Mask of Zorro*. The action is set in 1850, with the pair now married and parents to a ten-year-old boy (Adrian Alonso). Zorro swoops in to help the people of California who are being prevented from becoming the 31st state of the union by a mysterious medieval organisation. However, his exploits cause a domestic crisis, resulting in his wife divorcing him. The hero's drunken mooching that follows is tediously wasteful, but even when the action resumes, it's undermined by too much cheesy slapstick. SF DVD ☒

Antonio Banderas *Don Alejandro de la Vega/ Zorro* • Catherine Zeta-Jones *Elena de la Vega* • Rufus Sewell *Armand* • Julio Oscar Mechoso *Fray Felipe* • Adrian Alonso *Joaquin* • Nick Chinlund *Jacob McGivens* • Pedro Armendáriz *[Pedro Armendáriz Jr] Governor Don Pedro* ■ *Dir* Martin Campbell • *Scr* Roberto Orci, Alex Kurtzman, from a story by Orci, Kurtzman, Ted Elliott, Terry Rossio, from characters by Johnston McCulley

Legends of Oz: Dorothy's Return
★★ U

Animated musical adventure
2013 · US · Colour · 88min

This animated attempt to follow on from the classic L Frank Baum story is watchable but hardly wizard. It's based on a story by his great-grandson, Roger Stanton Baum, which sees Dorothy (*Glee*'s Lea Michele) and dog Toto getting carried back by rainbow to an Oz under threat from flying monkeys and diabolical jester Martin Short. It's a brash and thoroughly charmless affair, although the quality voice cast does give it pep and pace. DA DVD Blu-ray

Lea Michele *Dorothy* • Dan Aykroyd *Scarecrow* • Jim Belushi *[James Belushi] Cowardly Lion* • Kelsey Grammer *Tin Man* • Hugh Dancy *Marshal Mallow* • Martin Short *The Jester/The appraiser* • Bernadette Peters *Glinda* ■ *Dir* Will Finn, Daniel St Pierre • *Scr* Adam Balsam, Randi Barnes, from Roger S Baum's illustrated children's book

Legends of the Fall
★★★★ 15

Epic drama 1994 · US · Colour · 127min

In this fabulous throwback to the epic dramas of old, Anthony Hopkins plays a stern patriarch whose disgust at the actions of his own government during the Indian Wars leads him to bring up his three sons (Brad Pitt, Aidan Quinn and Henry Thomas) on a remote ranch in the Montana mountains. However, their idyllic life is thrown into turmoil by outside events and by the arrival of the beautiful Julia Ormond. Edward Zwick fashions a poetic hymn to values of loyalty and family ties, which only occasionally slips into melodramatic cliché. JF Violence, swearing, sex scenes, nudity. DVD

Brad Pitt *Tristan* • Anthony Hopkins *Ludlow* • Aidan Quinn *Alfred* • Julia Ormond *Susannah* • Henry Thomas *Samuel* • Karina Lombard *Isabel Two* • Tantoo Cardinal *Pet* • Gordon Tootoosis *One Stab* • Paul Desmond *Decker* • Christina Pickles *Isabel* ■ *Dir* Edward Zwick • *Scr* Susan Shilliday, Bill Wittliff, from the novella by Jim Harrison • *Cinematographer* John Toll

Legion
★★★ 15

Fantasy horror 2010 · US · Colour · 100min

Angels and demons battle it out for mankind's future in this feature debut from noted visual effects technician Scott Stewart. More than a little silly, it veers between high camp and supernatural hokum as an overqualified cast gives the portentous, Bible-based action far more conviction than it deserves. There's imposing Paul Bettany as a rogue archangel out to protect the new messiah; Dennis Quaid doing his grizzled best to defend his desert diner; and overtly macho Tyrese Gibson gunning down God's army of minions. The mock serious tone helps raise the entertainment value, but eventually this overblown tale becomes formulaic and far less fun. AJ Violence, swearing, sexual references. DVD ☒

Paul Bettany *Michael* • Lucas Black *Jeep Hanson* • Tyrese Gibson *Kyle Williams* • Adrianne Palicki *Charlie* • Charles S Dutton *Percy Walker* ■ *Dir* Scott Stewart • *Scr* Scott Stewart, Peter Schink

Legionnaire
★★ 15

Period action adventure
1998 · US · Colour · 94min

Jean-Claude Van Damme plays a boxer heading for Morocco to avoid some disgruntled punters in Paris. Riddled with implausibilities and acted with metronomic rigidity, it's notable for only one thing – Van Damme's isn't the worst performance on display. That honour goes to Steven Berkoff, whose extravagant posturing almost gives the film a cockeyed kudos. On the plus side, the training sequences and the battles with the Berbers are competently handled by director Peter MacDonald. DP DVD

Jean-Claude Van Damme *Alain Lefevre* • Adewale Akinnuoye-Agbaje *Luther* • Steven Berkoff *Steinkampf* • Nicholas Farrell *Mackintosh* • Jim Carter *Lucien Galgani* ■ *Dir* Peter MacDonald • *Scr* Sheldon Lettich, Rebecca Morrison, by Sheldon Lettich, by Jean-Claude Van Damme

The Lego Movie
★★★★ U

Animated comedy adventure
2014 · US/Den/Aus · Colour · 96min

After several small-scale DVD features, the first big-screen Lego adventure takes the fun – and merchandising possibilities – to a whole new level. Thankfully, *Cloudy with a Chance of Meatballs* directors Phil Lord and Christopher Miller have created a film every bit as imaginative, colourful and cleverly constructed as their plastic inspiration. The story centres on Emmet (voiced by Chris Pratt), a chirpy, rule-abiding construction worker for whom life is simply "awesome". That is, until he's chosen by a rebel group of master builders to stop President Business (Will Ferrell) executing his plan to keep the Lego populace exactly where he wants them. Ferrell enjoys the most memorable role, but there's great support from Morgan

Freeman, who plays a blind seer, and Will Arnett as a dour Batman. The action is literally block-busting and the gags come thick and fast, while the film's message about freedom of expression is positively inspiring. JH DVD Blu-ray ☒

Chris Pratt *Emmet* • Will Ferrell *Lord Business/ President Business/The man upstairs* • Elizabeth Banks (2) *Wyldstyle* • Liam Neeson *Bad Cop/ Good Cop/Pa Cop* • Morgan Freeman *Vitruvius* • Will Arnett *Batman* • Billy Dee Williams *Lando* • Anthony Daniels *C-3PO* ■ *Dir* Phil Lord, Christopher Miller [Chris Miller] • *Scr* Phil Lord, Christopher Miller, from a story by Miller, Lord, Dan & Kevin Hageman, from the Lego construction toys

Lemming
★★★ 15

Psychological drama 2005 · Fr · Colour · 124min

A quirky psychological drama that does its utmost to avoid genre pigeonholing, this plays like a Claude Chabrol mystery mutated into something ominous and twisted. Successful inventor Laurent Lucas enjoys a blissful, middle-class life in the south of France, with his wife Charlotte Gainsbourg. But following a squirm-inducing dinner with philandering boss André Dussollier and his poisonous-mouthed spouse (a creepy Charlotte Rampling), things start to fall apart. Suicide, obsession and, most bizarrely, bodily possession, ensue – a spooky string of events all apparently triggered by the discovery of a lemming blocking the young couple's kitchen sink. SF French +subtitles. Swearing, violence. DVD

Laurent Lucas *Alain Getty* • Charlotte Gainsbourg *Bénédicte Getty* • Charlotte Rampling *Alice Pollock* • André Dussollier *Richard Pollock* • Jacques Bonnaffé *Nicolas Chevalier* • Véronique Affholder *Francine* • Michel Cassagne *Vet* • Florence Desille *Nurse* ■ *Dir* Dominik Moll • *Scr* Dominik Moll, Gilles Marchand

Lemmy
★★★ 15

Music documentary 2010 · US · Colour · 111min

The legendary frontman of heavy metal band Motorhead is profiled in this affectionate film, as he records the group's 25th album, hangs out at his favourite Los Angeles bars and jams with equally noisy friends (Metallica, The Damned, Dave Grohl). Tracing his career from also-ran beat groups of the 1960s, through his fractious time with space rockers Hawkwind in the 70s, the release of *Ace of Spades* in 1980 and on to his current status as a rock icon, it's an entertaining portrait of a seemingly indestructible figure (he was born in 1945) still treading the boards night after night. TeS Swearing. DVD ☒

Lemmy • Dave Brock • Alice Cooper • Dave Grohl • Mick Jones • Slash ■ *Dir* Greg Olliver, Wes Orshoski

The Lemon Drop Kid
★★★

Drama 1934 · US · BW · 71min

This is an early adaptation of the Damon Runyon fable better known for the Bob Hope version made in 1951. This is tougher and more serious, closer in tone to Runyan's original, with Lee Tracy as the racetrack tipster who gets entangled with both the law and the underworld. Talented Tracy, a half-forgotten actor today, was a past-master at this sort of fast-talking, energetic role, and director Marshall Neilan keeps things moving and vividly captures Runyon's world of offbeat Broadway denizens. TV

Lee Tracy *Wally Brooks* • Helen Mack *Alice Deering* • William Frawley *The professor* • Minna Gombell *Maizie* • Baby LeRoy *The baby* • Robert McWade *Mr Griggsby* • Henry B Walthall *Jonas Deering* • Clarence H Wilson [Clarence Wilson] *Martin Potter* ■ *Dir* Marshall Neilan • *Scr* Howard J Green, JP McEvoy, from the short story by Damon Runyon

The Lemon Drop Kid
★★★

Musical comedy 1951 · US · BW · 91min

Bob Hope was no stranger to Damon Runyon's world of idiosyncratic, kind-hearted Broadway characters, having starred in *Sorrowful Jones*, one of many versions of *Little Miss Marker*. Here, he's a horse-racing tipster in debt to a gang boss,

who has his pals dress up as Father Christmas to raise the money he needs on the pretext of collecting for elderly "dolls". Hope himself even appears in drag as an old dear. It may not be real Runyon but it has enough bright quips and inventive moments to be good Hope. AE

Bob Hope *Lemon Drop Kid* • Marilyn Maxwell *Brainey Baxter* • Lloyd Nolan *Charlie* • Jane Darwell *Nellie Thursday* • Andrea King *Stella* • Fred Clark *Moose Moran* • Jay C Flippen *Straight Flush* • William Frawley *Gloomy Willie* ■ *Dir* Sidney Lanfield • *Scr* Edmund Hartmann [Edmund L Hartmann], Frank Tashlin, Robert O'Brien, from a story by Edmund Beloin, from the short story by Damon Runyon

Lemon Popsicle
★★★ 15

Drama 1978 · Is · Colour · 92min

One of the biggest grossing films ever made in Israel, Boaz Davidson's nostalgic comedy was more risqué than many of the rites-of-passage teen pictures being made in Hollywood at the same time. With every song on the radio echoing their adolescent pangs, Yiftach Katzur, Jonathan Segal and Zachi Noy resort to an ageing nymphomaniac and a diseased prostitute to satiate their rampaging urges. At least until Anat Atzmon appears on the scene. Brisk, bawdy and handled with a genuine fondness for the period and the characters, it breaks every rule in the PC handbook, but spawned six sequels. DP Hebrew +subtitles. Swearing, sexual references. DVD

Yiftach Katzur *Bentzi* • Anat Atzmon *Nili* • Jonathan Segal *Momo* • Zachi Noy *Yuda'leh* ■ *Dir* Boaz Davidson • *Scr* Boaz Davidson, Eli Tavor

The Lemon Sisters
★ 15

Comedy 1989 · US · Colour · 88min

Diane Keaton dropped her name as producer from the credits of this comedy drama, which shows she recognised it as the lemon it is. The story of three Atlantic City girlfriends – Keaton, Carol Kane and Kathryn Grody – trying to put their voices together as a singing group is a series of sorry sequences that are as banal as they are boring. TH

Diane Keaton *Eloise Hamer* • Carol Kane *Franki D'Angelo* • Kathryn Grody *Nola Frank* • Elliott Gould *Fred Frank* • Rubén Blades *CW* • Aidan Quinn *Frankie McGuinness* • Estelle Parsons *Mrs Kupchak* • Richard Libertini *Nicholas Panas* • Sully Boyar *Baxter O'Neil* ■ *Dir* Joyce Chopra • *Scr* Jeremy Pikser

Lemon Tree
★★★ PG

Drama based on a true story
2008 · Is/Ger/Fr · Colour · 101min

In this poignant but unduly optimistic parable, director Eran Riklis returns to a theme from previous movies *Cup Final* (1991) and *The Syrian Bride* (2004), namely that Palestinians and Israelis have just as many similarities as differences. Palestinian widow Salma (Hiam Abbass) insists on fighting her corner after the lemon grove she inherited from her father is fenced off to increase security around her new neighbour, the Israeli defence minister (Doron Tavory). However, she struggles to get support from the male leaders of her own community when she begins romancing a maverick lawyer (Ali Suliman), and only her neighbour's neglected wife (Rona Lipaz-Michael) seems to understand her frustration in the face of such cross-cultural chauvinistic oppression. DP Arabic, Hebrew, English +subtitles. DVD

Hiam Abbass *Salma Zidane* • Rona Lipaz-Michael *Mira Navon* • Ali Suliman *Ziad Daud* • Doron Tavory *Defense Minister Israel Navon* • Tarik Kopty *Abu Hussam* • Amos Lavie *[Amos Lavi] Captain Jacob* ■ *Dir* Eran Riklis • *Scr* Suha Arraf, Eran Riklis

Lemonade Mouth
★★★ U

Musical 2011 · US · Colour · 108min

It's not exactly rock 'n' roll, but music is the driving force of this cheerful tale of a high-school band. Watch out for British actress Naomi Scott as bass guitarist Mohini, teaming up with a bunch of misfit teenage musicians in detention class. This is another TV movie aiming to replicate the success of *Camp Rock*, and it does a fair job with a decent quota of drama. Most tweens will love it. GE

Bridgit Mendler *Olivia White* • Hayley Kiyoko *Stella Yamada* • Adam Hicks *Wendell "Wen" Gifford* • Naomi Scott *Mohini "Mo" Banjaree* • Blake Michael *Charlie Delgado* ■ *Dir* Patricia Riggen • *Scr* April Blair, from the novel for young adults by Mark Peter Hughes

Lemony Snicket's A Series of Unfortunate Events ★★★ PG

Fantasy comedy adventure
2004 · US/Ger · Colour · 103min

This visually inspired adaptation combines the first three titles in Lemony Snicket's bestselling series. A darkly humorous gothic fantasy, it unfolds like a Grimm fairy tale as imagined by Tim Burton. In another of his wildly over-the-top performances, Jim Carrey is the evil Count Olaf, an actor and master of disguise who's on a murderous mission to swindle three orphaned siblings out of their family fortune. The children are fabulous and, as they encounter everything from man-eating leeches to falling fridges, demonstrate real talent and charm. Although flawed, thanks to its quirkiness and whimsical Victorian styling, the film's still an enjoyable affair. SF *DVD*

Jim Carrey *Count Olaf* • Meryl Streep *Aunt Josephine* • Jude Law *Lemony Snicket* • Emily Browning *Violet Baudelaire* • Liam Aiken *Klaus Baudelaire* • Kara Hoffman *Sunny Baudelaire* • Shelby Hoffman *Sunny Baudelaire* • Timothy Spall *Mr Poe* • Billy Connolly *Uncle Monty* ■ *Dir* Brad Silberling • *Scr* Robert Gordon, from the books by Lemony Snicket

Lena: My 100 Children ★★★★ U

Drama based on a true story
1987 · US · Colour · 95min

This much-lauded TV movie is based on the true and deeply moving story of Lena Kuchler-Silberman, the extraordinary Polish Jew who risked her life to ensure a hundred Jewish children escaped from Poland to the Middle East just after the Second World War. The central role is wonderfully played by Linda Lavin who received many plaudits on the film's first transmission in 1987, the year Kuchler-Silberman died. A double-hanky movie. SH *DVD*

Linda Lavin *Lena Kuchler-Silberman* • Leonore Harris *Bella* • Cynthia Wilde *Rhea* • George Touliatos *Polonski* • John Evans *Sani* • Sam Malkin *Stefan* ■ *Dir* Ed Sherin [Edwin Sherin] • *Scr* Jonathan B Rintels Jr, Yabo Yablonsky, Maurice Hurley, from the non-fiction book *My Hundred Children* by Lena Kuchler-Silberman

Lena's Holiday ★★★ 12

Comedy drama 1990 · US · Colour · 93min

Hollywood has an unwritten law about luggage. If a suitcase gets accidentally switched, the replacement absolutely has to contain something valuable and the original's owner *must* endure all manner of dangers (comic or otherwise) before they, and their inevitable new-found love, retrieve their property and wave off the villains as they depart in a police car. But this tired old tale is lifted here by some perky performances, with Felicity Waterman and Chris Lemmon (son of Jack) clicking nicely. DP *DVD*

Felicity Waterman *Lena* • Chris Lemmon *Mike Camden* • Nick Mancuso *Corey Flynn* • Michael Sarrazin *Jan Mackenzie* • Noriyuki "Pat" Morita [Pat Morita] *Fred* ■ *Dir* Michael Keusch • *Scr* Michael Keusch, Deborah Tilton

Lenin in October ★★★

Historical drama 1937 · USSR · BW · 114min

Completed in just three months, to mark the 20th anniversary of the October Revolution, this propagandist biopic was designed less to celebrate historical fact than to reinforce the "cult of personality" that had been erected around the Bolshevik leader, VI Lenin. Yet, even this hagiographic purpose was of secondary consequence to extolling the part played by Stalin, not only in the overthrow of Tsarism, but also in helping Lenin secure power. BV Shchukin's amazing physical impersonation was based

on hours of studying agitprop newsreels. DP Russian +subtitles.

BV Shchukin *VI Lenin* • NP Okhlopkov [Nikolai P Okhlopkov] *Vasily* • Vasili Vanin *Factory manager* ■ *Dir* Mikhail Romm • *Scr* Aleksei Kapler

Leningrad Cowboys Go America ★★★★ 15

Comedy road movie 1989 · Fin · Colour · 75min

Proudly sporting the influence of Jim Jarmusch on his sleeve, Finnish director Aki Kaurismäki broke out of the art house ghetto and achieved cult status with this scattershot road movie. With their dead bassist travelling in his coffin and their Cadillac brimful of beer cans, the Leningrad Cowboys (whose hairstyles are more pointed than their winklepickers) fulfil their reputation as the world's worst rock band, as they lurch between disastrous stateside gigs before finally landing in Mexico. Yet, this isn't a *Spinal Tap*-type of picture, as it isn't the Cowboys that are under the microscope, but the deliriously ordinary folk they meet en route. An inferior sequel, *Leningrad Cowboys Meet Moses*, was released in 1993. DP English, Finnish +subtitles.

Matti Pellonpaa *Vladimir* • Kari Vaananen *Igor* • Nicky Tesco *Lost cousin* • Jim Jarmusch *Car salesman* ■ *Dir/Scr* Aki Kaurismäki

Lenny ★★★ 18

Biographical drama 1974 · US · BW · 106min

Whether you consider controversial American stand-up comedian Lenny Bruce a lost comic genius or a self-destructive chancer who caught the countercultural mood of the late 1950s and early 60s will dictate how much you enjoy Bob Fosse's mockumentary-styled biopic. Dustin Hoffman really comes alive during Bruce's improvised, convention-baiting routines (so much so that more people will have seen Hoffman than pre-video-age Bruce himself). Valerie Perrine is convincing, too, as his stripper wife. Fosse brilliantly captures Bruce's jazz-inflected style, and if the film, told in flashbacks, lacks a strong narrative arc, it compensates in style. AC Swearing, nudity. *DVD*

Dustin Hoffman *Lenny Bruce* • Valerie Perrine *Honey Bruce* • Jan Miner *Sally Marr* • Stanley Beck *Artie Silver* • Gary Morton *Sherman Hart* ■ *Dir* Bob Fosse • *Scr* Julian Barry, from his play • *Cinematographer* Bruce Surtees

Leo ★★ 15

Drama 2002 · US/UK · Colour · 103min

Director Mehdi Norowzian pursues two apparently separate stories: one of a young boy watching his mother descend into alcoholism after a family tragedy, while the other has a man (Joseph Fiennes) coming out of prison and attempting to rebuild his life. As the stories flash forwards and back, the identities of the characters and continuity of the plot become a little clearer. It's competently acted, moody, and often beautifully shot, but the fractured structure makes it impossible to engage emotionally with this sporadically intriguing curio. AS

Joseph Fiennes *Stephen* • Elisabeth Shue *Mary Bloom* • Justin Chambers *Ryan* • Deborah Kara Unger *Caroline* • Dennis Hopper *Horace* • Sam Shepard *Vic* • Jake Weber *Ben Bloom* • Mary Stuart Masterson *Brynne* ■ *Dir* Mehdi Norowzian • *Scr* Massy Tadjedin, Amir Tadjedin

Leo the Last ★★

Drama 1970 · UK · Colour · 103min

Although British director John Boorman won the best director award at Cannes for this calculatingly arty docu-fantasy, it's all too contrived for comfort, as convalescent aristocrat Leo (Marcello Mastroianni) sets up home in London's Notting Hill and gets to know the poverty-stricken residents who live there and who rent his properties. As an attempt at parable, it's obviously "let's-love-everyone" propaganda and comes out looking very banal. TH

Marcello Mastroianni *Leo* • Billie Whitelaw *Margaret* • Calvin Lockhart *Roscoe* • Glenna Forster-Jones *Salambo* • Graham Crowden *Max* • Gwen Ffrangcon-Davies *Hilda* • David De Keyser *David* ■ *Dir* John Boorman • *Scr* John Boorman, William Stair, from the play *The Prince* by George Tabori

Léolo ★★★★ 18

Comedy drama 1992 · Can/Fr · Colour · 106min

It reveals much about this unconventional but curiously convincing take on childhood that its young hero considers himself to have been conceived during his mother's encounter with a sperm-filled Sicilian tomato. Despite this, Maxime Collin is clearly the sanest member of his family, bearing in mind the sinister antics of his father and siblings. Employing expressionist tactics, Québecois director Jean-Claude Lauzon gives Collin's escapist and sexual fantasies a shoddy magic. DP French +subtitles. *DVD*

Gilbert Sicotte *Narrator* • Maxime Collin *Leo, aka Léolo* • Ginette Reno *Mother* • Julien Guiomar *Grandfather* • Pierre Bourgault *The Word Tamer* • Giudetta Del Vecchio *Bianca* • Denys Arcand *Career counsellor* ■ *Dir/Scr* Jean-Claude Lauzon

Leon ★★★★★ 18

Thriller 1994 · Fr · Colour · 110min

French director Luc Besson followed his hit *Nikita* with his first American-set movie, a haunting and compulsive thriller that explores the relationship between the emotionally stunted hitman of the title and his 12-year-old neighbour Natalie Portman. Jean Reno is reluctantly forced to befriend and protect the girl after her family is wiped out in a horrific drugs operation led by Gary Oldman. Reno ends up teaching Portman the tricks of his trade so that she can take revenge on the deranged cop. The two masterly central performances intelligently convey how the hitman's carefully constructed, reclusive existence falls apart as he lets feelings enter his life for the very first time. But it's the ultra-stylish action scenes that propel this into the suspense stratosphere as Besson redefines the action genre with a series of totally breathtaking set pieces. AJ Violence, swearing. *DVD* *Blu*

Jean Reno *Leon* • Gary Oldman *Stansfield* • Natalie Portman *Mathilda* • Danny Aiello *Tony* • Michael Badalucco *Mathilda's father* • Peter Appel *Malky* • Ellen Greene *Mathilda's mother* ■ *Dir/Scr* Luc Besson

Léon Morin, Priest ★★★★ PG

Second World War drama
1961 · Fr/It · BW · 111min

Few French film-makers have been as forthcoming about the Occupation as Jean-Pierre Melville. If his Resistance tribute, *L'Armée des Ombres*, is akin to *film noir*, this insight into the overpowering nature of love and faith recalls the restrained character studies of Robert Bresson. Reining in his natural exuberance, Jean-Paul Belmondo is holy yet human as the small-town priest whose ministrations elicit both spiritual and sexual responses from the previously agnostic Emmanuelle Riva. Utterly convincing in its period detail, this is a potent study of the mysteries of divine intervention. DP In French. *DVD*

Jean-Paul Belmondo *Léon Morin* • Emmanuelle Riva *Barny* • Irène Tunc *Christine* • Nicole Mirel *Sabine* • Marco Behar *Edelman* ■ *Dir* Jean-Pierre Melville • *Scr* Jean-Pierre Melville, from a novel by Beatrice Beck

Leon the Pig Farmer ★★★ 15

Comedy 1992 · UK · Colour · 99min

As a prime piece of crackling, this low-budget British comedy from Vadim Jean and Gary Sinyor isn't as hilarious as it thinks it is, but the story of a Jewish estate agent (Mark Frankel) discovering – shock! horror! – that his real father is a Yorkshire pig-breeder does have flashes of comic illumination to light up religious bigotry. The fantasy of a kosher pig is laboured, but there's still plenty of crisped flesh worth

flossing for, especially Brian Glover as the breeder. TH Swearing. *DVD* *Blu*

Mark Frankel *Leon Geller* • Janet Suzman *Judith Geller* • Brian Glover *Brian Chadwick* • Connie Booth *Yvonne Chadwick* • David De Keyser *Sidney Geller* • Maryam D'Abo *Madeleine* • Gina Bellman *Lisa* • Vincenzo Ricotta *Elliot Cohen* • Jean Anderson *Mrs Samuels* • John Woodvine *Vitelli* • Annette Crosbie *Doctor Johnson* • Burt Kwouk *Art collector* • Sean Pertwee *Keith Chadwick* ■ *Dir* Vadim Jean, Gary Sinyor • *Scr* Gary Sinyor, Michael Normand

Leonard Cohen: I'm Your Man ★★★ PG

Music documentary
2005 · US · Colour and BW · 103min

To some, gruff-voiced Montreal songwriter Leonard Cohen is one of the pop era's most romantic poets. To others, he's a musical enigma. Indeed, this documentary portrait might have been more revealing had director Lian Lunson concentrated on the compelling Cohen interviews. Instead, what emerges is that no one does his songs better than the man himself, as the action keeps cutting away to footage from the 70th birthday tribute concert held at Sydney Opera House, which features contributions by the likes of Nick Cave, Rufus Wainwright and Beth Orton. But, creditable though these performances are, they're neither a patch on Cohen's own rendition of *Tower of Song*, with U2, nor on his memoirs of how he went from New York cult celebrity to Zen isolation in a Californian monastery. DP

Leonard Cohen • Bono • Nick Cave • Jarvis Cocker • Martha Wainwright • Rufus Wainwright • Beth Orton ■ *Dir* Lian Lunson

Leonard, Part 6 ★ PG

Comedy 1987 · US · Colour · 81min

It's never a good sign when the star of a movie – in this case comedian Bill Cosby – warned audiences to give it a wide berth. Cosby is the ex-CIA man who comes out of retirement to find out why his former colleagues, counter-agents, are being assassinated by killer animals. Paul Weiland directed this lame, would-be Bond send-up, but to no great effect. TH

Bill Cosby *Leonard* • Tom Courtenay *Frayn* • Joe Don Baker *Snyderburn* • Gloria Foster *Medusa* • Moses Gunn *Giorgio* • Pat Colbert *Allison* • Victoria Rowell *Joan* • David Maier *Man Ray* • Grace Zabriskie *Jefferson* • Jane Fonda ■ *Dir* Paul Weiland • *Scr* Jonathan Reynolds, from a story by Bill Cosby

The Leopard ★★★★★ PG

Period drama 1962 · It · Colour · 180min

Beautifully photographed by master cameraman Giuseppe Rotunno, this opulent period classic sees director Luchino Visconti revisit the Risorgimento of the 1860s that he had previously explored in *Senso* (1954). Burt Lancaster is in tremendous form as the scion of a noble Italian family about to be brought down by a republican movement in this contemplation of Italian history and Visconti's own role - as an aristocratic Marxist - in it. The casting is splendid and some moments - such as the elaborate ballroom scene - are awash with visual splendour. The film, which deservedly won the Palme D'Or at Cannes, was dubbed and shortened for its American release. Visconti died in 1976, but Rotunno went on to supervise the film's restoration in the 1990s and this new print can now be seen in all its sumptuous widescreen glory. JA Italian +subtitles. *DVD* *Blu*

Burt Lancaster *Don Fabrizio, Prince of Salina* • Alain Delon *Tancredi, the Prince's nephew* • Claudia Cardinale *Angelica Sedara* • Paolo Stoppa *Don Calogero Sedara* • Rina Morelli *Maria Stella, wife of the Prince* • Romolo Valli *Father Pirrone* • Serge Reggiani *Don Ciccio Tumeo* • Leslie French *Cavalier Chevally* • Mario Girotti [Terence Hill] *Count Cavriaghi* ■ *Dir* Luchino Visconti • *Scr* Luchino Visconti, Suso Cecchi D'Amico, Pasquale Festa Campanile, Enrico Medioli, Massimo Franciosa, from the novel *Il Gattopardo* by Giuseppe Tomasi di Lampedusa • *Music* Nino Rota

The Leopard Man ★★★★

Thriller   1943 · US · BW · 66min

This unconventionally haunting masterpiece of "quiet horror", produced by B-movie auteur Val Lewton, is set in a small New Mexico town. A nightclub dancer attempts to upstage her rival by bringing a live leopard to the show, but the spooked animal escapes into the night and, soon after, mauled bodies begin to appear. All is not what it seems, however, in this splendidly old-school chiller that boasts some unforgettable scenes. Director Jacques Tourneur never bettered the moment in which a young girl's blood trickles under a locked door as she is attacked by an unseen force. AJ

Dennis O'Keefe *Jerry Manning* • Jean Brooks *Kiki Walker* • Margo *Clo-Clo* • Isabel Jewell *Maria* • James Bell *Dr Galbraith* • Margaret Landry *Teresa Delgado* ■ *Dir* Jacques Tourneur • *Scr* Ardel Wray, Edward Dein, from the novel *Black Alibi* by Cornell Woolrich • *Producer* Val Lewton

Lepke ★★★ 18

Biographical crime drama
1975 · US · Colour · 104min

This crime drama was designed to cash in on the gangster boom following the success of *The Godfather* and harked back to the golden age of James Cagney and Humphrey Bogart. Louis "Lepke" Buchalter was the Jewish hoodlum whose reign as the head of Murder Inc ended in the electric chair in 1944. Although he occasionally chews the scenery, Tony Curtis brings a disturbingly convincing megalomaniacal brutality to the title role, and he's well supported by Anjanette Comer as his put-upon wife and Milton Berle, in a rare non-comic role, as his father-in-law. DP

Tony Curtis *Louis "Lepke" Buchalter* • Anjanette Comer *Bernice Meyer* • Michael Callan *Robert Kane* • Warren Berlinger *Gurrah Shapiro* • Gianni Russo *Albert Anastasia* • Vic Tayback *Lucky Luciano* • Mary Wilcox *Marion* • Milton Berle *Mr Meyer* ■ *Dir* Menahem Golan • *Scr* Wesley Lau, Tamar Hoffs, from a story by Wesley Lau

Leprechaun ★ 15

Horror   1992 · US · Colour · 87min

This tacky debasement of a charming Irish legend is too juvenile for adult tastes and too gruesome for children. Three teenagers free nasty leprechaun (Warwick Davis) who's been trapped in a crate in a farmhouse for ten years and he then goes on the gory search for his stolen pot of gold. Made up of nothing but low points, the unfunny repartee, forced whimsicality and endless running around add shoddy insult to blarney injury. Sadly, four sequels followed. AJ Violence *DVD*

Warwick Davis *The Leprechaun* • Jennifer Aniston *Tory* • Ken Olandt *Nathan* • Mark Holton *Ozzie* • Robert Gorman [Robert Hy Gorman] *Alex* • John Sanderford *JD* ■ *Dir/Scr* Mark Jones (2)

Les Patterson Saves the World ★ 15

Comedy   1987 · Aus · Colour · 85min

Barry Humphries makes us laugh as Dame Edna Everage and as Australia's cultural attaché Sir Les Patterson, but this cinema outing is a catalogue of misfired jokes and rock bottom tastelessness. The beer-swilling Patterson racks up the sort of infantile puns that even the *Carry On* team would have thrown out. The plot about international espionage implies a sort of Bond send-up but to call it racist is to dignify it. Easily a candidate for the worst movie ever made. AT *DVD*

Barry Humphries *Sir Les Patterson/Dame Edna Everage* • Pamela Stephenson *Veronique Crudite* • Thaao Penghlis *Colonel Richard Godowni* • Andrew Clarke *Neville Thonge* • Henri Szeps *Dr Charles Herpes/Desiree* • Hugh Keays-Byrne *Inspector Farouk* • Garth Meade *Mustafa Toul* ■ *Dir* George Miller (1) • *Scr* Barry Humphries, Diane Millstead

Lesbian Vampire Killers ★★ 15

Comedy horror
2008 · UK/Can/Hun · Colour · 82min

Mathew Horne and James Corden were still riding high from hit comedy *Gavin & Stacey* when they collaborated on this horrid Hammer homage. However, their subsequent sketch show smacked of *The Emperor's New Clothes*, and this scatological traipse through Hammer iconography only confirms that assessment. Horne plays jilted wimp Jimmy, who goes hiking with priapic pal Corden to forget his ex and ends up in a village beset by Sapphic bloodsuckers. Comparisons to *Shaun of the Dead* are inevitable but that film succeeded in being both funny and gory. Despite the obvious love for the lurid sauciness of 1970s horror, the titters here are so telegraphed and hoary, they would barely have passed muster in that decade itself. JA Violence, swearing, sexual references. *DVD* *Blu-ray*

James Corden *Fletch* • Mathew Horne *Jimmy Maclaren/Baron Wolfgang Maclaren* • MyAnna Buring *Lotte* • Lucy Gaskell *Judy* • Ashley Mulheron *Trudi* • Louise Dylan *Anke* • Silvia Colloca *Carmilla* • Paul McGann *The Storyteller/Vicar* ■ *Dir* Phil Claydon • *Scr* Paul Hupfield, Stewart Williams

Less than Zero ★★ 18

Drama   1987 · US · Colour · 94min

The "Brat Pack" gets hedonistic in an overly glossy filming of Bret Easton Ellis's novel about rich kids living the wild life in Los Angeles. Robert Downey Jr is very convincing as a wealthy, charming cocaine addict on a slippery slope to rock bottom, and you'll struggle to find a sadder example of life imitating art. Andrew McCarthy and Jami Gertz are too lightweight for this material, though, and there's a lack of emotional involvement in what amounts to a pretty pop video about the perils of excess. RS *DVD*

Andrew McCarthy *Clay* • Jami Gertz *Blair* • Robert Downey Jr *Julian* • James Spader *Rip* • Tony Bill *Bradford Easton* • Nicholas Pryor *Benjamin Wells* • Donna Mitchell *Elaine Easton* • Michael Bowen *Hop* ■ *Dir* Marek Kanievska • *Scr* Harley Peyton, from the novel by Bret Easton Ellis

The Lesson ★★★★ 15

Comedy drama   2014 · Bul/Gre · Colour · 111min

Needs must is the lesson provincial Bulgarian teacher Margita Gosheva learns in this darkly funny thriller inspired by an actual event. Gosheva feels unable to ask her father for a loan to meet a mortgage payment and, after missing a deadline with a loan shark, the morally upright 30-something resorts to desperate measures. The film-makers subtly capture the claustrophobia and corruption of small-town life and, by keeping the camera close to Gosheva, they succeed in making her compelling. DP In Bulgarian, English. Swearing, sex references

Margita Gosheva *Nadezhda* • Ivan Burnev [Ivan Barnev] *Mladen* • Stefan Denolyubov *Money Lender* • Ivanka Bratoeva ■ *Dir/Scr* Kristina Grozeva, Petar Valchanov

A Lesson before Dying ★★★ 12

Period drama   1999 · US · Colour · 97min

Don Cheadle is the teacher attempting to restore dignity to a condemned man in this Emmy-winning TV movie set in rural 1940s Louisiana. Cheadle reluctantly visits a young African-American (Mekhi Phifer) due to be executed for a murder he did not commit. Unlike most movies in this genre, this is not about the search for an 11th-hour reprieve but rather an attempt to reconcile Phifer to his fate, however undeserved. The solid script, thoughtful direction and a first-rate cast, including veteran Cicely Tyson, make this memorable. MC *DVD*

Don Cheadle *Grant Wiggins* • Cicely Tyson *Tante Lou* • Mekhi Phifer *Jefferson* • Irma P Hall *Miss Emma* • Brent Jennings *Reverend Ambrose* ■ *Dir* Joseph Sargent • *Scr* Ann Peacock, from the novel by Ernest J Gaines

Lesson in Love ★★★ PG

Comedy   1954 · Swe · BW · 91min

Considering it was scripted within months of Ingmar Bergman divorcing his third wife, this is a surprisingly sprightly comedy of marital manners. However, it's the performances of Gunnar Björnstrand and Eva Dahlbeck, rather than the writing, that supply the sparkle in this story of the emotionally immature gynaecologist, who abandons a mistress to pursue his ex-wife to Copenhagen to witness her wedding to the sculptor she'd jilted at the altar once before. A minor charmer. DP Swedish +subtitles. *DVD*

Gunnar Björnstrand *David Erneman* • Eva Dahlbeck *Marianne Erneman* • Yvonne Lombard *Suzanne* • Harriet Andersson *Nix* ■ *Dir/Scr* Ingmar Bergman

Lessons in Love ★ 15

Romantic comedy drama
2014 · US · Colour · 99min

This amalgam of romantic comedy clichés is so dismal that it almost distracts from the smug chauvinism, as Cambridge poetry professor Pierce Brosnan relocates to Malibu after getting student Jessica Alba pregnant only to take a tilt at her older sister, Salma Hayek. Just when you think things can't get any worse, Brosnan's womanising father, Malcolm McDowell, arrives to drag this farrago to new lows. Reuniting after Brett Ratner's 2004 comic caper *After the Sunset*, Brosnan and Hayek lack chemistry, but their reluctance to put much effort in is perhaps understandable here. DP Swearing, sex

Pierce Brosnan *Richard Haig* • Jessica Alba *Kate* • Salma Hayek *Olivia* • Malcolm McDowell *Gordon* • Marlee Matlin *Cindy* ■ *Dir* Tom Vaughan (1) • *Scr* Matthew Newman • *Cinematographer* David Tattersall

Let 'Em Have It ★

Crime drama   1935 · US · BW · 98min

This cheap and plodding independent low-budget production was made simultaneously with James Cagney's much superior *"G" Men* in a new cycle that sought to glorify America's crime busters. Its demonstrations of the latest methods of scientific detection no longer enthral and Richard Arlen's federal agent is nowhere near as vital as Bruce Cabot's public enemy. AE

Richard Arlen *Mal Stevens* • Virginia Bruce *Eleanor Spencer* • Alice Brady *Aunt Ethel* • Bruce Cabot *Joe Keefer* • Harvey Stephens *Van Rensseler* • Eric Linden *Buddy Spencer* ■ *Dir* Sam Wood • *Scr* from a story by Joseph Moncure March, Elmer Harris

Let George Do It ★★★ U

Comedy   1940 · UK · BW · 79min

This is one of the best George Formby comedies, with Basil Dearden producing and co-scripting and Ronald Neame behind the camera. On screen, Formby is supported by Phyllis Calvert, as the homely girl who falls for his toothy charm, and Coral Browne, as a wicked seductress, as well as villain supreme Torin Thatcher. The story sees Formby do his first bit for the war effort, as he fetches up in Bergen instead of Blackpool and finds himself on the trail of Quislings and the Gestapo. DP

George Formby *George* • Phyllis Calvert *Mary* • Garry Marsh *Mendez* • Romney Brent *Slim* • Bernard Lee *Nelson* • Coral Browne *Ivy* • Diana Beaumont *Greta* ■ *Dir* Marcel Varnel • *Scr* John Dighton, Austin Melford, Angus MacPhail, Basil Dearden

Let Him Have It ★★★★ 15

Biographical crime drama
1991 · UK · Colour · 110min

Director Peter Medak followed his crime biopic *The Krays* with another *cause célèbre* torn from past headlines. The Derek Bentley case remains as much a classic crusading appeal against capital punishment today as it was back in 1952 when the mentally disabled teenage epileptic stood accused of inciting the shooting of a cop after a bungled factory burglary. With drab-chic production, Christopher Eccleston's marvellous central performance and a pop nostalgia soundtrack, the odious miscarriage of justice comes vividly to life to scandalise anew. AJ *DVD*

Chris Eccleston [Christopher Eccleston] *Derek Bentley* • Paul Reynolds *Chris Craig* • Tom Courtenay *William Bentley* • Tom Bell *Fairfax* • Eileen Atkins *Lilian Bentley* • Clare Holman *Iris Bentley* • Mark McGann *Niven Craig* • Michael Gough *Lord Goddard* • Serena Scott Thomas *Stella* • Ronald Fraser *Niven's judge* • Michael Elphick *Jack, the warder* ■ *Dir* Peter Medak • *Scr* Neal Purvis, Robert Wade

Let It Be ★★★★ U

Musical documentary
1970 · UK · Colour · 80min

Originally arranged as rehearsals for a one-off live show, the "Get Back" sessions proved to be the most directionless and destructive of the Beatles' career. With all four already pursuing personal projects, the tensions that would cause the final split were in evidence from the start. Yet, as Michael Lindsay-Hogg's *cinéma-vérité* record proves, the band was still capable of producing classical pop music, with the impromptu back-to-basics performance on the roof of the Apple building being the highlight. Astonishingly honest in its revelations, this underrated – and Oscar-winning – film provides a saddening insight into the end of a dream. DP

■ *Dir* Michael Lindsay-Hogg • *Executive Producers* John Lennon, Paul McCartney, George Harrison, Ringo Starr

Let It Be Me ★ 12

Romantic drama   1995 · US · Colour · 91min

This is a dance movie that fails to cut a rug. Campbell Scott wants to learn how to dance so he can impress his fiancée Jennifer Beals (of *Flashdance* fame). However, complications set in when both go to the same dancing instructor (Leslie Caron). An interesting supporting cast isn't enough to redeem this misfiring romance. FL Swearing.

Jennifer Beals *Emily* • Campbell Scott *Gabriel* • Yancy Butler *Corinne* • Jamie Goodwin *Bud* • Leslie Caron *Marguerite* • Patrick Stewart *John* • Elliott Gould *Sam* • Erika Burke *Meg* ■ *Dir/Scr* Eleanor Bergstein

Let Me In ★★★ 15

Fantasy horror
2010 · UK/US/Swe · Colour · 111min

For his retelling of the coming-of-age tale about a bullied boy (Kodi Smit-McPhee) and a vampire girl (Chloë Grace Moretz), *Cloverfield* director Matt Reeves retains the slow-building tension and chilling melancholy of the Swedish original *Let the Right One In*. Reeves's film answers more questions than the far subtler first film did, making for more standard Hollywood fare. Yet neat additions such as detective Elias Koteas, a terrific car crash filmed from inside the vehicle and an atmospheric score from Michael Giacchino (*Up*), combined with the fact that both child performers are heartbreakingly credible, make this retread much better than expected. AJ Violence, swearing. *DVD* *Blu-ray*

Kodi Smit-McPhee *Owen* • Chloë Grace Moretz *Abby* • Elias Koteas *The policeman* • Richard Jenkins *The father* • Cara Buono *Owen's mother* • Sasha Barrese *Virginia* • Dylan Kenin *Larry* • Dylan Minnette *Kenny* ■ *Dir* Matt Reeves • *Scr* Matt Reeves, from the novel *Let the Right One In* by John Ajvide Lindqvist • *Music* Michael Giacchino

Let No Man Write My Epitaph ★★★

Drama   1960 · US · BW · 105min

Adapted from the novel by Willard Motley, this sturdy social drama is the sequel to the same author's *Knock on Any Door*, filmed by Nicholas Ray in 1949. Set in Chicago's deprived South Side, it stars teenage idol

James Darren struggling to better himself, but getting involved with gangsters. British-born director Philip Leacock, whose Hollywood movies tackled strong themes, gets powerful performances from Burl Ives as a judge, and Shelley Winters as Darren's drug-addicted mother. Ella Fitzgerald not only gets to sing but also does a spot of acting. RB

Burl Ives *Judge Bruce Mallory* • Shelley Winters *Nellie Romano* • James Darren *Nick Romano* • Jean Seberg *Barbara Holloway* • Ricardo Montalban *Louie Ramponi* • Ella Fitzgerald *Flora* • Rodolfo Acosta *Max* ■ *Dir* Philip Leacock • *Scr* Robert Presnell Jr, from the novel by Willard Motley

Let the Devil Wear Black
★★ 18
Thriller   1999 · US · Colour · 91min

Stacy Title, who directed the wickedly funny *The Last Supper*, falters in this atmospheric but mannered crime tale, very loosely based on *Hamlet*. Title's husband Joseph Penner, who also co-wrote the script, is the young man haunted by his father's death who begins to take a closer interest in the dodgy family business. The cast can't be faulted, and Title's visuals evoke some brooding menace. However, the allusions are mannered and only serve to show up the deficiencies in the script. JF **DVD**

Jonathan Penner *Jack Lyne* • Jacqueline Bisset *Jack's mother* • Mary-Louise Parker *Julia* • Jamey Sheridan *Uncle Carl* • Philip Baker Hall *Saul Hirsch* ■ *Dir* Stacy Title • *Scr* Stacy Title, Jonathan Penner

Let the Good Times Roll
★★★★
Music documentary 1973 · US · Colour · 100min

An exhilarating blend of archive clips, fond memories and concert footage, this will prove irresistible to anyone who's ever tied on a blue suede shoe. Directors Robert Abel and Sid Levin frequently employ split screens to contrast "then" and "now", but the acts on display have lost none of the old hunger. Easy listeners will delight in The Five Satins and The Coasters, but hard-core rockers will be bouncing off the walls as Fats Domino, Chubby Checker, Bill Haley and Little Richard let rip. However, the highlight is Chuck Berry and Bo Diddley's rendition of *Johnny B Goode*. DP

Chuck Berry • Little Richard • Fats Domino ■ *Dir* Sidney Levin, Robert Abel

Let the Right One In
★★★★ 15
Horror   2008 · Swe/Nor · Colour · 109min

Set in the snowy urban wastes of Stockholm in the early 1980s, this Swedish vampire movie proves unexpectedly moving. It's a curious love story between bullied 12-year-old Oskar (Kare Hedebrant) and Eli (Lina Leandersson), a doe-eyed little girl who hides a dark secret. Based on John Ajvide Lindqvist's bestselling novel, *Let the Right One In* develops into a muted meditation on violence and vengeance as bloodsucker Eli convinces Oskar to strike back at his tormentors. It's undeniably frightening – much grisly bloodletting ensues as Eli's middle-aged helper Hakan (Per Ragnar) drains local youths for their haemoglobin – yet director Tomas Alfredson coaxes fragile performances from his two young leads, and his light touch adds soulful delicacy and a certain ambiguity to the proceedings. JR Swedish +subtitles. **DVD** **Blu-ray**

Kare Hedebrant *Oskar* • Lina Leandersson *Eli* • Per Ragnar *Hakan* • Henrik Dahl *Erik* • Karin Bergquist *Yvonne* • Peter Carlberg *Lacke* ■ *Dir* Tomas Alfredson • *Scr* John Ajvide Lindqvist, from his novel

Let Us Prey
★★ 18
Horror   2014 · UK/Ire · Colour · 92min

Bryan O'Malley's feature debut boasts an arresting opening and a frenziedly gory climax, so it's a shame everything else in between is underdeveloped. Enigmatic stranger Liam Cunningham is detained in the cells of a remote Scottish community and begins to infiltrate the minds of his fellow inmates and the police in charge. Only well-meaning rookie cop Pollyanna McIntosh on her first night shift is able to resist his evil influence. A stale and predictable exercise in outdated material, this is silly, not scary, half-baked nonsense. AJ Violence. **DVD**

Liam Cunningham *Six* • Pollyanna McIntosh *PC Rachel Heggie* • Bryan Larkin (2) *PC Jack Warnock* • Hanna Stanbridge *PC Jennifer Mundie* • Douglas Russell *Sgt MacReady* ■ *Dir* Brian O'Malley (2)

Lethal Tender
★★ 15
Action thriller   1996 · Can · Colour · 89min

Two of straight-to-video's finest, Gary Busey and Jeff Fahey, team up for this sly thriller that sensibly doesn't take itself too seriously while still delivering the goods on the action front. This time Fahey is the good-guy policeman who is conveniently visiting a dam when it is taken over by a gang of terrorists, led by Busey, who intend holding a city's water supply to ransom. Enjoyable enough. JF

Jeff Fahey *David Chase* • Kim Coates *Montessi* • Carrie-Anne Moss *Melissa Wilkins* • Gary Busey *Mr Turner* ■ *Dir* John Bradshaw • *Scr* Tony Johnston

Lethal Weapon
★★★★ 18
Action thriller   1987 · US · Colour · 112min

In this action-romp par excellence, each overblown set piece becomes ever more ludicrous – implausibility is, after all, a large part of the fun here. The basic buddy-buddy situation is very familiar, but stylishly delivered. Mel Gibson plays the reckless detective whose disregard for danger makes him a walking time bomb for criminals and colleagues alike. Mature family man Danny Glover is his by-the-book, ever-fretful partner. The pair investigate a drugs ring, and bring a great deal of spirit to the mindless mayhem. JM Violence, swearing, nudity. **DVD** **Blu-ray**

Mel Gibson *Martin Riggs* • Danny Glover *Roger Murtaugh* • Gary Busey *Joshua* • Mitchell Ryan *General McAllister* • Tom Atkins *Michael Hunsaker* • Darlene Love *Trish Murtaugh* • Traci Wolfe *Rianne Murtaugh* • Jackie Swanson *Amanda Hunsaker* • Damon Hines *Nick Murtaugh* • Ebonie Smith *Carrie Murtaugh* • Steve Kahan *Captain Ed Murphy* ■ *Dir* Richard Donner • *Scr* Shane Black

Lethal Weapon 2
★★★ 18
Action thriller   1989 · US · Colour · 112min

Let down by a tiresomely inconsistent script about South African drug runners and their crooked accountant, director Richard Donner here accents humour rather than explosive action. The result is an oddly toned, cartoon-like adventure with the comedy elements making the nasty violence seem even more gratuitous. However, Mel Gibson and Danny Glover's evident rapport continues to delight, as does Joe Pesci's fun turn. AJ Violence, swearing, nudity. **DVD** **Blu-ray**

Mel Gibson *Martin Riggs* • Danny Glover *Roger Murtaugh* • Joe Pesci *Leo Getz* • Joss Ackland *Arjen Rudd* • Derrick O'Connor *Pieter Vorstedt* • Patsy Kensit *Rika van den Haas* • Darlene Love *Trish Murtaugh* • Traci Wolfe *Rianne Murtaugh* • Steve Kahan *Captain Murphy* • Mark Rolston *Hans* ■ *Dir* Richard Donner • *Scr* Jeffrey Boam, from a story by Shane Black, Warren Murphy, from characters by Shane Black

Lethal Weapon 3
★★★ 15
Action comedy thriller 1992 · US · Colour · 115min

Mindless mayhem doesn't come slicker than in these action extravaganzas, and, even though the law of diminishing returns is starting to have an effect, the sheer scale of the set pieces will keep fans of the first two movies satisfied. This time around, Mel Gibson gets a girl after his own heart (cop Rene Russo), soon-to-retire partner Danny Glover looks more worried than ever, and Joe Pesci is the butt of the duo's jokes. JF Violence, swearing. **DVD** **Blu-ray** **CS**

Mel Gibson *Martin Riggs* • Danny Glover *Roger Murtaugh* • Joe Pesci *Leo Getz* • Rene Russo *Lorna Cole* • Stuart Wilson (1) *Jack Travis* • Steve Kahan *Captain Murphy* • Darlene Love *Trish Murtaugh* • Damon Hines *Nick Murtaugh* ■ *Dir* Richard Donner • *Scr* Jeffrey Boam, Robert Mark Kamen, from a story by Jeffrey Boam, from characters by Shane Black

Lethal Weapon 4
★★★ 15
Action comedy thriller 1998 · US · Colour · 120min

The fourth instalment in the action series has a "going through the motions" feel to it all. Mel Gibson and Danny Glover continue to bicker away amicably, Joe Pesci remains the butt of most of their jokes, while the pregnant Rene Russo is stuck largely on the sidelines. Chris Rock also jumps aboard the franchise, but the most notable addition is Jet Li, the Hong Kong action star whose awesome fighting skills leave the rest of the cast looking bemused. JF Swearing, violence, sex scenes, drug abuse. **DVD** **Blu-ray**

Mel Gibson *Martin Riggs* • Danny Glover *Roger Murtaugh* • Joe Pesci *Leo Getz* • Rene Russo *Lorna Cole* • Chris Rock *Lee Butters* • Jet Li *Wah Sing Ku* • Steve Kahan *Captain Murphy* • Kim Chan *Uncle Benny* • Darlene Love *Trish Murtaugh* • Traci Wolfe *Rianne* ■ *Dir* Richard Donner • *Scr* Channing Gibson, from a story by Jonathan Lemkin, Alfred Gough, Miles Millar, from characters by Shane Black

Let's Be Cops
★★ 15
Action comedy   2014 · US · Colour · 100min

New Girl co-stars Jake Johnson and Damon Wayans Jr play underachievers who go to a party as fancy-dress cops. When they are mistaken for real officers, they enjoy the attention and decide to keep the charade going – which throws them in the path of the Russian mob. Predictable from the start, this fake-cop comedy begins to grate once the novelty of the set-up fades. As likeable as the two on-screen losers are, the inevitability of their journey means both they and the impressive support cast career towards an eye-rolling finish. JL Violence, swearing, sexual references, drug abuse, brief nudity. **DVD** **Blu-ray**

Damon Wayans Jr *Justin Miller* • Jake Johnson *Ryan O'Malley* • Rob Riggle *Segars* • Nina Dobrev *Josie* • James D'Arcy *Mossi Kasic* • Andy Garcia *Brolin* ■ *Dir* Luke Greenfield • *Scr* Luke Greenfield, Nicholas Thomas

Let's Be Famous
★
Comedy   1939 · UK · BW · 83min

The chance to see *Coronation Street's* Betty Driver as a movie heroine is the only reason to catch this piffling Ealing comedy. Caught between the ambitions of her music-hall mother and strict chorister father, she catches the eye of Jimmy O'Dea, a chirpy Irish know-all who hopes to find fame on a radio programme. Only in 1930s Britain would anyone think that a spelling bee could be a source of hilarity. DP

Jimmy O'Dea *Jimmy Houlihan* • Betty Driver *Betty Pinbright* • Sonnie Hale *Finch* • Patrick Barr *Johnnie Blake* • Basil Radford *Watson* ■ *Dir* Walter Forde • *Scr* Roger MacDougal, Allan MacKinnon

Let's Dance
★★ U
Musical comedy   1950 · US · Colour · 112min

This is one of Fred Astaire's minor movies, in which the maestro is inexplicably second-billed to the studio's blonde bombshell, Betty Hutton. Their styles simply don't mesh: a cowboy dance routine is particularly embarrassing, with Hutton firing on all cylinders and the suave Astaire reduced to mere background. The plot's a nothing about a war widow and her son, but enjoy the Frank Loesser score and some nice Technicolor. TS

Betty Hutton *Kitty McNeil* • Fred Astaire *Donald Elwood* • Roland Young *Mr Edmund Pohlwhistle* • Lucile Watson *Serena Everett* • Ruth Warrick *Carola Everett* • Gregory Moffett *Richard "Richie" Everett* • Barton MacLane *Larry Channock* • Shepperd Strudwick *Timothy Bryant* • Melville Cooper *Mr Charles Wagstaffe* ■ *Dir* Norman Z McLeod • *Scr* Allan Scott, Dane Lussier, from the story *Little Boy Blue* by Maurice Zolotow

Let's Do It Again
★★★
Musical comedy   1953 · US · Colour · 94min

Columbia indulged in a little nostalgia with this musical remake of it's 1937 hit, *The Awful Truth*. Jane Wyman and Ray Milland are no Irene Dunne and Cary Grant, however, and their gallant attempts to whip up Mary Loos and Richard Sale's script into a frothy, light confection aren't helped by Ned Washington's decidedly uninspired songs. As the couple who divorce only to discover they were never so much in love, Wyman and Milland don't have the necessary lightness of touch. DP

Jane Wyman *Constance Stuart* • Ray Milland *Gary Stuart* • Aldo Ray *Frank McGraw* • Leon Ames *Chet Stuart* • Valerie Bettis *Lilly Adair* ■ *Dir* Alexander Hall • *Scr* Mary Loos, Richard Sale, from the play *The Awful Truth* by Arthur Richman • *Music/lyrics* Ned Washington

Let's Do It Again
★★★ U
Comedy   1975 · US · Colour · 112min

This hysterically funny follow-up to *Uptown Saturday Night* again teams Sidney Poitier and Bill Cosby (under Poitier's direction) as the two lodge brothers who hypnotise a puny pugilist into becoming a dynamite boxer in order to make a quick fortune in bets. The not-very-original plot's really a series of loosely tied sketches, accompanied by a terrific Curtis Mayfield soundtrack. The third film in this series was *A Piece of the Action*, but this is easily the best. TS

Sidney Poitier *Clyde Williams* • Bill Cosby *Billy Foster* • Calvin Lockhart *Biggie Smalls* • John Amos *Kansas City Mack* • Denise Nicholas *Beth Foster* • Lee Chamberlin *Dee Dee Williams* • Mel Stewart *Ellison* ■ *Dir* Sidney Poitier • *Scr* Richard Wesley, from a story by Timothy March

Let's Face It
★★ U
Musical comedy   1943 · US · BW · 76min

Fast-talking soldier Bob Hope lines up with loud-talking Betty Hutton in a farcical comedy of cheating husbands and fed-up wives. As a trawl of old jokes and lazy predictabilities, it's the sort of cannon fodder Paramount Studios turned out for troops' relaxation. But why, as it began life as a Cole Porter musical, are so few of his songs included? TH

Bob Hope *Jerry Walker* • Betty Hutton *Winnie Potter* • ZaSu Pitts *Cornelia Pidgeon* • Phyllis Povah *Nancy Collister* • Dave Willock *Barney Hilliard* • Eve Arden *Maggie Watson* ■ *Dir* Sidney Lanfield • *Scr* Harry Tugend, from the musical play by Dorothy Fields, Herbert Fields, Cole Porter, from the play *Cradle Snatchers* by Norma Mitchell, Russell G Medcraft

Let's Get Laid
★★ 18
Sex comedy   1977 · UK · Colour · 92min

Also known as *Love Trap*, this was Robin Askwith's farewell to the world of soft-core comedy. When you've been reduced to playing characters called Gordon Laid, it's easy to see how the novelty might have worn thin. The director is James Kenelm Clarke, whose involvement with the genre came after directing a BBC documentary on pornography. DP

Fiona Richmond *Maxine Lupercal* • Robin Askwith *Gordon Laid* • Anthony Steel *Moncrieff Dovecraft* • Graham Stark *Inspector Nugent* • Linda Hayden *Gloria* ■ *Dir* James Kenelm Clarke • *Scr* Michael Robson

Let's Get Lost
★★★ 15
Documentary   1988 · US · BW · 119min

Fashion photographer Bruce Weber produced and directed this documentary about the life and hard-drug times of jazz trumpeter Chet Baker. Because of his hard-living lifestyle Baker was described as the "James Dean of jazz". The talking-heads interviews with other musicians and some of Baker's lovers are interspersed with terrific jam sessions by the man whose edgy, bouncy music belied his inner tribulations. This is one of the most elegant biopics of a musical world unto itself. TH **DVD**

Chet Baker ■ *Dir* Bruce Weber • *Scr* Susan Stribling

Let's Hope It's a Girl
★★★ 15

Comedy 1985 · Fr/It · Colour · 119min

After his comic heist movie Big Deal On Madonna Street in 1958, it took Italian director Mario Monicelli almost 30 years to gain another world-wide success. This rather sprawling but entertaining semi-comic family saga with feminist undertones was helped by an excellent international cast, led by Sweden's Liv Ullmann. She plays an impoverished countess struggling to keep the family's decaying property. When the film sags occasionally, there is always the beautiful Catherine Deneuve and the ravishing Tuscan settings to distract one. RB French, Italian +subtitles.

Liv Ullmann *Elena Leonardo* · Catherine Deneuve *Claudia* · Philippe Noiret *Count Leonardo* · Giuliana De Sio *Franca* ■ *Dir* Mario Monicelli · *Scr* Leo Benvenuti, Piero De Bernadi, Suso Cecchi D'Amico, Tullio Pinelli, Mario Monicelli

Let's Live a Little
★★

Comedy 1948 · US · BW · 85min

This is the kind of frothy comedy that cries out for the likes of William Powell and Myrna Loy, but instead has to settle for Robert Cummings and Hedy Lamarr. Cummings seems more at home than his co-star with the endless round of misunderstandings and petty feuds, but the film suffers from a touch of the verbals whenever psychiatrist Lamarr gets to try out her couch-side manner on Cummings's neurotic advertising executive. DP

Hedy Lamarr *Dr JO Loring* · Robert Cummings *Duke Crawford* · Anna Sten *Michele Bennett* · Robert Shayne *Dr Richard Field* · Mary Treen *Miss Adams* · Harry Antrim *James Montgomery* ■ *Dir* Richard Wallace · *Scr* Howard Irving Young, Edmund Hartmann [Edmund L Hartmann], Albert J Cohen, from a story by Albert J Cohen, Jack Harvey

Let's Make It Legal
★★ U

Comedy 1951 · US · BW · 73min

Richard Sale directs this marital comedy about a couple (Claudette Colbert and Macdonald Carey) who decide to part after 20 years of wedded bliss. When, with divorce proceedings well under way, her old boyfriend from the distant past (Zachary Scott) turns up, her husband has second thoughts. A well-characterised screenplay and decent performances make for a proficient and mildly amusing film, in which starlet Marilyn Monroe flits through in a bathing suit. However, it's an autumnal echo of Colbert's glittering earlier outings in the genre, and the soufflé only rises half-way. RK

Claudette Colbert *Miriam* · Macdonald Carey *Hugh* · Zachary Scott *Victor* · Barbara Bates *Barbara Denham* · Robert Wagner *Jerry Denham* · Marilyn Monroe *Joyce* · Frank Cady *Ferguson* · Jim Hayward *Gardener* ■ *Dir* Richard Sale · *Scr* F Hugh Herbert, IAL Diamond, from the story by Mortimer Braus

Let's Make Love
★★★★ U

Romantic comedy 1960 · US · Colour · 113min

Marilyn Monroe's penultimate film has always been underrated by both critics and Monroe fans alike, but this musical actually contains some fabulous routines from the star. The lightweight plot – a trifle about a slumming billionaire – was originally created with Gregory Peck in mind. In the sophisticated hands of "woman's director" George Cukor, it becomes a fascinating study of Monroe's sexuality, helped by the fact that she and Peck's replacement, French heart-throb Yves Montand, were amorously involved in real life at the time. A delightful streak of satire runs through the film. TS DVD

Marilyn Monroe *Amanda* · Yves Montand *Jean-Marc Clement* · Tony Randall *Howard Coffman* · Frankie Vaughan *Tony Danton* · Wilfrid Hyde White *John Wales* · David Burns *Oliver Burton* · Michael David *Dave Kerry* · Bing Crosby · Gene Kelly · Milton Berle ■ *Dir* George Cukor · *Scr* Norman Krasna, Hal Kanter

Let's Make Music
★★ U

Musical 1940 · US · BW · 80min

Elderly spinster schoolteacher Elisabeth Risdon writes a song that is taken up by Bob Crosby, becomes a hit and gives her a new lease of life as a star on the musical entertainment circuit. Leslie Goodwins directs this inane and implausible diversion, designed as a showcase for Bing's younger brother, who makes a respectable job of playing himself. RK

Bob Crosby · Jean Rogers *Abby Adams* · Elisabeth Risdon *Malvina Adams* · Joseph Buloff *Joe Bellah* · Joyce Compton *Betty* · Bennie Bartlett *Tommy* · Louis Jean Heydt *Mr Stevens* ■ *Dir* Leslie Goodwins · *Scr* Nathanael West

Let's Spend the Night Together
★★ 15

Music documentary 1982 · US · Colour · 86min

You would not have expected Hal Ashby, the director responsible for the rich eccentricity of Harold and Maude and the poignancy of Coming Home, to have steered his career towards blandness, especially with a film about the Rolling Stones. How could he have resisted making witty or punchy comments on the five highly distinctive band members? Instead, he settles for the mundane, filming the Stones playing their hits in American arenas so vast that the energy is sapped by the size. Only Honky Tonk Woman and a handful of helicopter shots reach across the divide. JM

The Rolling Stones ■ *Dir* Hal Ashby

Let's Talk about the Rain
★★★★★ 12

Comedy drama 2008 · Fr · Colour · 94min

Agnès Jaoui and Jean-Pierre Bacri have always collaborated on literate and amusing films (Le Goût des Autres, Look at Me). But they have surpassed themselves here with this droll but edgy study of the delusions, deceptions and disappointments of everyday life. Returning to the south of France to announce her entry into politics, Jaoui's chic feminist Agathe is forced to confront her self-obsession and dislike of her birthplace while settling her late mother's affairs with uptight sister Florence (Pascale Arbillot). DP French +subtitles. DVD

Jean-Pierre Bacri *Michel Ronsard* · Jamel Debbouze *Karim* · Agnès Jaoui *Agathe Villanova* · Pascale Arbillot *Florence* · Guillaume De Tonquedec *Stéphane* · Frédéric Pierrot *Antoine* · Mimouna Hadji *Mimouna* · Florence Loiret-Caille [Florence Loiret Caille] *Aurélie* · Laurent Jarroir *Guillaume* · Anne Werner *Séverine* ■ *Dir* Agnès Jaoui · *Scr* Agnès Jaoui, Jean-Pierre Bacri

Let's Talk about Women
★★

Portmanteau comedy 1964 · Fr/It · BW · 110min

Having already forged his reputation as a screenwriter, Ettore Scola made his directorial debut with this episodic comedy, that showcased the versatility of Vittorio Gassman. He takes a different role in each of the eight vignettes, which were intended to explore the many facets of womankind. But such is his dominance of the proceedings that there's little room for co-stars of the calibre of Sylva Koscina and Antonella Lualdi to make much of an impact. Patchy and dated. DP In Italian.

Vittorio Gassman *Stranger/Practical joker/Client/ Lover/Impatient lover/Waiter/Timid brother/ Ragman/Prisoner* · Sylva Koscina *Reluctant girl* · Antonella Lualdi *Fiancée* · Walter Chiari *Philanderer* · Eleonora Rossi-Drago *Indolent lady* ■ *Dir* Ettore Scola · *Scr* Ettore Scola, Ruggero Maccari

The Letter
★★★

Drama 1929 · US · BW · 62min

The legendary Broadway star who died of a drug overdose in 1929, Jeanne Eagels (the subject of the 1957 biopic with Kim Novak) plays a murderous middle-class wife in Malaya, who pleads self-defence to cover up her killing of a would-be lover, in the first of several adaptations of W Somerset Maugham's play. The later film starring Bette Davis may be better, but it's worth

seeing this version because of the curiosity value. TH

Jeanne Eagels *Leslie Crosbie* · OP Heggie *Joyce* · Reginald Owen *Robert Crosbie* · Herbert Marshall *Geoffry Hammond* · Irene Browne *Mrs Joyce* ■ *Dir* Jean de Limur · *Scr* Garrett Fort, Monta Bell, Jean de Limur, from the play by W Somerset Maugham

The Letter
★★★★ PG

Drama 1940 · US · BW · 91min

As well as its startling opening sequence, this vehicle for Bette Davis also contains one of her best performances. The film is superbly controlled by director William Wyler, who also guided Davis to her Jezebel Oscar, not to mention having an ongoing relationship with the star. The original W Somerset Maugham tale of repressed passions and murder in Malaya is melodrama, pure and simple, but Davis uses her talent for turning tosh into art magnificently, and persuades us that this is a tragedy of untold dimensions rather than a formula product of the studio system. She is aided by atmospheric photography, an evocative score and excellent support from a sinister Gale Sondergaard. TS DVD

Bette Davis *Leslie Crosbie* · Herbert Marshall *Robert Crosbie* · James Stephenson *Howard Joyce* · Gale Sondergaard *Mrs Hammond* · Bruce Lester *John Withers* · Elizabeth Earl (I) *Adele Ainsworth* · Victor Sen Yung *Ong Chi Seng* · Doris Lloyd *Mrs Cooper* ■ *Dir* William Wyler · *Scr* Howard Koch, from the play by W Somerset Maugham · *Cinematographer* Tony Gaudio · *Music* Max Steiner

Letter from an Unknown Woman
★★★★ U

Romantic melodrama 1948 · US · BW · 83min

After one of the most tragic romantic openings in all movie history ("By the time you finish reading this letter I'll be dead"), this develops into a marvellously bittersweet tale. It's hauntingly played by Joan Fontaine and Louis Jourdan, and brilliantly and economically dramatised from Stefan Zweig's novel by émigré director Max Ophüls, who delivers that rare beast, a Hollywood art movie. For Ophüls, style was everything, but here the Zweig story harnesses his Viennese sensibility to a very real tale of an unrequited love so painful it tears at your heartstrings. It's very Viennese and very wonderful. TS DVD

Joan Fontaine *Lisa Berndle* · Louis Jourdan *Stefan Brand* · Mady Christians *Frau Berndle* · Marcel Journet *Johann Stauffer* · Art Smith *John* · Howard Freeman *Herr Kastner* · John Good *Lt Leopold von Kaltnegger* ■ *Dir* Max Ophüls · *Scr* Howard Koch, from the novel *Brief Einer Unbekannten* by Stefan Zweig

Letter of Introduction
★★★

Comedy drama 1938 · US · BW · 100min

John M Stahl produces and directs this enjoyable but slight comedy drama set in the world of theatre. It stars Adolphe Menjou as an ageing matinée idol who won't admit that aspiring young actress Andrea Leeds is actually his daughter. Adding to the pleasure are Ann Sheridan, wise-cracking Eve Arden, and ventriloquist Edgar Bergen (Candice's father) and his celebrated dummy Charlie McCarthy. RB

Adolphe Menjou *John Mannering* · Andrea Leeds *Kay Martin* · George Murphy *Barry Paige* · Rita Johnson *Honey* · Ann Sheridan *Lydia Hoyt* · Eve Arden *Cora* ■ *Dir* John M Stahl · *Scr* Sheridan Gibney, Leonard Spigelgass, from a story by Bernice Boone

Letter to Brezhnev
★★★★ 15

Comedy 1985 · UK · Colour · 88min

This is an endearingly wayward comedy, a sort of On the Town reworked for Liverpool, with the Beatles replacing Leonard Bernstein and Leonid Brezhnev replacing Miss Turnstiles. Frank Clarke's ingenious and surely ad-libbed script starts when a Soviet ship docks in Liverpool and decants two sailors (Alfred Molina and Peter Firth) for shore leave. Two scouse girls (Margi Clarke and Alexandra Pigg) pick them up, have a good time and one of them falls in

love, prompting the letter to the Kremlin. It's clever, vibrant, sexy and energetically performed. AT Swearing, nudity. DVD

Alfred Molina *Sergei* · Peter Firth *Peter* · Margi Clarke *Teresa King* · Alexandra Pigg *Elaine Spencer* · Susan Dempsey *Girl in yellow pedal pushers* · Ted Wood *Mick* · Ken Campbell *Reporter* ■ *Dir* Chris Bernard · *Scr* Frank Clarke

A Letter to Three Wives
★★★★ U

Drama 1949 · US · BW · 98min

This is a witty and sophisticated, though perhaps a shade too literary, slice of entertainment from writer/director Joseph L Mankiewicz, double Oscar winner (best director, best screenplay) for this movie. Today, the clever framing device may seem a little arch, but there's no denying the strength of the central idea of three women receiving a letter from the town floosie, who claims to have absconded with one of their husbands. You never see her, but her beautifully undulating voice is that of Celeste Holm. The plot carries you along in this intelligent, almost anti-Hollywood movie. Paul Douglas makes a fine film debut, and the other Douglas, Kirk, demonstrates his star potential, but the movie is stolen by clever Thelma Ritter. There was an unnecessary TV remake in 1985. TS DVD ⎯

Jeanne Crain *Deborah Bishop* · Linda Darnell *Lora May Hollingsway* · Ann Sothern *Rita Phipps* · Kirk Douglas *George Phipps* · Paul Douglas *Porter Hollingsway* · Barbara Lawrence *Babe* · Jeffrey Lynn *Brad Bishop* · Connie Gilchrist *Mrs Finney* · Florence Bates *Mrs Manleigh* · Hobart Cavanaugh *Mr Manleigh* · Celeste Holm *Addie Ross* ■ *Dir* Joseph L Mankiewicz · *Scr* Joseph L Mankiewicz, from the adaptation by Vera Caspary of the novel by John Klempner

A Letter to True
★★ PG

Documentary 2004 · US · Colour · 75min

Dog lovers and name-droppers will love photographer Bruce Weber's rattlebag documentary. However, those less impressed by his friendships with the likes of Elizabeth Taylor and Dirk Bogarde will be left to gaze upon the beauty of the canines and the lustre of the imagery while puzzling over the precise purpose of this exhibitionist trawl through some diverse and decidedly private obsessions. With over-produced torch songs oozing a sentimentality that seeps into Weber's handwritten musings to his labrador pooch, this is the most up-market home movie you will ever see. DP DVD

Bruce Weber *Narrator* · Julie Christie *Narrator* · Marianne Faithfull *Narrator* ■ *Dir/Scr* Bruce Weber

Letters from Iwo Jima
★★★ 15

Second World War drama 2006 · US · Colour · 134min

Clint Eastwood's Oscar-nominated companion piece to Flags of Our Fathers reconstructs the battle for the island of Iwo Jima from the perspective of the Japanese army. Shooting in Japanese, Eastwood focuses on a small group of soldiers commanded by Lieutenant General Kuribayashi (brilliantly played by The Last Samurai's Ken Watanabe), who face the overwhelming might of the invading US forces. This is a complex attempt to grapple with Japan's warrior culture, depicting an army where honour rules and suicide is preferable to surrender. In trying to humanise a once-demonised enemy, Eastwood's ambition is commendable, yet there's also something rather troubling about an American film-maker presuming to speak for the defeated side. JR Japanese, English +subtitles. DVD ⎯

Ken Watanabe *Lieutenant General Tadamichi Kuribayashi* · Kazunari Ninomiya *Saigo* · Tsuyoshi Ihara *Baron Nishi* · Ryo Kase *Shimizu* · Shidou Nakamura *Lieutenant Ito* · Hiroshi Watanabe *Lieutenant Fujita* · Takumi Bando *Captain Tanida* · Yuki Matsuzaki *Nozaki* ■ *Dir* Clint Eastwood · *Scr* Iris Yamashita, from a story by Yamashita, Paul Haggis, from the non-fiction book *Picture Letters from Commander In Chief* by Tadamichi Kuribayashi, edited by Tsuyoko Yoshida

Letters to Juliet ★★★★🄿🄶
Romantic drama 2010 · US · Colour · 100min

This slight but effective romantic drama packs an unexpected punch, thanks to Vanessa Redgrave's nuanced performance. She plays an Englishwoman who's on the trail of a long-lost lover in Verona, home of Shakespeare's Romeo and Juliet. She has returned to the city with her grandson (Christopher Egan) after a letter she wrote 50 years ago and posted into a crack in the wall beneath Verona's famous balcony is found by an aspiring novelist (Amanda Seyfried). The two women scour the Tuscan countryside, encountering all manner of false leads along the way. Nicely weighted performances and the beautiful Italian setting combine to make this an unassuming treat. KK *DVD* 🅱

Amanda Seyfried *Sophie* • Gael García Bernal *Victor* • Vanessa Redgrave *Claire* • Franco Nero *Lorenzo* • Christopher Egan *Charlie* • Oliver Platt *Bobby* ■ *Dir* Gary Winick • *Scr* José Rivera, Tim Sullivan

Leviathan ★★★🄸🄸
Science-fiction adventure
1989 · US/It · Colour · 93min

As trashy and outstandingly stupid as this underwater *Alien* is, director George Pan Cosmatos does a great job of disguising its huge credibility gaps with a diverting fast pace and superior production design. A team of deep-sea miners discover a Russian shipwreck containing a stash of vodka laced with a genetically-mutated virus that turns them into tentacled half-man, half-fish aqua-Draculas. An enjoyable monster scare. AJ

Peter Weller *Beck* • Richard Crenna *Doc* • Amanda Pays *Willie* • Daniel Stern *Sixpack* • Ernie Hudson *Jones* • Michael Carmine *DeJesus* • Lisa Eilbacher *Bowman* • Hector Elizondo *Cobb* • Meg Foster *Martin* ■ *Dir* George Pan Cosmatos • *Scr* David Webb Peoples, Jeb Stuart, from a story by David Webb Peoples

Leviathan ★★★
Documentary 2012 · Fr/UK/US · Colour · 86min

This rigorous documentary explores the blood-, sweat- and seawater-drenched world of the modern fishing industry. Shot in the North Atlantic on high-tech cameras, it follows various stern-faced American fishermen hauling nets, sorting catches and eventually nodding off in front of the TV below deck. Squeamish viewers may be upset by the sight of so many hacked piscine bodies, but there's nothing judgmental about the film-making style, which observes without comment. So viewers are left to draw their own conclusions about this arduous industry; highly mechanised, yet as old as civilisation. LF Swearing. *DVD* 🅱

■ *Dir* Lucien Castaing-Taylor, Véréna Paravel

Leviathan ★★★★★🄸🄸
Drama 2014 · Rus · Colour · 141min

Only time will tell if *Leviathan* turns out to be visionary director Andrey Zvyagintsev's finest film, but it's certainly his gutsiest, most overtly political. Ostensibly, it's about a legal battle between homeowner Alexei Serebryakov and the mayor of a small Northern town who wants to buy the prime real-estate on which his house is built. However, it's also an acid-etched parable on corruption that, through its epic scope and inspired cinematography and music, becomes a work of magisterial craftsmanship and sweep. LF Russian +subtitles. Swearing, a sex scene, brief nudity. *DVD* 🅱

Aleksey Serebryakov *Kolya* • Sergey Pokhodaev *Roma* • Roman Madyanov *Mayor* • Elena Lyadova *Lilya* • Vladimir Vdovichenkov *Dmitri Seleznev* ■ *Dir* Andrey Zvyagintsev • *Scr* Andrey Zvyagintsev, Oleg Negin

Levity ★★★🄸🄵
Drama 2002 · US/Fr · Colour · 96min

This sombre, low-key drama is a reflective film that treats its themes of redemption and forgiveness with almost pompous respect. In a performance as slow and plodding as the tale itself, Billy Bob Thornton plays a convicted killer who's released from prison after 22 years inside. Haunted by his crime, he tries to make amends by befriending his victim's sister (Holly Hunter). With its gentle stillness and muted visuals, the story skilfully conveys the quiet emotion at the heart of Thornton's spiritual quest. Although events occasionally feel contrived, the understated acting is appealing, and there's some wry dialogue. SF Swearing, sex scenes. *DVD*

Billy Bob Thornton *Manuel Jordan* • Morgan Freeman *Miles Evans* • Holly Hunter *Adele Easley* • Kirsten Dunst *Sofia Mellinger* • Dorian Harewood *Mackie Whittaker* • Geoffrey Wigdor *Abner Easley* • Luke Robertson *Young Abner Easley* • Billoah Greene *Don* ■ *Dir/Scr* Ed Solomon

The Liability ★★★🄸🄵
Thriller 2012 · UK · Colour · 82min

Tim Roth leads the way in this quirky road movie, playing a veteran hitman who hopes his latest job will be his last for ruthless boss Peter Mullan. However, he's forced to have Mullan's girlfriend's wayward son, Jack O'Connell, do the driving. Along the way, Roth schools O'Connell in the art of professional killing, but the lad finds the work is less glamorous than he thought. Director Craig Viveiros kicks off the action in the style of a reluctant buddy film, but steadily builds the tension with neat plot twists and a growing rapport between the two. TeS Violence, swearing. *DVD* 🅱

Tim Roth *Roy* • Jack O'Connell (2) *Adam* • Talulah Riley *The girl* • Peter Mullan *Peter* • Kierston Wareing *Nicky* ■ *Dir* Craig Viveiros • *Scr* John Wrathall

Une Liaison Pornographique ★★★★🄸🄵
Romantic drama
1999 · Fr/Bel/Swi · Colour · 77min

Nathalie Baye won the best actress prize at Venice for her work in this intriguing, intelligent study of modern sexual manners. Director Frédéric Fonteyne contrives to lock us out of the hotel room as Baye and Sergi Lopez engage in the fantasy she outlined in a lonely hearts ad. However, as feelings begin to creep into their coupling, we are permitted to become emotional voyeurs. The linking interview sequences are a touch intrusive, but the veracity of the performances makes the characters' parting a source of genuine regret. DP French +subtitles.

Nathalie Baye *Her* • Sergi Lopez *Him* ■ *Dir* Frédéric Fonteyne • *Scr* Philippe Blasband

Les Liaisons Dangereuses ★★★🄸🄵
Drama 1959 · Fr · BW · 104min

Roger Vadim directed (and co-wrote) this updated adaptation of Choderlos de Laclos's 18th-century epistolary novel. It coolly and poisonously exposes a very particular level of upper-class degeneracy in the sexual behaviour of Valmont and – in this version – his wife. Gérard Philipe (sadly nearing his premature death) and Jeanne Moreau co-star as the couple colluding in dangerous sexual adventures. Made with a measure of restraint and a nice feeling of irony by the generally showy Vadim. RK French +subtitles.

Gérard Philipe *Valmont de Merteuil* • Jeanne Moreau *Juliette de Merteuil* • Jeanne Valerie *Cecile Volanges* • Annette Vadim *Marianne Tourvel* • Simone Renant *Madame Volanges* • Jean-Louis Trintignant *Danceny* ■ *Dir* Roger Vadim • *Scr* Roger Vadim, Roger Vailland, Claude Brule, from the novel by Choderlos De Laclos

Liar ★★🄸🄸
Thriller 1997 · US · Colour · 97min

This game of psychological warfare isn't half as smart as it thinks it is. Tim Roth

heads a fairly strong cast in a narratively fractured tale of two cops (Chris Penn and Michael Rooker) who are trying to pin a murder on their sole suspect. The film is intense and sharply directed by the Pate brothers, but Roth isn't credible as the playboy who may be a killer, and the flurry of contrivances that cast suspicion on everyone are equally difficult to swallow. JC Violence, swearing. *DVD*

Tim Roth *Wayland* • Chris Penn *Braxton* • Michael Rooker *Kennesaw* • Renee Zellweger [Renée Zellweger] *Elizabeth* • Ellen Burstyn *Mook* • Rosanna Arquette *Mrs Kennesaw* • Michael Parks *Doctor Banyard* ■ *Dir* Josh Pate, Jonas Pate • *Scr* Jonas Pate, Josh Pate

Liar Liar ★★★★🄸🄸
Comedy 1997 · US · Colour · 82min

Jim Carrey stars as a ruthless lawyer and compulsive liar, who misses his son's birthday party and is "cursed" to tell the truth for 24 hours. Carrey's frenzied physical and vocal contortions provide lots of amusing comic moments, as well as a few riotous ones, in a role that's not only tailor-made for his rubber-faced antics but also gives him an opportunity to show a more human side. His bravura performance is one of his funniest to date. JC Some violence, swearing. *DVD* 🅱

Jim Carrey *Fletcher Reede* • Maura Tierney *Audrey Reede* • Justin Cooper *Max Reede* • Cary Elwes *Jerry* • Anne Haney *Greta* • Jennifer Tilly *Samantha Cole* • Amanda Donohoe *Miranda* • Jason Bernard *Judge Marshall Stevens* • Swoosie Kurtz *Dana Appleton* • Mitchell Ryan *Mr Allan* ■ *Dir* Tom Shadyac • *Scr* Paul Guay, Stephen Mazur

A Liar's Autobiography: the Untrue Story of Monty Python's Graham Chapman ★★🄸🄵
Animated biographical comedy
2012 · UK · Colour · 84min

Despite the involvement of three directors, more than a dozen animation houses and the vocal contributions of most of the remaining Pythons, this biopic of comedian Graham Chapman is sadly lacking in what made the anarchic troupe so great. Chapman was its most intriguing member, and was often cast as the bewildered "straight man" in sketches and films. Using audio recordings he made a few years before his death from cancer at the age of 48, the film sheds light on his homosexuality, struggles with alcoholism and, on the evidence here, a sex addiction. Some sections make for engaging viewing, but the sudden shifts in animation style are awkward and distracting. BP Swearing, sexual references, sex scenes, nudity. *DVD* 🅱🄳

Graham Chapman • John Cleese *Himself/ Exploding don/David Frost* • Terry Jones *Himself/ Mother/Biggles/Anatomy don/Enormous Peter* • Michael Palin *Himself/Father/Interview don 1/ Hibbern/Queen Mother* • Terry Gilliam *Interview don 2/Dr One Across/Pilot/Aleister Crowley/Jose* • Carol Cleveland *Masseuse/Singing telegram/ Stewardess* ■ *Dir* Bill Jones (2), Jeff Simpson, Ben Timlett • *Scr* Graham Chapman, from his *A Liar's Autobiography: Volume VI*

Liar's Moon ★★🄸🄵
Romantic drama 1982 · US · Colour · 100min

A young Matt Dillon stars in this endearingly dumb romantic drama - crammed with clichés, woodenly acted, and generally cornier than Kansas in August, September and October. Dillon and Cindy Fisher play eloped newlyweds, who find their relationship haunted by a family secret from the past. As a gimmick, the film was originally released with alternative endings - one happy, one sad. Nowadays, it's usually seen with just the happy one. Soapy tosh. DA

Matt Dillon *Jack Duncan* • Cindy Fisher *Ginny Peterson* • Christopher Connelly *Alex Peterson* • Yvonne De Carlo *Jeanene Dubois* • Hoyt Axton *Cecil Duncan* • Maggie Blye *Ellen "Babs" Duncan* • Broderick Crawford *Colonel Tubman* • Susan Tyrrell *Lora Mae Bouvier* ■ *Dir* David Fisher (2) • *Scr* David Fisher, from the story by Janice Thompson, Billy Hanna

Libel ★★★
Drama 1959 · UK · BW · 98min

This is one of Dirk Bogarde's better movies from the 1950s, when critics of the time were hoisting him into the Alec Guinness class. Bringing a libel action to clear his name against the man who doubts if he really was the prisoner of war he claims to have been, Bogarde's role is the teasing centre of a clever narrative. The context is artificial, but it's Bogarde you'll be watching, not too obvious on the sidelines. Compelling, if stagey. TH

Dirk Bogarde *Sir Mark Loddon/Frank Welney/ Number Fifteen* • Olivia de Havilland *Lady Maggie Loddon* • Paul Massie *Jeffrey Buckenham* • Robert Morley *Sir Wilfred* • Wilfrid Hyde White *Hubert Foxley* • Anthony Dawson *Gerald Loddon* • Richard Wattis *Judge* • Richard Dimbleby • Martin Miller *Dr Schrott* • Millicent Martin *Maisie* ■ *Dir* Anthony Asquith • *Scr* Anatole de Grunwald, Karl Tunberg, from the play by Edward Wooll

Libeled Lady ★★★★
Screwball comedy 1936 · US · BW · 98min

This marvellous comedy employs four great stars who play together with ease and show consummate professionalism in a wonderfully contrived farce. Spencer Tracy is the newspaper editor who can't concentrate on fiancée Jean Harlow while heiress Myrna Loy holds a libel action over him, so he uses smoothie William Powell in a counterplot. This is witty, sophisticated stuff, with the stars at their peaks. In real life, Harlow and Powell were an item, and their playing together is a joy to watch, while director Jack Conway maintains a terrific pace and the MGM gloss adds a quality finish. Remade in 1946 as *Easy to Wed*. TS

William Powell *Bill Chandler* • Myrna Loy *Connie Allenbury* • Jean Harlow *Gladys Benton* • Spencer Tracy *Warren Haggerty* • Walter Connolly *James B Allenbury* • Charley Grapewin *Hollis Bane* • Cora Witherspoon *Mrs Burns-Norvell* • EE Clive *Evans* ■ *Dir* Jack Conway • *Scr* Maurine Watkins, Howard Emmett Rogers, George Oppenheimer, from a story by Wallace Sullivan

Liberal Arts ★★★★🄸🄸
Romantic comedy drama
2011 · US · Colour · 93min

The second film by writer/director Josh Radnor, the genial star of TV's *How I Met Your Mother*, is an unexpected delight, dealing with intergenerational relationships in a funny and unusual way. Radnor plays Jesse, a coasting, 30-something New York academic who meets Zibby (Elizabeth Olsen), a pretty drama student 16 years his junior but surprisingly old for her age. What follows is a refreshing, realistic and, for once, genuinely romantic comedy, with two adorable leads whose chemistry is authentic and charming. But it's the supporting performances that seal the deal here, and if a stoner Zac Efron weren't enough, Allison Janney brings the house down as a predatory professor. DW Swearing, sexual references. *DVD* 🅱

Josh Radnor *Jesse Fisher* • Elizabeth Olsen *Zibby* • Richard Jenkins *Prof Peter Hoberg* • Allison Janney *Prof Judith Fairfield* • Elizabeth Reaser *Ana* • Zac Efron *Nat* ■ *Dir/Scr* Josh Radnor

The Liberation of LB Jones ★★★★
Drama 1970 · US · Colour · 102min

Directed by William Wyler, this story of racism in the American South tells of a black undertaker whose wife is sleeping with one of the town's racist cops. Divorce proceedings backfire, and the story ends in chilling violence and little glimmer of hope. It's far more radical and disturbing than *In The Heat of the Night* – Stirling Silliphant wrote both – but lacks the showy drama that turned *Heat* into an Oscar winner. Despite its intensity, this flopped and Wyler never directed another film. AT

Lee J Cobb *Oman Hedgepath* • Anthony Zerbe *Willie Joe Worth* • Roscoe Lee Browne *Lord Byron Jones* • Lola Falana *Emma Jones* • Lee Majors *Steve Mundine* • Barbara Hershey *Nella Mundine* • Yaphet Kotto *Sonny Boy Mosby* • Chill

L

Wills *Mr Ike* ■ *Dir* William Wyler • *Scr* Stirling Silliphant, Jesse Hill Ford, from the novel *The Liberation of Lord Byron Jones* by Jesse Hill Ford

Le Libertin ★★★ 15

Period comedy 2000 · Fr · Colour · 102min

Adapted with delicious romp and circumstance, this fragment from the life of 18th-century encyclopaedist Denis Diderot is both a classic French farce and a biting snipe at the hypocrisy of the Establishment. Director Gabriel Aghion's eye for a bawdy set piece ensures the encounter between the decadent Diderot (Vincent Perez), an ultra-conservative cardinal (Michel Serrault) and a sultry artist (Fanny Ardant) has its fair share of knockabout antics. However, the screenplay's epigrammatic quality is disappointing. DP French +subtitles.

Vincent Perez *Denis Diderot* • Fanny Ardant *Madame Therbouche* • Josiane Balasko *Baroness d'Holbach* • Michel Serrault *Cardinal* • Arielle Dombasle *Marquise de Jerfeuil* • Christian Charmetant *Marquis de Jerfeuil* • Françoise Lépine *Antoinette Diderot* ■ *Dir* Gabriel Aghion • *Scr* Gabriel Aghion, Eric-Emmanuel Schmitt, from a play by Eric-Emmanuel Schmitt

The Libertine ★★★★ 18

Period biographical drama
2004 · UK/US · Colour · 109min

Johnny Depp gives another remarkable performance as John Wilmot, Second Earl of Rochester, the 17th-century poet who drank and debauched his way to an early grave. Samantha Morton is marvellous as the girl embroiled in the Earl's life, while John Malkovich is an ambiguous King Charles II. Debuting director Laurence Dunmore gives the whole a simplicity of mood, enhanced by the music of Michael Nyman. But this is Johnny Depp's movie in that he eloquently and emotionally portrays the man who died at the age of 33, having exhausted what there was of life. TH Swearing, nudity, sex scenes. *DVD*

Johnny Depp *John Wilmot, second Earl of Rochester* • Samantha Morton *Elizabeth Barry* • John Malkovich *King Charles II* • Rosamund Pike *Elizabeth Malet* • Tom Hollander *George Etherege* • Johnny Vegas *Charles Sackville* • Kelly Reilly *Jane* • Jack Davenport *Harris* • Richard Coyle *Alcock* • Francesca Annis *Countess* ■ *Dir* Laurence Dunmore • *Scr* Stephen Jeffreys, from his play

Liberty Heights ★★★★ 15

Period drama 1999 · US · Colour · 122min

Barry Levinson has directed his share of large-scale productions, but he has always seemed happiest handling smaller, more personal films such as *Avalon* and this. The setting is Levinson's home town of Baltimore in the mid-1950s, when blacks, Jews and Gentiles led separate lives of mutual intolerance. The plot traces the family conflict caused when one of two Jewish brothers falls for a wealthy Protestant girl, while the other courts an African-American. Beautifully acted and crafted with a terrific eye for period detail, this is warm and uplifting. DA *DVD*

Adrien Brody *Van Kurtzman* • Ben Foster *Ben Kurtzman* • Orlando Jones *Little Melvin* • Bebe Neuwirth *Ada Kurtzman* • Joe Mantegna *Nate Kurtzman* ■ *Dir/Scr* Barry Levinson

Liberty Stands Still ★★ 15

Thriller 2002 · Can/Ger · Colour · 92min

Anyone who has seen the superior *Phone Booth* will be more than familiar with the execution and storyline of this tedious thriller. Centred around a single mobile phone call, it's another sniper revenge picture, only here it's bereaved father Wesley Snipes who's getting even for his daughter's fatal shooting. Snipes delivers a credible enough performance, but Linda Fiorentino is as ineffectual as the trapped character. SF *DVD*

Linda Fiorentino *Liberty Wallace* • Wesley Snipes *Joe* • Oliver Platt *Victor Wallace* • Martin Cummins *Russell Williams* • Jonathan Scarfe *Bill Tollman* • Hart Bochner *Hank Wilford* ■ *Dir/Scr* Kari Skogland

The Librarian: Quest for the Spear ★★ PG

Fantasy action adventure
2004 · US · Colour · 90min

Noah Wyle stars in this far-fetched fantasy action adventure (that was made for TV) as a brilliant but shy graduate who ends up guarding the world's most precious relics at the New York Metropolitan Library. When two members of a secret organisation come looking for the Spear of Destiny, Wyle realises that his job has hidden dangers. Wyle puts in a competent performance, as does the strong supporting cast. Followed in 2006 by *Return to King Solomon's Mines* and in 2008 by *The Curse of the Judas Chalice*, also starring Wyle. SuR

Noah Wyle *Flynn Carsen* • Kyle MacLachlan *Edward Wilde* • Sonya Walger *Nicole Noone* • Jane Curtin *Charlene* • Kelly Hu *Lana* • David Dayan Fisher *Rhodes* • Olympia Dukakis *Margie Carsen* • Bob Newhart *Judson* ■ *Dir* Peter Winther • *Scr* David Titcher

The Library Suicides ★★★ 15

Thriller 2016 · UK · Colour · 86min

In this taut, blood-soaked thriller, the National Library of Wales provides an unusual setting for a twisty tale of vengeance and murder. The story focuses on a pair of identical twins (both played by Catrin Stewart), devastated by the death of their mother. It's said to be suicide, but her last words suggest that she was murdered by a man she knew. After hearing this, the girls decide to take revenge. Stewart is impressive, and the film (though not especially gripping) offers enough intrigue to hold your attention. SC In Welsh. Violence, sex scenes, nudity, drug abuse, suicide references.

Catrin Stewart *Ana/Nan* • Sharon Morgan *Elena* • Dyfan Dwyfor *Dan* • Ryland Teifi *Eben* • Carwyn Glyn *Glyn* ■ *Dir* Euros Lyn • *Scr* Fflur Dafydd

Licence to Kill ★★★ 15

Spy adventure 1989 · US · Colour · 133min

Timothy Dalton followed his limp debut as James Bond in *The Living Daylights* with a tougher, more violent affair, which is well suited to his brooding incarnation of the superspy. More *Lethal Weapon* than 007, it sees Bond resign the day job to get the brutal drugs lord (Robert Davi), who's just turned his best mate into shark bait. It's a watchable adventure boosted by fearsome action sequences and a fiery climax with a bone-crunching punch-up. Pity Dalton didn't have another crack at proving his secret-agent credentials. JA Violence. *DVD*

Timothy Dalton *James Bond* • Carey Lowell *Pam Bouvier* • Robert Davi *Franz Sanchez* • Talisa Soto *Lupe Lamora* • Anthony Zerbe *Milton Krest* • Frank McRae *Sharkey* • Everett McGill *Killifer* • Wayne Newton *Professor Joe Butcher* • Benicio Del Toro *Dario* • Desmond Llewelyn *"Q"* • Robert Brown *"M"* • Caroline Bliss *Miss Moneypenny* ■ *Dir* John Glen • *Scr* Michael G Wilson, Richard Maibaum, from characters by Ian Fleming

License to Drive ★★ PG

Comedy 1988 · US · Colour · 86min

Corey Haim and Corey Feldman team up to make this dippy comedy about a teenager (Haim) who fails his driving test but continues cruising, and has no end of mishaps. There are some laughs to be had and the Coreys are fine, although it's clear that they were relying here more on their looks than their talent. JB Swearing. *DVD*

Corey Haim *Les* • Corey Feldman *Dean* • Carol Kane *Les's mother* • Richard Masur *Les's father* • Heather Graham *Mercedes* • Helen Hanft *Miss Heilberg* ■ *Dir* Greg Beeman • *Scr* Neil Tolkin

License to Wed ★★ 12

Romantic comedy 2007 · US · Colour · 87min

Dating, weddings, and even divorce have all made ripe subjects for movie comedies – but this may be one of the first to focus on a marriage-preparation course. Robin Williams slips into manic stand-up mode to play Reverend Frank, the semi-psychotic clergyman guiding engaged couple Sadie (Mandy Moore) and Ben (John Krasinski) down the aisle. Intent on teaching the

youngsters that marriage isn't a bed of roses, the rampaging Reverend bans sex, bugs their apartment and saddles them with two mewling, puking robot babies. Williams thunders through the proceedings, but when he's off-screen the film grinds to a halt and the dull romance between Sadie and Ben is revealed as little more than a prop for the comedian's patented schtick. JR *DVD* *BLU*

Robin Williams *Reverend Frank* • Mandy Moore *Sadie Jones* • John Krasinski *Ben Murphy* • Eric Christian Olsen *Carlisle* • Christine Taylor *Lindsey* • Josh Flitter *Choir boy* • DeRay Davis *Joel* ■ *Dir* Ken Kwapis • *Scr* Kim Barker, Tim Rasmussen, Vince Di Meglio, from a story by Barker, Wayne Lloyd

Licensed to Kill ★★

Spy spoof 1965 · UK · Colour · 96min

Tom Adams is Charles Vine, the "Second Best Secret Agent in the Whole Wide World". Part send-up of the Bond ethos and part B-thriller, it's about a plot to assassinate some Euro-boffin who has invented an anti-gravity machine to which the British government wants exclusive rights. While Vine isn't in Bond's league as a Romeo, he's quite convincing in the guns and fists department. Adams reprised the role in 1966's *Where Bullets Fly* and in 1967's *Somebody's Stolen Our Russian Spy*. AT

Tom Adams *Charles Vine* • Karel Stepanek *Henrik Jacobsen* • Veronica Hurst *Julia Lindberg* • Peter Bull *Masterman* • John Arnatt *Rockwell* • Francis De Wolff *Walter Pickering* ■ *Dir* Lindsay Shonteff • *Scr* Lindsay Shonteff, Howard Griffiths

The Lie ★★★★ 15

Drama 1992 · Fr · Colour · 84min

Following in the footsteps of many a key figure in French film history, François Margolin worked as a critic before taking his place behind the camera. In this, his debut feature, he explores the heartbreaking plight of innocents who become infected with the HIV virus through the irresponsibility of others. It's a subject that forces the viewer into taking sides, but Margolin might have allowed a few grey areas in the interests of both drama and truth. As the victim, Nathalie Baye gives a powerful performance. DP French +subtitles.

Nathalie Baye *Emma* • Didier Sandre *Charles* • Hélène Lapiower *Louise* • Marc Citti *Louis* • Dominique Besnéhard *Rozenberg* ■ *Dir* François Margolin • *Scr* Denis Saada, François Margolin, from an idea by Saada

Lie with Me ★★ 18

Erotic drama 2005 · Can · Colour · 89min

For a film about the emptiness of modern relationships, this is, err, pretty empty. The pouting Lauren Lee Smith and Eric Balfour are the bored 20-somethings with parental issues who are seemingly made for each other: both are more interested in sex than romance. However, they soon discover that lust alone cannot sustain a relationship. Unfortunately that's about as profound as it gets and the fact that the voiceover from Smith could have been lifted from pseuds corner doesn't exactly help. Clément Virgo's direction is stylishly provocative, but take out the lengthy and very explicit bonking scenes and all that's left are some moody, beautiful people in search of a fashion spread. JF *DVD*

Eric Balfour *David* • Lauren Lee Smith *Leila* • Don Francks *Joshua* • Polly Shannon • Kristen Lehman *Jay* ■ *Dir* Clément Virgo • *Scr* Tamara Faith Berger

Liebelei ★★★ U

Romantic drama 1932 · Ger · BW · 82min

Max Ophüls bade farewell to his native Germany with this bittersweet confection. Clearly still delighting in the novelty of sound and the gliding mobility of Franz Planer's camera, he settles for froth rather than dwelling on the text's ironic observations on the impermanence of love and the unendurable scars it leaves. Thus, the giddy whirl of imperial Viennese society is captured with subtle effervescence, as Magda Schneider falls for dashing

lieutenant Wolfgang Liebeneiner. But it's not all romantic sleigh rides, as cuckolded baron Gustaf Gründgens comes seeking revenge. DP In German.

Magda Schneider *Christine* • Wolfgang Liebeneiner *Fritz* • Luise Ullrich *Mitzi* • Olga Tschechowa *Baroness* • Gustaf Gründgens *Baron Eggerdorff* ■ *Dir* Max Ophüls • *Scr* Kurt Alexander, Hans Wilhelm, from the play by Arthur Schnitzler, adapted by Felix Salten

Liebestraum ★★★ 18

Mystery drama 1991 · US · Colour · 109min

When architectural journalist Kevin Anderson is called to the deathbed of the mother he never knew (Kim Novak), a chance encounter with an old college friend (Bill Pullman) provides an opportunity to study the site of a unique, soon-to-be-demolished department store. As passion flares between Anderson and Pullman's wife (Pamela Gidley), Novak's increasingly feverish reminiscences point to a dark secret contained within the condemned building's walls. The plot spirals out of sight, but still has a dizzying compulsion, and both the direction and cinematography are atmospheric. TH Swearing, sex scenes, nudity. *DVD*

Kevin Anderson *Nick Kaminsky* • Pamela Gidley *Jane Kessler* • Bill Pullman *Paul Kessler* • Kim Novak *Mrs Anderssen* • Graham Beckel *Sheriff Ricker* • Zach Grenier *Barnett Ralston IV* • Thomas Kopache *Dr Parker* ■ *Dir/Scr* Mike Figgis

Lies and Deception ★

Mystery thriller 2005 · Can/US · Colour · 85min

This suspense-free clunker sees Chicago widow Mädchen Amick employ the services of hunky private eye Andrew Walker when she discovers her doctor husband faked his own death five years earlier. Poor direction and an underdeveloped script ensure that their subsequent investigation is light on both action and explanation. SF

Mädchen Amick *Jean Brooks* • Andrew Walker [Andrew W Walker] *Eddie Fate* • Ellen Dubin *Charlotte Porter* • Joseph Kell *Chris Schwartzman* ■ *Dir* Louis Bélanger • *Scr* John Ireland

The Lies Boys Tell ★★★ PG

Drama 1994 · US · Colour · 87min

Writer Ernest Thompson won an Oscar for *On Golden Pond*, and he transfers its theme of child-parent reconciliation to the open road in this entertaining TV movie. Kirk Douglas plays a retired travelling salesman who embarks on one last adventure before he dies. Craig T Nelson, who digs deep to convince as the wayward son who goes along for the ride, prevents Douglas from dominating the film. Funny, provocative and touching. DP *DVD*

Kirk Douglas *Ed Reece* • Craig T Nelson *Larry Reece* • Eileen Brennan *Sada* • Bess Armstrong *Connie* • Bonnie Bartlett *Sylvia Reece* • Richard Gilliland *Russ Reece* • Ernest Thompson *Cal* ■ *Dir* Tom McLoughlin • *Scr* Ernest Thompson, from the novel by Lamar Herrin

Lies My Father Told Me ★★★

Period drama 1975 · Can · Colour · 102min

This screen version of writer Ted Allan's autobiographical opus about his early childhood is sympathetically directed by Czech émigré Jan Kadar. Benefitting hugely from a wonderfully warm performance from Yiddish actor Yossi Yadin as the young hero's grandfather, this Canadian film also features Allan himself (who wrote the script) playing old Mr Baumgarten. TS

Yossi Yadin *Zaida* • Len Birman *Harry Herman* • Marilyn Lightstone *Annie Herman* • Jeffrey Lynas *David Herman* • Ted Allan *Mr Baumgarten* • Barbara Chilcott *Mrs Tannenbaum* ■ *Dir* Jan Kadar • *Scr* Ted Allan, from his autobiography

Lies My Mother Told Me ★★

Crime drama 2004 · Can · Colour · 99min

Joely Richardson and Hayden Panettiere star in this unconvincing crime drama about a young girl's relationship with her serial conwoman mother. Inspired by a true story, it attempts to explore the complex ties that bind the duo over a deceit-riddled decade. While the film's themes are strong and occasionally poignant, too much ground is covered too quickly, making the narrative feel fragmented and insubstantial. **SF**

Joely Richardson *Laren Sims* • Colm Feore *Lucas Mackenzie* • Hayden Panettiere *Haylei Sims* • Jasmine Berg *Young Haylei Sims* • Tim Henry *Johnny* ■ *Dir* Christian Duguay • *Scr* Matt Dorff

Lt Robin Crusoe, USN ★★ U
Comedy adventure 1966 · US · Colour · 108min

This pretty feeble Dick Van Dyke vehicle for Disney, ostensibly a comic update of the Robinson Crusoe story, was made when the studio had seemingly lost touch with contemporary audiences. Fortunately, Disney bounced back, but movies such as this one, featuring a chimp from outer space, didn't help. **TS**

Dick Van Dyke *Lieutenant Robin Crusoe* • Nancy Kwan *Wednesday* • Akim Tamiroff *Tanamashu* • Arthur Malet *Umbrella Man* • Tyler McVey *Captain* ■ *Dir* Byron Paul • *Scr* Bill Walsh, Donald DaGradi, from a story by Retlaw Yensid [Walt Disney]

Life ★★ 15
Prison comedy 1999 · US · Colour · 104min

It's sad to see Eddie Murphy so completely unfunny in this cross between *The Shawshank Redemption* and *The Odd Couple*. Street-smart Murphy and bank clerk Martin Lawrence are framed by a Deep South sheriff for murder and sent to a Mississippi jail for life. Initially racist and brutal, the regime lightens up when warden Ned Beatty takes over and makes the pair his house-servants. The necessary chemistry between chalk-and-cheese Murphy and Lawrence is absent, so their banter is simply unpleasant. **TH** Swearing, violence. *DVD*

Eddie Murphy *Rayford Gibson* • Martin Lawrence *Claude Banks* • Obba Babatundé [Obba Babatunde] *Willie Long* • Ned Beatty *Dexter Wilkins* • Bernie Mac *Jangle Leg* • Miguel A Nunez [Miguel A Nunez Jr] *Biscuit* • Clarence Williams III *Winston Hancock* • Bokeem Woodbine *Can't Get Right* ■ *Dir* Ted Demme • *Scr* Robert Ramsey, Matthew Stone

Life ★★★★ 15
Drama 2015 · Can/UK/Ger/US/Aus · Colour · 111min

Dennis Stock's *Life* magazine image of James Dean, overcoat collar pulled up as he traverses a windswept Times Square, is the jumping-off point for this biographical drama. Robert Pattinson gives a nuanced performance as Stock, the photographer who realises that Dean's mix of melancholy and egomania, effectively rendered by actor Dane DeHaan, is something new. A quietly compelling drama, this reflects on the relationship between Hollywood, the talent and the media – and how much it's changed. **TJ** Sex, drug abuse

Robert Pattinson *Dennis Stock* • Dane DeHaan *James Dean* • Ben Kingsley *Jack Warner* • Joel Edgerton *John Morris* • Eva Fisher *Judy Garland* • Lauren Gallagher *Natalie Wood* ■ *Dir* Anton Corbijn • *Scr* Luke Davies • *Cinematographer* Charlotte Bruus Christensen

Life, above All ★★★ 12A
Drama 2010 · S Afr/Ger/Can/Fr · Colour · 105min

The subject matter is undeniably grim, but there's hope and forgiveness at the heart of this South Africa-set drama. In her first film role, Khomotso Manyaka gives a compelling performance as a 12-year-old girl attempting to keep her family together after her infant sister dies. Her mother (Lerato Mvelase) is too ill to care for her two other children, so strong-willed and intelligent Manyaka has to take on her role. The relationship between mother and daughter is beautifully depicted, and although the unremitting misery is capped with an uplifting (albeit unlikely) ending, this is still a simple, moving story about the power of love. **LB** Sotho, French +subtitles. Some swearing, sexual references.

Khomotso Manyaka *Chanda* • Lerato Mvelase *Lillian* • Harriet Manamela *Mrs Tafa* • Keaobaka Makanyane *Esther* • Tinah Mnumzana *Aunt*

Lizbet • Aubrey Poolo *Jonah* ■ *Dir* Oliver Schmitz • *Scr* Dennis Foon, from the novel *Chanda's Secrets* by Allan Stratton • *Cinematographer* Bernhard Jasper

Life after Beth ★★★ 15
Romantic horror comedy 2014 · UK · Colour · 85min

Just as the zombie genre refuses to die, this fitfully funny and well cast black comedy doesn't know when to stop either. Its lack of originality isn't really an issue, since the premise – high-school student Zach (Dane DeHaan) realises his girlfriend Beth (the excellent Aubrey Plaza) has returned from the grave – has its roots in myriad romantic horror comedies, from 1942's *I Married a Witch* onwards. And as a metaphor for fickle young relationships it works very well, too, as the once puppyish Zach grows out of love with the decomposing, erratic and increasingly clingy Beth. **DW** *DVD* *BL*

Aubrey Plaza *Beth Slocum* • Dane DeHaan *Zach Orfman* • John C Reilly *Maury Slocum* • Molly Shannon *Geenie Slocum* • Paul Reiser *Noah Orfman* • Anna Kendrick *Erica Wexler* ■ *Dir/Scr* Jeff Baena

The Life and Death of Colonel Blimp ★★★★★★ U
Period drama 1943 · UK · Colour · 156min

Winston Churchill ordered this film to be banned from exportation during the Second World War in case it gave the wrong impression of the British fighting man. Based on the comic-strip character created by David Low, Michael Powell and Emeric Pressburger's film does indeed take a pop at the complacency of the top brass, yet, thanks to Roger Livesey's astonishing performance in the lead, it is also a tribute to the more laudable peculiarities of the British character – honour, loyalty and a genius for making the most of a bad lot. Anton Walbrook also excels as Livesey's Prussian rival who becomes a lifelong friend, while a young Deborah Kerr makes her mark playing the three women in Livesey's life. One of British cinema's masterpieces. **DP** *DVD* *BL*

Roger Livesey *Clive Candy* • Deborah Kerr *Edith Hunter/Barbara Wyn/Johnny Cannon* • Anton Walbrook *Theo Kretschmar-Schuldorff* • James McKechnie *Spud Wilson* • Neville Mapp *Stuffy Graves* • Roland Culver *Colonel Betteridge* • David Hutcheson *Hoppy* • Spencer Trevor *Period Blimp* • AE Matthews *President of the Tribunal* ■ *Dir/Scr* Michael Powell, Emeric Pressburger

The Life and Death of Peter Sellers ★★★ 15
Biographical drama 2003 · US/UK · Colour · 121min

The fact that this biopic about one of British cinema's most familiar figures is so engaging owes much to an Oscar-worthy performance by Geoffrey Rush, who plays Peter Sellers as a volatile and selfish man struggling for a personality beyond his comic creations. The film begins with Sellers already at the height of his radio success with The Goons and concentrates on his relationship with his first wife Anne (Emily Watson) and a stormy second marriage to Britt Ekland (Charlize Theron). **BP** *DVD*

Geoffrey Rush *Peter Sellers* • Emily Watson *Anne Sellers* • Charlize Theron *Britt Ekland* • Miriam Margolyes *Peg Sellers* • John Lithgow *Blake Edwards* • Stephen Fry *Maurice Woodruff* • Stanley Tucci *Stanley Kubrick* • Peter Vaughan *Bill Sellers* • Sonia Aquino *Sophia Loren* • Nigel Havers *David Niven* ■ *Dir* Stephen Hopkins • *Scr* Christopher Markus, Stephen McFeely, from the book by Roger Lewis

Life and Debt ★★★ PG
Documentary 2001 · US · Colour · 82min

It's impossible to watch this documentary about the impact of globalisation on Jamaica without a rising sense of dismay. Director Stephanie Black refuses to pull her punches, and why should she, when she's got so much damning evidence at her disposal? Yet for all the eloquence of former Prime Minister Michael Manley and

the local labourers betrayed by faceless multinational fat cats and the International Monetary Fund, it's the extracts from Jamaica Kincaid's book, *A Small Place*, that make the most telling impact. Angry agitprop this may be, but it's irresistibly persuasive. **DP** *DVD*

Belinda Becker *Narrator* ■ *Dir* Stephanie Black • *Scr* Jamaica Kincaid, from her book *A Small Place*

The Life and Extraordinary Adventures of Private Ivan Chonkin ★★★ 15
Drama 1994 · Cz Rep/UK/Fr/Rus · Colour · 110min

Jiří Menzel, one of the key figures in the Czech film miracle of the 1960s, comes rather unstuck with this rough-and-ready adaptation of Russian writer Vladimir Voinovich's cult novel. This tale set just before the Second World War is so broad in its comedy, it often borders on farce. Paying scant regard to the themes of repression and resistance and missing the opportunity for some colourful character comedy, Menzel opts for a hectic pace and vulgar caricature. It's played with great vigour and is entertaining, but it's not one of the director's best. **DP** Czech +subtitles.

Gennadiy Nazarov *Ivan Chonkin* • Zoya Buryak *Nyura* • Vladimir Ilyin *Golubev* • Valeriy Dubrovin *Kilin* • Alexei Zharkov *Gladyshev* • Yuriy Dubrovin *Volkov* ■ *Dir* Jiří Menzel • *Scr* Zdenek Sverak, Vladimir Voinovich, from the novel by Vladimir Voinovich

Life & Lyrics ★★★ 15
Drama 2006 · UK · Colour · 95min

Former So Solid Crew rapper Ashley Walters delivers a smouldering performance in this likeably ambitious attempt to relocate the rap battles of Eminem's *8 Mile* to the south London '"hood". Walters plays a DJ who's about to compete in an "open mic" competition with his crew of mouthy MCs. As the title suggests, it's a film of two halves: acid-tongued rappers fight scathing lyrical battles on stage ("She looks suicidal/She's only here 'cos she got lost on the way to *Pop Idol*"), while Danny struggles to avoid the dangers of the ghetto between the breakbeats. Its street cred never entirely convinces, but Walters is a powerful presence, his brooding manner occasionally hinting at a heart of urban darkness beyond the reach of this movie. **JR** *DVD*

Ashley Walters *Danny Lewis* • Christopher Steward *Fable* • Akemnji Ndifornyen *Preach* • Louise Rose *Carmen* • Cat Simmons *Sista Twista* • Beau Baptist *Blitz* • Karl Collins *Winston Dimby* ■ *Dir* Richard Laxton • *Scr* Ken Williams

Life and Nothing But ★★★★ PG
Drama 1989 · Fr · Colour · 130min

Philippe Noiret gives one of his most memorable performances as a major in charge of the identification of shell-shocked survivors of the First World War. As well as helping the bereaved, the authorities have charged him with the task of finding a suitable Unknown Soldier. Shot in muted colours by Bruno De Keyzer, the film's atmosphere of loss and despair is deeply moving. Sabine Azéma and Pascale Vignal also impress as they search for missing lovers. **DP** French +subtitles.

Philippe Noiret *Dellaplane* • Sabine Azéma *Irène* • Pascale Vignal *Alice* • Maurice Barrier *Mercadot* • François Perrot *Perrin* ■ *Dir* Bertrand Tavernier • *Scr* Bertrand Tavernier, Jean Cosmos

The Life and Times of Judge Roy Bean ★★★ 15
Comedy western 1972 · US · Colour · 118min

Although this is very much a vehicle for star Paul Newman, he nevertheless seems a little ill at ease as the titular judge. Despite help from a notable supporting cast, director John Huston's rambling, incident-packed movie is overlong and actually rather dull. However, its wry humour and surreal moments can't help but endear this to most audiences. Casting has seldom

been more appropriate than Ava Gardner, in her late prime, as the embodiment of Lily Langtry, the object of the judge's affections. **TS** Violence.

Paul Newman *Judge Roy Bean* • Jacqueline Bisset *Rose Bean* • Ava Gardner *Lily Langtry* • Tab Hunter *Sam Dodd* • John Huston *Grizzly Adams* • Stacy Keach *Bad Bob* • Roddy McDowall *Frank Gass* • Anthony Perkins *Reverend Lasalle* • Victoria Principal *Marie Elena* • Ned Beatty *Tector Crites* ■ *Dir* John Huston • *Scr* John Milius

The Life and Times of Rosie the Riveter ★★★
Second World War documentary 1980 · US · Colour and BW · 65min

Forget the sham nostalgia of *Swing Shift*, as there was nothing romantic about working in America's munitions factories during the Second World War. Millions of women answered the call in 1941 and, for many of them, it was their first experience of full-time employment. Yet, rather than being welcomed with open arms by their male colleagues, they were patronised, marginalised and harassed. By shrewdly contrasting morale-boosting newsreel footage with whistleblowing personal testimonies, Connie Field is able to expose the conditions to which the "Rosies" were subjected without detracting from the scale of their achievement or their pride in it. **DP**

■ *Dir/Scr* Connie Field

The Life Aquatic with Steve Zissou ★★★ 15
Fantasy comedy drama 2004 · US · Colour · 113min

Director Wes Anderson's odd drama is centred on famous oceanographer Steve Zissou (played by Bill Murray and obviously inspired by marine pioneer Jacques Cousteau), who embarks on a Ahab-style quest to hunt and kill the mysterious sea creature that ate his best friend. Murray is so laid-back he sometimes seems to be asleep, but there's great support from Owen Wilson as Zissou's (apparently) long-lost son and Jeff Goldblum as a rival oceanographer. For some, Anderson's world is too strange to be affecting; for others, there's an irresistible charm to his eccentric characters. **AS** English, Italian, Tagalog +subtitles. Swearing. *DVD*

Bill Murray *Steve Zissou* • Owen Wilson *Ned Plimpton* • Cate Blanchett *Jane Winslett-Richardson* • Anjelica Huston *Eleanor Zissou* • Willem Dafoe *Klaus Daimler* • Jeff Goldblum *Alistair Hennessey* • Michael Gambon *Oseary Drakoulias* • Bud Cort *Bill Ubell* • Seu Jorge *Pelé dos Santos* • Noah Taylor *Vladimir Wolodarsky* • Seymour Cassel *Esteban du Plantier* ■ *Dir* Wes Anderson • *Scr* Wes Anderson, Noah Baumbach

Life as a House ★★ 15
Drama 2001 · US/Ger · Colour · 120min

Kevin Kline is a model-maker for an architectural firm who gets fired and informed he is dying in pretty short order. Kline then decides to spend his remaining months tearing down the shack his hated father left him, building his dream house on the same spot and patching things up with ex-wife Kristin Scott Thomas and son Hayden Christensen. This clumsy drama oozes schmaltz. **DP** *DVD*

Kevin Kline *George Monroe* • Kristin Scott Thomas *Robin Kimball* • Hayden Christensen *Sam* • Jamey Sheridan *Peter* • Sam Robards *David Dokos* • Scott Bakula *Kurt Walker* • Mary Steenburgen *Coleen Beck* ■ *Dir* Irwin Winkler • *Scr* Mark Andrus

Life as We Know It ★★ 12
Comedy drama 2010 · US · Colour · 109min

They can't stand each other, but they have to raise a child together. That's the premise of this unlikely, uneven and unlikeable comedy drama starring Katherine Heigl (*27 Dresses*) and Josh Duhamel (the *Transformers* films). They play warring acquaintances who become instant parents when their mutual best friends die and leave them as legal guardians of their daughter. The two leads have screen appeal, but the chemistry between them is thin, while the story is hackneyed and far-fetched. KK Sexual, drug references. **DVD** **Blu**

Katherine Heigl *Holly Berenson* • Josh Duhamel *Eric Messer* • Christina Hendricks *Alison Novack* • Josh Lucas *Sam* • Jean Smart *Helen Berenson* • Majandra Delfino *Jenna* ■ *Dir* Greg Berlanti • *Scr* Ian Deitchman, Kristin Rusk Robinson, Jon Harmon Feldman, Michael Green

Life at the Top ★★ 12
Drama 1965 · UK · BW · 110min

Having ridden roughshod over the citizens of Warnley in *Room at the Top*, Laurence Harvey leaves Yorkshire in search of the beautiful south in this hugely disappointing sequel. Mordecai Richler's adaptation and Ted Kotcheff's direction capture little of the spirit of swinging London, let alone the actions and emotions of a ruthlessly ambitious "angry young man". Harvey fails to rekindle the fire of his Oscar-nominated performance in the first film, and Jean Simmons is wasted as his put-upon wife. DP **DVD**

Laurence Harvey *Joe Lampton* • Jean Simmons *Susan Lampton* • Honor Blackman *Norah Hauxley* • Michael Craig *Mark* • Donald Wolfit *Abe Brown* • Robert Morley *Tiffield* ■ *Dir* Ted Kotcheff • *Scr* Mordecai Richler, from the novel by John Braine

The Life before Her Eyes ★★ 15
Psychological drama 2007 · US · Colour · 89min

The psychological impact of a Columbine-style high-school shooting is the central focus of this gorgeously shot but emotionally overwrought drama. Evan Rachel Wood plays rebellious teenager Diana in the build-up to the tragedy, and Uma Thurman portrays her 15 years later as a traumatised wife and mother who can't put the past behind her. Director Vadim Perelman (*House of Sand and Fog*) tackles Laura Kasischke's novel in a portentous manner, lacing everyday reality with a strangely soft-lit magical quality. While Wood's vivacious performance captures the boredom inherent in coming of age in a small town, Thurman's jittery mannerisms are less successful at conveying the corrosive effects of survivor guilt. JR Violence, swearing, brief drug abuse.

Uma Thurman *Diana (adult)* • Evan Rachel Wood *Diana (teen)* • Eva Amurri *Maureen* • Gabrielle Brennan *Emma* • Brett Cullen *Paul* • Oscar Isaac *Marcus* ■ *Dir* Vadim Perelman • *Scr* Emil Stern, from the novel by Laura Kasischke

The Life before This ★★★ 15
Drama 1999 · Can · Colour · 87min

A sombre meditation on fate, this Canadian drama is not without its faults, but is still well worth a look. The film opens with a shoot-out at a café in which innocent customers get caught in the crossfire. It then rewinds itself back to the beginning of the day and examines the interlinking stories of the individuals who by chance will find themselves at the coffee shop later that evening. The ensemble cast is superb, and although it is a tad too contrived for its own good, director Jerry Ciccoritti skilfully weaves together the various strands. JF

Catherine O'Hara *Sheena* • Stephen Rea *Brian* • Sarah Polley *Connie* • Joe Pantoliano *Jake Maclean* • Martha Burns *Gwen Maclean* • Emily Hampshire *Maggie* • Callum Keith Rennie *Martin Maclean* ■ *Dir* Jerry Ciccoritti • *Scr* Semi Chellas

Life Begins ★★
Drama 1932 · US · BW · 72min

Covering the events of a night in a maternity ward, this features among other mothers-about-to-be the lovely Loretta Young, as a woman serving a life sentence for murder. However it's excellent character actress Aline MacMahon as the head nurse, both controlling and compassionate, who holds the action together. Respectable, but downbeat. RK

Loretta Young *Grace Sutton* • Eric Linden *Jed Sutton* • Aline MacMahon *Miss Bowers* • Glenda Farrell *Florette* • Gilbert Roland *Tony* ■ *Dir* James Flood, Elliott Nugent • *Scr* Earl Baldwin, from the play by Mary M Axelson

Life Begins at 8.30 ★★
Comedy drama 1942 · US · BW · 84min

Ida Lupino sacrifices herself to care for her father, alcoholic actor Monty Woolley, until dashing composer Cornel Wilde arrives on cue to nurse him through a production of *King Lear*. Everything really depends on the charisma of Woolley and his ability to be actorly, grand and tragic at the same time, a man described as "a god on stage but a rat off". Woolley acquits himself reasonably well, given an overwritten script and leaden direction from Irving Pichel. AT

Monty Woolley *Madden Thomas* • Ida Lupino *Kathi Thomas* • Cornel Wilde *Robert* • Sara Allgood *Mrs Lothian* • Melville Cooper *Barty* • J Edward Bromberg *Gordon* • William Demarest *Officer* ■ *Dir* Irving Pichel • *Scr* Nunnally Johnson, from the play *The Light Of The Heart* by Emlyn Williams

Life Begins at 40 ★★★
Comedy 1935 · US · BW · 73min

In this charmingly folksy Will Rogers vehicle, the garrulous movie star-cum-philosopher is given acidic lines aplenty on the American way of life, though his well-practised lazy drawl seems deliberately to remove the sting in the barbs. This is one of his best pictures, with the star as a newspaper editor (Rogers contributed to a daily newspaper column and radio broadcasts in real life) bent on clearing an innocent young man's name. Director George Marshall manages to keep the sentiment at bay in this satisfying effort. ST

Will Rogers (1) *Kenesaw H Clark* • Rochelle Hudson *Adele Anderson* • Richard Cromwell *Lee Austin* • George Barbier *Colonel Joseph Abercrombie* • Jane Darwell *Ida Harris* • Slim Summerville *T Watterson Meriwether* • Sterling Holloway *Chris* ■ *Dir* George Marshall • *Scr* Lamar Trotti, Robert Quillen, Dudley Nichols, William M Conselman, from the novel by Walter B Pitkin

Life Begins for Andy Hardy ★★★ U
Comedy drama 1941 · US · BW · 101min

After ten episodes, MGM decided that Andy needed to grow up a bit. His country needed him but, no, he didn't go off to Guadalcanal, he has to decide between getting a job or going to college. He has a chat with dad and decides to go and "find himself" in New York, where he meets girlfriend Judy Garland. She drops into Andyworld for the third and last time, though MGM deleted her song from the final cut. Andy gets a job on a paltry salary, and Garland decides it's time to give dad a call. Working as a smart satire on big city business ethics, it's easily one of the best of the *Andy Hardy* series. AT

Mickey Rooney *Andy Hardy* • Lewis Stone *Judge James K Hardy* • Judy Garland *Betsy Booth* • Fay Holden *Mrs Emily Hardy* • Ann Rutherford *Polly Benedict* • Sara Haden *Aunt Milly* • Patricia Dane *Jennitt Hicks* • Ray McDonald *Jimmy Frobisher* ■ *Dir* George B Seitz • *Scr* Agnes Christine Johnston, from characters by Aurania Rouverol

Life Begins in College ★★★ U
Comedy 1937 · US · BW · 93min

Joan Davis co-stars with that blandest of crooners Tony Martin in one of those college romps where all the students look old enough to draw pensions. The zany Ritz Brothers are along for the ride, helping the college football team. Gloria Stuart is a charming ingénue, and Nat Pendleton gets much mileage as an Indian at college, though some may find it tasteless today. Originally released in the UK as *The Joy Parade*. TS

The Ritz Brothers [Al Ritz] *Ritz Brother* • The Ritz Brothers [Jimmy Ritz] *Ritz Brother* • The Ritz Brothers [Harry Ritz] *Ritz Brother* • Joan Davis *Inez* • Tony Martin (1) *Band Leader* • Gloria Stuart *Janet O'Hara* • Fred Stone *Coach O'Hara* • Nat Pendleton *George Black* • Dick Baldwin *Bob Hayner* ■ *Dir* William A Seiter • *Scr* Karl Tunberg, Don Ettlinger, Sidney Kuller, Ray Golden, Samuel Pokrass, from the stories by Darrell Ware

Life during Wartime ★★★ 15
Comedy drama 2009 · US · Colour · 97min

Taboo-challenging indie auteur Todd Solondz reopens old wounds with cut-throat precision in this loose sequel to his stinging black comedy *Happiness*. Revisiting the principal characters a decade on and with the shadow of paedophilia still hanging over the action, he uses an entirely new cast to focus on the still-dysfunctional Jordan sisters (Shirley Henderson, Allison Janney, Ally Sheedy), as they try to escape the ghosts of traumatic past relationships and create fulfilling futures. Ultimately, Solondz's determinedly left-field approach keeps his work an acquired taste, despite this being a welcome return to form after the unpalatable *Palindromes*. SF Violence, swearing, sex scenes, nudity, drug abuse.

Shirley Henderson *Joy Jordan* • Ciarán Hinds [Ciaran Hinds] *Bill Maplewood* • Allison Janney *Trish Maplewood* • Michael Lerner *Harvey Weiner* • Chris Marquette [Christopher George Marquette] *Billy Maplewood* • Charlotte Rampling *Jacqueline* • Ally Sheedy *Helen Jordan* ■ *Dir/Scr* Todd Solondz

Life for Ruth ★★ PG
Drama 1962 · UK · BW · 87min

Following *Sapphire* (on racism) and *Victim* (on homosexuality), Basil Dearden turned his attention to religious conviction in another of the social realism pictures he made at the turn of the 1960s. The story of a father with deep-seated religious beliefs who refuses to consent to the blood transfusion that will save his daughter's life is often too contrived to make the weighty impact that Dearden intends. The nationwide scandal whipped up by doctor Patrick McGoohan spoils the intricately developed and delicately played feud between the girl's parents (Michael Craig and Janet Munro). DP **DVD**

Michael Craig *John Harris* • Patrick McGoohan *Dr Jim Brown* • Janet Munro *Pat Harris* • Paul Rogers *Hart Jacobs* • Megs Jenkins *Mrs Gordon* • John Barrie *Mr Gordon* • Malcolm Keen *Mr Harris Sr* • Lynne Taylor *Ruth Harris* ■ *Dir* Basil Dearden • *Scr* Janet Green, John McCormick, from the play *Walk in the Shadow* by Janet Green

Life in a Day ★★★★ 12
Documentary 2011 · US · Colour · 91min

This ambitious documentary attempts nothing less than a snapshot portrait of life on Earth on 24 July 2010, edited down from over 80,000 clips submitted by YouTube contributors – a hefty 4,500 hours of material. Director Kevin Macdonald (*Touching the Void*, *The Last King of Scotland*) and his heroic editor Joe Walker show an average day unfolding around the globe, starting with sundry breakfast rituals and whisking us here and there, so we never know quite what's coming next. The result is witty, poignant, unexpected: all humanity is here, from birth to death, joy to sadness, delivered in fragments that give us a brief but illuminating glimpse into the varied experiences of others. True, the overbearing music sometimes feels like its massaging our emotions, but *Life in a Day* has the integrity never to cop out on the extremes of wealth and poverty that divide us – as well as the showmanship to remain thoroughly entertaining throughout. TJ Swearing, animal slaughter.

■ *Dir* Kevin Macdonald ■ *Editor* Joe Walker (2)

Life in a... METRO ★★ 12
Romantic drama 2007 · Ind · Colour · 126min

TV's *Celebrity Big Brother* may have made Bollywood actress Shilpa Shetty a household name, but this soap-style melodrama is likely to appeal to die-hard fans only. A clichéd tale of romance, lust and betrayal, it explores the entangled love lives of an interconnected group of Mumbai residents. Among them, housewife Shikha (a radiant Shetty) questions her unhappy marriage, while her virginal sister (Konkona Sen Sharma) hunts for Mr Right in all the wrong places. The performances are solid, despite the clumsy dialogue, and there's a good use of colour. But the film is overly

literal and emotionally unbalanced, and the inclusion of an Indian supergroup that intermittently bursts into song is particularly incongruous, rendering many sombre scenes hilarious. SF Hindi, English +subtitles. **DVD**

Shilpa Shetty *Shikha* • Shiney Ahuja *Akash* • Irrfan Khan [Irfan Khan] *Debu* • Kay Kay Menon *Ranjee* • Konkona Sen Sharma [Konkona Sensharma] *Shruti* • Sharman Joshi *Rahul* • Kangna Ranaut [Kangana Ranaut] *Neha* ■ *Dir* Anurag Basu • *Scr* Anurag Basu, Sanjeev Dutta

Life in Danger ★★
Thriller 1959 · UK · BW · 62min

As Alfred Hitchcock repeatedly demonstrated in films such as *The Wrong Man*, there is nothing more terrifying for the innocent than finding the evidence in a murder case irrefutably piling up against them while all attempts at establishing an alibi founder on the most unlikely caprices of fate. This is the situation confronting Derren Nesbitt in this passable low-budget drama, which is made even more alarming by its picturesque country setting. DP

Derren Nesbitt *The Man* • Julie Hopkins *Hazel Ashley* • Howard Marion-Crawford *Major Peters* • Victor Brooks *Tom Baldwin* • Jack Allen *Jack Ashley* • Christopher Witty *Johnny Ashley* • Carmel McSharry *Mrs Ashley* • Mary Manson *Jill Shadwell* • Bruce Seton *Landlord* ■ *Dir* Terry Bishop • *Scr* Malcolm Hulke, Eric Paice

Life in Emergency Ward 10 ★★ U
Medical drama 1959 · UK · BW · 82min

Two years after taking the nation by storm, ITV's soap smash made it to the big screen, and what a disappointment it was. The characters are caught up in the round of romantic entanglements and medical emergencies that were old hat at the time of MGM's *Dr Kildare* series. Michael Craig is dreadful as the Oxbridge General new boy playing fast and loose with the hearts of his patients and a colleague's neglected wife, and even the usually reliable Wilfrid Hyde White is off colour. DP

Michael Craig *Dr Stephen Russell* • Wilfrid Hyde White *Professor Bourne-Evans* • Dorothy Alison *Sister Janet Fraser* • Glyn Owen *Dr Paddy O'Meara* • Rosemary Miller *Nurse Pat Roberts* • Charles Tingwell *Dr Alan Dawson* • Frederick Bartman *Dr Simon Forrester* • Joan Sims *Mrs Pryor* ■ *Dir* Robert Day • *Scr* Tessa Diamond, Hazel Adair, from the TV series

A Life in the Balance ★★★
Thriller 1955 · US · BW · 71min

After *The Big Heat* and *The Wild One*, Lee Marvin was well established as a screen heavy when he made this thriller in Mexico City. It's a portrait of life in the slums, spiced up by the odd Buñuelian moment and the hunt for a serial killer with a religious fixation, played by Marvin. Ricardo Montalban plays the wrongly accused man, while Anne Bancroft is the love interest. AT

Ricardo Montalban *Antonio Gomez* • Anne Bancroft *Maria Ibinia* • Lee Marvin *The Murderer* • José Perez (1) *Paco Gomez* • Rodolfo Acosta *Lt Fernando* ■ *Dir* Harry Horner • *Scr* Robert Presnell Jr, Leo Townsend, from a story by Georges Simenon

A Life in the Theater ★★★★
Drama 1993 · US · Colour · 90min

As the veteran actor coming to the end of his career, that consummate professional Jack Lemmon savours every line of David Mamet's inspired dialogue in Gregory Mosher's version of Mamet's acclaimed play. It speaks volumes for Matthew Broderick that he stays the distance in his role as the promising newcomer who isn't simply prepared to listen and learn. The discussions on how certain scenes should be played are fascinating, but thanks to the passion of the performances they never become inaccessible. A touch highbrow, perhaps, but you don't often get to see acting of this calibre. DP

Jack Lemmon *Robert* • Matthew Broderick *John* ■ *Dir* Gregory Mosher • *Scr* David Mamet, from his play

U SUITABLE FOR ALL ∣ Uc SUITABLE ESPECIALLY FOR YOUNG CHILDREN (DVD ONLY) ∣ PG PARENTAL GUIDANCE ∣ 12A UNDER 12s TO BE ACCOMPANIED (CINEMA ONLY)

L

Life Is a Bed of Roses ★★★★ 12
Fantasy 1983 · Fr · Colour · 106min

The perfectibility of human existence is the awesome theme of director Alain Resnais's magical fable, structured in three parts. The first covers Ruggero Raimondi's pre-First World War project to create a "temple to happiness". In the second part (set in the present), a seminar examines the feasibility of creating Utopia. Finally, a medieval struggle between good and evil is played out through the imaginations of some children. Vittorio Gassman, Raimondi and Geraldine Chaplin set up the proposition with dramatic ardour, but some may find this intellectual puzzle rather heavy going. TH French +subtitles. *DVD*

Vittorio Gassman *Walter Guarini* · Ruggero Raimondi *Count Michel Forbek* · Geraldine Chaplin *Nora Winkle* · Fanny Ardant *Livia Cerasquier* · Sabine Azéma *Elisabeth Rousseau* ■ *Dir* Alain Resnais · *Scr* Jean Gruault

Life Is a Long Quiet River ★★★★ 15
Satirical comedy 1988 · Fr · Colour · 87min

A breaker of box-office records and the winner of a clutch of Césars (the French Oscars), this offbeat and often hilarious debut feature seems a prime candidate for a Hollywood makeover. That it has been spared such a fate is primarily due to the subtleties underlying the blackly comic surface, which would confound even the most astute American director. These acerbic asides on class, education and parental expectations superbly complement the broader humour about mixed-at-birth babies. However, like the river of the title, the initial sparkle and freshness gives way to rather too much meandering. DP French +subtitles.

Benoît Magimel *Momo* · Valerie Lalande *Bernadette* · Tara Romer *Million* · Jérôme Floc'h *Toc-Toc* · Sylvie Cubertafon *Ghislaine* · Emmanuel Cendrier *Pierre* ■ *Dir* Etienne Chatiliez · *Scr* Florence Quentin, Etienne Chatiliez

Life Is a Miracle ★★★ 15
Black comedy drama 2004 · Fr/Ser/Montenegro · Colour · 148min

No one unearths the absurdity in political tragedy with such melancholic vigour as Emir Kusturica. This frantic take on the Bosnian civil war stars Slavko Stimac as a Serbian railway engineer whose life is disrupted when his opera-singing wife leaves him and when his soccer-mad son (Vuk Kostic) is conscripted into the army. After Kostic is captured, Stimac intends to use Muslim nurse Natasa Solak as a bargaining chip for his son's return, but he falls in love with her. This is acerbic human drama, but it's almost a sideshow to the glorious set pieces. DP Serbian, German, Hungarian, English +subtitles. Swearing, nudity, drug abuse. *DVD*

Slavko Stimac *Luka* · Natasa Solak *Sabaha* · Vesna Trivalic *Jadranka* · Vuk Kostic *Milos* · Aleksandar Bercek *Veljo* · Stribor Kusturica *Captain Aleksic* · Nikola Kojo *Filipovic* ■ *Dir* Emir Kusturica · *Scr* Emir Kusturica, Ranko Bozic

Life Is Beautiful ★★★ PG
Second World War comedy drama 1997 · It · Colour · 111min

Is this a glowing tribute to humanity *in extremis*, or an ill-judged trivialisation of pitiless barbarism? Both verdicts have been passed on Roberto Benigni's multi-award-winning film. The opening section, charting Benigni's courtship of the imperious Nicoletta Braschi, is delightful. It also serves as a poignant backdrop for the nightmare to follow, as Benigni tries to shelter his son from the bitterest of truths. The result is courageous, humanistic film-making, but only a qualified success. DP Italian +subtitles. Violence. *DVD* *Blu-ray*

Roberto Benigni *Guido* · Nicoletta Braschi *Dora* · Giorgio Cantarini *Giosué* · Giustino Durano *Uncle* · Sergio Bustric *Ferruccio* · Marisa Paredes *Dora's mother* · Horst Buchholz *Dr Lessing* ■ *Dir* Roberto Benigni · *Scr* Roberto Benigni, Vincenzo Cerami, from their story · *Cinematographer* Tonino Delli Colli

Life Is Cheap... but Toilet Paper Is Expensive ★★★ 18
Comedy thriller 1990 · US · Colour · 86min

Wayne Wang, the director of such light dramas as *Dim Sum, The Joy Luck Club* and *Smoke*, shows the darker side of his cinematic sensibilities in an offbeat, graphically violent Hong Kong tour of some really nasty tourist sights. Wang's world is one of on-screen defecation, severed hands and dead ducks but the nastiness is made more palatable by some humorous touches (the film's courier hero is modelled on Clint Eastwood's "Man with No Name"). Considerably less warm than the director's American movies, this is an attention-grabbing film that deliberately shocks. JC

Chan Kim Wan *Duck Killer* · Spencer Nakasako *Man with No Name* · Victor Wong (2) *Blind man* · Cheng Kwan Min *Uncle Cheng* · Cora Miao *Money* · Chung Lam *Red Guard* · Allen Fong *Taxi driver* ■ *Dir* Wayne Wang · *Scr* Spencer Nakasako

Life Is Sweet ★★★★★ 15
Black comedy 1990 · UK · Colour · 98min

Writer/director Mike Leigh is on top form in this superbly observed satire on late-Thatcherite Britain. The wincingly funny and socially astute script touches on such issues as bulimia, free enterprise and social ambition without ever labouring the point. Alison Steadman and Jim Broadbent are outstanding as the thoroughly decent working-class couple, who watch their daughters develop with a mixture of pride and regret. Jane Horrocks does Essex slacker teen with great conviction, while Claire Skinner impresses as her tomboy sister, and Timothy Spall is sweatily repellent as a wannabe restaurateur. DP Swearing, sex scenes, nudity. *DVD* *Blu-ray*

Alison Steadman *Wendy* · Jim Broadbent *Andy* · Jane Horrocks *Nicola* · Claire Skinner *Natalie* · Stephen Rea *Patsy* · Timothy Spall *Aubrey* · David Thewlis *Nicola's lover* · Moya Brady *Paula* · David Neilson *Steve* ■ *Dir/Scr* Mike Leigh

Life Itself ★★★★
Documentary 2014 · US · Colour · 120min

This engaging documentary chronicles the life and times of celebrated American film critic Roger Ebert, who died in 2013. Narrated by passages from his own memoir, the film traces a path from Ebert's time as a fledgling journalist to the tragic battle with cancer that robbed him of his lower jaw and the ability to speak. The highlight is Ebert's antagonistic relationship with fellow critic Gene Siskel, but director Steve James (*Hoop Dreams*) makes great use of archive video clips and talking head interviews, as well as candid footage of Ebert during the last few months of his life. This is as much about life and the passage of time as it is about cinema and criticism. SC *DVD*

Roger Ebert · Martin Scorsese · Werner Herzog ■ *Dir* Steve James · *Scr* Based on the memoir *Life Itself* by Roger Ebert

Life Just Is ★★★ 15
Drama 2012 · UK · Colour · 102min

Anyone who has ever shared a student house will recognise the situations and conversations in this garrulous but intelligent drama. The film has much in common with Eric Rohmer's languid dramas, though here the action is often humdrum, while the performances frequently feel laboured. But director Alex Barrett allows his 20-something characters to discuss the kind of issues – friendship, commitment, faith – that preoccupy graduates faced with the decisions that will affect the rest of their lives. What sets this apart, however, is Barrett's innovative compositional style – the disconcerting shifts between static wide shots and intrusive close-ups ensures that the movie remains visually intriguing even when the scenario begins to flag. DP

Jack Gordon *Pete* · Nathaniel Martello-White *Tom* · Will de Meo *David* · Fiona Ryan *Claire* · Paul Nicholls *Bobby* · Jayne Wisener *Jay* ■ *Dir/Scr* Alex Barrett

A Life Less Ordinary ★★ 15
Romantic comedy 1997 · UK/US · Colour · 99min

Third time unlucky for the director, producer, writer and star quartet of *Shallow Grave* and *Trainspotting*. Desperate to regain his menial job in a giant American corporation, Ewan McGregor kidnaps his former boss's daughter, rich bitch Cameron Diaz. As the two go on the run, a pair of celestial cops (miscast Holly Hunter and Delroy Lindo) embark on a quest to make them fall in love. McGregor and Diaz are in good form, but this comes unstuck as the feel-good whimsy gets piled on. AJ *DVD* *CS*

Ewan McGregor *Robert* · Cameron Diaz *Celine Naville* · Holly Hunter *O'Reilly* · Delroy Lindo *Jackson* · Dan Hedaya *Gabriel* · Ian McNeice *Mayhew* · Frank Kanig *Ted* · Mel Winkler *Frank* ■ *Dir* Danny Boyle · *Scr* John Hodge

Life, Love and Tears ★★★
Drama 1984 · USSR · Colour · 103min

A respected actor/director of stage and screen, Nikolay Gubenko played a major role in the reorganisation of the Soviet cinema in the era of *perestroika*, first as a film-maker and then as minister of culture. This is a solid enough example of the *bytovye*, a genre of films dealing with the darker side of everyday life that would have been unthinkable in less enlightened times. Although packed with allegorical references to Mikhail Gorbachev's removal of the old Communist guard, this fascinating drama is anything but an unquestioning tribute. DP Russian +subtitles.

Zhanna Bolotova · Elena Fadeeva ■ *Dir/Scr* Nikolay Gubenko

Life of Crime ★★★ 15
Crime comedy 2013 · US · Colour · 98min

The last film to be adapted from an Elmore Leonard novel in his lifetime, this is an easygoing if unremarkable slice of sunny LA noir that plays like a less cartoonish version of *Ruthless People*. Mos Def and John Hawkes hatch a plan to kidnap Jennifer Aniston, the wife of rich property developer Tim Robbins. But Robbins has no interest in paying the ransom. A likeable if predictable black comedy, this feels like a Tarantino movie made by well-meaning committee. DW Violence, swearing, sex scenes. *DVD* *Blu-ray*

John Hawkes *Louis Gara* · Yasiin Bey [Mos Def] *Ordell Robbie* · Jennifer Aniston *Mickey Dawson* · Tim Robbins *Frank Dawson* · Isla Fisher *Melanie* · Will Forte *Marshall Taylor* ■ *Dir* Daniel Schechter · *Scr* Daniel Schechter, from Elmore Leonard's novel *The Switch*

The Life of David Gale ★★★ 15
Mystery drama 2003 · US/UK/Ger · Colour · 124min

Director Alan Parker's film about the fictional David Gale, a respected academic and opponent of the death penalty who's awaiting execution, never quite catches fire. It does, however, benefit from the astute casting of Kevin Spacey as the intellectual on death row who agrees to give an exclusive interview to tenacious reporter Kate Winslet. Despite some climactic twists and turns, this fails to provide tension or high drama. JC Violence, swearing, drug abuse, sex scenes, nudity. *DVD*

Kevin Spacey *David Gale* · Kate Winslet *Elizabeth "Bitsey" Bloom* · Laura Linney *Constance Harraway* · Gabriel Mann *Zack* · Matt Craven *Dusty* · Rhona Mitra *Berlin* · Leon Rippy *Braxton Belyeu* · Elizabeth Gast *Sharon Gale* ■ *Dir* Alan Parker · *Scr* Charles Randolph

The Life of Emile Zola ★★★★
Biographical drama 1937 · US · BW · 123min

This is one of a remarkable series of Warner Bros melodramatic biopics whose central performances were once considered prime examples of cinematic acting. Like Lon Chaney before him, Mr Paul Muni (as he liked to be billed), a former Yiddish Art Theater star, was never more convincing than when disguised with make-up and wigs, and here he makes a very creditable Zola in a distinguished movie that has only dated in its earnestness. Giving Muni a run for the acting honourr is Joseph Schildkraut as Captain Alfred Dreyfus. In its courageous exposé of anti-Semitism, this film can be seen today as part of the Warners social tradition. TS

Paul Muni *Emile Zola* · Gale Sondergaard *Lucie Dreyfus* · Joseph Schildkraut *Captain Alfred Dreyfus* · Gloria Holden *Alexandrine Zola* · Donald Crisp *Maître Labori* · Erin O'Brien-Moore *Nana* · Robert Barrat *Major Walsin-Esterhazy* ■ *Dir* William Dieterle · *Scr* Norman Reilly Raine, Heinz Herald, Geza Herczeg

A Life of Her Own ★★
Drama 1950 · US · BW · 108min

Lana Turner, appropriately cast as an innocent from the Midwest who becomes a top-flight fashion model, suffers nobly in this archetypal "woman's magazine" tear-jerker that can hardly be called original. George Cukor directs from a script that has Turner in love with married man Ray Milland, whose wife is crippled. The familiar territory is also inhabited by Tom Ewell as the model agency head, Louis Calhern as Milland's friend and lawyer and, best of all, Ann Dvorak as a model for whom things go badly wrong – as does the movie. RK

Lana Turner *Lily Brannel James* · Ray Milland *Steve Harleigh* · Tom Ewell *Tom Caraway* · Louis Calhern *Jim Leversoe* · Ann Dvorak *Mary Ashlon* · Barry Sullivan *Lee Gorrance* · Margaret Phillips *Nora Harleigh* · Jean Hagen *Maggie Collins* ■ *Dir* George Cukor · *Scr* Isobel Lennart, from the story *Abiding Vision* by Rebecca West

The Life of Oharu ★★★★★ PG
Period melodrama 1952 · Jpn · BW · 130min

One of the great works from the greatest of Japanese directors, this episodic, tragic melodrama traces the life of a woman living under the severe moral code of the Genroku era in late 17th-century Japan. Played by Kinuyo Tanaka (who appeared in 11 Mizoguchi films and later became the first woman to direct a Japanese film), Oharu suffers a catalogue of injustices, most of them arbitrary and accidental, others of her own doing. The film, which won the Silver Lion at Venice in 1952, is informed by a Buddhist view of the world that acknowledges the impermanence of everything, especially happiness. Shot in long, beautiful takes, it is more devastating than depressing. DO Japanese +subtitles. *DVD*

Kinuyo Tanaka *Oharu* · Toshiro Mifune *Katsunosuke* · Masao Shimizu *Kikuoji* · Ichiro Sugai *Shinzaemon* · Tsukue Matsuura *Tomo, mother* · Kiyoko Tsuji *Landlady of an inn* ■ *Dir* Kenji Mizoguchi · *Scr* Yoda Yoshikata, from the novel *Koshoku Ichidai Onna* by Saikaku Ihara · *Cinematographer* Yoshimi Hirano

Life of Pi ★★★ PG
Adventure drama 2012 · US/Tai/Aus/UK/Can · Colour · 121min

A spiritual journey at sea is the basis of this high-minded film from *Brokeback Mountain* director Ang Lee, based on Yann Martel's prize-winning novel. Thankfully, it's grounded with a good dose of humour and an endearing performance by newcomer Suraj Sharma as Pi, an Indian boy adrift at sea in a lifeboat with only a Bengal tiger for company. But apart from seeking safe passage, Pi is also looking for God. There are a few too many platitudes in the script, but the film's real strength is its stunning imagery, which evokes the mysteries of the universe and stirs great tension as Pi and a truly lifelike CGI tiger pussyfoot around each other on the way to enlightenment. SP *DVD* *Blu-ray* *3D*

Suraj Sharma *Pi Patel* · Irrfan Khan [Irfan Khan] *Adult Pi Patel* · Ayush Tandon *Young Pi* · Adil Hussain *Santosh Patel* · Tabu *Gita Patel* · Rafe Spall *The Writer* · Gérard Depardieu *Cook* ■ *Dir* Ang Lee · *Scr* David Magee, from Yann Martel's novel · *Cinematographer* Claudio Miranda · *Music* Mychael Danna · *Production Designers* David Gropman, Anna Pinnock

L

The Life of Riley ★★★★
Documentary 2012 · UK · Colour · 123min

Still playing half a decade after his farewell tour, Riley B King (better known as BB King) has more than earned his nickname "The King of the Blues". Born in Mississippi in 1925, he began recording in 1949 and influenced a generation of rock royalty, including Keith Richards, Mick Jagger, Ringo Starr, Eric Clapton and Bono, who all testify to his greatness here alongside Barack Obama. But this engrossing, Morgan Freeman-narrated profile puts King front and centre, and director Jon Brewer not only captures his musical genius, but also his tenacity in enduring decades of vicious and often violent racial prejudice. DP Some swearing, violent images. *DVD* Blu

BB King • Morgan Freeman *Narrator* ■ *Dir* Jon Brewer

Life of Riley ★★★★ 12
Comedy 2014 · Fr · Colour · 117min

Nonagenarian Alain Resnais returned to Alan Ayckbourn for what turned out to be his final feature. At its centre is an amateur production of Ayckbourn's *Relatively Speaking*, but all attention switches to the fate of dying (and entirely unseen) leading man Riley, as Sabine Azéma, Caroline Silhol and Sandrine Kiberlain compete to accompany him on a last holiday to Tenerife, regardless of the effect this will have on their respective partners. Making the most of every entrance and exit, the ensemble excels, while the script neatly merges dialogue from the play-within-the-film with ordinary conversation. DP French+subtitles. *DVD* Blu

Sabine Azéma *Kathryn* • Hippolyte Girardot *Colin* • Caroline Silhol [Caroline] *Tamara* • Michel Vuillermoz *Jack* • Sandrine Kiberlain *Monica* • André Dussollier *Simeon* ■ *Dir* Alain Resnais • *Scr* Laurent Herbiet, Alex Reval [Alain Resnais], Jean-Marie Besset, from the play *Life of Riley* by Alan Ayckbourn

The Life of Stuff ★★
Drama 1997 · UK · Colour · 87min

A strong British cast has a nasty night out in this shallow, static study of a Glasgow criminal holding a party for select friends and colleagues to celebrate the demise of a rival boss. Jason Flemyng, Ciaran Hinds, Gina McKee and Ewen Bremner try their hardest, but the characters aren't fleshed out and the incidents are so meaningless that they soon lose your attention. JC Violence, swearing, drug abuse.

Ewen Bremner *Fraser* • Liam Cunningham *Alec Sneddon* • Jason Flemyng *Willie Dobie* • Ciaran Hinds *David Arbogast* • Gina McKee *Janice* • Stuart McQuarrie *Leonard* ■ *Dir* Simon Donald • *Scr* Simon Donald, from his play

Life on a String ★★★★ PG
Drama 1991 · Chi/Ger/UK · Colour · 102min

Alighting on such themes as spirituality and sensuality, discipline and independence, salvation and delusion, this is Chen Kaige's least avant-garde use of the forbidding rural landscape. Yet, his almost avant-garde use of the forbidding rural landscape and the haunting soundtrack delicately underscore the enigmatic story of the musician and his disciple who overcome physical blindness to master their art. As the old man clinging to his mentor's promise that his sight will be restored when he breaks the thousandth string on his sanxian, Liu Zhongyuan displays an affecting trust that contrasts with the impetuosity of Huang Lei. DP Mandarin +subtitles.

Liu Zhongyuan *The Old Master* • Huang Lei *Shitou* • Xu Qing *Lanxiu* ■ *Dir* Chen Kaige • *Scr* Chen Kaige, from a short story by Shi Tiesheng

Life on Liberty Street ★★
Drama 2004 · US · Colour · 89min

This formulaic TV movie stars Annabeth Gish as a recently divorced nurse who leaves her job in an emergency room because procedure has become more important than patients. In a brain injury rehabilitation unit, she finds the inspiration to deal with her own issues. There was a real opportunity here to follow the example of a film like *Awakenings* and explore the problems facing those recovering from head trauma. But director David S Cass Sr is more interested in the heroic stance that Gish takes against Ed Begley Jr, the pushy lawyer father of a recuperating patient. DP

Annabeth Gish *Denise Garner* • Ethan Embry *Rick Spencer* • Wendy Phillips *Lucy* • Ed Begley Jr *Richard Spencer* • Brett Cullen *Dr Jake Mitchell* • Galvin Chapman *Sam* ■ *Dir* David S Cass Sr • *Scr* Deborah Jones

Life or Something like It ★★ 12
Romantic comedy drama
2002 · US · Colour · 99min

This would-be romantic comedy serves as evidence of Angelina Jolie's post-Oscar poor judgement. Here she plays a has-it-all Seattle TV reporter (great job, great boyfriend, great big hair) who is informed by a tramp known as Prophet Jack (Tony Shalhoub) that she has a week to live. Cue much re-evaluating of life goals and cod-philosophising with her hitherto loathed cameraman (Edward Burns). For much of the film, however, Jolie gives her character such a brittle, vain and shallow edge that it's hard to care. SuR Some violence, brief swearing. *DVD*

Angelina Jolie *Lanie Kerrigan* • Edward Burns *Pete* • Tony Shalhoub *Prophet Jack* • Christian Kane *Cal* • James Gammon *Lanie's father* • Melissa Errico *Andrea* • Stockard Channing *Deborah Connors* • Lisa Thornhill *Gwen* ■ *Dir* Stephen Herek • *Scr* John Scott Shepherd, Dana Stevens, from a story by Shepherd

Life-Size ★★ U
Fantasy comedy 2000 · US · Colour · 84min

Neglected by her father Jere Burns, who's become a workaholic following the death of his wife, young Lindsay Lohan hopes a book of spells will enable her to resurrect her mother. However, she succeeds only in animating her fashion doll, played by Tyra Banks, who is intent on enjoying herself. This Disney TV movie throws out so many intriguing themes, it's disappointing to see it settle for the usual feel-good resolution. DP *DVD*

Lindsay Lohan *Casey* • Tyra Banks *Eve* • Jere Burns *Ben* • Anne Marie Loder *Drew* • Garwin Sanford *Richie* ■ *Dir* Mark Rosman • *Scr* Mark Rosman, Stephanie Moore, from a story by Stephanie Moore

Life Stinks ★ 12
Comedy 1991 · US · Colour · 88min

The title tells all: the film stinks, as Mel Brooks tries to be Charlie Chaplin and fails miserably. As a billionaire, erecting a business monument to himself even if it means getting rid of a shantytown of vagrants, he's as callous and crass as expected. Then he takes a bet that he can't live as a derelict and the plot falls apart. TH Swearing, drug abuse. *DVD*

Mel Brooks *Goddard Bolt* • Lesley Ann Warren *Molly* • Jeffrey Tambor *Vance Crasswell* • Stuart Pankin *Pritchard* • Howard Morris *Sailor* • Rudy DeLuca *J Paul Getty* • Teddy Wilson (2) *Fumes* • Michael Ensign *Knowles* • Matthew Faison *Stevens* • Billy Barty *Willy* • Brian Thompson *Mean Victor* • Raymond O'Connor *Yo* • Carmine Caridi *Flophouse owner* • Sammy Shore *Reverend At Wedding* ■ *Dir* Mel Brooks • *Scr* Mel Brooks, Rudy DeLuca, Steve Haberman, from a story by Ron Clark, Mel Brooks, Rudy DeLuca, Steve Haberman

Life Upside Down ★★★★
Drama 1964 · Fr · BW · 94min

Alain Jessua made his feature debut with this piercing social critique, combining experimental techniques with a self-deprecating sense of irony. Ultimately, it's hard to disagree with 30-something estate agent Charles Denner's desire to withdraw from his banal life and begin existing only within himself. Frustrated fiancée Anna Gaylor has to resort to drastic measures to provoke a return to normalcy. Examining a viable alternative to urban living, this may be a curio, but it's compelling. DP French +subtitles.

Charles Denner *Jacques Valin* • Anna Gaylor *Viviane* • Guy Saint-Jean *Fernand* ■ *Dir/Scr* Alain Jessua

Life with Father ★★★★ U
Comedy 1947 · US · Colour · 117min

Warner Bros' movie version of the long-running Broadway hit is a rare charmer, beautifully directed by *Casablanca's* Michael Curtiz. If the whole seems slight and rather deliberately echoes MGM's 1944 hit *Meet Me in St Louis*, well, that's no bad thing. Watch for star-to-be Elizabeth Taylor (on loan to Warner Bros from MGM and looking radiant), and lovely support from Edmund Gwenn and ZaSu Pitts. Author Clarence Day Jr couldn't have wished for a better screen rendering of his reminiscences of family life in late 19th-century New York. TS *DVD*

William Powell *Clarence Day Sr* • Irene Dunne *Vinnie Day* • Elizabeth Taylor *Mary* • ZaSu Pitts *Cora* • Edmund Gwenn *Rev Dr Lloyd* • Jimmy Lydon [James Lydon] *Clarence Day Jr* • Martin Milner *John* • Derek Scott *Harlan* • Johnny Calkins *Whitney* • Emma Dunn *Margaret* ■ *Dir* Michael Curtiz • *Scr* Donald Ogden Stewart, from the play by Howard Lindsay, Russel Crouse, from the book by Clarence Day Jr

Life with Mikey ★★★ PG
Comedy 1993 · US · Colour · 91min

This is a perfect vehicle for the charms of Michael J Fox, who's on to every trick as the thespian who turns agent after the public stops finding him cute. What makes his performance particularly good is the grace with which he accepts the fact he's been set up to lose every scene to Christina Vidal, as the little urchin he steers to stardom. Their relationship is great fun to watch, but the jabs at celebrity are delivered without any real conviction. Originally released in the UK as *Give Me a Break*. DP *DVD*

Michael J Fox *Michael Chapman* • Christina Vidal *Angie Vega* • Nathan Lane *Ed Chapman* • Cyndi Lauper *Geena Briganti* • David Krumholtz *Barry Corman* • Christine Baranski *Carol* ■ *Dir* James Lapine • *Scr* Marc Lawrence

Life with the Lyons ★★ U
Comedy 1953 · UK · BW · 61min

Based on the second long-running radio show made in Britain by the American stars Ben Lyon and Bebe Daniels (after *Hi Gang!* in 1941), this is a lightweight domestic comedy whose cosy appeal has been attenuated by the passage of time. Their playing looks laboured, and the marshmallow script about a reluctant landlord doesn't help the cause. DP *DVD*

Bebe Daniels *Bebe* • Ben Lyon *Ben* • Barbara Lyon *Barbara* • Richard Lyon *Richard* • Horace Percival *Mr Wimple* • Molly Weir *Aggie* ■ *Dir* Val Guest • *Scr* Robert Dunbar, Val Guest, from the radio series by Bebe Daniels, Bob Block, Bill Harding

Lifeboat ★★★★ PG
Second World War drama
1944 · US · BW · 93min

Alfred Hitchcock's tense drama has the distinction of being shot on what looks like the smallest ever film set. The action takes place exclusively on board a lifeboat after a liner is torpedoed by a Nazi sub. As so often in Hitchcock's films, the suspense lies not in the audience being kept in the dark about the identity of the villain, but in making us watch and wait while the characters find it out for themselves. Tallulah Bankhead is the pick of an exceptional cast, but it's all about Hitch's matchless ability to create, shatter and re-create tension until our nerves are frayed. DP In English, German. *DVD* Blu

Tallulah Bankhead *Connie Porter* • William Bendix *Gus* • Walter Slezak *Willy, U-boat captain* • Mary Anderson *Alice* • John Hodiak *Kovak* • Henry Hull *Rittenhouse* • Heather Angel *Mrs Higgins* • Hume Cronyn *Stanley Garrett* • Canada Lee *George "Joe" Spencer* ■ *Dir* Alfred Hitchcock • *Scr* Jo Swerling, from the story by John Steinbeck

Lifeforce ★ 18
Science-fiction horror
1985 · UK · Colour · 111min

It's hard to believe that Tobe Hooper, director of the influential *The Texas Chain Saw Massacre*, came up with this laughably bad adaptation. Steve Railsback stars as one of a team of astronauts that discovers parasitic energy suckers on an invasion course for Earth in a strange craft lurking in the tail of Halley's Comet. Rather than the homage to vintage Hammer horror that Hooper wanted to make, this is more a cruel parody. AJ Violence, swearing, nudity. *DVD* Blu

Steve Railsback *Colonel Tom Carlsen* • Peter Firth *Colonel Colin Caine* • Frank Finlay *Dr Hans Fallada* • Mathilda May *Space girl* • Patrick Stewart *Dr Armstrong* • Michael Gothard *Bukovsky* • Nicholas Ball *Derebridge* ■ *Dir* Tobe Hooper • *Scr* Dan O'Bannon, Don Jakoby, from the novel *The Space Vampires* by Colin Wilson

Life's a Breeze ★★★ 15
Comedy drama 2013 · Ire/Swe · Colour · 83min

Writer/director Lance Daly's fifth feature is an enjoyable quest comedy that quirkily transfers an Israeli news story to recessional Dublin. Determined to do something nice for mother Fionnula Flanagan's 80th birthday, cash-strapped wastrel Pat Shortt coerces his siblings into tidying up her famously shambolic house. But he throws away a mattress containing the old lady's savings, and the hunt begins to find it before the hoards alerted by press rumours of a million-euro windfall. Some of the subplots clutter proceedings, but the twists are well judged and the main roles neatly played. DP Swearing.

Kelly Thornton *Emma* • Fionnula Flanagan *Nan* • Pat Shortt *Colm* • Eva Birthistle *Margaret* • Brian Gleeson *Hawk Man* • Lesley Conroy *Annie* ■ *Dir/Scr* Lance Daly

Lifespan ★★★ 18
Science-fiction thriller
1975 · US/Neth · Colour · 77min

This shoestring thriller posits an intriguing contrast between humanitarian hopes for the elimination of disease and the sinister medical experimentation undertaken by the Nazis. Representing enlightened science is Hiram Keller, who discovers that a dead colleague may have concocted an elixir for eternal life, while the forces of darkness summon up Klaus Kinski, as the deranged industrialist sponsoring the unnatural project. Writer/director Alexander Whitelaw makes atmospheric use of both his Amsterdam locations and the antiseptic interiors that contrast so tellingly with the gloriously gothic labs of expressionist horror. DP

Hiram Keller *Dr Ben Land* • Tina Aumont *Anna* • Klaus Kinski *Nicholas Ulrich* ■ *Dir* Alexander Whitelaw • *Scr* Alexander Whitelaw, Judith Rascoe, Alva Ruben

Lift to the Scaffold ★★★★ PG
Crime thriller 1957 · Fr · BW · 91min

Louis Malle made his feature directorial debut with this assured thriller, which recalled both the poetic realism of Marcel Carné and the brooding menace of American *films noirs*. In addition to making a star of Jeanne Moreau and giving a generation a phobia about elevators, the film also had a considerable influence on the nascent French New Wave through the moody naturalism of Henri Decaë's photography. The sublime jazz score was improvised by Miles Davis and a band of European musicians while the film played on a screen before them. DP French +subtitles. *DVD* Blu

Jeanne Moreau *Florence Carala* • Maurice Ronet *Julien Tavernier* • Georges Poujouly *Louis* • Yori Bertin *Véronique* • Jean Wall *Simon Carala* ■ *Dir* Louis Malle • *Scr* Louis Malle, from the novel *Ascenseur pour l'Echafaud* by Noël Calef

The Light across the Street ★★★
Drama 1956 · Fr · BW · 98min

Early in her career Brigitte Bardot created a stir on the art house circuit with her smouldering performance in this cheerless tale of repressed passion. However, the real acting here comes from Raymond Pellegrin, as the disabled husband who is prevented from consummating the marriage and has to watch with growing indignation as his bride succumbs to the muscular charms of garage owner Roger Pigaut. With its fetid atmosphere, this may be noir lite, but is compelling nonetheless. DP French +subtitles.

Brigitte Bardot Olivia Marceau • Raymond Pellegrin Georges Marceau • Roger Pigaut Pietri • Claude Romain Barbette ■ Dir Georges Lacombe • Scr Louis Chavance, René Masson, René Lefèvre, from the story La Lumière d'en Face by Jean-Claude Aurel

The Light at the Edge of the World ★ 15
Adventure
1971 • US/Sp/Liechtenstein • Colour • 122min

Some movies are just so awful you wonder how they could have been conceived in the first place. This overlong adaptation of a Jules Verne novel about a lighthouse that is beset by pirates is pathetic, geared for neither adults nor children, and has grievous trouble finding both style and tone. Star Kirk Douglas, villain Yul Brynner and female lead Samantha Eggar look uncomfortable, while director Kevin Billington seems out of his depth. TS Violence.

Kirk Douglas Will Denton • Yul Brynner Jonathan Kongre • Samantha Eggar Arabella • Jean-Claude Drouot Virgilio • Fernando Rey Captain Moriz ■ Dir Kevin Billington • Scr Tom Rowe, Rachel Billington, Bertha Dominguez, from the novel by Jules Verne

The Light in the Forest ★★★ U
Period drama
1958 • US • Colour • 88min

This intriguing period drama, which originated on Disney's The Wonderful World of Color series, should appeal to older children. James MacArthur stars as a white boy who, having been captured and raised by the Delaware Indians, is forced to go and live with a racist guardian under the terms of a 1764 peace treaty. Wendell Corey is utterly loathsome in an unusually unsympathetic role, while Carol Lynley makes an impressive film debut as his kindly servant. DP

James MacArthur Johnny Butler/True Son • Carol Lynley Shenandoe • Fess Parker Del Hardy • Wendell Corey Wilse Owens • Joanne Dru Milly Elder • Jessica Tandy Myra Butler • Joseph Calleia Chief Cuyloga • John McIntire John Elder ■ Dir Herschel Daugherty • Scr Lawrence Edward Watkin, from a novel by Conrad Richter

Light in the Piazza ★★★
Drama
1961 • US • Colour • 101min

This splendid late MGM melodrama was sumptuously produced in Europe, largely on Italian locations. It's based on a novel by Elizabeth Spencer about a mother caring for her mentally disabled daughter. As the daughter, Yvette Mimeux gives a performance of great subtlety under the direction of the still underrated Guy Green, and Olivia de Havilland is perfectly cast as the mother. George Hamilton makes a suave suitor, but the film's delicate tone is disrupted by the silly antics of Rossano Brazzi and Barry Sullivan. TS

Olivia de Havilland Margaret Johnson • Rossano Brazzi Signor Naccarelli • Yvette Mimieux Clara Johnson • George Hamilton Farizio Naccarelli • Barry Sullivan Noel Johnson • Isabel Dean Miss Hawtree ■ Dir Guy Green • Scr Julius J Epstein, from the novella The Light in the Piazza by Elizabeth Spencer

Light It Up ★★ 15
Drama
1999 • US • Colour • 95min

Picture The Breakfast Club in a Dangerous Minds kind of inner-city school against the backdrop of a Dog Day Afternoon siege and you've some idea of what to expect from this confrontational drama. Director Craig Bolotin strains to point out the latent militancy in today's "don't care" kids – providing they've got something to fight for. The reinstatement of popular teacher Judd Nelson proves to be such a cause. DP

Usher Raymond Lester Dewitt • Forest Whitaker Officer Dante Jackson • Rosario Dawson Stephanie Williams • Robert Ri'chard Zacharias "Ziggy" Malone • Judd Nelson Ken Knowles • Fredro Starr Rodney J Templeton • Sara Gilbert Lynn Sabatini • Clifton Collins Jr Robert "Rivers" Tremont ■ Dir Craig Bolotin • Scr Craig Bolotin, Druann Carlson

Light Sleeper ★★★ 15
Thriller
1991 • US • Colour • 98min

One of director Paul Schrader's more successful examinations of down-and-outs on society's fringe, this film features a top-notch performance from Willem Dafoe as a middle-league, middle-aged drug supplier who's come to a crossroads in his life. The "fun" era of designer drugs is over, crack and the cops have moved into his Manhattan manor, and he wants out. So, too, does his upper-class boss Susan Sarandon (equally excellent) to whom he looks to solve his career dilemma. Violent redemption awaits both in Schrader's leisurely paced, rewarding study of terminal addiction. AJ Swearing, violence, sex scenes, nudity. DVD

Willem Dafoe John LeTour • Susan Sarandon Ann • Dana Delany Marianne • David Clennon Robert • Mary Beth Hurt Teresa Aranow • Victor Garber Tis • Jane Adams (2) Randi ■ Dir/Scr Paul Schrader

The Light That Failed ★★★
Drama
1939 • US • BW • 87min

Ronald Colman is impeccably cast as the former soldier-turned-artist who, going blind from a war wound, is determined to finish his masterpiece – a portrait of his turbulent cockney model (Ida Lupino). Under the restrained and expert direction of William A Wellman, an excellent supporting cast, headed by Walter Huston as Colman's friend, reflects the quality of the leading performances and Robert Carson's screenplay, to make for a moving drama. RK

Ronald Colman Dick Heldar • Walter Huston Terpenhow • Muriel Angelus Maisie • Ida Lupino Bessie Broke • Dudley Digges The Nilghai • Ernest Cossart Beeton ■ Dir William A Wellman • Scr Robert Carson, from the story by Rudyard Kipling

The Light Touch ★★
Crime drama
1951 • US • BW • 106min

Writer/director Richard Brooks fails to bring a light touch to this predictable bag of clichés, which stars Pier Angeli as a young artist working for suave art dealer George Sanders. Sanders turns out not to be what he seems and, before she can say "palette-knife", the innocent girl finds herself involved with Stewart Granger (also not what he seems). The locations are rather more worthy of attention than the plot, which gets her mixed up with international art-thieving. RK

Stewart Granger Sam Conride • Pier Angeli Anna Vasarri • George Sanders Felix Guignol • Kurt Kasznar Mr Aramescu • Joseph Calleia Lt Massiro • Larry Keating Mr RF Hawkley ■ Dir Richard Brooks • Scr Richard Brooks, from a story by Jed Harris, Tom Reed

Light Up the Sky ★ PG
Second World War comedy drama
1960 • UK • BW • 85min

In this hackneyed theatrical hand-me-down, Victor Maddern heads a plane-spotting detail during the Second World War. His crew comprises Sydney Tafler who's mourning his son, Harry Locke who's short of money, lovesick Johnny Briggs and Tommy Steele who, in addition to going AWOL to do music-hall turns with Benny Hill, has made his mistress pregnant. Little relieves the incessant chat. DP DVD

Ian Carmichael Lieutenant Ogleby • Tommy Steele Eric McCaffey • Benny Hill Syd McCaffey • Sydney Tafler Ted Green • Victor Maddern Lance Bombardier Tomlinson • Harry Locke Roland Kenyon • Johnny Briggs Leslie Smith • Cyril Smith "Spinner" Rice • Dick Emery Harry the Driver • Cardew Robinson Compere • Sheila Hancock Theatre act ■ Dir Lewis Gilbert • Scr Vernon Harris, from the play Touch It Light by Robert Storey

Light Years ★★
Animated science-fiction
1988 • Fr • Colour • 83min

This space fantasy from French director René Laloux is a disappointingly weak attempt to blend adult science-fiction with children's fables. The Heavy Metal magazine-inspired animation is highly stylised and imaginative, but this tale of a young hero defending a Utopian land from destruction is too static and laboriously talky. Miramax's Harvey Weinstein directed the American version of the French original, which was scripted by Isaac Asimov. RS

Glenn Close Ambisextra • Christopher Plummer Metamorphis • Earl Hammond Blaminhor • Jennifer Grey Airelle • John Shea Sylvain • Bridget Fonda Historian/Head ■ Dir René Laloux, Harvey Weinstein • Scr Raphael Cluzel, Isaac Asimov (American version), from the novel Robots Against Gandahar by Jean-Pierre Andrevan, adapted by René Laloux

The Lighthorsemen ★★★ PG
First World War drama
1987 • Aus • Colour • 110min

The misuse of Australian soldiers by their British commanders during the First World War had been well chronicled by Peter Weir in Gallipoli. But Simon Wincer adds a new dimension to the cannon-fodder theme by examining the horrors endured by the horses roped into service during the same conflict. The cavalry charge essential to Anthony Andrews's cunning plan to seize a Turkish water supply is both exhilarating and disturbing, as classical and modern warfare clash head on. Wincer makes the most of both animals and scenery. DP Swearing.

Peter Phelps Dave Mitchell • Tony Bonner Colonel Bourchier • Gary Sweet Frank • John Walton Tas • Tim McKenzie Chiller • Jon Blake Scotty • Sigrid Thornton Anne • Anthony Andrews Major Meinertzhagen ■ Dir Simon Wincer • Scr Ian Jones

Lighthouse ★★★ 15
Horror
1999 • UK • Colour • 91min

This low-budget horror is a surprising gem. Set in an isolated island lighthouse, it follows an escaped serial killer hunting down survivors of a wrecked prison ship. Although the film is ambitious, it never exceeds its capabilities. Instead, it relies largely on atmosphere and old-fashioned suspense techniques to deliver a highly effective spinetingler. Shooting entirely at night, director Simon Hunter makes full use of shadows and gloom, creating some wonderful finger-chewing set pieces. Show-stealer Chris Adamson oozes menace as the head-lopping psycho. SF DVD

James Purefoy Richard Spader • Rachel Shelley Dr Kirsty McCloud • Chris Adamson [Christopher Adamson] Leo Rook • Paul Brooke Captain Campbell • Don Warrington Prison Officer Ian Goslet • Chris Dunne Chief Prison Officer O'Neil • Bob Goody Weevil ■ Dir/Scr Simon Hunter

Lightning in a Bottle ★★★ PG
Music documentary 2004 • US • Colour • 105min

Executive producer Martin Scorsese and former video director Antoine Fuqua wear their musical hearts on their sleeves in this passionate celebration of the blues. Capturing the atmospheric highs of a 2003 benefit concert, held at New York's Radio City Music Hall, it pays tribute to more than a century of sensational sounds. From blues legends such as Buddy Guy, Ruth Brown and the awesome BB King to contemporaries including Macy Gray and a stand-out Natalie Cole, the performances are an aural treat throughout. But although the event is occasionally interspersed with archival clips, interviews and rehearsals, this is no history lesson. Instead Fuqua allows the music to speak for itself. SF DVD

■ Dir Antoine Fuqua

Lightning Jack ★★ PG
Comedy western 1994 • Aus • Colour • 93min

Paul Hogan managed to raise the funds to make this spoof western via the Australian

Stock Exchange. If only he could have raised some laughs as well. There's very little return on the gag investment in this only moderately entertaining comedy about a legendary gunslinger teaching the tricks of his trade to mute misfit and aspiring outlaw Cuba Gooding Jr. AJ Violence, swearing.

Paul Hogan Lightning Jack Kane • Cuba Gooding Jr Ben Doyle • Beverly D'Angelo Lana • Kamala Dawson Pilar • Pat Hingle Marshall Kurtz • Richard Riehle Reporter • Frank McRae Mr Doyle • Roger Daltrey John T Coles • LQ Jones Local sheriff ■ Dir Simon Wincer • Scr Paul Hogan

Lightning over Water ★★★ 15
Documentary drama
1980 • W Ger/Swe • Colour • 86min

Nicholas Ray's mesmerising screen debut, They Live By Night (1948), heralded a dozen productive years which saw him make a dozen good, often great, movies. This final film, shown posthumously and co-directed with friend and colleague Wim Wenders, is therefore doubly painful to watch as we recall a tense, tall, energetic director now withering away on screen, succumbing to lung cancer. The film is not about his proposed fictional story of a dying painter, but about family, friendship and a last ditch attempt to resurrect a style of cinema that began to decline alongside Ray's career in the 1960s. BB DVD

■ Dir/Scr Nicholas Ray, Wim Wenders

Lightning Strikes Twice ★★
Mystery drama 1951 • US • BW • 91min

Director King Vidor has trouble sorting out the plot in this turgid Warner Bros melodrama. Richard Todd, in one of his first Hollywood movies, is cleared of murdering his wife but is still seen as guilty by his friends and neighbours, so he sets out to find the real killer with the help of new love Ruth Roman. It's neither film noir nor romance; Todd is excellent, as are Zachary Scott and Mercedes McCambridge, but Roman offers little in the crucial co-starring role. TS

Richard Todd Richard Trevelyan • Ruth Roman Shelley Carnes • Mercedes McCambridge Liza McStringer • Zachary Scott Harvey Turner • Frank Conroy JD Nolan • Kathryn Givney Myra Nolan • Rhys Williams Father Paul • Darryl Hickman String ■ Dir King Vidor • Scr Lenore Coffee, from the novel A Man without Friends by Margaret Echard

Lights in the Dusk ★★★★ PG
Drama
2006 • Fin/Ger/It/Swe/Fr • Colour • 74min

Finnish director Aki Kaurismäki is at his most laconic with the concluding episode of his "Loser" trilogy, following Drifting Clouds (1996) and The Man without a Past (2002). Yet there's a grim fascination with security guard Janne Hyytiainen's inevitable seduction by femme fatale Maria Jarvenhelmi. No one does deadpan melancholia quite like Kaurismäki, but there's also plenty of wry humour here. The film is made all the more compelling by Kaurismäki's calculated references to Charlie Chaplin, Alfred Hitchcock, Rainer Werner Fassbinder and Hollywood noir, as well as cinematographer Timo Salminen's allusions to the paintings of Edward Hopper. DP Finnish, Russian +subtitles. DVD

Janne Hyytiainen Koistinen • Maria Jarvenhelmi Mirja • Maria Heiskanen Aila • Ilkka Koivula Lindholm • Matti Onnismaa Shift boss • Sulevi Peltola Supervisor ■ Dir/Scr Aki Kaurismäki • Cinematographer Timo Salminen

Lights of New York ★★
Crime drama 1928 • US • BW • 57min

Billed by Warner Bros as "the first 100 per cent all-talking picture" – The Jazz Singer was only partly sound – they really should have spent more on voice coaching for the many vaudeville stars (Helene Costello, Cullen Landis) hired to make this gangster movie more viable and entertaining. Directed by Bryan Foy, with Gladys Brockwell as the gangster's moll and Robert

Elliott as the tough detective, the story flits from small-town integrity to "Great White Way" shenanigans, with sets dwarfing everyone and very few participants knowing how to project any kind of conviction. Still, it does have a certain novelty value. TH

Helene Costello *Kitty Lewis* • Cullen Landis *Eddie Morgan* • Gladys Brockwell *Molly Thompson* • Mary Carr *Mrs Morgan* • Wheeler Oakman *Hawk Miller* • Eugene Pallette *Gene* • Robert Elliott *Detective Crosby* • Tom Dugan (1) *Sam* ■ *Dir* Bryan Foy • *Scr* Hugh Herbert, Murray Roth, from a story by Charles R Gaskill

Lights Out ★★★ 15
Horror   2016 · US · Colour · 80min

Now you see it, now you don't in this horror where a family is terrorised by a visitation that only comes out in the dark. Turn the lights back on, and the ghoul goes out of sight again... but not out of mind. It's a conceit that most horror films take for granted, but it becomes a hugely effective scare tactic here, and director David F Sandberg (adapting his own short, which went viral on the web) does a terrific job of traumatising Teresa Palmer's errant, metal-head big sister and her plucky little brother Gabriel Bateman. TJ

Teresa Palmer *Rebecca* • Emily Alyn Lind *Teen Sophie* • Maria Bello *Sophie* • Billy Burke *Paul* ■ *Dir* David F Sandberg • *Scr* Eric Heisserer, from David F Sandberg's short film

The Lightship ★★ 15
Psychological thriller 1985 · US · Colour · 84min

After the success of films as diverse as *Mephisto* and *Out of Africa*, Austrian actor Klaus Maria Brandauer looked set to become an international star, but this laboured thriller was not a good showcase for his talents. Here he plays second fiddle to Robert Duvall, who leads a gang of psychos aboard Brandauer's rustbucket lightship. The trouble is, the captain's role is too passive and it's Duvall who has the lion's share of the action. TH *Violence, swearing.*

Robert Duvall *Caspary* • Klaus Maria Brandauer *Captain Miller* • Tom Bower *Coop* • Robert Costanzo *Stump* • Badja Djola *Nate* • William Forsythe *Gene* • Arliss Howard *Eddie* ■ *Dir* Jerzy Skolimowski • *Scr* William Mai, David Taylor, from the novel *Das Feuerschiff* by Siegfried Lenz

Like Crazy ★★ 12
Romantic drama   2011 · US · Colour · 90min

Wearing its heart prominently on its sleeve, this romance tries a little too hard to persuade its audience that they too should fall in love with its star-crossed protagonists. Anna (Felicity Jones) is a young English woman studying at university in Los Angeles. She fancies fellow student Jacob (Anton Yelchin) and before long they are head over heels in love. Their passion proves so all-consuming that she cannot bear to be parted from him and stays on in the US when her visa runs out. The problems that this faux pas ultimately throws up should come as no surprise to someone of Anna's intelligence, but viewers may regard her actions as charming or simply stupid. BP *Swearing.* DVD

Anton Yelchin *Jacob* • Felicity Jones *Anna* • Jennifer Lawrence (2) *Sam* • Charlie Bewley *Simon* • Alex Kingston *Jackie* • Oliver Muirhead *Bernard* ■ *Dir* Drake Doremus • *Scr* Drake Doremus, Ben York Jones

Like Father ★★★ 15
Drama   2001 · UK · Colour · 97min

A young Durham boy finds himself marginalised by his adult relations as social and domestic issues collide head on in this well-meaning portrait of a proud region in uneasy transition. Produced by the Amber film collective, this is an occasionally naive melodrama, which settles for an overly cosy resolution. Discarded miner Joe Armstrong drifts apart from wife Anna Gascoigne in seeking to rebuild his career as a club entertainer, while falling out with his dad, Ned Kelly, over a plan to redevelop the land on which his pigeon loft is located. DP

Ned Kelly *Arthur Elliott* • Joe Armstrong *Joe Elliott* • Jonathon Dent *Michael Elliott* • Anna Gascoigne *Carol Elliott*

Like Father, like Son ★★★ 15
Comedy   1987 · US · Colour · 95min

Apart from running out of funny things for Dudley Moore and son Kirk Cameron to do once they have traded places, this first of several late-1980s body-swap comedies is surprisingly good value. Giggling and scurrying for all he is worth, Moore whoops it up as the surgeon reliving his teens, and his performance is not a million miles behind the one that won Tom Hanks an Oscar nomination in *Big*. DP *Swearing.* DVD

Dudley Moore *Dr Jack Hammond* • Kirk Cameron *Chris Hammond* • Margaret Colin *Ginnie Armbruster* • Catherine Hicks *Dr Amy Larkin* • Patrick O'Neal (1) *Dr Armbruster* • Sean Astin *Trigger* • Cami Cooper [Camille Cooper] *Lori Beaumont* ■ *Dir* Rod Daniel • *Scr* Lorne Cameron, Steven L Bloom, from a story by Lorne Cameron

Like Father, like Son ★★★ PG
Drama   2013 · Jpn · Colour · 121min

The meaning of being a parent slowly dawns on a workaholic Tokyo architect in this charming but lightweight changeling drama. Masaharu Fukuyama plays the father who discovers that the hospital where his son was born made an error six years earlier, and that the boy is not his own flesh and blood. Accompanied by his dutiful wife, Fukuyama meets his real child, who has been raised in a much more relaxed manner in the suburbs. Director Hirokazu Koreeda's well-told tale makes some keen insights into the dynamics of the average Japanese household but the conclusions he reaches regarding the nature-versus-nurture debate are poignant if rather predictable. DP *Japanese +subtitles.*

Masaharu Fukuyama *Ryota Nonomiya* • Machiko Ono *Midorino Nonomiya* • Yoko Maki *Yukari Saiki* • Lily Franky *Yudai Saiki* ■ *Dir/Scr* Hirokazu Kore-eda [Hirokazu Koreeda]

Like It Is ★★★ 18
Comedy drama   1997 · UK · Colour · 95min

A young boxer from Blackpool (played by British amateur featherweight champion Steve Bell) finds love and disillusionment in London's gay clubland in first-time director Paul Oremland's good-natured production. Ian Rose is the record producer Bell follows to Soho after a one night stand, only to face harsh realities in the big city. Roger Daltrey is Rose's predatory boss and Dani Behr Daltrey's latest singing discovery, and both see Bell as a threat. Slightly awkward, this is has a naturalistic charm. AJ *Violence, sex scenes, swearing.* DVD

Steve Bell *Craig* • Roger Daltrey *Pop mogul* • Dani Behr *Paula* • Ian Rose *Matt* ■ *Dir* Paul Oremland • *Scr* Robert Cray

Like Mike ★★★ PG
Sports fantasy comedy   2002 · US · Colour · 95min

Pubescent rapper Lil' Bow Wow stars as an orphan who longs to be a basketball star. When the pair of trainers he is wearing (that he believes once belonged to Michael Jordan) are struck by a handy bolt of lightning, he's transformed him into an on-court whizz. As Lil' Bow Wow sets off on the road to NBA stardom, the film piles on the clichés, with his evil guardian (a typically offbeat Crispin Glover) seeking to exploit him. The movie redeems itself, however, with its light, playful tone and a winning central turn from Lil' Bow Wow. IF DVD

Lil' Bow Wow [Bow Wow] *Calvin Cambridge* • Morris Chestnut *Tracy Reynolds* • Jonathan Lipnicki *Murph* • Brenda Song *Reg Stevens* • Jesse Plemons *Ox* • Julius Charles Ritter *Marlon* • Crispin Glover *Stan Bittleman* • Anne Haney *Sister Theresa* ■ *Dir* John Schultz • *Scr* Michael Elliot, Jordan Moffet, from a story by Elliot

Like Minds ★★ 15
Crime thriller   2006 · Aus/UK · Colour · 104min

Toni Collette takes top billing in this initially intriguing but ultimately unsatisfying psychological thriller. The film's set primarily in Yorkshire, where forensic psychiatrist Collette is asked by cop Richard Roxburgh to interview a troubled public schoolboy (Eddie Redmayne). He has apparently murdered fellow student Tom Sturridge, but there's a lack of hard evidence. The dysfunctional relationship between the two boys is told in lengthy flashbacks and Redmayne, in particular, is convincing as the disturbed young man who may just be a victim rather than a killer. Gregory Read's confident direction generates a fair bit of menace, too, and he certainly keeps you guessing right to the end. However, the plotting is so artificial that by the finale you're unlikely to care either way. JF DVD

Toni Collette *Sally Rowe* • Eddie Redmayne *Alex Forbes* • Tom Sturridge *Nigel Colby* • Patrick Malahide *Dr Forbes* • Richard Roxburgh *Inspector Martin McKenzie* • Kate Maberly *Susan Mueller* • Jonathan Overton *Josh* ■ *Dir/Scr* Gregory J Read

Like Someone in Love ★★★ 12
Drama   2012 · Fr/Jpn · Colour · 105min

Appearances prove continually deceptive in Abbas Kiarostami's second fictional feature outside his native Iran. And again, as with *Certified Copy*, an unconventional relationship comes under scrutiny, this time between a twentysomething student (Rin Takanashi), who pays her tuition fees by escorting for a Tokyo pimp (Denden), and an ageing sociology professor (Tadashi Okuno), who is more interested in her as a companion than a lover. Katsumi Yanagijima's camera certainly lingers, but it is forever observant and the tiny details it lights upon are deftly counterpointed by Reza Narimizadeh's atmospheric sound design. The tale is inconsequential and the dénouement melodramatic, but as an exercise in conveying place, mood and human foible, this is consistently intriguing. DP *Japanese +subtitles. Some swearing, sexual references.* DVD Blu

Tadashi Okuno *Takashi Watanabe* • Rin Takanashi *Akiko* • Ryo Kase *Noriaki* • Denden *Hiroshi* • Reiko Mori *Nagisa* • Kaneko Kubota *Akiko's grandmother* ■ *Dir/Scr* Abbas Kiarostami • *Cinematographer* Katsumi Yanagijima

Like Water for Chocolate ★★★★ 15
Romantic fantasy   1993 · Mex · Colour · 111min

The combination of culinary art and magic realism that made Laura Esquivel's bestseller so distinctive is very much to the fore in husband Alfonso Arau's acclaimed adaptation. Set in Mexico at the turn of the century, this epic of a forbidden love consummated only through food has a sizzling story and committed performances, but Arau's direction is naively over-emphatic, with scenes of great erotic intensity sometimes missing their mark. DP *English, Spanish +subtitles.* DVD

Marco Leonardi *Pedro* • Lumi Cavazos *Tita* • Regina Torne *Mama Elena* • Mario Ivan Martinez *John Brown* • Ada Carrasco *Nacha* • Yareli Arizmendi *Rosaura* • Claudette Maille *Gertrudis* • Pilar Aranda *Chencha* ■ *Dir* Alfonso Arau • *Scr* Laura Esquivel, from her novel *Como Agua para Chocolate*

The Likely Lads ★★★ PG
Comedy   1976 · UK · Colour · 85min

This film version of the hit BBC sitcom has more in common with *Whatever Happened to the Likely Lads?*, and has poignant things to say about the cusp of middle age and the melancholy of beloved buildings being demolished. It's a worthwhile extension of the show (if a little bluer) and Rodney Bewes and James Bolam are as engaging as ever. AC DVD

Rodney Bewes *Bob Ferris* • James Bolam *Terry Collier* • Brigit Forsyth *Thelma Ferris* • Mary Tamm *Christina* • Sheila Fearn *Audrey* • Zena Walker *Laura* ■ *Dir* Michael Tuchner • *Scr* Dick Clement, Ian La Frenais

Li'l Abner ★★★★ U
Musical comedy   1959 · US · Colour · 75min

This is a sexy and witty adaptation of the brash and sassy Broadway show, highly stylised and superbly photographed by Daniel L Fapp in eye-popping Technicolor and VistaVision. The plot imposed on Al Capp's cartoon *Dogpatch* is classically simple: being the most worthless place in America the government wants to use it for nuclear testing. Cue for terrific songs, exhilarating dancing and a wonderful cast, including Stella Stevens as Apassionata Von Climax and Julie Newmar as Stupefyin' Jones. TS

Peter Palmer *Li'l Abner* • Leslie Parrish *Daisy Mae* • Stubby Kaye *Marryin' Sam* • Howard St John *General Bullmoose* • Julie Newmar *Stupefyin' Jones* • Stella Stevens *Appassionata Von Climax* • Alan Carney *Mayor Dawgmeat* • Jerry Lewis *Frank* ■ *Dir* Melvin Frank • *Scr* Norman Panama, Melvin Frank, from their musical, from characters in the comic strip *Dogpatch* created by Al Capp

Lilac Time ★★★
Silent First World War drama 1928 · US · BW · 79min

Misunderstandings bloom, along with the flowers, in this vastly romantic, hugely successful crowd-pleaser set during the First World War. French girl Colleen Moore endures the usual wartime romantic tribulations as she waits for dashing English pilot Gary Cooper to keep his promise to return to her. This lives up to its optimistic alternative title of *Love Never Dies*. TH

Colleen Moore *Jeannine Berthelot* • Gary Cooper *Capt Philip Blythe* • Burr McIntosh *Gen Blythe* • George Cooper (1) *Mechanic's helper* ■ *Dir* George Fitzmaurice • *Scr* Carey Wilson, Willis Goldbeck, from the play by Jane Cowl, Jane Murfin

Lilacs in the Spring ★★ U
Fantasy   1955 · UK · Colour · 87min

Unconscious as a result of a bomb explosion during the Blitz, a young entertainer with a boyfriend dilemma dreams of herself as Nell Gwynne, as Queen Victoria and as her own actress mother, who was killed en route to a reconciliation with her famous actor husband. A piece of romantic whimsy, produced and directed in Trucolor by Herbert Wilcox as a vehicle for his wife, Anna Neagle, who acquits herself well. Errol Flynn appears as her mother's estranged husband. RK DVD

Anna Neagle *Carole Beaumont/Lillian Grey/Queen Victoria/Nell Gwyn* • Errol Flynn *John Beaumont* • David Farrar *Charles King/King Charles* • Kathleen Harrison *Kate* • Peter Graves (1) *Albert Gutman/Prince Albert* • Helen Haye *Lady Drayton* • Sean Connery ■ *Dir* Herbert Wilcox • *Scr* Harold Purcell, from the play *The Glorious Days* by Robert Nesbitt

Lili ★★★★ U
Romantic musical drama   1953 · US · Colour · 80min

Gamine Leslie Caron stars as a waif who joins a carnival, while Mel Ferrer, in his most sympathetic role, is a self-pitying puppeteer who provides some of the film's most memorable moments. The score won an Oscar, and there's also a marvellously rich fantasy ballet sequence. Director Charles Walters makes superb use of MGM's French village set, beautifully photographed in Technicolor by Robert Planck, but children of all ages will gasp at the magic tricks performed by Jean-Pierre Aumont and Zsa Zsa Gabor. An absolute charmer. TS

Leslie Caron *Lili Daurier* • Mel Ferrer *Paul Berthalet* • Jean-Pierre Aumont *Marc* • Zsa Zsa Gabor *Rosalie* • Kurt Kasznar *Jacquot* • Amanda Blake *Peach Lips* ■ *Dir* Charles Walters • *Scr* Helen Deutsch, from the story by Paul Gallico • *Music* Bronislau Kaper

L

Lili Marleen ★★ 15
Second World War drama
1980 · W Ger · Colour · 111min

Rainer Werner Fassbinder intended this wartime weepie to be both a homage to the Hollywood romance and an assault on the lingering influence of Nazi gloss on modern German cinema. However, his evident lack of interest in the project meant that his most expensive picture was also among his worst. Hanna Schygulla is off-key as the second-rate chanteuse who risks her status within the Reich to help smuggle her Jewish beloved, composer Giancarlo Giannini, to safety. Garishly designed and lazily directed. DP

Hanna Schygulla *Wilkie Bunterberg* • Giancarlo Giannini *Robert Mendelssohn* • Mel Ferrer *David Mendelssohn* • Karl-Heinz von Hassel *Hans Henkel* • Erik Schumann *Von Strehlow* • Hark Bohm *Taschner* • Udo Kier *Drewitz* ■ *Dir* Rainer Werner Fassbinder • *Scr* Manfred Purzer, Joshua Sinclair, Rainer Werner Fassbinder, from the novel *Der Himmel Hat Viele Farben* by Lale Andersen

Lilies of the Field ★★★★ U
Drama
1963 · US · BW · 90min

Sidney Poitier won only the second Oscar for a black actor in 24 years – the first went to Hattie McDaniel in *Gone with the Wind* – for his role here as an itinerant handyman helping German nuns build a chapel on barren Arizona land. James Poe's simplistic screenplay might have become sluggishly sentimental without Ralph Nelson's discerning direction and Poitier's sharp humour, and the film also benefits from the distinguished performance of Lilia Skala as the mother superior. TH DVD

Sidney Poitier *Homer Smith* • Lilia Skala *Mother Maria* • Lisa Mann *Sister Gertrude* • Isa Crino *Sister Agnes* • Francesca Jarvis *Sister Albertine* • Pamela Branch *Sister Elizabeth* • Stanley Adams *Juan* • Dan Frazer *Father Murphy* • Ralph Nelson *Mr Ashton* ■ *Dir* Ralph Nelson • *Scr* James Poe, from the novel by William E Barrett

Lilith ★★★★
Drama
1964 · US · BW · 113min

This is a disturbing and poetic study of mental illness, with Warren Beatty as the therapist who becomes drawn to patient Jean Seberg. Shot in lustrous black and white, and the last film to be directed by Robert Rossen, this is a hypnotic experience, a movie which simmers suggestively but never comes fully to the boil. Trashed by most critics on release and a predictable box-office bomb, its reputation has grown over the years. AT

Warren Beatty *Vincent Bruce* • Jean Seberg *Lilith Arthur* • Peter Fonda *Stephen Evshevsky* • Kim Hunter *Bea Brice* • Anne Meacham *Yvonne Meaghan* • James Patterson *Dr Lavrier* • Jessica Walter *Laura* • Gene Hackman *Norman* • Robert Reilly *Bob Clayfield* • René Auberjonois *Howie* ■ *Dir* Robert Rossen • *Scr* Robert Rossen, from the novel by JR Salamanca

Lillian Russell ★★ U
Biographical musical
1940 · US · BW · 127min

Alice Faye takes the title role in this plodding biopic of a famous and colourful entertainer. Starting in the 1880s, the movie is lavishly mounted and costumed - it was Oscar-nominated for best interior decoration – and includes a clutch of pleasingly appropriate songs. But aside from some production number highlights, the dreary, cliché-strewn script sinks the enterprise. RK

Alice Faye *Lillian Russell* • Don Ameche *Edward Solomon* • Henry Fonda *Alexander Moore* • Edward Arnold *Diamond Jim Brady* • Warren William *Jesse Lewisohn* • Leo Carrillo *Tony Pastor* • Helen Westley *Grandma Leonard* • Dorothy Peterson *Cynthia Leonard* • Una O'Connor *Marie* ■ *Dir* Irving Cummings • *Scr* William Anthony McGuire • *Cinematographer* Leon Shamroy • *Costume Designer* Travis Banton • *Set Decorator* Thomas Little

Lilo & Stitch ★★★★ U
Animated science-fiction comedy
2002 · US · Colour · 81min

An innovative and quirky mix of comedy, family drama and action, this Disney fantasy is as lush and lovely as its Hawaiian setting. Accompanied by a foot-tapping Elvis Presley soundtrack, the film pushes a message of multicultural equality and tolerance so all-encompassing that it even embraces extraterrestrials. In doing so, it turns lonely youngster Lilo's friendship with cute but naughty alien fugitive Stitch into a candy-coloured morality tale. Followed by three straight-to-video/DVD spin-offs, *Stitch! The Movie* (2003), *Lilo & Stitch 2: Stitch Has a Glitch* (2005) and *Lilo & Stitch: Leroy & Stitch* (2006), and a TV series. SF DVD

Daveigh Chase *Lilo* • Christopher Michael Sanders [Chris Sanders (2)] *Stitch* • Tia Carrere *Nani* • David Ogden Stiers *Jumba* • Kevin McDonald *Pleakley* • Ving Rhames *Cobra Bubbles* • Zoe Caldwell *Grand Councilwoman* • Jason Scott Lee *David Kawena* ■ *Dir/Scr* Chris Sanders (2), Dean DeBlois

Lilting ★★★ 15
Drama
2014 · UK · Colour · 86min

Lilting traces the impact of a young man's sudden death on his partner (Ben Whishaw) and widowed mother (famed Chinese actress Cheng Pei Pei). In an attempt to pick up the pieces, Whishaw begins visiting the reserved Cheng at her care home – though matters are somewhat complicated by the fact that Cheng has no idea her son was gay, and can barely speak a word of English. Khaou's beautifully shot film is so ethereal in tone it occasionally risks evaporating altogether, though it is an undeniably heartfelt exploration of loss. SI English, Mandarin +subtitles. DVD

Ben Whishaw *Richard* • Cheng Pei Pei *Junn* • Andrew Leung *Kai* • Naomi Christie *Vann* • Peter Bowles *Alan* ■ *Dir/Scr* Hong Khaou

Lily in Love ★★ 15
Comedy
1985 · Hun/US · Colour · 102min

Despite bullish performances from Christopher Plummer and Maggie Smith, the idea that a wife would not recognise her husband beneath some risibly unconvincing greasepaint requires a suspension of disbelief that this stodgy film's smugness fails to persuade us to make. As the stage ham desperate to land the part of an Italian blonde in his screenwriter wife's new movie, Plummer sportingly debunks his own image. DP

Christopher Plummer *Fitzroy Wynn/Roberto Terranova* • Maggie Smith *Lily Wynn* • Elke Sommer *Alice Braun* • Adolph Green *Jerry Silber* • Szabo Sander *Teodor* ■ *Dir* Karoly Makk • *Scr* Frank Cucci, from the play *The Guardsman* by Ferenc Molnar

Lilya 4-Ever ★★★★ 18
Drama
2002 · Swe/Den · Colour · 104min

Teenager Oksana Akinishina excels in this sobering study of life on the bottom rung. As the eponymous Lilya, her naive vulnerability is readily evident whether she's being cheeky to the Russian mother who abandons her to emigrate to the United States, exchanging insults with the classmates who think she's turned to prostitution, or enduring the exploitation of the grotesques who populate her nightmare existence in Malmo. But it's in the company of the 14-year-old Volodya (Artiom Bogucharskij), a substance-abusing runaway, that the film finds the flicker of human warmth that makes its realism all the more tragic. DP Russian, English, Swedish +subtitles. DVD

Oksana Akinishina *Lilya* • Artiom Bogucharskij *Volodya* • Elina Benenson *Natasha* • Lilia Sinkarjova *Aunt Anna* • Pavel Ponomarjov *Andrei* • Tomas Neumann *Witek* • Ljubov Agapova *Lilya's mother* ■ *Dir/Scr* Lukas Moodysson

Limbo ★★ 15
Drama
1999 · US · Colour · 121min

John Sayles is on a pivotal indie director and mainstream screenwriter for hire, and the two sides are evident in this jarring blend of social study and outdoor adventure. When exploring the conflicting relationships within a small Alaskan coastal community, the film brims with life. However, contrivance takes over once former fisherman David Strathairn, torch singer Mary Elizabeth Mastrantonio and her troubled teenage daughter Vanessa Martinez are stranded on a remote island. The film's hard-won sense of spirituality is no substitute for the engrossing melodrama that precedes it. DP Swearing. DVD

Mary Elizabeth Mastrantonio *Donna De Angelo* • David Strathairn *Joe Gastineau* • Vanessa Martinez *Noelle De Angelo* • Kris Kristofferson *Smilin' Jack* • Casey Siemaszko *Bobby Gastineau* ■ *Dir/Scr* John Sayles

Limelight ★★
Musical
1936 · UK · BW · 65min

This British musical co-stars Arthur Tracy, popular on radio and record as the "Street Singer" but proving himself woefully inadequate as an actor, and Anna Neagle. Lavishly mounted by director Herbert Wilcox, the tale concerns a chorus girl (Neagle) who, in love with a busker (Tracy), helps him to success in the theatre, but complications ensue when he falls for a socialite. A syrupy and very British backstage drama. RK

Anna Neagle *Marjorie Kaye* • Arthur Tracy *Bob Grant* • Jane Winton *Ray Madison* • Ellis Jeffreys *Lady Madeleine* • Muriel George *Mrs Kaye* • Alexander Field *Alf Sparkes* • Antony Holles *Impresario* • William Freshman *Joe* ■ *Dir* Herbert Wilcox • *Scr* Laura Whetter

Limelight ★★★★ U
Comedy drama
1952 · US · BW · 132min

Meant as a summation of his life and art, Charles Chaplin's last American film has some stunning set pieces of vaudeville comedy - one featuring his great rival, Buster Keaton - but an inordinate degree of self-pity. As a drunken has-been entertainer, Chaplin saves young dancer Claire Bloom from suicide and nurses her to success, though his own comeback is doomed by a world which has no place for pantomime. Featuring five of his children, it's a very personal indulgence that works best as a celebration of British music hall, not as an exposé of Chaplin's own grievances. TH DVD

Charles Chaplin *Calvero* • Claire Bloom *Terry* • Nigel Bruce *Postant* • Buster Keaton *Piano accompanist* • Sydney Chaplin *Neville* • Norman Lloyd *Bodalink* • Andre Eglevsky *Harlequin* • Melissa Hayden *Columbine* • Charles Chaplin Jr *Clown* • Wheeler Dryden *Clown* • Marjorie Bennett *Mrs Alsop* • Geraldine Chaplin *Street urchin* • Michael Chaplin *Street urchin* • Josephine Chaplin *Street urchin* ■ *Dir/Scr* Charles Chaplin • *Music* Charles Chaplin

The Limey ★★★★ 18
Thriller
1999 · US · Colour · 85min

The past lives of Terence Stamp and Peter Fonda underline and illuminate this Steven Soderbergh thriller. Stamp plays Wilson, an English ex-con out for revenge, while Fonda is Valentine, a millionaire record producer whom Wilson thinks caused the death of his daughter. The former is shown as a much younger man in flashbacks taken from Ken Loach's *Poor Cow* (1967), while Fonda is now of an age when he has to hire minders to do his dirty work for him. With its Chandleresque dialogue and machine gun resonance, this requiem for the hard man is in the top flight of gangster movies. TH Violence, swearing. DVD

Terence Stamp *Wilson* • Peter Fonda *Terry Valentine* • Lesley Ann Warren *Elaine* • Melissa George *Jennifer "Jenny" Wilson* • Luis Guzman *Ed* • Barry Newman *Jim Avery* • Joe Dallesandro *Uncle John* • Nicky Katt *Stacy* ■ *Dir* Steven Soderbergh • *Scr* Lem Dobbs

Limitless ★★★★ 15
Science-fiction thriller
2011 · US · Colour · 100min

An illicit drug transforms struggling writer Eddie Morra (Bradley Cooper) from a man crippled by self-doubt and headed for the skids to a world-beater in Neil Burger's thriller. When an old friend slips him a dose of the untested substance, it prompts a massive rush of creativity, but its addictive downside also becomes frighteningly obvious and soon he's craving more of the so-called NZT. All looks set for a fairly standard cautionary tale on the pros and cons of narcotics, yet Burger generates maximum impact from the amiable Cooper's highs and lows, and poses interesting questions about whether the benefits accrued from such artificial assistance are earned or unearned. True, the film has some problematic loose ends and the female roles are largely underwritten, but otherwise this is punchy and witty entertainment. TJ Violence. DVD

Bradley Cooper *Eddie Morra* • Robert De Niro *Carl Van Loon* • Abbie Cornish *Lindy* • Anna Friel *Melissa* • Andrew Howard *Gennady* • Johnny Whitworth *Vernon* ■ *Dir* Neil Burger • *Scr* Leslie Dixon, from the novel *The Dark Fields* by Alan Glynn

The Limits of Control ★★ 15
Crime mystery thriller
2008 · US/Jpn · Colour · 110min

Writer/director Jim Jarmusch has here crafted a ponderous and pretentious thriller that's noticeably light on thrills. A mysterious loner (Isaach De Bankolé) travels across Spain on his way to a murderous assignment, meeting with a motley set of characters from whom he picks up instructions. There are fleeting appearances by Tilda Swinton, John Hurt and Bill Murray along the way, but these amount to little more than extended cameos for underdeveloped cameos. It's safe to say that Jarmusch was on more assured and accessible ground in his earlier Zen-assassin movie *Ghost Dog: the Way of the Samurai*. TeS English, Spanish, French, Hebrew +subtitles. Swearing, nudity. DVD

Isaach De Bankolé [Isaach de Bankole] *Lone man* • Bill Murray *American* • Tilda Swinton *Blonde* • John Hurt *Guitar* • Gael García Bernal *Mexican* • Luis Tosar *Violin* ■ *Dir/Scr* Jim Jarmusch

Lincoln ★★★★ 12
Biographical drama
2012 · US · Colour · 150min

Director Steven Spielberg originally intended this biopic to be a more expansive look at Lincoln's presidency; instead it concentrates on just four months in 1865, when he pushed the 13th Amendment through the House of Representatives, outlawing slavery and bringing an end to the Civil War. Abe is played with understated, folksy authority by an Oscar-winning Daniel Day-Lewis, and there are outstanding performances from Sally Field, who risks an unsympathetic role as the First Lady, and Tommy Lee Jones, relishing the rich dialogue as Radical Republican Thaddeus Stevens. The bulk of *Lincoln* takes place indoors, making the glimpses of war all the more stirring for their scarcity. Marked by oratory, anecdote and verbal jousting, Spielberg's epic brings to life a moment of 19th-century political brinkmanship in captivating style. AC Some violence, swearing. DVD

Daniel Day-Lewis *Abraham Lincoln* • Sally Field *Mary Todd Lincoln* • David Strathairn *William Seward* • Joseph Gordon-Levitt *Robert Lincoln* • James Spader *WN Bilbo* • Hal Holbrook *Francis Preston Blair* • Tommy Lee Jones *Thaddeus Stevens* ■ *Dir* Steven Spielberg • *Scr* Tony Kushner, from the non-fiction book *Team of Rivals* by Doris Kearns Goodwin • *Cinematographer* Janusz Kaminski • *Music* John Williams • *Production Designers* Rick Carter, Jim Erickson • *Costume Designer* Joanna Johnston

The Lincoln Lawyer ★★★ 15
Crime drama
2011 · US · Colour · 113min

Based on Michael Connelly's LA *noir* novel, this stars Matthew McConaughey as Mick Haller, a handsome, hard-drinking defence attorney who works from his chauffeured Lincoln town car - the one with the NTGUILTY vanity plate. Haller takes on the apparently straightforward and lucrative case of a rich kid (Ryan Phillippe) accused of the attempted murder of a prostitute, only to discover that what he's been told is anything but the truth. This is standard crime fare with almost too many twists, turns and surprises, but McConaughey more than holds his own in the lead and there's a solid supporting cast that includes

William H Macy and Marisa Tomei. KK Sexual violence. DVD BL

Matthew McConaughey *Mick Haller* • Marisa Tomei *Maggie McPherson* • Ryan Phillippe *Louis Roulet* • Josh Lucas *Ted Minton* • John Leguizamo *Val Valenzuela* • Michael Peña [Michael Pena] *Jesus Martinez* • Bryan Cranston *Detective Lankford* • William H Macy *Frank Levin* ■ *Dir* Brad Furman • *Scr* John Romano, from the novel by Michael Connelly

The Lindbergh Kidnapping Case ★★★

Drama based on a true story
1976 · US · Colour · 148min

Anthony Hopkins won an Emmy for his portrayal of Bruno Hauptmann, the man convicted of and executed for the kidnapping of aviator Charles Lindbergh's infant son. Director Buzz Kulik sets the scene well in this involving TV movie, outlining how Lindbergh (played by Cliff De Young) became a national hero and how the whole of America was appalled by the abduction. Yet, Kulik's approach to the investigation of the case is less sure-footed, as he adopts the official line in accepting the evidence without bothering to question its circumstantial nature. DP

Anthony Hopkins *Bruno Richard Hauptmann* • Joseph Cotten *Dr Joseph Francis Condon* • Cliff De Young *Charles Lindbergh* • Sian Barbara Allen *Anne Morrow Lindbergh* • Martin Balsam *Edward J Reilly* • Denise Alexander *Violet Sharpe* • Keenan Wynn *Fred Huisache* • Walter Pidgeon *Judge Trenchard* ■ *Dir* Buzz Kulik • *Scr* JP Miller

The Line ★★15

Crime thriller 2008 · Mex/US · Colour · 90min

In this disjointed narco-thriller, Ray Liotta plays a contract killer on the CIA's payroll tasked with stopping Taliban terrorists from using the line to run weapons of mass destruction into the US. Jittery editing and a convoluted, talky screenplay don't deliver the expected B-movie action; meanwhile, it's uncertain whether Liotta's permanently pained expression reflects his character's fractured mental state, or the actor's realisation that *GoodFellas* was a lifetime ago. JR In English, Spanish. DVD

Ray Liotta *Mark Shields* • Andy Garcia *Javier Salazar* • Esai Morales *Pelon* • Armand Assante *Padre Antonio* • Valerie Cruz *Olivia* • Danny Trejo *Mario* • Jason Connery *Randall* ■ *Dir* James Cotten • *Scr* R Ellis Frazier

The Lineup ★★★

Crime drama 1958 · US · BW · 86min

This riveting low-budget thriller, shot on location in San Francisco, was completely overlooked on its original release, being taken for a ripoff of a TV series to which it is only loosely connected. It teams Eli Wallach with veteran character actor Robert Keith, as two ruthless killers carrying on didactic conversations while tracking down passengers from a boat who have been unwitting heroin-carriers. Cleverly written by Stirling Silliphant and brilliantly staged by action director Don Siegel, the film is notable for its tense car chase along the uncompleted elevated freeway. AE

Eli Wallach *Dancer* • Robert Keith (1) *Julian* • Warner Anderson *Lieutenant Guthrie* • Richard Jaeckel *Sandy McLain* • Mary LaRoche *Dorothy Bradshaw* • William Leslie *Larry Warner* • Emile Meyer *Inspector Al Quine* ■ *Dir* Don Siegel • *Scr* Stirling Silliphant

Linewatch ★★15

Crime thriller 2008 · US · Colour · 85min

Set on the US/Mexico border, this strictly serviceable thriller gives Cuba Gooding Jr plenty to wrinkle his furrowed forehead over. The Oscar winner plays a veteran border cop whose search for a "coyote" smuggling illegal immigrants from Mexico leads him into a stark confrontation with his chequered past. Over-egging its plot with assorted redneck militia and 'gangsta' clichés, *Linewatch* proves bland indeed, while Gooding Jr glides through the proceedings like a man in search of an easy buck. JR In English, Spanish. Violence, swearing. DVD

Cuba Gooding Jr *Michael Dixon* • Omari Hardwick *Drake* • Sharon Leal *Angela Dixon* • Evan Ross *Little Boy* • Dean Norris *Warren* ■ *Dir* Kevin Bray • *Scr* David W Warfield

The Linguini Incident ★★15

Comedy drama 1991 · US · Colour · 104min

A designer restaurant called Dali is the setting for this bizarre and ultimately unsuccessful comedy. Bartender David Bowie, elegant as ever, is paired with a more quirky than usual Rosanna Arquette, who works as a waitress. Romance does blossom eventually, but not before cash-strapped Bowie has masterminded a robbery at the restaurant. Combine this with Arquette's Houdini-like desire to truss herself up in a tank full of water, and you have a plot as unappealing as a bowl of soggy pasta. LH DVD

Rosanna Arquette *Lucy* • David Bowie *Monte* • Eszter Balint *Vivian* • Andre Gregory *Dante* • Buck Henry *Cecil* • Viveca Lindfors *Miracle* • Marlee Matlin *Jeanette* • Lewis Arquette *Texas Joe* • Iman *Dali guest* ■ *Dir* Richard Shepard • *Scr* Richard Shepard, Tamara Brott

Linha de Passe ★★15

Social drama 2008 · US/UK/Bra · Colour · 109min

Four fatherless brothers try to escape the poverty of Sao Paolo's slums in this bleak realist drama from co-directors Walter Salles and Daniela Thomas. Vinicius de Oliveira (from Salles's *Central Station*) desperately seeks soccer fame; another sibling becomes religious; a third flirts with a life of street crime; while the youngest brother is obsessed with identifying his bus driver father. And matriarch Sandra Corveloni (a surprising Cannes 2008 best actress winner) is pregnant again. She attempts to hold her unruly family together in what is a sobering, slow and sometimes bittersweet snapshot of Brazil in social crisis. There are no resolutions to the issues raised here and for many it will prove a tough, depressing watch. AJ Portuguese +subtitles. DVD

Sandra Corveloni *Cleuza* • Vinicius de Oliveira *Dario* • Joao Baldasserini *Denis* • Jose Geraldo Rodrigues *Dinho* • Kaique de Jesus Santos *Reginaldo* ■ *Dir* Walter Salles, Daniela Thomas • *Scr* Daniela Thomas, George Moura, Braulio Mantovani

Link ★15

Horror thriller 1986 · UK · Colour · 99min

Ever wondered what a horror movie would look like made as PG Tips commercial? The answer lies here in this oddity, in which American zoologist Elisabeth Shue arrives at professor Terence Stamp's remote house-cum-laboratory to work on his revolutionary simian theories. On the brink of a major breakthrough, he disappears, and Shue is left in charge of three gifted chimpanzees. Her wards gradually revert to the laws of the jungle and start a campaign of ludicrous menace. AJ

Terence Stamp *Dr Steven Phillip* • Elisabeth Shue *Jane Chase* • Steven Pinner *David* • Richard Garnett *Dennis* • David O'Hara *Tom* • Kevin Lloyd *Bailey* • Locke *Link* ■ *Dir* Richard Franklin • *Scr* Everett DeRoche, from the story by Lee Zlotoff, Tom Ackerman

The Lion ★★U

Drama 1962 · UK · Colour · 95min

Concocted to indulge William Holden's love of Africa and its wildlife (he had his own private game ranch and co-owned the luxurious Mount Kenya Safari Lodge), this movie also indulges its star's interest in the actress Capucine. She plays his ex-wife, now married to white hunter Trevor Howard. There is also a heavily symbolic lion named "King" who befriends Holden's daughter. AT

William Holden (2) *Robert Hayward* • Trevor Howard *John Bullitt* • Capucine *Christine* • Pamela Franklin *Tina* ■ *Dir* Jack Cardiff • *Scr* Louis Kamp, Irene Kamp, from a novel by Joseph Kessel

The Lion Has Wings ★★★U

Second World War documentary drama 1939 · UK · BW · 72min

Produced with foresight by Alexander Korda, and hustled into cinemas a mere eight weeks after it started shooting, this propagandist feature attempts to predict what would happen if war broke out. The film falls into two halves. The first, brilliantly edited (by William Hornbeck) documentary section contrasts peaceful England with a Germany arming for war; the second, frankly ludicrous fictional section has Merle Oberon (Mrs Korda) fretting over RAF hubby Ralph Richardson. Still interesting to see today. TS

Merle Oberon *Mrs Richardson* • Ralph Richardson *Wing Commander Richardson* • June Duprez *June* • Robert Douglas *Briefing officer* ■ *Dir* Michael Powell, Brian Desmond Hurst, Adrian Brunel • *Scr* Adrian Brunel, EVH Emmett, from a story by Ian Dalrymple

The Lion in Winter ★★★★★12

Historical drama 1968 · UK · Colour · 128min

Katharine Hepburn is on Oscar-winning form and sparring verbally with Oscar-nominated Peter O'Toole in this adaptation of James Goldman's play about Henry II and Eleanor of Aquitaine. Set mostly within the austere castle ramparts over the Christmas festival, it's a story of a family squabble that has geopolitical import, a medieval dynastic war. While the script and the performances are simply dazzling, it is notable, too, for the screen debuts of Timothy Dalton and Anthony Hopkins who, like O'Toole, was a protégé of Hepburn's. John Barry's beautiful, melancholy score won an Oscar. AT DVD

Peter O'Toole *King Henry II* • Katharine Hepburn *Queen Eleanor* • Jane Merrow *Princess Alais* • John Castle *Prince Geoffrey* • Timothy Dalton *King Philip of France* • Anthony Hopkins *Prince Richard* • Nigel Stock *William Marshall* • Nigel Terry *Prince John* ■ *Dir* Anthony Harvey • *Scr* James Goldman, from his play • *Cinematographer* Douglas Slocombe

A Lion Is in the Streets ★★★PG

Political drama 1953 · US · Colour · 85min

James Cagney had a few run-ins with the guardians of the Hollywood Production Code before he managed to get the green light to adapt Adria Locke Langley's novel about political corruption in the Deep South. Loosely based on the life of Louisiana governor Huey Long, the film had to depart from the ending in the book to satisfy Hollywood's vision of the American Way. Cagney and director Raoul Walsh were old sparring partners, but this picture lacks the punch and pace of earlier outings, a fact attributable to Luther Davis's pedestrian script. DP

James Cagney *Hank Martin* • Barbara Hale *Verity Wade* • Anne Francis *Flamingo* • Warner Anderson *Jules Bolduc* • John McIntire *Jeb Brown* • Jeanne Cagney *Jennie Brown* • Lon Chaney Jr *Spurge* • Frank McHugh *Rector* ■ *Dir* Raoul Walsh • *Scr* Luther Davis, from the novel by Adria Locke Langley

The Lion King ★★★★U

Animated musical adventure 1994 · US · Colour · 84min

This crowd-pleasing cartoon musical from Walt Disney had enormous box-office appeal, and proved so popular that it was adapted as a spectacular stage show. For the children there's the story of how a lion cub, exiled by his wicked uncle, achieves his destiny; for grown-ups there's a visual feast of exciting animation work and some great Elton John songs. Voices range from Whoopi Goldberg to Rowan Atkinson, with Jeremy Irons a vocal standout as the evil uncle Scar. Two straight-to-video sequels (*The Lion King: Simba's Pride, The Lion 3: Hakuna Matata*) followed. TH DVD BL

Jonathan Taylor Thomas *Young Simba* • Matthew Broderick *Adult Simba* • James Earl Jones *Mufasa* • Jeremy Irons *Scar* • Moira Kelly *Adult Nala* • Niketa Calame *Young Nala* • Ernie Sabella *Pumbaa* • Nathan Lane *Timon* • Robert

Guillaume *Rafiki* • Rowan Atkinson *Zazu* • Madge Sinclair *Sarabi* • Whoopi Goldberg *Shenzi the Hyena* • Richard "Cheech" Marin *Banzai the Hyena* • Jim Cummings *Ed the Hyena* ■ *Dir* Roger Allers, Rob Minkoff • *Scr* Irene Mecchi, Jonathan Roberts, Linda Woolverton

The Lion King II: Simba's Pride ★★U

Animated musical adventure 1998 · US · Colour · 77min

Disney has become increasingly conservative in recent years, with family values ranking high on its list of plot priorities. So, while Simba's cub Kiara is allowed a moment of juvenile rebellion, she's soon roped into upholding the big cat equivalent of civic virtues, as she teams with her new pal, Kovu, to prevent his mum (Scar's embittered widow, Zira), from toppling her father from his position on Pride Rock. The graphics are less luxuriant, the songs less inspired, yet it still sold well on its direct-to-video release. DP DVD BL

Matthew Broderick *Simba* • Neve Campbell *Kiara* • Andy Dick *Nuka* • Robert Guillaume *Rafiki* • James Earl Jones *Mufasa* • Moira Kelly *Nala* • Jason Marsden *Kovu* • Suzanne Pleshette *Zira* ■ *Dir* Rob LaDuca, Darrell Rooney • *Scr* Flip Kobler, Cindy Marcus

Lion of Oz ★★U

Animated adventure 2000 · Can · Colour · 74min

This flimsy animated adventure – billed as a prequel to *The Wizard of Oz* – suffers from an excess of contrivance. Yet the vocal talents on duty are impressive. Jason Priestley voices the heroic circus lion who becomes increasingly cowardly on his travels, while Jane Horrocks plays the little girl who helps him resist the wiles of Lynn Redgrave's Wicked Witch of the East. DP DVD

Jason Priestley *The Lion* • Lynn Redgrave *The Witch* • Tim Curry *Captain Fitzgerald* • Kathy Griffin *Caroline* • Jane Horrocks *Wimsik* • Bob Goldthwait [Bobcat Goldthwait] *Silly Ozbul* • Dom DeLuise *Oscar Diggs* ■ *Dir* Tim Deacon • *Scr* Elana Lesser, Cliff Ruby, from the novel *The Lion of Oz and the Badge of Courage* by Roger S Baum

Lion of the Desert ★★★★15

War adventure 1981 · UK · Colour · 156min

Financed by Colonel Gaddafi, this paean to Libya's national hero, Omar Mukhtar, is often stirring stuff, shot in stunning desert scenery and with hordes of extras not seen since the days of *Lawrence of Arabia*. Mukhtar was a fervent nationalist and Bedouin peasant who resisted Mussolini's annexation of Libya in the 1930s. As Mukhtar, Anthony Quinn is predictable but believable. Rod Steiger is very Rod Steiger as Mussolini, while Oliver Reed is often chilling as Musso's muscle man. There's a silly love interest patched in, but overall this is a fine film that must have been a nightmare to make. AT DVD BL

Anthony Quinn *Omar Mukhtar* • Oliver Reed *General Rodolfo Graziani* • Irene Papas *Mabrouka* • Raf Vallone *Colonel Diodiece* • Rod Steiger *Benito Mussolini* • John Gielgud *Sharif El Gariani* • Andrew Keir *Salem* ■ *Dir* Moustapha Akkad • *Scr* HAL Craig

Lionheart ★★PG

Fantasy adventure 1986 · US · Colour · 100min

This curious drama attempts to interest younger viewers in a little medieval history. Sadly, neither director Franklin J Schaffner nor his star Eric Stoltz has any idea how to pitch the story of a knight who interrupts his quest to join King Richard in the Holy Land to help a gang of bedraggled kids from being sold into slavery by Gabriel Byrne. The result is a sort of live-action cartoon, but with none of the charm. DP

Eric Stoltz *Robert Nerra* • Gabriel Byrne *Black Prince* • Nicola Cowper *Blanche* • Dexter Fletcher *Michael* • Deborah Barrymore [Deborah Moore (1)] *Mathilda* • Nicholas Clay *Charles De Montfort* • Bruce Purchase *Simon Nerra* • Neil Dickson *King Richard* • Chris Pitt *Odo* ■ *Dir* Franklin J Schaffner • *Scr* Menno Meyjes, Richard Outten, from a story by Menno Meyjes

L

Lion's Den ★★★★ 15
Social drama
2008 · Arg/Bra/S Kor · Colour · 112min

How do you raise a child in prison? That urgent issue is one director Pablo Trapero tackles with affecting skill in an initially squalid yet ultimately uplifting social drama. Jailed for a murder she can't remember, Martina Gusman is aloof over impending motherhood (she is not even sure who made her pregnant). But, thanks to her growing love for her cell-born son, the struggle to provide what's best for him becomes a moving testament to parental resolve. This tough but touching gem features a luminous performance by Gusman (Trapero's wife). Her journey from trashy tart to Mother Courage holds such intense compassion, it proves impossible to resist. AJ Spanish +subtitles.

Martina Gusman *Julia* • Elli Medeiros *Sofia* • Rodrigo Santoro *Ramiro* • Laura Garcia *Marta* • Tomas Plotinsky [Tómas Plotinsky] *Tomás* ■ *Dir* Pablo Trapero • *Scr* Pablo Trapero, Alejandro Fadel, Martin Mauregui, Santiago Mitre

Lions for Lambs ★★ 15
Political drama 2007 · US · Colour · 87min

Robert Redford's film comprises three interlinked scenarios told in parallel: in California, an idealistic college professor (Redford) attempts to motivate a clever but apathetic student (Andrew Garfield); in Washington DC, Tom Cruise's hawkish presidential hopeful spars with Meryl Streep's TV reporter; in Afghanistan, two of Redford's former charges experience the cold, hard reality of military combat. Unfortunately, the sum of these three parts amounts to very little – a big subject boiled down to two conversations in two offices intercut with some fairly underwhelming military action in a snowstorm. Though Cruise and Streep bring much-needed charisma to the politics, their debate on military action is so balanced as to cancel itself out. AC *DVD*

Robert Redford *Dr Stephen Malley* • Meryl Streep *Janine Roth* • Tom Cruise *Senator Jasper Irving* • Michael Peña [Michael Pena] *Ernest* • Derek Luke *Arian* • Peter Berg *Lt Col Falco* • Andrew Garfield *Todd* ■ *Dir* Robert Redford • *Scr* Matthew Michael Carnahan • *Cinematographer* Philippe Rousselot

Lipstick ★★★ 18
Drama 1976 · US · Colour · 82min

This purported to be a serious drama about the crime of rape but is actually just an up-market exploitation movie, glossily directed by Lamont Johnson and featuring an eye-catching screen debut by Ernest Hemingway's grand-daughter, Margaux. She plays a fashion model who is raped by apparently nice music teacher Chris Sarandon. Margaux's sister, Mariel, also makes her screen debut as one of Sarandon's pupils. A schlocky resolution turns Margaux into Charles Bronson. AT

Margaux Hemingway *Chris McCormick* • Chris Sarandon *Gordon Stuart* • Perry King *Steve Edison* • Anne Bancroft *Carla Bondi* • John Bennett Perry *Martin McCormick* • Mariel Hemingway *Kathy McCormick* • Robin Gammell *Nathan Cartwright* ■ *Dir* Lamont Johnson • *Scr* David Rayfiel

Lipstick ★★★
Biographical comedy drama
2006 · US · Colour · 85min

Scrubs star Sarah Chalke is increasingly affecting here, as the 27-year-old New York journalist who uses her red lipstick as psychological armour against the world after being diagnosed with breast cancer. The dialogue has an unusual vitality that develops into something deeper once the harsh reality of chemotherapy takes effect, while Chalke's intimate performance candidly captures the emotional and physical facts of her character's condition. Inevitably, sentimentality does creep in, but it's the film's fighting spirit and overriding message of hope that dominate. SF

Sarah Chalke *Geralyn Lucas* • Patti LaBelle *Monisha* • Jay Harrington *Tyler Lucas* • Julie Khaner *Meredith* ■ *Dir* Peter Werner • *Scr* Nancy Silvers, from the autobiography *Why I Wore Lipstick to My Mastectomy* by Geralyn Lucas

Liquid Sky ★★ 18
Science-fiction fantasy
1982 · US · Colour · 107min

This is a dirty, funny, perverse and pretentiously overlong look at New York's punk-chic drug culture. An alien spacecraft lands on a Manhattan skyscraper and its inhabitants quickly get hooked on the powdered and sexual thrills indulged in by everyone populating the sordid landscape. Anne Carlisle, playing both male and female leads (don't ask, it's art!), then uses the aliens to vaporise her enemies. Indulgent and stylistically over the top to a distracting degree. AJ

Anne Carlisle *Margaret/Jimmy* • Paula Sheppard *Adrian* • Bob Brady *Owen* • Susan Doukas *Sylvia* • Otto von Wernherr *Johann* • Elaine C Grove *Katherine* ■ *Scr* Slava Tsukerman • *Dir* Slava Tsukerman, Nina V Kerova, Anne Carlisle

The Liquidator ★★ PG
Spy drama 1966 · UK · Colour · 104min

This is one of dozens of Bond ripoffs, right down to Shirley Bassey belting out the title number. Aussie actor Rod Taylor plays a hitman and former soldier who is hired by MI6, in the person of Trevor Howard, to do some liquidating. Taylor, currently a waiter in a Paris bistro, sub-contracts the work out, leading to various complications, including the near assassination of Prince Philip. Very swinging 1960s in tone, with jet-set locations, snazzy cartoon titles and willing ladies in mini-skirts. AT

Rod Taylor *Boysie Oakes* • Trevor Howard *Mostyn* • Jill St John *Iris MacIntosh* • Wilfrid Hyde White *Chief* • David Tomlinson *Quadrant* • Eric Sykes *Griffen* • Akim Tamiroff *Sheriek* • Derek Nimmo *Fly* • Jeremy Lloyd *Young man* ■ *Dir* Jack Cardiff • *Scr* Peter Yeldham, from the novel by John Gardner

Lisa and the Devil ★★★ 15
Horror 1974 · It · Colour · 91min

Mario Bava's subtle and sophisticated spellbinder is his most personal movie, one putting into focus his own dark obsessions and fears of manipulation. But for years the only available version of this movie was titled *The House of Exorcism* – the jumbled concoction it became when it was extensively recut and new footage added in a post-*Exorcist* frenzy. (Hence the Mickey Lion pseudonym Bava insisted on.) Yet Elke Sommer gives one of her most endearing performances as the tourist stumbling into a house filled with all manner of depravity in this demonic possession case history. AJ *DVD*

Telly Savalas *Leandro* • Elke Sommer *Lisa Reiner/Elena* • Sylva Koscina *Sophia Lehar* • Alida Valli *Max's mother* ■ *Dir* Mickey Lion [Mario Bava] • *Scr* Alfredo Leone, Cecilio Paniagua

Lisboa ★★★
Road movie thriller
1999 · Sp/Arg · Colour · 99min

Set along the Hispano-Portuguese border, Antonio Hernández's road thriller gets off to an arresting start, with Sergi Lopez's video salesman and Carmen Maura's runaway wife instantly developing a rapport that's every bit as intriguing as her seemingly implausible tale of financial misdeeds and callous assassinations. But as various members of her family (each one a sly Mafia caricature) catch up with them and mischievously muddy the water, the tension seeps away to be replaced by a more sinister tone. Diverting but underdeveloped. DP Spanish +subtitles.

Carmen Maura *Berta* • Sergi Lopez *Joao* • Federico Luppi *Jose Luis* • Laia Marull *Veronica* • Antonio Birabent *Carlos* • Saturnino Garcia *Bruno* ■ *Dir* Antonio Hernández • *Scr* Antonio Hernández, Enrique Braso

Lisbon ★★★ PG
Thriller 1956 · US · Colour · 86min

Republic sent star/producer/director Ray Milland to Portugal to unlock frozen funds and shoot this slack but enjoyable melodrama that made early use of the studio's own variant of CinemaScope, a process called Naturama. Milland chose Maureen O'Hara and suave Claude Rains as his co-stars, but it's a pity the story – a scheming O'Hara uses Milland through Rains to "rescue" her elderly husband from behind the Iron Curtain – isn't stronger. Nelson Riddle's adaptation of a Portuguese number for the title music is catchy. AE

Ray Milland *Captain Robert John Evans* • Maureen O'Hara *Sylvia Merrill* • Claude Rains *Aristides Mavros* • Yvonne Furneaux *Maria Maddalena Masanet* • Francis Lederer *Serafim* • Percy Marmont *Lloyd Merrill* • Jay Novello *Joao Casimiro Fonseca* ■ *Dir* R Milland [Ray Milland] • *Scr* John Tucker Battle, from a story by Martin Rackin

Lisbon Story ★★
Drama 1994 · Ger/Por · BW and Colour · 105min

Wim Wenders directs this movie about a sound editor who receives a postcard begging him to help his director friend, Patrick Bauchau, complete his movie in Portugal. Editor Rüdiger Vogler heads south in his battered car only to find the director's flat empty. He wanders through Lisbon, filming it and involving himself in the city's wonderful music, hoping for Bauchau to re-surface. A shaggy dog story minus incident, directed without humour or vitality. BB English, German, Portuguese +subtitles.

Rüdiger Vogler *Phillip Winter* • Patrick Bauchau *Friedrich Monroe* • Teresa Salgueiro *Teresa* • Manoel de Oliveira ■ *Dir/Scr* Wim Wenders

The List of Adrian Messenger ★★★ PG
Murder mystery 1963 · US · BW · 94min

John Huston's bizarre take on *Kinds Hearts and Coronets* – with stars such as Burt Lancaster, Robert Mitchum, Tony Curtis and Frank Sinatra behind make-up for cameo roles – is a gleeful black comedy for most of its running time. An unknown killer begins to eliminate 11 men who knew him as a wartime traitor, and is planning to kill the boy who is the only obstacle to his acquisition of a huge fortune. As the plot wobbles into self-indulgence, it becomes more of a hoot for the cast than the audience. TH *DVD*

George C Scott *Anthony Gethryn* • Dana Wynter *Lady Jocelyn Bruttenholm* • Clive Brook *Marquis of Gleneyre* • Herbert Marshall *Sir Wilfred Lucas* • Jacques Roux *Raoul LeBorg* • Bernard Archard *Inspector Pike* • Gladys Cooper *Mrs Karoudjian* • Walter Anthony Huston [Tony Huston] *Derek* • John Merivale *Adrian Messenger* • Marcel Dalio *Max* • John Huston *Huntsman* • Kirk Douglas *George Brougham* • Tony Curtis *Italian* • Burt Lancaster *Woman* • Robert Mitchum *Jim Slattery* • Frank Sinatra *Gypsy stableman* ■ *Dir* John Huston • *Scr* Anthony Veiller, from the novel by Philip MacDonald

Listen, Darling ★★★
Romantic comedy 1938 · US · BW · 72min

Mary Astor is a widowed mother struggling to support her children is tempted to marry a pompous, unattractive banker. Daughter Judy Garland and pal Freddie Bartholomew kidnap her in the family trailer to go in search of a more suitable match, and find two possibilities in devil-may-care Walter Pidgeon and kindly millionaire Alan Hale. Fresh and charming, this comedy has a reliable adult cast and terrific performances from Garland, Bartholomew and little Scotty Beckett as the incorrigible small brother. RK

Judy Garland *Pinkie Wingate* • Freddie Bartholomew *Buzz Mitchell* • Mary Astor *Dottie Wingate* • Walter Pidgeon *Richard Thurlow* • Alan Hale *JJ Slattery* • Scotty Beckett *Billie Wingate* ■ *Dir* Edwin L Marin • *Scr* Elaine Ryan, Anne Morrison Chapin, from a story by Katherine Brush

Listen to Me ★ 15
Drama 1989 · US · Colour · 105min

Roy Scheider oversees a bunch of squabbling students in a convoluted tale concerning a college debating competition. The final debate – on the morality of abortion – is due to be argued in front of Supreme Court judges, but this takes a back seat to the tribulations of the kids. A cliché-ridden waste of time. LH

Kirk Cameron *Tucker Muldowney* • Jami Gertz *Monica Tomanski* • Roy Scheider *Charlie Nichols* • Amanda Peterson *Donna Lumis* • Tim Quill *Garson McKellar* • George Wyner *Dean Schwimmer* • Anthony Zerbe *Senator McKellar* • Christopher Atkins *Bruce Arlington* ■ *Dir/Scr* Douglas Day Stewart

Listen to Me Marlon ★★★★ 15
Documentary
2015 · UK · Colour and BW · 98min

Maddening, magnificent, mercurial – all these views of Marlon Brando arise in a terrific tapestry of a great star's life. Documentary-maker Stevan Riley *Everything or Nothing: the Untold Story of 007*) lucked out when he gained access to the reclusive actor's self-therapy tapes, which provide a vivid and unique flavour to the director's masterful melding of archive and clips. Eerily introduced by Brando himself, by way of a digitised head, it chronicles a well-documented life... but it's no hagiography; this is Brando in the raw. JA Violence, swearing. *DVD* *Blu*

Marlon Brando ■ *Dir* Stevan Riley • *Scr* Stevan Riley, Peter Ettedgui

Listen Up Philip ★★★★ 15
Drama 2014 · US · Colour · 109min

This acerbic comedy is built around one of the most abrasive lead characters in recent memory. Philip Lewis Friedman (Jason Schwartzman) is a joyless, insensitive, narcissistic writer whose second novel is about to be published. Unable to work in the city, he decides to abandon his girlfriend (Elisabeth Moss) temporarily and spend the summer at a remote country house, where a respected author (Jonathan Pryce) is only too happy to act as his mentor. Some viewers will probably find it hard to get past Philip's prickliness, but beyond it is a witty, well-observed film about ego, relationships and social isolation. SC *Blu*

Jason Schwartzman *Philip Lewis Friedman* • Jonathan Pryce *Ike Zimmerman* • Elisabeth Moss *Ashley Kane* • Krysten Ritter *Melanie Zimmerman* • Eric Bogosian *Narrator* ■ *Dir/Scr* Alex Ross Perry

Listen Up: the Lives of Quincy Jones ★★★ 15
Music documentary 1990 · US · Colour · 110min

The first black composer to score mainstream Hollywood movies and the recipient of countless Grammys and six Oscar nominations, Quincy Jones has spent his career at the top. The same can't be said for his personal life. Deprived of his mother's love because of her mental illness, he has rarely enjoyed harmonious relationships with women, while he has twice required brain surgery. Ellen Weissbrod's documentary reveals Jones as a man of regrets behind the cheery façade. But, as fascinating as he is, the film lacks focus, meandering between recollections and tributes like a musical mystery tour. DP Swearing.

Quincy Jones • Ella Fitzgerald • Miles Davis ■ *Dir* Ellen Weissbrod

Lisztomania ★ 18
Biographical fantasy 1975 · UK · Colour · 101min

With *The Devils*, *The Music Lovers*, *Mahler* and *Tommy*, Ken Russell created a very powerful style that intimidated producers and divided the critics. However, he came a cropper with this ugly, migraine-inducing and mind-numbing bore. Liszt is here portrayed by pop idol Roger Daltrey of the Who; Paul Nicholas plays Richard Wagner, while Ringo Starr is a natural as the Pope.

The result is an epic of self-loathing, self-parody and self-destruction. AT *DVD*

Roger Daltrey *Franz Liszt* • Sara Kestelman *Princess Carolyn* • Paul Nicholas *Richard Wagner* • Fiona Lewis *Countess Marie* • Veronica Quilligan *Cosima* • Nell Campbell *Olga* • Andrew Reilly *Hans von Bulow* • Ringo Starr *Pope* ■ *Dir/Scr* Ken Russell • *Producers* Roy Baird, David Puttnam

Little Annie Rooney ★★★
Silent comedy drama 1925 · US · BW · 93min

A characteristic Mary Pickford picture, this piece of Irish-American whimsy presents her, at age 32, as the resourceful, impish, curly-headed 12-year-old who looks after her brother and her widowed father, a cop. When the latter is killed, little Annie and her band of neighbourhood ragamuffins capture the villains, while Annie gives blood to save the life of a wounded ruffian, played by William Haines. Under William Beaudine's directorial guidance, Pickford had another hit that condemned her to remain in curls. AE

Mary Pickford *Little Annie Rooney* • William Haines *Joe Kelly* • Walter James *Officer Rooney* • Gordon Griffith *Tim* ■ *Dir* William Beaudine • *Scr* Hope Loring, Louis D Lighton, from the story by Katherine Hennessey

Little Ashes ★★★ 15
Biographical drama 2008 · Sp/UK/US · Colour · 107min

Blind ambition destroys youthful integrity in British director Paul Morrison's visually stunning account of surrealist eccentric Salvador Dalí's student days in 1920s Madrid. It traces the artist's gradual transformation from shy dandy to outlandish celebrity narcissist, using his rumoured university romance with Spanish poet Federico García Lorca as a keystone. *Twilight* heart-throb Robert Pattinson shows impressive range as Dalí, whose anti-conformist stance attracts the friendship of fellow avant-garde scholars Lorca (striking newcomer Javier Beltrán) and film-maker Luis Buñuel (Matthew McNulty). But the overall lack of drama ultimately squanders the narrative's rich potential, resulting in a diluted finale. SF *DVD*

Robert Pattinson *Salvador Dalí* • Javier Beltrán *Federico García Lorca* • Matthew McNulty *Luis Buñuel* • Arly Jover *Gala* • Marina Gatell *Margarita* • Esther Nubiola *Adela* ■ *Dir* Paul Morrison • *Scr* Philippa Goslett

Little Big League ★★★ PG
Sports comedy 1994 · US · Colour · 115min

This amiable wish-fulfilment comedy is about a 12-year-old kid (Luke Edwards) who inherits a Minnesota baseball team and decides he could do a better job than their current manager. If you can accept that grown sportsmen would take orders from a little pipsqueak, then the film will touch a few bases. Edwards conveys a real passion for the game and the script has more time for character development than your average slice of sporting life. JC

Luke Edwards *Billy Heywood* • Timothy Busfield *Lou Collins* • John Ashton *Mac MacNally* • Ashley Crow *Jenny Heywood* • Kevin Dunn *Arthur Goslin* • Billy L Sullivan *Chuck Lobert* • Miles Feulner *Joey Smith* • Jonathan Silverman *Jim Bowers* • Dennis Farina *George O'Farrell* • Jason Robards *Thomas Heywood* ■ *Dir* Andrew Scheinman • *Scr* Gregory K Pincus, Adam Scheinman, from a story by Gregory K Pincus

Little Big Man ★★★★ 15
Epic western 1970 · US · Colour · 134min

Having presented an alternative view of the gangster era in *Bonnie and Clyde*, director Arthur Penn re-examined some of the most cherished myths of the Old West in this sprawling, handsome and ceaselessly sly tragicomedy. While Dustin Hoffman dominates the film as the 121-year-old who claims to be the sole survivor of Custer's last stand at the Little Bighorn, the dignified, Oscar-nominated performance of Chief Dan George is equally noteworthy. One or two of Hoffman's encounters with the mavericks, hypocrites and fools of the frontier hang heavy, but this is an

ambitious, offbeat and thoroughly provocative picture. DP *DVD*

Dustin Hoffman *Jack Crabb* • Faye Dunaway *Mrs Pendrake* • Martin Balsam *Allardyce T Merriweather* • Richard Mulligan *General George A Custer* • Chief Dan George *Old Lodge Skins* • Jeff Corey *Wild Bill Hickok* • Amy Eccles *(Aimee Eccles) Sunshine* • Kelly Jean Peters *Olga* ■ *Dir* Arthur Penn • *Scr* Calder Willingham, from the novel by Thomas Berger

Little Big Soldier ★★★ 15
Period action adventure 2010 · Chi/HK · Colour · 91min

Midnight Run's odd-couple formula is transplanted to ancient China in this breezy romp. Set during the final years of the Warring States Period, it sees Liang soldier Jackie Chan capture Wei general Wang Leehom and attempt to return him to Liang for a reward. Chan wrote the story 20 years ago and, maybe because of that wait, he puts in one of his more rounded performances, while his acrobatic moves are as fluid as ever. The pace slackens when the squabbling twosome are separated, but this is further proof - if any were needed - that Chan's work is at its most interesting away from Hollywood. JH Mandarin +subtitles. Violence. *DVD* *SL*

Jackie Chan *The soldier* • Wang Leehom *The general* • Steve Yoo *Prince Wen* • Lin Peng *Singer* • Du Yu Ming *Guard Wu* • Yu Rong Guang *Captain Yu* ■ *Dir* Ding Sheng • *Scr* Ding Sheng, from a story by Jackie Chan

Little Bigfoot ★★ PG
Fantasy adventure 1995 · US · Colour · 92min

This is a cheap and cheerful cash-in on *Bigfoot and the Hendersons*, with director Art Camacho upping the cuteness stakes by making the creature a baby. Ross Malinger plays the child who makes friends with Bigfoot Jr as the pair attempt to thwart the plans of a ruthless businessman. Children will love the cuddly creature. A dismal sequel appeared three years later. JF

Ross Malinger *Payton Shoemaker* • PJ Soles *Carolyn Shoemaker* • Kenneth Tigar *Mr Largo* • Joseph Gritto *Little Bigfoot* • Matt McCoy *Sheriff Cliffton* • Caitlin Barrett *Maggie Shoemaker* ■ *Dir* Art Camacho • *Scr* Richard Preston Jr, from a story by Scott McAboy

A Little Bit of Heaven ★★ 12
Romantic comedy drama 2011 · US · Colour · 102min

Kate Hudson struggles to break the kooky blonde mould here, playing cancer patient Marley, who is bubbly on the surface but inside is wallowing in the darkness of uncertainty. That is, until a burgeoning romance with her doctor (Gael García Bernal) forces her to open up. Hudson struggles to strike the balance between comedy and tragedy, and she and Bernal share little chemistry. What comedy there is stems mostly from Marley's relentless sarcasm, and the effect is all a bit wearying. SP Brief swearing, sexual references. *DVD* *SL*

Kate Hudson *Marley Corbett* • Gael García Bernal *Dr Julian Goldstein* • Kathy Bates *Beverly Corbett* • Whoopi Goldberg *God* • Lucy Punch *Sarah* • Treat Williams *Jack Corbett* • Romany Malco *Peter* ■ *Dir* Nicole Kassell • *Scr* Gren Wells

Little Black Book ★★ 12
Romantic comedy 2004 · US · Colour · 102min

If you can believe Brittany Murphy as the associate producer on a daytime talk show, you'll swallow any of this far-fetched nonsense. Murphy plays a dizzy 20-something who is egged on by her co-worker (Holly Hunter) to delve into the secrets held within her boyfriend's electronic organiser. Murphy's clumsy charm is engaging, while the role of self-serving confidante showcases Hunter's aptitude for comedy. But what starts off cute, if dumb, soon becomes cringeworthy. SF *DVD*

Brittany Murphy *Stacy Holt* • Holly Hunter *Barb* • Ron Livingston *Derek* • Julianne Nicholson *Joyce* • Kathy Bates *Kippie Kann* • Stephen Tobolowsky *Carl* • Kevin Sussman *Ira* ■ *Dir* Nick Hurran • *Scr* Melissa Carter, Elisa Bell, from a story by Melissa Carter

Little Boy Lost ★★★ U
Drama 1953 · US · BW · 94min

Bing Crosby acquits himself admirably in this non-musical (though he does perform a handful of songs) in one of his few dramatic roles. He plays an American news reporter who returns to France after the Second World War to find his "lost" son. Crosby is well supported by a splendid French cast, including Nicole Maurey and little Christian Fourcade, as the boy he finds in an orphanage and hopes is his son. Made in France, the film is a pleasant, but modest, tear-jerker. RB

Bing Crosby *Bill Wainwright* • Claude Dauphin *Pierre Verdier* • Christian Fourçade *Jean* • Gabrielle Dorziat *Mother Superior* • Nicole Maurey *Lisa Garret* • Collette Dereal *Nelly* • Georgette Anys *Madame Quilleboeuf* ■ *Dir* George Seaton • *Scr* George Seaton, from the novel by Marghanita Laski

Little Buddha ★★★ PG
Religious drama 1993 · Fr/UK · Colour · 117min

Bernardo Bertolucci's hymn to Buddhism comprises two parallel stories set 2,500 years apart: in one, Keanu Reeves plays Prince Siddhartha, who became the Buddha. In the other, an American boy is chosen as one of three children who could be the reincarnation of a lama. Although the contrast between the old and new cultures is handled well and Bertolucci's movie looks stunning, Reeves is horribly miscast in the pivotal role. TH *DVD*

Keanu Reeves *Prince Siddhartha* • Ying Ruocheng *Lama Norbu* • Chris Isaak *Dean Conrad* • Bridget Fonda *Lisa Conrad* • Alex Weisendanger *Jesse Conrad* • Raju Lal *Raju* ■ *Dir* Bernardo Bertolucci • *Scr* Rudy Wurlitzer, Mark Peploe, from a story by Bernardo Bertolucci • *Cinematographer* Vittorio Storaro • *Music* Ryuichi Sakamoto

Little Caesar ★★★★ PG
Crime drama 1931 · US · BW · 75min

This classic gangster picture established the legendary Edward G Robinson as one of the most unlikely movie stars, in a role based on real-life mobster Al Capone. This tough-as-nails crime melodrama consolidated the movie-making style begun by James Cagney's *The Public Enemy* the same year at Warner Bros, the studio that specialised in such tales. Robinson is so scene-stealingly good that one tends to forget the excellence of the rest of the cast, particularly carefree Douglas Fairbanks Jr and caustic Glenda Farrell. But nobody will ever forget the finale: "Mother of God, is this the end of Rico?" TS *DVD*

Edward G Robinson *Cesare Enrico Bandello* • Douglas Fairbanks Jr *Joe Massara* • Glenda Farrell *Olga Strassoff* • William Collier Jr *Tony Passa* • Ralph Ince *Diamond Pete Montana* • George E Stone *Otero* • Thomas Jackson [Thomas E Jackson] *Lieutenant Tom Flaherty* • Stanley Fields *Sam Vettori* ■ *Dir* Mervyn LeRoy • *Scr* Francis Edward Faragoh, Robert N Lee, from the novel by WR Burnett

A Little Chaos ★★★ 12A
Romantic period drama 2014 · UK · Colour · 117min

Romance blossoms between two landscape gardeners in this spirited costume drama, the directorial debut of Alan Rickman. The story takes place in the 17th century at the Palace of Versailles, where King Louis XIV (Rickman) is looking to develop the now-famous gardens. Chief designer Matthias Schoenaerts recruits strong-willed widow Kate Winslet to help with the task. If there's a criticism to be made it's that the central romance isn't as engaging as it needs to be, but all in all it's rather charming. SC *DVD* *SL*

Kate Winslet *Sabine De Barra* • Matthias Schoenaerts *Andre Le Notre* • Alan Rickman *King Louis XIV* • Helen McCrory *Madame Le Notre* • Stanley Tucci *Philippe, Duc d'Orleans* • Jennifer Ehle *Madame De Montespan* ■ *Dir* Alan Rickman • *Scr* Alison Deegan, Jeremy Brock, Alan Rickman

Little Children ★★★ 15
Black comedy drama 2006 · US · Colour · 131min

With his debut feature, *In the Bedroom*, director Todd Field explored the darker side of middle-class suburban angst, and he's still in the same territory for this follow-up. The setting is a tight-knit American community, into which convicted sex criminal Ronald McGorvey (an extraordinary turn by Jackie Earle Haley) has been released. We're then introduced to Sarah (Kate Winslet), a married mother who becomes fascinated with a charming - and equally married - father (Patrick Wilson) at the local playground. Passions flare, but McGorvey bubbles back to the surface as the stories mesh together, leading to an implausible finale that's not quite as profound as it thinks it is. Though its production values are impeccable and its performances pitch-perfect, *Little Children* feels more than a little exploitative of a hot-button subject. DW Swearing, sex scenes. *DVD*

Kate Winslet *Sarah Pierce* • Jennifer Connelly *Kathy Adamson* • Patrick Wilson *Brad Adamson* • Jackie Earle Haley *Ronald James McGorvey* • Noah Emmerich *Larry Hedges* • Gregg Edelman *Richard Pierce* • Phyllis Somerville *May McGorvey* • Raymond J Barry *Bullhorn Bob* • Jane Adams (2) *Sheila* ■ *Dir* Todd Field • *Scr* Todd Field, Tom Perrotta, from the novel by Perrotta

Little City ★★★ 15
Romantic comedy drama 1997 · US · Colour · 86min

Set in San Francisco instead of Manhattan, it's one of those easy-on-the-eye and easier-on-the-brain tales of couples breaking up and getting together that you imagine Woody Allen would write if he had had a frontal lobotomy. Jon Bon Jovi is cute as the guy sleeping with Annabella Sciorra, while she also sees his best friend (Josh Charles), and Penelope Ann Miller, Joanna Going and JoBeth Williams are just some of the other people entangled in this relationship confusion. JB

Jon Bon Jovi *Kevin* • Josh Charles *Adam* • Joanna Going *Kate* • Annabella Sciorra *Nina* • Penelope Ann Miller *Rebecca* • JoBeth Williams *Anne* ■ *Dir/Scr* Roberto Benabib

The Little Colonel ★★★ U
Musical drama 1935 · US · BW and Colour · 78min

Talented moppet Shirley Temple was a huge star when this glutinous confection was made, the first of four movies she released the same year. Temple herself is the "Little Colonel" of the title, having won the heart of a regiment. It's a hard heart that won't be moved by the child star bringing together crusty old Lionel Barrymore and sweet Evelyn Venable. TS *DVD*

Shirley Temple *Lloyd Sherman, The Little Colonel* • Lionel Barrymore *Colonel Lloyd* • Evelyn Venable *Elizabeth Lloyd Sherman* • John Lodge *Jack Sherman* • Sidney Blackmer *Swazey* • Alden Chase *Hull* • William Burress *Dr Scott* • David O'Brien [Dave O'Brien] *Frank Randolph* • Hattie McDaniel *Mom Beck* • Geneva Williams *Maria* ■ *Dir* David Butler • *Scr* William Conselman, from the story by Annie Fellows Johnston

Little Darlings ★★★ 15
Drama 1980 · US · Colour · 90min

At summer camp, streetwise tough Kristy McNichol and rich brat Tatum O'Neal bet on who can lose their virginity first. McNichol sets her sights on mumbling Matt Dillon while O'Neal tries to seduce Armand Assante, one of the camp instructors. Director Ronald F Maxwell's teen box-office hit veers from crude humour to cute sentimentality with such breathless aplomb that it takes the edge off what could have become merely exploitative material in less dextrous hands. Worth watching for McNichol alone who is funny and sensitive. AJ

Tatum O'Neal *Ferris Whitney* • Kristy McNichol *Angel Bright* • Armand Assante *Gary Callahan* • Matt Dillon *Randy* • Krista Errickson *Cinder* ■ *Dir* Ronald F Maxwell • *Scr* Kimi Peck, Dalene Young, from a story by Kimi Peck

Little Dieter Needs to Fly
★★★

Documentary 1997 · Fr/UK/Ger · Colour · 71min

Werner Herzog's personality always dominates his documentaries. Consequently, his curiosity is as much to the fore as Dieter Dengler's memory in this biographical study that will outrage the purists with its unconventional approach to truth. Raised in poverty in post-Nazi Germany, Dengler emigrated to the United States aged 18 to fulfil his flying ambitions. However, his stint in the USAF resulted in him being shot down over Laos and tortured by his captors before he managed to escape. Some of the reconstructions may seem extreme, but Dengler seems to trust the director implicitly and, moreover, they chime in with Herzog's perennial fixation with obsession. DP English, German +subtitles. *DVD*

Werner Herzog *Narrator* ■ *Dir/Scr* Werner Herzog

Little Dorrit
★★★★★ U

Period drama 1987 · UK · Colour · 343min

Running nearly six hours, this monumental reworking of Dickens is divided into two parts - *Nobody's Fault* and *Little Dorrit's Story* - with much of the action of the first half being repeated in the second, so that we see the unfolding drama from the different perspectives of its two main protagonists, the bashful Arthur Clennam and Little Dorrit herself, who has been raised by her father in the Marshalsea debtors' prison. Christine Edzard not only directed and scripted the film, but she also made many of the costumes and, along with her husband Richard Goodwin, built the sets at a warehouse in London's Rotherhithe. The huge cast is superb, with Derek Jacobi, Sarah Pickering and Alec Guinness outstanding. DP

Derek Jacobi *Arthur Clennam* · Alec Guinness *William Dorrit* · Sarah Pickering *Little Dorrit* · Cyril Cusack *Frederick Dorrit* · Joan Greenwood *Mrs Clennam* · Max Wall *Flintwinch* · Patricia Hayes *Affery* · Miriam Margolyes *Flora Finching* · Roshan Seth *Mr Pancks* ■ *Dir* Christine Edzard · *Scr* Christine Edzard, from the novel by Charles Dickens

The Little Drummer Girl
★★★ 15

Spy drama 1984 · US · Colour · 124min

Diane Keaton is still in eye-flutteringly winsome mode seven years after Woody Allen's *Annie Hall*, so she never quite convinces here as the politically-correct actress who's recruited by Israeli Intelligence to infiltrate a Palestinian terrorist group. John le Carré's bestseller, from which this is adapted, has many different character shades, but director George Roy Hill opts for broader strokes of near caricature that suit Klaus Kinski's strident performance as the Israeli agent in charge of Keaton's enrolment. Too much talk slows the pace from urgency to languor. TH

Diane Keaton *Charlie* · Klaus Kinski *Kurtz* · Yorgo Voyagis *Joseph* · Sami Frey *Khalil* · David Suchet *Mesterbein* · Eli Danker *Litvak* · Ben Levine *Dimitri* · Michael Cristofer *Tayeh* · Bill Nighy *Al* · Anna Massey *Chairwoman* ■ *Dir* George Roy Hill · *Scr* Loring Mandel, from the novel by John le Carré

Little Fish
★★★ 15

Drama 2005 · Aus · Colour · 109min

Cate Blanchett contributes a deeply moving portrayal to this consistently disconcerting Sydney-based drama about a reformed junkie's bid to put her life back on track. She's ably supported by Noni Hazlehurst, as her over-protective mother, and Hugo Weaving, as her bisexual stepfather, who relies on heroin provided by retiring gangster Sam Neill to cope with losing the fame he once enjoyed as a rugby league star. But while director Rowan Woods makes evocative use of the city's Little Saigon neighbourhood, he fails to integrate the drug deal subplot involving Blanchett's disabled brother, Martin Henderson, and

her Vietnamese ex-boyfriend, Dustin Nguyen. DP Swearing. *DVD*

Cate Blanchett *Tracy Heart* · Sam Neill *Brad "The Jockey" Thompson* · Hugo Weaving *Lionel Dawson* · Martin Henderson *Ray Heart* · Noni Hazlehurst *Janelle Heart* · Dustin Nguyen *Jonny* · Joel Tobeck *Steven Moss* ■ *Dir* Rowan Woods · *Scr* Jacquelin Perske

Little Fockers
★★★ 12

Comedy 2010 · US · Colour · 93min

The third instalment of the comedy franchise may not be as funny as *Meet the Parents*, but it is more amusing than *Meet the Fockers*, boldly expanding the family conflict to include the clan's youngest additions. Here, Greg Focker (Ben Stiller) is now a successful nurse and proud father of twins, heading his own dysfunctional brood despite continued interference from his ex-CIA father-in-law (Robert De Niro) and the sexual advances of a pharmaceutical saleswoman (Jessica Alba). The average script sags a little in the middle but mostly pings with laughs, thanks to exquisite comic timing from an impressive supporting cast. KK Sexual references. *DVD* *Blu*

Robert De Niro *Jack Byrnes* · Ben Stiller *Greg Focker* · Dustin Hoffman *Bernie Focker* · Barbra Streisand *Rozalin Focker* · Jessica Alba *Andi Garcia* · Teri Polo *Pamela Byrnes-Focker* · Laura Dern *Prudence* · Owen Wilson *Kevin Rawley* · Harvey Keitel *Randy Weir* ■ *Dir* Paul Weitz · *Scr* John Hamburg, Victoria Strouse, Larry Stuckey

The Little Foxes
★★★★ PG

Period drama 1941 · US · BW · 111min

It may have been something to do with the fact that director William Wyler and star Bette Davis were romantically involved that gave their many celluloid collaborations such an exciting buzz. This is a splendid example of Davis at the height of her powers as the deeply nasty Regina, the power-hungry schemer of a once wealthy southern clan. The critics always said of Wyler that he "understood women"; they meant that he was not afraid to give a talent like Davis's full flight while also managing to contain her worst histrionic excesses. The result here is a quite magnificent movie. SR

Bette Davis *Regina Hubbard Giddens* · Herbert Marshall *Horace Giddens* · Teresa Wright *Alexandra Giddens* · Richard Carlson *David Hewitt* · Patricia Collinge *Birdie Hubbard* · Dan Duryea *Leo Hubbard* · Charles Dingle *Ben Hubbard* · Carl Benton Reid *Oscar Hubbard* ■ *Dir* William Wyler · *Scr* Lillian Hellman, Arthur Kober, Dorothy Parker, Alan Campbell, from the play by Lillian Hellman

The Little Giant
★★

Crime comedy 1933 · US · BW · 70min

In one of the first gangster comedies, Edward G Robinson plays beer baron "Bugs" Ahearn, who at the end of Prohibition tries to establish himself as a respectable figure out west. Hiring Mary Astor's estate agent as his social adviser, he finds high society to be as full of crooks as the Chicago he left behind. Although briskly directed by Roy Del Ruth, this is small beer compared to Robinson's later send-ups of his tough-guy image (*A Slight Case of Murder, Brother Orchid*). AE

Edward G Robinson *James Francis "Bugs" Ahearn* · Mary Astor *Polly Cass* · Helen Vinson *Polly Cass* · Russell Hopton *Al Daniels* · Kenneth Thomson *John Stanley* · Shirley Grey *Edith Merriam* · Berton Churchill *Donald Hadley Cass* · Donald Dillaway *Gordon Cass* · Louise Mackintosh *Mrs Cass* ■ *Dir* Roy Del Ruth · *Scr* Wilson Mizner, Robert Lord

Little Giant
★★

Comedy 1946 · US · BW · 91min

On this occasion, Abbott and Costello take a radical departure from their usual routine of playing pals who find themselves in all sorts of hot water. Here they perform separately rather than as a double act. Costello plays a country bumpkin who leaves the big city to make enough money to marry his sweetheart. Abbott, in a double role, hires him on as a vacuum cleaner salesman. There's plenty of slapstick action in this film and it also

features appearances from Lou's brother Pat and former Marx Brothers straight woman Margaret Dumont. DF

Bud Abbott *Mr EL Morrison/Tom Chandler* · Lou Costello *Benny Miller* · Brenda Joyce *Ruby* · Jacqueline de Wit *Hazel Temple* · George Cleveland *Uncle Clarence Goodring* · Elena Verdugo *Martha Hill* · Mary Gordon *Anna Miller* · Pierre Watkin *President PS Van Loon* · Margaret Dumont *Mrs Hendrickson* ■ *Dir* William A Seiter · *Scr* Walter DeLeon, from a story by Paul Jarrico, from Richard Collins

Little Giants
★★ PG

Sports comedy drama 1994 · US · Colour · 101min

This is yet another story of misfit kids who defy all the odds to trounce the champions. The one twist this utterly predictable American football comedy has going for it is that the side has been assembled to give a girl the chance to parade her skills against some boneheaded boys. As the girl in question, Shawna Waldron gives a good account of herself. However, the same can't be said of Rick Moranis as her gormless dad. DP

Rick Moranis *Danny O'Shea* · Ed O'Neill *Kevin O'Shea* · Sam Horrigan *Spike Hammers* · Shawna Waldron *Becky O'Shea* · Mary Ellen Trainor *Karen O'Shea* · Devon Sawa *Junior Floyd* · Susanna Thompson *Patty Floyd* ■ *Dir* Duwayne Dunham, Brian Levant · *Scr* James Ferguson, Robert Shallcross, Tommy Swerdlow, Michael Goldberg, from a story by James Ferguson, Robert Shallcross

Little Girl from Hanoi
★★★

War drama 1974 · Viet · BW · 85min

Whereas American pictures made during the Vietnam War concentrated on gung-ho heroics, Nguyen Hai Ninh's Vietnamese drama focuses on the human cost of the conflict, as a 12-year-old girl goes looking for her family during the Christmas air raids on Hanoi, only to meet a kindly soldier, to whom she confides her memories of happier times. As all Vietnamese pictures were made in black and white until the mid-1980s, the action has a newsreel feel to it, which reinforces its propaganda value. DP Vietnamese +subtitles.

■ *Dir* Nguyen Hai Ninh · *Scr* Hoang Tich Chi, Nguyen Hai Ninh, Vuong Dan Hoang

Little Girl Lost: the Delimar Vera Story
★★

Drama based on a true story 2008 · US/Can · Colour · 120min

Based on a real case, this simple but effective story centres on an outstanding performance from *Scrubs* star Judy Reyes as a working-class Philadelphia woman who struggles for six years to convince her family and the authorities that her baby was abducted rather than killed in a house fire. Despite an overly neat finale that dabbles in sentimentality, the film remains consistently compelling. SF

Judy Reyes *Luz Cuevas* · Ana Ortiz *Valerie Valleja* · Hector Luis Bustamante *Pedro Vera* · Marlene Forte *Tatita* · A Martinez *Angel Cruz* · Jillian Bruno *Delimar Vera/Aaliyah* ■ *Dir* Paul A Kaufman · *Scr* Christopher Canaan, Maria Nation, from a story by Canaan

The Little Girl Who Lives Down the Lane
★★★ 15

Thriller 1976 · Can/Fr · Colour · 88min

This chilling oddity - a psychological thriller exploring serious themes - features an intuitive performance from 13-year-old Jodie Foster that hints at what was to come. Grief-stricken Foster murders her mother when her father commits suicide and then buries both corpses in the cellar. Unfortunately, her suspicious actions arouse the curiosity of landlady Alexis Smith and - worse - the interest of her child-molesting, psychopathic son (a startling turn by Martin Sheen). This macabre fairy tale becomes a captivating experience under Nicolas Gessner's sensitive direction. AJ *DVD*

Jodie Foster *Rynn Jacobs* · Martin Sheen *Frank Hallet* · Alexis Smith *Mrs Hallet* · Mort Shuman *Officer Miglioriti* · Scott Jacoby *Mario Podesta* ■ *Dir* Nicolas Gessner · *Scr* Laird Koenig, from his novel

The Little Hut
★

Comedy 1957 · US · Colour · 96min

There's nothing more tedious than Hollywood tease, as director Mark Robson attempts to film a French sex farce in the days when censorship permitted only talk and no action. Shipwrecked together on a deserted South Pacific island are Stewart Granger as a neglectful husband, Ava Gardner as his love-starved wife, David Niven as his best friend and her would-be lover. Gardner hated the picture and only took it to be near her current beau, Walter Chiari, who turns up as the randy ship's chef. AE

Ava Gardner *Susan* · Stewart Granger *Sir Philip Ashlow* · David Niven *Henry Brittingham-Brett* · Walter Chiari *Mario* · Finlay Currie *Reverend Brittingham-Brett* · Jean Cadell *Mrs Brittingham-Brett* ■ *Dir* Mark Robson · *Scr* F Hugh Herbert, from a play by André Roussin, Nancy Mitford

Little Lord Fauntleroy
★★★

Silent drama 1921 · US · BW · 111min

One of Mary Pickford's biggest box-office successes - and one of her own personal favourites - was this overlong version of Frances Hodgson Burnett's maudlin Victorian tale. As her own producer, Pickford elected to play both the widowed mother and her son, Cedric, whom she surrenders to an English castle for preparation to become the next Lord Fauntleroy. Under Alfred E Green's direction (with some help from Pickford's brother, Jack), Mary excelled both in another of her child roles, and as the mother forced to live apart from her precious son. The immaculate trick photography of the two together was quite an achievement at the time, and the vast castle set is memorable. AE

Mary Pickford *Cedric, Little Lord Fauntleroy/ Dearest, Cedric's mother* · Claude Gillingwater *The Earl of Dorincourt* · Joseph Dowling *Haversham, the Earl's Counsel* · James A Marcus *Hobbs, the grocer* · Frances Marion *Her son, the pretender* ■ *Dir* Alfred E Green, Jack Pickford · *Scr* Bernard McConville, from the novel by Frances Hodgson Burnett · *Cinematographer* Charles Rosher

Little Lord Fauntleroy
★★★

Drama 1936 · US · BW · 98min

David O Selznick proved the sceptics wrong when he chose this Victorian chestnut for his first independent production and had a critical and box-office success. He borrowed child star Freddie Bartholomew from MGM to portray the Brooklyn youngster who becomes a British lord and persuaded Dolores Costello to make a comeback, displaying radiant charm as the mother he calls "Dearest". Under John Cromwell's smooth direction, with C Aubrey Smith as the irritable earl who can't abide his American daughter-in-law, the sentimental story of the boy's arrival in England is as well told as it possibly could be. AE

Freddie Bartholomew *Ceddie Errol* · Dolores Costello Barrymore *[Dolores Costello] "Dearest", Mrs Errol* · C Aubrey Smith *Earl of Dorincourt* · Guy Kibbee *Mr Hobbs* · Henry Stephenson *Havisham* · Mickey Rooney *Dick* ■ *Dir* John Cromwell · *Scr* Hugh Walpole, from the novel by Frances Hodgson Burnett

Little Man
★ 12

Comedy 2006 · US · Colour · 93min

Scary Movie franchise creators the Wayans brothers continue to give lowbrow entertainment a bad name with this barrel-scraping comedy. A crude and cartoonish film that's even worse than their 2004 effort *White Chicks*, it adopts one vaguely amusing concept - a diminutive jewel thief masquerading as a baby to retrieve a diamond - and bleeds it dry long before the *Home Alone*-style finale. SF *DVD*

Marlon Wayans *Calvin Simms* · Shawn Wayans *Darryl Edwards* · Kerry Washington *Vanessa* · John Witherspoon *Pops* · Tracy Morgan *Percy* ·

Lochlyn Munro *Greg* • Chazz Palminteri *Walken* • Molly Shannon *Soccer Mom* ■ *Dir* Keenen Ivory Wayans • *Scr* Keenen Ivory Wayans, Marlon Wayans, Shawn Wayans

Little Man Tate ★★★★ PG

Drama   1991 · US · Colour · 95min

Jodie Foster made an impressive directorial debut with this touching drama about a young mother (played by Foster) who is determined to get the best for her exceptionally gifted six-year-old son (an enjoyable performance from Adam Hann-Byrd). While it has its clichéd moments, this is moving without being cloying. The film also features some nice supporting performances, notably from Dianne Wiest as a child psychologist, and from musician/actor Harry Connick Jr. JB *DVD*

Jodie Foster *Dede Tate* • Dianne Wiest *Dr Jane Grierson* • Adam Hann-Byrd *Fred Tate* • Harry Connick Jr *Eddie* • David Pierce [David Hyde Pierce] *Garth* • Debi Mazar *Gina* • PJ Ochlan *Damon Wells* • George Plimpton *Winston F Buckner* ■ *Dir* Jodie Foster • *Scr* Scott Frank

Little Man, What Now? ★★★

Drama   1934 · US · BW · 91min

With poverty and unemployment rife in Germany after the First World War, newlywed Douglass Montgomery loses his job, plunging himself and his pregnant wife Margaret Sullavan into a series of catastrophes. Sullavan glows at the centre of director Frank Borzage's film, rich in atmosphere and fascinating as a social document of the period. Viewed with hindsight, one is haunted by the knowledge of the Nazi regime to come. However, on the whole, this once popular and well-regarded film has dated badly, overdosing on sentimentality and with a rather weak hero. RK

Margaret Sullavan *Lämmchen* • Douglass Montgomery *Hans Pinneberg* • Alan Hale *Holger Jachman* • Catherine Doucet *Mia Pinneberg* • DeWitt Jennings *Emil Kleinholtz* • Muriel Kirkland *Marie Kleinholz* ■ *Dir* Frank Borzage • *Scr* William Anthony McGuire, Rudolph Ditzen [Hans Fallada]

Little Manhattan ★★★★ PG

Romantic comedy   2005 · US · Colour · 86min

Josh Hutcherson plays an angst-ridden 11-year-old who, quite literally, falls head over heels for Charlie Ray at karate class. Over the course of one languorous New York summer, he struggles to negotiate the protocols of dating and win her heart. Writer Jennifer Flackett allows access to Gabe's innermost thoughts with an amusingly precocious voiceover where he muses that love is "a terrible, ugly business". Hutcherson delivers the lines with total conviction in a charming film that doesn't patronise its young subject or his emotions. SP

Josh Hutcherson *Gabe* • Charlie Ray *Rosemary* • Bradley Whitford *Adam* • Cynthia Nixon *Leslie* • Willie Garson *Ralph* ■ *Dir* Mark Levin • *Scr* Jennifer Flackett

The Little Mermaid ★★★ U

Adventure   1976 · USSR · Colour · 77min

Vladimir Bychkov's live-action version of Hans Christian Andersen's celebrated story has a certain charm, reminiscent of that Eastern bloc TV classic, *The Singing Ringing Tree*. He unfussily extracts a little fairy-tale magic from the stylised backdrops against which unfolds the story of prince Valentin Nikulin, who falls in love with Vika Novikova, the mermaid who delivered him from the wiles of her singing sisters. The downbeat ending won't please everyone, but at least Bychkov has remained true to his source. DP In Russian.

Vika Novikova *The Little Mermaid* • Valentin Nikouline *Troubador* • Galina Artemova *Princess* • Yuri Senkevitch *Prince* • Galina Volchek *Witch* ■ *Dir* Vladimir Bychkov • *Scr* Victor Vitkovich, Grigory Lagfeld, from the fairy tale by Hans Christian Andersen

The Little Mermaid ★★★★★ U

Animated musical adventure   1989 · US · Colour · 85min

What a splash this adventure made on its release, marking as it did the beginning of a new "golden age" of Disney animated features. The story of the plucky Ariel (who set the tone for a new generation of Disney heroines) features impressive animation and a catchy, show-stopping score by Academy Award-nominated Alan Menken - including the instant hit *Under the Sea*, sung with Caribbean verve by Sebastian, composer to the court of King Triton and Ariel's reluctant minder. While some of the scenes could frighten very young children, especially those featuring the loathesome Ursula, this remains an enduring delight. KFS *DVD* *BL*

Jodi Benson *Ariel* • Samuel E Wright *Sebastian* • Jason Marin *Flounder* • Christopher Daniel Barnes *Eric* • Pat Carroll *Ursula* • Edie McClurg *Carlotta* • Buddy Hackett *Scuttle* • Kenneth Mars *Triton* • Ben Wright (1) *Grimsby* • René Auberjonois *Louis* ■ *Dir* John Musker, Ron Clements • *Scr* John Musker, Ron Clements, from the fairy tale by Hans Christian Andersen

The Little Mermaid II: Return to the Sea ★★★ U

Animated musical adventure   2000 · US · Colour · 72min

By the generally poor standards of straight-to-video Disney sequels, this second aquatic outing provides reasonable entertainment. The film's new heroine is Ariel's 12-year-old daughter Melody, whose underwater ancestry has been kept hidden to protect her from the evil influence of Ursula's bitter sister Morgana. The animation is unexceptional and the tunes aren't in the same Oscar winning league as the buoyant originals. On the positive side, the same voice cast returns. JC *DVD*

Jodi Benson *Ariel* • Samuel E Wright *Sebastian* • Tara Charendoff *Melody* • Pat Carroll *Morgana* • Buddy Hackett *Scuttle* • Kenneth Mars *King Triton* • Max Casella *Tip* • Stephen Furst *Dash* ■ *Dir* Jim Kammerud, Brian Smith (3) • *Scr* Elizabeth Anderson, Temple Mathews

The Little Minister ★★★

Period drama   1934 · US · BW · 104min

Adapted from a novel and play by JM Barrie, this screen incarnation of the tale (several silent versions were made) stars Katharine Hepburn as a gypsy girl, an exotic outsider in a strictly religious Scottish community. Her romantic relationship with new, handsome young minister John Beal causes a furore among the village congregation. Beal gives a competent portrayal of a rigid cleric gradually melting under the influence of love, while Hepburn offers one of her livelier performances. RK

Katharine Hepburn *Babbie* • John Beal *Gavin* • Alan Hale *Rob Dow* • Donald Crisp *Dr McQueen* • Lumsden Hare *Thammas* • Andy Clyde *Wearyworld* • Beryl Mercer *Margaret* ■ *Dir* Richard Wallace • *Scr* Jane Murfin, Sarah Y Mason, Victor Heerman, Mortimer Offner, Jack Wagner, from the play by JM Barrie

Little Miss Broadway ★★★ U

Musical   1938 · US · BW · 71min

This is a characteristic vehicle for the world's most famous child star, Shirley Temple, now a veteran at ten years old and looking a mite plump. The idiotic plot is a variation on a number of other Temple vehicles in which the little moppet brings sunshine into a dozen lives and melts the stoniest of hearts - in this case mean Edna May Oliver who wants to close the hotel for stage troupers where Temple, rescued from an orphanage, lives with the family that has adopted her. The precocious child is both ghastly and irresistible. RK

Shirley Temple *Betsy Brown* • George Murphy *Roger Wendling* • Jimmy Durante *Jimmy Clayton* • Phyllis Brooks *Barbara Shea* • Edna May Oliver *Sarah Wendling* • George Barbier *Pop Shea* • Edward Ellis *Pop Shea* • Jane Darwell *Miss Hutchins* ■ *Dir* Irving Cummings • *Scr* Harry Tugend, Jack Yellen

Little Miss Marker ★★★

Comedy   1934 · US · BW · 78min

This was the film that clinched Shirley Temple's claim to stardom. The diminutive phenomenon, six years old at the time, is utterly disarming and captivating as the moppet who is left with a bookie (Adolphe Menjou) as an IOU, and proceeds to reform the gambling fraternity with her charm. Based on a Damon Runyon story, the cast is peopled with the author's typically amusing guys and dolls. This is a warm and witty tale with the inestimable advantage of Temple's performance. TV

Adolphe Menjou *Sorrowful Jones* • Dorothy Dell *Bangles Carson* • Charles Bickford *Big Steve* • Shirley Temple *Miss Marker* • Lynne Overman *Regret* ■ *Dir* Alexander Hall • *Scr* William R Lipman, Sam Hellman, Gladys Lehman, from the story by Damon Runyon

Little Miss Marker ★ U

Comedy   1980 · US · Colour · 97min

This remake of the 1934 Shirley Temple vehicle is so sickly sweet it's guaranteed to give you toothache. Sara Stimson has the unenviable role of following Temple as the titular Little Miss, who is handed over by her father to Walter Matthau's bookie as the guarantee for a racing debt. Matthau soon becomes putty in her childish hands in an unconvincing tale of a cute kid softening a grumpy old man. Throw a simpering Julie Andrews and a mincing Tony Curtis into the melting pot and you'll have Damon Runyon turning in his grave. LH

Walter Matthau *Sorrowful Jones* • Julie Andrews *Amanda* • Tony Curtis *Blackie* • Bob Newhart *Regret* • Lee Grant *The Judge* • Brian Dennehy *Herbie* • Kenneth McMillan *Brannigan* • Sara Stimson *The Kid* ■ *Dir* Walter Bernstein • *Scr* Walter Bernstein, from the story by Damon Runyon

Little Miss Sunshine ★★★★ 15

Road movie comedy   2006 · US · Colour · 98min

Greg Kinnear leads a dysfunctional family on a road trip from New Mexico to California in this sparkling indie comedy. He's spot-on as the pompous dad who aspires to becoming a "success coach" despite being stalked by failure. Every role is brilliantly cast, but it's a tug-of-war for best performance between Kinnear and Steve Carell, as the suicidal brother-in-law. Co-directors Jonathan Dayton and Valerie Faris skilfully balance zany gags involving mislaid porn and a stashed corpse with genuinely touching family drama. Disarmingly funny and bold, it's a clever swipe at American values. SP Swearing, drug abuse. *DVD* *BL*

Greg Kinnear *Richard* • Steve Carell *Frank* • Toni Collette *Sheryl* • Alan Arkin *Grandpa* • Abigail Breslin *Olive* • Paul Dano *Dwayne* ■ *Dir* Jonathan Dayton, Valerie Faris • *Scr* Michael Arndt

Little Moon & Jud McGraw ★

Western   1978 · US · Colour · 92min

This comedy western was previously known by the even less appealing title *Bronco Busters*. James Caan finds himself in one of the many troughs that have characterised his rollercoaster career. He's the falsely accused Jud McGraw, trying to clear his name and track down the real villain. Unoriginal. DA

James Caan *Jud McGraw* • Aldo Ray *Nemo* • Stefanie Powers • Sammy Davis Jr ■ *Dir* Bernard Girard • *Scr* JAS McCombie, Douglas Stewart, Monroe Manning, Marcus Devian

Little Murders ★★★★

Black comedy   1971 · US · Colour · 108min

Satiric cartoonist Jules Feiffer adapted his play for the screen under the direction of actor Alan Arkin. Elliott Gould (who also co-produced) plays a young photographer who specialises in taking pictures of excrement. As a hardened New Yorker he's blithely unconcerned about crime and violence - even when he's the victim. Into this life of apathy comes optimist Marcia Rodd who thinks he will make ideal husband material.

This black comedy of Manhattan manners hasn't dated - if anything its chilling view of alienation and arbitrary violence is more relevant than when it was made. A wonderful cast makes this little-known, thought-provoking film worth seeking out. TH

Elliott Gould *Alfred Chamberlain* • Marcia Rodd *Patsy Newquist* • Vincent Gardenia *Mr Newquist* • Elizabeth Wilson *Mrs Newquist* • Jon Korkes *Kenny* • John Randolph *Mr Chamberlain* • Doris Roberts *Mrs Chamberlain* • Donald Sutherland *Minister* • Alan Arkin *Detective* ■ *Dir* Alan Arkin • *Scr* Jules Feiffer, from his play

Little Nellie Kelly ★★★ U

Musical drama   1940 · US · BW · 98min

Judy Garland was solo billed for the first time in this awkward slice of blarney, playing not only the young title character but also her dying mother! Today, some may well find this MGM adaptation rather mawkish and, as ever, delivers a wonderfully sincere performance, her talent shining through. George Murphy has the right surname but too bland a manner as Judy's husband/father. TS

Judy Garland *Nellie Kelly/Little Nellie Kelly* • George Murphy *Jerry Kelly* • Charles Winninger *Michael Noonan* • Douglas McPhail *Dennis Fogarty* • Arthur Shields *Timothy Fogarty* • Rita Page *Mary Fogarty* ■ *Dir* Norman Taurog • *Scr* Jack McGowan, from the musical comedy by George M Cohan

Little Nicky ★★★ 12

Comedy   2000 · US · Colour · 86min

This might be stupid, crass and vulgar, but it is also - in places - gloriously funny. For the first time, comedian Adam Sandler gets to perform his trademark moronic schtick against a backdrop of visually imaginative production values and devilishly good special effects. Sandler plays the son of Satan (Harvey Keitel), dispatched to Earth to bring his brothers (Rhys Ifans and Tom "Tiny" Lister Jr) back to the underworld before they can gather up enough evil souls to stage a coup in Hades. AJ Swearing, drug abuse. *DVD*

Adam Sandler *Nicky* • Patricia Arquette *Valerie* • Harvey Keitel *Dad* • Rhys Ifans *Adrian* • Allen Covert *Todd* • Tommy "Tiny" Lister Jr [Tom "Tiny" Lister Jr] *Cassius* • Quentin Tarantino *Deacon* • Rodney Dangerfield *Lucifer* ■ *Dir* Steven Brill • *Scr* Steven Brill, Tim Herlihy, Adam Sandler

A Little Night Music ★★★ 12

Musical   1977 · Austria/US/W Ger · Colour · 119min

Stephen Sondheim's Broadway musical *A Little Night Music* is brought to the screen here with glamorous Elizabeth Taylor and Diana Rigg as two of the guests at a country estate. Appropriately, Taylor is cast as an actress with a colourful past but now looking for some stability in her life. Other visitors include her current lover and his wife (Rigg) and a past beau with his new bride. Stage director Hal Prince can't replicate the pace of the Broadway show but fans of Stephen Sondheim will enjoy the music, and the costume design received an Oscar nomination. TH

Elizabeth Taylor *Desiree Armfeldt* • Diana Rigg *Charlotte Mittelheim* • Len Cariou *Frederick Egerman* • Lesley-Anne Down *Anne Egerman* • Hermione Gingold *Mme Armfeldt* • Laurence Guittard *Carl-Magnus Mittelheim* • Christopher Guard *Erich Egerman* • Chloe Franks *Fredericka Armfeldt* ■ *Dir* Harold Prince • *Scr* Hugh Wheeler, from the musical by Hugh Wheeler, Stephen Sondheim, from the film *Smiles of a Summer Night* by Ingmar Bergman • *Costume Designer* Florence Klotz

Little Nikita ★★★ 12

Spy thriller   1988 · US · Colour · 92min

Teenager River Phoenix has parents who are "sleepers" - spies planted in key locations with orders to live unremarkable lives until "activated". But when Phoenix applies to join the US Air Force, the suspicions of FBI agent Sidney Poitier are aroused. Director Richard Benjamin wastes the intriguing premise, and settles for a game of cat and mouse as Poitier and

L

Phoenix join forces to catch the real Soviet snakes. DP *DVD*

Sidney Poitier *Roy Parmenter* • River Phoenix *Jeff Grant* • Richard Jenkins *Richard Grant* • Caroline Kava *Elizabeth Grant* • Richard Bradford *Konstantin Karpov* • Richard Lynch *Scuba* ■ *Dir* Richard Benjamin • *Scr* John Hill, Bo Goldman, from a story by Tom Musca, Terry Schwartz

Little Noises ★★★ 15
Drama 1992 · US · Colour · 87min

This is an offbeat fable about greed, guilt and wanting more than you truly deserve. Struggling would-be writer Crispin Glover steals poems written by his friend Matthew Hutton who, though gifted with words, is actually mute. This unscrupulous behaviour brings Glover fame, fortune and success in the publishing world in director Jane Spencer's deliberately small-scale, character-driven opus. Fine work by Glover (who doesn't come across quite as strange as he usually does) and the eclectic cast make this ambitious chamber piece worth a look. AJ

Crispin Glover *Joey Kremple* • Tatum O'Neal *Stella Winslow* • John C McGinley *Stu Slovack* • Rik Mayall *Mathias Lichtenstein* • Steven Schub *Timmy Smith* • Tate Donovan *Elliott* • Nina Siemaszko *Dolores* • Matthew Hutton *Marty Slovack* • Carole Shelley *Aunt Shirley* ■ *Dir* Jane Spencer • *Scr* Jane Spencer, Jon Zeiderman, from the story by Anthony Brito, Jane Spencer

Little Norse Prince Valiant ★★★ U
Animated fantasy adventure
1968 · Jpn · Colour · 81min

This is the animation that has been credited as the first modern anime. Despite the Scandinavian setting, it's a Japanese production from the team that eventually formed Studio Ghibli, and is based around Japanese rather than Norse folklore. It's a simple tale of good versus evil, with young hero Hols pulling the Sword of the Sun from a rock giant and setting off on a journey that will lead him to battle against the Ice King. It was pulled from theatres in Japan after only ten days, but its combination of complex themes, technical skill and compelling adventure soon gained it a cult following. TF Japanese +subtitles. *DVD*

■ *Dir* Isao Takahata • *Scr* Kazuo Fukazawa

Little Odessa ★★★ 15
Crime thriller 1994 · US · Colour · 94min

In this intimate character study, chilly both in setting and in atmosphere, a hitman (Tim Roth) is forced to return to his old Russian-Jewish Brooklyn neighbourhood to carry out an execution. But contact with his family only serves to re-ignite old feuds. Writer/director James Gray, here making a promising debut, elicits meaty performances from Roth, Edward Furlong and Maximilian Schell. However, his tendency to swamp key moments with excessive visual stylistics does sometimes blunt this movie's dramatic edge. JC Violence, swearing, nudity.

Tim Roth *Joshua Shapira* • Edward Furlong *Reuben Shapira* • Moira Kelly *Alla Shustervich* • Vanessa Redgrave *Irina Shapira* • Maximilian Schell *Arkady Shapira* • Paul Guilfoyle (2) *Boris Volkoff* • Natasha Andreichenko *Natasha* • David Vadim *Sasha* ■ *Dir/Scr* James Gray

A Little of What You Fancy ★★★ U
Music documentary 1968 · UK · Colour · 68min

A treat for anyone who laments the passing of *The Good Old Days*. Using a variety of photographs, posters, theatre bills and other memorabilia, this slickly produced documentary traces the history of British music hall from 1854 to 1968. Although much of this nostalgic wallow is occupied by a glorified *son et lumière* show, director Robert Webb tacks on an interesting finale in which he explores how the music hall tradition survived in the pubs, clubs and cabarets of the late 1960s, thanks to such performers as Helen Shapiro and Barry Cryer. DP

Barry Cryer *Barry Cryer* • Helen Shapiro • Mark Eden ■ *Dir* Robert Webb [Robert D Webb] • *Scr* Ray Mackender

Little Old New York ★★★ U
Comedy drama 1940 · US · BW · 100min

The story of Robert Fulton, who, back in 1807, managed to achieve his dream of building the first ever steamboat, is turned here by 20th Century-Fox into a vehicle for Alice Faye. She plays a breezy Irish saloon-keeper torn between sturdy Fred MacMurray and callow but bright Richard Greene as Fulton. Director Henry King wisely concentrates on the boat-building sequences, which are actually rather good. But the eternal triangle plot is silly and this style of movie has dated rather badly. TS

Alice Faye *Pat O'Day* • Fred MacMurray *Charles Browne* • Richard Greene *Robert Fulton* • Brenda Joyce *Harriet Livingstone* • Andy Devine *Commodore* • Henry Stephenson *Chancellor Livingstone* ■ *Dir* Henry King • *Scr* Harry Tugend, from a story by John Balderson, from the play by Rita Johnson Young

Little Otik ★★★★ 15
Part-animated black comedy fantasy
2000 · Cz Rep/UK/Jpn · Colour · 126min

Veteran Czech surrealist Jan Svankmajer makes another foray into the world of dissatisfaction and decay in this deliriously macabre comedy. Unable to have children of their own, Prague couple Veronica Zilkova and Jan Hartl fashion a baby out of a tree stump, only for it to evolve into a flesh-eating monster. In giving a traditional fable a bitingly modern makeover, Svankmajer not only succeeds in satirising contemporary Czech society, but also in conveying an ecology-conscious subtext about the dangers of tinkering with the natural order. Uncompromising and provocative, this is an urban horror film of chilling simplicity and intelligence. DP Czech +subtitles. Nudity, some violence. *DVD*

Veronika Zilkova *Bozena Horakova* • Jan Hartl *Karel Horak* • Jaroslava Kretschmerova *Mrs Stadlerova* • Pavel Novy *Frantisek Stadler* • Kristina Adamcova *Alzbetka* ■ *Dir* Jan Svankmajer • *Scr* Jan Svankmajer, from his story

The Little Polar Bear ★★★ U
Animated adventure
2001 · Ger/Swi/US · Colour · 73min

This enchanting tale has the titular fur-covered cutie, Lars, taking a trip to the tropics courtesy of a drifting ice floe, while an eco-aware subplot has him tackling a sinister automated super-trawler that's decimating the local fish stocks. The animation has a nicely retro feel, the storyline is clear and simple, and Lars is a love – although a passle of terminally depressed lemmings manage to steal the show. This adventure is ideal for younger kids. DA German dubbed. *DVD*

Wesley Singerman *Lars* • Brianne Siddall *Robby* • Michael McConnohie *Mika* • Daran Norris *Brutus* • Neil Kaplan *Bert* • Tom Fahn *Boris* • Steve Kramer *Screenplay* ■ *Dir* Thilo Graf Rothkirch, Piet de Rycker • *Scr* Piet de Rycker, Thilo Rothkirch, Bert Schrickel, Thomas Wittenburg, from the books by Hans de Beer

The Little Polar Bear: the Mysterious Island ★★ U
Animated adventure
2005 · Ger · Colour · 77min

Young Lars the polar bear returns for a second animated feature based on the books by Hans de Beer. In keeping with the first movie's eco-friendly premise, he and his North Pole pals learn valuable lessons about preserving the balance of nature during a trip to the Galapagos Islands. Adults may yawn at the tale's visual and thematic simplicity, but at least it's short and sweet. SF German dubbed.

Anjella Macintosh *Lars* • Helena Roman *Greta* • Suzy Cooper *Robby* • Ben Bishop *Caruso* • Melanie Cooper *Maria* ■ *Dir* Thilo Graf Rothkirch, Piet de Rycker • *Scr* Bert Schrickel, Thomas Wittenburg, Piet de Rycker, Rolf Giesen, from the books by Hans de Beer

The Little Prince ★★ U
Musical 1974 · UK · Colour · 84min

Antoine de Saint-Exupéry's much loved allegory on the importance of childhood becomes a ponderous musical fable with few sparkling moments under Stanley Donen's stodgy direction. Pilot Richard Kiley crashes in the Sahara desert and is discovered by the Little Prince (Steven Warner), an emissary from another planet, who proceeds to teach him the true meaning of life through surreal intergalactic flashbacks. Lumbered with pointless songs by Alan Jay Lerner and Frederick Loewe, Donen's inability to meld the achingly real with the strangely fantastic turns this to heavy-handed whimsy. AJ *DVD*

Richard Kiley *Pilot* • Steven Warner *Little Prince* • Bob Fosse *Snake* • Gene Wilder *Fox* • Joss Ackland *Businessman* • Clive Revill *Businessman* • Victor Spinetti *Historian* • Graham Crowden *General* • Donna McKechnie *Rose* ■ *Dir* Stanley Donen • *Scr* Alan Jay Lerner, from the book *Le Petit Prince* by Antoine De Saint-Exupéry

The Little Princess ★★★★ U
Musical drama 1939 · US · Colour · 89min

Made when the career of dimpled darling Shirley Temple was waning, this is now considered her best film. A lovingly produced version of Frances Hodgson Burnett's classic story of a little rich girl moved to the cold attic of her boarding school when her father is reported dead. Beautifully crafted and filmed in gorgeous Technicolor, this is a little gem. Arthur Treacher accompanies the star in a delightful song and dance number. TV *DVD*

Shirley Temple *Sara Crewe* • Richard Greene *Geoffrey Hamilton* • Anita Louise *Rose* • Ian Hunter *Capt Crewe* • Cesar Romero *Ram Dass* • Arthur Treacher *Bertie Minchin* • Mary Nash *Amanda Minchin* • Sybil Jason *Becky* ■ *Dir* Walter Lang • *Scr* Ethel Hill, Walter Ferris, from the novel by Frances Hodgson Burnett

A Little Princess ★★★★★ U
Period fantasy drama 1995 · US · Colour · 93min

Simple for children to understand, yet sophisticated enough for adults to enjoy too, this wonderful adaptation of the novel by Frances Hodgson Burnett (who also wrote *The Secret Garden*) is an instant classic. The importance of magic and imagination in all our lives is engagingly conveyed through the entrancing tale of a schoolgirl escaping into exotic flights of fancy after news of her father's death. Mexican director Alfonso Cuarón gives his spellbinding fable a dazzling look and an astonishing atmosphere that prove hard to resist. You'll be enthralled by this little marvel from colourful start to heart-rending finish. AJ *DVD*

Eleanor Bron *Miss Minchin* • Liam Cunningham *Captain Crewe/Prince Rama* • Liesel Matthews *Sara Crewe* • Rusty Schwimmer *Amelia Minchin* • Arthur Malet *Charles Randolph* • Vanessa Lee Chester *Becky* • Errol Sitahal *Ram Dass* • Heather DeLoach *Ermengarde* ■ *Dir* Alfonso Cuarón • *Scr* Richard LaGravenese, Elizabeth Chandler, from the novel *Sara Crewe* and the play *The Little Princess* by Frances Hodgson Burnett

The Little Rascals ★ U
Comedy 1994 · US · Colour · 78min

Launched by Hal Roach in 1922, the Our Gang series ran until 1944, ending its days at MGM. A decade later, around 100 of these comic shorts resurfaced on TV under the title *The Little Rascals*. Having failed the previous year to capture the magic of *The Beverly Hillbillies* on film, director Penelope Spheeris thought she'd take a crack at bringing Alfalfa, Darla and Spanky to a new audience, only to miss the target again and by a much wider margin. DP *DVD*

Travis Tedford *Spanky* • Bug Hall *Alfalfa* • Brittany Ashton Holmes *Darla* • Kevin Jamal Woods *Stymie* • Zachary Mabry *Porky* • Ross Elliot Bagley *Buckwheat* • Sam Saletta *Butch* • Blake McIver Ewing *Waldo* • Mel Brooks *Mr Welling* • Whoopi Goldberg *Buckwheat's Mom* • Daryl Hannah *Miss Crabtree* • Donald Trump *Waldo's dad* • George Wendt *Lumberyard clerk* ■

Dir Penelope Spheeris
Dir Penelope Spheeris • *Scr* Paul Guay, Stephen Mazur, Penelope Spheeris, from a story by Penelope Spheeris, Robert Wolterstorff, Mike Scott, Paul Guay, Stephen Mazur

Little Red Flowers ★★★ 12
Comedy drama 2006 · Chi/It · Colour · 87min

It's never explicitly stated, but Zhang Yuan's schoolyard drama appears to be set in the 1950s during the early days of Chinese state Communism. A four-year-old tot is left at a boarding kindergarten for the offspring of Party officials where kids are treated like pint-sized military conscripts. Rebellious by nature, the boy proves quite the revolutionary, eventually overcoming his square-peg status to lead the other children in a rebellion. To enjoy this film to the full, it's necessary to have a soft spot for watching cute children running around, although its allegorical elements about nonconformity under Mao give it some thought-provoking depth. AC Mandarin +subtitles. Brief swearing. *DVD*

Dong Bowen *Fang Qiangqiang* • Ning Yuanyuan *Yang Nanyan* • Chen Manyuan *Yang Beiyan* • Zhao Rui *Ms Li* • Li Xiaofeng *Ms Tang* • Sun Yujia *Dou* • Du Ma Fa ■ *Dir* Zhang Yuan • *Scr* Ning Dai, Zhang Yuan, from the novel by Wang Shuo • *Cinematographer* Yang Tao

Little Red Monkey ★★★ PG
Spy drama 1955 · UK · BW · 71min

Ken Hughes honed his skills as a director of thrillers working on the Scotland Yard B-movie series. Consequently, this quota quickie has a great deal more substance and style than many of its contemporaries. A top Russian boffin defects and American agent Richard Conte must escort him across the Atlantic. Hughes keeps the action on the boil, while Russell Napier and Rona Anderson are fine as a Scotland Yard detective and his niece. DP *DVD*

Richard Conte *Bill Locklin* • Rona Anderson *Julia* • Russell Napier *Superintendent Harrington* • Colin Gordon *Martin* • Arnold Marlé *Dushenko* • Sylvia Langova *Hilde* • Donald Bisset *Editor* ■ *Dir* Ken Hughes • *Scr* Ken Hughes, James Eastwood, from the TV serial *Case of the Red Monkey* by Eric Maschwitz

The Little Riders ★★★
Second World War drama
1996 · US · Colour · 96min

A made-for-TV film, this features the British veteran Paul Scofield, with Malcolm McDowell in prime villain mode. The story centres on Noley Thornton who, trapped in Holland with her grandparents (Scofield and Rosemary Harris), is intent on preventing the town clock from falling into Nazi hands. McDowell is suitably nasty as the German leader set on destroying the timepiece and its "Little Riders" statues. It's compelling fare if tinged with Disney cuteness. LH Some violence.

Paul Scofield *Grandpa Pieter Roden* • Malcolm McDowell *Captain Kessel* • Rosemary Harris *Grandma Juliana Roden* • Noley Thornton *Joanne Hunter* • Benedick Blythe *Lieutenant Karl Braun* ■ *Dir* Kevin Connor • *Scr* Gerald DiPego, from the novel by Margaretha Shemin

A Little Romance ★★★ PG
Romantic comedy
1979 · US/Fr · Colour · 105min

That Laurence Olivier could ham it up with the best, or worst, of them is proved unquestionably as he takes on the role of a Maurice Chevalier-like boulevardier helping lovelorn youngsters to a happy ending. The adults (Sally Kellerman, Arthur Hill, David Dukes) are so overdrawn there's inevitable sympathy for Diane Lane, the American girl in Paris falling for Thelonious Bernard despite family pressure. Charming and entertaining fluff; watch for Broderick Crawford's abrasive cameo appearance. TH

Laurence Olivier *Julius Edmond Santorin* • Diane Lane *Lauren King* • Thelonious Bernard *Daniel Michon* • Arthur Hill *Richard King* • Sally Kellerman *Kay King* • Broderick Crawford • David Dukes *George de Marco* • Andrew Duncan *Bob Duryea* • Claudette Sutherland *Janet Duryea* ■ *Dir* George Roy Hill • *Scr* Allan Burns, from the novel *E=MC Mon Amour* by Patrick Cauvin

A Little Sex ★★ 15

Comedy · 1981 · US · Colour · 90min

Mary Tyler Moore became a major player behind the screen when she set up MTM Enterprises, which produced such hit series as Hill Street Blues, St Elsewhere and Lou Grant. Their first theatrical production stayed loyal to its small screen roots, featuring Tim Matheson as a successful director of TV commercials who is also a hit with the ladies. DF

Tim Matheson Michael · Kate Capshaw Katherine · Edward Herrmann Brother · John Glover Walter · Joan Copeland Mrs Harrison · Susanna Dalton Nancy ■ Dir Bruce Paltrow · Scr Robert DeLaurentiis

The Little Shop of Horrors ★★★ PG

Horror comedy · 1960 · US · BW · 72min

According to Hollywood legend, this riotous no-budget comic horror from cult director Roger Corman was shot in three days on a leftover set. Jonathan Haze plays the browbeaten florist's apprentice who breeds a carnivorous plant that starts terrorising the neighbourhood. Look out for Jack Nicholson, who's hilarious as Wilbur Force, the masochistic dental patient reading Pain magazine in the waiting room. AJ DVD

Jonathan Haze Seymour Krelboined · Jackie Joseph Audrey Fulguard · Mel Welles Gravis Mushnik · Myrtle Vail Winifred Krelboined · Leola Wendorff Mrs Shiva · Jack Nicholson Wilbur Force ■ Dir Roger Corman · Scr Charles B Griffith

Little Shop of Horrors ★★★★ PG

Musical black comedy horror
1986 · US · Colour · 89min

Frank Oz here brings Howard Ashman's off-Broadway musical to the big screen in a way that Roger Corman (who directed a 1960 version) could only have dreamed of. It's packed with great doo-wop songs, a killer line-up of stars (Steve Martin shines brightest as the sadistic dentist) and clever horticultural special effects that underline, but never swamp, the charming theatricality of the stylised whole. The Four Tops's Levi Stubbs voices the alien Venus People-Trap that causes deliciously nerdy Rick Moranis to hack up victims for plant food and impress his Monroe-inspired lover, Ellen Greene, who reprises her award-winning stage role. This memorably weird musical is in the grand old Hollywood tradition. AJ Violence, swearing. DVD

Rick Moranis Seymour Krelborn · Ellen Greene Audrey · Vincent Gardenia Mushnik · Steve Martin Orin Scrivello, DDS · Tichina Arnold Crystal · Tisha Campbell Chiffon · Michelle Weeks Ronette · James Belushi Patrick Martin · John Candy Wink Wilkinson · Christopher Guest First customer · Bill Murray Arthur Denton · Levi Stubbs Audrey II ■ Dir Frank Oz · Scr Howard Ashman, from his play, from the film by Charles B Griffith

Little Sparrows ★★★

Drama · 2010 · Aus · Colour · 88min

It may be an Australian film from a writer/director born in Taiwan, but Little Sparrows has a definite European sensibility, with its leisurely exploration of a middle-class family's problems. Susan (Nicola Bartlett), the mother of three grown daughters, is married to James (James Hagan), an actor who has been far from reliable as a husband and father. When Susan discovers that her breast cancer has returned, she gathers the family together for one last Christmas. The pace is a little too languid at times, but this is still a gentle, bittersweet tale held together by Bartlett's emotionally charged performance. LB

Nicola Bartlett Susan · Nina Deasley Nina · Melanie Munt Anna · James Hagan James ■ Dir/Scr Yu-Hsiu Camille Chen

The Little Theatre of Jean Renoir ★★★ U

Portmanteau drama
1969 · Fr/It/W Ger · Colour · 107min

Made for television, Jean Renoir's final feature is a delightful compendium, revisiting the humanist concerns that had preoccupied him for over forty years. In Le Dernier Reveillon, a homeless old couple find peace in companionship and dreams; Le Cireuse Electrique is a recitative denunciation of the evils of urban progress; Quand l'Amour Se Meurt is a musical interlude, sung by Jeanne Moreau in Belle Epoque costume; while Le Roi d'Yvetot centres on a cuckold forgiving both his wife and his best friend in a paean to the consoling joys of the countryside. It's a mixed bag, but ultimately a master's folly. DP French +subtitles.

Nino Fornicola Tramp · Minny Monti Tramp · Marguerite Cassan Isabelle · Pierre Olaf Gustave, her husband · Jeanne Moreau Singer · Fernand Sardou Duvallier · Françoise Arnoul Isabelle Duvallier · Jean Carmet Féraud · Jean Renoir Jean Renoir, master of ceremonies ■ Dir/Scr Jean Renoir

Little Treasure ★★★ 15

Comedy adventure · 1985 · US · Colour · 94min

Margot Kidder is a loudmouthed topless dancer, summoned to Mexico for a reunion with her father, Burt Lancaster. She spends most of her time hanging out with Ted Danson and pursuing some elusive stolen cash. These are characters at the end of the line, and in some way the movie resembles a softened-up, distaff version of Bring Me the Head of Alfredo Garcia. AT

Margot Kidder Margo · Ted Danson Eugene · Burt Lancaster Teschemacher · Joseph Hacker Norman Kane · Malena Doria Evangelina · John Pearce Joseph · Gladys Holland Sadie ■ Dir/Scr Alan Sharp

The Little Unicorn ★★ U

Fantasy adventure · 1998 · UK · Colour · 90min

Like Black Beauty before it, this story occasionally touches on darker issues, such as the death of the orphaned Brittney Bomann's beloved mare and the cruelty meted out to its unicorn foal by the dastardly Joe Penny. But this is primarily an uplifting fable, with shysters such as failed magician George Hamilton getting their just desserts and Bomann leading a rescue mission to save her stolen pet from the circus. DP DVD

Brittney Bomann Polly Regan · David Warner Grandfather · George Hamilton The Great Allonso · Joe Penny Tiny · Christopher Atkins Aunt Lucy's fiancé · Emma Samms Aunt Lucy ■ Dir/Scr Paul Matthews

The Little Vampire ★★★ U

Horror fantasy adventure
2000 · Ger/Neth/UK/US · Colour · 91min

A human boy helps a young vampire and his bloodsucking family escape the attentions of a vampire slayer in this entertaining adventure. Jonathan Lipnicki as the human and bright British newcomer Rollo Weeks as his undead friend turn in good performances, while Richard E Grant and Alice Krige camp it up as the vampire parents and Jim Carter is in slightly unhinged mode as the slayer. Witty and well written, this is that rarity – a children's film that doesn't patronise its audience. DA DVD

Jonathan Lipnicki Tony Thompson · Richard E Grant Frederick Sackville-Bagg · Jim Carter Rookery · Alice Krige Freda · Pamela Gidley Dottie Thompson · Tommy Hinkley Bob Thompson · Anna Popplewell Anna · Dean Cook Gregory · Rollo Weeks Rudolph · John Wood (2) Lord McAshton ■ Dir Uli Edel · Scr Karey Kirkpatrick, Larry Wilson, from the novels by Angela Sommer-Bodenburg

Little Vegas ★★★★ 15

Comedy · 1990 · US · Colour · 87min

This small-scale comedy drama compensates for a lack of stars with lovely ensemble playing from Anthony John Denison, Catherine O'Hara and Jerry Stiller. They're part of the community of oddballs

and eccentrics who live in in a Nevada trailer park. Bruce McGill dreams of turning the town into a mini gambling mecca, but he's opposed Stiller who has seen it all before with the pioneering mobsters of the real Vegas. Directed by Perry Lang, this intriguing story has director John Sayles in a small role. TH

Anthony John Denison Carmine · Catherine O'Hara Lexie · Anne Francis Martha · Michael Nouri Frank · Perry Lang Steve · Bruce McGill Harvey · Jerry Stiller Sam · John Sayles ■ Dir/Scr Perry Lang

Little Voice ★★★★ 15

Comedy drama · 1998 · UK · Colour · 92min

Jane Horrocks reprises her stage performance as the reclusive girl whose virtuoso impersonations of the great singers – among them Shirley Bassey and Judy Garland – contrast with her almost total shyness. Her talents are belatedly recognised by sleazy agent Michael Caine, who's prepared to endure the attentions of her sexually predatory mother (Brenda Blethyn) as long as he can make some money out of that voice. The brilliance of Horrocks is slightly undermined by director Mark Herman's crude depiction of working-class life in a northern seaside town, but there's good support from nightclub boss Jim Broadbent and Ewan McGregor. TH Swearing, nudity. DVD

Brenda Blethyn Mari Hoff · Jane Horrocks "LV" · Ewan McGregor Billy · Philip Jackson George · Annette Badland Sadie · Michael Caine Ray Say · Jim Broadbent Mr Boo ■ Dir Mark Herman · Scr Mark Herman, from the play The Rise and Fall of Little Voice by Jim Cartwright

Little White Lies ★★★ 15

Comedy drama · 2010 · Fr/Bel · Colour · 154min

This funny and warm French ensemble effort plays out like an early Woody Allen comedy, with its bourgeois characters, witty banter and relationship intrigues. Marion Cotillard rises above cliché as an angst-ridden woman, by turns detached and overwrought, who is one of a group of friends invited to stay at the seaside home of high-flyer Max (François Cluzet). The holiday comes after a devastating accident that leaves one of their number (Jean Dujardin) in a critical condition. After garnering acclaim with his taut 2006 thriller Tell No One, director Guillaume Canet lets the reins hang a bit loose this time, making for a surprisingly long running time. SP French +subtitles. Swearing. DVD SL

François Cluzet Max Cantara · Marion Cotillard Marie · Benoît Magimel Vincent Ribaud · Gilles Lellouche Eric · Jean Dujardin Ludo · Laurent Lafitte Antoine ■ Dir/Scr Guillaume Canet

Little Women ★★★★ U

Period drama · 1933 · US · BW · 110min

This is the first of three talkie versions of Louisa May Alcott's classic novel, starring Katharine Hepburn, Joan Bennett, Frances Dee and Jean Parker as the four sisters growing up in New England during the Civil War period. Director George Cukor had an early opportunity to show his affinity with the great female stars of the era. The film struck a chord with audiences at the time but lost out on the Oscars for best film and best director. This remains an entrancing movie, with Hepburn perfectly cast. AT DVD

Katharine Hepburn Jo · Joan Bennett Amy · Paul Lukas Prof Fritz Bhaer · Edna May Oliver Aunt March · Jean Parker Beth · Frances Dee Meg · Henry Stephenson Mr Laurence · Douglass Montgomery Laurie · John Davis Lodge [John Lodge] Brooke · Spring Byington Marmee ■ Dir George Cukor · Scr Sarah Y Mason, Victor Heerman, from the novel by Louisa May Alcott

Little Women ★★★ U

Period drama · 1949 · US · Colour · 121min

This lush adaptation of Louisa May Alcott's novel has the benefit of a good cast, but the studio settings and the MGM production requirements really get in the way of the storytelling. Elizabeth Taylor and Janet Leigh are far too knowing for their roles, and top-billed June Allyson is too coy (and

too old) for Jo. There's charm, certainly, whenever Margaret O'Brien and Peter Lawford are around, and this cotton-candy confection is very pretty to look at. TS

June Allyson Jo March · Peter Lawford Laurie Laurence · Margaret O'Brien Beth March · Elizabeth Taylor Amy March · Janet Leigh Meg March · Rossano Brazzi Professor Bhaer · Mary Astor Marmee March · Lucile Watson Aunt March · C Aubrey Smith Mr Laurence · Elizabeth Patterson Hannah · Leon Ames Mr March ■ Dir Mervyn LeRoy · Scr Andrew Solt, Sarah Y Mason, Victor Heerman, from the novel by Louisa May Alcott

Little Women ★★★ U

Period drama · 1994 · US · Colour · 113min

Mother hen Susan Sarandon dominates this adaptation of Louisa May Alcott's much-loved novel about four impoverished sisters growing up during the American Civil War. Australian director Gillian Armstrong jettisons some of the schmaltz that adorned the earlier film versions, allowing Winona Ryder, who's superbly cast as the spirited Jo, to emote like mad. As a result, this 1990s take on the tale is less cosy and, therefore, less memorable, despite its wonderful pedigree. TH DVD

Winona Ryder Jo March · Susan Sarandon Marmee March · Gabriel Byrne Professor Friedrich Baer · Eric Stoltz John Brooke · Samantha Mathis Amy, aged 16 · Trini Alvarado Meg · Kirsten Dunst Amy, aged 12 · Claire Danes Beth · Christian Bale Laurie · Mary Wickes Aunt March · Matthew Walker Mr March ■ Dir Gillian Armstrong · Scr Robin Swicord, from the novel by Louisa May Alcott

The Little World of Don Camillo ★★★★ U

Comedy · 1951 · Fr/It · BW · 102min

This was the first of Fernandel's five outings as the Po valley priest with a surfeit of sense and a hotline to God. With his equine features beaming bonhomie, he's perfectly cast in a role demanding comic charm and unforced humility. Yet, this is anything but a one-man show, as Gino Cervi more than holds his own as the communist mayor who delights in pitting his principles against his rival's religious beliefs, but also rallies round at times of crises. This time he helps with a tangled romance and Don Camillo's possible transfer. Filmed in French, Italian and English language versions. DP

Fernandel Don Camillo · Gino Cervi Peppone · Sylvie Christina · Vera Talchi Gina · Franco Interlenghi Mariolino · Orson Welles Narrator (American version) ■ Dir Julien Duvivier · Scr René Barjavel, Julien Duvivier, from stories by Giovanni Guareschi

The Littlest Horse Thieves ★★★ U

Period drama · 1976 · UK · Colour · 99min

This Disney period piece (also known as Escape from the Dark) provided Alastair Sim with his last screen role, and there are echoes of the unreformed Scrooge in his performance as an Edwardian mine owner. Director Charles Jarrott makes the most of the Yorkshire scenery, but the most exciting scenes take place underground as the three scamps who rescue the ponies use them to save some trapped miners. DP

Alastair Sim Lord Harrogate · Peter Barkworth Richard Sandman · Maurice Colbourne Luke Armstrong · Susan Tebbs Violet Armstrong · Geraldine McEwan Miss Coutts · Prunella Scales Mrs Sandman ■ Dir Charles Jarrott · Scr Rosemary Anne Sisson, from a story by Rosemary Anne Sisson, Burt Kennedy

The Littlest Rebel ★★★ PG

Musical war drama · 1935 · US · BW · 70min

This was a quintessential vehicle for Shirley Temple, made when the incredibly talented moppet was the top box-office attraction around the world. In this Civil War tale, Temple displays all the facets that made her so unique. The scene in which she pleads with President Lincoln to set her father free from a prisoner-of-war camp displays both humour and pathos, and she chirpily performs two dance duets with Bill

L

Robinson. Only those violently allergic to Temple could fail to warm to this. TV *DVD*

Shirley Temple *Virginia "Virgie" Houston Cary* • **John Boles** *Confederate Capt Herbert Cary* • **Jack Holt** *Union Colonel Morrison* • **Karen Morley** *Mrs Cary* • **Bill Robinson** *Uncle Billy* • **Guinn Williams** [Guinn "Big Boy" Williams] *Sgt Dudley* • **Willie Best** *James Henry* • **Frank McGlynn Sr** *President Abraham Lincoln* • **Bessie Lyle Mammy** ■ *Dir* David Butler • *Scr* Edwin Burke, Harry Tugend, from the play by Edward Peple

Live! ★★★ 15
Satirical comedy drama
2007 · US · Colour · 92min

The excesses of reality TV go under the microscope in this wry and all-too-plausible satire. Eva Mendes is impressive as the glamorous president of a US broadcasting network, who is determined to mount a Russian roulette show, in which contestants gamble with their lives for the chance to win $5 million. Meanwhile, a documentary crew led by David Krumholtz films her at work. Of course, the targets are obvious ones, yet it's impossible not to get wound up by the gut-wrenching spectacle or the deft, tastelessly sentimental mini-profiles of the competitors. And that's the entire point. AJ Swearing, sexual references, brief nudity. *DVD*

Eva Mendes *Katy* • **David Krumholtz** *Rex* • **Rob Brown** *Byron* • **Katie Cassidy** *Jewel* • **Jay Hernandez** *Pablo* • **Eric Lively** *Brad* • **Monet Mazur** *Abalone* • **Jeffrey Dean Morgan** *Rick* ■ *Dir/Scr* Bill Guttentag

Live a Little, Love a Little
★★ PG
Musical 1968 · US · Colour · 85min

This is an enjoyable romp, at least by Elvis Presley standards, with several tuneful songs. Elvis plays a photographer who digs himself into a hole when he tries to shuttle between two jobs for publishers with very different editorial policies – both in the same office building. Watch out for Rudy Vallee, a singing star from an earlier era, as a publisher. Frothy. JG

Elvis Presley *Greg* • **Michele Carey** *Bernice* • **Don Porter** *Mike Landsdown* • **Rudy Vallee** *Penlow* • **Dick Sargent** *Harry* • **Sterling Holloway** *Milkman* ■ *Dir* Norman Taurog • *Scr* Michael A Hoey, Dan Greenburg, from the novel *Kiss My Firm But Pliant Lips* by Dan Greenburg

Live and Let Die ★★★★ PG
Spy adventure 1973 · UK · Colour · 116min

Roger Moore's first tour of duty as James Bond, in the eighth of the licensed-to-kill series, has him up against the dark powers of voodoo in the bulky shape of Yaphet Kotto, while embracing the more curvaceous figure of tarot-reader Jane Seymour. Boasting as many cliff-hanging moments as a Saturday-matinée serial, this tale of a plan to turn everyone into drug addicts allows Bond's adversaries to be as mechanical as Moore himself. There are some splendid spasms of action, however, notably a speedboat leap that set a world record, as well as the usual hi-tech gadgetry. TH *DVD* *BL*

Roger Moore *James Bond* • **Yaphet Kotto** *Dr Kananga/Mr Big* • **Jane Seymour** (2) *Solitaire* • **Clifton James** *Sheriff Pepper* • **Julius W Harris** [Julius Harris] *Tee Hee* • **Geoffrey Holder** *Baron Samedi* • **David Hedison** *Felix Leiter* • **Gloria Hendry** *Rosie* • **Bernard Lee** *"M"* • **Lois Maxwell** *Miss Moneypenny* • **Ruth Kempf** *Mrs Bell* • **Joie Chitwood** *Charlie* • **Madeline Smith** *Miss Caruso* ■ *Dir* Guy Hamilton • *Scr* Tom Mankiewicz, from the novel by Ian Fleming

Live by Night
Period crime drama 2016 · US · Colour

This is a preview – no prints were available to review prior to publication: Ben Affleck goes back behind the camera with another adaptation of a Dennis Lehane novel, to follow 2007 thriller *Gone Baby Gone*. There's a more epic sprawl to this one, however, as it's set during the Prohibition Era with a classically pitched rags-to-riches tale of one man's rise through the criminal ranks in Boston. Affleck also stars as the ambitious Joe Coughlin whose life is fatefully changed after he crosses paths

with a seductive blonde (played by Sienna Miller). With the central romance being pivotal to the story, a lot will depend on the on-screen chemistry between Affleck and Miller. SP

Ben Affleck *Joe Coughlin* • **Sienna Miller** *Emma Gould* • **Zoe Saldana** [Zoë Saldana] *Graciella Corrales* • **Elle Fanning** *Loretta Figgis* • **Chris Cooper** *Chief Irving Figgis* ■ *Dir* Ben Affleck • *Scr* Ben Affleck, from Dennis Lehane's novel

Live Flesh ★★★★ 18
Black comedy thriller
1997 · Sp/Fr · Colour · 96min

Excruciatingly funny, fearlessly frank and gloriously ironic, Spanish director Pedro Almodóvar's engaging take on the Ruth Rendell thriller is a deliciously twisted tale of destiny, desire and death. Using the central concept of how a single bullet fired during a botched police investigation causes a ricochet effect through the lives of five different characters, the camp iconoclast serves up a cocktail of subversion and sexual tension where truth and humanity are used as clever red herrings. AJ Spanish +subtitles. Violence, swearing, sex scenes, nudity. *DVD*

Francesca Neri *Elena* • **Javier Bardem** *David* • **Liberto Rabal** *Víctor Plaza* • **José Sancho** *Sancho* • **Angela Molina** *Clara* • **Penélope Cruz** *Isabelle* • **Pilar Bardem** *Dona Centro* ■ *Dir* Pedro Almodóvar • *Scr* Pedro Almodóvar, Ray Loriga, Jorge Guerricaechevarría, from the novel by Ruth Rendell

Live Forever ★★ 15
Music documentary 2002 · UK · Colour · 82min

Britpop was a social phenomenon that heralded the dawn of New Labour. At least that's the contention of this lively, but narrowly focused, insight into the 1990s music scene. Ignoring the Spice Girls and the entire dance-music sector, first-time director John Dower concentrates on guitar bands with vague political agendas in a specious bid to celebrate a single cultural constituency that several of the interviewees actively deny. The issue of laddism is also airbrushed, yet the class fissures remain clearly evident. Damon Albarn, Jarvis Cocker and Noel Gallagher offer valuable analysis, but other contributions range from the peripheral to the downright embarrassing. DP *DVD*

■ *Dir* John Dower • *Cinematographer* Frédéric Fabre • *Editor* Jake Martin

Live from Baghdad ★★★ 15
Historical war drama
2002 · US · Colour · 108min

This award-winning TV movie tells the story of a group of CNN reporters who stayed to cover the unfolding Gulf War crisis in 1991 after all the other networks had pulled out of the Iraqi capital, Baghdad. Co-written by one of the key players, veteran CNN producer Robert Wiener (played by Michael Keaton), it seamlessly mixes genuine news footage with taut, well-shot and impressively acted drama. Though the film's gung-ho attitude and occasionally too convenient scenarios smack of low-level propaganda, there's no denying the power of the tale, which makes even the dullest mechanics of journalism exciting. SF Swearing. *DVD*

Michael Keaton *Robert Wiener* • **Helena Bonham Carter** *Ingrid Formanek* • **Lili Taylor** *Judy Parker* • **Bruce McGill** *Peter Arnett* • **David Suchet** *Naji Al-Hadithi* • **Robert Wisdom** *Bernard Shaw* • **Paul Guilfoyle** (2) *Ed Turner* ■ *Dir* Mick Jackson • *Scr* Robert Wiener, Richard Chapman, John Patrick Shanley, Timothy J Sexton, from the non-fiction book *Live from Baghdad: Making Journalism History behind the Lines* by Robert Wiener

Live It Up ★★ U
Musical comedy 1963 · UK · BW · 71min

You'd hardly know that the Beatles were in the process of transforming the British pop scene from some of the sounds presented in this determinedly traditional musical. Lance Comfort was a decent director, but he was hardly cutting edge and he handles the drama as unimaginatively as he stages the songs. Icon-in-waiting David Hemmings looks distinctly uncomfortable as the Post

Office messenger who defies trad dad Ed Devereux to bid for the top, prompting a hackneyed subplot about an audition and a big American producer. DP

David Hemmings *Dave Martin* • **Jennifer Moss** *Jill* • **John Pike** *Phil* • **Heinz Burt** *Ron* • **Stephen Marriott** [Steve Marriott] *Ricky* • **Joan Newell** *Margaret Martin* • **Ed Devereaux** *Herbert Martin* ■ *Dir* Lance Comfort • *Scr* Lyn Fairhurst, from his story, from an idea by Harold Shampan

Live, Love and Learn ★★★
Comedy 1937 · US · BW · 78min

Rich girl Rosalind Russell marries impoverished artist Robert Montgomery and the two enjoy bohemian bliss in Greenwich Village until success for the artist rears its corrupting head. The two stars are delightful in the early portions of this mixture of screwball comedy and melodrama, but get little help from the script when things get tougher. The stars, the MGM polish and a sterling supporting cast give the fluffy concoction some substance. TV

Robert Montgomery *Bob Graham* • **Rosalind Russell** *Julie Stoddard Graham* • **Robert Benchley** *Oscar* • **Helen Vinson** *Lily Chalmers* • **Monty Woolley** *Mr Charles C Bawltitude* • **EE Clive** *Mr Palmiston* • **Mickey Rooney** *Jerry Crump* ■ *Dir* George Fitzmaurice • *Scr* Charles Brackett, Cyril Hume, Richard Maibaum, from a story by Marion Parsonnet, Helen Grace Carlisle

Live Now – Pay Later
★★★★
Comedy 1962 · UK · BW · 103min

This is a remarkably cynical and revealing portrait of Britain shifting from postwar austerity into rampant consumerism and the Swinging Sixties. Ian Hendry plays a seedy, on-the-make, door-to-door salesman who pressurises his customers – usually housewives – into bed and into hock. Hendry's character is appalling, yet he is also sympathetic since he's the only person who ever does anything in a society built on inertia and the sense of defeat that only wartime victory can bring. AT

Ian Hendry *Albert Argyle* • **June Ritchie** *Treasure* • **John Gregson** *Callendar* • **Liz Fraser** *Joyce Corby* • **Geoffrey Keen** *Reggie Corby* • **Jeannette Sterke** *Grace* • **Peter Butterworth** *Fred* • **Nyree Dawn Porter** *Marjorie Mason* • **Ronald Howard** *Cedric Mason* • **Harold Berens** *Solly Cowell* ■ *Dir* Jay Lewis • *Scr* Jack Trevor Story, from the novel *All on the Never-Never* by Jack Lindsay

Live Virgin ★★ 15
Comedy 2000 · US/Fr · Colour · 83min

Mena Suvari finds herself at the centre of a tug-of-war between rival porn barons in this decidedly dubious comedy. Jean-Pierre Marois proposes a scathing satire on everything from pay-per-view to the internet and consenting smut, but his film rapidly descends into a bawdy farce. Robert Loggia and Bob Hoskins toss restraint to the winds, while Gabriel Mann's geeky boyfriend and Sally Kellerman's talk-show hostess are lazy clichés. As for Suvari, readying to lose her virginity on the cameras, better things were in store. DP *DVD*

Bob Hoskins *Joey* • **Mena Suvari** *Katrina* • **Robert Loggia** *Ronny* • **Gabriel Mann** *Brian* • **Sally Kellerman** *Quaint* • **Lamont Johnson** *Nick* ■ *Dir* Jean-Pierre Marois • *Scr* Ira Israel, Jean-Pierre Marois

Live Wire ★★★ 15
Thriller 1992 · US · Colour · 81min

Pierce Brosnan stars in this better-than-average TV movie with a strong cast and an ingenious storyline. The future 007 plays an FBI agent trying to stop the villainous Ben Cross blowing up Washington politicians. The twist here is that Cross has developed a liquid explosive that gives new meaning to the phrase "don't drink the water": if you do, you effectively become a human bomb. That's the cue for some truly stunning explosive effects. His dodgy American accent aside, Brosnan is as charismatic as ever. JF Swearing, violence, a sex scene.

Pierce Brosnan *Danny O'Neill* • **Ron Silver** *Frank Traveres* • **Ben Cross** *Mikhail Rashid* • **Lisa Eilbacher** *Terry O'Neill* • **Tony Plana** *Al-Red* • **Al Waxman** *James Garvey* • **Philip Baker Hall** *Senator Thyme* ■ *Dir* Christian Duguay • *Scr* Bart Baker

The Lives of a Bengal Lancer ★★★★ U
Action adventure 1935 · US · BW · 104min

A fabulous chunk of "Hollywood colonial", this wonderful, rip-roaring tale was a smash hit in its day and still manages to stir the hearts of adventure lovers. Gary Cooper, in a career-defining performance, and the urbane Franchot Tone are terrific as buddies on the North-West Frontier, fighting an array of evil, turbaned character actors, and looking after new recruit Richard Cromwell, who just happens to be the son of their commanding officer, Guy Standing. Multi-Oscar nominated, this has been highly influential. TS

Gary Cooper *Lieutenant Alan McGregor* • **Franchot Tone** *Lieutenant "Fort" Forsythe* • **C Aubrey Smith** *Major Hamilton* • **Richard Cromwell** *Lieutenant Donald Stone* • **Guy Standing** *Colonel Stone* • **Kathleen Burke** *Tania Volkanskaya* • **Douglass Dumbrille** *Mohammed Khan* • **Monte Blue** *Hamzulla Khan* • **Akim Tamiroff** *Emir of Gopal* • **J Carrol Naish** *Grand Vizier* ■ *Dir* Henry Hathaway • *Scr* Waldemar Young, John L Balderston, Achmed Abdullah, from the novel by Major Francis Yeats-Brown, adapted by Grover Jones, Wiliam Slavens McNutt

The Lives of Others ★★★★★ 15
Drama 2006 · Ger · Colour · 131min

Winner of the 2006 Oscar for best foreign language film, this meticulous portrait of compassion in the midst of oppression from director Florian Henckel von Donnersmarck is a riveting masterpiece. Intelligently written and sensitively directed, it's set in East Germany in 1984 when the Stasi (the country's secret police) used covert surveillance, imprisonment and torture to quash any hint of non-conformity. Ruthless Stasi agent Ulrich Mühe is ordered to bug the East Berlin apartment of loyal socialist playwright Sebastian Koch and his famous actress lover Martina Gedeck, but he soon finds their vibrant lives in stark contrast to his own sterile existence. Brilliantly told through exceptional performances and dynamic storytelling, this heart-wrenching thriller is a triumph. AJ German +subtitles. Sex scenes. *DVD* *BL*

Martina Gedeck *Christa-Maria Sieland* • **Ulrich Mühe** *Captain Gerd Wiesler* • **Sebastian Koch** *Georg Dreyman* • **Ulrich Tukur** *Lieutenant Colonel Anton Grubitz* • **Thomas Thieme** *Minister Bruno Hempf* • **Hans-Uwe Bauer** *Paul Hauser* • **Volkmar Kleinert** *Albert Jerska* • **Matthias Brenner** *Karl Wallner* ■ *Dir/Scr* Florian Henckel von Donnersmarck

The Lives of the Saints ★★ 15
Crime drama 2005 · UK · Colour · 95min

The feature debut of co-directors Chris Cottam and photographer Rankin is part of a trend in modern British cinema that glories not just in trying to be original but also in grotesque unpleasantness. From the outset, it's obvious the picture is out to shock, as early gangster Karva (played by a bald, bearded James Cosmo) receives sexual favours from his stepson Othello's girlfriend (Emma Pierson). However, the nub of the tale concerns the apparent ability of an abandoned, speechless boy to make dreams come true. Cosmo delivers a performance of scenery-chewing gusto that's out of tune with the rest of the cast, which is typical of a film that seems unsure of its intentions and ends up a sprawling, overwrought mess. BP *DVD*

James Cosmo *Mr Karva* • **David Leon** *Othello* • **Emma Pierson** *Tina* • **Bronson Webb** *Emilio* • **Sam MacLintock** *Child* • **Daon Broni** *Roadrunner* ■ *Dir* Rankin, Chris Cottam • *Scr* Tony Grisoni

The Living Daylights
★★★ PG

Spy adventure 1987 · UK · Colour · 130min

After the creaky pantomime of the late Roger Moore era, Timothy Dalton's take on 007 is a breath of fresh air. For a story that segues from Soviet defection and arms dealing to the struggles of the Mujahidin, this is an endearingly human Bond. He sweats, he bleeds and, unusually, he falls in love. It's a romantic adventure with a sweetly staged prologue, nods to the gadget brigade and a hair-raising aerial scrap. MB Violence, nudity. DVD BL

Timothy Dalton *James Bond* • Maryam d'Abo *Kara Milovy* • Jeroen Krabbé *General Georgi Koskov* • Joe Don Baker *Brad Whitaker* • John Rhys-Davies *General Leonid Pushkin* • Art Malik *Kamran Shah* • Andreas Wisniewski *Necros* • Thomas Wheatley *Saunders* • Desmond Llewelyn *"Q"* • Robert Brown *"M"* • Caroline Bliss *Miss Moneypenny* ■ *Dir* John Glen • *Scr* Richard Maibaum, Michael G Wilson, from a story by Ian Fleming

The Living Dead
★★★★

Horror fantasy 1932 · Ger · BW · 98min

Paul Wegener, the great German actor and director, notably of *The Golem* (1914 and 1920), made his talkie debut in one of the last films of the Expressionist movement. Set in a shadowy England, it was based on two Edgar Allan Poe stories and one from Robert Louis Stevenson's *The Suicide Club*. Wegener plays a crazed inventor who kills his wife accidentally and conceals her body in a wall. The film, which seems to herald incipient Nazism, contains effective scenes in a waxworks museum and in an asylum where the lunatics have taken over. RB German +subtitles.

Paul Wegener *The murderer* • Harald Paulsen *Frank Briggs* • Mary Parker *Briggs's fiancée* • Paul Henckels *Doctor* ■ *Dir* Richard Ornstein [Richard Oswald] • *Scr* Heinz Goldberg, Eugen Szatmari, from stories by Edgar Allan Poe and from a short story by Robert Louis Stevenson

The Living Dead at the Manchester Morgue ★★★ 18

Horror 1974 · Sp/It · Colour · 89min

Night of the Living Dead gets an extreme gore makeover in this high-level Spanish shocker from splatter-maestro Jorge Grau. An experimental pesticide developed by the government not only succeeds in killing bugs but also raising the corpses in a nearby Manchester hospital. Wooden Ray Lovelock is the hippy hero who tries to stop the flesh-eating hordes. There's a bleak twist involving fascist cop Arthur Kennedy, and although nauseatingly graphic, Grau's cannibal holocaust is stylishly presented. AJ DVD

Raymond Lovelock *George* • Christina Galbo *Edna* • Arthur Kennedy *Inspector McCormick* • Jeanine Mestre *Katie* • Jose Lifante *Martin* ■ *Dir* Jorge Grau • *Scr* Sandro Continenza, Marcello Coscia • *Music* Giuliano Sorgini

The Living Desert ★★★★ U

Documentary 1953 · US · Colour · 71min

Keen to exploit the success of the "True-Life Adventures" series, Walt Disney moved into feature documentaries with this Oscar-winning study of the wildlife that endures the climatic extremes of Death Valley, the Yuma sand dunes and the Salton Sea mud pots. Disney's regular distributor, RKO, was convinced the film would fail at the box-office and so Walt founded his own company, Buena Vista, to launch the phenomenally profitable picture. Critics denounced the fact that the bobcat's escape from some wild pigs was staged rather than "discovered", but with a lively commentary by Winston Hibler, it remains a classic of its kind. DP

Winston Hibler *Narrator* ■ *Dir* James Algar • *Scr* James Algar, Winston Hibler, Ted Sears, Jack Moffitt

The Living End ★★★ 18

Road movie 1992 · US · Colour · 82min

Shot on a shoestring by Gregg Araki, the *enfant terrible* of American independent cinema, this film gleefully advertised itself as an "irresponsible" black comedy about society's attitude towards HIV-positive gay men. While Araki sometimes tries a little too hard to shock and the acting is always the wrong side of raw, this is a film that is not ashamed to make a fool of itself in order to convey its audacious mix of comedy and anger. DP Violence, swearing, nudity.

Mike Dytri *Luke* • Craig Gilmore *Jon* • Mark Finch *Doctor* • Mary Woronov *Daisy* ■ *Dir/Scr* Gregg Araki

Living Free ★★ U

Wildlife adventure 1972 · UK · Colour · 88min

This sequel to the ever-popular *Born Free* follows the fate of Elsa the lioness's three cubs after their mother is killed. The scenery is stunning and the cubs are as cute as ever as the Adamsons embark on a struggle to keep their charges out of the zoo. Unfortunately, their 700-mile journey across the wilds of Kenya to the Serengeti National Park has too few moments of high drama. Richard Harris starred as George Adamson in an excellent follow-up film, 1999's *To Walk with Lions*. DP DVD

Nigel Davenport *George Adamson* • Susan Hampshire *Joy Adamson* • Geoffrey Keen *John Kendall* • Edward Judd *Game Warden Weaver* ■ *Dir* Jack Couffer • *Scr* Millard Kaufman, from the books by Joy Adamson

The Living Idol ★

Adventure 1955 · US · Colour · 100min

Director Albert Lewin's sixth and final movie was this preposterous Mexican-set fantasy. An archaeological expedition discovers a strange temple dedicated to the Mayan jaguar god; before long possession and reincarnation decimate the mission. Matinée idol Steve Forrest, bumbling British stalwart James Robertson-Justice and Broadway legend Liliane Montevecchi enliven the proceedings – but not by much. AJ

Steve Forrest *Terry Matthews* • Liliane Montevecchi *Juanita* • James Robertson-Justice *Dr Alfred Stones* • Sara Garcia *Elena* • Eduardo Noriega (1) *Manuel* ■ *Dir/Scr* Albert Lewin

Living in a Big Way ★★

Comedy drama 1947 · US · BW · 103min

Marrying in haste before being drafted overseas, a GI returns to repent at leisure when his wife turns out to be wealthy, pampered, intent on a good time and a totally unsuitable mate. A box-office disaster in its day and hardly seen since, this confused mix of comedy, drama, social message, and sentimentality is not without some entertainment value. Gene Kelly stars as the idealistic hero, Marie "The Body" McDonald is the wife, and the experienced Gregory La Cava directs with some style. RK

Gene Kelly *Leo Gogarty* • Marie McDonald *Margaud Morgan* • Charles Winninger *D Rutherford Morgan* • Phyllis Thaxter *Peggy Randall* • Spring Byington *Mrs Morgan* ■ *Dir* Gregory La Cava • *Scr* Gregory La Cava, Irving Ravetch, from a story by Gregory La Cava

Living in Oblivion ★★★★ 15

Comedy 1995 · US · Colour and BW · 86min

The tribulations of low-budget independent film-making are sent up with glorious wit in this low-budget independent film from director Tom DiCillo. Steve Buscemi is hilarious as the harassed director contending with egomaniacal leading man James LeGros, inept stagehands, back-stabbing assistants, off-screen love affairs and a temperamental dwarf, all in one day of production. Packed with movie-buff in-jokes, DiCillo's sparkling satire recalls François Truffaut's similarly themed 1973 movie *Day for Night*. AJ Swearing, sex scenes, nudity. DVD

Steve Buscemi *Nick Reve* • Catherine Keener *Nicole* • Dermot Mulroney *Wolf* • Danielle Von Zerneck *Wanda* • James LeGros *Chad Palomino* ■ *Dir/Scr* Tom DiCillo

Living It Up ★★★ U

Musical comedy 1954 · US · Colour · 90min

This good-natured Dean Martin and Jerry Lewis comedy is actually a remake of the 1937 black comedy movie *Nothing Sacred*. Lewis takes the Carole Lombard role as the victim of radiation poisoning, with smoothie Martin as Jerry's medic, and sexy Janet Leigh in the Fredric March part of the ambitious reporter. Highlights include Sheree North's sizzling performance of what was arguably the first rock 'n' roll number on celluloid. Very funny indeed. TS DVD

Dean Martin *Steve* • Jerry Lewis *Homer* • Janet Leigh *Wally Cook* • Edward Arnold *The Mayor* • Fred Clark *Oliver Stone* • Sheree North *Jitterbug dancer* ■ *Dir* Norman Taurog • *Scr* Jack Rose, Melville Shavelson, from the musical *Hazel Flagg* by Ben Hecht, Jule Styne, Bob Hilliard, from a story by James Street

Living Out Loud ★★★ 15

Comedy drama 1998 · US · Colour · 95min

Screenwriter Richard LaGravenese's directorial debut is a bittersweet comedy with Holly Hunter terrific as the chic Manhattan 40-something trying to make it on her own after her husband of 15 years leaves her. Ensconced in her deluxe highrise apartment, she passes the time of day with lift operator Danny DeVito and has imaginary conversations with singer Queen Latifah at a jazz bar. An interesting look at 1990s relationships and one woman's journey in particular, the film unfortunately loses its power towards the end. JB Swearing. DVD

Holly Hunter *Judith* • Danny DeVito *Pat* • Queen Latifah *Liz Bailey* • Martin Donovan (2) *Bob Nelson* • Richard Schiff *Philly* • Elias Koteas *The Kisser* • Suzanne Shepherd *Mary* • Mariangela Pino *Donna* ■ *Dir* Richard LaGravenese • *Scr* Richard LaGravenese, from stories by Anton Chekhov

Living Proof ★★★ PG

Biographical drama 2008 · US · Colour · 86min

A strong cast, solid acting and an emotive true story put this earnest melodrama well above the usual made-for-TV fare. In the sort of unashamed tear-jerker that both engages and educates, an impassioned Harry Connick Jr plays the oncologist whose war against breast cancer led to the development of a new life-saving drug treatment. The intricate interweaving of individual women's experiences gives the film its heart, as each of the actresses, from Regina King to Trudie Styler, delivers dignified and uplifting performances, resulting in a powerful picture that will strike a chord with many viewers. SF DVD

Harry Connick Jr *Dr Dennis Slamon* • Paula Cale Lisbe [Paula Lisbe] *Donna Slamon* • Angie Harmon *Lilly Tartikoff* • Bernadette Peters *Barbara* • Regina King *Ellie* • Amanda Bynes *Jamie* ■ *Dir* Dan Ireland • *Scr* Vivienne Radkoff, from the novel *Her-2* by Robert Bazell

Liz & Dick ★★

Biographical drama 2012 · US · Colour · 88min

Oh, dear. There's sadly little to recommend this take on the tumultuous romance between Elizabeth Taylor and Richard Burton, overshadowed as it is by the casting of Lindsay Lohan as Taylor. She pouts, she throws bottles, she cries, she has false eyelashes the size of Texas, but she's unable to breathe life into the legendary star. It's a car crash. Grant Bowler does marginally better as Burton; he's worked very hard on the voice, and his portrayal of an actor who drank away his promise has some pathos. GC

Lindsay Lohan *Elizabeth Taylor* • Grant Bowler *Richard Burton* • Theresa Russell *Sara Taylor* • David Hunt *Ifor Jenkins* • Bruce Nozick *Bernard* ■ *Dir* Lloyd Kramer • *Scr* Christopher Monger

Lizzie ★★★

Psychological drama 1957 · US · BW · 81min

Eleanor Parker is very fine as the woman with three personalities: one quiet and shy, another raunchy and boisterous and the third together and caring. Psychiatric treatment from a stolidly able Richard Boone swiftly ensues. Hugo Haas's rather humdrum and plodding movie has all the hallmarks of 1950s psychiatric knowledge and practice. SR

Eleanor Parker *Elizabeth Richmond* • Richard Boone *Dr Neal Wright* • Joan Blondell *Aunt Morgan* • Hugo Haas *Walter Brenner* • Ric Roman *Johnny Valenzo* • Dorothy Arnold *Elizabeth's mother* • John Reach *Robin* • Marion Ross *Ruth Seaton* • Johnny Mathis *Nightclub singer* ■ *Dir* Hugo Haas • *Scr* Mel Dinelli, from the novel *The Bird's Nest* by Shirley Jackson

The Lizzie McGuire Movie ★★ U

Part-animated comedy drama 2003 · US · Colour · 90min

Only ardent fans of the Disney Channel's sitcom princess will like director Jim Fall's retake on *Gidget Goes to Rome*. Everyone else should give this synthetic soap opera a wide berth. Fluffy to the point of nearly blowing off the screen, the clumsy TV eighth-grader (Hilary Duff) goes on a graduation school trip to the Eternal City where she's mistaken for the female half of a sensational Italian pop duo. This inane confection is sugar-coated blandness personified and not remotely funny. AJ DVD

Hilary Duff *Lizzie McGuire/Isabella* • Adam Lamberg *David "Gordo" Gordon* • Robert Carradine *Sam* • Hallie Todd *Jo* • Jake Thomas *Matt* • Yani Gellman *Paolo* • Ashlie Brillault *Kate* • Clayton Snyder *Ethan* ■ *Dir* Jim Fall • *Scr* Susan Estelle Jansen, Ed Decter, John J Strauss, from the TV series by Terri Minsky

The Llano Kid ★★

Western 1939 · US · BW · 69min

This mild little Paramount western features imported Latin-American crooner Tito Guizar as writer O Henry's legendary "kissing bandit", previously played by the great Gary Cooper in *The Texan*. This was made to cash in on the then-popular Cisco Kid style of exotic cowboy lead. Guizar has an interesting co-star in Jan Clayton, but since the other woman is evil Gale Sondergaard, her co-stars barely get a look-in. TS

Tito Guizar *The Llano Kid* • Alan Mowbray *John Travers* • Gale Sondergaard *Lora Travers* • Jan Clayton *Lupita* • Emma Dunn *Donna Teresa* • Minor Watson *Sheriff McLane* ■ *Dir* Edward Venturini • *Scr* Wanda Tuchock, from the short story *The Double-Dyed Deceiver* by O Henry

Lloyd's of London ★★★★

Historical epic 1936 · US · BW · 115min

No facet of history was safe from 20th Century-Fox, who managed to turn both Rothschild and Lloyd's into household names in America. The presence of the young Tyrone Power undeniably helped in the latter instance, and this is the movie that launched the matinée idol's stardom. Power's character begins, though, as an apprentice (played by Freddie Bartholomew) in the famous brokerage house. He grows up to vie with suave George Sanders for the beauteous Madeleine Carroll. It's extremely handsomely mounted and director Henry King treats it all as though it's a solid piece of Americana. TS

Freddie Bartholomew *Young Jonathan Blake* • Tyrone Power *Jonathan Blake* • Madeleine Carroll *Lady Elizabeth Stacy* • Sir Guy Standing [Guy Standing] *John Julius Angerstein* • George Sanders *Lord Everett Stacy* • C Aubrey Smith *Old "Q"* • Virginia Field *Polly* • Montagu Love *Hawkins* • Una O'Connor *Widow Blake* • JM Kerrigan *Brook Watson* ■ *Dir* Henry King • *Scr* Ernest Pascal, Walter Ferris, from a story by Curtis Kenyon

Loaded ★★ 18

Psychological thriller 1994 · UK/NZ · Colour · 91min

Anna Campion, sister of the Oscar-winning Jane, makes her directing debut with this modest, yet intriguing thriller. The story focuses on a vaguely pretentious group of Generation X school-leavers who travel to the country to make a horror film. Things go pear-shaped when they collectively drop some tabs of acid one night. Campion summons up an air of quiet menace, although it's hard to work up much sympathy for the self-centred characters. JF **DVD**

Oliver Milburn *Neil* • Nick Patrick *Giles* • Catherine McCormack *Rose* • Thandie Newton *Zita* • Matthew Eggleton *Lionel* • Danny Cunningham *Lance* • Biddy Hodson *Charlotte* ■ *Dir/Scr* Anna Campion

The Lobster ★★★ 15
Surreal romantic fantasy
2015 · Ire/UK/Gr/Fr/Neth · Colour · 118min

Yorgos Lanthimos's fearsomely strange, sporadically very funny satire on the mores of human mating has David (Colin Farrell) being dumped by his partner and being sent to what looks like an expensive spa. There he is informed that if he cannot find a mate after 45 days he will be transformed into an animal of his choosing, in David's case the titular Lobster. This is beautifully shot, and bravely acted – particularly by an impressive Colin Farrell, but satire's essential bite hinges on the quality of its target and here it's unclear. AS Swearing, sex scenes.

Colin Farrell (2) *David* • Rachel Weisz *Short-sighted woman* • Olivia Colman *Hotel manager* • Ashley Jensen *Biscuit woman* • John C Reilly *Lisping man* • Léa Seydoux *Loner leader* • Ben Whishaw *Limping man* ■ *Dir* Yorgos Lanthimos • *Scr* Yorgos Lanthimos, Efthimis Filippou

Lobster Man from Mars
★★ PG
Science-fiction comedy
1989 · US · Colour · 78min

Borrowing liberally from Mel Brooks's classic *The Producers*, this good-natured spoof of all those drive-in monster movies of the 1950s is just about tacky and smart enough to be intermittently enjoyable. Tony Curtis stars as movie mogul JP Shelldrake who, upon being told he needs a flop for tax purposes, sets out to make the biggest howler in Hollywood history. The performances are enthusiastic and suitably ripe, but director Stanley Sheff fails to maintain a high level of inspirational parody. RS

Tony Curtis *JP Shelldrake* • Deborah Foreman *Mary* • Anthony Hickox *John* • Tommy Sledge • Dean Jacobson *Stevie Horowitz* • Fred Holliday *Colonel Ankrum* • Bobby Pickett *King of Mars, the Astrologer* • SD Nemeth *Dreaded Lobster Man* ■ *Dir* Stanley Sheff • *Scr* Bob Greenberg

Local Hero ★★★★ PG
Comedy drama 1983 · UK · Colour · 107min

This comedy drama firmly established Bill Forsyth as a major British film-maker. It's a lyrical, almost mystical, tale that follows the attempts of Texas oilman Burt Lancaster and his minion Peter Riegert to buy up an isolated Scottish village in order to build an oil refinery, without bargaining on the village's integral strength of community. This avoids the relentless whimsy of Forsyth's previous outing, *Gregory's Girl*, while the scenery is gorgeous, and the performances funny, ironic and moving. SR Swearing. **DVD**

Peter Riegert *MacIntyre* • Burt Lancaster *Happer* • Denis Lawson *Urquhart* • Peter Capaldi *Oldsen* • Fulton Mackay *Ben* • Jenny Seagrove *Marina* • Jennifer Black *Stella* • Christopher Asante *Reverend MacPherson* • Rikki Fulton *Geddes* ■ *Dir/Scr* Bill Forsyth • *Cinematographer* Chris Menges

Loch Ness ★★★ PG
Fantasy drama 1995 · UK · Colour · 96min

There's more than a hint of *Local Hero* in this feel-good fantasy drama from director John Henderson. The script had been around for a decade before Ted Danson signed up as the scientist sent to the Highlands to disprove the existence of Nessie. Naturally, his investigation is sidetracked by romance and the self-interested schemes of the locals before he, too, becomes convinced by the legend. Although Danson is a touch bland, Joely Richardson turns in a doughty performance as the single mum whose daughter knows a

thing or two about "water kelpies". DP **DVD**

Ted Danson *Dempsey* • Joely Richardson *Laura* • Ian Holm *Water Bailiff* • Harris Yulin *Doctor Mercer* • James Frain *Adrian Foote* • Keith Allen *Gordon Shoals* • Nick Brimble *Andy Maclean* • Kirsty Graham *Isabel* • Harry Jones *Wee Wullie* • Philip O'Brien *Doctor Abernathy* ■ *Dir* John Henderson • *Scr* John Fusco

Lock, Stock and Two Smoking Barrels ★★★★ 18
Crime comedy 1998 · UK · Colour · 102min

Widely regarded as the best British crime movie since *The Long Good Friday*, this cheerfully amoral debut feature from Guy Ritchie has a youthful exuberance that's truly infectious. The superb cast is spiced up with the presence of celebrities such as Sting and, especially, Vinnie Jones in a well-received henchman-with-a-heart role. The action revolves around young cardsharp Eddy (Nick Moran), who loses £500,000 he doesn't have to crime king Hatchet Harry. With a week to come up with the shortfall, he and mates Dexter Fletcher, Jason Flemyng and Jason Statham plan to hijack the proceeds of a robbery hatched by their gangster neighbours. But things go horribly wrong very quickly. JF Violence, swearing, nudity, drug abuse. **DVD**

Nick Moran *Eddy* • Jason Flemyng *Tom* • Dexter Fletcher *Soap* • Jason Statham *Bacon* • Steven Mackintosh *Winston* • Nicholas Rowe *J* • Nick Marcq *Charles* • Charlie Forbes *Willie* • Vinnie Jones *Big Chris* • Lenny McLean *Barry the Baptist* • Peter McNicholl *Little Chris* • PH Moriarty *Hatchet Harry* • Stephen Marcus *Nick the Greek* • Vas Blackwood *Rory Breaker* • Sting *JD* ■ *Dir/Scr* Guy Ritchie

Lock Up ★★ 18
Prison drama 1989 · US · Colour · 104min

Sylvester Stallone opts for some grittier material after the cartoon heroics of his Rambo and Rocky characters, but this proves to be almost as disastrous as his forays into comedy. He plays a nice criminal on the verge of being released who is whisked away to a gothic prison hell presided over by a wildly over-the-top Donald Sutherland. Director John Flynn loses his way in a flood of testosterone and prison clichés. JF Swearing, violence. **DVD**

Sylvester Stallone *Frank Leone* • Donald Sutherland *Warden Drumgoole* • John Amos *Meissner* • Tom Sizemore *Dallas* • Frank McRae *Eclipse* • Sonny Landham *Chink* • Larry Romano *First Base* • Darlanne Fluegel *Melissa* ■ *Dir* John Flynn • *Scr* Richard Smith, Jeb Stuart, Henry Rosenbaum

Lock Up Your Daughters!
★★ 15
Period comedy 1969 · UK · Colour · 97min

The story of three sex-starved sailors on leave and at large isn't just confined to *On the Town*, as this adaptation of an 18th-century comedy demonstrates. This version of the London stage musical comes to the screen minus the songs. Despite its distinguished origins – and a cast that includes Christopher Plummer, Susannah York and Glynis Johns – it comes across as non-musical slapstick that's as loud and vulgar as a cheapjack panto. TH Violence, swearing, sex scenes.

Christopher Plummer *Lord Foppington* • Susannah York *Hilaret* • Glynis Johns *Mrs Squeezum* • Ian Bannen *Ramble* • Tom Bell *Shaftoe* • Elaine Taylor *Cloris* • Jim Dale *Lusty* • Kathleen Harrison *Lady Clumsey* • Roy Kinnear *Sir Tunbelly Clumsey* • Georgia Brown *Nell* • Roy Dotrice *Gossip* • Fenella Fielding *Lady Eager* ■ *Dir* Peter Coe • *Scr* Keith Waterhouse, Willis Hall, from the musical *Lock Up Your Daughters!* by Bernard Miles, Laurie Johnson, Lionel Bart, from the play *Rape upon Rape* by Henry Fielding and the play *The Relapse* by John Vanbrugh

Locke ★★★★ 15
Drama 2014 · US/UK · Colour · 81min

Tom Hardy gives the performance of a lifetime as a construction foreman caught in emotional turmoil in this self-contained tour de force. Shot almost completely inside a car on the motorway, this slice of real-

time drama is an unexpectedly thrilling treat. Hardy plays against type as Ivan Locke, who speaks with a heavy Welsh accent, wears a jumper and cares deeply about his wife, kids and job. Driving from work one evening, he fields a stretch of angst-filled phone calls (evocatively performed by a cast that includes Ruth Wilson, Andrew Scott and Olivia Colman). Locke is a rare hero in modern cinema, a moral action man and blazing beacon of heroic normalcy. As well as that, he's a paean to calm – despite the mounting pressure, he always keeps to the speed limit. KK **DVD** **Blu**

Tom Hardy *Ivan Locke* • Olivia Colman *Bethan* • Ruth Wilson *Katrina* • Andrew Scott *Donal* • Ben Daniels *Gareth* • Tom Holland (2) *Eddie* • Bill Milner *Sean* ■ *Dir/Scr* Steven Knight

The Locket ★★★
Film noir 1946 · US · BW · 85min

In this minor league *film noir*, tightly directed by John Brahm and starring Laraine Day, a little girl allegedly steals a locket and grows up to be a woman whose kleptomania leads to murder, suicide and nervous breakdowns for everyone around her. Every flashbacked scene is a crisis, every performance over the top. Day is convincingly neurotic, while Robert Mitchum gives her solid support as the first of her men to crack. AT **DVD**

Laraine Day *Nancy* • Robert Mitchum *Norman Clyde* • Brian Aherne *Dr Blair* • Gene Raymond *John Willis* • Sharyn Moffett *Nancy, aged 10* • Ricardo Cortez *Mr Bonner* • Henry Stephenson *Lord Wyndham* ■ *Dir* John Brahm • *Scr* Sheridan Gibney

Lockout ★★★ 15
Science-fiction action thriller 2012 · US/Fr · Colour · 91min

In this fast-paced futuristic thriller, violent inmates take over an experimental prison ship orbiting the Earth and hold the US president's humanitarian-worker daughter (Maggie Grace) among their hostages. So maverick government agent Snow (Guy Pearce) blasts off on a rescue mission. What might, on paper, look like a bog-standard "*Escape from New York* in space" variation quickly establishes its own character and personality, thanks mainly to Pearce's charismatic wisecracking hero and a pair of genuinely chilling adversaries in Vincent Regan and Joseph Gilgun. TeS Violence, swearing, sexual references. **DVD** **Blu**

Guy Pearce *Snow* • Maggie Grace *Emilie Warnock* • Peter Stormare *Langral* • Vincent Regan *Alex* • Lennie James *Shaw* ■ *Dir* James Mather, Stephen St Leger • *Scr* Luc Besson, James Mather, Stephen St Leger, from an idea by Besson

The Lodger ★★★★ PG
Classic silent thriller 1926 · UK · BW · 79min

Alfred Hitchcock once called this the "first true Hitchcock movie". In addition to being the first in which he explored his favourite theme of the innocent in danger, it also marked his debut before the camera in one of those celebrated fleeting cameos. Clearly reflecting the influence of German Expressionism, this was dismissed as a disaster by the distributors, but the critics proclaimed it the best British film made to date. The action is based on a novel about Jack the Ripper and is played with extravagance by matinée idol Ivor Novello. DP **DVD** **Blu**

Ivor Novello *The Lodger/Jonathan Drew* • June Daisy Bunting • Marie Ault *Mrs Bunting* • Arthur Chesney *Mr Bunting* • Malcolm Keen *Joe Betts* ■ *Dir* Alfred Hitchcock • *Scr* Alfred Hitchcock, Eliot Stannard, Ivor Montagu, from the novel by Marie Belloc-Lowndes

The Lodger ★★★★ PG
Thriller 1944 · US · BW · 79min

In his first big starring role, the massive young character actor Laird Cregar makes an excellent job of portraying the lodger in Victorian London who is really the notorious killer, Jack the Ripper. Merle Oberon is the singer living in the same house, and George Sanders is the Scotland

Yard inspector. A fine script is enhanced by the striking visual sense of director John Brahm and cameraman Lucien Ballard, who later married Oberon. Sadly, Cregar's promising career ended when he died from crash-dieting. AE **DVD**

Merle Oberon *Kitty* • George Sanders *John Garrick* • Laird Cregar *The Lodger* • Sir Cedric Hardwicke [Cedric Hardwicke] *Robert Burton* • Sara Allgood *Ellen* • Aubrey Mather *Supt Sutherland* • Queenie Leonard *Daisy* • David Clyde *Sgt Bates* ■ *Dir* John Brahm • *Scr* Barré Lyndon, from the novel by Marie Belloc-Lowndes

The Lodger ★★ 15
Horror thriller 2009 · US · Colour · 91min

A serial killer with Jack the Ripper pretensions is slicing his way through a host of Hollywood hookers in this dour update of Alfred Hitchcock's 1926 silent thriller. Alfred Molina is suitably brooding as the cop who risks his career to nab the maniac. Sadly, writer/director David Ondaatje is no Master of Suspense despite nods to the Hitchcock back catalogue and the use of pointedly Bernard Herrmann-like music. JA Swearing, violence, nudity.

Alfred Molina *Chandler Manning* • Hope Davis *Ellen* • Shane West *Street* • Rachael Leigh Cook *Amanda* • Simon Baker (1) *Malcolm* • Philip Baker Hall *Captain Smith* ■ *Dir* David Ondaatje • *Scr* David Ondaatje, from Marie Belloc-Lowndes's novel

Logan's Run ★★★ PG
Science-fiction thriller 1976 · US · Colour · 113min

Michael York and Jenny Agutter star in this tale that earnestly depicts a society that dooms those over the age of 30 to the myth of "renewal". Director Michael Anderson takes a while to make his point here, but puts on a real spurt when the runners head for the outside. Dale Hennesy and Robert De Vestel's Oscar-nominated imaginative designs compensate for the rather cumbersome plot. TH Violence, nudity. **DVD**

Michael York *Logan* • Jenny Agutter *Jessica* • Richard Jordan *Francis* • Roscoe Lee Browne *Box* • Farrah Fawcett-Majors [Farrah Fawcett] *Holly* • Peter Ustinov *Old man* • Michael Anderson Jr *Doc* • Gary Morgan *Billy* ■ *Dir* Michael Anderson • *Scr* David Zelag Goodman, from the novel by William F Nolan, George Clayton Johnson • *Costume Designer* Bill Thomas

Logan's War: Bound by Honor ★★ 15
Action drama 1998 · US · Colour · 87min

Chuck Norris sticks to pretty much to his usual formula here in a story co-written by his brother, Aaron. It's a no-nonsense drama with plenty of bruising fight sequences and even more corny dialogue. Accepting his advancing years, Norris passes the buck to Eddie Cibrian, who stars as an army ranger out to avenge his murdered family. DP **DVD**

Chuck Norris *Jake Fallon* • Eddie Cibrian *Logan Fallon* • Joe Spano *Agent Downing* • Jeff Kober *Sal Mercado* • RD Call *Al Talgorno* ■ *Dir* Michael Preece • *Scr* Walter Klenhard, from a story by Chuck Norris, Aaron Norris, Walter Klenhard

Lola ★★★★★ PG
Romantic comedy drama 1960 · Fr/It · BW · 83min

Dedicated to Max Ophüls but bearing the hallmarks of a Gene Kelly musical, Jacques Demy's debut feature is a charming paean to his home town of Nantes, here given a monochrome gloss by cinematographer Raoul Coutard that evokes both the poetic realism of the 1930s and the vibrancy of the *nouvelle vague*. Demy sweeps his camera around the port as cabaret dancer Anouk Aimée has love affairs while awaiting the return of her daughter's absentee father. Gleefully playing games with chance and coincidence, this fond satire on movie romance remains as fresh, enchanting and deliciously superficial as it seemed on its original release. Demy remade this in 1969 as *Model Shop* for his Hollywood debut. DP French +subtitles. **DVD**

Anouk Aimée *Lola* • Marc Michel *Roland* • Elina Labourdette *Mme Desnoyers* • Alan Scott *Frankie* • Annie Duperoux *Cecile* ■ *Dir/Scr* Jacques Demy

Lola ★★★★ 15
Black comedy 1982 · W Ger · Colour · 109min

Coming between *The Marriage of Maria Braun* and *Veronika Voss*, the second in Rainer Werner Fassbinder's trilogy is unusual in that it has a happy ending. Or, at least as happy as possible considering that brothel chanteuse Barbara Sukowa is bedding corrupt construction boss Mario Adorf within minutes of marrying idealistic town planner Armin Mueller-Stahl. Arguing that fascism did not die with Hitler, Fassbinder mischievously makes a hero of Adorf's petty dictator by having every citizen acquiesce so compliantly to his imposed conformity. A daringly dark comedy. DP German +subtitles.
Barbara Sukowa *Lola* • Armin Mueller-Stahl *Von Bohm* • Mario Adorf *Schuckert* • Matthias Fuchs *Esslin* • Helga Feddersen *Frau Hettich* • Karin Baal *Lola's mother* • Ivan Desny *Wittich* ■ *Dir* Rainer Werner Fassbinder • *Scr* Peter Marthesheimer, Pea Frohlich

Lola ★★★
Thriller 1986 · Sp · Colour · 106min

As the factory worker who escapes an abusive relationship to find all-too-brief contentment with her daughter, Angela Molina is both passionate and vulnerable, particularly in the early scenes with Feodor Atkine, the true love who reappears on the scene to investigate her seemingly respectable French husband, Patrick Bauchau. Packed with moments of graphic physicality, psychological intensity and sadistic violence, Bigas Luna's three-act melodrama is sordid and compelling in equal measure. DP Spanish dubbed.
Angela Molina *Lola* • Patrick Bauchau *Robert* • Feodor Atkine [Féodor Atkine] *Mario* • Assumpta Serna *Silvia* ■ *Dir* Bigas Luna • *Scr* Bigas Luna, Luis Herce, Enrique Viciano

Lola Montès ★★★★★ PG
Historical romantic drama
1955 · Fr/W Ger · Colour · 110min

Max Ophüls was inspired to film this story of the rise and fall of the famous mistress of King Ludwig I and Franz Liszt by Judy Garland's nervous breakdown and Zsa Zsa Gabor's romances. Ophüls's final film, his only work in colour, transcends the trappings of a conventional historical romance by his brilliant use of the CinemaScope screen and the virtuoso camerawork. Sadly, on its initial release, the producers reduced the 140-minute film to 90 minutes. It was not until 1969, when it was shown in a restored form, that the film was recognised as the masterpiece it is. RB French +subtitles. DVD
Martine Carol *Lola Montès* • Peter Ustinov *Circus Master* • Anton Walbrook *Ludwig I, King of Bavaria* • Ivan Desny *James* • Will Quadflieg *Liszt* • Oskar Werner *The Student* • Lise Delamare *Mrs Craigie* • Henri Guisol *Maurice* • Paulette Dubost *Joséphine* ■ *Dir* Max Ophüls • *Scr* Max Ophuls, Annette Wademant, Franz Geiger, from the novel *La Vie Extraordinaire de Lola Montès* by Cécil St Laurent, Jacques Natanson • *Cinematographer* Christian Matras

Lola Versus ★★ 15
Romantic comedy 2012 · US · Colour · 86min

In this typically unremarkable but watchable Hollywood romantic comedy, quirky Greta Gerwig plays Lola, a 29-year-old New Yorker who is dumped on the eve of their wedding by her longtime boyfriend (Joel Kinnaman). Essentially, she's that stock romantic comedy character: the over-dependent neurotic who feels she can't function without a fella. But Gerwig is a likeably offbeat comedy actress, and Bill Pullman and Debra Winger offer pleasing cameos as her laid-back parents. DA Swearing, drug abuse, sex scenes. DVD Blu-ray
Greta Gerwig *Lola* • Joel Kinnaman *Luke* • Hamish Linklater *Henry* • Zoe Lister Jones *Alice* • Bill Pullman *Lenny* • Debra Winger *Robin* ■ *Dir* Daryl Wein • *Scr* Daryl Wein, Zoe Lister Jones

Lolita ★★★★★ 15
Black comedy drama 1961 · UK · BW · 147min

"How did they ever make a film of *Lolita*?" asked the posters for this brilliant Stanley Kubrick film. Well, in Vladimir Nabokov's adaptation of his own famous novel about the professor and the 12-year-old girl, there are added layers of black comedy and only slight compromise: James Mason seems to love Sue Lyon rather than lust after her, and Lolita's age is increased to 15. Shelley Winters's hilarious and sad portrayal of Lolita's mother is American momism incarnate, while Peter Sellers as Clare Quilty is like a creepy chameleon. For economic and censorship reasons the picture was made in England, and because of this Nabokov's nightmare vision of urban America and its seedy motels is reduced to obvious back projection and even more obvious Elstree locations. AT DVD Blu-ray
James Mason *Humbert Humbert* • Sue Lyon *Lolita Haze* • Shelley Winters *Charlotte Haze* • Peter Sellers *Clare Quilty* • Diana Decker *Jean Farlow* • Jerry Stovin *John Farlow* • Gary Cockrell *Dick* • Marianne Stone *Vivian Darkbloom* ■ *Dir* Stanley Kubrick • *Scr* Vladimir Nabokov, from his novel

Lolita ★★★ 18
Black comedy drama
1997 · Fr/US · Colour · 131min

To be fair, this 1997 version of Vladimir Nabokov's notorious 1955 novel isn't as sacrilegious as it might have been with the flashy, superficial Adrian Lyne (*Fatal Attraction, Indecent Proposal*) at the helm. However, it is Lyne's bid for artistic "respectability" (the artful shots, the fidelity to the book) that is also the film's undoing. It looks good, but lacks danger. Despite a compelling, tortured turn from Jeremy Irons as Humbert – and a seductive one from Dominique Swain as Lolita – it's all a little too cosmetic and soft-focused. AC DVD CS
Jeremy Irons *Humbert Humbert* • Melanie Griffith *Charlotte Haze* • Frank Langella *Clare Quilty* • Dominique Swain *Lolita Haze* • Suzanne Shepherd *Miss Pratt* • Keith Reddin *Reverend Rigger* • Erin J Dean *Mona* • Joan Glover *Miss LeBone* ■ *Dir* Adrian Lyne • *Scr* Stephen Schiff, from the novel by Vladimir Nabokov

The Lolly-Madonna War ★★★
Drama 1973 · US · Colour · 105min

Let backwoods battle commence! Rod Steiger and Robert Ryan are the heads of the feuding families in this variable drama. The two sides have been brought to the brink of violence by a land dispute and matters come to a head with a bizarre case of mistaken identity involving Season Hubley as the presumed "Lolly-Madonna". Director Richard C Sarafian piles a lot of enthusiasm into the mayhem, and the cast is strong. Unfortunately, the film's mood-swings make it only a superior example of Peckinpah-lite. TH
Rod Steiger *Laban Feather* • Robert Ryan *Pap Gutshall* • Jeff Bridges *Zack Feather* • Scott Wilson *Thrush Feather* • Katherine Squire *Mrs Feather* • Tresa Hughes *Mrs Gutshall* • Season Hubley *Roonie Gill* • Randy Quaid *Finch Feather* • Gary Busey *Seb Gutshall* ■ *Dir* Richard C Sarafian • *Scr* Rodney Carr-Smith, Sue Grafton, from the novel by Sue Grafton

Londinium ★★
Comedy 1999 · US · Colour · 90min

Writer/director Mike Binder also stars in this misfiring comedy of marital manners. It all begins brightly enough, with Binder arriving in London to pen fading US star Mariel Hemingway's new TV series, and falling for French make-up artist Irène Jacob. But once Binder and Hemingway embark on an affair and try to pair off Jacob with Hemingway's husband (Colin Firth), the story begins to stutter. DP
Mike Binder *Ben Greene* • Colin Firth *Allen Portland* • Mariel Hemingway *Carly Matthews Portland* • Irène Jacob *Fiona Delgrazia* • Stephen Fry *Nigel* • Jack Dee *Glen* • Stephen Marcus *Davey* ■ *Dir/Scr* Mike Binder

London ★★★★ U
Documentary drama 1994 · UK · Colour · 81min

After a series of shorts, documentarist Patrick Keiller made his feature debut with this unique portrait of the English capital. With its highly literate commentary from Paul Scofield, this is essentially the story of three expeditions as the narrator and his friend Robinson go in search of London's literary past as well as exploring the reasons why the city sold its soul to suburbia. However, distractions abound as contemporary events such as the 1992 General Election and IRA bomb attacks intrude upon their musings. The juxtaposition of text and image is intriguing as Keiller lilts between travelogue, love letter and lament. Keiller's follow-up to this, a journey around England called *Robinson in Space*, is equally as fascinating. DP DVD
Paul Scofield *Narrator* ■ *Dir/Scr* Patrick Keiller

London after Midnight
Silent mystery 1927 · US · BW · 65min

Now sadly lost, this is on the American Film Institute's "most wanted" list. One of the first American films to deal with vampirism, this silent classic was a memorable collaboration between Lon Chaney and that other horror genius, producer/director Tod Browning. Chaney plays multiple roles in a complex plot about a pair of actors terrorising the inhabitants of a cursed Gothic mansion into believing a vampire stalks the premises. This seminal shocker was remade as *Mark of the Vampire* in 1935. AJ
Lon Chaney *Burke* • Marceline Day *Lucille Balfour* • Henry B Walthall *Sir James Hamlin* • Percy Williams *Butler* • Conrad Nagel *Arthur Hibbs* ■ *Dir* Tod Browning • *Scr* Tod Browning, Waldemar Young, from a story by Browning

London – Babylon ★★★★ 15
Documentary 2012 · UK · Colour · 127min

Chronicling a century of the capital's history, Julien Temple's rousing documentary makes exceptional use of a dazzling range of archive material to capture the personality of London and the changing face of the people who have shaped its destiny over the past 100 years. Opening with the recollections of 106-year-old Hackney resident Hetty Bower, the film celebrates the indomitability of the city's multifarious citizens, who have managed to keep calm and carry on in the face of sieges, rallies, wars and riots, as well as seismic social, political and cultural upheaval. A witty, trenchant and utterly compelling film. DP Swearing. DVD
■ *Dir* Julien Temple

London Belongs to Me ★★★ PG
Drama 1948 · UK · BW · 107min

Richard Attenborough as the mechanic charged with murder might be the central character in this Frank Launder and Sidney Gilliat production, but the film belongs fairly and squarely to Alastair Sim. As the fake medium desperately trying to dupe Joyce Carey into marriage, he is hilariously sinister, and the scenes can't pass quickly enough before he's back on the screen. For once, the US title, *Dulcimer Street*, is probably more apposite, as this is one of those sentimentalised "strength in the community" pictures that postwar British cinema was so fond of. DP DVD
Richard Attenborough *Percy Boon* • Alastair Sim *Mr Squales* • Fay Compton *Mrs Josser* • Stephen Murray *Uncle Henry* • Wylie Watson *Mr Josser* • Susan Shaw *Doris Josser* • Ivy St Helier *Connie* ■ *Dir* Sidney Gilliat • *Scr* Sidney Gilliat, JB Williams, from the novel by Norman Collins

London Boulevard ★★ 18
Crime thriller 2010 · US · Colour · 98min

Walking the straight and narrow isn't so simple for an ex-con in this moody crime drama. Colin Farrell is surprisingly understated as Mitchel, the old-school cockney wide-boy who lands a seemingly cushy job protecting a London starlet (Keira

Knightley, drawing on experience) from overzealous paparazzi. Seasoned Hollywood scriptwriter William Monahan (*The Departed*) is keen to celebrate an almost forgotten tradition of *noir*, where moral choices provide the pulse of the story rather than bullets and car chases. It's intriguing for that reason, but sadly, there's just too much meandering. SP Violence, swearing. DVD Blu-ray
Colin Farrell (2) *Harry "Mitch" Mitchel* • Keira Knightley *Charlotte* • David Thewlis *Jordan* • Anna Friel *Briony* • Ray Winstone *Gant* • Eddie Marsan *DI Bailey* • Jamie Campbell Bower *Whiteboy* ■ *Dir* William Monahan • *Scr* William Monahan, from the novel by Ken Bruen • *Cinematographer* Chris Menges

London by Night ★★★
Crime thriller 1937 · US · BW · 70min

Actor/dancer and future US senator George Murphy is the star of this snappy and suspenseful thriller from MGM. A well-crafted script, with punchy dialogue, has Murphy and sassy Rita Johnson (in her film debut) on the trail of a blackmailer who fakes two murders to build his reputation. Genuine English accents were provided by London-born Virginia Field and, as a Scotland Yard detective, Manchester-born George Zucco. RB
George Murphy *Michael Denis* • Rita Johnson *Patricia Herrick* • Virginia Field *Bessie* • Leo G Carroll *Correy* • George Zucco *Inspector Jefferson* • Montagu Love *Sir Arthur Herrick* ■ *Dir* William Thiele • *Scr* George Oppenheimer, from the play *The Umbrella Man* by Will Scott

London Fields
Mystery thriller 2015 · US/UK · Colour · 118min

This is a preview – no prints were available to review prior to publication: When Martin Amis's convoluted but compelling novel finally makes it to the screen, it will have survived an aborted attempt by David Cronenberg and legal difficulties between director Mathew Cullen and producers prior to release. Considered by many to be the author's best work, it's set in 1999 against a background of social degradation and tells the story of a woman (Amber Heard) who knows she will be murdered on her 35th birthday. It's blackly comic and populated by a cast of not particularly likeable characters but, with Johnny Depp and Billy Bob Thornton in town, they'll be desperately hoping for a good response. TP
Amber Heard *Nicola Six* • Billy Bob Thornton *Samson Young* • Jaimie Alexander *Hope Clinch* • Theo James *Guy Clinch* • Cara Delevingne *Kath Talent* • Johnny Depp *Chick Purchase* ■ *Dir* Mathew Cullen • *Scr* Roberta Hanley, from Martin Amis's novel

London Has Fallen ★★ 15
Action thriller 2016 · US/UK · Colour · 94min

This sequel to White House siege thriller *Olympus Has Fallen* relocates to London for a state funeral that is plunged into chaos by a terrorist attack. Caught up in the slaughter are agent Gerard Butler and US president Aaron Eckhart. Director Babak Najafi extracts some black comedy from all the pyrotechnics, but there's something nasty about this orgy of below-par CGI destruction. AC Violence, swearing DVD Blu-ray
Gerald Butler *Mike Banning* • Aaron Eckhart *President Benjamin Asher* • Morgan Freeman *Speaker Trumbull* • Charlotte Riley *MI6 Jacquelin Marshall* • Angela Bassett *Lynn Jacobs* ■ *Dir* Babak Najafi • *Scr* Katrin Benedikt, Christian Gudegast, Creighton Rothenberger, Chad St John, from a story by Benedikt, Rothenberger, from their characters

London Kills Me ★ 18
Comedy drama 1991 · UK · Colour · 102min

This is a disappointing directorial debut from Hanif Kureishi, the provocative writer of *My Beautiful Laundrette* and *Sammy and Rosie Get Laid*. Justin Chadwick is a Notting Hill drug-dealer of no fixed abode, who wants to get his life together, but needs a nice pair of shoes in order to land a waiter's job at a restaurant. Whatever Kureishi was trying to say about London criminal culture is lost among boring characters and the meaningless, uninvolving story. JC

Justin Chadwick *Clint* • Steven Mackintosh *Muffdiver* • Emer McCourt *Sylvie* • Roshan Seth *Dr Bubba* • Fiona Shaw *Headley* • Brad Dourif *Hemingway* • Tony Haygarth *Burns* • Stevan Rimkus *Tom Tom* • Eleanor David *Lily* • Alun Armstrong *Stone* • Nick Dunning *Faulkner* ■ *Dir/Scr* Hanif Kureishi

London Melody ★★
Musical romance 1937 · UK · BW · 75min

Anna Neagle, a street singer and dancer, attracts the attention of Tullio Carminati's wealthy, sophisticated diplomat who secretly pays for dancing lessons, enabling her to become a cabaret star. He even takes the blame for a mistake made by the cad (Robert Douglas) to whom she was engaged. Although started at Elstree, its one claim to fame is that it was the very first production to shoot on the sound stages of the new Pinewood Studios in September 1936. AE

Anna Neagle *Jacqueline* • Tullio Carminati *Marius Andreani* • Robert Douglas *Nigel Taplow* • Horace Hodges *Father Donnelly* ■ *Dir* Herbert Wilcox • *Scr* Florence Tranter, Monckton Hoffe, from a story by Ray Lewis

London River ★★★★12
Drama 2009 · UK/Fr/Alg · Colour · 84min

Writer/director Rachid Bouchareb (*Days of Glory*) uses the traumatic aftermath of the 7/7 London bombings as the setting for this compassionate, thoughtful drama. Brenda Blethyn and Malian actor Sotigui Kouyaté play the parents who meet in London while looking for their missing children. Blethyn, as ever, gives it her all, though the sad-eyed restraint of her co-star (who died in April 2010) is even more touching. The movie is an unexpected, yet sincere, response that draws positive values from tragic events. TJ French, English, Arabic +subtitles. *DVD*

Brenda Blethyn *Elisabeth* • otigui Kouyaté [Sotigui Kouyaté] *Ousmane* • Sami Bouajila *Imam* • Roschdy Zem *Butcher* • Francis Magee *Inspector* ■ *Dir* Rachid Bouchareb • *Scr* Rachid Bouchareb, Zoé Galeron, Olivier Lorelle

London Road ★★★★15
Musical based on a true story 2014 · UK · Colour · 91min

As a theatre piece, *London Road* was extraordinary enough, a "verbatim" musical based on the exact words of Ipswich locals from interviews conducted in the run-up to the conviction of serial killer Steve Wright in 2008. Rufus Norris's equally unique film is about the effect his crimes had on a normal suburban street. Trading up from the stage version, the movie benefits from well-known names like Olivia Colman, as the woman who unites the local residents, and Tom Hardy as a paranoid taxi driver. Not all the songs work, but when they do they chill the spine. DW Swearing, sex scenes. *DVD*

Olivia Colman *Julie* • Paul Thornley *Dodge* • Nick Holder *Ron* • Tom Hardy *Mark the taxi driver* • Anita Dobson *June* • Kate Fleetwood *Vicky* • Calvin Demba *Alec* • Gillian Bevan *Colette McBeth* ■ *Dir* Rufus Norris • *Scr* Alecky Blythe, from the musical by Blythe (story), Adam Cork (music & lyrics)

London to Brighton ★★★★18
Crime drama 2006 · UK · Colour · 82min

Powerful, harrowing and gripping, Paul Andrew Williams's feature debut is a brutally raw thriller. Reminiscent of Mike Leigh's *Naked* in its intensity and grimness, this assured crime drama finds prostitute Lorraine Stanley ordered by her pimp (Johnny Harris) to procure underage, homeless and desperate Georgia Groome for a millionaire gangster. What follows is a suspenseful build to a surprise twist, shot through with the seediest of atmospheres. The performances are frighteningly realistic, but it's the core relationship between Stanley and Groome, as they flee for their lives (making the journey of the title), that anchors the debased humanity with emotional heart. AJ Violence, swearing. *DVD*

Lorraine Stanley *Kelly* • Georgia Groome *Joanne* • Johnny Harris *Derek* • Sam Spruell *Stuart Allen* • Alexander Morton *Duncan Allen* • Nathan Constance *Chum* ■ *Dir/Scr* Paul Andrew Williams

London Town ★U
Musical comedy 1946 · UK · Colour · 127min

A comedian from the provinces arrives in London for his big break, only to find he has been hired as the understudy. Thanks to the devious machinations of his daughter, he goes on as the main comic attraction. A huge budget was lavished on this film, with American director Wesley Ruggles imported for the occasion. Unfortunately, it turned out a major disaster. The plot is unappealing, the script weak, the pace laboured and the film too long. RK

Sid Field *Jerry* • Greta Gynt *Mrs Barry* • Petula Clark *Peggy* • Sonnie Hale *Charlie* • Kay Kendall *Patsy* • Jerry Desmonde *George* ■ *Dir* Wesley Ruggles • *Scr* Elliot Paul, Val Guest, Siegfried Herzig, from a story by Wesley Ruggles

The Lone Hand ★★U
Western 1953 · US · Colour · 79min

This routine western from Universal has Joel McCrea posing as an outlaw to bring a criminal gang to justice. McCrea's stolid sturdiness nearly sinks the film; you keep wanting him to show more emotion, but, after all, he is in disguise, even from his own son. George Sherman's direction is undistinguished, but two subsequent TV stars make a creditable showing Barbara Hale from *Perry Mason* and *Gunsmoke*'s James Arness. TS

Joel McCrea *Zachary Hallock* • Barbara Hale *Sarah Jane Skaggs* • Alex Nicol *Jonah Varden* • Charles Drake *George Hadley* • Jimmy Hunt *Joshua Hallock* • Jim Arness [James Arness] *Gus Varden* • Roy Roberts *Mr Skaggs* ■ *Dir* George Sherman • *Scr* Joseph Hoffman, from a story by Irving Ravetch

The Lone Ranger ★★U
Western 1956 · US · Colour · 86min

Clayton Moore and Jay Silverheels filled a break from their long-running black-and-white TV series by starring in this deluxe Warner Bros western, still playing their usual characters of the masked avenger and his Indian sidekick, Tonto. The hills of Utah echo to the cry of "Hi-ho, Silver!" as the duo carry out more brave exploits, exposing rancher Lyle Bettger as the man stirring up the Indians to break their treaty so that he can mine the silver in their sacred mountain. AE *DVD*

Clayton Moore *Lone Ranger* • Jay Silverheels *Tonto* • Lyle Bettger *Reece Kilgore* • Bonita Granville *Welcome* • Perry Lopez *Ramirez* • Robert J Wilke *Cassidy* • John Pickard *Sheriff Kimberly* • Beverly Washburn *Lila* • Michael Ansara *Angry Horse* ■ *Dir* Stuart Heisler • *Scr* Herb Meadow, from characters by Fran Striker, George W Trendle

The Lone Ranger ★★★★12
Western action adventure 2013 · US · Colour · 143min

How did an idealistic Texas Ranger become the legendary masked man of mystery? His surviving partner Tonto relates their unusual meeting and past adventures - mainly ruining corrupt railway pioneer Tom Wilkinson's plans for invading Comanche territory - to a wide-eyed kid in a Wild West sideshow. Director Gore Verbinski whips up the same kind of engaging myth-making he created with the *Pirates of the Caribbean* franchise, with Johnny Depp making a wonderfully quirky native American and Armie Hammer perfect as his clean-cut cowboy foil. Once the iconic Rossini theme tune starts, the brilliantly staged runaway train action begins and the result is absolutely thrilling, top-flight epic escapism. AJ Some violence. *DVD* *3D*

Johnny Depp *Tonto* • Armie Hammer *John Reid/The Lone Ranger* • James Badge Dale *Dan Reid* • Tom Wilkinson *Latham Cole* ■ *Dir* Gore Verbinski • *Scr* Ted Elliott, Justin Haythe, Terry Rossio, from characters by Fran Striker, George W Trendle • *Music* Jack White

Lone Rider ★★
Western 2008 · US · Colour · 80min

Lou Diamond Phillips adds another forgettable TV movie to his deteriorating CV with this uninspired western. He plays a retired cavalry man who returns home to face a new war when he learns an old friend (Vincent Spano) has taken over the town and now has designs on his family's ranch. Phillips barely twitches his acting muscles, assuming town defender mode on autopilot and leaving it to Spano to chew the admittedly handsome scenery. SF

Lou Diamond Phillips *Bobby Hattaway* • Angela Alvarado *Serena Sanchez* • Timothy Bottoms *Gus* • Stacy Keach *Robert Hattaway* • Vincent Spano *Stu Croker* ■ *Dir* David S Cass Sr • *Scr* Frank Sharp

The Lone Rider in Ghost Town ★★U
Western 1941 · US · BW · 55min

Deemed the best of the 1941 *Lone Riders*, this was released first to whet the public appetite for a new cowboy hero. In 1944, however, star George Houston died of a heart attack in his mid-40s. The majority of the nine-strong series was directed by the prolific Sam Newfield, and produced by his brother Sigmund Neufeld, chief of production at PRC. The series waned rapidly in popularity, and the last few were released without the words "Lone Rider" in the actual titles. TS

George Houston *Tom Cameron* • Al St John *Fuzzy* • Alaine Brandes *Helen* • Budd Buster *Moosehide* • Frank Hagney *O'Shead* • Alden Chase *Sinclair* • Reed Howes *Gordon* • Charles King (2) *Roberts* • George Chesebro *Jed* • Edward Peil Sr *Clark* ■ *Dir* Sam Newfield • *Scr* Joe O'Donnell

Lone Star ★★U
Western 1952 · US · BW · 94min

This is a heavy-going saga of Texas in 1845 when the big question was whether it should become part of the United States or remain a republic. Clark Gable is the rancher favouring statehood, dispatched by Andrew Jackson (Lionel Barrymore) to scupper any possible deal with the Mexicans. His main adversary is Broderick Crawford, a staunch republican senator, while Ava Gardner is the newspaperwoman caught in the middle. Verbose. AE

Clark Gable *Devereaux Burke* • Ava Gardner *Martha Ronda* • Broderick Crawford *Thomas Craden* • Lionel Barrymore *Andrew Jackson* • Beulah Bondi *Minniver Bryan* • Ed Begley *Sen Anthony Demmett* • William Farnum *Sen Tom Crockett* • Lowell Gilmore *Capt Elliott* ■ *Dir* Vincent Sherman • *Scr* Borden Chase, from a stories by Howard Estabrook, Borden Chase

Lone Star ★★★★★15
Murder mystery drama 1995 · US · Colour · 129min

An engrossing storyline and a superb ensemble cast make this deeply textured account of the burden of history people carry with them a graceful slow-burner. Sheriff Chris Cooper discovers a skeleton buried in the desert outskirts of his Mexican border town and launches a murder investigation. So begins a multi-generation mosaic of family ties, local legend, interracial romance and political tinkering as he discovers the murky past of his own late father (Matthew McConaughey), also a cop. Confident direction combines with intelligent drama to craft a breathtaking and bittersweet delicacy. AJ Some violence. *DVD*

Chris Cooper *Sam Deeds* • Kris Kristofferson *Charlie Wade* • Matthew McConaughey *Buddy Deeds* • Elizabeth Peña *Pilar* • Clifton James *Hollis* • Miriam Colon *Mercedes Cruz* • Stephen Mendillo *Otis* • Frances McDormand *Bunny* • Ron Canada *Otis* • Joe Morton *Del* ■ *Dir/Scr* John Sayles

Lone Star State of Mind ★★12
Crime comedy 2002 · US · Colour · 84min

This mediocre chase comedy has plenty of plot, but far too few laughs. Joshua

Jackson works hard as the Texan asked by his stepsister-cum-fiancée to keep her cousin out of trouble while she's away. However, he struggles to convey the desperation of a man losing every semblance of control, as the cousin (DJ Qualls) and his dumb buddy (Ryan Hurst) fall foul of irate drug pushers. DP Swearing, violence. *DVD*

Jaime King *Baby* • Joshua Jackson *Earl Crest* • Matthew Davis *Jimbo* • Ryan Hurst *Tinker* • John Mellencamp *Wayne* • DJ Qualls *Junior* • Sam McMurray *Mr Smith* • Thomas Haden Church *Killer* ■ *Dir* David Semel • *Scr* Trevor Munson

Lone Survivor ★★★15
Action thriller based on a true story 2013 · US · Colour · 116min

Beautifully made but brutal and as gung ho as they come, Peter Berg's action movie is pure Viagra for anyone turned on by military hardware, soldier speak and noisy combat. Based on a true story, the film stars Mark Wahlberg, Emile Hirsch and Taylor Kitsch (a refugee from Berg's equally jingoistic *Battleship*) as members of a small Navy SEAL hit squad who are dropped deep behind enemy lines in Afghanistan to find and kill a top Taliban warlord. It's unrelenting stuff and rarely a pleasant watch, but those with a stomach for this kind of thing will find it hard to take their eyes off it. DA English, Pashto, Dari +subtitles. Violence, swearing, sexual references. *DVD* *BD*

Mark Wahlberg *Marcus Luttrell* • Taylor Kitsch *Michael Murphy* • Emile Hirsch *Danny Dietz* • Eric Bana *Erik Kristensen* • Ben Foster *Matt "Axe" Axelson* ■ *Dir* Peter Berg • *Scr* Peter Berg, from the non-fiction book by Marcus Luttrell, Patrick Robinson

Lone Wolf McQuade ★★★18
Action adventure 1983 · US · Colour · 102min

Probably the best movie action-man hero Chuck Norris has ever made. He's a Texas Ranger battling evil gunrunner David Carradine in this modern western, which is styled after the work of Italian maestro Sergio Leone. Barbara Carrera provides the love interest in a sticky subplot, but the thrust of director Steve Carver (another Roger Corman protégé) always remains geared towards the super-macho elements - strong, silent heroes and villains, loads of weaponry and self-styled enigmatic warriors playing rough. AJ Swearing, violence, brief nudity.

Chuck Norris *JJ McQuade* • David Carradine *Rawley Wilkes* • Barbara Carrera *Lola Richardson* • Leon Isaac Kennedy *Jackson* • Robert Beltran *Kayo* • LQ Jones *Dakota* ■ *Dir* Steve Carver • *Scr* BJ Nelson, from the story by H Kaye Dyal, BJ Nelson

The Lone Wolf Returns ★★★
Mystery adventure 1936 · US · BW · 64min

Although Warren William is most closely associated with the Lone Wolf role, it was Melvyn Douglas who played him in Columbia's first adventure featuring Louis Joseph Vance's troubleshooting sleuth. Directed by Roy William Neill (who would later handle Universal's Sherlock Holmes series), this is a rattling comedy thriller, in which Douglas's jewel thief is lured out of retirement by Gail Patrick's necklace. William took over for the third instalment from a final total of 15. DP

Melvyn Douglas *Michael Lanyard/"The Lone Wolf"/Col Thompson* • Gail Patrick *Marcia Stewart* • Tala Birell *Liane Mallison* • Henry Mollison *Mallison* • Thurston Hall *Crane* • Raymond Walburn *Jenkins* • Douglass Dumbrille *Morphew* ■ *Dir* Roy William Neill • *Scr* Joseph Krumgold, Bruce Manning, Lionel Houser, from the novel by Louis Joseph Vance

The Lone Wolf Spy Hunt ★★★
Mystery adventure 1939 · US · BW · 67min

Smoothly accomplished Warren William, out of the same mould as William Powell and Melvyn Douglas, plays Michael Lanyard, alias the Lone Wolf, a gentleman jewel thief turned sleuth, in this agreeably old-fashioned comedy-thriller which finds Lanyard tangling with a ruthless international spy ring. Columbia's modestly entertaining 19-picture Lone Wolf series, based on thriller-writer Louis Joseph Vance's creation, survived from 1926 to 1949, with a five-year gap. Bert Lytell played Lanyard from 1926 to 1930; Melvyn Douglas starred in *The Lone Wolf Returns* in 1936, followed by Francis Lederer in 1938 before William took over for nine in a row. After his departure, the formula ran out of steam and after three with the lacklustre Gerald Mohr the films ended with Ron Randell in *The Lone Wolf and His Lady*. RK

Warren William *Michael Lanyard, "The Lone Wolf"* • Ida Lupino *Val Carson* • Rita Hayworth *Karen* • Virginia Weidler *Patricia Lanyard* • Ralph Morgan *Spiro Gregory* • Tom Dugan (1) *Sgt Devan* ■ *Dir* Peter Godfrey • *Scr* Jonathan Latimer, from the novel *The Lone Wolf's Daughter* by Louis Joseph Vance

The Loneliness of the Long Distance Runner ★★★★★ 12
Drama   1962 · UK · BW · 99min

Having already scored successes with *Look Back in Anger* and *A Taste of Honey*, director Tony Richardson completed his outstanding "kitchen sink" collection with this stirring tale of the borstal boy who dares to buck the system just as it offers him a lifeline. Tom Courtenay delivers a remarkable debut performance as the embittered delinquent whose talent for running gives governor Michael Redgrave the means to raise the profile of his institution. Masterfully adapted by Alan Sillitoe and unobtrusively shot by Walter Lassally, this is as powerful and relevant today as it ever was. DP *DVD* *Blu-ray*

Tom Courtenay *Colin Smith* • Michael Redgrave *Governor* • Avis Bunnage *Mrs Smith* • Peter Madden *Mr Smith* • James Bolam *Mike* • Julia Foster *Gladys* • Topsy Jane *Audrey* ■ *Dir* Tony Richardson • *Scr* Alan Sillitoe, from his novel

Lonely Are the Brave ★★★★ PG
Western   1962 · US · BW · 102min

This moving story about a contemporary cowboy is Kirk Douglas's own favourite among his films. It highlights the dignity of the individual as Douglas's law-breaking loner is pursued across the mountains by sheriff Walter Matthau. Matthau's posse uses helicopters and mountain jeeps, making the power and speed of Douglas on his horse tragically irrelevant. The symbolism in former blacklisted writer Dalton Trumbo's script becomes a little too obvious, especially at the end, but the location photography (by Philip Lathrop) is stunning and the cast is superb. TS *DVD*

Kirk Douglas *Jack Burns* • Gena Rowlands *Jerri Bondi* • Walter Matthau *Sheriff Johnson* • Michael Kane *Paul Bondi* • Carroll O'Connor *Hinton* • William Schallert *Harry* • Karl Swenson *Reverend Hoskins* • George Kennedy *Guitierrez* ■ *Dir* David Miller (1) • *Scr* Dalton Trumbo, from the novel *Brave Cowboy* by Edward Abbey

The Lonely Guy ★★ 15
Comedy   1984 · US · Colour · 86min

After he finds his girlfriend in bed with another man, Steve Martin is escorted through the rather sad world of the "lonely guy" by a sympathetic Charles Grodin. It's slickly directed by Arthur Hiller and there are some genuinely funny passages. However, Martin is strangely subdued and the film is stolen from under his nose by the ever-excellent Grodin. JF Swearing, brief nudity. *DVD*

Steve Martin *Larry Hubbard* • Charles Grodin *Warren Evans* • Judith Ivey *Iris* • Steve Lawrence *Jack Fenwick* • Robyn Douglass *Danielle* • Merv Griffin *Dr Joyce Brothers* ■ *Dir* Arthur Hiller • *Scr* Ed Weinberger, Stan Daniels, from the novel *The Lonely Guy's Book of Life* by Bruce Jay Friedman, adapted by Neil Simon

Lonely Hearts ★★★★ 15
Romantic comedy   1981 · Aus · Colour · 91min

Paul Cox delivers another of his idiosyncratic insights into the soul of the misfit in this charming tale of late-life love.

Norman Kaye, harbouring fantasies that are both innocent and desperate, expertly assumes the mantle of the timid everyman, as he begins to live after years of tending to his mother. His impersonation of a blind piano teacher and his encounter with a smarmy toupee salesman are just dotty enough to come off. But it's his hesitant relationship with Wendy Hughes, who has waited until her 30s to rebel against her parents, that gives the film its heart. DP

Wendy Hughes *Patricia Curnov* • Norman Kaye *Peter Thompson* • Jon Finlayson *George* • Julia Blake *Pamela* • Jonathan Hardy *Bruce* ■ *Dir/Scr* Paul Cox

Lonely Hearts ★★ 15
Crime thriller   2006 · Ger/US · Colour · 103min

As with *The Black Dahlia*, this starry thriller is based on a crime case that shocked the US in the 1940s. But, disappointingly, this is all about surface authenticity – cool suits, hip jazz soundtrack, hard-boiled narration – rather than true *noir*. John Travolta plays a widowed homicide detective who, together with loyal partner James Gandolfini, is on the trail of a pair of murderous con artists. Jared Leto and Salma Hayek play the predatory pair who contact their victims via the lonely hearts columns. Writer/director Todd Robinson nails the period details perfectly, but the characters themselves never really ring true. JF *DVD*

John Travolta *Elmer C Robinson* • James Gandolfini *Charles Hildebrandt* • Salma Hayek *Martha Beck* • Jared Leto *Raymond Fernandez* • Laura Dern *Rene* • Scott Caan *Detective Reilly* • Alice Krige *Janet Long* ■ *Dir/Scr* Todd Robinson • *Cinematographer* Peter Levy

The Lonely Lady ★ 18
Drama   1983 · US · Colour · 87min

The fact that it's based on a novel by Harold Robbins should offer a big clue as to the quality of the material. The link between career success and sexual promiscuity is explored in the antics of aspiring screenwriter Pia Zadora, who's rescued from rapist Ray Liotta by successful writer Lloyd Bochner. Badly scripted, shot and acted, with turgid and offensive sex scenes, this is possibly one of the worst films of all time. LH

Pia Zadora *Jerilee Randall* • Lloyd Bochner *Walter Thornton* • Bibi Besch *Veronica Randall* • Joseph Cali *Vincent Dacosta* • Anthony Holland *Guy Jackson* • Jared Martin *George Ballantine* • Ray Liotta *Joe Heron* ■ *Dir* Peter Sasdy • *Scr* John Kershaw, Shawn Randall, from the novel by Harold Robbins, adapted by Ellen Shepard

The Lonely Man ★★★
Western   1957 · US · BW · 87min

Jack Palance and Anthony Perkins, as estranged father and son, try to out-smoulder each other in this taut, offbeat, psychological western. Perkins, who blames his long-absent father for the death of his mother, reluctantly links up with ex-bandit Palance. It turns out that Perkins isn't the only one who has a few old scores to settle with him. RB

Jack Palance *Jacob Wade* • Anthony Perkins *Riley Wade* • Neville Brand *King Fisher* • Robert Middleton *Ben Ryerson* • Elaine Aiken *Ada Marshall* • Elisha Cook Jr *Willie* • Claude Akins *Blackburn* • Lee Van Cleef *Faro* • Denver Pyle *Sheriff* ■ *Dir* Henry Levin • *Scr* Harry Essex, Robert Smith

The Lonely Passion of Judith Hearne ★★★ 15
Drama   1987 · UK · Colour · 111min

Nobody does it better than Maggie Smith when it comes to forlorn, middle-aged Irish spinsters trying to look on the bright side, but finding the silver gleam tarnished by experience. Director Jack Clayton counterbalances booze and religion as the most powerful passions in Judith Hearne's life, so that Bob Hoskins's flirtatious entrepreneur never really stands a chance. Too sombre for what little it has to say, but the performances manage to redeem it. TH Swearing, nudity.

Maggie Smith *Judith Hearne* • Bob Hoskins *James Madden* • Wendy Hiller *Aunt D'Arcy* • Marie Kean *Mrs Rice* • Ian McNeice *Bernard* • Alan Devlin *Father Quigley* • Rudi Davies *Mary* • Prunella Scales *Moira O'Neill* ■ *Dir* Jack Clayton • *Scr* Peter Nelson, from the novel by Brian Moore

A Lonely Place to Die ★★★ 15
Action horror thriller   2011 · UK · Colour · 95min

The Scottish Highlands make a breathtaking backdrop for horror here, as climber Melissa George and her friends discover a Serbian schoolgirl (Holly Boyd) in a forest pit and have to contend with murderous kidnappers Sean Harris and Stephen McCole, along with the hostile terrain. But the arrival of the girl's warlord father to handle negotiations and unleash a couple of mercenaries sparks a less inventive scramble for sanctuary. Alongside some solid performances, the mix of aerial swoops and handheld close-ups give this wilderness thriller a brisk energy. DP Violence, swearing. *DVD* *Blu-ray*

Melissa George *Alison* • Ed Speleers *Ed* • Eamonn Walker *Andy* • Karel Roden *Darko* • Sean Harris *Mr Kidd* • Kate Magowan *Jenny* ■ *Dir* Julian Gilbey • *Scr* Julian Gilbey, Will Gilbey

Lonely Woman Seeks Lifetime Companion ★★★
Romantic drama   1987 · USSR · Colour · 91min

This touching Moscow-set drama would have been unthinkable in the pre-*glasnost* era, but such *bytove* or "everyday" pictures became something of a staple of Soviet cinema in the late 1980s. Desperate to escape from her midlife cul-de-sac, Irina Kupchenko sticks lonely hearts advertisements to lampposts in the hope of finding Mr Right. Homeless, alcoholic ex-acrobat Aleksandr Zbruyev is hardly what she has in mind, but love comes in all guises. Shooting in a fly-on-the-wall style, director Vyacheslav Krishtofovich is rewarded with touching and believable performances. DP Russian +subtitles.

Irina Kupchenko *Kladvia* • Aleksandr Zbruev *Valentin* ■ *Dir* Vyacheslav Krishtofovich • *Scr* Viktor Merezhko

Lonelyhearts ★★
Drama   1958 · US · BW · 103min

Fans of Nathanael West's famous 1933 novella *Miss Lonelyhearts*, which deals in the despair of a male agony aunt columnist, will despair at this attempt to broaden and contemporise the story with earnest moral and political platitudes. That said, there are convincing performances from Montgomery Clift, sensitive in the title role, Robert Ryan as his hard-bitten editor, and Broadway actress Maureen Stapleton, making her screen debut (and earning an Oscar nomination) as the sexually frustrated wife of a crippled husband. RK

Montgomery Clift *Adam White* • Robert Ryan *William Shrike* • Myrna Loy *Florence Shrike* • Dolores Hart *Justy Sargent* • Maureen Stapleton *Fay Doyle* • Frank Maxwell *Pat Doyle* • Jackie Coogan *Gates* ■ *Dir* Vincent J Donehue • *Scr* Dore Schary, from the novella *Miss Lonelyhearts* by Nathanael West

Lonesome Cowboys ★★★ 18
Experimental western   1968 · US · Colour · 104min

One of the last films to feature artist Andy Warhol as director, this gay cowboy fantasy does raise the fundamental question conventional westerns have failed to address. If cowboys live, ride and die together, surely they must have sex with each other, too? The plot is a thin excuse to indulge in camp and erotic posing as Viva and Taylor Mead, both desperate for male company, pounce on Louis Waldon's homosexual gang when they ride into their desert town. By turn boring, bizarre and hilarious, this amateur Factory film captures the decadence and ennui of 1960s counterculture. AJ

Viva *Ramona Alvarez* • Tom Hompertz *Drifter* • Louis Waldon *Mickey, the eldest brother* • Eric Emerson *Eric* • Taylor Mead *Nurse* • Joe

Dallesandro *Little Joe* • Francis Francine *Sheriff* • Julian Burroughs *Julian, the brother* ■ *Dir/Scr* Andy Warhol

Lonesome Jim ★★★ 15
Romantic comedy drama   2005 · US · Colour · 87min

As admirers of Steve Buscemi's 1996 directorial debut, *Trees Lounge*, will know, his comedy is dry and his idea of romance can be a little gloomy. In this HD-shot romantic comedy, Buscemi casts Casey Affleck as the title character, an Indiana native who has failed in his bid to become a hip writer in New York and returned to the suffocating embrace of his family. Thankfully, his pasty-faced pout turns into a smile when he meets nurse Anika (Liv Tyler). At this point, the film doesn't take off, exactly, but it does throw down an honest emotional anchor that keeps the interest rooted as their tentative relationship develops. DW *DVD*

Casey Affleck *Jim* • Liv Tyler *Anika* • Mary Kay Place *Sally* • Seymour Cassel *Don* • Kevin Corrigan *Tim* • Jack Rovello *Ben* • Mark Boone Junior *Evil* • Rachel Strouse *Rachel* • Sarah Strouse *Sarah* ■ *Dir* Steve Buscemi • *Scr* James C Strouse

The Long Absence ★★★★ U
Drama   1961 · Fr/It · BW · 96min

The fact that it shared the Palme d'Or at Cannes with Luis Buñuel's *Viridiana*, at the height of New Wave euphoria, itself suggests the quality of this study of isolation and enduring love. Retaining the subtle melancholy of Marguerite Duras's orginal story, director Henri Colpi refuses to hurry the relationship between Alida Valli and Georges Wilson as the Parisian café owner and the amnesiac vagabond she believes to be the husband she lost in Germany during the war. Consequently, her hope and his confusion are conveyed with a painful delicacy. DP French +subtitles.

Alida Valli *Thérèse Langlois* • Georges Wilson *Tramp* • Jacques Harden *Truckdriver* • Diana Lepvrier *Martine* • Catherine Fontenay *Alice* ■ *Dir* Henri Colpi • *Scr* Marguerite Duras, Gérard Jarlot, from a story by Marguerite Duras

The Long and the Short and the Tall ★★★ PG
Second World War drama   1960 · UK · BW · 101min

Time hasn't been kind to this studio-bound version of a Royal Court Second World War play. The film, about a patrol deep in the Burmese jungle that takes a Japanese soldier prisoner, was shatteringly powerful in its day but seems rather weak now. There's a lack of realistic dialogue, phoney Elstree jungle sets and the uncomfortable star performance from Richard Todd, attempting a laboured regional accent. TS *DVD*

Richard Todd *Sergeant Mitchem* • Laurence Harvey *Private Bamforth* • Richard Harris *Corporal Johnstone* • Ronald Fraser *Lance-Corporal MacLeish* • John Meillon *Private Smith* • David McCallum (1) *Private Whitaker* • John Rees *Private Evans* • Kenji Takaki *Tojo* ■ *Dir* Leslie Norman • *Scr* Wolf Mankowitz, Willis Hall, from the play by Willis Hall

The Long Arm ★★★ U
Police drama   1956 · UK · BW · 92min

This rather glum insight into the policeman's lot was the final film made at Ealing Studios. Jack Hawkins wears a suitably hangdog expression as the detective faced with a series of robberies and a rocky marriage to neglected Dorothy Alison. Far from adding to the realism of the tale, the domestic crisis is a crashing bore and it's with evident relief that director Charles Frend abandons Bromley to head back to the side streets of Covent Garden and, finally, to the Festival Hall to provide an exciting conclusion to the case. DP *DVD*

Jack Hawkins *Detective Superintendent Tom Halliday* • Dorothy Alison *Mary Halliday* • Michael Brooke Jr *Tony Halliday* • John Stratton *Sergeant Ward* • Geoffrey Keen *Superintendent Malcolm* • Newton Blick *Commander Harris* • Ralph Truman *Colonel Blenkinsop* • Joss Ambler

Cashier • Ian Bannen *Workman* • Nicholas Parsons *Police Constable Bates* • Alec McCowen *Surgeon* ■ *Dir* Charles Frend • *Scr* Janet Green, Robert Barr, Dorothy Christie, Campbell Christie, from a story by Robert Barr

The Long Dark Hall ★
Crime thriller   1951 • UK • BW • 86min

Off-screen spouses (at the time) Rex Harrison and Lilli Palmer star in this risible courtroom drama in which Harrison stands trial for murder, while the real killer canoodles with his wilting wife. Co-director Anthony Bushell also plays Harrison's defence lawyer, but there are no sparks in his clashes with prosecutor Denis O'Dea. About as tense as snapped elastic. DP

Rex Harrison *Arthur Groome* • Lilli Palmer *Mary Groome* • Raymond Huntley *Chief Inspector Sullivan* • Anthony Dawson *The Man* • Denis O'Dea *Sir Charles Morton* • Anthony Bushell *Clive Bedford* ■ *Dir* Anthony Bushell, Reginald Beck • *Scr* Nunnally Johnson, WEC Fairchild [William Fairchild], from Edgar Lustgarten's novel *A Case to Answer*

The Long Day Closes ★★★★★ PG
Biographical drama   1992 • UK • Colour • 81min

Anyone who has ever been lost in wonder at the magic of the movies will find that this enchanting feature strikes repeated chords. In the second of his films set in the Liverpool of his childhood, Terence Davies fondly recalls those marvellous moments at the local fleapit when the drabness of everyday life receded the instant the opening credits appeared on screen. Leigh McCormack is absolutely superb as the 11-year-old whose life revolves around film and family, and his performance lends dramatic unity to this kaleidoscopic autobiography. Unmissable. DP *DVD*

Marjorie Yates *Mother* • Leigh McCormack *Bud* • Anthony Watson *Kevin* • Nicholas Lamont *John* • Ayse Owens *Helen* • Tina Malone *Edna* • Jimmy Wilde *Curly* ■ *Dir/Scr* Terence Davies

Long Day's Journey into Night ★★★ PG
Drama   1962 • US • BW • 161min

Set in 1912, Eugene O'Neill's epic play about a self-destructive Connecticut family is a challenge for any actor and, indeed, audience. Katharine Hepburn picked up an inevitable Oscar nomination as the morphine-addicted mother of alcoholic Jason Robards and tubercular Dean Stockwell, but the star turn here is Ralph Richardson as the head of the ill-fated clan. AT *DVD*

Katharine Hepburn *Mary Tyrone* • Ralph Richardson *James Tyrone Sr* • Jason Robards Jr [Jason Robards] *James Tyrone Jr* • Dean Stockwell *Edmund Tyrone* • Jeanne Barr *Cathleen* ■ *Dir* Sidney Lumet • *Scr* from the play by Eugene O'Neill

The Long Duel ★★ U
Period adventure   1967 • UK • Colour • 115min

It's big, it's British and it's trying very hard to be spectacular. Director Ken Annakin makes the 1920s Indian setting look authentic and keeps the conflict bubbling, but Yul Brynner's rebel tribal leader is prone to ranting and speechifying, police officer Trevor Howard conveys the feeling that he'd rather be in Tunbridge Wells, and the true-life story of obsessed antagonism rings false thanks to stilted dialogue and clichéd situations. TS

Yul Brynner *Sultan* • Trevor Howard *Freddy Young* • Harry Andrews *Stafford* • Andrew Keir *Gungaram* • Charlotte Rampling *Jane Stafford* • Virginia North *Champa* • Laurence Naismith *McDougal* • Maurice Denham *Governor* • Imogen Hassall *Tara* ■ *Dir* Ken Annakin • *Scr* Ernest Bornemann, Geoffrey Orme, Peter Yeldham, from a story by Ranveer Singh

The Long Good Friday ★★★★ 18
Crime drama   1979 • UK • Colour • 109min

Bob Hoskins got his big break playing the East End gangster who realises his gang is being ruthlessly picked off by an unknown rival. Owing something to American thrillers of the 1940s, and rather more to *Get Carter* and TV crime shows, John Mackenzie's film remains both an explosively violent thriller and a sharp evocation of the enterprise culture of the time (Hoskins's dream is to build a new city in London's Docklands with Mafia money). Helen Mirren offers seductive support, while Pierce Brosnan appears as an anonymous IRA hitman. AT Violence, swearing, nudity. *DVD* *BD*

Bob Hoskins *Harold Shand* • Helen Mirren *Victoria* • Eddie Constantine *Charlie* • Dave King *Parky* • Bryan Marshall *Harris* • George Coulouris *Gus* • Derek Thompson *Jeff* • Pierce Brosnan *First Irishman* ■ *Dir* John Mackenzie (1) • *Scr* Barrie Keefe

The Long Goodbye ★★★★★★ 18
Detective drama   1973 • US • Colour • 111min

This semi-spoof update of Raymond Chandler's novel from director Robert Altman ranks as one of the most intelligent adaptations of the celebrated thriller writer's work since *The Big Sleep* in 1946. Elliott Gould may seem an odd choice to play the world-weary Philip Marlowe, but his laid-back take on the legendary gumshoe is a masterstroke. By brilliantly deconstructing the standard private eye thriller with irony and affection, Altman comments on the changes in American society and the American Dream to starkly satirical effect. One of the finest films of the 1970s. AJ Violence, swearing, nudity. *DVD* *BD*

Elliott Gould *Philip Marlowe* • Nina Van Pallandt *Eileen Wade* • Sterling Hayden *Roger Wade* • Mark Rydell *Marty Augustine* • Henry Gibson *Dr Verringer* • David Arkin *Harry* • Jim Bouton *Terry Lennox* • Jack Knight *Mabel* ■ *Dir* Robert Altman • *Scr* Leigh Brackett, from the novel by Raymond Chandler

The Long Gray Line ★★★ U
Biographical comedy drama   1955 • US • Colour • 131min

One of director John Ford's most sentimental movies, this will only excite those who believe West Point Military Academy is an institution to be valued for its righteous place in the American way of life. A uniformed *Goodbye, Mr Chips*, it stars Tyrone Power, who arrives at the academy as a menial worker, becomes a cadet-instructor, marries Maureen O'Hara, and stays on teaching boys to be men, until time immemorial and a Ford-blessed sunset. Beautifully crafted, but appallingly banal. TH

Tyrone Power *Marty Maher* • Maureen O'Hara *Mary O'Donnell* • Robert Francis *James Sundstrom Jr* • Donald Crisp *Old Martin* • Ward Bond *Capt Herman J Koehler* • Betsy Palmer *Kitty Carter* • Phil Carey [Philip Carey] *Charles Dotson* • William Leslie *Red Sundstrom* • Harry Carey Jr *Dwight Eisenhower* • Patrick Wayne *Cherub Overton* ■ *Dir* John Ford • *Scr* Edward Hope, from the nove *Bringing up the Brass* by Marty Maher, Nardi Reeder Campion

The Long, Hot Summer ★★★★ PG
Drama   1958 • US • Colour • 111min

Two short stories and a novel by William Faulkner were glued together to form the script of this torrid Deep South melodrama with a simply marvellous cast. Paul Newman is the drifter and redneck who catches the eye of Lee Remick and wins the favour of her father-in-law, local tyrant Orson Welles, who tries to pair him off with daughter Joanne Woodward. Ludicrously overheated but magnificent with it, this was the first of several pictures Newman made with Woodward: the couple married after filming was completed. AT *DVD*

Paul Newman *Ben Quick* • Joanne Woodward *Clara Varner* • Orson Welles *Will Varner* • Anthony Franciosa *Jody Varner* • Lee Remick *Eula* • Richard Anderson *Alan Stewart* ■ *Dir* Martin Ritt • *Scr* Irving Ravetch, Harriet Frank Jr, from the stories *Barn Burning*, *The Spotted Horse*, and the novel *The Hamlet* by William Faulkner

The Long Island Incident ★★
Drama based on a true story   1998 • US • Colour • 120min

In 1993, a gunman's rampage on a crowded commuter train prompted one of the dead victim's wives to start a campaign for firearms control. This well-meaning TV drama re-enacts the true story, with Laurie Metcalf giving a gutsy performance as the ordinary suburban housewife transformed into a political crusader by tragedy. However, director Joseph Sargent tries too hard to cram everything into a film that should have packed a more provocative punch. SF Some violence.

Laurie Metcalf *Carolyn McCarthy* • MacKenzie Astin *Kevin McCarthy* • Tyrone Benskin *Colin Ferguson* • Cedric Smith *Tim Bobek* ■ *Dir* Joseph Sargent • *Scr* Maria Nation

Long John Silver ★★ U
Swashbuckling adventure   1954 • Aus • Colour • 105min

Fresh from hijacking Disney's *Treasure Island*, Robert Newton reprised the role of the infamous peg-legged pirate in this mediocre adventure that owes little to the genius of Robert Louis Stevenson. Martin Rackin's screenplay is a patchwork of episodes discarded from the original adaptation, making the action seem both confused and incidental. But the real problem is Newton, whose affinity for the bottle clearly clouded his judgement of tone, as he overplays every scene. DP

Robert Newton *Long John Silver* • Kit Taylor *Jim Hawkins* • Connie Gilchrist *Purity Pinker* • Lloyd Berrell *Captain Mendoza, "El Toro"* • Eric Reiman *Trip Fenner* • Syd Chambers *Ned Shill* ■ *Dir* Byron Haskin • *Scr* Martin Rackin, from characters by Robert Louis Stevenson

The Long Kiss Goodnight ★★★★ 18
Action thriller   1996 • US • Colour • 115min

This vehicle for Geena Davis is a loud, sassy and hugely entertaining action blockbuster. Directed by then-husband Renny Harlin, it's wonderfully over the top in virtually every respect, from *Lethal Weapon* scriptwriter Shane Black's barmy story and even crazier characters to the nonstop, reality defying action set pieces. Davis stars as a small-town housewife suffering from amnesia who discovers that she was once a ruthless assassin working for a shadowy government agency. JF Swearing, violence. *DVD* *BD*

Geena Davis *Samantha Caine/Charly Baltimore* • Samuel L Jackson *Mitch Hennessey* • Craig Bierko *Timothy* • Yvonne Zima *Caitlin* • Brian Cox (1) *Nathan* • Patrick Malahide *Perkins* • Tom Amandes *Hal* • David Morse *Luke/Daedalus* ■ *Dir* Renny Harlin • *Scr* Shane Black

Long Live the Lady! ★★★★ 15
Comedy   1987 • It • Colour • 106min

Six young graduates of a catering school are engaged to wait at table at a grand banquet being given in a medieval castle by a mysterious old lady. Like the bespectacled pimpled youth, through whose eyes we see the feast, the director Ermanno Olmi minutely observes, by turns fascinated and repulsed, the rituals of a strictly hierarchical, decaying society whose dominant symbol is the huge, ugly fish which the guests consume with relish. By the use of eloquent gestures, faces and looks, rather than dialogue, Olmi has created a witty and sharp satire on the haute bourgeoisie. RB Italian +subtitles.

Marco Esposito *Libenzio* • Simona Brandalise *Corinna* • Stefania Busarello *Anna* • Simone Dalla Rosa *Mao* • Lorenzo Paolini *Ciccio* • Tarcisio Tosi *Pigi* ■ *Dir/Scr* Ermanno Olmi

The Long, Long Trailer ★★ U
Comedy   1954 • US • Colour • 96min

After mediocre cinema careers, Lucille Ball and Desi Arnaz became household names on TV in *I Love Lucy*. They returned in triumph to MGM for this episodic comedy feature which essentially preserves their small screen images of madcap wife and long-suffering husband. Playing newlyweds, Lucille persuades Desi that they should invest in a mobile home and use it for their honeymoon trip, leading to scrapes and disasters. AE

Lucille Ball *Tacy Collini* • Desi Arnaz *Nicholas Carlos Collini* • Marjorie Main *Mrs Hittaway* • Keenan Wynn *Policeman* • Gladys Hurlbut *Mrs Bolton* • Moroni Olsen *Mr Tewitt* ■ *Dir* Vincente Minnelli • *Scr* Albert Hackett, Frances Goodrich, from the novel by Clinton Twiss

Long Lost Father ★★
Drama   1934 • US • BW • 64min

John Barrymore was never too choosy with his later screen roles, and this was one of his lesser efforts. Barrymore, in his world-weary manner, plays a man who deserted his family many years before but finds his grown-up daughter (Helen Chandler) working in the same nightclub as he is. Naturally, he wins back her love. The director Ernest B Schoedsack shows no feeling for the material. RB

John Barrymore *Carl Bellairs* • Helen Chandler *Lindsey Lane* • Donald Cook *Dr Bill Strong* • Alan Mowbray *Sir Anthony Gelding* • Claude King *Inspector* • EE Clive *Spot Hawkins* • Reginald Sharland *Lord Vivyan* ■ *Dir* Ernest B Schoedsack • *Scr* Dwight Taylor, from GB Stern's novel

The Long Memory ★★ PG
Thriller   1952 • UK • BW • 89min

Robert Hamer will always be remembered as the director of the classic Ealing comedy *Kind Hearts and Coronets*, but he also had an excellent eye for local detail. Here he cleverly captures the murky side of life in London's marshlands, but he is beaten from the start by the utterly predictable wrong man story. John Mills is badly miscast as an old lag desperate to discover who framed him for murder, while detective John McCallum is clueless. DP *DVD*

John Mills *Davidson* • John McCallum *Detective Inspector Lowther* • Elizabeth Sellars *Fay Lowther* • Eva Bergh *Elsa* • Geoffrey Keen *Craig* • Michael Martin-Harvey *Jackson* • John Chandos *Boyd* • John Slater *Pewsey* • Thora Hird *Mrs Pewsey* ■ *Dir* Robert Hamer • *Scr* Robert Hamer, Frank Harvey, from a novel by Howard Clewes

The Long Night ★★★ PG
Drama   1947 • US • BW • 96min

In this effective, more socially orientated version of *Le Jour Se Lève*, Henry Fonda performs sensitively as the ex-serviceman-turned-killer who keeps the police at bay during a long night in which he looks back on the disastrous sequence of events that have left him trapped. This aroused critical fury at the time when when it was (mistakenly) believed that the producers of the remake had destroyed every copy of Marcel Carné's great original film. AE *DVD*

Henry Fonda *Joe Adams* • Barbara Bel Geddes *Jo Ann* • Vincent Price *Maximilian* • Ann Dvorak *Charlene* • Howard Freeman *Sheriff* • Moroni Olsen *Chief of Police* • Elisha Cook Jr *Frank* • Queenie Smith *Janitor's wife* ■ *Dir* Anatole Litvak • *Scr* John Wexley, from the film *Le Jour Se Lève* by Jacques Viot

Long Pants ★★★★ U
Silent comedy   1927 • US • BW • 62min

This bizarre black comedy is the last of three silent features that display the full genius of baby-faced Harry Langdon, following *Tramp, Tramp, Tramp* and *The Strong Man*. Here he plays the boy who has just graduated to long pants and dreams of being a great lover. The attractions of long-time sweetheart Priscilla Bonner pale in comparison with Alma Bennett's more exciting big city vamp and our "hero" decides that drastic measures are required. Langdon's effectiveness stems from the astute direction of the young Frank Capra. When Langdon fired Capra and tried to go it alone, he wrecked his career. AE

L

12 15 18 PASSED FOR PEOPLE OF THESE AGES AND OVER   *DVD* RELEASED ON DVD   *BD* RELEASED ON BLU-RAY   *3D* RELEASED IN 3D   *CS* END CREDIT SEQUENCE   759

Harry Langdon *The boy* • Gladys Brockwell *His mother* • Alan Roscoe *His father* • Alma Bennett *The vamp* • Priscilla Bonner *Priscilla* ■ *Dir* Frank Capra • *Scr* Robert Eddy, from a story by Arthur Ripley

The Long Riders ★★★★ 15
Western   1980 · US · Colour · 99min

Powerful novelty casting and a superb score by guitar maestro Ry Cooder are major draws in this authentic-looking western that concerns the events surrounding the notorious Northfield, Minnesota, bank raid. Directed by Walter Hill, it's very reminiscent of *The Wild Bunch* in its use of slow-motion violence and flashbacks. Three Carradines (David, Keith and Robert) play the Younger brothers, with Stacy and James Keach as Frank and Jesse James; Randy and Dennis Quaid portray the less familiar Miller boys, while the Fords (Bob and Charlie) are brought to life by Nicholas and Christopher Guest. Not to be outdone by the siblings, Pamela Reed gives a heartfelt performance. TS Violence, swearing, nudity. *DVD* ⓑ

Stacy Keach *Frank James* • David Carradine *Cole Younger* • Keith Carradine *Jim Younger* • Robert Carradine *Bob Younger* • James Keach *Jesse James* • Dennis Quaid *Ed Miller* • Randy Quaid *Clell Miller* • Kevin Brophy *John Younger* • Harry Carey Jr *George Arthur* • Christopher Guest *Charlie Ford* • Nicholas Guest *Bob Ford* ■ *Dir* Walter Hill • *Scr* Bill Bryden, Steven Phillip Smith, Stacy Keach, James Keach, Ry Cooder

The Long Run ★★ 15
Sports drama   2000 · S Afr · Colour · 107min

This is another story about a disciplinarian coach who drives his prodigy to the edge in a bid to fulfil her athletic potential. But what sets Jean Stewart's drama apart is that it's set in democratic South Africa and that the budding champion in Armin Mueller-Stahl's care is Namibian refugee Nthati Moshesh. Stewart fully exploits the forbidding scenery, but she fails to generate any sense of sporting excitement. DP *DVD*

Armin Mueller-Stahl *Bertold "Berry" Bohmer* • Nthati Moshesh *Christine* • Paterson Joseph *Gasa* • Desmond Dube *Miso* ■ *Dir* Jean Stewart (2) • *Scr* Johann Potgieter

The Long Ships ★★ PG
Action adventure
1963 · UK/Yug · Colour · 120min

This eager co-production has almost everything you would expect of a lavish screen epic. There's plenty of action and more than a hint of sin, the costumes and sets are opulent, and Christopher Challis's colour photography shimmers with richness. But while Richard Widmark plays his Viking role with pantomimic brio, Sidney Poitier chooses to play the Moorish prince as a sort of medieval civil rights activist. In other words, like many epics before and since, it's too self-indulgent for its own good. DP

Richard Widmark *Rolfe* • Sidney Poitier *El Mansuh* • Rosanna Schiaffino *Aminah* • Russ Tamblyn *Orm* • Oscar Homolka *Krok* • Lionel Jeffries *Aziz* • Edward Judd *Sven* • Beba Loncar *Gerda* • Clifford Evans *King Harald* • Colin Blakely *Rhykka* • Gordon Jackson *Vahlin* • David Lodge *Olla* ■ *Dir* Jack Cardiff • *Scr* Berkely Mather, Beverley Cross, from the novel by Frans T Bengtsson

Long Shot ★★
Drama   1978 · UK · Colour · 85min

This unusual docu-comedy set in and around the Edinburgh Festival should be required viewing for any aspiring film-maker. Film producer and proud Scot Charles Gormley is attempting to find backers for his movie entitled *Gulf and Western*. Naturally this proves to be problematic but some farcical comedy ensues and movie buffs will enjoy spotting luminaries like Wim Wenders, Stephen Frears, John Boorman and Susannah York in the supporting cast. LH

Charles Gormley *Charlie* • Neville Smith *Neville* • Ann Zelda *Annie* • David Stone *Distributor* • Suzanne Danielle *Sue* • Ron Taylor (1) *American director* • Wim Wenders *Another director* • Stephen Frears *Biscuit Man* • Maurice Bulbulian

French-Canadian director • William Forsythe [Bill Forsyth] *Billie* • Alan Bennett *Neville's doctor* • Susannah York *Actress* • John Boorman *The Director* ■ *Dir* Maurice Hatton • *Scr* Eoin McCann, Maurice Hatton

The Long Shot ★★
Drama   2004 · US · Colour · 100min

Julie Benz plays an abandoned wife whose second chances at life always seem tantalisingly just out of reach. Benz regains a little self esteem at Marsha Mason's stables, but then the horse she enters in a competition goes blind and the prize money she needs to rebuild her life seems to be slipping from her grasp. Horse lovers might find something to enjoy in this sentimental TV drama, but others will find it far too melodramatic. DP

Julie Benz *Annie Garrett* • Marsha Mason *Mary Lou O'Brian* • Paul Le Mat *Guido Levits* • Gage Golightly *Taylor Garrett* • Christopher Cousins *John Oaks* • David Alexander *Monte Shelton* ■ *Dir* Georg Stanford Brown • *Scr* David Alexander

The Long Summer of George Adams ★★★★
Drama   1982 · US · Colour · 100min

Director Stuart Margolin excels himself here with an ambitious TV movie that stars his longtime pal James Garner as a married man suffering a midlife crisis. Joan Hackett, in one of her last roles, matches the masterful Garner and their beautifully modulated performances are the heart of this small-town drama. Unsentimental, humorous and intelligently scripted, this is a low-key work about an all too human relationship. BB

James Garner *George Adams* • Joan Hackett *Norma Adams* • Alex Harvey *Ernie Lankford* • Juanin Clay *Ann Sharp* • David Graf *Olin Summers* • Anjanette Comer *Venida Pierce* ■ *Dir* Stuart Margolin • *Scr* John Gay, from the novel by Weldon Hill

Long Time Dead ★ 15
Horror   2001 · UK/US · Colour · 90min

Everything about this south London-set *Scream* – featuring college students summoning up an ancient fire demon during a Ouija board session – is obvious, third-hand and bogus. Former *EastEnders* pin-up Joe Absolom and obligatory American "name" Lukas Haas add little to this supernatural tosh, which is further marred by a vague dénouement and some sloppy editing. AJ *DVD*

Lukas Haas *Webster* • Joe Absolom *Rob* • Lara Belmont *Stella* • Melanie Gutteridge *Annie* • James Hillier *Spence* • Alec Newman *Liam* • Tom Bell *Becker* ■ *Dir* Marcus Adams • *Scr* Eitan Arrusi, Daniel Bronzite, Chris Baker, Andy Day, from a story by Marcus Adams, Daniel Bronzite, James Gay-Rees

The Long Voyage Home ★★★★ PG
Second World War drama
1940 · US · BW · 100min

This near masterpiece from director John Ford was scripted from four one-act seafaring plays by Eugene O'Neill, and it bears that satisfying streak of grim melancholy that typifies the finest work of one of America's greatest writers. Although relentlessly studio bound, the magnificent photography captures the dangerous atmosphere as a freighter transports a cargo of dynamite across the Atlantic during the Second World War. John Wayne plays a Swedish merchant seaman, and he's backed up by an effective supporting cast. TS

John Wayne *Ole Olsen* • Thomas Mitchell *Aloysius Driscoll* • Ian Hunter *Smitty* • Barry Fitzgerald *Cocky* • Wilfrid Lawson *Captain* • Mildred Natwick *Freda* • John Qualen *Axel Swanson* • Ward Bond *Yank* ■ *Dir* John Ford • *Scr* Dudley Nichols, from four one-act plays by Eugene O'Neill • *Cinematographer* Gregg Toland

The Long Walk Home ★★★ PG
Period drama   1990 · US · Colour · 91min

Whoopi Goldberg plays Sissy Spacek's housemaid in this convincing drama set during the early years of the civil rights movement. Tensions rise in Spacek's Alabama household as blacks and whites grow further apart when the blacks boycott the segregated buses and the whites up the ante with an arson attack on Martin Luther King's house. Solid acting, a no-nonsense script, a convincing 1950s look and marvellous gospel music all distinguish this. AT

Whoopi Goldberg *Odessa Cotter* • Sissy Spacek *Miriam Thompson* • Dwight Schultz *Norman Thompson* • Ving Rhames *Herbert Cotter* • Dylan Baker *Tunker Thompson* • Erika Alexander *Selma Cotter* • Lexi Faith Randall [Lexi Randall] *Mary Catherine* • Richard Habersham *Theodore Cotter* • Jason Weaver *Franklin Cotter* ■ *Dir* Richard Pearce • *Scr* John Cork

A Long Way Down ★★ 15
Comedy drama   2013 · UK · Colour · 92min

Based on the novel by Nick Hornby, this lacklustre and manipulative black comedy centres on four suicidal Londoners who all decide to jump from the same tower block, but then agree to hold off taking the plunge. In the meantime, they bond, and director Pascal Chaumeil delves into their back stories. It's a pointless exercise as, even with a classy line-up that includes Pierce Brosnan, Toni Collette and Aaron Paul (of TV's *Breaking Bad*), you may find yourself wishing this depressed – and depressing – bunch had put an end to things a lot earlier. DA *DVD*

Pierce Brosnan *Martin Sharp* • Toni Collette *Maureen* • Aaron Paul *JJ* • Imogen Poots *Jess* • Rosamund Pike *Penny* • Sam Neill *Chris Crichton* ■ *Dir* Pascal Chaumeil • *Scr* Jack Thorne, from the novel by Nick Hornby

A Long Way from Home ★★★ 12
Romantic drama   2013 · UK/Fr · Colour · 78min

Virginia Gilbert's feature debut has vague echoes of father Brian's 1986 romantic comedy *The Frog Prince*. *Amour fou* provides the connection, as septuagenarian Joseph (James Fox) is captivated by the youth and vivacity of Suzanne (Natalie Dormer) when she comes to Nîmes on holiday and forges an unlikely friendship with Joseph and his feisty Irish wife (Brenda Fricker). But despite the polished performances, the narrative always seems contrived, though the views of the city are often sublime. DP *DVD*

James Fox *Joseph* • Natalie Dormer *Suzanne* • Paul Nicholls *Mark* • Brenda Fricker *Brenda* ■ *Dir/Scr* Virginia Gilbert

The Long Way Home ★★★★
Documentary
1996 · US · BW and Colour · 119min

The winner of the Oscar for best feature documentary, this is a devastating exposé of the events that followed the liberation of the European concentration camps at the end of the Second World War. Narrated by Morgan Freeman and combining archive footage, stills, interviews and personal testimonies, the shameful catalogue of oversights, errors and wilful acts of neglect can only astonish those unaware that the suffering of the Holocaust survivors did not end with the defeat of the Nazis. Conducting his exhaustive research in conjunction with Rabbi Marvin Hier, Mark Jonathan Harris had fashioned a fitting tribute to these victims. DP

Morgan Freeman *Narrator* ■ *Dir/Scr* Mark Jonathan Harris

The Long Way Home ★★★ PG
Drama   1998 · US · Colour · 87min

Jack Lemmon provides the extra bit of class that lifts this sudsy TV melodrama out of the ordinary. The veteran star plays a lonely widower, staying with his son and

daughter-in-law, who gets a new lease of life when his friendship with feisty young Sarah Paulson leads to a chance encounter. Lemmon relishes this juicy role, while director Glenn Jordan sidesteps the more sugary moments. JF *DVD*

Jack Lemmon *Tom Gerrin* • Betty Garrett *Veronica* • Sarah Paulson *Leanne Bossert* • Kristin Griffith *Bonnie Gerrin* • Garwin Sanford *Ken Gerrin* ■ *Dir* Glenn Jordan • *Scr* William Hanley, from the TV film *Thomas Guerin, Retraite* by Louise Vincent, Patrick Jamain

Long Weekend ★★ 15
Thriller   1977 · Aus · Colour · 94min

The eco-thriller is one of the coming genres of western cinema, but this is a pretty resistible early effort. In an attempt to save their failing marriage, John Hargreaves and Briony Behets decide to spend a weekend on a deserted stretch of the Australian coastline. As the forces of nature turn the weekend into a nightmare fight for survival, the bickering couple squabble even more, reinforcing the view that whatever happens to this ghastly pair is more than due. DP *DVD*

John Hargreaves *Peter* • Briony Behets *Marcia* ■ *Dir* Colin Eggleston • *Scr* Everett De Roche

Long Weekend ★★ 15
Horror thriller   2008 · Aus · Colour · 84min

The wrath of Mother Nature is unleashed on a vacationing couple in this efficient remake of a 1977 Aussie thriller. Jim Caviezel and Claudia Karvan play the bickering husband and wife who head for the country to relax at an idyllic beach hideaway and patch up their ailing marriage. However, their crass treatment of environment and animal alike soon sees them under siege from all manner of flora and fauna. Director Jamie Blanks goes for a sustained sense of dread rather than jolts and shocks, and though the tetchy twosome are an unlikeable pair, the shimmering location photography and ominous atmosphere keep things interesting. JA Violence, swearing. *DVD*

Jim Caviezel *Peter* • Claudia Karvan *Carla* • Robert Taylor (4) *Bartender* • John Brumpton *Old timer* • Roger Ward *Trucker* ■ *Dir* Jamie Blanks • *Scr* Everett De Roche, from the 1977 film • *Cinematographer* Karl von Möller [Karl von Moller]

The Longest Day ★★★★ PG
Second World War drama
1962 · US · BW · 168min

This war film has a lot going for it: a huge budget and masses of military co-operation; the clever idea of providing a composite picture of the Allied invasion of Occupied France on D-Day 6 June 1944 from the British, American, French Resistance and German viewpoints; well-known actors from each nationality to help audiences cope with the large number of characters; and black-and-white photography to convey a sense of newsreel authenticity. The picture holds its three-hour length well and is far from gung ho in highlighting the errors and miscalculations on both sides. The battle scenes are memorably staged and the major Hollywood stars fit in particularly well – but it's let down by overacting from many of the European players, some crude characterisation and pretentious vignettes. AE English, German +subtitles. *DVD* ⓑ

John Wayne *Col Benjamin Vandervoort* • Robert Mitchum *Brig Gen Norman Cota* • Henry Fonda *Brig Gen Theodore Roosevelt* • Robert Ryan *Brig Gen James Gavin* • Rod Steiger *Destroyer commander* • Robert Wagner *US ranger* • Richard Beymer *Schultz* • Mel Ferrer *Maj Gen Robert Haines* • Jeffrey Hunter *Sgt Fuller* • Paul Anka *US ranger* • Sal Mineo *Pte Martini* • Roddy McDowall *Pte Morris* • Stuart Whitman *Lt Sheen* • Eddie Albert *Col Newton* • Edmond O'Brien *Gen Raymond O Barton* • Fabian *Ranger* • Red Buttons *Pte Steel* • Tom Tryon *Lt Wilson* • Alexander Knox *Maj Gen Walter Bedell Smith* • Richard Burton *RAF pilot* • Kenneth More *Capt Maud* • Peter Lawford *Lord Lovat* • Richard Todd *Maj Howard* • Sean Connery *Pte Flanagan* • Christopher Lee *Bit* ■ *Dir* Andrew Marton, Ken

L

Annakin, Bernhard Wicki • *Scr* Cornelius Ryan, Romain Gary, James Jones, David Pursall, Jack Seddon, from the novel by Cornelius Ryan

The Longest Ride ★★ 12
Romantic drama 2015 · US · Colour · 123min

Devotees of Nicholas Sparks's work will no doubt be delighted with this bonanza offering: two preposterous love stories for the price of one! The first happens in the present day, when a student (Britt Robertson) falls for a swoonsome but obsessive bull-rider (Scott Eastwood). Their relationship seems doomed until the pair rescue a car-crash victim (Alan Alda), whose own marital ups and downs, shown in flashback, contain inspirational life lessons about true love and sacrifice. The leads are game enough, struggling against dialogue with the aroma of something that emerged from the wrong end of one of Eastwood's bovine opponents, while George Tillman Jr's clod-hopping direction means the movie is not much of a ride. AS Swearing, sex scenes. *DVD* 📀

Britt Robertson *Sophia Danko* • Scott Eastwood *Luke Collins* • Alan Alda *Ira Levinson* • Jack Huston *Young Ira* • Oona Chaplin *Young Ruth* • Melissa Benoist *Marcia* ■ *Dir* George Tillman Jr • *Scr* Craig Bolotin, from the novel by Nicholas Sparks

The Longest Week ★★ 15
Comedy drama 2014 · US · Colour · 86min

Following a cool reception for their debut production *Grace of Monaco* YRF Entertainment, the US subsidiary of Bollywood powerhouse Yash Raj Films, takes aim at the sort of smart comedy that Woody Allen made in the 1970s – and misses by a Manhattan mile. Its stars provide what power it has – Jason Bateman as the rich dilettante suddenly locked out of his trust fund, Olivia Wilde as the beauty-with-brains who injects meaning into his aimless life, and a particularly fine Billy Crudup as the louche gallerist pal who comes between the two of them. SvM *DVD*

Jason Bateman *Conrad Valmont* • Olivia Wilde *Beatrice Fairbanks* • Billy Crudup *Dylan Tate* • Tony Roberts *Barry the Therapist* ■ *Dir* Peter Glanz • *Scr* Peter Glanz, from a story by Glanz, Juan Iglesias

The Longest Yard ★★★ 12
Prison sports comedy
2005 · US · Colour · 108min

In this remake of 1974 Burt Reynolds comedy *The Mean Machine*, Adam Sandler plays a washed-up football star who lands in prison. Warden James Cromwell asks Sandler to train a group of convicts to take on a team of guards for a warm-up match but, encouraged by Chris Rock, the failed player sets his sights on winning the game. Lazy, predictable but warmly humorous, this eschews complex characterisation in favour of well-worn prison genre clichés, but is still entertaining. GM *DVD*

Adam Sandler *Paul "Wrecking" Crewe* • Chris Rock *Caretaker* • Burt Reynolds *Coach Nate Scarborough* • Nelly *Earl Megget* • James Cromwell *Warden Hazen* • William Fichtner *Captain Knauer* • Michael Irvin *Deacon Moss* ■ *Dir* Peter Segal • *Scr* Sheldon Turner, from the 1974 film by Tracy Keenan Wynn, from a story by Albert S Ruddy

Longtime Companion
★★★★ 15
Drama 1990 · US · Colour · 95min

This is the riveting, gut-wrenching account of eight friends' experiences from the day a newspaper reports "a rare cancer affecting the homosexual community" to the mounting impact Aids has on their lives. Charting the way affluent gays were shocked out of their Calvin Klein lifestyles into dealing with bigotry and misunderstanding as they coped with bewildering loss, this quasi-documentary is a most accessible Aids history lesson. Oscar-nominee Bruce Davison gives the stand-out performance in a powerful, courageous testament. AJ Swearing. *DVD*

Bruce Davison *David* • Campbell Scott *Willy* • Stephen Caffrey *Fuzzy* • Mark Lamos *Sean* • Patrick Cassidy *Howard* • Mary-Louise Parker *Lisa* • John Dossett *Paul* ■ *Dir* Norman René • *Scr* Craig Lucas

Look at Me ★★★★ 12
Comedy drama 2004 · Fr/It · Colour · 106min

Young music student Marilou Berry, a voluptuous beauty who is obsessed with her weight, pines for the affection of her self-absorbed novelist father Jean-Pierre Bacri. Director Agnès Jaoui plays a singing teacher, who is brought into the family's orbit when her own novelist husband befriends Bacri. Another half dozen characters, each lovelorn or damaged in some way, populate the seemingly casual but deftly constructed plot. This is a wise and elegant comedy in which the dialogue fizzes. LF French +subtitles. *DVD*

Marilou Berry *Lolita Cassard* • Agnès Jaoui *Sylvia Miller* • Jean-Pierre Bacri *Étienne Cassard* • Laurent Grévill *Pierre Miller* • Virginie Desarnauts *Karine* • Keine Bouhiza *Sébastien* • Grégoire Oestermann *Vincent* • Serge Riaboukine *Felix* • Michèle Moretti *Edith* ■ *Dir* Agnès Jaoui • *Scr* Jean-Pierre Bacri, Agnès Jaoui

Look Back in Anger
★★★★ PG
Drama 1959 · UK · BW · 95min

Richard Burton is on a whingeing streak as the ever-complaining Jimmy Porter in Tony Richardson's version of the John Osborne play, the epitome of the kitchen sink drama that heralded the liberated Swinging Sixties. As the downtrodden, middle-class wife taking the brunt of his tirades, Mary Ure poignantly deserves better from life than a husband who believes the world owes him a living, because Burton makes the man totally unsympathetic. As an emblem of its time, though, not to be missed. TH

Richard Burton *Jimmy Porter* • Claire Bloom *Helena Charles* • Mary Ure *Alison Porter* • Edith Evans *Mrs Tanner* • Gary Raymond *Cliff Lewis* • Glen Byam Shaw *Corporal Redfern* • Phyllis Nielson-Terry *Mrs Redfern* • Donald Pleasence *Hurst* • Jane Eccles *Miss Drury* ■ *Dir* Tony Richardson • *Scr* Nigel Kneale, John Osborne, from the play by John Osborne

Look Both Ways ★★★★ 12
Relationship drama 2005 · Aus · Colour · 96min

Animator Sarah Watt's first live-action feature is a visually inventive tale that explores attitudes towards mortality from the viewpoint of four anxiety-ridden protagonists. She elicits moving performances from a largely unknown cast – particularly William McInnes as a photographer who discovers he has cancer, and Justine Clarke, the paranoid artist with whom he establishes a fragile bond. This quietly affecting if sometimes disturbing drama dominated the 2005 Australian Film Institute awards, beating more starry productions like *The Proposition* (Guy Pearce, Ray Winstone) to scoop best film, best direction, best supporting actor and best original screenplay. JF *DVD*

William McInnes *Nick* • Justine Clarke *Meryl* • Leigh • Anthony Hayes *Andy* • Lisa Flanagan *Anna* • Andrew S Gilbert *Phil* • Daniela Farinacci *Julia* ■ *Dir/Scr* Sarah Watt • *Cinematographer* Ray Argall

Look for the Silver Lining
★★★ U
Musical biography 1949 · US · Colour · 106min

This is an underrated Warner Bros biopic of Broadway legend Marilyn Miller (after whom Marilyn Monroe was named), vivaciously played here by June Haver. Large chunks of Miller's New York hits *Sunny* and *Sally* are re-created, with highstepping Ray Bolger as her partner Jack Donahue, the man who taught Eleanor Powell to dance. In reality, Miller married three times, the second of her husbands being Mary Pickford's brother Jack, but here she's been given a fictional husband played by Gordon MacRae. David Butler directs it all with style. TS

June Haver *Marilyn Miller* • Ray Bolger *Jack Donahue* • Gordon MacRae *Frank Carter* • Charlie Ruggles [Charles Ruggles] *Pop Miller* • Rosemary

DeCamp *Mom Miller* • Lee Wilde *Claire Miller* • Lynn Wilde *Ruth Miller* • Will Rogers Jr *Will Rogers* ■ *Dir* David Butler • *Scr* Henry Ephron, Phoebe Ephron, Marian Spitzer, from the story *Life of Marilyn Miller* by Bert Kalmar, Harry Ruby

The Look of Love ★★★★ 18
Biographical comedy drama
2013 · UK · Colour and BW · 96min

The life and loves of adult entertainment pioneer Paul Raymond are handled with sensitivity in this biopic of the man who funnelled his porn profits into property to become the richest man in Britain. Beginning in the late 1950s, with the opening of the topless Raymond Revue Bar in the heart of sleazy Soho, the film offers decade-by-decade snapshots of his life until his retirement from the public eye in the early 90s. Steve Coogan gives a surprisingly moving performance as Raymond, who struggles to communicate with his first wife (Anna Friel), long-term lover (Tamsin Egerton) and daughter (Imogen Poots). Indeed, it's one of director Michael Winterbottom's more human films, a bittersweet study of heartbreak and a fable-like meditation on the true cost of success. DW Sex scenes, nudity, drug abuse. *DVD* 📀

Steve Coogan *Paul Raymond* • Anna Friel *Jean Raymond* • Imogen Poots *Debbie Raymond* • Tamsin Egerton *Amber St George/Fiona Richmond* • Chris Addison *Tony Power* • Matt Lucas *Matron behind bars* • David Walliams *Rev Edwyn Young* ■ *Dir* Michael Winterbottom • *Scr* Matt Greenhalgh, from the non-fiction book *Members Only: the Life and Times of Paul Raymond* by Paul Willetts

The Look of Silence
★★★★ 15
Documentary
2014 · Den/Fin/Indonesia/Nor/UK · Colour · 103min

Joshua Oppenheimer's extraordinary 2012 film *The Act of Killing* dealt with the bully boys and executioners of the anti-Communist regime during the Indonesian genocide of 1965-66. This film is concerned with their victims, focusing on Adi Rukun, whose older brother Ramli was butchered in the carnage. Now 44 and a travelling optician, Adi slyly uses the tools of his trade to get close to the men who took Ramli and destroyed his parents' lives. While *The Act of Killing* had a strong visual power, notably in the scenes where the subjects act out their sick and deluded dreams of glory, this film is much more muted. What we hear is shocking enough; thankfully Oppenheimer leaves most of these savage horrors to our imagination. DW Indonesian +subtitles.

■ *Dir* Joshua Oppenheimer (2)

Look Up and Laugh ★★ U
Comedy 1935 · UK · BW · 74min

Celebrated author JB Priestley supplied the story for this Gracie Fields vehicle. Gracie and her fellow market traders discover an ancient Royal Charter that enables them to declare independence from Britain and so confound the takeover plans of a department-store chain. Look out for an uncredited Kenneth More making his screen debut and Vivien Leigh in only her third film. DP

Gracie Fields *Grace Pearson* • Alfred Drayton *Belfer* • Douglas Wakefield *Joe Chirk* • Billy Nelson *Alf Chirk* • Harry Tate *Turnpenny* • Huntley Wright *Old Ketley* • Vivien Leigh *Marjorie Belfer* • Kenneth More ■ *Dir* Basil Dean • *Scr* Gordon Wellesley, from a story by JB Priestley

Look Who's Laughing ★★ U
Comedy 1941 · US · BW · 78min

Not many people manage to become national celebrities through a radio ventriloquism act. But that's what happened to Edgar Bergen, who teams once more with his cheeky dummy Charlie McCarthy for this slight, but tolerable flag-waver. He's joined by radio regulars Fibber McGee and Molly (Jim and Marian Jordan) and Harold Peary in one of his five film ventures as the Great Gildersleeve. DP

Edgar Bergen • Jim Jordan *Fibber McGee* • Marian Jordan *Molly McGee* • Lucille Ball *Julie Patterson* • Harold Peary *The Great Gildersleeve* ■ *Dir* Allan Dwan • *Scr* James V Kern, Don Quinn, Leonard L Levinson, Zeno Klinker, Dorothy Kingsley

Look Who's Talking ★★★ 12
Comedy 1989 · US · Colour · 95min

This is the smash hit that brought John Travolta back from the wilderness into the public eye and spawned two increasingly silly sequels. Kirstie Alley is the single mother on the lookout for the perfect husband, even though we know lowly taxi driver Travolta is the safe bet from the outset. Bruce Willis, the wisecracking voice of baby Mikey, has the best lines, although Travolta and Alley are an amiable pairing, and there's nice support from Olympia Dukakis and George Segal. JF Swearing, sexual references. *DVD*

John Travolta *James* • Kirstie Alley *Mollie* • Olympia Dukakis *Rosie* • George Segal *Albert* • Abe Vigoda *Grandpa* • Bruce Willis *Mikey* • Twink Caplan *Rona* ■ *Dir/Scr* Amy Heckerling

Look Who's Talking Too
★★ 15
Comedy 1990 · US · Colour · 76min

Although this sequel succeeded in reuniting the stars of the first movie, it is a pallid retread. The twist this time around is that precocious Mikey (voiced again by Bruce Willis) gets a baby sister (vocals courtesy of Roseanne Barr), but, just to be doubly sure, director Amy Heckerling throws in a couple of other big names – the voice talent of Damon Wayans and Mel Brooks. A worrying strain of sentimentality starts to seep through. JF Swearing. *DVD*

John Travolta *James* • Kirstie Alley *Mollie* • Olympia Dukakis *Rosie* • Elias Koteas *Stuart* • Twink Kaplan *Rona* • Neal Israel *Mr Ross* • Bruce Willis *Mikey* • Roseanne Barr *Julie* • Damon Wayans *Eddie* • Mel Brooks *Mr Toilet Man* ■ *Dir* Amy Heckerling • *Scr* Amy Heckerling, Neal Israel, from characters by Amy Heckerling

Look Who's Talking Now!
★★ 12
Comedy 1993 · US · Colour · 91min

The talking baby concept had been exhausted by the first two *Look Who's* films, so the makers moved on to animals for this second sequel. However, even the presence of Danny DeVito and Diane Keaton couldn't breathe life into a tired formula. John Travolta and Kirstie Alley go through the motions again as the bickering couple, while DeVito and Keaton, providing the voices for two dogs from different sides of the tracks, snap away in similar fashion. Good gags are thin on the ground. JF *DVD*

John Travolta *James Ubriacco* • Kirstie Alley *Mollie Ubriacco* • David Gallagher *Mikey Ubriacco* • Tabitha Lupien *Julie Ubriacco* • Lysette Anthony *Samantha* • Olympia Dukakis *Rosie* • Danny DeVito *Rocks* • Diane Keaton *Daphne* • George Segal *Albert* ■ *Dir* Tom Ropelewski • *Scr* Tom Ropelewski, Leslie Dixon, from characters by Amy Heckerling

Looker ★★★★ 15
Science-fiction thriller
1981 · US · Colour · 89min

This underrated blend of techno horror and suspense is a slick outing about subliminal advertising, in which plastic surgeon Albert Finney joins pin-up Susan Dey to investigate the deaths of his supermodel clients and their association with advertising agency chief James Coburn. Although it's confusing at times, the design is fabulous, and the time-continuum blaster gizmo is a brilliant device allowing Michael Crichton to indulge in some great visual effects. The acting, from Finney especially, is outstanding. AJ Nudity.

Albert Finney *Dr Larry Roberts* • James Coburn *John Reston* • Susan Dey *Cindy* • Leigh Taylor-Young *Jennifer Long* • Dorian Harewood *Lieutenant Masters* • Tim Rossovich *Moustache Man* ■ *Dir/Scr* Michael Crichton

L

Lookin' Italian ★★ 18

Crime drama   1994 · US · Colour · 97min

This is a rather embarrassing skeleton from *Friends* star Matt LeBlanc's closet. He is actually a supporting player here, appearing as the hot-headed nephew of the Mafia-connected Jay Acovone, who is attempting to begin a new peaceful life in Los Angeles. The performances are wildly over the top and Guy Magar's script is stacked with every gangster cliché in the book. JF DVD

Jay Acovone *Vinny Pallazzo* • Matt LeBlanc *Anthony Manetti* • Stephanie Richards *Danielle* • John LaMotta *Don Dinardo* • Ralph Manza *Manza* • Lou Rawls *Willy* ■ *Dir/Scr* Guy Magar

Looking for Eric ★★★★ 15

Comedy drama
2009 · UK/Fr/It/Bel/Sp · Colour · 111min

A luckless Manchester postman is taught life lessons by an apparition of football legend Eric Cantona in this charming and uplifting drama from director Ken Loach. Eric Bishop (Steve Evets) pines for the first wife (Stephanie Bishop) that he abandoned as a youth, while struggling to keep his wayward stepsons from his failed second marriage on the right side of the law. Enter his Old Trafford hero and namesake with reams of cod philosophy and Gallic arrogance. Loach revisits the grim kitchen-sink milieu of his earlier work, but casually wrong-foots the viewer by infusing the movie with fantasy elements and hilarious set pieces. TeS Swearing, drug abuse.
DVD BL S

Steve Evets *Eric Bishop* • Eric Cantona *Eric* • John Henshaw *Meatballs* • Stephanie Bishop *Lily* • Gerard Kearns *Ryan Bishop* • Lucy-Jo Hudson *Sam* • Stefan Gumbs *Jess Bishop* • Justin Moorhouse *Spleen* ■ *Dir* Ken Loach • *Scr* Paul Laverty

Looking for Hortense ★★★ 12A

Comedy   2012 · Fr · Colour · 100min

A bourgeois Parisian marriage hits troubled waters in this serio-comic affair. Yet again, Kristin Scott Thomas shines in a French role, playing a chain-smoking theatre director who is drawn to her hunky leading man. But she plays second fiddle to Jean-Pierre Bacri's university lecturer, a bit of a moocher with a certain charisma. The story leans towards a romantic comedy formula, except there's a bit too much on its plate, so that its underlying themes get a little lost. Still, there's plenty of Gallic sophistication to savour – and the two classy leads. TJ French +subtitles. Swearing.

Jean-Pierre Bacri *Damien* • Kristin Scott Thomas *Iva* • Isabelle Carré *Aurore* • Marin Orcand Tourrès *Noé Hauer* • Claude Rich *Sébastien Hauer* ■ *Dir* Pascal Bonitzer • *Scr* Agnes de Sacy, Pascal Bonitzer

Looking for Mr Goodbar ★★★★ 18

Drama   1977 · US · Colour · 130min

Although not the most obvious choice to play the man-hungry heroine in this adaptation of Judith Rossner's bestseller, Diane Keaton manages a wonderfully fraught performance in writer/director Richard Brooks's overcharged sexual melodrama. Keaton plays a teacher of deaf children who haunts singles bars at night, taking the sadistic rough (Richard Gere) with the decent smooth (William Atherton) until she meets a bisexual killer (Tom Berenger). Although reminiscent of the German classic *Pandora's Box*, this has a glib puritanism pervading the sleaze and, even if some aspects of the novel are glossed over, it's still very raw. TH Violence, sex scenes, swearing, drug abuse.

Diane Keaton *Theresa Dunn* • Tuesday Weld *Katherine Dunn* • Richard Gere *Tony Lopanto* • William Atherton *James Morrissey* • Richard Kiley *Mr Dunn* • Alan Feinstein *Professor Engle* • Tom Berenger *Gary Cooper White* ■ *Dir* Richard Brooks • *Scr* Richard Brooks, from the novel by Judith Rossner

Looking for Richard ★★★★ 12

Documentary drama 1996 · US · Colour · 107min

Al Pacino's unusual and very personal tribute to Shakespeare follows his attempts to adapt *Richard III* for the screen. It's partly a documentary (containing interviews with the likes of Kenneth Branagh and John Gielgud), partly a filmed adaptation of the play, as Pacino plays out scenes with fellow Americans Kevin Spacey, Winona Ryder, Aidan Quinn and Alec Baldwin. Demonstrating genuine love and understanding of the Bard as well as great skill as a Shakespearean actor, Pacino explores the classic text in a compelling and original way. LH Violence, swearing. DVD

Al Pacino *Richard III* • Alec Baldwin *Clarence* • Kevin Spacey *Buckingham* • Winona Ryder *Lady Anne* • Aidan Quinn *Richmond* • Kenneth Branagh • Kevin Kline • James Earl Jones • Derek Jacobi • Estelle Parsons *Margaret* ■ *Dir* Al Pacino

Looking for Trouble ★★

Crime drama   1934 · US · BW · 77min

Spencer Tracy and Jack Oakie play two telephone line repairmen in this action-packed and sometimes confusing drama from director William A Wellman. These macho stalwarts get involved in every kind of crisis from fire and earthquake, to robbery, romance and murder. Constance Cummings co-stars, and there are enough dramatics to keep the action moving and hold – if not exactly grip – one's attention. RK

Spencer Tracy *Joe Graham* • Jack Oakie *Casey* • Constance Cummings *Ethel Greenwood* • Morgan Conway *Dan Sutter* • Arline Judge *Maizie* ■ *Dir* William A Wellman • *Scr* Leonard Praskins, Elmer Harris, from a story by JR Bren

The Looking Glass War ★★★ 15

Spy drama   1969 · UK · Colour · 102min

The spymasters come out best, but that's because they're played by Ralph Richardson and Paul Rogers in this John le Carré adaptation in which a Polish refugee (Christopher Jones) is persuaded to enter East Germany to verify Russian missile sites. The foot soldiers of espionage (including a young Anthony Hopkins) have a tough time of it, and its Cold War climate now seems long ago and far away. TH Violence, swearing.

Christopher Jones *Leiser* • Pia Degermark *The Girl* • Ralph Richardson *Leclerc* • Anthony Hopkins *John Avery* • Paul Rogers *Haldane* • Susan George *Susan* • Ray McAnally *Starr* • Robert Urquhart *Johnson* ■ *Dir* Frank R Pierson [Frank Pierson] • *Scr* Frank R Pierson, from the novel by John le Carré

Looking on the Bright Side ★★★ U

Musical comedy   1931 · UK · BW · 78min

Gracie Fields hit the movie big time with this sprightly musical comedy, which was co-directed by theatre impresario Basil Dean and silent specialist Graham Cutts. As ever, she plays a spirited working lass, who keeps her wits around her, even when things are at their bleakest. Quitting her job as a manicurist, when the hairdresser she adores gets the chance to write songs for a superstar, she joins the police and not only rediscovers her self-esteem, but also arrives on stage to save her beau's flagging career. DP DVD

Gracie Fields *Gracie* • Richard Dolman *Laurie* • Julian Rose *Oscar Schultz* • Wyn Richmond *Miss Joy* ■ *Dir* Basil Dean, Graham Cutts • *Scr* Basil Dean, Archie Pitt, Brock Williams

The Lookout ★★★ 15

Crime drama   2007 · US · Colour · 94min

Joseph Gordon-Levitt (*Brick*) impresses again here in this offbeat thriller as Chris, a brain-damaged teenager whose lack of self-esteem sees him easily seduced into facilitating a heist at the small-town bank. The first half of the film, which concentrates on Chris's relationship with his irascible blind flatmate Lewis (the always watchable Jeff Daniels), is much the better of the two. In fact, debut director Scott Frank (writer of *Out of Sight*) might have done well to maintain the focus on this storyline. The second half, in which the robbery plans of a former schoolfriend (Matthew Goode) take centre stage, becomes rather too *Rambo*-like to be completely credible. Still, it's a decent first-time effort from Frank. DA DVD

Joseph Gordon-Levitt *Chris* • Pratt • Jeff Daniels *Lewis* • Matthew Goode *Gary Spargo* • Isla Fisher *Luvlee Lemons* • Carla Gugino *Janet* • Bruce McGill *Robert Pratt* • Alberta Watson *Barbara Pratt* • Alex Borstein *Mrs Lange* ■ *Dir/Scr* Scott Frank

The Lookout ★★ 15

Crime thriller 2012 · Fr/Bel/It · Colour · 85min

The focus here seems to be on a world-weary Parisian detective (Daniel Auteuil), as he pursues the masked sniper (Mathieu Kassovitz) who stopped him from nabbing a gang of bank robbers. But as the emphasis shifts, plot and character development become exceedingly clumsy, with strands about serial killers, the secret service and a fretful wife refusing to link together. But Auteuil and Kassovitz are always watchable, and the steely use of desaturated colour is highly atmospheric. DP French +subtitles. Violence, swearing, drug abuse, nudity.

Daniel Auteuil *Mattei* • Mathieu Kassovitz *Vincent Kaminski* • Olivier Gourmet *Franck* • Francis Renaud *Eric* • Nicolas Briaçon *Meyer* ■ *Dir* Michele Placido • *Scr* Denis Brusseaux, Cédric Melon

Looks and Smiles ★★★★ 15

Drama   1981 · UK · Colour · 103min

The rising damp of despair permeates this Ken Loach docudrama about the effect of redundancies on teenagers living in Sheffield, South Yorkshire. One boy opts for enlistment and ends up in Belfast; another stays at home, condemning himself to the futility of the job search and a relationship with shopgirl Carolyn Nicholson. Loach elicits marvellous performances from his three leads, all amateur actors behaving like true professionals. TH DVD

Graham Green *Mick Walsh* • Carolyn Nicholson *Karen Lodge* • Tony Pitts *Alan Wright* • Roy Haywood *Phil Adams* • Phil Askham *Mr Walsh* • Pam Darrell *Mrs Walsh* • Tracey Goodlad *Julie* ■ *Dir* Kenneth Loach [Ken Loach] • *Scr* Barry Hines

Looney Looney Looney Bugs Bunny Movie ★★★ U

Animation   1981 · US · Colour · 69min

Forty-one years after *A Wild Hare*, the most famous character in the Warner Bros cartoon stable returns in another greatest hits compilation. Bugs Bunny is always good value and the selection made here by Friz Freleng, one of the animators who first brought him to life (based on sketches by a story man named Bugs Hardaway, hence the name) is often very funny indeed. The highlight is *Knighty Knight Bugs*, which won the Oscar for best animated short subject in 1958. DP

Mel Blanc *Bugs Bunny/Daffy Duck/Sylvester/ Tweety Pie/Porky Pig* ■ *Dir* Friz Freleng, Gerry Chiniquy • *Scr* David Detiege, John W Dunn

Looney Tunes: Back in Action ★★ PG

Part-animated fantasy adventure
2004 · US · Colour · 87min

The live actors interact awkwardly with the animation in a dumb story that has studio security guard DJ Drake (Brendan Fraser), Daffy Duck and Bugs Bunny attempting to foil the world domination plans of Mr Chairman (Steve Martin). Director Joe Dante packs every frame with his brand of referential humour, but the most inspired moments of this uneven adventure come during a classic *Looney Tunes* chase through the Louvre. AJ DVD CS

Brendan Fraser *DJ Drake/Brendan Fraser* • Jenna Elfman *Kate Houghton* • Timothy Dalton *Damien Drake* • Joan Cusack *Mother* • Bill Goldberg *Mr Smith* • Heather Locklear *Dusty Tails* • Steve Martin *Mr Chairman* ■ *Dir* Joe Dante • *Scr* Larry Doyle

Looper ★★★★★ 15

Science-fiction action thriller
2012 · US · Colour · 113min

This fast-paced, gritty sci-fi thriller will satisfy not only those in search of popcorn thrills, but also those looking for an intelligent genre movie. Set in 2044, it stars Joseph Gordon-Levitt as Joe, a low-grade hitman charged with killing mob targets sent back through time from 30 years in the future. But when his older self (Bruce Willis) appears, and promptly escapes, Joe has to find and kill himself before the mob does. It sounds complex – and it is – but director Rian Johnson keeps the action pumping as the young Joe gets on the trail of older Joe, who is stalking a shadowy figure called the Rainmaker. Emily Blunt provides feisty love interest as the farm girl who takes pity on the young Joe, but it's Willis and Gordon-Levitt who sell the mind and muscle of an ingenious, witty film that simply brims with ideas and energy. DW Violence, swearing. DVD BL S

Joseph Gordon-Levitt *Joe* • Bruce Willis *Old Joe* • Emily Blunt *Sara* • Paul Dano *Seth* • Noah Segan *Kid Blue* • Piper Perabo *Suzie* • Jeff Daniels *Abe* ■ *Dir/Scr* Rian Johnson

Loophole ★★ PG

Crime drama   1980 · UK · Colour · 99min

Albert Finney and Susannah York star in this lacklustre heist caper. Martin Sheen is the obligatory American import, whose in-depth knowledge of bank security systems and hefty overdraft make him the ideal partner for Finney's mastermind. The blag itself is pretty routine, although the action picks up slightly when the gang's escape through the London sewers is hindered by a torrential downpour. Drably directed, not even Lalo Schifrin's score can enliven the proceedings. DP

Albert Finney *Mike Daniels* • Martin Sheen *Stephen Booker* • Susannah York *Dinah Booker* • Colin Blakely *Gardner* • Jonathan Pryce *Taylor* • Robert Morley *Godfrey* • Alfred Lynch *Harry* • Tony Doyle *Nolan* ■ *Dir* John Quested • *Scr* Jonathan Hales, from a novel by Robert Pollock

Loose Cannons ★ 15

Comedy   1990 · US · Colour · 90min

This dire buddy comedy marked a new low for the excellent Gene Hackman. He is the tough cop who finds himself reluctantly paired on a case with oddball detective Dan Aykroyd, who happens to suffer from a form of multiple personality disorder brought on by imminent danger. An unwatchable mess. JF Swearing, violence, nudity. DVD

Gene Hackman *Mac Stern* • Dan Aykroyd *Ellis Fielding* • Dom DeLuise *Harry "The Hippo" Gutterman* • Ronny Cox *Bob Smiley* • Nancy Travis *Riva* • Robert Prosky *Curt Von Metz* ■ *Dir* Bob Clark • *Scr* Richard Christian Matheson, Richard Matheson, Bob Clark

Loose Cannons ★★★ 12

Comedy drama   2010 · It · Colour · 112min

A duty-bound son learns the importance of being true to himself in this slick and bittersweet Italian comedy. Directed with panache by Turkey's Ferzan Ozpetek, the handsomely shot tale sees aspiring novelist Tommaso (*Romanzo Criminale's* Riccardo Scamarcio) caught up in a cross-generational tangle of guilt and self-sacrifice when his plan to escape the family pasta business by announcing he's gay is thwarted. Delightful performances and Ozpetek's gentle touch ensure the changes of tone work beautifully, particularly in the scenes between Tommaso and his wise-through-heartache grandmother (a wonderful Ilaria Occhini). SF Italian +subtitles. Swearing. DVD

Riccardo Scamarcio *Tommaso Cantone* • Nicole Grimaudo *Alba Brunetti* • Alessandro Preziosi *Antonio Cantone* • Ennio Fantastichini *Vincenzo Cantone* • Ilaria Occhini *Grandmother* ■ *Dir* Ferzan Ozpetek • *Scr* Ferzan Ozpetek, Ivan Cotroneo

Loose Connections ★★★ PG

Comedy   1983 · UK · Colour · 95min

This attempt by theatre director Richard Eyre to resurrect the screwball comedies of the 1930s has unlikely duo Lindsay Duncan and Stephen Rea as the protagonists. Duncan plays an uptight Germaine Greer type, driving through Germany with "co-pilot" Rea as her unfortunate companion. Their inability to see eye to eye fits well with the film's general depiction of the Brits abroad. Turns from Robbie Coltrane and Gary Olsen add to the fun and the two leads carry the film with style. Eyre doesn't quite obtain his objective. LH

Stephen Rea *Harry* • Lindsay Duncan *Sally* • Carol Harrison *Kay* • Frances Low *Laurie* • Andy de la Tour *Journalist* • David Purcell *Photographer* • Keith Allen *Keith* • Robbie Coltrane *Drunk* • Ruth Bruck *Wirtin* ▪ *Dir* Richard Eyre • *Scr* Maggie Brooks

Loot ★★★★ 15

Comedy   1970 · UK · Colour · 97min

Joe Orton's mordant play is about a bundle of stolen money hidden in a coffin that gets buried in the churchyard. It's a ruthless satire on authoritarianism as well as a send-up of the Agatha Christie-style whodunnit that had kept the British theatre ticking over for decades. The play had gone from disaster to prize-winning success but the film version flopped badly. Reworked by TV writers Ray Galton and Alan Simpson, it's wholly faithful to Orton's surreal sense of humour and the extreme tackiness of the characters, especially Richard Attenborough who clearly delights in playing the creepiest, kinkiest detective you'll ever see. AT

Richard Attenborough *Inspector Truscott* • Lee Remick *Fay* • Hywel Bennett *Dennis* • Roy Holder *Hal* • Milo O'Shea *Mr McLeavy* • Dick Emery *Mr Bateman* • Joe Lynch *Father O'Shaughnessy* • John Cater *Meadows* • Aubrey Woods *Undertaker* ▪ *Dir* Silvio Narizzano • *Scr* Ray Galton, Alan Simpson, from the play by Joe Orton

The Looters ★★

Crime drama   1966 · Fr/It · Colour · 102min

Ex-criminal Frederick Stafford falls for Jean Seberg, but finds that her gangster father has other plans for him. He's recruited to crack a safe and steal some gold owned by a would-be dictator who is planning a coup. Despite these political undertones, the film is a straightforward, not very lively crime caper. JG French, Italian dubbed.

Frederick Stafford *Sam Morgan* • Jean Seberg *Colleen O'Hara* • Mario Pisu *Patrick O'Hara* • Maria-Rosa Rodriguez *Estella* • Serge Gainsbourg *Clyde* ▪ *Dir* Jacques Besnard • *Scr* Pierre Foucaud, Michel Lebrun

Lorca and the Outlaws ★★ PG

Science fiction   1985 · UK · Colour · 86min

This is another dreary *Star Wars* clone with a bit of *Mad Max* thrown in. A miner's strike on a remote desert world is put down by militaristic police – the irony being that this British-financed production (shot in the Australian outback) was made in the year of Arthur Scargill's miners' strike – a fact seemingly lost on the film-makers. Despite killer robots and numerous fights and chases the whole affair is a chaotic bore. RS

John Tarrant *Lorca* • Donogh Rees *Abbie* • Deep Roy *Kid* • Cassandra Webb *Suzi* • Ralph Cotterill *Jowitt* • Hugh Keays-Byrne *Danny* ▪ *Dir* Roger Christian • *Scr* Roger Christian, Matthew Jacobs • *Music* Tony Banks

Lord Edgware Dies ★

Murder mystery   1934 · US · BW · 81min

Agatha Christie's 13th whodunnit was filmed the year after its publication. It was intended to be the start of a series of Hercule Poirot movie adventures, with Austin Trevor as the fastidious Belgian sleuth. But such was the wave of apathy that greeted this lacklustre adaptation that the plans were shelved. Trevor is wincingly bad, completely missing the trademark mannerisms of Poirot that later actors would bring to the character. DP

Austin Trevor *Hercule Poirot* • Jane Carr (1) *Lady Edgware* • Richard Cooper *Captain Hastings* • John Turnbull *Inspector Japp* • Michael Shepley *Captain Ronald Marsh* • Leslie Perrins *Bryan Martin* • CV France *Lord Edgware* • Esme Percy *Duke of Merton* ▪ *Dir* Henry Edwards • *Scr* H Fowler Mear, from the novel by Agatha Christie

Lord Jim ★★★★ PG

Period adventure   1965 · UK · Colour · 154min

Peter O'Toole gives one of his finest performances in this adaptation of Joseph Conrad's story about a merchant seaman branded a coward after jumping ship during a storm. His search for salvation in South East Asia results in action against a fanatical tyrant lording it over oppressed natives. Writer/director Richard Brooks allows the plot to meander out of control, but Freddie Young's photography of the mist-shrouded rivers and jungles emphasises the weird spirituality of Lord Jim's quest for redemption. TH *DVD*

Peter O'Toole *Lord Jim* • James Mason *Gentleman Brown* • Curt Jurgens *Cornelius* • Eli Wallach *The General* • Jack Hawkins *Marlow* • Paul Lukas *Stein* • Akim Tamiroff *Schomberg* • Daliah Lavi *The Girl* ▪ *Dir* Richard Brooks • *Scr* Richard Brooks, from the novel by Joseph Conrad

Lord Love a Duck ★★★

Black comedy   1966 · US · BW · 105min

George Axelrod made a notable directorial debut with this wickedly funny and beautifully acted satire on 1960s California lifestyles. It is centred on a bizarre high school, where clairvoyant Roddy McDowall grants wishes for the students, notably those of teen vamp Tuesday Weld. This is a real one-off: a wacky black comedy unfettered by taste, written and performed with great élan, with an interesting supporting cast including eccentric Ruth Gordon and Lola Albright as Weld's suicidal mom. TS

Roddy McDowall *Alan "Mollymauk" Musgrave* • Tuesday Weld *Barbara Ann Greene* • Lola Albright *Marie Greene* • Martin West *Bob Barnard* • Ruth Gordon *Stella Barnard* • Harvey Korman *Weldon Emmett* • Sarah Marshall *Miss Schwartz* ▪ *Dir* George Axelrod • *Scr* Larry H Johnson, George Axelrod, from the novel by Al Hine

Lord of Illusions ★★ 18

Horror   1995 · US · Colour · 116min

This unfocused and meandering dark fairy tale is directed by *Hellraiser* horror novelist Clive Barker and features his literary creation, the world-weary private eye Harry D'Amour (Scott Bakula). The troubled detective is on the trail of an evil cult spiritualist and his murder investigation takes him into the illusory world of professional theatre magicians. Barker's keen visual flair is evident throughout this gory intrigue, but there's far too much style and not enough content to fully engage the fear senses. AJ *DVD*

Scott Bakula *Harry D'Amour* • Famke Janssen *Dorothea Swann* • Trevor Edmond *Young Butterfield* • Daniel Von Bargen *Nix* • Kevin J O'Connor *Philip Swann* • Joseph Latimore *Caspar Quaid* ▪ *Dir/Scr* Clive Barker

Lord of the Flies ★★★★ PG

Drama   1963 · UK · BW · 87min

Novelist William Golding's fierce morality tale about schoolboys marooned on a desert island and reverting to religious savagery is given the larger-than-life treatment by theatrical director Peter Brook, who can't quite cope with cinematic character, but who keeps the tension tight as a crossbow. The wider implications of the idea, as a comment on mankind's original sin don't come across, but, taken as a parable limited to a bleak blueprint, it's vividly memorable. TH *DVD*

James Aubrey *Ralph* • Tom Chapin *Jack* • Hugh Edwards *Piggy* • Roger Elwin *Roger* • Tom Gaman *Simon* ▪ *Dir* Peter Brook • *Scr* Peter Brook, from the novel by William Golding

Lord of the Flies ★★★ 15

Drama   1990 · US · Colour · 87min

This is a worthy but misfiring attempt to feed William Golding's classic tale to the masses. The switch from British public schoolboys to American military cadets actually works better than it sounds and, at one level, makes the boys' savage transformation even more believable. Director Harry Hook coaxes wonderful performances out of a young, largely unknown cast led by Balthazar Getty. However, he doesn't quite succeed in recapturing the dark undercurrents of the novel. JF Swearing, violence. *DVD*

Balthazar Getty *Ralph* • Chris Furrh *Jack* • Daniel Pipoly *Piggy* • Gary Rule *Roger* • Terry Wells *Andy* • Braden MacDonald *Larry* ▪ *Dir* Harry Hook • *Scr* Sara Schiff, from the novel by William Golding

The Lord of the Rings ★★ PG

Animated fantasy adventure   1978 · US · Colour · 127min

Unlikely to satisfy fans of JRR Tolkien's novels, this animated version is also small beer compared to recent animated spectaculars. It seems less concerned with Tolkien than the West Coast druggie culture of the mid-1970s and as a herald of New Ageism. It's also rather slow and virtually impossible to follow unless you know the books. AT *DVD*

Christopher Guard *Frodo* • Michael Scholes *Samwise* • John Hurt *Aragorn "Strider"* • William Squire *Gandalf* • Simon Chandler *Merry* • Dominic Guard *Pippin* • Norman Bird *Bilbo* • Anthony Daniels *Legolas* ▪ *Dir* Ralph Bakshi • *Scr* Chris Conkling, Peter S Beagle, from the novels by JRR Tolkien

The Lord of the Rings: The Fellowship of the Ring ★★★★★ PG

Fantasy adventure   2001 · NZ/US · Colour · 171min

In the first chapter of director Peter Jackson's $300-million adaptation of JRR Tolkien's classic trilogy, Middle-earth is the fictional setting, but it's no backdrop; it's a living, breathing universe, in which mild-mannered hobbit Frodo Baggins (Elijah Wood) is forced to turn hero when he inherits the ring of absolute power. Assisted by powerful wizard Gandalf (a perfectly cast Ian McKellen) and a ragtag group of warriors and friends, he must journey across mountain, forest and plain to return the talisman to its source. The computer-generated images transform the New Zealand locations into views that will take your breath away and only someone with a pathological aversion to fantasy could fail to be absorbed and transported by this stunning, sincere and frequently terrifying adaptation. AC *DVD*

Elijah Wood *Frodo Baggins* • Ian McKellen *Gandalf the Grey* • Liv Tyler *Arwen Undómiel* • Viggo Mortensen *Aragorn/Strider* • Sean Astin *Samwise "Sam" Gamgee* • Cate Blanchett *Galadriel* • Hugo Weaving *Elrond* • Sean Bean *Boromir* • Ian Holm *Bilbo Baggins* • Christopher Lee *Saruman the White* • John Rhys-Davies *Gimli* • Billy Boyd (1) *Peregrin "Pippin" Took* • Dominic Monaghan *Meriadoc "Merry" Brandybuck* • Orlando Bloom *Legolas Greenleaf* • Andy Serkis *Sméagol/Gollum* ▪ *Dir* Peter Jackson • *Scr* Peter Jackson, Philippa Boyens, Fran Walsh, from the novel by JRR Tolkien • *Cinematographer* Andrew Lesnie • *Music* Howard Shore

The Lord of the Rings: The Two Towers ★★★★★ 12

Fantasy adventure   2002 · NZ/US/Ger · Colour · 171min

Under the assumption that everyone has seen *The Fellowship of the Ring*, director Peter Jackson jumps straight back into the action. With the fellowship fractured, the story diverges into three separate strands: Frodo and Sam's trek to Mordor, on which they are joined by the deranged Gollum; Gimli, Legolas and Aragorn's new allegiance with the imperilled kingdom of Rohan; and Merry and Pippin's affiliation with the sentient trees of Fangorn Forest. Darker and more urgent than the first film,

Jackson again displays an unparalleled grasp of storytelling on a grand scale – the siege of Helm's Deep in the final hour is as heroic and spectacular as any battle scene ever committed to film. The performances are uniformly excellent, but the most impressive contribution comes from Andy Serkis, who provides the creepy tones and fluid physical movements of Gollum, the most convincing CGI character created to date. JC *DVD* *BD*

Elijah Wood *Frodo Baggins* • Ian McKellen *Gandalf the White* • Liv Tyler *Arwen Undómiel* • Viggo Mortensen *Aragorn/Strider* • Sean Astin *Samwise "Sam" Gamgee* • Cate Blanchett *Galadriel* • John Rhys-Davies *Gimli/Treebeard* • Billy Boyd (1) *Peregrin "Pippin" Took* • Dominic Monaghan *Meriadoc "Merry" Brandybuck* • Orlando Bloom *Legolas Greenleaf* • Christopher Lee *Saruman the White* • Hugo Weaving *Elrond* • Miranda Otto *Eowyn of Rohan* • Bernard Hill *King Théoden* • Andy Serkis *Sméagol/Gollum* ▪ *Dir* Peter Jackson • *Scr* Peter Jackson, Philippa Boyens, Fran Walsh, Stephen Sinclair, from the novel by JRR Tolkien

The Lord of the Rings: The Return of the King ★★★★★ 12

Fantasy adventure   2003 · NZ/US/Ger · Colour · 192min

Peter Jackson deservedly won the best director Oscar for this powerful and enchanting concluding episode to his massively ambitious adaptation of JRR Tolkien's trilogy. It also became the first fantasy film to receive the best picture Oscar and won awards in all the categories for which it was nominated, equalling the record haul of 11 set by *Ben-Hur* and *Titanic*. One staggeringly beautiful sight follows another as the brilliant ensemble cast mix man, myth and magic together with astonishing scope and intoxicating invention. The action picks up from *The Two Towers* with Frodo crawling to Mount Doom to destroy the ring, while Aragorn enlists an army of the dead to help Gandalf defend the besieged city of Minas Tirith from the Witch-king and his armies. The ending does drag on with its series of teary farewells, but this is a minor gripe considering Jackson's towering achievement in creating a literate masterpiece. AJ *DVD* *BD*

Elijah Wood *Frodo Baggins* • Ian McKellen *Gandalf the White* • Liv Tyler *Arwen Undómiel* • Viggo Mortensen *Aragorn/Strider* • Sean Astin *Samwise "Sam" Gamgee* • Cate Blanchett *Galadriel* • John Rhys-Davies *Gimli* • Bernard Hill *King Théoden* • Billy Boyd (1) *Peregrin "Pippin" Took* • Dominic Monaghan *Meriadoc "Merry" Brandybuck* • Orlando Bloom *Legolas Greenleaf* • Hugo Weaving *Elrond* • Miranda Otto *Eowyn of Rohan* • David Wenham *Faramir* • John Noble *Denethor, Steward of Gondor* • Andy Serkis *Sméagol/Gollum* ▪ *Dir* Peter Jackson • *Scr* Peter Jackson, Fran Walsh, Philippa Boyens, from the novel by JRR Tolkien

Lord of War ★★★ 15

Black comedy action thriller   2005 · US · Colour · 116min

Writer/director Andrew Niccol takes a cynical swipe at the world arms trade in this sleek and confrontational thriller. Nicolas Cage plays an Ukrainian-American entrepreneur who sees an opportunity to escape his humdrum Brooklyn life by dealing in illegal weaponry. Recruiting wayward younger brother Jared Leto, Cage quickly finds himself running a global business, but success comes at a horrific price. The film is extremely smart and visually sophisticated, with some powerful action sequences. Yet the tale's cleverness and exactitude are also its undoing, making it feel soulless and fake. SF English, Russian, Spanish, Mandarin, Arabic +subtitles. Swearing, violence, drug abuse. *DVD* *BD*

Nicolas Cage *Yuri Orlov* • Jared Leto *Vitaly Orlov* • Bridget Moynahan *Ava Fontaine* • Ian Holm *Simeon Weisz* • Ethan Hawke *Jack Valentine* • Eamonn Walker *Andre Baptiste Senior* • Sammi Rotibi *Andre Baptiste Junior* ▪ *Dir/Scr* Andrew Niccol

L

The Lords of Discipline
★★★ 15

Drama 1983 · US · Colour · 98min

Having hanged himself in An Officer and a Gentleman, David Keith goes back to military school for this sinister thriller in which he combats the racist bigotry of a secret society known as "The Ten". Director Franc Roddam is comfortable with the sights and sounds of 1960s Carolina, but once the scene has been set he rather loses the plot, spending a disturbing amount of time on the acts of cruelty perpetrated upon the academy's first black cadet and not enough time sleuthing the culprits. DP Violence, swearing, brief nudity. DVD

David Keith Will McClean • Robert Prosky Colonel "Bear" Berrineau • GD Spradlin General Durrell • Barbara Babcock Abigail • Michael Biehn Alexander • Rick Rossovich Pig • John Lavachielli Mark • Judge Reinhold Macabbee • Bill Paxton Gilbreath • Jason Connery MacKinnon ■ Dir Franc Roddam • Scr Thomas Pope, Lloyd Fonvielle, from the novel by Pat Conroy

Lords of Dogtown
★★★ 15

Sports action drama
2005 · US · Colour · 105min

Stacy Peralta, who directed the documentary Dogtown and Z-Boys (2001) that charted the rise of three young skateboarders in California in the early 1970s, provides the script for this dramatisation of the same events. It's a fast, good-looking movie, thanks to director Catherine Hardwicke, who gives the film an intense immediacy. The weaknesses are all down to the script, with the young heroes walking a well-trodden path. However, the leads are charismatic and the soundtrack outstanding. GM DVD

Emile Hirsch Jay Adams • Victor Rasuk Tony Alva • John Robinson (3) Stacy Peralta • Michael Angarano Sid • Nikki Reed Kathy Alva • Heath Ledger Skip Engblom • Rebecca De Mornay Philaine • Johnny Knoxville Topper Banks ■ Dir Catherine Hardwicke • Scr Stacy Peralta

The Lords of Flatbush
★★★★ 15

Drama 1974 · US · Colour · 80min

Sylvester Stallone (in his first top-billed role), Happy Days star Henry Winkler, B-movie heart-throb Perry King and Paul Mace are members of a Brooklyn gang in this brilliant coming-of-age saga set in the late 1950s. Stallone sets the seal on his future success as a tough-talker pushed into marriage by his pregnant girlfriend when all he really wants to do is hang out with the guys and tend his pigeons. This evokes a strong sense of time and place, with a great nostalgic soundtrack. AJ

Perry King Chico Tyrell • Sylvester Stallone Stanley Rosiello • Henry Winkler Butchey Weinstein • Paul Mace Wimpy Murgalo • Susan Blakely Jane Bradshaw • Maria Smith Frannie Malincanico • Renee Paris Annie Yuckamanelli • Ray Sharkey Student • Paul Jabara Crazy Cohen ■ Dir Stephen Verona, Martin Davidson • Scr Stephen Verona, Martin Davidson, Gayle Gleckler, Sylvester Stallone

The Lords of Salem
★★ 18

Horror 2012 · US/UK/Can · Colour · 96min

This disjointed combination of The Witches of Eastwick and The Lair of the White Worm is a careless, scare-less farrago. Director Rob Zombie's regular muse, wife Sheri Moon, stars as a radio DJ who plays a record by the mysterious band Lords of Salem on air, and its droning tune, composed during the famous witch trials, spirals her back into a traumatic drug-addicted past. A wonderful cast of B-movie horror names can't disguise the fact that Zombie has absolutely no idea what he's doing or where his clichéd "weird for weirdness sake" story is going. AJ Violence, swearing, drug abuse, sex scenes, nudity.

Sheri Moon Zombie Heidi Hawthorne • Bruce Davison Francis Matthias • Jeffrey Daniel Phillips Herman "Whitey" Salvatore • Judy Geeson Lacy Doyle • Meg Foster Margaret Morgan • Ken Foree Herman Jackson ■ Dir/Scr Rob Zombie

Lore
★★★ 15

Wartime drama
2012 · Ger/Aus/UK · Colour · 104min

This visually striking but sombre drama focuses on a small group of children making their way through a ravaged Germany in the months after the collapse of the Third Reich. But it is more than a gruelling study of survival, for these children have been brought up to believe every grotesque lie the Nazis told and are now confronted with the appalling truth. After her parents are arrested by the Allies, 14-year-old Lore (Saskia Rosendahl) is left to care for her younger siblings. They set off for their grandmother's house in Hamburg, a long journey that will bring the war home to them for the first time. Australian co-writer and director Cate Shortland gets astounding performances from a very young cast in a film that is quietly shocking and offers no comforting answers. KK German, English +subtitles. DVD

Saskia Rosendahl Lore • Kai Malina Thomas • Nele Trebs Liesel • Ursina Lardi Mutti • Hans-Jochen Wagner Vati ■ Dir Cate Shortland • Scr Cate Shortland, Robin Mukherjee, from the novel The Dark Room by Rachel Seiffert

Lorenzo's Oil
★★★ 15

Biographical drama 1992 · US · Colour · 129min

This glossy, at times harrowing, heart-tugger is dominated by the towering performance of Susan Sarandon as the determined Michaela Odone, who takes on the medical establishment when her young son is diagnosed with a rare and normally fatal wasting disease. But Nick Nolte is less successful as the boy's father, Augusto, sporting a bizarre Italian accent. You'll either love or loathe this intelligent, well-made wallow that's ably directed by Mad Max veteran George Miller. SH DVD

Nick Nolte Augusto Odone • Susan Sarandon Michaela Odone • Peter Ustinov Professor Nikolais • Kathleen Wilhoite Deirdre Murphy • Gerry Bamman Doctor Judalon • Margo Martindale Wendy Gimble • Zack O'Malley Greenburg Lorenzo • Laura Linney Young teacher ■ Dir George Miller (2) • Scr George Miller, Nick Enright

Lorna
★★ 18

Satirical melodrama 1964 · US · BW · 79min

Part gothic melodrama, part sex morality play, this was the notorious Russ Meyer's first serious effort at "legitimate" film-making. Certainly it's his first plot-driven movie and casts buxom Lorna Maitland as the eponymous heroine, a backwoods wife who strays from her dull husband and begins an affair with an escaped con. Meyer, with his typically flamboyant editing and direction, does a pretty good job of things considering the mediocre acting talent and script at his disposal. RS Sex scenes, swearing, violence. DVD

Lorna Maitland Lorna • Mark Bradley (1) Fugitive • James Rucker James • Hal Hopper Luther • Doc Scott Jonah • James Griffith Prophet/Narrator ■ Dir Russ Meyer • Scr James Griffith, from a story by R Albion Meyer

Lorna Doone
★★★ U

Period drama 1934 · UK · BW · 82min

RD Blackmore's novel is a full-blooded melodrama set in 17th century Exmoor where two feuding families – the Doones and the Ridds – are at each other's throats. As in Romeo and Juliet, there is a cross-feudal romance between strappingly handsome John Ridd and pretty Lorna who, it transpires, isn't a Doone at all but a kidnapped aristocrat. Victoria Hopper, the wife of the producer/director Basil Dean, stars as Lorna. John Loder, as the hero Ridd, was always a rather wooden actor, though Margaret Lockwood, in her screen debut, is a ravishing beauty. AT

Victoria Hopper Lorna Doone • John Loder John Ridd • Margaret Lockwood Annie Ridd • Roy Emerton Carver Doone • Mary Clare Mistress Ridd • Edward Rigby Reuben Huckaback • Roger Livesey Tom Faggus • George Curzon King James II ■ Dir Basil Dean • Scr Dorothy Farnum, Miles Malleson, Gordon Wellesley, from the novel by RD Blackmore

Lorna Doone
★★ U

Period drama 1951 · US · Colour · 83min

Hollywood has a go at the classic yarn of a rustic feud, a hulking hero and a smart heroine who turns out to be a kidnapped heiress. It's made on a slimmed down budget and shot in the Yosemite National Park, California, rather than on Exmoor, but the studio did put up the money for Technicolor. B-movie director Phil Karlson treats it just like a western. AT

Barbara Hale Lorna Doone • Richard Greene John Ridd • Carl Benton Reid Sir Ensor Doone • William Bishop Carver Doone • Ron Randell Tom Faggus • Sean McClory Charleworth Doone • Onslow Stevens Counsellor Doone • Lester Matthews King Charles II ■ Dir Phil Karlson • Scr Jesse L Lasky Jr [Jesse Lasky Jr], Richard Schayer, from the novel by RD Blackmore

Loser
★ 12

Comedy romance 2000 · US · Colour · 91min

Teen films often plumb the depths of good taste, but rarely do they hit rock bottom like this one. Outrage and amorality have long been staples of the genre, but it's a fine line between chucklesome grossness and unfunny crassness. Date-rape drugs and under-age sex are just two of the areas mined for so-called mirth as callow country kid Jason Biggs bids to be accepted by his sex-obsessed, boorish roommates at a big-city college. DA DVD

Jason Biggs Paul Tannek • Mena Suvari Dora Diamond • Zak Orth Adam • Tom Sadoski Chris • Jimmi Simpson Noah • Greg Kinnear Professor Edward Alcott • Dan Aykroyd Dad ■ Dir/Scr Amy Heckerling

Loser Takes All
★ PG

Comedy drama 1956 · UK · Colour · 85min

Given that this screenplay was written by Graham Greene from his own book, its awfulness defies explanation. The casting of Glynis Johns and Rossano Brazzi as a newlywed couple honeymooning in Monte Carlo at the invitation of a vaguely characterised and only intermittently seen Robert Morley is a pairing so unlikely as to sink the enterprise on its own. However, the screenplay, about the husband developing a gambling obsession, is not much better. RK DVD

Rossano Brazzi Bertrand • Glynis Johns Cary • Robert Morley Dreuther • Felix Aylmer The Other ■ Dir Ken Annakin • Scr Graham Greene, from his novella

Loser Takes All
★ PG

Comedy 1990 · US · Colour · 81min

Robert Lindsay and Molly Ringwald take over from Rossano Brazzi and Glynis Johns as the British couple who are gifted a honeymoon in Monte Carlo, only for staid hubbie to become seduced by the casino. Lindsay does his best with the ploddingly predictable material but Ringwald is grievously miscast as his wife and even the presence of a distinguished supporting cast can't save it. JF

Robert Lindsay Ian Bertram • Molly Ringwald Cary Porter • John Gielgud Herbert Dreuther • Simon de la Brosse Philippe • Max Wall Bowles • Margi Clarke Bowles's nurse • Frances de la Tour Mrs De Vere ■ Dir James Scott • Scr James Scott, from the novella by Graham Greene

The Losers
★ 12

Action adventure
2010 · US/Fr/Ger · Colour · 92min

A covert group of US agents get double-crossed and left for dead in this Hollywood take on the graphic novel of the same name. There's a "men on a mission" template at work here that goes back at least as far as The Dirty Dozen, but this yarn proves a painfully undistinguished affair. It's just too formulaic for its own good, from the grizzled leader (Jeffrey Dean Morgan) to the wise-cracking comic relief (Chris Evans) and sleek, ruthless villain (Jason Patric). Avatar's Zoë Saldana is the token female interloper, providing curvaceous interest for teenage boys, as the shambling plot strings together a series of explosive set pieces rendered ineffective by mediocre digital effects. TJ DVD Blu-ray

Zoë Saldana Aisha • Jeffrey Dean Morgan Clay • Chris Evans Jensen • Idris Elba Roque • Jason Patric Max • Columbus Short Pooch • Holt McCallany Wade • Oscar Jaenada Cougar ■ Dir Sylvain White • Scr Peter Berg, James Vanderbilt, from the series of graphic novels by Andy Diggle, Jock

Losin' It
★★ 18

Comedy drama 1983 · US · Colour · 95min

Tom Cruise, in one of his earliest roles, adds curiosity value to an unexceptional coming-of-age tale about three teenagers heading for Tijuana to gain a broader perspective on life and lose their virginity. Shelley Long comes along for the ride as a woman hoping to get a quick divorce. AJ

Tom Cruise Woody • Jackie Earle Haley Dave • John Stockwell Spider • Shelley Long Kathy • John P Navin Jr Wendell the Wimp • Henry Darrow El Jefe, Sheriff • Hector Elias Chuey ■ Dir Curtis Hanson • Scr BWL Norton, from his story

Losing Isaiah
★★★ 15

Drama 1995 · US · Colour · 102min

This emotionally-charged drama examines the custody battle between a young black mother (Halle Berry), who three years earlier had abandoned her baby while high on drugs, and the loving white couple (Jessica Lange and David Strathairn) who have adopted him. The strong cast adds dramatic weight to a "TV movie of the week" plot. A tad contrived, but still believable. JC Violence, swearing, drug abuse. DVD

Jessica Lange Margaret Lewin • Halle Berry Khaila Richards • David Strathairn Charles Lewin • Cuba Gooding Jr Eddie Hughes • Daisy Eagan Hannah Lewin • Marc John Jeffries Isaiah • Samuel L Jackson Kadar Lewis ■ Dir Stephen Gyllenhaal • Scr Naomi Foner, from the novel by Seth J Margolis

The Loss of Sexual Innocence
★★ 18

Drama 1999 · US/UK · Colour · 105min

Specked with fascinating moments, this is an otherwise over-indulgent hobby horse from writer/director Mike Figgis. A fragmentary memoir of a movie producer called Nic (played variously by Jonathan Rhys Meyers and Julian Sands), it traces his development from school bullying and love on the Tyne to marital discord and tragedy in the Sahara. Alas, the decision to intercut the action with a mixed race re-telling of the Adam and Eve story is self-conscious. DP Sex scenes, nudity.

Julian Sands Nic (as an adult) • Saffron Burrows English twin/Italian twin • Stefano Dionisi Lucca • Kelly Macdonald Susan • Gina McKee Susan's mother • Jonathan Rhys Meyers Nic (age 16) • Bernard Hill Susan's father ■ Dir/Scr Mike Figgis

Lost
★★★

Crime drama 1955 · UK · Colour · 89min

This film succeeds because it confronts every parent's nightmare: what happens when you suddenly look away and find your child is missing when you look back? Of course, this being a class-riddled Rank picture, it's the nanny who loses the baby, but it's pretty harrowing nonetheless, despite the casting of insipid David Knight and Julia Arnall as the parents. Granite-faced cop David Farrar is on hand to bring grit to this earnest chase movie and Harry Waxman's colour location photography is superb. TS

David Farrar Inspector Craig • David Knight Lee Cochrane • Julia Arnall Sue Cochrane • Anthony Oliver Sergeant Lyel • Thora Hird Landlady • Eleanor Summerfield Sergeant Cook • Ann Paige Nanny • Anna Turner Mrs Robey ■ Dir Guy Green • Scr Janet Green

Lost
★★★

Psychological thriller
2005 · US · Colour · 86min

Dean Cain's post-Superman career has been pretty forgettable, but this nifty low-budget thriller ranks as one of his better efforts. He plays a slick businessman who gets lost in the Nevada desert on the way home to his family. At the same time, a gang of bank robbers are on the loose and it soon becomes apparent why he is in such a hurry. Cain is on screen for virtually the whole movie and acquits himself well, while writer/director Darren Lemke succeeds in wringing a few neat twists out of the road-trip-from-hell scenario. JF

Dean Cain *Jeremy Stanton* • Ashley Scott *Judy* • Danny Trejo *Archer* • Irina Bjorklund *Cora Stanton* • Justin Henry *Chester Gould* • Griffin Armstorff *Tyler Stanton* ■ *Dir/Scr* Darren Lemke

Lost and Found ★ 15
Romantic comedy
1979 · UK/US · Colour · 100min

Re-uniting George Segal and Glenda Jackson, the delightful duo of *A Touch of Class*, might have seemed like a good plan, but this story of a widowed American professor meeting a British divorcee on a skiing holiday, marrying, and living unhappily ever after makes us regret the very idea. Like a ski-run, the film heads downhill all the way. TH Swearing.

George Segal *Adam Watson* • Glenda Jackson *Patricia Brittenham* • Maureen Stapleton *Jemmy* • Hollis Mclaren *Eden* • John Cunningham (1) *Lenny* • Paul Sorvino *Reilly* • John Candy *Carpentier* • Martin Short *Engel* ■ *Dir* Melvin Frank • *Scr* Melvin Frank, Jack Rose

Lost & Found ★★ 12
Romantic comedy 1999 · US · Colour · 95min

Dependable comic actor David Spade finally cracked the big time with his role in the US sitcom *Just Shoot Me*. His success led to a starring role in this romantic comedy in which Spade plays a restaurateur who falls in lust with his attractive French neighbour Sophie Marceau. Spade's smarmy persona can be an acquired taste, so take one off if you're a fan, take one off if you find his bitchy asides and pointed sarcasm hard to take. DF Swearing, brief nudity.

David Spade *Dylan Ramsey* • Sophie Marceau *Lila Dubois* • Patrick Bruel *Rene* • Artie Lange *Wally* • Mitchell Whitfield *Mark Glidewell* • Martin Sheen *Millstone* • Jon Lovitz *Uncle Harry* ■ *Dir* Jeff Pollack • *Scr* David Spade, Marc Meeks, JB Cook

Lost Angel ★★★ U
Drama 1943 · US · BW · 90min

Foundling child Margaret O'Brien, made the subject of a scientific experiment, reveals herself as a genius by the age of six, but at the cost of the normal joys of childhood. The situation is remedied when police reporter James Craig takes her under his wing. The film demonstrates O'Brien's talent and appeal and, although an implausible exercise in sentimentality designed to tug at the heartstrings, its saccharine content is nicely modulated. RK

Margaret O'Brien *Alpha* • James Craig *Mike Regan* • Marsha Hunt *Katie Mallory* • Philip Merivale *Professor Peter Vincent* • Keenan Wynn *Packy* • Alan Napier *Dr Woodring* ■ *Dir* Roy Rowland • *Scr* Isobel Lennart, from an idea by Angna Enters

The Lost Boys ★★★ 15
Horror comedy 1987 · US · Colour · 93min

There's a nasty surprise in store for divorcee Dianne Wiest when she moves her family to a small town on the Californian coast. The local teenage gang is actually a pack of punk vampires with designs on her teenage sons (Jason Patric and Corey Haim). This quintessentially 1980s tale is a slick attempt to update the bloodsucking genre for the MTV generation and Kiefer Sutherland's role as the charismatic leader of the vampires is an early career highlight – he makes being undead seem very cool. While it's not quite as original or witty as it could have been, this unashamedly glossy take on vampire mythology has a clever script that's packed with twists, and builds to a surprisingly tense climax. AJ Swearing.
DVD 🅑

Jason Patric *Michael Emerson* • Kiefer Sutherland *David* • Corey Feldman *Edgar Frog* • Corey Haim *Sam Emerson* • Dianne Wiest *Lucy Emerson* • Barnard Hughes *Grandpa* • Edward Herrmann *Max* • Jami Gertz *Star* ■ *Dir* Joel

Schumacher • *Scr* Janice Fischer, James Jeremias, Jeffrey Boam, from a story by Janice Fischer, James Jeremias

The Lost City ★★ 15
Period drama 2005 · US · Colour · 144min

Andy Garcia directs and stars in this ode to pre-revolution Cuba. He plays Fico, the owner of top nightclub El Tropico and the eldest of three brothers whose loyalties are tested during the revolution that brought Castro to power in 1959. Garcia is always a compelling presence on screen, but he's less successful behind the camera. The film looks terrific, yet Garcia lets the story get away from him, especially when it comes to the romance between Fico and his dreary sister-in-law (Inés Sastre). Then there's Bill Murray as Fico's wisecracking sidekick, who has no obvious purpose except to make sardonic comments that undercut any real drama. SP Violence.

Andy Garcia *Fico Fellove* • Inés Sastre *Aurora Fellove* • Tomas Milian *Don Federico Fellove* • Richard Bradford *Don Donoso Fellove* • Nestor Carbonell *Luis Fellove* • Enrique Murciano *Ricardo Fellove* • Dustin Hoffman *Meyer Lansky* • Bill Murray *The writer* • Steven Bauer *Captain Castel* • William Marquez *Rodney* ■ *Dir* Andy Garcia • *Scr* G Cabrera Infante • *Music* Andy Garcia

The Lost City of Z
Period adventure based on a true story
2016 · US · Colour

This is a preview – no prints were available to review prior to publication: *Sherlock* star Benedict Cumberbatch was originally set to headline this period yarn about a real-life 1920s British explorer and his quest to find a legendary city in the Amazon jungle. But his fame has now skyrocketed thanks in no small way to his Oscar nomination for *The Imitation Game*, so scheduling conflicts mean replacement by *Sons of Anarchy's* Charlie Hunnam. *Twilight* heart-throb Robert Pattinson is still set to co-star, so this *Boys' Own* adventure remains a box-office draw for both genders. JA

Robert Pattinson *Henry Costin* • Sienna Miller *Nina Fawcett* • Charlie Hunnam *Colonel Percival Fawcett* ■ *Dir* James Gray • *Scr* James Gray, from David Grann's non-fiction book

The Lost Continent ★★ 12
Fantasy adventure 1968 · US · Colour · 83min

Director Leslie Norman probably heaved a huge sigh of relief when he parted company with this Hammer stinker just a few days into production. Michael Carreras took over and immediately ran the project on to the cinematic rocks. The script is wonderfully bizarre, with Eric Porter and his crew setting foot on an island ruled by the Spanish Inquisition. The monsters will have you shrieking with laughter. DP DVD

Eric Porter *Captain Lansen* • Hildegarde Neff *Eva* • Suzanna Leigh *Unity* • Tony Beckley *Harry Tyler* • Nigel Stock *Dr Webster* • Neil McCallum *First Officer Hemmings* ■ *Dir* Michael Carreras • *Scr* Michael Nash *[Michael Carreras]*, from the novel *Uncharted Seas* by Dennis Wheatley

The Lost Embrace ★★★ 15
Comedy drama
2003 · Arg/Sp/Fr/It · Colour · 99min

Set in a working-class, predominantly Jewish corner of Buenos Aires, Daniel Burman's affirming drama suggests that there's more to multiculturalism than racial tension and political correctness. Frustrated by his dead-end existence, college dropout Daniel Hendler is keen to acquire a Polish passport and start afresh, but most people around him are too busy making the most of every day to collude in his plans. Burman creates a sense of community that is reinforced by the splendid ensemble. DP Spanish +subtitles.

Daniel Hendler *Ariel* • Adriana Aizemberg *Sonia* • Jorge D'Elia *Elias* • Sergio Boris *Joseph* • Rosita Londner *Ariel's grandmother* • Diego Korol *Mitelman* • Silvina Bosco *Rita* • Melina Petriella *Estela* ■ *Dir* Daniel Burman • *Scr* Daniel Burman, Marcelo Birmajer

Lost Highway ★★★★ 18
Psychological thriller
1996 · US · Colour · 128min

David Lynch's narrative-defying psychological thriller is about a jazz saxophonist (an exemplary Bill Pullman) in a disturbed domestic limbo who suddenly and inexplicably transforms into a younger man (Balthazar Getty). Though never together in a scene, the men share what appears to be the same elusive, deceptive woman (Patricia Arquette). It's not the most accessible scenario, but the delivery is hypnotising. Painterly, impenetrable and creepy. DO Violence, swearing, sex scenes, nudity. DVD 🅑

Bill Pullman *Fred Madison* • Patricia Arquette *Renee Madison/Alice Wakefield* • Balthazar Getty *Pete Dayton* • Robert Blake *Mystery man* • Natasha Gregson Wagner *Sheila* • Robert Loggia *Mr Eddy/Dick Laurent* • Gary Busey *Bill Dayton* • Richard Pryor *Arnie* • Michael Massee *Andy* • Henry Rollins *Guard Henry* • Jack Nance *Phil* • Mink Stole *Forewoman* • Giovanni Ribisi *Steve "V"* ■ *Dir* David Lynch • *Scr* David Lynch, Barry Gifford • *Cinematographer* Peter Deming

Lost Holiday: the Jim and Suzanne Shemwell Story ★★
Adventure drama based on a true story
2007 · US · Colour · 120min

Dylan Walsh and Jami Gertz whine and bicker their way through this Christmas-set drama, playing an estranged couple who are forced to re-evaluate their lives and relationship when a blizzard traps them in the Idaho Mountains. But the focus on arguing over action becomes irritating rather quickly, and leaves the actors struggling to bring realism, and more importantly tension, to the true story-based events. SF

Dylan Walsh *Jim Shemwell* • Jami Gertz *Suzanne Shemwell* • Brooklynn Proulx *Taryn Shemwell* • Aaron Pearl *Blake* ■ *Dir/Scr* Gregory Goodell

The Lost Honour of Katharina Blum ★★★★ 12
Political thriller 1975 · W Ger · Colour · 105min

Slightly shifting the emphasis of Heinrich Böll's novel to inculcate the police, as well as the media, in the downfall of an innocent victim, Volker Schlöndorff and Margarethe von Trotta have created a chilling tale of state paranoia and tabloid sensationalism that remains a depressingly familiar tale for our times. Displaying dignity in the face of provocation, Angela Winkler is harrowingly credible as the apolitical woman whose one night stand with a suspected terrorist results in the ruination of her life. Filmed with a realism that adds to its menace, this is a key example of New German Cinema. DP DVD 🅑

Angela Winkler *Katharina Blum* • Mario Adorf *Beizmenne* • Dieter Laser *Werner Toetgess* • Heinz Bennent *Dr Blorna* • Hannelore Hoger *Trude Blorna* • Harald Kuhlmann *Moeding* • Karl Heinz Vosgerau *Alois Straubleder* • Jürgen Prochnow *Ludwig Götten* ■ *Dir* Volker Schlöndorff, Margarethe von Trotta • *Scr* Volker Schlöndorff, Margarethe von Trotta, from the novel by Heinrich Böll

Lost Horizon ★★★★★ U
Fantasy adventure 1937 · US · BW · 127min

Here's one of the great dream fulfilment movies, showing there is a better place, a heaven on Earth with lasting peace and happiness, tucked away in the Himalayas. In his enthusiasm to film James Hilton's novel, Columbia's ace director Frank Capra persuaded the studio to spend a record $2.5 million. The money was well utilised to create a Shangri-la of Art Deco cleanliness and simplicity populated with unfamiliar faces - most memorably Sam Jaffe as the 250-year-old High Lama - to contrast with the typecasting of Ronald Colman, Thomas Mitchell, Edward Everett Horton and others as the outsiders. Colman ensures the film's success - his sincerity and passion make believers of us all. AE DVD

Ronald Colman *Robert Conway* • Jane Wyatt *Sondra* • Edward Everett Horton *Alexander P Lovett* • John Howard (1) *George Conway* • Thomas Mitchell *Henry Barnard* • Margo *Maria* • Isabel Jewell *Gloria Stone* • HB Warner *Chang* • Sam Jaffe *High Lama* ■ *Dir* Frank Capra • *Scr* Robert Riskin, from the novel by James Hilton • *Music* Dimitri Tiomkin *[Dmitri Tiomkin]* • *Cinematographer* Joseph Walker • *Art Director* Stephen Goosson

Lost Horizon ★ U
Musical 1973 · US · Colour · 132min

In his 1937 adaptation, Frank Capra managed to make sense of the fanciful ideas raised in James Hilton's novel, but they are rendered risible in this ill-conceived musical remake. Aiming for the glossy sophistication he brought to his earlier projects, producer Ross Hunter presents Shangri-la as a Himalayan country club instead of a utopian sanctuary. Peter Finch, meanwhile, looks as though he's in purgatory as he exchanges trite truisms with High Lama Charles Boyer, though he's not alone in struggling with the dire ditties penned by Burt Bacharach and Hal David. DP

Peter Finch *Richard Conway* • Michael York *George Conway* • Liv Ullmann *Catherine* • Sally Kellerman *Sally Hughes* • George Kennedy *Sam Cornelius* • Olivia Hussey *Maria* • Bobby Van *Harry Lovett* • James Shigeta *Brother To-Lenn* • Charles Boyer *High Lama* • John Gielgud *Chang* ■ *Dir* Charles Jarrott • *Scr* Larry Kramer, from the novel by James Hilton

The Lost Hours ★★ U
Murder mystery 1952 · UK · BW · 70min

This is one of director David MacDonald's least distinguished ventures, being another of the dreaded quota quickies in which a third-rate Hollywood star gets to play the lead in a threadbare crime story, notable for the cheapness of the sets, the dismal dialogue and the eagerness of the supporting cast. Mark Stevens is the luckless Yank in this ham-fisted tale about amnesia, smuggling and jealousy, which is lifted only by Jean Kent's elegance and Garry Marsh as the dogged flatfoot. DP

Mark Stevens *Paul Smith* • Jean Kent *Louise Parker* • Garry Marsh *Foster* • John Bentley *Clark Sutton* • Dianne Foster *Dianne Wrigley* • Jack Lambert *John Parker* • Thora Hird *Maid* ■ *Dir* David MacDonald • *Scr* Steve Fisher, John Gilling

Lost in a Harem ★★★
Comedy 1944 · US · BW · 88min

Abbott and Costello are way out east as two prop men with a travelling show touring a desert kingdom. Thrown in jail along with the show's star Marilyn Maxwell, they are freed by dispossessed prince John Conte to help him recapture his lost kingdom. This is well up to standard for the boys and there's good value from Douglass Dumbrille as the villainous Sultan Nimativ - the funnier routines involve his hypnotic rings. DF

Bud Abbott *Peter Johnson* • Lou Costello *Harvey Garvey* • Marilyn Maxwell *Hazel Moon* • John Conte *Prince Ramo* • Douglass Dumbrille *Nimativ* ■ *Dir* Charles Reisner • *Scr* John Grant, Harry Crane, Harry Ruskin

Lost in Alaska ★ PG
Comedy 1952 · US · BW · 76min

This feels like a two-reeler that's been teased out (not to say tormented) to reach feature length. Abbott and Costello play a couple of San Franciscan firemen who head for the Yukon determined to track down the $2 million in gold that's been stolen from suicidal prospector Tom Ewell. The tunes intoned by saloon singer Mitzi Green were part-scored by Henry Mancini, who was making his movie debut here. DP

Bud Abbott *Tom Watson* • Lou Costello *George Bell* • Mitzi Green *Rosette* • Tom Ewell *Nugget Joe McDermott* • Bruce Cabot *Jake Stillman* • Emory Parnell *Sherman* • Jack Ingram *Henchman* ■ *Dir* Jean Yarbrough • *Scr* Martin A Ragaway *[Martin Ragaway]*, Leonard Stern, from a story by Elwood Ullman

L

Lost in America ★★★ 15
Comedy 1985 · US · Colour · 87min

Albert Brooks is one of Hollywood's most engaging, oddball talents, a sort of West Coast Woody Allen who writes, directs and stars in his own projects. In this satire, he's a nervously successful advertising executive in LA who, with wife Julie Hagerty, drops out and sets off to discover America "just like *Easy Rider*", he says. The story takes as many byways as highways and is always unpredictable and engaging, with weird characters seen through Brooks's askew lens. Maybe it lacks that extra bite – an easy ride, but always an enjoyable one. AT

Albert Brooks *David Howard* • Julie Hagerty *Linda Howard* • Maggie Roswell *Patty* • Michael Greene *Paul Dunn* • Tom Tarpey *Brad Tooley* • Raynold Gideon *Ray* ■ *Dir* Albert Brooks • *Scr* Albert Brooks, Monica Johnson

Lost in Karastan ★★★ 15
Comedy 2014 · UK/Ger/Rus/Georgia · BW and Colour · 95min

Despite co-writing with Pawel Pawlikowski (*My Summer of Love*), writer/director Ben Hopkins never quite nails this satire on movie-making and Eastern European politics. Matthew Macfadyen plays the fading director accepting a dictator's request to make an epic about his country. But bad casting, rebel assaults and sexual politics soon cause morale to sag. It's bullishly played by all, but Hopkins's first directorial work in five years raises more broad laughs than potent points about art and politics. DP Swearing, sex *DVD*

Matthew Macfadyen *Emil Forester* • MyAnna Buring *Chulpan* • Noah Taylor *Xan Butler* • Richard van Weyden *President Abashiliev* ■ *Dir* Ben Hopkins • *Scr* Ben Hopkins, Pawel Pawlikowski

Lost in La Mancha ★★★★ 15
Documentary 2002 · UK · Colour · 89min

Keith Fulton and Louis Pepe's compelling documentary charts the derailment of Terry Gilliam's film *The Man Who Killed Don Quixote*. The film opens with clips from Orson Welles's ill-fated attempt to bring the Cervantes classic to the screen, and from there draws upon over 80 hours of video footage, widescreen rushes and animated storyboards to tell the whole "un-making" of Gilliam's project. With Jean Rochefort as the eccentric knight and Johnny Depp as a time-traveller mistaken for Sancho Panza, everything looks set. But an air of *Munchausen* madness pervades both pre-production and the brief shoot, leaving one to lament the loss of a potential masterpiece and marvel at the terrifying unpredictability of the movie business. DP *DVD* *CS*

Jeff Bridges *Narrator* ■ *Dir/Scr* Keith Fulton, Louis Pepe

Lost in Siberia ★★★ 15
Period drama 1991 · UK/USSR · Colour · 103min

Among the first Russian films to consider the notorious gulags, this forceful drama may be set in the early days of the Cold War, but the implication is that matters scarcely improved in the intervening years. In a radical departure from his *Brideshead* image, Anthony Andrews gives one his strongest performances as the Russo-British geologist, who is wrongly arrested for spying on the Persian border and consigned to a Siberian labour camp. Alexander Mitta focuses on the empowerment the inmates derive from their unshakeable friendships. Made in both Russian and English versions. DP

Anthony Andrews *Andrei Miller* • Yelena Mayorova *Doctor Anna* • Vladimir Ilyin *Captain Malakhov* • Ira Mikhalyova *Lilka* • Yevgeni F Mironov [Yevgeni Mironov] *Volodya* ■ *Dir* Alexander Mitta • *Scr* Alexander Mitta, Valery Fried, Yuri Korotkov, James Brabazon (English version)

Lost in Space ★★ PG
Science-fiction adventure 1998 · US · Colour · 124min

This big-budget screen version of Irwin Allen's cult 1960s TV series is a charmless if flashy affair under the direction of Stephen Hopkins. The Robinson family's Earth migration experiment is sabotaged by evil Doctor Smith (Gary Oldman) and they are forced to land on a mysterious planet inhabited by mutated monster spiders. The special effects, nostalgic look, varying tone and acting never gel in what is basically a cynical marketing exercise. AJ *DVD* *SL*

Gary Oldman *Dr Smith* • William Hurt *John Robinson* • Matt LeBlanc *Don West* • Mimi Rogers *Maureen Robinson* • Heather Graham *Judy Robinson* • Lacey Chabert *Penny Robinson* • Jack Johnson *Will Robinson* • Jared Harris *Older Will* ■ *Dir* Stephen Hopkins • *Scr* Akiva Goldsman, from the TV series

Lost in the Stars ★★★ PG
Musical drama 1974 · US · Colour · 93min

This was the last musical score by *The Threepenny Opera*'s Kurt Weill, an operetta that translates Alan Paton's poignant anti-apartheid novel *Cry, the Beloved Country* into ironic harmonies. Brock Peters gives a fine performance as the black clergyman in search of his son in Johannesburg, who finds instead cruel racism and repression. While the music is memorable and the production sincere, this "stage record" also somewhat predictable and ponderous. TH Some violence. *DVD*

Brock Peters *Stephen Kumalo* • Melba Moore *Irina* • Raymond St Jacques *John Kumalo* • Clifton Davis *Absalom* • Paul Rogers *James Jarvis* • Paulene Myers *Grace* ■ *Dir* Daniel Mann • *Scr* Alfred Hayes, from the play by Maxwell Anderson, Kurt Weill, from the novel *Cry, the Beloved Country* by Alan Paton

Lost in Translation ★★★★★ 15
Romantic comedy drama 2003 · US · Colour · 97min

Bill Murray gives a delicately restrained and masterful performance in Sofia Coppola's marvellous follow-up to her debut movie *The Virgin Suicides*. He stars as a world-weary film actor who's in Japan to make a whisky commercial. There he meets Scarlett Johansson, equally good as an unhappily married young woman. Coppola wisely underpins the bittersweet soul-searching with a healthy dose of humour. She also expertly uses the neon-drenched backdrop of night-time Tokyo as an alien landscape against which the couple delicately explore each other's ambiguous feelings. A sad, funny, magical and irresistibly moving experience. AS *DVD* *SL*

Bill Murray *Bob Harris* • Scarlett Johansson *Charlotte* • Giovanni Ribisi *John* • Anna Faris *Kelly* • Fumihiro Hayashi *Charlie* • Catherine Lambert *Jazz singer* • Akiko Takeshita *Ms Kawasaki* ■ *Dir/Scr* Sofia Coppola

Lost in Yonkers ★★★ PG
Comedy drama 1993 · US · Colour · 109min

Richard Dreyfuss stars as a small-time gangster who returns to his childhood home in Yonkers to lie low, regaling his young nephews Brad Stoll and Mike Damus with tall tales of his life of crime. Grandma Irene Worth rules the household with a rod of iron that has broken the spirit of Dreyfuss's sister Mercedes Ruehl. This is another of playwright Neil Simon's semi-autobiographical dramas, but, despite some wonderful acting turns, this can be humdrum. TH *DVD*

Richard Dreyfuss *Louie* • Mercedes Ruehl *Bella* • Irene Worth *Grandma* • Brad Stoll *Jay* • Mike Damus *Arty* • David Strathairn *Johnny* ■ *Dir* Martha Coolidge • *Scr* Neil Simon, from his play

The Lost Lover ★★ PG
Drama 1999 · It/UK · Colour · 93min

For all its liberalism and committed playing, this is a morose and ultimately inconsequential melodrama from Italian director Roberto Faenza. Living in Israel after the death of his son, garage owner Ciaran Hinds goes in search of mysterious stranger Stuart Bunce in the hope of preventing his withdrawn wife, Juliet Aubrey, from drifting into another bout of depression. Neither enlightening nor engaging. DP

Ciaran Hinds *Adam* • Juliet Aubrey *Asya* • Stuart Bunce *Gabriel* • Clara Bryant *Dafi* • Erick Vazquez *Naim* • Phyllida Law *Grandmother* ■ *Dir* Roberto Faenza • *Scr* Sandro Petraglia, Roberto Faenza

The Lost Man ★★
Drama 1969 · US · Colour · 122min

Sidney Poitier plays a black radical who plans a robbery on a factory that only employs whites. The heist backfires and Poitier, with white love interest Joanna Shimkus, finds himself on the run. As the highly equivocal hero, partially modelled on Malcolm X, Poitier probably thought this was a brave movie to make, but it's hardly a radical movie, just another caper-gone-wrong action film. There's also a twist at the end that signals a rapid descent into treacle. AT

Sidney Poitier *Jason Higgs* • Joanna Shimkus *Cathy Ellis* • Al Freeman Jr *Dennis Laurence* • Michael Tolan *Hamilton* • Leon Bibb *Eddie Moxy* • Richard Dysart *Barnes* ■ *Dir* Robert Alan Aurthur • *Scr* Robert Alan Aurthur, from the novel *Odd Man Out* by FL Green

The Lost Moment ★★★
Period drama 1947 · US · BW · 88min

Henry James's novel *The Aspern Papers* is a highly theatrical, intimate and intriguing work. The simple story concerns the quest of a publisher for the letters of a famous poet, which are now in the possession of a very old woman who lives with her spinster niece. Set in a convincing and studio-built Venice, this film version stars Robert Cummings, a superb Agnes Moorehead as the old lady and, in an unexpected piece of casting, Susan Hayward as her niece. A compelling, stylised period drama, elegantly directed by Martin Gabel, and with a surprise dénouement. RK

Robert Cummings *Lewis Venable* • Susan Hayward *Tina* • Agnes Moorehead *Juliana* • Joan Lorring *Amelia* • John Archer *Charles* • Eduardo Ciannelli *Father Rinaldo* ■ *Dir* Martin Gabel • *Scr* Leonardo Bercovici, from the novel *The Aspern Papers* by Henry James

The Lost One ★★★
Drama 1951 · W Ger · BW · 97min

The wonderful character actor Peter Lorre only directed this one film and it has a melancholic sense of self-reference that probably would have been difficult to follow. He returned to Germany (from which he exiled himself in 1933) in the doldrums days of the postwar national cinema and starred in this harrowing work about a scientist who has been trapped into working for the Nazis. The consequences of the relationship bring death and betrayal to his existence and eventually lead him to seek salvation in a refugee camp. Lorre directs fluently in a somewhat dated expressionist style that is reminiscent of the great German master, Fritz Lang. BB German +subtitles.

Peter Lorre *Dr Karl Rothe* • Karl John *Hoesch* • Helmut Rudolf *Colonel Winkler* • Renate Mannhardt *Inge Hermann* • Johanna Hofer *Frau Hermann* • Eva-Ingeborg Scholz *Ursula Weber* ■ *Dir* Peter Lorre • *Scr* Peter Lorre, Benno Vigny, Axel Eggebrecht

The Lost Patrol ★★
First World War adventure 1934 · US · BW · 74min

In the Mesopotamian desert during the First World War, a small group of lost British cavalrymen search for their comrades while being gradually finished off by Arab snipers, the scorching sun and lack of water. As directed by John Ford, it's more of a western than a war movie and the climactic skirmish looks like Custer's Last Stand. AT

Victor McLaglen *Sergeant* • Boris Karloff *Sanders* • Wallace Ford *Morelli* • Reginald Denny *Brown* • JM Kerrigan *Quincannon* • Billy Bevan *Hale* • Alan Hale *Cook* ■ *Dir* John Ford • *Scr* Dudley Nichols, Garrett Fort, from the story *Patrol* by Philip MacDonald

The Lost People ★
Drama 1949 · UK · BW · 89min

Bridget Boland's play, *Cockpit*, which tackled the problem of Europeans left stateless and homeless after the Second World War, meant well and was excitingly experimental. This film version, still confined to one set, doesn't work. It's all talk and no action, and additional love scenes, written by Muriel Box, stick out like sore thumbs. Worse, the efforts of British officer Dennis Price to get people of many nationalities to co-operate with each other now come across as xenophobic. DM

Dennis Price *Captain Ridley* • Mai Zetterling *Lili* • Richard Attenborough *Jan* • Siobhan McKenna *Marie* • Maxwell Reed *Peter* • William Hartnell *Sgt Barnes* • Gerard Heinz *Professor* • Zena Marshall *Anna* ■ *Dir* Bernard Knowles, Muriel Box • *Scr* Bridget Boland, Muriel Box, from the play *Cockpit* by Bridget Boland

Lost River ★★★ 15
Fantasy thriller 2014 · US · Colour · 90min

Actor Ryan Gosling makes his writer/director debut with a twisted adult fairy tale heavily influenced by David Lynch and Nicolas Winding Refn. Financially strapped single mother Christina Hendricks is offered work in a club where torture mutilation acts top the bill, while her teenage son (splendid Iain De Caestecker) draws the attention of lip-severing psycho Matt Smith (the 11th Doctor) who runs their no-go neighbourhood. Gosling's parable of economic exploitation does boast some incredibly potent imagery, but it's indulgent and unfocused and is more concerned with its arresting look than any proper coherence. AJ *DVD*

Christina Hendricks *Billy* • Saoirse Ronan *Rat* • Iain De Caestecker *Bones* • Matt Smith *Bully* • Barbara Steele *Grandma* • Eva Mendes *Cat* • Ben Mendelsohn *Dave* ■ *Dir/Scr* Ryan Gosling

The Lost Son ★★ 18
Crime drama 1998 · UK/Fr · Colour · 98min

This is Daniel Auteuil's first English language film, but that's not the only problem here. This deeply ambitious movie, following Auteuil as an ex-cop turned private investigator who unearths a paedophile ring while on the trail of a missing son, is sadly flawed. Aside from the interestingly bleak nature of the story and Auteuil's watchability, the casting is bizarre. Billie Whitelaw, Ciaran Hinds – whose accent is so atrocious one is left wondering where he's supposed to be from – and Nastassja Kinski all fail to convince. LH Violence, sex scenes, swearing, nudity. *DVD*

Daniel Auteuil *Xavier Lombard* • Nastassja Kinski *Deborah* • Katrin Cartlidge *Emily* • Ciaran Hinds *Carlos* • Marianne Denicourt *Nathalie* • Bruce Greenwood *Friedman* • Billie Whitelaw *Mrs Spitz* • Cyril Shaps *Mr Spitz* ■ *Dir* Chris Menges • *Scr* Eric Leclere, Margaret Leclere, Mark Mills

Lost Souls ★★ 15
Supernatural horror thriller 2000 · US · Colour · 93min

This stars Winona Ryder as a traumatised victim of demonic possession, who learns that author Ben Chaplin is destined to be "reborn" as Christianity's arch-enemy. Ryder is a credible witness to events, but Chaplin faces impending reincarnation with all the foreboding of a man whose bus is late, while John Hurt (as a priest) seems to think that merely looking soulful will pass for acting. The directorial debut of Oscar-winning cinematographer Janusz Kaminski, this is visually striking but short on dramatic tension. TH *DVD*

Winona Ryder *Maya Larkin* • Ben Chaplin *Peter Kelson* • Philip Baker Hall *Father James* • Elias Koteas *John Townsend* • Sarah Wynter *Claire Van Owen* • John Beasley *Mike Smythe* • John Hurt *Father Lareaux* ■ *Dir* Janusz Kaminski • *Scr* Pierce Gardner, from a story by Pierce Gardner, Betsy Stahl

U SUITABLE FOR ALL   **Uc** SUITABLE ESPECIALLY FOR YOUNG CHILDREN (DVD ONLY)   **PG** PARENTAL GUIDANCE   **12A** UNDER 12s TO BE ACCOMPANIED (CINEMA ONLY)

The Lost Squadron ★★★★
Adventure drama   1932 · US · BW · 72min

This fascinating movie is a genuine cinematic equivalent of the great "lost generation" postwar writings of Ernest Hemingway and F Scott Fitzgerald. A group of First World War fighter pilots find themselves in postwar stunt flying in the movies under the direction of demented Erich von Stroheim. The atmosphere of disillusionment is quite palpable, thanks to a knowing original story by Dick Grace, himself a stunt flyer. The acting and the plot structure may seem creaky now, but the tone is brilliantly sustained and von Stroheim's performance – lampooning himself - is a tour de force. TS

Richard Dix *Captain Gibson* • Mary Astor *Follette Marsh* • Erich von Stroheim *Von Furst* • Joel McCrea *Red* • Robert Armstrong *Woody* • Dorothy Jordan *The Pest* ■ *Dir* George Archainbaud • *Scr* Wallace Smith, Herman J Mankiewicz, Robert Presnell, from a story by Dick Grace

The Lost Weekend ★★★★ PG
Drama   1945 · US · BW · 96min

Billy Wilder's ground-breaking drama about an alcoholic writer trying to kick the bottle won Oscars for best film, direction, screenplay and and actor. Ray Milland is the booze-afflicted antihero, suffering from writer's block and a frighteningly convincing case of the DTs. Despite the grim subject matter, there are glimpses of Wilder's characteristic mordant wit and the director's location work in New York's Third Avenue district is exemplary. Casting the hitherto bland Milland was a stroke of genius, but the scenes involving his brother (Phillip Terry) and girlfriend (Jane Wyman) are soft-centred and don't work. AT *DVD*
Blu-ray

Ray Milland *Don Birnam* • Jane Wyman *Helen St James* • Phillip Terry *Nick Birnam* • Howard Da Silva *Nat the bartender* • Doris Dowling *Gloria* ■ *Dir* Billy Wilder • *Scr* Charles Brackett, Billy Wilder, from the novel by Charles R Jackson • *Cinematographer* John F Seitz • *Music* Miklos Rozsa • *Special Effects* Farciot Edouart, Gordon Jennings

The Lost World ★★★ U
Silent fantasy adventure
1925 · US · BW · 92min

Of great historical interest, this film of Arthur Conan Doyle's novel was a smash hit in 1925 because of its sensational representation of prehistoric creatures by the special effects team headed by Willis O'Brien, who later perfected his skills on *King Kong*. Wallace Beery stars as Professor Challenger, leading an expedition to a South American plateau where an abundance of wild life previously thought extinct still lives. O'Brien combined live action and stop-action animation to convincing effect for the first time. AE *DVD*

Bessie Love *Paula White* • Lloyd Hughes *Edward J Malone* • Lewis Stone *Sir John Roxton* • Wallace Beery *Prof Challenger* • Arthur Hoyt *Prof Summerlee* • Margaret McWade *Mrs Challenger* ■ *Dir* Harry O Hoyt • *Scr* Marion Fairfax, from the novel by Sir Arthur Conan Doyle • *Cinematographer* Arthur Edeson • *Special Effects* Willis H O'Brien

The Lost World ★★★ PG
Fantasy adventure   1960 · US · Colour · 92min

Long before Steven Spielberg and Michael Crichton got there, the "master of disaster" Irwin Allen had already transported audiences to a lost world – author Sir Arthur Conan Doyle's South American plateau forgotten by time. In one of his later roles, Claude Rains leads the cast of lesser stars on an Amazon expedition where they confront a host of magnified pet-shop lizards with plastic fins in a glossy, if conventionally plotted, adventure with intermittent thrills. Clips from this would be a mainstay of Allen's TV fantasy series for years to come. AJ Blu-ray

Michael Rennie *Lord Roxton* • Jill St John *Jennifer Holmes* • David Hedison *Ed Malone* • Claude Rains *Professor Challenger* • Fernando Lamas *Gomez* • Richard Haydn *Professor*

Summerlee • Ray Stricklyn *David* ■ *Dir* Irwin Allen • *Scr* Irwin Allen, Charles Bennett, from the novel by Sir Arthur Conan Doyle

The Lost World: Jurassic Park ★★★ PG
Science-fiction adventure
1997 · US · Colour · 123min

There's another island full of genetically created dinosaurs in director Steven Spielberg's exuberantly calculated sequel to his own *Jurassic Park*. But while the cloned prehistoric package does elicit a sense of *déjà vu*, such feelings never get in the way of the excitement or special effects spectacle served up in deliciously scary dollops. With Richard Attenborough and Jeff Goldblum on hand once more to test the balance of nature off the coast of Costa Rica, Spielberg ensures his thrill-ride runs smoothly along well-oiled tracks. AJ
Violence, swearing. *DVD* Blu-ray

Jeff Goldblum *Dr Ian Malcolm* • Julianne Moore *Dr Sarah Harding* • Pete Postlethwaite *Roland Tembo* • Arliss Howard *Peter Ludlow* • Richard Attenborough *John Hammond* • Vince Vaughn *Nick Van Owen* ■ *Dir* Steven Spielberg • *Scr* David Koepp, from the novel by Michael Crichton

A Lot like Love ★★★ 12
Romantic comedy   2005 · US · Colour · 102min

Ashton Kutcher and Amanda Peet play the strangers who meet by joining the mile-high club, only to cross paths again (and again...) in a rollercoaster journey spanning seven years. Even when they're rubbing each other the wrong way, Kutcher and Peet create dazzling sparks. Direct Nigel Cole teases out human insecurities with humour and sensitivity, which, together with inspired casting, make this a fling worth embarking on. SP Sexual references. *DVD*

Ashton Kutcher *Oliver Martin* • Amanda Peet *Emily Friehl* • Kathryn Hahn *Michelle* • Kal Penn *Jeeter* • Ali Larter *Gina* • Taryn Manning *Ellen Geary* • Gabriel Mann *Peter* • Jeremy Sisto *Ben Miller* • Ty Giordano *Graham Martin* ■ *Dir* Nigel Cole • *Scr* Colin Patrick Lynch

Louder than Bombs ★★★★ 15
Drama   2015 · Nor/Fr/Den · Colour · 109min

This delicate, mournful drama follows a family that is haunted by loss. The story takes place three years after the death of Isabelle (Isabelle Huppert), a renowned war photographer who was killed in a car accident. Her husband, Gene (Gabriel Byrne), is concerned about his youngest son, Conrad (Devin Druid), a withdrawn teenager who barely speaks. Is Conrad ready to hear the truth about his mother's death? Conrad's older brother, Jonah (Jesse Eisenberg), thinks that this is a bad idea. You could argue that the film lacks focus, but it has plenty of potent scenes that ring true, and these combine to form a sensitive, quietly absorbing drama about grief and memory. SC In English, French. Swearing, brief nudity.

Gabriel Byrne *Gene Reed* • Jesse Eisenberg *Jonah Reed* • Isabelle Huppert *Isabelle Reed* • Devin Druid *Conrad Reed* ■ *Dir* Joachim Trier • *Scr* Joachim Trier, Eskil Vogt

Louise-Michel ★★★ 12A
Black comedy   2008 · Fr · Colour · 94min

This splendidly jet-black French farce offers up a novel riposte to the global economic meltdown. When the workers at a French factory are abruptly laid off, fearsome former employee Louise (Yolande Moreau) suggests that the staff pool their meagre redundancy pay and hire a hitman to get revenge on their duplicitous boss. However, her chosen assassin, the bumbling Michel (Bouli Lanners), turns out to be a less than lethal killer. Although directors Gustave Kervern and Benoît Delépine strike a little too hard at times for outrage, this is still wickedly funny. JF French +subtitles. Some violence, swearing.

Yolande Moreau *Louise* • Bouli Lanners *Michel* • Jacqueline Knuysen *Jackie* • Terence Debarle *Terence* • Benoît Poelvoorde *Guy* • Mathieu

Kassovitz *Farm owner* ■ *Dir/Scr* Gustave Kervern, Benoît Delépine • *Cinematographer* Hugues Poulain

Louisiana Purchase ★★★ U
Musical comedy   1941 · US · Colour · 94min

Hard, perhaps, to whip up much enthusiasm for a musical satire on the notoriously corrupt politicians of Louisiana, but this is worth a look. For most of the way, it is unusually faithful to the Broadway hit, with veteran comedian Victor Moore reprising his role as Senator Loganberry and featuring dancer Vera Zorina and others from the original cast. The major change is bringing in Bob Hope as the fall guy for the scheming politicians, but he filibusters his way out of trouble in style. AE *DVD*

Bob Hope *Jim Taylor* • Vera Zorina *Marina Von Minden* • Victor Moore *Sen Oliver P Loganberry* • Irene Bordoni *Madame Bordelaise* • Dona Drake *Beatrice* • Raymond Walburn *Colonel Davis Sr* • Maxie Rosenbloom *The Shadow* • Frank Albertson *Davis Jr* ■ *Dir* Irving Cummings • *Scr* Jerome Chodorov, Joseph Fields, from the musical by Morrie Ryskind, BG "Buddy" DeSylva • *Cinematographers* Ray Rennahan, Harry Hallenberger • *Music/lyrics* Irving Berlin

Louisiana Story ★★★ U
Documentary drama   1948 · US · BW · 77min

Documentary director Robert Flaherty (*Nanook of the North*) went to the bayou country of Louisiana and recruited non-professionals to tell a simple but affecting story of a small boy, whose father ekes out a living by hunting and fishing while oil prospectors set up a floating derrick and sink a well. With sparse dialogue and a notable score by Virgil Thomson, the film has little action other than the boy's fight with an alligator. Flaherty was backed by a major oil company, which must have been delighted by the entirely favourable impression the film gives of the oil drillers. AE

■ *Dir* Robert J Flaherty [Robert Flaherty] • *Scr* Robert J Flaherty, Frances Flaherty • *Cinematographer* Richard Leacock • *Music* Virgil Thomson

Loulou ★★★★ 18
Drama   1980 · Fr · Colour · 100min

This is an unforgettable exercise in street naturalism from director Maurice Pialat. Rarely has Paris looked less inviting as it provides the backdrop for the picaresque adventures of Gérard Depardieu's blue-collar boor and the bourgeois Isabelle Huppert, who abandons husband Guy Marchand out of boredom and unadulterated lust. This is much more than just an "odd couple" romance, as Pialat's accumulation of telling details exposes the soulless social and sexual state of contemporary France. DP French +subtitles.

Isabelle Huppert *Nelly* • Gérard Depardieu *Loulou* • Guy Marchand *André* • Humbert Balsan *Michel* ■ *Dir* Maurice Pialat • *Scr* Arlette Langmann, Maurice Pialat, from a story by Arlette Langmann

Lourdes ★★★★ U
Drama   2009 · Austria/Fr/Ger · Colour · 95min

The miraculous and the tacky coincide in Jessica Hausner's wry study of the hopes and hypocrisies of those visiting the Catholic shrine. Long confined to a wheelchair, Christine (Sylvie Testud) returns to Lourdes as much in need of a holiday as a cure for her multiple sclerosis. Frustrated by the coddling of an officious nurse and her devout roommate, she becomes intrigued by the romance between charity workers Marie and Kuno (Léa Seydoux and Bruno Todeschini). Hausner ponders the mysteries of faith with a respect that's teasingly tinged with irony, as she examines such thorny issues as divine intervention, piety and exploitation. DP French, English, German, Italian +subtitles. *DVD* Blu-ray

Sylvie Testud *Christine* • Léa Seydoux *Maria* • Gilette Barbier *Frau Hartl* • Gerhard Liebmann *Pater Nigl* • Bruno Todeschini *Kuno* • Elina Löwensohn [Elina Lowensohn] *Cécile* ■ *Dir/Scr* Jessica Hausner • *Cinematographer* Martin Gschlacht

The Lovable Cheat ★★ U
Comedy drama   1949 · US · BW · 78min

Charles Ruggles is the bankrupt Parisian who'll stop at nothing to keep his creditors at bay in this stagey comedy drama. Ruggles hopes that marrying off his daughter Peggy Ann Garner to a suitable suitor might be the answer to his problems. A strong cast (including Buster Keaton) do their best with the material but this has nothing new going for it apart from a fascination with money and the way it makes both love, and the world, go round – and wrong. TH

Charles Ruggles *Claude Mercadet* • Peggy Ann Garner *Julie Mercadet* • Richard Ney *Jacques Minard* • Alan Mowbray *Justin* • John Wengraf *Pierquin* • Curt Bois *Count de la Brive* • Buster Keaton *Goulard* ■ *Dir* Richard Oswald • *Scr* Richard Oswald, Edward Lewis, from the play *Mercadet le Faiseur* by Honoré de Balzac

Love ★★
Silent drama   1927 · US · BW · 97min

This silent version of Tolstoy's *Anna Karenina* from MGM was a box-office hit in its day, thanks to the starring of Greta Garbo as Anna and John Gilbert as Vronsky, the lover who ruins her. Directed by Edmund Goulding, it's not uninteresting, especially for Garbo fans, but has been long superseded by the studio's much superior sound remake *Anna Karenina* (1935) in which Garbo repeats the role under Clarence Brown's direction. RK

Greta Garbo *Anna Karenina* • John Gilbert (1) *Vronsky* • George Fawcett *Grand Duke* • Emily Fitzroy *Grand Duchess* • Brandon Hurst *Karenin* ■ *Dir* Edmund Goulding • *Scr* Frances Marion, Lorna Moon, from the novel *Anna Karenina* by Leo Nikolayevich Tolstoy

Love ★★★★ PG
Drama   1971 · Hun · BW · 84min

Set in the twilight of the Stalinist era, and passing sly asides on the cult of personality, this adroit study of the dissemination and reception of propaganda is cleverly couched in terms of a delicate chamber drama. Handled with great finesse by Karoly Makk, there's genuine affection in the relationship between a wife who tries to assuage her bedridden mother-in-law's fears about her son by fabricating letters about his Hollywood success, while hiding her own pain at the knowledge he's in a labour camp. Both Mari Torocsik and Lili Darvas, the widow of the famous playwright, Ferenc Molnar, are superb. DP Hungarian +subtitles. *DVD*

Lili Darvas *Mother* • Mari Torocsik *Luca, the wife* • Ivan Darvas *Janos, the son* ■ *Dir* Karoly Makk • *Scr* Tibor Dery, from his novella

Love ★★ 12
Science-fiction drama
2011 · US · Colour · 80min

William Eubank's ambitious small-scale sci-fi epic is a call to arms for low-budget film-making. Conceived as a series of music videos for an Angels and Airwaves album, it took on a life of its own, with the songs demoted to soundtrack status. After a beautiful but confusing Civil War-set opening, the story moves forward in time, as an astronaut contemplates his loneliness after he loses contact with Earth. It's definitely worth a look, but it also leaves a feeling of disappointment for what could have been. TF Swearing. *DVD* Blu-ray

Gunner Wright *Captain Lee Miller* • Corey Richardson *General McLain* • Bradley Horne *Captain Lee Briggs* ■ *Dir/Scr* William Eubank

Love ★★ 18
Romantic drama   2015 · Fr/Bel · Colour · 129min

Controversial director Gaspar Noé (*Irréversible*) employs 3D in his bid to depict "sentimental sexuality" in this teasingly semi-autobiographical, but underwhelming melodrama. He makes interesting use of space and texture, while achieving some neat transitions in the edit, but there's a 70s porno feel about a story involving an aspiring film-maker and his tangled liaisons with the estranged love of his life and the

L

mother of his child. The trio's struggle with improvised dialogue reinforces this impression, though they commit entirely to the coital sequences, photographed with a mix of prurience and sensitivity to capture unsimulated passion. DP Swearing, sex scenes. **DVD** **3D**

Aomi Muyock *Electra* • Karl Glusman *Murphy* • Klara Kristin *Omi* • Ugo Fox *Gaspar* • Juan Saavedra *Julio* ■ Dir/Scr Gaspar Noé

Love Actually ★★★ 15

Romantic comedy
2003 · UK/US/Fr · Colour · 129min

A film so drenched in upbeat sentiment that it makes Frank Capra seem emotionally reserved, this ensemble romantic comedy from writer Richard Curtis is an unashamedly saccharine proposition. In his debut behind the camera, Curtis unfurls eight ongoing stories, headed by Hugh Grant's new Prime Minister falling for junior staff member Martine McCutcheon, and writer Colin Firth enchanted by his Portuguese housekeeper. JC **DVD**

Alan Rickman *Harry* • Bill Nighy *Billy Mack* • Colin Firth *Jamie* • Emma Thompson *Karen* • Hugh Grant *David, the Prime Minister* • Laura Linney *Sarah* • Liam Neeson *Daniel* • Martine McCutcheon *Natalie* • Keira Knightley *Juliet* • Rowan Atkinson *Rufus* • Billy Bob Thornton *The US President* • Lucia Moniz *Aurelia Barros* ■ Dir/Scr Richard Curtis

Love Affair ★★

Romantic drama
1932 · US · BW · 68min

The main reason to watch this antique romantic drama is for an early performance from Humphrey Bogart. He's a handsome but impoverished aviator who attracts the attentions of an heiress who invests in the plane and then in Bogart himself. Further characters complicate the romantic situation which is resolved – naturally enough – aloft. AT

Dorothy Mackaill *Carol Owen* • Humphrey Bogart *Jim Leonard* • Jack Kennedy *Gilligan* • Barbara Leonard *Felice* • Astrid Allwyn *Linda Lee* • Bradley Page *Georgie* ■ Dir Thornton Freeland • Scr Jo Swerling, Dorothy Howell, from a story by Ursula Parrott

Love Affair ★★★★★ U

Romantic comedy drama
1939 · US · BW · 86min

Charles Boyer and Irene Dunne meet on an ocean liner bound for New York and, despite their determination to avoid involvement, fall hopelessly in love. They agree to meet six months later at an appointed time at the top of the Empire State Building if they still feel the same, but when the day comes, she is not there. One word suffices for Leo McCarey's film, which garnered six Academy Award nominations: perfect. Witty, sophisticated, romantic and poignant, it is extremely well written, immaculately directed, and beautifully played by the stars. It remains one of the best love stories ever to emerge from Hollywood, and McCarey remade it faithfully as *An Affair to Remember* (1957), with Cary Grant and Deborah Kerr, while Nora Ephron paid it tribute with *Sleepless in Seattle*. RK

Irene Dunne *Terry McKay* • Charles Boyer *Michel Marnet* • Maria Ouspenskaya *Grandmother Janou* • Lee Bowman *Kenneth Bradley* • Astrid Allwyn *Lois Clarke* • Maurice Moscovich *Maurice Cobert* ■ Dir Leo McCarey • Scr Delmer Daves, Donald Ogden Stewart, from a story by Leo McCarey, Delmer Daves, Mildred Cram

Love Affair ★★★ 12

Romantic drama
1994 · US · Colour · 103min

This remake of *Love Affair* and *An Affair to Remember* failed to impress the critics and never even got to cinemas in the UK. But it is an undeniably polished production and if Glenn Gordon Caron's direction is occasionally sluggish and Ennio Morricone's score is stiflingly lush, the story of the lovers who are torn apart by the cruellest twist of fate can still get the tears flowing. However, the most heartbreaking moment is the all-too-brief appearance of Katharine

Hepburn, gamely fighting against the effects of Parkinson's Disease. DP

Warren Beatty *Mike Gambril* • Annette Bening *Terry McKay* • Katharine Hepburn *Aunt Ginny* • Garry Shandling *Kip DeMay* • Chloe Webb *Tina Wilson* • Pierce Brosnan *Ken Allen* • Kate Capshaw *Lynn Weaver* • Brenda Vaccaro *Nora Stillman* • Paul Mazursky *Herb Stillman* ■ Dir Glenn Gordon Caron • Scr Robert Towne, Warren Beatty, from the 1939 film

Love among the Ruins ★★★★

Romantic comedy
1975 · US · Colour · 72min

This extremely classy made-for-television film from veteran director George Cukor stars Katharine Hepburn as a dowager in the early 20th century being sued by a young upstart. Sadly her defence barrister Laurence Olivier also has it in for her as she has failed to recollect their affair from years before. Olivier thus decides to portray the poor woman as short of her marbles throughout the court case. Comic, painful and insightful, Cukor extracts excellent performances from Hepburn and Olivier and it makes for a rare televisual treat. LH

Katharine Hepburn *Jessica Medlicott* • Laurence Olivier *Sir Arthur Granville-Jones* • Colin Blakely *JF Devine* • Richard Pierson *Druce* • Joan Sims *Fanny Pratt* • Leigh Lawson *Alfred Pratt* ■ Dir George Cukor • Scr James Costigan

Love and a .45 ★★★★ 18

Thriller
1994 · US · Colour · 97min

Although the Tarantino influences are clear to see, this matt-black trailer trash thriller is an impressively nasty treat. Gil Bellows is the nice-ish convenience store robber who is forced to go on the run with his devoted girlfriend (an electric early showing from Renee Zellweger) after a raid goes horribly wrong. The body count continues to multiply as they are pursued by Bellows's old partner in crime (Rory Cochrane) and two psycho debt collectors, along with massed ranks of law enforcement. CM Talkington's direction is hip and amoral and the performances uniformly good. JF **DVD**

Gil Bellows *Watty Watts* • Renee Zellweger [Renée Zellweger] *Starlene Cheatham* • Rory Cochrane *Billy Mack Black* • Jeffrey Combs *Dino Bob* • Jace Alexander *Creepy Cody* • Ann Wedgeworth *Thaylene* • Peter Fonda *Vergil* ■ Dir/Scr CM Talkington

Love & Basketball ★★★ 12

Romantic sports drama
2000 · US · Colour · 119min

Sanaa Lathan and Omar Epps are young athletes with a lifelong love of basketball and each other. The movie follows them from childhood games to professional careers, all the while contrasting the different challenges men and women face while playing the same sport. Gina Prince-Bythewood's feature debut captures the characters' passion for the game, though she struggles with scenes that take place off the court. While Lathan delivers a passionate, star-making performance, her fellow actors are hobbled by underdeveloped roles. ST **DVD**

Sanaa Lathan *Monica Wright* • Omar Epps *Quincy McCall* • Alfre Woodard *Camille Wright* • Dennis Haysbert *Zeke McCall* • Debbi Morgan *Mona McCall* • Harry Lennix *Nathan Wright* ■ Dir/Scr Gina Prince-Bythewood

Love and Bullets ★★ 15

Thriller
1978 · UK · Colour · 99min

Charles Bronson stars as an American policeman on a mission to break a crime syndicate in Switzerland, in director Stuart Rosenberg's dull and predictable thriller. Rather surprisingly, Bronson struggles to portray the toughness required of his role, while Rod Steiger goes way over the top as a Mafia boss. Only Jill Ireland impresses as the gangster's moll. Unintentional laughs can be had from watching Steiger in Mussolini-mode, and the Swiss locations are breathtaking. AT **DVD**

Charles Bronson *Charlie Congers* • Jill Ireland *Jackie Pruitt* • Rod Steiger *Joe Bomposa* • Henry Silva *Vittorio Faroni* • Strother Martin *Louis Monk*

• Bradford Dillman *Brickman* ■ Dir Stuart Rosenberg • Scr Wendell Mayes, John Melson, from a story by Wendell Mayes

Love and Death ★★★★ PG

Satirical comedy
1975 · US · Colour · 81min

Woody Allen's first forays into cinema as writer/director/star were essentially gag-packed genre spoofs, but this ambitious take on classic Russian literature displayed a new intellectual and philosophical appetite that in many ways drew a line under his "early, funny films". Here he plays Boris, an unlikely hero of the Russian Army during the Napoleonic Wars, who's characterised by his self-professed pacifism and cowardice – and modern, thick-rimmed glasses. However, the film is chiefly remembered for its cracking set pieces and rewarding nods to the novels of Tolstoy and Dostoyevsky, and the films of Ingmar Bergman and Sergei Eisenstein. Rarely has silly, knockabout comedy been so highbrow. AC **DVD**

Woody Allen *Boris Grushenko* • Diane Keaton *Sonja Volonska* • Harold Gould *Anton* • Olga Georges-Picot *Countess Alexandrovna* • Zvee Scooler *Father* • Despo Diamantidou *Mother* ■ Dir/Scr Woody Allen • Music Sergei Prokofiev

Love and Death on Long Island ★★★ 15

Comedy drama
1998 · UK/Can · Colour · 93min

John Hurt plays a naive, unworldly writer/scholar who becomes besotted with the American star (Jason Priestley) of *Hotpants College 2*, a low-budget teen movie he mistakenly wanders into. Hurt then travels to Long Island to meet what he thinks will be his true love. There is a sense of impending tragedy throughout but Hurt's wonderful performance ensures that it never slips into melodramatic gloom. Priestley has fun sending up his teen idol image, while Richard Kwietniowksi directs with affection. JF Swearing. **DVD**

John Hurt *Giles De'Ath* • Jason Priestley *Ronnie Bostock* • Fiona Loewi *Audrey* • Sheila Hancock *Mrs Barker* • Harvey Atkin *Lou* • Gawn Grainger *Henry, Giles's agent* • Elizabeth Quinn *Mrs Reed* • Maury Chaykin *Irving Buckmuller* ■ Dir Richard Kwietniowski • Scr Richard Kwietniowski, from the novel by Gilbert Adair

Love & Friendship ★★★★ U

Period comedy drama
2016 · US · Colour · 93min

Cult auteur Whit Stillman's effervescent adaptation of Jane Austen's neglected novella *Lady Susan* reunites the stars of his 1998 film *The Last Days of Disco*, Kate Beckinsale and Chloë Sevigny. Recently widowed and leaving a trail of scandal behind her, legendary flirt Lady Susan Vernon arrives to stay with her estranged in-laws. Beckinsale is a fine fit for the book's eponymous schemer, turning in a pristine performance as an arch-manipulator who remains amusingly unflappable in the face of hysteria and indignation, and she's well supported by Sevigny as her, now American, confidante. Embellishing the source material, Stillman toys with the traditional trappings of period drama, throwing out the stuffiness in favour of something terrifically fresh and oh-so wonderfully wicked. EAS

Kate Beckinsale *Lady Susan Vernon* • Chloë Sevigny *Alicia Johnson* • Xavier Samuel *Reginald DeCourcy* • Stephen Fry *Mr Johnson* • Jemma Redgrave *Lady DeCourcy* ■ Dir Whit Stillman • Scr Whit Stillman, from the novella *Lady Susan* by Jane Austen

Love + Hate ★★ 15

Romantic drama
2005 · UK · Colour · 82min

The self conscious "+" in the title of this love-across-the-racial-divide drama is presumably meant to bring to mind Baz Luhrmann's rejigged *Romeo + Juliet*. But, unlike that dynamic yarn of star-crossed lovers, this is a dull, disappointingly pedestrian tale. Set in an unnamed northern town, the soapy plot concerns teen racist Tom Hudson who falls for Muslim girl Samina Awan. Director Dominic Savage had his young cast improvise their

dialogue, and, despite their best efforts and some mildly promising new talent (particularly Awan), it often shows. AS Swearing, violence. **DVD**

Samina Awan *Naseema* • Tom Hudson *Adam* • Nichola Burley *Michelle* • Wasim Zakir *Yousif* • Dean Andrews *Derek* • Azara *Azara* • Peter O'Connor *Pete* • Ryan Leslie *Sean* ■ Dir/Scr Dominic Savage

Love and Human Remains ★★ 18

Drama
1993 · Can · Colour · 99min

The activities of a serial killer cast a shadow over this drama of modern relationships, as does the spectre of Aids. This was the first English language film from Québécois filmmaker Denys Arcand, director of the 1989 art house hit *Jesus of Montreal*. Though Arcand is widely regarded as being more comfortable working in his native French, this remains a watchable drama focusing on the sexual pursuits, fears and fetishes of a bunch of adult cityfolk. DA

Thomas Gibson *David* • Ruth Marshall *Candy* • Cameron Bancroft *Bernie* • Mia Kirshner *Benita* • Rick Roberts *Robert* • Joanne Vannicola *Jerri* • Matthew Ferguson *Kane* ■ Dir Denys Arcand • Scr Brad Fraser, from his play *Unidentified Human Remains and the True Nature of Love*

Love & Mercy ★★★ 12

Biographical drama
2014 · US · Colour and BW · 116min

This uneven biopic focuses on two significant periods in the life of Brian Wilson, the troubled singer-songwriter who co-founded the Beach Boys. Half the film takes place in the 1960s, and follows Brian (Paul Dano) as he tries to take the band in a different, somewhat experimental direction. The other half is set in the 1980s, when Brian (John Cusack) has become a fragile, overly medicated man-child. A fascinating biopic could be made about Brian Wilson, but this isn't it. SC Swearing, drug abuse. **DVD** **BD**

John Cusack *Brian Wilson, older* • Paul Dano *Brian Wilson* • Elizabeth Banks (2) *Melinda Ledbetter* • Paul Giamatti *Dr Eugene Landy* • Jake Abel *Mike Love* • Kenny Wormald *Dennis Wilson* ■ Dir Bill Pohlad • Scr Oren Moverman, Michael Alan Lerner

Love and Money ★★

Thriller
1982 · US · Colour · 90min

Director James Toback, presented with natural drama, doesn't know how to commit himself to his material and so turns what should be high octane into an afternoon stroll. Financier Ray Sharkey decides to inject some excitement into his life by getting mixed up with Klaus Kinski's business schemes. Sharkey, Ornella Muti (as his love interest) and Kinski perform adequately, but they are upstaged by an appearance from celebrated director King Vidor. JM Swearing.

Ray Sharkey *Byron Levin* • Ornella Muti *Catherine Stockheinz* • Klaus Kinski *Frederick Stockheinz* • Armand Assante *Lorenzo Prado* • King Vidor *Walter Klein* • Susan Heldfond *Vicky* ■ Dir/Scr James Toback • Music Aaron Copland

Love and Other Catastrophes ★★★ 15

Comedy drama
1996 · Aus · Colour · 75min

This spirited Australian comedy recounts an incident-packed day in the life of five college students. All human experience seems condensed into the 24-hour period as the protagonists cope with unrequited love, romantic entanglements and life-changing decisions. Reputedly shot in just 17 days, the speed of the production translates to the screen and the film whizzes by delightfully. A strong ensemble cast ensures that all the characters are well rounded and believable. DF Swearing, sex scenes.

Alice Garner *Alice* • Frances O'Connor *Mia* • Matthew Dyktynski *Ari* • Matt Day *Michael* • Radha Mitchell *Danni* • Suzi Dougherty *Savita* • Kim Gyngell *Professor Leach* ■ Dir Emma-Kate Croghan • Scr Emma-Kate Croghan, Yael Bergman, Helen Bandis, from a story by Stavros Andonis Efthymiou [Stavros Kazantzidis]

Love & Other Drugs ★★★ 15
Romantic comedy drama
2010 · US · Colour · 107min

This ribald, challenging and funny romance stars Jake Gyllenhaal as pharmaceutical salesman Jamie Randall, who's riding high in the mid-1990s boom, peddling a new pill called Viagra. He meets and immediately falls into bed with Maggie Murdock (Anne Hathaway), a beautiful, mysterious girl who seemingly only wants sex with no strings attached. But when the two become closer, Maggie is forced to make a painful revelation. While the film isn't entirely free of stereotypes, it does says something real about what happens when love is threatened by illness – with the copious amounts of nudity from the leads actually adding to its telling. It isn't quite *Love Story*, but comes close. KK Swearing, sex scenes, nudity. DVD BL

Jake Gyllenhaal *Jamie Randall* • Anne Hathaway *Maggie Murdock* • Oliver Platt *Bruce Winston* • Hank Azaria *Dr Stan Knight* • Josh Gad *Josh Randall* • Gabriel Macht *Trey Hannigan* • Judy Greer *Cindy* • George Segal *Dr James Randall* ■ *Dir* Edward Zwick • *Scr* Marshall Herskovitz, Charles Randolph, Edward Zwick, from the non-fiction book *Hard Sell: The Evolution of a Viagra Salesman* by Jamie Reidy

Love and Other Impossible Pursuits ★★ 15
Drama
2009 · US · Colour · 98min

A young mother's grief over the death of her baby threatens to derail her marriage in this sober drama from director Don Roos. It's the sort of subject tackled in average TV movies but this New York-set tale is spared from outright ordinariness by Natalie Portman's lead performance as the distraught wife Emilia. Burdened with guilt and her own family issues, Emilia struggles to bond with her highly strung stepson (Charlie Tahan) while fending off her husband's icy ex-wife (Lisa Kudrow, in a thankless role). The film has its moving moments, but some wit wouldn't have gone amiss to leaven the increasingly oppressive melodrama. After all, this is the director who gave Christina Ricci her breakout adult role in the darkly funny *The Opposite of Sex* back in 1998. JA Swearing, sex scenes. DVD BL

Natalie Portman *Emilia* • Scott Cohen *Jack* • Charlie Tahan *William* • Lisa Kudrow *Carolyn* • Lauren Ambrose *Mindy* ■ *Dir* Don Roos • *Scr* Don Roos, from Ayelet Waldman's novel

Love and Pain and the Whole Damn Thing ★★★★
Drama
1973 · US · Colour · 113min

Alan J Pakula's political thrillers *Klute* (1971), *The Parallax View* (1974) and *All the President's Men* (1976), make him seem a social warrior, but this is an out-of-character delight with unexpected and refreshing romanticism. Maggie Smith plays a terminally ill spinster in Spain whose heartbeats click like castanets when she meets youngster Timothy Bottoms. Despite the fatal-illness undercurrent, sentimentality is kept at bay in this rare gem. TH

Maggie Smith *Lila Fisher* • Timothy Bottoms *Walter Elbertson* • Emiliano Redondo *Spanish gentleman* • Charles Baxter *Dr Elbertson* • Margaret Modlin *Mrs Elbertson* • May Heatherly *Melanie Elbertson* ■ *Dir* Alan J Pakula • *Scr* Alvin Sargent

Love & Sex ★★★ 15
Romantic comedy
2000 · US · Colour · 82min

In this perceptive comedy from writer/director Valerie Breiman, Famke Janssen plays a magazine journalist who, while re-writing a feature about love and relationships, muses on her own experiences. Though she can recall a whole candelabra of old flames, Janssen's thoughts keep returning to a key romance with artist Jon Favreau. While Breiman doesn't cover any new ground, the combined energies of her snappy script and the two lead performances will have you nodding as you watch the pair. JB Sex scenes. DVD

Famke Janssen *Kate Welles* • Jon Favreau *Adam* • Noah Emmerich *Eric* • Ann Magnuson *Ms Steinbacher* • Cheri Oteri *Mary* • Josh Hopkins *Joey Santino* • Robert Knepper *Gerard* ■ *Dir/Scr* Valerie Breiman

Love at First Bite ★★★★ 15
Horror spoof
1979 · US · Colour · 91min

This very funny spoof of the Dracula legend has George Hamilton as the uprooted, undead count, who's trying to adjust to life in the modern Big Apple. Former MGM heart-throb Hamilton camps it up delightfully as he clumsily romances fashion model Susan Saint James, to the chagrin of her psychiatrist lover Richard Benjamin, who gets his vampire lore amusingly scrambled when he tries to intervene. It's fast and furious fun, superbly scripted by Robert Kaufman, and wonderfully pulled together by director Stan Dragoti. AJ Swearing.

George Hamilton *Count Dracula* • Susan Saint James *Cindy Sondheim* • Richard Benjamin *Dr Jeff Rosenberg* • Dick Shawn *Lieutenant Ferguson* • Arte Johnson *Renfield* • Sherman Hemsley *Reverend Mike* • Isabel Sanford *Judge* ■ *Dir* Stan Dragoti • *Scr* Robert Kaufman, from a story by Robert Kaufman, Mark Gindes

Love at Large ★★ 15
Crime drama
1990 · US · Colour · 93min

Tom Berenger's career took a downward turn with this daft, if imaginative, attempt at a light-hearted *film noir* by writer/director Alan Rudolph. A private detective, hired by a beautiful woman, ends up following the wrong man and is himself followed by a female detective. Still with us? Well, you won't be after an hour and a half of mistaken identities, tortuous plot twists and below-par acting. JB Violence, swearing.

Tom Berenger *Harry Dobbs* • Elizabeth Perkins *Stella Wynkowski* • Anne Archer *Miss Dolan* • Kate Capshaw *Ellen McGraw* • Annette O'Toole *Mrs King* ■ *Dir/Scr* Alan Rudolph

Love at Stake ★★★ 15
Comedy drama
1987 · US · Colour · 83min

Kelly Preston plays the town baker (Sara Lee!) in this farcical comedy set amid a colony of Puritans in 17th-century Salem. The local judge and mayor have devised a fiendish plan to steal villagers' land by accusing them of witchcraft. Very much *The Crucible* meets *The Naked Gun*, this is awash with toilet humour and screamingly bad gags. Barbara Carrera does a great turn as the only actual witch, and this will keep lovers of the genre heartily amused. LH

Patrick Cassidy *Miles* • Kelly Preston *Sara Lee* • Bud Cort *Parson Babcock* • David Graf *Nathaniel* • Stuart Pankin *Judge Samuel John* • Dave Thomas *Mayor Upton* • Barbara Carrera *Faith* ■ *Dir* John Moffitt • *Scr* Terrence Sweeney, Lanier Laney

Love at Twenty ★★★
Portmanteau drama
1962 · Fr/It/Jpn/W Ger/Pol · BW · 115min

The most significant entry in this portmanteau picture is *Antoine et Colette*, which furthered the Antoine Doinel cycle launched by François Truffaut in *The 400 Blows*. However, there's much to enjoy elsewhere. In Renzo Rossellini's *Rome* a rich woman fights to keep her lover from a beautiful innocent, while Marcel Ophüls's *Munich* sees a photographer develop a passion for the mother of his child. A factory worker murders the student who refuses his advances in Shintaro Ishihara's *Tokyo*, while in Andrzej Wajda's intriguing *Warsaw* a man's life changes after he rescues a child from the bear pit at the zoo. DP French +subtitles.

Jean-Pierre Léaud *Antoine Doinel* • Marie-France Pisier *Colette* • Eleonora Rossi-Drago *Valentina* • Koji Furuhata *Hiroshi* • Nami Tamura *Fukimo* • Christian Doermer *Tonio* • Barbara Frey *Ursula* • Barbara Lass *Basia* ■ *Dir* François Truffaut, Renzo Rossellini, Shintaro Ishihara, Marcel Ophüls, Andrzej Wajda • *Scr* François Truffaut, Yvon Samuel, Renzo Rossellini, Shintaro Ishihara, Marcel Ophüls, Jerzy Stefan Stawinski

Love before Breakfast ★★
Comedy
1936 · US · BW · 65min

A middle-of-the-road lightweight romantic comedy is given A-grade treatment in casting and production values. The title is meaningless and the flimsy plot concerns Cesar Romero and Preston Foster as suitors vying for the affections of New York socialite Carole Lombard. Foster schemes to get his rival out of the way – even out of the country – but Lombard smells a rat. Walter Lang directs what, in most circumstances, would be a waste of time, but anything starring the lovely Lombard is worth a look. RK

Carole Lombard *Kay Colby* • Preston Foster *Scott Miller* • Cesar Romero *Bill Wadsworth* • Janet Beecher *Mrs Colby* • Betty Lawford *Contessa Janie Campanella* ■ *Dir* Walter Lang • *Scr* Herbert Fields, from the novel *Spinster Dinner* by Faith Baldwin

Love Bite ★ 15
Comedy horror
2012 · UK · Colour · 90min

Aimed squarely at the more gormless elements of the *Inbetweeners* audience, this lowbrow British horror comedy is short on scares and seriously long on schoolboy smut. There's a werewolf on the loose in a small seaside town and it's feasting on virgins – and the place is full of them. With a full moon looming, teenager Jamie (*Eragon*'s Ed Speleers) has just 24 hours to have sex in order to avoid a grisly fate. This is ghastly, for all the wrong reasons. DA Violence, sexual references, brief nudity.

Ed Speleers *Jamie* • Jessica Szohr *Juliana* • Timothy Spall *Sid* • Luke Pasqualino *Kev* • Robert Pugh *Sergeant Rooney* • Kierston Wareing *Natalie* ■ *Dir* Andy de Emmony • *Scr* Cris Cole, Ronan Blaney

The Love Bug ★★★★ U
Comedy
1969 · US · Colour · 107min

In this classic Disney comedy, plain good fun is at the wheel, with its foot down to the floor. Herbie, the Volkswagen with as much bottle as throttle, is a brilliant invention, and Dean Jones, as his racing driver owner, and David Tomlinson, as Jones's ruthless rival, work wonders to stop the little Beetle running away with the film. Having shown a flair for fantasy with *Mary Poppins*, director Robert Stevenson here demonstrates a sure slapstick touch. *Herbie Rides Again*, the first of three of sequels, followed in 1974. DP DVD

Dean Jones *Jim Douglas* • Michele Lee *Carole Bennett* • David Tomlinson *Peter Thorndyke* • Buddy Hackett *Tennessee Steinmetz* • Joe Flynn *Havershaw* • Benson Fong *Mr Wu* ■ *Dir* Robert Stevenson • *Scr* Don DaGradi, Bill Walsh, from a story by Gordon Buford

The Love Cage ★★
Crime romance
1964 · Fr · BW · 96min

Jane Fonda, in her sex-kitten phase, stars in her first French movie, originally titled *Les Félins*. France's biggest star, Alain Delon, plays a gangster who is given refuge in a vast chateau by Fonda and her aunt, Lola Albright, whose lover, another gangster, has murdered her husband. It's a game of sexual charades – clothes come off and then a gun goes off, spoiling all the fun. AT French dubbed.

Alain Delon *Marc* • Jane Fonda *Melinda* • Lola Albright *Barbara* • Carl Studer *Loftus* • Sorrell Booke *Harry* • André Oumansky *Vincent* • Arthur Howard (2) *Rev Nielson* ■ *Dir* René Clément • *Scr* René Clément, Charles Williams, Pascal Jardin, from the novel *Joy House* by Day Keene

Love, Cheat & Steal ★★ 18
Revenge thriller
1994 · US · Colour · 91min

An unpleasant modern *film noir*, this features Eric Roberts as a vengeful escaped convict who shows-up at ex-wife Mädchen Amick's house posing as her estranged brother. John Lithgow is Amick's new, rich banker husband, whose vaults full of Colombian drug money are targeted by Roberts. The attractively elf-like, but fatally wooden, Amick goes through more skimpy costume changes than a fashion show. Things do perk up, however, in the satisfying, twist-laden robbery climax. JC Violence, swearing, sex scenes.

John Lithgow *Paul Harrington* • Eric Roberts *Reno Adams* • Mädchen Amick *Lauren Harrington* • Richard Edson *Billy Quayle* • Donald Moffat *Paul's father* • David Ackroyd *Tom Kerry* • Dan O'Herlihy *Hamilton Fisk* ■ *Dir/Scr* William Curran

Love Child ★★★ 18
Drama based on a true story
1982 · US · Colour · 92min

Amy Madigan made her big screen debut here as Terry Jean Moore, a condemned criminal who is initially sentenced to 15 years for robbery, increased to 20 years for starting a fire in jail. Moore campaigns for her right to keep her baby, who was fathered by one of the prison guards, played by Beau Bridges. The real-life case attracted a lot of press coverage in America, turning the volatile Moore into a celebrity and feminist icon. The approach is level-headed and semi-documentary in style. AT

Amy Madigan *Terry Jean Moore* • Beau Bridges *Jack Hansen* • Mackenzie Phillips *JJ* • Albert Salmi *Captain Ellis* • Joanna Merlin *Superintendent Sturgis* • Margaret Whitton *Jacki Steinberg* ■ *Dir* Larry Peerce • *Scr* Anne Gerard, Katherine Specktor, from a story by Anne Gerard

Love Crazy ★★★
Screwball comedy
1941 · US · BW · 98min

The favourite box-office team of William Powell and Myrna Loy (Nick and Nora Charles of the *Thin Man* series) are the beleaguered couple in this madcap farce. Instead of celebrating a wedding anniversary it looks as though they're heading for the rocks when her mother comes to stay and he meets up with an old flame. Directed at a rollicking pace by Jack Conway, this is complete nonsense and lots of fun. RK

William Powell *Steven Ireland* • Myrna Loy *Susan Ireland* • Gail Patrick *Isobel Grayson* • Jack Carson *Ward Willoughby* • Florence Bates *Mrs Cooper* • Sidney Blackmer *George Hennie* • Vladimir Sokoloff *Dr Klugle* • Kathleen Lockhart *Mrs Bristol* ■ *Dir* Jack Conway • *Scr* William Ludwig, Charles Lederer, David Hertz, from a story by David Hertz, William Ludwig

Love Crime ★★★ 15
Mystery thriller
2010 · Fr · Colour · 102min

A ruthless corporate executive exploits her female underling's hard work and takes the credit herself until the put-upon junior decides to fight back in this sleek boardroom thriller. Kristin Scott Thomas offers a masterclass in ruthless, elegant scheming, though Ludivine Sagnier's seemingly benign protégé proves a quick learner. This is never less than classy, but it's not a fully satisfying experience. However, the interplay between the two very different leads and the involving, increasingly dark story keep things moving along nicely. TJ French, English +subtitles. DVD BL

Ludivine Sagnier *Isabelle Guérin* • Kristin Scott Thomas *Christine* • Patrick Mille *Philippe* • Guillaume Marquet *Daniel* • Gérald Laroche *Gérard* • Julien Rochefort *The lawyer* ■ *Dir* Alain Corneau • *Scr* Alain Corneau, Natalie Carter

Love Crimes ★ 18
Erotic thriller
1991 · US · Colour · 86min

Director Lizzie Borden's unbelievable thriller has lawyer Sean Young going undercover to trap con artist Patrick Bergin, a man who preys on unsuspecting women by posing as a fashion photographer and offering them the chance of a modelling career. The ridiculous story makes little sense and wooden performances by both leads don't help much. AJ Violence, swearing, nudity.

Sean Young *Dana Greenway* • Patrick Bergin *David Hanover* • Arnetia Walker *Maria Johnson* • James Read *Stanton Gray* • Ron Orbach *Detective Eugene Tully* • Fern Dorsey *Colleen Dells* • Tina Hightower *Anne Winslow* ■ *Dir* Lizzie Borden • *Scr* Allan Moyle, Laurie Frank, from a story by Allan Moyle

L

Love Don't Cost a Thing ★★ 15

Romantic comedy   2003 · US · Colour · 97min

Having bought the remake rights to *Can't Buy Me Love*, director Troy Beyer clearly didn't have enough left over to pay for either a decent screenplay or a capable cast. There's virtually no spark between high-school nobody Nick Cannon and Christina Milian, as the girl who helps secure him an entrée to the in-crowd in return for repairing her mom's car. Beyer's choice of camera angles often beggars belief in this mixed-message movie. DP Sexual references. **DVD**

Nick Cannon *Alvin Johnson* • Christina Milian *Paris Morgan* • Steve Harvey *Alvin's dad* • Al Thompson *Big Ted* • Kal Penn *Kenneth* • Kenan Thompson *Walter* • Vanessa Bell Calloway *Mrs Johnson* • Melissa Schuman *Zoe* ■ *Dir* Troy Beyer • *Scr* Troy Beyer, Michael Swerdlick, from the film *Can't Buy Me Love* by Michael Swerdlick

Love etc ★★★ 15

Romantic drama   1997 · Fr · Colour · 99min

It's not just the title and setting that director Marion Vernoux jettisons in her Gallicisation of Julian Barnes's novel *Talking It Over*. The confessional narrative style is also reined in to permit a more traditionally structured account of the romantic triangle that forms between timid executive Yvan Attal, art restorer Charlotte Gainsbourg and the indolent Charles Berling. While fitfully amusing, this is essentially a rather sad story, marred by uncertain pacing. DP French +subtitles. Swearing, sex scenes. **DVD**

Charlotte Gainsbourg *Marie* • Yvan Attal *Benoît* • Charles Berling *Pierre* • Thibault de Montalembert *Bernard* • Elodie Navarre *Eléonore* ■ *Dir* Marion Vernoux • *Scr* Marion Vernoux, Dodine Henry, from the novel *Talking It Over* by Julian Barnes

Love Exposure ★★★★ 18

Romantic comedy drama
2008 · Jpn · Colour · 236min

The path to true love takes a circuitous form in this epic Japanese manga-inspired serio-comic fresco, where a young man searching for his own personal Virgin Mary tangles with the sinister Church of Zero, a cult seeking the extermination of human desire. At just shy of four hours, Sion Sono's film asks a lot of the viewer, but it delivers abundantly too for those who can look beyond its seeming frivolity. A work of undoubted excess, but startling originality, too. TJ Japanese +subtitles. Violence. **DVD**

Takahiro Nishijima *Yu* • Hikari Mitsushima *Yoko* • Sakura Ando *Koike* • Yutaka Shimizu *Yuji* • Hiroyuki Onoue *Takahiro* ■ *Dir/Scr* Sion Sono

Love Field ★★★★ 15

Romantic drama   1992 · US · Colour · 100min

Michelle Pfeiffer may have been nominated for an Oscar for her role in this neglected drama, but that still didn't guarantee it a cinema release in this country, where it slipped quietly straight to video. Pfeiffer is superb as the bleach-blonde Jackie Kennedy-obsessed housewife who walks out on her husband to travel to President Kennedy's funeral, and Dennis Haysbert (replacing Denzel Washington, who turned down the role) is equally watchable as the secretive black man travelling with his daughter, with whom she makes friends on the journey. Political intrigue aside, this is a fascinating tale of innocent enthusiasm in a bigoted world. JB Violence, swearing. **DVD**

Michelle Pfeiffer *Lurene Hallett* • Dennis Haysbert *Paul Cater* • Stephanie McFadden *Jonell Cater* • Brian Kerwin *Ray Hallett* • Louise Latham *Mrs Enright* • Peggy Rea *Mrs Heisenbuttal* • Beth Grant *Hazel* • Rhoda Griffis *Jacqueline Kennedy* ■ *Dir* Jonathan Kaplan • *Scr* Don Roos

Love Finds Andy Hardy ★★★

Comedy drama   1938 · US · BW · 87min

This is the fourth and one of the freshest films in the Andy Hardy series, with Mickey Rooney muddling dance dates and getting in a dreadful mess. Judy Garland makes the first of three appearances in the series – she sings three songs – and seems a natural when compared to the precocious Rooney. Another star-in-waiting, Lana Turner, plays one of Rooney's girlfriends. AT **DVD**

Mickey Rooney *Andy Hardy* • Lewis Stone *Judge James K Hardy* • Judy Garland *Betsy Booth* • Ann Rutherford *Polly Benedict* • Lana Turner *Cynthia Potter* • Cecilia Parker *Marian Hardy* • Fay Holden *Mrs Emily Hardy* • Betty Ross Clark [Betty Ross Clarke] *Aunt Milly* ■ *Dir* George B Seitz • *Scr* William Ludwig, from stories by Vivian R Bretherton, from characters by Aurania Rouverol

Love from a Stranger ★★★

Crime drama   1936 · UK · BW · 86min

Having come into a fortune but quarrelled with her fiancé, Ann Harding is swept off her feet into marriage by Basil Rathbone, whom she barely knows. They settle in luxury in Europe, only for her to be warned that he murders wealthy women. Directed by Rowland V Lee, this is a neat, smooth suspense drama, in which the stars give polished performances. RK

Basil Rathbone *Gerald Lovell* • Ann Harding *Carol Howard* • Binnie Hale *Kate Meadows* • Bruce Seton *Ronald Bruce* • Jean Cadell *Aunt Lou* • Bryan Powley *Dr Gribble* • Joan Hickson *Emmy* ■ *Dir* Rowland V Lee • *Scr* Frances Marion, from the play by Frank Vosper, from the short story *Philomel Cottage* by Agatha Christie in the collection *The Listerdale Mystery and Other Stories*

Love from a Stranger ★★

Period mystery   1947 · US · BW · 81min

Based on an Agatha Christie story *Philomel Cottage*, in which a wealthy young woman has a whirlwind courtship and marries a habitual wife murderer, this is a pointless and markedly inferior remake of the splendid 1936 version. Sylvia Sidney, her once great career by then in shreds but her talent intact, stars as the intended victim, with John Hodiak as the Bluebeard-style villain. RK

John Hodiak *Manuel Cortez/Pedro Ferrara* • Sylvia Sidney *Cecily Harrington* • Ann Richards *Mavis Wilson* • John Howard (1) *Nigel Lawrence* • Isobel Elsom *Auntie Loo-Loo* • Ernest Cossart *Billings* ■ *Dir* Richard Whorf • *Scr* Philip MacDonald, from the play *Love from a Stranger* by Frank Vosper, from the short story *Philomel Cottage* by Agatha Christie in the collection *The Listerdale Mystery and Other Stories*

The Love Goddesses ★★★★

Compilation   1965 · US · BW and Colour · 78min

This is a marvellous compilation of clips featuring Hollywood's finest sex symbols. Trouble is, the producers were obviously constrained by availability and copyright, so where you would perhaps expect more you might get less, and vice versa. Paramount stars are favoured, but, nevertheless, many of the great ladies of the silver screen are present and correct, and the makers refreshingly cast their nets wider than the US, including Hedy Lamarr (as Hedwig Keisler), famously nude in *Ecstasy*, and that wanton Lulu, Louise Brooks, abroad in Europe. There's even a sizeable chunk of *Expresso Bongo*, one of the most daring (and underrated) flicks of its day. Sylvia Syms a love goddess? You bet! TS Nudity.

Claudette Colbert • Bette Davis • Marlene Dietrich • Greta Garbo • Lillian Gish • Jean Harlow • Rita Hayworth • Audrey Hepburn • Sophia Loren • Marilyn Monroe • Barbara Stanwyck • Gloria Swanson • Elizabeth Taylor • Lana Turner • Mae West ■ *Dir/Scr* Saul J Turrell, Graeme Ferguson • *Editor* Howard Kuperman • *Music* Percy Faith

The Love Guru ★★★ 12

Comedy   2008 · US · Colour · 83min

Mike Myers lampoons New Age spirituality in debut director Marco Schnabel's snappy, colourful enlightenment spoof that will delight *Austin Powers* fans. Myers plays Guru Pitka, an American raised in an Indian ashram, returning to become the next big name on the lucrative self-help scene. The plot is tenuous – Pitka must get a dysfunctional Canadian hockey star back with his estranged wife before the finals – but it gives Myers the room to be vaguely profound, supremely silly, and even at times annoying and potentially offensive. Co-stars Jessica Alba, "Mini Me" actor Verne Troyer and Justin Timberlake keep up with the fast pace. Think Austin Powers with a beard and a kaftan and you won't be disappointed. KK **DVD BD**

Mike Myers *Guru Pitka* • Jessica Alba *Jane Bullard* • Justin Timberlake *Jacques Grande* • Romany Malco *Darren Roanoke* • Meagan Good *Prudence* • Omid Djalili *Guru Satchabigknoba* • Ben Kingsley *Guru Tugginmypuddha* • Verne Troyer *Cherkov* ■ *Dir* Marco Schnabel • *Scr* Graham Gordy, Mike Myers

Love Happens ★★ 12

Romantic drama
2009 · US/Can · Colour · 104min

Debut director (and co-writer) Brandon Camp squeezes a few laughs and a hint of romance from this otherwise serious and sorrowful drama. Bestselling self-help author Aaron Eckhart travels around America giving seminars to those coping with grief. But when he meets quirky florist Jennifer Aniston, some telling truths are revealed about his own life. Aniston and Eckhart struggle somewhat as they try to plumb deep emotional waters, and are further hampered by a flimsy plot. Although it's strikingly shot in and around Seattle and has a strong supporting cast, this is only a lightly effective story about moving through grief to new love. KK Sexual references. **DVD**

Aaron Eckhart *Burke Ryan* • Jennifer Aniston *Eloise Chandler* • Dan Fogler *Lane* • Judy Greer *Marty* • Joe Anderson (1) *Tyler* • John Carroll Lynch *Walter* • Martin Sheen *Silver* • Frances Conroy *Eloise's mom* ■ *Dir* Brandon Camp • *Scr* Brandon Camp, Mike Thompson

Love Happy ★★ U

Comedy   1949 · US · BW · 84min

The Marx Brothers' penultimate film together is hardly worth the effort – unless you hanker for a glimpse of Marilyn Monroe. Harpo wrote the story and gets most of the spotlight as the shoplifting member of a penniless group of actors who unwittingly picks up a sardine can filled with diamonds. Raymond Burr is one of the villains trying to get the jewels back and Vera-Ellen plays Harpo's love interest. Groucho fans should note that his appearance is a brief one. TH **DVD**

Harpo Marx *Harpo* • Chico Marx *Faustino the Great* • Ilona Massey *Madame Egilichi* • Vera-Ellen *Maggie Phillips* • Marion Hutton *Bunny Dolan* • Raymond Burr *Alphonse Zoto* • Melville Cooper *Lefty Throckmorton* • Paul Valentine *Mike Johnson* • Leon Belasco *Mr Lyons* • Eric Blore *Mackinaw* • Bruce Gordon (2) *Hannibal Zoto* • Marilyn Monroe *Grunion's client* • Groucho Marx *Detective Sam Grunion, narrator* ■ *Dir* David Miller (1) • *Scr* Frank Tashlin, Mac Benoff, from a story by Harpo Marx

Love Has Many Faces ★

Romantic drama   1965 · US · Colour · 105min

The title of this witless farrago is as unintentionally hilarious as its content. The many faces include Lana Turner as a millionairess in Acapulco and Cliff Robertson as her husband, a former beach lothario who married her for her money and is now lusting after Stefanie Powers. Turner has her hands full with bullfighter Jaime Bravo, and Hugh O'Brian – a gigolo on the make with both Lana and the equally wealthy Ruth Roman. RK

Lana Turner *Kit Jordan* • Cliff Robertson *Pete Jordan* • Hugh O'Brian *Hank Walker* • Ruth Roman *Margot Eliot* • Stefanie Powers *Carol Lambert* • Virginia Grey *Irene Talbot* ■ *Dir* Alexander Singer • *Scr* Marguerite Roberts

Love, Honour and Obey ★★ 18

Comedy drama   2000 · UK · Colour · 94min

This is the second film from the self-styled Fugitives, a loose artists' collective centred around actors Ray Winstone, Jude Law and Sadie Frost. Jonny Lee Miller, Rhys Ifans and Denise Van Outen play the trio in this tale of a courier who wheedles his way into a London crime family, only to embroil them in a deadly feud with a rival gang. The humour is laddish, lowbrow and not especially funny, while some improvised scenes should have been cut. DA **DVD**

Ray Winstone *Ray* • Jonny Lee Miller *Jonny* • Jude Law *Jude* • Kathy Burke *Kathy* • Sadie Frost *Sadie* • Sean Pertwee *Sean* • Denise Van Outen *Denise* • Rhys Ifans *Mathew* ■ *Dir/Scr* Dominic Anciano, Ray Burdis

Love Hurts ★★ 15

Comedy drama   1990 · US · Colour · 102min

Jeff Daniels's reluctant divorcee is the only believable character in this well-meaning comedy drama from veteran director Bud Yorkin. But Cloris Leachman is over the top playing the hero's zany mum, as this plodding effort attempts to look at the idea of civilised parting, what to do with the extended relatives and how to comfort the children. It's a good try, but it comes unstuck after the first reel and the inappropriately crass comedy all too often fails to hit the button. SR Violence, swearing.

Jeff Daniels *Paul Weaver* • Cynthia Sikes *Nancy Weaver* • Judith Ivey *Susan Volcheck* • John Mahoney *Boomer* • Cloris Leachman *Ruth Weaver* • Amy Wright *Karen Weaver* • Mary Griffin *Sarah Weaver* ■ *Dir* Bud Yorkin • *Scr* Ron Nyswaner

Love in Pawn ★ U

Comedy   1953 · UK · BW · 70min

Britain's popular radio (and later TV) imports from Canada, Bernard Braden and his wife Barbara Kelly, star in this indescribably puerile and unfunny comedy directed by Charles Saunders. It concerns a penniless artist who must prove his respectability in order to inherit a fortune from his wealthy uncle. Best forgotten, which it was. RK

Bernard Braden *Roger Fox* • Barbara Kelly *Jean Fox* • Jean Carson [Jeannie Carson] *Amber Trusslove* • Reg Dixon *Albert Trusslove* ■ *Dir* Charles Saunders • *Scr* Guy Morgan, Frank Muir, Denis Norden, from a story by Humphrey Knight

Love in the Afternoon ★★★★★ PG

Romantic comedy   1957 · US · BW · 124min

Filmed and set in Paris, Billy Wilder's romantic comedy will delight fans of his earlier *Sabrina*. Audrey Hepburn again stars, this time as the daughter of French private eye Maurice Chevalier who becomes obsessed by one of his targets: American businessman and serial adulterer Gary Cooper who lives at the Ritz and has a gypsy band serenade his love-making sessions. Critics at the time found the crinkly Cooper much too old to romance the gorgeous Hepburn, but that's precisely the point: she humanises and energises him with her European vivacity. This first collaboration between Wilder and co-writer IAL Diamond features some lovely scenes and a number of colourful secondary characters. AT

Gary Cooper *Frank Flannagan* • Audrey Hepburn *Ariane Chavasse* • Maurice Chevalier *Claude Chavasse* • John McGiver *Monsieur X* • Van Doude *Michel* • Lise Bourdin *Madame X* ■ *Dir* Billy Wilder • *Scr* Billy Wilder, IAL Diamond, from the novel *Ariane* by Claude Anet

Love in the Afternoon ★★★★ 15

Comedy drama   1972 · Fr · Colour · 93min

Eric Rohmer winds up his "Six Moral Tales" series with this delightful comedy drama, also known by its American title *Chloé in the Afternoon*. Rather than exploring the doubts that beset those contemplating marriage, Rohmer here considers the temptations that take the sheen off wedded bliss. Real-life husband and wife Bernard and Françoise Verley play a couple whose contentment is jeopardised by his secret meetings with old friend Zouzou. The acting is impeccable, and Rohmer's skilful use of location adds to the atmosphere and charm. DP French +subtitles. **DVD**

Zouzou *Chloë* • Bernard Verley *Frédéric* • Françoise Verley *Hélène* • Daniel Ceccaldi *Gérard* • Malvina Penne *Fabienne* • Babette Ferrier *Martine* • Frederique Hender *Madame M* ■ *Dir/Scr* Eric Rohmer

Love in the City ★★
Portmanteau comedy drama
1953 · It · BW · 110min

In the early 1950s, Italian cinema was arguably the liveliest and most innovative in Europe, and this brought together many of its major writers and directors. But, like most of these compilation films, it's a mixed blessing. The idea was to film real-life stories and real people, but Federico Fellini copped out and made a fantasy about a werewolf who uses a marriage agency because he thinks getting hitched will cure him. Michelangelo Antonioni offers some interviews with girls who attempted suicides. Other stories scour the gutter. AT Italian +subtitles.

■ *Dir* Michelangelo Antonioni, Federico Fellini, Alberto Lattuada, Carlo Lizzani, Francesco Maselli, Dino Risi, Cesare Zavattini • *Scr* Aldo Buzzi, Luigi Chiarini, Luigi Malerba, Tullio Pinelli, Vittorio Veltroni

Love in the Strangest Way ★★ 15
Thriller
1994 · Fr · Colour · 102min

Seeking to break with his amiable screen image, Thierry Lhermitte plays a ruthless debt collector whose dangerous liaison with a mystery woman can only lead to one thing. Devoid of passion, suspense or social grit, this mildly salacious film isn't worth the effort. DP French +subtitles. Violence, swearing, nudity.

Thierry Lhermitte *Julien Bernier* • Maruschka Detmers *Anne Bernier* • Nadia Farès *Angela Galli* • Johann Martel *Charles* • Umberto Orsini *Vienne* ■ *Dir* Christopher Frank • *Scr* Christopher Frank, Jean Nachbaur, from an idea by Jean-Marc Roberts

Love in the Time of Cholera ★★ 15
Romantic drama
2007 · US · Colour · 132min

This adaptation of Gabriel García Márquez's acclaimed novel should have been an epic flight of fancy, but feels more like a long trawl through a bog. Javier Bardem plays the Colombian telegraph clerk whose love for a local girl (Giovanna Mezzogiorno) goes unrequited across five decades. Bardem's gift for quiet pathos means that he retains his dignity, but only just, because director Mike Newell handles his transition from weeping virgin to debonair Don Juan with as much refinement as he might a high-school sex romp. Mezzogiorno gets to do plenty of wistful gazing in the role of the dutiful wife to an aristocratic doctor (Benjamin Bratt), but her character's innermost passions are also never really explored. Ultimately, this is a romance that doesn't have any heart. SP DVD

Javier Bardem *Florentino Ariza* • Giovanna Mezzogiorno *Fermina Daza Urbino* • Benjamin Bratt *Dr Juvenal Urbino* • Catalina Sandino Moreno *Hildebranda* • Hector Elizondo *Don Leo* • Liev Schreiber *Lotario Thugut* • Ana Claudia Talancón *Olimpia Zuleta* • Fernanda Montenegro *Transito Ariza* ■ *Dir* Mike Newell • *Scr* Ronald Harwood, from the novel by Gabriel García Márquez

Love Is a Ball ★★
Romantic comedy
1963 · US · Colour · 112min

The early 1960s was plagued with this kind of French Riviera tosh. Acres of bikini-clad bottoms, tinkling champagne glasses on clifftop terraces, Ferraris taking hairpin bends at ridiculous speeds and a plethora of Equity no-hopers make the entire "We're having a jolly privileged time" premise appear more wooden than a barn door. SH

Charles Boyer *Monsieur Etienne Pimm* • Glenn Ford *John Davis* • Hope Lange *Millie Mehaffey* • Ricardo Montalban *Gaspard* • Telly Savalas *Dr Gump* • Ruth McDevitt *Mathilda* ■ *Dir* David Swift • *Scr* David Swift, Tom Waldman, Frank Waldman, from the novel *The Grand Duke and Mr Pimm* by Lindsay Hardy

Love Is a Many-Splendored Thing ★★ U
Romantic drama
1955 · US · Colour · 97min

Despite having one of the most famous romantic titles of all time, this soap opera's distinction rests largely with its hit title ballad and director Henry King's imaginative use of early CinemaScope, which captures stars Jennifer Jones and William Holden horizontal at every possible opportunity. Trouble is, both Jones and Holden fail to convince in this occasionally trite tale of forbidden love, which is a shame, because the source book by Han Suyin is actually very moving. TS DVD

William Holden (2) *Mark Elliot* • Jennifer Jones *Han Suyin* • Torin Thatcher *Mr Palmer-Jones* • Isobel Elsom *Adeline Palmer-Jones* • Murray Matheson *Dr Tam* • Virginia Gregg *Ann Richards* • Richard Loo *Robert Hung* • Soo Young *Nora Hung* • Philip Ahn *Third Uncle* ■ *Dir* Henry King • *Scr* John Patrick, from the book *A Many Splendored Thing* by Han Suyin • *Music* Alfred Newman

Love Is a Racket ★★★
Crime comedy drama
1932 · US · BW · 72min

Douglas Fairbanks Jr is the Broadway gossip columnist who falls for an ambitious but financially irresponsible young actress (Frances Dee). She becomes indebted to a ruthless gangster, who then meets with an untimely death. Fairbanks is terrific as the cynical reporter with sudden stardust in his eyes, and he is well supported by a cast that includes Lee Tracy, Lyle Talbot and Ann Dvorak. A pacey comedy drama, smartly scripted and, under William A Wellman's immaculate direction, offering lots of New York nightlife atmosphere. RK

Douglas Fairbanks Jr *Jimmy Russell* • Ann Dvorak *Sally* • Frances Dee *Mary Wodehouse* • Lee Tracy *Stanley Fiske* • Lyle Talbot *Eddie Shaw* • George Raft *Stinky* ■ *Dir* William A Wellman • *Scr* Courtenay Terrett [Courtney Terrett], from the novel *Love Is a Racket* by Rian James

Love Is All ★★★ 12
Documentary
2014 · UK · Colour and BW · 73min

The most potent and mysterious of all emotional states comes under the microscope in this slim but enchanting documentary from British director Kim Longinotto. Combining archive footage with excerpts from features and shorts for a humorous, perhaps too frivolous, look at lust, crushes and courtship over the past century or so, this s a charming, appealingly orchestrated illustration of a simple message: times may change but love is eternal. EAS DVD

■ *Dir* Kim Longinotto

Love Is All There Is ★ 12
Comedy drama
1996 · US · Colour · 101min

An oafish update of *Romeo and Juliet*, with competing catering companies as the families linked by star-crossed love. Crass, loud and a lot less funny than it thinks it is, the main interest here is an early performance from Oscar winner Angelina Jolie as the "Juliet" character. Joseph Bologna (who also co-directed), Barbara Carrera and Paul Sorvino fill out the mid-quality cast. If food be the music of love, *don't pay up*! DA DVD

Lainie Kazan *Sadie* • Paul Sorvino *Piero* • Barbara Carrera *Maria* • Joseph Bologna *Mike* • Angelina Jolie *Gina* • Nathaniel Marston *Rosario* • Renee Taylor *Mona* • William Hickey *Monsignor* • Dick Van Patten *Dr Rondino* • Abe Vigoda *Rudy* • Connie Stevens *Miss DeLuca* • Blessed Roscoe ■ *Dir/Scr* Renee Taylor, Joseph Bologna

Love Is All You Need ★★★ 15
Romantic comedy
2012 · Den/Swe/It/Fr /Ger · Colour · 111min

Pierce Brosnan is a pleasingly humble sort of hero in this sprawling but sweet romantic comedy from director Susanne Bier (*Open Hearts, Brothers*), which blends British and Danish cultures against a pretty Italian backdrop. Brosnan and Trine Dyrholm overcome life-changing traumas to celebrate the marriage of their children and seize their own chance at happiness, too. But it's a bumpy road to love, littered with drunk exes and desperate in-laws. Bier has a knack for dissecting complicated relationships and the results are mostly very funny. The tears and tantrums on the big day are pure contrivance, but Brosnan and Dyrholm have a sparky rapport, and a sugary frosting of feel-good sentiment saves the day. SP In English, Danish, Italian. DVD

Pierce Brosnan *Philip* • Trine Dyrholm *Ida* • Kim Bodnia *Leif* • Paprika Steen *Benedikte* • Sebastian Jessen *Patrick* • Christiane Schaumburg-Müller *Tilde* ■ *Dir* Susanne Bier • *Scr* Anders Thomas Jensen

Love Is Better than Ever ★★ U
Romantic comedy
1951 · US · BW · 80min

A naive dance teacher comes to New York for a dance convention and meets a slick theatrical agent. He shows her around but she misinterprets his attentiveness as honorable intentions and falls in love with him. Directed by Stanley Donen, this wisp of a forgotten romantic comedy is definitely lower-half-of-the-bill stuff, even though the girl is a young Elizabeth Taylor. Her love interest is Larry Parks, starring in his last film before the McCarthy hearings destroyed his career. RK

Larry Parks *Jud Parker* • Elizabeth Taylor *Anastacia Macaboy* • Josephine Hutchinson *Mrs Macaboy* • Tom Tully *Mr Macaboy* • Ann Doran *Mrs Levoy* • Elinor Donahue *Pattie Marie Levoy* • Kathleen Freeman *Mrs Kahmey* • Doreen McCann *Albertina Kahrney* • Gene Kelly *Guest star* ■ *Dir* Stanley Donen • *Scr* Ruth Brooks Flippen

Love Is Colder than Death ★★★★ 15
Romantic crime comedy
1969 · W Ger · BW · 84min

Clearly taking up where Jean-Luc Godard had left off in his assault on traditional cinema, Rainer Werner Fassbinder made his remarkable debut with this micro-budget deconstruction of the crime thriller. Much of the action is staged as tableaux before a doggedly static camera. The minimalist plot is presented in fragmentary form, while lowlifes Ulli Lommel and Fassbinder (and Hanna Schygulla as the girl caught between them) scarcely exchange a word. It's almost wilfully obscure, but compelling nonetheless. DP German +subtitles.

Ulli Lommel *Bruno* • Hanna Schygulla *Johanna* • Rainer Werner Fassbinder *Franz* • Katrin Schaake *Lady in train* • Hans Hirschmüller *Peter* ■ *Dir/Scr* Rainer Werner Fassbinder

Love Is in the Air ★★ 15
Romantic comedy
2013 · Fr · Colour · 93min

This proves that even the French can make a mediocre romantic comedy. The premise is preposterously straightforward: sculptress Ludivine Sagnier is on a flight from New York to Paris to get married, but has her head turned en route by the caddish lawyer (Nicolas Bedos) she dumped three years earlier. It's difficult to sympathise with Sagnier, as not only did she go out with him in the first place, but she is now all-too-willing to be seduced by his chauvinist schtick all over again. The many flashbacks often slip ingeniously back into the present, but the situation is thuddingly familiar. DP French, English +subtitles. Swearing, sex scenes, drug abuse.

Ludivine Sagnier *Julie* • Nicolas Bedos *Antoine* • Jonathan Cohen *Hugo* • Arnaud Ducret *Franck* • Brigitte Catillon *Claire* • Jackie Berroyer *Arthur* ■ *Dir* Alexandre Castagnetti • *Scr* Xavier Nemo, Nirina Ralanto, Julien Simonet, Alexandre Castagnetti, Nicolas Bedos, Brigitte Bémol, from a screenplay by Vincent Angell

Love Is News ★★★
Screwball comedy
1937 · US · BW · 78min

This screwball battle-of-the-sexes romantic comedy pits heart-throb newshound Tyrone Power against beautiful heiress Loretta Young. Fed up with being chased by journalists, she takes her revenge on Power by announcing that she's leaving fiancé George Sanders for him, whereupon he's sacked by boss Don Ameche, and on goes a plot of escalating lunacy and pace. This is often hilarious fare, well cast and delightfully played. Remade as a beguiling Fox musical, *Sweet Rosie O'Grady*, in 1943, and again in 1948 as *That Wonderful Urge* (also starring Power). RK

Tyrone Power *Steve Leyton* • Loretta Young *Tony Gateson* • Don Ameche *Martin J Canavan* • Slim Summerville *Judge Hart* • Dudley Digges *Cyrus Jeffrey* • Walter Catlett *Eddie Johnson* • Pauline Moore *Lois Westcott* • Jane Darwell *Mrs Flaherty* • Stepin Fetchit *Penrod* • George Sanders *Count André de Guyon* • Elisha Cook Jr *Egbert Eggleston* ■ *Dir* Tay Garnett • *Scr* Harry Tugend, Jack Yellen, from a story by William R Lipman, Frederick Stephani

Love Is Strange ★★★ 15
Romantic comedy drama
2014 · US/Fr · Colour · 90min

Love is never easy, as a devoted single-sex couple discovers, in this poignant romantic comedy from Ira Sachs. After 39 years together, artist John Lithgow and teacher Alfred Molina decide to get married, but the news brings unemployment and then homelessness. The story does wander a bit, but Lithgow and Molina turn in nuanced and realistic performances as the chalk-and-cheese pair. Heartening, heart-warming and heartbreaking, *Love Is Strange* is a road trip through a durable, fascinating romance. KK DVD

John Lithgow *Ben* • Alfred Molina *George* • Marisa Tomei *Kate* • Charlie Tahan *Joey* ■ *Dir* Ira Sachs • *Scr* Ira Sachs, Mauricio Zacharias

Love Is the Devil: Study for a Portrait of Francis Bacon ★★★ 18
Biographical drama
1998 · UK · Colour · 86min

John Maybury's film is a highly stylised account of the painter's abrasive affair with reformed thief George Dyer. As lovers divided by culture and class, Derek Jacobi gives a remarkable physical impersonation of Bacon, while Daniel Craig is a model of repressed anger and bemused despair. The director's use of distorting lenses, reflective surfaces, angular close-ups and split-screen devices conveys both the couple's dislocated world and the style of Bacon's paintings. However, the film needs momentum, while the dialogue is pretentiously epigrammatic. DP Nudity, sex scenes, some swearing. DVD

Derek Jacobi *Francis Bacon* • Daniel Craig *George Dyer* • Anne Lambton *Isabel Rawsthorne* • Karl Johnson (2) *John Deakin* • Annabel Brooks *Henrietta Moraes* • Adrian Scarborough *Daniel Farson* • Tilda Swinton *Muriel Belcher* • Richard Newbold *Blonde Billy* ■ *Dir* John Maybury • *Scr* John Maybury, James Cohen, Don Jordan

Love Jones ★★★ 15
Romantic comedy
1997 · US · Colour · 104min

Writer Theodore Witcher made his directorial debut with this funny, funky tale of love among a group of Chicago middle-class African Americans. Nia Long and Larenz Tate are the star-crossed lovers who meet, make love and then part, leading to the usual romantic complications. Portraying blacks as successful urbanites rather than the usual clichéd, downbeat characters, this features superb performances from the leads. Stylishly shot and with a snappy script, this is a knowing look at the pitfalls of love and romance in the 1990s. JB Swearing, sexual references.

Larenz Tate *Darius Lovehall* • Nia Long *Nina Mosley* • Isaiah Washington *Savon Garrison* • Lisa Nicole Carson *Josie Nichols* • Bill Bellamy *Hollywood* ■ *Dir/Scr* Theodore Witcher

Love Kills ★★★ 18
Comedy
1998 · US · Colour · 90min

Mario Van Peebles stars a masseur and con artist who specialises in scamming recently widowed women in ingenious ways dreamed up by his insanely jealous girlfriend Loretta Devine. His new target is Lesley Ann Warren who is actually broke,

L

but whose flakey stepson (Donovan Leitch) is about to inherit jewels worth millions. Into this stew comes Daniel Baldwin as a *Columbo*-style cop who might not be what he seems. Glossily produced for indie fodder, this is worth checking out if only for Van Peebles's extraordinary dreadlocks. **JF** **DVD**

Mario Van Peebles *Poe Finklestein* • Lesley Ann Warren *Evelyn Heiss* • Daniel Baldwin *Danny Tucker* • Donovan Leitch *Dominique* • Alexis Arquette *James* • Louise Fletcher *Alena Heiss* • Loretta Devine *Sylvia Finklestein* • Melvin Van Peebles *Abel* ■ *Dir/Scr* Mario Van Peebles

Love Laughs at Andy Hardy ★★ U
Comedy drama   1946 · US · BW · 92min

This was the 15th and last genuine Andy Hardy movie (though there was a nostalgic straggler, *Andy Hardy Comes Home*, in 1958). Andy and his dad (Lewis Stone) had entertained America through the war years and kept alive small-town values, but Mickey Rooney couldn't conceal the fact that he was now 26 years old. This instalment sees Rooney back from the war and crushed when his fiancée (Bonita Granville) runs off with someone else. **AT** **DVD**

Mickey Rooney *Andy Hardy* • Lewis Stone *Judge James K Hardy* • Fay Holden *Mrs Emily Hardy* • Sara Haden *Aunt Milly* • Bonita Granville *Kay Wilson* ■ *Dir* Willis Goldbeck • *Scr* Harry Ruskin, William Ludwig, from a story by Howard Dimsdale, from characters by Aurania Rouverol

The Love Letter ★★ 15
Romantic comedy   1999 · US · Colour · 83min

This film about a divorced single mother is very much a family affair. Actress Kate Capshaw bought the rights to Cathleen Schine's novel in order to produce it for husband Steven Spielberg's DreamWorks company, while one of the Spielberg children, Sasha, has a walk-on role. Capshaw finds an anonymous letter written in amorously endearing terms and thinks it's for her. The film's romantic focus is unsteady and soapily blurred. **TH** Swearing, a sex scene, nudity. **DVD**

Kate Capshaw *Helen* • Blythe Danner *Lillian* • Ellen DeGeneres *Janet* • Geraldine McEwan *Miss Scattergoods* • Julianne Nicholson *Jennifer* • Tom Everett Scott *Johnny* • Tom Selleck *George* • Gloria Stuart *Eleanor* • Jessica Capshaw *Kelly* • Sasha Spielberg *Girl with sparkler* ■ *Dir* Peter Ho-Sun Chan • *Scr* Maria Maggenti, from the novel by Cathleen Schine

Love Letters ★★★
Melodrama   1945 · US · BW · 101min

Mogul David O Selznick loaned his protégée and future wife, Jennifer Jones, to producer Hal B Wallis and Paramount for this glitzy romantic soap opera. In Ayn Rand's screenplay, Jones suffers a number of shocks, including amnesia and the traumatic discovery that her treasured collection of love letters was written not by her husband (Robert Sully) but by co-star Joseph Cotten. This stylish and enjoyable nonsense was directed by William Dieterle and received several Oscar nominations including one for Jones (as best actress). **RK**

Jennifer Jones *Singleton* • Joseph Cotten *Alan Quinton* • Ann Richards *Dilly Carson* • Anita Louise *Helen Wentworth* • Cecil Kellaway *Mack* • Gladys Cooper *Beatrice Remington* • Byron Barr *Derek Quinton* • Robert Sully *Roger Morland* ■ *Dir* William Dieterle • *Scr* Ayn Rand, from the novel *Pity My Simplicity* by Chris Massie

Love Letters ★★★★ 18
Drama   1983 · US · Colour · 84min

This hugely impressive emotional drama is beautifully played and sensitively directed by Amy Jones. The story centres on a single woman who discovers evidence of an affair among her dead mother's letters, then takes up herself with a married man. The film intelligently probes the emotions of infidelity, and its frequent justification on the grounds that it's sometimes right to do the wrong thing. The starry cast includes

Jamie Lee Curtis, Amy Madigan, Bud Cort and James Keach. **DA**

Jamie Lee Curtis *Anna* • James Keach *Oliver* • Amy Madigan *Wendy* • Bud Cort *Danny* • Matt Clark *Winter* • Bonnie Bartlett *Mrs Winter* ■ *Dir/Scr* Amy Jones [Amy Holden Jones]

Love Letters ★★
Romantic drama   1999 · US · Colour · 85min

Fifteen years after his directorial career seemed to have ended ignominiously with *Blame It on Rio*, Stanley Donen made his TV-movie debut with this romantic drama. It's essentially a series of flashbacks tracing the correspondence between US senator Steven Weber and Laura Linney, his childhood friend who died without fulfilling her artistic ambitions. Donen directs with his usual style and geniality, but he overdoes the sentimentality. **DP**

Laura Linney *Melissa Gardner* • Steven Weber *Senator Andrew Ladd* • Kirsten Storms *Teenage Melissa* • Tim Redwine *Teenage Andy* • Isabella Fink *Young Melissa* • Stephen Joffe *Young Andy* ■ *Dir* Stanley Donen • *Scr* AR Gurney, from his play

Love Life ★★★ 15
Drama   2009 · Neth · Colour · 112min

Raymond van de Klundert's bestseller, *A Woman Goes to the Doctor*, made him a celebrity in his native Netherlands. But those unfamiliar with the story of a philandering husband who strays while his spouse is dying of breast cancer will find this a very tough watch. It's bad enough seeing advertising executive Barry Atsma playing away, as feisty Carice van Houten endures the agonies and humiliation of her ravaging treatment. But Reinout Oerlemans's flashy direction ensures it's almost impossible to empathise with the confusion and pain that Atsma feels as he seduces another woman to give him the strength to nurse his wife. It also imposes a superficiality that makes van Houten's poignant performance feel unduly melodramatic. **DP** Dutch +subtitles. Swearing, sex scenes.

Carice van Houten *Carmen* • Barry Atsma *Stijn* • Anna Drijver *Roos* ■ *Dir* Reinout Oerlemans • *Scr* Gert Embrechts, from the novel *A Woman Goes to the Doctor (Komt Een Vrouw Bij de Dokter)* by Kluun [Raymond van de Klundert]

Love, Life and Laughter ★★ U
Musical comedy drama   1934 · UK · BW · 81min

This self-conscious musical romance – a variation on *The Prince and the Showgirl* scenario – is not one of Gracie Fields's finest hours, as it sacrifices her trademark realism for neverland fantasy. Fields seems slightly inhibited as the actress who lures the heir to the throne away from his Ruritanian kingdom, and fiancée Norah Howard, but John Loder, as the prince, rises to the challenge admirably. The idea that movies have become the new fairy tales is a good one, however. **DP**

Gracie Fields *Nellie Gwyn* • John Loder *Prince Charles* • Norah Howard *Princess Grapfel* • Alan Aynesworth *King* • Esme Percy *Goebschen* • Veronica Brady *Mrs Gwyn* • Horace Kenney *Mr Gwyn* ■ *Dir* Maurice Elvey • *Scr* Robert Edmunds, from a story by Maurice Braddell

Love like Poison ★★★★ 15
Coming-of-age drama   2010 · Fr · Colour · 81min

Director Katell Quillévéré's feature debut is a sensitive, sensual and surprisingly spiritual account of an adolescent girl's coming of age. Happy to be away from her detested boarding school, Anna (Clara Augarde) arrives at her grandfather's Breton home just as her parents confirm their separation. With her mother (Lio) seeking solace from a local priest (Stefano Cassetti), Anna relies on a choirboy (Youen Leboulanger-Gourvil) to help make sense of her feelings as she prepares for her confirmation. Exquisitely photographed by Tom Harari with graceful camerawork that captures the atmosphere of a sleepy coastal village, this subtly episodic saga is perfectly paced by Quillévéré, whose courageous use of silence, impassivity and nudity makes the

flame-haired Augarde's performance all the more remarkable. **DP** French, Italian, English +subtitles. Nudity.

Clara Augarde *Anna* • Lio *Jeanne* • Michel Galabru *Jean* • Stefano Cassetti *Father François* • Youen Leboulanger-Gourvil *Pierre* • Thierry Neuvic *Paul* ■ *Dir* Katell Quillévéré • *Scr* Katell Quillévéré, Mariette Désert • *Cinematographer* Tom Harari

Love Liza ★★★ 15
Drama   2001 · US/Fr/Ger · Colour · 86min

Actor Philip Seymour Hoffman excels in a story that won his brother Gordy the prestigious Waldo Salt Screenwriting Award at the 2002 Sundance festival. As a widower coming to terms with his loss, Hoffman conveys the slow erosion of surface calm by inner turmoil, as he succumbs to sniffing petrol fumes to obliterate the guilt and rejection inspired by his wife's unexplained suicide. Some of his misadventures may seem eccentric, but the raw emotion of Hoffman's performance is authentic. **DP** **DVD**

Philip Seymour Hoffman *Wilson Joel* • Kathy Bates *Mary Ann Bankhead* • Jack Kehler *Denny* • Sarah Koskoff *Maura* • Stephen Tobolowsky *Tom Bailey* • Erika Alexander *Brenda* ■ *Dir* Todd Louiso • *Scr* Gordy Hoffman

The Love Lottery ★★★ U
Comedy   1953 · UK · Colour · 84min

David Niven is his usual smooth self and the part of a 1950s celluloid heart-throb was made for him. Charles Crichton directs with his tongue well placed in his cheek. The plot is about as daft as you can possibly get – Niven agrees to be first prize in a love lottery for fans – but nobody really cares as there's just enough satire to keep this fizzy romp afloat. **SR** **DVD**

David Niven *Rex Allerton* • Peggy Cummins *Sally* • Anne Vernon *Jane* • Herbert Lom *Amico* • Charles Victor *Jennings* • Gordon Jackson *Ralph* • Humphrey Bogart ■ *Dir* Charles Crichton • *Scr* Harry Kurnitz, from the story by Charles Neilson-Terry, Zelma Bramley-Moore

The Love Machine ★ 18
Drama   1971 · US · Colour · 103min

Jacqueline Susann hit paydirt with this tacky adaptation of her bestselling novel. The setting is the power-crazed, sexually torrid world of television news and if you can believe John Philip Law as the head honcho you will believe anything. Dyan Cannon pouts, Robert Ryan looks bored as a company chairman and David Hemmings plays a hyped-up photographer – a not very subtle in-joke about his role in *Blowup*. This lacks the really bad taste and send-up performances to make it even vaguely enjoyable. **AT**

John Phillip Law *Robin Stone* • Dyan Cannon *Judith Austin* • Robert Ryan *Gregory Austin* • Jackie Cooper *Danton Miller* • David Hemmings *Jerry Nelson* ■ *Dir* Jack Haley Jr • *Scr* Samuel Taylor, from the novel by Jacqueline Susann

Love, Marilyn ★★★ 12
Documentary   2012 · US · Colour · 103min

This slick mosaic about Marilyn Monroe uses famous faces such as Uma Thurman and Paul Giamatti to read out items from Monroe's recently discovered personal papers. Director Liz Garbus has a gift for revelation, having previously made *Bobby Fischer against the World*. This time, there is little fresh to say about Monroe, but new ephemera justify the jaunt through a standard biography. Excerpts from the notes of her therapists, friends and jotted thoughts about herself help to make the film a fragmented scrapbook of docu-tainment for a new generation of fans. **KK** Swearing. **DVD**

F Murray Abraham • Adrien Brody • Ellen Burstyn • Glenn Close • Paul Giamatti • Lindsay Lohan • Uma Thurman ■ *Dir/Scr* Liz Garbus

The Love Match ★★★ U
Comedy   1955 · UK · BW · 82min

Although this is an admirable enough comedy, it is also one of those unforgivably patronising pictures that bourgeois British film-makers believed presented an

authentic picture of working-class life. Arthur Askey stars as a football crazy railway employee whose passion for a team of no-hopers lands him in all sorts of trouble. Struggling against a shortage of genuinely funny situations, the cast does well to keep the action alive. The highlight is Askey's heckling of the referee, a wonderful moment of football hooliganism. **DP** **DVD**

Arthur Askey *Bill Brown* • Thora Hird *Sal Brown* • Glenn Melvyn *Wally Binns* • Robb Wilton *Mr Muddlecombe* • James Kenney *Percy Brown* • Shirley Eaton *Rose Brown* ■ *Dir* David Paltenghi • *Scr* Geoffrey Orme, Glenn Melvyn, from the play by Glenn Melvyn

Love Me If You Dare ★★★ 15
Romantic comedy drama   2003 · Fr/Bel · Colour · 89min

Taking a childhood game to adult extremes, Yann Samuell's anti-romance asks us to root for a couple destined to be together, but wilfully determined to remain apart. The dares that young Thibault Verhaeghe and Josephine Lebas Joly make to get them through the pain of growing up are mischievous and sweet. But the fact that Guillaume Canet and Marion Cotillard continue to disrupt each other's lives periodically over the next 15 years seems capricious, contrived and occasionally cruel. Technically accomplished, this is entertaining but never wholly engaging. **DP** French +subtitles. Swearing, sex scenes. **DVD**

Guillaume Canet *Julien* • Marion Cotillard *Sophie* • Thibault Verhaeghe *Julien, aged 8* • Josephine Lebas Joly *Sophie, aged 8* • Emmanuelle Grönvold *Julien's mother* • Gérard Watkins *Julien's father* • Gilles Lellouche *Sergei* • Julia Faure *Sophie's sister* • Laetizia Venezia *Christelle* • Elodie Navarre *Aurélie* ■ *Dir/Scr* Yann Samuell

Love Me or Leave Me ★★★★ PG
Biographical musical drama   1955 · US · Colour · 116min

This cracking biopic of 1920s chanteuse Ruth Etting was originally intended as a vehicle for Ava Gardner, but MGM wisely brought in Doris Day, giving her a sexy new image and pairing her with tough guy James Cagney, and, boy, how those sparks fly! Though censorship has diluted this tawdry saga of a kept woman and her obsessive and sexually inadequate gangster sponsor, the truth is not glossed over, despite the top-notch production values that make the tale less squalid than it was. Day is a knockout, performing the title number and *Ten Cents a Dance* with great understanding, but it's Cagney who walks away with the movie. **TS** **DVD**

Doris Day *Ruth Etting* • James Cagney *Martin "the Gimp" Snyder* • Cameron Mitchell *Johnny Alderman* • Robert Keith (1) *Bernard V Loomis* • Tom Tully *Frobisher* • Harry Bellaver *Georgie* • Richard Gaines *Paul Hunter* ■ *Dir* Charles Vidor • *Scr* Daniel Fuchs, Isobel Lennart, from a story by Daniel Fuchs

Love Me Tender ★★★ PG
Western   1956 · US · BW · 85min

When 20th Century-Fox made a cheap black-and-white CinemaScope western called *The Reno Brothers*, they couldn't possibly have foreseen how one lucky stroke of casting would bring their production costs back within the first three days of opening. For, as younger brother Clint Reno, rock 'n' roll sensation Elvis Presley made his screen debut, and the title of the movie was changed to that of its ballad, *Love Me Tender*. Elvis proved to be a natural screen presence and, although third-billed to stars Richard Egan and Debra Paget, effortlessly dominates the film. **TS** **DVD**

Richard Egan *Vance* • Debra Paget *Cathy* • Elvis Presley *Clint* • Robert Middleton *Siringo* • William Campbell *Brett Reno* • Neville Brand *Mike Gavin* • Mildred Dunnock *Mother* ■ *Dir* Robert D Webb • *Scr* Robert Buckner, from a story by Maurice Geraghty

Love Me Tonight ★★★★★★
Musical comedy   1932 · US · BW · 104min

This is one of Hollywood's most clever and influential film musicals, with a sublime Rodgers and Hart score illuminating director Rouben Mamoulian's successful attempt at freeing the production from its staid, stage-bound forerunner. The irrepressible Maurice Chevalier is "the son-of-a-gun who's nothing but a tailor" who falls for princess Jeanette MacDonald, long before MGM put her in a straitjacket opposite the sexless Nelson Eddy. And those songs - *Mimi, Lover, Isn't It Romantic?* - and, ooh, that risqué dialogue: make a note of Myrna Loy's pre-censorship response to "Could you go for a doctor?". TS

Maurice Chevalier *Maurice Courtelin* · Jeanette MacDonald *Princess Jeanette* · Myrna Loy *Countess Valentine* · Charlie Ruggles [Charles Ruggles] *Vicomte de Vareze* · C Aubrey Smith *Duke* · Charles Butterworth *Count de Savignac* · Joseph Cawthorn *Dr Armand de Fontinac* · Robert Greig *Flamond* ■ *Dir* Rouben Mamoulian · *Scr* Samuel Hoffenstein, Waldemar Young, George Marion Jr, from the play *Tailor in the Chateau* by Léopold Marchand, by Paul Armont

Love Nest ★★ U
Comedy   1951 · US · BW · 81min

This piece of harmless fluff stars sweet and pretty June Haver in one of her rare non-musical roles. She and bland William Lundigan are a married couple who have invested their life savings in an apartment building, but a number of problems arise. One of them comes in the comely shape of Marilyn Monroe - on the eve of stardom - tossed in to create jealousy. It's all ineptly contrived. RB *DVD*

June Haver *Connie Scott* · William Lundigan *Jim Scott* · Frank Fay *Charley Patterson* · Myrna Monroe *Roberta Stevens* · Jack Paar *Ed Forbes* · Leatrice Joy *Eadie Gaynor* ■ *Dir* Joseph M Newman · *Scr* IAL Diamond, from the novel by Scott Corbett

The Love of Jeanne Ney ★★★★
Silent romance   1927 · Ger · BW · 144min

Made in the heyday of UFA, the famed German production company, just prior to GW Pabst's best works, *Pandora's Box* and *Diary of a Lost Girl*, this epic love story deserves to be better known. A mixture of social realism and Hollywood-style romance, the rather complicated plot moves from the Crimea (studio sets) during the Russian Revolution to Paris, where sequences were shot in the streets. The lovers, portrayed by Edith Jehanne and Uno Henning, are outplayed by Fritz Rasp, a wonderfully sleazy villain, and Brigitte Helm, cast as a lonely blind girl. RB

Edith Jehanne *Jeanne Ney* · Brigitte Helm *Gabrielle Ney* · Hertha von Walther *Margot* · Uno Henning *Andreas Labov* · Fritz Rasp *Khalibiev* · Adolph Edgar Licho *Raymond Ney* · Eugen Jensen *Alfred Ney* · Hans Jaray *Emile Poitras* · Wladimir Sokoloff [Vladimir Sokoloff] *Zacharkiewitsch* ■ *Dir* GW Pabst · *Scr* Ladislao Vajda, Rudolph Leonhardt, Ilya Ehrenburg, from the novel *Die Liebe der Jeanne Ney* by Ilya Ehrenburg

The Love of Sumako the Actress ★★★
Biographical drama   1947 · Jpn · BW · 96min

Although he had much sympathy for geishas and others who suffered from patriarchal injustice, Kenji Mizoguchi was perhaps less astute in his handling of successful females. Consequently, although he stages this biopic of Sumako Matsui with a genuine feel for the Japanese theatre at a time when actresses and western techniques were virtually unknown, he is less certain in his presentation of the melodramatic events surrounding her affair with married director, Hogetsu Shimamura. DP Japanese +subtitles.

Kinuyo Tanaka *Sumako Matsui* · So Yamamura *Hogetsu Shimamura* · Eijiro Tono *Shoyo Tsubouchi* · Kikue Mori *Ichiko Shimamura* ■ *Dir* Kenji Mizoguchi · *Scr* Yoshikata Yoda, from the play *Karumen Yukinu* by Hideo Nagata

Love on the Dole ★★★★ PG
Drama   1941 · UK · BW · 94min

This dramatisation of Walter Greenwood's influential novel about working-class life stars Deborah Kerr as a mill girl caught on the horns of a classic 1930s dilemma: become a kept woman and escape poverty, or keep faith with the morality of her class. Director John Baxter has summoned all the usual slum-dwelling stereotypes - local sharp-suited bookie and cruel paterfamilias - yet the movie resonates with strong feeling for the harshness and brutal truths of life in Depression-era Salford, and Kerr is subtly affecting. SH *DVD* *BD*

Deborah Kerr *Sally Hardcastle* · Clifford Evans *Larry Meath* · Joyce Howard *Helen Hawkins* · George Carney *Mr Hardcastle* · Mary Merrall *Mrs Hardcastle* · Geoffrey Hibbert *Harry Hardcastle* · Frank Cellier *Sam Grundy* · Martin Walker *Ned Narkey* ■ *Dir* John Baxter · *Scr* Walter Greenwood, Barbara K Emary, Rollo Gamble, from Ronald Gow's play, from Greenwood's novel

Love on the Run ★★★
Comedy   1936 · US · BW · 80min

This is class. It may not seem very clever or original today, but it never really had to be. The stars are Joan Crawford and Clark Gable, and for many movie fans of the era that's all that matters. One of those globetrotting romances that never get off the backlot, this is whipped along ever-so-lightly by director WS Van Dyke ("One-take Woody"), an expert craftsman who knew exactly how to handle material like this. TS

Joan Crawford *Sally Parker* · Clark Gable *Michael Anthony* · Franchot Tone *Barnabas Pells* · Reginald Owen *Baron Spandermann* · Mona Barrie *Baroness* · Ivan Lebedeff *Prince Igor* ■ *Dir* WS Van Dyke · *Scr* John Lee Mahin, Manuel Seff, Gladys Hurlbut, from the story *Beauty and the Beast* by Alan Green, Julian Brodie

Love on the Run ★★★ 12
Comedy drama   1979 · Fr · Colour · 91min

The fifth, last and least of François Truffaut's films about his alter ego Antoine Doinel, first seen in the director's debut feature, *The 400 Blows*, made 20 years earlier. This is also a nostalgic movie, with many of Antoine's former female conquests making guest appearances, some in sequences from earlier films, as he prepares to write a novel of his romantic career. It's more than a shade indulgent, and some may find Jean-Pierre Léaud a real pain as the lead. Yet it's still a funny and humane movie. AT French +subtitles. *DVD* *BD*

Jean-Pierre Léaud *Antoine Doinel* · Marie-France Pisier *Colette* · Claude Jade *Christine* · Dani *Liliane* · Dorothée *Sabine* ■ *Dir* François Truffaut · *Scr* François Truffaut, Suzanne Schiffman, Marie-France Pisier, Jean Aurel

The Love Parade ★★★★
Musical comedy   1929 · US · BW · 107min

Soprano Jeanette MacDonald, the queen of screen operetta, made her film debut as Queen Louise, being wooed by Maurice Chevalier's Count Alfred Renard in Ernst Lubitsch's first talkie. His Gallic charm and her Anglo-Saxon reserve and self-mockery produced a seductive, piquant combination in this saucy fairy tale set in Paris and the fictional land of Sylvania. With its lavish settings, songs integrated into the scenario and sexual innuendo, it set the pattern for future Hollywood musicals. RB

Maurice Chevalier *Count Alfred Renard* · Jeanette MacDonald *Queen Louise* · Lupino Lane *Jacques* · Lillian Roth *Lulu* · Edgar Norton *Major-Domo* · Jean Harlow ■ *Dir* Ernst Lubitsch · *Scr* Ernst Vajda, Guy Bolton, from the play *The Prince Consort* by Leon Xanrof, Jules Chancel

The Love Pill ★ 18
Erotic comedy   1971 · UK · Colour · 79min

In the early 1970s, the pill was still held responsible in many quarters for the onset of the permissive society and so this crass picture takes the argument to its illogical conclusion by having dozens of women take a tablet that transforms them into nymphomaniacs. Instantly forgettable soft-core comedy. DP

Henry Woolf *Libido* · Toni Sinclair *Sylvia, Libido's secretary* · David Pugh *Arnold* · Melinda Churcher *Linda* · Kenneth Waller *Professor Edwards* ■ *Dir* Kenneth Turner · *Scr* from a story by John Lindsay

Love Potion No 9 ★★ PG
Romantic fantasy comedy   1992 · US · Colour · 92min

Taking its plot cues from the lyrics of the famous pop hit, this is silly, cute and randomly amusing. Tate Donovan and Sandra Bullock are the nerdy lab assistants who discover a spray formula that makes them irresistible to the opposite sex. The expected complications ensue. Writer/director Dale Launer knows his limitations and deftly creates an unassuming feel-good factor around them. Worth seeing for Anne Bancroft's uncredited mystic gypsy cameo. AJ *DVD*

Tate Donovan *Paul Matthews* · Sandra Bullock *Diane Farrow* · Mary Mara *Marisa* · Dale Midkiff *Gary Logan* · Hillary Bailey Smith *Sally* · Dylan Baker *Prince Geoffrey* · Anne Bancroft *Madame Ruth* (uncredited) ■ *Dir* Dale Launer · *Scr* Dale Launer, from a song by Jerry Leiber, Mike Stoller

The Love Punch ★★★★ 12
Romantic comedy caper   2013 · UK/Fr · Colour · 90min

Emma Thompson teams with Pierce Brosnan for a screwball caper full of fizz and pop, which tracks the bumbling efforts of a divorced couple to steal a diamond from the fat cat (Laurent Lafitte) who has squandered their pension fund. Writer/director Joel Hopkins may be courting an older audience here, but not necessarily a more mature one. Thompson and Brosnan are giddy as schoolkids on a mission that takes them to the French Riviera, where they scale cliff-faces, get into car chases, and, yes, fall in love with each other all over again. The chemistry is bang on, Celia Imrie and Timothy Spall provide sterling backup, and if the plot is a bit clumsy, that's more than made up for with sheer exuberance and plenty of cheeky banter. SP *DVD* *BD*

Emma Thompson *Kate* · Pierce Brosnan *Richard* · Timothy Spall *Jerry* · Celia Imrie *Penelope* · Louise Bourgoin *Manon Fontaine* · Tuppence Middleton *Sophie* ■ *Dir/Scr* Joel Hopkins

Love, Rosie ★★ 15
Romantic comedy   2014 · UK/US · Colour · 98min

Lily Collins and Sam Claflin play platonic best friends who seem destined for each other, but over the years life-changing events and their own misunderstandings conspire to keep them apart. The film exists in a world only found in romantic comedies - pretty people living out stories of increasing improbability in a chirpy soundtrack (here including Lily Allen). Children, marriages, even deaths are seen as nothing more than obstacles to this near-miss romance, to the point where you either get swept up in it all, or disengage completely. JL *DVD* *BD*

Lily Collins *Rosie Dunne* · Sam Claflin *Alex Stewart* · Christian Cooke *Greg* · Tamsin Egerton *Sally* · Suki Waterhouse *Bethany Williams* · Jaime Winstone *Ruby* ■ *Dir* Christian Ditter

A Love Song for Bobby Long ★★★
Drama   2004 · US · Colour · 119min

John Travolta tackles the inevitable fact of ageing in this tale of a young woman (Scarlett Johansson), who returns to her home after her mother's death only to find it occupied by a group of alcoholic literary types who have every intention of staying put. Despite Travolta's best efforts (and impressively silvered hair), he never quite convinces as an ageing, drunk writer, but what director Shainee Gabel's debut movie lacks slightly in dramatic credibility it more than makes up for in New Orleans atmosphere. AS

John Travolta *Bobby Long* · Scarlett Johansson *Pursy* · Gabriel Macht *Lawson* · Deborah Kara Unger *Georgianna* · Dane Rhodes *Cecil* · David Jensen (2) *Junior* · Clayne Crawford *Lee* ■ *Dir* Shainee Gabel · *Scr* Shainee Gabel, from the novel *Off Magazine Street* by Ronald Everett Capps

Love Songs ★★
Drama   1984 · Fr · Colour · 109min

The prospect of watching Christopher Lambert and Richard Anconina camp it up as wannabe rock stars will probably dissuade many from sticking with this showbiz melodrama, particularly as the ditties are hardly the finest. But the romance that develops between Lambert and record mogul Catherine Deneuve is not without interest. The leads' contrasting acting styles also add to this otherwise pedestrian picture. DP French dubbed.

Catherine Deneuve *Margaux* · Christopher Lambert *Jeremy* · Richard Anconina *Michel* · Jacques Perrin *Yves* · Dayle Haddon *Corinne* · Nick Mancuso *Peter* · Charlotte Gainsbourg *Charlotte* · Dominique Lavanant *Florence* · Lionel Rocheman *Gruber* ■ *Dir/Scr* Elie Chouraqui

Love Songs ★★★★ 15
Romantic musical drama   2007 · Fr · Colour · 91min

Having celebrated the ingenuity of the *nouvelle vague* in 2006's *Inside Paris*, writer/director Christophe Honoré recalls the glories of Jacques Demy (*The Umbrellas of Cherbourg*) here. He integrates 13 songs into a bittersweet storyline about Parisian Louis Garrel's struggle to cope with the sudden death of girlfriend Ludivine Sagnier. The musical is often condemned for persisting with the outmoded conceit of ordinary people bursting into song in everyday locations. But the melancholy lyrics to Alex Beaupain's tunes have a psychological significance that make the characters more, rather than less, credible. Staged with a real understanding of the genre, this is simply delightful. DP French +subtitles. *DVD*

Louis Garrel *Ismaël Bénoliel* · Ludivine Sagnier *Julie* · Chiara Mastroianni *Jeanne* · Clotilde Hesme *Alice* · Grégoire Leprince-Ringuet *Erwann* · Brigitte Roüan *Mother* ■ *Dir/Scr* Christophe Honoré · *Cinematographer* Rémy Chevrin · *Music* Alex Beaupain

Love Story ★★ U
Romantic melodrama   1944 · UK · BW · 108min

This is one of those tragic romances in which all concerned would have been spared a lot of tears if just one of the lovers had bothered to give the other an inkling of the truth. But with former pilot Stewart Granger keeping mum about his incipient blindness and pianist Margaret Lockwood equally reticent about her terminal illness, we are guaranteed angst aplenty. Stiff-upper-lipped hokum. DP

Margaret Lockwood *Lissa Campbell* · Stewart Granger *Kit Firth* · Patricia Roc *Judy Martin* · Tom Walls *Tom Tanner* · Reginald Purdell *Albert* · Moira Lister *Carol* · Dorothy Bramhall *Susie* · Vincent Holman *Prospero* · Joan Rees *Ariel* ■ *Dir* Leslie Arliss · *Scr* Leslie Arliss, Doreen Montgomery, Rodney Ackland, from the story by JW Drawbell

Love Story ★★★ PG
Romantic drama   1970 · US · Colour · 95min

This heady mixture of love and life-threatening illness was roundly condemned by critics in its day, but became a massive box-office hit nevertheless. Drown in the excess of it all, as the ill-starred romance between tragic Ali MacGraw and Ryan O'Neal takes its course and you'll require two boxes of Kleenex. On the other hand, bring even the remotest hint of cynicism to bear and it will grate like fingernails on a blackboard. A sequel, *Oliver's Story*, followed belatedly in 1978. SH Swearing, sex scenes. *DVD* *BD*

Ali MacGraw *Jenny Cavilleri* · Ryan O'Neal *Oliver Barrett IV* · John Marley *Phil Cavilleri* · Ray Milland *Oliver Barrett III* · Russell Nype *Dean Thompson* · Katherine Balfour *Mrs Oliver Barrett III* · Sydney Walker *Dr Shapeley* · Robert Modica *Dr Addison* · Tom Lee Jones [Tommy Lee Jones] *Hank* ■ *Dir* Arthur Hiller · *Scr* Erich Segal, from his novel · *Music* Francis Lai

L

The Love Test ★★★
Comedy 1935 · UK · BW · 63min

This early romantic comedy from director Michael Powell features one of Bernard Miles's first appearances, as well as an early outing for Googie Withers, whom Powell claimed "brings sunshine into dull lives, makes bald hair grow". Judy Gunn stars as a laboratory overseer up against her male employees. Initially successful, Gunn has to work to outwit her adversaries, who plot to oust her by making her fall in love. Only rediscovered in the late 1980s, this demonstrates Powell's fascination with strong women. LH

Judy Gunn *Mary* • Louis Hayward *John* • David Hutcheson *Thompson* • Morris Harvey *President* • Googie Withers *Minnie* • Aubrey Dexter *Vice-President* • Bernard Miles *Allan* ■ *Dir* Michael Powell • *Scr* Selwyn Jepson, from a story by Jack Celestin

Love the Beast ★★★ 15
Documentary 2008 · Aus · Colour · 88min

This documentary is actor and first-time director Eric Bana's loving tribute to his first car, a Ford GT Falcon Coupe, which he and his friends have painstakingly restored over the years and which he is about to race in a rally in Tasmania. Along the way, he takes time out to chat to fellow car freaks like Jay Leno and Jeremy Clarkson, along with his family and childhood friends, who remain his loyal pit crew. Although it helps to be a car nut to watch this, Bana's unpretentious passion is infectious and the only real missteps are the psychological insights provided by American TV shrink Dr Phil McGraw. One only hopes that his Aussie mates gave Bana a lot of stick over that. JF *DVD*

Eric Bana • Jeremy Clarkson • Jay Leno • Dr Phil McGraw ■ *Dir* Eric Bana • *Cinematographers* Rod Pollard, David Rose

L

Love Thy Neighbour ★ PG
Comedy 1973 · UK · Colour · 82min

The attitudes on display in this film based on the 1970s TV comedy series – about two neighbours, one black the other white, who are in constant conflict with one another – are so dated that they are more laughable than offensive. Time hasn't dimmed its spectacular unfunniness. JF *DVD*

Jack Smethurst *Eddie Booth* • Rudolph Walker *Bill Reynolds* • Nina Baden-Semper *Barbie* • Kate Williams *Joan Booth* ■ *Dir* John Robins • *Scr* Vince Powell, Harry Driver

Love Tomorrow ★★ PG
Romantic drama 2012 · UK · Colour · 76min

Ballet documentaries have demonstrated the levels of sacrifice and hard work needed to make it in such a highly competitive milieu. So director Christopher Payne's dance drama feels like a somewhat superfluous addition, especially as it so spends so long avoiding both dance and drama. Real-life dancers Cindy Jourdain and Arionel Vargas play a couple who swiftly become inseparable but when they do finally dance in a park, the effect is as enchanting as it is transient, and one is left wondering why Payne has chosen to play against the strengths of these professional dancers, who so clearly struggle to convey emotion through dialogue. DP Some swearing. *DVD*

Cindy Jourdain *Eva/Maya* • Arionel Vargas *Oriel* • Max Brown *Dominic* • Samuel Barnett *Cal* • John McArdle *Henry* ■ *Dir/Scr* Christopher Payne

Love! Valour! Compassion! ★★★ 15
Comedy drama 1997 · US · Colour · 109min

Joe Mantello's poignant adaptation of Terrence McNally's award-winning play explores the differing emotions and attitudes (sexual and otherwise) of eight gay men staying at a glorious country retreat. Set over three American holiday weekends, this is an involving if overly sentimental study of human relationships, with a talented ensemble cast. Despite the absence of any straight characters, the film's honesty and insight into human nature makes it accessible to all audiences. JC Swearing, nudity.

Jason Alexander *Buzz Hauser* • Randy Becker *Ramon Fornos* • Stephen Bogardus *Gregory Mitchell* • John Glover *John Jeckyll/James Jeckyll* • John Benjamin Hickey *Arthur Pape* • Justin Kirk *Bobby Brahms* • Stephen Spinella *Perry Sellars* ■ *Dir* Joe Mantello • *Scr* Terrence McNally, from his play

Love Walked In ★★ 15
Crime thriller 1997 · US/Arg · Colour · 87min

Having won an Emmy for *Life Stories*, director Juan José Campanella attempted a latterday *noir* here, as struggling pianist Denis Leary and singer wife Aitana Sanchez-Gijon conspire with sleazy private eye Michael Badalucco to sting wealthy Terence Stamp with a divorce scam. But, while the thriller elements are established efficiently, Campanella spends too much time on staging episodes from Leary's horror scribblings, which distracts from the action. DP Swearing, violence.

Denis Leary *Jack Morrisey* • Aitana Sanchez-Gijon *Vicky* • Terence Stamp *Fred Moore* • Michael Badalucco *Eddie* • Gene Canfield *Joey* • Marj Dusay *Mrs Moore* • Moira Kelly *Vera* • Neal Huff *Howard* ■ *Dir* Juan José Campanella • *Scr* Lynn Geller, Larry Golin, Juan José Campanella, from the novel *Ni el Tiro del Final* by Jose Pablo Feinmann

Love Will Keep Us Together ★★
Romantic drama 2010 · US · Colour · 107min

In this mediocre TV movie, a workaholic widower (David James Elliott) tries to reconnect with his two children following his redundancy. The result is a string of flimsy and predictable occurrences, thrown together to demonstrate the trials and tribulations of being a stay-at-home dad. Of course, we're meant to chuckle at his initial domestic ineptitude – and the fact his idea of "reconnecting" involves such far-fetched nonsense as food fights – but the scenario's been done better so many times before that it elicits neither amusement nor sympathy. SF

David James Elliott *Ben Westman* • Sharon Case *Hope Jensen* • Madison Davenport *Lindsay Westman* • Will Shadley *Dylan Westman* • Jay Huguley *Brian Westman* ■ *Dir* Bradford May • *Scr* Adam Rockoff

Love with the Proper Stranger ★★★★
Comedy drama 1963 · US · BW · 100min

After a one-night stand, demure Natalie Wood gets pregnant and jazz musician Steve McQueen does one of those wonderful, trademark double-takes when she tells him the news. This is a fresh and very touching drama, set against the religious and staunch family traditions of New York's Italian community. Even when the script begins to run out of ideas, the gorgeous Wood and McQueen have more than enough charisma to fill the screen without saying a word. AT

Natalie Wood *Angie Rossini* • Steve McQueen (1) *Rocky Papasano* • Edie Adams *Barbie, Barbara of Seville* • Herschel Bernardi *Dominick Rossini* • Tom Bosley *Anthony Colombo* • Harvey Lembeck *Julio Rossini* ■ *Dir* Robert Mulligan • *Scr* Arnold Schulman

Love Wrecked ★★ PG
Romantic comedy 2005 · US · Colour · 83min

Grease director Randal Kleiser targets the female pre-teen market with this inane wish-fulfilment fantasy. A slight and predictable vehicle for *She's the Man* star Amanda Bynes, it follows the comic deception that unfolds when smitten teen Jenny ends up shipwrecked with her rock idol, Jason Masters (Chris Carmack). But after discovering they're actually only a short distance away from their holiday resort, Jenny decides to keep quiet, hoping the singer will fall for her if they're left alone together. The clichés come thick and fast, with no stone left unturned in the ruthless quest for quick laughs. While under-13s probably won't see past the mischievously cheesy dialogue and frothy pop soundtrack, anybody older should look elsewhere for their fun. SF *DVD*

Amanda Bynes *Jenny Taylor* • Chris Carmack *Jason Masters* • Jamie-Lynn Sigler [Jamie-Lynn DiScala] *Alexis Manetti* • Jonathan Bennett *Ryan Howell* • Alfonso Ribeiro *Brent Hernandez* • Fred Willard *Mr Taylor* • Lance Bass *Dan* ■ *Dir* Randal Kleiser • *Scr* Stephen Langford

Loved ★ 15
Drama 1996 · US · Colour · 99min

This fumbles the sensitive subject of domestic violence. Writer/director Erin Dignam manages to turn in an almost insulting and poorly paced drama that does its well-meaning cast a disservice. Robin Wright Penn is the woman still in love with her ex-partner despite his abuse, who is asked to testify against him by DA William Hurt, after another of the man's lovers throws herself in front of a car. JB Some swearing, nudity. *DVD*

William Hurt *KD Dietrickson* • Robin Wright *Hedda* • Amy Madigan *Brett* • Joanna Cassidy *Elenore* • Paul Dooley *Leo* • Anthony Lucero *Defendent* • Jennifer Rubin *Debra* • Sean Penn *Michael* ■ *Dir/Scr* Erin Dignam

The Loved One ★★★
Black comedy 1965 · US · BW · 122min

Although he ranks among the most admired British novelists of the century, the cinema has not been kind to Evelyn Waugh. Given that this novel, set in a California pet cemetery, is overladen with scathing swipes at Hollywood and American notions of the afterlife, screenwriters Terry Southern and Christopher Isherwood (themselves acclaimed novelists) might have produced a darker, more bitingly satirical script. However, director Tony Richardson and his all-star cast make the most of their opportunities before events descend into broad farce. TH

Robert Morse *Dennis Barlow* • Rod Steiger *Mr Joyboy* • Jonathan Winters *Harry Glenworthy/Wilbur Glenworthy* • Anjanette Comer *Aimee Thanatogenos* • Dana Andrews *General Brinkman* • Milton Berle *Mr Kenton* • John Gielgud *Sir Francis Hinsley* • James Coburn *Immigration Officer* • Tab Hunter *Guide* • Liberace *Mr Starker* • Lionel Stander *Guru Brahmin* ■ *Dir* Tony Richardson • *Scr* Terry Southern, Christopher Isherwood, from the novel by Evelyn Waugh

The Loved Ones ★★★★ 18
Horror thriller 2009 · Aus · Colour · 80min

The torture-porn genre gets a Day-Glo makeover in this hilariously deranged Ocker shocker. Xavier Samuel stars as Brent, the unfortunate youth who makes the mistake of turning down a date to the school dance from Lola (Robin McLeavy). As revenge, she gets her adoring dad (John Brumpton) to kidnap him and then sets about re-creating the dance at her own house. The bodily harm inflicted by writer/director Sean Byrne on the hapless Brent is wince-inducing in the extreme, but the cheerful black humour means it's never nastily exploitative. The result is an instant cult classic. JF Violence, swearing, drug abuse, sex scenes, nudity. *DVD* *BL*

Xavier Samuel *Brent* • Robin McLeavy *Lola "Princess"* • John Brumpton *Daddy* • Richard Wilson *Jamie* • Victoria Thaine *Holly* ■ *Dir/Scr* Sean Byrne

Lovelace ★★★ 18
Biographical drama 2013 · US · Colour · 89min

Amanda Seyfried shimmers in this entertainingly sleazy, star-studded take on the late porn star Linda Lovelace's "true story". Growing up with a strict mother (Sharon Stone, virtually unrecognisable), Lovelace marries abusive Chuck Traynor (Peter Sarsgaard), a lowlife who forces her into pornographic films. *Deep Throat* makes her a star but the marital and career abuse continues. Humanising the story is Seyfried's remarkable performance in what is a surprisingly watchable and endearingly heartbreaking swipe at the truth. KK Violence, sex scenes. *DVD* *BL*

Amanda Seyfried *Linda Boreman, "Linda Lovelace"* • Peter Sarsgaard *Chuck Traynor* • Hank Azaria *Jerry Damiano* • James Franco *Hugh Hefner* • Robert Patrick *John Boreman* • Sharon Stone *Dorothy Boreman* ■ *Dir* Rob Epstein, Jeffrey Friedman • *Scr* Andy Bellin

The Loveless ★★ 15
Drama 1981 · US · Colour · 79min

Willem Dafoe's first major screen role was in this comatose existential biker movie. Dafoe and neo-rockabilly singer Robert Gordon are members of a rough-and-tumble biker gang who, on en route to Daytona, get stranded in a small southern town where they swagger and sneer a lot and put the narrow-minded locals' backs up. Worth a look for Dafoe alone. AJ Nudity.

Willem Dafoe *Vance* • Robert Gordon *Davis* • Marin Kanter *Telena* • J Don Ferguson *Tarver* • Tina L'Hotsky *Sportster Debbie* • Lawrence Matarese *LaVille* ■ *Dir* Monty Montgomery, Kathryn Bigelow • *Scr* Kathryn Bigelow

Lovely & Amazing ★★★ 15
Comedy 2001 · US · Colour · 87min

Writer/director Nicole Holofcener explores the emotional fallout that accrues when self-absorption meets low self-esteem in this caustic, expertly played and restrained comedy drama. Although widowed mother Brenda Blethyn is undergoing liposuction and younger sister Emily Mortimer is seized by doubts about her beauty despite a burgeoning acting career, it's the underachieving Catherine Keener who experiences the gravest identity crisis, as she veers from a loveless marriage into a romance with her teenage boss at a photo shop. DP Swearing, sex scenes, nudity. *DVD*

Catherine Keener *Michelle Marks* • Brenda Blethyn *Jane Marks* • Emily Mortimer *Elizabeth Marks* • Raven Goodwin *Annie Marks* • Aunjanue Ellis *Lorraine* • Clark Gregg *Bill* • Jake Gyllenhaal *Jordan* • James LeGros *Paul* • Michael Nouri *Dr Crane* • Dermot Mulroney *Kevin McCabe* ■ *Dir/Scr* Nicole Holofcener

The Lovely Bones ★★ 12
Fantasy drama 2009 · US/UK/NZ · Colour · 129min

After realising Middle-earth so solidly in the *Lord of the Rings* saga, director Peter Jackson spends too long in the clouds in this contemporary fantasy based on Alice Sebold's bestselling novel. A suitably wistful Saoirse Ronan plays the teenage girl who observes from on high the aftermath of her brutal murder and sees her killer (a rather too obvious Stanley Tucci) prepare for his next strike. And while Mark Wahlberg delivers a poignantly childlike performance to echo the loss of his daughter, Rachel Weisz, Susan Sarandon and Rose McIver (as mum, grandma and sister) feel superfluous. Consequently, the finale – though tense – lacks that visceral gut punch. SP Violence. *DVD* *BL*

Mark Wahlberg *Jack Salmon* • Rachel Weisz *Abigail Salmon* • Susan Sarandon *Grandma Lynn* • Saoirse Ronan *Susie Salmon* • Stanley Tucci *George Harvey* • Michael Imperioli *Len Fenerman* ■ *Dir* Peter Jackson • *Scr* Peter Jackson, Fran Walsh, Philippa Boyens, from the novel by Alice Sebold

Lovely Molly ★★ 15
Horror thriller 2012 · US · Colour · 96min

This intimate supernatural horror from *Blair Witch* co-writer/director Eduardo Sanchez stars Gretchen Lodge as newly married former heroin addict Molly, who finds her life unravelling when she moves back into the creaky old family home. It begins well, with an effectively nasty ambience, but quickly degenerates into all-out mumbo jumbo. The performances sell it well (especially Lodge), but quite what's going on in the final stretch is, quite frankly, anyone's guess. DW Violence, swearing, drug abuse, a sex scene, nudity. *DVD* *BL*

Gretchen Lodge *Molly* • Johnny Lewis *Tim* • Alexandra Holden *Hannah* • Katie Foster *Stacey* • Ken Arnold *Samuels* ■ *Dir* Eduardo Sanchez • *Scr* Eduardo Sanchez, Jamie Nash

Lovely to Look At ★★★ U
Musical comedy 1952 · US · Colour · 101min

This is the sumptuous MGM remake of the old RKO musical hit *Roberta*, an early vehicle for Fred Astaire and Ginger Rogers. It's the story of three friends who hope to finance a Broadway show with the proceeds from a Paris dress shop. The superb Jerome Kern score has been retained, and the songs, notably *Smoke Gets in Your Eyes* and *I Won't Dance*, still scintillate, especially when they're handled by such marvellous musical movie artists. **TS**

Kathryn Grayson *Stephanie* · Red Skelton *Al Marsh* · Howard Keel *Tony Naylor* · Marge Champion *Clarisse* · Gower Champion *Jerry Ralby* · Ann Miller *Bubbles Cassidy* · Zsa Zsa Gabor *Zsa Zsa* ■ *Dir* Mervyn LeRoy · *Scr* George Wells, Harry Ruby, Andrew Solt, from the musical *Roberta* by Jerome Kern, Dorothy Fields, Otto Harbach, from the novel *Roberta* by Alice Duer Miller

A Lovely Way to Go ★
Thriller 1968 · US · Colour · 103min

This is a lifeless, excessively complicated detective story that fails to deliver suspense, wit or romance. Kirk Douglas is wasted as the ex-cop hired by Eli Wallach's wily lawyer to protect Sylva Koscina, young unfaithful wife, on trial for murdering her husband. Douglas brings his usual vitality to bear but Koscina is bland and there is no energy between them. Look out for Ali MacGraw making her screen debut. **AE**

Kirk Douglas *Jim Schuyler* · Sylva Koscina *Rena Westabrook* · Eli Wallach *Tennessee Fredericks* · Kenneth Haigh *Jonathan Fleming* · Sharon Farrell *Carol* · Gordon Peters *Eric* · Martyn Green *Finchley* · Doris Roberts *Feeney* · Carey Nairnes *Harris* · Ralph Waite *Sean Magruder* · Ali MacGraw *Melody* ■ *Dir* David Lowell Rich · *Scr* AJ Russell

The Lover ★★ 18
Erotic drama 1992 · Fr/UK · Colour · 110min

Jean-Jacques Annaud raised a few eyebrows with this steamy tale of a girl's sexual awakening in 1920s Indo-China. It did feature young star Jane March in various states of undress, but there was really nothing much to get steamed up about. March plays a 15-year-old schoolgirl who loses more than her inhibitions with older man Tony Leung. Cue a voiceover by Jeanne Moreau, and a few meaningful moments which March is too out of her depth to convey. **JB** Sex scenes. **DVD**

Jane March *Young Marguerite Duras* · Tony Kar-Fai Leung [Tony Leung (1)] *Chinese man* · Frédérique Meininger *Mother* · Arnaud Giovaninetti *Elder brother* · Melvil Poupaud *Younger brother* · Lisa Faulkner *Hélène Lagonelle* ■ *Dir* Jean-Jacques Annaud · *Scr* Jean-Jacques Annaud, Gérard Brach, from the novel by Marguerite Duras

A Lover and His Lass ★★★
Comedy 1975 · Swe · Colour · 94min

This is the debut feature of Lasse Hallström, the Swedish director who went on to achieve international fame in Hollywood. Brasse Brännström (who also provided the story for the film) stars as a shiftless young man who is charm personified, but whose vocabulary does not include the words "fidelity" or "employment". Also known as *A Guy and His Gal*, this is a ribald, well-observed comedy, with winning performances. **DP** Swedish +subtitles.

Brasse Brännström *Lasse* · Mariann Rudberg *Lena* · Christer Jonsson *Bosse* · Börje Ahlstedt *Lasse's Brother* · Chatarina Larsson *Ulla* ■ *Dir* Lasse Hallström · *Scr* Lasse Hallström, from a story by Brasse Brännström

Lover Come Back ★★
Romantic comedy 1946 · US · BW · 91min

This romantic comedy has war correspondent George Brent returning from a couple of years away on assignment. Wife Lucille Ball's warm welcome is soon frozen by the discovery that her hubby hasn't lacked for female company and she takes off for a Vegas divorce. Naturally, he follows. Some zany shenanigans along the way pep up a mildly entertaining movie, disadvantaged by its dull leading man. **RK**

George Brent *Bill Williams* · Lucille Ball *Kay Williams* · Vera Zorina *Madeline Laslo* · Charles Winninger *Pa Williams* · Carl Esmond *Paul* · Raymond Walburn *JP Winthrop* · Elisabeth Risdon *Ma Williams* · Louise Beavers *Martha* ■ *Dir* William A Seiter · *Scr* Michael Fessier, Ernest Pagano

Lover Come Back ★★★ PG
Romantic comedy 1961 · US · Colour · 102min

This dig at the world of advertising features Doris Day, reuniting her with her *Pillow Talk* co-star Rock Hudson. This ultra-glossy romantic comedy is very much of its period, but the idea of Madison Avenue executives marketing a non-existent product (called VIP) remains a good one, and the anti-advertising jokes are still funny. Stanley Shapiro and Paul Henning's script was Oscar-nominated, though the finale is astoundingly tasteless. **TS** **DVD**

Rock Hudson *Jerry Webster* · Doris Day *Carol Templeton* · Tony Randall *Peter Ramsey* · Edie Adams *Rebel Davis* · Jack Oakie *J Paxton Miller* ■ *Dir* Delbert Mann · *Scr* Stanley Shapiro, Paul Henning · *Costume Designer* Irene

Loverboy ★★★ 15
Comedy 1989 · US · Colour · 94min

Patrick Dempsey is the pizza delivery boy bringing more than just a deep pan with extra cheese to a somewhat silly comedy from director Joan Micklin Silver. Carrie Fisher, Kirstie Alley and Barbara Carrera are just three of the women falling for his charms, and Dempsey is an engaging lead. Light-hearted and well played nonsense. **JB** Swearing.

Patrick Dempsey *Randy Bodek* · Kate Jackson *Diane Bodek* · Kirstie Alley *Joyce Palmer* · Carrie Fisher *Monica Delarcy* · Robert Ginty *Joe Bodek* · Nancy Valen *Jenny Gordon* · Charles Hunter Walsh *Jory Talbot* · Barbara Carrera *Alex Barnett* ■ *Dir* Joan Micklin Silver · *Scr* Robin Schiff, Tom Ropelewski, Leslie Dixon, from a story by Robin Schiff

The Lovers! ★★★
Comedy 1972 · UK · Colour · 88min

Lasting just 13 episodes on ITV in the early 1970s, this popular sitcom was another stepping stone in the careers of creator Jack Rosenthal and director Michael Apted. It didn't exactly harm the prospects of Richard Beckinsale or Paula Wilcox, either, as the couple who tiptoe towards commitment in spite of his passion for Manchester United and her refusal to entertain encounters with "Percy Filth". Hardly hilarious, but rather sweet. **DP**

Paula Wilcox *Beryl* · Richard Beckinsale *Geoffrey* · Joan Scott (1) *Beryl's mum* · Stella Moray *Geoffrey's mum* · Nikolas Simmonds *Roland* · Susan Littler *Sandra* · Anthony Naylor *Neville* · Bruce Watt *Jeremy* · John Comer *Geoffrey's dad* ■ *Dir* Herbert Wise · *Scr* Jack Rosenthal

Lovers ★★★ 18
Erotic thriller 1991 · Sp · Colour · 104min

Victoria Abril won the best actress award at Berlin for her performance in this re-enactment of a true-life *crime passionnel*. Set in mid-1950s Madrid, the film concentrates on the romantic entanglements of soldier Jorge Sanz, who honours fiancée Maribel Verdú's virginity by satiating his lust with landlady Abril. The action is beautifully shot but it lacks the sense of smouldering passion that might precipitate murder. **DP** Spanish +subtitles. Violence, swearing, nudity.

Victoria Abril *Luisa* · Jorge Sanz *Paco* · Maribel Verdú *Trini* · Enrique Cerro *Commandant* · Mabel Escano *Commandant's wife* ■ *Dir* Vicente Aranda · *Scr* Carlos Perez Merinero, Alvaro Del Amo, Vicente Aranda · *Cinematographer* José Luis Alcaine

Lovers ★★★
Romantic drama 1999 · Fr · Colour · 100min

The fifth film under the auspices of Dogme 95, and the first to be directed by a non-Dane, Jean-Marc Barr's movie owes as much to the stylistic devices of the French New Wave as it does to Lars von Trier's much vaunted Vow of Chastity. However, such is Barr's preoccupation with achieving spontaneous video visuals that he neglects the dramatic aspects of his disjointed, episodic tale. Deciding to live outside the law in order to love freely, bookseller Elodie Bouchez and painter Sergej Trifunovic (an illegal exile from the former Yugoslavia) are credibly desperate. But the jarringly edited hand-held footage undermines their efforts. **DP** French +subtitles.

Sergej Trifunovic *Dragan* · Elodie Bouchez *Jeanne* · Genevieve Page *Dragan Nikolic* · Thibault de Montalembert ■ *Dir* Jean-Marc Barr · *Scr* Jean-Marc Barr, Pascal Arnold

Lovers and Other Strangers ★★★★ 15
Comedy 1970 · US · Colour · 104min

This caustic and very funny wedding comedy shows what happens to a couple's extended family when they decide to get married. The cast contains so many exquisite performances that it seems invidious to single out anyone in particular. Gig Young, however, is simply terrific as the father of the bride (Bonnie Bedelia). Director Cy Howard knows when to step back and let the excellent script speak for itself. Meanwhile, look out for Diane Keaton in her screen debut. **TS**

Bonnie Bedelia *Susan Henderson* · Gig Young *Hal Henderson* · Michael Brandon *Mike Vecchio* · Beatrice Arthur *Bea Vecchio* · Richard Castellano *Frank Vecchio* · Robert Dishy [Bob Dishy] *Jerry* · Harry Guardino *Johnny* · Diane Keaton *Joan* ■ *Dir* Cy Howard · *Scr* Renee Taylor, Joseph Bologna, David Zelag Goodman, from a play by Taylor, Bologna

The Lovers of the Arctic Circle ★★★★ 15
Romantic drama 1998 · Sp/Fr · Colour · 104min

Basque director Julio Medem's metaphysical romance is one of his most inventive and accessible works to date. From the age of eight, Otto (Fele Martínez) and Ana (Najwa Nimri) know they are destined to be together. However, fate keeps intervening well into adulthood, forcing their on again/off again relationship to weather their being apart for long stretches. Employing an unusual narrative technique that blurs both lovers' perspectives together, and a dazzling style that confuses time periods and reveals certain key scenes, this dreamy rumination on unrequited love, chance and coincidence is a wonderfully rich and potent fable for our times. **AJ** Spanish +subtitles. Swearing, sex scenes. **DVD**

Fele Martínez *Otto* · Najwa Nimri *Ana* · Nancho Novo *Alvaro* · Maru Valdivielso *Olga* ■ *Dir/Scr* Julio Medem

Loves Kitchen ★★ 15
Romantic comedy drama 2010 · UK · Colour · 88min

Don't be distracted by a gimmicky cameo by Gordon Ramsay, as James Hacking's foodie comedy has more in common with Ealing whimsy than reality TV. Roused from a lengthy period of mourning by a stinging review of his restaurant, widowed chef Dougray Scott opens a gastro pub in the Hertfordshire countryside. There are too many minor characters for any to be drawn in depth and the storyline is as predictable as a greasy spoon menu. But off-screen marrieds Scott and Claire Forlani spark genially enough, while Simon Callow revels in playing a camp old soak. **DP** **DVD**

Dougray Scott *Rob Haley* · Claire Forlani *Kate Templeton* · Simon Callow *Guy Witherspoon* · Gordon Ramsay · Simon Hepworth *James Forester* · Michelle Ryan *Shauna* · Peter Bowles *Max Templeton* · Cherie Lunghi *Margaret* ■ *Dir/Scr* James Hacking · *Cinematographer* Jordan Cushing

Love's Labour's Lost ★★★ U
Romantic musical comedy 1999 · US/Fr/UK · Colour · 89min

Kenneth Branagh gives his Shakespearean adaptation a lift by combining this story of four sets of lovers with a host of 1930s and 40s song-and-dance numbers. Adrian Lester shines in a sublime musical set piece, and Natascha McElhone again demonstrates her depth and beauty. The film is flawed, though. The environment never transcends the feel of a studio, American stars Alicia Silverstone and Matthew Lillard are clumsy and miscast, and Branagh has lost some of the play's complexity by oversimplifying the text. **LH** **DVD**

Kenneth Branagh *Berowne* · Nathan Lane *Costard, the clown* · Adrian Lester *Dumaine* · Matthew Lillard *Longaville* · Natascha McElhone *Rosaline* · Alessandro Nivola *King* · Alicia Silverstone *Princess* · Timothy Spall *Don Armado* · Richard Briers *Nathaniel* · Richard Clifford *Boyet* · Carmen Ejogo *Maria* · Daniel Hill *Mercade* · Geraldine McEwan *Holofernia* · Emily Mortimer *Katherine* ■ *Dir* Kenneth Branagh · *Scr* Kenneth Branagh, from the play by William Shakespeare

The Loves of Carmen ★★★
Drama 1948 · US · Colour · 92min

There's no Bizet here, and hardly much of author Prosper Mérimée's great original either, as the director and stars of the immortal drama *Gilda* reunite to tell another tale of *amour fou* beneath blazing skies. Sadly, it doesn't quite gel. Not only is there no darker underside, but the 1940s Technicolor casts a bizarre and garish glow over the proceedings. Glenn Ford is arguably the most unlikely Don Jose ever, but Hayworth looks ravishing. **TS** **DVD**

Rita Hayworth *Carmen Garcia* · Glenn Ford *Don Jose* · Ron Randell *Andres* · Victor Jory *Garcia* · Luther Adler *Dancaire* · Arnold Moss *Colonel* · Joseph Buloff *Remendado* ■ *Dir* Charles Vidor · *Scr* Helen Deutsch, from the story *Carmen* by Prosper Mérimée

The Loves of Joanna Godden ★★★
Drama 1947 · UK · BW · 89min

This is a classic example of how the documentary-style story (so popular with postwar British film-makers) could result in pictures as crashingly dull as they were worthy. The story centres on Edwardian farmer Googie Withers, whose determination to make good as a sheep breeder and protect her spoiled sister (Jean Kent) forces her to discard a trio of eager beaus (John McCallum, Chips Rafferty and Derek Bond). There is plenty of incident, but the realism beloved of director Charles Frend is scarcely appropriate for such ripe melodrama. **DP**

Googie Withers *Joanna Godden* · Jean Kent *Ellen Godden* · John McCallum *Arthur Alce* · Derek Bond *Martin Trevor* · Henry Mollison *Harry Trevor* · Chips Rafferty *Collard* ■ *Dir* Charles Frend · *Scr* HE Bates, Angus MacPhail, from the novel *Joanna Godden* by Sheila Kaye-Smith

The Loves of Three Queens ★★
Drama 1954 · It/Fr · Colour · 90min

Having been frustrated by the cancellation of her comeback picture, *Queen Esther and the King of Egypt*, Hedy Lamarr signed up for this project for Marc Allégret. Originally intended to be a three-hour investigation into the mysteries of womanhood, the oft-altered screenplay had Lamarr question three male friends about which historical figure she should impersonate at a masquerade ball and then appear in vignettes prompted by their answers. Edgar G Ulmer shot some uncredited linking sequences and this was released to little acclaim. **DP**

Hedy Lamarr *Hedy Windsor/Helen of Troy/ Empress Josephine/Geneviève de Brabant* · Gérard Oury *Napoleon Bonaparte* · Massimo Serato *Paris* · Robert Beatty *Menelaus* · Cathy O'Donnell *Oenone* · Guido Celano *Jupiter* · Rico Glori *Priamus* · Seren Michelotti *Cassandra* · Alba Arnova *Venus* ■ *Dir* Marc Allégret · *Scr* Nino Novarese, Marc Allégret, Salka Viertel, from a story by Allégret, Aeneas MacKenzie, Vadim Plenianikov, Hugh Gray

Lovesick ★★★ 15

Romantic comedy 1983 · US · Colour · 91min

Long-time Woody Allen collaborator Marshall Brickman made his second outing as writer/director with this droll comedy in which psychiatrist Dudley Moore falls helplessly in love with patient Elizabeth McGovern. The unlikely pairing works a treat thanks to the coy performances and several nifty one-liners. There are also some knowing cameos from Ron Silver, Wallace Shawn and legendary director John Huston. DP

Dudley Moore *Saul Benjamin* • Elizabeth McGovern *Chloe Allan* • Alec Guinness *Sigmund Freud* • Renee Taylor *Mrs Mondragon* • Ron Silver *Ted Caruso* • Gene Saks *Frantic patient* • Christine Baranski *Nymphomaniac* • David Strathairn *Zuckerman* ■ *Dir/Scr* Marshall Brickman

Lovespell ★

Drama 1979 · US · Colour · 91min

Even die-hard Wagner fans will detest this incompetent retelling of the amorous tragedy of Tristan and Isolde. Richard Burton makes a splendid king, but Kate Mulgrew is rather too mature to play his Juliet-like bride. Filmed on lush Irish locations, the language is as parched as a desert, while Tom Donovan's direction is woefully lacking for a story that needs tender, loving care if audiences are to be convinced of its contemporary relevance. TH

Richard Burton *King Mark of Cornwall* • Kate Mulgrew *Iseult* • Nicholas Clay *Tristan* • Cyril Cusack • Geraldine Fitzgerald ■ *Dir* Tom Donovan • *Scr* Claire Labine

Loving ★★★

Comedy drama 1970 · US · Colour · 89min

It takes all George Segal's underused skill to touch our sympathy here, playing a character who is well out of charm's way – an ageing commercial artist heading for mental and marital breakdown. As his emotionally devoted but drained wife, Eva Marie Saint is outstandingly forbearing, enough to make us wonder why she married him in the first place. But then again, there is a glimmer in Segal that explains it. TH Swearing.

George Segal *Brooks Wilson* • Eva Marie Saint *Selma Wilson* • Sterling Hayden *Lepridon* • Keenan Wynn *Edward* • Nancie Phillips *Nelly* • Janis Young *Grace* • David Doyle *Will* • Paul Sparer *Marve* • Andrew Duncan *Willy* • Sherry Lansing *Susan* ■ *Dir* Irvin Kershner • *Scr* Don Devlin, from the novel *Brooks Wilson, Ltd* by JM Ryan

Loving ★★★★

Drama based on a true story 2016 · US/UK · Colour · 123min

Ruth Negga and Joel Edgerton deliver astonishingly nuanced performances in the compelling true story of interracial couple Mildred and Ruth Loving, whose marriage in Washington DC in 1958 (illegal in their home state of Virginia) sparked a Supreme Court legal battle. Director Jeff Nichols brings a beautiful restraint to this moving tribute to the Lovings' courage in the face of overwhelming adversity. With none of the clichés usually associated with such a hot-button topic, Nichols sidesteps expectations with tact and intelligence. AJ

Ruth Negga *Mildred Loving* • Joel Edgerton *Richard Loving* • Michael Shannon *Grey Villet* • Marton Csokas *Sheriff Brooks* • Nick Kroll *Bernie Cohen* ■ *Dir/Scr* Jeff Nichols

Loving Couples ★★

Romantic comedy 1980 · US · Colour · 97min

Shirley MacLaine and James Coburn are the middle-aged married couple who spice up their relationship with a spot of partner-swapping with younger (and more glamorous) Susan Sarandon and Stephen Collins. While MacLaine enjoys the charms of her toyboy, Coburn looks extremely uncomfortable with a woman almost young enough to be his daughter on his arm. All the embarrassing May-September clichés

are dredged up, and this never gets beyond the predictable. JB

Shirley MacLaine *Evelyn* • James Coburn *Walter* • Susan Sarandon *Stephanie* • Stephen Collins *Gregg* • Sally Kellerman *Mrs Liggett* ■ *Dir* Jack Smight • *Scr* Martin Donovan

Loving Vincent

Animated crime drama 2016 · UK/Pol · Colour

This is a preview – no prints were available to review as we went to press: Grown-up animation goes highbrow with a post-impressionistic portrait of van Gogh that speculates about his death. Directed by Polish painter and director Dorota Kobiela and Hugh Welchman (an Oscar winner for *Peter and the Wolf*), it tells his story using his own masterpieces and the characters that inhabit them. Helen McCrory, Saoirse Ronan, Douglas Booth, Chris O'Dowd and TV's *Poldark*, Aidan Turner, are all in the frame of this ambitious work – albeit as a series of artfully daubed paint smudges. SP

Saoirse Ronan *Margaret Gachet* • Aidan Turner *Boatman* • Douglas Booth *Armand Roulin* • Helen McCrory *Louise Chevalier* • Chris O'Dowd *Postman Roulin* • John Sessions *Pere Tanguy* ■ *Dir* Dorota Kobiela, Hugh Welchman • *Scr* Dorota Kobiela, Hugh Welchman, Jacek von Dehnel

Loving You ★★★ U

Musical drama 1957 · US · Colour · 101min

Elvis Presley's second movie (the first under famous producer Hal B Wallis) gives us a precious look at the King in his rock 'n' roll prime. The plot allows Presley to re-enact his rise to stardom, under the guidance here of director Hal Kanter, who studied Presley on stage beforehand for authenticity. Musical highlights include *Teddy Bear* and *Lonesome Cowboy* (the film's original title). Scorned in its day (but not by fans), this looks better by the decade, and Presley's natural screen presence reminds us of his early raw talent. TS DVD

Elvis Presley *Deke Rivers* • Lizabeth Scott *Glenda Markle* • Wendell Corey *Tex Warner* • Dolores Hart *Susan Jessup* • James Gleason *Carl Meade* ■ *Dir* Hal Kanter • *Scr* Herbert Baker, Hal Kanter, from the story *A Call from Mitch Miller* by Mary Agnes Thompson

The Low Down ★★★ 18

Drama 2000 · UK · Colour · 95min

This feature debut from writer/director Jamie Thraves has film-school experimentation written all over it, some of which works, some of which doesn't. Focusing on the excellent Aidan Gillen, one of a group of lost 20-something bohemian Londoners, the movie follows his burgeoning romance with Kate Ashfield, which parallels his journey out of a Peter Pan complex into adulthood. Honest, true and cinematographically original, this suffers from an all-too-familiar rites-of-passage plot with an overkill feel that's reminiscent of a Nick Hornby or Helen Fielding novel. LH DVD

Aidan Gillen *Frank* • Kate Ashfield *Ruby* • Dean Lennox Kelly *Mike* • Tobias Menzies *John* • Rupert Proctor *Terry* ■ *Dir/Scr* Jamie Thraves

A Low Down Dirty Shame ★★ 18

Action spoof 1994 · US · Colour · 100min

After scoring several direct hits with his blaxploitation spoof, *I'm Gonna Git You Sucka*, Keenen Ivory Wayans shoots high and wide with this scattergun parody of *film noir* crime pictures. Clearly spreading himself too thin, Wayans seems to be the only performer with real faith in his script, which is woefully predictable and too often settles for the easy (and occasionally offensive) gag. His direction is equally sloppy. DP

Keenen Ivory Wayans *Andre Shame* • Charles S Dutton *Sonny Rothmiller* • Jada Pinkett [Jada Pinkett Smith] *Peaches Jordan* • Salli Richardson *Angela Flowers* • Andrew Divoff *Ernesto Mendoza* • Corwin Hawkins *Wayman* • Gary Cervantes *Luis* • Gregory Sierra *Captain Nunez* • Kim Wayans *Diane* ■ *Dir/Scr* Keenen Ivory Wayans

The Low Life ★★

Comedy drama 1995 · US · Colour · 98min

Excellent central performances from a first-rate young cast can't save this depressing character study. There's no life in this tale of wannabe writer Rory Cochrane coming to LA only to find himself stuck in low-paying temp jobs and lumbered with a girlfriend (Kyra Sedgwick) uninterested in serious commitment. Occasionally funny and touching, ultimately this takes too long in getting nowhere in particular. RS

Rory Cochrane *John* • Kyra Sedgwick *Bevin* • Ron Livingston *Chad* • Christian Meoli *Leonard* • Sara Melson *Suzie* • James LeGros *Mike Jr* • Sean Astin *Andrew* • JT Walsh *Mike Sr* • Renee Zellweger [Renée Zellweger] *Poet* ■ *Dir* George Hickenlooper • *Scr* George Hickenlooper, from the story by John Enbom

Lower City ★★★ 18

Romantic drama 2005 · Bra · Colour · 94min

All-consuming passion is the key to this steamy *ménage à trois* that presents a sobering picture of Brazil's dispossessed underclass. But while free-spirited hooker Alice Braga's liaisons with best buddies Lazaro Ramos and Wagner Moura generate plenty of sparks, there's too little social or psychological depth to their story. This is highly cinematic, and there are obvious parallels with *Jules et Jim*, but as a human drama it lacks resonance. DP Portuguese +subtitles. Violence, sex scenes. DVD

Lazaro Ramos *Deco* • Wagner Moura *Naldinho* • Alice Braga *Karinna* • Maria Menezes *Luzinete* • Joao Miguel Leonelli *Drug store clerk* • Debora Santiago *Sirlene* • Karim Ainouz *Screenplay* ■ *Dir/Scr* Sergio Machado

The Lower Depths ★★★

Drama 1936 · Fr · BW · 95min

Having secured the dying Maxim Gorky's permission to rework parts of his celebrated socialist play, cinema's leading humanist, Jean Renoir, proceeded to produce his darkest film of the Popular Front period. Although there's a rapport between impoverished baron Louis Jouvet and petty thief Jean Gabin, the sense of community that existed in *Le Crime de Monsieur Lange* has been replaced by a survivalist individualism, as they seek to out-manoeuvre landlord Vladimir Sokoloff. As ever, Renoir's compositional flair is to the fore, with a strolling, deep-focus camera endlessly picking up significant expressions, gestures and details. DP French +subtitles.

Jean Gabin *Pépel* • Louis Jouvet *The baron* • Suzy Prim *Vassilissa* • Jany Holt *Nastia* • Vladimir Sokoloff *Kostyley* • André Gabriello *Commisaire Toptun* ■ *Dir* Jean Renoir • *Scr* Eugène Zamiatine, Jacques Companeez, Jean Renoir, Charles Spaak, from the play *Na Dne* by Maxim Gorky

The Lower Depths ★★★★ PG

Period drama 1956 · Jpn · BW · 119min

Maxim Gorky's claustrophobic play about slum dwellers is here transposed by Akira Kurosawa from Moscow to Edo, towards the end of the Tokugawa period. The action is confined to just two sets and the magnificent ensemble playing (he rehearsed for six weeks before the quick shoot) creates an unsentimental portrait of transitory lives, without hope. The ending is abrupt, when during a boisterous drinking session an announcement is made about the suicide of one of the group. There's a close-up, characteristic of the film's style, and another man says, "A pity just when the party was getting started". BB Japanese +subtitles.

Toshiro Mifune *Sutekichi, the thief* • Isuzu Yamada *Osugi, the landlady* • Ganjiro Nakamura *Rokubei, her husband* • Kyoko Kagawa *Okayo, her sister* • Bokuzen Hidari *Kahei, the priest* ■ *Dir* Akira Kurosawa • *Scr* Shinobu Hashimoto, Akira Kurosawa, Hideo Oguni, from the play *Na Dne* by Maxim Gorky

The Loyal 47 Ronin ★★★★

Historical epic 1941 · Jpn · BW · 222min

Threatened with closure for its failure to produce enough National Policy pictures, the Shochiku studio was

reprieved by Kenji Mizoguchi's offer to shoot the second part of this historical epic under its auspices. Set in the early 18th century, the action follows the revenge of Oishi and his fellow samurai on the evil warlord who tricked their master into committing hara-kiri. Large scale historicals were not the director's forte, but he opened out this fact-based Kabuki standard to spectacular effect. Originally released in two parts. DP Japanese +subtitles.

Chojuro Kawarazaki *Kuranosuke Oishi* • Yoshisaburo Arashi *Takuminokami, Lord Asano* • Mantoyo Mimasu *Kozunosuke, Lord Kira* • Kanemon Nakamura *Sukeemon Tomimori* • Utaemon Ichikawa *Tsunatoyo Tokugawa* • Mitsuko Miura *Yosenin, Lady Asano* ■ *Dir* Kenji Mizoguchi • *Scr* Kenichiro Hara, Yoshikata Yoda, from the play by Seika Mayama, from a well-known story that took place in 1703

Lucas ★★★★ 12

Comedy drama 1986 · US · Colour · 95min

Corey Haim gives an excellent performance in this sweet, simple and cliché-free study of first love. As the serious kid whom half the school wouldn't notice unless they tripped over him, he is witty and wise beyond his years, and his earnest conversations with heart's desire Kerri Green are small masterpieces of observation. But true love can never run smoothly, especially when there are sporty bozos like school football star Charlie Sheen bestriding the primrose path. Winona Ryder made her debut in this delightful comedy. DP Swearing. DVD

Corey Haim *Lucas Blye* • Kerri Green *Maggie* • Charlie Sheen *Cappie* • Courtney Thorne-Smith *Alise* • Winona Ryder *Rina* • Thomas E Hodges [Tom Hodges] *Bruno* • Ciro Poppiti *Ben* ■ *Dir/Scr* David Seltzer

Lucia ★★ 15

Opera drama 1998 · UK · Colour · 102min

Drawing on the old "life imitating art" formula, Don Boyd uses scenes from the opera *Lucia di Lammermoor* to comment on the doomed romance between soprano Amanda Boyd and tenor Richard Coxon. The pair are to co-star in *Lucia* just as she enters into a loveless marriage (sanctioned by her impoverished brother) to a dissolute millionaire. Essentially this is a feature-length opera video, with stylised visuals that often distract from the determinedly contemporary arrangements. Stiffly acted and archly staged, yet filmed with imagination and passion, this has its rewards. DP

Amanda Boyd *Kate Ashton, "Lucia"* • Richard Coxon *Sam Ravenswood, "Edgardo"* • Ann Taylor *Alice, "Alisa"* • John Daszak *Norman, "Normanno"* • Andrew Greenan *Raymond, "Raimondo"* • John Osborn *Oliver Hickox, "Arturo"* • Mark Holland *Hamish Ashton, "Enrico"* • Mark Shanahan *Conductor, London Studio* ■ *Dir* Don Boyd • *Scr* Don Boyd, from the opera *Lucia Di Lammermoor* by Gaetano Donizetti, from the novel *The Bride of Lammermoor* by Sir Walter Scott

Lucie Aubrac ★★ 12

Wartime drama based on a true story 1997 · Fr · Colour · 111min

Daniel Auteuil stars as a French resistance worker taken prisoner by the Gestapo, and Carole Bouquet is the devoted wife who risks all to save him. Surprisingly, considering the calibre of the cast and the intrinsic drama of storyline, the film is a plodding affair, with director Claude Berri more concerned with sticking to facts rather than exploiting the story's full cinematic potential. DA French +subtitles. DVD

Carole Bouquet *Lucie Bernard* • Daniel Auteuil *Raymond Samuel* • Patrice Chéreau *Max* • Eric Boucher *Serge* • Jean-Roger Milo *Maurice* • Heino Ferch *Klaus Barbie* • Jean Martin *Paul Lardanchet* • Andrzej Seweryn *Lieutenant Schlöndorff* • Pascal Greggory *Hardy* ■ *Dir* Claude Berri • *Scr* Claude Berri, Arlette Langmann, from the novel *Outwitting the Gestapo (Ils Partiront dans l'Ivresse)* by Lucie Aubrac, Claude Berri

Lucifer Rising ★★★ 15
Experimental movie 1981 · US · Colour · 27min

Using rather startling free-association imagery, such as flying saucers hovering over the Temple of Luxor, this is one of the better Kenneth Anger "visual music" avant-garde movies (with no plot or acting to speak of). Anger himself plays a Magus who invokes Lucifer, celebrating his rebirth with a birthday cake with Lucifer Mark VI written in pink icing. The eclectic cast includes Marianne Faithfull, director Donald Cammell, and Leslie Huggins, a hunky young Middlesbrough steel worker. An earlier version of the film, shot in 1966, was stolen and buried in the Mojave desert by the musician Bobby Beausoleil, currently serving a life sentence for murder. RB

Miriam Gibril *Isis* • Donald Cammell *Osiris* • Haydn Couts *The Adept* • Kenneth Anger *The Magus* • Sir Francis Rose *Chaos* • Marianne Faithfull *Lilith* • Leslie Huggins *Lucifer* ■ *Dir* Kenneth Anger • *Scr* Kenneth Anger, from the poem *Hymn to Lucifer* by Aleister Crowley

The Luck of Ginger Coffey ★★★
Drama 1964 · US/Can · BW · 99min

Robert Shaw and Mary Ure star as Irish immigrants in freezing Montreal, coping with his unemployment, their separation and their daughter's decision to live with her father. A slight story but an affecting one, due to the wealth of everyday detail created by writer Brian Moore and director Irvin Kershner. Shaw and Ure, a tempestuous married couple off-screen, give a satisfying portrayal of a love that somehow endures. AT

Robert Shaw *Ginger Coffey* • Mary Ure *Vera* • Liam Redmond *MacGregor* • Tom Harvey *Joe McGlade* • Libby McClintock *Paulie* • Leo Leyden *Brott* ■ *Dir* Irvin Kershner • *Scr* Brian Moore, from his novel

Luck of the Draw ★★
Action crime drama 2000 · US · Colour · 108min

This crime thriller opens promisingly, with a rattling gunfight involving rival French and American mobsters and a gang of corrupt cops. But, as James Marshall's ex-con witness makes off with the counterfeit $100 plates that the gangs are squabbling over, director Luca Bercovici fails to spot the obvious fact that his hero is incapable of holding the viewer's attention against the scene-chewing abilities of Dennis Hopper, Eric Roberts and Michael Madsen. Add to that the lack of novelty in plot and style, and the tale soon becomes humdrum. DP

Dennis Hopper *Gianni Ponti* • William Forsythe *Max Fenton* • James Marshall *Jack Sweeney* • Michael Madsen *Zippo* • Ice-T *Macneilly* • Eric Roberts *Carlo* • Frank Gorshin *Sterling Johnson* ■ *Dir* Luca Bercovici • *Scr* Namon Ami, Rick Joe Bloggs [Rick Bloggs], Kandice King

Luck, Trust & Ketchup ★★★ 15
Documentary 1994 · US · Colour · 89min

Try to excuse the lousy title, for this is a highly entertaining and informative documentary about director Robert Altman, his films and his methods. Recorded during the making of *Short Cuts*, it has a day-in-the-life feel that makes it an ideal companion piece to that film, but there are also dozens of little insights that have a bearing on Altman's entire output. Co-directed by longtime colleague Mike Kaplan, this also contains interviews with the principal members of the *Short Cuts* cast, not all of whom present themselves in the most favourable light. DP Swearing. *DVD*

Robert Altman • Anne Archer • Jennifer Jason Leigh • Jack Lemmon • Andie MacDowell ■ *Dir* Mike Kaplan, John Dorr

Lucky Break ★★★★ 12
Crime comedy 2001 · UK/Ger/US · Colour · 103min

It took director Peter Cattaneo four years to follow up *The Full Monty*, and he chose his next project wisely. On the surface, this brilliantly cast prison comedy has much in common with the Sheffield strippers – a

group of men bonding through showbiz (here, they stage a prison musical as cover for an escape) – but this is more of a character study than a social satire. Although the idea of the climactic amateur show acts as a magnet for grand farce moments, it's the more subtle relationships between the cons that give the film its depth. AC Swearing. *DVD*

James Nesbitt *Jimmy Hands* • Olivia Williams *Annabel Sweep* • Timothy Spall *Cliff Gumbell* • Bill Nighy *Roger Chamberlain* • Lennie James *Rudy Guscott* • Ron Cook *Perry* • Christopher Plummer *Governor Graham Mortimer* ■ *Dir* Peter Cattaneo • *Scr* Ronan Bennett

Lucky Devils ★★★
Action adventure 1933 · US · BW · 64min

Based on a story by stuntman Bob Rose, who also appears in the film, this is just an excuse for stuntmen William Boyd (later Hopalong Cassidy) and William Gargan to go through their paces. Boyd also gets the girl in the person of Dorothy Wilson. Among the cast is Lon Chaney Jr, credited under his real name of Creighton Chaney. The highlights of the movie are the spectacular stunts, including a climactic ride over a waterfall. RB

Bill Boyd [William Boyd (1)] *Skipper* • William Gargan *Bob* • Bruce Cabot *Happy* • William Bakewell *Slugger* • Creighton Chaney [Lon Chaney Jr] *Frankie* • Bob Rose *Rusty* • Dorothy Wilson *Fran* • Sylvia Picker *Toots* ■ *Dir* Ralph Ince • *Scr* Ben Markson, Agnes Christine Johnston, from a story by Casey Robinson, Bob Rose

Lucky Jim ★★★★ U
Comedy 1957 · UK · BW · 91min

Kingsley Amis's comic masterpiece was one of the most influential English novels of the 1950s. The Boulting brothers' film adaptation misses some of the subtle nuances, barbed satire and deliciously sly characterisation of the book, but you will find that this still makes for very agreeable entertainment. Ian Carmichael gives a good account of himself as Jim Dixon, the disaster-prone lecturer whose career in the red-bricked halls of academe gets off to the worst possible start, while those masters of comic support Hugh Griffith and Terry-Thomas are on form. DP *DVD*

Ian Carmichael *Jim Dixon* • Terry-Thomas *Bertrand Welch* • Hugh Griffith *Professor Welch* • Sharon Acker *Christine Callaghan* • Jean Anderson *Mrs Welch* • Maureen Connell *Margaret Peel* • Clive Morton *Sir Hector Gore-Urquhart* ■ *Dir* John Boulting • *Scr* Jeffrey Dell, Patrick Campbell, from the novel by Kingsley Amis

The Lucky Lady ★★
Silent romantic comedy 1926 · US · BW · 62min

This silent movie, directed by the admirable Raoul Walsh early in his career, has young princess Greta Nissen sneaking out of her convent school to see a travelling theatre show. There she meets youthful American William Collier Jr and falls in love with him. This doesn't go down well at the palace where they have lined up lecherous Lionel Barrymore as her future husband. Set in the fictional principality of San Guido, this romantic comedy has a certain charm, but it's well past its sell-by date for all but silent movie devotees. RK

Greta Nissen *Antoinette* • Lionel Barrymore *Count Ferarrzo* • William Collier Jr *Clarke* • Marc MacDermott *Franz Garletz* ■ *Dir* Raoul Walsh • *Scr* James T O'Donohoe, Robert Emmet Sherwood [Robert E Sherwood], from a story by Bertram Bloch • *Cinematographer* Victor Milner

Lucky Lady ★ 12
Comedy 1975 · US · Colour · 112min

Gene Hackman and Liza Minnelli were both recent Oscar winners, and Burt Reynolds was at the peak of his stardom. Yet audiences somehow sensed this was a stinker and stayed away in droves. The romantic rivalry between the two leading men, playing bootleg liquor smugglers, is negligible, while Minnelli never seems comfortable in her role as the nightclub singer they fall for. AT

Gene Hackman *Kibby* • Liza Minnelli *Claire* • Burt Reynolds *Walker* • Geoffrey Lewis *Captain Aaron Mosley* • John Hillerman *Christy McTeague* • Robby Benson *Billy Webber* • Michael Hordern *Captain Rockwell* • Anthony Holland *Mr Tully* ■ *Dir* Stanley Donen • *Scr* Willard Huyck, Gloria Katz

Lucky Luciano ★★★★ 18
Biographical crime drama 1973 · Fr/It · Colour · 105min

Francesco Rosi's sociological melodrama, set in America and Italy, reveals the criminal network – both legal and illegal – for which Lucky Luciano was the crime kingpin. While Rod Steiger was the leading gangster in *Al Capone* (1959), here it's Gian Maria Volonté. This is more complex than a simple dirty-rat-tat-tat view of the world, and Volonté is excellent, but Steiger's hardman performance upstages all the political nuances by sheer power. TH *DVD*

Gian Maria Volonté *Lucky Luciano* • Rod Steiger *Gene Giannini* • Charles Siragusa • Vincent Gardenia *American colonel* ■ *Dir* Francesco Rosi • *Scr* Francesco Rosi, Tonino Guerra

Lucky Me ★★ U
Comedy musical 1954 · US · Colour · 96min

Doris Day sings as delightfully as ever and acts with gusto, but this musical about showbusiness hopefuls – her penultimate film under her contract at Warner Bros – is substandard. Talents such as Phil Silvers, Nancy Walker and Eddie Foy are wasted, and Day is saddled with an inappropriate leading man in Robert Cummings. The songs, by the *Calamity Jane* team of Sammy Fain and Paul Francis Webster, also disappoint. TV *DVD*

Doris Day *Candy Williams* • Robert Cummings *Dick Carson* • Phil Silvers *Hap Snyder* • Eddie Foy Jr *Duke McGee* • Nancy Walker *Flo Neely* • Martha Hyer *Lorraine Thayer* • Bill Goodwin *Otis Thayer* • Marcel Dalio *Anton* • Hayden Rorke *Tommy Arthur* • Angie Dickinson *Party guest* ■ *Dir* Jack Donohue • *Scr* James O'Hanlon, Robert O'Brien, Irving Elinson, from a story by James O'Hanlon

Lucky Number Slevin ★★★ 18
Black comedy thriller 2006 · US · Colour · 105min

Paul McGuigan directs this playfully convoluted thriller starring Josh Hartnett as Slevin, a young smart mouth who seems to be the victim of a serious case of mistaken identity when he's dragged from a friend's flat by some thugs. Soon he finds himself in the middle of a war between two rival gang leaders (Morgan Freeman and Ben Kingsley), who each appear to be employing the same mysterious hitman (Bruce Willis). Jason Smilovic's script provides zingy one-liners for Hartnett, as well as scenery-chewing opportunities for both Freeman and Kingsley. AS Violence. *DVD* *Blu-ray*

Josh Hartnett *Slevin* • Morgan Freeman *The Boss* • Sir Ben Kingsley [Ben Kingsley] *Schlomo "The Rabbi"* • Bruce Willis *Goodkat* • Lucy Liu *Lindsey* • Stanley Tucci *Brikowski* ■ *Dir* Paul McGuigan • *Scr* Jason Smilovic

The Lucky One ★★ 12
Romantic drama 2012 · US · Colour · 96min

Zac Efron stars in this slick, corny, comfortingly undemanding romantic drama directed by *Shine*'s Scott Hicks from the novel by Nicholas Sparks (*The Notebook*, *Dear John*). A buff-looking Efron plays Logan, a US marine who attributes survival in Iraq to the photo of a woman that he found there, and comes home resolving to find out just who his guardian angel is. Efron looks good, and is a perfectly decent actor; co-star Taylor Schilling is even better and marks herself out as an actress to watch. However, the movie doesn't linger long in the memory. DA Violence, swearing, sex scenes. *DVD* *Blu-ray*

Zac Efron *Logan Thibault* • Blythe Danner *Ellie Green* • Taylor Schilling *Beth Green* • Riley Thomas Stewart *Ben* • Jay R Ferguson *Keith Clayton* ■ *Dir* Scott Hicks • *Scr* Will Fetters, from the novel by Nicholas Sparks

Lucky Partners ★★★ U
Comedy 1940 · US · BW · 99min

This frothy comedy is somewhat let down by the uncomfortable pairing of its two leads. Perky Ginger Rogers, then under contract to RKO and at her professional peak, and urbane Ronald Colman fail to spark in an American remake of Sacha Guitry's 1935 French film *Bonne Chance*. The romance seems too lightweight for Colman, under Lewis Milestone's experienced, if slightly heavy-handed, direction. Still, fans of the two great stars won't want to miss this. TS

Ginger Rogers *Jean Newton* • Ronald Colman *David Grant* • Jack Carson *Freddie* • Spring Byington *Aunt* • Cecilia Loftus *Mrs Sylvester* • Harry Davenport *Judge* • Billy Gilbert *Charles* ■ *Dir* Lewis Milestone • *Scr* Allan Scott, John Van Druten, from the film *Bonne Chance* by Sacha Guitry

The Lucky Star ★★★
Second World War drama 1980 · Can · Colour · 110min

A Texan twist on the idea of Nazi occupation makes this Canadian family adventure original, to say the least. A young Dutch Jew (Brett Marx), fascinated by westerns, sees his parents taken away by the Germans. So he sets about kidnapping the colonel (Rod Steiger) he holds responsible. Directed by Max Fischer from a script he co-wrote with TV playwright Jack Rosenthal, it manages to say something imaginative about this emotive period of history. TH

Rod Steiger *Col Gluck* • Louise Fletcher *Loes Bakker* • Lou Jacobi *Elia Goldberg* • Brett Marx *David Goldberg* • Helen Hughes *Rose Goldberg* ■ *Dir* Max Fischer • *Scr* Max Fischer, Jack Rosenthal, from an idea by Roland Topor

The Lucky Texan ★★ U
Western 1934 · US · BW · 53min

One of those irritating programme fillers that mixes contemporary icons – in this case a model "T" Ford in a chase sequence – with traditional western elements. The clean-cut John Wayne provides the heroism, and Lloyd Whitlock and stuntman Yakima Canutt the villainy. But really, unless these minor movies are your cup of tea, it's not very good. TS *DVD*

John Wayne *Jerry Mason* • Barbara Sheldon *Betty* • George Hayes [George "Gabby" Hayes] *Jake Benson* • Yakima Canutt *Cole* • Gordon DeMaine *Sheriff* ■ *Dir/Scr* Robert N Bradbury

Lucky Them ★★★ 15
Comedy drama 2013 · US · Colour · 92min

Toni Collette steals the show as a music journalist on a personal assignment. Helped by little more than rumours and an obnoxious film-maker (Thomas Hayden Church), she sets out to find her ex-boyfriend, a celebrated musician, on the tenth anniversary of his disappearance. At times feeling like a paint-by-numbers indie drama, this comic tale revels in its trendy Seattle setting, but fails to provide anything that truly engages beyond some well-cast leads. Fun while it lasts, but no more than that. JL Swearing, a sex scene, drug abuse

Toni Collette *Ellie Klug* • Thomas Haden Church *Charlie* • Oliver Platt *Giles* • Ryan Eggold *Lucas* • Johnny Depp *Matthew Smith* ■ *Dir* Megan Griffiths • *Scr* Huck Botko, Emily Wachtel, from an idea by Caroline Sherman

Lucky to Be a Woman ★★★
Comedy drama 1955 · It · BW · 95min

Marcello Mastroianni and Sophia Loren team up for what is, in many ways, a dry run for *La Dolce Vita*. Oozing languid charm, Mastroianni revels in the antiheroic antics of the scurrilous paparazzo whose cheeky snap of Loren's legs persuades lecherous aristocrat Charles Boyer to transform her into a movie star. Strewn with in-jokes and satirical pot-shots at the supposedly sophisticated worlds of film and high fashion, this polished comedy is as artificial as its target. But the smooth direction and the accomplished

L

performances give it an easy charm. DP In Italian.

Sophia Loren *Antoinette* • Charles Boyer *Count Gregorio* • Marcello Mastroianni *Corrado* • Nino Besozzi *Film producer* ■ *Dir* Alessandro Blasetti • *Scr* Suso Cecchi D'Amico, Ennio Flaiano, Alessandro Continenza, Alessandro Blasetti

Lucky You ★★ PG

Drama 2007 · US · Colour · 118min

In this brooding yarn from director Curtis Hanson, Eric Bana plays a professional gambler who keeps his cards close to his chest in the game of love. It's just unlucky for him that he's stuck with a lumbering script and a tepid leading lady in Drew Barrymore. She isn't just implausible in the role of a struggling lounge singer but downright irritating, serving up mindless platitudes and oozing so much sugary sweetness it would make even Mary Poppins choke. Her intimate scenes with Bana fall flat, providing little respite between the drawn-out action at the Las Vegas poker tables. Bana's grudge match with his errant father (Robert Duvall) offers more interest, but by that time it feels like too little too late. SP DVD CS

Eric Bana *Huck Cheever* • Drew Barrymore *Billie Offer* • Robert Duvall *LC Cheever* • Debra Messing *Suzanne Offer* • Horatio Sanz *Ready Eddie* • Charles Martin Smith *Roy Durucher* • Saverio Guerra *Lester* • Jean Smart *Michelle Carson* ■ *Dir* Curtis Hanson • *Scr* Eric Roth, Curtis Hanson, from a story by Roth • *Cinematographer* Peter Deming

Lucy ★★★

Biographical comedy drama
2003 · US · Colour and BW · 150min

Broadway actress Rachel York shines as comedian Lucille Ball in this warts-and-all biopic. Focusing largely on her turbulent marriage to philandering *I Love Lucy* co-star Desi Arnaz (Danny Pino), it takes an absorbing but superficial look at the highs and lows of their celebrity lifestyle. Despite neither lead really resembling their real-life counterpart, they both deliver convincing impersonations, with York completely nailing Ball's goofball public persona. SF

Rachel York *Lucille Ball* • Daniel Pino *Desi Arnaz* • La Chanze Sapp-Gooding [La Chanze] *Harriett* • Ann Dowd *Dede* • Rebecca Hobbs *Vivian Vance* • Madeline Zima *Teen Lucy* ■ *Dir* Glenn Jordan • *Scr* Katie Ford, TS Cook

Lucy ★★★ 15

Action adventure 2014 · Fr · Colour · 85min

Director Luc Besson wallows in the mind-blowing as much as the action in this collision of *Limitless* and *2001: a Space Odyssey*. Scarlett Johansson (whose languid blankness is ideal here) stars as the title heroine forced to be a drugs mule for a nasty crime boss. Trouble is, when she accidentally ingests the experimental substance, it expands her brain power to cosmic proportions. It's a barmy but enthralling ride in which action clichés are turned on their head to breathtaking effect. JA DVD BL

Scarlett Johansson *Lucy* • Morgan Freeman *Professor Norman* • Choi Min-sik *Mr Jang* • Julian Rhind-Tutt *The Limey* ■ *Dir/Scr* Luc Besson

Lucy Gallant ★★★ U

Drama 1955 · US · Colour · 104min

Dressmaker Jane Wyman devotes herself to work and becomes a successful female fashion-house mogul, but the price of her independence is a rocky ride in her love life. Charlton Heston is the man involved in this particular battle of the sexes. The supporting cast includes Thelma Ritter and Claire Trevor (both irresistible) and a rare on-screen appearance from Edith Head, winner of eight Oscars, who also designed the costumes. Haute couture, VistaVision and deft direction by Robert Parrish contribute to the enjoyment of this typical 1950s "woman's picture". RK

Jane Wyman *Lucy Gallant* • Charlton Heston *Casey Cole* • Claire Trevor *Lady MacBeth* • Thelma Ritter *Molly Basserman* • William Demarest *Charles Madden* • Wallace Ford *Gus Basserman* • Tom Helmore *Jim Wardman* • Gloria

Talbott *Laura Wilson* • Edith Head ■ *Dir* Robert Parrish • *Scr* John Lee Mahin, Winston Miller, from the novel *The Life of Lucy Gallant* by Margaret Cousins

Ludwig ★★ 12

Historical drama
1973 · It/W Ger/Fr · Colour · 227min

This is director Luchino Visconti's study of mad King Ludwig of Bavaria, whose obsession with Wagner's music inspired him to build a series of fairy-tale castles and lose what was already a tenuous hold on sanity before his operatic death by drowning. In the title role, Helmut Berger looks the part – pouting, wild and very pretty – and the castles themselves are stunning backdrops. Trevor Howard makes an honourable stab at Wagner and Romy Schneider is simply gorgeous as Ludwig's unhappy bride Empress Elizabeth. But Visconti's approach is rather too solemn, and the movie drags. AT In Italian. DVD

Helmut Berger *Ludwig* • Romy Schneider *Empress Elisabetta* • Trevor Howard *Richard Wagner* • Silvana Mangano *Cosima von Bulow* • Gert Fröbe *Father Hoffman* • Helmut Griem *Captain Durckeim* • Isabella Telezynska *Queen Mother* • Umberto Orsini *Count Von Holstein* ■ *Dir* Luchino Visconti • *Scr* Luchino Visconti, Enrico Medioli, Suso Cecchi D'Amico

Lullaby of Broadway ★★ U

Musical comedy 1951 · US · Colour · 88min

Despite its promising title and the presence of Doris Day, this tailor-made vehicle is one of Warner Bros' least effective movies. Still, there are points in its favour: the songs though seriously underperformed and staged, are nevertheless memorable, and the amiable and talented Gene Nelson is an effective leading man. Warners veteran Gladys George brings all her experience to bear playing Day's wayward mum, and presumably taught Day a trick or two about acting in the process, but, if ever a movie looked undirected, it's this one. TS

Doris Day *Melinda Howard* • Gene Nelson *Tom Farnham* • SZ Sakall *Adolph Hubbell* • Billy De Wolfe *"Lefty" Mack* • Gladys George *Jessica Howard* • Florence Bates *Mrs Hubbell* ■ *Dir* David Butler • *Scr* Earl Baldwin, from his story *My Irish Molly O*

Lulu Belle ★★★

Drama 1948 · US · BW · 86min

This tougher than usual melodrama marked an attempt to change Dorothy Lamour's screen image: the amoral chanteuse she plays here is as far removed from the saronged lovelies of the *Road* series as it's possible to be. Unfortunately, such a character is hard to like, though today's more cynical audiences might be better disposed to Lulu's manner of dealing with anyone who gets in her way. Lamour's early career as a singer provides her with real insights into the role and she proves how good an actress she could be, but she's not helped by the bland performance of leading man George Montgomery and Leslie Fenton's routine direction. TS

Dorothy Lamour *Lulu Belle* • George Montgomery *George Davis* • Albert Dekker *Mark Brady* • Otto Kruger *Harry Randolph* • Glenda Farrell *Molly Benson* • Greg McClure *Butch Cooper* • Charlotte Wynters *Mrs Randolph* ■ *Dir* Leslie Fenton • *Scr* Everett Freeman, Karl Kamb, from the play by Charles MacArthur, Edward Sheldon

Lulu on the Bridge ★

Romantic mystery drama
1998 · US · Colour · 103min

What begins promisingly – Harvey Keitel is a musician starting over after a shooting ends his career – quickly takes a turn for the bizarre. He finds a mysterious glowing stone, which not only leads him to aspiring actress Mira Sorvino but also causes them to fall in love. A first-rate cast is wasted in this esoteric and monotonous film. A twist ending doesn't help clear up any of the confusion, it just makes you happy that the movie is over. ST DVD

Harvey Keitel *Izzy Maurer* • Mira Sorvino *Celia Burns* • Willem Dafoe *Dr Van Horn* • Gina Gershon *Hannah* • Mandy Patinkin *Philip Kleinman* • Vanessa Redgrave *Catherine Moore* ■ *Dir/Scr* Paul Auster

La Luna ★★★

Drama 1979 · It · Colour · 141min

This deliberately artificial tale of an opera diva, her heroin-addicted son, their almost incestuous relationship and his search for a father figure caused quite a stir on its release. In the role of the diva, Jill Clayburgh seems to be mimicking Kiri Te Kanawa as she sings her way through the Verdi back catalogue. Sadly, the other performances are wooden. As always with a Bernardo Bertolucci film, the real star of the show is Vittorio Storaro's exquisite photography. AT

Jill Clayburgh *Caterina Silveri* • Matthew Barry *Joe* • Laura Betti *Ludovica* • Fred Gwynne *Douglas Winter* • Veronica Lazar *Marina* • Renato Salvatori *Communist* • Tomas Milian *Giuseppe* • Alida Valli *Giuseppe's mother* • Roberto Benigni *Upholsterer* ■ *Dir* Bernardo Bertolucci • *Scr* Bernardo Bertolucci, Giuseppe Bertolucci, Clare Peploe, George Malko, from a story by Franco Arcalli, Bernardo Bertolucci, Giuseppe Bertolucci • *Music* Ennio Morricone

Luna ★★★ 15

Fantasy drama 2014 · UK · Colour · 105min

Emotions run high during a weekend gathering by the sea in a typically singular movie from *MirrorMask* director Dave McKean. Freya (Stephanie Leonidas) and her older artist partner Dean (Michael Maloney) invite his art-school friends Christine (Dervla Kirwan) and Grant (Ben Daniels) to visit their splendid seaside house. However, it soon becomes clear there are deep differences and fissures between the various members of the quartet. It might sound like yet another oh-so-British middle-class angst movie, and it is in a way, but what's extraordinary is the way McKean threads fantasy elements in and out of the action. LF

Ben Daniels *Grant* • Dervla Kirwan *Christine* • Stephanie Leonidas *Freya* • Michael Maloney *Dean* • Maurice Roëves *Jacob, the doctor* ■ *Dir* Dave McKean • *Scr* Dave McKean, from a story by McKean, Allen Spiegel

Lunacy ★★★★ 18

Part-animated fantasy horror
2005 · Cz Rep/Slovakia/Jpn · Colour · 114min

Stuffed with moments of surreal horror and bleak satire, this mortifying allegory on the post-Soviet world ranks among writer/director Jan Svankmajer's finest achievements. Jean (Pavel Liska) suffers from a morbid fear of lunacy – his mother has recently died in the asylum at Charenton. Returning from her funeral, this tormented traveller has an eccentric encounter with a decadent aristocrat (Jan Triska), whose offer of hospitality plunges him into a nightmare that exposes the perils of both crushing oppression and untrammelled liberty. With stop-motion sequences of creeping flesh punctuating proceedings, this is a despondent vision of a world out of control. DP Czech +subtitles. DVD

Pavel Liska *Jean Berlot* • Jan Triska *Marquess* • Anna Geislerova *Charlota* • Martin Huba *Dr Coulmiere* • Jaroslav Dusek *Dr Murlloppe* • Stano Danciak [Stanislav Danciak] *Innkeeper* • Pavel Novy *Servant Dominic* ■ *Dir* Jan Svankmajer • *Scr* Jan Svankmajer, from ideas by Edgar Allan Poe and inspired by the writings of the Marquis de Sade

The Lunatic ★★ 15

Comedy 1992 · US · Colour · 94min

Lol Creme, founder member of the pop group 10CC and renowned rock video director, makes his feature debut with this genial oddity which boasts a low-key quirky charm. Paul Campbell is the resident idiot of a Jamaican village who has a fling with insatiable German tourist Julie T Wallace. But it's when she also starts having an affair with Rastafarian butcher Carl Bradshaw that the romantic complications begin, especially once he sucks them both into

burgling a white landowner. A film of minor appeal, but reasonably beguiling all the same. AJ

Julie T Wallace *Inga* • Paul Campbell (2) *Aloysius* • Reggie Carter *Busha/Voice of Strongheart Tree* • Carl Bradshaw *Service* • Winston Stona *Linstrom* • Linda Gambrill *Sarah* • Rosemary Murray *Widow Dawkins* • Lloyd Reckord *Judge* ■ *Dir* Lol Creme • *Scr* Anthony C Winkler, from his novel

Lunatics: a Love Story ★★★ 15

Black comedy romance
1991 · US · Colour · 83min

In this bizarre comedy about the relationship between a mismatched pair of kooks, Ted Raimi (Sam's brother) plays Hank, whose psychological problems include hallucinations about doctors trying to "treat" him with outsize needles, and an inability to leave his tin-foil lined apartment. The object of his affections is Deborah Foreman, who is convinced that she causes mayhem for anyone who comes into contact with her. Eccentric and surprisingly charming, the film puts a comedic rather than horrific spin on Raimi's visions. DA

Ted Raimi *Hank* • Deborah Foreman *Nancy* • Bruce Campbell *Ray* • George Aguilar *Comet* • Brian McCree *Presto* ■ *Dir/Scr* Josh Becker

Lunch Hour ★★ U

Comedy 1962 · UK · BW · 63min

John Mortimer adapted this well constructed but predictable bedroom farce from his own play. Tired of being interrupted during their midday trysts, wallpaper executive Robert Stephens and designer Shirley Anne Field book a hotel room, but then their problems really start. Directed at a fair lick by James Hill, this lively romp is admirably played, with Kay Walsh and Nigel Davenport's supporting turns particularly worthy of note, but there's often an excess of chat between the excruciating moments. DP DVD

Shirley Anne Field *Girl* • Robert Stephens *Man* • Kay Walsh *Manageress* • Hazel Hughes *Aunty* • Michael Robbins *Harris* • Nigel Davenport *Manager* ■ *Dir* James Hill • *Scr* John Mortimer, from his play

Lunch on the Grass ★★★ PG

Romantic drama 1959 · Fr · Colour · 88min

Jean Renoir, then 65, took 21 days to shoot this late work at Les Collettes, the house of his father Auguste, in the south of France. This hymn to nature is the great film director's only direct homage to his great Impressionist painter parent. Paul Meurisse is amusing as a supercilious biology professor experimenting with artificial insemination until he gets a beautiful peasant pregnant by conventional means. The rather reactionary satire also takes a dig at nuclear weapons, space travel and a united Europe, but delivers its message simplistically. RB French +subtitles. DVD

Paul Meurisse *Etienne* • Catherine Rouvel *Nenette* • Fernand Sardou *Nino* • Jacqueline Morane *Titine* • Jean-Pierre Granval *Ritou* ■ *Dir/Scr* Jean Renoir

The Lunchbox ★★★★ PG

Romantic drama
2013 · Ind/Fr/Ger/US · Colour · 100min

Writer/director Ritesh Batra's debut exudes wit, warmth and charm, as a delicious lunch is delivered in error to a grumpy, soon-to-retire claims accountant, instead of to the unfaithful husband for whom it was intended. Without fetishising the dishes, Batra keeps the focus on the food and the notion of variety being the spice of life. But it's the way he conveys urban alienation and aloneness that makes this beautifully acted picture so affecting. DP In Hindi, English. DVD BL

Irrfan Khan [Irfan Khan] *Saajan Fernandes* • Nimrat Kaur *Ila* • Nawazuddin Siddiqui *Shaikh* • Denzil Smith *Mr Shroff* ■ *Dir/Scr* Ritesh Batra

Lured ★★ PG
Crime drama   1947 · US · BW · 102min

This preposterous and bizarrely cast would-be thriller is over-plotted beyond redemption. It's not helped by director Douglas Sirk's ham-fisted direction of his players, particularly Cedric Hardwicke. The incredible story involves showgirl Lucille Ball being used by Scotland Yard to trap a killer in a London seemingly made up of leftover Hollywood sets. Along the way Ball falls for suspect George Sanders. TS **DVD**

George Sanders *Robert Fleming* • Lucille Ball *Sandra Carpenter* • Charles Coburn *Inspector Temple* • Boris Karloff *Artist* • Alan Mowbray *Maxwell* • Cedric Hardwicke *Julian Wilde* • George Zucco *Officer Barrett* ■ *Dir* Douglas Sirk • *Scr* Leo Rosten, from the 1939 film *Pièges* by Jacques Companeez, Ernest Neuville, Simon Gantillon

Lured Innocence ★★
Thriller   1999 · US · Colour · 99min

Marley Shelton valiantly attempts to smoulder as the southern small-town temptress who seeks to exploit both the ailing Talia Shire (delicately distressed) and her frustrated husband Dennis Hopper (gleefully *Grand Guignol*) in their mutual murder plans. But the weakest link is Devon Gummersall who plays the reporter returning to his home town to try to save his erstwhile sweetheart in some of the most tension-free courtroom scenes you'll ever see. DP

Dennis Hopper *Rick Chambers* • Marley Shelton *Elsie Townsend* • Devon Gummersall *Elden Tolbert* • Talia Shire *Marsha Chambers* • Cheri Oteri *Molly* • John M Sullivan II *Bill Beckman* ■ *Dir/Scr* Kikuo Kawasaki

Lush Life ★★★ 15
Drama   1993 · US · Colour · 101min

Forest Whitaker stars in this well-above-average TV movie. Jeff Goldblum co-stars as his sax-playing partner, living life to the full around the smoky clubs of New York, until Whitaker is diagnosed as having a brain tumour. But if you've gotta go, then what better way than with the mother of all jazz gigs. A little melancholy in places, but the stars make a fine team and Lennie Niehaus's music will keep your toes tapping. DP Swearing, sex scenes, drug abuse. **DVD**

Jeff Goldblum *Al Gorky* • Forest Whitaker *Buddy Chester* • Kathy Baker *Janice Gorky* • Tracey Needham *Sarah* • Lois Chiles *Lucy* • Don Cheadle *Jack* ■ *Dir/Scr* Michael Elias

Lust, Caution ★★★★ 18
Wartime romantic thriller
2007 · Tai/US/HK/Chi · Colour · 151min

Ang Lee's follow-up to gay cowboy drama *Brokeback Mountain* is equally daring. This sexually explicit spy thriller, set in Japanese-occupied Shanghai during the Second World War, is in part inspired by similar films of the 1940s, most notably Alfred Hitchcock's *Notorious*. The film focuses on a young Chinese acting student named Wong (Tang Wei), who is recruited by the resistance movement to infiltrate the social circle of despised collaborator Mr Yee (Tony Leung). Seduced by Yee in a series of dark, violent sex scenes that are both shocking and psychologically revealing, Wong finds herself playing a dangerous game, struggling to hold on to her true identity while facing a war on all fronts, not least from her cold, scheming revolutionary paymasters. Though slow in pace, Lee's beautiful and at times claustrophobic film has plenty to say about the painful complexities of human relationships. DW Mandarin, Cantonese, Shanghainese, English, Japanese +subtitles. Sex scenes. **DVD**

Tony Chiu-Wai Leung [Tony Leung (2)] *Mr Yee* • Tang Wei *Wong Chia Chi/Mrs Mak* • Joan Chen *Mrs Yee* • Wang Leehom *Kuang Yu Min* • Tou Chung Hua *Old Wu* • Chu Chih-ying *Lai Shu Jin* • Kao Ying-hsien *Huang Lei* • Ko Yue-Lin *Liang Jun Sheng* ■ *Dir* Ang Lee • *Scr* James Schamus, Wang Hui-Ling, from the story *Se, Jei* by Eileen Chang

Lust for a Vampire ★★ 18
Gothic horror   1970 · UK · Colour · 91min

Hammer veteran Jimmy Sangster called it "an embarrassment" in his autobiography, and Ralph Bates regretted ever starring in something so "tasteless". This is the second of Hammer's Karnstein trilogy (which began with *The Vampire Lovers*) inspired by Sheridan Le Fanu's story *Carmilla*, with gratuitous lesbianism thrown in. A shallow performance by Yutte Stensgaard and some pretty ragged sets fix the lurid tone even lower as terror stalks the corridors of an exclusive girls' finishing school. *Twins of Evil* completed the trilogy in 1971. AJ Nudity. **DVD**

Ralph Bates *Giles Barton* • Yutte Stensgaard *Mircalla/Carmilla* • Barbara Jefford *Countess Herritzen* • Suzanna Leigh *Janet Playfair* • Michael Johnson *Richard Lestrange* ■ *Dir* Jimmy Sangster • *Scr* Tudor Gates, from the story *Carmilla* by J Sheridan Le Fanu

Lust for Life ★★★★ PG
Biographical drama   1956 · US · Colour · 117min

This tale of tortured painter Vincent van Gogh is a superior example of the Hollywood biopic. Van Gogh is uncannily well played by Kirk Douglas, who seems to capture the very essence of the tormented artist, though it was actually Anthony Quinn's Gauguin that won the Oscar. It's lovingly crafted by brilliant director Vincente Minnelli, the superb colour and CinemaScope cinematography is by Russell Harlan and the great Freddie Young, while the authentic Arles location and a fine Miklos Rozsa score are also major plus points. This intelligent, beautifully made film was never a commercial success, but it acquired a cult following. TS **DVD**

Kirk Douglas *Vincent van Gogh* • Anthony Quinn *Paul Gauguin* • James Donald *Theo van Gogh* • Pamela Brown *Christine* • Everett Sloane *Dr Gachet* • Niall MacGinnis *Roulin* • Noel Purcell *Anton Mauve* • Henry Daniell *Theodorus van Gogh* • Madge Kennedy *Anna Cornelia van Gogh* • Jill Bennett *Willemien* ■ *Dir* Vincente Minnelli • *Scr* Norman Corwin, from the novel by Irving Stone

Lust in the Dust ★★ 15
Comedy western   1984 · US · Colour · 80min

Considering this lame parody of vintage American and spaghetti westerns was directed by *Eating Raoul* director Paul Bartel and features a fabulous cult cast, the end result should have been much wilder and funnier than it actually is. Greedy gunslinger Tab Hunter, fiery cantina owner Lainie Kazan, saloon singer Divine and desperado Geoffrey Lewis team up to search for gold. A lifeless and lewd lampoon. AJ

Tab Hunter *Abel Wood* • Divine *Rosie Velez* • Lainie Kazan *Marguerita Ventura* • Geoffrey Lewis *Hard Case Williams* • Henry Silva *Bernardo* • Cesar Romero *Father Garcia* • Woody Strode *Blackman* ■ *Dir* Paul Bartel (1) • *Scr* Philip John Taylor

Lust of the Vampire ★★★★ 12
Horror   1956 · It · BW · 77min

Director Riccardo Freda fought with the producers of this seminal vampire chiller, walked out, and left ace cinematographer Mario Bava to complete the undead saga in two days. The stunning result set the seal on the future of Italian horror and prompted Hammer to mine the same gothic vein in Britain. Beautiful "vampire" Gianna Maria Canale is kept artificially young by transfusions of blood from kidnapped girls in this haunting *Grand Guignol* tale of immortal obsession given the monstrously atmospheric spark of emotion by incredible black-and-white photography and amazing in-camera special effects. One of the most influential horror movies of all time. AJ In Italian. **DVD**

Gianna Maria Canale *Duchess Mararethe Du Grand* • Antoine Balpêtré *Professor Julien Du Grand* • Paul Muller *Joseph Signoret* ■ *Dir* Riccardo Freda • *Scr* Piero Regnoli, Rik Sjostrom • *Cinematographer* Mario Bava

The Lusty Men ★★★ U
Western   1952 · US · BW · 95min

This touching, realistic drama stars Robert Mitchum as the former rodeo champ forced to retire through injury, and Arthur Kennedy as the young man whom Mitchum coaches. Of course, there's also a woman – Susan Hayward, who's married to Kennedy and takes Bob's fancy. Mitchum extended his range considerably with this role, and Lee Garmes's sombre black-and-white photography mirrors the characters' drab existence. A critical and box-office failure at the time, it is now regarded as one of director Nicholas Ray's finest films. AT

Susan Hayward *Louise Merritt* • Robert Mitchum *Jeff McCloud* • Arthur Kennedy *Wes Merritt* • Arthur Hunnicutt *Booker Davis* • Frank Faylen *Al Dawson* • Walter Coy *Buster Burgess* • Carol Nugent *Rusty Davis* • Maria Hart *Rosemary Maddox* ■ *Dir* Nicholas Ray • *Scr* Horace McCoy, David Dortort, from a story by Claude Stanush

Luther ★★★
Biographical drama
1974 · US/UK · Colour · 111min

Playwright John Osborne's vivid portrayal of the religious revolutionary who famously broke with the Roman Catholic Church gets a rather lacklustre treatment here from director Guy Green, though Stacy Keach sweats a bundle as the cleric whose heavenly aspirations were always of the earthy variety. Osborne's deliberately matey dialogue is reduced to the level of tonsured chatter by a largely underused cast that includes Patrick Magee and Hugh Griffith, although Judi Dench is a rose among all those thorny tenets of faith. TH

Stacy Keach *Martin Luther* • Patrick Magee *Hans* • Hugh Griffith *Tetzel* • Robert Stephens *Von Eck* • Alan Badel *Cajetan* • Judi Dench *Katherine* • Leonard Rossiter *Weinand* • Maurice Denham *Staupitz* • Julian Glover *The Knight* ■ *Dir* Guy Green • *Scr* Edward Anhalt, from the play by John Osborne

Luv ★
Sex comedy   1967 · US · Colour · 95min

In this tasteless sex comedy, Jack Lemmon is saved from suicide by former schoolmate Peter Falk; he repays the favour by wooing and then wedding Falk's unwanted wife (Elaine May). After that, things get embarrassing for all concerned. This is an unmitigated disaster, not helped by the fact that Lemmon and Falk switched parts just days before shooting started. AT

Jack Lemmon *Harry Berlin* • Peter Falk *Milt Manville* • Elaine May *Ellen Manville* • Nina Wayne *Linda* • Eddie Mayehoff *Attorney Goodhart* ■ *Dir* Clive Donner • *Scr* Elliott Baker, from a play by Murray Schisgal

The Luzhin Defence ★★★ 12
Period romantic drama
2000 · UK/Fr/It/Hun/US · Colour · 104min

Adapted from a story by Vladimir Nabokov, this is both an emotional drama and a psychological thriller. Can unworldly chess master John Turturro suppress the doubts caused by his parents' failed marriage and find love with socialite Emily Watson, while also breaking the ruinous hold exerted over him by former mentor Stuart Wilson? Director Marleen Gorris was drawn to the project by the prospect of analysing a man torn between two passions. But she has also succeeded in exploiting the romantic beauty of Lake Como in the 1920s to fashion a moving love story, well played by an impressive cast. DP **DVD**

John Turturro *Alexander Luzhin* • Emily Watson *Natalia* • Geraldine James *Vera* • Stuart Wilson (1) *Valentinov* • Christopher Thompson *Stassard* • Fabio Sartor *Turati* • Peter Blythe *Ilya* ■ *Dir* Marleen Gorris • *Scr* Peter Berry, from the novel by Vladimir Nabokov

Lydia ★★★ U
Romantic drama   1941 · US · BW · 94min

Sumptuously mounted but leisurely paced, this is an unofficial Hollywood retread of the French classic *Un Carnet de Bal*, made by the same director, Julien Duvivier. Here he reworks and actively improves upon the original, working for the émigré Hungarian producer/director Alexander Korda, who provides Duvivier with a fine cast, headed by Merle Oberon (Mrs Korda), in the title role. Extravagantly romantic, and some would say overly sentimental, it nevertheless sustains a fine bittersweet tone. The marvellous score by the great Miklos Rozsa received an Oscar nomination. TS

Merle Oberon *Lydia MacMillan* • Edna May Oliver *Granny* • Alan Marshal *Richard Mason* • Joseph Cotten *Michael Fitzpatrick* • Hans Jaray *Frank Audry* • George Reeves *Bob Willard* • John Halliday *Fitzpatrick the Butler* ■ *Dir* Julien Duvivier • *Scr* Ben Hecht, Samuel Hoffenstein, from a story by Julien Duvivier, Laslo Bush-Fekete

Lying to Be Perfect ★★
Comedy drama   2010 · US/Can · Colour · 89min

Sisterhood, self-confidence and, sadly, skinniness prove the key to female fulfilment in this far-fetched, book-based fantasy, in which overweight editor Poppy Montgomery and her two best friends strive to "become the women we know we are inside". Initially, events are playful yet thought-provoking, but an abrupt tonal shift and seriously conflicting messages suck the fun out of the second half, making the simplistic, fairy tale-style climax feel patronising and hollow. SF

Poppy Montgomery *Nola Devlin/Belinda Apple* • Adam Kaufman *Chip/Alex* ■ *Dir* Gary Harvey • *Scr* Nancey Silvers, from the novel *The Cinderella Pact* by Sarah Strohmeyer

Lymelife ★★★★ 15
Drama   2008 · US · Colour · 90min

The mentally debilitating effect of Lyme disease is just one factor blighting a community in late 1970s Long Island in this well-cast indie drama. Derick Martini's first feature may inhabit similar territory to *The Ice Storm* and *American Beauty*, but it's not overshadowed by them. It's insightful, has a vivid sense of time and place, and offers fine actors like Alec Baldwin, Timothy Hutton and an excellent Rory Culkin some quality material to sink their teeth into. TJ **DVD**

Alec Baldwin *Mickey Bartlett* • Rory Culkin *Scott Bartlett* • Kieran Culkin *Jimmy Bartlett* • Jill Hennessy *Brenda Bartlett* • Timothy Hutton *Charlie Bragg* • Cynthia Nixon *Melissa Bragg* • Emma Roberts *Adrianna Bragg* • Adam Scarimbolo *Todd O'Leary* • *Scr* Derick Martini, Steven Martini

The Lyons in Paris ★★★ U
Comedy   1955 · UK · BW · 81min

The popular radio series, *Life with the Lyons*, starring Ben Lyon, Bebe Daniels and their troublesome children, Barbara and Richard, produced two film spin-offs. This, the second, looks suspiciously like three radio episodes joined together. Bebe mistakenly thinks Ben has forgotten their wedding anniversary, but he's secretly been planning a trip to Paris (there are some genuine location shots); Ben and Richard are wooed by a naughty demoiselle; Barbara falls in love with an existentialist (a bit of satire here). Director Val Guest maintains a brisk pace, and the Lyons are really rather endearing. DM **DVD**

Bebe Daniels *Bebe* • Ben Lyon *Ben* • Barbara Lyon *Barbara* • Richard Lyon *Richard* • Reginald Beckwith *Capt le Grand* • Martine Alexis *Fifi le Fleur* ■ *Dir* Val Guest • *Scr* Val Guest, from the radio series *Life with the Lyons* by Bebe Daniels, Bob Block, Bill Harding

LANDMARK FILM

Fritz Lang's first talkie sets a template for crime drama – and especially *film noir* – still utilised today

M
Classic crime drama ★★★★★ PG
1931 · Ger · BW · 110min

Peter Lorre is the most underrated actor in the history of Hollywood. In his later years, he was content to parody the sinister snivelling that made him so compelling to watch. Here, the familiar persona has a real edge of menace, as he plays the self-loathing child murderer whose crimes are always preceded by a chilling whistle. Making his talkie debut, Fritz Lang continues to fill the screen with the atmospheric expressionist images that made him Europe's pre-eminent silent director, but his use of sound is also inspired, whether in crowd scenes or details like the clicking-open of Lorre's knife. This is a genuine masterpiece. DP German +subtitles. *DVD* *BL*

Peter Lorre *Franz Becker* • Otto Wernicke *Inspector Lohmann* • Gustaf Gründgens *Safebreaker* • Theo Lingen *Con man* • Inge Landgut *Child* • Ellen Widmann *Mother* • Fritz Odemar *Cheat* • Theodore Loos [Theodor Loos] *Groeber* ■ *Dir* Fritz Lang • *Scr* Thea von Harbou, Paul Falkenberg, Karl Vash, Adolf Jansen, from an article by Egon Jacobson

M
Crime drama ★★★
1951 · US · BW · 88min

Independent producer Seymour Nebenzal was behind this Hollywood remake of his acclaimed 1931 German production. The idea of the underworld helping to catch a murderer of children doesn't ring true in a Los Angeles setting. Yet director Joseph Losey created a visually powerful picture with some brilliantly chosen locations and effective use of music, while David Wayne comes close to matching Peter Lorre as the pathetic murderer. AE

David Wayne *Martin Harrow* • Howard Da Silva *Carney* • Luther Adler *Langley* • Martin Gabel *Marshall* • Steve Brodie *Lt Becker* • Raymond Burr *Pottsy* • Glenn Anders *Riggert* • Karen Morley *Mrs Coster* • Jim Backus *Mayor* ■ *Dir* Joseph Losey • *Scr* Norman Reilly Raine, Leo Katcher, Waldo Salt, from the 1931 film, from an article by Egon Jacobson

M Butterfly
Drama ★★ 15
1993 · US · Colour · 96min

Director David Cronenberg came horribly unstuck with this insipid adaptation of David Henry Hwang's successful Broadway play about sexual deception and espionage. Jeremy Irons is a minor French diplomat in Beijing who falls under the spell of beautiful Chinese diva Song Liling. But not only is Song a spy, she's also a man! While it's obvious why Cronenberg would be attracted to such an operatic story of blurred identity, this should be filed under "interesting failure". AJ Violence, swearing, sex scenes.

Jeremy Irons *René Gallimard* • John Lone *Song Liling* • Barbara Sukowa *Jeanne Gallimard* • Ian Richardson *Ambassador Toulon* • Annabel Leventon *Frau Baden* • Shizuko Hoshi *Comrade Chin* • Richard McMillan *Embassy colleague* • Vernon Dobtcheff *Agent Etancelin* ■ *Dir* David Cronenberg • *Scr* David Henry Hwan, from his play

MGM's Big Parade of Comedy
Comedy compilation ★★★ U
1964 · US · BW · 89min

This patchy celebration of MGM's comic past is another of the compilation films

assembled by producer Robert Youngson. There are a couple of funny episodes featuring Laurel and Hardy and Buster Keaton, but neither did their best work for the studio and we are forced to spend too long in the company of performers such as Wallace Beery and Marie Dressler, whose brand of humour is now very dated. The high points are provided by William Powell, Myrna Loy, Jean Harlow and Marion Davies, who was a much better actress than critics at the time gave her credit for. DP

■ *Dir* Robert Youngson

Ma and Pa Kettle
Comedy ★★
1949 · US · BW · 76min

As the hillbilly couple of the 1947 hit comedy *The Egg and I*, Marjorie Main and Percy Kilbride scored so many laughs they were given a film of their own, which developed into a hugely successful annual series that ran until 1957. Here the Kettles, facing eviction from their ramshackle abode, win a futuristic new home in which to live with their 15 offspring. Their efforts to cope with its gadgets provide much of the slapstick humour. AE

Marjorie Main *Ma Kettle* • Percy Kilbride *Pa Kettle* • Richard Long *Tom Kettle* • Meg Randall *Kim Parker* • Patricia Alphin *Secretary* • Esther Dale *Mrs Birdie Hicks* • Barry Kelley *Mr Tomkins* • Harry Antrim *Mayor Swiggins* ■ *Dir* Charles Lamont • *Scr* Herbert Margolis, Louis Morheim, Al Lewis, from the characters by Betty MacDonald

Ma Femme Est une Actrice
★★★ 15
Comedy
2001 · Fr · Colour · 91min

Actor Yvan Attal makes his feature debut as director with this attractive French comedy that he also wrote and co-stars in. Attal's off-screen wife Charlotte Gainsbourg appears as the superstar actress whose success begins to make her sportswriter husband feel increasingly uneasy. This knowing satire lacks a certain sparkle, but with Terence Stamp preening himself as the suave English thespian Attal suspects as a romantic rival and the screenplay supplying some sly asides on both the male and artistic ego, it is eminently enjoyable. DP French +subtitles. *DVD*

Charlotte Gainsbourg *Charlotte* • Yvan Attal *Yvan* • Terence Stamp *John* • Noémie Lvovsky *Nathalie* • Laurent Bateau *Vincent* • Ludivine Sagnier *Géraldine* • Lionel Abelanski *Georges* • Keith Allen *David* ■ *Dir/Scr* Yvan Attal

ma ma
Drama ★★ 12
2015 · Sp/Fr · Colour · 111min

Painfully well-intentioned but frequently clunky, particularly in its final throes, *ma ma* is the latest feature from Spanish director Julio Medem (*Sex and Lucía*). Penélope Cruz is the recently unemployed teacher and devoted mother diagnosed with breast cancer, who's forced to grit her teeth and endure treatment alone as her husband cavorts with another woman. Cruz keeps things engaging but she's really up against it in a film that's mawkish, melodramatic and sometimes comically misjudged. EAS In Spanish. Some swearing, nudity, sex references

Penélope Cruz *Magda* • Luis Tosar *Arturo* • Asier Etxeandia *Julián* • Tea Planell *Dani* ■ *Dir/Scr* Julio Medem

Ma Mère
★★ 18
Drama
2004 · Fr/Sp/Austria · Colour · 107min

Isabelle Huppert here explores the dark heart of human sexuality, playing a licentious mother who falls for the physical charms of her 17-year-old son (Louis Garrel). Director Christophe Honoré goes all out to challenge contemporary taboos, depicting incest as just another form of decadent tension-relief in a holiday resort where everyone's bed-hopping. In trying so hard to shock, however, Honoré creates a voyeuristic movie that sadly never delves into the minds of its unrestrained protagonists. SF French +subtitles. Sex scenes. *DVD*

Isabelle Huppert *Hélène* • Louis Garrel *Pierre* • Emma de Caunes *Hansi* • Joana Preiss *Réa* • Jean-Baptiste Montagut *Loulou* • Dominique Reymond *Marthe* • Olivier Rabourdin *Robert* • Philippe Duclos *Father* ■ *Dir* Christophe Honoré • *Scr* Christophe Honoré, from the novel by Georges Battaille

Ma Saison Préferée
★★ 15
Drama
1993 · Fr · Colour · 121min

Daniel Auteuil and Catherine Deneuve are brother and sister brought together after many years to attend the imminent demise of their mother. The familial strife around a death-bed recalls those hothouse dramas by Tennessee Williams and Eugene O'Neill, and this effort offers few surprises. The main point of interest is the fact that Deneuve's daughter is played by her real-life daughter, Chiara, whose father was famed actor Marcello Mastroianni. AT French +subtitles.

Catherine Deneuve *Emilie* • Daniel Auteuil *Antoine* • Marthe Villalonga *Berthe* • Jean-Pierre Bouvier *Bruno* • Chiara Mastroianni *Anne* ■ *Dir* André Téchiné • *Scr* André Téchiné, Pascal Bonitzer

Ma Vie en Rose
★★★ 12
Drama
1997 · Fr/Bel/UK/Swi · Colour · 85min

Both director Alain Berliner and his young star, Georges Du Fresne, make auspicious debuts with this bittersweet tale of sexual confusion and bourgeois prudery. Berliner's clever shifts in colour, as reality intrudes upon the boy's Barbie-doll daydreams, are inspired, while as the pre-teen convinced he'll eventually turn into a girl, Du Fresne is so disingenuously trusting that he almost atones for the film's muddled blend of social satire and whimsical fantasy. Mother Michèle Laroque is so delightfully sympathetic that the trite ending has just the right ring of optimism. DP French +subtitles. *DVD*

Michèle Laroque *Hanna* • Jean-Philippe Ecoffey *Pierre* • Hélène Vincent *Elisabeth* • Georges Du Fresne *Ludovic* • Daniel Hanssens *Albert* • Laurence Bibot *Lisette* ■ *Dir* Alain Berliner • *Scr* Alain Berliner, from a story by Chris Vander Stappen

Ma Vie Sexuelle
★★★ 15
Drama
1996 · Fr · Colour · 172min

Directed with a genuine curiosity about his characters that is too rare in 1990s cinema, Arnaud Desplechin's leisurely study of Parisian 20-something angst has its moments, but too few to justify the running time. As the wannabe intellectual trapped in a dead-end teaching post, Mathieu Amalric creates an introspective loser. But his relationships with neglected girlfriend Emmanuelle Devos, unhinged student Marianne Denicourt and his cousin's lover, Chiara Mastroianni, only occasionally flicker into life. DP French +subtitles. *DVD*

Mathieu Amalric *Paul* • Emmanuelle Devos *Esther* • Emmanuel Salinger *Nathan* • Marianne Denicourt *Sylvia* • Chiara Mastroianni *Patricia* ■ *Dir* Arnaud Desplechin • *Scr* Arnaud Desplechin, Emmanuel Bourdieu

Ma Vraie Vie à Rouen
★★★ 15
Comedy drama
2002 · Fr · Colour · 100min

Olivier Ducastel and Jacques Martineau take a technical risk in presenting the whole of this teasingly self-reflexive picture from the camcorded perspective of an unprepossessing Rouen teenager. But what emerges is a touchingly honest portrait of a wannabe figure skater coming to terms with his sexuality and the fact that most of his dreams won't come true. Jimmy Tavares impresses in his limited screen time, but Ariane Ascaride excels as the doting, widowed mother both amused and irritated by his fixation with turning family and friends into characters in his personal soap. DP French +subtitles. *DVD*

Ariane Ascaride *Caroline* • Jonathan Zaccaï *Laurent* • Hélène Surgère *Grandmother* • Jimmy Tavares *Etienne* • Lucas Bonnifait *Ludovic* ■ *Dir/Scr* Olivier Ducastel, Jacques Martineau

Mac
★★★ 18
Period drama
1992 · US · Colour · 113min

Three brothers from Queens try to set themselves up as business contractors in actor John Turturro's accomplished directing debut. But fraternal rivalry rears its ugly head in an absorbing, 1950s-set ensemble piece that is brutal and warmly humorous by turns. Turturro plays Mac, the bullying perfectionist who wants to make his father proud, with a painful honesty that's both touching and believable. This is an intimate drama of great depth and keen observation. AJ

John Turturro *Niccolo "Mac" Vitelli* • Michael Badalucco *Vico Vitelli* • Carl Capotorto *Bruno Vitelli* • Katherine Borowitz *Alice Vitelli* • John Amos *Nat* • Olek Krupa *Polowski* • Ellen Barkin *Oona* ■ *Dir* John Turturro • *Scr* John Turturro, Brandon Cole

Mac and Me
★★ U
Adventure
1988 · US · Colour · 95min

After ET's jaunt to our planet captured the hearts of Earthlings of all ages, it was only to be expected that he would be followed by a positive star fleet of cute critters from outer space. Mac was not one of the more endearing, although there are moments when his relationship with Jade Calegory (who doesn't allow spina bifida to detract from her courageous performance) is quite touching. Director Stewart Raffill's film is otherwise an unashamed rip-off and only remembered as the picture that gave product placement a bad name. DP *DVD*

Christine Ebersole *Janet Cruise* • Jonathan Ward *Michael Cruise* • Katrina Caspary [Tina Caspary] *Courtney* • Lauren Stanley *Debbie* • Jade Calegory *Eric Cruise* • Vinnie Torrente *Mitford* • Martin West *Wickett* • Ivan Jorge Rado *Zimmerman* ■ *Dir* Stewart Raffill • *Scr* Stewart Raffill, Steve Feke

Macabre
★★
Horror
1958 · US · BW · 71min

The first gimmick horror movie from showman producer/director William Castle is more a mystery whodunnit than a ghoulish chiller, filled with fog-shrouded cardboard graveyards and numerous surprises. Doctor William Prince has just five hours to find his daughter, who has been buried alive as part of an elaborate charade. Castle arranged a $1,000 life insurance policy with Lloyd's of London to cover audience members from "death by fright" – a successful ploy that found him mounting ever more outlandish stunts over the next decade. AJ

William Prince *Dr Rodney Barrett* • Jim Backus *Jim Tyloe* • Jacqueline Scott *Polly Baron* • Philip Tonge *Jode Wetherby* • Ellen Corby *Miss Kushins* • Susan Morrow *Sylvia Stevenson* • Christine White *Nancy Wetherby* ■ *Dir* William Castle • *Scr* Robb White, from the novel by Theo Durrant

Macao
★★★ PG
Crime drama
1952 · US · BW · 77min

This piece of low-budget exotica was directed by Josef von Sternberg, who was at odds with some of his cast as well as the project as a whole. When Nicholas Ray, who also directed some sequences of Robert Mitchum's *The Racket*, was given credit for shooting some of the final scenes, von Sternberg denounced the film. It's a diversion, with Mitchum and Jane Russell beautifully matched as a fugitive from justice and a nightclub singer who become involved in a bid to ensnare a local crime boss. If only the story and script were on a par with them as well. AT

Robert Mitchum *Nick Cochran* • Jane Russell *Julie Benson* • William Bendix *Lawrence Trumble* • Thomas Gomez *Lt Sebastian* • Gloria Grahame *Margie* • Brad Dexter *Halloran* • Edward Ashley *Martin Stewart* ■ *Dir* Josef von Sternberg, Nicholas Ray • *Scr* Bernard C Schoenfeld, Stanley Rubin, from a story by Bob Williams

Macario
★★★★
Period fantasy
1960 · Mex · BW · 89min

Like the film that beat it to the Oscar for best foreign film, Ingmar Bergman's *The Virgin Spring*, this Mexican drama focuses on faith, superstition and death. But there's little optimism in Roberto Gavaldon's fantasy, evocatively shot by master cinematographer Gabriel Figueroa and drawing on the magic realist tradition. The story turns on the fate of starving woodsman, Ignacio Lopez Tarso who, having refused to share a turkey with either God or the Devil, is tricked into a pact with Death. DP In Spanish.

Ignacio Lopez Tarso *Macario* • Pina Pellicer *Macario's wife* • Enrique Lucero *Death* ■ *Dir* Roberto Gavaldon • *Scr* Roberto Galvadon, Emilio Carballido, from the story *The Third Guest* by Bruno Traven

Macaroni ★★★ PG
Comedy drama   1985 · It · Colour · 101min

It sounds so improbable it could never work. Yet, in the hands of Jack Lemmon and Marcello Mastroianni, Ettore Scola's tale of the surly businessman who rediscovers the simple joys of life from an eccentric Neapolitan exercises an irresistible charm right through to its closing note of quiet optimism. Discovering that Marcello has continued writing love letters to the heartbroken sister GI Jack jilted at the end of the war, Lemmon gratefully succumbs to the companionship absent from his troubled life. DP English, Italian +subtitles.

Jack Lemmon *Robert Traven* • Marcello Mastroianni *Antonio* • Daria Nicolodi *Laura* • Isa Danieli *Carmelina* • Patrizia Sacchi *Virginia* • Bruno Esposito *Giulio* • Giovanna Sanfilippo *Maria* ■ *Dir* Ettore Scola • *Scr* Ruggero Maccari, Furio Scarpelli, Ettore Scola

MacArthur ★★★ PG
Biographical drama   1977 · US · Colour · 123min

Though not in the same league as *Patton*, this solid, old-fashioned war epic deals with a similarly controversial and complex military commander. Gregory Peck is well cast as the martinet/genius, who famously said, "I will return" after being forced to evacuate Corregidor, the last American stronghold in the Philippines. He did go back, defeating the Japanese and later leading the US forces in Korea. AT *DVD*

Gregory Peck *General Douglas MacArthur* • Ivan Bonar *General Sutherland* • Dan O'Herlihy *President Roosevelt* • Ward Costello *General Marshall* • Nicolas Coster *Colonel Huff* • Marj Dusay *Mrs MacArthur* • Ed Flanders *President Harry S Truman* ■ *Dir* Joseph Sargent • *Scr* Hal Barwood, Matthew Robbins

Macbeth ★★★★ PG
Tragedy   1948 · US · BW · 102min

Orson Welles's rendition of *Macbeth* may be the least of his Shakespeare adaptations but, bearing in mind the brilliance of *Chimes at Midnight* and *Othello*, this can hardly be taken as a denunciation. Admittedly, the Scottish accents are often impenetrable thanks to the indifferent sound quality, and Jeanette Nolan may not be the incarnation of merciless ambition that is most people's idea of Lady Macbeth. But Welles gives a towering performance, vacillating between ambition, indecision and conscience with supreme skill. The film's design conveys an atmosphere of evil and unease far more effectively than the plush trappings of Roman Polanski's 1971 version. DP *DVD*

Orson Welles *Macbeth* • Jeanette Nolan *Lady Macbeth* • Dan O'Herlihy *Macduff* • Roddy McDowall *Malcolm* • Edgar Barrier *Banquo* • Erskine Sanford *Duncan* • John Dierkes *Ross* • Keene Curtis *Lennox* • Peggy Webber *Lady Macduff* • Alan Napier *A Holy Father* ■ *Dir* Orson Welles • *Scr* Orson Welles, from the play by William Shakespeare

Macbeth ★★★★ 15
Tragedy   1971 · UK · Colour · 134min

A controversial adaptation by Roman Polanski (with Kenneth Tynan advising), this sacrifices some of Shakespeare's bleak poetry in favour of great barbaric imagery. A bloody account of Macbeth (Jon Finch) and his intimidating wife (Francesca Annis) making their way to the top of the medieval heap via murder and treachery, it was Polanski's first film after the murder of his wife, Sharon Tate, and has a savagery that seems tinged with paranoia. Lady Macbeth's nude sleepwalking scene

resulted in critical flak and was seen as evidence of the malign influence of production company Playboy. It deserves better than that jibe. TH *DVD* *Blu*

Jon Finch *Macbeth* • Francesca Annis *Lady Macbeth* • Martin Shaw *Banquo* • Nicholas Selby *Duncan* • John Stride *Ross* • Stephan Chase *Malcolm* • Paul Shelley *Donalbain* • Terence Baylor *Macduff* ■ *Dir* Roman Polanski • *Scr* Roman Polanski, from the play by William Shakespeare • *Cinematographer* Gilbert Taylor

Macbeth ★★ 12
Tragedy   1997 · UK · Colour · 142min

This doggedly low-budget affair lacks the power or cinematic imagination of earlier efforts by Orson Welles, Akira Kurosawa (*Throne of Blood*) and Roman Polanski. As Macbeth, a role long coveted by his father, Jason Connery is suitably hesitant in his ambition, but there's a suspicion this owes more to his discomfort with the difficult dialogue than character insight. Helen Baxendale is similarly troubled as his scheming wife. Director Jeremy Freeston has some splendid locations to work with; a pity, then, he shoots much of the dialogue in suffocating close-up. DP *DVD*

Jason Connery *Macbeth* • Helen Baxendale *Lady Macbeth* • Graham McTavish *Banquo* • Kenny Bryans *Macduff* • Kern Falconer *Seyton* • Hildegard Neil *1st witch* • Brian Blessed *Edward the Confessor* ■ *Dir* Jeremy Freeston • *Scr* Bob Carruthers, Jeremy Freeston, from the play by William Shakespeare

Macbeth ★★ 15
Crime drama   2006 · Aus · Colour · 104min

Reinventing Shakespeare's famous tragedy as a mob drama may not be a bad idea, it's just not a particularly original one – see *Joe Macbeth* and *Men of Respect*. But what's most disappointing about *Romper Stomper* director Geoffrey Wright's first Australian film since 1994's *Metal Skin* is that the gangster elements fail to convince. Melbourne provides a suitably dark backdrop, but the action set pieces are clumsily staged, and purists won't be impressed with the truncated text and the jarring Aussie accents. To top it all, Sam Worthington lacks charisma in the title role. There are some nice touches, however – turning the three witches into saucy schoolgirls is a cheeky but inspired move. JF *DVD*

Sam Worthington *Macbeth* • Victoria Hill *Lady Macbeth* • Lachy Hulme *Macduff* • Steve Bastoni *Banquo* • Gary Sweet *Duncan* • Matt Doran *Malcolm* ■ *Dir* Geoffrey Wright • *Scr* Geoffrey Wright, Victoria Hill, from the play by William Shakespeare • *Cinematographer* Will Gibson

Macbeth ★★★★★ 15
Tragedy   2015 · UK · Colour · 112min

This masterful interpretation of the "Scottish play" delivers an onslaught of visual and emotional bravado, setting its story of spilt blood amid billowing smoke and red, raging fire. Eeriness abounds, with director Justin Kurzel liberally employing filmic audacity to reinvigorate an oft-told tale. The ferocious imagery complements the grandiose dialogue, every syllable of which is uttered with conviction by an exemplary cast. The setting is simple, the story well known, yet the film is so searing it'll have you pinned to your seat. EAS *DVD* *Blu*

Michael Fassbender *Macbeth* • Marion Cotillard *Lady Macbeth* • Paddy Considine *Banquo* • David Thewlis *Duncan* • Sean Harris *Macduff* • Elizabeth Debicki *Lady Macduff* ■ *Dir* Justin Kurzel • *Scr* Jacob Koskoff, Michael Lesslie, Todd Louiso, from Shakespeare's play

McCabe and Mrs Miller ★★★★ 15
Western   1971 · US · Colour · 115min

Warren Beatty stars as McCabe, a gambler who goes into business with English whorehouse madam Mrs Miller (Julie Christie), in a bleak western set against the backdrop of a developing town in the American North West. It's an interesting tale with all the classic elements of the genre, and the affair is given added weight

by the solid performances of Beatty and Christie. A reminder of just how good *Short Cuts* director Robert Altman could be when he was on form. JB *DVD*

Warren Beatty *John McCabe* • Julie Christie *Constance Miller* • René Auberjonois *Sheehan* • John Schuck *Smalley* • Bert Remsen *Bart Coyle* • Keith Carradine *Cowboy* • William Devane *Lawyer* • Corey Fischer *Mr Elliott* • Shelley Duvall *Ida Coyle* ■ *Dir* Robert Altman • *Scr* Robert Altman, Brian McKay, from the novel *McCabe* by Edmund Naughton

The McConnell Story ★★ U
Biographical drama   1955 · US · Colour · 102min

Alan Ladd was terrified of flying, but he had no qualms about playing Captain Joseph C McConnell Jr, a real-life pilot ace of the Korean War. It's standard stuff, with Ladd putting duty first and his patient wife (June Allyson) second, though the script had to be revised when McConnell was killed testing a new type of plane shortly before production started. The jingoistic embellishments are somewhat sickening, however. AE

Alan Ladd *Captain Joseph C "Mac" McConnell Jr* • June Allyson *"Butch"* • James Whitmore *Ty Whitman* • Frank Faylen *Sykes* • Robert Ellis *Bob* • Willis Bouchey *Newton Bass* ■ *Dir* Gordon Douglas • *Scr* Ted Sherdeman, Sam Rolfe, from a story by Ted Sherdeman

McCullin ★★★★ 15
Documentary   2012 · UK · Colour · 91min

London-born photographer Don McCullin, who's celebrated for his powerful images of the world's trouble spots in the 1960s and 70s, is himself the subject of David and Jacqui Morris's documentary portrait. He proves a forcefully articulate interviewee, taking the story from his tough upbringing in Finsbury Park to the realisation that his gift lay in capturing the violence and chaos of war. Archive news footage helps sketch in the historical background, while McCullin recalls the painful contradictions involved in seeking out the most awful suffering and then taking photos. TJ Violence. *DVD* *Blu*

Don McCullin ■ *Dir* David Morris (2), Jacqui Morris

MacGruber ★★ 15
Spoof action comedy   2010 · US · Colour · 90min

This knockabout comedy is based on the *Saturday Night Live* character created and played by comic Will Forte. Here the bumbling soldier of fortune comes out of retirement to thwart Val Kilmer's terrorist, who threatens to launch a stolen nuclear warhead on Washington. Forte is likeable as the renegade good guy – a parody of 1980s small-screen hero MacGyver – but the humour relies too heavily on blatantly telegraphed sight gags and villains with rude-sounding names. TeS Violence, swearing, sex scenes. *DVD* *Blu*

Will Forte *MacGruber* • Val Kilmer *Dieter Von Cunth* • Ryan Phillippe *Dixon Piper* • Kristen Wiig *Vicki St Elmo* • Maya Rudolph *Casey* ■ *Dir* Jorma Taccone • *Scr* John Solomon, Jorma Taccone, Will Forte

McHale's Navy ★★★ U
War comedy   1964 · US · Colour · 92min

McHale's Navy first aired on US TV in 1962 and was an immediate hit, showing the antics of the crew of a PT boat. This film version preserves the main cast and production team, giving Ernest Borgnine the plum role as Lt Cmdr Quinton McHale, the least likely officer in the Pacific. Very much a product of its times, it includes some genuinely funny, even surreal moments such as a Japanese peering through his periscope and seeing a racehorse on the bows of the PT boat. AT

Ernest Borgnine *Lt Cmdr Quinton McHale* • Joe Flynn *Capt Wallace Burton Binghamton* • Tim Conway *Ensign Charles Parker* • Carl Ballantine *Torpedoman Lester Gruber* • Gary Vinson *QM George "Christy" Christopher* ■ *Dir* Edward J Montagne • *Scr* Frank Gill Jr, G Carleton Brown, from a story by Si Rose

McHale's Navy ★★ PG
Comedy   1997 · US · Colour · 104min

Tom Arnold stars in this update of the 1960s TV series. Lt Cmdr Quinton McHale is lured out of retirement in the Caribbean to fight dangerous international terrorist Tim Curry, who is trying to build his own nuclear silo and fire a missile at the Pentagon. So much attention was paid to getting an impressive cast of B-movie actors that somebody forgot to write any jokes. ST Some swearing.

Tom Arnold *Lt Cmdr Quinton McHale* • Dean Stockwell *Capt Wallace B Binghampton* • Debra Messing *Lt Penelope Carpenter* • David Alan Grier *Ensign Charles T Parker* • Tim Curry *Major Vladikov* • Ernest Borgnine *Cobra* ■ *Dir* Bryan Spicer • *Scr* Peter Crabbe, from a story by Andy Rose, Peter Crabbe

Machan ★★★ 15
Sports comedy based on a true story
2008 · Ger/UK/It/Sri L · Colour · 102min

The true tale of the Sri Lankan slum dwellers whose dream of a life in the West was realised by inventing a handball team to play in a German tournament is a real winner, and *Full Monty* producer Uberto Pasolini's mix of professionals and non-actors gives the broad humour of the script a docudrama feel. The result is an entertaining, if a little overlong, movie that could even bring a smile to the face of a hardened border control official. TF Sinhala, English +subtitles. Swearing, a sex scene. *DVD*

Dharmapriya Dias *Stanley* • Gihan de Chickera *Manoj* • Dharshan Dharmaraj *Suresh* • Mahendra Perera *Ruan* ■ *Dir* Uberto Pasolini • *Scr* Uberto Pasolini, Ruwanthie de Chickera

Machete ★★★ 18
Action crime thriller   2010 · US · Colour · 100min

Danny Trejo plays the craggy ex-lawman with a tragic past who is tempted into carrying out a hit on a racist American senator (Robert De Niro) and winds up on the run from the FBI. This raucous romp throws several haphazard subplots into the mix, including one involving a gratuitously nude and lascivious Lindsay Lohan, before settling into a needlessly protracted chase that finds De Niro at his most hammy and least funny in years. Trejo rallies at the end to give the film a cool, satisfying send-off but, for the most part, this entertaining but often shambolic romp sorely needs his laconic presence throughout. DW Violence, nudity. *DVD* *Blu*

Danny Trejo *Machete* • Jessica Alba *Sartana* • Michelle Rodriguez *Luz* • Robert De Niro *Senator McLaughlin* • Steven Seagal *Torrez* • Lindsay Lohan *April Booth* • Cheech Marin *[Richard "Cheech" Marin] Padre* • Don Johnson *Von* ■ *Dir* Ethan Maniquis, Robert Rodriguez • *Scr* Robert Rodriguez, Álvaro Rodríguez

Machete Kills ★★★ 15
Action thriller   2013 · US · Colour · 103min

Robert Rodriguez's slicker if less pacey sequel to *Machete* comes across like an 007 adventure for a generation weaned on 1970s B-movie exploitation. Here, US President Charlie Sheen (credited under his birth name Carlos Estevez) enlists Machete (stone-faced Danny Trejo) to apprehend a crazed Mexican revolutionary aiming a nuclear bomb at Washington. There are some memorable turns among the jumble of bloody action, including Cuba Gooding Jr as a chameleonic hitman who also takes on the appearance of Lady Gaga and Antonio Banderas. AJ Violence, swearing, a sex scene. *DVD* *Blu* *CS*

Danny Trejo *Machete* • Michelle Rodriguez *Luz* • Sofia Vergara *Desdemona* • Amber Heard *Miss San Antonio* • Mel Gibson *Luther Voz* • Cuba Gooding Jr *El Camaleon 2* • Carlos Estevez [Charlie Sheen] *US President* • Jessica Alba *Sartana* • Alexa Vega *KillJoy* ■ *Dir* Robert Rodriguez • *Scr* Kyle Ward, from a story by Marcel Rodriguez, Robert Rodriguez, from a character by Robert Rodriguez

M

La Machine ★★★ 18
Science-fiction horror thriller
1994 · Fr/Ger · Colour · 91min

Gérard Depardieu plays a psychologist with a particular fascination for the criminal mind. He develops a machine that enables him to swap brains with Didier Bourdon, a man convicted of stabbing three women to death. Unfortunately, the experiment becomes permanent. But does his wife, Nathalie Baye, still recognise him? This exercise in schlock provides some effective jolts as Depardieu surfs someone else's brainwaves. **AT** French dubbed.

Gérard Depardieu *Marc* • Nathalie Baye *Marie* • Didier Bourdon *Zyto* • Natalia Woerner *Marianne* • Erwan Baynaud *Leonard* ■ *Dir* François Dupeyron • *Scr* François Dupeyron, from a novel by René Belletto

The Machine ★★★ 15
Science-fiction thriller
2013 · UK · Colour · 90min

This sleek artificial intelligence thriller stars Toby Stephens and Caity Lotz as computer boffins working for the Ministry of Defence. He wants to aid the disabled via cranial implants, while she is trying to create a machine that can make decisions for itself. Predictably, their ideals are in conflict with their shady MoD bosses, who simply want to create a robotic super-soldier. Writer/director Caradog James touches on some intriguing questions, but the film's content never quite matches its tremendous style (with visuals that belie a modest budget), and from an A-movie start it descends into a B-movie finish. **DA** Violence.

Toby Stephens *Vincent McCarthy* • Caity Lotz *Ava/The Machine* • Denis Lawson *Thomson* • Sam Hazeldine *James* • Pooneh Hajimohammadi *Suri* • John Paul Macleod *Paul Dawson* ■ *Dir/Scr* Caradog James

Machine Gun Kelly ★★★ 12
Biographical crime drama
1958 · US · BW · 83min

One of the first films to gain cult director Roger Corman international recognition and critical acclaim, this is a vivid and fast-moving biopic about the infamous 1930s bank robber. Charles Bronson (in his first starring role) brings an edgy intensity to Kelly, the audacious gangster who finally surrendered to the FBI rather than be killed in a shoot-out. Rapid-fire dialogue and effective characterisations all down the line make this a winner. **AJ** *DVD*

Charles Bronson *Machine Gun Kelly* • Susan Cabot *Flo* • Morey Amsterdam *Fandango* • Jack Lambert *Howard* • Wally Campo *Maize* ■ *Dir* Roger Corman • *Scr* R Wright Campbell

Machine Gun Preacher ★★ 15
Action drama based on a true story
2011 · US · Colour · 123min

He's flirted with romantic comedies, but Gerard Butler seems to have accepted that tough guy roles are his forte. Here's another, albeit one where he gets to show a sensitive side. Based on a true story, this lurid film sees Butler playing a drug-dealing biker who comes close to killing a man, then gets religion and changes his ways. On missionary work in the Sudan, he goes for his gun again in a crusade against the use of child soldiers by local warlords. It's a worthy film more than a remarkable one, with its foundation in fact perhaps restricting director Marc Foster when it came to heightening the drama. **DA** Violence, swearing, drug abuse. *DVD* BL

Gerard Butler *Sam Childers* • Michelle Monaghan *Lynn Childers* • Michael Shannon *Donnie* • Madeline Carroll *Paige Childers* • Kathy Baker *Daisy Childers* ■ *Dir* Marc Forster • *Scr* Jason Keller

The Machinist ★★★ 15
Psychological mystery thriller
2003 · Sp · Colour · 97min

The most astonishing thing about this bleak, underplayed psychological thriller is Christian Bale's incredible physical transformation. Bale deliberately withered to the point where his appearance is shockingly reminiscent of undernourished PoWs. Reportedly losing over 60 pounds to get into the role, Bale plays a factory worker whose emaciated condition and chronic insomnia may be linked to a mysterious stranger and a secret from his past. Director Brad Anderson cultivates a studied, effectively creepy atmosphere but his determination to move everything at a pace that would disgrace a slothful snail finally undermines some of the tension. **AS** Swearing, violence. *DVD* BL

Christian Bale *Trevor Reznik* • Jennifer Jason Leigh *Stevie* • Aitana Sanchez-Gijon *Marie* • John Sharian *Ivan* • Michael Ironside *Miller* • Larry Gilliard Jr *Jackson* • Reg E Cathey *Jones* • Anna Massey *Mrs Shrike* ■ *Dir* Brad Anderson • *Scr* Scott Kosar

Machuca ★★★ 15
Period drama
2004 · Chil/Sp/UK/Fr · Colour · 115min

Andrés Wood's emotive drama was a huge success in the director's native Chile and is set against the fall of the Allende government in 1973. It shrewdly views events from a child's perspective, charting the growing friendship between pampered Matías Quer and shantytown kid Ariel Mateluna, after the latter is awarded a place at Quer's prestigious school. Quer develops a crush on Mateluna's cousin Manuela Martelli, who divides her time between menial jobs and social protest. Wood captures the period mood well, but he laces the occasionally fraught melodrama with some bombastic political rhetoric. **DP** Spanish +subtitles. Swearing. *DVD*

Matías Quer *Gonzalo Infante* • Ariel Mateluna *Pedro Machuca* • Manuela Martelli *Silvana* • Aline Küppenheim *María Luisa Infante* • Federico Luppi *Roberto Ochagavía* • Ernesto Malbrán *Father McEnroe* • Tamara Acosta *Juana* • Francisco Reyes *Patricio Infante* ■ *Dir* Andrés Wood • *Scr* Andrés Wood, Roberto Brodsky, Mamoun Hassan

Mack the Knife ★ 15
Musical drama
1989 · US · Colour · 117min

An all-star British cast gives support to Raul Julia's MacHeath in this version of Bertolt Brecht and Kurt Weill's *Threepenny Opera*. However, the impressive line-up conceals an appalling travesty of a theatrical classic that's totally alien to the spirit of the original. Set in deprived Victorian London, this is a forced affair, full of turgid scenes and dialogue. It's no surprise to learn that Anthony Hopkins walked off set complaining of "creative differences"; the real mystery is why everybody else didn't follow suit. **LH**

Raul Julia *MacHeath* • Julia Migenes-Johnson *Jenny* • Richard Harris *Mr Peachum* • Julie Walters *Mrs Peachum* • Roger Daltrey *Street singer* • Rachel Robertson *Polly Peachum* • Clive Revill *Money Matthew* • Miranda Garrison *Esmerelda* ■ *Dir* Menahem Golan • *Scr* Menahem Golan, from the musical *The Threepenny Opera* by Bertolt Brecht, Kurt Weill

Mackenna's Gold ★★★ 15
Western
1969 · US · Colour · 122min

How could this possibly fail – a western about hidden Apache gold with more stars in the cast than there are twists, swindles and red herrings in the plot? Yet fail it did, and there was nothing that such powerhouse performers as Gregory Peck, Omar Sharif and Edward G Robinson could do about it. Carl Foreman's script may be cliché ridden, but J Lee Thompson's direction is vigorous. **DP** Violence, swearing. *DVD*

Gregory Peck *Mackenna* • Omar Sharif *Colorado* • Telly Savalas *Sergeant Tibbs* • Camilla Sparv *Inga* • Keenan Wynn *Sanchez* • Julie Newmar *Heshke* • Ted Cassidy *Hachita* • Lee J Cobb *Editor* • Raymond Massey *Preacher* • Burgess Meredith *Storekeeper* • Anthony Quayle *Older Englishman* • Edward G Robinson *Old Adams* • Eli Wallach *Ben Baker* ■ *Dir* J Lee Thompson • *Scr* Carl Foreman, from the novel by Will Henry [Heck Allen]

The McKenzie Break ★★★★ 12
Second World War drama
1970 · UK · Colour · 105min

This unusual slant on the prisoner-of-war escape movie has members of a German U-boat crew in a Scottish internment camp plan to make their getaway. Brian Keith's intelligence officer finds himself opposing Helmut Griem's fanatical Nazi, who is willing to sacrifice others for the glory of the Fatherland. Directed by Lamont Johnson, this rare and interesting movie acknowledges that guards can only run such lock-ups efficiently with the tacit permission of the prisoners. Keith and Griem turn in admirable performances, and the tense script ensures a nail-biting finish. **TH** Violence, swearing. *DVD*

Brian Keith *Captain Jack Connor* • Helmut Griem *Kapitan Schluetter* • Ian Hendry *Major Perry* • Jack Watson *General Kerr* • Patrick O'Connell *Sergeant Major Cox* • Horst Janson *Neuchl* • Alexander Allerson *Von Sperrle* • John Abineri *Kranz* ■ *Dir* Lamont Johnson • *Scr* William Norton, from the novel *The Bowmanville Break* by Sidney Shelley

The Mackintosh Man ★★ 15
Spy thriller
1973 · UK · Colour · 95min

This movie has everything you would expect of a Cold War thriller – and therein lies its problem. Walter Hill has made a smooth enough job of adapting Desmond Bagley's novel, but John Huston handles the cleverly crafted frame-up, the ingenious escapes and the finale in Malta with little conviction. Paul Newman and James Mason seem equally distracted as, respectively, the undercover agent and the high-ranking MP who is not what he seems. **DP**

Paul Newman *Joseph Rearden* • James Mason *Sir George Wheeler* • Dominique Sanda *Mrs Smith* • Harry Andrews *Angus Mackintosh* • Nigel Patrick *Soames-Trevelyan* • Ian Bannen *Slade* • Peter Vaughan *Brunskill* • Roland Culver *Judge* • Michael Hordern *Brown* ■ *Dir* John Huston • *Scr* Walter Hill, (uncredited) William Fairchild, from Desmond Bagley's novel *The Freedom Trap*

McLibel ★★★
Documentary
2005 · UK · Colour · 86min

Barmaid Helen Steel and postman Dave Morris here receive a decent tribute to their heroic stance against the might of McDonald's despite this documentary having a somewhat home-made look to it. Yet, for all its flaws as a film, this feature-length version of Fran Armstrong's 1998 account of their libel proceedings – which now boasts some rather perfunctory courtroom sequences by Ken Loach – really does capture the enormity of the couple's victory in the face of the multinational's financial clout and the vagaries of the British legal system. The issues raised about fast food and the human, animal and environmental exploitation involved in its production are as persuasive as the science on the damaging effects of a bad diet. **DP** *DVD*

■ *Dir* Franny Armstrong, Ken Loach • *Scr* Franny Armstrong

McLintock! ★★★ U
Comedy western
1963 · US · Colour · 122min

This rollicking John Wayne vehicle is a real Wayne family affair: it co-stars one son, Patrick, and another, Michael, produced the movie. He also issued it in varying forms, shortened, and with different music, but the best version, is the full two hours-plus Panavisioned opus. It's basically a rewrite of *The Taming of the Shrew*, with all the pre-feminist attitudes endemic to that Shakespeare comedy – attitudes, one suspects, held by the Duke himself. Rowdy, rude and rather dated. **TS** *DVD*

John Wayne *George Washington McLintock* • Maureen O'Hara *Katherine McLintock* • Yvonne De Carlo *Louise Warren* • Patrick Wayne *Devlin Warren* • Stefanie Powers *Becky McLintock* • Jack Kruschen *Birnbaum* • Chill Wills *Drago* ■ *Dir* Andrew V McLaglen • *Scr* James Edward Grant

The Macomber Affair ★★★
Romantic drama
1947 · US · BW · 89min

Based on a brilliant story by Ernest Hemingway, this is a serious – perhaps too serious – film attempt at translating the author's prose to the silver screen. Gregory Peck is wooden in the lead, but Robert Preston and Joan Bennett have a rare intelligence as a sparky married couple who are on safari under Peck's wing. A hard film to like, but an easy one to admire, and a must for collectors of filmed Hemingway. **TS**

Gregory Peck *Robert Wilson* • Robert Preston *Francis Macomber* • Joan Bennett *Margaret Macomber* • Reginald Denny *Captain Smollet* • Carl Harbord *Coroner* ■ *Dir* Zoltan Korda • *Scr* Casey Robinson, Seymour Bennett, Frank Arnold, from the story *The Short Happy Life of Francis Macomber* by Ernest Hemingway

Macon County Line ★★★
Crime drama
1973 · US · Colour · 88min

Max Baer Jr (*The Beverly Hillbillies*) wrote, produced and co-starred in this minor drive-in classic. Two footloose brothers, one of whom is about to go into the army, pick up a girl and go on one last hellraising spree in 1950s Georgia, only to run foul of a redneck sheriff who hunts them down for a murder they didn't commit. Supposedly based on a true story, this isn't your average "good ol' boy" flick. Although director Richard Compton has much to say about gun use and small-town mores, the melodrama of the piece swamps any message. Compton directed a disappointing sequel, *Return to Macon County* (1975). **RS**

Alan Vint *Chris Dixon* • Cheryl Waters *Jenny* • Geoffrey Lewis *Hamp* • Joan Blackman *Carol Morgan* • Jesse Vint *Wayne Dixon* • Max Baer Jr *Deputy Morgan* • Sam Gilman *Deputy Bill* ■ *Dir* Richard Compton • *Scr* Max Baer Jr, Richard Compton, from a story by Max Baer Jr

McQ ★★ 15
Thriller
1974 · US · Colour · 106min

Star John Wayne and director John Sturges were both past their action prime when they collaborated on this ill-conceived excursion into *Dirty Harry* territory. Cop Wayne hands in his badge as he pursues the truth about his murdered pal. The car-chase finale on the beach is particularly poorly staged, but this will come as no surprise. Shot in Seattle, this is watchable mainly for the scenery and the solid supporting performances. **TS** Violence, swearing.

John Wayne *Detective Lt Lon McQ* • Eddie Albert *Capt Ed Kosterman* • Diana Muldaur *Lois Boyle* • Colleen Dewhurst *Myra* • Clu Gulager *Franklin Toms* • David Huddleston *Edward M "Pinky" Farrow* ■ *Dir* John Sturges • *Scr* Lawrence Roman

McVicar ★★ 18
Prison drama
1980 · UK · Colour · 107min

This is an ill-conceived account, based on his autobiography, of folk hero John McVicar's escape from Durham prison. The Who's Roger Daltrey was one of the producers and the band had a hand in the noisy, inappropriate rock score. Daltrey also attempts the role of McVicar, while another pop singer, Adam Faith, plays his mate Walter. Tom Clegg directs it all in slam-bang *Sweeney* style. **DM** *DVD*

Roger Daltrey *John McVicar* • Adam Faith *Walter Probyn* • Cheryl Campbell *Sheila McVicar* • Billy Murray *Joey Davis* • Georgina Hale *Kate* • Ian Hendry *Hitchens* • Steven Berkoff *Ronnie Harrison* ■ *Dir* Tom Clegg • *Scr* Tom Clegg, John McVicar, from the autobiography *McVicar by Himself* by John McVicar

Mad about Mambo ★★★ 12
Romantic comedy
1999 · UK/US · Colour · 88min

Actor Gabriel Byrne executive produced this agreeable fairy-tale romance, set in Belfast, about a talented schoolboy footballer (William Ash). Inspired by the words of a Brazilian player who says "we don't run with the ball, we dance", he starts taking samba lessons in order to find some rhythm. Soon he is catching the eye of pretty dance champion Keri Russell, but their class differences, and her football commitments and her ex-boyfriend threaten to ruin the happy ending. This feel-good confection is engagingly played by the two young stars. JC *DVD*

William Ash *Danny Mitchell* • Keri Russell *Lucy McLoughlin* • Brian Cox (1) *Sidney McLoughlin* • Theo Fraser Steele *Oliver* • Julian Littman *Rudi Morelli* • Maclean Stewart *Mickey* ■ *Dir/Scr* John Forte

Mad about Men ★★ U
Fantasy   1954 · UK · Colour · 81min

Director Ralph Thomas, so effective with the *Doctor* series, is out of his depth with this slice of outdated hokum, a cliché-ridden story that's a sequel to the first mermaid movie *Miranda*. Glynis Johns still looks good as the aquatic star, swapping roles with a sports mistress who's going on holiday, but this is certainly not the equal of the charming original. TH *DVD*

Glynis Johns *Miranda/Caroline* • Anne Crawford *Barbara* • Donald Sinden *Jeff Saunders* • Margaret Rutherford *Nurse Cary* • Dora Bryan *Berengaria* • Nicholas Phipps *Barclay Sutton* • Peter Martyn *Ronald* • Noel Purcell *Old Salt* • Joan Hickson *Mrs Forster* • Irene Handl *Madame Blanche* ■ *Dir* Ralph Thomas • *Scr* Peter Blackmore

Mad about Music ★★★ U
Drama   1938 · US · BW · 91min

In her third starring role, Deanna Durbin plays the daughter of a vain actress (Gail Patrick) who keeps her hidden away at a Swiss school. There the parentless girl invents a romantic explorer father and regales her fellow pupils with his exploits. When her deception looks about to be revealed, she dragoons a bemused but co-operative Herbert Marshall into impersonating her fantasy. Like all of Durbin's vehicles, this is charming, delightful nonsense. RK *DVD*

Deanna Durbin *Gloria Harkinson* • Herbert Marshall *Richard Todd* • Arthur Treacher *Tripps* • Gail Patrick *Gwen Taylor* • William Frawley *Dusty Rhodes* • Jackie Moran *Tommy* • Helen Parrish *Felice* ■ *Dir* Norman Taurog • *Scr* Bruce Manning, Felix Jackson, from a story by Marcella Burke, Frederick Kohner

Mad City ★★★★ 12
Crime drama   1997 · US · Colour · 110min

John Travolta is the museum security guard who resorts to the desperate measure of holding a group of children hostage after he loses his job. In this 1990s version of *Ace in the Hole*, Dustin Hoffman is the ageing newsman in need of a career break, who decides to manipulate Travolta for his own ends. Surprisingly dark for a Hollywood movie, this works exceptionally well thanks to a well thought-out script, subtle direction and superb performances from Travolta, Hoffman and Alan Alda as his news rival. JB Swearing, violence. *DVD*

Dustin Hoffman *Max Brackett* • John Travolta *Sam Baily* • Alan Alda *Kevin Hollander* • Mia Kirshner *Laurie Callahan* • Ted Levine *Alvin Lemke* • Robert Prosky *Lou Potts* • Blythe Danner *Mrs Banks* • William Atherton *Dohlen* ■ *Dir* Costa-Gavras • *Scr* Tom Matthews, Eric Williams, from a story by Tom Matthews

Mad Cows ★ 15
Comedy   1999 · UK · Colour · 86min

Kathy Lette's bestselling comic novel transfers to the screen with tiresomely over-the-top characters, amateurish direction and a witless script. Anna Friel nails the accent as Australian single mum Maddy, but her gamine looks and limited skills render her character unconvincing. If the poor performances and stupid story don't drive you mad, the heavy-handed, "wacky" camerawork should finish the job. JC Drug abuse, nudity. *DVD*

Anna Friel *Maddy* • Joanna Lumley *Gillian* • Anna Massey *Dwina Phelps* • Phyllida Law *Lady Drake* • Greg Wise *Alex* • John Standing *Johnny Vaguelawn* • Prunella Scales *Dr Minny Stinkler* • Mohamed Al-Fayed *Harrods doorman* • Meg Mathews *Harrods shopper* ■ *Dir* Sara Sugarman • *Scr* Sasha Hails, Sara Sugarman, from the novel by Kathy Lette

Mad Detective ★★★ 15
Crime thriller   2007 · HK · Colour · 85min

In this offbeat crime thriller from co-directors Johnnie To and Wai Ka-Fai, eccentric but gifted former detective Lau Ching Wan is enlisted by ex-colleague Andy On to solve the mystery of a missing cop whose gun has been used in a number of crimes. This engaging thriller is undermined somewhat by the muddled script and the directors never quite solve the problem of how to depict the "invisible personalities" that Lau can somehow see within the damaged psyche of the missing cop's partner. Still, the film does feature several imaginative and stylish set pieces. DP Cantonese, English +subtitles. Violence. *DVD BD*

Lau Ching Wan *Inspector Chan Kwai Bun* • Andy On *Inspector Ho Ka On* • Lam Ka Tung *Ko Chi-Wai* • Kelly Lin *May Cheung* ■ *Dir* Johnnie To, Wai Ka-Fai • *Scr* Wai Ka-Fai, Au Kin Yee [Kin Yee Au]

The Mad Doctor of Market Street ★★★
Drama   1942 · US · BW · 60min

Slyly derivative of HG Wells's *The Island of Dr Moreau*, this schlocky drama stars Lionel Atwill as a deranged doctor forced to quit his plush New York surgery for indulging in strange practices. Fleeing by boat, he is shipwrecked on a desert island with a bunch of survivors whom he decides to turn into zombies. Cult director Joseph H Lewis keeps his tongue firmly in cheek, but his film has quite a narrative pull. TH

Una Merkel *Aunt Margaret* • Lionel Atwill *Dr Benson* • Nat Pendleton *"Red"* • Claire Dodd *Patricia Wentworth* ■ *Dir* Joseph H Lewis • *Scr* Al Martin

Mad Dog ★★★★ 15
Biographical action drama   1976 · Aus · Colour · 98min

Australia, 1854, and young Dennis Hopper, partaking of opium in Chinatown, survives a massacre and is sentenced to a dozen years after stealing some clothing. Raped in jail, he gets out after six years and becomes a legendary outlaw, Mad Dog Morgan. With his boomerang-throwing, didgeridoo-playing partner, played by David Gulpilil from *Walkabout*, Hopper is every inch the social bandit, and writer/director Philippe Mora surely skews a few facts to make us regard him as a hero. Superbly shot and pacily directed. AT *DVD*

Dennis Hopper *Daniel Morgan* • Jack Thompson *Detective Manwaring* • David Gulpilil *Billy* • Frank Thring *Superintendent Cobham* • Michael Pate *Superintendent Winch* • Wallas Eaton *Macpherson* • Bill Hunter *Sgt Smith* ■ *Dir* Philippe Mora • *Scr* Philippe Mora, from the book *Morgan the Bold Bushranger* by Margaret Carnegie

Mad Dog and Glory ★★★ 15
Romantic drama   1992 · US · Colour and BW · 97min

In this intriguing oddity, Robert De Niro stars as the "Mad Dog" of the title, a shy, quiet police forensics photographer who saves the life of mobster and aspiring stand-up comedian Bill Murray. In return, he gets a "present" – Uma Thurman – but the arrangement becomes complicated when the mismatched duo fall in love. The direction from John McNaughton is subtle, even though he has difficulty keeping the diverse elements of the story together, but he's helped by an understated performance from De Niro, and a rather strange one from Murray. JF Violence, swearing, nudity. *DVD*

Robert De Niro *Wayne Dobie* • Uma Thurman *Glory* • Bill Murray *Frank Milo* • David Caruso *Mike* • Mike Starr *Harold* • Tom Towles *Andrew* • Kathy Baker *Lee* ■ *Dir* John McNaughton • *Scr* Richard Price

Mad Dog Coll ★★
Biographical crime drama   1961 · US · BW · 87min

Initially rejected by the British censor, this violent biopic of the eponymous gangster marked the film debut of Gene Hackman, in

a small role as a policeman. The eagle-eyed will also spot early screen appearances by a hirsute Telly Savalas and a youthful Vincent Gardenia. The movie was one of a handful directed by Burt Balaban, an ex-marine and combat cameraman, who died in 1965. BB

John Davis Chandler *Vincent Coll* • Kay Doubleday *Clio* • Brooke Hayward *Elizabeth* • Neil Nephew *Rocco* • Jerry Orbach *Joe* • Telly Savalas *Lieutenant Darrell* • Vincent Gardenia *Dutch Schultz* • Gene Hackman *Cop* ■ *Dir* Burt Balaban • *Scr* Edward Schreiber, from material by Leo Lieberman

Mad Dogs and Englishmen ★ 18
Thriller   1994 · UK · Colour · 93min

The links between drug addiction and the privileged classes form the basis of this completely misguided thriller. In an awful performance, Elizabeth Hurley plays an upper-class heroin addict who floats through stately homes surrounded by pompous twits and listless "Hooray Henriettas". Joss Ackland puts in an even worse turn as the investigating cockney policeman, while everyone else gamely tries to make sense of the dreadful dialogue. AJ Swearing, violence, drug abuse, sex scenes.

Elizabeth Hurley *Antonia Dyer* • C Thomas Howell *Mike Stone* • Joss Ackland *Inspector Sam Stringer* • Claire Bloom *Liz Stringer* • Jeremy Brett *Tony Vernon-Smith* • Frederick Treves *Sir Harry Dyer* • Andrew Connolly *Clive Nathan* ■ *Dir* Henry Cole • *Scr* Tim Sewell, from a story by Henry Cole

The Mad Game ★★★
Crime drama   1933 · US · BW · 73min

When the former partners-in-crime of imprisoned bootlegger Spencer Tracy kidnap the children of the judge (Ralph Morgan) who put him away, Tracy is let loose to help track down the guilty men. Directed by Irving Cummings and co-starring Claire Trevor as a reporter who takes a shine to Tracy, this routine crime movie is kept very watchable by the star. RK

Spencer Tracy *Edward Carson* • Claire Trevor *Jane Lee* • Ralph Morgan *Judge Penfield* • J Carrol Naish *Chopper Allen* • John Miljan *William Bennett* ■ *Dir* Irving Cummings • *Scr* William Conselman, Henry Johnson

The Mad Genius ★★★
Drama   1931 · US · BW · 81min

Matinée idol John Barrymore had tremendous success with the movie version of *Svengali*, and Warner Bros ordered an immediate follow-up. This virtual sequel was released later the same year, and, helped by a better director in Michael Curtiz, Barrymore is sensational. This movie does seem freer than *Svengali* in dealing with similar themes, though its plot is based on the bizarre relationship between ballet impresario Diaghilev and his star dancer Nijinsky. TS

John Barrymore *Ivan Tzarakov* • Marian Marsh *Nana* • Donald Cook *Fedor* • Charles Butterworth *Karinsky* • Luis Alberni *Serge Bankieff* • Carmel Myers *Preskoya* • André Luguet *Bartag* • Frankie Darro *Fedor as a boy* • Boris Karloff *Fedor's father* ■ *Dir* Michael Curtiz • *Scr* J Grubb Alexander, Harvey Thew, from the play *The Idol* by Martin Brown

Mad Love ★★★★
Horror   1935 · US · BW · 67min

Peter Lorre made his American debut in this, one of the all-time classic horror stories, the first sound remake of the 1925 silent shocker *The Hands of Orlac*. Colin Clive is the concert pianist given the hands of an executed killer when his own are lost in an accident. Lorre brilliantly conveys twisted compassion and obsessive madness as the surgeon who performs the operation because he loves the pianist's actress wife. A real chiller about psychological fear, made even more effective by Karl Freund's hard-edged poetic direction, way ahead of its time for atmosphere, eerie visuals and imaginative camera technique. AJ

Peter Lorre *Doctor Gogol* • Frances Drake *Yvonne Orlac* • Colin Clive *Stephen Orlac* • Ted Healy *Reagan* • Sara Haden *Marie* • Edward Brophy *Rollo* • Henry Kolker *Prefect Rosset* • May Beatty *Françoise* ■ *Dir* Karl Freund • *Scr* Guy Endore, PJ Wolfson, John L Balderston, from the novel *Les Mains d'Orlac* by Maurice Renard • *Cinematographers* Gregg Toland, Chester Lyons

Mad Love ★★ 15
Romantic drama   1995 · US · Colour · 92min

British director Antonia Bird made her Hollywood debut with this uninspired reworking of the tired teens-on-the-run theme. She puts her foot on the emotional pedal just as the action needs to be approached with care, with the consequence that Drew Barrymore's increasingly unpredictable behaviour becomes irritating rather than harrowing. Without depth, Paula Milne's script is a hotch-potch of half-digested clichés. DP Violence, swearing, nudity. *DVD*

Chris O'Donnell *Matt* • Drew Barrymore *Casey* • Matthew Lillard *Eric* • Richard Chaim *Duncan* • Robert Nadir *Coach* • Joan Allen *Margaret* • Jude Ciccolella *Richard* • Amy Sakasitz *Joanna* ■ *Dir* Antonia Bird • *Scr* Paula Milne

The Mad Magician ★★★
Horror   1954 · US · BW · 72min

When *House of Wax* became a huge hit, Vincent Price was thrown into a quickie imitation with a similar turn-of-the-century setting, fantastic plot and lurid murders. He hams it up endearingly as a deranged illusionist who kills the rival who stole his outrageous tricks, and then assumes his identity. Wonderfully over-the-top nonsense, with Price badly dubbed each time he's in disguise. It was originally shot in 3D, which explains some of the weirder effects. AJ

Vincent Price *Gallico* • Mary Murphy (1) *Karen Lee* • Eva Gabor *Claire* • John Emery *Rinaldi* • Donald Randolph *Ross Ormond* • Lenita Lane *Alice Prentiss* • Patrick O'Neal (1) *Bruce Allen* ■ *Dir* John Brahm • *Scr* Crane Wilbur

M

Mad Max ★★★★★ 18
Futuristic action adventure   1979 · Aus · Colour · 88min

Despite its low budget, this highly inventive, violent action picture became an international hit, made a star of Mel Gibson and spawned two sequels. Gibson is at his mean and moody best as a heroic cop, one of the few who are left trying to hold together a disintegrating society in a bleak and desolate future. What the film lacks in repartee, it makes up for in rip-roaring spectacle, marvellous chase sequences, terrific stunts and natty leather costumes, setting an early example of grunge chic. In his debut feature, director George Miller exhibits a striking visual style. AJ Violence, swearing, nudity. *DVD BD*

Mel Gibson *Max Rockatansky* • Joanne Samuel *Jessie* • Hugh Keays-Byrne *Toecutter* • Steve Bisley *Jim Goose* • Tim Burns (1) *Johnny the Boy* • Roger Ward *Fifi Macaffee* • Vince Gil *Nightrider* • Geoff Parry *Bubba Zanetti* ■ *Dir* George Miller • *Scr* George Miller, James McCausland, from a story by George Miller, Byron Kennedy

Mad Max 2 ★★★★ 18
Futuristic action adventure   1981 · Aus · Colour · 95min

After the low-budget nihilism of the original movie, director George Miller moved up a gear and the result was this violent, slick and exhilarating action thriller that further helped launch Mel Gibson into superstardom. His police days now well behind him, Mel the road warrior comes to the aid of a peace-loving group that owns a valuable source of fuel and is being threatened by the voracious gangs that patrol the highways of the future. Gibson is charismatic as the hero, and Miller doesn't take his foot off the accelerator for a second. JF Violence, swearing, a sex scene, nudity. *DVD BD*

Mel Gibson *Max Rockatansky* • Bruce Spence *Gyro captain* • Vernon Wells *Wez* • Mike Preston [Michael Preston] *Pappagallo* • Emil Minty *Feral Kid* • Kjell Nilsson *Humungus* • Virginia Hey

Warrior woman • Syd Heylen *Curmudgeon* ■ *Dir* George Miller (2) • *Scr* Terry Hayes, George Miller, Brian Hannant

Mad Max beyond Thunderdome ★★★ 15

Futuristic action adventure
1985 · Aus · Colour · 102min

The third in Mel Gibson's sci-fi series is the weakest, but it remains a hugely entertaining futuristic spectacular. This time around Gibson finds himself a reluctant surrogate father to a lost tribe of youngsters, as well as getting mixed up with gladiatorial battles in the thunderdome of the wild city of Bartertown, ruled over by the extraordinary Tina Turner. Directors George Miller and George Ogilvie stage some exhilarating set pieces and keep the action bustling along nicely, even if there are also some daft dollops of new ageism. JF Violence, swearing. DVD SD

Mel Gibson *Mad Max* • Tina Turner *Aunty Entity* • Bruce Spence *Jedediah* • Adam Cockburn *Jedediah Jr* • Frank Thring *The collector* • Angelo Rossitto *The master* • Paul Larsson *The blaster* • Angry Anderson *Ironbar* ■ *Dir* George Miller (2), George Ogilvie • *Scr* Terry Hayes, George Miller

Mad Max: Fury Road ★★★★ 15

Futuristic action adventure
2015 · Aus/US · Colour · 115min

George Miller brings the futuristic franchise thundering back to life, a lot less lean but just as mean, more than three decades after Mel Gibson donned the leathers. Miller puts a feminist spin on it, too, by placing Charlize Theron in the driving seat as Furiosa while Max (this time played by Tom Hardy) is her wingman. They embark on what is essentially one big, bone-rattling chase through the desert to escape tribal leader Immortan Joe (Hugh Keays-Byrne who played Toecutter in the original 1979 film) and his hot-wheeled henchmen. Theron's Furiosa is the beating heart at the centre of all this chaos, and balancing her fury is the quietly magnetic Hardy as the machismo and machine-based mayhem keep the adrenaline pumping. SP Violence. DVD SD SD

Tom Hardy *Max Rockatansky* • Charlize Theron *Imperator Furiosa* • Nicholas Hoult *Nux* • Hugh Keays-Byrne *Immortan Joe* • Zoë Kravitz *Toast* • Rosie Huntington-Whiteley *Splendid* ■ *Dir* George Miller (2) • *Scr* Nick Lathouris, Brendan McCarthy, George Miller (2)

The Mad Miss Manton ★★★ U

Screwball comedy murder mystery
1938 · US · BW · 80min

Barbara Stanwyck is a delight as the Manhattan debutante and amateur detective, and so is Henry Fonda as the obsessive but romantically rather awkward newspaper editor who finds they are both chasing the same murder story. There are borrowings from *The Thin Man* and any number of screwball comedies here, and the result is slight and completely artificial. Thanks to the appeal of its stars, it's slyly enjoyable. AT DVD

Barbara Stanwyck *Melsa Manton* • Henry Fonda *Peter Ames* • Sam Levene *Lieutenant Brent* • Frances Mercer *Helen Frayne* • Stanley Ridges *Edward Norris* • Whitney Bourne *Pat James* • Vicki Lester *Kit Beverly* • Hattie McDaniel *Hilda* ■ *Dir* Leigh Jason • *Scr* Phillip J Epstein, Hal Yates, from a story by Wilson Collison

Mad Money ★★★ 12

Crime comedy 2008 · US/UK · Colour · 99min

Girl power gets greedy in this fast-paced crime caper about a trio of women who rob a Kansas City bank. Diane Keaton stars as a debt-ridden desperate housewife who takes a job as a cleaner in the high-tech, high-security bank and recruits co-workers Queen Latifah (sassy) and Katie Holmes (dippy) for a cunning plan: the women will steal used notes scheduled for shredding and sneak them out in their knickers. Zipping along with plenty of panache, this chick flick gets by on the novelty pairing of its three unlikely leads and the incongruous

sight of Keaton in a jumpsuit, scrubbing toilets. JR Swearing, sexual references. DVD

Diane Keaton *Bridget Cardigan* • Queen Latifah *Nina Brewster* • Katie Holmes *Jackie Truman* • Ted Danson *Don Cardigan* • Stephen Root *Glover* • Chris McDonald *Bryce Arbogast* ■ *Dir* Callie Khouri • *Scr* Glenn Gers

Mad Monster Party ★★★ U

Animated comedy horror
1966 · US · Colour · 91min

Baron Boris von Frankenstein (voiced by Boris Karloff) throws a retirement party and invites all his celebrity monster friends in this fun animated feature, filmed in the "Animagic" process using stop-motion puppets. Co-written by Harvey Kurtzman, the creator of *Mad* magazine, the film also includes contributions by Forrest J Ackerman, editor of *Famous Monsters of Filmland*. Dracula, the Creature from the Black Lagoon, Dr Jekyll and Mr Hyde, the Mummy, the Invisible Man and the Hunchback of Notre Dame all make the guest list in an enchanting blend of horror and comedy. AJ

Boris Karloff *Baron Boris von Frankenstein* • Ethel Ennis • Gale Garnett *Francesca* • Phyllis Diller *Frankenstein's wife* • Allen Swift *Felix Flankin/Dracula/Invisible Man/Dr Jekyll/Mr Hyde* • Jack Davis *Puppet Designer* ■ *Dir* Jules Bass • *Scr* Len Korobkin, Harvey Kurtzman, Forrest J Ackerman (uncredited), from a story by Arthur Rankin Jr

Mad Wednesday ★★★ U

Comedy 1950 · US · BW · 76min

Originally released in 1947 as *The Sin of of Harold Diddlebock*, Preston Sturges's film was re-edited and re-released in 1950 as this. The brilliant premise has elegant silent movie clown Harold Lloyd (in his final role) in a story showing what has happened to one of his earlier creations, the football hero star of *The Freshman* (1925). Thus two comic giants were united on one project and, although this is not a masterpiece, it still features some wonderful comic moments. The longer (89-minute) original merits another star. DF

Harold Lloyd *Harold Diddlebock* • Frances Ramsden *Miss Otis* • Jimmy Conlin *Wormy* • Raymond Walburn *EJ Waggleberry* • Edgar Kennedy *Jake, the bartender* • Arline Judge *Manicurist* • Franklin Pangborn *Formfit Franklin* • Lionel Stander *Max* • Margaret Hamilton *Flora* ■ *Dir/Scr* Preston Sturges

Mad, Sad & Bad ★ 15

Comedy drama 2009 · UK · Colour · 90min

Their mother's death provides a moment for reflection in the tangled lives of three British Asian siblings in this modest comedy drama. Meera Syal plays the sad sister – a spinster forced to change her ways when her mum throws her out of the house – and makes something from her ugly duckling role, but everyone else is left high and dry by the painfully thin material. It's uninspired and thoroughly uninvolving. TJ Violence, swearing, sex scenes.

Meera Syal *Rashmi* • Nitin Ganatra *Atul* • Zubin Varla *Hardeep* • Leena Dhingra *Usha* • Tony Gardner *Graham* • Ayesha Dharkar *Roxy* ■ *Dir/Scr* Avie Luthra

Madagascar ★★★ U

Animated comedy adventure
2005 · US · Colour · 82min

In this entertaining family film, Chris Rock and Ben Stiller provide the voices for Marty the zebra and Alex, a preening lion, who enjoy a comfortable existence in Manhattan's Central Park Zoo until Marty expresses a desire to return the wild. What follows is a predictable but engaging series of mishaps that land the pair in Africa, along with a neurotic giraffe (David Schwimmer) and a no-nonsense hippo (Jada Pinkett Smith). The pace drags in the last third of the movie, but the film is always marvellous to look at and the sight gags come thick and fast. GM DVD SD

Ben Stiller *Alex the Lion* • Chris Rock *Marty the Zebra* • David Schwimmer *Melman the Giraffe* • Jada Pinkett Smith *Gloria the Hippo* • Sacha Baron Cohen *King Julien* • Cedric the Entertainer

Maurice • Andy Richter *Mort* ■ *Dir* Eric Darnell, Tom McGrath • *Scr* Mark Burton, Billy Frolick, Eric Darnell, Tom McGrath

Madagascar: Escape 2 Africa ★★ PG

Animated comedy adventure
2008 · US · Colour · 85min

Hit films invariably spawn sequels and here we rejoin Alex the Lion, Marty the Zebra and the rest of the menagerie, who are still stranded in Madagascar. For the first 20 minutes, this follow-up does seem well worth a second visit, as the scene-stealing penguins fix up a crashed plane in an attempt to get back home. But then, just like the aircraft, the film rather runs out of gas. The plane goes down on the African plains, where Alex meets his long-lost family, and the story then becomes yet another riff on the *The Lion King*. Still, there are enough witty lines and cute animated animals for the target audience. DA DVD SD

Ben Stiller *Alex the Lion* • Chris Rock *Marty the Zebra* • David Schwimmer *Melman the Giraffe* • Jada Pinkett Smith *Gloria the Hippo* • Sacha Baron Cohen *King Julien* • Cedric the Entertainer *Maurice* • Bernie Mac *Zuba* • Alec Baldwin *Makunga* ■ *Dir* Eric Darnell, Tom McGrath • *Scr* Eric Darnell, Tom McGrath, Etan Cohen

Madagascar 3: Europe's Most Wanted ★★★ PG

Animated comedy adventure
2012 · US · Colour · 89min

In this good-looking but hyperactive film, Alex the Lion and co are still animals abroad, and desperate to get back home to their New York zoo. But, courtesy of encounters with a travelling circus and a dogged French animal-control officer voiced by Frances McDormand, they soon discover that you have to be careful what you wish for – because you just might get it. As ever, the "mobster" penguins effortlessly steal a show that lurches maniacally from one haphazard scene to another. It may lack a little in charm and warmth, but the technical brilliance goes some way towards compensating. The *Penguins of Madagascar* is due in late 2014. DA

Ben Stiller *Alex* • Chris Rock *Marty* • David Schwimmer *Melman* • Jada Pinkett Smith *Gloria* • Jessica Chastain *Gia* • Martin Short *Stefano* • Sacha Baron Cohen *King Julien XIII* ■ *Dir* Tom McGrath, Conrad Vernon, Eric Darnell • *Scr* Noah Baumbach, Eric Darnell, from characters by Darnell, Mark Burton, Billy Frolick, Tom McGrath

Madagascar Skin ★★★ 15

Drama 1995 · UK · Colour · 91min

Slow-moving and often wordless, director Chris Newby's follow-up to the enigmatic *Anchoress* is a weird boy-meets-boy fable. Bored with the big city, John Hannah (his face covered with a birthmark in the shape of Madagascar) heads for the coast where he discovers cheeky Bernard Hill buried up to his neck in sand. When the two outcasts set up home together in a semi-derelict cottage, this strangely endearing chamber piece becomes an inventive and brave drama. AJ Swearing.

Bernard Hill *Flint* • John Hannah *Harry* • Mark Anthony *Adonis* • Mark Petit *Lover* • Danny Earl *Lover* • Robin Neath *Thug* • Simon Bennett *Thug* ■ *Dir/Scr* Chris Newby

Madam Satan ★

Comedy musical 1930 · US · BW · 80min

Directed by Cecil B DeMille, this must be one of the most bizarre films ever made. It begins as a supposed comedy of manners, with socialite Kay Johnson catching on to the fact that her frivolous husband, Reginald Denny, is having an affair with good-time girl Lillian Roth. Played as a mind-numbingly unfunny and badly acted farce for the first half, it becomes a characteristic DeMille extravaganza in the second. RK

Kay Johnson *Angela Brooks* • Reginald Denny *Bob Brooks* • Roland Young *Jimmy Wade* • Lillian Roth *Trixie* • Elsa Peterson *Martha* ■ *Dir* Cecil B DeMille • *Scr* Jeanie Macpherson, Gladys Unger, Elsie Janis

Madame ★★

Period comedy 1961 · Fr/It/Sp · Colour · 100min

Sophia Loren plays the woman who does Napoleon's laundry, though this is before he started to own most of Europe. This adaptation, directed by swashbuckler specialist Christian-Jaque, is a pleasantly frothy affair, with Loren falling for Robert Hossein's nobleman, marrying him and generally leading from the front in the manner of her Italian comedies. AT Italian dubbed.

Sophia Loren *Madame Catherine Hubscher* • Robert Hossein *Lefebvre* • Julien Bertheau *Napoleon Bonaparte* • Marina Berti *Elisa* • Carlo Giuffrè *Jerome* ■ *Dir* Christian-Jaque • *Scr* Henri Jeanson, Ennio De Concini, Christian-Jaque, Franco Solinas, Jean Ferry, from the play *Madame Sans-Gêne* by Emile Moreau, Victorien Sardou

Madame Bovary ★★★★

Period romance 1933 · Fr · BW · 101min

What a tragedy that the producers of this fascinating adaptation of Flaubert's classic novel should have felt the need to cut over an hour from the three-hour original in the interests of commercial viability. Director Jean Renoir had attempted to translate the novel's subtle symbolism into cinematic terms and, through his pioneering use of deep-focus photography, he succeeded in visibly locating his heroine in the stifling provincial surroundings that so repressed her spirit. You'll either love or loathe Valentine Tessier's Emma Bovary, but there's no doubting the quality of Renoir's elder brother Pierre's performance as the insensitive doctor. A remarkable film. DP French +subtitles.

Valentine Tessier *Emma Bovary* • Pierre Renoir *Charles Bovary* • Fernand Fabre *Rodolphe Boulanger* • Daniel Lecourtois *Leon* • Pierre Larquey *Hippolyte* • Christiane Dor *Madame Le François* • Monette Dinay *Félicité* • Alice Tissot *Madame Bovary, Charles's mother* ■ *Dir* Jean Renoir • *Scr* Jean Renoir, from Gustave Flaubert's novel

Madame Bovary ★★★

Period romance 1949 · US · BW · 114min

James Mason, as author Gustave Flaubert, defends his renowned tale in flashback from a Paris court in which he finds himself accused of violating contemporary morality. The story he recounts is dressed in MGM's finest 1940s production values, and directed by master of style Vincente Minnelli, whose wonderful ball sequence is one of the cinema's great unrecognised set pieces. Unfortunately, Jennifer Jones lacks the range for Emma Bovary, but she tries gamely, while Van Heflin and Louis Jourdan as her husband and lover respectively are both perfectly cast. This film was critically abused in its day, but now stands up well against other screen versions. TS

Jennifer Jones *Emma Bovary* • James Mason *Gustave Flaubert* • Van Heflin *Charles Bovary* • Louis Jourdan *Rodolphe Boulanger* • Christopher Kent [Alf Kjellin] *Leon Dupuis* • Gene Lockhart *J Homais* • Frank Allenby *L'hereux* • Gladys Cooper *Madame Dupuis* ■ *Dir* Vincente Minnelli • *Scr* Robert Ardrey, from the novel by Gustave Flaubert

Madame Bovary ★★★ PG

Period romance 1991 · Fr · Colour · 136min

Isabelle Huppert's third movie collaboration with Claude Chabrol promised much. But their fidelity to Flaubert's novel makes this a less effective film than previous adaptations by Jean Renoir and Vincente Minnelli. As the doctor's wife tempted into adultery by the tedium of rural life, Huppert brilliantly conveys the stifled passions that bring about her ruin, while Chabrol uses all his skill at psychological dissection to expose the social and moral rigidity of the mid-19th century. DP French +subtitles. DVD

Isabelle Huppert *Emma Bovary* • Jean-François Balmer *Charles Bovary* • Jean Yanne *Monsieur Homais, Pharmacist* • Christophe Malavoy *Rodolphe Boulanger* • Lucas Belvaux *Leon Dupuis* • Jean-Louis Maury *L'heureux* ■ *Dir* Claude Chabrol • *Scr* Claude Chabrol, from the novel by Gustave Flaubert

Madame Bovary ★★
Period melodrama 2014 · US · Colour · 118min

Mia Wasikowska is striking in this retelling of the classic novel, playing a 19th century doctor's wife who goes to desperate lengths to find excitement both romantically and socially. Director Sophie Barthes's interpretation strips Bovary's world down to the essentials, with dark rooms lit by candlelight to match the film's often overwhelmingly dour tone. But, for all the charisma in Wasikowska's performance, the story lacks passion and as a result Bovary's downfall doesn't grab the viewer as it should. JL

Mia Wasikowska *Emma Bovary* • Paul Giamatti *Monsieur Homais* • Rhys Ifans *Monsieur Lheureux* • Ezra Miller *Leon Dupuis* • Logan Marshall-Green *The Marquis* • Laura Carmichael *Henriette* ■ *Dir* Sophie Barthes • *Scr* Sophie Barthes, Rose Barreneche, from Gustave Flaubert's novel

Madame Butterfly ★
Drama 1932 · US · BW · 86min

Paramount came a cropper with this film version of the classic tragedy, an updated presentation told as straight melodrama. Directed at a snail's pace by Marion Gering, with Cary Grant not at his best as Lieutenant Pinkerton, it's a turgid bore. Sylvia Sidney has the perfect face and sad soulful eyes for Butterfly, the Japanese girl whose heart is broken by Pinkerton's desertion. In the end, though, it's just not enough. RK

Sylvia Sidney *Cho-cho San* • Cary Grant *Lt BF Pinkerton* • Charlie Ruggles [Charles Ruggles] *Lt Barton* • Irving Pichel *Yamadori* • Helen Jerome Eddy *Cho-cho San's mother* • Edmund Breese *Cho-cho San's grandfather* • Louise Carter *Suzuki* ■ *Dir* Marion Gering • *Scr* Josephine Lovett, Joseph Moncure March, from the play by David Belasco, from the novel by John Luther Long

Madame Curie ★★★ U
Biographical drama 1943 · US · BW · 124min

Two hours of MGM gloss canonising the discoverer of radium might be a bit much for modern palates, but this thoughtful and finely acted biopic was the epitome of taste in its day. Greer Garson and Walter Pidgeon – as Marie and Pierre Curie – X-ray themselves into dramatic bliss, with hardly a thought for the side effects. It still represents the studio at its worthy, educational and sincere best. TS

Greer Garson *Madame Marie Curie* • Walter Pidgeon *Pierre Curie* • Robert Walker *David LeGros* • Dame May Whitty *Madame Eugene Curie* • Henry Travers *Eugene Curie* • C Aubrey Smith *Lord Kelvin* • Albert Basserman *Professor Jean Perot* ■ *Dir* Mervyn LeRoy • *Scr* Paul Osborn, Paul H Rameau, from a biography by Eve Curie

Madame de... ★★★★ U
Drama 1953 · Fr/It · BW · 95min

Although Max Ophüls's penultimate film was Oscar-nominated for its costumes, it really should have brought him a direction award, as he sends his camera on a series of gliding shots around the luxurious haunts of the idle rich, revealing their every secret and laying bare their empty souls. Danielle Darrieux is the unnamed noblewoman of the title, whose precious earrings, which she has already sold, return to her via husband Charles Boyer's mistress and her own lover, Vittorio De Sica. The script is witty, the performances beyond sophistication. This is just about as polished as European cinema gets. DP French +subtitles.

Danielle Darrieux *Countess Louise De...* • Charles Boyer *General André De...* • Vittorio De Sica *Baron Fabrizio Donati* • Mireille Perrey *Madame De...'s nurse* • Jean Debucourt *Monsieur Rémy, the jeweller* • Serge Lecointe *Jérome, his son* • Lia Di Léo *Lola, the general's mistress* • Jean

Galland *Monsieur De Bernac* ■ *Dir* Max Ophüls • *Scr* Marcel Achard, Max Ophüls, Annette Wademant, from the novel by Louise de Vilmorin

Madame Du Barry ★★
Historical drama 1934 · US · BW · 79min

Here are the life and times of Louis XV's court at Versailles, seen through the eyes of his famed mistress from the time the king takes her up to her banishment when Louis XVI succeeds to the throne. Dolores Del Rio is ravishingly beautiful, as befits the legendary Du Barry. Sadly, though, she lacks the personality required to carry this lavishly mounted but dull historical romance. Reginald Owen is the king, while a large cast impersonates the figures of the period. RK

Dolores Del Rio *Mme Du Barry* • Reginald Owen *King Louis XV* • Victor Jory *Duke D'Aiguillon* • Osgood Perkins *Richelieu* • Verree Teasdale *Duchess De Granmont* • Henry O'Neill *Duc De Choiseul* • Anita Louise *Marie Antoinette* ■ *Dir* William Dieterle • *Scr* Edward Chodorov

Madame du Barry ★★★
Historical drama 1954 · Fr/It · Colour · 110min

Martine Carol was France's leading sex symbol and top box-office attraction in the years preceding the rise of Brigitte Bardot, and many of her greatest hits were directed by her husband Christian-Jaque. Though the director was not a favourite with the critics, the public loved his work. This example has a typical mix of gorgeous settings, exuberant performances and an emphasis on entertainment rather than history. TV In French.

Martine Carol *Madame Du Barry* • André Luguet *Louis XV* • Daniel Ivernel *Count Du Barry* • Gianna-Maria Canale *Madame Gramont* ■ *Dir* Christian-Jaque • *Scr* Christian-Jaque, Albert Valentin, Henri Jeanson

Madame Pimpernel ★★
Wartime drama 1945 · US · BW · 97min

Gracie Fields's final feature betrays how little Hollywood understood the war in Europe. Also known as *Paris Underground* and re-creating a neverland French, Gregory Ratoff's romp depicts Gracie using an antiques shop as cover to help Constance Bennett smuggle airmen back to Blighty. They're highly fortunate in the fact that the Nazis are incredibly inept and even when the intrepid pair are finally captured, they are spared the usual fate for resistance activity. This did little to restore Fields's reputation with British audiences, who felt she had betrayed them by relocating to Hollywood in 1943. DP

Constance Bennett *Kitty de Mornay* • Gracie Fields *Emmyline Quayle* • George Rigaud *Andre de Mornay* • Kurt Kreuger *Captain Kurt von Weber* ■ *Dir* Gregory Ratoff • *Scr* Boris Ingster, Gertrude Purcell, from the novel *Paris Underground* by Etta Shiber • *Cinematographer* Lee Garmes

Madame Rosa ★
Drama 1977 · Fr · Colour · 105min

This is sentimental and manipulative rubbish about an Auschwitz survivor and ex-prostitute who lives out her final days in Paris cared for by an Arab youth (Samy Ben Youb). The movie is full of Arab-Israeli pieties, flashbacks to the Holocaust and a performance from Simone Signoret that was calculated to win prizes and publicity. The movie's badness didn't stop it from winning an Oscar for best foreign language film. AT French +subtitles.

Simone Signoret *Madame Rosa* • Samy Ben Youb Mohammed, "Momo" • Claude Dauphin *Dr Katz* • Gabriel Jabbour *Monsieur Hamil* • Michal Bat-Adam *Madame Nadine* • Costa-Gavras *Ramon* ■ *Dir* Moshe Mizrahi • *Scr* Moshe Mizrahi, from the novel *Momo* by Emile Ajar [Romain Gary]

Madame Sin ★★ PG
Spy thriller 1972 · US · Colour · 86min

Made for television originally, but released theatrically in the UK, this cramped-looking melodrama offers a splendid character part to Bette Davis, who loses no opportunity to chew all the scenery in sight. Co-star Robert Wagner has little to do but observe this

awesome spectacle, while director David Greene has the good sense to stand well back and let Davis queen it over a batch of English worthies. The plot, by the way, is some tortuous spy stuff about flogging off a Polaris submarine. TS

Bette Davis *Madame Sin* • Robert Wagner *Tony Lawrence* • Denholm Elliott *Malcolm* • Gordon Jackson *Commander Teddy Cavandish* • Dudley Sutton *Monk* • Catherine Schell *Barbara* • Paul Maxwell *Connors* • Roy Kinnear *Holidaymaker* ■ *Dir* David Greene • *Scr* David Greene, Barry Oringer

Madame Sousatzka ★★★ 15
Drama 1988 · UK · Colour · 115min

Rather lost in the crowd on its release, this an engaging picture that slowly draws you into the quietly tragic lives of the inhabitants of Peggy Ashcroft's run-down London house. As the imperious piano teacher of the title, Shirley MacLaine beautifully combines the wistful regret for her own disappointments with a commitment to the future of her students. Navin Chowdhry is an excellent foil as her teenage prodigy, while Twiggy and Geoffrey Bayldon do well as fellow tenants worn down by their everyday lives. DP Swearing.
DVD

Shirley MacLaine *Madame Sousatzka* • Peggy Ashcroft *Lady Emily* • Twiggy *Jenny* • Navin Chowdhry *Manek Sen* • Shabana Azmi *Sushila Sen* • Leigh Lawson *Ronnie Blum* • Geoffrey Bayldon *Mr Cordle* • Lee Montague *Vincent Pick* ■ *Dir* John Schlesinger • *Scr* Ruth Prawer Jhabvala, John Schlesinger, from the novel by Bernice Rubens

Madame X ★★
Melodrama 1929 · US · BW · 95min

After a romantic indiscretion, a Parisian wife is thrown out by her eminent but unbending lawyer husband. Forbidden to see her beloved son, she sinks into a life of alcoholic degradation. This classic melodrama fascinated film-makers and audiences for decades. The title role is here played by the splendid Broadway actress Ruth Chatterton, with Lewis Stone as the husband. Both Chatterton and director Lionel Barrymore were Oscar-nominated, but the film now seems slow, mannered and stagey. RK

Ruth Chatterton *Jacqueline* • Lewis Stone *Floriot* • Raymond Hackett *Raymond* • Holmes Herbert *Noel* • Eugenie Besserer *Rose* ■ *Dir* Lionel Barrymore • *Scr* Willard Mack, from the play *La Femme X* by Alexandre Bisson

Madame X ★★★★
Melodrama 1937 · US · BW · 75min

Gladys George takes the title role in the second, and best, talkie version of the melodrama to end them all. She meets the challenge head on in a powerful performance that pulls no punches, and the film as a whole is played with a seriousness that undercuts the soap opera, at least until the sentimental histrionics of the courtroom finale. Warren William is perfectly cast as George's husband, while Henry Daniell is suitably slimy as the conman who undoes her. RK

Gladys George *Jacqueline Fleuriot* • John Beal *Raymond Fleuriot* • Warren William *Bernard Fleuriot* • Reginald Owen *Maurice Dourel* • Henry Daniell *Lerocle* • Jonathan Hale *Hugh Fariman Sr* • William Henry *Hugh Fariman Jr* ■ *Dir* Sam Wood • *Scr* John Meehan, from the play *La Femme X* by Alexandre Bisson

Madame X ★★
Melodrama 1966 · US · Colour · 100min

This is the last – to date – cinema version (there was a TV-movie remake in 1981 starring Tuesday Weld) of Alexandre Bisson's play about a woman on trial for murder unknowingly defended by her son. Here producer Ross Hunter casts Lana Turner in the leading role; trouble is, Turner seems to have aged suddenly, and the lame direction also does her no favours. Still, there's a super support cast, including Constance Bennett in her last screen appearance. TS

Lana Turner *Holly Parker* • John Forsythe *Clay Anderson* • Ricardo Montalban *Phil Benton* • Burgess Meredith *Dan Sullivan* • Constance Bennett *Estelle* • Teddy Quinn *Clay Jr as a child* • Keir Dullea *Clay Jr as an adult* ■ *Dir* David Lowell Rich • *Scr* Jean Holloway, from the play *La Femme X* by Alexandre Bisson

The Maddening ★★ 18
Horror thriller 1995 · US · Colour · 92min

Mia Sara's trip to see her sister turns nasty when she takes a short cut proposed to her by shifty gas station owner Burt Reynolds. That's because Reynolds is a nutcase who kidnaps Sara and her daughter to keep his own deranged wife (Angie Dickinson) and child company. This slickly produced thriller is fairly well acted, but it's too exploitative and sordid to provide much entertainment. ST

Burt Reynolds *Roy Scudder* • Angie Dickinson *Georgina Scudder* • Mia Sara *Cassie Osborne* • Brian Wimmer *David Osborne* • Josh Mostel *Chicky Ross* • William Hickey *Daddy* ■ *Dir* Danny Huston • *Scr* Henry Slesar, Leslie Greif

Made ★★ 15
Crime comedy drama 2001 · US · Colour · 90min

Containing an uncharacteristically showy performance by Vince Vaughn, this irritates and annoys as it explores the dual themes of male friendship and loyalty. Vaughn and Jon Favreau play boxing buddies who moonlight as muscle for the local Mob. When they're sent on simple courier duty to New York, it's a recipe for trouble. Favreau just wants to get the job done, and then get back to keeping other people's paws off his stripper girlfriend Famke Janssen. Vaughn, by contrast, sees the job as his chance to take a step up the Mob hierarchy. Contrasting ambitions lead to Laurel and Hardy-style humour. DA *DVD*

Jon Favreau *Bobby* • Vince Vaughn *Ricky* • Sean Combs *Ruiz* • Famke Janssen *Jessica* • Peter Falk *Max* ■ *Dir/Scr* Jon Favreau

Made for Each Other ★★★ U
Comedy drama 1939 · US · BW · 90min

A besotted young couple who marry in indecent haste face a mounting series of travails in the form of her difficult mother-in-law (Lucile Watson), his failure to gain promotion in his law firm and, climactically, the potentially fatal illness of their baby son. James Stewart and Carole Lombard star, while Charles Coburn is terrific as the crusty law boss; the director is John Cromwell, a master of soap opera. Although certainly not one of the best of its kind (Stewart's self-deprecating persona is almost irritating here), the formula is gold-plated. RK *DVD*

Carole Lombard *Jane Mason* • James Stewart *Johnny Mason* • Charles Coburn *Judge Joseph Doolittle* • Lucile Watson *Mrs Mason* • Harry Davenport *Dr Healy* • Ruth Weston *Eunice Doolittle* ■ *Dir* John Cromwell • *Scr* Jo Swerling, Frank Ryan

Made in America ★★ 12
Romantic comedy 1993 · US · Colour · 106min

The central idea of this comedy has potential – a young black teenager discovers that her biological father is white because of a mix-up at the sperm bank – and the cast just about makes it watchable. Whoopi Goldberg and Ted Danson turn in engaging performances as the unsuspecting parents, and Nia Long is entirely believable as their confused offspring, while Will Smith provides confident support. Sadly, the finished product is low on laughs and thin on content, with merely workmanlike direction. JF Swearing. *DVD*

Whoopi Goldberg *Sarah Mathews* • Ted Danson *Hal Jackson* • Nia Long *Zora Mathews* • Will Smith *Tea Cake Walters* • Paul Rodriguez *Jose* • Jennifer Tilly *Stacy* • Peggy Rea *Alberta* • Clyde Kusatsu *Bob Takashima* ■ *Dir* Richard Benjamin • *Scr* Holly Goldberg Sloan, from a story by Marcia Brandwynne, Nadine Schiff, Holly Goldberg Sloan

M

Made in Dagenham ★★★★ 15

Comedy drama based on a true story
2010 · UK/Ire · Colour · 108min

There seems to be a fail-safe formula for creating successful British films: take some plucky working-class Brits, mix with a situation that tests their mettle, sprinkle in some gritty social history, and you have a surefire hit on your hands. *Made in Dagenham* follows that recipe to a T, and is entertaining and touching in equal measure. Set in 1968, it focuses on the struggle of women machinists at Dagenham's Ford factory to gain the same pay as their "skilled" male colleagues, a breakthrough moment of the 1960s. *Calendar Girls* director Nigel Cole's film is paced for smiles, not political punches, but the performances are superb, especially Miranda Richardson stealing every scene as cabinet minister Barbara Castle. **AIS** Swearing, sex scene. *DVD*

Sally Hawkins *Rita O'Grady* • Bob Hoskins *Albert* • Rosamund Pike *Lisa Hopkins* • Miranda Richardson *Barbara Castle* • Daniel Mays *Eddie O'Grady* • Robbie Kay *Graham O'Grady* • Geraldine James *Connie* • Jaime Winstone *Sandra* • Roger Lloyd Pack *George* • John Sessions *Prime Minister Harold Wilson* ■ *Dir* Nigel Cole • *Scr* William Ivory

Made in Heaven ★★★ U

Comedy   1952 · UK · Colour · 81min

This sprightly comedy was inspired by the ancient English custom of the "Dunmow Flitch", in which married couples sought to win a sizeable side of bacon by swearing on Whit Monday to an uninterrupted year of wedded bliss. However, the chances of the ideally suited Petula Clark and David Tomlinson take a dip when they employ pouting Hungarian maid Sonja Ziemann. Vicar Richard Wattis and his stern sister Athene Seyler add to the fun, which is glossily photographed by Geoffrey Unsworth. **DP**

Petula Clark *Julie Topham* • David Tomlinson *Basil Topham* • Sonja Ziemann *Marta* • AE Matthews *Grandpa* • Charles Victor *Mr Topham* • Sophie Stewart *Mrs Topham* • Richard Wattis *Vicar* • Athene Seyler *Miss Honeycroft* ■ *Dir* John Paddy Carstairs • *Scr* William Douglas Home, George H Brown

Made in Heaven ★★ PG

Romantic fantasy
1987 · US · Colour and BW · 98min

This quirky fantasy was cult director Alan Rudolph's bid for a box-office hit, but he too often strains for effect. Timothy Hutton stars as a dead man who meets his future love (Kelly McGillis) in heaven when she's not yet been born. It looks good, like most Rudolph movies, and Hutton handles the comedy with aplomb. Hutton's then wife Debra Winger gives an uncredited performance as the male administrative head of heaven. **DP**

Timothy Hutton *Mike Shea/Elmo Barnett* • Kelly McGillis *Annie Packert/Ally Chandler* • Maureen Stapleton *Aunt Lisa* • Ann Wedgeworth *Annette Shea* • James Gammon *Steve Shea* • Mare Winningham *Brenda Carlucci* • Don Murray *Ben Chandler* • Timothy Daly *Tom Donnelly* ■ *Dir* Alan Rudolph • *Scr* Bruce A Evans, Raynold Gideon

Made in Hong Kong ★★★★ 15

Crime drama   1997 · HK · Colour · 104min

Fruit Chan's searching study of a community in transition was shot on discarded scraps of film stock and makes powerful use of its authentic locations and unfamiliar performers. Prone to technical gimmickry and overdoing the political symbolism, Chan nevertheless brings an abrasive energy to this story of a Triad wannabe imprisoned by both his social circumstances and fate. Sam Lee captures the disillusion shared by many Hong Kong youths as he tries to protect both his slow-witted mate and his dying girlfriend, while haunted by the memory of a suicide victim he never knew. **DP** Cantonese +subtitles. Swearing, violence, sexual references.

Sam Lee Chan-Sam [Sam Lee] *To Chung-Chau, "Moon"* • Neiky Hui-Chi Yim *Lam Yuk-Ping, "Ping"* • Wenbers Tung-Chuen Li *Ah-Lung, "Sylvester"* • Amy Ka-Chuen Tam *Hui Bo-San, "Susan"* ■ *Dir/Scr* Fruit Kuo Chan [Fruit Chan]

Made in USA ★★★ 18

Crime drama   1966 · Fr · Colour · 78min

There is a story of sorts – Anna Karina on the trail of her lover's killer – but this Jean-Luc Godard movie shows the director moving inexorably and often excitingly away from conventional narrative. As a piece of 1960s pop art, this movie takes some beating but today's viewers, largely unaware of the impact Godard made on world cinema, will soon tire of his playing with the medium, his political slogans and passing thoughts on JFK and the Algerian war. By the time the film was made, Karina and Godard were divorced; this was their final film together. **AT** French +subtitles. *DVD*

Anna Karina *Paula Nelson* • Laszlo Szabo *Richard Widmark* • Jean-Pierre Léaud *Donald Siegel* • Yves Alfonso *David Goodis* • Ernest Menzer *Edgar Typhus* ■ *Dir* Jean-Luc Godard • *Scr* Jean-Luc Godard, from the novel *The Juggler* by Richard Stark [Donald E Westlake]

Made Men ★★★ 15

Action thriller   1999 · US · Colour · 86min

In this derivative though solidly made action thriller, James Belushi is forced to flee from the gangster he not only shopped to the cops, but from whom he also pilfered the tidy sum of $12 million. Director Louis Morneau's previous picture, *Bats*, was disappointing, but this time round there are dramatic fireworks to match the explosions, as Belushi finds that the head of a backwoods drugs racket and corrupt sheriff Timothy Dalton are also on his tail. **DP** *DVD*

James Belushi *Bill Manucci* • Timothy Dalton *Sheriff Dex Drier* • Michael Beach *Miles* • Steve Railsback *Kyle* • Carlton Wilborn *Felix* • Vanessa Angel *Debra* ■ *Dir* Louis Morneau • *Scr* Robert Franke, Miles Millar, Alfred Gough

Made of Honor ★★ 12

Romantic comedy   2008 · US · Colour · 97min

Patrick Dempsey (with his career on the up thanks to TV's *Grey's Anatomy*) stars in this routine, and rather daftly titled, romantic comedy. He plays Tom, a ladies' man whose best friend is the lovely Hannah (Michelle Monaghan). When she's sent away to Scotland for a six-week business trip, Tom realises that she's also the woman of his dreams. His plans for the future are scuppered when Hannah returns, and reveals her engagement to hunky Scotsman Colin (Kevin McKidd). She asks Tom to be her maid of honour, a role he accepts – but only in order to win her for himself. The film boasts decent performances from an amiable cast, but they deserve rather better material to work with than this slog through overly familiar territory. **DA** Swearing, sexual references. *DVD* *Blu-ray*

Patrick Dempsey *Tom* • Michelle Monaghan *Hannah* • Kevin McKidd *Colin* • Kathleen Quinlan *Joan* • Sydney Pollack *Thomas Sr* • Busy Philipps *Melissa* • Kadeem Hardison *Felix* • James Sikking [James B Sikking] *Reverend Foote* ■ *Dir* Paul Weiland • *Scr* Harry Elfont, Deborah Kaplan, Adam Sztykiel, from a story by Sztykiel

Made of Stone ★★★★ 15

Music documentary
2013 · UK · Colour and BW · 96min

Shane Meadows was a teenage fan when the Stone Roses shook the world with their potent blend of psychedelic rock and swaggering Mancunian groove, but he never saw them live. Therefore, this potentially conventional feature-length chronicle of their 2011/12 reunion becomes something more personal. Meadows gains access all areas as he shadows the well-preserved four-piece on the road to triumphant shows at Greater Manchester's Heaton Park – his camera often skulking in corridors and dressing rooms. And while the band are at the top of their game musically, the director puts the largely middle-aged fans centre stage; their heart-warming stories dominating the section that captures a joyous secret gig at Warrington. The result is a witty, honest and valuable tribute. **AC** Swearing. *DVD* *Blu-ray*

Ian Brown • John Squire • Gary Mounfield *Gary "Mani" Mounfield* • Alan Wren *Alan "Reni" Wren* ■ *Dir* Shane Meadows

Madeleine ★★ U

Drama   1949 · UK · BW · 109min

Only two films blot David Lean's otherwise immaculate copybook (*The Passionate Friends* is the other), and both feature Ann Todd, whom he married in 1949. Todd was never the most expressive of actresses, but here her face is a blank and her delivery as modulated as the speaking clock. Uncomfortable with the courtroom format and confounded by the deadliness of dialogue drawn from original trial transcripts, Lean allows love to cloud his judgement, at the expense of what might otherwise have been an intriguing tale of murder in Victorian Glasgow. **DP** *DVD*

Ann Todd *Madeleine Smith* • Norman Wooland *William Minnoch* • Ivan Desny *Emile l'Angelier* • Leslie Banks *James Smith* • Edward Chapman *Dr Thompson* • Barbara Everest *Mrs Smith* • André Morell *Dean* • Barry Jones *Lord Advocate* ■ *Dir* David Lean • *Scr* Stanley Haynes, Nicholas Phipps

Madeline ★★★ U

Comedy   1998 · US/Ger · Colour · 85min

This sweet, but not entirely successful, children's film is based on Ludwig Bemelmans's books. Hatty Jones is cute as the young orphan, but adults are more likely to be charmed by a warm turn from Frances McDormand as the engaging Miss Clavel, who runs the girls' school and dispenses wisdom to her charges. This well-meaning entertainment for young girls may get overlooked in favour of big-budget productions full of special effects, but it will certainly hold its target audience's attention on a rainy afternoon. **JB** *DVD*

Frances McDormand *Miss Clavel* • Nigel Hawthorne *Lord Covington* • Hatty Jones *Madeline* • Ben Daniels *Leopold, the tutor* • Stéphane Audran *Lady Covington* ■ *Dir* Daisy von Scherler Mayer • *Scr* Mark Levin, Jennifer Flackett, from a story by Malia Scotch Marmo, Mark Levin, Jennifer Flackett, from the books by Ludwig Bemelmans

Madeline: Lost in Paris ★★

Animated adventure 1999 · US · Colour · 76min

Following a mixed reception for Columbia's live-action adaptation of Ludwig Bemelmans's popular books, Disney returned to the original graphic style for this dark, but always engaging adventure. Orphan Madeline, the smallest of the 12 girls residing at Miss Clavel's Parisian school, thinks she's finally found a family when a long-lost Viennese uncle comes to claim her. This should keep younger viewers entertained, but the grown-ups might wince at the songs. **DP**

Lauren Bacall *Madame Lacroque* • Jason Alexander *Uncle Horst/Henri* • Christopher Plummer *Narrator* • Andrea Libman *Madeline* • Stephanie Louise Vallance *Miss Clavel* ■ *Dir* Stan Phillips • *Scr* from the character created by Ludwig Bemelmans

Mademoiselle ★★★ 15

Psychological drama 1966 · Fr/UK · BW · 99min

Scripted by Jean Genet, the controversial French playwright, this has Jeanne Moreau in the title role as a sexually frustrated schoolmarm in a French farming community. Her secret acts of terrorism – arson, the poisoning of a water supply, flooding fields – lead the hatred of the village to be directed at the object of her desires, an Italian woodcutter (Ettore Manni). It has a weird compulsion, but director Tony Richardson's over-decorative style is too ponderous for the subject. **TH** English, Italian +subtitles. *DVD*

Jeanne Moreau *Mademoiselle* • Ettore Manni *Manou* • Keith Skinner *Bruno* • Umberto Orsini *Antonio* • Jane Beretta *Annette* • Mony Reh *Vievotte* ■ *Dir* Tony Richardson • *Scr* Jean Genet, Bernard Frechtman

Mademoiselle C ★★★ 12

Documentary   2013 · Fr · Colour · 88min

In the wake of *The September Issue* shining a light on to American *Vogue* and its formidable editor, Anna Wintour, this documentary offers a more personable portrait of her French counterpart, Carine Roitfeld. In 2012, Roitfeld chose to go it alone and release her own fashion magazine, *CR Fashion Book*, with director Fabien Constant following her every step of the way. Roitfeld comes across as a warm and well-liked person in an industry as fleeting and insincere as all those air kisses. But aside from shenanigans from her former employers, the production of *CR* proves to be a less-than-bumpy affair. Dedicated followers of fashion are sure to find this fascinating, but those less blinded by the bling may feel everything here is as carefully styled as a cover shot. **JH** English, French +subtitles. *DVD*

Carine Roitfeld ■ *Dir* Fabien Constant

Mademoiselle Chambon ★★★ 12A

Romantic drama   2009 · Fr · Colour · 101min

The eloquence of silence is readily evident in Stéphane Brizé's poignant dramatisation of an Eric Holder novel about the hesitant romance between a small-town builder and his son's teacher. Vincent Lindon and Sandrine Kiberlain were formerly married in real life, and achieve a palpable charge here as the ruggedly taciturn Jean and the primly demure Mlle Chambon. The shifts in the couple's emotions are superbly controlled by the two leads, and the movie builds to a courageous, albeit slightly anticlimactic, denouement. **DP** French +subtitles. A sex scene.

Vincent Lindon *Jean* • Sandrine Kiberlain *Véronique Chambon* • Aure Atika *Anne-Marie* • Jean-Marc Thibault *Jean's father* ■ *Dir* Stéphane Brizé • *Scr* Florence Vignon, Stéphane Brizé, from Eric Holder's novel

Mademoiselle Docteur ★★★★

First World War spy drama
1936 · Fr · BW · 86min

This melodramatic account of Germany's most famous spy, Anne-Marie Lesser, is given distinction by a fine cast and the evocative direction of GW Pabst. The plotting and assignations during the First World War are vividly re-created in salons, cabarets and railway stations, while delicately beautiful Dita Parlo makes an ethereal heroine. An English language version was made simultaneously by Edmond T Gréville with Erich von Stroheim in the role played by here Louis Jouvet. The same story had been filmed by MGM in 1934 as *Stamboul Quest* with Myrna Loy, but this is by far the better version. **TV** French +subtitles.

Dita Parlo *Anne-Marie Lesser/Mademoiselle Docteur* • Pierre Blanchar *Gregor Courdane/Condoyan* • Pierre Fresnay *Capt Georges Carrère* • Louis Jouvet *Simonis* • Charles Dullin *Col Matthesius* • Viviane Romance *Gaby* ■ *Dir* GW Pabst • *Scr* Irma von Cube, Georges Neveux, Leo Birinski, Herman J Mankiewicz, Jacques Natanson

Madhouse ★★★ 18

Horror spoof   1974 · UK · Colour · 87min

In the early 1970s, Vincent Price came to the UK for a string of delightfully black horror comedies, among them *Theatre of Blood* and the *Dr Phibes* movies. *Madhouse* is not in the same class, but it's an entertaining enough romp all the same. The horror legend plays a distinguished actor whose return to the small screen coincides with a series of brutish murders. There is a sterling support cast, and director Jim Clark delivers enough gory chuckles to keep Price fans more than happy. **JF** Swearing.

Vincent Price *Paul Toombes* • Peter Cushing *Herbert Flay* • Robert Quarry *Oliver Quayle* • Adrienne Corri *Faye Flay* • Natasha Pyne *Julia* • Michael Parkinson *Television interviewer* • Linda Hayden *Elizabeth Peters* ■ *Dir* Jim Clark • *Scr* Greg Morrison, Ken Levison, from the novel *Devilday* by Angus Hall

Madhouse ★★★ 15
Comedy   1990 · US · Colour · 86min

The unwanted guest has long been a staple of cinematic comedy. The situation is taken to its extreme in this uneven farce, in which Kirstie Alley and John Larroquette find their new love nest overrun by the kind of relatives you hope you only see at weddings and funerals. The contrast between down-on-their-luck John Diehl and Jessica Lundy and wealthy wife Alison LaPlaca makes for contrived satire, but Tom Ropelewski comes up with a couple of cracking moments. DP Swearing.

John Larroquette *Mark Bannister* • Kirstie Alley *Jessie Bannister* • Alison LaPlaca *Claudia* • John Diehl *Fred* • Jessica Lundy *Bernice* • Bradley Gregg *Jonathan* • Dennis Miller *Wes* • Robert Ginty *Dale* ■ *Dir/Scr* Tom Ropelewski

Madhouse ★★ 15
Horror   2004 · US · Colour · 86min

There are more clichés than corpses in this predictable and rather anaemic psychological horror about strange and deadly happenings in a mental health facility. Consequently, you may have guessed the ultimate big twist early on, as Joshua Leonard's eager young psychiatric intern arrives at the decrepit institute and soon starts seeing ghosts. Unfortunately, weak scripting and acting alongside lazy direction, mean events are never genuinely tense or scary. SF *DVD*

Joshua Leonard *Clark Stevens* • Lance Henriksen *Dr Franks* • Jordan Ladd *Sara* • Natasha Lyonne *Alice* ■ *Dir* William Butler • *Scr* William Butler, from a story by Aaron Strongoni

Madhumati ★★★★ U
Mystery drama   1958 · Ind · BW · 165min

Contemporary critics were appalled that director Bimal Roy had succumbed to commercialism with this flashback tale of doomed love and pitiless revenge. But the combination of Ritwick Ghatak's intricate screenplay, Salil Choudhury's enchanting score and Dilip Gupta's atmospheric photography gives this reincarnation saga a sophistication that few Bollywood films of the time could match. Dilip Kumar and Vyjayantimala excel in their multiple roles, and Pran also impresses as the villainous boss of a timber firm, whose fury at the couple's happiness provokes a tragedy whose cause is exposed in an elaborate deception. It's pure, melodramatic escapism. DP Hindi +subtitles. *DVD*

Dilip Kumar *Anand/Devendra* • Vyjayantimala [Vyjayantimala] *Madhumati/Madhavi/Radha* • Johny Walker [Johnny Walker] *Charandas* • Pran *Raja Ugra Narayan* • Jayant *Pawan Raja (Madhumati's father)* • Tiwari *Bir Singh* ■ *Dir* Bimal Roy • *Scr* Rajinder Singh Bedi, from a story by Ritwick Ghatak [Ritwik Ghatak]

Madigan ★★★★ 12
Crime drama   1968 · US · Colour · 96min

Gifted director Don Siegel amassed a critical and cult following with such hard-boiled movies as this terrific New York-based crime drama. The superb Richard Widmark gives one of his finest performances in the title role, but the laconic Henry Fonda is more than a match for him as the troubled police commissioner. There's a marvellously gritty supporting cast, and the film contains its fair share of sex and violence. Only the cheapness of Universal's Techniscope process disappoints, though the inherent grain oddly suits the night scenes. TS

Richard Widmark *Det Dan Madigan* • Henry Fonda *Commissioner Anthony Russell* • Inger Stevens *Julia Madigan* • Harry Guardino *Det Rocco Bonaro* • James Whitmore *Chief Inspector Charles Kane* • Sheree North *Jonesy* ■ *Dir* Don Siegel • *Scr* Henri Simoun, Harry Kleiner, Abraham Polonsky, from the novel *The Commissioner* by Richard Dougherty

Madigan's Millions ★
Crime caper   1967 · Sp/It · Colour · 78min

This Dustin Hoffman film was made in Italy in 1966, before he made *The Graduate* and shot to stardom. It's a caper comedy, with Hoffman playing a US tax inspector sent to Europe to look into a murdered mobster's murky accounts. Cesar Romero plays the gangster (he replaced George Raft in the role), while Elsa Martinelli plays his daughter. AT In English, Spanish, Italian.

Dustin Hoffman *Jason Fister* • Elsa Martinelli *Vicky Shaw* • Cesar Romero *Mike Madigan* ■ *Dir* Stanley Prager, Dan Ash, Giorgio Gentili • *Scr* James Henaghan, Jose Luis Bayonas

Madison Avenue ★★★ U
Drama   1962 · US · BW · 93min

This is a late round-up of once major 20th Century-Fox stars, in a turgid but still entertaining melodrama set in the world of advertising. Dana Andrews stars as an ambitious executive who's fired, but is determined to succeed regardless of the consequences. Co-stars Jeanne Crain and Eleanor Parker shine as though they knew this was going to be one of the last gasps of the studio system. Directing his final feature, H Bruce Humberstone uses the black-and-white photography very effectively. TS

Dana Andrews *Clint Lorimer* • Eleanor Parker *Anne Tremaine* • Jeanne Crain *Peggy Shannon* • Eddie Albert *Harvey Ames* • Howard St John *JD Jocelyn* • Henry Daniell *Stipe* • Kathleen Freeman *Miss Haley* • David White (1) *Stevenson Brock* ■ *Dir* H Bruce Humberstone • *Scr* Norman Corwin, from the novel *The Build-Up Boys* by Jeremy Kirk

Madman ★ 18
Horror   1981 · US · Colour · 88min

Supposedly based on the legend of Madman Marz, who took an axe to his family and then escaped the local lynch mob to disappear without a trace, this is a derivative bore. The disfigured maniac returns and soon the leafy glades are splattered with blood as headless corpses, strangulation victims and mutilated bodies are dragged back to the Marz shack to be meat-hooked. AJ *DVD*

Alexis Dubin *Betsy* • Tony Fish *TP* • Harriet Bass *Stacey* • Seth Jones *Dave* • Jan Claire *Ellie* ■ *Dir/Scr* Joe Giannone

The Madness of King George ★★★★★ PG
Biographical historical drama
1995 · UK · Colour · 105min

Nigel Hawthorne gives an inspired, funny and deeply moving performance in the title role of this celebrated, Oscar-winning film of Alan Bennett's play. The king is married to Charlotte (Helen Mirren), dallying with Lady Pembroke (Amanda Donohoe), and is not only father of 15 children but also of a nation and an empire. Problem is, Farmer George – a nickname the king delights in – is showing signs of madness, or at least that's the official diagnosis. Surgeon Ian Holm is brought in to put the king into a straitjacket. Behind the sardonic jokes and colloquialisms that are Bennett's trademark is a serious study of 18th-century politics and the monarchy. Immaculately directed by Nicholas Hytner, this is an unmissable treat. AT Swearing. *DVD*

Nigel Hawthorne *George III* • Helen Mirren *Queen Charlotte* • Ian Holm *Willis* • Rupert Graves *Greville* • Amanda Donohoe *Lady Pembroke* • Rupert Everett *Prince of Wales* • Julian Rhind-Tutt *Duke of York* • Julian Wadham *Pitt* • Jim Carter *Fox* • Geoffrey Palmer *Warren* ■ *Dir* Nicholas Hytner • *Scr* Alan Bennett, from his play • *Production Designer* Ken Adam

Madness of the Heart ★★ PG
Drama   1949 · UK · BW · 85min

Margaret Lockwood's career was already in terminal decline by the time she made this unpersuasive melodrama. As the London lass convinced she's been blinded by lust, she does what she can with a preposterous plot that has her marrying her French lover, Paul Dupuis, only to become the target of a mysterious assassin. Kudos to the supporting cast for keeping straight faces throughout. DP

Margaret Lockwood *Lydia Garth* • Paul Dupuis *Paul De Vandiere* • Maxwell Reed *Joseph Rondolet* • Thora Hird *Rosa* • Kathleen Byron *Verite Faimont* • Raymond Lovell *Comte De Vandiere* • Maurice Denham *Dr Simon Blake* ■ *Dir* Charles Bennett • *Scr* Charles Bennett, from the novel by Flora Sandstrom

Madness: Take It or Leave It ★★★ PG
Music documentary   1981 · UK · Colour · 83min

Shot on a shoestring, this is a fanciful but largely factual account of how a north London combo known as the Invaders evolved into Morris and the Minors and then Madness. Re-enacting key moments from the mid-1970s up to 1981, the band members revisit the dead-end jobs that sustained them through the early rehearsals, the landmark gigs and the changes that eventually saw "Suggs", "Woody" and "Bedders" join the line-up. Rough and ready, but revealing and often self-deprecatingly hilarious, this is a must for all Nutty Boy fans. DP

Graham "Suggs" McPherson *Suggs* • Mark Bedford *Bedders* • Dan Woodgate *Woody* ■ *Dir* Dave Robinson • *Scr* Dave Robinson, Phil McDonald

Mado ★★★★
Melodrama   1976 · Fr · Colour · 135min

This scathing snapshot of France under President Giscard d'Estaing is a typically perceptive study of the country's disconcerted, middle-aged middle classes from director Claude Sautet. Shaken by the suicide of his partner, Michel Piccoli gets lured into Julien Guiomar's attempt to swindle Charles Denner. More important than the real estate MacGuffin, however, are Piccoli's relationships with Ottavia Piccolo, a prostitute at the centre of the scam, and Romy Schneider, whose desperate loyalty to this confused yet undeserving man is heartbreaking. Riveting and revealing. DP French +subtitles.

Michel Piccoli *Simon* • Ottavia Piccolo *Mado* • Jacques Dutronc *Pierre* • Romy Schneider *Helene* • Charles Denner *Manecca* • Julien Guiomar *Boss* ■ *Dir* Claude Sautet • *Scr* Claude Sautet, Claude Néron • *Cinematographer* Jean Boffety

Madonna of the Seven Moons ★★★ U
Romantic drama   1944 · UK · BW · 105min

A huge box-office success in its day, this Gainsborough costume drama divided the critics, with many denouncing it as a piece of overblown twaddle. Director Arthur Crabtree was a first-class cinematographer, and he brings a lurid glamour to the proceedings. However, he is all at sea where plotting and pacing are concerned. Only the experience of his cast, particularly Phyllis Calvert as the gentlewoman leading a double life as a gypsy, prevents the more melodramatic passages becoming even more over-the-top. DP *DVD*

Phyllis Calvert *Maddalena Lambardi/Rosanna* • Stewart Granger *Nino Barucci* • Patricia Roc *Angela Lambardi* • Peter Glenville *Sandro Barucci* • John Stuart *Giuseppi Lambardi* • Jean Kent *Vittoria* • Nancy Price *Madame Barucci* • Peter Murray Hill *Logan* ■ *Dir* Arthur Crabtree • *Scr* Roland Pertwee, Brock Williams, from the novel by Margery Lawrence

La Madre Muerta ★★★★ 18
Thriller   1993 · Sp · Colour · 106min

Exploring dark and dangerous themes, Juanma Bajo Ulloa's intense film treads a fine line between the disturbing and the distasteful with an agility remarkable for a director making only his second feature. Set in the Basque region, the film considers the controversial topic of sex and the emotionally arrested through the eyes of both a killer (who kidnaps, years later, the mute daughter of his victim to prevent her from identifying him) and his lover (whose jealousy of the girl becomes more threatening than his fear). The acting is excellent, but it's Bajo Ulloa's relentless direction that makes this so troubling. DP Spanish +subtitles.

Karra Elejalde *Ismael Lopez De Matauko* • Ana Alvarez *Leire* • Lio *Maite* • Silvia Marso *Blanca* • Elena Irureta *Female director* • Ramón Barea *Nightclub owner* • Gregoria Mangas *Mrs Millas* • Marisol Sez *Mother* ■ *Dir* Juanma Bajo Ulloa • *Scr* Juanma Bajo Ulloa, Eduardo Bajo Ulloa

Madron ★★ 12
Western   1970 · US · Colour · 91min

Richard Boone gives one of the craggiest of his many craggy performances in this western about a glowering gunslinger with a soft spot for the kindly nun (Leslie Caron) he's escorting through hostile Apache territory. Shot on location in Israel's Negev desert, there are shades of *The Wild Bunch* in the way the action unfolds; the occasional brutality is another thing it shares with Sam Peckinpah's film. PF Violence *DVD*

Richard Boone *Madron* • Leslie Caron *Sister Mary* • Paul Smith *Gabe Price* • Gabi Amrani *Angel* • Chaim Banai *Sam Red* ■ *Dir* Jerry Hopper • *Scr* Edward Chappell, Leo McMahon, from a story by Leo McMahon

The Madwoman of Chaillot ★ U
Comedy   1969 · US · Colour · 142min

An eccentric Parisian countess (Katharine Hepburn) and her batty companions (Margaret Leighton, Edith Evans and Giulietta Masina) foil a fiendish plan to turn the city into a giant oilfield in this wordy, repetitive and boring tale. It's not helped either by the overloading of the cast with star names in even the smallest of the many roles. The opulent sets and costumes, reminiscent of Versailles rather than modern Paris, fail to rescue a misconceived enterprise. RK

Katharine Hepburn *Countess Aurelia* • Charles Boyer *The Broker* • Claude Dauphin *Dr Jadin* • Edith Evans *Josephine* • John Gavin *Reverend* • Paul Henreid *The General* • Oscar Homolka *Commissar* • Margaret Leighton *Constance* • Giulietta Masina *Gabrielle* • Nanette Newman *Irma* • Richard Chamberlain *Roderick* • Yul Brynner *Chairman* • Donald Pleasence *Prospector* • Danny Kaye *Ragpicker* ■ *Dir* Bryan Forbes • *Scr* Edward Anhalt, from the play *La Folle de Chaillot* by Jean Giraudoux

Maelström ★★★
Psychological drama
2000 · Can · Colour · 95min

The curious caprices of life inform this handsomely atmospheric but self-consciously surreal melodrama. Boutique owner Marie-Josée Croze's brushes with death and her fortuitous discovery of a reason to live are chronicled with an unnervingly bleak optimism. But it's difficult to see how they gain any intensity or macabre irony by being narrated by a soon-to-be-slaughtered fish. Ambitious, but lacking finesse. DP French, Norwegian, English +subtitles.

Marie-Josée Croze *Bibianne Champagne* • Jean-Nicolas Verreault *Evian Karlsen* • Stephanie Morgenstern *Claire Gunderson* • Pierre Lebeau *Fish* • Klimbo *Head-Annstein Karlsen* ■ *Dir/Scr* Denis Villeneuve

Il Maestro ★
Drama   1989 · Fr/Bel · Colour · 90min

British Malcolm McDowell and French Charles Aznavour co-star as Italians. It's a convoluted story about an orchestra conductor (McDowell) who gets a touch of the vapours when rehearsing *Madame Butterfly*. This leads to a flashback to an era when both McDowell and Aznavour were on the run from the Nazis. The result is a dramatic mess. AT

Malcolm McDowell *Goldberg* • Charles Aznavour *Romualdi* • Andréa Ferréol *Dolores* • Francis Lemaire *Administrator* • Carmela Locantore *Paola* • Pietro Pizzuti *Father Superior* • Serge-Henri Valcke *Major Wyatt* • Chen Qilian *Margerita* ■ *Dir* Marion Hänsel • *Scr* Marion Hänsel, from the story *La Giacca Verde* by Mario Soldati

M

The Magdalene Sisters ★★★★ 15

Period drama 2002 · UK/Ire · Colour · 114min

Religious repression and moral hypocrisy are targeted by writer/director Peter Mullan in this bitter indictment of the Magdalene Asylums – convent laundries that were run like workhouses – into which "fallen women" were forced in order to cleanse their "sins". Following three wayward teenagers sent to one such asylum in the 1960s, Mullan's fictionalised version of actual events keeps soapy sentimentality at bay, thanks mainly to the compelling performances of a young cast of unknowns – Eileen Walsh is especially outstanding as the tragic Crispina – while Geraldine McEwan is frighteningly good as the bullying Mother Superior. AJ DVD

Geraldine McEwan *Sister Bridget* · Anne-Marie Duff *Margaret* · Nora-Jane Noone *Bernadette* · Dorothy Duffy *Rose/Patricia* · Eileen Walsh *Crispina* · Mary Murray *Una* · Britta Smith *Katy* · Frances Healy *Sister Jude* ■ *Dir/Scr* Peter Mullan

The Maggie ★★★★ U

Comedy 1953 · UK · BW · 88min

Ostensibly, this most underestimated of Ealing comedies is a whimsical story about a crew of canny Clydebankers giving a brash American a torrid time after being assigned to carry his property aboard their clapped-out steamer. Don't be fooled, however, by the leisurely pace, the gentle humour and the relatively good-natured conclusion. This is a wicked little satire on the mutual contempt that underlies Euro-American relations, and few could have handled it with such incisive insight as American-born Scot Alexander Mackendrick. Cruel rather than quaint. DP DVD Blu

Paul Douglas *Marshall* · Alex Mackenzie *Skipper* · James Copeland *Mate* · Abe Barker *Engineer* · Tommy Kearins *Wee boy* · Hubert Gregg *Pusey* · Geoffrey Keen *Campbell* · Dorothy Alison *Miss Peters* ■ *Dir* Alexander Mackendrick · *Scr* William Rose, from a story by Alexander Mackendrick

Maggie ★★★★ 15

Horror thriller 2015 · Swi/US · Colour · 94min

Contrary to popular belief, Arnold Schwarzenegger is an effective actor if you give him a half-decent film and not too much dialogue to deal with. *Maggie* is easily one of his best works. Essentially, it's a zombie film, but with a sombre tone, in which Arnie plays a doting dad who is forced to choose between confinement at home and a government-run quarantine-cum-concentration camp for his teenage daughter (Abigail Breslin), who has fallen victim to a global pandemic of "necroambulism". Gripping and genuinely moving, *Maggie* is a film of subtlety with a different kind of horror that tears at the heartstrings. DA DVD Blu

Arnold Schwarzenegger *Wade Vogel* · Abigail Breslin *Maggie Vogel* · Joely Richardson *Caroline* · Douglas M Griffin *Ray* · JD Evermore *Holt* ■ *Dir* Henry Hobson · *Scr* John Scott 3

Maggie's Plan ★★★ 15

Romantic comedy 2016 · US · Colour · 98min

Playing out like old-school Woody Allen, writer/director Rebecca Miller's screwball comedy is a consistently engaging diversion. A winning Greta Gerwig is the insecure kook of the title who plans to have a baby whether she finds Mr Right or not. After settling on a pickle-selling sperm donor (Travis Fimmel), she then clicks with a married novelist (Ethan Hawke). Gerwig's offbeat charm effortlessly navigates the themes of destiny and best intentions in a sharp comedy full of funny one-liners. AJ Swearing

Greta Gerwig *Maggie* · Ethan Hawke *John* · Julianne Moore *Georgette* · Bill Hader *Tony* · Maya Rudolph *Felicia* ■ *Dir* Rebecca Miller · *Scr* Rebecca Miller, from a story by Karen Rinaldi · *Cinematographer* Sam Levy

Magic ★★ 15

Thriller 1978 · US · Colour · 106min

This low-key update of the old "ventriloquist taken over by his evil dummy" theme is scripted by William Goldman. Richard Attenborough overstretches an already thin premise and deliberately minimises the horror elements by placing the emphasis on warped entertainer Anthony Hopkins's unbalanced psychological condition. The result is a sadly sentimental effort, lacking both suspense and atmosphere. AJ Swearing, some violence.

Anthony Hopkins *Corky/"Fats"* · Ann-Margret *Peggy Ann Snow* · Burgess Meredith *Ben Greene* · Ed Lauter *Duke* · EJ André *Merlin* · Jerry Houser *Cab driver* · David Ogden Stiers *George Hudson Todson* · Lillian Randolph *Sadie* ■ *Dir* Richard Attenborough · *Scr* William Goldman, from his novel

Magic beyond Words: the JK Rowling Story ★★

Biographical drama 2011 · US · Colour · 90min

The story of how Harry Potter creator JK Rowling became one of the world's most celebrated authors is reduced to a string of visual bullet points in this extremely episodic and poorly researched biopic. From her richly imaginative childhood to her struggles as a mum on benefits, Rowling's significant moments are trotted out minus detail, realism or atmosphere, robbing both tragedies and triumphs of emotional impact. Poppy Montgomery does her best to convey the writer's relentless passion for writing, but sadly can't prevent the overall drama feeling unconvincing. SF

Poppy Montgomery *Joanne Rowling* · Antonio Cupo *Jorge* · Janet Kidder *Anne Rowling* · Lisa Norton *Jill* · Wesley MacInnes *Sean* · Madison Desjarlais *Joanne Rowling at 17* ■ *Dir* Paul A Kaufman · *Scr* Jeffrey Berman, Tony Caballero, from the biography *JK Rowling* by Sean Smith

The Magic Bow ★★ U

Biographical drama 1946 · UK · BW · 101min

The few facts that have been retained in this biopic of the violin virtuoso Niccolo Paganini have been submerged in melodramatic scenes that are notable only for a certain pomposity of dialogue, while such invented details as the duel and the pawning of his Stradivarius betray the penny-dreadful imagination of the scriptwriters. Yet somehow this film still manages to get under the skin, thanks to the vigorous vulgarity of Stewart Granger's performance and Yehudi Menuhin's vibrant playing on the soundtrack. DP DVD

Stewart Granger *Paganini* · Phyllis Calvert *Jeanne* · Jean Kent *Bianchi* · Dennis Price *Paul De La Roche* · Cecil Parker *Germi* · Felix Aylmer *Pasini* ■ *Dir* Bernard Knowles · *Scr* Roland Pertwee, Norman Ginsbury, from the novel by Manuel Komroff

The Magic Box ★★★★ U

Biographical drama 1951 · UK · Colour · 103min

Produced for the Festival of Britain, this biopic of William Friese-Greene is more a piece of wishful thinking than an accurate portrait of Britain's pre-eminent cinema pioneer. So what if Friese-Greene failed in his attempt to project moving images, and who cares if he "borrowed" many of his ideas from forgotten collaborators like John Rudge and Mortimer Evans? This is charming and thoroughly entertaining myth-making, made all the more palatable by the engaging performance of Robert Donat. DP DVD

Robert Donat *William Friese-Greene* · Maria Schell *Helena* · Margaret Johnston *Edith Friese-Greene* · Robert Beatty *Lord Beaverbrook* · Renée Asherson *Miss Tagg* · Michael Redgrave *Mr Lege* · Richard Attenborough *Jack Carter* · Laurence Olivier *Second Holborn policeman* · Eric Portman *Arthur Collings* · Glynis Johns *May Jones* · Margaret Rutherford *Lady Pond* · Peter Ustinov *Industry man* · Stanley Holloway *Broker's man* ■ *Dir* John Boulting · *Scr* Eric Ambler, from the book *Friese-Greene, Close-up of an Inventor* by Ray Allister

The Magic Bubble ★★★ 12

Fantasy comedy 1992 · US · Colour · 90min

In a thought-provoking film, a downtrodden mum who's just turned 40 is finally able to stick two fingers up to her bullying hubby after a magic bubble grants her deepest desire, and she finds she can no longer remember her age. Renewed "youthfulness" leads to changes in appearance, personality and permissiveness. Diane Salinger and John Calvin star, but the main cast interest resides in an early role for George Clooney. DA DVD

Diane Salinger *Julia Cole* · John Calvin *Charles Cole* · Priscilla Pointer *Grandma* · George Clooney *Mac* · Colleen Camp *Deborah* · Wallace Shawn *Dr Block* · Shera Danese *Letty* ■ *Dir* Deborah Ringel, Alfredo Ringel · *Scr* Meridith Baer, Geoff Prysirr

The Magic Christian ★★ 15

Comedy 1969 · UK · Colour · 88min

Admiring Terry Southern's satirical novel of 1959, Peter Sellers sent it to Stanley Kubrick who liked its humour so much he hired Southern to work on *Dr Strangelove*. Then Sellers reunited with Southern for this comedy about the richest man in the world who adopts a drop-out son, Ringo Starr, to prove his and the rest of humanity's worthlessness. A dreadful mess, very much part of the Swinging Sixties culture, this film is also unmissable for its eye-popping cast. AT DVD

Peter Sellers *Sir Guy Grand* · Ringo Starr *Youngman Grand* · Richard Attenborough *Oxford coach* · Leonard Frey *Psychiatrist on ship* · Laurence Harvey *Hamlet* · Christopher Lee *Ship's vampire* · Spike Milligan *Traffic warden #27* · Yul Brynner *Lady singer* · Roman Polanski *Man listening to lady singer* · Raquel Welch *Priestess of the Whip* · Wilfrid Hyde White *Ship's captain* · Graham Chapman *Oxford stroke* · John Cleese *Director in Sotheby's* · Clive Dunn *Sommelier* · Hattie Jacques *Ginger Horton* ■ *Dir* Joseph McGrath · *Scr* Terry Southern, Joseph McGrath, Peter Sellers, Graham Chapman, John Cleese from the novel by Terry Southern

The Magic Donkey ★★★ PG

Fantasy 1970 · Fr · Colour · 85min

Following their exemplary collaboration on *The Umbrellas of Cherbourg*, director Jacques Demy and composer Michel Legrand reunited for this adaptation of Charles Perrault's distinctly dubious fairy tale. The film achieves its neverland atmosphere through the enchanting decor and some glorious colour photography from Ghislain Cloquet. However, it's hard to identify with the story of a king (Jean Marais) whose promise to his dying queen that he will only marry someone of comparable beauty sets him after his daughter (Catherine Deneuve). DP French +subtitles. DVD

Catherine Deneuve *Peau d'Ane/Queen* · Jacques Perrin *Prince* · Jean Marais *King* · Delphine Seyrig *Fairy* · Fernand Ledoux *Red King* · Micheline Presle *Red Queen* ■ *Dir* Jacques Demy · *Scr* Jacques Demy, from the fairy tales *Les Contes de Ma Mère l'Oye* by Charles Perrault

Magic Fire ★★

Biographical drama 1956 · US · Colour · 112min

Long-delayed in reaching the screen, then barely released, this biography of composer Richard Wagner proved to be too ambitious for Republic Studios. Despite a finely upholstered look and a flamboyant performance from Alan Badel, the film is scuppered by his wooden Argentinian co-star Carlos Thompson and leaden direction from veteran William Dieterle. TS

Alan Badel *Richard Wagner* · Yvonne De Carlo *Minna* · Carlos Thompson *Franz Liszt* · Rita Gam *Cosima* · Valentina Cortese *Mathilde* · Peter Cushing *Otto Wesendonk* · Frederick Valk *Minister von Moll* · Gerhard Riedmann *King Ludwig II* ■ *Dir* William Dieterle · *Scr* Bertita Harding, EA Dupont, David Chantler, from the novel by Harding · *Music* Erich Wolfgang Korngold · *Cinematographer* Ernest Haller

The Magic Flute ★★★ U

Opera 1974 · Swe · Colour · 134min

Aiming both to re-create the contemporary experience of watching Mozart's final operatic masterpiece and make opera accessible to viewers of all races and ages, Ingmar Bergman's stylised staging only fitfully succeeds. A surfeit of audience reaction shots and some rather twee backstage docu-snaps interfere with the flow of the story. However, the studio re-creation of the handsome Drottningholm Theatre and its 18th-century paraphernalia is delightful, while the cast is admirable. DP Swedish +subtitles.

Josef Köstlinger *Tamino* · Irma Urrila *Pamina* · Hakan Hagegard *Papageno* · Elisabeth Eriksson *Papagena* · Ulrik Cold *Sarastro* ■ *Dir* Ingmar Bergman · *Scr* Ingmar Bergman

The Magic Flute ★★★ PG

Opera 2006 · UK/Fr · Colour · 133min

Kenneth Branagh's bold update of Mozart's opera relocates the story of Tamino (Joseph Kaiser) and Pamina (Amy Carson) to the trenches of the First World War. The $27 million budget allows Branagh to turn the trenches into a fantasy realm, where walls of sandbags transform into a chorus of singing faces, while squadrons of cartoon-like biplanes swoop above. Sadly, the romance of the original love story is swamped by computer-generated effects and the lyrics of Stephen Fry's witty English-language libretto are sometimes hard to hear. Ironically, this worthy attempt to bring Mozart to a popular audience will be enjoyed most by those well-versed enough in opera to appreciate the songs that Branagh intermittently shows. JR DVD

Joseph Kaiser *Tamino* · Amy Carson *Pamina* · Benjamin Jay Davis *Papageno* · Silvia Moi *Papagena* · René Pape *Sarastro* · Lyubov Petrova *Queen of the Night* · Tom Randle *Monostatos* · Liz Smith *Old Papagena* ■ *Dir* Kenneth Branagh · *Scr* Kenneth Branagh, Stephen Fry, from the opera by Wolfgang Amadeus Mozart, Emanuel Schikaneder

Magic Hunter ★★★

Fantasy 1994 · Hun/Swi/Fr/Can · Colour · 106min

Executive produced by David Bowie and starring Gary Kemp and Sadie Frost, this is a surreal though beautiful treatise from director Ildiko Enyedi. Set in medieval Hungary and contemporary Budapest, the film interweaves two tales. One tells the story of a policeman (Kemp) who loses his ability to shoot on target just when he is assigned to protect a chess master from assassination. The other involves a painting of the Virgin Mary (Natalie Conde) coming to life. LH Hungarian +subtitles.

Gary Kemp *Max* · Sadie Frost *Eva* · Alexander Kaidanovsky *Maxim* · Peter Vallai *Kaspar* · Mathias Gnadinger *Police chief* · Alexandra Wasscher *Lili* · Ildiko Toth *Lina* · Natalie Conde *Virgin Mary* ■ *Dir* Ildiko Enyedi · *Scr* Ildiko Enyedi, Laszlo Revesz, from the opera *Der Freischutz* by Carl Maria von Weber

Magic in the Moonlight ★★ 12

Romantic comedy drama 2014 · US · Colour · 93min

Woody Allen's jazz-age drama is seductively set during a summer on the Côte d'Azur, where Emma Stone is thrilling the chattering classes with her alleged gift as a psychic, while conjuror Colin Firth debunks mediums for fun. Unfortunately, a miserable Firth lacks the quiet smoulder that made his Darcy so compelling, while Stone simply simpers. Eileen Atkins does bring humour as his aunt, but everyone else is cast in a dim light. SP DVD Blu

Emma Stone *Sophie* · Colin Firth *Stanley* · Simon McBurney *Howard Burkan* · Eileen Atkins *Aunt Vanessa* · Hamish Linklater *Brice* · Marcia Gay Harden *Mrs Baker* ■ *Dir/Scr* Woody Allen

Magic in the Water ★★★ 🅿🄶
Fantasy adventure
1995 · Can/US · Colour · 96min

Mark Harmon and Harley Jane Kozak star in this charming family film about a mythical water creature that helps a psychiatrist realise he's so wrapped up in his work that he's making a mess of his life. Rick Stevenson's film wisely goes easy on the special effects, emphasising instead the magic inherent in the basic scenario. Delightfully escapist. **DA** 𝘿𝙑𝘿

Mark Harmon *Jack Black* • Joshua Jackson *Joshua Black* • Harley Jane Kozak *Dr Wanda Bell* ■ *Dir* Rick Stevenson • *Scr* Rick Stevenson, Icel Dobell Massey, from a story by Ninian Dunnett, Stevenson, Dobell Massey

Magic Magic ★★🄵
Psychological thriller
2013 · US/Chil/Arg · Colour · 94min

This exasperating thriller sees fragile Juno Temple on holiday on a Chilean island with cousin Emily Browning. But Browning is called away, leaving Temple at the mercy of strangers, including creepy Michael Cera (in a disturbing departure from his likeable geek persona). Is the desperate girl being driven mad? Maybe it's lack of sleep, drugs or even supernatural possession that ails her? Temple is convincingly wild-eyed, but the film veers off on such an odd tangent, you'll be left frustrated. **JA** Swearing, sex scene, nudity. 𝘿𝙑𝘿

Juno Temple *Alicia* • Michael Cera *Brink* • Emily Browning *Sara* • Catalina Sandino Moreno *Bárbara* ■ *Dir/Scr* Sebastián Silva

Magic Mike ★★★🄵
Comedy drama
2012 · US · Colour · 105min

Steven Soderbergh's surprisingly sweet-natured tale of Florida male strippers stars Alex Pettyfer as the naive 19-year-old introduced to the steamy world of stripping by superstar Channing Tatum. The movie is beautifully shot and skilfully acted, with Tatum showing an almost irresistible screen charm, as well as baby-smooth glutes. Dramatically, however, it's a little underpowered: apart from a somewhat lackadaisical foray into a *Boogie Nights*-style drug deal gone awry, not much of any interest actually happens. **AS** Swearing, sexual references, drug abuse, nudity. 𝘿𝙑𝘿 🅱

Channing Tatum *Mike* • Alex Pettyfer *Adam "The Kid"* • Matthew McConaughey *Dallas* • Cody Horn *Brooke* • Olivia Munn *Joanna* • Matt Bomer *Ken* • Riley Keough *Nora* • Joe Manganiello *Big Dick Richie* ■ *Dir* Steven Soderbergh • *Scr* Reid Carolin • *Cinematographer* Steven Soderbergh

Magic Mike XXL ★★🄵
Comedy drama
2015 · US · Colour · 110min

Channing Tatum returns as the Florida stripper with aspirations, here living down to some of the expectations that *Magic Mike* defied. But, because Mike had decided to grow up and left the club scene behind, director Gregory Jacobs has nowhere to go with the story except backwards. Putting Mike on the road with the other "Kings of Tampa" (minus Matthew McConaughey) only gives the impression of movement, and the initial banter between the lads - some of which is actually quite funny - eventually gives way to cheesy scenes designed to titillate rather than tickle the funny bone. **SP** Swearing, sexual references, drug abuse.

Channing Tatum *Mike* • Matt Bomer *Ken* • Joe Manganiello *Big Dick Richie* • Kevin Nash *Tarzan* • Amber Heard *Zoe* • Elizabeth Banks (2) *Paris* • Andie MacDowell *Nancy* • Jada Pinkett Smith *Rome* ■ *Dir* Gregory Jacobs • *Scr* Reid Carolin • *Editor* Steven Soderbergh

The Magic of Lassie ★★🅄
Drama
1978 · US · Colour · 99min

Not even the presence of James Stewart, Mickey Rooney and Alice Faye can save this otherwise unremarkable attempt to resurrect the world's most famous collie. Director Don Chaffey sticks closely to the story of the original *Lassie Come Home*, as nasty Pernell Roberts takes Lassie away from a debt-ridden family. The 1943 classic was genuinely uplifting - this is just cloyingly sentimental. **JF** 𝘿𝙑𝘿

James Stewart *Clovis Mitchell* • Mickey Rooney *Gus* • Alice Faye *Alice* • Pernell Roberts *Jamison* • Stephanie Zimbalist *Kelly Mitchell* • Michael Sharrett *Chris Mitchell* ■ *Dir* Don Chaffey • *Scr* Jean Holloway, Robert B Sherman, Richard M Sherman

The Magic Pudding ★★★🅄
Animated fantasy adventure
2000 · Aus · Colour · 75min

Norman Lindsay was the controversial Australian artist whose story was retold in *Sirens*. Surprisingly, he was also the author of the children's favourite on which this animated feature is based. Some of the continent's finest performers contribute voices to the story of Bunyip Bluegum (Geoffrey Rush), a koala who is joined in the search for his missing parents by Bill Barnacle the sailor (Hugo Weaving) and the penguin, Sam Sawnoff (Sam Neill). With Jack Thompson as the wicked wombat Buncle, who tries to steal Albert (John Cleese), the pudding that never runs out, this should keep the whole family amused. **DP**

John Cleese *Albert the Magic Pudding* • Geoffrey Rush *Bunyip Bluegum* • Sam Neill *Sam Sawnoff* • Hugo Weaving *Bill Barnacle* • Toni Collette *Meg Bluegum* • Jack Thompson *Buncle* ■ *Dir* Karl Zwicky • *Scr* Harry Cripps

The Magic Roundabout ★★★🅄
Animated fantasy adventure
2005 · UK/Fr · Colour · 78min

The much loved children's TV classic is re-imagined for 21st-century youngsters in this attractive computer-animated adventure. Using the original characters as a springboard, the film broadens and updates their escapades to satisfy contemporary tastes. The result is a colourful tribute to the eccentric 1960s show, in which Dougal the dog inadvertently releases imprisoned sorcerer Zeebad (voiced by Tom Baker). The dialogue and comic scenarios still have their knowing undertones, while the slightly beefed-up characters retain their simple charm. **SF** 𝘿𝙑𝘿

Tom Baker *Zeebad* • Jim Broadbent *Brian* • Joanna Lumley *Ermintrude* • Kylie Minogue *Florence* • Robbie Williams *Dougal* • Ian McKellen *Zebedee* • Bill Nighy *Dylan* • Ray Winstone *Soldier Sam* • Lee Evans *Train* ■ *Dir* Dave Borthwick, Jean Duval, Frank Passingham • *Scr* Paul Bassett, Raolf Sanoussi, Stephane Sanoussi, from characters by Serge Danot, Martine Danot

The Magic Sword ★★★
Fantasy
1962 · US · Colour · 80min

This medieval fantasy never really takes off, coming across as a blunt version of *Excalibur*. Gary Lockwood plays a young knight who sets out to rescue princess Anne Helm from wicked sorcerer Basil Rathbone. The latter is magnificent, as usual, while Estelle Winwood's witch is a wonderful piece of dithery expertise. Otherwise, though, this not really cutting-edge material, despite some neat special effects by Milt Rice. **TH**

Basil Rathbone *Lodac* • Estelle Winwood *Sybil* • Gary Lockwood *St George* • Anne Helm *Princess Helene* • Liam Sullivan *Sir Branton* • John Mauldin *Sir Patrick* • Jacques Gallo *Sir Dennis* • Leroy Johnson *Sir Ulrich* ■ *Dir* Bert I Gordon • *Scr* Bernard Schoenfeld, from a story by Bert I Gordon

The Magic Sword: Quest for Camelot ★★★🅄
Animated period adventure
1997 · US · Colour · 82min

The daughter of a murdered knight searches for King Arthur's magic sword, Excalibur, which has been stolen and is lost in a mythic wood. Adapted from the novel *The King's Damosel* by British writer Vera Chapman, it's hot on character but rather devoid of action. There's an interesting cast of voices, from Gary Oldman's evil Sir Ruber to John Gielgud's magical Merlin, and Pierce Brosnan is a very smooth-talking King Arthur. **TH** 𝘿𝙑𝘿

Cary Elwes *Garrett* • Bryan White *Garrett* • Jessalyn Gilsig *Kayley* • Andrea Corr *Kayley* • Gary Oldman *Sir Ruber* • Eric Idle *Devon* • Don Rickles *Cornwall* • Pierce Brosnan *King Arthur* • John Gielgud *Merlin* ■ *Dir* Frederik Du Chau • *Scr* Kirk De Micco, William Schiffrin, Jacqueline Feather, David Seidler, from the novel *The King's Damosel* by Vera Chapman

Magic Town ★★★🅄
Comedy drama
1947 · US · BW · 98min

This intriguing comedy drama, deftly directed by William A Wellman, provides a fascinating insight into small-town America. James Stewart is convinced that the white-picket-fence haven of Grandview can be used as a statistical yardstick for the country as a whole, while Jane Wyman's strong newspaper editor seeks positive social change. The old and new vie for supremacy in postwar society, and Wellman uses his film as a metaphor for the debate while staying in touch with the human story. **SH** 𝘿𝙑𝘿

James Stewart *Lawrence Rip Smith* • Jane Wyman *Mary Peterman* • Kent Smith *Hoopendecker* • Ned Sparks *Ike Sloan* • Wallace Ford *Lou Dicketts* • Regis Toomey *Ed Weaver* • Ann Doran *Mrs Weaver* • Donald Meek *Mr Twiddle* ■ *Dir* William A Wellman • *Scr* Robert Riskin, from a story by Robert Riskin, Joseph Krumgold

Magic Trip: Ken Kesey's Search for a Kool Place ★★★🄵
Documentary
2011 · US · Colour and BW · 107min

In 1964, author Ken Kesey (of *One Flew over the Cuckoo's Nest* fame) replaced pen with camera and, along with a group of friends, embarked on a journey from California to the New York World's Fair. The meandering trip was destined to become the stuff of counter-culture legend, as the LSD-fuelled group in their psychedelic painted bus driven by Neal Cassady (immortalised as Dean Moriarty in Jack Kerouac's Beat milestone *On the Road*) challenged conventional thinking wherever they went. This fascinating film pieces together randomly shot and previously unseen footage, and blends it seamlessly with new material to create a kaleidoscopic snapshot of those heady days. **TP**

Ken Kesey • Allen Ginsberg • Stanley Tucci *The Interviewer* • Neal Cassady ■ *Dir/Scr* Alex Gibney, Alison Ellwood

The Magician ★★★🅿🄶
Fantasy drama
1958 · Swe · BW · 96min

Winner of the special jury prize at Venice, Ingmar Bergman's gothic drama has been described as a comedy without jokes and a horror film without chills. Focusing on the artist's value to society and exploring such themes as illusion, faith, science and truth, this has the feel of a man trying too hard to repeat the success of the previous year's masterpieces. Max von Sydow gives a bravura performance as the 19th-century mesmerist Vogler, while Gunnar Fischer's photography creates the right mood of uncertainty. **DP** Swedish +subtitles. 𝘿𝙑𝘿

Max von Sydow *Vogler* • Ingrid Thulin *Manda* • Gunnar Björnstrand *Dr Vergerus* • Naima Wifstrand *Grandmother* • Bengt Ekerot *Spegel* • Bibi Andersson *Sara* • Gertrud Fridh *Ottilia* • Lars Ekborg *Simson* • Erland Josephson *Egerman* ■ *Dir/Scr* Ingmar Bergman • *Cinematographer* Gunnar Fischer

The Magician ★★★🄵
Crime black comedy
2005 · Aus · Colour · 81min

The mock documentary has emerged as a very useful format for low budget film-makers, and, in his feature debut, Australian Scott Ryan displays enough canny touches to lift this variation above the ordinary. As well as writing, producing and directing, Ryan also takes the lead role of the Melbourne villain who allows his largely unseen friend (Massimiliano Andrighetto) to record his life as a hitman-for-hire. Despite being a remorseless killer and borderline sociopath, Ryan makes for oddly sympathetic character and there are plenty of laughs to be had in the banter with his cameraman. **JF** Swearing, sex scenes.

Scott Ryan *Ray Shoesmith* • Ben Walker *Tony Rickards* • Massimiliano Andrighetto *Massimo "Max" Totti* • Kane Mason *Benny* • Nathaniel Lindsay *Edna* ■ *Dir/Scr* Scott Ryan

The Magician of Lublin ★★★🄵
Period drama
1979 · Is/W Ger · Colour · 108min

Isaac Bashevis Singer's novel gets a halfway decent adaptation from, of all people, ex-Cannon boss and trash director Menahem Golan. Alan Arkin stars as a Jewish entertainer who becomes the toast of late 19th and early 20th-century Warsaw society, thanks to his talent as an ace illusionist and escape artist. But greed, lust and his giant ego soon cause his rapid fall from grace. A good cast invests this rarefied period piece with a high-tone atmosphere and its unusual fantasy elements provide a surprising conclusion. **AJ**

Alan Arkin *Yasha Mazur* • Louise Fletcher *Emilia* • Valerie Perrine *Zeftel* • Shelley Winters *Elizabeta* • Maia Danziger *Magda* • Linda Bernstein *Esther* • Lou Jacobi *Wolsky* ■ *Dir* Menahem Golan • *Scr* Irving S White, Menahem Golan, from the novel by Isaac Bashevis Singer

Magician: the Astonishing Life and Work of Orson Welles ★★★★
Documentary
2014 · US · Colour and BW · 91min

There's no such thing as a dull anecdote about Orson Welles (who would have turned 100 in 2015), especially when it is related in stentorian tones by the man himself. Consequently, Chuck Workman's documentary is stuffed with fascinating details about the multifarious achievements of the wunderkind. For those unfamiliar with tales about *War of the Worlds* radio broadcast, the clashes with RKO over *Citizen Kane* and *The Magnificent Ambersons*, and the lengthy nomadic period that resulted in Welles becoming the accidental godfather of independent cinema, this is a fine place to start and a fitting centenary tribute. **DP** 𝘿𝙑𝘿

Orson Welles • Peter Bogdanovich ■ *Dir* Chuck Workman

Magicians ★★🄵
Comedy
2007 · UK · Colour · 86min

David Mitchell and Robert Webb, the stars of TV's *Peep Show*, are well cast as rival magicians in this British comedy, scripted by the show's writers Sam Bain and Jesse Armstrong. Harry (Mitchell) and Karl (Webb) are a once popular magic act who fell out when Harry discovered Karl's affair with his wife (the act's assistant) and accidentally killed her on stage. Four years later the pair are still not on speaking terms, until the lure of a large cash prize at an international magic contest brings them reluctantly back together. The familiar acts and corrupt officials are expected but effective. While the story is predictable, there are some witty flashes in the script and Mitchell displays well-rounded comic timing. **KK** 𝘿𝙑𝘿 🄲🅂

David Mitchell (3) *Harry* • Robert Webb *Karl* • Jessica Stevenson *Linda* • Darren Boyd *Otto* • Steve Edge *Tony White* • Peter Capaldi *Mike Francis* • Andrea Riseborough *Dani* • Rosie Fellner *Shelly* ■ *Dir* Andrew O'Connor • *Scr* Jesse Armstrong, Sam Bain

The Magnet ★★🅄
Comedy
1950 · UK · BW · 74min

This was one of Ealing superscribe TEB Clarke's least distinguished efforts. The story of a young boy who steals a magnet and becomes the toast of his community after his accidental heroics is contrived, but it's the totally false characters that let it down. Moreover, director Charles Frend fails to exploit the run-down urban locations. William Fox would later change his first name to James and become a star. DP *DVD*

Stephen Murray *Dr Brent* • Kay Walsh *Mrs Brent* • William Fox [James Fox] *Johnny Brent* • Meredith Edwards *Harper* • Gladys Henson *Nannie* • Thora Hird *Nannie's friend* • Michael Brooke Jr *Kit* • Wylie Watson *Pickering* ■ *Dir* Charles Frend • *Scr* TEB Clarke

The Magnificent Ambersons ★★★★★ U

Classic period drama   1942 · US · BW · 84min

Orson Welles's follow-up to *Citizen Kane* is one of cinema's flawed masterpieces. Adapted from Booth Tarkington's novel, it tells the compelling story of the decline of a once-proud family in the face of sprawling industrialisation. We shall never see the director's version, as executives at RKO felt the film was too long and depressing, and so ordered over 40 minutes of cuts, destroyed the footage and tacked on a happy ending directed by production manager Freddie Fleck. Out of the country on location, Welles was powerless to do anything about it. It says much for his genius that this is still a brilliant exercise in nostalgia and film technique. DP *DVD*

Joseph Cotten *Eugene Morgan* • Agnes Moorehead *Fanny Minafer* • Dolores Costello *Isabel Amberson Minafer* • Anne Baxter *Lucy Morgan* • Tim Holt *George Amberson Minafer* • Don Dillaway [Donald Dillaway] *Wilbur Minafer* • Ray Collins *Jack Amberson* • Richard Bennett (1) *Major Amberson* • Erskine Sanford *Roger Bronson* • Charles Phipps *Uncle John* • Orson Welles *Narrator* ■ *Dir* Orson Welles • *Scr* Orson Welles, from the novel by Booth Tarkington • *Cinematographer* Stanley Cortez • *Editor* Robert Wise • *Music* Bernard Herrmann • *Costume Designer* Edward Stevenson • *Production Designer* Mark-Lee Kirk

The Magnificent Ambersons ★★

Period drama   2001 · US · Colour · 150min

Orson Welles's 1942 attempt to adapt Booth Tarkington's novel was butchered by the studio and Alfonso Arau fares no better in his $16 million, made-for-TV bid to realise the master's original screenplay. The meticulously re-created period trappings count for nought, as a quality cast passes blithely through a project in which it appears to have little pride or faith. DP

Bruce Greenwood *Eugene Morgan* • Madeleine Stowe *Isabelle Amberson Minafer* • Jonathan Rhys Meyers *George Minafer Amberson* • Gretchen Mol *Lucy Morgan* • Jennifer Tilly *Aunt Fanny Minafer* • James Cromwell *Major Amberson* • William Hootkins *Uncle George Amberson* • Dina Merrill *Mrs Johnson* ■ *Dir* Alfonso Arau • *Scr* from Orson Welles's screenplay for the 1942 film, from the novel by Booth Tarkington

Magnificent Doll ★

Historical drama   1946 · US · BW · 90min

One of the great romantic dramas of American history is rendered flatter than a pancake by grotesque miscasting and direction that completely fails the subject matter. Ginger Rogers is spectacularly wrong as Dolly Payne Madison, one of the White House's great ladies, in a screenplay by Irving Stone that plays fast and loose with the facts. David Niven, as Aaron Burr, gives a truly awful performance. TS

Ginger Rogers *Dorthea "Dolly" Payne Madison* • David Niven *Aaron Burr* • Burgess Meredith *James Madison* • Horace McNally [Stephen McNally] *John Todd* • Peggy Wood *Mrs Payne* • Frances Williams *Amy, the maid* • Grandon Rhodes *Thomas Jefferson* ■ *Dir* Frank Borzage • *Scr* Irving Stone, from his story

The Magnificent Dope ★★ U

Comedy drama   1942 · US · BW · 83min

Henry Fonda stars as a lazy country hick who arrives in New York and teaches everyone how to chill out, relax and take things easy. This amazes city slicker Don Ameche and charms starlet Lynn Bari, a starlet whom 20th Century-Fox promoted as the "girl with the million dollar figure" as well as "the woo woo girl": American GIs apparently rated her second only to Betty

Grable in pin-up power. As corny as Kansas in August, but entertaining enough. AT

Henry Fonda *Tad Page* • Lynn Bari *Claire* • Don Ameche *Dawson* • Edward Everett Horton *Horace Hunter* • George Barbier *Barker* • Frank Orth *Messenger* • Roseanne Murray *Dawson's secretary* • Marietta Canty *Jennie* ■ *Dir* Walter Lang • *Scr* George Seaton, from a story by Joseph Schrank

A Magnificent Haunting ★★★ 15

Fantasy comedy
2012 · It · Colour and BW · 101min

Once an edgy provocateur, Turkish-born director Ferzan Ozpetek has recently shown a gentler side and it is very much to the fore in this witty if slight ghost story. Moving to Rome from Sicily to pursue his acting ambitions, Elio Germano's Pietro discovers he's sharing his cheap digs with the ghostly members of a theatrical troupe, who are convinced it's 1943 and they are still fighting a covert rearguard against Fascism. Ozpetek's mix of comedy, romance and historical soul-searching is often sentimental, but it's charmingly played by a fine ensemble cast. DP Italian +subtitles. Swearing, sexual references.

Elio Germano *Pietro* • Margherita Buy *Lea Marni* • Vittoria Puccini *Beatrice Marni* • Giuseppe Fiorello *Filippo Apollonio* ■ *Dir* Ferzan Ozpetek • *Scr* Ferzan Ozpetek, Federica Pontremoli

Magnificent Obsession ★★★★

Melodrama   1935 · US · BW · 112min

Directed by a master of the soap opera, Universal's John M Stahl, this romantic melodrama has Robert Taylor as a wealthy, irresponsible playboy who is partly responsible for the death of a revered doctor and, subsequently, for an accident that blinds the doctor's widow Irene Dunne, with whom he falls in love. Filled with remorse, Merrick becomes a Nobel Prize-winning brain surgeon and, years later, finds her again, hoping to redeem himself. Beautifully made and well-acted, it's a more restrained and credible version than the Douglas Sirk remake, but not half as much fun! RK

Irene Dunne *Helen Hudson* • Robert Taylor (1) *Bobby Merrick* • Charles Butterworth *Tommy Masterson* • Betty Furness *Joyce Hudson* • Sara Haden *Nancy Ashford* • Ralph Morgan *Randolph* • Henry Armetta *Tony* • Gilbert Emery *Dr Ramsay* ■ *Dir* John M Stahl • *Scr* George O'Neil, Sarah Y Mason, Victor Heerman, Finley Peter Dunne, from the novel by Lloyd C Douglas

Magnificent Obsession ★★★★ U

Classic melodrama   1954 · US · Colour · 103min

This luscious, glorious Technicolor entry from Universal's memorable Ross Hunter/ Douglas Sirk cycle of no-holds-barred melodramas is the one that turned beefcake Rock Hudson into a romantic superstar. Adapted from the syrupy novel by Lloyd C Douglas, it was a box-office hit the first time around (in 1935). This time an Oscar-nominated Jane Wyman plays the woman who loses her husband and then goes blind, partly through Hudson's irresponsibility. While she is cared for by Agnes Moorehead, he mends his ways and becomes a brilliant surgeon before seeking her out years later. RK *DVD*

Jane Wyman *Helen Phillips* • Rock Hudson *Bob Merrick* • Barbara Rush *Joyce Phillips* • Agnes Moorehead *Nancy Ashford* • Otto Kruger *Randolph* • Gregg Palmer *Tom Masterson* ■ *Dir* Douglas Sirk • *Scr* Robert Blees, Wells Root, from the 1935 film, from the novel by Lloyd C Douglas

The Magnificent Rebel ★★ U

Biographical drama
1961 · US/W Ger · Colour · 94min

Karlheinz Böhm plays a brooding and intense Ludwig van Beethoven in this Disney biography, shot in Germany. It was originally shown in two parts on American television, but released as a film elsewhere. Böhm does well, but the screenplay is poor, the direction turgid and the dubbing

distracting. However, the photography and, of course, the music make this very watchable. TS German dubbed.

Karlheinz Böhm *Ludwig van Beethoven* • Giulia Rubini *Giulietta* • Ivan Desny *Lichnowsky* • Peter Arens *Amenda* • Oliver Grimm *Stefan* ■ *Dir* Georg Tressler • *Scr* Joanne Court [Joan Scott] • *Cinematographer* Göran Strindberg

The Magnificent Seven ★★★★★ PG

Classic western   1960 · US · Colour · 122min

Director John Sturges was extremely fortunate in securing a near-perfect cast for this enduringly popular western reworking of Japanese classic *Seven Samurai*. Not content with forging a new iconic image for Yul Brynner as a black-clad gunslinger, he also created key star-making roles for 1960s sensations Steve McQueen, James Coburn and Charles Bronson. The use of Panavision landscape is glorious to behold, Eli Wallach is a suitably slimy villain and the action sequences are tremendously exciting. There's also one of the greatest musical themes ever written for a movie, in an altogether fine brass-led score by composer Elmer Bernstein. Three sequels followed, beginning with *Return of the Seven* in 1966 and *Guns of the Magnificent Seven* (1969). TS Violence. *DVD* *SD*

Yul Brynner *Chris* • Steve McQueen (1) *Vin* • Eli Wallach *Calvera* • Horst Buchholz *Chico* • Charles Bronson *O'Reilly* • Robert Vaughn (1) *Lee* • Brad Dexter *Harry Luck* • James Coburn *Britt* • Vladimir Sokoloff *Old man* • Rosenda Monteros *Petra* ■ *Dir* John Sturges • *Scr* William Roberts, Walter Bernstein, Walter Newman (uncredited) • *Cinematographer* Charles Lang Jr [Charles Lang]

The Magnificent Seven

Western   2016 · US · Colour

This is a preview - no prints were available to review as we went to press: Three sequels and a 1998 TV series couldn't match the classic 1960 western (itself a remake of Kurosawa's *Seven Samurai*), so this retread from Antoine Fuqua (known for urban thrillers like *The Equalizer*) is an intriguing proposition. The cast led by Denzel Washington (in his first western), Ethan Hawke and Chris Pratt may not quite match Yul Brynner, Steve McQueen or James Coburn for superstar quality, but the story of seven gunmen swatting baddies away from a village can't really go wrong. JA

Denzel Washington *Sam Chisolm* • Chris Pratt *Josh Farraday* • Ethan Hawke *Goodnight Robicheaux* • Peter Sarsgaard *Bartholomew Bogue* • Vincent D'Onofrio *Jack Horne* • Haley Bennett *Emma Cullen* ■ *Dir* Antoine Fuqua • *Scr* John Lee Hancock, Nic Pizzolatto, from the 1954 film *Seven Samurai*

The Magnificent Seven Deadly Sins ★★ PG

Comedy   1971 · UK · Colour · 103min

Having packed his short film *Simon*, *Simon* with cameos by his famous friends, comic actor Graham Stark enticed even more comedians and comic writers to contribute to this, his only feature. It comprises seven sketches, each one a mildly amusing illustration of a deadly sin. The film is very much a product of its time, with familiar television faces performing glorified sitcom (two of the segments are adaptations of TV episodes), while busty starlets remove their clothes. DM *DVD* *SD*

Bruce Forsyth • Joan Sims • Roy Hudd • Harry Secombe • Leslie Phillips • Julie Ege • Harry H Corbett • Ian Carmichael • Alfie Bass • Spike Milligan • Ronald Fraser ■ *Dir* Graham Stark • *Scr* Marty Feldman, Graham Stark, Ray Galton, Alan Simpson, Barry Cryer, John Esmonde, Graham Chapman, Dave Freeman, Bob Larbey, Spike Milligan

The Magnificent Seven Ride! ★★★ PG

Western   1972 · US · Colour · 96min

Not really, they don't. This is the fourth and last outing for the famous title and, as in the previous sequel, no members of the original cast are to be found. Still, Lee Van Cleef makes a perfectly acceptable

substitute for Yul Brynner, and the theme remains true to the original's concept. Here the bandits kidnap Van Cleef's wife and the seven are rounded up to seek vengeance, but the real star is Elmer Bernstein's score. TS *DVD*

Lee Van Cleef *Chris* • Stefanie Powers *Laurie Gunn* • Mariette Hartley *Arilla* • Michael Callan *Noah Forbes* • Luke Askew *Skinner* • Pedro Armendáriz Jr *Pepe Carral* • Ralph Waite *Jim Mackay* • William Lucking *Walt Drummond* ■ *Dir* George McCowan • *Scr* Arthur Rowe • *Music* Elmer Bernstein

The Magnificent Showman ★★★ U

Action adventure   1964 · US · Colour · 131min

This entertaining big-top saga features John Wayne as a circus owner whose business faces a variety of crises. Begun as *Circus World* by director Frank Capra, the film was then entrusted to the much more suitable Henry Hathaway, who makes the lengthy tale race by in a jiffy. The climactic fire and the capsize of the circus ship (special effects by Alex Weldon) were amazingly effective. And what other movie features Rita Hayworth and Claudia Cardinale as mother and daughter, each trying to upstage the other? TS *DVD*

John Wayne *Matt Masters* • Rita Hayworth *Lili Alfredo* • Claudia Cardinale *Toni Alfredo* • Lloyd Nolan *Cap Carson* • Richard Conte *Aldo Alfredo* • John Smith *Steve McCabe* • Henri Dantes *Emile Schuman* • Wanda Rotha *Mrs Schuman* ■ *Dir* Henry Hathaway • *Scr* Ben Hecht, Julian Halevy [Julian Zimet], James Edward Grant, from the story by Philip Yordan, Nicholas Ray

The Magnificent Two ★★ PG

Comedy   1967 · UK · Colour · 91min

Like most British comedians of the 1960s and 1970s, Morecambe and Wise failed to make it in movies because the situations that made their TV series so successful simply could not be sustained beyond an hour or the confines of a studio setting. Here Eric and Ernie do their utmost to kick-start this poor comedy of errors about travelling salesmen caught up in a South American revolution. But the plot is paper thin, the jokes aren't funny and the use of a bikini-clad army to install Margit Saad as president is unworthy of the duo. DP *DVD*

Eric Morecambe *Eric* • Ernie Wise *Ernie* • Margit Saad *Carla* • Cecil Parker *British ambassador* • Virgilio Teixeira *Carillo* • Isobel Black *Juanita* • Martin Benson *President Diaz* ■ *Dir* Cliff Owen • *Scr* SC Green, RM Hills, Michael Pertwee, Peter Blackmore

The Magnificent Yankee ★★★ U

Biographical drama   1950 · US · BW · 88min

Oliver Wendell Holmes (1841-1935), a Supreme Court judge, was famous for his witticisms and his espousal of liberal causes, which earned him the nickname "The Great Dissenter". This biopic charts Holmes's career between the presidencies of two Roosevelts, taking in such key historical events as the Great War and the Depression. As Holmes, Louis Calhern has to age considerably, dispense justice *and* have a private life with his wife (Ann Harding). No wonder his performance earned him an Oscar nomination. A stagey, talky movie that oozes prestige. AT

Louis Calhern *Oliver Wendell Holmes* • Ann Harding *Fanny Bowditch Holmes* • Eduard Franz *Judge Louis Brandeis* • Philip Ober *Mr Owen Wister* • Ian Wolfe *Mr Adams* • Edith Evanson *Annie Gough* • Richard Anderson *Reynolds* ■ *Dir* John Sturges • *Scr* Emmet Lavery, from the play by Emmet Lavery, from the novel *Mr Justice Holmes* by Francis Biddle

Magnolia ★★★★★ 18

Drama   1999 · US · Colour · 180min

Paul Thomas Anderson sealed his growing reputation as one of Hollywood's most ambitious and audacious film-makers with this dark, daring and dazzling take on Robert Altman's *Short Cuts*. Boldly tossing aside storytelling conventions, Anderson's offbeat epic charts 24 hours in the weird lives of a dozen San Fernando Valley

M

inhabitants. The cast is just superb, with Tom Cruise's supremely arrogant sex guru standing out. But Jason Robards, Julianne Moore, Melora Walters, John C Reilly and William H Macy are also brilliant in their one-of-a-kind roles. Although the running time is a little indulgent, the film's increasingly frantic pace, manic camerawork and unpredictable scenarios command the attention. JC Violence, swearing, sex scenes, drug abuse, nudity. *DVD*

Tom Cruise *Frank TJ Mackey* • Julianne Moore *Linda Partridge* • William H Macy *Quiz Kid Donnie Smith* • Philip Seymour Hoffman *Phil Parma* • Melora Walters *Claudia Wilson Gator* • John C Reilly *Jim Kurring* • Jason Robards *Earl Partridge* • Philip Baker Hall *Jimmy Gator* • Melinda Dillon *Rose Gator* • Luis Guzman *Luis* • Orlando Jones *Worm* • Alfred Molina *Solomon Solomon* • Henry Gibson *Thurston Howell* ■ *Dir/Scr* Paul Thomas Anderson • *Cinematographer* Robert Elswit

Magnum Force ★★★ 18
Crime thriller　1973 · US · Colour · 117min

"Dirty" Harry Callahan's shoot-first-ask-questions-later modus operandi comes back to haunt him in this watchable sequel to the seminal 1971 thriller. As usual, Clint Eastwood's San Francisco cop is meting out justice in his own inimitable fashion, until the execution of local felons puts his no-nonsense methods, and indeed Harry himself, in the spotlight. Eastwood oozes laconic cool, even if the storyline here is more brutally violent, and the climactic showdown on a deserted aircraft carrier is superbly staged. *The Enforcer* (1976) continued the series. JA Violence, swearing. *DVD*

Clint Eastwood *Harry Callahan* • Hal Holbrook *Lieutenant Briggs* • Felton Perry *Early Smith* • Mitchell Ryan *Charlie McCoy* • David Soul *Davis* • Tim Matheson *Sweet* • Robert Urich *Grimes* ■ *Dir* Ted Post • *Scr* John Milius, Michael Cimino, from a story by Milius, from original material by Harry Julian & RM Fink

The Magus ★ PG
Fantasy drama　1968 · UK · Colour · 101min

Asked whether he would do everything the same if he had to live his life all over again, Peter Sellers thought for a moment and said: "Yes. But I would not see *The Magus*." Here's a movie so pretentious, it's worth sampling a reel or two just to confirm that, yes, they *can* make them as bad as this. The producers committed a double whammy by choosing an unfilmable novel and then getting its author – John Fowles – to adapt it himself. It's about a British schoolteacher (played by Michael Caine) cast sexually and metaphysically adrift on a Greek island. Anthony Quinn is in it, with Candice Bergen and Anna Karina. AT *DVD*

Anthony Quinn *Maurice Conchis* • Michael Caine *Nicholas Urfe* • Candice Bergen *Lily* • Anna Karina *Anne* • Julian Glover *Anton* • Takis Emmanuel *Kapetan* ■ *Dir* Guy Green • *Scr* John Fowles, from his novel

Mahal ★★★★ PG
Romantic mystery thriller
1949 · Ind · BW · 141min

This beguiling romantic mystery thriller marked Kamal Amrohi's directorial debut and made a star of both its leading lady, Madhubala, and uncredited playback singer, Lata Mangeshkar. Madhubala radiates ethereal beauty as the spectre who so entrances Ashok Kumar when he moves into an abandoned manor that he is willing to ruin his marriage to the trusting Vijayalaxmi to possess her. For all its melodramatics and debt to such Hollywood sagas as *The Ghost and Mrs Muir*, this is still deeply affecting. DP Hindi, Urdu +subtitles. *DVD*

Ashok Kumar *Hari Shankar* • Madhubala *Kamini/Mallan* • Vijayalaxmi *Ranjana* • Kanu Roy *Shrinath* ■ *Dir/Scr* Kamal Amrohi

Mahler ★★★ 15
Biographical drama　1974 · UK · Colour · 110min

This was one of the more successful and less outré outings from Ken Russell, in which he returned to familiar turf, having directed a series of television

dramatisations of famous composers' lives during the 1960s. Gustav Mahler is played with some depth and subtlety by Robert Powell and there's excellent support from Georgina Hale as his self-sacrificing wife. The director here considerably tones down the cinematic excesses for which he has become notorious, and this is a brief, interesting, finely scripted film. SH *DVD*

Robert Powell *Gustav Mahler* • Georgina Hale *Alma Mahler* • Richard Morant *Max* • Lee Montague *Bernhard Mahler* • Rosalie Crutchley *Marie Mahler* • Benny Lee *Uncle Arnold* • Miriam Karlin *Aunt Rosa* • Angela Down *Justine* ■ *Dir/Scr* Ken Russell

Mahogany ★
Melodrama　1975 · US · Colour · 108min

The only good thing to come out of this mess is the theme song, the Diana Ross classic *Do You Know Where You're Going To*. Ross stars as a humble Chicago secretary who becomes a fashion model, then a fashion designer with the help of fruitcake photographer Anthony Perkins. Pitched as a full-blooded melodrama, it's banality has to be seen to be believed. AT

Diana Ross *Tracy/Mahogany* • Billy Dee Williams *Brian* • Anthony Perkins *Sean* • Jean-Pierre Aumont *Christian Rosetti* • Beah Richards *Florence* • Nina Foch *Miss Evans* • Marisa Mell *Carlotta Gavina* ■ *Dir* Berry Gordy Jr • *Scr* John Byrum, from a story by Toni Amber

The Maid ★★ PG
Romantic comedy　1991 · US/Fr · Colour · 86min

This soft-centred romantic comedy wastes the talents of its stars, Martin Sheen and Jacqueline Bisset. The former is a besotted businessman who poses as a servant to be with his newly discovered true love Bisset. There are some nice role-reversal moments, but the script lacks bite and there is little to work with. Supporting players Jean-Pierre Cassel and James Faulkner fare the best, but it's slim pickings all round. JF *DVD*

Martin Sheen *Anthony Wayne* • Jacqueline Bisset *Nicole Chantrelle* • Victoria Shalet *Marie* • Jean-Pierre Cassel *CP Oliver* • James Faulkner *Laurent Leclair* • Dominique Varda *Nicole's secretary* ■ *Dir* Ian Toynton • *Scr* Timothy Prager

The Maid ★★★★ 15
Drama　2009 · Chil/Mex · Colour · 92min

Sebastián Silva's second feature is an exceptional study of the emotional investment that domestics make in the families they serve. After 23 years of devotion to one family, Raquel (Catalina Saavedra) begins to fear that she's being taken for granted. She resists all attempts at lightening her workload, but the arrival of the resilient Lucy (Mariana Loyola) has a more transformative effect. Saavedra is mesmerising as she shifts from subservient to scheming, with Silva's delicate touch ensuring that she remains sympathetic, even at her most comically cruel. DP Spanish +subtitles. Swearing. *DVD*

Catalina Saavedra *Raquel* • Claudia Celedón *Pilar* • Alejandro Goic *Mundo* • Andrea García-Huidobro *Camila* • Mariana Loyola *Lucy* • Agustín Silva *Lucas* ■ *Dir* Sebastián Silva • *Scr* Sebastián Silva, Pedro Peirano

Maid in Manhattan ★★ PG
Romantic comedy　2002 · US · Colour · 100min

Director Wayne Wang swaps originality and sophistication for feel-good froth in this predictable Cinderella story. Ralph Fiennes piles on the charm as a would-be senatorial candidate who falls for Manhattan hotel maid and single parent Jennifer Lopez in the mistaken belief she's a socialite. Comic mishaps and schmaltzy soul-searching ensue, but the two leads are unconvincing. SF *DVD* 🆂

Jennifer Lopez *Marisa Ventura* • Ralph Fiennes *Christopher Marshall* • Natasha Richardson *Caroline Lane* • Stanley Tucci *Jerry Siegel* • Bob Hoskins *Lionel Bloch* • Tyler Garcia Posey *Ty Ventura* • Frances Conroy *Paula Burns* • Chris Eigeman *John Bextrum* ■ *Dir* Wayne Wang • *Scr* Kevin Wade, from a story by Edmond Dantes [John Hughes]

Maid to Order ★★★ 15
Comedy　1987 · US · Colour · 89min

This is a story of wish fulfilment, but if the majority of the cast were given the chance they would probably have wished for a sharper script than this one, in which poor little rich girl Ally Sheedy learns about life the hard way after she is erased from her father's memory. Sheedy is too nice to convince as a spoilt brat, but Valerie Perrine and Dick Shawn are good value as the vulgar wannabes who hire her as their maid. DP

Ally Sheedy *Jessie Montgomery* • Beverly D'Angelo *Stella* • Michael Ontkean *Nick McGuire* • Valerie Perrine *Georgette Starkey* • Dick Shawn *Stan Starkey* • Tom Skerritt *Charles Montgomery* • Merry Clayton *Audrey James* • Begona Plaza *Maria* ■ *Dir* Amy Jones [Amy Holden Jones] • *Scr* Amy Jones [Amy Holden Jones], Perry Howze, Randy Howze

Maidan ★★★★ 12A
Documentary　2014 · Ukr/Neth · Colour · 133min

Belarusian director Sergei Loznitsa returns to his documentary roots for this mesmerising account of the events that transformed Ukraine in late 2013/early 2014. Positioning his camera on Kiev's Maidan Nezalezhnosti (or Independence Square), Loznitsa allows the scene to unfold before him, with a carnival atmosphere surrounding the protests against pro-Russian president Viktor Yanukovych. As the fervour of patriotic and parodic songs gives way to the shouts and screams of the defiant and the terrified, there is something painterly about the digital imagery, and the sound mix is equally inspired. DP

■ *Dir* Sergey Loznitsa [Sergei Loznitsa]

The Maids ★★ 12
Drama　1974 · UK/Can · Colour · 90min

This is a dull screen version of the dreary Jean Genet play about two Parisian maids who concoct a sadomasochistic plan to murder their hated mistress, but then never actually go through with it. It's that sort of play, and film. The main interest resides in the quality acting from a top-notch British cast. DA *DVD*

Glenda Jackson *Solange* • Susannah York *Claire* • Vivien Merchant *Madame* • Mark Burns *Monsieur* ■ *Dir* Christopher Miles • *Scr* Robert Enders, Christopher Miles, from the play *Les Bonnes* by Jean Genet

Maid's Night Out ★★★
Comedy　1938 · US · BW · 64min

To win a bet with his self-made father, millionaire Allan Lane becomes a milkman for a month and falls for rich girl Joan Fontaine whom he thinks is the maid. RKO dropped their budding star Fontaine the same year she made this jolly little film, played and directed (by Ben Holmes) with evident enjoyment; she would shortly bounce back by making *Rebecca* for Hitchcock. Gossip columnist Hedda Hopper, who began her career as an actress, is in the supporting cast. RK

Joan Fontaine *Sheila Harrison* • Allan Lane *Bill Norman* • Hedda Hopper *Mrs Harrison* • George Irving *Rufus Norman* • William Brisbane *Wally Martin* • Billy Gilbert *Papalapoulas* • Cecil Kellaway *Geoffrey* ■ *Dir* Ben Holmes • *Scr* Bert Granet, from a story by Willoughby Speyers

Maigret Sets a Trap ★★★
Detective drama　1957 · Fr · BW · 110min

The work of Georges Simenon – especially that featuring Inspector Maigret – has reputedly been more often adapted to the screen than those of any other 20th-century writer. This entertaining whodunnit benefits from the presence of the incomparable Jean Gabin, who brings grace and gravitas to the role of the detective in pursuit of a night stalker and killer. BB In French.

Jean Gabin *Inspector Jules Maigret* • Annie Girardot *Yvonne Maurin* • Jean Desailly *Marcel Maurin* • Olivier Hussenot *Inspector Lagrume* • Jeanne Boitel *Mme Maigret* • Lucienne Bogaert

Mme Maurin ■ *Dir* Jean Delannoy • *Scr* RM Arlaud, Michel Audiard, Jean Delannoy, from a novel by Georges Simenon

Mail Order Bride ★★★
Western　1963 · US · Colour · 83min

In this slight but rather charming western, Buddy Ebsen tries to tame Keir Dullea, the hotheaded son of a dead friend, by making him marry Lois Nettleton, a widow with a young son. Writer/director Burt Kennedy's dialogue is splendid, and he extracts fine performances from his cast; his use of the camera could have been more dynamic, though. Warren Oates contributes some colourful work as the villain, while Marie Windsor figures nicely as the saloon keeper. AE

Buddy Ebsen *Will Lane* • Keir Dullea *Lee Carey* • Lois Nettleton *Annie Boley* • Warren Oates *Jace* • Barbara Luna *Marietta* • Paul Fix *Jess Linley* • Marie Windsor *Hanna* • Denver Pyle *Preacher Pope* ■ *Dir* Burt Kennedy • *Scr* Burt Kennedy, from the story *Mail-Order Bride* by Van Cort in *The Saturday Evening Post*

The Main Attraction ★★
Romantic drama　1962 · UK · Colour · 89min

Keen to kick against his clean-cut image, American crooner Pat Boone hightailed it to Europe for this ludicrous circus melodrama, in which he trifles with the affections of ventriloquist Mai Zetterling, while holding a candle for bareback rider Nancy Kwan. Yet Boone isn't the most miscast member of this sorry ensemble. That honour goes to Lionel Blair as the clown who becomes pathologically jealous of Boone's relationship with Zetterling. DP

Pat Boone *Eddie* • Nancy Kwan *Tessa* • Mai Zetterling *Gina* • Yvonne Mitchell *Elenora* • Kieron Moore *Ricco* • John Le Mesurier *Bozo* • Warren Mitchell *Proprietor* • Lionel Blair *Clown* ■ *Dir* Daniel Petrie • *Scr* John Patrick

The Main Event ★★ 15
Romantic comedy　1979 · US · Colour · 104min

This is one of those self-centred films that Barbra Streisand produces, in which she takes her favourite role of sexual predator. Her target is Ryan O'Neal but the stars fail to re-create the comic success they had in *What's Up, Doc?* Streisand plays the bankrupt owner of a perfume company whose only asset is washed-up boxer O'Neal. Sadly, director Howard Zieff's comedy falls a long way short of going the distance. TH *DVD*

Barbra Streisand *Hillary Kramer* • Ryan O'Neal *Eddie "Kid Natural" Scanlon* • Paul Sand *David* • Whitman Sand *Percy* • Patti D'Arbanville *Donna* • Chu Chu Malave *Luis* • Richard Lawson *Hector Mantilla* ■ *Dir* Howard Zieff • *Scr* Gail Parent, Andrew Smith

Main Street to Broadway ★★
Romantic comedy　1953 · US · BW · 101min

The professional struggles of aspiring young playwright Tom Morton and his involvement with actress Mary Murphy offer a flimsy excuse for fleeting appearances by just about every star on MGM's books. The result is a dull and uninteresting look at Broadway's backstage life, marginally enlivened by Tallulah Bankhead's guest turn. RK

Tom Morton *Tony Monaco* • Mary Murphy (1) *Mary Craig* • Agnes Moorehead *Mildred Waterbury* • Herb Shriner *Frank Johnson* • Rosemary DeCamp *Mrs Craig* • Clinton Sundberg *Mr Craig* • Tallulah Bankhead • Ethel Barrymore ■ *Dir* Tay Garnett, Joel Newton • *Scr* Samson Raphaelson, from a story by Robert E Sherwood

Les Mains Sales ★★
Drama　1951 · Fr · BW · 106min

Jean-Paul Sartre co-adapted his once controversial play to the screen, ensuring – given the date – that the inherent conflict between disillusioned politico Pierre Brasseur and dedicated young communist and potential assassin Daniel Gélin was retained. Sadly, Fernand Rivers displays little filmic invention so we're left with a talkative battle between the revolutionaries,

M

past and present, when the younger man, accompanied by his wife (Monique Artur) agrees to murder his colleague, who might compromise their cause. Plenty of discussion and no resolution. **BB** French +subtitles.

Pierre Brasseur *Hoederer* • Daniel Gélin *Hugo* • Claude Nollier *Olga* • Monique Artur *Jessica* • Jacques Castelot *Prince* • Marcel André *Karski* ■ *Dir* Fernand Rivers • *Scr* Jacques-Laurent Bost, Fernand Rivers, Jean-Paul Sartre, from the play by Jean-Paul Sartre

Maisie ★★★
Comedy 1939 · US · BW · 74min

MGM cast Ann Sothern in this programmer about a curly-headed showgirl stranded without a dime in a one-horse rodeo town. After a chapter of accidents and misadventures involving taciturn ranch manager Robert Young, she cons her way into a job as maid to the owner (Ian Hunter) and his faithless wife (Ruth Hussey). Directed by Edwin L Marin, the success of this fresh, breezy and inconsequential film spawned a ten-picture series, making Maisie/Sothern a 1940s institution. Seen in our jaded age, the picture is both sociologically fascinating and enormous good fun. **RK**

Robert Young (1) *"Slim" Martin* • Ann Sothern *Maisie Ravier* • Ruth Hussey *Sybil Ames* • Ian Hunter *Clifford Ames* • Cliff Edwards *Shorty* • Anthony Allan [John Hubbard] *Richard Raymond* • Art Mix *"Red"* • George Tobias *Rico* ■ *Dir* Edwin L Marin • *Scr* Mary C McCall Jr, from the novel *Dark Dame* by Wilson Collison

Maîtresse ★★★18
Erotic black comedy 1976 · Fr · Colour · 108min

Walking the tightrope between titillation and tact, this study of sadomasochism stars Bulle Ogier as a "mistress" or dominatrix, who inflicts pain and various sorts of humiliation upon her clients. Coming into this secret world is petty crook Gérard Depardieu, who becomes not only Ogier's lover but also her willing assistant. Through the perversion, the purity of Ogier and Depardieu's affair emerges and enters a surreal zone of its own. **AT** French +subtitles. *DVD*

Gérard Depardieu *Olivier* • Bulle Ogier *Ariane* • André Rouyer *Mario* • Nathalie Keryan *Lucienne* ■ *Dir* Barbet Schroeder • *Scr* Barbet Schroeder, Paul Voujargol

The Majestic ★★★PG
Romantic comedy drama
2001 · US/Aus · Colour · 146min

This unashamedly Capra-esque film endorses the values of small-town America and their redemptive effects. Jim Carrey stars as a blacklisted screenwriter in 1950s Hollywood who – in a state of drunken despair – accidentally drives his car off a bridge and is later found washed up on the shores of a proverbial small town, suffering from amnesia. He closely resembles the missing soldier son of Martin Landau, who owns the town's Majestic cinema. With his part in the renovation of the crumbling movie-house, Carrey is able to find his true worth and the town's spirit is revived. Overlong, but caring. **TH** *DVD*

Jim Carrey *Peter Appleton/Luke Trimble* • Martin Landau *Harry Trimble* • Laurie Holden *Adele Stanton* • David Ogden Stiers *Doc Stanton* • James Whitmore *Stan Keller* • Jeffrey DeMunn *Ernie Cole* • Hal Holbrook *Congressman Doyle* • Bob Balaban *Majority Counsel Elvin Clyde* • Allen Garfield *Leo Kubelsky* ■ *Dir* Frank Darabont • *Scr* Michael Sloane

The Major and the Minor ★★★U
Romantic comedy 1942 · US · BW · 96min

A 12-year-old girl on a train awakens the concern of army officer Ray Milland. She also awakens his sexual interest and that of the boys at the military academy where he's stationed. This romantic comedy marked Billy Wilder's Hollywood directing debut. The girl, of course, is not underage at all, but Ginger Rogers masquerading to avoid paying full fare. Famous wit and sometime character actor Robert Benchley

offers support, and Ginger's real-life mother Lela plays her mom. Daft, sparkling entertainment. **RK** *DVD*

Ginger Rogers *Susan Applegate* • Ray Milland *Maj Kirby* • Rita Johnson *Pamela Hill* • Robert Benchley *Mr Osborne* • Diana Lynn *Lucy Hill* • Edward Fielding *Col Hill* • Frankie Thomas *Cadet Osborne* • Raymond Roe *Cadet Wigton* • Lela Rogers *Mrs Applegate* ■ *Dir* Billy Wilder • *Scr* Billy Wilder, Charles Brackett, from the play *Connie Goes Home* by Edward Childs Carpenter, from the story *Sunny Goes Home* by Fannie Kilbourne

Major Barbara ★★★★PG
Satirical comedy 1941 · UK · BW · 115min

This is a superbly cast adaptation of George Bernard Shaw's morality study of the Salvation Army and armaments manufacture. Wendy Hiller in the title role, Rex Harrison as her admirer and a marvellous array of British stage and screen names acquit themselves with distinction. The only flawed performance comes from Robert Morley, who plays Hiller's capitalist father as a fool. Although direction is originally credited to the Hungarian producer Gabriel Pascal, who had acquired the sole rights to film Shaw, this was in fact an early directorial effort by the young David Lean and Harold French. Deborah Kerr looks radiant in an early appearance, and the sophistication of the comedy is perfectly balanced by Ronald Neame's photography and Vincent Korda's splendid interior sets. **TS** *DVD*

Wendy Hiller *Major Barbara Undershaft* • Rex Harrison *Adolphus Cusins* • Robert Morley *Andrew Undershaft* • Emlyn Williams *Snobby Price* • Robert Newton *Bill Walker* • Sybil Thorndike *The General* • Deborah Kerr *Jenny Hill* • David Tree *Charles Lomax* ■ *Dir* Gabriel Pascal, Harold French, David Lean • *Scr* Anatole de Grunwald, George Bernard Shaw, from the play by George Bernard Shaw

Major Dundee ★★★PG
Western 1965 · US · Colour · 130min

Sam Peckinpah's third feature stars Charlton Heston as a Union officer leading a wild bunch of Confederate prisoners, including Richard Harris, to capture an even wilder bunch of marauding Apaches. While Peckinpah had in mind a dark, violent epic about the Civil War, Columbia wanted a breezy cavalry and Indians adventure. When Columbia threatened to fire the director mid-shoot, Heston backed him up and offered to return his $200,000 fee. The studio, of course, accepted this rash offer and let Peckinpah continue, though it still cut 40 minutes of footage. **AT** *DVD*

Charlton Heston *Major Amos Dundee* • Richard Harris *Captain Benjamin Tyreen* • Senta Berger *Teresa Santiago* • Jim Hutton *Lieutenant Graham* • James Coburn *Samuel Potts* • Michael Anderson Jr *Tim Ryan* • Brock Peters *Aesop* ■ *Dir* Sam Peckinpah • *Scr* Harry Julian Fink, Oscar Saul, Sam Peckinpah, from a story by Harry Julian Fink

Major League ★★★15
Sports comedy 1989 · US · Colour · 101min

In this amiable but predictable sporting comedy, the players of a deadbeat baseball team, led by Tom Berenger, decide to fight back when they discover that their new boss (Margaret Whitton) is determined to see them finish bottom of the league. The misfits include the short-sighted pitcher Charlie Sheen and the hopelessly vain Corbin Bernsen. This gets by on star power alone. **JF** Swearing.

Tom Berenger *Jake Taylor* • Charlie Sheen *Rickie Vaughn* • Corbin Bernsen *Roger Dorn* • Margaret Whitton *Rachel Phelps* • James Gammon *Lou Brown* • Rene Russo *Lynn Wells* • Wesley Snipes *Willie Mays Hayes* ■ *Dir/Scr* David S Ward

Major League II ★★PG
Sports comedy 1994 · US · Colour · 100min

Five years after the Cleveland Indians baseball team stepped out in Major League, the same sorry crew (minus Wesley Snipes and Rene Russo) reassembles for another season, with the team's original nemesis, owner Margaret Whitton, once again determined to dismantle the club. The

acting is minor league, while the bawdy locker-room banter and the endless on-the-field foul-ups become tiresome. **DP** Swearing.

Charlie Sheen *Rick "Wild Thing" Vaughn* • Tom Berenger *Jake Taylor* • Corbin Bernsen *Roger Dorn* • Dennis Haysbert *Pedro Cerrano* • James Gammon *Lou Brown* • Omar Epps *Willie Mays Hayes* • Margaret Whitton *Rachel Phelps* ■ *Dir* David S Ward • *Scr* RJ Stewart, from a story by Tom S Parker, Jim Jennewein, RJ Stewart

Major League: Back to the Minors ★★12
Sports comedy 1998 · US · Colour · 95min

It's strike three for this baseball comedy franchise, and it's out – of ideas. Scott Bakula should have been suspicious when even the non-selective Charlie Sheen declined to return for this second sequel. Slimy Corbin Bernsen is back, though, offering ex-player Bakula the job of managing the worst team in the league. **JC** Swearing.

Scott Bakula *Gus Cantrell* • Corbin Bernsen *Roger Dorn* • Takaaki Ishibashi *Taka Tanaka* • Ted McGinley *Leonard Huff* • Bob Uecker *Harry Doyle* • Dennis Haysbert *Pedro Cerrano* ■ *Dir/Scr* John Warren (2)

A Majority of One ★U
Comedy drama 1961 · US · Colour · 153min

The unlikely love affair between a middle-aged Jewish widow and a Japanese diplomat is the subject of this movie, adapted by Leonard Spigelgass from his hit Broadway play. The film, however, directed by Mervyn LeRoy at interminable length, falls flat on its face, due in no small part to disastrous miscasting. **RK**

Rosalind Russell *Mrs Jacoby* • Alec Guinness *Koichi Asano* • Ray Danton *Jerome Black* • Madlyn Rhue *Alice Black* • Mae Questel *Mrs Rubin* ■ *Dir* Mervyn LeRoy • *Scr* Leonard Spigelgass, from his play

Make It Happen ★★PG
Dance drama 2008 · US/Can · Colour · 86min

Mary Elizabeth Winstead stars as Lauryn, who quits her life in a small Indiana town to become a dance sensation in the big city. But she soon finds herself having to gyrate at Ruby's burlesque club after her hopes of being accepted at the Chicago School of Music & Dance are dashed. Winstead makes an appealing heroine, but the join-the-dots plot recycles clichés that were hoary even in Busby Berkeley's heyday. The supporting actors also have less to do, with Tessa Thompson as the heart-of-gold gal who befriends Winstead after her audition implodes and Julissa Bermudez as the haughty star of Ruby's who soon finds herself upstaged. However, Riley Smith's drippy turn as the club DJ who helps Lauryn discover her potential fails to register at all. **DP** *DVD*

Mary Elizabeth Winstead *Lauryn* • Riley Smith *Russ* • John Reardon *Joel* • Tessa Thompson *Dana* • Ashley Roberts *Brooke* • Julissa Bermudez *Carmen* ■ *Dir* Darren Grant • *Scr* Duane Adler, Nicole Avril, from a story by Adler

Make Me a Star ★★★
Comedy drama 1932 · US · BW · 86min

Stuart Erwin stars as the screen-struck hick who goes to Hollywood and becomes a movie star when cast in a comedy western that he thinks is a serious film. Great fun, with Joan Blondell the sympathetic co-star, ZaSu Pitts and Ben Turpin in support, and a host of the famous (Claudette Colbert, Tallulah Bankhead, Gary Cooper, Charlie Ruggles, Fredric March et al) flitting through Paramount studios as themselves. **RK**

Joan Blondell *"Flips" Montague* • Stuart Erwin *Merton Gill* • ZaSu Pitts *Mrs Scudder* • Ben Turpin *Ben* • Charles Sellon *Mr Gashwiler* • Florence Roberts *Mrs Gashwiler* ■ *Dir* William Beaudine • *Scr* Sam Mintz, Walter DeLeon, Arthur Kober, from the play *Merton of the Movies* by George S Kaufman, Marc Connelly, from the novel *Merton of the Movies* by Harry Leon Wilson

Make Mine a Million ★★★U
Comedy 1959 · UK · BW · 78min

Diminutive funster Arthur Askey had often spoofed the BBC on radio and in films and, when he made the transition from the BBC to ITV (in 1956), he likewise took the rise out of his new employers. In this satire on TV advertising, Arthur Askey is a make-up man who falls under the influence of dodgy promoter Sidney James and becomes the star of soap powder commercials. A pacey romp. **DF** *DVD*

Arthur Askey *Arthur Ashton* • Sidney James *Sid Gibson* • Dermot Walsh *Martin Russell* • Sally Barnes *Sally* • Olga Lindo *Mrs Burgess* • Bernard Cribbins *Jack* • Kenneth Connor *Anxious husband* ■ *Dir* Lance Comfort • *Scr* Peter Blackmore, Talbot Rothwell, Arthur Askey, from a story by Jack Francis

Make Mine Mink ★★U
Comedy 1960 · UK · BW · 96min

This is so awash with whimsy that the comedy only occasionally manages to bob to the surface. But, while it's not an uproarious laughfest, there's still plenty to enjoy as the dependable Terry-Thomas masterminds a series of robberies for his gang of old dears in order to raise money for a children's home. Athene Seyler, Elspeth Duxbury and Hattie Jacques are good value as the respectable rogues, and Kenneth Williams is fun as their fence. But Billie Whitelaw is less convincing as the reformed delinquent. **DP** *DVD*

Terry-Thomas *Major Albert Rayne* • Hattie Jacques *Nanette Parry* • Athene Seyler *Dame Beatrice Appleby* • Billie Whitelaw *Lily* • Elspeth Duxbury *Elizabeth Pinkerton* • Irene Handl *Madame Spolinski* • Kenneth Williams *Freddy Warrington* ■ *Dir* Robert Asher • *Scr* Michael Pertwee, Peter Blackmore, from the play *Breath of Spring* by Peter Coke

Make Mine Music ★★★★U
Musical animation 1946 · US · Colour · 74min

This was Walt Disney's attempt to do for popular music what his studio's animation had achieved for classical music in *Fantasia*, but he failed to meet with similar box-office success. This beautifully crafted film is by no means as well known as it should be. As with *Fantasia*, the crass populism of this episodic treat divided critics and delighted children, and today there's even more to enjoy, not least the glorious period Technicolor and the display of major 1940s talent, including the Benny Goodman Orchestra, the Andrews Sisters, Dinah Shore and Nelson Eddy. **TS** *DVD*

Nelson Eddy • Dinah Shore • Jerry Colonna • Andy Russell • Sterling Holloway ■ *Dir* Jack Kinney, Clyde Geronimi, Hamilton Luske, Robert Cormack, Joshua Meador • *Scr* Homer Brightman, Dick Huemer, Dick Kinney, John Walbridge, Tom Oreb, Dick Shaw, Eric Gurney, Sylvia Holland, T Hee, Dick Kelsey, Jesse Marsh, Roy Williams, Erdman Penner, James Bodrero, Cap Palmer, Erwin Graham • *Music* Lillian Henley

Make More Noise! Suffragettes in Silent Film ★★★PG
Silent compilation 2015 · UK · BW · 74min

The BFI examines the struggle for women's suffrage with this impeccably researched compilation. In addition to newsreel clips of the demonstrations led by the Pankhursts, it also explores how women were portrayed in comic shorts that suggest they were socially emancipated long before they were enfranchised. The footage of Emily Davison's funeral following her fatal injury at the 1913 Epsom Derby along with a couple of war effort documentaries have great historical value. **DP**

Make Way for Tomorrow ★★★★U
Comedy drama 1937 · US · BW · 91min

There aren't many films on the painful subject of growing old and becoming a burden to one's offspring: Yasujiro Ozu's *Tokyo Story*, *Kotch* with Walter Matthau and this heart-rending Leo McCarey picture, a genuine tear-jerker thanks to its acute understanding of human nature. Victor Moore and Beulah Bondi play the retired couple who lose their home and are forced to separate when none of their children will take them in. The old pair are shown realistically, being quite difficult at times, but their continuing optimism makes their plight all the worse. AE 🅱️ 🔵

Victor Moore *Barkley Cooper* • Beulah Bondi *Lucy Cooper* • Fay Bainter *Anita Cooper* • Thomas Mitchell *George Cooper* • Porter Hall *Harvey Chase* • Barbara Read *Rhoda Cooper* • Maurice Moscovitch [Maurice Moscovich] *Max Rubens* • Elisabeth Risdon *Cora Payne* • Leo McCarey *Passerby/Man in overcoat/Carpet sweeper* ■ *Dir* Leo McCarey • *Scr* Viña Delmar [Vina Delmar], from the unpublished play *Years Are So Long* by Helen Leary, Nolan Leary, from the novel *Years Are So Long* by Josephine Lawrence

The Maker ★★★ 18
Crime drama 1997 · US · Colour · 94min

Director Tim Hunter made his name with the startling *River's Edge*, a harrowing portrait of disaffected youth, and this sees him covering similar ground. Jonathan Rhys Meyers plays a teenage slacker who, along with his friends fills his days by hanging around malls and indulging in petty crime. Then his long-lost older brother Matthew Modine turns up out of the blue and initiates him into burglary. The thriller elements don't quite come off but Hunter still has a sharp eye for adolescent trauma. JF Swearing, violence. **DVD**

Matthew Modine *Walter Schmeiss* • Mary-Louise Parker *Officer Emily Peck* • Jonathan Rhys Meyers *Josh Minnell* • Michael Madsen *Skarney* • Fairuza Balk *Bella Sotto* • Kate McGregor-Stewart *Mother Minnell* • Lawrence Pressman *Father Minnell* ■ *Dir* Tim Hunter • *Scr* Rand Ravich

Making Contact ★★★ 15
Supernatural adventure
1985 · W Ger · Colour · 75min

This early film from director Roland Emmerich was made a decade before he went big and blockbustery with *Stargate*, *Independence Day* and *Godzilla*. Emmerich brings flair and imagination to this superior kids' film about a boy whose grief at his dad's death activates previously hidden telekinetic powers. DA

Joshua Morrell *Joey* • Eva Kryll *Laura, Joey's mother* • Jan Zierold *Martin, Joey's father* • Tammy Shields *Sally* • Barbara Klein *Dr Haiden* ■ *Dir* Roland Emmerich • *Scr* Hans J Haller, Thomas Lechner

Making Love ★★ 15
Drama 1982 · US · Colour · 106min

Kate Jackson gets a shock when her doctor husband Michael Ontkean confesses he is in love with another. The other happens to be a man (Harry Hamlin). Arthur Hiller's restrained account of a repressed man coming out of the closet was something of a ground-breaking film for Hollywood at the time. But because such care has been taken not to offend anyone, this never rises above the uncomplicated, routine level of a soap opera. AME **DVD**

Michael Ontkean *Zack* • Kate Jackson *Claire* • Harry Hamlin *Bart McGuire* • Wendy Hiller *Winnie Bates* • Arthur Hill *Henry* • Nancy Olson *Christine* • John Dukakis *Tim* ■ *Dir* Arthur Hiller • *Scr* Barry Sandler, from a story by A Scott Berg

Making Mr Right ★★★ 15
Science-fiction satire
1987 · US · Colour · 94min

This quirky satire was Susan Seidelman's next movie after her big hit, *Desperately Seeking Susan*. John Malkovich plays both an inventor and the android he has created, while Ann Magnuson is a wacky PR whizz hired to promote the robot but soon falling in love with it. Zany stuff, combining shades of vintage B-movies with punk hairstyles and postmodern sensibilities. Less than the sum of its rather too diverse parts. PF **DVD**

John Malkovich *Dr Jeff Peters/Ulysses* • Ann Magnuson *Frankie Stone* • Glenne Headly *Trish* • Ben Masters *Congressman Steve Marcus* • Laurie

Metcalf *Sandy* • Polly Bergen *Estelle Stone* • Harsh Nayyar *Dr Ravi Ramdas* • Susan Berman *Ivy Stone* ■ *Dir* Susan Seidelman • *Scr* Floyd Byars, Laurie Frank

The Makioka Sisters ★★★★
Drama 1983 · Jpn · Colour and BW · 140min

Adapted from Junichiro Tanizaki's novel, this is a sprawling study of Japanese society in the days preceding the Second World War. Bound by family wealth, but divided on everything else – from politics and progress to the role of women within an increasingly militaristic state – the four Makioka sisters take some time getting to know. But once Kon Ichikawa has established their attitudes and alliances, their ambitions, fears, romances and rivalries begin to engross. The result is impeccably played and beautifully designed and photographed. DP Japanese +subtitles.

Keiko Kishi *Tsuruko, oldest sister* • Yoshiko Sakuma *Sachiko, second oldest sister* • Sayuri Yoshinaga *Yukiko, third oldest sister* • Yuko Kotegawa *Taeko, youngest sister* • Juzo Itami *Tsuruko's husband* ■ *Dir* Kon Ichikawa • *Scr* Kon Ichikawa, Shinya Hidaki, from the novel by Junichiro Tanizaki • *Production Designer* Shinobu Muraki • *Cinematographer* Kiyoshi Hasegawa

Malachi's Cove ★★ U
Period adventure 1973 · UK · Colour · 85min

Set in 19th-century Cornwall, this benefits from ripe, eye-rolling performances from Donald Pleasence and Peter Vaughan. But the direction and underwritten screenplay by Henry Herbert leave much to be desired, and this tale of a plucky young girl trying to make a living barely received a cinema release. Nevertheless, Veronica Quilligan and Dai Bradley are well cast as the youngsters and Walter Lassally's location photography is attractive. TS

Donald Pleasence *Malachi* • Dai Bradley [David Bradley (3)] *Barty* • Veronica Quilligan *Mally* • Peter Vaughan *Mr Gunliffe* • Lilias Walker *Mrs Gunliffe* • Arthur English *Jack Combes* ■ *Dir* Henry Herbert • *Scr* Henry Herbert, from a story by Anthony Trollope

Malaga ★ U
Action adventure 1954 · UK · Colour · 88min

Tangier comes across vividly enough as the exotic setting for this British-produced thriller. Maureen O'Hara certainly looks gorgeous, but the queen of the redheads takes some swallowing as a modern Mata Hari working for the American government to expose a dope-smuggling ring. Macdonald Carey is flabby and uninspiring as her co-star. AE

Maureen O'Hara *Joanna Dane* • Macdonald Carey *Van Logan* • Binnie Barnes *Frisco* • Guy Middleton *Soames Howard* • Hugh McDermott *Richard Farrell* • James Lilburn *Danny Boy* ■ *Dir* Richard Sale • *Scr* Robert Westerby

Malaya ★★★
Second World War adventure
1949 · US · BW · 94min

Enjoyable tosh from MGM, this has an amazing cast, though in the end it's not much more than a B-movie. Spencer Tracy and James Stewart play a convict and a reporter hired to smuggle rubber out of Japanese-occupied Malaya. (The fact that this was a British theatre of war doesn't seem to enter into the equation.) Sydney Greenstreet runs a bar in the jungle where Valentina Cortese sings while waiting to see which star she ends up with in the end. AT

Spencer Tracy *Carnahan* • James Stewart *John Royer* • Valentina Cortese *Luana* • Sydney Greenstreet *Dutchman* • John Hodiak *Keller* • Lionel Barrymore *John Manchester* • Gilbert Roland *Romano* • DeForest Kelley *Lt Glenson* ■ *Dir* Richard Thorpe • *Scr* Frank Fenton, from a story by Manchester Boddy

Malcolm ★★★ 12
Crime comedy 1986 · Aus · Colour · 82min

This comedy tells the gently contrived story of Colin Friels, a simple, inarticulate man whose Heath Robinson-like constructions help his lodgers (John Hargreaves and Lindy Davies) pursue a career in remote-controlled crime. The directorial debut of

Nadia Tass, whose husband, David Parker, wrote the script, it has a quaintness of observation that is never coy. It's a tribute to the actors that they are never upstaged by the scene-stealing inventions. TH **DVD**

Colin Friels *Malcolm* • John Hargreaves *Frank* • Lindy Davies *Judith* • Chris Haywood *Willy* • Judith Stratford *Jenny* • Beverly Phillips *Mrs T* ■ *Dir* Nadia Tass • *Scr* David Parker

Malcolm X ★★★ 15
Biographical drama 1992 · US · Colour · 193min

To describe a film as "worthy" is to damn it with faint praise. But, as much as one admires the ambition of Spike Lee's picture, it is surprisingly conventional and, at times, downright dull. There are speeches, reams and reams of them, and Denzel Washington as the black militant leader of the 1960s copes with them as best he can. Washington looks impressive and he has undoubted charisma, like Malcolm X himself, but he's stuck in a huge epic that lumbers on through the decades, continents and events. AT Violence, swearing. **DVD** 🔵

Denzel Washington *Malcolm X* • Angela Bassett *Betty Shabazz* • Albert Hall *Baines* • Al Freeman Jr *Elijah Muhammad* • Delroy Lindo *West Indian Archie* • Spike Lee *Shorty* • Theresa Randle *Laura* • Kate Vernon *Sophia* • Lonette McKee *Louise Little* • Tommy Hollis *Earl Little* ■ *Dir* Spike Lee • *Scr* Arnold Perl, Spike Lee, from *The Autobiography of Malcolm X, as told to Alex Haley*

The Maldonado Miracle ★★★
Drama 2003 · US · Colour · 99min

Salma Hayek makes a decent directorial debut with this adaptation of Theodore Taylor's novel. Set in a Californian backwater, the action centres on drops of blood that appear on the crucifix of the local church. But while disillusioned priest Peter Fonda despairs at the miracle frenzy whipped up by the media, diner owner Mare Winningham and her bar-room beau Ruben Blades discover that the blood's source was wounded Mexican illegal kid Eddy Martin and they protect him from the cynics who want him silenced to sustain the town's much-needed revival. Undoubtedly sentimental, this is still a thoughtful study of faith in secular times. DP

Peter Fonda *Father Russell* • Mare Winningham *Maisie* • Rubén Blades *Cruz* • Eddy Martin *José Maldonado* • Bill Sage *Lyle* • Soledad St Hilaire *Josephina* • Jesse Borrego *Hector Maldonado* • Christina Cabot *Stella* ■ *Dir* Salma Hayek • *Scr* Paul W Cooper, from the novel by Theodore Taylor

Male and Female ★★★★
Silent satire 1919 · US · BW · 115min

Before Cecil B DeMille discovered the Bible, the flamboyant producer/director explored sex in a series of enjoyably risqué comedies, six of them with Gloria Swanson. In this free adaptation of JM Barrie's *The Admirable Crichton*, Swanson plays one of a group of shipwrecked aristocrats who find themselves dependent on their butler (Thomas Meighan). DeMille remade it in 1934 as *Four Frightened People*. RB

Thomas Meighan *Crichton* • Gloria Swanson *Lady Mary Lasenby* • Lila Lee *Tweeny* • Theodore Roberts *Lord Loam* • Raymond Hatton *Honorable Ernest Wolley* • Mildred Reardon *Agatha Lasenby* • Bebe Daniels *The King's favourite* ■ *Dir* Cecil B DeMille • *Scr* Jeanie Macpherson, from the play *The Admirable Crichton* by JM Barrie

The Male Animal ★★★★
Comedy 1942 · US · BW · 100min

A punchy, apposite comedy, regarded as highly sophisticated in its day, this still stands the test of time. Henry Fonda is excellent as the college professor about to lose his wife Olivia de Havilland to old flame Jack Carson, and his job, if he reads a controversial letter written by anarchists to his students. All three leads are splendid, giving great light and shade to their characters and so immediately drawing us into the complex plot. SH

Henry Fonda *Tommy Turner* • Olivia de Havilland *Ellen Turner* • Joan Leslie *Patricia Stanley* • Jack Carson *Joe Ferguson* • Eugene Pallette *Ed Keller* • Herbert Anderson *Michael Barnes* • Hattie McDaniel *Cleota* • Ivan Simpson *Dr Damon* ■ *Dir* Elliott Nugent • *Scr* Julius J Epstein, Philip G Epstein, Stephen Morehouse Avery, from the play by James Thurber, Elliott Nugent

Male Hunt ★★
Comedy 1964 · Fr/It · BW · 92min

Edouard Molinaro, who later made *La Cages aux Folles*, directs this sex comedy about bachelors on the run from beautiful women. A big hit in France, this is worth seeing only for its astonishing cast: the raffish charm of Jean-Claude Brialy is complemented by Jean-Paul Belmondo doing his trademark petty criminal act. The women are even more eye-catching and include Catherine Deneuve and her sister Françoise Dorléac, who died so tragically in a car crash in 1967. AT French +subtitles.

Jean-Paul Belmondo *Fernand* • Jean-Claude Brialy *Tony* • Bernard Blier *Mons Heurtin* • Catherine Deneuve *Denise* • Françoise Dorléac *Sandra* • Micheline Presle *Isabelle* • Claude Rich *Julien* • Marie Laforêt *Gisèle* • Bernadette Lafont *Flora* ■ *Dir* Edouard Molinaro • *Scr* France Roche, Michel Audiard, from an idea by Yvon Guezel, from stories by Albert Simonin, Michel Duran

Maleficent ★★★ PG
Fantasy 2014 · US · Colour · 93min

One of Disney's most memorable villains gets to tell her side of the story of *Sleeping Beauty* in this enjoyable reworking of the fairy tale. Angelina Jolie stars as Maleficent, the protector of the fairy realm, who is betrayed by her childhood sweetheart, Stefan (Sharlto Copley), and takes her revenge by cursing his first-born child, Aurora. Jolie, clad in black with chiselled cheekbones, devilish horns and blood-red lipstick, is undoubtedly the star of the show, while Elle Fanning makes a winsome if rather vacuous Aurora. While *Maleficent* may not leave you spellbound, there's still plenty to enchant and entertain. JH **DVD** 🔵 🅂🄳

Angelina Jolie *Maleficent* • Sharlto Copley *Stefan* • Elle Fanning *Aurora* • Sam Riley *Diaval* • Imelda Staunton *Knotgrass* • Juno Temple *Thistlewit* • Lesley Manville *Flittle* ■ *Dir* Robert Stromberg • *Scr* Linda Woolverton, from the film *Sleeping Beauty* by Erdman Penner, from the fairy tale *La Belle au Bois Dormant* by Charles Perrault • *Cinematographer* Dean Semler • *Music* James Newton Howard

Malena ★★★ 15
Second World War romantic drama
2000 · It/US · Colour · 88min

Set in a picturesque, fictional Sicilian town, Giuseppe Tornatore's two-toned rite-of-passage picture is set against the changing fortunes of the Second World War. Debuting Giuseppe Sulfaro manages a naivety that tempers his furtive imaginings, as the teenager besotted with local beauty Malena (Monica Bellucci). Tornatore revels in a gallery of Italianate caricatures, but the film belongs to Bellucci, who almost wordlessly conveys allure, vulnerability, brassiness and courage. DP Italian +subtitles. Violence, swearing, sex scenes. **DVD** 🔵

Monica Bellucci *Malena Scordia* • Giuseppe Sulfaro *Renato Amoroso* • Luciano Federico *Renato's father* • Matilde Piana *Renato's mother* • Pietro Notarianni *Professor Bonsignore* • Gaetano Aronica *Nino Scordia* ■ *Dir* Giuseppe Tornatore • *Scr* Giuseppe Tornatore, from a story by Luciano Vincenzoni • *Music* Ennio Morricone • *Cinematographer* Lajos Koltai

Malibu's Most Wanted ★★ 15
Comedy 2003 · US · Colour · 82min

As a skit on his TV comedy series, *The Jamie Kennedy Experiment*, Jamie Kennedy's portrayal of a white teen who acts like a black rap artist had plenty of comic scope. But stretched out for a full feature, the joke soon wears thin. Though B-Rad's gangsta posturing is amusing in his over-privileged Malibu environment, once

M

transposed to the LA "ghetto" the film becomes a Caucasian pastiche of black urban life. It gets tedious watching the same old ethnic clichés, while the repetitive gags are as transparent as the plotline. SF Swearing, violence. **DVD**

Jamie Kennedy *B-Rad* • Taye Diggs *Sean* • Anthony Anderson *P J* • Blair Underwood *Tom Gibbons* • Regina Hall *Shondra* • Damien Dante Wayans [Damien Wayans] *Tec* • Ryan O'Neal *Bill Gluckman* • Snoop Dogg *Ronnie Rizzat* • Bo Derek *Bess Gluckman* • Jeffrey Tambor *Dr Feldman* ▪ *Dir* John Whitesell • *Scr* Fax Bahr, Adam Small, Jamie Kennedy, Nick Swardson, from the character created by Jamie Kennedy

Malice ★★★ 15
Psychological thriller
1993 · US · Colour · 102min

Nicole Kidman has surprised the cynics by forging a very individual career of her own. Here she plays the seemingly innocent young newlywed who ensnares nice-but-dim husband Bill Pullman and charismatic surgeon Alec Baldwin in a deadly scam. Kidman is smart and sexy as the *femme fatale* figure, while Baldwin, always better at being bad, excels as the arrogant doctor. The screenplay is a mite too tortuous, but director Harold Becker has fun piling on the red herrings. JF Violence, swearing, sex scenes, nudity. **DVD**

Alec Baldwin *Jed Hill* • Nicole Kidman *Tracy Safian* • Bill Pullman *Andy Safian* • Bebe Neuwirth *Dana* • George C Scott *Dr Kessler* • Anne Bancroft *Claire Kennsinger* • Peter Gallagher *Dennis Riley* • Gwyneth Paltrow *Paula Bell* ▪ *Dir* Harold Becker • *Scr* Aaron Sorkin, Scott Frank, from a story by Aaron Sorkin, Jonas McCord

Malice in Wonderland ★★ 15
Fantasy drama 2009 · UK · Colour · 83min

It won't come as much of a surprise that this is a variation on Lewis Carroll's timeless fantasy. The twist here is that it's an updated urban spin on his work. Maggie Grace (from TV's *Lost*) stars as an amnesiac Alice whose version of Wonderland is the neon-lit North East of England, where she's taken by London cabbie Whitey (Danny Dyer) after he hits her with his taxi. The film has a lively cast of recognisable small-screen stars (Paul Kaye, Nathaniel Parker, *Peep Show*'s Matt King), but Alice's adventures lose something in their contemporary translation, and there is very little to care about. It's nicely shot, though, in the style of a 1980s music video. JA **DVD**

Maggie Grace *Alice* • Danny Dyer *Whitey* • Nathaniel Parker *Harry Hunt* • Matt King *Gonzo* • Bronagh Gallagher *Hattie* • Paul Kaye *Caterpillar* • Gary Beadle *Felix Chester* • Pam Ferris *Doochey* ▪ *Dir* Simon Fellows • *Scr* Jayson Rothwell, inspired by the illustrated children's books *Alice's Adventures in Wonderland/Through the Looking Glass* by Lewis Carroll

Mallrats ★★★ 18
Comedy 1995 · US · Colour · 91min

Director Kevin Smith's follow-up to his no-budget independent hit *Clerks* was this underrated comic look at pop Americana, junk culture and adolescent angst that gained enormously from the use of a professional cast (Shannen Doherty, Claire Forlani, Ben Affleck). Focusing on a pair of slackers mooching around the local shopping mall after being dumped by their girlfriends, Smith's vulgar and amusing diversion is equally irreverent and desperately spot-on as its predecessor. AJ **DVD**

Shannen Doherty *Rene* • Jeremy London *TS Quint* • Jason Lee *Brodie Bruce* • Claire Forlani *Brandi Svenning* • Ben Affleck *Shannon Hamilton* • Joey Lauren Adams *Gwen Turner* • Renee Humphrey *Tricia Jones* • Jason Mewes *Jay* • Stan Lee • Kevin Smith (2) *Silent Bob* ▪ *Dir/Scr* Kevin Smith (2)

Malone ★★ 18
Action drama 1987 · US · Colour · 87min

Burt Reynolds is in standard macho form as a former CIA agent on the trail of a baddie who's busy building his personal paramilitary empire. Apart from the fact

that Reynolds and co-star Cliff Robertson know their way around the all-action scenario like maps of their home town, there's nothing much of merit here. SH Swearing, violence.

Burt Reynolds *Malone* • Cliff Robertson *Delaney* • Cynthia Gibb *Jo Barlow* • Scott Wilson *Paul Barlow* • Kenneth McMillan *Hawkins* • Lauren Hutton *Jamie* ▪ *Dir* Harley Cokliss • *Scr* Christopher Frank, from the novel *Shotgun* by William Wingate

Malpertuis ★★★★ 18
Horror fantasy
1971 · Fr/W Ger/Bel · Colour · 91min

A triumph of conception and design that's slightly betrayed by its execution, this is, nevertheless, a dazzlingly audacious attempt to realise Jean Ray's fantasy novel, in which the deities of Mount Olympus eke out a woeful bourgeois existence inside a labyrinthine mansion. Director Harry Kümel cleverly uses the fabulous gothic sets to generate a real sense of earthbound ethereality, which is reinforced by cinematographer Gerry Fisher's confident use of texture and colour. But, while Orson Welles and Charles Janssens invest their roles with knowing humour, Mathieu Carrière's sailor and Susan Hampshire's Gorgon are markedly less successful. DP Flemish, French +subtitles. **DVD**

Orson Welles *Cassavius* • Susan Hampshire *Nancy/Euryale/Alice/Nurse* • Michel Bouquet *Dideloo* • Mathieu Carrière *Jan* • Jean-Pierre Cassel *Lampernisse* • Charles Janssens *Philarette* • Daniel Pilon *Mathias Crook* ▪ *Dir* Harry Kümel • *Scr* Jean Ferry, from the novel by Jean Ray

Malpractice ★★
Thriller 2001 · US · Colour · 90min

This New Orleans-based thriller is a melodramatic though proficient puzzler, in which medical lawyer Stephanie Zimbalist goes up against her mentor, Michael Arata, to sue the hospital that recently suspended her seriously depressed husband (Markus Flanagan) for surgical negligence. The case itself is only mildly diverting, largely because of the padding that reduces the pace. But Zimbalist turns in a serviceable display of unfussy professionalism. The director is Monkees drummer Micky Dolenz. DP

Stephanie Zimbalist *Beth Garrett* • Gabrielle Carteris *Ellen Robertson* • Michael Arata *Doug* • Ritchie Montgomery *Bradley* • John McConnell *Walter* • Adriana Bate *Victoria* ▪ *Dir* Micky Dolenz • *Scr* Stuart Alexander

Malta Story ★★★ U
Second World War drama
1953 · UK · BW · 99min

Intended as a cinematic tribute to the island that was awarded the George Cross for its courage during the Second World War, this is a remarkably restrained drama in comparison to other British-made accounts of wartime heroics. Blending romance and intrigue with convincing combat sequences, director Brian Desmond Hurst presents a moving human story without slipping into melodrama. Alec Guinness is overly subdued as the photographer, but Flora Robson is superb as the mother whose children experience the sharply contrasting fortunes of war. DP **DVD**

Alec Guinness *Peter Ross* • Jack Hawkins *Air Commanding Officer* • Anthony Steel *Bartlett* • Muriel Pavlow *Maria* • Flora Robson *Melita* • Renée Asherson *Joan* • Ralph Truman *Banks* • Reginald Tate *Payne* ▪ *Dir* Brian Desmond Hurst • *Scr* William Fairchild, Nigel Balchin, Thorold Dickinson, Peter de Sarigny

The Maltese Bippy ★
Comedy 1969 · US · Colour · 91min

At the height of their TV fame with *Laugh In*, comedians Dan Rowan and Dick Martin parlayed one of their catchphrases – "You bet your sweet bippy" – into a brainless, feature-length horror send-up. Rowan plays a nudie movie producer who takes his lead star, Martin, to a Long Island haunted house. Cue lots of alternative endings, none of which is funny. AJ

Dan Rowan *Sam Smith* • Dick Martin *Ernest Grey* • Carol Lynley *Robin Sherwood* • Julie Newmar *Carlotta Ravenswood* • Mildred Natwick *Molly Fletcher* • Fritz Weaver *Mr Ravenswood* • Robert Reed *Lt Tim Crane* ▪ *Dir* Norman Panama • *Scr* Everett Freeman, Ray Singer, from a story by Everett Freeman

The Maltese Falcon ★★★★★ PG
Classic film noir 1941 · US · BW · 96min

Superb cinematic entertainment, this third version of Dashiell Hammett's hard-boiled crime drama completely obliterated memories of the two perfectly fine earlier films (*Dangerous Female* and *Satan Met a Lady*) and created a brand new movie icon in Humphrey Bogart's cynical private detective Sam Spade. This was the beginning of a beautiful friendship between Bogie and John Huston, who was then a screenwriter making his feature debut as director, and whose tart screenplay retains most of the sharp dialogue and sleazy amorality of Hammett's original. The supporting cast is an extraordinary combination that couldn't be bettered – stage actor Sydney Greenstreet made his screen debut as Gutman, lusting after the Black Bird; Peter Lorre is the whiny, effeminate Joel Cairo; and Mary Astor is cast against type as *femme fatale* supreme. TS **DVD** **Blu**

Humphrey Bogart *Samuel Spade* • Mary Astor *Brigid O'Shaughnessy/Miss Wonderly* • Gladys George *Iva Archer* • Peter Lorre *Joel Cairo* • Barton MacLane *Lt of Detectives Dundy* • Lee Patrick *Effie Perine* • Sydney Greenstreet *Kasper Gutman* • Ward Bond *Det Tom Polhaus* • Jerome Cowan *Miles Archer* • Elisha Cook Jr *Wilmer Cook* ▪ *Dir* John Huston • *Scr* John Huston, from the novel by Dashiell Hammett • *Cinematographer* Arthur Edeson • *Music* Adolph Deutsch

Mama ★★ 15
Horror 2013 · Sp/Can/US · Colour · 99min

The debut feature of director Andy Muschietti – expanding on his 2008 short – has spooky atmosphere to spare even if the plot bears too many stretch marks. After a car crash, two little girls lost in the woods are sustained by a deranged ghost consumed with possessive motherly love. Rescued years later, they go to live with their uncle (Nikolaj Coster-Waldau) and his girlfriend (Jessica Chastain) whose efforts to bond with the children are disrupted by the evil presence. CGI-augmented *[Rec]* actor Javier Botet certainly looks the part, lurking under beds and in the closet. But there aren't enough scares and the final swerve into an unconvincing fairy-tale finale undercuts the primal terror once and for all. AJ Violence. **DVD** **Blu**

Jessica Chastain *Annabel* • Nikolaj Coster-Waldau *Lucas/Jeffrey* • Megan Charpentier *Victoria* • Isabelle Nélisse *Lilly* • Javier Botet *Mama* ▪ *Dir* Andy Muschietti [Andres Muschietti] • *Scr* Neil Cross, Andy Muschietti [Andres Muschietti], Barbara Muschietti

Mamá Cumple 100 Años ★★★
Black comedy 1979 · Sp · Colour · 95min

In *Anna and the Wolves*, Carlos Saura used Rafaela Aparicio's three sons to symbolise what he considered to be the primary evils of Franco's Spain: religion, sexual repression and authoritarian fascism. This Oscar-nominated follow-up shows the two surviving siblings joining with the rest of Aparicio's grasping family to celebrate her centenary, though they soon abandon their false bonhomie to scrap for a chunk of her fortune. The satire is ferocious, yet the caricatures grotesque, with Saura more intent on amusing than denouncing. DP Spanish +subtitles.

Geraldine Chaplin *Anna* • Amparo Muñoz *Natalia* • Rafaela Aparicio *Mother* • Fernando Fernán Gómez *Fernando* • Norman Briski *Antonio* • Charo Soriano *Luchi* ▪ *Dir/Scr* Carlos Saura

La Maman et la Putain ★★★★★ 18
Drama 1973 · Fr · BW · 208min

A sprawling study of sexual politics and smug 1960s intellectualism, Jean Eustache's masterpiece was the last hurrah of the French New Wave. Based on actual conversations, the screenplay was delivered verbatim by a superb cast that deserves considerable credit for making every line seem so spontaneous – particularly Françoise Lebrun, a first-time non-professional whose epic speech about the futility of sex without love is remarkable for its power and intensity. But Jean-Pierre Léaud's indolent student and his sensible girlfriend, Bernadette Lafont, are equally impressive in a brilliantly observed portrait that remains as compelling as it is controversial. DP French +subtitles. Swearing, sex scenes.

Bernadette Lafont *Marie* • Jean-Pierre Léaud *Alexandre* • Françoise Lebrun *Veronika* • Isabelle Weingarten *Gilberte* ▪ *Dir/Scr* Jean Eustache

Mama's Dirty Girls ★ 18
Black comedy 1974 · US · Colour · 76min

A witless melange of attempted murders and inane seduction, this supposed black comedy was another nail in the coffin of one-time Hollywood *femme fatale* Gloria Grahame's illustrious career. She plays a black widow who, after dispatching one idiot husband, lures another allegedly rich man into marrying her. Moribund and yawn-inducing. AJ

Gloria Grahame *Mama Love* • Paul Lambert *Harold* • Sondra Currie *Addie* • Candice Rialson *Becky* • Christopher Wines *Sheriff* ▪ *Dir* John Hayes • *Scr* Gil Lasky

Mambo Italiano ★★ 15
Comedy 2003 · Can · Colour · 85min

The dramatic impetus of this adaptation is provided by wannabe TV writer Luke Kirby's gradual acceptance of his homosexuality. However, the thematic emphasis is firmly on the socio-cultural mores of Kirby's traditionalist Italian family. It's a pity, therefore, that both Paul Sorvino (as Kirby's father) and Mary Walsh (as the mother of Kirby's Italian-Canadian policeman lover) overdo the ethnic caricatures as they strive to come to terms with the relationship of their sons. Both the social commentary and the sitcom-style humour lack bite. DP Swearing. **DVD**

Ginette Reno *Maria Barberini* • Sophie Lorain *Pina Lunetti* • Paul Sorvino *Gino Barberini* • Luke Kirby *Angelo Barberini* • Peter Miller (3) *Nino Paventi* • Mary Walsh *Lina Paventi* • Claudia Ferri *Anna Barberini* • Pierrette Robitaille *Rosetta* • Dino Tavarone *Giorgio* ▪ *Dir* Emile Gaudreault • *Scr* Emile Gaudreault, Steve Galluccio, from the play by Steve Galluccio

The Mambo Kings ★★★★ 15
Musical drama 1992 · US/Fr · Colour · 99min

Antonio Banderas made the jump from Spanish star to international hunk with this, his first big English-language movie, a musical drama based on the Pulitzer Prize-winning novel by Oscar Hijuelos. Banderas and Armand Assante star as two Cuban musicians who arrive in postwar America seeking love, fame and fortune. The film positively sizzles when the music gets going, and the mambo itself is as much a character in the movie as the actors. Debut director Arne Glimcher went on to make the Sean Connery thriller *Just Cause*. JB **DVD**

Armand Assante *Cesar Castillo* • Antonio Banderas *Nestor Castillo* • Cathy Moriarty *Lanna Lake* • Maruschka Detmers *Delores Fuentes* • Pablo Calogero *Ramon* • Scott Cohen *Bernadito* • Mario Grillo *Mario* ▪ *Dir* Arne Glimcher • *Scr* Cynthia Cidre, from the novel *The Mambo Kings Play Songs of Love* by Oscar Hijuelos

Mame ★ PG
Musical comedy 1974 · US · Colour · 125min

You need a better voice than Lucille Ball's to carry this dreary, predictable and almost embarrassing paean to American matriarchy at its most egocentric. Lumbered with a weak plotline and sketchy characterisation, the original show relied on one great, thumping performance to win the day, and Gene Saks's film is no different. There are plenty of musical stars who could have pulled it off, but this sitcom queen is not one of them. **SH**

Lucille Ball *Mame* • Robert Preston *Beauregard* • Beatrice Arthur *Vera* • Bruce Davison *Older Patrick* • Joyce Van Patten *Sally Cato* • Don Porter *Mr Upson* • Audrey Christie *Mrs Upson* ■ *Dir* Gene Saks • *Scr* Paul Zindel, from the musical Jerome Lawrence, Jerry Herman, Robert E Lee, from the play *Auntie Mame* by Jerome Lawrence, Robert E Lee, from the novel *Auntie Mame* by Patrick Dennis

Mamma Mia! ★★★★PG
Musical romantic comedy
2008 · UK/US · Colour · 104min

This happy romantic comedy set to Abba's greatest hits proved a winning formula on stage and with this big-screen adaptation it's been taken up another notch. Meryl Streep sings her heart out as ageing rock chick-turned-hotel owner Donna, whose daughter Sophie (Amanda Seyfried) is about to get married. But the wedding is thrown into chaos when three of Donna's ex-lovers (Pierce Brosnan, Colin Firth and Stellan Skarsgård) turn up. Each has a case for being Sophie's father, but only one stakes a claim on Donna's heart. It's a feather-light story, but that's entirely fitting when the film is populated with big, brash disco numbers like *Dancing Queen* and *Voulez-Vouz*. The fun is in watching usually straight actors like Streep, Brosnan and company throwing caution to the wind and making up for weak vocals with infectious gusto. **SP** *DVD*

Meryl Streep *Donna* • Colin Firth *Harry Bright* • Pierce Brosnan *Sam Carmichael* • Amanda Seyfried *Sophie* • Stellan Skarsgård *Bill* • Julie Walters *Rosie* • Christine Baranski *Tanya* • Dominic Cooper *Sky* ■ *Dir* Phyllida Lloyd • *Scr* Catherine Johnson

Mamma Roma ★★★★15
Drama 1962 · It · BW · 101min

Following the acclaim for *Accatone*, Pier Paolo Pasolini refined his unique blend of Marxism, Catholicism, kitchen sink naturalism, classicism and street poetry in this unforgettable portrait of a Rome that never makes the guide books. As the only professional in an outstanding cast, Anna Magnani gives a typically extrovert performance as the prostitute whose bid to prevent her beloved teenage son from being sucked into the perilous underworld of vice and crime is hamstrung by her grasping pimp. This has none of the sentimentality that so clouded the neorealist vision. **DP** Italian +subtitles.
DVD

Anna Magnani *Mamma Roma* • Ettore Garofolo *Ettore* • Franco Citti *Carmine* • Silvana Corsini *Bruna* • Luisa Loiano *Biancofiore* • Paolo Volponi *Priest* • Luciano Gonini *Zacaria* ■ *Dir/Scr* Pier Paolo Pasolini • *Cinematographer* Tonino Delli Colli

Mammoth ★★★15
Drama 2009 · Swe/Ger/Den · Colour · 120min

Like Alejandro González Iñárritu's *Babel*, this compassionate but superficial film is a study of parents, children and the widening chasm between the world's rich and poor. Surgeon Michelle Williams frets about her Filipino nanny's growing influence on her seven-year-old daughter, while her millionaire husband (Gael García Bernal) jets off to sign a lucrative contract in Thailand where he experiences pangs of conscience while exploiting a prostitute. Ably contrasting cinematographer Marcel Zyskind's urban interiors and exotic vistas, director Lukas Moodysson slickly cuts between the storylines. But there's a surfeit of exposition, and the socio-political themes are occasionally stressed at the expense of believable dialogue. **DP** English, Tagalog, Thai +subtitles. Swearing, sexual references. *DVD*

Gael García Bernal *Leo* • Michelle Williams *Ellen* • Marife Necesito *Gloria* • Sophie Nyweide *Jackie* • Run Srinikornchot *Cookie* ■ *Dir/Scr* Lukas Moodysson

Mammuth ★★15
Comedy drama 2010 · Fr · Colour · 91min

This eccentric road movie sees a generously proportioned Gérard Depardieu play a retired meat packer who goes in search of documents that will enable him to claim his full state pension. The title derives from the trusty Münch motorbike on which this hapless lump of a man criss-crosses rural France. The film's would-be madcap wit doesn't always take flight, although Depardieu is really rather lovable as the permanently confused protagonist. **TJ** French +subtitles. Swearing, some sex scenes.

Gérard Depardieu *Serge, "Mammuth"* • Yolande Moreau *Catherine* • Isabelle Adjani *Yasmine* • Miss Ming • Bouli Lanners *Recruiting agent* ■ *Dir/Scr* Gustave Kervern, Benoît Delépine • *Cinematographer* Hugues Poulain

Mammy ★★
Musical comedy
1930 · US · BW and Colour · 83min

This is a star vehicle for Al Jolson, here playing the leading light of a touring minstrel act. Unjustly accused of shooting the troupe's MC (Lowell Sherman), the two-timing fiancé of Lois Moran, Jolson briefly goes on the run and visits the mother he adores (Louise Dresser) before returning for the happy ending. A smash hit in its day, this boasts a score by Irving Berlin, but it has dated badly. **RK**

Al Jolson *Al Fuller* • Lois Moran *Nora Meadows* • Louise Dresser *Mrs Fuller* • Lowell Sherman *Westy* • Hobart Bosworth *Meadows* • Tully Marshall *Slats* ■ *Dir* Michael Curtiz • *Scr* Joseph Jackson, Gordon Rigby, from the play *Mr Bones* by Irving Berlin, James Gleason

The Man ★★★
Drama 1972 · US · Colour · 93min

When the US president and Speaker of the House are killed in a freak accident and the Vice-President is rendered insensible by a stroke, senate leader James Earl Jones becomes the first black man to live in the White House. Based on the bestselling novel by Irving Wallace, the drama skips rather nervously over several key issues, including apartheid in South Africa. Jones, though, is impressive as the unelected president fighting for acceptance. **AT**

James Earl Jones *Douglas Dilman* • Martin Balsam *Jim Talley* • Burgess Meredith *Senator Watson* • Lew Ayres *Noah Calvin* • William Windom *Arthur Eaton* • Barbara Rush *Kay Eaton* • Georg Stanford Brown *Robert Wheeler* • Janet MacLachlan *Wanda* • Jack Benny ■ *Dir* Joseph Sargent • *Scr* Rod Serling, from a novel by Irving Wallace

The Man ★★12
Action comedy 2005 · US · Colour · 79min

In this wayward comedy, Eugene Levy plays a naive dental-supplies salesman who becomes involved in an investigation with federal agent Samuel L Jackson. Relying on Levy's cartoonish expressions and Jackson's clichéd hardman antics for interest, this sagging caper is only redeemed (and then only partially) by the incidental detail. Former pop star Luke Goss shows a nifty sense of comic timing. **KK** *DVD*

Eugene Levy *Andy Fidler* • Samuel L Jackson *Derrick Vann* • Luke Goss *Joey* • Miguel Ferrer *Agent Peters* • Anthony Mackie *Booty* • Susie Essman *Lt Cabrone* • Horatio Sanz *Diaz* • Rachael Crawford *Dara Vann* ■ *Dir* Les Mayfield • *Scr* Jim Piddock, Margaret Oberman, Steve Carpenter

A Man, a Woman and a Bank ★★15
Comedy thriller 1979 · Can · Colour · 101min

In this loopy heist movie, Donald Sutherland and Paul Mazursky plug in their computer to a new electronic bank, hoping to transfer $4 million to their hideaway in Macao. Despite some very funny scenes and the engaging performances, including Brooke Adams as Sutherland's romantic interest, the movie is rather too ramshackle for its own good, though its predictions about

computerised banking procedures seem right on the money. **AT**

Donald Sutherland *Reese Halperin* • Brooke Adams *Stacey Bishop* • Paul Mazursky *Norman Barrie* • Allan Migicovsky *Peter* • Leigh Hamilton *Marie* • Nick Rice *Gino* • Peter Erlich *Jerry* ■ *Dir* Noel Black • *Scr* Ronald Gideon, Bruce A Evans, Stuart Margolin

A Man about the House ★★PG
Period thriller 1947 · UK · BW · 89min

Two English spinster sisters (Margaret Johnston, Dulcie Gray) take up residence in a Neapolitan villa they have inherited and are charmed by the handsome young Italian (Kieron Moore) who is caring for the place. He marries Johnston, but all is not bliss. A suitably brooding British-made melodrama, directed by Leslie Arliss, this seems rather drearily predictable now. **RK** *DVD* *BD*

Margaret Johnston *Agnes Isit* • Dulcie Gray *Ellen Isit* • Kieron Moore *Salvatore* • Guy Middleton *Sir Benjamin Dench* • Felix Aylmer *Richard Sanctuary* • Lilian Braithwaite *Mrs Armitage* ■ *Dir* Leslie Arliss • *Scr* Leslie Arliss, JB Williams, from the play by John Perry, from the novel by Francis Brett Young

Man about the House ★★PG
Comedy 1974 · UK · Colour · 85min

Not the product you would normally associate with Hammer, this spin-off from the popular TV series was the kind of project the House of Horror was forced to resort to as the fright business took a down turn in the mid-1970s. The material is thinner than a bedsit wall as housemates Richard O'Sullivan, Sally Thomsett and Paula Wilcox team up with their inimitable landlords Brian Murphy and Yootha Joyce to see off unscrupulous property developers. **DP** *DVD*

Richard O'Sullivan *Robin Tripp* • Paula Wilcox *Chrissy* • Sally Thomsett *Jo* • Brian Murphy *Mr Roper* • Yootha Joyce *Mrs Roper* • Doug Fisher *Larry Simmonds* • Peter Cellier *Morris Pluthero* • Patrick Newell *Sir Edmund Weir* • Spike Milligan • Arthur Lowe *Spiros* ■ *Dir* John Robins • *Scr* Johnnie Mortimer, Brian Cooke

Man about Town ★★★★
Period romantic comedy
1947 · Fr/US · BW · 89min

René Clair's first French film for over a decade is a bittersweet, regretful look at the silent cinema in which he began his career. Maurice Chevalier plays an ageing ex-actor, now a director, who teaches his assistant (François Périer) the arts of seduction, unaware that they are both in love with the same young girl (an insipid Marcelle Derrien). The re-creation of the era is rather more convincing than the plot, but Chevalier shows a rare depth. **RB** French dubbed.

Maurice Chevalier *Emile Clément* • François Périer *Jacques* • Marcelle Derrien *Madeleine Célestin* • Mme Dany Robin [Dany Robin] *Lucette* ■ *Dir* René Clair • *Scr* René Clair, Robert Pirosh, from a story by Clair

A Man Alone ★★★U
Western 1955 · US · Colour · 95min

Ray Milland joined up with Republic as a producer, director and star, and acquitted himself well on all three counts in making this offbeat western. Milland doesn't say a word for the first third of the film, which casts him as a mysterious loner who arrives in town, only to be accused of committing a stagecoach robbery. The house he takes refuge in belongs to sheriff Ward Bond, who's quarantined with yellow fever. Although it becomes more routine towards the end, this is still a jump ahead of most westerns of the time, especially Republic's. **AE**

Ray Milland *Wes Steele* • Mary Murphy (1) *Nadine Corrigan* • Ward Bond *Gil Corrigan* • Raymond Burr *Stanley* • Arthur Space *Dr Mason* • Lee Van Cleef *Clantin* • Alan Hale [Alan Hale Jr] *Anderson* ■ *Dir* Ray Milland • *Scr* John Tucker Battle, from a story by Mort Briskin

A Man and a Woman: 20 Years Later ★★15
Romantic drama 1986 · Fr · Colour · 107min

Two decades after racing driver Jean-Louis Trintignant and script girl Anouk Aimée parted in *Un Homme et une Femme*, Claude Lelouch reunited them for this self-reflexive look at how film shapes life for its own ends. Trintignant is now scouting for younger talent and big-shot producer Aimée is so desperate for a hit that she resorts to a musical version of her own *amour fou*. This glossily explicit confection is overwhelmed by a stupid subplot, gratuitous structural gimmickry and a gloating sense of cinematic significance. **DP** French +subtitles.

Anouk Aimée *Anne Gauthier* • Jean-Louis Trintignant *Jean-Louis Duroc* • Evelyne Bouix *Françoise* • Marie-Sophie L Pochat *Marie-Sophie* ■ *Dir* Claude Lelouch • *Scr* Claude Lelouch, Pierre Uytterhoeven, Monique Lange, Jérôme Tonnerre • *Music* Francis Lai

A Man Apart ★★18
Crime action thriller
2003 · US/Ger · Colour · 105min

Vin Diesel doesn't display any acting muscle in this by-the-numbers action thriller. Diesel's DEA agent reluctantly enlists the help of an imprisoned drugs lord in order to track down the mysterious new cartel boss who may be responsible for the murder of his wife. As bland as its title, this isn't helped by unbelievable characters and action scenes of perfunctory viciousness. **AJ** English, Spanish +subtitles. Violence, swearing, drug abuse. *DVD*

Vin Diesel *Sean Vetter* • Larenz Tate *Demetrius Hicks* • Timothy Olyphant *"Hollywood" Jack Slayton* • Jacqueline Obradors *Stacy Vetter* • Geno Silva *Memo Lucero* • Juan Fernandez *Mateo Santos* • Steve Eastin *Ty Frost* ■ *Dir* F Gary Gray • *Scr* Christian Gudegast, Paul T Scheuring

Man at the Top ★★★15
Drama 1973 · UK · Colour · 88min

Still ruthlessly ambitious and sexually voracious, working-class social climber Joe Lampton (from 1958's *Room at the Top*) is now a high-flyer at a drugs company, until the suicide of his predecessor casts a shadow over his future. Kenneth Haigh starred as Lampton in the 1970s TV series, and here in the spin-off movie he wears his 70s tache well and exhibits blunt, northern nankiness with aplomb. The film certainly has plenty of curio value – cameos from champion boxer John Conteh and stand-up comedian Charlie Williams, and a distinctively twangy score from composer Roy Budd – that make it worthwhile. **JA** Swearing, sex scenes, nudity. *DVD*

Kenneth Haigh *Joe Lampton* • Nanette Newman *Alex* • Harry Andrews *Lord Clive Ackerman* • Clive Swift *Massey* • William Lucas *Marshall* ■ *Dir* Mike Vardy • *Scr* Hugh Whitemore, John Junkin, from characters by John Braine

Man Beast ★★
Adventure 1956 · US · BW · 60min

Virginia Maynor and Lloyd Nelson mount an expedition to the Himalayas to search for her missing brother, only to uncover a dastardly plot by Abominable Snowmen to lure women into their domain. Cobbled together by cheapskate producer/director Jerry Warren from Mexican-shot location footage, with a cast full of game has-beens and men in Yeti suits, this is dumb fun in a non-scary way. **AJ**

Rock Madison *Lon Raynon* • Virginia Maynor *Connie Hayward* • Tom Maruzzi *Steve Cameron* • Lloyd Nelson *Trevor Hudson* • George Wells Lewis *Dr Erickson* ■ *Dir* Jerry Warren • *Scr* B Arthur Cassidy

The Man behind the Gun ★★U
Western adventure 1953 · US · Colour · 82min

Set in Los Angeles on the eve of the Civil War, this convoluted adventure sees star Randolph Scott arriving in town to investigate a conspiracy. He's soon feuding with testy army captain Philip Carey for the

affections of schoolteacher Patrice Wymore and colluding with a Mexican gunrunner to expose the political machinations of the local elite. The script is mediocre, but the performances are fair and Bert Glennon's Technicolor cinematography is a treat. DP
Randolph Scott *Major Ransome Callicut* • Patrice Wymore *Lora Roberts* • Philip Carey *Capt Roy Giles* • Lina Romay (1) *Chona Degnon* ■ *Dir* Felix E Feist • *Scr* John Twist, from a story by Robert Buckner

A Man Betrayed ★★ U
Crime drama   1941 · US · BW · 81min

John Wayne became Republic's biggest asset thanks to the good films he made elsewhere. But his home studio repeatedly let him down with feeble pictures such as this, also known as *Citadel of Crime* and *Wheel of Fortune*, which tries to combine an exposé of crooked politics with doses of screwball comedy and fails on both counts. On the plus side, Wayne is appealing as a crusading lawyer, while Frances Dee is vivacious as a corrupt politician's daughter. AE
John Wayne *Lynn Hollister* • Frances Dee *Sabra Cameron* • Edward Ellis *Tom Cameron* • Wallace Ford *Casey* • Ward Bond *Floyd* ■ *Dir* John H Auer • *Scr* Isabel Dawn, Tom Kilpatrick, from a story by Jack Moffitt

The Man Between ★★ U
Spy drama   1953 · UK · BW · 94min

Set in partitioned Berlin at the height of the Cold War, this is a less than convincing return to *Third Man* territory by Carol Reed. Using some of the most outrageously oblique camera angles of his career to suggest a city out of kilter and its citizens beset by fear and doubt, Reed strains for a visual edginess that might atone for the flatness of this melodramatic and suspenseless tale. Recognising that their characters have no depth, the members of the cast fail to rouse themselves, although James Mason is as watchable as ever. DP
James Mason *Ivo Kern* • Claire Bloom *Susanne Mallison* • Hildegarde Neff *Bettina* • Geoffrey Toone *Martin Mallison* • Aribert Wäscher *Halendar* • Ernst Schroeder [Ernst Schröder] *Kastner* ■ *Dir* Carol Reed • *Scr* Harry Kurnitz, Eric Linklater, from the novel *Susanne in Berlin* by Walter Ebert

Man Bites Dog ★★★★ 18
Satirical black comedy
1992 · Bel · Colour · 92min

A prize winner at Cannes, this searing satire caused a storm of protest on its original release. Were its co-directors exposing our lust for media sensationalism? Or were they merely getting away with explicit scenes of rape and slaughter in the name of social commentary? Many will bridle at the graphic imagery, while others will resent the cockiness of the approach as documentarists André Bonzel and Rémy Belvaux play an increasingly active role in the crimes of serial killer Benoît Poelvoorde. Yet this is an undeniably bold contribution to the debate on screen violence and the responsibilities of both film-makers and audiences. DP French +subtitles. *DVD*
Benoît Poelvoorde *Ben* • Rémy Belvaux *Reporter* • André Bonzel *Cameraman* • Jacqueline Poelvoorde-Pappaert *Ben's mother* ■ *Dir* Rémy Belvaux, André Bonzel, Benoît Poelvoorde • *Scr* Rémy Belvaux, André Bonzel, Benoît Poelvoorde, Vincent Tavier, from an idea by Rémy Belvaux

A Man Called Adam ★★
Drama   1966 · US · Colour · 103min

Trying to yoke an allegory about race to this story of a black trumpeter (Ossie Davis) battling discrimination and feelings of inadequacy makes for a rather queasy mix. The guest stars make it enjoyable, though – Sammy Davis Jr, Louis Armstrong and Mel Tormé – while Cicely Tyson shines in a supporting role. The director is Leo Penn, father of Chris and Sean. TH
Sammy Davis Jr *Adam Johnson* • Ossie Davis *Nelson Davis* • Cicely Tyson *Claudia Ferguson* • Louis Armstrong *Willie "Sweet Daddy" Ferguson* • Frank Sinatra Jr *Vincent* • Peter Lawford *Manny* • Mel Tormé ■ *Dir* Leo Penn • *Scr* Tina Rome, Les Pine

A Man Called Gannon ★★
Western   1969 · US · Colour · 105min

This is a quite pointless Universal remake of its own minor classic *Man without a Star*. Here, talented director James Goldstone does what he can, but the hyper-erotic elements of the original torrid western are missing and the cast, headed by Tony Franciosa as the drifter who gets involved in a range war, has little to get its teeth into. TS
Tony Franciosa [Anthony Franciosa] *Gannon* • Michael Sarrazin *Jess Washburn* • Judi West *Beth* • Susan Oliver *Matty* • John Anderson *Capper* • David Sheiner *Sheriff Polaski* • James Westerfield *Amos* • Gavin Macleod *Lou* ■ *Dir* James Goldstone • *Scr* Gene Kearney, Borden Chase, DD Beauchamp, from the novel by Dee Linford

A Man Called Hero ★★ 15
Period martial arts fantasy
1999 · HK/Chi · Colour · 102min

In this period actioner, Andrew Lau succeeds in evoking a time of fear and despair, when arrivals at New York's Ellis Island were as likely to find themselves entering a nightmare as embarking on the American Dream. The fight sequences are staged with typical ebullience, but the flashback structure complicates an already tortuous plot, in which Ekin Cheng is eventually joined by his son, Nicholas Tse, in his bid to find the Japanese ninjas responsible for the murder of his wife. DP Cantonese +subtitles. *DVD*
Ekin Cheng *Hero Hua* • Shu Qi *Mu* • Kristy Yang *Jade* • Nicholas Tse *Sword Hua* • Yuen Biao *Yuen Mo* ■ *Dir* Andrew Lau • *Scr* Manfred Wong, from a comic book by Ma Wing Shing

A Man Called Horse ★★★ 15
Western   1970 · US · Colour · 109min

This key film in the trend towards a more realistic depiction of life in the Old West provides a thorough study of the Sioux tribe's mores as experienced by an English aristocrat who is unfortunate enough to become his prisoner. Richard Harris gives a compelling performance as the man who is tortured, ridiculed and turned into a beast of burden before finding ways to improve his lot. You'll need a strong stomach to watch Harris undergoing the elaborate (and accurately depicted) Sun Vow ceremony in which he is impaled by hooks. Followed in 1976 by *Return of a Man Called Horse*, the first of two sequels. AE *DVD*
Richard Harris *Lord John Morgan* • Judith Anderson *Buffalo Cow Head* • Manu Tupou *Yellow Hand* • Jean Gascon *Batise* • Corinna Tsopei *Running Deer* • Dub Taylor *Joe* • William Jordan *Bent* ■ *Dir* Elliot Silverstein • *Scr* Jack DeWitt, from the story by Dorothy M Johnson

A Man Called Peter ★★★ U
Biographical drama   1955 · US · Colour · 119min

This is a solidly mounted biopic about Peter Marshall, the Scottish cleric who began as an assistant at the Church of the Presidents and rose to become chaplain to the US Senate. Richard Todd brings dignity and zeal to the part of the Presbyterian whose uncompromising sermons did not always endear him to listeners at opposite ends of the political spectrum, while Jean Peters is quiet and loyal as his wife Catherine. DP
Richard Todd *Peter Marshall* • Jean Peters *Catherine Marshall* • Marjorie Rambeau *Miss Fowler* • Jill Esmond *Mrs Findlay* • Les Tremayne *Senator Harvey* • Robert Burton *Mr Peyton* • Gladys Hurlbut *Mrs Peyton* • Gloria Gordon *Barbara* ■ *Dir* Henry Koster • *Scr* Eleanore Griffin, from the memoirs by Catherine Marshall

A Man Could Get Killed ★★★ U
Spy spoof   1966 · US · Colour · 98min

James Garner's air of suave bafflement comes in handy for this spoof thriller, in which he plays a businessman in Portugal suspected of being a secret agent. The cast is a curious mix of nationalities – Greek spitfire Melina Mercouri fizzes exotically, while Cecil Parker and Dulcie Gray keep the British end up – though a better-balanced plot would have been more to the point. TH
James Garner *William Beddoes* • Melina Mercouri *Aurora-Celeste da Costa* • Sandra Dee *Amy Franklin* • Tony Franciosa [Anthony Franciosa] *Steve-Antonio* • Robert Coote *Hatton-Jones* • Roland Culver *Dr Mathieson* • Grégoire Aslan *Florian* • Cecil Parker *Sir Huntley Frazier* • Dulcie Gray *Mrs Mathieson* • Jenny Agutter *Linda Frazier* ■ *Dir* Ronald Neame, Cliff Owen • *Scr* Richard Breen [Richard L Breen], TEB Clarke, from the novel *Diamonds for Danger* by David Esdaile Walker

Man Dancin' ★★ 15
Crime drama   2003 · UK · Colour · 109min

Norman Stone directs this ambitious, but leadenly symbolic gangland parable. Ex-con Alex Ferns, bristling with compassion and righteous anger, accepts the lead in priest Tom Georgeson's Passion play – his participation being a condition of his parole. But Ferns's former boss James Cosmo and bent copper Kenneth Cranham suspect his motives, and a modern-day tragedy that mirrors the trials of Christ unfolds. An improvement on many recent British crime flicks, this drama doesn't always avoid the genre's clichés. DP Violence, drug abuse. *DVD*
Alex Ferns *Jimmy Kerrigan* • Tom Georgeson *Father Gabriel Flynn* • Kenneth Cranham *Detective Inspector "Pancho" Villers* • James Cosmo *Donnie McGlone* • Jenny Foulds *Maria Gallagher* • Cas Harkins *Terry Kerrigan* • Tam White *Johnny Bus-Stop* ■ *Dir* Norman Stone • *Scr* Sergio Casci

A Man Escaped ★★★★★ U
Prison drama   1956 · Fr · BW · 95min

Robert Bresson's story of an imprisoned and condemned French Resistance fighter who plans an escape with his teenage cellmate is one of the great classics of European art cinema. As usual, Bresson uses non-professional actors and a technique that is utterly hypnotic despite being almost totally devoid of stylistic flourish. Many subsequent prison movies are deeply indebted to it – most notably *Birdman of Alcatraz*, *Escape from Alcatraz* and *The Shawshank Redemption*, all of which attempted to evoke the director's peculiar mood of quietude and contemplation as the two men conduct their meticulous plan of escape. AT French +subtitles. *DVD*
François Leterrier *Fontaine* • Charles Le Clainche *Jost* • Roland Monod *Priest* • Jacques Ertaud *Orsini* • Maurice Beerblock *Blanchet* ■ *Dir* Robert Bresson • *Scr* Robert Bresson, from the articles by André Devigny

A Man for All Seasons ★★★★ U
Historical drama   1966 · UK · Colour · 115min

Fred Zinnemann's Oscar-laden version of Robert Bolt's 1960 play, with Paul Scofield as Sir Thomas More, who wins the moral argument but loses the more vital one, concerning custody of his head, to Henry VIII. Robert Shaw's Henry is a man of formidable intelligence and political skill, while Orson Welles's Cardinal Wolsey is a beached, purple whale and John Hurt (in his first major role) is eloquent in Parliament. But it's Scofield's picture – an inspired performance of virtue with a dash of vanity. AT *DVD*
Paul Scofield *Thomas More* • Wendy Hiller *Alice More* • Leo McKern *Thomas Cromwell* • Robert Shaw *King Henry VIII* • Orson Welles *Cardinal Wolsey* • Susannah York *Margaret More* • Nigel Davenport *Duke of Norfolk* • John Hurt *Richard Rich* • Corin Redgrave *William Roper* • Colin Blakely *Matthew* • Vanessa Redgrave *Anne Boleyn* ■ *Dir* Fred Zinnemann • *Scr* Robert Bolt, from the play by Robert Bolt

A Man for All Seasons ★★★ PG
Historical drama   1988 · US · Colour · 148min

A creditable television version of Robert Bolt's fine play, previously filmed by Fred Zinnemann. The director this time out, unusually, is Charlton Heston, who also plays the leading role of Sir Thomas More. Heston's creased features and distinguished tones are well suited to the part, and his innate integrity shines through. He's well served by a distinguished British support cast that includes John Gielgud, Vanessa Redgrave and, notably, Roy Kinnear. TS
Charlton Heston *Sir Thomas More* • Vanessa Redgrave *Lady Alice More* • John Gielgud *Cardinal Wolsey* • Richard Johnson *Duke of Norfolk* • Roy Kinnear *The Common Man* • Benjamin Whitrow *Thomas Cromwell* • Adrienne Thomas *Margaret More* • Martin Chamberlain *King Henry VIII* • John Hudson (2) *William Roper* ■ *Dir* Charlton Heston • *Scr* Robert Bolt, from his play

Man Friday ★★ PG
Adventure   1975 · UK · Colour · 109min

In revising Daniel Defoe's 1719 novel, *Robinson Crusoe*, screenwriter Adrian Mitchell clearly intended both to denounce the idea of the white man's burden and to preach a code of racial equality. Unfortunately, he has succeeded only in destroying the narrative tension of the original. Jack Gold's hesitant direction doesn't help, while Peter O'Toole and Richard Roundtree have nothing to do but mouth platitudes. DP
Peter O'Toole *Robinson Crusoe* • Richard Roundtree *Friday* • Peter Cellier *Carey* • Christopher Cabot *McBain* • Sam Seabrook *Young girl* ■ *Dir* Jack Gold • *Scr* Adrian Mitchell, from his play by Adrian Mitchell, from the novel *The Adventures of Robinson Crusoe* by Daniel Defoe

The Man from Bitter Ridge ★★ U
Western   1955 · US · Colour · 80min

Despite the presence of distinguished cameraman Russell Metty, this Universal western is nothing special. It stars former Tarzan Lex Barker as a lawman investigating stagecoach robberies. His chief suspects are Stephen McNally and John Dehner, while Mara Corday provides the glamour. Directing his first western, Jack Arnold keeps the pace up and the bullets flying. TS
Lex Barker *Jeff Carr* • Mara Corday *Holly Kenton* • Stephen McNally *Alec Black* • John Dehner *Ranse Jackman* • Trevor Bardette *Walter Dunham* ■ *Dir* Jack Arnold • *Scr* Lawrence Roman, Teddi Sherman, from the novel by William MacLeod Raine

The Man from Button Willow ★★ U
Animated western   1965 · US · Colour · 77min

Set in the 1860s, this is a so-so children's animated tale about a rancher who leads a double life as a secret agent. Young children may be entertained, but it's unlikely that anyone brought up on the new generation of Disney animation will be too impressed. Dale Robertson and Howard Keel are among the actors lending their voices. JB
Dale Robertson *Justin Eagle* • Edgar Buchanan *Sorry* • Barbara Jean Wong *Stormy* • Howard Keel ■ *Dir/Scr* David Detiege

The Man from Cairo ★ U
Crime drama   1953 · US/It · BW · 81min

The man in question is George Raft, and he's in Algiers, not Cairo, turning the Casbah upside down in a search for Nazi gold. Along the way he meets all the usual suspects: black marketeers, shady café owners, torch singers, Arab pickpockets and shifty spies. Raft's career was then in terminal decline due to his underworld connections, failing casinos and a flop TV series that he financed himself. AT
George Raft *Mike Canelli* • Gianna Maria Canale *Lorraine* • Massimo Serato *Basil Constantine* • Irene Papas *Yvonne* • Guido Celano *Emile Touchard* ■ *Dir* Ray Enright • *Scr* Eugene Ling, Janet Stevenson, Philip Stevenson, from a story by Ladislas Fodor

The Man from Colorado
★★★ **PG**

Psychological western
1948 · US · Colour · 94min

Before he adopted a crew cut for *The Blackboard Jungle* and went Method, Glenn Ford was seldom more than mildly interesting. Here, unusually, he portrays a sadistic military tyrant, appointed as judge to govern Colorado. Ford's unstable character is confronted by a likeable hero in the shape of the pre-*Sunset Blvd* William Holden. The story by Borden Chase can be read as an allegory of the brutalising effect the Second World War had on its returning veterans, and the insinuations are clearly there if you look for them. **TS** **DVD**

Glenn Ford *Colonel Owen Devereaux* • William Holden (2) *Captain Del Stewart* • Ellen Drew *Caroline Emmett* • Ray Collins *Big Ed Carter* • Edgar Buchanan *Doc Merriam* • Jerome Courtland *Johnny Howard* • James Millican *Sergeant Jericho Howard* • Jim Bannon *Nagel* ■ *Dir* Henry Levin • *Scr* Robert D Andrews, Ben Maddow, from a story by Borden Chase

The Man from Dakota ★★★

Western
1940 · US · BW · 75min

In this American Civil War tale, a couple of Yankee soldiers escape from imprisonment in the South, become spies and hook up with a glamorous Russian refugee while they're on the run. This unlikely, not to mention fanciful, idea sounds like a Bob Hope spoof, but it's actually an action-packed period adventure. The men are Wallace Beery and John Howard; the lady is Dolores Del Rio. **RK**

Wallace Beery *Sgt Barstow* • John Howard (1) *Oliver Clark* • Dolores Del Rio *Eugenia, "Jenny"* • Donald Meek *Mr Vestry* • Robert Barrat *Parson Summers* • Addison Richards *Provost Marshal* • Frederick Burton *Leader* ■ *Dir* Leslie Fenton • *Scr* Laurence Stallings, from the novel *Arouse and Beware* by MacKinlay Kantor

The Man from Down Under
★★

Drama
1943 · US · BW · 103min

Charles Laughton stars as an Australian army sergeant who adopts two orphaned Belgian children after the Great War and takes them back with him to Oz, raising one of them to become a boxing champion. The film was produced by a certain Orville O Dull and lives up to his name. That said, Laughton's Australian accent is good for a laugh. **AT**

Charles Laughton *Jocko Wilson* • Binnie Barnes *Aggie Dawlins* • Richard Carlson *"Nipper" Wilson* • Donna Reed *Mary Wilson* • Christopher Severn *Young "Nipper"* • Clyde Cook *Ginger Gaffney* • Horace McNally [Stephen McNally] *"Dusty" Rhodes* • Arthur Shields *Father Polycarp* ■ *Dir* Robert Z Leonard • *Scr* Wells Root, Thomas Seller, from a story by Bogart Rogers, Mark Kelly

The Man from Elysian Fields
★★★ **15**

Drama
2001 · US · Colour · 101min

In this intelligent, involving drama from director George Hickenlooper (*Mayor of the Sunset Strip*, *Factory Girl*), Andy Garcia plays Byron Tiller, a novelist whose commerical success hasn't matched his critical acclaim. With no publisher for his latest book, and ashamed that he can't support his wife and young son, he's intrigued when he meets ageing lothario Luther Fox (Mick Jagger). Fox runs male escort agency Elysian Fields, catering mostly to ladies of a certain age. But when Byron – who doesn't need much convincing to join Luther's books – meets his first client, she's young and beautiful ... and married to an elderly Pulitzer Prize-winning author. What follows is rather implausible, but is made up for by the complex and believably human characters portrayed by the fine ensemble cast. Jagger in particular delivers his lines with relish and is surprisingly touching as a man facing his twilight years. **LB** Swearing. **DVD**

Andy Garcia *Byron Tiller* • Mick Jagger *Luther Fox* • Julianna Margulies *Dena Tiller* • Olivia Williams *Andrea Allcott* • James Coburn *Tobias*

Allcott • Anjelica Huston *Jennifer Adler* ■ *Dir* George Hickenlooper • *Scr* Jayson Philip Lasker

The Man from Hong Kong ★

Martial arts action
1975 · Aus/HK · Colour · 103min

Jimmy Wang Yu – a sort of low-rent Bruce Lee – stars in this action mess with erstwhile 007 George Lazenby, cast more for gimmick value than anything else. The tiresome Wang is a Hong Kong cop who travels to Sydney to apprehend a drugs baron (Lazenby) who also happens to run a kung fu academy. To describe Lazenby as wooden is an understatement – he's an entire forestry commission. **AT**

Jimmy Wang Yu [Wang Yu (1)] *Inspector Fang Sing-Ling* • George Lazenby *Jack Wilton* • Frank Thring *Willard* • Hugh Keays-Byrne *Morrie Grosse* ■ *Dir/Scr* Brian Trenchard-Smith

The Man from Laramie
★★★★ **U**

Western
1955 · US · Colour · 98min

In partnership with director Anthony Mann, James Stewart helped change the very nature of the western. Considerably tougher than Mann's other psychological entries in the genre, this is a tale of vengeance, as Stewart seeks the man responsible for supplying the Apaches with the guns that killed his brother. The infighting between rancher Donald Crisp and sons Alex Nicol and Arthur Kennedy (one natural, one adopted) dominates the action, but the scenes in which Stewart is shot in the hand and the final shoot-out on the cliffs are the ones you'll remember. **DP** **DVD**

James Stewart *Will Lockhart* • Arthur Kennedy *Vic Hansbro* • Donald Crisp *Alec Waggoman* • Cathy O'Donnell *Barbara Waggoman* • Alex Nicol *Dave Waggoman* • Aline MacMahon *Kate Canaday* • Wallace Ford *Charley O'Leary* • Jack Elam *Chris Boldt* ■ *Dir* Anthony Mann • *Scr* Philip Yordan, Frank Burt, from a story by Thomas T Flynt

The Man from Left Field
★★ **15**

Sports drama
1993 · US · Colour · 92min

Burt Reynolds directs and stars in this tale of an amnesiac drifter reluctantly recruited to coach a Little League baseball team. He rallies his players and falls in love with the homespun mother of one of the kids (recording star Reba McEntire). Implausible situations and a stone-faced performance by Reynolds keep this TV movie tale of redemption from getting to first base. **MC**

Burt Reynolds *Jack* • Reba McEntire *Nancy Lee Prinzi* • Kauwela Acocella *Beau* • Derek Baxter *Malcolm* • Adam Cronan *Bama* ■ *Dir* Burt Reynolds • *Scr* Wayne A Rice

The Man from London
★★★ **12A**

Crime drama
2007 · Hun/Fr/Ger/Swi · BW · 139min

Had anyone else made this adaptation of Georges Simenon's crime novel, it would probably have been hailed as an impeccable exercise in cinematic artistry. But there's a vacuum at the centre of director Bela Tarr's slow-burning, existentialist *noir*. World-weary railway signalman Miroslav Krobot witnesses a dockside murder, and decides to steal the money he recovers from the victim. Both this dilemma and his strained relationships with wife Tilda Swinton and daughter Erika Bok are depicted with such detachment that it's not easy to empathise with the anti-hero. Add to that the impenetrably impassive action and this becomes tantalising but never compelling. **DP** French, English +subtitles.

Miroslav Krobot *Maloin* • Tilda Swinton *Maloin's wife* • Erika Bok *Henriette* • Janos Derzsi *Brown* • Agi Szirtes *Mrs Brown* • Istvan Lenart *Inspector Morrison* ■ *Dir* Bela Tarr • *Scr* Bela Tarr, Laszlo Krasznahorkai, from the novel *L'Homme de Londres* by Georges Simenon

The Man from Morocco ★★

Second World War adventure
1944 · UK · BW · 117min

What should have been an intriguing drama of espionage is rendered tedious thanks to the moribund direction of Max Greene. Even the usually watchable Anton Walbrook, playing a Czech refugee who is interned by the Vichy regime and sent as slave labour to help build the Saharan railroad for the Germans, is defeated by the film's lack of pace. **TS**

Anton Walbrook *Karel Langer* • Margaretta Scott *Manuela* • Mary Morris *Sarah Duboste* • Reginald Tate *Ricardi* • Peter Sinclair *Jock Sinclair* • David Horne *Dr Duboste* • Hartley Power *Colonel Bagley* ■ *Dir* Max Greene • *Scr* Edward Dryhurst, Marguerite Steen, Warwick Ward, from a story by Rudolf Cartier

The Man from Planet X
★★★

Science-fiction drama
1951 · US · BW · 70min

Shot in six days by B-movie maven Edgar G Ulmer, this mini-classic was one of the first science-fiction movies to accent sombre and serious issues above gung-ho fantasy. A lonely alien seeking assistance for his freezing planet finds a similar coldness in humanity when he lands his spaceship on the Scottish moors. Ulmer's odd camera angles create a real sense of unease in this decent cosmic fable, while the extraterrestrial – a bubble-headed midget with an immobile white face and chest-plate speaker – is one of sci-fi's most haunting creations. **AJ**

Robert Clarke *Lawrence* • Margaret Field *Enid Elliot* • Raymond Bond *Prof Elliot* • William Schallert *Mears* • Roy Engel *Constable* • Charles Davis (1) *Geordie* ■ *Dir* Edgar G Ulmer • *Scr* Aubrey Wisberg, Jack Pollexfen

The Man from Snowy River
★★★ **PG**

Adventure
1982 · Aus · Colour · 103min

Based on AB "Banjo" Paterson's poem (known to every Australian from an early age), this epic from Down Under offers a surprising dual role to Kirk Douglas, who plays both the grizzled mountain man and his autocratic landowner brother. Jack Thompson has little to do in support and youthful co-star Tom Burlinson can't quite carry the picture. Behind the camera is the "other" George Miller, not the *Mad Max/ Lorenzo's Oil* director of the same name, and he makes the most of the impressive locations. **TS** **DVD** **BL**

Kirk Douglas *Harrison/Spur* • Tom Burlinson *Jim Craig* • Sigrid Thornton *Jessica* • Jack Thompson *Clancy* • Lorraine Bayly *Rosemary* • Chris Haywood *Curly* • Tony Bonner *Kane* • Gus Mercurio *Frew* • David Bradshaw *AB "Banjo" Paterson* ■ *Dir* George Miller (1) • *Scr* John Dixon, Fred Cullen, from the poem by AB "Banjo" Paterson

Man from Tangier
★★ **U**

Crime drama
1957 · UK · BW · 66min

This barely acceptable B-thriller was made at a time when British cinemas habitually ran supporting features to give you time to buy your soft drinks and popcorn. Directed by the indefatigable Lance Comfort, it's a forgery caper involving shifty foreigners, an international criminal mastermind, a lady without a passport and a film stuntman, played by Robert Hutton (an American actor whose Hollywood career never took off). **AT**

Robert Hutton *Chuck Collins* • Lisa Gastoni *Michele* • Martin Benson *Voss* • Leonard Sachs *Heinrich* • Robert Raglan *Inspector Meredith* • Derek Sydney *Darracq* • Jack Allen *Rex* • Richard Shaw *Johnny* ■ *Dir* Lance Comfort • *Scr* P Manning O'Brine

The Man from the Alamo
★★★ **U**

Western
1953 · US · Colour · 76min

Glenn Ford is branded a coward after surviving the massacre at the Alamo, but proves himself a hero by fighting Victor Jory's band of rampaging renegades. This vigorous western has a rather perfunctory

script, but director Budd Boetticher and cameraman Russell Metty stage the exciting action scenes with some real imagination, while Julie Adams is a forceful leading lady. **AE** **DVD**

Glenn Ford *John Stroud* • Julia Adams [Julie Adams] *Beth Anders* • Chill Wills *John Gage* • Victor Jory *Jess Wade* • Hugh O'Brian *Lieutenant Lamar* • Jeanne Cooper *Kate Lamar* ■ *Dir* Budd Boetticher • *Scr* Steve Fisher, DD Beauchamp, from a story by Niven Busch, Oliver Crawford

The Man from the Diner's Club
★★

Comedy
1963 · US · BW · 96min

Telly Savalas is a mobster, while Danny Kaye plays the eponymous man from the Diner's Club. Both men share a physical peculiarity – one foot bigger than the other – which gives Savalas the idea of faking his own death with the help of Kaye's corpse. There's a gentle (read toothless) satire here about American capitalism, life on credit and the growing importance of computerisation. **AT**

Danny Kaye *Ernie Klenk* • Cara Williams *Sugar Pye* • Martha Hyer *Lucy* • Telly Savalas *Foots Pulardos* • Everett Sloane *Martindale* • Kay Stevens *Bea Frampton* • Howard Caine *Bassanio* • George Kennedy *George* • Harry Dean Stanton *First beatnik* ■ *Dir* Frank Tashlin • *Scr* Bill Blatty [William Peter Blatty], from a story by John Fenton Murray, Bill Blatty [William Peter Blatty]

The Man from UNCLE
★★ **12A**

Spy adventure
2015 · US · Colour · 116min

CIA operative Henry Cavill and KGB agent Armie Hammer team up in this lame origin story inspired by the popular Swinging Sixties TV series. Director Guy Ritchie piles on self-conscious hipness and half-hearted action in this mismatched Bond meets *La Dolce Vita* affair that motors through every tiresome spy-fi cliché, yet completely lacks the charm or light touch that made the spoof espionage show so enjoyable. The straining pop art production design only increases the feel of a frantic, thrown-together mess. **AJ** **DVD** **BL**

Henry Cavill *Napoleon Solo* • Armie Hammer *Illya Kuryakin* • Hugh Grant *Waverly* • Elizabeth Debicki *Victoria Vinciguerra* • Jared Harris *Sanders* ■ *Dir* Guy Ritchie • *Scr* Guy Ritchie, Lionel Wigram, from a story by Jeff Kleeman, David Campbell Wilson, Ritchie, Wigram, from the TV series by Sam Rolfe

The Man from Utah ★★ **U**

Western
1934 · US · BW · 51min

This is a very routine example of John Wayne's B-western output, from his period at Monogram Studios. Despite the estimable Yakima Canutt as villain, the rodeo setting holds no surprises, and nor does a plot which features the Duke turning down the offer of sheriff in order to enter a horse race. Very average, but the fist-fight at the beginning is a corker. **TS** **DVD**

John Wayne *John Weston* • Polly Ann Young *Marjorie Carter* • George "Gabby" Hayes *George Higgins* • Yakima Canutt *Cheyenne Kent* • Edward Peil Sr *Barton* • Anita Campillo *Aurora* • Lafe McKee *Judge Carter* • George Cleveland *Sheriff* ■ *Dir* Robert N Bradbury • *Scr* Lindsley Parsons, from his story

The Man from Yesterday
★★

First World War romance
1932 · US · BW · 68min

The "yesterday" of the title is more a matter of "yesteryear", when British officer Clive Brook married American Claudette Colbert and went off to fight in the First World War, but does not return. Years later he reappears, but when it becomes apparent that his wife loves army surgeon Charles Boyer, he bravely vanishes again. This lachrymose melodrama strains credibility and lacks interest, despite the top-notch trio of leads. **RK**

Claudette Colbert *Sylvia Suffolk* • Clive Brook *Tony Clyde* • Charles Boyer *Rene Goudin* • Andy Devine *Steve Hand* • Alan Mowbray *Dr Waite* • Greta Meyer *Proprietress of Swiss inn* ■

M

Dir Berthold Viertel • *Scr* Oliver HP Garrett, from the play *The Wound Stripe* by Nell Blackwell, Rowland G Edwards

Man Hunt ★★★ PG

Second World War spy drama
1941 · US · BW · 98min

From its riveting opening, as Walter Pidgeon, perched on a ridge above Hitler's "Eagle's Nest" at Berchtesgaden, fixes the Führer in his rifle sight and prepares to pull the trigger, this fine adaptation of Geoffrey Household's *Rogue Male* substantially changes the tenor of the original. Under the direction of Fritz Lang, the Germans, including svelte George Sanders and gaunt John Carradine, are genuinely chilling, but heroine Joan Bennett's English accent leaves a lot to be desired. Pidgeon was seldom better. Peter O'Toole starred in an inferior TV-movie remake. TS DVD

Walter Pidgeon *Captain Thorndike* • Joan Bennett *Jerry* • George Sanders *Quive-Smith* • John Carradine *Mr Jones* • Roddy McDowall *Vaner* • Ludwig Stossel *Doctor* • Heather Thatcher *Lady Risborough* • Frederic Worlock [Frederick Worlock] *Lord Risborough* ■ *Dir* Fritz Lang • *Scr* Dudley Nichols, from the novel *Rogue Male* by Geoffrey Household

The Man I Killed ★★★

Drama   1932 · US · BW · 77min

Phillips Holmes is a young Frenchman who seeks out the family of a German soldier he killed during the war. Pretending he was a friend of their son's, he falls in love with the dead man's fiancée (Nancy Carroll). Though sombre and oversentimental at times, this sensitively wrought and perfectly crafted drama is, surprisingly, the work of Ernst Lubitsch, straying far from his usual territory. Critics acclaimed it, but audiences stayed away, and the great director of romantic comedy never made another serious film. RK

Lionel Barrymore *Dr Holderlin* • Nancy Carroll *Elsa* • Phillips Holmes *Paul* • Tom Douglas *Walter Holderin* • ZaSu Pitts *Anna* ■ *Dir* Ernst Lubitsch • *Scr* Ernest Vajda, Samson Raphaelson, Reginald Berkeley, from the play *L'Homme Que J'ai Tué* by Maurice Rostand

The Man I Love ★★★★

Musical drama   1946 · US · BW · 96min

This Ida Lupino/Robert Alda vehicle is a glittering, highly professional potboiler that grabs its audience by the scruff of the neck and refuses to let go. Lupino is suitably sassy as the charismatic nightclub singer relentlessly chased by Alda's feckless hood. There are more holes in the plot than in Nora Batty's tights, but who cares? Sit back and enjoy. SH

Ida Lupino *Petey Brown* • Robert Alda *Nicky Toresca* • Andrea King *Sally Otis* • Martha Vickers *Virginia Brown* • Bruce Bennett *Sam Thomas* • Alan Hale *Riley* • Dolores Moran *Gloria O'Connor* ■ *Dir* Raoul Walsh • *Scr* Catherine Turney, Jo Pagano, from the novel *Night Shift* by Maritta Wolff

The Man I Married ★★★★

Second World War drama
1940 · US · BW · 77min

This riveting topical drama features Joan Bennett as the American wife of handsome Francis Lederer, who returns to Germany on holiday only to be swept up on a tide of Nazi propaganda. Oliver HP Garrett's clever screenplay is unsparing in its depiction of Hitler's prewar regime, and the plot, in which Lederer discovers that his own grandmother is Jewish, is brilliantly constructed. Twentieth Century-Fox's stark black-and-white studio look suits this film very well. TS

Joan Bennett *Carol* • Francis Lederer *Eric Hoffman* • Lloyd Nolan *Kenneth Delane* • Anna Sten *Freda Heinkel* • Otto Kruger *Heinrich Hoffman* • Maria Ouspenskaya *Frau Gerhardt* • Ludwig Stossel *Dr Hugo Gerhardt* • Johnny Russell *Ricky* ■ *Dir* Irving Pichel • *Scr* Oliver HP Garrett, from the articles *I Married a Nazi* by Oscar Schisgall

The Man in Grey ★★★ PG

Period drama   1943 · UK · BW · 111min

This rip-roaring costume drama thrilled war-weary audiences with its shameless depiction of the lawlessness and lasciviousness of Regency England. No longer likely to set pulses racing, this remains an excellent example of the kind of bodice-ripping escapism churned out by Gainsborough Studios. Directed with gusto by Leslie Arliss, the picture sags when the virtuous Phyllis Calvert and Stewart Granger are on screen, but from the moment Margaret Lockwood and James Mason take centre stage, the action begins to smoulder. DP DVD

James Mason *Rohan* • Phyllis Calvert *Clarissa* • Margaret Lockwood *Hesther Shaw* • Stewart Granger *Rokeby* • Nora Swinburne *Mrs Fitzherbert* • Martita Hunt *Miss Patchett* • Raymond Lovell *Prince Regent* ■ *Dir* Leslie Arliss • *Scr* Margaret Kennedy, Doreen Montgomery, Leslie Arliss, from the novel by Lady Eleanor Smith

A Man in Love ★★ 18

Romantic drama   1987 · Fr · Colour · 105min

This French production filmed in Italy was the first mainly English-language film from Diane Kurys, the award-winning French writer/director, but it is not, unfortunately, among her finest efforts. Greta Scacchi brings her usual sensuality to some passionate scenes with Peter Coyote but, despite moments of intelligence and insight, the tale about love and adultery on a movie set in Rome ultimately outstays its welcome. PF English, French, Italian +subtitles.

Greta Scacchi *Jane Steiner* • Peter Coyote *Steve Elliott* • Peter Riegert *Michael Pozner* • Claudia Cardinale *Julia Steiner* • John Berry *Harry Steiner* • Vincent Lindon *Bruno Schlosser* • Jamie Lee Curtis *Susan Elliott* ■ *Dir/Scr* Diane Kurys

Man in the Attic ★★★

Horror mystery   1953 · US · BW · 79min

Marie Belloc-Lowndes's novel *The Lodger*, about a man suspected of being Jack the Ripper, was filmed twice in Britain with Ivor Novello, then again in Hollywood with Laird Cregar. Fox dug out its old script, had a new writer make some unhelpful alterations and turned out this modestly budgeted thriller to exploit Jack Palance's sudden rise to villainous stardom. He's too obviously sinister and the other players are weak, but the story is virtually fool-proof and director Hugo Fregonese whips up some chills and a good Victorian atmosphere. AE

Jack Palance *Slade* • Constance Smith *Lily Bonner* • Byron Palmer *Paul Warwick* • Frances Bavier *Helen Harley* • Rhys Williams *William Harley* ■ *Dir* Hugo Fregonese • *Scr* Robert Presnell Jr, Barre Lyndon, from the novel *The Lodger* by Marie Belloc-Lowndes

The Man in the Back Seat ★★★

Thriller   1961 · UK · BW · 57min

The phrase "quota quickie" was synonymous with cheaply made, under-plotted films notable only for the ineptitude of the acting. It's a rare treat, therefore, to stumble across a British B with an intriguing idea that's been ingeniously executed. Director Vernon Sewell outdoes himself with this haunting story that obviously has its roots in the Banquo's ghost segment of *Macbeth*. Derren Nesbitt and Keith Faulkner turn in creditable performances as the two young thieves trying to rob a bookmaker, who has his bag of money chained to his wrist. DP

Derren Nesbitt *Tony* • Keith Faulkner *Frank* • Carol White *Jean* • Harry Locke *Joe Carter* ■ *Dir* Vernon Sewell • *Scr* Malcolm Hulke, Eric Paice, from the novel by Edgar Wallace

The Man in the Brown Suit ★ PG

Murder mystery   1989 · US · Colour · 91min

It's safe to assume this raucous blend of mirth, mystery and mayhem was not what Agatha Christie had in mind when she wrote the original book. The decision to shift the murder from Hyde Park Tube station to Cairo Airport should give you some idea of how overblown this made-for-TV whodunnit has become. However, the fact that Stephanie Zimbalist is transformed from spirited amateur sleuth into the kind of heroine Kathleen Turner played in *Romancing the Stone* is the real giveaway. Directed by Alan Grint with no feeling for the Crime Queen's unique style, this ranks among the poorest Christie adaptations. DP

Rue McClanahan *Suzanne Blair* • Tony Randall *Minks* • Edward Woodward *Sir Eustace Pedlar* • Stephanie Zimbalist *Anne Beddingfeld* • Ken Howard *Gordon Race* • Nickolas Grace *Guy Underhill* • Simon Dutton *Harry Lucas* ■ *Dir* Alan Grint • *Scr* Carla Jean Wagner, from the novel by Agatha Christie

Man in the Chair ★★ 12A

Comedy drama
2006 · US · Colour and BW · 109min

There's an old-fashioned feel to writer/director Michael Schroeder's comedy drama, in which a technician from Hollywood's Golden Age helps teenager Michael Angarano shoot a film for a school competition. But the amusing references to Orson Welles's *Citizen Kane* and *Touch of Evil* are swamped by the melodramatics of a contrived storyline and bombastic performances. Christopher Plummer veers between drunken self-pity and tetchy sentimentality as he coerces washed-up writer M Emmet Walsh and wife-stealing producer Robert Wagner into collaborating on the project. DP Brief swearing.

Christopher Plummer *Flash Madden* • Michael Angarano *Cameron Kincaid* • Robert Wagner *Taylor Moss* • M Emmet Walsh *Mickey Hopkins* • Joshua Boyd *Murphy White* • George Murdock *Richard Butler* • Mimi Kennedy *Mama Judy Kincaid* • Taber Schroeder *Brett Raven* ■ *Dir/Scr* Michael Schroeder

The Man in the Gray Flannel Suit ★★★ 12

Drama   1956 · US · Colour · 146min

In an overlong, self-important yet compelling melodrama, Gregory Peck stars as the appealingly flawed hero choosing between his family and a high-powered but time-consuming job. To add to his woes, his marriage to Jennifer Jones is undermined by the revelation that he fathered a child in Italy during the war. The excellent Peck and Jones are joined by the ever-reliable Fredric March and Lee J Cobb, as well as Marisa Pavan, twin sister of Pier Angeli. AT DVD

Gregory Peck *Tom Rath* • Jennifer Jones *Betsy Rath* • Fredric March *Ralph Hopkins* • Marisa Pavan *Maria* • Ann Harding *Mrs Hopkins* • Lee J Cobb *Judge Bernstein* • Keenan Wynn *Caesar Gardella* • Gene Lockhart *Hawthorne* ■ *Dir* Nunnally Johnson • *Scr* Nunnally Johnson, from the novel by Sloan Wilson

The Man in the Iron Mask ★★★ U

Period adventure   1939 · US · BW · 111min

Louis Hayward gives a riveting performance in this adaptation of Alexandre Dumas's splendid swashbuckling tale about the twin heirs to the throne of France. Under the sympathetic direction of the great James Whale, Hayward exhibits just the right amount of baroque arrogance as Louis XIV plus a genuine feeling of romantic helplessness as the imprisoned Philippe. Warren William is fine as D'Artagnan, Philippe's guardian, but the other musketeers are blithely cast, as is Joan Bennett as Maria Theresa. Watch closely for Peter Cushing in his movie debut. TS

Louis Hayward *Louis XIV/Philippe* • Joan Bennett *Maria Theresa* • Warren William *D'Artagnan* • Joseph Schildkraut *Fouquet* • Alan Hale *Porthos* • Miles Mander *Aramis* • Bert Roach *Athos* • Walter Kingsford *Colbert* • Peter Cushing *King's messenger* ■ *Dir* James Whale • *Scr* George Bruce, from the novel by Alexandre Dumas

The Man in the Iron Mask ★★★ PG

Period adventure
1977 · US/UK · Colour · 100min

In this sprightly adaptation of the classic Alexandre Dumas adventure, Richard Chamberlain plays both Louis XIV and his imprisoned twin. Money was obviously thrown at the production and it stuck: it looks good. There's a strong supporting cast, plus zippy direction. AT DVD

Richard Chamberlain *Philippe/Louis XIV* • Patrick McGoohan *Fouquet* • Louis Jourdan *D'Artagnan* • Jenny Agutter *Louise de la Valliere* • Ian Holm *Duval* • Ralph Richardson *Colbert de Voliere* • Vivien Merchant *Queen Maria Theresa* • Brenda Bruce *Anne of Austria* ■ *Dir* Mike Newell • *Scr* William Bast, from the novel by Alexandre Dumas

The Man in the Iron Mask ★★★ 12

Period adventure   1997 · US · Colour · 126min

Leonardo DiCaprio has a dual role as both the wicked King Louis XIV and his mistreated twin Phillippe. The three musketeers (Jeremy Irons, John Malkovich, Gérard Depardieu) ride to the rescue, while D'Artagnan (Gabriel Byrne) decides to support Louis, despite riots in the street and rats in the court. The performances are uniformly good in this rousing version, and the French locations are beautifully shot by cinematographer Peter Suschitzky. TH DVD Blu

Leonardo DiCaprio *King Louis/Phillippe* • Jeremy Irons *Father Aramis* • John Malkovich *Athos* • Gérard Depardieu *Porthos* • Gabriel Byrne *D'Artagnan* • Anne Parillaud *Queen Anne* • Judith Godrèche *Christine Balfour* • Hugh Laurie *King's advisor* ■ *Dir* Randall Wallace • *Scr* Randall Wallace, from the novel by Alexandre Dumas

The Man in the Mirror ★★ U

Fantasy comedy   1936 · UK · BW · 78min

Lugubrious Edward Everett Horton, American master of the double-take, stars in this low-rent British fantasy as a dithering businessman whose looking-glass alter ego takes over his battles in life. Interesting more for the social assumptions of its time than for any cinematic adroitness, it was directed by Maurice Elvey, who made more than 300 unmemorable features in his career. TH DVD

Edward Everett Horton *Jeremy Dike* • Genevieve Tobin *Helen* • Garry Marsh *Tarkington* • Ursula Jeans *Veronica* • Alastair Sim *Interpreter* • Aubrey Mather *Bogus of Bokhara* • Renée Gadd [Renee Gadd] *Miss Blake* ■ *Dir* Maurice Elvey • *Scr* McGrew Willis, Hugh Mills, from the novel by William Garrett

Man in the Moon ★★ U

Comedy   1960 · UK · BW · 98min

Apart from an amiable performance by Kenneth More as the test pilot whose A1 fitness makes him the ideal candidate to become Britain's first astronaut, this British spoof on the Nasa space programme never leaves the launch pad. Seemingly stuck for ideas, writers Michael Relph and Bryan Forbes fall back on that old plot stand-by, the rival with his nose out of joint, to enliven the scenes of More's training with a few acts of unfunny sabotage. Mildly amusing. DP

Kenneth More *William Blood* • Shirley Anne Field *Polly* • Norman Bird *Herbert* • Michael Hordern *Dr Davidson* • John Glyn-Jones *Dr Wilmot* • John Phillips (1) *Professor Stephens* • Charles Gray *Leo* ■ *Dir* Basil Dearden • *Scr* Michael Relph, Bryan Forbes

The Man in the Moon ★★★ PG

Period drama   1991 · US · Colour · 95min

To Kill a Mockingbird director Robert Mulligan is an old hand at dealing with coming-of-age stories. Here he lovingly re-creates rural America of the 1950s in a tasteful, if somewhat anachronistic drama. Reese Witherspoon, making her feature film debut, is the troubled adolescent who has a crush on an older teen equally smitten by her older sister. There are memorable performances from the youngsters, and nicely underplayed supporting turns. JF *DVD*

Sam Waterston *Matthew Trant* • Tess Harper *Abigail Trant* • Gail Strickland *Marie Foster* • Reese Witherspoon *Dani Trant* • Jason London *Court Foster* • Emily Warfield *Maureen Trant* • Bentley Mitchum *Billy Sanders* ■ *Dir* Robert Mulligan • *Scr* Jenny Wingfield

The Man in the Road ★★ U
Spy mystery   1957 · UK · BW · 86min

A surprisingly fine cast was assembled for this unremarkable quickie adapted from the espionage thriller by Anthony Armstrong. Derek Farr stars as a scientist whose loss of memory alone prevents a vital secret from falling into the hands of the communists who have abducted him. Donald Wolfit was knighted the same year, but surely not on the strength of his performance here as a blustering professor. DP

Derek Farr *Ivan Mason* • Ella Raines *Rhona Ellison* • Donald Wolfit *Professor Cattrell* • Lisa Daniely *Mitzi* • Karel Stepanek *Dmitri Palenkov* • Cyril Cusack *Dr Kelly* • Olive Sloane *Mrs Lemming* • Bruce Beeby *Dr Manning* ■ *Dir* Lance Comfort • *Scr* Guy Morgan, from the novel *He Was Found in the Road* by Anthony Armstrong

Man in the Saddle ★★★★ PG
Western   1951 · US · Colour · 83min

This excellent Randolph Scott western has the star somewhat unusually cast in a love triangle involving Joan Leslie and Alexander Knox. Directed by the underrated Andre De Toth, the film contains some marvellous Technicolor night scenes. John Russell is a terrific tight-lipped villain and has a great punch-up with Scott, while Ellen Drew's schoolmarm makes a very sexy other woman. Great stuff. TS *DVD*

Randolph Scott *Owen Merritt* • Joan Leslie *Laure Bidwell* • Ellen Drew *Nan Melotte* • Alexander Knox *Will Isham* • Richard Rober *Fay Dutcher* • John Russell *Hugh Clagg* ■ *Dir* Andre De Toth • *Scr* Kenneth Gamet, from the novel by Ernest Haycox

Man in the Shadow ★★★ U
Western   1957 · US · BW · 99min

This modern western pits new sheriff Jeff Chandler against Orson Welles as the rancher who owns everything as far as the eye can see. Chandler insists on investigating the death of a Mexican labourer and eventually topples Welles's empire. Producer Albert Zugsmith and director Jack Arnold use Gene L Coon's script as a springboard for some action that was considered rather violent for its time, while Welles's posturing performance overwhelms both the picture and Colleen Miller, who plays his appalled daughter. The film was retitled *Pay the Devil* for its original UK release. AE

Jeff Chandler *Ben Sadler* • Orson Welles *Virgil Renchler* • Colleen Miller *Skippy Renchler* • Barbara Lawrence *Helen Sadler* • Ben Alexander *Ab Begley* • John Larch *Ed Yates* • Royal Dano *Aiken Clay* • James Gleason *Hank James* ■ *Dir* Jack Arnold • *Scr* Gene L Coon

The Man in the Sky ★★ U
Drama   1956 · UK · BW · 85min

Although he excelled at playing principled everymen, Jack Hawkins was never at his most convincing when called upon to express emotion. Thus, he contributes a rather uneven performance to this mediocre Ealing outing about the trials and tribulations of a test pilot. While at the controls of a prototype aeroplane, he's every inch the action hero, particularly during the final test flight. But once Hawkins gets home to demanding wife Elizabeth Sellars, Charles Crichton's melodrama loses direction. DP

Jack Hawkins *John Mitchell* • Elizabeth Sellars *Mary Mitchell* • Walter Fitzgerald *Conway* • Eddie Byrne *Ashmore* • John Stratton *Peter Hook* • Victor Maddern *Joe Biggs* • Lionel Jeffries *Keith* • Donald Pleasence *Crabtree* ■ *Dir* Charles Crichton • *Scr* John Eldridge, William Rose, from a story by William Rose

Man in the Trunk ★★★
Comedy drama   1973 · Fr · Colour · 100min

Georges Lautner pulls off the tricky task of finding the lighter side of the Arab-Israeli conflict, without offending anyone's political sensibilities, in this lively spy spoof. Mireille Darc gives a customarily lively performance as the music-hall chanteuse who joins with embassy official Michel Constantin to help Israeli agent Jean-Pierre Marielle flee Tunisia during an airport strike. Lautner does well to raise a few unexpected smiles. DP French dubbed.

Mireille Darc *Françoise* • Michel Constantin *Augier* • Jean-Pierre Marielle *Bloch* • Jean Lefebvre *Baggage controller* • Amidou *Abdul* • Raoul Saint-Yves *Ambassador* ■ *Dir* Georges Lautner • *Scr* Francis Veber

The Man in the White Suit ★★★★★ U
Classic satire   1951 · UK · BW · 81min

Telling the story of a scientist who is undone by the seeming perfection of his own invention, Alexander Mackendrick's astute film is the only Ealing comedy to bare its teeth. Capitalist greed, professional jealousy, the spectre of unemployment and a fear of progress are just some of the provocative themes explored in this razor-sharp satire that spurns the studio's customary whimsy. Alec Guinness is wonderfully unworldly as the boffin whose indestructible cloth unites the textile industry against him, while Joan Greenwood is also impressive as the spirited daughter of mill owner Cecil Parker. DP *DVD* Blu

Alec Guinness *Sidney Stratton* • Joan Greenwood *Daphne Birnley* • Cecil Parker *Alan Birnley* • Michael Gough *Michael Corland* • Ernest Thesiger *Sir John Kierlaw* • Vida Hope *Bertha* • Howard Marion-Crawford *Cranford* • Miles Malleson *Tailor* • Henry Mollison *Hoskins* ■ *Dir* Alexander Mackendrick • *Scr* Roger MacDougall, John Dighton, Alexander Mackendrick, from the play by Roger MacDougal • *Cinematographer* Douglas Slocombe

Man in the Wilderness ★★ PG
Period adventure   1971 · US/Sp · Colour · 100min

Richard Harris here exhibits the same sort of macho masochism he affected in *A Man Called Horse*, enduring the rigours of both nature and native American tribal rituals as a 19th-century fur trapper left to die after being mauled by a bear and vowing revenge. The resemblance is not surprising as this movie was made by the same team that sparked up *Horse*. Allegedly based on a true story, it's all very predictable. TH

Richard Harris *Zachary Bass* • John Huston *Captain Filmore Henry* • Henry Wilcoxon *Indian chief* • Percy Herbert *Fogarty* • Dennis Waterman *Lowrie* • Prunella Ransome *Grace* • Norman Rossington *Ferris* ■ *Dir* Richard C Sarafian • *Scr* Jack DeWitt

The Man Inside ★★★
Crime drama   1958 · UK · Colour · 96min

This old-fashioned yarn has Nigel Patrick on the lam with a priceless diamond and Hollywood hunk Jack Palance as the private eye in hot pursuit. This dashes from one eye-catching European capital to the next, picking up the statuesque Anita Ekberg en route. With Anthony Newley as a Spanish cabbie, Donald Pleasence as an organ grinder and Sid James as a wideboy, the cast alone makes this worth watching, even if the plot is as old as the hills. AT

Jack Palance *Milo Marsh* • Anita Ekberg *Trudie Hall* • Nigel Patrick *Sam Carter* • Anthony Newley *Ernesto* • Bonar Colleano *Martin Lomer* • Sean Kelly *Rizzio* • Sidney James *Franklin* • Donald Pleasence *Organ grinder* ■ *Dir* John Gilling • *Scr* David Shaw, John Gilling, Richard Maibaum, from a novel by ME Chaber

The Man Inside ★★ 15
Crime thriller   2012 · UK · Colour · 95min

This is a cheery little tale of teen violence, domestic abuse - and boxing. Rapper/actor Ashley "Bashy" Thomas plays a promising young boxer whose biggest fight is with the fear that he will grow up to be like his abusive father.(*Homeland*'s David Harewood). Thomas makes a decent fist of his role, and there's solid support from Peter Mullan as his trainer and Harewood, who hams it up shamelessly. Overall, it's a well made movie, but it's so mired in melodrama that it fails to deliver the knockout punch. DA Violence, swearing, racist language. *DVD* Blu

Ashley "Bashy" Thomas *Clayton Murdoch* • Peter Mullan *Gordon Sinclair* • David Harewood *Eugene Murdoch* • Michelle Ryan *Alexia Sinclair* • Jason Maza *Danny Lee* • Theo Barklem-Biggs *Karl Lee* ■ *Dir/Scr* Dan Turner

Man Made Monster ★★★
Science-fiction horror   1941 · US · BW · 56min

Lon Chaney Jr made his horror acting debut in this above-average Universal B-movie, which lacks the verve and gusto of the studio's earlier genre hits. Chaney is circus sideshow performer "Dynamo Dan, the Electric Man", and ever-reliable Lionel Atwill is the mad doctor who wants to turn up his voltage and convert him into a zombie killer with a lethal touch. Make-up genius Jack Pierce provided Chaney's fiendish look as the natty rubber-suited "atomic monster" (the film's re-release title). AJ

Lionel Atwill *Dr Paul Rigas* • Lon Chaney Jr *Dan McCormick* • Anne Nagel *June Lawrence* • Frank Albertson *Mark Adams* • Samuel S Hinds *Dr Lawrence* ■ *Dir* George Waggner • *Scr* Joseph West [George Waggner], from the short story *The Electric Man* by HJ Essex, Sid Schwartz, Len Golos

The Man Next Door ★★ 15
Horror   1998 · US · Colour · 94min

Movie legend Virginia Mayo adds a little undeserved value to this otherwise undistinguished straight-to-video horror flick, which revolves around a troubled young woman who develops a worrying fixation on a beau from her youth; the problem is that he's no longer the sweet young boy from next door. Mayo and veteran character actor David Huddleston stand out among the otherwise unknown cast. JF *DVD*

Laura Lael Ellis *Vivian* • John Hardison *Clayton* • Virginia Mayo *Lucia* • John Furlong *George* • Karen Carlson *Grace* • Ricky Simpson *Carey* • David Huddleston *Sheriff Dawkins* ■ *Dir/Scr* Rod C Spence

Man of a Thousand Faces ★★★ PG
Biographical drama   1957 · US · BW · 121min

The life and work of silent actor and special make-up genius Lon Chaney is brought into less than sharp focus in a heavily fictionalised biopic starring the impressive James Cagney. It's a typical rags-to-riches saga of the humble boy raised by deaf-mute parents whose talent for playing grotesquely deformed screen villains made him a Hollywood legend. Cagney gets to appear in re-creations of Chaney's two most famous roles – the Phantom of the Opera and the Hunchback of Notre Dame – in a hokey but reasonably entertaining tribute. AJ *DVD*

James Cagney *Lon Chaney* • Dorothy Malone *Cleva Creighton Chaney* • Jane Greer *Hazel Bennet* • Marjorie Rambeau *Gert* • Jim Backus *Clarence Logan* • Robert Evans *Irving Thalberg* • Celia Lovsky *Mrs Chaney* • Jeanne Cagney *Carrie Chaney* ■ *Dir* Joseph Pevney • *Scr* R Wright Campbell, Ivan Goff, Ben Roberts, from a story by Ralph Wheelwright

Man of Africa ★★★ U
Documentary drama   1954 · UK · Colour · 84min

Although this tale of the Ugandan bush was made 20 years after Robert Flaherty's seminal *Man of Aran*, it's a shade disappointing to see how little producer John Grierson had moved away from that style of drama documentary. Still, his influence is considerably more evident than that of his acolyte, Cyril Frankel. Following the migration of the Bakija and Batwa tribes, the action centres on farming couple Frederick Bijuerenda and Violet Mukabuerza as they endure everything from malaria and internecine strife to marauding elephants and pygmies. DP

Violet Mukabuerza *Violet* • Frederick Bijuerenda *Jonathan* ■ *Dir* Cyril Frankel • *Scr* Montagu Slater

Man of Aran ★★★ U
Documentary   1934 · UK · BW · 73min

Having pioneered the feature documentary with *Nanook of the North* (1922), Robert Flaherty unintentionally highlighted its shortcomings with this poetic realist re-creation of a bygone way of life that he passed off as contemporary fact. Keen to depict shark hunting off the Irish coast, Flaherty spent a year on Aran selecting photogenic locals and teaching them techniques that had not been used for generations. There's no denying the dramatic and visual power of the action, but sadly this tribute to heroic fortitude will always be remembered more for its artifice than its artistry. DP *DVD*

Colman King *A man of Aran* • Maggie Dirrane *His wife* • Michael Dillane *Their son* ■ *Dir* Robert J Flaherty [Robert Flaherty] • *Scr* John Goldman, Robert and Frances Flaherty • *Cinematographers* John Goldman, Robert J Flaherty [Robert Flaherty]

Man of Flowers ★★★ 18
Drama   1984 · Aus · Colour · 86min

After making his name as one of Australia's most respected photographers and documentarists, Dutch-born film-maker Paul Cox brought his distinctive, compassionate take on alienation and eccentricity to his adopted country's cinema resurgence. Here Norman Kaye is a lonely, mother-fixated bachelor who finds quiet delight in gardening and the artist's model (Alyson Best) he employs to undress for him once a week. Renowned German director Werner Herzog plays Kaye's fearsome father in the flashbacks. AME

Norman Kaye *Charles Bremer* • Alyson Best *Lisa* • Chris Haywood *David* • Sarah Walker *Jane* • Julia Blake *Art teacher* • Bob Ellis *Psychiatrist* • Werner Herzog *Father* ■ *Dir* Paul Cox • *Scr* Paul Cox, Bob Ellis

Man of Iron ★★★★ 12
Drama   1981 · Pol · Colour · 146min

The winner of the Palme d'Or at Cannes, this semi-sequel sees Krystyna Janda return to the documentary fray, this time to chart the career of her husband, a Solidarity leader and the son of her subject in *Man of Marble*. But the main focus falls on Marian Opania, a broken-down reporter whose mission to spy on the rebellious Gdansk shipworkers is undermined by his growing politicisation. Capturing history in the making and neatly weaving it into his fictional tale, Andrzej Wajda expertly manages to convey the optimism of Lech Walesa's working class heroes without losing a sense of perspective. DP Polish +subtitles. *DVD*

Jerzy Radziwilowicz *Tomczyk* • Krystyna Janda *Agnieszka* • Marian Opania *Winkiel* • Irene Byrska *Anna Hulewicz's mother* ■ *Dir* Andrzej Wajda • *Scr* Aleksandar Scibor-Rylski

Man of La Mancha ★ PG
Musical   1972 · US · Colour · 123min

The Broadway show was a massive hit, but this movie adaptation bungles everything, including the big number – *The Impossible Dream* – and the moment when Don Quixote tilts at the windmills. Peter O'Toole fights a losing battle as both Miguel de Cervantes and the hopelessly idealistic knight. Arthur Hiller's direction is heavy-going, tricksy and self-consciously arty, while Sophia Loren unwisely sings her own songs. A costly dud. AT *DVD*

Peter O'Toole *Miguel de Cervantes/Don Quixote/Quijana* • Sophia Loren *Aldonza/Alonso Dulcinea* • James Coco *Manservant/Sancho Panza* • Harry Andrews *Governor/Innkeeper* • John Castle *Duke/Dr Carrasco/Black Knight/Knight of the Mirrors* • Brian Blessed *Pedro* ■ *Dir* Arthur Hiller • *Scr* Dale Wasserman, from his play *Man of La Mancha*, from the novel *El Ingenioso Hidalgo Don Quijote de la Mancha* by Miguel de Cervantes Saavedra

Man of Marble ★★★★ U

Drama　1977 · Pol · Colour · 153min

Employing a "talking heads" style redolent of both *Citizen Kane* and the polemics of Jean-Luc Godard, this is a superbly controlled treatise on the power of the Party, the transience of reputation and the veracity of visual evidence. Expertly manufacturing "contemporary" newsreel footage, Andrzej Wajda turns a pseudo-documentary into a disturbing thriller as film student Krystyna Janda relentlessly investigates the part played by the Communist authorities in the tragedy of Mateusz Birkut, a Stakhanovite hero of the 1950s who was destroyed when his influence became too great. DP Polish +subtitles.

Jerzy Radziwilowicz *Mateusz Birkut* • Krystyna Janda *Agnieszka* • Tadeusz Lomnicki *Jerzy Burski* • Jacek Lomnicki *Younger Burski* • Michal Tarkowski *Witek* ■ *Dir* Andrzej Wajda • *Scr* Aleksandar Sciber-Rylski

Man of Miracles ★★ PG

Drama　1999 · US · Colour · 91min

John Ritter plays a preacher and volunteer fireman whose struggles with his faith, family and community are put into perspective by an incident at burning building. Its budget doesn't allow for much spectacle, but this TV movie, aimed at a family audience, is old-fashioned and heartfelt. SF *DVD*

John Ritter *Joe Cass* • Meredith Baxter *Annie Cass* • Linda Purl *Joan Wolrod* • David Tom *David Cass* • Kayla Campbell *Aimiee Cass* • Joanna Garcia *Joyce Cass* ■ *Dir* Larry Peerce • *Scr* Edmond Keenan Wynn [Ned Wynn]

A Man of No Importance

★★★★ 15

Drama　1994 · UK/Ire · Colour · 94min

Albert Finney gives a great performance as the eccentric Alfie, the poetry-loving Dublin bus conductor with a tenacious dream to stage Oscar Wilde's play *Salome* in the local village hall, an ambition that sets off a train of unfortunate events. One of the film's splendidly handled central themes is the painful comparison between Finney's ebullient public face and his sexually repressed, private hell. Dublin in 1963 is realistically brought to life in this major treat. SH A sex scene, violence .

Albert Finney *Alfie Byrne* • Rufus Sewell *Robbie Fay* • Brenda Fricker *Lily Byrne* • Tara FitzGerald *Adele Rice* • Michael Gambon *Carney* • Patrick Malahide *Carson* • Anna Manahan *Mrs Grace* ■ *Dir* Suri Krishnamma • *Scr* Barry Devlin

Man of Steel ★★★ 12

Fantasy adventure　2013 · US · Colour · 137min

Spurred on by the success of Christopher Nolan's Batman trilogy and Marvel's blockbuster output, DC's archetypal superhero is back in the strapping shape of buff Brit Henry Cavill. This first adventure melds the plots of the first two Christopher Reeve epics – origins story meets Kryptonian bad-guy invasion. While Cavill certainly looks the part, the moment he dons the supersuit is rather muted, and the rest of the cast has little to do, which is a shame when you have the likes of Amy Adams (as Lois Lane) and Laurence Fishburne to call on. Snyder's failure to create sustained emotional depth feels like a lost opportunity, but the climactic smackdown in Metropolis makes the end of *Avengers Assemble* look like a minor fracas. Let's hope any sequel has script and direction that's a little more superpowered. JA *DVD* ʙʟ

Henry Cavill *Clark Kent/Kal-El* • Amy Adams *Lois Lane* • Michael Shannon *General Zod* • Kevin Costner *Jonathan Kent* • Diane Lane *Martha Kent* • Russell Crowe *Jor-El* ■ *Dir* Zack Snyder • *Scr* David S Goyer, from a story by Goyer, Christopher Nolan, from characters by Joe Shuster, Jerry Siegel • *Production Designer* Alex McDowell • *Music* Hans Zimmer

Man of Tai Chi ★★ 15

Martial arts drama
2013 · US/Chi/HK · Colour · 100min

Keanu Reeves reteams with some of the talents behind his hit *Matrix* series for this moody Far Eastern action movie, which also marks the star's debut as director. Stuntman-turned-actor Chen Hu gives an impressively agile performance as the tai chi student who takes businessman Reeves up on his lucrative offer of competing in an illegal fight club. The story seems curiously old-fashioned despite its modern-day setting, but to his credit, Reeves has fashioned an authentic-looking martial arts movie. Sadly, the simplistic way in which it is resolved is more eye-rolling than heart-pounding. JH English, Mandarin, Cantonese +subtitles.

Chen Hu *"Tiger" Chen Lin Hu* • Keanu Reeves *Donaka Mark* • Karen Mok *Inspector Suen Jing Si* • Simon Yam *Superintendent Wong* ■ *Dir* Keanu Reeves • *Scr* Michael G Cooney

Man of the East ★★ 12

Spaghetti western comedy
1972 · Yug/Fr/It · Colour · 120min

Terence Hill stars here in another of his jokey spaghetti western outings, playing an English gent who follows in his dead father's footsteps and heads to the Wild West. But his foppish ways soon cause a stir, and it's left to his pop's three outlaw buddies to whip him into shape. The action meanders along towards a showdown between Hill's blue-eyed boy and the sharp-shooting varmint who wants him out of town. At two hours, the film certainly overstays its welcome, but Hill's transformation from wet Brit to rugged cowpoke is quite fun, while the lush Yugoslav locations are pleasing on the eye. JH Some violence, sexual references. *DVD*

Terence Hill *Sir Thomas Fitzpatrick Phillip Moore* • Gregory Walcott *Bull Schmidt* • Dominic Barto *Monkey Smith* • Harry Carey [Harry Carey Jr] *Holy Joe* ■ *Dir/Scr* EB Clucher [Enzo Barboni]

Man of the House ★★ U

Comedy　1994 · US · Colour · 92min

Well-meaning Chevy Chase, reprising his now familiar nice-but-dim persona, moves in with girlfriend Farrah Fawcett and attempts to bond with her son (Jonathan Taylor Thomas) with disastrous consequences. There's a syrupy undertone to much of the juvenile slapstick and not even *Cheers* star George Wendt can wring many laughs out of the dull script. JF *DVD*

Chevy Chase *Jack Sturges* • Farrah Fawcett *Sandra Archer* • Jonathan Taylor Thomas *Ben Archer* • George Wendt *Chet Bronski* • David Shiner *Lloyd Small* • Art LaFleur *Red Sweeney* ■ *Dir* James Orr • *Scr* James Orr, Jim Cruickshank, from a story by David Peckinpah, Richard Jefferies

Man of the House ★★ 12

Action comedy　2005 · US · Colour · 95min

Tommy Lee Jones plays a lawman again, this time babysitting a bunch of college cheerleaders who are the only eyewitnesses to a Mob hit. Predictably, when crusty cop meets exuberant airheads, it's a learning experience for all. As lowbrow comedy, this is breezy enough, but there's something rather sad about seeing an actor of Jones's calibre slumming it in such mediocrity. DA Violence. *DVD*

Tommy Lee Jones *Roland Sharp* • Anne Archer *Professor Molly McCarthy* • Brian Van Holt *Eddie Zane* • Christina Milian *Anne* • Paula Garcés *Teresa* • Monica Keena *Evie* • R Lee Ermey *Captain Nichols* • Cedric the Entertainer *Percy Stevens* • Vanessa Ferlito *Heather* ■ *Dir* Stephen Herek • *Scr* Robert Ramsey, Matthew Stone, John J McLaughlin, from a story by John J McLaughlin, Scott Lobdell

Man of the Moment ★★★ U

Comedy　1955 · UK · BW · 85min

Norman Wisdom is almost at the peak of his powers in this typically silly comedy, in which slapstick and sentiment jostle for centre stage. Norman is a Whitehall nobody who suddenly finds himself a target for foreign agents after he stalls the entire United Nations with his support for the island of Tarawaki. Although we usually think of Norman as a bashful bungler, he also did a nice line in cockiness, and it's surprisingly amusing to watch Whitehall and Geneva dance to his tune. Jerry Desmonde again proves to be the supreme stooge. DP *DVD*

Norman Wisdom *Norman* • Lana Morris *Penny* • Belinda Lee *Sonia* • Jerry Desmonde *Jackson* • Karel Stepanek *Lom* • Garry Marsh *British delegate* • Inia Te Wiata *Toki* • Evelyn Roberts *Sir Horace* ■ *Dir* John Paddy Carstairs • *Scr* Vernon Sylvaine, John Paddy Carstairs, from a story by Maurice Cowan

Man of the West ★★★★ 12

Western　1958 · US · Colour · 95min

This fine, relentlessly grim western was given scant critical approval on its original release. A study of choice and injustice, it stars Gary Cooper, whose haggard, ageing features lend the tale of a reformed gunslinger an almost biblical intensity. Director Anthony Mann's use of CinemaScope is exemplary, although the sometimes savage story suffered cuts, particularly the rape of saloon singer Julie London. The screenplay, by *12 Angry Men* writer Reginald Rose, is highly literate, and Lee J Cobb's ferocious study in villainy is wonderful. TS *DVD* ʙʟ

Gary Cooper *Link Jones* • Julie London *Billie Ellis* • Lee J Cobb *Dock Tobin* • Arthur O'Connell *Sam Beasley* • Jack Lord *Coaley* • John Dehner *Claude* • Royal Dano *Trout* • Robert Wilke [Robert J Wilke] *Ponch* ■ *Dir* Anthony Mann • *Scr* Reginald Rose, from the novel *The Border Jumpers* by Will C Brown

Man of the World ★★★

Drama　1931 · US · BW · 71min

Smooth, sophisticated gigolo-turned-blackmailer William Powell chooses fellow Americans in Paris as his victims. But he comes unstuck when he falls in love with one of them (Carole Lombard) and is threatened with exposure by his hard-boiled mistress Wynne Gibson. Scripted by Herman J Mankiewicz, this high society drama, characteristic of the period, more than gets by thanks to its star casting. Powell is impeccable, while Lombard – his off-screen wife from 1931 to 1933 – is clearly on her way to major stardom. RK

William Powell *Michael Trevor* • Carole Lombard *Mary Kendall* • Wynne Gibson *Irene Hoffa* • Guy Kibbee *Harold Taylor* • Lawrence Gray *Frank Thompson* • Andre Cheron *Victor* ■ *Dir* Richard Wallace, Edward Goodman • *Scr* Herman J Mankiewicz, from his story

Man of the Year ★★★ 15

Drama documentary　1995 · US · Colour · 85min

Playgirl's 1992 Man of the Year, actor/model-turned-film-maker Dick Shafer, blends fact and fiction to good effect in this tale of his year as every woman's fantasy, while hiding the fact that he was gay. Because Shafer is so involved in the movie, it sometimes becomes a bit of a vanity project. But there are also a lot of interesting comments about sexual stereotypes and prejudices, as well as plenty of self-deprecating humour on the part of Shafer that makes this an interesting and unusual documentary. JB

Dirk Shafer *Dirk Schafer* • Vivian Paxton • Claudette Sutherland *Tammy Shafer* • Michael Ornstein *Mike Miller* • Calvin Bartlett [Cal Bartlett] *Ken Shafer* • Beth Broderick *Kelly Bound* ■ *Dir/Scr* Dirk Shafer

The Man of the Year

★★★ 15

Crime action comedy
2002 · Bra · Colour · 104min

Working with a screenplay by his father Rubem, debutant director José Enrique Fonseca delves into the murky layer of corruption, decadence and violence that insulates Brazilians aspiring to bourgeois respectability from those existing in backstreet squalor. The tone vacillates between bleak comedy and urban parable, but the story of an accidental hero who is duped into becoming the people's vigilante tries to cover too much ground. It's intriguing, but not wholly convincing. DP Portuguese +subtitles. Drug abuse, swearing, violence. *DVD*

Murilo Benicio *Maiquel Jorge* • Claudia Abreu *Cledir* • Natalia Lage *Erica* • Jorge Doria *Dr Carvalho* • José Wilker *Silvio* • Agildo Ribeiro *Zilmar* ■ *Dir* José Henrique Fonseca • *Scr* Rubem Fonseca, from the novel *O Matador [The Killer]* by Patricia Melo

Man of the Year ★★ 12

Comedy　2006 · US · Colour · 110min

Dispirited by the line-up of candidates for the US Presidency, a Jon Stewart-like talk-show host (Robin Williams) decides to throw his hat into the ring and is astonished when he actually wins the election. What he doesn't know is that the electronic voting machines have a glitch – one that only software programmer Laura Linney knows about. Her bosses, who include an oily Jeff Goldblum, are determined to shut her up, and it's then that this comedy changes gear and turns into a conspiracy thriller. It's a shame because Williams appears to relish a return to his stand-up roots and the concept – a comedian in the White House – is certainly ripe with comic potential. JF *DVD*

Robin Williams *Tom Dobbs* • Christopher Walken *Jack Menken* • Laura Linney *Eleanor Green* • Lewis Black *Eddie Langston* • Jeff Goldblum *Stewart* • David Alpay *Danny* • Tina Fey • Amy Poehler ■ *Dir/Scr* Barry Levinson

Man on a Ledge ★★ 12

Thriller　2012 · US · Colour · 98min

The plot of this thriller is as wobbly as Nick Cassidy (Sam Worthington), the eponymous man who, it seems, has no intention of jumping. That's a shame, if only because it removes a lot of tension which director Asger Leth tries to replace by having Nick's little brother Joey (Jamie Bell) simultaneously engaged in a break-in. As far as the performances go, Bell is the more entertaining actor to watch, as Worthington just doesn't have a commanding presence, even shouting from halfway up a skyscraper. In every way, this film oversteps the mark. SP Brief swearing. *DVD* ʙʟ

Sam Worthington *Nick Cassidy* • Elizabeth Banks (2) *Lydia Mercer* • Jamie Bell *Joey Cassidy* • Ed Harris *David Englander* • Anthony Mackie *Mike Ackerman* • Kyra Sedgwick *Suzie Morales* ■ *Dir* Asger Leth • *Scr* Pablo Fenjves [Pablo F Fenjves]

Man on a Tightrope ★★★ PG

Drama based on a true story
1953 · US · BW · 105min

This professionally made and absorbing drama is based on real-life events, about a circus troupe escaping across the border from communist Czechoslovakia to Austria. This is well acted, particularly by Fredric March and Robert Beatty, and effectively directed by Elia Kazan, but the fact that this was the movie Kazan was working on when he shamefully "named names" to the House Un-American Activities Committee makes the story ironic. TS *DVD*

Fredric March *Karel Cernik* • Terry Moore *Tereza Cernik* • Gloria Grahame *Zama Cernik* • Cameron Mitchell *Joe Vosdek* • Adolphe Menjou *Fesker* • Robert Beatty *Barovic* • Alex D'Arcy *Rudolph* ■ *Dir* Elia Kazan • *Scr* Robert E Sherwood, from the story *International Incident* by Neil Peterson

Man on Fire ★★ 18

Thriller　1987 · It/Fr · Colour · 87min

In an often unintentionally funny mix of big-blast set pieces and patently ludicrous plot shenanigans, Scott Glenn plays a former CIA agent, now pacifist, who becomes a Rambo-style avenger when the 12-year-old girl in his charge is kidnapped. Alongside Glenn, Jonathan Pryce, Danny Aiello and Joe Pesci are confounded by the mediocrity of the project. JM Swearing, violence.

Scott Glenn *Chris Creasy* • Jade Malle *Samantha "Sam" Balletto* • Joe Pesci *David* • Brooke Adams *Jane Balletto* • Jonathan Pryce *Michael* • Paul Shenar *Ettore Balletto* • Danny Aiello *Conti* •

Laura Morante *Julia* ▪ *Dir* Elie Chouraqui • *Scr* Elie Chouraqui, Sergio Donati, from the novel by AJ Quinnell

Man on Fire ★★★ 18

Action thriller 2004 · US/UK · Colour · 140min

Denzel Washington excels here as a burned-out former US government agent, who reluctantly takes a job in Mexico City as bodyguard to Dakota Fanning, the child of wealthy parents who needs protection during a wave of kidnappings. Director Tony Scott hits the right notes early on when the girl's charm begins to win over her emotionally closed-off protector. But once Fanning is kidnapped, this becomes a drawn-out revenge thriller, as the second half of the film degenerates into a showcase of imaginative ultra-violence. GM English, Spanish +subtitles. Violence. *DVD*

Denzel Washington *John Creasy* • Dakota Fanning *Lupita "Pita" Martin Ramos* • Marc Anthony *Samuel Ramos* • Radha Mitchell *Lisa Martin Ramos* • Christopher Walken *Rayburn* • Giancarlo Giannini *Manzano* • Rachel Ticotin *Mariana* • Mickey Rourke *Jordan Kalfus* ▪ *Dir* Tony Scott • *Scr* Brian Helgeland, from the novel by AJ Quinnell

The Man on the Eiffel Tower ★★ PG

Detective thriller 1949 · US · Colour · 88min

Charles Laughton stars as Georges Simenon's Inspector Maigret, with Franchot Tone as his fiendish and arrogant adversary. Burgess Meredith plays an impoverished knife-grinder and directed most of the picture, filmed in Paris using the untried Ansco Color process. Laughton directed some scenes, including the one in which Meredith turns burglar and comes upon two women stabbed to death in the bedroom. There are some striking touches but not much suspense. AE *DVD*

Charles Laughton *Inspector Maigret* • Franchot Tone *Johann Radek* • Burgess Meredith *Joseph Huertin* • Robert Hutton *Bill Kirby* • Jean Wallace *Edna Wallace* • Patricia Roc *Helen Kirby* • Belita *Gisella* • George Thorpe *Comelieu* • Wilfrid Hyde White *Prof Grollet* ▪ *Dir* Burgess Meredith • *Scr* Harry Brown, from the novelette *La Tête d'un Homme (A Battle of Nerves)* by Georges Simenon

Man on the Flying Trapeze ★★ U

Comedy 1935 · US · BW · 63min

WC Fields, who dreamed up the storyline with Sam Hardy, is the characteristically curmudgeonly star of this misleadingly titled comedy, released more accurately in Britain as *The Memory Expert*. Fields plays a man who capitalises on his astonishing feats of memory to reduce all those around him, including his nagging wife, to gibbering submission. The sole exception is his daughter, played by Mary Brian. Clyde Bruckman directs what is essentially a showcase for a series of Fields gags. RK *DVD*

WC Fields *Ambrose Wolfinger* • Mary Brian *Hope Wolfinger* • Kathleen Howard *Leona Wolfinger* • Grady Sutton *Claude Neselrode* • Vera Lewis *Mrs Cordelia Neselrode* • Lucien Littlefield *Mr Peabody* • Walter Brennan *"Legs" Garnett* ▪ *Dir* Clyde Bruckman • *Scr* Ray Harris, Sam Hardy, Jack Cunningham, Bobby Vernon, from a story by Sam Hardy, Charles Bogle [WC Fields]

Man on the Moon ★★★★ 15

Biographical comedy drama 1999 · US · Colour · 113min

The strange, self-destructive career of comedian Andy Kaufman is re-created by Jim Carrey and director Milos Forman in this challenging, off-the-wall biography. Carrey gives everything he's got to portray the man who found fame as the squeaky-voiced Latka in 1980s sitcom *Taxi*. In an audacious piece of casting, Kaufman's *Taxi* co-star Danny DeVito portrays his manager, and he too is first-rate. From the bizarre credits scene onwards, Forman keeps the audience unsure of how to perceive Kaufman, a decision that prompted some

critics to complain he does not allow enough insight into the man. JC *DVD*

Jim Carrey *Andy Kaufman* • Danny DeVito *George Shapiro* • Courtney Love *Lynne Margulies* • Paul Giamatti *Bob Zmuda* • Vincent Schiavelli *Maynard Smith* • Jerry Lawler • Gerry Becker *Stanley Kaufman* • Leslie Lyles *Janice Kaufman* ▪ *Dir* Miles Forman • *Scr* Scott Alexander, Larry Karaszewski

Man on Wire ★★★★★ 12

Drama documentary 2007 · UK · Colour · 93min

A jaw-dropping blend of traditional talking-head interviews, archive footage and meticulous period re-creation, this charts one man's determination from childhood to walk a tightrope between the Twin Towers of the World Trade Center in New York, a dream that finally came true over the rooftops of Manhattan in 1974. Its subject, a charismatic Frenchman named Philippe Petit is a joy to watch, an ebullient mix of elegant mime artist Marcel Marceau and cartoon dervish Roadrunner, and the film offers a deceptively sturdy sounding board for his often crazy ideas. Sadly, no footage exists of Petit's 47-minute walk, but director James Marsh expertly captures the vertiginous thrills of that incredible day, leaving one with a sense of wonder and admiration for the rigorous preparation and heady commitment that made it all possible. DW English, French +subtitles. *DVD*

Philippe Petit • Jean-Louis Blondeau • Annie Allix • Jean-François Heckel *Jean-François Heckel* • Paul McGill *Philippe Petit* • David Demato *Jean-Louis Blondeau* • Arcis Campbell *Annie Allix* • Aaron Haskell *Jean-François Heckel* ▪ *Dir* James Marsh • *Scr* Inspired by the autobiography *To Reach the Clouds* by Philippe Petit

Man-Proof ★★★

Comedy drama 1937 · US · BW · 74min

Shenanigans among the sophisticated set as an uncharacteristically predatory Myrna Loy sets her sights on Walter Pidgeon and keeps them there, even when he marries her rival (Rosalind Russell). Rescue, however, is at hand in the shape of Franchot Tone, a mildly diverting romantic comedy drama, directed by Richard Thorpe, that holds the attention thanks to the easy expertise of the classy cast. RK

Myrna Loy *Mimi Swift* • Franchot Tone *Jimmy Kilmartin* • Rosalind Russell *Elizabeth Kent* • Walter Pidgeon *Alan Wythe* • Rita Johnson *Florence* • Nana Bryant *Meg Swift* • Ruth Hussey *Jane* • Leonard Penn *Bob* ▪ *Dir* Richard Thorpe • *Scr* George Oppenheimer, Vincent Lawrence, Waldemar Young, from the novel *The Four Marys* by Fanny Heaslip Lea

Man Push Cart ★★★ 15

Drama 2005 · US · Colour · 86min

Despite its pertinent message and poignant imagery, this gentle tale of New York street life is undermined by some stilted acting. When he's hauling his coffee kiosk through the nocturnal streets, Ahmad Razvi seems genuinely weighed down by the twin burdens of having lost his wife (and been parted from his son by her parents) and his career as a singer back in Pakistan. But his encounters with self-serving yuppie Charles Daniel Sandoval and lonely Spanish news vendor Leticia Dolera lack authenticity, let alone humanity. The invisibility of the immigrant within the urban landscape is an intriguing theme, but while Iranian-American director Ramin Bahrani clearly has a cinematic eye, his handling of the cast and dialogue is less assured. DP

Ahmad Razvi *Ahmad* • Leticia Dolera *Noemi* • Charles Daniel Sandoval *Mohammad* • Ali Reza Manish • Farooq "Duke" Muhammad *Duke* • Panicker Upendran *Noori* ▪ *Dir/Scr* Ramin Bahrani

The Man They Could Not Hang ★★★

Horror 1939 · US · BW · 64min

While not exactly the "holocaust of horror" promised at the time, this incredibly prophetic sci-fi thriller is laced with enough sinister menace to get by. British bogeyman Boris Karloff plays a crazed scientist

dabbling in heart transplant surgery who is sentenced to death by the medical authorities. After his execution, his own technology is used to turn him into a vengeful maniac with a mechanical ticker. As usual, kindly Karloff elevates standard fear fare with wit, grace and presence. AJ

Boris Karloff *Dr Henryk Savaard* • Lorna Gray *Janet Saavard* • Robert Wilcox *Scoop Foley* • Roger Pryor *District Attorney Drake* • Don Beddoe *Lt Shane* ▪ *Dir* Nick Grinde • *Scr* Karl Brown, from a story by Leslie T White, George W Sayre

Man Trouble ★★ 15

Romantic comedy 1992 · US · Colour · 95min

Proof that even the most talented actors – in this case, Jack Nicholson and Ellen Barkin – can make bad choices and turn in mediocre performances in a below-par film. When opera singer Barkin thinks she's being stalked, she enlists the help of oddball dog trainer Nicholson to find her an attack dog. Naturally, the pair are soon sparring along the path to true love. Ridiculous and insignificant complications ensue. JB *DVD*

Jack Nicholson *Harry Bliss* • Ellen Barkin *Joan Spruance* • Harry Dean Stanton *Redmond Layls* • Beverly D'Angelo *Andy Ellerman* • Michael McKean *Eddy Revere* • Saul Rubinek *Laurence Moncrief* ▪ *Dir* Bob Rafelson • *Scr* Carole Eastman

Man Up ★★★★ 15

Romantic comedy 2015 · UK/Fr · Colour · 84min

Nancy (Lake Bell) steals someone else's blind date, Jack (Simon Pegg), from under a clock at Waterloo Station, and the lie leads to major mayhem in this feel-good comedy. There's a screwball rhythm to the action and a snappy, wordy script that gallops past the "meet-cute" concept to redeem itself with a credible romance. *Man Up* is heaped with wit and insight, and has a smart script, sharp direction and crisp performances. Bell's English accent is pretty good, too. KK *DVD*

Lake Bell *Nancy* • Simon Pegg *Jack* • Rory Kinnear *Sean* • Sharon Horgan *Elaine* • Olivia Williams *Hilary* • Stephen Campbell Moore *Ed* • Harriet Walter *Fran* • Ophelia Lovibond *Jessica/Girl on train* • Dean-Charles Chapman *Harry* ▪ *Dir* Ben Palmer • *Scr* Tess Morris

The Man Upstairs ★★★ PG

Drama 1958 · UK · Colour · 84min

Le Jour Se Lève (1939) starred Jean Gabin as a killer who barricades himself in his attic flat. It was remade in 1947 as *The Long Night* with Henry Fonda, and this too is a remake, with Richard Attenborough going bonkers upstairs while the police downstairs try to calm him down. The motivation has changed (he blames himself for his fiancée's brother's death), but the dramatic set-up is identical and makes for some agreeable tension. AT

Richard Attenborough *Peter Watson, the man* • Bernard Lee *Inspector Thompson* • Donald Houston *Sanderson* • Dorothy Alison *Mrs Barnes* • Patricia Jessel *Mrs Lawrence* • Virginia Maskell *Helen Grey* ▪ *Dir* Don Chaffey • *Scr* Alun Falconer, Robert Dunbar, Don Chaffey, from a story by Alun Falconer

The Man Who Broke the Bank at Monte Carlo ★★

Comedy 1935 · US · BW · 70min

The popular song is played over the titles, but this movie is initially set in Paris where Russian émigré Ronald Colman works as a cab driver. He decides to try his luck in Monte Carlo and lands a multi-million franc windfall at the tables. Joan Bennett is the casino employee sent to woo him and his winnings back. This would-be sophisticated comedy fall flats under the heavy-handed direction of former stuntman Stephen Roberts. AT

Ronald Colman *Paul Gallard* • Joan Bennett *Helen Berkeley* • Colin Clive *Bertrand Berkeley* • Nigel Bruce *Ivan* • Montagu Love *Director* • Ferdinand Gottschalk *Office man* ▪ *Dir* Stephen Roberts • *Scr* Howard Ellis Smith, Nunnally Johnson, from the play *Monsieur Alexandre, Igra, Lepy and the Gamble* by Illia Surgutchoff, Frederick Albert Swann

The Man Who Came to Dinner ★★★★ U

Comedy 1941 · US · BW · 116min

New York character actor Monty Woolley transferred his stage role to the screen, playing irascible lecturer Sheridan Whiteside in this sparkling Warner Bros comedy based on the Broadway hit. Incapacitated after slipping on ice outside the home of Grant Mitchell, Woolley becomes an unwelcome guest who takes control of the house, leaving a respectable family totally bewildered. Despite Woolley's screen-hogging, the presence of the dynamic Bette Davis and Ann Sheridan lends Woolley the star power he personally lacks. The result is splendid entertainment. TS

Bette Davis *Maggie Cutler* • Monty Woolley *Sheridan Whiteside* • Ann Sheridan *Lorraine Sheldon* • Richard "Dick" Travis [Richard Travis] • Bert Jefferson • Jimmy Durante *Banjo* • Reginald Gardiner *Beverly Carlton* • Billie Burke *Mrs Stanley* • Mary Wickes *Miss Preen* ▪ *Dir* William Keighley • *Scr* Julius J Epstein, Philip G Epstein, from the play by George S Kaufman, Moss Hart

The Man Who Captured Eichmann ★★★★ PG

Historical drama 1996 · US · Colour · 92min

A great actor was needed to find a shred of humanity in Nazi Adolf Eichmann and this made-for-cable movie has that actor in Robert Duvall. He portrays the bureaucrat who sent millions of people to the gas chambers as an aged, infirm exile, kidnapped in Argentina by masterspy Peter Malkin (Arliss Howard) and taken to Israel to face trial. Concentrating on the excitement of the chase, the film nevertheless carries the horror of the Holocaust across the years. TH

Robert Duvall *Adolf Eichmann* • Arliss Howard *Peter Malkin* • Jeffrey Tambor *Isser Harel* • Jack Laufer *Uzi* • Nicolas Surovy *Hans* ▪ *Dir* William A Graham • *Scr* Lionel Chetwynd, from the memoirs *Eichmann in My Hands* by Peter Malkin, Harry Stein

The Man Who Changed His Mind ★★★ U

Science-fiction thriller 1936 · UK · BW · 62min

Boris Karloff is up to his brain transference tricks again in this seldom-seen British chiller. As Dr Laurience, he's in love with lab assistant Anna Lee. Unfortunately, she's planning to marry John Loder. So Karloff plans to switch brains with him using the usual strange scientific apparatus so popular in 1930s borderline sci-fi melodrama. Karloff gives one of his best performances in the amusing leading role. AJ *DVD*

Boris Karloff *Dr Laurience* • Anna Lee *Dr Claire Wyatt* • John Loder *Dick Haslewood* • Frank Cellier *Lord Haslewood* • Donald Calthrop *Clayton* • Cecil Parker *Dr Gratton* • Lyn Harding *Professor Holloway* ▪ *Dir* Robert Stevenson • *Scr* L DuGarde Peach, Sidney Gilliat, John L Balderston

The Man Who Could Cheat Death ★★ 12

Horror 1959 · UK · Colour · 82min

A 104-year-old doctor is able to look like a 30-year-old thanks to annual glandular transplants taken from living donors. When he murders his own doctor, however, things starts to unravel. This strange Hammer horror has its moments, but not very many. That said, it does provide a starring role to Anton Diffring, who usually played sadistic SS officers. AT *DVD*

Anton Diffring *Dr Georges Bonnet* • Hazel Court *Janine* • Delphi Lawrence *Margo* • Christopher Lee *Dr Pierre Gerard* • Francis De Wolff *Inspector Legris* ▪ *Dir* Terence Fisher • *Scr* Jimmy Sangster, from the play *The Man in Half Moon Street* by Barré Lyndon

The Man Who Could Work Miracles ★★ U

Fantasy comedy 1936 · UK · BW · 69min

Having produced HG Wells's *Things to Come*, British movie mogul Alexander Korda went straight on to another Wells story, a rather corny fantasy about a bashful draper's assistant (Roland Young) who acquires miraculous powers when the gods look kindly upon him. The comedy soon gives way to pomposity, as Young gathers world leaders and tells them to be nice to each other. While Ralph Richardson is delightfully eccentric throughout, it's embarrassingly dated and simplistic. AT *DVD*

Roland Young *George McWhirter Fotheringay* • Ralph Richardson *Colonel Winstanley* • Edward Chapman *Major Grigsby* • Ernest Thesiger *Mr Maydig* • Joan Gardner *Ada Price* • Sophie Stewart *Maggie Hooper* • Robert Cochran *Bill Stoker* • Lawrence Hanray *Mr Bamfylde* ■ *Dir* Lothar Mendes • *Scr* HG Wells, Lajos Biró, from the short story by HG Wells

The Man Who Cried ★★ 12

Period romantic drama
2000 · UK/Fr/US · Colour · 95min

Set mostly in France just prior to Nazi occupation, this theatrically staged romance follows Christina Ricci's Jewish émigré as she moves from her native Russia to London then Paris, dependent on the kindness of others, notably showgirl Cate Blanchett. Ricci falls in love with Johnny Depp's unintentionally comic gypsy horseman, although their on-screen chemistry is nil. The characters in Sally Potter's colourful film are little more than chocolate-box cut-outs. AC Violence, sex scenes. *DVD*

Christina Ricci *Suzie* • Cate Blanchett *Lola* • John Turturro *Dante Domino* • Johnny Depp *Cesar* • Oleg Yankovskiy *Father* • Harry Dean Stanton *Felix Perlman* • Miriam Karlin *Madame Goldstein* ■ *Dir/Scr* Sally Potter

The Man Who Fell to Earth ★★★★ 18

Cult science-fiction drama
1976 · UK · Colour · 133min

This typically eccentric and multidimensional movie from director Nicolas Roeg transforms Walter Tevis's novel into an enigmatic and chilling mosaic of corporate satire and effective science fiction. In his feature debut, David Bowie is exactly right as the Swiftian starman who becomes fabulously wealthy from his intergalactic inventions, but soon gets corrupted by such earthbound vices as alcohol, television and sex. Already an established sci-fi classic, this is a fascinating new-age fairy tale, with Bowie's "fall" open to numerous allegorical interpretations. AJ Violence, swearing, sex scenes, nudity. *DVD* ◄►

David Bowie *Thomas Jerome Newton* • Rip Torn *Nathan Bryce* • Candy Clark *Mary-Lou* • Buck Henry *Oliver Farnsworth* • Bernie Casey *Peters* • Jackson D Kane *Professor Canutti* • Rick Riccardo *Trevor* • Tony Mascia *Arthur* ■ *Dir* Nicolas Roeg • *Scr* Paul Mayersburg, from the novel by Walter Tevis

The Man Who Finally Died ★ PG

Drama   1962 · UK · BW · 96min

Stanley Baker goes to Bavaria to find out about his long-lost German father; while there, he gets involved in espionage. This routine spy thriller based on a TV series plods more than it surprises, though the actors deserve some credit for delivering the deathless lines with a conviction that's way beyond the call of duty. AJ *DVD*

Stanley Baker *Joe Newman* • Peter Cushing *Dr von Brecht* • Eric Portman *Hofmeister* • Mai Zetterling *Lisa* • Niall MacGinnis *Brenner* • Nigel Green *Hirsch* • Barbara Everest *Martha* ■ *Dir* Quentin Lawrence • *Scr* Lewis Greifer, Louis Marks, from a story by Lewis Greifer

The Man Who Had Power over Women ★

Comedy   1970 · UK · Colour · 89min

This awful, cringe-inducing story about a public relations executive and his obnoxious pop star client was filmed at the fag end of the Swinging Sixties, and it has dated very badly. Although the film toys around with the moral issue of abortion, it never achieves more than a glossy vacuity. AT

Rod Taylor *Peter Reaney* • Carol White *Jody Pringle* • James Booth *Val Pringle* • Penelope Horner *Angela Reaney* • Charles Korvin *Alfred Felix* • Alexandra Stewart *Frances* ■ *Dir* John Krish • *Scr* Allan Scott, Chris Bryant, Andrew Meredith, from the novel by Gordon M Williams

The Man Who Haunted Himself ★★★ PG

Thriller   1970 · UK · Colour · 88min

This wonderfully improbable chiller affords the rare opportunity to see Roger Moore being acted off the screen – by Roger Moore! The respectable business executive whose life is transformed by a car crash is a drip of the first order, but the sinister alter ego who escapes while he is unconscious is a rip-roaring cad. Veteran director Basil Dearden just manages to sustain the eerie atmosphere and, even though the mistaken identity card is overplayed, it's very watchable. DP *DVD* ◄►

Roger Moore *Harold Pelham* • Hildegard Neil *Eve Pelham* • Alastair Mackenzie (1) *Michael* • Hugh Mackenzie *James* • Kevork Malikyan *Luigi* • Thorley Walters *Bellamy* • Anton Rodgers *Tony Alexander* • Olga Georges-Picot *Julie* ■ *Dir* Basil Dearden • *Scr* Basil Dearden, Michael Relph, from the short story *The Case of Mr Pelham* by Anthony Armstrong

The Man Who Knew Infinity ★★★ 12A

Biographical drama 2015 · UK · Colour · 108min

Marigold Hotel star Dev Patel has few blessings to count in this earnest portrait of genius mathematician Srinivasa Ramanujan, whose pioneering research didn't protect him from racist treatment at Cambridge University. On the eve of the First World War, Ramanujan is brought from India to England, where Professor GH Hardy (Jeremy Irons) is keen to work with him. Patel has a natural warmth that tempers his character's slight egotism and ultimately brings home the tragedy of Ramanujan's short life. SP In English, Tamil. Offensive language

Dev Patel *Srinivasa Ramanujan* • Jeremy Irons *GH Hardy* • Toby Jones *Littlewood* • Stephen Fry *Sir Francis Spring* • Jeremy Northam *Bertrand Russell* ■ *Dir* Matt Brown • *Scr* Matt Brown, from Robert Kanigel's biography

The Man Who Knew Too Little ★★★ 12

Spy comedy   1997 · US/Ger · Colour · 89min

As the parodic Hitchcock title suggests, this sweet-natured Bill Murray comedy is an entertaining throwback to the espionage thrillers of yesteryear. Naive Murray is visiting brother Peter Gallagher in London and unwittingly becomes entangled in an assassination plot, the inspired twist being that Murray thinks it's all part of a participatory drama group. Enjoyable, but the one-joke premise does eventually lose its lustre. JC Violence, swearing.

Bill Murray *Wallace Ritchie* • Peter Gallagher *James Ritchie* • Joanne Whalley-Kilmer [Joanne Whalley] *Lori* • Alfred Molina *Boris, the Butcher* • Richard Wilson (3) *Sir Roger Daggenhurst* • Geraldine James *Dr Ludmilla Kropotkin* • John Standing *Gilbert Embleton* • Anna Chancellor *Barbara Ritchie* ■ *Dir* Jon Amiel • *Scr* Robert Farrar, Howard Franklin, from the novel *Watch That Man* by Robert Farrar

The Man Who Knew Too Much ★★★★ U

Thriller   1934 · UK · BW · 79min

With a finale inspired by the 1911 Sidney Street siege, this early Hitchcock – the only film he remade – was originally devised as a case for Bulldog Drummond. A taut, twisting thriller, the film sweeps from Switzerland to London's Albert Hall as Leslie Banks and Edna Best seek to rescue kidnapped daughter Nova Pilbeam and prevent a political assassination. Laced with gallows humour, this expertly structured tale marked the English-language debut of Peter Lorre, whose delight in his own villainy is tempered with a touch of humanity. DP *DVD* ◄►

Leslie Banks *Bob Lawrence* • Edna Best *Jill Lawrence* • Peter Lorre *Abbott* • Frank Vosper *Ramon Levine* • Hugh Wakefield *Clive* • Nova Pilbeam *Betty Lawrence* • Pierre Fresnay *Louis Bernard* • Cicely Oates *Nurse Agnes* ■ *Dir* Alfred Hitchcock • *Scr* Edwin Greenwood, AR Rawlinson, Emlyn Williams, Charles Bennett, DB Wyndham-Lewis, from a story by DB Wyndham-Lewis

The Man Who Knew Too Much ★★★ PG

Thriller   1956 · US · Colour · 114min

Alfred Hitchcock once told François Truffaut that his 1934 version of this exciting thriller – about a family innocently involved in an assassination plot – was "the work of a talented amateur and the second was made by a professional". There's no doubt that this colour remake is technically more accomplished, while the deft tinkering with the finale adds to the suspense. Not all of the additional minutes are as well spent. *Que Sera, Sera* might have won the Oscar, but its inclusion was solely to mollify Doris Day fans. The storytelling is occasionally over-deliberate, but James Stewart is superb. DP *DVD* ◄►

James Stewart *Dr Ben McKenna* • Doris Day *Jo McKenna* • Bernard Miles *Mr Drayton* • Brenda de Banzie *Mrs Drayton* • Ralph Truman *Buchanan* • Daniel Gélin *Louis Bernard* • Reggie Nalder *Rien, the assassin* • Mogens Wieth *Ambassador* • Alan Mowbray *Val Parnell* • Hillary Brooke *Jan Peterson* ■ *Dir* Alfred Hitchcock • *Scr* John Michael Hayes, Angus MacPhail, from a story by DB Wyndham-Lewis, Charles Bennett

The Man Who Laughs ★★★★

Silent period drama   1928 · US · BW · 110min

The third of four moody and mysterious films German-born director Paul Leni made in Hollywood was released a year after it was made in order to add music and sound effects. Based on Victor Hugo's tale, it tells of a man whose face is distorted into a hideous grin. Becoming a circus clown, he falls in love with a blind girl. Conrad Veidt plays the protagonist, while Mary Philbin is touching as his beloved. RB

Conrad Veidt *Gwynplaine* • Mary Philbin *Dea* ■ *Dir* Paul Leni • *Scr* J Grubb Alexander, Charles E Whittaker, Marion Ward, May McLean, Walter Anthony (titles), from the novel *L'Homme Qui Rit* by Victor Hugo

The Man Who Liked Funerals ★★ PG

Comedy   1959 · UK · BW · 57min

Leslie Phillips landed his first starring role in this sleek B-picture. Reining in the trademark charm, he plays a printer who attempts to fill the coffers of a struggling boys' club by blackmailing the relatives of recently departed bigwigs, whose scandalous (albeit forged) memoirs he threatens to publish. However, it all goes horribly wrong when he picks on the family of a notorious gangster. The film is nothing to get excited about, but it does raise the odd smile. DP *DVD*

Leslie Phillips *Simon Hurd* • Brian Tyler (1) *Nutter* • Anthony Green *Tommy* • Shaun O'Riordan *Reverend Pitt* • Susan Beaumont *Stella* • Bill Fraser *Jeremy Bentham* ■ *Dir* David Eady • *Scr* Margot Bennett, from a story by C Finn, Joan O'Connor

The Man Who Lived Twice ★★★

Crime drama   1936 · US · BW · 73min

Before Ralph Bellamy became cast as the typical "other man" – notably in 1937's *The Awful Truth* – he was known as a useful and recognisable tough lead. Here, he's excellent as a murderer who has brain and facial surgery which turns him into quite literally another person. Never a big hit, this average feature has an interesting period sheen. TS

Ralph Bellamy *James Blake/Slick Rawley* • Marian Marsh *Janet Haydon* • Thurston Hall *Dr Schuyler* • Isabel Jewell *Peggy Russell* • Nana Bryant *Mrs Margaret Schuyler* • Ward Bond

Gloves Baker ■ *Dir* Harry Lachman • *Scr* Tom Van Dycke, Fred Niblo Jr, Arthur Strawn, from the story by Tom Van Dycke, Henry Altimus

The Man Who Loved Cat Dancing ★ 18

Western   1973 · US · Colour · 118min

Rumour has it that Robert Bolt did a bit of script doctoring to improve this western, which starred his wife Sarah Miles and Burt Reynolds. Imagine how awful it must have been before he got hold of it. Directed with no sense of narrative, let alone the old West, what starts out as a revenge story soon turns into a soppy romance. Lee J Cobb and Jack Warden are left cooling their heels while Reynolds and Miles make little effort to hide their obvious antipathy towards one another. DP

Burt Reynolds *Jay Grobart* • Sarah Miles *Catherine Crocker* • Lee J Cobb *Lapchance* • Jack Warden *Dawes* • George Hamilton *Crocker* • Bo Hopkins *Billy* • Robert Donner *Dub* • Jay Silverheels *The Chief* ■ *Dir* Richard C Sarafian • *Scr* Eleanor Perry, from the novel by Marilyn Durham

The Man Who Loved Redheads ★★★ PG

Comedy   1954 · UK · Colour · 86min

An elegant and witty screenplay by Terence Rattigan, based on his play, helps make this extremely civilised and sophisticated entertainment. It also benefits immensely from an early Eastmancolor process and photography by the great Georges Périnal, a combination that proved ideal for showing off the titian tresses of Moira Shearer. The idea is nicely bittersweet, as Shearer plays all the "other" women in the recollections of John Justin, married to Gladys Cooper in the film. The dénouement is moving, and a marvellous line-up of supporting players speeds the slight tale pleasurably on its way. TS *DVD*

Moira Shearer *Sylvia/Daphne/Olga/Colette* • John Justin *Mark St Neots* • Roland Culver *Oscar* • Gladys Cooper *Caroline* • Denholm Elliott *Denis* • Harry Andrews *Williams* • Patricia Cutts *Bubbles* • John Hart *Sergei* ■ *Dir* Harold French • *Scr* Terence Rattigan, from his play *Who Is Sylvia?*

The Man Who Loved Women ★★★ 15

Comedy   1977 · Fr · Colour · 114min

Attacked for its chauvinism, François Truffaut's wry comedy is actually a shrugging admission that men are little boys who don't deserve the women who love them. As he recalls each pair of legs that has enticed him, Charles Denner emerges less as a manipulative cad and more a sad man who has missed so many opportunities to live a fuller life. Unfortunately, Truffaut turns his memoirs into a long series of flashbacks, which prevents him from exploring Denner's motives and emotions. A touch more gravitas might have made his tale more poignant. DP French +subtitles. *DVD*

Charles Denner *Bertrand Morane* • Brigitte Fossey *Geneviève Bigey* • Nelly Borgeaud *Delphine Grezel* • Geneviève Fontanel *Helene* • Nathalie Baye *Martine Desdoits* • Sabine Glaser *Bernadette* • Leslie Caron *Vera* ■ *Dir* François Truffaut • *Scr* François Truffaut, Michel Fermaud, Suzanne Schiffman

The Man Who Loved Women ★★ 15

Comedy   1983 · US · Colour · 105min

This is an early example of the American trend of adapting (and usually ruining) a French success for the US market. Director Blake Edwards takes François Truffaut's minor film and balloons it into something grander, yet emptier. Burt Reynolds works well as a women-obsessed sculptor whose story is played out via flashbacks at his funeral. Julie Andrews is the psychiatrist to whom Reynolds confesses all. The cast is pleasing, but this fails to hit the mark. DF

Burt Reynolds *David* • Julie Andrews *Marianna* • Kim Basinger *Louise* • Marilu Henner *Agnes* • Cynthia Sikes *Courtney* • Sela Ward *Janet* ■

---

802   U SUITABLE FOR ALL   Uc SUITABLE ESPECIALLY FOR YOUNG CHILDREN (DVD ONLY)   PG PARENTAL GUIDANCE   12A UNDER 12s TO BE ACCOMPANIED (CINEMA ONLY)

Dir Blake Edwards • Scr Blake Edwards, Milton Wexler, Geoffrey Edwards, from the 1977 film by François Truffaut

The Man Who Never Was
★★★ U

Second World War spy drama
1955 · UK · Colour · 102min

This is a lacklustre Second World War espionage caper about a plan to fool the Nazis into believing that the Allies had no interest in invading Sicily from North Africa. Scripted by Nigel Balchin, the plan hinges on a corpse, a British one, washed ashore with secret papers marking Greece as the invasion site. But the Germans aren't so easily convinced and send Irish agent Stephen Boyd to London to investigate. Stodgily directed by Ronald Neame, this is less a thriller than a game of wartime charades. AT

Clifton Webb *Lt Cmdr Ewen Montagu* • Gloria Grahame *Lucy* • Stephen Boyd *O'Reilly* • Robert Flemyng *George Acres* • Josephine Griffin *Pam* • André Morell *Sir Bernard Spilsbury* • Laurence Naismith *Admiral Cross* • Michael Hordern *General Coburn* ■ Dir Ronald Neame • Scr Nigel Balchin, from the book by Ewen Montagu

The Man Who Played God
★★★★

Drama
1932 · US · BW · 81min

The great George Arliss, with his death's-head face, effete elegance and mannered theatrical style, might at first strike modern audiences as faintly comical. However, in this intriguing fable about love, faith and redemption, he is mesmerising as a wealthy international concert pianist who becomes an embittered recluse after going deaf from a bomb explosion. Eventually, he learns to lip-read the conversations of passers-by and uses his wealth to play God. Bette Davis made her striking Warner Bros debut as his youthful and passionate disciple, and John Adolfi directed this compelling drama with imagination and sensitivity. It was embarrassingly updated in 1955 as *Sincerely Yours*, a starring vehicle for Liberace. RK

George Arliss *Montgomery Royale* • Violet Heming *Mildred Miller* • Ivan Simpson *Battle* • Louise Closser Hale *Florence Royale* • Bette Davis *Grace Blair* • André Luguet *The King* • Donald Cook *Harold Van Adam* • Charles E Evans *The Doctor* ■ Dir John G Adolfi • Scr Julien Josephson, Maude Howell, from the play by Jules Eckert Goodman, from the short story *The Silent Voice* by Gouverneur Morris

The Man Who Saved the World
★★★ 15

Documentary
2013 · Den · Colour · 109min

On 26 September 1983, the Soviet Union's early warning system indicated that US missiles were heading for Moscow. However, duty officer Stanislav Petrov wasn't convinced that the threat was real, so he decided not to confirm the attack, thereby preventing all-out war. Three decades later, these incredible events are documented to sobering effect by Danish director Peter Anthony, who follows Petrov on a cathartic trip Stateside. The resulting footage is distractingly shot like a traditional feature, but Petrov's story is fascinating and deserves to be told. SC In Russian, English. Swearing.

Kevin Costner • Matt Damon • Robert De Niro • Stanislav Petrov ■ Dir/Scr Peter Anthony

The Man Who Shot Liberty Valance
★★★★★ U

Western
1962 · US · BW · 118min

In this key late John Ford western, top-billed James Stewart plays a US senator who returns to the town of Shinbone for the funeral of rancher John Wayne. The bulk of the story unfolds in flashback, culminating in a twist that only a spoilsport would reveal. The skilfully written screenplay makes the complexity of its themes appear so simple and the film clearly shows the impact of the arrival of literacy on an innocent, more primitive west. Wayne and Stewart create indelible

western icons, and a superb Lee Marvin offers memorable support as the Liberty Valance of the title. But perhaps this neglected masterpiece is best summed up by its most famous quote, "When the legend becomes the fact, print the legend!" TS **DVD** **BL**

James Stewart *Ransom Stoddard* • John Wayne *Tom Doniphon* • Vera Miles *Hallie Stoddard* • Lee Marvin *Liberty Valance* • Edmond O'Brien *Dutton Peabody* • Andy Devine *Link Appleyard* • Woody Strode *Pompey* • Ken Murray *Doc Willoughby* • John Carradine *Major Cassius Starbuckle* ■ Dir John Ford • Scr Willis Goldbeck, James Warner Bellah, from a story by Dorothy M Johnson • Cinematographer William H Clothier [William Clothier]

The Man Who Sued God
★★★ 15

Comedy drama
2001 · Aus · Colour · 96min

Unashamedly Capra-esque in its championing of the little feller against the system, Mark Joffe's comedy provides a charming, but acute indictment of the self-serving attitudes of established religion and the insurance industry. Angered at the decision that the destruction of his boat by lightning was an act of God, fisherman Billy Connolly teams up with journalist Judy Davis to challenge establishment truisms . The romantic subplot sugars the pill. DP Swearing. **DVD**

Billy Connolly *Steve Myers* • Judy Davis *Anna Redmond* • Colin Friels *David Myers* • Bille Brown *Gerry Ryan* • Wendy Hughes *Jules Myers* • Blair Venn *Les* • Emily Browning *Rebecca Myers* ■ Dir Mark Joffe • Scr Don Watson, from a screenplay (unproduced) by John Clarke, from an idea by Patrick McCarville

The Man Who Understood Women
★★

Satirical drama
1959 · US · Colour · 135min

Leslie Caron and Henry Fonda make up a May-December partnership in this overlong mix of comedy, romance and drama. Fonda is a film-maker who finds popular success by turning his new love, Caron, into a star. When she becomes involved with pilot Cesare Danova, however, Fonda gets jealous, and what could have been a hilarious satire on Hollywood turns into an unconvincing melodrama. The stars are good, but Nunnally Johnson, who writes, produces *and* directs, seems to lose his focus and his grip. RK

Leslie Caron *Ann Garantier* • Henry Fonda *Willie Bauche* • Cesare Danova *Marco Ranieri* • Myron McCormick *Preacher* • Marcel Dalio *Le Marne* • Conrad Nagel *GK* ■ Dir Nunnally Johnson • Scr Nunnally Johnson, from the novel *The Colors of Day* by Romain Gary

The Man Who Wasn't There
★★★★ 15

Period crime drama
2001 · US/UK · BW · 106min

It would be simplistic to call this Coen brothers' movie a pastiche of *film noir*. Certainly it is set in small-town California in 1949 and involves an ordinary Joe embroiled in a murder plot – and presented in period black and white – but the veneer of homage masks something far more complex and clever. The story, in which Billy Bob Thornton's inscrutable barber attempts to escape from his humdrum life through blackmail, is typical of the Coens. With its dash of flying-saucer paranoia, it's tempting to interpret the film as a broader examination of existential themes. There is sublime acting from Thornton and Coen regular Frances McDormand, aided by the stunning photography of Roger Deakins. AC Violence, swearing. **DVD**

Billy Bob Thornton *Ed Crane* • Frances McDormand *Doris Crane* • Michael Badalucco *Frank* • James Gandolfini *Big Dave* • Katherine Borowitz *Ann Nirdlinger* • Jon Polito *Creighton Tolliver* • Scarlett Johansson *Birdy Abundas* • Richard Jenkins *Walter Abundas* • Tony Shalhoub *Freddy Riedenschneider* ■ Dir Joel Coen • Scr Joel Coen, Ethan Coen

The Man Who Watched Trains Go By
★★★ PG

Mystery
1952 · UK · Colour · 77min

Adapted from the novel by the prolific Georges Simenon, this was one of Claude Rains's rare assignments in his homeland. Notwithstanding the dreadful colour, the tale of a clerk who takes advantage of the accidental death of crooked boss Herbert Lom quickly involves, with director Harold French capturing the atmosphere of provincial France and Rains essaying the decent little man with ease. DP **DVD**

Claude Rains *Kees Popinga* • Michael Nightingale *Clerk* • Felix Aylmer *Merkemans* • Herbert Lom *Julius de Koster Jr* • Gibb McLaughlin *Julius de Koster Sr* • Marius Goring *Lucas* • Marta Toren *Michele* ■ Dir Harold French • Scr Harold French, from the novel by Georges Simenon

The Man Who Would Be King
★★★★★ PG

Period adventure
1975 · US · Colour · 123min

This colourful movie version of Rudyard Kipling's right royal 19th-century adventure stars Sean Connery and Michael Caine as the veteran army squaddies who bamboozle a remote mountain tribe in Afghanistan into accepting Connery's regal credentials. Greed and circumstances topple the comic elements of the tale into a serious fable about the vanity of human endeavour and the folly of imperialism. Director John Huston matches character to action in masterly fashion, aided by the brief bonus of an aloof commentary on the situation by Christopher Plummer, as Kipling himself. Packed with sly dialogue and memorable scenes, plus a stirring score from Maurice Jarre. TH Violence, swearing. **DVD**

Sean Connery *Daniel Dravot* • Michael Caine *Peachy Carnehan* • Christopher Plummer *Rudyard Kipling* • Saeed Jaffrey *Billy Fish* • Karroum Ben Bouih *Kafu-Selim* • Jack May *District commissioner* • Doghmi Larbi *Ootah* • Shakira Caine *Roxanne* ■ Dir John Huston • Scr John Huston, Gladys Hill, from the story by Rudyard Kipling • Cinematographer Oswald Morris • Music Maurice Jarre

The Man Who Wouldn't Die
★★★ PG

Mystery
1995 · US · Colour · 88min

Why aren't there more TV movies with the same dark sense of fun as this one? Take one crime novelist, have him meet a waitress (who is also a medium) and have her announce that the supposedly dead villain on whom he based one of his characters is not only very much alive, but is busy re-enacting the killings his monarchy-mad murderer perpetrated on the page. Cracking stuff, directed at full tilt by Bill Condon with hammy performances from Roger Moore, Malcolm McDowell and Nancy Allen. DP Violence.

Roger Moore *Thomas Grace/Fullbright* • Malcolm McDowell *Bernard Drake/Morrissey* • Nancy Allen *Jesse Gallardo* • Michael Puttonen *Frank* • Wendy Van Riesen *Ingrid* • Scott Bellis *Boris* • Don MacKay *Henry Graham* • Eric McCormack *Bill Sullivan* ■ Dir Bill Condon • Scr David Amann

The Man Who Wouldn't Talk
★★★

Crime drama
1940 · US · BW · 72min

Lloyd Nolan has one of his strongest roles playing the mysterious figure who confesses to killing a businessman, yet steadfastly refuses to reveal his true identity or motive. This entertaining Fox B-feature was the second screen version of a 1920s play, having previously served as the basis of Paul Muni's film, *The Valiant* (1929), but the previously tragic ending is discarded. AE

Lloyd Nolan *Joe Monday* • Jean Rogers *Alice Stetson* • Richard Clarke (1) *Steve Phillips* • Onslow Stevens *Frederick Keller* • Eric Blore *Horace Parker* ■ Dir David Burton (1) • Scr Robert Ellis, Helen Logan, Lester Ziffren, Edward Ettinger, from the play *The Valiant* by Holworthy Hall, Robert M Middlemass

The Man Who Wouldn't Talk
★★ U

Courtroom drama
1957 · UK · BW · 93min

Producer/director Herbert Wilcox makes a moderately entertaining film out of this courtroom drama in which Anthony Quayle's American scientist, accused of murder, refuses to testify in his own defence. Wilcox's wife, Anna Neagle, gives another of her great lady portraits as Britain's leading Queen's Counsel, demonstrating her deductive brilliance in spotting a bullet hole in a witness's window pane and her oratorical skills in a dramatic five-minute courtroom address. AE **DVD**

Anthony Quayle *Dr Frank Smith* • Anna Neagle *Mary Randall QC* • Zsa Zsa Gabor *Eve Trent* • Katherine Kath *Yvonne Delbeau* • Dora Bryan *Telephonist* • Patrick Allen *Kennedy* • Hugh McDermott *Bernie* ■ Dir Herbert Wilcox • Scr Edgar Lustgarten, from the book by Stanley Jackson

The Man with a Cloak
★★ U

Period drama
1951 · US · BW · 80min

In 19th-century New York, villainous housekeeper Barbara Stanwyck schemes to murder Louis Calhern and cheat innocent young Leslie Caron out of her inheritance. Mysterious stranger Joseph Cotten arrives on the scene to save the day, turning out, quite inexplicably, to be Edgar Allan Poe. A bemusing period farrago, directed by Fletcher Markle, that would deserve to sink without trace were it not for Stanwyck's characteristically uncompromising performance. RK

Joseph Cotten *Dupin* • Barbara Stanwyck *Lorna Bounty* • Louis Calhern *Thevenet* • Leslie Caron *Madeline Minot* • Joe De Santis *Martin* • Jim Backus *Flaherty* • Margaret Wycherly *Mrs Flynn* • Richard Hale *Durand* ■ Dir Fletcher Markle • Scr Frank Fenton, from a story by John Dickson Carr

LANDMARK FILM
Dziga Vertov's vibrant documentary offers a masterclass in artistic technique

Man with a Movie Camera
★★★★★

Silent experimental documentary
1928 · USSR · BW · 70min

Dziga Vertov claimed that his purpose in making this remarkable panorama of Moscow life – the workers, shoppers, holidaymakers and machines that keep the city moving – was to film "life as it is". To achieve this, Vertov displayed all the techniques of cinema at his disposal: split-screen, dissolves, slow-motion and freeze frames. Indeed, it's the camera that is the hero of this influential documentary. Born Denis Kaufman, Vertov took his name from the Ukrainian words meaning spinning, turning or, more appropriately, revolution. The film was shot (sometimes perilously) by his brother, Mikhail; a third brother, Boris Kaufman, became an Oscar-winning cinematographer. RB **DVD** **BL**

■ Dir/Scr Dziga Vertov • Cinematographer Mikhail Kaufman

The Man with Bogart's Face
★★★

Detective comedy mystery
1980 · US · Colour · 111min

This is an enjoyable, unassuming movie about a second-rate private eye called Sam Marlow who has plastic surgery to make him look like his role model, Humphrey Bogart. It's a neat idea, and Bogart clone Robert Sacchi could certainly be mistaken for Bogie on a darkly lit mean street. The *Maltese Falcon*-style plot involves Alexander the Great's sapphires, with Victor Buono and Herbert Lom in the Greenstreet and Lorre roles. AT

Robert Sacchi *Sam Marlow* • Michelle Phillips *Gena* • Franco Nero *Hakim* • Olivia Hussey *Elsa* • Victor Buono *Commodore Anastas* • Herbert Lom *Mr Zebra* • George Raft *Petey Cane* ■ Dir Robert Day • Scr Andrew J Fenady, from his novel

M

The Man with One Red Shoe ★★ PG

Comedy 1985 · US · Colour · 88min

Hollywood has no qualms about trawling foreign climes for inspirational ideas and turning them into blandly inoffensive pap. This time around, however, the source is the French farce *The Tall Blond Man with One Black Shoe*, which itself limps along unfunnily in the slow lane. Unsurprisingly, so does the remake, making little use of Tom Hanks's comic talents. Marooned by inanity and mistiming, he plays a violinist who is mistaken for a spy. JM **DVD**

Tom Hanks *Richard* • Dabney Coleman *Cooper* • Lori Singer *Maddy* • Charles Durning *Ross* • Carrie Fisher *Paula* • Edward Herrmann *Brown* • Jim Belushi [James Belushi] *Morris* ■ *Dir* Stan Dragoti • *Scr* Robert Klane, from the film *The Tall Blond Man with One Black Shoe* by Francis Veber, Yves Robert

The Man with the Deadly Lens ★★★ 15

Satirical thriller 1982 · US · Colour · 112min

This thriller finds roving TV journalist Sean Connery uncovering a hornet's nest of conspiracies and terrorist links at the heart of the US government. The tone is often satirical but there are so many plots, subplots and red herrings that it's hard to figure out if it's a mess or immensely sophisticated. However, Connery is an anchorman in every respect, giving the film a firm foundation. AT **DVD**

Sean Connery *Patrick Hale* • George Grizzard *President Lockwood* • Robert Conrad *General Wombat* • Katharine Ross *Sally Blake* • GD Spradlin *Philindros* • John Saxon *Homer Hubbard* • Henry Silva *Rafeeq* • Leslie Nielsen *Mallory* ■ *Dir* Richard Brooks • *Scr* Richard Brooks, from the novel *The Better Angels* by Charles McCarry

The Man with the Golden Arm ★★★★ 15

Drama 1955 · US · BW · 119min

This is to drug addiction what *The Lost Weekend* was to alcoholism – a trailblazer. From Saul Bass's opening credits to Elmer Bernstein's jazzy score, Otto Preminger's movie boasts its modernity in its unflinching approach to the story of an aspiring musician and heroin addict. In the clean-cut Eisenhower era, this movie shocked audiences deeply. Frank Sinatra's Oscar-nominated performance still impresses, as do those of Eleanor Parker as his wife and Kim Novak as Sinatra's object of desire. AT **DVD** Blu

Frank Sinatra *Frankie Machine* • Kim Novak *Molly* • Eleanor Parker *Zosch Machine* • Arnold Stang *Sparrow* • Darren McGavin *Louie* • Robert Strauss *Schwiefka* • George Mathews *Williams* • John Conte *Drunky* ■ *Dir* Otto Preminger • *Scr* Walter Newman, Lewis Meltzer, from the novel by Nelson Algren

The Man with the Golden Gun ★★★ PG

Spy adventure 1974 · UK · Colour · 119min

This is an improvement on Ian Fleming's novel, with Christopher Lee making a fine villain, sporting a golden gun, a third nipple and a tiny henchman called Nick Nack, wittily played by Herve Villechaize. Britt Ekland is funny, too, sending herself up as Bond's clueless assistant and surviving the most sexist scene in the entire 007 series. There are major faults as well – notably the repeat of the pre-credit scene for the climax (borrowing from Orson Welles's *The Lady from Shanghai*). Thailand's Phang-Nga Bay was a stunning choice of location, though it was soon to become a tourist trap. AT **DVD** Blu

Roger Moore *James Bond* • Christopher Lee *Scaramanga* • Britt Ekland *Mary Goodnight* • Maud Adams *Andrea* • Herve Villechaize *Nick Nack* • Clifton James *Sheriff JW Pepper* • Soon Taik Oh [Soon-Teck Oh] *Hip* • Richard Loo *Hai Fat* • Bernard Lee *"M"* • Lois Maxwell *Miss Moneypenny* • Marc Lawrence (1) *Rodney* • Desmond Llewelyn *"Q"* ■ *Dir* Guy Hamilton • *Scr* Richard Maibaum, Tom Mankiewicz, from the novel by Ian Fleming

Man with the Gun ★★★ PG

Western 1955 · US · BW · 80min

One of Robert Mitchum's strengths was his ability to grab a western like this by its throat and turn it into a personal statement. Mitchum plays a brooding gunman who cleans up a town to try to win back his estranged wife, played by the excellent Jan Sterling. There's a fair amount of sadism on show, and the mood and tone are satisfyingly grim. It's an impressive directorial debut from former Orson Welles associate Richard Wilson, featuring fine photography from the great Lee Garmes. TS **DVD**

Robert Mitchum *Clint Tollinger* • Jan Sterling *Nelly Bain* • Karen Sharpe *Stella Atkins* • Henry Hull *Marshal Sims* • Emile Meyer *Saul Atkins* • John Lupton *Jeff Castle* • Angie Dickinson *Kitty* ■ *Dir* Richard Wilson (1) • *Scr* NB Stone Jr, Richard Wilson

The Man with the Iron Fists ★★ 18

Martial arts action thriller 2012 · US/HK · Colour · 91min

If you are fan of the 1970s-era kung fu action adventures in the Shaw Brothers tradition, then this heady concoction from hip-hop superstar RZA – who directs, stars and co-writes (with gore guru Eli Roth) – hits the target. But beware otherwise, because it's just average genre fare. RZA plays a village blacksmith in 19th-century China, whose forearms are replaced with death-dealing iron contraptions after they are severed by the evil Lion Clan. With the aid of mercenary Russell Crowe, warrior Rick Yune and brothel madam Lucy Liu, he sets out for revenge. Crowe and Liu bring an entertaining gusto to their formulaic roles, while RZA (making his directorial debut) enlivens a predictable finale with operatic melodrama and split-screen techniques. AJ Violence, some swearing, drug abuse, sexual references. **DVD** Blu

Russell Crowe *Jack Knife* • Lucy Liu *Madam Blossom* • RZA *The Blacksmith* • Jamie Chung *Lady Silk* • Cung Le *Bronze Lion* • Rick Yune *Zen Yi/The X-Blade* • Pam Grier *Jane* ■ *Dir* RZA • *Scr* RZA, Eli Roth, from a story by RZA

The Man with the X-Ray Eyes ★★★★ PG

Science-fiction thriller 1963 · US · Colour · 75min

Ray Milland plays one of his best remembered roles in Roger Corman's pocket-sized, yet highly potent, sci-fi shocker. He is scientist Dr Xavier, who experiments on himself and gains the power to see through solid materials. But as his sight gets stronger, so do the side-effects – Corman's cue to move from playful sideshow terror to mystical allegory, with plenty of engaging surreal imagery along the way. The Bible provided the inspiration for this cult classic, something clearly evident in the unforgettable revival-meeting climax. AJ **DVD**

Ray Milland *Dr James Xavier* • Diana Van Der Vlis *Dr Diane Fairfax* • Harold J Stone *Dr Sam Brant* • John Hoyt *Dr Willard Benson* • Don Rickles *Crane* • Lorie Summers *Carnival owner/party dancer* • Vicki Lee *Young girl patient* • Kathryn Hart *Mrs Mart* ■ *Dir* Roger Corman • *Scr* Robert Dillon, Ray Russell, from the story by Ray Russell

The Man with Two Brains ★★★★★ 15

Comedy 1983 · US · Colour · 85min

There have been more accomplished Steve Martin films – *Roxanne*, *LA Story* – but this dazzlingly inventive comedy remains his finest hour. Martin is Doctor Hfuhruhurr, the brilliant brain surgeon who marries black widow Kathleen Turner but falls for a disembodied brain, voiced by Sissy Spacek. Turner hilariously sends up the *femme fatale* persona she established in *Body Heat*, David Warner co-stars as a fellow mad scientist, and there is also a surprise cameo in the form of the Elevator Killer. Sublime. JF Some violence, swearing, brief nudity. **DVD**

Steve Martin *Dr Michael Hfuhruhurr* • Kathleen Turner *Dolores Benedict* • David Warner *Dr Necessiter* • Paul Benedict *Butler* • Richard Brestoff *Dr Pasteur* • James Cromwell *Realtor* • George Furth *Timon* • Peter Hobbs *Dr Brandon* • Earl Boen *Dr Conrad* • Sissy Spacek *Anne Uumellmahaye* ■ *Dir* Carl Reiner • *Scr* Steve Martin, Carl Reiner, George Gipe

The Man Within ★★★

Period adventure 1947 · UK · BW · 87min

Set in 19th-century Sussex, Graham Greene's first published novel tells the story of an orphaned teenager, played by Richard Attenborough, who shops his guardian (Michael Redgrave), a smuggler. Greene thought this tale of guilt, identity and moral redemption was "embarrassingly sentimental", and he dismissed Bernard Knowles's film version as a treachery. AT

Michael Redgrave *Richard Carlyon* • Jean Kent *Lucy* • Joan Greenwood *Elizabeth* • Richard Attenborough *Francis Andrews* • Francis L Sullivan *Mr Braddock* • Felix Aylmer *Priest* • Ronald Shiner *Cockney Harry* • Basil Sydney *Sir Henry Merriman* • Ernest Thesiger *Farne* ■ *Dir* Bernard Knowles • *Scr* Muriel Box, Bernard Box, from the novel by Graham Greene

The Man without a Country ★★★

Period drama 1973 · US · Colour · 78min

At a time when patriotism and nationalism are becoming increasingly confused, this period drama – the first feature-length adaptation of Edward Everett Hale's celebrated 1863 novel - is a truly perceptive insight into what love of country is actually about. Giving one of his best performances, Cliff Robertson ages impressively, playing the naval officer who renounces his nationality at his court martial and is sentenced to spend the remainder of his life aboard a ship sailing within tantalising distance of his homeland. DP

Cliff Robertson *Philip Nolan* • Beau Bridges *Frederick Ingham* • Peter Strauss *Arthur Danforth* • Robert Ryan *Lieutenant Commander Vaughan* • Walter Abel *Colonel AB Morgan* • Geoffrey Holder *Slave on ship* ■ *Dir* Delbert Mann • *Scr* Sidney Carroll, from the novel by Edward Everett Hale

The Man without a Face ★★★ 12

Drama 1993 · US · Colour · 114min

Mel Gibson marked his directorial debut with this low-key, coming-of-age drama set in the late 1960s. Gibson plays the horribly scarred former teacher, who lives a reclusive life away from the gossip of his small-town neighbours. He is gradually drawn out of his shell by an unhappy young boy (Nick Stahl), but their close relationship eventually comes back to haunt him. Gibson takes a back seat to his young lead, and Stahl doesn't disappoint, delivering a moving, intense performance. Although the direction sometimes errs on the side of sentimentality, it remains an assured debut. JF Violence, swearing. **DVD**

Mel Gibson *Justin McLeod* • Margaret Whitton *Catherine* • Fay Masterson *Gloria* • Gaby Hoffman [Gaby Hoffmann] *Megan* • Geoffrey Lewis *Chief Stark* • Richard Masur *Carl* • Nick Stahl *Chuck Norstadt* • Michael DeLuise *Douglas Hall* ■ *Dir* Mel Gibson • *Scr* Malcolm MacRury, from the novel by Isabelle Holland

The Man without a Past ★★★★ 12

Romantic comedy drama 2002 · Fin/Ger/Fr · Colour · 93min

Although Timo Salminen's lustrous photography and Aki Kaurismäki's ripe dialogue evoke the Hollywood melodramas of yesteryear, this has a distinctively Finnish feel. Deadpan delivery, quirky humour and compassion for ordinary people quietly striving to get by are established Kaurismäki trademarks, but there's nothing predictable about the way in which Markku Peltola recovers his sense of identity, notably through his chaste relationship with Salvation Army member, Kati Outinen. The community on the outskirts of Helsinki belongs to a rock 'n' roll fairy tale, but Kaurismäki's detached style is too rooted in reality to proffer unfettered escapism. DP Finnish +subtitles. Violence. **DVD**

Markku Peltola *M* • Kati Outinen *Irma* • Juhani Niemela *Nieminen* • Sakari Kuosmanen *Anttila* ■ *Dir/Scr* Aki Kaurismäki

Man without a Star ★★★★ PG

Western 1955 · US · Colour · 85min

This fine Technicolor western was made by King Vidor and features the wonderful Kirk Douglas in an all-grinning, all-snarling portrayal, the kind of role he was born to play. There's tremendous sexual tension generated between Douglas and manipulative ranch owner Jeanne Crain, and the psychological slant is also cleverly integrated, as juvenile William Campbell idolises the no-good Douglas. Remade, poorly, in 1969 as *A Man Called Gannon*. TS **DVD**

Kirk Douglas *Dempsey Rae* • Jeanne Crain *Reed Bowman* • Claire Trevor *Idonee* • Richard Boone *Steve Miles* • William Campbell *Jeff Jimson* • Jay C Flippen *Strap Davis* • Myrna Hansen *Tess Cassidy* • Mara Corday *Moccasin Mary* • Eddy C Waller [Eddy Waller] *Bill Cassidy* ■ *Dir* King Vidor • *Scr* Borden Chase, DD Beauchamp, from the novel by Dee Linford

Man, Woman and Child ★★★ PG

Drama 1983 · US · Colour · 96min

Adapting his own novel, Erich Segal teamed with David Zelag Goodman for this unashamed weepie. It provides an unusually soft-centred role for Martin Sheen as the happily married man who discovers that the French dalliance of a decade ago resulted in a son. But it's Blythe Danner who will have you reaching for the tissues as the wife trying to come to terms with the new member of her family. DP

Martin Sheen *Robert Beckwith* • Blythe Danner *Sheila Beckwith* • Craig T Nelson *Bernie Ackerman* • David Hemmings *Gavin Wilson* • Nathalie Nell *Nicole Guerin* • Maureen Anderman *Margo* ■ *Dir* Dick Richards • *Scr* Erich Segal, David Zelag Goodman, from the novel by Segal

Management ★★ 15

Romantic comedy 2008 · US · Colour · 89min

First-time writer/director Stephen Belber's off-kilter romantic comedy finds a shy motel worker falling for one of his guests, a sales rep dealing in the sort of paintings only ever seen in hotel rooms. Steve Zahn skilfully portrays the aching vulnerability of his socially maladjusted nerd (whose idea of a chat-up line is "You have a great butt"), while Jennifer Aniston convinces as the seemingly hoity-toity businesswoman who responds to her gawky suitor's utter lack of guile. But the central love story is buried under a welter of would-be quirkiness and the essentially sweet-natured tale rather outstays its welcome. TJ Swearing. **DVD** Blu

Jennifer Aniston *Sue* • Steve Zahn *Mike* • Margo Martindale *Trish* • Fred Ward *Jerry* • James Hiroyuki Liao [James Liao] *Al* • Woody Harrelson *Jango* ■ *Dir/Scr* Stephen Belber

Manchester United: beyond the Promised Land ★ PG

Documentary 2000 · UK/US · Colour · 80min

Even the diehards are going to find this self-congratulatory tribute to MUFC plc hard to swallow. Less a documentary than a corporate video designed to attract potential investors, it's more about selling a brand than chronicling a season. Strenuous attempts are made to demonstrate the club's sensitivity to its sponsors, the internationalism of its fans and how much fun Sir Alex Ferguson really is. But fan-friendly issues such as player crises and United's farcical involvement in Fifa's World Club Championship are glossed over. Crude cinematic spin-doctoring. DP **DVD**

Alex Ferguson • David Beckham • Ryan Giggs • Roy Keane ■ *Dir* Bob Potter • *Cinematographer* Ferdia de Buitléar • *Editor* Paul Doyle Jr

U SUITABLE FOR ALL   Uc SUITABLE ESPECIALLY FOR YOUNG CHILDREN (DVD ONLY)   PG PARENTAL GUIDANCE   12A UNDER 12s TO BE ACCOMPANIED (CINEMA ONLY)

The Manchurian Candidate
★★★★★ 15

Psychological thriller 1962 · US · BW · 121min

Director John Frankenheimer's masterpiece of Cold War paranoia was withdrawn from circulation in the wake of the death of JFK, its assassination plot a chilling mirror to contemporary events. Over 50 years on, it has lost none of its ability to thrill and provoke. Laurence Harvey has returned from the Korean War a hero, the saviour of his platoon. Why, then, is his former commanding officer (Frank Sinatra) plagued by nightmares in which the repressed Harvey coolly kills one of his comrades under the orders of a Chinese general? Harvey is perfectly cast, while Sinatra has one of his very best roles as the tormented officer. But stealing the show is Angela Lansbury as Harvey's mother (though she was just 37 to Harvey's 34) – monstrous, manipulative and completely power-crazed, she is an unforgettable creation. AR *DVD* *Blu*

Frank Sinatra *Bennett Marco* • Laurence Harvey *Raymond Shaw* • Janet Leigh *Rosie* • Angela Lansbury *Raymond's mother* • Henry Silva *Chunjin* • James Gregory *Senator John Iselin* • Leslie Parrish *Jocie Jordon* • John McGiver *Senator Thomas Jordon* ■ *Dir* John Frankenheimer • *Scr* George Axelrod, John Frankenheimer, from the novel by Richard Condon • *Cinematographer* Lionel Lindon • *Art Director* Richard Sylbert

The Manchurian Candidate
★★★★ 15

Psychological thriller 2004 · US · Colour · 124min

This intelligent update of John Frankenheimer's classic 1962 film relocates the military conflict at the heart of the story from Communist Korea to the first Gulf War in Kuwait. Denzel Washington steps into Frank Sinatra's shoes, playing a tormented US Army major who unwittingly becomes the key to a complex political conspiracy. Jonathan Demme's controlled direction is exhilarating, and he elicits brilliant performances from a fine cast. Liev Schreiber finally gets a part to sink his teeth into, as Washington's former sergeant who becomes a vice presidential candidate, but it's Meryl Streep, as Schreiber's unscrupulous senator mother, who leaves the deepest impression. SF Violence, swearing. *DVD* *Blu*

Denzel Washington *Bennett "Ben" Marco* • Meryl Streep *Senator Eleanor Prentiss Shaw* • Liev Schreiber *Raymond Shaw* • Jon Voight *Senator Thomas Jordan* • Kimberly Elise *Rosie* • Jeffrey Wright *Al Melvin* • Ted Levine *Colonel Howard* • Bruno Ganz *Richard Delp* • Miguel Ferrer *Colonel Garret* • Dean Stockwell *Mark Whiting* ■ *Dir* Jonathan Demme • *Scr* Daniel Pyne, Dean Georgaris, from the film by George Axelrod, from the novel by Richard Condon

Mandalay
★★

Melodrama 1934 · US · BW · 65min

Good-time girl Kay Francis, doctor Lyle Talbot and gunrunner Ricardo Cortez are all up the Irrawaddy without a paddle in this Warner Bros melodrama. Set in a Burma that exists only on the studio backlot, Michael Curtiz's film seems to draw most of its inspiration from MGM's *Red Dust*, in which Clark Gable got all steamed up over Jean Harlow. Unfortunately, the creaky plot and arthritic performances mean that *Mandalay* is really showing its age. AT

Kay Francis *Tanya Borisoff/Spot White* • Ricardo Cortez *Tony Evans* • Warner Oland *Nick* • Lyle Talbot *Dr Gregory Burton* • Ruth Donnelly *Mrs Peters* • Reginald Owen *Police commissioner* • Shirley Temple *Betty Shaw* ■ *Dir* Michael Curtiz • *Scr* Austin Parker, Charles Kenyon, from a story by Paul Hervey Fox

Mandela
★★★★ PG

Biographical documentary 1995 · US · Colour · 117min

This Oscar-nominated documentary about the father of the new South Africa benefits immeasurably from having much of it fronted by Mandela himself. Afforded apparently unlimited access to the man and his mind, the film-makers trace Mandela's life from his humble village origins, through his early ANC involvement and lengthy incarceration by the country's white minority government, right up to his distancing from second wife Winnie. Particularly moving are Mandela's returns to the village of his birth and the cell where he was imprisoned for almost three decades. DA

Nelson Mandela • Nomzamo Winnie Mandela ■ *Dir* Jo Menell, Angus Gibson

Mandela and de Klerk
★★★ PG

Political drama 1997 · US · Colour · 109min

One of the problems of making a film about recent events is that the screenwriter has to tiptoe around the sensibilities of extant characters. Consequently, this worthy TV movie can only tell part of the story of how Nelson Mandela and FW de Klerk jointly earned the Nobel Peace Prize for their efforts in bringing about democracy in South Africa. As the ANC leader who is thrust back into the limelight after 27 years' imprisonment, Sidney Poitier has the requisite dignity and determination. But Michael Caine's Afrikaaner president is the more grounded performance. DP

Sidney Poitier *Nelson Mandela* • Michael Caine *FW de Klerk* • Tina Lifford *Winnie Mandela* • Gerry Maritz *PW Botha* • Terry Norton *Marike de Klerk* ■ *Dir* Joseph Sargent • *Scr* Richard Wesley

Mandela: Long Walk to Freedom
★★★ 12

Biographical drama 2013 · S Afr/UK · Colour · 146min

Adapted from Nelson Mandela's 1995 autobiography, this handsome but prosaic life story of the great South African statesman pivots on a performance of controlled grace from the statuesque Idris Elba. British director Justin Chadwick is evidently aiming for the historical grandeur of *Gandhi*, but, even at two-and-a-half hours, the film's 50-year span – from anti-apartheid activism to high office – feels episodic. Any deeper understanding of Mandela the man is undermined by facile recourse to newsreel to fill in the gaps. AC *DVD*

Idris Elba *Nelson Mandela* • Naomie Harris *Winnie Madikizela* • Tony Kgoroge *Walter Sisulu* • Gys de Villiers *FW De Klerk* ■ *Dir* Justin Chadwick • *Scr* William Nicholson, from the autobiography *Long Walk to Freedom* by Nelson Mandela

Manderlay
★★★ 15

Period drama 2005 · Den/Swe/Fr/ JK/Ger/Neth/It · Colour · 132min

Lars von Trier goes for the American jugular with this second drama in his USA trilogy. Resuming the story where *Dogville* left off, in 1933, it sees gangster's daughter Grace (Bryce Dallas Howard, competently replacing Nicole Kidman) forcibly liberating an Alabama cotton plantation that still relies on slavery 70 years after Abolition. What follows is a lazy attack on US democracy and culture, as Grace's naive attempts to make amends for the black slaves' abuse have terrible consequences. Technically, the feature excels, but this lacks its predecessor's startling power. SF Swearing, violence, nudity, a sex scene. *DVD*

Bryce Dallas Howard *Grace* • Willem Dafoe *Grace's father* • Danny Glover *Wilhelm* • Isaach de Bankolé [Isaach de Bankole] *Timothy* • Michael Abiteboul *Thomas* • Lauren Bacall *Mam* • Jean-Marc Barr *Mr Robinson* • Geoffrey Bateman *Bertie* • Virgile Bramly *Edvard* • Ruben Brinkman *Bingo* ■ *Dir/Scr* Lars von Trier

Mandingo
★★★★ 18

Period drama 1975 · US · Colour · 120min

Hollywood always had a romantic and sanitised view of what really went on in the Old South. This full-blooded excursion into American Gothic puts the lie to all that. Plantation owner James Mason festers away in a rotten old mansion, his feet resting on a black boy so that his disease will feed from him to the child. Mason's son (Perry King) keeps a harem of women slaves, while his wife, a sweaty Susan George, has sex with one of the slaves Mason trains to be a fighter. Vilified by most critics at the time, this is a head-on examination of the period; it's also one of the bravest American movies of the 1970s. Don't bother with the dire 1976 sequel, *Drum*. AT

James Mason *Warren Maxwell* • Susan George *Blanche* • Perry King *Hammond Maxwell* • Richard Ward *Agamemnon* • Brenda Sykes *Ellen* • Ken Norton *Mede* • Lillian Hayman *Lucrezia Borgia* ■ *Dir* Richard Fleischer • *Scr* Norman Wexler, from the play by Jack Kirkland, from the novel by Kyle Onstott

Mandragora
★★★ 18

Crime drama 1997 · Cz Rep/UK · Colour · 129min

According to legend, the mandragora is a plant that grows under the gallows from the sperm of dead men. It's a powerful symbol for this harrowing, fact-based study of Prague's gay sex market, as each youth is condemned as soon as he steps on to the streets. Miroslav Caslavka heads a largely non-professional cast (many of whom are rent boys) that pumps itself with drink and drugs to withstand the exploitation of tourists and the brutality of their pimps. Directed with an unerring sense of pity by Wiktor Grodecki. DP Czech +subtitles. *DVD*

Miroslav Caslavka *Marek Nedela* • David Svec *David* • Pavel Skripal *Honza* • Kostas Zedraloglu *Krysa* • Miroslav Breu *Libor* • Jiri Kodet *Otec* ■ *Dir* Wiktor Grodecki • *Scr* Wiktor Grodecki, David Svec

Mandy
★★★★ PG

Drama 1952 · UK · BW · 89min

Whisky Galore! director Alexander Mackendrick's only non-comedy during his stay at Ealing is a highly intelligent film with much to say about the generation gap. Mandy Miller gives a performance of remarkable charm and insight as the deaf-mute child whose silent world is opened up by committed headmaster Jack Hawkins. An unusually unsympathetic Phyllis Calvert and Terence Morgan do well as Mandy's feuding parents and there is a stand-out turn from Godfrey Tearle as her embittered grandfather. DP

Phyllis Calvert *Christine* • Jack Hawkins *Searle* • Terence Morgan *Harry* • Godfrey Tearle *Mr Garland* • Mandy Miller (1) *Mandy* • Marjorie Fielding *Mrs Garland* • Nancy Price *Jane Ellis* • Edward Chapman *Ackland* ■ *Dir* Alexander Mackendrick • *Scr* Nigel Balchin, Jack Whittingham, from the novel *The Day is Ours* by Hilda Lewis

Manglehorn
★★ 12

Drama 2014 · US · Colour · 93min

Al Pacino plays AJ Manglehorn, a Texas locksmith who lives alone with his cat, has a fractious relationship with his son (Chris Messina) and flirts with local bank teller Holly Hunter. But when Hunter tries to step things up, Pacino backs away – rather obviously for a story about a locksmith, his emotions are all chained up. But for how much longer? Essentially a character piece, this trite, predictable love story lurches through various oddball set pieces to its cloying, sentimental climax. DW *DVD* *Blu*

Al Pacino *AJ Manglehorn* • Holly Hunter *Dawn* • Chris Messina *Jacob* • Harmony Korine *Gary* ■ *Dir* David Gordon Green • *Scr* Paul Logan (2)

The Mangler
★★ 18

Horror 1994 · US · Colour · 101min

This Stephen King-based nonsense is about a possessed speed-ironing machine at a rural laundry that demands a virgin sacrifice every so often if the town's bigwigs want to remain prosperous. Horror icon Robert Englund chews the scenery in this shock-less wonder as the crotchety laundry owner, covered in old-age make-up and wearing leg braces, who made a pact with the Devil years before. The direction is also on crutches. AJ *DVD*

Robert Englund *Bill Gartley* • Ted Levine *John Hunton* • Daniel Matmor *Mark Jackson* • Jeremy Crutchley *Pictureman Mortician* • Vanessa Pike *Sherry Ouelette* ■ *Dir* Tobe Hooper • *Scr* Tobe Hooper, Stephen Brooks, Peter Welbeck [Harry Alan Towers], from a story by Stephen King

Manhatta
★★★

Silent experimental documentary 1921 · US · BW · 9min

Although Hollywood dominated the mainstream, experimental cinema was largely the preserve of European artists during the silent era. However, that changed with the release of this portrait of New York, which anticipated the "city symphony" style that would reach its apogee in Walter Ruttmann's *Berlin, Symphony of a Great City* (1927). Accompanied by extracts from a poem by Walt Whitman, the photographic vistas assembled by Charles Sheeler and Paul Strand are meticulously composed. But there's little action within the frame and less sense of urban rhythm. Shown as a trailer in the States and exhibited at a French Dadaist happening, it was subsequently hailed as the keystone of the American avant-garde. DP

■ *Dir* Paul Strand, Charles Sheeler

Manhattan
★★★★★ 15

Romantic comedy 1979 · US · BW · 92min

This early masterpiece from Woody Allen celebrates his beloved New York. Allen stars as a neurotic TV writer who's taken up with 17-year-old Mariel Hemingway, but who's being diverted by fast-talking Diane Keaton and – more dangerously – by the book written about him by his lesbian ex-wife Jill (Meryl Streep). Allen and his fellow New Yorkers swan in and out of the cultural byways of the Big Apple, indulging in psychiatric therapy that's never quite the cure-all they crave. The characters could have become over-articulate bores, but Allen invests them with the saving grace of humanity. A wonderful film, with a George Gershwin score that adds just the right amount of poignancy. TH Swearing. *DVD* *Blu*

Woody Allen *Isaac Davis* • Diane Keaton *Mary Wilke* • Michael Murphy (1) *Yale* • Mariel Hemingway *Tracy* • Meryl Streep *Jill* • Anne Byrne *Emily* • Karen Ludwig *Connie* • Michael O'Donoghue *Dennis* • Wallace Shawn *Jeremiah* ■ *Dir* Woody Allen • *Scr* Woody Allen, Marshall Brickman • *Cinematographer* Gordon Willis

Manhattan Melodrama
★★

Crime drama 1934 · US · BW · 93min

On 22 July 1934, John Dillinger went to see *Manhattan Melodrama* at the Biograph in Chicago. He was shot dead by government agents on leaving the cinema. The film he saw is a heavily moralistic drama featuring Mickey Rooney in a childhood flashback that explains why Blackie Gallagher (Clark Gable) became a racketeer and killer. While this has its wisecracking, stylish moments, it's mostly cringe-inducing – though it does mark the first teaming of William Powell and Myrna Loy, who went on to make the successful and popular *Thin Man* films. AT

Clark Gable *Blackie Gallagher* • William Powell *Jim Wade* • Myrna Loy *Eleanor* • Leo Carrillo *Father Joe* • Nat Pendleton *Spud* • George Sidney (1) *Poppa Rosen* • Mickey Rooney *Blackie as a boy* ■ *Dir* WS Van Dyke II [WS Van Dyke] • *Scr* Oliver HP Garrett, Joseph L Mankiewicz, from the story *Three Men* by Arthur Caesar

Manhattan Murder Mystery
★★★★ PG

Comedy thriller 1993 · US · Colour · 103min

This lightweight comedy clearly bears the hallmark of being an uncontentious romp that would keep Woody Allen occupied while he awaited his day in court with ex-partner Mia Farrow. Another couple of hours pounding away at the typewriter clearly wouldn't have gone amiss, but this is a hugely enjoyable little film that slyly mocks the pretensions of Manhattan's well-heeled intelligentsia. The role originally intended for Farrow is taken by Diane Keaton, and the ease with which she and

Allen combine leaves you longing for just one more reunion. AC Violence, swearing. *DVD*

Alan Alda *Ted* • Woody Allen *Larry Lipton* • Diane Keaton *Carol Lipton* • Anjelica Huston *Marcia Fox* • Jerry Adler *Paul House* • Joy Behar *Marilyn* • Ron Rifkin *Sy* • Lynn Cohen *Lillian House* • *Dir* Woody Allen • *Scr* Woody Allen, Marshall Brickman

Manhunter ★★★★ 18
Thriller   1986 · US · Colour · 116min

Whether or not, as some contend, this is a better movie than *The Silence of the Lambs*, the second and more celebrated film adaptation of novelist Thomas Harris's source material, it is undoubtedly a gripping psycho-chiller. William Petersen plays the former FBI whizz, hauled from retirement to help hunt a sophisticated serial murderer. Strong performances, especially from Brian Cox as Hannibal Lecktor, combine with a clever plot and top-notch direction by Michael Mann to produce an atmospheric and arresting thriller. PF Violence, swearing. *DVD* *BL*

William Petersen [William L Petersen] *Will Graham* • Brian Cox (1) *Dr Hannibal Lecktor* • Dennis Farina *Jack Crawford* • Kim Greist *Molly Graham* • Stephen Lang *Freddie Lounds* • Tom Noonan *Francis Dollarhyde* • Joan Allen *Reba* • Benjamin Hendrickson *Dr Chilton* ■ *Dir* Michael Mann • *Scr* Michael Mann, from the novel *Red Dragon* by Thomas Harris

Maniac ★★★
Psychological thriller   1962 · UK · BW · 88min

This psychological horror film is a typical Hammer programme filler of the 1960s. The convoluted mystery takes ages to set up, but some of the shocks (most memorably an attempted murder by blowtorch) have stood the test of time, and the twist ending is brilliant. Kerwin Mathews plays an American artist who becomes involved with a young woman (Liliane Brousse) and her stepmother (Nadia Gray) and agrees to help them spring Brousse's father (Donald Houston) from the loony bin. Not a good idea. DM

Kerwin Mathews *Geoff Farrell* • Nadia Gray *Eve Beynat* • Donald Houston *Georges Beynat* • Liliane Brousse *Annette Beynat* • George Pastell *Inspector Etienne* ■ *Dir* Michael Carreras • *Scr* Jimmy Sangster

Maniac ★★★
Crime drama   1977 · US · Colour · 84min

In this solid crime drama, a psychotic killer starts to bump off a small town's populace before demanding a million-dollar ransom to stop. The town's richest man isn't having any of it, though, and hires a mercenary to kill the killer. Oddball but interesting casting sees the likes of Stuart Whitman and Deborah Raffin acting opposite Oliver Reed. The film has its dull spots, but it remains watchable. DA Violence.

Oliver Reed *Nick McCormick* • Deborah Raffin *Cindy Simmons* • Stuart Whitman *William Whitaker* • Jim Mitchum [James Mitchum] *Tracker* • John Ireland *Chief Haliburton* ■ *Dir* Richard Compton • *Scr* John C Broderick, Ron Silkosky

Maniac ★★★ 18
Horror   2012 · Fr/US · Colour · 85min

While nowhere near as sleazy as the 1980 original, director Franck Khalfoun's update treads the same lurid exploitation path. A scarcely believable Elijah Wood plays the deranged psycho who was subject to years of motherly abuse and now vents his rage on the female population of downtown Los Angeles, killing them and placing their scalps on dummies in his mannequin store. Not that you see the wild-eyed Wood much, because the stalking is done from his point of view, so you only glimpse him in shop windows, mirrors and CCTV footage. It's a remarkable technical challenge that Khalfoun cleverly pulls off, and it goes a long way to refreshing all the gory stabbings and seedy heavy-breathing. AJ Violence, swearing, sex scenes, nudity, drug abuse. *DVD* *BL*

Elijah Wood *Frank Zito* • Nora Arnezeder *Anna* • Geneviève Alexandra *Jessica* • Jan Broberg *Rita* • Megan Duffy *Lucie 86* ■ *Dir* Franck Khalfoun • *Scr* Alexandre Aja, Grégory Levasseur, from the 1980 film

Maniac Cop ★★ 18
Action horror   1988 · US · Colour · 90min

True to its title, this features a maniac in a policeman's uniform loose on the streets of New York City, killing any innocent people who stray into his path and giving the NYPD a bad reputation they don't deserve. (Stop laughing!) Bruce Campbell is the cop who takes the fall for the true killer and eventually hunts him down. Fairly well written (by Larry Cohen of *It's Alive* fame), but the acting can't keep up and *Evil Dead* star Campbell is given too little to do. ST *DVD* *BL*

Tom Atkins *Lieutenant Frank McCrae* • Bruce Campbell *Jack Forrest* • Laurene Landon *Theresa Mallory* • Richard Roundtree *Commissioner Pike* • William Smith *Captain Ripley* • Robert Z'Dar *Matt Cordell* ■ *Dir* William Lustig • *Scr* Larry Cohen

Maniac Cop 2 ★★ 18
Action horror   1990 · US · Colour · 83min

An undead ex-cop goes on another gruesome killing rampage in this sequel, this time in concert with a serial killer who targets strippers – presumably to get the maximum amount of skin on screen. Screenwriter Larry Cohen decides to clean up the killer's image this time: now we're told he was an honest cop who was willing to prosecute powerful people, as opposed to the first movie, in which he was known for violating suspects' civil rights. ST *DVD*

Robert Davi *Detective Sean McKinney* • Claudia Christian *Susan Riley* • Michael Lerner *Edward Doyle* • Bruce Campbell *Jack Forrest* • Laurene Landon *Teresa Mallory* • Robert Z'Dar *Matt Cordell* • Clarence Williams III *Blum* ■ *Dir* William Lustig • *Scr* Larry Cohen

Manic ★★ 15
Drama   2001 · US · Colour · 96min

First-time director Jordan Melamed tips his hat to the Dogme school of film-making with this gruelling exploration of teen psychosis. Shot on hand-held digital video, this unfolds in the adolescent wing of a psychiatric institution, where teenager Joseph Gordon-Levitt has been sent after viciously attacking a classmate. Under the watchful eye of a recovering drug addict doctor (an impressive Don Cheadle), the patients confront their personal demons during group therapy. Although the performances are accomplished, the film remains sterile and tediously banal. SF *DVD*

Joseph Gordon-Levitt *Lyle* • Michael Bacall *Chad* • Zooey Deschanel *Tracey* • Cody Lightning *Kenny* • Elden Henson *Michael* • Sara Rivas *Sara* • Don Cheadle *Dr David Monroe* ■ *Dir* Jordan Melamed • *Scr* Michael Bacall, Blayne Weaver

The Manitou ★★ 15
Horror   1978 · US · Colour · 99min

Something very nasty is growing on Susan Strasberg's neck in this preposterous *Exorcist* clone. This time around, the demon is a 400-year-old witch doctor seeking reincarnation in modern-day San Francisco. Tony Curtis, as a fake medium suddenly flung into the real world of the supernatural, is always worth watching, while the monster's first appearance has a certain visceral impact. The title derives from the native American word for a human's spirit inhabiting all things. RS *DVD*

Tony Curtis *Harry Erskine* • Michael Ansara *Singing Rock* • Susan Strasberg *Karen Tandy* • Stella Stevens *Amelia Crusoe* • Jon Cedar *Dr Jack Hughes* • Ann Sothern *Mrs Karmann* ■ *Dir* William Girdler • *Scr* William Girdler, Jon Cedar, Tom Pope, from the novel by Graham Masterson

Mannequin ★★★
Drama   1937 · US · BW · 92min

The fabulous Joan Crawford works her way out of the Lower East Side slums and into

the arms of Spencer Tracy. Crawford, whose exquisite gowns come complete with influential Adrian shoulder pads, is totally miscast as the lower-class working girl. But this is an MGM star vehicle, with all that that implies: you've never seen such glossy tenements! Director Frank Borzage seems at home with this corny melodrama, which audiences loved. DP

Joan Crawford *Jessie Cassidy* • Spencer Tracy *John L Hennessey* • Alan Curtis *Eddie Miller* • Ralph Morgan *Briggs* • Mary Phillips [Mary Philips] *Beryl* • Oscar O'Shea *"Pa" Cassidy* • Elisabeth Risdon *Mrs Cassidy* • Leo Gorcey *Clifford* ■ *Dir* Frank Borzage • *Scr* Lawrence Hazard, from the play *Marry For Money* by Katherine Brush • *Costume Designer* Adrian

Mannequin ★★ PG
Comedy   1987 · US · Colour · 87min

Sculptor Andrew McCarthy falls for a shop window dummy (Kim Cattrall). To everybody else, however, Cattrall is just an ordinary mannequin, which makes for a rather tricky romance. It requires a light, frothy touch, but director Michael Gottlieb instead takes it as a cue for some helpless mugging and crude slapstick. McCarthy is even more plastic than Cattrall, Meshach Taylor is a gruesome caricature as his sympathetic co-worker, while James Spader simply looks embarrassed. JF *DVD*

Andrew McCarthy *Jonathan Switcher* • Kim Cattrall *Emmy* • Estelle Getty *Claire Timkin* • James Spader *Richards* • GW Bailey *Felix* • Carole Davis *Roxie* • Stephen Vinovich [Steve Vinovich] *BJ Wert* • Meshach Taylor *Hollywood* ■ *Dir* Michael Gottlieb • *Scr* Edward Rugoff, Michael Gottlieb

Mannequin on the Move ★ PG
Comedy   1991 · US · Colour · 91min

If ever a movie didn't need a sequel, it was *Mannequin*. In another story of a lovesick woman returning from the past as a shop dummy, statuesque beauty Kristy Swanson asks us to spot when she's acting and when she's deliberately being inanimate. It's not all her fault: the script is so full of old gags it must have been chiselled on stone tablets. DP

Kristy Swanson *Jessie* • William Ragsdale *Jason Williamson/Prince William* • Meshach Taylor *Hollywood Montrose/Doorman* • Terry Kiser *Count Spretzle/Sorcerer* • Stuart Pankin *Mr James* ■ *Dir* Stewart Raffill • *Scr* Edward Rugoff, David Isaacs, Ken Levine, Betsy Israel, from characters by Edward Rugoff, Michael Gottlieb

Manon des Sources ★★★ U
Drama   1952 · Fr · BW · 144min

Even though Marcel Pagnol was working from his own screenplay (later expanded into a novel, *L'Eau des Collines*), this poetic, over-ambitious adaptation is never as captivating as Claude Berri's 1986 remake. Originally running nearly five hours, the action meanders as Pagnol places a lyrical emphasis on the beauty of the landscape at the expense of taut storytelling. His wife, Jacqueline, struggles to convince in the title role, as she seeks revenge on the Soubeyrans for the death of her hunchbacked father. DP In French.

Jacqueline Pagnol *Manon Cadoret* • Raymond Pellegrin *Maurice, the schoolteacher* • Rellys *Ugolin* • Robert Vattier *Monsieur Belloiseau* • Henri Poupon *Le Papet, the uncle* • Henri Vilbert *The Priest* ■ *Dir/Scr* Marcel Pagnol

Manon des Sources
★★★★ PG
Period drama   1986 · Fr/It/Swi · Colour · 108min

The conclusion to Claude Berri's adaptation of Marcel Pagnol's *L'Eau des Collines* takes place ten years after the death of Jean de Florette. Once more the photography borders on the sublime and the direction is paced to suit life under the scorching sun. The script is less convincing, however, with melodrama seeping into too many scenes and an uncomfortable number of loose ends being neatly tied up in the closing moments. Yves Montand and Daniel Auteuil maintain the quality of their performances, with the latter impressive as he tries to atone for the wrong done to Manon

(Emmanuelle Béart) and her family. DP French +subtitles. *DVD*

Yves Montand *César Soubeyran, le Papet* • Daniel Auteuil *Ugolin Soubeyran* • Emmanuelle Béart *Manon Cadoret* • Elisabeth Depardieu *Aimée Cadoret* • Hippolyte Girardot *Bernard Olivier* • Margarita Lozano *Baptistine* • Gabriel Bacquier *Victor* • Ernestine Mazurowna *Young Manon* ■ *Dir* Claude Berri • *Scr* Gérard Brach, Claude Berri, from the novel *L'Eau des Collines* by Marcel Pagnol • *Cinematographer* Bruno Nuytten

Manorama Six Feet Under ★★★ 15
Crime drama   2007 · Ind · Colour · 137min

Debut director Navdeep Singh pays tribute to Roman Polanski's classic *Chinatown* in this twisting Indian thriller. A slow-burning yet meaty mix of murder, deceit and corruption, it sees Abhay Deol's struggling crime novelist turn detective for real after an irrigation minister's wife hires him to collect evidence against her unfaithful husband. The complex jigsaw that results simmers with mystery and unease, as the amateur sleuth discovers nothing is as it seems in the atmospheric desert locales of backwater Rajasthan. Understated central performances help give the downbeat ending its satisfying punch. SF Hindi +subtitles. Violence, sexual references. *DVD*

Abhay Deol *Satyaveer* • Gul Panag [Gul Kirat Panag] *Nimmi* • Raima Sen *Sheetal* • Sarika *Manorama* ■ *Dir* Navdeep Singh • *Scr* Devika Bhagat, Navdeep Singh, Manoj Tapadia, from a story by Bhagat, Singh

Manpower ★★★
Drama   1941 · US · BW · 102min

Two power linesmen, Edward G Robinson and George Raft, compete for the favours of seductive café hostess Marlene Dietrich, with fatal results. While not an unfamiliar tale, it's given heavyweight treatment thanks to the three-way star chemistry and tough direction by Raoul Walsh. It plays like a gangster movie, slightly marred by some misfiring attempts at comic relief. The sassy Eve Arden is featured in support. RK

Edward G Robinson *Hank McHenry* • Marlene Dietrich *Fay Duval* • George Raft *Johnny Marshall* • Alan Hale *Jumbo Wells* • Frank McHugh *Omaha* • Eve Arden *Dolly* • Barton MacLane *Smiley Quinn* • Ward Bond *Eddie Adams* ■ *Dir* Raoul Walsh • *Scr* Richard Macaulay, Jerry Wald

Man's Best Friend ★★ 15
Science-fiction thriller
1993 · US · Colour · 83min

You'd have thought Stephen King's *Cujo* was the last word on mad dogs. Not according to this sci-fi thriller, in which reporter Ally Sheedy rescues a big pooch from a laboratory, only to discover there's a reason why scientist Lance Henriksen keeps it in a cage. It's because the initially lovable canine has been genetically mutated and is now a furry killer! Daftly enjoyable. JB

Ally Sheedy *Lori Tanner* • Lance Henriksen *Dr Jarret* • Robert Costanzo *Detective Kovacs* • Fredric Lehne *Perry* ■ *Dir/Scr* John Lafia

Man's Castle ★★★
Romantic drama   1933 · US · BW · 70min

This marvellously romantic view of love during the Depression was fashioned by one of Hollywood's most sensitive directors, the double Academy Award-winner Frank Borzage. His acute romanticising is sometimes hard to stomach, and Spencer Tracy's aggressively macho character ultimately becomes grating. But Loretta Young is genuinely charming and gives a lovely, winsome performance. On the downside, the shantytown setting looks relentlessly studio-bound, and the use of miniatures still looks phoney. TS

Spencer Tracy *Bill* • Loretta Young *Trina* • Glenda Farrell *Fay LaRue* • Walter Connolly *Ira* • Arthur Hohl *Bragg* • Marjorie Rambeau *Flossie* • Dickie Moore *Joie* • Harvey Clark *Café manager* ■ *Dir* Frank Borzage • *Scr* Jo Swerling, from a play by Lawrence Hazard

Man's Favorite Sport?
★★★★ U

Screwball comedy   1964 · US · Colour · 115min

This is one of the great underrated American comedies, with a simple plot and layer upon layer of delicious sexual innuendo. Director Howard Hawks has fashioned a film that's the true successor to his comic masterpiece *Bringing Up Baby*. Filmed in glossy Technicolor, it features Rock Hudson as a fishing expert who can't fish. Paula Prentiss, an unfairly overlooked actress, is simply fabulous as Hudson's nemesis, determined to expose him, and the supporting cast is genuinely funny. **TS** *DVD*

Rock Hudson *Roger Willoughby* • Paula Prentiss *Abigail Page* • Maria Perschy *Isolde "Easy" Mueller* • Charlene Holt *Tex Connors* • John McGiver *William Cadwalader* • Roscoe Karns *Major Phipps* • Forrest Lewis *Skaggs* • Norman Alden *John Screaming Eagle* ■ *Dir* Howard Hawks • *Scr* John Fenton Murray, Steve McNeil, from the story *The Girl Who Almost Got Away* by Pat Frank

Man's Hope
★★★★

War drama   1945 · Sp/Fr · BW · 72min

Based on his novel *L'Espoir*, the only feature directed by André Malraux began shooting in Barcelona in 1938, but was interrupted when General Franco took the city. Completed in a studio in Paris, it was not shown until after the Second World War, with different editing. Malraux, who was still at the front, was not consulted; indeed, when he saw the film for the first time, he did not recognise the cutting. Nevertheless, despite the professional actors and the studio work, this semi-documentary about a small group of Republican fighters in the Spanish Civil War attempting to blow up a bridge gives the impression that the actual war is being filmed. **RB** Spanish +subtitles.

Andres Mejutc *Capt Munoz* • Nicolas Rodriguez *Pilot Marquez* • Jose Lado *The peasant* ■ *Dir* André Malraux • *Scr* André Malraux, from his novel *L'Espoir*

A Man's Story
★★ 15

Documentary   2010 · UK · Colour · 93min

It's remarkable that Varon Bonicos's profile of menswear designer Ozwald Boateng is even vaguely coherent, considering it was edited from 420 hours of footage shot over ten years. However, this documentary is very much a greatest clips compilation that celebrates the triumphs of the first black tailor to have a shop on London's prestigious Savile Row, rather than an exploration of the prejudices and setbacks that shaped both his personality and his career. **DP** Swearing. *DVD*

Ozwald Boateng • Giorgio Armani ■ *Dir* Varon Bonicos

Mansfield Park
★★★★ 15

Period drama   1999 · UK/US · Colour · 107min

Writer/director Patricia Rozema looks beyond Jane Austen's third novel for inspiration and uses the author's own letters and journals to beef up this cleverly constructed and lively update. Frances O'Connor dazzles as Fanny Price, plucked from poverty and sent to live with her wealthy relatives on the Mansfield Park estate. There she must choose between true love and social duty. Austen purists may be offended by the liberties taken, but Rozema's bracing rumination on class hypocrisy and social hierarchy is a compelling revision of traditional costume drama. **AJ** Violence, a sex scene, nudity. *DVD*

Frances O'Connor *Fanny Price* • Embeth Davidtz *Mary Crawford* • Jonny Lee Miller *Edmund Bertram* • Alessandro Nivola *Henry Crawford* • Harold Pinter *Sir Thomas Bertram* • Lindsay Duncan *Lady Bertram/Frances Price* • Sheila Gish *Mrs Norris* • James Purefoy *Tom Bertram* ■ *Dir* Patricia Rozema • *Scr* Patricia Rozema, from the novel by Jane Austen

Mansion of the Doomed ★ 15

Horror   1975 · US · Colour · 83min

This utterly repugnant horror film at least has the courage of its gruesome convictions. An eminent surgeon abducts victims and removes their eyes in the hope of restoring the sight of his daughter, blinded in a car wreck. Director Michael Pataki piles on the banality and reduces Richard Basehart and Gloria Grahame to embarrassed shells of their former selves. Squeamish viewers beware! **RS** *DVD*

Richard Basehart *Dr Leonard Chaney* • Trish Stewart *Nancy Chaney* • Gloria Grahame *Katherine* • Lance Henriksen *Dr Dan Bryan* ■ *Dir* Michael Pataki • *Scr* Frank Ray Perilli

Manslaughter
★★

Drama   1930 · US · BW · 85min

The lives of a district attorney (Fredric March) and the rich and idle society girl (Claudette Colbert) with whom he is in love are complicated when she runs over a traffic cop and kills him, forcing March to send her to jail. Written and directed by George Abbott, this updated version of a more flamboyant silent made by Cecil B DeMille in 1922 is notable mainly for Colbert's fine performance. **RK**

Claudette Colbert *Lydia Thorne* • Fredric March *Dan O'Bannon* • Emma Dunn *Miss Bennett* • Natalie Moorhead *Eleanor* • Richard Tucker *Albee* • Hilda Vaughn *Evans* • G Pat Collins *Drummond* ■ *Dir* George Abbott • *Scr* George Abbott, from the story by Alice Duer Miller

The Manson Family   ★★ 18

Horror based on a true story
2003 · US/UK · Colour · 91min

Fifteen years in the making, maverick director Jim VanBebber's legendary micro-budget horror (originally titled *Charlie's Family*) is an ultra-graphic and often powerful examination of the 1969 Tate-La Bianca slayings. This manic meditation draws on court transcriptions from the murder trial and restages interviews from the 1972 documentary *Manson* to reconstruct the Manson Family's infamous attack on director Roman Polanski's house, which left his pregnant wife (the actress Sharon Tate) and four others dead. The amateur acting and deliberate evocation of the 1970s exploitation Z-movie style severely hampers the director's choppy, celluloid orgy. **AJ** Sex scenes, drug abuse. *DVD*

Marcelo Games *Charlie* • Marc Pitman *Tex* • Leslie Orr *Patty* • Maureen Allisse *Sadie* • Amy Yates *Leslie* • Jim VanBebber *Bobbi* ■ *Dir/Scr* Jim VanBebber

Mantrap
★★★

Silent comedy drama   1926 · US · BW · 66min

Bored to tears with her marriage to small-town businessman Ernest Torrence, sexy flapper Clara Bow falls into the arms of visiting lawyer Percy Marmont and plans to run off with him to the big city. One of Bow's more substantial vehicles, adapted for the silent screen from a novel by Sinclair Lewis and directed by her then-lover, Victor Fleming. A good example of the screen persona that made the "It Girl" box-office dynamite in the 1920s. **RK**

Ernest Torrence *Joe Easter* • Clara Bow *Alverna* • Percy Marmont *Ralph Prescott* • Eugene Pallette *E Wesson Woodbury* • Tom Kennedy *Curly Evans* • Josephine Crowell *Mrs McGavity* • William Orlamond *Mr McGavity* • Charles Stevens *Lawrence Jackfish* ■ *Dir* Victor Fleming • *Scr* Adelaide Heilbron, Ethel Doherty, George Marion Jr (titles), from a novel by Sinclair Lewis

Mantrap
★★

Thriller   1952 · UK · BW · 78min

Paul Henreid, that oily smoothie from *Casablanca* and *Now, Voyager*, here washes up in the torrid, tawdry, cheapskate world of the British quota quickie. Lois Maxwell plays a wife who changes her name and begins a new life after her husband is convicted of murder. When he escapes, she goes to private detective Henreid for help. Maxwell later found fame as Miss Moneypenny in the Bond films. **AT**

Paul Henreid *Hugo Bishop* • Lois Maxwell *Thelma Tasman* • Kieron Moore *Mervyn Speight* • Hugh Sinclair *Maurice Jerrard* ■ *Dir* Terence Fisher • *Scr* Paul Tabori, Terence Fisher, from the novel *Queen in Danger* by Elleston Trevor

Manuela
★★ PG

Romantic drama   1957 · UK · BW · 89min

This unlikely shipboard romance was later gently lampooned in *Carry On Jack*. Director Guy Hamilton does a fair job of reining in Trevor Howard's natural bullishness, coming as close as anyone ever did to discovering vulnerability in his gruff make-up. Elsa Martinelli never really convinces in her boyish disguise, but it's clear to see why tipsy Captain Howard would fall for her. This frippery is beneath the cast, but it still has an easy charm. **DP** *DVD*

Trevor Howard *James Prothero* • Elsa Martinelli *Manuela* • Leslie Weston *Bleloch* • Donald Pleasence *Evans* • Jack MacGowran *Tommy* • Warren Mitchell *Moss* • Pedro Armendáriz *Mario Constanza* ■ *Dir* Guy Hamilton • *Scr* William Woods, Guy Hamilton, Ivan Foxwell, from the novel by William Woods

Manufacturing Dissent: Uncovering Michael Moore
★★★ 15

Documentary   2007 · Can · Colour · 96min

Intended as an admiring portrait of icon of the political left Michael Moore, Debbie Melnyk and Rick Caine's film becomes a search for the truth behind Moore's most famous documentaries. They speak to colleagues of Moore's as well as journalists, cineastes and political commentators, and the picture that emerges is of someone who is driven to get things done by any means necessary. From manipulating his interviewees to misrepresenting the facts, Moore is accused of taking liberties with the truth and the chronology of events for greater dramatic effect. Yet, despite the abundance of such damning testimony, the message loses much of its resonance in the muddled presentation. If Melnyk and Caine had studied the clarity and structure of Moore's work more carefully, their own film might have made more of an impact. **SuR** *DVD*

Michael Moore (2) *Michael Moore* • Debbie Melnyk • John Pierson • Ralph Nader • Harlan Jacobson • Noam Chomsky • Al Franken • Janeane Garofalo • Christopher Hitchens • Mick Jagger ■ *Dir* Rick Caine, Debbie Melnyk • *Scr* Debbie Melnyk, Rick Caine

The Manxman
★★ U

Silent drama   1929 · UK · BW · 79min

Alfred Hitchcock's last silent film is a brooding melodrama concerning a love triangle that ends in tragedy. Anny Ondra is loved by two men who are best friends – fisherman Carl Brisson and lawyer Malcolm Keen. She loves Brisson but when her father forbids marriage, he leaves the island and Keen steps in. Unfamiliar territory for present-day Hitchcock fans, this is competently done and atmospheric, but too old-fashioned to be of more than limited interest. **RK**

Carl Brisson *Pete Quilliam* • Malcolm Keen *Philip Christian* • Anny Ondra *Kate Cregeen* ■ *Dir* Alfred Hitchcock • *Scr* Eliot Stannard, from the novel by Sir Hall Caine

The Many Adventures of Winnie the Pooh   ★★★★ U

Animated adventure   1977 · US · Colour · 70min

AA Milne's enduringly entertaining tales are retold with considerable charm in a compilation of three stories that were originally released by Disney as shorts. *Winnie the Pooh and the Honey Tree* (1966) sees the bear of little brain (wonderfully voiced by Sterling Holloway) trying to disguise himself as a rain cloud before getting stuck in Rabbit's doorway. The Oscar-winning *Winnie the Pooh and the Blustery Day* (1968) brings Piglet and Tigger to the Hundred Acre Wood, as a storm brings down Owl's house. Finally there's *Winnie the Pooh and Tigger Too!* (1974), in which Rabbit is taught about tolerance. It's cleverly linked, amusingly told and timeless in its appeal. **DP** *DVD*

Sterling Holloway *Winnie the Pooh* • Paul Winchell *Tigger* • Sebastian Cabot *Narrator* • Clint Howard *Roo* • Dir John Lounsbery, Wolfgang Reitherman • *Scr* From the *Winnie the Pooh* books by AA Milne

Many Rivers to Cross
★★★ U

Comedy western   1955 · US · Colour · 94min

This good-natured buckskin-clad MGM pre-western frontier comedy was sold on the back of the similarly themed *Seven Brides for Seven Brothers*. Robert Taylor and Eleanor Parker make an attractively spunky pair, but the script lets them down, being neither as hilarious nor as perceptive about the female condition as it thinks it is. Underrated director Roy Rowland does what he can, but the constant need to roister defeats him and exhausts the audience's patience. Lovely to look at, though. **TS**

Robert Taylor (1) *Bushrod Gentry* • Eleanor Parker *Mary Stuart Cherne* • Victor McLaglen *Cadmus Cherne* • Jeff Richards *Fremont* • Russ Tamblyn *Shields* • James Arness *Esau Hamilton* • Alan Hale Jr *Luke Radford* ■ *Dir* Roy Rowland • *Scr* Harry Brown, Guy Trosper, from a story by Steve Frazee

Map of the Human Heart
★★★★ 15

Drama   1992 · UK/Aus/Can/Fr · Colour · 105min

Spanning several decades and told as an elongated flashback to cartographer John Cusack, this is a rare blend of imagination and insight. Memorable moments abound, from a plane landing on the Arctic ice to Inuit Jason Scott Lee and mixed-race Anne Parillaud finally consummating their on-off affair atop a deflating barrage balloon. It would be too easy to say that it is only the stunning visuals that prevent this romantic triangle drama from lapsing into sentimental platitude, but it has the intelligence and humanity to make its tale seem like life, not contrivance. **DP** *DVD*

Jason Scott Lee *Avik* • Robert Joamie *Young Avik* • Anne Parillaud *Albertine* • Annie Galipeau *Young Albertine* • Patrick Bergin *Walter Russell* • Clotilde Courau *Rainee* • John Cusack *Mapmaker* • Jeanne Moreau *Sister Banville* ■ *Dir* Vincent Ward • *Scr* Louis Nowra, from a story by Vincent Ward

A Map of the World
★★★★ 15

Drama   1999 · US · Colour · 120min

Sigourney Weaver gives what is perhaps the finest performance of her career as a rural housewife not just on the verge of a nervous breakdown, but engulfed by it. She's the lone bright woman in a Wisconsin farming community, but her mundane life is disturbed when a neighbour's two-year-old daughter drowns while in her care and young local Marc Donato accuses her of sexual abuse. Director Scott Elliott loses his grip in the second half, but Weaver's performance transcends the flaws. **TH** *DVD*

Sigourney Weaver *Alice Goodwin* • Julianne Moore *Theresa Collins* • David Strathairn *Howard Goodwin* • Ron Lea *Paul Reverdy* • Chloë Sevigny *Carole Mackessy* • Louise Fletcher *Nellie* • Marc Donato *Robbie* ■ *Dir* Scott Elliott • *Scr* Peter Hedges, Polly Platt, from the novel by Jane Hamilton

Mapantsula
★★★★ 15

Crime drama   1988 · S Afr · Colour · 99min

With its title coming from the Soweto slang for "spiv", this was one of the few South African films of the apartheid era to background the political situation and eschew fashionable Caucasian liberalism. Thomas Mogotlane excels as the thief who reveals levels of determination and dignity as he endures the same sadistic brutality as the militant activists with whom he shares a cell. The township sequences teem with life, drawing additional authenticity from the fact that Mogotlane doesn't care which side of the racial divide he operates. **DP** Sotho, Zulu, Afrikaans +subtitles.

Thomas Mogotlane *Panic* • Marcel Van Heerden *Stander* • Thembi Mtshali *Pat* • Dolly Rathebe *Ma Mobise* • Peter Sephuma *Buma* • Darlington Michaels *Dingaan* • Eugene Majola *Sam* ■ *Dir* Oliver Schmitz • *Scr* Oliver Schmitz, Thomas Mogotlane

Mapplethorpe 18

Biography drama 2016 · US · Colour · 108min

This is a preview - no prints were available to review as we went to press: While he was famous for his celebrity portraits (including of close friend Patti Smith) and sensitive images of flowers, controversial US photographer Robert Mapplethorpe (played here by Britain's Matt Smith) achieved notoriety through his nudes of men and women (but mainly men) and images of sado masochism and androgyny. Questions were even raised on the floor of the US Senate about the content of his work. He died in 1989 having lived life completely on his own terms. It promises to be a fascinating story. **TP**

Matt Smith *Robert Mapplethorpe* • Zosia Mamet *Patti Smith* ■ *Dir* Ondi Timoner • *Scr* Ondi Timoner, with additional material by Bruce Goodrich

Mapplethorpe: Look at the Pictures ★★★18

Documentary
2016 · US · Colour and BW · 108min

In this documentary about photographer Robert Mapplethorpe, viewers are urged to look again at pictures that were branded as pornographic and recognise their artistic merit. The likes of Debbie Harry and Brooke Shields gush over his works, while critics, models and friends discuss Mapplethorpe's floral still lifes in the context of his Catholic background and New York heyday. No question, the B&W close-ups of male genitalia and BDSM gear are visually striking and politically strident. The question of their beauty lies very much in the eye of the beholder. **DP** Swearing, sex scenes, nudity. *DVD*

Debbie Harry [Deborah Harry] *Debbie Harry* • Brooke Shields • Robert Mapplethorpe • Edward Mapplethorpe ■ *Dir* Fenton Bailey, Randy Barbato

Maps to the Stars ★★★★18

Drama 2014 · Can/Fr/Ger · Colour · 107min

David Cronenberg's latest offering appears to be an acerbic satire on the Hollywood ego along the lines of Robert Altman's *The Player*, but it soon sheds its superficially satirical surface to reveal a fiercely original take on the nightmare that lurks beneath the Hollywood sign. An excellent Julianne Moore is a fading actress desperate for a role in a remake of a film in which her own abusive film-star mother, who died in a fire (a theme of the movie), originally starred. Beautifully shot in the blazing Californian sunshine, this gleefully perverse, haunting film fuses elements of *Mommie Dearest* and the dreamy surreality of *Mulholland Drive* into a twisted Hollywood fairy tale with a heart-rending tragedy at its dark core. **AS** Violence, swearing, nudity, drug abuse. *DVD* ☐

Julianne Moore *Havana Segrand* • Mia Wasikowska *Agatha Weiss* • Robert Pattinson *Jerome Fontana* • Olivia Williams *Cristina Weiss* • John Cusack *Dr Stafford Weiss* ■ *Dir* David Cronenberg • *Scr* Bruce Wagner

Mara Maru ★★

Adventure 1952 · US · BW · 97min

Approaching the end of his romantic swashbuckler career, but still making a handsome fist of it, Errol Flynn stars as a deep-sea diver who knows the whereabouts of a bejewelled cross, sunk on a PT boat in the China Seas during the Second World War. Flynn is hired by wealthy villain Raymond Burr to retrieve the treasure, and sets out on a voyage rife with deception and chicanery. Mildly entertaining. **RK**

Errol Flynn *Gregory Mason* • Ruth Roman *Stella Callahan* • Raymond Burr *Brock Benedict* • Paul Picerni *Steven Ranier* • Richard Webb *Andy*

Callahan ■ *Dir* Gordon Douglas • *Scr* N Richard Nash, from a story by Philip Yordan, Sidney Harmon, Hollister Noble

Maracaibo ★

Adventure drama 1958 · US · Colour · 88min

In this disjointed mess, Cornel Wilde struggles manfully to douse a fire in an undersea oil well in Venezuela. Then Wilde has to give his real-life wife, Jean Wallace, something to do. So a second plot is trumped up about an American woman novelist who learns about the personal tragedy of the owner of the blazing well. The two halves quickly come unglued in a welter of travelogue footage of watersports and flamenco dancing. **AT**

Cornel Wilde *Vic Scott* • Jean Wallace *Laura Kingsley* • Abbe Lane *Elena Holbrook* • Francis Lederer *Senor Miguel Orlando* • Michael Landon *Lago* • Joe E Ross *Milt Karger* ■ *Dir* Cornel Wilde • *Scr* Ted Sherdeman, from a novel by Stirling Silliphant

Marat/Sade ★★

Historical drama
1966 · UK · BW and Colour · 115min

The Marquis de Sade (Patrick Magee) directs his insane asylum inmates in a morality play-within-a-play about the assassination of French Revolutionary leader Jean-Paul Marat (Ian Richardson). The bedlam governor (Clifford Rose) continually stops the performance to demand cuts in the polemic. Arty and worthy, with de Sade and Marat mainly shouting political rhetoric at each other, Peter Brook's hard-going film adaptation adds extra Brechtian close-up nuance to his controversial stage hit. **AJ**

Ian Richardson *Jean-Paul Marat* • Patrick Magee *Marquis de Sade* • Glenda Jackson *Charlotte Corday* • Clifford Rose *M Coulmier* • Brenda Kempner *Mme Coulmier* • Ruth Baker *Mlle Coulmier* • Michael Williams *Herald* • Freddie Jones *Cucurucu* ■ *Dir* Peter Brook • *Scr* Adrian Mitchell, from the play *The Persecution and Assassination of Jean-Paul Marat as Performed by the Inmates of the Asylum of Charenton under the Direction of the Marquis de Sade* by Peter Weiss, as translated by Geoffrey Skelton, Adrian Mitchell of the play *Die Verfolgung und Ermordung Jean Paul Marats, Dargestellt durch die Schauspielgruppe des Hospizes zu Charenton unter Anleitung des Herrn de Sade*

Marathon Man ★★★★15

Thriller 1976 · US · Colour · 120min

Dustin Hoffman stars as the bewildered New York student training to run a marathon who inadvertently becomes mixed up in a hunt for a haul of Nazi diamonds in director John Schlesinger's gripping thriller. Laurence Olivier is the essence of evil as the former concentration camp sadist who leaves South America to claim his legacy - the priceless gems taken from Jewish victims during the war. Also making an impact is Roy Scheider as Hoffman's secret agent older brother. Schlesinger's film is not without its flaws - it takes rather too long to get started and is too dislocated - but it's a very classy package. **TH** Violence, a sex scene, swearing, nudity. *DVD* ☐

Dustin Hoffman *Babe Levy* • Laurence Olivier *Szell* • Roy Scheider *Doc Levy* • William Devane *Janeway* • Marthe Keller *Elsa* • Fritz Weaver *Professor Biesenthal* • Richard Bright *Karl* • Marc Lawrence (1) *Erhard* • Allen Joseph *Babe's father* ■ *Dir* John Schlesinger • *Scr* William Goldman, from his novel

Marcello Mastroianni: I Remember ★★★★★

Documentary 1997 · It · Colour and BW · 198min

Although directed by his partner, Anna Maria Tato, this is essentially a cinematic self-portrait from Marcello Mastroianni, who amassed over 170 credits in his glittering yet ceaselessly questing career. He emerges from these glorious clips and monologues as a charming, erudite, cosmopolitan gentleman, with a love of literature, a pride in his career and a passion for life. Lamenting the artistic decline of mainstream cinema, he fondly recalls collaborations with Vittoria De

---

Sica, Federico Fellini and Marco Ferreri, while deriding his international reputation as a Latin lover. However, these mercurial memoirs also provide many personal insights that make them as invaluable as Mastroianni is irreplaceable. **DP** Italian +subtitles.

■ *Dir* Anna Maria Tato

The March Hare ★★★U

Drama 1956 · UK · Colour · 84min

Best remembered (if at all) for Philip Green's jaunty theme music, this British Lion horse-racing romp gains from the fact that it was photographed in colour and CinemaScope by the great Jack Hildyard. It also has good-looking leads in handsome Terence Morgan and sultry Peggy Cummins who, together with a sly performance from Cyril Cusack, keep the whole thing a good deal more watchable than it deserves to be. **TS**

Peggy Cummins *Pat McGuire* • Terence Morgan *Sir Charles Hare* • Martita Hunt *Lady Anne* • Cyril Cusack *Lazy Mangan* • Wilfrid Hyde White *Colonel Keene* • Charles Hawtrey *Fisher* ■ *Dir* George More O'Ferrall • *Scr* Gordon Wellesley, Paul Vincent Carroll, Allan Mckinnon, from the novel *Gamblers Sometimes Win* by TH Bird

March of the Penguins ★★★★U

Documentary 2005 · US/Fr · Colour · 76min

Director Luc Jacquet's disarmingly simple documentary follows a flock of emperor penguins as they make the arduous journey to their annual breeding ground, and then endure the Antarctic's extreme winter until their chicks are hatched. The avian protagonists' comical ungainliness on land and deadpan manner make for adorable viewing, while the austere, glacial landscape is consistently breathtaking. Originally, the film had a soppy dialogue track in which French actors voiced the penguins' "thoughts". The English-language version ditches most of the anthropomorphism in favour of a drier, factual narration by Morgan Freeman, which marvels at the penguins' stamina, dedication as parents and serial monogamy. **LF** *DVD* ☐

Morgan Freeman *Narrator* ■ *Dir* Luc Jacquet • *Scr* Luc Jacquet, Michel Fessler, Jordan Roberts (English-language narration), from a story by Jacquet • *Cinematographers* Laurent Chalet, Jérôme Maison

March or Die ★★PG

Adventure 1977 · UK · Colour · 102min

Producer Lew Grade's good intentions often led to disappointing results. So it proved in this *Beau Geste*-style tale about the French Foreign Legion. Much of the blame must lie with Terence Hill, who got by in comic westerns where his accent and lack of ability weren't too apparent. Alongside such talents as Gene Hackman and Max von Sydow, however, he is totally lost, slowing the pace down to a snail's crawl. Catherine Deneuve looks radiant, though, while John Alcott's photography is a treat. **TS** *DVD*

Gene Hackman *Major William Sherman Foster* • Terence Hill *Marco Segrain* • Catherine Deneuve *Simone Picard* • Max von Sydow *François Marneau* • Ian Holm *El Krim* • Jack O'Halloran *Ivan* ■ *Dir* Dick Richards • *Scr* David Zelag Goodman, from a story by Goodman, Dick Richards

The March Sisters at Christmas ★★

Comedy 2012 · US · Colour · 85min

Louisa May Alcott's *Little Women* is done no favours in this flimsy and charmless update of the literary classic. Peppered with sexual references and with the siblings' virtues almost lost amid their booze-swilling and exaggeratedly modern behaviour, the throwaway TV movie sees the quartet out to prevent the selling of their family home in the run-up to Christmas. The result is a contrived, Christmas Eve finale that brings predictable happy endings but none of the warmth associated with Alcott's beloved original story. **SF**

Julie Marie Berman *Jo March* • Kaitlin Doubleday *Meg March* • Melissa Farman *Beth March* • Molly Kunz *Amy March* • John Shea *Mr Lawrence* ■ *Dir* John Stimpson • *Scr* Jennifer Maisel, from the novel *Little Women* by Louisa May Alcott

Marci X ★★15

Comedy 2003 · US · Colour · 80min

Lisa Kudrow plays a Jewish New York socialite who enters into the world of hard-core rap artist Damon Wayans to save her ailing father's company. In a role far removed from her small screen character in *Friends*, Kudrow is endearing and sassy, but, like Wayans, she's wasted in an imprudent film that tries too hard to be hip and trendy. The picture is often patronising and stereotypical; consequently, most of the laughs come from the questionable taste of Richard Benjamin's subject matter. **SF** Swearing, drug abuse. *DVD*

Lisa Kudrow *Marci Feld* • Damon Wayans *Dr S* • Richard Benjamin *Ben Feld* • Christine Baranski *Sen Mary Ellen Spinkle* • Paula Garcés *Yolanda Quinones* • Billy Griffith *Tubby Fenders* • Jane Krakowski *Lauren* ■ *Dir* Richard Benjamin • *Scr* Paul Rudnick

Marco ★★★

Period musical 1973 · US · Colour · 109min

The exploits of the medieval explorer Marco Polo have proved unlucky for film-makers. This little-known musical version of Marco Polo's travels is in fact the best of the lot, with the benefit of actual Oriental locations, serviceable songs and a pleasing cast. Desi Arnaz Jr has youthful exuberance as the explorer and Zero Mostel is a scene-stealing Kublai Khan. **TV**

Desi Arnaz Jr *Marco Polo* • Zero Mostel *Kublai Khan* • Jack Weston *Maffio Polo* • Win Cie Cie *Aigiarm* • Aimee Eccles *Kuklatoi* • Fred Sadoff *Niccolo Polo* ■ *Dir* Seymour Robbie • *Scr* Romeo Muller • *Music* Maury Laws

The Marcus-Nelson Murders ★★★15

Crime drama 1973 · US · Colour · 137min

A superb Telly Savalas made his first appearance as the no-nonsense detective Theo Kojak in this gritty pilot episode of the influential 1970s police series. Providing the driving force in an otherwise slow-moving affair, he finds himself fighting for justice after suspecting colleagues of trying to frame a black youth for double murder. While TV film-maker Joseph Sargent (subsequent director of the original *The Taking of Pelham One Two Three*) excels in capturing the atmosphere, look and attitude of 1960s New York, some poor dialogue and sluggish pacing reduce the drama's overall impact. **SF**

Telly Savalas *Lt Theo Kojak* • Marjoe Gortner *Teddy Hopper* • José Ferrer *Jake Weinhaus* • Ned Beatty *Det Dan Corrigan* • Allen Garfield *Mario Portello* • Lorraine Gary *Ruthie* ■ *Dir* Joseph Sargent • *Scr* Abby Mann, from a novel by Selwyn Raab

Mardi Gras ★★U

Musical 1958 · US · Colour · 107min

It must have seemed a good idea to team pop idols Pat Boone and Tommy Sands with Gary Crosby (son of Bing) as military cadets on a spree in New Orleans. Frankly, however, 20th Century-Fox could have come up with a better plot. This one's some hokum about winning a date on a raffle, which wouldn't matter too much if the songs were any good, but they're not. This empty piece of entertainment marked the downward spiral of Boone's movie career as his amiable, ingratiating smile was becoming tiresome. **TS**

Pat Boone *Pat Newell* • Christine Carère *Michelle Marton* • Tommy Sands *Barry Denton* • Sheree North *Eadie West* • Gary Crosby *Tony Runkle* • Fred Clark *Hal Curtis* • Richard Sargent [Dick Sargent] *Dick Saglon* ■ *Dir* Edmund Goulding • *Scr* Winston Miller, Hal Kanter, from a story by Curtis Harrington

---

U SUITABLE FOR ALL Uc SUITABLE ESPECIALLY FOR YOUNG CHILDREN (DVD ONLY) PG PARENTAL GUIDANCE 12A UNDER 12s TO BE ACCOMPANIED (CINEMA ONLY)

Mare Nostrum ★★★
Silent First World War drama
1926 · US · BW · 102min

Directed by Rex Ingram, a master at epic romances, this tragic First World War love story touched nerves as well as hearts with its story of a German spy (Alice Terry, Ingram's wife) who falls in love with a Spanish captain (Antonio Moreno). Nowadays, of course, it feels dreadfully dated, but the film still has a narrative charge that still appeals. TH

Alice Terry *Freya Talberg* · Antonio Moreno *Ulysses Ferragut* · Uni Apollon *The Triton* ■ *Dir* Rex Ingram (1) · *Scr* Willis Goldbeck, from the novel by Vicente Blasco Ibañez

Marebito ★★ 18
Horror
2004 · Jpn · Colour · 91min

Shot on grainy digital video in eight days, *The Grudge* director Takashi Shimizu's haphazard horror is an empty exercise in unease that never builds into anything coherently creepy. Shinya Tsukamoto plays a news cameraman obsessed with understanding the true nature of fear. He follows the ghost of a suicide into the Tokyo netherworld and returns with a vampire girl whom he is compelled to feed with the blood of murdered victims. AJ Japanese +subtitles. *DVD*

Shinya Tsukamoto *Masuoka* · Tomomi Miyashita · Kazuhiro Nakahara · Shun Sugata ■ *Dir* Takashi Shimizu · *Scr* Chiaka Konaka

Margaret ★★ 15
Drama
2008 · US · Colour · 143min

As a child actress, Anna Paquin won an Oscar for *The Piano*. As an adult, she went on to headline the hit TV show *True Blood*. Here, she returns to the big screen for a drama about unintended consequences. She plays an attractive high-school student who inadvertently distracts the driver of a passing bus (Mark Ruffalo). The bus crashes a red light, and a pedestrian is graphically killed. Tormented by a peculiarly teenage sense of guilt, she sets out to make amends by bringing the bus driver to book. Paquin plays the teen with spunk and spark, and the supporting stars, including Matt Damon and Jean Reno, are fine, too. But, at 150 minutes, the film is way too long, with several superfluous scenes and subplots. On top of all that, moments of overwrought opera and high melodrama suggest that it has an over-inflated sense of its own importance. DA *DVD*

Anna Paquin *Lisa Cohen* · J Smith-Cameron *Joan* · Mark Ruffalo *Maretti* · Jeannie Berlin *Emily* · Jean Reno *Ramon* · Allison Janney *Monica Patterson* · Kieran Culkin *Paul* · Matt Damon *Mr Aaron* · Matthew Broderick *John* ■ *Dir/Scr* Kenneth Lonergan

Margaret's Museum ★★★ 15
Period drama
1995 · Can/UK · Colour · 95min

This powerful period piece is set in a Canadian coal-mining community during the 1940s. Helena Bonham Carter is Margaret, whose father and brother have already perished down the mines, and who is determined that the new love in her life, a bagpipe-playing, Gaelic-speaking dishwasher, won't follow suit. But times are hard, jobs are scarce and history looks bound to repeat itself. Clive Russell and Kate Nelligan offer strong support, but it's Bonham Carter's film. DA Sex scenes.

Helena Bonham Carter *Margaret MacNeil* · Clive Russell *Neil Currie* · Craig Olejnik *Jimmy MacNeil* · Kate Nelligan *Catherine MacNeil* · Kenneth Welsh *Angus MacNeil* · Andrea Morris *Marilyn Campbell* ■ *Dir* Mort Ransen · *Scr* Mort Ransen, Gerald Wexler, from the short story *The Glace Bay Miner's Museum* by Sheldon Currie

Margie ★★★★ U
Musical comedy
1946 · US · Colour · 93min

In the wake of MGM's *Meet Me in St Louis*, the other studios dusted off their songbooks and petticoats, and 20th Century-Fox produced this little Technicolored charmer, which set a style and standard that endured at the studio for well over a decade. Set in the 1920s, the era of the raccoon coat and the charleston, this is a captivating work, lovingly directed, and starring Jeanne Crain in the role of her career. Completely evading the schmaltz and vulgarity that hampered later entries in the same vein, this remains a model of wit, taste and good musical sense. TS

Jeanne Crain *Margie McDuff* · Glenn Langan *Professor Ralph Fontayne* · Lynn Bari *Miss Isabelle Palmer* · Alan Young *Roy Hornsdale* · Barbara Lawrence *Marybelle Tenor* · Conrad Janis *Johnny Green* · Esther Dale *Grandma McSweeney* · Hattie McDaniel *Cynthia* ■ *Dir* Henry King · *Scr* F Hugh Herbert, from a story by Ruth McKinney, Richard Bransten

Margin Call ★★★★ 15
Drama
2011 · US · Colour · 102min

Following the factual dramatisation of the 2008 US financial meltdown in HBO's fine *Too Big to Fail*, *Margin Call* plays the fictionalised card, focusing on the rapid reaction of a Lehmans-like investment bank to the crisis over a 36-hour period. In an assured feature debut, writer/director JC Chandor drives the action by way of a USB stick handed to Zachary Quinto's whizzkid junior by Stanley Tucci, who plays a bitter risk manager being escorted from the building during a cull. News of the information therein travels up through the ranks until it reaches elusive CEO Jeremy Irons (who gives a deliciously vulpine performance). The movie is mostly shot at night in a New York skyscraper, and the claustrophobic isolationism of the financial services industry is cleverly implied, as the central disaster s humanised by individual ones – notably Kevin Spacey's conflicted middle manager. AC Swearing. *DVD* *Blu-ray*

Kevin Spacey *Sam Rogers* · Paul Bettany *Will Emerson* · Jeremy Irons *John Tuld* · Zachary Quinto *Peter Sullivan* · Penn Badgley *Seth Bregman* · Simon Baker *Jared Cohen* · Demi Moore *Sarah Robertson* · Stanley Tucci *Eric Dale* ■ *Dir/Scr* JC Chandor

Margin for Error ★★★ PG
Black comedy
1943 · US · BW · 71min

After an unhappy start in Hollywood as a producer turned director, Otto Preminger returned to Broadway. Among the most successful plays he directed was this black comedy by Clare Boothe about the Nazi consul in Brooklyn and the Jewish policeman ordered to protect him. Preminger played the role of the arrogant Nazi himself and repeats it on screen, typecasting himself forever in the process, while future TV comedian Milton Berle plays the cop. To improve the script Preminger hired Samuel Fuller, who worked without credit while he was on leave from the army. AT *DVD*

Joan Bennett *Sophie Baumer* · Milton Berle *Moe Finkelstein* · Otto Preminger *Karl Baumer* · Carl Esmond *Baron Max von Alvenstor* · Howard Freeman *Otto Horst* · Poldy Dur *Frieda Schmidt* ■ *Dir* Otto Preminger · *Scr* Lillie Hayward, Samuel Fuller, from the play by Clare Boothe [Clare Boothe Luce]

Margot at the Wedding ★★★ 15
Comedy drama
2007 · US · Colour · 88min

After a clutch of underwhelming blockbusters (*The Invasion*, *The Golden Compass*), Nicole Kidman wisely found a more intimate vehicle for her talents with this low-key comedy drama from director Noah Baumbach. Kidman plays meddling New York writer Margot, whose surprise appearance at the wedding of her free-spirited sister Pauline (Jennifer Jason Leigh) quickly causes seeds of doubt to be sown about Pauline's husband-to-be (a nicely understated Jack Black). Following the critical acclaim of his previous feature *The Squid and the Whale*, Baumbach proves he is no flash in the pan here, with a well-acted piece of low-budget film-making. DA *DVD*

Nicole Kidman *Margot Zeller* · Jennifer Jason Leigh *Pauline* · Jack Black *Malcolm* · John Turturro *Jim* · Ciaran Hinds *Dick Koosman* · Zane Pais *Claude Zeller* ■ *Dir/Scr* Noah Baumbach

Marguerite ★★★ 15
Period drama
2015 · Fr/Cz Rep/Bel · Colour · 128min

A thoughtful piece on talent, class, sycophancy and truth, this takes its cues from the life of Florence Foster Jenkins (portrayed by Meryl Streep in the eponymous 2016 biopic). Set in Paris in 1921, the story centres on French aristocrat Marguerite Dumont (Catherine Frot), whose patronage is so crucial to a musical society that its members indulge her delusion she's a gifted diva. A subplot involving an aspiring singer never quite slots into place, but Frot is superb as the oblivious chanteuse. DP French +subtitles. Sex scenes, nudity.

Catherine Frot *Marguerite Dumont* · André Marcon *Georges Dumont* · Michel Fau *Atos Pezzini* · Denis Mpunga *Madelbos* ■ *Dir* Xavier Giannoli · *Scr* Xavier Giannoli, Marcia Romano

Marguerite de la Nuit ★★★
Drama
1955 · Fr · Colour · 130min

Complete with Art Deco backdrops from Max Douy and plenty of photographic tricks from Jacques Natteau, this is a stylish, if dramatically unsatisfactory updating of the Faust myth to the mid-1920s. Shifting the emphasis of Goethe's story away from the ageing doctor who signs away his soul to regain his youth, director Claude Autant-Lara concentrates instead on the relationship between the satanic Pigalle drug-dealer and Marguerite, the long-suffering object of Faust's affections. Jean-François Calvé is out of his depth, but Yves Montand and Michèle Morgan generate plenty of spark. DP In French.

Michèle Morgan *Marguerite* · Yves Montand *M Léon* · Jean-François Calvé *Georges Faust* · Massimo Girotti *Valentin* · Fernand Sardou *Le patron du café* · Pierre Palau *Dr Faust* ■ *Dir* Claude Autant-Lara · *Scr* Ghislaine Autant-Lara, Gabriel Arout, from the novel *Marguerite de la Nuit* by Pierre Mac Orlan [Pierre Dumarchais], from the writings *Faust* by Johann Wolfgang von Goethe

Maria Chapdelaine ★★★
Romantic drama
1982 · Can/Fr · Colour · 108min

Clearly intent on commenting on Quebec's nationalist aspirations throughout the 20th century, Gilles Carle gives Carole Laure's romantic quandary an allegorical edge that intensifies an already engrossing drama. Torn between timid farmer Pierre Curzi, swarthy trapper Nick Mancuso and dapper sophisticate Donald Lautrec, Laure spiritedly personifies Québecois fervour. Pierre Mignot's images of the forbidding far north also impress. DP French +subtitles.

Carole Laure *Maria Chapdelaine* · Nick Mancuso *François Paradis* · Claude Rich *Father Cordelier* · Amulette Garneau *Laura Chapdelaine* · Yoland Guérard *Samuel Chapdelaine* · Pierre Curzi *Eutrope Gagnon* · Donald Lautrec *Lorenzo Suprenant* ■ *Dir* Gilles Carle · *Scr* Gilles Carle, Guy Fournier, from the novel by Louis Hémon

Maria do Mar ★★★★
Silent drama
1930 · Por · BW · 104min

The reputation of Manoel de Oliveira casts such a long shadow over Portuguese cinema that it's easy to forget that there were not only accomplished film-makers who predated him, but also those whose work inspired his own. Two things are significant about José Leitao de Barros's silent melodrama. Firstly, it marries the Soviet visual style with the authenticity that would characterise both the British documentary movement and Italian neorealism. But, secondly, this tale of feuding fisherfolk is impassioned to the point of provocation, with the non-professionals of Nazaré revelling in their roles, while also providing an invaluable record of everyday life. DP

Rosa Maria *Maria do Mar* · Oliveira Martins *Manuel* · Adelina Abranches *Aunt Aurélia* · Alves da Cunha *Falacha* · Perpetua dos Santos *Falacha's wife* ■ *Dir* José Leitão de Barros · *Scr* José Leitão de Barros, Norberto Lopes (titles)

Maria Full of Grace ★★★ 15
Crime drama
2003 · US/Col/Ecu · Colour · 96min

Writer/director Joshua Marston's first feature – the story of drug mule Maria (Catalina Sandino Moreno) – is told with a forensic eye for detail and a sure sense of suspense. Frustrated by the lack of opportunities in her rural Colombian community, the pregnant 17-year-old elects to ingest a consignment of heroin for trafficker Jaime Osorio Gomez. Her journey from Bogota to New York is both riveting and revealing. The subtlety of Moreno's Oscar-nominated performance conveys the pressures that drive the dispossessed to take such potentially fatal risks. DP Spanish, English +subtitles. Swearing. *DVD*

Catalina Sandino Moreno *Maria* · Yenny Paola Vega *Blanca* · Giulied Lopez *Lucy* · Jhon Alex Toro *Franklin* · Patricia Rae *Carla* · Orlando Tobon *Don Fernando* ■ *Dir/Scr* Joshua Marston

Maria Larsson's Everlasting Moments ★★★★★ 15
Period drama based on a true story
2008 · Swe/Den/Nor/Fin/Ger · Colour · 106min

Veteran Swedish director Jan Troell's beautifully observed drama explores how a working-class family woman snatches some respite from her everyday struggles by taking photos with a simple box camera. It's an unfashionably leisurely account of times past and time passing, which nevertheless draws us into the world it depicts through sheer storytelling skill. Maria Heiskanen's doughty central performance holds it all together as she sticks by her boozy, lovable lout of a husband (Mikael Persbrandt), and discovers unexpected self-worth when she peers through the viewfinder. Her talent to select the decisive moment that gives an image lasting life is a skill shared by Troell, who delivers a masterpiece with this composed, affecting window on our common humanity. TJ Swedish +subtitles. Violence, swearing. *DVD*

Maria Heiskanen *Maria Larsson* · Mikael Persbrandt *Sigfrid Larsson* · Jesper Christensen *Sebastian Pedersen, "Piff Paff Puff"* · Callin Ohrvall *Maja Larsson (15-22 years)* · Ghita Norby *Miss Fagerdal* · Amanda Ooms *Matilda* ■ *Dir* Jan Troell · *Scr* Niklas Radstrom, Jan Troell, Agneta Ulfsater Troell, from her story

Maria Marten, or the Murder in the Red Barn ★★ PG
Melodrama
1935 · UK · BW · 63min

Based on a true story, this creaky melodrama tells of a rotten squire who gets a young innocent girl pregnant, then murders her. Director Milton Rosmer strives unsuccessfully for a suitably gothic air, but the cast (Eric Portman and Tod Slaughter in their movie debuts, and Sophie Stewart) has a fine time hamming things up. JF *DVD*

Tod Slaughter *Squire William Corder* · Sophie Stewart *Maria Marten* · DJ Williams *Farmer Marten* · Clare Greet *Mrs Marten* · Eric Portman *Carlos* · Gerrard Tyrell *Tim* · Ann Trevor *Nan* · Antonia Brough *Maud Sennett* ■ *Dir* Milton Rosmer · *Scr* Randall Faye

El Mariachi ★★★ 15
Action adventure
1992 · US · Colour · 81min

Carlos Gallardo, the *mariachi* of the title, is an innocent musician mistaken for a lethal killer who's gunning for Mob boss Peter Marquardt. Robert Rodriguez's debut feature is a no-budget, no-frills effort but the director carries off the action set pieces with confidence and style. *Desperado*, the Hollywood remake, may have had more money and Antonio Banderas as the hero, but this is still the more endearing film. AJ Spanish +subtitles. *DVD*

Carlos Gallardo *El Mariachi* · Consuelo Gomez *Domino* · Jaime De Hoyos *Bigoton* · Peter Marquardt *Mauricio (Moco)* · Reinol Martinez *Azul* · Ramiro Gomez *Cantinero* · Jesus Lopez *Viejo clerk* ■ *Dir/Scr* Robert Rodriguez

M

Mariachi Gringo ★★★
Romantic comedy
2012 · US/Mex · Colour · 95min

The folk music style that has become a Mexican cultural advert is given its place in the spotlight in this charming if slight rite of passage. Awkward Kansas 30-something Shawn Ashmore crosses the Rio Grande to learn more about what he had always dismissed as clappy party music. Easing him through the culture clash is Martha Higareda, who has returned to Guadalajara after studying stateside. Director Tom Gustafson settles for too many stereotypes and clichés in explaining the soul, passion and complexity of mariachi. But the sense of place is undeniably persuasive and the music quite irresistible. DP
Shawn Ashmore *Edward* • Martha Higareda *Lilia* • Kate Burton *Anne* • Adriana Barraza *Magdalena* • Fernando Becerril *Alberto* • Lila Downs *Sophia* ■ *Dir* Tom Gustafson • *Scr* Cory James Krueckeberg

Marianne de Ma Jeunesse ★★★
Fantasy romantic drama
1955 · Fr · BW · 105min

This was a huge hit with adolescent French audiences in the mid-1950s, though critics were more restrained in their enthusiasm. However, Marianne Hold is delightfully coquettish as the mysterious young girl who persuades student Pierre Vaneck (who's been locked in an eerie Bavarian castle as an initiation prank by his classmates) that she is being held captive by a pitiless ogre. Equally, there's no denying the visual fascination of Julien Duvivier's fantasy, while special effects wizard Eugen Schüfftan's trickery enhances Léonce-Henry Burel's atmospheric photography. DP In French.
Marianne Hold *Marianne* • Pierre Vaneck *Vincent* • Isabella Pia *Lise* • Gil Vidal *Manfred* ■ *Dir* Julien Duvivier • *Scr* Julien Duvivier, from the novel *Douloureuse Arcadie* by P De Mendelssohn

Maria's Lovers ★★★ 15
Romantic drama
1984 · US · Colour · 104min

Traumatised Second World War veteran John Savage cannot consummate his marriage to childhood sweetheart Nastassja Kinski, so she runs off with various men, including Keith Carradine. The plot sounds a little like Tennessee Williams, but it's actually far less melodramatic than that. Indeed, the mining community setting, the Russian émigré community and the presence of Savage makes Soviet director Andrei Konchalovsky's American debut tender, touching and well acted. AT DVD
Nastassja Kinski *Maria Bosic* • John Savage *Ivan Bibic* • Robert Mitchum *Ivan's father* • Keith Carradine *Clarence Butts* • Anita Morris *Mrs Wynic* • Bud Cort *Harvey* • Karen Young *Rosie* • John Goodman *Frank* ■ *Dir* Andrei Konchalovsky • *Scr* Andrei Konchalovsky, Gérard Brach, Paul Zindel, Marjorie David

Marie: a True Story ★★★ 15
Biographical drama
1985 · US · Colour · 106min

Sissy Spacek gives an impressive performance as Marie Ragghianti, a single mother with three kids who attempts to rid Tennessee's parole board of corruption. This utter paragon actually existed, and Roger Donaldson's well paced biography zings with some great performances and truthful set pieces which grip from the word go. There are a few dull patches, however, largely due to the fact that Donaldson can't bear to speak ill of the put-upon. SH DVD
Sissy Spacek *Marie Ragghianti* • Jeff Daniels *Eddie Sisk* • Keith Szarabajka *Kevin McCormack* • Don Hood *Governor Ray Blanton* • Morgan Freeman *Charles Traughber* • Lisa Banes *Toni Greer* ■ *Dir* Roger Donaldson • *Scr* John Briley, from the book by Peter Maas

Marie Antoinette ★★★★
Biographical romantic epic
1938 · US · Sepia · 160min

This highly romanticised version of the life of France's most famous queen is, in a word, sumptuous. An Oscar-nominated Norma Shearer takes the title role, dazzlingly dressed by Adrian and lovingly photographed by William Daniels under the direction of WS Van Dyke II. Robert Morley (also Oscar-nominated) plays her husband, Tyrone Power is her self-sacrificing lover, Joseph Schildkraut makes a devious Duke of Orleans and Gladys George is the infamous Madame DuBarry. This is MGM at its most extravagant. RK
Norma Shearer *Marie Antoinette* • Tyrone Power *Count Axel de Fersen* • John Barrymore *King Louis XV* • Gladys George *Mme DuBarry* • Robert Morley *King Louis XVI* • Anita Louise *Princess DeLamballe* • Joseph Schildkraut *Duke of Orleans* • Henry Stephenson *Count Mercey* ■ *Dir* WS Van Dyke II [WS Van Dyke], Julien Duvivier • *Scr* Claudine West, Donald Ogden Stewart, Ernest Vajda, F Scott Fitzgerald, from the book by Stefan Zweig

Marie Antoinette ★★★
Biographical drama
1956 · Fr · Colour · 120min

Tracing Marie Antoinette's life from her leave of Austria, through her affair with a dashing ambassador, to her dignified appearance before the Revolutionary Tribunal, this is markedly less melodramatic than the Norma Shearer vehicle. Filmed simultaneously in French and English, Jean Delannoy's lavish biopic is strong on period detail, but, just as Michèle Morgan's regality errs towards coldness, so the screenplay tends dryly towards the academic. DP
Michèle Morgan *Marie Antoinette* • Richard Todd *Count Axel De Fresen* • Jacques Morel *Louis XVI* • Aimé Clariond *Louis XV* • Jeanne Boitel *Madame Campan* • Guy Tréjan *Lafayette* • Marina Berti *Comtesse de Polignac* • Madeleine Rousset *Madame de Tourzel* ■ *Dir* Jean Delannoy • *Scr* Jean Delannoy, Bernard Zimmer, Philippe Erlanger

Marie Antoinette ★★★ 12
Biographical historical drama
2005 · US/Fr/Jpn · Colour · 117min

Think Valley Girl in 18th-century dress and you'll have some idea of director Sofia Coppola's modernist take on the infamous "Let them eat cake" royal. Although based on Antonia Fraser's respected biography, hard fact gives way to a "Queens just want to have fun" superficial portrait of the feisty Austrian princess (a coquettish Kirsten Dunst) as she heads to Versailles to marry the shy dauphin (a blank Jason Schwartzman). Ravishing to look at, but its frothy, clumsy charm eventually wears thin. AJ DVD
Kirsten Dunst *Marie Antoinette* • Jason Schwartzman *Louis XVI* • Judy Davis *Comtesse de Noailles* • Rip Torn *Louis XV* • Asia Argento *Comtesse du Barry* • Shirley Henderson *Aunt Sophie* • Marianne Faithfull *Maria Teresa* • Steve Coogan *Ambassador Mercy* • Aurore Clément *Duchesse de Chartres* ■ *Dir* Sofia Coppola • *Scr* Sofia Coppola, from the biography *Marie Antoinette: The Journey* by Antonia Fraser

Marie Galante ★★ PG
Spy adventure
1934 · US · BW · 84min

Cinematographer John F Seitz's mastery of moody atmosphere gives this pulp novel adaptation some unmerited class. The project was intended to showcase the talents of French import Ketti Gallian, as a kidnap victim who becomes embroiled in a plot to sabotage the Panama Canal. However, she's upstaged at every turn by Spencer Tracy as the pugnacious secret agent who falls for her charms. The supporting cast is unfussily proficient, but wisecracking adventure clearly isn't director Henry King's forte. DP DVD
Spencer Tracy *Crawbett* • Ketti Gallian *Marie Galante* • Ned Sparks *Plosser* • Helen Morgan (1) *Tapia* • Sig Rumann [Sig Ruman] *Brogard* • Leslie Fenton *Tenoki* • AS Byron [Arthur Byron] *General Phillips* ■ *Dir* Henry King • *Scr* Reginald Berkeley, from a novel by Jacques Deval

Les Mariés de l'An Deux ★★★
Period adventure
1971 · Fr · Colour · 98min

Jean-Paul Rappeneau likened this rousing costume adventure to a collaboration between Mozart and bullish Hollywood director Raoul Walsh. Certainly, there's plenty of Walsh brio about the proceedings, which see anti-royalist Jean-Paul Belmondo return from New World exile to revolutionary France to secure the divorce he needs to marry an American heiress. He's soon entangled in the schemes of his duplicitous wife Marlène Jobert. Smartly satirising period politics, this keeps the action light and furious. DP French dubbed.
DVD Blu-ray
Jean-Paul Belmondo *Nicolas* • Marlène Jobert *Charlotte* • Laura Antonelli *Pauline* • Michel Auclair *Prince* • Sami Frey *Marquis* • Pierre Brasseur *Gosselin* ■ *Dir* Jean-Paul Rappeneau • *Scr* Daniel Boulanger, Jean-Paul Rappeneau, Claude Sautet, Maurice Clavel

Marigold ★★★ PG
Romantic musical comedy
2007 · US/Ind/UK · Colour · 107min

In a bid to resurrect his career, the irrepressible and often controversial Salman Khan teams up with *Heroes* star Ali Larter in an honest attempt at an east-west comedy crossover. Larter plays self-centred Hollywood actress Marigold Lexton who travels to India for stardom, but soon finds herself cast in a traditional Bollywood musical and falling for charismatic choreographer Prem (Khan). There's a refreshing lack of cynicism here, and director Willard Carroll's bemusement with the kitscher side of Bollywood is also strongly reflected in several colourful musical interludes and some sumptuous visuals. OA In English, Hindi. DVD
Salman Khan *Prem* • Ali Larter *Marigold Lexton* • Vikas Bhalla *Raj* • Simone Singh *Shazia* • Suchitra Pillai *Rani* • Vijendra Ghatge [Vijayendra Ghatge] *Mahendra* ■ *Dir/Scr* Willard Carroll

Marilyn ★★
Crime drama
1953 · UK · BW · 69min

Having already been unofficially adapted by Luchino Visconti as *Ossessione* (1942), James M Cain's hard-boiled novel *The Postman Always Rings Twice* was apparently plundered again for this bleak British B-movie. It's a solid enough study in lust, despair and avarice, with Sandra Dorne oozing cynical sensuality as the unhappy wife whose liaison with mechanic Maxwell Reed leads to the death of her grouchy, garage-owning husband Leslie Dwyer. DP
Sandra Dorne *Marilyn Saunders* • Leslie Dwyer *George Saunders* • Maxwell Reed *Tom Price* • Vida Hope *Rosie* • Ferdy Mayne *Nicky Everton* • Kenneth Connor *Customer* ■ *Dir/Scr* Wolf Rilla

Marilyn Hotchkiss Ballroom Dancing & Charm School ★★★ 12
Romantic comedy drama
2005 · US · Colour · 92min

This expanded version of writer/director Randall Miller's 1990 short is a shameless feel-good movie, blessed with a warm-hearted script and a talented ensemble cast. Widower Frank (Robert Carlyle) is delivering bread when he encounters car-crash victim Steve (John Goodman). The dying man was on his way to keep a 40-year-old promise to meet up with his childhood sweetheart at the eponymous ballroom dancing school, so he enlists Frank to go in his place. On his quest, this good samaritan meets one-legged shrinking violet Meredith (Marisa Tomei), and he is soon waltzing his way back to happiness. The tale is cloying, but never nauseating, which is enough to make up for the dramatic missteps. JR DVD
Robert Carlyle *Frank Keane* • Marisa Tomei *Meredith Morrison* • John Goodman *Steve Mills* • Mary Steenburgen *Marienne Hotchkiss* • Sean Astin *Kip Kipling* • Donnie Wahlberg *Randall Ipswitch* • David Paymer *Rafael Horowitz* • Danny DeVito *Booth* ■ *Dir* Randall Miller • *Scr* Randall Miller, Jody Savin, from the short film by Miller

Marine Raiders ★★
Second World War drama
1944 · US · BW · 90min

This Second World War adventure salutes the marines who trained and then fought for the island of Guadalcanal in the South Pacific. Filmed in pseudo-documentary style, it takes a handful of marines, led by blokeish Pat O'Brien, and plonks them down in California for basic training before showing how they fare in battle. Australia serves as a halfway house, where there's time for romance for Robert Ryan and Ruth Hussey. AT
Robert Ryan *Capt Dan Craig* • Pat O'Brien *Major Steve Lockhard* • Ruth Hussey *Ellen Foster* • Frank McHugh *Sgt Louis Leary* • Barton MacLane *Sgt Maguire* • Richard Martin (1) *Jimmy* • Edmund Glover *Miller* ■ *Dir* Harold Schuster • *Scr* Warren Duff, from a story by Warren Duff, Martin Rackin

Marius ★★★★
Drama
1931 · Fr · BW · 125min

Alexander Korda directed *Marius* in France, written and produced by Marcel Pagnol. Rich in depth of characterisation and exquisitely played, it launched the famous Marseille trilogy that continued with *Fanny* (1932), and *César* (1936). Throughout, the same actors play the principal roles: blunt but lovable café owner César (Raimu); his son Marius (Pierre Fresnay); Fanny, Marius' sweetheart (Orane Demazis); and elderly widower Panisse (Fernand Charpin). Establishing the relationships for what is to come, Marius here pursues his dream of going to sea and joins the merchant navy, unknowingly leaving Fanny pregnant with their child. RK French +subtitles.
Pierre Fresnay *Marius* • Orane Demazis *Fanny* • Raimu *César* • Alida Rouffe *Honorine* • Fernand Charpin *Panisse* • Paul Dullac *Escartefigue* ■ *Dir* Alexander Korda • *Scr* Marcel Pagnol, from his play

Marius ★★★★ 12A
Drama
2012 · Fr · Colour · 93min

Marcel Pagnol's Marseille trilogy gets a fresh celluloid revamp thanks to actor-director Daniel Auteuil, who re-creates the city's old port in the 1930s to unfurl a tale of love, longing and the call of the sea. Old-fashioned this might be, but the material itself remains utterly charming, as barman's son Marius (Raphaël Personnaz) dreams of adventure while secretly carrying a torch for Fanny (Victoire Bélézy), the girl at the shellfish stall. This hugely enjoyable combination of Mediterranean sun and wise humanity closes with a cliff-hanger, compelling you to see the simultaneously released second instalment, *Fanny*. TJ French +subtitles. Sexual references, brief nudity.
Daniel Auteuil *César* • Raphaël Personnaz *Marius* • Jean-Pierre Darroussin *Panisse* • Victoire Bélézy *Fanny* • Marie-Anne Chazel *Honorine* • Nicolas Vaude *M Brun* ■ *Dir* Daniel Auteuil • *Scr* Daniel Auteuil, from the play by Marcel Pagnol • *Music* Alexandre Desplat

Marius et Jeannette ★★★★ 15
Romantic comedy drama
1997 · Fr · Colour · 97min

Set in a Marseille backwater, this kitchen sink romance resembles both Marcel Pagnol's famous *Marius* trilogy and the poetic realist films of Vigo, Renoir and René Clair. Soft-centred spitfire Ariane Ascaride is superb as the single mum struggling to provide for her kids and make sense of her relationship with taciturn nightwatchman Gérard Meylan. Touching on everything from the failure of communism to the overlapping doctrines of Christianity and Islam, this bristling pageant is observed with a keen eye by underrated director Robert Guédiguian. DP French +subtitles. Swearing, nudity.
Ariane Ascaride *Jeannette* • Gérard Meylan *Marius* • Pascale Roberts *Caroline* • Jacques Boudet *Justin* • Frédérique Bonnal *Monique* • Pierre Banderet *M Ebrard* ■ *Dir* Robert Guédiguian • *Scr* Robert Guédiguian, Jean-Louis Milesi

Marjorie Morningstar ★★★ U
Drama
1958 · US · Colour · 122min

Natalie Wood stars as a New York Jewish princess with unconventional ambitions who falls for the supposed glamour of showbusiness, as represented by the producer of a summer stock theatrical company, played by Gene Kelly. Irving Rapper's film underplays the sex and Jewish angles and ends up as a rather bland "woman's picture", though Wood is very good and Kelly is fine in a non-musical role. RK

Natalie Wood *Marjorie* • Gene Kelly *Noel Airman* • Claire Trevor *Rose* • Carolyn Jones *Marsha* • Ed Wynn *Uncle Samson* • Everett Sloane *Arnold* • Martin Milner *Wally* • Martin Balsam *Dr David Harris* ■ *Dir* Irving Rapper • *Scr* Everett Freeman, from the novel by Herman Wouk

The Mark ★★★ 15
Crime drama 1961 · UK · BW · 121min

An apparently reformed paedophile starts a relationship with a young widow who has a little daughter. Things begin to unravel, however, when the press start taking an interest in his new life. Pitched as a rather sentimentalised melodrama, this is still an unusually frank and adult treatment of a serious topic, set in Britain but performed by two major Hollywood stars: an Oscar-nominated Stuart Whitman and Rod Steiger, who plays the hero's psychiatrist. AT *DVD*

Maria Schell *Mrs Ruth Leighton* • Stuart Whitman *Jim Fuller* • Rod Steiger *Dr Edmund McNally* • Brenda de Banzie *Mrs Cartwright* • Donald Houston *Austin, reporter* • Donald Wolfit *Mr Clive* ■ *Dir* Guy Green • *Scr* Sidney Buchman, Stanley Mann, from the novel by Charles Israel

The Mark of Cain ★★ PG
Period crime drama 1947 · UK · BW · 84min

This morose melodrama never wrestles free of its penny-dreadful origins. One reason for this is the heavy-handed direction of Brian Desmond Hurst. But, primarily, there's simply no spark between the leads. Distraught that her French manners don't appeal to bluff northern industrialist Patrick Holt, Sally Gray seeks advice from brother-in-law, Eric Portman. However, he's got plans for her himself, although they don't involve being charged with her husband's murder. DP

Sally Gray *Sarah Bonheur* • Eric Portman *Richrad Howard* • Patrick Holt *John Howard* • Dermot Walsh *Jerome Thorn* • Denis O'Dea *Sir William Godfrey* • Edward Lexy *Lord Rochford* ■ *Dir* Brian Desmond Hurst • *Scr* Christianna Brand, Francis Crowdy, WP Lipscomb, from the novel *Airing in a Closed Carriage* by Joseph Shearing

Mark of the Devil ★★ 18
Horror 1970 · W Ger/UK · Colour · 96min

The plot of this notorious "sex and sadism" shocker revolves around witchfinder Herbert Lom and assistant Udo Kier, who falls in love with a suspected witch. But Michael Armstrong's film is essentially a succession of graphically violent scenes "justified" by spurious historical references. When the film was released in the US, cinema patrons were issued with sick bags and the result was a huge box office success (and a sequel in 1972). DM German dubbed. *DVD* *Blu-ray*

Herbert Lom *Count Cumberland* • Olivera Vuco *Vanessa* • Udo Kier *Christian* • Reggie Nalder *Albino* • Herbert Fux *Chief executioner* ■ *Dir* Michael Armstrong • *Scr* Sergio Casstner [Michael Armstrong], Percy Parker [Adrian Hoven]

Mark of the Phoenix ★ U
Thriller 1957 · UK · BW · 77min

This dismal low-budget thriller has a corkscrew plot involving rare metals, jewel thieves, international blackmail, the Cold War and much else. Made in 1957, it was shelved for two years until a suitably worthy main feature was found to accompany it. The mediocre cast is typical of British B-movies of the period, with the sole exception of Anton Diffring. AT

Julia Arnall *Petra* • Sheldon Lawrence *Chuck Martin* • Anton Diffring *Inspector Schell* • Eric Pohlmann *Duser* • George Margo *Emilson* • Michael Peake *Koos* • Martin Miller *Brunet* ■ *Dir* Maclean Rogers • *Scr* Norman Hudis, from a story by Desmond Cory

Mark of the Vampire ★★★
Horror 1935 · US · BW · 60min

Bela Lugosi is on chilling form in this stylish horror from Tod Browning. It's a remake of Browning's own silent classic *London after Midnight*. Lionel Barrymore is the vampire hunter, and his over-the-top performance prompted critics to acclaim the film as an astute parody. Carol Borland looks bemused as Lugosi's accomplice, which is hardly surprising since her part had been slashed after the censors detected references to incest. DP

Bela Lugosi *Count Mora* • Lionel Barrymore *Professor Zelen* • Lionel Atwill *Inspector Neumann* • Elizabeth Allan *Irena Borotyn* • Holmes Herbert *Sir Karell Borotyn* • Jean Hersholt *Baron Otto Von Zinden* • Carol Borland *Luna Mora* • Dona d Meek *Dr Doskil* ■ *Dir* Tod Browning • *Scr* Guy Endore, Bernard Schubert

The Mark of Zorro ★★★
Silent swashbuckling adventure
1920 · US · BW · 89min

Don Diego Vega is a sort of American-Mexican Scarlet Pimpernel who leads a double life as Zorro, a masked avenger and expert swordsman, waging war on tyranny. Combining adventure with a dash of romance and comedy, the film gave Douglas Fairbanks the first of the swashbuckling roles that earned him immortality. Directed by Fred Niblo, it co-stars Marguerite De La Motte as the woman who has no time for Don Diego, but is in love with Zorro. Fairbanks returned as Zorro in 1925's *Don Q, Son of Zorro*. RK

Douglas Fairbanks *Don Diego Vega/Señor Zorro* • Noah Beery *Sergeant Pedro* • Charles Hill Mailes *Don Carlos Pulido* • Claire McDowell *Don Catalina, his wife* • Marguerite De La Motte *Lolita* • Robert McKim *Captain Juan Ramon* ■ *Dir* Fred Niblo • *Scr* Eugene Miller, from the short story *The Curse of Capistrano* by Johnston McCulley

The Mark of Zorro ★★★★ U
Swashbuckling adventure
1940 · US · BW · 89min

This wonderful, definitive adaptation of the great romantic legend stars matinée idol Tyrone Power as the swashbuckling Don Diego Vega, alias the masked avenger known as Zorro. Amazingly, Power is the equal (well, almost) of predecessor Douglas Fairbanks Sr in this lavish black-and-white 20th Century-Fox spectacular. Basil Rathbone makes a superb villain, and the swordfights are terrific. For schoolboys of all ages. TS *DVD*

Tyrone Power *Don Diego Vega* • Linda Darnell *Lolita Quintero* • Basil Rathbone *Captain Esteban Pasquale* • Gale Sondergaard *Inez Quintero* • Eugene Pallette *Fra Felipe* • J Edward Bromberg *Don Luis Quintero* • Montagu Love *Don Alejandro Vega* • Janet Beecher *Senora Isabella Vega* ■ *Dir* Rouben Mamculian • *Scr* John Tainton Foote, Garrett Fort, Bess Meredyth, from the novel *The Curse of Capistrano* by Johnston McCulley

The Mark of Zorro ★★
Swashbuckling adventure
1974 · US · Colour · 78min

Frank Langella parries and thrusts to good effect in the title role in this TV movie, although his adversary, Ricardo Montalban, is much more fun to watch. A young Anne Archer does little but look demure, while veterans Gilbert Roland and Yvonne De Carlo ham it up a treat. DP

Frank Langella *Don Diego/Zorro* • Ricardo Montalban *Captain Esteban* • Gilbert Roland *Don Alejandro Vega* • Yvonne De Carlo *Isabella Vega* • Louise Sorel *Inez Quintero* • Robert Middleton *Don Luis Quinterc* • Anne Archer *Teresa* ■ *Dir* Don McDouga l • *Scr* Brian Taggert, from the novel *The Curse of Capistrano* by Johnston McCulley

Marked for Death ★★★ 18
Action thriller 1990 · US · Colour · 89min

Steven Seagal plays a former Drug Enforcement Agency operative who gets involved in a war between local drug dealers and Jamaican Yardies when he "retires" to his home town of Chicago. Basil Wallace is wildly over the top as the bizarrely named Yardie leader Screwface,

and female leads Joanna Pacula and Elizabeth Gracen are given little to do. But the action sequences are superbly choreographed and it's efficiently directed by Dwight H Little. JF Violence, nudity, swearing, drug abuse. *DVD*

Steven Seagal *John Hatcher* • Basil Wallace *Screwface* • Keith David *Max* • Tom Wright *Charles* • Joanna Pacula *Leslie* • Elizabeth Gracen *Melissa* • Bette Ford *Kate Hatcher* • Danielle Harris *Tracey* ■ *Dir* Dwight H Little • *Scr* Michael Grias, Mark Victor

Marked Woman ★★★★ PG
Crime drama 1937 · US · BW · 91min

This terrific Warner Bros crime exposé melodrama is based on the real-life case of a group of prostitutes testifying against their gangland boss. No punches are pulled in this taut dramatisation, which stars Bette Davis as a battered victim of the hoodlum, and Humphrey Bogart on the right side of the law as a crusading attorney. Neither star had yet found their respective trademark style, but both display a compulsively watchable dynamic presence. Eduardo Ciannelli is particularly persuasive as the slimy hood, and the screenplay is surprisingly explicit. TS

Bette Davis *Mary Dwight* • Humphrey Bogart *David Graham* • Jane Bryan *Betty Strauber* • Eduardo Ciannelli *Johnny Vanning* • Isabel Jewell *Emmy Lou Egan* • Allen Jenkins *Louie* • Mayo Methot *Estelle Porter* • Lola Lane *Gabby Marvin* ■ *Dir* Lloyd Bacon • *Scr* Robert Rossen, Abem Finkel, Seton I Miller

Marlene ★★★ PG
Biographical documentary
1984 · W Ger · Colour and BW · 92min

A mesmerising documentary from actor/director Maximilian Schell about the legendary Marlene Dietrich, this is based on a series of tape-recorded interviews. She wouldn't let him point the camera at her, but had no objection to the sound rolling. Although the image is necessarily blunted, Dietrich's comments are utterly revelatory, and Schell utilises film clips and archive material to flesh out his unseen subject. The style palls after a while, but this is still essential viewing for film students and quite unmissable for fans. TS In English, German. *DVD*

Marlene Dietrich • Maximilian Schell ■ *Dir* Maximilian Schell • *Scr* Maximilian Schell, Meir Dohnal

Marley ★★★ 15
Music documentary
2012 · US/UK · Colour · 139min

Reggae superstar Bob Marley died of cancer at the age of 36 in 1981, but his legend lives on through his music and iconic image. After several false starts with other directors, the Marley family approved Kevin Macdonald's approach, which traces the story using carefully selected archive footage and interviews. Running to nearly two and a half hours, it's a simple, leisurely look at the Jamaican musician and celebrity who could quell riots by his very presence. This feel-good primer is sure to bring his music to a new audience. KK Drug abuse. *Blu-ray*

Bob Marley • Rita Marley • Neville "Bunny Wailer" Livingston • David "Ziggy" Marley [Ziggy Marley] *David "Ziggy" Marley* • Cedella Marley • Jimmy Cliff ■ *Dir* Kevin Macdonald

Marley & Me ★★★ PG
Comedy drama based on a true story
2008 · US · Colour · 110min

The antics of Marley, a misbehaving labrador, provide the comic impetus for this appealing tale from David Frankel (*The Devil Wears Prada*). Owen Wilson plays real-life journalist John Grogan, who moves to Florida with his wife (Jennifer Aniston), where he ends up acquiring a dog and penning a column about his life with a four-legged force-of-nature. The movie version of Grogan's book wins us over early on with lots of cute canine naughtiness, but the focus is just as much on the ups and downs of the Grogans' marriage. Inevitably, the lifestyle depicted here is a little idealised,

but the film's approach is more grown-up than you'd expect. A prequel was made in 2011, *Marley & Me: the Puppy Years*, but with no Jen or Owen. TJ *DVD* *Blu-ray*

Owen Wilson *John Grogan* • Jennifer Aniston *Jenny Grogan* • Eric Dane *Sebastian* • Kathleen Turner *Ms Kornblut* • Alan Arkin *Arnie Klein* • Nathan Gamble *Patrick, aged 10* • Haley Bennett *Lisa* ■ *Dir* David Frankel • *Scr* Scott Frank, Don Roos, from memoirs by John Grogan

Marlowe ★★★
Mystery thriller 1969 · US · Colour · 95min

Raymond Chandler always preferred Dick Powell to Humphrey Bogart as his great private eye, but had he been alive he may well have liked James Garner's quizzical, slightly bemused charm. Taking on a missing persons case, chivalrous Marlowe tries to track down Sharon Farrell's brother. Bruce Lee, in his first American movie, makes a big impression as the heavy. TH Drug abuse.

James Garner *Philip Marlowe* • Gayle Hunnicutt *Mavis Wald* • Carroll O'Connor *Lt Christy French* • Rita Moreno *Dolores Gonzales* • Sharon Farrell *Orfamay Quest* • William Daniels (2) *Mr Crowell* • HM Wynant *Sonny Steelgrave* • Jackie Coogan *Grant W Hicks* • Bruce Lee *Winslow Wong* ■ *Dir* Paul Bogart • *Scr* Sterling Silliphant, from the novel *The Little Sister* by Raymond Chandler

Marmaduke ★★★ U
Comedy 2010 · US · Colour · 84min

Great dane Marmaduke talks the talk in this effects-assisted family frolic, which uses clever lip-synching to illustrate the dog's conversational skills. Along with his owners, the galumphing hound attempts to adjust to moving from Kansas to California where dad (Lee Pace) has started working for a pet-food tycoon (William H Macy). The movie's real purpose is keeping younger viewers happy with lots of furry mischief, but Owen Wilson's witty voiceover will have the grown-ups smiling. TJ *DVD* *Blu-ray*

Owen Wilson *Marmaduke* • Lee Pace *Phil Winslow* • Judy Greer *Debbie Winslow* • William H Macy *Don Twombly* • Emma Stone *Mazie* • Sam Elliott *Chupadogra* • Fergie *[Stacy Ferguson] Jezebel* • Kiefer Sutherland *Bosco* • Steve Coogan *Raisin* • David Walliams *Anton Harrison* ■ *Dir* Tom Dey • *Scr* Tim Rasmussen, Vince Di Meglio, from the comic book by Brad Anderson, Phil Leeming

Marnie ★★★★ 15
Psychological drama 1964 · US · Colour · 130min

Rumours abounded that Grace Kelly would be making a comeback before this adaptation of Winston Graham's novel went into production. Her icy aloofness would have been perfect for the tale of kleptomania, frigidity, fetishism and suppressed anxiety, and Tippi Hedren was considered no substitute by contemporary critics. Hindsight has established this as one of Hitchcock's more fascinating "misfires". Some of the conspicuously artificial set design and back projection may not suit all tastes, but watch for Robert Burks's suave colour photography and the mental duel between a man (Sean Connery) turned on by crime and a woman who steals to forget. DP *DVD* *Blu-ray*

"Tippi" Hedren [Tippi Hedren] *Marnie Edgar* • Sean Connery *Mark Rutland* • Diane Baker *Lil Mainwaring* • Martin Gabel *Sidney Strutt* • Louise Latham *Bernice Edgar* • Bob Sweeney *Cousin Bob* • Milton Selzer *Man at the track* • Alan Napier *Mr Rutland* • Mariette Hartley *Susan Clabon* • Bruce Dern *Sailor* • S John Launer *Sam Ward* ■ *Dir* Alfred Hitchcock • *Scr* Jay Presson Allen, from the novel by Winston Graham.

Maroc 7 ★★
Crime drama 1966 · UK · Colour · 91min

The heavily insured legs of Cyd Charisse are on display in this lacklustre crime caper about an international jewel thief and a priceless medallion, with a support cast that includes such acting luminaries as Elsa Martinelli and Leslie Phillips. One of those misfires that makes you wonder why someone in the production line didn't cry out "Stop, abandon ship". SH

Gene Barry *Simon Grant* • Elsa Martinelli *Claudia* • Cyd Charisse *Louise Henderson* • Leslie Phillips *Raymond Lowe* • Denholm Elliott *Inspector Barrada* • Alexandra Stewart *Michele Craig* ■ *Dir* Gerry O'Hara • *Scr* David Osborn, from his story

Marooned ★★★ U

Science-fiction adventure
1969 · US · Colour · 123min

Winner of the Oscar for best special visual effects, this astute blend of science fact and fiction eerily anticipated the kind of lost-in-space crisis that would actually occur during the *Apollo 13* mission. Gene Hackman, Richard Crenna and James Franciscus successfully combine public confidence with private misgivings as the stranded crew, while Gregory Peck heads the Nasa operation with typical reserve. Director John Sturges makes the most of his space hardware but never gets the domestic drama off the ground, with Lee Grant and the other wives being reduced to mere cardboard cutouts. DP *DVD*

Gregory Peck *Charles Keith* • Richard Crenna *Jim Pruett* • David Janssen *Ted Dougherty* • James Franciscus *Clayton Stone* • Gene Hackman *Buzz Lloyd* • Lee Grant *Celia Pruett* • Nancy Kovack *Teresa Stone* • Mariette Hartley *Betty Lloyd* ■ *Dir* John Sturges • *Scr* Mayo Simon, from the novel by Martin Caidin • *Special Effects* Lawrence Butler, Donald C Glouner, Robie Robinson

Marquis ★★★ 18

Satirical historical fantasy
1989 · Bel/Fr · Colour · 79min

It's hard to know whether to applaud this for its sheer audacity or to decry its many misfiring ideas. Certainly, director Henri Xhonneux and his designer Roland Topor can't be accused of taking a traditional approach to the Marquis de Sade's last days in the Bastille, as scenes from his books are presented as claymation diversions, while their much-maligned author spends most of the time in conversation with his penis, a human-faced member named Colin. All the cast wear symbolic animal heads, while the dialogue could have come from a bawdy pantomime. DP French +subtitles.

François Marthouret *Marquis/Dog* • Valérie Kling *Colin/Colin's Sex* • Michel Robin *Ambert/Rat* • Isabelle Canet-Wolfe *Justine/Cow* ■ *Dir* Henri Xhonneux • *Scr* Roland Topor, Henry Xhonneux, from the novel *Justine* by the Marquis de Sade

The Marquise of O ★★★★ PG

Period drama   1976 · W Ger/Fr · Colour · 98min

One of Eric Rohmer's extremely rare departures from France and the present, this elegant version of Heinrich von Kleist's classic novella is set during the Franco-Prussian War. A virtuous widow is drugged, then raped by an officer in the invading Russian army. When she finds herself pregnant, she marries the man, not realising it was he who raped her. Rohmer seems perfectly at ease with the ironic nuances of the delicate story; he and his cinematographer Nestor Almendros were inspired by German Romantic painters and bathe the interiors in an unearthly light. RB German +subtitles. *DVD*

Edith Clever *Marquise* • Bruno Ganz *Count* • Peter Lühr *Marquise's father* • Edda Seippel *Marquise's mother* • Otto Sander *Marquise's brother* • Ruth Drexel *Midwife* ■ *Dir* Eric Rohmer • *Scr* Eric Rohmer, from a novella by Heinrich von Kleist

The Marriage Circle ★★★★★

Silent comedy   1924 · US · BW · 90min

The first, and perhaps best, of the six silent films Ernst Lubitsch made at Warner Bros in his first years in Hollywood is a daring and sophisticated comedy of manners. Set in Vienna, the scenario (by Paul Bern, later married to Jean Harlow) tells of the intricate intrigues between two married couples and their suspicions of infidelity, both justified and unjustified. What distinguishes the "Lubitsch touch" is the way he works by suggestion rather than direct statement, coupled with casually significant close-ups of objects. The playing, notably by Florence Vidor (recently separated from director King Vidor), Marie

Prevost and Adolphe Menjou, is particularly subtle. RB

Florence Vidor *Charlotte Braun* • Monte Blue *Dr Franz Braun* • Marie Prevost *Mizzie Stock* • Creighton Hale *Dr Gustav Mueller* • Adolphe Menjou *Prof Josef Stock* ■ *Dir* Ernst Lubitsch • *Scr* Paul Bern, from the play *Nur ein Traum, Lustspiel in 3 Akten (Only a Dream)* by Lothar Schmidt [Lothar Goldschmidt]

The Marriage-Go-Round ★★

Romantic comedy   1960 · US · Colour · 98min

The marriage of James Mason and Susan Hayward is upset when Swedish beauty Julie Newmar comes to stay. Newmar decides that the brains of brilliant anthropology professor Mason, combined with her physical attributes, would make for the perfect child. In adapting his play for the screen, Leslie Stevens mislays the laugh quotient, resulting in a faintly embarrassing comedy that falls flat on its face. Hayward is terrific, however. RK

Susan Hayward *Content Delville* • James Mason *Paul Delville* • Julie Newmar *Katrin Sveg* • Robert Paige *Dr Ross Barnett* • Jane Clayworth *Flo Granger* • Joe Kirkwood Jr *Henry* • Mary Patton *Mamie* ■ *Dir* Walter Lang • *Scr* Leslie Stevens, from his play

Marriage Is a Private Affair ★★★

Romantic comedy   1944 · US · BW · 116min

A spoilt but insecure New York beauty (Lana Turner), fearful of following in the footsteps of her shallow, much-married mother, makes a hasty wartime marriage to a stuffed-shirt air force officer (John Hodiak) and has a baby. Tempted to commit infidelity with an old flame (James Craig), she finally grows up and finds herself. Under Robert Z Leonard's direction, the inexperienced Turner does well in this intelligent drama, slightly marred by extraneous and silly excesses. RK

Lana Turner *Theo Scofield West* • James Craig *Captain Miles Lancing* • John Hodiak *Lieutenant Tom West* • Frances Gifford *Sissy Mortimer* • Hugh Marlowe *Joseph I Murdock* • Keenan Wynn *Major Bob Wilton* ■ *Dir* Robert Z Leonard • *Scr* David Hertz, Lenore Coffee, from the novel by Judith Kelly

Marriage – Italian Style ★★ 12

Comedy drama   1964 · Fr/It · Colour · 95min

Businessman Marcello Mastroianni hires a prostitute to double as his live-in lover and his aged mother's nursemaid. Years later, she traps him into marriage by pretending she's terminally ill; in fact, she's hiding three children, one of whom may be Mastroianni's. Male chauvinist pigs may admire Mastroianni's behaviour, while feminists will revel in Loren's sly scheming. Few will laugh, though. AT In Italian. *DVD*

Sophia Loren *Filomena Marturano* • Marcello Mastroianni *Domenico Soriano* • Aldo Puglisi *Alfredo* • Tecla Scarano *Rosalie* • Marilu Tolo *Diane* ■ *Dir* Vittorio De Sica • *Scr* Eduardo De Filippo, Renato Castellani, Tonino Guerra, Leo Benvenuti, Piero De Bernardi, from the play *Filumena Marturano* by Eduardo De Filippo

The Marriage of Maria Braun ★★★★ 15

Romantic drama   1978 · W Ger · Colour · 115min

Hanna Schygulla won the best actress prize at Berlin for her work in Rainer Werner Fassbinder's most avowedly commercial film. This owes much to the glossy 1950s melodramas of Douglas Sirk and works just as well as soap opera as socio-political treatise. The choices Maria makes to survive during her husband's prolonged absences clearly reflect those made by Germany in the post-Hitler era, and Fassbinder evidently disapproves of Maria's (and the nation's) notion of paradise postponed. Accessible, yet also complex and ambiguous. DP German, English +subtitles. *DVD*

Hanna Schygulla *Maria Braun* • Klaus Löwitsch *Hermann Braun* • Ivan Desny *Karl Oswald* • Gottfried John *Willi Klenze* ■ *Dir* Rainer Werner

Fassbinder • *Scr* Peter Marthesheimer, Pea Fröhlich, Rainer Werner Fassbinder, from a story by Rainer Werner Fassbinder

Marriage on the Rocks ★★ PG

Comedy   1965 · US · Colour · 104min

This unfunny and tasteless farrago looks like an attempt by Frank Sinatra and Dean Martin to have a holiday on location in Mexico away from fellow clan members, while dragging along an awkwardly cast Deborah Kerr. There's a moderately entertaining turn from Cesar Romero, plus a motley collection of supporting players including Sinatra's daughter Nancy. Beautifully photographed by Garbo's cameraman William H Daniels, it's not entirely without interest either, but it's surprisingly underdirected by one-time dance supremo Jack Donohue. TS *DVD*

Frank Sinatra *Dan Edwards* • Deborah Kerr *Valerie Edwards* • Dean Martin *Ernie Brewer* • Cesar Romero *Miguel Santos* • Hermione Baddeley *Jeannie MacPherson* • Tony Bill *Jim Blake* • John McGiver *Shad Nathan* • Nancy Sinatra *Tracy Edwards* • Trini Lopez ■ *Dir* Jack Donohue • *Scr* Cy Howard

The Marriage Playground ★★★

Drama   1929 · US · BW · 70min

This was the fourth of five films made in 1929 by the undeservedly neglected German director, Lothar Mendes. Elegantly adapted from an Edith Wharton novel, it also confirmed Broadway actor Fredric March as a Hollywood fixture. As the wealthy American touring Italy, he comes to the rescue of young Mary Brian, who has been left by her pleasure-loving parents (Huntley Gordon and Lilyan Tashman) to care for her siblings. Ben Kingsley starred in the 1990 remake, *The Children*. DP

Fredric March *Martin Boyne* • Mary Brian *Judith Wheater* • Lilyan Tashman *Joyce Wheater* • Huntley Gordon *Cliffe Wheater* • Kay Francis *Zinnia La Crosse* ■ *Dir* Lothar Mendes • *Scr* J Walter Ruben, Doris Anderson, from the novel *The Children* by Edith Wharton

Married Life ★★ PG

Romantic crime drama
2007 · US/Can · Colour · 87min

In this drama of tangled relationships set at the end of the 1940s, Pierce Brosnan plays Richard, a ladies' man with a dull best friend called Harry (Chris Cooper, delivering a customarily subtle characterisation). Harry is supposedly blissfully married to Pat (Patricia Clarkson), but has fallen head over heels for the younger Kay (Rachel McAdams). When Richard is introduced to Kay, he finds himself smitten, too. Intended as a homage to 40s melodramas, it has little sense of period and occasionally teeters on the brink of farce. Worse still is Brosnan's infuriating voice-over narration that explains what's already on screen, presumably for the hard of thinking. BP *DVD*

Pierce Brosnan *Richard Langley* • Chris Cooper *Harry Allen* • Patricia Clarkson *Pat Allen* • Rachel McAdams *Kay* • David Wenham *John O'Brien* ■ *Dir* Ira Sachs • *Scr* Ira Sachs, Oren Moverman, from the novel *Five Roundabouts to Heaven* by John Bingham

Married to the Mob ★★★★ 15

Comedy thriller   1988 · US · Colour · 99min

Michelle Pfeiffer proves she's a deft hand at light-hearted fare in Jonathan Demme's gangster comedy thriller. She plays the widow of mobster Alec Baldwin, who decides to make a new life for herself and her child, but doesn't allow for the attentions of crime boss Dean Stockwell and the FBI's Matthew Modine. The cast is superb – especially Mercedes Ruehl in over-the-top mode as Stockwell's brassy, jealous wife – and Demme keeps both the action and the laughs perfectly tuned. JB Swearing, violence, nudity. *DVD*

Michelle Pfeiffer *Angela De Marco* • Matthew Modine *Mike Downey* • Dean Stockwell *Tony "The Tiger" Russo* • Alec Baldwin *Frank "The*

Cucumber" De Marco • Mercedes Ruehl *Connie Russo* • Joan Cusack *Rose Boyle* ■ *Dir* Jonathan Demme • *Scr* Barry Strugatz, Mark R Burns

Married/Unmarried ★★ 18

Drama   2001 · UK/US/Aus · Colour · 98min

Already an established director, Noli demonstrates an edgy flair for cinema in his directorial debut. His use of colour and close-up are admirable, but he fails to create the intimacy that the frank sexual actions and revelations of two bed-hopping couples require. Ben Daniels's brutal humiliation of lover Kristen McMenamy always feels self-consciously shocking, while his mistress Gina Bellman's crisis-riven marriage to Paolo Seganti seems blissfully dull by comparison. DP Swearing. *DVD*

Paolo Seganti *Paul* • Ben Daniels *Danny* • Gina Bellman *Amanda* • Kristen McMenamy *Kim* • Denis Lavant *Love* • Lidija Zovkic *Tania* ■ *Dir* Noli • *Scr* Noli, from his play

The Married Woman ★★★★ 15

Drama   1964 · Fr · BW · 91min

Jean-Luc Godard's movie gained immediate notoriety for its sex scenes – the director shoots intertwined legs, arms and bodies in artful close-up – and no less a personage than General De Gaulle objected to the morality of its heroine. Macha Méril is married to a pilot, has an affair with an actor and seems to fill her head with glamorous images from magazines. As with all Godard movies, this is like a scrapbook of bits and pieces that, glued together, reveal the impact of the consumer society. AT French +subtitles. *DVD* *BL*

Macha Méril *Charlotte Giraud* • Bernard Noël *Robert, the lover* • Philippe Leroy *Pierre, the husband* • Roger Leenhardt • Rita Maiden *Madame Celine* ■ *Dir/Scr* Jean-Luc Godard

Marry Me Again ★★★

Comedy   1953 · US · BW · 73min

Writer/director Frank Tashlin's cartooning experience intermittently livens up this tame satire in which garage hand Robert Cummings leaves blonde scatterbrain Marie Wilson at the altar to become a Korean War hero, then won't marry her because she's inherited a fortune. Tashlin, who married supporting player Mary Costa at the end of shooting, has mild fun with nutty psychiatrists, empty shoes and the vogue for 3D movies, but it's a far cry from his best work. AE

Robert Cummings *Bill* • Marie Wilson *Doris* • Ray Walker *Mac* • Mary Costa *Joan* • Jess Barker *Jenkins* • Lloyd Corrigan *Mr Taylor* • June Vincent *Miss Craig* • Richard Gaines *Dr Pepperdine* ■ *Dir* Frank Tashlin • *Scr* Frank Tashlin, from a story by Alex Gottlieb

Marry Me! Marry Me! ★★★

Comedy drama   1968 · Fr · Colour · 89min

Years before his tragic rural masterpieces, *Jean de Florette* and *Manon des Sources* (both 1986), writer/producer/director Claude Berri allowed himself a little levity about this inconsequential trifle about Parisienne love and marriage. Berri stars as an encyclopedia salesman wavering between two women. Airy, but nicely ventilated. TH In French.

Claude Berri *Claude* • Elisabeth Wiener *Isabelle Schmoll* • Luisa Colpeyn *Louisa Colpeyn/ Madame Schmoll* • Grégoire Aslan *Monsieur Schmoll* • Régine *Marthe Schmoll* ■ *Dir/Scr* Claude Berri

The Marrying Kind ★★★★

Comedy drama   1952 · US · BW · 92min

A post office worker (Aldo Ray) and his ex-secretary wife (Judy Holliday) are on the brink of divorce. As they tell their story to an understanding judge (one-time silent screen star Madge Kennedy), we watch their relationship in flashback, from first meeting through marriage and children. Well directed by George Cukor, this is a perfect vehicle for the quirky, brilliant Holliday. Overlaid with incisive wit and beautifully played by both stars, this combination of domestic drama and comedy is a winner all the way. RK

Judy Holliday *Florence Keefer* • Aldo Ray *Chet Keefer* • Madge Kennedy *Judge Carroll* • Sheila Bond *Joan Shipley* • John Alexander (1) *Howard Shipley* • Rex Williams *George Bastian* • Phyllis Povah *Mrs Derringer* • Peggy Cass *Emily Bundy* ■ *Dir* George Cukor • *Scr* Ruth Gordon, Garson Kanin

Mars Attacks! ★★★★ 12
Satirical science fiction comedy
1996 · US · Colour · 101min

Little green men from the angry red planet launch a flying-saucer attack on Earth in director Tim Burton's slow-starting space oddity, based on a bubble-gum card storyline from the 1960s. In both a tribute to and a spoof of 1950s B-movies, Burton stumbles as many times as he succeeds in playing with the back catalogue of lurid pulp sci-fi references. But once the computer-generated bug-eyed Martians arrive and strut their evil stuff, this daffy *Independence Day* lampoon comes alive. Among an amazing roster of stars, Pierce Brosnan is hilarious as a presidential adviser and Lisa Marie is weirdly creepy as a disguised alien temptress. AJ DVD

Jack Nicholson *President James Dale/Art Land* • Glenn Close *Marsha Dale* • Annette Bening *Barbara Land* • Pierce Brosnan *Donald Kessler* • Danny DeVito *Rude gambler* • Martin Short *Jerry Ross* • Sarah Jessica Parker *Nathalie Lake* • Michael J Fox *Jason Stone* • Rod Steiger *General Decker* • Tom Jones • Lisa Marie *Martian girl* • *Dir* Tim Burton • *Scr* Jonathan Gems, from his story, from the illustrated card series by the Topps Company

Mars Needs Moms ★★ PG
Animated science-fiction comedy
2011 · US · Colour · 84min

Mars may need moms, but does Earth need this movie? Because, by Disney's high standards, this animated sci-fi comedy is distinctly charmless. Disciplinarian moms are being whipped away to Mars to "control" Martian mites. Toss into the motion-captured mix Earth kid Milo (Seth Green) who wants his mom (Joan Cusack) back, a couple of cute robo-bots, and an "astronut" buddy who's creepy, but not in a good way, and you have an OK piece of kids entertainment, but not one that is likely to be added to the pantheon of Disney classics. DA Some violence. DVD 3D

Seth Green *Milo* • Joan Cusack *Mom* • Elisabeth Harnois *Ki* • Dan Fogler *Gribble* • Mindy Sterling *The supervisor* • Kevin Cahoon *Wingnut* ■ *Dir* Simon Wells • *Scr* Simon Wells, Wendy Wells, from the illustrated children's book by Berkeley Breathed

La Marseillaise ★★★ PG
Historical drama
1938 · Fr · BW · 125min

Sponsored by the trades union movement, this is the "official" film of the French Revolution. It's not one of Renoir's greatest films: he seems torn between the need to make a big populist epic and his own instinct to produce a humane document, in which both the doomed aristocracy and the revolting peasantry are accorded a sympathetic hearing. Thus the king has toothache and worries about his wig; the approaching army has foot sores; and, when the national anthem is first heard, someone says how awful it is. AT French +subtitles. DVD

Pierre Renoir *Louis XVI* • Lise Delamare *Marie Antoinette* • Léon Larive *Picard* • William Aguet *La Rochefoucauld-Liancourt* • Louis Jouvet *Roederer* ■ *Dir* Jean Renoir • *Scr* Jean Renoir, Carl Koch, N Martel Dreyfus, Mme Jean-Paul Dreyfus

The Marseille Contract ★★ 15
Thriller
1974 · UK/Fr · Colour · 87min

Despite an endearing performance from Michael Caine as a hitman, this carefree slice of mayhem involving drug smuggling, an assassination attempt and executive double-crosses never quite gets into top gear. Only the presence of Anthony Quinn and James Mason, along with some eye-catching Paris and Marseille locations, adds

any interest to the stereotypical characters and familiar plot. TH

Michael Caine *Deray* • Anthony Quinn *Steve Ventura* • James Mason *Brizard* • Maureen Kerwin *Lucianne* • Marcel Bozzuffi *Calmet* • Catherine Rouvel *Erizard's mistress* • Maurice Ronet *Inspector Briac* • André Oumansky *Marsac* • Alexandra Stewart *Rita* ■ *Dir* Robert Parrish • *Scr* Judd Bernard, from his story *What Are Friends For?*

The Marsh ★★ 15
Horror thriller
2006 · Can · Colour · 88min

In this cheesy, by-the-numbers ghost story, nightmare-plagued children's writer Gabrielle Anwar rents a haunted farmhouse that predictably holds the secret to her past. Cue a catalogue of fright-flick clichés: heightened sound, false jolts and a sinister score filling in for genuine scares. Think sub-Stephen King meets *Stir of Echoes* and you'll guess exactly what's going on. Forest Whitaker puts the rest of the twitchy supporting cast to shame, playing an investigator who helps Anwar. SF Swearing. DVD

Gabrielle Anwar *Claire Holloway* • Forest Whitaker *Geoffrey Hunt* • Justin Louis *Noah Pitney* • Niamh Wilson *Little Claire/Rose* ■ *Dir* Jordon Barker • *Scr* Michael Stokes

Marshland ★★★★ 15
Crime thriller
2014 · Sp · Colour · 101min

This is a grim, atmospheric and thrillingly well-made slice of Euro noir. Raúl Arévalo is a police detective sent to the dense, poverty-stricken marshlands of Spain's deep south, where he slowly unearths a horrific cluster of murders of young women. Pleasing echoes of classic Hollywood police tales – *Chinatown*, *Blood Simple* – abound, and the cast is uniformly excellent, the pitch-perfect performances and sharply realised locale rendering this unmissable thriller as dense and sinister as its setting. AS Spanish +subtitles. DVD

Raúl Arévalo *Pedro* • Javier Gutiérrez *Juan* • Antonio de la Torre *Rodrigo* • Nerea Barros *Rocío* ■ *Dir* Alberto Rodríguez • *Scr* Alberto Rodríguez, Rafael Cobos

Martha ★★★ 15
Thriller
1973 · W Ger · Colour · 111min

Rainer Werner Fassbinder laid waste the "woman's picture" with this highly stylised study of the dark desires that lurk behind even the most respectable façades. Sunny, naturalistic compositions take on unexpectedly sinister aspects, as Karlheinz Böhm dominates and then destroys Margit Carstensen, the 30-something virgin whose yearning for romance contributes to her own downfall. Littering the Hollywood-style melodrama with Freudian dream symbols and allusions to Germany's fascist past, Fassbinder also encourages a florid performance from Carstensen. DP German +subtitles.

Margit Carstensen *Martha* • Karlheinz Böhm *Helmut Salomon* • Barbara Valentin *Marianne* • Peter Chatel *Kaiser* • Gisela Fackeldey *Mother* ■ *Dir/Scr* Rainer Werner Fassbinder

Martha and I ★★★★
Period drama
1990 · W Ger/It/Fr · Colour · 106min

Set on the eve of the Second World War, this is a moving and unforced plea for tolerance. Defying conventional wisdom about class, race and physical appearance, Michel Piccoli marries the family's portly maid (Marianne Sägebrecht) and finds a contentment that young Ondrej Vetchy immediately appreciates when he is sent to stay with his uncle by his haughty parents in the hope that he will be cured of a similar obsession. DP German +subtitles.

Marianne Sägebrecht *Martha* • Michel Piccoli *Dr Ernst Fuchs* • Vaclav Chalupa *Emil as a teenager* • Ondrej Vetchy *Emil as an adult* ■ *Dir/Scr* Jiri Weiss

Martha Marcy May Marlene ★★★★ 15
Mystery drama
2011 · US · Colour · 97min

Questions of identity, love and loyalty are at the heart of writer/director Sean Durkin's haunting mystery drama. Martha (Elizabeth Olsen) comes to stay with her sister Lucy (Sarah Paulson) and posh British husband (Hugh Dancy), but seems strangely unable to cope with normal life. That's because she has just escaped after two years with a cult, where charismatic leader John Hawkes named her Marcy May. But will he let her go that easily? Olsen is simply mesmerising, perfectly capturing the brainwashed Martha's disorientation and conflicting emotions. The rest of the cast is equally impressive, in particular Hawkes as the manipulative, Svengali-like cult leader. It's an intelligent, hypnotic and compelling film. LB Swearing, sex scenes. DVD Blu

Elizabeth Olsen *Martha* • Sarah Paulson *Lucy* • Hugh Dancy *Ted* • John Hawkes *Patrick* • Brady Corbet *Watts* • Maria Dizzia *Katie* ■ *Dir/Scr* Sean Durkin

Martha – Meet Frank, Daniel and Laurence ★★★ 15
Romantic comedy drama
1997 · UK · Colour · 83min

Three hapless British chaps (Rufus Sewell, Joseph Fiennes and Tom Hollander) fall for gorgeous American Monica Potter when she arrives in London hoping to start a new life. There's the odd rough patch, but the witty script uses coincidence as a springboard for plot, and shows that a British movie can be both romantic and funny. Potter is an adept comedian, and, despite its dreadful title, this deserves attention. SR Swearing. DVD

Monica Potter *Martha* • Rufus Sewell *Frank* • Tom Hollander *Daniel* • Joseph Fiennes *Laurence* • Ray Winstone *Pedersen* ■ *Dir* Nick Hamm • *Scr* Peter Morgan (1)

The Martian ★★★★ 12
Science-fiction drama
2015 · US · Colour · 141min

Life on Mars requires ingenuity and a keen sense of humour if Ridley Scott's film is anything to go by. An Oscar-nominated Matt Damon is the astronaut left for dead who must make do and mend on the Red Planet, accompanied only by disco records belonging to his commanding officer (Jessica Chastain). There are few dark moments in a survival story that went on to win a Golden Globe in the best comedy/musical category– Damon lives by his wits and trades on witticisms to get by, as he cheerfully sets his mind to growing potatoes and re-opening lines of communication – and the use of "real science" adds a fascinating dimension to the story. SP Swearing. DVD Blu

Matt Damon *Mark Watney* • Jessica Chastain *Melissa Lewis* • Kristen Wiig *Annie Montrose* • Jeff Daniels *Teddy Sanders* • Michael Peña [Michael Pena] *Rick Martinez* • Kate Mara *Beth Johanssen* • Sean Bean *Mitch Henderson* ■ *Dir* Ridley Scott • *Scr* Drew Goddard, from Andy Weir's novel • *Editor* Pietro Scalia • *Production Designer* Arthur Max

Martin ★★★★ 18
Horror
1978 · US · Colour and BW · 90min

Is teenager John Amplas a sexually repressed oddball with a Dracula fixation, or an octogenarian kept youthful by blood? George A Romero doesn't give the game away easily, instead telling his highly intelligent story with overdoses of atmosphere, gore and jet-black humour. The film also features a splendid central performance from Amplas, who stalks suburbia killing frenziedly with razor blades instead of the traditional fangs. Not everyone's cup of tea (or blood), this is well worth a look for horror addicts with a craving for the offbeat. RS DVD

John Amplas *Martin* • Lincoln Maazel *Tati Cuda* • Christine Forrest *Christina* • Elayne Nadeau *Mrs Santini* • Tom Savini *Arthur* • George A Romero *Father Howard* ■ *Dir/Scr* George A Romero

Martin and Lewis ★★
Biographical comedy drama
2002 · US · Colour · 92min

The questionable casting of Sean Hayes (*Will & Grace*) opposite clipped Brit Jeremy Northam undermines this TV biopic of the legendary comedy double-act, Jerry Lewis and Dean Martin. Northam occasionally catches Dino's laid-back approach, but Hayes singularly fails to re-create the madcap schtick that made Lewis the entertainment king of France. DP

Jeremy Northam *Dean Martin* • Sean Hayes *Jerry Lewis* • Paula Cale *Betty Martin* • Sarah Manninen *Patti Lewis* • Kate Levering *Jeanne Martin* ■ *Dir* John Gray • *Scr* John Gray, from the biography *Everybody Loves Somebody Sometime* by Arthur Marx

Martin Roumagnac ★★
Crime drama
1946 · Fr · BW · 88min

Directed by Georges Lacombe, this French drama concerns an affair between Jean Gabin, a provincial builder, and Marlene Dietrich, a sophisticated new arrival from the city for whom he is building a house. On discovering that she is a high-class whore, Gabin murders her. The potentially erotic pairing of Dietrich and Gabin promises much. Sadly, it delivers little more than a run-of-the-mill courtroom drama, with the story of the affair told in flashback. RK

Marlene Dietrich *Blanche Ferrand* • Jean Gabin *Martin Roumagnac* • Margo Lion *Martin's sister* • Marcel Herrand *Consul* • Jean d'Yd *Blanche's uncle* ■ *Dir* Georges Lacombe • *Scr* Pierre Véry, from a novel by Pierre-René Wolf

The Martins ★★★ 15
Black comedy drama
2001 · UK · Colour · 83min

Crassly sold as a knockabout comedy, this fares better if approached as a tragic drama about social exclusion. The eponymous family are Hatfield's "neighbours from hell": unemployable dad, pregnant 14-year-old daughter, et al. It is to the credit of writer/first-time director Tony Grounds that these apparent undesirables elicit such sympathy. A nicely understated Lee Evans loves Kathy Burke and both would do anything for their family. This stretches to armed robbery, and thus we have the film's essentially comedic, runaway plot. But this is sad rather than hilarious, and richer for it. AC DVD

Lee Evans *Robert Martin* • Kathy Burke *Angie Martin* • Linda Bassett *Anthea* • Frank Finlay *Mr Heath* • Ray Winstone *Mr Marvel* • Lorraine Ashbourne *Lil* • Barbara Leigh-Hunt *Mrs Heath* ■ *Dir/Scr* Tony Grounds

Martin's Day ★★ 15
Drama
1984 · Can · Colour · 94min

This Canadian drama managed to attract a notable cast (Richard Harris, Linday Wagner, James Coburn, Karen Black) but little attention. Director Alan Gibson struggles with the emotionally driven material, which revolves around an escaped convict and his adventures with his young hostage, and he doesn't manage to get even half the performance out of Justin Henry that Robert Benton did in *Kramer vs Kramer*. NF

Richard Harris *Martin Steckert* • Lindsay Wagner *Dr Mennen* • James Coburn *Lieutenant Lardner* • Justin Henry *Martin* • Karen Black *Karen* • John Ireland *Brewer* ■ *Dir* Alan Gibson • *Scr* Allan Scott, Chris Bryant

Marty ★★★★★ U
Romantic drama
1955 · US · BW · 88min

Beginning life as a TV drama, Paddy Chayefsky's slice-of-life tale became part of the fabric of the 1950s and won Oscars for best picture, Delbert Mann's direction, Chayefsky's marvellous screenplay and Ernest Borgnine's performance. Audiences used to seeing Borgnine in more menacing roles in films warmed to his sympathetic portrayal of the Bronx butcher with low self-esteem. Equally good is Betsy Blair as the vulnerable schoolteacher Marty falls in love with. This moving film was a major triumph for its uncredited co-producer Burt

Lancaster, who, allegedly, made it as a tax loss. TS *DVD*

Ernest Borgnine *Marty* • Betsy Blair *Clara* • Esther Minciotti *Mrs Pilletti* • Joe Mantell *Angie* • Augusta Ciolli *Catherine* • Karen Steele *Virginia* • Jerry Paris *Thomas* • Frank Sutton *Ralph* ■ *Dir* Delbert Mann • *Scr* Paddy Chayefsky, from his TV play

Martyrs ★★★★ 18
Horror   2008 • Fr/Can • Colour • 95min

Few horror movies rock the genre in such a contentiously divisive way as this disturbingly violent film from French writer/director Pascal Laugier. It tells of the twisted revenge taken by psychologically devastated Lucie (Mylène Jampanoï) on a family she's convinced constantly abused her and kept her captive in her youth. But as her best friend Anna (Morjana Alaoui) finds out, the truth is a far more complex proposition. Veering through *Switchblade Romance* and *Hellraiser* territory for a harshly surreal and often repulsive experience, Laugier's visceral audacity will for many be overpoweringly shocking. Yet as unpredictably nasty as it gets, there is a stark controversial point to the strangely beautiful excess as well as an astonishingly profound conclusion. AJ French +subtitles. Violence. *DVD*

Morjana Alaoui *Anna* • Mylène Jampanoï *Lucie* • Catherine Bégin *Mademoiselle* • Robert Toupin *Father* • Patricia Tulasne *Mother* ■ *Dir/Scr* Pascal Laugier

Martyrs ★★ 18
Horror thriller   2015 • US • Colour • 82min

A groundbreaking French horror film is hacked to pieces and given a Hollywood sheen in this pointless "re-imagining". They over-explain the backstory, de-claw the visceral, hardcore shocks and radically change the controversial plot. A decade after escaping kidnappers who tortured her, Troian Bellisario sets out to find her abductors. This is nothing less than a trashy desecration of a masterpiece. AJ Strong violence

Troian Bellisario *Lucie* • Bailey Noble *Anna* • Kate Burton *Eleanor* • Caitlin Carmichael *Sam* • Melissa Tracy *The Creature* ■ *Dir* Kevin Goetz, Michael Goetz • *Scr* Mark L Smith, from characters by Pascal Laugier

Marvel Avengers Assemble ★★★★★ 12
Action fantasy adventure
2012 • US • Colour • 137min

The storyline that's underpinned Marvel Comics adaptations since *Iron Man* (2008) reaches big-screen fruition with this hugely entertaining superhero epic from writer/director Joss Whedon. Iron Man, Thor, Captain America, the Hulk, Black Widow and Hawkeye are brought together in a cosmos-spanning adventure, and Whedon immediately unleashes the action as rogue Asgardian god Loki (Tom Hiddleston) infiltrates spy agency Shield to help an alien race invade Earth. Samuel L Jackson's SHIELD boss Nick Fury mobilises this bickering team of heroes, and the result is a city-wrecking slugfest that puts the bombastic *Transformers* franchise in the shade. But what raises this escapade above the merely awesome is a script brimming with snappy, laugh-out-loud banter and moments, and evident chemistry between the principals, who all get their moment in the sun. A sequel again directed by Whedon is due in 2015. JA Some violence, swearing. *DVD* *Blu-ray* *CS*

Robert Downey Jr *Tony Stark/Iron Man* • Samuel L Jackson *Nick Fury* • Mark Ruffalo *Bruce Banner/Hulk* • Chris Evans *Steve Rogers/Captain America* • Chris Hemsworth *Thor* • Scarlett Johansson *Natasha Romanoff/Black Widow* • Jeremy Renner *Clint Barton/Hawkeye* • Tom Hiddleston *Loki* • Jenny Agutter *Council member* • Gwyneth Paltrow *Pepper Potts* • Stellan Skarsgård *Professor Erik Selvig* • Harry Dean Stanton *Security guard* • Powers Boothe *Council member* • Stan Lee • Jerzy Skolimowski *Georgi Luchkov* ■ *Dir* Joss Whedon • *Scr* Joss Whedon, from a story by Whedon, Zak Penn • *Cinematographer* Seamus McGarvey

Marvin and Tige ★
Drama   1983 • US • Colour • 104min

John Cassavetes stars as a middle-aged dropout reduced to earning a little cash by collecting the deposits on discarded bottles. For company he ties up with 11-year-old Gibran Brown, a street urchin whom he saves from committing suicide. Working like one of the corniest, most manipulative products of the Depression era, this eminently missable tear-jerker has a banality that is hard to top. AT

John Cassavetes *Marvin Stewart* • Billy Dee Williams *Richard Davis* • Denise Nicholas-Hill [Denise Nicholas] *Vanessa Jackson* • Gibran Brown *Tige Jackson* • Fay Hauser *Brenda Davis* ■ *Dir* Eric Weston • *Scr* Wanda Dell, Eric Weston, from a novel by Frankcina Glass

Marvin's Room ★★★★ 12
Drama   1996 • US • Colour • 94min

Based on the play by Scott McPherson, who adapted his work for the screen, this character-driven tale benefits from restrained and impressive performances. Diane Keaton plays a carer who has been looking after her bedridden father for years, but who is forced to ask her estranged sister, Meryl Streep, for help after she is told she has leukaemia. To complicate family relations further, Streep arrives with her two sons, Hal Scardino and Leonardo DiCaprio. Keaton was nominated for an Oscar for her portrayal of the proud spinster battling a debilitating disease, but kudos should go to the entire cast. JB Swearing. *DVD*

Meryl Streep *Lee* • Leonardo DiCaprio *Hank* • Diane Keaton *Bessie* • Robert De Niro *Dr Wally* • Hume Cronyn *Marvin* • Gwen Verdon *Ruth* • Hal Scardino *Charlie* • Dan Hedaya *Bob* ■ *Dir* Jerry Zaks • *Scr* Scott McPherson, from his play

Mary and Max ★★★★ 12
Animated comedy drama
2008 • Aus • BW and Colour • 88min

The first full-length animated feature from Australian director Adam Elliot (an Oscar winner for his short *Harvie Krumpet*) is a dark yet poignant account of the pen-pal friendship that develops between a shy Melbourne girl and a grumpy middle-aged man from New York. It's lovingly rendered in traditional claymation with a voice cast led by Toni Collette as the grown-up girl and Philip Seymour Hoffman as her Asperger's-suffering correspondent. Listen out, too, for Eric Bana and Barry Humphries, who narrates. Note, however, that the melancholy story isn't really suitable for children. JF In English, Yiddish. Suicide references, drug abuse. *DVD*

Toni Collette *Mary Daisy Dinkle* • Philip Seymour Hoffman *Max* • Jerry Horowitz • Eric Bana *Damian Cyril Popodopolous* • Barry Humphries *Narrator* • Bethany Whitmore *Young Mary* ■ *Dir/Scr* Adam Elliot

Mary Higgins Clark's Let Me Call You Sweetheart ★★★ 12
Murder mystery   1997 • US • Colour • 88min

A sinister plastic surgeon and a long-closed murder case lie at the heart of this convoluted but surprisingly effective TV thriller from the pen of Mary Higgins Clark. Attorney Meredith Baxter's pursuit of the "Sweetheart Killer" isn't without its clichés, however, as she falls headlong for her sidekick, Victor Garber, and risks her boss's political future by delving into the trial on which her reputation is based. But the doppelganger aspect of the plot is decidedly creepy, as are Baxter's nightmares. DP *DVD*

Meredith Baxter *DA Kerry McGrath* • Sophie Lang *Robin McGrath* • Tony LoBianco *Dr Charles Smith* • Victor Garber *Geoff Dorso* • Nick Mancuso *Bob Kinellen* ■ *Dir* Bill Corcoran • *Scr* Christopher Lofton, from the novel by Mary Higgins Clark

Mary Higgins Clark's Pretend You Don't See Her ★★ PG
Thriller   2002 • US/UK/Can • Colour • 90min

Emma Samms over-emotes her way through this undemanding thriller, playing a Manhattan real estate agent who's forced to relocate after witnessing a client's murder. Though based on author Mary Higgins Clark's bestselling suspense novel, the film is atmospherically barren, lacking any form of tension or indeed realism. Events unfold like a poorly written soap opera, with forgettable supporting performances only emphasising the cardboard characters and unnatural dialogue. SF

Emma Samms *Lacey Farrell* • Hannes Jaenicke *Curtis Caldwell Blake* • Beau Starr *Detective Ed Sloan* • Stewart Bick *Ken Lynch* • Russell Paul Batty *Darren Marinkovitch* • Laura Press *Chantal Greco* • Reiner Schöne *Jimmy Greco* ■ *Dir* René Bonnière • *Scr* Donald Hounam, from the novel by Mary Higgins Clark

Mary Higgins Clark's The Cradle Will Fall ★★ 12
Mystery thriller   2004 • US • Colour • 89min

Doubtless, Mary Higgins Clark fans will settle into this Rob King-directed adaptation with ready expectation. Yet there's a by-the-numbers feel about the story of a plucky lawyer whose overnight stay in hospital convinces her that a doctor with a reputation for curing infertility is up to no good. The sequence in which a drugged Angie Everhart thinks she sees a woman's body being bundled into a car is eerily done, but the character interaction lacks suspense. DP *DVD*

Angie Everhart *Katie DeMaio* • John Ralston *Dr Edgar Highley* • Philippe Brenninkmeyer *Dr Richard Carroll* • William B Davis *District Attorney Alex Myerson* • Alan C Peterson *Detective Charley Newkirk* • Stephen Spender *Chris Lewis* • Carol Higgins Clark *Molly* ■ *Dir* Rob W King • *Scr* John Benjamin Martin, from the novel by Mary Higgins Clark

Mary Higgins Clark's Try to Remember ★★ 15
Crime mystery   2004 • US • Colour • 89min

Mary Higgins Clark's books may not be the most demanding whodunnits ever committed to print, but they certainly rattle along and this adaptation of one of her mysteries is no exception – although fans of *Silent Witness* may feel it's a tad trite. Gabrielle Anwar is credible enough, playing the forensics expert who's trying to find out why the witnesses to her best friend's murder 15 years earlier are being methodically bumped off (including her own mother). Sadly, the twist in the tale will hardly come as a surprise. DP *DVD*

Gabrielle Anwar *Lisa Monroe* • Max Martini *Joe* • Gary Chalk *Stuart Kling* • Diego Wallraff *Jake Mitchell* • David Richmond-Peck *Benny Thomason* • Kevin Foley *Unseen man* • Gerald Lenton-Young *Fred Rand* ■ *Dir* Jeff Beesley • *Scr* Jeff Martel, John Benjamin Martin, from the novel by Mary Higgins Clark

Mary Higgins Clark's We'll Meet Again ★★ 12
Mystery   2002 • Can • Colour • 90min

Baywatch's Brandy Ledford and *Melrose Place*'s Laura Leighton join forces in this proficient but wholly predictable adaptation of Mary Higgins Clark's whodunnit. Paroled after serving six years for murdering her wealthy husband, Ledford calls on school pal Leighton to help prove her innocence. Devoid of intrigue and racked by contrivance, this is one for the author's fans only. DP *DVD*

Laura Leighton *Fran Simmons* • Brandy Ledford *Molly Lasch* • Gedeon Burkhard *Dr Peter Gaines* • Andrew Jackson *Nick Whitehall* • Anne Openshaw *Jenna Whitehall* ■ *Dir* Michael Storey • *Scr* Michael Thoma, John Benjamin Martin, from the novel by Mary Higgins Clark

Mary, Mary ★★
Comedy   1963 • US • Colour • 126min

This rather dour comedy is based on the play by Jean Kerr (whose own life was filmed as *Please Don't Eat the Daisies*) about a divorced couple bent on destroying each other's future happiness. Brash Debbie Reynolds is miscast, and the men in her life – amiable Barry Nelson and gaunt Michael Rennie – are colourless. Director Mervyn LeRoy fails to disguise the theatrical origins. TS

Debbie Reynolds *Mary McKellaway* • Barry Nelson *Bob McKellaway* • Michael Rennie *Dirk Winston* • Diane McBain *Tiffany Richards* • Hiram Sherman *Oscar Nelson* ■ *Dir* Mervyn LeRoy • *Scr* Richard Breen [Richard L Breen], from the play *Mary, Mary* by Jean Kerr

Mary of Scotland ★★★ U
Historical drama   1936 • US • BW • 118min

Despite sterling work by Katharine Hepburn in the title role, and moody, shadowy photography by the great Joseph H August, director John Ford fails to make this screen version of the Maxwell Anderson play very cinematic. Fredric March (as the Earl of Bothwell) and Mrs Fredric March, Florence Eldridge (as Queen Elizabeth I), are too contemporary and therefore feel miscast, though John Carradine and Donald Crisp – the only member of the cast with a genuine Scottish accent – seem quite at home at court. TS *DVD*

Katharine Hepburn *Mary Stuart* • Fredric March *Bothwell* • Florence Eldridge *Elizabeth Tudor* • Douglas Walton *Darnley* • John Carradine *Rizzio* • Robert Barrat *Morton* • Gavin Muir *Leicester* • Donald Crisp *Huntley* ■ *Dir* John Ford • *Scr* Dudley Nichols, from the play by Maxwell Anderson

Mary Poppins ★★★★★ U
Classic musical fantasy
1964 • US • Colour • 133min

This is easily the best of Disney's experiments in combining animation and live action, and one of the studio's best-loved films. The last feature overseen by Walt Disney before his death, it was nominated for 13 Oscars and scooped five, including best actress for Julie Andrews in her screen debut. She is splendid as the prim nanny who transforms the lives of her young charges through their visits to her charming fantasy world. Quite why Dick Van Dyke was not even nominated for his performance as Bert the chimney sweep remains a mystery, as his energy is one of the picture's main assets (though his cockney accent does leave something to be desired). Packed with unforgettable sequences, adorable cartoon characters and timeless songs, it's quite simply supercalifragilistic-expialidocious. DP *DVD* *Blu-ray*

Julie Andrews *Mary Poppins* • Dick Van Dyke *Bert/Mr Dawes Sr* • David Tomlinson *Mr Banks* • Glynis Johns *Mrs Banks* • Hermione Baddeley *Ellen* • Karen Dotrice *Jane Banks* • Matthew Garber *Michael Banks* • Reta Shaw *Mrs Brill* • Elsa Lanchester *Katie Nanna* • Arthur Treacher *Constable Jones* • Reginald Owen *Admiral Boom* • Ed Wynn *Uncle Albert* • Jane Darwell *Bird woman* ■ *Dir* Robert Stevenson • *Scr* Bill Walsh, Don DaGradi, from the *Mary Poppins* books by PL Travers • *Costume Designer* Tony Walton • *Music/lyrics* Richard M Sherman, Robert B Sherman

Mary, Queen of Scots ★★★★
Historical drama   1971 • UK • Colour • 126min

Here the great Tudor power play is laid out like a richly embroidered carpet with, in the blue corner, Glenda Jackson as Elizabeth I and, in the red corner, Vanessa Redgrave as her deeply principled cousin Mary Stuart. In short, two of Britain's finest actresses shine in tailor-made roles. There are a few liberties taken with historical fact, but who cares? This is a splendid costume drama with the stars ably assisted by the likes of Ian Holm, Nigel Davenport and Trevor Howard. Wonderful stuff. SH *DVD*

Vanessa Redgrave *Mary, Queen of Scots* • Glenda Jackson *Queen Elizabeth I* • Patrick McGoohan *James Stuart* • Timothy Dalton *Henry, Lord Darnley* • Nigel Davenport *Lord Bothwell* • Trevor Howard *William Cecil* • Ian Holm *David Riccio* • Daniel Massey *Robert Dudley, Earl of Leicester* ∎ *Dir* Charles Jarrott • *Scr* John Hale

Mary Reilly ★★★ 15

Psychological horror 1995 · US · Colour · 103min

This is a clever twist on *Dr Jekyll and Mr Hyde*, as seen through the eyes of his housemaid, played by a totally miscast but oddly touching Julia Roberts. As the famous split personality, John Malkovich gives a typical complex and powerful performance. Director Stephen Frears's lavish, black-bricked and gaslit production is satisfying both as a meditation on a literary classic and as an old-fashioned Victorian horror story. But this was a jinxed production, virtually disowned by the studio that financed it. AT *DVD*

Julia Roberts *Mary Reilly* • John Malkovich *Dr Jekyll/Mr Hyde* • George Cole *Mr Poole* • Michael Gambon *Mary's father* • Kathy Staff *Mrs Kent* • Glenn Close *Mrs Farraday* • Michael Sheen *Bradshaw* • Bronagh Gallagher *Annie* ∎ *Dir* Stephen Frears • *Scr* Christopher Hampton, from the novel by Valerie Martin, from the story *The Strange Case of Dr Jekyll and Mr Hyde* by Robert Louis Stevenson

Mary Shelley's Frankenstein ★★ 15

Horror 1994 · US · Colour · 118min

Kenneth Branagh's version of the much-filmed story is as pompous as it is perverse in the way it wastes not only his own talents (as Victor Frankenstein), but also those of Robert De Niro (who boasts a few moving moments as the man-made monster) and Helena Bonham Carter. The creation of the creature is undoubtedly spectacular, but the rest of the movie is not a fraction as frightening nor as funny as the 1931 classic. TH Violence, nudity. *DVD*

Robert De Niro *Creature/Sharp-featured man* • Kenneth Branagh *Victor Frankenstein* • Tom Hulce *Henry* • Helena Bonham Carter *Elizabeth* • Aidan Quinn *Captain Walton* • Ian Holm *Victor's father* • Richard Briers *Grandfather* • John Cleese *Prof Waldman* • Robert Hardy *Prof Krempe* ∎ *Dir* Kenneth Branagh • *Scr* Steph Lady, Frank Darabont, from the novel by Mary Shelley

Maryland ★★★ U

Drama 1940 · US · Colour · 91min

This is one of a seemingly unending series of 20th Century-Fox horse-racing sagas, superbly photographed in breathtaking Technicolor. Veteran director Henry King extracts the maximum drama from an awkward plot about a mother who won't let her son ride because that's how his father died. Vapid John Payne plays the son, but Fay Bainter and Walter Brennan ride out the grimmer moments and prove to be more than a match for the scenery. TS

Walter Brennan *William Stewart* • Fay Bainter *Charlotte Danfield* • Brenda Joyce *Linda* • John Payne *Lee Danfield* • Charles Ruggles *Dick Piper* • Hattie McDanie *Hattie* • Marjorie Weaver *Georgie Tomlin* • Sidney Blackmer *Spencer Danfield* ∎ *Dir* Henry King • *Scr* Ethel Hill, Jack Andrews • *Cinematographers* George Barnes, Ray Rennahan

Masala ★★★ 18

Comedy drama 1991 · Can · Colour · 105min

Srinivas Krishna makes an impressive debut with this deceptively serious study of the problems facing Asians settling in the New World. Besides the black comedy and the pastiches of Bollywood's trademark musical sequences, what gives the film its appeal is the superb characterisation, whether it's Krishna himself as the outsider who scandalises his adoptive family with his attitude to sex and drugs; Zohra Segal, who uses her VCR to communicate with the gods; or Saeed Jaffrey as both Krishna's grasping uncle and the impoverished father of the girl he loves. Quirky, inventive and socially astute. DP

Saeed Jaffrey *Lalu Bhai Solanki/Mr Tikkoo/Lord Krishna* • Zohra Segal *Grandma Tikkoo* • Srinivas Krishna *Krishna* • Sakina Jaffrey *Rita Tikkoo* ∎ *Dir/Scr* Srinivas Krishna

Mascara ★★ 18

Psychological thriller 1987 · Bel/Neth/Fr/US · Colour · 94min

An unabashed exploitation movie, with oodles of sex and swearing, this is about a kinky relationship between a brother and his sister. Charlotte Rampling and Michael Sarrazin star in a film that one suspects doesn't exactly hold pride of place on their respective CVs. Lurid and nasty. DA

Charlotte Rampling *Gaby Hart* • Michael Sarrazin *Bert Sanders* • Derek De Lint *Chris Brine* • Jappe Claes *Colonel March* • Herbert Flack *David Hyde* • *Scr* Hugo Claus, Pierre Drouot, Patrick Conrad, from an idea by Patrick Conrad

Masculine Feminine ★★★ 15

Romantic drama 1966 · Fr/Swe · Colour · 99min

Jean-Pierre Léaud is best known for playing Antoine Doinel, the shambolic but incurable romantic in a series of Truffaut films. In this, his first of many films for Jean-Luc Godard, Léaud plays a more politicised version of the same character: demobbed from the army, dallying with several girls and dabbling with radical politics. Fans at the time hailed this as a vital Godard masterpiece about 1960s youth; others saw it as a self-indulgent mess. AT French +subtitles. *DVD*

Jean-Pierre Léaud *Paul* • Chantal Goya *Madeleine* • Marlène Jobert *Elisabeth* • Michel Debord *Robert* • Catherine-Isabelle Duport [Catherine Duport] *Catherine* • Brigitte Bardot ∎ *Dir* Jean-Luc Godard • *Scr* Jean-Luc Godard, from the short stories *La Femme de Paul* and *Le Signe* by Guy de Maupassant

The Masculine Mystique ★★★

Documentary drama 1984 · Can · Colour · 87min

This intriguing example of docudrama, by Canadian film-makers John N Smith and Giles Walker, has a style and structure that has rarely been pursued since. Four men discuss the impact of women's lib on their attitudes, re-enacting situations to echo those reactions. These days TV does this sort of thing better, and it's easy to dismiss it all as glib. But the intention is sincere, and the technique is skilful, and the witty quartet manage to save the picture from pretentiousness. TH

Stefan Wodoslawsky *Blue* • Char Davies *Amurie* • Sam Grana *Alex* • Eleanor MacKinnon *Shelley* • Mort Ransen *Mort* • Annebet Zwartsenberg *Bet* • Ashley Murray *Ashley* ∎ *Dir* John N Smith, Giles Walker • *Scr* John N Smith, Giles Walker, David Wilson

MASH ★★★★★ 15

Wartime black comedy 1969 · US · Colour · 111min

The quality of Robert Altman's acerbic study of life in a Korean War field hospital has been too often overlooked because of the popularity of the TV series it spawned. It takes a while to get used to Donald Sutherland in the role of Hawkeye that Alan Alda later made his own; similarly, you keep expecting Loretta Swit and not Sally Kellerman to appear whenever "Hot Lips" is mentioned. But the glorious wit of Ring Lardner Jr's Oscar-winning script soon has you under its spell. Altman and Kellerman were both rewarded with Oscar nominations, only to lose out to Franklin J Schaffner and Helen Hayes, while the film lost to *Patton*. DP Swearing, brief nudity. *DVD*

Donald Sutherland *Hawkeye Pierce* • Elliott Gould *Trapper John McIntyre* • Tom Skerritt *Duke Forrest* • Sally Kellerman *Major "Hot Lips" Houlihan* • Robert Duvall *Major Frank Burns* • Jo Ann Pflug *Lieutenant Dish* • René Auberjonois *Dago Red* • Roger Bowen *Colonel Henry Blake* • Gary Burghoff *Radar O'Reilly* ∎ *Dir* Robert Altman • *Scr* Ring Lardner Jr, from the novel by Richard Hooker

Mask ★★★★ 15

Biographical drama 1985 · US · Colour · 114min

This emotional real-life tale features what is perhaps Cher's finest role. She plays the mother of Rocky Dennis (Eric Stoltz), a teenager with a rare bone disease who is trying to cope with his disfigurement and the prospect of imminent death. Peter Bogdanovich's direction shrewdly reveals the strengths and weaknesses of both mother and son as Cher tries to give him the confidence he lacks, encouraging him to follow her example and live life to the full. The end result is both an enormously moving and life-affirming experience. TH Swearing. *DVD*

Cher *Rusty Dennis* • Eric Stoltz *Rocky Dennis* • Sam Elliott *Gar* • Estelle Getty *Evelyn* • Richard Dysart *Abe* • Laura Dern *Diana* • Micole Mercurio *Babe* • Harry Carey Jr *Red* • Dennis Burkley *Dozer* ∎ *Dir* Peter Bogdanovich • *Scr* Anna Hamilton Phelan

The Mask ★★★★★ PG

Fantasy comedy 1994 · US · Colour · 97min

Jim Carrey consolidated his "Ace Ventura" position as America's most successful comedian with this stunning tribute to the zany style of Tex Avery and other Warner Bros animators from the golden age of cartoons. Amazing computer-generated special effects drive this slick showcase for Carrey's explosively unpredictable talents, as he plays a mild-mannered banker who turns into a wild and crazy superhero when he finds a magical ancient mask. Highlights include the Bugs Bunny-style *Cuban Pete* routine, Carrey's pet dog donning the mask and gorgeous Cameron Diaz as the star's love interest. But mainly it's an excuse for Carrey to move with whirlwind speed, pop his eyeballs and swap parts of his anatomy for the cartoon equivalents in hysterically funny and tremendously imaginative ways. AJ *DVD* *Blu-ray*

Jim Carrey *Stanley Ipkiss/The Mask* • Cameron Diaz *Tina Carlyle* • Peter Riegert *Lieutenant Mitch Kellaway* • Peter Greene *Dorian* • Amy Yasbeck *Peggy Brandt* • Richard Jeni *Charlie Schumaker* • Orestes Matacena *Niko* • Timothy Bagley *Irv* ∎ *Dir* Charles Russell [Chuck Russell] • *Scr* Mike Werb, from a story by Michael Fallon, Mark Verheiden

The Mask of Dimitrios ★★★★

Spy drama 1944 · US · BW · 95min

Peter Lorre and Sydney Greenstreet, those beloved character actors best known for *Casablanca* and *The Maltese Falcon*, co-star in this marvellous *film noir*. Terrifically directed by *Johnny Belinda's* Jean Negulesco, it's a scorching adaptation of Eric Ambler's novel that provides a fine example of Warner Bros literacy at work. Dimitrios himself is played by Zachary Scott in his screen debut – his acting ability would later earn him the nickname "The Eyebrow". TS

Sydney Greenstreet *Mr Peters* • Zachary Scott *Dimitrios* • Faye Emerson *Irana Preveza* • Peter Lorre *Cornelius Latimer Leyden* • George Tobias *Fedor Muishkin* ∎ *Dir* Jean Negulesco • *Scr* Frank Gruber, from the novel *A Coffin for Dimitrios* by Eric Ambler

Mask of Dust ★ U

Sports drama 1954 · UK · BW · 74min

Hammer's American partner imposed a Hollywood scriptwriter and sent over not one, but two minor US stars for this cheap action drama. British racing drivers such as Stirling Moss appear as themselves and double for lead Richard Conte and other players in this cliché-ridden tale. The intercut footage of real races shows up the artificiality of the studio work. AE *DVD*

Richard Conte *Peter Wells* • Mari Aldon *Pat Wells* • George Coulouris *Dallapiccola* • Peter Illing *Bellario* • Alec Mango *Guido Rizetti* • Meredith Edwards *Lawrence* • Jimmy Copeland [James Copeland] *Johnny* • Jeremy Hawk *Martin* ∎ *Dir* Terence Fisher • *Scr* Richard Landau, Paul Tabori, from the novel *The Last Race* by Jon Manchip White

The Mask of Fu Manchu ★★★

Horror adventure 1932 · US · BW · 72min

Boris Karloff only played Sax Rohmer's ruthless Asian madman once, but the result is a wonderfully outrageous exercise in campy exotica. Forget the story – something about stealing Genghis Khan's ceremonial mask and sword to take over the world. Just marvel at the fabulous sets and costumes artfully and stylishly employed to disguise the thin content. A death ray, crocodile pits, dungeons and assorted torture devices provide this classic "Yellow Peril" adventure with enough colourful incident to pack an entire 1930s serial. AJ

Boris Karloff *Dr Fu Manchu* • Lewis Stone *Nayland Smith* • Karen Morley *Sheila Barton* • Charles Starrett *Terence Granville* • Myrna Loy *Fah Lo See* • Jean Hersholt *Professor Von Berg* • Lawrence Grant *Sir Lionel Barton* ∎ *Dir* King Vidor, Charles Brabin • *Scr* Irene Kuhn, Edgar Allen Woolf, John Willard, from the novel by Sax Rohmer

The Mask of Satan ★★★★ 15

Horror 1960 · It · BW · 83min

For his directing debut, Italian cinematographer Mario Bava cast British starlet Barbara Steele as the soul-snatching witch Asa and shot the whole grisly tale of vengeance from beyond the grave in stunning black and white. He created an instant horror classic that established his cutting-edge reputation, confirmed over the next two decades. A masterpiece of the macabre, it had censors worldwide up in arms over its still powerful opening torture sequence, in which a mask of nails is hammered onto Steele's screaming face. Steele launched an entire career playing vamps, vampires and victims on the strength of her impact in this atmospheric stunner. AJ Italian dubbed. *DVD* *Blu-ray*

Barbara Steele *Katia/Asa* • John Richardson *Dr Andrej Gorobek* • Ivo Garrani *Prince Vajda* • Andrea Checchi *Dr Kruvajan* • Arturo Dominici *Javutich* • Clara Bindi *Innkeeper* • Enrico Olivieri *Constantine* • Mario Passante *Nikita* ∎ *Dir* Mario Bava • *Scr* Mario Bava, Marcello Coscia, Ennio De Concini, Mario Serandrei, from the story *The Vij* by Nikolay Vasilyevich Gogol [Nikolai Gogol]

The Mask of Zorro ★★★★ PG

Swashbuckling action adventure 1998 · US · Colour · 131min

Zorro may wear a mask, but there's no disguising the fact that this is a splendid swashbuckler. Anthony Hopkins plays the original righter of wrongs who hands over his rapier, and his mission, to a younger man, Antonio Banderas, while Catherine Zeta-Jones, as the fiery heroine, proves she's a match for the men in the action sequences. Director Martin Campbell makes the most of the dramatic swordplay and paces the film perfectly to its explosive conclusion. TH Violence. *DVD* *Blu-ray*

Antonio Banderas *Alejandro Murrieta/Zorro* • Anthony Hopkins *Zorro/Don Diego de la Vega* • Stuart Wilson [1] *Don Rafael Montero* • Catherine Zeta-Jones *Elena* • Matt Letscher *Captain Harrison Love* • Maury Chaykin *Prison warden* • LQ Jones *Three-Fingered Jack* ∎ *Dir* Martin Campbell • *Scr* John Eskow, Ted Elliott, Terry Rossio, from a story by Randall Johnson, from characters by Johnston McCulley

Masked and Anonymous ★ 12

Drama 2003 · US/UK · Colour · 101min

Written by Bob Dylan with director Larry Charles under pseudonyms (hence the title), this a vacuous, self-indulgent mess, set in a futuristic, post-revolutionary America. John Goodman and Jessica Lange play dodgy promoters who spring Dylan's aging rocker from prison to give a charity benefit concert. What follows is the most pretentious ego trip, in which a host of cameoing stars spout his hideously pompous dialogue, while wandering apathetically through the unstructured

M

scenes. A criminal waste of a fantastic cast. SF DVD

Jeff Bridges *Tom Friend* • Penélope Cruz *Pagan Lace* • Bob Dylan *Jack Fate* • John Goodman *Uncle Sweetheart* • Jessica Lange *Nina Veronica* • Luke Wilson *Bobby Cupid* ■ *Dir* Larry Charles • *Scr* Sergei Petrov [Bob Dylan], Rene Fontaine [Larry Charles]

Le Masque de Fer ★★★
Historical swashbuckling adventure
1962 · Fr/It · Colour · 127min

In his efforts to install Louis XIV's identical brother on the throne, D'Artagnan proves invincible with a sword but perilously susceptible to feminine wiles in this rousing adventure. The period trappings and historical characters are just an exotic backdrop against which Jean Marais can demonstrate his dashing athleticism and irresistibility to Claudine Auger and Sylva Koscina. DP In French.

Jean Marais *D'Artagnan* • Jean-François Poron *Louis XIV/Henri* • Germaine Montero *Anne d'Autriche* • Claudine Auger *Isabelle de Saint-Mars* • Jean Rochefort *Lastreaumont* • Jean Davy *Marchal de Turenne* • Sylva Koscina *Marion* ■ *Dir* Henri Decoin • *Scr* Cécil Saint-Laurent, Gerard Devries, from the novel *The Man in the Iron Mask* by Alexandre Dumas

The Masque of the Red Death ★★★★ 15
Horror 1964 · UK/US · Colour · 85min

This is easily the finest of director Roger Corman's Edgar Allan Poe adaptations, with Vincent Price the very essence of evil as the sadistic devil-worshipper trying to keep the plague at bay in 12th-century Italy by indulging in degenerate revels. While there are touches of deliciously wicked humour, the aura of terror comes from the doom-laden tone Corman creates by reaching as much into sombre Ingmar Bergman territory (crimson-cloaked Death stalking through fog-shrouded woods) as atmospheric Hammer shock. AJ DVD

Vincent Price *Prince Prospero* • Hazel Court *Juliana* • Jane Asher *Francesca* • David Weston *Gino* • Patrick Magee *Alfredo* • Nigel Green *Ludovico* ■ *Dir* Roger Corman • *Scr* Charles Beaumont, R Wright Campbell, from the short stories by Edgar Allan Poe • *Cinematographer* Nicolas Roeg

Masquerade ★★ U
Comedy adventure 1965 · UK · Colour · 99min

This slack send-up of British imperialism and James Bondism has Jack Hawkins and Cliff Robertson as British and American agents involved in the kidnapping of an Arab oil sheik. The plot is sometimes impossible to follow, so one is left half-smiling at the familiar turns from the likes of Bill Fraser, John Le Mesurier and Charles Gray. Robertson, who was brought in at the last minute to replace Rex Harrison, enlisted screenwriter William Goldman to rewrite his scenes. AT

Cliff Robertson *David Frazer* • Jack Hawkins *Col Drexel* • Marisa Mell *Sophie* • Michel Piccoli *Sarrasin* • Bill Fraser *Dunwoody* • Charles Gray *Benson* • John Le Mesurier *Sir Robert* ■ *Dir* Basil Dearden • *Scr* Michael Relph, William Goldman, from the novel *Castle Minerva* by Victor Canning

Masquerade ★★ 18
Thriller 1988 · US · Colour · 87min

Director Bob Swaim's misfiring attempt at a Hitchcock-style thriller set among the Long Island yachting fraternity has the advantage of good performances by Rob Lowe and Meg Tilly. Otherwise, it's a rather dumb and violent affair as timid heiress Tilly is married to gigolo Lowe as part of a long-term plot to kill her and get her millions. Sleek boats and beautiful beaches give it the glossy look of a holiday commerical, but out-of-the-blue character changes make it implausible. TH Violence, swearing, sex scenes, nudity. DVD

Rob Lowe *Tim Whalan* • Meg Tilly *Olivia Lawrence* • Kim Cattrall *Brooke Morrison* • Doug Savant *Mike McGill* • John Glover *Tony Gateworth* • Dana Delany *Anne Briscoe* • Erik Holland *Chief of police* • Brian Davies *Granger Morrison* ■ *Dir* Bob Swaim • *Scr* Dick Wolf

The Masquerader ★★★ PG
Drama 1933 · US · BW · 73min

Suave Ronald Colman essays a dual role in a virtual rehearsal for *The Prisoner of Zenda* four years later. He plays a drug-addicted MP who hires his cousin to impersonate him and make a major speech in parliament. Of course, this has a knock-on effect on his love life (can the lovely Elissa Landi tell them apart?) and his conniving butler (brilliant Halliwell Hobbes). Intelligent stuff, though a little creaky. TS

Ronald Colman *Sir John Chilcote/John Loder* • Elissa Landi *Eve Chilcote* • Juliette Compton *Lady Joyce* • Halliwell Hobbes *Brock* • David Torrence *Fraser* • Creighton Hale *Lakely* ■ *Dir* Richard Wallace • *Scr* Howard Estabrook, from the play by John Hunter Booth, from the novel by Katherine Cecil Thurston

Masques ★★★★ 12
Thriller 1987 · Fr · Colour · 96min

The name of Alfred Hitchcock is often bandied around during the discussion of suspense thrillers, but French director Claude Chabrol has consistently demonstrated a near-understanding of the master's style and preoccupations. This isn't Chabrol at his best, but the tale of writer Robin Renucci trying to uncover the guilty secret of game show host Philippe Noiret's country chateau is endlessly entertaining. Flashy, but littered with delicious moments. DP French +subtitles.

Philippe Noiret *Christian Legagneur* • Robin Renucci *Roland Wolf* • Bernadette Lafont *Patricia Marquet* • Monique Chaumette *Colette* • Anne Brochet *Catherine* • Roger Dumas *Manuel Marquet* ■ *Dir* Claude Chabrol • *Scr* Odile Barski, Claude Chabrol

Mass Appeal ★★★ 15
Comedy drama 1984 · US · Colour · 95min

Not quite as funny as *The Apartment*, this is another film comedy with a theatrical feel and Jack Lemmon in the lead. Directed by Glenn Jordan, it's an enjoyable screen adaptation of Bill C Davis's hit Broadway play, in which a live wire theology student (Zeljko Ivanek) challenges an easy-going, affable priest (played by the ever-excellent Lemmon). The picture has appeal, though not necessarily of the mass variety. PF

Jack Lemmon *Father Farley* • Zeljko Ivanek *Mark Dolson* • Charles Durning *Monsignor Burke* • Louise Latham *Margaret* • Alice Hirson *Mrs Hart* • Helene Heigh *Mrs Hart's mother* • Sharee Gregory *Marion Hart* ■ *Dir* Glenn Jordan • *Scr* Bill C Davis, from his play

Massacre in Rome ★ 15
Wartime drama based on a true story
1973 · It/Fr · Colour · 99min

Richard Burton, as the German commandant in Rome, and Marcello Mastroianni, as a priest trying to prevent mass executions, have to gargle with some awful dialogue here. The pace would make a snail itch with impatience, and this was a resounding flop everywhere except Italy. AT Violence, some swearing.

Richard Burton *Col Kappler* • Marcello Mastroianni *Father Pietro Antonelli* • Leo McKern *General Kurt Maelzer* • John Steiner *Colonel Dollmann* • Delia Boccardo *Elena* ■ *Dir* George Pan Cosmatos • *Scr* George Pan Cosmatos, Robert Katz, from the novel *Death in Rome* by Robert Katz

The Master ★★★★ 15
Drama 2012 · US · Colour · 131min

After the oil-rush epic *There Will Be Blood*, writer/director Paul Thomas Anderson conjures another richly evoked American period drama here. The postwar optimism and material upswing of the early 1950s have bypassed the demobbed, mentally damaged sailor Freddie Quell (Joaquin Phoenix), who, after a chance meeting, is taken under the wing of Lancaster Dodd (Philip Seymour Hoffman), persuasive leader of psychobabbling self-help organisation The Cause. A spellbinding, forcefully physical Phoenix imbues his short-fused alcoholic with sufficient guileless charisma to explain the enduring mentor-pupil relationship that drives the narrative. But what might have been Anderson's latest masterpiece fails to fully take dramatic flight in an unsatisfying final act. It remains, however, vital, character-driven film-making. AC Swearing, sex scenes. DVD Blu-ray

Joaquin Phoenix *Freddie Quell* • Philip Seymour Hoffman *Lancaster Dodd* • Amy Adams *Peggy Dodd* • Laura Dern *Helen* • Ambyr Childers *Elizabeth Dodd* • Rami Malek *Clark* ■ *Dir/Scr* Paul Thomas Anderson

Master and Commander: the Far Side of the World ★★★★ 12
Period adventure drama
2003 · US · Colour · 132min

Like the much loved series of novels by Patrick O'Brian, Peter Weir's film immerses the audience in the day-to-day life on board a 19th-century British warship as it pursues a "phantom" French vessel. Purists will endlessly discuss the casting of Russell Crowe as Captain Aubrey (here deploying his self-described "RSC two pints after lunch" English accent) and Paul Bettany as his ship's doctor and best friend, Maturin, but both give full-blooded performances. It might be a little repetitive but thankfully the likeable characters, Weir's meticulous attention to period detail and the stunningly realised action more than compensate. AS Violence, swearing. DVD Blu-ray

Russell Crowe *Captain Jack Aubrey* • Paul Bettany *Dr Stephen Maturin* • Billy Boyd (1) *Barrett Bonden* • James D'Arcy *First Lt Thomas Pullings* • Lee Ingleby *Hollom* • George Innes *Joe Plaice* • Mark Lewis Jones *Mr Hogg* • Chris Larkin *Captain Howard* ■ *Dir* Peter Weir • *Scr* Peter Weir, John Collee, from the novels *Master and Commander* and *The Far Side of the World* by Patrick O'Brian

The Master Gunfighter ★
Western 1975 · US · Colour · 110min

This sloppy western is credited to Frank Laughlin, the nine-year-old son of real director and star Tom Laughlin. That family in-joke sets the tone for a painfully self-indulgent mess. Laughlin is a gun expert pitted against a Mexican warlord. There are obvious nods to Vietnam, the peace movement and native American consciousness amid the clumsily shot blood-letting. AT Violence.

Tom Laughlin *Finley McCloud* • Ron O'Neal *Paulo* • Lincoln Kilpatrick *Jacques St Charles* • Geo Anne Sosa *Chorika* • Barbara Carrera *Eula* • Victor Campos *Maltese* • Hector Elias *Juan* ■ *Dir* Frank Laughlin [Tom Laughlin] • *Scr* Harold Lapland, from the film *Goyokin* by Kei Tasaka, Hideo Gosha

The Master of Ballantrae ★★★ PG
Period swashbuckling adventure
1953 · US/UK · Colour · 85min

Errol Flynn was beginning to look old and tired when he made this colourful adaptation of the Robert Louis Stevenson story (changed almost beyond recognition) in Europe. Nevertheless, with the help of Warner Bros veteran director William Keighley, the ailing star revived enough to make his mark in a movie that's not entirely without charm. There's a fine British cast and a lovely leading lady in Beatrice Campbell. TS DVD

Errol Flynn *James Durrisdeer* • Roger Livesey *Colonel Francis Burke* • Anthony Steel *Henry Durrisdeer* • Beatrice Campbell *Lady Alison* • Yvonne Furneaux *Jessie Brown* • Jacques Berthier *Arnaud* • Felix Aylmer *Lord Durrisdeer* • Mervyn Johns *MacKellar* • Gillian Lynne *Marianne* ■ *Dir* William Keighley • *Scr* Herb Meadow, Harold Medford, from the novel by Robert Louis Stevenson

The Master of Bankdam ★★★
Period drama 1947 · UK · BW · 105min

This is a thunderingly good melodrama spanning virtually the entire Victorian era. Tom Walls is all accent and folly as the head of a mill-owning northern family who entrusts the business to the wrong son. But the feud between swaggering Stephen Murray and his gritty brother Dennis Price is nothing compared to the rivalry between the foppish David Tomlinson and the down-to-earth Jimmy Hanley. DP

Anne Crawford *Annie Pickersgill* • Dennis Price *Joshua Crowther* • Tom Walls *Simeon Crowther Sr* • Stephen Murray *Zebediah Crowther* • Linden Travers *Clara Baker* • Jimmy Hanley *Simeon Crowther Jr* • Nancy Price *Lydia Crowther* • David Tomlinson *Lancelot Handel Crowther* ■ *Dir* Walter Forde • *Scr* Edward Dryhurst, Moie Charles, from the novel *The Crowthers of Bankdam* by Thomas Armstrong

The Master of Disguise ★ PG
Fantasy comedy 2002 · US · Colour · 76min

This lamentably limp comedy cruelly demonstrates why Dana Carvey does not enjoy the superstar status of his *Wayne's World* co-star Mike Myers. Carvey plays a sheltered Italian youth who discovers that he has amazing powers of disguise and uses them to rescue his parents from the clutches of evil mastermind Brent Spiner. The nearest thing to a genuine joke is the bad guy's propensity for breaking wind whenever he laughs. AS DVD CS

Dana Carvey *Pistachio Disguisey* • Jennifer Esposito *Jennifer* • Harold Gould *Grandfather* • James Brolin *Fabbrizio* • Brent Spiner *Devlin Bowman* • Edie McClurg *Mother* • Maria Canals *Sophia* • Bo Derek ■ *Dir* Perry Andelin Blake • *Scr* Dana Carvey, Harris Goldberg

Master of the House ★★★★★ U
Silent romantic drama 1925 · Den · BW · 91min

This domestic tragicomedy with a feminist slant was Danish director Carl Th Dreyer's seventh feature and anticipates his greatest films. The deceptively simple story tells of a husband whose disregard for his wife's feelings causes her to become ill. When she is sent away to recuperate, his old nanny moves in and teaches him to mend his ways. Dreyer filmed in an exact replica of a real two-roomed flat built in a studio, using its limitations to his advantage. A film of close-ups and gestures, it contains a wonderful performance from Mathilde Nielsen as the nanny. RB DVD

Johannes Meyer *Victor Frandsen* • Astrid Holm *Ida, his wife* • Karin Nellemose *Karen Frandsen* • Clara Schonfeld *Alvilda Kryger* • Mathilde Nielsen *Mads* ■ *Dir* Carl Th Dreyer • *Scr* Carl Th Dreyer, Svend Rindom, from the play *Tyraennens Fald (The Fall of a Tyrant)* by Svend Rindom

Master of the World ★★ U
Fantasy adventure 1961 · US · Colour · 98min

With his usual suave and sinister panache, Vincent Price plays a 19th-century inventor who plans to destroy all of mankind's weapons from a flying airship in this uneven adaptation of two Jules Verne novels. Spiced up with stock battle footage taken from other costume epics, it's a cheap and cheerful fantasy that comes across as a highly moralistic anti-war fable. AJ

Vincent Price *Robur* • Charles Bronson *Strock* • Henry Hull *Prudent* • Mary Webster *Dorothy* • David Frankham *Philip* • Richard Harrison *Alistair* • Vito Scotti *Topage* ■ *Dir* William Witney • *Scr* Richard Matheson, from the novels *Master of the World* and *Robur, the Conqueror* by Jules Verne

The Master Plan ★★★ U
Spy drama 1954 · UK · BW · 77min

Blacklisted in Hollywood during the communist witch-hunt, South African-born Cy Endfield worked uncredited on three British thrillers with Charles De Lautour. This was his first solo venture in exile, made under the pseudonym Hugh Raker. It's an above-average quota quickie, with war hero and B-movie stalwart Wayne Morris as a government troubleshooter fighting against the double agent who is leaking secrets to the enemy. DP

Wayne Morris *Major Brent* • Tilda Thamar *Helen* • Norman Wooland *Colonel Cleaver* • Mary Mackenzie *Miss Gray* • Arnold Bell *General Goulding* • Marjorie Stewart *Yvonne* • Laurie Main *Johnny Sowell* • Frederick Schrecker *Dr Morgan Stern* ■ *Dir* Hugh Raker [Cy Enfield] • *Scr* Hugh Raker [Cy Enfield], Donald Bull, from the TV play *Operation North Star* by Harold Bratt

M

The Master Race ★★
Second World War drama
1944 · US · BW · 01min

In a bizarre wartime curio, a Nazi officer hides out in Belgium and tries to keep the fascist fires burning by causing dissent among the newly liberated countries. Made promptly after the D-Day landings, it's a heavy slice of peace propaganda, with George Coulouris deeply sinister as the villain. Director Herbert J Biberman, blacklisted in 1948 as a result of his communist sympathies, was one of the original Hollywood Ten. AT

George Coulouris *Von Beck* • Stanley Ridges *Phil Carson* • Osa Massen *Helena* • Carl Esmond *Andrei* • Nancy Gates *Nina* • Morris Carnovsky *Old Man Bartoc* • Lloyd Bridges *Frank* ■ *Dir* Herbert J Biberman • *Scr* Herbert J Biberman, Anne Froelick, Rowland Leigh, from a story by Herbert J Biberman

Master Spy ★ U
Spy drama
1964 · UK · BW · 70min

There isn't an atom of suspense in Montgomery Tully's tepid thriller about spying scientists. Indeed, the most exciting moments are the games of chess during which defector Stephen Murray passes vital secrets to communist squire, Alan Wheatley. There's a valiant attempt to put a sting in the tail, but only lab assistant June Thorburn fails to see through the slenderest web of deception. DP

Stephen Murray *Boris Turganev* • June Thorburn *Leila* • Alan Wheatley *Paul Skelton* • John Carson *Richard Colman* • John Bown *John Baxter* • Jack Watson *Captain Foster* ■ *Dir* Montgomery Tully • *Scr* Maurice J Wilson, from the story *They Also Serve* by Gerald Anstruther, Paul White

Mastermind ★★★
Spoof detective drama
1976 · US · Colour · 131min

Shot in 1969 and left on the shelf for seven years, this curiosity is worth seeking out. It's a Charlie Chan parody, with the great blacklisted clown Zero Mostel as a bumbling Oriental detective, and a sterling supporting cast including a last appearance from *On the Town's* Jules Munshin. Plus there's a knockout car chase and some voluble slapstick, too. TS

Zero Mostel *Inspector Hoku* • Bradford Dillman *Jabez Link* • Keiko Kishi *Nikki Kono* • Gawn Grainger *Nigel Crouchback* • Jules Munshin *Israeli agent* ■ *Dir* Alex March • *Scr* Terence Klein, Ian McLellan Hunter, from a story by Terence Klein

Masterminds ★ 12
Action adventure
1997 · US · Colour · 100min

It's hard to understand why accomplished actor Patrick Stewart agreed to appear in this odious adventure movie. Stewart poses as a security expert, installing surveillance systems at a posh private school in order to hold a small number of the wealthiest kids in the world hostage. But he doesn't count on the school's biggest troublemaker, who has the school rigged for his own mischievous ends. ST Violence.

Patrick Stewart *Rafe Bentley* • Vincent Kartheiser *Ozzie* • Brenda Fricker *Principal Claire Maloney* • Brad Whitford [Bradley Whitford] *Miles Lawrence* • Matt Craven *Jake Paxton* ■ *Dir* Roger Christian • *Scr* Floyd Byars, from a story by Alex Siskin, Chris Black, Floyd Byars

Masterminds ★ 12A
Crime comedy based on a true story
2015 · US · Colour · 94min

Masterminds, a caper flick based loosely on a real-life heist gone belly-up, manages to miss the mark on almost all counts, delivering neither laughs nor anything resembling a compelling story. *Napoleon Dynamite* director Jared Hess misjudges almost every element – from the baffling casting of Owen Wilson against type to the injection of a criminally misjudged gross-out sequence, this is a symphony of comedic bum notes. Sadly for those involved, they certainly ain't comedy masterminds. AS Violence, sexual references.

Kristen Wiig *Kelly* • Zach Galifianakis *David* • Owen Wilson *Steve* • Jason Sudeikis *Mike McKinney* • Mary Elizabeth Ellis *Michelle* ■ *Dir* Jared Hess • *Scr* Chris Bowman, Jody Hill, Danny McBride (2), Hubbel Palmer

The Masters ★★★
Mystery drama
1975 · It · Colour · 113min

A naive schoolmistress (Jennifer O'Neill), newly arrived in a tiny Sicilian town, is insulted by a local peasant who is then murdered by the local Mafia. It's all to do with the corrupt police, but the teacher takes a long time to figure out exactly what's going on. Director Luigi Zampa gives the mystery more credibility than it deserves, while James Mason supplies a menacing turn. TH Italian dubbed.

James Mason *Antonio Bellocampo* • Franco Nero *Prof Belcore* • Jennifer O'Neill *Elena Bardi* • Orazio Orlando • Claudio Gora ■ *Dir* Luigi Zampa • *Scr* Piero Bernard, from the novel by Giuseppe Fava

Masters of the Universe ★★ PG
Fantasy adventure
1987 · US · Colour · 101min

It is difficult to make convincing live-action versions of cult cartoon strips, and this big-screen version of the momentarily popular TV series is one of the least successful attempts. Dolph Lundgren has the necessary physique for He-Man, and Frank Langella has been splendidly made-up for the role of Skeletor. But the story – about a cosmic key that will enable its holder to become master of the universe – is uninspired, while the effects look painfully cheap. DP CS

Dolph Lundgren *He-Man* • Frank Langella *Skeletor* • Meg Foster *Evil-Lyn* • Billy Barty *Gwildor* • Courteney Cox *Julie Winston* • Robert Duncan McNeill *Kevin* ■ *Dir* Gary Goddard • *Scr* David Odell

Mata Hari ★★★★ PG
Spy melodrama
1931 · US · BW · 85min

Greta Garbo's transcendent persona found an ideal outlet as the First World War spy who operates above all laws yet is brought down by a fatally romantic detour. The film is sensual and atmospheric and ranks as one of the few vehicles actually worthy of the celluloid goddess. Director George Fitzmaurice and cameraman William Daniels capture the story in stylishly visual terms, while there is a poignant chemistry between Garbo and the intense Ramon Novarro. And revealing a contradiction that is at once fascinating and modern, Garbo applies her customary sense of elsewhere to situations that call for desire, drive and purpose in a mercenary role. DO DVD

Greta Garbo *Mata Hari* • Ramon Novarro *Lt Alexis Rosanoff* • Lionel Barrymore *General Serge Shubin* • Lewis Stone *Andriani* • C Henry Gordon *Dubois* • Karen Morley *Carlotta* ■ *Dir* George Fitzmaurice • *Scr* Benjamin Glazer, Leo Birinski, Doris Anderson, Gilbert Emery

Mata Hari ★ 18
Spy drama
1985 · US · Colour · 103min

This soft-core sex version of the old First World War yarn has Sylvia Kristel (*Emmanuelle*) as the French spy, taking off her clothes at the drop of a proverbial hat. Christopher Cazenove is her opposite number in Germany – the spy who loved her. Director Curtis Harrington may have intended a satire but the producers wanted a bit of hot stuff. AT

Sylvia Kristel *Mata Hari* • Christopher Cazenove *Karl Von Byerling* • Oliver Tobias *Captain Ladoux* • Gaye Brown *Fraulein Doktor* • William Fox *Maître Clunet* ■ *Dir* Curtis Harrington • *Scr* Joel Ziskin

Matador ★★★ 18
Black comedy drama
1986 · Sp · Colour · 101min

Flashy, trashy and vibrantly colourful, Pedro Almodóvar's film explores the links between eroticism and violence. Antonio Banderas gives a courageous performance as the trainee bullfighter whose overpowering fantasies and his own sexual misdemeanours prompt him to confess to a series of kinky killings. Some of the dialogue is laughably pretentious, while Almodóvar's emphasis on voyeuristic titillation and cheap black comedy comes at the expense of developing some interesting themes. DP Spanish +subtitles. Violence, nudity. DVD

Assumpta Serna *Maria Cardenal* • Antonio Banderas *Angel Giminez* • Nacho Martinez *Diego Montes* • Eva Cobo *Eva* • Julieta Serrano *Berta* • Chus Lampreave *Pilar* • Carmen Maura *Julia* ■ *Dir* Pedro Almodóvar • *Scr* Pedro Almodóvar, Jesus Ferrero, from a story by Pedro Almodóvar

The Matador ★★★ 15
Black comedy drama
2005 · US/Ger/Ire · Colour · 93min

Pierce Brosnan plays a hitman undergoing a midlife crisis of conscience in this blackish comedy. Meeting Greg Kinnear's crestfallen businessman by chance in a Mexico City hotel bar, Brosnan takes solace in the everyday problems of this average Joe, and an odd friendship soon develops. Brosnan overplays his part, while Greg Kinnear underplays his, but striking just the right balance is Hope Davis, who is wonderful as Kinnear's slightly wacky wife. The film could perhaps have been a little sharper, but it's entertaining stuff. DA Swearing, sexual references. DVD

Pierce Brosnan *Julian Noble* • Greg Kinnear *Danny Wright* • Hope Davis *Carolyn "Bean" Wright* • Philip Baker Hall *Mr Randy* • Dylan Baker *Lovell* • Adam Scott *Phil Garrison* ■ *Dir/Scr* Richard Shepard

The Match ★★★ 15
Comedy drama
1999 · UK/US/Ire · Colour · 92min

Apparently an attempt at reviving the spirit of the Ealing comedy, this tells the story of young Scottish milkman Max Beesley, looking forward to the return of girlfriend Laura Fraser from university. Despite Beesley's physical disadvantages, he finds himself involved in a soccer match-cum-feud between two local watering holes. An amiable movie with no pretensions, this presents a host of familiar British faces and plenty of cosy characters. TH Swearing. DVD

Max Beesley *Wullie Smith* • Isla Blair *Sheila Bailey* • James Cosmo *Billy Bailey* • Laura Fraser *Rosemary Bailey* • Richard E Grant *Gorgeous Gus* • Ian Holm *Big Tam* • Tom Sizemore *Buffalo* • Pierce Brosnan *John McGee* ■ *Dir/Scr* Mick Davis

The Match Factory Girl ★★★ 15
Drama
1990 · Fin/Swe · Colour · 66min

Finnish film-maker Aki Kaurismäki claimed that this picture was intended to make Robert Bresson seem like the director of epic action movies. While it certainly shares the French master's minimalist style, the story of a plain Jane who defies the harshest of odds, finally to take control of her life, lacks the compassion that characterised even the bleakest Bresson scenario. But Kati Outinen is superb in the title role, overcoming the odd improbable plot twist to convince you that she is one of the countless Eleanor Rigbys totally dependent on dreams to sweeten their bitter reality. DP Finnish +subtitles. DVD

Kati Outinen *Iris* • Elina Salo *Mother* • Esko Nikkari *Stepfather* • Vesa Vierikko *Aarne* • Reijjo Taipale *Singer* • Silu Seppala *Brother* • Outi Maenpaa *Workmate* • Marja Packalen *Doctor* ■ *Dir/Scr* Aki Kaurismäki

Match Point ★★★★ 12
Romantic thriller
2005 · UK/US/Lux · Colour · 118min

The role of luck in life is the theme of this morality fable from Woody Allen, his first film to be set in the United Kingdom. The cream of British acting talent surrounds superbly cast *femme fatale* Scarlett Johansson in a confidently layered tragedy that's spiked with mordant humour. Permanently grey London skies underscore the dark undercurrents in this story of a tennis coach (Jonathan Rhys Meyers) who marries into the wealthy elite and is prepared to do anything to stay there. The script offers up a neat balance of sporting analogies and philosophical questions that continues right up to the surprising ending. AJ Sex scenes. DVD

Jonathan Rhys Meyers *Chris Wilton* • Scarlett Johansson *Nola Rice* • Emily Mortimer *Chloe Hewett Wilton* • Brian Cox (1) *Alec Hewett* • Matthew Goode *Tom Hewett* • Penelope Wilton *Eleanor Hewett* • Ewen Bremner *Inspector Dowd* • James Nesbitt *Detective Banner* ■ *Dir/Scr* Woody Allen

The Matchmaker ★★★ U
Period comedy
1958 · US · BW · 96min

This is *Hello, Dolly!* without the tunes or, indeed, Barbra Streisand. Shirley Booth is Dolly Levi, the widowed, interfering busybody who arranges marriages like flowers in a vase. In her own sights is Paul Ford's merchant; getting tangled up in her plans are Shirley MacLaine and Anthony Perkins. The performances are perfectly attuned to the 1880s ambience, which is nicely enhanced when the actors address the camera directly. AT DVD

Shirley Booth *Dolly Levi* • Anthony Perkins *Cornelius Hackl* • Shirley MacLaine *Irene Molloy* • Paul Ford *Horace Vandergelder* • Robert Morse *Barnaby Tucker* • Wallace Ford *Malachi Stack* • Perry Wilson *Minnie Fay* ■ *Dir* Joseph Anthony • *Scr* John Michael Hayes, from the play by Thornton Wilder

The Matchmaker ★★★ 15
Romantic comedy
1997 · Ire/UK/US · Colour · 97min

The underrated Janeane Garofalo gets to flex her acting muscles as Marcy, dispatched to the Emerald Isle to round up a US senator's ancestors. Inadvertently she finds herself at a matchmaking festival, where sparks are soon flying between her and gauche barman David O'Hara. Matchmaker Milo O'Shea bets he can get them together and sends them on a wild goose chase to the Aran islands. It's unfortunate that the movie begins and ends in America, but what's in between has all the charm that Ireland can offer. LH

Janeane Garofalo *Marcy Tizard* • David O'Hara *Sean Kelly* • Milo O'Shea *Dermot O'Brien* • Jay O Sanders *Senator John McGlory* • Denis Leary *Nick* ■ *Dir* Mark Joffe • *Scr* Karen Janszen, Louis Nowra, Graham Linehan, from a screenplay (unproduced) by Greg Dinner

Matchstick Men ★★★ 12
Crime comedy drama
2003 · US · Colour · 111min

Director Ridley Scott's low-key movie stars Nicolas Cage as a conman who is also afflicted by an obsessive-compulsive disorder that makes him nervous and a cleanliness freak. That this is at odds with his lifestyle choice does stretch credibility, but it also allows Scott to indulge in all sorts of appropriately edgy cuts and compositions. Cage and partner Sam Rockwell embark on a high-stakes scam, just as the former discovers he has a bright teenage daughter (Alison Lohman). The bonding scenes are played beautifully, yet the script cheapens this sharp set-up with a predictable con of its own. JC Swearing, violence. DVD

Nicolas Cage *Roy Waller* • Sam Rockwell *Frank Mercer* • Alison Lohman *Angela* • Bruce McGill *Chuck Frechette* • Bruce Altman *Dr Harris Klein* • Sheila Kelley (1) *Kathy* • Beth Grant *Laundry lady* ■ *Dir* Ridley Scott • *Scr* Ted Griffin, Nicholas Griffin, from the novel by Eric Garcia

Material Girls ★★ PG
Comedy drama
2006 · US · Colour · 93min

Any hopes that this would be some wicked send-up of the antics of the Hilton sisters and their ilk is pretty much dashed when you discover that chirpy Disney favourites Hilary and Haylie Duff are the siblings in question here. They play heiresses to a cosmetics empire whose easy life is upset when their late father's company is sued and all their assets are frozen. Ostracised by their friends, they are schooled in real life by their housekeeper (Maria Conchita Alonso). While there are a few digs at the shallowness of the lifestyles of the young, rich and famous, it's pretty toothless, Cinderella-in-reverse stuff and Martha Coolidge's direction is as bland as the two leads. Even Anjelica Huston as a rival cosmetics magnate struggles to inject any venom into the proceedings. JF *DVD*

Hilary Duff *Tanzie Marchetta* • Haylie Duff *Ava Marchetta* • Anjelica Huston *Fabiella* • Brent Spiner *Tommy Katzenbach* • Maria Conchita Alonso *Inez* • Lukas Haas *Henry Baines* • Marcus Coloma *Rick* ■ *Dir* Martha Coolidge • *Scr* John Quaintance, Jessica O'Toole, Amy Rardin

Matewan ★★★★ 15

Historical drama 1987 · US · Colour · 127min

When the local coal company cuts the pay of its mainly white workforce and begins using blacks and Italian immigrants at cheaper rates, tensions run high in the West Virginian mining town of Matewan. Union organiser Joe Kenehan (Chris Cooper) arrives to sort out the increasingly violent confrontation. Set in the 1920s, this resembles a western: the good, the bad and the ugly characters are clearly delineated, even if John Sayles often gives them speeches instead of dialogue. Films about the American labour movement are rare, so this uncompromising, fact-based drama is to be savoured. The glowing cinematography is by Haskell Wexler. AT Swearing. *DVD*

Chris Cooper *Joe Kenehan* • James Earl Jones *"Few Clothes" Johnson* • Will Oldham *Danny Radnor* • Jace Alexander *Hillard* • Ken Jenkins *Sephus Purcell* • Bob Gunton *CE Lively* • Gary McCleery *Ludie* • Kevin Tighe *Hickey* ■ *Dir/Scr* John Sayles

Matilda ★★ U

Sports comedy 1978 · US · Colour · 87min

This is a screen version of the Paul Gallico book about a boxing kangaroo and the small-time theatrical agent who becomes the marsupial's manager. The budget obviously didn't stretch to special effects, so the kangaroo is played by a man in a costume. This cute comedy looks a little dated these days, but kids might want to hop along to see it. Elliott Gould and Robert Mitchum head the humans, while Gary Morgan is the guy in the suit. DA

Elliott Gould *Bernie Bonnelli* • Robert Mitchum *Duke Parkhurst* • Harry Guardino *Uncle Nono* • Clive Revill *Billy Baker/Narration* • Lionel Stander *Pinky Schwab* • Karen Carlson *Kathleen Smith* • Gary Morgan ■ *Dir* Daniel Mann • *Scr* Albert S Ruddy, Timothy Galfas, from the novel by Paul Gallico

Matilda ★★★★ PG

Comedy fantasy 1996 · US · Colour · 94min

Director Danny DeVito revels in the black comedy of this typically dark Roald Dahl story, in which monstrous adults consider children as inconvenient accessories. DeVito – who also stars as Matilda's boorish dad – cleverly emphasises the point by shooting much of the film from a child's-eye view, making people and buildings alike look forbidding and cold. Mara Wilson is excellent in the lead, while Embeth Davidtz prevents beloved teacher Miss Honey from being too sweet. But stealing the acting honours is Pam Ferris, who brings vicious Miss Trunchbull to terrifying life. DP *DVD* *Blu-ray*

Mara Wilson *Matilda* • Danny DeVito *Harry Wormwood* • Rhea Perlman *Zinnia Wormwood* • Embeth Davidtz *Miss Honey* • Pam Ferris *Agatha Trunchbull* • Paul Reubens *FBI agent* ■ *Dir* Danny DeVito • *Scr* Nicholas Kazan, Robin Swicord, from Roald Dahl's illustrated children's book

Matinee ★★★★ PG

Comedy drama 1993 · US · Colour · 94min

This glorious coming-of-age saga from Joe Dante is a paean to growing up in the early 1960s, using the twin backdrops of nuclear bomb paranoia and "Atom Age" monster flicks. It's also a loving tribute to legendary producer/director William Castle, the schlock showman responsible for gimmick B-movies such as *The Tingler* and *House on Haunted Hill*. Charming John Goodman is the Castle clone launching his new giant insect horror film in Key West during the Cuban missile crisis, and it's the contrast between fake movie scares and real-life

ones that makes Dante's nostalgic film so engaging. AJ *DVD* *Blu-ray* *CS*

John Goodman *Lawrence Woolsey* • Cathy Moriarty *Ruth Corday/Carole* • Simon Fenton *Gene Loomis* • Omri Katz *Stan* • Kellie Martin *Sherry* • Lisa Jakub *Sandra* • Lucinda Jenney *Anne Loomis* • Jesse Lee *Dennis Loomis* ■ *Dir* Joe Dante • *Scr* Charlie Haas, from a story by Jerico, Charlie Haas

The Matinee Idol ★★ U

Silent comedy 1928 · US · BW · 65min

A Broadway star catches a Civil War drama performed by a theatrical troupe out in the boondocks. It's so badly done that he takes it to the city as a comedy and has a hit. Bessie Love is the appealing star of this silent, the second to be directed for Columbia by Frank Capra. Romance blossoms between Love and the actor who plays a black soldier and only declares his affection when rain washes off his make-up. Although Capra could have given more weight to the fact that the actors have been made fools of, the film is frequently very funny. RK

Bessie Love *Ginger Bolivar* • Johnnie Walker *Don Wilson/Harry Mann* • Lionel Belmore *Col Jasper Bolivar* ■ *Dir* Frank Capra • *Scr* Peter Milne, Elmer Harris, from the story *Come Back to Aaron* by Robert Lord

The Mating Game ★★★★ U

Comedy 1959 · US · Colour · 96min

The Darling Buds of May is better known here as the popular TV series that introduced us to Catherine Zeta-Jones. But this MGM version of HE Bates's novel is actually much funnier and more faithful to the spirit of the original. The cast is also much classier: Paul Douglas is a truly estimable father to Debbie Reynolds, the farm girl who falls for taxman Tony Randall, while director George Marshall keeps it all zipping along. TS

Debbie Reynolds *Mariette Larkin* • Tony Randall *Lorenzo Charlton* • Paul Douglas *Pop Larkin* • Fred Clark *Oliver Kelsey* • Una Merkel *Ma Larkin* ■ *Dir* George Marshall • *Scr* William Roberts, from the novel *The Darling Buds of May* by HE Bates

The Mating Habits of the Earthbound Human ★ 15

Romantic comedy 1999 · US · Colour · 86min

David Hyde Pierce is the narrator (an anthropologist from an alien world) in this awful comedy, helping us to understand how humans relate and mate. Badly written, woodenly performed and, overall, an ill-advised and badly directed disaster. JB

David Hyde Pierce *Narrator* • MacKenzie Astin *Billy Masterson* • Carmen Electra *Jenny Smith* • Lucy Liu *Jenny's friend* • Marcus Redmond *Billy's friend* • Lisa Rotondi *Jenny's friend* • Marc Blucas *Jenny's ex-boyfriend* ■ *Dir/Scr* Jeff Abugov

The Mating Season ★★ U

Comedy 1951 · US · BW · 101min

Working man John Lund ascends the social ladder through marriage to Gene Tierney, daughter of an ambassador, whose family is unaware of his humble origins. His mother Thelma Ritter pretends to be a servant and comes to work for the newlyweds. Given his somewhat lifeless co-stars and a workmanlike script, director Mitchell Leisen wisely lets Thelma Ritter walk away with this comedy. Her performance earned her the second of her record six Oscar nominations for best supporting actress. RK

Gene Tierney *Maggie Carleton* • John Lund *Van McNulty* • Miriam Hopkins *Fran Carleton* • Thelma Ritter *Ellen McNulty* • Jan Sterling *Betsy* • Larry Keating *Mr Kallinger Sr* ■ *Dir* Mitchell Leisen • *Scr* Charles Brackett, Walter Reisch, Richard Breen [Richard L Breen]

The Matrix ★★★★★ 15

Science-fiction action thriller 1999 · US · Colour · 136min

Keanu Reeves reclaims his action hero crown in the Wachowski brothers' super-smart science-fiction action adventure set across two dimensions. Thematically complex, yet intelligently integrating eastern philosophy, Lewis Carroll and ancient mysticism, the film has Reeves as Neo, a reclusive computer hacker who may just be the one to save the world from the evils of cyberspace slavery. Taking a quantum leap beyond anything the fantasy sensation seeker has seen before in the special effects department, this mixes ultra-cool visuals, vertigo-inducing kung fu and a deliciously paranoid scenario for an adrenaline-pumping rollercoaster ride of extraordinary vision and power. AJ Violence, swearing. *DVD* *Blu-ray*

Keanu Reeves *Thomas A Anderson/Neo* • Carrie-Anne Moss *Trinity* • Laurence Fishburne *Morpheus* • Hugo Weaving *Agent Smith* • Joe Pantoliano *Cypher* • Marcus Chong *Tank* • Gloria Foster *Oracle* ■ *Dir/Scr* Larry Wachowski [Lana Wachowski], and Andy Wachowski [Lilly Wachowski]

The Matrix Reloaded ★★★ 15

Science-fiction action thriller 2002 · US/Aus · Colour · 132min

Creating a sequel to the superlative sci-fi action blockbuster *The Matrix* was always going to be a Herculean task. The Wachowski brothers set themselves such a high standard that the second chapter in their epic man-versus-machines trilogy was never likely to match the impact of the first. The duo add a handful of fantastic – though underused – new villains and deliver an array of astonishing set pieces, as Neo (Keanu Reeves) and his associates fight to save Zion, Earth's last human enclave. Disappointingly, however, such elements fail to lift a film that suffers from stilted dialogue, cheesy scripting and a plodding pace. SF Violence. *DVD* *Blu-ray* *CS*

Keanu Reeves *Thomas A Anderson/Neo* • Laurence Fishburne *Morpheus* • Carrie-Anne Moss *Trinity* • Hugo Weaving *Agent Smith* • Jada Pinkett Smith *Niobe* • Gloria Foster *Oracle* • Monica Bellucci *Persephone* • Collin Chou *Seraph* • Nona Gaye *Zee* • Randall Duk Kim *Keymaker* ■ *Dir/Scr* Larry Wachowski [Lana Wachowski], Andy Wachowski [Lilly Wachowski]

The Matrix Revolutions ★★★ 15

Science-fiction action thriller 2003 · US · Colour · 123min

Continuing straight on from the events of *Reloaded*, the first hour of this more substantial second sequel plays like an extended version of the previous film: annoyingly cryptic conversations, overfamiliar acrobatic shoot-outs and inert pacing. But, in a great second half, the Wachowski Brothers get the trilogy back on track, as humans in huge combat armour battle valiantly to protect their Zion stronghold against a million robotic Sentinels. Both technically and artistically, this extended siege is perhaps the most impressive set piece of the series. JC Violence. *DVD* *Blu-ray*

Keanu Reeves *Thomas A Anderson/Neo* • Carrie-Anne Moss *Trinity* • Laurence Fishburne *Morpheus* • Hugo Weaving *Agent Smith* • Jada Pinkett Smith *Niobe* • Mary Alice *The Oracle* • Tanveer Atwal *Sati* • Monica Bellucci *Persephone* ■ *Dir/Scr* Larry Wachowski [Lana Wachowski], Andy Wachowski [Lilly Wachowski]

The Mattei Affair ★★★★ U

Historical crime drama 1972 · It · Colour · 115min

Dubbed by *Time* magazine "the most powerful Italian since Augustus Caesar", Enrico Mattei was a wartime hero who rose through the ranks of the AGIP utility to head ENI, a state-sponsored body that he moulded into an operation capable of transforming the nation's petro-chemical

industry. However, his ambitions died with him in a plane crash in 1962. Delving into the murky worlds of international capitalism and postwar Italian politics, Francesco Rosi's compelling, Palme d'Or-winning reconstruction seeks to prove that this deeply flawed man (impeccably played by Gian Maria Volonté) was the victim of a conspiracy inspired by corruption. DP Italian +subtitles.

Gian Maria Volonté *Enrico Mattei* • Luigi Squarzina *Journalist* • Gianfranco Ombuen Ferrari • Edda Ferronao *Mrs Mattei* ■ *Dir* Francesco Rosi • *Scr* Francesco Rosi, Tonino Guerra, Nerio Minuzzo, Tito Di Stefano

A Matter of Dignity ★★★

Drama 1957 · Gr · BW · 102min

Michael Cacoyannis's fourth feature is an exacting domestic melodrama centring on the morality of three very different women. Ellie Lambetti drew the most plaudits as the daughter of an impoverished household who contemplates marrying a man she detests for his money. However, there's much to admire in the supporting performances of both Athena Michaelidou, as her grasping, snobbish mother, and Eleni Zafiriou, as the maid who has endured exploitation and incurred ruinous debts in order to care for her ailing son. DP Greek +subtitles.

Ellie Lambetti *Chloé* • Georges Pappas *Cléon Pellas* • Athena Michaelidou *Roxane* • Eleni Zafiriou *Katerina* ■ *Dir/Scr* Michael Cacoyannis

A Matter of Life and Death ★★★★★ U

Romantic fantasy 1946 · UK · BW and Colour · 99min

The theatrical stylisation of Michael Powell and Emeric Pressburger sometimes deflected their thematic purpose, but in this dazzling fantasy they succeed in marrying the two to perfection. David Niven stars as an RAF pilot who has a conversation with American servicewoman Kim Hunter as his plane is going down. After his miraculous survival, the two meet and fall in love but he is then told he was meant to die and must defend himself in heaven. Although the film was intended to celebrate the Anglo-American alliance that had prevailed in the Second World War, it delivered a barbed allegory that called into question the strength of the ties between the Allies and Britain's status as a world power. Its political outspokenness, visual audacity and mannered playing now make it one of the most fondly recalled British movies. DP *DVD*

David Niven *Squadron Leader Peter Carter* • Kim Hunter *June* • Roger Livesey *Dr Reeves* • Robert Coote *Bob Trubshawe* • Marius Goring *Conductor 71* • Raymond Massey *Abraham Farlan* • Kathleen Byron *Angel* • Richard Attenborough *English pilot* • Bonar Colleano *American pilot* • Joan Maude *Chief recorder* ■ *Dir/Scr* Michael Powell, Emeric Pressburger • *Cinematographer* Jack Cardiff • *Production Designer* Alfred Junge

A Matter of Time ★ PG

Drama 1976 · It/US · Colour · 99min

Movie star Liza Minnelli recalls her encounters with aged contessa Ingrid Bergman whose rambling tales of her life inspired the young girl. Made up of a series of utterly confusing flashbacks-within-flashbacks, this maudlin rubbish is not helped by Minnelli's undisciplined, edgy performance – or that of Bergman, done up as a dessicated crone. Isabella Rossellini has a cameo as the old contessa's nurse. RK

Liza Minnelli *Nina* • Ingrid Bergman *Contessa Sanziani* • Charles Boyer *Count* • Spiros Andros *Mario* • Tina Aumont *Valentina* • Gabriele Ferzetti *Antonio Vicari* • Isabella Rossellini *Sister Pia* ■ *Dir* Vincente Minnelli • *Scr* John Gay, from the novel *The Film of Memory* by Maurice Druon

Maurice ★★★ 15

Period drama 1987 · UK · Colour · 134min

EM Forster's autobiographical novel about homosexuals at Cambridge was written in 1914, but withheld from publication until after his death in 1970. From its opening scenes, in which Simon Callow campily tells the young Maurice what great things he can expect from his body, James Ivory's film skips rather gingerly around the subject matter. The older Maurice, now played by James Wilby, goes up to Cambridge where Hugh Grant awaits; eventually, though, he ends up with a bit of rough trade, played by Rupert Graves. It's impeccably mounted, prim and a tad dull. AT DVD

James Wilby *Maurice Hall* • Hugh Grant *Clive Durham* • Denholm Elliott *Dr Barry* • Simon Callow *Mr Ducie* • Billie Whitelaw *Mrs Hall* • Ben Kingsley *Lasker-Jones* • Judy Parfitt *Mrs Durham* • Rupert Graves *Alec Scudder* ■ *Dir* James Ivory • *Scr* Kit Hesketh-Harvey, James Ivory, from the novel by EM Forster

Mausoleum ★ 18
Horror 1983 · US · Colour · 91min

Self-styled sleaze starlet Bobbie Bresee plays a housewife who, due to a family curse, becomes possessed by a demon that turns her into a ritually homicidal nymphomaniac. Bresee dances around topless a lot and, in the film's only fun moment, reveals her breasts have teeth. Otherwise the special effects are cheesy (Bresee sports glowing green eyes when feeling lustful), the acting amateurish and the dialogue dreadful. AJ

Marjoe Gortner *Oliver Farrell* • Bobbie Bresee *Susan Farrell* • Norman Burton *Dr Simon Andrews* • Maurice Sherbanee *Ben, the gardener* • LaWanda Page *Elsie* ■ *Dir* Michael Dugan • *Scr* Robert Madero, Robert Barich, from a story by Katherine Rosenwink

Mauvais Sang ★★★ 15
Romantic thriller 1986 · Fr · Colour · 114min

For all his visual flair, director Leos Carax's storytelling skills leave a lot to be desired. There's a carelessly pulpy quality about this futuristic thriller, in which Denis Lavant's commitment to the theft of a serum that cures a fatal disease afflicting only the romantically insincere is diminished by his growing obsession with Juliette Binoche, the mistress of fellow gang member, Michel Piccoli. Away from the plot's comic book sensibilities, however, the compositions recall the pictorial genius of film-makers as different as Fritz Lang and Jean-Luc Godard. Fascinating, but frustrating. DP French +subtitles. DVD BL

Denis Lavant *Alex* • Juliette Binoche *Anna* • Michel Piccoli *Marc* • Hans Meyer *Hans* • Julie Delpy *Lise* • Carroll Brooks *The American* • Hugo Pratt *Boris* • Serge Reggiani *Charlie* ■ *Dir/Scr* Leos Carax

Maverick ★★★ PG
Comedy western 1994 · US · Colour · 121min

Despite the attention of master scriptwriter William Goldman, this gentle tribute to the hit comedy western TV series missed a golden opportunity for a razor-sharp spoof. Mel Gibson and Jodie Foster spark nicely as the eponymous gambler and the con artist who is more than his match. But it's left to James Garner (who played the original Bret Maverick), saddled with a role that is little more than a clumsy in-joke, to demonstrate what comic acting is really all about. Fans of westerns, both small screen and big screen, should keep an eye out for the familiar faces around the riverboat poker tables. DP Violence. DVD

Mel Gibson *Bret Maverick* • Jodie Foster *Annabelle Bransford* • James Garner *Zane Cooper* • James Coburn *Commodore Duval* • Alfred Molina *Angel* • Graham Greene (2) *Joseph* • Geoffrey Lewis *Matthew Wicker* • Dub Taylor *Room clerk* ■ *Dir* Richard Donner • *Scr* William Goldman, from the TV series by Roy Huggins

Mavis! ★★★ PG
Music documentary 2015 · US · Colour · 80min

Mavis Staples has one of the most distinctive voices in modern music. Yet she remains relatively unknown, struggling to establish herself as a solo artist outside the family band. In fact, following her father's death in 2000, Mavis was more interested in releasing an album of his last recordings than she was in working on her own material. Frustratingly, debuting documentarist Jessica Edwards fails to

capture the 70-something's potency during the live interludes, but the revelation about Bob Dylan's marriage proposal atones somewhat. DP

Mavis Staples ■ *Dir* Jessica Edwards

Max ★★★
Drama 1994 · Can · Colour · 94min

This intelligent and involving drama takes an occasionally bitter look at how the ideals of the 1960s have been sold out by the 1990s. The film follows a family's bid to escape the tensions and dangers of the city by settling in the desert, only to discover that their new environment brings new problems. RH Thomson and Denise Crosby head a credible cast. JF

RH Thomson *Andy Blake* • Denise Crosby *Jayne Blake* • Walter Dalton *Jayne's Dad* • Garwin Sanford *Doctor Kaye* • Don Davis [Don S Davis] *Earl* ■ *Dir/Scr* Charles Wilkinson

Max ★★ 15
Period drama 2002 · Hun/Can/UK · Colour · 104min

Menno Meyjes's feature debut is a brave and, at least thematically, fascinating work. Controversially focusing on Adolf Hitler the man, Meyjes offers a fictional account of the early events that set a demobbed soldier and frustrated artist on the road to genocide. Fellow First World War veteran and Jewish art dealer John Cusack befriends the obnoxious young Adolf (Noah Taylor) and tries to persuade him to put as much passion into his painting as he does into his embryonic hate politics. While the drama is well shot and Taylor gives a striking performance, the film is too contrived and simplistic. SF DVD

John Cusack *Max Rothman* • Noah Taylor *Adolf Hitler* • Leelee Sobieski *Liselore* • Molly Parker *Nina Rothman* • Ulrich Thomsen *Captain Mayr* • David Horovitch *Max's father* • Janet Suzman *Max's mother* • Peter Capaldi *David Cohn* ■ *Dir/Scr* Menno Meyjes

Max ★★★ 12
Adventure 2015 · US · Colour · 106min

The hero of this movie is a military trained German shepherd, who is repatriated with the canine equivalent of post-traumatic stress after his handler Kyle is killed in an Afghan ambush. Lodged with Kyle's grieving family, Max's mental rehabilitation centres on the bond he establishes with Kyle's teenage brother, Justin. The pet/weepie combination makes for a movie that's decent family entertainment, especially for anyone who's down with dogs. DA DVD BL

Thomas Haden Church *Ray Wincott* • Robbie Amell *Kyle Wincott* • Luke Kleintank *Tyler Harne* • Jay Hernandez *Sergeant Reyes* ■ *Dir* Boaz Yakin • *Scr* Boaz Yakin, Sheldon Lettich

Max Dugan Returns ★★★ PG
Comedy 1983 · US · Colour · 93min

This Neil Simon comedy stars his then wife, Marsha Mason, as a widow struggling against the foibles of modern life to bring up her 15-year-old son (Matthew Broderick). Just as we get to know them and their world – a world in which every domestic appliance is against them – Jason Robards shows up as Mason's father. He abandoned her when she was nine; now he's terminally ill and stinking rich. Easy on the eye and the mind, with a very attractive cast. AT

Marsha Mason *Nora* • Jason Robards *Max Dugan* • Donald Sutherland *Brian* • Matthew Broderick *Michael* • Dody Goodman *Mrs Litke* • Sal Viscuso *Coach* • Panchito Gomez *Luis* • Kiefer Sutherland *Bill* ■ *Dir* Herbert Ross • *Scr* Neil Simon

Max Keeble's Big Move ★★ PG
Comedy 2001 · US · Colour · 82min

Alex D Linz plays the boy trying to get by at school without being bullied, or caught out by the mean-minded principal. But when dad Robert Carradine announces the family is decamping to Chicago, Linz has just a week to wreak revenge on bullying Noel Fisher, unprincipled principal Larry Miller and grumpy ice-cream man Jamie Kennedy,

while also trying to impress dream-girl Zena Grey. Frantic, dumbed-down fun with neither charm nor credibility. DP

Alex D Linz *Max Keeble* • Larry Miller *Principal Jindraike* • Jamie Kennedy *Evil Ice Cream Man* • Zena Grey *Megan* • Josh Peck *Robe* • Nora Dunn *Lily Keeble* • Robert Carradine *Don Keeble* ■ *Dir* Tim Hill • *Scr* Jonathan Bernstein, Mark Blackwell, James Greer, from a story by David Watts, Jonathan Bernstein, Mark Blackwell, James Greer

Max Mon Amour ★★ 18
Black comedy 1986 · Fr/US · Colour · 93min

Director Nagisa Oshima tries to follow in Luis Buñuel's surreal footsteps by taking apart the hypocrisies of the French bourgeoisie. Charlotte Rampling is the diplomat's deeply bored wife in Paris who takes a chimpanzee as a lover, and Anthony Higgins is her non-plussed husband who is determined to take it on the stiff upper lip and chin. The satire fails to bite, however, owing to a pair of stultifying performances from the main stars, though Max the chimp is actually rather good. SH French, English +subtitles. DVD

Charlotte Rampling *Margaret Jones* • Anthony Higgins *Peter Jones* • Bernard-Pierre Donnadieu *Archibald* • Victoria Abril *Maria* • Anne-Marie Besse *Suzanne* • Nicole Calfan *Hélène* ■ *Dir* Nagisa Oshima • *Scr* Nagisa Oshima, Jean-Claude Carrière, from an idea by Jean-Claude Carrière

Max Payne ★★ 15
Action crime drama 2008 · US/Can · Colour · 95min

Max Payne is yet another big-screen adaptation of a video game that fails to impress. Mark Wahlberg, who can sometimes be unexpectedly good, is at his inert worst as a stony-faced, grieving New York cop seeking revenge for the murders of his wife and child. There's also a sub-plot that revolves around a drug that conjures up giant winged demons, which may or may not be real. The gimmick of the computer game was that the player could slow down time at certain points. The movie, despite its flashy visuals, manages the same trick – its 90-odd-minute running time feels twice as long. AS In English, Spanish. DVD BL

Mark Wahlberg *Max Payne* • Mila Kunis *Mona Sax* • Beau Bridges *BB Hensley* • Chris "Ludacris" Bridges *Jim Bravura* • Chris O'Donnell *Jason Colvin* • Donal Logue *Alex Balder* ■ *Dir* John Moore (3) • *Scr* Beau Thorne, from characters by Sam Lake (2)

Maxie ★★★ PG
Comedy fantasy 1985 · US · Colour · 93min

In this old-fashioned fantasy, Glenn Close is the bishop's secretary whose body is taken over by a free spirit from the 1920s called Maxie Malone. Close has fun with the dual role of the conservative working wife and the jazz-age flapper, but it is *Chicago Hope's* Mandy Patinkin who, as Close's husband, comes across as most at home with the light romantic comedy. Slight but enjoyable. JB

Glenn Close *Jan/Maxie* • Mandy Patinkin *Nick* • Ruth Gordon *Mrs Lavin* • Barnard Hughes *Bishop Campbell* • Valerie Curtin *Miss Sheffer* • Googy Gress *Father Jerome* ■ *Dir* Paul Aaron • *Scr* Patricia Resnick, from the novel *Marion's Wall* by Jack Finney

Maximum Overdrive ★★ 18
Horror 1986 · US · Colour · 93min

Horror writer Stephen King decided his neon-lit prose needed his neon-lit direction. It's a courageous debut, with the machinery in a North Carolina small town coming to lethal life and besieging a group headed by Emilio Estevez and Pat Hingle. The trouble is that writer King should have explained to director King that you must not outpace your audience's interest, however well-managed the action. TH Violence, swearing. DVD

Emilio Estevez *Bill Robinson* • Pat Hingle *Hendershot* • Laura Harrington *Brett* • Yeardley Smith *Connie* • John Short *Curt* • Ellen McElduff *Wanda June* ■ *Dir* Stephen King • *Scr* Stephen King, from his story.

Maximum Risk ★★ 18
Action thriller 1996 · US · Colour · 96min

In *Double Impact*, we suffered the agony of two Jean-Claude Van Dammes for the entire movie. Here, thankfully, his twin gets bumped off in the opening few minutes. It's still hard work, but at least in the hands of Hong Kong director Ringo Lam (*City on Fire*) there are plenty of tremendous action set pieces to relish as Van Damme takes on the might of the Russian Mafia with the help of his late sibling's girlfriend (Natasha Henstridge from *Species*). JF Violence, swearing, a sex scene and nudity. DVD BL

Jean-Claude Van Damme *Alain/Mikhail* • Natasha Henstridge *Alex* • Jean-Hugues Anglade *Sebastien* • Zach Grenier *Ivan* • Stéphane Audran *Chantal Moreau* ■ *Dir* Ringo Lam • *Scr* Larry Ferguson

may i kill u? ★★ 15
Black comedy 2012 · UK · Colour · 87min

This low-budget black comedy stars Kevin Bishop as a bicycle policeman who's seen as a figure of fun on London's mean streets – until, that is, a bash on the bonce during the 2011 riots turns the well-mannered pedalling plod into an equally politic vigilante killer. Posting the footage on social media networks turns him from cycle-beat zero to internet hero, though he keeps his identity a secret. Better in concept than in execution, this has its chucklesome moments, but writer/director Stuart Urban struggles to sustain interest throughout. DA Violence, swearing, sexual references, brief nudity.

Kevin Bishop *Baz* • Jack Doolan *Seth* • Frances Barber *Bernice* • Rosemary Leach *Mags* • Kasia Koleczek *Maya* ■ *Dir/Scr* Stuart Urban

May Wine ★★★ 15
Romantic comedy 1990 · Fr/US · Colour · 80min

Lara Flynn Boyle is on good form here as a troublesome daughter whose refusal to dump an unsuitable boyfriend prompts mother Joanna Cassidy to sweep her off to Paris. No sooner have they arrived than they both fall for the same doctor, Guy Marchand. Cassidy is one of Hollywood's more underrated actresses, while Marchand is among French cinema's most accomplished supporting players. Consequently, the cast brings out the best in director Carol Wiseman's frothy script. DP Swearing, nudity.

Joanna Cassidy *Lorraine* • Lara Flynn Boyle *Camille* • Guy Marchand *Dr Paul Charmant* • Paul Freeman *Tom* • Andre Penvern *Concierge* • Emmanuel Fouquet *Porter* ■ *Dir* Carol Wiseman • *Scr* Carol Wiseman, from a screenplay (unproduced) by Peter Lefcourt

Maya ★★★ 15
Drama 1992 · Ind/UK · Colour · 121min

Ketan Mehta emerged as one of India's foremost directors with *Mirch Masala* and he further enhanced his reputation with this imaginative adaptation of Flaubert's *Madame Bovary*. Set in the days following independence from Britain, Mehta manages to be faithful to the spirit of the novel while also developing his own themes, using Deepa Sahi's passionate fantasies and unrewarding affairs to highlight the mood of the Indian people in 1949, torn between the notion of nationhood and nostalgia for the Raj. DP Hindi +subtitles.

Deepa Sahi *Maya* • Farooque Sheikh *Charudatta Das* • Raj Babbar *Rudrapratap Singh* • Shah Rukh Khan *Lalit Kumar* • Satyadev Dubey *Old interrogator* • Shrivallabh Vyas *Young interrogator* • Dr Shree Ram Lagoo *Maya's father* ■ *Dir* Ketan Mehta • *Scr* Sitanshu Yashashchandra, Ketan Mehta

Maya the Bee ★★ U
Animated comedy adventure 2014 · Aus/Ger · Colour · 84min

Maya the Bee has been a screen regular since Waldemar Bonsels published his beloved children's book in 1912, with a 1924 German feature made with real bees. Here, an Australian cast puts a new spin on a story that sees the rebellious Maya (voiced by Coco Jack Willies) being turfed out of

M

the hive by the villainous Buzzlina (Jacki Weaver).Younger viewers will be amused, especially by a pair of goofy army ants. **DP**

Coco Jack Gillies *Maya* • Miriam Margolyes *The Queen* • Jacki Weaver *Buzzlina Von Beena* • Kodi Smit-McPhee *Willy* ■ *Dir* Alexs Stadermann • *Scr* Fin Edquist, Marcus Sauermann, from the children's books *Maya the Bee and Her Adventures/Heaven Folk* by Waldemar Bonsels

Maybe Baby ★ 🔞
Romantic comedy 1999 · UK · Colour · 100min

Debut writer/director Ben Elton tries and fails to step into the winning comedy shoes of erstwhile *Blackadder* partner Richard Curtis. Revolving around Hugh Laurie and Joely Richardson's attempts to have a child, this is a clichéd, caricatured and dreadfully acted tale, which even Elton's direction is colourless. **JC** *DVD*

Hugh Laurie *Sam Bell* • Joely Richardson *Lucy Bell* • Adrian Lester *George* • James Purefoy *Carl Phipps* • Tom Hollander *Ewan Proclaimer* • Joanna Lumley *Sheila* • Emma Thompson *Druscilla* • Rowan Atkinson *Mr James* • Dawn French *Charlene* ■ *Dir/Scr* Ben Elton

Mayerling ★★★★
Historical romance 1936 · Fr · BW · 96min

This is an exquisite account of one of history's most famous and poignant love affairs: that of Crown Prince Rudolph, heir to the Austro-Hungarian throne, and the youthful Marie Vetsera, a well-born commoner. Denied a release from his loveless marriage, Rudolph and Marie escape for a 24-hour idyll to Mayerling, his hunting lodge, at the end of which he shoots her and then himself in a suicide pact. Charles Boyer and Danielle Darrieux are faultlessly cast as the ill-fated lovers under Anatole Litvak's stylish and sensitive direction. The film led to a Hollywood contract for Litvak and made an international heart-throb of Boyer. **RK** In French.

Charles Boyer *Archduke Rudolph of Austria* • Danielle Darrieux *Marie Vetsera* • Suzy Prim *Countess Larisch* • Jean Dax *Emperor Franz Joseph* • Gabrielle Dorziat *Empress Elizabeth* • Jean Debucourt *Count Taafe* • Marthe Régnier *Baroness Vetsera/Helene* ■ *Dir* Anatole Litvak • *Scr* Joseph Kessel, Irma Von Cube, from the novel by Claude Anet

Mayerling ★★ 🅿🅶
Historical romance 1968 · Fr/UK · Colour · 132min

Despite a fine cast, this take on the tragic love affair between Crown Prince Rudolf of Austria and Maria Vetsera is too heavy-handed. Relating the story of Rudolf's doomed romance with his mistress, director Terence Young's version is both overblown and overlong. The presence of James Mason, Ava Gardner and Genevieve Page merely adds surface gloss to the slow trickle of syrup. **RK**

Omar Sharif *Crown Prince Rudolf* • Catherine Deneuve *Baroness Maria Vetsera* • James Mason *Emperor Franz Josef* • Ava Gardner *Empress Elizabeth* • James Robertson-Justice *Edward, Prince of Wales* • Genevieve Page *Countess Larisch* ■ *Dir* Terence Young • *Scr* Terence Young, Denis Cannan, Joseph Kessel, from the novel by Claude Anet and the novel *The Archduke* by Michael Arnold

Mayflower: the Pilgrims' Adventure ★★
Historical drama 1979 · US · Colour · 97min

There's a distinct made-for-schools feel to this simple and extremely dated historical drama about the English Pilgrims escape to America in 1620. A slow-moving TV movie that's neither convincing nor meaty, it takes almost a third of the running time for the persecuted Puritans to set sail, and then stays onboard the problem-plagued Mayflower for the remainder. For contemporary UK audiences, a youthful Anthony Hopkins will be the only draw, playing the ship's terse captain and delivering some inadvertently amusing dialogue. The rest of the cast, including dodgily accented love interests Jenny Agutter and Michael Beck, and Richard Crenna as Reverend William Brewster, are

as bland as the events, which fail to convey the real hell of the 66-day voyage. **SF**

Anthony Hopkins *Captain Jones* • Richard Crenna *William Brewster* • Jenny Agutter *Priscilla Mullins* • Michael Beck *John Alden* ■ *Dir* George Schaefer • *Scr* James Lee Barrett

The Mayor of Hell ★★
Crime drama 1933 · US · BW · 85min

This typical Warner Bros social melodrama stars James Cagney as a racketeer who suddenly takes an interest in a reform school and the conditions of the youngsters inside. Will he corrupt them or does he become a do-gooder? Despite Cagney's energy, the picture is hopelessly dated, full of mawkish moments, dire knockabout humour and bouts of violence as Cagney carries on with his profession. **AT**

James Cagney *Patsy Gargan* • Madge Evans *Dorothy Griffith* • Arthur Byron *Judge Gilbert* • Allen Jenkins *Mike* • Dudley Digges *Thompson* • Frankie Darro *Jimmy Smith* • Sheila Terry *The girl* ■ *Dir* Archie Mayo • *Scr* Edward Chodorov, from a story by Islin Auster

Maytime ★★★★ 🆄
Romantic musical 1937 · US · Sepia · 131min

Singing duo Jeanette MacDonald and Nelson Eddy were in their prime in this splendid version of Rida Johnson Young and Sigmund Romberg's melancholy operetta, and the theme song *Will You Remember?* became for ever identified with them. The classy MGM production is particularly lavish, and director Robert Z Leonard manages a marvellous tragic tone, as a former opera singer looks back on her career. The film is further enhanced by the presence of the great John Barrymore, in one of his last worthwhile roles. **TS** *DVD*

Jeanette MacDonald *Miss Morrison/Marcia Morney* • Nelson Eddy *Paul Allison* • John Barrymore *Nicolai Nazaroff* • Herman Bing *August Archipenco* • Tom Brown *Kip Stuart* • Lynn Carver [Lynne Carver] *Barbara Roberts* • Rafaela Ottiano *Ellen* ■ *Dir* Robert Z Leonard • *Scr* Noel Langley, from the operetta by Rida Johnson Young, Sigmund Romberg

Maytime in Mayfair ★★★ 🆄
Romantic musical 1949 · UK · Colour · 98min

This is virtually a remake of the previous year's Anna Neagle/Michael Wilding smash hit *Spring in Park Lane*. The plot resembles an earlier Neagle movie, *Irene*, with its dress-shop rivalry, once so fashionable and today so dated. Neagle looks rather too old and staid to partner the charming Wilding, but a hard-working supporting cast keeps the fun bubbling. **TS**

Anna Neagle *Eileen Grahame* • Michael Wilding *Michael Gore-Brown* • Peter Graves (1) *D'Arcy Davenport* • Nicholas Phipps *Sir Henry Hazelrigg* • Thora Hird *Janet* • Michael Shepley *Shepherd* • Tom Walls *Inspector* ■ *Dir* Herbert Wilcox • *Scr* Nicholas Phipps

The Maze ★★★
Horror 1953 · US · BW · 80min

Filmed in monochrome 3D (but since made available in a duo-colour print), this adaptation was an early venture into stereoscopy. As you'd expect of someone with William Cameron Menzies's genius for art design, this atmospheric shocker, set in an isolated Scottish castle, looks superb, in spite of some of the more gimmicky shots. However, there's little tension in Veronica Hurst's pursuit of runaway fiancé Richard Carlson, who is now a prematurely aged recluse. Moreover, the supposedly Kafka-esque resolution is more than slightly preposterous. **DP**

Richard Carlson *Gerald McTeam* • Veronica Hurst *Kitty Murray* • Katherine Emery *Mrs Murray* • Michael Pate *William* • John Dodsworth *Dr Bert Dilling* ■ *Dir* William Cameron Menzies • *Scr* Dan Ullman [Daniel B Ullman] , from a novel by Maurice Sandoz

The Maze Runner ★★★★ 🔢
Science-fiction thriller 2014 · US/UK/Can · Colour · 108min

The Hunger Games meets *Lord of the Flies* in this fast-paced and enjoyably moody teen thriller adapted from the bestselling novel.

It's a star-making role for Dylan O'Brien, the latest in a line of boys to be dumped in a clearing at the centre of a giant maze while suffering from a bad case of amnesia. Power struggles ensue when our hero announces his intention to run the maze and find a way out. There are plenty of twists and turns to keep the momentum building, and a well-balanced combination of politics, action and mystery draws you deeper into the story. **SP** *DVD* *BL*

Dylan O'Brien (1) *Thomas* • Kaya Scodelario *Teresa* • Will Poulter *Gally* • Thomas Brodie-Sangster *Newt* • Aml Ameen *Alby* • Ki Hong Lee *Minho* • Patricia Clarkson *Ava Paige* ■ *Dir* Wes Ball • *Scr* Noah Oppenheim, TS Nowlin, Grant Pierce Myers, from James Dashner's novel

Maze Runner: The Scorch Trials ★★★ 🔢
Science-fiction thriller 2015 · US · Colour · 125min

Dylan O'Brien returns as dashing teen savior Thomas who, after leading a ragtag bunch of kids out of a giant mechanical maze, encourages them to bust out of a high-security facility into a post-apocalyptic world. Back in the director's chair, Wes Ball makes the most of a bigger canvas. The action set pieces come thick and fast, and the tone is a shade darker. But Thomas lacks complexity, while the absence of Will Poulter is keenly felt. Owing to an on-set accident involving O'Brien, part 3 (*The Death Cure*) is delayed to January 2018. **SP** Violence. *DVD* *BL*

Dylan O'Brien (1) *Thomas* • Kaya Scodelario *Teresa* • Thomas Brodie-Sangster *Newt* • Giancarlo Esposito *Jorge* • Aidan Gillen *Janson* ■ *Dir* Wes Ball • *Scr* TS Nowlin, from James Dashner's novel

McFarland, USA ★★ 🅿🅶
Sports drama based on a true story 2015 · US · Colour · 128min

New Zealand director Niki Caro would seem an odd choice for this very American underdog drama. However, Kevin Costner is perfectly cast as the uncompromising football coach who decides to form a running team after discovering that some of his students are pretty quick on their feet. Despite Caro's good intentions, Costner's battle to win over the students, along with the neglect of his own family, are threads that unfold with depressing predictability. **JF** In English, Spanish.

Kevin Costner *Jim White* • Morgan Saylor *Julie White* • Martha Higareda *Lupe* • Michael Aguero *Damacio Diaz* ■ *Dir* Niki Caro • *Scr* Christopher Cleveland, Bettina Gilois, Grant Thompson, from a story by Cleveland, Gilois

Me and Earl and the Dying Girl ★★★★ 🔢
Drama 2015 · US · Colour · 98min

Too-cool quirkiness eventually gives way to poignancy when Thomas Mann's mother forces him to hang out with Olivia Cooke because she's been diagnosed with leukaemia. A friendship develops based on their shared sense of surreal humour, expressed through spoofs of classic movies ("A Sockwork Orange"). And as their relationship matures in a surprising way, eschewing romantic melodrama, the delivery of a heart-rending finish is testament to Jesse Andrews's sensitive adaptation of his own novel. **SP** Swearing, sexual/drug references. *DVD*

Thomas Mann (2) *Greg Gaines* • Olivia Cooke *Rachel Kushner* • RJ Cyler *Earl* • Nick Offerman *Greg's dad* ■ *Dir* Alfonso Gomez-Rejon • *Scr* Jesse Andrews, from the novel

Me & Isaac Newton ★★★
Documentary 2000 · US · Colour · 105min

Although he's had his share of blockbusters, Michael Apted has never forgotten his roots in documentary. Here he turns his attention to scientific genius in this lively and accessible survey. It's a talking heads affair, but this is anything but dry and academic. There are genuinely touching moments, like Nobel laureate Gertrude Elion's recollection of the fiancé whose death sparked her interest in chemistry. But everyone has something interesting to say, whether it's

Steven Pinker ascribing his love of language to his argumentative parents or string-theorist Michio Kaku considering the therapeutic benefits of ice skating. **DP**

■ *Dir* Michael Apted

Me and My Gal ★★★
Comedy drama 1932 · US · BW · 78min

This charming but creaky 20th Century-Fox comedy drama is given a lift by its tart dialogue and the naturalistic playing of stars Spencer Tracy and Joan Bennett. The bulk of the plot turns out to be some nonsense about Bennett's sister falling for a gangster, with Tracy playing a cop who's keen on Bennett. Director Raoul Walsh tries to keep sentimentality at bay, but the whole turns out to be rather ramshackle, if short and sweet. **TS**

Spencer Tracy *Danny Dolan* • Joan Bennett *Helen Riley* • Marion Burns *Kate Riley* • George Walsh *Duke Castenega* • J Farrell MacDonald *Pat "Pop" Riley* • Noel Madison *Baby Face* • Henry B Walthall *Sarge* • Bert Hanlon *Jake* ■ *Dir* Raoul Walsh • *Scr* Arthur Kober, Frank J Dolan (uncredited), Philip Dunne (uncredited), Charles Vidor (uncredited), Al Cohn (uncredited), from a story by Barry Connors, from a story by Phillip Klein

Me and Orson Welles ★★ 🔢
Period drama 2008 · UK · Colour · 108min

High School Musical star Zac Efron is ill-served both by screenplay and director in this fictional account of a young actor's encounter with Orson Welles (Christian McKay). Efron is the wannabe actor who lucks into a small role in Welles's famous 1937 theatre production of *Julius Caesar*, and in the process falls for ambitious company member Claire Danes. Richard Linklater, the indie director who hit the big time with *The School of Rock*, never seems to get to grips with his actors and leaves Efron high and dry. The highlight is McKay, who conjures the bluster and charisma of Welles, as well as bearing an uncanny physical resemblance to the boy-genius. **AS** Swearing, sexual references. *DVD*

Zac Efron *Richard Samuels* • Claire Danes *Sonja Jones* • Christian McKay *Orson Welles* • Ben Chaplin *George Coulouris* • Eddie Marsan *John Houseman* • James Tupper *Joseph Cotten* ■ *Dir* Richard Linklater • *Scr* Holly Gent Palmo, Vince Palmo, from the novel by Robert Kaplow

Me and the Colonel ★★★ 🆄
Second World War comedy 1958 · US · BW · 105min

Danny Kaye gained new admirers with his subdued performance and altered appearance in this serious comedy, playing one half of an odd couple: a self-effacing, resourceful Jew fleeing the German occupation of Paris in 1940. Joining the journey of escape is an arrogant, aristocratic Polish colonel, played by Curt Jurgens, who ultimately overcomes his anti-Semitism. Director Peter Glenville draws finely judged performances from his leads, and there are some expert supporting performances. **AE** *DVD*

Danny Kaye *SL Jacobowsky* • Curt Jurgens *Colonel Tadeusz Boleslav Prokoszny* • Nicole Maurey *Suzanne Roualet* • Françoise Rosay *Madame Bouffier* • Akim Tamiroff *Szabuniewicz* • Martita Hunt *Mother Superior* • Alexander Scourby *Major Von Bergen* ■ *Dir* Peter Glenville • *Scr* George Froeschel, SN Behrman, from the play *Jacobowsky and the Colonel* by Franz Werfel

Me and the Kid ★★
Crime comedy drama 1993 · US · Colour · 97min

In this plodding semi-comedy, bungling burglars break into a rich man's home, find the safe empty and decide to kidnap the rich guy's neglected kid instead. The thieves fall out when one decides to return the boy, only to find that he prefers his new life and doesn't want to go back. Poor pacing makes the film heavy going. **DA** Some swearing.

Danny Aiello *Harry* • Alex Zuckerman *Gary Feldman* • Joe Pantoliano *Roy* • Cathy Moriarty *Rose* • David Dukes *Victor Feldman* • Anita Morris *Mrs Feldman* ■ *Dir* Dan Curtis • *Scr* Richard Tannenbaum, from the novel *Taking Gary Feldman* by Stanley Cohen

🆄 SUITABLE FOR ALL 🆄🄴 SUITABLE ESPECIALLY FOR YOUNG CHILDREN (DVD ONLY) 🅿🅶 PARENTAL GUIDANCE 🄸🄰 UNDER 12s TO BE ACCOMPANIED (CINEMA ONLY)

Me and You ★★★ 15

Drama 2012 · It/Swi · Colour · 96min

In director Bernardo Bertolucci's rites-of-passage story, a teenage loner (Jacopo Olmi Antinori) uses the excuse of a class skiing trip to fool his overprotective mum into thinking he's away, when in fact he's holed up in the basement. However, the surprise arrival of his half-sister (Tea Falco) soon changes his perspective. Much more modest than his past glories like multi-Oscar winner *The Last Emperor*, Bertolucci's film unfolds as a chamber piece. Nevertheless, it works well on its own terms, building our understanding of why these privileged kids should feel so ill at ease. Also, brilliant use of David Bowie's *Space Oddity* shows that Bertolucci's insight and dramatic flair are still intact, but operating on a more intimate scale. TJ
Italian +subtitles. Swearing. DVD BD

Jacopo Olmo Antinori *Lorenzo* • Tea Falco *Olivia* • Sonia Bergamasco *Arianna* • Veronica Lazar *Grandmother* ■ *Dir* Bernardo Bertolucci • *Scr* Bernardo Bertolucci, Niccolo Ammaniti, Umberto Contarello, Francesca Marciano, from the novel by Ammaniti

Me and You and Everyone We Know ★★★★ 15

Comedy drama 2005 · US/UK/Jpn · Colour · 87min

Performance artist Miranda July's accomplished feature debut weaves together the stories of lonely suburbanites struggling to connect in southern California. Shoe salesman John Hawkes is so distraught when his wife dumps him, he sets fire to his own hand. Literally and figuratively scarred, he's hesitant to respond to romantic overtures from a kooky artist-cum-cab driver (writer/director July). Some viewers might feel a little uncomfortable about subplots involving Hawkes's teenage son Miles Thompson discovering oral sex and even younger son Brandon Ratcliff entering into a salacious online relationship with a stranger. However, July handles such material with sensitivity as well as humour, and her film is characterised by sharp writing and abundant heart. LF Swearing. DVD

Miranda July *Christine Jesperson* • John Hawkes *Richard Swersey* • Miles Thompson *Peter Swersey* • Brandon Ratcliff *Robby Swersey* • Carlie Westerman *Sylvie* • Hector Elias *Michael* • Brad William Henke *Andrew* • Natasha Slayton *Heather* ■ *Dir/Scr* Miranda July

Me before You ★★★ 12A

Romantic drama 2016 · US · Colour · 110min

Emilia Clarke is the chirpiest of romantic leads in this story about a young woman who falls for the man she is employed to care for, a paralysed and wealthy young man named Will (Sam Claflin). This all-out weepie may annoy some with its relentless attempts to put lumps in throats. However, a chick flick is only as good as its leads, and this is where director Thea Sharrock's debut feature comes up trumps. JL

Emilia Clarke *Louisa "Lou" Clark* • Sam Claflin *Will Traynor* • Janet McTeer *Camilla Traynor* • Charles Dance *Stephen Traynor* • Jenna Coleman *Katrina "Treena" Clark* ■ *Dir* Thea Sharrock • *Scr* Jojo Moyes, from her novel

Me, Myself & Irene ★★★ 15

Comedy 2000 · US · Colour · 116min

As a Rhode Island state trooper, Jim Carrey's sweet-hearted loser falls in love with Renée Zellweger, even though he's lumbered with three delightful grown-up black sons from his wife's adulterous liaison. Unfortunately, his vicious alter-ego has also fallen for her, and comic mayhem ensues as when Jekyll wrestles with Hyde for Zellweger's affections. The jokes are outrageously tasteless, but the movie delivers its vulgarity with almost surreal panache. TH Violence, swearing, nudity. DVD BD CS

Jim Carrey *Charlie Baileygates/Hank* • Renée Zellweger *Irene P White* • Chris Cooper *Lieutenant Gerke* • Robert Forster *Colonel Partington* ■ *Dir* Bobby Farrelly, Peter Farrelly • *Scr* Peter Farrelly, Mike Cerrone, Bobby Farrelly

Me, Myself and Mum ★★★ 15

Comedy 2013 · Fr/Bel · Colour · 86min

Guillaume Gallienne's autobiographical play about a gender misfit reaches the screen co-written, directed by and starring its creator. On stage Gallienne created all the characters, but on film – while retaining the framing device of a live performance – he merely plays himself and his elegant but brittle and reserved mother. He is witty and compelling in both roles, delivering what's probably the finest cross-dressing turn since Dustin Hoffman in *Tootsie*, though the connecting narrative of his misadventures proves somewhat sketchy. TJ In French, English, Spanish, German.

Guillaume Gallienne *Guillaume/Mum* • André Marcon *Dad* • Françoise Fabian *Babou* • Nanou Garcia *Paqui* • Diane Kruger *Ingeborg* ■ *Dir* Guillaume Gallienne • *Scr* Guillaume Gallienne, Claude Mathieu, Nicolas Vassiliev

Me Myself I ★★★★ 15

Romantic comedy fantasy 1999 · Fr/Aus · Colour · 100min

Rachel Griffiths delivers an engaging performance as a single 30-something journalist who wonders what would have happened if she had married her former sweetheart David Roberts and settled down to the life of a housewife and mother. After a freak (and never explained) occurrence, she wakes up to discover that her old life has disappeared and she is *that* woman, complete with annoying children and a sexless marriage. Brilliantly written and directed by Pip Karmel, this realistically presents the pros and cons of both of lives, while Griffiths proves she has a deft comic touch. JB

Rachel Griffiths *Pamela* • David Roberts (2) *Robert* • Sandy Winton *Ben* • Yael Stone *Stacey* • Shaun Loseby *Douglas* • Trent Sullivan *Rupert* • Rebecca Frith *Terri* • Felix Williamson *Geoff* ■ *Dir/Scr* Pip Karmel

Me without You ★★★★ 15

Comedy drama 2001 · UK/Ger · Colour · 103min

This film about female friendship was a deserved hit for director Sandra Goldbacher at the Venice film festival. Detailing the relationship between childhood friends Anna Friel and Michelle Williams, the film follows the girls from 1970s spacehoppers through teenage sex, drugs and rock 'n' roll, to university and into the present day. The fabulous attention to period detail is matched by equally strong emotional observation, as the difference between Friel's brittle bitch and Williams's bright but delicate innocent gets more exaggerated and the friendship disintegrates from undying loyalty to an almost claustrophobic curse. LH DVD

Anna Friel *Marina* • Michelle Williams *Holly* • Kyle MacLachlan *Daniel* • Oliver Milburn *Nat* • Trudie Styler *Linda* • Marianne Denicourt *Isabel* • Nicky Henson *Ray* ■ *Dir* Sandra Goldbacher • *Scr* Sandra Goldbacher, Laurence Coriat

Me, You, Them ★★★ PG

Comedy drama 2000 · Bra/US/Por · Colour · 102min

This is an amiable, if unambitious, attempt to explore socio-sexual mores in a tightly knit Brazilian community. Regina Case romps through the fact-based proceedings as the jilted bride amassing a motley collection of beaus and babies. But much of the humour is centred on cuckolded chauvinist Lima Duarte and Stenio Garcia, the poacher who turns gamekeeper when Case begins spending her lunch hours cavorting in the fields with handsome drifter Luiz Carlos Vasconcelos. Andrucha Waddington employs camera and character intelligently, but this is largely undemanding fare. DP Portuguese +subtitles. DVD

Regina Case *Darlene* • Lima Duarte *Osias Linhares* • Stenio Garcia *Zezinho* • Luiz Carlos Vasconcelos *Ciro* • Nilda Spencer *Raquel* ■ *Dir* Andrucha Waddington • *Scr* Elena Soarez

Mea Culpa ★★★ 15

Action thriller 2012 · Fr/Bel · Colour and BW · 86min

Fans of fast-paced action movies will find much to enjoy in this bruising French thriller. It centres on the haunted figure of Simon (Vincent Lindon), a taciturn former cop whose old skill set is required when his little boy is targeted by a gang of murderous criminals. Deciding that attack is the best form of defence, Simon teams up with his loyal ex-partner (Gilles Lellouche) and takes the fight to them. The numerous chases and shoot-outs that follow are staged with finesse, and they boast an impressive sense of driving momentum. SC French +subtitles. Violence, swearing.

Vincent Lindon *Simon* • Gilles Lellouche *Franck Vasseur* • Nadine Labaki *Alice* • Gilles Cohen *Pastor* • Max Baissette de Malglaive *Théo, aged 10* ■ *Dir* Fred Cavayé • *Scr* Fred Cavayé, Guillaume Lemans, from an idea by Olivier Marchal

Mea Maxima Culpa: Silence in the House of God ★★★ 15

Documentary 2012 · US · Colour · 106min

Only the victims emerge with any credit in Alex Gibney's harrowing exposé of child abuse within the Roman Catholic Church. The central case is built around the activities of Father Lawrence Murphy, who assaulted boys at St John's School for the Deaf in Wisconsin for a quarter of a century before four ex-students decided to take a stand in the 1970s. The evidence Gibney presents is persuasive and is backed up by plenty of compelling first-hand testimony, but the melodramatic methods employed to reconstruct Murphy's predatory prowling distract from the appalling revelations. DP English, Italian +subtitles. References to child sexual abuse.

Terry Kohut • Arthur Budzinski • Gary Smith • Pat Kuehn • Jamey Sheridan *Terry Kohut* • John Slattery *Arthur Budzinski* • Chris Cooper *Gary Smith* • Ethan Hawke *Pat Kuehn* ■ *Dir/Scr* Alex Gibney

Mean Creek ★★★★ 15

Thriller 2004 · US · Colour · 86min

Rory Culkin gives a more-than-competent performance in this compelling tale of teenage revenge, playing an unremarkable schoolkid who is harassed by bully Josh Peck. When his older brother (Trevor Morgan) finds out about it, he cooks up a plan for some payback with town bad boy Scott Mechlowicz. This is a gripping, original thriller that boasts an unusual level of moral engagement and is studded with outstanding performances. Jacob Aaron Estes, in his debut feature, takes what could have been hackneyed material and transforms it into something surprising and serious. AS Swearing, sexual references. DVD

Rory Culkin *Sam* • Ryan Kelley *Clyde* • Scott Mechlowicz *Marty* • Trevor Morgan *Rocky* • Josh Peck *George* • Carly Schroeder *Millie* • James W Crawford *Tom* ■ *Dir/Scr* Jacob Aaron Estes

Mean Girls ★★★ 12

Comedy 2004 · US · Colour · 92min

Inspired by a real life high-school survival manual for teenage girls and their mothers, this is a bracingly dark comedy. Lindsay Lohan stars as a bright, pretty kid who has been home-schooled in Africa by her anthropologist parents, and is thrown in at the deep end when she attends high school in the US for the first time. Befriended by the geek clique, she also infiltrates the "plastics" – a troika of Barbie-like popular girls. Despite descending into slightly saccharine moralising towards the end, this is a snappily written, acerbic account of the American high-school experience. AS Swearing, sexual references. DVD

Lindsay Lohan *Cady Heron* • Rachel McAdams *Regina George* • Tina Fey *Ms Norbury* • Tim Meadows *Mr Duvall* • Amy Poehler *Mrs George* • Ana Gasteyer *Betsy Heron* • Lacey Chabert *Gretchen Wieners* • Lizzy Caplan *Janis Ian* • Daniel Franzese *Damian* • Neil Flynn *Chip Heron* ■ *Dir* Mark S Waters [Mark Waters (1)] • *Scr* Tina Fey, from the non-fiction book *Queen*

Bees and Wannabes: Helping Your Daughter Survive Cliques, Gossip, Boyfriends and Other Realities of Adolescence by Rosalind Wiseman

The Mean Machine ★★★★ 15

Prison sports comedy 1974 · US · Colour · 121min

This is the film that fixed Burt Reynolds's "good old boy" image in the minds of audiences everywhere and helped propel him to superstardom. Reynolds exudes star quality as an imprisoned football pro who's forced to organise a team of convicts for a match against their guards. Full of references to *The Dirty Dozen* and the corrupt regime of President Nixon, Robert Aldrich's feature is a little heavy-handed as a political satire. But as a boisterous comedy, with a few choice asides on dignity, loyalty and liberty, it's pretty hard to beat. Released in the US as *The Longest Yard*, the UK DVD release is also under this title. DP DVD

Burt Reynolds *Paul Crewe* • Eddie Albert *Warden Hazen* • Ed Lauter *Captain Knauer* • Michael Conrad *Nate Scarboro* • Jim Hampton [James Hampton] *Caretaker* • Harry Caesar *Granville* • John Steadman *Pop* • Charles Tyner *Unger* ■ *Dir* Robert Aldrich • *Scr* Tracy Keenan Wynn, from a story by Albert S Ruddy

Mean Machine ★★★ 15

Prison sports comedy 2001 · US/UK · Colour · 95min

Vinnie Jones doesn't stray too far from home for his first leading part, starring in this remake of Robert Aldrich's 1974 movie. If you can overlook the rather thin characters and simplistic plot, the film's final third – an ill-tempered soccer match between warders and inmates – is very well filmed and entertaining. Jones isn't bad in a made-to-measure role, though the best shots come from Jason Statham's maverick keeper and Jason Flemyng's unconventional commentator. JC DVD

Vinnie Jones *Danny Meehan* • David Kelly *Doc* • David Hemmings *Governor* • Ralph Brown (2) *Burton* • Vas Blackwood *Massive* • Robbie Gee *Trojan* • Jason Flemyng *Bob Likely* • Jason Statham *Monk* ■ *Dir* Barry Skolnick • *Scr* Barry Fletcher, Chris Baker, Andrew Day, from the 1974 film by Tracy Keenan Wynn, from a story by Albert S Ruddy

The Mean Season ★★★ 15

Thriller 1985 · US · Colour · 99min

This is a cracker of a thriller, marred only by some seriously duff moments, most notably supplied by poor Mariel Hemingway, who is saddled with the weak "girlfriend under threat from a psychopath" role. Her boyfriend is cynical journalist Kurt Russell, who gives a mesmerising performance as a man who finds himself dragged further into his latest crime story than is comfortable. A taut, atmospheric and potentially distressing movie, with the odd dull spell. SH Violence, swearing, nudity. DVD

Kurt Russell *Malcolm Anderson* • Mariel Hemingway *Christine Connelly* • Richard Jordan *Alan Delour* • Richard Masur *Bill Nolan* • Joe Pantoliano *Andy Porter* • Richard Bradford *Phil Wilson* • Andy Garcia *Ray Martinez* ■ *Dir* Phillip Borsos • *Scr* Leon Piedmont, from the novel *In the Heat of the Summer* by John Katzenbach

LANDMARK FILM
Scorsese's breakthrough film showcases his future trademarks and is the first of eight collaborations with Robert De Niro

Mean Streets ★★★★ 18

Drama 1973 · US · Colour · 107min

In his breakthrough film, director Martin Scorsese drew on his upbringing in New York's Little Italy for this semi-autobiographical story about two friends. Harvey Keitel is the older of the two and a debt-collector for the Mob, while tearaway hoodlum Robert De Niro is in hock to loan sharks. This explicitly European-influenced film establishes Scorsese's masterful use of music, mixing a 1960s pop soundtrack with grubby pool-hall violence. This keystone of 1970s American cinema hinges on the power of its lead performances; Keitel exhibits simmering anguish as he struggles to reconcile his religion and lifestyle while

M

dating the epileptic Amy Robinson against his boss's wishes, while the freewheeling De Niro is full of edgy humour, life and barely concealed danger. **AC** English, Italian +subtitles. Violence, swearing, nudity. **DVD**

Harvey Keitel *Charlie* • Robert De Niro *Johnny Boy* • David Proval *Tony* • Amy Robinson *Teresa* • Richard Romanus *Michael* • Cesare Danova *Giovanni* • Vic Argo [Victor Argo] *Mario* • Robert Carradine *Assassin* ■ *Dir* Martin Scorsese • *Scr* Martin Scorsese, Mardik Martin, from a story by Martin Scorsese

The Meanest Man in the World ★★★ U

Comedy 1943 · US · BW · 57min

This is a cracking vehicle for the inimitable partnership of Jack Benny and Eddie "Rochester" Anderson. Few comics could milk a gag as well as Benny, whose expression, as he steals a lollipop from a child in an effort to prove to both his prospective father-in-law and millionaire Edmund Gwenn that he is a lawyer to be reckoned with, is priceless. Priscilla Lane is under-used as Benny's fiancée, but Anne Revere is splendid as his wavering secretary. **DP**

Jack Benny *Richard Clark* • Priscilla Lane *Janie Brown* • Eddie "Rochester" Anderson *Shufro* • Edmund Gwenn *Frederick P Leggitt* • Matt Briggs *Mr Brown* • Anne Revere *Kitty Crockett* • Margaret Seddon *Mrs Leggitt* • Harry Hayden *Mr Chambers* ■ *Dir* Sidney Lanfield • *Scr* George Seaton, Allan House, from a play by Augustin MacHugh, George M Cohan

The Measure of a Man ★★★ PG

Drama 2015 · Fr · Colour · 91min

The pressures of the employment situation in France are depicted in such low-key detail here that it feels like a staged reality show, but with little glamour. Vincent Lindon stars as a laid-off factory worker in his 50s who needs a job to support his wife and disabled son. At last employed as a security guard, it's now Lindon's turn to observe those taking desperate measures to supplement their meagre wages. It all ends rather abruptly, but Lindon's dignified performance drives a beautifully shot and edited slice of modern blue-collar life. **DW** French +subtitles. Some swearing.

Vincent Lindon *Thierry Taugourdeau* • Yves Ory *Employment agent* • Karine De Mirbeck *Katherine, Thierry's wife* • Matthieu Schaller *Mathieu, Thierry's son* ■ *Dir* Stéphane Brizé • *Scr* Stéphane Brizé, Olivier Gorce

Meatballs ★★ 15

Comedy 1979 · Can · Colour · 89min

This early collaboration of *Ghost Busters* director Ivan Reitman and Bill Murray is solely dependent on its star for laughs, and there aren't that many. Murray plays a goofy counsellor at a Canadian summer camp who takes a young loner under his wing. No better or worse than dozens of other similarly plotted comedies, although Reitman has the good sense to get Murray on screen as often as possible. Further films followed in the 1980s and early 90s, but three sequels later, this mix of smut and slapstick looked very dated indeed. **JC**

Bill Murray *Tripper* • Harvey Atkin *Morty* • Kate Lynch *Roxanne* • Russ Banham *Crockett* • Kristine DeBell *AL* • Sarah Torgov *Candace* • Jack Blum *Spaz* • Keith Knight *Fink* ■ *Dir* Ivan Reitman • *Scr* Len Blum, Dan Goldberg, Janis Allen, Harold Ramis

The Mechanic ★★★ 15

Action thriller 1972 · US · Colour · 95min

No-frills direction from Michael Winner creates the right tone of seething disquiet for star Charles Bronson in this forerunner to *Death Wish*. No one is better at suggesting silent menace than Bronson, who here plays a hitman capable of making his messy work look accidental and training a young pretender to the throne. Winner, though sometimes disrupting the action with unnecessary gloss, keeps his film

suspenseful and violent. **JM** Swearing. **DVD**

Charles Bronson *Arthur Bishop* • Jan-Michael Vincent *Steve McKenna* • Keenan Wynn *Harry McKenna* • Jill Ireland *Prostitute* • Linda Ridgeway *Louise* • Frank De Kova *Syndicate head* • Lindsay H Crosby *Policeman* ■ *Dir* Michael Winner • *Scr* Lewis John Carlino

The Mechanic ★★ 15

Action thriller 2011 · US · Colour · 88min

A professional assassin finds his life at crisis point when he starts training his mentor's volatile son, in this remake of Michael Winner's 1972 thriller. Jason Statham is astute casting to take over from Charles Bronson in the title role, and he acquits himself well as the taciturn killer – quiet when he needs to be, suitably fleet-footed when the competent action scenes require it. There are problems elsewhere, however, especially a miscast Ben Foster as the protégé learning the ropes from an ice-cool loner. Unwisely, director Simon West (*Con Air*) jettisons the existential musings that made the original a surprisingly thoughtful entry in the Bronson canon and replaces them with Tony Goldwyn's scenery-chewing turn as a covert agency schemer, although Donald Sutherland adds class in his cameo as Statham's ill-fated handler. A sequel with Statham is due in 2016. **TJ** Violence, swearing, a sex scene, nudity. **DVD**

Jason Statham *Arthur Bishop* • Ben Foster *Steve McKenna* • Donald Sutherland *Harry McKenna* • Tony Goldwyn *Dean Sanderson* • Jeff Chase *Burke* • Mini Anden *Sarah* • James Logan *Jorge Lara* • John McConnell *Vaughn* ■ *Dir* Simon West • *Scr* Richard Wenk, from the 1972 film

Mechanic: Resurrection 15

Action crime thriller 2016 · US/Thai/Fr · Colour · 98min

This is a preview – no prints were available to review as we went to press: Films whose release dates keep getting bounced tend to be duffers. Will that be the case with Jason Statham's return in the latest of the all-action franchises that keep him so busy? Fans will remember the original 2011 *Mechanic* as being one long bluffing face-off between Statham and Ben Foster. It did not end well for one of them. This time around, he's joined by Jessica Alba, Tommy Lee Jones and Michelle Yeoh, and it's set to be one hell of a shakedown **SvM**

Jason Statham *Arthur Bishop* • Jessica Alba *Gina* • Tommy Lee Jones *Max Adams* • Michelle Yeoh *Mei* ■ *Dir* Dennis Gansel • *Scr* Philip Shelby, Tony Mosher, Rachel Long, Brian Pittman

A Medal for Benny ★★★ U

Satirical drama 1945 · US · BW · 80min

Though Benny himself is never seen, his trouble-making has got him evicted from the small town on the California coast, home to Mexican immigrants. Then his shamed family and the townspeople learn he's a war hero, having killed 100 Japanese single-handed before being killed himself. Interesting, untypical casting and a semi-satirical script that manages (just) to veer off easy sentimentality make this little-known picture well worth a look. The story, partly by John Steinbeck, was Oscar-nominated. **AT**

Dorothy Lamour *Lolita Sierra* • Arturo de Cordova *Joe Morales* • J Carrol Naish *Charley Martin* • Mikhail Rasumny *Raphael Catalina* • Fernando Alvarado *Chito Sierra* • Charles Dingle *Zach Mibbs* • Frank McHugh *Edgar Lovekin* • Douglass Dumbrille *General* ■ *Dir* Irving Pichel • *Scr* Frank Butler, Jack Wagner, from a story by Jack Wagner, John Steinbeck

The Medallion ★ PG

Action fantasy 2003 · HK/US · Colour · 84min

In a Jackie Chan film only two elements really matter: the chemistry between the two inevitable buddies/partners and the quality of the action. Sadly both are well below par in this Dublin-set farrago. Chan stars as a cop whose search for evil crime lord Julian Sands leads to the discovery of an ancient medallion and a kidnapped boy. Looking like it was edited on a bacon slicer, this mess couldn't possibly get any worse

until Lee Evans applies the tin lid with an excruciating performance. **AS** **DVD**

Jackie Chan *Eddie Yang* • Lee Evans *Arthur Watson* • Claire Forlani *Nicole James* • Julian Sands *Snakehead* • John Rhys-Davies *Commander Hammerstock-Smythe* • Anthony Wong (1) *Lester Wong* ■ *Dir* Gordon Chan • *Scr* Bey Logan, Gordon Chan, Alfred Cheung, Bennett Joshua Davlin, Paul Wheeler, from a story by Alfred Cheung, from characters by Alfred Cheung

The Meddler ★★★★ 12A

Comedy drama 2015 · US · Colour · 103min

The title refers to Marnie Minervini (Susan Sarandon), an upbeat widow who has moved to LA to be closer to her daughter, Lori (Rose Byrne). Marnie is kind and well-meaning, but she's also intrusive and overbearing. And when Lori leaves for New York, Marnie channels her energy into helping people she barely knows, her way of coping with the death of her husband. This is beautifully conveyed by Sarandon, who oozes likeability while allowing us to see glimpses of Marnie's grief. **SC** Some swearing, drug abuse

Susan Sarandon *Marnie Minervini* • Rose Byrne *Lori Minervini* • JK Simmons *Zipper* • Jerrod Carmichael *Freddy/Fredo* • Cecily Strong *Jillian* ■ *Dir/Scr* Lorene Scafaria

Medea ★★ 12

Tragedy 1970 · It/Fr/W Ger · Colour · 106min

Following his 1967 adaptation of Sophocles's *Oedipus Rex*, this was Pier Paolo Pasolini's second venture into Greek mythology. But this version of Euripides's play suffers as much from miscasting as it does from lacklustre direction. Opera legend Maria Callas is stripped of much of her power by the fact that her voice is dubbed, while Giuseppe Gentile brings little but physique to the part of Jason. The locations have been exploited to the full, but Pasolini's overambitious mix of myth, Marxism and psychology makes for heavy going. **DP** Italian +subtitles.

Maria Callas *Medea* • Giuseppe Gentile *Jason* • Massimo Girotti *Creon* • Laurent Terzieff *Centaur* • Margareth Clementi *Glauce* ■ *Dir* Pier Paolo Pasolini • *Scr* Pier Paolo Pasolini, from the play by Euripides

Medea ★★★

Tragedy 1988 · Den · Colour · 75min

Danish director Lars von Trier's version of Euripides's classical tragedy about the woman who took revenge on Jason has an icy calm and muted colours that give this locations an unworldly feel. Working from an unproduced 1960s screenplay by influential Danish director Carl Th Dreyer and poet Preben Thomsen, von Trier artfully uses his video camera to approximate Dreyer's atmospheric austerity. But the bravura technique and liberal interpretation are pure von Trier. **DP** Danish +subtitles.

Kirsten Olesen *Medea* • Udo Kier *Jason* ■ *Dir* Lars von Trier • *Scr* Lars von Trier, from a screenplay (unproduced) by Preben Thomsen, Carl Theodor [Carl Th] Dreyer, from the play by Euripides

Medicine Man ★★ PG

Drama 1992 · US · Colour · 100min

Giving an effortlessly charismatic performance, Sean Connery overcomes an unfocused script and an even worse ponytail. He plays a grumpy scientist who has discovered a cure for cancer deep in the heart of the South American rainforest, but is now unable to reproduce it. He also has to cope with the twin threats of destructive developers and Lorraine Bracco (badly miscast), who has been sent to supervise him. **JF**

Sean Connery *Dr Robert Campbell* • Lorraine Bracco *Dr Rae Crane* • José Wilker *Dr Miguel Ornega* • Rodolfo De Alexandre *Tanaki* • Francisco Tsirene Tsere Rereme *Jahausa* • Elias Monteiro Da Silva *Palala* • Edinei Maria Serrio Dos Santos *Kalana* ■ *Dir* John McTiernan • *Scr* Tom Schulman, Sally Robinson

Mediterraneo ★★★★ 15

Comedy drama 1991 · It · Colour · 86min

As with so many recent winners of the Oscar for best foreign language film, this is an undemanding picture closer to the Hollywood brand of light entertainment than to art house gravitas. Set in a largely forgotten theatre of the Second World War, the action centres on eight Italian soldiers sent to guard the strategically negligible Greek island of Kastellorizo. The interaction between the mismatched squad and its increasingly amicable relationship with the islanders throws up few novel situations, but everything is done with such sleepy good humour that it makes for easy watching. **DP** Italian +subtitles. **DVD**

Claudio Bigagli *Lieutenant Montini* • Giuseppe Cederna *Farina* • Claudio Bisio *Noventa* • Gigio Alberti *Strazzabosco* • Ugo Conti *Colosanti* • Memo Dini *Felice Munaron* • Vasco Mirondola *Libero Munaron* ■ *Dir* Gabriele Salvatores • *Scr* Vincenzo Monteleone

Medium Cool ★★★★★

Drama 1969 · US · Colour · 110min

The Oscar-winning cameraman Haskell Wexler turned director with this semi-documentary study of America's political temperature in the turbulent late-1960s. Robert Forster plays a TV news cameraman who covers various major events, notably the riots at the Democratic Convention in Chicago, while trying to prevent his personal life from falling apart. Much of the movie's thrust derives from media pundit Marshall McLuhan's dictum that "the medium is the message". The film's flaws are obvious, but this is still a provocative and hugely influential movie that ends on a note of deep pessimism with the chant, "The whole world is watching". **AT** **DVD**

Robert Forster *John Cassellis* • Verna Bloom *Eileen Horton* • Peter Bonerz *Gus* • Marianna Hill *Ruth* • Harold Blankenship *Harold Horton* • Sid McCoy *Frank Baker* ■ *Dir* Haskell Wexler • *Scr* Haskell Wexler, from the novel *The Concrete Wilderness* by Jack Couffer • *Cinematographer* Haskell Wexler

The Medusa Touch ★★★ PG

Supernatural thriller 1978 · UK/Fr · Colour · 104min

This is a quietly effective thriller that combines the kinetic thrills of a disaster movie with *Omen*-style shocks. Richard Burton is a novelist driven to the brink of insanity by his murderous mental powers, while Lee Remick is the psychiatrist attempting to piece together the puzzle. Director Jack Gold keeps this amiable tosh ticking along, aided by some spectacular disaster footage and an impressive roster of British support players. **RS** **DVD**

Richard Burton *John Morlar* • Lee Remick *Dr Zonfeld* • Lino Ventura *Detective Inspector Brunel* • Harry Andrews *Assistant Commissioner* • Marie-Christine Barrault *Patricia Morlar* • Michael Hordern *Atropos* • Gordon Jackson *Dr Johnson* • Derek Jacobi *Townley* ■ *Dir* Jack Gold • *Scr* John Briley, Jack Gold, from a novel by Peter Van Greenaway

Mee-Shee: the Water Giant ★★ PG

Fantasy adventure 2005 · Ger/UK/US · Colour · 90min

This family-orientated "creature feature" treads similar territory to *Magic in the Water* and *Loch Ness*. Ten-year-old Mac (Daniel Magder) is disappointed when he has to put his holiday plans on hold to accompany his dad, an oil-company recovery expert, to a remote Canadian lake. While dad (the dependable Bruce Greenwood) attempts to retrieve a priceless lost drill bit from the lake's bottom, Mac is befriended by Mee-Shee, a Nessie-type lake monster. But soon a pair of bad guys are on the scene. Adults will enjoy the scenery but might baulk at some dodgy special effects and predictable characters, while younger children are sure to enjoy the cute Mee-Shee itself, a product of the Jim Henson Creature Shop. **DA** **DVD**

Bruce Greenwood *Sean Campbell* • Daniel Magder *Mac Campbell* • Rena Owen *"Crazy" Norma* • Jacinta Wawatai *Pawnee Custer* • Phyllida Law *Mrs Coogan* • Luanne Gordon *Laura Simmons* ■ *Dir* John Henderson • *Scr* Barry Authors • *Cinematographer* John Ignatius

Meek's Cutoff ★★★★ PG
Western   2010 · US · Colour · 98min

Director Kelly Reichardt's atmospheric and feminist frontier fable follows a wagon train across Oregon's unyielding Cascade Mountains in 1845. Led by Bruce Greenwood's arrogant mountain man Meek, the settlers are initially divided into a traditional patriarchal power dynamic, with the husbands making the decisions while the wives – including feisty Michelle Williams – make dinner. But as supplies run out and a lone Cayuse Indian is brought into the group, Meek's authority is challenged. Convincingly acted and sparingly scripted, this is a prairie tale that vividly immerses the audience in an unforgiving landscape. AC *DVD*

Michelle Williams *Emily Tetherow* • Bruce Greenwood *Stephen Meek* • Will Patton *Solomon Tetherow* • Zoe Kazan *Millie Gately* • Paul Dano *Thomas Gately* • Shirley Henderson *Glory White* ■ *Dir* Kelly Reichardt • *Scr* Jon Raymond [Jonathan Raymond]

The Meerkats ★★★ PG
Drama documentary   2007 · UK/US · Colour · 83min

Taking its cue from *March of the Penguins*, this cute if rather contrived wildlife documentary justifies its elevation to the big screen thanks to charming narration, voiced by the late Paul Newman and written by Alexander McCall Smith (author of the *No 1 Ladies' Detective Agency* books). Familiar to many thanks to the BBC's *Meerkat Manor* series, the adorable Kalahari-dwelling creatures are naturals before the camera, making this thoroughly engaging for younger viewers – but be warned, there are some scary sequences involving snakes, scorpions and eagles. DA

Paul Newman *Narrator* ■ *Dir* James Honeyborne • *Scr* Alexander McCall Smith, from a story by James Honeyborne

Meet Boston Blackie ★★★
Detective drama   1941 · US · BW · 60min

Pulp novelist Jack Boyle's thief-turned-troubleshooter debuted on screen in 1918. But this film, directed with aplomb by Robert Florey, launched Columbia's 14-strong B series, which boasted Chester Morris as the wisecracking maverick with an eye for the girls and a nose for trouble. Richard Lane was ever present as the perpetually suspicious Inspector Farraday (here as Faraday), as was Morris's sidekick, The Runt (played here by Charles Wagenheim and later by George E Stone and then Sid Tomack, for the franchise finale). Lloyd Corrigan had an occasional role in the series as thrill-seeking playboy Arthur Manleder. Diamonds, jailbreaks and murder feature strongly, as does Morris's penchant for magic. DP

Chester Morris *Boston Blackie/Horatio Black* • Rochelle Hudson *Cecelia Bradley* • Richard Lane *Inspector Faraday* • Charles Wagenheim *The Runt* • Constance Worth *Marilyn Howard* • Nestor Paiva *Martin Vestrick* ■ *Dir* Robert Florey • *Scr* Jay Dratler, from a story by Jay Dratler, from the character created by by Jack Boyle

Meet Danny Wilson ★★★ PG
Musical drama   1952 · US · BW · 84min

Frank Sinatra stars a crooner who rises to the top through his ultimately disastrous association with a racketeering thug (Raymond Burr). Playing a role that, in the context of the star's own life, is pretty close to the bone, Ol' Blue Eyes does justice to his twin talents as actor and singer in a tight drama, directed by Joseph Pevney and laced with some of Frank's best-loved standards. Shelley Winters is the girl caught between Sinatra and his best friend, Alex Nicol. RK *DVD*

Frank Sinatra *Danny Wilson* • Shelley Winters *Joy Carroll* • Alex Nicol *Mike Ryan* • Raymond Burr *Nick Driscoll* • Tommy Farrell *Tommy Wells* •

Vaughn Taylor *TW Hatcher* • Donald MacBride *Sergeant* • Barbara Knudson *Marie* • Tony Curtis *Man in nightclub* ■ *Dir* Joseph Pevney • *Scr* Don McGuire, from his story

Meet Dave ★★ PG
Science-fiction comedy   2008 · US · Colour · 86min

Following the below-the-belt comedy of *Norbit*, Eddie Murphy remains in lowbrow mode with this lame sci-fi comedy. Once again Murphy appears in dual roles; as a spaceship disguised as a human (the Dave of the title) and as the captain of the tiny aliens that operate him. Dave and its crew land in New York City to plunder Earth's resources in an effort to save their own planet. Needless to say, a spaceship disguised as a man finds it hard to fit in with modern Earth ways and all sorts of hilarious consequences fail to ensue. The moments of toilet humour may raise a giggle among some small children, but adults are advised to steer clear of Dave's orbit. DA *DVD*

Eddie Murphy *Dave/Captain* • Elizabeth Banks (2) *Gina Morrison* • Gabrielle Union *No 3 - Cultural Officer* • Scott Caan *Dooley* • Ed Helms *No 2 - 2nd In Command* • Mike O'Malley *Knox* ■ *Dir* Brian Robbins • *Scr* Rob Greenberg, Bill Corbett

Meet Dr Christian ★★★ U
Medical drama   1939 · US · BW · 63min

This is the first in a six-film series spun-off from a long-running radio show inspired by the exploits of Allan Dafoe, the Canadian medic who famously delivered the Dionne Quintuplets. Having played the good doctor in three previous films, Jean Hersholt (the Danish star after whom the Oscar people named their Humanitarian Award) was the natural choice to headline these sentimental B-movies, in which his folksy wisdom was as crucial to the citizens of River's End, Minnesota, as his surgical skill. Nurse Dorothy Lovett's complicated love life, housekeeper Maude Eburne's kvetching and storekeeper Edgar Kennedy's irritability leavened Hersholt's saintliness with some much-needed human foibles. DP

Jean Hersholt *Dr Christian* • Dorothy Lovett *Judy Price* • Robert Baldwin *Roy Davis* • Enid Bennett *Anne Hewitt* • Paul Harvey *John Hewitt* • Marcia Mae Jones *Marilee* ■ *Dir* Bernard Vorhaus • *Scr* Ian McLellan Hunter, Ring Lardner Jr, Harvey Gates, from a story by Harvey Gates

Meet Joe Black ★★ 12
Romantic fantasy drama   1998 · US · Colour · 172min

Brad Pitt stars as the Grim Reaper in this remake of the 1930s classic *Death Takes a Holiday*, giving ailing media magnate Anthony Hopkins an offer he can't refuse – extra life, provided Death can spend a few days living among mortals. However, no one is more startled by Pitt's arrival than Hopkins's daughter Claire Forlani, because Death has taken over the body of the stranger she met earlier in a coffee shop. Nicely played but ridiculously overlong. JF A sex scene, swearing. *DVD*

Brad Pitt *Joe Black/Young man in coffee shop* • Anthony Hopkins *William Parrish* • Claire Forlani *Susan Parrish* • Jake Weber *Drew* • Marcia Gay Harden *Allison* • Jeffrey Tambor *Quince* ■ *Dir* Martin Brest • *Scr* Ron Osborn, Jeff Reno, Kevin Wade, Bo Goldman, from the film *Death Takes a Holiday* by Maxwell Anderson, Gladys Lehman, Walter Ferris, from the play *Death Takes a Holiday* by Alberto Casella

Meet John Doe ★★ U
Drama   1941 · US · BW · 122min

This sombre fantasy from Frank Capra starts off interesting, but by the end it's almost unwatchable. Capra failed to solve the film's structural problems and allegedly shot five different endings. Gary Cooper and Barbara Stanwyck head a fine cast, but Capra provides no colour and far too much worthy dialogue. "John Doe" is here the signature on a powerful letter from a mystery man promising to commit suicide by Christmas and atone for the sins of the world. TS *DVD*

Gary Cooper *John Doe/Long John Willoughby* • Barbara Stanwyck *Ann Mitchell* • Edward Arnold *DB Norton* • Walter Brennan *The "Colonel"* • Spring Byington *Mrs Mitchell* • James Gleason *Henry Connell* • Gene Lockhart *Mayor Lovett* ■ *Dir* Frank Capra • *Scr* Robert Riskin, Myles Connolly (uncredited), from the short story *A Reputation* by Richard Connell in *Century Magazine*

Meet Me after the Show ★★ U
Musical comedy   1951 · US · Colour · 86min

This feeble Betty Grable vehicle has precious little to recommend it. A perfunctory plot and appallingly static direction from Richard Sale battle in vain to hold the attention, though Grable's co-stars Macdonald Carey and Rory Calhoun are likeable. More of the healthy vulgarity that characterised Grable's other Fox features would have helped, and the faked amnesia plot is strictly for the birds. TS

Betty Grable *Delilah* • Macdonald Carey *Jeff* • Rory Calhoun *David Hemingway* • Eddie Albert *Christopher Leeds* • Fred Clark *Tim* • Lois Andrews *Gloria Carstairs* ■ *Dir* Richard Sale • *Scr* Mary Loos, Richard Sale, from a story by Erna Lazarus, W Scott Darling

Meet Me at Dawn ★★
Romantic comedy   1946 · UK · BW · 98min

After making his name with *Flying down to Rio*, this was something of a crash-landing for American director Thornton Freeland. His understanding of the peculiarities of British humour seems to have deserted him after his wartime sojourn in Hollywood, for he misses every laughter cue (and goodness knows there are precious few) in this feeble comedy. His fellow Yank in exile, William Eythe, looks increasingly uncomfortable as this tale of duelling and duplicity develops. DP

William Eythe *Charles Morton* • Stanley Holloway *Emile* • Hazel Court *Gabrielle Vermorel* • George Thorpe *Senator Philipe Renault* • Irene Browne *Madame Renault* • Beatrice Campbell *Margot* • Basil Sydney *Georges Vermorel* • Margaret Rutherford *Madame Vermorel* ■ *Dir* Thornton Freeland, Peter Cresswell • *Scr* Lesley Storm, James Seymour, from the play *La Tueur* by Marcel Achard, Anatole Litvak

Meet Me at the Fair ★★★ U
Musical romantic drama   1952 · US · Colour · 87min

When a travelling show's medicine man (Dan Dailey) takes in an orphan boy (Chet Allen) who has run away from a cruel institution, he is accused of kidnapping and must battle with a politician's social worker fiancée (Diana Lynn). No prizes for guessing how things are resolved in this amiable, folksy musical directed by Douglas Sirk, which combines a dose of drama with romance and features some pleasing numbers. RK

Dan Dailey *"Doc" Tilbee* • Diana Lynn *Zerelda Wing* • Chet Allen *"Tad" Bayliss* • Scatman Crothers *Enoch Jones* • Hugh O'Brian *Chilton Corr* • Carole Mathews *Clara Brink* • Rhys Williams *Pete McCoy* ■ *Dir* Douglas Sirk • *Scr* Irving Wallace, Martin Berkeley, from the novel *The Great Companions* by Gene Markey

Meet Me in Las Vegas ★★★ U
Musical   1956 · US · Colour · 112min

This late MGM musical is a delight. A showcase for Vegas itself, the negligible plot (every time Dan Dailey holds Cyd Charisse's hand he comes up trumps) serves as a framing device for a whole slew of talent: here are on-screen numbers from Lena Horne and Frankie Laine, and uncredited guest slots from some of the biggest stars of the day. Charisse dances up a storm, but the sizzle is stolen by Cara Williams, who lights up the screen. Better known here by its British title *Viva Las Vegas!* TS

Dan Dailey *Chuck Rodwell* • Cyd Charisse *Maria Corvier* • Agnes Moorehead *Miss Hattie* • Lili Darvas *Sari Hatvani* • Jim Backus *Tom Culdane* • Oscar Karlweis *Loisi* • Liliane Montevecchi *Lilli* •

George Kerris [George Chakiris] *Young groom* • Betty Lynn *Young bride* ■ *Dir* Roy Rowland • *Scr* Isobel Lennart

Meet Me in St Louis ★★★★★ U
Classic musical   1944 · US · Colour · 108min

This portrayal of a perfect American family was too sugary for some critical tastes at the time, but it can be viewed today as a vintage MGM musical. Whatever the film's minor flaws, they are more than made up for by some dazzling musical numbers – such as *Have Yourself a Merry Little Christmas*, *The Trolley Song* and *Skip to My Lou* – enhanced by the masterly direction of Vincente Minnelli at the top of his form. Providing a romanticised but still uplifting depiction of life in St Louis at the beginning of the 20th century, with Mary Astor as mom and Judy Garland as one of four daughters, this is a tale that only works against the backdrop of a more innocent age. PF *DVD* Blu-ray

Judy Garland *Esther Smith* • Margaret O'Brien *"Tootie" Smith* • Mary Astor *Mrs Anna Smith* • Lucille Bremer *Rose Smith* • Leon Ames *Mr Alonzo "Lon" Smith* • Tom Drake *John Truett* • Marjorie Main *Katie, the maid* • Harry Davenport *Grandpa Prophater* • June Lockhart *Lucille Ballard* • Henry H Daniels Jr *Lon Smith Jr* • Joan Carroll *Agnes Smith* ■ *Dir* Vincente Minnelli • *Scr* Irving Brecher, Fred F Finklehoffe, from the novel by Sally Benson • *Cinematographer* George Folsey • *Costume Designer* Irene

Meet Me Tonight ★★ PG
Portmanteau comedy   1952 · UK · Colour · 80min

This below par portmanteau picture comprises three one-act plays written by Noël Coward. There are too few examples of the urbane Coward wit to atone for the banality of the stories, while the observations on the types produced by the British class system are shallow to the point of platitude. However, the performances stand up rather well. DP

Kay Walsh *Lily Pepper* • Ted Ray *George Pepper* • Stanley Holloway *Henry Gow* • Betty Ann Davies *Doris Gow* • Valerie Hobson *Stella Cartwright* • Nigel Patrick *Toby Cartwright* • Jack Warner *Murdoch* ■ *Dir* Anthony Pelissier • *Scr* Noël Coward, from his play *Tonight at 8:30*

Meet Mr Lucifer ★★ U
Fantasy comedy   1953 · UK · BW · 82min

For every Ealing comedy gem there is at least one poor imitation, packed with cosy caricatures and devoid of the usual satirical bite. This tepid assault on television has Stanley Holloway as a pantomime demon who is sent as an emissary from hell to ensure that TV sets throughout the nation bring nothing but misery. DP *DVD*

Stanley Holloway *Sam Hollingsworth/Mr Lucifer* • Peggy Cummins *Kitty Norton* • Jack Watling *Jim Norton* • Barbara Murray *Patricia Pedelty* • Joseph Tomelty *Mr Pedelty* • Kay Kendall *Lonely hearts singer* • Gordon Jackson *Hector McPhee* ■ *Dir* Anthony Pelissier • *Scr* Monja Danischewsky, Peter Myers, Alec Graham, from the play *Beggar My Neighbour* by Arnold Ridley

Meet Monica Velour ★★ 15
Comedy   2011 · US · Colour · 93min

When dorky 17-year-old Tobe (Dustin Ingram) learns that Monica Velour (a porn star from the 1980s) is making a personal appearance in an Indiana strip joint, he sets out to meet the object of his infatuation – even though she is now a seedy alcoholic and old enough to be his granny. The film is intended as a comedy drama, but its principals seem to be acting in two different movies, with Kim Cattrall playing it like Tennessee Williams. The problem is that this odd couple are not sweet, funny or even particularly interesting. BP Swearing, sex scenes, nudity, drug abuse.

Kim Cattrall *Linda Romanoli* • Dustin Ingram *Tobe* • Brian Dennehy *Pop Pop* • David Keith *Claude* ■ *Dir/Scr* Keith Bearden

M

Meet Nero Wolfe ★★★ U
Detective murder mystery
1936 · US · BW · 71min

Edward Arnold plays the corpulent gourmet and orchid cultivator Nero Wolfe, who solves most of his cases from the comfort of his own home. Directed by Herbert Biberman with Lionel Stander, Victor Jory and Rita Cansino (later Hayworth) in the cast, this neat little thriller finds the sleuth connecting and solving the murders of a college president and a mechanic. Columbia intended to build a series around Rex Stout's popular detective, but there was just one more picture, *League of Frightened Men* (1937). RK

Edward Arnold *Nero Wolfe* · Lionel Stander *Archie Goodwin* · Joan Perry *Ellen Barstow* · Victor Jory *Claude Roberts* · Nana Bryant *Sarah Barstow* · Rita Cansino [Rita Hayworth] *Maria Maringola* ■ *Dir* Herbert Biberman [Herbert J Biberman] · *Scr* Howard J Green, Bruce Manning, Joseph Anthony, from a novel by Rex Stout, from his novel *Fer-de-Lance*

Meet the Applegates
★★★★ 15
Satirical fantasy 1991 · US · Colour · 86min

Giant insects take on human form and move to Ohio from the Amazon rainforest to take revenge on humanity for destroying their home in director Michael Lehmann's surreal send-up of 1950s monster insect flicks, environmental issues and life in semi-detached suburbia. But while their creepy-crawly spirits are willing, their flesh-and-blood disguises are weak and soon they succumb to human nature: sex, drugs and drink ("grasshopper cocktail, anyone?"). It's a stinging satire on brainless pop culture and trashy Americana, and great fun, too. AJ Swearing.

Ed Begley Jr *Dick Applegate* · Stockard Channing *Jane Applegate* · Dabney Coleman *Aunt Bea* · Bobby Jacoby *Johnny Applegate* · Cami Cooper [Camille Cooper] *Sally Applegate* · Glenn Shadix *Greg Samson* · Susan Barnes *Opal Withers* · Adam Biesk *Vince Samson* ■ *Dir* Michael Lehmann · *Scr* Redbeard Simmons, Michael Lehmann

Meet the Baron ★★
Comedy 1933 · US · BW · 65min

Complete with his catchphrase "Vas you dere, Sharlie?", Jack Pearl was a big star on American radio in the 1930s. So Louis B Mayer surrounded him with impressive backstage talents to ensure his feature debut was a roaring success. But the story of an opportunist who masquerades as the celebrated fabulist Baron Munchausen fails to gel, despite the presence of the ever-willing Jimmy Durante. DP

Jack Pearl *Julius/Baron Munchausen* · Jimmy Durante *Joe McGoo* · ZaSu Pitts *ZaSu* · Ted Healy *Ted* · Edna May Oliver *Dean Primrose* · Henry Kolker *Baron Munchausen* · Moe Howard · Jerry Howard · Larry Fine ■ *Dir* Walter Lang · *Scr* Allen Rivkin, PJ Wolfson, from a story by Herman J Mankiewicz, from a story by Norman Krasna

Meet the Deedles ★ PG
Comedy 1998 · US · Colour · 90min

This downmarket cousin to *Bill & Ted's Excellent Adventure* has two surf-bum twins (Paul Walker and Steve Van Wormer) accidentally becoming rangers in Yellowstone National Park. There they are given the task of thwarting former employee Dennis Hopper, who plans to sabotage the landscape with help from a pack of prairie dogs. Only for teenagers with nothing better to do. LH DVD

Steve Van Wormer *Stew Deedle* · Paul Walker *Phil Deedle* · AJ Langer *Jesse Ryan* · John Ashton *Captain Douglas Pine* · Dennis Hopper *Frank Slater* · Eric Braeden *Elton Deedle* · Robert Englund *Nemo* ■ *Dir* Steve Boyum · *Scr* Jim Herzfeld, Dale Pollock

Meet the Feebles ★★ 18
Puppet black comedy 1989 · NZ · Colour · 96min

In the sickest and most offensive puppet movie ever made, Peter Jackson presents his muppets as violent, perverted and just plain unpleasant. Taking the form of an animal backstage musical, the unhinged creatures and debauched behaviour are often amusing, mainly because you can't believe someone made a fluffy animal movie this twisted. JC DVD

■ *Dir* Peter Jackson · *Scr* Peter Jackson, Frances Walsh [Fran Walsh], Stephen Sinclair, Daniel Mulheron

Meet the Fockers ★★★ 12
Comedy 2004 · US · Colour · 110min

In this sequel to *Meet the Parents*, Robert De Niro's anal ex-CIA man returns to spar with accident-prone, soon-to-be son-in-law Ben Stiller and travels to Florida to meet Stiller's mother and father. It is testament to the cracking performances of Dustin Hoffman and Barbra Streisand as Stiller's parents that they steal the film from De Niro. In their roles as earth mother sex therapist and hippy househusband, Streisand and Hoffman are utterly credible, while playing everything for the broadest of laughs. The least successful parts of the film are those that depend on knowledge of the original or that simply reuse the same jokes. AC Some swearing. DVD BD

Robert De Niro *Jack Byrnes* · Ben Stiller *Greg Focker* · Dustin Hoffman *Bernie Focker* · Barbra Streisand *Roz Focker* · Blythe Danner *Dina Byrnes* · Teri Polo *Pam Byrnes* · Tim Blake Nelson *Officer Le Flore* · Owen Wilson *Kevin Rawley* ■ *Dir* Jay Roach · *Scr* Jim Herzfeld, John Hamburg, from a story by Jim Herzfeld, Marc Hyman, from characters by by Greg Glienna, Mary Ruth Clarke

Meet the Parents ★★★★ 12
Comedy 2000 · US · Colour · 103min

Teri Polo takes her potential groom Ben Stiller home to meet her parents. In the course of the weekend, he loses the cat, floods the garden and has his various weaknesses painfully exposed by her father, a former CIA operative. Given the set-up, this comedy could have been predictable and cliché-ridden, but the sheer class of the cast elevates this into something really special. Ben Stiller gives the unfortunate beau humanity and realism; Robert De Niro's gravitas makes "dad" an intimidating presence and Blythe Danner is a quirky prospect as the mother-in-law. Ridiculously funny and somehow rather endearing. LH Swearing. DVD BD

Robert De Niro *Jack Byrnes* · Ben Stiller *Greg Focker* · Teri Polo *Pam Byrnes* · Blythe Danner *Dina Byrnes* · Owen Wilson *Kevin Rawley* · Nicole DeHuff *Debbie Byrnes* · Jon Abrahams *Denny Byrnes* · James Rebhorn *Larry Banks* ■ *Dir* Jay Roach · *Scr* John Hamburg, from a story by Greg Glienna, Mary Ruth Clarke · *Music* Randy Newman

Meet the People ★★★ U
Musical comedy 1944 · US · BW · 100min

Masquerading as a minor MGM musical, this is a delight, featuring such period entertainers as frozen-faced Virginia O'Brien, crooner Vaughn Monroe and vaudevillian (and Cowardly Lion) Bert Lahr. The plot is extraordinarily liberal, with committed activist Dick Powell causing Broadway star Lucille Ball to abandon showbusiness and work as a riveter in the shipyards. Well, it was wartime, but even so, this is pre-McCarthy era political dynamite. TS

Lucille Ball *Julie Hampton* · Dick Powell *William "Swanee" Swanson* · Virginia O'Brien *"Woodpecker" Peg* · Bert Lahr *Commander* · Rags Ragland *Mr Smith* · June Allyson *Annie* ■ *Dir* Charles Reisner · *Scr* SM Herzig, Fred Saidy, from a story by Sol Barzman, Ben Barzman, Louis Lantz

Meet the Robinsons ★★ U
Animated adventure 2006 · US · Colour · 90min

In this brash and charmless animated adventure from Disney (also available in a 3D version), boy genius Lewis is whisked off to the future so that his gee-wizardry with gadgets can help a dysfunctional family in distress. But pretty soon his journey hits a snag when he encounters a baddie who threatens his chances of getting home. Coming across as two parts *Jimmy Neutron* and one part *Robots*, this unoriginal tale has little to distinguish it from the ever-increasing number of computer-generated children's films. Technically it's spot-on, but despite boasting the vocal talents of Tom Selleck and Laurie Metcalf, this is too complex and cluttered for kids, and lacks the wit and warmth to endear it to accompanying adults. DA DVD BD Sp

Daniel Hansen *Lewis* · Jordan Fry *Lewis* · Wesley Singerman *Wilbur Robinson* · Tom Selleck *Cornelius Robinson* · Nicole Sullivan *Franny Robinson* · Stephen Anderson (2) *Grandpa Bud/Bowler Hat Guy* · Laurie Metcalf *Lucille Krunklehorn* · Ethan Sandler *Doris/CEO/Uncle Spike/Uncle Dimitri/Cousin Laszlo/Uncle Fritz/Aunt Petunia* · Tom Kenny *Mr Willerstein* · Adam West *Uncle Art* · Angela Bassett *Mildred* ■ *Dir* Stephen Anderson (2) · *Scr* Jon Bernstein, Michelle Spitz, Don Hall, Nathan Greno, Aurian Redson, Joe Mateo, Stephen Anderson (2), from the illustrated children's book *A Day with Wilbur* by William Joyce

Meet the Santas ★★
Comedy drama 2005 · US · Colour · 96min

Following the success of *Single Santa Seeks Mrs Claus*, director Harvey Frost reassembled the cast for this sequel, in which Steve Guttenberg has to marry LA advertising executive Crystal Bernard before Christmas Eve or his father's plans for him to take over at the North Pole will be ruined. However, even though Guttenberg can call on the services of his faithful factotum, Armin Shimerman, he hasn't banked on the interference of Bernard's haughty society mother, Mariette Hartley. Echoes of *Three Men and a Little Lady* reverberate throughout the action, which is occasionally guilty of a little inverted snobbery. DP

Steve Guttenberg *Nick* · Crystal Bernard *Beth* · Marcia Ann Burrs *Mrs Claus* · Mariette Hartley *Beth's mother* · Dominic Scott Kay *Jake* · Armin Shimerman *Ernest* ■ *Dir* Harvey Frost · *Scr* Pamela Wallace

Meet the Spartans ★ 12
Spoof epic 2008 · US · Colour · 82min

After enduring the torturously unfunny *Date Movie* and *Epic Movie*, one could be forgiven for concluding that the art of cinematic parody was in terminal decline. This latest instalment in Jason Friedberg and Aaron Seltzer's franchise hammers a final nail into the coffin. The backbone of *Meet the Spartans* takes pot shots at high-camp historical war movie *300*, as King Leonidas (Sean Maguire) leads his army of 13 soldiers (287 short) against Persian invader Xerxes (Ken Davitian). The resulting barrage of homophobic jokes about men in codpieces is moronic and offensive. Junk-food cinema at its worst. JR Some violence, swearing, sexual references. DVD BD

Sean Maguire *Leonidas* · Carmen Electra *Queen Margo* · Ken Davitian *Xerxes* · Kevin Sorbo *Captain* · Diedrich Bader *Traitoro* · Method Man *Persian Emissary* ■ *Dir/Scr* Jason Friedberg, Aaron Seltzer

Meeting at Midnight ★★ PG
Mystery 1944 · US · BW · 62min

Originally released as *Black Magic*, this is the third in Monogram's Charlie Chan series. When his daughter, Frances Chan, is caught up in the murder of a medium, Chinese sleuth Sidney Toler sets out to expose the victim's fraudulent operation and discover the significance of events that happened almost a decade before in London. Too much time is devoted to the slapstick antics of Mantan Moreland, but the sequence in which Toler teeters on a rooftop under the influence of a mind-controlling drug is effective. DP DVD

Sidney Toler *Charlie Chan* · Mantan Moreland *Birmingham Brown* · Frances Chan · Joseph Crehan *Matthew* · Jacqueline de Wit *Justine Bonner* · Ralph Peters *Rafferty* · Helen Beverly *Norma Duncan* · Richard Gordon [Dick Gordon] *Bonner* ■ *Dir* Phil Rosen · *Scr* George Callahan, from characters by Earl Derr Biggers

Meeting Venus ★★★ 15
Satirical romantic drama
1990 · UK · Colour · 114min

Kiri Te Kanawa provides the arias for Glenn Close's Swedish high diva in director István Szabó's up-market romantic comedy drama. Close has fun as the man-eating prima donna whose infamous temperament threatens the career-enhancing project of young conductor Niels Arestrup. Wagner's music ponderously matches the melodrama, as hardline politics are exposed along with naked ambition. Szabó keeps a tight rein on his cast as the backstage passions flare, and if you can't stand the tantrums, the soundtrack is marvellous. TH

Glenn Close *Karin Anderson* · Niels Arestrup *Zoltan Szanto* · Marian Labuda *Von Schneider* · Maite Nahyr *Maria Krawiecki* · Victor Poletti *Stefano Del Sarto* · Jay O Sanders *Stephen Taylor* ■ *Dir* István Szabó · *Scr* István Szabó, Michael Hirst

Meetings with Remarkable Men ★★ U
Biographical drama 1979 · UK · Colour · 102min

With Gilbert Taylor's camera rejoicing in the beauty of the Afghan mountainscapes, this is an uncomfortable combination of the gloriously cinematic and the doggedly theatrical. In electing to employ his famous technique of "forced improvisation" to adapt the memoirs of GI Gurdjieff, Peter Brook conveys something of the assiduity of the mystic's lifelong search for enlightenment. But neither his ideas nor his unique methods of meditation make for riveting viewing. DP

Dragan Maksimovic *Gurdjieff* · Terence Stamp *Prince Lubovedsky* · Athol Fugard *Professor Skridlov* · Warren Mitchell *Gurdjieff's father* · Natasha Parry *Vitvitskaia* ■ *Dir* Peter Brook · *Scr* Peter Brook, Jeanne DeSalzmann, from the book by GI Gurdjieff

Mega Piranha ★★ 15
Science-fiction horror
2010 · US · Colour · 88min

Gigantic, genetically modified piranha chomp their way down Venezuela's Orinoco River in this deliberately over-the-top creature feature, and it's up to a female scientist (1980s pop star Tiffany) and a special agent (Paul Logan) to try to prevent them reaching Florida. While the leads compete for the title of "most hammy performance", a brainless script and ludicrously un-special effects recall the worst excesses of 1950s B-movies. Those who follow the "so bad it's good" school of thought will probably love it - anyone else should avoid. SF In English, Spanish. Violence, nudity. DVD

Paul Logan *Special Forces Agent Jason Fitch* · Tiffany *Sarah Monroe* · Barry Williams *Bob Grady* · David Labiosa *Diaz* · Jude Gerard Prest *Higgins* ■ *Dir/Scr* Eric Forsberg

Mega Shark vs Giant Octopus ★ 15
Science-fiction action drama
2008 · US · Colour · 85min

After thousands of years under the ice, two prehistoric monsters are freed by illegal underwater testing to terrorise the planet and ultimately face each other in lethal combat. Despite all singer Debbie (now Deborah) Gibson's efforts at serious acting, this is so bad, it's unintentionally hilarious. If you get the chance to watch the trailer, then do, as it contains the best bits of the film and almost makes them look well-made. When it comes to the feature itself, however, no such luck. SuR Swearing. DVD

Lorenzo Lamas *Allan Baxter* · Deborah Gibson *Emma MacNeil* · Vic Chao *Dr Seiji Shimada* · Sean Lawlor *Lamar Sanders* ■ *Dir/Scr* Jack Perez

Megamind ★★★★ PG
Animated comedy adventure
2010 · US · Colour · 91min

This fast-paced animated adventure will delight kids of all ages, while also appealing to grown-ups - and superhero comic-book fans. Blue bulbous-headed extraterrestrial villain Megamind (voiced by Will Ferrell) finally defeats his longtime nemesis Metro Man (Brad Pitt), but grows tired of having no one to fight and creates a new adversary, Tighten. But when Tighten crosses over to the dark side, Megamind has to come to the rescue of Metro City. Director Tom McGrath packs in countless sight gags and whip-smart one-liners, poking specific fun at the Christopher Reeve Superman movies along the way (watch out for Ferrell's Marlon Brando impression). It's terrific fun from start to finish, even if it doesn't quite match the good-versus-evil japes of *The Incredibles* or *Despicable Me*. TeS DVD ▣ ▣ ▣

Will Ferrell *Megamind* • Brad Pitt *Metro Man* • Jonah Hill *Hal Stewart/Tighten* • Tina Fey *Roxanne Ritchi* • David Cross (2) *Minion* • Justin Theroux *Megamind's father* • Ben Stiller *Bernard* • Jessica Schulte *Megamind's mother* ■ *Dir* Tom McGrath • *Scr* Alan Schoolcraft [Alan J Schoolcraft], Brent Simons

Melancholia ★★★★▣
Political thriller
1989 · UK/W Ger · Colour · 83min

It may look distinctly unpromising and yet this political thriller is extremely well made and becomes increasingly exciting. Jeroen Krabbé plays a German art critic whose old anarchist fervour is reignited by the opportunity to assassinate a member of the Chilean military, but with escalating consequences. Surprisingly, this suspenseful movie is the only feature directed by Andi Engel, a larger-than-life film distributor with a wealth of cinematic knowledge. Camera shots are full of sleek, clean lines, while well-chosen London locations make the city look great. DM

Jeroen Krabbé *David Keller* • Ulrich Wildgruber *Manfred* • Susannah York *Catherine* • Kate Hardie *Rachel* • Jane Gurnett *Sarah Yelin* • Saul Reichlin *Dr Vargas* ■ *Dir* Andi Engel • *Scr* Andi Engel, Lewis Rodia

Melancholia ★★★★▣
Science-fiction drama
2011 · Den/Swe/Fr/Ger/It · Colour · 129min

This operatic meditation on the apocalypse from Danish auteur Lars von Trier is visually ravishing and highly cinematic, and so is a world apart from his avant-garde Dogme 95 work. The opulent country-house wedding reception of Kirsten Dunst and Alexander Skarsgård descends from social farce into nightmare when her mental illness asserts itself. Later, the rogue planet of the title is revealed to be on a collision course with Earth – a case of narrative threat acting as a metaphor for depression – as Dunst's sister Charlotte Gainsbourg nurses her through a debilitating dark mood. Applying Wagner's *Tristan und Isolde* to underline the doom, von Trier creates gorgeous tableaux and mines symbolism from prophetic nightmares and portents. Never mind *Armageddon*, this is a cerebral kind of disaster movie with imagery and themes that prove much harder to shake. AC Nudity. DVD ▣

Kirsten Dunst *Justine* • Charlotte Gainsbourg *Claire* • Kiefer Sutherland *John* • Alexander Skarsgård *Michael* • Stellan Skarsgård *Jack* • Charlotte Rampling *Gaby* • John Hurt *Dexter* ■ *Dir/Scr* Lars von Trier

Melinda and Melinda ★★★▣
Comedy drama
2004 · US · Colour · 95min

Cleverly structured, Woody Allen's comedy drama runs along parallel plotlines - one tragic, one comic - that are both initiated by a troubled woman named Melinda (Radha Mitchell), who subtly disrupts the lives of those around her. In one tale, Melinda falls for a suave pianist (Chiwetel Ejiofor), but finds herself betrayed by a close friend. In the other, Melinda's upstairs neighbour - a married, out-of-work actor played by Will Ferrell - falls for her. Trying to keep the separate stories unravelled can be a little confusing, but that's the point: that sadness and joy are inextricably entwined. LF Sexual references. DVD

Radha Mitchell *Melinda* • Will Ferrell *Hobie* • Jonny Lee Miller *Lee* • Amanda Peet *Susan* • Chiwetel Ejiofor *Ellis Moonsong* • Chloë Sevigny *Laurel* • Wallace Shawn *Sy* • David Aaron Baker *Steve* ■ *Dir/Scr* Woody Allen

Mélo ★★★★▣
Romantic drama
1986 · Fr · Colour · 105min

Surprisingly opting for a traditionally linear (and rather theatrical) approach, Alain Resnais explores his perennial theme of memory by peeling away the sophisticated veneer to reveal the genuine pain felt by Sabine Azéma, the adulterous wife of violinist Pierre Arditi, who is driven to suicide by the loyalty of his more celebrated virtuoso friend, André Dussolier. Impeccably played and outwardly old-fashioned, this is a powerful study of ruthless decency and emotional anguish. DP French +subtitles. DVD

Sabine Azéma *Romaine Belcroix* • Pierre Arditi *Pierre Belcroix* • André Dussollier *Marcel Blanc* • Fanny Ardant *Christiane Levesque* • Jacques Dacqmine *Dr Remy* • Catherine Arditi *Yvonne* ■ *Dir* Alain Resnais • *Scr* Alain Resnais, from the play by Henri Bernstein

Melody ★★▣
Romantic comedy
1971 · UK · Colour · 102min

David Puttnam's first production – from Alan Parker's first script – was retitled *SWALK*, as in *Sealed with a Loving Kiss*. Puttnam had bought the rights to a handful of songs by the Bee Gees, which had to be incorporated into a story. So Parker came up with this tale of two kids (played by Jack Wild and Mark Lester) at a south London comprehensive whose friendship is tested when a pretty girl comes into their social orbit. AT DVD

Jack Wild *Ornshaw* • Mark Lester (2) *Daniel* • Tracy Hyde *Melody* • Colin Barrie *Chambers* • Billy Franks *Burgess* • Ashley Knight *Stacey* • Craig Marriott *Dadd's* ■ *Dir* Waris Hussein • *Scr* Alan Parker, Andrew Birkin

Melody Cruise ★★
Musical comedy
1933 · US · BW · 76min

Phil Harris - the voice of Disney favourites Baloo the bear and O'Malley the alley cat - stars as a millionaire pursued by a shipful of gold diggers in this likeable comedy. Stealing the show, however, is flustered *farceur* Charles Ruggles as the minder hired to keep Harris on the straight and narrow. Mark Sandrich overdoes the camera trickery, but he handles the song and dance routines with some flair. DP

Charles Ruggles *Pete Wells* • Phil Harris *Alan Chandler* • Greta Nissen *Ann* • Helen Mack *Laurie Marlowe* • Chick Chandler *Steward* • Betty Grable *Stewardess* ■ *Dir* Mark Sandrich • *Scr* Mark Sandrich, Ben Holmes, Allen Rivkin, RG Wolfson, from a story by Mark Sandrich, Ben Holmes

Melody Time ★★▣
Animation
1948 · US · Colour · 71min

In this hit-and-miss Disney short story collection each tale is inspired by a popular tune. Whereas *Fantasia* was founded on established pieces from the classical repertoire, this relies on numbers that have not stood the test of time, and younger viewers may struggle to identify with the songs. Best of the bunch is *Little Toot* about a mischievous tugboat, and *Bumble Boogie*, a jazz variation on The Flight of the Bumble Bee. DP DVD

■ *Dir* Clyde Geronimi, Hamilton Luske, Jack Kinney, Wilfred Jackson

Melvin and Howard ★★★★▣
Comedy drama
1980 · US · Colour · 90min

In 1976, hard-up, much-married Melvin Dummar learned he had been left $156 million in the will of a man he barely knew. And all, according to this delightful film from Jonathan Demme, because Melvin treated the reclusive tycoon Howard Hughes to a slice of real life just when he needed it most. Jason Robards is typically bluff as the bedraggled eccentric, while Paul Le Mat is so good as the amiable everyman it's hard to fathom why his career has never

really taken off. Mary Steenburgen won the Oscar for best supporting actress. DP

Paul Le Mat *Melvin Dummar* • Jason Robards *Howard Hughes* • Mary Steenburgen *Lynda Dummar* • Elizabeth Cheshire *Darcy Dummar* • Chip Taylor *Clark Taylor* • Michael J Pollard *Little Red* • Denise Galik *Lucy* • Gloria Grahame *Mrs Sisk* ■ *Dir* Jonathan Demme • *Scr* Bo Goldman

The Member of the Wedding ★★★
Drama
1952 · US · BW · 89min

This interesting drama would have been wonderful if it had shifted up a gear. Carson McCullers's highly intelligent novel and stage play are transferred delicately to the screen and directed with some flair by Fred Zinnemann. Julie Harris is sublime as the unworldly child forced to face reality as the arrangements for her brother's wedding gather steam; it was her film debut, and she was nominated for an Oscar. Well worth catching for the beautifully rendered, claustrophobic atmosphere. SH

Ethel Waters *Berenice Sadie Brown* • Julie Harris (2) *Frankie Addams* • Brandon de Wilde *John Henry* • Arthur Franz *Jarvis* • Nancy Gates *Janice* • William Hansen *Mr Addams* • James Edwards *Honey Camden Brown* ■ *Dir* Fred Zinnemann • *Scr* Edna Anhalt, Edward Anhalt, from the novel and play by Carson McCullers

The Member of the Wedding ★★★
Drama
1997 · US · Colour · 93min

Carson McCullers's novel is vividly brought to life by Oscar winner Anna Paquin. In Georgia during the summer of 1944, a feisty, 12-year-old tomboy comes of age with the guidance of family housekeeper Alfre Woodard, who offers wisdom and solace. As her family prepare for the girl's beloved older brother's wedding, she must cope with her feelings of abandonment and jealousy. This made-for-TV movie is more straightforward and perfunctory than the 1952 film version, but the timeless material retains enough magic to charm all ages. MC

Alfre Woodard *Berenice Sadie Brown* • Anna Paquin *Frankie Addams* • Pat Hingle *Officer Wyle* ■ *Dir* Fielder Cook • *Scr* David W Rintels, from the novel and play by Carson McCullers

Memento ★★★★★▣
Thriller
2000 · US · Colour and BW · 108min

This dazzling, highly original "anti-thriller" has a complex narrative that moves backwards in time. Thus we begin with the climactic murder, then regress through the events that led up to it. Matters are complicated by the fact that the person investigating the killing (Guy Pearce) suffers from a rare form of amnesia, leaving him with no short-term memory. The mystery requires a lot of concentration, but the stunning final scene is ample reward. The ingenious structure makes the point that memory, although unreliable, is what we depend upon for our sense of reality. Writer/director Christopher Nolan's first film, the similar *Following*, signalled his brilliantly individual talent. DM Violence, swearing. DVD ▣

Guy Pearce *Leonard Shelby* • Carrie-Anne Moss *Natalie* • Joe Pantoliano *Teddy* • Mark Boone Junior *Burt* • Stephen Tobolowsky *Sammy Jankis* • Harriet Sansom Harris *Mrs Jankis* • Callum Keith Rennie *Dodd* ■ *Dir* Christopher Nolan • *Scr* Christopher Nolan, from a short story by Jonathan Nolan

Memoirs of a Geisha ★★★★▣
Period romantic drama
2005 · US · Colour · 139min

Director Rob Marshall's tender coming-of-age story is almost Dickensian in its portrait of a girl wrenched from her home in late-1920s Japan to endure the luxuries and privations of life as a geisha. Ziyi Zhang's porcelain beauty is ideally suited to the lead role of Sayuri, who must utilise all her skills and femininity, without revealing her emotions to the men she entertains. There are smouldering performances, too, from Ken Watanabe and Michelle Yeoh, but it's Suzuka Ohgo, playing Zhang's character as

a young girl, who really anchors the story with a sense of purity and idealism. Although Marshall does allow the story to lapse into melodrama, the fine acting together with opulent visuals will appeal to lovers of dazzling spectacle. SP Sex scenes. DVD

Ziyi Zhang [Zhang Ziyi] *Sayuri* • Ken Watanabe *The Chairman* • Michelle Yeoh *Mameha* • Koji Yakusho *Nobu* • Youki Kudoh *Pumpkin* • Kaori Momoi *Mother* • Tsai Chin *Auntie* • Cary-Hiroyuki Tagawa *The Baron* • Suzuka Ohgo *Chiyo* • Gong Li *Hatsumomo* • Kenneth Tsang *General* ■ *Dir* Rob Marshall • *Scr* Robin Swicord, from the novel by Arthur Golden

Memoirs of an Invisible Man ★★★▣
Comedy thriller
1992 · US · Colour · 94min

Director John Carpenter returned to the Hollywood mainstream with this flawed thriller. While Carpenter ensures that the action whips along at a cracking pace and the effects are stunning, the main problem is the uncertainty of tone. Chevy Chase, the innocent man who inadvertently becomes invisible, looks at home with the comic elements but is less convincing as a straightforward action hero. JF DVD

Chevy Chase *Nick Halloway* • Daryl Hannah *Alice Monroe* • Sam Neill *David Jenkins* • Michael McKean *George Talbot* • Stephen Tobolowsky *Warren Singleton* • Jim Norton *Dr Bernard Wachs* • Pat Skipper *Morrissey* • Paul Perri *Gomez* ■ *Dir* John Carpenter • *Scr* Robert Collector, Dana Olsen, William Goldman, from the novel by HF Saint

Memories of Matsuko ★★★▣
Musical drama
2006 · Jpn · Colour · 129min

Adapted from a novel by Muneki Yamada, this engaging musical drama lampoons the "fallen woman" stories popular with postwar Japanese audiences. Desperate for approval to compensate for her father's neglect, Miki Nakatani devotes herself to several undeserving men before ending up a recluse in a shabby Tokyo apartment. Yet, for all its pathos, this is an often exhilarating picture, thanks to Masakazu Ato's luminous photography and the Gabriele Roberto production numbers. DP Japanese +subtitles. Violence, swearing, sexual references. DVD ▣

Miki Nakatani *Matsuko* • Eita Sho • Yusuke Iseya *Ryu Yoichi* • Mikako Ichikawa *Kumi* • Asuka Kurosawa *Megumi* ■ *Dir* Tetsuya Nakashima • *Scr* Tetsuya Nakashima, from a novel by Muneki Yamada

Memories of Me ★▣
Comedy drama
1988 · US · Colour · 98min

When funny man Billy Crystal is good, he's very good, but when he's bad, he's terrible. This mawkish comedy drama falls in the latter category, as Crystal tries to put his life in order after a mind-altering heart attack. This means searching out his estranged father - the cue for even more sickly sentiment and some hopelessly artificial, angst-ridden emotion. The laughs are certainly there, but they're mostly unintentional. AJ DVD

Billy Crystal *Dr Abbie Polin* • Alan King *Abe Polin* • JoBeth Williams *Lisa McConnell* • Sean Connery • Janet Carroll *Dorothy Davis* • David Ackroyd *First assistant director* ■ *Dir* Henry Winkler • *Scr* Eric Roth, Billy Crystal

Memories of Murder ★★★▣
Murder mystery based on a true story
2003 · S Kor · Colour · 130min

Inspired by the unsolved crimes of South Korea's first serial killer, Bong Joon-ho's simmering police procedural focuses as much on the relationship between incompetent small-town cop Song Kang-ho and his city superior, Kim Sang-kyung, as it does on the search for the brutal rapist who has claimed ten victims on a sadistic spree. Initially, there's a comic edge to the town-and-country posturing, but the tone grows darker once female officer Koh Seo-hee establishes a link with a radio request show. DP Korean +subtitles. Swearing, violence. DVD

Song Kang-ho *Detective Park Doo-man* • Kim Sang-kyung *Detective Seo Tae-yoon* • Kim Rwe-ha *Detective Cho Yong-koo* • Song Jae-ho *Sergeant Shin Dong-chul* • Byun Hee-bong *Sergeant Koo Hee-bong* • Koh Seo-hee *Officer Kweon Kwi-ok* ■ *Dir* Bong Joon-ho • *Scr* Bong Joon-ho, Shim Sung-bo, from a story by Kim Gwang-rim

Memories of Underdevelopment
★★★★ 15

Political drama   1968 · Cub · BW · 93min

Already acclaimed for 1966's *Death of a Bureaucrat*, Cuban director Tomás Gutiérrez Alea came of age with this scathing satire, in which bourgeois intellectual Sergio Corrieri refuses the chance to flee to Miami. Instead he finds himself caught between his socialist ideals, European aspirations and the comfortable trappings of his lifestyle as he tries to sustain a love affair and assimilate to the new regime. Slotting newsreel footage into the exhilarating visuals, this is a shrewd insight into a society struggling to come to terms with its post-colonial identity. DP Spanish +subtitles. *DVD*

Sergio Corrieri *Sergio* • Daisy Granados *Elena* ■ *Dir* Tomás Gutiérrez Alea • *Scr* Tomás Gutiérrez Alea, Edmundo Desnoes, from a novel by Desnoes

The Memory Keeper's Daughter
★★ PG

Drama   2008 · US · Colour · 85min

In this poignant but over-ambitious TV movie, a doctor (Dermot Mulroney) secretly gives away one of his newborn twins after discovering the baby has Down's syndrome. It's an impulsive mistake bringing lasting consequences, both for him and his wife (Gretchen Mol), and also the compassionate nurse (Emily Watson) who takes in the child. The film has a simplistic and uneven feel, while bland performances compound these faults, leaving it to the heart-tugging conclusion to make amends. SF *DVD*

Emily Watson *Caroline Gill* • Dermot Mulroney *Dr David Henry* • Gretchen Mol *Nora Henry* • Krystal Hope Nausbaum *Phoebe* • Hugh Thompson *Al* ■ *Dir* Mick Jackson • *Scr* John Pielmeier, from the novel by Kim Edwards

Memory Run
★★ 18

Science-fiction action thriller
1995 · US · Colour · 89min

This unnecessarily complicated slice of sci-fi sees Karen Duffy going on the run from an evil corporate empire after she discovers that its executives have been literally playing with her mind. Saul Rubinek and Matt McCoy add respectability, but this one is for genre fans only. JF *DVD*

Karen Duffy *Celeste/Josette* • Saul Rubinek *Dr Munger* • Matt McCoy *Gabriel* • Chris Makepeace *Andre Fuller* ■ *Dir* Allan A Goldstein • *Scr* David Gottlieb, Dale Hildebrand, from the novel *Season of the Witch* by Hank Stine

Memphis Belle
★★★★ U

Second World War documentary
1943 · US/UK · Colour · 39min

This is one of the finest combat documentaries of the Second World War. The Flying Fortress *Memphis Belle* had flown 24 successful missions and this daylight bombing raid was to be its last. Director William Wyler's pulsating short film uses diagrams to explain the mission and then takes us on board as the crew encounters flak and enemy fighters before hitting its targets. Footage from the film was used in the 1990 feature of the same name, which was co-produced by Wyler's daughter, Catherine. DP

Eugene Kern *Narrator* • Corp John Beal *Narrator* ■ *Dir* Lt Col William Wyler [William Wyler] • *Scr* Capt Edwin Gilbert, Tech Sgt Lester Koenig • *Cinematographer* Major William Clothier [William Clothier], Lt Col William Wyler [William Wyler], Lt Harold Tannenbaum [Harold Tannenbaum]

Memphis Belle
★★★ PG

Historical Second World War drama
1990 · UK · Colour · 102min

Co-producer David Puttnam was the force behind this moving and nostalgic trip back to the Second World War. The focus is upon the crew of a B-17 bomber bidding to complete its final mission. It's a bit too predictable – the usual "Will they make it back or not?" heroics – but the characters, all slickly played by a strong cast including Matthew Modine and Eric Stoltz, are endearing and the crew's final flight is grippingly filmed. Most of the plaudits, though, must go to the stunning aerial effects and photography. NF Some violence, swearing. *DVD* SF

Matthew Modine *Dennis Dearborn* • John Lithgow *Colonel Bruce Derringer* • Eric Stoltz *Danny Daly* • Sean Astin *Richard "Rascal" Moore* • Harry Connick Jr *Clay Busby* • Reed Edward Diamond [Reed Diamond] *Virgil* • Tate Donovan *Luke Sinclair* • DB Sweeney *Phil Rosenthal* • Billy Zane *Val Kozlowski* • Jane Horrocks *Faith* ■ *Dir* Michael Caton-Jones • *Scr* Monte Merrick • *Cinematographer* David Watkin

The Men
★★★★ PG

Drama   1950 · US · BW · 86min

This film is now remembered for the remarkable screen debut of Marlon Brando, who changed the very nature of screen acting with his mesmerising, naturalistic, self-pitying performance as a paraplegic war veteran. Brando first appears after the notable opening address by doctor Everett Sloane, a clever ploy used by director Fred Zinnemann to set the tone and prepare the audience for what follows. The sexual aspect of the tale is superbly circumvented (made necessary by the censors) in Carl Foreman's sensitive screenplay and it may all seem dated and overly melodramatic today. TS *DVD*

Marlon Brando *Ken "Bud" Wilozek* • Teresa Wright *Ellen* • Everett Sloane *Dr Brock* • Jack Webb *Norm Butler* • Richard Erdman *Leo* • Arthur Jurado *Angel* • Virginia Farmer *Nurse Robbins* ■ *Dir* Fred Zinnemann • *Scr* Carl Foreman, from his story

Men & Chicken
★★★ 15

Black comedy   2015 · Den/Ger · Colour · 99min

Like the mansion where most of the action unfolds, writer/director Anders Thomas Jensen's fourth feature brims with mutant creatures, bestial desires and warped family feelings. Seriously strange but also oddly enchanting, this Danish black comedy revolves around two brothers (Mads Mikkelsen, David Dencik) who discover strange truths when, on the death of their father, they go searching for their past. LF Danish +subtitles. Strong sex references *DVD* SF

Mads Mikkelsen *Elias* • David Dencik *Gabriel* • Nikolaj Lie Kaas *Gregor* • Soren Malling *Franz* ■ *Dir/Scr* Anders Thomas Jensen

Men Are Not Gods
★★ U

Drama   1936 · UK · BW · 79min

Here's a chance to see a youthful Rex Harrison in a supporting role in this languid luvvie yarn about an actor (Sebastian Shaw) playing Othello, who takes his work too seriously and attempts to strangle his wife Gertrude Lawrence (who's playing Desdemona) because he's fallen for Miriam Hopkins. Essentially an excuse to look at the incestuous antics within a theatre company, this is daft from the portentous title onwards. SH

Miriam Hopkins *Ann Williams* • Gertrude Lawrence *Barbara Halford* • Sebastian Shaw *Edmund Davey* • Rex Harrison *Tommy Stapleton* • AE Matthews *Skeates* • Val Gielgud *Producer* • Laura Smithson *Katherine* ■ *Dir* Walter Reisch • *Scr* GB Stern, Iris Wright, Walter Reisch

Men at Work
★★ 15

Comedy thriller   1990 · US · Colour · 94min

Emilio Estevez wrote and directed this comedy action tale about two dustbin men (played by Estevez and his brother Charlie Sheen) who uncover a corpse on their daily clean-up route. Together with a nutty Vietnam vet (Keith David), they attempt to solve the crime. Unsurprisingly, Sheen and Estevez have a chemistry that charms, but this is basically brainless. LH *DVD*

Charlie Sheen *Carl Taylor* • Emilio Estevez *James St James* • Leslie Hope *Susan Wilkins* • Keith David *Louis Fedders* • Dean Cameron *Pizza man* • John Getz *Maxwell Potterdam III* ■ *Dir/Scr* Emilio Estevez

Men Don't Leave
★★★★ 15

Drama   1990 · US · Colour · 109min

Jessica Lange gives another powerful performance as a mother coping with starting life anew after the death of her husband. Trying to pay off mounting debts and reduced to living in a small apartment with her sons (Charlie Korsmo and Chris O'Donnell, in one of his first roles), she also tries to begin a new relationship while battling against depression. Honest and absorbing, this confirms Lange as one of the best actresses of her generation. Watch out, too, for strong supporting turns from the excellent Joan Cusack and Kathy Bates. JB Violence, swearing.

Jessica Lange *Beth Macauley* • Chris O'Donnell *Chris Macauley* • Charlie Korsmo *Matt Macauley* • Arliss Howard *Charles Simon* • Tom Mason *John Macauley* • Joan Cusack *Jody* • Kathy Bates *Lisa Coleman* ■ *Dir* Paul Brickman • *Scr* Barbara Benedek, Paul Brickman, from a story by Barbara Benedek, suggested by the film *La Vie Continue*

Men in Black
★★★★ PG

Science-fiction comedy
1997 · US · Colour · 93min

This smash-hit science-fiction comedy, based on a short-lived 1980s comic strip, has secret agent Tommy Lee Jones and new recruit Will Smith as part of a top-secret agency responsible for regulating all extraterrestrial activity on Earth. While investigating an alien sighting the pair become involved in the search for a missing galaxy to appease an interstellar force and avert the Earth's destruction. Great special effects, inventive alien designs and Smith and Jones's hip, hilarious double act make director Barry Sonnenfeld's *Lethal Weapon*-style buddy picture a fast-paced pleasure. AJ Some violence, swearing. *DVD* BL

Tommy Lee Jones *K* • Will Smith *J* • Linda Fiorentino *Laurel* • Vincent D'Onofrio *Edgar* • Rip Torn *Zed* • Tony Shalhoub *Jeebs* ■ *Dir* Barry Sonnenfeld • *Scr* Ed Solomon, from the comic book by Lowell Cunningham

Men in Black 2
★★ PG

Science-fiction comedy
2002 · US · Colour · 84min

The smart-suited alien immigration agents Jay (Will Smith) and Kay (Tommy Lee Jones) return to save the planet, along with other familiar supporting players (including the hilarious talking pug Frank). This time, however, it's a super sexy Lara Flynn Boyle who's causing the cosmic chaos as evil alien queen Serleena. Her restrained performance lacks depth and menace, and adds no meat to an already emaciated plot. But there are enough flashy special effects and sharp humour to keep fans happy. SF Violence, swearing. *DVD* BL

Tommy Lee Jones *Agent Kay* • Will Smith *Agent Jay* • Lara Flynn Boyle *Serleena* • Johnny Knoxville *Scrad/Charlie* • Rosario Dawson *Laura* • Tony Shalhoub *Jeebs* • Rip Torn *Zed* • Patrick Warburton *Agent Tee* ■ *Dir* Barry Sonnenfeld • *Scr* Robert Gordon, Barry Fanola, from a story by Robert Gordon, from characters by Lowell Cunningham

Men in Black 3
★★★★ PG

Science-fiction comedy
2012 · US · Colour · 101min

After a disappointing second instalment, the men in black are back on top form in this madcap caper. Here, Agent J (Will Smith) is forced back to 1969 to keep partner K (Tommy Lee Jones) from getting killed by an alien fugitive (a truly flesh-crawling Jemaine Clement). Smith is just as wisecrackingly cool and Jones is his curmudgeonly self. But it's Josh Brolin who really lights up the screen with a rib-tickling tour de force as K's younger incarnation. The chemistry is just right and director

Barry Sonnenfeld exploits this – and when the script is just as sharp, the adventure is much more satisfying. SP Brief violence, swearing. *DVD* BL 3D

Will Smith *Agent J* • Tommy Lee Jones *Agent K* • Josh Brolin *Young Agent K* • Emma Thompson *O* • Alice Eve *Young Agent O* • Jemaine Clement *Boris* • Bill Hader *Andy Warhol* • Nicole Scherzinger *Lilly* • Michael Stuhlbarg *Griffin* • Justin Bieber • Tim Burton ■ *Dir* Barry Sonnenfeld • *Scr* Etan Cohen, from a comic book by Lowell Cunningham

The Men in Her Life
★★

Drama   1941 · US · BW · 89min

An ambitious former circus performer rises to become a famous ballerina and has several romances, at the cost of her relationship with her daughter. This trite and unconvincing melodrama stars the lovely but totally miscast Loretta Young. The under-characterised men in her life are Dean Jagger, John Shepperd (a pseudonym for Shepperd Strudwick) and Conrad Veidt as the strict ballet master who helps her to the top. Gregory Ratoff directs more stylishly than one might expect. RK

Loretta Young *Lina Varasvina/Polly Varley* • Conrad Veidt *Stanislas Rosing* • Dean Jagger *David Gibson* • Eugenie Leontovich *Marie* • John Shepperd [Shepperd Strudwick] *Sir Roger Chevis* • Otto Kruger *Victor* • Ann Todd [Ann E Todd] *Rose* ■ *Dir* Gregory Ratoff • *Scr* Frederick Kohner, Michael Wilson, Paul Trivers, from the novel *Ballerina* by Lady Eleanor Smith

Men in War
★★★ PG

War drama   1957 · US · BW · 98min

One of those minor war movies that were thick on the ground in the 1950s. But this account of a US infantry platoon in Korea is given distinction by the intelligent script and Anthony Mann's in-your-face direction, while the music by Elmer Bernstein is also a bonus. Robert Ryan's battle-exhausted lieutenant is a character whose attitude says more about war's futility than many a major epic. TH

Robert Ryan *Lieutenant Benson* • Aldo Ray *Montana* • Robert Keith (1) *Colonel* • Phillip Pine *Riordan* • Vic Morrow *Zwickley* • Nehemiah Persoff *Lewis* • LQ Jones *Editor* ■ *Dir* Anthony Mann • *Scr* Philip Yordan (front for Ben Maddow), from the novel *Combat* by Van Van Praag

Men in White
★★★

Drama   1934 · US · BW · 80min

Clark Gable is a brilliant and dedicated young intern who is chosen to work with veteran physician Jean Hersholt – Hollywood's resident kindly doctor – to the distress of his socialite fiancée Myrna Loy. This modest, decently-made drama is a flag-waver for the medical profession. Gable's tragic involvement with a student nurse (marvellously played by Elizabeth Allan) strays into unconvincing melodrama, but the rest is believable and absorbing. RK

Clark Gable *Dr Ferguson* • Myrna Loy *Laura* • Jean Hersholt *Dr Hochberg* • Elizabeth Allan *Barbara* • Otto Kruger *Dr Levine* ■ *Dir* Richard Boleslawski • *Scr* Waldemar Young, from the play by Sidney Kingsley

Men o' War
★★★★ U

Comedy   1929 · US · BW · 19min

One of 100-plus movie appearances for beloved comedy double act Laurel and Hardy, this 20-minute short is one of the team's best talkies. It's especially important for being the film that demonstrated that the duo could succeed with sound. The boys play sailors on leave enjoying a series of comic encounters – in a park, at an ice cream parlour and on a lake in a rowing boat. DF *DVD*

Stan Laurel *Stan* • Oliver Hardy *Ollie* • James Finlayson *Soda jerk* ■ *Dir* Lewis R Foster • *Scr* HM Walker

Men of Boys Town
★

Drama   1941 · US · BW · 106min

In an unspeakably yucky farrago, Spencer Tracy reprises his Oscar-winning role as Father Edward J Flanagan, first seen in *Boys Town*, who seems to think there's a saint in every delinquent. At one point,

Tracy even employs a pet pooch to help win over the kids. Tracy's rehabilitation of cute little Mickey Rooney from an unforgiving reform school will probably leave today's audiences nauseous. **AT**

Spencer Tracy *Father Flanagan* • Mickey Rooney *Whitey Marsh* • Bobs Watson *Pee Wee* • Larry Nunn *Ted Martley* • Darryl Hickman *Flip* • Henry O'Neill *Mr Maitland* • Lee J Cobb *Dave Morris* ■ *Dir* Norman Taurog • *Scr* James Kevin McGuinness

Men of Honor ★★★ 15
Action drama based on a true story
2000 · US · Colour · 123min

This earnest but enjoyable film is based on the experiences of Carl Brashear, who joined the US Navy in the late 1940s, just as segregation was abolished. In George Tillman Jr's film, Brashear (played by Cuba Gooding Jr) sets his sights on becoming the first African-American deep-sea navy diver. Sent to boot camp, he finds himself under the strict regime of hostile diving master Billy Sunday (Robert De Niro), and so begins a long struggle to win respect and achieve his goal. There are some spectacular underwater sequences, but they tend to overshadow the performances of both leads. **LH** *DVD* ~~

Robert De Niro *Billy Sunday* • Cuba Gooding Jr *Carl Brashear* • Charlize Theron *Gwen* • Aunjanue Ellis *Jo* • Hal Holbrook *Mr Pappy* • David Keith *Capt Hartigan* • Michael Rapaport *Snowhill* • Powers Boothe *Capt Pullman* ■ *Dir* George Tillman Jr • *Scr* Scott Marshall Smith

Men of Respect ★★ 18
Crime drama　1990 · US · Colour · 108min

The idea of translating William Shakespeare's "Scottish play" to the Mafia underworld is a good one but this film, like 1956's *Joe Macbeth*, fails to capitalise on the high concept. Writer/director William Reilly's dialogue teeters between the clever and the unintentionally hysterical. As the hood who becomes head of the Mob by bumping off his rivals, John Turturro is occasionally very sinister, and Katherine Borowitz (as his wife) eggs him on with sadistic glee. But there are just too many sniggers for a tough crime drama. **DP** Violence, swearing.

John Turturro *Mike Battaglia* • Katherine Borowitz *Ruthie Battaglia* • Rod Steiger *Charlie D'Amico* • Peter Boyle *Duffy* • Dennis Farina *Bankie Como* • Stanley Tucci *Mal* ■ *Dir* William Reilly • *Scr* William Reilly, from the play *Macbeth* by William Shakespeare

Men of Sherwood Forest ★★ U
Adventure　1954 · UK · Colour · 77min

In a cheap and cheerful Hammer outing to Sherwood, American nobody Don Taylor lacks both the dash and the devilment to convince as he leads his Merrie Men on a mission to aid Richard the Lionheart. Leonard Sachs similarly makes a lightweight Sheriff of Nottingham, while Eileen Moore provides some rather soppy love interest. Val Guest directs with little feel for the boisterous action. **DP**

Don Taylor *Robin Hood* • Reginald Beckwith *Friar Tuck* • Eileen Moore *Lady Alys* • David King-Wood *Sir Guy Belton* • Patrick Holt *King Richard* • John Van Eyssen *Will Scarlett* • Leonard Sachs *Sheriff of Nottingham* ■ *Dir* Val Guest • *Scr* Allan MacKinnon

Men of Texas ★★★ U
Western　1942 · US · BW · 82min

Chicago reporter Robert Stack is sent to investigate the aftermath of the Civil War in Texas and confronts Broderick Crawford, who refuses to admit defeat. The interesting interplay between the characters suggests that the pen is mightier than the sword, a strange concept to be advocating in the dark days of the Second World War. This is a good-looking western, pacily directed by Ray Enright, with Anne Gwynne making a very attractive leading lady, while Leo Carrillo supplies the humour as Stack's photographer sidekick. **TS**

Robert Stack *Barry Conovan* • Broderick Crawford *Henry Clay Jackson* • Jackie Cooper *Robert Houston Scott* • Anne Gwynne *Jane Baxter Scott* • Ralph Bellamy *Major Lamphere* • Leo Carrillo *Sam Sawyer* ■ *Dir* Ray Enright • *Scr* Harold Shumate, Richard Brooks, from the story *Frontier* by Harold Shumate • *Cinematographer* Milton Krasner

Men of the Fighting Lady ★
War drama　1954 · US · Colour · 79min

This is a commie-bashing Korean war yarn about a US aircraft carrier, *The Fighting Lady*, and the brave men who fly her bombers, aim their rockets at the enemy's railway network, then return to base to exchange some of the corniest dialogue ever to emerge from the MGM studio. Louis Calhern plays author James A Michener, whose reports in *The Saturday Evening Post* formed the basis for the script. **AT**

Van Johnson *Lieutenant Howard Thayer* • Walter Pidgeon *Commander Kent Dowling* • Louis Calhern *James A Michener* • Dewey Martin *Ensign Kenneth Schechter* • Keenan Wynn *Lieutenant Commander Ted Dodson* • Frank Lovejoy *Lieutenant Commander Paul Grayson* • Robert Horton *Ensign Neil Conovan* • Bert Freed *Lieutenant Andrew Szymanski* ■ *Dir* Andrew Marton • *Scr* Art Cohn, from the stories *The Forgotten Heroes of Korea* by James A Michener and *The Case of the Blind Pilot* by Commander Harry A Burns

Men on the Bridge ★★★★ 15
Drama
2009 · Ger/Tur/Neth/Fin · Colour · 86min

This perceptive debut from writer/director Asli Ozge views contemporary Turkey through the eyes of three men linked by the Bosphorus Bridge that unites Europe and Asia. The storylines involve a teenage slacker who illegally sells roses while fantasising about a better life; a lonesome cop who turns to the internet to find love; and an industrious cabby who strives to raise the cash to afford a new apartment to satisfy his aspirational spouse. However, Istanbul is the real star here, with Ozge and her cinematographer Emre Erkmen capturing the vibrancy, venality and vulgarity of a city that thrums with life. **DP** In Turkish, English, German. Swearing. *DVD*

Umut Ilker *Umut* • Fikret Portakal *Fikret* • Murat Tokgoz *Murat* • Cemile Ilker *Cemile* ■ *Dir/Scr* Asli Ozge • *Cinematographer* Emre Erkmen

The Men Who Stare at Goatsx ★★ 15
Wartime comedy
2009 · US/UK · Colour · 89min

This movie is based on the eccentric investigation by British journalist Jon Ronson into New Age psychological techniques within US military intelligence, but it may confound fans of his book and the accompanying 2004 TV documentary. What was intriguing source material is converted into a wacky, *Catch 22*-style war comedy set in Iraq, with Ewan McGregor as the bemused reporter who takes off with reactivated "psychic spy" George Clooney on a suitably vague desert mission. Aside from a few slapstick set pieces and the welcome presence of Jeff Bridges and Kevin Spacey, the film is dominated by expository narration, merely encouraging the audience to stare at an all-star cast for 90 minutes. **AC** Swearing, brief nudity. *DVD* ~~

George Clooney *Lyn Cassady* • Ewan McGregor *Bob Wilton* • Jeff Bridges *Bill Django* • Kevin Spacey *Larry Hooper* • Stephen Lang *Brigadier General Dean Hopgood* • Robert Patrick *Todd Nixon* • Rebecca Mader *Debora Wilton* ■ *Dir* Grant Heslov • *Scr* Peter Straughan, from the non-fiction book by Jon Ronson

Men with Guns ★★★★★ 15
Drama　1997 · US · Colour · 127min

John Sayles, one of America's most impressive and enterprising independent film-makers, makes this Spanish-language film a socially significant fable about tyranny. An elderly doctor (Federico Luppi) goes to visit former students working in poor Latin American villages, only to find they've been killed by the dictatorial regime. Made with a feeling and sincerity that is never undermined by sentimentality, it's a poignant reminder of how we all turn a blind eye to that which would inconvenience us. **TH** Spanish +subtitles.

Federico Luppi *Doctor Humberto Fuentes* • Damián Alcázar *Padre Portillo, the priest* • Tania Cruz *Graciela, the mute girl* • Damian Delgado *Domingo, the soldier* • Dan Rivera González *Conejo, the boy* • Iguandili Lopez *Mother* • Mandy Patinkin *Andrew* ■ *Dir* John Sayles • *Scr* John Sayles, inspired by a character in *The Long Night of White Chickens* by Francisco Goldman

Men with Wings ★★
Drama　1938 · US · Colour · 105min

Starting with a re-enactment of the Wright Brothers' first manned flight in 1903, this flying epic from *Wings* director William "Wild Bill" Wellman isn't nearly exciting enough. Childhood buddies Fred MacMurray and Ray Milland grow up to become aerial obsessives, building and inventing planes, fighting in the wars and having a protracted and rather dull dogfight over Louise Campbell. The end result was an expensive flop. **AT**

Fred MacMurray *Patrick Falconer* • Ray Milland *Scott Barnes* • Louise Campbell *Peggy Ranson* • Andy Devine *Joe Gibbs* • Lynne Overman *Hank Rinebow* • Porter Hall *Hiram F Jenkins* • Walter Abel *Nick Ranson* • Virginia Weidler *Peggy Ranson, as a child* • Donald O'Connor *Pat Falconer, as a child* ■ *Dir* William A Wellman • *Scr* Robert Carson

Men without Women ★★★
Drama　1930 · US · BW · 77min

Filmed as an early talkie but apparently surviving only in the alternative silent version, director John Ford's first collaboration with writer Dudley Nichols is the compelling drama of the attempts to rescue the crew of a crippled American submarine from the floor of the China Sea. John Wayne has a bit part as a sailor relaying messages with earphones and mouthpiece. Kenneth MacKenna and Frank Albertson are the stars, but it's Ford masterly direction that is the film's main attraction now. **AE**

Kenneth MacKenna *Chief Torpedoman Burke* • Frank Albertson *Ens Price* • Paul Page *Handsome* • Walter McGrail *Cobb* • Warren Hymer *Kaufman* • John Wayne ■ *Dir* John Ford • *Scr* Dudley Nichols, from a story by John Ford, James Kevin McGuinness

Men, Women: a User's Manual ★★★ 12
Satire　1996 · Fr · Colour · 118min

Disregard the title. Look instead to the subtitle, *An Inhuman Comedy*, to find a clue to this wry tale about a cruel practical joke. The perpetrator is doctor Alessandra Martines, whose long-harboured lover's grudge prompts her to inform oversexed tycoon Bernard Tapie that he is terminally ill, while telling dying cop Fabrice Luchini the opposite. In spite of the plot's preposterous contrivance, you are still drawn to director Claude Lelouch's rather resistible characters, although the subplots are less successful. **DP** French +subtitles.

Bernard Tapie *Benoît Blanc* • Fabrice Luchini *Fabio Lini* • Alessandra Martines *Doctor Nitez* • Pierre Arditi *Dr Pierre Lerner* • Caroline Céllier *Madame Blanc* • Ophélie Winter *Pretty blonde of Crillon* • Anouk Aimée *The widow* ■ *Dir* Claude Lelouch • *Scr* Claude Lelouch, René Bonnell, Jean-Phillipe Chatrier

Men, Women & Children ★★★ 15
Comedy drama　2014 · US · Colour · 119min

It doesn't physically exist, but the internet is still as real a place to us as Starbucks – a paradox explored in this ambitious film. Adam Sandler and Rosemarie DeWitt are the Trubys, both bored and looking for online kicks. He uses porn, she a dating site for love cheats, and through their son (Travis Tope) we enter the dog-eat-dog world of high school. As one might imagine from the director of *Juno*, this is where the meat of the film really lies, with a comic turn by Jennifer Garner as an overprotective mother. **DW** Swearing, sexual references.

Adam Sandler *Don Truby* • Rosemarie DeWitt *Helen Truby* • Jennifer Garner *Patricia Beltmeyer* • Emma Thompson *Narrator* • Ansel Elgort *Tim Mooney* • Judy Greer *Donna Clint* • Travis Tope *Chris Truby* ■ *Dir* Jason Reitman • *Scr* Erin Cressida Wilson, Jason Reitman, from Chad Kultgen's novel

Mena
Crime thriller　2017 · US · Colour

This is a preview – no prints were available to review as we went to press: Thirty years after *Top Gun* Tom Cruise is back in the cockpit in *Mena*, but he's not a fighter pilot this time. This is the true story of a TWA pilot who smuggled drugs for an infamous Colombian cartel in the 1970s until he was busted by the authorities and turned informant. On the face of it, this looks like Cruise muddying his good guy image, but don't be surprised if he finds redemption through his later work for the CIA. **SP**

Tom Cruise *Barry Seal* • Domhnall Gleeson *Monty Schafer* • Jayma Mays *Dana Sibota* • Sarah Wright *Lucy Seal* • Caleb Landry Jones *Bubba* ■ *Dir* Doug Liman • *Scr* Gary Spinelli

Menace II Society ★★★ 18
Drama　1993 · US · Colour · 97min

This is asearing portrait of life in the 'hood from Allen and Albert Hughes, twins who were just 20 at the time it was made. Tyrin Turner is the surly adolescent, the son of a junkie mother and a drug-pushing dad, who's torn between nice single mom Jada Pinkett or a life of drive-by shootings and petty crime. There's no denying the visceral power of the Hughes brothers' vision, but – with the exception of Pinkett – it's hard to have sympathy for any of the characters. **JF** *DVD* ~~

Jada Pinkett [Jada Pinkett Smith] *Ronnie* • Tyrin Turner *Caine* • Larenz Tate *O-Dog* • Charles S Dutton *Mr Butler* • Bill Duke *Detective* • Samuel L Jackson *Tat Lawson* ■ *Dir* Allen Hughes, Albert Hughes • *Scr* Tyger Williams, Allen Hughes, Albert Hughes, from their story

The Men's Club ★ 18
Drama　1986 · US · Colour · 96min

This static and stagey bore focuses on seven men who meet up to swap sexual stories, throw knives at a wall and howl like wolves before heading off to the weirdest brothel in the US. One-dimensional, misogynistic garbage, with flat direction and unengaging performances. **JC**

David Dukes *Phillip* • Richard Jordan *Kramer* • Harvey Keitel *Solly Berliner* • Frank Langella *Harold Canterbury* • Roy Scheider *Cavanaugh* • Craig Wasson *Paul* • Treat Williams *Terry* • Stockard Channing *Nancy* • Jennifer Jason Leigh *Teensy* ■ *Dir* Peter Medak • *Scr* Leonard Michaels, from his novel

Mental ★★★ 15
Comedy drama　2012 · US/Aus · Colour · 111min

Julie Andrews haunts this intermittently hilarious Aussie comedy, in which a downtrodden politician's wife (Rebecca Gibney) is committed to an institution for wanting to be Maria Von Trapp and singing songs from *The Sound of Music*. And there's more than a whiff of Mary Poppins about Shaz (Toni Collette), the charismatic "crazy" hired to look after her eccentrically neurotic daughters. But there's as much "Crocodile" Dundee as magic nanny about the wacky tactics that she uses to bring the kids to a self-confident "state of Shaz." At just under two hours, the film's too long but director PJ Hogan (*Muriel's Wedding*) does manage to elicit a good number of laugh-out-loud moments. **DA** Swearing, drug abuse, brief nudity. *DVD* ~~

Toni Collette *Shaz* • Liev Schreiber *Trevor Blundell* • Anthony LaPaglia *Barry Moochmore* • Rebecca Gibney *Shirley Moochmore* • Kerry Fox *Nancy* • Caroline Goodall *Doris* • Deborah Mailman *Sandra* ■ *Dir/Scr* PJ Hogan

M

Mephisto ★★★★★ 15
Drama 1981 · Hun · Colour · 138min

Winner of the Oscar for best foreign film, this was the first in István Szabó's loose trilogy on the theme of treachery and ambition. As in the subsequent *Colonel Redl* and *Hanussen*, Klaus Maria Brandauer plays a character who sells his soul for power, here as an actor who blithely ignores the implications of Nazi patronage to achieve stardom. Klaus Mann's source novel is essentially a revision of the Faust legend, but Szabó never loses a sense of historical perspective and delineates the seductive allure of fascism with chilling detachment to make its evil tenets all the more hideous. Brandauer is majestic and this is a masterpiece. DP German +subtitles. DVD

Klaus Maria Brandauer *Hendrik Höfgen* · Ildiko Bansagi *Nicoletta von Niebuhr* · Rolf Hoppe *General* · Gyorgy Cserhalmi *Hans Miklas* · Peter Andorai *Otto Ulrichs* · Karin Boyd *Juliette Martens* · Christine Harbort *Lotte Lindenthal* ■ *Dir* István Szabó · *Scr* Peter Dobai, István Szabó, Klaus Mann

The Mephisto Waltz ★★★
Horror drama 1971 · US · Colour · 108min

This underrated occult thriller blends urban gothic trappings with psychological insights. Dying concert pianist Curt Jurgens uses black magic to possess journalist Alan Alda's body in this unnerving shocker. It's when Alda's wife, Jacqueline Bisset, finds out what's going on that things start getting really scary. Director Paul Wendkos uses soap-opera clichés and dazzling psychedelic colours to distort the boundary between reality and fantasy in this diabolical tale of enigmatic paranoia. AJ

Alan Alda *Myles Clarkson* · Jacqueline Bisset *Paula Clarkson* · Barbara Parkins *Roxanne* · Curt Jurgens *Duncan Ely* · Brad Dillman [Bradford Dillman] *Bill* · William Windom *Dr West* · Kathleen Widdoes *Maggie West* · Pamelyn Ferdin *Abby Clarkson* ■ *Dir* Paul Wendkos · *Scr* Ben Maddow, from the novel by Fred Mustard Stewart

Le Mépris ★★★ 15
Satire 1963 · Fr/It · Colour · 98min

Jean-Luc Godard's weird satire on Hollywood's invasion of Europe stars Jack Palance as the American producer who says: "When I hear the word culture I reach for my cheque book." Fritz Lang plays the director of an intended version of Homer's *Odyssey*, while the sex interest is provided by – who else? – Brigitte Bardot. It sounds relatively straightforward, and probably would be if Godard didn't veer off at tangents in a desperate attempt not to be swamped by his biggest budget and cast to date. AT English, French, German, Italian +subtitles. Swearing, nudity DVD ▷

Brigitte Bardot *Camille Javal* · Michel Piccoli *Paul Javal* · Jack Palance *Jeremy Prokosh* · Fritz Lang · Giorgia Moll *Francesca Vanini* ■ *Dir/Scr* Jean-Luc Godard

Mercenary for Justice ★ 18
Action thriller 2006 · Aruba/US/S Afr · Colour · 92min

Asinine action movie in which Steven Seagal plays an ex-CIA mercenary who's so dispassionate that he could be auditioning for a role in one of George A Romero's zombie films. The overly convoluted plot shifts from a war-torn African island and on to American soil, then to a bank robbery and prison break in Cape Town, as Seagal searches for the elusive CIA villain (Luke Goss) who's betrayed him. JR Violence, swearing. DVD ▷

Steven Seagal *John Seeger* · Jacqueline Lord *Maxine Barnol* · Roger Guenveur Smith *Anthony Chapel* · Luke Goss *John Dresham* · Adrian Galley *Bulldog* ■ *Dir* Don E FauntLeRoy · *Scr* Steve Collins

The Merchant of Four Seasons ★★★★ 15
Drama 1971 · W Ger · Colour · 84min

Recalling the fate of his own uncle, Rainer Werner Fassbinder explores the emotional tyranny of women in this archly realist melodrama. Having failed in the Foreign Legion and the police, been neglected by his mother, jilted by his romantic ideal and humiliated by his jealous wife, greengrocer Hans Hirschmüller is trapped in an irrelevant, drink-sodden existence. Fassbinder employs a series of perfectly judged flashbacks to piece together this life just as it's falling apart. What results is both a sympathetic portrait of a far from blameless nobody and a pessimistic vision of everyday life. DP German +subtitles. DVD

Hans Hirschmüller *Hans Epp* · Irm Hermann *Irmgard Epp* · Hanna Schygulla *Anna* · Andrea Schober *Renate Epp* ■ *Dir/Scr* Rainer Werner Fassbinder

Merci Docteur Rey ★ 15
Comedy drama 2002 · UK/Fr · Colour · 88min

Andrew Litvack's debut feature is a gross miscalculation that is woefully over-written and shamefully overplayed. Dianne Wiest is primarily culpable as the operatic diva whose return to the Parisian stage is blighted by the murder of her ex-husband (Simon Callow). She's blithely unaware that her gay son Stanislas Merhar witnessed the crime and is seeking the killer while hiding out with Jane Birkin. Pretentious, preposterous and embarrassing. DP English, French +subtitles. Drug abuse, swearing. DVD

Dianne Wiest *Elisabeth Beaumont* · Jane Birkin *Penelope* · Stanislas Merhar *Thomas Beaumont* · Bulle Ogier *Claude Sabrie* · Karim Saleh *Murderer* · Didier Flamand *Detective* · Jerry Hall *Sybil* · Simon Callow *Bob* · Vanessa Redgrave ■ *Dir/Scr* Andrew Litvack

Merci la Vie ★★★ 18
Surreal fantasy drama 1991 · Fr · Colour and BW · 113min

At times dazzling, Bertrand Blier's film teems with ideas, but too often finds itself at a loss with what to do with them. Charlotte Gainsbourg and Anouk Grinberg give spellbinding performances as the social misfits confronted with a melange of maladjusted males, including doctor Gérard Depardieu and Nazi officer Jean-Louis Trintignant. Challenging, violent and often outrageously funny. DP French +subtitles. Violence, swearing, sex scenes. DVD

Charlotte Gainsbourg *Camille* · Anouk Grinberg *Joëlle* · Gérard Depardieu *Marc Antoine* · Michel Blanc *young man* · Jean Carmet *Old father* · Catherine Jacob *Young mother* · Thierry Frémont *François* · François Perrot *Maurice, the film director* · Jean-Louis Trintignant *Officer* ■ *Dir/Scr* Bertrand Blier

Merci pour le Chocolat ★★★ PG
Crime thriller 2000 · Fr/Swi · Colour · 96min

Alfred Hitchcock always wanted to set a film in a Swiss chocolate factory and he would doubtless have been amused by this realisation of his dream by his most fervent disciple, Claude Chabrol. A typically rich mixture of malice and mockery, his ultra-cool approach perhaps removes some of the spice from the tale, making the central pursuit (by an undetected murderess, Isabelle Huppert, of her pianist husband's new protégée) somewhat lacking in suspense. Yet Chabrol's talent for social satire remains undimmed and the clinical way in which he exposes the murderess's bourgeois foibles is deliciously excruciating to watch. DP French +subtitles. DVD

Isabelle Huppert *Marie-Claire "Mika" Muller* · Jacques Dutronc *André Polonski* · Anna Mouglalis *Jeanne Pollet* · Rodolphe Pauly *Guillaume Polonski* · Michel Robin *Patou Dufreigne* · Mathieu Simonet *Axel* ■ *Dir* Claude Chabrol · *Scr* Claude Chabrol, Caroline Eliacheff, from the novel *The Chocolate Cobweb* by Charlotte Armstrong

Mercury Rising ★★★ 15
Action thriller 1998 · US · Colour · 106min

Bruce Willis stars as a renegade government operative who becomes protector of an autistic child (Miko Hughes) who has cracked the supposedly impenetrable Mercury security code; Alec Baldwin is the crooked national security man hunting them down. Director Harold Becker manages to impart a little depth to the relationship between Willis and Hughes – in between the chases and shoot-outs – but the psychological backdrop is too contrived. JF Swearing, violence. DVD ▷

Bruce Willis *Art Jeffries* · Alec Baldwin *Nicholas Kudrow* · Miko Hughes *Simon Lynch* · Chi McBride *Tommy B Jordan* · Kim Dickens *Stacey* · Robert Stanton *Dean Crandell* ■ *Dir* Harold Becker · *Scr* Lawrence Konner, Mark Rosenthal, from the novel *Simple Simon* by Ryne Douglas Pearson

Mercy ★★ 18
Erotic detective thriller 2000 · US · Colour · 112min

Ellen Barkin is the cop investigating the murders of a series of women who have been tortured to death, while socialite Peta Wilson and therapist Julian Sands (giving his usual wooden performance) are two of her chief suspects. The cast is more interesting than the plot, which goes from "erotic" to "moralistic" just when it was looking intriguing – but there are nice performances here even if the script isn't up to much. JB

Ellen Barkin *Catherine Palmer* · Wendy Crewson *Bernadine Mello* · Peta Wilson *Vickie Kittrie* · Karen Young *Mary* · Julian Sands *Dominick Broussard* · Stephen Baldwin *Mechanic* · Marshall Bell *Gil Reynolds* · Beau Starr *Lt Frisch* ■ *Dir* Damian Harris · *Scr* Damian Harris, from the novel by David L Lindsey

The Mercy
Drama based on a true story 2016 · UK · Colour

This is a preview - no prints were available to review as we went to press: Colin Firth and Rachel Weisz star in this biopic based on the strange demise of British sailor Donald Crowhurst. After a bad start in the 1968 Golden Globe Race, the amateur yachtsman attempted to dupe the world into believing he had gone ahead and circled the globe. Crowhurst's self-built boat was discovered adrift some months later, but his body was never found. Director James Marsh is the latest in a relatively long line of film-makers to explore the mystery. BB

Rachel Weisz *Clare Crowhurst* · Colin Firth *Donald Crowhurst* · David Thewlis *Rodney Hallworth* · Jonathan Bailey *Wheeler* ■ *Dir* James Marsh · *Scr* Scott Z Burns

Merlin the Return ★★ PG
Action fantasy 2000 · UK · Colour · 87min

As dumbed-down derring do for the kids, this has its entertaining moments. The plot has King Arthur's evil half-brother, Mordred, concocting an escape from the Netherworld, while Merlin tries to awaken the slumbering King Arthur and his knights so that they can face their old foe. Craig Sheffer makes a nicely hissable Mordred, but Rik Mayall plays Merlin as if he were auditioning to be the next Doctor Who. The film has one genuinely scary sequence, and there's enough action hokum to please the under-tens. DA DVD

Rik Mayall *Merlin* · Tia Carrere *Joan Maxwell, a scientist* · Patrick Bergin *King Arthur* · Adrian Paul *Lancelot* · Craig Sheffer *Mordred* · Julie Hartley *Guinevere* ■ *Dir/Scr* Paul Matthews

Mermaid ★★
Drama based on a true story 2000 · US · Colour · 95min

Ellen Burstyn was nominated for a Daytime Emmy for her work in this touching melodrama from director Peter Masterson. But she's completely upstaged by Jodelle Ferland, who gives an amazingly mature performance as Burstyn's five-year-old granddaughter, who becomes increasingly depressed at receiving no reply to the letters she sends to her recently deceased father. This is shamelessly sentimental, but forgivably so, especially as it's based on real events. DP

Samantha Mathis *Rhonda* · Ellen Burstyn *Trish* · Jodelle Ferland *Desi* · David Kaye *Wade* · Peter Flemming *Steve* ■ *Dir* Peter Masterson · *Scr* Todd Robinson

Mermaid ★★★ 15
Romantic fantasy comedy 2016 · Chi · Colour · 93min

The Little Mermaid gets a novel reworking in this daffy eco fable, which broke all box-office records in its native China. Newcomer Jelly Lin plays Shan, a mermaid tasked with seducing tycoon Liu Xuan (Deng Chao), who plans to develop the unspoilt coastline where she and her fish-tailed friends live. The final confrontation between the mer-people and developers is surprisingly brutal but, overall, this is short, sweet and charming. JH Mandarin +subtitles.

Jelly Lin *Shan* · Deng Chao *Liu Xuan* · Show Lo *Octopus* · Zhang Yu Qi *Li Ruo-lan* ■ *Dir* Stephen Chow

Mermaids ★★★★ 15
Romantic comedy 1990 · US · Colour · 105min

In this gentle film, Richard Benjamin coaxes a deft performance from Winona Ryder as a confused 1960s teen, caught between her lust for a local handyman (Michael Schoeffling) and her desire to be a nun. Her eccentric mother (Cher) is having an on-off relationship with a local shopkeeper (Bob Hoskins), while her younger sister (Christina Ricci) practises being a swimmer by holding her breath in the bath. This is a curious, light-hearted tale, with Ryder the greatest surprise. DP Some swearing. DVD

Cher *Mrs Flax* · Bob Hoskins *Lou Landsky* · Winona Ryder *Charlotte Flax* · Michael Schoeffling *Joe Peretti* · Christina Ricci *Kate Flax* · Caroline McWilliams *Carrie* · Jan Miner *Mother Superior* · Betsey Townsend *Mary O'Brien* ■ *Dir* Richard Benjamin · *Scr* June Roberts, from the novel by Patty Dann

Merrill's Marauders ★★★★ U
Second World War drama 1962 · US · Colour · 94min

Grey-haired Jeff Chandler never made it to the top rung of Hollywood stardom, and this, his last and finest movie, makes us wonder why. As Brigadier General Frank Merrill, he's a vivid and boisterous leader of a top US Army unit in 1942 Burma. What marks it out from other battle movies is William Clothier's dramatic photography and director Samuel Fuller's understanding of soldiers in action. He knows that war is hell but that the heat of action can strengthen character. TH

Jeff Chandler *Brig Gen Frank Merrill* · Ty Hardin *Lieutenant Lee Stockton* · Peter Brown *Bullseye* · Andrew Duggan *Major "Doc" Nemeny* · Will Hutchins *Chowhound* · Claude Akins *Sergeant Kolowicz* · Luz Valdez *Burmese girl* · John Hoyt *General Stilwell* · Charles Briggs *Muley* ■ *Dir* Samuel Fuller · *Scr* Samuel Fuller, Milton Sperling, from the novel by Charlton Ogburn Jr

Merrily We Go to Hell ★★★
Comedy 1932 · US · BW · 78min

Sylvia Sidney once commented that she had been "paid by the tear", and her on-screen suffering was indeed relentless. At least this melodrama allowed her to leave the milieu of poverty and crime in which she was so often placed. Here she plays an heiress whose marriage to attractive writer Fredric March disintegrates as a result of his alcoholism and womanising. Deft direction and the strong presence of the stars rescue a plot that is short on substance. Look out for Cary Grant in a bit part. RK

Sylvia Sidney *Joan Prentice* · Fredric March *Jerry Corbett* · Adrianne Allen *Claire Hempstead* · Richard "Skeets" Gallagher *Buck* · Cary Grant *Charlie Baxter* ■ *Dir* Dorothy Arzner · *Scr* Edwin Justus Mayer, from the story *I, Jerry, Take Thee, Joan* by Cleo Lucas

Merrily We Live ★★★
Screwball comedy 1938 · US · BW · 90min

This delightful screwball comedy might be better known if the plot were not so similar to *My Man Godfrey*, made only two years earlier. The earlier film had a crazy rich family employing as a butler an educated bum who tames the spoilt daughter, while this has a crazy family (headed by Billie

Burke) employing as a chauffeur an educated bum (Brian Aherne) who tames the spoilt daughter (Constance Bennett). The pacing is a little off, but the timing of the cast cannot be faulted. **RB**

Constance Bennett *Jerry Kilbourne* • Brian Aherne *Wade Rawlins* • Billie Burke *Mrs Emily Kilbourne* • Alan Mowbray *Grosvenor* • Patsy Kelly *Cook* • Ann Dvorak *Minerva Harlan* • Tom Brown *Kane Kilbourne* • Bonita Granville *Marion Kilbourne* ■ *Dir* Norman Z McLeod • *Scr* Eddie Noran, Jack Jevne

Merry Andrew ★★★ U
Musical romantic comedy
1958 · US · Colour · 102min

This is by no means the funniest Danny Kaye vehicle, but it is energetic and good-humoured. Kaye is a teacher at a stuffy boys' school in England who sets out on an archaeological dig but ends up joining a circus, where he falls in love with Pier Angeli. Saul Chaplin and Johnny Mercer's score includes *The Square on the Hypotenuse* and *Salud*, the latter given a spirited production number with some dazzling dancing by Tommy Rall. **TV**

Danny Kaye *Andrew Larabee* • Pier Angeli *Selena* • Salvatore Baccaloni *Antonio Gallini* • Robert Coote *Dudley Larabee* • Noel Purcell *Matthew Larabee* • Patricia Cutts *Letitia Fairchild* • Rex Evans *Gregory Larabee* • Tommy Rall ■ *Dir* Michael Kidd • *Scr* Isobel Lennart, IAL Diamond, from the story *The Romance of Henry Menafee* by Paul Gallico

Merry Christmas ★★★ 12
First World War drama
2005 · Fr/Ger/UK/Bel/Rom · Colour · 111min

A touching tale of camaraderie and common sense in the midst of carnage and military madness, this is based on the now legendary ceasefire of Christmas 1914, when frontline French, German and Scottish troops spontaneously fraternised in the no man's land between their trenches, sang carols and played football. Here, the catalyst for this brief respite from hostilities is German opera singer Benno Fürmann, who gives a rendition of *Silent Night* for his visiting girlfriend (Diane Kruger). The film boasts glossy production values, and there's some decent stiff-upper-lip acting from an international cast, but this ladles on the sentimentality. **DA** English, German, French +subtitles. Violence, swearing, sex scenes.
DVD

Diane Kruger *Anna Sörensen* • Benno Fürmann *Nikolaus Sprink* • Guillaume Canet *Audebert* • Gary Lewis *Palmer* • Dany Boon *Ponchel* • Daniel Brühl *Horstmayer* • Alex Ferns *Gordon* • Steven Robertson *Jonathan* • Ian Richardson *Bishop* ■ *Dir/Scr* Christian Carion

Merry Christmas Mr Lawrence ★★★★ 15
Second World War drama
1982 · UK/Jpn · Colour · 118min

Nagisa Oshima, the most controversial director of the Japanese New Wave, made his English-language debut with this affecting story set in a PoW camp during the Second World War. Tom Conti stars as a bilingual prisoner who is forced to act as intermediary between commandant Ryuichi Sakamoto and his sadistic number two Takeshi "Beat" Kitano, and the blustering British CO Jack Thompson. Treading carefully in matters of duty and culpability, Oshima creates credible and complex characters, played with distinction by his international cast. **DP** Swearing, violence.
DVD Blu-ray

David Bowie *Major Jack "Straffer" Celliers* • Tom Conti *Colonel John Lawrence* • Ryuichi Sakamoto *Captain Yonoi* • Takeshi [Takeshi Kitano] *Sergeant Gengo Hara* • Jack Thompson *Group Captain Hicksley* • Johnny Okura *Kanemoto* • Alistair Browning *De Jong* ■ *Dir* Nagisa Oshima • *Scr* Nagisa Oshima, Paul Mayersberg, from the novel *The Seed and the Sower* and the stories *A Bar of Shadow* and *The Sword and the Doll* by Laurens van der Post

The Merry Gentleman ★★ 15
Romantic crime drama
2009 · US · Colour · 92min

Michael Keaton makes his directorial debut with, and stars in, this tepid romantic thriller. The nebulous plot sees hitman Frank Logan (Keaton) saved, unknowingly, from suicide by receptionist Kate (Kelly Macdonald). Frank inexplicably strikes up a relationship with Kate, an abused wife who has run away from her husband. Macdonald's perky performance is a distinct plus, especially because Keaton's character is so enigmatic he's unfathomable, while the movie's lack of pace is only partly offset by some very subtle camerawork. **DA** Violence, swearing. **DVD**

Michael Keaton *Frank Logan* • Kelly Macdonald *Kate Frazier* • Tom Bastounes *Dave Murcheson* • Darlene Hunt *Diane* • Guy Van Swearingen *Billy Goldman* • William Dick *Mr Weiss* • Bobby Cannavale *Michael* ■ *Dir* Michael Keaton • *Scr* Ron Lazzeretti

Merry-Go-Round ★★★
Romance
1956 · Hun · BW · 100min

Zoltan Fabri emerged as a leading figure in Hungarian "New Course" cinema with this rural *Romeo and Juliet* fable. Although the film's main purpose was to extol the virtues of collective farming, the romance between Bela Barsi and the debuting Mari Torocsik is full of touching moments, particularly during their whirlwind fairground courtship. Yet, in spite of the vivacious performances, Fabri's direction is stickily sentimental. **DP** Hungarian +subtitles.

Mari Torocsik *Pataki Mari* • Imre Soos *Mate* • Bela Barsi *Pataki Istvan* ■ *Dir* Zoltan Fabri • *Scr* Zoltan Fabri, from a novel by Imre Sarkadi

The Merry Monahans ★★★
Musical comedy
1944 · US · BW · 90min

This seen-it-all-before but delightfully nostalgic musical details the ups and downs, onstage and backstage, of the Monahans, a family of vaudeville entertainers. Jam-packed with musical favourites, the movie stars pint-sized dancing powerhouse Donald O'Connor, Jack Oakie and Peggy Ryan as the family in question. Ann Blyth, soon to play Joan Crawford's monster daughter in *Mildred Pierce*, turns up in more winsome mode. **RK**

Donald O'Connor *Jimmy Monahan* • Peggy Ryan *Patsy Monahan* • Jack Oakie *Pete Monahan* • Ann Blyth *Sheila DeRoyce* • Rosemary DeCamp *Lillian Rice DeRoyce* • John Miljan *Arnold Pembroke* • Gavin Muir *Weldon Laydon* • Isabel Jewell *Rose Monahan* ■ *Dir* Charles Lamont • *Scr* Michael Fessier, Ernest Pagano

The Merry Widow ★★★★
Silent romantic drama
1925 · US · BW · 110min

Erich von Stroheim transforms the Ruritanian romance of Franz Lehar's operetta into an erotic black comedy that carries with it a whiff of decay. Von Stroheim dwells on the lechery of Prince Danilo (John Gilbert) before he is sent to Paris to woo a wealthy American widow (Mae Murray) and thereby save his bankrupt country. Despite the fact that von Stroheim and Murray fought throughout the shooting, she gave one of her best performances, and the lavish pre-sound musical was a great success with both the public and the critics. **RB**

Mae Murray *Sally O'Hara* • John Gilbert (1) *Prince Danilo* • Roy D'Arcy *Crown Prince Mirko* • Tully Marshall *Baron Sadoja* ■ *Dir* Erich von Stroheim • *Scr* Erich von Stroheim, Benjamin Glazer, from the operetta *Die Lustique Witwe* by Victor Leon, Leo Stein, Franz Lehar

The Merry Widow ★★★★
Musical comedy
1934 · US · BW · 99min

This scintillating version of Franz Lehar's operetta includes all the favourite tunes and a fabulous pairing of the great Maurice Chevalier and Jeanette MacDonald. If you only know MacDonald for the films she made with Nelson Eddy, you'll find she's a revelation here - a very merry widow indeed! The film's wit, style and polish is down to the talents of brilliant director

Ernst Lubitsch, whose risqué "touch" is apparent in every scene. This is a real pleasure, dated only in its fashions and its view of a Europe that is long gone. **TS**

Maurice Chevalier *Prince Danilo* • Jeanette MacDonald *Sonia* • Edward Everett Horton *Ambassador Popoff* • Una Merkel *Queen Dolores* • George Barbier *King Achmed* • Minna Gombell *Marcelle* • Ruth Channing *Lulu* • Sterling Holloway *Mischka* ■ *Dir* Ernst Lubitsch • *Scr* Samson Raphaelson, Ernest Vajda, from the operetta *Die Lustique Witwe* by Victor Leon, Leo Stein, Franz Lehar

The Merry Widow ★★ U
Musical
1952 · US · Colour · 104min

Oodles of MGM money and all-stops-out Technicolor were lavished on this version of Franz Lehar's much loved operetta, set in the fantasy principality of Marshovia, but to little avail. A new and pedestrian screenplay, heavy-handed direction and the casting of an unsubtle Lana Turner (dubbed by Trudy Erwin) and a stereotypical Fernando Lamas drains the material of its romantic charm. **RK**

Lana Turner *Crystal Radek* • Fernando Lamas *Count Danilo* • Una Merkel *Kitty Riley* • Richard Haydn *Baron Popoff* • Thomas Gomez *King of Marshovia* ■ *Dir* Curtis Bernhardt • *Scr* Sonya Levien, William Ludwig, from the operetta *Die Lustique Witwe* by Victor Leon, Leo Stein, Franz Lehar

Merton of the Movies ★★ U
Comedy
1947 · US · BW · 81min

The George S Kaufman-Marc Connelly play about a small-town youth, who crashes Hollywood on a mission to be a movie star, would seem to be a splendid vehicle for comedian Red Skelton, but it just fails to ignite. Gloria Grahame, Virginia O'Brien and Alan Mowbray are among the fine talents on parade here, but this is generally a lifeless affair. **TV**

Red Skelton *Merton Gill/Clifford Armitage* • Virginia O'Brien *Phyllis Montague* • Gloria Grahame *Beulah Baxter* • Leon Ames *Lawrence Rupert* • Alan Mowbray *Frank Mulvaney* ■ *Dir* Robert Alton • *Scr* George Wells, Lou Breslow, from the play by George S Kaufman, Marc Connelly, from the novel by Harry Leon Wilson

Meru ★★ 15
Documentary
2015 · Ind/US · Colour · 90min

The Himalayan peak of Mount Meru may not have the notoriety of an Everest or a K2, but it's no less tough or dangerous to ascend. This documentary charts the attempts by a trio of US climbers to scale Meru via a sheer cliff ominously called the Shark's Fin. Some may feel there's too much talk in this chronicle of the preparations, setbacks and attempted ascents of three "big wall" climbers using a mix of fly-on-the-wall footage and talking-head interviews. But the climb itself is something to behold thanks to some spectacular footage **DA** Swearing. **DVD** Blu-ray

Jimmy Chin • Conrad Anker ■ *Dir* Jimmy Chin, Elizabeth Chai Vasarhelyi

Mesmerized ★★ 15
Period drama
1984 · Aus/NZ/UK · Colour · 94min

In this sluggish and visually uninspired film, young innocent Jodie Foster is forced into marrying an older man (John Lithgow) in 19th-century New Zealand. Unable to tolerate his sexual peccadillos, Foster kills him in self-defence and has to stand trial as a result. Foster delivers a strong performance, but this is not one of her better efforts. **LH** **DVD**

Jodie Foster *Victoria* • John Lithgow *Oliver Thompson* • Michael Murphy (1) *Reverend Wilson* • Harry Andrews *Old Thompson* • Dan Shor *George Thompson* • Philip Holder *Dr Finch* • Reg Evans *Mr Simmons* • Beryl Te Wiata *Mrs Simmons* ■ *Dir* Michael Laughlin • *Scr* Michael Laughlin, from a treatment by Jerzy Skolimowski

Mesrine: Killer Instinct ★★★★ 15
Biographical crime drama
2008 · Fr/Can/It · Colour · 108min

A notorious figure in his native France and beyond, Jacques Mesrine led such a wild life that it's taken two films to pack it all in. This first instalment opens with his shooting in 1979, before returning to his formative army years in Algeria, and a subsequent trail of criminality across 1960s France, Spain and Canada. Gérard Depardieu is on imposing form as a Parisian crime boss, Cécile de France sparkles as a *femme fatale*, but it's an electric Vincent Cassel who owns this movie as Mesrine himself. Director Jean-François Richet keeps up a cracking pace throughout, contrasting Mesrine's charismatic contempt for authority with a shocking ruthlessness. **TJ** French, Spanish, English, Arabic +subtitles. Violence, swearing, sex scenes. **DVD** Blu-ray

Vincent Cassel *Jacques Mesrine* • Cécile de France *Jeanne Schneider* • Gérard Depardieu *Guido* • Gilles Lellouche *Paul* • Roy Dupuis *Jean-Paul Mercier* • Elena Anaya *Sofia* ■ *Dir* Jean-François Richet • *Scr* Jean-François Richet, Abdel Raouf Dafri, from the autobiography *L'instinct de Mort* by Jacques Mesrine

Mesrine: Public Enemy No 1 ★★★★ 15
Biographical crime drama
2008 · Fr/Can · Colour · 127min

The second instalment of the two-part *Mesrine* chronicle finds Vincent Cassel's armed robber back in French custody (not for long, of course) where he realises his criminal exploits have made him a legend - a legend he feels he has to live up to. So, we're set for another series of escapes, heists, and flagrant grandstanding from a man whose pretence that he was rebelling against capitalism and state authority comes to sound increasingly like the delusions of a trigger-happy narcissist. The tone is darker than the previous film (which you probably will need to see to really appreciate this one), not least because we already know the violent fate awaiting Mesrine, whose increasing use of trickery and disguise allows leading man Cassel to deliver a central performance in the De Niro class. **TJ** French, English +subtitles. Violence, swearing, sex scenes, nudity. **DVD** Blu-ray

Vincent Cassel *Jacques Mesrine* • Ludivine Sagnier *Sylvie Jeanjacquot* • Mathieu Amalric *François Besse* • Gérard Lanvin *Charlie Bauer* • Samuel Le Bihan *Michel Ardouin* ■ *Dir* Jean-François Richet • *Scr* Abdel Raouf Dafri, Jean-François Richet

Message in a Bottle ★★★ 12
Romantic drama
1998 · US · Colour · 125min

Kevin Costner stars as a strong, silent and sensitive boat builder living in North Carolina, who's tracked down by newspaper researcher Robin Wright Penn after she finds a heart-rending love letter to his late wife in a bottle on the seashore. Her hard-nosed reporter's edge soon softens as she decides to learn more about the man. Although the inevitable happens - with a twist! - the beauty of director Luis Mandoki's intelligent tear-jerker is how all the emotions ring true. This is warm-hearted stuff, with a scene-stealing performance from Paul Newman as Costner's grizzled father. **AJ** A sex scene. **DVD**

Kevin Costner *Garret Blake* • Robin Wright Penn [Robin Wright] *Theresa Osborne* • Paul Newman *Dodge Blake* • John Savage *Johnny Land* • Illeana Douglas *Lina Paul* • Robbie Coltrane *Charlie Toschi* • Jesse James *Jason Osborne* ■ *Dir* Luis Mandoki • *Scr* Gerald DiPego, from the novel by Nicholas Sparks

A Message to Garcia ★★
War adventure
1936 · US · BW · 77min

It's the Hollywood version of the Spanish-American war, as army envoy John Boles goes in search of the titular general, surrounded by a cast of fine character actors, all of whom, alas, look quite out of place in the phoney Cuban setting.

M

Unfortunately, George Marshall's direction lacks the vitality this type of film really needs, but it's entertaining enough. Rogue Wallace Beery and Barbara Stanwyck are the leads helping bland Boles deliver that message. TS

Wallace Beery *Sergeant Dory* • Barbara Stanwyck *Raphaelita Maderos* • John Boles *Lieutenant Andrew Rowan* • Herbert Mundin *Henry Piper* • Martin Garralaga *Rodriquez* • Juan Torena *Luis Maderos* • Alan Hale *Dr Krug* • Enrique Acosta *General Garcia* ■ *Dir* George Marshall • *Scr* WP Lipscomb, Gene Fowler, Sam Hellman, Gladys Lehman, from the non-fiction book by Lieutenant Andrew S Rowan and an essay by Elbert Hubbard

Message to Love ★★★ 18
Concert documentary
1995 · US/UK · Colour · 138min

Proof that the dying embers of the 1960s were still flickering into the next decade is provided in this account of the 1970 Isle of Wight rock festival. Britain's answer to Woodstock (in organisational, as well as musical terms), the five-day jamboree drew a crowd of some 600,000, of whom only 50,000 actually paid. Twenty-five years later, film-maker Murray Lerner finally secured the funds to complete his film, albeit without the Bob Dylan footage. However, there's still a chance to see the flipside of flower power and keynote performances by Jimi Hendrix, the Who, Joan Baez, Donovan, Kris Kristofferson and the Doors. DP *DVD*

Jimi Hendrix • The Who • Donovan ■ *Dir* Murray Lerner

Messages ★ 15
Supernatural thriller 2007 · UK · Colour · 92min

Horror movies are often considered an easy genre for up-and-coming film-makers to cut their teeth on. This execrable third feature from advertising photographer-turned-director David Fairman proves how wrong that assumption can be. Jeff Fahey stars as a forensic pathologist struggling to come to terms with the loss of his wife, who starts receiving messages from what appear to be the victims of a serial killer on the loose in rural England. Stilted acting and amateurish production values don't help the film's yawning credibility gap or its lack of scares. JR

Jeff Fahey *Dr Richard Murray* • Kim Thomson *Frances Beale* • Jon-Paul Gates *Father Randall* • Martin Kove *DCI Collins* • Bruce Payne *Dr Robert Golding* • Geraldine Alexander *Carol* • Eileen Daly *Denise* ■ *Dir* David Fairman • *Scr* Wayne Kinsey, Ivan Levene • *Cinematographer* Simon Dennis

The Messenger ★★★★ 15
Wartime romantic drama
2009 · US/Aus/British Virgin Islands · Colour · 112min

This worthwhile drama reports from the home front as the war on terror continues. It follows military captain Woody Harrelson and his new cohort Ben Foster as their work for the US Army's casualty notification service takes its toll on those who bring the bad news as well as those unfortunate enough to receive it. Director Oren Moverman's film has an almost documentary immediacy, founded on tremendous performances from Oscar-nominated Harrelson (at odds with himself because he'd rather be overseas seeing action) and Foster (still wound-up tight after a traumatic tour in Iraq). A poignant turn from Samantha Morton as a young widow rounds out this fine character study, which, unlike a lot of Hollywood fare, is positively wary of overdoing the melodrama. TJ Swearing, sex scenes. *DVD* *Blu*

Ben Foster *Staff Sergeant Will Montgomery* • Jena Malone *Kelly* • Eamonn Walker *Colonel Stuart Dorsett* • Woody Harrelson *Captain Tony Stone* • Steve Buscemi *Dale Martin* • Samantha Morton *Olivia Pitterson* ■ *Dir* Oren Moverman • *Scr* Oren Moverman, Alessandra Camon

The Messenger ★★ 15
Horror mystery 2015 · UK · Colour · 96min

This supernatural drama tells the story of Jack, a young man (Robert Sheehan) who can see dead people. Jack is unable to live a normal life, since the deceased are constantly pestering him to deliver messages to their loved ones. "They never go away", he complains, exhibiting behaviour that suggests he is about to reach breaking point. Sheehan provides a strong, committed performance in his depiction of a haunted loner, but the film falls flat. SC Swearing, violence, sex

Robert Sheehan *Jack* • Lily Cole *Emma* • Joely Richardson *Psychiatrist* • Tamzin Merchant *Sarah* • Andrew Tiernan *Jack's dad* ■ *Dir* David Blair (4) • *Scr* Andrew Kirk

Messenger of Death ★★★ 18
Crime thriller 1988 · US · Colour · 92min

The title promises the usual Charles Bronson bloodfest, but the script is by Paul Jarrico, a mild-mannered intellectual who was blacklisted and then produced the provocative, Union-financed *Salt of the Earth*. Bronson plays a Denver crime reporter whose snooping into a multiple killing leads him into Mormon society and a family who seem to be ritualistically following the examples of Cain and Abel. Director J Lee Thompson juggles the various elements - mystery, biblical allegory, bloody thriller - with great assurance. AT *DVD*

Charles Bronson *Garret Smith* • Trish Van Devere *Jastra Watson* • Laurence Luckinbill *Homer Foxx* • Daniel Benzali *Chief Barney Doyle* • Marilyn Hassett *Josephine Fabrizio* • Charles Dierkop *Orville Beecham* ■ *Dir* J Lee Thompson • *Scr* Paul Jarrico, from the novel *The Avenging Angel* by Rex Burns

The Messengers ★★ 15
Horror thriller
2007 · US · Colour and BW · 86min

Ghost stories don't get much more formulaic than this disappointing Hollywood debut from Hong Kong film-makers Danny and Oxide Pang. Far removed from their innovative 2002 chiller *The Eye*, it's an uninspired tale that seems stitched together from other horror movies. There are references to everything from *The Birds* to *The Grudge*, as suburban couple Dylan McDermott and Penelope Ann Miller uproot their two children and move to a secluded North Dakota farm. The picture opens promisingly with a genuinely scary black-and-white pre-credit sequence that stylishly demonstrates the Pang brothers' talents. Yet while the creepy atmospherics and quick-hit jolts continue throughout, they seem like cheap and empty trickery the more the déjà vu narrative unfolds. SF *DVD*

Kristen Stewart *Jess Solomon* • Dylan McDermott *Roy Solomon* • Penelope Ann Miller *Denise Solomon* • John Corbett *John Burwell* • Evan Turner *Ben* • Theodore Turner *Ben* • Dustin Milligan *Bobby* ■ *Dir* Danny Pang, Oxide Pang • *Scr* Mark Wheaton, from a story by Todd Farmer • *Cinematographer* David Geddes

Messidor ★★★
Crime drama 1978 · Swi/Fr · Colour · 122min

Alain Tanner's road movie caused a stir not just because of the amorality of its hitch-hiking heroines, but also because of its unflattering portrait of his native Switzerland. From the moment student Clémentine Amouroux and shop assistant Catherine Rétoré decide to embark on a robbery spree, Tanner is less concerned with the nature of their crimes or their impact upon the women themselves than with the response of this unrepentantly capitalist country. DP French +subtitles.

Clémentine Amouroux *Jeanne* • Catherine Rétoré *Marie* • Franziskus Abgottspon • Gérald Battiaz ■ *Dir/Scr* Alain Tanner

Metal: a Headbanger's Journey ★★★ 15
Music documentary 2005 · Can · Colour · 94min

This entertaining music documentary looks at heavy metal, arguably the most popular youth-music genre of the last 35 years. The front man is Canadian anthropologist and metal fan Sam Dunn, who also co-directed. His tour guides comprise a motley crew of heavy metal heroes, from legends such as Alice Cooper, Tony Iommi of Black Sabbath, Iron Maiden's Bruce Dickinson and, of course, Motörhead's inimitable Lemmy. Exploring the scene from Los Angeles all the way to Birmingham (UK), Dunn also takes in more obscure "black metal" outfits. Dunn treats them all with equal seriousness, though audiences may find themselves grinning at the odd moment of *Spinal Tap* pomposity. DA Swearing, nudity.

■ *Dir/Scr* Sam Dunn, Scot McFadyen, Jessica Joy Wise

Metallica: Some Kind of Monster ★★★ 15
Music documentary 2004 · US · Colour · 140min

Those expecting insights into the creative process behind global rock brand Metallica or looking for a few *Spinal Tap*-style laughs at the expense of stadium-sized egos will walk away happy from this curiously affecting rock 'n' roll chronicle. Film-makers Joe Berlinger and Bruce Sinofsky first met the band while filming a documentary, *Paradise Lost: the Child Murders at Robin Hood Hills*, about three Metallica fans accused of "ritual" murders. But this is no fanboy tribute. The band's ridiculous behaviour is at times hilariously exposed as they struggle to record the album *St Anger* - unfortunately not one of their best - amid walkouts, stints in rehab, ego clashes, belly-aching and group therapy sessions. TH *DVD* *Blu*

■ *Dir* Joe Berlinger, Bruce Sinofsky

Metallica: Through the Never ★★★ 15
Action fantasy 2013 · US · Colour · 92min

As Metallica play to a packed house, young roadie Trip (Dane DeHaan) goes on a perilous, dreamlike journey trying to retrieve a mysterious leather satchel. Breathtaking concert footage will make this a must-see for any fan of the band, cycling through hits with all the confidence you would expect of rock stars with several decades' experience at the top. The story that weaves in and out of their show is harder to grasp - an odd, near silent tear through riotous city streets that looks good but doesn't really lead anywhere. JL Swearing. 3D

Dane DeHaan *Trip* • James Hetfield • Lars Ulrich • Kirk Hammett ■ *Dir* Nimrod Antal • *Scr* Nimrod Antal, Kirk Hammett, James Hetfield, Robert Trujillo, Lars Ulrich

Meteor ★ PG
Disaster movie 1979 · US · Colour · 102min

Director Ronald Neame here places the planet on star-studded collision course with a gigantic asteroid. Spectacle has never looked cheaper or more pathetic than the tidal waves, avalanches and mud-slides on view in this celluloid catastrophe that reaches an apex of absurdity when America (in the person of Sean Connery) and Russia (Natalie Wood) bury the hatchet to nuke the big rock. AJ

Sean Connery *Dr Paul Bradley* • Natalie Wood *Tatiana Donskaya* • Karl Malden *Harry Sherwood* • Brian Keith *Dr Dubov* • Martin Landau *General Adlon* • Trevor Howard *Sir Michael Hughes* • Richard Dysart *Secretary of Defense* • Henry Fonda *President* ■ *Dir* Ronald Neame • *Scr* Stanley Mann, Edmund H North, from a story by Edmund H North

The Meteor Man ★★ PG
Science-fiction comedy
1993 · US · Colour · 95min

After *Hollywood Shuffle* and *The Five Heartbeats*, this was third time unlucky for young, gifted and black actor/writer/director Robert Townsend. It's certainly about time we had more non-Caucasian superheroes, but there's something a little too fallible about this emerald-clad warrior whose powers have a nasty habit of waning at crucial moments. Similarly, although tackling the neighbourhood drug barons is a worthy mission, the heavy-handed social commentary provides few laughs or thrills. DP

Robert Townsend *Jefferson Reed* • Marla Gibbs *Mrs Reed* • Eddie Griffin *Michael* • Robert Guillaume *Mr Reed* • James Earl Jones *Mr Moses* • Roy Fegan *Simon* • Bill Cosby *Marvin* ■ *Dir/Scr* Robert Townsend

Metro ★★ 18
Action thriller 1997 · US · Colour · 112min

Eddie Murphy returns to the genre that made him a star with this misfiring action vehicle. It has a harder centre than usual as negotiator Murphy uses his motormouth talents to haggle with hostage takers. However, his persuasive charms are tested when he comes up against psychopathic jewel thief Michael Wincott. The highlight set piece is a car chase involving a runaway tram, but otherwise director Thomas Carter displays little flair in the action department. JF Violence, swearing, nudity. *DVD*

Eddie Murphy *Scott Roper* • Michael Rapaport *Kevin McCall* • Kim Miyori *Detective Kimura* • James Carpenter *Officer Forbes* • Art Evans *Lieutenant Sam Baffert* • Michael Wincott *Michael Korda* ■ *Dir* Thomas Carter • *Scr* Randy Feldman

Metro Manila ★★★ 15
Crime drama 2013 · UK/Phil · Colour · 114min

Early scenes suggest English director Sean Ellis's third feature is going to be an earnest depiction of the plight of the poor in the Philippines. But suddenly the film shifts towards John Woo territory, with a secret stash of cash, lethal gunplay and the sort of disfigured villain that would not look out of place in a James Bond movie. The film is impressively tight and clever as it gathers pace towards a strong conclusion, though some plot points do raise queries. But, on the whole, Ellis has produced an engaging and satisfying thriller. BP Tagalog +subtitles. *DVD* *Blu*

Jake Macapagal *Oscar Ramirez* • John Arcilla *Douglas Ong* • Althea Vega *Mai Ramirez* • Ana Aba-Santos *Dora Ong* ■ *Dir* Sean Ellis • *Scr* Sean Ellis, Frank E Flowers, from a story by Ellis

Metroland ★★ 18
Drama 1997 · UK/Fr/Sp · Colour · 96min

Philip Saville directs this disappointing adaptation of Julian Barnes's knowing novel. Every choice is so safe, whether it's a tell-tale period detail or an Identikit character trait. As a result, there's no urgency in bored suburbanite Christian Bale's dilemma after his hippy friend Lee Ross reappears and tries to persuade him to leave his wife (Emily Watson) and return to the hedonistic lifestyle they shared ten years before. DP Sex scenes, swearing. *DVD*

Christian Bale *Chris Lloyd* • Emily Watson *Marion Lloyd* • Lee Ross *Toni* • Elsa Zylberstein *Annick* • Rufus *Henri* ■ *Dir* Philip Saville • *Scr* Adrian Hodges, from the novel by Julian Barnes

LANDMARK FILM
Thanks to its seminal design, Fritz Lang's sci-fi fantasy classic casts the longest shadow in the genre

Metropolis ★★★★★ PG
Silent science-fiction fantasy
1926 · Ger/US · BW · 119min

No sooner had it been premiered - at approximately 153 minutes in length - than Fritz Lang's sci-fi masterpiece was subjected to commercially inspired abridgement. This 119-minute version was compiled from the various extant prints and released in 2002. What remains still stands as a monument to both the ingenuity of the UFA art department and Lang's vision as a film-maker. The muddled political message of the film - in which the master of a futuristic city attempts to quell the simmering discontent among his workforce - has been the subject of much conjecture, but few can deny the majesty of the cityscapes and the inhumanity of the subterranean caverns. Among the most famous and influential silent films ever made, *Metropolis* has lost none of its ability to inspire awe and provoke debate. Discovery of further, presumed lost footage led to a more complete cut of the film being released in 2010. DP *DVD* *Blu*

Alfred Abel *John Fredersen* • Gustav Fröhlich *Freder* • Rudolf Klein-Rogge *Rotwang* • Brigitte Helm *Maria/Robot* • Fritz Rasp *Slim* • Theodor Loos *Josaphat/Joseph* ■ *Dir* Fritz Lang • *Scr* Fritz Lang, Thea von Harbou, from the novel by Thea von Harbou • *Cinematographers* Karl Freund, Günther Rittau

Metropolis ★★★ PG
Animated futuristic drama
2001 · Jpn · Colour · 103min

Re-imagining the core of Fritz Lang's 1926 silent masterpiece as an *anime* feature was always going to be a considerable challenge. Like its illustrious namesake, Metropolis is a grand city of the future; however the Japanese model comprises a strictly divided society of humans and robots, not thinkers and workers as in the German original. Into this chaotic mix are pitched a pair of detectives who are on the trail of a renegade robot scientist and his latest creation. Despite a script by *Akira* auteur Katsuhiro Otomo, this fails to live up to expectations. DP Japanese +subtitles. **DVD**

Dave Mallow *Pero* • Scott Weinger *Atlas* • Rebecca Olkewski *Tima* • Dave Whittenberg *Rock* • Tony Pope *Shunsaku Ban* ■ *Dir* Tarô Rin [Rintaro] • *Scr* Katsuhiro Otomo, from the comic strip by Osamu Tezuka

Metropolitan ★★★ 15
Comedy
1990 · US · Colour · 98min

Director Whit Stillman sold his Manhattan apartment to raise the budget for his debut movie. Using a cast of unknowns, it tells the story of a group of young, privileged New Yorkers who call themselves the SFRP (Sally Fowler Rat Pack, named after a party hostess) and do little during the Christmas season other than attending debutante balls, having party postmortems, swapping bons mots and courting each other. It's the world of F Scott Fitzgerald caught in a time warp, complete with social interloper Edward Clements. Stillman's witty, sophisticated screenplay was Oscar-nominated. AT **DVD**

Edward Clements *Tom Townsend* • Carolyn Farina *Audrey Rouget* • Christopher Eigeman [Chris Eigeman] *Nick Smith* • Taylor Nichols *Charlie Black* • Allison Rutledge-Parisi *Jane Clarke* • Dylan Hundley *Sally Fowler* ■ *Dir/Scr* Whit Stillman

The Mexican ★★★ 15
Comedy drama
2001 · US · Colour · 118min

Audiences wishing to see Julia Roberts and Brad Pitt sizzle for more than two hours will be disappointed to find they only spend 15 minutes together on screen. However, this offbeat comedy thriller does have an ace script and quirkily appealing performances from the two leads. Pitt is a useless Mafia appendage, trying to extricate himself from the Mob by doing one last job: retrieving an antique pistol, the "Mexican" of the title. Meanwhile, James Gandolfini kidnaps his girlfriend Roberts to ensure Pitt will return, gun in hand. LH Violence, swearing. **DVD**

Brad Pitt *Jerry Welbach* • Julia Roberts *Samantha* • James Gandolfini *Leroy* • Bob Balaban *Bernie Nayman* • Gene Hackman *Arnold Margolese* ■ *Dir* Gore Verbinski • *Scr* JH Wyman

Mexican Bus Ride ★★★★ PG
Comedy drama
1951 · Mex · BW · 74min

Esteban Marquez plays a young man dragged away on his wedding night by his avaricious elder brothers, who need his endorsement of their dying mother's will. A perilous and incident-packed mountain bus trip ensues, during which a woman gives birth and Marquez has to fend off the attentions of the local floozy. From Spain's great Luis Buñuel, who based this deftly-made film on a real journey made by his poet friend Altolaguirre, it's one of the director's lightest works. RB Spanish +subtitles. **DVD**

Lilia Prado *Raquel* • Carmelita Gonzalez *Oliviero's wife* • Esteban Marquez *Oliviero* • Manuel Donde *Eladio Gonzales* • Roberto Cobo *Juan* • Luis Aceves Castañeda *Silvestre* ■ *Dir* Luis Buñuel • *Scr* Manuel Altolaguirre, Luis Buñuel, Juan De La Cabada

Mexican Spitfire ★★ U
Comedy
1940 · US · BW · 67min

The spitfire of the title is Lupe Velez, married to Donald Woods's advertising executive and fighting off efforts by his disapproving aunt (Elisabeth Risdon) and jealous ex-fiancée (Linda Hayes) to break them up. Based on characters introduced in *The Girl from Mexico*, this cleverly orchestrated, lowbrow farce has Leon Errol as both a benevolent uncle and a visiting English whisky baron. The pie-throwing finale recalls Mack Sennett in his prime. Six sequels followed. AE

Lupe Velez *Carmelita Lindsay* • Leon Errol *Uncle Matt Lindsay/Lord Basil Epping* • Donald Woods *Dennis Lindsay* • Linda Hayes *Elizabeth* • Cecil Kellaway *Chumley* • Elisabeth Risdon *Aunt Della Lindsay* ■ *Scr* Leslie Goodwins • *Scr* Joseph Fields, Charles E Roberts, from a story by Joseph Fields

Mi Vida Loca ★★★ 15
Drama
1993 · US · Colour · 91min

Allison Anders's third feature is a much tougher picture than her poignantly moving *Gas, Food, Lodging*, being closer to the uncompromising portrait of inner-city life presented in the films of the African-American new wave. Although some of the dialogue recalls the work of longtime friend Quentin Tarantino, their concerns could not be more diverse, with Anders showing how religion and pulp romance sustain Hispanic teenage girls in a world where violence and loss are commonplace. The use of real street gangsters adds to the urgency and authenticity, although the dramatic quality suffers. DP Swearing, substance abuse.

Angel Aviles *Sad girl* • Seidy Lopez *Mousie* • Jacob Vargas *Ernesto* • Marlo Marron *Giggles* • Jesse Borrego *El Duran* • Magali Alvarado *La Blue Eyes* ■ *Dir/Scr* Allison Anders

Mia Madre ★★★ 15
Drama
2015 · It/Fr · Colour · 106min

A return to the wry family dramas Nanni Moretti used to make for domestic audiences, this exploration of loss is sweet but slight. Margherita Buy is the director dealing with issues on set – like her star (John Turturro on fine form), romantic breakdown and her mother's fatal illness. Cross-cutting Buy and her inconsolable brother's emotional crises, it's all done in upper register, with light relief from insecure Turturro, making for a distinctly variable tone in a lethargic (by Moretti's standards) exercise in irony. AJ In Italian, English.

Margherita Buy *Margherita* • John Turturro *Barry Huggins* • Giulia Lazzarini *Ada* • Nanni Moretti *Giovanni* ■ *Dir* Nanni Moretti • *Scr* Nanni Moretti, Valia Santella, Francesco Piccolo, from a story by Moretti, Santella, Gaia Manzini, Chiara Valerio

Miami Blues ★★★★ 18
Crime thriller
1990 · US · Colour · 92min

Alec Baldwin has never been better than as a vicious ex-con who takes up with naive hooker Jennifer Jason Leigh in Miami. Things get complicated when he steals investigating cop Fred Ward's gun, badge and false teeth and sets about robbing and shooting just about everyone in his path, while masquerading as a police officer. An absorbing, gripping (and often very violent) battle of wits, this has some wonderfully dark comic moments and superb performances. JB **DVD**

Fred Ward *Sergeant Hoke Moseley* • Alec Baldwin *Frederick J Frenger Jr* • Jennifer Jason Leigh *Susie Waggoner* • Nora Dunn *Ellita Sanchez* • Charles Napier *Sergeant Bill Henderson* • Obba Babatunde *Blink Willie* ■ *Dir* George Armitage • *Scr* George Armitage, from the novel by Charles Willeford

Miami Rhapsody ★★★ 15
Romantic comedy
1995 · US · Colour · 91min

You could be forgiven here for thinking that you are watching a Woody Allen comedy. The setting may be Miami, not Manhattan, but there is the central character (Sarah Jessica Parker) bemoaning her lot, a dysfunctional family and Mia Farrow in a co-

starring role as Parker's mother. But as the action develops, it's clear that writer/director David Frankel is more of a Woody wannabe than a genuine pretender to the throne. If this lacks the deft touches that make Allen's work so uniquely enjoyable, it's still a clever and satisfying counterfeit. DP Swearing.

Sarah Jessica Parker *Gwyn Marcus* • Gil Bellows *Matt* • Antonio Banderas *Antonio* • Mia Farrow *Nina Marcus* • Paul Mazursky *Vic Marcus* • Kevin Pollak *Jordan Marcus* • Barbara Garrick *Terri* • Naomi Campbell *Kaia* ■ *Dir/Scr* David Frankel

Miami Vice ★★ 15
Action crime thriller
2006 · US · Colour · 126min

Writer/director Michael Mann returns to the scene of his 1980s pop culture classic here but with grittier, darker intentions. Mann executive produced the TV series between 1984 and 1989, and presents a TV episode plotline that is overblown with garbled confusion. The same old hard-bitten cops, Sonny Crockett (Colin Farrell) and Ricardo Tubbs (Jamie Foxx), go undercover to infiltrate a sophisticated drug cartel when an FBI sting backfires horribly. Serious and seriously violent, the film will have Mann fans applauding his decision to axe the pastels and neon of the TV series for a harder attitude and updated style, though others may not be so forgiving of the unintelligible dialogue and lack of ending. To add to the disappointment, the morose Farrell/Foxx partnership isn't even as memorable as that of Don Johnson and Philip Michael Thomas. AJ **DVD** **Blu-ray**

Colin Farrell (2) *Sonny Crockett* • Jamie Foxx *Ricardo Tubbs* • Gong Li *Isabella* • Luis Tosar *Montoya* • Naomie Harris *Trudy Joplin* • Ciaran Hinds *FBI Agent Fujima* • Barry Shabaka Henley [Barry "Shabaka" Henley] *Lieutenant Martin Castillo* • Justin Theroux *Zito* ■ *Dir* Michael Mann • *Scr* Michael Mann, from characters by Anthony Yerkovich

Michael ★★★ PG
Fantasy comedy
1996 · US · Colour · 100min

John Travolta stars as an angel living in backwoods Iowa. Even though he comes with feathers on his back, he's close to being trailer trash, but when some journalists arrive to write a story about him Travolta turns their hard-boiled hearts into slush. William Hurt is dependably strange and often very funny as one of the hacks, but Bob Hoskins is embarrassing as Hurt's editor and Andie MacDowell fails to make her mark as the female lead. AT Some swearing.

John Travolta *Michael* • Andie MacDowell *Dorothy Winters* • William Hurt *Frank Quinlan* • Bob Hoskins *Vartan Malt* • Robert Pastorelli *Huey Driscoll* • Jean Stapleton *Pansy Milbank* • Teri Garr *Judge Esther Newberg* ■ *Dir* Nora Ephron • *Scr* Nora Ephron, Delia Ephron, Pete Dexter, Jim Quinlan, from a story by Pete Dexter, Jim Quinlan

Michael ★★★ 18
Drama
2011 · Austria · Colour · 92min

Austrian writer/director Markus Schleinzer makes an accomplished debut with this study of the relationship between a 30-something paedophile and his ten-year-old captive, inspired by the infamous cases of Wolfgang Priklopil and Josef Fritzl. It's a remarkable film, but the steely detachment, precise composition and bleak wit come at a price. Schleinzer avoids depicting the abuse Wolfgang (David Rauchenberger) suffers at the hands of Michael (Michael Fuith), but a disconcerting air of exploitation lingers nonetheless. So while this is brilliantly played, gruesomely compelling and often as tense as it is unnerving, it also feels more like an exercise in stylistic restraint than a considered treatise on everyday evil. DP German +subtitles. **DVD** **Blu-ray**

Michael Fuith *Michael* • David Rauchenberger *Wolfgang* • Christine Kain *Mother* • Ursula Strauss *Sister* • Victor Tremmel *Brother-in-law* ■ *Dir/Scr* Markus Schleinzer

Michael Clayton ★★★★ 15
Conspiracy thriller
2007 · US · Colour · 114min

For an actor renowned for having a twinkle in his eye, George Clooney takes quite a risk in this downbeat but gripping legal thriller. He barely raises a smile as the eponymous "fixer" for a huge Manhattan legal firm, who's struggling with a failed marriage, a gambling habit and crushing debts following an ill-advised investment. When top attorney Tom Wilkinson suffers a breakdown and switches sides during a long-running case involving an agrochemical giant, Clooney is dispatched to deal with the fallout. First-time director Tony Gilroy (who won his spurs writing the *Bourne* trilogy) handles the mostly wordy action with confidence – unravelling much of the story in flashback and drip-feeding the facts. Clooney is magnificently moody and troubled, and Tilda Swinton and Sydney Pollack provide knockout support as, respectively, conniving counsel and Clooney's boss. It's not quite up there with the similarly themed *Erin Brockovich*, but this is still powerful, intelligent adult fare. AC Swearing, sexual references. **DVD** **Blu-ray**

George Clooney *Michael Clayton* • Tilda Swinton *Karen Crowder* • Tom Wilkinson *Arthur Edens* • Sydney Pollack *Marty Bach* • Michael O'Keefe *Barry Grissom* • Sean Cullen *Gene Clayton* • Denis O'Hare *Mr Greer* • Robert Prescott *Mr Verne* ■ *Dir/Scr* Tony Gilroy • *Music* James Newton Howard • *Editor* John Gilroy

Michael Collins ★★★★ 15
Biographical drama
1996 · US/UK · Colour · 126min

Michael Collins was the founder of the IRA, an intellectual who virtually invented urban terrorism and bombed his way to talks in Downing Street before being assassinated by his own side in 1922. Neil Jordan's biopic begins with an impressively filmed Easter uprising, yet there's also an even-handedness when it comes to depicting and simplifying the political struggle for Irish independence. As Collins, Liam Neeson is both charming and menacing, while Alan Rickman is superbly cast as Eamon De Valera. Julia Roberts, however, looks lost. AT Swearing, violence. **DVD** **Blu-ray**

Liam Neeson *Michael Collins* • Julia Roberts *Kitty Kiernan* • Aidan Quinn *Harry Boland* • Ian Hart *Joe O'Reilly* • Stephen Rea *Ned Broy* • John Kenny *Patrick Pearse* • Alan Rickman *Eamon De Valera* • Charles Dance *Soames* ■ *Dir/Scr* Neil Jordan

Michael Jackson's This Is It ★★★ PG
Music documentary
2009 · US · Colour · 111min

Giving the ardent admirer everything they could wish for and the cynics much to ponder, this curiously bittersweet tribute to the late Michael Jackson is better than expected, especially considering its fast turnaround after his untimely death. Director, choreographer and friend Kenny Ortega (*High School Musical*) assembles a heartfelt celebration from over 100 hours of auditions, interviews and rehearsal footage taken from the "King of Pop's" preparations for his ill-fated London concert series. AJ **DVD** **Blu-ray**

Michael Jackson (3) *Michael Jackson* ■ *Dir* Kenny Ortega • *Choreographer* Kenny Ortega

Michael Shayne, Private Detective ★★
Crime mystery
1940 · US · BW · 76min

The first in an interesting series of programme fillers from 20th Century-Fox, this is important today because it featured a tough, resilient and self-reliant private eye before the popularity of those moody Humphrey Bogart movies later on in the decade. Shayne was incarnated on screen by the excellent Lloyd Nolan, an actor whose very persona suggested he brooked no nonsense. This pilot movie is abrasive, sexy and watchable within its B-budget. Nolan reprised the role in two further films. TS

M

Lloyd Nolan *Michael Shayne* • Marjorie Weaver *Phyllis Brighton* • Joan Valerie *Marsha Gordon* • Walter Abel *Elliott Thomas* • Elizabeth Patterson *Aunt Olivia* • Donald MacBride *Chief Painter* • Douglass Dumbrille *Gordon* ■ *Dir* Eugene Forde • *Scr* Stanley Rauh, Manning O'Connor, from a novel by Brett Halliday

Mickey Blue Eyes ★★★ 15
Comedy 1999 · US/UK · Colour · 97min

Hugh Grant is sublimely ridiculous as an English auctioneer in New York, who learns that marrying sweetheart Jeanne Tripplehorn means getting spliced to the Mob. Tripplehorn's father, James Caan, is the local don and Grant quickly finds himself up to his neck in linguine as he fakes the identity of out-of-town mobster "Mickey Blue Eyes". This is gently entertaining. LH Swearing, violence. *DVD*

Hugh Grant *Michael Felgate* • James Caan *Frank Vitale* • Jeanne Tripplehorn *Gina Vitale* • Burt Young *Vito Graziosi* • James Fox *Philip Cromwell* • Joe Viterelli *Vinnie* • Gerry Becker *Agent Connell* • Maddie Corman *Carol* ■ *Dir* Kelly Makin • *Scr* Mark Lawrence, Adam Scheinmann, Robert Kuhn

Mickey One ★★★
Crime drama 1965 · US · BW · 92min

Warren Beatty made *Mickey One* right after *Lilith* and the result was another flop. It's easy to see why. Essentially a thriller about a nightclub comic, the plot fragments into a psychological drama about the Mob. The style, though, is something else. This is an American art movie, incredibly flash and tricksy, with a melodramatic Hurd Hatfield as a homosexual club owner and oblique references to the Kennedy assassination and Jack Ruby. A fascinating mess. AT

Warren Beatty *Mickey One* • Alexandra Stewart *Jenny* • Hurd Hatfield *Castle* • Franchot Tone *Ruby Lopp* • Teddy Hart *Berson* • Jeff Corey *Fryer* • Kamatari Fujiwara *Artist* ■ *Dir* Arthur Penn • *Scr* Alan M Surgal

Micki & Maude ★ PG
Comedy 1984 · US · Colour · 112min

Dudley Moore's cinematic career reached its height with the movies *10* and *Arthur*, but by the time this weak Blake Edwards comedy was made in 1984 it was in a trough as deep as the Grand Canyon. This farcical tale of a man who wants to marry his pregnant mistress while still remaining married to his equally expectant wife didn't help matters, and the blame has to be laid at the feet of the similarly out-of-luck Edwards. JB

Dudley Moore *Rob Salinger* • Amy Irving *Maude Guillory* • Ann Reinking *Micki Salinger* • Richard Mulligan *Leo Brody* • George Gaynes *Dr Eugene Glztski* • Wallace Shawn *Dr Elliot Fibel* • John Pleshette *Hap Ludlow* • HB Haggerty *Barkhas Guillory* ■ *Dir* Blake Edwards • *Scr* Jonathan Reynolds

Micmacs ★★★★★ 12
Revenge comedy 2009 · Fr · Colour · 100min

Adopting the same stylised, magical view of Paris as *Amélie*, coupled with the visual invention of *Delicatessen*, director Jean-Pierre Jeunet's whimsical comedy is a deliciously smart satire on the arms trade. French superstar Dany Boon is exemplary as the deadpan Buster Keaton-like vagrant who takes inspired revenge on the weapons manufacturers responsible for his plight. Chock full of Jeunet's distinctive set designs, supreme sight gags, quirky characters (such as a human cannonball played by Jeunet regular Dominique Pinon) and luminous cinematography, this "*Steptoe and Son in Wonderland*" offers limitless scope for the director's unique imagination. AJ French +subtitles. Violence, sexual references. *DVD* Blu

Dany Boon *Bazil* • André Dussollier *Nicolas Thibault De Fenouillet* • Nicolas Marié *François Marconi* • Jean-Pierre Marielle *Slammer* • Dominique Pinon *Buster* ■ *Dir* Jean-Pierre Jeunet • *Scr* Jean-Pierre Jeunet, Guillaume Laurant

Microbe & Gasoline ★★ 15
Comedy 2015 · Fr · Colour · 99min

The spirits of François Truffaut and Louis Malle permeate Michel Gondry's curiously old-fashioned rites-of-passage road trip, except that it feels languid and wordy. Misfits Ange Dargent and Théophile Baquet pal up at the Versailles school where the long-haired Dargent is teased for his size and the quirkily self-assured Baquet for his odour. So they head south after building a car using a lawnmower engine and a garden shed. Sadly, these teen heroes are completely resistible. DP In French. Strong sex references

Ange Dargent *Daniel* • Théophile Baquet *Théo* • Diane Besnier *Laura* • Audrey Tautou *Marie-Thérèse* ■ *Dir/Scr* Michel Gondry

Microcosmos ★★★★ U
Documentary 1996 · Fr/Swi/It · Colour · 72min

Directors Claude Nuridsany and Marie Pérennou redefine the boundaries of the nature documentary with this astounding look at the insect life in a French meadow. Filmed over three years using revolutionary camera and sound equipment, it presents a bug's-eye view of the world in a series of visually amazing close-ups highlighting a stag beetle battle, an ant colony hatching and the deliberate movement of a caterpillar. The soundtrack contains the startling noises of the insects themselves and an eclectic array of music, and the result is an overpowering experience to delight nature lovers. AJ *DVD*

Kristin Scott Thomas *Narrator* ■ *Dir* Claude Nuridsany, Marie Pérennou

Midas Run ★★
Crime mystery 1969 · US · Colour · 106min

Swedish actor/director Alf Kjellin - so memorable in *Torment* (1944), a tale of troubled adolescence - comes a cropper with this Hollywood hokum about an elderly spymaster determined to steal a load of gold bullion. (Hence the alternative title, *A Run on Gold*.) It has a splendid job-lot of class actors: Fred Astaire, Richard Crenna, Ralph Richardson, Cesar Romero. They don't help much, though. TH

Richard Crenna *Mike Warden* • Anne Heywood *Sylvia Giroux* • Fred Astaire *John Pedley* • Roddy McDowall *Wister* • Ralph Richardson *Henshaw* • Cesar Romero *Dodero* • Adolfo Celi *Aldo Ferranti* • Maurice Denham *Crittenden* • John Le Mesurier *Wells* ■ *Dir* Alf Kjellin • *Scr* James Buchanan, Ronald Austin, Berne Giler, from a story by Berne Giler

Middle Age Crazy ★★★ 15
Comedy drama 1980 · Can · Colour · 89min

Bruce Dern has a midlife crisis, though his gangling frame, thinning hair, buck teeth and country hick voice make him look a little unhinged to begin with. He's a Texan architect - nothing fancy, just fast food stands - who has just clocked 40. So when his dad dies, he buys a Porsche, dresses like JR Ewing, leaves his wife (played by the wittily voluptuous Ann-Margret) and runs off with sexy Deborah Wakeham. All the clichés of a movie marriage on the rocks fall into place, but it's none the worse for that. AT

Bruce Dern *Bobby Lee* • Ann-Margret *Sue Ann* • Graham Jarvis *JD* • Eric Christmas *Tommy* • Helen Hughes *Ruth* • Geoffrey Bowes *Greg* • Deborah Wakeham *Nancy* ■ *Dir* John Trent • *Scr* Carl Kleinschmitt, from the song by Jerry Lee Lewis

The Middleman ★★★★
Satirical drama 1975 · Ind · BW · 122min

This knowing satire from Satyajit Ray on the corruption that grips all aspects of Indian commerce completes the Calcutta trilogy that began with *The Adversary* and *Company Limited*. Providing an unflattering picture of both the middle classes and inner-city life, the film focuses on the shady dealings of a university graduate as he searches for an escort for a client. Deftly switching between comedy and social comment, Ray draws a fine performance from Pradip Mukherjee as the ambitious 20-

something who has been reduced to behaving like the Arthur Daley of Calcutta. DP Bengali +subtitles.

Pradip Mukherjee *Somnath Bannerji* • Satya Bannerji [Satya Bannerjee] *Somnath's father* • Dipankar Dey *Bhombol* • Lily Chakravarty *Kamala* • Aparna Sen *Somnath's girlfriend* • Goutam Chakravarti *Sukumar, Somnath's friend* ■ *Dir* Satyajit Ray • *Scr* Satyajit Ray, from the novel by Shankar

Middleton's Changeling ★ 18
Tragedy 1997 · UK · Colour · 85min

Based on the classic Jacobean tragedy about doomed love, betrayal and madness, director Marcus Thompson's film is a total bore. His interpretation involves much poetic license with the text and period (heroine Amanda Ray-King wears sneakers under her petticoats). Although such gimmickry is shrouded in visually arresting images, the film remains an infuriating curiosity. AJ Swearing, sex scenes, violence. *DVD*

Ian Dury *De Flores* • Amanda Ray-King *Beatrice Joanna* • Colm O Maonlai *Alsemero* • Billy Connolly *Alibius* • Campbell Morrison *Lollio* • Moya Brady *Isabella* • Richard Mayes *Vermandero* ■ *Dir* Marcus Thompson • *Scr* Marcus Thompson, from the play by Thomas Middleton, William Rowley

Middletown ★★ 15
Drama 2006 · UK/Ire · Colour · 85min

Religious zealotry in postwar Ireland is the theme of this bleak yet unconvincing drama. Matthew Macfadyen stars as Gabriel Hunter, a minister who returns to his home town to preach fire and brimstone. His new flock doesn't appreciate his passion, though, especially since they like nothing better than supping Guinness and watching cockfights in the local pub. Charged with Gothic atmosphere, *Middletown*'s story of religious mania encourages a brooding performance from Macfadyen, his character's unhinged temperament leading to scenes of ever more extreme behaviour. An unrelentingly glum aesthetic lends a suitable touch of misery but Gabriel's inevitable descent into outright psychosis as he becomes the Lord's avenging angel is far too melodramatic for its own good. JR *DVD*

Matthew Macfadyen *Gabriel Hunter* • Daniel Mays *Jim Hunter* • Eva Birthistle *Caroline Hunter* • Gerard McSorley *Bill Hunter* • Richard Dormer *Ned* • David Wilmot *Sammy* • Sorcha Cusack *Mrs Lennon* ■ *Dir* Brian Kirk • *Scr* Daragh Carville

Midgets vs Mascots ★ 18
Comedy documentary
2008 · US · Colour · 81min

Barrel-scraping non-PC laughs are all this crude mockumentary has to offer. Falling over itself to shock, the *Jackass*-style production unleashes a brainless torrent of pranks and humiliations, as five "little people" (including *Diff'rent Strokes* actor Gary Coleman) compete against a team of absurdly-costumed human mascots to inherit the fortune of a dead porn-star dwarf. Drinking games, alligator wrestling and fight-club bouts are among the dignity-trampling challenges captured with puerile glee. The repetitive, visual-based gags quickly wear thin, while the lazy racial and sizeist slurs, flatulence and copious bodily fluids serve to emphasise the film's lack of imagination and wit. SF Sex scenes, nudity. *DVD* Blu

Gary Coleman *Gary* • Jason Mewes *Jason* • Scottie Pippen • Ron Jeremy *Ron* ■ *Dir* Ron Carlson • *Scr* Kevin Andounian

Midnight ★★ PG
Drama 1934 · US · BW · 73min

A crime of passion repeats itself: just as a jury foreman announces the guilty verdict that sends a woman to the electric chair, his daughter shoots her lover to stop him going away. The daughter is Sidney Fox, and the lover is a racketeer played by the young Humphrey Bogart. The film is rather pretentious, and Bogart is quite unremarkable in his small role – though that didn't stop an American distributor

reissuing it in 1947 as *Call It Murder*, billing Bogie as the star. AE

Humphrey Bogart *Gar Boni* • Henry Hull *Bob Nolan* • Sidney Fox *Stella Weldon* • OP Heggie *Edward Weldon* • Richard Whorf *Arthur Weldon* ■ *Dir* Chester Erskine • *Scr* Chester Erskine, from a play by Paul & Claire Sifton

Midnight ★★★★★
Classic comedy 1939 · US · BW · 94min

Written by the incomparable team of Charles Brackett and Billy Wilder, starring Claudette Colbert, Don Ameche and John Barrymore (in one of his best late roles), this is right up there with *Ninotchka*, another Wilder and Brackett classic. Add Mary Astor and Rex O'Malley in support and expert direction from Mitchell Leisen, and the result is one of the most stylish and enduring comedies of the era. The story involves an American girl (Colbert) who arrives penniless in Paris at midnight. After catching the eye of a Hungarian taxi driver (Ameche), she finds herself masquerading as a baroness, hired by a wealthy man (Barrymore) to lure away his wife's lover. Sophisticated and hilarious. RK

Claudette Colbert *Eve Peabody/"Baroness Czerny"* • Don Ameche *Tibor Czerny* • John Barrymore *Georges Flammarion* • Francis Lederer *Jacques Picot* • Mary Astor *Helene Flammarion* • Elaine Barrie *Simone* • Hedda Hopper *Stephanie* • Rex O'Malley *Marcel* • Monty Woolley *Judge* ■ *Dir* Mitchell Leisen • *Scr* Charles Brackett, Billy Wilder, from a story by Edwin Justus Mayer, Franz Shulz

Midnight ★ 15
Horror satire 1989 · US · Colour · 81min

Low-grade horror rubbish, this is a lame lampoon on showbiz. Lynn Redgrave plays an Elvira-style TV horror hostess, complete with frizzy wig and gothic costume, whose entourage is being killed off. There's good support from Tony Curtis as her greedy network boss and Frank Gorshin as a double-crossing agent, but director Norman Thaddeus Vane generates no suspense. RS

Lynn Redgrave *Midnight (Vera)* • Tony Curtis *Mr B* • Steve Parrish *Mickey Modine* • Rita Gam *Heidi* • Gustav Vintas *Siegfried* • Karen Witter *Mitty* • Frank Gorshin *Ron* ■ *Dir/Scr* Norman Thaddeus Vane

Midnight ★★★
Drama 1998 · Bra/Fr · Colour · 76min

Walter Salles's follow-up to *Central Station* may be set on Millennium Eve, but by the time an escaped prisoner and an abandoned teacher meet on a Rio rooftop, it's clear this is no nostalgic paean to the passing century or expression of hope for the future. Instead it's a grim reminder that, for all the high-minded resolutions of the establishment, life grinds on for those ordinary people caught in time's relentless mechanism. DP Portuguese +subtitles.

Fernanda Torres *Maria* • Luiz Carlos Vasconcelos *Joao* • Carlos Vereza *Pedro* ■ *Dir* Walter Salles, Daniela Thomas • *Scr* Daniela Thomas, José de Carvalho, Walter Salles, Joao Emanuel Carneiro

Midnight at Madame Tussaud's ★★
Thriller 1936 · UK · BW · 66min

Made at Highbury studios, this creaky old chiller benefits from some superb sets, but the story, about a famous explorer who hopes to reduce his debts by betting he can spend the night in the famous Chamber of Horrors, is pretty limp. Not even a subplot involving his daughter's shady love life can pep it up. Bernard Miles is good value as the ghoulish sculptor, but James Carew as the explorer is less animated than the exhibits. DP

James Carew *Sir Clive Cheyne* • Lucille Lisle *Carol Cheyne* • Charles Oliver *Harry Newton* • Kim Peacock *Nick Frome* • Patrick Barr *Gerry Melville* • William Hartnell *Stubbs* • Bernard Miles *Modeller* ■ *Dir* George Pearson • *Scr* Kim Peacock, Roger MacDougall, from a story by James S Edwards, MacDougall

A Midnight Clear ★★★★ 15
Second World War drama
1991 · US · Colour · 103min

The shifting group dynamics of a Second World War infantry squad are put under the psychological microscope in director Keith Gordon's gripping morality play about the personal price exacted by battle. It's when the GIs meet some German soldiers, just back from the disastrous campaign on the Russian front, that the main thrust of this insightful drama snaps into focus. The ensemble cast shines in a powerful tragedy full of surprises and visual style. AJ DVD ◐

Peter Berg *Bud Miller* • Kevin Dillon *Mel Avakian* • Arye Gross *Stan Shutzer* • Ethan Hawke *Will Knott* • Gary Sinise *"Mother" Wilkins* • Frank Whaley *"Father" Mundy* • John C McGinley *Major Griffin* • Larry Joshua *Lieutenant Ware* ■ *Dir* Keith Gordon · *Scr* Keith Gordon, from the novel by William Wharton

Midnight Cop ★★★ 18
Thriller
1988 · W Ger · Colour · 92min

This passable police thriller benefits enormously from Armin Mueller-Stahl's strong central performance as an eccentric, ageing Berlin cop hunting down a vicious serial killer. Director Peter Patzak works wonders with a meandering storyline and deserves a medal for the sheer temerity of casting TV soap bimbette Morgan Fairchild as a call girl who acts as a decoy to trap the killer. RS

Armin Mueller-Stahl *Inspector Alex Glas* • Morgan Fairchild *Lisa* • Michael York *Karstens* • Frank Stallone *Jack Miskowski* • Julia Kent *Shirley* ■ *Dir* Peter Patzak · *Scr* Julia Kent, Paul Nicholas, Peter Patzak

Midnight Cowboy ★★★★★ 18
Drama
1969 · US · Colour · 108min

This tawdry, strident yet deeply affecting tale of a naive Texas stud striking up a relationship with a tubercular conman deservedly won several Oscars. British film-maker John Schlesinger was the perfect director to cast an alien eye on Manhattan's sexual permissiveness and Warhol weirdness, and exposes the jaundiced stratum beneath the hip surface with scalpel-sharp precision. Jon Voight and Dustin Hoffman are a perfectly matched odd couple adrift on the sea of amorality in a warped buddy picture that cleverly walks a fine line between warmth and cruelty. AJ Violence, swearing, sex scenes, drug abuse, nudity. DVD ◐

Dustin Hoffman *Ratso Rizzo* • Jon Voight *Joe Buck* • Sylvia Miles *Cass* • Brenda Vaccaro *Shirley* • John McGiver *Mr O'Daniel* • Barnard Hughes *Towny* • Ruth White *Sally Buck* • Jennifer Salt *Annie* ■ *Dir* John Schlesinger · *Scr* Waldo Salt, from the novel by James Leo Herlihy · *Music* John Barry (1)

Midnight Crossing ★★ 18
Thriller
1988 · US · Colour · 92min

Faye Dunaway demonstrates here that even the most illustrious career can suffer a nose dive. Daniel J Travanti takes blind wife Dunaway on a Caribbean holiday; unbeknown to her, though, he's actually there to recover some stolen money. The plot gets seriously twisted as everyone starts crossing and double-crossing each other, but the script and the performances don't generate much interest. JB DVD

Faye Dunaway *Helen Barton* • Daniel J Travanti *Morely Barton* • Kim Cattrall *Alexa Schubb* • Ned Beatty *Ellis* • John Laughlin *Jeffrey Schubb* • Pedro De Pool *Capt Mendoza* • Doug Weiser *Miller* ■ *Dir* Roger Holzberg · *Scr* Roger Holzberg, Doug Weiser, from a story by Roger Holzberg

Midnight Express ★★★★★ 18
Biographical drama
1978 · UK/US · Colour · 115min

It's hard to counter some of the criticisms about the sympathetic depiction of drug traffickers, the pitiless violence, the stereotypical representation of the Turkish jailers and the over-simplistic approach to the key issues raised that greeted this film on its release. Yet it is still a superbly staged drama, which exploits its excesses to force the viewer into considering the broader moral and humanitarian themes, as well as the harrowing events on the screen. Scripted by Oliver Stone from the memoirs of Billy Hayes, it is directed with power and intelligence by Alan Parker, while Brad Davis is outstanding in the lead. DP Violence, swearing, sex scenes, drug abuse, nudity. DVD ◐

Brad Davis *Billy Hayes* • Randy Quaid *Jimmy Booth* • John Hurt *Max* • Irene Miracle *Susan* • Bo Hopkins *Tex* • Paolo Bonacelli *Rifki* • Paul Smith *Hamidou* • Norbert Weisser *Erich* ■ *Dir* Alan Parker · *Scr* Oliver Stone, from the non-fiction book by Billy Hayes, William Hoffer

Midnight in Paris ★★★★ 12
Romantic comedy
2011 · Sp/US · Colour · 90min

A Hollywood hack struggling with his first novel finds magical inspiration in the French capital in this whimsical time-travelling comedy from Woody Allen. Owen Wilson is unexpected casting in the central role, yet proves utterly delightful as the befuddled scribe who can't quite confess to his shrewish fiancée (Rachel McAdams) he's been zapping back to the 1920s to spend his evenings with Hemingway and F Scott Fitzgerald – Americans in Paris during a more gilded age. Yes, it helps to know the literary and painterly references, but Allen's deliciously dotty plot construction ensures that seriousness never takes over. Bravo, monsieur Woody! TJ Sexual references. DVD

Owen Wilson *Gil* • Marion Cotillard *Adriana* • Rachel McAdams *Inez* • Michael Sheen *Paul* • Kathy Bates *Gert* • Tom Hiddleston *Mr Fitzgerald* ■ *Dir/Scr* Woody Allen

Midnight in St Petersburg ★★ 15
Thriller
1995 · UK/Can/Rus · Colour · 85min

Harry Palmer really should have stayed in retirement, but Michael Caine was persuaded to resurrect the bespectacled spy character that made his name back in the 1960s for two new adventures, shot back-to-back on location in Russia. However, his heart doesn't really seem in it and the result is the worst sort of Euro-pudding. This is the second of the two films (following *Bullet to Beijing*), with Harry running a security firm in Moscow. JF Violence, swearing. DVD

Michael Caine *Harry Palmer* • Jason Connery *Nick* • Michael Sarrazin *Craig* • Michael Gambon *Alex Alexovich* • Michelle Rene Thomas [Michelle Burke] *Brandy* • Tanya Jackson *Tatiana* • Yuri Limonty *Circus clown* • Michael Scherer *Mafioso* ■ *Dir* Doug Jackson [Douglas Jackson] · *Scr* Peter Welbeck [Harry Alan Towers], from the novel by Len Deighton

Midnight in the Garden of Good and Evil ★★★★ 15
Crime drama
1997 · US · Colour · 148min

John Berendt's bestseller was an audacious blend of travel journalism and true-life crime that gave a tremendous boost to the tourist industry of Savannah, Georgia. Clint Eastwood's long and leisurely adaptation is so seduced by the town's sultry, seedy atmosphere that the plot sometimes seems incidental. John Cusack is the naive New York journalist who stumbles into Savannah's sinister underbelly, meeting Kevin Spacey's wealthy antiques dealer and getting lost in a demimonde of soirées, rent boys and murder. Underrated by most critics, this grows in stature and lingers long in the memory. AT Swearing, violence. DVD

Kevin Spacey *Jim Williams* • John Cusack *John Kelso* • Jack Thompson *Sonny Seiler* • Irma P Hall *Minerva* • Jude Law *Billy Hanson* • Alison Eastwood *Mandy Nichols* • Paul Hipp *Joe Odom* • The Lady Chablis [Lady Chablis] *Chablis Deveau* ■ *Dir* Clint Eastwood · *Scr* John Lee Hancock, from the novel by John Berendt

Midnight Lace ★★ PG
Psychological thriller
1960 · US · Colour · 103min

With Doris Day and Rex Harrison, one expects a comedy. But this is a thriller in which Day, married to businessman Harrison, is stalked, receives abusive phone calls and is nearly pushed under a bus. The police think she's fibbing; Harrison claims she's losing her marbles. Set in London and filmed entirely in Hollywood, the supporting cast is a bonus. AT DVD

Doris Day *Kit Preston* • Rex Harrison *Tony Preston* • John Gavin *Brian Younger* • Myrna Loy *Aunt Bea* • Roddy McDowall *Malcolm* • Herbert Marshall *Charles Manning* • Natasha Parry *Peggy Thompson* • John Williams *Inspector Byrnes* • Hermione Baddeley *Dora* ■ *Dir* David Miller (1) · *Scr* Ivan Goff, Ben Roberts, from the play *Matilda Shouted Fire* by Janet Green · *Costume Designer* Irene

Midnight Madness ★★ PG
Comedy
1980 · US · Colour · 107min

This Disney campus comedy is a juvenile take on *It's a Mad Mad Mad World*, with five teams of student stereotypes – nerds, jocks, sorority girls, slobs – cavorting around Los Angeles in a 24-hour scavenger hunt for the clues deposited by the uncharismatic Alan Solomon. Michael J Fox fans will wince at the sight of the 18-year-old debuting as a pre-teen. DP

David Naughton *Adam* • Debra Clinger *Laura* • Eddie Deezen *Wesley* • Brad Wilkin *Lavitas* • Maggie Roswell *Donna* • Stephen Furst *Harold* • Michael J Fox *Scott* • Alan Solomon *Leon* ■ *Dir* Michael Nankin, David Wechter · *Scr* David Wechter, Michael Nankin

The Midnight Meat Train ★★★ 18
Horror thriller
2008 · US · Colour · 98min

Director Ryuhei Kitamura's viscerally mesmerising horror is based on a short story from Clive Barker's *Books of Blood* series, and remains true to the core dread of Barker's best works. When struggling photographer Bradley Cooper snaps a subway mugging for an art exhibition, it puts him on the trail of serial killer Vinnie Jones, who is butchering late-night commuters on subway trains. Kitamura's ultra-gory, white-knuckle suspense ride terrifies to the end of the line, where a supernatural twist lurks. A strong stomach is required, although it's the consistently repellent tone and unsettling atmosphere that most rattle the nerves. Thankfully, Jones remains almost silent throughout, giving far more power to his ominous presence. AJ Violence, sex scenes, nudity DVD ◐

Bradley Cooper *Leon* • Leslie Bibb *Maya* • Brooke Shields *Susan Hoff* • Vinnie Jones *Mahogany* • Roger Bart *Jurgis* • Tony Curran *Driver* • Barbara Eve Harris *Det Lynn Hadley* ■ *Dir* Ryuhei Kitamura · *Scr* Jeff Buhler, from the short story by Clive Barker

Midnight Movies: from the Margins to the Mainstream ★★★ 18
Documentary
2005 · Can/US · Colour and BW · 85min

Between 1970 and 1977, six low-budget movies transformed the way audiences watched underground films and how the industry marketed them. Alexandro Jodorowsky's *El Topo*, David Lynch's *Eraserhead*, George A Romero's *Night of the Living Dead*, Perry Henzell's *The Harder They Come*, John Waters's *Pink Flamingos* and Richard O'Brien's brainchild *The Rocky Horror Picture Show* found their niche in midnight slots, programmed by adventurous cinema managers. That counterculture phenomenon is given lightweight handling in this clips-and-talking-heads overview from Stuart Samuels. AJ DVD

Alexandro Jodorowsky • George Romero [George A Romero] *George Romero* • Perry Henzel • John Waters (2) *John Waters* • Richard O'Brien • David Lynch ■ *Dir/Scr* Stuart Samuels

Midnight Run ★★★★ 18
Comedy thriller
1988 · US · Colour · 121min

Robert De Niro played this action picture for laughs and, as a result, had his first hit in years. It's a variant on the odd-couple theme, as De Niro's bounty hunter goes on the run with an accountant who has embezzled $15 million from the Mob. The accountant is Charles Grodin, whose underplaying is an absolute joy. A simple air trip from New York to LA turns into a saga of trains and automobiles, car crashes and skirmishes with the FBI and a dozen other interested parties in this first-class road movie. AT Swearing, violence. DVD ◐

Robert De Niro *Jack Walsh* • Charles Grodin *Jonathan Mardukas* • Yaphet Kotto *Alonzo Mosely* • John Ashton *Marvin Dorfler* • Dennis Farina *Jimmy Serrano* • Joe Pantoliano *Eddie Moscone* • Richard Foronjy *Tony Darvo* ■ *Dir* Martin Brest · *Scr* George Gallo

Midnight Son ★★★ 18
Horror drama
2011 · US · Colour · 88min

Writer/director Scott Leberecht's feature debut is a poignant study of a reluctant vampire's fear that his growing appetite for human blood will ruin his burgeoning romance. Zak Kilberg stars as the anaemic security guard who works the night shift and spends his spare time painting sunsets until he gets a chance taste of blood and falls for a vivacious cigarette girl (Maya Parish). Cinematographer Lyn Moncrief's views of the lesser-seen side of Los Angeles reinforce the sense of melancholic dread, and Leberecht is well served by the neurotic Kilberg and feisty Parish. DP Violence, swearing, drug abuse, sex scenes, nudity.

Zak Kilberg *Jacob* • Maya Parish *Mary* • Jo D Jonz *Marcus* • Larry Cedar *Detective Ginslegh* ■ *Dir/Scr* Scott Leberecht

Midnight Special ★★★★ 12A
Science-fiction drama
2015 · US · Colour · 111min

An unconventional road movie that channels Spielberg's *Close Encounters* and Carpenter's *Starman* to create a top-flight, enigmatic fantasy. Michael Shannon plays the dad on the run with his gifted eight-year-old son (Jaeden Lieberher), who is being hunted down by a Bible Belt cult and federal agents convinced he can pull satellites out of orbit. This sensitive metaphor for parenthood builds slowly through wrenching family drama to an imaginative sci-fi finale. AJ Some violence

Michael Shannon *Roy* • Joel Edgerton *Lucas* • Kirsten Dunst *Sarah Tomlin* • Jaeden Lieberher *Alton* • Sam Shepard *Calvin Meyer* ■ *Dir/Scr* Jeff Nichols

Midnight Sting ★★★ 15
Sports drama
1992 · US · Colour · 93min

This sparky comedy drama packs such a punch, that it's hard to believe it sank without trace on its British cinema release. This boxing variation on *The Sting* bristles with sassy dialogue, dynamic fight sequences and truly dastardly villainy (provided by the ever-hissable Bruce Dern). As the cons who hope to clean up with a boxing scam in a small rural backwater, James Woods, Louis Gossett Jr and Oliver Platt are bang on form, but director Michael Ritchie lets the side down by wasting time on a tiresome romantic interlude and a sentimental subplot. DP DVD

James Woods *Gabriel Caine* • Louis Gossett Jr *"Honey" Roy Palmer* • Bruce Dern *John Gillon* • Oliver Platt *Fitz* • Heather Graham *Emily Forrester* • Randall "Tex" Cobb *Wolf Forrester* • Thomas Wilson Brown *Robby Gillon* • Duane Davis *Hambone Busby* ■ *Dir* Michael Ritchie · *Scr* Steven McKay, from the novel *The Diggstown Ringers* by Leonard Wise

The Midnight Story ★★★ PG
Crime mystery
1957 · US · BW · 85min

Traffic cop Tony Curtis is refused a transfer to homicide, so he resigns from the force in order to investigate the murder of his best friend, the Catholic priest who raised him as an orphan. Curtis's main quarry is restaurateur Gilbert Roland, who invites him to lodge at his house. Set in the Italian community of San Francisco, it's as much about Curtis's need for a family, a faith and a sense of belonging as it is a whodunit. Unpretentious, compelling and with a neat twist at the end. AT DVD

M

Tony Curtis *Joe Martini* • Marisa Pavan *Anna Malatesta* • Gilbert Roland *Sylvio Malatesta* • Jay C Flippen *Sergeant Jack Gillen* • Argentina Brunetti *Mama Malatesta* ■ *Dir* Joseph Pevney • *Scr* John Robinson, Edwin Blum, from a story by Edwin Blum

Midnight's Children ★★★ 12

Drama   2012 · Can/UK/US · Colour · 139min

Salman Rushdie himself wrote the script for this adaptation of his prize-winning novel about a group of Indian children with superpowers whose lives interweave with the history of the subcontinent in the decades after independence. And that is the main problem. It's as if Rushdie has tried to pack too much of the novel into the film. At the same time Rushdie rather loses his focus on the children, whose powers resemble those of traditional comic-book superheroes, though their environment could not be farther from Batman's Gotham City. The most glaring misjudgement, however, is Rushdie's voiceover, which continually describes what's actually being shown on screen. Nonetheless the film is stunningly beautiful. And the story retains at least some of the elements that made the novel so special in its imagination, ambition and scope. **BP** English, Hindi, Urdu +subtitles. *DVD*

Satya Bhabha *Saleem Sinai* • Shahana Goswami *Amina Sinai nee Mumtaz Aziz* • Rajat Kapoor *Aadam Aziz* • Seema Biswas *Mary Pereira* ■ *Dir* Deepa Mehta • *Scr* Salman Rushdie, from his novel • *Cinematographer* Giles Nuttgens

Midshipman Easy ★★★ U

Comedy adventure   1935 · UK · BW · 79min

Opportunity knocked for 15-year-old Hughie Green in this lively Thorold Dickinson-produced Ealing adaptation of Captain Frederick Marryat's popular maritime adventure set in the 1790s. Spiritedly adapted by Anthony Kimmins, the action barrels along, as Green seeks to impress captain Roger Livesey and the crew of HMS *Harpy* by having an opinion on everything. The swordfighting is splendidly staged, but there is precious little chemistry between Green and damsel in distress Margaret Lockwood. **DP** *DVD*

Hughie Green [Hugh Green] *Midshipman Easy* • Margaret Lockwood *Donna Agnes* • Harry Tate *Mr Biggs* • Robert Adams *Mesty* • Roger Livesey *Captain Wilson* ■ *Dir* Carol Reed • *Scr* Anthony Kimmins, from the novel *Mr Midshipman Easy* by Frederick Marryat

A Midsummer Night's Dream ★★★★ U

Romantic comedy fantasy   1935 · US · BW · 111min

One of the pottiest movies ever made in Hollywood – a loose rendition of Shakespeare's play, set amid lavish and fantastical woodland sets and with some extraordinary performances from James Cagney as Bottom, Olivia de Havilland as Hermia, Dick Powell as Lysander and Mickey Rooney as Puck. Warner Bros gave theatre maestro Max Reinhardt carte blanche to create a masterwork and, when he set too slow a pace and got into a muddle, decided to give him a co-director, studio hack William Dieterle. From the mess came two Oscars, the debut of a movie composer Erich Wolfgang Korngold, and a breathtaking, if kitsch classic. **AT**

James Cagney *Bottom, the weaver* • Dick Powell *Lysander* • Mickey Rooney *Puck, or Robin Goodfellow* • Joe E Brown *Flute, the bellows-mender* • Victor Jory *Oberon* • Ian Hunter *Theseus, Duke of Athens* • Verree Teasdale *Hippolyta* • Hobart Cavanaugh *Philostrate* • Ross Alexander (I) *Demetrius* • Olivia de Haviland [Olivia de Haviland] *Hermia* • Jean Muir *Helena* • Grant Mitchell *Egeus* • Frank McHugh *Quince* • Anita Louise *Titania* • Kenneth Anger *Changeling prince* ■ *Dir* Max Reinhardt, William Dieterle • *Scr* Charles Kenyon, Mary C McCall Jr, from the play by William Shakespeare • *Cinematographers* Hal Mohr, Ernest Haller • *Art Director* Anton Grot

A Midsummer Night's Dream ★★★★

Animated romantic fantasy   1961 · Cz · Colour · 76min

Three years in the making, Jiri Trnka's masterpiece seeks to dispense with the Shakespearean text and tell the still-enchanting story by means of pantomimic puppetry and dance. Trnka and his co-animator, Bretislav Pojar, lavished considerable care on both the costumes and the forest settings. For all the richness of the visual detail, though, there was still room for the simple exhilaration created by Puck and the mechanicals. The balletic quality of the action left international audiences confused, however, and a voiceover quoting from and commenting on the Bard's play was added against Trnka's wishes. **DP**

Richard Burton *Narrator* • Tom Criddle *Lysander* • Ann Bell *Hermia* • Michael Meacham *Demetrius* • John Warner *Egeus* • Barbara Leigh-Hunt *Helena* • Hugh Manning *Theseus* • Joss Ackland *Quince* • Alec McCowen *Bottom* • Stephen Moore *Flute* • Barbara Jefford *Titania* • Jack Gwillim *Oberon* ■ *Dir* Jiri Trnka, Howard Sackler • *Scr* Jiri Trnka, Jiri Brdecka, Howard Sackler, from the play by William Shakespeare

A Midsummer Night's Dream ★★ U

Romantic comedy fantasy   1969 · UK · Colour · 119min

Sir Peter Hall's early attempt at translating this Shakespearean classic from stage to screen is too close to the original RSC production to achieve a new lease of life on film. Diana Rigg, Helen Mirren, Judi Dench and Ian Richardson star in this tale of four lovers and a "rude mechanical", lost in the forest and at the mercy of mischievous fairies. Hall, an opera and theatre veteran, betrays his lack of film experience by making some very strange editing and sound choices. **LH**

Derek Godfrey *Theseus* • Barbara Jefford *Hippolyta* • Hugh Sullivan *Philostrate* • Nicholas Selby *Egeus* • David Warner *Lysander* • Michael Jayston *Demetrius* • Diana Rigg *Helena* • Helen Mirren *Hermia* • Ian Richardson *Oberon* • Judi Dench *Titania* • Ian Holm *Puck* ■ *Dir* Peter Hall • *Scr* from the play by William Shakespeare

A Midsummer Night's Dream ★★ PG

Romantic comedy fantasy   1996 · UK · Colour · 99min

The great tragedy of this screen version of director Adrian Noble's Royal Shakespeare Company production is that, on stage, it would be absolutely electrifying. The hanging light bulbs that comprise the Athenian forest, the stylised costumes and the glittery make-up help convey some of the play's magic. But the fairies in glowing wigs and the tacky conceit of having the whole thing dreamed by a young boy are ghastly misjudgements. The leaden camera movements are matched only by the clumsiness of the editing. **DP** *DVD*

Lindsay Duncan *Hippolyta/Titania* • Alex Jennings *Theseus/Oberon* • Desmond Barrit *Nick Bottom* • Barry Lynch *Puck/Philostrate* • Monica Dolan *Hermia* • Kevin Doyle *Demetrius* • Daniel Evans *Lysander* • Emily Raymond *Helena* ■ *Dir* Adrian Noble • *Scr* Adrian Noble, from the play by William Shakespeare

A Midsummer Night's Dream ★★★ PG

Romantic comedy fantasy   1999 · US · Colour · 120min

Kevin Kline steals the show as Bottom in this stilted version of Shakespeare's ode to blighted love. As played by Kline, not only is Bottom a garrulous bumbler, but he's also far – when transformed into a donkey by Oberon (Rupert Everett) to fool Titania (Michelle Pfeiffer) – an object of abject poignancy. Updated to 19th-century Italy, Michael Hoffman's film looks most elegant – Calista Flockhart makes a beautiful Helena, and Stanley Tucci's Puck should get a prize for the best-dressed fairy – but without a core

of real magic the result is simply a pretty enchantment. **TH** *DVD*

Kevin Kline *Nick Bottom* • Michelle Pfeiffer *Titania* • Rupert Everett *Oberon* • Stanley Tucci *Puck* • Calista Flockhart *Helena* • Anna Friel *Hermia* • Christian Bale *Demetrius* • Dominic West *Lysander* • Sophie Marceau *Hippolyta* • Bernard Hill *Egeus* • John Sessions *Philostrate* ■ *Dir* Michael Hoffman • *Scr* Michael Hoffman, from the play by William Shakespeare

A Midsummer Night's Sex Comedy ★★★★ 15

Comedy   1982 · US · Colour · 84min

Woody Allen pays homage to Ingmar Bergman in this re-vamp of *Smiles of a Summer Night*, in which six characters gather at a turn-of-the-century farmhouse in search of sexual satisfaction. José Ferrer is the pedantic scholar engaged to Mia Farrow; Allen is the stockbroker trying to bed his frigid wife, Mary Steenburgen. The jokes come thin and slow for a Woody movie, with the result that Allen's oddball inventions (which include a flying bicycle) are at least as interesting as the oddball people. Gordon Willis's photography is exquisite, however. **TH** *DVD*

Woody Allen *Andrew* • Mia Farrow *Ariel Weymouth* • José Ferrer *Leopold* • Julie Hagerty *Dulcy Ford* • Tony Roberts *Maxwell* • Mary Steenburgen *Adrian* • Michael Higgins *Reynolds* • Adam Redfield *Student Foxx* ■ *Dir/Scr* Woody Allen

Midwives ★★ PG

Drama   2001 · US · Colour · 88min

The story of a Vermont midwife who performs a caesarean section in the middle of a snowstorm to save a dead mother's baby is classic TV-movie fodder. After this momentous opening, director Glenn Jordan piles on the melodrama as the grieving husband accuses the midwife of killing his wife. It's saved from complete disaster by Sissy Spacek's typically strong performance as the midwife fighting for her future, with Peter Coyote suitably combative as her lawyer. **DP**

Sissy Spacek *Sibyl Danforth* • Peter Coyote *Stephen Hastings* • Terry Kinney *Rand Danforth* • Alison Pill *Constance "Connie" Danforth* • Susannah Hoffman *Charlotte Bedford* • Piper Laurie *Cheryl Visco* ■ *Dir* Glenn Jordan • *Scr* Cynthia Saunders, from the novel by Chris Bohjalian [Christopher A Bohjalian]

Mifune ★★★ 15

Romantic comedy drama   1999 · Swe/Den · Colour · 101min

Less abrasive than earlier Dogme outings, this surprisingly traditional comedy is similar in storyline and tone to the 1998 Dutch film *The Polish Bride*. Spurning the shock tactics and hand-held camera style of *Festen* and *The Idiots*, director Søren Kragh-Jacobsen uses the beautiful Lolland light to bring a pleasing rustic ambience to the piece. The tale centres on the romance between prostitute Iben Hjejle and Anders W Berthelsen, a newly married yuppie who hides his country origins. A predictable but rather pleasing little film. **DP** Danish +subtitles. Swearing.

Anders W Berthelsen *Kresten* • Jesper Asholt *Rud* • Iben Hjejle *Liva Psilander* • Sofie Grabol *Claire* • Emil Tarding *Bjarke Psilander* ■ *Dir* Søren Kragh-Jacobsen • *Scr* Søren Kragh-Jacobsen, Anders Thomas Jensen

The Mighty ★★★★ PG

Fantasy drama   1998 · US · Colour · 96min

Lumbering outcast Elden Henson doesn't fit in with the other kids in school, but he finally finds a friend when Kieran Culkin is instructed to tutor him. Culkin is a disabled hunchback, but he is also a lover of stories who introduces Henson to an imaginary life outside their own depressing existence. Both boys are superb, and they are ably supported by a cast which includes Sharon Stone, Gena Rowlands, Gillian Anderson and Harry Dean Stanton. A moving, wonderfully-played tale. **JB** *DVD*

Sharon Stone *Gwen Dillon* • Harry Dean Stanton *Grim* • Gena Rowlands *Gram* • Kieran Culkin *Kevin Dillon* • Gillian Anderson *Loretta Lee* •

Elden Henson *Maxwell Kane* • Meat Loaf Aday [Meat Loaf] *Iggy* ■ *Dir* Peter Chelsom • *Scr* Charles Leavitt, from the novel *Freak the Mighty* by Rodman Philbrick

Mighty Aphrodite ★★★ 15

Comedy   1995 · US · Colour · 90min

Woody Allen audaciously lays on an actual Greek chorus for this good-natured comedy of Manhattan neuroses. Allen plays a sports writer who adopts a baby boy because his gallery-owner wife (Helena Bonham Carter) can't afford to take a year out of her life to have one of her own. As the marriage crumbles, Allen seeks out the boy's birth mother, who turns out to be Mira Sorvino's blonde hooker (an Oscar-winning turn). Their developing relationship forms the rest of the story, as he tries to get her out of the game. **AC** *DVD*

Woody Allen *Lenny* • Helena Bonham Carter *Amanda* • Mira Sorvino *Linda* • F Murray Abraham *Chorus leader* • Claire Bloom *Amanda's mother* • Olympia Dukakis *Jocasta* • Michael Rapaport *Kevin* • David Ogden Stiers *Laius* ■ *Dir/Scr* Woody Allen

The Mighty Barnum ★★★

Biographical drama   1934 · US · BW · 87min

Wallace Beery made Phineas T Barnum his own in this breezy 20th Century-Fox biography of the self-styled greatest showman of them all. Beery seemed born to espouse Barnum's phrases and philosophy, such as "There's one born every minute", and if the plot errs a little on the fanciful side, that would have been just dandy for old Phineas. Adolphe Menjou makes an unlikely reluctant partner. Virginia Bruce, as the "Swedish Nightingale" Jenny Lind, is lovely. **TS**

Wallace Beery *Phineas T Barnum* • Adolphe Menjou *Mr Bailey Walsh* • Virginia Bruce *Jenny Lind* • Rochelle Hudson *Ellen* • Janet Beecher *Nancy Barnum* • Tammany Young *Todd* • Lucille La Verne *Joyce Heth* • Herman Bing *Farmer Schultz* • George Brasno *General Tom Thumb* ■ *Dir* Walter Lang • *Scr* Gene Fowler, Bess Merdeyth, from their story

The Mighty Celt ★★ 15

Drama   2005 · Ire/UK · Colour · 78min

Robert Carlyle and Gillian Anderson star in this affable if underwhelming canine variation on Barry Hines's novel *A Kestrel for a Knave*. Tyrone McKenna shows promise as an idealistic youngster, and there are plenty of *Full Monty* moments, too, as Carlyle's ex-IRA man has to face up to his past in seeking to start afresh with Anderson, an old flame and McKenna's mum. Meanwhile, Ken Stott provides some effective villainy as the dog trainer. **DP** Swearing. *DVD*

Robert Carlyle *O* • Gillian Anderson *Kate* • Ken Stott *Good Joe* • Tyrone McKenna *Donal* • Sean McGinley *"I'm a cripple"* ■ *Dir/Scr* Pearse Elliott

The Mighty Ducks ★★ PG

Sports comedy   1992 · US · Colour · 99min

Playing a disgraced lawyer coaching the world's worst ice-hockey team as part of his community service, Emilio Estevez makes the best of what, the ice apart, could hardly be called a cool assignment. This is *The Bad News Bears* with skates on, and you know from the first face-off how it's going to end. But director Stephen Herek pitches every gag and moment of melodrama at just the right level. Originally released in the UK as *Champions*; two sequels (*D2: the Mighty Ducks* and *D3: the Mighty Ducks*) followed. **DP** *DVD*

Emilio Estevez *Gordon Bombay* • Joss Ackland *Hans* • Lane Smith *Coach Reilly* • Heidi Kling *Casey* • Josef Sommer *Gerald Ducksworth* • Joshua Jackson *Charlie Conroy* • Elden Ratliff *Fulton Reed* • Shaun Weiss *Goldberg* ■ *Dir* Stephen Herek • *Scr* Steven Brill

A Mighty Heart ★★★★ 15

Biographical drama   2007 · US/UK · Colour · 103min

In 2002, Daniel Pearl, an American *Wall Street Journal* reporter in Karachi, was kidnapped by Pakistani jihadists. Throughout Pearl's captivity, his heavily

U SUITABLE FOR ALL   Uc SUITABLE ESPECIALLY FOR YOUNG CHILDREN (DVD ONLY)   PG PARENTAL GUIDANCE   12A UNDER 12s TO BE ACCOMPANIED (CINEMA ONLY)

pregnant wife Mariane (Angelina Jolie) made eloquent appeals for his release. British director Michael Winterbottom captures the realities of the story with grim precision, staccato editing and handheld cameras, propelling us into the chaotic whirlwind around Mariane, as competing authorities attempt to negotiate her husband's release. On one level it plays as a tense, beat-the-clock thriller; except we already know the tragic ending. On another level it's rather simplistic reportage that retreads real life, while adding little more than the presence of a Hollywood star. Winterbottom brings his customary intelligence to bear on the subject, creating a film that is undeniably moving. JR Swearing. **DVD** **SD**

Angelina Jolie *Mariane Pearl* • Dan Futterman *Daniel "Danny" Pearl* • Archie Panjabi *Asra Nomani* • Irrfan Khan [Irfan Khan] *Javed Nabib, "Captain"* • Will Patton *Randall Bennett* • Adnan Siddiqui *Dost Aliani* • Gary Wilmes *Steve LeVine* ■ *Dir* Michael Winterbottom • *Scr* John Orloff, from the non-fiction book *A Mighty Heart: the Brave Life and Death of My Husband Danny Pearl* by Mariane Pearl, Sarah Crichton • *Cinematographer* Marcel Zyskind

Mighty Joe Young ★★★ U
Fantasy adventure 1949 · US · BW · 93min

As an emasculated *King Kong*, this variation on the monster theme is, nevertheless, entertaining enough. Terry Moore is persuaded to bring her enormous pet gorilla from Africa to America to become part of a nightclub act which includes, in superlatively kitsch style, her playing *Beautiful Dreamer* while being held aloft by the gorilla. Directed by Ernest B Schoedsack, who co-directed *King Kong*, with special effects by *King Kong* originator Willis O'Brien and, among others, Ray Harryhausen, it's excruciatingly schmaltzy but keeps its innocence intact. TH

Terry Moore *Jill Young* • Robert Armstrong *Max O'Hara* • Ben Johnson (1) *Gregg Ford* • Frank McHugh *Press agent* • Douglas Fowley *Jones* ■ *Dir* Ernest B Schoedsack • *Scr* Ruth Rose, from a story by Merian C Cooper

Mighty Joe Young ★★★ PG
Fantasy adventure 1998 · US · Colour · 109min

This entertaining remake of the 1949 family drama has beautiful Charlize Theron as the woman who befriends a colossal but cute gorilla hidden in the deepest jungle. Of course, Joe doesn't remain concealed for long after explorer Bill Paxton discovers him, and he's soon pursued by nasty hunters who want to capture him for some rich collector's amusement. It's a fun romp with some impressive ape effects and luscious scenery. JB **DVD**

Charlize Theron *Jill Young* • Bill Paxton *Gregg O'Hara* • Rade Serbedzija *Strasser* • Peter Firth *Garth* • David Paymer *Harry Ruben* • Regina King *Cecily Banks* • Robert Wisdom *Kweli* • Naveen Andrews *Pindi* ■ *Dir* Ron Underwood • *Scr* Mark Rosenthal, Lawrence Konner, from the 1949 film

Mighty Morphin Power Rangers: the Movie ★★★ PG
Science-fiction adventure
1995 · US · Colour · 91min

A few years ago, these superheroes in vinyl tights were the hottest thing around. Now the tie-in toys are about as fashionable as Cabbage Patch dolls. Here the Power Rangers battle their old enemy Rita Repulsa, fight off slime creatures and squash the world domination plans of evil Ivan Ooze. This colourful junk will while away a couple of very mindless hours. A second film, *Power Rangers 2*, followed. AJ **DVD**

Karan Ashley *Aisha/Yellow Ranger* • Johnny Yong Bosch *Adam/Black Ranger* • Stephen Antonio Cardenas *Rocky/Red Ranger* • Jason David Frank *Tommy/White Ranger* • Amy Jo Johnson *Kimberly/Pink Ranger* • David Harold Yost *Billy/Blue Ranger* • Paul Schrier *Bulk* • Paul Freeman *Ivan Ooze* • Julia Cortez *Rita Repulsa* ■ *Dir* Bryan Spicer • *Scr* Arne Olsen, from a story by John Kamps, Arne Olsen

The Mighty Quinn ★★★ 15
Detective drama 1989 · US · Colour · 94min

Denzel Washington hasn't made many wrong moves in his movie career, but he nearly came a cropper with this lightweight Caribbean thriller. He is his usual charismatic self as the determined police chief on a small former colony who gets mixed up in murder and political corruption, and there is a solid enough supporting cast. But director Carl Schenkel seems to have been seduced by the beautiful locations and laid-back lifestyle, as there is little in the way of suspense. JF Swearing. **DVD**

Denzel Washington *Xavier Quinn* • James Fox *Elgin* • Mimi Rogers *Hadley* • Robert Townsend *Maubee* • M Emmet Walsh *Miller* • Sheryl Lee Ralph *Lola* • Art Evans *Jump* • Esther Rolle *Ubu Pearl* ■ *Dir* Carl Schenkel • *Scr* Hampton Fancher, from the novel *Finding Maubee* by AHZ Carr

A Mighty Wind ★★★★ 12
Satirical comedy 2003 · US · Colour · 88min

This Is Spinal Tap's Christopher Guest takes the mickey out of the folk music scene in this musical satire. Director and co-writer Guest is called upon to reform acoustic trio The Folksmen for a memorial concert for the late promoter Irving Steinbloom. Headlining the event above the ridiculously upbeat New Main Street Singers are Mitch & Mickey (played by Eugene Levy and Catherine O'Hara), once the sweethearts of the folk world, who haven't spoken to each other for nearly three decades following a messy divorce. This can't match the satirical bite of the classic *Spinal Tap*, but there are still many laugh-out-loud moments. TH **DVD**

Bob Balaban *Jonathan Steinbloom* • Ed Begley Jr *Lars Olfen* • Jennifer Coolidge *Amber Cole* • Christopher Guest *Alan Barrows* • John Michael Higgins *Terry Bohner* • Eugene Levy *Mitch Cohen* • Jane Lynch *Laurie Bohner* • Michael McKean *Jerry Palter* • Catherine O'Hara *Mickey Crabbe* • Parker Posey *Sissy Knox* • Harry Shearer *Mark Shubb* • Fred Willard *Mike LaFontaine* ■ *Dir* Christopher Guest • *Scr* Christopher Guest, Eugene Levy

Mignon Has Left ★★★ 12
Drama 1988 · It/Fr · Colour · 98min

Italian director Francesca Archibugi made a considerable impact with this, her debut feature. Ostensibly a tale of two cities, the story focuses on Céline Beauvallet, a chic Parisian teen who is sent to stay with working-class relatives in Rome when her father is jailed. Beauvallet's abrupt awakening and her bashful cousin's achingly true-to-life crush are delicately handled, but it's the upward struggle of her put-upon aunt (the excellent Stefania Sandrelli) that gives this drama its poignancy and credibility. DP Italian +subtitles.

Stefania Sandrelli *Mama* • Jean-Pierre Duriez *Federico* • Leonardo Ruta *Giorgio* • Céline Beauvallet *Mignon* • Francesca Antonelli *Chiara* • Lorenzo De Pasqua *Cacio* • Eleonora Sambiagio *Antonella* ■ *Dir* Francesca Archibugi • *Scr* Francesca Archibugi, Gloria Malatesta, Claudia Sbarigia

The Mikado ★★★ U
Operetta 1939 · UK · Colour · 86min

American Victor Schertzinger, a composer himself, faithfully directs this lavish British production of the famed Gilbert and Sullivan Savoy operetta. Also imported from the States was radio crooner Kenny Baker to star as Nanki-Poo, and he seems ill-at-ease among the D'Oyly Carte players, notably Martyn Green as Ko-Ko and Sydney Granville as Pooh-Bah, playing as if born to their roles. The marvellous use of early Technicolor makes this rather dull adaptation very watchable today. TS **DVD**

Kenny Baker (1) *Nanki-Poo* • Martyn Green *Ko-Ko* • Sydney Granville *Pooh-Bah* • John Barclay *The Mikado* • Gregory Stroud *Pish-Tush* • Jean Collin *Yum-Yum* • Constance Willis *Katisha* • Elizabeth Paynter *Pitti-Sing* ■ *Dir* Victor Schertzinger • *Scr* Geoffrey Toye, from the operetta by WS Gilbert, Arthur Sullivan • *Cinematographers* William Skall [William V Skall], Bernard Knowles

Mike and Dave Need Wedding Dates ★★ 15
Comedy 2016 · US · Colour · 98min

Sadly, there are very few laughs to be found in this raunchy, vulgar comedy. Loosely based on a true story, it follows two brothers – Mike (Adam Devine) and Dave (Zac Efron) – who ruin every family gathering with their booze-fuelled antics. As their sister prepares to get married, the boys are instructed to be on their best behaviour, with their parents insisting that each of them bring a nice, respectable girl to the wedding. So the boys place an ad on the internet. The result is semi-amusing, but most of the gags fall flat. SC Swearing, sexual references, drug abuse, nudity.

Zac Efron *Dave Stangle* • Adam Devine [Adam Devine] *Mike Stangle* • Anna Kendrick *Alice* • Aubrey Plaza *Tatiana* ■ *Dir* Jake Szymanski • *Scr* Andrew Jay Cohen, Brendan O'Brien

Mike Bassett: England Manager ★★★ 15
Sports satire 2001 · UK · Colour · 85min

Thanks to the minimal use of on-field action football sequences, we are spared the embarrassment of watching players who can't act and actors who can't play in this funny sports satire. Instead, the film focuses on the boardroom, back-room and dressing-room shenanigans that ensue after a lower-league soccer boss is made England manager. Ricky Tomlinson plays Bassett with a nice mix of humour and pathos. When the team flukes its way into the World Cup in Brazil, Bassett is faced with the task of turning his individual allsorts into a winning side. DA Violence, swearing, brief nudity. **DVD**

Ricky Tomlinson *Mike Bassett* • Amanda Redman *Karine Bassett* • Philip Jackson *Lonnie Urquart* • Bradley Walsh *Dave Dodds* • Phill Jupitus *Tommo Thompson* • Ulrich Thomsen *Professor Shoegaarten* • Pelé • Gabby Logan ■ *Dir* Steve Barron • *Scr* Rob Sprackling, JRN Smith

Mike's Murder ★★ 18
Psychological thriller
1984 · US · Colour · 104min

Long-delayed and barely released, this murky thriller reunites Debra Winger with her *Urban Cowboy* director, James Bridges. Here she's sleuthing over a drug deal that went wrong – though not half as wrong as the movie itself, which spent a couple of years being edited, restructured, cut again and then finally dubbed in England. TS Swearing.

Debra Winger *Betty Parrish* • Mark Keyloun *Mike* • Paul Winfield *Phillip* • Darrell Larson *Pete* • Brooke Alderson *Patty* • Robert Crosson *Sam* ■ *Dir/Scr* James Bridges • *Music* Joe Jackson, John Barry (1)

The Milagro Beanfield War ★★★★ 15
Drama 1988 · US · Colour · 112min

With *Quiz Show* and *Ordinary People*, former heart-throb Robert Redford revealed himself to be one of America's finest directors of actors. Here he proves adept at handling a large ensemble cast in this adaptation of John Nichols's whimsical novel about a New Mexican farmer (Chick Vennera), who deflects water from a housing development to start his own beanfield. Watch out for Melanie Griffith, John Heard and Christopher Walken, enjoy Dave Grusin's Oscar-winning score, and don't be put off by that title. TS Swearing. **DVD**

Rubén Blades *Sheriff Bernabe Montoya* • Richard Bradford *Ladd Devine* • Sonia Braga *Ruby Archuleta* • Julie Carmen *Nancy Mondragon* • James Gammon *Horsethief Shorty* • Melanie Griffith *Flossie Devine* • John Heard *Charlie Bloom* • Christopher Walken *Kyril Montana* ■ *Dir* Robert Redford • *Scr* David Ward, John Nichols, from the novel by John Nichols

Mildred Pierce ★★★★★ PG
Classic film noir melodrama
1945 · US · BW · 106min

Although it will forever be known as the movie that relaunched Joan Crawford's flagging career, there is much more to this classic "woman's picture" than an Oscar-winning performance. Crawford is fabulous as the woman who, after the breakdown of her marriage, goes to work to pay for her daughters' education and builds up a successful business. Tragedy, naturally, awaits. While it reworks the original plot, Ranald MacDougall's script retains the sharp edge of James M Cain's novel, while Michael Curtiz's cool direction keeps the action moving and Crawford, Ann Blyth and Zachary Scott away from caricature. Ernest Haller's moody photography and Anton Grot's sets (which, at a glance, convey Mildred's changing social status) are also outstanding. Screen suffering was never so sophisticated. DP **DVD**

Joan Crawford *Mildred Pierce* • Jack Carson *Wally Fay* • Zachary Scott *Monte Beragon* • Eve Arden *Ida Corwin* • Ann Blyth *Veda Pierce* • Bruce Bennett *Bert Pierce* • Lee Patrick *Mrs Maggie Biederhof* • Moroni Olsen *Inspector Peterson* • Jo Ann Marlowe *Kay Pierce* • Butterfly McQueen *Lottie* ■ *Dir* Michael Curtiz • *Scr* Ranald MacDougall, from the novel by James M Cain • *Music* Max Steiner

Miles Ahead ★★★ 15
Music biography 2015 · US · Colour · 100min

Legendary jazz musician Miles Davis is the subject of this appropriately mercurial biopic, which marks the directorial debut of Don Cheadle. Most of the film takes place during the late 1970s, depicting Davis (Cheadle) as a prickly, cocaine-addled recluse whose best days are behind him. Holed up in his apartment, he receives a visit from a pushy journalist (Ewan McGregor) who wants to write a "comeback story". Cheadle deserves plenty of credit, but his performance veers towards caricature. SC Violence, swearing, drug abuse, nudity.

Don Cheadle *Miles Davis* • Ewan McGregor *Dave Braden* • Emayatzy Corinealdi *Frances Taylor* • Lakeith Lee Stanfield [Keith Stanfield] *Junior* • Michael Stuhlbarg *Harper Hamilton* ■ *Dir* Don Cheadle • *Scr* Don Cheadle, Steven Baigelman, from a story by Stephen J Rivele, Christopher Wilkinson, Cheadle, Baigelman

Miles from Home ★★★ 15
Drama 1988 · US · Colour · 103min

Richard Gere, whose career was somewhat in the doldrums at the time, made a stab for credibility with this worthy, if uneven, rural drama. Gere is the farmer whose property is in danger of being seized by the banks, forcing him into increasingly drastic action. Actor Gary Sinise here directs ably, but it is the playing that really makes the picture; if Gere is not entirely convincing in the leading role, Kevin Anderson, as his younger brother, is terrific, while the supporting turns more than compensate for the weaknesses in the script. JF Violence, swearing, drug abuse.

Richard Gere *Frank Roberts Jr* • Kevin Anderson *Terry Roberts* • Brian Dennehy *Frank Roberts Sr* • Jason Campbell *Young Frank* • Austin Bamgarner *Young Terry* • Larry Poling *Nikita Khrushchev* • Laurie Metcalf *Ellen* • John Malkovich *Barry Maxwell* ■ *Dir* Gary Sinise • *Scr* Chris Gerolmo

Miles to Go ★★★ 15
Drama 1986 · US · Colour · 89min

Jill Clayburgh was so good in films like *Gable and Lombard* and *An Unmarried Woman* that her place among American cinema's elite seemed assured. But Hollywood has always had problems accommodating intelligent actresses and the roles she deserved simply didn't come her way. She's easily the best thing in this TV movie, playing a dying woman trying to find a replacement wife and mother for her family. Prolific TV-movie director David Greene, who made the screen version of the hit musical *Godspell*, directs with a sensitive touch. DP

Jill Clayburgh *Moira Browning* • Tom Skerritt *Stuart Browning* • Mimi Kuzyk *Suzanne* • Rosemary Dunsmore *Cynthia* • Cyndy Preston *Jani Browning* • Andrew Bednarski *Brad Browning* • Peter Dvorsky *Dr Michael Kosberg* • Caroline Arnold *Centre woman* ■ *Dir* David Greene • *Scr* Beverly Levitt, Stuart Fischoff, from a story by Levitt

M

Military Policeman ★★ U
Comedy   1953 · US · BW · 90min

The Bob Hope style of wise-cracking comedy was showing some strain by the time of this effort, and 1953 was the last year in which he figured in the top ten box-office stars. His teaming with the exuberant Mickey Rooney does not always gel, either, but there are sufficient laughs to make this a pleasant enough time-passer. Eddie Mayehoff shines as a military policeman who despairs at Hope's ineptitude, playing a boxer's manager stuck with a term in the army. TV

Bob Hope *Wally Hogan* • Mickey Rooney *Herbert Tuttle* • Marilyn Maxwell *Connie Curtis* • Eddie Mayehoff *Karl Danzig* • Stanley Clements *Bullet Bradley* • Jack Dempsey ■ *Dir* George Marshall • *Scr* Hal Kanter, Jack Sher, from a story by Hal Kanter

Militia ★★ 15
Action thriller   2000 · US · Colour · 85min

TV's Superman Dean Cain has not made much of an impact on the movie scene and, despite a better than average cast, the main problem here is the typically sloppy direction of Jim Wynorski. Cain is the Government agent who is paired with former right-wing extremist Frederic Forrest to infiltrate a shadowy new militia headed by crazy Stacy Keach. JF *DVD*

Dean Cain *Ethan Carter* • Jennifer Beals *Julie Sanders* • Frederic Forrest *William Fain* • Stacy Keach *Mr Montgomery* • Brett Butler *Bobbie* ■ *Dir* Jay Andrews [Jim Wynorski] • *Scr* Steve Latshaw, William Carson

Milius ★★★★ 15
Documentary   2013 · US · Colour · 103min

He may have been part of the same wave of maverick film-makers that spawned the likes of Francis Ford Coppola and Martin Scorsese, but writer/director John Milius has never been afforded the same recognition. Joey Figueroa and Zak Knutson go part of the way to explaining why, in this engrossing portrait of an outspoken right-wing rebel and his many clashes with studio bosses. Beyond the films he made himself, Milius brought his writing talent – uncredited and credited – to *Jaws* and *Apocalypse Now*. But his larger-than-life personality was often his undoing, not least after the controversy surrounding the Soviet-baiting *Red Dawn*. TeS

John Milius ■ *Dir* Joey Figueroa, Zak Knutson

Milk ★★ 15
Black comedy   1999 · UK/Aus · Colour · 92min

An enviable British ensemble is under-employed in William Brookfield's directorial debut. James Fleet is rather swept away by the grasping relatives who descend on his Wiltshire dairy farm following the death of his martinet mother. Consequently, we're much more interested in the antics of such scene-stealers as Peter Jones and Dawn French than in Fleet's machinations and his tentative relationship with back-packer, Clotilde Courau. This is never macabre nor comic enough. DP *DVD*

James Fleet *Adrian* • Phyllida Law *Veronica* • Joss Ackland *Vicar* • Clotilde Courau *Ilaria* • Peter Jones *Harry* • Francesca Annis *Harriet* • Dawn French *Virginia* • Lesley Manville *Fiona* • Richard Johnson *John* ■ *Dir/Scr* William Brookfield

Milk ★★★★★ 15
Biographical drama
2008 · US · Colour and BW · 122min

Sean Penn delivers an unexpected gem of a performance in Gus Van Sant's humane, intelligent biopic of Harvey Milk, who, in 1978, became the first openly gay man to be elected to public office. Milk remained in the closet until he was 40, before moving from New York to San Francisco with a younger boyfriend (James Franco) and discovering a passion for activism. Penn plays him as a warm, attractive character, and an astute politician with none of the tortured angst more typical of his previous roles. However, Milk's growing political success comes at the expense of his personal life and his relationships with his

colleagues, particularly a tightly wound Josh Brolin. Van Sant, reminding us here that he is capable of conventional storytelling as well as such experimental fare as *Elephant* (2003), wonderfully re-creates the milieu of 1970s San Francisco and handles the material with great skill. AS Swearing. *DVD* *BL*

Sean Penn *Harvey Milk* • Emile Hirsch *Cleve Jones* • Josh Brolin *Dan White* • Diego Luna *Jack Lira* • James Franco *Scott Smith* • Alison Pill *Anne Kronenberg* • Victor Garber *Mayor Moscone* • Lucas Grabeel *Danny Nicoletta* ■ *Dir* Gus Van Sant • *Scr* Dustin Lance Black

Milk Money ★★★ 12
Romantic comedy   1994 · US · Colour · 104min

Four years after *Pretty Woman* came another implausible "prostitute finds love with a nice man" romantic comedy. This is more warm-hearted than the successful Julia Roberts film, with Melanie Griffith sexy and down-to-earth as the hooker brought home by a young boy as a prospective wife for his lonely dad (Ed Harris). Both Harris and Griffith give nice, unshowy performances, while Malcolm McDowell is convincingly nasty as the pimp who's after Griffith. Utterly preposterous, but thoroughly enjoyable entertainment. JB *DVD*

Melanie Griffith *V* • Ed Harris *Tom Wheeler* • Michael Patrick Carter *Frank Wheeler* • Malcolm McDowell *Waltzer* • Anne Heche *Betty* • Casey Siemaszko *Cash* • Philip Bosco *Jerry the Pope* • Brian Christopher *Kevin Clean* ■ *Dir* Richard Benjamin • *Scr* John Mattson

The Milk of Sorrow ★★★★ 12A
Drama   2009 · Sp/Peru · Colour · 98min

Peru's traumatic past keeps a young woman shackled by fear in writer/director Claudia Llosa's Oscar-nominated drama. Magaly Solier is quietly poignant as the troubled slum-dweller Fausta, whose relatives believe she inherited her anxieties through the milk of her now dying mother, a 1980s civil war rape victim. This legacy of sexual violence impacts deeply on Fausta, but she eventually finds a voice in her improvised singing to the volatile pianist (Susi Sanchez) she begins working for. Despite its sombre themes, Llosa's narrative remains hope-fuelled, enriched with natural performances and vivid atmospherics. The result is a slice of magical realism whose power lies in symbolism and subtlety rather than heavy-handed sensationalism. SF Spanish, Quechua +subtitles.

Magaly Solier *Fausta* • Susi Sanchez *Señora Aida* • Efrain Solis Noe • Marino Ballon *Tio Lucido* • Barbara Lazon *Perpetua* • Delci Heredia *Tia Carmela* • Karla Heredia *Severina* ■ *Dir/Scr* Claudia Llosa

The Milky Way ★★★★ U
Sports comedy   1936 · US · BW · 87min

Perhaps the last great Harold Lloyd comedy classic (this was later remade as *The Kid from Brooklyn* with Danny Kaye, becoming blandly pasteurised in the process). Lloyd plays a mild-mannered milkman who, mistaken for a potential world boxing champion, gets caught up with a gang of crooked fixers. Adolphe Menjou, Helen Mack and Lionel Stander provide wonderful back-up for his endeavours. TH *DVD*

Harold Lloyd *Burleigh "Tiger" Sullivan* • Adolphe Menjou *Gabby Sloan* • Verree Teasdale *Ann Westley* • Helen Mack *Mae Sullivan* • William Gargan *Elwood "Speed" MacFarland* • George Barbier *Wilbur Austin* • Dorothy Wilson *Polly Pringle* • Lionel Stander *Spider Schultz* ■ *Dir* Leo McCarey • *Scr* Grover Jones, Frank Butler, Richard Connell, from a play by Lynn Root, Harry Clork

The Milky Way ★★★★★ 12
Drama   1968 · Fr/It · Colour · 97min

This pilgrim's regress by the great surrealist master Luis Buñuel, while being among his most anti-clerical and enigmatic movies, is still marvellously accessible even for those not in tune with Catholic concerns. His two tramps, progressing from Paris to a shrine

in Spain, slip through time to encounter the Devil, the Virgin Mary and many zealots. They conclude, on their road to religious ruin, that intolerance is next to godliness. Buñuel, who was always on the side of the heretics, makes his points with sarcastic compassion. TH French +subtitles. *DVD*

Laurent Terzieff *Jean* • Paul Frankeur *Pierre* • Delphine Seyrig *Prostitute* • Edith Scob *Virgin Mary* • Bernard Verley *Jesus* • Georges Marchal *Jesuit* • Jean Piat *Jansenist* • Pierre Clémenti *The Devil* ■ *Dir* Luis Buñuel • *Scr* Luis Buñuel, Jean-Claude Carrière

The Mill on the Floss ★★
Period drama   1937 · UK · BW · 82min

Director Tim Whelan was also one of four writers attempting to adapt George Eliot's famous novel about the tragic feud between the Tullivers and the Wakems, and the resulting Victorian period piece is to be recommended for its polished British cast. The poignancy of the novel does make itself felt. RK

Geraldine Fitzgerald *Maggie Tulliver* • James Mason *Tom Tulliver* • Felix Aylmer *Mr Wakem* • Frank Lawton *Philip Wakem* • Fay Compton *Mrs Tulliver* • Griffith Jones *Stephen Guest* • Mary Clare *Mrs Moss* • Victoria Hopper *Lucy Deane* ■ *Dir* Tim Whelan • *Scr* Tim Whelan, John Drinkwater, Garnett Weston, Austin Melford, from the novel by George Eliot

Millennium ★★ PG
Science-fiction drama
1989 · US · Colour · 101min

Based on an interesting short story, this doesn't have enough meat on it for a feature and it's a struggle to stay watching to the end. Kris Kristofferson is the investigator trying to work out what happened after an air disaster, who discovers that the passengers were whisked off by time traveller Cheryl Ladd before the crash. Unfortunately, a promising premise gets lost among the clichés and B-movie performances. JB

Kris Kristofferson *Bill Smith* • Cheryl Ladd *Louise Baltimore* • Daniel J Travanti *Arnold Mayer* • Robert Joy *Sherman* • Lloyd Bochner *Walters* • Brent Carver *Coventry* • Maury Chaykin *Roger Keane* ■ *Dir* Michael Anderson • *Scr* John Varley, from the short story *Air Raid* by John Varley

Miller's Crossing ★★★★★ 18
Period crime drama   1990 · US · Colour · 114min

The Coen brothers' sublime Prohibition-era gangster saga is a magnificent display of compelling acting, spellbinding storytelling and fine film-making. A dark-hued, richly operatic mood piece, with machine-gun-fire dialogue and twisted meaty substance to spare, it focuses on the friendship between politician Albert Finney and Gabriel Byrne, the power behind his throne, and the bloody Mob war that erupts when they fall in love with the same woman (Marcia Gay Harden). The title refers to a lonely, leafy glade where somebody's murder will take place. Byrne is simply outstanding as the cool, calculating catalyst around whom the spectacle revolves. AJ Violence, sex scenes, swearing, nudity. *DVD* *BL*

Gabriel Byrne *Tom Reagan* • Marcia Gay Harden *Verna* • John Turturro *Bernie Bernbaum* • Jon Polito *Johnny Caspar* • JE Freeman *Eddie Dane* • Albert Finney *Leo* • Mike Starr *Frankie* • Al Mancini *Tic-Tac* • Steve Buscemi *Mink* ■ *Dir* Joel Coen • *Scr* Joel Coen, Ethan Coen • *Cinematographer* Barry Sonnenfeld

The Miller's Wife ★
Period comedy   1955 · It · Colour · 94min

The governor of Naples (Vittorio De Sica), lusting after the sexy wife (Sophia Loren) of the local miller (Marcello Mastroianni), has the man arrested on a trumped-up charge, then offers the wife her husband's release in return for her favours. A melodramatic plot is the basis for a vulgar and unfunny Neapolitan farce, directed without a trace of inspiration. RK In Italian.

Vittorio De Sica *The Governor* • Marcello Mastroianni *Luca, the miller* • Sophia Loren *Carmela* • Paolo Stoppa *Gardunia* ■ *Dir* Mario

Camerini • *Scr* Mario Camerini, Ennio De Concini, Augusto Camerini, Alessandro Continenza, Ivo Perilli, from the play by Pedro DeAlacon

Le Million ★★★★
Comedy   1931 · Fr · BW · 85min

René Lefèvre stars as a poor painter who wins a fortune on the lottery, only to discover that the ticket is in the pocket of an old jacket that's been stolen. His chase across Paris to recover it, which lands him on the stage of the opera house, forms the delightfully funny substance of this famously charming, innovative and influential early sound film from French director René Clair. The lovely Annabella and the fluent camera of future cinematographic ace Georges Périnal contribute to the stylishness. RK In French.

Annabella *Beatrice* • René Lefèvre *Michel* • Paul Olivier *"Father Tulipe" Crochard, a gangster* • Louis Allibert *Prosper* ■ *Dir* René Clair • *Scr* René Clair, from the musical by Georges Berr, M Guillemaud

Million Dollar Arm ★★★ PG
Sports drama   2014 · US · Colour · 118min

In this true-story fish-out-of-water tale Jon Hamm plays a sports agent who recruits two young cricket players from India to convert to baseball stars in America. But the change in sports and cultures proves harder than all three had first thought. Predictable yet charming, it's delicately handled by director Craig Gillespie. It may be just another feel-good sports movie, but what it does, it does well. JL In English, Hindi. Some swearing, sexual references. *DVD* *BL*

Jon Hamm *JB Bernstein* • Lake Bell *Brenda* • Suraj Sharma *Rinku* • Madhur Mittal *Dinesh* • Alan Arkin *Ray Poitevint* • Bill Paxton *Tom House* ■ *Dir* Craig Gillespie • *Scr* Thomas McCarthy

Million Dollar Baby ★★
Romantic comedy   1941 · US · BW · 100min

This modest little comedy was one of eight movies in which Warner Bros paired sparky and wholesome Priscilla Lane with handsome Jeffrey Lynn. The plot has Lane inheriting a million dollars from crotchety May Robson, only to arrive at the unrealistic conclusion that money doesn't bring happiness. Along the way she dallies with Ronald Reagan, improbably cast as a concert pianist. RB

Priscilla Lane *Pamela McAllister* • Jeffrey Lynn *James Amory* • Ronald Reagan *Peter Rowan* • May Robson *Cornelia Wheelwright* • Lee Patrick *Josie LaRue* • Helen Westley *Mrs Galloway* ■ *Dir* Curtis Bernhardt • *Scr* Casey Robinson, Richard Macaulay, Jerry Wald, from the story *Miss Wheelwright Discovers America* by Leonard Spigelgass

Million Dollar Baby ★★★★★ 12
Sports drama   2004 · US · Colour · 127min

For those who thought *Unforgiven* was the masterpiece of Clint Eastwood's autumn years, this sharp, moving and brutally bleak drama proves that he can bring the same grizzled genius to the sports arena. Eastwood stars as a washed-up coach whose fighters abandon him as soon as they hit the big time. Dumped by his latest slugger, he reluctantly turns his attentions to Hilary Swank, a 31-year-old waitress who turns up at his gym begging for lessons. Eastwood tutors Swank to success, but then this otherwise standard underdog story takes a shocking turn in its final third that gives the movie an unexpected depth and immense power. Morgan Freeman is impressive as the trainer's crumpled sidekick, and Swank is terrific, too, but this is Clint's film, both as its tortured hero and as a great director. DW Violence, swearing. *DVD* *BL*

Clint Eastwood *Frankie Dunn* • Hilary Swank *Maggie Fitzgerald* • Morgan Freeman *Eddie "Scrap-Iron" Dupris* • Anthony Mackie *Shawrelle Berry* • Jay Baruchel *Danger Barch* • Mike Colter *Big Willie Little* • Lucia Rijker *Billie "The Blue Bear"* • Brian F O'Byrne [Brian O'Byrne] *Father*

Horvak ■ *Dir* Clint Eastwood • *Scr* Paul Haggis, from the short stories *Rope Burns: Stories from the Corner* by FX Toole

The Million Dollar Duck ★★★ U

Comedy 1971 · US · Colour · 92min

Disney's unofficial remake of the Douglas Fairbanks Jr vehicle, *Mr Drake's Duck*, provides yet another twist on the nutty professor story. Dean Jones is a scientist whose experiments on the behaviour of ducks go haywire when his prize specimen, Charley, dips his beak into some radioactive apple sauce and begins laying golden eggs. From then on, it's the familiar tale of bungling baddies and government agents seeking to snatch the remarkable bird from the prof and his young friends. DP

Dean Jones *Professor Albert Dooley* • Sandy Duncan *Katie Dooley* • Joe Flynn *Finley Hooper* • Tony Roberts *Fred Hines* • James Gregory *Rutledge* • Lee Harcourt Montgomery [Lee Montgomery] *Jimmy Dooley* • Jack Kruschen *Dr Gottlieb* ■ *Dir* Vincent McEveety • *Scr* Roswell Rogers, from a story by Ted Key

The Million Dollar Hotel ★ 15

Comedy drama 1999 · Ger/US · Colour · 116min

Director Wim Wenders applies his art house touch to this Hollywood tale of an FBI agent investigating a suspicious death at a bizarre, bohemian hotel. Kept simple, it could have worked; unfortunately, Wenders cloaks everything in needless complexity and wilful obscurity. Mel Gibson, whose company Icon Entertainment produced the film, plays the agent and looks less than a million dollars. DA *DVD*

Jeremy Davies *Tom Tom* • Milla Jovovich *Eloise* • Mel Gibson *Skinner* • Jimmy Smits *Geronimo* • Peter Stormare *Dixie* • Amanda Plummer *Vivien* • Bud Cort *Shorty* • Julian Sands *Terence Scopey* • Tim Roth *Izzy Goldkiss* ■ *Dir* Wim Wenders • *Scr* Nicholas Klein, from a story by Bono, Nicholas Klein

Million Dollar Legs ★★ U

Comedy 1932 · US · BW · 64min

As the President of Klopstokia, a mythical principality that's bankrupt, WC Fields plays very much second fiddle to Jack Oakie in this nonsensical slapstick farce. Oakie is a visiting American brush salesman, who falls in love with the President's daughter and comes up with the money-making scheme of entering Klopstokia in the Los Angeles Olympics. Directed by Edward Cline, it plays like an inferior version of a Marx Brothers excursion into silliness, with pratfalls, non-sequiturs and really terrible gags. RK

Jack Oakie *Migg Tweeny* • WC Fields *The President of Klopstokia* • Andy Clyde *The Major-domo* • Lyda Roberti *Mata Machree* • Susan Fleming *Angela* ■ *Dir* Edward Cline • *Scr* Henry Myers, Nick Barrows, from a story by Joseph L Mankiewicz

Million Dollar Legs ★★ U

Comedy 1939 · US · BW · 64min

A college student takes up a collection and bets the money on a horse named Million Dollar Legs, thus raising the cash to buy badly needed equipment for the college rowing team. This is most interesting for a cast that includes future stars Betty Grable, 14-year-old Donald O'Connor and William Holden, in a two-word bit part. Also cast was Jackie Coogan, the real-life husband of Grable, whose stardom ended with his coming of age. RK

Betty Grable *Carol Parker* • John Hartley *Greg Melton* • Donald O'Connor *Sticky Boone* • Jackie Coogan *Russ Simpson* • Larry Crabbe [Larry "Buster" Crabbe] *Coach Baxter* ■ *Dir* Nick Grinde • *Scr* Lewis R Foster, Richard English, from a story by Lewis R Foster

Million Dollar Mermaid ★★★ U

Biographical drama 1952 · US · Colour · 115min

Who else but the divine water-goddess of MGM, Esther Williams, this time afloat in a highly fictionalised biopic of her predecessor, silent screen sensation Annette Kellerman? Of course, this being MGM, the plot is just an excuse for some wonderfully ornate Busby Berkeley routines, which today seem hilarious or camp. Williams is as radiant as ever, but the period sense is nonexistent. TS

Esther Williams *Annette Kellerman* • Victor Mature *James Sullivan* • Walter Pidgeon *Frederick Kellerman* • David Brian *Alfred Harper* • Donna Corcoran *Annette, aged ten* • Jesse White *Doc Cronnel* • Maria Tallchief *Pavlova* • Howard Freeman *Aldrich* ■ *Dir* Mervyn LeRoy • *Scr* Everett Freeman

Million Dollar Murder ★★

Drama based on a true story 2004 · Can · Colour · 88min

Drawing on a true-life murder case, Jerry Ciccoritti's TV movie makes the most of its opulent settings, but rarely rises above soap-opera melodrama. Poppy Montgomery gives a bravura performance as the mentally unstable wife whose jealousy of millionaire banker husband David Sutcliffe prompts her to accuse him of adultery, luring electrician Shawn Christian into her demented schemes. Too much story and not enough character. DP Violence.

Poppy Montgomery *Generosa Rand* • David Sutcliffe *Ted Amron* • Shawn Christian *Danny Pelosi* • Maxim Roy *Lindy Fisher* ■ *Dir* Jerry Ciccoritti • *Scr* Robert L Freedman

The Million Pound Note ★★★★ U

Classic satirical comedy 1953 · UK · Colour · 84min

In this lovely comedy, Gregory Peck plays a bankrupt American abroad, who is given the title bank note and told to keep it intact for a month. As the butt of a joke between two rich gamblers, Peck has problems at first, but then finds the note means he never has to spend a penny because his credit rating is so good. Set in Edwardian London, the picture has a lot of charm and humour, owing to Peck's delight in the role and to Ronald Neame's unobtrusive direction. The witty script was based on the story by Mark Twain. AT *DVD*

Gregory Peck *Henry Adams* • Jane Griffiths *Portia Lansdowne* • Ronald Squire *Oliver Montpelier* • Wilfrid Hyde White *Roderick Montpelier* • Joyce Grenfell *Duchess of Cromarty* • Reginald Beckwith *Rock* • Hartley Power *Hastings* • Brian Oulton *Lloyd* ■ *Dir* Ronald Neame • *Scr* Jill Craigie, from the story by Mark Twain

A Million to One ★★★

Drama 1937 · US · BW · 59min

One of the main functions of film is as a recording medium, and this artless, fictionalised true story is of real value as a social record, featuring 1932 Olympic shot-putter Herman Brix as an athlete preparing for an Olympic decathlon. If Brix looks vaguely familiar, it's because he did actually become a film star, initially as Tarzan, and latterly changing his name to Bruce Bennett. A young Joan Fontaine rather sweetly plays a society lass who falls for Brix, and the film has a overall charm, despite static direction and a pace which may well deter all but the hardiest of Olympic fans. TS

Herman Brix [Bruce Bennett] *Johnny Kent* • Joan Fontaine *Joan Stevens* • Reed Howes *Duke Hale* • Monte Blue *John Kent Sr* • Kenneth Harlan *William Stevens* • Suzanne Kaaren *Pat Stanley* • Ed Piel Mac • Ben Hall *Joe* • *Dir* Lynn Shores • *Scr* John T Neville

A Million Ways to Die in the West ★★★★★ 15

Comedy western 2014 · US · Colour · 111min

Take *Blazing Saddles*, throw in a bucketful of modern expletives and you've got a future classic. Director, co-writer and star Seth MacFarlane (*Ted*) plays a frontier nerd who loses his girl (Amanda Seyfried) to the town's wealthy moustache emporium owner (Neil Patrick Harris). MacFarlane's modern view of the Wild West is actually very subtle, even if the laughs seem to hinge mostly on death, sheep and bodily functions – and they come fast and thick... and not to everyone's taste. KK Violence, swearing, sexual references, drug abuse.
DVD *Blu-ray*

Seth MacFarlane *Albert* • Charlize Theron *Anna* • Amanda Seyfried *Louise* • Liam Neeson *Clinch* • Giovanni Ribisi *Edward* • Neil Patrick Harris *Foy* • Sarah Silverman *Ruth* ■ *Dir* Seth MacFarlane • *Scr* Seth MacFarlane, Alec Sulkin, Wellesley Wild • *Cinematographer* Michael Barrett (3)

A Millionaire for Christy ★★★★ U

Romantic comedy 1951 · US · BW · 91min

A good old-fashioned madcap comedy has always been a pleasing way to pass the time and this latter-day screwball provides more than its fair share of laughs. Fred MacMurray gives a droll performance as a folksy radio celebrity who becomes the target of legal secretary Eleanor Parker after he unexpectedly becomes a millionaire. Adding to the fun is MacMurray's on/off wedding with Kay Buckley and his chaotic pursuit of absconded best man Richard Carlson. Ken Englund's script brings plenty of verbal wit to the breezy situations, while director George Marshall outdoes himself with the hilarious beach scene. DP

Fred MacMurray *Peter Ulysses Lockwood* • Eleanor Parker *Christy Sloane* • Richard Carlson *Dr Roland Cook* • Kay Buckley *June Chandler* • Una Merkel *Patsy* • Douglass Dumbrille *AK Thompson* • Raymond Greenleaf *Benjamin Chandler* • Nestor Paiva *Mr Rapello* ■ *Dir* George Marshall • *Scr* Ken Englund, from a story by Robert Harari

The Millionairess ★★★ U

Comedy 1960 · UK · Colour · 86min

An important film for British comedy actor Peter Sellers, this would give him his first real international audience. Sophia Loren was already a Sellers fan and was happy to have him play the Indian doctor opposite her spoiled heiress in this adaptation of the George Bernard Shaw play. Sellers brings a gentle charm to his character and avoids taking the easy route to laughter by racial caricature. Loren is stunning and excels at the light comedy. Romance blossomed on set between the two and perhaps helped to make plausible the unlikely on-screen romance. DF *DVD*

Sophia Loren *Epifania Parerga* • Peter Sellers *Dr Ahmed el Kabir* • Vittorio De Sica *Joe* • Alastair Sim *Sagamore* • Dennis Price *Dr Adrian Bond* • Gary Raymond *Alastair* • Alfie Bass *Fish Curer* • Miriam Karlin *Mrs Joe* ■ *Dir* Anthony Asquith • *Scr* Wolf Mankowitz, Riccardo Aragno, from the play by George Bernard Shaw

Millions ★★★★ 12

Comedy drama 2004 · UK · Colour · 94min

Two schoolboy brothers have a week to spend a load of stolen sterling before the UK switches to the euro in this charming comedy drama from director Danny Boyle. Alex Etel is wonderful as the angel-faced seven-year-old whose hilarious visitations from saints lead him to believe that the mislaid robbery loot that lands in his lap is actually a gift from God. But while he wants to use the money for worthy causes, his nine-year-old brother Lewis McGibbon favours entirely personal consumption, leading to a clash of wills that attracts the wrong kind of attention. Boyle handles the material deftly, delivering a sweet morality tale. SF *DVD*

James Nesbitt *Ronnie Cunningham* • Daisy Donovan *Dorothy* • Alex Etel *Damian Cunningham* • Lewis McGibbon *Anthony Cunningham* • Christopher Fulford *The Man* • Pearce Quigley *Community policeman* • Jane Hogarth *Mum* • Alun Armstrong *St Peter* ■ *Dir* Danny Boyle • *Scr* Frank Cottrell Boyce

Millions like Us ★★★★ U

Second World War drama 1943 · UK · BW · 98min

Frank Launder and Sidney Gilliat are better known for their comedies, but here they produced one of the finest home-front dramas of the Second World War. Adopting the docudramatic approach that characterise many British flag-wavers, the co-directors present a nation pulling together in spite of class differences. The sequences in the factory and at the workers' dormitory are fascinating for the way in which they depict the emergence of both a new kind of woman and a new social order. Patricia Roc and Eric Portman stand out in the excellent cast. DP *DVD*

Eric Portman *Charlie Forbes* • Patricia Roc *Celia Crowson* • Gordon Jackson *Fred Blake* • Anne Crawford *Jennifer Knowles* • Joy Shelton *Phyllis Crowson* • Megs Jenkins *Gwen Price* • Terry Randall *Annie Earnshaw* • Basil Radford *Charters* • Naunton Wayne *Caldicott* ■ *Dir/Scr* Frank Launder, Sidney Gilliat

Milou en Mai ★★★ 15

Black comedy 1989 · Fr · Colour · 102min

Louis Malle's final French film may not stand comparison with his earlier classics, but it is still a polished piece from a director whose willingness to tackle the more controversial aspects of France's recent past established him as one of the most fascinating artists to emerge from the New Wave era of the early 1960s. He handles the family flirting and bickering with assurance, but fumbles the serious and satirical political themes. DP French +subtitles.
DVD

Michel Piccoli *Milou* • Miou-Miou *Camille* • Michel Duchaussoy *Georges* • Dominique Blanc *Claire* • Harriet Walter *Lily* • Bruno Carette *Grimaldi* • François Berléand *Daniel* • Martine Gautier *Adèle* ■ *Dir* Louis Malle • *Scr* Louis Malle, Jean-Claude Carrière • *Music* Stéphane Grappelli [Stephane Grappelli]

Milwaukee, Minnesota ★★★ 15

Comedy drama 2002 · US · Colour · 91min

With Bernd Heinl's camera evocatively capturing the frozen desolation of small-town Wisconsin, this is a quirky film in the true indie tradition. Yet, Allan Mindel is occasionally over-conscious of the need to operate in left field; consequently, the scramble for the affections of unworldly champion ice fisherman Troy Garity by various exploitative predators feels like an assemblage of set pieces rather than a cogent narrative. However, Bruce Dern and Randy Quaid seize the opportunity to act to the hilt, while Alison Folland impresses as a street-smart con artist. DP Swearing, violence. *DVD*

Troy Garity *Albert Burroughs* • Alison Folland *Tuey Stites* • Bruce Dern *Sean McNally* • Mark Harris *Stan Stites* • Debra Monk *Edna Burroughs* • Josh Brolin *Gary* • Holly Woodlawn *Transvestite* • Randy Quaid *Jerry James* ■ *Dir* Allan Mindel • *Scr* RD Murphy [Richard Murphy (2)]

Mimic ★★★ 15

Science-fiction horror 1997 · US · Colour · 101min

Mira Sorvino stars as an entomologist determined to find out what has invaded the New York subway system. It's preposterous stuff, but the tale of oversized insects (a genetically enhanced species developed to eradicate an epidemic-spreading breed of cockroaches) is suitably gruesome and atmospheric thanks to director Guillermo del Toro's dark direction. Sorvino is believably tough, too, and smartly supported by Jeremy Northam, Charles S Dutton and Josh Brolin as potential monster munchies. Two video sequels followed. JB Violence, swearing.
DVD *Blu-ray*

Mira Sorvino *Dr Susan Tyler* • Jeremy Northam *Dr Peter Mann* • Josh Brolin *Josh Maslow* • Giancarlo Giannini *Manny* • Alexander Goodwin *Chuy* • Alix Koromzay *Remy* • F Murray Abraham *Doctor Gates* • Charles S Dutton *Leo* ■ *Dir* Guillermo del Toro • *Scr* Matthew Robbins, Guillermo del Toro, from a story by Matthew Robbins, Guillermo del Toro, Donald A Wollheim

Min and Bill ★★★

Comedy drama 1930 · US · BW · 66min

Dated but of considerable historical interest, this comedy drama was MGM's biggest hit of 1930 and won Marie Dressler an Academy Award for best actress. Dressler portrays the hard-boiled owner of a waterfront hotel who kills to protect the waif she has raised (Dorothy Jordan). Cast as her fisherman sweetheart, Wallace Beery registered so well opposite her that they were teamed in another smash hit, *Tugboat Annie*. AE

Marie Dressler *Min Divot* • Wallace Beery *Bill* • Dorothy Jordan *Nancy Smith* • Marjorie Rambeau *Bella Pringle* • Donald Dillaway *Dick Cameron* • DeWitt Jennings *Groot* ■ *Dir* George Hill • *Scr* Frances Marion, Marion Jackson, from the novel *Dark Star* by Lorna Moon

Mina Tannenbaum ★★★★ 12
Drama   1993 · Fr/Bel/Neth · Colour · 123min

Martine Dugowson made her directorial debut with this tragicomic rites-of-passage story. Tackling such diverse topics as heredity, conformity, compatibility, Jewishness and the nature of friendship in a competitive world, the film employs an impressive range of cinematic devices, including jump cuts, speeches direct to camera, Truffaut-like movie references and trick photography. Romane Bohringer and Elsa Zylberstein are superb as the lifelong friends, while Jean-Philippe Ecoffey stands out among the dreadful men they encounter over the years. DP French +subtitles. Swearing.

Romane Bohringer *Mina Tannenbaum* • Elsa Zylberstein *Ethel Bénégui* • Nils Tavernier *François* • Stéphane Slima *Didier* • Florence Thomassin *The cousin* • Chantal Krief *Daisy* • Jany Gastaldi *Gisèle* • Jean-Philippe Ecoffey *Jacques Dana* ■ *Dir/Scr* Martine Dugowson

The Mind Benders ★★ 12
Science-fiction drama   1963 · UK · BW · 104min

Ahead of its time in 1963 and now hopelessly dated, this melodrama about spying, brainwashing and Oxford dons was ill-fated from the start. Dirk Bogarde is just one of the scientists who spends a few hours in an isolation tank and ends up even more unpleasant than he was before. The film boasts some fine performances – not to mention the screen debut of Edward Fox – but Basil Dearden's direction is far too straightforward for such a bizarre story. AT
DVD

Dirk Bogarde *Dr Henry Longman* • Mary Ure *Oonagh Longman* • John Clements *Major Hall* • Michael Bryant *Dr Tate* • Wendy Craig *Annabelle* • Harold Goldblatt *Professor Sharpey* • Geoffrey Keen *Calder* • Terry Palmer *Norman* • Edward Fox *Stewart* ■ *Dir* Basil Dearden • *Scr* James Kennaway

The Mind of Mr Soames ★★★★
Science-fiction thriller
1970 · UK · Colour · 97min

A thought-provoking psychological study of human behaviour, director Alan Cooke's sensitive work signalled an exciting new direction for Amicus, Hammer's nearest British rival, as they entered the horror-swamped 1970s. Terence Stamp is brought out of a 30-year coma by neurosurgeon Robert Vaughn and, following a crash course in the ways of society, is sent into the terrifying outside world. In one of his finest roles, Stamp is outstanding; his subtle character shadings ooze a captivating truth. An overlooked, intelligent thriller. AJ

Terence Stamp *John Soames* • Robert Vaughn (1) *Dr Michael Bergen* • Nigel Davenport *Dr Maitland* • Donal Donnelly *Dr Joe Allen* • Christian Roberts *Thomas Fleming* • Vickery Turner *Naomi* • Scott Forbes *Richard Bannerman* • Judy Parfitt *Jenny Bannerman* ■ *Dir* Alan Cooke (1) • *Scr* John Hale, Edward Simpson, from the novel by Charles Eric Maine

The Mind Reader ★★★
Drama   1933 · US · BW · 68min

Warren William stars as a failed carnival grifter who turns fake clairvoyant, gets into trouble, and then tries to go straight for the sake of the wife who believes in him. This is a rather curious but watchable mix of satirical humour, sentimentality and near melodrama, distinguished by a first-rate performance from William and an excellent supporting cast, including the classy Constance Cummings as the loyal wife. RK

Warren William *Chandra Chandler/Dr Munro* • Constance Cummings *Sylvia* • Allen Jenkins *Frank* • Natalie Moorhead *Mrs Austin* • Mayo Methot *Jenny* • Clarence Muse *Sam* ■ *Dir* Roy Del Ruth • *Scr* Robert Lord, Wilson Mizner, from a story by Vivian Crosby

The Mind Snatchers ★★ 15
Drama   1972 · US · Colour · 92min

In this slow-moving drama, army scientists use controversial shock therapy on overly aggressive soldiers who find it difficult to conform to army life. Ronny Cox and a pre-stardom Christopher Walken play two victims who respond to the pleasure-centre brain treatment in differing ways. Despite powerful moments, the movie never fully conquers its stage play origins, although it does manage to put across the trauma inherent in the experimental euphoria. AJ
DVD

Christopher Walken *Private James Reese* • Joss Ackland *Dr Frederick* • Ralph Meeker *Major* • Ronny Cox *Miles* • Marco St John *Orderly* ■ *Dir* Bernard Girard • *Scr* Ron Whyte, from the play by Dennis Reardon

Mindhunters ★★ 15
Crime thriller
2003 · US/Neth/UK/Fin · Colour · 101min

A group of FBI trainees is sent to a remote island for an elaborate exercise by their predictably unorthodox mentor, Val Kilmer. They are joined at the last minute by police officer LL Cool J and new recruit Christian Slater, who falls victim to a possible serial killer. But the characters are so bland and Renny Harlin's direction so full of meaningless slow-motion gloss that it's difficult to care. GM Violence, swearing.
DVD

James Todd Smith [LL Cool J] *Gabe Jensen* • Jonny Lee Miller *Lucas Harper* • Kathryn Morris *Sara Moore* • Patricia Velasquez *Nicole Willis* • Val Kilmer *Jake Harris* • Christian Slater *JD Reston* ■ *Dir* Renny Harlin • *Scr* Wayne Kramer, Kevin Brodbin, from a story by Kramer

Mindscape ★★ 15
Psychological thriller
2013 · US/Sp/Fr · Colour · 94min

Director Jorge Dorado makes his feature debut with a film that encroaches on *Inception* territory as it explores the darker recesses of the mind. Mark Strong stars as a psychic who is called in to help hunger-striking teenager Taissa Farmiga. But during their sessions together, sinister secrets from her past come to light. Any attempt to build atmosphere is let down by the clichéd dialogue, and Strong in particular fails to bring any intensity to his role. SaO *DVD*

Mark Strong *John* • Taissa Farmiga *Anna* • Saskia Reeves *Michelle Greene* • Richard Dillane *Robert* ■ *Dir* Jorge Dorado • *Scr* Guy Holmes, from a story by Guy & Martha Holmes

Mine Own Executioner ★★★
Psychological drama   1947 · UK · BW · 104min

A nerve-shattered former prisoner of war, who has tried to kill the wife he loves, is treated by a lay psychiatrist with problems of his own. This is a brave and intelligent piece of film-making, which allowed Nigel Balchin to adapt his novel with almost no box-office concessions. The psychiatrist becomes Canadian to suit American actor Burgess Meredith, but he plays the part brilliantly. Under the direction of Anthony Kimmins, Kieron Moore is also excellent as the disturbed man. The climax on the ledge of a high building will make your feet tingle. AE *DVD*

Burgess Meredith *Felix Milne* • Dulcie Gray *Patricia Milne* • Kieron Moore *Adam Lucian* • Barbara White *Molly Lucian* • Christine Norden *Barbara Edge* • John Laurie *Dr James Garsten* • Michael Shepley *Peter Edge* • Lawrence Hanray *Dr Lefage* ■ *Dir* Anthony Kimmins • *Scr* Nigel Balchin, from his novel

Minions ★★★ U
Animated comedy   2015 · US · Colour · 87min

Despicable Me's lovable yellow sidekicks get their own movie in this prequel that sends a trio of intrepid Minions to Sixties London in search of a truly evil leader. There's very little point to it, but it's hard to deny that the charmingly stupid leads and some clever comedy make for an enjoyable experience, aided in no small part by a killer classic rock soundtrack. Of the new additions, Sandra Bullock throws herself into voicing maniacally insecure villain Scarlett Overkill, while Jon Hamm gets some of the biggest laughs as her sidekick/husband. JL *DVD* *BL* *3D*

Sandra Bullock *Scarlett Overkill* • Pierre Coffin *Minions Kevin, Bob and Stuart* • Jon Hamm *Herb Overkill* • Michael Keaton *Walter Nelson* • Allison Janney *Madge Nelson* • Steve Coogan *Professor Flux/Tower Guard* ■ *Dir* Kyle Balda, Pierre Coffin • *Scr* Brian Lynch

Ministry of Fear ★★★ PG
Spy drama   1945 · US · BW · 82min

Paramount snapped up the rights to Graham Greene's novel because they liked the title. The plot that came with it was largely disposable, and the book was turned into a pursuit thriller starring Ray Milland as a mental patient who has spent two years in an insane asylum for murdering his wife. Fritz Lang turns this into a creepily effective work, full of bravura set pieces and subtle suggestions, and somehow creating, in Hollywood, an impression of the London Blitz. AT *DVD*

Ray Milland *Stephen Neale* • Marjorie Reynolds *Carla Hilfe* • Carl Esmond *Willi Hilfe* • Hillary Brooke *Mrs Bellane* • Percy Waram *Inspector Prentice* • Dan Duryea *Cost/Travers* • Alan Napier *Dr Forrester* • Erskine Sanford *Mr Rennit* ■ *Dir* Fritz Lang • *Scr* Seton I Miller, from the novel by Graham Greene

The Miniver Story ★ U
Drama   1950 · UK/US · BW · 104min

MGM's *Mrs Miniver* (1942) won six Oscars and was a famous beacon of patriotic light in the darkest days of the Second World War. This disastrously ill-judged sequel brings back the stars, with a new cast playing the now grown-up Miniver children. Directed by HC Potter, this irrelevant follow-up is a second-rate soap opera, bleak and depressing. RK

Greer Garson *Kay Miniver* • Walter Pidgeon *Clem Miniver* • John Hodiak *Spike Romway* • Leo Genn *Steve Brunswick* • Cathy O'Donnell *Judy Miniver* • Reginald Owen *Mr Foley* • Anthony Bushell *Dr Kanesley* • Peter Finch *Polish officer* ■ *Dir* HC Potter • *Scr* Ronald Millar, George Froeschel, from characters by Jan Struther

Minnie and Moskowitz ★★★ 12
Comedy drama   1971 · US · Colour · 112min

Two sad and lonely people meet and fall in love against the hectic, heedless backdrop of the big city. Minnie (Gena Rowlands) works in a museum; Moskowitz (Seymour Cassel) is a car park attendant. The setting, Los Angeles, is important, since the movie is about the ribbon of dreams that people tie up their lives with. As always with writer/director John Cassavetes, the film goes out of its way to show how different it is from conventional Hollywood fare. AT

Gena Rowlands *Minnie Moore* • Seymour Cassel *Seymour Moskowitz* • Val Avery *Zelmo* • Timothy Carey *Morgan* • Katherine Cassavetes *Sheba Moskowitz* • Elizabeth Deering *Girl* • Elsie Ames *Florence* • Lady Rowlands *Georgia Moore* ■ *Dir/Scr* John Cassavetes

Minor Mishaps ★★★★ 15
Drama   2002 · Den · Colour · 104min

With its improvised approach to dysfunction, there's more than a hint of Mike Leigh about Annette K Olesen's directorial debut. Yet, this Danish domestic drama also contains elements of those Dogme favourites, *Festen* and *Italian for Beginners*, as the various everyday and extraordinary crises facing a working-class Copenhagen family combine both the pugnacity of a soap and the geniality of a sitcom. Focusing on the frustrations of middle age, it also succeeds in presenting widower Jorgen Kill's unprepossessing offspring – reclusive chef Maria Würgler Rich, overworked contractor Henrik Prip and eccentric artist, Jannie Faurschou – without ever demonising or patronising them. A minor triumph. DP Danish +subtitles. *DVD*

Jorgen Kill *John Olsen, father* • Maria Würgler Rich *Marianne Olsen, younger daughter* • Jannie Faurschou *Eva Olsen, older daughter* • Henrik Prip *Tom Olsen, John's son* • Jesper Christensen *Soren Olsen, John's brother* • Karen-Lise Mynster *Hanne, Soren's wife* • Tina Gylling Mortensen *Ellen* • Julie Wieth *Lisbeth, Tom's wife* • Vigga Bro *Ulla Olsen, mother* ■ *Dir* Annette K Olesen • *Scr* Kim Fupz Aakeson

Minority Report ★★★★ 12
Futuristic action thriller
2002 · US · Colour · 139min

Steven Spielberg's masterfully sleek vision of the future is an awesome mix of skewed science fiction, twisty Hitchcock-style thrills, stunning blue-grey tinged photography and outstanding design. Set in 2054, when police use precognitive mutants to detect homicides before they're committed, the plot sees top "Pre-cop" Tom Cruise identified as a future killer and forced to go on the run to discover why he's been set up and by whom. Adroitly realised by Spielberg, this is what sci-fi cinema should always be about but rarely is – mind-boggling images and a literate, witty script skilfully working together in perfect harmony. AJ Some violence, swearing, drug abuse, brief sex scenes. *DVD* *BL*

Tom Cruise *Chief John Anderton* • Colin Farrell (2) *Danny Witwer* • Samantha Morton *Agatha* • Max von Sydow *Director Lamar Burgess* • Lois Smith *Dr Iris Hineman* • Peter Stormare *Dr Solomon Eddie* • Tim Blake Nelson *Gideon* ■ *Dir* Steven Spielberg • *Scr* Scott Frank, Jon Cohen, from the story by Philip K Dick

The Minus Man ★★★★ 15
Psychological thriller
1999 · US · Colour · 106min

This is a low-key tension-builder of the unbearable kind. The pleasant boy-next-door manner of drifter Owen Wilson hides the fact that he's a serial killer. It's when he lodges with troubled marrieds Brian Cox and Mercedes Ruehl that fate selects his next mark, and his precarious union with postal worker Janeane Garofalo suggests his poisoning days might be numbered. A very creepy, jet-black psychological thriller, this is made more unsettling by having Wilson meditate on his actions in comically toned voiceover. A true original steeped in macabre chills and tightly-coiled emotions. AJ Swearing, drug abuse. *DVD*

Owen Wilson *Vann Siegert* • Janeane Garofalo *Ferrin* • Brian Cox (1) *Doug* • Mercedes Ruehl *Jane* • Dwight Yoakam *Blair* • Dennis Haysbert *Graves* • Sheryl Crow *Caspar* • Eric Mabius *Gene* ■ *Dir* Hampton Fancher • *Scr* Hampton Fancher, from the novel by Lew McCreary

Mio in the Land of Faraway ★★ U
Fantasy adventure
1987 · Swe/USSR/Nor · Colour · 94min

This is the kind of tosh that gives sword and sorcery a bad name. Young Nicholas Pickard's bid to defeat evil knight Christopher Lee has all the necessary quest ingredients. But director Vladimir Grammatikov assembles them too slowly and Lee arrives too late to revive flagging interest. Lacking in charm, but suffused with shoestring mediocrity, it's Tolkein for *Tweenie* tots. DP

Nicholas Pickard *Mio* • Christian Bale *Yum-Yum* • Christopher Lee *Wicked knight* • Timothy Bottoms *King* • Susannah York *Weaver woman* ■ *Dir* Vladimir Grammatikov • *Scr* William Aldridge, from the novel *Mio, My Son* by Astrid Lindgren

The Miracle ★★★★ 15
Drama   1990 · UK · Colour · 92min

Set in a small Irish seaside town, Neil Jordan's wonderful drama is often overlooked. Teenagers Lorraine Pilkington and Niall Byrne spend most of their time imagining the secret lives of their neighbours. Then glamorous actress Beverly D'Angelo turns up and pulls them into a real world of romance and mystery. Deliciously affecting, this was a small-scale comeback for Jordan after a couple of American disasters. JB

Beverly D'Angelo *Renee* • Donal McCann *Sam* • Niall Byrne *Jimmy* • Lorraine Pilkington *Rose* • JG Devlin *Mr Beausang* • Cathleen Delaney *Miss Strange* ■ *Dir/Scr* Neil Jordan

Miracle ★★★ PG
Sports drama based on a true story
2004 · US · Colour · 130min

You don't need to be a sports fan to enjoy this real-life hockey drama. A rousing strength-through-adversity tale, it shows how a team of American underdogs managed to defeat the seemingly invincible Soviet Union side in the 1980 Winter Olympics. The gruelling training and accompanying emotional fall-out are compelling, giving the movie a very human core. Kurt Russell is particularly good as unorthodox coach Herb Brooks, but as strong as his performance is, it's the well-shot action sequences that steal the show. SF *DVD*

Kurt Russell *Herb Brooks* • Patricia Clarkson *Patty Brooks* • Noah Emmerich *Craig Patrick* • Sean McCann *Walter Bush* • Kenneth Welsh *Doc Nagobads* • Eddie Cahill *Jim Craig* • Patrick O'Brien Demsey *Mike Eruzione* • Michael Mantenuto *Jack O'Callahan* • Nathan West *Rob McClanahan* ■ *Dir* Gavin O'Connor • *Scr* Eric Guggenheim

Miracle in Milan ★★★ U
Fantasy drama
1950 · It · BW · 92min

Vittorio De Sica's follow-up to the internationally acclaimed *Bicycle Thieves* is a modern biblical parable that begins with the words, "Once upon a time". Abandoned in a cabbage patch, the hero, Toto, is brought up by a kindly old lady. The boy grows up to become one of life's saints, and the poverty that surrounds him in the shanty town outside Milan only sharpens his faith in human nature. Like a piece of 16th-century art seen through a neorealist lens, this will probably seem very corny and simplistic to modern audiences. AT Italian +subtitles. *DVD* *BD*

Branduani Gianni *Little Toto, aged 11* • Francesco Golisano *Good Toto* • Paolo Stoppa *Bad Rappi* • Emma Gramatica *Old Lolatta* • Guglielmo Barnabo *Mobbi the rich man* ■ *Dir* Vittorio De Sica • *Scr* Cesare Zavattini, Vittorio De Sica, Suso Cecchi D'Amico, Mario Chiari, Adolfo Franci, from the story *Toto Il Buono* by Cesare Zavattini

Miracle in Soho ★★ U
Drama
1957 · UK · Colour · 97min

Emeric Pressburger's screenwriting outings in Britain without Michael Powell were few and far between, and this dour little drama might go some way to explaining why. Pressburger's script aims for the sort of semi-documentary tone that had become fashionable at the time, but this romance between a roadsweeper and an Italian girl needed a little local colour to buck it up, not grey sociological pronouncements. The grim images of Soho do have a certain historical value, however, DP

John Gregson *Michael Morgan* • Belinda Lee *Julia Gozzi* • Cyril Cusack *Sam Bishop* • Rosalie Crutchley *Mafalda Gozzi* • Peter Illing *Papa Gozzi* • Marie Burke *Mama Gozzi* • Ian Bannen *Filippo Gozzi* • Brian Bedford *Johnny* ■ *Dir* Julian Amyes • *Scr* Emeric Pressburger • *Cinematographer* Christopher Challis

Miracle in the Rain ★★ U
Romantic drama
1956 · US · BW · 107min

Fine performances from stars Jane Wyman (as a timid office girl) and the ever-dependable Van Johnson (as an extrovert soldier) keep this soapy melodrama watchable, but its ending takes an awful lot of swallowing. Director Rudolph Maté sketches a credible working class New York, unusual for a period in American cinema when gloss ruled. The film is well made, but it comes across as either very moving or rather tacky. TS

Jane Wyman *Ruth Wood* • Van Johnson *Arthur Hugenon* • Peggie Castle *Millie Kranz* • Fred Clark *Stephen Jalonkik* • Eileen Heckart *Grace Ullman* • Josephine Hutchinson *Agnes Wood* • Alan King

Sgt Gil Parker • Barbara Nichols *Arleene* ■ *Dir* Rudolph Maté • *Scr* Ben Hecht, from a novel by Ben Hecht

The Miracle Maker ★★★ U
Biblical animation
1999 · UK/Rus · Colour · 86min

This co-production uses clay puppets and Wallace and Gromit-style techniques to tell the tale of Christ's life, his eventual crucifixion, resurrection and ascension. The puppets are beautifully made, if a tad creepy, while the stop-motion animation is state of the art, especially during crowd scenes that feature dozens of little figures pootling about. However, this is somewhat dull and on the reverential side. DA *DVD*

Ralph Fiennes *Jesus* • Michael Bryant *God/The Doctor* • Julie Christie *Rachel* • Richard E Grant *John the Baptist* • Ian Holm *Pilate* • William Hurt *Jairus* • Bob Peck *Joseph of Arimathea* • Miranda Richardson *Mary Magdalene* • Antony Sher *Ben Azra* • David Thewlis *Judas* ■ *Dir* Derek Hayes, Stanislav Sokolov • *Scr* Murray Watts

Miracle Mile ★★★ 15
Science-fiction drama
1989 · US · Colour · 83min

Anthony Edwards plays a musician who accidentally intercepts a phone call in which a man reveals that a nuclear Armageddon is on its way, with an hour to go before the world's destruction. Writer/director Steve De Jarnatt specifically zeroes in on Edwards to capture the impact of the bad news. The man is caught between his moral responsibilities and his desire to see his new love (Mare Winningham) one last time. JF

Anthony Edwards *Harry Washello* • Mare Winningham *Julie Peters* • John Agar *Ivan Peters* • Lou Hancock *Lucy Peters* • Mykelti Williamson *Wilson* • Kelly Minter *Kelly Jo Minter* *Charlotta* • Kurt Fuller *Gerstead* • Denise Crosby *Landa* ■ *Dir/Scr* Steve De Jarnatt

The Miracle of Bern ★★★★ PG
Sports drama based on a true story
2003 · Ger · Colour · 113min

In 1954, the West German team staged one of the most remarkable comebacks in World Cup football history. Having been battered 8-3 by Hungary in the group stages, they exacted their revenge by beating them 3-2 in the final held in Bern, Switzerland. Director Sönke Wortmann satisfyingly relates the story of the unexpected triumph, but this is not just a feel-good sports movie. t is also a moving domestic drama, as young footie fan Louis Klamroth tries to get to know his father who has just returned from a Soviet labour camp, 11 years after being taken prisoner in the war. The performances are splendid, but even more impress ve are the soccer sequences. DP German +subtitles. *DVD*

Peter Lohmeyer *Richard Lubanski* • Louis Klamroth *Matthias Lubanski* • Lucas Gregorowicz *Paul Ackermann* • Katharina Wackernagel *Annette Ackermann* • Johanna Gastdorf *Christa Lubanski* • Mirko Lang *Bruno Lubanski* • Birthe Wolter *Ingrid Lubanski* • Sascha Göpel *Helmut Rahn* ■ *Dir* Sönke Wortmann • *Scr* Sönke Wortmann, Rochus Hahn

The Miracle of Dommatina ★★
Drama
2009 · US · Colour · 93min

Car trouble in Mexico leads an LA couple to reassess their personal problems in this far-fetched though heartening drama. Teri Polo and Jason Priestley play the childless husband and wife whose obsession with having a baby is put into perspective after they break down in a small town. Soon the locale's vitality is transforming their relationship. The downbeat drama of the earlier scenes and a stream of button-pushing sentimentality make way for inspiring positivity and the inevitable happy ending. SF

Jason Priestley *Pete Stanhope* • Teri Polo *Donna Stanhope* • Cheech Marin *Cheech "Cheech" Marin* *Father Arturo* • Shalim Ortiz *Juan* • Rebeka Montoya *Magdalena* ■ *Dir* Steve Gomer • *Scr* Donald Davenport

The Miracle of Morgan's Creek ★★★★★
Classic comedy
1943 · US · BW · 98min

With its controversial (at the time) subject matter, the real miracle was that this film was allowed to be made in the first place. Writer/director Preston Sturges thumbed his nose at the Hays Office (administrators of the film censorship code) delivering a fast-paced story of a girl (Betty Hutton) who finds herself pregnant after attending a GI party and has no idea of the identity of the father from the men present. Sturges was the great Hollywood satirist of the 1940s and he made a slew of trailblazing films that remain some of the period's finest. This is a blistering comedy with marvellous moments and terrific interplay between the leads. DF

Eddie Bracken *Norval Jones* • Betty Hutton *Trudy Kockenlocker* • Diana Lynn *Emmy Kockenlocker* • William Demarest *Officer Kockenlocker* • Porter Hall *Jacob Woodson, Justice of the Peace* • McGinty [Brian Donlevy] *Governor McGinty* • The Boss [Akim Tamiroff] *Boss* ■ *Dir/Scr* Preston Sturges • *Cinematographer* John F Seitz

The Miracle of Our Lady of Fatima ★★★ U
Religious drama
1952 · US · Colour · 102min

Never approaching the Oscar-winning standard of *The Song of Bernadette*, this is, nevertheless, a sincere account of the 1917 apparition of the Virgin Mary at the Cova of Iria outside the Portuguese village of Fatima. The trio claim to have heard prophecies from a "lady in the sky" on the 13th of six consecutive months. But even though director John Brahm makes such moments as the cure of the lame and blind truly inspirational, the reverential approach will be harder to take for many than the episode's religious implications. DP

Gilbert Roland *Hugo Da Silva* • Susan Whitney *Lucia Dos Santos* • Sherry Jackson *Jacinta Marto* • Sammy Ogg *Francisco Marto* • Angela Clark *Maria Rosa* • Frank Silvera *Arturo Dos Santos* • Jay Novello *Antonio* • Richard Hale *Father Ferreira* ■ *Dir* John Brahm • *Scr* Cran Wilbur, James O'Hanlon

The Miracle of the Bells ★★★ U
Drama
1948 · US · BW · 119min

This is definitely one for those who like religious themes tied up in a neat parcel and featuring bearded men on fluffy clouds. Frank Sinatra, Fred MacMurray and Alida Valli star in an undemanding slice of whimsy, in which movie star Valli is laid to rest in her mining home town to rather dramatic effect. It's all a shade too sugary and daft, with stereotypes firmly in place, but still charming. SH *DVD*

Fred MacMurray *Bill Dunnigan* • Valli [Alida Valli] *Olga Treskovna* • Frank Sinatra *Father Paul* • Lee J Cobb *Marcus Harris* • Jim Nolan *Ted Jones* • Veronika Pataky *Anna Klovna* • Philip Ahn *Ming Gow* ■ *Dir* Irving Pichel • *Scr* Ben Hecht, Quentin Reynolds, DeWitt Bodeen, from the novel by Russell Janney

Miracle of the White Stallions ★★★ U
Wartime adventure based on a true story
1963 · US · Colour · 89min

In this real-life adventure, the famous white Lippizaner stallions of the Spanish Riding School in Vienna are evacuated to the countryside during the final days of the war. The head of the school leads the horses to safety and puts on a show for General Patton, thus securing American protection from the advancing Russians. The Disney brand might induce a certain cynicism, but this is a fairly straight, sugar-free yarn. AT

Robert Taylor [] *Colonel Podhajsky* • Lilli Palmer *Verena Podhajsky* • Curt Jurgens *General Tellheim* • Eddie Albert *Rider Otto* • James Franciscus *Major Hoffman* • John Larch *General Patton* ■ *Dir* Arthur Hiller • *Scr* AJ Carothers, from the non-fiction book *The Dancing White Stallions of Vienna* by Colonel Alois Podhajsky

Miracle on Main Street ★★★
Seasonal drama
1940 · US · BW · 76min

A tight little Columbia programme filler, this derives great strength from the performance of Margo, who stars as a dance-hall girl who finds an abandoned baby on Christmas Eve in a Los Angeles alley. Director Steve Sekely keeps sentiment at bay, and Jane Darwell and Veda Ann Borg provide potent cameos. TS

Margo *Maria Porter* • Walter Abel *Jim Foreman* • William Collier Sr *Doctor Miles* • Jane Darwell *Mrs Herman* • Lyle Talbot *Dick Porter* • Wynne Gibson *Sade "Coochie" Blake* • Veda Ann Borg *Flo* • Pat Flaherty *Detective* ■ *Dir* Steve Sekely • *Scr* Frederick Jackson, from a story by Samuel Ornitz, Boris Ingster

Miracle on the 17th Green ★★
Drama
1999 · US · Colour · 100min

The likeable, prolific Robert Urich holds this dubious midlife crisis TV drama together. He plays the 50-something advertising executive who picks himself up after being fired and pursues his lifelong dream on the Seniors pro golf tour. Director Michael Switzer never comes to grips with the emotional themes of the movie and seems happiest shooting the golfing footage. DP

Robert Urich *Mitch McKinley* • Meredith Baxter *Susan McKinley* • Donnelly Rhodes *Peter McKinley* • Matthew Walker *Father McNaughton* ■ *Dir* Michael Switzer • *Scr* Wesley Bishop, from the novel by James Patterson, Peter De Jong

Miracle on 34th Street ★★★★★ U
Seasonal comedy fantasy
1947 · US · BW · 96min

Natalie Wood is a jaded youngster who knows there's no such thing as Father Christmas because her mother, Maureen O'Hara, organises a New York department store's yearly parade, and Wood has always seen Santa played by drunken old men. The great plot was rightly awarded Oscars for best screenplay and original story, while Edmund Gwenn also won as best supporting actor. Indeed, Gwenn became so identified with the role of Kris Kringle that every holiday he found himself hired to hand out presents at the houses of such Hollywood notables as Louis B Mayer. Utterly beguiling. TS *DVD*

Maureen O'Hara *Doris Walker* • John Payne *Fred Gailey* • Edmund Gwenn *Kris Kringle* • Natalie Wood *Susan Walker* • Gene Lockhart *Judge Henry X Harper* • Porter Hall *Mr Sawyer* • William Frawley *Charles Halloran* • Jerome Cowan *Thomas Mara* • Philip Tonge *Mr Shellhammer* • James Seay *Dr Pierce* ■ *Dir* George Seaton • *Scr* George Seaton, from a story by Valentine Davies

Miracle on 34th Street ★★★ U
Christmas fantasy
1994 · US · Colour · 109min

Richard Attenborough plays Kriss Kringle in this remake of the classic 1947 fantasy. He positively twinkles in the role in an attempt to convince moppet Mara Wilson and the audience, that he is a living legend. Yet, although the film as a whole is a much more glamorous affair, and Wilson and Elizabeth Perkins as her mother are charming, it does lack some of the magic of the original. TH *DVD*

Richard Attenborough *Kriss Kringle* • Elizabeth Perkins *Dorey Walker* • Dylan McDermott *Bryan Bedford* • JT Walsh *Ed Collins* • Mara Wilson *Susan Walker* • James Remar *Jack Duff* • Jane Leeves *Alberta Leonard* • Simon Jones *Shellhammer* ■ *Dir* Les Mayfield • *Scr* John Hughes, from the 1947 film, from a story by Valentine Davies

The Miracle Woman ★★★
Drama
1931 · US · BW · 90min

Its theme of fake evangelism made this extraordinary early work from director Frank Capra a controversial film in its day, based as it was on a play featuring a thinly disguised portrait of popular evangelist Aimée Semple McPherson. Barbara Stanwyck gives a remarkable performance, combining rare delicacy with great strength of purpose. Interestingly, this movie was produced in the days before the Hays Code censored such dialogue and sequences dealing with religious issues. Only a few years later such content would not be deemed fit material for US audiences. TS

Barbara Stanwyck *Florence "Faith" Fallon* • David Manners *John Carson* • Sam Hardy *Bob Hornsby* • Beryl Mercer *Mrs Higgins* • Russell Hopton *Bill Welford* • Charles Middleton *Simpson* • Eddie Boland *Collins* • Thelma Hill *Gussie* ■ *Dir* Frank R Capra [Frank Capra] • *Scr* Dorothy Howell, Jo Swerling, from the play *Bless You Sister* by John Meehan

The Miracle Worker ★★★★★ PG

Biographical drama   1962 · US · BW · 102min

This is a marvellously moving biopic about the youth of deaf, dumb and blind Helen Keller, and her remarkable teacher Annie Sullivan. There are outstanding Oscar-winning performances from Anne Bancroft as Sullivan and Patty Duke as Keller, while Arthur Penn's direction is superb, remaining solidly unsentimental throughout. Unsettling and thought-provoking, this is a fine American humanitarian work, brilliantly photographed in harsh black and white by Ernesto Caparros. Duke later played the Sullivan role in a 1979 TV movie remake. TS *DVD*

Anne Bancroft *Annie Sullivan* • Patty Duke *Helen Keller* • Victor Jory *Captain Keller* • Inga Swenson *Kate Keller* • Andrew Prine *James Keller* • Kathleen Comegys *Aunt Ev* • Beah Richards *Viney* ■ *Dir* Arthur Penn • *Scr* William Gibson, from his play, from the non-fiction book *The Story of My Life* by Helen Keller

Miracles ★★ PG

Comedy   1985 · US · Colour · 83min

In this predictable, frantic caper, Teri Garr and her ex-husband Tom Conti suffer various indignities in the South American desert. Conti gives us his floppy-haired, shyly charming act, while Garr, a passably talented actress on occasion, is once again handed a script requiring little more than constant hysterics. If you're in a tolerant mood, this piece of visual chewing gum may amuse. SH

Tom Conti *Roger* • Teri Garr *Jean* • Christopher Lloyd *Harry* • Paul Rodriguez *Juan* • Adalberto Martinez *Kayum, witch doctor* • Jorge Russek *Judge* • Paco Morayta *Sgt Gomez* ■ *Dir/Scr* Jim Kouf

Miracles for Sale ★★

Murder mystery   1939 · US · BW · 71min

This is a change of pace for director Tod Browning, best known for controversial cult favourite *Freaks*, with a story about a magician (Robert Young) who gets involved in some supernatural murders. Browning plays it fairly straight in his final film but builds the tension nicely, aided by the capable performances of his cast. JF

Robert Young (1) *Michael Morgan* • Florence Rice *Judy Barclay* • Frank Craven *Dad Morgan* • Henry Hull *Dave Duvallo* • Lee Bowman *La Clair* • Cliff Clark *Inspector Gavigan* • Astrid Allwyn *Zelma La Clair* • Walter Kingsford *Colonel Watrous* ■ *Dir* Tod Browning • *Scr* Harry Ruskin, Marion Parsonnet, James Edward Grant, from the novel *Death from a Top Hat* by Clayton Rawston

Miracles from Heaven ★★ 12A

Drama based on a true story
2016 · US · Colour · 108min

Though unquestionably a film of faith, *Miracles from Heaven* doesn't ram its religiosity down your throat. Not until a horribly over-fluffy finale, that is. Based on real events, it's the story of a 10-year-old Texan girl whose potentially fatal digestive illness defies all medical treatments. The drama takes its time. It feels long, too, but it is well made and acted (led by Jennifer Garner), and director Patricia Riggen (*The 33*) explores guts and goodness as much as it does grace and God. Until that over-the-top ending, anyway. DA

Jennifer Garner *Christy Beam* • Kylie Rogers *Anna Beam* • Martin Henderson *Kevin Beam* • John Carroll Lynch *Pastor Scott* • Eugenio Derbez *Dr Nurko* • Queen Latifah *Angela* ■ *Dir* Patricia Riggen • *Scr* Randy Brown, from the non-fiction book by Christy Beam

Mirage ★★★★

Mystery thriller   1965 · US · Colour · 108min

Corkscrew plots come no screwier than in this corker. The story is unfathomable, and it's not certain whether that's deliberate or simply a symptom of poor film-making. Gregory Peck stars as an amnesiac who finds himself in a variety of tense situations, aided, abetted and threatened by a fine supporting cast of spooks. One could regard this paranoid nightmare as a reflection of director Edward Dmytryk's experience of the Hollywood blacklist. This was remade three years later as *Jigsaw*. AT

Gregory Peck *David Stillwell* • Diane Baker *Sheila* • Walter Matthau *Ted Caselle* • Kevin McCarthy *Josephson* • Jack Weston *Lester* • Leif Erickson *Major Crawford* • Walter Abel *Charles Calvin* • George Kennedy *Willard* ■ *Dir* Edward Dmytryk • *Scr* Peter Stone, from the novel *Fallen Angel* by Walter Ericson [Howard Fast]

Miral ★★ 12

Drama
2010 · Fr/Is/It/Ind · Colour and BW · 107min

Envisaged as a humanitarian take on the Israeli-Palestinian divide, this sprawling would-be epic is quickly sunk by flat direction, stilted dialogue and *very* ill-advised casting. The film is about Palestinian rebel Miral (Freida Pinto), but throws in a history lesson about the displacement of Palestinian children after the founding of Israel in 1948 before following the heroine from childhood to her teenage political awakening in the late 1980s. Considering the director is Julian Schnabel (*The Diving-Bell and the Butterfly*), you would expect a subtle and complex piece of work; instead, *Miral* develops a clumsy, brutally simplistic monotone, and Pinto just doesn't have the acting chops to carry the last third. DW Violence, swearing. *DVD*

Freida Pinto *Miral* • Willem Dafoe *Eddie* • Vanessa Redgrave *Bertha Spafford* • Alexander Siddig *Jamal* • Hiam Abbass *Hind Husseini* • Omar Metwally *Hani* ■ *Dir* Julian Schnabel • *Scr* Rula Jebreal, from her novel

Miranda ★★★

Comedy fantasy   1947 · UK · BW · 79min

Glynis Johns gives one of the best performances of her career as Miranda the mermaid, in this fishy tale that had more than a passing influence on the Ron Howard hit *Splash*. Griffith Jones is something of a stuffed shirt as the doctor who pulls her out of the sea and gives her the run of his bathroom, but Googie Withers is good value as his suspicious wife, yet no one can compare with the marvellous Margaret Rutherford as the local nurse. Never exactly funny, but enjoyable all the same. A sequel, *Mad about Men*, followed in 1954. DP

Glynis Johns *Miranda* • Googie Withers *Clare Marten* • Griffith Jones *Dr Paul Marten* • John McCallum *Nigel Hood* • Margaret Rutherford *Nurse Cary* • David Tomlinson *Charles* • Yvonne Owen *Betty* • Sonia Holm *Isobel* ■ *Dir* Ken Annakin • *Scr* Peter Blackmore, Denis Waldock, from the play by Peter Blackmore

Miranda ★ 15

Romantic thriller
2001 · UK/Ger · Colour · 88min

Grubby, artificial and showcasing one of Christina Ricci's worst performances to date, this dull embarrassment is supposedly a comedy romance, but features little of either. John Simm is a librarian who falls in love with the enigmatic Ricci, only to learn she's a conwoman. When director Marc Munden shifts this listless mediocrity into tepid thriller territory the whole farrago becomes indigestible. AJ *DVD*

Christina Ricci *Miranda* • John Simm *Frank* • Kyle MacLachlan *Nailor* • John Hurt *Christian* • Julian Rhind-Tutt *Rod* • Cavan Clerkin *Gerry* • Matthew Marsh *Charles* ■ *Dir* Marc Munden • *Scr* Rob Young

Mirch Masala ★★★ 15

Drama   1987 · Ind · Colour · 119min

Although it loses track of its intellectual purpose and ends up being a rather bland melodrama, this political allegory made the international reputation of Indian director Ketan Mehta. Naseeruddin Shah plays the Raj-obsessed tax collector, or subedar, whose passion for Smita Patil is drawn with considerable ferocity. Om Puri is also impressive as the sage watchman who protects the frightened Patil in an otherwise all-female spice factory. It's beautifully photographed, but much of the symbolism will lack significance for western audiences. DP Hindi +subtitles.

Naseeruddin Shah *Subedar* • Smita Patil *Sonbai* • Suresh Oberoi *Mukhi* • Om Puri ■ *Dir* Ketan Mehta

Mirror ★★★★ U

Experimental biographical drama
1974 · USSR · Colour and BW · 101min

Cinema doesn't get much more personal than this. Casting his mother as the old woman and using his famous father, Arseni Tarkovsky's poetry on the soundtrack, director Andrei Tarkovsky draws on childhood memories, artistic fantasies and actual events to explore the ways in which the history of his country impinged on the lives of three generations of his family. It's a bewildering blend of documentary footage and stylised imagery, that can only be described as cinematic poetry. Some of the references are decidedly obscure and demand concentration to keep in step, but it is an awesome achievement, nevertheless. DP Russian +subtitles. *DVD*

Margarita Terekhova *Alexei's mother/Natalia* • Ignat Daniltsev *Ignat/Alexei, aged 12* • Maria Tarkovskaya *Alexei's mother, as an old woman* • Alla Demidova *Lisa* • Fillip Yankovsky *Alexei, aged five* • Oleg Yankovsky *Father* ■ *Dir* Andrei Tarkovsky • *Scr* Andrei Tarkovsky, Aleksandr Misharin

The Mirror Crack'd ★★ PG

Murder mystery   1980 · UK · Colour · 101min

This mediocre mystery gave Angela Lansbury the chance to rehearse her role as a crime-solving novelist in *Murder, She Wrote*. Here, she takes on the mantle of Agatha Christie's Miss Marple. Frankly, with the clash of the titans going on between Elizabeth Taylor and Kim Novak, nobody else really gets a look in, not even Tony Curtis and Rock Hudson (in his penultimate picture). DP *DVD*

Angela Lansbury *Miss Marple* • Elizabeth Taylor *Marina Rudd* • Tony Curtis *Marty N Fenn* • Edward Fox *Inspector Craddock* • Rock Hudson *Jason Rudd* • Geraldine Chaplin *Ella Zielinsky* • Kim Novak *Lola Brewster* ■ *Dir* Guy Hamilton • *Scr* Jonathan Hales, Barry Sandler, from the novel by Agatha Christie

The Mirror Has Two Faces ★★★ 15

Romantic comedy   1996 · US · Colour · 121min

Barbra Streisand directs and stars in this so-so romantic comedy. She plays a dowdy professor who agrees to have a purely platonic relationship with Jeff Bridges, which is his solution to years of empty sexual romances. Of course, Babs secretly fancies the pants off him, so she decides to turn herself into a sensual swan and seduce him. While Streisand and Bridges fumble with their roles, the movie is stolen out from under them by supporting cast members Mimi Rogers, as Barbra's glamour-puss sister, and Lauren Bacall as her critical mother. JB *DVD*

Barbra Streisand *Rose Morgan* • Jeff Bridges *Gregory Larkin* • Lauren Bacall *Hannah Morgan* • George Segal *Henry Fine* • Mimi Rogers *Claire* • Pierce Brosnan *Alex* • Brenda Vaccaro *Doris* • Austin Pendleton *Barry* • Elle Macpherson *Candy* ■ *Dir* Barbra Streisand • *Scr* Richard LaGravenese, from his story, from the film *Le Miroir a Deux Faces* by André Cayatte, Gérard

Oury • *Music* Marvin Hamlisch • *Cinematographers* Dante Spinotti, Andrzej Bartkowiak

Mirror Mirror ★★ PG

Fantasy adventure   2012 · US · Colour · 101min

This is a shallow re-imagining of the Snow White fairy tale from *Immortals* director Tarsem Singh, with Julia Roberts as the wicked stepmother who steals the kingdom from Snow White (a bland but effective Lily Collins). The seven dwarves are recast as forest-dwelling rebels, led by our plucky heroine in an attempt to win back her birthright. Paling in comparison to more famous retellings, this minor chintzy fantasy has all the depth of a pop-up storybook. AJ *DVD* *BL*

Sean Bean *The King* • Lily Collins *Snow White* • Julia Roberts *The Queen* • Armie Hammer *Prince Alcott* • Nathan Lane *Brighton* • Mare Winningham *Baker Margaret* ■ *Dir* Tarsem Singh • *Scr* Jason Keller, Marc Klein, from a story by Melisa Wallack, from the Snow White fairy tale by Jacob and Wilhelm Grimm

MirrorMask ★★ PG

Fantasy adventure   2004 · US · Colour · 96min

Longtime comic book collaborators Dave McKean and Neil Gaiman transfer their creative talents to celluloid for this ambitious fantasy adventure. Combining live action and digital animation, it's the surreal tale of a Brighton circus owner's daughter (Stephanie Leonidas) who becomes trapped in a magical world ruled over by the opposing queens of Light and Shadows (both played by Gina McKee). The events are visually handsome, but the clumsy execution is compounded by an underdeveloped storyline and flat performances. SF *DVD*

Stephanie Leonidas *Helena/Anti-Helena* • Gina McKee *Joanne/Queen of LIght/Queen of Shadows* • Rob Brydon *Morris Campbell/Prime Minister* • Jason Barry *Valentine* • Dora Bryan *Nan* • Robert Llewellyn *Gryphon* • Andy Hamilton *Small Hairy* • Stephen Fry *Librarian* • Nik Robson *Pingo/Bing* • Lenny Henry *Cops 1-4* ■ *Dir* Dave McKean • *Scr* Neil Gaiman, from the book by Neil Gaiman, Dave McKean

Mirrors ★★ 18

Horror   2008 · US/Ger · Colour · 106min

Director Alexandre Aja follows his 2006 remake of *The Hills Have Eyes* with this update of the 2003 Korean horror *Into the Mirror*. Kiefer Sutherland plays a disgraced cop who takes a job as a night security guard at a fire-ravaged department store. Soon he begins to see grotesque images in the building's mirrors, including violent visions of himself being tortured. Although it's bigger and grander than the original and boasts a neat twist, the jumble of expository clues and explanations becomes increasingly contrived. AJ *DVD* *BL*

Kiefer Sutherland *Ben Carson* • Paula Patton *Amy Carson* • Amy Smart *Angela Carson* • Cameron Boyce *Michael Carson* • Erica Gluck *Daisy Carson* • Mary Beth Peil *Anna Esseker* • John Shrapnel *Lorenzo Sapelli* • Jason Flemyng *Larry Byrne* • Julian Glover *Robert Esseker* ■ *Dir* Alexandre Aja • *Scr* Alexandre Aja, Gregory Levasseur [Grégory Levasseur], from the 2003 film *Into the Mirror*

The Misadventures of Margaret ★★ 15

Romantic comedy
1998 · Fr/UK/US · Colour · 88min

The art of screwball comedy was dead long before writer/director Brian Skeet banged this nail into its coffin. As she attempts valiantly to impersonate Katharine Hepburn, star Parker Posey succeeds only in being irritatingly overeager in the role of the novelist whose marriage, to genial academic Jeremy Northam, begins to unravel as she researches her latest book. Despite a few clever touches and its strong cast, this is a misadventure from start to finish. DP Swearing, sex scenes. *DVD*

Parker Posey *Margaret Nathan* • Jeremy Northam *Edward Nathan* • Craig Chester *Richard Lane* • Elizabeth McGovern *Till Turner* • Brooke Shields *Lily* • Corbin Bernsen *Art Turner* • Justine

U SUITABLE FOR ALL   Uc SUITABLE ESPECIALLY FOR YOUNG CHILDREN (DVD ONLY)   PG PARENTAL GUIDANCE   12A UNDER 12s TO BE ACCOMPANIED (CINEMA ONLY)

Waddell *Young girl* ■ *Dir* Brian Skeet • *Scr* Brian Skeet, from the novel *Rameau's Niece* by Cathleen Schine

The Misadventures of Merlin Jones ★★ U

Comedy 1964 · US · Colour · 90min

In this pleasant, undemanding Disney comedy, Tommy Kirk plays a college genius who accidentally develops a means of reading minds. Turning this new ability to good use - in contrast to the way some of us might be tempted to exploit it - he tries to solve crimes, but winds up in court himself. The characters returned in a 1965 sequel, *The Monkey's Uncle*. JG

Tommy Kirk *Merlin Jones* • Annette Funicello *Jennifer* • Leon Ames *Judge Holmby* • Stuart Erwin *Police Capt Loomis* • Alan Hewitt *Prof Shattuck* • Connie Gilchrist *Mrs Gossett* ■ *Dir* Robert Stevenson • *Scr* Tom August [Alfred Lewis Levitt], Helen August [Helen Levitt], from a story by Bill Walsh

Mischief Night ★★★★ 15

Comedy drama 2006 · UK · Colour · 89min

Penny Woolcock's Leeds-set comedy drama offers a wonderfully vibrant take on contemporary Britain. Shot in Beeston and largely cast with non-professional actors, it feels refreshingly authentic. Kelli Hollis (star of Woolcock's made-for-TV *Tina Goes Shopping* and *Tina Takes a Break*) again plays single mum Tina. As the traditional celebration of Mischief Night approaches, tensions are simmering between whites and Asians, and Tina and old flame Immie (Ramon Tikaram) are caught on the racial fault line. Woolcock's not afraid of tackling taboos, from radical Islam to heroin addiction, and manages to make no problem seem impossible of being salved - if not solved - by the power of laughter. JR English, Urdu +subtitles. Swearing, racist references. *DVD*

Kelli Hollis *Tina* • Holly Kenny *Kimberley* • Michael Taylor (3) *Tyler* • Jake Hayward *Macauley* • Ramon Tikaram *Immie* • Sarah Byrne *Sarina* • Qasim Akhtar *Asif* • James Foster *Kev* ■ *Dir/Scr* Penny Woolcock

Misconduct ★★★ 15

Thriller 2016 · US · Colour · 101min

This twisty legal thriller features two Hollywood legends in the form of Al Pacino and Anthony Hopkins. Importantly, though, neither gets a huge amount of screen time. Instead, the lead role belongs to Josh Duhamel (from the *Transformers* franchise), who plays rising lawyer Ben Cahill. After Ben presents evidence incriminating billionaire Hopkins to his boss Pacino, the film serves up a series of twists and turns, some of which aren't entirely convincing. SC Swearing, violence, sex references

Josh Duhamel *Ben Cahill* • Anthony Hopkins *Arthur Denning* • Al Pacino *Charles Abrams* • Alice Eve *Charlotte Cahill* • Malin Akerman *Emily Hynes* • Julia Stiles *Jane Clemente* ■ *Dir* Shintaro Shimosawa • *Scr* Adam Mason, Simon Boyes

Les Misérables ★★★★★ U

Period epic 1934 · Fr · BW · 104min

Since 1909, there have been nearly two dozen film versions of Victor Hugo's vast novel. The story is trifling yet monumental. After serving a massive prison sentence for petty theft, Jean Valjean's spiritual transformation into a pillar of society is undermined by Javert, the policeman who obsessively pursues him. Add to this an epic panorama of French Revolutionary history and a doomed love affair, and you have a humanist masterpiece that works on a multitude of levels. Raymond Bernard's epic version of 1934 might be compared to Abel Gance's *Napoleon* (it shares the same cameraman, Jules Krüger): it's slow, unfailingly faithful to the source, and contains towering performances by Harry Bauer and Charles Vanel. AT French +subtitles. *DVD* *BL*

Harry Baur *Jean Valjean* • Charles Vanel *Javert* • Henry Krauss *Monseignor Myriel* • Odette Florelle [Florelle] *Fantine* ■ *Dir* Raymond Bernard • *Scr* Raymond Bernard, Andre Lang, from the novel by Victor Hugo • *Music* Arthur Honnegger

Les Misérables ★★★★

Period epic 1935 · US · BW · 111min

Victor Hugo's classic novel had been filmed several times in the silent era, and there was an impressive French version in 1934. Despite cuts to the text, however, this lavish 20th Century-Fox production (which imported MGM talent for the occasion) is considered to be one of the best. Fredric March, as the criminal Jean Valjean, gives a solid and noble performance, but the film is dominated by Charles Laughton as the policeman Javert, a magnificent portrayal of obsession. The film's emotional and ironic climax was regarded by Laughton as "the finest thing I have ever been able to accomplish on the screen". AT

Fredric March *Jean Valjean* • Charles Laughton *Javert* • Cedric Hardwicke *Bishop Bienvenu* • Rochelle Hudson *Big Cosette* • Marilyn Knowlden *Little Cosette* • Frances Drake *Eponine* • John Beal *Marius* • Jessie Ralph *Madame Magloire* ■ *Dir* Richard Boleslawski • *Scr* WP Lipscomb, from the novel by Victor Hugo • *Cinematographer* Gregg Toland

Les Misérables ★★

Period epic 1946 · It · BW · 120min

This Italian version of the Victor Hugo story puts the emphasis not on Jean Valjean (Gino Cervi) and Inspector Javert (Hans Hinrich), but on Valentina Cortese, who plays both Fantine and her daughter Cosette. Original versions were in two parts - *Manhunt* and *Storm over Paris* - of 90 minutes each. A foreign version, with lamentable English dubbing, was released in 1952 at 140 minutes; it was later cut to two hours. AT Italian dubbed.

Valentina Cortese *Fantine/Cosette* • Gino Cervi *Jean Valjean* • Hans Hinrich *Inspector Javert* • Aldo Nicodemi *Marius* ■ *Dir* Riccardo Freda • *Scr* Riccardo Freda, Mario Monicelli, Stefano Vanzina, from the novel by Victor Hugo • *Cinematographer* Rodolfo Lombardi

Les Misérables ★★★ U

Period epic 1952 · US · BW · 101min

Lewis Milestone's film is a faithful but undeniably pedestrian version of Victor Hugo's masterpiece. Michael Rennie makes a decent Valjean, but he comes in some way behind Harry Baur, Fredric March and Jean Gabin, all of whom invested the part with considerably more truth and emotion. Robert Newton plays Javert as an eye-rolling villain whose fanaticism is at odds with Milestone's contention that personality has no part to play in the enforcement of the law. Edmund Gwenn alone captures the novel's humanity as a benevolent bishop. DP *DVD*

Michael Rennie *Jean Valjean* • Robert Newton *Javert* • Debra Paget *Cosette* • Edmund Gwenn *Bishop* • Sylvia Sidney *Fantine* • Cameron Mitchell *Marius* • Elsa Lanchester *Madame Magloire* • James Robertson-Justice *Robert* ■ *Dir* Lewis Milestone • *Scr* Richard Murphy, from the novel by Victor Hugo

Les Misérables ★★

Period epic 1957 · E Ger/It/Fr · Colour · 210min

Despite the presence of France's greatest screen actor, Jean Gabin, this version of Victor Hugo's classic is likely to lose many viewers during the course of its three-and-a-half hours. Gabin's performance as the petty criminal turned saintly hero Jean Valjean is perfectly adequate, and Bernard Blier is also good as Javert, the cop who obsessively haunts him. The problem lies in the stolid direction by former Resistance fighter Jean-Paul Le Chanois, while filming in the state-run studios of communist East Germany benefited only the budget. AT French +subtitles.

Jean Gabin *Jean Valjean* • Bernard Blier *Javert* • Bourvil *Thenardier* • Danièle Delorme *Fantine* • Fernand Ledoux *Myriel* • Béatrice Altariba *Cosette* • Gianni Esposito *Marius* • Silvia Montfort

Eponine ■ *Dir* Jean-Paul Le Chanois • *Scr* Jean-Paul Le Chanois, Michel Audiard, René Barjavel, from the novel by Victor Hugo,

Les Misérables ★★★ PG

Period epic 1978 · US · Colour · 137min

Richard Jordan and Anthony Perkins take on the challenging roles of Valjean (the hunted) and Javert (the hunter) in Victor Hugo's classic tale, investing this impressive TV movie with intelligence and depth. Director Glenn Jordan, a TV movie specialist whose early career was in the theatre, gives a luxurious (and thus ironic) feel to the claustrophobic world of Hugo's characters, providing plenty of room for his stars to shine. JM *DVD*

Richard Jordan *Jean Valjean* • Anthony Perkins *Inspector Javert* • Cyril Cusack *Fauchelevent* • Claude Dauphin *Bishop Myriel* • John Gielgud *Gillenormand* • Ian Holm *Thenardier* • Celia Johnson *Sister Simplice* • Flora Robson *Prioress* ■ *Dir* Glenn Jordan • *Scr* John Gay, from the novel by Victor Hugo

Les Misérables ★★★

Period epic 1982 · Fr · Colour · 180min

A middling *Misérables*, better than the 1957 version with Jean Gabin, but not in the same league as the 1934 and 1935 versions or Claude Lelouch's radical update of 1995. Made for French TV and shown in six 50-minute episodes (a cinema version of three hours was shown first), Robert Hossein's exhaustive and exhausting effort boasts an excellent Valjean and Javert in the charismatic, Bogart-like Lino Ventura and the creepy Michel Bouquet. It's a bit like a primer for students, but some of it is spectacular to look at, with marvellous use of the medieval town of Sarlat. AT French +subtitles.

Lino Ventura *Jean Valjean* • Michel Bouquet *Inspector Javert* • Jean Carmet *Thenardier* • Françoise Seigner *La Thenardier* • Evelyne Bouix *Fantine* • Christine Jean *Cosette* ■ *Dir* Robert Hossein • *Scr* Robert Hossein, Alain Decaux, from the novel by Victor Hugo

Les Misérables ★★★★ 12

Period epic 1995 · Fr · Colour · 167min

Director Claude Lelouch makes an ambitious attempt to update Victor Hugo's tale to the 20th century. Although he provides a provocative portrait of France under the Nazi occupation, this sprawling epic is very much a picaresque adventure, with Jean-Paul Belmondo outstanding as the former boxer for whom the task of keeping a Jewish family out of the clutches of the Nazis is no less daunting than completing Hugo's mammoth tome. Brimming with incident and with excellent support from Annie Girardot, this is both exhilarating and moving. DP French +subtitles.

Jean-Paul Belmondo *Henri Fortin/Jean Valjean* • Michel Boujenah *André Ziman* • Alessandra Martines *Elise Ziman* • Salomé [Salomé Lelouch] *Salomé Ziman* • Annie Girardot *Théardière farmer woman* • Philippe Léotard *Thénardier* ■ *Dir* Claude Lelouch • *Scr* Claude Lelouch, from the novel by Victor Hugo

Les Misérables ★★ 12

Period epic 1997 · US · Colour · 128min

Liam Neeson stars as the reformed criminal, Jean Valjean; Geoffrey Rush the obsessive detective, Javert; Uma Thurman and Claire Danes play the women Valjean cares for. On paper, this is an impressive cast; on screen, though, the performances are distinctly underwhelming. Bille August's production, mostly shot in Prague, looks like a TV mini-series that's been hacked down for cinema release and the rhythm is all wrong. AT Some swearing, violence. *DVD*

Liam Neeson *Jean Valjean* • Geoffrey Rush *Javert* • Uma Thurman *Fantine* • Claire Danes *Cosette* • Hans Matheson *Marius* • Reine Brynolfsson *Captain Beauvais* • Peter Vaughan *Bishop* ■ *Dir* Bille August • *Scr* Rafael Yglesias, from the novel by Victor Hugo

Les Misérables ★★★ 12

Period musical 2012 · UK · Colour · 151min

The long-running stage sensation emerges as a well-mounted film "poperetta" in the hands of *King's Speech* director Tom Hooper. He takes an episodic approach to Victor Hugo's epic saga that revolves around Jean Valjean (Hugh Jackman), a thief-turned-good Samaritan who is pursued through 19th-century France by the intractable officer Javert (Russell Crowe). There are some rousing anthems (performed live, with no studio enhancements) such as *Bring Him Home* and Anne Hathaway's powerfully moving rendition of *I Dreamed a Dream*, but Hooper doesn't really vary their presentation. A grimy look and overliteral rhyming in the mundane libretto also makes it rather heavy going. Still, fans of the stage version will find it built to please. AJ Some violence. *DVD* *BL*

Hugh Jackman *Jean Valjean* • Anne Hathaway *Fantine* • Russell Crowe *Inspector Javert* • Helena Bonham Carter *Madame Thénardier* • Amanda Seyfried *Cosette* • Sacha Baron Cohen *Monsieur Thénardier* • Eddie Redmayne *Marius* • Samantha Barks *Eponine* ■ *Dir* Tom Hooper • *Scr* William Nicholson, from a musical by Alain Boubil (libretto), Herbert Kretzmer (lyrics), Claude-Michel Schonberg (music), from Victor Hugo's novel • *Costume Designer* Paco Delgado • *Production Designers* Eve Stewart, Anna Lynch-Robinson

Misery ★★★★ 18

Psychological thriller 1990 · US · Colour · 103min

Director Rob Reiner's superb adaptation of Stephen King's bestseller deals with the trappings of celebrity, fanatical devotion, artistic dilemmas and the worthiness of commercial fiction within a psychological suspense context. Kathy Bates deservedly won an Oscar for her monstrously scary performance as novelist James Caan's "Number One Fan", turning from caring nurse to insane torturer after learning he's killed off her favourite character. Reiner's adept exercise in chilling claustrophobia contains numerous jolts, with the "hobbling" scene certain to evoke screams of revulsion. AJ Violence, swearing. *DVD* *BL*

James Caan *Paul Sheldon* • Kathy Bates *Annie Wilkes* • Richard Farnsworth *Buster, Sheriff* • Frances Sternhagen *Virginia* • Lauren Bacall *Marcia Sindell* • Graham Jarvis *Libby* • Jerry Potter *Pete* ■ *Dir* Rob Reiner • *Scr* William Goldman, from the novel by Stephen King • *Cinematographer* Barry Sonnenfeld

Misery Loves Comedy ★★★

Comedy documentary 2015 · US · Colour · 94min

It is well documented that some comedians are depressives, but this star-studded cavalcade of talking heads largely from the American comedy circuit (plus Steve Coogan, Stephen Merchant and candid Aussie Jim Jeffries) takes that generalisation to its logical conclusion, positing that they're all wracked with self-doubt and self-loathing, and perversely thrive on it. Edited from 60 hours of footage, this unpretentious doc is hamstrung by amateurish graphics and a lack of background information beyond the occasional still, but the insight shines through. AC

Jon Favreau • Matthew Perry • Janeane Garofalo • Whoopi Goldberg • Judd Apatow • Christopher Guest • Stephen Merchant ■ *Dir* Kevin Pollak

The Misfits ★★★★ PG

Drama 1961 · US · BW · 124min

The last film of both Marilyn Monroe and Clark Gable, and some might say containing the last real performance from Montgomery Clift, it went from box-office flop to cult status within the space of a year. Written by Monroe's then husband, Arthur Miller, it's a grey, solemn and at times pretentious piece about three drifters who hunt horses destined to become pet food. Somehow the flat, arid Nevada landscape mirrors the characters' bleak existence and sets the

M

overall mood of despair and depression. John Huston's film is easy to admire but hard to enjoy fully. AT DVD Blu-ray

Clark Gable *Gay Langland* • Marilyn Monroe *Roslyn Taber* • Montgomery Clift *Perce Howland* • Eli Wallach *Guido* • Thelma Ritter *Isabelle Steers* • James Barton *Old man in bar* • Estelle Winwood *Church lady* • Kevin McCarthy *Raymond Taber* ■ *Dir* John Huston • *Scr* Arthur Miller

Mishima: a Life in Four Chapters ★★★★ 15

Biographical drama
1985 · US/Jpn · Colour and BW · 115min

This is an astonishing portrait by Paul Schrader of the life and works of Yukio Mishima, the Japanese literary icon who committed *seppuku* (ritual suicide) on 25 November 1970. Audaciously cutting between the events of that day, monochrome flashbacks and stylised excerpts from Mishima's writings, Schrader produces a film of exemplary control and penetrating insight – a feat made all the more impressive by the fact that Mishima's widow forbade any explicit reference to her late husband's sexuality and controversial politics. Exquisitely designed, the scenes from Mishima's works are mesmerisingly beautiful and enlightening. DP English, Japanese +subtitles.

Ken Ogata *Yukio Mishima* • Masayuki Shionoya *Morita* • Junkichi Orimoto *General Mashita* • Naoko Otani *Mother* • Go Riju *Mishima, aged 18-19* • Masato Aizawa *Mishima, aged 9-14* • Yuki Nagahara *Mishima, aged 5* • Haruko Kato *Grandmother* ■ *Dir* Paul Schrader • *Scr* Leonard Schrader, Paul Schrader, Chieko Schrader, from various literary works by Yukio Mishima • *Production Designer* Eiko Ishioka

Miss Annie Rooney ★★ U

Drama
1942 · US · BW · 86min

At the age of 14, former childhood sweetheart Shirley Temple was having trouble sustaining her popularity, and this is one of the mild vehicles she found herself in after leaving Fox. The star sings and jitterbugs, but its chief selling point was the fact that Temple received her first screen kiss (though it's little more than a peck on the cheek). It was given by another former child star Dickie Moore, who would state that the kiss was a first for him, too. Moore couldn't dance, so those scenes were performed by Roland Dupree, wearing a rubber face-mask in the image of his co-star. TV

Shirley Temple *Annie Rooney* • William Gargan *Tim Rooney* • Guy Kibbee *Grandpop Rooney* • Dickie Moore *Marty White* • Peggy Ryan *Myrtle* • Roland DuPree *Joey* • Jonathan Hale *Mr White* • Gloria Holden *Mrs White* ■ *Dir* Edwin L Marin • *Scr* George Bruce

Miss Bala ★★★★ 15

Crime drama
2011 · Mex · Colour · 108min

Gerardo Naranjo's uncompromising exposé of Mexican drug cartels – and the corruption of those entrusted with busting them – is shocking in both its grim authenticity and explosive stylisation. Wannabe beauty queen Stephanie Sigman suddenly finds herself at the mercy of a ruthless drug lord (Noe Hernandez), who helps her win a pageant so as to smuggle arms and drugs to a US contact (James Russo). Although Sigman's role lacks depth, the film remains devastatingly dramatic, especially the audacious shootouts. DP Spanish +subtitles. Violence, swearing, sex scenes. DVD

Stephanie Sigman *Laura Guerrero* • Noe Hernandez *Lino Valdez* • James Russo *Jimmy* • Lakshmi Picazo *Suzu* ■ *Dir* Gerardo Naranjo • *Scr* Gerardo Naranjo, Mauricio Katz

Miss Congeniality ★★★★ 12

Action comedy
2000 · US · Colour · 105min

Sandra Bullock returned to form in director Donald Petrie's energetic comedy that focuses on the world of beauty pageants. Bullock's determinedly unfeminine FBI agent is drafted in as a beauty contestant after warnings of a bomb attack on the Miss United States competition. Pampered and preened by contest expert Michael Caine,

Bullock uncovers her own feminine side and has some of her preconceptions shattered. Her relationship with FBI colleague Benjamin Bratt sparkles with sexual chemistry and the gags come thick and fast. The antics of the competition's hosts, Candice Bergen and William Shatner, are slightly overplayed, but on the whole this is great fun. LH Swearing, some violence. DVD

Sandra Bullock *Gracie Hart* • Michael Caine *Victor Melling* • Benjamin Bratt *Eric Matthews* • Candice Bergen *Kathy Morningside* • William Shatner *Stan Fields* • Ernie Hudson *McDonald* • Heather Burns *Cheryl "Rhode Island"* ■ *Dir* Donald Petrie • *Scr* Marc Lawrence (2), from a story by Katie Ford, Caryn Lucas, Marc Lawrence

Miss Congeniality 2: Armed & Fabulous ★★ 12

Action comedy
2005 · US/Aus · Colour · 110min

Sandra Bullock returns as clumsy FBI agent Gracie Hart in this lazy sequel. Picking up where the original movie left off, the story involves Hart reluctantly accepting a PR role after her new-found fame makes it impossible for her to operate undercover. Groomed to perfection, the Bureau's poster girl soon begins to relish her position, much to the distaste of her tough new bodyguard (Regina King). Were it not for Bullock's natural comic timing, this would fall apart. SF Violence. DVD

Sandra Bullock *Gracie Hart* • William Shatner *Stan Fields* • Heather Burns *Cheryl* • Regina King *Sam Fuller* • Ernie Hudson *McDonald* • Treat Williams *Collins* ■ *Dir* John Pasquin • *Scr* Marc Lawrence (2)

Miss Evers' Boys ★★★★

Period drama based on a true story
1997 · US · Colour · 118min

This Emmy Award-winning true story brilliantly dramatises a dark and shameful chapter in America's recent past. Alfre Woodard stars as a caring nurse who tries to alleviate her patients' suffering while working on a federal health project in 1930s Alabama. The study, intended to monitor and treat syphilis among poor African-American men, instead lapses into a heartless experiment on patients deteriorating into madness from the untreated disease. Writer Walter Bernstein's sensitive adaptation, Joseph Sargent's direction and a distinguished cast make this TV movie a drama of rare power and eloquence. MC Swearing.

Alfre Woodard *Eunice Evers* • Laurence Fishburne *Caleb Humphries* • Craig Sheffer *Dr Douglas* • Joe Morton *Dr Brodus* • Ossie Davis *Mr Evers* • EG Marshall *Senate chairman* ■ *Dir* Joseph Sargent • *Scr* Walter Bernstein, from the play by David Feldshuh

Miss Firecracker ★★★ PG

Comedy drama
1989 · US · Colour · 98min

Dazzling Holly Hunter is full of energetic snap, crackle and pop as she re-creates the part she made her own on stage. It's Hunter's dream to win the Yazoo City beauty contest, and the tale of how she makes it to the finals against all the odds is beautifully told by director Thomas Schlamme. This gentle, offbeat comedy is filled with southern eccentrics brought to scene-stealing life by the likes of Mary Steenburgen, Alfre Woodard and Tim Robbins. AJ DVD

Holly Hunter *Carnelle Scott* • Mary Steenburgen *Elain Rutledge* • Tim Robbins *Delmount Williams* • Alfre Woodard *Popeye Jackson* • Scott Glenn *Mac Sam* • Veanne Cox *Tessy Mahoney* • Ann Wedgeworth *Miss Blue* ■ *Dir* Thomas Schlamme • *Scr* Beth Henley, from her play

Miss Grant Takes Richmond ★★★ U

Crime comedy
1949 · US · BW · 88min

An archetypal dumb blonde takes a job as a secretary in a real-estate office, unaware that it's a fake outfit fronting a crooked betting syndicate. When she concerns herself with the problems of the homeless, her boss finds himself organising a low-cost housing scheme as a way of paying off his bad gambling debts. A lightweight comedy,

directed with a suitably light touch by Lloyd Bacon, the movie's main attraction is Lucille Ball in a role tailor-made for her kooky talents. She's ably supported by a personable William Holden as her boss. RK

Lucille Ball *Ellen Grant* • William Holden (2) *Dick Richmond* • Janis Carter *Peggy Donato* • James Gleason *J Hobart Gleason* • Gloria Henry *Helen White* • Frank McHugh *Kilcoyne* ■ *Dir* Lloyd Bacon • *Scr* Nat Perrin, Devery Freeman, Frank Tashlin, from the story by Everett Freeman

Miss Hokusai ★★★ 12A

Animated period drama
2015 · Jpn · Colour · 89min

Artist Katsushika Hokusai is renowned for his views of Mount Fuji and the iconic *The Great Wave off Kanagawa*. But the focus of this animated dramatisation falls on his 23-year-old daughter, O-Ei, who was not only his trusted assistant but also a fine painter in her own right. This is an intriguing memoir of a significant female artist, but, despite the precision of the character design and the elegance of the computer-generated backdrops, Keiichi Hara's portrait never quite captures the imagination. DP Japanese +subtitles. DVD Blu-ray

Yutaka Matsushige *Katsushika Hokusai* • Kumiko Aso *Sayogoromo* • An *O-Ei* • Gaku Hamada *Zenjiro* ■ *Dir* Keiichi Hara • *Scr* Miho Maruo, from the manga *Sarusuberi* by Hinako Sugiura

Miss Julie ★★★★

Period drama
1951 · Swe · BW · 90min

Considered shocking in its day for the eroticism of its exchanges, Alf Sjöberg's adaptation of August Strindberg's one-act play shared the Grand Prix at Cannes with Vittorio De Sica's *Miracle in Milan*. Defying her inexperience, Anita Björk gives a wickedly wilful performance as the spoilt daughter who takes out the resentment she feels towards her ex-fiancé (and men in general) by goading the family's misanthropic valet, Ulf Palme, into seducing her. The flashback/flash forward structure dissipates the intensity, but enables Sjöberg to explore the attitudes Björk inherited from her mother, and the price she pays for her cruelty. DP In Swedish.

Anita Björk *Miss Julie* • Ulf Palme *Jean* • Inger Norberg *Miss Julie as a child* • Jan Hagerman *Jean as a child* ■ *Dir* Alf Sjöberg • *Scr* Alf Sjöberg, from the play by August Strindberg

Miss Julie ★★★ 15

Period drama
1999 · UK/US · Colour · 96min

Mike Figgis directs this screen adaptation of August Strindberg's play as a vehicle for the statuesque Saffron Burrows. She plays the eponymous Julie, the spoilt daughter of a wealthy family, whose nocturnal dalliance with footman Peter Mullan threatens to bring destruction down on both their heads. Claustrophobically filmed on a single set, this virtual two-hander (the third main character, played by Maria Doyle Kennedy, sleeps through most of the action) suffers from a marked height imbalance between the leads, which renders much of their interaction faintly ludicrous. Mullan, however, brings an intensity and rage to the upstart Jean. NS Swearing, a sex scene. DVD

Saffron Burrows *Miss Julie* • Peter Mullan *Jean* • Maria Doyle Kennedy *Christine* ■ *Dir* Mike Figgis • *Scr* Helen Cooper, from the play by August Strindberg

Miss Julie ★★ 12A

Period drama
2014 · Nor/UK/Fr/Ire · Colour · 130min

Colin Farrell and Jessica Chastain play servant and mistress in this screen adaptation of Swedish playwright August Strindberg's talky tale of social and sexual shenanigans. It's adapted and directed by the Swedish actress Luv Ullmann who, for reasons best known to herself, relocates the action from Sweden to Ireland. Farrell and Chastain both give it some welly as the socially ambitious valet and repressed nobleman's daughter, but Ullmann's direction, though competent, doesn't open

things out for cinema. DA Some swearing, sexual references.

Jessica Chastain *Miss Julie* • Colin Farrell (2) *John* • Samantha Morton *Kathleen* • Nora McMenamy *Little Miss Julie* ■ *Dir* Liv Ullmann • *Scr* Liv Ullmann, from August Strindberg's play

Miss London Ltd ★★★ U

Musical comedy
1943 · UK · BW · 94min

This was the first feature film directed by Val Guest, who had written several scripts for comics Will Hay and Arthur Askey. For this lively musical, Guest also co-wrote the script and provided the lyrics for the eight Manning Sherwin melodies. The story - perky blonde Evelyn Dall inherits half of a run-down escort agency and sets out to make it a success with partner Askey – is an excuse for songs and lots of comic business. TV DVD

Arthur Askey *Arthur Bowman* • Evelyn Dall *Terry Arden* • Anne Shelton *Gail Martin* • Richard Hearne *Commodore* • Max Bacon *Romeo* • Jack Train *Joe Nelson* • Peter Graves (1) *Capt Rory O'More* ■ *Dir* Val Guest • *Scr* Val Guest, Marriott Edgar

Miss March ★ 15

Comedy
2009 · US · Colour · 86min

Left in a coma for four years by an accident that prevented him from consummating his relationship with his high-school sweetheart, a young man awakes to discover that his beloved is now a *Playboy* centrefold and sets off to win her back. It's described as a comecy, but stars Zach Cregger and Trevor Moore (who also write and direct) conjure up not a single laugh in the process. As performers, Cregger's whiny sincerity (he's the one just out of hospital) is almost as grating as partner Moore's one-note man-child zaniness. As writers, their efforts to milk humour from the crassest of targets fall by the wayside, while their directorial ineptitude mis-times any gag that had even a hope of garnering a smile. TJ Swearing, sex scenes, drug abuse. DVD

Zach Cregger *Eugene Bell* • Trevor Moore *Tucker Cleigh* • Raquel Alessi *Cindi Whitehall* • Molly Stanton *Candace* • Craig Robinson *Horsedick.MPEG* ■ *Dir* Zach Cregger, Trevor Moore • *Scr* Zach Cregger, Trevor Moore, from a story by Dennis Haggerty, Ryan Homchick, Thomas Mimms

Miss Mary ★★★ 15

Drama
1986 · Arg/US · Colour · 95min

One of those strange but all too vacuous roles that the highly politicised Julie Christie took on during the 1980s. She plays a sexually repressed but simmering governess, employed by an aristocratic Argentinian family in the late 1930s. The pot never boils over sufficiently to make it interesting. Christie looks great in high-cut, flouncy collars and the scenery is spectacular. SH English, Spanish +subtitles. Some swearing.

Julie Christie *Mary Mulligan* • Nacha Guevara *Mecha* • Luisina Brando *Perla* • Eduardo Pavlovsky *Alfredo* • Gerardo Romano *Ernesto* • Iris Marga *Grandmother* • Guillermo Battaglia *Grandfather* • Sofia Viruboff *Carolina* ■ *Dir* Maria Luisa Bemberg • *Scr* Maria Luisa Bemberg, Jorge Goldenberg

Miss Nobody ★★★

Drama
1997 · Pol · Colour · 98min

Few of Andrzej Wajda's films have focused solely on female protagonists, and an uncertainty of tone undermines the account of rural teenager Anna Wielgucka's tempestuous relationships with the girls at her Warsaw school. These include New Age devotee Anna Mucha and Anna Powierza, whose brusque cynicism arouses rebellious emotions. Overstressing the allegorical undertones and uncomfortable with both the philosophical and sexual aspects of the story, this is one of Wajda's lesser achievements. DP In Polish.

Anna Wielgucka *Marysia Kawaczak* • Anna Mucha *Kasia* • Anna Powierza *Ewa* • Stanislawa Celinska *Marysia's mother* ■ *Dir* Andrzej Wajda • *Scr* Radoslaw Piwowarski, from a novel by Tomek Tryzna

Miss Oyu ★★★ PG
Drama   1951 · Jpn · Colour · 93min

Kenji Mizoguchi's first collaboration with cinematographer Kazuo Miyagawa disappointed the critics and the director alike. However, this had little to do with the long, fluid takes, or the intensity of the performances. The problem lies with Junichiro Tanizaki's source novel, which offered Mizoguchi little chance to explore his usual social and gynocentric themes. The film stars Kinuyo Tanaka as the respectable widow who persuades her younger sister, Nobuko Otowa, to marry the wealthy Yuji Hori so that she can continue their affair while protecting her son's inheritance. DP In Japanese. _DVD_

Kinuyo Tanaka *Oyu Kayukawa* • Nobuko Otowa *Shizu* • Yuji Hori *Shinnosuke Seribashi* • Kiyoko Hirai *Osumi* ■ *Dir* Kenji Mizoguchi • *Scr* Yoshikata Yoda, from the novel *Ashikari* by Junichiro Tanizaki • *Cinematographer* Kazuo Miyagawa

Miss Peregrine's Home for Peculiar Children
Fantasy   2016 · US · Colour

This is a preview – no prints were available to review prior to publication: Director Tim Burton adds to his catalogue of dark fairy tales, this time taking inspiration from a young adult novel by Ransom Riggs. Asa Butterfield, the pale-faced child from *The Boy in the Striped Pyjamas*, has been cast as the teenager (he's 18 now) who happens upon a children's home on a Welsh island that once housed supernaturally gifted kids – among them, his murdered grandfather. The more he digs, the more the mystery deepens. Expect haunting visuals, especially as the story was initially built around a collection of vintage photographs. SP

Eva Green *Miss Peregrine* • Samuel L Jackson *Barron* • Asa Butterfield *Jacob Portman* • Allison Janney *Dr Golan* ■ *Dir* Tim Burton • *Scr* Jane Goldman, from Ransom Riggs's novel

Miss Pettigrew Lives for a Day ★★★ PG
Romantic comedy drama
2007 · UK/US · Colour · 87min

Love and laughter are all-important in this romantic comedy set in London just prior to the Second World War. Frances McDormand stars as the engagingly prim and proper Miss Pettigrew, an impoverished governess who soon finds herself employed as "social secretary" to flighty American starlet Delysia Lafosse (Amy Adams). While trying to show Delysia the error of her ways, Pettigrew is forced to reassess her own love life and indulges in a flirtation with a world-weary bachelor (Ciaran Hinds). The dialogue is whip smart, but director Bharat Nalluri tends to move the action along at the pace of a Merchant Ivory drama. Ultimately, though, it's the sterling performances that win the day. SP _DVD_

Frances McDormand *Miss Guinevere Pettigrew* • Amy Adams *Delysia Lafosse* • Lee Pace *Michael Pardue* • Ciaran Hinds *Joe Blumfield* • Shirley Henderson *Edythe DuBarry* • Mark Strong *Nick Colderelli* ■ *Dir* Bharat Nalluri • *Scr* David Magee, Simon Beaufoy, from the novel by Winifred Watson

Miss Potter ★★★ PG
Biographical period drama
2006 · UK/US · Colour · 88min

Beatrix Potter (Renée Zellweger) didn't just write and illustrate world-famous children's books; she was a proto-feminist – making a fortune in a man's world – and an early environmentalist – saving her beloved Lake District from property development. That's the spin of *Babe* director Chris Noonan's heart-warming but overly sentimental costume drama, in which Zellweger gurns a lot through her portrayal of the creative Victorian free spirit. What makes the film work is Ewan McGregor's effortless charm as the timid publisher who shares her vision of *The Tale of Peter Rabbit* and becomes her first romance in the bestselling process. A sweet and lightweight treat. AJ _DVD_

Renée Zellweger *Beatrix Potter* • Ewan McGregor *Norman Warne* • Emily Watson *Millie Warne* • Barbara Flynn *Helen Potter* • Bill Paterson *Rupert Potter* • Matyelok Gibbs *Miss Wiggin* • Lloyd Owen *William Heelis* • Anton Lesser *Harold Warne* • Phyllida Law *Mrs Warne* ■ *Dir* Chris Noonan • *Scr* Richard Maltby Jr • *Cinematographer* Andrew Dunn (1)

Miss Robin Hood ★★ U
Comedy   1952 · UK · BW · 71min

This disappointing comedy gave the much loved Margaret Rutherford a rare chance to star. Considering the infectious enthusiasm of her performance as the mischievous Miss Honey, she deserved better material than this slight skirmish with a gang of crooks over a valuable whisky recipe. There are solid turns from Sid James and James Robertson-Justice, but writers Val Valentine and Patrick Campbell have over-diluted the mixture for most tastes. DP _DVD_

Margaret Rutherford *Miss Honey* • Richard Hearne *Henry Wrigley* • Michael Medwin *Ernest* • Peter Jones *Lidstone* • James Robertson-Justice *McAllister* • Sidney James *Sidney* • Dora Bryan *Pearl* ■ *Dir* John Guillermin • *Scr* Val Valentine, Patrick Campbell, from a story by Reed de Rouen

Miss Rose White ★★★★
Drama   1992 · US · Colour · 95min

Kyra Sedgwick stars as a Polish Jew in a moving story of two sisters exiled in New York - one who escaped the Holocaust and one who survived it. Describing her terrifying experiences with heart-rending conviction, Amanda Plummer will surprise those used to seeing her in more manic roles, while Maximilian Schell and Maureen Stapleton provide solid support. This won three Emmys, for outstanding made-for-TV movie, Plummer (supporting actress) and director Joseph Sargent. DP

Kyra Sedgwick *Reyzel Weiss/Rose White* • Amanda Plummer *Lusia* • Penny Fuller *Miss Ryan* • Maureen Stapleton *Tanta Perla* • Maximilian Schell *Mordechai* • DB Sweeney *Dan* • Milton Selzer *Shimon* • Gina Gershon *Angie* ■ *Dir* Joseph Sargent • *Scr* Anna Sandor, from the play *A Shayna Maidel* by Barbara Lebow

Miss Sadie Thompson ★★★
Drama   1953 · US · Colour · 90min

It's Somerset Maugham's *Rain* again, this time with sexy Rita Hayworth in the title role as the hooker who floors a religious fanatic, filmed in glorious Technicolor with some terrific songs added to boot. Originally this movie was made in 3D and composed for widescreen, so if watching on TV you see too many floors and ceilings and a lot of room above the actors' heads in close-up. Try to ignore all that, and enjoy instead an over-the-top performance from José Ferrer. TS

Rita Hayworth *Sadie Thompson* • José Ferrer *Alfred Davidson* • Aldo Ray *Sergeant Phil O'Hara* • Russell Collins *Dr Robert MacPhail* • Diosa Costello *Ameena Horn* • Harry Bellaver *Joe Horn* • Wilton Graff *Governor* • Charles Buchinsky [Charles Bronson] *Edwards* ■ *Dir* Curtis Bernhardt • *Scr* Harry Kleiner, from the short story *Rain* by W Somerset Maugham

Miss Susie Slagle's ★★★
Period drama   1945 · US · BW · 87min

Lillian Gish runs a boarding house in Baltimore for medical students training at the famed John Hopkins institution and keeps a motherly eye on their concerns and love affairs. John Berry, a newcomer to film but an alumnus of Orson Welles and John Houseman's Mercury Theatre company, directs. A charming and gentle period piece set in 1910, this is illuminated, as always, by the presence of Gish. She'd been in film for three decades and had another four to go. RK

Veronica Lake *Nan Rogers* • Sonny Tufts *Pug Prentiss* • Joan Caulfield *Margaretta Howe* • Ray Collins *Dr Elijah Howe* • Billy De Wolfe *Ben Mead* • Lillian Gish *Miss Susie Slagle* • Lloyd Bridges *Silas Holmes* ■ *Dir* John Berry • *Scr* Anne Froelick, Hugo Butler, Theodore Strauss, Adrian Scott, from the novel by Augusta Tucker

Miss Tatlock's Millions ★★★★ U
Comedy   1948 · US · BW · 100min

One of the brighter comedies of the late 1940s, this verges perilously close to bad taste, with lead John Lund pretending to be an idiot for most of the picture. Hired to attend the reading of a will, Lund continues the deception after the lunatic he is portraying unexpectedly becomes co-heir to a fortune. Character actor Richard Haydn proves an astute choice of director, milking the situations for all their worth as the family endures Lund's outrageous behaviour to remain in his favour. AE

John Lund *Burke* • Wanda Hendrix *Nan Tatlock* • Barry Fitzgerald *Denno Noonan* • Monty Woolley *Miles Tatlock* • Ilka Chase *Cassie Van Alen* • Robert Stack *Nickey Van Alen* • Ray Milland • Richard Rancyd [Richard Haydn] *Fergel* ■ *Dir* Richard Haydn • *Scr* Charles Brackett, Richard Breen [Richard L Breen], from the play *Oh – Brother* by Jacques Deval

Miss Violence ★★★ 18
Drama   2013 · Gr · Colour · 98min

As the title suggests, this modern Greek tragedy – whose opening scene coolly depicts the apparent suicide of an 11-year-old girl at her own birthday party – doesn't pull its punches. Its grim tension comes from the unravelling of the mystery behind the girl's untimely death and its effect on her dysfunctional family. As the unsurprisingly ugly truth emerges, writer/director Alexandros Avranas pulls back the curtain to reveal brutal, explicit scenes that owe more to the nightmarish extremes of X-rated horror. Viscerally intense but far from subtle, it's an approach many will find gratuitously shocking, but others will see as boldly unflinching. SI Greek +subtitles. Violence, nudity. _DVD_

Eleni Roussinou *Eleni* • Themis Panou *Father* • Reni Pittaki *Mother* • Chloe Bolota *Angeliki* • Konstantinos Athanasiades *Filippos* • Sissy Toumasi *Myrto* ■ *Dir* Alexandros Avranas • *Scr* Alexandros Avranas, Kostas Peroulis

Miss You Already ★★★★ 12A
Romantic comedy drama
2015 · UK · Colour · 107min

Drew Barrymore and Toni Collette, both on top form, play best friends in a dyed-in-the-wool British weepie that targets the tear ducts with laser precision. The friends since childhood find their bond truly put to the test when Milly (Collette) is diagnosed with aggressive breast cancer. In spite of its subject matter, *Miss You Already* is no laugh-free zone. There's plenty of humour, not all of it black. And there's much-needed positivity too in a parallel storyline of Jess (Barrymore) finding herself pregnant after years of trying. DA Sex, some swearing _DVD_ _Blu-ray_

Toni Collette *Milly* • Drew Barrymore *Jess* • Dominic Cooper *Kit* • Paddy Considine *Jago* • Jacqueline Bisset *Miranda* ■ *Dir* Catherine Hardwicke • *Scr* Morwenna Banks

Missing ★★★★ 15
Drama based on a true story
1981 · US · Colour · 117min

The US State Department denounced Costa-Gavras's uncompromising human drama when it was first released because of possible political repercussions. But then the director of *Z* and *State of Siege* was used to causing controversy, and this riveting true saga proved to be his most accessible Kafka-esque nightmare. What happened to American writer Charles Horman, who disappeared during the military coup that overthrew the Allende government of Chile in 1973? That's what his liberal wife Sissy Spacek and staunchly conservative father Jack Lemmon try to find out in a compelling moral tale. AJ Swearing, nudity. _DVD_

Jack Lemmon *Ed Horman* • Sissy Spacek *Beth Horman* • Melanie Mayron *Terry Simon* • John Shea *Charles Horman* • Charles Cioffi *Captain Ray Tower* • David Clennon *Consul Phil Putnam* • Richard Venture *US Ambassador* • Jerry Hardin

Colonel Sean Patrick ■ *Dir* Costa-Gavras • *Scr* Costa-Gavras, Donald Stewart, from a non-fiction book by Thomas Hauser • *Music* Vangelis

The Missing ★★ 15
Western   2003 · US · Colour · 131min

After a moderately promising start, director Ron Howard's stab at creating an epic western soon degenerates into a bloated chase movie. Cate Blanchett stars as an unmarried frontier woman whose hard life gets a whole lot harder when her estranged father (Tommy Lee Jones) turns up on her doorstep, and her eldest daughter is kidnapped by slave traders. Blanchett gives an agreeable performance, while Jones makes the most of his ludicrous role as a mystical wanderer. AS Violence. _DVD_ _Blu-ray_

Tommy Lee Jones *Samuel Jones* • Cate Blanchett *Maggie Gilkeson* • Eric Schweig *Chidin* • Evan Rachel Wood *Lilly Gilkeson* • Jenna Boyd *Dot Gilkeson* • Steve Reevis *Two Stone* • Ray McKinnon *Russell J Wintick* • Val Kilmer *Lt Jim Ducharme* ■ *Dir* Ron Howard • *Scr* Ken Kaufman, from the novel *The Last Ride* by Thomas Eidson

The Missing Gun ★★★ 12
Comedy thriller   2002 · Chi · Colour · 86min

Lu Chuan makes confident, if occasionally careless use of film speeds, camera angles and intriguing inserts in this directorial debut. But it's the performance of Jiang Wen, as a rural Chinese policeman searching for the service revolver he lost at a drunken wedding, that melds the plot's gently satirical social critique and murder mystery sub-plot into a satisfying whole. With Wu Yujuan, as his teacher wife, heading an impeccable ensemble, this is a captivating study of character and community. DP Mandarin +subtitles. Swearing, violence. _DVD_

Jiang Wen *Ma Shan* • Ning Jing • Shi Liang ■ *Dir* Lu Chuan • *Scr* Lu Chuan, from the story *The Search for a Missing Gun* by Fan Yiping

Missing in Action ★★ 15
Action thriller   1984 · US · Colour · 97min

Chuck Norris is an American soldier who was held illegally in a Vietnamese PoW camp for seven years after the war ended. Now he returns to Vietnam to prove that other Americans are still being held. When diplomatic means fail, Norris arms himself and goes on a one-man commando mission to liberate the GIs. Stupid and simplistic, but with lots of action and posturing by Norris. ST Violence, swearing. _DVD_

Chuck Norris *Colonel Braddock* • M Emmet Walsh *Tuck* • David Tress *Senator Porter* • Lenore Kasdorf *Ann* • James Hong *General Tran* ■ *Dir* Joseph Zito • *Scr* James Bruner, from a story by John Crowther, Lance Hool, from characters by Arthur Silver, Larry Levinson, Steve Bing

Missing in Action 2: the Beginning ★ 18
Action adventure   1985 · US · Colour · 91min

This prequel, which shows us the origins of Colonel Braddock, Norris's self-righteous, gun-toting patriot, is even more blockheaded than the first film. Norris may be the one being tortured by scheming commanders and brutal guards, but you'll beg for mercy long before he does. A second sequel, *Braddock: Missing in Action III* followed in 1988. ST _DVD_

Chuck Norris *Colonel Braddock* • Soon-Teck Oh *Colonel Yin* • Cosie Costa *Mazilli* • Steven Williams *Captain David Nester* • David Chung *Dou Chou* • Joe Michael Terry *Opelka* ■ *Dir* Lance Hool • *Scr* Arthur Silver, Larry Levinson, Steve Bing

Missing Link ★★ PG
Prehistoric documentary drama
1989 · US · Colour · 87min

The travails of the last apeman, doomed to extinction by Man's invention of the axe circa one million years BC, provide the basis for this odd, non-dialogue "mockumentary". Gifted mime artist Peter Elliott, who choreographed the primates in *Greystoke*, brings a savage wistfulness to a prehistory lesson resembling the "Dawn of Man" prologue from *2001* in both look and tone. Shot on stunning Namibian locations, it

M

contains unsubtle ecological messages and dire warnings, but fans of nature shows will love the wildlife footage. AJ

Peter Elliott *Apeman* • Michael Gambon *Narrator* ■ *Dir/Scr* David Hughes (3), Carol Hughes (2) • *Cinematographers* David Hughes (3), Carol Hughes (2)

The Mission ★★★ PG
Historical drama 1986 · UK · Colour · 119min

Winner of the Palme d'Or at Cannes, but accorded a mixed critical reception, this is a studied, elegant and very moving drama set in 18th-century South America. There's no denying the existence of longueurs in the script, a certain flabbiness in the direction and a detached contribution from a curiously cast Robert De Niro. However, Jeremy Irons gives a performance of great sincerity as the head of a Jesuit mission under threat from the greed of Iberian slavers and the whim of Ray McAnally's cardinal. Chris Menges's Oscar-winning photography is glorious, while Ennio Morricone's score sends shivers down the spine. DP Violence, some nudity. DVD CS

Robert De Niro *Mendoza* • Jeremy Irons *Father Gabriel* • Ray McAnally *Altamirano* • Aidan Quinn *Felipe* • Cherie Lunghi *Carlotta* • Ronald Pickup *Hontar* • Liam Neeson *Fielding* • Chuck Low *Cabeza* ■ *Dir* Roland Joffé • *Scr* Robert Bolt, from his story

Mission: Impossible
★★★★ PG

Action spy thriller 1996 · US · Colour · 105min

Superstar Tom Cruise and director Brian De Palma join forces for this thrilling extravaganza of jaw-dropping special effects and amazing stunts. Based on the cult 1960s TV series about a covert strike force designing situations villains believe to be real, it's best to forget the complicated plot – something about Cruise clearing his name and proving to the CIA he's not a treacherous mole – and simply enjoy the epic rollercoaster ride that De Palma brings to life with his customary brilliance. AJ Violence, swearing DVD

Tom Cruise *Ethan Hunt* • Jon Voight *Jim Phelps* • Emmanuelle Béart *Claire* • Henry Czerny *Kittridge* • Jean Reno *Krieger* • Ving Rhames *Luther* • Kristin Scott Thomas *Sarah Davies* • Vanessa Redgrave *Max* • Dale Dye *Frank Barnes* • Marcel Iures *Golitsyn* ■ *Dir* Brian De Palma • *Scr* David Koepp, Robert Towne, from a story by David Koepp, Steven Zaillian, from the TV series by Bruce Geller

Mission: Impossible 2
★★★★ 15

Action spy thriller 1999 · US · Colour · 118min

By replacing the tired spy shenanigans of the original TV series with the slick, slow-motion mayhem that has become his trademark, John Woo creates a sequel very different from the first *Mission: Impossible*. Admittedly, there's a distinct shortage of pulse-quickening, slam-bang action in the first hour, which finds Tom Cruise wooing lithe lady thief Thandie Newton before heading Down Under to stop bad guy Dougray Scott holding the world to ransom. Around the halfway mark, though, Woo cranks the pace up a gear. If it's adrenaline you're after, look no further. NS DVD

Tom Cruise *Ethan Hunt* • Dougray Scott *Sean Ambrose* • Thandie Newton *Nyah Hall* • Ving Rhames *Luther Stickel* • Richard Roxburgh *Hugh Stamp* • John Polson *Billy Baird* • Anthony Hopkins *Mission Commander Swanbeck* ■ *Dir* John Woo • *Scr* Robert Towne, Ronald D Moore, from a story by Brannon Braga, from the TV series by Bruce Geller • *Cinematographer* Jeffrey L Kimball

Mission: Impossible III
★★★ 12

Action spy thriller 2006 · US · Colour · 120min

Impossible Missions Force agent Ethan Hunt (Tom Cruise) springs into action for a third time as the mega-budget espionage franchise rolls on. Newly betrothed Hunt is called out of retirement to rescue a former trainee who's been kidnapped by a ruthless arms dealer (an under-used Philip Seymour Hoffman). But when the assignment goes wrong, it's Hunt's new wife (Michelle Monaghan) who's the primary target for revenge. The race against time that follows is fast-paced and slick, yet for all the film's visual intensity, the formula itself feels stale and mechanical. SF DVD

Tom Cruise *Ethan Hunt* • Philip Seymour Hoffman *Owen Davian* • Michelle Monaghan *Julia* • Ving Rhames *Luther* • Billy Crudup *Musgrave* • Jonathan Rhys Meyers *Declan* • Keri Russell *Lindsey* • Laurence Fishburne *John Brassel* • Maggie Q *Zhen* • Simon Pegg *Benji Dunn* ■ *Dir* JJ Abrams • *Scr* JJ Abrams, Alex Kurtzman, Roberto Orci, from the TV series by Bruce Geller

Mission: Impossible – Ghost Protocol ★★★★ 12

Action spy thriller 2011 · US · Colour · 127min

The Incredibles director Brad Bird transfers his dazzling and dynamic skills to the live-action format superbly in his gripping rejuvenation of the spy action franchise. Agent Ethan Hunt (Tom Cruise) and his crack team are blamed for a botched mission, and the entire Impossible Missions Force is disbanded (the ghost protocol of the title). Cut off from all support, the agents must attempt to stop a rogue extremist scientist (Michael Nyqvist) from causing a nuclear armageddon. The story may sound familiar, but the gadgets are more outlandish than ever, the spectacle absolutely amazing and the special effects as high-end as they come. It's an inventive, relentless and tension-laden caper. AJ Violence. DVD

Tom Cruise *Ethan Hunt* • Paula Patton *Jane* • Simon Pegg *Benji* • Jeremy Renner *Brandt* • Michael Nyqvist *Hendricks* • Vladimir Mashkov *Anatoly Sidirov* • Samuli Edelmann *Wistrom* • Anil Kapoor *Brij Nath* • Léa Seydoux *Sabine Moreau* • Josh Holloway *Hanaway* • Ving Rhames *Luther Stickell* • Michelle Monaghan *Julia Meade* ■ *Dir* Brad Bird • *Scr* Josh Appelbaum, André Nemec, from the TV series by Bruce Geller • *Cinematographer* Robert Elswit

Mission: Impossible – Rogue Nation ★★★★ 12

Action spy adventure 2015 · US · Colour · 131min

Dismantled by the CIA, the IMF (Impossible Missions Force) covertly reforms and struggles to neutralise The Syndicate, an insidious global threat that those in authority refuse to believe exists, in the fifth solidly satisfying episode of the spy thriller franchise. On impressive form, Tom Cruise is once more the master of all he surveys whether agilely putting himself in harm's way – the much-touted aeroplane stunt, done for real – or sending himself up as "the living manifestation of destiny". With ace support from menacing villain Sean Harris, this sleek well-oiled machine is a fast and furious delight. AJ Some violence. DVD

Tom Cruise *Ethan Hunt* • Jeremy Renner *William Brandt* • Simon Pegg *Benji Dunn* • Rebecca Ferguson *Ilsa Faust* • Ving Rhames *Luther Stickell* • Sean Harris *Solomon Lane* ■ *Dir* Christopher McQuarrie • *Scr* Drew Pearce, Christopher McQuarrie

Mission to Lars ★★★★
Documentary 2012 · UK/US · Colour · 74min

The premise of this documentary is wholly contrived, but it's made with sincerity. Filmmaker Will Spicer and his journalist sister Kate (best known as a food critic) aim to get to know their autistic brother Tom a bit better on a road trip across the States to meet his hero, Metallica drummer Lars Ulrich. A potentially intrusive and sentimental scenario is tackled with great compassion and wit in a film that illustrates why disability should never be a handicap. It also reveals the softer side of hard rock. DP DVD

Kate Spicer • Tom Spicer • Lars Ulrich ■ *Dir* William Spicer, James Moore

Mission to Mars ★★★ PG
Science-fiction drama
1999 · US · Colour · 108min

Brian De Palma slums it with his first science-fiction melodrama, which comes loaded with sentiment, camp moments and risible dialogue. However, while there's nothing new in this red planet space opera, the *Carrie* director covers its drawbacks with pristine craftsmanship, trademark suspense sequences and a full quota of sharp computer visuals. Nasa astronauts Gary Sinise and Tim Robbins embark on a rescue mission to the planet and make an extraordinary discovery. AJ DVD

Gary Sinise *Jim McConnell* • Don Cheadle *Mission Commander Luke Graham* • Connie Nielsen *Mars Rescue Mission specialist Dr Terri Fisher* • Tim Robbins *Commander Woody Blake* • Jerry O'Connell *Mission Specialist Phil Ohlmyer* • Armin Mueller-Stahl *Ray Beck* ■ *Dir* Brian De Palma • *Scr* John Thomas, Jim Thomas, Graham Yost, from a story by John Thomas, Jim Thomas, Lowell Cannon

Mission to Moscow★★★★ U
Drama 1943 · US · BW · 121min

This prestigious Warner Bros epic is based on US ambassador Joseph E Davies's bestseller about his pre-Second World War years in the Soviet Union, and is introduced by Davies himself. What lends it particular piquancy today is its documentary-style depiction of a pre-Cold War, pre-Red Scare Russia, filmed at an impressive pace by director Michael Curtiz. Walter Huston is ideally cast as the avuncular Davies, and it's sobering to realise that in subsequent years the film was denounced as pro-Communist propaganda because of its view of Stalin as a benevolent ruler. TS

Walter Huston *Ambassador Joseph E Davies* • Ann Harding *Mrs Davies* • Oscar Homolka *Maxim Litvinov* • George Tobias *Freddie* • Gene Lockhart *Vyacheslav Molotov* • Frieda Inescort *Madame Molotov* • Eleanor Parker *Emlen Davies* • Richard Travis *Paul Grosjean* ■ *Dir* Michael Curtiz • *Scr* Howard Koch, from the non-fiction book by Joseph E Davies

The Missionary ★★★ 15
Period comedy 1982 · UK · Colour · 77min

In his first solo film venture away from the Pythons, Michael Palin came up with this saucy comedy. Palin is pleasing enough as an innocent abroad in the crinoline jungle of Edwardian prostitution, but the supporting cast has all the fun, with Maggie Smith in fine fettle as a frustrated aristocrat. Palin struggles to sustain the comedy, but Richard Loncraine lashes on the period style to good effect. DP Swearing. DVD

Michael Palin *Reverend Charles Fortescue* • Maggie Smith *Lady Ames* • Trevor Howard *Lord Ames* • Denholm Elliott *The Bishop* • Michael Hordern *Slatterthwaite* • Graham Crowden *Reverend Fitzbanks* • Phoebe Nicholls *Deborah* • Tricia George *Ada* ■ *Dir* Richard Loncraine • *Scr* Michael Palin

Mississippi ★★
Musical comedy 1935 · US · BW · 80min

To escape accusations of cowardice, a creamy-voiced Southerner joins a showboat on the Mississippi, finds true love and rescues his reputation. Directed by A Edward Sutherland as a vehicle for Bing Crosby, this rambling period musical is partly redeemed by several Rodgers and Hart numbers, while WC Fields is splendid as the boat's captain. RK

Bing Crosby *Tom Grayson/Col Steele* • WC Fields *Commodore Orlando Jackson* • Joan Bennett *Lucy Rumford* • Queenie Smith *Alabam'* • Gail Patrick *Elvira Rumford* ■ *Dir* A Edward Sutherland • *Scr* Francis Martin, Jack Cunningham, Claude Binyon, Herbert Fields, from the play *Magnolia* by Booth Tarkington

Mississippi Burning
★★★★ 18

Drama based on a true story
1988 · US · Colour · 122min

In this powerful drama from director Alan Parker, Gene Hackman gives a mesmerising performance as a Southern States FBI agent fighting racism with local knowledge and canny psychology. Willem Dafoe is equally impressive, if more restrained, as his rule-obsessed Ivy League partner. Parker's wonderful creation crackles with dramatic tension and simmering violence that often reaches boiling point. Loosely based on a true story and shot with great visual flair (Peter Biziou won the Oscar for best cinematography), this is a gripping evocation of the early days of the civil rights movement. SH Violence, swearing. DVD

Gene Hackman *Rupert Anderson* • Willem Dafoe *Alan Ward* • Frances McDormand *Mrs Pell* • Brad Dourif *Deputy Pell* • R Lee Ermey *Mayor Tilman* • Gailard Sartain *Sheriff Stuckey* • Stephen Tobolowsky *Townley* • Michael Rooker *Frank Bailey* • Pruitt Taylor Vince *Lester Cowens* ■ *Dir* Alan Parker • *Scr* Chris Gerolmo

The Mississippi Gambler
★★★ U

Adventure 1953 · US · Colour · 98min

Matinée idol Tyrone Power stars as a handsome and honest riverboat gambler, forced to jump ship with partner John McIntire to chase comely Piper Laurie in New Orleans. The studio sets and location photography look superb, but the leads are dull and the plot unnecessarily complicated. TS

Tyrone Power *Mark Fallon* • Piper Laurie *Angelique Duroux* • Julia Adams [Julie Adams] *Ann Conant* • John McIntire *Kansas John Polly* • William Reynolds *Pierre* • Paul Cavanagh *Edmund Duroux* • John Baer *Laurent Duroux* ■ *Dir* Rudolph Maté • *Scr* Seton I Miller

Mississippi Grind ★★★★ 15
Drama 2015 · US · Colour · 108min

A brace of fine turns from Ben Mendelsohn and Ryan Reynolds are at the heart of this bittersweet buddy movie that pleasingly brings to mind great character-driven dramas like John Schlesinger's *Midnight Cowboy*. Mendelsohn plays an increasingly desperate gambling addict in hock to the local loan shark (an icily brilliant Alfre Woodard) so he plans escape with a free-spirited stranger (Reynolds). Mendelsohn skilfully and subtly sketches a complex character, but it's Reynolds who really breaks out, delivering a layered, careful performance. AS Swearing.

Ryan Reynolds *Curtis* • Ben Mendelsohn *Gerry* • Sienna Miller *Simone* • Alfre Woodard *Sam* ■ *Dir/Scr* Ryan Fleck, Anna Boden

Mississippi Masala★★★★ 15
Romantic drama 1991 · US · Colour · 112min

A masala is a culinary collection of hot and colourful spices used in curry dishes. Here, though, it's a good word to describe the Mississippi community where black American Denzel Washington falls in love with Asian woman Sarita Choudhury, causing tension between their families. As a mix of romance and racism, Mira Nair's follow-up to *Salaam Bombay!* (1988) ends on an ingenuously optimistic note. Roshan Seth is powerfully credible as Choudhury's bigoted father, however. TH

Denzel Washington *Demetrius* • Sarita Choudhury *Mina* • Roshan Seth *Jay* • Sharmila Tagore *Kinnu* • Charles S Dutton *Tyrone* • Joe Seneca *Williben* • Ranjit Chowdhry *Anil* ■ *Dir* Mira Nair • *Scr* Sooni Taraporevala

Mississippi Mermaid ★★ 12
Romantic mystery 1969 · Fr/It · Colour · 117min

Catherine Deneuve arrives on the island of Réunion to marry plantation owner Jean-Paul Belmondo in this adaptation of a Cornell Woolrich novel, transformed by François Truffaut into a lavish study of obsessive love. Things turn darker when the tropics give way to winter in the French Alps and romance turns to murder. This was the director's first major flop, originally released abroad in a slightly cut and badly dubbed version that rendered the dialogue risible. AT French +subtitles. DVD

Jean-Paul Belmondo *Louis Mahé* • Catherine Deneuve *Marion/Julie Roussel* • Michel Bouquet *Comolli* • Nelly Borgeaud *Berthe Roussel* • Marcel Berbert *Jardine* ■ *Dir* François Truffaut • *Scr* François Truffaut, from the novel *Waltz into Darkness* by William Irish [Cornell Woolrich]

The Missouri Breaks
★★★★ 15
Western 1976 · US · Colour · 120min

This film has a shambles of a plot but is still exciting stuff because of the ego battle between Marlon Brando and Jack Nicholson. Brando plays a hired bounty hunter, pitting his wits against horse-thief Nicholson amid the conflict between Montana ranchers and rustlers, and both actors twitch their way through an upstaging duel that is as mesmerising as it is arrogant. Director Arthur Penn seems to stand back from this clash of the titans, though his view of pioneer days is still so fascinatingly uncluttered and fresh that you can almost smell the raw wood of log cabins. TH Violence, swearing. *DVD*

Marlon Brando *Robert E Lee Clayton* · Jack Nicholson *Tom Logan* · Randy Quaid *Little Tod* · Kathleen Lloyd *Jane Braxton* · Frederic Forrest *Cary* · Harry Dean Stanton *Calvin* · John McLiam *David Braxton* ■ *Dir* Arthur Penn · *Scr* Thomas McGuane · *Music* John Williams

The Mist
★★★ 15
Science-fiction horror 2007 · US · Colour · 120min

Smoke machines and B-movie clichés go into overdrive in a Stephen King adaptation that's actually more interested in metaphors than monsters. Thomas Jane plays a small-town resident who is trapped in a grocery store with a ragtag group of locals when a mysterious mist rolls in. As monstrous tentacles and mutant insects emerge from the fog, the captive townsfolk split into factions, with a batty old maid (Marcia Gay Harden) preaching fire and brimstone while Jane's resourceful hero prefers a more hands-on approach to their dilemma. Unlike Frank Darabont's previous King adaptations (*The Green Mile*, *The Shawshank Redemption*), this is more of a 1950s monster movie with McCarthyite panic replaced by warnings about the dangers of religious fanaticism. The claustrophobic setting and committed ensemble cast give it a certain frisson, but it's difficult to reconcile the wordy screenplay with the slightly ludicrous giant bugs. JR *DVD* Blu

Thomas Jane *David Drayton* · Marcia Gay Harden *Mrs Carmody* · Laurie Holden *Amanda Dumfries* · André Braugher *Brent Norton* · Toby Jones *Ollie Weeks* · William Sadler *Jim Grondin* · Jeffrey DeMunn *Dan Miller* · Frances Sternhagen *Irene Reppler* ■ *Dir* Frank Darabont · *Scr* Frank Darabont, from the novella by Stephen King

Mistaken for Strangers
★★★ 15
Music documentary 2013 · US · Colour · 74min

Tom Berninger's candid, funny and surprisingly touching documentary charts his experiences as a roadie with his older brother Matt's band, moody US indie rockers The National, as they embark on a year-long world tour. But it's clear from the start that this affable but gaff-prone, heavy metal-lovin' guy is very much the square peg in the operation: his inept handling of his duties (including losing the celebrity guest at the band's LA gig), hard-partying ways and general lack of tour etiquette make him more of a liability than a help. It's not until we see Berninger's efforts to bring the material together that the film offers its satisfying pay-off. JH Swearing.

Tom Berninger · Matt Berninger · Aaron Dessner · Bryce Dessner ■ *Dir* Tom Berninger

Mr and Mrs Bridge
★★★ PG
Period drama 1990 · UK · Colour · 125min

The winning Merchant Ivory partnership is off target in this pretty but ultimately disappointing vehicle for Paul Newman and his wife Joanne Woodward. It's another of director James Ivory's polite studies of emotional repression, but the rambling, episodic tale of American family life in the 1930s and 1940s lacks cohesion. However, the two stars are superb as the eponymous married couple: Newman all starched conservatism as the stiff-necked lawyer, stubbornly resisting the changes around

him; and Woodward the devoted wife attempting in her own quiet way to open his eyes. JF

Paul Newman *Walter Bridge* · Joanne Woodward *India Bridge* · Robert Sean Leonard *Douglas Bridge* · Margaret Welsh *Carolyn Bridge* · Kyra Sedgwick *Ruth Bridge* · Blythe Danner *Grace Barron* · Simon Callow *Dr Alex Sauer* ■ *Dir* James Ivory · *Scr* Ruth Prawer Jhabvala, from the novels *Mr Bridge* and *Mrs Bridge* by Evan S Connell

Mr and Mrs '55
★★★★ U
Romantic comedy drama 1955 · Ind · BW · 129min

Even Busby Berkeley would have been proud of the musical numbers in this classic Bollywood masala from Guru Dutt. Ostensibly a satire at the expense of the urban upper echelons, this is also a delightfully romantic comedy, in which Dutt is hired as a groom by heiress Madhubala for the wedding of convenience that will fulfil the terms of her father's will. Don't look for any plot sophistication, just revel in the joyous performances of the leads and the wholly cinematic, endlessly inventive song-and-dance routines. DP Hindi +subtitles. *DVD*

Madhubala *Anita* · Lalita Pawar *Seeta Devi* · Guru Dutt *Preetam Kumar* · Johnny Walker *Johnny* · Tuntun *Lily D'Silva* ■ *Dir* Guru Dutt · *Scr* Abrar Alvi, Majrooh Sultanpuri

Mr and Mrs Loving
★★★
Drama based on a true story 1993 · US · Colour · 104min

Timothy Hutton stars in this powerful, made-for-TV, civil rights drama, set in the 1950s and based on a true story. Hutton and Lela Rochon play a couple in breach of local laws following their interracial marriage. The resulting benchmark trial by the Supreme Court is given the right degree of gravitas by director Richard Friedenberg, and he is well served by his two leads. TH

Timothy Hutton *Richard Loving* · Lela Rochon *Mildred "Bean" Jeter* · Ruby Dee *Sophia* · Bill Nunn *Leonard* · Corey Parker *Bernie Cohen* · Isaiah Washington *Blue* · Lawrence Dane *Sheriff* ■ *Dir/Scr* Richard Friedenberg

Mr and Mrs Smith
★★★ U
Screwball comedy 1941 · US · BW · 90min

Carole Lombard had always wanted to star in an Alfred Hitchcock film and, although situation comedy was far from Hitchcock's forte, he agreed to take the assignment as a favour for a friend. The result is a patchy farce in which Lombard and Robert Montgomery discover that their marriage is invalid and set about trying to outdo each other in their pleasure at being single. Even a screwball maestro like Howard Hawks would have been pushed to do much with the clunky script, and Hitch's lack of interest is apparent. Lombard took over the director's chair for Hitch's obligatory cameo in which he plays a drunk asking for money. DP *DVD*

Carole Lombard *Ann Smith* · Robert Montgomery *David Smith* · Gene Raymond *Jeff* · Jack Carson *Chuck* · Philip Merivale *Mr Custer* · Lucile Watson *Mrs Custer* · William Tracy *Sammy* · Charles Halton *Mr Deever* ■ *Dir* Alfred Hitchcock · *Scr* Norman Krasna

Mr & Mrs Smith
★★★ 15
Romantic action comedy 2005 · US · Colour · 115min

In this enjoyably daft action comedy, Brad Pitt and Angelina Jolie play a married couple who are bored with each other (to many, the movie's most preposterous conceit) and also professional killers (unknown to one another) hired to rub each other out. Director Doug Liman combines wit with stylish mayhem to great effect here, though some will feel that he lurches into overkill in the last half hour. Although it's supremely silly, Pitt and Jolie look outrageously good in their roles and it's fun while it lasts. AS Violence, swearing, sex scenes. *DVD* Blu

Brad Pitt *John Smith* · Angelina Jolie *Jane Smith* · Vince Vaughn *Eddie* · Adam Brody *Benjamin Danz* · Kerry Washington *Jasmine* · Keith David

Father · Chris Weitz *Martin Coleman* · Rachael Huntley *Suzy Coleman* · Michelle Monaghan *Gwen* ■ *Dir* Doug Liman · *Scr* Simon Kinberg

Mr Baseball
★★ 15
Comedy 1992 · US · Colour · 103min

Tom Selleck was never much of an actor for detail and here paints his has-been hero with too broad a brush. Even though his character, a faded baseball player transferred to Japan, is meant to be annoying the locals because of his arrogance, Selleck just can't resist letting his natural charm wash over the screen. Director Fred Schepisi reduces the pace to a tepid canter. JM Swearing.

Tom Selleck *Jack Elliot* · Ken Takakura *Uchiyama* · Aya Takanashi *Hiroko Uchiyama* · Dennis Haysbert *Max "Hammer" Dubois* · Toshi Shioya *Yoji Nishimura* · Kosuke Toyohara *Toshi Yamashita* · Toshizo Fujiwara *Ryoh Mukai* ■ *Dir* Fred Schepisi · *Scr* Gary Ross, Kevin Wade, Monte Merrick, Theo Pelletier, John Junkerman

Mr Bean's Holiday
★★★ PG
Comedy 2007 · UK · Colour · 85min

A little Mr Bean definitely goes a long way. That said, ten years after his first big-screen appearance, this second film outing for Rowan Atkinson's slightly creepy comic creation is, for the first hour at least, really rather good. Bean, who has won a Côte d'Azur holiday in a church raffle, heads off to Paris by train and proceeds to bumble his way across France. Its only real purpose seems to be to offer a somewhat lost-looking Willem Dafoe the chance to guest-star as a pretentious film director, while Bean is needlessly turned from zero to hero. In this case, a little less of a good thing would have been rather more. DA *DVD* Blu CS

Rowan Atkinson *Mr Bean* · Max Baldry *Stepan* · Emma de Caunes *Sabine* · Willem Dafoe *Carson Clay* · Karel Roden *Emil* · Jean Rochefort *Maitre d'* · Steve Pemberton *Vicar* ■ *Dir* Steve Bendelack · *Scr* Robin Driscoll, Hamish McColl, from a story by Simon McBurney, from a character created by Richard Curtis, Rowan Atkinson

Mr Belvedere Goes to College
★★ U
Comedy 1949 · US · BW · 82min

Clifton Webb had made a spectacular success playing the egocentric genius Lynn Belvedere in the previous year's *Sitting Pretty*, and this was the first of two sequels in which he played the same character. Proposing to earn a four-year degree in one year, he enters college; alas, his escapades are too predictable to generate the amusement intended. Shirley Temple, nearing the end of her film career, and Tom Drake provide romance. TV

Clifton Webb *Lynn Belvedere* · Shirley Temple *Ellen Baker* · Tom Drake *Bill Chase* · Alan Young *Avery Brubaker* · Jessie Royce Landis *Mrs Chase* · Kathleen Hughes *Kay Nelson* ■ *Dir* Elliott Nugent · *Scr* Richard Sale, Mary Loos, Mary McCall Jr, from the character created by Gwen Davenport

Mr Belvedere Rings the Bell
★★★ U
Comedy 1951 · US · BW · 87min

Former Broadway musical star Clifton Webb (and his infamous mother, who went with him everywhere) had been around since the silent days, but it took his portrayal of the sour-tongued misanthrope Belvedere in 1948's *Sitting Pretty* to actually endear him to movie audiences. In this light-hearted second sequel, Belvedere takes up residence in an old people's home to prove age is no barrier to living a full life. TS

Clifton Webb *Lynn Belvedere/Oliver Erwenter* · Joanne Dru *Miss Tripp* · Hugh Marlowe *Reverend Watson* · Zero Mostel *Emmett* · William Lynn *Mr Beebe* · Doro Merande *Mrs Hammer* · Frances Brandt *Miss Hoadley* ■ *Dir* Henry Koster · *Scr* Ranald MacDougall, from the play *The Silver Whistle* by Robert C McEnroe and the character created by Gwen Davenport

Mr Billion
★★ PG
Action adventure 1977 · US · Colour · 88min

Spaghetti western star Terence Hill got his Hollywood break with this road-movie take on *Mr Deeds Goes to Town*. He plays an amiable Italian mechanic who inherits a fortune but must go to the US to get it. Of course, there are diversions (including Valerie Perrine's buxom detective) to slow him down, but the star lacks the knockabout charm of, say, Burt Reynolds to carry off what is only mildly watchable. JA

Terence Hill *Guido Falcone* · Valerie Perrine *Rosi Jones* · Jackie Gleason *John Cutler* · Slim Pickens *Duane Hawkins* · William Redfield *Leopold Lacy* · Chill Wills *Colonel Clayton T Winkle* · Dick Miller *Bernie* · RG Armstrong *Sheriff TC Bishop* ■ *Dir* Jonathan Kaplan · *Scr* Ken Friedman, Jonathan Kaplan

Mr Blandings Builds His Dream House
★★★★ U
Comedy 1948 · US · BW · 94min

Many viewers will identify with the plight of Cary Grant and Myrna Loy in this sublime comedy. As the married couple who move to the countryside and do, quite literally, what the title states, Grant and Loy get conned by every cowboy builder along the way. The film was remade in 1985 as *The Money Pit*, but it wasn't as funny or stylish as this original, as neither Tom Hanks nor Shelley Long could compete with Grant and Loy at their best – just watch Loy recite her proposed colour scheme! TS

Cary Grant *Jim Blandings* · Myrna Loy *Muriel Blandings* · Melvyn Douglas *Bill Cole* · Sharyn Moffett *Joan Blandings* · Connie Marshall *Betsy Blandings* · Louise Beavers *Gussie* · Harry Shannon *Mr Tesander* ■ *Dir* HC Potter · *Scr* Norman Panama, Melvin Frank, from the novel by Eric Hodgins

Mr Brooks
★★★ 18
Psychological thriller 2007 · US/Aus · Colour · 115min

The chief delight in this shamelessly overwrought but sporadically entertaining thriller is watching two of Hollywood's finest actors dally with material obviously beneath them and fashion it into something above the routine. Kevin Costner (beautifully cast both to and against type) is Earl Brooks, a respected businessman who is attempting to give up a secret addiction – namely, to random murder. But his alter ego (a lightly sinister William Hurt) slyly coaxes him into further slaughter. Events are further complicated by a blackmailer who wants to join in the bloody mayhem. It all spins off the rails in the last act, and Demi Moore is shriekingly irritating as a Clarice Starling-style detective. But a few effective twists and shocks are enough to make it worth suspending your disbelief. AS *DVD*

Kevin Costner *Earl Brooks* · Demi Moore *Detective Tracy Atwood* · Dane Cook *Mr Smith* · William Hurt *Marshall* · Marg Helgenberger *Emma Brooks* · Ruben Santiago-Hudson *Hawkins* · Danielle Panabaker *Jane Brooks* · Aisha Hinds *Nancy Hart* · Lindsay Crouse *Captain Lister* · Jason Lewis *Jesse Vialo* ■ *Dir* Bruce A Evans · *Scr* Bruce A Evans, Raynold Gideon

Mr Calzaghe
★★★ 15
Sports documentary 2015 · UK · Colour · 89min

The title of this film portrait refers to undefeated Welsh-Italian boxer Joe Calzaghe, the longest-reigning super middleweight world champion in history. But, though he is the headline act here, it's his charismatic dad Enzo (also his trainer) who dominates this stylish and literally hard-hitting documentary. For the most part, Joe lets his fists do the talking via quality ring footage from his most famous matches. Slickly made though thoroughly non-critical, it should appeal to fans of the *Italian Dragon* even if it is a bit light on its feet. DA Swearing. *DVD* Blu

Joe Calzaghe · Michael J Fox · Mike Tyson ■ *Dir* Vaughan Sivell

M

Mr Corbett's Ghost ★★ PG
Fantasy drama   1986 · UK · Colour · 54min

Directed by Danny Huston (John Huston's son) this is a slapdash adaptation of Leon Garfield's superb story about transferred identities and eerie disappearances. Starring Paul Scofield, it was supervised by John Huston – who also acted in it – but its period atmosphere is TV-fustian and it never takes on the book's elaborate tension. That is probably why it was never theatrically released. TH *DVD*

Paul Scofield *Mr Corbett* • John Huston *Soul collector* • Burgess Meredith *Mad Tom* • Mark Farmer *Benjamin Partridge* ■ *Dir* Danny Huston • *Scr* Terry Wilson, from Leon Garfield's novel

Mister Cory ★★★
Drama   1957 · US · Colour · 92min

Tony Curtis emerges from the slums of Chicago, becomes a dishwasher at a swish country club, teams up with gambler Charles Bickford and ends up owning a casino. It's a rags-to-riches tale, which helped move Curtis out of the matinée idol, sword-and-sandal ghetto. As written by Blake Edwards – this was also his third directing stint – the story is shot through with cynicism. The use of CinemaScope and colour, though, tends to blunt the film's sharp edge. AT

Tony Curtis *Cory* • Martha Hyer *Abby Vollard* • Charles Bickford *Biloxi* • Kathryn Grant *Jen Vollard* • William Reynolds *Alex Wyncott* • Henry Daniell *Earnshaw* • Russ Morgan *Ruby Matrobe* ■ *Dir* Blake Edwards • *Scr* Blake Edwards, from a story by Leo Rosten

Mr Death: the Rise and Fall of Fred A Leuchter Jr ★★★★
Documentary   1999 · US · Colour · 90min

Errol Morris has always fed on obsessional outsiders, but none has been so dangerously deluded as Fred A Leuchter, the American "execution expert" whose vanity led to his becoming a reviled apologist for Holocaust denial. But Morris avoids mockery, as he demonstrates Leuchter's commitment to bringing humanity and efficiency to the various death penalty procedures, before following him to Auschwitz, where he spent his honeymoon illicitly and inexpertly collecting evidence to support Ernst Zündel's theories denying the existence of the gas chambers. Chilling and compelling. DP

■ *Dir* Errol Morris • *Cinematographers* Peter Donohue, Robert Richardson

Mr Deeds ★ 12
Comedy   2002 · US · Colour · 92min

In this remake of *Mr Deeds Goes to Town* , comedian Adam Sandler takes on the Gary Cooper role of the country bumpkin who inherits a business empire. Whereas Cooper was an Everyman, Sandler is just the man in the street, and director Steven Brill is no Frank Capra; he has replaced wit with smut and sentiment with saccharin. StH Swearing, violence. *DVD*

Adam Sandler *Longfellow Deeds* • Winona Ryder *Babe Bennett/Pam Dawson* • Peter Gallagher *Chuck Cedar* • Jared Harris *Mac McGrath* • John Turturro *Emilio Lopez* • Conchata Ferrell *Jan* • Steve Buscemi *Crazy Eyes* ■ *Dir* Steven Brill • *Scr* Tim Herlihy, from the film *Mr Deeds Goes to Town* by Robert Riskin, from the story *Opera Hat* by Clarence Budington Kelland

Mr Deeds Goes to Town ★★★★ U
Comedy   1936 · US · BW · 110min

A popular and critical success in its day, this slight morality tale won an Oscar for director Frank Capra, but today's more cynical audience might find it too full of Capra-corn. Lanky Gary Cooper is wonderful as Longfellow Deeds, the tuba-playing "Cinderella Man" who inherits a small fortune. But the character of the investigative reporter played by Jean Arthur rings false, as do the myriad minor roles, although many are well cast. While it lacks a truly convincing climax, it's still very

funny and struck a blow for recognition of the ordinary Joe as movie hero. TS *DVD*

Gary Cooper *Longfellow Deeds* • Jean Arthur *Louise "Babe" Bennett* • George Bancroft *MacWade* • Lionel Stander *Cornelius Cobb* • Douglass Dumbrille *John Cedar* • Raymond Walburn *Walter* • HB Warner *Judge Walker* • Margaret Matzenauer *Madame Pomponi* • Warren Hymer *Bodyguard* ■ *Dir* Frank Capra • *Scr* Robert Riskin, from the story *Opera Hat* by Clarence Budington Kelland

Mr Denning Drives North ★★★
Comedy thriller   1951 · UK · BW · 93min

John Mills looked brooding in the startling red-and-black poster for this film, and audiences might have found themselves somewhat disappointed by this genteel drama. Mills is excellent as the father who accidentally bumps off his daughter's devious lover, but acting honours are stolen by Sam Wanamaker as the truth-seeking boyfriend, and there's an excellent supporting cast of stalwarts. TS

John Mills *Tom Denning* • Phyllis Calvert *Kay Denning* • Eileen Moore *Liz Denning* • Sam Wanamaker *Chick Eddowes* • Herbert Lom *Mados* • Raymond Huntley *Wright* • Russell Waters *Harry Stopes* • Wilfrid Hyde White *Woods* • Bernard Lee *Inspector Dodds* ■ *Dir* Anthony Kimmins • *Scr* Alec Coppel, from his novel

Mr Destiny ★★ PG
Comedy drama   1990 · US · Colour · 105min

You might expect this fantasy to live up to its wistful plotline, as Michael Caine's bartender dispenses what-if potions to a baseball fan (James Belushi) who regrets the day all those years ago when he missed a home run. Yet as Belushi lives his life again, more successful but wishing he was still married to Linda Hamilton rather than his new wife (Rene Russo), it's hard not to see him as a tedious slob who can't make up his mind. TH *DVD*

James Belushi *Larry Burrows* • Linda Hamilton *Ellen Burrows* • Michael Caine *Mike* • Jon Lovitz *Clip Metzler* • Hart Bochner *Niles Pender* • Bill McCutcheon *Leo Hansen* • Rene Russo *Cindy Jo* • Jay O Sanders *Jackie Earle* • Maury Chaykin *Guzelman* ■ *Dir* James Orr • *Scr* James Orr, Jim Cruickshank

Mr Drake's Duck ★★★ U
Comedy   1950 · UK · BW · 85min

A bright, breezy comedy from British writer/director Val Guest about a duck that lays uranium eggs, this was filmed in an innocent era when the long-term effects of radiation poisoning were still unknown. Mrs Guest, the blonde and perky Yolande Donlan, plays Mrs Drake, who's married to suave Douglas Fairbanks Jr and who, together with her husband, breeds ducks on their Sussex farm, one of which turns out to be a source of possible riches. Very enjoyable, and popular in its day. TS

Douglas Fairbanks Jr *Don Drake* • Yolande Donlan *Penny Drake* • Howard Marion-Crawford *Major Travers* • Reginald Beckwith *Mr Boothby* • Wilfrid Hyde White *Mr May* • John Boxer *Sergeant* • Jon Pertwee *Reuben* • Peter Butterworth *Higgins* ■ *Dir* Val Guest • *Scr* Val Guest, from the play by Ian Messiter

Mister 880 ★★★ U
Comedy drama   1950 · US · BW · 89min

Amazingly based on a true story, this is a delightful light comedy about an old codger who has forged dollar bills for years and bewilderingly left the authorities in his wake. Lovable Edmund Gwenn, everybody's favourite Santa, is the junk collector with his own printing press, and Burt Lancaster, on the cusp of stardom, is all teeth and shoulders as the federal agent chasing him. TS

Burt Lancaster *Steve Buchanan* • Dorothy McGuire *Ann Winslow* • Edmund Gwenn *Skipper Miller* • Millard Mitchell *Mac* • Minor Watson *Judge O'Neil* • Howard St John *Chief* • Hugh Sanders *Thad Mitchell* • James Millican *Olie Johnson* ■ *Dir* Edmund Goulding • *Scr* Robert Riskin, from the *New Yorker* article *Old Eight Eighty* by St Clair McKelway

Mister Frost ★★ 15
Horror   1990 · Fr/UK · Colour · 99min

Jeff Goldblum makes an unlikely Satan in this tale about a mass murderer whose countryside estate is littered with mutilated victims. Arrested and sent to a mental institution, he confides to psychiatrist Kathy Baker that he is in fact the Devil. His mission is simple: to get her to kill him. Policeman Alan Bates is also involved, making for an overly earnest and rather ridiculous film. LH

Jeff Goldblum *Mister Frost* • Alan Bates *Felix Detweiler* • Kathy Baker *Dr Sarah Day* • Roland Giraud *Raymond Reynhardt* • François Négret *Christophe Kovac* • Jean-Pierre Cassel *Inspector Correlli* ■ *Dir* Philippe Setbon • *Scr* Philippe Setbon, Brad Lynch

Mr Hobbs Takes a Vacation ★★★ U
Comedy   1962 · US · Colour · 114min

James Stewart made some amiable movies during the 1960s, lightweight fluff that warmed the heart without stretching the brain. Here he's married to the lovely Maureen O'Hara, and the slight plot is encapsulated in the title. Contemporary heart-throbs Fabian and John Saxon add to the period charm, and the ingénue is Cliff Richard's flame from *Summer Holiday*, Lauri Peters. It's all rather endearing in a ramshackle kind of way. TS

James Stewart *Mr Hobbs* • Maureen O'Hara *Peggy Hobbs* • Fabian *Joe* • Lauri Peters *Katey* • Lili Gentle *Janie* • John Saxon *Byron* • John McGiver *Martin Turner* • Marie Wilson *Emily Turner* ■ *Dir* Henry Koster • *Scr* Nunnally Johnson, from the novel *Hobb's Vacation* by Edward Streeter

Mr Holland's Opus ★★★★ PG
Drama   1995 · US · Colour · 136min

Richard Dreyfuss strikes just the right note of sentiment and truth as music teacher Glenn Holland, who wonders if 30 years at the high school chalkface have been worthwhile, especially as he sacrificed his ambitions to be a composer. A shrewd mix of *Goodbye Mr Chips* and *It's a Wonderful Life*, it adds harsher ingredients including Mr Holland's neglect of his wife and hearing-impaired son to further the education of his students. The way Richard Dreyfuss lightens up his character makes the film satisfyingly accessible to young and old. TH Some swearing. *DVD*

Richard Dreyfuss *Glenn Holland* • Glenne Headly *Iris Holland* • Jay Thomas *Bill Meister* • Olympia Dukakis *Principal Jacobs* • William H Macy *Vice Principal Wolters* • Alicia Witt *Gertrude Lang* • Terrence Howard *Louis Russ* • Damon Whitaker *Bobby Tidd* ■ *Dir* Stephen Herek • *Scr* Patrick Sheane Duncan

Mr Holmes ★★★★ PG
Crime mystery   2014 · UK/US/Aus · Colour · 99min

This mystery takes a sympathetic look at the agonies of old age, as it finds one of the great fictional minds failing. Sherlock Holmes (Ian McKellen) is now a frail 93-year-old retiree living with housekeeper Laura Linney and her young son (Milo Parker). Haunted by scattershot memories, Holmes pieces together the fragments of his final case, in a story told partly in flashbacks. McKellen communicates Holmes's complex psychology through a range of scowls, sneers and scoffs, while the lively Parker makes for a delightful companion and Linney delivers dramatic conviction aplenty. *Mr Holmes* works its way deep under the skin and resists the sensational reveals of traditional murder mysteries, opting for more moving conclusions. EAS In English, Japanese. *DVD* BL

Ian McKellen *Sherlock Holmes* • Laura Linney *Mrs Munro* • Milo Parker *Roger* • Roger Allam *Dr Barrie* • Frances de la Tour *Madame Schirmer* • Hattie Morahan *Ann Kelmot* ■ *Dir* Bill Condon • *Scr* Bill Condon, Jeffrey Hatcher, from the novel *A Slight Trick of the Mind* by Mitch Cullin, from characters by Sir Arthur Conan Doyle

Mr Imperium ★ U
Drama   1951 · US · Colour · 86min

Lana Turner stars as a glamorous vocalist with a cowboy quartet who falls in love with European prince Ezio Pinza. When he inherits the throne, though, he can't consort with a commoner. Marking the screen debut of Metropolitan Opera star Pinza, this cardboard drivel was a disastrous bomb. Directed by Don Hartman, it boasts good-looking locations and sumptuous clothes, while Pinza is in good voice on the rare occasions he's permitted to sing. RK

Lana Turner *Fredda Barlo* • Ezio Pinza *Mr Imperium* • Marjorie Main *Mrs Cabot* • Barry Sullivan *Paul Hunter* • Cedric Hardwicke *Prime Minister Bernard* • Keenan Wynn *Motor cop* • Debbie Reynolds *Gwen* ■ *Dir* Don Hartman • *Scr* Don Hartman, Edwin H Knopf, from a play by Edwin H Knopf

Mr In-Between ★ 15
Romantic thriller   2001 · UK · Colour · 94min

Atom Egoyan's regular cinematographer Paul Sarossy makes his directorial debut with this disappointing adaptation. Much of the problem lies in Peter Waddington's plodding script and the lifeless performance of Andrew Howard as the dispassionate hitman whose ruthless streak is softened by a chance re-acquaintance with the object of his teenage affection, Geraldine O'Rawe. But the pitilessly sadistic sequences involving gentleman bad guys David Calder, Saeed Jaffrey and Clive Russell also undermine Sarossy's attempts to imbue proceedings with a sense of pessimistic realism. DP *DVD*

Andrew Howard *Jon* • Geraldine O'Rawe *Cathy* • David Calder *The Tattooed Man* • Andrew Tiernan *Andy* • Mark Benton *Phil* • Clive Russell *Mr Michaelmas* • Clint Dyer *Rickets* • Peter Waddington *Priest* • Saeed Jaffrey *Mr Basmati* ■ *Dir* Paul Sarossy • *Scr* Peter Waddington, from the novel by Neil Cross

Mr Jealousy ★★★
Romantic comedy drama   1997 · US · Colour · 105min

Eric Stoltz plays the mister of the title, a guy permanently obsessed about his dates' fidelity. His latest flame is Annabella Sciorra, but his relentless stalking and green-eyed psychology work against him. Director Noah Baumbach is sadly too concerned with "clever" pastiches of François Truffaut and Woody Allen to create a focused film. His script is good, as is his depiction of a generation of 30-year-olds refusing to grow old gracefully, but the end result is mixed. LH

Eric Stoltz *Lester Grimm* • Annabella Sciorra *Ramona Ray* • Chris Eigeman *Dashiell Frank* • Carlos Jacott *Vince* • Marianne Jean-Baptiste *Lucretia* • Brian Kerwin *Stephen* • Peter Bogdanovich *Dr Poke* • Bridget Fonda *Irene* ■ *Dir/Scr* Noah Baumbach

Mister Jerico ★★ U
Comedy crime caper   1969 · US · Colour · 81min

This run-of-the-mill comedy is chiefly of interest today for fans of Patrick Macnee, better known even then as John Steed in *The Avengers*. The usual ingredients of diamonds, crooks and blonde sirens can't make up for the lack of plot, although Herbert Lom is on hand to remind viewers of the *Pink Panther* capers. JA *DVD*

Patrick Macnee *Dudley Jerico* • Connie Stevens *Susan* • Herbert Lom *Victor Russo* • Marty Allen *Wally* • Leonardo Pieroni *Angelo* ■ *Dir* Sidney Hayers • *Scr* Philip Levene, from an idea by David T Chantler

Mister John ★★★★ 15
Drama   2013 · Ire/UK/Sing · Colour · 91min

As with their undervalued 2008 film *Helen*, writer/directors Joe Lawlor and Christine Molloy create a disconcerting character study here. Gerry (Aidan Gillen) travels to Singapore after the mysterious death of his brother John, an expat who ran a hostess bar, and he soon realises that he can slip into his brother's life as easily as his clothes. The success of this fascinating examination of masculinity and identity is due to Gillen, whose subtle central performance is utterly compelling. LB Swearing, sexual references. **DVD**

Aidan Gillen *Gerry Devine* • Zoe Tay *Kim Devine* • Claire Keelan *Kathleen Devine* • Michael Thomas Lester • Ashleigh Judith White *Isadora Devine* ■ *Dir/Scr* Joe Lawlor, Christine Molloy

Mister Johnson ★★★ PG

Period drama 1991 · US · Colour · 96min

Following on from *Driving Miss Daisy*, Bruce Beresford returned to the idea of a white master and a black servant, possibly hoping to garner the best director Oscar he didn't get the year before. It's colonial West Africa in the 1920s, and Mr Johnson (Maynard Eziashi) is the clerk of English administrator Harry Rudbeck. Unfortunately, this slight film has none of the depth of the Joyce Cary novel upon which it is based, and much of the blame can be laid at the director's door. Although Beresford peppers the movie with beautiful landscapes, there is not enough characterisation to really engage the viewer. JB

Pierce Brosnan *Harry Rudbeck* • Maynard Eziashi *Mister Johnson* • Edward Woodward *Sargy Gollup* • Beatie Edney *Celia Rudbeck* • Denis Quilley *Bulteen* • Nick Reding *Tring* ■ *Dir* Bruce Beresford • *Scr* William Boyd, Bruce Beresford, from the novel by Joyce Cary

Mr Jones ★★ 15

Romantic drama 1993 · US · Colour · 109min

Here's one Jones that audiences won't want to keep up with, as manic-depressive Richard Gere suffers a Freudian slip-up by having an affair with his psychiatrist, Lena Olin. Gere's mood-swinging hero displays surprising energy and verve, which was probably not the original intention: studio executives ordered extensive recutting in order to lighten up what was by all accounts a sombre movie, and the result makes uncomfortable viewing. TH Swearing. **DVD**

Richard Gere *Mr Jones* • Lena Olin *Dr Libbie Bowen* • Anne Bancroft *Dr Catherine Holland* • Tom Irwin *Patrick* • Delroy Lindo *Howard* • Bill Pullman *Construction site foreman* ■ *Dir* Mike Figgis • *Scr* Eric Roth, Michael Cristofer, from a story by Eric Roth

Mr Kingstreet's War ★★★

Adventure drama 1970 · US · Colour · 92min

Former Alfred Hitchcock leading lady Tippi Hedren became a lady with a cause after marrying African safari ecologist Noel Marshall, and made a worthy series of movies espousing wildlife campaigns. This film, not thought good enough for a cinema release in the UK, is an unusual and fascinating study of pre-Second World War Africa, where, despite the encroachment of the opposing Italian and British forces, the wildlife sanctuaries are preserved by a determined couple. In spite of its amateur origins, the casting of former heart-throbs John Saxon and Rossano Brazzi keeps the movie watchable. TS

John Saxon *Jim Kingstreet* • Tippi Hedren *Mary Kingstreet* • Rossano Brazzi *Count Ugo Bernadelli* • Brian O'Shaughnessy *Morgan* ■ *Dir* Percival Rubens

Mr Klein ★★★★ 12

Second World War thriller
1976 · Fr · Colour · 118min

Set in Paris during the Nazi occupation, this thriller by director Joseph Losey is one of his most poignant and Kafka-esque. Alain Delon is the Roman Catholic antiques dealer who fleeces Jews desperate to flee France. His world starts to unravel when he is mistaken for another Robert Klein, a Jew who is using his identity as a cover for subversive activities. Delon gives one of his greatest performances in this undervalued drama. TH French dubbed. **DVD**

Alain Delon *Mr Klein* • Jeanne Moreau *Florence* • Suzanne Flon *Concierge* • [Michel Lonsdale] *Pierre* • Juliet Berto *Janine* ■ *Dir* Joseph Losey • *Scr* Franco Solinas

Mister Lonely ★★ 15

Comedy drama
2007 · UK/Fr/Ire/US/Jpn · Colour · 111min

Director Harmony Korine's third film after *Gummo* and *julien donkey-boy* is an eccentric tale about celebrity impersonators. Diego Luna gives a quietly tragic turn as a Michael Jackson lookalike who joins a commune of faux celebrities after a chance encounter with Marilyn Monroe (Samantha Morton). The sight of the King of Pop frolicking with *Seven Year Itch*-era Monroe is decidedly surreal. However, beyond a few clumsy stabs at the dangers of celebrity adulation, the film's never much more than a rambling series of semi-improvised longueurs about the group's attempt to put on a variety show. A self-indulgent fancy dress party gone horribly wrong. JR **DVD** **BD**

Diego Luna *Michael Jackson* • Samantha Morton *Marilyn Monroe* • Denis Lavant *Charlie Chaplin* • James Fox *The Pope* • Werner Herzog *Father Umbrillo* • Leos Carax *Renard* • Richard Strange *Abraham Lincoln* • Anita Pallenberg *The Queen of England* ■ *Dir* Harmony Korine • *Scr* Harmony Korine, Avi Korine

Mr Lucky ★★★ U

Comedy 1943 · US · BW · 99min

Cary Grant stars as a cynical professional gambler who romances heiress Laraine Day. Having cheated the American War Relief Society, he redeems himself by turning his gambling ship into a vessel laden with medical supplies. It sounds tacky, and it is a bit, but the movie was a big hit in 1943 and Grant always rated it as one of his favourites "because the character I played was more like the real Cary Grant than any before". First-time screenwriter Milton Holmes was in fact a pro at the Beverly Hills Tennis Club who pitched the idea to Grant in the parking lot. AT

Cary Grant *Joe Adams* • Laraine Day *Dorothy Bryant* • Charles Bickford *Hard Swede* • Gladys Cooper *Capt Steadman* • Alan Carney *Crunk* • Henry Stephenson *Mr Bryant* • Paul Stewart *Zepp* ■ *Dir* HC Potter • *Scr* Milton Holmes, Adrian Scott, from the story *Bundles for Freedom* by Milton Holmes

Mr Magoo ★ PG

Comedy 1997 · US · Colour · 83min

The main joke of the original cartoon was the myopia of its hero, the lugubrious Magoo. In a squirm-inducing sop to political correctness, a title at the end of this live-action feature points out that short-sighted people are not being ridiculed – which, of course, they are. As Magoo, Leslie Nielsen shows his limitations as a comedian: he barely raises a smile, let alone a laugh. The plot, about the chase for a stolen jewel, is pathetic. AT Some violence. **DVD**

Leslie Nielsen *Mr Magoo* • Kelly Lynch *Luanne* • Matt Keeslar *Waldo* • Nick Chinlund *Bob Morgan* • Stephen Tobolowsky *Agent Chuck Stupak* • Ernie Hudson *Agent Gus Anders* • Jennifer Garner *Stacey* • Malcolm McDowell *Austin Cloquet* ■ *Dir* Stanley Tong • *Scr* Pat Proft, Tom Sherohman

Mr Magorium's Wonder Emporium ★★ U

Fantasy comedy drama
2007 · US · Colour · 90min

Stranger than Fiction writer Zach Helm makes his directorial debut with this family-friendly tale of an enchanted toy store. Dustin Hoffman hams it up as the eponymous 243-year-old proprietor, whose time on Earth's running out. He plans to pass the baton to his young assistant (a cutesy turn by Natalie Portman), but she has her heart set on becoming a composer. As you'd expect, the setting allows Helm to conjure up a colourful array of bells and whistles, but the paper-thin yarn fails to draw you in. Sadly, there's just not enough magic here to make it memorable. SP **DVD** **BD**

Natalie Portman *Molly Mahoney* • Dustin Hoffman *Mr Magorium* • Jason Bateman *Henry Weston* • Zach Mills *Eric Applebaum* • Ted Ludzik *Bellini* • Jonathan Potts *Dr Dunn* • Marcia Bennett *Lora* ■ *Dir/Scr* Zach Helm

Mr Majestyk ★★ 18

Action thriller 1974 · US · Colour · 99min

Charles Bronson is cast here in the unlikely role of a melon farmer. But when the Mafia starts interfering with his peaceful rural life, the star soon resorts to his violent ways to protect his workers and his harvest. Director Richard Fleischer has come up with a sort of *Death Wish* in Colorado – a combination that doesn't really work despite decent performances. Notably, the screenplay is written by Elmore Leonard. TS Violence, swearing. **DVD** **BD**

Charles Bronson *Vince Majestyk* • Al Lettieri *Frank Renda* • Linda Cristal *Nancy Chavez* • Lee Purcell *Wiley* • Paul Koslo *Bobby Kopas* • Taylor Lacher *Gene Lundy* • Frank Maxwell *Det Lt McAllen* • Alejandro Rey *Larry Mendoza* ■ *Dir* Richard Fleischer • *Scr* Elmore Leonard

Mr Mom ★★ PG

Comedy drama 1983 · US · Colour · 87min

In this role-reversal comedy, a dad gets fired from his high-powered job and winds up as a househusband while his wife goes out to work. Probably something of a novelty back in 1983, nowadays the tendency would be to tell "Mr Mom" to stop flapping and start coping. Michael Keaton and Teri Garr star, with support from Christopher Lloyd and Martin Mull, and they're all likeable enough, but the film takes the easy options, plumping for farce and slapstick. DA **DVD**

Michael Keaton *Jack Butler* • Teri Garr *Caroline Butler* • Frederick Koehler *Alex Butler* • Taliesin Jaffe *Kenny Butler* • Courtney White *Megan Butler* • Brittany White *Megan Butler* • Martin Mull *Ron Richardson* • Christopher Lloyd *Larry* ■ *Dir* Stan Dragoti • *Scr* John Hughes

Mr Morgan's Last Love ★★ 12

Comedy drama
2013 · Ger/ US/Bel/Fr · Colour · 110min

Michael Caine stars as Matthew, an American widower living in Paris whose cycle of grief is interrupted when he meets Pauline (Clémence Poésy), a young woman with whom he has an instant connection. But, with little in the way of development, the mood turns maudlin and this initially interesting liaison becomes increasingly static. Despite a shaky American accent, Caine is as watchable as ever and the flashbacks with Matthew and his wife (Jane Alexander) are heartbreaking at times. But, Caine's heart-rending flourish aside, this mawkish drama struggles to make a point. JL In English, French. Brief swearing. **DVD**

Michael Caine *Matthew Morgan* • Clémence Poésy *Pauline Laubie* • Gillian Anderson *Karen Morgan* • Jane Alexander *Joan Morgan* • Justin Kirk *Miles Morgan* ■ *Dir* Sandra Nettelbeck • *Scr* Sandra Nettelbeck, from the novel *La Douceur Assassine* by Françoise Dorner

Mr Moto in Danger Island ★★★

Detective drama 1939 · US · BW · 63min

The last filmed of the *Mr Moto* series (that began in 1937 with *Think Fast, Mr Moto*), although it was released before *Mr Moto Takes a Vacation*. Beginning to look bored with the part of the wily Japanese troubleshooter, Peter Lorre finds himself in Puerto Rico, where he loads the evidence against himself in order to lure a gang of murderous diamond smugglers into the open. There was a belated attempt to revive the detective in 1965 with *The Return of Mr Moto*. DP

Peter Lorre *Mr Moto* • Jean Hersholt *Sutter* • Amanda Duff *Joan Castle* • Warren Hymer *Twister McGurk* • Richard Lane *Commissioner Gordon* • Leon Ames *Commissioner Madero* • Douglass Dumbrille *Commander La Costa* ■ *Dir* Herbert I Leeds • *Scr* Peter Milne, from ideas by John Reinhardt, George Bricker, from the novel *Murder in Trinidad* by John W Vandercook, from the character created by JP Marquand

Mr Moto Takes a Chance ★★

Detective drama 1938 · US · BW · 63min

Inspired by JP Marquand's stories, the *Mr Moto* movies are hardly known for the clarity of their storylines. This one, though, is impenetrable. On his fourth outing as the Japanese detective, Peter Lorre finds himself in Cambodia in order to discover the secret of the caverns beneath a ruined temple. J Edward Bromberg has a ball as the chieftain. DP

Peter Lorre *Mr Moto* • Rochelle Hudson *Victoria Mason* • Robert Kent *Marty Weston* • J Edward Bromberg *Rajah Ali* • Chick Chandler *Chick Davis* • George Regas *Boker, High Priest* ■ *Dir* Norman Foster • *Scr* Lou Breslow, John Patrick, from a story by Willis Cooper, Norman Foster, from the character created by JP Marquand

Mr Moto Takes a Vacation ★★★ PG

Detective drama 1939 · US · BW · 59min

One of the last entries in the *Mr Moto* series; by the end of 1939, with Japan flexing its military muscles in South East Asia, the character was considered unsuitably heroic. This time, JP Marquand's master meddler is asked to protect an ancient African crown before it falls into the hands of a collector who has already nabbed some of the crown jewels. DP **DVD**

Peter Lorre *Mr Moto* • Joseph Schildkraut *Hendrik Manderson* • Lionel Atwill *Professor Hildebrand* • Virginia Field *Eleanor Kirke* • John King *Howard Stevens* • Iva Stewart *Susan French* ■ *Dir* Norman Foster • *Scr* Norman Foster, Philip MacDonald, from the character created by JP Marquand

Mr Moto's Gamble ★★★ PG

Detective drama 1938 · US · BW · 69min

Returning for the third time to the role of the wily Japanese detective, Peter Lorre cruises through this undemanding boxing mystery, originally intended as a case for Charlie Chan. However, Keye Luke, who played Chan's "Number One Son", puts in a welcome appearance alongside Maxie Rosenbloom as a trainee sleuth. The latter helps Moto discover how poison got on the gloves of contender Dick Baldwin during a bout on which gangster Douglas Fowley had placed a sizeable bet. DP **DVD**

Peter Lorre *Mr Moto* • Keye Luke *Lee Chan* • Dick Baldwin *Bill Steele* • Lynn Bari *Penny Kendall* • Douglas Fowley *Nick Crowder* • Jayne Regan *Linda Benton* ■ *Dir* James Tinling • *Scr* Charles Belden, Jerry Cady [Jerome Cady], from the character created by JP Marquand

Mr Moto's Last Warning ★★★

Detective drama 1938 · US · BW · 71min

The sixth in the series featuring Peter Lorre as JP Marquand's Japanese sleuth sees Mr Moto in the Middle East, doing battle with spies intent on sabotaging French ships in the Suez canal and blaming it on the British. The formula is B-movie basic, with lots of rat-a-tat chat, plenty of plot twists and a scarcity of clues. The supporting cast is premier league calibre. DP

Peter Lorre *Mr Moto* • Ricardo Cortez *Fabian* • Virginia Field *Connie Porter* • John Carradine *Danforth* • George Sanders *Eric Norvel* • Joan Carol *Mary Delacour* • Robert Coote *Rollo Venables* ■ *Dir* Norman Foster • *Scr* Philip MacDonald, Norman Foster, from the character created by JP Marquand

Mr Murder ★★ 15

Thriller 1998 · US/Ger/Neth · Colour · 126min

Though based on a book by horror maestro Dean R Koontz, this TV thriller places the emphasis on action rather than chills. Stephen Baldwin plays a writer of bizarre murder mysteries who becomes embroiled in a deadly real-life game, when a mix-up involving blood samples during a shady genetics experiment results in the creation of Baldwin's evil clone. The end result is enjoyable, if a tad unbelievable. JF Violence, swearing, nudity. **DVD**

Stephen Baldwin *Marty Stillwater/Alfie* • Julie Warner *Paige Stillwater* • Bill Smitrovich *Lieutenant Lowbock* • James Coburn *Drew Oslett Sr* • Thomas Haden Church *Drew Oslett Jr* ■ *Dir* Dick Lowry • *Scr* Stephen Tolkin, from a novel by Dean R Koontz

Mr Music ★★★ U
Musical   1950 · US · BW · 114min

This agreeable musical remake of 1935's *Accent on Youth*, itself based on a play, was tailor-made for the easy-going talents of Bing Crosby. Bing, who plays a middle-aged songwriter who would rather play off than write songs, gets to sing several lively Burke/Van Heusen numbers. However, the film – under the direction of prissy comic actor Richard Haydn is even more laid-back than its star. It's also far too long for its flimsy subject matter. The guest stars, including Peggy Lee and Groucho Marx, perk things up considerably. RB

Bing Crosby *Paul Merrick* • Nancy Olson *Katherine Holbrook* • Charles Coburn *Alex Conway* • Ruth Hussey *Lorna* • Robert Stack *Jefferson* • Ida Moore *Aunt Amy* • Tom Ewell *Haggerty* ■ *Dir* Richard Haydn • *Scr* Arthur Sheekman, from the play *Accent on Youth* by Samson Raphaelson

Mr Nanny ★★ PG
Comedy   1992 · US · Colour · 80min

This is the one where "Hulk" Hogan gets to dress up like a ballerina and aims to entertain what one assumes is his main fan base: young children. In a variation on the concept of youngsters inflicting humiliation on grown-ups, Hogan plays a former wrestler who winds up as bodyguard-cum-nanny to two troublesome brats, whose father is under threat because he has invented a super microchip. JF Some swearing, violence.

Terry "Hulk" Hogan [Hulk Hogan] *Sean Armstrong* • Sherman Hemsley *Bert Wilson* • Austin Pendleton *Alex Mason Sr* • Robert Gorman [Robert Hy Gorman] *Alex Mason Jr* • Madeline Zima *Kate Mason* • Raymond O'Connor *Frank Olsen* • Mother Love *Corinne* ■ *Dir* Michael Gottlieb • *Scr* Edward Rugoff, Michael Gottlieb

Mr Nice ★★★ 18
Biographical comedy drama
2010 · UK · Colour and BW · 115min

It makes a change to see a movie about criminality that doesn't romanticise male bonding and violence. And by glossing over some of the nastier aspects of the illegal hashish trade, director Bernard Rose's film works very nicely as an elegant if somewhat fey alternative. Essentially it's a biopic, with Rhys Ifans as Howard Marks, the highly intelligent Welsh Oxford graduate who, in the 1970s, became the world's most prolific drug smuggler. The scenes leading up to Marks's comeuppance are exciting and darkly comic, though the movie becomes frustratingly busy in the final scenes. But it gives a very good sense of why a bright young man would leave teacher training to become the most wanted man in Britain. DW Drug abuse. DVD BD

Rhys Ifans *Howard Marks* • Chloë Sevigny *Judy Marks* • David Thewlis *Jim McCann* • Omid Djalili *Salem Malik* • Luis Tosar *Craig Lovato* • Christian McKay *Hamilton McMillan* ■ *Dir* Bernard Rose • *Scr* Bernard Rose, from Howard Marks's autobiography

Mr Nice Guy ★★ 15
Martial arts action comedy
1996 · HK · Colour · 84min

This Melbourne-set vehicle for Hong Kong action star Jackie Chan may have been shot in English, but something definitely got lost in the translation. Chan plays a TV chef who gets mixed up with journalist Gabrielle Fitzpatrick's investigation into a drugs ring led by Richard Norton. The fight sequences are as inventive as ever, but all the performances border on the hysterical. JF DVD

Jackie Chan *Jackie* • Richard Norton *Giancarlo "The Saint" Lucchetti* • Miki Lee *Miki* • Karen McLymont *Lakeisha* • Gabrielle Fitzpatrick *Diana* • Vince Poletto *Romeo Baggio* ■ *Dir* Sammo Hung • *Scr* Edward Tang, Fibe Ma

Mr North ★★★ PG
Period comedy drama
1988 · US · Colour · 88min

An exceptional amalgam of American greats – Robert Mitchum, Lauren Bacall, a script co-written by John Huston – adds much to this gently amusing tale. Anthony Edwards performs healing miracles among the Newport elite in the 1920s and finds himself going head to head with the local doctor. Very much a family affair – executive produced by Huston, the film stars his daughter Anjelica and is directed by his son Danny – this is a quality period fare and well worth watching. LH

Anthony Edwards *Theophilus North* • Robert Mitchum *James McHenry Bosworth* • Lauren Bacall *Mrs Amelia Cranston* • Harry Dean Stanton *Henry Simmons* • Anjelica Huston *Persis Bosworth-Tennyson* • Mary Stuart Masterson *Elspeth Skeel* • Virginia Madsen *Sally Boffin* • David Warner *Dr McPherson* ■ *Dir* Danny Huston • *Scr* Janet Roach, John Huston, James Costigan, from the novel *Theophilus North* by Thornton Wilder

Mr Peabody & Sherman ★★★★ U
Animated science-fiction adventure
2013 · US · Colour · 92min

Take one genius (who just happens to be a talking dog), add his adopted human son and a time machine, and what do you get? A crazy, irreverent history lesson that's terrific family entertainment. Courtesy of Mr Peabody's WABAC invention, the canine and his kid are able to go back in time to meet history's greats. But when Sherman breaks the rules in a bid to impress a girl, the space-time continuum gets all messed-up, and it's left to our heroes to disentangle things. Part time-trip extravaganza, part father/son bonding story, Rob Minkoff's film is cleverly written, warm-hearted, fast-paced and fun. DA DVD BD 3D

Ty Burrell *Mr Peabody* • Max Charles *Sherman* • Ariel Winter *Penny Peterson* • Stephen Colbert *Mr Peterson* • Allison Janney *Miss Grunion* • Stanley Tucci *Leonardo da Vinci* • Mel Brooks *Albert Einstein* ■ *Dir* Rob Minkoff • *Scr* Craig Wright, from characters by Ted Key

Mr Peabody and the Mermaid ★★★ U
Comedy fantasy   1948 · US · BW · 89min

This gentle and now-forgotten romantic comedy was the first mermaid movie to make postwar movie censors tremble. Not that there is much to worry about, since lovely Ann Blyth is a most provocative, but totally covered-up, former denizen of the deep. William Powell catches her while fishing, and his urbanity makes this Nunnally Johnson-scripted tosh acceptable, though it would have benefited from a stronger director than Irving Pichel. TS

William Powell *Mr Peabody* • Ann Blyth *Mermaid* • Irene Hervey *Polly Peabody* • Andrea King *Cathy Livingston* • Clinton Sundberg *Mike Fitzgerald* • Art Smith *Dr Harvey* ■ *Dir* Irving Pichel • *Scr* Nunnally Johnson, from the novel *Peabody's Mermaid* by Guy Jones, Constance Jones

Mr Perrin and Mr Traill ★★★
Drama   1948 · UK · BW · 91min

Hugh Walpole's novel becomes a well-performed but obvious drama of life in a boys' public school. Marius Goring plays the stuffy, frustrated, ageing housemaster, while David Farrar is the virile and popular new games teacher. The problems start when they clash disastrously over Greta Gynt's glamorous school nurse. Lacking the subtlety of the later, rather similar *The Browning Version*, this swaps any sense of tragedy for melodrama. AE

Marius Goring *Vincent Perrin* • David Farrar *David Traill* • Greta Gynt *Isobel Lester* • Raymond Huntley *Moy-Thompson* • Edward Chapman *Birkland* • Mary Jerrold *Mrs Perrin* • Ralph Truman *Comber* • Finlay Currie *Sir Joshua Varley* ■ *Dir* Lawrence Huntington • *Scr* LAG Strong, TJ Morrison, from the novel by Hugh Walpole

Mr Popper's Penguins ★★★ PG
Comedy   2011 · US · Colour · 90min

There are high jinks in Manhattan when real-estate developer Jim Carrey inherits half a dozen penguins from his explorer father in this enjoyable comedy. After his initial bewilderment, Popper forms a bond with the birds and sets about turning his up-market apartment into a winter wonderland, learning valuable lessons about family and friendship along the way. The much-loved children's book of the 1930s has been given a flashy modern-day overhaul, and director Mark Waters maintains a lively pace, with the undeniably adorable penguins at the heart of the action. But this is ultimately standard family fare that will keep children happy without really making a lasting impression. TeS DVD BD

Jim Carrey *Tom Popper* • Carla Gugino *Amanda* • Madeline Carroll *Janie Popper* • Angela Lansbury *Mrs Van Gundy* • Ophelia Lovibond *Pippi* • Philip Baker Hall *Franklin* ■ *Dir* Mark Waters (1) • *Scr* Sean Anders, John Morris, Jared Stern, from the illustrated children's book by Richard and Florence Atwater

Mister Quilp ★★ U
Musical   1975 · UK · Colour · 122min

Anthony Newley plays the mean-spirited, hunchbacked money-lender Quilp in this film version of Charles Dickens's *The Old Curiosity Shop*. The star also composed the songs in the manner of Lionel Bart's *Oliver!*. This is principally a sanitised, Americanised, family-orientated affair that nevertheless preserves some of the darker elements of the original. The performances, particularly Newley's, put the emphasis on grotesquerie. AT

Anthony Newley *Daniel Quilp* • David Hemmings *Richard Swiveller* • David Warner *Sampson Brass* • Michael Hordern *Grandfather/Edward Trent* • Paul Rogers *Single gent/Henry Trent* • Jill Bennett *Sally Brass* • Mona Washbourne *Mrs Jarley* ■ *Dir* Michael Tuchner • *Scr* Louis Kamp, Irene Kamp, from the novel *The Old Curiosity Shop* by Charles Dickens

Mr Reliable ★★★★ 15
Comedy drama based on a true story
1996 · Aus · Colour · 108min

Down Under in the late 1960s, dim-witted crook Colin Friels and his new girlfriend, single mum Jacqueline McKenzie, scare off an irritating policeman with a shotgun, sparking a full-scale hostage crisis. However, much to the embarrassment of the local Establishment, the fair dinkum general public are firmly on the lovestruck couple's side. Friels and McKenzie are terrific as the dopey heroes, and all the characters are fleshed out with great affection. A beaut. JF Swearing, violence, some sex scenes.

Colin Friels *Wally Mellish* • Jacqueline McKenzie *Beryl Muddle* • Paul Sonkkila *Norman Allan* • Fred Gallacher *Don Fergusson* • Lisa Hensley *Penny Wilberforce* ■ *Dir* Nadia Tass • *Scr* Don Catchlove, Terry Hayes

Mr Ricco ★★ 15
Crime drama   1975 · US · Colour · 93min

This humdrum crime drama gave Dean Martin his last leading role before his career lapsed into the occasional wry cameo appearance. As a liberal lawyer in San Francisco, he successfully defends a black militant accused of murder who then appears to be responsible for a vicious killing spree. No Matt Helm dramatics here, this film's tired Dino is a lonely widower who keeps a shaggy dog to retrieve his golf balls, drinks milk, and has a lady friend of a suitable age – neatly portrayed by Geraldine Brooks. AE

Dean Martin *Joe Ricco* • Eugene Roche *George Cronyn* • Thalmus Rasulala *Frankie Steele* • Denise Nicholas *Irene Mapes* • Cindy Williams *Jamison* • Geraldine Brooks *Katherine Fremont* • Philip Thomas [Philip Michael Thomas] *Purvis Mapes* ■ *Dir* Paul Bogart • *Scr* Robert Hoban, from a story by Ed Harvey, Francis Kiernan

Mister Roberts ★★★★★ U
Comedy drama   1955 · US · Colour · 115min

This magnificent adaptation of the hit Broadway comedy sees Henry Fonda returning to the screen after a long absence to re-create his stage role as a supply-ship officer who longs to be part of the action during the Second World War. Fonda clashed with original director John Ford over how to play the part, which led to director Mervyn LeRoy taking over, but the transfer was seamless and the qualities of the play were retained. The film has a cast to die for: James Cagney as the captain, William Powell (his last movie) as the wise old doc, and young Jack Lemmon, winning his first Oscar as the brash, irresistible and irrepressible Ensign Pulver. Perhaps if Lemmon had reprised the role in 1964's disappointing spin-off *Ensign Pulver* that might have been a better movie. This, however, is a great one. TS

Henry Fonda *Lieutenant Doug Roberts* • James Cagney *Captain* • Jack Lemmon *Ensign Frank Thurlowe Pulver* • William Powell *Doc* • Betsy Palmer *Lieutenant Ann Girard* • Ward Bond *Chief Petty Officer Dowdy* ■ *Dir* John Ford, Mervyn LeRoy • *Scr* Joshua Logan, Frank S Nugent, from the play by Joshua Logan, Thomas Heggen, from the novel by Thomas Heggen

Mr Sardonicus ★★★ 12
Horror   1961 · US · BW · 86min

Director William Castle worked overtime on this unofficial reworking of the 1928 chiller *The Man Who Laughs*. Having personally introduced the picture, Castle concluded proceedings with a Punishment Poll, in which the audience decided the fate of Guy Rolfe as Sardonicus, the 19th-century aristocrat who kidnaps Audrey Dalton to compel her surgeon sweetheart, Ronald Lewis, to operate on his face, which was frozen in childhood into a hideous grin. Eerily shot by Burnett Guffey, with a surprisingly literate script from Ray Russell. DP

Ronald Lewis *Sir Robert Cargrave* • Audrey Dalton *Maude Sardonicus* • Guy Rolfe *Sardonicus Father* • Oscar Homolka *Krull* • Vladimir Sokoloff ■ *Dir* William Castle • *Scr* Ray Russell, from a short story by Ray Russell

Mr Saturday Night ★★★ 15
Comedy drama   1992 · US · Colour · 114min

Billy Crystal builds on a character he developed during his early stand-up days for this affectionate, fictional biopic. Crystal's Buddy Young Jr is a stand-up comedian whose career spans more than 50 years; however, he is less successful with personal relationships, notably with his brother and manager David Paymer. The best bits are the scenes of his initial bids for success on stage; the dramatic elements are less successfully incorporated into the picture. JF Swearing. DVD

Billy Crystal *Buddy Young Jr* • David Paymer *Stan Yankelman* • Julie Warner *Elaine* • Helen Hunt *Annie* • Mary Mara *Susan* • Jerry Orbach *Phil Gussman* • Ron Silver *Larry Meyerson* • Jerry Lewis ■ *Dir* Billy Crystal • *Scr* Billy Crystal, Lowell Ganz, Babaloo Mandel

Mr Skeffington ★★★★ U
Melodrama   1944 · US · BW · 140min

A narcissistic, selfish, faithless and rich society woman marries a loyal, dignified and adoring businessman to protect her feckless brother's reputation, and treats him like dirt. Retribution arrives when diphtheria ravages her looks, redemption when he returns blind from a Nazi concentration camp. It's well directed by Vincent Sherman on opulent sets and contains fabulous performances from the Oscar-nominated Bette Davis and Claude Rains, who are both at the height of their powers. RK DVD

Bette Davis *Fanny Trellis* • Claude Rains *Job Skeffington* • Walter Abel *George Trellis* • Richard Waring *Trippy Trellis* • George Coulouris *Dr Byles* • Marjorie Riordan *Young Fanny* • Robert Shayne *MacMahon* ■ *Dir* Vincent Sherman • *Scr* Philip G Epstein, Julius J Epstein, James Leicester, from the novel by "Elizabeth" [Mary Annette Beauchamp Russell] • *Music* Franz Waxman • *Art Director* Robert Haas

Mr Smith Goes to Washington ★★★★★ U

Political comedy drama 1939 · US · BW · 124min

This superb discourse on corruption in American politics is one of Hollywood's finest achievements. Director Frank Capra remarkably (for him) keeps sentimentality at bay in his film of Lewis R Foster's Oscar-winning original story (adapted by Sidney Buchman) about an idealistic young senator who finally realises that he is not his own man. Washington hated this movie, but the public flocked to see James Stewart in, arguably, his finest hour. Few movies are as well cast: the bell-voiced Jean Arthur is wonderful as a super-cynical secretary, but veteran western star Harry Carey is quite magnificent as the vice president, one of the greatest supporting roles in all cinema, and alone a reason for viewing. TS **DVD**

Jean Arthur *Clarissa Saunders* • James Stewart *Jefferson Smith* • Claude Rains *Senator Joseph Paine* • Edward Arnold *Jim Taylor* • Guy Kibbee *Governor Hubert Hopper* • Thomas Mitchell *Diz Moore* • Eugene Pallette *Chick McGann* • Beulah Bondi *Ma Smith* • HB Warner *Senate majority leader* • Harry Carey *President of the Senate* ■ *Dir* Frank Capra • *Scr* Sidney Buchman, Myles Connolly, from the story *The Gentleman from Montana* by Lewis R Foster

Mr Sycamore ★ PG

Comedy drama 1974 · US · Colour · 84min

They don't make them like this any more, with good reason. A fine cast is ill-used in this whimsical comedy about one man's attempt to escape the rat race. A mild-mannered postman (Jason Robards), under the heel of his overbearing wife, decides to become a tree. Luckily for Robards, his cinema career perked up shortly afterwards with an Oscar-winning role in *All the President's Men*. JG

Jerome Thor *Higgins* • Jason Robards *John Gwilt* • Sandy Dennis *Jane Gwilt* • Jean Simmons *Estelle Benbow* • Robert Easton *Fred Staines* • Brenda Smith *Daisy* ■ *Dir* Pancho Kohner • *Scr* Pancho Kohner, Ketti Frings, from a story by Robert Ayre, from a play by Ketti Frings

Mister Ten Per Cent ★★ U

Comedy 1967 · UK · Colour · 85min

For all his success on TV, Charlie Drake has failed to make an impact on the big screen, with only four movies in 13 years before this flop. Co-scripted by Drake and Norman Hudis, it's a comedy about the deliberate staging of a box-office bomb to claim the insurance, which predated Mel Brooks's similarly themed *The Producers* by a year. In spite of an accomplished cast, it's killed stone dead by Drake himself, who was so hurt by its failure that he went into temporary retirement. DP

Charlie Drake *Percy Pointer* • Derek Nimmo *Tony* • Wanda Ventham *Kathy* • John Le Mesurier *Jocelyn Macauley* • Anthony Nicholls *Casey* • Noel Dyson *Mrs Gorman* • John Hewer *Townsend* ■ *Dir* Peter Graham Scott • *Scr* Norman Hudis, Charlie Drake

Mr 3000 ★★ 12

Sports comedy 2004 · US · Colour · 99min

Bernie Mac plays a retired baseball superstar known as "Mr 3000" after scoring what he believes is a record 3,000 hits. However, years later he discovers that a clerical error has left him three shots short of the spectacular total, and he must return to the game at the age of 47 to achieve his record. Mac is rather good as the thwarted pro and so is Angela Bassett as his former girlfriend, but neither is well-served by the formulaic script and by-numbers direction. SF Brief swearing. **DVD**

Bernie Mac *Stan Ross* • Angela Bassett *Mo* • Michael Rispoli *Boca* • Brian White *T-Rex* • Ian Anthony Dale *Fukuda* ■ *Dir* Charles Stone III • *Scr* Eric Champnella, Keith Mitchell, Howard Michael Gould, from a story by Champnella, Mitchell

Mr Topaze ★★ U

Comedy 1961 · UK · Colour · 96min

Peter Sellers directed himself in this adaptation of a Marcel Pagnol play, so he has only himself to blame. He plays an ex-schoolmaster in a small French town who falls among thieves and comes up wealthy. Beset by the likes of Herbert Lom, Leo McKern and Nadia Gray, Sellers makes an endearing innocent at large. Alas, his direction lacks the edge the idea needed. TH

Peter Sellers *Mr Topaze* • Nadia Gray *Suzy* • Herbert Lom *Castel Benac* • Leo McKern *Muche* • Martita Hunt *Baroness* • John Neville *Roger* • Billie Whitelaw *Ernestine* • Michael Gough *Tamise* • Joan Sims *Colette* ■ *Dir* Peter Sellers • *Scr* Pierre Rouve, from the play *Topaze* by Marcel Pagnol

Mr Turner ★★★★★ 12

Period biographical drama 2014 · UK/Fr/Ger · Colour · 143min

Mike Leigh's beautifully limned portrait of the 19th-century British artist William Turner focuses largely on the later years of the painter's life, when he was already a fêted name with eccentric habits and a complicated private life. Timothy Spall delivers arguably his most majestic performance in a rich career, capturing both Turner's quicksilver intelligence and energy but also his coarse manners, while Mike Leigh's deft handling of actors and humour is palpable throughout – some might even consider it his best film to date. LF **DVD**

Timothy Spall *JMW Turner* • Paul Jesson *William Turner* • Dorothy Atkinson *Hannah Danby* • Ruth Sheen *Sarah Danby* • Lesley Manville *Mary Somerville* • Roger Ashton-Griffiths *Henry William Pickersgill* • Joshua McGuire *John Ruskin* • James Norton *Francis Willoughby* • Jamie Thomas King *David Roberts* ■ *Dir/Scr* Mike Leigh

Mr Vampire ★★★★ 15

Comedy horror 1986 · HK · Colour · 93min

Slapstick comedy, mystic martial arts and astonishing gore appear in the first of a long line of popular, and much copied, period Chinese horror films. Lam Ching Ying is the voodoo priest hired to exorcise his bouncing bloodsucker father. Complications arise thanks to Lam's two over-enthusiastic apprentices, lured by lonely ghosts into exhausting nights of spectral passion, and the eight zombies left in his undertaking care. This is oriental knockabout horror at its most entertaining. AJ Cantonese +subtitles. **DVD**

Ricky Hui *Man Chor* • Moon Lee *Ting Ting* • Lam Ching Ying *Master* • Pauline Wong *Jade Ah Wai* • Anthony Chan *Brother* ■ *Dir* Ricky Lau • *Scr* Wong Ching, Szeto Cheuk Hon

Mr Winkle Goes to War ★

Second World War drama 1944 · US · BW · 79min

In one of the crassest wartime propaganda movies ever made, Edward G Robinson stars as a meek bank clerk who's bullied by his wife (Ruth Warrick) – until he's drafted, that is. This same little man becomes a hero when he fetches up on a Pacific island and drives a bulldozer straight through the Japanese defences. Give that man a medal and watch his wife dissolve with pride. The manipulative calculation of this movie has to be seen to be believed. Released as *Arms and the Woman* in the UK. AT

Edward G Robinson *Wilbert George Winkle* • Ruth Warrick *Amy Winkle* • Ted Donaldson *Barry* • Bob Haymes *Jack Pettigrew* • Richard Lane *Sgt "Alphabet"* • Robert Mitchum *Corporal* ■ *Dir* Alfred E Green • *Scr* Waldo Salt, George Corey, Louis Solomon, from a novel by Theodore Pratt

Mr Wonderful ★★★ 15

Romantic drama 1992 · US · Colour · 95min

Director Anthony Minghella made his American debut with this quaint comedy that scores so heavily on the performance level that you can forgive it its contrived plot and odd lapses in logic. Matt Dillon's plans to open a bowling alley depend entirely on cutting the alimony paid to ex-wife Annabella Sciorra, but she's dating married academic William Hurt and has no plans to tie the knot. What follows is obvious, but romantics will not be disappointed. DP

Matt Dillon *Gus* • Annabella Sciorra *Lee* • Mary-Louise Parker *Rita* • William Hurt *Tom* • Vincent D'Onofrio *Dominic* • David Barry Gray *Pope* • Dan Hedaya *Harvey* ■ *Dir* Anthony Minghella • *Scr* Anthony Minghella, from a screenplay (unproduced) by Amy Schor, Vicki Polon

Mr Woodcock ★★ 12

Comedy 2007 · US · Colour · 83min

Following *School for Scoundrels* and *Bad Santa*, Billy Bob Thornton provides another exercise in snarling comic villainy. Years after suffering through gym class with Thornton's malevolent PE teacher Mr Woodcock, John Farley (Seann William Scott) has overcome his chubby child misery with a bestselling self-help book about getting over one's past. But when Farley returns home, he discovers that his mum (Susan Sarandon) is now dating the bullying educator. A less-than-hilarious battle of wits ensues. Thornton can play this kind of role in his sleep, and that's pretty much what he does in this formulaic comedy. JR **DVD** **Blu-ray**

Billy Bob Thornton *Mr Woodcock* • Seann William Scott *John Farley* • Susan Sarandon *Beverly* • Amy Poehler *Maggie* • Melissa Sagemiller *Tracy* • Ethan Suplee *Nedderman* • Jacob Davich *Nedderman's brother* • Kyley Baldridge *Young Farley* ■ *Dir* Craig Gillespie • *Scr* Michael Carnes, Josh Gilbert

Mr Wrong ★★★ 15

Thriller 1985 · NZ · Colour · 88min

This psycho-thriller concerns a woman who buys a Jaguar car that turns out to be haunted. Alfred Hitchcock himself once showed interest in filming Elizabeth Jane Howard's story and, while this is not in the master's class, it is still a skilful and enjoyable feature debut by former documentary-maker Gaylene Preston. PF

Heather Bolton *Meg* • David Letch *Mr Wrong* • Margaret Umbers *Samantha* • Suzanne Lee *Val* • Gary Stalker *Bruce* • Danny Mulheron *Wayne* ■ *Dir* Gaylene Preston • *Scr* Gaylene Preston, Geoff Murphy, Graeme Tetley, from a story by Elizabeth Jane Howard

Mr Wrong ★ 12

Romantic comedy 1996 · US · Colour · 92min

You will discover how truly unfunny a comedy can be if you subject yourself to this unfortunate fare, made as a big-screen vehicle for TV star Ellen DeGeneres. She's the lonely single woman who meets hunky Bill Pullman and discovers, too late, what a loser he really is – by which point she can't seem to get rid of him. Unfortunately, director Nick Castle lets this tedious tale amble along, and DeGeneres and Pullman and Joan Cusack can't save it. JB Swearing.

Ellen DeGeneres *Martha Alston* • Bill Pullman *Whitman Crawford* • Joan Cusack *Inga* • Dean Stockwell *Jack Tramonte* • Joan Plowright *Mrs Crawford* • John Livingston *Walter* • Robert Goulet *Dick Braxton* • Ellen Cleghorne *Jane* • Hope Davis *Annie* ■ *Dir* Nick Castle • *Scr* Chris Matheson, Kerry Ehrin, Craig Munson

The Mistle-Tones ★★

Musical 2012 · US · Colour · 90min

Sweet if predictable, this yuletide tale goes for perkiness rather than substance in its blend of musical and romantic comedy. Talented songbird Tia Mowry-Hardrict plays the founder of a singing group after she's denied a place in diva Tori Spelling's quintet. Recruiting from work colleagues, she heads for a climactic sing-off, resulting in carolling montages, hissy fits from Spelling, and love, naturally. The final scene is cute, but you'll need to be in a festive mood to appreciate the rest of it. SF

Tia Mowry-Hardrict [Tia Mowry] *Holly* • Tori Spelling *Marci* • Jonathan Patrick Moore *Nick* • Reginald VelJohnson *Holly's dad* ■ *Dir* Paul Hoen • *Scr* Jed Elinoff, Scott Thomas

Mistress ★★ 15

Satirical comedy 1992 · US · Colour · 105min

This Tinseltown comedy keeps threatening to blow the lid off the whole movie-making business. Yet, while the script wickedly captures the nitty-gritty of wheeler-dealing, the story lacks originality and direction. As the trio willing to back Robert Wuhl's film (providing there are starring roles for their mistresses), Eli Wallach, Danny Aiello and Robert De Niro are hugely disappointing, although Martin Landau shines as a producer. DP

Robert Wuhl *Marvin Landisman* • Martin Landau *Jack Roth* • Jace Alexander *Stuart Stratland Jr* • Robert De Niro *Evan M Wright* • Laurie Metcalf *Rachel Landisman* • Eli Wallach *George Lieberhoff* • Danny Aiello *Carmine Rasso* • Christopher Walken *Warren Zell* ■ *Dir* Barry Primus • *Scr* Barry Primus, JF Lawton, from a story by Barry Primus

Mistress America ★★★★★ 15

Comedy 2015 · US · Colour · 84min

A New York student with literary ambitions finds ample material when she befriends a scatterbrained socialite in this serio-comic frolic co-written – like *Frances Ha* before it – by director Noah Baumbach and leading lady Greta Gerwig. As the film recalls 1930s screwball comedy and the young Katharine Hepburn, the hilarious and poignant story feels both old and new at the same time. Gerwig's delightful turn is the dominating presence, her eccentric wit masking an underlying desperation to succeed. TJ Swearing, sexual references, drug abuse.

Lola Kirke *Tracy* • Greta Gerwig *Brooke* • Matthew Shear *Tony* • Jasmine Cephas Jones *Nicolette* ■ *Dir* Noah Baumbach • *Scr* Noah Baumbach, Greta Gerwig

Misunderstood ★★

Drama 2014 · It/Fr · Colour

Asia Argento's third disappointing feature is self-absorbed navel-gazing of the most enervating kind. Although Argento adamantly says it's not autobiographical, most events depicting 9-year-old Aria (Asia's birth name) and her decision to run away from her constantly arguing artist parents are clearly based on the tortuous relationship she had with her real ones, including horror film maestro Dario Argento and his actress muse Daria Nicolodi (so-so Gabriel Garko and Charlotte Gainsbourg on screen). There's a touching climax revealing Aria's true goal in life. If only it wasn't such a drawn-out and tedious journey getting there. AJ In Italian, French.

Anna Lou Castoldi *Donatina* • Charlotte Gainsbourg *Madre* • Gabriel Garko *Padre* • Max Gazzé *Manuel Ginori* ■ *Dir* Asia Argento • *Scr* Asia Argento, Barbara Alberti

Mitsuko Delivers ★★★★ PG

Comedy 2011 · Jpn · Colour · 108min

In this quirky comedy from Yuya Ishii (*Sawako Decides*), a young woman in the ninth month of her pregnancy changes the lives of her friends and neighbours in a run-down Tokyo tenement. Star of the show here is Riisa Naka's determined heroine, who's something of a social outcast since she's carrying the child of her African-American ex-boyfriend, yet is absolutely set on improving the fortunes of the eccentric support group that has formed around her. The deceptively whimsical storyline has much to say about Japanese emotional reticence and the postwar victim mentality. But most of all, it's a heart-warming portrait of ordinary folk battling through testing circumstances. TJ Japanese +subtitles. Brief sexual references. **DVD**

Riisa Naka *Mitsuko* • Aoi Nakamura *Yoichi* • Ryo Ishibashi *Jiro* ■ *Dir/Scr* Yuya Ishii

Mix Me a Person ★★ 12

Crime drama 1962 · UK · BW · 103min

Like most early British pop stars, Adam Faith appeared in a few movies. Unlike the majority, though, he didn't shy away from meatier roles more usually reserved for "proper" actors. In this routine courtroom drama, he rather woodenly plays a teenage

M

garage mechanic convicted of killing a policeman. Anne Baxter is the psychiatrist wife of his barrister Donald Sinden who sets out to prove his innocence. Faith sings the title song in this pedestrian thriller. **AJ** *DVD*

Anne Baxter *Dr Anne Dyson* • Donald Sinden *Philip Jukes QC* • Adam Faith *Harry Jukes* • David Kernan *Socko* • *Dir* Leslie Norman • *Scr* Ian Dalrymple, Roy Kerridge, from the novel by Jack Trevor Story

Mixed Nuts ★★ 12

Comedy   1994 · US · Colour · 93min

An off-form Steve Martin stars as the manager of a struggling telephone help-line that's about to be disconnected in this California-set adaptation of French comedy *Le Père Noël Est une Ordure*. It's so tasteless you'd scarcely believe it's by Nora Ephron, director of that eminently inoffensive romantic comedy *Sleepless in Seattle*. There's also little to warm the heart in the bleak Christmas context. **TH** Swearing. *DVD*

Steve Martin *Philip* • Rita Wilson *Catherine* • Madeline Kahn *Mrs Munchnik* • Robert Klein *Mr Lobel* • Anthony LaPaglia *Felix* • Juliette Lewis *Gracie* • Rob Reiner *Dr Kinsky* • Garry Shandling *Stanley* • Adam Sandler *Louie* • Liev Schreiber *Chris* ■ *Dir* Nora Ephron • *Scr* Nora Ephron, Delia Ephron, from the 1982 film *Le Père Noël est une Ordure*

Mo' Better Blues ★★★ 15

Drama   1990 · US · Colour · 123min

Spike Lee suffers under the weight of his own ambition here, trying to cram his film with so many ideas (the nature of obsession, the avoidance of reality, the conflict between art and life) that it comes unglued at an early stage, especially as there's not enough plot to shore it up. Yet Denzel Washington, as a single-minded trumpeter, gingerly steps over the cracks to provide plenty of powerful scenes. He is helped by Wesley Snipes and Lee himself, and the lack of coherence is offset by vigorous, stylish camerawork and a killer jazz score. **JM** Violence, swearing, sex scenes, nudity.

Denzel Washington *Bleek Gilliam* • Spike Lee *Giant* • Wesley Snipes *Shadow Henderson* • Joie Lee *Indigo Downes* • Cynda Williams *Clarke Bentancourt* • Dick Anthony Williams *Big Stop Gilliam* • Giancarlo Esposito *Left Hand Lacey* ■ *Dir/Scr* Spike Lee

Mo' Money ★ 15

Action comedy   1992 · US · Colour · 89min

Written and executive produced by its star, Damon Wayans, this is a ridiculous and gratuitously violent action movie which also professes to be a comedy. Wayans tries to impress his girlfriend (Stacey Dash) by getting a lowly job at the credit card company where she works. In no time at all, he's up to his neck in fraud. **LH** *DVD*

Damon Wayans *Johnny Stewart* • Stacey Dash *Amber Evans* • Joe Santos *Lt Raymond Walsh* • John Diehl *Keith Heading* • Harry J Lennix [Harry Lennix] *Tom Dilton* • Marlon Wayans *Seymour Stewart* ■ *Dir* Peter MacDonald • *Scr* Damon Wayans

Moana ★★★★

Silent documentary   1926 · US · BW · 77min

Because of the success of Robert Flaherty's first feature, *Nanook of the North* (1922), Paramount asked the ethnological director to make a "Nanook of the South Seas". So, with an unlimited budget, Flaherty spent two years in the Samoan islands making *Moana*. He returned with a lyrical, beautifully photographed, idealised picture of an island paradise where noble savages hunt, fish and cook. Although it did not as successful as the earlier film, it inspired British film producer John Grierson to coin the word "documentary". **RB**

■ *Dir* Robert Flaherty • *Scr* Robert Flaherty, Julian Johnson (titles) • *Cinematographer* Robert Flaherty

The Mob ★★★

Crime drama   1951 · US · BW · 86min

When talented, underrated director Robert Parrish worked as an editor, he managed to help pull together the shambles that was *All the King's Men*, not only winning himself an Oscar nomination (with Al Clark), but securing the best picture award and the best actor statuette for star Broderick Crawford. Crawford paid back the debt by lending his considerable (and bulky) presence to this, Parrish's second film as a director. Crawford brings great credibility to the role of a cop passing for a thug, and is especially good at the sexy repartee with forgotten actress Lynne Baggett. **TS**

Broderick Crawford *Johnny Damico* • Betty Buehler *Mary Kiernan* • Richard Kiley *Thomas Clancy* • Otto Hulett *Lieutenant Banks* • Matt Crowley *Smoothie* • Neville Brand *Gunner* • Ernest Borgnine *Joe Castro* • Charles Buchinski [Charles Bronson] *Jack* • *Dir* Robert Parrish • *Scr* William Bowers, from the novel *Waterfront* by Ferguson Findley

The Mobster ★★

Crime drama   1958 · US · BW · 79min

After gaining critical attention with *Machine Gun Kelly*, director Roger Corman quickly followed up that historical gangster thriller with one set in the modern era. Told in flashback to a Senate investigating committee, it charts the rise and fall of gangland leader Steve Cochran, from his lowly slum beginnings working a numbers racket and dealing drugs to becoming head of the syndicate. While the script is nowhere near as strong as *Kelly*, Corman captures the grimy criminal atmosphere in broad strokes and with swift action pacing. **AJ**

Steve Cochran *Joe Sante* • Lita Milan *Teresa Porter* • Robert Strauss *Black Frankie* • Celia Lovsky *Mrs Sante* • Lili St Cyr • John Brinkley *Ernie Porter* • Yvette Vickers *Blonde* • Grant Withers *Joe Moran* ■ *Dir* Roger Corman • *Scr* Steve Fisher, from the novel *I, Mobster* by Joseph Hilton Smyth

Mobsters ★★ 18

Crime thriller   1991 · US · Colour · 120min

It is extraordinary that, with gangster-era America providing such a natural source of drama, director Michael Karbelnikoff should turn gritty reality into such an empty tale. Hampered by inanity and a tortuous plot, Christian Slater (as "Lucky" Luciano), Patrick Dempsey (Meyer Lansky) and Richard Grieco ("Bugsy" Siegel) still look credible in period suits, while Anthony Quinn and Michael Gambon, as two hard mobsters, supply the flair and fire. **JM** Sex scenes, swearing, violence, nudity. *DVD*

Christian Slater *Charlie "Lucky" Luciano* • Patrick Dempsey *Meyer Lansky* • Richard Grieco *Benjamin "Bugsy" Siegel* • Costas Mandylor *Frank Costello* • Anthony Quinn *Don Masseria* • F Murray Abraham *Arnold Rothstein* • Michael Gambon *Don Faranzano* • Lara Flynn Boyle *Mara Motes* ■ *Dir* Michael Karbelnikoff • *Scr* Michael Mahern, Nicholas Kazan, from a story by Michael Mahern

Moby Dick ★★

Adventure drama   1930 · US · BW · 75min

A bowdlerised version of Herman Melville's classic novel, this has Captain Ahab (John Barrymore) losing his leg to a whale as a result of being pushed overboard by an evil stepbrother who is after the preacher's daughter (Joan Bennett) Ahab loves. Directed by Lloyd Bacon, the sequences where Ahab hunts the whale are let down by the clumsily obvious model of the predator. Barrymore almost holds the nonsensically melodramatic plot together with a fine performance. **RK**

John Barrymore *Captain Ahab* • Joan Bennett *Faith* • Lloyd Hughes *Derek* • May Boley *Whale Oil Rosie* • Walter Long *Stubbs* • Tom O'Brien *Starbuck* • Nigel de Brulier *Elijah* ■ *Dir* Lloyd Bacon • *Scr* J Grubb Alexander, from the novel by Herman Melville

Moby Dick ★★★ PG

Adventure drama   1956 · UK/US · Colour · 110min

John Huston's long-cherished adaptation of Herman Melville's novel has some wonderful scenes but must be counted as a noble failure. The great white whale always looks phoney; it performed badly in high seas off the coasts of Ireland and the Canaries, pushing the budget through the roof. Gregory Peck as Captain Ahab is miscast, lacking the required demonic presence. Wags at the time joked that Orson Welles should have played the whale, while Peck himself thought that Huston should have played Ahab. **AT** *DVD*

Gregory Peck *Captain Ahab* • Richard Basehart *Ishmael* • Leo Genn *Starbuck* • Orson Welles *Father Mapple* • Friedrich Ledebur *Queequeg* • Harry Andrews *Stubb* • Bernard Miles *Manxman* • James Robertson-Justice *Captain Boomer* ■ *Dir* John Huston • *Scr* John Huston, Ray Bradbury, from the novel by Herman Melville • *Cinematographers* Oswald Morris, Freddie Francis

Moby Dick ★★ PG

Adventure drama   1998 · US · Colour · 173min

Reduced to feature length from a 240-minute mini-series, this adaptation of Herman Melville's seafaring classic has been carefully made by Franc Roddam, but it lacks the messy magnificence of John Huston's version. Patrick Stewart proves a worthy successor to Gregory Peck as the obsessive Captain Ahab, while Peck himself turns in a confident performance as the sermonising reverend so blusteringly played in the 1950s by Orson Welles. Costing $20 million, the production took advantage of mechanical and digital technology to create the great white whale, though this is still one masterpiece that sits better on the page than the screen. **DP** *DVD*

Patrick Stewart *Captain Ahab* • Henry Thomas *Ishmael* • Gregory Peck *Father Mapple* • Piripi Waretini *Queequeg* • Michael Jackson (1) *Shantyman* ■ *Dir* Franc Roddam • *Scr* Franc Roddam, Anton Diether, from the novel by Herman Melville

The Mod Squad ★ 15

Crime action drama   1999 · US · Colour · 90min

This remake of the popular 1960s TV series about three former criminals who become undercover cops is a good example of how not to make a movie. It spends 40 minutes establishing the hipness of its trio of main characters before getting to the plot, and then buries the rest in a mishmash of atmospherics and 20-something angst. **ST** Swearing, violence. *DVD*

Claire Danes *Julie Barnes* • Giovanni Ribisi *Pete Cochrane* • Omar Epps *Linc Hayes* • Josh Brolin *Billy Waites* • Dennis Farina *Captain Adam Greer* • Steve Harris *Detective Briggs* ■ *Dir* Scott Silver • *Scr* Scott Silver, Stephen Kay, Kate Lanier, from characters by Buddy Ruskin

The Model and the Marriage Broker ★★★

Comedy drama   1951 · US · BW · 103min

This minor but charming movie from "women's director" George Cukor is slightly overdependent on the undoubted talents and weather-beaten features of character actress and notorious scene-stealer Thelma Ritter. Ritter is marvellous, trying to pair friend Jeanne Crain with handsome radiographer Scott Brady, while trying not to let Crain know matchmaking is her real profession. Others in the marriage market include a pre-blacklist Zero Mostel. **TS**

Jeanne Crain *Kitty Bennett* • Scott Brady *Matt Hornbeck* • Thelma Ritter *Mae Swazey* • Zero Mostel *Wixted* • Michael O'Shea (1) *Doberman* • Helen Ford *Emmy Swazey* • Frank Fontaine *Johannson* ■ *Dir* George Cukor • *Scr* Charles Brackett, Walter Reisch, Richard Breen [Richard L Breen]

Model Shop ★

Romantic comedy drama   1969 · US/Fr · Colour · 97min

Jacques Demy made some fine films in France, but his Hollywood debut was a mistake from start to finish. Made in LA during the time of anti-Vietnam demos, the counterculture and the sexual revolution, it's a frivolous thing about fashion design and photography. Gary Lockwood has all the personality of a paper cup, while Anouk Aimée, who revives her 1960 character from Demy's *Lola*, does little but stare vacantly into the middle distance. **AT**

Anouk Aimée *Lola* • Gary Lockwood *George Matthews* • Alexandra Hay *Gloria* • Carol Cole *Barbara* • Severn Darden *Portly man* • Tom Fielding *Gerry* ■ *Dir* Jacques Demy • *Scr* Jacques Demy, Adrien Joyce

Modern Life ★★★★

Documentary   2008 · Fr · Colour · 86min

Following *L'Approche* (2001) and *Le Quotidien* (2005), the third in Raymond Depardon's fascinating *Profils Paysans* series shows how tough farm life has become in the hamlets around La Villaret in mid-southern France. Goatherd Amandine Valla can no longer raise her young children on mediocre cheese sales and is contemplating selling up. Daniel Roy would love to follow his siblings out of the beautiful if benighted area, but feels as duty-bound to his parents' run-down property as ageing couple Marcel and Germaine Challaye do to their dwindling milk herd. However, the main focus falls on querulous octogenarian brothers Marcel and Raymond Privat, who take out their frustrations on Cécile, nephew Alain Rouvière's new wife from Calais. This is documentary cinema at its most sincere and compassionate. **DP** French, Occitan +subtitles. *DVD*

■ *Dir* Raymond Depardon

Modern Love ★★ 15

Romantic comedy   1990 · US · Colour · 104min

This lame, hackneyed look at the problems of modern relationships and the family adds nothing new to the great American middle income debate. Robby Benson co-opted his real-life wife, Karla DeVito, and their own daughter to play his family, which gives the whole plodding affair a smug, incestuous air. Benson cobbled this one together as part of a university film course; he should have listened to the old maxim "those who can, do; those who can't, teach". **SH**

Robby Benson *Greg* • Karla DeVito *Dr Billie Parker* • Burt Reynolds *Colonel Frank Parker* • Debra Port *Annabell* • Cliff Bemis *Dirk Martin* • Rue McClanahan *Evelyn* • Frankie Valli *Mr Hoskins* ■ *Dir/Scr* Robby Benson

Modern Problems ★

Comedy   1981 · US · Colour · 90min

Stressed-out air traffic controller Chevy Chase is driving along the freeway when a truck carrying nuclear waste springs a leak, drenching our hero in radioactive slime. Instead of making him grow an extra head or simply killing him, the incident causes Chase to develop telekinetic powers. These help him sort out the problems in his life and enable him to take sweet revenge on his enemies. An idea that might have occupied a five-minute sketch on a TV show is overstretched to feature-film length. **AT**

Chevy Chase *Max* • Patti D'Arbanville *Darcy* • Mary Kay Place *Lorraine* • Nell Carter *Dorita* • Brian Doyle-Murray *Brian* • Dabney Coleman *Mark* • Mitch Kreindel *Barry* ■ *Dir* Ken Shapiro • *Scr* Ken Shapiro, Tom Sherohman, Arthur Sellers

Modern Romance ★★★ 15

Romantic comedy   1981 · US · Colour · 89min

This is a neglected and totally original comedy from co-writer/director/star Albert Brooks. He plays a film editor, and the sequences involving the cutting process are insightful and truthful, as he and the excellent Bruno Kirby go to work on a sci-fi flick with the mercilessly hamming George Kennedy as space leader Zeron. The man behind the camera for the schlock movie is played by real-life director James L Brooks, who would later offer Albert (no relation) the role of his career in *Broadcast News*. The plot's slight, but the film is enjoyable and interesting, especially for movie buffs. **TS** Swearing.

  U SUITABLE FOR ALL   **Uc** SUITABLE ESPECIALLY FOR YOUNG CHILDREN (DVD ONLY)   **PG** PARENTAL GUIDANCE   **12A** UNDER 12s TO BE ACCOMPANIED (CINEMA ONLY)

Albert Brooks *Robert Cole* • Kathryn Harrold *Mary Harvard* • Tyann Means *Waitress* • Bruno Kirby *Jay* • Jane Hallaren *Ellen* • Karen Chandler *Neighbour* • James L Brooks *David* • George Kennedy *Zeron* ■ *Dir* Albert Brooks • *Scr* Albert Brooks, Monica Johnson

Modern Times ★★★★★ U
Comedy   1936 · US · Colour · 86min

Charles Chaplin's ridiculing of an increasingly mechanised and mechanical society is an inspired assembly line of gags, similar to *A Nous la Liberté* by the French director René Clair, who declared he had always been inspired by Chaplin, so was honoured if "the master" had been inspired by him. As machines chew up our hero and spit him out, Charlie finds solace in the love of Paulette Goddard and a sunset stroll into a happy-ever-after. Naive this may be, but what else could Chaplin do? He was in the business of redemption and this was the only way out he could find in darkening days. TH *DVD*

Charlie Chaplin [Charles Chaplin] *Factory worker* • Paulette Goddard *Gamine* • Henry Bergman *Café owner* • Stanley Sanford [Tiny Sanford] *Big Bill/Worker* • Chester Conklin *Mechanic* ■ *Dir/Scr* Charlie Chaplin [Charles Chaplin] • *Cinematographers* Rollie Totheroh, Ira Morgan

The Moderns ★★★ 15
Period drama
1988 · US · Colour and BW · 121min

Alan Rudolph's wry study of the cabal that gathered itself around Ernest Hemingway in 1920s Paris is short on drama, but stuffed with arch academic allusions. As convincingly fake as the pictures Keith Carradine is commissioned to paint, the neverland of bons mots and chic cafés is superbly sustained by the brilliance of the screenplay and Rudolph's lightness of touch, which enables his cast to shine without dazzling. With Wallace Shawn impressive as the journalist feeding off the "lost generation" and Linda Fiorentino as Carradine's ex-wife, this is both ambitious and accessible. DP Nudity.

Keith Carradine *Nick Hart* • Linda Fiorentino *Rachel Stone* • Geneviève Bujold *Libby Valentin* • Geraldine Chaplin *Nathalie de Ville* • Wallace Shawn *Oiseau* • John Lone *Bertram Stone* • Kevin J O'Connor *Ernest Hemingway* • Elsa Raven *Gertrude Stein* • Ali Giron *Alice B Toklas* ■ *Dir* Alan Rudolph • *Scr* Alan Rudolph, John Bradshaw

Modesty Blaise ★★ 12
Spy spoof   1966 · UK · Colour · 114min

With its dizzy set designs and flamboyant costumes, Joseph Losey's misguided screen adaptation of Peter O'Donnell's seminal cartoon strip is a paean to the excesses of the mid-1960s. The years have not been kind, however, and the film now exists in a pop art time-bubble of its own making. In a plot that makes virtually no sense, Monica Vitti is miscast as the sexy female spy, a sort of earthbound Barberella out to thwart effete arch fiend Dirk Bogarde (in a silver wig and sunglasses). RS Some violence. *DVD*

Monica Vitti *Modesty Blaise* • Dirk Bogarde *Gabriel* • Terence Stamp *Willie Garvin* • Michael Craig *Paul Hagan* • Harry Andrews *Sir Gerald Tarrant* • Rossella Falk *Mrs Fothergill* • Scilla Gabel *Melina* • Clive Revill *McWhirter/Sheik Abu Tahir* • Joe Melia *Crevier* ■ *Dir* Joseph Losey • *Scr* Evan Jones, from a story by Peter O'Donnell, Stanley Dubens, from the comic strip by Peter O'Donnell, Jim Holdaway

Moebius ★★★★ 18
Satirical drama   2013 · S Kor · Colour · 88min

An angry wife fails to emasculate her philandering hubby with a hunting knife, but their teenage son is not quite so lucky. As extreme as this sounds, this drama-cum-satire from South Korean provocateur Kim Ki-Duk plays out like the blackest comedy, and much of the mayhem is implied rather than shown. Kim's device of removing the dialogue so characters communicate in grunts emphasises the fable-like aspect of the story, and this is challenging and effective in the way it gets us to reconsider

the basic tenets of family and sexuality. TJ In Korean.

Cho Jae-Hyeon *Father* • Lee Eun-woo *Mother/A young woman* • Seo Young-ju *Son* ■ *Dir/Scr* Kim Ki-Duk

Mogambo ★★★ U
Romantic adventure 1953 · US · Colour · 111min

In 1932, Clark Gable made a picture for MGM called *Red Dust*, and very steamy it was, too. A story of lust set in the jungles of south-east Asia, it featured Gable as a rubber planter choosing between temptress Jean Harlow and demure Mary Astor. *Mogambo*, directed by John Ford, is the remake, transposed to Africa with Gable again, plus Ava Gardner and Grace Kelly. Gone is the steaminess of the original: this is a Technicolor adventure romp fit for the postwar Eisenhower era of healthy living. AT *DVD*

Clark Gable *Victor Marswell* • Ava Gardner *Eloise Y Kelly* • Grace Kelly *Linda Nordley* • Donald Sinden *Donald Nordley* • Philip Stainton *John Brown Pryce* • Eric Pohlmann *Skipper* • Laurence Naismith *Skipper* ■ *Dir* John Ford • *Scr* John Lee Mahin, from the play *Red Dust* by Wilson Collison

The Moguls ★★★ 15
Comedy   2005 · US/UK/Ger · Colour · 92min

In this sketchy exploration of middle-aged angst lifted by a cheeky veneer, Jeff Bridges stars as the insecure, divorced dad who's desperate to compete financially with his son's wealthy stepfather. Suddenly hitting on a supposedly perfect solution, he persuades his nerdy friends to help shoot a locally recruited porn flick. Of course, everything that could go wrong invariably does, unleashing bursts of goofy humour. A daftly likeable romp. SF Swearing. *DVD*

Jeff Bridges *Andy Sargentee* • Tim Blake Nelson *Barney* • Joe Pantoliano *Some Idiot* • William Fichtner *Otis* • Ted Danson *Moose* • Patrick Fugit *Emmett* • Glenne Headly *Helen* • Lauren Graham *Peggy* • Jeanne Tripplehorn *Thelma* • Isaiah Washington *Homer* ■ *Dir/Scr* Michael Traeger

Mohabbatein ★★★ PG
Romantic musical drama
2000 · Ind · Colour · 215min

Aditya Chopra's second feature is a titanic battle of generational wills. Veteran superstar Amitabh Bachchan confirms he's made the transition from action hero with a glaring display as the unbending head of a prestigious college who vents his wrath on music teacher Shah Rukh Khan, after he dares not only to encourage six of his amorous students to pair off, but also to make eyes at Bachchan's daughter, Aishwarya Rai. DP Hindi +subtitles. *DVD*

Amitabh Bachchan *Narayan Shankar* • Shah Rukh Khan *Raj Aryan* • Uday Chopra *Vicky* • Shamita Shetty *Ishika* • Jugal Hansraj *Sameer* • Kim Sharma *Sanjana* • Jimmy Shergill *Karan* • Preeti Jhangiani *Kiran* • Aishwarya Rai *Megha, Narayan Shankar's daughter* ■ *Dir/Scr* Aditya Chopra

Mohawk ★★ PG
Western   1956 · US · Colour · 79min

This is splendidly camp stuff, as a quintessential bevy of 1950s movie icons throw themselves at devil-may-care artist Scott Brady. Director Kurt Neumann's baroque style was way ahead of contemporary audiences' tastes – this film is really for collectors only. Despite the presence of Neville Brand in the cast, true western devotees should steer clear. TS *DVD*

Scott Brady *Jonathan Adams* • Rita Gam *Onida* • Neville Brand *Rokhawah* • Lori Nelson *Cynthia Stanhope* • Allison Hayes *Greta* • John Hoyt *Butler* • Vera Vague [Barbara Jo Allen] *Aunt Agatha* ■ *Dir* Kurt Neumann • *Scr* Maurice Geraghty, Milton Krims

Mojave ★★★ 15
Thriller   2014 · US · Colour · 92min

Writer William Monahan doubles up as director for this good-looking psycho-thriller. Garrett Hedlund is the jaded film director who's so disenchanted with LA life that he goes into the desert to find himself,

Unfortunately, he also finds Oscar Isaac's spooky drifter. A pure stalker horror this is not, however: Monahan (through Isaac) takes the opportunity to have a dig at Hollywood. Some will feel all the existential soul-searching is a bit pretentious but the locations are well used and Isaac is one of the most watchable actors around. JA Violence, swearing. *DVD* *BD*

Oscar Isaac *Jack* • Garrett Hedlund *Thomas* • Mark Wahlberg *Norman* • Walton Goggins *Jim* ■ *Dir/Scr* William Monahan

Mojave Moon ★★ 15
Romantic comedy   1996 · US · Colour · 91min

This determinedly "difficult" indie movie has a decent cast trying desperately to make sense of a wilfully wacky script and coping manfully with indifferent direction. Danny Aiello plays a lovelorn LA car salesman who drives a young woman back to her Mojave desert home. There, he's drawn into the weird world of the girl's mom and her paranoid boyfriend. The superb cast includes Angelina Jolie in an early screen appearance. DA Violence, nudity, swearing, drug abuse, sexual situations. *DVD*

Danny Aiello *Al* • Angelina Jolie *Ellie* • Anne Archer *Julie* • Jack Noseworthy *Kaiser* • Alfred Molina *Sal* • Michael Biehn *Boyd* ■ *Dir* Kevin Dowling • *Scr* Leonard Glasser

Mojo ★★ 15
Period drama   1998 · UK · Colour · 92min

Revealing the dark underside of London in the late 1950s, this brutal Soho-set drama by Jez Butterworth was a big hit at London's Royal Court theatre. But, in spite of a nervously energetic camera and diverse directorial flourishes, this adaptation remains a stubbornly theatrical experience. There's a laudable eagerness about the performances, as ambitious henchman Ian Hart gets embroiled in Harold Pinter's scheme to move in on a singing sensation at Ricky Tomlinson's seedy club. DP Swearing, violence.

Ian Hart *Mickey* • Ewen Bremner *Skinny Luke* • Aidan Gillen *Baby* • Martin Gwynn Jones *Sweets* • Hans Matheson *Silver Johnny* • Andy Serkis *Sid Potts* • Ricky Tomlinson *Ezra* • Harold Pinter *Sam Ross* ■ *Dir* Jez Butterworth • *Scr* Jez Butterworth, Tom Butterworth, from the play by Jez Butterworth

The Mole People ★★
Science fiction   1956 · US · BW · 77min

Anthropologists John Agar and Hugh Beaumont fall into a deep cave in Asia, discover a lost Sumerian city, and get captured by albino natives who have Mole Men as slaves. Armed with only flashlights to keep the sunlight-hating race at bay, they make their escape when the Mole Men stage a revolt. This nonsensical pulp is made more fun thanks to the weird rubber Mole suits, Agar and Beaumont making a hilarious hero team and a few fanciful directorial glimmers by Virgil Vogel. A minor cult classic. AJ

John Agar *Dr Roger Bentley* • Cynthia Patrick *Adad Gizelle* • Hugh Beaumont *Dr Jud Bellamin* • Alan Napier *Elinu High Priest* • Nestor Paiva *Prof Etienne Lafarge* ■ *Dir* Virgil Vogel [Virgil W Vogel] • *Scr* Laszlo Gorog

Molière ★★★ 12
Period comedy drama
2006 · Fr · Colour · 115min

In 1644, actor/playwright Jean Baptiste Poquelin, aka Molière, disappeared following imprisonment for non-payment of debts. It's a historical mystery co-writer/director Laurent Tirard uses for frothy speculation to suggest this formative episode inspired the French dramatist to write his classic farce *The Misanthrope*. Arch characters, ludicrous disguises and contrived situations fill this ravishing and often highly amusing costume romp, in which Molière (Romain Duris) poses as a priest to give acting lessons to wealthy, and married, bourgeois Jourdain (Fabrice Luchini) to aid his seduction of a widowed marquise. Duris subtly captures Molière as a wide-eyed observer, mining human frailties

for comic potential, while Laura Morante is hilariously droll as Jourdain's wife and provides the touching ending. AJ French +subtitles. *DVD*

Romain Duris *Jean-Baptiste Poquelin/Molière* • Fabrice Luchini *Jourdain* • Laura Morante *Elmire Jourdain* • Édouard Baer [Edouard Baer] *Dorante* • Ludivine Sagnier *Célimène* • Fanny Valette *Henriette Jourdain* ■ *Dir* Laurent Tirard • *Scr* Grégoire Vigneron, Laurent Tirard • *Cinematographer* Gilles Henry

Moll Flanders ★★★ 12
Period drama   1995 · US · Colour · 117min

Daniel Defoe's story of the hard-edged young woman with dubious virtues gets the Hollywood treatment in a classy, if sometimes yawn-inducing reworking of the 18th-century romp. Robin Wright is well cast as Moll, whose sad, eventful life is recounted to her abandoned daughter Aisling Corcoran by manservant Morgan Freeman. Far grittier than you would expect from a Tinseltown interpretation, director Pen Densham's convincing period evocation is bolstered by Wright's terrific work as the abused heroine. JC Some swearing, sexual situations.

Robin Wright *Moll Flanders* • Morgan Freeman *Hibble* • Stockard Channing *Mrs Allworthy* • John Lynch *Fielding* • Brenda Fricker *Mrs Mazzawatti* • Geraldine James *Edna* • Aisling Corcoran *Flora* ■ *Dir* Pen Densham • *Scr* Pen Densham, from the novel by Daniel Defoe

Molly ★ 15
Drama   1999 · US · Colour · 98min

Elisabeth Shue plays a 28-year-old autistic woman who undergoes an operation that brings her out of her shell. Unfortunately, the changed persona does little to improve the star's performance, which is so over-the-top it's embarrassing. Worse still are their attempts to punctuate the drama with various kinds of offensive humour. KB

Elisabeth Shue *Molly McKay* • Aaron Eckhart *Buck McKay* • Thomas Jane *Sam* • Jill Hennessy *Susan Brookes* • DW Moffett *Mark Cottrell* • Elizabeth Mitchell *Beverly Trehare* ■ *Dir* John Duigan • *Scr* Dick Christie

Molly and Lawless John ★★★
Western   1972 · US · Colour · 97min

There's an ingenious storyline and a distinct feminist slant to this undiscovered western, directed by TV-movie expert Gary Nelson. Vera Miles plays the unhappy, 40-something wife of staid local sheriff John Anderson who has blond and dashing young outlaw Sam Elliott in his jail. Elliott persuades Miles to organise his escape and they run off together, though it's not long before Miles begins to despise her new man. AT

Vera Miles *Molly Parker* • Sam Elliott *Johnny Lawler* • Clu Gulager *Deputy* • John Anderson *Sheriff Parker* • Cynthia Myers *Dolly* ■ *Dir* Gary Nelson • *Scr* Terry Kingsley-Smith

Molly and Me ★★★
Musical comedy   1945 · US · BW · 76min

Gracie Fields and Monty Woolley co-star in this engaging variation of the *Pollyanna* story, in which Our Gracie and a bunch of "resting" entertainers transform Woolley's staid existence while working as his servants. Brightly directed by Lewis Seiler, the film is as interesting for its supporting cast as it is for its leads. DP

Gracie Fields *Molly* • Monty Woolley *Graham* • Roddy McDowall *Jimmy Graham* • Reginald Gardiner *Peabody* • Natalie Schafer *Kitty* • Edith Barrett *Julia* • Clifford Brooke *Pops* • Aminta Dyne *Musette* • Queenie Leonard *Lily* • Doris Lloyd *Mrs Graham* ■ *Dir* Lewis Seiler • *Scr* Leonard Praskins, Roger Burford, from the novel by Frances Marion

The Molly Maguires ★★ PG
Period drama   1970 · US · Colour · 119min

With a cast that features Sean Connery as a rebellious coal miner, Richard Harris as a mining company *agent provocateur* and Samantha Eggar as Harris's above-the-ground love interest, it's sad that the end result proves so disappointing. All the effort

M

here has gone into the depiction of mining conditions in 19th-century Pennsylvania, but the script seems to have been written by a mechanical digger. Every scene rams home some kind of message, and Martin Ritt directs from a soapbox. **AT** Violence, swearing. **DVD**

Richard Harris *James McParlan/McKenna* • Sean Connery *Jack Kehoe* • Samantha Eggar *Mary Raines* • Frank Finlay *Captain Davies* • Anthony Zerbe *Dougherty* • Bethel Leslie *Mrs Kehoe* • Art Lund *Frazier* ■ *Dir* Martin Ritt • *Scr* Walter Bernstein, from the novel *Lament for the Molly Maguires* by H Arthur Lewis

Molly Moon and the Incredible Book of Hypnotism ★★★

Adventure   2015 · UK · Colour · 98min

Clunkingly old-fashioned, but also cute and kinda fun, this magical fantasy stars newcomer Raffey Cassidy as Molly, a young orphan girl who stumbles across an ancient book on hypnotism, and discovers that she has the uncanny knack of putting its theories into practice. She uses her powers to kid Britain's TV audience into believing she's a singing sensation. Boasting more British stars than you can shake a stick at, this is easy to criticise but hard to hate, providing perfect fantasy fulfilment for pre-teen girls. **DA**

Raffey Cassidy *Molly Moon* • Dominic Monaghan *Nockman* • Emily Watson *Miss Trinklebury* • Tom Wisdom *Charlie Cooper* • Anne-Marie Duff *Lucy* • Joan Collins *Nockman's mother* • Celia Imrie *Edna* ■ *Dir* Christopher N Rowley • *Scr* Tom Butterworth, Chris Hurford, from Georgia Byng's novel • *Cinematographer* Remi Adefarasin

Moloch ★★★12

Historical drama
1999 · Rus/Ger/Fr · Colour · 107min

Owing a visual debt to the German Romantic artist Caspar David Friedrich, Aleksandr Sokurov's Berchtesgaden dissertation on the nature of power also nods, occasionally, in the direction of the Reich's official film-maker, Leni Riefenstahl. However, instead of presenting a revealing portrait of the Führer through the eyes of his long-suffering mistress, Eva Braun, Sokurov succeeds only in presenting an illustrated digest of the table talk of Adolf Hitler. **DP** German +subtitles. **DVD**

Leonid Mozgovoy *Adolf Hitler* • Elena Rufanova *Eva Braun* • Leonid Sokol *Josef Goebbels* • Elena Spiridonova *Magda Goebbels* • Vladimir Bogdanov *Martin Bormann* ■ *Dir* Aleksandr Sokurov • *Scr* Yuri Arabov, Marina Koreneva

Mom and Dad Save the World ★PG

Science-fiction comedy
1992 · US · Colour · 86min

When middle-class parents Teri Garr and the wonderful Jeffrey Jones are spirited away to a far distant planet whose ruler intends making Garr his bride, Jones is forced into warrior mode to oust the tyrant and put rightful heir Eric Idle onto the throne. With its tasteless sets and rubber-suited monsters, the film's modest budget is flaunted as if it were a selling point. Yet director Greg Beeman can't disguise the lamentable script. **RS** **DVD**

Teri Garr *Marge Nelson* • Jeffrey Jones *Dick Nelson* • Jon Lovitz *Tod Spengo* • Dwier Brown *Sirk* • Kathy Ireland *Semage* • Thalmus Rasulala *General Afir* • Wallace Shawn *Sibor* • Eric Idle *Raff* ■ *Dir* Greg Beeman • *Scr* Ed Solomon, Chris Matheson

Mom at Sixteen ★★

Drama   2005 · US · Colour · 86min

A decent cast makes the most of the melodramatic material in this preachy TV movie. Danielle Panabaker plays the pregnant high-school student who decides to keep her baby and agrees to let mother Mercedes Ruehl pretend the child is hers. The deception involves moving house and school, and their new life puts pressure on the family that's not helped by the friendly persistence of a school health councillor (Jane Krakowski). The movie clearly means

well, but the moralising is decidedly off-putting. **DP**

Mercedes Ruehl *Terry Jeffries* • Danielle Panabaker *Jacey Jeffries* • Jane Krakowski *Donna Cooper* • Clare Stone *Macy* • Tyler Hynes *Brad* • Colin Ferguson *Bob* • Hollis McLaren *Marlene* • Megan Edwards *Linda* ■ *Dir* Peter Werner • *Scr* Nancey Silvers

Moment by Moment ★

Romantic comedy   1978 · US · Colour · 93min

Jane Wagner writes and directs this embarrassing romance, a vehicle for her longtime companion and collaborator, Lily Tomlin. The latter stars as a bored Malibu housewife whose juices are stirred by John Travolta, playing a drifter with the hilarious name of Strip. Alas, audiences showed little interest in their May-December relationship. **FL**

Lily Tomlin *Trisha Rawlings* • John Travolta *Strip* • Andra Akers *Naomi* • Bert Kramer *Stu Rawlings* • Shelley R Bonus *Peg* • Debra Feuer *Stacie* ■ *Dir/Scr* Jane Wagner

Un Moment d'Egarement ★★

Comedy   1977 · Fr · Colour · 85min

It's hard to forgive this comedy since it spawned one of the most charmless movies ever made, *Blame It on Rio*. The story hinges on two friends, Jean-Pierre Marielle – newly divorced – and Victor Lanoux, holidaying together in the South of France, each with their 17-year-old daughters in tow. When Marielle has a brief affair with Agnes Soral, the premise turns farcical, as her outraged father mistakes another man as the seducer. Glamorous locations and French panache stop the film lapsing into crass vulgarity. **BB** French +subtitles.

Jean-Pierre Marielle *Pierre* • Victor Lanoux *Jacques* • Christine Dejoux *Martine* • Agnes Soral *Françoise* ■ *Dir/Scr* Claude Berri

Moment of Danger ★★

Crime drama   1960 · UK · BW · 97min

Meek locksmith and cuckolded husband Trevor Howard is recruited by debonair Edmund Purdom to rob a Mayfair jewellers. After the robbery, Purdom vanishes with all the swag so Howard pursues him to Spain with Purdom's jilted girlfriend, Dorothy Dandridge. Part thriller, part romantic tangle, this is produced by Douglas Fairbanks Jr and directed by Laslo Benedek. **AT**

Trevor Howard *John Bain* • Dorothy Dandridge *Gianna* • Edmund Purdom *Peter Carran* • Michael Hordern *Inspector Farrell* • Paul Stassino *Juan Montoya* ■ *Dir* Laslo Benedek • *Scr* David Osborn, Donald Ogden Stewart, from the novel *The Scent of Danger* by Donald MacKenzie

A Moment of Innocence ★★★

Comedy drama
1996 · Iran/Fr/Swi · Colour · 77min

Iranian cinema's preoccupation with the mechanics of movie-making once again comes to the fore in this teasing treatise on idealism, love, coincidence and the selectivity of memory. Recalling an incident from the days of the Shah when he stabbed a policeman, Mohsen Makhmalbaf cross-cuts between this moment of revolutionary zeal and the production of a film re-creating the event. With the actual cop, Mirhadi Tayebi, playing himself and coaching his young alter ego, the action challenges the viewer to question the motives of participants and the relevance of distinguishing between fact and fiction. **DP** Farsi +subtitles.

Mirhadi Tayebi *The policeman* • Mohsen Makhmalbaf *The director* • Ali Bakhshi *The young director* • Ammar Tafti *The young policeman* ■ *Dir/Scr* Mohsen Makhmalbaf

The Moment of Truth ★★★★

Drama   1964 · It/Sp · Colour · 105min

The infamous "sport" of bullfighting is depicted here, although it could equally be boxing or professional football that entices the poor with nothing but nerves and

strength to offer in return for wealth and fame. In Francesco Rosi's superb docudrama, a poor Andalusian boy (played by then famous matador "Miguelin"), living in arid poverty, determines to confront beasts rather than live like one. Making his name in the *corrida*, he becomes a minnow among sharks as entrepreneurs and the wealthy, who respect his skill not his life, encircle him. Rosi depicts society in a harsh glare and finds it wanting, while the cameramen, led by Gianni Di Venanzo, help capture the perverse glamour and cruelty. **BB** In Italian.

"Miguelin" [Miguel "Miguelin" Mateo] *Miguel* • Pedro Basauri *Maestro Pedrucho* • Jose Gomez Sevillano *Impresario* • Linda Christian *American woman* ■ *Dir* Francesco Rosi • *Scr* Francesco Rosi, Pedro Portabella, Ricardo Muñoz Suay, Pedro Beltran, Raffaele La Capria, from a story by Rosi

Moment to Moment ★★

Romantic thriller   1966 · US · Colour · 107min

A psychiatrist's wife, left alone on the French Riviera during her husband's frequent absences, becomes involved with a young officer who is later shot and left for dead. The result is a ludicrous brew of adultery and attempted murder, directed by Mervyn LeRoy, dressed by Yves Saint-Laurent and photographed by Harry Stradling. Alas, the overlay of gloss and glamour fails to disguise the dreadful script or the inert performances. **RK**

Jean Seberg *Kay Stanton* • Honor Blackman *Daphne Fields* • Sean Garrison *Mark Dominic* • Arthur Hill *Neil Stanton* • Peter Robbins *Timmy Stanton* • Grégoire Aslan *Edward DeFargo* • Donald Woods *Mr Singer* • Walter Reed *Hendricks* ■ *Dir* Mervyn LeRoy • *Scr* John Lee Mahin, Alec Coppel, from the short story *Laughs With a Stranger* by Alec Coppel

Momentum ★★★★15

Action thriller   2015 · S Afr/ US · Colour · 91min

Clint Eastwood's go-to camera operator Stephen S Campanelli makes an impressive directorial debut with this fast-paced thriller. From its attention-grabbing bank heist opening to the exciting chase finale through Cape Town's Byzantine airport, the breathless cat-and-mouse action never lets up. It's also well-choreographed and laced with flashy violence as CIA assassin James Purefoy relentlessly tracks glamorous jewel thief Olga Kurylenko. Sure, it's a kick-ass *Bourne* on a budget, but it has a strikingly mature sense of style, slick wall-to-wall stunts, plus wit and suspense. **AJ** Swearing, violence, sex **DVD** **BL**

Olga Kurylenko *Alex Farraday* • James Purefoy *Mr Washington* • Morgan Freeman *Senator* • Hlomla Dandala *Mr Madison* • Lee-Anne Summers *Penny* ■ *Dir* Stephen S Campanelli • *Scr* Adam Marcus, Debra Sullivan

Momma's Man ★★15

Drama   2008 · US · Colour · 98min

A midlife crisis sees a grown-up son seeking refuge in his ageing parents' bohemian New York loft in this observant but unsatisfying indie drama. While his wife and baby are back in California, stressed middle-manager Mikey (Matt Boren) suddenly can't face returning to his responsibilities, and spends his days in his old bedroom, leafing through the detritus of his adolescence. Azazel Jacobs's camera indefatigably records these becalmed moments, slowing the action down to a crawl, which will test the patience of all but the most dedicated. There is a degree of poignancy from knowing that the parents on screen are Jacobs's real-life mum and dad, Ken and Flo Jacobs – Ken is a legend in the avant-garde New York art scene – and the house is the one he grew up in. **TJ**

Matt Boren *Mikey* • Flo Jacobs *Mom* • Ken Jacobs *Dad* • Richard Edson *Tom* • Eleanor Hutchins *Brigitte* ■ *Dir/Scr* Azazel Jacobs

Mommie Dearest ★★★★15

Biographical drama   1981 · US · Colour · 122min

This riveting melodrama about Joan Crawford is based on her daughter Christina's vengeful memoir. Faye Dunaway

is astonishing as Crawford, risen from rags to bitches, who still scrubs the floors, runs rings around studio bosses and creates a living hell for her daughter (brilliantly played by young Mara Hobel and, later, by Diana Scarwid). This is lavish and pretty accurate as far as Hollywood lore is concerned, but Dunaway makes Norma Desmond look like Doris Day. **AT** Violence, swearing. **DVD**

Faye Dunaway *Joan Crawford* • Diana Scarwid *Christina Crawford* • Steve Forrest *Greg Savitt* • Howard Da Silva *Louis B Mayer* • Mara Hobel *Christina as a child* • Rutanya Alda *Carol Ann* • Harry Goz *Al Steele* ■ *Dir* Frank Perry • *Scr* Frank Yablans, Frank Perry, Tracy Hotchner, Robert Getchell, from the memoirs by Christina Crawford

Mommy ★★★★★15

Drama   2014 · Can · Colour · 132min

Once better known for being young, gay, outspoken, prolific (five feature films before the age of 25) and handsomely coiffured, French-Canadian director Xavier Dolan establishes himself as a serious talent with this superb, Palme d'Or-nominated drama. Anne Dorval stars as Diane "Die" Després, a Quebec widow whose unruly teenage son Steve (Antoine Olivier Pilon) has a violent form of ADHD. Steve's mood swings put a strain on his mother's life, but he can also be sweet and adorable. Dolan's charming and artful film keeps us involved via an oddly effective range of screen ratios (mostly the square 1:1 to reflect its characters' isolated intimacy) and frequent bursts of joyous FM pop music. It borders on pretentious but never is, thanks largely to Dorval's wonderful, authentic performance as the titular everywoman. **DW** French, English +subtitles. Swearing, sexual references. **DVD**

Anne Dorval *Diane (Die) Després* • Antoine Olivier Pilon *Steve O'Connor Després* • Suzanne Clément *Kyla* • Patrick Huard *Paul Béliveau* • Alexandre Goyette *Patrick* • Viviane Pascal *Marthe* ■ *Dir/Scr* Xavier Dolan

The Mommy Market ★★PG

Fantasy comedy   1994 · US · Colour · 79min

Sissy Spacek's virtuosity isn't enough to save this lame satire on children's expectations of their parents, adapted by Tia Brelis from her mother Nancy's 1966 novel. Anna Chlumsky plays one of a trio of siblings whose dissatisfaction with their mother prompts them to trade her in at a magical market. But each alternative (played with mischievous insight by Spacek) falls short of their exacting standards. It should have been fun, but it will barely raise a smile. **DP**

Sissy Spacek *Mrs Martin/Maman/Mom/Natasha* • Anna Chlumsky *Elizabeth* • Aaron Michael Metchik *Jeremy* • Asher Metchik *Harry* • Maureen Stapleton *Mrs Cavour* ■ *Dir* Tia Brelis • *Scr* Tia Brelis, from the novel *The Mommy Market* by Nancy Brelis

Mon Homme ★★★18

Drama   1996 · Fr · Colour · 95min

In a typically outrageous and undisciplined effort from Bertrand Blier, Anouk Grinberg is the proverbial tart with a heart who decides to rescue the homeless man (Gérard Lanvin) living in the garbage dump of her apartment block. After she cooks for him and sleeps with him, he becomes her pimp. Buried beneath the sexual frolics, however, there lies a chaste tale of redemption. **AT** French +subtitles.

Anouk Grinberg *Marie* • Gérard Lanvin *Jeannot* • Valéria Bruni-Tedeschi *Sanguine* • Olivier Martinez *Jean-François* • Sabine Azéma *Bérangère* • Mathieu Kassovitz *Client* • Jean-Pierre Léaud *Claude* ■ *Dir/Scr* Bertrand Blier

Mon Oncle ★★★★★U

Satirical comedy   1958 · Fr · Colour · 105min

Jacques Tati revived Monsieur Hulot for this typically gentle yet incisive satire on the mechanised madness of the modern world. Although shot in widescreen for the maximum democracy of viewing and patterned with plenty of symbolic colour, Hulot's baffled encounter with his sister's soulless, state-of-the-art residence depends as much on the meticulously constructed soundtrack as the visual humour for its comic impact. Belying hours of punctilious preparation, each gag seems positively spontaneous as Tati puts progress in its place by exto ling the virtues of human contact. Two versions were actually shot simultaneous y, although the English one is some ten minutes shorter than the French. DP French +subtitles. *DVD* *BL*

Jacques Tati *Monsieur Hulot* • Jean-Pierre Zola *Monsieur Arpel* • Adrienne Servantie *Madame Arpel* • Alain Bécourt *Gérard* • Lucien Frégis *Monsieur Pichard* • Betty Schneider *Betty* • Yvonne Arnaud *Georgette, the maid* • Dominique Marie *Neighbour* ■ *Dir* Jacques Tati • *Scr* Jacques Tati, Jacques Lagrange, Jean L'Hote

Mon Oncle d'Amérique ★

Drama   1980 · Fr · Colour · 123min

We all know that life is a rat race. To underline the point, though, Alain Resnais uses the staggeringly original device of filming rats scurrying about! He also indulges animal behaviourist Dr Henri Laborit as he laboriously passes comment on the three main characters: a suicidal middle manager (Gérard Depardieu), an actress (Nicole Garcia) and a TV executive (Roger Pierre). A complete waste of time. AT In French.

Gérard Depardieu *Rene Ragueneau* • Nicole Garcia *Janine Carnier* • Roger Pierre *Jean Le Gall* • Marie Dubois *Therese Ragueneau* • Nelly Borgeaud *Arlette Le Gall* • Henri Laborit ■ *Dir* Alain Resnais • *Scr* Jean Gruault, from the works of Henri Laborit

Mon Père Ce Héros ★★★★ PG

Romantic comedy   1991 · Fr · Colour · 99min

There are moments in this boisterous French comedy that will cause many politically correct brows to knit in disapproval. However, without ever atoning for its lapses, Gérard Lauzier's one-joke comedy rather creeps up on you, almost solely on account of the performance of Gérard Depardieu as the indulgent father who becomes the talk of a holiday hotel when his 14-year-old daughter tells all and sundry he is her lover. Marie Gillain bristles with coquettish charm, but the pace dips when Depardieu is off screen. Consequently he was the obvious choice for the 1994 Hollywood remake, *My Father the Hero*. DP French +subtitles. *DVD*

Gérard Depardieu *André* • Marie Gillain *Véronique* • Patrick Mille *Benjamin* • Catherine Jacob *Christelle* • Charlotte De Turckheim *Irina* • Jean-François Rangasamy *Pablo* • Koomaren Chetty *Karim* ■ *Dir/Scr* Gérard Lauzier

Mon Roi ★★★ 15

Road movie drama   2015 · Fr · Colour · 120min

Maïwenn's latest feature film is one of those works that will only appeal to those with a high tolerance for French drama where the central couple fight, fret and fornicate a lot. The basic points along the narrative arc are pretty predictable, but the performances are completely committed. Maïwenn and her collaborators clearly understand who these people are, what kind of clothes they wear, what food they eat, and so on, which sometimes makes this feel a bit too much like lifestyle porn for Francophiles. LF In French. *DVD* *BL*

Vincent Cassel *Georgio* • Emmanuelle Bercot *Tony* • Louis Garrel *Solal* ■ *Dir* Maïwenn • *Scr* Maïwenn, Etienne Comar

Mona Lisa ★★★★ 15

Crime drama   1986 · UK · Colour · 99min

In this haunting, if often disturbing, London-set thriller, Bob Hoskins manages to convey some deeper emotion than his more usual thuggery. As the gangster's chauffeur madly in love with Cathy Tyson's detached, emotionally bruised prostitute, Hoskins brings rich pathos to a plot not overloaded with such feelings. Neil Jordan directs with great flair and insight, and the photography lingers long in the mind. Summing up a certain 1980s soullessness, this is still a

thought-provoking gem. SH Violence, swearing, sex scenes, nudity. *DVD* *BL*

Bob Hoskins *George* • Cathy Tyson *Simone* • Michael Caine *Mortwell* • Robbie Coltrane *Thomas* • Clarke Peters *Anderson* • Kate Hardie *Cathy* • Zoe Nathenson *Jeannie* • Sammi Davis *May* • Joe Brown (2) *Dudley* ■ *Dir* Neil Jordan • *Scr* Neil Jordan, David Leland • *Cinematographer* Roger Pratt

Mona Lisa Smile ★★★ 12

Period drama   2003 · US · Colour · 114min

Julia Roberts stars as an unconventional teacher in an emotionally manipulative chick flick with a quasi-intellectual veneer. Kirsten Dunst, Julia Stiles and a vampy Maggie Gyllenhaal are among the students at a New England girls' college in 1953 whose lives are changed by the arrival of art history lecturer Roberts and her scandalous free-spirited ways. Though the characters are all recognisable stereotypes, they're solidly performed, while Roberts makes a sympathetic lead, despite her often anachronistic behaviour and appearance. SF Swearing. *DVD* *BL*

Julia Roberts *Katherine Ann Watson* • Kirsten Dunst *Betty Warren* • Julia Stiles *Joan Brandwyn* • Maggie Gyllenhaal *Giselle Levy* • Dominic West *Bill Dunbar* • Juliet Stevenson *Amanda Armstrong* • Marcia Gay Harden *Nancy Abbey* • Ginnifer Goodwin *Connie Baker* • John Slattery *Paul Moore* ■ *Dir* Mike Newell • *Scr* Lawrence Konner, Mark Rosenthal

Monarch ★★★★ 15

Biographical drama   1996 · UK · Colour · 83min

In this low-budget but fascinating little gem, that fine Irish actor TP McKenna takes on the larger-than-life role of Henry VIII, a big-actor part if ever there was one. Set in the final year of the old king's reign, it explores what happens when an ailing Henry is forced to take refuge in a seemingly deserted country house following an assassination attempt. It's a true labour of love for writer/director John Walsh, who remastered the picture years after the original negative went missing. He makes the most of a haunting score and the spacious location of Charlton House in Greenwich to create his own crown jewel. JA Violence, brief nudity. *DVD*

TP McKenna *King Henry VIII* • Jean Marsh *The Queens* • James Coombes *Thorn* • Peter Miles Duncan ■ *Dir/Scr* John Walsh

Monday Morning ★★★★ PG

Comedy drama   2002 · Fr/It · Colour · 122min

Otar Iosseliani won the Best Director prize at Berlin for this midlife satire, which suggests that the grass is rarely greener regardless of the location of the fence. Irked by the petty restrictions and domestic vexations that blight his existence, factory worker and frustrated artist Jacques Bidou heads to Venice to look up an old pal. But Arrigo Mozzo's life is no better, despite the beauty of the city and the eccentric presence of a bogus aristocrat (played with delicious pomposity by Iosseliani himself). Comprised of small moments and wry smiles, this is observational comedy at its most congenial. DP French, Italian, Romanian +subtitles. *DVD*

Jacques Bidou *Vincent* • Arrigo Mozzo *Carlo* • Anne Kravz-Tarnavsky *Josephine* • Narda Blanchet *Vincent's mother* • Otar Iosseliani *Enzo di Martini* ■ *Dir/Scr* Otar Iosseliani

Mondays in the Sun ★★★ 15

Drama   2002 · Sp/Fr/It · Colour · 113min

Fernando Léon de Aranoa relies on a solid ensemble cast and some downbeat realism to explore the social and psychological pressures borne by a group of working-class men who've been deprived of the dignity of labour. The story centres on Javier Bardem's rebellious shipbuilder, who's been reduced to babysitting for pocket money. But Luis Tosar's gnawing envy at wife Nieve de Medina's soul-destroying job at a tuna-canning factory and José Angel Egido's pathetic attempts to cut it in a younger man's world are equally affecting. DP Spanish +subtitles. Swearing.

Javier Bardem *Santa* • Luis Tosar *José* • José Angel Egido *Lino* • Nieve de Medina *Ana* • Enrique Villén *Reina* • Celso Bugallo *Amador* • Joaquín Climent *Rico* • Aida Folch *Nata* ■ *Dir* Fernando León de Aranoa • *Scr* Fernando León de Aranoa, Ignacio del Moral

Le Monde du Silence ★★★★ U

Documentary   1956 · Fr · Colour · 85min

The first feature of Jacques-Yves Cousteau, the famous French oceanographer, diver and documentary film-maker, is an exploration of the fascinating fauna and flora of the ocean's depths. Cousteau and his underwater cameramen went beyond the bounds of a scientific documentary by capturing the poetry of the "silent world". Cousteau's co-director was 24-year-old Louis Malle, getting his first director's credit. His work on the film caused him ear problems for the rest of his life. RB In French. *DVD* *BL*

■ *Dir* Jacques-Yves Cousteau, Louis Malle • *Scr* James Dugan (commentary)

Mondo Trasho ★★

Satirical melodrama   1970 · US · BW · 94min

The first widely-seen feature from John Waters, the "Pope of Trash", was made on a shoestring budget of $2,000 with no synchronised sound. An engagingly overwrought porn parody, it details a single day in the lives of hit-and-run driver Divine and her tormented victim, Mary Vivian Pearce. Foot fetishism, 1950s rock 'n' roll, visions of the Virgin Mary and a tacky homage to Tod Browning's controversial horror film *Freaks* are thrown around with gay abandon in this Fellini-esque lampoon. AJ

Mary Vivian Pearce *Girl* • John Leisenring *Shrimper* • Sharon Sandrock *Stepsister* • Berenica Cipcus *Stepsister/Nurse* • Divine *Hit-and-run driver* • Margie Skidmore *Madonna* • Mink Stole *Tapdancer* • David Lochary *Dr Coathanger* ■ *Dir/Scr* John Waters (2)

Mondovino ★★★★ PG

Documentary   2004 · US/Fr · Colour · 131min

It's clear where director Jonathan Nossiter's sympathies lie in this fascinating study of how globalisation has impinged upon something as traditionally localised as wine-making. He may mistrust the motives and methods of the California-based Mondavi corporation, but he allows them to reveal their own agenda. The French producers who are holding out against what they consider cultural imperialism are essentially depicted as maverick heroes. But Nossiter's film is also even-handed enough to recognise why impoverished farmers in Latin America could succumb to the Napa Valley invaders. A sequel, *Natural Resistance*, was released in 2014. DP English, French, Italian, Portuguese, Spanish +subtitles. *DVD*

■ *Dir/Scr* Jonathan Nossiter

Money for Nothing ★★ 15

Black comedy based on a true story
1993 · US · Colour · 96min

The problem with this black comedy is that it's based on actual events that are anything but amusing. Joey Coyle's decision to keep the $1.2 million he found after it fell out of a casino security van was the worst he ever made. Not only did he have to resort to a plea of temporary insanity to escape jail, but he committed suicide shortly before this film was released. John Cusack has the task of playing the docker, but not even his geniality can save this frantic misfire. DP Swearing. *DVD*

John Cusack *Joey Coyle* • Debi Mazar *Monica Russo* • Michael Madsen *Detective Pat Laurenzi* • Benicio Del Toro *Dino Palladino* • Michael Rapaport *Kenny Kozlowski* • Maury Chaykin *Vincente Goldoni* • James Gandolfini *Billy Coyle* • Fionnula Flanagan *Mrs Coyle* ■ *Dir* Ramon Menendez • *Scr* Ramon Menendez, Tom Musca, Carol Sobieski

Money from Home ★★ U

Comedy   1953 · US · Colour · 100min

Dean Martin and Jerry Lewis meet Damon Runyon in this rather weak entry in the Paramount canon, its combination of racetrack high jinks and comic Arabs defeating even Martin and Lewis. It certainly seemed funnier and more convincing in its original 3D format, but it was shown "flat" on release in the UK. This largely uninspired and rather juvenile romp is really just fan fodder. TS

Dean Martin *"Honey Talk" Nelson* • Jerry Lewis *Virgil Yokum* • Marjie Millar *Phyllis Leigh* • Pat Crowley *Autumn Claypool* • Richard Haydn *Bertie Searles* • Robert Strauss *Seldom Seen Kid* ■ *Dir* George Marshall • *Scr* Hal Kanter, James Allardice, from a story by Damon Runyon

Money Monster ★★ 15

Thriller   2016 · US · Colour · 98min

Hollywood's latest drama to take a dim view of the financial sector is named after a fictional cable TV show hosted by a bullish George Clooney, who's taken hostage by a gun-wielding Jack O'Connell whose life savings have been lost thanks to Clooney's "sure" tip. Producer Julia Roberts must balance the threat with the lure of a ratings spike. Promising a blend of *Network* and *The Wolf of Wall Street*, instead this uneven film wobbles tonally between satire and thriller, and despite a surfeit of talent, collapses under its own weight. AC Swearing, sex scenes.

George Clooney *Lee Gates* • Julia Roberts *Patty Fenn* • Caitriona Balfe *Diane Lester* • Jack O'Connell (2) *Kyle Budwell* • Dominic West *Walt Camby* ■ *Dir* Jodie Foster • *Scr* Alan DiFiore, Jim Kouf, Jamie Linden

The Money Pit ★★★ 12

Comedy   1985 · US · Colour · 90min

There are belly laughs aplenty in this unofficial remake of *Mr Blandings Builds His Dream House*, but director Richard Benjamin eventually runs out of inspiration. In this home renovation comedy, Tom Hanks does enough to remind us of what we've been missing since he made his mark in serious drama, while Shelley Long's perfect timing leaves you wondering why she has never quite made the transition from sitcom to cinema. DP Swearing. *DVD* *BL*

Tom Hanks *Walter Fielding* • Shelley Long *Anna Crowley* • Alexander Godunov *Max Beissart* • Maureen Stapleton *Estelle* • Joe Mantegna *Art Shirk* • Philip Bosco *Curly* • Josh Mostel *Jack Schnittman* ■ *Dir* Richard Benjamin • *Scr* David Giler

Money Talks ★★ 18

Action comedy   1997 · US · Colour · 91min

This mediocre action comedy sees complete opposites Chris Tucker and Charlie Sheen forced to rely on each other when the former, a small-time crook, crosses a gang of jewel thieves. Sheen is a TV reporter who sees the unfolding story as a way to save his ailing career. Endless explosions, tedious car chases and brainless shoot-outs punctuate a drearily crass plot whose appeal wholly depends on one's reaction to helium-voiced comedian Tucker. AJ Swearing, violence. *DVD*

Chris Tucker *Franklin Hatchett* • Charlie Sheen *James Russell* • Heather Locklear *Grace Cipriani* • Paul Sorvino *Guy Cipriani* • Veronica Cartwright *Connie Cipriani* • David Warner *Barclay* • Paul Gleason *Detective Bobby Pickett* ■ *Dir* Brett Ratner • *Scr* Joel Cohen, Alec Sokolow

Money Train ★★ 18

Comedy thriller   1995 · US · Colour · 105min

Die Hard meets *Speed*, but with the brakes on, as transport cop Wesley Snipes tries to stop his flaky foster brother Woody Harrelson robbing the New York subway transit system. Lightning doesn't strike twice for the *White Men Can't Jump* dynamic duo, and director Joseph Ruben's recycling of exhausted gags is lacklustre in the extreme. On the plus side, Jennifer Lopez is dynamite as the Hispanic rookie

M

cop. AJ Swearing, violence, sex scenes. *DVD*

Wesley Snipes *John* • Woody Harrelson *Charlie* • Robert Blake *Patterson* • Jennifer Lopez *Grace Santiago* • Chris Cooper *Torch* ■ *Dir* Joseph Ruben • *Scr* Doug Richardson, David Loughery, from a story by Doug Richardson

Moneyball ★★★★ 12
Sports drama based on a true story
2011 · US · Colour · 127min

This engrossing drama is based on the true story of the Oakland A's baseball team general manager Billy Beane's pioneering system, which used statistics and computer analysis to build a trophy-winning side. From what may seem, on the surface, to be dry subject matter, director Bennett Miller delivers a wordy but well-paced and thrilling film, closer to co-writer Aaron Sorkin's *The Social Network* than *Field of Dreams*. Brad Pitt brings a winning blend of charisma and daring enthusiasm to the lead role, ably supported by Jonah Hill as Beane's deputy, and a scene-stealing Philip Seymour Hoffman. TeS Swearing. *DVD* *BD*

Brad Pitt *Billy Beane* • Jonah Hill *Peter Brand* • Philip Seymour Hoffman *Art Howe* • Robin Wright *Sharon* • Chris Pratt *Scott Hatteberg* ■ *Dir* Bennett Miller • *Scr* Steven Zaillian, Aaron Sorkin, from a story by Stan Chervin, from the non-fiction book *Moneyball: the Art of Winning an Unfair Game* by Michael Lewis • *Cinematographer* Wally Pfister

Mongol ★★★ 15
Historical drama
2007 · Rus/Ger/Swi/Kaz/Mongolia · Colour · 120min

This sweeping historical drama is the first part of director Sergei Bodrov's planned trilogy about Temudjin, alias Genghis Khan, the 12th-century Mongol who rose from the humblest of beginnings to become ruler of a mighty empire. Beautifully filmed on location in Mongolia, China and Kazakhstan, it's the grand and enthralling tale of the legendary warrior's early life, his rise to power and his relationship with wife Borte. Japanese actor Tadanobu Asano gives a fine performance in the lead, but there's little insight here into the reasons behind his quest for world domination, and some doubts about the film's historical accuracy. It's an old-fashioned epic with enough blood in the numerous battle scenes to entertain those who value action over authenticity. DA Mongolian +subtitles. *DVD* *BD*

Tadanobu Asano *Temudjin* • Sun Honglei *Jamukha* • Khulan Chuluun *Borte* • Odnyam Odsuren *Young Temudjin* • Aliya *Oelun* • Bayertsetseg Erdenebat *Young Borte* ■ *Dir* Sergei Bodrov • *Scr* Sergei Bodrov, Arif Aliyev

The Mongols ★★
Historical drama 1961 · Fr/It · Colour · 105min

Jack Palance stars as Ogotai, son of Genghis Khan, who invades Europe in AD 1240 and gets as far as Cracow, Poland, where the local bigwig, Franco Silva, tries to negotiate peace. Also in the invasion party is the absurdly statuesque Anita Ekberg. Palance goes from one outlandish act of cruelty to the next, grinning madly. Such sadism, though, doesn't quite prepare us for the masochism of the climax. Made in Italy by three directors, it has the usual hilarious dubbing. AT Italian dubbed.

Jack Palance *Ogotai* • Anita Ekberg *Huluna* • Antonella Lualdi *Amina* • Franco Silva *Stephen* • Gianni Garko *Henry* • Roldano Lupi *Genghis Khan* ■ *Dir* Andre De Toth, Leopoldo Savona • *Scr* Ugo Guerra, Luciano Martino, Ottavio Alessi, Alessandro Ferrau

The Monk ★★★
Drama 1972 · Fr/W Ger/It · Colour · 92min

Luis Buñuel and Jean-Claude Carrière attempted to film Matthew Lewis's famous gothic novel in the mid-1960s, but the project was shelved for lack of funds. Their screenplay was used in this multinational production, with Buñuel's friend, Greek surrealist Ado Kyrou, in the director's chair. Franco Nero stars as the intellectual cleric whose attempts to resist the allure of novice Nathalie Delon draw him into the world of magic and an alliance with Satan.

All Buñuel's preoccupations with religious hypocrisy and repressed sexuality are present and correct, but Kyrou's direction lacks the master's touch. DP In French.

Franco Nero *Ambrosio* • Nathalie Delon *Mathilde* • Nicol Williamson *Duke of Talamur* • Nadja Tiller *Elvira* • Elisabeth Wiener *Nun* • Eliana De Santis *Antonia* ■ *Dir* Ado Kyrou • *Scr* Luis Buñuel, Jean-Claude Carrière, from the novel by Matthew Lewis

The Monk ★★★ 15
Period thriller 2011 · Sp/Fr · Colour · 100min

Luis Buñuel's unrealised adaptation of Matthew Lewis's 1796 gothic saga is one of cinema's more tantalising frustrations, but here Dominik Moll makes a decent stab at capturing its anti-clerical sensationalism. The theme of corrupted goodness remains, as firebrand preacher Ambrosio (Vincent Cassel) is lured into a satanic pact that enables him to possess a local beauty loved by a young nobleman. The sins may seem a touch tame now, but Cassel burns with debauched ardour and the contrast between the film's dark interiors and the sun-scorched Catalan landscape is superb. However, Moll struggles to tap into the text's simmering malevolence, while his attempts to draw comparisons between the Catholic Church's past and present peccadilloes seem strained. It's slick and atmospheric, but lacks edge. DP French +subtitles. Nudity.

Vincent Cassel *Ambrosio* • Déborah François *Valerio* • Joséphine Japy *Antonia* • Sergi López *The debaucherer* • Catherine Mouchet *Elvira* • Jordi Dauder *Father Miguel* • Geraldine Chaplin *Mother Superior* ■ *Dir* Dominik Moll • *Scr* Dominik Moll, Anne-Louise Trividic, from the novel by Matthew G Lewis

Monk Dawson ★★ 18
Religious drama 1997 · UK · Colour · 107min

This is a mildly entertaining tale of a monk who rapidly falls into bad habits when he quits cloistered monastery life and re-enters the real world. John Michie makes an engaging hero, and there's strong support from Martin Kemp. The film's "real" world never convinces, however, and the tone is wildly inconsistent. It's as if debut director Tom Waller wasn't really sure what sort of movie he wanted to make. DA Some swearing, sex scenes. *DVD*

John Michie *Eddie Dawson* • Ben Taylor *Bobby Winterman* • Paula Hamilton *Jenny Stanten* • Martin Kemp *David Allenby* • Rupert Vansittart *Father Timothy* • Frances Tomelty *Mrs Carter* ■ *Dir* Tom Waller • *Scr* James Magrane, from a novel by Piers Paul Read

Monkey Business ★★★★ U
Comedy 1931 · US · BW · 74min

This is the one in which Groucho Marx dances the tango (with Thelma Todd) and Zeppo gets tough with a gangster. One of the funniest early Marx Brothers comedies, it was the first to be written for the screen (by SJ Perelman among others) instead of being adapted from their stage routines. As stowaways on an ocean liner, the brothers have to keep on the move from cabin to cabin to avoid being clapped in irons. Harpo works in a Punch and Judy show, while Chico tickles the ivories. TH *DVD*

Groucho Marx *Groucho* • Harpo Marx *Harpo* • Chico Marx *Chico* • Zeppo Marx *Zeppo* • Thelma Todd *Lucille* • Tom Kennedy *Gibson* • Ruth Hall *Mary Helton* • Rockliffe Fellowes *Joe Helton* ■ *Dir* Norman Z McLeod • *Scr* Arthur Sheekman, from a story by SJ Perelman, WB Johnstone, Roland Pertwee

Monkey Business ★★★★★ U
Screwball comedy 1952 · US · BW · 92min

One of the funniest, smartest and most underrated Hollywood comedies, this has never secured the reputation it deserves, considering its pedigree. It was made by Howard Hawks, arguably Hollywood's greatest studio director, who was also responsible for the scatty *Bringing Up Baby* and dynamic *His Girl Friday*. Hawks is reunited here with his star from those films, Cary Grant, who gives a sublime performance as a man reduced to juvenility for arcane plot reasons too complex to

divulge. Ginger Rogers is a great foil, but it's Marilyn Monroe who steals the movie. Hawks jazzes up the story with witty optical effects, and this is a humdinger. TS *DVD*

Cary Grant *Professor Barnaby Fulton* • Ginger Rogers *Edwina Fulton* • Charles Coburn *Mr Oliver Oxley* • Marilyn Monroe *Lois Laurel* • Hugh Marlowe *Harvey Entwhistle* • Henri Letondal *Dr Siegfried Kitzel* ■ *Dir* Howard Hawks • *Scr* Ben Hecht, Charles Lederer, IAL Diamond, from a story by Harry Segall

A Monkey in Winter ★★★
Comedy drama 1962 · Fr · BW · 104min

Having vowed to remain teetotal if he survives the war, Jean Gabin's innkeeper is tempted off the straight and narrow by Jean-Paul Belmondo, a stranger who needs a drop of courage before visiting his daughter at the local school. Henri Verneuil's attention is fixed on these cinematic icons, but he also recognises the importance of character to establishing the rural Norman atmosphere and so Gabin's wife, Suzanne Flon, the eccentric Noël Roquevert and the chauffeur Charles Bouillaud are all excellent. DP French +subtitles.

Jean Gabin *Albert Quentin* • Jean-Paul Belmondo *Gabriel Fouquet* • Suzanne Flon *Suzanne Quentin* • Noël Roquevert *Landru* • Paul Frankeur *Esnault* • Gabrielle Dorziat *Victoria* • Charles Bouillaud *Chauffeur* ■ *Dir* Henri Verneuil • *Scr* François Boyer, Michel Audiard, from the novel *Un Singe en Hiver* by Antoine Blondin

Monkey Shines ★★★★ 18
Horror 1988 · US · Colour · 108min

This provocative shocker from *Night of the Living Dead* director George A Romero contains some of his finest and most disturbing visions. Jason Beghe is the wheelchair-using student who gradually realises the genetically brain-altered monkey trained to assist him is acting out his darkest desires and revenge impulses. Intense yet surprisingly tender, Romero's confident chiller is an intelligent nail-biter that takes a highly unusual look at the warped laws of the jungle one man must combat. AJ *DVD*

Jason Beghe *Allan Mann* • John Pankow *Geoffrey Fisher* • Kate McNeil *Melanie Parker* • Joyce Van Patten *Dorothy Mann* • Christine Forrest *Maryanne Hodges* • Stephen Root *Dean Burbage* • Stanley Tucci *Dr John Wiseman* • Janine Turner *Linda Aikman* ■ *Dir* George A Romero • *Scr* George A Romero, from the novel by Michael Stewart

Monkey Trouble ★★★ U
Action comedy 1994 · US · Colour · 92min

A cute family film from director Franco Amurri, this stars accomplished child actress Thora Birch *American Beauty*) as the young girl who finds and adopts a capuchin monkey, unaware the creature is actually a trained jewel thief belonging to petty criminal Harvey Keitel. Quite what the hard-as-nails star of *Reservoir Dogs* and *Bad Lieutenant* is doing in this comedy adventure is anyone's guess, but his performance will delight adults as much as the monkey business will enchant young children. JB *DVD*

Harvey Keitel *Azro* • Mimi Rogers *Amy* • Thora Birch *Eva* • Christopher McDonald *Tom* • Adrian Johnson *Jack* ■ *Dir* Franco Amurri • *Scr* Franco Amurri, Stu Krieger

Monkeybone ★★★ 12
Part-animated fantasy comedy
2000 · US · Colour · 88min

Quirky comedy and gallows humour mix uncomfortably in this strange little film from director Henry Selick. Brendan Fraser stars as a cartoonist who, following a freak accident, ends up comatose and trapped in a nightmare populated by weird creatures – including his cuddly but slightly racy creation, Monkeybone. Some of the humour is very juvenile and even Fraser's comic talents can't stop the film from sliding into complete silliness. However, the mix of animation and live action is strikingly done. JB Violence. *DVD*

Brendan Fraser *Stu Miley* • Bridget Fonda *Julie McElroy* • Chris Kattan *Stu, organ donor* • Dave Foley *Herb* • Giancarlo Esposito *Hypnos* • Lisa Zane *Medusa* • John Turturro *Monkeybone* • Whoopi Goldberg *Death* ■ *Dir* Henry Selick • *Scr* Sam Hamm, from the graphic novel *Dark Town* by Kaja Blackley

Monkeys, Go Home! ★★ U
Comedy 1966 · US · Colour · 86min

Maurice Chevalier bade movies farewell with this Disney offering that will have animal activists reaching for their placards. The sight of four chimps being trained to harvest olives might have delighted youngsters in the mid-1960s, but it's doubtful whether it will have quite the same quaint impact today. The studio spared no expense to re-create Provence in its backyard, even planting its own olive grove. But the story of Dean Jones's contretemps with his disgruntled French neighbours is less than gripping. DP

Maurice Chevalier *Father Sylvain* • Dean Jones *Hank Dussard* • Yvette Mimieux *Maria Riserau* • Bernard Woringer *Marcel Cartucci* • Clément Harari *Emile Paraulis* ■ *Dir* Andrew V McLaglen • *Scr* Maurice Tombragel, from the short story *The Monkeys* by GK Wilkinson

The Monkey's Mask ★★★ 18
Erotic thriller
2000 · Aus/Fr/Jpn/It · Colour · 89min

This Australian thriller has a plot that suggests yet another steamy entry in the late-night TV schedules – yet fortunately Samantha Lang's film is a lot more interesting than that. In classic *noir* style, a private investigator is hired by a Sydney family to find their student daughter and is soon drawn into a liaison with the prime suspect in the girl's murder. The twist here is that the detective (played by Susie Porter) is a gay woman, instantly attracted to Kelly McGillis, a married poetry lecturer with a penchant for cigarettes and illicit sex. This is a stylish movie that relies more on atmosphere than narrative coherence. JF *DVD*

Susie Porter *Jill Fitzpatrick* • Kelly McGillis *Diana* • Marton Csokas *Nick* • Abbie Cornish *Mickey* • Jean-Pierre Mignon *Tony Brach* • Caroline Gillmer *Barbara Brach* ■ *Dir* Samantha Lang • *Scr* Anne Kennedy, from the verse novel by Dorother Porter

A Monkey's Tale ★ U
Animated adventure
1999 · Fr/UK/Ger/Hun · Colour · 75min

This European attempt to board the Disney bandwagon boasts a hackneyed plot, a clutch of dreadful songs and some ghastly animation. A tree-dwelling ape takes up residence with his "civilised" brethren, though it's not long before he becomes embroiled in a plot to usurp the monkey throne. NS *DVD*

Matt Hill *Kom* • John Hurt *Chancellor Sebastian* • Michael York *The King* • Sally Ann Marsh *Gina* • Rik Mayall *Gerard* • Michael Gambon *Master Martin* • Shirley Anne Field *Governess* • French Tickner *Korkonak* ■ *Dir* Jean-François Laguionie • *Scr* Norman Hudis, Jean-François Laguionie

The Monkey's Uncle ★★ U
Comedy 1965 · US · Colour · 86min

A chimpanzee called Stanley is the real star of this droopy Disney sequel to *The Misadventures of Merlin Jones*, in which young inventor Tommy Kirk helps two kids pass a test and constructs a bike-powered flying machine. The chimp gets the best of it, spending most of the movie in the arms Annette Funicello. TH

Tommy Kirk *Merlin Jones* • Annette [Annette Funicello] *Jennifer* • Leon Ames *Judge Holmsby* • Frank Faylen *Mr Dearborne* • Arthur O'Connell *Darius Green III* • Leon Tyler *Leon* • Norman Grabowski *Norman* ■ *Dir* Robert Stevenson • *Scr* Tom August [Alfred Lewis Levitt], Helen August [Helen Levitt]

The Monolith Monsters ★★★ PG
Science fiction 1957 · US · Colour · 76min

Meteor fragments land on Earth, absorb moisture and grow to epic proportions.

After a rainstorm, they start covering the world like living skyscrapers. An effective minor entry from sci-fi's golden era, based on a story by 1950s icon Jack Arnold (*The Incredible Shrinking Man*, *Creature from the Black Lagoon*) and set in his favourite small-town desert locale. AJ

Grant Williams *Dave Miller* • Lola Albright *Cathy Barrett* • Les Tremayne *Martin Cochrane* • Trevor Bardette *Arthur Flanders* • Phil Harvey *Ben Gilbert* • William Flaherty *Police Chief Dan Corey* ■ *Dir* John Sherwood • *Scr* Norman Jolley, Robert M Fresco, from a story by Jack Arnold, Fresco

Monsieur Beaucaire ★★★
Comedy　　　　　　　1946 · US · BW · 93min

Made at the peak of Bob Hope's popularity, this remake of a Rudolph Valentino silent (based on a novel by Booth Tarkington) is played strictly for laughs as Hope, a barber at the court of Louis XV, is forced to masquerade as a great lover and swordsman. Joan Caulfield makes a colourless leading lady, but those scene-stealing stalwarts Joseph Schildkraut and Constance Collier add to the fun. TV

Bob Hope *Mons Beaucaire* • Joan Caulfield *Mimi* • Patric Knowles *Duc de Chandre* • Marjorie Reynolds *Princess Maria of Spain* • Cecil Kellaway *Count D'Armand* • Joseph Schildkraut *Don Francisco* • Reginald Owen *King Louis XV of France* • Constance Collier *The Queen* ■ *Dir* George Marshall • *Scr* Melvin Frank, Norman Panama, from the novel by Booth Tarkington

Monsieur Hire ★★★★★ 15
Thriller　　　　　1989 · Fr · Colour · 75min

Previously filmed by Julien Duvivier as *Panique*, Georges Simenon's chilling tale of murder and obsession is turned into a tender and compelling love story by Patrice Leconte. The director's insight, restraint and humanity is reinforced by Michael Nyman's achingly beautiful score and echoed in the superb performances. Never has the pain of loneliness been more truthfully depicted on screen than by Michel Blanc as the timid little man who willingly sacrifices all to assist his stunning neighbour, Sandrine Bonnaire. A must-see. DP French +subtitles. *DVD*

Michel Blanc *Monsieur Hire* • Sandrine Bonnaire *Alice* • Luc Thuillier *Emile* • André Wilms *Inspector* ■ *Dir* Patrice Leconte • *Scr* Patrice Leconte, Patrick Dewolf, from the novel *Les Fiançailles de M Hire* by Georges Simenon

LANDMARK FILM
Jacques Tati's masterpiece rediscovers the precision and purity of silent cinema, with individual episodes hilariously capturing life in all its eccentric glory

Monsieur Hulot's Holiday
★★★★★ U
Satirical comedy　　　1953 · Fr · BW · 83min

Inspired by the sophisticated silent clowning of Max Linder and Buster Keaton, Jacques Tati's masterpiece is a sublime blend of satire, slapstick and character comedy that was itself a key influence on the *nouvelle vague*. With the genial Hulot invariably at its centre, much of the hilarious seaside action was filmed in long shot - not only to allow the gags to develop in their own time and space, but also to enable audiences to discover for themselves Tati's intuitive use of the film frame, his acute understanding of human behaviour, and his gently mocking appreciation of the absurdities of life. DP French +subtitles. *DVD* ☒

Jacques Tati *Monsieur Hulot* • Nathalie Pascaud *Martine* • Michèle Rolla *Aunt* • Raymond Carl *Waiter* • Lucien Frégis *Hotel proprietor* • Valentine Camax *Englishwoman* ■ *Dir* Jacques Tati • *Scr* Jacques Tati, Henri Marquet, Pierre Aubert, Jacques Lagrange

Monsieur Ibrahim and the Flowers of the Koran ★★★
Drama　　　　　　2003 · Fr · Colour · 94min

As a Turkish shopkeeper with a wise word for every occasion, Omar Sharif gives his most accomplished performance in years in this genial, if ultimately fanciful meeting of clashing cultures. Director François Dupeyron ably establishes the strained relationship between teenager Pierre Boulanger and his inconsolable single father, Gilbert Melki. But the closer the Jewish boy and the kindly Muslim grow, the less credible their friendship becomes. DP French, Turkish +subtitles.

Omar Sharif *Monsieur Ibrahim* • Pierre Boulanger *Momo* • Gilbert Melki *Momo's father* • Isabelle Renauld *Momo's mother* • Lola Naynmark *Myriam* • Anne Suarez *Sylvie* • Mata Gavin *Fatou* • Céline Samie *Eva* • Isabelle Adjani *"La Star"* ■ *Dir* François Dupeyron • *Scr* François Dupeyron, Eric-Emmanuel Schmitt, from the play *Monsieur Ibrahim et les Fleurs du Coran* by Eric-Emmanuel Schmitt

Monsieur Lazhar ★★★★ 12
Drama　　　　　2011 · Can · Colour · 91min

The inspirational teacher is a stock Hollywood archetype. But this gentle, low-budget nominee for the best foreign-language Oscar from Quebec deftly avoids the clichés. Suspension of disbelief is required to swallow the premise of a beatific Algerian immigrant with no papers securing employment at a Montreal elementary school. But in a deeply sympathetic, warm-blooded portrayal from Mohamed Fellag, Lazhar convinces in his ability to connect with his pupils. It's the very lack of neat resolution that makes this hugely watchable and tear-jerking fable linger in the memory. AC French, English, Arabic +subtitles. *DVD*

Fellag [Mohamed Fellag] *Bachir Lazhar* • Sophie Nélisse *Alice* • Emilien Néron *Simon* • Marie-Eve Beauregard *Marie Frédérique* • Danielle Proulx *Ms Vaillancourt* ■ *Dir* Philippe Falardeau • *Scr* Philippe Falardeau, from a play by Evelyne de la Cheneliere

Monsieur N ★★★★ 12
Historical mystery thriller
2003 · Fr/UK/S Afr · Colour · 123min

Concentrating on the latter days of Napoleon, Antoine de Caunes's historical conspiracy thriller may not be entirely credible, but remains utterly intriguing. Philippe Torreton captures Bonaparte's complexities with a finesse that is slightly lacking in Richard E Grant's British governor. But the aristocratic ensemble trapped on the island of St Helena, from motives of selfishness and self-interest, also excels and the period look and feel is impeccable. DP English, French +subtitles. Nudity.

Philippe Torreton *Napoleon* • Richard E Grant *Sir Hudson Lowe* • Jay Rodan *Basil Heathcote* • Elsa Zylberstein *Albine de Montholon* • Roschdy Zem *Marshal Bertrand* • Bruno Putzulu *Cipriani* • Stéphane Freiss *General Montholon* • Frédéric Pierrot *General Gourgaud* ■ *Dir* Antoine de Caunes • *Scr* René Manzor, from an idea by Pierre Kubel

Monsieur Verdoux ★★★★ PG
Black comedy　　　1947 · US · BW · 123min

One of the best of the latter-day sound movies by Charles Chaplin, this is a chilling black comedy in which a bank clerk (watch him riffling through those bank-notes!) turns to killing wealthy women. Sentiment sneaks in with the appearance of the waifish Marilyn Nash, but it's soon dispelled by the vulgarity of Martha Raye as an intended victim. There's a fastidious cruelty about it all, reflecting Chaplin's deep-seated contempt for the middle-class, and the final speech allies the bank clerk's Bluebeard tendencies with the activities of the major political powers. Adapted from an idea by Orson Welles, this is an astringent treat. TH *DVD*

Charles Chaplin *Henri Verdoux/Varney/Bonheur/Floray/Narrator* • Mady Correll *Mona Verdoux* • Allison Roddan *Peter Verdoux* • Robert Lewis (1) *Maurice Bottello* • Martha Raye *Annabella* ■ *Dir* Charles Chaplin • *Scr* Charles Chaplin, from an idea by Orson Welles • *Cinematographer* Rollie Rotheroh

Monsieur Vincent ★★★★
Biographical religious drama
1947 · Fr · BW · 118min

The winner of only the second Oscar awarded to the best foreign film, this inspirational biopic also enabled Pierre Fresnay to land the best actor prize at the Venice film festival for his self-abasing performance as Vincent de Paul, the saintly priest who used his influence with the aristocracy to help relieve poverty in 17th-century France. Considering it was made with the backing of the Catholic Church, it's anything but a hagiography. Indeed, director Maurice Cloche is as keen to expose the disregard of Cardinal Richelieu's regime as to extol the cleric's compassion for the poor. DP French +subtitles.

Pierre Fresnay *Saint Vincent de Paul* • Lise Delamare *Countess de Gondi* • Aimé Clariond *Cardinal de Richelieu* • Gabrielle Dorziat *Mme Groussault* • Jean Debucourt *Count de Philippe de Gondi* • Germaine Dermoz *Queen Anne of Austria* • Pierre Dux *Chancellor Seguier* ■ *Dir* Maurice Cloche • *Scr* Jean Anouilh, Maurice Cloche, Jean Bernard Luc

Monsignor ★★★ 15
Drama　　　　　1982 · US · Colour · 116min

Christopher Reeve stars as an ambitious young priest who greases his way up the Vatican's slippery pole and faces various temptations along the way, including lusty nuns and Mafia gangsters. This dizzying melodrama rests on a knife edge between schlock and solemnity. AT

Christopher Reeve *Flaherty* • Geneviève Bujold *Clara* • Fernando Rey *Santoni* • Jason Miller *Appolini* • Joe Cortese *Varese* • Adolfo Celi *Vinci* • Leonardo Cimino *Pope* ■ *Dir* Frank Perry • *Scr* Abraham Polonsky, Wendell Mayes, from the novel by Jack Alain Leger

Monsoon Wedding ★★★★ 15
Comedy drama
2001 · US/It/Ger/Fr · Colour · 109min

This was a surprise winner of the Golden Lion at Venice, but, while the emphasis here is on fun - as Punjabi Vasundhara Das prepares for her nuptials with US-based engineer Parvin Dabas - there's still social comment to add backbone to the comedy. Celebrating the wisps of tradition that hold Indian society together while also exposing its less salubrious facets, Mira Nair draws vigorous performances from an impeccable ensemble cast and bathes the action in an irresistible Holly/Bollywood glow. DP English, Hindi, Punjabi +subtitles. Swearing. *DVD*

Naseeruddin Shah *Lalit Verma* • Lillete Dubey *Pimma Verma* • Shefali Shetty *Ria Verma* • Vijay Raaz *PK Dubey* • Tillotama Shome *Alice* • Vasundhara Das *Aditi Verma* • Kulbhushan Kharbanda *CL Chadha* • Parvin Dabas *Hemant Rai* ■ *Dir* Mira Nair • *Scr* Sabrina Dhawan

The Monster ★★★
Silent horror comedy　1925 · US · BW · 71min

One of Lon Chaney's more tongue-in-cheek horror films, this is a delight, if less memorable than *The Unholy Three* and *The Phantom of the Opera*, released in the same year. Here he's without elaborate make-up as the dapper Dr Ziska, a mad surgeon who arranges car accidents on a lonely road, thereby obtaining subjects for his experiments to discover the secret of life. Director Roland West handles the story with humour. AE

Lon Chaney *Dr Ziska* • Johnny Arthur *Under clerk* • Gertrude Olmsted *Betty Watson* • Hallam Cooley *Watson's head clerk* • Charles A Sellon [Charles Sellon] *Constable* ■ *Dir* Roland West • *Scr* Willard Mack, Albert Kenyon, from a play by Crane Wilbur • *Cinematographer* Hal Mohr

Monster ★★★ 18
Horror comedy　　1980 · US · Colour · 76min

Pollution-spawned creatures go on a carnal rampage in a lively update of the concepts Roger Corman adeptly used for his own cult films of the 1950s. Director Barbara Peeters complained producer Corman spliced in the sensationalised rape scenes after she had finished with the project, but they only add to the lurid, lip-smacking sleaze of the whole enjoyably tacky enterprise. AJ

Doug McClure *Jim Hill* • Ann Turkel *Dr Susan Drake* • Vic Morrow *Hank Slattery* • Cindy Weintraub *Carol Hill* • Anthony Penya *Johnny Eagle* • Denise Galik *Linda Beale* ■ *Dir* Barbara Peeters • *Scr* Frederick James, from a story by Frank Arnold, Martin B Cohen

Monster ★★★★ 18
Crime drama based on a true story
2003 · US/Ger · Colour · 104min

More an intense portrait of doomed romance than a serial-killer thriller, writer/director Patty Jenkins's brutal biopic of prostitute turned multiple murderer Aileen Wuornos burrows deep into the woman's psyche with the help of an Oscar-winning turn from Charlize Theron. Theron's performance goes beyond the weight-gain and dental prosthetics, finding both compassion and coldness in Wuornos's descent into homicidal mania, as she fights both to survive and to protect the naive outcast lesbian Selby (a superbly understated Christina Ricci). Tender, chilling, heartbreaking. IF *DVD*

Charlize Theron *Aileen Wuornos* • Christina Ricci *Selby Wall* • Bruce Dern *Thomas* • Lee Tergesen *Vincent Corey* • Annie Corley *Donna Tentler* • Marco St John *Evan/"undercover john"* • Pruitt Taylor Vince *Gene/"stuttering john"* • Scott Wilson *Horton/"last john"* ■ *Dir/Scr* Patty Jenkins

A Monster Calls
Fantasy drama　　2016 · US/Sp · Colour

This is a preview - no prints were available to review as we went to press: Terminal illness usually makes for good box office, so blend with a little bit of fantasy as in this tale of a boy who seeks the help of a tree monster to help save his mum and producers will hope they are on to a winner. Toby Kebbell stars alongside Liam Neeson and Felicity Jones, Neeson at last taking a break from killing people who threaten his family, and Jones hoping that her success in *The Theory of Everything* will help the box office of this effort. TP

Felicity Jones *Mum* • Liam Neeson *The Monster* • Toby Kebbell *Dad* • Sigourney Weaver *Grandma* ■ *Dir* JA Bayona [Juan Antonio Bayona] • *Scr* Patrick Ness

The Monster Club ★★★ 15
Horror　　　　　1980 · UK · Colour · 93min

John Carradine (as famed horror writer R Chetwynd-Hayes) travels to a Transylvanian disco where bloodsucker Vincent Price (playing a vampire for the first and only time) relates three macabre stories of varying quality in a shaky anthology based on Chetwynd-Hayes's tales of terror and complicated ghoul genealogy. Included in the pseudo-hip monster mash is a Shadmock whose silent whistle is fatal to mortals, a band of Mafia-type undead chasers with stakes in their violin cases, and the Humgoos who wreak havoc on a film director looking for a creepy location. Worth watching for the all-star cast alone. AJ Brief nudity. *DVD* ☒

Vincent Price *Erasmus* • John Carradine *R Chetwynd-Hayes* • James Laurenson *Raven* • Barbara Kellerman *Angela* • Simon Ward *George* • Geoffrey Bayldon *Psychiatrist* • Donald Pleasence *Pickering* • Britt Ekland *Lintom's mother* • Richard Johnson *Lintom's father* ■ *Dir* Roy Ward Baker • *Scr* Edward Abraham, Valerie Abraham, from the short story collection by R Chetwynd-Hayes

Monster from Green Hell
★★ PG
Science-fiction adventure
1958 · US · BW · 67min

Jim Davis leads an expedition of scientists through the African jungle, courtesy of stock footage from *Stanley and Livingstone* (1939) and some cheap backlot trimmings. He's looking for a crashed space probe and its cargo of radioactively enlarged wasps, but he needn't have bothered: after going on a weakly rendered trail of destruction, the inept wasps eventually stumble into an erupting volcano. An enjoyable, thick-witted trek through 1950s clichés. AJ

Jim Davis (1) *Quent Brady* • Robert E Griffin [Robert Griffin] *Dan Morgan* • Barbara Turner *Lorna Lorentz* • Eduardo Ciannelli *Mahri* • Vladimir Sokoloff *Dr Lorentz* • Joel Fluellen *Arobi* ■ *Dir* Kenneth Crane • *Scr* Louis Vittes, Endre Boehm

M

Monster House ★★★★ PG
Animated comedy horror
2006 · US · Colour · 86min

Upgrading the motion-capture animation process that Robert Zemeckis pioneered in *The Polar Express*, first-time director Gil Kenan creates an animated comedy horror with terrific success. As Halloween approaches, youngsters DJ (Mitchel Musso), Chowder (Sam Lerner) and Jenny (Spencer Locke) must unlock the secret of a creepy haunted house before it swallows the neighbourhood's trick-or-treaters. Executive produced by Zemeckis and Steven Spielberg (with Jason Clark), it's a fun and thrilling if slightly scary ride for kids, full of smart jokes for adults, and has plenty of sharp, imaginative detail to delight both. With a distinctive storybook look that's unique, it's an irresistible adventure. AJ Scary scenes, some swearing. *DVD* BL

Steve Buscemi *Nebbercracker* · Nick Cannon *Officer Lister* · Maggie Gyllenhaal *Zee* · Jon Heder *Reginald "Skull" Skulinski* · Kevin James *Officer Landers* · Jason Lee *Bones* · Catherine O'Hara *Mom* · Kathleen Turner *Constance* · Mitchel Musso *DJ Walter* · Sam Lerner *Chowder* · Spencer Locke *Jenny* ■ *Dir* Gil Kenan · *Scr* Dan Harmon, Pamela Pettler, Rob Schrab, from a story by Harmon, Schrab

Monster in a Box ★★★ PG
Biographical documentary
1991 · US · Colour · 89min

Following the success of *Swimming to Cambodia*, writer/actor Spalding Gray embarked upon a second one-man show. The film tells of the interruptions Gray experienced while writing his autobiographical novel, *Impossible Vacation*, including an account of a trip to the Soviet Union along with several Hollywood stars for a Soviet film festival. Shot in London by Nick Broomfield, the UK's master documentarist, the film suffers from audience laughter intruding into the soundtrack. DP *DVD*

■ *Dir* Nick Broomfield · *Scr* Spalding Gray

Monster-in-Law ★★★ 12
Romantic comedy 2005 · US · Colour · 97min

It's Gucci handbags at dawn for Jane Fonda and Jennifer Lopez in this comedy with bite from director Robert Luketic. While it stumbles a little during the corny courtship between J-Lo's bohemian babe and well-heeled doctor Michael Vartan, once Fonda turns up, the battle – and laughter – lines are very quickly drawn. After a 15-year sabbatical from movies, Fonda relishes the role of manic mommy, displaying a surprising gift for physical humour. The ending is sappy, but Lopez holds her own. SP *DVD*

Jennifer Lopez *Charlotte "Charlie" Cantilini* · Jane Fonda *Viola Fields* · Michael Vartan *Kevin Fields* · Wanda Sykes *Ruby* · Adam Scott *Remy* · Monet Mazur *Fiona* · Annie Parisse *Morgan* · Elaine Stritch *Gertrude* ■ *Dir* Robert Luketic · *Scr* Anya Kochoff

A Monster in Paris ★★★ U
Animated musical fantasy
2011 · Fr · Colour · 86min

Paris in 1910 is flooded and gloomy, and to make matters worse there's a scary creature on the loose. But, as this charming fantasy from the director of *Shark Tale* reveals, he's more of a misunderstood musician than a savage beast. Director Bibo Bergeron (who returned to his native France after making his name in Hollywood) has crafted a beautiful love letter to Paris – the city's landmarks are shown off to great effect, and there's a keen sense of period. He gets good performances from his voice cast, and also cleverly references early horror movies. While the attempts at humour occasionally fall flat, there's plenty of excitement in the chase scenes and a refreshing lack of sentiment, and the movie is topped by bewitchingly memorable songs. LB *DVD* BL SP

Adam Goldberg *Raoul* · Vanessa Paradis *Lucille* · Danny Huston *Commissioner Maynott* · Jay Harrington *Emile* · Sean Lennon *Francoeur* · Bob

Balaban *Pâté* ■ *Dir* Bibo Bergeron [Eric "Bibo" Bergeron] · *Scr* Bibo Bergeron, Stéphane Kazandjian

Monster in the Closet ★★ 15
Horror comedy 1983 · US · Colour · 85min

Released by Troma (though produced independently), this amusing update of 1950s horror movies works because its earnest cast deliver their absurd dialogue in a relatively straight fashion. Across the land, people are being killed by a monster (Kevin Peter Hall) who pops out of their closets. Rookie reporter Donald Grant pounds the streets for an answer and helps save the day when the monster comes out into the open. Lots of cameos add to the nostalgic feel. KB

Donald Grant *Richard Clark* · Denise DuBarry *Diane Bennett* · Claude Akins *Sheriff Ketchum* · Howard Duff *Father Finnegan* · Henry Gibson *Dr Pennyworth* · Donald Moffat *General Turnbull* · Paul Dooley *Roy Crane* · Stella Stevens *Margo Crane* · John Carradine *Old Joe* · Kevin Peter Hall *Monster* ■ *Dir* Bob Dahlin · *Scr* Bob Dahlin, from a story by Peter Bergquist, Bob Dahlin

The Monster Maker ★
Horror 1944 · US · BW · 62min

This repellent horror movie – more closely allied to surgical fiction than imaginative fantasy – casts J Carrol Naish (later to play Charlie Chan on TV) as a mad scientist who infects his enemies with distorting bacteria. Directed by Sam Newfield and co-starring Ralph Morgan and Wanda McKay, it has little to recommend it apart from its freak-show novelty and an audience-pulling title. TH

J Carrol Naish *Dr Igor Markoff* · Ralph Morgan *Lawrence* · Tala Birell *Maxine* · Wanda McKay *Patricia Lawrence* · Terry Frost *Blake* · Glenn Strange *Giant* ■ *Dir* Sam Newfield · *Scr* Pierre Gendron, Martin Mooney, from a story by Lawrence Williams

Monster Man ★★ 18
Comedy horror 2003 · US · Colour · 91min

Redneck clichés flow as freely as the gore in this derivative comedy horror. Wimpy Eric Jungmann and his obnoxious buddy Justin Urich find a cross-country road trip turning to terror when they become the target of a disfigured fiend driving a monster truck. Throw in a scantily clad hitch-hiker (Aimee Brooks), the occult and puerile female genitalia jokes, and you've got a daft genre hybrid best suited to teenagers and fans of trashy B-movies. Yet the film still has a few effective moments. SF *DVD*

Eric Jungmann *Adam* · Justin Urich *Harley* · Aimee Brooks *Sarah* · Joe Goodrich *Brother Fred* · Michael Bailey Smith *Brother Bob/Monster Man* · Bobby Ray Shafer [Robert R Shafer] *Deputy Dang* ■ *Dir/Scr* Michael Davis (3)

The Monster of Highgate Ponds ★★ U
Fantasy adventure 1961 · UK · BW · 56min

Although Michael Balcon usually gets all the credit for the creative stature of Ealing Studios, the director Alberto Cavalcanti was the major force, pouring oil on troubled waters and encouraging brilliance from the film-makers. This is a lacklustre example of his work in decline, a children's film set in north London and featuring Roy Vincente and Ronald Howard. Although it includes some neat touches, which show the talent that Cavalcanti was, it's too obviously aimed at its target audience of youngsters. TH *DVD*

Roy Vincente *The monster* · Ronald Howard *Uncle Dick* · Rachel Clay *Sophie* · Michael Wade *David* · Terry Raven *Chris* · Frederick Piper *Sam* · Michael Balfour *Bert* ■ *Dir* Alberto Cavalcanti · *Scr* Mary Cathcart Borer, from a story by Joy Batchelor

The Monster Squad ★★★ 15
Comedy horror 1987 · US · Colour · 78min

This horror movie scares just enough and amuses quite a lot. A well-cast Duncan Regehr is Count Dracula, journeying to suburban America to search for a mysterious amulet with the help of Frankenstein's monster and the Wolf Man,

among others. But he reckons without a group of excitable children who are soon rustling up a few stakes in woodwork class. Enormous fun. SH

André Gower *Sean Crenshaw* · Robby Kiger *Patrick* · Stephen Macht *Del Crenshaw* · Duncan Regehr *Count Dracula* · Tom Noonan *Frankenstein's monster* · Brent Chalem *Horace* · Ryan Lambert *Rudy* ■ *Dir* Fred Dekker · *Scr* Shane Black, Fred Dekker

The Monster That Challenged the World ★★★
Science-fiction horror 1957 · US · BW · 84min

In this fun, low-budget sci-fi horror movie, the eggs of an extinct sea monster are released during an earthquake and hatch as giant snail-like creatures that kill humans for their blood and water. Tim Holt came out of retirement to play the naval officer teaming up with Hans Conried's boffin to prevent the monsters breeding and spreading. An effective piece of film-making results from the good script, suspenseful direction and convincing monsters. AE

Tim Holt *Lieutenant Commander John Twilinger* · Audrey Dalton *Gail MacKenzie* · Hans Conried *Dr Jess Rogers* · Harlan Warde *Lieutenant Bob Clemens* · Casey Adams [Max Showalter] *Tad Johns* ■ *Dir* Arnold Laven · *Scr* Pat Fielder, from a story by David Duncan

Monster Trucks
Science-fiction action adventure
2015 · US · Colour · 122min

This is a preview – no prints were available to review prior to publication: This is listed as director Chris Wedge's "first live action film" – which it will be, sort of. The plot has echoes of *ET* and will be a blend of live-action and CGI special effects. Former X-Man Lucas Till and Danny Glover head the cast in what is sure to be knockabout fun from the man who gave us *Ice Age* and *Robots* and who have worked on *Kung Fu Panda* and *Alvin and the Chipmunks*. TP SP

Rob Lowe · Thomas Lennon (3) · Amy Ryan · Jane Levy *Meredith* · Barry Pepper ■ *Dir* Chris Wedge · *Scr* Derek Connolly, from a story by Jonathan Aibel, Glenn Berger, Matthew Robinson (3)

Monsters ★★★★ 12
Science-fiction drama
2010 · UK · Colour · 90min

In the wake of an alien infestation that has rendered the US-Mexico border a no-go area, two travellers attempt to traverse the danger zone in this blend of sci-fi and character drama. An enterprising debut from British writer/director Gareth Edwards, the film cannily deploys its modest budget to convince us that towering squid-like aliens are indeed stalking the earth. Mixing road movie, romance and ETs might sound unlikely, yet this makes something suspenseful and affecting from it. Moreover, the chemistry between the leads is obviously authentic, since they have now tied the knot in real-life. TJ Some swearing. *DVD* BL

Whitney Able *Samantha "Sam" Wynden* · Scoot McNairy *Andrew Kaulder* ■ *Dir/Scr* Gareth Edwards

Monsters: Dark Continent ★★★★ 15
Science-fiction thriller
2014 · UK · Colour · 114min

On a par with the affecting original, debut director Tom Green's inspirational vision uses the original ethos while expanding the sci-fi myth in extraordinarily thrilling and thought-provoking ways. Ten years after the events in *Monsters*, the infected zones have spread worldwide and the squid-like ETs may not be the deadliest threat after all. A powerful metaphor for the human condition during wartime, executed with remarkable skill, confidence and an astute fantasy feel. AJ Violence, swearing, sex scenes, nudity. *DVD* BL

Johnny Harris *Noah Frater* · Joe Dempsie *Frankie Maguire* · Kyle Soller *Karl Inkelaar* · Sofia Boutella *Ara* ■ *Dir* Tom Green (2) · *Scr* Jay Basu, Tom Green (2)

Monster's Ball ★★★★ 15
Romantic crime drama
2001 · US · Colour · 108min

The complexities of the heart are examined against a background of bigotry, despair and redemption in German-born director Marc Forster's blistering Deep South drama. Anchored by the compelling and provocative performances of Billy Bob Thornton and Oscar winner Halle Berry, the story focuses on the relationship between a grieving black widow and the white prison guard who presided over her convict husband's execution. A film of rare emotional depth and power, this is so centred on the irrationalities of human sentiment that many of the plot's implausibilities can be forgiven. SF Violence, a sex scene, swearing, nudity. *DVD*

Billy Bob Thornton *Hank Grotowski* · Halle Berry *Leticia Musgrove* · Heath Ledger *Sonny Grotowski* · Peter Boyle *Buck Grotowski* · Sean Combs *Lawrence Musgrove* · Mos Def *Ryrus Cooper* ■ *Dir* Marc Forster · *Scr* Milo Addica, Will Rokos

Monsters, Inc ★★★★★ U
Animated comedy adventure
2001 · US · Colour · 88min

In this frantic, funny and very furry animated feature from computer animation pioneers Pixar, the focus is on the creatures that lurk inside the bedroom closets of children and who terrify their human prey when the lights are off. The creatures are employees of Monsters Inc, a power provider for the city of Monstropolis which is fuelled by the screams of human children. Then Sulley (voiced by John Goodman) accidentally lets a little girl into a realm where kids are believed to be highly toxic. Packed with artistry and storytelling panache. JC *DVD* BL CS

John Goodman *James P "Sulley" Sullivan* · Billy Crystal *Michael "Mike" Wazowski* · Mary Gibbs *Boo* · Steve Buscemi *Randall Boggs* · James Coburn *Henry J Waternoose* · Jennifer Tilly *Celia* · Bob Peterson *Roz* · John Ratzenberger *Yeti* · Frank Oz *Fungus* ■ *Dir* Pete Docter · *Scr* Andrew Stanton, Daniel Gerson, from a story by Pete Docter, Jill Culton, Jeff Pidgeon, Ralph Eggleston

Monsters University ★★★★ U
Animated comedy 2013 · US · Colour · 99min

This gag-packed prequel takes the heroes of Pixar's *Monsters, Inc* back to their college days, before Mike (voiced by Billy Crystal) and Sulley (John Goodman) became best buddies. They're set a series of tasks under the watchful eye of Dean Hardscrabble (Helen Mirren) to prove they're worthy of graduating with the scariest of the scarers. The nods to live-action frat comedies down the years come thick and fast, but they never detract from what Pixar does so well time and again: telling a great story. TeS *DVD* BL CS

Billy Crystal *Mike Wazowski* · John Goodman *James P "Sulley" Sullivan* · Steve Buscemi *Randall Boggs* · Helen Mirren *Dean Hardscrabble* · Alfred Molina *Professor Knight* · Dave Foley *Terry* · Joel Murray *Don Carlton* · Peter Sohn *Scott "Squishy" Squibbles* · John Ratzenberger *The Abominable Snowman* ■ *Dir* Dan Scanlon · *Scr* Dan Scanlon, Daniel Gerson, Robert L Baird, from their story

Monsters vs Aliens ★★★★ PG
Animated science-fiction comedy
2009 · US · Colour · 90min

Five freaks of nature, not unlike those classic science-fiction icons Mothra, the Blob, the 50 Foot Woman, the Fly and the Gillman, are released from US government security to stave off an alien invasion in this charming, funny and ingeniously detailed cartoon caper from DreamWorks. The film is a valentine to B-movie creature features, with smart scripting and superior craftsmanship. Discerning adults and demanding children alike will be entranced by the action-packed dazzle and visually enthralling delights, including a stunning battle on San Francisco's Golden Gate Bridge. And for sci-fi buffs, the references will prove delicious, taking in the likes of *Close Encounters of the Third Kind, ET* and *Men in Black*. AJ **DVD** **Blu-ray**

Reese Witherspoon *Susan Murphy/Ginormica* • Seth Rogen *B.O.B.* • Hugh Laurie *Dr Cockroach, PhD* • Will Arnett *The Missing Link* • Kiefer Sutherland *General WR Monger* • Rainn Wilson *Gallaxhar* • Paul Rudd *Derek Dietl* ■ *Dir* Rob Letterman, Conrad Vernon • *Scr* Maya Forbes, Wally Wolodarsky, Jonathan Aibel, Glenn Berger, Rob Letterman, from a story by Conrad Vernon, Letterman

Montana ★★ PG
Western 1950 · US · Colour · 73min

A routine western in glorious Technicolor, this stars an amiable Errol Flynn as the sheep farmer daring to seek grazing land in cattle country. The film lacks any real bite, suffering in particular from the absence of an authoritative villain. Douglas Kennedy does his best, but it is the redheaded cattle queen played by Alexis Smith who wants to shoot it out with him at the end. AE

Errol Flynn *Morgan Lane* • Alexis Smith *Maria Singleton* • SZ "Cuddles" Sakall [SZ Sakall] *Poppa Schultz* • Douglas Kennedy *Rodney Ackroyd* • James Brown (1) *Tex Coyne* • Ian MacDonald *Slim Reeves* • Paul E Burns *Tecumseh Burke* ■ *Dir* Ray Enright • *Scr* James R Webb, Borden Chase, Charles O'Neal, from a story by Ernest Haycox

Montana ★★ 18
Crime drama 1997 · US · Colour · 92min

Though directed by a woman and centring around a female assassin (Kyra Sedgwick) framed by mobsters, this crime drama doesn't have any ambitions to offer a feminist perspective. The focus is more on dialogue and character than violence, though, which makes the shoot-outs seem out of place. The most original parts of the movie are its bizarre flashes of humour, while the cast is certainly worth a look. KB **DVD**

Kyra Sedgwick *Claire* • Stanley Tucci *Nick* • Robin Tunney *Kitty* • John Ritter *Dr Wexler* • Robbie Coltrane *The Boss* • Philip Seymour Hoffman *Duncan* ■ *Dir* Jennifer Leitzes • *Scr* John & Erich Hoeber

Monte Carlo ★★★
Musical comedy 1930 · US · BW · 90min

On the French Riviera, a count (Jack Buchanan) poses as a hairdresser and woos a countess (Jeanette MacDonald) in this feather-light musical romance from Ernst Lubitsch. What follows is enjoyable and characteristically stylish, though not as good as those to come which paired MacDonald with Maurice Chevalier. English stage star Buchanan is witty and appealing but lacks Chevalier's Gallic charm. RK

Jack Buchanan *Count Rudolph Falliere* • Jeanette MacDonald *Countess Vera von Conti* • ZaSu Pitts *Maria, Vera's maid* • Claude Allister [Claud Allister] *Prince Otto von Seibenheim* • Lionel Belmore *Duke Gustave von Seibenheim, his father* • Tyler Brooke *Armand, Rudolph's friend* ■ *Dir* Ernst Lubitsch • *Scr* Ernest Vajda, Vincent Lawrence, from the play *The Blue Coast* by Hans Muller and the novel *Monsieur Beaucaire* by Booth Tarkington

Monte Carlo ★★ PG
Romantic comedy adventure
2011 · US/Lux/Hun/Fr/Mon · Colour · 104min

Filmed largely in Hungary, with Budapest doubling for both Paris and Monte Carlo, this unremarkable romp stars Selena Gomez as the American teen in Paris who is mistaken for lookalike Cordelia (also Gomez), a spoiled British heiress, and is whisked off with her two companions (*Gossip Girl*'s Leighton Meester and Katie Cassidy) to a life of super-luxury in Monte Carlo. It's predictable and corny, but pre-teen Disney Channel fans probably won't care. DA **Blu-ray**

Selena Gomez *Grace Bennett/Cordelia Winthrop Scott* • Leighton Meester *Meg* • Katie Cassidy *Emma* • Cory Monteith *Owen* • Andie MacDowell *Pam* • Catherine Tate *Alicia Winthrop Scott* ■ *Dir* Thomas Bezucha • *Scr* Thomas Bezucha, April Blair, Maria Maggenti, from a story by Kelly Bowe, from the novel *Headhunters* by Jules Bass

Monte Carlo or Bust! ★★★ PG
Comedy 1969 · Fr/UK/It · Colour · 119min

This is a well-intentioned sequel to the massively popular *Those Magnificent Men in Their Flying Machines* from the same director, Ken Annakin, and with many of the same cast, only this time it's about a 1,500-mile car race. It's a long haul, but star Tony Curtis makes the most of the journey and there's a rare opportunity to see Peter Cook and Dudley Moore in the same movie, plus accomplished turns from the likes of Terry-Thomas, Eric Sykes and the splendid Bourvil. TS

Tony Curtis *Chester Schofield* • Susan Hampshire *Betty* • Terry-Thomas *Sir Cuthbert* • Peter Cook *Major Dawlish* • Dudley Moore *Lt Barrington* • Eric Sykes *Perkins* • Gert Frobe [Gert Fröbe] *Willi Schickel/Horst Muiler* • Hattie Jacques *Lady journalist* • Mireille Darc *Marie-Claude* • Jack Hawkins *Count Levinovitch* • Bourvil *Monsieur Dupont* ■ *Dir* Ken Annakin, Sam Itzkovitch • *Scr* Ken Annakin, Jack Davis

The Monte Carlo Story ★★ U
Comedy drama 1957 · It/US · Colour · 101min

Italian count Vittorio De Sica, bankrupted by gambling, looks for a rich woman to finance his "system" at the tables. He falls in love with Marlene Dietrich, but they part when he discovers she is also penniless. Writer/director Samuel Taylor trespasses into Lubitsch territory with this well-worn tale, but he lacks the latter's gift for transforming this kind of story and setting into witty and romantic magic. The result is a desperately overplotted affair. RK

Marlene Dietrich *Marquise Maria de Crevecoeur* • Vittorio De Sica *Count Dino della Fiaba* • Arthur O'Connell *Mr Hinkley* • Jane Rose *Mrs Freeman* • Clelia Matania *Sophia* • Alberto Rabagliati *Albert* • Mischa Auer *Hector* ■ *Dir* Sam Taylor • *Scr* Samuel Taylor, from a story by Marcello Girosi, Dino Risi

Monte Walsh ★★★ PG
Western 1970 · US · Colour · 94min

This evocative, painterly and melancholy western marks the directing debut of William A Fraker, the cameraman on *Bullitt* and *Paint Your Wagon*. It was the star of the latter, Lee Marvin, who enabled Fraker to make this movie about two cowboy friends, Marvin and Jack Palance, who see their way of life ending yet find their attempts to forge domesticated lives also doomed. It's a pity that Fraker's directing career all but fizzled out after this striking, beautifully cast first feature. AT

Lee Marvin *Monte Walsh* • Jack Palance *Chet Rollins* • Jeanne Moreau *Martine Bernard* • Mitch Ryan [Mitchell Ryan] *Shorty Austin* • Jim Davis (1) *Cal Brennan* • John Hudkins *Sonny Jacobs* • Raymond Guth *Sunfish Perkins* • John McKee *Petey Williams* ■ *Dir* William A Fraker • *Scr* David Z Goodman [David Zelag Goodman], Lukas Heller, from the novel by Jack Schaefer

Monte Walsh ★★★
Western 2003 · US · Colour · 150min

Based on a novel by Jack Schaefer (who also wrote *Shane*), this is a gritty lament for the passing of the Old West. But, like William Fraker before him, director Simon Wincer eschews rose-tinted romanticism to show both how tough life was on the range and how dangerous it could be in the insular frontier towns of the 1890s. While not in the same league as Lee Marvin in the 1970 original, Tom Selleck turns in a manly performance as the cowhand whose days of roaming Wyoming seem numbered. DP

Tom Selleck *Monte Walsh* • Isabella Rossellini *"Countess" Martine* • Keith Carradine *Chester "Chet" Rollins* • George Eads *Frank "Shorty" Austin* • Robert Carradine *Sunfish Perkins* • Barry Corbin *Bob the Storekeeper* • James Gammon *"Fighting" Joe Hooker/Albert Miller* • William Devane *Cal Brennan* ■ *Dir* Simon Wincer • *Scr* Michael Brandman, Robert B Parker, from the 1970 film by David Z Goodman [David Zelag Goodman], Lukas Heller, from the novel by Jack Schaefer • *Music/Lyrics* Keith Carradine

Montenegro ★★ 18
Surreal comedy 1981 · Swe/UK · Colour · 92min

It's not often that a scene involving a toy tank and a stripper provides the most arresting moment in a film, but that's the case with this comedy. Serbian director Dusan Makavejev coaxes a vibrant performance out of Susan Anspach as the bored housewife who gets to sample the wild side of life after missing a flight. But chauvinistic husband Erland Josephson is less impressive, and the symbolism is heavy-handed. DP Swearing, sex scenes, nudity.

Susan Anspach *Marilyn Jordan* • Erland Josephson *Martin Jordan* • Jamie Marsh *Jimmy* • Per Oscarsson *Dr Pazardjian* • Bora Todorovic *Alex* • Marianne Jacobi *Cookie* ■ *Dir/Scr* Dusan Makavejev

Monterey Pop ★★★★
Music documentary 1968 · US · Colour · 79min

This breakthrough concert movie, which paved the way for *Woodstock* with its ground-breaking, *cinéma vérité* style, was directed by DA Pennebaker, who made the Bob Dylan documentary *Don't Look Back* one year earlier. Over 45 hours of 16mm film was shot at the 1967 Monterey International Pop Festival and edited into the first major rock festival documentary, capturing some of the greatest music legends of the hippy era. In between shots of sexy chicks, arrays of sleeping bags and queues for the toilets, Janis Joplin wails her way through *Ball and Chain*, the Who trash sound equipment to *My Generation*, Otis Redding warbles *I've Been Loving You Too Long* and Jimi Hendrix sets his guitar aflame to *Wild Thing* – the highlight. AJ

■ *Dir/Scr* DA Pennebaker

A Month by the Lake ★★★ PG
Period romantic drama
1994 · UK/US · Colour · 87min

John Irvin's period drama is a *ménage à quatre* set on the shores of Italy's Lake Como on the eve of the Second World War. Vanessa Redgrave's flirtation with English major Edward Fox becomes more serious thanks to the intervention of American nanny Uma Thurman and the attentions of Italian youth Alessandro Gassman, who has a taste for older women. There's little emotional depth, but the acting is impeccable. TH **DVD**

Vanessa Redgrave *Miss Bentley* • Edward Fox *Major Wilshaw* • Uma Thurman *Miss Beaumont* • Alida Valli *Signora Fascioli* • Alessandro Gassman *Vittorio Balsari* • Carlo Cartier *Mr Bonizzoni* • Paolo Lombardi *Enrico* • Riccardo Rossi *Guido* • Sonia Martinelli *Maria* ■ *Dir* John Irvin • *Scr* Trevor Bentham, from the novella by HE Bates

A Month in the Country ★★★★ PG
Drama 1987 · UK · Colour · 91min

This moving and sensitive meditation on the aftereffects of the First World War shows shell-shocked survivors Colin Firth and Kenneth Branagh learning to live with each other's idiosyncracies and quirks of sexual nature while preserving and restoring relics from a bygone age. Working from Simon Gray's adaptation of JL Carr's book, director Pat O'Connor fashions a poignant gem with a very moving finale. TH **DVD** **Blu-ray**

Colin Firth *Tom Birkin* • Kenneth Branagh *Charles Moon* • Natasha Richardson *Alice Keach* • Patrick Malahide *Reverend Keach* • Jim Carter *Ellerbeck* • Richard Vernon *Colonel Hebron* ■ *Dir* Pat O'Connor • *Scr* Simon Gray, from the novel by JL Carr

Montparnasse 19 ★★★
Biographical drama 1958 · Fr/It · BW · 108min

What an ill-fated film! Having developed the project, Max Ophüls died before shooting, while both his replacement, Jacques Becker, and star, Gérard Philipe, would be dead within three years. Philipe was only 36 when he died, one year older than Amedeo Modigliani, the reckless artist he portrays here. The film revels in both his various addictions and the cut-throat nature of bohemian Paris in the early 20th century, but Becker leaves too little room for drama by refusing to stray from the facts. DP French +subtitles.

Gérard Philipe *Amedeo Modigliani* • Lilli Palmer *Béatrice Hastings* • Anouk Aimée *Jeanne Hébuterne* • Gérard Séty *Sborowski* • Lila Kedrova *Mme Sborowski* • Lea Padovani *Rosalie* • Jean Lanier *Monsieur Hébuterne* ■ *Dir* Jacques Becker • *Scr* Henri Jeanson, Max Ophüls, Jean Cocteau, from the novel *Les Montparnos* by Georges-Michel Michel

Monty Python and the Holy Grail ★★★★ 15
Comedy 1975 · UK · Colour · 85min

Complete with some inspired digressions and shorn of some of the weaker sketches, the soundtrack album of the Pythons' first story-based feature is even funnier than the film itself. Yet this remains a wonderfully inventive comedy that brilliantly debunks the Dark Ages and the legends of chivalry through King Arthur's encounters with an anarcho-syndicalist commune, the Black Knight, God (courtesy of Terry Gilliam) and the "knights who say ni". The *Camelot* and *Sir Robin* songs also get beneath the visor, but the highlights are the trial of Connie Booth's witch and the Holy Hand Grenade of Antioch sequence. Re-released in a sing-along version for its 40th anniversary. DP Swearing, some violence, nudity. **DVD** **Blu-ray**

Graham Chapman *King Arthur* • John Cleese *Black Knight/Sir Lancelot* • Terry Gilliam *Patsy/Green Knight* • Eric Idle *Sir Robin/Brother Maynard* • Terry Jones *Dennis' mother/Sir Bedevere* • Michael Palin *Dennis/Sir Galahad* • Connie Booth *Witch* ■ *Dir* Terry Gilliam, Terry Jones • *Scr* Graham Chapman, John Cleese, Terry Gilliam, Eric Idle, Terry Jones, Michael Palin • *Music/lyrics* Neil Innes

Monty Python Live at the Hollywood Bowl ★★★ 15
Comedy 1982 · UK · Colour · 77min

Suffering from writer's block during the scripting on *Monty Python's The Meaning of Life*, the Pythons decided to play the famous open-air Hollywood Bowl to revive their creative spirits. Under-rehearsed and prone to fits of giggles, the team still ran through such favourites as the *The Ministry of Silly Walks*, the *Bruces*, the *Four Yorkshiremen* and the *Lumberjack Song* with consummate skill. It's a mixed bag but, because HandMade decided to cut parts of the show for the film version, it's all over far too soon. DP Swearing.

Graham Chapman • John Cleese • Terry Gilliam • Eric Idle • Terry Jones • Michael Palin • Neil Innes • Carol Cleveland ■ *Dir* Terry Hughes, Ian MacNaughton • *Scr* Graham Chapman, John Cleese, Terry Gilliam, Eric Idle, Terry Jones, Michael Palin

Monty Python's Life of Brian ★★★★ 15
Comedy 1979 · UK · Colour · 89min

The controversy that surrounded this inspired send-up of religious epics overshadows the fact that this is the Monty Python team's most assured work. Graham Chapman ("he's not the Messiah, he's just a naughty boy") is the Judaean whose life bears some resemblance to a certain carpenter's around the same time, although the shambling story serves mainly as an excuse to take pot shots at some of their favourite targets and serve up some joyfully juvenile gags. Michael Palin gets some memorable roles, notably the Roman governor with a speech impediment ("Welease Wodewick"); Spike Milligan makes a very funny and quite irrelevant cameo. JF Violence, swearing, nudity. **DVD** **Blu-ray**

Terry Jones *The Virgin Mandy/The mother of Brian, a ratbag/Colin/Simon the holy man/Saintly passer-by* • Graham Chapman *First Wise Man/Brian called Brian/Biggus Dickus* • Michael Palin *Second Wise Man/Mr Big Nose/Francis, a Revolutionary/Mrs A, who casts the second stone/Ex-leper/Ben, an ancient prisoner/Pontius Pilate, Roman governor/A boring prophet/Eddie/Nisus Wettus* • John Cleese *Third Wise Man/Reg, leader of the Judean People's Front/Jewish*

M

official at the stoning/Centurion of the Yard/ Deadly Dirk/Arthur • Eric Idle Mr Cheeky/Stan called Loretta, a confused revolutionary/Harry the Haggler, beard and stone salesman/Culprit Woman, who casts the first stone/Intensely dull youth/Otto, the Nazarene jailer's assistant/Mr Frisbee III • Terry Gilliam Another person further forward/Revolutionaries and masked commandos/A blood and thunder prophet/ Geoffrey/Jailer ■ Dir Terry Jones • Scr Graham Chapman, John Cleese, Terry Gilliam, Eric Idle, Terry Jones, Michael Palin

Monty Python's The Meaning of Life ★★★ 18

Comedy   1983 · UK · Colour · 86min

A pick 'n' mix selection of comedy sketches by the anarchic, surrealistic team of John Cleese, Terry Gilliam, Eric Idle, Terry Jones, Michael Palin and Graham Chapman. Exploring the stages of human existence, ranging from conception to death, this is British humour at its most tasteless and occasionally brilliant – the sequence in which a financial institution is boarded by swashbuckling pirates is superb, while the one in which a glutton explosively overeats is wholly nasty. TH Violence, swearing, brief nudity. *DVD* Blu

Graham Chapman • John Cleese • Terry Gilliam • Eric Idle • Terry Jones • Michael Palin ■ Dir Terry Jones • Scr Terry Jones (HYF), Graham Chapman, John Cleese, Terry Gilliam, Eric Idle, Michael Palin

The Monuments Men ★★ 12

Wartime drama based on a true story
2013 · US · Colour · 113min

George Clooney directs, co-writes and stars in this wartime drama whose remarkable premise – a 1945 Allied "treasure hunt" for millions of paintings and sculptures stolen by the Nazis – is let down by dry fidelity to the facts and superficially etched characters. It's presented as an affectionate mission caper in the Dirty Dozen mould, but the terrific cast is underused and the film plods from leadenly comic vignette to jarringly serious interlude without cohering into a satisfying whole. AC Violence, swearing. *DVD* Blu

George Clooney Frank Stokes • Matt Damon James Granger • Bill Murray Richard Campbell • Cate Blanchett Claire Simone • John Goodman Walter Garfield • Hugh Bonneville Donald Jeffries • Jean Dujardin Jean Claude Clermont ■ Dir George Clooney • Scr George Clooney, Grant Heslov, from the non-fiction book The Monuments Men: Allied Heroes, Nazi Thieves and the Greatest Treasure Hunt in History by Robert M Edsel, Bretter Witter • Music Alexandre Desplat

The Moo Man ★★★★ U

Documentary   2013 · UK/Ger · Colour · 97min

Andy Heathcote and Heike Bachelier's perceptive look at the state of British agriculture contains plenty of wit, wisdom and compassion, as well as bucolic charm. The movie follows Sussex dairy farmer Stephen Hook, who, infuriated by the trading practices of the supermarket chains, makes a living by selling his unpasteurised milk on the doorstep and at markets. Hook insists on a humane approach that gives his cattle longer lives and gives the film a genuinely affecting poignancy. DP

Steve Hook • Heike Bachelier ■ Dir Andy Heathcote, Heike Bachelier

Mood Indigo ★★★★ 12

Fantasy drama   2013 · Fr/Bel · Colour · 90min

French director Michel Gondry (Eternal Sunshine of the Spotless Mind) is a purveyor of endearingly DIY flights of fantasy, so adapting Boris Vian's cult 1947 novel about a feckless fop trying to survive in an Orwellian world seems a perfect fit. And for an hour, this borders on genius with its playful visuals and unbelievable effects: a piano composes cocktails, a slow boogie makes its dancers' legs grow and the screen is cut in half to create a half-sunny, half-rainy picnic. However, it then takes a darker turn that caters more to serious fans than anyone hoping for a light French fancy. DW French +subtitles. *DVD* Blu

Romain Duris Colin • Audrey Tautou Chloé • Gad Elmaleh Chick • Omar Sy Nicolas • Aïssa Maïga Alise • Charlotte Le Bon Isis • Alain Chabat Gouffé ■ Dir Michel Gondry • Scr Luc Bossi, Michel Gondry, from the novel L'Écume des jours by Boris Vian

Moolaadé ★★★★ 15

Social drama
2004 · Sen/Burkina Faso/Mor/Tun/Cameroon/ Fr/Ger/Swi · Colour · 119min

The subject of female genital mutilation, which is still practised in many African countries, has been tackled before, but no film has emphasised the human aspect of this bitter dispute with such compassion and poetry as the continent's finest film-maker, Ousmane Sembene. A violent showdown ensues between the elders of a Burkina Faso village and the courageous Collé (Fatoumata Coulibaly) when she refuses to hand over four young girls for ritual "purification". Sembene captures the tensions between the Islamic patriarchs and womenfolk with an irresistible satirical power. DP Wolof, various African languages, French +subtitles. *DVD*

Fatoumata Coulibaly Collé Ardo Gallo Sy • Hélène Diarra Hadjatou Maïmouna • Salimata Traoré Amasatou • Dominique T Zeïda Mercenary • Mah Campaoré Leader of the purifiers • Aminata Dao Alima Ba ■ Dir/Scr Ousmane Sembene

Moomins on the Riviera ★★★ U

Animated comedy
2014 · Fin/Fr · Colour · 73min

Finland's famous cartoon characters finally make their first British cinema appearance in this sweet if odd sea adventure that takes the hippo-faced creatures from idyllic Moominvalley to the warmer, more exciting climes of the south of France. Hand-drawn and episodic, the film flies in the face of the current trend for computer-generated excess. Aimed at younger kids, it may sadly prove too slow for them, with its quirks and subtleties probably best appreciated by adults. DA Finnish dubbed. *DVD*

Russell Tovey Moomin • Nathaniel Parker Moominpappa • Tracy-Ann Oberman Moominmamma • Stephanie Winiecki Snorkmaiden • Ruth Gibson Little My ■ Dir Xavier Picard, Hanna Hemila • Scr Leslie Stewart, Annina Enckell, Hanna Hemila, Xavier Picard, Beata Harju, from the comic strip by Tove Jansson

Moon ★★★★ 15

Science-fiction drama
2008 · UK · Colour · 93min

Duncan Jones (who, as David Bowie's son, was once known as Zowie Bowie) made his directorial debut with this intelligent, poignant science-fiction tale. Sam Rockwell gives an excellent performance as Sam Bell, a lone mining engineer stuck incommunicado on the dark side of the Moon and about to complete his three-year contract. His only company is Gerty, a somewhat anodyne robot (voiced by Kevin Spacey), but as time goes on Sam begins to suspect that things, and even he, are not what they seem. The screenplay by Jones and Nathan Parker delicately and intriguingly investigates the themes of loneliness and humanity, and together with Jones's assured direction, makes for a hugely impressive first feature. AS Swearing. *DVD* Blu

Sam Rockwell Sam Bell • Kevin Spacey Gerty • Dominique McElligott Tess Bell • Kaya Scodelario Eve Bell • Benedict Wong Thompson • Matt Berry Overmeyers • Malcolm Stewart Technician ■ Dir Duncan Jones • Scr Nathan Parker, from a story by Duncan Jones

The Moon and Sixpence ★★★

Melodrama   1942 · US · BW and Colour · 88min

George Sanders stars as a London stockbroker who becomes a painter in Paris, goes all bohemian and then drops out in the South Seas. Somerset Maugham's novel was partly inspired by Gauguin and his sojourn in the Marquesas Islands, but Sanders's performance is more Oscar Wilde than Maugham. (It's certainly far removed

from Anthony Quinn's piratical Gauguin in Lust for Life.) Don't look for luscious location photography either; this is an effete, studio-bound exploration of artistic temperament. AT

George Sanders Charles Strickland • Herbert Marshall Geoffrey Wolfe • Steve Geray [Steven Geray] Dirk Stroeve • Doris Dudley Blanche Stroeve • Eric Blore Captain Nichols • Albert Basserman Doctor Coutras ■ Dir Albert Lewin • Scr Albert Lewin, from the novel by W Somerset Maugham

Moon 44 ★ 15

Science-fiction action drama
1990 · W Ger/US · Colour · 95min

Before his Hollywood successes, Roland Emmerich directed this German-financed sci-fi thriller about cop Michael Paré going undercover as a convict on an industrial planet to investigate ongoing sabotage. Over-plotted, cliché-ridden and highly derivative. JC

Michael Paré Felix Stone • Lisa Eichhorn Terry Morgan • Dean Devlin Tyler • Malcolm McDowell Major Lee • Brian Thompson Jake O'Neal • Stephen Geoffreys Cookie ■ Dir Roland Emmerich • Scr Dean Heyde, Oliver Eberle, from a story by Dean Heyde, Eberle, Roland Emmerich, PJ Mitchell

The Moon in the Gutter ★★★ 18

Mystery romance   1983 · Fr/It · Colour · 132min

Critically panned and reviled by even its star, Gérard Depardieu, director Jean-Jacques Beineix's follow-up to Diva is another glittering visual delight that suffers from a cumbersome and pretentious plot. Depardieu is a poor stevedore searching for the man who raped his sister. While on his traumatic odyssey, he ends up pursuing rich Nastassja Kinski who is, literally, the girl of his dreams. Deliriously obscure and dazzlingly superficial by turns, this contains the most erotic images of Kinski, Depardieu and Victoria Abril ever captured on film. AJ French +subtitles.

Gérard Depardieu Gerard • Nastassja Kinski Loretta • Victoria Abril Bella • Vittorio Mezzogiorno Newton Channing • Dominique Pinon Frank • Bertice Reading Lola ■ Dir Jean-Jacques Beineix • Scr Jean-Jacques Beineix, Olivier Mergault, from the novel by David Goodis

The Moon Is Blue ★★★ PG

Romantic comedy   1953 · US · BW · 95min

William Holden meets actress Maggie McNamara on top of the Empire State Building, only for McNamara to be pursued by older man David Niven. This mildly amusing comedy of romantic errors was a huge box-office success when director Otto Preminger defied the censor and released the film with dialogue that was considered extreme for its day. Preminger also gave a boost to Niven's career simply by casting him. Niven had broken with a vindictive Sam Goldwyn and was described by this film's production company, United Artists, as "all washed up". Given the chance to prove himself once again, Niven rose to the challenge brilliantly. TH

William Holden (2) Donald Gresham • David Niven David Slater • Maggie McNamara Patty O'Neill • Tom Tully Michael O'Neill • Dawn Addams Cynthia Slater ■ Dir Otto Preminger • Scr F Hugh Herbert, from his play

The Moon Is Down ★★

Second World War drama
1943 · US · BW · 90min

This clumsy piece of wartime propaganda sees some plucky Norwegians overcome the might of the Nazis. Doubtless such acts of selfless heroism occurred throughout the Second World War, but Hollywood (particularly its European exiles) could never resist setting them in fairy-tale towns populated by quaint characters. Cedric Hardwicke credits his Nazi commander with having some intelligence, but he's no match for Henry Travers, who's armed to the teeth with decency. DP

Cedric Hardwicke Colonel Lanser • Henry Travers Mayor Orden • Lee J Cobb Dr Winter • Dorris Bowdon Molly Morden • Margaret Wycherly

Madame Orden • Peter Van Eyck Lieutenant Tonder • Irving Pichel Innkeeper ■ Dir Irving Pichel • Scr Nunnally Johnson, from the novel by John Steinbeck

Moon Man ★★★ U

Animated fantasy
2012 · Fr/Ger/Ire · Colour · 91min

Based on the 1966 children's book by illustrious illustrator Tomi Ungerer, this gently entertaining fantasy goes against the grain of the majority of Hollywood's animated fare. The story of a bored Man in the Moon who catches a comet to Earth to find some excitement is depicted via old-school hand-drawn animation. There are the obligatory messages for children about love, trust and friendship, but there are also plenty of amusing sight gags, beautifully rendered visuals and an eclectic music score. Sentimental it is not, just charming and quaintly unassuming. JA *DVD*

Katharina Thalbach Moon Man • Pat Laffan Bunsen • Michael McElhatton President • Paul McLoone Father • Tomi Ungerer Narrator ■ Dir Stephan Schesch, Sarah Clara Weber • Scr Stephan Schesch, from the illustrated children's book by Tomi Ungerer

Moon over Miami ★★★ U

Musical   1941 · US · Colour · 87min

This is one of the very best of the 20th Century-Fox Technicolor Betty Grable vehicles – a pleasingly bright, garish and utterly unsophisticated version of Fox's great stand-by plot about money-hungry gals on a spree. There's some fun dancing here from Jack Cole and the Condos Brothers, and some nice songs, such as You Started Something and the title tune. Easy on the eye and ear, this is prime viewing for nostalgists. TS

Don Ameche Phil O'Neil • Betty Grable Kay Latimer • Robert Cummings Jeff Bolton • Charlotte Greenwood Aunt Susie Latimer • Jack Haley Jack O'Hara • Carole Landis Barbara Latimer • Cobina Wright Jr Connie Fentress ■ Dir Walter Lang • Scr Vincent Lawrence, Brown Holmes, George Seaton, Lynn Starling, from the play Three Blind Mice by Stephen Powys

Moon over Parador ★★ 15

Comedy   1988 · US · Colour · 99min

Director Paul Mazursky, whose instinct for comic mores is usually razor-sharp, resorts to a lazy trawl through a decent comedy idea, blunting the edges of any comic potential in the process. However, Richard Dreyfuss puts plenty of energy into his scenes as a frustrated actor turned South American despot, using his nervy tics and schoolboy charm to advantage, and there are a handful of pointed barbs at the expense of dictatorship. JM Swearing.

Richard Dreyfuss Jack Noah • Raul Julia Roberto Strausmann • Sonia Braga Madonna • Jonathan Winters Ralph • Fernando Rey Alejandro • Sammy Davis Jr • Michael Greene Clint • Charo Madame Loop ■ Dir Paul Mazursky • Scr Leon Capetanos, Paul Mazursky, from a story by Charles G Booth

Moon Pilot ★★★ U

Science-fiction comedy
1962 · US · Colour · 98min

In one of the better Disney live-action pictures of this period, Tom Tryon is selected to become the first man in space by a test-flight chimpanzee. The unwilling Tryon's resolve to remain on Earth is reinforced when he falls for Dany Saval, but when he discovers that she is a visitor from another planet, his feelings about outer space quickly change. The leads are engaging, and there are plenty of jokes at the expense of Nasa. DP

Tom Tryon Captain Richmond Talbot • Brian Keith Maj Gen John Vanneman • Edmond O'Brien McClosky • Dany Saval Lyrae • Bob Sweeney Senator McGuire ■ Dir James Neilson • Scr Maurice Tombragel, from a story by Robert Buckner

The Moon-Spinners ★★★ U

Mystery   1964 · US/UK · Colour · 113min

Walt Disney fashioned numerous star vehicles for young Hayley Mills, and here she's involved, along with Joan Greenwood, in some likeable nonsense about jewel thieves in Crete. But it's the supporting cast that makes this worth watching: silent screen vamp Pola Negri came out of retirement to play the mysterious Madame Habib, only to be upstaged by the evil Eli Wallach and Greek star Irene Papas as his sister. Unfortunately, it doesn't come off as a Hitchcock-style mystery, and Mary Stewart's original novel should have been reworked. TS

Hayley Mills *Nikky Ferris* • Eli Wallach *Stratos* • Pola Negri *Madame Habib* • Peter McEnery *Mark Camford* • Joan Greenwood *Aunt Frances* • Irene Papas *Sophia* • Sheila Hancock *Cynthia Gamble* • Michael Davis (2) *Alexis* • John Le Mesurier *Anthony Chelmscott Gamble* ■ *Dir* James Neilson • *Scr* Michael Dyne, from the novel by Mary Stewart

Moon Zero Two ★★ U
Science-fiction adventure
1969 · UK · Colour · 100min

In an effort to diversify, Hammer attempted this U certificate space western, in which James Olson and Ori Levy do battle with the bad guys for prospecting rights on a somewhat bleak-looking moon. It's exactly what you might expect from a western set on the moon, complete with shoot-outs, ambushes and dancing girls. The plot and dialogue are terrible, though there are a few thrills for the kids. DM

James Olson *Bill Kemp* • Catherina von Schell [Catherine Schell] *Clementine Taplin* • Warren Mitchell *JJ Hubbard* • Adrienne Corri *Liz Murphy* • Ori Levy *Karminski* • Dudley Foster *Whitsun* • Bernard Bresslaw *Harry* ■ *Dir* Roy Ward Baker • *Scr* Michael Carreras, from a story by Gavin Lyall, Frank Hardman, Martin Davison

Moonfleet ★★★
Period adventure 1955 · US · Colour · 86min

While a long way from being the best film on director Fritz Lang's illustrious CV, this adaptation of J Meade Falkner's swashbuckling classic still makes for rousing entertainment. Set in Dorset in the 1770s, the fast-moving tale of smuggling and secret identities provides Stewart Granger with the chance to add a touch of devilment to the expected romantic dash and derring-do. George Sanders gives his usual performance of silky smooth malevolence in this solid piece of old-fashioned escapism. DP

Stewart Granger *Jeremy Fox* • Joan Greenwood *Lady Ashwood* • George Sanders *Lord Ashwood* • Viveca Lindfors *Mrs Minton* • Jon Whiteley *John Mohune* • Liliane Montevecchi *Gypsy* ■ *Dir* Fritz Lang • *Scr* Jan Lustig, Margaret Fitts, from the novel by J Meade Falkner

Moonlight and Valentino ★★★ 15
Drama 1995 · US · Colour · 100min

This is a talky but well-acted adaptation of Ellen Simon's stage play about the struggles of a young widow to cope with life without her husband. Elizabeth Perkins's moving performance as the widow is the centrepiece of this beautifully shot, intimately detailed drama, but the supporting cast is equally praiseworthy, with special mention for star-in-the-making Gwyneth Paltrow as Perkins's eccentric sister. The sluggish, grief-drenched first half is pretty heavy going, though the tone is lightened by the introduction of charismatic rock star turned actor Jon Bon Jovi, who helps to re-awaken Perkins. JC Some sex scenes, swearing. *DVD*

Elizabeth Perkins *Rebecca Trager Lott* • Whoopi Goldberg *Sylvie Morrow* • Gwyneth Paltrow *Lucy Trager* • Kathleen Turner *Alberta Russell* • Jon Bon Jovi *The painter* • Peter Coyote *Paul* ■ *Dir* David Anspaugh • *Scr* Ellen Simon, from her play

Moonlight Mile ★★★ 15
Drama 2002 · US · Colour · 112min

Brad Silberling's polished drama blends a simple premise (grieving parents take in their murdered daughter's fiancé) with more complex emotional undercurrents. While the veteran actors – Dustin Hoffman and Susan Sarandon, in roles written

especially for them – credibly convey the emotional highs and lows, it's Jake Gyllenhaal's awkwardness and vulnerability that connects most satisfyingly. Silberling's final-act catharsis for every character is laid on too thickly, but there's no doubting the film-maker's sincerity. JC Swearing. *DVD*

Jake Gyllenhaal *Joe Nast* • Dustin Hoffman *Ben Floss* • Susan Sarandon *JoJo Floss* • Holly Hunter *Mona Camp* • Ellen Pompeo *Bertie Knox* • Richard T Jones *Ty* • Allan Corduner *Stan Michaels* • Dabney Coleman *Mike Mulcahey* ■ *Dir/Scr* Brad Silberling

Moonlight Sonata ★★ U
Romantic drama 1937 · UK · BW · 83min

A plane makes a forced landing in the grounds of a Swedish country house owned by the music-loving Baroness Lindenborg (Marie Tempest). The passengers needing refuge include a fortune-hunting cad (Eric Portman), who sweeps the baroness's granddaughter off her feet. This film exists only as an excuse for the great pianist Ignace Jan Paderewski to make his screen debut at the age of 77 as one of the passengers. RK *DVD*

Ignace Jan Paderewski • Charles Farrell (1) *Eric Molander* • Marie Tempest *Baroness Lindenborg* • Barbara Greene *Ingrid* • Eric Portman *Mario de la Costa* • Graham Browne *Dr Broman* • Queenie Leonard *Margit, his niece* • Lawrence Hanray *Bishop* ■ *Dir* Lothar Mendes • *Scr* Edward Knoblock, EM Delafield, from a story by Hans Rameau

The Moonlighter ★★ U
Western 1953 · US · BW · 77min

Barbara Stanwyck and Fred MacMurray, the doomed lovers from the classic *Double Indemnity*, are reunited in a western that was originally released in 3D. The weird plot is about a cattle rustler (MacMurray) who escapes a lynch mob and robs a bank. He is then pursued by his girlfriend (Stanwyck), who also happens to be the sheriff. The title derives from western lore that says rustlers work only in moonlight. AT 🔲

Barbara Stanwyck *Rela* • Fred MacMurray *Wes Anderson* • Ward Bond *Cole* • William Ching *Tom Anderson* • John Dierkes *Sheriff Daws* • Morris Ankrum *Prince* • Jack Elam *Strawboss* ■ *Dir* Roy Rowland • *Scr* Niven Busch

Moonlighting ★★★★ 15
Political drama 1982 · UK · Colour · 93min

Directed with vigour and assurance by the exiled Polish director Jerzy Skolimowski, this razor-sharp satire brilliantly equates the experiences of a crew of moonlighting Polish builders in Thatcherite London with the plight of the workers in the Gdansk shipyard at the height of the Solidarity uprising. As the leader of the gang, Jeremy Irons gives a fine performance as he imposes curfews and news blackouts to prevent his colleagues learning of the momentous events back home before the job is done. The shoplifting sequence is the highlight of an enthralling and intelligent picture. DP

Jeremy Irons *Nowak* • Eugene Lipinski *Banaszak* • Jiri Stanislaw *Wolski* • Eugeniusz Haczkiewicz *Kudaj* ■ *Dir/Scr* Jerzy Skolimowski

The Moonraker ★★★ U
Period adventure 1957 · UK · Colour · 78min

Although it lacks a decent budget and big stars, this is still an enjoyable romp. George Baker is the Cavalier who keeps the future Charles II out of the clutches of Oliver Cromwell (portrayed with visible relish by John Le Mesurier). Sylvia Syms provides the glamour and *Doctor Who* fans will recognise Patrick Troughton, who played the time traveller in his second incarnation. DP *DVD*

George Baker *Earl Anthony of Dawlish, "the Moonraker"* • Sylvia Syms *Anne Wyndham* • Peter Arne *Edmund Tyler* • Marius Goring *Colonel Beaumont* • Clive Morton *Lord Harcourt* • Gary Raymond *Prince Charles Stuart* • John Le Mesurier *Oliver Cromwell* • Patrick Troughton *Captain Wilcox* ■ *Dir* David MacDonald • *Scr* Robert Hall, Wilfrid Eades, Alistair Bell, from the play by Arthur Watkyn

Moonraker ★★ PG
Spy adventure 1979 · UK · Colour · 121min

The 11th Bond movie jettisons Ian Fleming's marvellous novel and sends 007 into space. Weighed down by its often clunky special effects and non-existent plotting, the movie seems to be merely an attempt to update Bond in the wake of *Star Wars*. Roger Moore is at his least convincing as Bond, Michael Lonsdale makes a lacklustre master criminal and Jaws, the towering sub-villain from *The Spy Who Loved Me*, makes a return appearance. Too much of the budget is wasted on overblown spectacle, without enough attention being given to the basics. AT *DVD* 🔵

Roger Moore *James Bond* • Lois Chiles *Holly Goodhead* • Michael Lonsdale [Michel Lonsdale] *Hugo Drax* • Richard Kiel *Jaws* • Corinne Cléry *Corinne Dufour* • Bernard Lee *"M"* • Desmond Llewelyn *"Q"* • Lois Maxwell *Miss Moneypenny* ■ *Dir* Lewis Gilbert • *Scr* Christopher Wood, from the novel by Ian Fleming • *Music* John Barry (1)

Moonrise ★★★★ PG
Film noir 1948 · US · BW · 86min

This sombre but compelling rural drama is a tribute to the skill of director Frank Borzage, a fine example of his tender feelings for young lovers in adversity. Dane Clark gives his best performance as the murderer's son who kills one of his tormentors, while Gail Russell brings her fragile beauty to the part of the girl who believes in him. Though tracked by the sheriff and his posse, his biggest enemy is himself. The film is a visual treat, and a true mood piece. AE

Dane Clark *Danny Hawkins* • Gail Russell *Gilly Johnson* • Ethel Barrymore *Grandma* • Allyn Joslyn *Clem Otis* • Henry Morgan [Harry Morgan] *Billy Scripture* • Rex Ingram (2) *Mose* ■ *Dir* Frank Borzage • *Scr* Charles Haas, from the novel by Theodore Strauss

Moonrise Kingdom ★★★ 12
Drama 2012 · US · Colour · 89min

In this typically oddball tale from director Wes Anderson (*The Royal Tenenbaums*), two troubled 12-year-olds retreat to nature and grapple with their primal instincts. Jared Gilman is suitably precocious as orphaned boy scout Sam, who escapes from his tent (*Shawshank Redemption*-style) to run away with bookish but rebellious girlfriend Suzy (Kara Hayward). They're tracked by Sam's scout peers and various concerned grown-ups, including Edward Norton's scoutmaster, stoical local cop Bruce Willis, and Suzy's self-absorbed parents (Bill Murray and Frances McDormand). Anderson's familiar mannered approach ensures plenty of laughs, but it also means his stabs at pathos miss the mark. This is a joyously silly, sweet and very cerebral coming-of-age yarn, but it never touches the heart. SP Some violence, swearing, sexual references. *DVD* 🔵

Edward Norton *Scout Master Ward* • Bruce Willis *Captain Sharp* • Bill Murray *Walt Bishop* • Harvey Keitel *Commander Pierce* • Tilda Swinton *Social Services* • Frances McDormand *Laura Bishop* • Jason Schwartzman *Cousin Ben* • Kara Hayward *Suzy Bishop* • Jared Gilman *Sam Shakusky* ■ *Dir* Wes Anderson • *Scr* Wes Anderson, Roman Coppola

The Moon's Our Home ★★★
Romantic comedy 1936 · US · BW · 80min

The major attraction of this romantic comedy is the pairing of Margaret Sullavan and Henry Fonda, two of Hollywood's most attractive and gifted stars of the 1930s, who were married in real life for a stormy couple of years from 1931 to 1933. She plays a movie star, he's a writer and explorer; they fly in the face of temperamental incompatibility and marry. The rest of the film, directed by William A Seiter from a witty script that includes contributions from Dorothy Parker, is concerned with how they sort out their differences. Warm and charming. RK

Margaret Sullavan *Sarah Brown/Cherry Chester* • Henry Fonda *John Smith/Anthony Amberton* • Charles Butterworth *Horace Van Steedan* • Beulah Bondi *Mrs Boyce Medford* • Margaret

Hamilton *Mitty Simpson* • Henrietta Crosman *Lucy Van Steedan* ■ *Dir* William A Seiter • *Scr* Isabel Dawn, Boyce DeGaw, Dorothy Parker, Alan Campbell, from the story by Faith Baldwin

The Moonstone ★★
Mystery 1934 · US · BW · 62min

Wilkie Collins's novel has always been a hard nut for film-makers to crack, so it comes as no surprise to learn that there have been no film versions since this one (although there have been some made-for-TV efforts). David Manners makes a stiff and unappealing hero, though the result does have some historical interest. Collins fared much better with Warner Bros' 1948 version of *The Woman in White*, which came complete with all the requisite gothic trimmings. TS

David Manners *Franklin Blake* • Phyllis Barry *Anne Verinder* • Jameson Thomas *Godfrey Ablewhite, rare book dealer* • Gustav von Seyffertitz *Septimus Lucker, money-lender* • Herbert Bunston *Sir John Verinder* ■ *Dir* Reginald Barker • *Scr* Adele Buffington, from the novel by Wilkie Collins

Moonstruck ★★★★ PG
Romantic comedy 1987 · US · Colour · 97min

This unashamedly romantic comedy established once and for all that Cher could act. She gives an Oscar-winning performance as a widow who looks set for a safe marriage to Danny Aiello, but falls instead for his moody younger brother Nicolas Cage. John Patrick Shanley, who won an Oscar for best original screenplay, paints a warm and affectionate picture of Italian-American life, and there are enough quirky touches to prevent it from toppling into treacle. Norman Jewison directs subtly, allowing the splendid cast to make the most of Shanley's fine writing. JF *DVD* 🔵

Cher *Loretta Castorini* • Nicolas Cage *Ronny Cammareri* • Olympia Dukakis *Rose Castorini* • Vincent Gardenia *Cosmo Castorini* • Danny Aiello *Mr Johnny Cammareri* • Julie Bovasso *Rita Cappomaggi* • John Mahoney *Perry* ■ *Dir* Norman Jewison • *Scr* John Patrick Shanley

Moontide ★★★
Drama 1942 · US · BW · 94min

Jean Gabin is a heavy-drinking, rootless Frenchman who wanders from job to job in dockside towns supporting "buddy" Thomas Mitchell, who has a hold over him and clings like a leech. Gabin saves Ida Lupino from suicide, setting in motion a chain of dramatic events. In a modest, grittily effective and absorbing drama, French idol Gabin is impressive and Lupino appealing. Mitchell is excellent as the weak and scummy villain, while Claude Rains is unlikely but sympathetic as an educated night watchman. Archie Mayo's direction is uneven, but there are some fine sequences of brooding tension – doubtless explained by the fact that an uncredited Fritz Lang directed some of the film. RK

Jean Gabin *Bobo* • Ida Lupino *Anna* • Thomas Mitchell *Tiny* • Claude Rains *Nutsy* • Jerome Cowan *Dr Frank Brothers* • Helene Reynolds *Woman on boat* • Ralph Byrd *Rev Wilson* ■ *Dir* Archie Mayo • *Scr* John O'Hara, from the novel by Willard Robertson

Moonwalker ★★★ PG
Musical fantasy 1988 · US · Colour · 88min

Made when Michael Jackson was still the biggest pop star in the world, this is, unfortunately, a bit of a mess. However, fans will still love the music and the innovative pop promo interludes, while some older viewers might enjoy the discomfort of Joe Pesci as the evil Mr Big. Look out for Sean Lennon as one of Jackson's chums. JF *DVD* 🔵

Michael Jackson (3) *Michael* • Joe Pesci *Mr Big* • Sean Lennon *Sean* • Kellie Parker *Katie* • Brandon Adams *Zeke/"Baby Bad" Michael* ■ *Dir* Colin Chilvers, Jerry Kramer • *Scr* David Newman, from a story by Michael Jackson

More ★ 18
Drama 1969 · Lux/Fr · Colour · 111min

The fag end of the Swinging Sixties, as seen by debutant director Barbet Schroeder.

M

More soft-core porn than social comment, it's about a German lad who hitch-hikes across Europe, gets into drugs and ends up in Ibiza with Mimsy Farmer. This is the full druggie nightmare, complete with acid trips, skinny-dipping, hippy speak and a music score by Pink Floyd. AT *DVD*

Mimsy Farmer *Estelle* • Klaus Grunberg *Stefan* • Heinz Engelmann *Wolf* • Michel Chanderli *Charlie* • Louise Wink *Cathy* • Henry Wolf *Henry* ■ *Dir* Barbet Schroeder • *Scr* Paul Gegauff, Barbet Schroeder, from a story by Barbet Schroeder

More American Graffiti ★★ 12

Comedy drama   1979 · US · Colour · 106min

How do you follow a modern masterpiece like *American Graffiti*? Not with this plodding, inferior sequel, which catches up with the Class of 1962 as they live through the Vietnam-dominated, hippy 1960s. The only saving grace is yet another brilliant soundtrack, featuring golden oldies from the Supremes, Mary Wells, the Byrds, Bob Dylan and Cream. Wolfman Jack and Country Joe and the Fish also make appearances in this aimlessly directed failure. AJ *DVD* *BL*

Candy Clark *Debbie Dunham* • Bo Hopkins *Little Joe* • Ron Howard *Steve Bolander* • Paul Le Mat *John Milner* • Mackenzie Phillips *Carol Rainbow* • Charles Martin Smith *Terry the Toad* • Cindy Williams *Laurie Bolander* • Harrison Ford *Motorcycle cop* ■ *Dir* BWL Norton [Bill L Norton] • *Scr* BWL Norton, from characters by George Lucas, Gloria Katz, Willard Huyck

More Sex & the Single Mom ★★

Romantic drama   2005 · US · Colour · 120min

Three years after doctor Grant Show returned to his wife in *Sex & the Single Mom*, divorced lawyer Gail O'Grady has fallen for office colleague Rick Roberts. So it's hardly the best time for the newly divorced Show to reappear and discover that he's the father of a son that O'Grady omitted to tell him about. There's nothing particularly original in this TV-movie sequel, although some adolescent viewers might be surprised to learn that grown-ups are also prone to irrational urges where sex is concerned. DP

Gail O'Grady *Jess Gradwell* • Grant Show *Alex Lofton* • Chelsea Hobbs *Sara Gradwell* • Rick Roberts *Steve* • Lucas Bryant *Gabe Emerson* • Larissa Laskin *Megan* ■ *Dir* Don McBrearty • *Scr* Judith Paige Mitchell

More than a Miracle ★★★ U

Romantic fantasy drama
1967 · It/Fr · Colour · 103min

Sophia Loren and Omar Sharif are paired in this film about a Spanish aristocrat who falls in love with a peasant girl. The path of true love, however, runs anything but smoothly. Despite being weakened by a running time that's a little too long to support the tale, this is a charming mix of romance, social comment and whimsy, directed and played with a suitably light touch and photographed in the style of an illustrated fairy tale. RK Italian dubbed.

Sophia Loren *Isabella* • Omar Sharif *Prince Ramon* • Dolores Del Rio *Queen Mother* • Georges Wilson *Monzu* • Leslie French *Brother Joseph of Copertino* • Carlo Pisacane *Witch* • Marina Malfatti *Devout princess* ■ *Dir* Francesco Rosi • *Scr* Francesco Rosi, Tonino Guerra, Raffaele La Capria, Giuseppe Patroni-Griffi • *Cinematographer* Pasquale De Santis [Pasqualino De Santis]

More than Honey ★★★★

Documentary
2012 · Swi /Ger/Austria · Colour · 91min

The politics of bee-keeping isn't exactly well-trodden ground for film-makers, but Swiss director Markus Imhoof explores similar territory to 2009's *Vanishing of the Bees* in this tenacious investigation into the causes of this vital insect's ever-diminishing population. Imhoof works hard to keep this potentially downbeat subject brimming with life, travelling across four continents and always keeping an eye out for interesting characters and perspectives along the way.

The movie comes complete with some eye-popping visuals, giving unrivalled glimpses of the sophisticated bee world and its secrets. It's a surprisingly stimulating movie. ReP *DVD* *BL*

John Hurt *Narrator* ■ *Dir* Markus Imhoof • *Scr* Markus Imhoof, Kerstin Hoppenhaus

More than Just a Game ★★ 12

Sports drama based on a true story
2007 · S Afr · Colour · 89min

Presley Chweneyagae (*Tsotsi*) stars in this awkward docudrama that chronicles how a love of the beautiful game transformed the lives of political prisoners in apartheid-era South Africa. Focusing on five former inmates of Robben Island (where Nelson Mandela was held), the film combines talking-head reminiscences with sanitised re-enactments of the quintet's struggle to form an organised football league. It's a remarkable and inspirational story, but barely done justice by director Junaid Ahmed's dull and choppy format. SF Some swearing. *DVD*

Presley Chweneyagae *Mark Shinners* • Wright Ngubeni *Anthony Suze* • Az Abrahams *Sedick Isaacs* • Tshepo Maseko *Lizo Sitoto* • Merlin Balie Marcus Solomon ■ *Dir* Junaid Ahmed • *Scr* Tom Eaton

More than Meets the Eye: the Joan Brock Story ★★

Drama based on a true story
2003 · US · Colour · 95min

An Iowa teacher for the blind has to radically reassess her life after losing her own sight in this inspirational, true story-based drama. Carey Lowell gives a poignant turn as the eponymous Joan, capturing the woman's determination and resilience as she faces first her own health setback and then the death of her husband. Director Mike Robe resists the temptation to wallow in the double tragedy, so when events and dialogue do inevitably swing towards the syrupy it's easily overlooked, diluted by the positive message and subtle performances. SF

Carey Lowell *Joan Brock* • Dylan Walsh *Jim Brock* • Jon Ted Wynne *Mr Mason* • Jamie Johnston *Cory Mason* • Rea Kavanagh *Cory's mother* • Jennifer Pisana *Joy* • Robert Bockstael *Dr Corbett* ■ *Dir* Mike Robe • *Scr* Susan Nanus, from the non-fiction book *More than Meets the Eye* by Joan Brock, Derek L Gill

The More the Merrier ★★★★ U

Comedy   1943 · US · BW · 99min

The wartime housing shortage in Washington DC forces government employee Jean Arthur and Joel McCrea to share an apartment with kindly businessman Charles Coburn. Part screwball comedy, part message movie about the need to pull together, it's a piece of fluff effortlessly carried by the charm of its stars and by George Stevens's elegant direction. A scene on the steps of the apartment, when McCrea makes a pass at Arthur, aroused a good deal of comment at the time for being shockingly sexy. There was a 1966 remake, *Walk, Don't Run*, set in Tokyo with Cary Grant in the Coburn role. AT

Jean Arthur *Connie Milligan* • Joel McCrea *Joe Carter* • Charles Coburn *Benjamin Dingle* • Richard Gaines *Charles J Pendergast* • Bruce Bennett *Evans* • Frank Sully *Pike* • Clyde Fillmore *Senator Noonan* ■ *Scr* George Stevens • *Scr* Robert Russell, Frank Ross, Richard Flournoy, Lewis R Foster, from a story by Robert Russell, Frank Ross, Garson Kanin

The More Things Change ★★★ PG

Comedy drama   1985 · Aus · Colour · 90min

Robyn Nevin was already one of Australia's most respected theatrical directors when she embarked on this, her debut as a film director. She is evidently more at home with coaching her cast than she is with moving a camera and creating dramatic tension through editing, but the strength of

---

the story carries the day. Judy Morris and Barry Otto impress as the couple whose relationship becomes strained when he drops out of city life to renovate a run-down farm. Deftly handled, but the melodramatic subplot involving their pregnant teenage nanny gets in the way. DP

Judy Morris *Connie* • Barry Otto *Lex* • Victoria Longley *Geraldine* • Lewis Fitz-Gerald *Barry* • Peter Carroll *Roley* • Louise Le Nay *Lydia* • Owen Johnson *Nicholas* • Brenda Addie *Angela* ■ *Dir* Robyn Nevin • *Scr* Moya Wood

Morgan

Science-fiction thriller   2016 · US · Colour

This is a preview – no prints were available to review as we went to press: The title comes from the unit of recombinant frequency in genetics, so it will be no surprise that Luke Scott's directing debut is a piece of hard sci-fi. Luke is son of director Ridley and there's a faint echo of *Blade Runner* in the plotline about a company wonk (Kate Mara) determining whether she should pull the plug on a life-form created in the lab. And as Morgan is played by *The Witch*'s Anya Taylor-Joy, we can expect emotional nuance. SvM

Rose Leslie *Amy* • Anya Taylor-Joy *Morgan* • Kate Mara *Lee Weathers* • Jennifer Jason Leigh • Paul Giamatti ■ *Dir* Luke Scott • *Scr* Seth W Owen

Morgan – a Suitable Case for Treatment ★★★ PG

Comedy drama   1966 · UK · Colour · 92min

Angry young men were abundant in the British cinema of the 1960s, but they were never so irate as working-class artist David Warner, who tries to sabotage the second marriage of his middle-class ex-wife Vanessa Redgrave to art dealer Robert Stephens by rewiring their house and dressing in a gorilla suit. Adapted from David Mercer's television play, it's really a fable about the class society. Yet its dream sequences and surreal touches make it more odd than meaningful, and it now feels dated. TH *DVD*

Vanessa Redgrave *Leonie Delt* • David Warner *Morgan Delt* • Robert Stephens *Charles Napier* • Irene Handl *Mrs Delt* • Newton Blick *Mr Henderson* • Nan Munro *Mrs Henderson* • Bernard Bresslaw *Policeman* ■ *Dir* Karel Reisz • *Scr* David Mercer, from his TV play *A Suitable Case for Treatment*

Morgan the Pirate ★★ U

Swashbuckling adventure
1960 · It/Fr · Colour · 95min

Bodybuilder Steve Reeves shakes off the loincloth of his usual Greek heroes and dons the costume of legendary pirate Henry Morgan. Reeves sticks in the craw of the Spanish, launches a raid on Panama and sweeps the governor's daughter off her feet. His performance is fairly gormless but he's got a bigger chest than his leading ladies and a jawline that would make a crocodile shed tears. AT

Steve Reeves *Sir Henry Morgan* • Valérie Lagrange *Dona Inez* • Lidia Alfonsi *Dona Maria* • Chelo Alonso *Concepcion* • Armand Mestral *L'Olannais* • Ivo Garrani *Governor* ■ *Dir* Andre De Toth, Primo Zeglio • *Scr* Andre De Toth, Primo Zeglio, Filippo Sanjust

Morituri ★★★★ 12

Spy drama   1965 · US · BW · 118min

Despite the clashing egos on the set of *Mutiny on the Bounty*, Marlon Brando and Trevor Howard signed on for another shipboard drama. A Second World War spy drama, Brando plays a German pacifist recruited by British agent Howard to destroy a German supply vessel, skippered by Yul Brynner. While Brynner is far from being a card-carrying Nazi, Brando impersonates an SS officer, setting up a complex relationship based on moral deception. This is a claustrophobic, often very tense movie that deserves to be better known. AT *DVD*

Marlon Brando *Robert Crain* • Yul Brynner *Captain Mueller* • Janet Margolin *Esther* • Trevor Howard *Colonel Statter* • Martin Benrath *Kruse* •

Hans Christian Blech *Donkeyman* • Wally Cox *Dr Ambach* ■ *Dir* Bernhard Wicki • *Scr* Daniel Taradash, from a novel by Werner Jorg Luddecke

The Morning After ★★★ 15

Thriller   1986 · US · Colour · 102min

Sidney Lumet is best known for his New York stories of civic crime and corruption. This, though, was the first film he directed that was set in Los Angeles and he gives it an abstract gloss and uses some bizarre locations, including a Gaudi-esque house that hides away behind Rodeo Drive. The plot is rather more ordinary: alcoholic actress Jane Fonda wakes up next to a man with a knife through his chest. She hasn't a clue what happened, so ex-cop Jeff Bridges helps her out. There are false trails, red herrings and Raul Julia as Fonda's hairdresser husband; for Lumet, it's a rare exercise in style and mood. AT Swearing, violence.

Jane Fonda *Alex Sternbergen* • Jeff Bridges *Turner Kendall* • Raul Julia *Joaquin "Jacky" Manero* • Diane Salinger *Isabel Harding* • Richard Foronjy *Sergeant Greenbaum* • Geoffrey Scott *Bobby Korshack* ■ *Dir* Sidney Lumet • *Scr* James Hicks

Morning Departure ★★★ PG

Drama   1950 · UK · BW · 97min

An atmospheric "confined space" drama, this has John Mills in one of his best roles as the commander of a submarine, holed by a mine and plunging to the sea bed. Twelve crew members survive the initial impact, but only eight will be able to use the escape equipment. A spot of bother, in other words, but everyone makes you proud to be British, apart from Richard Attenborough, playing a weak-willed stoker with his trademark intensity. PF

John Mills *Lieutenant Commander Armstrong* • Helen Cherry *Helen* • Richard Attenborough *Stoker Snipe* • Lana Morris *Rose Snipe* • Nigel Patrick *Lieutenant Harry Manson* • Andrew Crawford *Warrant Officer McFee* • Michael Brennan *Chief Petty Officer Barlow* ■ *Dir* Roy Baker [Roy Ward Baker] • *Scr* WEC Fairchild [William Fairchild], from Kenneth Woollard's play

Morning Glory ★★★

Drama   1933 · US · BW · 74min

"The calla lilies are in bloom again" in Katharine Hepburn's stunningly mannered performance, which won her the first of her unequalled (and likely to remain so) four best actress Oscars. Cast as young Broadway hopeful Eva Lovelace, she's all angles and angst in this adaptation of Zoe Akins's play about a starry-eyed Cinderella. Despite Hepburn's worthy co-stars, who include Adolphe Menjou as a lecherous producer and Douglas Fairbanks Jr as an earnest playwright, the movie belongs totally to Kate. Remade in 1958 as *Stage Struck*. TS *DVD*

Katharine Hepburn *Eva Lovelace* • Douglas Fairbanks Jr *Joseph Sheridan* • Adolphe Menjou *Louis Easton* • Mary Duncan *Rita Vernon* • C Aubrey Smith *Robert Harley Hedges* ■ *Dir* Lowell Sherman • *Scr* Howard J Green, from the play by Zoe Akins

Morning Glory ★★★ 12

Comedy   2010 · US/UK · Colour · 103min

Harrison Ford and Rachel McAdams make an unlikely but likeable team in *Notting Hill* director Roger Michell's lively comedy. She's a perky TV producer saddled with a failing morning show, while he's the station's veteran news anchor who's forced to front it. Michell's seamless, steady direction lets McAdams's energy shine through and allows Ford and his fellow news anchor Diane Keaton to craft beautifully timed comedic performances, including their ongoing feud regarding who says the final on-air "goodbye". And watch out for Matt Malloy, who almost steals the show as a nerdy weatherman. KK Some swearing, sexual references. *DVD* *BL*

Harrison Ford *Mike Pomeroy* • Rachel McAdams *Becky Fuller* • Diane Keaton *Colleen Peck* • Patrick Wilson *Adam Bennett* • Jeff Goldblum *Jerry Barnes* • Curtis "50 Cent" Jackson ■ *Dir* Roger Michell • *Scr* Aline Brosh McKenna

---

Morocco ★★★★★ U
Romance 1930 · US · BW · 88min

This is screen goddess Marlene Dietrich's first American-made movie, sumptuously directed by her *Blue Angel* mentor Josef von Sternberg and ravishingly photographed by the great Lee Garmes and Lucien Ballard. Dietrich's romantic partner is handsome foreign legionnaire Gary Cooper, and the audience is left wondering whether she'll choose between him or dapper, worldly Adolphe Menjou. Dietrich makes her displaced cabaret chanteuse very real and touching, and her first appearance in the Moroccan nightclub is an ultra-sophisticated piece of staging that is as ornate as it is outrageous. TS 𝗗𝗩𝗗
Marlene Dietrich *Amy Jolly* · Gary Cooper *Tom Brown* · Adolphe Menjou *Le Bessier* · Ullrich Haupt *Adjutant Caesar* · Juliette Compton *Anna Dolores* · Francis McDonald *Cpl Tatoche* ■ *Dir* Josef von Sternberg · *Scr* Jules Furthman, from the novel *Amy Jolly* by Benno Vigny · *Art Director* Hans Dreier

Morons from Outer Space ★ PG
Science-fiction spoof 1985 · UK · Colour · 86min

Mel Smith and Griff Rhys Jones's lamentable lampoon is a shambling spoof with little wit. Directed by Mike Hodges, who really should have known better, the pathetic story concerns aliens from the planet Blob crash-landing on Earth and forming a glam-rock band. But the end result wouldn't have made the grade during the Oxbridge duo's student rag week. AJ Swearing. 𝗗𝗩𝗗
Mel Smith *Bernard* · Griff Rhys Jones *Graham Sweetley* · James B Sikking *Col Laribee* · Dinsdale Landen *Cdr Matteson* · Jimmy Nail *Desmond* · Joanne Pearce *Sandra* · Paul Bown *Julian* ■ *Dir* Mike Hodges · *Scr* Mel Smith, Griff Rhys Jones, Bob Mercer

Morris: a Life with Bells On ★★ 12A
Comedy 2009 · UK · Colour · 101min

Rarely has a British comedy worked so hard at being genial and quirky as actress Lucy Akhurst's directorial debut. Unfortunately, the effort is all-too-apparent and this mockumentary about a West Country morris-dancing troupe struggles to raise more than a handful of smiles. Screenwriter Charles Thomas Oldham stars as the maverick squire of the Millsham Morris, who is barred from attempting the mythical Threeple Hammer Damson and seeks a more willing audience for "New Morris" in the United States. The cast couldn't be more willing, but the satire simply isn't sharp or amusing enough. DP Swearing, sexual references.
Derek Jacobi *Quentin Neeley* · Greg Wise *Miloslav Villandry* · Ian Hart *Endeavour Hungerfjord-Welsh* · Naomie Harris *Sonja Walton* · Dominique Pinon *Jean Baptiste Poquelin* · Sophie Thompson *Glenda Frosser* · Harriet Walter *Professor Compton Chamberlayne* ■ *Dir* Lucy Akhurst · *Scr* Charles Thomas Oldham

Mortal Fear ★★ 12
Medical thriller 1994 · US · Colour · 86min

This TV thriller based on the novel by Robin Cook bears a remarkable similarity to his earlier bestseller, *Coma*. Joanna Kerns is the high-flying medic who suspects something is not quite right when her hospital begins to lose patients at a rate even an overworked junior doctor might notice. You've seen it all before. DP 𝗗𝗩𝗗
Joanna Kerns *Dr Jennifer Kessler* · Gregory Harrison *Philip Montgomery* · Robert Young *Dr Ralph Wanamaker* · Max Gail *Det Michael Curran* · Rebecca Schull *Dr Danforth* ■ *Dir* Larry Shaw · *Scr* Rob Gilmer, Roger Young, from the novel by Robin Cook

The Mortal Instruments: City of Bones ★★★ 12
Supernatural action drama 2013 · US/Ger · Colour · 124min

This sprawling action fantasy with franchise pretensions is packed with supernatural creatures, humour that blunts its more horrific edges and leather-clad actors from goth-lite central casting. The plot-heavy story boils down to Brooklyn teen Lily Collins learning she's a powerful Shadowhunter, part of a secret society tasked with protecting humanity from destructive demonic forces. Director Harald Zwart always keeps things interesting among the impressive CGI swirls of werewolves, vampires, runic spells and a *Stargate*-style dimensional portal. Once its relentless self-aggrandisement subsides, the story becomes quite absorbing as a love triangle moves centre stage and dark destinies point to further sequels. AJ 𝗗𝗩𝗗
Lily Collins *Clary Fray* · Jamie Campbell Bower *Jace Wayland* · Robert Sheehan *Simon Lewis* · Kevin Zegers *Alec Lightwood* · Lena Headey *Jocelyn Fray* · Jonathan Rhys Meyers *Valentine Morgenstern* · Jared Harris *Hodge Starkweather* · Jemima West *Isabelle Lightwood* ■ *Dir* Harald Zwart · *Scr* Jessica Postigo, from Cassandra Clare's novel

Mortal Kombat ★★★ 15
Martial arts action adventure 1995 · US · Colour · 97min

At the time this film was made, *Mortal Kombat* was the world's biggest-selling game franchise, so it was a natural choice for a Hollywood makeover. And unlike other games-inspired turkeys (*Super Mario Bros*, *Street Fighter*), this one actually works, thanks mainly to director Paul Anderson's single-minded dedication to nonstop, expertly choreographed martial arts action. Christopher Lambert is the nominal star, but the best work comes from Cary-Hiroyuki Tagawa, who steals the show with a typically charismatic performance. JF Violence, some swearing. 𝗗𝗩𝗗
Christopher Lambert *Lord Rayden* · Bridgette Wilson *Sonya Blade* · Linden Ashby *Johnny Cage* · Talisa Soto *Princess Kitana* · Cary-Hiroyuki Tagawa *Shang Tsung* ■ *Dir* Paul Anderson (1) · *Scr* Kevin Droney, from the computer game by Ed Boon, John Tobias

Mortal Kombat: Annihilation ★★ 15
Martial arts action adventure 1997 · US · Colour · 90min

The martial arts arcade game spawns a second movie incarnation that offers even bigger helpings of action and special effects than the original. Robin Shou is back from the first outing, though Christopher Lambert's role is now taken by James Remar. Evil warlords from the sinister Outworld are bent on dominating Earth again, and only a handful of fearless heroes can save the day. Undemanding fun. JF Violence. 𝗗𝗩𝗗
Robin Shou *Liu Kang* · Talisa Soto *Princess Kitana* · James Remar *Lord Rayden* · Sandra Hess *Sonya Blade* ■ *Dir* John R Leonetti · *Scr* Brent V Friedman, Bryce Zabel, from a story by John Tobias, Lawrence Kasanoff, Joshua Wexler, from the computer game by Ed Boon, John Tobias

The Mortal Storm ★★★
Drama 1940 · US · BW · 100min

This version was daring in its time for alerting American audiences to the dangers of Nazism, though the horror is softened by the casting of resolutely all-American types as Germans and by a very Culver City Reich. Director Frank Borzage does not keep sentimentality at bay, but his drama is nevertheless moving and tragic by turns. It also features the marvellous Margaret Sullavan and the lanky but lovable James Stewart. Frank Morgan is genuinely touching as the father who watches his family disintegrate, and there's a chilling early cameo from later dance master Dan Dailey. TS
Margaret Sullavan *Freya Roth* · James Stewart *Martin Brietner* · Robert Young (1) *Fritz Marlberg* · Frank Morgan *Professor Roth* · Robert Stack *Otto Von Rohn* · Bonita Granville *Elsa* · Irene Rich *Mrs Roth* · William T Orr *Erich Von Rohn* ■ *Dir* Frank Borzage · *Scr* Claudine West, Anderson Ellis, George Froeschel, from the novel by Phyllis Bottome

Mortal Thoughts ★★★ 18
Thriller 1991 · US · Colour · 98min

Told in flashback, this drama (co-produced by star Demi Moore) follows two women friends (Moore and Glenne Headly) who are both unhappy in their marriages, and who end up being linked with the murder of Headly's husband (Bruce Willis). The acting from the three protagonists, and Harvey Keitel as the investigating detective, is superb, lifting what could have been a depressing tale into an intriguing mystery. JB Swearing, violence. 𝗗𝗩𝗗
Demi Moore *Cynthia Kellogg* · Glenne Headly *Joyce Urbanski* · Bruce Willis *James Urbanski* · John Pankow *Arthur Kellogg* · Harvey Keitel *Detective John Woods* · Billie Neal *Linda Nealon* · Frank Vincent *Dominic Marino* · Karen Shallo *Gloria Urbanski* · Crystal Field *Jeanette Marino* ■ *Dir* Alan Rudolph · *Scr* William Reilly, Claude Kerven

Mortdecai ★★ 12
Comedy crime caper 2015 · US · Colour · 102min

Johnny Depp is in danger of being upstaged by his own moustache in this knockabout crime caper. His dodgy British art dealer benefits from the actor's roguish charm but, like the film as a whole, it's a performance comprised of affectations, anachronisms and ostentatious facial hair. Director David Koepp aims for *Jeeves and Wooster*-inspired satire, but without the olde worlde backdrop, this is just a tepid fish-out-water farce. Gwyneth Paltrow and Ewan McGregor try to make Mortdecai seem less conspicuous with their own overly plummy accents but, except for the odd chuckle here and there, the talented cast struggles to inject much comedy value. SP 𝗗𝗩𝗗 𝗕𝗹𝘂
Johnny Depp *Charlie Mortdecai* · Gwyneth Paltrow *Johanna Mortdecai* · Ewan McGregor *Inspector Alistair Martland* · Paul Bettany *Jock Strapp* · Olivia Munn *Georgina Krampf* · Michael Culkin *Sir Graham Archer* ■ *Dir* David Koepp · *Scr* Eric Aronson, from the novel *Don't Point That Thing at Me* by Kyril Bonfiglioli

Morvern Callar ★★★★ 15
Drama 2001 · UK/Can · Colour · 93min

Based on Alan Warner's cult novel, this is director Lynne Ramsay's follow-up to her acclaimed debut *Ratcatcher*. Preserving the novel's quirky and oblique originality, Ramsay relates the tale of the eponymous Oban shopgirl (an intelligent and compelling performance from Samantha Morton) who wakes on Christmas morning to find that her boyfriend has committed suicide. Morvern casually dismembers and buries his body, and then deletes her boyfriend's name from the novel he has bequeathed her, keys in her own and sends it to a publisher. Using money from his bank account, she departs for a hedonistic holiday in Spain, where the film shifts gear. With its assured directorial style, this confirms Ramsay's reputation as a true cinematic artist. AC 𝗗𝗩𝗗
Samantha Morton *Morvern Callar* · Kathleen McDermott *Lanna* · Raife Patrick Burchell *Boy in room 1022* · Dan Cadan *Dazzer* · Carolyn Calder *Tequila Sheila* · Jim Wilson (3) *Tom Boddington* · Dolly Wells *Susan* · Ruby Milton *Couris Jean* ■ *Dir* Lynne Ramsay · *Scr* Lynne Ramsay, Liana Dognini, from the novel by Alan Warner

Moscow Distrusts Tears ★★★
Romantic comedy drama 1979 · USSR · Colour · 147min

A surprise winner of the Oscar for best foreign film, Vladimir Menshov's "that was then, this is now" melodrama harks back to the ensemble "women's pictures" made in Hollywood in the 1950s. Beginning in a Moscow factory hostel in the Khrushchev era, the action jumps forward 20 years to see how socially ambitious Irina Muravyova, conservative Raisa Ryazanova and ditzy Vera Alentova made out. Despite the broken marriages, illegitimate births, compromises and disappointments, the trio remain inseparable. DP Russian +subtitles.
Vera Alentova *Katya* · Alexei Batalov *Goscha* · Irina Muravyova *Ludmilla* · Raisa Ryazanova *Antonia* · Yuri Vasilyev *Rudolf* ■ *Dir* Vladimir Menshov · *Scr* Valentin Chernykh

Moscow Nights ★★
Drama 1935 · UK · BW · 100min

The daughter of impoverished Russian aristocrats (a colourless Penelope Dudley Ward), forced into marriage with a boorish but wealthy tradesman (Harry Baur), really loves a handsome army officer (Laurence Olivier). In debt to her husband after losing a card game, the officer's efforts to pay up lead him into the spy game and a charge of treason. This tangled and creaky brouhaha offers good performances from Olivier and the splendid French actor Baur, but is curiously uninteresting. RK
Harry Baur *Brioukow* · Laurence Olivier *Capt Ignatoff* · Penelope Dudley Ward *Natasha* · Robert Cochran *Polonsky* · Morton Selten *Kovrin* · Athene Seyler *Mme Sabline* ■ *Dir* Anthony Asquith · *Scr* Anthony Asquith, Erich Seipmann, from the novel *Les Nuits de Moscou* by Pierre Benoit

Moscow on the Hudson ★★★ 15
Comedy drama 1984 · US · Colour · 112min

There's a gentle, sweet-natured core to Robin Williams's screen personality that is too often camouflaged by the hysteria that forms the basis of his performances. This rather melancholy comedy lets that attractive side surface to good effect, with Williams playing a Soviet circus musician who defects while shopping in New York. He then finds, once he's part of the immigrant experience, that life is as racist and rancid as back home, with freedom as a meagre bonus. Director Paul Mazursky gallops off in too many directions, but Williams's performance is a real treat. TH Swearing, violence, nudity. 𝗗𝗩𝗗
Robin Williams *Vladimir Ivanoff* · Maria Conchita Alonso *Lucia Lombardo* · Cleavant Derricks *Lionel Witherspoon* · Alejandro Rey *Orlando Ramirez* · Savely Kramarov *Boris* · Oleg Rudnik *Yury* ■ *Dir* Paul Mazursky · *Scr* Paul Mazursky, Leon Capetanos

Moses ★★ 12
Biblical epic 1975 · UK/It · Colour · 288min

Burt Lancaster does everything you'd expect as Moses: he orders up plagues, leads his people out of Egypt, parts the Red Sea, climbs Mount Sinai and comes back down with the Ten Commandments. This Lew Grade production was originally a six-hour mini-series, partly written by Anthony Burgess; the latter also composed his own music score, but it was rejected in favour of one from Ennio Morricone. However, where Cecil DeMille's *The Ten Commandments* (1965) was a ponderous but occasionally juicy religious epic, this is more of a dreary historical drama. AT 𝗗𝗩𝗗
Burt Lancaster *Moses* · Anthony Quayle *Aaron* · Ingrid Thulin *Miriam* · Irene Papas *Zipporah* · Mariangela Melato *Princess Bithia* · William Lancaster *Young Moses* ■ *Dir* Gianfranco de Bosio · *Scr* Anthony Burgess, Victorio Bonicelli, Gianfranco de Bosio

Moshi Monsters: the Movie ★★★ U
Animated adventure 2013 · UK · Colour · 81min

Moshi Monsters are this generation's Pokémon, only they're British, not Japanese. Their website world of customisable "pets" has now expanded to movies with a tale in which arch baddie Dr Strangeglove steals the mystical Great Moshling Egg as part of his fiendish plan to take over Monstro City. It's colourful, sort of cute, weirdly surreal and thoroughly impenetrable to anyone aged over eight. Ask younger kids to explain it to you. DA
Emma Tate *Katsuma/Luvli* · Tom Clarke Hill *Furi/Roary* · Ashley Slater *Dr Strangeglove/Zommer* · Boris Hiestand *Fishlips/Newsreader* ■ *Dir* Wip Vernooij, Morgan Francis · *Scr* Jocelyn Stevenson, Steve Cleverley

The Mosquito Coast
★★★★ PG

Drama   1986 · US · Colour · 113min

This absorbing journey into the heart of darkness provides Harrison Ford with one of the most unsympathetic characters of his film career. He plays an idealistic, obsessive inventor who begins a slow slide into madness when he moves his family to Central America in a doomed attempt to bring ice to the jungle. Paul Schrader intelligently adapts Paul Theroux's source novel and, if director Peter Weir loses his way a little, the performances are uniformly superb. Ford is surprisingly convincing as the outwardly charming control freak, while River Phoenix gives a portrayal beyond his years as his troubled son. JF Violence. *DVD*

Harrison Ford *Allie Fox* • Helen Mirren *Mother* • River Phoenix *Charlie* • Jadrien Steele *Jerry* • Hilary Gordon *April* • Rebecca Gordon *Clover* • Jason Alexander *Clerk* • Martha Plimpton *Emily Spellgood* ■ *Dir* Peter Weir • *Scr* Paul Schrader, from the novel by Paul Theroux

Mosquito Squadron
★★ PG

Second World War adventure
1968 · UK · Colour · 89min

A host of familiar faces that you can't quite put a name to keep their upper lips stiff as our boys try to destroy a French chateau containing the Nazis' super-duper doodlebug, the V3, in this derivative war adventure. David McCallum plays an RAF pilot who must comfort his missing friend's wife and lead the mission. Only some nice flying sequences and the support of Charles Gray pass muster. DP *DVD*

David McCallum (1) *Quint Munroe* • Suzanne Neve *Beth Scott* • David Buck *Squadron Leader David Scott* • David Dundas *Flight Lieutenant Douglas Shelton* • Dinsdale Landen *Wing Commander Penrose* • Charles Gray *Air Commodore Hufford* • Michael Anthony *Father Bellague* ■ *Dir* Boris Sagal • *Scr* Donald S Sanford, Joyce Perry

Moss Rose
★★

Period detective drama   1947 · US · BW · 81min

Who is murdering Victor Mature's lovers and leaving behind the clue of a bible marked with a dried moss rose? Vincent Price plays the sly detective in charge of the cryptic case, proving he could be just as convincing on the right side of the law as he would soon be on the wrong. Mature isn't interesting or enigmatic enough in this muddled whodunnit, but solid trouping by a good supporting cast gives it a much needed lift. AJ

Peggy Cummins *Belle Adair* • Victor Mature *Sir Alexander Sterling* • Ethel Barrymore *Lady Sterling* • Vincent Price *Inspector Clinner* • Margo Woode *Daisy Arrow* • George Zucco *Craxton* • Patricia Medina *Audrey Ashton* • Felippa Rock *Liza* ■ *Dir* Gregory Ratoff • *Scr* Jules Furthman, Tom Reed, Niven Busch, from the novel by Joseph Shearing

The Most Dangerous Game
★★★★ 12

Classic horror   1932 · US · BW · 62min

Originally released in the UK as *The Hounds of Zaroff*, this teaming of star Fay Wray and co-director Ernest B Schoedsack predates their classic *King Kong*, and traverses similar action territory, with the genius of composer Max Steiner vividly illuminating both movies. Richard Connell's story was a natural for filming, but none of the subsequent versions live up to the sheer exuberance of this cracker. Leslie Banks's mad Count Zaroff remains hard to replicate and the theme of hunting human game was never quite so chilling as here. Robert Wise directed a modest version in 1945, but no question, this is the best movie take on the tale. TS *DVD*

Joel McCrea *Bob Rainsford* • Fay Wray *Eve Trowbridge* • Leslie Banks *Count Zaroff* • Robert Armstrong *Martin Trowbridge* • Steve Clemento *Tartar servant* • Noble Johnson *Tartar servant* ■ *Dir* Ernest B Schoedsack, Irving Pichel • *Scr* James A Creelman, from the story by Richard Connell

The Most Dangerous Man Alive
★

Science-fiction thriller
1961 · US · Colour · 80min

Escaped convict Ron Randell is accidentally exposed to radiation by a cobalt bomb explosion and becomes an unstoppable superman, hell-bent on revenge against the gangsters who framed him. The last film directed by silent pioneer Allan Dwan is a poverty-row mix of science-fiction thriller and Mob melodrama. AJ

Ron Randell *Eddie Candell* • Debra Paget *Linda Marlow* • Elaine Stewart *Carla Angelo* • Anthony Caruso *Andy Darmon* • Gregg Palmer *Lt Fisher* ■ *Dir* Allan Dwan • *Scr* James Leicester, Phillip Rock, from the story *The Steel Monster* by Michael Pate, Phillip Rock

The Most Dangerous Man in America: Daniel Ellsberg and the Pentagon Papers
★★★★

Documentary   2009 · US · Colour · 94min

A compelling, multilayered and now Oscar-nominated film about military analyst Daniel Ellsberg, who helped to plan and promote the war in Vietnam but, overcome by guilt about the horror being wrought and the lies being told, leaked a devastating top-secret dossier to the press. This film coolly gets across the enormity of what Ellsberg did. Yet just as striking as the precedents Ellsberg set is what he didn't achieve – much of what he exposed has been forgotten. JkS

■ *Dir* Judith Ehrlich, Rick Goldsmith • *Scr* Michael Chandler, Judith Ehrlich, Rick Goldsmith, Lawrence Lerew

The Most Desired Man
★★★ 18

Romantic comedy   1994 · Ger · Colour · 90min

Highly rated by those who know their German movies, *The Most Desired Man* is proof that the phrase "German comedy" isn't always an oxymoron. The film concerns a heterosexual man and incorrigible womaniser who, having been booted out of his girlfriend's flat, moves in with a gay friend. When the girlfriend discovers she's pregnant, she sets out to get him back, ignorant of the circle he now moves in. DA German +subtitles.

Til Schweiger *Axel Feldheim* • Katja Riemann *Doro Feldheim* • Joachim Król *Norbert Brommer* • Antonia Lang *Elke Schmitt* ■ *Dir* Sönke Wortmann • *Scr* Sönke Wortmann, from the comic books *Der Bewegte Mann* and *Pretty Baby* by Ralf König

The Most Fertile Man in Ireland
★★ 15

Romantic comedy
1999 · UK/Ire · Colour · 92min

Debutant director Dudi Appleton opts for a broad and bawdy approach to the discovery that dating agent Kris Marshall has the potency to impregnate even the most infertile female. Consequently, the round of comic couplings soon loses its novelty, while subplots involving Marshall's crush on undertaker's assistant Kathy Keira Clarke and his brush with angry Orangeman James Nesbitt prompt a shift in tone that deflates the fun without adding much insight. DP *DVD*

Kris Marshall *Eamon Manley* • Kathy Keira Clarke *Rosie* • Bronagh Gallagher *Millicent* • James Nesbitt *"Mad Dog" Billy Wilson* • Kenneth Cranham *Da* • Olivia Nash *Ma* • Pauline McLynn *Maeve* • Toyah Willcox *Dr Johnson* ■ *Dir* Dudi Appleton • *Scr* Jim Keeble

A Most Violent Year
★★★★ 15

Crime thriller   2014 · US · Colour · 119min

Set in 1981, one of the most violent years in New York's history, this follows ice-cool immigrant entrepreneur Oscar Isaac as he attempts to seal the deal that will make him a fortune. However, with only a month to complete it, Isaac's dreams of expanding his heating-oil business are beset by disparate forces that threaten to destroy him. After his fabulous turn in *Inside Llewyn Davis*, Isaac gives another magnetic performance – like a young Al Pacino in looks and simmering intensity – while Chastain sinks her teeth into the juicy role of his hard-boiled Brooklyn spouse. It's a tense, subtly evocative Big Apple tale that could crown JC Chandor as a worthy successor to quintessential New York director Sidney Lumet. JA Violence, swearing. *DVD*

Oscar Isaac *Abel Morales* • Jessica Chastain *Anna Morales* • David Oyelowo *Lawrence* • Alessandro Nivola *Peter Forente* • Albert Brooks *Andrew Walsh* • Elyes Gabel *Julian* ■ *Dir/Scr* JC Chandor

Most Wanted
★★★ 15

Action adventure   1997 · US · Colour · 94min

In the conspiracy thriller stakes, this is minor league stuff, but very entertaining nonetheless. In a more serious role than usual, writer/star Keenen Ivory Wayans plays a former army sniper recruited into a shadowy government organisation, only to find himself framed for the murder of the First Lady. The political machinations don't bear close scrutiny, but director David Glenn Hogan stages some immaculate action set pieces and the cast is top quality. JF Some swearing, violence. *DVD*

Keenen Ivory Wayans *James Dunn* • Jon Voight *Casey/General Woodward* • Jill Hennessy *Dr Victoria Constantini* • Paul Sorvino *CIA Deputy Director Kenny Rackmill* • Robert Culp *Donald Bickhart* ■ *Dir* David Glenn Hogan [David Hogan] • *Scr* Keenen Ivory Wayans

A Most Wanted Man
★★★ 15

Spy thriller   2013 · UK/US/Ger · Colour · 116min

Philip Seymour Hoffman, in one of his final performances, presents us with another of John le Carré's world-weary agents – a rumpled, unshaven operative called Günther Bachmann, who likes his whisky and has seemingly been shunted downwards after some previous cock-up. After a mystery man dramatically emerges from a river in Hamburg, Bachmann struggles to make sense of the situation, while keeping one step ahead of rival agencies. Hoffman heads an impressive cast and the plot is well crafted, even if the characters and moral uncertainties seem very familiar and the message remains the same – it's a grubby business, trust no one. BP Swearing. *DVD*

Philip Seymour Hoffman *Günther Bachmann* • Rachel McAdams *Annabel Richter* • Willem Dafoe *Thomas Brue*, *"Tommy"* • Robin Wright *Martha Sullivan* • Daniel Brühl *Maximilian* • Nina Hoss *Irna Frey* ■ *Dir* Anton Corbijn • *Scr* Andrew Bovell, from John le Carré's novel

Motel Blue
★★ 18

Erotic thriller   1997 · US · Colour · 90min

Sean Young was briefly on the cusp of great things, but now she camps it up in soft-focus romps that tend to raise titters rather than titillate. Here she plays a top-level scientist, whose request for additional security clearance sparks a government inquiry that reveals much more than trade secrets. Soleil Moon Frye is out of her depth alongside such inveterate scene-stealers as Robert Vaughn and Seymour Cassel. DP

Sean Young *Lana Hawking* • Soleil Moon Frye *Agent Kyle Rivers* • Seymour Cassel *Old priest* • Robert Vaughn (1) *Chief MacIntyre* ■ *Dir* Sam Firstenberg • *Scr* Cormac Wibberley, Marianne Wibberley

Motel Hell
★★★ 18

Cult black comedy horror
1980 · US · Colour · 101min

This gory horror spoof successfully walks the fine line between bad taste and nutty wit, Amicus alumnus Kevin Connor's remarkable slice of backwoods American Gothic is a classy shocker that stands out from the usual stalk-and-slash pack. Farmer Rory Calhoun ambushes passers-by at his roadside motel, buries them alive up to their necks, fattens them up and then uses their flesh for his famous spicy smoked meats. Explicit, gruesome, harrowing (the human harvesting is very nasty) and outrageously funny (mainly because of Calhoun's nonchalant performance). AJ *DVD*

Rory Calhoun *Vincent Smith* • Paul Linke *Bruce Smith* • Nancy Parsons *Ida Smith* • Nina Axelrod *Terry* • Wolfman Jack *Reverend Billy* • Elaine Joyce *Edith Olson* ■ *Dir* Kevin Connor • *Scr* Robert Jaffe, Steven-Charles Jaffe

The Motel Life
★★★ 15

Thriller   2012 · US · Colour · 89min

This low-key, *noir*-ish thriller stars Stephen Dorff and Emile Hirsch as two orphaned brothers who drift from town to town across Nevada. But when Jerry Lee (Dorff) is involved in a hit-and-run accident, he and sibling Frank (Hirsch) are soon on the run. First-time directors (and real-life brothers) Gabe and Alan Polsky offer up a sombre parable about loyalty and redemption. The two leads work well in tandem, and there's strong support from Dakota Fanning as Frank's ex-girlfriend and Kris Kristofferson as a surrogate father figure. TeS Violence, swearing, sex scenes, drug abuse, nudity. *DVD*

Emile Hirsch *Frank* • Stephen Dorff *Jerry Lee* • Kris Kristofferson *Earl Hurley* • Dakota Fanning *Annie James* • Joshua Leonard *Tommy* ■ *Dir* Alan Polsky, Gabe Polsky • *Scr* Micah Fitzerman-Blue, Noah Harpster, from Willy Vlautin's novel

The Moth Diaries
★★ 15

Horror   2010 · Can/Ire · Colour · 78min

Rachel Klein's 2002 young adult novel was ahead of its time – it predated the whole *Twilight* teen vampire sensation by several years – but this belated film adaptation arrives a little too late. Sarah Bolger plays a troubled 16-year-old at a posh boarding school, whose best friend (Sarah Gadon) falls under the spell of mysterious new student Lily Cole, who never seems to eat, loves the night and whose enemies have a nasty habit of turning up dead. Mary Harron saturates the film in gothic tones, teenage angst and Sapphic references, but it's a little too ethereal for its own good and meanders to an unsatisfying climax. JF Swearing, sex scenes, drug abuse, brief nudity. *DVD*

Sarah Bolger *Rebecca* • Lily Cole *Ernessa* • Sarah Gadon *Lucy* • Scott Speedman *Mr Davies* • Judy Parfitt *Miss Rood* • Valerie Tian *Charley* ■ *Dir* Mary Harron • *Scr* Mary Harron, from the novel by Rachel Klein

Mother
★★★★★

Silent drama   1926 · USSR · BW · 106min

Vsevolod Pudovkin's first feature is one of the classics of the golden age of Russian cinema. The tightly constructed narrative, adapted from Maxim Gorky's rambling novel, concerns a mother (the extraordinary Vera Baranovskaya) who, at the time of the abortive revolution of 1905, accidentally gives up her communist son to the police. The superb cast is made up of members of the Moscow Arts Theatre, with Pudovkin himself playing the interrogating officer. By an ingenious juxtaposition of images, the director creates an illusion of sound, and the emotional impact has not diminished with time. RB

Vera Baranovskaya *Pelageya Vlasova, the mother* • A Tchistyakova *Vlasov, her husband* • Nikolai Batalov *Pavel, her son* • Vsevolod I Pudovkin *Police officer* ■ *Dir* Vsevolod I Pudovkin • *Scr* Nathan Zarkhi, Vsevolod Pudovkin, from the novel *Mat* by Maxim Gorky

Mother
★★★ 12

Comedy   1996 · US · Colour · 99min

Albert Brooks writes, directs and stars in this uneven but intermittently hilarious ode to mothers. He plays a writer who returns to his childhood home when his relationship and career go down the pan, only to be driven over the edge by his mom (hilariously played by Debbie Reynolds) and her sly, sarcastic comments. Brooks gives a nice performance, but this is Reynolds's film, and she steals every scene she's in. JB

Albert Brooks *John Henderson* • Debbie Reynolds *Beatrice Henderson* • Rob Morrow *Jeff Henderson* • Lisa Kudrow *Linda* • John C

McGinley *Carl* • Paul Collins *Lawyer* • Laura Weekes *Karen Henderson* ■ *Dir* Albert Brooks • *Scr* Albert Brooks, Monica Johnson

The Mother ★★★★ 15
Romantic drama 2003 · UK · Colour · 107min

Not since *Harold and Maude* has a film so affectionately addressed the controversial theme of autumn–spring romance. While visiting her children in West London, recently widowed grandmother Anne Reid gradually finds herself in lust with Daniel Craig, the much younger handyman renovating her son's house. Craig happens to be having an affair with Reid's daughter (Cathryn Bradshaw), but it's not long before Reid and Craig begin a sexual relationship of their own. Roger Michell's film thankfully avoids the pitfalls of its toy-boy premise, and it challenges taboos insightfully, with great emotional maturity. TH Swearing, drug abuse. *DVD*

Anne Reid *May* • Cathryn Bradshaw *Paula* • Daniel Craig *Darren* • Steven Mackintosh *Bobby* • Oliver Ford Davies *Bruce* • Anna Wilson-Jones *Helen* • Peter Vaughan *Toots* • Harry Michell *Harry* • Rosie Michell *Rosie* ■ *Dir* Roger Michell • *Scr* Hanif Kureishi

Mother ★★★★ 15
Crime thriller 2009 · S Kor · Colour · 123min

Maternal devotion is taken to startling extremes in this rewarding Hitchcockian thriller from Korean director Bong Joon-ho (*The Host*). Beautifully shot and grippingly plotted, the film sees doting mother Kim Hye-ja prepared to go to any lengths to clear her adult son's name after the feeble-minded young man (Won Bin) is accused of murder. A seam of absurd humour adds to the ostensibly simple story, but it's the slow-burning marriage of suspense and melodrama that proves most effective, amplified by Kim's subtle performance. SF Korean +subtitles. Violence, swearing, sex scenes. *DVD* *BL*

Kim Hye-ja *Mother* • Won Bin *Yoon Do-joon* • Jin Goo *Jin-tae* • Yoon Jae-Moon [Yoon Je-moon] *Je-mun* • Jun Mi-sun *Mi-sun* • Lee Young-suck *Ragman* ■ *Dir* Bong Joon-ho • *Scr* Bong Joon-ho, Park Eun-kyo, from a story by Bong

Mother and Child ★★★ 15
Drama 2009 · US · Colour · 121min

This dyed-in-the-wool weepie from director Rodrigo Garcia (*Nine Lives*) follows the interconnected worlds of three women with baby trouble. Annette Bening plays Karen, a 50-year-old still haunted by her decision as a teenage mum to give up her daughter for adoption. Naomi Watts plays Elizabeth, that daughter, now a high-flying lawyer. And Kerry Washington plays Lucy, a childless young wife looking to adopt. Their stories converge when the death of Karen's mum prompts her to plumb her past. The three leads are excellent, but at over two hours in length, this is strictly for patient, as well as sensitive, souls. DA Swearing, sex scenes. *DVD* *BL*

Naomi Watts *Elizabeth* • Annette Bening *Karen* • Kerry Washington *Lucy* • Samuel L Jackson *Paul* • Jimmy Smits *Paco* • S Epatha Merkerson *Ada* • David Morse *Tom* ■ *Dir/Scr* Rodrigo Garcia

Mother and Son ★★★★ U
Drama 1997 · Ger/Rus · Colour · 70min

The agony of seeing a loved one draw close to death is presented in such intimate detail in this meticulous Russian drama, that watching it feels like an intrusion on the grief of the ailing mother and her devoted son. Considering neither Gudrun Geyer nor Alexei Ananishnov are professionals, they give performances of remarkable power and simplicity as they explore their mutual dependence. Rarely has silence been so poignant. DP Russian +subtitles. *DVD*

Gudrun Geyer *Mother* • Alexei Ananishnov *Son* ■ *Dir* Aleksandr Sokurov • *Scr* Yuri Arabov

Mother India ★★★★ U
Drama 1957 · Ind · Colour · 159min

Regarded by some as Bollywood's *Gone with the Wind*, Mehboob Khan's film shows a heartbroken mother winning the support of her neighbours, thus becoming a symbol of national pain and perseverance. The action is told as an extended flashback, as Nargis remembers the hardships that ultimately drove her to kill her own rebellious son, Sunil Dutt (Nargis's future husband). Sacrificing realism for epic spectacle, the film was nominated for the best foreign film Oscar. DP Hindi +subtitles. *DVD*

Nargis *Radha* • Sunil Dutt *Birju* • Rajendra Kumar *Ramu* • Raaj Kumar *Shamoo* • *Dir* Mehboob Khan • *Scr* S Ali Raza, Vajahat Mirza, Mehboob Khan

Mother Is a Freshman ★★★ U
Comedy 1949 · US · Colour · 80min

This utterly charming Loretta Young vehicle has a very silly plot but is so ravishingly filmed in that rich and garish 1940s Technicolor that it hardly matters if mother Loretta or daughter Betty Lynn ends up with charmer Van Johnson. Veteran director Lloyd Bacon, responsible for *42nd Street*, just lets the laughs fall where they may, and there's a nice supporting turn from the one-time king of the megaphone Rudy Vallee. TS

Loretta Young *Abigail "Abby" Fortitude Abbott* • Van Johnson *Professor Richard Michaels* • Rudy Vallee *John Heaslip* • Barbara Lawrence *Louise Sharpe* • Robert Arthur (1) *Beaumont Jackson* • Betty Lynn *Susan Abbott* ■ *Dir* Lloyd Bacon • *Scr* Mary Loos, Richard Sale, from a story by Raphael Blau

Mother, Jugs & Speed ★★★ 15
Black comedy 1976 · US · Colour · 98min

Guess who's who in the title roles as Bill Cosby, Harvey Keitel and Raquel Welch charge around as private ambulance drivers in this dark comedy with slapstick moments from *Bullitt* director Peter Yates. The cast acquits itself well, and there's an especially funny pre-JR Larry Hagman playing a randy driver, but the whole enterprise really comes to a halt thanks to the lack of narrative. TS Some violence, swearing, drug abuse.

Bill Cosby *Mother* • Raquel Welch *Jugs* • Harvey Keitel *Speed* • Aller Garfield *Harry Fishbine* • LQ Jones *Davey* • Bruce Davison *Leroy* • Dick Butkus *Rodeo* • Larry Hagman *Murdoch* ■ *Dir* Peter Yates • *Scr* Tom Mankiewicz, from a story by Stephen Manes, Tom Mankiewicz

Mother Küsters Goes to Heaven ★★★★
Drama 1975 · W Ger · Colour · 108min

Banned from the Berlin film festival for its scathing exposé of the self-seeking agendas of both political activists and the press, Rainer Werner Fassbinder's bitterly ironic fable was filmed in a remarkable 20 days. Widowed after her working-class husband kills both his boss and himself, Brigitte Mira is cast into isolation before being besieged by new exploitative "friends". That she emerges having discovered both herself and her fate owes much to Mira's astute performance and to Fassbinder's world-weary cynicism. DP German +subtitles.

Brigitte Mira *Mother Küsters* • Ingrid Caven *Corinna Corinne* • Armin Meier *Ernst* • Irm Hermann *Helene* • Gottfried John *Journalist* • Karlheinz Böhm *Thalmann* • Margit Carstensen *Mrs Thalmann* ■ *Dir* Rainer Werner Fassbinder • *Scr* Rainer Werner Fassbinder, Kurt Raab, from a story by Heinrich Zille

Mother Night ★★★ 15
Drama 1996 · US · Colour and BW · 109min

Kurt Vonnegut's source novel about a Nazi war criminal – a sort of Lord Haw-Haw figure – standing trial in Israel, whose memoirs claim he was in fact an American spy, proves a hard nut to crack. It's a diffuse story told in flashback that stretches over five decades and also deals with racism in Harlem in the 1950s. Director Keith Gordon's film is brave and ambitious but not completely successful, though Nick Nolte is excellent in an especially demanding central role, and there is strong support from John Goodman and Alan Arkin. AT *DVD*

Nick Nolte *Howard Campbell* • Sheryl Lee *Helga Noth/Resi Noth* • Alan Arkin *George Kraft* • John Goodman *Major Frank Wirtanen* • Kirsten Dunst *Young Resi Noth* • Arye Gross *Abraham Epstein* ■ *Dir* Keith Gordon • *Scr* Robert B Weide, from the novel by Kurt Vonnegut Jr

Mother Wore Tights ★★★ U
Musical 1947 · US · Colour · 106min

An immensely popular Betty Grable musical, in which she's teamed with the likeable and talented Dan Dailey at 20th Century-Fox tells the story of the early days of vaudeville in garish Technicolor. Neither clever nor sophisticated, this effortlessly whiles away the time. It also has the benefit of a superb Oscar-winning Alfred Newman/Charles Henderson score, and contains a rare opportunity to see the great ventriloquist Senor Wences on celluloid. The story itself, however, which is held together by off-screen narration from Anne Baxter, rambles rather and lacks any real climax. TS

Betty Grable *Myrtle McKinley Burt* • Dan Dailey *Frank Burt* • Mona Freeman *Iris Burt* • Connie Marshall *Mikie Burt* • Vanessa Brown *Bessie* • Robert Arthur (1) *Bob Clarkman* • Sara Allgood *Grandmother McKinley* • William Frawley *Mr Schneider* • Ruth Nelson *Miss Ridgeway* • Anne Baxter *Narrator* ■ *Dir* Walter Lang • *Scr* Lamar Trotti, from the novel by Miriam Young

Motherhood ★★★ 15
Black comedy 1993 · US · Colour · 86min

There are equal parts gore and guffaw in this spirited horror romp, notable for a cast that includes the cream of America's wackier character actors. Tombstone-toothed Steve Buscemi plays a mummy's boy who'll do anything to bring his dearly departed back from the dead. Trouble is, anything works and back mum comes. But now she's dead different, her new appetite for insects being a particular bugbear. DA *DVD*

Steve Buscemi *Ed Chilton* • Miriam Margolyes *Mother* • Ned Beatty *Uncle Benny* • John Glover *AJ Pattie* • Sam Jenkins *Storm Reynolds* ■ *Dir* Jonathan Wacks • *Scr* Chuck Hughes

Motherhood ★★ 15
Comedy 2009 · US · Colour · 85min

A day in the life of a hassled mum is the subject of this mediocre comedy. Uma Thurman stars as the former writer-turned-blogger who lives with flaky hubby Anthony Edwards and their two kids in Manhattan's Greenwich Village, but struggles to face up to the daily slog of being a mother. It's a well-meaning film, but the attempts at amusing insights into the everyday life of a full-time mum are hamstrung by the 24-hour time frame and some ill-judged bad language. Not to mention the irritating nature of the film's characters. JA Swearing, sexual references. *DVD*

Uma Thurman *Eliza Welsh* • Anthony Edwards *Avery Welsh* • Minnie Driver *Sheila* • Daisy Tahan *Clara* • Arjun Gupta *Nikesh* • Stephanie Szostak *Sandrine Dumas* • Jodie Foster ■ *Dir/Scr* Katherine Dieckmann

Mother's Boys ★★ 15
Thriller 1993 · US · Colour · 91min

Psycho-mum Jamie Lee Curtis is the disturbed ex-wife of Peter Gallagher, and she doesn't like the way his new partner, Joanne Whalley-Kilmer, has taken over her former role. Yves Simoneau's direction is competent, but it's not really nasty enough to please ardent chiller fans and the ending is just plain daft. JF Swearing, violence, brief nudity.

Jamie Lee Curtis *Jude* • Peter Gallagher *Robert* • Joanne Whalley-Kilmer [Joanne Whalley] *Callie* • Vanessa Redgrave *Lydia* • Luke Edwards *Kes* • Colin Ward *Michael* • Joey Zimmerman *Ben* • Joss Ackland *Lansing* • Paul Guilfoyle (2) *Mark Kaplan* ■ *Dir* Yves Simoneau • *Scr* Barry Schneider, Richard Hawley, from the novel by Bernard Taylor

Mother's Day ★★★★ 18
Horror thriller 2010 · US · Colour · 107min

If you have the stomach for it, occasional *Saw* franchise director Darren Lynn Bousman's gory update of the trashy 1980 original Troma production is an intense, horrifying experience. Three brothers flee a botched bank robbery and head for their childhood home to hide, only to find the new owners celebrating their housewarming. It's a highly assured fusion of B-movie exploitation lore and home-invasion terror, and the slick tensions escalate early as the captives struggle to placate their intimidators. Some plot twists barely hold water, but that doesn't upset the exciting climactic stretch after the commanding Rebecca De Mornay arrives on the scene. AJ Violence. *DVD* *BL*

Rebecca De Mornay *Mother* • Jaime King *Beth Sohapi* • Patrick Flueger *Ike Koffin* • Warren Kole *Addley Koffin* • Deborah Ann Woll *Lydia Koffin* • Matt O'Leary *Johnny Koffin* • Briana Evigan *Annette Langston* ■ *Dir* Darren Lynn Bousman • *Scr* Scott Milam, based on the 1980 film by Charles Kaufman and Warren D Leight

Mother's Day ★★ 12A
Comedy 2016 · US · Colour · 117min

The third part of a star-studded series with *Valentine's Day* (2010) and *New Year's Eve* (2011), this comedy follows several overwrought mothers (including Jennifer Aniston, Kate Hudson and Julia Roberts) as they negotiate family traumas leading up to Mother's Day. Like the previous instalments, this is a drab mix of every romantic comedy convention that is neither realistic nor engaging. JL Swearing, sexual references.

Jennifer Aniston *Sandy* • Kate Hudson *Jesse* • Julia Roberts *Miranda* • Jason Sudeikis *Bradley* • Britt Robertson [Brittany Robertson] *Kristin* • Timothy Olyphant *Henry* • Hector Elizondo *Lance Wallace* ■ *Dir* Garry Marshall • *Scr* Tom Hines, Anya Kochoff Romano, Matt Walker, from a story by Walker, Hines, Lily Hollander, Garry Marshall

A Mother's Gift ★★
Western drama 1995 · US · Colour · 120min

Based on Bess Streeter Aldrich's 1928 novel *A Lantern in Her Hand*, this made-for-TV western approaches the harsh realities of frontier life from a woman's perspective. Tutored in music and art, Nancy McKeon has social ambitions, but, despite his promises, sweetheart Adrian Pasdar returns from the American Civil War and informs her that they are going to raise their family on a homestead in the middle of untamed Nebraska. Although it tries to depict the covered wagon trek, the extremes of the prairie climate and the dangers posed by native Americans as authentically as possible, this presents a highly romanticised vision throughout. DP

Nancy McKeon *Margaret Deal* • Adrian Pasdar *William Deal* • Lucy Deakins *Isobelle as an adult* • Adam Storke *Ed Matthews* • Max Wright *Herman Mandelbrot* • James Prince *Henry Lutz* ■ *Dir* Jerry London • *Scr* Earl Hamner [Earl Hamner Jr], Don Sipes, Joe Wiesenfeld, from the novel *A Lantern In Her Hand* by Bess Streeter Aldrich

Mother's Milk ★★★ 15
Drama 2012 · UK · Colour · 98min

This engaging saga accompanies well-heeled Jack Davenport to Provence for a holiday with his wife and their two sons in the villa that his Alzheimer's-afflicted mother has gifted to a New Age charlatan. When she requests his help to arrange her assisted suicide, Davenport is forced to rouse himself from his booze-fuelled stupor. Adapted by Edward St Aubyn from the Booker-nominated fourth instalment of his *Melrose Cycle*, the movie always feels like the continuation of an ongoing story. But the performances are fine and director Gerald Fox ably captures the local ambience and the distorted perspectives generated by Davenport's debilitating self-pity. DP Swearing. *DVD*

Jack Davenport *Patrick Melrose* • Annabel Mullion *Mary Melrose* • Adrian Dunbar *Seamus O'Dorke* • Margaret Tyzack *Eleanor Melrose* •

Diana Quick *Kettle* • Annette Badland *Margaret* ■ *Dir* Gerald Fox (2) • *Scr* Gerald Fox (2), Edward St Aubyn, from St Aubyn's novel

The Mothman Prophecies ★★★ 12

Supernatural thriller 2001 · US · Colour · 113min

The presence of Richard Gere in this paranormal thriller (based on "true" events) may suggest a rather mainstream approach to the material. Yet this eerie and engrossing movie is far from conventional, combining off-kilter camerawork and spooky sound mixing with enough narrative ambiguity to fill several David Lynch movies. Gere plays a political reporter who one night inexplicably drives hundreds of miles out of his way to a small West Virginia town. He discovers that the confused inhabitants are plagued by strange visitations from a large winged creature that seem to foreshadow disaster. JC

DVD

Richard Gere *John Klein* • Laura Linney *Connie Parker* • Will Patton *Gordon Smallwood* • Lucinda Jenney *Denise Smallwood* • Debra Messing *Mary Klein* • Alan Bates *Dr Alexander Leek* ■ *Dir* Mark Pellington • *Scr* Richard Hatem, from the non-fiction book by John A Keel

Mothra ★★★

Monster horror 1962 · Jpn · Colour · 90min

This introduction to one of Japan's most famous radioactive monsters was one of Toho Studios' best efforts, boasting colourful photography, a more ambitious story and good special effects. Surprisingly, Mothra here stays in egg or caterpillar form for most of the movie before finally growing wings, leaving less time than usual for monster mayhem. Much of the movie instead concerns Mothra's guardians – two tiny twin girls – and the greedy businessman who covets them. This is cute, though a sober reminder of the campness that would later give the genre a bad name. KB *Japanese dubbed.*

Frankie Sakai *"Bulldog" Tsinchan/Junichiro Fukada* • Hiroshi Koizumi *Dr Shinichi Chujo* • Kyoko Kagawa *Photographer Michi Hanamura* • Emi Ito *Mothra's priestess* • Yumi Ito *Mothra's priestess* ■ *Dir* Ishiro Honda [Inoshiro Honda] • *Scr* Shinichi Sekizawa, Robert Myerson (English dialogue), from a story by Shinichiro Nakamura, Takehiko Fukunaga, Yoshie Hotta as published in *Asahi Shimbun*

Motor Psycho ★★ 18

Crime drama 1965 · US · BW · 72min

In this slightly more tasteful companion to sexploitation director Russ Meyer's legendary *Faster, Pussycat! Kill! Kill!*, a three-man gang of bikers led by deranged Vietnam veteran Stephen Oliver bring terror, rape and mayhem to a small town. Country vet Alex Rocco teams up with Meyer regular Haji to take revenge on the hoodlums. Not as wild or as sordid as your typical Meyer melodrama, this homage to *The Wild One* is one of the mammary maestro's less memorable offerings. AJ *Violence, sexual situations, swearing.* **DVD**

Haji *Ruby Bonner* • Alex Rocco *Cory Maddox* • Stephen Oliver *Brahmin* • Joseph Cellini *Dante* ■ *Dir* Russ Meyer • *Scr* William E Sprague, Russ Meyer, from a story by Russ Meyer, James Griffith, Hal Hopper • *Cinematographer* Russ Meyer

Motorama ★★★★ 15

Fantasy road movie comedy 1991 · US · Colour · 85min

Director Barry Shils's weird and wonderful road movie is an undervalued gem. Starring a Who's Who of B-movie cultdom, this highly engaging oddity follows the bizarre exploits of ten-year-old Gus (Jordan Christopher Michael) who drives across a mythical kingdom in a car customised with wooden leg extenders (so he can reach the pedals) in search of cards given free at Chimera gas stations. If he collects the eight cards that spell the word "motorama" he'll win $1 million. He traverses the strange terrain populated by eccentric adults, ageing all the time as his innocence is

destroyed by the darkly comic encounters. AJ

Jordan Christopher Michael *Gus* • Martha Quinn *Bank teller* • Susan Tyrrell *Bartender* • John Diehl *Phil* • Robert Picardo *Jerry the policeman* • Michael J Pollard *Lou* • Sandy Baron *Kidnapping husband* • Mary Woronov *Kidnapping wife* • Drew Barrymore *Fantasy girl* • Meat Loaf *Vern* • Jack Nance *Motel clerk* ■ *Dir* Barry Shils • *Scr* Joseph Minion

The Motorcycle Diaries ★★★★★ 15

Biographical road movie drama 2004 · US/UK/Fr · Colour · 120min

It started as a fun road trip around South America for two Argentinian friends in 1952, but the social struggles and injustices witnessed en route awakened their political consciousness – and in the case of Ernesto "Che" Guevara de la Serna sealed his future as a revolutionary icon. Director Walter Salles's remarkably involving biography humanises Che, portraying the man rather than a propagandist myth. By turns funny (witness the duo's pick-up lines), lyrical (the gorgeously photographed locations in Argentina, Chile and Peru) and moving (their ultimate destination, the leper colony), Salles's film is astonishing in its emotional and physical scope. AJ *Spanish +subtitles. Swearing.* **DVD** **Blu**

Gael García Bernal *Ernesto Guevara de la Serna* • Rodrigo de la Serna *Alberto Granado* • Mía Maestro *Chichina Ferreyra* • Gustavo Bueno *Dr Hugo Pesce* • Jorge Chiarella *Dr Bresciani* • Mercedes Morán *Celia de la Serna* ■ *Dir* Walter Salles • *Scr* José Rivera, from the memoirs by Ernesto Che Guevara, from the memoirs *With Che through Latin America* by Alberto Granado

Motorcycle Gang ★ PG

Drama 1957 · US · BW · 77min

Four years after Marlon Brando terrorised a town in *The Wild One*, this film breezed into drive-in cinemas, double-billed with Roger Corman's *Sorority Girl*. Compared to the Brando picture, this is a pink Lambretta with a puncture – a daft, woodenly-acted and underwritten saga about teenagers and a police-organised bikers' club. AT *Violence, swearing.* **DVD**

Anne Neyland *Terry* • Steven Terrell *Randy* • John Ashley *Nick* • Carl Switzer [Carl "Alfalfa" Switzer] *Speed* • Raymond Hatton *Uncle Ed* • Russ Bender *Joe* • Jean Moorhead *Marilyn* ■ *Dir* Edward L Cahn • *Scr* Lou Rusoff

Mouchette ★★★★★ 15

Tragedy 1966 · Fr · BW · 77min

A documentary fidelity underpins Robert Bresson's rigorous, though accessible, adaptation of Georges Bernanos's novel. Mouchette (Nadine Nortier) inhabits a world of spiritual and physical brutality. School and family offer nothing, and the comfort of strangers leads to rejected charity and rape, providing solace through cruelty. With sparse dialogue, this elliptical film never sentimentalises and contains Bresson's most lyrical sequence when, from a single act of generosity, Nortier relishes a dodgem ride, rebelling against her pious, alcoholic father and God. The climax is devastating, compassionate and powerful. BB *French +subtitles. Swearing, violence, a sex scene.* **DVD** **Blu**

Nadine Nortier *Mouchette* • Marie Cardinal *Mother* • Paul Hébert *Father* • Jean Vimenet *Mathieu* • Jean-Claude Guilbert *Arsène* ■ *Dir* Robert Bresson • *Scr* Robert Bresson, from the novel *Nouvelle Histoire de Mouchette* by Georges Bernanos

Moulin Rouge ★★

Silent melodrama 1928 · UK · BW · 90min

Using German production facilities and creative personnel and opening with a long portrait of Paris by night, this silent drama – one of the costliest ever made in Britain – turns into a melodrama about a stripper whose aristocratic boyfriend plans to marry her own daughter, then decides to kill himself in his racing car. The film was heavily cut between its European and American premieres; when the original version was restored, it was given a jazz

soundtrack specially composed by Mike Westbrook and performed by the Matrix Ensemble. AT

Olga Tschechowa *Parysia* • Eve Gray *Margaret, her daughter* • Jean Bradin *Andre* • Georges Treville *Father* ■ *Dir/Scr* EA Dupont

Moulin Rouge ★★★★ PG

Biographical drama 1952 · US/UK · Colour · 114min

The first 20 minutes of this movie are truly exhilarating, with cancan dancers, amazing lookalike re-creations of period characters and a magnificent sense of the vibrancy of 1880s Paris. This segment is one of director John Huston's finest achievements, and rightly helped the film win its Oscars for best art direction and best costume design. The film then goes on to tell the morbid tale of artist Henri de Toulouse-Lautrec, memorably played by José Ferrer. The women in his life are well cast, notably an unusually credible Zsa Zsa Gabor, but the real co-star is Georges Auric's lovely main theme. TS **DVD**

José Ferrer *Henri de Toulouse-Lautrec/Comte de Toulouse-Lautrec* • Colette Marchand *Marie Charlet* • Suzanne Flon *Myriamme Hayem* • Zsa Zsa Gabor *Jane Avril* • Katherine Kath *La Goulue* • Claude Nollier *Countess de Toulouse-Lautrec* ■ *Dir* John Huston • *Scr* Anthony Veiller, John Huston, from the novel by Pierre La Mure • *Cinematographer* Oswald Morris • *Art Directors* Paul Sheriff, Marcel Vertes • *Costume Designer* Marcel Vertes

Moulin Rouge! ★★★★ 12

Musical romantic drama 2001 · US/Aus · Colour · 122min

This opulent, no-holds-barred and multilayered musical revolves around a simple story: struggling writer Ewan McGregor falls in love with beautiful courtesan Nicole Kidman at the famous Parisian nightclub of the title, but their love is threatened by her tuberculosis, as well as the fact she is betrothed to unscrupulous duke Richard Roxburgh. This is wrapped up in an audacious mix of traditional and contemporary song and staged with a near-insane visual ambition by Baz Luhrmann. You will either fall in love with every camp flourish, or find yourself soon exhausted. A singular achievement either way. AC *Some violence, sexual references.* **DVD** **Blu**

Nicole Kidman *Satine* • Ewan McGregor *Christian* • John Leguizamo *Toulouse-Lautrec* • Jim Broadbent *Zidler* • Richard Roxburgh *Duke of Worcester* • Kylie Minogue *Green Fairy* ■ *Dir* Baz Luhrmann • *Scr* Baz Luhrmann, Craig Pearce • *Music* Craig Armstrong • *Production Designer* Catherine Martin • *Costume Designers* Catherine Martin, Angus Strathie

The Mountain ★★★ U

Drama 1956 · US · Colour · 104min

When a plane crashes on top of a mountain, vile wastrel Robert Wagner plans to loot it with the help of his older brother, Spencer Tracy. What follows is a well-made, heavily symbolic drama about greed and the nature of heroism, further complicated by the fact that one person survives the plane crash. The survivor, an Indian girl, is played by Anna Kashfi, who was chosen for the part because she was skinny, and therefore less of a burden for Tracy to carry down the mountain. Shortly afterwards Kashfi became Mrs Marlon Brando, though the marriage was short-lived. AT

Spencer Tracy *Zachary Teller* • Robert Wagner *Chris Teller* • Claire Trevor *Marie* • William Demarest *Father Belacchi* • Barbara Darrow *Simone* • Richard Arlen *Rivial* • EG Marshall *Solange* • Anna Kashfi *Hindu girl* ■ *Dir* Edward Dmytryk • *Scr* Ranald MacDougall, from the novel by Henri Troyat

The Mountain Road ★★ U

Second World War drama 1960 · US · BW · 102min

The great James Stewart is always worth watching, but even he could be defeated by weak material and feeble direction. He does what he can here, but this overlong war drama set in a very Hollywood-backlot China as the Second World War nears its end remains one of his least successful

vehicles. Director Daniel Mann has problems with the tone, and Stewart looks uncomfortable. TS

James Stewart *Major Baldwin* • Lisa Lu *Madame Sue-Mei Hung* • Glenn Corbett *Collins* • Harry Morgan *Michaelson* • Frank Silvera *General Kwan* • James Best *Niergaard* ■ *Dir* Daniel Mann • *Scr* Alfred Hayes, from the novel by Theodore White

Mountains of the Moon ★★★ 15

Historical adventure 1989 · US · Colour · 130min

Five Easy Pieces director Bob Rafelson is not perhaps the first film-maker you would associate with a tale of Victorian explorers bonding manfully in the search for the source of the Nile. Yet he turned this long-cherished project into a stirring, offbeat and often compelling adventure. Patrick Bergin (as the adventurer Richard Burton) and Iain Glen (as the aristocratic John Hanning Speke) are both excellent, and there are neat turns from Richard E Grant and Bernard Hill as Dr Livingstone. DP *Violence, nudity.* **DVD**

Patrick Bergin *Richard Burton* • Iain Glen *John Hanning Speke* • Richard E Grant *Laurence Oliphant* • Fiona Shaw *Isabel Arundell* • John Savident *Lord Murchison* • James Villiers *Lord Oliphant* • Adrian Rawlins *Edward* • Peter Vaughan *Lord Houghton* • Delroy Lindo *Mabruki* • Bernard Hill *Dr Livingstone* ■ *Dir* Bob Rafelson • *Scr* William Harrison, Bob Rafelson, from the novel by William Harrison and the journals by Richard Burton, John Hanning Speke

Mourning Becomes Electra ★★★

Melodrama 1947 · US · BW · 159min

A heavy-duty adaptation of Eugene O'Neill's Civil War play based on Aeschylus's *Oresteia*, this is an impressive but over-ambitious and terribly stagey attempt from director Dudley Nichols. Rosalind Russell is miscast in the lead, having neither the range nor the intensity for Lavinia, and the mix 'n' match gathering of distinguished US and European thespians doesn't gel, but there's no denying that, for Hollywood, getting this made at all ranked as a major achievement. TS

Rosalind Russell *Lavinia Mannon* • Michael Redgrave *Orin Mannon* • Raymond Massey *Ezra Mannon* • Katina Paxinou *Christine Mannon* • Leo Genn *Adam Brent* • Kirk Douglas *Peter Niles* • Nancy Coleman *Hazel Niles* • Henry Hull *Seth Beckwith* ■ *Dir* Dudley Nichols • *Scr* Dudley Nichols, from the play by Eugene O'Neill

The Mouse and His Child ★★ U

Animation 1977 · US · Colour · 80min

Animation is at its best when propelled by imaginative action. But American animators Charles Swenson and Fred Wolf, perhaps worshipping at the shrine of British costume drama, overdo the chitchat in this feature-length cartoon about two toy mice and their attempts to become self-winding. There are some sequences which border on the lively, though, and the distinctive vocal intelligence of Peter Ustinov also freshens up the character of Manny the rat. JM

Peter Ustinov *Manny* • Cloris Leachman *Euterpe* • Sally Kellerman *Seal* • Andy Devine *Frog* • Alan Barzman *Mouse* • Marcy Swenson *Mouse child* ■ *Dir* Fred Wolf, Chuck Swenson [Charles Swenson] • *Scr* Carol Mon Pere, from the novel by Russell Hoban

The Mouse on the Moon ★★ U

Comedy 1963 · UK · Colour · 86min

The combination of a witty Michael Pertwee script, the exuberant direction of Richard Lester and the unique talents of Margaret Rutherford would normally have been enough to guarantee comic gold. But, perhaps because Peter Sellers in a triple role was a hard act to follow, this sequel to *The Mouse That Roared* never gets off the ground. Fitfully amusing, it wastes a splendid cast. DP

Margaret Rutherford *The Grand Duchess Gloriana* • Ron Moody *Mountjoy* • Bernard Cribbins *Vincent* • David Kossoff *Kokintz* • Terry-

Thomas *Spender* • June Ritchie *Cynthia* • John Le Mesurier *British delegate* ■ *Dir* Richard Lester • *Scr* Michael Pertwee, from the novel by Leonard Wibberley

The Mouse That Roared ★★★ⓤ

Comedy 1959 · UK · Colour · 79min

This wry little comedy opens brightly, but quickly loses direction as its one joke is stretched to breaking point. The idea of a tiny country declaring war on America to benefit from aid in defeat is a lovely one, but not even Peter Sellers in three widely differing roles can compensate for the longueurs that occupy the film's final hour. Jean Seberg is wasted in decorous support. DP *DVD*

Peter Sellers *Tully Bascombe/Grand Duchess Gloriana XII/PM Count Mountjoy* • Jean Seberg *Helen* • David Kossoff *Professor Kokintz* • William Hartnell *Will* • Leo McKern *Benter* • MacDonald Parke *Snippet* • Timothy Bateson *Roger* ■ *Dir* Jack Arnold • *Scr* Roger MacDougall, Stanley Mann, from the novel *The Wrath of Grapes* by Leonard Wibberley

Mousehunt ★★★★ⓅⒼ

Comedy 1997 · US · Colour · 93min

In this energetic and highly inventive comedy, hapless brothers Nathan Lane and Lee Evans inherit a valuable old house but find it is already occupied by a pesky rodent. There's stacks of Laurel and Hardy-style visual comedy as the pair wreak havoc in their bid to rid themselves of the furry fiend, though adults may prefer Christopher Walken's hilarious turn as an exterminator. The darker touches might upset younger children, and the film is definitely not for viewers with a phobia of rodents. But for sheer verve, this family entertainment is hard to beat. JB Swearing. *DVD*

Nathan Lane *Ernie Smuntz* • Lee Evans *Lars Smuntz* • Christopher Walken *Caesar* • Maury Chaykin *Alexander Falko* • Vicki Lewis *April Smuntz* • Eric Christmas *The lawyer* • William Hickey *Rudolf Smuntz* ■ *Dir* Gore Verbinski • *Scr* Adam Rifkin

The Mouth Agape ★★★★⑫

Drama 1974 · Fr · Colour · 83min

Shot in a series of intense long takes, this movingly natural drama explores the effect the news that she has terminal cancer has on 50-year-old Monique Mélinand's philandering husband and impotent son. Exploring the connection between sex and death and the inextricable bonds that somehow keep unhappy couples together, Maurice Pialat's analysis of physical and emotional pain is never moralistic or sentimental. DP French +subtitles. *DVD*

Monique Melinand *Mother* • Hubert Deschamps *Father* • Philippe Léotard *Philippe* • Nathalie Baye *Nathalie* ■ *Dir/Scr* Maurice Pialat

Mouth to Mouth ★★★

Black comedy thriller 1995 · Sp · Colour · 97min

Actor Javier Bardem, after a spell of unemployment, devotes his talent to a phone sex company. Unfortunately, his most regular callers are all male! When Aitana Sanchez-Gijon suggests a rendezvous, he jumps at the opportunity – and walks straight into a ploy to enrage her unfaithful husband. Director Manuel Gomez Pereira gives his Spanish peer Almodóvar a real run for his money with a compelling, cheeky and genuinely funny film. LH Spanish +subtitles.

Javier Bardem *Victor Ventura* • Jose Maria Flotats *Ricardo/Bill* • Aitana Sanchez-Gijon *Amanda* • Maria Barranco *Angela* • Myriam Mézières *Sheila* • Fernando Guillen-Cuervo *Raul* ■ *Dir* Manuel Gomez Pereira • *Scr* Manuel Gomez Pereira, Joaquín Oristrell, Juan Luis Iborra, Naomi Wise

Mouth to Mouth ★★⑮

Social drama 2005 · UK/Ger · Colour · 107min

Ellen Page proves that her Oscar nomination for *Juno* was anything but a fluke with her performance in writer/director Alison Murray's well-meaning feature debut. Page overcomes the shortcomings of the material to impress as

a rootless teenager travelling around Europe who finds a purpose in Berlin within a cultish group. Drawing on her own experiences living with various political activist groups, Murray is at her most persuasive when exploring the crises that drove the various group members into dropping out. DP Swearing, sex scenes, drug references. *DVD*

Ellen Page *Sherry* • Natasha Wightman *Rose* • Eric Thal *Harry* • August Diehl *Tiger* • Diana Greenwood *Dog* • Beatrice Brown *Nancy* ■ *Dir/Scr* Alison Murray

Move Over, Darling ★★★★ⓤ

Comedy 1963 · US · Colour · 99min

This Doris Day classic – a remake of 1940's *My Favorite Wife* – features the star as a woman who returns from a desert island to find that her husband James Garner has remarried. Providing perfect support for Day and Garner are Polly Bergen as the "other woman" and Chuck Connors as the hunk who was marooned with Day. Stealing the show, however, is the wonderful Thelma Ritter as Day's outspoken mother-in-law. Day's popularity suffered from the onset of the sexual revolution in the mid-1960s when her wholesome image seemed out of step with the time, but this film shows how her great talent has endured. SH *DVD*

Doris Day *Ellen Wagstaff Arden* • James Garner *Nicholas Arden* • Polly Bergen *Bianca Steele Arden* • Thelma Ritter *Grace Arden* • Elliott Reid *Dr Herman Schlick* • Don Knotts *Shoe salesman* • Chuck Connors *Stephen "Adam" Burkett* • Fred Clark ■ *Dir* Michael Gordon • *Scr* Hal Kanter, Jack Sher, from the film *My Favorite Wife* by Bella Spewack, Samuel Spewack, from a story by Leo McCarey, Samuel Spewack, Bella Spewack

Movers and Shakers ★⑮

Comedy 1985 · US · Colour · 76min

Charles Grodin is undoubtedly a superb comic actor who never really gets the material worthy of his talents. With this woeful comedy, however, he really only has himself to blame, as he wrote and co-produced it. A wonderful cast (Walter Matthau, Steve Martin, Gilda Radner, Vincent Gardenia) is reduced to mugging furiously in a supposedly satirical look at the movie business. JF Swearing.

Walter Matthau *Joe Mulholland* • Charles Grodin *Herb Derman* • Vincent Gardenia *Saul Gritz* • Tyne Daly *Nancy Derman* • Steve Martin *Fabio Longio* • Bill Macy *Sid Spokane* • Gilda Radner *Livia Machado* • Michael Lerner *Arnie* • Penny Marshall *Reva* ■ *Dir* William Asher • *Scr* Charles Grodin

Movie Crazy ★★★ⓤ

Comedy 1932 · US · BW · 79min

One of the great silent film clowns, Harold Lloyd was a master of physical comedy whose exploits delighted and thrilled early audiences. Made later in his career, this is undoubtably his best talkie. Lloyd plays Harold Hall, an unassuming type who yearns to be in the movies and gets his break when he meets starlet Constance Cummings. The brilliant set pieces include the famous sequence in which Lloyd wears a magician's suit to a swanky ball, only to find it contains more than he bargained for. DF

Harold Lloyd *Harold Hall* • Constance Cummings *Mary Sears* • Kenneth Thomson *Vance, a gentleman heavy* ■ *Dir* Clyde Bruckman • *Scr* Agnes Christine Johnston, John Grey, Felix Adler, Vincent Lawrence

Movie 43 ★★⑮

Comedy 2013 · US · Colour · 94min

If you can leave moral outrage at the cinema door, you'll likely laugh like a drain at this star-packed scatological collection of fake clips, skits and ads. With twelve directors, including Peter Farrelly (*There's Something about Mary*) and Brett Ratner (*Rush Hour*), it's inevitably a hit-and-miss hotchpotch of a film, with a paper-thin wraparound plot. But it does prove that Hugh Jackman, Halle Berry, Kate Winslet, Richard Gere, Gerard Butler, Emma Stone,

Naomi Watts, Uma Thurman and the rest have a sense of humour – though maybe one that somewhat outstrips their sense of taste. DA Swearing, sexual references, some violence, nudity. *DVD* *BL*

Hugh Jackman *Davis* • Kate Winslet *Beth* • Naomi Watts *Samantha* • Anna Faris *Vanessa* • Emma Stone *Veronica* • Uma Thurman *Lois Lane* • Halle Berry *Emily* • Gerard Butler *Chaun* • Richard Gere *Boss* ■ *Dir* Peter Farrelly, Will Graham, Steve Carr, Griffin Dunne, James Duffy, Brett Ratner, Steven Brill, Elizabeth Banks (2), James Gunn (2), Rusty Cundieff, Patrik Forsberg, Jonathan van Tulleken • *Scr* Rocky Russo, Jeremy Sosenko et al

Movie Movie ★★★ⓅⒼ

Comedy 1978 · US · BW and Colour · 101min

Stanley Donen's attempt to recapture the spirit of 1930s double-bills is in the form of two B-movies – a boxing melodrama, *Dynamite Hands*, and a backstage musical, *Baxter's Beauties of 1933*. Donen even offers a trailer in the middle. It's a smart idea that all film buffs will warm to, even if the execution doesn't quite do justice to the concept. It was one of several movies at the time – such as *Nickelodeon* and *Silent Movie* – that cashed in on the perceived nostalgia for old movies, but all that this inspired was some bad jokes from critics – "Lousy, Lousy", for instance. It's actually better than that and the musical sequence has some delectable moments. AT

George C Scott *Gloves Malloy/Spats Baxter* • Trish Van Devere *Betsy McGuire/Isobel Stewart* • Barbara Harris *Trixie Lane* ■ *Dir* Stanley Donen • *Scr* Larry Gelbart, Sheldon Keller

Moving ★⑮

Comedy 1988 · US · Colour · 85min

Director Alan Metter appears perfectly content to replace bona fide comedy with Richard Pryor's exaggerated racket in this lame suburban farce. Showing off is no substitute for acting, and letting Pryor roam free is a big mistake. Desperation sinks its jaws into this mediocrity at an early stage, as director and star latch on to anything in the vain hope of laughter. Children, removal men and Randy Quaid (playing a lawn-trimming slob) are all pushed into service, to meagre effect. JM Swearing.

Richard Pryor *Arlo Pear* • Beverly Todd *Monica Pear* • Dave Thomas *Gary Marcus* • Dana Carvey *Brad Williams* • Randy Quaid *Frank/Cornell Crawford* • Stacey Dash *Casey Pear* • Raphael Harris *Marshall Pear* • Ishmael Harris *Randy Pear* ■ *Dir* Alan Metter • *Scr* Andy Breckman

Moving Violations ★⑮

Comedy 1985 · US · Colour · 85min

It takes some skill to aim even more downmarket than *Police Academy*, but this dire cash-in certainly succeeds in that respect. The story revolves around the usual lovable collection of anarchic misfits who run rings around the establishment when they are sentenced to traffic school. James Keach, Sally Kellerman and Jennifer Tilly have doubtless erased this from their CVs. JF Swearing.

John Murray *Dana Cannon* • Jennifer Tilly *Amy Hopkins* • James Keach *Deputy Halik* • Sally Kellerman *Judge Nedra Henderson* • Brian Backer *Scott Greeber* • Ned Eisenberg *Wink Barnes* • Clara Peller *Emma Jean* ■ *Dir* Neal Israel • *Scr* Neal Israel, Pat Proft, from a story by Paul & Sharon Boorstin

Mozart's Sister ★★★⑫Ⓐ

Period drama 2010 · Fr · Colour · 120min

Like *Amadeus*, this wintry, melancholic period piece addresses a little known aspect of Mozart's life, but this one takes fewer liberties with the facts. It's set in the 1760s when Wolfgang (David Moreau) is still a child prodigy and on the road in Europe performing at various royal courts with talented older sister Nannerl (Marie Féret). It's a moving account of frustrated artistic ambition, and Féret is terrific in what is very much a family affair; it's written and directed by her father René, while her little sister Lisa plays her best friend Louise, one of the French king's forgotten children. JF In French. Swearing, a sex scene.

Marie Féret *Nannerl Mozart* • Marc Barbé *Leopold Mozart* • Delphine Chuillot *Anna-Maria Mozart* • David Moreau *Wolfgang Mozart* • Clovis Fouin *Le Dauphin* • Lisa Féret *Louise de France* ■ *Dir/Scr* René Féret

Mrs 'arris Goes to Paris ★★★

Comedy 1992 · US · Colour · 97min

This is one of those projects that spent decades doing the Hollywood rounds before finally being made as a TV movie. Angela Lansbury is the housekeeper who saves and saves so she can fulfil her lifelong dream of going to Paris and buying a Christian Dior dress. Lightweight stuff indeed, but Lansbury and co-stars Diana Rigg and Omar Sharif all seem to be having so much fun you can't help but laugh along with them. JB

Angela Lansbury *Mrs Harris* • Omar Sharif *Marquis DeChassange* • Diana Rigg *Madame Colbert* • Lothaire Bluteau *André* • John Savident *Armand* • Lila Kaye *Mrs Butterfield* • Tamara Gorski *Natasha* ■ *Dir* Anthony Shaw [Anthony Pullen Shaw] • *Scr* John Hawkesworth, from the novella by Paul Gallico

Mrs Brown ★★★★★ⓅⒼ

Historical drama
1997 · UK/US/Ire · Colour · 100min

Judi Dench and Billy Connolly are a wonderfully regal double-act in this perceptive blend of fact and fiction. The story examines the relationship between Queen Victoria and her Scottish gillie John Brown, who audaciously dispelled her gloom after the death of Prince Albert and with whom she became so close that gossips gave her his name. The Oscar-nominated Dench provides a wonderfully dignified counter-balance to comedian Connolly, whose forthright bluntness causes consternation among her tradition-bound household staff. Director John Madden and scriptwriter Jeremy Brock have created an engrossing account of an attachment that might have fulfilled itself romantically had it not been for the conventions of the time. TH *DVD*

Judi Dench *Queen Victoria* • Billy Connolly *John Brown* • Antony Sher *Benjamin Disraeli* • Geoffrey Palmer *Henry Ponsonby* • Richard Pasco *Doctor Jenner* • David Westhead *Bertie, Prince of Wales* • Gerard Butler *Archie Brown* • Bridget McConnel *Lady Ely* • Georgie Glen *Lady Churchill* ■ *Dir* John Madden • *Scr* Jeremy Brock, from an idea by George Rosie

Mrs Brown's Boys D'Movie ★★★⑮

Comedy 2014 · Ire/UK · Colour · 90min

Those who dislike the sitcom won't like "d'movie", but there is more to *Mrs Brown* than meets the eye. Brendan O'Carroll's alter ego is brash and slightly off-putting to look at, but she is also a likeable heroine despite her coarse manners and potty mouth because she puts her kids first. And, in this big screen outing, she tries to save Dublin's historic Moore Street Market, too. The absence of an audience robs the formula of some of its fizz, but the spirit of anarchy remains to keep fans tickled. SP Swearing, sexual references, brief nudity. *DVD* *BL*

Brendan O'Carroll *Agnes Brown* • Jennifer Gibney *Cathy Brown* • Fiona O'Carroll *Maria Brown* • Eilish O'Carroll *Winnie McGoogan* ■ *Dir* Ben Kellett • *Scr* Brendan O'Carroll

Mrs Caldicot's Cabbage War ★★⑫

Comedy drama 2000 · UK · Colour · 106min

This adaptation of Vernon Coleman's novel has the feel of an overgrown, overfamiliar sitcom. Initially the story shows promise, with the formerly browbeaten Pauline Collins embracing widowhood with vengeful gusto. However, once avaricious son Peter Capaldi consigns her to John Alderton's rest home, the gallows humour is replaced by a glutinous plea for a revision of society's attitude towards the elderly. DP *DVD*

M

Pauline Collins *Thelma Caldicot* • Peter Capaldi *Derek Caldicot, her son* • Anna Wilson-Jones *Veronica Caldicot* • Gwenllian Davies *Audrey* • Sheila Reid *Joyce* • Frank Mills *Leslie* • Frank Middlemass *Bernard* • John Alderton *Hawksmoor* ■ *Dir* Ian Sharp • *Scr* Malcolm Stone, from the novel by Vernon Coleman

Mrs Dalloway ★★★ PG
Period drama
1997 · US/UK/Neth · Colour · 93min

A day in the life of Vanessa Redgrave, the emotionally troubled wife of an MP, and Rupert Graves, a shell-shocked war veteran. They never meet, but fate still brings them together at the end of a series of flashbacks that sketch in Redgrave's early life and feature Natascha McElhone as her younger self. Adapting Virginia Woolf's intricate novel, Eileen Atkins juggles time and emotional choices with skill, while the performances are uniformly excellent. Yet it's also rather smug. AT Brief nudity. *DVD*

Vanessa Redgrave *Mrs Clarissa Dalloway* • Natascha McElhone *Young Clarissa Dalloway* • Rupert Graves *Septimus Warren Smith* • Michael Kitchen *Peter Walsh* • Alan Cox *Young Peter Walsh* • Sarah Badel *Lady Rosseter* • Lena Headey *Young Sally* • John Standing *Richard Dalloway* ■ *Dir* Marleen Gorris • *Scr* Eileen Atkins, from the novel by Virginia Woolf

Mrs Delafield Wants to Marry ★★★★
Romantic comedy 1986 · US · Colour · 94min

This delightful romantic TV comedy features the incomparable Katharine Hepburn as a rich, high society widow who scandalises her friends and family when she decides to marry her divorced, Jewish doctor (Harold Gould). As usual, Hepburn is watchable in a role created for her by Broadway playwright James Prideaux. The premise is hardly original, but the execution is deft and the underlying issues of race and class bigotry are dealt with in an entertaining way. MC

Katharine Hepburn *Mrs Delafield* • Harold Gould *Dr Marvin Elias* • Denholm Elliott *George Parker* • Brenda Forbes *Gladys Parker* • David Ogden Stiers *Horton* ■ *Dir* George Schaefer • *Scr* James Prideaux

Mrs Doubtfire ★★★★ PG
Comedy drama 1993 · US · Colour · 120min

This knowing blend of comedy and common sense is family entertainment par excellence. Aided by Oscar-winning make-up, Robin Williams gives one of the performances of his career as an actor who disguises himself as a Scottish nanny to be close to his children after he splits from wife Sally Field. Director Chris Columbus reins in the Williams exuberance, while retaining enough of his quick-fire personality to ensure that just about every gag hits its target. DP Swearing. *DVD* *Blu*

Robin Williams *Daniel Hillard/Mrs Doubtfire* • Sally Field *Miranda Hillard* • Pierce Brosnan *Stu* • Harvey Fierstein *Frank* • Polly Holliday *Gloria* • Lisa Jakub *Lydia Hillard* • Matthew Lawrence *Chris Hillard* • Mara Wilson *Natalie Hillard* ■ *Dir* Chris Columbus • *Scr* Randi Mayem Singer, Leslie Dixon, from the novel *Alias Mrs Doubtfire* by Anne Fine • *Make-up* Ve Neill, Greg Cannom, Yolanda Toussieng

Mrs Henderson Presents ★★★ 12
Period drama based on a true story
2005 · UK/US · Colour · 98min

Stephen Frears directs this benign and only occasionally downbeat drama. Judi Dench stars as a wealthy widow with a gleeful sense of adventure, who buys a decrepit London theatre in 1937. With the help of impresario Vivian Van Damm (Bob Hoskins), she turns it into a money-spinner by showing nonstop vaudeville shows. When business slackens, the unlikely partners launch Britain's first all-nude revue. Dench delivers every one-liner with a tart but impish twinkle that's consistently winning, while Hoskins is also very effective. LF Swearing. *DVD*

Judi Dench *Mrs Laura Henderson* • Bob Hoskins *Vivian Van Damm* • Will Young *Bertie* • Christopher Guest *Lord Cromer* • Kelly Reilly

Maureen • Thelma Barlow *Lady Conway* • Anna Brewster *Doris* • Rosalind Halstead *Frances* ■ *Dir* Stephen Frears • *Scr* Martin Sherman, from the books *We Never Closed* by Sheila Van Damm and *Tonight and Every Night* by Vivian Van Damm, from an idea by David Rose, Kathy Rose

Mrs Lambert Remembers Love ★★★ PG
Drama 1991 · US · Colour · 89min

This heartfelt TV movie explores the strains placed on the bonds of family by Alzheimer's disease. Ellen Burstyn stars as a grandmother who flees from the authorities rather than be separated from her nine-year-old orphaned grandson. The performances of Burstyn and co-star Walter Matthau, as her close friend, elevate what could have been a mawkish melodrama, and it's capably directed by Matthau's son, Charles. MC

Walter Matthau *Clifford* • Ellen Burstyn *Lil Lambert* • Ryan Todd *Jared Lambert* • William Schallert *Sheriff Pomeroy* • Kathleen Garrett *Darlene* • Sherry Hursey *Etta Crue* ■ *Dir* Charles Matthau • *Scr* Janet Heaney

Mrs Mike ★★
Romantic drama 1949 · US · BW · 98min

At the end of the 19th century, Boston girl Evelyn Keyes ventures to the rugged north-west of Canada, where she meets and falls in love with Mountie Dick Powell. They marry, and our heroine sets about adjusting to an unfamiliar way of life. Louis King directs this sentimental drama that's neither memorable nor absorbing, but does have believable performances. RK

Dick Powell *Sergeant Mike Flannigan* • Evelyn Keyes *Kathy O'Fallon* • JM Kerrigan *Uncle John* • Angela Clarke *Sarah Carpentier* • John Miljan *Mr Howard* • Nan Boardman *Georgette Beauclaire* • Will Wright *Dr McIntosh* ■ *Dir* Louis King • *Scr* Alfred Lewis Levitt, DeWitt Bodeen, from the novel by Benedict Freedman, Nancy Freedman

Mrs Miniver ★★★★★ U
Classic wartime drama 1942 · US · BW · 128min

This superb wartime melodrama was "more valuable than the combined efforts of six army divisions", according to Winston Churchill. Greer Garson and Walter Pidgeon play the British couple suffering in the Second World War, bringing this country's plight to the American public, and today this MGM production is best viewed in that propagandist light. The film won six Oscars, including best picture, best actress and best direction for William Wyler, and it's easy to understand why. Trivia buffs might like to note that Garson's real-life lover at the time, Richard Ney, plays her son in this movie – the couple married the following year. The sequel *The Miniver Story*, filmed eight years later, is nowhere near as good. TS *DVD*

Greer Garson *Mrs Miniver* • Walter Pidgeon *Clem Miniver* • Teresa Wright *Carol Beldon* • Dame May Whitty *Lady Beldon* • Reginald Owen *Foley* • Henry Travers *Mr Ballard* • Richard Ney *Vin Miniver* • Henry Wilcoxon *Vicar* • Christopher Severn *Toby Miniver* ■ *Dir* William Wyler • *Scr* Arthur Wimperis, George Froeschel, James Hilton, Claudine West, from the novel by Jan Struther • *Cinematographer* Joseph Ruttenberg

Mrs Miracle ★★
Seasonal romantic fantasy
2009 · US · Colour · 95min

In this message-laden Christmas fantasy, Doris Roberts (*Everybody Loves Raymond*) stars as the multitasking housekeeper-cum-modern-day Mary Poppins, who works excessively speedy magic on an emotionally wounded widower (James Van Der Beek) and his unruly six-year-old twins. While the family's problems are solved in a rush, the film itself is surprisingly lethargic - even if Van Der Beek does enjoy the opportunity to showcase his sensitive side. SF

Doris Roberts *Mrs Emily Merkle* • James Van Der Beek *Seth Webster* • Erin Karpluk *Reba Maxwell* ■ *Dir* Michael M Scott [Michael Scott] • *Scr* David Golden, from the novel by Debbie Macomber

Mrs O'Malley and Mr Malone ★★★
Comedy mystery 1950 · US · BW · 69min

Outspoken Montana widow Marjorie Main, en route to collect a prize from a radio show, and small-time lawyer James Whitmore, chasing a client for money, meet on the train to New York, where they turn amateur sleuths when his errant client turns up as a corpse. A snappy, enjoyable comedy thriller with an excellent supporting cast, and a memorably eccentric rendition by Main (best known as Ma Kettle) of *Possum up a Gum Stump*. RK

Marjorie Main *Hattie O'Malley* • James Whitmore *John J Malone* • Ann Dvorak *Connie Kepplar* • Phyllis Kirk *Kay* • Fred Clark *Tim Marino* • Dorothy Malone *Lola Gillway* • Douglas Fowley *Steve Kepplar* ■ *Dir* Norman Taurog • *Scr* William Bowers, from a story by Craig Rice, Stuart Palmer

Mrs Palfrey at The Claremont ★★★ PG
Comedy drama 2005 · UK · Colour · 103min

In this genteel comedy drama, an elderly widow (Joan Plowright) checks in to a London hotel in the hope of gaining some independence. The fusty Claremont is not what she'd hoped for, but a chance meeting with a young writer (Rupert Friend) opens up her restricted world. Plowright is magnificent in her touching depiction of the loneliness, vulnerability and stoicism of old age. The problem, however, of such an affecting central performance is that it draws attention to every imperfection in her younger, less talented co-star. SuR *DVD*

Joan Plowright *Mrs Palfrey* • Rupert Friend *Ludovic Meyer* • Zoe Tapper *Gwendolyn* • Anna Massey *Mrs Arbuthnot* • Robert Lang *Mr Osborne* • Marcia Warren *Mrs Post* • Millicent Martin *Mrs De Salis* • Lorcan O'Toole *Desmond* ■ *Dir* Dan Ireland • *Scr* Ruth Sacks, from the novel by Elizabeth Taylor (2)

Mrs Parker and the Vicious Circle ★★★★ 15
Biographical drama
1994 · US · Colour and BW · 119min

You'll either love or loathe Jennifer Jason Leigh's mannered performance here as Dorothy Parker in this brilliant wit of the 1920s and 30s. But her portrayal is still a constant delight of looks and language in director Alan Rudolph's biographical drama about the Algonquin hotel's Round Table (which consisted of writers and celebrities who gathered around Parker). Her affair with Charles MacArthur (played here by Matthew Broderick) and her subsequent affairs and fractured marriage chime a note of doom and despair that counters the show-off cleverness of the rest. TH Swearing, nudity.

Jennifer Jason Leigh *Dorothy Parker* • Campbell Scott *Robert Benchley* • Matthew Broderick *Charles MacArthur* • Andrew McCarthy *Eddie Parker* • Tom McGowan *Alexander Woollcott* • Nick Cassavetes *Robert Sherwood* ■ *Dir* Alan Rudolph • *Scr* Alan Rudolph, Randy Sue Coburn

Mrs Parkington ★★
Drama 1944 · US · BW · 123min

This drama gained Greer Garson an Oscar nomination more deserved by the make-up department. She starts the picture as an octagenarian widow and matriarch who suffers from flashback disease, thereby revealing her early life as the brash mining-town girl who married Pidgeon's millionaire and became a society figure. In the original American version, Edward, Prince of Wales (played by Cecil Kellaway) is entranced by Garson, but British audiences were given Hugo Haas as a Balkan monarch to avoid offending Buckingham Palace. AE

Greer Garson *Susie Parkington* • Walter Pidgeon *Maj Augustus Parkington* • Edward Arnold *Amory Stilham* • Frances Rafferty *Jane Stilham* • Agnes Moorehead *Aspasia Conti* • Selena Royle *Mattie Trounsen* • Gladys Cooper *Alice, Duchess de Brancourt* • Lee Patrick *Madeleine* • Dan Duryea *Jack Stilham* ■ *Dir* Tay Garnett • *Scr* Robert Thoeren, Polly James, from the novel by Louis Bromfield • *Costume Designer* Irene

Mrs Pollifax - Spy ★
Spy comedy adventure
1970 · US · Colour · 110min

This unfunny parody brought Rosalind Russell's big screen career to an end. She had only herself and husband Frederick Brisson to blame, though, since she wrote it pseudonymously and he produced it and employed the undistinguished Leslie Martinson to direct. Russell plays a middle-aged woman who joins the CIA and embarks on a series of unlikely and over-energetic adventures. BB

Rosalind Russell *Emily Pollifax* • Darren McGavin *Johnny Farrell* • Nehemiah Persoff *General Berisha* • Harold Gould *Colonel Nexdhet* • Albert Paulsen *General Perdido* • John Beck *Sgt Lulash* ■ *Dir* Leslie Martinson [Leslie H Martinson] • *Scr* CA McKnight [Rosalind Russell], from the novel *The Unexpected Mrs Pollifax* by Dorothy Gilman

Mrs Ratcliffe's Revolution ★★★ 12
Period comedy drama
2007 · UK/Hun · Colour · 98min

After *Starter for 10* and *Sixty Six*, TV comedian Catherine Tate finally gets a major role in this adaptation of a true story. Like director Billie Eltringham (billed here as Bille), she comfortably balances comedy and tragedy as a humble Yorkshire housewife whose family relocates to communist East Germany in the late 1960s. Her husband (Iain Glen), a self-styled champion of the downtrodden working classes, spares little thought for his wife's struggle to raise two daughters under the oppressive regime. It's the domestic conflict rather than the political content that keeps you watching - a battle of wills between mum and elder daughter (Brittany Ashworth) is one of the stronger elements - and while the energy sometimes wavers, there's enough here to entertain the masses. SP Brief swearing. *DVD*

Catherine Tate *Dorothy Ratcliffe* • Iain Glen *Frank Ratcliffe* • Katharina Thalbach *Anna* • Brittany Ashworth *Alex Ratcliffe* • Jessica Barden *Mary Ratcliffe* • Heike Makatsch *Frau Unger* • Christian Brassington *Thomas* ■ *Dir* Bille Eltringham [Billie Eltringham] • *Scr* Bridget O'Connor, Peter Straughan, from a story by Maggie Norris

Mrs Santa Claus ★★★ U
Seasonal musical 1996 · US · Colour · 86min

Jerry Herman, the man responsible for *Hello Dolly* and *Mame*, composed the songs for this brisk TV musical comedy that tempers its seasonal mush with a little social history. Set in 1910, its central themes are women's suffrage and child labour. But don't be put off, because Angela Lansbury is in fine fettle as Santa's feisty wife, whose determination to prove the efficiency of her star map lands her in the backstreets of New York. DP *DVD*

Angela Lansbury *Mrs Santa Claus* • Michael Jeter *Arvo* • Charles Durning *Santa Claus* • Terrence Mann *Augustus P Tavish* • Lynsey Bartilson *Nora* ■ *Dir* Terry Hughes • *Scr* Mark Saltzman

Mrs Soffel ★★★ PG
Biographical drama 1984 · US · Colour · 106min

Based on the true story of a prison warden's wife who fell in love with an inmate and plotted his escape, this turn-of-the-century costume romance is too dour for its own good. Australia's Gillian Armstrong directs the potentially passionate content with a cool detachment that mirrors the wintry landscapes across which the lovers flee, while Diane Keaton's contemporary style is also at odds with the piece. But there's plenty of appeal in the young Mel Gibson, appropriately seductive as the convicted murderer, and Matthew Modine is nicely cast as his dimwit brother. AME

Diane Keaton *Kate Soffel* • Mel Gibson *Ed Biddle* • Matthew Modine *Jack Biddle* • Edward Herrmann *Peter Soffel* • Trini Alvarado *Irene Soffel* • Jennie Dundas *Margaret Soffel* • Danny Corkill *Eddie Soffel* ■ *Dir* Gillian Armstrong • *Scr* Ron Nyswaner

Mrs Wiggs of the Cabbage Patch ★★

Melodrama   1934 · US · BW · 80min

Director Norman Taurog's film recounts the poverty-stricken but incident-packed existence of Pauline Lord and her five children, whose father has disappeared without trace. Always cheerful in the face of struggle, the family is helped by a local rich girl (Evelyn Venable). At times Dickensian in flavour, at others Chaplinesque, it's at its best in the second half when WC Fields arrives on the scene and courts family friend ZaSu Pitts. RK

Pauline Lord *Mrs Elvira Wiggs* · WC Fields *Mr C Ensworth Stubbins* · ZaSu Pitts *Miss Tabitha Hazy* · Evelyn Venable *Lucy Olcott* · Kent Taylor *Bob Redding* · Charles Middleton *Mr Bagby* · Donald Meek *Mr Hiram Wiggs* · Clara Lou Sheridan [Ann Sheridan] *Girl* ■ *Dir* Norman Taurog · *Scr* William Slavens McNutt, Jane Storm, from the play by Anne Crawford Flexner, from the novel by Alice Hegan Rice

Mrs Winterbourne ★★★ 12

Romantic comedy   1996 · US · Colour · 101min

This comic remake of the far more serious *No Man of Her Own* stars US talk-show queen Ricki Lake as a young girl with a baby on the way who, following a train crash, adopts the identity of the late Patricia Winterbourne. She is promptly whisked off to meet the rich Winterbourne family, who had never met their dead son's bride. Shirley MacLaine steals the show as the *grande dame* of the family, but Lake holds her own and there is nice support from Brendan Fraser as the brother-in-law with whom she falls in love. JB Swearing, sexual references. *DVD*

Shirley MacLaine *Grace Winterbourne* · Ricki Lake *Connie Doyle* · Brendan Fraser *Bill Winterbourne/Hugh Winterbourne* · Miguel Sandoval *Paco* · Loren Dean *Steve DeCunzo* · Peter Gerety *Father Brian* · Jane Krakowski *Christine* ■ *Dir* Richard Benjamin · *Scr* Phoef Sutton, Lisa-Marie Radano, from the novel *I Married a Dead Man* by Cornell Woolrich

Ms 45 ★★★ 18

Crime drama   1981 · US · Colour · 75min

Abel Ferrara was once Public Enemy No 1 as far as the UK censors were concerned: his first two movies ended up on the banned list. The notorious *Driller Killer* was the first; *Ms 45* was the second, and it's a far more accomplished affair. Zoe Tamerlis plays a mute woman who, after being raped twice in one day, decides to get her own back on mankind. It was billed as a feminist *Death Wish*, but it's a lot more disturbing than that, even if Ferrara and his regular scriptwriter Nicholas St John once again go overboard on the religious guilt. It was eventually approved for release, with a few minor cuts. JF

Zoe Tamerlis *Thana* · Bogey *Phil* · Albert Sinkys *Albert* · Darlene Stuto *Laurie* · Jimmy Laine [Abel Ferrara] *First rapist* · Peter Yellen *Second rapist* ■ *Dir* Abel Ferrara · *Scr* Nicholas St John

Much Ado about Nothing ★★★★ PG

Comedy drama   1993 · UK · Colour · 106min

In a real luvvies outing, the then married Kenneth Branagh and Emma Thompson decamp to Tuscany with pals to film an exciting, joyful and rollicking version of William Shakespeare's tale of frenetic wooing. Branagh, who stars and directs, gives the story an enormous *joie de vivre* and is aided by a star-studded supporting cast that includes Thompson's mother Phyllida Law, Imelda Staunton, Ben Elton, Keanu Reeves and Denzel Washington. SH Brief nudity. *DVD* *BL*

Kenneth Branagh *Benedick* · Richard Briers *Leonato* · Michael Keaton *Dogberry* · Denzel Washington *Don Pedro* · Robert Sean Leonard *Claudio* · Keanu Reeves *Don John* · Emma Thompson *Beatrice* · Kate Beckinsale *Hero* · Imelda Staunton *Margaret* · Phyllida Law *Ursula* · Ben Elton *Verges* ■ *Dir* Kenneth Branagh · *Scr* Kenneth Branagh, from the play by William Shakespeare

Much Ado about Nothing ★★★ 12

Romantic comedy   2012 · US · BW · 104min

Fans of *Buffy the Vampire Slayer* and *Angel* are likely to enjoy this resolutely lo-fi take on Shakespeare from Joss Whedon, the creator of those TV shows. The whimsical romance is all filmed in Whedon's own house and grounds, played out in modern dress (but with the original text) and filmed in luminous black and white, with Amy Acker and Alexis Denisof (who both appeared in *Angel*) as bickering exes Beatrice and Benedick. It may not be as sun-kissed or as star-laden as Kenneth Branagh's 1993 version, but this particular home movie wins on ensemble acting and sheer charm. GC Some swearing, a sex scene, drug abuse. *DVD* *BL*

Amy Acker *Beatrice* · Alexis Denisof *Benedick* · Nathan Fillion *Dogberry* · Sean Maher *Don John* · Fran Kranz *Claudio* · Jillian Morgese *Hero* ■ *Dir* Joss Whedon · *Scr* Joss Whedon, from Shakespeare's play · *Music* Joss Whedon

Much Too Shy ★★ U

Comedy   1942 · UK · BW · 88min

Although he was still Britain's biggest box-office attraction, George Formby was already showing signs of the novelty fatigue that would result in the collapse of his screen career four years later. Too bashful to paint anything below the neck, he gets into hot water when his portraits of three village matrons end up in a soap advertisement attached to nude torsos. The cheeky wit that informed so many of Formby's songs is to the fore in this contrived comedy. DP *DVD*

George Formby *George Andy* · Kathleen Harrison *Amelia Peabody* · Hilda Bayley *Lady Driscoll* · Eileen Bennett *Jackie Somers* · Joss Ambler *Sir George Driscoll* ■ *Dir* Marcel Varnel · *Scr* Ronald Frankau

Mud ★★★★ 12

Drama   2012 · US · Colour · 124min

Two 14-year-old boys encounter a fugitive hiding out on a small island in this rites-of-passage story from writer/director Jeff Nichols (*Take Shelter*). Continuing his transformation from heart-throb to compelling character actor, Matthew McConaughey plays the wanted man, who asks the lads (Tye Sheridan and Jacob Lofland) to help him reconnect with his longtime sweetheart (Reese Witherspoon). This is a junior adventure story echoing *Huckleberry Finn* and *Stand by Me*, a tale which is in no hurry to unfold, but which is beautifully done, exquisitely performed, and filled with terror and wonder. TJ Some violence, swearing, sexual references. *DVD* *BL*

Matthew McConaughey *Mud* · Tye Sheridan *Ellis* · Reese Witherspoon *Juniper* · Jacob Lofland *Neckbone* · Sam Shepard *Tom Blankenship* · Michael Shannon *Galen* ■ *Dir/Scr* Jeff Nichols

Muddy River ★★★★ PG

Drama   1981 · Jpn · BW · 103min

Clearly inspired by Yasujiro Ozu's delightful studies of childhood friendship, Kohei Oguri's Oscar-nominated debut makes striking use of its black-and-white imagery to evoke a sense of both nostalgic innocence and the grinding poverty that so many Japanese experienced, even at the height of the 1950s boom. As the nine-year-old son of comfortable restaurateurs, Nobutaka Asahara is touchingly awestruck as he learns some harsh lessons about class and sex from the widow who works as a prostitute on the houseboat she shares with her kids. Dramatically satisfying, visually authentic and beautifully played. DP Japanese +subtitles.

Nobutaka Asahara *Nobuo* · Takahiro Tamura *Shinpei* · Yumiko Fujita *Nobuo's mother* · Minoru Sakurai *Kiichi* ■ *Dir* Kchei Oguri · *Scr* Takako Shigemuri, from the novel by Teru Miyamoto

Mudhoney ★★★★ 18

Melodrama   1965 · US · BW · 92min

This early film by soft porn maestro Russ Meyer has been hailed as an undiscovered masterpiece, and it's easy to see why. Apart from some brief glimpses of nudity, this Southern melodrama, set in the Prohibition era, could easily have been made by any of Hollywood's all-time greats. The plot (desperate men feuding over sex and power on a farm) is straight out of a dime novel, but the action builds to a rivetingly horrible dénouement, while the high standard of photography and performances has rarely been equalled in low-budget exploitation. Among the best of its kind. DM *DVD*

Hal Hopper *Sidney Brenshaw* · Lorna Maitland *Clara Belle* · Antoinette Cristiani *Hannah Brenshaw* · John Furlong *Calif McKinney* · Stuart Lancaster *Lute Wade* ■ *Dir* Russ Meyer · *Scr* Raymond Friday Locke, William E Sprague · *Cinematographer* Walter Schenk

The Mudlark ★★★ U

Period drama   1950 · UK · BW · 99min

This achieved minor notoriety for its relatively daring casting, with noted Hollywood *grande dame* Irene Dunne playing Queen Victoria to Alec Guinness's elegant Disraeli. Dunne acquits herself well enough, and Guinness is superb, particularly in a long speech that seems to be uninterrupted by cutting - bravura screen acting indeed. The story is about one of those Oliver Twist-like foundlings, played here by Andrew Ray, and the sentimental plot is hard to take seriously. TS

Irene Dunne *Queen Victoria* · Alec Guinness *Benjamin Disraeli* · Andrew Ray *Wheeler, the mudlark* · Beatrice Campbell *Lady Emily Prior* · Finlay Currie *John Brown* · Anthony Steel *Lieutenant Charles McHatten* · Raymond Lovell *Sergeant Footman Naseby* ■ *Dir* Jean Negulesco · *Scr* Nunnally Johnson, from the novel by Theodore Bonnet

Mugabe and the White African ★★★ 12A

Documentary   2009 · UK · Colour · 94min

The collapse of Zimbabwe is a tragedy that's rarely reported as it's almost impossible to film there. This documentary is the exception, charting the courageous legal fight of an ageing white farmer who bought his farm after independence in 1980, spent 20 years paying off the loan and was then told that under President Mugabe's Land Reform Programme he must hand it over to the son of a government minister. It's a portrait of cruel folly, dressed up as reparation for colonial rule. But, by the end, you can't help wishing a documentary this powerful could be made about the plight of the majority of Zimbabweans, suffering as much if not more. DB *DVD*

■ *Dir* Lucy Bailey, Andrew Thompson

Mughal-e-Azam ★★★★ PG

Period epic   1960 · Ind · Colour and BW · 197min

Re-creating the feud between the Emperor Akbar and his son Salim over his passion for the low-born dancer, Anarkali, this is one of the undisputed classics of Bollywood cinema. It's also one of the most sensual, with the lavish period trappings providing a fabulous setting for the intense love scenes between Dilip Kumar and Madhubala. Indeed, it's this unforced juxtaposition between scale and intimacy that characterises K Asif's direction, although he's not slow to recognise the emotional value of a grandiose, full-colour set piece. DP Hindi +subtitles. *DVD*

Dilip Kumar *Prince Salim* · Madhubala *Anarkali* · Prithviraj [Prithviraj Kapoor] *Emperor Akbar* · Durga Khote *Empress Jodha Bai* ■ *Dir* K Asif · *Scr* Aman, K Asif, Kamal Amrohi, Wajahat Mirza, Ehsan Rizvi

Muhammad Ali: King of the World ★ PG

Biographical sports drama 2000 · US · Colour · 89min

This TV movie is the weakest of the plethora of Ali biopics. The sporting focus here is on the Cassius Clay era, as the former Olympic champion gears up for his tilt at the title against world heavyweight legend, Sonny Liston. Compelling material, but melodramatic, with neither Terrence

Dashon Howard nor Gary Dourdan credible as the boxer and his mentor. DP *DVD*

Terrence Howard *Cassius Clay* · Gary Dourdan *Malcolm X* · Saint Adeogba *Betty X* · Rodger Boyce *Bill McDonald* · Darryl Cox *Howard Cosell* · Blue Deckert *Gorgeous George* ■ *Dir* John Sacret Young · *Scr* John Sacret Young, from the non-fiction book *King of the World: Muhammad Ali and the Rise of an American Hero* by David Remnick

Muhammad Ali, the Greatest ★★★★ PG

Documentary   1974 · Fr · Colour and BW · 110min

The first segment of William Klein's seminal portrait of a sporting legend begins in the monochrome days of 1964 and chronicles the furore that surrounded the then Cassius Clay at the time of his notorious bouts with Sonny Liston. Accompanying him on the road and into the changing rooms, director Klein produces Direct Cinema at its most immediate and provides an intimate insight into the fighter's lifestyle, emerging showmanship and growing potency as a black superstar in the Civil Rights era. The second half of this superb biography was filmed a decade after Clay's triumphs over Liston, by which time he was known as Muhammad Ali and on his way to his greatest victory at the "Rumble in the Jungle" in Zaire. DP *DVD*

Muhammad Ali · George Foreman ■ *Dir* William Klein · *Cinematographer* [William Klein]

Mujhse Shaadi Karogi ★★★ PG

Romantic comedy   2004 · Ind · Colour · 156min

David Dhawan, known as Bollywood's king of comedy, directs this sparky romantic comedy set in the coastal town of Goa. Salman Khan and Akshay Kumar are the hunky lifeguard and his free-spirited flatmate who find themselves competing for the affections of aspiring designer Priyanka Chopra. The leads bounce off each other to good effect, but Rajpal Yadav steals the show in the dual role of an astrologer and his troublemaking biker twin. DP Hindi +subtitles. *DVD*

Salman Khan *Samir* · Priyanka Chopra *Rani* · Amrish Puri *Colonel Dugraj Singh* · Akshay Kumar *Sunny* · Satish Shah *Surya Prakash* · Rajpal Yadav *Raj/Paul* ■ *Dir* David Dhawan · *Scr* Anees Bazmee, Rumi Jaffrey

Mulan ★★★★ U

Animated musical adventure
1998 · US · Colour · 87min

Set in ancient China, this recounts the adventures of the eponymous heroine who dons men's clothes and goes to war to save her family honour. Some splendid set pieces, the inevitable love between Mulan and her brave captain, and the often uproarious presence of a snappy little dragon (voiced by Eddie Murphy) are the highlights. Aspects of the story go a bit over young children's heads, but it's an enthralling narrative for everyone else and there's plenty of slapstick fun to keep youngsters happy. A startling addition to the Disney studio's catalogue. A belated straight-to-video sequel followed in 2004. TH *DVD* *BL*

Ming-Na *Mulan* · Eddie Murphy *Mushu* · Lea Salonga *Mulan* · BD Wong *Shang* · Donny Osmond *Shang* · Miguel Ferrer *Shan-Yu* · Harvey Fierstein *Yao* · Miriam Margolyes *Matchmaker* · Pat Morita *Emperor* · George Takei *First ancestor* ■ *Dir* Barry Cook, Tony Bancroft · *Scr* Rita Hsiao, Christopher [Chris] Sanders, Philip LaZebnik, Raymond Singer, Eugenia Bostwick-Singer, from a story by Robert D San Souci

Mulan II ★★ U

Animated musical adventure
2004 · US · Colour · 75min

This amiable if underwhelming animated sequel set in ancient China sees plucky female warrior Mulan and her fiancé Shang called upon to help safeguard the empire from Mongol invaders. The main voice cast from the original film returns, with Mark Moseley doing a fair job of filling in for Eddie Murphy as the wise-cracking dragon Mushu. The themes of love, duty and

M

sacrifice are easy to digest, but the songs and action sequences are somewhat lacking in spark this time around. And it's disappointing that the feisty Mulan ends up here as just another damsel in distress. JH
DVD

Ming-Na *Mulan* • BD Wong *Shang* • Mark Moseley *Mushu* • Lucy Liu *Mei* • Harvey Fierstein *Yao* • Sandra Oh *Ting Ting* • Pat Morita *Emperor* • George Takei *First ancestor* ■ *Dir* Darrell Rooney, Lynne Southerland • *Scr* Michael Lucker, Chris Parker, Roger SH Schulman, from characters by Robert D San Souci

Mule Train ★★ U
Western   1950 · US · Sepia · 70min

The song of the title was a million-selling pop hit for Frankie Laine, and this Gene Autry programme filler was made quickly to capitalise on the song's success. But threading a plot around the lyrics wasn't easy and resulted in this loose thriller about the construction of a dam and, bizarrely, cement claim jumping. The popular Autry is his usual likeable self, but Robert Livingston's evil freight shipper is actually far more interesting than the bland hero. The movie was originally filmed in the now forgotten screen process of Sepiatone. TS
Gene Autry • Pat Buttram *Smokey Argyle* • Sheila Ryan *Carol Bannister* • Robert Livingston *Sam Brady* • Frank Jacquet *Clayton Hodges* • Vince Barnett *Barber Mulkey* • Syd Saylor *Skeeter* • Sandy Sanders *Bud* ■ *Dir* John English • *Scr* Gerald Geraghty, from a story by Alan James

Mulholland Drive ★★★★★ 15
Psychological thriller   2001 · US/Fr · Colour · 140min

As twisted as the Los Angeles road it takes its name from, David Lynch's film is a typically weird and wonderful rumination on the American Dream, the Hollywood nightmare and the mysterious grey area in between. Lynch's dazzling thriller reaches new heights of mesmeric fascination thanks to scintillating visuals and an offbeat emotional intensity. Although many plot strands are thrown into the suspenseful mix, the main focus is on the bizarre relationship between amnesiac movie star Laura Elena Harring and wannabe actress Naomi Watts, who slowly helps the accident victim recover her memory and identity. With a sensational performance by Watts, it's a triple-strength masterpiece. AJ *DVD*
BD

Naomi Watts *Betty Elms/Diane Selwyn* • Laura Elena Harring [Laura Harring] *Rita/Camilla Rhodes* • Justin Theroux *Adam Kesher* • Ann Miller *Coco Lenoix* • Dan Hedaya *Vincenzo Castigliane* • Mark Pellegrino *Joe* • Brent Briscoe *Detective Domgaard* • Robert Forster *Det Harry McKnight* • Lee Grant *Louise Bonner* • Michael J Anderson *Mr Rocque* • Billy Ray Cyrus *Gene* • Chad Everett *Jimmy Katz* • Angelo Badalamenti *Luigi Castigliane* ■ *Dir/Scr* David Lynch

Mulholland Falls ★★★ 18
Period thriller   1996 · US · Colour · 102min

Nick Nolte heads a very starry cast as the hard-nosed head of the Hat Squad – a group of detectives prepared to take the law into their own hands to deal with mobsters. Nolte becomes entangled in a political conspiracy when investigating the death of a beautiful woman (Jennifer Connelly) who had been his lover. Director Lee Tamahori stylishly evokes the sleazy glamour of postwar Los Angeles and elicits excellent performances from the cast, but all are let down by a muddled script. JF
Violence, swearing, nudity, sex scenes.
DVD

Nick Nolte *Hoover* • Melanie Griffith *Katherine* • Chazz Palminteri *Coolidge* • Michael Madsen *Eddie Hall* • Chris Penn *Arthur* • Treat Williams *Fitzgerald* • Jennifer Connelly *Allison Pond* • John Malkovich *Timms* ■ *Dir* Lee Tamahori • *Scr* Pete Dexter, from a story by Floyd Mutrux, Pete Dexter

Multiple Maniacs ★★ 18
Satirical melodrama   1970 · US · BW · 90min

John Waters, the self-styled "Sovereign of Sleaze", dubbed this early work a "celluloid atrocity", while its title is a homage to the

---

1964 gorefest *Two Thousand Maniacs!* Waters's most overtly Catholic tale to date centres on "Lady Divine's Cavalcade of Perversions", a travelling freak show that pitches its tent in Baltimore. The moral is that the world at large contains far worse horrors than those featured in Divine's ghoulish gallery. An eye-opening gutter parable that comes complete with the Infant of Prague. AJ
Divine *Lady Divine* • David Lochary *Mr David* • Mary Vivian Pearce *Bonnie* • Mink Stole • Cookie Mueller *Cookie* • Paul Swift *Steve* • Rick Morrow *Ricky* • Michael Renner Jr *Infant of Prague* ■ *Dir/Scr* John Waters (2)

Multiplicity ★★★ 12
Fantasy comedy   1996 · US · Colour · 112min

Director Harold Ramis's inventive comedy is a sprightly romp that benefits from Michael Keaton's very funny multiple performances. Keaton finds his time stretched to the limit between his wife, career and family, until he meets a scientist who offers to clone him. Of course, one clone ends up not being enough and soon he has an attic full of them – all played by Keaton and each with a different personality – while his wife (Andie MacDowell) wonders what is going on. JB
Swearing. *DVD*

Michael Keaton *Doug Kinney* • Andie MacDowell *Laura Kinney* • Zack Duhame *Zack Kinney* • Katie Schlossberg *Jennifer Kinney* • Harris Yulin *Dr Leeds* • Richard Masur *Del King* • Eugene Levy *Vic* • Ann Cusack *Noreen* ■ *Dir* Harold Ramis • *Scr* Chris Miller, Mary Hale, Lowell Ganz, Babaloo Mandel, from a short story by Chris Miller

Mum & Dad ★★★ 18
Horror   2008 · UK · Colour · 84min

This gruesome British horror about a husband-and-wife serial-killer team living in the shadow of Heathrow airport is a twisted family drama for those with very strong stomachs. Partly inspired by the notorious story of Fred and Rose West, it stars owl-faced character actor Perry Benson (*Somers Town*) as a suburban father whose net curtains cover his murderous hobbies. It begins with a Polish cleaning girl being led into Dad's clutches by dutiful daughter Birdie (Ainsley Howard). The nightmare that befalls her, however, isn't simply another exercise in torture porn, and writer/director Steven Sheil's micro-budget movie has plenty of wicked things to say about the dynamics of the supposedly normal family unit. DW *DVD*

Perry Benson *Dad* • Dido Miles *Mum* • Olga Fedori *Lena* • Ainsley Howard *Birdie* • Toby Alexander *Elbie* ■ *Dir/Scr* Steven Sheil

Mumbai Matinee ★★★ 12
Comedy   2003 · Ind · Colour · 125min

This enjoyable comedy from Anant Balani takes something of a Bollywood risk by focusing on the subject of virginity. Star Rahul Bose is suitably despairing as the 32-year-old innocent who accidentally becomes a porn star through the underhand dealings of immoral fixer Vijay Raaz and down-at-heel director Saurabh Shukla, while Perizaad Zorabian co-stars as the unflappable journalist who rescues Bose's flagging reputation. DP Hindi, English +subtitles. *DVD*
Rahul Bose *Debashish Chatterjee* • Perizaad Zorabian *Sonali Verma* • Vijay Raaz *Baba Hindustani* • Saurabh Shukla *Nitin Kapoor* ■ *Dir/Scr* Anant Balani

Mumford ★★ 15
Comedy drama
1999 · US · Colour and BW · 107min

Though advertised as a riotous comedy, this story of a small-town psychiatrist with a deep secret and his wondrous effect on the locals is really more of a light-hearted drama. While never boring, and filled with moments both touching and humorous, it moves at a snail's pace. Relieved of its multiple subplots, the film might have felt less congested. Even then, some unexplained changes in the characters – particularly Martin Short's – would remain. KB Drug abuse, sex scenes, nudity, swearing. *DVD*

Loren Dean *Mumford* • Hope Davis *Sofie Crisp* • Jason Lee *Skip Skipperton* • Alfre Woodard *Lily* • Mary McDonnell *Althea Brockett* • Pruitt Taylor Vince *Henry Follett* • Zooey Deschanel *Nessa Watkins* • Martin Short *Lionel Dillard* • Ted Danson *Jeremy Brockett* • Robert Stack ■ *Dir/Scr* Lawrence Kasdan

The Mummy ★★★ 15
Horror   1932 · US · BW · 70min

Boris Karloff's next film after *Frankenstein* shows what a subtle actor he was compared with the walking-dead performances of the supporting cast. He plays the ancient Egyptian Im-Ho-Tep who was buried alive for trying to restore life to his beloved princess. Brought back to life in the present day, he pursues his lost love, believing her to be reincarnated as the fiancée of a member of an archaeological expedition. Master photographer Karl Freund directs without shock tactics, apart from the burying alive scene, but with images worthy of Edgar Allan Poe. TH
DVD *BD*

Boris Karloff *Imhotep/Ardeth Bey* • Zita Johann *Helen Grosvenor/Princess Ankh-es-en-Amon* • David Manners *Frank Whemple* • Arthur Byron *Sir Joseph Whemple* • Edward Van Sloan *Doctor Muller* • Bramwell Fletcher *Ralph Norton* • Eddie Kane *Doctor* ■ *Dir* Karl Freund • *Scr* John L Balderston, from the story *Cagliostro* by Nina Wilcox Putnam, Richard Schayer

The Mummy ★★★ PG
Horror   1959 · UK · Colour · 84min

After its huge success with Dracula and Frankenstein, Hammer turned to another vintage Universal monster for its scream dream team of Peter Cushing, Christopher Lee and director Terence Fisher. Although rather talky and undemanding plotwise, Cushing is marvellously crisp as the tomb-desecrating archaeologist, fending off the malevolent attentions of gauze-wrapped Lee. And, unlike your usual shambling mummy, Lee captures the murderously powerful ferocity of the bandaged reincarnation as he stomps through foggy London. AJ *DVD* *BD*

Peter Cushing *John Banning* • Christopher Lee *Kharis, the Mummy* • Yvonne Furneaux *Isobel Banning/Princess Ananka* • Eddie Byrne *Inspector Mulrooney* • Felix Aylmer *Stephen Banning* • Raymond Huntley *Joseph Whemple* ■ *Dir* Terence Fisher • *Scr* Jimmy Sangster, from the 1932 film

The Mummy ★★★ 12
Period horror adventure   1999 · US · Colour · 119min

In the good old days, the Mummy merely met Abbott and Costello. Now, thanks to the wizards of the special effects industry, this digitally manipulated villain can meet his adversaries in a world of vibrant action adventure. Stephen Sommers has embroidered the original story to excess at times, with flesh-eating beetles and battling zombie slaves just two of the gruesome modern additions. Yet Brendan Fraser does his goofy macho best and Arnold Vosloo has the perfect bone structure for the brooding menace returned from the dead. AJ *DVD* *BD*

Brendan Fraser *Rick O'Connell* • Rachel Weisz *Evelyn* • John Hannah *Jonathan* • Arnold Vosloo *Imhotep* • Kevin J O'Connor *Beni* • Jonathan Hyde *Egyptologist* • Oded Fehr *Ardeth Bay* • Omid Djalili *Warden* ■ *Dir* Stephen Sommers • *Scr* Stephen Sommers, from a story by Lloyd Fonvielle, Kevin Jarre, Stephen Sommers

The Mummy
Action fantasy   2017 · US · Colour

This is a preview - no prints were available to review as we went to press: The Mummy returns from the dead once again, this time as a Tom Cruise action adventure set in modern day London. Co-starring with Sofia Boutella, Cruise plays a Navy SEAL sent to investigate a bunker in the Iraqi desert that turns out to be an ancient tomb. After *Dracula Untold*, *The Mummy* will be the second of several monster movie reboots set in the shared fictional universe dreamt up by Universal in 2014. Expect more action and less horror, an overturned number 25 bus and a bonus cameo from Russell Crowe. BB

Tom Cruise *Tyler Colt* • Sofia Boutella *Mummy* • Annabelle Wallis *Jenny* • Russell Crowe *Dr Henry Jekyll* ■ *Dir* Alex Kurtzman • *Scr* Jon Spaihts

The Mummy Returns ★★★ 12
Period horror adventure   2001 · US · Colour · 129min

You have to admire them for getting a sequel into the cinemas just two years after the first *Mummy* became a surprise hit. This sense of continuity pulls the franchise in line with the *Indiana Jones* films, to which this owes so much with its tomb-raiding themes, period colour and deft mix of comedy and action. To praise it faintly as more of the same does a disservice to the slick bravado of writer/director Stephen Sommers and the wizardry of Industrial Light and Magic, who created the screen-dominating CGI effects. AC *DVD* *BD*

Brendan Fraser *Rick O'Connell* • Rachel Weisz *Evelyn/Nefertiri* • John Hannah *Jonathan* • Arnold Vosloo *Imhotep* • Oded Fehr *Ardeth Bay* • Patricia Velasquez *Meela/Anck-Su-Namun* • The Rock [Dwayne Johnson] *The Scorpion King* ■ *Dir/Scr* Stephen Sommers

The Mummy: Tomb of the Dragon Emperor ★★ 12
Period horror adventure   2008 · Ger/Chi/US · Colour · 107min

What a difference a decade makes in this second sequel (discounting series spin-off *The Scorpion King*) to Stephen Sommers's 1999 hit. Brendan Fraser is back but much of the vigour of his original performance is gone, as he and wife Maria Bello (replacing Rachel Weisz) get drawn into a plot to resurrect the ruthless Emperor Han (Jet Li) and restore him to power. The poor dialogue and dreadful acting – Bello's wayward English accent, Fraser's cringeworthy tête-à-tête with son Luke Ford – are forgivable in an action movie. But the much-anticipated fight between Li and Michelle Yeoh is too brief, the action is badly choreographed and John Hannah's comedy sidekick is such a tiresome embarrassment. SuR *DVD* *BD*

Brendan Fraser *Rick O'Connell* • Jet Li *Emperor Han* • Maria Bello *Evelyn O'Connell* • John Hannah *Jonathan Carnahan* • Michelle Yeoh *Zi Yuan* • Luke Ford *Alex O'Connell* • Anthony Wong Chau-Sang [Anthony Wong (1)] *General Yang* • Isabella Leong *Lin* ■ *Dir* Rob Cohen • *Scr* Miles Millar, Alfred Gough, from characters by Lloyd Fonvielle, Kevin Jarre

The Mummy's Curse ★ PG
Horror   1944 · US · BW · 57min

This carbon copy chiller finds Kharis the Mummy (Lon Chaney Jr in his third and last bandaged big-screen outing) once more terrorising swamp dwellers and archaeologists in the monotonous search for the reincarnation of his Princess Ananka (Virginia Christine). The striking opening – the only sequence given any visual flair by director Leslie Goodwins – has Ananka dug out of the quicksand she sank into during the finale of *The Mummy's Ghost*. Otherwise, this is a slow-moving, predictable potboiler. AJ

Lon Chaney [Lon Chaney Jr] *Kharis, the Mummy* • Peter Coe *Dr Ilzor Zandaab* • Virginia Christine *Princess Ananka* • Kay Harding *Betty Walsh* • Dennis Moore *Dr James Halsey* • Martin Kosleck *Ragheb* ■ *Dir* Leslie Goodwins • *Scr* Bernard Schubert, Leon Abrams, Dwight V Babcock, from a story by Leon Abrams, Dwight V Babcock

The Mummy's Ghost ★ PG
Horror   1944 · US · BW · 57min

This creaky programme filler is carelessly directed with little originality on show. Priest George Zucco sends disciple John Carradine to New England to help Kharis the Mummy (Lon Chaney Jr, in his second bandaged appearance after 1942's *The Mummy's Tomb*) find the Princess Ananka. Her soul has been reincarnated in student Ramsay Ames. Musty and murky. AJ

John Carradine *Yousef Bey* • Lon Chaney [Lon Chaney Jr] *Kharis, the Mummy* • Robert Lowery *Tom Hervey* • Ramsay Ames *Amina Mansouri* • Barton MacLane *Inspector Walgreen* • George

---

M

Zucco *High priest* • Frank Reicher *Professor Matthew Norman* ▪ *Dir* Reginald LeBorg [Reginald Le Borg] • *Scr* Griffin Jay, Henry Sucher, Brenda Weisberg, from a story by Griffin Jay, Henry Sucher

The Mummy's Hand ★★
Horror   1940 · US · BW · 67min

This first sequel to Boris Karloff's *The Mummy* plagiarises its predecessor and is a cheap and cheerful precursor to a series of cumbersome follow-ups. The head of the Cairo Museum (George Zucco) balefully revives the 3,000-year-old Kharis (Tom Tyler) as a prelude to Mummy mayhem. Predictably, Universal spent little money, making use of sets from earlier movies, and there's minimal shock-horror as the bandaged threat lurches into view with only a dodgy left leg and memories of things long past to propel his murderous ambitions. BB

Dick Foran *Steve Banning* • Peggy Moran *Marta Solvani* • Wallace Ford *Babe Jenson* • Eduardo Cianelli [Eduardo Ciannelli] *High priest* • George Zucco *Andoheb* • Cecil Kelloway [Cecil Kellaway] *Mr Solvani* • Tom Tyler *Kharis, the Mummy* ▪ *Dir* Christy Cabanne • *Scr* Griffin Jay, Maxwell Shane, from a story by Griffin Jay

The Mummy's Shroud ★★ PG
Horror   1966 · UK · Colour · 86min

Hammer could never resist dabbling with the dark forces of ancient Egypt, but this third descent into the mummy's tomb was one of the studio's least accomplished horrors. After dwelling a bit too long in the land of the pharaohs, the action shifts to 1920 as André Morell's expedition ventures into the vault. We know it's doomed because: a) it's sponsored by treasure-seeking rogue John Phillips; and b) local malcontent Roger Delgado knows the spell to revive the avenging mummy. There are some grisly murders and a terrific finale, but it's mostly dry as dust. DP *DVD* *Blu*

André Morell *Sir Basil Walden* • John Phillips (1) *Stanley Preston* • David Buck *Paul Preston* • Elizabeth Sellars *Barbara Preston* • Maggie Kimberley *Claire de Sangre* • Michael Ripper *Longbarrow* • Roger Delgado *Hasmid Ali* ▪ *Dir* John Gilling • *Scr* John Gilling, from a story by John Elder [Anthony Hinds]

The Mummy's Tomb ★★ PG
Horror   1942 · US · BW · 58min

The tedious cost-cutting sequel to *The Mummy's Hand* features flashbacks to that 1940 potboiler, angry villager scenes borrowed from *Frankenstein* and, despite being promoted on Lon Chaney Jr's rising horror appeal, stuntman Eddie Parker doubled for the overweight star as the bandaged Kharis in numerous shots. Ageing high priest George Zucco sends disciple Turhan Bey to America with Kharis to wreak vengeance on the expedition members who defiled his Egyptian resting place. An uninspired addition to the musty formula that should have stayed under wraps. AJ

Lon Chaney [Lon Chaney Jr] *Kharis, the Mummy* • Dick Foran *Stephen A Banning* • John Hubbard *John Banning* • Elyse Knox *Isobel Evans Banning* • George Zucco *Andoheb* • Wallace Ford *Babe Hanson* • Turhan Bey *Mehemet Bey* ▪ *Dir* Harold Young • *Scr* Griffin Jay, Henry Sucher, from a story by Neil P Varnick

Mumsy, Nanny, Sonny & Girly ★ 15
Horror thriller   1970 · UK · Colour · 101min

The title promises rubbish, and the film obliges. Michael Bryant falls prey to a weird gang - a mother, two children and a maid - who kidnap men, play with them and then kill them. Neither comedy nor horror, this is merely a mess. The director is Freddie Francis, a former house cameraman for Hammer Films who would later collaborate with David Lynch on *Dune* and *The Elephant Man*. AT *DVD*

Michael Bryant *"New Friend"* • Ursula Howells *Mumsy* • Pat Heywood *Nanny* • Howard Trevor *Sonny* • Vanessa Howard *Girly* • Robert Swann *Soldier* • Imogen Hassall *Girlfriend* • Michael

Ripper *Zoo attendant* ▪ *Dir* Freddie Francis • *Scr* Brian Comport, from Maisie Mosco's play *The Happy Family*

Munchie ★★ PG
Fantasy comedy   1992 · US · Colour · 77min

In this first sequel to 1987's *Munchies*, a magical furry creature (voiced by Dom DeLuise) befriends a precocious young boy struggling to adjust at his new school. Munchie's appearance may actually frighten kids, especially since the puppetry is so poor that his lip movements rarely match DeLuise's voice. Loni Anderson plays the kid's mom, but it rather looks as if she's doing a favour for pal DeLuise. ST Drug abuse.

Loni Anderson *Cathy* • Dom DeLuise *Munchie* • Andrew Stevens *Elliott* • Jaime McEnnan *Gage Dobson* • Arte Johnson *Professor Cruikshank* • Mike Simmrin *Leon* • Scott Ferguson *Ashton* • Love Hewitt [Jennifer Love Hewitt] *Andrea* ▪ *Dir* Jim Wynorski • *Scr* Jim Wynorski, RJ Robertson

Munchie Strikes Back ★★ PG
Fantasy comedy   1994 · US · Colour · 85min

In this second sequel to the poor man's *Gremlins*, the troublesome space creature gets one final chance to do some good on Earth when he is assigned to the household of Lesley-Anne Down. Andrew Stevens, Loni Anderson and Dom DeLouise return from the first sequel, with *WKRP Cincinnati* alumnus Howard Hesseman providing the voice of Munchie. Director Jim Wynorksi keeps the action racing along and undemanding children may like it. JF

Lesley-Anne Down *Linda McClelland* • Howard Hesseman *Munchie* • Angus Scrimm *Kronus* • Trenton Knight *Chris* • Corey Mendelsohn *Brett Carlisle* • Andrew Stevens *Shelby* • Loni Anderson • Dom DeLuise ▪ *Dir* Jim Wynorski • *Scr* Jim Wynorski, RJ Robertson

Munchies ★ PG
Comedy horror   1987 · US · Colour · 78min

What's worse than a rip-off of *Gremlins*? A rip-off of *Gremlins* with Harvey Korman in multiple roles, of course. Alien-hunter Korman thinks he's found definitive proof in the form of a cute little creature who eats junk food. His evil brother (Korman again) gets hold of the little guy and, before you know it, there are scads of them, causing trouble for everyone. Two sequels followed. ST

Harvey Korman *Cecil/Simon Waterman* • Charles Stratton [Charlie Stratton] *Paul* • Nadine Van Der Velde *Cindy* • Alix Elias *Melvis* • Charlie Phillips *Eddie* • Hardy Rawls *Big Ed* • Jon Stafford *Dude* • Robert Picardo *Bob Marvelle* ▪ *Dir* Bettina Hirsch • *Scr* Lance Smith

Munich ★★★★ 15
Drama based on a true story
2005 · US · Colour · 156min

Steven Spielberg's bold and brooding thriller begins with the tragedy of the 1972 Munich Olympics when 11 Israeli athletes were taken hostage by Black September terrorists, and a botched rescue mission left them all dead. Spielberg pulls no punches here, but rather than sensationalise the atrocity, he uses it as an echo of the moral questions raised when Israeli intelligence subsequently orders the assassination of the Palestinian ringleaders. Eric Bana and his hit squad eliminate their targets one-by-one, but when doubts creep in, so does a palpable sense of urgency. SP In English, German, Italian, French, Arabic, Hebrew. Swearing, violence. *DVD*

Eric Bana *Avner* • Daniel Craig *Steve* • Ciaran Hinds *Carl* • Mathieu Kassovitz *Robert* • Hanns Zischler *Hans* • Ayelet Zurer *Daphna* • Geoffrey Rush *Ephraim* • Michael Lonsdale [Michel Lonsdale] *Papa* • Mathieu Amalric *Louis* ▪ *Dir* Steven Spielberg • *Scr* Tony Kushner, Eric Roth, from the non-fiction book *Vengeance* by George Jonas

Munster, Go Home! ★★★ U
Comedy   1966 · US · Colour · 96min

Popular sitcoms rarely make the grade when they are extended to feature-film length. Here's one of the few exceptions,

originally made for television but deemed good enough for theatrical release. The family inherits an English estate that is being used by their nefarious relatives as the centre of a counterfeiting ring. When they turn up to inspect Munster Hall, their aristocratic next-of-kin (under the deliciously plummy command of Hermione Gingold) try to scare them away with fake apparitions and musty scares. Terry-Thomas and genre veteran John Carradine enter into the spirit of a charming, colourful and funny affair. AJ *DVD*

Fred Gwynne *Herman* • Yvonne De Carlo *Lily* • Al Lewis *Grandpa* • Butch Patrick *Eddie* • Debbie Watson *Marilyn* • Terry-Thomas *Freddie* • Hermione Gingold *Lady Effigie* • Robert Pine *Roger* • John Carradine *Cruikshank* • Richard Dawson *Joey* ▪ *Dir* Earl Bellamy • *Scr* George Tibbles, Joe Connelly, Bob Mosher, from the TV series *The Munsters*

The Muppet Movie ★★★★ U
Comedy adventure   1979 · US · Colour · 91min

Jim Henson's beloved, zany puppets made their feature debut in this entertaining adventure relating Kermit's inspirational journey from Georgia swamp tadpole to Hollywood star frog. Director James Frawley imposes pleasing order on the charming proceedings, while Henson and his long-time associate Frank Oz delightfully dominate as the manipulators and voices of Kermit and Miss Piggy. An indication of how big the Muppets were at the time is the more than a dozen silly star cameos. The only letdown is the below-par score. 2011 sees the relaunch of the franchise, with *The Muppets* starring Amy Adams and Jason Segel. AME *DVD* CS

Jim Henson *Kermit the Frog/Rowlf/Dr Teeth/ Waldorf* • Frank Oz *Miss Piggy/Fozzie Bear/ Animal/Sam the Eagle* • Jerry Nelson *Floyd Pepper/Crazy Harry/Robin the Frog/Lew Zealand* • Richard Hunt *Scooter/Statler/Janice/ Sweetums/Beaker* • Dave Goelz *Gonzo/Zoot/Dr Bunsen Honeydew* ▪ *Dir* James Frawley • *Scr* Jerry Juhl, Jack Burns

The Muppets Take Manhattan ★★★ U
Comedy   1984 · US · Colour · 93min

The third big-screen outing for Jim Henson's puppets has playwright Kermit frog-marching his pals to New York to stage his college show on Broadway. Alas, he finds that biting the Big Apple can leave a sour taste in the mouth. It's not quite up to the standards of the two earlier outings, but the bouncy songs and clever use of Manhattan locations are bonuses. Muppet movies always feature a vast array of guest stars: watch out here for cameos from Liza Minnelli, Brooke Shields, Joan Rivers and Gregory Hines, among others. SuR *DVD*

Jim Henson *Kermit the Frog/Rowlf/Dr Teeth/ Ernie/Muppet newsman/Swedish chef/Animal* • Frank Oz *Miss Piggy/Fozzie Bear/Animal/Sam the Eagle/Bert/Cookie Monster* • Dave Goelz *Gonzo/Chester Rat/Bill the Frog/Dr Bunsen Honeydew/Zoot* • Steve Whitmire *Rizzo the Rat/ Gil the Frog* • Juliana Donald *Jenny* • Lonny Price *Ronnie* • Louis Zorich *Pete* ▪ *Dir* Frank Oz • *Scr* Frank Oz, Tom Patchett, Jay Tarses, from a story by Patchett, Tarses

The Muppet Christmas Carol ★★★★ U
Comedy fantasy   1992 · US · Colour · 85min

With Michael Caine as Scrooge, Kermit and Miss Piggy as the Cratchits, and Gonzo as Dickens, this is quite simply corking Christmas entertainment. Although the story has been Muppetised (with Fozzie Bear as Fozziwig, the owner of a rubber chicken factory), no attempt has been made to water down the story, and the poignancy of the moral tale is as affecting as ever. Caine hasn't been this good in years, and his scenes with those hecklers supreme Statler and Waldorf, as the Marley brothers, are the highlight of the film. DP *DVD*

Michael Caine *Scrooge* • Steve Whitmire *Bob Cratchit (Kermit)/Rizzo/Beaker / Bean Bunny/ Belinda Cratchit* • Frank Oz *Miss Piggy (Miss Piggy)/Sam Eagle/Animal/Fozziwig (Fozzie Bear)* • Dave Goelz *Charles Dickens (The Great Gonzo)/ Bunsen Honeydew/Waldorf/Zoot/Betina Cratchit*

• David Rudman *Peter Cratchit/Swedish Chef/Old Joe* • Jerry Nelson *Statler/Floyd/Ma Bear/Tiny Tim/The Ghost of Christmas Present* ▪ *Dir* Brian Henson • *Scr* Jerry Juhl, from the story by Charles Dickens

Muppet Treasure Island ★★★★ U
Comedy adventure   1996 · US · Colour · 95min

The Muppets take on Robert Louis Stevenson in their inimitable way in this rollicking musical version of the pirate saga. Using the bare bones of the classic story as a framework, director Brian Henson press-gangs the likes of Billy Connolly, Jennifer Saunders and Tim Curry into service for a series of hilarious cameos, accompanied by some rousing songs and the now customary "romance" between Miss Piggy and Kermit. Adults may find the voyage a long haul, but children will love it. AJ *DVD*

Steve Whitmire *Captain Abraham Smollet (Kermit the Frog)/Rizzo the Rat* • Frank Oz *Benjamina Gunn (Miss Piggy)* • Tim Curry *Long John Silver* • Kevin Bishop *Jim Hawkins* • Billy Connolly *Billy Bones* • Jennifer Saunders *Mrs Bluveridge* • Dave Goelz *The Great Gonzo* ▪ *Dir* Brian Henson • *Scr* Jerry Juhl, Kirk R Thatcher, James V Hart

Muppets from Space ★★★★ U
Science-fiction comedy adventure
1999 · UK/US · Colour · 84min

Although more earthbound than the title suggests, this achieves a high chuckle factor. Nasally challenged Gonzo believes his long-lost family are aliens and that they're coming to take him home. Aspiring TV reporter Miss Piggy and assorted government agents, led by Jeffrey Tambor, want to abduct him for their own ends. Movies from *Close Encounters* to *The Shawshank Redemption* are wickedly parodied, while F Murray Abraham, Ray Liotta and Andie MacDowell have a great time. SR *DVD*

Frank Oz *Miss Piggy/Fozzie Bear/Animal/Sam Eagle* • Dave Goelz *Gonzo/Bunsen Honeydew/ Waldorf/The Birdman* • Steve Whitmire *Kermit the Frog/Rizzo the Rat/Beaker/Cosmic Fish No 1* • Bill Barretta *Pepe the Prawn/Bobo as Rentro/ Bubba the Rat/Johnny Fiama/Cosmic Fish No 2* • Jerry Nelson *Robin/Statler/Ubergonzo* • Jeffrey Tambor *K Edgar Singer* • F Murray Abraham *Noah* • Ray Liotta *Gate guard* • Andie MacDowell *Shelley Snipes* ▪ *Dir* Tim Hill • *Scr* Jerry Juhl, Joseph Mazzarino, Ken Kaufman

The Muppets' Wizard of Oz ★★ U
Comedy musical fantasy
2005 · US · Colour · 95min

The Muppets make their least convincing foray into classic literature with this update of the classic story. Ashanti interacts well enough with Kermit's Scarecrow, Fozzie's Cowardly Lion and Gonzo's "Tin Thing", while Miss Piggy makes a splendidly hammy Wicked Witch. But the peppering of the dialogue with unsuitably grown-up gags seems as ill-judged as the excess of decidedly mediocre songs. Equally perplexing is the guest appearance of Quentin Tarantino. DP *DVD*

Ashanti *Dorothy* • Jeffrey Tambor *The Wizard* • Quentin Tarantino • David Alan Grier *Uncle Henry* • Queen Latifah *Auntie Em* • Steve Whitmire *Kermit the Frog/Rizzo the Rat/Beaker/Bean Bunny/Statler* • Dave Goelz *Gonzo/Dr. Bunsen Honeydew/Waldorf/Zoot* • Bill Barretta *Pepe the Prawn/Johnny Fiama/Dr Teeth/Lew Zealand/ Swedish Chef/Rowlf* • Eric Jacobson *Miss Piggy/ Fozzie Bear/Animal/Sam the Eagle* ▪ *Dir* Kirk R Thatcher • *Scr* Adam F Goldberg, Tom Martin, from a story by Debra Frank, Steve L Hayes, from the novel *The Wonderful Wizard of Oz* by L Frank Baum

The Muppets ★★★★ U
Musical comedy   2011 · US · Colour · 98min

Kermit the Frog rounds up the gang to save the Muppets' derelict old theatre from a ruthless tycoon in this laugh-out-loud return to the enduring TV characters' roots. Aided by a couple of humans (co-writer Jason Segel and an adorable Amy Adams) and their new Muppet pal Walter, our furry

M

heroes struggle to stage a money-spinning telethon on the site of their former triumphs. But will an indifferent modern-day public take them to their hearts again? Although he aims the laughs primarily at a younger audience, director James Bobin (TV's *Flight of the Conchords*) packs the film with just enough retro references and subversive humour to strike a chord with grown-ups who will remember the show from their own childhood. TeS **DVD** **BL**

Jason Segel *Gary* • Amy Adams *Mary* • Peter Linz *Walter* • Chris Cooper *Tex Richman* • Rashida Jones *Veronica* • Steve Whitmire *Kermit/Beaker/Statler/Rizzo/Link Hogthrob/The Newsman* • Eric Jacobson *Miss Piggy/Fozzie Bear/Animal/Sam Eagle/Marvin Suggs* • Dave Goelz *Gonzo/Bunsen/Zoot/Beauregard/Waldorf/ Kermit Moopet* • Jack Black • Zach Galifianakis *Hobo Joe* ■ *Dir* James Bobin • *Scr* Jason Segel, Nicholas Stoller

Muppets Most Wanted ★★★ **U**

Crime comedy adventure
2014 · US · Colour · 102min

Self-deprecation is one of the key weapons in the Muppets' arsenal of charm so perhaps we are meant to demur when they sing about how this sequel is not quite as good as the last film – but alas it's true. Kermit gets mistaken for Russian criminal Constantine and is sent to a gulag overseen by a hammy Tina Fey. Meanwhile, his dastardly doppelganger goes on a European tour with the rest of the gang, which provides the perfect cover for Constantine and sidekick Dominic Badguy (Ricky Gervais) to carry out a heist. There's a goodly quantity of amusing gags but fewer belly laughs this time round, and a lot more star cameos, as if to distract attention away from the plot. LF **DVD** **BL**

Ricky Gervais *Dominic Badguy* • Ty Burrell *Jean Pierre Napoleon* • Tina Fey *Nadya* • Steve Whitmire *Kermit the Frog/Foo Foo/Statler/ Beaker/Lips/Rizzo the Rat/Link Hogthrob/ Newsman* • Eric Jacobson *Miss Piggy/Fozzie Bear/Sam Eagle/Animal* • Dave Goelz *The Great Gonzo/Dr Bunsen Honeydew/Zoot/Beauregard/ Waldorf* • Céline Dion [Celine Dion] *Piggy Fairy Godmother* • Lady Gaga • Tom Hiddleston *Great Escapo* • James McAvoy *UPS guy* • Christoph Waltz ■ *Dir* James Bobin • *Scr* James Bobin, Nicholas Stoller • *Cinematographer* Don Burgess

Murder ★★★ **PG**

Mystery
1930 · UK · BW · 99min

Alfred Hitchcock's third talkie is a creaky murder mystery, co-adapted by Hitch's wife, Alma Reville. Herbert Marshall does well in only his second sound film as a juror who conducts his own inquiries after he suspects an actress isn't a killer. Without giving too much away, the dénouement was considered rather daring in its day, as was the use of a stream-of-consciousness voiceover, which established Hitchcock as one of the most inventive of sound directors. The acting now seems rather stagey and the whodunnit isn't particularly taxing, but it's still fascinating. DP

Herbert Marshall *Sir John Menier* • Norah Baring *Diana Baring* • Phyllis Konstam *Dulcie Markham* • Edward Chapman *Ted Markham* • Miles Mander *Gordon Druce* • Esme Percy *Handel Fane* ■ *Dir* Alfred Hitchcock • *Scr* Alma Reville, Walter C Mycroft, Alfred Hitchcock, from the novel and play *Enter Sir John* by Clemence Dane, Helen Simpson

Murder à la Mod ★★★

Mystery comedy drama 1968 · US · BW · 80min

After several acclaimed shorts, Brian De Palma moved into features with *The Wedding Party*, which he co-directed with Cynthia Munroe and Wilford Leach in 1966. However, by the time it was released, three years later, he had completed his solo feature bow with this enigmatic comedy thriller. Centred on the murder of a pornographer's lover, this is a Rashomonesque exercise, with each segment reflecting the lifestyle of the protagonist – soap opera for the victim, Hitchcock-inspired thriller for the blackmailed husband and silent slapstick for

the deaf-mute horror actor. The result is intriguing, but inconsistent. DP

Margo Norton *Karen* • Andra Akers *Tracy* • Jared Martin *Christopher* • William Finley *Otto* • Ken Burrows *Wiley* ■ *Dir/Scr* Brian De Palma

Murder Ahoy ★★★ **U**

Murder mystery comedy
1964 · UK · BW · 88min

The final entry in Margaret Rutherford's Miss Marple casebook is the only one not reworked from a story by Agatha Christie. While David Pursall and Jack Seddon's original screenplay has all the characteristics of a Christie whodunnit, closer scrutiny reveals too many offbeat characters, a glut of inconsequential chat and more comedy than you'd ever find in a well-stocked shelf of the great Dame's mysteries. Having said that, it's neatly staged and the solution is neither blatantly obvious nor buried under a mass of clues. DP **DVD**

Margaret Rutherford *Miss Marple* • Lionel Jeffries *Captain de Courcy Rhumstone* • Charles Tingwell *Detective Inspector Craddock* • William Mervyn *Commander Breeze-Connington* • Joan Benham *Matron Alice Fanbraid* • Stringer Davis *Mr Stringer* • Nicholas Parsons *Dr Crump* • Miles Malleson *Bishop Faulkner* • Henry Oscar *Lord Rudkin* • Derek Nimmo *Sub-Lt Humbert* ■ *Dir* George Pollock • *Scr* David Pursall, Jack Seddon, from the character created by Agatha Christie

Murder among Friends ★★

Detective drama 2001 · US · Colour · 88min

This offbeat comedy thriller may lack star wattage, but it partially atones for that in brio. Greg Evigan is still best known for TV series like *BJ and the Bear* and *My Two Dads*, while Donnamarie Recco will be vaguely familiar from playing Sheila in *Analyze This* (1999) and *Analyze That* (2002). But they make a tolerable team, as Recco's Sophia Loren wannabe joins forces with Evigan's world-weary detective after one of her acting school classmates is arrested for the murder of his father. The real culprit is pretty obvious, but the movie makes no claims to Agatha Christie-sophistication. DP

Greg Evigan *Steve Alder* • Donnamarie Recco *Isabella Dellarocca* • Jennie Raymond *Alicia Carlisle* • Jeff Geddis *Dylan White* • Andrew Kraulis *Jamie Stockard* • James Thomas Brandon Walden ■ *Dir* Michael Kennedy • *Scr* Matthew Weisman, from a story by Edgar Lyall

Murder at Devil's Glen ★★★ **15**

Thriller 1999 · US · Colour · 88min

This nifty made-for-TV variation on *I Know What You Did Last Summer* makes up for what it lacks in thrills with some cunning plotting. The film opens with four students burying a body in the deserted Devil's Glen. Fast forward eight years and one of the number (Rick Schroder) emerges from prison with some bad news for his now respectable buddies: their burial ground is about to be redeveloped and they need to move the body. JF Violence, swearing. **DVD**

Rick Schroder *Henry* • Jack Noseworthy *Oliver* • Jayce Bartok *Doc* • Michael Easton *Charlie* • Tara Reid *Girl* ■ *Dir* Paul Shapiro • *Scr* Eric Harlacher

Murder at 1600 ★★ **15**

Political thriller 1997 · US · Colour · 102min

Wesley Snipes delivers another of his one-note tough guys in an uninspired, cliché-ridden action thriller about a Washington DC cop called in to investigate a murder at the White House. As he delves deeper into the crime with the help of Secret Service agent Diane Lane, he uncovers a conspiracy which may reach all the way to the President himself. Director Dwight H Little's routine mystery generates little suspense and even less interest. AJ Violence, swearing, a sex scene. **DVD**

Wesley Snipes *Detective Harlan Regis* • Diane Lane *Nina Chance* • Alan Alda *Alvin Jordan* • Daniel Benzali *Nick Spikings* • Dennis Miller

Detective Stengel • Ronny Cox *President Jack Neil* • Diane Baker *Kitty Neil* ■ *Dir* Dwight H Little • *Scr* Wayne Beach, David Hodgin

Murder at the Gallop ★★★ **U**

Murder mystery comedy 1963 · UK · BW · 77min

Robert Morley and Flora Robson add a touch of class to the list of suspects as Miss Marple investigates the murder of a rich recluse. While detective Charles Tingwell scratches his head in bewilderment, the divine Margaret Rutherford lures the killer into a trap using herself as bait. Director George Pollock effortlessly blends clues and comedy in Rutherford's second outing as the doyenne of St Mary Mead (after 1961's *Murder She Said*), but the most striking thing about this lively whodunnit is that it was inspired by the novel *After the Funeral*, in which the case was actually solved by Hercule Poirot! DP **DVD**

Margaret Rutherford *Miss Marple* • Stringer Davis *Mr Stringer* • Robert Morley *Hector Enderby* • Flora Robson *Miss Gilchrist* • Charles Tingwell *Det Insp Craddock* • Gordon Harris *Sgt Bacon* • Robert Urquhart *George Crossfield* • Katya Douglas *Rosamund Shane* • James Villiers *Michael Shane* • Noel Howlett *Mr Trundell* • Finlay Currie *Old Enderby* ■ *Dir* George Pollock • *Scr* James P Cavanagh, David Pursall, Jack Seddon, from the novel *After the Funeral* by Agatha Christie

Murder at the Presidio ★★ **15**

Murder mystery based on a true story 2005 · US · Colour · 84min

Lou Diamond Phillips is on an emotional rollercoaster as an angst-riddled military detective in this by-numbers murder mystery. Alternating between surly tough guy and haunted neurotic, he's forced to face his own demons while investigating the alleged robbery-related killing of a sergeant's wife on a prestigious US army base. There's not much actual action and the pieces come together far too easily despite the plodding pace. SF Violence, a sex scene, nudity. **DVD**

Lou Diamond Phillips *CWO James Chandler* • Victoria Pratt *Cpl Tara Jeffries* • Martin Cummins *Barry Atkins* • Eugene Clark *Captain Donovan* • Kim Hawthorne [Kimberly Hawthorne] *Barbara Owens* • Leslie Easterbrook *Thelma "Bunny" Atkins* • Jason Priestley *Tom* ■ *Dir* John Fasano • *Scr* Alison Graham

Murder between Friends ★★★ **15**

Crime drama based on a true story 1993 · US · Colour · 91min

This TV movie tells the story of a perplexing murder in Louisiana, based on true events. Stephen Lang and Martin Kemp play friends who are spotted leaving the house where Lang's wife has been beaten to death; both then insist the other is guilty of the murder, and it's left to assistant district attorney Timothy Busfield to unravel the mystery. It borders on the melodramatic, but Lang and Kemp deliver chilling performances. JF **DVD**

Timothy Busfield *Assistant DA John Thorn* • Stephen Lang *Kerry Meyers* • Martin Kemp *Bill Fontanille* • Lisa Blount *Janet Myers* • O'Neal Compton *Detective Easby* • Alex Courtney *Rene LeGallais* ■ *Dir* Waris Hussein • *Scr* Philip Rosenberg

Murder by Contract ★★★

Thriller 1958 · US · BW · 80min

Here's a real gem and total justification for the existence of the B-movie. X-certificated in the UK on release, this darkly sinister plot masks a deeply original screenplay proffering philosophical insights into what makes hitman Vince Edwards tick. Ostensibly he wants more cash on discovering that his victim is female, but really he begins to ruminate on himself and his ambitions. Stunningly directed by Irving Lerner and cleverly produced on a shoestring, this is original, clever and absorbing. TS

Vince Edwards *Claude* • Phillip Pine *Marc* • Herschel Bernardi *George* • Michael Granger *Moon* • Caprice Toriel *Billie Williams* ■ *Dir* Irving Lerner • *Scr* Ben Simcoe

Murder by Death ★★ **PG**

Detective spoof 1976 · US · Colour · 90min

A bizarre hotch-potch of greats, also-rans and has-beens combine to pay the mortgage in one of those whodunnits in a big house. Truman Capote has gathered together the world's top sleuths to present them with a slaying due to take place at midnight, and only Maggie Smith is worth watching as the hands creep round. This one belongs firmly in the genre that maintains that as long as you can get enough famous names on the poster the public will accept anything. Not true. SH **DVD**

Peter Sellers *Sidney Wang* • Peter Falk *Sam Diamond* • David Niven *Dick Charleston* • Maggie Smith *Dora Charleston* • Alec Guinness *Butler Bensonmum* • Truman Capote *Lionel Twain* • Eileen Brennan *Tess Skeffington* • James Coco *Milo Perrier* • Elsa Lanchester *Jessica Marbles* ■ *Dir* Robert Moore • *Scr* Neil Simon

Murder by Decree ★★ **12**

Period detective drama 1978 · Can/UK · Colour · 118min

Rather than having Holmes and Watson plod wearily around London, director Bob Clark gives them a surprisingly imaginative lift. The film proposes politicians, freemasons and royalty as links to the Jack the Ripper murders. Such speculation is made with a fair degree of gothic credibility, even though the flabby plot wanders off up too many byways. Also, Donald Sutherland is not the best choice as a fruitcake visionary. Still, even during moments of slack, Christopher Plummer and James Mason interpret their roles as Holmes and Watson with plenty of heart. JM **DVD**

Christopher Plummer *Sherlock Holmes* • James Mason *Dr Watson* • David Hemmings *Inspector Foxborough* • Anthony Quayle *Sir Charles Warren* • Geneviève Bujold *Annie Crook* • Frank Finlay *Inspector Lestrade* • John Gielgud *Prime Minister* • Donald Sutherland *Robert Lees* ■ *Dir* Bob Clark • *Scr* John Hopkins, from a story by Bob Clark, from characters by Sir Arthur Conan Doyle

Murder by Numbers ★★ **15**

Detective thriller 2002 · US · Colour · 115min

Michael Pitt and Ryan Gosling play bored teenagers who kill a defenceless woman simply to get away with it. Of course, their mistake is to underestimate unconventional homicide detective Sandra Bullock who smells a rat and confronts a few skeletons in her own cupboard to come after them. Bullock plays the maverick detective rather well, but there's little else to get excited about in this dull and predictable thriller. LH Violence, swearing, sex scenes, drug abuse. **DVD**

Sandra Bullock *Cassie Mayweather* • Ben Chaplin *Sam Kennedy* • Ryan Gosling *Richard Haywood* • Michael Pitt *Justin Pendleton* • Agnes Bruckner *Lisa Mills* • Chris Penn *Ray* • RD Call *Captain Rod Cody* ■ *Dir* Barbet Schroeder • *Scr* Tony Gayton

Murder by Phone ★★ **15**

Mystery thriller 1982 · Can · Colour · 89min

If you answer the phone in this picture you end up dead. The killer has devised a system that sends an electric pulse down the line, which sends the brain into immediate meltdown. Richard Chamberlain is the science lecturer investigating the death of a student, John Houseman is a glorified telephone engineer and Sara Botsford an artist who taps into phone company files to trap the killer. AT

Richard Chamberlain *Nat Bridger* • John Houseman *Dr Stanley Markowitz* • Sara Botsford *Ridley Taylor* • Robin Gammell *Noah Clayton* • Gary Reineke *Detective Meara* • Barry Morse *Fred Waits* ■ *Dir* Michael Anderson • *Scr* Michael Butler, Dennis Shryack, John Kent Harrison

Murder, He Says ★★★

Comedy 1945 · US · BW · 94min

This slapstick comedy is one of the most bizarre pictures made in Hollywood, a kind of *Arsenic and Old Lace* in hillbilly country that's either very funny or totally unendurable, depending on your point of view. Fred MacMurray stars as the insurance investigator who runs into

Marjorie Main's mad brood in a house where poisoned food glows in the dark (along with anyone foolish enough to eat it) and secret passages lead to hidden treasure. Veteran director George Marshall claimed to have made it up as he went along. AE

Fred MacMurray *Pete Marshall* • Helen Walker *Claire Mathews* • Marjorie Main *Marnie Johnson* • Jean Heather *Eany Fleagle* • Porter Hall *Mr Johnson* • Peter Whitney *Mert Fleagle/Bert Fleagle* ■ *Dir* George Marshall • *Scr* Lou Breslow, from a story by Jack Moffitt

Murder in a Small Town
★★★

Period murder mystery
1999 · US · Colour · 100min

In addition to headlining, Gene Wilder also co-wrote this pleasing TV whodunnit, which is given additional charm by its 1930s setting. Self-exiled from Broadway following the murder of his wife, Wilder's impresario takes to managing a small theatre in Connecticut. However, when an anti-Semitic industrialist is found murdered, Wilder uses his understanding of character motivation to help detective Mike Starr solve the case. This was successful enough for Wilder to reprise the role in *The Lady in Question*. DP

Gene Wilder *Larry "Cash" Carter* • Mike Starr *Tony* • Cherry Jones *Mimi* • Frances Conroy *Martha Lassiter* ■ *Dir* Joyce Chopra • *Scr* Gene Wilder, Gilbert Pearlman

Murder in Greenwich ★★15

Drama based on a true story
2002 · US · Colour · 88min

Over 20 years after the 1975 murder of 15-year-old Martha Moxley, cop Mark Fuhrman reopened the case in his new role as a private investigator. Fuhrman found evidence pointing towards the Skakel brothers, Michael and Tommy, who are related to the Kennedys and who were interviewed by the police back in 1975. Considering the salacious material at his disposal, director Tom McLoughlin fails to generate much interest in this TV-movie reconstruction. DP Swearing, drug abuse. *DVD*

Christopher Meloni *Mark Fuhrman* • Robert Forster *Steve Carroll* • Maggie Grace *Martha Moxley* • Jon Foster (1) *Michael Skakel* • Toby Moore (1) *Tommy Skakel* • Liddy Holloway *Dorothy Moxley* ■ *Dir* Tom McLoughlin • *Scr* Dave Erickson, from a book by Mark Fuhrman

Murder in Mind ★★★18

Psychological thriller
1996 · US/UK · Colour · 84min

Nigel Hawthorne leads an impressive cast as a respected psychiatrist who uses hypnosis to question a disturbed Mary-Louise Parker, the prime suspect in the murder of her husband. As the mind games are played out, the lines between victim, suspect and investigator become blurred. It's a claustrophobic, sometimes erratic affair, but there are striking supporting turns from Jimmy Smits and Jason Scott Lee. JF Violence, swearing, nudity. *DVD*

Nigel Hawthorne *Dr Ellis* • Mary Louise Parker [Mary-Louise Parker] *Caroline* • Jimmy Smits *Peter* • Jason Scott Lee *Holloway* • Gailard Sartain *Charlie* • Jon Cedar *Superior officer* ■ *Dir* Andrew Morahan • *Scr* Michael Cooney, from his play

Murder in Mississippi
★★★★15

Drama based on a true story
1990 · US · Colour · 92min

This US TV movie was made just two years after Alan Parker's Oscar-nominated *Mississippi Burning*. However, while Parker's movie was only loosely based on truth, this small-screen film sticks more closely to the known facts about the murder of three civil rights activists by the Ku Klux Klan in the Deep South. Parker's movie was a hard act to follow yet, thanks to a strong narrative, superior acting and a mournful score, this powerful and violent stab at the story makes almost equally compelling viewing. PF

Tom Hulce *Mickey Schwerner* • Blair Underwood *James Chaney* • Josh Charles *Andrew Goodman* • Jennifer Grey *Rita Schwerner* • Eugene Byrd *Ben Chaney Jr* • Donzaleigh Abernathy *Sue Brown* • CCH Pounder *Fannie Lee Chaney* ■ *Dir* Roger Young • *Scr* Stanley Weiser, from an article by Ben Stein • *Music* Mason Daring

Murder in New Hampshire
★★15

Crime drama based on a true story
1991 · US · Colour · 89min

This TV movie is based on an infamous real-life case in which a small-town schoolteacher plans to murder her husband with the help of her student lover. Helen Hunt attacks her role with gusto and even though the whole farrago has a rather "filming by numbers" feel, it still packs a generous punch. SH *DVD*

Helen Hunt *Pamela Smart* • Chad Allen *Billy Flynn* • Michael Learned *Judy Smart* • Ken Howard *Bill Smart* • Howard Hesseman *DA Paul Maggiotto* • Larry Drake *Mark Sisti* ■ *Dir* Joyce Chopra • *Scr* William Wood, Joe Cacaci

Murder in the Cathedral
★★PG

Religious drama
1952 · UK · BW · 109min

TS Eliot's play about Thomas à Becket and the political and theosophical complexities surrounding his murder by Henry II's henchmen was first performed in 1935. Negligible as a piece of cinema, this film version preserves Eliot's text and allows us to see National Theatre actors much as theatre audiences would have seen them. We hear Eliot himself, as the "Fourth tempter", goading Henry into killing his Archbishop. AT *DVD*

John Groser *Thomas à Becket* • Alexander Gauge *King Henry II* • David Ward *First tempter* • George Woodbridge *Second tempter* • Basil Burton *Third tempter* • TS Eliot *Fourth tempter* • Donald Bisset *First priest* • Clement McCallin *Second priest* • Leo McKern *Third knight* ■ *Dir* George Hoellering • *Scr* George Hoellering, from the play by TS Eliot

Murder in the First
★★★★15

Drama based on a true story
1994 · US · Colour · 122min

Kevin Bacon gives an outstanding performance in this sensational assault on the prison system. Based on the actual experiences of Henri Young, Marc Rocco's uncompromising picture alternates between Alcatraz and a forbidding courtroom, as lawyer Christian Slater tries to pin Bacon's murder of a fellow inmate on the regime that maltreated him to the verge of madness. A little over-intense at times, this is essentially a showcase for its two leads, although Gary Oldman is terrifyingly sinister as the nasty Warden Glenn. Exhausting but enthralling. DP Swearing, violence, a sex scene. *DVD*

Christian Slater *James Stamphill* • Kevin Bacon *Henri Young* • Gary Oldman *Associate Warden Glenn* • Embeth Davidtz *Mary McCasslin* • Bill Macy [William H Macy] *William McNeil* • Stephen Tobolowsky *Mr Henkin* • Brad Dourif *Byron Stamphill* • R Lee Ermey *Judge Clawson* ■ *Dir* Marc Rocco • *Scr* Dan Gordon

Murder Man
★★★

Crime drama
1935 · US · BW · 70min

From a time when newspapermen were the folk heroes that psychiatrists and counter-agents became in later years, comes this low-budget but gutsy crime drama. Spencer Tracy is the boozy reporter who plots the perfect revenge for the crooks who ruined his father and caused the suicide of his estranged wife, while Virginia Bruce is the girl who loves him. The great Lionel Atwill articulates authority with every word, while a briefly-glimpsed James Stewart is starting to drawl his way to stardom. TH

Spencer Tracy *Steve Gray* • Virginia Bruce *Mary Shannon* • Lionel Atwill *Capt Cole* • Harvey Stephens *Henry Mander* • James Stewart *Shorty* • William Demarest *Rod McGuire* ■ *Dir* Tim Whelan • *Scr* Tim Whelan, John C Higgins, from a story by Tim Whelan, Guy Bolton

The Murder Men ★★

Crime drama
1961 · US · BW · 74min

Dorothy Dandridge's fortunes dwindled rapidly after starring in lover Otto Preminger's disappointing version of *Porgy and Bess*. Bankrupt and limited in her options by cinema's strict rules on mixed-race romance, she ended up giving her farewell (and pathetically poignant) performance in this melancholy melodrama about a washed-up jazz singer that was originally made for television. DP

Mark Richman [Peter Mark Richman] *Nick Cain* • Dorothy Dandridge *Norma Sherman* • James Coburn *Arthur Troy* • Joe Mantell *Maury Troy* • Ivan Dixon *Joe Sherman* • Edward Asner *Dan Keller* ■ *Dir* John Peyser • *Scr* Mel Goldberg

Murder Most Foul ★★★U

Murder mystery　　1964 · UK · BW · 86min

Margaret Rutherford dons the tweed twinset of Miss Marple for the third time after *Murder She Said* and *Murder at the Gallop* in this rather contrived adaptation of *Mrs McGinty's Dead*, the second Hercule Poirot case to be reworked as a vehicle for Agatha Christie's spinster sleuth. Having hung a jury during a murder trial, Miss M treads the boards with a shambolic theatre company to find the real culprit. Ron Moody is over the top as a temperamental thespian, but director George Pollock sustains the suspense and there is solid support from Rutherford's real-life husband, Stringer Davis. DP *DVD*

Margaret Rutherford *Miss Marple* • Ron Moody *Driffold Cosgood* • Charles Tingwell *Detective Inspector Craddock* • Andrew Cruickshank *Justice Crosby* • Megs Jenkins *Mrs Thomas* • Ralph Michael *Ralph Summers* • James Bolam *Bill Hanson* • Stringer Davis *Mr Stringer* • Francesca Annis *Sheila Upward* ■ *Dir* George Pollock • *Scr* David Pursall, Jack Seddon, from the novel *Mrs McGinty's Dead* by Agatha Christie

A Murder of Crows ★★★15

Murder mystery thriller
1998 · US · Colour · 96min

This slick if barely credible suspense yarn has Cuba Gooding Jr as a disbarred lawyer-turned-writer who appropriates a dead man's unpublished novel and passes it off as his own. The novel's a huge hit, but Gooding Jr is hauled up on homicide charges when killings in the book are found to mirror real-life murders and include details that only the killer himself could have known. Some of the dialogue tries too hard to sound hard-boiled, but this TV movie is stylishly made and well acted by a quality cast. DA *DVD*

Cuba Gooding Jr *Lawson Russell* • Tom Berenger *Clifford Dubose* • Eric Stoltz *Thurman Parks III* • Marianne Jean-Baptiste *Elizabeth Pope* • Ashley Lauren [Ashley Laurence] *Janine DeVrie* • Doug Wert *Billy Ray* ■ *Dir/Scr* Rowdy Herrington

Murder on a Bridle Path ★★

Comedy mystery　　1936 · US · BW · 63min

It took two directors and four writers to fashion this fourth entry in the Hildegarde Withers RKO series, which began in 1932 with *The Penguin Pool*. This time Helen Broderick takes over as the sleuthing schoolmarm from the redoubtable Edna May Oliver, but to lesser effect. James Gleason is still aboard as cigar-chomping cop Oscar Piper, but unfortunately is lumbered here with some very silly dialogue. That and the slowish pace make this a weaker entry in the series. TS

James Gleason *Inspector Oscar Piper* • Helen Broderick *Hildegarde Withers* • Louise Latimer *Barbara Foley* • Owen Davis Jr *Eddie Fry* • John Arledge *Joey* ■ *Dir* William Hamilton, Edward Killy • *Scr* Dorothy Yost, Thomas Lennon (1), Edmund H North, James Gow, from the novel by Stuart Palmer

Murder on a Honeymoon
★★★

Mystery　　1935 · US · BW · 75min

The third film in RKO's splendid series featuring schoolteacher sleuth Hildegarde Withers (played by Edna May Oliver in her last appearance in the role) and detective

partner Oscar Piper (James Gleason). Wittily co-scripted by famed humorist Robert Benchley, it has the distinction of actually being filmed on location on Catalina Island off the coast of California. Very enjoyable indeed. Helen Broderick took over the role in 1936's *Murder on a Bridle Path*. TS

Edna May Oliver *Hildegarde Withers* • James Gleason *Inspector Oscar Piper* • Lola Lane *Phyllis La Font* • Chick Chandler *Pilot French* • George Meeker *Kelsey* • Dorothy Libaire *Kay Deving* • Harry Ellerbe *Marvin Deving* ■ *Dir* Lloyd Corrigan • *Scr* Seton I Miller, Robert Benchley, from the novel *Puzzle of the Pepper Tree* by Stuart Palmer

Murder on a Sunday Morning ★★★12

Documentary　　2001 · US/Fr · Colour · 111min

French director Jean-Xavier de Lestrade won an Oscar for this account of black teenager Brenton Butler's ordeal after being charged with the murder of a 65-year-old woman in a Florida motel. Outrage is the initial response, but indignant jubilation takes over as public defender Pat McGuinness exposes both the institutional racism within the Jacksonville police department and the flaws in a legal system that could allow such a prosecution to reach trial. Lestrade clearly takes sides, but his concern for the boy and his pious parents is evident and his presentation of the courtroom revelations is highly suspenseful. DP *DVD*

■ *Dir* Jean-Xavier de Lestrade

Murder on the Blackboard
★★

Mystery　　1934 · US · BW · 71min

In the second, after *The Penguin Pool*, of RKO's series based on Stuart Palmer's stories, Edna May Oliver and James Gleason as Hildegarde Withers and Oscar Piper investigate the death of a schoolteacher. Also returning from the first film is delightful character actor Edgar Kennedy, as one of Gleason's colleagues. Not as good as the original, but still fun. TS

Edna May Oliver *Hildegarde Withers* • James Gleason *Inspector Oscar Piper* • Bruce Cabot *Asst principal Addison Stevens* • Gertrude Michael *Janey Davis* • Regis Toomey *Smiley* • Edgar Kennedy *Detective Donahue* • Tully Marshall *MacFarland* • Jackie Searle *Leland Jones* ■ *Dir* George Archainbaud • *Scr* Willis Goldbeck, from the story by Stuart Palmer

Murder on the Orient Express ★★★★PG

Murder mystery　　1974 · UK · Colour · 122min

Easily the best screen adaptation of an Agatha Christie whodunnit and, for those unfamiliar with either book or film, the solution will take your breath away. Albert Finney makes fussy Belgian detective Hercule Poirot seem every bit as preposterous as Christie intended he was and earned an Oscar nomination for his wonderful performance. The supporting cast does everything that is expected of it, with Ingrid Bergman's Oscar-winning turn just about the pick of a stellar selection. Praise should also go to director Sidney Lumet for keeping you guessing right to the end. DP Violence, swearing. *DVD*

Albert Finney *Hercule Poirot* • Lauren Bacall *Mrs Hubbard* • Martin Balsam *Bianchi* • Ingrid Bergman *Greta Ohlsson* • Jacqueline Bisset *Countess Andrenyi* • Jean-Pierre Cassel *Pierre Paul Michel* • Sean Connery *Colonel Arbuthnot* • John Gielgud *Beddoes* • Wendy Hiller *Princess Dragomiroff* • Anthony Perkins *Hector McQueen* • Vanessa Redgrave *Mary Debenham* • Rachel Roberts (1) *Hildegarde Schmidt* • Richard Widmark *Ratchett* • Michael York *Count Andrenyi* • Colin Blakely *Hardman* ■ *Dir* Sidney Lumet • *Scr* Paul Dehn, from the novel by Agatha Christie

Murder on the Orient Express ★★

Murder mystery　　2001 · US · Colour · 100min

Agatha Christie's classic whodunnit had already been brought to the screen with aplomb by Sidney Lumet, so it was hard to fathom the need for this TV-movie remake. With the exception of Leslie Caron, the cast list is nowhere near as star-studded and the characters are much less subtly drawn, with the result that Alfred Molina's Poirot seems all the more eccentric. Just as damaging, however, is the decision to update the action to the present day. **DP**

Alfred Molina *Hercule Poirot* • Meredith Baxter *Mrs Caroline Hubbard* • Leslie Caron *Senora Alvarado* • Amira Casar *Helena von Strauss* • Peter Strauss *Mr Samuel Ratchett* • David Hunt *Bob Arbuthnot* ■ *Dir* Carl Schenkel

Murder 101   ★★
Murder mystery   2006 · US · Colour · 105min

Dick Van Dyke reunites with his *Diagnosis Murder* director Christian Nyby II for this routine murder mystery. Bringing his customary charm to the role of bumbling criminology expert Dr Jonathan Maxwell, Van Dyke stars alongside his real-life son, Barry (who plays a private eye). Together, the duo enjoy an easy chemistry as they try to prove the innocence of a reporter who's accused of blowing up a successful executive. **SF** Some violence.

Dick Van Dyke *Prof Jonathan Maxwell* • Barry Van Dyke *Mike Bryant* • Tracey Needham *Cheryl Collins* • William Allen Young *Lt Dietrich* ■ *Dir* Christian I Nyby II • *Scr* Dean Hargrove

Murder She Said   ★★ PG
Murder mystery   1961 · UK · BW · 82min

Through the window of a passing train, Miss Marple (Margaret Rutherford) spots a woman being murdered. When no corpse can be found, however, her suspicions are dismissed as the ravings of an eccentric elderly spinster. Determined to solve the mystery, she takes a job as a maid at the estate of James Robertson-Justice. The first screen adaptation to star Rutherford as Agatha Christie's amateur sleuth only holds the interest now because of its star's unique persona and comic timing. **RK** DVD

Margaret Rutherford *Miss Marple* • Arthur Kennedy *Dr Quimper* • Muriel Pavlow *Emma Ackenthorpe* • James Robertson-Justice *Mr Ackenthorpe* • Charles Tingwell *Inspector Craddock* • Thorley Walters *Cedric Ackenthorpe* • Joan Hickson *Mrs Kidder* ■ *Dir* George Pollock • *Scr* David Pursall, Jack Seddon, David Osborn, from the novel *4.50 from Paddington* by Agatha Christie

Murder without Conviction
                                  ★★
Mystery thriller   2004 · US · Colour · 120min

A bigger budget and a more competent director could have made this a gripping mystery thriller. Instead, Lee Harris's well-plotted source novel is downgraded into a rambling and largely unconvincing affair, in which a sleuthing former nun (Megan Ward) tries to exonerate autistic twins, accused of murdering their mother decades earlier. Ward lacks presence, but it's the weak direction that's most damaging. **SF**

Megan Ward *Christine Bennett* • Morgan Weisser *Det Jack Brooks* • Rutanya Alda *Dr Virginia McAlpin* • David Proval *James Talley/Edward Talley age 55* • Patty Duke *Mother Joseph* • Rafael Feldman *James Talley age 24* • Daryl Sabara *James Talley age 10* ■ *Dir* Kevin Connor • *Scr* Bruce Franklin Singer, from the novel *The Good Friday Murder* by Lee Harris

Murder without Crime ★★ 12
Crime thriller   1950 · UK · BW · 73min

Director J Lee Thompson was also a playwright, and this is his own adaptation of his play, *Double Error*. It's basically a four-hander about a marriage, a murder and a third party who sees an opportunity for blackmail. The result is a film of modest budget and ambition with a nice performance by Dennis Price, as suave and duplicitous as ever. **AT** DVD

Derek Farr *Stephen* • Dennis Price *Matthew* • Patricia Plunkett *Jan* • Joan Dowling *Grena* ■ *Dir* J Lee Thompson • *Scr* J Lee Thompson, from his play *Double Error*

Murderball   ★★★★ 15
Sports documentary
2005 · US/Can · Colour · 82min

Co-directors Henry Alex Rubin and Dana Adam Shapiro lift the lid on the ferociously competitive sport of quadriplegic rugby in this revealing documentary. The film is structured around the intense rivalry between the USA and Canadian teams – beginning at the 2002 World Championships and climaxing at the 2004 Paralympics in Athens – and focuses on the bad blood between intimidating US star player Mark Zupan and American hero-turned-Canadian-coach Joe Soares. Glimpses into teams' lives are combined with candid interviews about their disabilities and particularly the impact on their sex lives. Both the vicious matches and the background stories are presented with an absence of pity that is inspiring, thrilling and humbling. **AJ** Swearing. DVD

■ *Dir* Henry Alex Rubin, Dana Adam Shapiro • *Scr* From the article by Dana Adam Shapiro

Murders in the Rue Morgue
                              ★★★ 12
Horror   1932 · US · BW · 57min

Director Robert Florey plunders German expressionism and atmospheric shocks while allowing plenty of room for Bela Lugosi to enjoy his Dr Caligari-esque mad scientist role. Lugosi runs an offbeat carnival attraction featuring a giant gorilla by day. By night, however, he's engaged in diabolical blood transfusion experiments involving apes and beautiful virgins. Although far removed from its Edgar Allan Poe inspiration, the lurid overtones of the pulp plot are handled with candour. **AJ**

Bela Lugosi *Dr Mirakle* • Sidney Fox *Camille* • Leon Waycoff [Leon Ames] *Pierre Dupin* • Bert Roach *Paul* • Brandon Hurst *Prefect of Police* • Noble Johnson *Janos* ■ *Dir* Robert Florey • *Scr* Tom Reed, Dale Van Every, John Huston, from the story by Edgar Allan Poe

Murders in the Rue Morgue
                                  ★★★
Horror   1971 · US · Colour · 87min

Director Gordon Hessler's fourth collaboration with Hammer scriptwriter Christopher Wicking is one of the most undervalued horror movies of the 1970s. A superb Eurotrash cast populate this clever revenge story, in which a series of grisly murders strikes members of Jason Robards's *Grand Guignol* theatre company while they are presenting a stage version of the Edgar Allan Poe classic. Hessler's suspense shocker is packed with sophisticated insight, surrealistic poetry and a nightmarish delirium. **AJ**

Jason Robards *Cesar Charron* • Herbert Lom *Marot* • Christine Kaufmann *Madeleine* • Adolfo Celi *Vidocq* • Lilli Palmer *Madeleine's mother* • Maria Perschy *Genevre* ■ *Dir* Gordon Hessler • *Scr* Christopher Wicking, Henry Slesar, from the story by Edgar Allan Poe

Murders in the Zoo   ★★
Horror   1933 · US · BW · 60min

Lionel Atwill overacts a storm as a sadistic zookeeper using the animals in his care to kill anyone who so much as looks at his gorgeous wife, Kathleen Burke. Lions, snakes and alligators are called on to do their worst by the insanely jealous warden, but it's the moment where he sews up the mouth of one paramour which provides the most chills. Randolph Scott is the hero and Charles Ruggles provides the comic relief in a menacing melodrama that was considered highly shocking and tasteless in its day. **AJ**

Charles Ruggles *Peter Yates* • Lionel Atwill *Eric Gorman* • Gail Patrick *Jerry Evans* • Randolph Scott *Dr Woodford* • John Lodge *Roger Hewitt* • Kathleen Burke *Evelyn Gorman* • Harry Beresford *Professor Evans* ■ *Dir* Edward Sutherland [A Edward Sutherland] • *Scr* Phillip Wylie, Seton I Miller

Muriel   ★★★★
Drama   1963 · Fr/It · Colour · 115min

With her stepson Jean-Baptiste Thierrée home from army service in Algeria, Delphine Seyrig invites her erstwhile lover Jean-Pierre Kérien, together with his niece Nita Klein, to visit her in Boulogne. The son is haunted by memories of a dead girl called Muriel, while the ex-lovers are similarly caught in memories of their past. From the unique poetic and metaphysical imagination of French director Alain Resnais, this is an opaque mix of memory and imagination, past and present. Faultlessly assembled, acted and photographed, it's certainly intriguing and generally regarded as one of Resnais's masterworks. **RK** In French.

Delphine Seyrig *Helene Aughain* • Jean-Pierre Kérien *Alphonse Noyard* • Nita Klein *Françoise* • Jean-Baptiste Thierrée *Bernard* • Laurence Badie *Claudie* • Martine Vatel *Marie-Dominique* ■ *Dir* Alain Resnais • *Scr* Jean Cayrol, from his story

Muriel's Wedding   ★★★★ 15
Comedy drama   1994 · Aus · Colour · 101min

The Ugly Duckling is given a delightful Down Under spin in this congenial comedy. Flabby Muriel (Toni Collette) lives in a frothy fantasy world of Abba songs, husband-shopping and wedding-dress dreams. It's when she leaves her small-minded home town under a cloud to flat-share with an old acquaintance from school (snappily played by Rachel Griffiths), that the initially hilarious humour begins to turn a shade more poignant. Collette is tremendously affecting as the mousey no-mark who spends her life flicking through bridal catalogues, while PJ Hogan (*My Best Friend's Wedding*) directs with a breezy touch. **AJ** Swearing, nudity.

Toni Collette *Muriel Heslop* • Bill Hunter *Bill Heslop* • Rachel Griffiths *Rhonda* • Jeanie Drynan *Betty Heslop* • Gennie Nevinson *Deidre* • Matt Day *Brice* ■ *Dir* PJ Hogan • *Scr* PJ Hogan, from a story by PJ Hogan, Jocelyn Moorhouse

Murphy's Law   ★★ 18
Action thriller   1986 · US · Colour · 96min

The Defiant Ones meets *Death Wish* in a formula Charles Bronson crime thriller, which casts him as an alcoholic cop framed for murdering his estranged wife by a psychopathic criminal with a grudge. There's lots of shouting and shooting, as Bronson escapes arrest handcuffed to a female offender, but not much in the way of gripping suspense. **AJ**

Charles Bronson *Jack Murphy* • Kathleen Wilhoite *Arabella McGee* • Carrie Snodgress *Joan Freeman* • Robert F Lyons *Art Penney* • Richard Romanus *Frank Vincenzo* • Bill Henderson *Ben Wilcove* ■ *Dir* J Lee Thompson • *Scr* Gail Morgan Hickman

Murphy's Romance ★★★ 15
Drama   1985 · US · Colour · 103min

Six years after she won the best actress Oscar for *Norma Rae*, Sally Field teamed up with director Martin Ritt again for this easy-going comedy about a May to December-style romance between an ambitious young trainer and a widowed pharmacist. The result? Her rugged love interest, twinkle-eyed James Garner, gained a first-time nomination instead. Quite why is the question; while eager to please, this is flimsy stuff that lacks the director's usual hard edge. **AJ**

James Garner *Murphy Jones* • Sally Field *Emma Moriarty* • Brian Kerwin *Bobby Jack Moriarty* • Corey Haim *Jake Moriarty* • Dennis Burkley *Freeman Coverly* • Georgann Johnson *Margaret* • Carole King *Tillie* ■ *Dir* Martin Ritt • *Scr* Harriet Frank Jr, Irving Ravetch, from the novella by Max Schott

Murphy's War   ★★★ 12
Second World War action adventure
1971 · UK · Colour · 101min

This trifle has hints of *The African Queen*, with Peter O'Toole as a manic Irish seaman teaming up with a Quaker missionary (O'Toole's then wife, Sian Phillips) and a French oil engineer, convincingly played by Philippe Noiret. O'Toole's scheme is to

repair an old plane and use it to sink a German U-boat down on the Orinoco delta. Shot in the jungles of Venezuela, the film is a blend of whimsy and battle, skilfully handled by director Peter Yates, who was riding high on the success of *Bullitt*. **AT** Some swearing. DVD

Peter O'Toole *Murphy* • Sian Phillips *Dr Hayden* • Philippe Noiret *Louis Brezan* • Horst Janson *Kapitan Lauchs* • John Hallam *Lieutenant Ellis* • Ingo Mogendorf *Lieutenant Voght* ■ *Dir* Peter Yates • *Scr* Stirling Silliphant, from the novel by Max Catto

Musashi Miyamoto ★★★ PG
Drama   1944 · Jpn · BW · 93min

This was the first film made by Kenji Mizoguchi after his wife, Chieko, was declared insane and committed to the asylum where she was to spend the rest of her life. Yet his lack of interest in the project owes as much to the fact that he had little empathy for either the samurai genre or the nationalist sentiments that lay behind it. Mizoguchi was incapable of making an unwatchable film, however, and so it proves here. The story shows how Kinuyo Tanaka and Kigoro Ikushima's determination to avenge the murder of their father leads to a showdown between two legendary swordsmen. **DP** In Japanese.

Chojuro Kawarazaki *Musashi Miyamoto* • Kinuyo Tanaka *Shinobu Nonomiya* • Kanemon Nakamura *Kojiro Sasaki* • Kigoro Ikushima *Genichiro Nonomiya* ■ *Dir* Kenji Mizoguchi • *Scr* Matsutaro Kawaguchi, from a serialised story by Kan Kikuchi in the newsapaper *Mainichi Shinbun*

Muscle Beach Party   ★★
Musical   1964 · US · Colour · 94min

This one is so dated that it practically has cobwebs hanging off it. The quiffed crooner Frankie Avalon starred in a plethora of these jivin' beach party movies, in which everyone hops around in shorts shaking their heads wildly to truly terrible music. The original *Beach Party* was a big teen success, so the producers came up with this lacklustre sequel. Avalon warbles horribly, Annette Funicello dances as if she has a live octopus attached to her derrière, while the plot involves clashing teenage rivals. **SH**

Frankie Avalon *Frankie* • Annette Funicello *Dee Dee* • Luciana Paluzzi *Julie* • John Ashley *Johnny* • Don Rickles *Jack Fanny* • Peter Turgeon *Theodore* • Jody McCrea *Deadhead* • Little Stevie Wonder [Stevie Wonder] • Peter Lorre *Mr Strangdour* ■ *Dir* William Asher • *Scr* Robert Dillon, from a story by Robert Dillon, William Asher

Muscle Shoals   ★★★★
Music documentary   2013 · US · Colour · 111min

This somewhat uneven but often truly uplifting documentary tells the story of the local, racially integrated music scene in Muscle Shoals, Alabama, "the small town with the big sound". The name may be unfamiliar, though it's the place where the Rolling Stones recorded *Brown Sugar* in the late 1960s. Soul giants Aretha Franklin, Wilson Pickett and Percy Sledge all laid down classic tracks there, usually with funky house band the Swampers, an unassuming bunch of musicians who shocked the industry when it was revealed they were, in fact, all white. The real star of the show, though, is moustachioed Muscle Shoals impresario Rick Hall, whose love of music enabled him to escape a childhood of poverty and tragedy. **DW** Some swearing. DVD

■ *Dir* Greg "Freddy" Camalier

The Muse   ★★★ PG
Satirical comedy   1999 · US · Colour · 92min

American satirist Albert Brooks casts his waspish eye over the film business, writing, directing and starring in this tale of a screenwriter who has lost his touch. Though he is sceptical when successful writer chum Jeff Bridges claims to be inspired by a real-life muse, Brooks nonetheless woos the temperamental Sharon Stone, only to find her turning his life with wife Andie MacDowell upside down. Despite Brooks's ever-present cynicism about life, his film is full of lovely, gentle humour, while film fans will love the cameos from Stone's other "clients", among them James Cameron and Martin Scorsese. SR **DVD**

Albert Brooks *Steven Phillips* • Sharon Stone *Sarah Liddle/Christine* • Andie MacDowell *Laura Phillips* • Jeff Bridges *Jack Warrick* • Mark Feuerstein *Josh Martin* • Steven Wright *Stan Spielberg* ■ *Dir* Albert Brooks • *Scr* Albert Brooks, Monica Johnson

Museum Hours ★★★★ 12
Drama   2012 · Austria/US · Colour · 102min

Vienna in winter provides the sublime setting for this beguiling and often moving treatise on the relationship between art and life. Mary Margaret O'Hara plays a Canadian visiting the Austrian capital to see a relative who has lapsed into a coma. There, she forges a friendship with Bobby Sommer, who translates for her at the hospital, accompanies her on walks, and arranges for her to visit the galleries at the museum where he works. The performances by the non-professional leads are warm and authentic, while the exteriors (shot on 16mm film) and interiors (captured digitally) brilliantly contrast the details in the paintings with the drama, beauty, humour and poignancy of everyday existence. DP English, German +subtitles. **DVD**

Mary Margaret O'Hara *Anne* • Bobby Sommer *Johann* • Ela Piplits *Gerda* ■ *Dir/Scr* Jem Cohen

Music and Lyrics ★★ PG
Romantic comedy   2007 · US/Aus · Colour · 99min

Hugh Grant and Drew Barrymore fail to hit any high notes in this humdrum romantic comedy from writer/director Marc Lawrence (*Two Weeks Notice*). Grant plays a washed-up 1980s pop idol who's competing for the chance to contribute a song to a new album. Sadly, lyrics aren't his forte, but his "plant carer" Sophie (Barrymore) proves to have a way with words. Grant gets his share of snappy one-liners, but his incessant glibness becomes tiresome. His budding relationship with Barrymore is largely unconvincing and it doesn't help matters that she's in constant danger of being upstaged by the vegetation around her. And frankly, the less said about the soundtrack, the better. SP Some swearing, sexual references. **DVD** **Blu-ray**

Drew Barrymore *Sophie Fisher* • Hugh Grant *Alex Fletcher* • Brad Garrett *Chris Riley* • Kristen Johnston *Rhonda Fisher* • Campbell Scott *Sloan Cates* • Haley Bennett *Cora Corman* ■ *Dir/Scr* Marc Lawrence (2) • *Cinematographer* Xavier Pérez Grobet

The Music Box ★★★★★ U
Classic comedy   1932 · US · BW · 28min

Perhaps the best-loved of all the Laurel and Hardy shorts (albeit a longish one, at just under 30 minutes), it won the pair an Oscar and rightly so. In this classic outing they must deliver a piano to an address at the top of a vast flight of steps, and the duo certainly deliver the comedy, with assorted variations on the theme of the instrument jangling down the stairs in its box, and some fine slapstick involving an ornamental pond. Even when they finally get it inside Professor von Schwarzenhoffen's (Billy Gilbert) house, the trouble isn't over. The result is a definitive (and partly improvised) display. AC **DVD**

Stan Laurel *Stan* • Oliver Hardy *Ollie* • Billy Gilbert *Professor Theodore von Schwarzenhoffen* • William Gillespie *Piano salesman* • Charlie Hall *Postman* ■ *Dir* James Parrott • *Scr* HM Walker

Music Box ★★★★ 15
Drama   1989 · US · Colour · 120min

In Costa-Gavras's political melodrama, Jessica Lange stars as a lawyer who defends her blue-collar Hungarian father (Armin Mueller-Stahl) from a charge of being the leader of an SS-run death squad during the Second World War. Courtroom battles generally make riveting viewing and this is no exception. We are kept on a knife-edge of suspense as we wonder if the now kindly veteran could have been a hideous

monster in his past. The film raises more questions than it answers and Costa-Gavras's direction is perhaps a little too detached, but the intensity of Lange and Mueller-Stahl more than makes amends. TH Swearing. **DVD**

Jessica Lange *Ann Talbot* • Armin Mueller-Stahl *Mike Laszlo* • Frederic Forrest *Jack Burke* • Donald Moffat *Harry Talbot* • Lukas Haas *Mikey Talbot* • Cheryl Lynn Bruce *Georgine Wheeler* ■ *Dir* Costa-Gavras • *Scr* Joe Eszterhas

Music for Millions ★★★
Musical drama   1944 · US · BW · 117min

Child prodigy Margaret O'Brien co-stars with June Allyson in this family entertainment from MGM that mixes wartime sentiments and tear-jerking sentimentality with comedy, songs and classical music. O'Brien is the younger sister dispensing comfort to pregnant older sibling Allyson, a cellist with José Iturbi's orchestra whose husband is away fighting in the Pacific. Pianist Iturbi supplies outpourings of Debussy, Tchaikovsky, Dvorak and Grieg, while Jimmy Durante (as the maestro's manager) leavens the mix with a couple of characteristic numbers. RK

Margaret O'Brien *"Mike"* • José Iturbi *Jose Iturbi* • June Allyson *Barbara "Babs" Ainsworth* • Jimmy Durante *Andy Andrews* • Marsha Hunt *Rosalind* • Hugh Herbert *Uncle Ferdinand, "Bish"* ■ *Dir* Henry Koster • *Scr* Myles Connolly • *Costume Designer* Irene

Music from Another Room ★★★ 12
Romantic comedy drama   1998 · US · Colour · 99min

Jude Law stars in this whimsical, watchable romance with a high-calibre cast. As a small boy, Law's character helps his doctor father deliver Brenda Blethyn's latest baby, a girl. Years later, Law sets out to woo the girl (Gretchen Mol), who's engaged to be married to Jon Tenney. Various distractions include a dying Blethyn, a blind sister (Jennifer Tilly) and assorted other dysfunctional siblings. This is either engagingly offbeat or irritatingly quirky, depending on your point of view, but the cast merits attention, even if the material is lightweight and contrived. DA **DVD**

Jude Law *Danny* • Jennifer Tilly *Nina Swan* • Gretchen Mol *Anna Swan* • Martha Plimpton *Karen Swan* • Brenda Blethyn *Grace Swan* • Jon Tenney *Eric* • Jeremy Piven *Billy* ■ *Dir/Scr* Charlie Peters

Music Hath Charms ★ U
Musical   1935 · UK · BW · 65min

Henry Hall merits his place in musical legend for that children's classic *The Teddy Bears' Picnic*. However, he goes down in cinematic infamy for this dismal collection of sketches in which people around the world have their cares soothed away by the soporific melodies of Henry and his orchestra. Strictly for nostalgia nuts. DP **DVD**

Henry Hall (2) • WH Berry *Basil Turner* • Carol Goodner *Mrs Norbray* • Arthur Margetson *Alan Sterling* • Lorna Hubbard *Marjorie Turner* • Antoinette Cellier *Joan* • Billy Milton *Jack Lawton* • Aubrey Mallalieu *Judge* ■ *Dir* Thomas Bentley, Alexander Esway, Walter Summers, Arthur Woods [Arthur B Woods] • *Scr* Jack Davies, Courtney Terrett, from a story by L DuGarde Peach

Music in Manhattan ★★
Musical comedy   1944 · US · BW · 80min

Song-and-dance hopeful Anne Shirley is mistaken for war hero Phillip Terry's bride when she visits Washington to promote her act with Dennis Day in this professionally produced, albeit lacklustre musical comedy. There are lots of songs, but few are any good, though it's a pleasant enough period piece that includes a rare appearance by Charlie Barnet and his band. TS

Anne Shirley *Frankie* • Dennis Day *Stanley* • Phillip Terry *Johnny* • Raymond Walburn *Professor* • Jane Darwell *Mrs Pearson* • Patti Brill *Gladys* ■ *Dir* John H Auer • *Scr* Lawrence Kimble, from a story by Maurice Tombragel, Hal Smith, Jack Scholl

Music in My Heart ★★
Musical   1940 · US · BW · 69min

Someone once described Tony Martin as a "singing tuxedo". Although he was rather a stiff actor, he was handsome and charming, with a winning, dimpled smile and, most importantly, a mellifluous tenor voice. In the silly paper-thin plot of this low-budget musical, Martin plays a foreign singer fighting deportation from the US. He's given a few pleasant songs and a lovely partner in Rita Hayworth, in her first musical for Columbia. RB

Tony Martin (1) *Robert Gregory* • Rita Hayworth *Patricia O'Malley* • Edith Fellows *Mary O'Malley* • Alan Mowbray *Charles Gardner* • Eric Blore *Griggs* • George Tobias *Sascha* ■ *Dir* Joseph Santley • *Scr* James Edward Grant, from his story *Passport to Happiness*

The Music Lovers ★★★ 15
Historical drama   1970 · UK · Colour · 118min

Summing up director Ken Russell's output in the 1970s, the phrase "nothing succeeds like excess" comes to mind, and this biopic of Tchaikovsky is no exception. Here, Richard Chamberlain portrays the great Russian composer as a tortured bisexual, trapped in a loveless marriage with nymphomaniac wife Nina (Glenda Jackson), and he's actually rather good. Jackson has a less prominent role but is nevertheless memorable, not least as Nina's dysfunctional relationship with Tchaikovsky sees her descend into madness. And, of course, with any biopic from Russell, the music is allowed to reign supreme, accompanied by some of the most vivid imagery in British cinema. JA **DVD**

Richard Chamberlain *Tchaikovsky* • Glenda Jackson *Nina Milyukova* • Max Adrian *Nicholas Rubenstein* • Christopher Gable *Chiluvsky* • Isabella Telezynska *Madame Von Meck* • Kenneth Colley *Modeste Tchaikovsky* ■ *Dir* Ken Russell • *Scr* Melvyn Bragg, from the novel *Beloved Friend* by Catherine Drinker Bowen, Barbara von Meck

The Music Man ★★★★ U
Musical comedy   1962 · US · Colour · 144min

Morton DaCosta, who directed Meredith Willson's hit musical on Broadway, was given carte blanche by Jack Warner to re-create it on the screen. He did so with the aid of his Broadway leading man, the dynamic Robert Preston, and came up with an Oscar-winning blockbuster. Preston plays the energetic, charming and silver-tongued conman who charms the elders of River City, Iowa, to finance a band. Also involved is Shirley Jones, the romantic interest and subject of the song *Marian the Librarian*. Onna White's electric choreography and a score that includes *Till There Was You* and *76 Trombones* contribute to an invigorating experience. Matthew Broderick starred in a made-for-TV remake in 2003. RK **DVD**

Robert Preston *Harold Hill* • Shirley Jones *Marian Paroo* • Buddy Hackett *Marcellus Washburn* • Hermione Gingold *Eulalie Mackechnie Shinn* • Paul Ford *Mayor Shinn* • Pert Kelton *Mrs Paroo* • Timmy Everett *Tommy Djilas* • Susan Luckey *Zaneeta Shinn* • Ronny Howard [Ron Howard] *Winthrop Paroo* ■ *Dir* Morton Da Costa • *Scr* Marion Hargrove, from the musical by Meredith Willson, Franklin Lacey

The Music of Chance ★★★ 15
Drama   1993 · US · Colour · 94min

This is a beguiling adaptation of Paul Auster's disquieting novel from ex-documentary director Philip Haas, who extracts every ounce of intelligence, wit and insight from a slight tale without ever straining for effect. He is well served by some exceptional performances, notably from James Spader and Mandy Patinkin as the gamblers forced to build a medieval stone wall to pay off a debt. The conclusion is disappointing, but this neglected curio is worth watching. DP Swearing. **DVD**

James Spader *Jack Pozzi* • Mandy Patinkin *James Nashe* • Charles Durning *Bill Flower* • Joel Grey *Willie Stone* • M Emmet Walsh *Calvin Murks* • Samantha Mathis *Tiffany* • Chris Penn *Floyd* •

Pearl Jones *Louise* ■ *Dir* Philip Haas • *Scr* Philip Haas, Belinda Haas, from the novel by Paul Auster

Music of the Heart ★★ PG
Biographical drama   1999 · US · Colour · 118min

Horror maestro Wes Craven's first non-fantasy is a bland bust. The true story of violin teacher Roberta Guaspari (Meryl Streep), who brought music and hope to the school kids of East Harlem, gets nothing more than a vacuous TV-movie treatment under Craven's restrained direction. Streep merely plays a parody of herself in this mix of *Fame* and *Dangerous Minds*, while salsa superstar Gloria Estefan couldn't have made a more ineffectual feature debut. AJ **DVD**

Meryl Streep *Roberta* • Angela Bassett *Janet* • Aidan Quinn *Brian* • Cloris Leachman *Assunta* • Gloria Estefan *Isabel* • Jane Leeves *Dorothea* • Itzhak Perlman • Isaac Stern ■ *Dir* Wes Craven • *Scr* Pamela Gray

The Music Room ★★★ U
Drama   1958 · Ind · BW · 100min

In addition to scripting the majority of his pictures, Bengali director Satyajit Ray also regularly composed the soundtracks. Few films better showcased his command of Indian music than this poignant tale of an aristocrat who spends everything he has on a concert to serenade a passing age. There is much to admire in Chhabi Biswas's mournful performance and the way in which Ray maintains the delicate balance between progress and decay. But you really need an ear for Indian classical music to fully appreciate this. DP Hindi +subtitles.

Chhabi Biswas *Bishwambar Roy* • Padmadevi *Roy's wife* • Pinaki Sengupta *Khoka* • Tulsi Lahiri *Manager of Roy's estate* ■ *Dir* Satyajit Ray • *Scr* Satyajit Ray, from a short story by Tarashankar Bannerjee

The Music Teacher ★★ U
Drama   1988 · Bel · Colour · 93min

The director Gérard Corbiau has received an Oscar nomination each time he has ventured into the world of opera. Snippets from Verdi, Mozart, Schubert and Bellini pop up like selections from a classical jukebox, as retiring tenor José Van Dam pits his pickpocketing protégé against bisexual prince Patrick Bauchau's toyboy baritone. The action is often pretentious, but the art direction and cinematography look good enough to eat. DP French +subtitles. **DVD**

José Van Dam *Joachim Dallayrac* • Anne Roussel *Sophie* • Philippe Volter *Jean* • Sylvie Fennec *Estelle* • Patrick Bauchau *Prince Scotti* • Johan Leysen *François* ■ *Dir* Gérard Corbiau • *Scr* Gérard Corbiau, André Corbiau, from a story by Luc Jabon, Gérard Corbiau • *Cinematographer* Walther van den Ende

The Music Teacher ★★
Drama   2012 · Can · Colour · 111min

Fans of *Glee* will probably appreciate this cheesy and sentimental TV movie that sees adult former pupils rallying to help their much-loved old music teacher (an occasionally overbearing Annie Potts) when budget cuts threaten her after-school classes. Naturally, it's their regrettably toe-curling performing skills that the group decides to utilise, which leads to an underwhelming fundraising show in which all the key characters get to belt out a number. Fortunately, the acting overall is better than the singing, especially Richard Thomas's small but sympathetic turn as Potts's romantically frustrated boyfriend. SF

Annie Potts *Alyson Daley* • Kerry James *Zack* • Shawn Roberts *Jace* • Moneca Delain *Karen* • Rukiya Bernard *Sheila* • Richard Thomas *Ray* ■ *Dir* Ron Oliver • *Scr* Ronald Parker

The Musketeer ★ PG
Swashbuckling action adventure   2001 · Ger/US/UK/Lux · Colour · 100min

Falling flat from the clumsy opening titles, this fails entirely in its aim to update Alexandre Dumas's classic by adding *Matrix*-style fight choreography. The

M

confrontation sequences between Justin Chambers's vengeful musketeer and Cardinal Richelieu's henchman Tim Roth are tension free, while the ludicrous collection of mullet haircuts, beards and inconsistent accents adds an extra air of farce to a movie crammed with hammy dialogue and wooden performances. **SF** **DVD**

Catherine Deneuve *The Queen* • Mena Suvari *Francesca* • Stephen Rea *Cardinal Richelieu* • Tim Roth *Febre* • Justin Chambers *D'Artagnan* • Nick Moran *Aramis* • Bill Treacher *Bonacieux* ■ *Dir* Peter Hyams • *Scr* Gene Quintano, Fabrice Ziolkowski, from the novel *Les Trois Mousquetaires* by Alexandre Dumas

The Musketeers of Pig Alley ★★★★
Silent drama 1912 · US · BW · 17min

Advertised as "a depiction of the gangster evil", the finest of DW Griffith's short films is also one of the first gangster pictures. Lillian Gish, whom Griffith was to make into one of the silent screen's greatest stars, in only her third film, shines as a young wife who becomes the object of a hoodlum's attentions. This realistic drama, which reflected the director's interest in social concerns, was shot in authentic locations and is of lasting historical interest as a picture of New York's slums in 1912. **RB**

Lillian Gish *Little Lady* • Elmer Booth *Snapper Kid, "Chief of the Musketeers"* • Walter Miller *A musician* • Harry Carey ■ *Dir* DW Griffith • *Scr* DW Griffiths, Anita Loos

Must Love Dogs ★★ 12
Romantic comedy 2005 · US · Colour · 93min

John Cusack and Diane Lane star as the date-shy divorcees who meet via internet personal ads placed by friends and family, and then conduct a constantly sidetracked courtship, sparked initially by their mutually feigned love of dogs. It's a watchable enough diversion, but both leads deserve better. After a few pithy early lines, this degenerates into a routine piece of forgettable fluff. **DA** **DVD**

Diane Lane *Sarah Nolan* • John Cusack *Jake Anderson* • Elizabeth Perkins *Carol* • Dermot Mulroney *Bob Connor* • Christopher Plummer *Bill* • Stockard Channing *Dolly* ■ *Dir* Gary David Goldberg • *Scr* Gary David Goldberg, from the novel by Claire Cook

Mustang ★★★★ 15
Drama
2015 · Fr/Ger/Tur/Qatar · Colour · 93min

Part social-realist slice of contemporary rural Turkish life, part fairy tale, this striking debut from co-writer/director Deniz Gamze Erguven has a close cousin in Sofia Coppola's *The Virgin Suicides*. In both, a group of five sisters are grounded by overprotective families with pressure-cooker results. Honoured at Cannes and the Césars, *Mustang* never quite conforms to expectation, and some of the tonal shifts from comic to tragic jar, but it's a confident, illuminating debut. **AC** Turkish +subtitles. Swearing, sexual references. **DVD** **SB**

Gunes Nezihe Sensoy [Gunes Sensoy] *Lale* • Doga Zeynep Doguslu *Nur* • Tugba Sunguroglu *Selma* • Elit Iscan *Ece* • Ilayda Akdogan *Sonay* • Nihal Koldas [Nihal G Koldas] *Grandmother* ■ *Dir* Deniz Gamze Erguven • *Scr* Deniz Gamze Erguven, Alice Winocour

Mustang Country ★★ U
Western 1976 · US · Colour · 79min

There's more than a little biographical irony in this solidly crafted western. The action is set in 1925, around the time that a young hopeful named Joel McCrea was working as a movie stuntman and horse wrangler. Here, 51 years on, McCrea is making his final appearance in a distinguished screen career, playing a retired rodeo star and rancher who helps a native American lad track down and tame a wild horse in time for a big meet. **DP**

Joel McCrea *Dan Treego* • Nika Mina *Nika* • Robert Fuller *Griff* • Patrick Wayne *Tee Jay* ■ *Dir/Scr* John C Champion

Mutant ★★ 18
Science-fiction horror
1984 · US · Colour · 95min

A small midwestern town is menaced by zombie mutants who have been contaminated by a toxic waste spill. As usual, the local corporation is trying to cover up the scandal that has endangered the whole community. Although the zombies do little more than lunge at people with outstretched arms, the movie is well paced, but it lacks the tension and suspense of the *Living Dead* landmarks that it's so clearly trying to copy. **AJ** **DVD**

Wings Hauser *Josh Cameron* • Bo Hopkins *Sheriff Will Stewart* • Jody Medford *Holly Pierce* • Lee Montgomery *Mike Cameron* • Marc Clement *Albert* • Cary Guffey *Billy* • Jennifer Warren *Dr Myra Tate* ■ *Dir* John "Bud" Cardos • *Scr* Peter Orton, Michael Jones, from a story by John Kruize

Mutant Chronicles ★★ 18
Science-fiction action adventure
2008 · US/UK · Colour · 106min

Inspired by the successful role-playing game, the action takes place in the 23rd century, when the Earth is being ravaged by blade-wielding creatures. As the population flees the planet, soldier Major Mitch Hunter (Thomas Jane) and a band of battle-scarred veterans are recruited by the Keeper of the Chronicles, Brother Samuel (a red-robed Ron Perlman), for a suicide mission to stem the mutant tide. Corny dialogue and cheap CGI special effects don't raise the credibility stakes, although a couple of competent action set pieces may drum up a modicum of cult momentum among undemanding genre fans. **JR** **DVD** **SB**

Thomas Jane *Major Mitch Hunter* • Ron Perlman *Brother Samuel* • Devon Aoki *Duval* • John Malkovich *Constantine* • Sean Pertwee *Nathan Rooker* • Benno Fürmann *Steiner* • Anna Walton *Severian* • Tom Wu *Juba* ■ *Dir* Simon Hunter • *Scr* Philip Eisner, from the role-playing game created by Target Games

The Mutations ★★ 18
Horror 1973 · UK · Colour · 88min

Veteran cinematographer-turned-director Jack Cardiff's mind-boggling mad scientist extravaganza triumphantly embraces bad taste to provide queasy *frissons* rarely witnessed in British horror. Demented biologist Donald Pleasence crosses humans with plants and sends his gruesome failures to Michael Dunn, a dwarf who runs a circus sideshow. His most successful hybrid is a man-sized Venus fly trap (Scott Antony) who ingests a tramp before traumatising Jill Haworth and Julie Ege. Mixing genuinely deformed performers with made-up actors, the discomfiting template may be that of *Freaks*, but its prurient atmosphere is rooted in 1970s British sleaze. **AJ**

Donald Pleasence *Dr Nolter* • Tom Baker *Lynch* • Brad Harris *Brian* • Julie Ege *Hedi* • Michael Dunn *Burns* • Scott Antony *Tony* • Jill Haworth *Lauren* ■ *Dir* Jack Cardiff • *Scr* Robert D Weinbach, Edward Mann

Mute Witness ★★★★ 18
Thriller 1995 · UK/Ger · Colour · 92min

A mute special-effects make-up artist accidentally sees a "snuff" movie being filmed in a Moscow studio, then spends the rest of this supercool thriller running for her life. Reminiscent of early Brian De Palma shockers, Anthony Waller's witty fright stuff revitalises the "woman in peril" genre with jet-black humour, tons of superbly controlled style, grisly corkscrew twists and the sinister appearance of Alec Guinness as "the Reaper". The Russian locations only add to the atmosphere. **AJ** Violence, swearing, sex scenes, nudity. **DVD**

Marina Sudina *Billie Hughes* • Fay Ripley *Karen Hughes* • Evan Richards *Andy Clarke* • Oleg Jankowski [Oleg Jankowski] *Larsen* • Igor Volkov *Arkadi* • Sergej Karlenkov *Lyosha* • Alexander Buriev *Strohbecker* • Alec Guinness *"The Reaper"* ■ *Dir/Scr* Anthony Waller

Mutiny ★★ U
Period adventure 1952 · US · Colour · 77min

This rousing adventure is set aboard a war ship on the high seas during the War of 1812. An event-filled plot involves a heroic sea captain (Mark Stevens), a mutinous English sailor (Patric Knowles), and a duplicitous firebrand (Angela Lansbury) who is the object of both their affections. Mutiny, gold bullion, the sinking of British ships, and a horde of colourful peg-leg and one-eyed pirates all add to the excitement. **RK**

Mark Stevens *James Marshall* • Angela Lansbury *Leslie* • Patric Knowles *Ben Waldridge* • Gene Evans *Hook* • Rhys Williams *Redlegs* ■ *Dir* Edward Dmytryk • *Scr* Sidney Harmon, Philip Yordan, from a story by Hollister Noble

Mutiny on the Bounty ★★★★ PG
Classic historical adventure
1935 · US · BW · 132min

Clark Gable squirmed at the idea of wearing a pigtail, knickerbockers and shoes with silver buckles to play the part of Fletcher Christian in what was to be his first costume movie. But he and Charles Laughton (as Captain Bligh) teamed to bracing effect in this lavish and stirring adventure on the high seas, based, of course, on the famous real-life mutiny. Director Frank Lloyd won best director Oscars (for *The Divine Lady* and *Cavalcade*), but this may be his best movie of all. The Academy certainly thought so: they voted it best picture. **PF** **DVD**

Charles Laughton *Captain William Bligh* • Clark Gable *Fletcher Christian* • Franchot Tone *Roger Byam* • Herbert Mundin *Smith* • Eddie Quillan *Ellison* • Dudley Digges *Bacchus* • Donald Crisp *Burkitt* • Henry Stephenson *Sir Joseph Banks* • James Cagney • David Niven ■ *Dir* Frank Lloyd • *Scr* Talbot Jennings, Jules Furthman, Carey Wilson, from the novels *Mutiny on the Bounty* and *Men against the Sea* by Charles Nordhoff, James Norman Hall

Mutiny on the Bounty ★★★★ 12
Historical adventure 1962 · US · Colour · 177min

This version of the famous nautical adventure from Lewis Milestone is a memorable successor to the Oscar-winning 1935 movie. Milestone deserves credit for surviving laborious re-shoots and difficulties caused by Marlon Brando's temperament. Though controversial, Brando's performance as Fletcher Christian is impressive as he moves from arrogant fop to gallant hero, despite his somewhat strangulated English accent. Trevor Howard is fine as the sadistic Captain Bligh, but the Tahiti interlude is a sequence to be missed. **TH** **DVD**

Marlon Brando *Fletcher Christian* • Trevor Howard *Captain William Bligh* • Richard Harris *John Mills* • Hugh Griffith *Alexander Smith* • Richard Haydn *William Brown* • Tarita *Maimiti* • Tim Seely *Edward Young* • Percy Herbert *Matthew Quintal* • Gordon Jackson *Edward Birkett* ■ *Dir* Lewis Milestone • *Scr* Charles Lederer, Eric Ambler, William L Driscoll, Borden Chase, John Gay, Ben Hecht, from the novel by Charles Nordhoff, James Norman Hall

Mutiny on the Buses ★ PG
Comedy 1972 · UK · Colour · 84min

Things must have been bad at Hammer for the once-famous horror studio to resort to big screen TV spin-offs such as this woefully unfunny comedy based on the popular ITV series. You'd have thought there was simply no more mileage left in the jokes about Blakey's schedules, Olive and Arthur's marriage and Stan and Jack's allergy to work, but they managed to squeeze out a third movie – *Holiday on the Buses* – the following year. **DP** **DVD**

Reg Varney *Stan Butler* • Doris Hare *Mrs Butler* • Anna Karen *Olive* • Michael Robbins *Arthur* • Bob Grant *Jack* • Stephen Lewis *Inspector Blake* ■ *Dir* Harry Booth • *Scr* Ronald Wolfe, Ronald Chesney

Mutual Appreciation ★★★ 15
Comedy 2005 · US · BW · 108min

Just as he had done in the splendidly offbeat *Funny Ha Ha*, maverick auteur Andrew Bujalski apes Eric Rohmer in his latest loquacious study of self-obsessed but emotionally stunted youth. The influence of John Cassavetes, Woody Allen and Jim Jarmusch is also evident in this low-key comedy that centres on Alan (Justin Rice), a musician who arrives in New York to ponder the future after splitting from his indie bandmates. Alan's rambling detachment from reality might strike some as frustrating, but this quirky, semi-improvised film develops a sense of unease that's squirmingly compelling. **DP** **DVD**

Justin Rice *Alan* • Rachel Clift *Ellie* • Andrew Bujalski *Lawrence* • Seung-min Lee *Sara* • Kevin Micka *Dennis* • Bill Morrison *Walter* • Pamela Corkey *Patricia* ■ *Dir/Scr* Andrew Bujalski

My Afternoons with Margueritte ★★★ 15
Comedy drama 2010 · Fr · Colour · 82min

In this cosy but lightweight small-town tale, illiterate handyman Germain (Gérard Depardieu) and elderly Margueritte (Gisèle Casadesus) become friends when they meet while feeding pigeons in the park. Slowly, Margueritte fosters Germain's love of literature by spending her afternoons reading aloud to him on their favourite bench. But beguiling though the leads are, when Margueritte's sight begins to fail and her relatives scheme to deposit her in a cheap hostel in Belgium, director Jean Becker can't quite prevent things from slipping into melodrama. **DP** French +subtitles. Swearing.

Gérard Depardieu *Germain Chazes* • Gisèle Casadesus *Margueritte* • Sophie Guillemin *Annette* • Patrick Bouchitey *Landremont* • Jean-François Stévenin *Jojo* • Claire Maurier *Germain's mother* ■ *Dir* Jean Becker • *Scr* Jean Becker, Jean-Loup Dabadie, from the novel *La Tête en Friche* by Marie-Sabine Roger

My Ain Folk ★★★★ PG
Biographical drama 1973 · UK · BW · 52min

The second part of Bill Douglas's autobiographical trilogy (that began the previous year with *My Childhood*) owes more to the style of the Soviet cinema of the 1920s and 1930s than the others in the series. Extreme close-ups leave us nowhere to hide from the misery Stephen Archibald experiences as he goes to stay with his father's parents after his maternal grandma dies and his half-brother is packed off to a home. Such is the loveless nature of the relationship between his grandparents and the bitterness they feel towards the boy's mother that you are left with that uncomfortable feeling you get when you hear the neighbours having a blazing row. The concluding segment is *My Way Home*. **DP** **DVD**

Stephen Archibald *Jamie* • Hughie Restorick *Tommy* • Jean Taylor-Smith *Grandmother* • Bernard McKenna *Tommy's father* • Mr Munro *Jamie's grandfather* • Paul Kermack *Jamie's father* ■ *Dir/Scr* Bill Douglas

My American Cousin ★★★ PG
Comedy drama 1985 · Can · Colour · 85min

This delightful coming-of-age tale was made and set in Canada. It's the summer of 1959, and all there is to do is some cherry picking until a pre-teen girl's Californian cousin rides into town in his red Cadillac and sets everyone's hearts a-flutter. The film won six Genies (the Canadian equivalent of the Oscar), and it's easy to see why, thanks to the charming script and enjoyable performances by a relatively unknown cast. An equally charming sequel, *American Boyfriends*, followed in 1989. **JB**

Margaret Langrick *Sandy* • John Wildman *Butch Walker* • Richard Donat *Major Wilcox* • Jane Mortifee *Kitty Wilcox* • TJ Scott *Lenny McPhee* • Camille Henderson *Shirley Darling* ■ *Dir/Scr* Sandy Wilson

My Architect ★★★★ PG
Documentary   2003 · US · Colour · 116min

In this meditative and poetic documentary, Nathaniel Kahn - one of two illegitimate children that the architect Louis Kahn had with two different women - seeks to find out who his late father really was. In interviews with architectural greats such as IM Pei and Frank Gehry, we learn of Kahn's brilliance and the respect accorded to him by his peers. Unfortunately, the film-maker shies away from asking tough questions of the women who could perhaps give more insight into Kahn's private life. Like Nathaniel (who was only 11 when his father died), we are left to discover what we can of the man through his influential work, which includes the impressive Capital building in Bangladesh. Almost as fascinating is how Louis Kahn's own journey took him from greatness to bankruptcy and a lonely death from a heart attack in the men's room at New York's Penn Station in 1974. GM *DVD*

Nathaniel Kahn *Narrator* ▪ *Dir/Scr* Nathaniel Kahn · *Cinematographer* Bob Richman

My Beautiful Laundrette ★★★★★ 15
Drama   1985 · UK · Colour · 93min

This seminal 1980s movie launched a plethora of now distinguished careers, including those of director Stephen Frears and Daniel Day-Lewis. The latter shines here in his first major role as the scabrous punk and friend to Gordon Warnecke's entrepreneurial Asian, who dreams of creating the most glittering launderette in London. The movie's undoubted importance lies in the way it takes many of the decade's Thatcherite characteristics - grafting in the free market, the desire for material acquisitions, the establishment of stability - and turns everything on its head with a merciful lack of polemic. SH Violence, swearing, sex scenes, nudity. *DVD*

Daniel Day-Lewis *Johnny* · Gordon Warnecke *Omar* · Saeed Jaffrey *Nasser* · Roshan Seth *Papa* · Derrick Branche *Salim* · Shirley Anne Field *Rachel* · Rita Wolf *Tania* ▪ *Dir* Stephen Frears · *Scr* Hanif Kureishi

My Best Fiend ★★★ 15
Documentary
1999 · Ger/UK/US · Colour and BW · 98min

Even though the tensions that existed between them bordered on genuine hatred, director Werner Herzog and actor Klaus Kinski made five quite remarkable films together. Yet, as Herzog recalls in this bittersweet documentary memoir, he only prevented the native Indians from killing his star on the Amazonian set of *Fitzcarraldo* because he needed him for a few more scenes. Almost fondly philosophical about the tantrums and abuse, Herzog recalls them at length, and he virtually regards the infrequent ceasefires as wasted opportunities. This is clearly only one side of the story, but it's still a fascinating one. DP German +subtitles. Swearing. *DVD*

Werner Herzog *Narrator* · Klaus Kinski · Claudia Cardinale · Eva Mattes · Beat Presser ▪ *Dir* Werner Herzog

My Best Friend ★★★ 12
Comedy   2006 · Fr · Colour · 90min

Patrice Leconte's whimsical French comedy stars Daniel Auteuil as François, a selfish middle-aged antiques dealer who suddenly realises that he has no real friends. Goaded into accepting a bet from his business partner (Julie Gayet), he has just ten days to produce his best mate or forfeit an expensive Greek vase. All looks lost, until François realises that Bruno (Dany Boon), the talkative taxi driver who's been ferrying him around, seems to have a gift for making people like him. A tactfully underplayed performance from Auteuil holds this otherwise lightweight film together - his hangdog expressions perfectly capturing a certain kind of middle-aged misanthropy. It all leads to a delightful climax on the French *Who Wants to Be a Millionaire?* JR French +subtitles. Some swearing. *DVD*

Daniel Auteuil *François* · Dany Boon *Bruno* · Julie Gayet *Catherine* · Julie Durand *Louise* · Jacques Mathou *M Bouley, Bruno's father* · Marie Pillet *Mme Bouley, Bruno's mother* · Elizabeth Bourgine *Julia* ▪ *Dir* Patrice Leconte · *Scr* Jérôme Tonnerre, Patrice Leconte, from a story by Olivier Dazat · *Cinematographer* Jean-Marie Dreujou

My Best Friend's Girl ★★ 18
Comedy   2008 · US · Colour · 112min

In this humdrum romantic comedy, Dane Cook plays a guy so good at being gross that dumped men pay him to date their exes and be so disgusting that the women run right back to them. The dull, dated and oh-so-predictable plot has the next jilted man being Cook's best friend, Jason Biggs. The object of his affection is Kate Hudson, who has decided to enjoy life as a single girl. This is just slick and soulless entertainment, saved only by Alec Baldwin's all-too-brief role as Cook's womanising father. DA Swearing, sexual references, nudity. *DVD* *Blu-ray*

Dane Cook *Tank* · Kate Hudson *Alexis* · Jason Biggs *Dustin* · Alec Baldwin *Professor Turner* · Diora Baird *Rachel* · Lizzy Caplan *Ami* ▪ *Dir* Howard Deutch · *Scr* Jordan Cahan

My Best Friend's Wedding ★★★★ 12
Romantic comedy   1997 · US · Colour · 104min

This sparkling comedy proved to be a career-resurrecting movie for Julia Roberts, and for once she plays someone who may not get the guy. When she hears her best friend and former lover (Dermot Mulroney) is getting married to Cameron Diaz, Roberts realises she wants to be more than just friends after all. What makes this film work so well is that it's not just "The Julia Roberts Show". While she does the bumbling, adorable stuff she's best at, the stunning Diaz and superb Rupert Everett (as Roberts's gay friend and accomplice) battle it out for best supporting performance (and both win). JB *DVD* *Blu-ray*

Julia Roberts *Julianne Potter* · Dermot Mulroney *Michael O'Neal* · Cameron Diaz *Kimmy Wallace* · Rupert Everett *George Downes* · Philip Bosco *Walter Wallace* · M Emmet Walsh *Joe O'Neal* · Rachel Griffiths *Samantha Newhouse* · Carrie Preston *Mandy Newhouse* ▪ *Dir* PJ Hogan · *Scr* Ronald Bass

My Best Girl ★★★ U
Silent romantic comedy   1927 · US · BW · 66min

Made for her own production company under the auspices of United Artists, which she co-founded with Douglas Fairbanks, Charlie Chaplin and DW Griffith, this was one of Mary Pickford's last silent films. As the only normal member of a hopelessly irresponsible family, Pickford works in a Five-and-Dime and becomes romantically involved with the new clerk (Charles "Buddy" Rogers), who is really the boss's son. Other than asking us to believe that the 34-year-old "Little Mary" is 18, this is sweetly pleasing, if inconsequential. RK

Mary Pickford *Maggie Johnson* · Charles "Buddy" Rogers *Joe Grant* · Sunshine Hart *Ma Johnson* · Lucien Littlefield *Pa Johnson* · Carmelita Geraghty *Liz Johnson* ▪ *Dir* Sam Taylor · *Scr* Hope Loring, Allen McNeil, Tim Whelan, from a story by Kathleen Norris

My Big Fat Greek Wedding ★★★ PG
Romantic comedy
2002 · US/Can · Colour · 91min

This perky, low-budget romantic comedy - adapted from star Nia Vardalos for her autobiographical one-woman stage show - was the unexpected success story of 2002. Vardalos shines as a frumpy waitress at her Greek family's restaurant who goes against her father's traditionalist views when she finds a new job, gets a confidence-boosting makeover and hooks handsome teacher John Corbett. While the happy couple-to-be - who share charming screen chemistry - are played relatively straight, Vardalos's in-your-face relatives are a source of buoyant comic vitality. A sequel is due in early 2016. JC English, Greek +subtitles. *DVD*

Nia Vardalos *Toula Portokalos* · John Corbett *Ian Miller* · Michael Constantine *Gus Portokalos* · Lainie Kazan *Maria Portokalos* · Andrea Martin *Aunt Voula* · Joey Fatone *Angelo* · Gia Carides *Nikki* · Louis Mandylor *Nick* · Ian Gomez *Mike* ▪ *Dir* Joel Zwick · *Scr* Nia Vardalos, from her one-woman show

My Big Fat Greek Wedding 2 ★★★ 12
Romantic comedy   2016 · US · Colour · 89min

Fourteen years after the first film became the highest grossing romantic comedy ever, writer/star Nia Vardalos revisits life on the street where Toula's family live side-by-side. The jokes feel familiar, but Vardalos draws you back in with the same big heart as Toula strives to put the spark back into her marriage with Ian (John Corbett). Amid extreme silliness, Vardalos's script makes pointed observations about the suffocating nature of a close-knit family, and she creates an infectious feel that helps you forgive the flaws. SP Sexual references. *DVD* *Blu-ray*

Nia Vardalos *Toula Miller* · John Corbett *Ian Miller* · Elena Kampouris *Paris Miller* · Lainie Kazan *Maria* · Michael Constantine *Gus* ▪ *Dir* Kirk Jones · *Scr* Nia Vardalos

My Blood Runs Cold ★★
Thriller   1965 · US · BW · 103min

This chiller has an intriguing enough premise, with Troy Donahue attempting to worm his way into heiress Joey Heatherton's bank account by claiming they were lovers in a previous life. However, with both directorial and actorly restraint at a premium, the reincarnation angle is soon forgotten and the psychopathic Donahue embarks on the inevitable stalk-and-slash mission. DP

Troy Donahue *Ben Gunther* · Joey Heatherton *Julie Merriday* · Barry Sullivan *Julian Merriday* · Nicolas Coster *Harry Lindsay* · Jeanette Nolan *Aunt Sarah* ▪ *Dir* William Conrad · *Scr* John Mantley, from the story *The Girl Who Was Two* by John Meredyth Lucas

My Bloody Valentine ★★ 15
Horror   1981 · Can · Colour · 86min

This 1981 slasher horror was one of a slew of derivative movies (*Friday the 13th*, *Prom Night*, *The Burning*) that followed in the wake of John Carpenter's *Halloween*. Set in a small mining town during a Valentine's Day celebration, the film follows the tried-and-tested formula of horny, partying teenagers being stalked like lambs to the slaughter by a hack-happy boogeyman (in this case, a pickaxe-wielding miner). There's the odd creepy moment, particularly when the death-dealing moves to a genuine mine. But the bland characters and sub-par scares and gore (the movie was reputedly slashed by US censors and the UK version seems shorn of full-on bloodletting) just go to show how good Carpenter's 1978 classic really is. JA *DVD*

Paul Kelman *Jessie "TJ" Hanniger* · Lori Hallier *Sarah* · Neil Affleck *Axel* · Don Francks *Chief Newby* ▪ *Dir* George Mihalka · *Scr* John Beaird, from a story by Stephen A Miller

My Bloody Valentine ★★★ 18
Horror thriller   2009 · US · Colour · 96min

George Mihalka's 1981 *Halloween* wannabe receives a highly respectable reboot here, with canny 3D coating (the first horror to be shot in the digital Real D process) giving extra flinch value to the standard-issue slasher clichés. Ten years after a mining tragedy caused a seriously injured survivor to turn psycho and go on the rampage, a new series of brutal slayings begins when Jensen Ackles (from TV's *Supernatural*) returns to the small community to sell his creepy colliery inheritance. Director/co-editor Patrick Lussier ensures the pace stays lively and the demented miner's pickaxe remains the thing to dodge, among the eyeballs, brains and blood that seemingly fly from the screen in impressively orchestrated ways. AJ *DVD* *Blu-ray*

Jensen Ackles *Tom Hanniger* · Jaime King *Sarah Palmer* · Kerr Smith *Axel Palmer* · Kevin Tighe *Ben Foley* · Edi Gathegi *Deputy Martin* · Tom Atkins *Sheriff Burke* · Betsy Rue *Irene* · Megan Boone *Megan* ▪ *Dir* Patrick Lussier · *Scr* Todd Farmer, Zane Smith, from the 1981 film, from a story by Stephen A Miller

My Blue Heaven ★★★ U
Musical comedy   1950 · US · Colour · 92min

This teaming of Betty Grable and Dan Dailey from 20th Century-Fox follows the surprise success of 1947's *Mother Wore Tights*. This isn't bad, but its plot about vaudevillians wanting to adopt a child may seem a little tasteless, and, frankly, it's hard to accept Grable drooling over a baby and admitting that she wants to wash nappies! The songs are nice, the Technicolor is ravishing and the result is fairly typical of a Fox musical. TS *DVD*

Betty Grable *Molly Moran* · Dan Dailey *Jack Moran* · David Wayne *Walter Pringle* · Jane Wyatt *Janet Pringle* · Mitzi Gaynor *Gloria Adams* · Una Merkel *Miss Gilbert* · Louise Beavers *Selma* ▪ *Dir* Henry Koster · *Scr* Lamar Trotti, Claude Binyon, from the story *Storks Don't Bring Babies* by SK Lauren

My Blue Heaven ★★ PG
Comedy   1990 · US · Colour · 91min

With Steve Martin and Rick Moranis in the leads and a script by Nora Ephron, this satire on suburban America promises much. Sadly, it delivers very little, largely because the supply of gags runs out too quickly and Martin rather overdoes it as a hood hidden away prior to testifying in a Mob murder trial. Moranis's FBI agent won't be the only one not to see the funny side as Martin commits a few crimes for old time's sake. DP Swearing, violence.

Steve Martin *Vinnie Antonelli* · Rick Moranis *Barney Coopersmith* · Joan Cusack *Hannah Stubbs* · Melanie Mayron *Crystal Rybak* · William Irwin [Bill Irwin] *Kirby* · Carol Kane *Shaldeen* · William Hickey *Billy Sparrow* · Deborah Rush *Linda* · Daniel Stern *Will Stubbs* ▪ *Dir* Herbert Ross · *Scr* Nora Ephron

My Blueberry Nights ★★★ 12
Romantic drama
2007 · HK/Fr/Chi · Colour · 91min

Hong Kong art house director Wong Kar-Wai brings an outsider's perspective to the American road-trip genre in his first English-language movie. Singer Norah Jones plays a New York lonelyheart who takes off on a voyage of self-discovery to Memphis and Las Vegas. In the first - and flimsiest - section, Jones befriends ex-pat café owner Jude Law, whose kindness masks a deeper affection. Moving west, she meets a boozy southern belle (Rachel Weisz), whose rocky relationship with a cop (David Strathairn) takes a tragic turn. In the more satisfying home stretch, Jones hooks up with a brazen gambler (Natalie Portman) who has daddy issues. Though lovely to look at, and well played, this poetic journey is undermined by the director's tin ear for dialogue. DW Brief swearing. *DVD* *Blu-ray*

Norah Jones *Elizabeth* · Jude Law *Jeremy* · David Strathairn *Arnie* · Rachel Weisz *Sue Lynne* · Natalie Portman *Leslie* · Chan Marshall *Katya* · Katya Blumenberg *Girlfriend* · Chad Davis [Chad R Davis] *Boyfriend* ▪ *Dir* Wong Kar-Wai · *Scr* Wong Kar-Wai, Lawrence Block, from a story by Wong

My Body, My Child ★★★
Drama based on a true story
1982 · US · Colour · 100min

Based on a true story, this "moral dilemma of the week" TV movie may not have the most original premise in the world, but it is well told and directed by Marvin J Chomsky. Vanessa Redgrave gives one of her strongest recent performances as a middle-aged Catholic schoolteacher who must wrestle with the mother of all decisions when she finds herself pregnant with what may be a deformed foetus. Joseph Campanella convinces as Redgrave's equally confused husband, while Jack Albertson won a posthumous Emmy for his final performance as her invalid dad. PF

M

Vanessa Redgrave *Leenie Cabrezi* • Joseph Campanella *Joe Cabrezi* • Stephen Elliott (1) *Dr Gallagher* • James Naughton *Dr Dan Berenson* • Gail Strickland *Adele* • Jack Albertson *Poppa MacMahon* • Sarah Jessica Parker *Katy* ■ *Dir* Marvin J Chomsky • *Scr* Louisa Burns-Bisogno

My Bodyguard ★★★ PG

Drama   1980 · US · Colour · 92min

School bully Matt Dillon persecutes rich kid Chris Makepeace, who retaliates by attempting to hire the morose and overgrown Adam Baldwin as his personal bodyguard. First-time director Tony Bill creates a believable atmosphere at this Chicago school while gradually shifting attention away from Makepeace's plight to Baldwin's troubled past. Cameos from Ruth Gordon and John Houseman, plus the screen debut of Joan Cusack, are bonuses. AT *DVD*

Chris Makepeace *Clifford* • Adam Baldwin *Linderman* • Matt Dillon *Moody* • Paul Quandt *Carson* • Joan Cusack *Shelley* • Dean R Miller *Hightower* • Richard Bradley *Dubrow* • Ruth Gordon *Gramma* • John Houseman *Dobbs* ■ *Dir* Tony Bill • *Scr* Alan Ormsby

My Boss's Daughter ★ 12

Romantic comedy   2003 · US · Colour · 86min

David Zucker's clunker of a comedy is utterly devoid of wit. Publishing researcher Ashton Kutcher finds himself housesitting for his boss (Terence Stamp), who also happens to be the scrupulous father of his heart's desire, Tara Reid. But none of the misfortunes that befall Stamp's prized home are the remotest bit amusing and it's hard to see how a cast this stellar could be attracted to a project this dire. DP *DVD*

Ashton Kutcher *Tom Stansfield* • Tara Reid *Lisa Taylor* • Jeffrey Tambor *Ken* • Andy Richter *Red Taylor* • Michael Madsen *TJ* • Jon Abrahams *Paul* • David Koechner *Speed* • Carmen Electra *Tina* • Terence Stamp *Jack Taylor* ■ *Dir* David Zucker • *Scr* David Dorfman

My Boyfriend's Back ★★★★ PG

Comedy drama   1989 · US · Colour · 93min

Sandy Duncan, Judith Light and Jill Eikenberry star as the members of a 1960s trio who reunite 25 years on for a television music concert in a TV movie that does more than just skate across the surface. The three leads give carefully layered performances, personal and social insights abound, real emotion is built into every frame and drama is fused seamlessly with wit. Actual pop stars of the 1960s appear, including Mary Wells, Gary Puckett and the Penguins. JM

Sandy Duncan *Chris Henry* • Jill Eikenberry *Deborah McGuire* • Judith Light *Vicki Vine* • John Sanderford *Harry Simons* • Stephen Macht *Joseph, Deborah's boyfriend* ■ *Dir* Paul Schneider (1) • *Scr* Lindsay Harrison, from a story by April Campbell, Bruce Jones

My Boyfriend's Back ★ 15

Comedy   1993 · US · Colour · 81min

As naff and dreadful as the title suggests, this gross comedy regurgitates that old chestnut about the high school geek who woos the prettiest girl in school. Andrew Lowery is the bespectacled teen who gets shot just before his dream prom date with Traci Lind. In absolute absurdist style, he returns from the dead and goes to the ball regardless. Things go from bad to worse when his body parts start dropping off. LH *DVD*

Andrew Lowery *Johnny Dingle* • Traci Lind *Missy McCloud* • Danny Zorn *Eddie* • Edward Herrmann *Mr Dingle* • Mary Beth Hurt *Mrs Dingle* • Jay O Sanders *Sheriff McCloud* • Libby Villari *Camille McCloud* • Matthew Fox *Buck* ■ *Dir* Bob Balaban • *Scr* Dean Lorey

My Brilliant Career ★★★★ U

Period drama   1979 · Aus · Colour · 95min

A key film in the Australian film renaissance of the 1970s, this sensitive story of a fiercely independent young woman with aspirations to be a writer in male-dominated turn-of-the-century Australia made international reputations for director Gillian Armstrong and her remarkably assured 23-year-old star, Judy Davis. With Sam Neill and Wendy Hughes providing attractive support, the one drawback is being expected to believe any woman in her right mind would turn down Neill's charming, wealthy suitor. AME *DVD*

Judy Davis *Sybylla Melvyn* • Sam Neill *Harry Beecham* • Wendy Hughes *Aunt Helen* • Robert Grubb *Frank Hawdon* • Max Cullen *Mr McSwat* • Patricia Kennedy *Aunt Gussie* ■ *Dir* Gillian Armstrong • *Scr* Eleanor Witcombe, from the novel by Miles Franklin

My Brother Is an Only Child ★★★ 15

Period comedy drama   2006 · It/Fr · Colour · 101min

Daniele Luchetti's deft, funny examination of Italy's recent past is set in Mussolini's purpose-built town of Latina in the 1960s and 70s. Troublesome younger brother Accio (Elio Germano) returns home after being expelled from a seminary and becomes involved with a fascist group. Meanwhile, his older brother Manrico (Riccardo Scamarcio) is a committed left-wing activist. The domestic and political conflicts that follow could have made for heavy-handed drama, but Luchetti's breezy direction and some beautifully balanced performances make us understand and care about these characters – even if we don't like them. The soundtrack's use of nifty Italian pop songs of the period combines with costumes, location and set design to create a knowing look at a troubled era in the country's history. KK Italian +subtitles. Violence, swearing. *DVD*

Elio Germano *Accio* • Riccardo Scamarcio *Manrico* • Angela Finocchiaro *Accio's mother* • Massimo Popolizio *Accio's father* • Alba Rohrwacher *Violetta* ■ *Dir* Daniele Luchetti • *Scr* Daniele Luchetti, Sandro Petraglia, Stefano Rulli, from their story, from the novel *Il Fasciocomunista* by Antonio Pennacchi

My Brother Jonathan ★★ U

Drama   1947 · UK · BW · 103min

Time has not been kind to the films featuring husband and wife Michael Denison and Dulcie Gray. Yet Denison's clipped tones and stiff acting style and Gray's mousey loyalty turned this into a respectable hit. It follows the fortunes of Black Country doctor Denison, whose ambitions to become a surgeon are thwarted by family ties. Harold French directs steadily, but without a feel for small-town life. Polished but sterile. DP *DVD*

Michael Denison *Jonathan Dakers* • Dulcie Gray *Rachel Hammond* • Stephen Murray *Doctor Craig* • Ronald Howard *Harold Dakers* • Mary Clare *Mrs Dakers* • Finlay Currie *Doctor Hammond* • James Robertson-Justice *Eugene Dakers* ■ *Dir* Harold French • *Scr* Leslie Landau, Adrian Alington, from the novel by Francis Brett Young

My Brother Talks to Horses ★★★ U

Comedy   1946 · US · BW · 92min

This MGM co-feature served to show off the burgeoning talent of director Fred Zinnemann, who would later make such Oscar-winning classics as *High Noon*, *From Here to Eternity* and *A Man for All Seasons*. There's not much sign of the promise to come in this silly but charming picture, however, which is succinctly summed up by its title. Young Jackie "Butch" Jenkins plays the original horse whisperer, and there's interesting period support, but the central gimmick becomes tiresome and the plot has nowhere to go. TS

"Butch" Jenkins [Jackie "Butch" Jenkins] *Lewis Penrose* • Peter Lawford *John S Penrose* • Spring Byington *Mrs Penrose* • Beverly Tyler *Martha* • Edward Arnold *Mr Bledsoe* • Charlie Ruggles [Charles Ruggles] *Richard Pennington Roeder* ■ *Dir* Fred Zinnemann • *Scr* Morton Thompson

My Brother the Devil ★★★ 15

Crime drama   2012 · UK/Egy/US · Colour · 107min

A myriad influences go into making this stylish British gangster tale rather more distinctive than the norm. Though the trimmings of urban drama may seem grimly familiar – young east Londoner Mo (Fady Elsayed) desperately wants to follow his respected, drug-dealing brother Rashid (James Floyd) into a life of crime - the story plays out as anything but. The feature debut of Welsh-Egyptian director Sally El Hosaini handles issues of sexuality and roots boldly, for once actually probing the macho and territorial nature of gang culture rather than simply reflecting it. Also, the look of the film presents the high-rise blocks of the capital's scruffier streets with a refreshing feel. DW Violence, swearing, sex scenes, drug abuse. *DVD* *BL*

Saïd Taghmaoui *Sayyid* • James Floyd *Rashid* • Fady Elsayed *Mo* • Aymen Hamdouchi *Repo* • Ashley Thomas [Ashley "Bashy" Thomas] *Lenny* ■ *Dir/Scr* Sally El Hosaini

My Brother the Pig ★★ PG

Comedy fantasy   1999 · US · Colour · 91min

Scarlett Johansson has found fame since she starred in this comedy fantasy about a boy's accidental transformation into a pig. Though Johansson has the starring role, much of the focus falls on Eva Mendes, playing the nanny whose magical powers bring misfortune upon the curious Nick Fuoco. It's a predictable romp, but the Mexican setting is interesting. DP *DVD*

Nick Fuoco *George Caldwell* • Scarlett Johansson *Kathy Caldwell* • Judge Reinhold *Richard Caldwell* • Romy Walthall [Romy Windsor] *Dee Dee Caldwell* • Eva Mendes *Matilda* • Alex D Linz *Freud* ■ *Dir* Erik Fleming • *Scr* Matthew Flynn

My Brother Tom ★★★ 18

Romantic drama   2001 · UK/Ger · Colour · 104min

Dom Rotheroe's debut feature is an interesting psychodrama that takes a walk on the wilder side of teenage love. Jenna Harrison is a Home Counties schoolgirl who falls for loner Ben Whishaw, and the two adolescents seek refuge in their own private world. Photographed on digital video by *Breaking the Waves* cameraman Robby Müller, the film has an aura of sullen inevitability that hangs over the couple like a cloud, though their love-in-a-mist attitude is redeemed by some wonderful acting. The later lurch into murder and melodrama is a step too far. TH Violence.

Jenna Harrison *Jessica* • Ben Whishaw *Tom* • Adrian Rawlins *Jack* • Judith Scott *Jessica's mum* • Richard Hope *Jessica's dad* ■ *Dir* Dom Rotheroe • *Scr* Dom Rotheroe, Alison Beeton-Hilder

My Brother's Keeper ★★

Drama   1948 · UK · BW · 86min

A decade before Tony Curtis and Sidney Poitier played *The Defiant Ones*, Jack Warner and George Cole starred as a couple of convicts whose escape is hindered by the fact that they are handcuffed together. Replacing the racial theme is the neat twist that only one of the runaways is guilty. Under the direction of Alfred Roome and Roy Rich, however, their perils are often predictable. DP

Jack Warner *George Martin* • George Cole *Willie Stannard* • Jane Hylton *Nora Lawrence* • David Tomlinson *Ronnie Waring* • Bill Owen *Syd Evans* • Yvonne Owen *Margaret "Meg" Waring* • Raymond Lovell *Bill Wainwright* ■ *Dir* Alfred Roome, Roy Rich • *Scr* Frank Harvey, from a story by Maurice Wiltshire

My Brother's Keeper ★★

Drama   1995 · US · Colour · 94min

Having portrayed sinister siblings in Brian De Palma's mischievous thriller *Raising Cain*, John Lithgow plays brothers again in this well-meaning if somewhat strained TV movie that seeks to expose the folly of demonising Aids. Lithgow earned an Emmy nomination for his dual performance as a small-town teacher who discovers that he's HIV positive and the twin brother who challenges an insurance company in the courts over a life-saving bone marrow transplant. Lithgow's performance is matched by those of Ellen Burstyn, Veronica Cartwright and Annette O'Toole, as the bourgeois neighbours who overcome their prejudices to give the brothers their wholehearted support. DP

John Lithgow *Bob Bradley/Tom Bradley* • Ellen Burstyn *Helen* • Annette O'Toole *Joann* • Veronica Cartwright *Pat* • Brian Doyle-Murray *Curtis* • Zeljko Ivanek *Dr Hill* • Richard Masur *Morley* ■ *Dir* Glenn Jordan • *Scr* Gregory Goodell

My Chauffeur ★★ 15

Comedy   1986 · US · Colour · 97min

Feisty Deborah Foreman stars as a girl who makes it in the predominantly male profession of limousine driving. Picking up a depressed and drunk millionaire's son, she is dismissed when he wakes up the next day on her couch. An inconsequential attempt at screwball comedy and farce, with a truly terrible combination of bad jokes thrown in. LH

Deborah Foreman *Casey Meadows* • Sam J Jones [Sam Jones] *Battle Witherspoon* • Sean McClory *O'Brien* • Howard Hesseman *McBride* • EG Marshall *Witherspoon* • Penn Jillette *Bone* • Teller *Abdul* ■ *Dir/Scr* David Beaird

My Childhood ★★★ PG

Biographical drama   1972 · UK · BW · 44min

Costing some £4,000 to make and lasting less than an hour, this is the first part of director Bill Douglas's autobiographical trilogy, one of the most painful evocations of childhood ever brought to the screen. Set in a run-down Scottish mining village, the film explores the strained relationships between an eight-year-old boy, his half-brother, his uncompromising grandmother and a kindly German prisoner of war. Stephen Archibald gives a remarkable performance as Douglas's alter ego, while Jean Taylor-Smith sends shivers as the very antithesis of a loving granny. *My Ain Folk* (1973) continues his story. DP *DVD*

Stephen Archibald *Jamie* • Hughie Restorick *Tommy* • Jean Taylor-Smith *Grandmother* • Karl Fieseler *Helmuth* • Bernard McKenna *Tommy's father* • Paul Kermack *Jamie's father* ■ *Dir/Scr* Bill Douglas

My Cousin Rachel ★★★

Romantic mystery   1952 · BW · 98min

Based on Daphne du Maurier's novel, this overwrought melodrama has Richard Burton first detesting, then obsessively loving Olivia de Havilland, who married and may have murdered his beloved cousin. Set on the clifftops of 19th-century Cornwall, it puts the story of *Rebecca* into reverse gear and delivers great dollops of emotion. The dashingly handsome, brooding Burton picked up the first of his seven unsuccessful Oscar nominations for his first Hollywood role. AT

Olivia de Havilland *Rachel Ashley* • Richard Burton *Philip Ashley* • Audrey Dalton *Louise* • Ronald Squire *Nick Kendall* • George Dolenz *Rainaldi, Rachel's lawyer* • John Sutton *Ambrose Ashley* • Tudor Owen *Seecombe* ■ *Dir* Henry Koster • *Scr* Nunnally Johnson, from the novel by Daphne du Maurier

My Cousin Rachel

Romantic mystery   2017 · US · Colour

This is a preview – no prints were available to review as we went to press: In 1952, it was Richard Burton plotting to kill his older cousin (Olivia De Havilland) as revenge for his guardian's death. How will a drama about a man knocked off course by beauty play out now that Sam Claflin and Rachel Weisz are the leads? With the gothic making a comeback, Daphne Du Maurier's dark story could find appreciative audiences. What's more, director Roger Michell has shown himself to be a master of depicting twisted relationships. SvM

Rachel Weisz *Rachel* • Sam Claflin *Philip* • Holliday Grainger • Iain Glen • Simon Russell Beale ■ *Dir* Roger Michell • *Scr* Roger Michell, from Daphne du Maurier's novel

My Cousin Vinny ★★★★🅸🅵

Comedy 1992 · US · Colour · 114min

Joe Pesci plays the Vinny of the title, an extremely inept lawyer (who has never tried a case in court), who comes to the rescue of his young cousin (Ralph Macchio) when the lad runs into a bit of trouble with the law in the Deep South. Pesci has great fun with his role but the biggest surprise is Marisa Tomei, who plays his coarse Brooklyn girlfriend. Although she's great in what was her first major role, there was widespread surprise when she walked off with the best supporting actress Oscar. JB Swearing. *DVD* *BD*

Joe Pesci *Vinny Gambini* • Marisa Tomei *Mona Lisa Vito* • Ralph Macchio *Bill Gambini* • Mitchell Whitfield *Stan Rothenstein* • Fred Gwynne *Judge Chamberlain Haller* • Lane Smith *Jim Trotter III* • Austin Pendleton *John Gibbons* • Bruce McGill *Sheriff Farley* ■ *Dir* Jonathan Lynn • *Scr* Dale Launer

My Darling Clementine ★★★★★🅸

Classic western 1946 · US · BW · 98min

In this classic western, Henry Fonda's Wyatt Earp and Victor Mature's Doc Holliday are heading for that close shave at the OK Corral. Owing rather less to historical accuracy than more recent movies, this John Ford picture boasts some fine sequences. The best is a dance in an unfinished church, a fine symbol of the "garden being fashioned from the wilderness" by the strong-arm methods of Fonda's self-righteous lawman. Filmed in expressive black and white against Monument Valley backdrops, the picture combines both the grandeur and the folksiness so typical of its director. AT *DVD* *BD*

Henry Fonda *Wyatt Earp* • Victor Mature *Doc Holliday* • Linda Darnell *Chihuahua* • Walter Brennan *Old Man Clanton* • Cathy Downs *Clementine* • Tim Holt *Virgil Earp* • Ward Bond *Morgan Earp* • John Ireland *Billy Clanton* ■ *Dir* John Ford • *Scr* Samuel G Engel, Winston Miller, from a story by Sam Hellman, from the novel *Wyatt Earp, Frontier Marshal* by Stuart N Lake • *Cinematographer* Joe MacDonald

My Date with Drew ★★🅿🅶

Documentary 2003 · US · Colour · 90min

Fanboy obsession combines with shameless self-promotion in this breezy documentary in which aspiring film-maker Brian Herzlinger tries to secure a date with his idol Drew Barrymore. Restricted finances and a 30-day returns policy on his camera complicate this Herculean quest, prompting the goofy optimist to plump for a "six degrees of separation" approach to achieve his dream. But in interviewing anyone with even the slightest link to Barrymore, Herzlinger overstretches the concept, making an initially quirky and endearing exercise increasingly wearing. SF *DVD*

■ *Dir* Jon Gunn, Brian Herzlinger, Brett Winn

My Dear Secretary ★★🅄

Romantic comedy 1948 · US · BW · 89min

Bestselling novelist Kirk Douglas, who suffers from an irresistible drive to make passes at his secretaries, gets more than he bargained for when he hires Laraine Day. He ends up marrying her – whereupon she becomes jealous of her replacement. This mindless variant on the familiar wife-versus-secretary idea, directed by Charles Martin from his own thin script, is made thinner still by Douglas's lack of comic flair. What laughs there are come from Keenan Wynn and Rudy Vallee. RK *DVD*

Kirk Douglas *Owen Waterbury* • Laraine Day *Stephanie Gaylord* • Keenan Wynn *Ronnie Hastings* • Helen Walker *Elsie* • Rudy Vallee *Charles Harris* • Florence Bates *Mrs Reeves* ■ *Dir/Scr* Charles Martin

My Demon Lover ★★🅸🅵

Horror comedy 1987 · US · Colour · 83min

This typical 1980s horror comedy is enlivened by an enthusiastic cast and some good make-up effects. Brat Pack wannabe Scott Valentine is subject to an ancient curse that turns him into a whole menagerie of monsters whenever he is sexually aroused. Shot on location in New York, one wonders if director Charles Loventhal has ever been there, especially when he places a huge gothic castle straight out of a Bela Lugosi movie slap-bang in the middle of Central Park. RS

Scott Valentine *Kaz* • Michelle Little *Denny* • Arnold Johnson *Fixer* • Robert Trebor *Charles* • Alan Fudge *Captain Phil Janus* ■ *Dir* Charles Loventhal • *Scr* Leslie Ray

My Dinner with Andre ★★★🄵

Drama 1981 · US · Colour · 106min

Few films polarise critical opinion more than this love it or loathe it chat-fest from director Louis Malle. Your response to the film depends entirely on whether you consider avant-garde theatre director Andre Gregory to be a man of charm, imagination and questing intellect, or a pompous narcissist in love with the sound of his own voice. Wallace Shawn is altogether easier to take as Gregory's straight man with a nice line in barbed quippery. Drawn from the pair's actual conversations, the adventures and ideas Gregory relates range from the fascinating to the preposterous. DP *DVD*

Wallace Shawn *Wally* • Andre Gregory *Andre* • Jean Lenauer *Waiter* ■ *Dir* Louis Malle • *Scr* Wallace Shawn, Andre Gregory

My Dog Skip ★★★🄴

Biographical drama 1999 · US · Colour · 95min

Though corny at times, this is less sentimental than most boy-and-dog movies. Against the backdrops of the Second World War and Deep South segregation, this heart-warming family film traces the bonding between an eight-year-old Mississippi youngster (Frankie Muniz) and a Jack Russell terrier. It's old-fashioned entertainment for adults and older children, though the under-tens may find it a touch slow and talky. DA *DVD*

Frankie Muniz *Willie Morris* • Diane Lane *Ellen Morris* • Luke Wilson *Dink Jenkins* • Kevin Bacon *Jack Morris* • Mark Beech *Army buddy* ■ *Dir* Jay Russell • *Scr* Gail Gilchriest, from the memoir by Willie Morris

My Dog Tulip ★★★🄵🄰

Animated drama 2009 · US · Colour · 81min

The first animated feature to be drawn and painted entirely using paperless computer technology is also the second picture inspired by writer JR Ackerley's relationship with a possessive Alsatian bitch after *We Think the World of You* in 1988. Whereas that tale was primarily fictional, this is a moving personal memoir of Tulip's rescue from her original owners and the determination of Ackerley (voiced by Christopher Plummer) to find her the best possible mate. Unlike most tales about man's best friend, this study in dedication, defecation and reproduction sometimes feels like an intrusion into a very private affair. But the gentle humour is emphasised more than the misanthropy and John Avarese's score retains the lightness of tone even as the images expose the less cosy aspects of pet ownership. DP Some sexual references, nudity.

Christopher Plummer *JR Ackerley* • Lynn Redgrave *Nancy/Greengrocer's wife* • Isabella Rossellini *Ms Canvenini* • Peter Gerety *Mr Plum/Pugilist* • Brian Murray *Captain Pugh/Mr Blandish* • Paul Hecht *Army vet* ■ *Dir* Paul Fierlinger, Sandra Fierlinger • *Scr* Paul Fierlinger, from the memoirs by JR Ackerley

My Dream Is Yours ★★★

Musical 1949 · US · Colour · 99min

Doris Day stars in this extremely pleasant Warner Bros film, a very gentle satire on radio, with a swipe at the movies. Day and co-star Jack Carson clown and croon sweetly under Michael Curtiz's competent direction. Scene-stealing honours go to Warners veteran Bugs Bunny, who appears in a super dream sequence. TS

Jack Carson *Doug Blake* • Doris Day *Martha Gibson* • Lee Bowman *Gary Mitchell* • Adolphe Menjou *Thomas Hutchins* • Eve Arden *Vivian Martin* • SZ Sakall *Felix Hofer* • Selena Royle *Freda Hofer* • Edgar Kennedy *Uncle Charlie* ■ *Dir* Michael Curtiz • *Scr* Harry Kurnitz, Dane Lussier, Allen Rivkin, Laura Kerr, from the story *Hot Air* by Jerry Wald, Paul Moss

My Fair Lady ★★★★★🅄

Classic musical 1964 · US · Colour · 166min

This sumptuous adaptation of Lerner and Loewe's smash Broadway version of George Bernard Shaw's play *Pygmalion* won eight well-deserved Oscars. It boasts superb performances from Rex Harrison repeating his stage success as Henry Higgins and Stanley Holloway as Alfred P Doolittle. At the time, there was criticism that Julie Andrews didn't re-create her original Broadway role, but Audrey Hepburn is still quite wonderful as Eliza. If not coarse enough for the Covent Garden flower girl, nobody, but nobody, could ever blossom as beautifully as Hepburn does in the Cecil Beaton costumes later on, and, despite being dubbed in the songs by Marni Nixon, her portrayal is funny and heart-warming in equal doses. A more visually inspired director might have brought a little more élan to the work, but George Cukor rightly preserves the theatricality of the enterprise and provides a film to savour again and again. TS *DVD* *BD*

Audrey Hepburn *Eliza Doolittle* • Rex Harrison *Professor Henry Higgins* • Stanley Holloway *Alfred P Doolittle* • Wilfrid Hyde White *Colonel Hugh Pickering* • Gladys Cooper *Mrs Higgins* • Jeremy Brett *Freddy Eynsford-Hill* • Theodore Bikel *Zoltan Karpathy* • Isobel Elsom *Mrs Eynsford-Hill* • Mona Washbourne *Mrs Pearce* ■ *Dir* George Cukor • *Scr* Alan Jay Lerner, from the musical by Alan Jay Lerner, Frederick Loewe, from the play *Pygmalion* by George Bernard Shaw • *Cinematographer* Harry Stradling • *Art Directors* Cecil Beaton, Gene Allen • *Music Director* Andre Previn [André Previn]

My Fair Madeline ★★★🄴

Animated adventure 2002 · US · Colour · 70min

Inspired by Ludwig Bemelmans's books, this charming animated adventure has Whoopi Goldberg as Miss Clavel. The action opens with Madeline being sent to an English finishing school after her bid to thwart some thieves in the Louvre is misinterpreted as bad behaviour. However, she gets her chance for revenge when she discovers that the same gang is after the Crown Jewels. The songs are so-so, but, otherwise, this is fun. DP *DVD*

Whoopi Goldberg *Miss Clavel* • Chantal Strand *Madeline* • Jim Byrnes *Mayor of Paris* • Shannon Chan-Kent *Chloe* • Chris Gaze [Christopher Gaze] *Narrator* ■ *Dir* Scott Heming • *Scr* Shelley Zellman, from a story by Phil Harnage, from characters by Ludwig Bemelmans

My Fake Fiancé ★★

Romantic comedy 2009 · US · Colour · 95min

Dishonesty has predictable romantic consequences in this flimsy and unevenly paced comedy, in which cash-strapped acquaintances pretend to get married so they can split the presents and money. But despite enthusiastic performances and a few bursts of quick-fire wit, former teen stars Melissa Joan Hart and Joseph Lawrence lack the charm and chemistry to compensate for the entirely formulaic plotting. Lame, unsubtle humour and hammy support compound the overall forced air. SF

Melissa Joan Hart *Jennifer* • Joey Lawrence *Vince* • Steven R Schirripa [Steve Schirripa] *Monkey* • Nicole Tubiola *Courtney* ■ *Dir* Gil Junger • *Scr* Howard March

My Family ★★★★🅸🅵

Drama 1994 · US · Colour · 121min

Writer/director Gregory Nava's drama charts the trials, triumphs and tribulations of a family of Mexican immigrants in Los Angeles over three generations. What sets this picture apart from other such films are the striking performances from the cast, which includes Jimmy Smits, Esai Morales and Edward James Olmos, plus an admirable lack of sentimentality from Nava. Both moving and funny, this is a treat. JB

Jimmy Smits *Jimmy Sanchez* • Esai Morales *Chucho* • Edward James Olmos *Paco* • Eduardo Lopez Rojas *Jose Sanchez* • Jenny Gago *Maria Sanchez* • Elpidia Carrillo *Isabel Magana* ■ *Dir* Gregory Nava • *Scr* Gregory Nava, Anna Thomas

My Family's Secret ★★

Crime thriller 2010 · Can · Colour · 90min

Multiple Personality Disorder receives heavy-handed treatment in another by-the-numbers thriller. Nicholle Tom (the eldest of the *Beethoven* children) is the devoted wife seeking financial help from mysterious brother-in-law Philip Riccio after her husband attempts suicide. But her subsequent probing into the siblings' traumatic childhood causes the obviously unbalanced Riccio to unravel. It culminates in a big confrontation, though it's all very rushed and underwhelming. SF

Nicholle Tom *Lara Darcie* • Philip Riccio *Grady Darcie* • Dylan Neal *Jason Darcie* • Paul McCarthy-Boyington *William* ■ *Dir* Curtis Crawford • *Scr* Christine Conradt

My Father and the Man in Black ★★🅸🅵

Drama documentary 2012 · Can · Colour · 87min

This heartfelt documentary promises a new angle on the Johnny Cash story, but in essence is about one man's search for the father he barely knew. Jonathan Holiff is that man and his father was Saul Holiff, Cash's manager, who was on the road for years, leaving a void in his son's life. He eventually committed suicide in 2005, so Holiff Jr attempts to piece the past together using a series of tapes and Cash memorabilia found in a storage unit after his death. Sadly, the research raises more questions than it answers in a frustrating film that gets lost down too many side roads. TeS

Jonathan Holiff • Johnny Cash • Saul Holiff • June Carter Cash ■ *Dir/Scr* Jonathan Holiff

My Father, My Son ★★★🅸🅵

Drama based on a true story 1988 · US · Colour · 88min

The tragic consequences of duty versus family give terrific power to this TV movie about a US Navy admiral whose order to use toxic defoliant "Agent Orange" in Vietnam apparently caused his own son's subsequent cancer. The fine, unsentimental script by Jacqueline Feather and David Seidler, Jeff Bleckner's sensitive direction and strong performances by Karl Malden and Keith Carradine make this unusual story of guilt and love between father and son seem vividly real. MC

Karl Malden *Admiral Elmo R Zumwalt* • Keith Carradine *Lt Elmo R Zumwalt Jr* • Margaret Klonk *Kathy Zumwalt* • Michael Horton *Martin* • Dirk Blocker *Nairmore* • Grace Zabriskie *Mouza Zumwalt* ■ *Dir* Jeff Bleckner • *Scr* Jacqueline Feather, David Seidler

My Father the Hero ★★★🅿🅶

Comedy drama 1994 · US · Colour · 86min

If you enjoyed the French original, *Mon Père Ce Héros*, then steer well clear of this Hollywood remake. However, if you are coming to the film with an open mind, there's every chance you will glean some enjoyment from this frivolous comedy in which Katherine Heigl tries to impress the admiring Dalton James by pretending that her father, Gérard Depardieu, is really her sugar daddy. The film has the distinction of being the only American remake of a Gallic hit to retain the original star, but Depardieu is obviously aware of the gulf between the two pictures. DP *DVD*

Gérard Depardieu *André* • Katherine Heigl *Nicole* • Dalton James *Ben* • Lauren Hutton *Megan* • Faith Prince *Diana* • Stephen Tobolowsky *Mike* •

M

Ann Hearn *Stella* ■ *Dir* Steve Miner • *Scr* Francis Veber, Charlie Peters, from the film *Mon Père Ce Héros* by Gérard Lauzier

My Favorite Blonde ★★★★

Comedy 1942 · US · BW · 78min

Vaudeville entertainer Bob Hope meets gorgeous blonde Madeleine Carroll who, it turns out, is a British spy being pursued by Nazi villains, notably the sinister duo of George Zucco and glamorous Gale Sondergaard. It's Bob to the rescue in one of his best vehicles. Directed at a laugh a minute and a thrilling pace by Sidney Lanfield, this is a glorious spoof on the espionage-chase films so beloved of Alfred Hitchcock. **RK**

Bob Hope *Larry Haines* • Madeleine Carroll *Karen Bentley* • Gale Sondergaard *Mme Stephanie Runick* • George Zucco *Dr Hugo Streger* • Lionel Royce *Karl* • Walter Kingsford *Dr Faber* • Bing Crosby *Man giving directions* ■ *Dir* Sidney Lanfield • *Scr* Don Hartman, Frank Butler, from a story by Melvin Frank, Norman Panama

My Favorite Brunette ★★★ PG

Comedy mystery 1947 · US · BW · 86min

In this entertaining comedy, Bob Hope plays a man who, mistaken for a Philip Marlowe-type private eye, decides to live out the role in order to help mysterious Dorothy Lamour, who's in a spot of bother involving gangsters. Only moderately successful as a spoof of the Raymond Chandler school, it's still amusing enough. It was Hope's first starring role for his own production company, Hope Enterprises. **RK** *DVD*

Bob Hope *Ronnie Jackson* • Dorothy Lamour *Carlotta Montay* • Peter Lorre *Kismet* • Lon Chaney Jr *Willy* • Charles Dingle *Major Simon Montague* • John Hoyt *Dr Lundau* • Reginald Denny *James Collins* • Jack LaRue *Tony* • Bing Crosby *Executioner* • Alan Ladd *Sam McCloud* ■ *Dir* Elliott Nugent • *Scr* Edmund Beloin, Jack Rose

M My Favorite Martian ★ PG

Science-fiction comedy
1999 · US · Colour · 93min

This farce is a pointless farrago that's nowhere near as fun as the 1960s TV series that inspired it, despite an in-joke appearance by original Martian Ray Walston. Here, unemployed TV-news producer Jeff Daniels hides crash-landed alien Christopher Lloyd in his car as the manic shape-shifter searches for spaceship spare parts. A highly talented cast drowns in a mass of bad quips, slapstick pratfalls and shameless mugging. **AJ** *DVD*

Jeff Daniels *Tim O'Hara* • Christopher Lloyd *Uncle Martin* • Elizabeth Hurley *Brace Channing* • Daryl Hannah *Lizzie* • Christine Ebersole *Mrs Lorelei Brown* • Wallace Shawn *Coleye* • Michael Lerner *Mr Channing* • Jeremy Hotz *Billy* • Ray Walston *Armitan* ■ *Dir* Donald Petrie • *Scr* Deanna Oliver, Sherri Stoner, from the TV series by John L Greene

My Favorite Spy ★ U

Musical comedy 1942 · US · BW · 85min

Bandleader/comedian Kay Kyser is an acquired taste, and though some of his films prove ingenuous fun, this is the weakest of the five films he made for RKO in the early 1940s. Produced by former silent star Harold Lloyd with too much reliance on Kyser's minimal flare for comedy, it has surprisingly lifeless direction by Tay Garnett. Pleasant songs by Jimmy Van Heusen and Johnny Burke provide some respite from the antics of Kyser as a bandleader chosen by Army Intelligence to infiltrate a spy ring. **TV**

Kay Kyser *Jane Wyman Connie* • Ellen Drew *Terry Kyser* • Robert Armstrong *Harry Robinson* • Helen Westley *Aunt Jessie* • Una O'Connor *Cora* ■ *Dir* Tay Garnett • *Scr* William Bowers, Sig Herzig, from a story by M Coates Webster

My Favorite Spy ★★★

Comedy 1951 · US · BW · 93min

This is Bob Hope's third *My Favorite* outing, directed this time by Norman Z McLeod, and with the stunningly beautiful Hedy Lamarr following in the footsteps of

---

Madeleine Carroll and Dorothy Lamour as the comedian's co-star. The nonsensical plot has Hope as a minor-league vaudeville comic being persuaded to take the place of an agent in Tangier and foil a conspiracy. While this is less funny than its predecessors, it does offer some adroit slapstick and fans will enjoy it. **RK**

Bob Hope *Peanuts White/Eric Augustine* • Hedy Lamarr *Lily Dalbray* • Francis L Sullivan *Karl Brubaker* • Arnold Moss *Tasso* • John Archer *Henderson* • Luis Van Rooten *Hoenig* • Stephen Chase (1) *Donald Bailey* ■ *Dir* Norman Z McLeod • *Scr* Edmund Hartmann [Edmund L Hartmann], Jack Sher, Edmund Beloin, Lou Breslow, Hal Kanter, from a story by Edmund Beloin, Lou Breslow

My Favorite Wife ★★★★ U

Romantic comedy 1940 · US · BW · 88min

Irene Dunne, having disappeared seven years earlier in a shipwreck, shows up alive and well just after her husband, Cary Grant, has remarried (to Gail Patrick). With a screenplay that burns brightly for most of the way and a cast that scintillates to the last, this hit romantic comedy remains a delight. Producer Leo McCarey had directed the 1937 Dunne-Grant smash *The Awful Truth* and was due to direct this one, but had to let Garson Kanin take over after being involved in a serious car crash. It was remade in 1963 as *Move Over, Darling*, with Doris Day and James Garner. **RK** *DVD*

Cary Grant *Nick Arden* • Irene Dunne *Ellen Arden* • Randolph Scott *Stephen Burkett* • Gail Patrick *Bianca* • Ann Shoemaker *Ma* • Scotty Beckett *Tim Arden* • Mary Lou Harrington *Chinch Arden* • Donald MacBride *Hotel clerk* ■ *Dir* Garson Kanin • *Scr* Sam Spewack, Bella Spewack, from a story by Sam Spewack, Bella Spewack, Leo McCarey

My Favorite Year ★★★★ PG

Comedy 1982 · US · Colour · 88min

Peter O'Toole's deliciously unbalanced portrayal of a legendary Hollywood star falling off the wagon is one of the joys of this farcical excursion to the relatively early days (1954) of American TV. There are lots of echoes here, as naive writer Mark Linn-Baker tries to keep the Errol Flynn-like hero sober for a television interview in the way Budd Schulberg was minder for F Scott Fitzgerald. The show's despotic boss, Joseph Bologna, has more than a touch or two of comedian Sid Caesar. **TH** Swearing.

Peter O'Toole *Alan Swann* • Mark Linn-Baker *Benjy Stone* • Jessica Harper *KC Downing* • Joseph Bologna *King Kaiser* • Bill Macy *Sy Benson* • Lainie Kazan *Belle Carroca* • Anne De Salvo *Alice Miller* • Basil Hoffman *Herb Lee* • Lou Jacobi *Uncle Morty* ■ *Dir* Richard Benjamin • *Scr* Norman Steinberg, Dennis Palumbo, from a story by Dennis Palumbo

My Fellow Americans ★★★ 12

Satirical comedy 1996 · US · Colour · 96min

In this clever twist on *The Odd Couple* format, two grouchy ex-Presidents – one Democrat, the other Republican – hit the road pursued by the Secret Service. Old-timers Jack Lemmon and James Garner squabble for the best lines in this gentle satire on American politics and middle America. The notable supporting cast includes Dan Aykroyd and John Heard, while Lauren Bacall makes a memorable ex-First Lady. **AT** Swearing.

Jack Lemmon *Russell P Kramer* • James Garner *Matt Douglas* • John Heard *Ted Matthews* • Dan Aykroyd *William Haney* • Sela Ward *Kaye Griffin* • Wilford Brimley *Joe Hollis* • Lauren Bacall *Margaret Kramer* ■ *Dir* Peter Segal • *Scr* E Jack Kaplan, Richard Chapman, Peter Tolan, from a story by E Jack Kaplan, Richard Chapman

My First Mister ★★★ 15

Drama 2001 · US/Ger · Colour · 104min

A sweet film about the relationship between two lonely people, this benefits from superb performances from leads Albert Brooks and Leelee Sobieski. She plays the alienated teenager who spends her days wandering around the mall until she sees a middle-aged man rearranging the window of a men's clothing shop. She asks for a job, and once she's agreed to tone down her

---

appearance to work there, the two become friends. Writer Jill Franklyn loses courage about the relationship before the film ends, and we are left with a contrived plot twist. **JB** Swearing, drug abuse. *DVD*

Albert Brooks *Randall, "R"* • Leelee Sobieski *Jennifer, "J"* • Desmond Harrington *Randy* • Carol Kane *Mrs Benson* • Mary Kay Place *Patty, nurse* • John Goodman *Benjamin* ■ *Dir* Christine Lahti • *Scr* Jill Franklyn

My First Wife ★★★★ 15

Drama 1984 · Aus · Colour · 97min

This frankly autobiographical tale from writer/director Paul Cox is a harrowing and highly personal account of marital break-up. Memories and emotions tumble over each other as DJ/composer John Hargreaves learns that not only is his father dying, but his wife is also having an affair. As Hargreaves resorts to increasingly desperate measures to keep his family together, it would have been easy for Cox to turn Wendy Hughes's character into a callous bitch. However, such is the honesty and intensity of this curiously poetic treatise on desire we are too shattered to take sides. **DP**

John Hargreaves *John* • Wendy Hughes *Helen* • Lucy Angwin *Lucy* • David Cameron *Tom* ■ *Dir* Paul Cox • *Scr* Paul Cox, Bob Ellis

My Foolish Heart ★★★ U

Romantic drama 1949 · US · BW · 94min

Susan Hayward gives one of her least mechanical performances here as the wife and mother unhappily married to Kent Smith and remembering past moments with pilot Dana Andrews. Written by Julius J and Philip G Epstein from a JD Salinger short story, this weepie has the customary gloss associated with its producer, Samuel Goldwyn, but the direction (by Mark Robson) never really achieves the emotional depth required. Sadly, Salinger was so unhappy with this adaptation that he decided against agreeing to any further films of his work. **TH**

Dana Andrews *Walt Dreiser* • Susan Hayward *Eloise Winters* • Kent Smith *Lew Wengler* • Lois Wheeler *Mary Jane* • Jessie Royce Landis *Martha Winters* • Robert Keith (1) *Henry Winters* ■ *Dir* Mark Robson • *Scr* Julius J Epstein, Philip G Epstein, from the short story *Uncle Wiggily in Connecticut* by JD Salinger

My Forbidden Past ★ U

Drama 1951 · US · BW · 70min

With the starry line-up of beautiful Ava Gardner, cool Robert Mitchum and debonair Melvyn Douglas, you'd assume this RKO feature would be well nigh unmissable. Actually it's a Deep South potboiler of staggering banality, not even raised above its own low level by the stars. Director Robert Stevenson has to be held partly responsible for the slow pace and lack of action. The casual attitude accorded this New Orleans-set melodrama is indicated by the fact that nobody even attempts a southern accent. **TS** *DVD*

Robert Mitchum *Dr Mark Lucas* • Ava Gardner *Barbara Beaurevel* • Melvyn Douglas *Paul Beaurevel* • Lucile Watson *Aunt Eula* • Janis Carter *Corinne* • Gordon Oliver *Clay Duchesne* ■ *Dir* Robert Stevenson • *Scr* Marion Parsonnet, Leopold Atlas, from the novel *Carriage Entrance* by Polan Banks

My Friend Flicka ★★★★ U

Drama 1943 · US · Colour · 85min

This is one of those films for all the family carelessly referred to by hardened hacks as heartwarming. But it really is. Roddy McDowall is the lonely son of Rocky Mountain rancher Preston Foster, whose dearest wish comes true when he is entrusted with raising his own horse. The story is simply irresistible, the photography glows and the scenes in which McDowall trains the animal and nurses it through sickness put the film up among the best of its kind. McDowall returned for a sequel, *Thunderhead – Son of Flicka* two years later. **DP** *DVD*

Roddy McDowall *Ken McLaughlin* • Preston Foster *Rob McLaughlin* • Rita Johnson *Nell* • James Bell *Gus* • Jeff Corey *Tim Murphy* • Diana Hale *Hildy* • Arthur Loft *Charley Sargent* ■ *Dir* Harold Schuster • *Scr* Lillie Hayward, Frances Edwards Faragoh

My Friend Irma ★★ U

Comedy 1949 · US · BW · 103min

Based on a hit radio show starring Marie Wilson as the ultimate dumb blonde (a characterisation exceedingly sexist by today's standards), this mild comedy is notable only for marking the screen debut of Dean Martin and Jerry Lewis. They raise more laughs than Wilson, whose predictably daffy reactions as she tries to help her larcenous boyfriend (John Lund) in his money-making schemes lack the sublimely convoluted logic of the more endearingly eccentric Gracie Allen. **TV**

John Lund *Al* • Diana Lynn *Jane Stacey* • Don DeFore *Richard Rhinelander* • Marie Wilson *Irma Peterson* • Dean Martin *Steve Baird* • Jerry Lewis *Seymour* • Hans Conried *Prof Kropotkin* • Kathryn Givney *Mrs Rhinelander* ■ *Dir* George Marshall • *Scr* Cy Howard, Parke Levy, from a radio series by Cy Howard

My Friend Irma Goes West ★★ U

Comedy 1950 · US · BW · 90min

This sequel to *My Friend Irma* (1949) has dumb blonde Marie Wilson heading for California with her friends to try their luck in movies. It is marginally superior to its predecessor, due mainly to the extra time given to the comedy team of Dean Martin and Jerry Lewis, who had received an enthusiastic response from audiences with their debut in the earlier film. **TV**

John Lund *Al* • Marie Wilson *Irma Peterson* • Diana Lynn *Jane Stacey* • Dean Martin *Steve Baird* • Jerry Lewis *Seymour* • Corinne Calvet *Yvonne Yvonne* • Lloyd Corrigan *Sharpie* ■ *Dir* Hal Walker • *Scr* Cy Howard, Parke Levy, from a radio series by Cy Howard

My Friend Ivan Lapshin ★★★★ 15

Period drama
1982 · USSR · Colour and BW · 98min

Adapted from his father Yuri's stories, Alexei Gherman's third feature is a compelling, understated portrait of Soviet provincial life in the days before the Stalinist purges. Opening in colour, the action flashes back into atmospheric monochrome to follow police chief Andrei Boltnev as he divides his time between tracking down an unscrupulous gang and pursuing actress Nina Ruslanova. Even the subplots, focusing on his relationships with a recently widowed friend and a neighbour and his nine-year-old son, are packed with acute observations that not only evoke the everyday, but also suggest the carnage to come. **DP** Russian +subtitles.

Andrei Boltnev *Ivan Lapshin* • Nina Ruslanova *Natasha Adashova* • Andrei Mironov *Khanin* • Z Adamovich *Patrikeyevna* ■ *Dir* Alexei German • *Scr* Eduard Volodarsky, from stories by Yuri Gherman

My Friend Joe ★★

Drama 1996 · UK/Ger/Ire · Colour · 100min

In this self-consciously provocative drama, Stephen McHattie, a soured ex-acrobat, insists on raising his orphaned niece, Schuyler Fisk, as a nephew. The friendship between the young American and John Cleere's timid Irish outcast is pleasingly developed, but once Fisk's secret emerges, the mood shifts and director Chris Bould settles for a sentimental solution. **DP** Swearing.

Schuyler Fisk *Joe* • John Cleere *Chris Doyle* • Stephen McHattie *Curt* • Stanley Townsend *Mr Doyle* • Pauline Mulls *Ms Doyle* ■ *Dir* Chris Bould • *Scr* David Howard

My Gal Sal ★★★ U

Biographical musical drama
1942 · US · Colour · 103min

They really don't make 'em like this any more: a musical, set in the 1890s, that bounces along on enough high-octane energy to run the National Grid for a week. Rita Hayworth is at her most luscious and appealing as the chanteuse love object of Victor Mature, playing popular songwriter Paul Dresser, whose wonderful old songs give this warm, engaging movie its fuel. What unites the movie's feel-good ingredients is the sublime choreography of Hermes Pan, the man partly responsible for Fred Astaire's legendary routines, and Val Raset. SH

Rita Hayworth *Sally Elliott* • Victor Mature *Paul Dresser* • John Sutton *Fred Haviland* • Carole Landis *Mae Colfns* • James Gleason *Pat Hawley* • Phil Silvers *Wiley* ■ *Dir* Irving Cummings • *Scr* Seton I Miller, Darrell Ware, Karl Tunberg, from the biography *My Brother Paul* by Theodore Dreiser

My Geisha ★★
Romantic comedy 1962 · US · Colour · 119min

When a movie director (Yves Montand) refuses to cast his wife (Shirley MacLaine) in his film of *Madame Butterfly*, she disguises herself as a geisha girl in order to change his mind. Produced in Japan by Steve Parker as a vehicle for his wife MacLaine, and directed by Oscar-winning cinematographer Jack Cardiff, the film looks gorgeous. The mildly amusing idea fails to take fire, however, and what should have been a sprightly comedy becomes a big yawn. RK

Shirley MacLaine *Lucy Dell/Yoko Mori* • Yves Montand *Paul Robaix* • Edward G Robinson *Sam Lewis* • Bob Cummings [Robert Cummings] *Bob Moore* ■ *Dir* Jack Cardiff • *Scr* Norman Krasna

My Giant ★★PG
Comedy 1998 · US · Colour · 99min

Billy Crystal plays a second-rate talent agent who, while in Romania to visit his latest signing, has a close encounter with a seven-foot-seven giant (basketball player Gheorghe Muresan). Crystal sees potential in this soft-hearted titan and promptly whisks him off to America, promising to reunite him with his childhood sweetheart. What follows is a less than scintillating mawkish family flick. NS Some swearing.

Billy Crystal *Sammy* • Kathleen Quinlan *Serena* • Gheorghe Muresan *Max* • Joanna Pacula *Lillianna* • Zane Carney *Nick* • Jere Burns *Weller* • Harold Gould *Milt* • Dan Castellaneta *Partlow* ■ *Dir* Michael Lehmann • *Scr* David Seltzer, from a story by Billy Crystal, David Seltzer

My Girl ★★PG
Romantic drama 1991 · US · Colour · 98min

Macaulay Culkin doesn't have much screen time in this occasionally charming tale. Anna Chlumsky plays a young tomboy who is trying to come to terms with life and the fact that her mortician father (Dan Aykroyd) is starting a relationship with the woman (Jamie Lee Curtis) who makes up the bodies at his funeral parlour. It's one for the less cynical members of the family, although younger viewers may find some moments distressing. JB Swearing. *DVD*

Dan Aykroyd *Harry Sultenfuss* • Jamie Lee Curtis *Shelly DeVoto* • Macaulay Culkin *Thomas J Sennett* • Anna Chlumsky *Vada Sultenfuss* • Richard Masur *Phil Sultenfuss* • Griffin Dunne *Mr Bixler* ■ *Dir* Howard Zieff • *Scr* Laurice Elehwany

My Girl 2 ★★PG
Drama 1994 · US · Colour · 94min

This unthreatening, absolutely redundant sequel has the now adolescent Anna Chlumsky trekking off to Los Angeles to find out what her real mother (who died during childbirth) was like. The nominal adult leads (Dan Aykroyd and Jamie Lee Curtis) are left stuck at home with little to do but wring their hands with concern. JF *DVD*

Dan Aykroyd *Harry Sultenfuss* • Jamie Lee Curtis *Shelly Sultenfuss* • Anna Chlumsky *Vada Sultenfuss* • Austin O'Brien *Nick Zsigmond* • Richard Masur *Phil Sultenfuss* • Christine Ebersole *Rose Zsigmond* • John David Souther [JD Souther] *Jeffrey Pommeroy* ■ *Dir* Howard Zieff • *Scr* Janet Kovalcik

My Girl Tisa ★★★U
Drama 1948 · US · BW · 95min

This is a starring vehicle for Lilli Palmer, who successfully combined beauty, intelligence and acting ability. She plays a young immigrant trying to bring her father to America, a role which must have had many resonances for Palmer, who herself grew up in Germany, the daughter of a Jewish surgeon, and fled with her sister Irene to Paris to avoid the persecution of the Jews by the Nazis. Here she co-stars with other noted refugees Sam Wanamaker, Akim Tamiroff and Hugo Haas in a deeply committed movie that doesn't quite reach the heights of social realism to which it aspires. TS

Lilli Palmer *Tisa Kepes* • Sam Wanamaker *Mark Denek* • Akim Tamiroff *Mr Grumbach* • Alan Hale Dugan • Hugo Haas *Tescu* • Gale Robbins *Jenny Kepes* • Stella Adler *Mrs Faludi* ■ *Dir* Elliott Nugent • *Scr* Allen Boretz, from the play *Ever the Beginning* by Lucille S Prumbs, Sara B Smith

My Girlfriend's Boyfriend ★★★★PG
Comedy drama 1987 · Fr · Colour · 99min

Eric Rohmer effortlessly blends the old and the new in this typically deft study of the inconsequential love lives of his youthful, self-obsessed protagonists. Inspired by the social wit of the 18th-century playwright, Marivaux, yet set against the futuristic landscape of the antiseptic Parisian suburb of Cergy-Pontoise, the focus falls on Emmanuelle Chaulet, who finds herself irresistibly drawn to her best friend's swain, Eric Viellard. While the characters endlessly analyse emotions that seem as artificial as their surroundings, Rohmer experiments with colour and language as he explores the nature of fidelity and friendship. A delight. DP French +subtitles. *DVD*

Emmanuelle Chaulet *Blanche* • Sophie Renoir *Léa* • Anne-Laure Meury *Adrienne* • Eric Viellard *Fabien* • François-Eric Gendron *Alexandre* ■ *Dir/Scr* Eric Rohmer

My Heroes Have Always Been Cowboys ★★★
Western 1991 · US · Colour · 106min

It would be all too easy to write off Stuart Rosenberg's film as a pale imitation of Sam Peckinpah's rodeo classic, *Junior Bonner*. But that would be unfair to a fine ensemble cast that rises above a formulaic screenplay to create some highly credible characters. There's a real air of disappointment about Scott Glenn's battle-scarred rider, while Kate Capshaw makes light of the clichés as a woman torn between the thrill of love and the pain of bitter experience. Ben Johnson steals the show as Glenn's cantankerous father. DP Violence, swearing.

Scott Glenn *HD Dalton* • Kate Capshaw *Jolie Meadows* • Ben Johnson (1) *Jesse Dalton* • Tess Harper *Cheryl Hornby* • Paul Balthazar Getty [Balthazar Getty] *Jud Meadows* • Gary Busey *Clint Hornby* • Mickey Rooney *Junior* • Clarence Williams III *Virgil* • Dub Taylor *Gimme Cap* ■ *Dir* Stuart Rosenberg • *Scr* Joel Don Humphreys

My House in Umbria ★★★12
Drama 2002 · US/UK/It · Colour · 98min

Maggie Smith won an Emmy Award for her typically mannered performance as an English romance novelist in this adaptation of William Trevor's 1991 novella. On a trip to Milan, Smith's train compartment is wrecked by an explosion and she is one of the few survivors. She invites the others to recover at her palatial country house in Umbria. Director Richard Loncraine's HBO cable movie features glorious vistas but is weak-kneed and overly sentimental. Best to forget the artificiality of the lazy plot and focus on the high standard of acting. AJ Sexual references. *DVD*

Maggie Smith *Mrs Emily Delahunty* • Chris Cooper *Thomas "Tom" Riversmith* • Timothy Spall *Quinty* • Benno Fürmann *Werner* • Ronnie Barker *The General* • Giancarlo Giannini *Inspector Girotti* • Libero De Rienzo *Dr Innocenti* ■ *Dir* Richard Loncraine • *Scr* Hugh Whitemore, from the novella by William Trevor

My Hustler ★★
Drama 1965 · US · BW · 79min

One of 18 films Andy Warhol made in 1965, this has, unusually for Warhol, some sort of plot. It concerns a young hustler, hired for the weekend through "Dial-a-Hustler", who bronzes himself on Fire Island beach while a trio of admirers bitch and banter about who will seduce him first. Be advised that the sexually explicit film also contains lengthy shots of men shaving. Mainly for Warhol fans. PF

Paul America *Young hustler* • Ed Hood *The "John"* • Joseph Campbell *Sugar Plum Fairy* • John MacDermott *Houseboy* ■ *Dir* Andy Warhol • *Scr* Chuck Wein

My Kid Could Paint That ★★12
Documentary 2007 · US/UK · Colour · 80min

Amir Bar-Lev's documentary focuses on Marla Olmstead, a precociously talented four-year-old whose abstract paintings led to her being dubbed "a budding Picasso". Midway through the making of the film, allegations surfaced that Marla's dad, an amateur painter, might have also been a dab hand at helping his daughter. Although Bar-Lev is ideally placed to either support or scupper her status as a painting prodigy, he unfortunately misses the opportunity and instead blunders about inconclusively. This is a good yarn, but in the hands of a more experienced film-maker it could have been so much better. DA *DVD*

Marla Olmstead • Mark Olmstead • Laura Olmstead • Anthony Brunelli • Elizabeth Cohen • Michael Kimmelman • Amir Bar-Lev ■ *Dir* Amir Bar-Lev

My Kidnapper ★★★
Documentary 2010 · UK · Colour · 82min

In September 2003, TV producer Mark Henderson was kidnapped along with seven other tourists while visiting the ancient Colombian city of Ciudad Perdida. He was released after 101 days and suffered from post-traumatic stress disorder on his return to Britain. A few months later, however, he received an email from one of his abductors and, in 2009, he consented to return to the scene of his ordeal with three fellow captives. This vérité record of the trip is clearly designed to be cathartic, and it's a compelling story. But the structure of the film is haphazard, and it's also deeply and disconcertingly personal. DP *DVD*

■ *Dir* Mark Henderson, Kate Horne

My Kingdom ★★★18
Crime drama 2001 · It/UK · Colour · 111min

King Lear meets *Get Carter* in this entertaining tribute to the British gangster movie from director Don Boyd. As the Liverpool hood realising his day is done in the wake of his wife's murder, Richard Harris produces a display of rage and despair that's all the more powerful for its restraint. Every aspect of this pitiless family feud drips with corrosive criminality, whether it's scheming sisters Louise Lombard and Lorraine Pilkington fighting over bent cop Aiden Gillen, or their husbands, Paul McGann and Jimi Mistry, vying for supremacy. DP Violence, swearing. *DVD*

Richard Harris *Sandeman* • Lynn Redgrave *Mandy* • Louise Lombard *Kath* • Lorraine Pilkington *Tracy* • Emma Catherwood *Jo* • Paul McGann *Dean* • Jimi Mistry *Jughinder "Jug" Singh* • Aidan Gillen *Detective Sergeant Barry Puttnam* • Tom Bell *Richard Quick* ■ *Dir* Don Boyd • *Scr* Nick Davies, Don Boyd

My Last Five Girlfriends ★★12
Romantic comedy 2009 · UK · Colour · 83min

Based loosely on philosopher Alain de Botton's novel *Essays in Love*, this ragged, low-budget romantic comedy is essentially one long flashback during the suicidal last moments of romantic failure Duncan (Brendan Patricks). By glancing back into Duncan's past love life, director Julian Kemp treads similar ground to *(500) Days*

of Summer, but does so in a contrived visual style coupled with an overlong narrative and extremely low production values. The cast doesn't have the material with which to shine, and only a surprising cameo by Michael Sheen brightens an otherwise below-average offering. KK *DVD*

Brendan Patricks *Duncan Anderson* • Naomie Harris *Gemma* • Cécile Cassel *Rhona* • Kelly Adams *Wendy* • Jane March *Olive* • Edith Bukovics *Natalie* • Michael Sheen *Detective Burnam* ■ *Dir* Julian Kemp • *Scr* Julian Kemp, from the novel *Essays in Love* by Alain de Botton

My Learned Friend ★★★★PG
Comedy 1943 · UK · BW · 71min

Will Hay's last film is a devilishly black comedy in which he not only stars, but also co-directs with Basil Dearden. Reduced to writing begging letters after he's disbarred, shyster lawyer Hay joins forces with bungling barrister Claude Hulbert to end the reign of terror being waged by Mervyn Johns, an ex-jailbird bent on taking murderous revenge on all who convicted him for forgery. Hay is on tip-top form and Johns indulges himself as the eye-rolling maniac. There are laughs aplenty and the Big Ben finale skilfully marries Hitchcock and Harold Lloyd. DP *DVD*

Will Hay *William Fitch* • Claude Hulbert *Claude Babbington* • Mervyn Johns *Grimshaw* • Laurence Hanray [Lawrence Hanray] *Sir Norman* • Aubrey Mallalieu *Magistrate* • Charles Victor *"Safety" Wilson* ■ *Dir* Will Hay, Basil Dearden • *Scr* John Dighton, Angus MacPhail

My Left Foot ★★★★★15
Biographical drama 1989 · UK/Ire · Colour · 98min

This superb movie chronicles the life of writer and artist Christy Brown, who was born with cerebral palsy, portrayed with astonishing passion and sensitivity by Daniel Day-Lewis. All concerned were rightly showered with praise and plaudits at the time, including Oscars for Day-Lewis and Brenda Fricker as Christy's stoical mum. There were some low rumblings that Day-Lewis's role should have been given to a disabled actor, a view which won some sympathy, but nothing can be taken away from this all-round great movie. It's also notable for the penultimate screen appearance of the marvellous Ray McAnally. SH Swearing. *DVD*

Daniel Day-Lewis *Christy Brown* • Ray McAnally *Mr Brown* • Brenda Fricker *Mrs Brown* • Ruth McCabe *Mary Carr* • Fiona Shaw *Dr Eileen Cole* • Eanna MacLiam *Benny* • Alison Whelan *Sheila* • Hugh O'Conor *Younger Christy* ■ *Dir* Jim Sheridan • *Scr* Shane Connaughton, Jim Sheridan, from the autobiography by Christy Brown • *Music* Elmer Bernstein

My Life ★★★15
Drama 1993 · US · Colour · 112min

The directorial debut of screenwriter Bruce Joel Rubin, who won an Oscar for his screenplay for *Ghost*, and a passable effort it is, too. Michael Keaton is very effective as the hotshot public relations executive given only months to live, and Nicole Kidman is nicely sparky as his newly pregnant wife. Rubin keeps everything just the right side of pathos until the final reel, when he jettisons all semblance of reality. The film is at its most endearing and revealing, however, when Keaton videotapes messages to leave to his unborn child. SH Swearing. *DVD*

Michael Keaton *Bob Jones* • Nicole Kidman *Gail Jones* • Bradley Whitford *Paul* • Queen Latifah *Theresa* • Michael Constantine *Bill* • Rebecca Schull *Rose* • Mark Lowenthal *Doctor Mills* • Lee Garlington *Carol Sandman* • Haing S Ngor *Mr Ho* ■ *Dir/Scr* Bruce Joel Rubin

My Life as a Dog ★★★★PG
Period comedy drama 1985 · Swe · Colour · 101min

Oscar-nominated Lasse Hallström invests this delightful rites-of-passage picture with as many autobiographical references as he does incidents from Reidar Jonsson's popular novel to produce a film of great

M

warmth and wit. He shows a keen appreciation of the workings of a young mind, as he chronicles the misadventures of an imaginative 12-year-old packed off by his tubercular mother to stay with his uncle in the southern Swedish countryside of the 1950s. Hallström elicits a performance of innocence and spirit from Anton Glanzelius, who is wonderfully natural. DP Swedish +subtitles. *DVD*

Anton Glanzelius *Ingemar Johansson* • Anki Liden *Ingemar's mother* • Tomas von Brömssen *Uncle Gunnar* • Manfred Serner *Erik Johansson* ■ *Dir* Lasse Hallström • *Scr* Lasse Hallström, Brasse Brännström, Pelle Berglund, Reidar Jonsson, from the novel *Mitt Liv som Hund* by Reidar Jonsson

My Life So Far ★★★ 12
Period drama   1999 · UK/US · Colour · 90min

This is a small, intimate portrait of one eccentric family in the Scottish highlands of the 1920s. Shot from the perspective of the family's ten-year-old son, the movie follows the traumatic events of one tumultuous year as the boy's madcap inventor dad (Colin Firth) has a fling with a visiting uncle's French fiancée (Irène Jacob). Crammed with quirkily memorable characters, the film's subject matter may be too twee for some tastes, though others will enjoy its fine evocation of an era long gone. DA

Colin Firth *Edward Pettigrew* • Rosemary Harris *Gamma Macintosh* • Irène Jacob *Heloise* • Tcheky Karyo *Gabriel Chenoux* • Mary Elizabeth Mastrantonio *Moira Pettigrew* • Malcolm McDowell *Uncle Morris Macintosh* • Kelly Macdonald *Elspeth Pettigrew* • Robert Norman *Fraser Pettigrew* ■ *Dir* Hugh Hudson • *Scr* Simon Donald, from the memoir *Son of Adam* by Sir Denis Forman

My Life with Caroline ★★
Romantic comedy   1941 · US · BW · 80min

When his wife (British actress Anna Lee in her Hollywood debut) decides that she might be better off married to either Reginald Gardiner or Gilbert Roland, Ronald Colman must constantly woo her to retain her affections. Considering the talents involved – playwright John Van Druten wrote it, Lewis MIlestone directs – this misfiring romantic comedy is remarkably devoid of amusement. It's always a pleasure to watch the elegant Colman, though. RK

Ronald Colman *Anthony Mason* • Anna Lee *Caroline Mason* • Charles Winninger *Bliss* • Reginald Gardiner *Paul Martindale* • Gilbert Roland *Paco Del Valle* • Katherine Leslie *Helen* ■ *Dir* Lewis Milestone • *Scr* John Van Druten, Arnold Belgard, from the play *Train to Venice* by Louis Verneuil, Georges Berr

My Life without Me ★★★★ 15
Drama   2002 · Sp/Can · Colour · 101min

The small details we take for granted in everyday life are celebrated with passion in this warm and bittersweet drama. It follows a 23-year-old working-class mother of two (Sarah Polley) who learns to appreciate the value of existence when she's diagnosed as terminally ill. This beautifully shot tale is a wonderfully perceptive, wryly amusing and occasionally surreal experience. Spanish writer/director Isabel Coixet's soulful heroine is as much an eternal optimist as she is a realist, despite her convict father, work-shy husband and resentful mother (singer Deborah Harry). Heart-rending and joyfully uplifting. SF *DVD*

Sarah Polley *Ann* • Amanda Plummer *Laurie* • Scott Speedman *Don* • Leonor Watling *Neighbour Ann* • Deborah Harry *Ann's mother* • Maria de Medeiros *Hairdresser* • Mark Ruffalo *Lee* • Julian Richings *Dr Thompson* • Alfred Molina *Ann's father* ■ *Dir* Isabel Coixet • *Scr* Isabel Coixet, from the short story *Pretending the Bed Is a Raft* by Nanci Kincaid

My Little Chickadee ★★★ PG
Comedy western   1940 · US · BW · 80min

The teaming of WC Fields and Mae West should have resulted in one of the funniest wisecracking movies of all time, but this never comes close to hilarity and ends up as merely rollicking fun. Returning to the screen after two years, West (aided by Fields) penned a script that suited her style of precisely timed innuendo, but which also reined in Fields's brand of off-the-cuff rambling. There are some memorable moments, but the linking narrative is ponderous. DP *DVD*

Mae West *Flower Belle Lee* • WC Fields *Cuthbert J Twillie* • Joseph Calleia *Jeff Badger* • Dick Foran *Wayne Carter* • Ruth Donnelly *Aunt Lou* • Margaret Hamilton *Mrs Gideon* • Donald Meek *Amos Budge* • Fuzzy Knight *Cousin Zeb* ■ *Dir* Edward Cline • *Scr* Mae West, WC Fields

My Little Eye ★★★ 18
Horror   2002 · UK/US/Fr/Can · Colour · 91min

Five "lucky" strangers are put under constant 24-hour surveillance for an internet reality show. The group will all win $1 million if they live together in a remote, snowbound Nova Scotia house for six months with their every move being watched. As the deadline approaches, a mysterious stranger arrives, causing sexual havoc and pushing this bleak chiller into an unrelenting frenzy of intense, bloody carnage. Too many genre clichés early on test the patience but the grainy fly-on-the-wall style builds up a disturbing atmosphere. AJ *DVD*

Jennifer Sky *Charlie* • Stephen O'Reilly *Danny* • Laura Regan *Emma* • Sean CW Johnson *Matt* • Kris Lemche *Rex* • Bradley Cooper *Travis Patterson* ■ *Dir* Marc Evans • *Scr* David Hilton, James Watkins, from a story by David Hilton

My Little Girl ★★★ 15
Drama   1986 · US · Colour · 112min

A little contrived and a tad sentimental, this well-meaning melodrama marked Connie Kaiserman's directorial debut. As the poor little rich girl spending her summer in a hostel for underprivileged kids, Mary Stuart Masterson conveys something of a teenager's confusion at coming face to face with the real world. She's well supported by James Earl Jones, who adds some down-to-earth dignity to the proceedings as the hostel's director. DP Violence, swearing.

James Earl Jones *Ike Bailey* • Geraldine Page *Molly* • Mary Stuart Masterson *Franny Bettinger* • Anne Meara *Mrs Shopper* • Pamela Payton-Wright *Cordelia "Delly" Bettinger* • Peter Michael Goetz *Norman Bettinger* ■ *Dir* Connie Kaiserman • *Scr* Connie Kaiserman, Nan Mason

My Love Has Been Burning ★★★★
Political drama   1949 · Jpn · BW · 96min

Made quickly and cheaply, yet anticipating director Kenji Mizoguchi's mature style, this film à clef was based on the autobiography of the 19th-century women's rights campaigner, Hideko Kageyama. As played by Kinuyo Tanaka, Eiko is a typical Mizoguchi heroine: she sees her school closed down on account of her political views, suffers imprisonment and then marries a prominent liberal who refuses to support her demand for female suffrage. The action, inspired by the postwar art of Picasso, is unexpectedly violent. DP Japanese +subtitles.

Kinuyo Tanaka *Eiko Hirayama* • Mitsuko Mito *Chiyo* • Eitaro Ozawa *Hayase* • Ichiro Sugai *Kentaro Omoi* • Kuniko Miyake *Toshiko Kishida* ■ *Dir* Kenji Mizoguchi • *Scr* Yoshikata Yoda, Kaneto Shindo, from the autobiography *Warawa no Hanshogai (My Half Life)* by Hideko Kageyama

My Lucky Star ★★★
Musical comedy   1938 · US · BW and Tinted · 63min

This minor Sonja Henie vehicle has a nice Mack Gordon-Harry Revel score and a daft plot that gives the dimpled skater plenty of opportunity to strut her stuff. Henie plays a department store clerk who catches the eye of the boss's son, Cesar Romero; the latter's wife is played by Louise Hovick, better known as Gypsy Rose Lee. The rest of the supporting cast is way above par, though leading man Richard Greene is a bit bland. The *Alice in Wonderland* ice ballet was originally tinted pink. TS

Sonja Henie *Kristina Nielson* • Richard Greene *Larry Taylor* • Joan Davis *Mary Dwight* • Cesar Romero *George Cabot Jr* • Buddy Ebsen *Buddy* • Arthur Treacher *Whipple* • George Barbier *George Cabot Sr* • Louise Hovick [Gypsy Rose Lee] *Marcelle La Verne* • Billy Gilbert *Nick* • Elisha Cook Jr *Waldo* ■ *Dir* Roy Del Ruth • *Scr* Harry Tugend, Jack Yellen, from the story *They Met in Chicago* by Karl Tunberg, Don Ettlinger

My Man Godfrey ★★★★ U
Screwball comedy   1936 · US · BW · 89min

A derelict (William Powell) finds himself rescued by a wealthy Fifth Avenue family's irrepressible younger daughter (Carole Lombard) and installed as the latest in a succession of butlers. Who he really is, and how he withstands the pressure of the family's insane antics, is the stuff of this classic comedy. It would be faultless if the family's farcical behaviour didn't strain credibility. Yet it's no surprise that both stars, director Gregory La Cava and the screenplay he co-wrote were all nominated for Oscars, as were Alice Brady for her portrayal of the featherbrained mother of the clan and Mischa Auer as the latter's posturing protégé. RK *DVD*

William Powell *Godfrey Parke* • Carole Lombard *Irene Bullock* • Alice Brady *Angelica Bullock* • Gail Patrick *Cornelia Bullock* • Jean Dixon *Molly* • Eugene Pallette *Alexander Bullock* • Alan Mowbray *Tommy Gray* • Mischa Auer *Carlo* • Franklin Pangborn *Master of ceremonies* ■ *Dir* Gregory La Cava • *Scr* Morrie Ryskind, Eric Hatch, Robert Presnell, Zoë Akins [Zoe Akins], from the novel by Eric Hatch

My Man Godfrey ★★ U
Comedy   1957 · US · Colour · 91min

Perhaps it was a mistake to try to recapture the atmosphere of the well-loved original, a classic 1930s screwball comedy, but Universal did try gamely here, casting David Niven and June Allyson and throwing in the dubious benefits of colour and CinemaScope. To be fair, if you've never seen the 1936 movie, this may pass the time well enough, especially if you're a fan of either star. Trouble is, Niven is too often reduced to eyebrow-raising double takes, while Allyson is outclassed by her leading man. TS

David Niven *Godfrey* • June Allyson *Irene* • Jessie Royce Landis *Angelica* • Robert Keith (1) *Mr Bullock* • Eva Gabor *Francesca* • Jay Robinson *Vincent* • Martha Hyer *Cordelia* • Herbert Anderson *Hubert* ■ *Dir* Henry Koster • *Scr* Everett Freeman, Peter Berneis, William Bowers, from the 1936 film, from the novel *1101 Park Avenue* by Eric Hatch

My Mother Frank ★★★ 15
Comedy drama   2000 · Aus · Colour · 90min

This is an astute Australian comedy about an overbearing Catholic mother who undergoes a transformation on enrolling at her son's university. Sinead Cusack's conversion is made all the more enjoyable by the fact that it's partly brought about by her dismissively arrogant tutor, who is played with typically self-effacing nonchalance by Sam Neill. Admittedly, there are distinct echoes of *Educating Rita*, but writer/director Mark Lamprell is smart enough to muffle them with a subplot involving Cusack's son Matthew Newton. DP *DVD*

Sinead Cusack *Frances "Frank" Kennedy* • Matthew Newton *David Kennedy* • Sam Neill *Professor Mortlock* • Celia Ireland *Maggie* • Rose Byrne *Jenny* ■ *Dir/Scr* Mark Lamprell

My Mother's Courage ★★★★ 12
Wartime biographical drama   1995 · Ger/UK/Austria · Colour · 90min

This is a powerful, moving and decidedly different telling of a true Holocaust tale about the deportation of 4,000 Hungarian Jews from Budapest to Auschwitz in 1944. Told in flashback, the film focuses on the narrator's mother (Pauline Collins), who survived due to a mix of coincidence, courage and help from a most unexpected quarter. Director Michael Verhoeven also made *The Nasty Girl* (1990), and there are similar touches of surrealism here. DA

Pauline Collins *Elsa Tabori* • Ulrich Tukur *SS officer* • Heribert Sasse *Kelemen* • Natalie Morse *Maria* • Robert Giggenbach *Cornelius Tabori* • Günter Bothur *"Moustache"* • Simon Verhoeven *Young SS man* ■ *Dir* Michael Verhoeven • *Scr* Michael Verhoeven, from the novel by George Tabori

My Name Is Bill W ★★★★
Drama based on a true story   1989 · US · Colour · 100min

This is a generally impressive TV drama about the founding of Alcoholics Anonymous. Few of the familiar Hollywood clichés about drunks are present in the script, and Daniel Petrie's direction is sensitive and well tuned to the remarkable actors. James Woods is compelling as Bill Wilson, living and drinking himself to an early grave until he meets Dr Bob Smith, another alcoholic, played by James Garner. Together they put the cork in the bottle and start the famous meetings. AT

James Woods *Bill Wilson* • JoBeth Williams *Lois Wilson* • James Garner *Dr Bob Smith* • Gary Sinise *Ebby Thatcher* • George Coe *Frank Shaw* • Fritz Weaver *Dr Burnham* ■ *Dir* Daniel Petrie • *Scr* William G Borchert

My Name Is Bruce ★ 15
Comedy horror   2008 · US · Colour · 84min

Director/star Bruce Campbell's comedy horror is a grindingly unfunny love letter to his own B-movie career. The cult hero of *Bubba Ho-tep* and the *Evil Dead* films admittedly turns on his offbeat charisma full blast here. Yet even that charm wears thin in a tiresome spoof that apes the lousy production values of his worst films. AJ *DVD* *BL*

Bruce Campbell • Grace Thorsen *Kelly Graham* • Taylor Sharpe *Jeff* • Ted Raimi *Mills Toddner* • Ben McCain *Mayor* • Ellen Sandweiss *Cheryl* ■ *Dir* Bruce Campbell • *Scr* Mark Verheiden

My Name Is Joe ★★★★★ 15
Drama   1998 · UK/Ger/Fr/It/Sp · Colour · 100min

This trawl through the Glaswegian underworld by director Ken Loach tells the story of Joe (Peter Mullan), a recovering alcoholic who falls in love with a social worker (Louise Goodall). However, his past comes back to haunt him when he vainly tries to help a young friend and his junkie wife who are being threatened by local gangsters. Downbeat and buoyant by turns, Loach's poignant drama boasts laugh-out-loud moments and a host of splendid performances. TH Violence, swearing, a sex scene, drug abuse. *DVD*

Peter Mullan *Joe* • Louise Goodall *Sarah* • Gary Lewis *Shanks* • Lorraine McIntosh *Maggie* • David McKay *Liam* • Annemarie Kennedy *Sabine* • Scott Hannah *Scott* ■ *Dir* Ken Loach • *Scr* Paul Laverty

My Name Is Julia Ross ★★★
Film noir   1945 · US · BW · 64min

With unusual acumen, the bosses at Columbia realised they had a rather good little thriller on their hands and gave this a major launch, earning some rave reviews despite the lack of box-office names. Nina Foch takes the principal role of the secretary who is given a new identity against her will and imprisoned in a remote mansion. Dame May Whitty plays against type as the villainess, supported by the ever-sinister George Macready as her murderous son. The setting is Hollywood's idea of England, but it's still an entertaining picture that helped director Joseph H Lewis climb out of B-features. AE

Nina Foch *Julia Ross* • May Whitty [Dame May Whitty] *Mrs Williamson Hughes* • George Macready *Ralph Hughes* • Roland Varno *Dennis Bruce* • Anita Bolster *Sparkes* • Doris Lloyd *Mrs Mackie* ■ *Dir* Joseph H Lewis • *Scr* Muriel Roy Bolton, from the novel *The Woman in Red* by Anthony Gilbert

My Name Is Khan ★★★ 12
Romantic drama
2010 · Ind/HK/US · Colour · 154min

Bollywood superstar Shah Rukh Khan tugs heartstrings as an Indian Muslim with Asperger's syndrome in this deeply moving if overstuffed Hindi tale about the tragic effects of racial intolerance in post-9/11 America. Drawing together a film of two tonally distinct halves, Khan brings impressive warmth and increasingly contrived melodrama goes from his playfully depicted relationship with a single mum and her young son in San Francisco to his desperate mission to meet the President after their happy family life is destroyed. Ultimately, the emotional impact of events reduces the film's believability. SF Hindi, English +subtitles. *DVD*

Shah Rukh Khan *Rizvan Khan* • Kajol *Mandira Khan* • Katie Amanda Keane *Sarah Garrick* • Kenton Duty *Reese Garrick* ■ *Dir* Karan Johar • *Scr* Shibani Bathija

My Name Is Nobody ★★★ 12
Spaghetti western
1973 · It/Fr/W Ger · Colour · 111min

Sergio Leone produced this spaghetti western and again cast Henry Fonda, the star of *Once upon a Time in the West*, as a notorious gunfighter who plans to take an ocean liner from New Orleans and retire in Europe. Terence Hill plays "Nobody", who idolises Fonda and seduces him into one last showdown. The story has epic pretensions, but the knockabout mood is poorly judged, while Hill is no substitute for Clint Eastwood. Leone's involvement is clear from the gunfights, huge close-ups and Ennio Morricone score. AT Some dialogue dubbed. *DVD*

Henry Fonda *Jack Beauregard* • Terence Hill *Nobody* • Jean Martin *Sullivan* • Piero Lulli *Sheriff* • Leo Gordon *Red* • RG Armstrong *Honest John* ■ *Dir* Tonino Valerii • *Scr* Ernesto Gastaldi, from a story by Fulvio Morsella, Ernesto Gastaldi, from an idea by Sergio Leone

My Name Is Salt ★★★★ U
Documentary
2013 · Swi · Colour · 91min

A gruelling way of life is depicted in Farida Pacha's compelling documentary, which opens fittingly with a quote from Albert Camus's essay *The Myth of Sisyphus*. Each year, Sanabhai Pagi takes his family to the Little Rann of Kutch in the Indian state of Gujarat, where they live in a small shack to harvest the salt crystals that are left behind when the retreating sea turns the coastline into a saline desert. Pacha makes no attempt to construct a narrative from their existence; instead, she and cameraman Lutz Konermann maintain a discreet distance to capture a unique trade in mesmerising detail. DP Gujarati +subtitles.

■ *Dir/Scr* Farida Pacha • *Cinematographer* Lutz Konermann

My Nazi Legacy ★★★ PG
Documentary 2015 · UK · Colour and BW · 91min

"What would it be like to grow up the son of a mass murderer?" That's the dilemma facing the sons of two high-ranking Nazis (one Hitler's lawyer, the other a local governor) in a sobering but absorbing film. Brought together by human rights advocate Philippe Sands, the aged pair's opposing views of their fathers define the narrative. It's eventually knocked off course and loses momentum, but this is still a valuable look at the battle between responsibility and loyalty, set against events that should never be taken for granted. JA *DVD*

Niklas Frank • Philippe Sands • Horst von Wächter ■ *Dir* David Evans • *Scr* Philippe Sands

My Neighbor's Keeper ★★
Mystery thriller 2007 · Can · Colour · 91min

Nothing rings true in this flat and badly written TV movie that sees childless Laura Harring (*Mulholland Drive*) among the suspects when her best friend, a mother of two, is murdered. But following a sluggish set-up designed to establish her apparent motive to kill, the "did she or didn't she?"

angle soon peters out in favour of a predictable plotline involving the dead pal's husband (a one-note Linden Ashby). Incompatible story threads make this feel unfocused and unsatisfying. SF

Laura Harring *Kate Powell* • Linden Ashby *Mike Harding* • Ken Tremblett *Tim Powell* • Brenda Campbell *Ann Harding* ■ *Dir* Walter Klenhard • *Scr* Lindsay Macadam

My Neighbor's Secret ★★
Crime thriller 2009 · Can · Colour · 91min

Architect Nicholas Brendon flips between sensitive and psychopathic following his wife's murder in this routine and poorly paced tale of lies, revenge and obsession. Offered support by neighbours Vincent Ventresca and Chandra West, he becomes fixated on West and resolves to steal her for himself. Brendon (who played Xander in *Buffy the Vampire Slayer* for seven years) shines in a stereotypical nutcase role, capturing his character's fractured personality with chilling precision. But the insipid plotting results in even the confrontational climax falling flat. SF Violence.

Nicholas Brendon *Brent* • Chandra West *Casey* • Vincent Ventresca *Jason* • Dakota Goyo *Austin Hest* ■ *Dir* Leslie Hope • *Scr* Michael Murray

My Neighbour Totoro ★★★★ U
Animated fantasy adventure
1988 · Jpn · Colour · 82min

Set in the 1950s, this charming tale draws on the childhood experiences of director Hayao Miyazaki (*Spirited Away*). Left alone while their father frets over their sick mother, Satsuki (voiced by Dakota Fanning) and her younger sister Mei (Dakota's little sister, Elle) have fantastical woodland adventures with soot balls known as "dustbunnies", a 12-legged cat bus and furry giant Totoro. Despite the minimalist storyline, everything sings of the wonderment of youth and the graphics are an utter delight. DP Japanese dubbed.
DVD Blu

Dakota Fanning *Satsuki* • Elle Fanning *Mei* ■ *Dir* Hayao Miyazaki • *Scr* Hayao Miyazaki, with Cindy Davis Hewitt, Donald H Hewitt (2005 Disney redubbed version)

My Neighbours the Yamadas ★★★ PG
Animated comedy 1999 · Jpn · Colour · 103min

Anyone expecting Studio Ghibli's wide-eyed animé style will be surprised at the strip-cartoon quality of this quirky look at Japanese domestic life. For studio co-founder Isao Takahata is in the chair, and he has a more experimental take on his art than colleague Hayao Mayazaki. It's beautifully rendered and water-coloured, surprisingly all done on computer, as the family - scatty parents, inquisitive children and hard-talking grandma - survive a series of mildly diverting scenarios. TF Japanese +subtitles. *DVD* Blu

Hayato Isobata *Noboru Yamada* • Masako Araki *Shige Yamano* • Naomi Uno *Nonoko Yamada* ■ *Dir* Isao Takahata • *Scr* Isao Takahata, from the comic strip *Nono-chan* by Hisaichi Ishii

My New Gun ★★★ 15
Black comedy 1992 · US · Colour · 94min

This charming, eccentric slice of Americana provides Diane Lane with one of her best roles to date, playing an ordinary suburban housewife who strikes up a curious relationship with wild neighbour James LeGros. When LeGros steals the gun Lane's husband Stephen Collins bought her for protection, a series of events unfolds that changes her life for ever. Writer/director Stacy Cochran, in her first feature, pokes some wry fun at the American obsession with weaponry, and there are winning performances from Lane, LeGros, Tess Harper and the cast-against-type Collins. JF Swearing.

Diane Lane *Debbie Bender* • James LeGros *Skippy* • Stephen Collins *Gerald Bender* • Tess Harper *Kimmy Hayes* • Bill Raymond *Andrew* •

Bruce Altman *Irwin* • Maddie Corman *Myra* • Philip Seymour Hoffman *Chris* ■ *Dir/Scr* Stacy Cochran

My Night with Maud ★★★★ U
Drama 1969 · Fr · BW · 105min

Oscar-nominated for best foreign language film, this is one of Eric Rohmer's few films to boast a star-studded cast. It is an engrossing study of temptation and moral rectitude, with a delicious twist in which Rohmer questions the validity of religious and philosophical conviction in the face of human caprice. As the staunchly Catholic engineer, Jean-Louis Trintignant gives one of his finest performances as he resists the seduction of sophisticated divorcee Françoise Fabian out of fidelity to Marie-Christine Barrault, a woman he adores silently from afar. DP French +subtitles. *DVD*

Jean-Louis Trintignant *Jean-Louis/Narrator* • Françoise Fabian *Maud* • Marie-Christine Barrault *Françoise* • Antoine Vitez *Vidal* • Leonide Kogan *Concert violinist* ■ *Dir/Scr* Eric Rohmer • *Cinematographer* Nestor Almendros

My Old Lady ★★★ 12A
Comedy drama
2014 · US/Fr/UK · Colour · 106min

Maggie Smith capitalises on the success of *Downton Abbey* here, playing another wealthy old dowager, Madame Girard. However, Girard's stiff upper lip conceals some loose morals, which are gradually revealed when a smart-mouthed New Yorker (Kevin Kline) comes to take possession of his grand Parisian home, but is dismayed to find that by law he is obliged to let her stay. Smith and Kline have excellent chemistry but skeletons tumble out of the closet in a clumsy fashion, so it's just as well the refined cast is able to put some meat on those old bones. SP *DVD*
Blu

Maggie Smith *Mathilde Girard* • Kevin Kline *Mathias Gold* • Kristin Scott Thomas *Chloé Girard* • Dominique Pinon *Monsieur Lefebvre* ■ *Dir* Israel Horovitz • *Scr* Israel Horovitz, from his play

My Own Private Idaho ★★★★ 18
Drama 1991 · US · Colour · 99min

A narcoleptic rent boy's doomed quest to find his mother is all the story director Gus Van Sant needs to explore the meaning of home and family in this unsettling tone poem. Using hallucinatory dream sequences, *cinéma vérité* confessions with male hustlers, artful sexual posing and impressionistic effects to hammer home the disturbed state of River Phoenix's mind, Van Sant also manages to extract a mould-breaking performance from Keanu Reeves (playing the object of Phoenix's affections). Audacious, controversial, directional, important and totally unique, you'll either love it or hate it. But see it! AJ Swearing, sex scenes, drug abuse, nudity. *DVD*

River Phoenix *Mike Waters* • Keanu Reeves *Scott Favor* • James Russo *Richard Waters* • William Richert *Bob Pigeon* • Rodney Harvey *Gary* • Chiara Caselli *Carmella* • Michael Parker *Digger* • Jessie Thomas *Denise* • Grace Zabriskie *Alena* ■ *Dir* Gus Van Sant • *Scr* Gus Van Sant, with additional dialogue by William Shakespeare

My Pal Trigger ★★ U
Western 1946 · US · BW · 79min

Roy Rogers declared this a favourite among his westerns, though it's hard to see why - except for the fact that it gives Trigger more prominence than usual. Horse breeding is central to the dramatic storyline, which sees one champion steed shot dead, Rogers accused of the crime, and a mare being injured by a mountain lion while protecting her offspring. Former star Jack Holt plays the lead heavy. AE

Roy Rogers • George "Gabby" Hayes *Gabby Kendrick* • Dale Evans *Susan* • Jack Holt *Brett Scoville* • LeRoy Mason *Carson* • Roy Barcroft *Hunter* • Kenne Duncan *Croupier* ■ *Dir* Frank McDonald • *Scr* Jack Townley, John K Butler, from a story by Paul Gangelin

My Reputation ★★
Melodrama 1946 · US · BW · 92min

In this typical vehicle, Barbara Stanwyck plays a widow who creates a scandal by dating too soon after her husband's death (hence the title). She's got two suitors, one of whom is George Brent, playing against type as a womaniser, and there are no real surprises, except for the fact that Stanwyck fairly drips with furs and jewellery when rolling bandages for the local Red Cross. Eve Arden as Stanwyck's best friend steals the movie, but it's petty larceny. TS

Barbara Stanwyck *Jessica Drummond* • George Brent *Major Scott Landis* • Warner Anderson *Frank Everett* • Lucile Watson *Mrs Kimball* • John Ridgely *Cary Abbott* • Eve Arden *Ginna Abbott* • Jerome Cowan *George Van Orman* ■ *Dir* Curtis Bernhardt • *Scr* Catherine Turney, from the novel *Instruct My Sorrows* by Clare Jaynes

My Science Project ★★ 15
Science-fiction adventure
1985 · US · Colour · 90min

This laugh-free comedy typifies the problems that the Disney studios have always had in producing films for kids who've outgrown their cartoons. The plot is OK: high school students get their hands on an extraterrestrial gizmo that lets them summon up objects from the past and future. But its development, especially the emphasis on clumsily portrayed and badly integrated adolescent sex, leaves a nasty taste in the mouth. Dennis Hopper, however, is truly funny as an ageing hippy science teacher. DA *DVD*

John Stockwell *Michael Harlan* • Danielle Von Zerneck *Ellie Sawyer* • Fisher Stevens *Vince Latello* • Raphael Sbarge *Sherman* • Dennis Hopper *Bob Roberts* • Barry Corbin *Lew Harlan* • Richard Masur *Detective Isadore Nulty* ■ *Dir/Scr* Jonathan Betuel

My Scientology Movie
Documentary 2015 · UK/US · Colour

This is a preview - no prints were available to review as we went to press: The title of Louis Theroux's documentary all but acknowledges the fact that we've already had one exposé on Scientology - Paul Haggis's *Going Clear: Scientology and the Prison of Belief*. But Theroux has a different line of attack than Haggis, preferring to use humour, role-play and dramatic reconstruction plus many shots of uneasy Scientologists filming Louis filming them to add flavour to what might otherwise be a dry re-run. SvM

Louis Theroux • Rob Alter *Tom Cruise* • Andrew Perez *David Miscavige* • Paz de la Huerta ■ *Dir* John Dower • *Scr* John Dower, Louis Theroux

My Sin ★★★
Drama 1931 · US · BW · 77min

About to marry into wealthy New York society, former nightclub singer Tallulah Bankhead, who shot and killed a man in Panama, is confronted by her murky hidden past when the lawyer (Fredric March) who defended her appears on the scene. This was Paramount's second attempt in a year (the first was *Tarnished Lady*) to turn stage, society and gossip-column legend Tallulah into a big-time movie star. However, the wild girl's charismatic sex appeal once again failed to transfer itself to celluloid in this rather creaky melodrama. RK

Tallulah Bankhead *Carlotta/Ann Trevor* • Fredric March *Dick Grady* • Harry Davenport *Roger Metcalf* • Scott Kolk *Larry Gordon* • Anne Sutherland *Mrs Gordon* • Margaret Adams *Paula Marsden* • Lily Cahill *Helen Grace* ■ *Dir* George Abbott • *Scr* Owen Davis, Adelaide Heilbron, George Abbott, from the play *Her Past* by Frederick Jackson

My Sister Eileen ★★★ U
Comedy 1942 · US · BW · 96min

This film version of the hit play was a great success in its day, though it seems somewhat forced and strident now. Yet Rosalind Russell's expert comic timing is a joy to behold in her role as an aspiring writer, trying her luck in Manhattan and finding opportunity comes more easily to her beautiful sister (Janet Blair). Russell

M

won an Oscar nomination for her performance, which she re-created to enormous acclaim in the stage musical *Wonderful Town*. Columbia, however, who owned the rights to the original play, made a completely different musical of the property in 1955. **TV**

Rosalind Russell *Ruth Sherwood* • Brian Aherne *Robert Baker* • Janet Blair *Eileen Sherwood* • George Tobias *Landlord Appopolous* • Allyn Joslyn *Chick Clark* • Richard Quine *Frank Lippincott* • *Dir* Alexander Hall • *Scr* Joseph Fields, Jerome Chodorov, from their play, from the stories by Ruth McKenney

My Sister Eileen ★★★ U
Musical comedy   1955 · US · Colour · 96min

This charming musical remake of the 1942 comedy details the adventures of two girls from the Ohio backwoods getting to grips with the fleshpots of New York. Starring a whole host of early 1950s faces, the whole enterprise zings with an amiable kookiness. Betty Garrett in particular shines as the plain elder sister with a heart of fractured gold. **SH**

Janet Leigh *Eileen Sherwood* • Betty Garrett *Ruth Sherwood* • Jack Lemmon *Bob Baker* • Robert Fosse [Bob Fosse] *Frank Lippencott* • Kurt Kasznar *Appopolous* • Richard York [Dick York] *"Wreck"* • Lucy Marlow *Helen* • Tommy Rall *Chick Clark* • *Dir* Richard Quine • *Scr* Blake Edwards, Richard Quine, from the play by Joseph Fields, Jerome Chodorov, from the stories by Ruth McKenney

My Sister, My Love ★★
Period romantic drama   1966 · Swe · BW · 97min

The story of Bibi Andersson's incestuous relationship with long-absent brother Per Oscarsson labours under the misapprehension that it's a serious and shocking work of art, when it's actually a shoddy bodice-ripper that fritters away its hard-working cast and forbidding setting, as well as the fascinating contrast between the godless decadence of the reign of Enlightenment monarch Gustaf III with the 1960s breakdown in traditional morality. Undeterred, Vilgot Sjöman went on to confirm his reputation as the bad boy of Swedish cinema with *I Am Curious – Yellow*. **DP**

Per Oscarsson *Jacob* • Bibi Andersson *Charlotte* • Jarl Kulle *Alsmeden* • Gunnar Björnstrand *Count Schwartz* • Tina Hedström *Ebba Livin* • Berta Hall *Mrs Kuller* ■ *Dir* Vilgot Sjöman • *Scr* Vilgot Sjöman, inspired by the play *Tis Pity She's a Whore* by John Ford

My Sister's Keeper ★★ 12
Drama   2009 · US · Colour · 104min

Based on the bestselling novel by Jodi Picoult, this drama has Cameron Diaz as the frantic mother of two daughters, one (Abigail Breslin) conceived specifically to donate blood cells to her sister, who is dying of leukaemia. Writer/director Nick Cassavetes can't keep the story from feeling maudlin at times, but the casting of Breslin (*Little Miss Sunshine*) as the donor child certainly helps. Her candid remarks challenge the softly-softly approach of her parents, especially when she decides that she doesn't want to give up a kidney, going so far as to hire a lawyer (Alec Baldwin). While there are touching and sincere moments, even these are undermined by an unlikely last-minute twist. **SP** Brief swearing. *DVD* *BLU*

Cameron Diaz *Sara Fitzgerald* • Alec Baldwin *Campbell Alexander* • Abigail Breslin *Anna Fitzgerald* • Joan Cusack *Judge De Salvo* • Thomas Dekker *Taylor Ambrose* • Sofia Vassilieva *Kate Fitzgerald* • Jason Patric *Brian Fitzgerald* • Evan Ellingson *Jesse Fitzgerald* ■ *Dir* Nick Cassavetes • *Scr* Nick Cassavetes, Jeremy Leven, from the novel by Jodi Picoult • *Cinematographer* Caleb Deschanel

My Six Loves ★★★ U
Romantic comedy   1962 · US · Colour · 100min

As a film director, ace choreographer Gower Champion never achieved the heights he reached on Broadway. Nor did he equal his popularity as half of the dance team of Marge and Gower Champion who appeared in a series of superbly

entertaining MGM features. Here he reunites with another MGM alumnus, Debbie Reynolds, in a likeable tale of theatrical folk. This is either mawkish or genuinely sentimental, but certainly professional. **TS**

Debbie Reynolds *Janice Courtney* • Cliff Robertson *Rev Jim Larkin* • David Janssen *Martin Bliss* • Eileen Heckart *Ethel Swenson* • Jim Backus *The Sheriff* • Pippa Scott *Diane Soper* • John McGiver *Judge Harris* • Hans Conried *Kingsley Cross* ■ *Dir* Gower Champion • *Scr* John Fante, Joseph Calvelli, William Wood, from the novel by Peter VK Funk

My Son John ★ U
Drama   1952 · US · BW · 121min

A patriotic American family goes into shock when they learn their beloved son is a communist. All is forgiven when he recants and dies. An abysmal anti-Red movie, directed by Leo McCarey. Helen Hayes returned to the screen after a long absence to play the mother, while Robert Walker died before the film's completion, forcing the production to fill in the gaps with footage from *Strangers on a Train*. To the astonishment of many, McCarey was Oscar-nominated for his original story, which presents an unbalanced picture of bigotry. **RK**

Helen Hayes *Lucille Jefferson* • Van Heflin *Stedman of the FBI* • Robert Walker *John Jefferson* • Dean Jagger *Dan Jefferson* • Minor Watson *Dr Carver* • Frank McHugh *Father O'Dowd* • Richard Jaeckel *Chuck Jefferson* • James Young (2) *Ben Jefferson* ■ *Dir* Leo McCarey • *Scr* Myles Connolly, Leo McCarey, John Lee Mahin, from a story by Leo McCarey

My Son, My Son! ★★★★
First World War drama   1940 · US · BW · 116min

A solid and stellar cast, under Charles Vidor's sober and well-judged direction, brings Howard Spring's powerful bestseller to life. Brian Aherne plays William Essex who, born into a poverty-stricken background, has pulled himself up by the bootstraps to become a successful novelist. He dotes on his son (Louis Hayward), but the latter grows into cruel, unfeeling manhood, mocking his father, destroying his own childhood sweetheart (Laraine Day) and attempting to seduce the woman his father loves (Madeleine Carroll). An absorbing drama of the highest order. **RK**

Madeleine Carroll *Livia Vaynol* • Brian Aherne *William Essex* • Louis Hayward *Oliver Essex* • Laraine Day *Maeve O'Riordan* • Henry Hull *Dermot O'Riordan* • Josephine Hutchinson *Nellie Moscrop Essex* • Sophie Stewart *Sheila O'Riordan* • Bruce Lester *Rory O'Riordan* ■ *Dir* Charles Vidor • *Scr* Leonore Coffee, from the novel by Howard Spring

My Son, My Son, What Have Ye Done ★★★ 15
Crime thriller based on a true story
2009 · US/Ger · Colour · 91min

Werner Herzog fans will undoubtedly enjoy spotting allusions to his past works in this quirky crime thriller. The less committed, however, are likely to be utterly bemused by its contrived structure and mannered performances. Willem Dafoe and Michael Peña play the cops who are summoned when Brad Macallum (Michael Shannon) murders his mother and barricades himself inside his home. They then begin piecing together Macallum's backstory from testimonies provided by his fiancée (Chloë Sevigny) and others. The nods to *Aguirre, Wrath of God* and *Fitzcarraldo* won't go unnoticed, but the more obtuse touches that bear the stamp of executive producer David Lynch may prove too eccentric. **DP** Swearing, gore. *DVD*

Willem Dafoe *Detective Hank Havenhurst* • Michael Shannon *Brad Macallum* • Chloë Sevigny *Ingrid* • Michael Peña [Michael Pena] *Detective Vargas* • Udo Kier *Lee Meyers* • Brad Dourif *Uncle Ted* • Grace Zabriskie *Mrs Macallum* • Irma Hall [Irma P Hall] *Mrs Roberts* • Loretta Devine *Miss Roberts* ■ *Dir* Werner Herzog • *Scr* Werner Herzog, Herbert Golder

My Son the Fanatic ★★★ 15
Drama   1997 · UK · Colour · 83min

Caricature and cliché come close to scuppering this Yorkshire-based drama from screenwriter Hanif Kureishi. But such is the excellence of leads Om Puri and Rachel Griffiths that this study of religious intolerance, class snobbery and the seeming impossibility of social integration is never less than absorbing. As the immigrant cab driver whose hopes for acceptance are dashed by his son's involvement with a strict Islamic sect, Puri strikes up a rapport with Griffiths's harassed prostitute and thus deepens his crisis. **DP** Sex scenes, swearing, drug abuse. *DVD*

Om Puri *Parvez* • Rachel Griffiths *Bettina* • Stellan Skarsgård *Schitz* • Akbar Kurtha *Farid* • Gopi Desai *Minoo* • Harish Patel *Fizzy* • Bhasker Patel [Bhasker] *The Maulvi* • Sarah Jane Potts *Madelaine* ■ *Dir* Udayan Prasad • *Scr* Hanif Kureishi, from his short story

My Soul to Take ★★ 18
Horror thriller   2010 · US · Colour · 102min

Legendary horror director Wes Craven is on shaky form in this mild shocker about a small-town homocidal maniac who puts a curse on the seven children born the same night of his demise, vowing to return and kill them all. Then, 16 years later, the kids are gruesomely murdered one by one. On paper, this contains many of the elements needed for a thrill-a-minute horror. But Craven seems unable to crank up the tension or deliver the spooks required. A pivotal plot twist is telegraphed within the opening 20 minutes, and the script relies heavily on scenes of laboured clunky dialogue to move it forward. **TeS** *DVD* *BLU*

Max Thieriot *Bug* • Frank Grillo *Detective Frank Paterson* • Emily Meade *Fang* • Denzel Whitaker *Jerome* • Zena Grey *Penelope* • Nick Lashaway *Brandon* ■ *Dir/Scr* Wes Craven

My Spy ★ 12
Action comedy   2008 · US/Ger · Colour · 93min

Falling directly into the "What were they thinking?" category, this all-star disaster has Colin Hanks's young FBI agent discover that his once obese mother has turned into a middle-aged hottie (Meg Ryan). She's also dating Latin charmer Antonio Banderas, an art thief that Hanks is ordered to put under 24-hour surveillance. The talents of a cast that also includes Selma Blair are wasted by the puerile script. **JF** Swearing, sexual references. *DVD*

Antonio Banderas *Tommy* • Meg Ryan *Marty Durand* • Selma Blair *Emily* • Colin Hanks *Henry Durand* • Trevor Morgan *Eddie* ■ *Dir/Scr* George Gallo

My Stepmother Is an Alien ★★★ 15
Science-fiction comedy
1988 · US · Colour · 103min

"Barbarella Goes Shopping" is the premise of this clunky cosmic satire, saved by Kim Basinger's untapped flair for light comedy. She plays a gorgeous ET who shacks up with scientist slob Dan Aykroyd to save her planet from destruction. Forget the plot, just settle down and watch a series of goofy culture-clash sketches revolving around Basinger coping with suburban life on Earth armed only with her talking alien handbag. Fine moments of inspired lunacy jostle with predictably slight comic relief, but Basinger's eager-to-please freshness and verve make this muddle impossible to dislike. **AJ** Swearing. *DVD*

Dan Aykroyd *Dr Steven Mills* • Kim Basinger *Celeste Martin* • Jon Lovitz *Ron Mills* • Alyson Hannigan *Jessie Mills* • Joseph Maher *Dr Lucas Budlong* • Seth Green *Fred Glass* • Wesley Mann *Grady* • Adrian Sparks *Dr Morosini* ■ *Dir* Richard Benjamin • *Scr* Jerico, Herschel Weingrod, Timothy Harris, Jonathan Reynolds

My Stuff ★★★ 15
Documentary   2013 · Fin · Colour · 82min

A man runs naked through the frozen streets of Helsinki. His name is Petri Luukkainen, and his streaking ends at a

storage facility where he picks out a warm coat. It's the first item of his "stuff" (comprising not just his clothes but also the entire contents of his flat) that he will allow himself to retrieve on a daily basis for a year-long "experiment". This artfully shot film often feels like a fiction (and is ripe to be adapted as one), but the amusing premise does wane after his immediate home comforts are restored. **JH** Finnish +subtitles.

■ *Dir/Scr* Petri Luukkainen • *Cinematographer* Jesse Jokinen

My Summer of Love ★★★★ 15
Drama   2004 · UK · Colour · 82min

This loose adaptation of Helen Cross's Yorkshire-set novel makes several astute contrasts between surface illusion and bitter reality. Ryszard Lenczewski's cinematography perfectly captures a balmy atmosphere of rural contentment, as working-class teenager Natalie Press falls for well-heeled Emily Blunt. The intensity of their relationship soon threatens to overwhelm them, and seems as fragile as Paddy Considine's fervent, prison-inspired dalliance with born-again Christianity. The naive optimism of the central characters is sensitively conveyed, but the assault on religion is heavy-handed and the dialogue occasionally ponderous. **AC** Swearing, sex scenes. *DVD*

Natalie Press *Mona* • Emily Blunt *Tamsin* • Paddy Considine *Phil* • Dean Andrews *Ricky* • Michelle Byrne *Ricky's wife* • Paul Antony-Barber *Tamsin's father* • Lynette Edwards *Tamsin's mother* • Kathryn Summer *Sadie* ■ *Dir* Pawel Pawlikowski • *Scr* Pawel Pawlikowski, Michael Wynne, from the novel by Helen Cross

My Super Ex-Girlfriend ★★★ 12
Romantic fantasy comedy
2006 · US · Colour · 92min

Breaking up is hard to do but when your superhero girlfriend can shoot lasers from her eyes, it's even harder. That's the premise of this amusing high-concept comedy starring Uma Thurman and Luke Wilson. It boasts at least some of the good-natured mischief and mayhem of *Ghost Busters*, which put Ivan Reitman on the A-list of Hollywood directors in the 1980s. With his hangdog handsomeness and tendency for self-effacing humour, Wilson is perfect as the boyfriend who is slowly emasculated by atomic-fuelled scorn. Thurman is also convincing as G-Girl, but it's a shame that in the second half of the movie, Don Payne's script abandons all sympathy for her. **SP** *DVD* *BLU*

Uma Thurman *Jenny Johnson/G-Girl* • Luke Wilson *Matt Saunders* • Anna Faris *Hannah Lewis* • Eddie Izzard *Professor Bedlam/Barry* • Wanda Sykes *Carla Dunkirk* • Rainn Wilson *Vaughn* ■ *Dir* Ivan Reitman • *Scr* Don Payne • *Cinematographer* Don Burgess

My Sweet Little Village ★★★ PG
Comedy   1986 · Cz · Colour · 99min

Touching obliquely on bureaucratic corruption, the underdevelopment of the countryside and the shortage of decent housing, this is one of Jirí Menzel's mildest political allegories. It's a benign gaze that falls upon the villagers of a muddle-along collective, where the doctor is accident-prone, a bashful student becomes besotted with his teacher, a young wife strays from nuptial bliss and a truck driver and his doltish assistant fall out over repeated bungling. Amiable entertainment. **DP** In Czech.

Janos Ban *Otik Rakosnik* • Marian Labuda *Pavek* • Rudolf Hrusinsky *Dr Skruzny* • Petr Cepek *Turek* ■ *Dir* Jirí Menzel • *Scr* Zdenek Sverak

My Teenage Daughter ★ PG
Drama   1956 · UK · BW · 96min

Anna Neagle stars in this ludicrous and staggeringly awful melodrama about the problems of motherhood in the 1950s. Neagle plays a magazine editor whose teenage daughter (Sylvia Syms) gets a new boyfriend and ends up in jail for manslaughter. The villain of the piece is jive dancing, while everyone speaks with Mayfair accents and seems to think they're making a statement about youth. AT **DVD**

Anna Neagle *Valerie Carr* • Sylvia Syms *Janet Carr* • Wilfrid Hyde White *Sir Joseph* • Norman Wooland *Hugh Manning* • Kenneth Haigh *Tony Ward Black* • Julia Lockwood *Poppet Carr* • Helen Haye *Aunt Louisa* ■ *Dir* Herbert Wilcox • *Scr* Felicity Douglas

My Tutor ★★ 18
Comedy drama   1983 · US · Colour · 92min

A desperately dated and awful teen comedy drama, this is only saved by a wacky supporting performance from Crispin Glover. Matt Lattanzi stars as the teenager whose father hires him a tutor so he can get into Yale and luckily for him, Caren Kaye is blonde and beautiful. Director George Bowers tries to handle their relationship sympathetically rather than gratuitously, but it is overshadowed by a silly subplot. JB

Caren Kaye *Terry* • Matt Lattanzi *Bobby Chrystal* • Kevin McCarthy *Mr Chrystal* • Clark Brandon *Billy* • Bruce Bauer *Don* • Arlene Golonka *Mrs Chrystal* • Crispin Glover *Jack* • Kitten Natividad *Ana Maria* ■ *Dir* George Bowers • *Scr* Joe Roberts, from the story by Mark Tenser

My Uncle Antoine ★★★
Drama   1971 · Can · Colour · 110min

This small-scale, 1940s-set rural drama is sometimes regarded as one of the best Canadian films ever made. Dealing with life and death in a Québec village, it gently juggles a gallery of characters, focusing on teenage Jacques Gagnon and his uncle (Jean Duceppe), the local undertaker. Director Claude Jutra has a small role as the town clerk, but his career was tragically cut short by Alzheimer's disease. In 1986, he vanished; a year later, his decomposed body was found in the frozen St Lawrence river with a note to identify himself. AT French +subtitles.

Jacques Gagnon *Benoît* • Lyne Champagne *Carmen* • Jean Duceppe *Antoine* • Monique Mercure *Alexandrine* • Lionel Villeneuve *Joseph Poulin* • Olivette Thibault *Cecile* • Claude Jutra *Fernand* ■ *Dir* Claude Jutra • *Scr* Clement Perron, Claude Jutra, from a story by Clement Perron

My Voyage to Italy ★★★★ 12
Documentary   1999 · It/US · Colour · 236min

This insightful documentary provides as much of a window into the thematic and stylistic preoccupations of Martin Scorsese as a history of Italian cinema prior to 1963. Some might find the choice of the films that illuminated Scorsese's Little Italy boyhood a touch conservative. But the director's decision to stick to the critical classics enables him to show in admirable detail (and with lengthy clips) how neorealism shaped the increasingly personal work of Federico Fellini and Michelangelo Antonioni, and the lengthy clips allow the audience to catch Scorsese's infectious enthusiasm. DP **DVD**

■ *Dir* Martin Scorsese

My Way Home ★★★★ 15
Biographical drama   1978 · UK · BW · 68min

Having endured endless poverty and rejection, Stephen Archibald emerges from the dark tunnel of his childhood in the concluding part of Bill Douglas's magnificent film autobiography, that began with *My Childhood* (1972). After all the pain of family life, it is, unsurprisingly, a stranger whom Archibald meets on National Service in Egypt who transforms the boy's life. Taken together, Douglas's trilogy is one of the finest achievements in British cinema history. DP **DVD**

Stephen Archibald *Jamie* • Paul Kermack *Jamie's father* • Jessie Combe *Father's wife* • William Carrol *Archie* • Morag McNee *Father's girlfriend* • Lennox Milne *Grandmother* ■ *Dir/Scr* Bill Douglas

My Week with Marilyn ★★★★ 15
Drama based on a true story   2011 · US/UK · Colour · 94min

In 1956, the press was agog that screen siren Marilyn Monroe had sensationally been paired with theatre giant Laurence Olivier in the British movie *The Prince and the Showgirl*, but the drama that unfolded backstage offers greater intrigue. Their clash of styles is revealed in this beguiling adaptation of a memoir by Colin Clark (played by a wide-eyed Eddie Redmayne), who was a production runner on the film and became a confidante/companion to the isolated movie star during her stay in England. Michelle Williams captivates as Marilyn, matching her childlike lust for life with a darker, destructive nature. But the standouts are a hilarious Kenneth Branagh, whose Olivier is always ready with a scathing one-liner, and Judi Dench, who plays Dame Sybil Thorndike like a fussing aunt. It oozes with romance, too, but most of all it's delightfully evocative of a bygone era of film-making. SP Swearing, brief nudity. **DVD** **Blu-ray**

Michelle Williams *Marilyn Monroe* • Eddie Redmayne *Colin Ciark* • Kenneth Branagh *Sir Laurence Olivier* • Julia Ormond *Vivien Leigh* • Dougray Scott *Artnur Miller* • Judi Dench *Dame Sybil Thorndike* • Dominic Cooper *Milton Greene* • Emma Watson *Lucy* ■ *Dir* Simon Curtis • *Scr* Adrian Hodges, from the diaries by Colin Clark

My Wife's Lodger ★★ PG
Comedy   1952 · UK · BW · 76min

Few things date quicker than humour and Maurice Elvey's northern farce certainly belongs to another era. Dominic Roche stars as a hen-pecked soldier returning from war service to find wife Olive Sloane flirting with lodger Leslie Dwyer and daughter Diana Dors besotted with GI Alan Sedgwick. However, a night's drinking encourages some home truths. The humour is broad, the musical interludes dismal, but the cast's enthusiasm is infectious. DP **DVD** **Blu-ray**

Dominic Roche *Willie Higginbotham* • Olive Sloane *Maggie Higginbotham* • Leslie Dwyer *Roger the lodger* • Diana Dors *Eunice Higginbotham* • Alan Sedgwick *Tex* • Vincent Dowling *Norman Higginbotham* ■ *Dir* Maurice Elvey • *Scr* Stafford Dickens, from the play by Dominic Roche

My Wild Irish Rose ★★ U
Biographical musical   1947 · US · Colour · 100min

The subject of this rather feeble biopic is Chauncey Olcott, an Irish-American tenor who co-wrote the title song, *Mother Machree* and *When Irish Eyes Are Smiling*. The songs are well sung by charming Dennis Morgan, who plays the composer with a wobbly Irish brogue. If the film is to be believed (and it isn't), Olcott was enamoured with glamorous singer Lillian Russell (Andrea King) before settling down with his wife. The latter is portrayed by beautiful redhead Arlene Dahl. RB

Dennis Morgan *Chauncey Olcott/Jack Chancellor* • Arlene Dahl *Rose Donovan* • Andrea King *Lillian Russell* • Alan Hale *John Donovan* • George Tobias *Nick Popolis* • George O'Brien *William "Duke" Muldoon* • Sara Allgood *Mrs Brennan* ■ *Dir* David Butler • *Scr* Peter Milne, Edwin Gilbert, Sidney Fields, from the story *Song in His Heart* by Rita Olcott

My Winnipeg ★★★★ 12
Fantasy documentary   2007 · Can/US · BW and Colour · 76min

Guy Maddin (*The Saddest Music in the World*) delights in pastiching past cinematic styles, and here he draws on everything from silent montage to *film noir*. The Canadian auteur creates a mesmerising "docu fantasia" about his birthplace of Winnipeg, which mischievously blends snippets of autobiography, local myth and facetious fiction to droll but dark effect. Maddin evokes a universal sense of home-town nostalgia through anecdotes about his childhood as the son of an ice hockey manager and a beautician, faux news

stories and a horse race that ends in tragedy in a frozen river. This inspired movie is alternately angry, melancholy and hilarious, but it's never less than compelling. DP **DVD**

Guy Maddin *Narrator* • Darcy Fehr *Guy Maddin* • Ann Savage *Mother* • Amy Stewart *Janet Maddin* • Louis Negin *Mayor Cornish* • Brendan Cade *Cameron Maddin* • Wesley Cade *Ross Maddin* ■ *Dir* Guy Maddin • *Scr* Guy Maddin, George Toles (dialogue) • *Cinematographer* Jody Shapiro • *Production Designer* Réjean Labrie

My Year without Sex ★★★
Comedy drama   2009 · Aus · Colour · 92min

Having made an eye-catching debut with animation-strewn drama *Look Both Ways* (2005), Sarah Watt confirmed the good impression with this darkly comic domestic saga that sees Melbourne 30-something Sacha Horler being advised to avoid orgasms while recovering from a brain aneurysm. The saucy chapter headings are a touch superfluous, but the performances are splendid, with Horler particularly shining as the disgruntled survivor who's able to give everyday trivialities and big issues alike a wry but incisive spin. DP Swearing.

Sacha Horler *Natalie* • Matt Day *Ross* • Jonathan Segat *Louis* • Portia Bradley *Ruby* ■ *Dir/Scr* Sarah Watt

Myra Breckinridge ★★★ 18
Comedy   1970 · US · Colour and BW · 90min

Time has tempered the scandalised revulsion that initially greeted director Michael Sarne's ultra-melodramatic adaptation of Gore Vidal's transsexual satire. Clouded by the controversy, contemporary critics failed to see it as a rather sly essay on gender, all-American movie-star stereotypes and vintage Hollywood nostalgia. Despite Mae West's comeback after a 27-year absence from the big screen to play a tentle-entendre "talent agent", the movie belongs to Raquel Welch in her most underrated role. AJ Swearing, nudity. **DVD**

Mae West *Leticia Van Allen* • John Huston *Buck Loner* • Raquel Welch *Myra Breckinridge* • Rex Reed *Myron Breckinridge* • Farrah Fawcett *Mary-Ann Pringle* • Roger C Carmel *Dr Randolph Spencer Montag* • Roger Herren *Rusty* • Jim Backus *Doctor* • John Carradine *Surgeon* • Andy Devine *Coyote Bill* • Tom Selleck *Stud* ■ *Dir* Michael Sarne • *Scr* Michael Sarne, David Giler, from the novel by Gore Vidal

Le Mystère Picasso ★★★★ U
Documentary   1956 · Fr · BW and Colour · 77min

Pablo Picasso creates 15 original artworks in this majestic study of a genius at work. However, as they were all destroyed after the documentary was finished, they exist only as moving sketches that are captured with graceful simplicity through a transparent canvas by cinematographer Claude Renoir (whose grandfather was the Impressionist, Auguste Renoir). Director Henri-Georges Clouzot occasionally tinkers with time-lapse and at one point splendidly shifts into widescreen when the Spaniard complains that he needs more space. But, essentially, he keeps his distance to allow Picasso's personality and inspiration to mesmerise and delight, even when he produces a muddled misfire. DP In French.

■ *Dir* Henri-Georges Clouzot • *Cinematographer* Claude Renoir • *Music* Georges Auric

Mysteries of Lisbon ★★★★★ PG
Mystery drama   2010 · Por/Fr · Colour · 255min

Adapted from a 19th-century doorstopper novel, this four-hour extravaganza offers a Dickensian level of storytelling richness while unfurling the tangled personal history of a teenage boy seeking the truth about his parentage. Deposited in the care of a kindly priest by his aristocratic mother, young Pedro's desire to learn the identity of his father sets in motion an epic saga of tragic romance, murder and betrayal, in which everyone has a coincidence-packed tale to tell. In the expert directorial hands of

maverick Chilean exile Raúl Ruiz, the result is not only a pleasurably convoluted and elegantly appointed costume drama, but also a reflection on the flexibility of social identity. A masterly swan song from a film-maker who never failed to provoke and excite, this represents the extravagant pleasures of 19th-century fiction with as much cinematic aplomb as anything since Stanley Kubrick's *Barry Lyndon*. TJ Portuguese, French +subtitles. **DVD**

Adriano Luz *Father Dinis* • Maria João Bastos *Angela de Lima* • Ricardo Pereira *Alberto de Magalhães* • Clotilde Hesme *Elisa de Montfort* • Afonso Pimentel *Pedro da Silva as an adult* • João Luis Arrais *Pedro da Silva as a child* ■ *Dir* Raúl Ruiz [Raúl Ruiz] • *Scr* Carlos Saboga, from the novel *Mistérios de Lisboa* by Camilo Castelo Branco

The Mysteries of Paris ★★★ U
Period adventure   1962 · Fr · Colour · 95min

This lavish production was adapted from Eugène Sue's story of kidnap and murder, set during the reign of Louis Philippe. The novel's socio-political themes have been excised to leave a lively adventure in which master of disguise Jean Marais sweeps through the Paris underworld avenging evil and rewarding good. Packed with reformed crooks, vile urchins, mischievous artists and gullible do-gooders, André Hunebelle's film blends thrills and laughs to good effect, while Marais is suitably mysterious amid the splendid period trappings. DP French dubbed.

Jean Marais *Rodolphe De Sambreuil* • Dany Robin *Irene* • Raymond Pellegrin *Baron De Lansignac* • Jill Haworth *Marie* • Pierre Mondy *Le Chourineur* • Renée Gardes *"The Witch"* ■ *Dir* André Hunebelle • *Scr* Jean Halain, Pierre Foucaud, Diego Fabbri, from a novel by Eugène Sue

Mysterious Island ★★★ U
Fantasy adventure   1961 · UK/US · Colour · 96min

Based on Jules Verne's sequel to *20,000 Leagues under the Sea*, this enjoyable British production blends Sinbad-style giant monster thrills, pirates, volcanic eruptions and, of course, Captain Nemo (not James Mason this time, but Herbert Lom). As ever, stop-frame animation maestro Ray Harryhausen's monstrous menagerie provides most of the film's highlights, as oversized bees and colossal crabs threaten the health of Michael Craig, Joan Greenwood and their companions. Although the rather colourless cast doesn't do much to raise excitement levels, Harryhausen's fine work and Bernard Herrmann's atmospheric score make this fantasy worthwhile. SG **DVD**

Michael Craig *Captain Cyrus Harding* • Joan Greenwood *Lady Mary Fairchild* • Michael Callan *Herbert Brown* • Gary Merrill *Gideon Spilett* • Herbert Lom *Captain Nemo* • Beth Rogan *Elena* ■ *Dir* Cy Endfield • *Scr* John Prebble, Daniel Ullman, Crane Wilbur, from the novel *L'Ile Mysterieuse* by Jules Verne

The Mysterious Lady ★★ U
Silent romantic drama   1928 · US · BW · 89min

In her sixth Hollywood film, Greta Garbo stars as a Russian spy who has an affair with Austrian officer Conrad Nagel in order to steal some secret documents. But she falls in love with him for real, eventually betraying her masters. Competently directed by Fred Niblo to capitalise on the camera's love affair with Garbo, it's actually the most risible nonsense, only good for a giggle and an opportunity for her fans to gaze upon her beauty and savour her mysterious persona. RK **DVD**

Greta Garbo *Tania* • Conrad Nagel *Karl von Heinersdorff* • Gustav von Seyffertitz *General Alexandroff* • Albert Pollet *Max* ■ *Dir* Fred Niblo • *Scr* Bess Meredyth, Marian Ainslee (titles), Ruth Cummings (titles), from the novel *Der Krieg im Dunkel* by Ludwig Wolff

M

Mysterious Mr Moto ★★★
Detective drama   1938 · US · BW · 62min

Master of disguise and intrepid meddler in other people's business, Mr Moto sweeps from Scotland Yard to Devil's Island in pursuit of an international crime ring in one of the weaker entries in 20th Century-Fox's amiable B-movie series. The production has an all-expenses-spared feel about it and the plot is hardly out of the top drawer. But such is the pace of Norman Foster's direction that you barely have time to notice. DP

Peter Lorre *Mr Moto* • Mary Maguire *Ann Richman* • Henry Wilcoxon *Anton Darvak* • Erik Rhodes *David Scott-Frensham* • Harold Huber *Ernst Litmar* • Leon Ames *Paul Brissac* ■ *Dir* Norman Foster • *Scr* Norman Foster, Philip MacDonald, from the character created by JP Marquand

Mysterious Skin ★★★ 18
Drama   2004 · US/Neth · Colour · 100min

A poignant and disturbing exploration of paedophilia and its emotional fallout, this poetic and elegantly constructed drama is Gregg Araki's most accessible work to date, and also his most perceptive. In powerful performances, Joseph Gordon-Levitt and Brady Corbet play polar-opposite teens, linked together by an unsettling experience that they shared aged eight. The painful journey that each young man undertakes is difficult to watch, addressing extreme facets of abuse in an impartial manner that some viewers will find offensive. SF Violence, swearing, sexual abuse, drug abuse. *DVD*

Brady Corbet *Brian Lackey* • Joseph Gordon-Levitt *Neil McCormick* • Michelle Trachtenberg *Wendy Peterson* • Jeff Licon *Eric Preston* • Bill Sage *Coach Heider* • Mary Lynn Rajskub *Avalyn Friesen* • Elisabeth Shue *Mrs McCormick* • Billy Drago *Zeke* ■ *Dir* Gregg Araki • *Scr* Gregg Araki, from the novel by Scott Heim

Mystery, Alaska ★★★ 15
Sports comedy drama
1999 · US · Colour · 113min

Russell Crowe heads an ensemble cast in this offbeat sporting tale from *Meet the Parents* director Jay Roach. An uneasy mix of cheeky comedy and button-pushing drama, it charts the small-town frenzy that follows when a backwater Alaskan ice-hockey team gets the chance to compete against the mighty New York Rangers. The end result plays more like an episode of TV's *Northern Exposure* than a Hollywood feature, but it's an enjoyable diversion nonetheless. I SF *DVD*

Russell Crowe *John Biebe* • Hank Azaria *Charles Danner* • Mary McCormack *Donna Biebe* • Burt Reynolds *Judge Walter Burns* • Colm Meaney *Mayor Scott Pitcher* • Lolita Davidovich *Mary Jane Pitcher* • Maury Chaykin *Bailey Pruitt* • Mike Myers *Donnie Shulzhoffer* • Little Richard ■ *Dir* Jay Roach • *Scr* David E Kelley, Sean O'Byrne

Mystery Date ★★ 15
Comedy thriller   1991 · US · Colour · 93min

What's the real reason behind Ethan Hawke's shady older brother organising a blind date for him with the sexy next door neighbour? Could it have something to do with the corpse in his car? This is wildly uneven, but is still a fun black comedy with many surprising touches, not least how endearing Hawke proves to be in a thankless role. AJ Swearing, violence. *DVD*

Ethan Hawke *Tom McHugh* • Teri Polo *Geena Matthews* • Brian McNamara *Craig McHugh* • Fisher Stevens *Dwight* • BD Wong *James Lew* • Tony Rosato *Sharpie* ■ *Dir* Jonathan Wacks • *Scr* Terry Runte, Parker Bennett

Mystery Men ★★★ PG
Comedy action adventure
1999 · US · Colour · 116min

An eclectic cast adds a quality sheen to this mildly diverting superhero spoof, based on the Dark Horse comic. The gimmick is that these saviours of Champion City possess abilities that are of no use whatsoever – fork-throwing expertise, shovel-wielding skills, noxious bodily odours and so on. At a shade over two hours, Kinka Usher's film is much too long to sustain the script's slender humour quota. However, with actors of the calibre of William H Macy, Greg Kinnear, Ben Stiller, Wes Studi and Geoffrey Rush, it's never short of quirky appeal. JC *DVD*

Hank Azaria *The Blue Raja* • Janeane Garofalo *The Bowler* • William H Macy *The Shoveler* • Kel Mitchell *Invisible Boy* • Paul Reubens *The Spleen* • Ben Stiller *Mr Furious* • Wes Studi *The Sphinx* • Greg Kinnear *Captain Amazing/Lance* ■ *Dir* Kinka Usher • *Scr* Neil Cuthbert, from the comic book by Bob Burden

The Mystery of a Hansom Cab ★★
Period murder mystery
2012 · Aus · Colour · 100min

The class divide is the underlying concern of this mundane and insubstantial Aussie whodunnit, based on 19th-century writer Fergus Hume's much-adapted detective novel. Set in Melbourne in 1886, the obviously made-for-TV production sees blame quickly attributed when a member of high society is murdered in the back of the horse-drawn carriage of the title. Though the film has the right visual look for the era (especially in its scenes of poverty), stagey acting and unsubtle direction sadly negate its stab at realism. SF

John Waters (3) *Mark Frettlby* • Marco Chiappi *Duncan Calton* • Shane Jacobson *Detective Samuel Gorby* • Jessica De Gouw *Madge* • Oliver Ackland *Brian Fitzgerald* ■ *Dir* Shawn Seet • *Scr* Glen Dolman, from Fergus Hume's novel

Mystery of Chess Boxing ★★★ 18
Martial arts adventure
1979 · HK · Colour · 86min

Also known as *Ninja Checkmate* (despite not featuring a single ninja), this relentless kung fu caper introduced one of the genre's most memorable bad guys in the shape of the Ghost Face Killer, out for revenge on the clan leaders who plotted against him. Not a ground-breaking story, then; but who needs plot when you've got such stunning fight choreography? GR Cantonese dubbed. *DVD*

Simon Lee [Li Yi-min] *Ah Pao* ■ *Dir* Joseph Kuo

The Mystery of Edwin Drood ★★★
Mystery   1935 · US · BW · 87min

Faced with the unenviable prospect of concocting a credible finale to the tale Charles Dickens left unfinished at his death, John L Balderston and his fellow screenwriters wisely place the emphasis on character in this atmospheric adaptation of the novelist's most sinister opus. The exceptional cast thrives under Stuart Walker's generous direction, with Claude Rains responding particularly well as the opium-addled chorister whose love for Heather Angel spells disaster for her fiancé, David Manners. The stylised gothic sets add to the overall sense of unease, but the wildly melodramatic ending undermines an otherwise effective production. DP

Claude Rains *John Jasper* • Douglass Montgomery *Neville Landless* • Heather Angel *Rosa Bud* • David Manners *Edwin Drood* • Valerie Hobson *Helena Landless* • Francis L Sullivan *Mr Crisparkle* • Walter Kingsford *Hiram Grewigious* • EE Clive *Thomas Sapsea* ■ *Dir* Stuart Walker • *Scr* John L Balderston, Gladys Unger, Leopold Atlas, Bradley King, from the novel by Charles Dickens

The Mystery of Edwin Drood ★ 15
Mystery   1993 · UK · Colour · 97min

Filming Charles Dickens's unfinished novel presents two distinct, but equally difficult challenges: to capture the style of what is a decidedly atypical tome, and to devise a feasible finale. Timothy Forder fails to come close on either count, shooting the opening section with stuffy reverence before launching into a hand-held Hammer pastiche that lacks both imagination and credibility. DP

Robert Powell *John Jasper* • Nanette Newman *Mrs Crisparkle* • Gemma Craven *Miss Twinkleton* • Rosemary Leach *Mrs Tope* • Finty Williams *Rosa* • Glyn Houston *Grewgious* • Ronald Fraser *Dean* ■ *Dir* Timothy Forder • *Scr* Timothy Forder, from the novel by Charles Dickens

The Mystery of Natalie Wood ★★
Biographical drama
2004 · Aus/US · Colour · 172min

Director Peter Bogdanovich explores the troubled life and tragic death by drowning of actress Natalie Wood in this unnecessarily melodramatic TV movie. Bolstering an episodic narrative with extensive archive material and talking-head reminiscences, the film has Wood (played in adulthood by a well-cast Justine Waddell) progress from child performer to serious acting sensation, crossing paths with the likes of Marilyn Monroe and James Dean along the way. But once her neuroses and unhappy relationships with drink, pills and men – particularly Michael Weatherly's self-centred Robert Wagner – kick in, events become a relentless endurance test that reaches a climax with the dragged-out imagining of her final moments. SF

Justine Waddell *Natalie Wood* • Michael Weatherly *Robert Wagner* • Colin Friels *Nick Gurdin* • Alice Krige *Maria Gurdin* • Malcolm Kennard *Christopher Walken* • Matthew Settle *Warren Beatty* ■ *Dir* Peter Bogdanovich • *Scr* Elizabeth Egloff, from *Natasha: the Biography of Natalie Wood* by Suzanne Finstad and the biography *Natalie & RJ: Hollywood's Star-Crossed Lovers* by Warren G Harris

Mystery of the Wax Museum ★★★★ PG
Horror   1933 · US · Colour · 74min

Lionel Atwill stars in this golden-era fright classic as a mad sculptor repopulating his burnt-down museum with wax-covered murder victims. Fay Wray supplies the screams, plus the magic moment where she cracks Atwill's false face to reveal the scars beneath. Glenda Farrell also shines, as a wise-cracking reporter. The inspiration for the later *House of Wax*, this *Grand Guignol* outing boasts fabulous sets, zippy pacing, surprising frankness and marvellously evocative early two-strip Technicolor. AJ *DVD*

Lionel Atwill *Ivan Igor* • Fay Wray *Charlotte Duncan* • Glenda Farrell *Florence Dempsey* • Frank McHugh *Jim* • Gavin Gordon *Harold Winton* • Edwin Maxwell *Joe Worth* ■ *Dir* Michael Curtiz • *Scr* Don Mullally, Carl Erickson, from a play by Charles S Belden [Charles Belden] • *Art Director* Anton F Grot [Anton Grot]

Mystery Road ★★★ 15
Crime drama   2013 · Aus · Colour · 116min

The wide open glory of the outback settings may give this brooding Australian thriller the feel of an Ocker western, but its depiction of the plight of remote Aboriginal communities roots it very much in the present day. The all-star Aussie cast is headed by Aaron Pedersen, who plays a detective just returned to the small Queensland town where he grew up. His investigation into the murder of a teenage Aboriginal girl causes waves in a redneck community divided by race. The mystery at the centre is a little undercooked, but writer/director Ivan Sen makes some telling points about these ghetto-like communities. JF Violence, swearing. *DVD* Blu-ray

Aaron Pedersen *Jay Swan* • Hugo Weaving *Johnno* • Jack Thompson *Mr Murray* • Ryan Kwanten *Pete* • Tony Barry *Sergeant* • Tasma Walton *Mary* ■ *Dir/Scr* Ivan Sen

Mystery Science Theater 3000: the movie ★★★ PG
Science-fiction comedy
1996 · US · Colour · 70min

In this big-screen version of the long-running American cable television series, we eavesdrop on Michael J Nelson and his two robot friends (voiced by Trace Beaulieu and Kevin Murphy) as they watch the 1950s sci-fi movie *This Island Earth*. Mike and the droids are adept at poking fun at the bad movies they're forced to watch by evil scientist Dr Forrester (also played by Beaulieu), though *This Island Earth* is cut above most of the films shown on the original TV show. ST Blu-ray

Trace Beaulieu *Dr Clayton Forrester/Crow T Robot* • Michael J Nelson *Mike Nelson* • Jim Mallon *Gypsy* • Kevin Murphy *Tom Servo* • John Brady *Benkitnorf* ■ *Dir* Jim Mallon • *Scr* Michael J Nelson, Trace Beaulieu, Jim Mallon, Kevin Wagner Murphy [Kevin Murphy], Mary Jo Pehl, Paul Chaplin, Bridget Jones, from the TV series by Joel Hodgson

Mystery Street ★★★
Crime thriller   1950 · US · Colour · 92min

MGM's B-movies were quite unlike any other studio's: they had a professional, glossy look to them and often featured players who would be quite at home in costlier fare. This is a rattlingly good example: a tight little caper tale expertly directed by John Sturges, who over the next decade-and-a-half would be producing such heavyweight movies as *Gunfight at the OK Corral*, *The Magnificent Seven* and *The Great Escape*. Sturges does well by the Boston setting, and he's helped by an expert cast headed by the versatile Ricardo Montalban. TS

Ricardo Montalban *Lieutenant Peter Moralas* • Sally Forrest *Grace Shanway* • Bruce Bennett *Dr McAdoo* • Elsa Lanchester *Mrs Smerrling* • Marshall Thompson *Henry Shanway* • Jan Sterling *Vivian Heldon* ■ *Dir* John Sturges • *Scr* Sydney Boehm, Richard Brooks, from a story by Leonard Spiegelgass

Mystery Submarine ★ U
Spy drama   1950 · US · BW · 78min

Of interest only to close observers of the career of its director, Douglas Sirk, this minor work was his first as a contract director at Universal. The extravagant plot has Robert Douglas's U-boat captain, who has survived the Second World War in South America along with his vessel, kidnapping a German atomic scientist and offering him for sale to a foreign power. Fortunately, Macdonald Carey's US agent has infiltrated the crew. AE

Macdonald Carey *Dr Brett Young* • Marta Toren *Madeline Brenner* • Robert Douglas *Comdr Eric Von Molter* • Carl Esmond *Lt Heldman* • Ludwig Donath *Dr Adolph Guernitz* ■ *Dir* Douglas Sirk • *Scr* George W George, George F Slavin, from a story by George W George, George F Slavin, Ralph Dietrich

Mystery Train ★★★★ 15
Comedy drama   1989 · US/Jpn · Colour · 105min

Demonstrating his customary, quirky genius for character, director Jim Jarmusch effortlessly weaves together three stories set in a moth-eaten Memphis hotel, which is little more than a seedy shrine to Elvis Presley, whose spirit pervades the entire picture. The scenes involving Japanese rock pilgrims Masatoshi Nagase and Youki Kudoh are a delight, while the postmortem into Joe Strummer and Steve Buscemi's bungled robbery is tantamount to a Tarantino prototype. Capping the lot are the exchanges between night clerk Screamin' Jay Hawkins and bellboy Cinque Lee. DP English, Japanese, Italian +subtitles. Violence, swearing, nudity, drug abuse. *DVD* Blu-ray

Masatoshi Nagase *Jun* • Youki Kudoh *Mitzuko* • Screamin' Jay Hawkins *Night clerk* • Cinqué Lee *Bellboy* • Nicoletta Braschi *Luisa* • Elizabeth Bracco *Dee Dee* • Joe Strummer *Johnny* • Steve Buscemi *Charlie* • Tom Waits *Voice of radio DJ* ■ *Dir/Scr* Jim Jarmusch

Mystery Woman ★★
Murder mystery   2003 · US · Colour

Whodunnit enthusiast Kellie Martin turns amateur sleuth to investigate an apparent suicide in this flimsy pilot for a series of TV movies. Having inherited her late uncle's bookshop specialising in mystery novels, she puts his stock and her own extensive knowledge to use trying to prove that her former professor (Robert Wagner) was murdered. The resulting "eureka" moments are overly convenient and the plot's too action-light for its running time. SF

Kellie Martin *Samantha Kinsey* • Robert Wagner *Jack Stenning* • Constance Zimmer *Cassie* • Amy Locane *Tracy Stenning* • JE Freeman *Ian Philby* ■ *Dir* Walter Klenhard • *Scr* Michael Sloan

The Mystic Masseur ★★★ PG
Period satirical drama
2001 · UK/Ind · Colour · 113min

Ismail Merchant's previous directorial offerings have been tainted by a tendency to gild the lily. But while this adaptation of VS Naipaul's novel is admirably restrained in its depiction of Asian society in Trinidad, it misses the nuances of the original prose and instead opts for broad satire. Aasif Mandvi's rise from poet to politician seems more like a pantomime than a parable, with Om Puri reduced to caricature as the village grocer seduced by his son-in-law's celebrity. Entertaining enough. DP *DVD*

Om Puri *Ramlogan* • James Fox *Mr Stewart* • Aasif Mandvi *Ganesh* • Sanjeev Bhaskar *Beharry* • Ayesha Dharkar *Leela* ■ *Dir* Ismail Merchant • *Scr* Caryl Phillips, from the novel by VS Naipaul

Mystic Pizza ★★★★ 15
Romantic comedy
1988 · US · Colour · 103min

This coming-of-age tale contains one of Julia Roberts's first major roles, and it's still one of her best. It follows the ups and downs of Roberts, pal Lili Taylor and sister Annabeth Gish, who get into trouble with love while working at a pizza parlour in their home town of Mystic, Connecticut. Director Donald Petrie serves up a fine films, successfully interlacing the story of the girls' problems with some delightfully comic moments and astute observations. Hard to believe now, but Gish was the bigger star at the time. JB Swearing, sex scenes. *DVD*

Julia Roberts *Daisy Araujo* • Annabeth Gish *Kat Araujo* • Lili Taylor *Jojo Barboza* • Vincent D'Onofrio *[Vincent D'Onofrio]* • Bill Montijo • William R Moses *Tim Travers* • Adam Storke *Charles Gordon Winsor* • Conchata Ferrell *Leona Valsouano* • Joanna Merlin *Margaret* ■ *Dir* Donald Petrie • *Scr* Amy Jones [Amy Holden Jones], Perry Howze, Randy Howze, Alfred Uhry, from a story by Amy Jones [Amy Holden Jones]

Mystic River ★★★★ 15
Murder mystery drama
2003 · US/Aus · Colour · 132min

This ambitious, well-crafted drama is a welcome return to form for Clint Eastwood the director. It features sterling performances from an excellent cast and only just misses greatness by a whisker. Sean Penn, Tim Robbins and Kevin Bacon play childhood friends whose lives are shattered when Penn's daughter is brutally murdered, an event that forces them to confront a horrific episode from their own shared past. Eastwood directs with crisp efficiency but Brian Helgeland's screenplay somehow fails to convince, emerging as a sequence of well-written individual scenes rather than an integrated whole. Judged to the highest standards then, this is a flawed piece of work, but it still ranks as must-see, grown-up cinema. AS Swearing, violence. *DVD* *Blu-ray*

Sean Penn *Jimmy Markum* • Tim Robbins *Dave Boyle* • Kevin Bacon *Sean Devine* • Laurence Fishburne *Whitey Powers* • Marcia Gay Harden *Celeste Boyle* • Laura Linney *Annabeth Markum* • Kevin Chapman *Val Savage* • Emmy Rossum *Katie Markum* • Spencer Treat Clark *Silent Ray Harris* • Tom Guiry *Brendan Harris* ■ *Dir* Clint Eastwood • *Scr* Brian Helgeland, from the novel by Dennis Lehane

The Myth of Fingerprints ★★★ 15
Drama
1996 · US · Colour · 86min

Julianne Moore and *ER*'s Noah Wyle are two of four grown-up siblings who return to their New England home for the traditional Thanksgiving dinner. Cue the airing of family grudges, secrets and emotions in this sly and subdued drama from writer/director Bart Freundlich. Blythe Danner and Roy Scheider stand out as the overwrought parents, but what is most attractive about the film is that it offers no jaw-dropping

revelations or happily-ever-after resolutions. JB Swearing, sex scenes.

Roy Scheider *Hal* • Julianne Moore *Mia* • Blythe Danner *Lena* • Noah Wyle *Warren* • Hope Davis *Margaret* • James LeGros *Cezanne* • Brian Kerwin *Elliot* • Laurel Holloman *Leigh* ■ *Dir/Scr* Bart Freundlich

The Myth of the American Sleepover ★★ 15
Comedy drama 2010 · US · Colour · 96min

In his feature debut, Indie film-maker David Robert Mitchell conjures a hormonally charged Neverland that owes more to movies than real life. The multistranded story unfolds over the course of one balmy summer night in a Detroit curiously devoid of modern gadgets and disapproving adults, but none of the vignettes is particularly engaging. Mitchell strives for a dreamy "salad days" atmosphere by overloading it with gauche French New Wave tropes, but this only emphasises the awkwardness of the acting. DP Swearing, brief nudity.

Claire Sloma *Maggie* • Marlon Morton *Rob Salvati* • Amanda Bauer *Claudia* • Annette DeNoyer *Beth* • Brett Jacobsen *Scott Holland* ■ *Dir/Scr* David Mitchell [David Robert Mitchell]

The Myth of the Male Orgasm ★★
Comedy 1993 · Can · Colour · 90min

Director John Hamilton made his debut with this satire that was barely seen outside his native Canada. Bruce Dinsmore stars as a college professor who is so bewildered by his failure to attract the opposite sex that he agrees to be a guinea pig for a study of male attitudes being conducted by a group of feminist psychologists. There are one or two amusing moments, but that's about it. DP Swearing.

Bruce Dinsmore *Jimmy Ruvinsky* • Miranda de Pencier *Jane Doe* • Mark Camacho *Tim* • Burke Lawrence *Sean* • Ruth Marshall *Mimi* • Macha Grenon *Paula* ■ *Dir* John Hamilton • *Scr* John Hamilton, David Reckziegel

NYC: Tornado Terror ★ 12
Disaster thriller 2008 · Can · Colour · 86min

The Big Apple comes under threat yet again in this cliché-riddled disaster movie. This time it's mini tornados causing made-for-TV chaos, leaving deputy mayor Sebastian Spence and his meteorologist wife Nicole de Boer racing to save the day. Realism is the first casualty of this global-warming fallout, as sudden gusts of abysmal computer effects compete for unintended laughs alongside beyond-stupid dialogue. SF *DVD*

Nicole de Boer *Cassie Lawrence* • Sebastian Spence *James Lawrence* • Jerry Wasserman *Mayor Leonardo* • Colby Johannson *Brian Flynn* • Tegan Moss *Lori* ■ *Dir* Tibor Takacs • *Scr* TS Cook

Naach ★★ PG
Musical romantic drama
2004 · Ind · Colour · 134min

Simply shot but technically sound, this charts the growing relationship between struggling actor Abhishek Bachchan and aspiring choreographer Antara Mali, as they both try to further their careers in the film industry. Talented cinematographer (and co-director) Kiran Reddy paints every scene with cloying emotion, but the absence of chemistry between the two leads and a dreary screenplay scupper the film. OA In Hindi. *DVD*

Abhishek Bachchan *Abhi* • Antara Mali *Rewa* ■ *Dir* Ram Gopal Varma, Kiran Reddy

Naayak ★★★ PG
Drama 1966 · Ind · BW · 112min

Satyajit Ray was often accused of being apolitical and this study of a film star's emotional state as he pours out his heart to the female journalist he hopes will revive his flagging fortunes has often been derided for its narrow focus. But, in packing a train compartment en route to Delhi with representatives of Bengal's new bourgeoisie, Ray succeeds in showing how all strata of the Establishment lose touch with their constituents once they have tasted wealth and power. Uttam Kumar ably conveys the desperation of a celebrity forced to confront his true nature as his carefully manicured façade cracks. But, as is often the case, it's Ray's humanism that makes the deepest impression. DP Bengali +subtitles. *DVD*

Uttam Kumar *Arindam Mukherjee* • Sharmila Tagore *Aditi* • Bireswar Sen *Mukunda Lahiri* • Somen Bose *Sankar* • Nirmal Ghosh *Jyoti* ■ *Dir/Scr* Satyajit Ray

Nacho Libre ★★★ 12
Sports comedy 2006 · US/Ger · Colour · 88min

The creators of *Napoleon Dynamite*, Jared and Jerusha Hess, team up with offbeat comedian Jack Black for another endearing slice of comic eccentricity. Ignacio (Black) is an orphan who has been raised by friars at a Mexican monastery, but leads a double life as the masked wrestler Nacho to raise cash for his monastery orphans and (hopefully) impress the lovely Sister Encarnación (Ana de la Reguera). Black, with his stretchy outfits, insane fighting flair and outrageous accent, makes a highly appealing, sweetly goofy underdog, and he's well complemented by deadpan Héctor Jiménez as his tag-team sidekick. AJ *DVD* *Blu-ray*

Jack Black *Ignacio/Nacho* • Ana de la Reguera *Sister Encarnación* • Héctor Jiménez *Esqueleto* • Darius A Rose *Chancho* • Moisés Arias *Juan Pablo* • Diego Eduardo Gómez *Chuy* • Carlos

Maycotte *Segundo Núñez* • Richard Montoya *Guillermo* ■ *Dir* Jared Hess • *Scr* Jared Hess, Jerusha Hess, Mike White

Nada ★★★ 18
Political crime drama
1974 · Fr/It · Colour · 107min

Claude Chabrol here adopts the style of the exciting political thrillers of Costa-Gavras, though he adds his special brand of cynicism and black humour and refuses to take sides. Nada, the Spanish for "nothing", is the name of a group of anarchists who decide to kidnap the American ambassador in Paris during his weekly visit to a high-class bordello. This overlong film came as a surprise after Chabrol's series of domestic murder stories featuring his wife, Stéphane Audran. RB French +subtitles. *DVD*

Fabio Testi *Buenaventura Diaz* • Michel Duchaussoy *Marcel Treufais* • Maurice Garrel *André Epaulard* • Michel Aumont *Goémond* • Lou Castel *D'Arey* ■ *Dir* Claude Chabrol • *Scr* Claude Chabrol, Jean-Patrick Manchette, from a novel by Manchette

Nader and Simin, a Separation ★★★★ PG
Drama 2011 · Iran · Colour · 117min

Iranian film-maker Asghar Farhadi's convoluted tale of class envy, religious division and domestic deceit starts when Nader (Peyman Moadi) refuses to emigrate, prompting his wife Simin (Leila Hatami) to seek a divorce. The lead quartet shared the acting honours at the Berlin film festival, where Farhadi's supremely controlled direction also helped the movie picked up the Golden Bear. DP Farsi +subtitles. Some swearing. *DVD* *Blu-ray*

Leila Hatami *Simin* • Peyman Moadi *Nader* • Shahab Hosseini *Hodjat* • Sareh Bayat *Razieh* • Sarina Farhadi *Termeh* ■ *Dir/Scr* Asghar Farhadi

Nadine ★★ PG
Comedy thriller 1987 · US · Colour · 79min

Director Robert Benton scores something of a misfire with this well-intentioned but uneven comedy. The story of a manicurist who witnesses a murder and teams up with her soon-to-be ex-husband to solve the crime has its moments. But the problems lie mainly with Kim Basinger and Jeff Bridges, neither of whom makes this broad comedy work. JB Violence, swearing.

Jeff Bridges *Vernon Hightower* • Kim Basinger *Nadine Hightower* • Rip Torn *Buford Pope* • Gwen Verdon *Vera* • Glenne Headly *Renee* • Jerry Stiller *Raymond Escobar* • Jay Patterson *Dwight Estes* ■ *Dir/Scr* Robert Benton

Nadja ★★★★ 15
Horror 1995 · US · BW · 88min

David Lynch (who pops up in a cameo as a mortuary attendant) executive-produced this erotic vampire thriller, stylishly shot in black and white. Elina Lowensohn is the Nadja of the title, an enthusiastic creature of the night who just happens to be the daughter of Dracula. She prowls the clubs of New York for her prey, but vampire-hunter Van Helsing (Peter Fonda) is on her trail. It's a bizarre update of the vampire legend by independent film-maker Michael Almereyda, a deft hand at powerful visual images. JB

Elina Lowensohn *Nadja* • Suzy Amis *Cassandra* • Peter Fonda *Dracula/Dr Van Helsing* • Martin Donovan (2) *Jim* • Galaxy Craze *Lucy* • Karl Geary *Renfield* • Jared Harris *Edgar* ■ *Dir/Scr* Michael Almereyda

Naked ★★★★ 18
Drama 1993 · UK · Colour · 125min

Mike Leigh prowls new working class territory with this grim tale about a Mancunian misfit who turns up at his ex-girlfriend's London flat and proceeds to tell the naked truth regarding the city's uncaring society by lashing out unmercifully at everyone he meets. David Thewlis is outstanding as a deeply nasty 1990s version of Alfie, and Leigh's bravura mix of comedy, tragedy, violence and warmth marks this uncompromising exposé as

British film-making at its finest. **AJ** Swearing, drug abuse, nudity.

David Thewlis *Johnny* • Lesley Sharp *Louise* • Katrin Cartlidge *Sophie* • Greg Cruttwell *Jeremy* • Claire Skinner *Sandra* • Peter Wight *Brian* • Ewen Bremner *Archie* • Susan Vidler *Maggie* ■ *Dir/Scr* Mike Leigh

Naked Alibi ★★

Crime drama   1954 · US · BW · 85min

After he is dismissed for harassing suburban baker Gene Barry whom he's convinced is a violent killer, senior cop Sterling Hayden continues to hunt his quarry. When he finds himself in trouble in a Mexican bordertown, he is helped by Barry's girlfriend Gloria Grahame. Directed by Jerry Hopper, this mix of detective thriller, gangster movie and *film noir* starts promisingly enough but degenerates about a third of the way through as a result of a derivative screenplay and some unconvincing characterisation. **RK**

Sterling Hayden *Joseph Conroy* • Gloria Grahame *Marianna* • Gene Barry *Al Willis* • Marcia Henderson *Helen Willis* • Casey Adams [Max Showalter] *Lieutenant Parks* • Billy Chapin *Petey* • Chuck Connors *Captain Owen Kincaide* ■ *Dir* Jerry Hopper • *Scr* Lawrence Roman, from the story *Cry Copper* by J Robert Breen, Gladys Atwater

The Naked and the Dead ★★★ PG

Second World War drama
1958 · US · Colour · 130min

Since it was clearly impossible to film the vigorous intensity, not to mention the language, of Norman Mailer's superb anti-war first novel, director Raoul Walsh opted for a virtual remake of his 1955 Warners Bros hit *Battle Cry*, although this time the characters are not realistic enough. Aldo Ray is Mailer's sadistic sergeant, handling most of the diatribes and virtually holding the long movie together by himself. The battle scenes are fine and interestingly shot through a green night filter. **TS**

Aldo Ray *Croft* • Cliff Robertson *Hearn* • Raymond Massey *General Cummings* • Lili St Cyr *Lily* • Barbara Nichols *Mildred* • William Campbell *Brown* • Richard Jaeckel *Gallagher* • James Best *Ridges* • Joey Bishop *Roth* ■ *Dir* Raoul Walsh • *Scr* Denis Sanders, Terry Sanders, from the novel by Norman Mailer • *Cinematographer* Joseph LaShelle

The Naked City ★★★★ PG

Crime drama   1948 · US · BW · 91min

Hugely influential, thanks to its innovative documentary style and character-driven treatment, of an otherwise conventional cop drama (murdered blonde in bathtub, homicide squad gets moving). The movie is hard-hitting, gripping and a hymn to the excitement of New York City, where it was shot entirely on location. Narrated by its producer, former crime reporter Mark Hellinger, it stars Barry Fitzgerald as the police lieutenant heading the murder investigation. There were Oscars for cinematography and editing, and the voiceover proclaiming "there are eight million stories in the naked city" passed into popular culture, thanks to the long-running TV series. **RK** DVD

Barry Fitzgerald *Lt Dan Muldoon* • Howard Duff *Frank Niles* • Dorothy Hart *Ruth Morrison* • Don Taylor *Jimmy Halloran* • Ted De Corsia *Garzah* • House Jameson *Dr Stoneman* • Mark Hellinger *Narrator* ■ *Dir* Jules Dassin • *Scr* Albert Maltz, Malvin Wald, from a story by Malvin Wald • *Music* Miklos Rozsa, Frank Skinner • *Cinematographer* William Daniels (1) • *Editor* Paul Weatherwax

The Naked Country ★★★ 15

Thriller   1985 · Aus · Colour · 87min

Set in the Australian outback, this is a gripping outdoors thriller from Tim Burstall, one of the key directors of the 1970s "new wave". Based on the novel by Morris West, it's about a ranch owner who gets caught up in a bitter struggle with an unruly tribe of Aborigines. Burstall conjures up a taut, well paced drama that builds up nicely to a tense chase climax. **NF** Violence.

John Stanton *Lance Dillon* • Rebecca Gilling *Mary Dillon* • Ivar Kants *Sergeant Neil Adams* • Tommy Lewis *Mundaru* • Simon Chilvers *Inspector Poole* • John Jarratt *Mick Conrad* ■ *Dir* Tim Burstall • *Scr* Ross Dimsey, Tim Burstall, from the novel by Morris West

The Naked Dawn ★★★

Crime drama   1955 · US · Colour · 82min

Arthur Kennedy plays the likeable Mexican bandit whose booty tempts the impoverished farmer he befriends, and whose way of life appeals to the farmer's dissatisfied young wife. This character study was made on a shoestring in Mexico by the low-budget maestro Edgar G Ulmer, who shapes the material into a moving study of salvation. It could have been an intense, brooding piece, but it's shot in colour and displays a generosity of spirit that is ultimately moving. **AE**

Arthur Kennedy *Santiago* • Betta St John *Maria* • Eugene Iglesias *Manuel* • Charlita *Tita* • Roy Engel *Guntz* ■ *Dir* Edgar G Ulmer • *Scr* Nina Schneider, Herman Schneider (fronts for Julian Zimet)

The Naked Edge ★★

Mystery thriller   1961 · UK · BW · 103min

This bleak and undistinguished thriller, about an American businessman based in London whose wife (Deborah Kerr) comes to suspect him of murder, marked a most unfitting end to Gary Cooper's illustrious career. The actor died shortly after giving one last wooden performance and floundering among the plot's red herrings. **RK**

Gary Cooper *George Radcliffe* • Deborah Kerr *Martha Radcliffe* • Eric Portman *Jeremy Clay* • Diane Cilento *Mrs Heath* • Hermione Gingold *Lilly Harris* • Peter Cushing *Mr Wrack* • Michael Wilding *Morris Brooke* • Ray McAnally *Donald Heath* ■ *Dir* Michael Anderson • *Scr* Joseph Stefano, from the novel *First Train to Babylon* by Max Ehrlich

The Naked Face ★★ 18

Crime thriller   1984 · US · Colour · 100min

Psychiatrist Roger Moore is the prime suspect when one of his patients is murdered in director Bryan Forbes's tepid adaptation of an early Sidney Sheldon bestseller. When it becomes clear he's the next target, he takes the law into his own hands to unmask the killer, despite the suspicions of cops Rod Steiger and Elliott Gould. Reasonably well-acted, the complex plot has too many red herrings to be completely satisfying. **AJ** Swearing, violence, nudity.

Roger Moore *Dr Judd Stevens* • Rod Steiger *Lieutenant McGreavy* • Elliott Gould *Angeli* • Art Carney *Morgens* • Anne Archer *Ann Blake* • David Hedison *Dr Hadley* • Deanna Dunagan *Mrs Hadley* ■ *Dir* Bryan Forbes • *Scr* Bryan Forbes, from the novel by Sidney Sheldon

Naked Fury ★ U

Crime drama   1959 · UK · BW · 64min

As with many other crime capers of the late 1950s, this gives the impression of being a routine TV episode that has had a bit of money thrown at it. It's a sordid little tale about a gang of safe-crackers who are forced to kill a night watchman and kidnap his daughter to make good their escape. Director Charles Saunders and his cast are left high and dry by the desperate script. **DP**

Leigh Madison *Carol* • Reed De Rouen *Eddy* • Kenneth Cope *Johnny* • Arthur Lovegrove *Syd* • Thomas Eytle *Steve* • Alexander Field *Vic* ■ *Dir* Charles Saunders • *Scr* Brock Williams, from a story by Guido Coen

The Naked Gun ★★★★★ 15

Comedy   1988 · US · Colour · 81min

The team behind *Airplane!* first turned their wicked talents on to the police force with the short-lived cult TV series *Police Squad!*, but it took this feature-length version to make Leslie Nielsen's inspired Frank Drebin a worldwide star. He is wonderfully stone-faced as he proceeds to wreak havoc in Los Angeles while investigating the shooting of a colleague. The supporting players – George Kennedy as his captain and Priscilla Presley as the equally clumsy love interest – are delightfully deadpan, and the determinedly juvenile gags never stop flowing. **JF** Swearing. DVD

Leslie Nielsen *Lieutenant Frank Drebin* • Priscilla Presley *Jane Spencer* • Ricardo Montalban *Vincent Ludwig* • George Kennedy *Captain Ed Hocken* • OJ Simpson *Nordberg* • Nancy Marchand *Mayor* ■ *Dir* David Zucker • *Scr* Jerry Zucker, Jim Abrahams, David Zucker, Pat Proft, from the TV series *Police Squad!* by David Zucker, Jerry Zucker, Jim Abrahams

The Naked Gun 2½: the Smell of Fear ★★★★ 15

Comedy   1991 · US · Colour · 81min

This second instalment from the files of *Police Squad!* is deliriously funny. Leslie Nielsen, as the steadfastly stupid Frank Drebin, starts off by wrecking a White House reception, then proceeds to blunder his way through an investigation into a group of corrupt businessmen plotting to stave off radical new changes to the energy industry. Many of the original cast return for this sequel, and while it's not quite up to the standard set by the first film, it's still a treat. **AJ** Swearing. DVD CS

Leslie Nielsen *Lieutenant Frank Drebin* • Priscilla Presley *Jane Spencer* • George Kennedy *Ed Hocken* • Robert Goulet *Quentin Hapsburg* • Richard Griffiths *Dr Meinheimer/Earl Hacker* • OJ Simpson *Nordberg* • Anthony James *Hector Savage* • Lloyd Bochner *Baggett* • Tim O'Connor *Fenzwick* ■ *Dir* David Zucker • *Scr* David Zucker, Pat Proft, from the TV series *Police Squad!* by David Zucker, Jerry Zucker, Jim Abrahams

Naked Gun 33⅓: the Final Insult ★★★★ 12

Comedy   1994 · US · Colour · 79min

The first two *Naked Guns* were comedy classics, but this is only very, very funny. Leslie Nielsen and the team return for another endearingly silly, gag-filled spoof in which house-husband Frank Drebin comes out of retirement to pursue a lethal bomber. Although it trades a little too casually on the jokes and slapstick of the first two, Nielsen delivers another wonderfully deadpan performance, and there are a host of neat cameos. **JF** Swearing. DVD

Leslie Nielsen *Lieutenant Frank Drebin* • Priscilla Presley *Jane Spencer* • George Kennedy *Ed Hocken* • OJ Simpson *Nordberg* • Fred Ward *Rocco* • Kathleen Freeman *Muriel* • Anna Nicole Smith *Tanya* • Ellen Greene *Louise* ■ *Dir* Peter Segal • *Scr* David Zucker, Pat Proft, Robert LoCash, from the TV series *Police Squad!* by David Zucker, Jerry Zucker, Jim Abrahams

Naked in New York ★★★ 15

Romantic comedy   1994 · US · Colour · 87min

This is an autobiographical first feature by Daniel Algrant, who got Martin Scorsese to executive produce – in other words, help raise the money and encourage some big names to guest star. The story is slight enough: Eric Stoltz grows up without a dad, decides to be a playwright and becomes a magnet to women. But it's the guest appearances that make the most impact – Tony Curtis, Timothy Dalton and Kathleen Turner, camping it up as a Broadway star. **AT**

Eric Stoltz *Jake Briggs* • Mary-Louise Parker *Joanne White* • Ralph Macchio *Chris* • Jill Clayburgh *Shirley Briggs* • Tony Curtis *Carl Fisher* • Timothy Dalton *Elliot Price* • Kathleen Turner *Dana Coles* • Whoopi Goldberg *Tragedy Mask* • Quentin Crisp ■ *Dir* Dan Algrant [Daniel Algrant] • *Scr* Dan Algrant [Daniel Algrant], John Warren

The Naked Jungle ★★★★ 12

Adventure drama   1953 · US · Colour · 91min

Charlton Heston is the South American plantation owner battling both his red-haired wife (Eleanor Parker) and a plague of red ants, which provides a spectacular climax to this riveting blend directed by Byron Haskin. Both an adventure and a thought-provoking drama, the movie is beautifully photographed by Ernest Laszlo and remains one of Heston's most interesting early films. **JB** DVD

Eleanor Parker *Joanna Leiningen* • Charlton Heston *Christopher Leiningen* • William Conrad *Commissioner* • Romo Vincent *Boat captain* • Douglas Fowley *Medicine man* • John Dierkes *Gruber* • Leonard Strong *Kutina* ■ *Dir* Byron Haskin • *Scr* Philip Yordan (front for Ben Maddow), Ranald MacDougall, from the story *Leiningen versus the Ants* by Carl Stephenson

The Naked Kiss ★★★★ 18

Cult drama   1964 · US · BW · 86min

This is a typically bleak and brutal tale from maverick American independent director Samuel Fuller, who this time turns his cynical eye to the corrupt values lurking beneath small-town life. Constance Towers gives a dignified performance as a former prostitute who attempts to build a new life in a new town, but finds her past coming back to haunt her when she tries to establish a relationship with the local leading citizen. The storyline is pure melodrama, but the harsh photography and startling images make this a cult classic. **JF** DVD

Constance Towers *Kelly* • Anthony Eisley *Griff* • Michael Dante *Grant* • Virginia Grey *Candy* • Patsy Kelly *Mac* • Betty Bronson *Miss Josephine* • Marie Devereux *Buff* • Karen Conrad *Dusty* ■ *Dir/Scr* Samuel Fuller • *Cinematographer* Stanley Cortez

Naked Lunch ★★★ 18

Fantasy drama   1991 · UK/Can · Colour · 110min

This is one to admire more than enjoy – only horror maestro David Cronenberg could have filmed William S Burroughs's notorious cult novel as an intellectual paranoid acid trip through the creative writing process. Cronenberg underlines Burroughs's autobiographical concerns over abuses of power (metaphorically disguised as fantasy drug addiction and surreal sexual acts), crafting a uniquely slanted mind-blower with more than a hint of highbrow inaccessibility. **AJ** Violence, swearing, sex scenes, drug abuse, nudity. DVD

Peter Weller *William Lee* • Judy Davis *Joan Frost/Joan Lee* • Ian Holm *Tom Frost* • Julian Sands *Yves Cloquet* • Roy Scheider *Dr Benway* • Monique Mercure *Fadela* • Nicholas Campbell *Hank* • Michael Zelniker *Martin* ■ *Dir* David Cronenberg • *Scr* David Cronenberg, from the novel by William S Burroughs

The Naked Maja ★★

Biographical drama
1959 · US/It · Colour · 111min

Despite the title, there's nothing particularly revelatory in this account of the life of the Spanish painter Goya (Anthony Franciosa), who grew from peasant stock to become a painter of royalty. The script revolves around Goya's scandalous nude portrait of a duchess (Ava Gardner), but director Henry Koster gives no more than a surface gloss to the proceedings. Movies about artists were all the rage at the time, but this one is a still life in more ways than one. **TH**

Ava Gardner *Duchess of Alba* • Anthony Franciosa *Francisco Goya* • Amedeo Nazzari *Manuel Godoy* • Gino Cervi *King Carlos IV* • Lea Padovani *Queen Maria Luisa* ■ *Dir* Henry Koster, Mario Russo • *Scr* Norman Corwin, Giorgio Prosperi, from a story by Oscar Saul, Talbot Jennings

The Naked Prey ★★★ 12

Adventure   1966 · US · Colour · 95min

Filmed entirely in South Africa, this offbeat adventure was directed by ex-matinée idol Cornel Wilde, who also stars as a 19th-century white hunter whose safari expedition is captured and tortured by tribesmen. Set free in a skimpy loincloth that would make even Johnny Weissmuller blush, Wilde is then relentlessly hunted down like prey. Bolstered by a documentary-style realism, if dated in its African stereotypes, this remains a riveting tale of survival. Wilde gives a fine performance, despite being ill for much of the filming. **RS** Violence DVD

Cornel Wilde *Man* • Gert Van Den Bergh *Second man* • Ken Gampu *Warrior leader* • Patrick Mynhardt *Safari overseer* ■ *Dir* Cornel Wilde • *Scr* Clint Johnston, Don Peters

U SUITABLE FOR ALL   Uc SUITABLE ESPECIALLY FOR YOUNG CHILDREN (DVD ONLY)   PG PARENTAL GUIDANCE   12A UNDER 12s TO BE ACCOMPANIED (CINEMA ONLY)

The Naked Runner ★★ PG
Spy drama 1967 · UK · Colour · 99min

This Stanley Mann-scripted slice of Cold War shenanigans is bland, thanks to unappealing characters and a far-fetched narrative. Frank Sinatra stars as a wartime crack shot reluctantly reactivated for an assassination plot in East Germany; Edward Fox and Peter Vaughan represent British intelligence. Sidney J Furie's gimmicky direction is jarring, while Sinatra can do nothing with a monotonous role that merely requires him to be shunted around like a pawn on a chessboard. RS

Frank Sinatra *Sam Laker* • Peter Vaughan *Martin Slattery* • Derren Nesbitt *Colonel Hartmann* • Nadia Gray *Karen Gisevius* • Toby Robins *Ruth* • Inger Stratton *Anna* • Cyril Luckham *Cabinet minister* • Edward Fox *Ritchie Jackson* ■ *Dir* Sidney J Furie • *Scr* Stanley Mann, from the novel by Francis Clifford

Naked Souls ★ 18
Erotic science-fiction thriller 1995 · US · Colour · 81min

Pamela Anderson's main assets unsurprisingly play a prominent role in this daft erotic science-fiction thriller. The pneumatic former *Baywatch* babe portrays an artist – don't laugh – whose geeky scientist boyfriend Brian Krause gets into trouble when he starts playing around with the memories of dead serial killers and messing with sinister rival David Warner. JF Violence, sex scenes, swearing, nudity. *DVD*

Pamela Anderson Lee [Pamela Anderson] *Britanny "Brit" Clark* • Brian Krause *Edward Adams* • David Warner *Everett Longstreet* • Dean Stockwell *Duncan Ellis* ■ *Dir* Lyndon Chubbuck • *Scr* Frank Dietz

The Naked Spur ★★★★ PG
Western 1953 · US · Colour · 91min

In the third of the great collaborations between James Stewart and director Anthony Mann, Stewart stars as a neurotic bounty hunter on the trail of Robert Ryan, hoping to make enough money to buy a ranch in California, but threatened by madness. This melodramatic western aspires to Greek or Shakespearean tragedy and, set in the truly Olympian Rocky Mountains of Colorado, the characters look suitably puny and pitiful. Janet Leigh, however, looks gorgeous. AT

James Stewart *Howard Kemp* • Robert Ryan *Ben Vandergroat* • Janet Leigh *Lina Patch* • Ralph Meeker *Roy Anderson* • Millard Mitchell *Jesse Tate* ■ *Dir* Anthony Mann • *Scr* Sam Rolfe, Harold Jack Bloom

The Naked Street ★★
Crime drama 1955 · US · BW · 84min

In this lurid melodrama, Anthony Quinn is the racketeer who, not unlike Paul Muni in *Scarface*, has an almost unhealthy fixation with his sister, played by Anne Bancroft. When she becomes pregnant by Farley Granger's two-bit hood, Quinn gets him off a murder rap and tries to make him go straight. Maxwell Shane draws effective performances from his three lead players but the contrived plot deprives this of tragic force. AE

Farley Granger *Nicky Bradna* • Anthony Quinn *Phil Regal* • Anne Bancroft *Rosalie Regalzyk* • Peter Graves (2) *Joe McFarland* • Else Neft *Mrs Regalzyk* • Jerry Paris *Latzi Franks* • Frank Sully *Nutsy* • John Dennis *Big Eddie* ■ *Dir* Maxwell Shane • *Scr* Maxwell Shane, from a story by Leo Katcher

Naked Tango ★★ 18
Period erotic thriller 1990 · US/Arg · Colour · 88min

This overheated and rather silly melodrama is set in Argentina in the days when Rudolph Valentino was "tango-ing" a swooning female audience. Mathilda May is the young wife en route to South America who takes on a new identity and ends up being fought over by gangster Esai Morales and "dirty dancer" Vincent D'Onofrio. It's beautifully designed, and the much put-upon May delivers a sensual performance. Unfortunately, D'Onofrio lacks charisma

and Leonard Schrader's script drips with pretension. JF Swearing, violence, sex scenes, nudity.

Vincent D'Onofrio *Cholo* • Mathilda May *Stephanie/Alba* • Esai Morales *Zico Borenstein* • Fernando Rey *Judge Torres* • Josh Mostel *Bertoni the jeweller* ■ *Dir* Leonard Schrader • *Scr* Leonard Schrader, from the works of Manuel Puig

The Naked Truth ★★★★ U
Black comedy 1957 · UK · BW · 88min

This early Peter Sellers comedy supplied him with some of his funniest and finest material. He plays a crowd-pleasing TV host who's being blackmailed by smarmy Dennis Price, editor of a muck-raking magazine. Terry-Thomas and Peggy Mount are among the victims who gang up against their persecutor. Based on class and sex, as the best British humour often is, it's satisfyingly scripted by Michael Pertwee and directed with superb timing by Mario Zampi. TH *DVD*

Peter Sellers *Sonny MacGregor* • Terry-Thomas *Lord Mayley* • Peggy Mount *Flora Ransom* • Dennis Price *Michael Dennis* • Shirley Eaton *Belinda Wright* • Georgina Cookson *Lady Mayley* • Joan Sims *Ethel Ransom* ■ *Dir* Mario Zampi • *Scr* Michael Pertwee

The Name of the Rose ★★★★ 18
Period mystery 1986 · It/W Ger/Fr · Colour · 126min

Sean Connery is in majestic form as the Franciscan friar who, with novice Christian Slater, investigates a series of murders in a remote 14th-century abbey, incurring the wrath of vicious inquisitor F Murray Abraham in the process. Director Jean-Jacques Annaud has decoded Umberto Eco's cryptic bestseller with an eye-blinkingly ornate visual style. While the inhabitants of the abbey are mostly as grotesque as gargoyles, the Holmesian figure of Connery dominates and elucidates with the kind of deductive brilliance that Conan Doyle's sleuth was to display centuries later. TH Violence, nudity, a sex scene. *DVD*

Sean Connery *William of Baskerville* • F Murray Abraham *Bernardo Gui* • Christian Slater *Adso of Melk* • Elya Baskin *Severinus* • Feodor Chaliapin Jr *Jorge de Burgos* • William Hickey *Ubertino de Casale* • Ron Perlman *Salvatore* ■ *Dir* Jean-Jacques Annaud • *Scr* Andrew Birkin, Gérard Brach, Howard Franklin, Alain Godard, from the novel *Il Nome Della Rosa* by Umberto Eco

The Namesake ★★★ 12
Romantic comedy drama 2006 · US/Ind/Jpn · Colour · 117min

This ambitious adaptation of Jhumpa Lahiri's novel spans two generations and two continents, and continues *Monsoon Wedding* director Mira Nair's fascination with culture clash. Irrfan Khan plays a young Bengali man who returns from Calcutta to his adopted New York with his new wife (Tabu) during the 1970s. The namesake of the title is their son, Gogol, who is named after the Russian author by his father. Stark juxtapositions between colourful India-set scenes and the grey realities of living as an immigrant in the First World let Nair create an epic tale of dual identities and family history, as the adult Gogol (Kal Penn) struggles to find his place in the world. JR English, Bengali, Hindi +subtitles.

Kal Penn *Gogol Ganguli* • Tabu *Ashima Ganguli* • Irrfan Khan [Irfan Khan] *Ashoke Ganguli* • Jacinda Barrett *Maxine* • Zuleika Robinson [Zuleikha Robinson] *Moushumi Mazumdar* • Brooke Smith *Sally* • Nair Sahira *Sonia* ■ *Dir* Mira Nair • *Scr* Sooni Taraporevala, from the novel by Jhumpa Lahiri • *Cinematographer* Frederick Elmes

Namu, the Killer Whale ★★★ U
Adventure based on a true story 1966 · US · Colour · 85min

Laslo Benedek directs this factually-based drama, superbly photographed on location in Puget Sound off the Washington State

coast. The film follows the struggle of marine biologist Robert Lansing to prevent local fishermen from killing the trapped whale which is threatening their livelihood. The story can't fail to stir the emotions, but Benedek deserves credit for presenting the case for both sides with admirable fairness. DP *DVD*

Robert Lansing *Hank Donner* • John Anderson *Joe Clausen* • Robin Mattson *Lisa Rand* • Richard Erdman *Deke* • Lee Meriwether *Kate Rand* ■ *Dir* Laslo Benedek • *Scr* Arthur Weiss • *Cinematographer* Lamar Boren

Nana ★★★
Silent period drama 1926 · Fr · BW · 161min

Jean Renoir distils Zola's novel via just three characters, Nana, Vandeuvres and Muffat, while sumptuously re-creating the end of the Second Empire. The story follows Nana's brief success as an "actress", her period as a courtesan and grim death. Catherine Hessling, the director's wife, gives a somewhat laboured performance but there are many pleasures in this apprentice work. Although well received critically, *Nana* was badly distributed and cost Renoir a million francs of an inheritance from his father, whose visual influence is apparent in the film. BB

Catherine Hessling *Nana* • Werner Krauss *Comte Muffat* • Jean Angelo *Comte de Vandeuvres* • Raymond Guérin-Catelain *Georges Hugon* • Pierre Philippe [Pierre Lestringuez] *Bordenave* • Pierre Champagne *La Faloise* ■ *Dir* Jean Renoir • *Scr* Pierre Lestringuez, Jean Renoir, from the novel by Emile Zola

Nana ★★★ PG
Period romantic melodrama 1934 · US · BW · 83min

Dorothy Arzner was one of the few women directors working in Hollywood during its Golden Age. Her films have recently been given a feminist slant, but it is hard to see this loose adaptation of Emile Zola's novel as anything other than pure melodrama. In place of Zola's gritty naturalism is producer Samuel Goldwyn's glossy sensationalism, as waif Anna Sten plunges into the seedy world of the French music hall and finds herself torn between amorous brothers Lionel Atwill and Phillips Holmes. DP

Anna Sten *Nana* • Phillips Holmes *Lieutenant George Muffat* • Lionel Atwill *Colonel André Muffat* • Richard Bennett (1) *Gaston Greiner* • Mae Clarke *Satin* • Muriel Kirkland *Mimi* ■ *Dir* Dorothy Arzner • *Scr* Willard Mack, Harry Wagstaff Gribble, from the novel by Emile Zola

Nancy Drew ★★ PG
Mystery adventure 2007 · US · Colour · 95min

Pitched between *Clueless* and Miss Marple, *The Craft* director Andrew Fleming's lame attempt to modernise Carolyn Keene's literary teen sleuth couldn't be more wooden or lacklustre. Squeaky clean Nancy Drew (Emma Roberts) leaves her home town of River Heights and heads for Hollywood, where she sets about solving the long dormant mystery of a movie star's murder. It's all here: a creepy old mansion with secret passageways; cardboard cut-out villains; an enigmatic handyman; Chinese boxes with false bottoms; shoals of red herrings; and floorboards that creak as much as the slight plot. Roberts (Julia's niece) plays wholesome well, but on every other level this fails to engage. AJ Brief swearing, violence. *DVD*

Emma Roberts *Nancy Drew* • Josh Flitter *Corky* • Max Thieriot *Ned Nickerson* • Rachael Leigh Cook *Jane Brighton* • Tate Donovan *Carson Drew* • Barry Bostwick *Dashiel Biedermeyer* • Laura Elena Harring [Laura Harring] *Dehlia Draycott* • Bruce Willis *Bruce* ■ *Dir* Andrew Fleming • *Scr* Andrew Fleming, Tiffany Paulsen, from a story by Paulsen, from characters by Carolyn Keene [Mildred Wirt Benson] • *Cinematographer* Alexander Gruszynski

Nancy Drew – Detective ★★★ U
Mystery adventure 1938 · US · BW · 66min

Warners launched its four-film series based on Carolyn Keene's popular teenage mysteries, with the gymslip sleuth being

played by Bonita Granville. Partnered by devoted sidekick Frankie Thomas, the gutsy Granville cracks cases with an energy and ingenuity that typical of the studio's no-nonsense ethos. Here she tries to stop a house owned by two elderly ladies from falling into the hands of some ruthless gangsters. The films are bracingly enjoyable, but journeyman director William Clemens's attitude to the crude realities of crime was surprisingly uncompromising. DP

Bonita Granville *Nancy Drew* • John Litel *Carson Drew* • James Stephenson *Challon* • Frankie Thomas *Ted Nickerson* • Frank Orth *Inspector Milligan* • Charles Trowbridge *Hollister* ■ *Dir* William Clemens • *Scr* Kenneth Gamet, from the novel *The Password to Larkspur Lane* by Carolyn Keene

Nancy Goes to Rio ★★★ U
Musical 1950 · US · Colour · 99min

MGM's resident soubrette, pert and pretty Jane Powell, was the true successor to Deanna Durbin, as underlined by this remake of Durbin's *It's a Date* (1940). This time around, instead of a trip to Hawaii and black and white, Powell and her actress mother (Ann Sothern) are on a luxury liner on their way to Rio in glorious Technicolor. There are some good numbers, especially *Shine on Harvest Moon*, sung by Powell, Sothern and (unexpectedly) Louis Calhern. RB

Jane Powell *Nancy Barklay* • Ann Sothern *Frances Elliott* • Barry Sullivan *Paul Berten* • Carmen Miranda *Marina Rodriguez* • Louis Calhern *Gregory Elliott* ■ *Dir* Robert Z Leonard • *Scr* Sidney Sheldon, from a story by Jane Hall, Frederick Kohner, Ralph Block

Nancy Steele Is Missing ★★★
Drama 1937 · US · BW · 84min

Lindbergh baby kidnapper Bruno Hauptmann had been sent to the electric chair the year before this film opened, so the timing could not have been entirely coincidental. Nunnally Johnson's rambling production confronts the Hays Office head on by using lovable Victor McLaglen as a sympathetic abductor who eventually ends up as a gardener after reuniting his victim with her real father. George Marshall's direction is on the slow side, but McLaglen keeps it watchable. TS

Victor McLaglen *Dannie O'Neill* • Walter Connolly *Michael Steele* • Peter Lorre *Professor Sturm* • June Lang *Sheila O'Neill/Nancy Steele* • Robert Kent *Jimmie Wilson* • Shirley Deane *Nancy* • John Carradine *Harry Wilkins* ■ *Dir* George Marshall • *Scr* Hal Long, Gene Fowler, from the story *Ransom* by Charles Francis Coe

The Nanny ★★★ 15
Thriller 1965 · UK · BW · 89min

The first of two movies Bette Davis made for Britain's Hammer films is a genuinely chilling horror tale, with a clever plot written by Hammer regular Jimmy Sangster. However, movie purists may well object to the fact that the flashbacks reveal incidents that never actually happened, manipulating the expectations of the audience. Despite valiant work from Davis and director Seth Holt, the narrative weaknesses and the general unpleasantness of the piece spoil what could have been an interesting addition to the genre. TS *DVD*

Bette Davis *Nanny* • Wendy Craig *Virgie Fane* • Jill Bennett *Pen* • James Villiers *Bill Fane* • William Dix *Joey* • Pamela Franklin *Bobby* • Jack Watling *Dr Medman* • Alfred Burke *Dr Wills* • Maurice Denham *Dr Beamaster* ■ *Dir* Seth Holt • *Scr* Jimmy Sangster from a novel by Evelyn Piper

The Nanny Diaries ★★★ 12
Comedy drama 2007 · US · Colour · 100min

Scarlett Johansson stars in this entertaining but unexceptional adaptation of the satirical bestseller about nannying on New York's snooty Upper East Side. She plays a New Jersey anthropology student who gets mistaken for a nanny, and winds up child-rearing for over-moneyed but under-mannered Big Apple couple Laura

Linney and Paul Giamatti. It's slavery without the whips and shackles, but with all the attendant humiliation and lack of freedom. The humour of *The Nanny Diaries* is blunt and broad, and a voiceover subjecting events to cod-anthropological analysis is an irritant, not an asset. But Johansson confirms her growing comic promise and the film is a mild diversion for the more easily amused. DA *DVD*

Scarlett Johansson *Annie Braddock* • Laura Linney *Mrs X* • Paul Giamatti *Mr X* • Nicholas Reese Art *Grayer* • Alicia Keys *Lynette* • Chris Evans *Harvard Hottie* • Donna Murphy *Judy Braddock* • Nathan Corddry *Calvin* • *Dir* Shari Springer Berman, Robert Pulcini • *Scr* Shari Springer Berman, Robert Pulcini, from the novel by Emma McLaughlin, Nicola Kraus

The Nanny Express ★★
Comedy drama 2008 · US · Colour · 120min

If only real-life problems were as easily resolved as they are in this simplistic family drama. God-fearing trainee teacher Vanessa Marcil offers her childcare services to a dishy widower whose offspring have driven away every nanny he's hired. Though the ultimate outcome is obvious from the second she gets the job, what's unexpected is the rapid speed at which Marcil's excessively saintly behaviour works its magic. SF

Natalie Dreyfuss *Emily Chandler* • Uriah Shelton *Ben Chandler* • Vanessa Marcil *Kate Hewitt* • Brennan Elliott *David Chandler* • Dean Stockwell *Jerry Hewitt* • Peter Dobson *Ray* • *Dir* Bradford May • *Scr* Judith Heiman Kriegsman, Stephen Langford, Riley Weston

Nanny McPhee ★★★ U
Period fantasy adventure
2005 · UK/US/Fr · Colour · 94min

This lively fantasy, adapted by and starring Emma Thompson, is the story of seven Victorian youngsters whose behaviour is so beastly that they've driven away 17 nannies. Their conduct worsens when they learn that their widowed father (Colin Firth) is planning to remarry; however, salvation is at hand in the form of stern and comically ugly Nanny McPhee (Thompson). Armed with a magic stick, mysterious McPhee turns her charges' antics against them in a series of darkly amusing sequences. Younger viewers will love its imaginative mayhem and mischievous dialogue, but the conclusion may seem mawkish and predictable. SF *DVD* *BLU*

Emma Thompson *Nanny McPhee* • Colin Firth *Mr Cedric Brown* • Kelly Macdonald *Evangeline* • Celia Imrie *Mrs Quickly* • Derek Jacobi *Mr Wheen* • Patrick Barlow *Mr Jowls* • Imelda Staunton *Mrs Blatherwick* • Thomas Sangster [Thomas Brodie-Sangster] *Simon Brown* • Angela Lansbury *Aunt Adelaide* • *Dir* Kirk Jones • *Scr* Emma Thompson, from the *Nurse Matilda* books by Christianna Brand

Nanny McPhee & the Big Bang ★★★★ U
Period fantasy adventure
2010 · UK/Fr · Colour · 104min

It's the Second World War and three usually very nice children are running rings around their mother (Maggie Gyllenhaal, complete with refined English accent) and fighting with their spoilt evacuee cousins. Meanwhile, mother is desperate to save her farm from the clutches of her avaricious brother-in-law (Rhys Ifans), while trying to keep absent-minded local shopkeeper Maggie Smith from turning her shop floor into a treacle pudding. Enter Nanny McPhee (Emma Thompson) to find order in the chaos. Adapted by Thompson from Christianna Brand's *Nurse Matilda* books, this magical first sequel is bursting with humour and warmth. Schmaltzy and twee, this is definitely not for the cynical, but small children will love it - especially the synchronised swimming piglets. SuR *DVD* *BLU*

Emma Thompson *Nanny McPhee* • Maggie Gyllenhaal *Mrs Green* • Maggie Smith *Mrs Docherty* • Rhys Ifans *Uncle Phil* • Asa Butterfield *Norman Green* • Lil Woods *Megsie Green* • Oscar Steer *Vincent Green* • Eros Vlahos *Cyril Gray* • Rosie Taylor-Ritson *Celia Gray* • Bill Bailey (2)

Farmer *Macreadie* • Ralph Fiennes *Lord Gray* ■ *Dir* Susanna White • *Scr* Emma Thompson, from the *Nurse Matilda* books by Christianna Brand

A Nanny's Secret ★★
Mystery thriller 2008 · Can · Colour · 90min

Snooze-worthy plotting and a bland character do Hilary Duff's big sister Haylie a major disservice in this insubstantial TV-movie crime tale. Still, she throws herself into it, emoting earnestly as a devoted nanny whose loyalty is tested after her wayward brother is suspected of murdering her boss's dad. Naturally, she insists he's innocent. Ultimately, if it weren't for the overdramatic score you'd forget this is a thriller, until the cat-and-mouse climax finally brings a dash of excitement. SF

Haylie Duff *Claudia* • Jessica Steen *Julia* • Eric Johnson (3) *Drew* • Dillon Casey *Carter* • Jon McLaren *Jace* ■ *Dir* Douglas Jackson • *Scr* Christine Conradt

LANDMARK FILM
Robert Flaherty records the everyday life of the Inuit and becomes known as the "Father of the documentary"

Nanook of the North ★★★ U
Classic silent documentary
1922 · US · BW · 49min

Sponsored by furriers Revillon Frères, shot in the frozen wastes of Hudson Bay and re-edited in 1948 with commentary and music added, this remains a historic, groundbreaking work by the great pioneering documentarist Robert Flaherty. According his subject matter the dignity it deserves, Flaherty recorded, with insight and touches of humour, the life of Inuit Nanook, his wife Nyla and their family and their harsh daily struggle for survival. A truthful, unembellished account of Inuit life - building an igloo, capturing a seal, fishing in ice for food - the film looks undeniably primitive by today's standards, but present-day documentarists owe it a debt. RK

■ *Dir* Robert Flaherty • *Scr* Robert Flaherty, Carl Stearns Clancy (titles), Robert Flaherty (titles) • *Cinematographer* Robert Flaherty

LANDMARK FILM
Using a forerunner of the split-screen process, audacious camerawork is viewed on three screens simultaneously

Napoléon ★★★★★ U
Silent historical drama 1927 · Fr · BW · 223min

Intended as the first instalment of a six-part biography, Abel Gance's factitious account of Bonaparte's life from military school to the Italian campaign originally ran for over five hours. Achieving his audacious movements by variously attaching the camera to a galloping horse's back, a pendulum and a flying football, Gance pushed the technology of silent cinema to its limits, even shooting several scenes in a triptych process called Polyvision. His energetic metaphorical editing was also endlessly innovative, at one point filling the screen with 16 superimposed images. Albert Dieudonné gives a spirited performance in the title role, but the accolades belong to the director. DP *DVD*

Albert Dieudonné *Napoléon Bonaparte* • Gina Manès *Josephine de Beauharnais* • Vladimir Roudenko *Young Napoleon* • Alexandre Koubitzky *Georges Jacques Danton* • Antonin Artaud *Jean-Paul Marat* • Abel Gance *Louis Saint-Just* • *Dir/Scr* Abel Gance

Napoléon ★★★★
Biographical drama 1955 · Fr · Colour · 190min

One of the most entertaining of Sacha Guitry's witty all-star extravaganzas, this features the 70-year-old actor/writer/director as Talleyrand, recounting a series of anecdotes about the life and loves of Napoléon Bonaparte (played first by Daniel Gélin and then Raymond Pellegrin). The film, which cost $1.8 million, then a record for a French film, was shot at the Parc des Expositions because no studio was large enough to accommodate the sets. Yet the three-hour film has an intimate feel as Guitry holds court, introducing a mouth-watering cast that includes Michèle Morgan as Joséphine, Erich von Stroheim as

---

Beethoven and Orson Welles as Napoléon's jailer. RB French +subtitles.

Jean-Pierre Aumont *Renault de Saint-Jean d'Angely* • Pierre Brasseur *Barras* • Danielle Darrieux *Eleonore Denuelle* • Jean Gabin *Marshal Lannes* • Daniel Gélin *Bonaparte* • Sacha Guitry *Talleyrand* • Jean Marais *Count de Montholon* • Yves Montand *Marshal Lefebvre* • Michèle Morgan *Joséphine de Beauharnais* • Raymond Pellegrin *Napoléon* • Serge Reggiani *Lucien Bonaparte* • Maria Schell *Marie-Louis d'Autriche* • Erich von Stroheim *Beethoven* • Orson Welles *Hudson Lowe* ■ *Dir/Scr* Sacha Guitry

Napoleon ★★★ U
Adventure 1995 · Aus/Jpn/US · Colour · 77min

This Australian adventure will delight those who prefer their animal magic with a touch of authenticity. The encounters of a golden-retriever puppy who runs away to join the outback's wild dogs are often gleefully eccentric - whether they're with a psycho cat, a Dame Edna Everage-voiced kangaroo or with Joan Rivers's mother kangaroo. Cannily directed, it's cute, but never tacky. DP

Adam Wylie *Muffin/Napoleon* • Bronson Pinchot *Birdo Lucci* • Dame Edna Everage [Barry Humphries] *Kangaroo* • Carol Kane *Spider* • Joan Rivers *Mother Penguin* • David Ogden Stiers *Koala/Owl* • Blythe Danner *Mother Dingo* ■ *Dir* Mario Andreacchio • *Scr* Mario Andreacchio, Michael Bourchier, Mark Saltzman

Napoleon and Samantha ★★★ U
Adventure 1972 · US · Colour · 91min

Just think how much it would cost to team Michael Douglas and Jodie Foster today. Back in 1972, Disney had to shell out next to nothing to land the relatively unknown Douglas and the debuting Foster for this amiable adventure about a couple of runaway kids and their pet lion. No one will be able to resist Major, the retired circus lion who was also a veteran of several movies and TV episodes opposite Ron Ely's Tarzan. DP

Michael Douglas (1) *Danny* • Will Geer *Grandpa* • Arch Johnson *Chief of Police* • Johnny Whitaker *Napoleon Wilson* • Jodie Foster *Samantha* • Henry Jones *Mr Gutteridge* ■ *Dir* Bernard McEveety • *Scr* Stewart Raffill

Napoleon Dynamite ★★★ PG
Comedy 2004 · US · Colour · 89min

Like the central character's bizarre name, there's something self-consciously quirky about this whimsical tale of a super-nerd's small-town life. Tthe eponymous Napoleon (Jon Heder), a blank-faced teen with carrot-coloured hair and seriously underdeveloped interpersonal skills, tries to help his equally nerdish best friend (Efren Ramirez) win the school elections. Heder's performance is entertainingly eccentric, while the supporting characters are amusing though a tad one-dimensional. Nevertheless, there are some genuine laugh-out-loud moments and an uplifting ending. AS *DVD*

Jon Heder *Napoleon Dynamite* • Jon Gries [Jonathan Gries] *Uncle Rico* • Aaron Ruell *Kip* • Efren Ramirez *Pedro* • Tina Majorino *Deb* • Diedrich Bader *Rex* • Haylie Duff *Summer Wheatly* ■ *Dir* Jared Hess • *Scr* Jared Hess, Jerusha Hess

Narc ★★★ 18
Police thriller 2001 · US · Colour · 100min

Joe Carnahan deftly manipulates all the clichés of the hard-boiled cop thriller in this intriguing example of the genre. Jason Patric is suspended after a drugs surveillance operation ends with him accidentally shooting a pregnant woman. Almost two years later, he returns to the force to investigate the homicide of a colleague. The dead man's partner, played with hair-raising energy by Ray Liotta, seems to be quite willing to break all the rules to get the killer, but Patric begins to suspect his motives. While the overfamiliar plot often fails to convince, strong performances by the well-matched leads hold the attention. AS Violence, swearing, drug abuse. *DVD*

Ray Liotta *Lt Henry Oak* • Jason Patric *Nick Tellis* • Chi McBride *Capt Cheevers* • Busta Rhymes *Darnell "Big D" Beery* • Anne Openshaw *Katherine Calvess* • John Oritz *Octavio Ruiz* ■ *Dir/Scr* Joe Carnahan

Narcopolis ★ 15
Science-fiction thriller
2014 · UK · Colour · 91min

In 2024, recreational drugs are legally controlled by the mysterious Ambro company. But dangerous narcotics are still available and that's what brusque cop Elliot Cowan (unable to make his caricature gumshoe character remotely believable) is cracking down on before being assigned a tangential case involving a mutilated corpse. Drenched in futuristic trappings this may be, but the unnecessary time travelling is too simplistic and confusing, and the tension slack and careless. AJ Swearing, drug abuse

Elliot Cowan *Frank Grieves* • Elodie Yung *Eva Gray* • Jonathan Pryce *Yuri Sidorov* • Robert Bathurst *Kim Nolan* • Nicky Henson *Chief Ballard* ■ *Dir/Scr* Justin Trefgarne

The Narrow Margin ★★★★ PG
Crime thriller 1952 · US · BW · 71min

This rattlingly good train thriller epitomises the very best of the style now known and recognised as *film noir*, directed with a wonderful sense of the claustrophobic by Richard Fleischer and terrifically performed by tough guy Charles McGraw. He's the cop taking floozy Marie Windsor to testify to the grand jury, with evidence that will send a mobster gang to the chair. Naturally enough, they don't want her to squeal. The suspense is acute, nobody is quite who they seem to be, and the action is riveting. A classic B-movie. TS

Charles McGraw *Walter Brown* • Marie Windsor *Mrs Neil* • Jacqueline White *Ann Sinclair* • Gordon Gebert *Tommy Sinclair* • Queenie Leonard *Mrs Troll* • David Clarke *Kemp* • Peter Virgo *Densel* ■ *Dir* Richard Fleischer • *Scr* Earl Fenton, from a story by Martin Goldsmith, Jack Leonard

Narrow Margin ★★★ 15
Thriller 1990 · US · Colour · 92min

Gene Hackman stars as the assistant district attorney who faces a nightmarish train journey when he escorts a key witness (Anne Archer) to a Mob trial in this efficient remake of Richard Fleischer's cracking 1950s B-movie. Director Peter Hyams doesn't bring anything particularly new or innovative to his update, but the cat-and-mouse games between Hackman and chief assassin James B Sikking are a delight, and the action sequences on the roof of the speeding train are exhilaratingly shot. JF Violence, swearing. *DVD*

Gene Hackman *Robert Caulfield* • Anne Archer *Carol Hunnicut* • James B Sikking *Nelson* • JT Walsh *Michael Tarlow* • M Emmet Walsh *Sergeant Dominick Benti* • Susan Hogan *Kathryn Weller* ■ *Dir* Peter Hyams • *Scr* Peter Hyams, from the 1952 film

LANDMARK FILM
Ensemble films and TV series are indebted to Robert Altman's ambitious drama, with its overlapping dialogue, multiple storylines and innovative technique

Nashville ★★★★★ 15
Comedy drama 1975 · US · Colour · 160min

Produced in time for the American bicentennial, this is Robert Altman's magnum opus, breathtaking in its scope and ambition. Set in Nashville, it is less a story than a mosaic with two dozen characters who connect, disconnect and reflect aspects of America, notably its music and politics. Ronee Blakley is one of the principal characters, supported by, among others, Geraldine Chaplin, Shelley Duvall and Ned Beatty, with cameos from Elliott Gould and Julie Christie. Its blend of country and western music, comedy and tragedy is never less than dazzling, and represents a major technical achievement for its visual and sound editors. AT Violence, swearing, nudity. *DVD* *BLU*

David Arkin *Norman* • Barbara Baxley *Lady Pearl* • Ned Beatty *Delbert Reese* • Karen Black *Connie White* • Ronee Blakley *Barbara Jean* • Timothy Brown *Tommy Brown* • Keith Carradine *Tom Frank* • Geraldine Chaplin *Opal* • Robert DoQui *Wade* • Shelley Duvall *LA Joan* • Allen Garfield *Barnett* • Henry Gibson *Haven Hamilton* • Lily Tomlin *Linnea Reese* • Jeff Goldblum *Tricycle man* ◾ *Dir* Robert Altman • *Scr* Joan Tewkesbury

Nasty Baby ★★★★ 🔟

Drama 2016 · Chil/US · Colour · 96min

Even by Chilean director Sebastián Silva's usual standards, this tale of a gay couple (Silva himself, Tunde Adebimpe) and their female friend (Kristen Wiig) trying to have a baby – takes a startlingly unpredictable turn in the third act. It's a brilliant twist that transforms the wry, naturalistic drama into something far more abrasive and challenging. Silva captures the boho hipster milieu of the Brooklyn setting, but adds a sense of unease in the guise of a man with mental health issues, a challenging presence in the neighbourhood. WI In English, Spanish. Swearing, violence, sex

Sebastián Silva *Freddy* • Kristen Wiig *Polly* • Tunde Adebimpe *Mo* • Reg E Cathey *The Bishop* • Anthony Chisholm *Mo's father* ◾ *Dir/Scr* Sebastián Silva

The Nasty Girl ★★★★ 🔟

Political satire based on a true story
1990 · W Ger · Colour and BW · 90min

Barely seen in this country on its original release, this bitingly brilliant film is a searing study of the way in which modern Germany has assuaged its conscience following the Nazi era. Writer/director Michael Verhoeven based his script on the experiences of Anja Rosmus, whose rummaging into the history of her own town led to her becoming a social outcast. The dazzling use of back projection and the unexpected transitions between scenes give the film a vibrancy that both invigorates and disturbs. DP German +subtitles. Swearing, some violence. *DVD*

Lena Stolze *Sonja* • Monika Baumgartner *Maria* • Michael Garr *Paul Rosenberger* • Fred Stillkrauth *Uncle* • Elisabeth Eertram *Grandmother* ◾ *Dir/Scr* Michael Verhoeven • *Cinematographer* Axel de Roche

Nasty Habits ★★ 🅟🅖

Comedy 1976 · US/UK · Colour · 87min

This is an appropriate title for a mildly sacrilegious comedy, about nuns attempting to rig the election of the new abbess at their Philadelphia convent. As the nuns smoke, drink, swear and cheat their way to the ballot, it gradually becomes apparent that the events are mimicking those of the Watergate scandal. Today, though, few people will appreciate the political references. In a noteworthy cast, Glenda Jackson seems to have little interest in the proceedings, but Sandy Dennis is very funny DM

Glenda Jackson *Sister Alexandra* • Melina Mercouri *Sister Gertrude* • Geraldine Page *Sister Walburga* • Sandy Dennis *Sister Winifred* • Anne Jackson *Sister Mildred* • Anne Meara *Sister Geraldine* • Susan Penhaligon *Sister Felicity* ◾ *Dir* Michael Lindsay-Hogg • *Scr* Robert Enders, from the novel *The Abbess of Crewe* by Muriel Spark

Nasty Neighbours ★★ 🔟

Black comedy 2000 · UK · Colour · 85min

Ricky Tomlinson plays a pompous Middle Englander whose quiet life in semi-detached suburbia conceals the turmoil of job problems and mounting debts. When moneyed wide boy Phil Daniels and his wife Rachel Fielding move next door, it's hate at first sight, with mutual loathing escalating into a war of words, and worse. Director Debbie Isitt's black comedy was adapted from her own stage play and features some good performances, but it's a one-note film. DA Violence, swearing, drug abuse.

Ricky Tomlinson *Harold Peach* • Phil Daniels *Robert Chapman* • Rachel Fielding *Ellen Chapman* • Hywel Bennett *The boss* • Debbie Isitt *Pauline Peach* ◾ *Dir* Debbie Isitt • *Scr* Debbie Isitt, from her play

Nathalie... ★★★ 🔟

Drama 2003 · Fr/Sp · Colour · 101min

In this intense psychological drama, middle-aged gynaecologist Fanny Ardant pays sex-club hostess Emmanuelle Béart to lure her errant husband (Gérard Depardieu) into an affair. Ardant is motivated by revenge for a casual fling and meets Béart after each of the encounters with her husband for an explicit recounting of events. The conceit depends on a surprise ending that might have worked in a novel, but which is glaringly apparent on screen. DP French +subtitles. Swearing. *DVD*

Fanny Ardant *Catherine* • Emmanuelle Béart *Nathalie/Marlène* • Gérard Depardieu *Bernard* • Wladimir Yordanoff *François* • Judith Magre *Catherine's mother* • Rodolphe Pauly *Thierry* ◾ *Dir* Anne Fontaine • *Scr* Jacques Fieschi, Anne Fontaine, François-Olivier Rousseau, from an idea by Philippe Blasband

The National Health ★★★ 🅟🅖

Comedy 1973 · UK · Colour · 92min

This adaptation of Peter Nichols's play shows the United Kingdom in intensive care. The setting is a run-down, ramshackle hospital, where the grisly reality of life on a men's ward contrasts with the slippery fiction of a TV soap opera entitled *Nurse Norton's Affair*. Director Jack Gold assembles some sprightly set pieces and fine actors (Donald Sinden, Lynn Redgrave, Jim Dale) who give real clout to the sometimes contrived satire. TH

Lynn Redgrave *Nurse Sweet/Betty* • Donald Sinden *Mr Carr/Dr Boyd* • Jim Dale *Barnet/Neil* • Eleanor Bron *Nurse McFee/Sister Mary* • Colin Blakely *Loach* • Clive Swift *Ash* • Bob Hoskins *Foster* ◾ *Dir* Jack Gold • *Scr* Peter Nichols, from his play

LANDMARK FILM
This first and best crude campus comedy inspires a legion of unfunny cash-ins

National Lampoon's Animal House ★★★★ 🔟

Comedy 1978 · US · Colour · 104min

It spawned a number of puerile spin-offs, but this cheerfully vulgar offering deserves the status of comedy classic. As well as providing John Belushi with his best ever role, it also helped launch the career of a number of rising young actors (Kevin Bacon, Tom Hulce, Peter Riegert), not to mention director John Landis and co-writer Harold Ramis. There's not much of a plot to speak of: at a US college in the early 1960s, dean John Vernon decides to remove the depraved Delta House fraternity from the campus; Belushi and his fellow students decide to fight back. The film is crammed with smart sight gags and one-liners. JF Swearing, nudity. *DVD* 🅱🅡

John Belushi *John "Bluto" Blutarsky* • Tim Matheson *Eric "Otter" Stratton* • John Vernon *Dean Vernon Wormer* • Verna Bloom *Marion Wormer* • Thomas Hulce [Tom Hulce] *Larry "Pinto" Kroger* • Peter Riegert *Donald "Boon" Schoenstein* • Stephen Furst *Kent "Flounder" Dorfman* • Kevin Bacon *Chip Diller* ◾ *Dir* John Landis • *Scr* Harold Ramis, Douglas Kenney, Chris Miller • *Music* Elmer Bernstein

National Lampoon's Christmas Vacation ★★ 🅟🅖

Comedy 1989 · US · Colour · 92min

Following on from the funnier *National Lampoon's Vacation* and *European Vacation*, the plot here again revolves around the Griswold family, led by Chevy Chase and Beverly D'Angelo. This time the family stays at home, and, of course, is beset by a series of disasters during the Christmas holiday. Silly in the extreme, it is only saved by Randy Quaid's performance as an obnoxious relative. A TV-movie sequel followed in 2003. JB Swearing. *DVD* 🅱🅡

Chevy Chase *Clark W Griswold Jr* • Beverly D'Angelo *Ellen Griswold* • Randy Quaid *Cousin Eddie* • Miriam Flynn *Catherine, Eddie's wife* •

Johnny Galecki *Rusty Griswold* • Juliette Lewis *Audrey Griswold* • John Randolph *Clark W Griswold Sr* • Diane Ladd *Nora Griswold* • EG Marshall *Art, Ellen's father* • Doris Roberts *Frances, Ellen's mother* ◾ *Dir* Jeremiah S Chechik [Jeremiah Chechik] • *Scr* John Hughes

National Lampoon's Class Reunion ★ 🔞

Comedy horror 1982 · US · Colour · 85min

An appalling comedy horror, this has a bunch of obnoxious ex-students locked in at their class reunion and stalked by a psychopathic killer. The script is so inept, repulsive and agonisingly humour-free that it's hard to believe it was written by the usually dependable John Hughes. The cast wanders from room to room, while we cross our fingers hoping that the maniac will butcher them all. JC *DVD*

Gerrit Graham *Bob Spinnaker* • Michael Lerner *Dr Robert Young* • Fred McCarren *Gary Nash* • Miriam Flynn *Bunny Packard* • Stephen Furst *Hubert Downs* • Marya Small *Iris Augen* ◾ *Dir* Michael Miller (2) • *Scr* John Hughes

National Lampoon's European Vacation ★★★ 🔟

Comedy 1985 · US · Colour · 90min

Amy Heckerling's politically incorrect comedy should be dismissed without hesitation. But there is something endearing about the Griswold family, and Chevy Chase and Beverly D'Angelo's infectious enthusiasm manages to sweep you along on this cliché-ridden package tour. Every conceivable national stereotype is pressed into service, as polite British cyclists, rude French waiters, aggressive Germans in lederhosen and Mafia hitmen are trotted out with soothing predictability. DP Swearing, nudity.

Chevy Chase *Clark W Griswold* • Beverly D'Angelo *Ellen Griswold* • Dana Hill *Audrey Griswold* • Jason Lively *Rusty Griswold* • John Astin *Quiz host* • Eric Idle *Bike rider* • Mel Smith *Hotel manager* • Robbie Coltrane *Man in bathroom* • Maureen Lipman *Lady In bed* ◾ *Dir* Amy Heckerling • *Scr* John Hughes, Robert Klane, from a story by John Hughes

National Lampoon's Loaded Weapon 1 ★★★ 🅟🅖

Comedy 1993 · US · Colour · 79min

This bid by the *National Lampoon* team to cash in with some *Naked Gun*-style spoofery lacks the brainless invention of those films but still manages to score quite a few laughs. The *Lethal Weapon* series is its main target, with Emilio Estevez taking over the Mel Gibson role and Samuel L Jackson standing in for Danny Glover. Often the targets and gags are far too obvious, but much of the fun is in watching out for the cameos. JF Violence, swearing. *DVD*

Emilio Estevez *Jack Colt* • Samuel L Jackson *Wes Luger* • Tim Curry *Jigsaw* • Jon Lovitz *Becker* • Kathy Ireland *Destiny Demeanor* • William Shatner *General Mortars* • Frank McRae *Captain Doyle* • F Murray Abraham *Harold Leacher* ◾ *Dir* Gene Quintano • *Scr* Don Holley, Gene Quintano, from a story by Don Holley, Tori Tellem

National Lampoon's Movie Madness ★ 🔟

Comedy 1981 · US · Colour · 85min

This is one of the worst films in the series: a bloated, desperately unfunny trilogy of mini-spoofs which unforgivably wastes the talents of an exceptional cast. Personal growth films, cop movies and soaps are the predictable targets; a fourth segment on disaster movies never saw the light of day. JF Swearing.

Christopher Lloyd *Samuel Starkman* • Robby Benson *Brent Falcone* • Richard Widmark *Stan Nagurski* • Barry Diamond *Junkie* • Elisha Cook Jr *Mousy* • Julie Kavner *Mrs Falcone* • Henny Youngman *Lawyer* • Robert Culp *Paul Everest* • Olympia Dukakis *Helena Naxos* • Peter Riegert *Jason Cooper* • Diane Lane *Liza* ◾ *Dir* Henry Jaglom, Bob Giraldi • *Scr* Tod Carroll, Shary Slenniken

National Lampoon's Senior Trip ★ 🔟

Comedy 1995 · US · Colour · 87min

Each successive entry in this once hilariously irreverent series is denounced as its nadir, but this risible comedy has stronger claims than most. Every character is a walking cliché, while every gag is designed to be cheap, and often offensive, rather than funny. Satire is at a premium as a gang of high school students write to the President lamenting the state of the nation and receive an invitation to the White House. Inept twaddle. DP Swearing.

Matt Frewer *Principal Moss* • Valerie Mahaffey *Miss Tracy Milford* • Lawrence Dane *Senator John Lerman* • Tommy Chong *Red* • Jeremy Renner *Mark "Dags" D'Agostino* • Rob Moore *Reggie* ◾ *Dir* Kelly Makin • *Scr* Roger Kumble, I Marlene King

National Lampoon's Vacation ★★★ 🔟

Comedy 1983 · US · Colour · 94min

National Lampoon's first outing (1978's *Animal House*) is still the funniest by far, but this is a decent effort. Chevy Chase is the put-upon dad who sets off to take his family across America to an amusement park, encountering numerous mishaps and disasters along the way. Director Harold Ramis keeps the silliness coming fast and furious, and he is ably abetted by a strong supporting cast. JB Drug abuse, swearing, nudity. *DVD*

Chevy Chase *Clark Griswold* • Beverly D'Angelo *Ellen Griswold* • Imogene Coca *Aunt Edna* • Randy Quaid *Cousin Eddie* • Anthony Michael Hall *Rusty Griswold* • Dana Barron *Audrey Griswold* • Eddie Bracken *Roy Walley* • James Keach *Motorcycle cop* • John Candy *Lasky* • Christie Brinkley *Girl in red Ferrari* ◾ *Dir* Harold Ramis • *Scr* John Hughes

National Security ★★ 🔟

Action comedy 2002 · US/UK · Colour · 84min

This poorly executed buddy movie is a vehicle for Martin Lawrence and Steve Zahn. Lawrence plays a wannabe cop who's booted out of the academy and becomes a security guard; Zahn is an ex-policeman who was sent down for six months after being falsely accused, by Lawrence, of a racist assault and is also forced to find work as a guard. They are thrown together and end up on the trail of the ruthless crooks who were responsible for the death of Zahn's partner. Dumb, tasteless and short on laughs. JC *DVD* 🅱🅡

Martin Lawrence *Earl Montgomery* • Steve Zahn *Hank Rafferty* • Colm Feore *Det Frank McDuff* • Bill Duke *Lt Washington* • Eric Roberts *Nash* • Timothy Busfield *Charlie Reed* • Robinne Lee *Denise* • Matt McCoy *Robert Barton* ◾ *Dir* Dennis Dugan • *Scr* Jay Scherick, David Ronn

National Treasure ★★ 🅟🅖

Action adventure 2004 · US · Colour · 125min

This is part historical detective story, part conspiracy thriller and part *Boys' Own* adventure, but director Jon Turteltaub never quite finds a successful way to marry all these elements together. Nicolas Cage sleepwalks his way through the role of Benjamin Franklin Gates, who embarks on a cross-country treasure hunt to discover the whereabouts of booty hidden by the Founding Fathers of the United States. En route, there are some limp action moments, colourless characters and sluggish storytelling, but this Jerry Bruckheimer production still has enough to keep the undemanding interested. IF *DVD* 🅱🅡

Nicolas Cage *Benjamin Franklin Gates* • Jon Voight *Patrick Gates* • Harvey Keitel *Agent Sadusky* • Diane Kruger *Dr Abigail Chase* • Sean Bean *Ian Howe* • Justin Bartha *Riley Poole* • Christopher Plummer *John Adams Gates* • Hunter Gomez *Young Ben Gates* ◾ *Dir* Jon Turteltaub • *Scr* Jim Kouf, Cormac Wibberley, Marianne Wibberley, from a story by Jim Kouf, Oren Aviv, Charles Segars

N

National Treasure: Book of Secrets ★★★ PG

Action adventure · 2007 · US · Colour · 119min

Nicolas Cage returns as treasure hunter Ben Gates in this sequel to 2004's *National Treasure*. This time the plot finds him searching for a fabled lost City of Gold and trying to clear his family's name after an ancestor is implicated in the assassination of President Abraham Lincoln. Following the clues again are his father Patrick (Jon Voight), National Archive curator and now ex-girlfriend Abigail (Diane Kruger) and geeky sidekick Riley (Justin Bartha). Newcomer to the cast Helen Mirren brings an element of comedy to the proceedings as Ben's mother, a linguistics expert. With intriguing puzzles, interesting locations (including our own Buckingham Palace), and stunning set pieces, the film delivers plenty of excitement and fun – enough to make you overlook some distinctly hammy acting by Cage and Voight. KK DVD BL

Nicolas Cage *Ben Gates* · Justin Bartha *Riley Poole* · Diane Kruger *Abigail Chase* · Jon Voight *Patrick Gates* · Helen Mirren *Emily Appleton* · Ed Harris *Mitch Wilkinson* · Harvey Keitel *Sadusky* · Bruce Greenwood *The President* ■ *Dir* Jon Turteltaub · *Scr* The Wibberleys [Cormac and Marianne Wibberley], from a story by the Wibberleys, Gregory Poirier, Ted Elliott, Terry Rossio, from characters by Jim Kouf, Oren Aviv, Charles Segars

The National Tree ★★

Seasonal drama · 2009 · US · Colour · 88min

A majestic Sitka spruce helps gruff widower Andrew McCarthy reconnect with his teenage son (Evan Williams) in this yuletide road movie. Originally planted by McCarthy's character to celebrate his boy's birth, it's now being driven 3,000 miles cross-country by the antagonistic pair, after it's selected as the official White House Christmas tree. What's meant to be a thought-provoking father-child bonding tale ends up as a bitty and rather cheesy travelogue, which makes the occasional bursts of drama seem excessively contrived. SF

Andrew McCarthy *Corey Burdock* · Evan Williams *Rock Burdock* · Kari Matchett *Faith* · Paula Brancati *Katie* · Jayne Eastwood *Lana* · *Dir* Graeme Campbell · *Scr* JB White, from a story by Lloyd Fonvielle, from David Kranes's novel

National Velvet ★★★★ U

Classic sports drama · 1944 · US · Colour · 11min

In this adaptation of Enid Bagnold's novel, 12-year-old Elizabeth Taylor gives a star-making performance as the girl who dreams of racing her horse in the Grand National. Director Clarence Brown knows how to tug at the heartstrings and this film has become a classic, even though the story has to be taken with a large pinch of salt. Thanks to a strong performance from Mickey Rooney, an Oscar-winning one from Anne Revere, and the appeal of Taylor herself, this is a richly satisfying movie. A misguided sequel, *International Velvet*, followed in 1978. TS DVD

Mickey Rooney *Mi Taylor* · Donald Crisp *Mr Herbert Brown* · Elizabeth Taylor *Velvet Brown* · Anne Revere *Mrs Brown* · Angela Lansbury *Edwina Brown* · Jackie "Butch" Jenkins *Donald Brown* · Juanita Quigley *Malvolia Brown* · Arthur Treacher *Race patron* · Reginald Owen *Farmer Ede* · Norma Varden *Miss Simms* ■ *Dir* Clarence Brown · *Scr* Theodore Reeves, Helen Deutsch, from the novel by Enid Bagnold

Nationale 7 ★★★★ 15

Comedy drama · 1999 · Fr · Colour · 95min

Director/co-writer Jean-Pierre Sinapi avoids any patronising pitfalls in this droll drama, which was inspired by the experiences of his nursing sister and a dying friend with a lust for life. Indeed, Olivier Gourmet's wheelchair-using socialist is so human he's unbearable, at least until nurse Nadia Kaci agrees to chaperone his visits to a prostitute in a Nationale 7 lay-by. The theme may be physical, racial, sexual and religious acceptance, but Sinapi never preaches and succeeds in affirming life

however it's lived. DP French +subtitles. Swearing, sexual references.

Nadia Kaci *Julie* · Olivier Gourmet *René* · Lionel Abelanski *Roland* · Chantal Neuwirth *Sandrine* ■ *Dir* Jean-Pierre Sinapi · *Scr* Jean-Pierre Sinapi, Anne-Marie Catois

Native Land ★★★ PG

Documentary drama · 1942 · US · BW · 88min

Based on testimony given to the US Senate Civil Liberties Committee, this docudrama focuses on the cruel irony entailed in the American boast to be the Land of the Free. With narration by Paul Robeson, episodes set in a Midwest farm, a bustling metropolis, a Southern village and a factory town proffer a potent amalgam of rhetoric, image and score. But in depicting those who demean the Bill of Rights as the "enemy within" and those striving for labour representation as the "new pioneers", Leo Hurwitz and Paul Strand betray the naivety of their political stance. DP

Paul Robeson *Narrator/Singer* · Fred Johnson *Fred Hill, the farmer* · Mary George *Farmer's wife* · John Rennick *Farmer's son* · *Dir* Leo Hurwitz, Paul Strand · *Scr* David Wolff [Ben Maddow], Leo Hurwitz, Paul Strand

Native Son ★★

Crime drama · 1951 · US/Arg · BW · 91min

The work of American author Richard Wright probably offers the harshest portrait of the South ever published. Shortly after he exiled himself to Paris in 1950, Wright was persuaded by director Pierre Chenal to star in his own adaptation of his most famous novel, about a boy from the slums who gets a job as a chauffeur to a white family. When the daughter of the family gets drunk, the youngster tries to keep her quiet and accidentally kills her. Sadly, Wright was no actor and he was twice the age of his protagonist so this tame version failed. BB

Richard Wright *Bigger Thomas* · Jean Wallace *Mary Dalton* · Nicholas Joy *Mr Dalton* · Gloria Madison *Bessie Mears* ■ *Dir* Pierre Chenal · *Scr* Pierre Chenal, Richard Wright, from the novel by Richard Wright

Native Son ★★★ 15

Drama · 1986 · US · Colour · 106min

Native Son has an impressive pedigree. It began as a 1940 novel by Richard Wright about a maladjusted, malcontented black youth who is taken for a night out by his employer's pretty daughter and her boyfriend. Both are active communists who make a show of equality. Later he accidentally murders the girl, incinerates the body and gets sentenced to death. This 1986 adaptation is pitched as a full-blooded melodrama and is worth seeing for its splendid cast: Carroll Baker as the blind mother, Elizabeth McGovern and Matt Dillon as the young communists, Victor Love as the central character and Oprah Winfrey in a cringe-making final scene. AT

Carroll Baker *Mrs Dalton* · Akosua Busia *Bessie* · Matt Dillon *Jan* · Art Evans *Doc* · John Karlen *Max* · Victor Love *Bigger Thomas* · Elizabeth McGovern *Mary Dalton* · John McMartin *Mr Dalton* · Geraldine Page *Peggy* · Oprah Winfrey *Mrs Thomas* ■ *Dir* Jerrold Freedman · *Scr* Richard Wesley, from the novel by Richard Wright

Nativity! ★★★ U

Comedy · 2009 · UK · Colour · 101min

This spirited comedy from writer/director Debbie Isitt (*Confetti*) revolves around a Coventry teacher who creates a sensation when word leaks out that a Hollywood film company is coming to film his primary school's nativity play. Unfortunately for Martin Freeman's Mr Maddens, the rumour isn't true. Freeman's practised delivery of much-hassled decency provides a sturdy anchor for this family farce that rather stumbles its way through a predictable triumph-of-the-underdog plot, but cajoles splendid turns from seasoned professionals and school-aged talent alike. TJ DVD BL

Martin Freeman *Paul Maddens* · Marc Wootton *Mr Poppy* · Jason Watkins *Gordon Shakespeare* · Ashley Jensen *Jennifer Lore* · Pam Ferris *Mrs Bevan* · Ricky Tomlinson *Lord Mayor* ■ *Dir/Scr* Debbie Isitt

Nativity 2: Danger in the Manger! ★★ U

Seasonal comedy · 2012 · UK · Colour · 105min

Nativity 2 is aimed shamelessly at the most sentimental of movie-goers and is only saved from tipping right over into awfulness by its clever, if manipulative, use of adorable non-actors in the schoolkid roles. David Tennant (replacing Martin Freeman from the first film) plays hapless teacher Mr Peterson, while Marc Wootton returns as creepy classroom assistant Mr Poppy. All hell breaks loose after Mr Poppy persuades Mr Peterson to take his pupils on an unsanctioned coach trip to a Christmas song competition in rural Wales. What happens next is utterly predictable, frenetic and wildly overplayed. A second sequel, this time starring Catherine Tate, is due in cinemas in late 2014. DA

David Tennant *David Peterson/Roderick Peterson* · Joanna Page *Mrs Peterson* · Jessica Hynes [Jessica Stevenson] *Angel Matthews* · Marc Wootton *Mr Poppy* · Pam Ferris *Mrs Bevan* ■ *Dir/Scr* Debbie Isitt

Nativity 3: Dude Where's My Donkey ★ U

Comedy · 2014 · UK · Colour · 109min

This second sequel has more fun and games from the kids of St Bernadette's and their oh-so-creepy classroom assistant, Mr Poppy (Marc Wootton), but the comedy returns are definitely diminishing. Martin Clunes plays a hapless new teacher who loses both his memory and the school donkey before the kids can say, "please, sir", leaving Poppy and co to save the day. This is desperately poor, juvenile in the extreme and thoroughly unfunny. DA

Martin Clunes *Mr Shepherd* · Catherine Tate *Sophie* · Marc Wootton *Mr Poppy* · Celia Imrie *Mrs Keen* · Adam Garcia *Bradley Finch* · Ralf Little *Sophie's brother* ■ *Dir/Scr* Debbie Isitt

The Nativity Story ★★ PG

Religious drama · 2006 · US · Colour · 96min

After crashing onto the indie scene with the dynamic and controversial growing-pains chronicle *Thirteen*, director Catherine Hardwicke shows much more decorum for *The Nativity Story*. Unfortunately her retelling of the Christmas story is rather too reverential, full of po-faced performances from a cast that includes Keisha Castle-Hughes as the Virgin Mary. Considering that Mary is a young teenager at the time she falls miraculously pregnant, she has surprisingly little awe or curiosity about her predicament (qualities that Castle-Hughes exuded in abundance in coming-of-age yarn *Whale Rider*). SP DVD

Keisha Castle-Hughes *Mary* · Oscar Isaac *Joseph* · Hiam Abbass *Anna* · Shaun Toub *Joaquim* · Ciaran Hinds *King Herod* · Shohreh Aghdashloo *Elizabeth* · Stanley Townsend *Zechariah* · Alexander Siddig *The Angel Gabriel* ■ *Dir* Catherine Hardwicke · *Scr* Mike Rich · *Cinematographer* Elliot Davis

The Natural ★★★★ PG

Sports drama · 1984 · US · Colour · 116min

Based on Bernard Malamud's 1952 novel, this is a wistful and often memorable look at the world of baseball by director Barry Levinson. Robert Redford is at his beautiful best as the player who experiences the highs and lows of the game in a film that's more *Field of Dreams* than *Bull Durham*. Baseball here is seen as something magical – Redford has a mystical bat named "Wonderboy", which he fashioned from a tree struck by lightning – rather than merely a sport. If you can suspend disbelief, you'll be rewarded with an emotional and heart-warming experience. JB Swearing. DVD

Robert Redford *Roy Hobbs* · Robert Duvall *Max Mercy* · Glenn Close *Iris* · Kim Basinger *Memo Paris* · Wilford Brimley *Pop Fisher* · Barbara Hershey *Harriet Bird* · Robert Prosky *The Judge* · Richard Farnsworth *Red Blow* · Joe Don Baker

The Whammer ■ *Dir* Barry Levinson · *Scr* Roger Towne, Phil Dusenberry, from the novel by Bernard Malamud

Natural Born Killers ★★★★ 18

Crime drama · 1994 · US · Colour and BW · 114min

Woody Harrelson and Juliette Lewis are serial killers turned into folk heroes by media excesses in this striking movie, criticised by original story author Quentin Tarantino after being largely rewritten by director Oliver Stone and others. Ambitious, unrelenting and inventive, Stone's controversial landmark film excites the intellect while bludgeoning the senses, blending naturalistic violence with stylised visuals, and commandeering every available cinematic trick to put across its searing message. A dazzling display of technique underscoring the media's obsession with violent crime, this is the most provocative addition to the debate since *A Clockwork Orange*. AJ Violence, sex scenes, swearing, nudity. DVD BL

Woody Harrelson *Mickey Knox* · Juliette Lewis *Mallory Knox* · Robert Downey Jr *Wayne Gale* · Tommy Lee Jones *Dwight McClusky* · Tom Sizemore *Jack Scagnetti* · Rodney Dangerfield *Mallory's dad* ■ *Dir* Oliver Stone · *Scr* David Veloz, Richard Rutowski, Oliver Stone, from a story by Quentin Tarantino

Natural Resistance ★★★ 12

Documentary · 2014 · It/Fr · Colour · 82min

Having castigated the French wine industry for marginalising mavericks in *Mondovino*, film-maker Jonathan Nossiter turns his focus to Italy in this charming if scattershot survey. Travelling around the country, Nossiter seeks the opinions of various wine-makers . But, while these rebels against EU and regional directives fight standardisation and commercialism, Nossiter is distracted by connections between viniculture and film preservation. So, just as oenophiles will enjoy the bucolic atmosphere, cineastes can relish 60s rarities about rural illiteracy scored by Nino Rota. DP Italian +subtitles. Brief nudity. DVD

■ *Dir* Jonathan Nossiter

Naughty but Nice ★★★ U

Musical · 1939 · US · BW · 89min

Crooner Dick Powell's last movie under his Warner Bros contract is an amiable lightweight tale, in which Powell – courtesy of some demon rum – plays a Jekyll-and-Hyde music professor. This loose satire on Tin Pan Alley is really a vehicle for top-billed Ann Sheridan, the lovely and talented Texas sophisticate who Warners tagged the "Oomph Girl". But even she can't salvage this silly movie, in which the only satirical content is a look at how popular songs always steal from the classics. Look out for an early appearance from a callow Ronald Reagan. TS

Ann Sheridan *Zelda Manion* · Dick Powell *Professor Hardwick* · Gale Page *Linda McKay* · Helen Broderick *Aunt Martha* · Allen Jenkins *Joe Dirk* · ZaSu Pitts *Aunt Penelope* · Ronald Reagan *Ed Clark* ■ *Dir* Ray Enright · *Scr* Richard Macaulay, Jerry Wald, from their story *Always Leave Them Laughing*

Naughty Marietta ★★★

Musical · 1935 · US · BW · 103min

This was the first movie to team "America's Sweethearts", Jeanette MacDonald and Nelson Eddy. The somewhat sickly mixture of Nelson as a lecherous rake and Jeanette as a maligned loose woman might seem old hat today, but there's no denying the sheer panache of the production, and the undoubted pleasure (if you like that sort of thing) of a Victor Herbert score that includes *Tramp, Tramp, Tramp* and *Ah, Sweet Mystery of Life*. Louis B Mayer liked it so much that he willed MacDonald to sing *Sweet Mystery* at his funeral. She did. TS

Jeanette MacDonald *Princess Marie de Namours de la Bonfain/"Marietta Franini"* · Nelson Eddy *Captain Richard Warrington* · Frank Morgan *Governor Gaspard d'Annard* · Elsa Lanchester *Madame d'Annard* · Douglass Dumbrille *Prince de Namours de la Bonfain* ■ *Dir* WS Van Dyke II [WS

U SUITABLE FOR ALL · Uc SUITABLE ESPECIALLY FOR YOUNG CHILDREN (DVD ONLY) · PG PARENTAL GUIDANCE · 12A UNDER 12s TO BE ACCOMPANIED (CINEMA ONLY)

Van Dyke] • *Scr* John Lee Mahin, Frances Goodrich, Albert Hackett, from the operetta by Victor Herbert, Rida Johnson Young

The Naughty Nineties ★★
Period comedy   1945 · US · BW · 76min

Bud and Lou: names that terrorise hardened movie-goers or evoke rapture at the prospect of their comic antics. While they lack the genius of Stan and Ollie - it's slapstick and music hall, not sublime comedies of errors - Abbott and Costello were once the highest paid comics in Hollywood. Often they are best remembered for incident rather than narrative, which here involves the duo helping out an elderly steamboat owner. The highlight for many will be the six-minute "Who's on First" dualogue, about the playing order of the St Louis baseball team. It's a routine that defies description and eschews a question mark. BB

Bud Abbott *Dexter Broadhurst* • Lou Costello *Sebastian Dinwiddie* • Alan Curtis *Crawford* • Rita Johnson *Bonita Farrow* • Henry Travers *Captain Sam Jackson* • Lois Collier *Caroline Jackson* ■ *Dir* Jean Yarbrough • *Scr* Edmund L Hartmann, John Grant, Edmund Joseph, Hal Fimberg, Felix Adler

Nausicaa of the Valley of the Wind ★★★ PG
Animated science-fiction fantasy
1984 · Jpn · Colour · 117min

Spirited Away director Hayao Miyazaki delivers a strong environmental message in this vibrant animated sci-fi fantasy set in a future where toxic spores threaten Earth's few human inhabitants. The storyline is ambitious, exploring darker themes reminiscent of Miyazaki's *Princess Mononoke*, yet it's frustratingly underdeveloped. Fortunately, visual fluidity and beauty offer compensation, even if the artwork isn't as refined as in his later work. SF Japanese +subtitles. DVD BD

■ *Dir/Scr* Hayao Miyazaki

Navajo Joe ★★ 15
Spaghetti western   1966 · It/Sp · Colour · 88min

Burt Reynolds made this spaghetti western shortly after he saw his friend Clint Eastwood in *A Fistful of Dollars*. "They'll love you in Italy," Eastwood told Reynolds. "You're quarter Indian, you can ride a horse like no one I know and you like to hug people." Reynolds plays a Navajo Indian who exacts bloody revenge after his entire tribe murdered, including the woman he loves. That's all there is to it. AT Italian dubbed. DVD

Burt Reynolds *Joe* • Aldo Sambrell *Marvin "Vee" Duncan* • Nicoletta Machiavelli *Estella* • Tanya Lopert *Maria* • Fernando Rey *Rattigan* • Franca Polesello *Barbara* • Peter Cross [Pierre Cressoy] *Dr Chester Lynne* ■ *Dir* Sergio Corbucci • *Scr* Dean Craig [Mario Pierotti], Fernando Di Leo, from a story by Ugo Pirro • *Music* Leo Nichols [Ennio Morricone]

The Navigator ★★★★ U
Classic silent comedy   1924 · US · BW · 57min

This gorgeous Buster Keaton comedy is set aboard a real ocean liner - the SS *Buford*, which was destined for the scrapyard before Keaton turned it into a marvellous prop. The story has Keaton playing Rollo Treadway - "heir to the Treadway fortune and and living proof that every family tree must have its sap" - who becomes adrift on the ship with his girlfriend. There are encounters with cannibals, an impromptu duel between swordfish, and an extraordinary underwater sequence with Keaton in full frogman's gear, filmed in 20 feet of water in Lake Tahoe, Nevada. AT DVD

Buster Keaton *Rollo Treadway* • Kathryn McGuire *Betsy O'Brien* • Frederick Vroom *John O'Brien* • Clarence Burton *Spy* • HM Clugston *Spy* • Noble Johnson *Cannibal chief* ■ *Dir* Donald Crisp, Buster Keaton • *Scr* Clyde Bruckman, Joseph Mitchell, Jean Havez

The Navigator - a Medieval Odyssey ★★★★ PG
Fantasy adventure
1988 · Aus/NZ · Colour and BW · 87min

An outstanding fable from New Zealand director Vincent Ward, this switches in time between Cumbria in the Middle Ages and the Antipodes of today. A medieval village threatened by the plague sends a group on a journey to find a miraculous church located on the other side of the world. The intrepid miners, however, burrow through the earth and end up in 20th-century New Zealand. The story could have been the basis for a knockabout time-travel comedy; indeed, there are some nice gags. Yet Ward is more interested in creating a mythical tale that subtly alludes to the Aids crisis and the nuclear apocalypse. JF

Bruce Lyons *Connor* • Hamish McFarlane *Griffin* • Noel Appleby *Ulf* • Marshall Napier *Searle* • Chris Haywood *Arno* • Paul Livingston *Martin* ■ *Dir/Scr* Vincent Ward

The Navigators ★★★ 15
Political drama
2001 · UK/Ger/Sp/It/Fr · Colour · 92min

New Labour may be in the ascendancy, but little has changed for the average worker according to Ken Loach in this stinging swipe at post-socialist Britain. Joe Duttine and Tom Craig demonstrate Yorkshire grit as the rail gangers whose livelihoods and self-esteem are jeopardised by privatisation. The humanity that gave Loach's earlier socio-dramas an integrity to match their commitment has been replaced by a more strident politicking. DP DVD

Joe Duttine *Paul* • Tom Craig *Mick* • Dean Andrews *John* • Steve Huison *Jim* • Venn Tracey *Gerry* • Andy Swallow *Len* ■ *Dir* Ken Loach • *Scr* Rob Dawber

Navy Blue and Gold ★★ U
Drama   1937 · US · BW · 93min

This is one of dozens of movies set in the naval training academy of Annapolis. There's a football game coming up against the army, and a question mark hangs over James Stewart's vital participation. It seems he slipped into Annapolis under an assumed name, because his navy father had a major blemish on his career. Can Stewart redeem his family name and get to the game on time? AT

Robert Young (1) *Roger Ash* • James Stewart *John "Truck" Cross* • Lionel Barrymore *Capt "Skinny" Dawes* • Florence Rice *Patricia Gates* • Billie Burke *Mrs Alyce Gates* • Tom Brown *Richard Arnold Gates Jr* • Samuel S Hinds *Richard A Gates Sr* ■ *Dir* Sam Wood • *Scr* George Bruce, from his novel

The Navy Comes Through ★★ U
Second World War drama
1942 · US · BW · 81min

There's a convoy heading across the ocean, and it's Pat O'Brien's job to sink the enemy subs, shoot the fighters out of the sky and keep George Murphy guessing about his promotion prospects. That's because Murphy has been having an affair with O'Brien's sister (Jane Wyatt), who also happens to be aboard. The action scenes mainly comprise stock footage from a dozen other RKO efforts. AT

Pat O'Brien *Mallory* • George Murphy *Sands* • Jane Wyatt *Myra* • Jackie Cooper *Babe* • Carl Esmond *Kroner* • Max Baer *Berringer* • Desi Arnaz *Tarriba* ■ *Dir* A Edward Sutherland • *Scr* Earl Baldwin, Roy Chanslor, John Twist, Aeneas MacKenzie, from the story *Pay to Learn* by Borden Chase

The Navy Lark ★★ U
Comedy   1959 · UK · BW · 82min

The Navy Lark was a BBC Home Service comedy show that tickled people pink throughout the 1950s. Filmed in CinemaScope and running three times its normal length, it's a nostalgia trip for those who remember and a baffling experience for those who don't. The idea was to show naval life as a jolly jape, so the plot deals with life aboard a mine sweeper whose

skipper invents an outbreak of yellow fever. What follows is wrapped up in *Carry On*-style puns and saucy seaside postcard situations. AT

Cecil Parker *Commander Stanton* • Ronald Shiner *CPO Banyard* • Leslie Phillips *Lieutenant Pouter* • Elvi Hale *Leading Wren Heather* • Nicholas Phipps *Captain Povey* • Cardew Robinson *Lieutenant Binns* • Gordon Jackson *Leading Seaman Johnson* • Hattie Jacques *Fortune teller* ■ *Dir* Gordon Parry • *Scr* Sid Colin, Laurie Wyman, from the radio series by Laurie Wyman

Navy SEALs ★★ 15
Action thriller
1990 · US · Colour · 108min

Charlie Sheen has proved to be more convincing sending up action heroes (namely in the *Hot Shots!* films) than playing it straight, and this uninspired adventure yarn is a perfect case in point. Sheen is the slightly crazy crack commando who, with colleagues such as Michael Biehn and Rick Rossovich, sets out to rid the world of baddies. Director Lewis Teague lets off the requisite number of explosions, but the script is riddled with clichés and Sheen is hardly a charismatic lead. JF Swearing, violence. DVD

Charlie Sheen *Lieutenant Dale Hawkins* • Michael Biehn *Lieutenant Commander James Curran* • Joanne Whalley-Kilmer [Joanne Whalley] *Claire Verens* • Rick Rossovich *Leary* • Bill Paxton *Dane* ■ *Dir* Lewis Teague • *Scr* Chuck Pfarrer, Gary Goldman

The Navy Steps Out ★★★ U
Comedy   1941 · US · BW · 90min

Produced by the great silent comedian Harold Lloyd, this lightweight farce starts merrily enough as stenographer Lucille Ball and her wacky family and friends show stuffed-shirt tycoon Edmond O'Brien how to get some fun out of life. The rapid pace and slapstick situations keep the fun bubbling until the last reel. Worth a look, if only to see Ball displaying the assurance and talent that Hollywood took so long to acknowledge. TV

Lucille Ball *Dot Duncan* • Edmond O'Brien *Stephen Herrick* • George Murphy *Coffee Cup* • George Cleveland *Pokey* • Henry Travers *Abel Martin* • Franklin Pangborn *Pet shop owner* • Kathleen Howard *Jawme* ■ *Dir* Richard Wallace • *Scr* Bert Granet, Frank Ryan, from a story by Grover Jones

The Navy vs the Night Monsters ★★ 12
Science-fiction drama
1966 · US · Colour · 85min

Antarctic vegetable samples replanted on an island naval base grow into acid-bleeding, walking trees and terrorise the inhabitants of a South Seas navy base. But most of the cast are too busy ogling 1950s blonde bombshell Mamie Van Doren to even notice. A terrible script, awful direction and ham acting from a bunch of Z-movie celebrities make this mind-boggling misfire a camp must-see. AJ

Mamie Van Doren *Lt Nora Hall* • Anthony Eisley *Lt Charles Brown* • Pamela Mason [Pamela Kellino] *Maria, a scientist* • Billy Gray *Petty Officer Fred Twining* • Bobby Van *Ens Rutherford Chandler* ■ *Dir* Michael A Hoey • *Scr* Michael A Hoey, from the novel *Monster from Earth's End* by Murray Leinster

Naya Daur ★★★ U
Drama   1957 · Ind · BW · 161min

Directed by BR Chopra, this is a solid example of the politically conscious movie known as the "masala social". Just about every problem besetting the inhabitants of India's outlying rural communities comes under the microscope in this relentless melodrama, in which the arrival of new technology blows the lid off a long-simmering class and caste crisis. As if this wasn't enough to be getting on with, there is also a romantic triangle, a villain and a handful of those extravagant song-and-dance routines that make Indian cinema so unique. Re-released in cinemas in 2007 in a digitally remastered colourised version. DP Hindi +subtitles.

Jeevan *Kundan* • Dilip Kumar *Shankar* • Ajit (1) *Krishna* • Nasir Hussain (1) *Seth Maganlal* ■ *Dir* BR Chopra • *Scr* Akhtar Mirza

Nazarín ★★★★ 12
Religious drama   1958 · Mex · BW · 94min

Rejecting the chance to adapt *The House of Bernarda Alba*, Luis Buñuel instead chose to direct this distressing odyssey through rural Mexico, which is sufficiently ambiguous to be claimed as both a scathing attack on the Catholic Church and a humanist lament at the impossibility of evangelising a determinedly secular world. Francisco Rabal wears an increasingly haunted look as his journey (which frequently echoes events from the Gospels) reveals the virtual irrelevance of religion. DP In Spanish. Some swearing. DVD

Francisco Rabal *Nazarín* • Marga Lopez *Beatriz* • Rita Macedo *Andara* • Ignacio Lopez Tarso *Sacrilegist* • Ofelia Guilmain *Chanfa* ■ *Dir* Luis Buñuel • *Scr* Luis Buñuel, Julio Alejandro, from a novel by Benito Perez Galdos

Nazi Hunter: the Beate Klarsfeld Story ★★★★
Drama based on a true story
1986 · US · Colour · 100min

Every now and then a star pulls out a performance that leaves you dumbfounded because you simply didn't think they had it in them. Farrah Fawcett is the performer working wonders here, in the title role of this genuinely affecting TV movie about the capture of the Butcher of Lyons, Klaus Barbie, who, at the end of the war, had fled into exile in Bolivia. Director Michael Lindsay-Hogg also draws expert performances from Tom Conti as Fawcett's devoted husband, and Geraldine Page as a camp survivor whose testimony helps nail the fugitive. It's just a shame it dips too frequently into melodrama. DP

Farrah Fawcett *Beate Klarsfeld* • Tom Conti *Serge Klarsfeld* • Geraldine Page *Itta Halaunbrenner* • Catherine Allégret *Madame Simone Lagrange* • Féodor Atkine *Luc Pleyel* • Helene Vallier *Raissa Klarsfeld* • Vincent Gauthier *Barbie in 1944* ■ *Dir* Michael Lindsay-Hogg • *Scr* Frederic Hunter

N

Near Dark ★★★★ 18
Horror   1987 · US · Colour · 94min

An undead revamp of *Bonnie and Clyde*, director Kathryn Bigelow's tense road movie combines the western and horror genres in one visually stunning and frightening package. Adrian Pasdar is the farm boy inducted by Jenny Wright into her itinerant family of gangster bloodsuckers as they manage to keep one step ahead of the law and daylight. Bigelow spins a genuinely scary tale, slickly examining the violent lifestyle of the outlaw gang, with Lance Henriksen and Bill Paxton giving stand-out performances. AJ Violence, swearing. DVD BD

Adrian Pasdar *Caleb Colton* • Jenny Wright *Mae* • Lance Henriksen *Jesse* • Bill Paxton *Severen* • Jenette Goldstein *Diamondback* • Joshua Miller [Joshua John Miller] *Homer* • Marcie Leeds *Sarah Colton* • Tim Thomerson *Loy Colton* • Kenny Call *Deputy Sheriff* ■ *Dir* Kathryn Bigelow • *Scr* Eric Red, Kathryn Bigelow

Near Mrs ★★ 15
Romantic comedy   1990 · Fr/US · Colour · 89min

Judge Reinhold strains every sinew to amuse as the hi-tech executive whose bigamous double life is exposed when he persuades doltish Casey Siemaszko to stand in for him on the annual Army Reserve fortnight while he romances his latest mistress. The farce that follows Siemaszko's kidnap by the Soviets is laboured, in spite of the pace. DP Swearing.

Judge Reinhold *Claude Jobert* • Casey Siemaszko *Colin Phipps* • Cécile Paoli *Molly* • Rebecca Pauly *Maggie* • Muriel Combeau *Toni* • Katarzyna Figura *Sasha* ■ *Dir* Baz Taylor • *Scr* Peter I Baloff [Peter Baloff], David W Wollert

The Near Room ★★ 18
Thriller   1995 · UK · Colour · 85min

The third feature from actor/director David Hayman (*Silent Scream*, *The Hawk*) is a rather grim thriller about a gutter-press journalist (Adrian Dunbar) on the trail of his long-lost teenage daughter. The search takes him through child sex rackets, pornography rings and other underworld horrors. Some viewers may find the relentless squalor, thick accents and foul language hard to take. **AT**

Adrian Dunbar *Charlie Colquhoun* • David O'Hara *Harris Hill* • David Hayman *Dougie Patterson* • Julie Graham *Elise Grey* ■ *Dir* David Hayman • *Scr* Robert Murphy

Nearest and Dearest ★★

Comedy 1972 · UK · Colour · 84min

Responsible for some of Hammer's most grisly horrors, Michael Carreras was perhaps a surprise choice to produce this spin-off from the long-running ITV comedy series. Released the year before this fondly remembered sitcom departed our screens, it provides a worthy record of the word-mangling sniping between Hylda Baker and Jimmy Jewel as they try to suppress their sibling rivalry and make a go of their father's pickle factory. Bawdy entertainment. **DP**

Hylda Baker *Nellie Pledge* • Jimmy Jewel *Eli Pledge* • Eddie Malin *Walter* • Madge Hindle *Lily* • Joe Gladwin *Stan* • Norman Mitchell *Vernon Smallpiece* • Pat Ashton *Freda* • Yootha Joyce *Mrs Rowbottom* ■ *Dir* John Robins • *Scr* Tom Brennand, Roy Bottomley, from the TV series

Nearly a Nasty Accident ★★★ U

Comedy 1961 · UK · BW · 89min

Jimmy Edwards teams with Kenneth Connor for this old-fashioned blend of slapstick and bluster. Although Edwards, his handlebar moustache bristling with indignation, is the nominal star as the RAF officer whose cushy lifestyle is shattered by the arrival of an accident-prone mechanic, it's Connor's talent for timidity and catastrophe that makes this catalogue of disasters so amusing. Don Chaffey directs with undue fuss, and there's practised support from some stalwart players. **DP**

Jimmy Edwards *Group Captain Kingsley* • Kenneth Connor *AC2 Alexander Wood* • Shirley Eaton *Jean Briggs* • Ronnie Stevens *Fl Lt Pocock* • Richard Wattis *Wagstaffe* • Jon Pertwee *General Birkenshaw* • Eric Barker *Minister* • Peter Jones *Fl Lt Winters* ■ *Dir* Don Chaffey • *Scr* Jack Davies, Hugh Woodhouse, from the play *Touch Wood* by David Stringer

'Neath the Arizona Skies ★★ U

Western 1934 · US · BW · 51min

There's little to get excited about here in a very routine John Wayne Monogram programme filler, except for a spectacular, waterlogged fistfight between the Duke and stuntman Yakima Canutt at the climax. The rest of the tale is flimsily plotted around a far-fetched case of mistaken identity. This is for Wayne fans only, and even they might blanch at such a minor opus. **TS** DVD

John Wayne *Chris Morrell* • Sheila Terry *Clara Moore* • Jay Wilsey [Buffalo Bill Jr] *Jim Moore* • Shirley Ricketts [Shirley Jane Ricketts] *Nina* • George "Gabby" Hayes *Matt Downing* • Yakima Canutt *Sam Black* ■ *Dir* Harry Fraser • *Scr* Burl Tuttle, from his story

Nebraska ★★★★★ 15

Road movie comedy 2013 · US · BW · 114min

Though shot in arty monochrome and featuring some starkly beautiful images of the US Midwest, this is actually a wittily observant film about family life. Bruce Dern thinks he's won a million dollars so son Will Forte agrees to drive him to collect his "winnings". It's at this point that this lovely and poignant comedy finds its feet, revealing itself as an exquisite study of past lives and roots; in particular, in the form of Stacy Keach's horribly overbearing neighbour, the people we quite deliberately leave behind. **DW** DVD

Bruce Dern *Woody Grant* • Will Forte *David Grant* • Stacy Keach *Ed Pegram* • June Squibb *Kate Grant* • Bob Odenkirk *Ross Grant* ■ *Dir* Alexander Payne • *Scr* Bob Nelson

Necronomicon ★★ 18

Horror 1993 · US · Colour · 92min

Pacts with sea devils, mad scientists searching for eternal life and alien sacrifices are the themes of this trilogy of terror based on the works of HP Lovecraft. Nothing too remarkable is on offer here, although the gothic lyricism of Christophe Gans's episode *The Drowned* is noteworthy and the gruesome Edgar Allan Poe poetry of Shu Kaneko's *The Cold* gets a lift from the manic performance of David Warner. Brian Yuzna's *Whispers* is the goriest and daftest of the three. **AJ**

Jeffrey Combs *HP Lovecraft* • Tony Azito *Librarian* • Brian Yuzna *Cabbie* • Bruce Payne *Edward de la Poer* • Richard Lynch *Jethro de la Poer* • David Warner *Dr Madden* ■ *Dir* Christophe Gans, Shu Kaneko [Shusuke Kaneko], Brian Yuzna • *Scr* Brent V Friedman, Christophe Gans, Kazunori Ito, Brian Yuzna, from stories by HP Lovecraft

Ned Kelly ★★ 15

Biographical drama 1970 · UK · Colour · 99min

One of the unfortunate temptations of hiring a rock star to carry a film is for the director to rely rather lazily on that star's charisma instead of trying to mould him into a character. Witness Mick Jagger, here cast as Australia's most memorable outlaw, who is so similar to his stage image that you half expect him to start shrieking, "Thank you, Sydney, you've been a great audience!". Director Tony Richardson's handling sometimes obscures the message and buries the drama. **JM** Swearing, violence. DVD

Mick Jagger *Ned Kelly* • Allen Bickford *Dan Kelly* • Geoff Gilmour *Steve Hart* • Mark McManus *Joe Byrne* • Serge Lazareff *Wild Wright* • Peter Sumner *Tom Lloyd* • Ken Shorter *Aaron Sherritt* • James Elliott *Pat O'Donnell* ■ *Dir* Tony Richardson • *Scr* Tony Richardson, Ian Jones

Ned Kelly ★★★ 15

Biographical drama 2003 · Aus/UK/US/Fr · Colour · 105min

Gregor Jordan's film about Australia's famous outlaw casts as rosy a light as possible on the outback legend. Heath Ledger gives a growling performance as Kelly, while the oppressive nature of the world in which he lived is evocatively presented. Misjudged and set up by the police, especially Superintendent Hare (Geoffrey Rush), he is forced to go on the run and form a gang. The outback is filmed in tones as sumptuous as any tourist brochure, but the idolisation of Kelly rings only as true as the stature accorded to Billy the Kid. **TH** DVD

Heath Ledger *Ned Kelly* • Orlando Bloom *Joe Byrne* • Geoffrey Rush *Superintendent Francis Hare* • Naomi Watts *Julia Cook* • Laurence Kinlan *Dan Kelly* • Philip Barantini *Steve Hart* • Joel Edgerton *Aaron Sherritt* • Kiri Paramore *Alex Fitzpatrick* ■ *Dir* Gregor Jordan • *Scr* John Michael McDonagh, from the novel *Our Sunshine* by Robert Drewe

Neds ★★★ 18

Coming-of-age drama 2010 · UK · Colour · 118min

A teenager's inability to escape his hoodlum brother's shadow has devastating consequences in writer/director Peter Mullan's raw and intense coming-of-age drama. Evoking the angry realism of Alan Clarke and Ken Loach, it's a visceral account of how hope-filled young lives can be destroyed by oppression, brutality and social prejudice, as working-class bookworm John McGill (played superbly by Conor McCarron) tragically slips into the gang-centred world of the Neds (Non-Educated Delinquents) in 1970s Glasgow. There's a well-balanced seam of jet-black humour that keeps the escalating grimness bearable, but the film loses its grip in the incongruous final act. **SF** Violence, swearing. DVD

Conor McCarron *John McGill, aged 14* • Louise Goodall *Theresa McGill* • Peter Mullan *Mr McGill* • Greg Forrest *John McGill, aged 10* • Joe Szula *Benny McGill* • John Joe Hay *Fergie* ■ *Dir/Scr* Peter Mullan

Need for Speed ★★ 12

Action thriller 2014 · US · Colour · 125min

Aaron Paul and Dominic Cooper go head to head in a cross-country supercars race in this speedfreak extravaganza loosely based on the popular video game. It's aimed fairly and squarely at the *Fast & Furious* crowd, and it's entertaining enough in its lowbrow way. The characters are cornily cardboard, but the cars are unquestionably super, and the racing rather exciting. **DA** Swearing, brief nudity. DVD BL

Aaron Paul *Tobey Marshall* • Dominic Cooper *Dino Brewster* • Scott Mescudi *Benny* • Imogen Poots *Julia Maddon* • Ramon Rodriguez *Joe Peck* ■ *Dir* Scott Waugh • *Scr* George Gatins, from a story by John & Gatins, from the computer game series by Electronic Arts

Needful Things ★★ 15

Horror 1993 · US · Colour · 115min

The Devil arrives in the sleepy coastal town of Castle Rock to open a curiosity shop selling bric-a-brac with nasty surprises attached. Director Fraser C Heston's adaptation of the Stephen King novel is overlong, if mechanically efficient, and the script can't make up its mind whether to mine the humour or the horror. Despite capable performances, this fails to generate any sympathy for its characters, and the episodic format is annoying. **AJ** Swearing, violence. DVD

Max von Sydow *Leland Gaunt* • Ed Harris *Sheriff Alan Pangborn* • Bonnie Bedelia *Polly Chalmers* • Amanda Plummer *Nettie Cobb* • JT Walsh *Danforth Keeton III* • Ray McKinnon *Deputy Norris Ridgewick* • Duncan Fraser *Hugh Priest* ■ *Dir* Fraser C Heston • *Scr* WD Richter, from the novel by Stephen King

Nefertite, Queen of the Nile ★★★

Historical epic 1961 · It · Colour · 97min

Part of a deal made by 20th Century-Fox with Italian studios, this is a negligible trip to Ancient Egypt. Contract player Edmund Purdom is the sculptor who falls for the high priest's daughter (Jeanne Crain) and is sentenced to death. She's meant to be a bride of the new pharaoh so it's a case of "less majesty" if she loses her virginity. There are some cherishable lines, but otherwise it's a very dull excursion to the past. **TH** Italian dubbed.

Jeanne Crain *Tanit/Nefertite* • Vincent Price *Benakon* • Edmund Purdom *Tumos* • Amedeo Nazzari *Amenophis IV* • Liana Orfei *Merith* ■ *Dir* Fernando Cerchio • *Scr* John Byrne, Ottavio Poggi, Fernando Cerchio

The Negotiator ★★★★ 15

Action drama 1998 · US/Ger · Colour · 133min

Cluttered with clichés from other thrillers, this is still efficiently exciting cinema because of the electrifying chemistry between Samuel L Jackson and Kevin Spacey as Chicago police negotiators – cops skilled at talking hostage-takers out of the dead ends into which they put themselves. Jackson, fresh from persuading a madman not to kill his daughter, is accused of stealing from police funds. So he takes captives until his name is cleared, and Spacey has the job of "talking him down". It's that stand-off that director F Gary Gray makes such a cunningly dramatic centrepiece. **TH** Swearing, violence. DVD

Samuel L Jackson *Danny Roman* • Kevin Spacey *Chris Sabian* • David Morse *Commander Adam Beck* • Ron Rifkin *Commander Grant Frost* • John Spencer *Chief Al Travis* • JT Walsh *Terence Niebaum* • Siobhan Fallon *Maggie* • Paul Giamatti *Rudy Timmons* ■ *Dir* F Gary Gray • *Scr* James DeMonaco, Kevin Fox

Neighbors ★★★★ U

Silent comedy 1920 · US · BW · 17min

Set amid run-down city tenements, this tale of thwarted lovers provides the impetus for some of Buster Keaton's most inspired sight gags. The sequence in which he uses a washing-line to escape from Virginia Fox's third-storey apartment is a masterclass in gymnastic slapstick, which culminates in

him careering back into his beloved's room and straight into the arms of her seething pop, Joe Roberts. The clothes-line shenanigans with his own father, Joe Keaton, were a glorious throwback to their vaudeville days. **DP**

Buster Keaton *Boy* • Joe Keaton *His father* • Virginia Fox *Girl* • Joe Roberts *Her father* • Eddie Cline [Edward Cline] *Cop* ■ *Dir/Scr* Buster Keaton, Eddie Cline [Edward Cline]

Neighbors ★★★ 15

Comedy 1981 · US · Colour · 91min

This swan song of the John Belushi/Dan Aykroyd partnership is a flawed but fascinating stab by the comedians at breaking away from their traditional knockabout slapstick. The two stars even swap their usual comic personae, with Belushi playing a geeky, mild-mannered suburbanite who is slowly being driven mad by his crazy neighbours (Aykroyd and Cathy Moriarty). Director John G Avildsen shows little affinity for the material, but Aykroyd and especially Belushi are excellent and make it worth a look. **JF** Swearing.

John Belushi *Earl Keese* • Dan Aykroyd *Vic* • Kathryn Walker *Enid Keese* • Cathy Moriarty *Ramona* • Igors Gavon *Chic* ■ *Dir* John G Avildsen • *Scr* Larry Gelbart, from the novel by Thomas Berger

Neighbouring Sounds ★★★★ 15

Drama 2012 · Bra/Neth · Colour and BW · 131min

This assured slice-of-life drama from Brazil sees a private security firm arrive in a well-heeled suburb, but their avowed intention to protect the residents' property may hide a darker motive. The film follows various storylines, a little like a TV soap opera, flitting between a disgruntled wife, an uneasy love affair and the secret machinations of the local landowner. In doing so, confident first-time writer/director Kleber Mendonça Filho delivers a portrait of the national psyche, whose lingering class and ethnic divisions still underpin everyday affairs. What's so fascinating, though, is that we're allowed to read the signs for ourselves. This is a disarming and utterly delightful original that will reward the adventurous and perceptive viewer. **TJ** Portuguese, English, Mandarin +subtitles.

Irandhir Santos *Clodoaldo* • Gustavo Jahn *Joao* • Maeve Jinkings *Beatriz "Bia" Linhares* • WJ Solha *Francisco* • Irma Brown *Sofia* ■ *Dir/Scr* Kleber Mendonça Filho

Neil Young: Heart of Gold ★★★★ PG

Music documentary 2006 · US · Colour · 99min

Jonathan Demme is no stranger to the work of Neil Young, having previously made the 30-minute film *The Complex Sessions*, which showcased tracks from his 1994 album *Sleeps with Angels*. Here, Demme explores the Canadian country/folk legend's gentler side with an elegant record of the Nashville shows that were held to premiere his critically acclaimed release *Prairie Wind*. As well as marking an extraordinary comeback for the artist after his brain aneurysm, the concert serves as a moving tribute to Young's late father, who inspired much of his most recent album. Demme's unobtrusive direction confirms his reputation as one of the most sympathetic music film directors working today. **JF** DVD

Neil Young (1) *Neil Young* • Emmylou Harris ■ *Dir* Jonathan Demme • *Cinematographer* Ellen Kuras

Neil Young Journeys ★★★ PG

Music documentary 2011 · US · Colour · 74min

This documentary about the legendary Canadian rocker intersperses live footage of him on stage in Toronto with scenes of him driving across Ontario on his way to the venue. As he travels through small towns and revisits old haunts, Young recalls boyhood adventures and family functions

with warmth and wit, offering some insight into the inspiration for his music. However, director Jonathan Demme spends just a fraction of the film's running time on the "journey", opting instead to concentrate on the performance. TeS
Neil Young ■ *Dir* Jonathan Demme

Neither the Sea nor the Sand ★★

Fantasy drama   1972 · UK · Colour · 95min

Based on the novel by one-time newsreader Gordon Honeycombe, this romantic ghost story is a genuine oddity that was sadly overlooked at the time. Susan Hampshire retreats to Jersey where she meets and falls in love with lighthouse keeper Michael Petrovitch. When he dies, her friends and family (including Anthony Booth, Cherie's dad) are dismayed to find that death is no barrier to their love. FL
Susan Hampshire *Anna Robinson* • Michael Petrovitch *Hugh Dabernon* • Frank Finlay *George Dabernon* • Michael Craze *Collie* • Jack Lambert *Dr Irving* • David Garth *Mr Mackay* • Betty Duncan *Mrs Mackay* • Anthony Booth *Delamare* ■ *Dir* Fred Burnley • *Scr* Gordon Honeycombe, Rosemary Davies, from the novel by Gordon Honeycombe

Nell ★★★ 12

Drama   1994 · US · Colour · 110min

Jodie Foster plays a young woman living in the North Carolina woods who has never seen the outside world and speaks a strange indecipherable language. Psychologist Natasha Richardson wants to take her into psychiatric care for research; sympathetic local doctor Liam Neeson believes she should be left alone. Although Foster is perhaps a little too showy in the title role (and was again Oscar-nominated for her pains), she still delivers a marvellous performance, and director Michael Apted, making the most of the stunning locations, keeps the syrup at bay. JF Some swearing, brief nudity.
Jodie Foster *Nell* • Liam Neeson *Jerome Lovell* • Natasha Richardson *Paula Olsen* • Richard Libertini *Alexander Paley* • Nick Searcy *Todd Peterson* • Robin Mullins *Mary Peterson* • Jeremy Davies *Billy Fisher* ■ *Dir* Michael Apted • *Scr* William Nicholson, Mark Handley, from Handley's play *Idioglossia*

Nell Gwyn ★★★ U

Historical drama   1934 · UK · BW · 71min

The American censors were appalled when Herbert Wilcox's bawdy historical drama about Charles II's mistress was presented to them. In addition to 35 cuts, they suggested that a much more suitable ending would be to have Nell marry the king! A box-office smash in this country, the film benefits from a script by Miles Malleson (who also appears) that took much of its dialogue from Samuel Pepys's famous diary. Cedric Hardwicke has a rare old time as Charles, but Anna Neagle is just a touch too refined as Nell and comes off second best to Jeanne de Casalis. DP **DVD**
Anna Neagle *Nell Gwyn* • Cedric Hardwicke *King Charles II* • Miles Malleson *Chiffinch* • Esme Percy *Samuel Pepys* • Jeanne de Casalis *Duchess of Portsmouth* • Lawrence Anderson *Duke of York* • Helena Pickard *Mrs Pepys* ■ *Dir* Herbert Wilcox • *Scr* Miles Malleson, from the diaries of Samuel Pepys

Nelly & Monsieur Arnaud
★★★★★ PG

Drama   1995 · Fr/It/Ger · Colour · 106min

Director Claude Sautet's distinctively cool style is wonderfully suited to this melancholy study of a young woman (Emmanuelle Béart) who becomes involved in a fragile, unfulfilled relationship with the elderly businessman (Michel Serrault) for whom she works as a secretary. There are more emotional insights than you find in many a so-called romantic movie, while the tale of obsession is told so discreetly it makes the film all the more haunting. TH French +subtitles.

Emmanuelle Béart *Nelly* • Michel Serrault *Monsieur Arnaud* • Jean-Hugues Anglade *Vincent* • Claire Nadeau *Jacqueline* • Françoise Brion *Lucie* ■ *Dir* Claude Sautet • *Scr* Claude Sautet, Jacques Fieschi

Nemesis ★ 18

Science-fiction action thriller
1993 · US · Colour · 91min

Cyborg ex-cop Olivier Gruner is forced by police chief Tim Thomerson into stopping a band of techno-terrorists planning to disrupt a summit meeting. If he refuses, he'll die from a bomb implanted in his body. Schlockmeister Albert Pyun has had a long fascination with stories involving cyborgs, but this effort is just as threadbare and unconvincing as all his other attempts. Sue Price took over as the lead for three sequels. KB **DVD**
Olivier Gruner *Alex Rain* • Tim Thomerson *Farnsworth* • Deborah Shelton *Julian* • Marjorie Monaghan *Jared* • Merle Kennedy *Max Impact* • Cary-Hiroyuki Tagawa *Angie Liv* ■ *Dir* Albert Pyun • *Scr* Rebecca Charles

Nénette ★★★ PG

Documentary   2010 · Fr · Colour · 70min

Seasoned documentarian Nicolas Philibert (*Etre et Avoir*) originally intended this profile of a 40-year-old orangutan at Paris's Jardin des Plantes to be a short film. However, he became so intrigued by Nénette's wistful gazes, bursts of activity and interaction with her son Tübo that he extended the study to incorporate the voiceover insights of her keepers and visitors. Philibert's observational sensitivity is never in doubt, but it's difficult not to feel pity for a creature clearly affected by its captivity and the film prompts a discussion as to the value of zoos. Yet, while the minimalist close-up technique used is audacious and the vocal interjections are alternately educational, amusing, sentimental and provocative, this is never entirely compelling. DP French +subtitles.
DVD
■ *Dir* Nicolas Philibert

The Neon Bible ★★★ 15

Drama   1995 · UK/US · Colour · 87min

This measured, beautifully photographed but harrowing study of family angst in Georgia around the time of the Second World War marked the American debut of director Terence Davies. He breathes some new life into the familiar small-town formula, thanks to his keen eye for detail and a supremely assured performance from Gena Rowlands as the nightclub singer aunt who shakes up the lives of ten-year-old Drake Bell and his parents Diana Scarwid and Denis Leary. DP Violence, swearing.
Gena Rowlands *Aunt Mae* • Diana Scarwid *Sarah* • Denis Leary *Frank* • Jacob Tierney *David aged 15* • Leo Burmester *Bobbie Lee Taylor* • Frances Conroy *Miss Scover* • Peter McRobbie *Reverend Watkins* • Joan Glover *Flora* • Drake Bell *David aged ten* ■ *Dir* Terence Davies • *Scr* Terence Davies, from the novel by John Kennedy Toole • *Cinematographer* Mick Coulter

The Neon Demon ★★★ 18

Horror thriller   2016 · Den/Fr · Colour · 117min

Fans of *Drive* director Nicolas Winding Refn's recent output will find plenty to chew on in this graphic, gothic-psychological horror movie, which stars Elle Fanning as teenage model Jesse, who moves to LA to start a modelling career. Taken by some to be a lurid satire on the fashion world, this is really a cerebral tribute to 1980s slasher films that's better seen as a psychedelic meditation on fame, with a trippy score by Cliff Martinez that helps soften the narrative lurches between each striking set piece. DW Violence, swearing, sex scenes, nudity, sexual violence.
Elle Fanning *Jesse* • Jena Malone *Ruby* • Bella Heathcote *Gigi* • Abbey Lee *Sarah* • Keanu Reeves *Hank* • Christina Hendricks *Roberta Hoffman* ■ *Dir* Nicolas Winding Refn • *Scr* Nicolas Winding Refn, Mary Laws, Polly Stenham, from Refn's story • *Music* Cliff Martinez

The Nephew ★★ 12

Drama   1997 · Ire · Colour · 104min

In yet another Irish rural saga, a young American man returns to the village from which his deceased mother came, sending the residents into a turmoil. Sounds familiar? The only twist in the tale is that the man is black, but that's not enough to keep you entertained throughout this well-meaning but cliché-ridden tale. Taking a break from the Bond films, Pierce Brosnan is one of the film's producers, and he also stars as the local publican. JB Swearing, violence. **DVD**
Pierce Brosnan *Joe Brady* • Donal McCann *Tony Egan* • Sinead Cusack *Brenda O'Boyce* • Hill Harper *Chad Egan-Washington* • Aislin McGuckin *Aislin Brady* • Niall Toibin *Sean Post* ■ *Dir* Eugene Brady • *Scr* Jacqueline O'Neill, Sean P Steele, from a story by Eugene Brady, Douglas Mayfield, Jacqueline O'Neill

The Neptune Factor ★ U

Science-fiction adventure
1973 · Can · Colour · 98min

"The most fantastic undersea odyssey ever filmed," bragged the poster. Hardly – the producers should have been done under the trades description act for this feeble slice of aquatic sci-fi. Ben Gazzara and Ernest Borgnine are in charge of a mini-submarine that offers the only chance of rescuing the crew of a sea-lab trapped by an earthquake on the ocean floor. A huge letdown. RS
Ben Gazzara *Commander Adrian Blake* • Yvette Mimieux *Leah Jansen* • Walter Pidgeon *Dr Samuel Andrews* • Ernest Borgnine *"Mack" MacKay* • Chris Wiggins *Captain Williams* ■ *Dir* Daniel Petrie • *Scr* Jack DeWitt

Neptune's Daughter ★★★ U

Musical comedy   1949 · US · Colour · 92min

A super-fun all-star MGM Technicolor musical, this is as good-natured as they come. Metro's aqua-queen Esther Williams stars along with Red Skelton, Ricardo Montalban and the ever-wonderful Betty Garrett, and she gets to sing one of the nicest numbers ever to win the Academy Award for best song, Frank Loesser's catchy *Baby, It's Cold Outside*. The mistaken-identity plot is purely functional, but keep a beady eye out for a rare appearance on screen of the great Mel Blanc, the voice of all the Warner Bros cartoon characters. TS
Esther Williams *Eve Barrett* • Red Skelton *Jack Spratt* • Ricardo Montalban *Jose O'Rourke* • Betty Garrett *Betty Barrett* • Keenan Wynn *Joe Backett* • Xavier Cugat • Mike Mazurki *Mac Mozolla* • Mel Blanc *Julio* ■ *Dir* Edward Buzzell • *Scr* Dorothy Kingsley, Ray Singer, Dick Chevillat

Nerve ★★★ 15

Thriller   2016 · US · Colour · 96min

This neon-bathed thriller follows Vee (Emma Roberts), a teenager who embarks on a series of risky smart-phone games with co-player Ian (Dave Franco). The two of them do well, and rise through the game's ranks. But the moral of the story from co-directors Henry Joost and Ariel Schulman (who made social media exposé *Catfish*) is that by gaining followers they lose control over their lives. Roberts has easy chemistry with Franco, which is key to this fast-moving if never entirely credible film's appeal. SC
Emma Roberts *Vee* • Dave Franco *Ian* • Juliette Lewis *Nancy* ■ *Dir* Henry Joost, Ariel Schulman • *Scr* Jessica Sharzer, from Jeanne Ryan's novel

The Net ★★ U

Spy drama   1953 · UK · BW · 82min

This tepid thriller might have enjoyed more box-office success under its American title, *Project M7*. Although best known for his literary adaptations, director Anthony Asquith was no stranger to suspense movies but he plods through this story about aviation espionage with little enthusiasm. The surprisingly strong cast probably deserved better, and only Herbert Lom manages to give a good account of himself. DP

Phyllis Calvert *Lydia Heathly* • James Donald *Michael Heathly* • Robert Beatty *Sam Seagram* • Herbert Lom *Alex Leon* • Muriel Pavlow *Caroline Cartier* • Noel Willman *Dr Dennis Bord* • Maurice Denham *Carrington* ■ *Dir* Anthony Asquith • *Scr* William Fairchild, from John Pudney's novel

The Net ★★ 12

Thriller   1995 · US · Colour · 109min

Sandra Bullock's star charisma raises this mediocre computer-age paranoia fantasy to the level of watchable entertainment. The *Speed* heroine plays a lonely hacker who uncovers a criminal conspiracy. How she copes with the threat of cyberspace annihilation from an unknown assassin turns an already slow-moving thriller into a predictable game of hide-and-seek. AJ Violence, swearing. **DVD**
Sandra Bullock *Angela Bennett* • Jeremy Northam *Jack Devlin* • Dennis Miller *Dr Alan Champion* • Diane Baker *Mrs Bennett* • Wendy Gazelle *Imposter* • Ken Howard *Bergstrom* • Ray McKinnon *Dale* ■ *Dir* Irwin Winkler • *Scr* John Brancato, Michael Ferris

Network ★★★★ 15

Drama   1976 · US · Colour · 116min

This was a thunderous, strangely eerie swan song for Peter Finch, who plays a bilious and increasingly demented TV anchorman, ranting on air against his powerlessness. It's is a bravura performance from Finch – who was awarded a posthumous Oscar – given full flight by Paddy Chayefsky's daring, sumptuously satirical script, which throws a continuous hail of barbs at the electronic eye. Sidney Lumet directs with wild aplomb, allowing Finch free rein and keeping up a furious pace. Criticised by some at the time for a certain naivety and lack of subtlety, this remains one of the most devastating condemnations of the media's urge to exploit. SH Swearing. **DVD** **SD**
Peter Finch *Howard Beale* • Faye Dunaway *Diana Christensen* • William Holden (2) *Max Schumacher* • Robert Duvall *Frank Hackett* • Wesley Addy *Nelson Chaney* • Ned Beatty *Arthur Jensen* • Beatrice Straight *Louise Schumacher* ■ *Dir* Sidney Lumet • *Scr* Paddy Chayefsky

Nevada ★★ U

Western   1944 · US · BW · 61min

After RKO signed up Robert Mitchum in 1946, it tested his starring potential in a couple of B westerns as a replacement for Tim Holt who was away in the Armed Services. Mitchum is drearily deadpan and uncharismatic as a cowboy who is almost lynched after stumbling across the body of a murdered miner. Between chatting up not one, but two, leading ladies, Anne Jeffreys and Nancy Gates, he exposes the villain out to collar some hidden silver deposits. AE
Bob Mitchum [Robert Mitchum] *Jim "Nevada" Lacy* • Anne Jeffreys *Julie Dexter* • Nancy Gates *Hattie Ide* • Craig Reynolds *Crash Burridge* • Guinn "Big Boy" Williams *Dusty* • Richard Martin (1) *Chito Rafferty* ■ *Dir* Edward Killy • *Scr* Norman Houston, from the novel *Nevada* by Zane Grey

Nevada Smith ★★★ 15

Western   1966 · US · Colour · 125min

An epic western with a fascinating premise – a young man tracks down the outlaws who killed his white father and Indian mother – is suffocated by lethargic direction from veteran Henry Hathaway, though the film is redeemed by Lucien Ballard's lush photography and an outstanding supporting cast. A miscast Steve McQueen brings star presence to a film that was backed by his own production company, Solar, and was a major hit. RS **DVD**
Steve McQueen (1) *Nevada Smith/Max Sand* • Karl Malden *Tom Fitch* • Brian Keith *Jonas Cord* • Arthur Kennedy *Bill Bowdre* • Suzanne Pleshette *Pilar* • Raf Vallone *Father Zaccardi* • Janet Margolin *Neesa* • Pat Hingle *Big Foot* • Howard Da Silva *Warden* • Martin Landau *Jesse Coe* ■ *Dir* Henry Hathaway • *Scr* John Michael Hayes, from characters by Harold Robbins

N

Never a Dull Moment

★★★ **U**

Comedy   1950 · US · BW · 89min

A Manhattan lady songwriter and a widowed farmer meet at a charity show and fall in love. Transplanted to his rustic ranch, she has to cope with her precocious stepdaughters as well as the living conditions, the horses and the local characters. Irene Dunne and Fred MacMurray co-star in this good-natured, sometimes near-farcical romantic comedy. It's a lot of fun and didn't deserve the scathing critical reception it received upon release. **RK**

Irene Dunne *Kay* • Fred MacMurray *Chris* • William Demarest *Mears* • Andy Devine *Orvie* • Gigi Perreau *Tina* • Natalie Wood *Nan* • Philip Ober *Jed* • Jack Kirkwood *Papa Dude* ■ *Dir* George Marshall • *Scr* Lou Breslow, Doris Anderson, from the novel *Who Could Ask for Anything More* by Kay Swift

Never Apologize

★★ **15**

Documentary   2007 · UK · Colour and BW · 111min

Few people worked more closely with Lindsay Anderson than actor Malcolm McDowell. He's the ideal choice, therefore, for this intimate memoir – in the form of a one-man show – that draws on the maverick director's letters and diaries to supplement anecdotes from the sets of *if...* (1968), *O Lucky Man!* (1973) and *Britannia Hospital* (1982) – all of which starred McDowell. Yet, for all the vigour of McDowell the raconteur, Mike Kaplan's record of the performance rather dies a death, with too many jokes failing to elicit suitable amusement from a largely movie-colony crowd. **DP** *DVD*

Malcolm McDowell • Lindsay Anderson ■ *Dir* Mike Kaplan

Never Back Down

★★ **12**

Martial arts action drama   2008 · US · Colour · 108min

Clichés abound in this slick, brutal "slugfest". Jake Tyler (Sean Faris) is struggling to deal with the death of his dad and with fitting in at his new school. Fortunately, salvation is at hand, as coach Roqua (Djimon Hounsou, who deserves better) initiates Jake into mixed martial arts, which combines moves from several disciplines including wrestling, kick-boxing and karate. Fans of the *Karate Kid* series will recognise the basic plot in which a troubled teen is taken under the wing of a martial-arts master. And, like those films, *Never Back Down* pays lip service to such lofty ideals as self-worth and anger management. Basically though, this is just glossy entertainment for lovers of crash-bang-wallop movies. **DA** Violence *DVD*

Sean Faris *Jake Tyler* • Djimon Hounsou *Jean Roqua* • Amber Heard *Baja* • Leslie Hope *Margot* • Cam Gigandet *Ryan McCarthy* • Evan Peters *Max* • Wyatt Smith *Charlie* ■ *Dir* Jeff Wadlow • *Scr* Chris Hauty

Never Been Kissed

★★★ **12**

Romantic comedy   1999 · US · Colour · 107min

Drew Barrymore does what she does best – cute, funny romance – in this simple teen comedy about a bumbling young copy editor who gets a chance to prove herself as a reporter when she's sent under cover to a high school to find out just what sort of nefarious things students get up to nowadays. It also gives her the chance to rewrite her own painful school memories – she was the class nerd. Thanks to Barrymore's captivating performance and a fun turn from David Arquette as her older brother, this is enjoyably sweet fare. **JB**
DVD ⁍

Drew Barrymore *Josie Geller* • David Arquette *Rob Geller* • Michael Vartan *Sam Coulson* • Molly Shannon *Anita* • John C Reilly *Gus* • Garry Marshall *Rigfort* • Leelee Sobieski *Aldys* ■ *Dir* Raja Gosnell • *Scr* Abby Kohn, Marc Silverstein, Jenny Bicks

Never Cry Devil

★★ **18**

Horror   1989 · US · Colour · 87min

Strange that a film boasting Satanists, hookers, ritual butchery and voyeurism should prove such a dull watch. Yet this proves to be the case with Rupert Hitzig's uninspired slant on the boy-who-cried-wolf story. Derek Rydall stars as a school kid given to outrageous lies who witnesses the murder of a neighbourhood prostitute. Police captain Richard Roundtree doesn't believe him, so Rydall turns to retired cop Elliott Gould for help. An awkward blend of thrills and cheap laughs. **RS**

Elliott Gould *Ron Devereaux* • Richard Roundtree *Captain Crane* • Allen Garfield *Zachary Willard* • Michael J Pollard *Stanley Willard* • Derek Rydall *Billy Colton* • Teresa Van Der Woude *Kelly Fremont* • Shannon Tweed *Lisa Grace* ■ *Dir* Rupert Hitzig • *Scr* Randal Viscovich

Never Cry Wolf

★★★ **PG**

Adventure based on a true story 1983 · US · Colour · 100min

After his directorial debut with the superb *Black Stallion*, Carroll Ballard spent two years on location in British Columbia making this captivating adaptation of Farley Mowat's account of his time spent with a pack of wolves. Charles Martin Smith plays Tyler, a young scientist who, with the help of the Inuit who saved his life, not only learns all about the frozen wilderness and its people, but also discovers who is responsible for ravaging the local caribou herds. As you'd expect of Ballard, a cameraman on *Star Wars*, the photography is awesome. **DP** Brief nudity.

Charles Martin Smith *Tyler* • Brian Dennehy *Rosie* • Zachary Ittimangnaq *Ootek* • Samson Jorah *Mike* • Hugh Webster *Drunk* ■ *Dir* Carroll Ballard • *Scr* Curtis Hanson, Sam Hamm, Richard Kletter, Charles Martin Smith, Eugene Corr, Christina Luescher, from the non-fiction book by Farley Mowat

Never Die Alone

★★★ **18**

Crime drama   2004 · US · Colour · 84min

Director Ernest Dickerson gives a hackneyed topic an interesting spin in this gritty gangster thriller based on the novel by career criminal Donald Goines. Centred around a strong performance from rapper DMX, it tells the posthumous story of a drug dealer and all-round brute. Thematically there's nothing new in the cocktail of guns, addiction and crime, but it's the film's stylish execution that makes its mark. The urban *noir* atmosphere as aspiring reporter David Arquette unravels events has a pulpy appeal, while the unusually inventive visuals help offset the plot's predictability. **SF** Violence, swearing, drug abuse. *DVD*

DM X *King David* • David Arquette *Paul* • Michael Ealy *Mike* • Clifton Powell *Moon* • Reagan Gomez-Preston *Juanita* • Jennifer Sky *Janet* • Antwon Tanner *Blue* ■ *Dir* Ernest Dickerson [Ernest R Dickerson] • *Scr* James Gibson, from the novel *Holloway House* by Donald Goines

Never Give a Sucker an Even Break

★★★★ **U**

Comedy   1941 · US · BW · 67min

Although only credited (as Otis Criblecoblis) with devising the story, WC Fields actually scripted his final feature because director Edward Cline felt the rewrite imposed by the Universal front office was abysmal. In addition to being a dart directed at the empty heart of Hollywood, this is also a joyously anarchic assault on the sort of film narrative that Tinseltown held dear. By linking a series of bizarre, unrelated incidents and by blurring the line between reality and fantasy, Fields was way ahead of his time. A blistering parting gesture to an industry that failed to appreciate his genius. **DP** *DVD*

WC Fields *The Great Man, WC "Uncle Bill" Fields* • Gloria Jean *His niece, Gloria Jean* • Leon Errol *His rival, Leon Errol* • Butch [Billy Lenhart] *Heckler* • Buddy [Kenneth Brown] *Heckler* • Margaret Dumont *Mrs Hemogloben* • Susan Miller *Ouliotta Hemogloben* • Franklin Pangborn *Producer, Franklin Pangborn* • Mona Barrie *Producer's wife* • Anne Nagel *Madame*

Gorgeous ■ *Dir* Edward Cline • *Scr* John T Neville, Prescott Chaplin, from a story by Otis Criblecoblis [WC Fields]

Never Let Go

★ **PG**

Crime drama   1960 · UK · BW · 87min

What was intended to be a gritty insight into the brutality of the underworld ends up being a tatty melodrama in this misfire from director John Guillermin. Peter Sellers is cast against type as the leader of a stolen car racket, whose ruthless methods prompt victim Richard Todd and street punk Adam Faith to forge an unlikely alliance against him. Alun Falconer's script does nobody any favours, with Sellers reduced to embarrassing histrionics in the bid to shed his comic image. **DP** *DVD*

Richard Todd *John Cummings* • Peter Sellers *Lionel Meadows* • Elizabeth Sellars *Anne Cummings* • Adam Faith *Tommy Towers* • Carol White *Jackie* • Mervyn Johns *Alfie Barnes* • Peter Jones *Alec Berger* • John Le Mesurier *Pennington* ■ *Dir* John Guillermin • *Scr* Alun Falconer, from a story by John Guillermin, Peter De Sarigny

Never Let Me Go

★★★ **U**

Romantic adventure   1953 · US/UK · BW · 93min

An American news reporter in Russia falls in love with a ballerina and marries her, only for him to be deported by the authorities. A middle-aged Clark Gable and the glamorous Gene Tierney are the stars in this love story, which turns into a rescue drama halfway through. Directed by Delmer Daves, it was made by MGM's British arm, which explains the presence of Kenneth More, Bernard Miles and Frederick Valk in the cast. No surprises, but respectably escapist. **RK**

Clark Gable *Philip Sutherland* • Gene Tierney *Marya Lamarkina* • Richard Haydn *Christopher Wellington St John Denny* • Bernard Miles *Joe Brooks* • Belita *Valentina Alexandrovna* • Kenneth More *Steve Quillan* • Karel Stepanek *Commissar* • Theodore Bikel *Lieutenant* • Frederick Valk *Kuragin* ■ *Dir* Delmer Daves • *Scr* Ronald Millar, George Froeschel, from the novel *Came the Dawn* by Roger Bax

Never Let Me Go

★★★ **12**

Romantic science-fiction drama 2010 · UK/US · Colour · 99min

Mark Romanek (*One Hour Photo*) opens his third feature film in a boarding school for children, who are obviously in some way different. Onto this framework is grafted a doomed three-way romance, involving Carey Mulligan, Andrew Garfield and Keira Knightley. Most stories where the lives of individuals or society in general are controlled by draconian laws, major scientific advances or powerful but generally unseen rulers – from *1984* and *Fahrenheit 451* to *Logan's Run* and *Zardoz* – lead almost inevitably to some sort of act of rebellion, but the notion of revolt is oddly lacking here. Maybe that is the point. But while the film has powerful individual scenes and the performances of Mulligan and Garfield convey the anguish of their plight, the work as a whole remains curiously uninvolving. **BP** Sex scenes, nudity. *DVD* ⁍

Carey Mulligan *Kathy* • Keira Knightley *Ruth* • Andrew Garfield *Tommy* • Sally Hawkins *Miss Lucy* • Charlotte Rampling *Miss Emily* ■ *Dir* Mark Romanek • *Scr* Alex Garland, from the novel by Kazuo Ishiguro • *Cinematographer* Adam Kimmel

Never on Sunday

★★★ **PG**

Comedy drama   1960 · Gr · BW · 98min

Melina Mercouri won the best actress prize at Cannes for her boisterous performance in this rarified romp that owes more than a little to the Pygmalion myth. As the waterfront prostitute who receives a cultural crash course from a besotted American professor, she gleefully casts restraint to the winds, much to the approval of her director, co-star and future husband, Jules Dassin. Although Dassin successfully soaks up the local atmosphere, his script too often errs on the side of laboured bons mots and intellectual snobbery. Manos Hadjidakis's bouzouki music is an acquired

taste, but his theme song landed him an Oscar. **DP** *DVD*

Melina Mercouri *Ilya* • Jules Dassin *Homer* • George Foundas *Tonio* • Titos Vandis *Jorgo* ■ *Dir/Scr* Jules Dassin

Never Say Die

★★ **U**

Comedy   1939 · US · BW · 75min

This is a lesser effort for Bob Hope, playing an eccentric millionaire who, believing he has only weeks to live, marries Martha Raye so that she can inherit his money. Though the script (co-written by Preston Sturges) has its fair share of gags, too much of the film is silly and Raye tries to compensate with a surfeit of mugging. Alan Mowbray provides some of the best moments with his droll underplaying of a disagreeable prince. **TV**

Martha Raye *Mickey Hawkins* • Bob Hope *John Kidley* • Andy Devine *Henry Munch* • Alan Mowbray *Prince Smirnov* • Gale Sondergaard *Juno* • Sig Rumann [Sig Ruman] *Poppa Ingleborg* • Ernest Cossart *Jeepers* • Paul Harvey *Jasper Hawkins* ■ *Dir* Elliott Nugent • *Scr* Don Hartman, Frank Butler, Preston Sturges, from a play by William H Post

Never Say Goodbye

★★

Romantic comedy   1946 · US · BW · 97min

The small daughter (Patti Brady) of a devil-may-care commercial artist (Errol Flynn) and a Park Avenue mother (Eleanor Parker) must live alternately with each of her recently divorced parents who, of course, still really love each other. Directed by James V Kern, this romantic comedy, while admittedly a collection of recycled clichés devoid of substance and populated by stereotypes, is nonetheless an entertainingly breezy affair. **RK**

Errol Flynn *Phil Gayley* • Eleanor Parker *Ellen Gayley* • Lucile Watson *Mrs Hamilton* • SZ "Cuddles" Sakall [SZ Sakall] *Luigi* • Forrest Tucker *Fenwick Lonkowski* • Donald Woods *Rex DeVallon* • Hattie McDaniel *Cozy* • Patti Brady *Phillippa "Flip" Gayley* ■ *Dir* James V Kern • *Scr* James V Kern, IAL Diamond, Lewis R Foster, from the story *Don't Ever Leave Me* by Ben Barzman, Norma Barzman

Never Say Goodbye

★★ **U**

Romantic drama   1955 · US · Colour · 95min

American doctor Rock Hudson marries Cornell Borchers in Europe, but later walks out on her, taking their small daughter with him. Reconciliation is prevented by her incarceration in a Russian labour camp, but he runs into her ten years later in America. A shameless attempt by Universal to recycle the hit formula of their five-handkerchief weepie *Magnificent Obsession*, right down to Hudson operating on Borchers after she is hit by a truck in Chicago! The result is a cornucopia of wilted clichés. **RK**

Rock Hudson *Dr Michael Parker* • Cornell Borchers *Lisa Gosting/Dorian Kent* • George Sanders *Victor* • Ray Collins *Dr Bailey* • David Janssen *Dave* • Shelley Fabares *Suzy Parker* ■ *Dir* Jerry Hopper, Douglas Sirk • *Scr* Charles Hoffman, from the film *This Love of Ours* by Bruce Manning, John Klorer, Leonard Lee, from the play *Come Prima Meglio di Prima* by Luigi Pirandello

Never Say Never Again

★★★ **PG**

Spy adventure   1983 · UK · Colour · 128min

By the time this movie was released the Bond franchise had become steeped in self-parody, aided hugely by the smirking frivolity of Roger Moore, and it was down to Sean Connery, returning to the role after 12 years, to balance the comic hysteria with action-man authenticity. Connery, ever-aware that he's at the centre of a big, expensive joke, still makes you believe that he's heroic to the core. His well-groomed presence holds the screen with ease and he's flanked here by three charismatic ne'er-do-wells, Klaus Maria Brandauer, Max von Sydow and Barbara Carrera. The plot, which owes much to *Thunderball*, lurches at times. **JM** *DVD* ⁍

Sean Connery *James Bond* • Klaus Maria Brandauer *Largo* • Max von Sydow *Blofeld* • Barbara Carrera *Fatima Blush* • Kim Basinger *Domino* • Bernie Casey *Felix Leiter* • Alec McCowen *"Q"/Algy* • Edward Fox *"M"* • Pamela Salem *Miss Moneypenny* ■ *Dir* Irvin Kershner • *Scr* Lorenzo Semple Jr, from a story by Kevin McClory, Jack Whittingham, Ian Fleming

Never So Few ★★PG
Second World War drama
1959 · US · Colour · 116min

This MGM drama about wartime activity in Burma is notable mainly for its use of Ceylon locations. But the discussion of key moral issues is quickly discarded for the sake of a hot romance between Frank Sinatra and Gina Lollobrigida. Today, this film is a fascinating relic of a studio in decline. The story is undimmed by the star casting of Sinatra, who had yet to acquire the image that would undermine his credibility in such roles forever. TS **DVD**

Frank Sinatra *Captain Tom C Reynolds* • Gina Lollobrigida *Carla Vesari* • Peter Lawford *Captain Grey Travis* • Steve McQueen (1) *Bill Ringa* • Richard Johnson *Captain Danny de Mortimer* • Paul Henreid *Nikko Regas* • Brian Donlevy *General Sloane* • Dean Jones *Sergeant Jim Norby* • Charles Bronson *Sergeant John Danforth* ■ *Dir* John Sturges • *Scr* Millard Kaufman, from the novel by Tom T Chamales

Never Steal Anything Small ★★★★
Musical crime drama 1959 · US · Colour · 94min

This terrific semi-musical starring James Cagney is based on a play about trade unionism that never made it to Broadway. It's colourful and funny stuff, classily shot in CinemaScope and with some knockout production numbers, especially from moll Cara Williams. Cagney shines throughout, though, in truth, he's a mite old for the role. Shirley Jones is just a little too sweet to be Cagney's other half, but there's super character work from the likes of Nehemiah Persoff and Royal Dano. TS

James Cagney *Jake MacIllaney* • Shirley Jones *Linda Cabot* • Roger Smith *Dan Cabot* • Cara Williams *Winnipeg* • Nehemiah Persoff *Pinelli* • Royal Dano *Words Cannon* • Anthony Caruso *Lieutenant Tevis* • Horace McMahon *OK Merritt* ■ *Dir* Charles Lederer • *Scr* Charles Lederer, from the play *The Devil's Hornpipe* by Maxwell Anderson, Rouben Mamoulian

Never Take No for an Answer ★★★U
Drama 1951 · UK/It · BW · 83min

Awash with sentimentality, yet rejoicing in the innocence and faith of its young hero, Paul Gallico's novel, *The Small Miracle*, is given a light coating of neorealism by its joint directors Maurice Cloche and Ralph Smart. As Peppino, the seven-year-old war orphan convinced that his ailing donkey will be cured if they visit the tomb of St Francis, the patron saint of animals, Vittorio Manunta is miraculously natural. DP

Vittorio Manunta *Peppino* • Denis O'Dea *Father Damico* • Guido Celano *Strotti* • Nerio Bernardi *Father Superior* ■ *Dir* Maurice Cloche, Ralph Smart • *Scr* Paul Gallico, Pauline Gallico, Maurice Cloche, Ralph Smart, from the novella *The Small Miracle* by Paul Gallico

Never Take Sweets from a Stranger ★★★
Drama 1960 · UK · BW · 91min

An extremely audacious film for its time, this deals with the problem of paedophilia and builds towards a surprisingly grim and disturbing climax. The story concerns an English family who emigrate to a small town in Canada. The father, Patrick Allen, takes up the post of headmaster at a school, but then his nine-year-old daughter is sexually abused by a local bigwig, played by Felix Aylmer. It's made by Hammer Films, so the movie walks a tightrope between seriousness and sensation. AT

Gwen Watford *Sally Carter* • Patrick Allen *Peter Carter* • Felix Aylmer *Clarence Olderberry Sr* • Niall MacGinnis *Defense counsel* • Alison Leggatt *Martha* • Bill Nagy *Clarence Olderberry Jr* ■ *Dir* Cyril Frankel • *Scr* John Hunter, from the play *The Pony Cart* by Roger Garis

Never Too Late ★★★
Comedy 1965 · US · Colour · 103min

Adapting his own Broadway hit, Sumner Arthur Long succeeds better than most in opening out a play for the big screen. He's helped in no small measure by Paul Ford and Maureen O'Sullivan, who expertly reprise their stage roles as the not exactly youthful couple whose ordered existence is thrown into turmoil by an unexpected pregnancy. Less effective, however, are Connie Stevens and Jim Hutton as their self-obsessed daughter and son-in-law, who milk the gags their elders time to perfection. DP

Paul Ford *Harry Lambert* • Maureen O'Sullivan *Edith Lambert* • Connie Stevens *Kate Clinton* • Jim Hutton *Charlie Clinton* • Jane Wyatt *Grace Kimbrough* • Henry Jones *Doctor Kimbrough* ■ *Dir* Bud Yorkin • *Scr* Sumner Arthur Long, from his play

Never Too Late ★PG
Comedy drama 1996 · Can · Colour · 92min

This takes the talents of Olympia Dukakis, Cloris Leachman and Jan Rubes, then buries their performances under a pile of bizarre plot twists and uneven farce. All you need to know is that the old folks include a manic depressive and a paraplegic lesbian, Corey Haim brings S&M to the proceedings and Matt Craven overacts to the point of absurdity as the retirement home's suspicious manager. Terrible stuff. JB

Olympia Dukakis *Rose* • Cloris Leachman *Olive* • Jan Rubes *Joseph* • Jean Lapointe *Woody* • Corey Haim *Max* • Matt Craven *Carl O'Neal* ■ *Dir* Giles Walker • *Scr* Donald Martin

Never Too Young to Rock ★★U
Musical 1975 · UK · Colour · 101min

This crucial guide to mid-1970s glam rock features the tinsel tonsils of the Rubettes, Mud and the Glitter Band. Heart-throb Peter Noone (of Herman's Hermits) bridges the generation gap in the daftest plot imaginable. But the whole point to this sequined extravaganza is hearing such jukebox jives as *Angel Face*, *Tiger Feet* and the classic *Sugar Baby Love* again. AJ

Peter Denyer *Hero* • Freddie Jones *Mr Rockbottom* • Sheila Steafel *Café proprietress* • Joe Lynch *Russian soldier* • John Clive *Bandsman* • Peter Noone *Army captain* ■ *Dir* Dennis Abey • *Scr* Ron Inkpen, Dennis Abey

Never Wave at a WAC ★★★
Comedy 1952 · US · BW · 87min

In this delightful, light-hearted farce, a divorced Washington hostess joins the Women's Army Corps in order to get to Paris and meet her boyfriend. Rosalind Russell has fun playing the unworldly heroine – when she goes to sign up, she takes her secretary with her to fill in the forms – and when not in uniform she wears a succession of eye-catching James Galanos gowns. When the script flags, the top-flight cast keeps things bubbling. TV

Rosalind Russell *Jo McBain* • Paul Douglas *Andrew McBain* • Marie Wilson *Clara Schneiderman* • William Ching *Lt Col Schuyler Fairchild* • Leif Erickson *Sgt Noisy Jackson* • Arleen Whelan *Sgt Toni Wayne* • Charles Dingle *Senator Tom Reynolds* • Lurene Tuttle *Capt Murchison* ■ *Dir* Norman Z McLeod • *Scr* Ken Englund, from the story *The Private Wore Skirts* by Frederick Kohner, Fred Brady

The NeverEnding Story ★★★★U
Fantasy adventure 1984 · W Ger · Colour · 91min

German director Wolfgang Petersen is now perhaps best known for action-packed blockbusters, but in his first English-language movie he proves to be equally at home in the world of fantasy. Barret Oliver plays the young boy drawn by a magical book into a wondrous alternative world that is threatened by evil forces. The story is a touch simplistic, but Petersen's direction is assured and children will be dazzled by the imaginative effects and stunning sets. JF **DVD Blu**

Noah Hathaway *Atreyu* • Barret Oliver *Bastian* • Tami Stronach *Childlike empress* • Moses Gunn *Cairon* • Patricia Hayes *Urgl* • Gerald McRaney *Bastian's father* • Thomas Hill *Koreander* ■ *Dir* Wolfgang Petersen • *Scr* Wolfgang Petersen, Herman Weigel, from the novel by Michael Ende

The NeverEnding Story II: the Next Chapter ★★U
Fantasy adventure 1991 · Ger/US · Colour · 85min

Bastian returns (albeit in a different guise) for another adventure in the imaginary land of Fantasia in this frankly disappointing sequel. Australian director George Miller (not the *Mad Max* one) assumes the storyteller's chair only to find that, for all its empresses, towers and enchanted creatures, he's been given a dull tale to relate. He does what he can with some engaging special effects, but Jonathan Brandis is too feeble a hero to get excited about. DP

Jonathan Brandis *Bastian* • Kenny Morrison *Atreyu* • Clarissa Burt *Xayide* • Alexandra Johnes *Childlike empress* • Martin Umbach *Nimbly* • John Wesley Shipp *Barney Boy* ■ *Dir* George Miller (1) • *Scr* Karin Howard, from the novel *The NeverEnding Story* by Michael Ende

The NeverEnding Story III ★★U
Fantasy adventure 1994 · Ger · Colour · 91min

By now, the *NeverEnding Story* franchise was, well, heading towards an end. This one is more firmly anchored in real life, possibly to its detriment, with young Bastian being badly bullied at school by a bunch of no-gooders called the "Nasties". His only sanctuary is the library where he can escape to the world of Fantasia via the storybook. JF

Jason James Richter *Bastian Bux* • Melody Kay Nicole • Freddie Jones *Mr Coreander/Old Man of Wandering Mountain* • Jack Black *Slip* • Ryan Bollman *Dog* • Carole Finn *Mookie* ■ *Dir* Peter MacDonald • *Scr* Jeff Lieberman, from a story by Karin Howard, from characters by Michael Ende

The New Adventures of Pinocchio ★★PG
Fantasy adventure 1999 · US/Lux · Colour · 84min

Veteran director Michael Anderson may seem an odd choice to handle this special effects-laden fairy tale. But he invests the "sequel" to Carlo Collodi's classic story with a certain old-fashioned charm. Now a real 12-year-old boy, Gabriel Thompson is transformed back into a puppet after drinking a potion given to him by a carnival crone, who turns out to be sinister puppeteer Udo Kier. Technically, it's quietly impressive. If only the same could be said for the song-and-dance routines. DP **DVD**

Martin Landau *Geppetto* • Udo Kier *Mme Flambeau/Lorenzini* • Gabriel Thompson *Pinocchio* • Gemma Gregory *Blue Fairy* • Warwick Davis *Dwarf* ■ *Dir* Michael Anderson • *Scr* Sherry Mills, Tom Sheppard, from characters by Carlo Collodi

The New Adventures of Pippi Longstocking ★U
Adventure 1988 · US · Colour · 96min

There was absolutely no point whatsoever in Americanising the popular creation of Swedish children's novelist Astrid Lindgren, whose character had already featured in several home-grown film versions. Despite a much publicised quest to find a new Pippi, this new movie barely saw the light of day. Leaden and unwatchable. TS

Tami Erin *Pippi Longstocking* • David Seaman Jr *Tommy* • Cory Crow *Annika* • Eileen Brennan *Miss Bannister* • Dennis Dugan *Mr Settigren* • Dianne Hull *Mrs Settigren* ■ *Dir* Ken Annakin • *Scr* Ken Annakin, from the books by Astrid Lindgren

The New Adventures of Tarzan ★★★PG
Adventure 1935 · US · BW · 70min

The jungle swinger from Edgar Rice Burroughs's famous yarns goes to Guatemala to rescue an old friend and encounters a dangerous cult religion. Also known as *Tarzan and the Lost Goddess*, this B-picture was originally a Saturday matinée serial, but was later released as a feature. It lacks sophistication, but is still mildly compelling. Tarzan is played by Herman Brix, who later changed his name to Bruce Bennett. TH

Herman Brix [Bruce Bennett] *Tarzan* • Frank Baker (1) *Major Martling, archaeologist* • Dale Walsh *Alice Martling* • Harry Ernest *Gordon Hamilton* • Lewis Sargent *George* • Ula Holt *Ula Vale* • Don Castello *Raglan* ■ *Dir* Edward Kull, WF McGaugh • *Scr* Edwin Blum, Charles Francis Royal, from the novels by Edgar Rice Burroughs

The New Age ★★18
Satire 1994 · US · Colour · 107min

Since arriving in Hollywood from Australia in the early 1990s, Judy Davis has all too rarely been given the chance to show what she can do. Given that it was written and directed by *The Player* screenwriter Michael Tolkin, this should have been the perfect vehicle – an LA couple's yuppie lifestyle takes a turn for the worse, ushering the pair in to running their own upmarket fashion boutique. Tolkin infuriatingly misses the target. Davis and *RoboCop* star Peter Weller are splendid as the downwardly spiralling husband and wife, but what should have been a savage satire emerges merely as a collection of clever ideas gone sadly awry. DP

Peter Weller *Peter Witner* • Judy Davis *Katherine Witner* • Patrick Bauchau *Jean Levy* • Rachel Rosenthal *Sarah Friedberg* • Adam West *Jeff Winter* • Paula Marshall *Alison Gale* ■ *Dir/Scr* Michael Tolkin

The New Babylon ★★★U
Silent political drama 1929 · USSR · BW · 76min

Babylon is a fashionable Paris department store where salesgirl Elena Kuzmina works for the capitalist bourgeoisie. A significant silent film from the influential Soviet partnership of Grigori Kozintsev and Leonid Trauberg, this utilises the montage techniques that characterised the films of Eisenstein. Satirical, cynical and inventive, the film is also episodic and emblematic – capitalists are cowardly and greedy, the workers patriotic and brave – as it observes the devastating effects of the Franco-Prussian war through a Marxist/Stalinist eye. RK

Elena Kuzmina *Louise Poirier* • Pyotr Sobolevsky *Jean, a soldier* • David Gutman *Grasselin* • Sophie Magarill *An actress* • Sergei Gerasimov *Lutro, journalist* ■ *Dir/Scr* Grigori Kozintsev, Leonid Trauberg

The New Centurions ★★★★15
Police drama 1972 · US · Colour · 98min

Virtually dismissed on release, this cracking crime drama is violent and humorous by turns and superbly directed by the estimable Richard Fleischer from a top-notch screenplay by Stirling Silliphant. The real star of the movie, despite competition from a high-calibre cast, is cop-turned-author Joseph Wambaugh, whose own police experiences form the basis of the movie. Many of the cast went on to play similar roles in TV series; this one, though, is the real thing, with star George C Scott particularly outstanding. TS

George C Scott *Sergeant Kilvinsky* • Stacy Keach *Roy Fehler* • Jane Alexander *Dorothy Fehler* • Scott Wilson *Gus* • Rosalind Cash *Lorrie* • Erik Estrada *Sergio* • Clifton James *Whitey* • Richard Kalk *Milton* • James Sikking [James B Sikking] *Sergeant Anders* ■ *Dir* Richard Fleischer • *Scr* Stirling Silliphant, from the novel by Joseph Wambaugh

The New Daughter ★★15
Horror thriller 2009 · US · Colour · 103min

Kevin Costner makes a rare foray into horror territory, playing a single father in a new town who finds himself up against the unknown when a paranormal entity threatens to consume his teenage daughter. Director Luis Berdejo ticks off several worn-out clichés (a haunted house, creepy dolls, even creepier children) and while he brings a lingering sense of

foreboding to the action, it moves at a pace that leaves you begging for urgency. **JL**
DVD *BL*

Kevin Costner *John James* • Ivana Baquero *Louisa James* • Gattlin Griffith *Sam James* • Samantha Mathis *Cassandra Parker* • Noah Taylor *Professor Evan White* ■ *Dir* Luis Berdejo • *Scr* John Travis, from a short story by John Connolly

New Faces ★★★

Musical comedy revue
1954 · US · Colour · 98min

No attempt was made to open out this hit-and-miss filmed record of the popular Broadway revue, and CinemaScope only enhanced the feeling of a proscenium arch. Yet it's interesting to see a cast of talented newcomers headed by Eartha Kitt, who sings (or rather purrs) five wittily sexy songs. Comedienne Alice Ghostley has an ironic number called *Boston Beguine*, while Carol Lawrence sings and dances. **RB**

Ronny Graham • Eartha Kitt • Robert Clary • Carol Lawrence • Alice Ghostley • June Carroll • Paul Lynde ■ *Dir* Harry Horner • *Scr* Melvin Brooks [Mel Brooks], Ronny Graham, Paul Lynde, Luther Davis, John Cleveland, from the revue *New Faces of 1952* by Leonard Sillman

New Faces of 1937 ★★🅄

Musical 1937 · US · BW · 98min

A theatrical producer sells 85 per cent of a show to four backers, then tries to make sure it's a flop so he can pocket the surplus. Yes, it's the plot of *The Producers* some 30 years earlier, though this version lacks both the wit and the flair of the Mel Brooks classic, with even the great Milton Berle straining to compensate for poor material. An undistinguished score is no help, but musical fans will find it watchable for the variety acts. **TV**

Joe Penner *Seymore Semor* • Milton Berle *Wellington Wedge* • Parkyakarkus *Parky* • Harriet Hilliard [Harriet Nelson] *Patricia* • William Brady *Jimmy* • Jerome Cowan *Robert Hunt* • Thelma Leeds *Elaine* • Lorraine Krueger *Suzy* • Ann Miller ■ *Dir* Leigh Jason • *Scr* Nat Perrin, Philip G Epstein, Irving S Brecher, Harold Kusell, Harry Clork, Howard J Green, David Freedman, from the story *Shoestring* by George Bradshaw

The New Girlfriend ★★★🅂

Drama 2014 · Fr · Colour · 103min

In this quirky tale of love and attraction from director François Ozon, Claire (Anaïs Demoustier) promises to look after her dead best friend's husband David (Romain Duris) and their daughter. But those caring feelings are soon challenged when she discovers David has a cross-dressing alter ego. Loosely based on a Ruth Rendell story, this colourful, Almodóvar-like tale could be judged fluffy and fun by some, or irritating and ridiculous by others. But Ozon unashamedly sails straight into the incredible, with fantasies and twists to at least keep us guessing. **KK** French +subtitles. *DVD*

Romain Duris *David/Virginia* • Anaïs Demoustier *Claire* • Raphaël Personnaz *Gilles* • Isild Le Besco *Laura* ■ *Dir* François Ozon • *Scr* François Ozon, from the short story *The New Girlfriend* by Ruth Rendell

The New Gulliver ★★★★

Puppet fantasy 1935 · USSR · BW · 85min

Russian special effects expert Alexander Ptushko chose Jonathan Swift's satire *Gulliver's Travels* as the basis for the world's first feature-length puppet film. The laborious process - it took Ptushko almost three years to complete - also made it one of the last of the genre. Effective use is made of tiny, grotesque wax puppets, created in conjunction with an actor playing Gulliver, while the tale itself was adapted to fit the Soviet ideology of the time. **RB** Russian +subtitles.

Vladimir Konstantinov *Gulliver* ■ *Dir* Alexander Ptushko • *Scr* Alexander Ptushko, Grigori Roshal, from the novel *Gulliver's Travels* by Jonathan Swift • *Puppet Maker* Sarra Mokil

The New Guy ★🔟

Comedy 2002 · US · Colour · 84min

Directed by *There's Something about Mary* co-writer Ed Decter, this excruciating teen comedy is a formulaic jumble of crass visual gags, limp dialogue and social stereotyping. DJ Qualls plays drippy senior Dizzy, who reinvents himself as the epitome of high-school cool and, of course, gets the hottest girl (Eliza Dushku) with the assistance of a black convict with attitude. It's blatantly unfunny and infuriatingly repetitious, underscoring its faults with a saccharine ending that patronisingly proclaims "it's OK to be an outcast". **SF** *DVD*

DJ Qualls *Dizzy Gillespie Harrison/Gil Harris* • Eliza Dushku *Danielle* • Zooey Deschanel *Nora* • Lyle Lovett *Bear* • Jerod Mixon *Kirk* • Illeana Douglas *Kiki Pierce* ■ *Dir* Ed Decter • *Scr* David Kendall

New in Town ★🔟

Romantic comedy
2008 · US/Can · Colour · 92min

Even Renée Zellweger in full-on perky mode can't save this terminally unappealing romantic comedy. She plays a high-powered corporate executive who's dispatched from Miami to deepest Minnesota with instructions to downsize a newly acquired dairy-products factory. Naturally, she finds the general tweeness of the place jarring at first, but it's not long before she warms to the hardy locals' homespun ways - and especially pick-up driving, beer-drinkin', plaid-wearin' widower Harry Connick Jr. It may adhere to a well-worn formula, but the yawning lack of wit, inspiration or emotional engagement here is so pronounced it's quite startling. **TJ** *DVD* *BL*

Renée Zellweger *Lucy Hill* • Harry Connick Jr *Ted Mitchell* • JK Simmons *Stu Kopenhafer* • Siobhan Fallon Hogan [Siobhan Fallon] *Blanche Gunderson* • Mike O'Brien *Lars Ulstead* • Frances Conroy *Trudy Van Uuden* ■ *Dir* Jonas Elmer • *Scr* Kenneth [Ken] Rance, C Jay Cox

New Jack City ★★★★🔞

Action drama 1991 · US · Colour · 96min

Mario Van Peebles made his directorial debut with this hard-hitting mix of crime thriller and social drama, which is as indebted to the urban realism of Spike Lee as it is to gangster movies such as Brian De Palma's *Scarface*. Based on actual events, the film suggests that the problems facing black inner-city kids are often as much caused by exploitative drugs barons as they are by racial discrimination. Wesley Snipes achieves a chilling mix of arrogance and malevolence as a ruthless drugs lord, while Van Peebles and fellow cops Ice-T and Judd Nelson successfully convey a sense of crusade rather than mere law enforcement. **DP** Swearing, violence, sex scenes. *DVD*

Wesley Snipes *Nino Brown* • Ice-T *Scotty Appleton* • Allen Payne *Gee Money* • Chris Rock *Pookie* • Mario Van Peebles *Detective Stone* • Michele Michele *Selina* • Bill Nunn *Duh Duh Duh Man* • Judd Nelson *Officer Nick Peretti* ■ *Dir* Mario Van Peebles • *Scr* Barry Michael Cooper, Thomas Lee Wright, from a story by Thomas Lee Wright

A New Kind of Love ★★

Comedy 1963 · US · Colour · 110min

Paul Newman has had his moments as a screen comedian, but this is not one of them. In this undistinguished battle of the sexes, he plays a struggling writer who makes his name penning a newspaper column based on the romantic exploits of a smart Parisienne, unaware that she is the tomboy fashion designer he met on the plane. While not in the screwball class of a Katharine Hepburn, Joanne Woodward is nevertheless highly engaging as both the dippy career girl and the fibbing socialite. **DP**

Paul Newman *Steve Sherman* • Joanne Woodward *Samantha Blake* • Thelma Ritter *Lena O'Connor* • Eva Gabor *Felicianne Courbeau* • George Tobias *Joseph Bergner* ■ *Dir/Scr* Melville Shavelson

The New Land ★★★★

Adventure drama 1972 · Swe · Colour · 160min

Having survived the perilous passage depicted in *The Emigrants*, Swedish farmer Max von Sydow and his wife, Liv Ullmann, endeavour to make their mark upon the unrelenting plains of Minnesota in this concluding part of Jan Troell's epic adaptation of Vilhelm Moberg's literary saga. As before, Troell's refusal to romanticise either the landscape or the daily grind heightens the authenticity of the struggle, as well as its dramatic intensity. Von Sydow is superb as he tries to comprehend both his kinsmen's lust for gold and the complex politics that will plunge his adopted nation into civil war. **DP** Swedish +subtitles. *DVD* *BL*

Max von Sydow *Karl Oskar* • Liv Ullmann *Kristina* • Eddie Axberg *Robert* • Hans Alfredson *Jonas Petter* • Halvar Bjork *Anders Mansson* • Allan Edwall *Danjel* ■ *Dir* Jan Troell • *Scr* Bengt Forslund, Jan Troell, from the novel *The Emigrants* by Vilhelm Moberg

A New Leaf ★★★★🅄

Black comedy 1971 · US · Colour · 101min

In a sophisticated, cynical black comedy from writer/director/star Elaine May, middle-aged playboy Walter Matthau who, lacking the resources to sustain his extravagant lifestyle, decides to marry wealthy wallflower Elaine May to keep himself in the luxury to which he's accustomed. Matthau intends to bump his new bride off, only to find himself afflicted by a guilty conscience. This is a wonderfully mordant Manhattan fairy tale. **TH** *DVD* *BL*

Walter Matthau *Henry Graham* • Elaine May *Henrietta Lowell* • Jack Weston *Andrew McPherson* • George Rose *Harold* • James Coco *Uncle Harry* • Doris Roberts *Mrs Traggert* • Renee Taylor *Sharon Hart* • William Redfield *Beckett* ■ *Dir* Elaine May • *Scr* Elaine May, from the short story *The Green Heart* by Jack Ritchie

A New Life ★★★🔟

Comedy drama 1988 · US · Colour · 99min

Alan Alda, still trying to break free from his *MASH* TV image, here takes control of his career by writing and directing, as well as starring in, this comedy drama. He and his screen wife Ann-Margret divorce after more than 20 years, leaving Alda to drink and wisecrack his way through a series of one-night stands before both he and Ann-Margret start up relationships with younger people (Veronica Hamel and John Shea). It's all sub-Woody Allen stuff, but the performances are amiable. **JB** Swearing.

Alan Alda *Steve Giardino* • Ann-Margret *Jackie Giardino* • Hal Linden *Mel Arons* • Veronica Hamel *Dr Kay Hutton* • John Shea *Doc* • Mary Kay Place *Donna* ■ *Dir/Scr* Alan Alda

New Moon ★★★🅄

Musical 1940 · US · BW · 104min

A splendid and popular Jeanette MacDonald/Nelson Eddy version of Sigmund Romberg's operetta, which was filmed a decade earlier with Metropolitan Opera stars Grace Moore and Lawrence Tibbett. MGM changed the setting from pre-revolutionary Russia to a very anti-British New Orleans, but it makes no difference. The terrific score includes *Softly as in a Morning Sunrise*, *Lover Come Back* and *One Kiss*, all with marvellous Oscar Hammerstein lyrics. **TS**

Jeanette MacDonald *Marianne de Beaumanoir* • Nelson Eddy *Charles Mission/Duc de Villiers* • Mary Boland *Valerie de Rossac* • George Zucco *Vicomte de Ribaud* • HB Warner *Father Michel* • Richard Purcell [Dick Purcell] *Alexander* • Stanley Fields *Tambour* • Bunty Cutler *Julie the maid* ■ *Dir* Robert Z Leonard • *Scr* Jacques Deval, Robert Arthur, from the operetta by Sigmund Romberg, Oscar Hammerstein II, Frank Mandel, Lawrence Schwab

New Moon ★★🔟

Romantic horror fantasy
2009 · US · Colour · 125min

The second instalment of the hugely successful *Twilight* series sees heroine Bella (Kristen Stewart) in a deep funk, which

unfortunately sets the tone for the entire film. Her vampire beau Edward (Robert Pattinson) must leave town, and in his absence Bella begins riding motorbikes, but only because the danger allows her to see visions of her love - which is just as well for Pattinson's army of fans. Taylor Lautner makes for a bland substitute as Jacob, Bella's hunky rebound guy, who also happens to be a werewolf. The bike stunts and werewolf-versus-vampire scenes only drag out the wait until Edward reappears, along with a camp Michael Sheen as the vampire overlord who decides their fate. *Eclipse* followed, and a further instalment, *Breaking Dawn*, is being released in two parts in 2011 and 2012. **SP** Violence. *DVD* *BL*

Kristen Stewart *Bella Swan* • Robert Pattinson *Edward Cullen* • Taylor Lautner *Jacob Black* • Ashley Greene *Alice Cullen* • Rachelle Lefevre *Victoria* • Billy Burke *Charlie Swan* • Peter Facinelli *Dr Carlisle Cullen* • Nikki Reed *Rosalie Hale* ■ *Dir* Chris Weitz • *Scr* Melissa Rosenberg, from the novel by Stephenie Meyer

New Police Story ★★★🔢

Crime action thriller
2004 · HK/Chi · Colour · 117min

Technically, this isn't a sequel to Jackie Chan's original *Police Story* movies, but it still counts as a satisfactory return to his Hong Kong roots. He plays a veteran cop who descends into alcoholic self-pity after his unit is wiped out by some extreme-sports-loving, hi-tech thieves. However, a persistent young man (Nicholas Tse) posing as his new partner eventually raises him from his stupor and together they set out to track down the gang. At times, this thriller may be a little too melodramatic for its own good, but after the lightweight fluff Chan gets stuck with in Hollywood, that actually makes a pleasant change. **JF** Cantonese, Mandarin, English +subtitles. *DVD*

Jackie Chan *Chan Kwok-Wing* • Nicholas Tse *Frank* • Charlie Young *Ho Yee* • Charlene Choi *Sa Sa* • Daniel Wu *Joe* • Wang Chieh *Sam* • Andy On *Tin Tin* ■ *Dir* Benny Chan • *Scr* Alan Yuen

New Port South ★★★🔟

Drama 2001 · US · Colour · 89min

This John Hughes-produced exploration of the cause and effect of youthful idealism is a sophisticated affair. Stylishly shot and featuring strong performances, it's a well-executed, non-patronising movie with a powerful message. Events unfold in a suburban Chicago high school, where a former pupil's escape from a mental institute prompts student Blake Shields to investigate his mysterious case. Believing that the school's restrictive rules were to blame for the boy's incarceration, Shields persuades his friends to initiate a campaign against their teachers. **SF** *DVD*

Blake Shields *Maddox* • Todd Field *Mr Walsh* • Will Estes *Chris* • Melissa George *Amanda* • Raymond J Barry *Edwards* ■ *Dir* Kyle Cooper • *Scr* James Hughes

New Rose Hotel ★

Science-fiction drama
1998 · US · Colour · 91min

Based on a William Gibson short story, cult director Abel Ferrara's cyberpunk *Pygmalion* is an incomprehensible mess. It's an arrogantly arty sci-fi reverie about Willem Dafoe's life unravelling as the dirty deals he's involved in finally catch up with him and he anguishes over the true meaning of love. A murkily shot, pretentious drone. **AJ**

Christopher Walken *Fox* • Willem Dafoe *X* • Asia Argento *Sandii* • Yoshitaka Amano *Hiroshi* • Annabella Sciorra *Madame Rosa* ■ *Dir* Abel Ferrara • *Scr* Christi Zois, Abel Ferrara, from a short story by William Gibson

New Town Killers ★★★🔢

Thriller 2009 · UK · Colour · 96min

A game of hide-and-seek is taken to deadly extremes in writer/director Richard Jobson's visceral fourth feature. In a tense cat-and-mouse thriller that fuses biting socio-economic commentary with breakneck action, callous investment banker Alistair (Dougray Scott) and his new apprentice (Alastair Mackenzie) make violent sport of Edinburgh's unfortunates. Their latest victim is jobless teen Sean (James Anthony Pearson), who's offered cash in return for being the quarry in a manhunt through the night-time streets. Although Jobson occasionally neglects his dialogue and disregards the characters' frequently implausible behaviour, the performances from Pearson and Scott remain strong. **SF** Violence, swearing. **DVD** **BL**

Dougray Scott *Alistair Roskolnikov* • Alastair Mackenzie (2) *Jamie Stewart* • James Anthony Pearson *Sean MacDonald* • Liz White *Alice Kelly* • Charles Mnene *Sam* • Shelley Conn *Julie Stewart* ■ *Dir/Scr* Richard Jobson

New Town Original ★★15
Drama 2004 · UK · Colour · 86min

The banality of estate life in Blair's Britain is exposed in this ambitious but undistinguished independent feature. Set in the concrete jungle that is Basildon, writer/director Jason Ford's first movie is a low-budget tale about everyman Elliott Jordan, who becomes convinced that he's in danger after sleeping with the ex-girlfriend (Katharine Peachey) of local hard man Paul McNeilly. Sadly, it's impossible to ignore the inexperience of the young cast, whose overplaying tips the tone from gritty realism into amateurish melodrama. **DP** Swearing, sex scenes, violence.

Elliott Jordan *Mick* • Nathan Thomas *Johnno* • Katharine Peachey *Nicki* • Richard Gooch *Ozzy* • Kai Aise *Bal* • Paul McNeilly *Si Naylor* • Steve Gibbs *Dave Milner* • Terry Bird *Darren Tutt* ■ *Dir/Scr* Jason Ford

The New World ★★★★12
Historical adventure
2005 · US · Colour · 129min

Terrence Malick's fourth feature in 32 years centres on the legendary romance between disgraced soldier of fortune Captain John Smith (a poignantly gentle Colin Farrell) and native American princess Pocahontas (Q'Orianka Kilcher), following the foundation of the English settlement of Jamestown, Virginia, in 1607. Farrell and Kilcher exude an intense chemistry and it's through the purity of their characters' experiences that the extreme gulfs separating the old and new cultures become most apparent. But, while the universally strong performances anchor the free-flowing tale, it's Malick's rich and self-indulgent vision that sustains this languid epic. **SF** Violence. **DVD** **BL**

Colin Farrell (2) *Captain John Smith* • Christopher Plummer *Captain Christopher Newport* • Christian Bale *John Rolfe* • August Schellenberg *Powhatan* • Wes Studi *Opechancanough* • David Thewlis *Captain Edward Wingfield* • Yorick van Wageningen *Captain Argall* • Q'Orianka Kilcher *Pocahontas* • Raoul Trujillo *Tomocomo* • Michael Greyeyes *Rupwew* ■ *Dir/Scr* Terrence Malick

New World Disorder ★★18
Action thriller 1999 · US · Colour · 89min

If this computer thriller is anything to go by, villainy is clearly not Andrew McCarthy's forte. Rutger Hauer plays the veteran detective forced to learn new tricks from his tech-savvy partner Tara FitzGerald as they track down evil hacker McCarthy. Director Richard Spence hurls his actors through a series of barely competent set pieces while forcing them to spout risible dialogue. **DP**

Rutger Hauer *David Marx* • Andrew McCarthy *Kurt Bishop* • Tara FitzGerald *Kris Paddock* • Hari Dhillon *Mark Ohai* ■ *Dir* Richard Spence • *Scr* Jeffrey Smith, Ehren Kruger

New Year's Day ★★18
Drama 1999 · UK/Fr · Colour · 97min

In this low-budget British attempt to explore the adolescent response to loss, Andrew Lee-Potts and Bobby Barry play the sole survivors of a tragic accident that killed all their schoolfriends and put their teacher in a coma. The two friends embark on a series of therapeutic, but increasingly

preposterous pranks with the intention of committing cliff-top suicide in a year's time. Unfortunately the courageous performances of the two lead actors are compromised throughout by a calculating blend of social realism, macabre comedy and overt sentimentality. **DP** **DVD**

Marianne Jean-Baptiste *Veronica* • Anastasia Hille *Shelley* • Andrew Lee Potts *Jake* • Bobby Barry *Steven* • Michael Kitchen *Robin* • Sue Johnston *Mrs Fisher* • Jacqueline Bisset *Geraldine* ■ *Dir* Suri Krishnamma • *Scr* Ralph Brown

New Year's Eve ★★12
Romantic comedy 2011 · US · Colour · 113min

In *Pretty Woman* director Garry Marshall's schmaltzy follow-up to *Valentine's Day*, a huge string of stars fails to light up a trawl through New York on the eve of 2012. Michelle Pfeiffer is the highlight as a bitter frump who aims, with the help of a relentlessly upbeat Zac Efron, to make all her dreams come true before midnight. But Marshall struggles to balance the fluff with a weightier storyline that features Robert De Niro as a dying man who – for no credible reason – endeavours to see the famous ball drop in Times Square one last time. **SP** Swearing. **DVD** **BL**

Robert De Niro *Stan* • Ashton Kutcher *Randy* • Michelle Pfeiffer *Ingrid* • Halle Berry *Nurse Aimee* • Sarah Jessica Parker *Kim* • Hilary Swank *Claire* • Katherine Heigl *Laura* • Jessica Biel *Tess* • Zac Efron *Paul* ■ *Dir* Garry Marshall • *Scr* Katherine Fugate, from a story by Fugate, Abby Kohn, Marc Silverstein

New York Confidential ★★★12
Crime drama 1955 · US · BW · 87min

This gangster thriller, a precursor to *The Godfather*, was among the first to show the Mafia as a business linked as much by blood as bloodiness. Written by Clarence Greene and Russell Rouse, who also directs, it marked the end of an era for Warner Bros, home of Cagney, Bogart and Robinson, and the beginning of a new one. Broderick Crawford is the godfather, Anne Bancroft is his daughter, while Richard Conte is the assassin. **TH** **DVD**

Broderick Crawford *Charlie Lupo* • Richard Conte *Nick Magellan* • Marilyn Maxwell *Iris Palmer* • Anne Bancroft *Kathy Lupo* • J Carrol Naish *Ben Dagajanian* ■ *Dir* Russell Rouse • *Scr* Clarence Greene, Russell Rouse, from a book by Jack Lait, Lee Mortimer

New York Doll ★★★★12
Documentary 2005 · US · Colour · 74min

Caught between glam rock and punk, the New York Dolls were one of the most outrageous American bands of the 1970s. Yet, while the spotlight invariably fell on extrovert frontman David Johansen, bassist Arthur "Killer" Kane became an accidental icon because of his cultish stage inertia. Surviving a booze-inspired suicide attempt following the band's inevitable split, Kane joined the Mormons and passed his days at their Family History Center in Los Angeles until Morrissey reunited the surviving Dolls for the 2004 Meltdown festival in London. The sheer pleasure that this last moment in the spotlight afforded the genial, gentle "Killer" is a joy to behold. Greg Whiteley's bittersweet memoir is a compelling confounding of rock expectations that's given added poignancy by Kane's unexpected demise soon after the band's brief reconciliation. **DP** **DVD**

Morrissey • Bob Geldof • Chrissie Hynde • Iggy Pop • Mick Jones ■ *Dir* Greg Whiteley

New York, I Love You ★★15
Portmanteau drama
2009 · Fr/US · Colour · 103min

As with *Paris, Je T'Aime* (it's from the same producer, Emmanuel Benbihy), the sheer diversity of this portmanteau movie is both a curse and a blessing. With its 11 directors (including Fatih Akin, Shekhar Kapur, Mira Nair and Jiang Wen) and stellar cast (Natalie Portman, Orlando Bloom, Shia LaBeouf, Julie Christie etc etc), there's no shortage of award-winning talent. But it's

Brett Ratner's tale of a memorable prom date between a teenage boy (Anton Yelchin) and a young wheelchair user (Olivia Thirlby) that hits the spot. **JF** English, Russian, Yiddish +subtitles. Swearing, sexual references. **DVD**

Hayden Christensen *Ben* • Natalie Portman *Rifka* • Orlando Bloom *David* • Ethan Hawke *Writer* • Robin Wright Penn [Robin Wright] *Anna* • Olivia Thirlby *Actress* • Anton Yelchin *Boy in the park* • Bradley Cooper *Gus* • Julie Christie *Isabelle* • Shia LaBeouf *Jacob* • Burt Young *Landlord* • Eli Wallach *Abe* • John Hurt *Bellhop* ■ *Dir* Jiang Wen, Mira Nair, Shunji Iwai, Yvan Attal, Brett Ratner, Allen Hughes, Shekhar Kapur, Natalie Portman, Fatih Akin, Joshua Marston • *Scr* Jiang Wen, Suketu Mehta, Shunji Iwai, Yvan Attal, Brett Ratner, Xan Cassavetes [Alexandra Cassavetes], Anthony Minghella, Natalie Portman, Fatih Akin and others, from a feature concept by Emmanuel Benbihy

New York Minute ★★PG
Comedy adventure 2004 · US · Colour · 87min

This action comedy is the project that twins Mary-Kate and Ashley Olsen selected as their first "grown-up" movie, building on their successful careers as child actors. Aiming to demonstrate the teens' very individual personalities, the film sees Mary-Kate's school-skipping rebel heading to New York to try to slip her rock band's demo to music executives, accompanied by her overachieving sibling who's there to compete for a university scholarship. Too predictable and cutesy to appeal much beyond its adolescent audience. **SF** **DVD**

Ashley Olsen *Jane Ryan* • Mary-Kate Olsen *Roxy Ryan* • Eugene Levy *Max Lomax* • Andy Richter *Bennie Bang* • Riley Smith *Jim, the bike messenger* • Jared Padalecki *Trey Lipton* • Dr Drew Pinsky *Dr Ryan* • Darrell Hammond *Hudson McGill* • Andrea Martin *Sen Anne Baxter-Lipton* ■ *Dir* Dennie Gordon • *Scr* Emily Fox, Adam Cooper, Bill Collage, from a story by Emily Fox

New York, New York ★★★★PG
Musical drama 1977 · US · Colour · 156min

This neglected gem from Martin Scorsese traces the love/hate relationship of saxophonist Robert De Niro and singer Liza Minnelli. The action fairly swings along from the couple's first meeting on VJ Day, through De Niro's rise to bandleader and the birth of their baby, to Minnelli's big break in the movies. Although the tempo drops occasionally, Scorsese's re-creation of the postwar era is faultless, and he handles the musical numbers with considerable aplomb. De Niro packs plenty of swaggering sax appeal, but Minnelli steals the spotlight with a series of showstoppers. **DP** Swearing. **DVD** **BL**

Robert De Niro *Jimmy Doyle* • Liza Minnelli *Francine Evans* • Lionel Stander *Tony Harwell* • Mary Kay Place *Bernice* • George Memmoli *Nicky* • Murray Moston *Horace Morris* • Barry Primus *Paul Wilson* • Georgie Auld *Frankie Harte* ■ *Dir* Martin Scorsese • *Scr* Earl MacRauch, Mardik Martin, from a story by Earl MacRauch

New York Stories ★★★15
Portmanteau movie 1989 · US · Colour · 119min

A word to the wise. As soon as Martin Scorsese's *Life Lessons* episode ends, you have 33 minutes to yourself – unless, of course, you feel you really have to sit through Francis Coppola's atrocious aberration *Life without Zoe*. Scorsese's contribution, on the other hand, is a superbly controlled drama focusing on artist Nick Nolte's relationship with his muse, Rosanna Arquette. But the real showstopper comes from Woody Allen, whose *Oedipus Wrecks* is one of the funniest things he's ever done, thanks largely to a monstrous performance from mother-from-hell Mae Questel. **DP** Swearing. **DVD**

Nick Nolte *Lionel Dobie* • Rosanna Arquette *Paulette* • Steve Buscemi *Gregory Stark* • Peter Gabriel • Heather McComb *Zoe* • Talia Shire *Charlotte* • Giancarlo Giannini *Claudio* • Woody Allen *Sheldon Mills* • Mia Farrow *Lisa* • Julie Kavner *Treva* • Mae Questel *Sadie Millstein* ■ *Dir* Martin Scorsese, Francis Coppola [Francis

Ford Coppola], Woody Allen • *Scr* Richard Price, Francis Coppola [Francis Ford Coppola], Sophia Coppola, Woody Allen

A New York Winter's Tale ★★12
Romantic fantasy 2014 · US · Colour · 118min

Akiva Goldsman, the Oscar-winning screenwriter of *A Beautiful Mind*, makes an ambitious directorial debut with a romantic fantasy injected with heavy doses of magical realism. Even leading man Colin Farrell looks a little dizzied by the plot: he's a petty thief who falls in love with an ailing heiress (*Downton Abbey*'s Jessica Brown Findlay) in the early 20th century, but is still walking the streets of New York a hundred years later. Russell Crowe is the hammy villain bent on spoiling the couple's happiness. The scope of Goldsman's vision is to be admired, but despite so much epic sweep, the story from Mark Helprin's doorstop-sized novel ends up feeling small and silly. **SP** **DVD** **BL**

Colin Farrell (2) *Peter Lake* • Russell Crowe *Pearly Soames* • Jessica Brown Findlay *Beverly Penn* • Jennifer Connelly *Virginia Gamely* • Will Smith *Lucifer* • Eva Marie Saint *Adult Willa* • William Hurt *Isaac Penn* ■ *Dir* Akiva Goldsman • *Scr* Akiva Goldsman, from Mark Helprin's novel *Winter's Tale* • *Cinematographer* Caleb Deschanel

Newman's Law ★★
Police drama 1974 · US · Colour · 98min

George Peppard stars in this suitably dour and predictable cop movie. Squaring up against big city politics and corrupt police colleagues, he's framed and then suspended for getting too close to a drug kingpin. Director Richard T Heffron deals efficiently with the requisite physical action and bolsters the routine good cop/bad cop plot with diverting insights into bureaucratic police methods. **RS**

George Peppard *Vince Newman* • Roger Robinson *Garry* • Eugene Roche *Reardon* • Gordon Pinsent *Eastman* • Abe Vigoda *Dellanzia* • Louis Zorich *Falcone* • Michael Lerner *Frank Acker* • Victor Campos *Jimenez* ■ *Dir* Richard T Heffron • *Scr* Anthony Wilson

News from the Good Lord ★★★
Black comedy
1996 · Fr/Swi/Por · Colour · 100min

Didier Le Pêcheur's debut rewards patient attention with a surfeit of audaciously original thinking and some bravura performances. Convinced they are characters in a badly written celestial novel, Christian Charmetant and his passionate sister, Marie Trintignant, set off in search of God to query his literary prowess. However, the idea that moral responsibility lies with one's creator is somewhat sidetracked by the designer violence of a road movie crime spree. **DP** French +subtitles.

Marie Trintignant *Evangila* • Maria de Medeiros *Karenina* • Christian Charmetant *North* • Isabelle Candelier *Edwarda* • Michel Vuillermoz *Zhivago* • Jean Yanne *God* • Mathieu Kassovitz ■ *Dir* Didier Le Pêcheur • *Scr* Didier Le Pêcheur, from his novel

Newsfront ★★★★
Drama 1978 · Aus · Colour and BW · 110min

Set during the 1940s and 1950s, this is a humane, witty and affectionate tribute to Australia's cinema newsreel cameramen. It beautifully conveys the mood of a nation, still tied emotionally and politically to Britain, and details both domestic crises and national disasters such as the Maitland floods. Clever use of black-and-white archive footage and a strong central performance from the burly, no-nonsense Bill Hunter distinguishes this fine movie from other first features. It's the movie directing debut of Phillip Noyce, who has since rather squandered his talent on Hollywood action blockbusters. **AT**

John Dease *Ken* • Wendy Hughes *Amy McKenzie* • Gerard Kennedy *Frank Maguire* • John Ewart *Charlie* • Angela Punch McGregor *Fay Maguire* • Bryan Brown *Geoff* • Bill Hunter *Len Maguire* ■ *Dir* Phillip Noyce • *Scr* Phillip Noyce, Bob Ellis, from an idea by David Elfick, Philippe Mora

N

The Newton Boys ★★★ 15
Biographical crime drama
1998 · US · Colour · 117min

In the early 1920s, the four Texan-born Newton brothers were the most successful bank robbers in history. *Slacker* director Richard Linklater gives this little-known piece of Americana a pumped-up modern spin and crafts a well constructed, highly entertaining adventure. Matthew McConaughey, Skeet Ulrich, Ethan Hawke and Vincent D'Onofrio make the boys a personable bunch with their differing traits, and Dwight Yoakam's nervous explosives expert is a blast. AJ *DVD*

Matthew McConaughey *Willis Newton* • Skeet Ulrich *Joe Newton* • Ethan Hawke *Jess Newton* • Gail Cronauer *Ma Newton* • Vincent D'Onofrio *Dock Newton* • Julianna Margulies *Louise Brown* • Dwight Yoakam *Brentwood Glasscock* • Bo Hopkins *KP Aldrich* ■ *Dir* Richard Linklater • *Scr* Richard Linklater, Claude Stanush, Clark Lee Walker, from a story by Willis Newton, Joe Newton, from the book *The Newton Boys: Portrait of an Outlaw Gang* by Claude Stanush, David Middleton

Next ★★ 12
Science-fiction thriller
2007 · US · Colour · 91min

After the disastrous *Paycheck* and *Impostor*, another terrible Philip K Dick adaptation comes along to swell the ranks. In director Lee Tamahori's crass take on the *Blade Runner* writer's short story *The Golden Man*, Nicolas Cage plays a Las Vegas magician who can see two minutes into the future. FBI counter-terror agent Julianne Moore needs to use his talent to thwart a nuclear attack on Los Angeles. Cage and Moore coast through the mediocre sci-fi action while Jessica Biel, as Cage's pre-destined love interest, gives the best performance. AJ *DVD* *SL*

Nicolas Cage *Cris Johnson* • Julianne Moore *Callie Ferris* • Jessica Biel *Liz* • Thomas Kretschmann *Mr Smith* • Peter Falk *Irv* • Tory Kittles *Cavanaugh* • Jim Beaver *Wisdom* ■ *Dir* Lee Tamahori • *Scr* Gary Goldman, Jonathan Hensleigh, Paul Bernbaum, from a story by Goldman, from the short story *The Golden Man* by Philip K Dick

The Next Best Thing ★★ 12
Comedy drama
2000 · US · Colour · 103min

Madonna stars in this humdrum comedy drama, as an LA yoga instructor whose life takes a dramatic turn when she sleeps with her gay best friend (Rupert Everett) and ends up pregnant. The couple set up house together for the good of their son, but problems arise when she falls for hunky Benjamin Bratt and Everett sues for custody. Director John Schlesinger handles his stars with kid gloves, and both deliver self-conscious performances. NS *DVD*

Madonna *Abbie* • Rupert Everett *Robert* • Illeana Douglas *Elizabeth Ryder* • Michael Vartan *Kevin* • Josef Sommer *Richard Whittaker* • Malcolm Stumpf *Sam* • Lynn Redgrave *Helen Whittaker* • Benjamin Bratt *Ben Cooper* • Neil Patrick Harris *David* ■ *Dir* John Schlesinger • *Scr* Thomas Ropelewski, Leslie Dixon, Rupert Everett, Mel Bordeaux

Next Friday ★★ 15
Comedy
1999 · US · Colour · 94min

Rapper-turned-actor Ice Cube grabs writing, producing and performing credits for this follow-up to his hit US comedy *Friday*. Just as lowbrow in its laughs, but sadly lacking the original's darkish hue, this has Cube's street-savvy character hiding out in an affluent LA suburb where, thanks to a lottery win, his uncle is the richest man on the block. Add gangsters, a curvy señorita and a doped-up dog, and you have the recipe for some undemanding hokum. DA *DVD*

Ice Cube *Craig Jones* • Mike Epps *Day-Day* • Justin Pierce *Roach* • John Witherspoon *Mr Jones* • Don "D C" Curry *Uncle Elroy* ■ *Dir* Steve Carr • *Scr* Ice Cube, from characters by Ice Cube, DJ Pooh

The Next Karate Kid ★★ PG
Martial arts adventure
1994 · US · Colour · 102min

Ralph Macchio may have departed, but at least the fourth instalment in this series could still call on the services of Pat Morita. Essentially, this is a case of "same stunts, different sex", as future Oscar winner Hilary Swank becomes Morita's prize pupil. A few pre-prom dance lessons are the only significant departure from the chop-socky formula, although Michael Ironside is good value as Swank's sinister gym teacher. DP *DVD*

Noriyuki "Pat" Morita [Pat Morita] *Mr Miyagi* • Hilary Swank *Julie Pierce* • Michael Ironside *Colonel Dugan* • Constance Towers *Louisa* • Chris Conrad *Eric* • Arsenio "Sonny" Trinidad *Abbot Monk* ■ *Dir* Christopher Cain • *Scr* Mark Lee, from characters by Robert Mark Kamen

The Next Man ★★ 15
Thriller
1976 · US · Colour · 99min

This confused thriller is a long way from Sean Connery's best, while the plot certainly takes a lot of swallowing. A hired killer (Cornelia Sharpe) is sent to murder a high-flying Arab diplomat (Connery), but finds herself falling for his charms. However, Connery is charismatic even when sleepwalking through a role and the locations are certainly exotic. JF

Sean Connery *Khalil Abdul Muhsen* • Cornelia Sharpe *Nicole Scott* • Albert Paulsen *Hamid* • Adolfo Celi *Al Sharif* • Marco St John *Justin* • Ted Beniades *Dedario* ■ *Dir* Richard C Sarafian • *Scr* Mort Fine, Alan Trustman, David M Wolf, Richard C Sarafian, from a story by Martin Bregman, Alan Trustman

Next of Kin ★★★★ PG
Second World War propaganda drama
1942 · UK · BW · 95min

Thorold Dickinson's eerily credible account of Fifth Column activity started life as a propaganda short, only to be expanded (at the MOI's behest) into a feature on the dangers of careless talk. Mervyn Johns gives a chillingly unassuming performance as the Nazi agent whose dual ability to invite confidences and blend into the background enables him to learn key secrets about an impending commando raid on a continental stronghold. Dickinson planned to use the failure of the attack to ram home his message. But Churchill intervened, fearing the film's effect on morale, and insisted the assault succeeded, but with heavy casualties. DP

Mervyn Johns *Mr Davis, No 23* • Basil Sidney *Naval captain* • Frederick Leister *Colonel* • John Chandos *Davis's contact, No 16* • Sqn/Ldr Reginald Tate [Reginald Tate] *Major Richards* • 2nd Lt Jack Hawkins [Jack Hawkins] *Brigade Major Harcourt* • Torin Thatcher *German general* • Thora Hird *ATS girl* ■ *Dir* Thorold Dickinson • *Scr* Thorold Dickinson, Basil Bartlett, Angus MacPhail, John Dighton

Next of Kin ★★ 15
Crime drama
1989 · US · Colour · 103min

From the days when Liam Neeson was serving his Hollywood apprenticeship, this sleazy muddle of a movie at least gives him a chance to flex his acting muscles as the hillbilly brother of Chicago cop Patrick Swayze. They unite in vengeance when another brother is killed by the Mob. British director John Irvin seems to have little idea of movie momentum or the way characters are developed, but these weaknesses may also be the fault of the banal script. TH Swearing, violence.

Patrick Swayze *Truman Gates* • Liam Neeson *Briar Gates* • Adam Baldwin *Joey Rossellini* • Helen Hunt *Jessie Gates* • Andreas Katsulas *John Isabella* • Bill Paxton *Gerald Gates* • Ben Stiller *Lawrence Isabella* ■ *Dir* John Irvin • *Scr* Michael Jenning, Jeb Stuart

Next Stop, Greenwich Village ★★★
Comedy
1976 · US · Colour · 111min

Set in New York in 1953, aspiring actor Lenny Baker has finally escaped his momma, Shelley Winters. Or so he thinks, for Winters shows up to steal a scene and to give her son some maternal advice and clean underwear. That makes the movie funny, but the evocation of bohemian New York is also splendidly realised. Of course, it's autobiographical since writer/director Paul Mazursky lived this life himself, brushed up against Brando, Strasberg and Actors' Studio types and finally went to Hollywood. AT

Lenny Baker *Larry Lapinsky* • Shelley Winters *Mrs Lapinsky* • Ellen Greene *Sarah* • Lois Smith *Anita* • Christopher Walken *Robert* • Dori Brenner *Connie* • Antonio Fargas *Bernstein* ■ *Dir/Scr* Paul Mazursky

Next Stop Murder ★★
Thriller
2010 · US · Colour · 90min

Alfred Hitchcock's *Strangers on a Train* is the apparent basis for this watchable TV movie, in which law student Brigid Brannagh faces an escalating nightmare when a disgruntled rich girl (Allison Lange) she meets on a bus suggests they solve their personal problems by killing someone for each other. Despite predominantly unconvincing performances, events remain reasonably atmospheric, with a couple of decent twists filling in the plot holes to set up a tense and dramatic finale. SF

Brigid Brannagh *Molly* • Allison Lange *Sophie* • Brian Krause *Jeff* • Rosa Blasi *Heather* ■ *Dir* John Murlowski • *Scr* Johnson Chan, Steven Palmer Peterson, from a story by George Stelzner

Next Stop Wonderland ★★★★
Romantic comedy
1998 · US · Colour · 111min

This terrific romantic comedy is all the more laudable for being the first feature from up-and-coming indie director Brad Anderson. Hope Davis plays Erin, a Boston night-shift nurse who swears off men after she's dumped by her boyfriend. Her mother, though, has other ideas and places a personal ad on her daughter's behalf. The film then chronicles Erin's reluctant return to the meet market. Philip Seymour Hoffman (*Happiness*) is the best-known face among the supporting cast. DA

Hope Davis *Erin Castleton* • Alan Gelfant *Alan Monteiro* • Victor Argo *Frank* • Jon Benjamin *Eric* • Cara Buono *Julie* • Larry Gilliard Jr *Brett* • Philip Seymour Hoffman *Sean* ■ *Dir* Brad Anderson • *Scr* Brad Anderson, Lyn Vaus

The Next Three Days ★★★ 12
Crime drama
2010 · US · Colour · 133min

Paul Haggis's drama, freely adapted from the French thriller *Anything for Her*, follows mild-mannered academic John Brennan (Russell Crowe) as he attempts to break his wife Lara (Elizabeth Banks) out of a maximum security jail after she is convicted for a murder she says she didn't commit. What follows is a kind of escape procedural, with Haggis delivering a host of interesting details about lock-picking and the faking of passports. But what really happened on the night that Lara's boss was killed, and is John setting free a cold-blooded murderer? Crowe is serviceable as the driven husband but what could have been the film's real strength - the innocence or otherwise of Lara - isn't exploited nearly as effectively as it could have been. AS Violence, swearing. *DVD* *SL*

Russell Crowe *John Brennan* • Elizabeth Banks (2) *Lara Brennan* • Lennie James *Lieutenant Nabulsi* • Liam Neeson *Damon Pennington* • Olivia Wilde *Nicole* • Brian Dennehy *George Brennan* • Daniel Stern *Meyer Fisk* • Kevin Corrigan *Alex* ■ *Dir* Paul Haggis • *Scr* Paul Haggis, from the film *Anything for Her* by Fred Cavayé, Guillaume Lemans • *Cinematographer* Stéphane Fontaine

Next Time We Love ★★★ U
Romantic melodrama
1936 · US · BW · 86min

The marriage between a Broadway actress and a news correspondent suffers from a conflict in career interests. A top-billed Margaret Sullavan co-stars with James Stewart in his first important role, while Ray Milland plays a stalwart friend of the couple who nurses an unrequited love for the wife. Beautifully mounted and superbly cast, this has all the makings of a first-class movie. Under Edward H Griffith's direction, though, it just plods along, just about held together by the polish and personality of the stars. RK *DVD*

Margaret Sullavan *Cicely Tyler* • James Stewart *Christopher Tyler* • Ray Milland *Tommy Abbott* • Grant Mitchell *Michael Jennings* • Robert McWade *Frank Carteret* ■ *Dir* Edward H Griffith • *Scr* Melville Baker, Preston Sturges, from the novel *Say Goodbye Again* by Ursula Parrott

Next to Her ★★★★ 15
Drama
2014 · Is · Colour · 89min

Basing her screenplay on her own experiences, Liron Ben-Shlush presents some poignant insights into dealing with a sister with severe learning difficulties in husband Asaf Korman's debut feature. Determined to protect her mentally disabled sister by locking her in their jumbled Haifa apartment while she works as a school security guard, Ben-Shlush is finally coerced into letting her attend a day-care centre. This is a discreet and compellingly authentic study of misplaced devotion that makes oppressive use of claustrophobic interiors to capture a dependency that is both affecting and unsettling. DP Hebrew +subtitles. Swearing, sex scenes, nudity.

Liron Ben-Shlush *Chelli* • Dana Ivgy *Gabby* • Yaakov Zada Daniel *Zohar* • Sophia Ostrisky *Sveta* • Carmit Messilati-Kaplan *Jenny* • Varda Ben Hur *Zohar's mother* ■ *Dir* Asaf Korman • *Scr* Liron Ben-Shlush, Sari Ezouz Berger

Next to No Time ★★★ U
Comedy
1958 · UK · Colour · 92min

This whimsical comedy was something of a disappointment considering it marked the reunion of director Henry Cornelius with his *Genevieve* star Kenneth More. Sadly, it proved to be Cornelius's last picture before his tragically early death the same year during the production of *Law and Disorder*. More is curiously out of sorts as an engineer who uses a voyage on the *Queen Elizabeth* to persuade wealthy Roland Culver to back his latest project. His romantic interest is provided by Betsy Drake, who was then married to Cary Grant. DP

Kenneth More *David Webb* • Betsy Drake *Georgie Brant* • Harry Green *Saul* • Patrick Barr *Jerry* • Maureen Connell *Mary* • Bessie Love *Becky* • Reginald Beckwith *Warren* • Roland Culver *Sir Godfrey Cowan* ■ *Dir* Henry Cornelius • *Scr* Henry Cornelius, from the story *The Enchanted Hour* by Paul Gallico

The Next Voice You Hear ★★★
Drama
1950 · US · BW · 82min

MGM's new studio head Dore Schary had made some interesting, relevant, and mildly liberal (by MGM standards) programme fillers during his tenure at RKO, and attempted to raise the thought and quality content at Metro, with varying degrees of success. This oddity, produced by Schary himself, concerns the effects on an allegorical US town when no less than the voice of God is heard over the radio. It's a fascinating idea, but action director William A Wellman handles it like a tub of molasses. TS

James Whitmore *Joe Smith* • Nancy Davis *Mary Smith* • Gary Gray *Johnny Smith* • Lillian Bronson *Aunt Ethel* • Art Smith *Mr Brannan* • Tom D'Andrea *Hap Magee* • Jeff Corey *Freddie* ■ *Dir* William A Wellman • *Scr* Charles Schnee, from a story by George Sumner Albee

Ngati ★★★
Drama
1987 · NZ · Colour · 88min

Made by a predominantly Maori cast and crew, this was the first feature produced anywhere by an indigenous community resident within a primarily white country. Set in 1948 and tackling the age-old theme of tradition versus progress, Barry Barclay's drama demonstrates the importance of ethnic unity by linking three distinct plot strands, concerning a dying child, an obsolete meat-freezing depot and an Australian doctor making a pilgrimage to the place of his birth. This may be rough around the edges, but the political points are soundly made. DP

Michael Tibble *Tione* • Oliver Jones *Ropata* • Judy McIntosh *Jenny Bennett* • Ross Girven *Greg Shaw* • Wi Kuki Kaa *Iwi, Ropata's father* ■ *Dir* Barry Barclay • *Scr* Tama Poata

Niagara ★★★★ PG
Thriller 1953 · US · Colour · 85min

If ever a film poster could be said to have created a stars image, it was the one for this movie – Marilyn Monroe draped across said falls with a certain look in her eye and a come-on caption to match her décolletage: "A raging torrent of emotion that even nature can't control!" Monroe, top-billed for the first time in her career, plays the faithless wife of Joseph Cotten who plots his murder at the honeymoon resort of Niagara Falls. She is sensational, but the film itself verges on melodrama, daft and clever by turns. There's a fine performance from Cotten and some great location shots of the falls, but this is Monroe's star-making movie and, boy, does she know it. TS DVD 🔵

Marilyn Monroe *Rose Loomis* • Joseph Cotten *George Loomis* • Jean Peters *Polly Cutler* • Casey Adams [Max Showalter] *Ray Cutler* • Denis O'Dea *Inspector Sharkey* • Richard Allen *Patrick* • Don Wilson *Mr Kettering* • Lurene Tuttle *Mrs Kettering* ■ *Dir* Henry Hathaway • *Scr* Charles Brackett, Walter Reisch, Richard Breen [Richard L Breen]

Niagara Motel ★★ 15
Black comedy drama
2005 · Can · Colour · 84min

A run-down motel in the honeymoon destination of Niagara Falls is the fitting focal point for this ramshackle black comedy drama tracing the interweaving lives and crises of a group of disparate individuals. Unfortunately, the film offers no warmth, making the characters so unsympathetic that it's hard to care about their all-too-predictable plights. The clumsy dialogue and stilted execution don't help either. SF DVD

Craig Ferguson *Paillie* • Anna Friel *Denise* • Kevin Pollak *Michael* • Wendy Crewson *Lily* • Caroline Dhavernas *Loretta Bourgogne* • Peter Keleghan *Henry* • Kristen Holden-Ried *RJ* • Tom Barnett *Dave* ■ *Dir* Gary Yates (1) • *Scr* Dani Romain, George F Walker, from the play *Suburban Motel* by George F Walker

Niagara Niagara ★★ 15
Romantic drama 1997 · US · Colour · 90min

Playing a victim of Tourette syndrome, Robin Tunney won the best actress prize at Venice for her convincing outbursts and involuntary acts of violence. But there are too many echoes of other road movies to elevate Bob Gosse's film above the crowd. Travelling with the taciturn Henry Thomas, it's only a matter of time before Tunney's lack of medication renders her increasingly unpredictable and the pair turn to crime. DP DVD

Robin Tunney *Marcy* • Henry Thomas *Seth* • Stephen Lang *Pharmacist* • John MacKay *Seth's father* • Michael Parks *Walter* ■ *Dir* Bob Gosse • *Scr* Matthew Weiss

The Nibelungen ★★★★ PG
Silent fantasy epic 1924 · Ger · BW · 280min

Fritz Lang's adaptation of the 13th-century German saga is a superb example of the craftsmanship at the UFA studios. Paul Richter is Siegfried, married to Margarete Schön; together the two journey from Iceland to Burgundy with Hanna Ralph, who is to be the bride of Theodor Loos. Adventures, magical and otherwise, death and revenge all ensue. The stylised sets create a mysterious beauty, especially the misty forest (constructed in a Zeppelin hangar) and the romantic castles. There is also a wonderful dragon that the hero slays early in Part I (*Siegfried*) and a massively staged battle to end Part II (*Kriemhild's Revenge*). The characters are deliberately

one-dimensional as befits the epic mode. RB DVD

Paul Richter *Siegfried* • Margarete Schön *Kriemhild* • Theodor Loos *King Gunther* • Hanna Ralph *Brunhild* ■ *Dir* Fritz Lang • *Scr* Fritz Lang, Thea von Harbou, from the anonymous 13th-century German poem *Das Nibelungenlied* and various Norse legends

Nice Girl? ★★★ U
Musical comedy 1941 · US · BW · 93min

Nice Deanna Durbin is at her most charming as a small-town girl who falls for a much older man (36-year-old Franchot Tone), a New York roué, because the boy next door (Robert Stack) is more interested in cars than in her. The situation, redolent with sexual possibilities, is rendered as innocently as possible, making the question mark in the title unnecessary. Among the pleasures here are the casting of humorist Robert Benchley as Deanna's father and Walter Brennan as a lovesick postman. RB DVD

Deanna Durbin *Jane Dana* • Franchot Tone *Richard Calvert* • Walter Brennan *Hector Titus* • Robert Stack *Don Webb* • Robert Benchley *Oliver Dana* • Helen Broderick *Cora Foster* • Ann Gillis *Nancy Dana* ■ *Dir* William A Seiter • *Scr* Richard Connell, Gladys Lehman, from the play by Phyllis Duganne

A Nice Girl like Me ★ 12
Comedy 1969 · UK · Colour · 86min

In this abysmal comedy, Barbara Ferris goes to France and Italy and comes back pregnant both times. If you want to see it as an allegory about Britain's thwarted desire to join the Common Market, the film has significance and irony; but seen as a comedy its ability to send its audience into a deep sleep is unrivalled. As the liberated young woman, proud of her right to choose her mate, Ferris is a real pain, while the supporting cast suggests an amateur rep production. AT DVD

Barbara Ferris *Candida* • Harry Andrews *Savage, caretaker* • Gladys Cooper *Aunt Mary* • Bill Hinnant *Ed* • James Villiers *Freddie* • Joyce Carey *Aunt Celia* • Christopher Guinee *Pierre* ■ *Dir* Desmond Davis • *Scr* Anne Piper, Desmond Davis, from the novel *Marry at Leisure* by Anne Piper

The Nice Guys ★★★★ 15
Crime comedy thriller
2016 · US · Colour · 115min

LA in 1977 is the setting and the death of a porn star is the catalyst that brings gumshoe Ryan Gosling into contact with mafia muscle Russell Crowe, drawing them into a missing-person mystery involving the adult entertainment industry, colourful Mob killers and municipal corruption. Beautifully shot and combining action, danger and comedy to exhilarating effect, this boasts great chemistry between the stars (Gosling has a ball playing the fool, Crowe proves a fabulous straight man), snappy dialogue and laugh-out-loud moments. JA Violence, swearing, nudity.

Russell Crowe *Jackson Healy* • Ryan Gosling *Holland March* • Angourie Rice *Holly* • Kim Basinger *Judith Kuttner* • Matt Bomer *John Boy* • Keith David *Older Guy* • *Dir* Shane Black • *Scr* Shane Black, Anthony Bagarozzi • *Cinematographer* Philippe Rousselot

A Nice Little Bank That Should Be Robbed ★★ U
Crime comedy 1958 · US · BW · 87min

Despite its whimsical title, a script by one of Fox's star writers (Sydney Boehm) and the presence of Mickey Rooney and Tom Ewell, this is a rather pathetic attempt at heist comedy. Two incompetent crooks rob a small-town bank, then buy a racehorse that is just as much of a loser as they are. Henry Levin directs with little of the flair such a subject needs, while the stars seem to know they're in a stinker. TH

Tom Ewell *Max Rutgers* • Mickey Rooney *Gus Harris* • Mickey Shaughnessy *Harold "Rocky" Baker* • Dina Merrill *Margie Solitaire* • Madge Kennedy *Grace Havens* • Frances Bavier *Mrs Solitaire* ■ *Dir* Henry Levin • *Scr* Sydney Boehm, from an article by Evan Wylie

Nicholas and Alexandra ★★★ PG
Historical drama 1971 · UK · Colour · 180min

This sumptuous, if overlong epic about the last days of the Russian Romanov dynasty, before the Bolsheviks executed Tsar Nicholas II and his family, shows the stretchmarks of too much padding, though Michael Jayston and Janet Suzman, as the Tsar and Tsarina, are a poignant reminder that a royal marriage can be both faithful and true. It overwhelms us with its detail, though Tom Baker is a lot of fun as the leering mystic Rasputin, and there are cameo appearances from Laurence Olivier and Michael Redgrave among others. TH DVD

Michael Jayston *Tsar Nicholas II* • Janet Suzman *Empress Alexandra* • Fiona Fullerton *Princess Anastasia* • Tom Baker *Rasputin* • Candace Glendenning *Princess Marie* • Lynne Frederick *Princess Tatiana* • Ania Marson *Princess Olga* • Roderic Noble *Prince Alexis* • John McEnery *Kerensky* ■ *Dir* Franklin Schaffner [Franklin J Schaffner] • *Scr* James Goldman, Edward Bond, from a non-fiction book by Robert K Massie

Nicholas' Gift ★★ PG
Drama based on a true story
1998 · It/US · Colour · 86min

As true weepies go, this TV movie is definitely in the premier league, if only for the top quality cast. Jamie Lee Curtis and Alan Bates play tourists on holiday in Italy whose young son is seriously wounded when they are attacked by jewel thieves. With the child given no chance of surviving, the grieving couple agree to donate his organs. Unbeknown to them, though, Italy has an appalling record in this area of medicine, and they come up against a brick wall of bureaucracy. Sentimentality runs riot. JF DVD

Jamie Lee Curtis *Maggie Green* • Alan Bates *Reginald Green* • Gene Wexler *Nicholas Green* • Hallie Kate Eisenberg *Eleanor Green* • *Dir* Robert Markowitz • *Scr* Christine Berardo

Nicholas Nickleby ★★★★ U
Period drama 1947 · UK · BW · 102min

Alberto Cavalcanti was the Brazilian-born film-maker who joined Michael Balcon's famous team of Ealing directors after helping to develop the documentary movement at the GPO Film Unit. One of his infrequent outings as a director, this was to be overshadowed by David Lean's *Oliver Twist* and *Great Expectations*, but it still deserves attention as a screen version of a Dickens fable that has relevance today. Derek Bond is hopelessly wooden as Nicholas, but Alfred Drayton is suitably loathsome as the head of Dotheboys Hall and Cedric Hardwicke is an Uncle Ralph of diabolical villainy. TH DVD

Derek Bond *Nicholas Nickleby* • Cedric Hardwicke *Ralph Nickleby* • Stanley Holloway *Vincent Crummles* • Alfred Drayton *Wackford Squeers* • Cyril Fletcher *Alfred Mantalini* • Bernard Miles *Newman Noggs* • Sally Ann Howes *Kate Nickleby* • Mary Merrall *Mrs Nickleby* • Sybil Thorndike *Mrs Squeers* ■ *Dir* Alberto Cavalcanti • *Scr* John Dighton, from the novel by Charles Dickens

Nicholas Nickleby ★★★★ PG
Period drama 2002 · US/UK · Colour · 127min

The actors in any film of a novel by Charles Dickens have to guard against caricature – so extreme in vice or virtue are his characters. Not a chance of parody, though, with this bustling, personality-packed account. Young Nicholas (Charlie Hunnam) is the innocent at large in a world controlled by Uncle Ralph (Christopher Plummer), one of the most evil men in English literature. First there is the tour to the lower depths of educational hell at Dotheboys Hall, run by Wackford Squeers (Jim Broadbent) and his wife (Juliet Stevenson). Then there is light at the end of the tunnel with the Cheeryble brothers (Timothy Spall and Gerard Horan) and the hope of love with Madeline (Anne Hathaway). Written and directed by Douglas McGrath, the original tale has been slightly truncated, but this is still a treat. TH DVD

Charlie Hunnam *Nicholas Nickleby* • Christopher Plummer *Ralph Nickleby* • Jamie Bell *Smike* • Jim Broadbent *Wackford Squeers* • Tom Courtenay *Newman Noggs* • Edward Fox *Sir Mulberry Hawk* • Juliet Stevenson *Mrs Squeers* • Nathan Lane *Vincent Crummles* • Dame Edna Everage [Barry Humphries] *Mrs Crummles* • Timothy Spall *Charles Cheeryble* • Alan Cumming *Mr Folair* • Anne Hathaway *Madeline Bray* • Gerard Horan *Ned Cheeryble* • Stella Gonet *Mrs Nickleby* ■ *Dir* Douglas McGrath • *Scr* Douglas McGrath, from the novel by Charles Dickens

Nick & Norah's Infinite Playlist ★★★ 12
Comedy drama 2008 · US · Colour · 85min

More indebted to *After Hours* than *Superbad*, this late-night tour of Manhattan stars Michael Cera and Kat Dennings and aims to be a smarter alternative to the usual youth movie. Yet in its tale of three teens dragged off-course in their search for a gig venue by a series of increasingly frantic mishaps, it fails to find the magical charm it needs to work properly. Instead it coasts leisurely by on its nicely mismatched central couple, gay-friendly supporting characters and name-checking of bands like Vampire Weekend and Band of Horses. JR DVD 🔵

Michael Cera *Nick* • Kat Dennings *Norah* • Alexis Dziena *Tris* • Ari Graynor *Caroline* • Aaron Yoo *Thom* • Rafi Gavron *Dev* ■ *Dir* Peter Sollett • *Scr* Lorene Scafaria, from the novel by Rachel Cohn, David Levithan

Nick Carter, Master Detective ★★
Detective spy drama 1939 · US · BW · 58min

This polished MGM B-feature was the first of three films in which Walter Pidgeon played the screen incarnation of a popular dime-novel sleuth. The topical story has Carter preventing blueprints of a new high-speed plane falling into the hands of spies. The film gives director Jacques Tourneur little chance to display the skill he would later bring to *Cat People* and *I Walked with a Zombie*, but it moves briskly and painlessly through its brief duration. *Phantom Raiders* and *Sky Murder*, both 1940, followed. AE

Walter Pidgeon *Nick Carter/Robert Chalmers* • Rita Johnson *Lou Farnsby* • Henry Hull *John A Keller* • Stanley C Ridges [Stanley Ridges] *Dr Frankton* • Donald Meek *Bartholomew* ■ *Dir* Jacques Tourneur • *Scr* Bertram Millhauser, from a story by Bertram Millhauser, Harold Buckley

Nick of Time ★★ 15
Action thriller 1995 · US · Colour · 85min

In director John Badham's weak suspense thriller, accountant Johnny Depp is told he has 90 minutes, and six bullets, to murder the governor of California or his daughter will be killed. Supposedly playing out his shock predicament in real-time, with lots of close-ups of clocks, Badham fluffs the tension by accenting the preposterous plot contrivances rather than creating any real emotional empathy with the plight of the characters. AJ DVD

Johnny Depp *Gene Watson* • Christopher Walken *Mr Smith* • Courtney Chase *Lynn Watson* • Charles S Dutton *Huey* • Roma Maffia *Ms Jones* • Marsha Mason *Governor Eleanor Grant* • Peter Strauss *Brendan Grant* • Gloria Reuben *Krista Brooks* ■ *Dir* John Badham • *Scr* Patrick Sheane Duncan

Nickelodeon ★★★ U
Comedy 1976 · US · Colour · 117min

Critic-turned-director Peter Bogdanovich intended this tribute to the early days of film-making to be his masterwork, but it turned out to be one of his biggest flops. Ryan O'Neal plays the director, Burt Reynolds the handsome star, Stella Stevens a vamp and Brian Keith a fledgeling movie mogul. It was a critical and commercial disaster, but it's still a charmer, with nice performances and impeccable period atmosphere. AT DVD

Ryan O'Neal *Leo Harrigan* • Burt Reynolds *Buck Greenway* • Tatum O'Neal *Alice Forsyte* • Brian Keith *HH Cobb* • Stella Stevens *Marty Reeves* • John Ritter *Franklin Frank* • Jane Hitchcock

Kathleen Cooke • Harry Carey Jr *Dobie* ■ *Dir* Peter Bogdanovich • *Scr* Peter Bogdanovich, WD Richter

Nico ★★ 18
Martial arts action thriller
1988 · US · Colour · 94min

Despite his obvious limitations as an actor, Steven Seagal's rock-fisted martial arts style made this action debut a massive video hit and paved the way for his lengthy career in similar biff-em-ups. He's a cop whose massive drug bust is suddenly stolen from under his nose by pushy FBI men for complex, and possibly criminal, reasons. Providing the actual acting talent are Pam Grier, Sharon Stone and villainous Henry Silva. Also known as *Above the Law*. JF Drug abuse, swearing, violence. **DVD** Ⓑ
Steven Seagal *Nico Toscani* • Pam Grier *Delores Jackson* • Henry Silva *Zagon* • Sharon Stone *Sara Toscani* • Daniel Faraldo *Salvano* ■ *Dir* Andrew Davis • *Scr* Steven Pressfield, Ronald Shusett, Andrew Davis, from a story by Steven Seagal, Andrew Davis

Nico the Unicorn ★★★
Fantasy drama
1998 · Can · Colour · 90min

This Canadian gem based on the Frank Sacks novel allows both children and adults to share something magical. Anne Archer moves house after her husband is killed and her son Kevin Zegers is crippled in the same accident. Feeling alone and somewhat bitter, the son visits a nearby circus and cajoles his mother into buying a neglected pony. When it gives birth to a unicorn, both their lives take a turn for the better. AJ
Anne Archer *Julie Hastings* • Kevin Zegers *Billy Hastings* • Michael Ontkean *Tom Gentry* ■ *Dir* Graeme Campbell • *Scr* Frank Sacks, from his novel

Night after Night ★★
Comedy drama
1932 · US · BW · 70min

Ex-prizefighter George Raft, looking to make something of his life, buys a ritzy nightclub, mingles with the smart set and falls in love with a socialite. Constance Cummings and Alison Skipworth co-star in this small-scale drama, which is long on Prohibition-era atmosphere but short on interesting content. The film is remembered, however, for promoting Raft to leading man status, and is unforgettable for marking the screen debut of Mae West. "Goodness, what diamonds!" remarks a hatcheck girl as she makes her entrance. "Goodness had nothing to do with it, dearie," Mae replies. RK
George Raft *Joe Anton* • Constance Cummings *Jerry Healy* • Wynne Gibson *Iris Dawn* • Mae West *Maudie Triplett* • Alison Skipworth *Mrs Mabel Jellyman* ■ *Dir* Archie Mayo • *Scr* Vincent Lawrence, Kathryn Scola, Mae West, from the novel *Single Night* by Louis Bromfield

Night and Day ★★★ Ⓤ
Musical biography
1946 · US · Colour · 122min

This is a mawkish yet mesmerising Warner Bros musical biopic, whose casting of Cary Grant as Cole Porter completely eliminated any suggestion of Porter's homosexuality. It also reduced his tragic riding accident (Porter eventually lost a leg) to Grant using a walking stick to get around. But the truth doesn't matter much in this kind of movie, and director Michael Curtiz does a smashing job, helped by ravishing Technicolor and a marvellous cast. TS
DVD
Cary Grant *Cole Porter* • Alexis Smith *Linda Lee Porter* • Monty Woolley • Ginny Simms *Carole Hill* • Jane Wyman *Gracie Harris* • Eve Arden *Gabrielle* • Victor Francen *Anatole Giron* • Alan Hale *Leon Dowling* • Dorothy Malone *Nancy* ■ *Dir* Michael Curtiz • *Scr* Charles Hoffman, Leo Townsend, William Bowers, from a biography by Jack Moffit

Night and Day ★★★★ 15
Romantic drama
1991 · Bel/Fr/Swi · Colour · 95min

Bearing the influence of François Truffaut (to whom the film is dedicated), Chantal Akerman's delicately-played morality tale continues her fascination with the way emotion reveals itself through the banalities of everyday life. Radiant in the atmospheric nocturnal photography, Guilaine Londez gives a disarmingly truthful performance as the girl whose love for cabbie Thomas Langmann is supplanted by a passion for François Négret, who drives the same taxi on the day shift. Thanks to Akerman's interest in her characters, the dialogue is as authentic as the resolution. DP French +subtitles.
Guilaine Londez *Julie* • Thomas Langmann *Jack* • François Négret *Joseph* • Nicole Colchat *Jack's mother* • Pierre Laroche *Jack's father* ■ *Dir* Chantal Akerman • *Scr* Chantal Akerman, Pascal Bonitzer

Night and the City ★★★★ PG
Crime drama
1950 · UK/US · BW · 91min

Here's a really interesting crime drama: a genuine 20th Century-Fox *film noir* set and filmed entirely in London, with imported American stars and a British supporting cast. Surprisingly, it works, largely because of star Richard Widmark's brilliant portrayal of a hustler on the edge, and skilled director Jules Dassin's atmospheric use of London locations and controlled pacing. The plot hangs on a wrestling fix, and is both adult and original. TS **DVD** Ⓑ
Richard Widmark *Harry Fabian* • Gene Tierney *Mary Bristol* • Googie Withers *Helen Nosseross* • Hugh Marlowe *Adam Dunn* • Francis L Sullivan *Phil Nosseross* • Herbert Lom *Kristo* • Stanley Zbyszko [Stanislaus Zbyszko] *Gregorius* • Mike Mazurki *Strangler* ■ *Dir* Jules Dassin • *Scr* Jo Eisinger, from the novel by Gerald Kersh

Night and the City ★★★ 15
Crime drama
1992 · US · Colour · 99min

A respectful update of Jules Dassin's 1950 classic, with the setting switched from London to New York. Robert De Niro takes the Richard Widmark role of the small-time promoter desperately trying to hustle his way to the big time, while Jessica Lange is the woman who gets too close to his dreams. Irwin Winkler's direction is functional, but he is smart enough to surround himself with an impressive array of talent. JF Violence, swearing. **DVD**
Robert De Niro *Harry Fabian* • Jessica Lange *Helen* • Cliff Gorman *Phil* • Alan King *"Boom Boom" Grossman* • Jack Warden *Al Grossman* • Eli Wallach *Peck* • Barry Primus *Tommy Tessler* • Gene Kirkwood *Resnick* • Pedro Sanchez [Ignazio Spalla] *Cuda Sanchez* ■ *Dir* Irwin Winkler • *Scr* Richard Price, from the 1950 film

A Night at the Cinema in 1914 ★★★★ Ⓤ
Silent compilation
2014 · US/UK · BW · 84min

Curated to mark the centenary of the outbreak of the Great War, this is an intriguing look at the kind of programme British audiences could have expected in the days before features. The 14 snippets range from topical items to travelogues and slapstick shorts featuring the likes of Florence Turner and Charlie Chaplin, while news stories document such timely events as Shackleton's preparations for an expedition, suffragette Emmeline Pankhurst protesting at Buckingham Palace and the Austrian royal family mourning Archduke Ferdinand. DP
• *Music* Stephen Horne

Night at the Museum ★★★ PG
Fantasy action comedy
2006 · US · Colour · 104min

Ben Stiller heads a cast of A-list comedy actors ranging from the likes of Mickey Rooney and Dick Van Dyke to Robin Williams in this raucous romp through history. Stiller plays the patsy once again as night watchman Larry Daley, who has to run for his life when an ancient curse causes the exhibits at the Museum of Natural History in New York to come to life. Stiller does a sterling job here and there's a witty use of visual effects. Meanwhile, Ricky Gervais pops up as an officious museum director who's not a million miles away from David Brent. Director Shawn Levy is not always in control of his storyline, but there are enough exciting stunts and larger-than-life performances to provide entertainment for kids and old relics alike. SP **DVD** Ⓑ
Ben Stiller *Larry Daley* • Carla Gugino *Rebecca* • Dick Van Dyke *Cecil* • Mickey Rooney *Gus* • Bill Cobbs *Reginald* • Jake Cherry *Nick Daley* • Ricky Gervais *Dr McPhee* • Steve Coogan *Octavius* • Owen Wilson *Jedidiah* ■ *Dir* Shawn Levy • *Scr* Robert Ben Garant, Thomas Lennon (3), from a story by Garant, Lennon, from the novel *The Night at the Museum* by Milan Trenc • *Cinematographer* Guillermo Navarro

Night at the Museum 2 ★★★ PG
Fantasy action comedy
2009 · US/Can · Colour · 100min

This snappy comedy sequel sees night watchman-turned-entrepreneur Larry Daley (Ben Stiller) return to his old haunts at New York's Museum of Natural History only to find that his exhibit pals (Owen Wilson and Steve Coogan) are headed for permanent storage at the Smithsonian Institution in Washington. He's summoned by a phone call from the bowels of the archive warning of a plot by egotistical Egyptian prince Kahmunrah (Hank Azaria on top form) to take over the museum. It's all fun and games as Larry exchanges quips with Kahmunrah and his cohorts (Napoleon, Al Capone and Ivan the Terrible), takes advice from Einstein and falls for Amelia Earhart (Amy Adams). The film has a broader scope and more imagination than the original, but it's the delightful special effects that impress the most. KK **DVD** Ⓑ Ⓒ
Ben Stiller *Larry Daley* • Amy Adams *Amelia Earhart* • Owen Wilson *Jedidiah* • Hank Azaria *Kahmunrah* • Robin Williams *Teddy Roosevelt* • Steve Coogan *Octavius* • Christopher Guest *Ivan the Terrible* • Alain Chabat *Napoleon Bonaparte* • Ricky Gervais *Dr McPhee* ■ *Dir* Shawn Levy • *Scr* Robert Ben Garant, Thomas Lennon (3), from characters by Garant, Lennon

Night at the Museum: Secret of the Tomb ★★ 12
Fantasy comedy
2014 · US · Colour · 97min

In this uneven third instalment in the series, Larry (Ben Stiller), night guard at New York's Natural History Museum, comes to the British Museum to refresh the ancient curse that brings museum exhibits to life at night. With his cohort of historical characters, Larry must also deal with Rebel Wilson as a suspicious guard and Dan Stevens as a rampaging Sir Lancelot. Robin Williams, Steve Coogan, Owen Wilson and Ricky Gervais are as funny as ever, but director Shawn Levy must rely on a peeing monkey and Stiller in a dual role as a Neanderthal to wring some laughs from the material. This is still worth watching, though, for some stellar cameos, a superb supporting cast (including Williams and Mickey Rooney in their final film performances) and wonderful views of beloved museums. KK **DVD** Ⓑ Ⓢ
Ben Stiller *Larry Daley* • Robin Williams *Teddy Roosevelt* • Owen Wilson *Jedidiah* • Dan Stevens *Sir Lancelot* • Ben Kingsley *Merenkahre* • Steve Coogan *Octavius* • Ricky Gervais *Dr McPhee* • Rebel Wilson *Tilly* • Skyler Gisondo *Nick Daley* • Rami Malek *Ahkmenrah* • Mickey Rooney *Gus* ■ *Dir* Shawn Levy • *Scr* David Guion, Michael Handelman, from a story by Guion, Handelman, Mark Friedman, from characters by Robert Ben Garant, Thomas Lennon (3)

A Night at the Opera ★★★★★ Ⓤ
Classic comedy
1935 · US · BW · 87min

At Paramount, the Marx Brothers had specialised in zany, freewheeling comedies that owed much to the anarchic antics of their vaudeville shows. This first outing for MGM was also honed on the stage, but producer Irving Thalberg used the three-week pre-production tour to chip away at the rough edges that made their humour so unique. But the Brothers' anarchic spirit triumphs, and the plot involving Groucho's bid to introduce wealthy Margaret Dumont into society through opera is almost an irrelevance. Certainly the romantic interludes with songbirds Allan Jones and Kitty Carlisle are. The madcap lunacy is unforgettable - whether it's the shenanigans inside Groucho's cabin or the slapstick ruination of *Il Trovatore*. DP **DVD**
Groucho Marx *Otis B Driftwood* • Chico Marx *Fiorello* • Harpo Marx *Tomasso* • Margaret Dumont *Mrs Claypool* • Allan Jones *Riccardo Baroni* • Kitty Carlisle *Rosa Castaldi* • Siegfried "Sig" Rumann [Sig Ruman] *Herman Gottlieb* ■ *Dir* Sam Wood • *Scr* George S Kaufman, Morrie Ryskind, Al Boasberg, Bert Kalmar, Harry Ruby, from a story by James Kevin McGuinness

A Night at the Roxbury ★ 15
Comedy
1998 · US · Colour · 81min

Beware movies based on comedy sketches as, with very few exceptions (*Wayne's World* being one), they are rarely very good. This tale, based on a *Saturday Night Live* skit about two dumber-than-dumb, sexist brothers trying to get into the coolest clubs in LA, is utterly devoid of any redeeming features. The actors are irritating, the script is humourless, and at under an hour-and-a-half it is still 80 minutes too long. JB Sexual references, some swearing.
Will Ferrell *Steve Butabi* • Chris Kattan *Doug Butabi* • Richard Grieco • Loni Anderson *Barbara Butabi* • Dan Hedaya *Kamehl Butabi* ■ *Dir* John Fortenberry • *Scr* Steven Koren, Will Ferrell, Chris Kattan

The Night Before ★ 15
Comedy
1988 · US · Colour · 86min

Keanu Reeves's first starring vehicle was understandably shelved for two years before its minuscule release. The future star of *The Matrix* shows no charisma as he stumbles through this *After Hours* for the adolescent crowd, playing a prom-bound teenager who retraces his steps after he wakes up in an alley with no car, no date and no memory of how he got there. The surreal touches are self-conscious and distracting and do not blend well with the movie's comic tone. KB
Keanu Reeves *Winston Connelly* • Lori Loughlin *Tara Mitchell* • Theresa Saldana *Rhonda* • Trinidad Silva *Tito* • Suzanne Snyder *Lisa* • Morgan Lofting *Mom* • Gwil Richards *Dad* ■ *Dir* Thom Eberhardt • *Scr* Gregory Scherick, Thom Eberhardt, from a story by Gregory Scherick

The Night Before ★★★ 15
Seasonal comedy
2015 · US · Colour · 97min

Three friends facing up to various adult responsibilities decide to end their tradition of going out partying on Christmas Eve, but not before one final wild night. What follows is a stoner comedy wrapped in tinsel, with the plot much further down the list of priorities than the comedy. Seth Rogen is a force of nature as the soon-to-be father with a box full of party drugs; while Joseph Gordon-Levitt and Anthony Mackie have enough charm and sincerity to make their sophomoric antics relatable. JL Swearing, nudity, drug abuse **DVD** Ⓑ
Joseph Gordon-Levitt *Ethan* • Seth Rogen *Isaac* • Anthony Mackie *Chris* • Jillian Bell *Betsy* • Lizzy Caplan *Diana* ■ *Dir* Jonathan Levine • *Scr* Evan Goldberg, Kyle Hunter, Jonathan Levine, Ariel Shaffir

Night Boat to Dublin ★★
Second World War spy drama
1946 · UK · BW · 91min

This B-thriller is worth seeing for its treatment of a topical theme - atomic weapons - and the performance of Robert Newton, then on the cusp of stardom. Newton plays a British Secret Service agent who travels to Dublin, where a Swedish scientist is giving atomic secrets to the Nazis. AT
Robert Newton *Captain David Grant* • Raymond Lovell *Paul Faber* • Guy Middleton *Captain Tony Hunter* • Muriel Pavlow *Marion Decker* • Herbert Lom *Keitel* • John Ruddock *Bowman* • Martin Miller *Professor Hansen* • Marius Goring *Frederick Jannings* ■ *Dir* Lawrence Huntington • *Scr* Robert Hall, Lawrence Huntington

The Night Caller ★★
Science-fiction thriller 1965 · UK · BW · 83min

You are an alien sent to Earth to find women to help repopulate your planet. How would you go about recruiting them? A wanted advert in *Bikini Girl* magazine, of course. This cheerful piece of nonsense has John Saxon as the scientist who is called in to investigate the arrival of a mysterious pod, and Alfred Burke as the copper unable to explain a spate of disappearances of young women. DP

John Saxon *Jack Costain* • Maurice Denham *Professor Morley* • Patricia Haines *Ann Barlow* • Alfred Burke *Superintendent Hartley* • John Carson *Major* • Jack Watson *Sergeant Hawkins* • Warren Mitchell *Lilburn* ■ *Dir* John Gilling • *Scr* Jim O'Connolly, from the novel *The Night Callers* by Frank Crisp

Night Creatures ★★★ 12
Horror adventure 1962 · UK · Colour · 78min

Skulduggery in the Romney Marsh of the 1790s is the theme of this good-looking curio from Hammer Studios. Horror stalwart Peter Cushing is typically sinister as a seeming y harmless vicar who double life as the head of a smuggling ring is jeopardised. Though based on classic adventure *Dr Syn*, alterations had to be made to avoid clashing with the Disney version released in the same year. But busty wenches, loutish sailors and the marauding Marsh Phantoms keep the mood up, while a young Oliver Reed cuts a dash as a preening local squire. JA Violence.

Peter Cushing *Rev Dr Blyss* • Patrick Allen *Captain Collier* • Yvonne Romain *Imogene* • Oliver Reed *Harry Cobtree* ■ *Dir* Peter Graham Scott • *Scr* John Elder [Anthony Hinds], from the novel *Dr Syn* by Russell Thorndike

Night Crossing ★★ PG
Adventure based on a true story
1981 · UK/US · Colour · 102min

Disney attempts to impose cuteness on a true Cold War story about two East German families who float perilously over the border to western life, liberty and the pursuit of capitalism in a home-made balloon. Director Delbert Mann conveys little of the truth of what must have been a strange and terrifying business. John Hurt, Jane Alexander and Beau Bridges give their all, but ultimately it is so much hot air. TH DVD

John Hurt *Peter Strelzyk* • Jane Alexander *Doris Strelzyk* • Doug McKeon *Frank Strelzyk* • Keith McKeon *Fitscher Strelzyk* • Beau Bridges *Gunter Wetzel* • Glynnis O'Connor *Petra Wetzel* ■ *Dir* Delbert Mann • *Scr* John McGreevey

Night Eyes ★★ 18
Erotic thriller 1990 · US · Colour · 94min

This is the first in what has turned out to be a very profitable franchise, spawning three very similar sequels. Called in to protect Tanya Roberts Andrew Stevens plays a security guard whose voyeuristic tendencies get the better of him. The sex and thrills are strictly soft-core and the performances little more than adequate. JF Violence, swearing, nudity.

Andrew Stevens *Will* • Tanya Roberts *Nikki* • Cooper Huckabee *Ernie* • Veronica Henson-Phillips *Lauretta* • Stephen Meadows *Michael Vincent* • Karen Elise Baldwin *Ellen* • Warwick Sims *Brian Walker* ■ *Dir* Jag Mundhra • *Scr* Tom Citrano, Andrew Stevens

Night Falls on Manhattan ★★ 15
Crime drama 1997 · US · Colour · 108min

Assistant DA Andy Garcia finds himself promoted following his successful, high-profile prosecution of a big-time drug dealer and cop killer. Then a skeleton is hauled out of the river, opening a hornet's nest of corruption. Despite some good performances this is really just another drive around the block for Sidney Lumet: he not only lets the pace slacken, but also sanctions a corny romance between Garcia and legal rival Lena Olin that turns the gritty realism into soapy melodrama. AT Violence, swearing. DVD

Andy Garcia *Sean Casey* • Richard Dreyfuss *Sam Vigoda* • Lena Olin *Peggy Lindstrom* • Ian Holm *Liam Casey* • James Gandolfini *Joey Allegretto* • Colm Feore *Elihu Harrison* ■ *Dir* Sidney Lumet • *Scr* Sidney Lumet, from the novel *Tainted Evidence* by Robert Daley

Night Flight ★★
Adventure 1933 · US · BW · 84min

MGM wheeled out a lot of stars for this flying yarn: two Barrymores, Clark Gable, Robert Montgomery and two fine leading ladies, Myrna Loy and Helen Hayes. The story is about the setting up of a company that delivers mail across the high Andes. In the air, it's all turbulence, fog and mountain peaks; on the ground, it's all macho posturing and romantic clinches. Its box-office success spawned a whole series of imitators. AT

John Barrymore *Riviere* • Helen Hayes *Mme Fabian* • Clark Gable *Jules* • Lionel Barrymore *Robineau* • Robert Montgomery *Auguste Pellerin* • Myrna Loy *Brazilian pilot's wife* ■ *Dir* Clarence Brown • *Scr* Oliver HP Garrett, from the story by Antoine de Saint-Exupéry

Night Games ★ 18
Erotic thriller 1979 · US · Colour · 101min

This is risible erotica from Roger Vadim, the man who "discovered", then married Brigitte Bardot and Jane Fonda (though not at the same time). Vadim's protégée Cindy Pickett isn't bad in her feature debut, playing a Beverly Hills housewife terrified of sexual contact due to a traumatic childhood incident. When she's reduced to having sex with a man dressed as a bird, though, it's fatally unclear whether Vadim is being mocking or serious. RS

Cindy Pickett *Valerie St John* • Joanna Cassidy *Julie Miller* • Barry Primus *Jason St John* • Paul Jenkins *Sean Daniels* • Gene Davis *Timothy* • Juliet Fabriga *Alicia* • Clem Parsons *Jun* • Mark Hanks *"The Phantom"* ■ *Dir* Roger Vadim • *Scr* Anton Diether, Clarke Reynolds, from a story by Barth Jules Sussman, Anton Diether

Night Has a Thousand Eyes ★★
Mystery 1948 · US · BW · 81min

The assumption that a vaudeville show clairvoyant (Edward G Robinson) is a fake turns out to be unfounded when he proves he really can foretell the future. John Farrow directs this efficiently made but bland entertainment, which co-stars Gail Russell, John Lund, Virginia Bruce and William Demarest. RK

Edward G Robinson *John Triton* • Gail Russell *Jean Courtland* • John Lund *Elliott Carson* • Virginia Bruce *Jenny* • William Demarest *Lt Shawn* • Richard Webb *Peter Vinson* ■ *Dir* John Farrow • *Scr* Barre Lyndon, Jonathan Latimer, from a novel by Cornell Woolrich

The Night Has Eyes ★★★ PG
Thriller 1942 · UK · BW · 75min

The saturnine side of James Mason's screen persona was exploited to the full in this studio-bound melodrama, set on the Yorkshire moors. Mason plays a reclusive composer and wounded veteran of the Spanish Civil War who is subject to fits. He could well be a threat to Joyce Howard, one of two female teachers taking refuge from a storm. On the other hand, there's something not quite right about Wilfrid Lawson and Mary Clare, the couple who run the house. Director Leslie Arliss develops the sinister atmosphere with some skill. AE DVD

James Mason *Stephen Deremid* • Joyce Howard *Marian Ives* • Wilfrid Lawson *Sturrock* • Mary Clare *Mrs Ranger* • Tucker McGuire *Doris* • John Fernald *Dr Barry Randall* ■ *Dir* Leslie Arliss • *Scr* John Argyle, Leslie Arliss, Alan Kennington, from a story by Alan Kennington

The Night Holds Terror ★★
Crime drama 1955 · US · BW · 85min

Watch this and you'll spend the night checking all locks and doors three times over. One of those post-*film noir* movies where everything is shadow and promised substance, but you get little more than a lot of characters with their mouths hanging

open and jauntily angled fedoras. Here, a family is held to ransom by crooks John Cassavetes (in only his second major role), Vince Edwards and David Cross. Quite exciting for the first 20 minutes, and immensely tedious thereafter. SH

Jack Kelly *Gene Courtier* • Hildy Parks *Doris Courtier* • Vince Edwards *Victor Gosset* • John Cassavetes *Robert Batsford* • David Gross *Luther Logan* • Edward Marr [Eddie Marr] *Captain Cole* ■ *Dir* Andrew Stone [Andrew L Stone] • *Scr* Andrew Stone

A Night in Casablanca ★★★ U
Comedy 1946 · US · BW · 81min

While it has none of the sustained genius of their earlier outings, this Marx Brothers' picture has enough moments of inspired lunacy to merit a place on most viewers' "must see" lists. Although freed from the constraints placed upon them by MGM, the trio (ending a five-year screen exile) are forced to play second fiddle to a contrived plot about spies and buried treasure, which was supposed to invite cheeky comparisons with the classic Bogart/Bergman drama. Groucho goes into one-liner overdrive to compensate for the absence of Margaret Dumont, but Harpo has the best gag. DP DVD

Groucho Marx *Ronald Kornblow* • Harpo Marx *Rusty* • Chico Marx *Corbaccio* • Lisette Verea *Beatrice Reiner* • Charles Drake *Pierre* • Lois Collier *Annette* • Dan Seymour *Captain Brizzard* • Sig Rumann [Sig Ruman] *Count Pfefferman* ■ *Dir* Archie Mayo • *Scr* Joseph Fields, Roland Kibbee

A Night in Heaven ★★ 18
Romantic drama 1983 · US · Colour · 79min

College professor Lesley Ann Warren goes to a male strip club and finds that the featured dancer is Christopher Atkins, who happens to be one of her more problematic students. A contrived May-December romantic drama, this coasts along thanks mainly to Warren's captivating turn and "Heaven", the Chippendales-style locale. Watch out for Andy Garcia in his first screen role. AJ

Christopher Atkins *Rick* • Lesley Ann Warren *Faye* • Robert Logan *Whitney* • Deborah Rush *Patsy* • Deney Terrio *Tony* • Sandra Beall *Slick* • Alix Elias *Shirley* • Carrie Snodgress *Mrs Johnson* • Amy Levine *Eve* • Andy Garcia *TJ* ■ *Dir* John G Avildsen • *Scr* Joan Tewkesbury

A Night in the Life of Jimmy Reardon ★★★ 15
Drama 1988 · US · Colour · 88min

River Phoenix strayed from his usual thoughtful pubescent role to play a romeo teenager with a gravity-defying hairdo in this hit-and-miss comedy. Although Phoenix is as engaging as ever, he seems ill at ease playing such an extrovert character. Nonetheless, the movie has its moments, notably Phoenix's assignations with older woman Ann Magnuson. JB Swearing. DVD

River Phoenix *Jimmy Reardon* • Meredith Salenger *Lisa* • Matthew L Perry [Matthew Perry] *Fred* • Ione Skye *Denise* • Ann Magnuson *Joyce* • Louanne *Suzie* • Paul Koslo *Mr Reardon* • Jane Hallaren *Mrs Reardon* ■ *Dir* William Richert • *Scr* William Richert, from his novel *Aren't You Even Gonna Kiss Me Goodbye?*

A Night in the Woods ★★★ 15
Horror 2011 · UK · Colour and BW · 79min

The *Blair Witch Project* template - three people vanish from a haunted wood with only recorded footage left to mark their passing - receives a surprisingly eerie British twist. An Anglo-American couple (Anna Skellern, *Monsters* star Scoot McNairy) and the woman's cousin (Andrew Hawley) dare to go camping on Dartmoor. But a potent mix of jealousy, paranoia and old wives' tales soon quickens the pulse as relations between the tric deteriorate. It's derivative stuff, but the improvised performances, beautiful yet isolated location and dynamic camerawork keep

things watchable. JA Violence, swearing, sexual references, drug abuse. DVD

Scoot McNairy *Brody Cartwright* • Anna Skellern *Kerry Hastings* • Andrew Hawley *Leo* ■ *Dir/Scr* Richard Parry

Night Is My Future ★★★ PG
Drama 1948 · Swe · BW · 84min

Ingmar Bergman's fourth feature was the first to turn a profit. His mentor, producer Lorens Marmstedt, insisted he adhered closely to the storyline, even though it was awash with sentimentality: from the fact that Birger Malmsten is blinded while trying to rescue a puppy from a firing range, to the final reunion with a radiantly waifish Mai Zetterling. However, there's a poetic realism about the picture, with the dream sequence allowing Bergman to break out of the film's melodramatic straitjacket. DP In Swedish. DVD

Mai Zetterling *Ingrid Olofsdotter* • Birger Malmsten *Bengt* • Bengt Eklund *Ebbe* ■ *Dir* Ingmar Bergman • *Scr* Dagmar Edqvist, from her novel

The Night Listener ★★ 15
Mystery thriller 2006 · US · Colour · 77min

Robin Williams is an actor who polarises opinions: some find his sentimental tomfoolery irresistible, while others might prefer to stick their heads into a bucket of bees rather than endure his tediously tearful antics. But even his detractors may have been pleasantly surprised by his convincing performances in *One Hour Photo* and *Insomnia*, in which he played directly against type. He's impressive again here as night-time radio phone-in host Gabriel Noone, who strikes up a long-distance relationship with Pete (Rory Culkin). Williams is effectively understated, but is ultimately let down by a plodding screenplay and shoddy direction by Patrick Stettner, who attempts to generate tension when there is none and fails to explore the characters or their situation with any real insight. AS DVD

Robin Williams *Gabriel Noone* • Toni Collette *Donna D Logand* • Bobby Cannavale *Jess* • Joe Morton *Ashe* • John Cullum *Pap Noone* • Rory Culkin *Pete D Logand* • Sandra Oh *Anna* ■ *Dir* Patrick Stettner • *Scr* Armistead Maupin, Terry Anderson, Patrick Stettner, from the novel by Armistead Maupin

Night Mail ★★★★★
Documentary 1936 · UK · BW · 23min

The jewel of British cinema in the 1930s was the documentary movement presided over by John Grierson (the man who coined the term "documentary" for factual films). Grierson and Stuart Legg provide the commentary for this evocative short, directed by Harry Watt and Basil Wright for the GPO Film Unit. Never have the dry statistics about the operation of the London-Glasgow mail train been presented with such flair. The beautiful shots of steaming engines, the rhythmic cutting, Benjamin Britten's pulsing score and WH Auden's adroit verses combine to form a film poem that delights both the ear and the eye. DP DVD

■ *Dir* Harry Watt, Basil Wright • *Scr* WH Auden, Basil Wright, Harry Watt

'Night, Mother ★★★★ 15
Drama 1986 · US · Colour · 92min

Sissy Spacek, who won an Oscar six years earlier for her performance in *Coal Miner's Daughter*, tells her mother she's going to commit suicide in this drama based on Marsha Norman's Pulitzer Prize-winning play. Both Spacek and Anne Bancroft (an Academy Award-winner herself for *The Miracle Worker*) are excellent, and though this character-driven piece sometimes feels a bit stagey, the performances are mesmerising enough to keep you riveted. JB DVD

Sissy Spacek *Jessie Cates* • Anne Bancroft *Thelma Cates* • Ed Berke *Dawson Cates* • Carol Robbins *Loretta Cates* • Jennifer Roosendahl *Melodie Cates* • Michael Kenworthy *Kenny Cates* ■ *Dir* Tom Moore • *Scr* Marsha Norman, from her play

N

Night Moves ★★★★ 18
Mystery thriller 1975 · US · Colour · 95min

Despite its title, this brilliantly self-conscious gumshoe movie by director Arthur Penn lights up a time of post-Watergate confusion as weary private eye Gene Hackman seeks a client's lost daughter (Melanie Griffith, in her third screen role) and his own lost honour. It's a bleak, pointless quest, encapsulated by the final shot of a boat going round in circles, but along the way there's plenty of sour wit in Alan Sharp's sparkling script. An enigmatic, entirely cinematic masterwork. TH Violence, swearing.

Gene Hackman *Harry Moseby* • Jennifer Warren *Paula* • Edward Binns *Joey Ziegler* • Harris Yulin *Marty Heller* • Kenneth Mars *Nick* • Janet Ward *Arlene Iverson* • James Woods *Quentin* • Anthony Costello *Marv Ellman* • John Crawford *Tom Iverson* • Melanie Griffith *Delly Grastner* • Susan Clark *Ellen Moseby* ■ *Dir* Arthur Penn • *Scr* Alan Sharp

Night Moves ★★★★ 15
Thriller 2013 · US · Colour · 112min

It's bold to borrow your title from a classic of new Hollywood – here, Arthur Penn's 1975 thriller – but after a string of intelligent US indies, Kelly Reichardt has paid her dues. Ostensibly one of her more ambitious productions (three young eco-activists try to blow up a hydroelectric dam), this focuses on the paranoid bubble they find themselves in rather than the outside world. Things get a little overheated between jittery Dakota Fanning and the loose cannon Jesse Eisenberg, but the direction stays cool and Reichardt earns her 70s stripes with a perfect, understated ending. DW *DVD*

Jesse Eisenberg *Josh* • Dakota Fanning *Dena* • Peter Sarsgaard *Harmon* • Alia Shawkat *Surprise* • Katherine Waterston *Anne* ■ *Dir* Kelly Reichardt • *Scr* Kelly Reichardt, Jonathan Raymond

Night Must Fall ★★★★
Thriller 1937 · US · BW · 116min

Emlyn Williams's famous shocker has had many incarnations, but this MGM version is very good indeed, largely due to the casting against type of the totally plausible Robert Montgomery as the suspected killer, and a marvellous performance from Rosalind Russell as the woman who slowly but surely discovers the killer's identity for herself. Several of the cast MGM employed had played their parts on stage in both London and New York, and the film is especially notable for the appearance of May Whitty, in one of her first talking roles, as a foolish, isolated old woman. TS

Robert Montgomery *Danny* • Rosalind Russell *Olivia* • May Whitty [Dame May Whitty] *Mrs Bransom* • Alan Marshal *Justin* • Merle Tottenham *Dora* • Kathleen Harrison *Mrs Terence* ■ *Dir* Richard Thorpe • *Scr* John van Druten, from the play by Emlyn Williams

Night Must Fall ★★★
Thriller 1964 · UK · BW · 104min

Emlyn Williams's popular, if shakily plotted, stage thriller was originally filmed in 1937. In this flashy remake, Susan Hampshire steps into the shoes of the woman who gradually comes to realise who is responsible for a series of countryside killings. Director Karel Reisz's attempts to explore the murderer's mental instability through camera movements and cross-cuts are undone by the staginess of the dialogue. Yet Freddie Francis's photography is highly atmospheric and Albert Finney's performance is occasionally electrifying. DP

Albert Finney *Danny* • Susan Hampshire *Olivia* • Mona Washbourne *Mrs Bramson* • Sheila Hancock *Dora* • Michael Medwin *Derek* • Joe Gladwin *Dodge* ■ *Dir* Karel Reisz • *Scr* Clive Exton, from the play by Emlyn Williams

The Night My Number Came Up ★★★ PG
Drama 1955 · UK · BW · 91min

This intriguing film bears more than a passing resemblance to the James Stewart airplane melodrama *No Highway*. Similarly held together by a first-rate central performance, the film features Michael Redgrave intent on grounding his flight to Tokyo as events alarmingly begin to resemble those in a nightmare. Exploring with a keen intelligence the coincidences and implausibilities generated by fear, RC Sherriff's tense screenplay is full of unsympathetic, self-obsessed characters, played to a nicety by a model supporting cast. DP *DVD*

Michael Redgrave *Air Marshal John Hardie* • Sheila Sim *Mary Campbell* • Alexander Knox *Owen Robertson* • Denholm Elliott *Flight Lieutenant McKenzie* • Ursula Jeans *Mrs Robertson* • Michael Hordern *Commander Lindsay* • Ralph Truman *Lord Wainwright* ■ *Dir* Leslie Norman • *Scr* RC Sherriff, from an article by Air Marshal Sir Victor Goddard

Night Nurse ★★★
Crime drama 1931 · US · BW · 62min

This fast-moving melodrama has a great cast headed by Barbara Stanwyck and Joan Blondell, who were accused by contemporary critics of boosting the film's audiences by spending an inordinate amount of screen time dressing and undressing. Ben Lyon is the co-star, but the screen is well and truly stolen by a young actor in the supporting role of sadistic chauffeur: Clark Gable on the road to stardom. This kind of tough, sexy drama vanished with the coming of the restrictive Hays Code, and it's always interesting to see what Hollywood could get away with before. TS

Barbara Stanwyck *Lora Hart* • Ben Lyon *Mortie* • Joan Blondell *Maloney* • Charles Winninger *Dr Arthur Bell* • Charlotte Merriam *Mrs Ritchey* • Edward Nugent *Eagan* • Blanche Frederici *Mrs Maxwell* ■ *Dir* William A Wellman • *Scr* Oliver HP Garrett, Charles Kenyon, from the novel by Dora Macy [Grace Perkins Oursler]

The Night of Counting the Years ★★★★
Historical drama 1969 · Egy · Colour · 102min

Recalling the actual theft by members of the Horrabat tribe of artefacts from a tomb in Thebes in 1881, this stunningly photographed picture considers whether an impoverished people should sell its antiquities to survive or resist the export of its heritage. Shadi Abdelsalam's background in art direction is evident in his hypnotic selection of deep-focus shots and his control of light and contrasting colours. Yet he also manages to keep this slow-moving story absorbing throughout. DP Arabic +subtitles.

Ahmed Marei *Wanniss* • Zouzou El Hakim *Mother* • Ahmad Hegazi *Brother* • Nadia Loutfy *Zeena* • Gaby Karraz *Maspero* ■ *Dir/Scr* Shadi Abdelsalam

Night of Dark Shadows ★★
Horror 1971 · US · Colour · 93min

The presence of Jonathan Frid as Barnabas the vampire is greatly missed in this second film sequel (after *House of Dark Shadows*) to the cult TV daytime serial *Dark Shadows*. The tale of the haunting of a newlywed couple who have recently moved in to their infamous ancestral home unfolds in haphazard fashion. Barking more than terrifying, this will be best enjoyed by fans of the soap opera and its misbegotten 1990s update. AJ

David Selby *Quentin Collins/Charles Collins* • Grayson Hall *Carlotta Drake* • John Karlen *Alex Jenkins* • Nancy Barrett *Claire Jenkins* • Lara Parker *Angélique* • Kate Jackson *Tracy Collins* • James Storm *Gerard Styles* • Diana Millay *Laura Collins* • Christopher Pennock *Gabriel Collins* • Thayer David *Reverend Strack* ■ *Dir* Dan Curtis • *Scr* Sam Hall, from a story by Sam Hall, Dan Curtis, from the TV series created by Dan Curtis, Art Wallace

The Night of San Lorenzo ★★★★ 12
Second World War drama 1981 · It · Colour · 102min

Told as an extended flashback by a woman who was just six when Tuscany was liberated by the Allies, this pacifist drama draws on both the Taviani brothers' own memories of the summer of 1944 and their cinematic influences to create an unforgettable, neorealist fairy tale. Against the visual poetry, small instances of surrealist fantasy and warm moments of simple humanity, however, is set the horror of war, as the Nazis and their Italian collaborators deal peremptorily with the partisans undermining their defence of San Martino. Thus the film's glowing romanticism lies less in the hard-won victory than in the people's unity and indomitability. DP Italian +subtitles. *DVD* *BD*

Paolo Hendel *Dilvo* • Omero Antonutti *Galvano* • Margarita Lozano *Concetta* • Claudio Bigagli *Corrado* • Massimo Bonetti *Nicola* • Norma Martelli *Ivana* ■ *Dir* Vittorio Taviani, Paolo Taviani • *Scr* Paolo Taviani, Vittorio Taviani, Giuliani G De Negri, Tonino Guerra

Night of Silence ★★★ PG
Drama 2012 · Tur · Colour · 91min

Turkish writer/director Reis Celik's intriguing update of the *Arabian Nights* sees Dilan Aksut as the 14-year-old coerced into an arranged marriage to end a blood feud. The middle-aged groom has recently been released from jail and feels humiliated at being made to marry a child. Celik confines most of the action to the bedroom, as Aksut realises that Salman is as reluctant a partner as herself, but each knows that proof of their consummation is required. It's an intimate, intense but always discreet dissection of antiquated patriarchal custom. DP Turkish +subtitles.

Ilyas Salman *Groom* • Dilan Aksut *Bride* ■ *Dir/Scr* Reis Celik

Night of the Big Heat ★★ 15
Science-fiction horror 1967 · UK · Colour · 90min

The ever-reliable team of Peter Cushing and Christopher Lee put a crisp British cast through its paces as mystified islanders are plagued by a winter heatwave caused by energy-starved aliens. Most of the action takes place at a local inn, where the helpless survivors get on each other's nerves. However, the final arrival of the monsters signals a few tepid thrills, even if they do resemble badly fried eggs with spaghetti innards. AJ Violence.

Christopher Lee *Hanson* • Peter Cushing *Dr Stone* • Patrick Allen *Jeff Callum* • Sarah Lawson *Frankie Callum* • Jane Merrow *Angela Roberts* • William Lucas *Ken Stanley* • Kenneth Cope *Tinker Mason* ■ *Dir* Terence Fisher • *Scr* Ronald Liles, Pip Baker, Jane Baker, from the novel by John Lymington

Night of the Comet ★★★ 15
Science-fiction thriller 1984 · US · Colour · 94min

Full of fun scares, gleeful unease and touching warmth, director Thom Eberhardt's tongue-in-cheek cult item pastes together numerous ideas from other science-fiction flicks and takes them the full distance. The same comet that wiped out the dinosaurs reappears to make most of mankind extinct this time. Catherine Mary Stewart and Kelli Maroney are two tough talking Valley girls who survive to take on the remaining flesh-eating zombies, marauding punks and sinister scientists in this upbeat and funky metaphor for maturity. AJ *DVD* *BD*

Catherine Mary Stewart *Regina* • Robert Beltran *Hector* • Kelli Maroney *Samantha* • Geoffrey Lewis *Carter* • Mary Woronov *Audrey* ■ *Dir/Scr* Thom Eberhardt

Night of the Demon ★★★★ PG
Horror 1957 · UK · BW · 91min

A remarkably well-constructed essay on the realm of the supernatural, *Cat People* director Jacques Tourneur's classic devil-cult chiller is a superb adaptation of the MR James short story *Casting the Runes*. Pitting rational scientist Dana Andrews against sinister mystic Niall MacGinnis, this top-notch suspense drama works marvellously well, despite studio interference insisting that the scary demon Tourneur wanted to avoid showing be included at the last minute. Edge-of-the-seat stuff, with a truly memorable climax. Released on video as *Curse of the Demon*. AJ *DVD*

Dana Andrews *John Holden* • Peggy Cummins *Joanna Harrington* • Niall MacGinnis *Dr Karswell* • Maurice Denham *Professor Harrington* • Athene Seyler *Mrs Karswell* • Liam Redmond *Mark O'Brien* • Reginald Beckwith *Mr Meek* • Ewan Roberts *Lloyd Williamson* ■ *Dir* Jacques Tourneur • *Scr* Charles Bennett, Hal E Chester, from the story *Casting the Runes* by MR James

Night of the Demons ★★ 18
Horror 1988 · US · Colour · 85min

A high schoolers' Halloween party at the local spook house goes predictably wrong in this goofy 1980s horror film. Think *The Breakfast Club* crossed with *The Evil Dead* and you'll get the basic idea. Sadly, it's nowhere near as funny as the first, or as scary as the second. Scream queen Linnea Quigley provides most of the requisite nudity, while Steve Johnson (Quigley's future husband) supplies the gore. There are a few bright moments, but mostly it's the same old schtick. ST *DVD*

Lance Fenton *Jay* • Cathy Podewell *Judy* • Alvin Alexis *Roger* • Hal Havins *Stooge* • Amelia Kinkade *Angela* • Linnea Quigley *Suzanne* ■ *Dir* Kevin S Tenney • *Scr* Joe Augustyn • *Special Effects* Steve Johnson

Night of the Demons ★★ 18
Horror 2010 · US · Colour · 108min

Director Adam Gierasch's remake of the trashy 1988 B-movie horror is more technically adept and better acted by an experienced cast (that includes *American Pie's* Shannon Elizabeth and *Terminator 2's* Edward Furlong). The plot is virtually identical to Kevin Tenney's cult original: a Halloween party in a haunted house turns deadly when drooling demons knock off drunken revellers. But patience with the braindead script's predictability runs thin as the pacing slackens off and the contrived sickness continually fails to shock. AJ Violence, sex scenes, nudity. *DVD* *BD*

Edward Furlong *Colin* • Shannon Elizabeth *Angela* • Monica Keena *Maddie Curtis* • Bobbi Sue Luther *Suzanne* ■ *Dir* Adam Gierasch • *Scr* Adam Gierasch, Jace Anderson, from the 1988 film

Night of the Demons 2 ★★★
Horror 1994 · US · Colour · 96min

This belated follow-up to the 1988 film is actually a more imaginative and outrageous ride, despite the clichéd plot about a group of brattish students holding a Halloween bash in a creepy old house. Director Brian Trenchard-Smith plays it for laughs at every opportunity and throws a smidgen of gratuitous nudity and gore into the teen-slasher brew. There are some truly inspired moments, such as when a nun saves the day using holy water in a squirt gun Uzi. A third instalment, *Demon House*, followed in 1997. RS

Cristi Harris *Bibi* • Bobby Jacoby *Perry* • Merle Kennedy *Mouse* • Amelia Kinkade *Angela* • Rod McCary *Father Bob* • Johnny Moran *Johnny* • Rick Peters *Rick* ■ *Dir* Brian Trenchard-Smith • *Scr* Joe Augustyn, from a story by James Penzi, Augustyn

Night of the Eagle ★★★ 12
Horror 1961 · UK · BW · 83min

A woman uses witchcraft to further her husband's career in this nifty adaptation of Fritz Leiber Jr's classic tale. Despite being over-melodramatic at times, Sidney Hayers's solid direction creates a great deal of terror out of the unseen to make it above average in the spine-tingling department. You'll still be unnerved even though you can glimpse the wires on the stone eagle as it comes to life in the eerie coda. AJ *DVD*

Peter Wyngarde *Norman Taylor* • Janet Blair *Tansy Taylor* • Margaret Johnston *Flora Carr* • Anthony Nicholls *Harvey Sawtelle* • Colin Gordon *Professor Lindsay Carr* • Kathleen Byron *Evelyn Sawtelle* • Reginald Beckwith *Harold Gunnison* • Jessica Dunning *Hilda Gunnison* ■ *Dir* Sidney

U SUITABLE FOR ALL   Uc SUITABLE ESPECIALLY FOR YOUNG CHILDREN (DVD ONLY)   PG PARENTAL GUIDANCE   12A UNDER 12s TO BE ACCOMPANIED (CINEMA ONLY)

Hayers • Scr Charles Beaumont, Richard Matheson, George Baxt, from the novel *Conjure Wife* by Fritz Leiber Jr

The Night of the Following Day ★★ 18

Crime thriller   1968 · UK/US · Colour · 89min

Marlon Brando wears a blond wig and a black T-shirt to show off his shockingly lithe figure in this deservedly obscure thriller, shot in Normandy under conditions of considerable chaos and tension, not least due to Brando's on-off relationship with co-star Rita Moreno. British actress Pamela Franklin is kidnapped by drug addict Moreno, tough cookie Richard Boone and chauffeur Brando. It's around this point that the movie becomes extremely arty in a way that suggests the director had been watching too much Godard. **AT**

Marlon Brando *Bud the chauffeur* • Richard Boone *Leer* • Rita Moreno *Vi* • Pamela Franklin *Girl* • Jess Hahn *Wally* ■ *Dir* Hubert Cornfield • *Scr* Hubert Cornfield, Robert Phippeny, from the novel *The Snatchers* by Lionel White

The Night of the Generals ★★★ 15

Second World War drama
1966 · UK/Fr · Colour · 138min

Three Nazi generals are the prime suspects following a series of Jack the Ripper-style murders in this lurid Second World War drama. Omar Sharif heads the inquiry while Peter O'Toole is top-billed as one of the officers under investigation. Director Anatole Litvak gives up on the whodunnit element early on and the plot just about muddles through, with Tom Courtenay representing the powerless ordinary soldier. **TH**

Peter O'Toole *General Tanz* • Omar Sharif *Major Grau* • Tom Courtenay *Corporal Hartmann* • Donald Pleasence *General Kahlenberge* • Joanna Pettet *Ulrike von Seidlitz-Gabler* • Philippe Noiret *Inspector Morand* • Charles Gray *General von Seidlitz-Gabler* • Coral Browne *Eleanore von Seidlitz-Gabler* ■ *Dir* Anatole Litvak • *Scr* Joseph Kessel, Paul Dehn, from the novels *Die Nacht der Generale* by Hans Helmut Kirst and *The Wary Transgressor* by James Hadley Chase

Night of the Ghouls ★ PG

Horror   1959 · US · BW · 66min

Even by the standards of Edward D Wood Jr, generally acknowledged as the worst director ever, this is woeful stuff. In this sequel of sorts to *Bride of the Monster*, Kenne Duncan, in a role originally written for Bela Lugosi, plays a fake medium who unwittingly resurrects the dead. The opening shot of Criswell arising from his coffin to warn the audience of things that go bump in the night is funnier than every Abbott and Costello film put together. This was one of Wood's last movies, though it was never released in his lifetime. **RS**

Criswell • Kenne Duncan *Dr Acula* • Maila Nurmi [Vampira] *Black ghost* • Tor Johnson *Lobo* • Valda Hansen *Fake ghost* • Lon Chaney Jr ■ *Dir/Scr* Edward D Wood Jr

The Night of the Hunter ★★★★★ 12

Classic thriller   1955 · US · BW · 88min

Charles Laughton's only film as a director is one of the great masterpieces of American cinema, a movie so strangely repellent, so poetic and so utterly hypnotic that it sadly never found an audience. It features Robert Mitchum's finest screen performance as a bogus priest and psychopath who has "love" and "hate" tattooed on his knuckles. Mitchum's always imposing, menacing presence is heightened by Laughton to an extraordinary degree, and this stunning collaboration is enhanced by Lillian Gish's portrayal of a gun-toting spinster. Set during the Depression in a rural backwater, this is a fairy tale turned into a dark night of the soul. Remade, unnecessarily, in 1991 as a TV movie. **AT** DVD 🔵

Robert Mitchum *Preacher Harry Powell* • Shelley Winters *Willa Harper* • Lillian Gish *Rachel* • Evelyn Varden *Icey Spoon* • Peter Graves (2) *Ben Harper* • Billy Chapin *John* • Sally Jane Bruce *Pearl* •

James Gleason *Birdie* ■ *Dir* Charles Laughton • *Scr* James Agee, from the novel by Davis Grubb • *Cinematographer* Stanley Cortez

The Night of the Iguana ★★★ 12

Melodrama   1964 · US · BW · 112min

It says much for the quality of the performances here that, from a cast that includes Richard Burton, Ava Gardner and Deborah Kerr, it was the little-known Grayson Hall who was nominated for an Oscar. As you would expect of a Tennessee Williams play, every performer has something to sink their teeth into. Yet Burton's defrocked cleric, Gardner's hotelier and Kerr's artist owe more to polished technique than flesh and blood. This may have something to do with director John Huston viewing this steamy story from his own laconic perspective. **DP** DVD

Richard Burton *Rev T Lawrence Shannon* • Ava Gardner *Maxine Faulk* • Deborah Kerr *Hannah Jelkes* • Sue Lyon *Charlotte Goodall* • James Ward *Hank Prosner* • Grayson Hall *Judith Fellowes* • Cyril Delevanti *Nonno* ■ *Dir* John Huston • *Scr* Anthony Veiller, John Huston, from the play by Tennessee Williams

Night of the Juggler ★★ 18

Action thriller   1980 · US · Colour · 96min

This overblown urban thriller achieves the rare feat of making New York look even uglier than it is in real life. When his daughter is mistakenly kidnapped by a candidate for "psycho of the month", ex-cop James Brolin trashes the city looking for her. Director Robert Butler brings technical craft to the numerous scenes of car crashes, but he seems rather less interested in the human beings in the cast. **RS**

James Brolin *Sean Boyd* • Cliff Gorman *Gus Soltic* • Richard Castellano *Lieutenant Tonelli* • Abby Bluestone *Kathy Boyd* • Dan Hedaya *Sergeant Otis Barnes* • Julie Carmen *Marie* • Mandy Patinkin *Cabbie* ■ *Dir* Robert Butler • *Scr* William Norton Sr, Rick Natkin, from the novel by William P McGivern

Night of the Living Dead ★★★★★ 15

Classic horror   1968 · US · BW · 91min

Director George A Romero redefined the meaning of horror for fear-sated audiences in the 1960s with this seminal classic. It starts suddenly with a jolting attack in a cemetery and continues on a relentless downward spiral of frantic despair as terrified people take fragile shelter in a secluded house to fight off an army of cannibalistic zombies. Conveying visceral terror through an unrelieved black-and-white documentary atmosphere, Romero's graphic cult chiller no longer scares the daylights out of viewers because of its countless imitations. But the director's radical style and lethal wit still impress. Five sequels, *Dawn of the Dead* (1978), *Day of the Dead* (1985), *Land of the Dead* (2005), *Diary of the Dead* (2007) and *Survival of the Dead* (2009) continue the masterful series. **AJ** DVD 🔵

Judith O'Dea *Barbara* • Russell Streiner *Johnny* • Duane Jones *Ben* • Karl Hardman *Harry Cooper* • Keith Wayne *Tom* ■ *Dir* George A Romero • *Scr* John A Russo, from a story by George A Romero

Night of the Living Dead ★★★★ 18

Horror   1990 · US · Colour · 84min

This highly acceptable remake of George A Romero's 1968 horror classic sticks close to the events of the original, as a group of people becomes trapped inside a farmhouse by a gang of flesh-eating zombies. However, the masterstroke here is to keep the viewer off-guard by introducing some fresh slants, courtesy of Romero (who updated his own script). Well acted and shot in atmospheric muted colours, this succeeds thanks to director Tom Savini's sure hand, bringing flair, intelligence and imagination to the task. **AJ** Violence, swearing. DVD

Tony Todd *Ben* • Patricia Tallman *Barbara* • Tom Towles *Harry* • McKee Anderson *Helen* • William Butler *Tom* • Katie Finneran *Judy Rose* • Bill Mosley [Bill Moseley] *Johnnie* • Heather Mazur *Sarah* ■ *Dir* Tom Savini • *Scr* George A Romero, from the 1968 film

Night of the Prowler ★ U

Crime drama   1962 · UK · BW · 61min

British director Francis Searle had the distinction of making only one bill-topping feature in his entire 27-film career, the daft comedy *A Girl in a Million*. The remainder of his output consisted of B-movies, including this offering. Devotees of laughably bad low-budget crime movies should enjoy this tawdry tale of ambition, murder and deceit, set in the cut-throat world of the motor trade! **DP**

Patrick Holt *Robert Langton* • Colette Wilde *Marie Langton* • Bill Nagy *Paul Conrad* • Mitzi Rogers *Jacky Reed* • John Horsley *Inspector Cameron* • Marianne Stone *Mrs Cross* ■ *Dir* Francis Searle • *Scr* Paul Erickson

Night of the Running Man ★★★ 18

Thriller   1994 · US · Colour · 88min

Andrew McCarthy stars in this decent enough crime thriller, which reunites him with Mark L Lester, his director on the previous year's *Extreme Justice*. Scott Glenn plays a hitman sent to wipe out cabbie McCarthy after he absconds with a cool million stolen from a Las Vegas casino. Lester is no stranger to this kind of action tale, but he too often allows the pace to drop to a canter. **DP** Violence, swearing, sex scenes.

Andrew McCarthy *Jerry Logan* • Scott Glenn *David Eckhart* • Janet Gunn *Chris Altman* • John Glover *Derek Mills* • Kim Lankford *Waitress* ■ *Dir* Mark L Lester • *Scr* Rodney Vaccaro, from the novel by Lee Wells

The Night of the Sunflowers ★★★★ 15

Crime thriller
2006 · Sp/Por/Fr · Colour · 118min

Writer/director Jorge Sánchez-Cabezudo exploits the sinister atmosphere of the countryside and exposes the perils of vigilante justice in this compelling Spanish *noir*. Unfolding in six chapters, the fractured timeline opens with the discovery of one body before shifting to travelling salesman Manuel Morón's attempted rape of city dweller Judith Diakhate. In his feature debut Sánchez-Cabezudo does occasionally lapse into melodrama as the story lurches from one act of bestial violence to another, but he also captures the characters' societal prejudices and debased morality with a chilling precision that makes the dénouement sordidly satisfying. **DP** Spanish +subtitles. DVD

Carmelo Gómez *Esteban* • Judith Diakhate *Gabi* • Celso Bugallo *Amadeo* • Mariano Alameda *Pedro* • Cesáreo Estébanez *Cecilio* • Vicente Romero *Tomás* • Manuel Morón *Salesman* ■ *Dir/Scr* Jorge Sánchez-Cabezudo

The Night of Truth ★★★ 18

Revenge drama
2004 · Burkina Faso/Fr · Colour · 95min

Set in an unnamed African country, the action in this sobering study of the ethnic tensions centres around the reconciliation rituals organised by Nayak president Adama Ouédraougo and the leader of the rebel Bonandé tribe, Moussa Cissé. However, the psychologically unstable First Lady, Naky Sy Savane, cannot forgive the slaughter of her son and her desire for revenge simmers beneath the stiffly cordial proceedings. While the dénouement is hardly a surprise, its savagery is genuinely shocking. **DP** French +subtitles. DVD

Naky Sy Savane *Edna* • Moussa Cissé *Colonel Theo* • Georgette Paré *Soumari* • Adama Ouédraougo [Adama Ouédraogo] *President Miossoune* • Rasmané Ouéd'aougo [Rasmane Ouedraogo] *Tomoto* ■ *Dir* Fanta Régina Nacro • *Scr* Marc Gautron, Fanta Régina Nacro

Night on Earth ★★★ 15

Comedy drama   1992 · US · Colour · 123min

Five taxi rides take place on the same night in Los Angeles, New York, Paris, Rome and Helsinki. In each cab, a moving story about life's little ironies unfolds. While the two American-based tales in Jim Jarmusch's highly accessible compendium fall flat, the European segments - Roberto Benigni confessing all to his priest-passenger, blind Béatrice Dalle teaching her cabbie a thing or two - hit the right note of quirkiness that has become the art house director's trademark. **AJ** English, French, Finnish, Italian +subtitles. DVD 🔵

Winona Ryder *Corky* • Gena Rowlands *Victoria Snelling* • Giancarlo Esposito *Yoyo* • Armin Mueller-Stahl *Helmut Grokenberger* • Rosie Perez *Angela* • Isaach de Bankole *Driver* • Béatrice Dalle *Blind woman* • Roberto Benigni *Gino* ■ *Dir/Scr* Jim Jarmusch

A Night on the Town ★★★ 15

Comedy   1987 · US · Colour · 102min

Also known as *Adventures in Babysitting*, this is one of the lightweight comedies Chris Columbus made before he directed the blockbusting hit *Home Alone*. It's a daft but fun teen movie with Elisabeth Shue as a girl who has a series of ridiculous adventures on the streets of Chicago one night with the children she's supposed to be babysitting. **JB** Violence, swearing. DVD CS

Elisabeth Shue *Chris Parker* • Maia Brewton *Sara Anderson* • Keith Coogan *Brad Anderson* • Anthony Rapp *Daryl Coopersmith* • Calvin Levels *Joe Gipp* • Vincent D'Onofrio [Vincent D'Onofrio] *Dawson* • Penelope Ann Miller *Brenda* ■ *Dir* Chris Columbus • *Scr* David Simkins

Night Passage ★★ U

Western   1957 · US · Colour · 86min

James Stewart, director Anthony Mann and writer Borden Chase already had a whole string of hit westerns under their belt when they started work on this below-par effort. Mann quit after a few days, sensing that the script wasn't quite ready, and made way for TV director James Neilson. Stewart plays a former railroad man who comes up against his own brother, train robber Audie Murphy, when he is hired to deliver a payroll. **AT** DVD

James Stewart *Grant McLaine* • Audie Murphy *Utica Kid* • Dan Duryea *Whitey Harbin* • Dianne Foster *Charlotte Drew* • Elaine Stewart *Verna Kimball* • Brandon de Wilde *Joey Adams* ■ *Dir* James Neilson • *Scr* Borden Chase, from a story by Norman A Fox

Night People ★★

Spy drama   1954 · US · Colour · 92min

Gregory Peck plays an American intelligence officer who flies to Berlin to secure the release of a US soldier kidnapped by the communists. There he runs into a giant conspiracy involving the young man's father, an influential magnate (Broderick Crawford), and the failed assassination plot against Hitler. This blend of Cold War jitters and Nazi hangover makes for a moderately gripping thriller that uses the real bombed-out city as its location, though gritty black and white might have served the story better than touristy Technicolor. **AT**

Gregory Peck *Colonel Van Dyke* • Broderick Crawford *Leatherby* • Anita Björk *Hoffy* • Rita Gam *Miss Cates* • Buddy Ebsen *Sergeant McColloch* • Walter Abel *Foster* ■ *Dir* Nunnally Johnson • *Scr* Nunnally Johnson, from a story by Jed Harris, Thomas Reed

Night People ★★★ 15

Drama   2005 · UK · Colour · 94min

First-time director Adrian Mead attempts to do for Edinburgh and its denizens what *Crash* and *Short Cuts* did for Los Angeles, taking several different stories and weaving them together in a single film. Mead also presents himself with the challenge of containing all his action within a single night, which certainly helps focus the material. Inevitably some episodes, some characters - and indeed some actors - are

N

better than others. A storyline involving a dim-witted father, a streetwise daughter and a stolen pedigree dog has some of the whimsical charm of Bill Forsyth, but at other times the drama seems rather flat – topics such as homelessness, drugs and rent boys have become overfamiliar in Scottish cinema. BP **DVD**

Katrina Bryan *Jane* • Alan McCafferty *Stewart* • Cara Shandley *Kelly* • Anthony Beselle *Matthew* • Kellyanne Farquhar *Mary* • Anthony Martin *David* • Neil Mackay *Josh* ■ *Dir* Adrian Mead • *Scr* Adrian Mead, Jack Dickson

The Night Porter ★★★ 18
Drama 1973 · It · Colour · 112min

What happens when former SS officer Dirk Bogarde and concentration camp inmate Charlotte Rampling meet years later and pick up their sadomasochistic sexual relationship more or less where they left off? Not quite the examination of the Nazi legacy in political and allegorical terms that director Liliana Cavani probably hoped for; hence the reason why her celebration of self-disgust and degradation so preoccupied the censors. Mere sexploitation or a serious analysis of guilty repression? The debate still rages. AJ Violence, nudity. **DVD** **BL**

Dirk Bogarde *Max* • Charlotte Rampling *Lucia* • Philippe Leroy *Klaus* • Gabriele Ferzetti *Hans* • Giuseppe Addobbati *Stumm* • Isa Miranda *Countess Stein* ■ *Dir* Liliana Cavani • *Scr* Liliana Cavani, Italo Moscati, from a story by Liliana Cavani, Barbara Alberti, Amedeo Pagani

The Night Runner ★★★
Film noir 1957 · US · BW · 78min

Ray Danton, who went on to play the title role in *The Rise and Fall of Legs Diamond* (1960), is well cast in this short, sharp shocker about a schizophrenic mental patient who takes up with Colleen Miller, much to the displeasure of her father. Abner Biberman directs with occasional flashes of insight to light up the murk, but the film never lets Danton show off his acting skills. TH

Ray Danton *Roy Turner* • Colleen Miller *Susan Mayes* • Merry Anders *Amy Hansen* • Willis Bouchey *Loren Mayes* • Harry Jackson *Hank Hansen* • Robert Anderson (2) *Ed Wallace* ■ *Dir* Abner Biberman • *Scr* Gene Levitt, from a story by Owen Cameron

Night Shift ★★★★ 15
Comedy 1982 · US · Colour · 101min

It was intended as a vehicle for director Ron Howard's old *Happy Days* chum Henry "the Fonz" Winkler, but future Batman Michael Keaton steals the show. Winkler is the shy mortuary attendant who gets involved in a call-girl operation run from the morgue by sharp-talking Keaton. The broad script doesn't attempt to milk the black opportunities in the scenario, but it is still very funny. This also gave early exposure to a number of other future stars, including Shelley Long and Kevin Costner. JF Violence, swearing, nudity.

Henry Winkler *Chuck Lumley* • Michael Keaton *Bill Blazejowski* • Shelley Long *Belinda Keaton* • Gina Hecht *Charlotte Koogle* • Pat Corley *Edward Koogle* • Bobby DiCicco *Leonard* • Clint Howard *Jefferey* • Kevin Costner *Frat boy* • Shannen Doherty *Bluebird* ■ *Dir* Ron Howard • *Scr* Lowell Ganz, Babaloo Mandel

Night Song ★★★ U
Romantic drama 1947 · US · BW · 102min

Merle Oberon gets to weep buckets in this sudsy melodrama in which she poses as a blind young woman to help her sightless protégé Dana Andrews fulfil his potential as a composer. Director John Cromwell could churn out this kind of sentimental nonsense in his sleep, and he knows just when to play on the heartstrings or lighten the atmosphere through the moving performances of Ethel Barrymore and Hoagy Carmichael. The best part is watching Artur Rubinstein and the New York Philharmonic treating Andrews's lousy tune as a classical masterpiece. DP

Dana Andrews *Dan* • Merle Oberon *Cathy* • Ethel Barrymore *Miss Willey* • Hoagy Carmichael *Chick* • Artur Rubinstein • Jacqueline White *Connie* ■

Dir John Cromwell • *Scr* DeWitt Bodeen, Frank Fenton, Dick Irving Hyland, from a story by Dick Irving Hyland

Night Sun ★★★ 15
Historical drama 1990 · It/Fr/W Ger · Colour · 107min

Tolstoy's story *Father Sergius* is translated to 18th-century Italy in this handsome yet minimalist study of asceticism, idealism and the perils of pride and fame. Quitting the Neapolitan court on discovering that his bride-to-be, Nastassja Kinski, was once the king's mistress, ennobled trooper Julian Sands embraces desert monasticism, only to be beset by worldly temptation (in the form of the minxish Charlotte Gainsbourg) after he's hailed as a miracle worker by pilgrims to Mount Petra. DP Italian +subtitles.

Julian Sands *Sergio Giuramondo* • Charlotte Gainsbourg *Matilda* • Nastassja Kinski *Cristina* • Massimo Bonetti *Prince Santobuono* • Margarita Lozano *Sergio's mother* • Patricia Millardet *Aurelia* ■ *Dir* Paolo Taviani, Vittorio Taviani • *Scr* Paolo Taviani, Vittorio Taviani, Tonino Guerra, from the story *Father Sergius* by Leo Tolstoy

The Night that Panicked America ★★★
Drama based on a true story 1975 · US · Colour · 100min

On October 30 1938, Orson Welles and his company broadcast a version of HG Wells's *The War Of The Worlds* on the radio – and millions took it seriously as a warning of alien invasion. Director Joseph Sargent's made-for-TV docudrama shows how some people fled to the hills, while others prayed in the streets; it was as near to a state of emergency as America has ever been. Paul Shenar, Vic Morrow and Eileen Brennan poignantly fictionalise some of the real-life stories that unfolded that night. TH

Paul Shenar *Orson Welles* • Vic Morrow *Hank Muldoon* • Cliff De Young *Stefan Grubowski* • Michael Constantine *Jess Wingate* • Walter McGinn *Paul Stewart* • Eileen Brennan *Ann Muldoon* • Meredith Baxter *Linda Davis* • Tom Bosley *Norman Smith* ■ *Dir* Joseph Sargent • *Scr* Nicholas Meyer, Anthony Wilson

The Night the Lights Went Out in Georgia ★ 15
Drama 1981 · US · Colour · 107min

Appealing performances by Dennis Quaid and Kristy McNichol can't save this road movie. They play sibling country and western singers. McNichol is trying to invest her rowdy brother with some of her Nashville ambition, but he's more interested in the women he gets to meet backstage. Stereotypical situations, barely functional dialogue and directional incompetence doesn't give the fine cast any chance at all. AJ

Kristy McNichol *Amanda Child* • Dennis Quaid *Travis Child* • Mark Hamill *Conrad* • Don Stroud *Seth* • Arlen Dean Snyder *Andy* ■ *Dir* Ronald F Maxwell • *Scr* Bob Bonney, from the song by Bobby Russell

The Night They Raided Minsky's ★★★ 12
Comedy 1968 · US · Colour · 94min

An amiably eccentric story of America's burlesque theatre has Norman Wisdom (yes, our Norm!) upstaging everyone, including Jason Robards. It's an atmospheric comedy with Britt Ekland as the Amish girl who eventually rebels against her father and takes off her clothes on a commercial basis. The scattershot narrative never quite gets its act together, but director William Friedkin, injects enough enthusiasm to make it enjoyable, if boisterous viewing. TH Brief nudity. **DVD**

Jason Robards *Raymond Paine* • Britt Ekland *Rachel Schpitendavel* • Norman Wisdom *Chick Williams* • Forrest Tucker *Trim Houlihan* • Harry Andrews *Jacob Schpitendavel* • Joseph Wiseman *Louis Minsky* • Denholm Elliott *Vance Fowler* • Elliott Gould *Billy Minsky* • Jack Burns *Candy Butcher* ■ *Dir* William Friedkin • *Scr* Arnold Schulman, Sidney Michaels, Norman Lear, from the novel by Rowland Barber

A Night to Remember ★★★ PG
Comedy thriller 1942 · US · BW · 88min

This witty and clever mystery tale has Brian Aherne and Loretta Young cast as a husband and wife trying to solve a murder. He is an author of whodunnits who knows he has a romantic novel in him; she is simply radiant and for some will be the whole reason for watching this sub-*Thin Man* opus. Director Richard Wallace lacks the requisite style to bring anything special to the mix, but he lets the stars shine and marshals a fine supporting cast of suspects. TS

Loretta Young *Nancy Troy* • Brian Aherne *Jeff Troy* • Jeff Donnell *Ann Carstairs* • William Wright *Scott Carstairs* • Sidney Toler *William Wright* • Gale Sondergaard *Mrs Devoe* • Lee Patrick *Polly Franklin* ■ *Dir* Richard Wallace • *Scr* Richard Flournoy, Jack Henley, from the story by Kelly Roos

A Night to Remember ★★★★ PG
Historical disaster drama 1958 · UK · BW · 117min

While this drama about the sinking of the *Titanic* can't compete in terms of spectacle with James Cameron's blockbuster, it still presents the facts of the disaster in a deeply moving and compelling manner. Director Roy Baker opts for a documentary style that focuses on the human interest angle without recourse to melodramatics. The result is a gripping account of the tragedy, impeccably acted by a sterling British cast, with Kenneth More excelling as heroic second officer Herbert Lightoller. DP **DVD** **BL**

Kenneth More *Herbert Lightoller* • Ronald Allen *Clarke* • Honor Blackman *Mrs Lucas* • Anthony Bushell *Captain Rostron (Carpathia)* • John Cairney *Murphy* • David McCallum (1) *Bride* • Robert Ayres *Peuchen* • Jill Dixon *Mrs Clarke* • Sean Connery *Deck hand* ■ *Dir* Roy Baker [Roy Ward Baker] • *Scr* Eric Ambler, from the book by Walter Lord

Night Train ★★ 15
Romantic drama 1998 · Ire · Colour · 89min

Brenda Blethyn plays a timid spinster who strikes up a friendship with ex-con John Hurt when he rents a room in her house. Hurt, who's on the run from some gangsters, has a passion for model trains and uses them to worm his way into Blethyn's heart. The two stars are fine, but this uneasy mix of crime thriller and romance takes some swallowing. NS **DVD**

John Hurt *Michael Poole* • Brenda Blethyn *Alice Mooney* • Pauline Flanagan *Mrs Mooney* • Lorcan Cranitch *Billy* ■ *Dir* John Lynch • *Scr* Aodhan Madden

Night Train to Lisbon ★★★ 12A
Romantic mystery thriller 2013 · Ger/Swi/Por · Colour · 111min

An ageing academic embarks on a journey of self-discovery in this old-fashioned thriller. Adapted from Pascal Mercier's bestselling novel, it invites us into the life of Raimund Gregorius (Jeremy Irons), a lonely Swiss teacher who prevents a young woman from committing suicide, and then becomes captivated by a book she left behind. Travelling to Portugal in an attempt to track down the author, the film switches from past to present to tell Portugal's story of fascism. These segments don't offer much tension, while the modern day scenes are undermined by convenience and contrivance. Still, the story is serviceable and Irons is an uncommonly engaging performer. SC Violence.

Jeremy Irons *Raimund Gregorius* • Mélanie Laurent *Young Estefania* • Jack Huston *Amadeu de Prado* • Martina Gedeck *Mariana* • Tom Courtenay *Old Joao Eca* • August Diehl *Young Jorge O'Kelly* • Bruno Ganz *Older Jorge O'Kelly* • Lena Olin *Older Estefania* ■ *Dir* Bille August • *Scr* Greg Latter, Ulrich Herrmann, from the novel by Pascal Mercier

Night Train to Munich ★★★★
Spy thriller 1940 · UK · BW · 90min

Witty and suspenseful, Frank Launder and Sidney Gilliat's screenplay about a missing Czech scientist bears an uncanny resemblance to the earlier classic they had a hand in, Alfred Hitchcock's *The Lady Vanishes*. Reinforcing the link is the reappearance of Basil Radford and Naunton Wayne as the cricket-mad eccentrics Charters and Caldicott. The dashing Rex Harrison evidently enjoys himself as the bemused British spy and Margaret Lockwood is the scientist's daughter does well to keep up with him. It's fast, furious and funny but, even with that master of atmosphere Carol Reed as director, it could have done with a couple of fresh tricks to keep us guessing. DP

Margaret Lockwood *Anna Bomasch* • Rex Harrison *Gus Bennett* • Paul Henreid *Karl Marsen* • Basil Radford *Charters* • Naunton Wayne *Caldicott* • James Harcourt *Axel Bomasch* ■ *Dir* Carol Reed • *Scr* Sidney Gilliat, Frank Launder, from a story by Gordon Wellesley

Night Train to Venice ★ 18
Thriller 1993 · Ger · Colour · 71min

Journalist and neo-Nazi expert Hugh Grant is victimised by skinheads during his train trip from Munich to Venice and spends the rest of the film agonising over his plight. Malcolm McDowell is "the stranger" who looks on with smug delight. Of course, the skinheads aren't finished with him just yet. Erratically edited and incoherently directed, this is as repulsive as it sounds. ST

Hugh Grant *Martin Gamil* • Tahnee Welch *Vera Cortese* • Malcolm McDowell *Stranger* • Samy Langs *Pedro* ■ *Dir* Carlo U Quinterio • *Scr* Leo Tichat, Toni Hirtreiter

Night unto Night ★★
Romantic drama 1949 · US · BW · 92min

Directed by Don Siegel, this obviously well-intended movie emerges as verbose, portentous claptrap that criminally wastes the gifts of the beautiful and talented Swedish-born actress Viveca Lindfors (Siegel's wife from 1949–53). She stars as a woman grieving over her husband's death, whose suffering is temporarily relieved by a lot of introspective talk with a troubled epileptic scientist, played by Ronald Reagan. RK

Ronald Reagan *John* • Viveca Lindfors *Ann* • Broderick Crawford *Shawn* • Rosemary DeCamp *Thalia* • Osa Massen *Lisa* • Craig Stevens *Tony* ■ *Dir* Don Siegel • *Scr* Kathryn Scola, from the novel by Philip Wylie

The Night Visitor ★★★
Suspense thriller 1970 · Swe/US · Colour · 101min

Very odd and rarely shown, this intriguing, arty horror movie was shot in Sweden and stars a handful of Ingmar Bergman's repertory company of actors. Max von Sydow is a farmer accused of murder he didn't commit, who ingeniously escapes from his insane asylum prison nightly to kill the people who put him there. This spooky gothic thriller has a compelling atmosphere that's most unusual. AJ

Max von Sydow *Salem* • Trevor Howard *Inspector* • Liv Ullmann *Esther Jenks* • Per Oscarsson *Dr Anton Jenks* • Rupert Davies *Clemens, the attorney* • Andrew Keir *Dr Kemp* ■ *Dir* Laslo Benedek • *Scr* Guy Elmes, from the short story *Salem Came to Supper* by Samuel Roecca

The Night Walker ★★
Horror thriller 1964 · US · BW · 85min

Barbara Stanwyck's last theatrical feature is a lame *Psycho* imitation from producer/director William Castle, who lit up the 1950s with such ingenious gimmick flicks as *Homicidal* and *The Tingler*. Starring with her real-life ex-husband Robert Taylor, Stanwyck is a widow suffering from recurring dreams about her dead spouse (Hayden Rorke). This is a tepid chiller with laughable special effects; Stanwyck is great value, though. AJ

Barbara Stanwyck *Irene Trent* • Robert Taylor (1) *Barry Morland* • Hayden Rorke *Howard Trent* • Lloyd Bochner *The man in the dream* • Judith Meredith *[Judi Meredith] Joyce* • Rochelle Hudson *Hilda* • Ted Durant *Narrator* ∎ *Dir* William Castle • *Scr* Robert Bloch, from the story *Witches' Friday* by Elizabeth Kata

Night Was Our Friend ★★
Psychological drama   1951 · UK · BW · 61min

Michael Gough is best known now for playing butler Alfred in the *Batman* movies. But this dowdy little drama from his dim and distant past is one picture he'd probably prefer to forget. Long believed to have perished in the Brazilian jungle, he returns to haunt wife Elizabeth Sellars and her new beau Ronald Howard. DP

Michael Gough *Martin Raynor* • Elizabeth Sellars *Sally Raynor* • Ronald Howard *Dr John Harper* • Marie Ney *Emily Raynor* • Edward Lexy *Arthur Glanville* • Nora Gordon *Kate* • Felix Felton *Jury foreman* ∎ *Dir* Michael Anderson • *Scr* Michael Pertwee, from his play

Night Watch ★★★ 15
Mystery thriller   1973 · UK · Colour · 98min

Reminiscent of *Gaslight*, this thriller stars Elizabeth Taylor as a woman recovering from a nervous breakdown who thinks she sees a corpse outside her window. Could it be the work of her husband (Laurence Harvey in his final film), who may or may not be having an affair with her best friend (Billie Whitelaw)? The actors give the tired plot all they've got, but director Brian G Hutton is more concerned with action than atmosphere, abbreviating tension where it should be given time to accumulate. TH
DVD

Elizabeth Taylor *Ellen Wheeler* • Laurence Harvey *John Wheeler* • Billie Whitelaw *Sarah Cooke* • Robert Lang *Appleby* • Tony Britton *Tony* • Bill Dean *Inspector Walker* ∎ *Dir* Brian G Hutton • *Scr* Tony Williamson, Evan Jones, from a play by Lucille Fletcher

Night Watch ★★ 15
Crime thriller   1995 · UK/US · Colour · 94min

This leaden caper is forced by budgetary constraint to serve up an uninvolving combination of hi-tech gadgetry and bruising stuntwork. A sub-007 adventure, it was Pierce Brosnan's last assignment before his debut as James Bond. Reprising the role that he played in *Death Train*, Brosnan turns art detective in a bid to recover a Rembrandt painting before it falls into the hands of a Hong Kong crime lord. DP Violence, swearing. *DVD*

Pierce Brosnan *Mike Graham* • Alexandra Paul *Sabrina Carver* • William Devane *Nick Caldwell* • Michael J Shannon *Martin Schrader* • Lim Kay Siu *Mao Yixin* • Irene Ng *Myra Tang* ∎ *Dir* David S Jackson • *Scr* David S Jackson, from the novel by Alistair MacLean

Night Watch ★★★ 15
Fantasy horror thriller   2004 · Rus · Colour · 109min

One of the highest-grossing Russian movies of all time, this is a horror fantasy about an ancient truce being broken between the forces of Light and Darkness, and the prophesised coming of the "Great Other" whose choice between them will tip the outcome of the final battle. Director Timur Bekmambetov flings special effects around, but his lightning pace rarely bothers to explain the plot, probably a good thing because it's essentially very silly. However, stylised subtitling adds to the experience, often becoming its own artistic statement. AJ Russian +subtitles. *DVD*
Blu-ray

Konstantin Khabensky *Anton Gorodetsky* • Vladimir Menshov *Boris Geser* • Valery Zolotukhin *Kostya's father* • Maria Poroshina *Svetlana* • Galina Tunina *Olga* • Viktor Verzhbitsky *Zavulon* • Gosha Kutsenko *Ignat* • Alexei Chadov *Kostya* • Zhanna Friske *Alisa* ∎ *Dir* Timur Bekmambetov • *Scr* Sergei Lukyanenko, Timur Bekmambetov, from the novel by Sergei Lukyanenko

The Night We Called It a Day ★★★ 15
Drama based on a true story   2003 · Aus/US · Colour · 91min

Dennis Hopper delivers a credible turn as the legendary crooner Frank Sinatra in this engaging romp. The year is 1974 and a small-time Australian rock promoter (Joel Edgerton) lands the coup of the decade when he convinces Ol' Blue Eyes to come to Australia for some live shows. However, Sinatra falls foul of the local media and the war of words escalates into a full-blown crisis involving the local trade unions, led by future prime minister Bob Hawke (David Field). But although there are some lovely moments, Paul Goldman's direction lacks fizz and the pace flags towards the end. JF Swearing.

Dennis Hopper *Frank Sinatra* • Melanie Griffith *Barbara Marx* • Portia de Rossi *Hilary Hunter* • Joel Edgerton *Rod Blue* • Rose Byrne *Audrey Rose Appleby* • David Hemmings *Mickey Rudin* • David Field *Bob Hawke* • Victoria Thaine *Penny* ∎ *Dir* Paul Goldman • *Scr* Michael Thomas, Peter Clifton

The Night We Dropped a Clanger ★★ U
Second World War comedy   1959 · UK · BW · 84min

This identity switch picture set during the Second World War tends to stretch its comic notions to breaking point. More disciplined comic timing would have provided an effective cure for the problem. However, farce king Brian Rix is a sensible choice for this wartime foolishness and he switches convincingly from military rigour (in one guise) to gormlessness (in the other). JM *DVD*

Brian Rix *Arthur Atwood/Wing Commander Blenkinsop* • Cecil Parker *Sir Bertram* • William Hartnell *Sergeant Bright* • Leslie Phillips *Squadron Leader Thomas* • Leo Franklyn *Sergeant Belling* • John Welsh *Squadron Leader Grant* • Toby Perkins *Flight Lieutenant Spendal* • Liz Fraser *Lulu* ∎ *Dir* Darcy Conyers • *Scr* John Chapman

The Night We Got the Bird ★ PG
Comedy   1960 · UK · BW · 78min

Your heart will go out to the splendid cast that found itself lumbered with this turkey. Ronald Shiner has the most luck, as he at least gets to spend much of the picture as a reincarnated parrot, thus leaving doltish egghead Brian Rix to carry the can for his misdemeanours as an antiques forger. With bedroom mix-ups, courtroom chaos and a break-in at a top-secret space lab, there's enough going on, but it's all dismally unfunny. DP *DVD*

Brian Rix *Bertie Skidmore* • Dora Bryan *Julie Skidmore* • Leo Franklyn *Victor* • Irene Handl *Ma* • Liz Fraser *Fay* • John Slater *Wolfie Green* • Reginald Beckwith *Chippendale Charlie* • Robertson Hare *Dr Vincent* • John Le Mesurier *Court clerk* • Ronald Shiner *Cecil Gibson* • Terry Scott *PC Lovejoy* ∎ *Dir* Darcy Conyers • *Scr* Ray Cooney, Tony Hilton, Darcy Conyers, from the play *The Love Birds* by Basil Thomas

The Night We Never Met ★★★★ 15
Romantic comedy   1993 · US · Colour · 94min

This is a sharp and cute study of young New Yorkers sharing a studio apartment on an alternate-days rota. Writer/director Warren Leight tinges the light comedy with a touch of Woody Allen-style angst, but whenever the story gets down-hearted his three leads (Kevin Anderson, yuppie slob; Annabella Sciorra, bored housewife; Matthew Broderick, dumped nice guy) perk it up with ensemble acting that dovetails perfectly. Love among the skyscrapers has rarely been such a delight. TH Swearing, nudity.
DVD

Matthew Broderick *Sam Lester* • Annabella Sciorra *Ellen Holder* • Kevin Anderson *Brian McVeigh* • Justine Bateman *Janet Beehan* • Jeanne Tripplehorn *Pastel* • Michael Mantell *Aaron Holder* • Christine Baranski *Lucy* ∎ *Dir/Scr* Warren Leight

Night Will Fall ★★★★ 15
Documentary   2014 · UK/Ger/Fr/US/Is · BW and Colour · 75min

Once Allied troops uncovered the ghastly secrets of the concentration camps at the end of the Second World War, the Supreme Allied Command was keen to make a record of the atrocities to ensure that such inhumanity was never repeated. André Singer reveals in this compelling documentary that diplomatic concerns soon impinged upon the production of *German Concentration Camps Factual Survey* and the project was abandoned. But the survivors and liberators interviewed here have never forgotten their experiences, and this crucial account of a dark episode in history stands as a chillingly eloquent memorial. DP English, Russian, Hebrew +subtitles. *DVD*

Helena Bonham Carter *Narrator* • Alfred Hitchcock *Alfred Hitchcock* • Sidney Bernstein *Sidney Bernstein* ∎ *Dir* André Singer • *Scr* Lynette Singer

Night without Stars ★★★ U
Crime drama   1951 · UK · BW · 82min

David Farrar is virtually blind and retires to the Riviera where he falls in love with Nadia Gray. Then he tangles with murderers, blackmailers and forgers when he discovers she is the widow of a resistance fighter. He's pushed off a cliff which forces him to get his sight restored and - very smart this - return to the Riviera still claiming to be blind so that he can trap the dirty rotters. Winston Graham adapted his own novel for this enjoyable little thriller. AT

David Farrar *Giles Gordon* • Nadia Gray *Alix Delaisse* • Maurice Teynac *Louis Malinay* • Gilles Quéant *Deffand* • Gérard Landry *Pierre Chaval* ∎ *Dir* Anthony Pelissier • *Scr* Winston Graham, from his novel

Night Zoo ★★★ 18
Crime drama   1987 · Can/Fr · Colour · 116min

Time hasn't been particularly kind to Jean-Claude Lauzon's award-winning, uncompromising study of the Montreal underworld. The 1980s look has dated very badly and Gilles Maheu's attempts to look mean and moody leave him occasionally looking like a third-rate Fonz impersonator. However, the story of a jailbird's bid to build bridges with both forgiving father Roger Le Bel and girlfriend-turned-hooker Lynne Adams - in the face of hostility from a couple of corrupt cops after their share of a drugs stash - still simmers with sexual and criminal menace. DP French +subtitles. Violence, nudity, sex scenes.

Roger Le Bel *Albert* • Gilles Maheu *Marcel* • Lorne Brass *Georges* • Germaine Houde *Charlie* • Lynne Adams (2) *Julie* ∎ *Dir/Scr* Jean-Claude Lauzon

Nightbreaker ★★★ 15
Historical drama   1989 · US · Colour · 95min

After such hits as *Stakeout* and *Young Guns*, Emilio Estevez opted for a change of pace and appeared alongside his father Martin Sheen in this modest, worthy drama. The subject matter concerns the postwar nuclear tests in the Nevada desert and the tragic consequences for the unwitting soldiers forced to witness them. Estevez plays the naive young doctor who gets involved in the test programme, with Sheen playing the same character in the 1980s. It's a tad overwrought at times, but the two leads are excellent. JF *DVD*

Martin Sheen *Dr Alexander Brown (present)* • Emilio Estevez *Dr Alexander Brown (past)* • Lea Thompson *Sally Matthews* • Melinda Dillon *Paula Brown* • Joe Pantoliano *Jack Russell* • Nicholas Pryor *Colonel William Devereau* ∎ *Dir* Peter Markle • *Scr* TS Cook, from the novel *Atomic Soldiers* by Howard Rosenberg

Nightbreed ★★★ 18
Horror   1990 · US · Colour · 97min

Hellraiser established Clive Barker as a major force in modern horror, but nothing he's done since has ever quite matched its unique visceral power. The trump up Barker's sleeve this time is the casting of cult horror director David Cronenberg as a malevolent shrink. He dupes a patient into believing that he's a serial killer and then tracks him down to the netherworld of Midian, a secret sanctuary for mutants and freaks. While this is self-indulgent, the imagination impresses. RS

Craig Sheffer *Boone* • Charles Haid *Captain Eigerman* • David Cronenberg *Dr Decker* • Anne Bobby *Lori* • Hugh Quarshie *Detective Joyce* ∎ *Dir* Clive Barker • *Scr* Clive Barker, from his novel *Cabal*

The Nightcomers ★★ 18
Thriller   1972 · UK · Colour · 92min

Marlon Brando is at his most loutishly sexual, tearing the clothes off Stephanie Beacham in this prequel to Henry James's *The Turn of the Screw*. It's a cod-Freudian exercise in sadomasochism, with Brando playing the groundsman and Beacham the governess to the two children destined to see ghosts later. Filmed with a distinct lack of subtlety and stretching early 1970s permissiveness to the limit, it was the last picture Brando made before he revived his flagging fortunes with *The Godfather* and *Last Tango in Paris*. It's trashily enjoyable, though. AT Sex scenes, some swearing, violence. *DVD* *Blu-ray*

Marlon Brando *Quint* • Stephanie Beacham *Miss Jessel* • Thora Hird *Mrs Grose* • Verna Harvey *Flora* • Christopher Ellis *Miles* • Harry Andrews *Master of the house* ∎ *Dir* Michael Winner • *Scr* Michael Hastings, from characters by Henry James

Nightcrawler ★★★★★ 15
Crime drama   2013 · US · Colour · 112min

On the surface, *Nightcrawler* is a state-of-the-nation address that uses California - with its lurid news reports of car crashes, homicides and shoot-outs - as the rest of the USA in microcosm. However, at its heart, this entertaining neo-*noir* is a fascinating character study, with a dramatically skinny Jake Gyllenhaal as its antihero Louis Bloom. A loner searching for work, Bloom sees his chance by investing in a camera and selling his wares to Rene Russo's TV station manager. As Bloom's media empire takes off, ethics quickly fall by the wayside, and director Dan Gilroy's feature debut begins to reveal itself as a terrifying modern morality tale. DW Violence, swearing. *DVD* *Blu-ray*

Jake Gyllenhaal *Louis Bloom* • Rene Russo *Nina Romina* • Riz Ahmed *[Rizwan Ahmed] Rick* • Bill Paxton *Joe Loder* • Kevin Rahm *Frank Kruse* ∎ *Dir/Scr* Dan Gilroy • *Music* James Newton Howard

Nightfall ★★★
Crime drama   1956 · US · BW · 78min

Aldo Ray was a briefly glimpsed star who burned himself out all too quickly, but he was a formidable presence even as the "wronged man" in this pacey thriller by *noir*-meister Jacques Tourneur. It's an early outing for scriptwriter Stirling Silliphant from a cult-pulp by David Goodis, and he's fashioned a bleak morality tale about a man who thinks he can't win after being framed for murder and robbery, but then discovers gleams of hope. Anne Bancroft is particularly good as the ambiguous figure of salvation. TH

Aldo Ray *James Vanning* • Brian Keith *John* • Anne Bancroft *Marie Gardner* • Jocelyn Brando *Laura Fraser* • James Gregory *Ben Fraser* • Frank Albertson *Dr Edward Gurston* ∎ *Dir* Jacques Tourneur • *Scr* Stirling Silliphant, from a novel by David Goodis

Nighthawks ★★★ 18
Action thriller   1981 · US · Colour · 95min

At this stage in his career Sylvester Stallone was not known as an action star, and in some ways this is his first real stab at the genre with which he is now most closely associated. Stallone and Billy Dee Williams play two New York cops who are sent scampering all over the Big Apple on the trail of a vicious international terrorist (Rutger Hauer, making an electrifying Hollywood debut). Director Bruce Malmuth keeps the action zipping along at a pleasing pace. JF Swearing, violence, nudity. *DVD*

Sylvester Stallone *Deke DaSilva* • Billy Dee Williams *Matthew Fox* • Lindsay Wagner *Irene* • Persis Khambatta *Shakka* • Nigel Davenport *Peter Hartman* • Rutger Hauer *Wulfgar* • Hilarie Thompson *Pam* ■ *Dir* Bruce Malmuth • *Scr* David Shaber, from a story by David Shaber, Paul Sylbert

A Nightingale Sang in Berkeley Square ★★★ PG
Comedy thriller 1979 · UK · Colour · 105min

This pleasing, if predictable, heist caper boasts an extraordinary cast. Giving one of the better performances of his twilight years, David Niven plays a criminal mastermind who blackmails old lag Richard Jordan into joining his audacious assault on a swanky bank. Making his first film in five years, veteran director Ralph Thomas fails to impose himself on the familiar sequence of events, but coaxes a splendid performance from Gloria Grahame. DP *DVD*

Richard Jordan *Pinky Green* • David Niven *Ivan the Terrible* • Oliver Tobias *Foxy* • Gloria Grahame *Ma* • Elke Sommer *Miss Pelham* • Richard Johnson *Inspector Watford* • Joss Ackland *Governor* • Michael Angelis *Pealer Bell* ■ *Dir* Ralph Thomas • *Scr* Guy Elmes

Nightmare ★★★★
Crime drama 1956 · US · BW · 89min

Director Maxwell Shane here remakes his 1947 film *Fear in the Night*. Kevin McCarthy gives a good performance as the musician who becomes convinced he's a murderer, but Edward G Robinson is better as the detective who sees the flaw in what appears to be an open-and-shut case. Cameraman Joseph Biroc's moody photography adds real menace to the disturbing idea, and there's a jazz score by Herschel Burke Gilbert that's as jumpy as a neurotic's bad dream. TH

Edward G Robinson *Rene Bressard* • Kevin McCarthy *Stan Grayson* • Connie Russell *Gina* • Virginia Christine *Sue* • Rhys Williams *Torrence* • Gage Clarke *Belknap* ■ *Dir* Maxwell Shane • *Scr* Maxwell Shane, from the short story by William Irish [Cornell Woolrich]

Nightmare ★★★
Horror 1963 · UK · BW · 82min

Ace cameraman Freddie Francis directs this Hammer-financed production, with English rose Jennie Linden having terrible nightmares about being tossed into a loony bin. The poor dear is taken to one of those dark, foreboding country houses where things go bump in the night. It isn't too long before the knives come out and everyone starts screaming. Brimming with sexual imagery and the odd reference to Henry James's *The Turn of the Screw*, this is let down by a pallid hero (David Knight) but pulls off quite a few decent shocks. AT

David Knight *Henry Baxter* • Moira Redmond *Grace* • Brenda Bruce *Mary* • Jennie Linden *Janet* • George A Cooper (2) *John* ■ *Dir* Freddie Francis • *Scr* Jimmy Sangster

Nightmare Alley ★★★ PG
Horror 1947 · US · BW · 106min

Tyrone Power, 20th Century-Fox's most bankable and romantic leading man at the time, gave his image a jolt with this bizarre study of mental breakdown, in which he was reunited with his *Razor's Edge* director, Edmund Goulding. Power is a bogus mind-reader in a small-time carnival who revives Joan Blondell and Ian Keith's long forgotten act as a means to get rich, with tragic results. The script, by Jules Furthman, is based on a novel by William Lindsay Gresham, a writer obsessed with the emotional nakedness of circus performance, who eventually committed suicide. AT *DVD*

Tyrone Power *Stanton Carlisle* • Joan Blondell *Zeena* • Coleen Gray *Molly* • Helen Walker *Dr Lilith Ritter* • Taylor Holmes *Ezra Grindle* • Mike Mazurki *Bruno* • Ian Keith *Pete* • Julia Dean *Mrs Peabody* ■ *Dir* Edmund Goulding • *Scr* Jules Furthman, from the novel by William Lindsay Gresham

The Nightmare before Christmas ★★★★★ PG
Animated musical fantasy 1993 · US · Colour · 73min

Producing here, Tim Burton called on the services of innovative animation director Henry Selick and composer Danny Elfman (a regular Burton collaborator, who wrote the ten surreal songs and lends his singing voice to the lead character) for this wonderfully weird fable that's packed with scary spooks, gags and dazzling decor. It enchants with every busy frame as spindly Jack Skellington, the mastermind behind Halloween, hijacks Christmas out of boredom, becoming a frightening Santa delivering nasty surprises instead of presents to terrified children. Its affectionate trashing of Christmas traditions is clever enough to please every generation. An unmissable treat that is now also available in 3D. AJ *DVD*

Danny Elfman *Jack Skellington* • Chris Sarandon *Jack Skellington* • Catherine O'Hara *Sally/Shock* • William Hickey *Evil scientist* • Glenn Shadix *Mayor* • Paul Reubens *Lock* • Ken Page *Oogie Boogie* • Ed Ivory *Santa* ■ *Dir* Henry Selick • *Scr* Caroline Thompson, from a story and characters by Tim Burton

Nightmare in Chicago ★★★★
Crime drama 1968 · US · Colour · 80min

Robert Altman was working in television when he directed this tale of a serial killer known to the police and press as the Georgie Porgie killer. Featuring Philip Abbott, Ted Knight and Charles McGraw, it was shot entirely on location in Chicago and has the creepy atmosphere of an authentic bad dream. TV movies don't come much better than this. TH

Charles McGraw *Georgie Porgie* • Robert Ridgely • Ted Knight • Philip Abbott ■ *Dir* Robert Altman • *Scr* David Moessinger, from the novel *Killer on the Turnpike* by William P McGivern

Nightmare in the Sun ★★
Crime drama 1964 · US · Colour · 81min

This innocent-on-the-run thriller finds the sexy wife (Ursula Andress) of a rich ranch owner picking up a hitch-hiker (John Derek, her then real-life husband) and bringing him home. The hitch-hiker decides to leave, but in a fit of rage the ranch boss kills Andress, leaving the drifter blamed for the murder by a corrupt, blackmailing sheriff. Less suspenseful than it sounds, but there are some early walk-ons from the likes of Robert Duvall and Richard Jaeckel. JG

Ursula Andress *Marsha* • John Derek *Hitch-hiker* • Aldo Ray *Sheriff* • Arthur O'Connell *Sam Wilson* • Sammy Davis Jr *Truck driver* • Allyn Joslyn *Junk dealer* • Keenan Wynn *Song-and-dance misfit* • Chick Chandler *Tavern owner* • Richard Jaeckel *Motorcyclist* • Robert Duvall *Motorcyclist* ■ *Dir* Marc Lawrence (1) • *Scr* Ted Thomas, Fanya Lawrence, from a story by Marc Lawrence, Fanya Lawrence, George Fass

A Nightmare on Elm Street ★★★★ 18
Horror 1984 · US · Colour · 87min

Four teenagers experience identical nightmares and are haunted by shockingly popular supernatural fiend Freddy Krueger (known here as Fred) in this pioneering fright flick from director Wes Craven. Craven's merging of dreams with reality is ingenious, as Heather Langenkamp realises she can only save her friends by staying awake and keeping the razor-fingered maniac at bay. Bloody and suspenseful murders disguise a somewhat weak script, but the engaging performances (look for Johnny Depp in his screen debut) and chilling concept make it a terror classic that spawned six sequels, a television series and a 2010 re-imagining starring Jackie Earle Haley. AJ Violence, swearing, drug abuse, nudity. *DVD*

Robert Englund *Fred Krueger* • John Saxon *Lt Thompson* • Ronee Blakley *Marge Thompson* • Heather Langenkamp *Nancy Thompson* • Amanda Wyss *Tina Gray* • Johnny Depp *Glen Lantz* ■ *Dir/Scr* Wes Craven

A Nightmare on Elm Street ★★ 18
Horror 2010 · US · Colour · 95min

Music video director Samuel Bayer's blandly efficient remake of Wes Craven's seminal horror retains the core concept (if you die in your dreams, you die in real life), but where the 1984 film was joltingly inventive and disturbing, this is just second-hand fright. Many of the original's iconic moments remain, but heroine Rooney Mara isn't the initial focus of the slightly tweaked terror, and that dilutes any empathy we might have with her past trauma. It's glossy and visually artful, but ultimately pointless without Craven's wickedly humorous touch. AJ Violence. *DVD*

Jackie Earle Haley *Freddy Krueger* • Katie Cassidy *Kris Fowles* • Kyle Gallner *Quentin Smith* • Rooney Mara *Nancy Holbrook* • Thomas Dekker *Jesse Braun* • Kellan Lutz *Dean Russell* • Clancy Brown *Alan Smith* ■ *Dir* Samuel Bayer • *Scr* Wesley Strick, Eric Heisserer, from a story by Strick, from characters by Wes Craven

A Nightmare on Elm Street 2: Freddy's Revenge ★ 18
Horror 1985 · US · Colour · 81min

Mark Patton moves into the sinister Elm Street house, and Freddy Krueger just as quickly moves into his dreams in this damp squib of a sequel. Surprisingly homoerotic in content, Jack Sholder's substandard shocker replaces clever dream imagery with the more conventional theme of possession, while Patton creates a vacuum with his one-expression performance. AJ *DVD*

Mark Patton *Jesse Walsh* • Robert Englund *Freddy Krueger* • Kim Myers *Lisa Webber* • Robert Rusler *Ron Grady* • Clu Gulager *Mr Walsh* • Hope Lange *Mrs Walsh* ■ *Dir* Jack Sholder • *Scr* David Chaskin, from a character created by Wes Craven

A Nightmare on Elm Street 3: Dream Warriors ★★★ 18
Horror 1987 · US · Colour · 92min

Anything can happen, and does, in this imaginative sequel that stretches the boundaries of 1980s horror to new limits with wildly inventive and brilliantly executed mayhem. Thanks to the psychic ability of Patricia Arquette, a group of youngsters terrorised by Freddy Krueger take part in a controlled experiment where they enter each other's nightmares on a time-share basis to exorcise his malevolent spirit. Full of great special effects, this is a rollercoaster ride from the opening Edgar Allan Poe quotation to the final Ray Harryhausen homage. AJ *DVD*

Heather Langenkamp *Nancy Thompson* • Patricia Arquette *Kristen Parker* • Larry Fishburne [Laurence Fishburne] *Max* • Priscilla Pointer *Dr Elizabeth Simms* • Craig Wasson *Dr Neil Goldman* • Robert Englund *Freddy Krueger* ■ *Dir* Chuck Russell • *Scr* Wes Craven, Bruce Wagner, Chuck Russell, Frank Darabont, from a story by Wes Craven, Bruce Wagner, from characters by Wes Craven

A Nightmare on Elm Street 4: The Dream Master ★★★ 18
Horror 1988 · US · Colour · 88min

Lisa Wilcox goes through the blood-stained looking glass in this strong Freddy Krueger episode, given a wonderfully different European art-horror feel by future blockbuster director Renny Harlin, who puts a fresh spin on the recurring nightmare cliché. Wilcox takes on the talents of her deceased friends to become the Dream Master, the ancient guardian of positive scenarios, poised to counterattack Freddy's negative nightmares in this beautifully photographed redefinition of the pop-culture formula. AJ *DVD*

Robert Englund *Freddy Krueger* • Lisa Wilcox *Alice* • Rodney Eastman *Joey* • Danny Hassel *Danny* • Andras Jones *Rick* • Tuesday Knight *Kristen Parker* ■ *Dir* Renny Harlin • *Scr* Brian Helgeland, Scott Pierce, from a story by William Kotzwinkle, Brian Helgeland, from a character created by Wes Craven

A Nightmare on Elm Street 5: The Dream Child ★★ 18
Horror 1989 · US · Colour · 86min

Lisa Wilcox thinks she's banished Freddy Krueger from her life until she's made pregnant by college jock Danny Hassel. According to the jumbled script, a foetus can dream a few days after conception, and Freddy seizes this chance to enter her subconscious once more and finger-blade her unbelieving friends to death. Director Stephen Hopkins valiantly tries to paper over the huge cracks in the derivative low-energy thrills by replacing vapid gore with furious pacing, sudden shock cuts and rock video-style cartoonish imagery. The series continued with two further sequels – *Freddy's Dead: the Final Nightmare* (1991) and *Wes Craven's New Nightmare* (1994). AJ *DVD*

Robert Englund *Freddy Krueger* • Lisa Wilcox *Alice Johnson* • Danny Hassel *Dan* • Kelly Jo Minter *Yvonne* • Erika Anderson *Greta* • Joe Seely *Mark* ■ *Dir* Stephen Hopkins • *Scr* Leslie Bohem, from a story by John Skip, Craig Spector, Leslie Bohem, from a character created by Wes Craven

Nightmares ★★ 15
Science-fiction horror 1983 · US · Colour · 94min

This uneven four-part anthology is more miss than hit. A housewife under murderous threat, a deadly video game obsessing Emilio Estevez, a priest losing faith on the eve of battling a possessed truck, and a giant rat terrorising a suburban family jostle for attention in a workmanlike collection accenting substandard eeriness and few scares. While the first two tales are OK, the other two are dire. AJ

Emilio Estevez *JJ Cooney* • Cristina Raines *Lisa* • Joe Lambie *Phil* • Anthony James *Clerk* • Clare Nono *Newswoman* • Raleigh Bond *Neighbour* • Robert Phelps *Newsman* • Dixie Lynn Royce *Little girl* ■ *Dir* Joseph Sargent • *Scr* Christopher Crowe, Jeffrey Bloom

Nightmaster ★ 15
Martial arts action thriller 1987 · Aus/Can · Colour · 87min

You need a masochistic taste for awful movies to watch this shoddily made, vaguely futuristic action thriller (also known as *Watch the Shadows Dance*). A tedious plodder, it focuses on teen students whose late night ninja-style war games take on a deadly dimension when two of them discover sinister secrets about their martial arts tutor. Only notable for an early screen role for Nicole Kidman. SF *DVD*

Tom Jennings *Robby Mason* • Nicole Kidman *Amy Gabriel* • Joanne Samuel *Sonia Spane* • Vince Martin *Steve Beck* • Craig Pearce *Guy Duncan* • Doug Parkinson *Pete "Pearly" Gates* • Jeremy Shadlow *Simon* ■ *Dir* Mark Joffe • *Scr* Michael McGennan

Nights in Rodanthe ★★ PG
Romantic drama 2008 · US/Aus · Colour · 92min

The mature pairing of Richard Gere and Diane Lane lends credence to this otherwise gooey portrait of midlife romance. Lane plays a woman who is estranged from her husband after an infidelity. When the opportunity arises, she agrees to look after a friend's North Carolina beachfront inn, the sole guest of which is a dedicated doctor (Gere) with problems of his own. The predictable ensues, with the two strangers opening up to one another and life-changing decisions being made. Based on the popular book by Nicholas Sparks (*The Notebook*), the weak script is rife with corny, clanging dialogue. But the movie should still satisfy die-hard romantics, equipped as it is with a full set of love clichés, though hankies are strictly optional. KK *DVD*

Richard Gere *Dr Paul Flanner* • Diane Lane *Adrienne Willis* • Scott Glenn *Robert Torrelson* • Viola Davis *Jean* • Christopher Meloni *Jack Willis* • Pablo Schreiber *Charlie Torrelson* • Mae Whitman *Amanda Willis* • James Franco *Mark*

Flanner ■ *Dir* George C Wolfe • *Scr* Ann Peacock, John Romano, from the novel by Nicholas Sparks

Nights of Cabiria ★★★★★ 15
Drama 1957 · It · BW · 106min

Often dismissed as grating and sentimental, this is one of Federico Fellini's most accessible films, which harks back to his days as a screenwriter during Italy's neorealist phase. The winner of the 1957 Oscar for best foreign film, it boasts a bravura performance from the director's wife, Giulietta Masina, as the childlike prostitute who is misused by everyone she encounters, yet still has the sense of self-worth to come bouncing back. Every bit as vulnerable as Shirley MacLaine in the Hollywood musical remake, *Sweet Charity*, Masina eschews sentiment to meet fate with grace. DP In Italian. *DVD*

Giulietta Masina *Cabiria* • François Périer *Oscar D'Onofrio, accountant* • Amedeo Nazzari *Alberto Lazzari, movie star* • Aldo Silvani *Hypnotist* ■ *Dir* Federico Fellini • *Scr* Federico Fellini, Ennio Flaiano, Tullio Pinelli, Pier Paolo Pasolini (additional dialogue) • *Music* Nino Rota • *Art Director* Piero Gherardi

Nightshift ★★★ 15
Psychological drama 2000 · Fr · Colour · 92min

Director Philippe Le Guay's unusually low-key blue-collar psychodrama is deliberately gloss-free and was shot using naturalistic lighting - elements that add enormous realism to its central story of a power struggle between co-workers. When Gérald Laroche switches to the lucrative nightshift in a glass factory, he becomes the target of a sadistic colleague's motiveless and increasingly brutal practical jokes. Striking a menacing and disorientating chord, Le Guay brilliantly explores the oddly compelling - even homoerotic - relationship between the two men, superbly portrayed by Laroche and Marc Barbé. AJ French +subtitles. *DVD*

Gérald Laroche *Pierre* • Marc Barbé *Fred* • Bernard Ballet *Franck* • Michel Cassagne *Alain* • Alexandre Carrière *Danny* • Jean-François Lapalus *Mickey* ■ *Dir/Scr* Philippe Le Guay

Nightwatch ★★★★ 18
Thriller 1994 · Den · Colour · 102min

A young student becomes night watchman at a mortuary where sinister things are happening and, before long, he's suspected of being a serial killer. Danish director Ole Bornedal's tense chiller is a quality genre item full of slow-burning suspense and high shock value. Everything good about this nerve-racking original was dumbed down for Bornedal's JS remake. AJ Danish +subtitles. *DVD*

Nikolaj Coster-Waldau *Martin Bork* • Sofie Gråbøl *Kalinka Martens* • Kim Bodnia *Jens Arnkiel* ■ *Dir/Scr* Ole Bornedal

Nightwatch ★★ 18
Horror thriller 1997 · US · Colour · 96min

Director Ole Bornedal takes his original 1994 Danish terror masterpiece - about a rookie morgue night watchman suspected of being a serial killer - and replaces the scary tension with formula gruesome shocks. The artful blend of hairy humour and creepy horror that graced the original doesn't quite survive in this good-looking poor relation. Ewan McGregor is fine, but Nick Nolte and Patricia Arquette sleepwalk through their roles. AJ Violence, swearing, sex scenes. *DVD*

Ewan McGregor *Martin* • Nick Nolte *Inspector Thomas Cray* • Patricia Arquette *Katherine* • Josh Brolin *James* • Lauren Graham *Marie* • Brad Dourif *Duty doctor* ■ *Dir* Ole Bornedal • *Scr* Steven Soderbergh, Ole Bornedal, from the 1994 film

Nightwing ★★ 15
Horror 1979 · US · Colour · 100min

The native Americans of New Mexico are in an uproar thanks to nightly raids by swarms of vampire bats that leave their cattle dead and their people horribly mutilated. Time to call in bat biologist David Warner, who's had it in for the beasts ever since they ate his

father. Arthur Hiller's uninspired direction and the absurd fake bats (built by Carlo Rambaldi of *ET* fame) doom this laughable version of Martin Cruz Smith's bestseller. AJ

Nick Mancuso *Youngman Duran* • David Warner *Phillip Payne* • Kathryn Harrold *Anne Dillon* • Stephen Macht *Walker Chee* • Strother Martin *Selwyn* ■ *Dir* Arthur Hiller • *Scr* Steve Shagan, Bud Shrake, Martin Cruz Smith, from the novel by Martin Cruz Smith

Nijinsky ★★★★ 15
Biographical drama 1980 · UK · Colour · 119min

Originally a Ken Russell project, this biopic of the tormented Russian ballet dancer has enough sex, angst and controversy to keep it boiling. Based on Nijinsky's diaries and Mrs Nijinsky's memoirs, it stars George De La Pena as the dancer and Alan Bates as his jilted inamorata, the impresario Diaghilev. As a study of life, art and ego, it's often close to Powell and Pressburger's *The Red Shoes* - powerfully acted and convincingly staged, with wonderful music. AT

Alan Bates *Sergei Diaghilev* • George De La Pena *Vaslav Nijinsky* • Leslie Browne *Romola DePulsky* • Alan Badel *Baron De Gunzberg* • Carla Fracci *Tamara Karsavina* • Colin Blakely *Vassili* • Ronald Pickup *Igor Stravinsky* ■ *Dir* Herbert Ross • *Scr* Hugh Wheeler, from the memoirs by Romola Nijinsky and the diary by Vaslav Nijinsky

Nikita ★★★★ 18
Thriller 1990 · Fr/It · Colour · 112min

After being involved in a robbery, vicious junkie Anne Parillaud is reprogrammed as an assassin for a secret government agency in French director Luc Besson's extremely exciting thriller with a feminist slant. In paying homage to American action movies, Besson goes one better than his clear inspirations, to craft a beautifully stylised, enthralling and very violent comic strip. Parillaud (married to Besson at the time) is tremendous as the unscrupulous hit woman and Jeanne Moreau's Charm Teacher cameo is a gem. Besson's boldly modern approach to traditional *film noir* material makes this elemental mind-blower striking. A Hollywood remake (*Point of No Return*) followed in 1993, starring Bridget Fonda. AJ French +subtitles. Violence, swearing. *DVD* *Blu-ray*

Anne Parillaud *Nikita* • Jean-Hugues Anglade *Marco* • Tcheky Karyo *Bob* • Jeanne Moreau *Amande* • Jean Reno *Victor the cleaner* • Marc Duret *Rico* • Philippe Leroy-Beaulieu *Grossman* ■ *Dir/Scr* Luc Besson

Nil by Mouth ★★★★★ 18
Drama 1997 · UK/US · Colour · 128min

A harrowing directorial debut by actor Gary Oldman, this centres on violence and alcoholism within a working-class south London family. Although the film is not specifically autobiographical, Oldman has drawn from his own background to create a portrait of dysfunctional domestic life that is both convincing and compelling. Ray Winstone hulks brilliantly in the central role as the alienated husband and father trapped in a descending spiral of drunken rage. Kathy Burke matches Winstone's intensity - and won the best actress award at Cannes - for her performance as the brutalised wife. *Nil by Mouth* tempers its bleakness with tender understanding and wounding insight. TH Swearing, sexual references, violence. *DVD*

Ray Winstone *Raymond* • Kathy Burke *Valerie* • Charlie Creed-Miles *Billy* • Laila Morse *Janet* • Edna Doré *Kath* • Chrissie Cotterill *Paula* ■ *Dir/Scr* Gary Oldman

Nim's Island ★★★ U
Fantasy adventure 2008 · US · Colour · 92min

Abigail Breslin earned an Oscar nomination for *Little Miss Sunshine* and once again lights up the screen as the young heroine of this tropical escapade. Breslin plays Nim who lives with her scientist father (Gerard Butler) on a remote island, and spends her days playing with her exotic animal friends and reading the adventure stories of Alex Rover. When her dad doesn't return from a boat trip, Nim looks to Rover for help, but

what she doesn't realise is that the author is actually Alexandra Rover (Jodie Foster), a phobia-ridden woman who hasn't left her home in months. The film's focus is awkwardly split between Nim's life on the island, her father lost at sea and the comical efforts of Alexandra to rescue the young girl. Fortunately, the sheer pluckiness of Breslin keeps proceedings fun. SP *DVD* *Blu-ray*

Abigail Breslin *Nim Rusoe* • Jodie Foster *Alexandra Rover* • Gerard Butler *Jack Rusoe/Alex Rover* • Michael Carman *Captain* • Mark Brady *Purser* • Anthony Simcoe *First mate* ■ *Dir* Jennifer Flackett, Mark Levin • *Scr* Jennifer Flackett, Joseph Kwong, Mark Levin, Paula Mazur, from the novel by Wendy Orr

Nina Takes a Lover ★★ 18
Romantic comedy 1993 · US · Colour · 93min

This initially intriguing romantic comedy has Laura San Giacomo as a young married woman who decides to have an affair with a photographer (played by Welsh actor Paul Rhys) while her husband is away. The story is related in flashbacks with San Giacomo relating the tale of her fling to a journalist, and it soon becomes clear that things are not quite as they seem. But the main weakness of this run-of-the-mill movie is the fact that all the characters come across as so self-absorbed. JB Swearing, nudity. *DVD*

Laura San Giacomo *Nina* • Paul Rhys *Photographer* • Michael O'Keefe *Journalist* • Fisher Stevens *Paulie* ■ *Dir/Scr* Alan Jacobs

Nina's Heavenly Delights ★★★ PG
Comedy drama 2006 · UK · Colour · 90min

An unlikely concoction of Indian cuisine and issues of ethnic and sexual diversity is served up in this Glasgow-set comedy that's as light as a soufflé. Nina (Shelley Conn), a young Scottish-Asian woman, returns home for the funeral of her father, with whom she fell out over her last-minute refusal to marry the son of his rival restaurateur Raj (Art Malik) and unite the city's two great curry houses. She soon forms a close bond with Lisa (Laura Fraser), who is now part-owner of the family restaurant. Director Pratibha Parmar's film seems determined to challenge expectations at every turn. Yet the basic philosophy of this inoffensive tale will probably appeal to the same audience that made *Billy Elliot* and *Bend It like Beckham* into major hits. BP *DVD*

Laura Fraser *Lisa* • Shelley Conn *Nina Shah* • Art Malik *Raj Khanna* • Ronny Jhutti *Bobbi* • Veena Sood *Suman Shah* • Atta Yaqub *Kary Shah* • Raji James *Sanjay Khanna* ■ *Dir* Pratibha Parmar • *Scr* Andrea Gibb, from a story by Pratibha Parmar

Nine ★★ 12
Musical drama 2009 · US · Colour and BW · 113min

Acclaimed Italian film director Guido Contini (a charmless Daniel Day-Lewis) suffers from both writer's block and a midlife crisis in *Chicago* director Rob Marshall's star-packed but pretentious and emotionally static movie. It's based on the Tony award-winning Broadway musical, itself adapted from Federico Fellini's 1963 film *8½*. This version is ravishingly executed in full early 1960s "Cinema Italiano" style but it's fatally misconceived, becoming little more than a tiresome series of music videos with the women in Contini's life (including Penélope Cruz and Nicole Kidman) singing of their frustration over his errant ways. Not even Sophia Loren's much-needed flash of authenticity helps the retro hollowness. AJ Swearing, sexual references. *DVD* *Blu-ray*

Daniel Day-Lewis *Guido Contini* • Penélope Cruz *Carla* • Marion Cotillard *Luisa Contini* • Nicole Kidman *Claudia Jenssen* • Judi Dench *Lilli* • Sophia Loren *Mamma* • Kate Hudson *Stephanie* ■ *Dir* Rob Marshall • *Scr* Anthony Minghella, Michael Tolkin, from the musical by Arthur L Kopit, Maury Yeston, Mario Fratti, from the play *Six Passionate Women* by Fratti, from the 1963 film *8½* • *Production Designers* John Myhre, Gordon Sim • *Costume Designer* Colleen Atwood

9 ★★★ 12
Animated fantasy adventure 2009 · US/Lux · Colour · 75min

This dark, charmingly grungy film is set in a post-apocalypse future when a group of small automatons - numbered 1 to 9 and all with distinct personalities - attempt to survive on an Earth destroyed by machines. Debuting director Shane Acker has expanded his own 11-minute short to produce a dystopian adventure that is blessed with quality vocal performances from Christopher Plummer, John C Reilly, and Elijah Wood as neophyte rebel leader 9. An ethereal, otherworldly look at the dangers of warfare technology, this is imaginative and melancholy but ultimately heart-warming. KK Some violence. *DVD* *Blu-ray*

Elijah Wood *9* • John C Reilly *5* • Jennifer Connelly *7* • Crispin Glover *6* • Martin Landau *2* • Christopher Plummer *1* • Fred Tatasciore *8* • Alan Oppenheimer *Scientist* ■ *Dir* Shane Acker • *Scr* Pamela Pettler, from a story by Shane Acker

Nine ½ Weeks ★★ 18
Erotic drama 1985 · US · Colour · 112min

Despite the high production values and a starry cast, this remains mild, soft-core entertainment. Kim Basinger is the career woman who falls under the spell of the mysterious Mickey Rourke and finds herself being led into dangerous sexual waters. It's complete tosh, of course, and the storyline is so slim that it just becomes a series of beautifully composed nude encounters. JF Sex scenes, violence, swearing. *DVD* *Blu-ray*

Mickey Rourke *John* • Kim Basinger *Elizabeth* • Margaret Whitton *Molly* • David Margulies *Harvey* • Christine Baranski *Thea* • Karen Young *Sue* • William De Acutis *Ted* ■ *Dir* Adrian Lyne • *Scr* Patricia Knop, Zalman King, Sarah Kernochan, from the novel by Elizabeth McNeill

9 Dead Gay Guys ★★ 18
Crime comedy 2001 · UK · Colour · 79min

Lab Ky Mo's debut seeks to shock with its politically incorrect caricatures and self-conscious bad taste. But, in fact, it's nowhere near outrageous enough, either to work as a black comedy or as an in-joke on the London gay scene. Most successful is the running gag about Irish rent boys Brendan Mackey and Glenn Mulhern's insistence that they're straight while seeking an enormous pile of money following the deaths of wealthy queen Michael Praed and kinky widower Steven Berkoff. Crude and lacking wit. DP Swearing. *DVD*

Glenn Mulhern *Kenny* • Brendan Mackey *Byron* • Steven Berkoff *Jeff* • Michael Praed *The Queen* • Vas Blackwood *Donkey-Dick Dark* ■ *Dir/Scr* Lab Ky Mo

Nine Lives ★★ PG
Comedy 2016 · Fr/Chi · Colour · 86min

In a fluff-ball feline comedy, workaholic billionaire Kevin Spacey buys his daughter a cat as a last-minute birthday gift and fate intervenes so that his spirit becomes trapped inside it. Enigmatic cat-whisperer Christopher Walken has quite a bit to do with it as the owner of a somewhat spooky pet shop. After an opening-credits sequence of internet cat videos, the laughs are rare and thereafter, the story plods. The digital effects also prove an awkward match in a film that should have been so much better. TJ

Kevin Spacey *Tom Brand/Mr Fuzzypants* • Jennifer Garner *Lara Brand* • Robbie Amell *David Brand* • Cheryl Hines *Madison Camden* • Christopher Walken *Felix Perkins* ■ *Dir* Barry Sonnenfeld • *Scr* Matt Allen, Dan Antoniazzi, Gwyn Lurie, Ben Shiffrin, Caleb Wilson

The Nine Lives of Fritz the Cat ★ 18
Animated erotic comedy 1974 · US · Colour · 76min

This uninspired sequel to *Fritz the Cat* finds the stoned feline imagining his other lives in the past and future. The astute social comment of both Robert Crumb's original strips and the first film directed by Ralph

Bakshi is mostly gone, and instead the animators seem more intent on creating psychedelic effects. DM DVD

Skip Hinnant *Fritz* • Reva Rose *Fritz's old lady* ■ *Dir* Robert Taylor (3) • *Scr* Fred Halliday, Eric Monte, Robert Taylor

The Nine Lives of Tomas Katz ★ 15
Fantasy 1999 · UK/Ger · BW · 84min

Set in a monochrome London on the eve of a possible apocalypse, this ambitious but wholly unsatisfactory fantasy is hamstrung by the juvenile humour and self-serving flamboyance of its director. Such is Ben Hopkins's eagerness to show off his familiarity with everything from expressionism to MTV, that his misadventures of alien Tomas Katz (Thomas Fisher) almost become an irrelevance. This is a muddle of obscure symbols and half-baked ideas. DP DVD

Thomas Fisher [Tom Fisher] *No/Tomas Katz* • Ian McNeice *The inspector* • Tim Barlow *Mr Browne* • Janet Henfrey *Janice Waily* • Tony Maudsley *Taxi driver* ■ *Dir* Ben Hopkins • *Scr* Ben Hopkins, Thomas Browne, from a story by Ben Hopkins, Robert Cheek

Nine Months ★★★
Comedy 1994 · Fr · Colour · 107min

This French comedy is infinitely superior to its Hollywood remake, primarily because it is less coy in its depiction of the sexual and gynaecological aspects of pregnancy than Chris Columbus's film. It is therefore able to develop its relationships and shifting attitudes on more than a superficially comic level. Similarly, Patrick Braoudé is less mannered than Hugh Grant and genuinely appears to be perturbed by the prospect of fatherhood, despite the assurances of his long-suffering wife, Philippine Leroy-Beaulieu. DP

Philippine Leroy-Beaulieu *Mathilde* • Catherine Jacob *Dominique* • Patrick Braoudé *Samuel* • Daniel Russo *Georges* • Patrick Bouchitey *Marc* ■ *Dir/Scr* Patrick Braoudé

Nine Months ★★ 12
Comedy 1995 · US · Colour · 98min

This attempt to cement Hugh Grant's reputation as the Cary Grant of the 1990s following the massive international success of *Four Weddings and a Funeral* collapses under sentimental crudity, as child psychologist Grant tries to come to terms with his fear of impending fatherhood when girlfriend Julianne Moore announces she is pregnant. TH Swearing. DVD

Hugh Grant *Samuel Faulkner* • Julianne Moore *Rebecca Taylor* • Tom Arnold *Marty Dwyer* • Joan Cusack *Gail Dwyer* • Jeff Goldblum *Sean Fletcher* • Robin Williams *Dr Kosevich* ■ *Dir* Chris Columbus • *Scr* Chris Columbus, from the 1994 film by Patrick Braoudé

The Nine Muses ★★★★ PG
Documentary 2010 · Gha/UK · Colour · 96min

Ghana-born John Akomfrah has been acclaimed by many as Britain's leading black film-maker. Here, taking his cue from Homer's *The Odyssey* and combining lustrous new digital imagery by Dewald Aukema with clips from features, newsreels and TV shows, Akomfrah and editor Miikka Leskinen create an alien backdrop to accompany quotations from such authors as Shakespeare, Joyce, Beckett, Dylan Thomas and Emily Dickinson. Their aim is to show how the postwar immigrants overcame seemingly insurmountable challenges to integrate into an unwelcoming society and gradually find something closer to acceptance. It's tough, demanding stuff but it's also thoughtful, poetic and utterly compelling. DP

■ *Dir* John Akomfrah • *Cinematographer* Dewald Aukema • *Editor* Miikka Leskinen

919 Fifth Avenue ★★
Mystery drama 1995 · US · Colour · 120min

Vanity Fair columnist Dominick Dunne is well known for chronicling the real-life misdeeds of the rich and infamous in novel form, but this original screenplay probably

won't do much to enhance his reputation. The cast credentials are impressive, with Denise Richards rubbing shoulders with TV regulars Barry Bostwick, Lisa Eilbacher and Brian Krause. But not even a murder at a charity bash can enliven the storyline, which centres around a biographer delving into the secrets of Manhattan's Van Degen dynasty. DP

Barry Bostwick *Lawrence Van Degen* • Reed Diamond *Ben Constant* • Lisa Eilbacher *Janet Van Degen* • Fionnula Flanagan *Brighty* • Brian Krause *Court Van Degen* • Denise Richards *Cathy Damore* ■ *Dir* Neil Hagar • *Scr* James Duff, Dominick Dunne

Nine Queens ★★★★ 15
Crime drama 2000 · Arg · Colour · 109min

Initially an entry in a screenwriting contest, Fabian Bielinsky's debut feature is dextrously assured. The story is set in Argentina and hinges on the meeting of incompetent con Gaston Pauls and experienced swindler Ricardo Darin. Their dubious deal involves a tycoon who's about to be deported and a forged set of priceless stamps. The endlessly inventive twists and turns are baffling, but the performances will keep you watching, with Darin outstanding as the small-time operator dripping with seedy charisma. Brisk without being brash, slick but never smug, this deftly handled tale is destined for cult status. An American remake, *Criminal*, was released in 2004. DP Spanish +subtitles. DVD

Gaston Pauls *Juan* • Ricardo Darin *Marcos* • Leticia Bredice *Valeria* • Tomas Fonzi *Federico* ■ *Dir/Scr* Fabian Bielinsky

9.79* ★★★★ PG
Documentary 2012 · US · Colour · 82min

9.79 seconds is the time set by Canadian sprinter Ben Johnson when he smashed the 100m world record in the final at the 1988 Seoul Olympics, annihilating a brilliant field that included our own Linford Christie and American golden boy Carl Lewis. The race subsequently became the most notorious in Olympic history after Johnson was disqualified for drug use, and most of the eight finalists have had issues with drugs since. Daniel Gordon's documentary discloses some stark revelations about the pervasiveness of doping. Access to all the protagonists (each erudite and plain speaking) is a major bonus and there's plenty of crisply edited footage (accompanied by the distinctive tones of ace commentator David Coleman), making this a worthy and informative addition to the chronicle of sport. JA Some swearing. DVD

Carl Lewis • Linford Christie • Ben Johnson (4) *Ben Johnson* • David Harewood *Narrator* ■ *Dir* Daniel Gordon • *Scr* Daniel Gordon, Nick Packer

976-EVIL ★ 18
Horror 1988 · US · Colour · 94min

Nerdy Stephen Geoffreys calls a "horrorscope" hot line and obtains supernatural powers that enable him to take revenge on his tormentors. A confusing mess directed by horror icon Robert Englund who falls back on Freddy Krueger wisecracks and other lifts from *A Nightmare on Elm Street* to beef up his demonic disaster. Sandy Dennis as Geoffreys's kooky religious aunt makes this stale tale almost worthwhile. AJ

Patrick O'Bryan *Spike* • Sandy Dennis *Aunt Lucy* • Stephen Geoffreys *Hoax* • Jim Metzler *Marty Palmer* • Maria Rubell *Angella Martinez* • Lezlie Deane *Suzie* ■ *Dir* Robert Englund • *Scr* Rhet Topham, Brian Helgeland

976-EVIL 2 ★ 18
Horror 1992 · US · Colour · 86min

In this awful sequel to the 1988 original, a serial killer is revealed to be a rotting zombie who murders via astral projection. Completely devoid of imagination, apart from one sequence where a victim is trapped in a black-and-white mix of *Night of the Living Dead* and *It's a Wonderful Life*,

this horror cheapie is royally fouled up by director Jim Wynorski. AJ

Patrick O'Bryan *Spike* • René Assa *Professor Grubeck* • Debbie James *Robin* • Brigitte Nielsen ■ *Dir* Jim Wynorski • *Scr* Erik Anjou

9 Songs ★★ 18
Erotic drama 2004 · UK · Colour · 66min

Heralded as the first British film featuring "frequent strong real sex" to receive an 18 rating, *9 Songs* is director Michael Winterbottom's ode to physical love. Unfolding against the backdrop of a series of concerts, this explores the sexual relationship between lanky American student Margo Stiller and British research scientist Keiran O'Brien. Instead of a lesson in how hedonistic two people can be, their romp-fuelled four months together demonstrates how a generation deals with loneliness. This is very much an exercise in style over content and, as such, some will find it a rewarding art house experiment with much to recommend it. Others watching simply for the explicit and unsimulated lovemaking may well find it boring and pretentious. KK DVD

Margo Stilley *Lisa* • Kieran O'Brien *Matt* ■ *Dir* Michael Winterbottom • *Cinematographer* Marcel Zyskind

Nine to Five ★★★ 15
Comedy 1980 · US · Colour · 109min

Dolly Parton makes her movie debut and belts out the Oscar-nominated title song in this cheery comedy, which went on to spawn a sitcom series of the same name. Parton, Lily Tomlin and Jane Fonda play three office colleagues who scheme revenge on their chauvinist boss when Tomlin is unfairly denied a promotion. It was Fonda who came up with the idea of making a Hollywood version of a feminist comedy, but it is Tomlin and Parton whose performances impress more. PF Drug abuse, some swearing. DVD

Jane Fonda *Judy Bernly* • Lily Tomlin *Violet Newstead* • Dolly Parton *Doralee Rhodes* • Dabney Coleman *Franklin Hart Jr* • Sterling Hayden *Russell Tinsworthy* • Elizabeth Wilson *Roz Keith* • Henry Jones *Hinkle* ■ *Dir* Colin Higgins • *Scr* Colin Higgins, Patricia Resnick, from a story by Patricia Resnick

The Nines ★★ 15
Mystery thriller 2007 · US · Colour · 95min

John August's film begins promisingly with a TV star (Ryan Reynolds) placed under house arrest after burning down his home, only to become convinced that his temporary domicile is haunted. In the second story, a writer (Reynolds again, as each tale features the same cast) endures development hell as his TV series collapses around him; while in the third instalment a video game designer finds himself stranded on a deserted country road with a mysterious woman for company. What begins as an intriguing and atmospheric mystery rapidly soon degenerates into nothing more than a middling episode of *Tales of the Unexpected*. AS Swearing, drug abuse DVD

Ryan Reynolds *Gary/Gavin/Gabriel* • Hope Davis *Sarah/Susan/Sierra* • Melissa McCarthy *Margaret/Melissa/Mary* • Elle Fanning *Noelle* • Dahlia Salem ■ *Dir/Scr* John August

1918 ★★★
Period drama 1985 · US · Colour · 91min

A fact-based period drama, set in rural Texas, this chronicles the death and despair brought to one small town by the killer flu epidemic that swept much of the US in the year of the title. Adapted from a Horton Foote play, the film seems understandably stagey at times. Nonetheless, the innate strength of story and some powerful performances carry it through. Look out for an early screen appearance by a young Matthew Broderick. Followed by a number of sequels. DA

William Converse-Roberts *Horace Robedaux* • Hallie Foote *Elizabeth Robedaux* • Rochelle Oliver *Mrs Vaughn* • Matthew Broderick *Brother* • Jeannie McCarthy [Jeanne McCarthy] *Bessie* •

Bill McGhee *Sam* • Horton Foote Jr *Jessie* ■ *Dir* Ken Harrison • *Scr* Horton Foote, from his play

1984 ★★★
Futuristic drama 1955 · UK · BW · 89min

Michael Anderson's adaptation of George Orwell's dystopian novel is reasonably faithful to its source, concentrating on the possibility of love and humanity in a totalitarian state ruled by a powerful bureaucratic elite, a world of "Big Brother", "Thought Police" and "Doublethink". It's not quite the equal of Michael Radford's 1984 version, but both pale beside the chilling, authentically Orwellian vision of Terry Gilliam's *Brazil*. AT

Edmond O'Brien *Winston Smith* • Michael Redgrave *O'Connor* • Jan Sterling *Julia* • David Kossoff *Charrington* • Mervyn Johns *Jones* • Donald Pleasence *Parsons* ■ *Dir* Michael Anderson • *Scr* William P Templeton [William Templeton], Ralph Bettinson, from the novel by George Orwell

Nineteen Eighty-Four ★★★★ 15
Futuristic drama 1984 · UK · Colour · 110min

Inspired less by Soviet tyranny than the paranoia induced by British wartime censorship and propaganda, George Orwell's study of a dystopian future has lost none of its pessimism and dread. Much bleaker than the 1955 version, Michael Radford's superbly designed return to Oceania holds out little hope that the human spirit will be able to withstand the onset of totalitarianism. John Hurt is perfectly cast as the government cog who enters into a relationship with co-worker Suzanna Hamilton as an act of rebellion. But it's his encounter with Richard Burton, as the personification of "Big Brother's" omnipresence, that provides the dramatic highlight. DP Violence, nudity. DVD

John Hurt *Winston Smith* • Richard Burton *O'Brien* • Suzanna Hamilton *Julia* • Cyril Cusack *Charrington* • Gregor Fisher *Parsons* • James Walker *Syme* • Andrew Wilde *Tillotson* • Phyllis Logan *Telescreen announcer* • Roger Lloyd Pack *Waiter* ■ *Dir* Michael Radford • *Scr* Michael Radford, Jonathan Gems, from the novel by George Orwell

1911 ★★ 15
Historical action drama
2011 · Chi/HK · Colour and BW · 95min

Jackie Chan's 100th movie release also celebrates the centenary of China's 1911 Xinhai Revolution, which marked the country's bloody transition from feudal empire to republic. As you might expect, it's a suitably epic, attractively shot drama that portrays the revolution and its martyrs in the most sympathetic of lights. Chan gives a convincing dramatic performance as revolutionary general Huang Xing, but the one that really stands out is Sun Chun's playful turn as general/politician Yuan Shikai, a self-serving opportunist who plays the revolutionaries and the Empress Dowager (a brittle Joan Chen) off against each other – and somehow comes out on top. JH Mandarin, English, French +subtitles. DVD BD

Jackie Chan *Huang Xing* • Winston Chao *Sun Yat-Sen* • Lee Bingbing [Bingbing Li] *Xu Zonghan* • Sun Chun [Chun Sun] *Yuan Shikai* • Joan Chen *Empress Longyu* ■ *Dir* Zhang Li • *Scr* Wang Xingdong, Chen Baoguang

1941 ★★★ 12
Comedy 1979 · US · Colour · 114min

Widely regarded as the one Steven Spielberg disaster, this sprawling comedy never deserved all the flak. True, it's a messy, hysterical affair and many of the gags are strictly puerile. However, the sentimentality that mars many of Spielberg's more acclaimed works is nowhere to be seen, and there is a mischievous, anarchic edge to the story of how LA collapsed into chaos over fear of Japanese invasion following Pearl Harbor. JF Swearing. DVD BD

Dan Aykroyd *Sergeant Tree* • Ned Beatty *Ward Douglas* • John Belushi *Wild Bill Kelso* • Lorraine Gary *Joan Douglas* • Murray Hamilton *Claude* • Christopher Lee *Von Kleinschmidt* • Tim Matheson *Birkhead* • Toshiro Mifune *Commander Mitamura* • Warren Oates *Maddox* • Robert Stack *General Stilwell* • Treat Williams *"Stretch" Sitarski* • Nancy Allen *Donna* • John Candy *Foley* • Elisha Cook [Elisha Cook Jr] *Patron* • Slim Pickens *Hollis Wood* • Sam Fuller [Samuel Fuller] *Interceptor commander* • John Landis *Mizerany* • Mickey Rourke *Reese* ■ *Dir* Steven Spielberg • *Scr* Robert Zemeckis Bob Gale, from a story by Zemeckis, Gale, John Milius

1942: a Love Story ★★★ 12
Drama   1994 · Ind · Colour · 151min

As the Quit India movement gathered momentum at the height of the Second World War, the British response to the growing unrest (much of which came in the form of the passive resistance advocated by Gandhi) was often swift and brutal. Packed with songs that topped the Indian charts, this Romeo and Juliet story stars Anil Kapoor and Manisha Koirala as a Himalayan couple whose fathers are on opposite sides in the conflict. Director Vidhu Vinod Chopra combines the human and the historical elements well. DP Hindi +subtitles. *DVD*

Anil Kapoor *Nandu* • Manisha Koirala *Rajjo* • Brian Glover *General Douglas* ■ *Dir* Vidhu Vinod Chopra • *Scr* Kamna, Chandra, Shiv Subrahmanyam, Vidhu Vinod Chopra

1900 ★★★★ 18
Epic period drama   1976 · It · Colour · 326min

This stunning but demanding Marxist epic spans 45 years of Italian political history. Tracing the rise and fall of Fascism, Bernardo Bertolucci uses characters to symbolise entire social groups. Gérard Depardieu and Robert De Niro are born on the same day in the year 1901, in the same rural region, one to poor sharecroppers, the other to landowners. As they grow from childhood friends to antagonistic men, Depardieu becomes an inspirational Communist leader. His nemesis, Donald Sutherland, is the local blackshirt and De Niro's foreman. Operatically staged and swollen with symbolism, this is a flawed masterpiece, best viewed as polemic as much as history. AC Italian +subtitles. *DVD*

Burt Lancaster *Alfredo Sr* • Robert De Niro *Alfredo Jr* • Gérard Depardieu *Olmo* • Donald Sutherland *Attila* • Dominique Sanda *Ada* • Sterling Hayden *Leo Dalco* • Stefania Sandrelli *Anita* • Alida Valli *Signora Pioppi* • Laura Betti *Regina* ■ *Dir* Bernardo Bertolucci • *Scr* Bernardo Bertolucci, Franco Arcalli, Giuseppe Bertolucci • *Music* Ennio Morricone

1919 ★★★
Period drama   1983 · Sp · Colour · 85min

Despite its visual lustre, this is a markedly less nostalgic picture than its predecessor, *Valentina*. Again recounted by a Republican PoW at the end of the Spanish Civil War, the story has now moved on to 1919, with Miguel Molina assuming the role of the young poet, Pepe. The hero is still devoted to his childhood sweetheart, Emma Suarez, but his passion is compromised by an encounter with Cristina Marsillach, the domestic he meets while studying in Zaragoza. DP Spanish +subtitles.

Anthony Quinn *Mosen Joaquin* • Miguel Molina *Pepe* • Cristina Marsillach *Isabelita* • Saturno Cerra *Don Jose* • Conchita Leza *Doña Luisa* • Walter Vidarte *Checa* • Emma Suarez *Valentina* ■ *Dir* Antonio Jose Betancor • *Scr* Lautaro Murúa, Antonio José Betancor, Carlos Escobedo, Javier Moro, from the novel *Crónica del Alba (Days Of Dawn)* by Ramón J Sender

Nineteen Nineteen ★★ 15
Drama   1984 · UK · Colour · 98min

Paul Scofield and Maria Schell co-star in this very solemn movie about Freudian analysis. The leads meet up in Vienna and recall their separate consultations with Dr Freud, given voice (but not a physical presence) by Frank Finlay. Scofield remembers the war, his marriage and his impossible love objects; Schell relives her lesbian relationship, marriage and divorce. AT

Maria Schell *Sophie Ruben* • Paul Scofield *Alexander Scherbatov* • Frank Finlay *Dr Freud* • Diana Quick *Anna* • Clare Higgins *Young Sophie* • Colin Firth *Young Alexander* ■ *Dir* Hugh Brody • *Scr* Hugh Brody, Michael Ignatieff

1991: The Year Punk Broke ★★
Music documentary   1992 · US · Colour · 99min

This documentary records Sonic Youth's 1991 European tour as they moved from small club venues to the outdoor festival circuit. Nicely shot and edited, but rather dull overall; other bands featured include Nirvana, Dinosaur Jr and the Ramones. Gumball and Babes in Toyland also appear, but neither group shows the talent or class of Sonic Youth, despite frontman Thurston Moore failing to live up to his legendary image as a vicious wit. AJ

■ *Dir* Dave Markey

1971 ★★★★
Documentary   2014 · US · Colour and BW

On 8 March 1971, members of the Citizens' Commission to Investigate the FBI broke into a Bureau office and stole evidence of J Edgar Hoover's counterintelligence programme to infiltrate and disrupt various political groups. Director Johanna Hamilton coaxes the co-conspirators into reliving their exploits over archival footage and slick reconstructions of the raid. Her film grips like a thriller but it also amuses with its accounts of FBI agents disguising themselves as hippies in an effort to nail the perpetrators. DP

■ *Dir* Johanna Hamilton • *Scr* Johanna Hamilton, Gabriel Rhodes

1969 ★★★ 15
Drama   1988 · US · Colour · 91min

This is an effective and often moving portrayal of life in America at the end of the 1960s, with Kiefer Sutherland and Robert Downey Jr as two friends who find themselves on opposite sides of US involvement in Vietnam. Downey takes a moral stance; Sutherland loses himself in drink and drugs while waiting for his number to come up on Nixon's Vietnam draft lottery. Although clichéd in places and definitely slow towards the middle, it's an interesting look at the war that never should have been. JB Violence, swearing, nudity. *DVD*

Robert Downey Jr *Ralph Carr* • Kiefer Sutherland *Scott Denny* • Bruce Dern *Cliff Denny* • Mariette Hartley *Jessie Denny* • Winona Ryder *Beth Carr* • Joanna Cassidy *Ev Carr* ■ *Dir/Scr* Ernest Thompson

99 and 44/100% Dead ★★ 15
Crime comedy   1974 · US · Colour · 97min

Arguably cinema's first pop-art gangster movie, this offbeat black comedy matches up to the strangeness of its title. In a role meant for Robert Mitchum, the always superb Richard Harris plays a hitman who is hired by a gang leader struggling for supremacy over a criminal colleague. A below-par John Frankenheimer brings a comic book feel to the various bloody shoot-outs and keeps the action moving at a fair clip, but he gets lost amid the nonsense. RS

Richard Harris *Harry Crown* • Edmond O'Brien *Uncle Frank* • Bradford Dillman *Big Eddie* • Ann Turkel *Buffy* • Constance Ford *Dolly* • David Hall *Tony* • Katherine Baumann *Baby* • Chuck Connors *Marvin "Claw" Zuckerman* ■ *Dir* John Frankenheimer • *Scr* Robert Dillon

99 Homes ★★★ 15
Drama   2014 · US · Colour · 107min

Spider-man gets an urgent lesson in capitalist economics in this thoughtful but emotionally schematic drama. Andrew Garfield takes up Michael Shannon's offer of working in his property firm, but soon finds that evicting and dispossessing others is a price he might not be willing to pay to save his mother's house. As moral sagas go, it's timely and sincere, but just as the Devil has all the best tunes, so the wily, reptilian

Shannon often hijacks our attention away from the earnest but no so interesting Garfield. DW *DVD* *Blu-ray*

Andrew Garfield *Dennis Nash* • Michael Shannon *Rick Carver* • Laura Dern *Lynn Nash* • Tim Guinee *Frank Green* • JD Evermore *Mr Tanner* ■ *Dir* Ramin Bahrani • *Scr* Ramin Bahrani, Amir Naderi, from a story by Bahrani, Bahareh Azimi

99 River Street ★★★
Film noir   1953 · US · BW · 83min

Peggie Castle, the wife of boxer-turned-cab driver John Payne, deserts him for jewel thief Brad Dexter. When Dexter grows bored with the blonde, he kills her and leaves the corpse in Payne's cab. Payne, with help from Evelyn Keyes, has to run the gauntlet of the seedy underworld and its gun-happy dangers in an effort to prove his innocence. A modest but taut, tough and atmospheric crime movie. RK

John Payne *Ernie Driscoll* • Evelyn Keyes *Linda James* • Brad Dexter *Victor Rawlins* • Frank Faylen *Stan Hogan* • Peggie Castle *Pauline Driscoll* ■ *Dir* Phil Karlson • *Scr* Robert Smith, from a story by George Zuckerman

92 in the Shade ★★★
Comedy drama   1975 · US/UK · Colour · 83min

Peter Fonda stars in this amiable coast-along playing a fishing guide in the Florida Keys at odds with the captain of another boat. He's in the company of such specialists in eccentricity as Warren Oates, Margot Kidder, Burgess Meredith and Harry Dean Stanton, and this makes up for directorial inexperience with atmosphere and quirkiness. TH

Peter Fonda *Tom Skelton* • Warren Oates *Nichol Dance* • Margot Kidder *Miranda* • Burgess Meredith *Goldsboro* • Harry Dean Stanton *Carter* • Sylvia Miles *Bella* • Elizabeth Ashley *Jeannie Carter* • William Hickey *Mr Skelton* ■ *Dir* Thomas McGuane • *Scr* Thomas McGuane, from his novel

Ninja Assassin ★ 18
Martial arts action adventure
2009 · US · Colour and BW · 94min

Martial arts and CGI carnage combine when rival ninjas clash in this underwhelming action flick. Naomie Harris plays the Berlin-based police researcher who twigs that ninjas have been involved in a string of assassinations. The fights are all digitally conjured up, so genuine thrills are at a minimum and the copious sprays of pixelated blood quickly pall. TJ Violence, swearing. *DVD* *Blu-ray*

Rain *Raizo* • Naomie Harris *Mika Coretti* • Ben Miles *Ryan Maslow* • Sho Kosugi *Lord Ozunu* • Rick Yune *Takeshi* • Sung Kang *Hollywood* ■ *Dir* James McTeigue • *Scr* Matthew Sand, J Michael Straczynski, from a story by Sand

Ninotchka ★★★★★ U
Comedy   1939 · US · BW · 105min

This is without doubt one of the funniest, most original screen comedies ever made, and from the greatest year in Hollywood's history. Director Ernst Lubitsch brings his magic touch to bear on this inspired tale of a Russian emissary (the great Greta Garbo in a startling change of image) sent to Paris to retrieve three errant communists who have fallen in love with the ways of the West. Of course, it's just a matter of time before Garbo melts and falls in love, in her case with debonair count Melvyn Douglas. Witty, sophisticated, immaculately cast and superbly performed, this film was advertised in its day simply as "Garbo laughs!" That she does, and so will you, long and loud, especially at the utterly charming café scene. TS

Greta Garbo *Ninotchka, Nina Ivanova Yakushova* • Melvyn Douglas *Count Leon d'Algout* • Ina Claire *Grand Duchess Swana* • Bela Lugosi *Commissar Razinin* • Sig Rumann [Sig Ruman] *Iranoff* • Felix Bressart *Bu'janoff* • Alexander Granach *Kopalski* • Gregory Gaye *Count Alexis Rakonin* ■ *Dir* Ernst Lubitsch • *Scr* Charles Brackett, Billy Wilder, Walter Reisch, from a story by Melchior Lengyel • *Cinematographer* William Daniels (1) • *Costume Designer* Adrian

9th Company ★★★ 15
War drama
2005 · Fin/Rus/Ukr · Colour · 133min

On the surface, this looks like just another war film. A raggle-taggle bunch of raw recruits are brought together, trained and packed off to the nearest war zone. The difference is that *9th Company* is Russian, its soldiers are Soviet and the war-torn land in which they find themselves is the Afghanistan of 1989. This is a fine mix of character and immense battle set pieces – and a timely reminder that war is hell, wherever you are from and whatever language you speak. DA Russian +subtitles. *DVD*

Alexei Chadov *Vorobey* • Artur Smolyaninov [Artur Smolianinov] *Lyutaev* • Konstantin Kryukov *Gioconda* • Ivan Kokorin *Chugun* • Artem Mikhalkov *Stas* • Fyodor Bondarchuk *Khokhol* ■ *Dir* Fyodor Bondarchuk • *Scr* Yuri Korotkov

The Ninth Configuration ★★★ 15
Psychological thriller 1979 · US · Colour · 113min

Produced, directed and scripted by *The Exorcist* creator William Peter Blatty, this surreal exercise in Freudian vaudeville stars Stacy Keach as a psychiatrist who provides radical therapy to possibly insane military veterans in a remote Gothic mansion. Of course, Keach has a gruesome secret and is going through his own apocalyptic catharsis. At times absolutely bewildering, at others completely gripping and harrowing, this overly literate and obtuse thriller has become the thinking man's cult classic. AJ Swearing, violence. *DVD* *Blu-ray*

Stacy Keach *Colonel Hudson Kane* • Scott Wilson *Captain Billy Cutshaw* • Jason Miller *Lieutenant Reno* • Ed Flanders *Colonel Fell* • Neville Brand *Major Groper* • Moses Gunn *Major Nammack* • Robert Loggia *Lieutenant Bennish* ■ *Dir* William Peter Blatty • *Scr* William Peter Blatty, from the novel *Twinkle, Twinkle, Killer Kane* by William Peter Blatty

The Ninth Gate ★★★ 15
Supernatural thriller
1999 · Fr/Sp/US · Colour · 127min

This is a largely successful return to the horror genre by Roman Polanski, and features sardonic wit, subtle suspense tricks and razor-sharp irony. Johnny Depp stars as a rare books expert hired by billionaire Frank Langella to authenticate his copy of an ancient tome that was supposedly written in conjunction with the Devil. This gothic chiller has moody atmosphere and a stunning score (from Wojciech Kilar), but the hallucinatory climax is a disappointment. AJ Violence, a sex scene, nudity. *DVD*

Johnny Depp *Dean Corso* • Frank Langella *Boris Balkan* • Lena Olin *Liana Telfer* • Emmanuelle Seigner *The girl* • Barbara Jefford *Baroness Kessler* • Jack Taylor *Victor Fargas* • James Russo *Bernie* ■ *Dir* Roman Polanski • *Scr* Enrique Urbizu, John Brownjohn, Roman Polanski, from the novel *El Club Dumas* by Arturo Pérez-Reverte

Nirvana ★★★★
Science-fiction thriller
1996 · It/Fr/UK · Colour · 115min

This stunning cyber-fantasy, rich in design and innovative ideas, intellectually engages the mind while always remaining enjoyable on the purest pulp levels. Superstar video game inventor Christopher Lambert creates a new game called Nirvana, then realises his virtual-reality hero (Italian matinée idol Diego Abatantuono) has a human consciousness. How he tries to erase the game before its mass-market Christmas release, which would condemn Abantuono to a never-ending existence, pits Lambert against a ruthless multinational corporation and takes him through the seedy underworlds of a future metropolis known as the Northern Agglomerate. AJ In Italian.

Christopher Lambert *Jimi* • Diego Abatantuono *Solo* • Sergio Rubini *Joystick* • Emmanuelle Seigner *Lisa* • Stefania Rocca *Naima* ■ *Dir* Gabriele Salvatores • *Scr* Gabriele Salvatores, Gloria Corica, Pino Cacucci

N

Nishant ★★★ 15
Crime drama 1975 · Ind · Colour · 136min

Shabana Azmi stars in Shyam Benegal's examination of the hypocrisy and corruption of rural society. The story centres on teacher Girish Karnad's determination to avenge the abduction and rape of his wife by Naseeruddin Shah, the youngest son of a feared landowner. Despite Benegal owing more to Satyajit Ray's style of cinema than the mainstream, this powerful, realist tale nevertheless turned the debuting Shah into a Bollywood legend, while Azmi confirmed her status as one of India's finest actresses. But it's Amrish Puri who dominates proceedings as Shah's vicious brother. **DP** Hindi +subtitles.

Girish Karnad *Schoolmaster* • Shabana Azmi *Sushila* • Anant Nag *Anjaiya* • Amrish Puri *Eldest Zamindar* • Satyadev Dubey *Priest* • Smita [Smita Patil] *Rukmani* • Mohan Agashe *Prasad* • Kulbhushan Kharbanda *Policeman Patel* • Naseeruddin Shah *Vishwam* ■ *Dir* Shyam Benegal • *Scr* Vijay Tendulkar

Nixon ★★★★ 15
Biographical drama
1995 · US · Colour and BW · 182min

Near the end of this biographical drama, the disgraced President gazes at a painting of John Kennedy and says, "When people look at you, they see what they want to be. When they look at me, they see what they are." That's a great line, the key to Oliver Stone's movie, which, like his earlier *JFK*, is three hours of brilliance, provocation and information overload. The movie makes great demands on the viewer and on Anthony Hopkins, whose brave performance is more an impression than an impersonation. At one point Paul Sorvino's sinister Henry Kissinger says, "He had greatness within his grasp but he had the defects of his qualities." Much the same can be said of this mesmerising movie. **AT** Swearing. *DVD*

Anthony Hopkins *Richard Milhous Nixon* • Joan Allen *Pat Nixon* • Powers Boothe *Alexander Haig* • Ed Harris *E Howard Hunt* • Bob Hoskins *J Edgar Hoover* • EG Marshall *John Mitchell* • David Paymer *Ron Ziegler* • David Hyde Pierce *John Dean* • Paul Sorvino *Henry Kissinger* • Mary Steenburgen *Hannah Nixon* • JT Walsh *John Ehrlichman* • James Woods *HR Haldeman* • Brian Bedford *Clyde Tolson* ■ *Dir* Oliver Stone • *Scr* Stephen J Rivele, Christopher Wilkinson, Oliver Stone

No ★★★ 15
Drama
2012 · Chil/Fr/US · Colour and BW · 112min

In 1988, after 15 years in power, Chilean dictator Augusto Pinochet staged a referendum to try to give his regime greater international legitimacy. It looked like he would win, despite widespread stories of torture, disappearances and the killing of opponents. In this drama, inspired by real events, Gael García Bernal plays the advertising executive brought in as campaign director for Pinochet's opponents, who prompts outrage when he suggests the "No" campaign should downplay the misery and employ the language of TV advertising. Director Pablo Larraín (*Tony Manero*) shot on old-fashioned videotape, enabling him to blend archive news footage into the story, which gives it a rough-edged authenticity. **BP** Spanish +subtitles. Swearing. *DVD*

Gael García Bernal *René Saavedra* • Alfredo Castro *Lucho Guzman* • Luis Gnecco *Urrutia* • Antonia Zegers *Verónica* • Marcial Tagle *Costa* ■ *Dir* Pablo Larraín • *Scr* Pedro Peirano, from the play *The Referendum* by Antonio Skarmeta

No Blade of Grass ★★★ 15
Science-fiction drama
1970 · UK · Colour · 91min

This bleak but affecting eco-message drama from director Cornel Wilde casts Nigel Davenport and, in her last film, Jean Wallace (Wilde's real-life wife) as parents leading their family across a British countryside devastated by environmental pollution and blighted by anarchy. Wilde's rough-edged handling of the material oddly gives it a semi-documentary feel that's intermittently effective. It's a sober, well-meaning film that, despite not quite coming off, is well worth catching. **RS**

Nigel Davenport *John Custance* • Jean Wallace *Ann Custance* • John Hamill *Roger Burnham* • Lynne Frederick *Mary Custance* • Patrick Holt *David Custance* • Anthony May *Andrew Pirrie* • Wendy Richard *Clara* ■ *Dir* Cornel Wilde • *Scr* Sean Forestal, Jefferson Pascal, from the novel *The Death of Grass* by John Christopher

No Code of Conduct ★★ 18
Crime action drama 1998 · US · Colour · 85min

Martin and Charlie Sheen are together again in this distinctly average crime drama. This time around, Charlie plays a maverick cop who's prepared to use any means necessary to bust a gigantic heroin ring, while Martin is a police executive waging his own war against high-level corruption. Expect the body count to mount rapidly. **JF** Swearing, violence. *DVD*

Martin Sheen *Bill Peterson* • Charles Sheen [Charlie Sheen] *Jake Peterson* • Bret Michaels *Shane* • Mark Dacascos *Paul DeLucca* • Joe Lando *Willdog* • Meredith Salenger *Rebecca Peterson* ■ *Dir* Bret Michaels • *Scr* Bill Gucwa, Ed Masterson, Bret Michaels, Charlie Sheen, Shane Stanley

No Country for Old Men
★★★★★ 15
Crime thriller 2007 · US · Colour · 117min

There's a lot of money being chased in this masterful, multi-faceted thriller from the Coen brothers, but it's not really what's at stake. Set in Texas in 1980, it begins with Vietnam veteran Llewelyn Moss (Josh Brolin) stumbling across a desert drug deal gone wrong and escaping with a suitcase containing $2 million. A game of cat and mouse ensues, as Moss is pursued by a ruthless assassin armed with a cattle stun gun (Javier Bardem), various Mexican drug dealers and an ageing police sheriff (Tommy Lee Jones), whose despairing take on the state of America provides the movie's moral heart. Adapting Cormac McCarthy's terse *noir* novel for the screen, the Coens marry the writer's apocalyptic sense of social breakdown with their own blackly comic sensibility and deliver a complex, utterly riveting thriller. The result is a terrific crime movie that bears comparison with their other career high points, *Blood Simple* and *Fargo*. **JR** Violence. *DVD*

Tommy Lee Jones *Ed Tom Bell* • Javier Bardem *Anton Chigurh* • Josh Brolin *Llewelyn Moss* • Woody Harrelson *Carson Wells* • Kelly Macdonald *Carla Jean Moss* • Garret Dillahunt *Wendell* • Tess Harper *Loretta Bell* • Barry Corbin *Ellis* ■ *Dir* Ethan Coen, Joel Coen • *Scr* Ethan Coen, Joel Coen, from the novel by Cormac McCarthy • *Cinematographer* Roger Deakins • *Music* Carter Burwell

No Deposit No Return ★★ U
Comedy 1976 · US · Colour · 106min

This Disney live-action picture is basically fine, with a couple of kids co-operating in their own kidnap in an attempt to avoid spending the summer with their uncaring grandfather. But it takes much more than a car chase, a pet skunk and David Niven hanging upside down by his heels to please kids. Darren McGavin and Don Knotts do their best as the dim-witted kidnappers, but the result isn't up to much. **DP**

David Niven *JW Osborne* • Darren McGavin *Duke* • Don Knotts *Bert* • Herschel Bernardi *Sergeant Turner* • Barbara Feldon *Carolyn* • Kim Richards *Tracy* • Brad Savage *Jay* ■ *Dir* Norman Tokar • *Scr* Arthur Alsberg, Don Nelson, from a story by Joe L McEveety

No Distance Left to Run
★★★ 15
Music documentary 2009 · UK · Colour · 104min

Blur band members Damon Albarn, Graham Coxon, Alex James and Dave Rowntree have clearly seen enough rockumentaries to know that they wanted this record of their 2009 reunion to look more like *Metallica: Some Kind of Monster* than *This Is Spinal Tap*. But while all four are guardedly nostalgic in chronicling the combo's journey from an Essex comprehensive to headliners at the Glastonbury festival, they let slip enough affection and frankness to provide a fascinating insight into the dynamics of one of British music's most chameleonic bands. **DP**

Damon Albarn • Graham Coxon • Alex James • Dave Rowntree ■ *Dir* Dylan Southern, Will Lovelace

No Down Payment ★★★
Drama 1957 · US · BW · 100min

Four couples who seek upward mobility by buying homes in a suburban housing estate must face the reality of paying the mortgage and must cope with the dramas that arise as their lives intersect. Some commentators consider the movie significant as an accurate picture of 1950s suburban America; as entertainment, it's a compendium of soap opera clichés. **RK**

Joanne Woodward *Leola Boone* • Sheree North *Isabelle Flagg* • Tony Randall *Jerry Flagg* • Jeffrey Hunter *David Martin* • Cameron Mitchell *Troy Boone* • Patricia Owens *Jean Martin* • Barbara Rush *Betty Kreitzer* • Pat Hingle *Herman Kreitzer* ■ *Dir* Martin Ritt • *Scr* Philip Yordan (front for Ben Maddow), from the novel by John McPartland

No Drums, No Bugles ★★★
Drama 1971 · US · Colour · 86min

In a fascinating, low-budget movie, Martin Sheen plays a Civil War soldier who, sickened by the killing, deserts and goes to live in the depths of the West Virginian forests. Vowing never to kill a living thing, Sheen turns into a mountain man with flowers in his hair and eco-awareness in his veins. This Vietnam allegory is artfully made – Sheen is the only real character, although others are briefly glimpsed or heard – and probably influenced by the Oscar-winning 1963 short, *Incident at Owl Creek*. **AT**

Martin Sheen *Ashby Gatrell* • Davey Davison *Callie Gatrell* • Rod McCary *Lieutenant* • Denine Terry *Sarah* ■ *Dir/Scr* Clyde Ware

No End ★★★ 15
Drama 1984 · Pol · Colour · 103min

Watched by the ghost of lawyer Jerzy Radziwilowicz, his widow, Grazyna Szapolowska, and his trade unionist client, Artur Barcis, face impossible moral dilemmas. She agonises over dishonouring his memory through physical need, while he debates whether to compromise his principles for freedom or become a martyr for the cause of liberty. Made in 1984, director Krzysztof Kieslowski's first collaboration with screenwriter Krzysztof Piesiewicz was withheld for two years from international release because of its pro-Solidarity sentiments. **DP** Polish +subtitles. *DVD*

Grazyna Szapolowska *Ula Zyro* • Maria Pakulnis *Joanna* • Aleksander Bardini *Labrador* • Jerzy Radziwilowicz *Antoni "Antek" Zyro* • Artur Barcis *Darius* ■ *Dir* Krzysztof Kieslowski • *Scr* Krzysztof Kieslowski, Krzysztof Piesiewicz

No Escape ★★★ 15
Futuristic action thriller
1994 · US · Colour · 118min

Ray Liotta gives it his best shot in this cheerfully trashy futuristic thriller from British director Martin Campbell. In the 21st century, Liotta finds himself imprisoned on an isolated island where the convicts have split into caring hippies and warmongering tribesmen. Lance Henriksen and Stuart Wilson ham it up for all they're worth as the leaders of the rival factions and, although his direction is a little erratic, Campbell delivers some satisfying set pieces. **JF** Swearing, violence. *DVD*

Ray Liotta *Robbins* • Lance Henriksen *The Father* • Stuart Wilson (1) *Marek* • Kevin Dillon *Casey* • Kevin J O'Connor *Stephano* • Don Henderson *Killian* • Ian McNeice *King* • Jack Shepherd *Dysart* ■ *Dir* Martin Campbell • *Scr* Michael Gaylin, Joel Gross, from the novel *The Penal Colony* by Richard Herley

No Escape ★★ 15
Thriller 2014 · US · Colour · 98min

Owen Wilson and Lake Bell are parents on the run for their life in John Erick Dowdle's thriller, after they find themselves targets following a revolution in their new Asian home. Patchy storytelling and far-fetched scenarios take the sting out of the tale, and Wilson is miscast in the everyman lead. Pierce Brosnan is bizarre but fun in a fleeting appearance in what is, overall, an occasionally thrilling but mostly formulaic thriller. **JL** Violence, swearing. *DVD*

Owen Wilson *Jack Dwyer* • Pierce Brosnan *Hammond* • Lake Bell *Annie Dwyer* • Sterling Jerins *Lucy Dwyer* ■ *Dir* John Erick Dowdle • *Scr* John Erick Dowdle, Drew Dowdle

No Fixed Abode ★★
Thriller 2012 · UK · Colour · 80min

Middle-class husband and father Patrick Baladi wakes up one morning in a hostel for the homeless, and proves unable to explain how he got there, in this low-budget British mystery drama. The film does a decent job of demonstrating that homelessness is not some remote issue by encouraging us to put ourselves in Baladi's position. But the question of whether he's experiencing a *Twilight Zone* nightmare fantasy or something closer to the real world is a tad confusing and seriously weakens the impact of a potentially powerful story. **TJ**

Patrick Baladi *Adam Smith* • David Sterne *Old John* • Saskia Butler *Jane Smith* • Simon Lowe *Dan* • Laurence Saunders *PC Mullen* • David Proud *Graham* ■ *Dir/Scr* Steve Rainbow

No Good Deed ★★ 15
Crime thriller
2002 · Can/US/Ger · Colour · 93min

Based on Dashiell Hammett's short story *The House on Turk Street* (the film's original title), this mediocre crime thriller has Samuel L Jackson's cello-playing detective kidnapped by bank robbers after he stumbles on their lair while hunting for a friend's missing daughter. The talents of the attractive cast are undermined by an increasingly preposterous script and this disappointment belies director Bob Rafelson's illustrious past. **SF** Swearing, violence, nudity. *DVD*

Samuel L Jackson *Jack Friar* • Milla Jovovich *Erin* • Stellan Skarsgård *Tyrone* • Doug Hutchison *Hoop* • Joss Ackland *Mr Quarre* • Grace Zabriskie *Mrs Quarre* • Jonathan Higgins *David Brewster* ■ *Dir* Bob Rafelson • *Scr* Christopher Canaan, Steve Barancik, from the short story *The House on Turk Street* by Dashiell Hammett

No Good Deed ★★ 15
Thriller 2014 · US · Colour · 83min

This tense thriller sees Taraji P Henson play a mother fighting to get through the night when an escaped killer (Idris Elba) turns up on her doorstep during a storm. So often the antihero, Elba makes the most of his imposing stature and voice to create an effective villain. He faces off with Henson's believable (if naive) heroine, and the pair carry the film ably. It's a shame, then, that these charismatic performances are at the service of an utterly unoriginal story. While serviceable as a late-night thrill, it falls into a trap of genre familiarity from which it cannot escape. **JL**

Idris Elba *Colin Evans* • Taraji P Henson *Terri* • Leslie Bibb *Meg* • Kate del Castillo *Alexis* • Henry Simmons *Jeffrey* ■ *Dir* Sam Miller • *Scr* Aimee Lagos

No Greater Glory ★★★ U
Thriller 1934 · US · BW · 73min

Frail young George Breakston gains courage, confidence and happiness when he is allowed into a gang, but his life is cut tragically short. No, this is not a juvenile crime movie, but a poignant, sensitive portrait of courage and love. Based on an autobiographical novel by Hungarian-born playwright Ferenc Molnar, Frank Borzage's film is acutely scripted by Jo Swerling and makes for a compelling, if sentimental, little drama. **RK**

George Breakston *Nemecsek* • Jimmy Butler *Boka* • Jackie Searl [Jackie Searle] *Gereb* • Frankie Darro *Feri Ats* • Donald Haines *Csonakos* • Rolf Ernest *Ferdie Pasztor* ■ *Dir* Frank Borzage • *Scr* Jo Swerling, from the novel *The Paul Street Boys* by Ferenc Molnar

No Greater Love ★★★★
Documentary   2009 · UK · Colour · 100min

Michael Whyte's respectful documentary profiles the Carmelite sisters residing in the Monastery of the Most Holy Trinity in Notting Hill. Although they take their vows very seriously, the order has allowed a little modernity to facilitate a regimen focused on praying for those too preoccupied with everyday troubles to find time for God. Whyte captures the humanity of the nuns, whether they are doing their chores, shopping online for groceries, playing ceilidh music or singing in the chapel. But it's the personal revelations about doubt, self-discovery, seclusion and divine love that make Prioress Mary of St Philip and her charges so inspirational. DP
■ *Dir* Michael Whyte

No Higher Love ★★PG
Drama   1999 · US · Colour · 86min

In this sentimental TV-movie, Katey Sagal plays a happily married woman with a career in real estate who is diagnosed with terminal cancer shortly after giving birth to a daughter. Annabeth Gish plays the divorced nurse who comes into their lives and gives the family hope for the future. Even though it's based on a true story, it's a very contrived scenario, full of brave smiles and lachrymose lapses calculated to leave the viewer misty eyed. DP *DVD*
Katey Sagal *Ellen Young* • Annabeth Gish *Claire Hutton* • Tom Irwin *Brian Young* • Alison Pill *Samantha Hutton* • Katie Boland *Lindsay Hutton* • Brenda Bazinet *Sandy Russo* • Roger Dunn *Bill Young* ■ *Dir* Michael Switzer • *Scr* Richard Leder

No Highway ★★★U
Thriller   1951 · UK · BW · 98min

James Stewart is in his best absent-minded professor mode as a scientist whose obstinacy prevents a series of flying disasters in this watchable thriller, based on Nevil Shute's novel. It's about a boffin (Stewart) who can't find his own front door, but who confidently predicts metal fatigue in a new type of British aircraft. Naturally, he's branded a loony. Marlene Dietrich has an inflated part as a film star who believes in him, along with Glynis Johns as a friendly stewardess and Janette Scott as his daughter. Directed by Henry Koster, this is much better than the family comedies he later made with Stewart. AE
James Stewart *Theodore Honey* • Marlene Dietrich *Monica Teasdale* • Glynis Johns *Marjorie Corder* • Jack Hawkins *Dennis Scott* • Ronald Squire *Sir John* • Janette Scott *Elspeth Honey* ■ *Dir* Henry Koster • *Scr* RC Sherriff, Oscar Millard, Alec Coppel, from the novel by Nevil Shute

No Home Movie ★★★★
Documentary   2015 · Bel/Fr · Colour · 115min

Chantal Akerman's final film is both a tribute to a dying mother and the last testament of a director who would take her own life just months after, aged 65. But there's nothing maudlin about this deeply personal profile of an octogenarian who had fled Poland and survived Auschwitz before raising Chantal and her sister and becoming housebound in her Brussels flat. Some will find this frustratingly introspective, but it encapsulates the themes that dominated Akerman's work and her sense of self as an individual and as a daughter. DP In French, English.
Natalia Akerman • Chantal Akerman ■ *Dir/Scr* Chantal Akerman

No Impact Man ★★★15
Documentary   2009 · US · Colour · 91min

Even after 90-odd minutes in the company of Manhattanite Colin Beavan, it's difficult to know whether this is a documentary about a sincere green activist attempting to reduce his carbon footprint, or yet another

opportunity for a remorseless self-publicist to seize some limelight. However, even cynics will enjoy watching Beavan's business-journalist wife Michelle Conlin slowly switch from mocking his new-found enthusiasm to accepting such developments as shopping in a farmers' market, going without electricity and hosting compost worms in her cosy apartment. DP Swearing.
Colin Beavan • Michelle Conlin ■ *Dir* Laura Gabbert, Justin Schein • *Cinematographer* Justin Schein

No Kidding ★★PG
Comedy drama   1960 · UK · BW · 83min

The *Carry On* team of producer Peter Rogers and director Gerald Thomas are responsible for this wallow in whimsy in which a couple inherit a large house and convert it into a holiday home for rich kids. As the house fills up with the offspring of oil sheikhs, royals and sundry millionaires, the locals speak up for the underprivileged kids in the area. Leslie Phillips and Geraldine McEwan play the couple who kick off the plot, Joan Hickson is their conspiratorial cook, while Irene Handl is the local busybody. AT *DVD*
Leslie Phillips *David Robinson* • Geraldine McEwan *Catherine Robinson* • Julia Lockwood *Vanilla* • Noel Purcell *Tandy* • Irene Handl *Mrs Spicer* • Joan Hickson *Cook* • Francesca Annis *Priscilla* • Christopher Witty *Richard Robinson* ■ *Dir* Gerald Thomas • *Scr* Norman Hudis, Robin Estridge, from the novel *Beware of Children* by Verily Anderson

No Limit ★★PG
Comedy   1935 · UK · BW · 77min

This was George Formby's debut for Associated Talking Pictures, but the star struggles to impose his inimitable personality on a plot that resembles an episode of the *Wacky Races* cartoon series. Sabotaged throughout the Isle of Man's famous TT Races, George eventually wins the day, thanks to the love of Florence Desmond and the assistance of a donkey. DP
George Formby *George Shuttleworth* • Florence Desmond *Florrie Dibney* • Howard Douglas *Turner* • Beatrix Fielden-Kaye *Mrs Horrocks* • Peter Gawthorne *Mr Higgins* • Alf Goddard *Norton* • Florence Gregson *Mrs Shuttleworth* • Jack Hobbs *Bert Tyldesley* ■ *Dir* Monty Banks • *Scr* Fred Thompson, from a story by Walter Greenwood

No Looking Back ★★15
Romantic comedy drama
1998 · US · Colour · 92min

Waitress Lauren Holly must decide between safe and dependable mechanic boyfriend Jon Bon Jovi, or her ex-lover, an exciting but unreliable drifter (played by director Edward Burns). Although the stars have charm, this is bland and risk-free. The script and performances aren't bad – it's just difficult to distinguish it from hundreds of similar movies. JC Swearing, sex scenes.
Lauren Holly *Claudia* • Edward Burns *Charlie* • Jon Bon Jovi *Michael* • Connie Britton *Kelly* • Nick Sandow *Goldie* • Kaili Vernoff *Alice* • Shari Albert *Shari* • Blythe Danner *Claudia's mother* ■ *Dir/Scr* Edward Burns

No Love for Johnnie ★★★★12
Political drama   1960 · UK · BW · 105min

Labour win the general election but Peter Finch MP is overlooked for the cabinet post he was expecting. Instead, his communist wife leaves him, he falls in with shifty communist-leaning MP Donald Pleasence and has a passionate affair with Mary Peach, a fashion model. Based on a novel by a Labour MP, this prefigures the Profumo affair with its then outspoken blend of sex and politics and remains eminently watchable and wholly plausible, due mainly to Finch's totally believable, award-winning portrayal. AT *DVD*
Peter Finch *Johnnie Byrne* • Stanley Holloway *Fred Andrews* • Mary Peach *Pauline West* • Donald Pleasence *Roger Renfrew* • Billie Whitelaw *Mary* • Dennis Price *Flagg* • Hugh

Burden *Tim Maxwell* • Rosalie Crutchley *Alice Byrne* ■ *Dir* Ralph Thomas • *Scr* Nicholas Phipps, Mordecai Richler, from the novel by Wilfred Fienburgh

No Man of Her Own ★★
Comedy drama   1932 · US · BW · 80min

Clark Gable, on loan to Paramount from MGM, co-stars with Carole Lombard in this tale of romance between a shady New York gambler and a librarian in the small town where he hides out. Wesley Ruggles directs an essentially routine script, elevated by the personalities of the attractive stars and their evident chemistry. (They would marry a few years later.) Dorothy Mackaill is the jealous woman whose threats to destroy Gable have a beneficial outcome. RK
Clark Gable *Jerry "Babe" Stewart* • Carole Lombard *Connie Randall* • Dorothy Mackaill *Kay Everly* • Grant Mitchell *Charlie Vane* • George Barbier *Mr Randall* • Elizabeth Patterson *Mrs Randall* ■ *Dir* Wesley Ruggles • *Scr* Maurine Watkins, Milton Gropper, from a story by Edmund Goulding, Benjamin Glazer

No Man of Her Own ★★★
Melodrama   1950 · US · BW · 97min

Barbara Stanwyck fires on all cylinders as the unmarried mother-to-be who adopts the identity of an also pregnant but much wealthier woman after the latter dies in a train crash. Just as she's enjoying her new life of deception, her baby's father shows up and starts blackmailing her. Given that the story is complete and utter tosh, and that John Lund is a lummox as Stanwyck's new beau, this *film noir* is gripping stuff. Remade 46 years later as *Mrs Winterbourne*, with the unlikely Ricki Lake in the Stanwyck role. AT
Barbara Stanwyck *Helen Ferguson* • John Lund *Bill Harkness* • Jane Cowl *Mrs Harkness* • Phyllis Thaxter *Patrice Harkness* • Lyle Bettger *Stephen Morley* • Henry O'Neill *Mr Harkness* • Richard Denning *Hugh Harkness* ■ *Dir* Mitchell Leisen • *Scr* Sally Benson, Catherine Turney, from the novel *I Married a Dead Man* by William Irish [Cornell Woolrich]

No Manifesto: A Film about Manic Street Preachers
★★★15
Music documentary   2015 · US · Colour · 115min

This candid, partisan portrait of agitprop South Wales trio Manic Street Preachers by American film-maker Elizabeth Marcus captures them writing, rehearsing, recording and touring their eighth studio album *Send Away the Tigers*, released in 2007. Closely shadowing singer/guitarist James Dean Bradfield, bassist Nicky Wire and drummer Sean Moore, it's a snapshot of their lives at the time, but financial pressure delayed completion of the film, rendering it several albums out of date on release. It still remains a valuable document for fans, though. AC
James Dean Bradfield • Nicky Wire • Sean Moore ■ *Dir* Elizabeth Marcus

No Man's Land ★★★15
Thriller   1987 · US · Colour · 102min

Welcome to the "chop shop", a scrapyard where stolen cars are broken up and reassembled as new. This stylish use of the locale has rookie cop DB Sweeney going undercover in a Porsche garage. He becomes a close friend of crooked proprietor Charlie Sheen, a fast-lane traveller who dazzles our hero not only with his lifestyle, but also with his sister (Lara Harris). A low-budget thriller that makes a big impact. TH Swearing, violence. *DVD*
Charlie Sheen *Ted Varrick* • DB Sweeney *Benjy Taylor* • Randy Quaid *Lieutenant Vincent Bracey* • Lara Harris *Ann Varrick* • Bill Duke *Malcolm* • M Emmet Walsh *Captain Haun* ■ *Dir* Peter Werner • *Scr* Dick Wolf

No Man's Land ★★★15
Satirical black comedy
2001 · Bosnia/Fr/It/UK/Bel · Colour · 93min

Winner of the Oscar for best foreign film, this is a bleak Balkan satire in which the intransigence of the combatants is both

maddening and devastatingly funny. Trapped in a bunker with a booby-trapped corpse, Bosnian Branko Djuric and Serb Rene Bitorajac engage in pointless bouts of brinkmanship, while the media and the United Nation's peace-keeping forces look on with a dispiriting mix of self-aggrandisement and indifference. Debutant writer/director Danis Tanovic's observations on the nature of warfare in general and this conflict in particular are fairly orthodox, but his chronicling of the escalating chaos and its cynical resolution is astute. DP Bosnian, Croatian, English, French, Serbian, Serbo-Croat +subtitles. *DVD*
Branko Djuric *Chiki* • Rene Bitorajac *Nino* • Filip Sovagovic *Cera* • Georges Siatidis *Sergeant Marchand* • Serge-Henri Valcke *Captain Dubois* • Sacha Kremer *Michel* ■ *Dir/Scr* Danis Tanovic

No Mercy ★★★18
Thriller   1986 · US · Colour · 103min

Richard Gere here stars to real effect in the film that prompted critics to note how much greyer, older and better he was. He plays a Chicago cop seeking vengeance in New Orleans following the death of his partner. Crime lord Jeroen Krabbé is his target and Kim Basinger is the gangster's reluctant moll, with whom Gere takes off into the Louisiana bayous for the rousing action finale. It's predictable hokum, but director Richard Pearce spins an artful story, helped by Gere's slick performance. TH Swearing, violence, sex scenes, drug abuse. *DVD*
Richard Gere *Eddie Jillette* • Kim Basinger *Michel Duval* • Jeroen Krabbé *Losado* • George Dzundza *Capt Stemkowski* • Gary Basaraba *Joe Collins* • Ray Sharkey *Angles Ryan* • William Atherton *Allan Deveneux* • Terry Kinney *Paul Deveneux* ■ *Dir* Richard Pearce • *Scr* Jim Carabatsos

No Minor Vices ★★
Comedy   1948 · US · BW · 95min

This is a slight piece about an eccentric artist who attempts to separate a stuffy paediatrician from his wife. The doctor is Dana Andrews, the artist is dashing foreigner Louis Jourdan, and the lady in question is the charming Lilli Palmer. Oh, and Jane Wyatt's in there, too, as Andrews's devoted assistant. This type of time-wasting tosh needs a far lighter touch than that of Lewis Milestone. TS
Dana Andrews *Dr Perry Aswell* • Lilli Palmer *April Aswell* • Louis Jourdan *Otavio Quaglini* • Jane Wyatt *Miss Darlington* • Norman Lloyd *Dr Sturdivant* • Bernard Gorcey *Mr Zitzfleisch* ■ *Dir* Lewis Milestone • *Scr* Arnold Manoff

No My Darling Daughter ★★PG
Romantic comedy   1961 · UK · BW · 92min

The quality cast deserves something far better than this tepid British comedy. Juliet Mills does a feisty turn as the tomboy daughter of Michael Redgrave, whose romance with an American student leads to scandal. Both Redgrave and Roger Livesey are totally wasted as director Ralph Thomas squeezes all the fun out of a screwball plot that would have been meat and drink to even the most plodding Hollywood hack. DP *DVD*
Michael Redgrave *Sir Matthew Carr* • Michael Craig *Thomas Barclay* • Juliet Mills *Tansy Carr* • Roger Livesey *General Henry Barclay* • Rad Fulton *Cornelius Allingham* • Renee Houston *Miss Yardley* • Joan Sims *Second typist* • Peter Barkworth *Charles* ■ *Dir* Ralph Thomas • *Scr* Frank Harvey, from the play *Handful of Tansy* by Harold Brooke, Kay Bannerman

No Name on the Bullet ★★★★U
Western   1959 · US · Colour · 76min

A mean and moody Audie Murphy is brilliantly cast in this study in paranoia as a gunman on the prowl, threatening a whole town, whose inhabitants each seem to have a guilty reason to be the assassin's potential victim. Director Jack Arnold keeps the action tense and the supporting cast, particularly Whit Bissell, is excellent. This Universal western contains plenty to watch even if you don't care for baby-faced war hero Murphy. **TS**

Audie Murphy *John Gant* • Joan Evans *Anne Benson* • Charles Drake *Dr Luke Canfield* • RG Armstrong *Asa Canfield* • Virginia Grey *Mrs Fraden* • Warren Stevens *Lou Fraden* • Whit Bissell *Thad Pierce* • Karl Swenson *Earl Stricker* ■ *Dir* Jack Arnold • *Scr* Gene L Coon, from a story by Howard Amacker

No, No, Nanette ★★ U
Musical　　　　　　　　1940 · US · BW · 96min

In the early 1940s, British producer/director Herbert Wilcox and Anna Neagle (who married in 1943) landed a contract with RKO, but their combined career in Hollywood was short-lived. Not surprising given this filming of the 1925 Broadway musical, in which the best things were songs such as *Tea for Two* and *I Want to Be Happy*. Unwisely, Wilcox relegated the score to the background at the expense of the silly plot about a young woman who helps her uncle out of his financial and amorous difficulties. **RB**

Anna Neagle *Nanette* • Richard Carlson *Tom* • Victor Mature *William* • Roland Young *Mr Smith* • Helen Broderick *Mrs Smith* • ZaSu Pitts *Pauline* • Eve Arden *Winnie* • Tamara *Sonya* • Billy Gilbert *Styles* ■ *Dir* Herbert Wilcox • *Scr* Ken Englund, from the musical by Frank Mandel, Otto Harbach, Emil Nyitray, Vincent Youmans

No, Not Yet ★★ PG
Drama　　　　　　1993 · Jpn · Colour · 134min

This meditation on death was the final film directed by famed Japanese director Akira Kurosawa, then aged 83. The film's hero is a university professor who decides to give up teaching for writing. The setting, though, is the Second World War and its aftermath, during which the professor and his wife lose their home in a bombing raid, though most drama comes from the heartache caused by a missing cat. It's a long, philosophical and very talkative movie that may entrance the director's admirers but will test the patience of more casual viewers. **AT** In Japanese. *DVD*

Hisashi Igawa *Takayama* • Kyoko Kagawa *Professor's wife* • Tatsuo Matsumura *Professor Hyakken Uehida* • George Tokoro *Amaki* ■ *Dir/Scr* Akira Kurosawa

No Nukes ★★
Concert documentary
1980 · US · Colour · 103min

Over five nights at Madison Square Garden in September 1979, and at an outdoor rally in Battery Park, a socially conscious group of rockers got together for pro-solar energy, anti-nuclear benefit concerts. Despite an impressive list of artists – including Bruce Springsteen, Carly Simon, Bonnie Raitt, Jackson Browne – this well-intentioned rockumentary is a thinly stretched effort, with only Bruce Springsteen shaking any life into the "right on" blandness. **AJ**

Bruce Springsteen • James Taylor *James Taylor* • Carly Simon ■ *Dir* Julian Schlossberg, Danny Goldberg [Dan Goldberg], Anthony Potenza

No One Knows about Persian Cats ★★★ 12A
Music drama　　　2009 · Iran · Colour · 106min

Western music is officially banned in Iran, and here Kurdish director Bahman Ghobadi celebrates the sound of youth and its growing mood of resistance in a whirlwind survey of Tehran's underground rock scene. Made in just 17 days, the film focuses on twentysomething musicians Ashkan Koshanejad and Negar Shaghaghi, who seek to secure the documentation needed to play abroad, while also trying to record an album and organise a secret gig. The linking episodes aren't always as satirical or trenchant as they might be, but this does serve as a showcase for a wonderfully diverse selection of Iranian bands. **DP** Farsi +subtitles.

Hamed Behdad *Nader* • Ashkan Koshanejad *Ashkan* • Negar Shaghaghi *Negar* • Hichkas • Hamed Seyyed Javadi ■ *Dir* Bahman Ghobadi • *Scr* Bahman Ghobadi, Hossein M Abkenar, Roxana Saberi • *Cinematographer* Turaj Aslani

No One Lives ★★★★ 18
Horror thriller　　　2012 · US · Colour · 82min

The Midnight Meat Train director Ryuhei Kitamura continues his American gothic adventure with this ingenious, ultra-stylish shocker. After screwing up a mansion heist, hillbilly robbers take out their frustration by mugging a couple in a car instead. Bad idea. Because the driver (charismatic Luke Evans) is a mass murderer with a kidnapped heiress in his clutches. From there on in, it's psychos vs psycho in a taut, tense cat-and-mouse chiller that sees each side attempting to outdo the other in terms of entrapment, torture and terror. Genuinely striking and unnerving, the film manages to ramp up the fright factor to such overly intense levels that uneasy laughter provides the only release. **AJ** Violence, swearing, a sex scene, nudity. *DVD*

Luke Evans *Driver* • Adelaide Clemens *Emma* • Lee Tergesen *Hoag* • Laura Ramsey *Betty* • Derek Magyar *Flynn* ■ *Dir* Ryuhei Kitamura • *Scr* David Cohen

No One Man ★
Drama　　　　　1932 · US · BW · 71min

Wealthy Florida divorcee Carole Lombard, eager to snare a new husband, is torn between two contenders: Ricardo Cortez, handsome and oozing charm but a feckless creature of questionable character, and the less dazzling but decent and dependable Paul Lukas, an Austrian physician. How Lombard, her natural charms dulled under the weight of a trivial, unconvincing and boring script, makes her choice takes up the thankfully short running time of Lloyd Corrigan's pointless film. **RK**

Carole Lombard *Penelope Newbold* • Ricardo Cortez *Bill Hanaway* • Paul Lukas *Dr Karl Bemis* • Juliette Compton *Sue Folsom* • George Barbier *Alfred Newbold* • Virginia Hammond *Mrs Newbold* ■ *Dir* Lloyd Corrigan • *Scr* Sidney Buchman, Agnes Brand Leahy, Percy Heath, from the novel by Rupert Hughes

No One Writes to the Colonel ★★★
Period drama
1999 · Mex/Sp/Fr · Colour · 118min

While this compassionate study of love in a time of adversity is restrained by his usual baroque standards, Mexican director Arturo Ripstein still overcooks this adaptation of Gabriel García Márquez's novel. Driven to the brink of despair by the murder of his son, Fernando Lujan's melancholic optimist invests heavily in his cock-fighting dreams and the overdue military pension that his asthmatic wife, Marisa Paredes, knows will never come. The acting is impeccable, while Ripstein expertly captures the ambience of their 1940s coastal town. Yet the director allows inconsequential subplots and slack pacing to dissipate the story's dramatic intensity. **DP** In Spanish.

Fernando Lujan *The Colonel* • Salma Hayek *Julia* • Marisa Paredes *Lola* • Ernesto Yanez *Don Sabas* • Rafael Inclan *Father Angel* ■ *Dir* Arturo Ripstein • *Scr* Paz Alicia Garciadiego, from the novel by Gabriel García Márquez

No Orchids for Miss Blandish ★
Crime drama　　　1948 · UK · BW · 104min

This British gangster film was once vilified for its violence and immorality – banned in many parts of Britain and naturally a huge hit everywhere else. George Melachrino's score is apt, but most of the dialogue and acting are phoney, the plot developments are ludicrous and the film never begins to explore the sexual attraction that Linden Travers's spoiled brat feels for her kidnapper, Jack LaRue. The same story forms the basis of Robert Aldrich's *The Grissom Gang*. **AE**

Jack LaRue *Slim Grisson* • Hugh McDermott *Fenner* • Linden Travers *Miss Blandish* • Walter Crisham *Eddie* • Leslie Bradley *Bailey* • Sidney James *Ted/Barman* • Lily Molnar *Ma Grissom* ■ *Dir* St John L Clowes • *Scr* St John L Clowes, from the novel by James Hadley Chase

No Ordinary Baby ★★★
Medical drama　　　2001 · US · Colour · 96min

Human cloning is taken out of the realms of science fiction and into everyday life in this thoughtful medical drama. Bridget Fonda stars as a fame-hungry local reporter on the trail of a desperate couple attempting to "replace" their dead daughter via a revolutionary new genetic process. It's a contentious topic, though surprisingly well handled for a TV movie, sensitively interweaving broad facts with poignant emotion and just a dash of syrupy manipulation. **SF** Some violence.

Bridget Fonda *Linda Sanclair* • Mary Beth Hurt *Dr Amanda Gordon* • Valerie Mahaffey *Virginia Hytner* • Philip Bosco *Dr Ed Walden* • Adam LeFevre *Chris Hytner* ■ *Dir* Peter Werner • *Scr* Richard Kletter, from a short story by Richard Kadrey

No Place for Jennifer ★★ PG
Drama　　　　　1949 · UK · BW · 86min

It's hard to believe that this tosh was one of the biggest box-office hits of 1949. Eleven-year-old Janette Scott (daughter of Thora Hird) plays the girl whose vanishing act brings about a change of heart in divorcing parents Leo Genn and Rosamund John. Scriptwriter and future director J Lee Thompson obviously had little enthusiasm for the task of adapting this penny-dreadful, while director Henry Cass fails to inject any sense of urgency into the search. **DP** *DVD*

Leo Genn *William* • Rosamund John *Rachel Kershaw* • Beatrice Campbell *Paula* • Guy Middleton *Brian Stewart* • Janette Scott *Jennifer* • Anthony Nicholls *Baxter* ■ *Dir* Henry Cass • *Scr* J Lee Thompson, from the novel *No Difference to Me* by Phyllis Hambledon

No Place to Hide ★★★ 18
Thriller　　　　　1992 · US · Colour · 92min

Some critics claim that Kris Kristofferson is so wooden, you can get splinters just watching him. But that's unfair. The country singer may not be the most dynamic of actors, but he boasts a certain screen presence which is evident in this fast-moving thriller, where his gruff manliness is in nice contrast to Drew Barrymore's precocious chirpiness. He's a rough, tough cop; she's a kid hunted by a murderer who's already slaughtered her sister. **DA**

Kris Kristofferson *Joe Garvey* • Drew Barrymore *Tinsel Hanley* • Martin Landau *Frank McCay* • OJ Simpson *Allie Wheeler* • Dey Young *Karen* • Bruce Weitz *Captain Nelson Silva* ■ *Dir/Scr* Richard Danus

No Problem! ★★★
Comedy　　　　　1975 · Fr · Colour · 105min

This rousing romp tosses slapstick and farce into the road movie formula to produce an hilarious and surprisingly sophisticated chase comedy. Heading for a Swiss rendezvous, Jean Lefebvre's womanising innocent is blissfully unaware of the corpse his son (Bernard Menez) has stashed in the boot of his car. The son sets off in hot pursuit with the stranger (Miou-Miou) who had asked him to dispose of the body. Maintaining a cracking pace, director Georges Lautner keeps the gag count high without sacrificing too much character depth. **DP** French dubbed.

Miou-Miou *Anita* • Jean Lefebvre *Michalon* • Bernard Menez *Jean-Pierre* • Henri Guybet *Daniel* • Anny Duperey *Janis* ■ *Dir* Georges Lautner • *Scr* Jean-Marie Poiré

No Regrets for Our Youth ★★★★ PG
Political drama based on a true story
1946 · Jpn · BW · 105min

Even though its critical reception was decidedly mixed, Akira Kurosawa's sixth feature marked his breakthrough as a major film-maker. Political subjects were never to be his strong point, but his conviction that postwar Japanese society needed to rediscover its self-respect drew him to the fact-based story of the young city sophisticate (played with a mix of romantic innocence and indomitable spirit by Setsuko Hara) who finds the will to

survive while slaving as a peasant after her father is dismissed from his university post for his communist views and her lover is executed as a spy. **DP** Japanese +subtitles. *DVD*

Denjiro Okochi *Professor Yagihara* • Eiko Miyoshi *Madame Yagihara, his wife* • Setsuko Hara *Yukie Yagihara, his daughter* • Susumu Fujita *Ryukichi Noge* ■ *Dir* Akira Kurosawa • *Scr* Eijiro Hisaita, Akira Kurosawa

No Reservations ★★★ PG
Romantic comedy drama
2007 · US/Aus · Colour · 99min

Opposites attract for Catherine Zeta-Jones and Aaron Eckhart in this affable remake of the 2001 romantic comedy *Mostly Martha*. Kate Armstrong (Zeta-Jones) is a no-nonsense chef who keeps a lid on her emotions, even after her sister dies and leaves daughter Zoe (Abigail Breslin) in her care. Eckhart plays the laid-back sous-chef who eventually begins to melt the heart of our uptight heroine. Zeta-Jones is initially tough to like – it's not until Breslin (*Little Miss Sunshine*) moves in that the mood of the movie is raised. Generally, director Scott Hicks (*Shine*) balances the bitter and the sweet beautifully, although the romance with Eckhart's too-good-to-be-true hunk does have its cloying moments. But the sincerity of Hicks's approach makes the occasional cheesy moment more palatable. **SP** *DVD* Blu-ray

Catherine Zeta-Jones *Kate Armstrong* • Aaron Eckhart *Nick Palmer* • Abigail Breslin *Zoe* • Patricia Clarkson *Paula* • Jenny Wade *Leah* • Bob Balaban *Therapist* • Brian F O'Byrne *Sean* ■ *Dir* Scott Hicks • *Scr* Carol Fuchs (2), from the film *Mostly Martha* by Sandra Nettelbeck • *Music* Philip Glass

No Resting Place ★★
Drama　　　　　1950 · UK · BW · 85min

Pioneer film historian and left-wing documentary maker Paul Rotha's film has as its strongest aspect the creation of a realistic background to the story, the fanciful tale of Irish tinker Michael Gough, who accidentally kills a gamekeeper. After a brawl with the police, he's heading for the gallows, but he escapes, briefly, to enjoy a reunion with his wife and child. Despite sympathetic observation and good performances, it is rather naive and cannot compare with Rotha's earlier documentary work. **BB**

Michael Gough *Alec Kyle* • Eithne Dunne *Meg Kyle* • Noel Purcell *Guard Mannigan* • Brian O'Higgins *Tom Kyle* • Jack MacGowran *Billy Kyle* • Diana Campbell *Bess Kyle* • Maureen O'Sullivan *Nan Kyle* ■ *Dir* Paul Rotha • *Scr* Gerard Healy, Colin Lesslie, Michael Orrom, Paul Rotha, from the novel by Ian Niall

No Retreat, No Surrender ★★ 15
Martial arts action drama
1985 · US/HK · Colour · 94min

With a plot reminiscent of *The Karate Kid*, this has Kurt McKinney as a martial arts enthusiast. He is victimised by his peers until he acquires an unexpected ally – the ghost of Bruce Lee. Almost charming in its silliness, the movie gets close to the so-bad-it's-good level but too often takes itself too seriously. This is most noteworthy as Jean-Claude Van Damme's first real role; two sequels followed. **KB** *DVD*

Kurt McKinney *Jason Stillwell* • Jean-Claude Van Damme *Karl Brezdin/Ivan the Russian* • JW Fails *RJ Madison* • Kathie Sileno *Kelly Reilly* • Kent Lipham *Scott* ■ *Dir* Corey Yuen • *Scr* Keith Strandberg, from a story by Ng See Yuen, Corey Yuen

No Road Back ★★
Crime melodrama　　1957 · UK · BW · 62min

Sean Connery had been a lifeguard and a coffin polisher before he began acting. He must have doubted the wisdom of giving up the day job after his first experience of film-making, as this is almost an Identikit "quota quickie". The lead is a skid-row American star (Skip Homeier), the plot is a threadbare crime caper, the sets are cheap and much of the action takes place in dank inner-city backstreets. Crooks Connery and Alfie Bass are convincing enough, with their botched robbery causing Homeier to question the honesty of his blind and deaf, club-owning ma. DP

Skip Homeier *John Railton* • Paul Carpenter *Clem Hayes* • Patricia Dainton *Beth* • Norman Wooland *Inspector Harris* • Margaret Rawlings *Mrs Railton* • Alfie Bass *Rudge Haven* • Sean Connery *Spike* ■ *Dir* Montgomery Tully • *Scr* Charles Leeds, Montgomery Tully, from the play *Madame Tictac* by Falkland D Cary, Philip Weathers

No Room at the Inn ★★★
Second World War drama
1948 · UK · BW · 82min

A group of child evacuees in Second World War England find themselves in the care of the cruelly unsympathetic, alcoholic Freda Jackson, who keeps them in conditions of squalor, neglect and semi-starvation while she imbibes a steady diet of gin. Poet Dylan Thomas co-wrote the screenplay for this nasty but effective view of human nature at its worst, in which Jackson (repeating her successful West End performance) is compelling. RK

Freda Jackson *Mrs Voray* • Joy Shelton *Judith Drave* • Hermione Baddeley *Mrs Waters* • Joan Dowling *Norma Bates* • Ann Stephens *Mary O'Rane* • Harcourt Williams *Reverend Allworth* • Dora Bryan ■ *Dir* Daniel Birt • *Scr* Ivan Foxwell, Dylan Thomas, from the play by Joan Temple

No Room for the Groom ★★ U
Comedy 1952 · US · BW · 82min

Piper Laurie is the young wife of a GI who moves in with her family while he is off on duty. When her husband (Tony Curtis) returns, he finds himself surrounded by her relatives, including Spring Byington as the mother trying to marry her off to someone else (Don DeFore). The breezy and attractive young leads help to keep this idiotic, frenzied and only mildly amusing comedy alive. RK

Tony Curtis *Alvah Morrell* • Piper Laurie *Lee Kingshead* • Don DeFore *Herman Strople* • Spring Byington *Mamma Kingshead* • Jack Kelly *Will Stubbins* ■ *Dir* Douglas Sirk • *Scr* Joseph Hoffman, from the novel *My True Love* by Darwin L Teilhet

No Sad Songs for Me ★★★
Melodrama 1950 · US · BW · 88min

The wistful Margaret Sullavan was a rare and special talent, and this was her last film, a Columbia melodrama about a dying woman preparing her family for her untimely but inevitable death. Sullavan makes this trite material unbearably moving, and there is real truth in her portrayal: tragic but uplifting, sad yet inspirational. Wendell Corey and Natalie Wood play the rest of the family, and Viveca Lindfors is admirable in support, but the film belongs totally to Sullavan. TS

Margaret Sullavan *Mary Scott* • Wendell Corey *Brad Scott* • Viveca Lindfors *Chris Radna* • Natalie Wood *Polly Scott* • John McIntire *Dr Ralph Frene* • Ann Doran *Louise Spears* • Richard Quine *Brownie* • Jeanette Nolan *Mona Frene* ■ *Dir* Rudolph Maté • *Scr* Howard Koch, from a story by Ruth Southard

No Saints for Sinners ★★★ 15
Crime thriller 2010 · US · Colour · 84min

This tale of gangsters, drugs and guns may offer few genuine surprises, but a likeable lead, brisk pacing and incident-packed plot ensure that it remains a satisfying entry in an overcrowded genre. Heading a low-key cast, Rick Crawford stars as Mickey, an IRA man with a conscience, who's forced to flee Belfast and makes a fresh start in LA. But when his girlfriend's wannabe-player brother ends up in debt to a drug dealer, Mickey must revert to his violent ways to keep him from being killed. JH DVD

Rick Crawford *Mickey* • Collin Sutton *Jimmy* • Marty Maguire *Mercer* • Kate Tomlinson *Nina* • James Cosmo *Murphy* ■ *Dir* Nathan Frankowski • *Scr* Kevin Miller, Nathan Frankowski, Chris Benzoni, from a story by Rick Crawford, Benzoni

No Sex Please – We're British ★★ PG
Comedy 1973 · UK · Colour · 84min

One of the West End's longest running comic farces arrived on the screen virtually intact, but with a significantly different leading man. Whereas Michael Crawford had consolidated both career and image by instigating the gawky, inadvertent gauche lead on stage, in the film the role went to the diminutive British comedian Ronnie Corbett. Corbett does well by the hackneyed plot, and underrated director Cliff Owen keeps up the pace. TS DVD

Ronnie Corbett *Brian Runnicles* • Beryl Reid *Bertha* • Arthur Lowe *Mr Bromley* • Ian Ogilvy *David Hunter* • Susan Penhaligon *Penny Hunter* • David Swift *Inspector Paul* • Cheryl Hall *Daphne* • Michael Bates *Needham* ■ *Dir* Cliff Owen • *Scr* Anthony Marriott, Johnnie Mortimer, Brian Cooke, from the play by Anthony Marriott, Alistair Foot

No Smoking ★★ U
Comedy 1954 · UK · BW · 72min

A small-town boffin comes up with a swallowable version of the nicotine patch, and then wonders why the tobacco giants will stop at nothing to put a stop to his discovery. Notable only for its anti-smoking theme in a period where no one bothered about puffing away on a cigarette, this gentle comedy ends up a wasted opportunity, though the cast give their all. JF

Reg Dixon *Reg Bates* • Belinda Lee *Miss Tonkins* • Lionel Jeffries *George Pogson* • Myrtle Rowe *Milly* • Ruth Trouncer *Joyce* • Peter Martyn *Hal* ■ *Dir* Henry Cass • *Scr* Kenneth R Hayles, Phil Park, from a TV play by Rex Rientis, George Moresby-White

No Strings Attached ★★★ 15
Romantic comedy 2011 · US · Colour · 103min

In this romantic comedy with a contemporary twist, medical intern Natalie Portman and aspiring TV scriptwriter Ashton Kutcher agree to remain sexual partners without any longer-term commitment. But this convenient arrangement gets more complicated when they start wanting a little bit more out of the relationship. Portman does seem a bit too brittle and neurotic for this sort of easy-going fluff, but Kutcher proves right at home. There's also a delightful array of supporting turns, including Kevin Kline as Kutcher's reprobate dad, Greta Gerwig as Portman's sceptical work colleague, plus Jake Johnson and Chris "Ludacris" Bridges as Kutcher's mates. Admittedly, we never quite buy the emotional reality of the central duo's dilemma, but it's all so amusing that it's never a deal-breaker. TJ
Swearing, sex scenes. DVD

Natalie Portman *Emma Kurtzman* • Ashton Kutcher *Adam Franklin* • Cary Elwes *Dr Metzner* • Kevin Kline *Alvin* • Greta Gerwig *Patrice* • Chris "Ludacris" Bridges *Wallace* • Jake Johnson *Eli* ■ *Dir* Ivan Reitman • *Scr* Elizabeth Meriwether, from a story by Meriwether, Mike Samonek

No Surrender ★ 15
Black comedy 1985 · UK · Colour · 98min

This offensive little tale purports to be black comedy but verges on the tasteless. A Liverpool nightclub owner plays host to a party of Irish OAPs with entertainment provided by, among others, Elvis Costello (in a cameo role). Problem is, they're a warring bunch of Catholics and Protestants, and the evening threatens to be explosive. Alan Bleasdale's script isn't bad as much as misdirected – as is Joanne Whalley. LH
DVD

Michael Angelis *Mike Moriarty* • Avis Bunnage *Martha Gorman* • JG Devlin *George Gorman* • James Ellis *Paddy Burke* • Tom Georgeson *Mr Ross* • Bernard Hill *Bernard* • Ray McAnally *Billy McRacken* • Joanne Whalley *Cheryl* • Elvis Costello *Rosco De Ville* ■ *Dir* Peter K Smith • *Scr* Alan Bleasdale

No Time for Comedy ★★★
Comedy drama 1940 · US · BW · 92min

One of those romantic comedies set in the cosy world of Broadway theatreland, this stars James Stewart as a playwright who's down in the dumps because of a midlife crisis that has leaked into his work. Rosalind Russell co-stars as his acerbic but uncomplaining wife. It's directed by William Keighley with the same smooth-paced energy that he brought to many gangster movies. TH

James Stewart *Gaylord Esterbrook* • Rosalind Russell *Linda Esterbrook* • Charlie Ruggles [Charles Ruggles] *Philo Swift* • Genevieve Tobin *Amanda Swift* • Allyn Joslyn *Morgan Carrel, theatrical director* • Clarence Kolb *Richard Benson* ■ *Dir* William Keighley • *Scr* Julius J Epstein, Philip G Epstein, from the play by SN Behrman

No Time for Love ★★★ U
Romantic comedy 1943 · US · BW · 83min

Claudette Colbert and Fred MacMurray star in yet another romantic comedy that revolves around hostility which is really true love. This time around, she's a professional photographer and he's the foreman of a tunnel-digging crew who becomes her assistant, inevitably leading to complications. The snappy screenplay, tailor-made for the two attractive stars, veers slightly more towards slapstick than sophistication, but is lent gloss by Paramount's first-rung production values and direction from the stylish Mitchell Leisen. RK

Claudette Colbert *Katherine Grant* • Fred MacMurray *Jim Ryan* • Ilka Chase *Hoppy Grant* • Richard Haydn *Roger, composer* • Paul McGrath *Henry Fulton, magazine publisher* • June Havoc *Darlene, chorus girl* ■ *Dir* Mitchell Leisen • *Scr* Claude Binyon, Warren Duff, from a story by Robert Lees

No Time for Sergeants ★★★ U
Comedy 1958 · US · BW · 114min

Andy Griffith starred in the long-running Broadway play and in this screen adaptation, using his Carolina drawl to good effect as the simple-minded hillbilly drafted into the air force. He teams up with Nick Adams and they both manage to fall out of their plane and then attend their own military funeral. Directed by Mervyn LeRoy, there's a touch of Laurel and Hardy, as well as the Marx Brothers' brand of irreverence, about this comic caper. AT

Andy Griffith *Will Stockdale* • Myron McCormick *Sergeant King* • Nick Adams *Ben Whitledge* • Murray Hamilton *Irvin Blanchard* • Howard Smith *General Bush* • Will Hutchins *Lieutenant Bridges* • Don Knotts *Manual Dexterity Corporal* ■ *Dir* Mervyn LeRoy • *Scr* John Lee Mahin, from the play by Ira Levin, from the novel by Mac Hyman

No Time for Tears ★★ U
Medical drama 1957 · UK · Colour · 85min

What else could you call a film whose sole intention is to have you blubbing your eyes out from the off? Anna Neagle stars in this mawkish account of life in a children's hospital. If the triumphs and tragedies of the kiddies don't have you reaching for tissues, then the torrid love life of nurse Sylvia Syms certainly will. The members of the cast work minor miracles despite the string of clichés. DP

Anna Neagle *Matron Eleanor Hammond* • George Baker *Nigel Barnes* • Sylvia Syms *Margaret* • Anthony Quayle *Dr Seagrave* • Flora Robson *Sister Birch* • Alan White *Dr Hugh Storey* • Joan Sims *Sister O'Malley* ■ *Dir* Cyril Frankel • *Scr* Anne Burnaby

No Time to Die ★★ U
Second World War drama
1958 · UK · Colour · 104min

Set during the campaign in the Libyan desert, American hunk Victor Mature plays an American who serves as a sergeant in the British army. He organises an escape from an Italian PoW camp and is then captured and tortured by a shifty sheikh in league with the Nazis. Every racial

stereotype in the book stands to attention as Mature lurches from one heroic deed to the next, culminating in a joust with a Panzer tank. AT

Victor Mature *Sgt David Thatcher* • Leo Genn *Sgt Kendall* • Anthony Newley *Tiger Noakes* • Bonar Colleano *Pole* • Luciana Paluzzi *Carola* • Anne Aubrey *Italian girl* ■ *Dir* Terence Young • *Scr* Richard Maibaum, Terence Young

No Trace ★★★
Crime thriller 1950 · UK · BW · 75min

This is a better-than-average "quota quickie" from John Gilling, in which crime writer Hugh Sinclair tries to cover his tracks (and delude snooping cop John Laurie) after he kills a blackmailer from his gangland past. As we know from the outset that he won't get away with it, the fun lies in watching him make the slips that give him away to secretary Dinah Sheridan and her admirer Barry Morse. DP

Hugh Sinclair *Robert Southley* • Dinah Sheridan *Linda* • John Laurie *Inspector MacDougall* • Barry Morse *Harrison* • Dora Bryan *Maisie* ■ *Dir/Scr* John Gilling

No Trees in the Street ★★ PG
Drama 1958 · UK · BW · 92min

Although a stalwart of stage and TV, screenwriter Ted Willis worked less in movies and in rather shows in this ludicrously sentimental adaptation of his own play. It was unlucky enough to be released in the same year that British cinema entered its great "kitchen sink" phase, but this thin-cut slice of street life could never feel anything but stale. Herbert Lom tries to inject a little menace as a small-time hoodlum, but, confronted with sickly sweet Sylvia Syms and teen tearaway Melvyn Hayes, he succumbs to the mediocrity. DP DVD

Sylvia Syms *Hetty* • Herbert Lom *Wilkie* • Ronald Howard *Frank* • Stanley Holloway *Kipper* • Joan Miller *Jess* • Melvyn Hayes *Tommy* ■ *Dir* J Lee Thompson • *Scr* Ted Willis, from his play

No Way Back ★ 18
Crime thriller 1996 · US/Jpn · Colour · 87min

In this preposterous crime thriller, Russell Crowe plays an FBI agent who, after a sting operation goes wrong in the most unbelievable manner, tries to bring a yakuza boss (Etsushi Toyokawa) from New York to Los Angeles on a commercial flight. The boss gets loose and forces the plane down on a small field in the mountains. Somehow the agent, the crime boss and a stewardess (Helen Slater) end up pushing a broken car around the desert. ST DVD

Russell Crowe *Zack Grant* • Helen Slater *Mary* • Etsushi Toyokawa *Yuji* • Michael Lerner *Frank Serlano* • Kyusaku Shimada *Tetsuro* • Kristopher Logan *Mr Contingency* ■ *Dir/Scr* Frank Cappello

No Way Home ★★★ 18
Crime drama 1996 · US · Colour · 96min

A grim yet uplifting story of rehabilitation and redemption, this is shot through with a dynamic tone and moody atmosphere by independent director Buddy Giovinazzo. Fresh out of prison, Tim Roth moves in with his older brother James Russo in an attempt to go straight. Alas, he's soon sucked back into the criminal life. Almost Pinteresque in the way silences convey as much heart-rending truth as the succinct dialogue, this touching moral tale is an uncompromising character study given a poignant level of honesty. AJ DVD

Tim Roth *Joey* • James Russo *Tommy* • Deborah Kara Unger *Lorraine* • Bernadette Penotti *Ronnie* • Larry Romano *Carter* ■ *Dir/Scr* Buddy Giovinazzo

No Way Out ★★★
Drama 1950 · US · BW · 101min

Joseph L Mankiewicz's drama about racial prejudice features Sidney Poitier, launching his career as a persecuted doctor at a municipal hospital. The head of Fox, Darryl

F Zanuck, said the picture would be as "real as sweat, dealing with the absolute blood and guts of negro hating." Mankiewicz said it was "the first time racial violence was shown on the screen except for *Birth of a Nation* in modern times." Both were rather overblown statements, and so is the picture, not least because of Richard Widmark's snarling, racist villain and the contrived, if ironic conclusion. AT

Richard Widmark *Ray Biddle* • Linda Darnell *Edie* • Stephen McNally *Dr Wharton* • Sidney Poitier *Dr Luther Brooks* • Mildred Joanne Smith *Cora* • Harry Bellaver *George Biddle* ■ *Dir* Joseph L Mankiewicz • *Scr* Joseph L Mankiewicz, Lesser Samuels

No Way Out ★★★★15

Thriller 1986 · US · Colour · 109min

Famous for its limousine sex scene, this Kevin Costner spy thriller provides a gripping insight into the corridors of US power. This is a highly intelligent, intriguing movie containing some wonderful performances, most notably from Gene Hackman as an icily manipulative politician. For once, Costner's tendency to stay emotionally removed from his character pays dividends as we are left guessing about the man right up to the final reel. The "surprise" twist is a trifle daft, but overall this is a major treat. SH Swearing, violence, nudity. *DVD*

Kevin Costner *Lieutenant Commander Tom Farrell* • Gene Hackman *David Brice* • Sean Young *Susan Atwell* • Will Patton *Scott Pritchard* • Howard Duff *Senator Willy Duvall* • George Dzundza *Dr Sam Hesselman* • Jason Bernard *Major Donovan* • Iman *Nina Beka* • Fred Dalton Thompson *Marshall* ■ *Dir* Roger Donaldson • *Scr* Robert Garland, from the novel *The Big Clock* by Kenneth Fearing

No Way to Treat a Lady ★★★★

Black comedy 1968 · US · Colour · 107min

Romantic comedies don't come much blacker than this immensely enjoyable tale of a serial strangler, incarnated in several guises by Rod Steiger. George Segal plays a Jewish cop, hysterically henpecked by his mother Eileen Heckart, while co-star Lee Remick has never looked lovelier as the sophisticated Lincoln Center guide who graduates from witness to intended victim. New York's the star, too, thanks to Jack Priestley's glossy photography, which includes interiors in both Joe Allen's and Sardi's. TS

Rod Steiger *Christopher Gill* • Lee Remick *Kate Palmer* • George Segal *Morris Brummel* • Eileen Heckart *Mrs Brummel* • Murray Hamilton *Inspector Haines* • Michael Dunn *Mr Kupperman* ■ *Dir* Jack Smight • *Scr* John Gay, from the novel by William Goldman

Noah ★★★12

Biblical epic 2014 · US · Colour · 137min

An Old Testament favourite is given a blockbuster makeover by *Black Swan* director Darren Aronofsky. Russell Crowe stars as the man chosen by God to undertake a momentous rescue mission before apocalyptic floods consume the Earth. Yet Noah is tormented by the big questions, not least why he should be the one chosen as saviour. It's an impressive spectacle – the ark itself is built to scale – but is occasionally unsure of whether to be epic or relevant, while Crowe is powerfully charismatic throughout. TeS *DVD* *BL*

Russell Crowe *Noah* • Jennifer Connelly *Naameh* • Ray Winstone *Tubal-cain* • Emma Watson *Ila* • Anthony Hopkins *Methuselah* • Logan Lerman *Ham* • Douglas Booth *Shem* ■ *Dir* Darren Aronofsky • *Scr* Darren Aronofsky, Ari Handel, John Logan • *Music* Clint Mansell

Nob Hill ★★

Musical 1945 · US · Colour · 95min

Nob Hill is where the nobs used to live in San Francisco, an area now the preserve of the city's swishest hotels. But this brash Fox musical is pretty downmarket, starring George Raft as the saloon owner who jilts torch singer Vivian Blaine for socialite Joan Bennett. The songs are strictly B-sides and

Henry Hathaway's direction doesn't have the necessary light touch. Another drawback is Raft, never a convincing leading man, though he once laid claim to being the world's fastest Charleston dancer. AT

George Raft *Johnny Angelo* • Joan Bennett *Harriet Carruthers* • Vivian Blaine *Sally Templeton* • Peggy Ann Garner *Katie Flanagan* • Falstaff Openshaw [Alan Reed] *Dapper Jack Harrigan* • BS Pully *Joe the bartender* • Emil Coleman *Pianist* ■ *Dir* Henry Hathaway • *Scr* Wanda Tuchock, Norman Reilly Raine, from a story by Eleanore Griffin

Nobody Knows ★★★★12

Drama 2003 · Jpn · Colour · 140min

In 1988, what was dubbed the "Affair of the Four Abandoned Children of Nishi-Sugamo" scandalised Japan and inspired Hirokazu Kore-eda's screenplay, which took 15 years to bring to the screen. The wait proved worthwhile, as this is a deeply moving study of juvenile endurance that earned Yuya Yagira the best actor prize at Cannes. As the oldest of the siblings left to fend for themselves by their mother, the 12-year-old displays both ingenuity and insecurity in trying to keep his secret from the outside world. Even more impressive, however, is Kore-eda's disjointed directorial style which mirrors the household's increasing pressures. DP Japanese +subtitles. *DVD*

Yuya Yagira *Akira* • Ayu Kitaura *Kyoko* • Hiei Kimura *Shigeru* • Momoko Shimizu *Yuki* • Hanae Kan *Saki* ■ *Dir/Scr* Hirokazu Kore-eda [Hirokazu Koreeda]

Nobody Lives Forever ★★★

Romantic drama 1946 · US · BW · 99min

Before method acting, John Garfield was doing it for real with a tough-talking style that seemed ad-libbed. It's that hard-bitten personality which saves this romance from sentimental stickiness. The star plays a conman who swindles rich widow Geraldine Fitzgerald, only to fall in love with his victim. Mills and Boon stuff, though Garfield transforms it into near-credible drama. TH

John Garfield *Nick Blake* • Geraldine Fitzgerald *Gladys Halvorsen* • Walter Brennan *Pop Gruber* • Faye Emerson *Toni* • George Coulouris *Doc Ganson* • George Tobias *Al Doyle* ■ *Dir* Jean Negulesco • *Scr* WR Burnett, from his story *I Wasn't Born Yesterday*

Nobody Runs Forever ★★PG

Thriller 1968 · UK · Colour · 97min

Rank threw together a motley array of B-list actors, plus Rod Taylor and Christopher Plummer, and let them fight it out among themselves with scant direction for this over-complicated yet weakly scripted thriller. The thrills are in distinctly short supply as an Australian cop is sent to London to arrest a dastardly diplomat for murder. SH

Rod Taylor *Scobie Malone* • Christopher Plummer *Sir James Quentin* • Lilli Palmer *Sheila Quentin* • Camilla Sparv *Lisa Pretorius* • Daliah Lavi *Madame Cholon* • Franchot Tone *Ambassador Townsend* • Clive Revill *Joseph* • Lee Montague *Denzil* ■ *Dir* Ralph Thomas • *Scr* Wilfred Greatorex, from the novel *The High Commissioner* by Jon Cleary

Nobody's Child ★★★★

Drama based on a true story 1986 · US · Colour · 100min

The haunting isolation of mental illness is made vividly personal by the breathtaking performance of Marlo Thomas in this TV movie about Marie Balter, a woman who spent 20 harrowing years in a mental hospital until a compassionate doctor helped her regain her sanity. The first-rate script by Mary Gallagher and Ara Watson, sensitive direction by Lee Grant and Thomas's single-minded commitment to telling the story make this memorable and moving. MC

Marlo Thomas *Marie Balter* • Ray Baker *Joe Balter* • Caroline Kava *Dr Blackwell* • Kathy Baker *Lucy* • Blanche Baker *Shari* ■ *Dir* Lee Grant • *Scr* Mary Gallagher, Ara Watson

Nobody's Daughter Haewon ★★★12

Drama 2013 · S Kor · Colour · 90min

Korean director Hong Sangsoo's musings on relationships (*In Another Country, Woman on the Beach*) definitely inhabit the low-budget art-house camp. The titular heroine of this leisurely, lilting drama is a young student (Jung Eunchae) who is in the doldrums after her mother moves away to Canada and decides to rekindle an affair with an older, married film professor. Fans of Eric Rohmer will lap up the languorous tone of the piece, but for some it may just be too emotionally uninvolving. JA Korean, English +subtitles. Swearing. *DVD*

Jung Eunchae *Haewon* • Lee Sunkyun [Lee Seon-gyun] *Seongjun* • Kim Jaok *Jinju* • Kim Euisung *Jungwon* • Jane Birkin *Tourist* • Yu Junsang *Jungshik* ■ *Dir/Scr* Hong Sangsoo [Hong Sang-soo]

Nobody's Fool ★★★15

Romantic comedy 1986 · US · Colour · 102min

This modest portrait of Arizona small-town life stars Rosanna Arquette as a waitress, aspiring actress and local "celebrity" learning to live with her chequered past. As she searches for love and redemption, Arquette's performance becomes a three-ring circus – funny here, touching there, veering off balance elsewhere. Sharply written by Beth Henley and co-starring Oscar winner Louise Fletcher, it's a pleasing diversion, if lacking dramatic fireworks. AT Swearing.

Rosanna Arquette *Cassie* • Eric Roberts *Riley* • Mare Winningham *Pat* • Jim Youngs *Billy* • Louise Fletcher *Pearl* • Gwen Welles *Shirley* • Stephen Tobolowsky *Kirk* • Lewis Arquette *Mr Fry* ■ *Dir* Evelyn Purcell • *Scr* Beth Henley

Nobody's Fool ★★★★15

Drama 1994 · US · Colour · 105min

Director Robert Benton's pleasingly low-key film stars Paul Newman as a grouchy town rogue who is forced to face up to his family responsibilities when his long-neglected son turns up for Thanksgiving. An old hand at this kind of heart-warming fare, Benton doesn't swamp it with sentimentality, allowing the crumpled charisma of Newman to carry the drama effortlessly. He is also well served by a starry cast in which the likes of Bruce Willis and Melanie Griffith line up with venerable character actors such as Jessica Tandy and Josef Sommer. JF Swearing, brief nudity.

Paul Newman *Donald Sullivan* • Jessica Tandy *Miss Beryl* • Bruce Willis *Carl Roebuck* • Melanie Griffith *Toby Roebuck* • Dylan Walsh *Peter* • Pruitt Taylor Vince *Rub Squeers* • Gene Saks *Wirf* • Josef Sommer *Clive Peoples Jr* ■ *Dir* Robert Benton • *Scr* Robert Benton, from the novel by Richard Russo

Les Noces Rouges ★★★15

Drama based on a true story 1973 · Fr/It · Colour · 92min

Another variation on Claude Chabrol's pet theme of infidelity leading to murder, this was part of the cycle of films in which Stéphane Audran, Chabrol's then-wife, added spice by playing either the victim or cause of the crime. Chabrol based his own screenplay on a newspaper account of a *crime passionnel*, which got the film banned for a while as it concerned a real murder case. The film is elegant, cool and blackly humorous, and the playing of the unsympathetic characters is impeccable. RB French +subtitles. *DVD*

Michel Piccoli *Pierre Maury* • Stéphane Audran *Lucienne Delamare* • Claude Piéplu *Paul Delamare* • Eliana De Santis *Hélène* • Pipo Merisi *Berthier* ■ *Dir/Scr* Claude Chabrol

Nocturnal Animals

Thriller 2016 · US · Colour

This is a preview – no prints were available to review as we went to press: After studying architecture, Tom Ford wound up as creative director at Gucci and YSL before launching his own label. His debut film, *A Single Man*, won star Colin Firth an Oscar nomination. No wonder his follow-up

is hotly anticipated – an adaptation of cult thriller *Tony and Susan* about a divorcee reading a draft of her husband's new novel and wondering if it isn't about their failed relationship. Amy Adams and Jake Gyllenhaal take the leads – and the fashion will be by Ford, no doubt. SvM

Jake Gyllenhaal *Tony Hastings* • Isla Fisher *Laura Hastings* • Amy Adams *Susan Morrow* • Aaron Taylor-Johnson [Aaron Johnson] *Stranger* • Armie Hammer *Walker Morrow* • Laura Linney *Anne Sutton* ■ *Dir* Tom Ford • *Scr* Tom Ford, from the novel *Tony and Susan* by Austin Wright

Nocturne ★★★

Crime drama 1946 · US · BW · 87min

A wealthy, cold-blooded composer is shot, bringing a verdict of suicide. Detective George Raft sets out to investigate further and comes to suspect glamorous starlet Lynn Bari of killing him. This glossy *film noir*, slickly directed by Edwin L Marin, offers an appealing performance from Raft in cultivated good-guy mode; it also features a catch of well-played red herrings, led by Virginia Huston, Joseph Pevney and Diana Dors lookalike Myrna Dell. The nocturne of the title, composed by Leigh Harline, features heavily in the plot. RK

George Raft *Lt Joe Warne* • Lynn Bari *Frances Ransom* • Virginia Huston *Carol Page* • Joseph Pevney *Fingers* • Myrna Dell *Susan* ■ *Dir* Edwin L Marin • *Scr* Jonathan Latimer, from a story by Frank Fenton, Rowland Brown • *Music* Leigh Harline

Noel ★★PG

Seasonal drama 2004 · US · Colour · 92min

Susan Sarandon is prominent among a semi-starry line-up playing despairing New Yorkers whose lonely lives intertwine in the most unlikely of ways. Director Chazz Palminteri tries to build a case for modern miracles, but the half-baked revelations and saccharine sentiment are tedious to watch. SP *DVD*

Penélope Cruz *Nina* • Susan Sarandon *Rose* • Paul Walker *Mike* • Alan Arkin *Artie* • Marcus Thomas *Jules* • Chazz Palminteri *Arizona* • Robin Williams *Charlie Boyd* ■ *Dir* Chazz Palminteri • *Scr* David Hubbard

Noi Tre ★★★PG

Biographical comedy drama 1984 · It · Colour · 85min

In this interesting, but inconsistent, Italian feature, director Pupi Avati tries to create an adolescence for musical genius Mozart by following the course of a summer stay with a country aristocrat and his mischievous teenage kin. Although it impressively conveys a sense of the crushing level of expectation placed on Mozart's shoulders, the film falls down in its portrayal of the youthful brawls and pranks, and the romantic stirrings that could have made it more engaging. DP In Italian.

Christopher Davidson *Wolfgang Amadeus Mozart* • Lino Capolicchio *Leopoldo* • Gianni Cavina *Cousin* • Carlo Delle Piane *Count Pallovicini* • Ida DiBenedetto *Maria Caterino* • Dario Parisini *Giuseppe* • Barbara Rebeschini *Antonia-Leda* ■ *Dir* Pupi Avati • *Scr* Pupi Avati, Antonio Avati, Cesare Bornazzini

Noir et Blanc ★★★18

Drama 1986 · Fr · BW · 80min

Claire Devers won the Caméra d'Or at Cannes for this debut feature. Shooting in monochrome, Devers explores the grey area between pain and pleasure as she chronicles the abrasive relationship between timid health centre accountant Francis Frappat and muscular masseur Jacques Martial. A study in sensuality without the sensationalism, this is an admirably controlled film. DP In French.

Francis Frappat *Antoine* • Jacques Martial *Dominique* • Josephine Fresson *Josy* • Marc Berman *Monsieur Roland* ■ *Dir* Claire Devers • *Scr* Claire Devers, Alain Bergala, from the story *Desire and the Black Masseur* by Tennessee Williams

Noises Off ★★★15

Comedy 1992 · US · Colour · 99min

Robbed of its essentially theatrical device – the comic contrast between off-stage chaos and on-stage calculation – this American adaptation of Michael Frayn's West End play provides more than enough laughs to skim over the potholes of improbability. Peter Bogdanovich's quick-fire direction is matched and aided by some wondrously staccato performances, notably from Carol Burnett, Michael Caine and Christopher Reeve. Luvvies at play have never been so pompously vulnerable or so sympathetic. TH *DVD*

Carol Burnett *Dotty Otley/Mrs Clackett* • Michael Caine *Lloyd Fellowes* • Denholm Elliott *Selsdon Mowbray/Burglar* • Julie Hagerty *Poppy Taylor* • Marilu Henner *Belinda Blair/Flavia Brent* • Mark Linn-Baker *Tim Allgood* • Christopher Reeve *Frederick Dallas/Philip Brent* • John Ritter *Garry Lejeune/Roger Tramplemain* ■ *Dir* Peter Bogdanovich • *Scr* Marty Kaplan, from the play by Michael Frayn

Noma: My Perfect Storm ★★★ 15
Documentary 2015 · UK · Colour · 99min

Film-maker Pierre Deschamps certainly got the timing right when he embarked upon this portrait of Noma, Copenhagen's avant-garde foodie shrine, and its charismatic chef René Redzepi. Named "Best Restaurant in the World" three years running, the establishment was hit in 2013 by a serious norovirus outbreak.Foremost in this fly-on-the-wall report is the fascinating contradiction of Redzepi himself, whose abrasive perfectionism appears to be prompted by the prejudice he suffered in his youth. TJ In Albanian, Danish, English, French, Spanish, Swedish. Swearing

René Redzepi • *Dir/Scr* Pierre Deschamps

Nomads ★★★ 18
Supernatural thriller 1985 · US · Colour · 88min

This fascinating and ambitious directorial debut from John McTiernan bypasses the 1980s fad for excessive gore and sex and focuses instead on atmosphere and dramatic visual scares. Pierce Brosnan gives a restrained performance as a French anthropologist working in Los Angeles drawn to a disparate gang of street punks, led by one-time pop idol Adam Ant, who are in reality nomadic demons roaming the earth. McTiernan apparently based his tale on Inuit legends, though his intriguing supernatural chiller might perhaps have worked better as a shorter, made-for-TV movie. RS

Pierce Brosnan *Pommier* • Lesley-Anne Down *Dr Flax* • Anna Maria Montecelli *Niki* • Adam Ant *Number One* • Hector Mercado *Ponytail* • Josie Cotton *Silver Ring* ■ *Dir/Scr* John McTiernan

Non-Stop ★★★ 12
Action thriller 2014 · US · Colour · 106min

This solid thriller stars Liam Neeson as a veteran air marshal on a flight from New York to London who receives a text telling him a passenger will die every 20 minutes unless $150 million is transferred to a secret account. Aided by frequent flyer Julianne Moore and plucky flight attendant Michelle Dockery, Neeson plays a cat-and-mouse game above the Atlantic while trying to keep the body count to a minimum. The premise is intriguing, and there are intermittent thrills, although Neeson's not helped by a script that lays on the hammy dialogue a little too thick. TeS In English, German. *DVD* *Blu-ray*

Liam Neeson *Bill Marks* • Julianne Moore *Jen Summers* • Michelle Dockery *Nancy* • Lupita Nyong'o *Gwen* • Nate Parker *Zack* • Scoot McNairy *Tom* ■ *Dir* Jaume Collet-Serra • *Scr* Chris Roach, John W Richardson, Ryan Engle, from a story by Richardson, Roach

None but the Brave ★★★ U
Adventure drama 1960 · US · Colour · 84min

Danny Bravo is a young native American boy who enters his horse in a race so he can win the prize money to build a new church. It's enough to bring tears to the eyes of local priest Richard Basehart, local doctor Stuart Erwin and, indeed, to Bravo's horse, but no one has told the local mountain lion (who does everything but

wear a black hat) that little Danny is off limits as prey. But let us not be cynical: this is a story that celebrates the human spirit, directed with Bressonian intensity by George Sherman. AT

Richard Basehart *Father Phelan* • Stuart Erwin *Dr Mills* • Arthur Shields *Father Walsh* • Armando Silvestre *Tony Eagle* • Elsa Cardenas *Mrs Eagle* • Michael Steckler *Ty Corbin* • Rex Allen • Danny Bravo *Michael* ■ *Dir* George Sherman • *Scr* DD Beauchamp

None but the Brave ★★ PG
Second World War drama
1965 · US/Jpn · Colour · 101min

You'd think Frank Sinatra might have chosen a better project for his only foray into direction than this wartime morality chestnut about enemy US and Japanese troops forced to co-exist on a remote Pacific island. As director, Sinatra succeeds moderately well, but the proceedings lose credibility during his moments on screen. TS *DVD*

Frank Sinatra *Chief Pharmacist's Mate Maloney* • Clint Walker *Captain Dennis Bourke* • Tommy Sands *Second Lieutenant Blair* • Brad Dexter *Sergeant Bleeker* • Tony Bill *Air Crewman Keller* • Tatsuya Mihashi *Lieutenant Kuroki* ■ *Dir* Frank Sinatra • *Scr* John Twist, Katsuya Susaki, from a story by Kikumaru Okuda • *Producer* Frank Sinatra

None but the Lonely Heart ★★ U
Drama 1944 · US · BW · 108min

The great Cary Grant was surprisingly nominated for an Oscar for this pretentious drama, in which he's hopelessly miscast as the cockney drifter Ernie Mott, a punk philosopher who drifts easily into crime because of the poverty of his circumstances. The star found an affinity between Mott and his own upbringing and insisted the left-wing playwright Clifford Odets be hired as director. Unfortunately, the result is turgid and earnest. TS

Cary Grant *Ernie Mott* • Ethel Barrymore *Ma Mott* • Barry Fitzgerald *Twite* • June Duprez *Ada* • Jane Wyatt *Aggie Hunter* • George Coulouris *Jim Mordinoy* • Dan Duryea *Lew Tate* ■ *Dir* Clifford Odets • *Scr* Clifford Odets, from the novel by Richard Llewellyn

None Shall Escape ★★★
Drama 1944 · US · BW · 85min

A very interesting and extremely clever movie, this examines in depth the career of a high-ranking German officer during his trial for war crimes. The film, though set after the First World War, was made and released before the end of the Second World War, and proved to be extraordinarily prescient. Director Andre De Toth keeps the story suspenseful and elicits excellent performances from Marsha Hunt and Henry Travers. TS

Marsha Hunt *Marja Pacierkowski* • Alexander Knox *Wilhelm Grimm* • Henry Travers *Father Warecki* • Erik Rolf *Karl Grimm* • Richard Crane *Willie Grimm as a man* • Dorothy Morris *Janina* • Richard Hale *Rabbi Levin* ■ *Dir* Andre De Toth • *Scr* Lester Cole, from a story by Alfred Neumann, Joseph Than

Noose ★★★
Crime thriller 1948 · UK · BW · 95min

This is a sterling slice of British *film noir*, starring American sex symbol Carole Landis. As the fashion journalist who gets mixed up in the murky underworld of London's black market, Landis bravely goes up against spivs and wide-boy racketeers in this well-made little thriller. While blonde bombshell Landis provides the glamour, the best performance is by Nigel Patrick as the fast-talking, charismatic villain. On a sad note, Landis committed suicide shortly after completing the film. She was 29. DF

Carole Landis *Linda Medbury* • Joseph Calleia *Sugiani* • Derek Farr *Captain Jumbo Hoyle* • Stanley Holloway *Inspector Rendall* • Nigel Patrick *Bar Gorman* ■ *Dir* Edmond T Gréville • *Scr* Richard Llewellyn, Richard Dryhurst, from the play *The Silk Noose* by Richard Llewellyn

Noose ★★★ 18
Crime drama 1997 · US · Colour · 89min

Mystifyingly straight-to-video here, this brutish tale of "boys from the O'Hood" is a cracking tale of bullets and blarney, carried along by a good cast. Set in Boston, it stars Denis Leary as the small-time car thief who is forced to examine his loyalty to local crime boss Colm Meaney when one of his relatives (Billy Crudup) falls foul of the gangster. With the supporting players including Famke Janssen, Ian Hart, Martin Sheen and Jeanne Tripplehorn, this is a classy affair directed with some sympathy by Ted Demme. JF Swearing, violence. *DVD*

Denis Leary *Bobby O'Grady* • Jason Barry *Seamus* • Billy Crudup *Teddy* • Ian Hart *Moose Murphy* • Famke Janssen *Katy O'Connor* • Colm Meaney *Jackie O'Hara* • Martin Sheen *Hanlon* • Jeanne Tripplehorn *Annie* ■ *Dir* Ted Demme • *Scr* Mike Armstrong

The Noose Hangs High ★★ U
Comedy 1948 · US · BW · 76min

Just when the fortunes of comedians Bud Abbott and Lou Costello seemed at their lowest, director Charles Barton brought in Leon Errol as guest star: a balding ditherer from countless B-pictures whose take on the double take was something to behold. Errol was the kind of trouper one could rely on, and he certainly raised the laughs in this predictable yarn about window cleaners mistaken for gamblers. TH

Bud Abbott *Ted Higgins* • Lou Costello *Homer Hinchcliffe* • Cathy Downs *Carol Scott* • Joseph Calleia *Mike Craig* • Leon Errol *Julius Caesar McBride* • Mike Mazurki *Chuck* ■ *Dir* Charles Barton • *Scr* John Grant, Howard Harris, from a story by Daniel Taradash, Julian Blaustein, Bernard Feins

Nor the Moon by Night ★★ U
Adventure 1958 · UK · Colour · 92min

Guy Elmes was one of the busiest British screenwriters of the 1950s and 1960s. In addition to penning several sword-and-sandal adventures in Italy, he also adapted the Graham Greene short story *The Stranger's Hand* for producer John Stafford, with whom he reunited for this rather scrappy melodrama. There's little to be said in defence of either the acting or the story, in which the warden of an African game reserve finally meets his pen pal only to discover she's not the person he expected her to be. DP

Belinda Lee *Alice Lang* • Michael Craig *Rusty Miller* • Patrick McGoohan *Andrew Miller* • Anna Gaylor *Thea Boryslawski* • Eric Pohlmann *Anton Boryslawski* • Pamela Stirling *Mrs Boryslawski* ■ *Dir* Ken Annakin • *Scr* Guy Elmes, from the novel by Joy Packer

Nora ★★ 15
Biographical drama
1999 · UK/Ire/Ger/It · Colour · 102min

Director Pat Murphy's exploration of James Joyce's relationship with his wife, Nora Barnacle, boasts a tour de force performance from Susan Lynch in the title role. She excels as a passionate woman rebelling against a repressive existence while struggling to understand her selfish, obsessive, literary genius of a husband. Telling Joyce's story from Nora's point of view is a clever stroke, but the movie is let down by Ewan McGregor's risible portrait of the artist. Slow and unbalanced, the result falls well short of the mark. LH *DVD*

Ewan McGregor *James Joyce* • Susan Lynch *Nora Barnacle* • Peter McDonald *Stanislaus Joyce* • Roberto Citran *Roberto Prezioso* • Andrew Scott *Michael Bodkin* • Vincent McCabe *[Vinnie McCabe] Uncle Tommy* • Veronica Duffy *Annie Barnacle* ■ *Dir* Pat Murphy • *Scr* Pat Murphy, Gerard Stembridge, from the biography by Brenda Maddox

Nora Prentiss ★★★
Crime melodrama 1947 · US · BW · 111min

This glossy "women's picture" romp can be enjoyed by all – if you leave your brains

behind. Nightclub chanteuse Ann Sheridan ruins doctor Kent Smith when he falls for her and assumes the identity of a dead patient. Allegedly based on an actual insurance scandal, this is high-camp entertainment, with a technical crew of the very best to ensure that every ludicrous moment seems credible. It's a little overlong for its plot, but don't miss Sheridan's two solos. TS

Ann Sheridan *Nora Prentiss* • Kent Smith *Dr Richard Talbot* • Bruce Bennett *Dr Joel Merriam* • Robert Alda *Phil McDade* • Rosemary DeCamp *Lucy Talbot* • John Ridgely *Walter Bailey* • Robert Arthur (1) *Gregory Talbot* ■ *Dir* Vincent Sherman • *Scr* N Richard Nash, Philip McDonald, from the story *The Man Who Died Twice* by Paul Webster, Jack Sobell

Nora Roberts' Carnal Innocence ★★ 15
Mystery thriller 2011 · US · Colour · 93min

A town called Innocence proves to be a deadly hotbed of secrets, lies and old family feuds in this pedestrian Deep South potboiler. Combining unconvincing romance with a clumsy whodunnit, it sees burnt-out concert violinist Gabrielle Anwar become dangerously entangled in a serial-killer case when she falls for privileged local lothario – and prime suspect – Colin Egglesfield. There's a sprinkling of tension when the murderer's finally unmasked, but poor pacing and melodramatic performances make this decidedly unsatisfactory. SF Violence, a sex scene. *DVD*

Gabrielle Anwar *Caroline Waverly* • Colin Egglesfield *Tucker Longstreet* • Pancho Demmings *Sheriff Burke* • Shirley Jones *Della Duncan* ■ *Dir* Peter Markle • *Scr* Donald Martin, from Nora Roberts's novel

Nora Roberts' High Noon ★★ 15
Romantic suspense drama
2009 · US · Colour · 87min

Emilie de Ravin of TV's *Lost* is the main attraction in this otherwise bland take on Nora Roberts's bestseller. Working hard to animate her unconvincing character, she plays an expert hostage negotiator who becomes the target of a vengeful killer. The storyline and its execution are so dull that it's difficult to muster any enthusiasm or empathy for anyone involved. SF Violence, sex scenes. *DVD*

Emilie de Ravin *Lt Phoebe McNamara* • Ivan Sergei *Duncan Swift* • Chris Aanderson *Detective "Bull" Sykes* • Cybill Shepherd *Essie McNamara* ■ *Dir* Peter Markle • *Scr* Terri Kopp, from the novel by Nora Roberts

Nora Roberts' Midnight Bayou ★★ 15
Mystery romantic drama
2009 · US · Colour · 87min

New Orleans post-Katrina provides a striking backdrop for this atmospheric but clumsy adaptation of the Nora Roberts bestseller. Combining a haunted-house mystery with a rushed romance, it sees bland northern lawyer Jerry O'Connell and sultry southerner Lauren Stamile forced to confront both literal and metaphorical ghosts after O'Connell buys an old Louisiana mansion to use as a legal aid practice. Despite its juicy themes, the tale ends up disappointingly underwhelming, thanks to weak, cliché-riddled scripting and pedestrian direction. SF Violence. *DVD*

Jerry O'Connell *Declan Fitzpatrick* • Lauren Stamile *Lena Simone* • Faye Dunaway *Odette Simone* ■ *Dir* Ralph Hemecker • *Scr* Stephen Tolkin, from the novel by Nora Roberts

Nora Roberts' Northern Lights ★★ 12
Mystery drama 2009 · US/Can · Colour · 87min

Small town, big secrets is the clichéd concept behind this pedestrian adaptation. The predictable romantic mystery sees Eddie Cibrian's Baltimore cop trying to escape past tragedy by becoming police chief of the bizarrely named town of Lunacy in Alaska. Naturally, the snowbound locale isn't as sleepy as he'd hoped, quickly

N

throwing up a long-undiscovered murder that brings him closer to the victim's feisty pilot daughter (country singer LeAnn Rimes, now Mrs Cibrian). An over-convenient "eureka" moment adds to the mediocrity to produce a truly ridiculous climax. SF Violence, sexual references. *DVD*

Eddie Cibrian *Nate Burns* • LeAnn Rimes *Meg Galligan* • Greg Lawson *Ed Woolcott* • Rosanna Arquette *Charlene Galligan* ■ *Dir* Mike Robe • *Scr* Janet Brownell, from the novel by Nora Roberts

Nora Roberts' Tribute ★★ 12
Mystery drama　2009 · US · Colour · 87min

An oddly flippant Brittany Murphy plays a former child star who stirs up old ghosts when she begins renovating the dilapidated Virginia home of her famous, late grandmother. Cue a flimsy and uneven mix of murder mystery and gooey romance, as haunting dreams and increasingly disturbing bursts of vandalism suggest gran's death wasn't suicide. The ensuing hunt for the truth is dull and slow moving, made worse by far too much time being spent on Murphy's sugary love games with neighbour Jason Lewis (*Sex and the City*). SF *DVD*

Brittany Murphy *Cilla McGowan* • Jason Lewis *Ford Sawyer* • Christian Oliver *Steve Chensky* • Diana Scarwid *Cathy Morrow* • Tippi Hedren *Mrs Hennessey* ■ *Dir* Martha Coolidge • *Scr* Gary Tieche, from the novel by Nora Roberts

Norbit ★ 12
Romantic comedy　2007 · US · Colour · 97min

Eddie Murphy continues the fat-suit antics he started in *The Nutty Professor* in this atrocious and offensive comedy. The star plays three roles: dorky, Afro-sporting Norbit, his gargantuan wife Rasputia and Mr Wong, proprietor of the orphanage where Norbit grew up. The save-the-orphanage plot and 12A certificate suggest a kids movie, but it's debatable whether parents really want to subject their offspring to ribald gags about oral sex, bikini-line waxing or plans to turn the orphanage into a "titty bar". Best avoided, despite Thandie Newton's role as Norbit's childhood sweetheart. JR Swearing, sexual references. *DVD* *BD*

Eddie Murphy *Norbit/Rasputia/Mr Wong* • Thandie Newton *Kate* • Terry Crews *Big Jack* • Clifton Powell *Earl* • Lester "Rasta" Speight *Blue* • Cuba Gooding Jr *Deion Hughes* • Eddie Griffin *Pope Sweet Jesus* • Katt Williams *Lord Have Mercy* • Marlon Wayans *Buster* ■ *Dir* Brian Robbins • *Scr* Jay Scherick, David Ronn, Eddie Murphy, Charles [Charlie] Murphy, from a story by Eddie and Charles Murphy

Norm of the North ★★ U
Animated comedy adventure
2016 · Ind/US · Colour · 86min

There's a commendable eco-friendly message here, as a polar bear (voiced by Rob Schneider) and his little lemming friends head to New York to thwart an evil property developer's plans to turn the Arctic into "Dubai on ice". There are strange detours and oddly random, incomplete dance sequences, which make it all fine without being too exciting. The voice cast give it some welly, but it's the mute lemmings – like the Minions they're blatantly modelled on – that steal this rather modest show. DA *DVD* *BD*

Rob Schneider *Norm* • Heather Graham *Vera* • Ken Jeong *Mr Greene* • Bill Nighy *Socrates* • Colm Meaney *Grandfather* • Loretta Devine *Tamecia* ■ *Dir* Trevor Wall • *Scr* Daniel Altiere, Steven Altiere, Malcolm T Goldman

Norma Jean & Marilyn
★★ 15
Biographical drama　1996 · US · Colour · 108min

The rise and fall of a 20th-century legend forms the basis of yet another TV-movie biography, which charts the life of Marilyn Monroe from her poor, rootless childhood as Norma Jean Baker to her final, tragic failure to resist her demons. The unusual approach of having two actresses – Ashley Judd and Mira Sorvino – play the same

character fails to hide the fact that this a leering, pointless fantasy on the life of one of Hollywood's most discussed yet least understood icons – these girls can wear Marilyn's clothes but they can't fill her shoes. MC *DVD*

Ashley Judd *Norma Jean Baker* • Mira Sorvino *Marilyn Monroe* • David Dukes *Arthur Miller* • Josh Charles *Eddie Jordan* • Ron Rifkin *Johnny Hyde* • Peter Dobson *Joe DiMaggio* • Taylor Nichols *Fred Karger* • John Rubinstein *Darryl Zanuck* ■ *Dir* Tim Fywell • *Scr* Jill Isaacs

Norma Rae ★★★★ PG
Drama based on a true story
1979 · US · Colour · 109min

Director Martin Ritt's last important film is typical of his best work. Based on the true story of a reluctant real-life heroine, this sincere drama with a social conscience makes its union cause authentic, heartfelt and grittily entertaining. Determinedly shedding her image as a perennially cute, bubbly comedian, Sally Field deservedly won her first Oscar for her committed performance as the widowed Southern textile worker who nervously allies herself with New York labour organiser Ron Leibman to fight appalling conditions and, with growing gumption, takes on the mill owners. There are fine performances all round, including Beau Bridges as her boorish man, but it's Field's triumph. AME *DVD*

Sally Field *Norma Rae* • Beau Bridges *Sonny Webster* • Ron Leibman *Reuben* • Pat Hingle *Vernon* • Barbara Baxley *Leona* • Gail Strickland *Bonnie Mae* • Morgan Paull *Wayne Billings* • Robert Broyles *Sam Bolen* ■ *Dir* Martin Ritt • *Scr* Irving Ravetch, Harriet Frank Jr

Normal ★★ 18
Comedy drama　2002 · US · Colour · 112min

Jane Anderson directs this polished adaptation of her stage play in this TV movie about transsexuality. However, in striving to de-sensationalise Tom Wilkinson's decision to end his 25-year marriage to Jessica Lange and undergo gender realignment, Anderson overcompensates by suppressing his inner turmoil and highlighting instead the prejudice of his family and friends. DP Swearing. *DVD*

Jessica Lange *Irma* • Tom Wilkinson *Roy* • Hayden Panettiere *Patty Ann* • Clancy Brown *Frank* • Joe Sikora *Wayne* • Randall Arney *Reverend Muncie* ■ *Dir* Jane Anderson • *Scr* Jane Anderson, from her play *Looking for Normal*

The Normal Heart ★★★★
Drama based on a true story
2014 · US · Colour · 128min

Mark Ruffalo gives a heart-rending performance as a gay rights activist attempting to raise awareness of the HIV/AIDS crisis in the early 1980s. His story, drawing inevitable comparisons with *Angels in America* (2003), offers a much more straightforward document that vividly captures a moment in history at the beginning of the epidemic. Director Ryan Murphy (*American Horror Story*, *Glee*) occasionally has difficulty converting the style of the original play to the screen, but his passion for the subject is evident. JL

Mark Ruffalo *Ned Weeks* • Matt Bomer *Felix Turner* • Taylor Kitsch *Bruce Niles* • Jim Parsons *Tommy Boatwright* • Julia Roberts *Emma Brookner* • Alfred Molina *Ben Weeks* ■ *Dir* Ryan Murphy • *Scr* Larry Kramer, from his play

Normal Life ★★ 18
Crime drama　1995 · US · Colour · 102min

Director John McNaughton, of *Henry: Portrait of a Serial Killer* and *Wild Things* fame, here delivers a sub-*Badlands* drama whose ending is obvious even before the opening credits have finished. Strait-laced cop Luke Perry finds his world unravelling after he falls for wild child Ashley Judd and gets caught up in credit card fraud and bank robbery. JB

Ashley Judd *Pam Anderson* • Luke Perry *Chris Anderson* • Bruce Young [Bruce A Young] *Agent Parker* • Jim True *Mike Anderson* • Dawn Maxey *Eva* • Tom Towles *Frank Anderson* ■ *Dir* John McNaughton • *Scr* Peg Haller, Bob Schneider

Norman Loves Rose ★★★
Comedy　1982 · Aus · Colour · 97min

A typically offbeat Australian comedy, this has a lovestruck teenager (Tony Owen) becoming enamoured of his sexy sister-in-law (Carol Kane). When the latter gets pregnant, it's less a case of how's-your-father than who's-the-father. The unsavoury-sounding plot actually raises more than its fair share of laughs, while Warren Mitchell (TV's Alf Garnett) shines in a supporting role. DA

Carol Kane *Rose* • Tony Owen *Norman* • Warren Mitchell *Morris* • Myra De Groot *Norman's mother* • David Downer *Michael* ■ *Dir/Scr* Henri Safran

The Norseman ★ PG
Period adventure　1978 · US · Colour · 86min

In this pathetic would-be period adventure, Lee Majors is a Viking who goes overseas looking for his lost father (played by Mel Ferrer). It's the sort of movie where men wear horns on their heads and say "Vrolop thar, gravad lax" to each other before hacking their enemies to pieces. The violence is of the slo-mo variety, the budget clearly nonexistent. Charles B Pierce writes, directs and produces at the sort of crass level that makes *Erik the Viking* look like a masterpiece. AT

Lee Majors *Thorvald Helge* • Cornel Wilde *Ragnar* • Mel Ferrer *King Eurich* • Jack Elam *Death Dreamer* • Chris Connelly [Christopher Connelly] *Rolf* • Deacon Jones *Thrall* ■ *Dir/Scr* Charles B Pierce

El Norte ★★★★ 15
Drama　1983 · US · Colour · 133min

Hailed as the "first American independent epic", Gregory Nava's compassionate film eschews political sermonising to concentrate on the human aspect of the arduous trek undertaken by so many Latinos to that pitiless promised land to the north. Adeptly using a docudramatic style to ward off overt sentimentality, Nava draws wondrously naturalistic performances from David Villalpando and Zaide Silvia Gutierrez. They play a brother and sister who, following the murder of their peasant father, experience both the despair of the refugee and the optimism of the immigrant after quitting their remote Guatemalan village. An irresistibly involving drama. DP English, Spanish +subtitles.

Ernesto Gómez Cruz *Arturo Xuncax* • David Villalpando *Enrique Xuncax* • Zaide Silvia Gutierrez *Rosa Xuncax* • Alicia del Lago *Lupe Xuncax* ■ *Dir* Gregory Nava • *Scr* Gregory Nava, Anna Thomas

North ★★ PG
Fantasy comedy drama
1994 · US · Colour · 83min

Tired of saving the world, Bruce Willis is out to save the soul of 11-year-old Elijah Wood. However, the casting of Willis as a guardian angel dressed as a pink bunny rabbit is laughably typical of the misjudgements in Rob Reiner's fantastical extravaganza. Wood "divorces" his selfish parents and sets out on a worldwide odyssey to audition possible alternatives. Meanwhile, the school swot has set up a kids-v-adults political power base on the strength of Wood's revolution. TH

Elijah Wood *North* • Bruce Willis *Narrator* • Jason Alexander *North's dad* • Julia Louis-Dreyfus *North's mom* • Mathew McCurley *Winchell* • Jon Lovitz *Arthur Belt* • Alan Arkin *Judge Buckle* • Dan Aykroyd *Pa Tex* ■ *Dir* Rob Reiner • *Scr* Alan Zweibel, Andrew Scheinman, from the novel by Alan Zweibel

North by Northwest
★★★★★ PG
Classic spy thriller　1959 · US · Colour · 130min

This Hitchcock classic contains extra helpings of the ingredients that make his films so unmissable. Action, intrigue, romance and comedy are blended

throughout with consummate skill; the attack by the crop-dusting plane and the finale on Mount Rushmore are simply the icing on the cake. Rarely did Hitchcock have as much fun with his favourite "innocent in peril" theme or make such inventive use of famous landmarks. In his fourth and final collaboration with the "Master of Suspense", Cary Grant is the personification of suaveness as he tackles a nest of enemy agents, led by James Mason. DP *DVD* *BD*

Cary Grant *Roger Thornhill* • Eva Marie Saint *Eve Kendall* • James Mason *Phillip Vandamm* • Jessie Royce Landis *Clara Thornhill* • Leo G Carroll *Professor* • Philip Ober *Lester Townsend* • Martin Landau *Leonard* • Adam Williams *Valerian* ■ *Dir* Alfred Hitchcock • *Scr* Ernest Lehman • *Cinematographer* Robert Burks • *Music* Bernard Herrmann

North Country ★★★ 15
Social drama　2005 · US · Colour · 121min

Charlize Theron brings her familiar combination of softness and steel to a yarn loosely based on America's first class-action lawsuit for sexual harassment. Theron returns to her home town in northern Minnesota after the break-up of her marriage and finds work in the mines. After suffering abuse from her male colleagues, she decides to take a stand. Director Niki Caro (*Whale Rider*) piles on the melodrama in the final stages, but gritty performances from Theron and the supporting cast make this a worthy effort. SP Swearing, violence, sexual references. *DVD*

Charlize Theron *Josey Aimes* • Frances McDormand *Glory* • Sean Bean *Kyle* • Richard Jenkins *Hank* • Jeremy Renner *Bobby Sharp* • Michelle Monaghan *Sherry* • Woody Harrelson *Bill White* • Sissy Spacek *Alice* • Rusty Schwimmer *Big Betty* ■ *Dir* Niki Caro • *Scr* Michael Seitzman, from the non-fiction book *Class Action: The Landmark Case That Changed Sexual Harassment Law* by Clara Bingham, Laura Leedy Gansler

North Dallas Forty ★★★ 18
Sports drama　1979 · US · Colour · 113min

This all-American sports saga stars Nick Nolte, looking the part of the professional American football player, now almost over the hill and wanting to escape the steroid culture and corruption surrounding the game. Since the National Football League declined to assist in the production, action footage is minimal until the climax, but this turns the spotlight on the characters involved and, it must be said, the clichés about heroism, role models and the girls on the sidelines. AT Swearing, drug abuse, nudity.

Nick Nolte *Phillip Elliott* • Mac Davis *Maxwell* • Charles Durning *Coach Johnson* • Dayle Haddon *Charlotte* • Bo Svenson *Jo Bob Priddy* • Steve Forrest *Conrad Hunter* • Dabney Coleman *Emmett* ■ *Dir* Ted Kotcheff • *Scr* Frank Yablans, Ted Kotcheff, Peter Gent, from the novel by Peter Gent

The North Face ★★★ 12A
Adventure drama based on a true story
2008 · Ger/Austria/Swi · Colour · 126min

This meticulous re-creation of the epic 1936 attempt to scale the north face of the Eiger ably captures the spirit of athletic endeavour that the Nazis fostered in Germany prior to the Berlin Olympics. However, a semi-romantic subplot involving a reporter covering the story proves a distraction from the tensions of the climb itself, which sees a pair of German friends (Benno Fürmann and Florian Lukas) being followed up their audacious route by two Austrian rivals. This is sufficiently rooted in the conventions of its genre and the attitudes of the time to guarantee an engrossing depiction of endeavour, heroism and sacrifice. DP German +subtitles.

Benno Fürmann *Toni Kurz* • Johanna Wokalek *Luise Fellner* • Florian Lukas *Andreas "Andi" Hinterstoisser* • Simon Schwarz *Willy Angerer* • Georg Friedrich *Edi Rainer* • Ulrich Tukur *Henry Arau* ■ *Dir* Philipp Stölzl • *Scr* Christoph Silber, Rupert Henning, Philipp Stölzl, Johannes Naber, from a screenplay (unproduced) by Benedikt Roeskau

North of the Great Divide
★★

Western 1950 · US · Colour · 67min

The Oseka tribe is starving after a new salmon cannery over-fishes a river but, with Roy Rogers as the friendly Indian agent, it's all sorted out before the natives take to the warpath. Roy Barcroft and a whip-cracking Jack Lambert dispense the villainy, while Penny Edwards is an attractive field nurse. With its conservation theme, colour photography and three songs, this is a tolerable late entry in a long-running series. AE

Roy Rogers • Penny Edwards *Ann Keith* • Gordon Jones *Splinters* • Roy Barcroft *Banning* • Jack Lambert *Stagg* ■ *Dir* William Witney • *Scr* Eric Taylor

North Sea Hijack
★★ 15

Action adventure 1979 · UK · Colour · 95min

Presumably because it was assumed that American audiences might not know where the North Sea was, this action caper was retitled *ffolkes* for the US market. Roger Moore is the frogman hero, James Mason is an admiral and Anthony Perkins is planning to hijack a North Sea oil rig. It's sub-Bond, sub-Forsyth, even sub-Alistair MacLean. ffeeble. AT Swearing, violence. **DVD**

Roger Moore *Rufus Excalibur Ffolkes* • James Mason *Admiral Sir Francis Brinsden* • Anthony Perkins *Lou Kramer* • Michael Parks *Shulman* • David Hedison *King* • Jack Watson *Olafsen* • Faith Brook *Prime Minister* ■ *Dir* Andrew V McLaglen • *Scr* Jack Davies, from his novel *Esther, Ruth and Jennifer*

North Shore
★★ PG

Action drama 1987 · US · Colour · 91min

This is a daft attempt to construct a youth-orientated surfer movie while maintaining an Elvis Presley-style innocence. The result? Anodyne nonsense. Matt Adler is the top surfer in Arizona who hitches to Hawaii to do battle with the famous Oahu waves. Adler falls in love, but his inamorata's family is none too keen. The script stinks, but the screen comes alive once surf's up. SH

Matt Adler *Rick Kane* • Gregory Harrison *Chandler* • Nia Peeples *Kiani* • John Philbin *Turtle* • Gerry Lopez *Vince* ■ *Dir* William Phelps • *Scr* William Phelps, Tim McCanlies, from a story by William Phelps, Randall Kleiser

The North Star
★★★ PG

Second World War drama
1943 · US · B/W · 99min

This Second World War drama is lifted above the mundane by a fine Lillian Hellman script (from her own story) and some strong playing from Walter Huston as a Ukrainian village doctor and Erich von Stroheim as his urbane Nazi counterpart. When the action is concentrated on the battle of words, this is a multilayered, complex film that contains some insights on the struggle against oppression, but there are far too many lengthy and tedious scenes of combat. SH

Anne Baxter *Marina* • Farley Granger *Damian* • Jane Withers *Claudia* • Eric Roberts (1) *Grisha* • Dana Andrews *Kolya* • Walter Brennan *Karp* • Walter Huston *Dr Kurin* • Erich von Stroheim *Dr Otto Von Harden* ■ *Dir* Lewis Milestone • *Scr* Lillian Hellman, from her story • *Music* Aaron Copeland

North Star
★ 15

Period adventure
1996 · Fr/It*Nor/UK · Colour · 84min

During the 1899 Alaskan Gold Rush, prospector James Caan battles Indian Christopher Lambert for land and the love of Cather ne McCormack. Directed by the Norwegian Nils Gaup, this contrived action adventure is weak on both plot and logic, resulting in a freeze-dried potboiler with little to recommend it apart from some spectacular locations. AJ

Christopher Lambert *Hudson Saanteek* • James Caan *Sean McLennon* • Catherine McCormack *Sarah* • Jacques François *Colonel Johnson* ■ *Dir* Nils Gaup • *Scr* Sergio Donati, Lorenzo Donati, Paul Ohl, from a story by Gilles Behat, Philippe Schwartz, from Heck Allen's novel

North to Alaska
★★★★ U

Comedy adventure 1960 · US · Colour · 116min

This splendid comedy adventure boasts a sparkling cast. John Wayne stars as a gold prospector, with the always underrated Stewart Granger as his wily partner. The eclectic casting also includes teen idol Fabian as Granger's unlikely sibling, and the acerbic Ernie Kovacs as a confidence trickster. Director Henry Hathaway keeps up the pace and humour, and the movie contains one of the wackiest bar-room brawls in Hollywood history. TS **DVD**

John Wayne *Sam McCord* • Stewart Granger *George Pratt* • Ernie Kovacs *Frankie Canon* • Fabian *Billy Pratt* • Capucine *Michelle, "Angel"* • Mickey Shaughnessy *Peter Boggs* ■ *Dir* Henry Hathaway • *Scr* John Lee Mahin, Martin Rackin, Claude Binyon, Wendell Mayes (uncredited), from an idea by John Kafka, from the play *Birthday Gift* by Laszlo Focor

North West Frontier
★★★ U

Adventure 1959 · UK · Colour · 124min

This adventure, directed with great pace and precision by J Lee Thompson, proves that an old-fashioned, all-action drama can still keep you on the edge of your seat without the benefit of flashy special effects. It could almost be called an "eastern", transplanting the old western plot of a railroad journey through hostile territory to turn-of-the-century India. Kenneth More gives an assured performance as the soldier entrusted with the safety of a Hindu prince. DP **DVD**

Kenneth More *Captain Scott* • Lauren Bacall *Catherine Wyatt* • Herbert Lom *Van Leyden* • Wilfrid Hyde White *Bridie* • IS Johar *Gupta* • Ursula Jeans *Lady Windham* • Eugene Deckers *Peters* • Ian Hunter *Sir John Windham* • Jack Gwillim *Brigadier Ames* ■ *Dir* J Lee Thompson • *Scr* Robin Estridge, Frank S Nugent, from a story by Patrick Ford, Will Price

North West Mounted Police
★★ U

Period adventure 1940 · US · Colour · 125min

Cecil B DeMille's flat-footed tribute to the Mounties has Gary Cooper as the Texas Ranger-turned-Mountie who, in the 1880s, helps suppress a 15-year revolt by settlers, many of whom are of mixed race. From these historical skirmishes came the Mounties' motto of always getting their man (or woman). A box-office blockbuster, this was shot on sound stages and in Oregon when DeMille's preferred location in the Canadian Rockies proved to be too expensive. AT

Gary Cooper *Dusty Rivers* • Madeleine Carroll *April Logan* • Paulette Goddard *Louvette Corbeau* • Preston Foster *Sgt Jim Brett* • Robert Preston *Constable Ronnie Logan* • George Bancroft *Jacques Corbeau* • Lynne Overman *Tod McDuff* • Akim Tamiroff *Dan Duroc* ■ *Dir* Cecil B DeMille • *Scr* A an LeMay, Jesse Lasky Jr, C Gardner Sullivan, from the book *Royal Canadian Mounted Police* by RC Fetherston-Haugh

Northern Pursuit
★★

Second World War adventure
1943 · US · BW · 93min

The idea of Nazi saboteurs secretly entering Canada had been cleverly explored in the British film *49th Parallel*, but here it gets a juvenile treatment by Warner Bros. Errol Flynn is the Mountie of German descent who goes undercover, foiling a German scheme to assemble a bomber and attack the Panama Canal. Made just after Flynn's acquittal on charges of rape, the film goes lightly on the romance with Julie Bishop. AE

Errol Flynn *Steve Wagner* • Julie Bishop *Laura McBain* • Helmut Dantine *Von Keller* • John Ridgely *Jim Austin* • Gene Lockhart *Ernst* • Tom Tully *Inspector Barnett* ■ *Dir* Raoul Walsh • *Scr* Frank Gruber, Alvah Bessie, from the story *Five Thousand Trojan Horses* by Leslie T White

Northern Soul
★★★★ 15

Drama 2012 · UK · Colour · 101min

The lives of two Lancashire lads change for ever after they discover the sounds of rare American soul music. It's 1974, Wigan Casino is the place to dance all night, and the two mates dream of scouring America for enough rare grooves to become the hottest DJs on the burgeoning Northern Soul scene. Like a British *Saturday Night Fever*, this captures the look and energy of 1970s youth culture. The soundtrack, including Frankie Valli, Edwin Starr and Marvin Gaye, is another delight in a tonally precise, multifaceted gem. AJ **DVD** **Blu**

Elliot James Langridge *John Clark* • Joshua Whitehouse *Matt* • Antonia Thomas *Angela* • Jack Gordon *Sean* • James Lance *Ray Henderson* ■ *Dir/Scr* Elaine Constantine

The Northerners
★★★★ 15

Surreal comedy drama
1992 · Neth · Colour · 102min

Director Alex Van Warmerdam first came to the attention of British audiences with his 1986 black comedy *Abel*. This is an equally offbeat offering, which presents a surreal and, ultimately, macabre portrait of life on an incomplete Dutch housing estate in 1960. Among the eccentric inhabitants are a sexually frustrated butcher and his saintly wife, a short-sighted forest ranger with delusions of grandeur, a couple of travelling missionaries and a postman (played by the director himself) who hides away in the forest to read people's mail. DP Dutch +subtitles.

Leonard Lucieer *Thomas* • Jack Wouterse *Jacob the butcher* • Rudolf Lucieer *Anton the ranger* • Alex Van Warmerdam *Simon the postman* • Annet Malherbe *Martha* ■ *Dir* Alex Van Warmerdam • *Scr* Alex Van Warmerdam, Aat Ceelen

Northfork
★★ PG

Period drama 2002 · US · Colour · 99min

Writer/directors Mark and Michael Polish's film is a wonky study in magical realism that places absurdist tone and somnambulant pacing over cohesive plotting or interesting characterisation. It's 1955 and the small Montana town of Northfork will be flooded when a nearby dam is built. Six men in black attempt to evacuate the remaining stragglers, including a modern-day Noah who has turned his house into an ark and a dying orphan having visions of angels. A pretentious biblical allegory. AJ **DVD**

Peter Coyote *Eddie* • Anthony Edwards *Happy* • Duel Farnes *Irwin* • Daryl Hannah *Flower Hercules* • Kyle MacLachlan *Mr Hope* • Nick Nolte *Father Harlan* • James Woods *Walter O'Brien* • Mark Polish *Willis O'Brien* • Graham Beckel *Marvin* • Jon Gries [Jonathan Gries] *Arnold* ■ *Dir* Michael Polish • *Scr* Michael Polish, Mark Polish

Northwest
★★★★ 15

Crime drama 2013 · Den · Colour · 86min

In this intelligent and good-looking drama set in the struggling suburbs of Copenhagen, charismatic teenager Casper (Gustav Dyekjaer Giese) is a petty criminal making ends meet to support his family when he is recruited by a local drug baron. This sets in motion a turf war with serious consequences for the boy. Gangster-movie boxes are duly ticked – hookers and cocaine are in plentiful supply – but this feels real and immediate, with Casper's youth and naivety bringing a rare sense of danger. DW In Danish. Swearing, drug abuse, some violence. **DVD**

Gustav Dyekjaer Giese *Casper* • Oscar Dyekjaer Giese *Andy* • Lene Maria Christensen *Olivia* • Annemieke Bredahl Peppink *Freja* • Nicholas Westwood Kidd *Robin* ■ *Dir* Michael Noer • *Scr* Michael Noer, Rasmus Heisterberg

Northwest Passage
★★★ PG

Epic adventure 1940 · US · Colour · 121min

A richly textured, beautifully shot adventure tale from MGM, this is pretty sturdy stuff, featuring a rugged Spencer Tracy as Robert Rogers himself, setting out to find the passage of the title. Director King Vidor spares nothing, with the river sequences particularly well-filmed, and there is a genuinely epic feel to the whole endeavour. The ending (shot by uncredited director Jack Conway) certainly leaves you wanting more, but all that followed was a feeble TV series in the late 1950s. TS

Spencer Tracy *Major Robert Rogers* • Robert Young (1) *Langdon Towne* • Walter Brennan *Hunk Marriner* • Ruth Hussey *Elizabeth Browne* • Nat Pendleton *Captain Huff* • Louis Hector *Reverend Browne* • Robert Barrat *Humphrey Towne* • Lumsden Hare *General Amherst* • Donald MacBride *Sergeant McNott* ■ *Dir* King Vidor • *Scr* Laurence Stallings, Talbot Jennings, from the novel by Kenneth Roberts

Norwegian Wood
★★ 15

Romantic drama 2010 · Jpn · Colour · 128min

A man (Kenichi Matsuyama) reflects on events during his life as a student in the late 1960s, when he became close to the ex-partner (Rinko Kikuchi) of a friend who committed suicide, in this gorgeous-looking adaptation of a supposedly unfilmable novel. It's ravishingly shot by Lee Ping-Bin, while Radiohead's Jonny Greenwood provides a subtly evocative score. Yet although director Tran Anh Hung delivers a beautiful, often atmospheric film, the story is too slight and relentlessly glum. Perhaps like most other unfilmable novels, this would have been best left alone. AS Japanese +subtitles. **DVD** **Blu**

Rinko Kikuchi *Naoko* • Kenichi Matsuyama [Ken'ichi Matsuyama] *Toru Watanabe* • Kiko Mizuhara *Midori* • Tetsuji Tamayama *Nagasawa* ■ *Dir* Tran Anh Hung • *Scr* Tran Anh Hung, from the novel by Haruki Murakami • *Cinematographer* Lee Ping-Bin [Mark Lee (3)] • *Music* Jonny Greenwood

LANDMARK FILM
This seminal movie establishes the vampire iconography that still persists today

Nosferatu, a Symphony of Horrors
★★★★★ PG

Classic silent horror
1922 · Ger · Tinted and BW · 80min

Celebrated German director FW Murnau plundered Bram Stoker's *Dracula* without permission for this 1922 ground-breaker, and was successfully sued by Stoker's wife. All prints were ordered to be destroyed, but a few survived. The result is the most frightening incarnation of the vampire count in horror history. With his grasping claws, pointed fangs, bald pate and white cadaverous features, Count Orlock, played by the hideous Max Schreck, creeps through Murnau's archetypal silent imagery with a mesmerising authority that retains a surprising amount of tension. The chilling finale, highlighted by Schreck's terrifying shadow outside his victim's door, packs a powerful punch even by today's standards. AJ **DVD**

Max Schreck *Count Orlock, Nosferatu* • Alexander Granach *Knock, an estate agent* • Gustav von Wangenheim *Hutter, his employee* • Greta Schroeder *Ellen, his wife* • GH Schnell *Harding, ship owner* • Ruth Landshoff *Annie, his wife* ■ *Dir* Friedrich W Murnau [FW Murnau] • *Scr* Henrik Galeen, from the novel *Dracula* by Bram Stoker

Nosferatu, the Vampyre
★★★ 15

Horror 1979 · Fr/W Ger · Colour · 107min

Director Werner Herzog took a risk remaking Murnau's 1922 silent horror masterpiece. Indeed, how could you compete with iconic Max Schreck as the cadaverous, world-weary vampire? Not to be deterred, Herzog cast volatile Klaus Kinski, who brings some tragic sadness to the part, as he seeks to possess object of desire Isabelle Adjani. Remakes of classics can fail, but there is a haunting quality that allows this magnificent-looking interpretation to exist on its own terms. JA German +subtitles. **DVD** **Blu**

Klaus Kinski *Count Dracula* • Isabelle Adjani *Lucy Harker* • Bruno Ganz *Jonathan Harker* • Roland Topor *Renfield* • Walter Ladengast *Dr Van Helsing* • Dan Van Husen *Warden* ■ *Dir* Werner Herzog • *Scr* Werner Herzog, from the 1922 film by Henrik Galeen, from the novel *Dracula* by Bram Stoker

Nostalgia
★★★★ 15

Drama 1983 · USSR/It · Colour and BW · 120min

In rejecting a possible affair and his intellectual researches to undertake the eternal quest for enlightenment, Oleg

N

Yankovsky finds redemption of sorts as he rises to the symbolic challenge of carrying a lighted candle across a sulphurous spa - a challenge posed by Erland Josephson, the apocalypse-obsessed resident of a Tuscan shrine town. Contrasting monochrome flashbacks with desaturated colour landscapes, Andrei Tarkovsky (in his first non-Soviet picture) poetically employs langorous takes which not only convey Yankovsky's fragile mental and spiritual condition, but also heighten the mesmerising mysticism of this metaphysical allegory. DP Italian +subtitles. *DVD*

Oleg Yankovsky *Andrei Gorchakov* • Erland Josephson *Domenico* • Domiziana Giordano *Eugenia* • Patrizia Terreno *Gorchakov's wife* ■ *Dir* Andrei Tarkovsky • *Scr* Andrei Tarkovsky, Tonino Guerra

Nostalgia for the Light
★★★★12

Documentary
2010 · Fr/Ger/Chil/US · Colour · 93min

Veteran Chilean film-maker Patricio Guzmán's latest, award-winning work takes a more abstract approach than his *Battle of Chile* trilogy, but it still packs a political punch. Guzmán's spare, eloquent narration tells the story of his country's "disappeared", the thousands who were taken under the rule of Augusto Pinochet, and incarcerated in concentration camps in the Atacama desert. Intensely moving and stunning to look at, this poetic meditation on the political importance of memory leaves the viewer with much to think about. AC Spanish, English +subtitles.
DVD BL

■ *Dir/Scr* Patricio Guzmán

Nostradamus
★★★15

Biographical drama
1993 · UK/Ger · Colour · 114min

Director Roger Christian paints the charismatic 16th-century rebel doctor as a person shaken by the relevance of his dreams, but whose reputation for accuracy eventually attracts the patronage of French queen Catherine de'Medici. Using bursts of newsreel footage depicting African famine, atomic bomb testing, re-creations of the Second World War and space travel to visualise Nostradamus's predictions, Christian's po-faced venture is a genuine oddity. AJ

Tcheky Karyo *Nostradamus* • F Murray Abraham *Scalinger* • Rutger Hauer *Mystic Monk* • Amanda Plummer *Catherine de'Medici* • Julia Ormond *Marie* • Assumpta Serna *Anne* • Anthony Higgins *King Henry II* • Diana Quick *Diane de Portier* ■ *Dir* Roger Christian • *Scr* Kurt Boeser, from a story by Piers Ashworth, Roger Christian

Not Another Happy Ending
★★★12

Romantic comedy
2013 · UK · Colour · 97min

This light tale about writer's block stars Karen Gillan as an author who has drawn on her traumatic early years to write a bestseller. The problem for her dishy publisher (Stanley Weber) is that, on the back of her success, Gillan is happy and is suffering from a serious case of writer's block. So he sets out to sabotage her life in order to make her productive again. Gillan is utterly charming, but it's impossible to believe in her as a bestselling author - and Weber is so mean-spirited that it is difficult to see his attractions. However, despite the film's flaws, Gillan's passion, director John McKay's nice touches and some attractive Glasgow locations just about save the day. BP Swearing, sexual references. *DVD*

Karen Gillan *Jane Lockhart* • Stanley Weber *Thomas Duval* • Iain De Caestecker *Roddy* • Amy Manson *Darsie* • Henry Ian Cusick *Willie* ■ *Dir* John McKay • *Scr* David Solomons

Not Another Teen Movie
★15

Parody
2001 · US · Colour · 85min

This is a contender for the title of the year's most puerile and vulgar film. A popular teen makes a bet he can get the plainest girl to attend the prom with him, and this pathetic

excuse for humour reinforces every possible negative social stereotype. Former MTV producer and first-time director Joel Gallen throws incest, aneurysms and an avalanche of human waste into the tasteless equation. SF *DVD* CS

Chyler Leigh *Janey Briggs (The Pretty Ugly Girl)* • Chris Evans *Jake Wyler (The Popular Jock)* • Jaime Pressly *Priscilla (The Bitchy Cheerleader)* • Eric Christian Olsen *Austin (The Cocky Blond Guy)* • Mia Kirshner *Catherine (The Cruellest Girl in School)* • Deon Richmond *Malik (The Token Black Guy)* • Mr T *Wise janitor* • Molly Ringwald *Flight attendant* • Randy Quaid *Mr Briggs* ■ *Dir* Joel Gallen • *Scr* Michael G Bender, Adam Jay Epstein, Andrew Jacobson, Phil Beauman, Buddy Johnson

Not as a Stranger
★★★

Medical drama
1955 · US · BW · 136min

After producing many key films, Stanley Kramer turned director with this melodrama. It's about impoverished medical student Robert Mitchum, who marries Swedish nurse Olivia de Havilland because she can pay his tuition fees. Then Mitchum steps out with Gloria Grahame. Containing lots of lurid detail about surgical procedures, this is an occasionally lumpen effort, but the cast is always worth watching. AT

Olivia de Havilland *Kristina Hedvigson* • Robert Mitchum *Lucas Marsh* • Frank Sinatra *Alfred Boone* • Gloria Grahame *Harriet Lang* • Broderick Crawford *Dr Aarons* • Charles Bickford *Dr Runkleman* • Myron McCormick *Dr Snider* • Lon Chaney Jr *Job Marsh* • Lee Marvin *Brundage* ■ *Dir* Stanley Kramer • *Scr* Edna Anhalt, Edward Anhalt, from the novel by Morton Thompson

Not Easily Broken
★★PG

Drama
2009 · US · Colour · 99min

A once-loving marriage is put to the test in this soapy drama set in LA's black community. Morris Chestnut stars as a husband whose baseball career was ended by injury and who now scrapes along as a self-employed builder playing second-fiddle to his acquisitive estate-agent wife (Taraji P Henson). She puts her career first, leaving him unable to play the role of father and provider, as the film trots out a conservative line that everything will be all right if men are allowed to be men, couples pay heed to their church fathers, and wives keep their shrewish mothers at a safe distance. To be fair, this adaptation of a novel by evangelist pastor TD Jakes is undeniably sincere in its aims, but as a movie it's as trite as a greeting card verse and almost as predictable. TJ

Morris Chestnut *Dave Johnson* • Taraji P Henson *Clarice Clark* • Maeve Quinlan *Julie Sawyer* • Kevin Hart *Tree* • Wood Harris *Darnell* • Eddie Cibrian *Brock Houseman* • Jenifer Lewis *Mary "Mama" Clark* ■ *Scr* Brian Bird, from the novel by TD Jakes

Not for Publication
★★★15

Comedy
1984 · US · Colour · 83min

Nancy Allen works for *The Informer*, at one time a crusading newspaper run by her father, but now a sleazy scandal sheet. Sent to interview the mayor of New York (Laurence Luckinbill), Allen finds his campaign plans in a mess and agrees to help out - without revealing his links to the muckraking *Informer*. This 1980s attempt to capture the flavour and style of a 1940s screwball comedy never quite comes off, but delivers plenty of fun along the way. DF

Nancy Allen *Lois Thorndyke* • Laurence Luckinbill *Mayor Claude Franklyn* • David Naughton *Barry Denver* • Alice Ghostley *Doris* • Don Peoples *Cy Katz* • Richard Blackburn *Jim* • Cork Hubbert *Odo* ■ *Dir* Paul Bartel (1) • *Scr* Paul Bartel, John Meyer

Not Here to Be Loved
★★★★15

Comedy
2005 · Fr · Colour · 93min

Lonely 50-something bailiff Patrick Chesnais finds unexpected affection in Stéphane Brizé's slow-burning charmer. Small details are key to this studied portrait of a son whose devotion to his ingrate father (Georges Wilson) not only extends to visiting him at his care home each Sunday,

but also to taking over the detested family business. However, a change at work makes Chesnais realise he has been wasting his life. Exquisitely capturing the melancholy of a stagnating existence, this deft character study is played with an insight and restraint that makes the suppressed passion all the more touching and intense. DP French +subtitles.

Patrick Chesnais *Jean-Claude Delsart* • Anne Consigny *Françoise* • Georges Wilson *Jean-Claude's father* • Lionel Abelanski *Thierry, Françoise's fiancé* • Cyril Couton *Jean-Claude's son* • Marie-Sohna Condé *Rose Diakité* • Anne Benoît *Secretary* ■ *Dir* Stéphane Brizé • *Scr* Juliette Sales, Stéphane Brizé

Not Now, Comrade
★12

Comedy
1976 · UK · Colour · 85min

It's hard to envisage anyone wanting to film any British stage farce. Yet what is so unforgivable about this woeful farrago is that it has been done in such a visually uninteresting way that it comes over as little more than illustrated radio. The fault lies squarely with Ray Cooney, who not only wrote and co-directed, but also co-stars in this horrid comedy of errors about a defecting Russian ballet dancer. DP *DVD*

Leslie Phillips *Commander Rimmington* • Roy Kinnear *Hoskins* • Windsor Davies *Constable Pulford* • Don Estelle *Bobby Hargreaves* • Michele Dotrice *Nancy Rimmington* • Ray Cooney *Mr Laver* • June Whitfield *Janet Rimmington* ■ *Dir* Ray Cooney, Harold Snoad • *Scr* Ray Cooney

Not Now Darling
★★PG

Comedy
1972 · UK · Colour · 90min

What an appalling waste of a remarkable cast that provides a comic link between the golden age of music hall and the *Carry Ons*. Popular 1930s husband-and-wife team Jack Hulbert and Cicely Courtneidge were reunited on screen for the first time in 12 years for this clumsy version of Ray Cooney's long-running West End farce. Leslie Phillips holds this threadbare piece together, as the furrier up to his neck in girlfriends and cheap minks, but it's all rather tatty. DP *DVD*

Leslie Phillips *Gilbert Bodley* • Ray Cooney *Arnold* • Moira Lister *Maude Bodley* • Julie Ege *Janie* • Joan Sims *Miss Tipdale* • Derren Nesbitt *Harry* • Barbara Windsor *Sue* • Jack Hulbert • Cicely Courtneidge ■ *Dir* Ray Cooney, David Croft • *Scr* John Chapman, from the play by Ray Cooney

Not of This Earth
★★★PG

Science-fiction horror
1956 · US · BW · 68min

Cult director Roger Corman mixes science-fiction, horror and humour in his classic alien invasion quickie with vampiric overtones. Paul Birch is a visitor from the planet Davanna on the trail of human blood because his own race is facing extinction from nuclear anaemia. Death rays are generated whenever he removes his black sunglasses. Corman's elegantly styled, fast-paced gem was the first of his prolific output to lace comedy with suspense successfully, inspiring him to continue in the same vein. The head-crushing bat monster is a fine example of pure 1950s pulp sci-fi. AJ *DVD*

Paul Birch *Paul Johnson* • Beverly Garland *Nadine Story* • Morgan Jones (1) *Harry Sherbourne* • William Roerick *Dr Rochelle* • Jonathan Haze *Jeremy Perrin* • Richard Miller [Dick Miller] *Joe Piper* ■ *Dir* Roger Corman • *Scr* Charles Griffith, Mark Hanna

Not of This Earth
★18

Science-fiction horror
1988 · US · Colour · 77min

Ex-porn queen Traci Lords tried to go respectable in this dire remake of Roger Corman's 1956 cult favourite. After opening, for no apparent reason, with numerous clips from the New World Pictures back catalogue, director Jim Wynorski's laughably cheap effort tells exactly the same story as the original: a vampire from outer space checks out Earthlings' blood types for possible invasion purposes. Trash, no flash. AJ

Traci Lords *Nadine Story* • Arthur Roberts *Mr Johnson* • Lenny Juliano *Jeremy* • Ace Mask *Dr Rochelle* • Roger Lodge *Harry* • Michael Delano *Vacuum cleaner salesman* • Rebecca Perle *Davanna Girl* ■ *Dir* Jim Wynorski • *Scr* Jim Wynorski, RJ Robertson, from the 1956 film

Not One Less
★★★★U

Comedy drama
1999 · Chi · Colour · 102min

This sentimental but engaging drama from Zhang Yimou is wryly humanist but politically outspoken, and won the Golden Lion at Venice. It starts out by castigating the shoddiness of the Chinese education system, especially in the poor rural regions. However, once 13-year-old stand-in teacher Wei Minzhi sets off to retrieve the runaway student who can deprive her of a bonus for keeping all 28 charges in class, the focus of protest switches to the exploitation of child labour on the urban black market. DP Mandarin +subtitles. *DVD*

Wei Minzhi • Zhang Huike • Tian Zhenda *Village chief* • Gao Enman *Teacher Gao* ■ *Dir* Zhang Yimou • *Scr* Shi Xiangsheng

Not Quite Hollywood
★★★18

Documentary
2008 · Aus/US · Colour · 98min

The golden age of Australian cinema wasn't just about starchy Victorian dramas, as this eye-opening documentary proves. Beginning in the early 1970s, it celebrates the cheap, lurid and frequently outrageous exploitation ("Ozploitation") films that entertained domestic audiences and thrilled overseas grindhouse fans. Actors, critics and film-makers reminisce about "ocker" comedies, horror and action flicks, accompanied by numerous clips of nudity, gratuitous gore and death-defying stunts. The retro-style graphics and refreshingly tongue-in-cheek tone make this a riotous if not exactly subtle trawl through a neglected corner of Aussie culture. SS *DVD*

Quentin Tarantino • Christopher Lee • George Lazenby • Dennis Hopper • Jamie Lee Curtis • Barry Humphries ■ *Dir/Scr* Mark Hartley

Not Quite Jerusalem
★★15

Comedy drama
1985 · UK · Colour · 109min

This old-fashioned romance from Lewis Gilbert is a pleasant enough yarn about multinational volunteers working on an Israeli kibbutz and the budding relationship that develops between young American Sam Robards and local girl Joanna Pacula. The pacing is a little pedestrian, but it's still the sort of low-key love story that very easy to get lost in. DA

Joanna Pacula *Gila* • Sam Robards *Mike* • Kevin McNally *Pete* • Todd Graff *Rothwell T Schwartz* • Selina Cadell *Carrie* • Bernard Strother *Dave* ■ *Dir* Lewis Gilbert • *Scr* Paul Kember, from his play

Not the Messiah: He's a Very Naughty Boy
★★★PG

Concert documentary
2009 · UK · Colour · 87min

And now for something completely different: filmed in the Royal Albert Hall in October 2009, this "comic oratorio in five parts" is inspired by Monty Python's *The Life of Brian*. Former Python Eric Idle (who co-wrote and acts as narrator) leads the BBC Symphony Orchestra and Chorus through a musical romp that takes the mickey out of Handel and recycles classic gags like "What have the Romans ever done for us?" as comic arias. The inevitable limitations of the staging mean *He's Not the Messiah* rarely raises more than a chortle. Still, you don't have to be a diehard Python fan to smile at the incongruity of it all. JR Some swearing, sexual references. *DVD* BL

Eric Idle *Baritonish* • Michael Palin • Terry Jones • Terry Gilliam • Shannon Mercer *Soprano* • Rosalind Plowright *Mezzo* ■ *Dir* Aubrey Powell • *Scr* Eric Idle, John Du Prez

Not Wanted on Voyage
★U

Comedy
1957 · UK · BW · 70min

A story about a luxury liner and a stolen necklace - sounds familiar? The script of *Titanic* might not be poetry, but it's a darn sight better than the drivel that passes for dialogue in this dismal comedy. Co-screenwriter Michael Pertwee enjoyed considerable success both before and after making a contribution to this venture, which is so unfunny that even gallant troupers Ronald Shiner and Brian Rix cannot conceal their dismay. DP *DVD*

Ronald Shiner *Steward Albert Higgins* • Brian Rix *Steward Cecil Hollebone* • Griffith Jones *Guy Harding* • Catherine Boyle *Julie Haines* • Fabia Drake *Mrs Brough* • Michael Brennan *Chief Steward* ■ *Dir* Maclean Rogers • *Scr* Michael Pertwee, Evadne Price, Roland Pertwee, Jack Marks, from a screenplay (unproduced) by Dudley Sturrock, from the play *Wanted On Voyage* by Evadne Price, Ken Attiwill

Not with My Wife, You Don't! ★★★
Romantic comedy 1966 · US · Colour · 118min

George C Scott, usually associated with heavyweight drama rather than lightweight fluff, here proves his comic strength when he muscles in on the uneasy marriage of US Air Force aide Tony Curtis and Virna Lisi, intent on carrying off the woman for whom he and Curtis once vied when they were Korean War comrades. Comic director Norman Panama and co-writers Larry Gelbart and Peter Barnes make the nonstop contrivance of the situation appear seamless. TH

Tony Curtis *Tom Ferris* • Virna Lisi *Julie Ferris* • George C Scott *"Tank" Martin* • Carroll O'Connor *General Parker* • Richard Eastham *General Walters* • Eddie Ryder *Sgt Gilroy* • George Tyne *Sgt Dogerty* ■ *Dir* Norman Panama • *Scr* Norman Panama, Larry Gelbart, Peter Barnes, from a story by Norman Panama, Melvyn Frank

Not without My Daughter ★★15
Biographical drama 1990 · US · Colour · 111min

A real-life nightmare is turned into an overwrought soap. Betty Mahmoody, played by Sally Field, went to Iran with her doctor husband and their daughter, only to find him becoming a violent tyrant and all rights being taken from her. It took an underground chain of helpers to aid her and her daughter's escape. Sympathy for Field's character is distanced by her hysterical performance, and not even the usually impressive Alfred Molina can believably convey the husband's personality switch. TH Some violence, swearing. *DVD*

Sally Field *Betty Mahmoody* • Alfred Molina *Moody* • Sheila Rosenthal *Mahtob* • Roshan Seth *Houssein* • Sarah Badel *Nicole* • Mony Rey *Ameh Bozorg* • Georges Corraface *Mohsen* ■ *Dir* Brian Gilbert • *Scr* David W Rintels, from the non-fiction book by Betty Mahmoody, William Hoffer

The Notebook ★★★12
Romantic drama 2003 · US · Colour · 118min

A shameless tear-jerker, this skilfully pushes all the right emotional buttons. The movie opens in the present day with elderly James Garner reading to nursing-home resident Gena Rowlands from an old notebook. We then flash back 60 years to an ill-starred teenage romance between poor country boy Ryan Gosling and Rachel McAdams, daughter of rich city folk. The film is slickly made by Rowlands's son, Nick Cassavetes, and the acting is uniformly excellent, but the director should have taken his foot slightly off the slush pedal. DA *DVD*

Ryan Gosling *Noah Calhoun* • Rachel McAdams *Allie Hamilton* • James Garner *Duke* • Gena Rowlands *Allie Calhoun* • James Marsden *Lon* • Kevin Connolly *Fin* • David Thornton *John Hamilton* • Joan Allen *Anne Hamilton* • Sam Shepard *Frank Calhoun* ■ *Dir* Nick Cassavetes • *Scr* Jeremy Leven, Jan Sardi, from a novel by Nicholas Sparks

Notebook on Cities and Clothes ★★★U
Documentary 1989 · W Ger · Colour · 78min

Although this is not as engaging, amusing or as insightful as the somewhat similar *Unzipped*, this documentary by German director Wim Wenders nonetheless provides an astute look at the work and creative process of innovative Japanese fashion designer Yohji Yamamoto. We see him contemplating the relationship between cities, identity and the future of cinema in the digital age. The film culminates in a Paris spring catwalk show at the Louvre and the way in which Wenders draws comparisons between his own work and Yamamoto's high-chic designs is a fascinating exercise. An English language version was also released. AJ In German. *DVD*

Wim Wenders *Narrator* • Yohji Yamamoto ■ *Dir* Wim Wenders • *Scr* Wim Wenders, from an idea by François Burkhardt

Notes on a Scandal ★★★★15
Psychological drama 2006 · UK/US · Colour · 87min

Judi Dench reunites with *Iris* director Richard Eyre to give one of the most intense performances of her career in this gritty, observational drama based on Zoë Heller's bestselling novel. The Oscar-nominated Dench injects malignant spite into the role of Barbara Covett, a lonely teacher who develops a dark obsession with her spirited new colleague Sheba (fellow nominee Cate Blanchett). Dench and Blanchett sink their teeth into their meaty characters, clearly relishing *Closer* writer Patrick Marber's deliciously acerbic script. The film's climax packs less of a punch, but this is still satisfying adult viewing, complemented by a mood-enhancing, Oscar-nominated Philip Glass score. SF Swearing, sexual references. *DVD* *BLU*

Judi Dench *Barbara Covett* • Cate Blanchett *Sheba Hart* • Bill Nighy *Richard Hart* • Andrew Simpson *Steven Connolly* • Phil Davis [Philip Davis] *Brian Bangs* • Michael Maloney *Sandy Pabblem* ■ *Dir* Richard Eyre • *Scr* Patrick Marber, from the novel by Zoë Heller • *Cinematographer* Chris Menges • *Music* Philip Glass

Notes on Blindness ★★★★U
Drama documentary 2016 · UK · Colour · 90min

Sort of a documentary, kind of a drama, an essay of sorts, this isn't quite like any film you've ever seen, unless of course you've seen Clio Barnard's wonderful *The Arbor* which, like this, features actors lip-synching to audio recordings of real people talking about their lives. The life and voice at the centre of this richly evocative and thought-provoking film is that of John Hull, an Australian academic theologian living in the UK who went blind in 1980, and died, aged 80, in 2015. Determined to make sense of his experience, he started an audio diary. LF

Dan Renton Skinner *John Hull* • Simone Kirby *Marilyn Hull* • John Hull • Marilyn Hull ■ *Dir* Pete Middleton, James Spinney

Nothing but a Man ★★★12
Drama 1964 · US · BW · 92min

This engrossing drama stars Ivan Dixon as the black railroad worker in a small Southern town who takes on racist bully-boys so that he can stand tall in front of his wife and family. By making the dilemma small and intimate instead of loud and declamatory, director Michael Roemer ensures the issues involved are relevant to all. TH *DVD*

Ivan Dixon *Duff Anderson* • Abbey Lincoln *Josie Dawson* • Gloria Foster *Lee* • Julius Harris *Will Anderson* • Yaphet Kotto *Jocko* ■ *Dir* Michael Roemer • *Scr* Michael Roemer, Robert Young

Nothing but the Best ★★★★
Black comedy satire 1963 · UK · Colour · 97min

Scripted by Frederic Raphael, photographed by Nicolas Roeg and directed by Clive Donner, this has all the credentials to be one of the best British big-screen satires. There's no denying it's a very funny film, a sort of *School for Scoundrels* in a *Room at the Top* but the brushstrokes are so broad that there is no room for the finer detail that would have made it a classic. Alan Bates is splendid as a working-class wannabe but Denholm Elliott steals every scene as an indolent aristocrat who tutors him in the delicate art of being a cad. DP

Alan Bates *Jimmy Brewster* • Denholm Elliott *Charlie Prince* • Harry Andrews *Mr Horton* • Millicent Martin *Ann Horton* • Pauline Delany *Mrs March* • Godfrey Quigley *Coates* • Alison Leggatt *Mrs Brewster* ■ *Dir* Clive Donner • *Scr* Frederic Raphael, from the short story *The Best of Everything* by Stanley Ellin

Nothing but the Night ★★12
Supernatural murder mystery 1972 · UK · Colour · 87min

The first and last production from Christopher Lee's own company, Charlemagne, is a silly, supernatural variant on *Village of the Damned*. The brooding atmosphere of John Blackburn's possession novel goes awry under horror stalwart Peter Sasdy's confusing direction, leading to a complete absence of menace or suspense. A patchy affair. AJ *DVD*

Christopher Lee *Colonel Bingham* • Peter Cushing *Sir Mark Ashley* • Diana Dors *Anna Harb* • Georgia Brown *Joan Foster* • Keith Barron *Dr Haynes* • Gwyneth Strong *Mary Valley* • Fulton Mackay *Cameron* • John Robinson (1) *Lord Fawnlee* • Michael Gambon *Inspector Grant* ■ *Dir* Peter Sasdy • *Scr* Brian Hayles, from the novel by John Blackburn

Nothing but the Truth ★★★
Comedy 1941 · US · BW · 90min

This has a sure-fire plot in its story of a young man who vows to tell the absolute truth for 24 hours. Though slow to start, it pays off in the second half during a party on a yacht at which the hero's dilemma becomes increasingly farcical. Bob Hope was a master at this sort of thing and the vivacious Paulette Goddard always teamed well with him – this was their third film together. TV

Bob Hope *Steve Bennett* • Paulette Goddard *Gwen Saunders* • Edward Arnold *TT Ralston* • Leif Erickson *Tom Van Deusen* • Helen Vinson *Linda Graham* • Willie Best *Samuel* • Clarence Kolb *Mr James P Van Deusen* ■ *Dir* Elliott Nugent • *Scr* Don Hartman, Ken Englund, from the play by James Montgomery, from the novel by Frederick S Isham

Nothing but Trouble ★★U
Comedy 1944 · US · BW · 66min

A mawkish late entry from Laurel and Hardy working for a studio (MGM) which didn't understand their needs, so straitjacketed them into an oddly unlikeable story. Stan and Ollie are descendants of a long line of butlers and chefs whose own culinary disasters make them pariahs. They befriend boy king David Leland, who is in peril from his uncle Philip Merivale. The attempted murder puts the glooms on Stan and Ollie's light-hearted spirits. TH *DVD*

Stan Laurel *Stan* • Oliver Hardy *Oliver* • Mary Boland *Mrs Elvira Hawkley* • Philip Merivale *Prince Saul* • Henry O'Neill *Mr Basil Hawkley* • David Leland *King Christopher* • John Warburton *Ronetz* ■ *Dir* Sam Taylor • *Scr* Russell Rouse, Ray Golden, Bradford Ropes, Margaret Gruen, from an idea by Robert Halff

Nothing but Trouble ★15
Fantasy comedy 1991 · US · Colour · 89min

"Wasn't Worth the Trouble" might have been a more suitable title for a lousy comedy that rips off the premise of Peter Weir's cult classic, *The Cars That Ate Paris*. Dan Aykroyd wrote and directed this calamity, in which he also stars as a sadistic judge who delights in tormenting unsuspecting motorists. Chevy Chase and Demi Moore deserve no sympathy: they read the script before they signed on. DP

Chevy Chase *Chris Thorne* • Dan Aykroyd *"JP"/ Bobo* • John Candy *Dennis/Eldona* • Demi Moore *Diane Lightson* • Taylor Negron *Fausto* • Bertila Damas *Renalda* ■ *Dir* Dan Aykroyd • *Scr* Dan Aykroyd, from a story by Peter Aykroyd

Nothing in Common ★★15
Drama 1986 · US · Colour · 114min

Once the king of American TV comedy, Jackie Gleason stars as the washed-up rag trader who foists himself on his yuppie son (Tom Hanks) after his wife of 36 years, Eva Marie Saint, walks out on him. Director Garry Marshall treats the veteran Gleason with far too much respect, allowing him to get away with a hugely self-indulgent performance. Even Hanks is below his best. DP Swearing. *DVD*

Tom Hanks *David Basner* • Jackie Gleason *Max Basner* • Eva Marie Saint *Lorraine Basner* • Hector Elizondo *Charlie Gargas* • Barry Corbin *Andrew Woolridge* • Bess Armstrong *Donna Mildred Martin* • Sela Ward *Cheryl Ann Wayne* ■ *Dir* Garry Marshall • *Scr* Rick Podell, Michael Preminger

Nothing Lasts Forever ★★★15
Comedy 1984 · US · Colour and BW · 155min

This is a rather bizarre but entertaining comedy shot in colour and black and white, with Zach Galligan as an artist experiencing life in the New York of the future. Most notable for its quirky cast, this was produced by *Saturday Night Live*'s Lorne Michaels, but is far stranger than anything that appeared on that innovative show. Not to everyone's taste, but definitely worth a look. JB

Zach Galligan *Adam Beckett* • Lauren Tom *Ely* • Apollonia Van Ravenstein *Mara Hofmeier* • Dan Aykroyd *Buck Heller* • Imogene Coca *Daisy Schackman* • Eddie Fisher • Mort Sahl *Uncle Mort* • Bill Murray ■ *Dir* Tom Schiller • *Scr* Tom Schiller

Nothing Personal ★★★15
Drama 1995 · UK/Ire · Colour · 81min

In striving for balance, Thaddeus O'Sullivan's pre-Irish peace process drama fails to deliver its intended statement and ends up merely reinforcing the clichés and stereotypes that exist on either side of the divide, while its murderous conclusion is cheaply manipulative. John Lynch is too familiar as the father who finds himself on the front line, while Ian Hart is wildly over-the-top as a trigger-happy bigot. Yet the solid work of Michael Gambon and James Frain, makes it worth watching. DP Violence, swearing. *DVD*

Ian Hart *Ginger* • John Lynch *Liam* • James Frain *Kenny* • Michael Gambon *Leonard* • Gary Lydon *Eddie* • Ruaidhri Conroy *Tommy* ■ *Dir* Thaddeus O'Sullivan • *Scr* Daniel Mornin, from his novel *All Our Fault*

Nothing Sacred ★★★U
Screwball comedy 1937 · US · Colour · 73min

A cynical black comedy from the acid pen of former journalist Ben Hecht, this is terrifically acted by Fredric March as a tabloid reporter and Carole Lombard as a Vermont girl whose last wish before she dies of radium poisoning is to see New York. Of course, she isn't really dying, but that doesn't stop March from exploiting her case to the hilt, and allowing Hecht to take swipes at his former profession. Tasteless, certainly, and not quite as funny as it thinks it is. TS

Carole Lombard *Hazel Flagg* • Fredric March *Wally Cook* • Charles Winninger *Dr Downer* • Walter Connolly *Stone* • Sig Rumann [Sig Ruman] *Dr Eggelhoffer* • Frank Fay *Master of Ceremonies* • Maxie Rosenbloom *Max Levinsky* • Hattie McDaniel *Mrs Walker* • Hedda Hopper *Dowager* ■ *Dir* William Wellman [William A Wellman] • *Scr* Ben Hecht, Ring Lardner Jr, Budd Schulberg, from the story *Letter to the Editor* by James H Street [James Street]

Nothing to Lose ★★15
Action comedy 1997 · US · Colour · 93min

Tim Robbins stars in this glossy but empty-headed buddy movie. He plays a stressed-out exec who thinks his wife (Kelly Preston) is having an affair with his boss (Michael McKean). Seeking revenge, he finds an unlikely ally in petty thief Martin Lawrence. The two stars do their best with the comic crumbs they are handed, but they are hampered by the fact that this is an action comedy where nothing really happens. JF Swearing, violence, a sex scene. *DVD* *CS*

Martin Lawrence *T Paul* • Tim Robbins *Nick Beam* • John C McGinley *Davis "Rig" Lanlow* • Giancarlo Esposito *Charlie Dunt* • Kelly Preston *Ann* • Michael McKean *Phillip Barrow* ■ *Dir/Scr* Steve Oedekerk

Notorious ★★★★★ U

Classic romantic thriller 1946 · US · BW · 97min

Scripted by hard-boiled veteran Ben Hecht and boasting a highly topical uranium MacGuffin, this isn't as thematically complex or technically audacious as some of Alfred Hitchcock's later classics. But it's still hard to beat for pure, polished entertainment. Cary Grant and Ingrid Bergman are perfectly paired as an American agent and the high-living daughter of a Nazi sympathiser whom he has under surveillance. Yet they're almost upstaged by Claude Rains, who invests his treacherous villain with a modicum of humanity. Hitch permits himself one moment of visual virtuosity (a stunning crane shot swooping towards a key in Bergman's hand), but mostly confines himself to spinning his yarn with customarily mischievous skill. DP *DVD*

Cary Grant *TR Devlin* • Ingrid Bergman *Alicia Huberman* • Claude Rains *Alexander Sebastian* • Louis Calhern *Paul Prescott* • Madame Konstantin [Leopoldine Konstantin] *Mme Anna Sebastian* • Reinhold Schünzel *Dr Anderson/Otto Rensler* ■ *Dir* Alfred Hitchcock • *Scr* Ben Hecht • *Cinematographer* Ted Tetzlaff

Notorious ★★ 15

Biographical drama 2009 · US · Colour · 122min

In this rags-to-riches true story, Jamal Woolard fits snugly into the extra-large shoes of Brooklyn-born rapper Christopher Wallace, better known as The Notorious BIG. The singer's mother Voletta co-produced the film with, among others, Sean "P Diddy" Combs (sharply portrayed here by Derek Luke), the man who gave the ex-drug dealer a record deal and sang a chart-topping tribute to him following his murder in 1997. The fatal shooting was seen as reprisal for the gunning down of LA rapper-turned-actor Tupac Shakur months earlier. Unfortunately, director George Tillman Jr doesn't get to the root of the trouble between one-time friends "Biggie" and Tupac (Anthony Mackie), preferring instead to wheel out the clichés of the "player" lifestyle. SP *DVD*

Angela Bassett *Voletta Wallace* • Jamal Woolard *Christopher "Biggie" Wallace* • Derek Luke *Sean "Puffy" Combs* • Anthony Mackie *Tupac Shakur* • Antonique Smith *Faith Evans* • Naturi Naughton *Lil' Kim* • Sean Ringgold *Suge Knight* • *Dir* George Tillman Jr • *Scr* Reggie Rock Bythewood, Cheo Hodari Coker

The Notorious Bettie Page ★★★ 18

Biographical drama
2005 · US · BW and Colour · 90min

A pin-up icon in the 1950s, Bettie Page comes under the spotlight in this shallow yet breezy biopic. Centred on a deliciously radiant performance by Gretchen Mol, it explores how the God-fearing Nashville girl shot to fame as a fetish model, only to return to normal life after being targeted in a 1955 US Senate crusade against pornography. Mol's purity-oozing Page is just one of a host of frothy characters that give the picture its charm and sunny atmosphere. But visual superficialities rather than perceptive insights drive the flimsy narrative, with the end result being a nostalgic slice of ocular titillation that scarcely scratches the surface of its subject. SF Sexual violence, swearing, nudity. *DVD*

Gretchen Mol *Bettie Page* • Chris Bauer *Irving Klaw* • Jared Harris *John Willie* • Sarah Paulson *Bunny Yeager* • Cara Seymour *Maxie* • David Strathairn *Estes Kefauver* • Lili Taylor *Paula Klaw* • Jonathan Woodward [Jonathan M Woodward] *Marvin* ■ *Dir* Mary Harron • *Scr* Mary Harron, Guinevere Turner, from the biography *The Real Bettie Page* by Richard Foster

The Notorious Landlady ★★★

Comedy mystery 1962 · US · BW · 126min

This eccentric comedy mystery set principally in London boasts a sparkling cast led by Jack Lemmon, Kim Novak and, briefly, Fred Astaire. Lemmon plays a newly arrived diplomat whose landlady, Miss Novak, is suspected of murdering her husband who has vanished. When the husband does appear, Novak promptly shoots him. After that twist the plot thickens. London was created entirely on studio sets, giving the film an arch theatricality. AT

Kim Novak *Carlye Hardwicke* • Jack Lemmon *William Gridley* • Fred Astaire *Franklyn Ambruster* • Lionel Jeffries *Inspector Oliphant* • Estelle Winwood *Mrs Dunhill* • Maxwell Reed *Miles Hardwicke* • Philippa Bevans *Mrs Brown* ■ *Dir* Richard Quine • *Scr* Larry Gelbart, Blake Edwards, from a story by Margery Sharp

The Notorious Mr Bout ★★★★ 12

Documentary 2014 · Rus/US · Colour · 86min

In real life, Russian arms dealer Viktor Bout seems more like a Sacha Baron Cohen creation than the avaricious monster depicted by Nicolas Cage in Andrew Niccol's 2005 film á clef, *Lord of War*. Seizing upon the opportunities presented by the fall of Communism, Bout became a millionaire by the age of 25, with a fleet of cargo planes delivering goods around the world. But he was also happy to deliver weapons, seemingly without a hint of conscience. As Tony Gerber and Maxim Pozdorovkin's riveting documentary unfolds, it becomes easier to equate this roguish buffoon with the banality of evil. DP In Russian, English. Swearing.

■ *Dir* Tony Gerber, Maxim Pozdorovkin

Notre Musique ★★★ 12

Political drama
2004 · Fr/Swi · Colour and BW · 76min

The opening montage of harrowing war footage culled from both fictional and documentary sources is reason enough to tackle this typically provocative offering from director Jean-Luc Godard. But his modern variation on Dante's *Divine Comedy* also throws up all manner of contentious social and political issues, as Jewish journalist Sarah Adler seeks answers and inspiration at a literary conference in postwar Sarajevo. Godard consistently demonstrates a passion for cinema and imaginative use of imagery, and the result is eclectic and demanding. DP French, English, Spanish, Arabic, Serbo-Croat +subtitles. *DVD*

Sarah Adler *Judith Lerner* • Nade Dieu *Olga Brodsky* • Jean-Luc Godard *The Film-maker* • Rony Kramer *Ramos Garcia* • Georges Aguilar *American Indian* • Leticia Gutiérrez *American Indian* • Simon Eine *Ambassador* ■ *Dir/Scr* Jean-Luc Godard

La Notte ★★★★★ 12

Drama 1961 · Fr/It · BW · 116min

Michelangelo Antonioni's famous study of a marriage on the rocks stars Marcello Mastroianni as a novelist who blames his wife, Jeanne Moreau, for his lack of inspiration. She, in turn, feels ignored and patronised. After visiting a friend in hospital, Mastroianni and Moreau have an argument and separate. She spends the night wandering through the ugly bits of Milan; she goes to a party and pursues a virtually catatonic Monica Vitti. Mastroianni and Moreau loathed their parts, their director and the favouritism that he showed to Vitti, who was then his mistress. Yet this is, first and foremost, a director's film: rigidly controlled, very slow and with dazzling shots of the modern city that seem to infect the characters' despair and alienation. Dated it may be, but *La Notte* remains a mesmeric movie that cracks open the shell of the human soul. AT In Italian. *DVD*

Marcello Mastroianni *Giovanni Pontano* • Jeanne Moreau *Lidia Pontano* • Monica Vitti *Valentina Gherardini* • Bernhard Wicki *Tommaso* ■

Dir Michelangelo Antonioni • *Scr* Michelangelo Antonioni, Ennio Flaiano, Tonino Guerra, from a story by Michelangelo Antonioni

Notting Hill ★★★★ 15

Romantic comedy
1999 · US/UK · Colour · 123min

The *Four Weddings* team produced another smash with this charming tale of bumbling bookshop owner Hugh Grant falling for the "most famous actress in the world", Julia Roberts. Inevitably, the course of true love is a bumpy road, with friends, family and flatmates getting in the way, but that's the cue for a series of screamingly funny scenarios. Saturated with wit and well directed by Roger Michell, the film was bashed by sceptics for its fluffiness and lack of realism (for a racially mixed area of London, there's not a black face to be seen). But, if you can accept the context as 100 per cent white middle class, it's an intensely enjoyable experience. LH Swearing. *DVD* *SD*

Julia Roberts *Anna Scott* • Hugh Grant *William Thacker* • Hugh Bonneville *Bernie* • Emma Chambers *Honey* • James Dreyfus *Martin* • Rhys Ifans *Spike* • Tim McInnerny *Max* • Gina McKee *Bella* • Richard McCabe *Tony* ■ *Dir* Roger Michell • *Scr* Richard Curtis

Nous Sommes Tous des Assassins ★★★

Drama 1952 · Fr · BW · 107min

From the early 1950s, André Cayatte's popular films – more radical in content than form – tackled such topics as euthanasia, juvenile delinquency, police corruption and, until the film was suppressed, false arrest. This movie about French complacency towards the death penalty evoked heated debate in its depiction of the experiences of several men on death row. One of them – a war hero – is accused of killing a policeman, but we never learn his fate or whether or not he is guilty. The emphatic title leaves us in no doubt about Cayatte's attitude to "legalised murder". The film won the special jury prize at Cannes. BB In French.

Marcel Mouloudji *René Le Guen* • Raymond Pellegrin *Gino* • Antoine Balpêtré *Dr Albert Dutoit* • Claude Laydu *Philippe Arnaud* • Paul Frankeur *Leon* ■ *Dir* André Cayatte • *Scr* André Cayatte, Charles Spaak

La Nouvelle Eve ★★★ 18

Romantic drama 1998 · Fr · Colour · 88min

A lifeguard with a fierce sense of independence may sound like an unlikely *femme fatale*, but that's exactly what Karin Viard plays in this quirky romantic comedy, set in the new Eden of 1990s Paris. However, in ambitiously updating notions of the stock literary heroine, director Catherine Corsini tempers Viard's pursuit of a politically active family man (Pierre-Loup Rajot) by adopting the rosy view that everyone's soulmate is out there somewhere. DP French +subtitles. Sex scenes. *DVD*

Karin Viard *Camille* • Pierre-Loup Rajot *Alexis* • Catherine Frot *Isabelle* • Sergi Lopez *Ben* • Laurent Lucas *Emile* • Mireille Roussel *Louise* • Nozha Khouadra *Solveig* • Valentine Vidal *Sophie* ■ *Dir* Catherine Corsini • *Scr* Catherine Corsini, Marc Syrigas, Emmanuel Bourdieu, Denyse Rodriguez-Tome

Nouvelle-France ★ 12

Historical drama
2004 · Can/Fr/UK · Colour · 137min

Witchcraft, deceit, betrayal, Voltaire... everything's thrown into this slow-moving tale of doomed romance set against a backdrop of England's 18th-century battle for French Canada. Yet despite its epic intentions, the historically inaccurate drama is flat and unconvincing, as dying Quebec priest Gérard Depardieu confesses to the tragedy he caused by trying to separate socially disparate lovers Noémie Godin-Vigneau and David La Haye. The resulting flashback-narrative looks and feels like a cheap TV movie. SF In English, French. Violence, sex scenes. *DVD*

Noémie Godin-Vigneau *Marie-Loup Carignan* • David La Haye *Francois Le Gardeur* • Sebastien Huberdeau *Xavier Maillard* • Juliette Gosselin *France Carignan, age ten* • Irène Jacob *Angelique de Roquebrune* • Tim Roth *William Pitt* • Gérard Depardieu *Father Thomas Blondeau* • Jason Isaacs *General James Wolfe* ■ *Dir* Jean Beaudin • *Scr* Pierre Billon

Nouvelle Vague ★★★

Drama 1990 · Swi/Fr · Colour · 90min

Seducing us with some lustrous visuals before disarming our expectations with a melodramatic storyline and dialogue taken from a range of literary, philosophical and cinematic sources, this is something of a curate's egg from Jean-Luc Godard. Despite his dual involvement, Alain Delon looks curiously detached from the proceedings as he returns to wreak his revenge on murderous aristocrat Domiziana Giordano. Everything from socio-political allegory to morality tale is there if you can be bothered to scour the stylised imagery. DP In French.

Alain Delon *Roger Lennox/Richard Lennox* • Domiziana Giordano *Countess Elena Torlato-Favrini* • Roland Amstutz *Jules the gardener* ■ *Dir/Scr* Jean-Luc Godard

November Christmas ★★★

Drama 2010 · US · Colour

Compassionate acts have a snowball effect across a small-town community in this simple but huge-hearted festive tale about healing and the magic of human kindness. Directed with warmth and sensitivity by veteran film-maker Robert Harmon (*The Hitcher*), the short story-based feature allows the delightfully natural performances to speak for themselves, as perceptive farmer Sam Elliott helps a seriously ill child and her family celebrate Halloween. Elliott's relaxed charm and his character's innate goodness really make this a TV movie to remember. SF

Sam Elliott *Jess Sanford* • John Corbett *Tom Marks* • Sarah Paulson *Beth Marks* • Emily Alyn Lind *Vanessa Marks* ■ *Dir* Robert Harmon • *Scr* Pnenah Goldstein, from a short story by Greg Coppa

The November Man ★★★ 15

Spy thriller 2014 · US · Colour · 107min

Twelve years on from his last 007 adventure, Pierce Brosnan returns to the world of espionage, playing a retired operative looking for answers after one last mission goes awry. With spectacular car chases, sleazy Eastern European contacts and a mission of revenge, this is a Brosnan-era Bond in all but name. However, the star clearly relishes getting back in the action and delivers an interestingly cold, ruthless antihero who bounds between set pieces with ageless enthusiasm. The plot is by the numbers, but the movie is a welcome return for Brosnan to the genre that made him famous. JL Violence, swearing, a sex scene, drug abuse, brief nudity.

Pierce Brosnan *Peter Devereaux* • Luke Bracey *David Mason* • Olga Kurylenko *Alice Fournier* • Eliza Taylor *Sarah* • Caterina Scorsone *Celia* • Bill Smitrovich *John Hanley* ■ *Dir* Roger Donaldson • *Scr* Michael Finch, Karl Gajdusek, from Bill Granger's novel *There Are No Spies*

Novocaine ★★ 15

Black comedy mystery
2001 · US · Colour · 90min

Director David Atkins bites off more than he can chew in this numbingly mediocre comedy. Opening improbably and becoming increasingly implausible by the minute, the story turns on respectable dentist Steve Martin's dangerous liaison with tearaway Helena Bonham Carter and her drug-dealing brother, Scott Caan. Only Laura Dern, as Martin's fiancée, makes an impression. DP *DVD*

Steve Martin *Dr Frank Sangster* • Helena Bonham Carter *Susan Ivey* • Laura Dern *Jean Noble* • Elias Koteas *Harlan Sangster* • Scott Caan *Duane* • Keith David *Detective Lunt* • Lynne Thigpen *Pat* • Kevin Bacon *Lance Phelps* ■ *Dir* David Atkins • *Scr* David Atkins, from a story by David Atkins, Paul Felopulos

Now and Forever ★★
Comedy drama 1934 · US · BW · 81min

Gary Cooper steals some jewellery and hides it in the teddy bear belonging to his small daughter. When they're discovered, his mistress, Carole Lombard, takes the blame, and Cooper allows the owner of the gems to adopt his child. This is a run-of-the-mill affair, with neither star shining too brightly. Its main attraction is the appearance of six-year-old Shirley Temple as Coop's daughter. RK

Gary Cooper *Jerry Day* • Carole Lombard *Toni Carstairs* • Shirley Temple *Penelope Day* • Guy Standing *Felix Evans* • Charlotte Granville *Mrs JHP Crane* • Gilbert Emery *James Higginson* ■ *Dir* Henry Hathaway • *Scr* Vincent Lawrence, Sylvia Thalberg, from the story *Honor Bright* by Jack Kirkland, Melville Baker

Now and Then ★★★ PG
Drama 1995 · US · Colour · 98min

Demi Moore co-produced this female version of *Stand by Me*, which follows four young girls (Gaby Hoffmann, Christina Ricci, Thora Birch, Ashleigh Aston Moore) in 1970 as they attempt to solve the mystery of the death of a local boy. It's a simple, small-town story, bookended by the present-day revelations of the girls, now grown up into Moore, Melanie Griffith, Rita Wilson and Rosie O'Donnell. A sweet 1970s nostalgia trip. JB Swearing. *DVD*

Demi Moore *Samantha Albertson* • Melanie Griffith *Tina "Teeny" Tercell* • Rosie O'Donnell *Roberta Martin* • Rita Wilson *Christina "Chrissy" Dewitt* • Christina Ricci *Young Roberta* • Thora Birch *Young Teeny* • Gaby Hoffmann *Young Samantha* • Ashleigh Aston Moore *Young Chrissy* ■ *Dir* Lesli Linka Glatter • *Scr* I Marlene King

Now Barabbas Was a Robber ★★★
Prison drama 1949 · UK · BW · 84min

"Elsie's Dad is inside again" reads the chalk message on a prison wall, one of several humorous touches in an otherwise sombre story of prison life. The assorted inmates include a bigamist, an embezzler, an Irish terrorist (strikingly portrayed by Richard Burton in his second screen role) and a well-mannered murderer about to be executed (a likeable performance by Richard Greene). Ably directed by Gordon Parry, this film version of William Douglas Home's play argues against the death penalty, but had the development of a homosexual relationship cut by the censor. AE

Richard Greene *Tufnell* • Cedric Hardwicke *Governor* • Kathleen Harrison *Mrs Brown* • Ronald Howard *Roberts, bank cashier* • Stephen Murray *Chaplain* • William Hartnell *Warder Jackson* • Beatrice Campbell *Kitty* • Richard Burton *Paddy* • Kenneth More *Spencer* • Dora Bryan *Winnie* ■ *Dir* Gordon Parry • *Scr* Gordon Parry, from the play by William Douglas Home

NOW: In the Wings on a World Stage ★★★
Documentary 2014 · US · Colour · 96min

Despite the surfeit of effusively erudite platitudes, this backstage account of the Old Vic's 2011-12 tour of Richard III offers genuine insights into the rigours and romance of the theatre. Mounted by Kevin Spacey and Sam Mendes, the Anglo-American production played to packed houses around the world. But, while there is overlap with Al Pacino's *Looking for Richard* (1996) in the textual analysis, debutant Jeremy Whelehan concentrates on the mechanics of taking a large company on the road. It's just a pity we get to see so little of the wittily staged Shakespeare. DP Swearing. *DVD*

Kevin Spacey • Sam Mendes ■ *Dir* Jeremy Whelehan

Now Is Good ★★ 12
Romantic drama 2012 · UK/Fr · Colour · 98min

Despite his terrific cast and solid production values, writer/director Ol Parker fumbles the potential of Jenny Downham's young adult novel *Before I Die* in this overlong, meandering mush of a movie. Dakota

Fanning's cut-glass accent never slips as the American plays a glazed-over English teenager who's dying from leukemia but chooses to do so on her own terms. This mopey soap may find an audience with young teens and fans of weepies, but everyone else may be find it all a bit cringe-making. KK Swearing, drug abuse, sexual references. *DVD*

Dakota Fanning *Tessa Scott* • Jeremy Irvine *Adam* • Paddy Considine *Father* • Kaya Scodelario *Zoey* • Olivia Williams *Mother* • Patrick Baladi *Richard* ■ *Dir* Ol Parker • *Scr* Ol Parker, from the novel *Before I Die* by Jenny Downham

Now, Voyager ★★★★★ PG
Classic romantic melodrama 1942 · US · BW · 113min

Bette Davis gives a consummate performance as the lifelong spinster emerging from her confining chrysalis into the arms of Paul Henreid in this lush, beautifully acted movie. One of the all-time great weepies, it has gone down in the annals of cinema history for Henreid's lighting of two cigarettes scene and a tear-jerking speech from Davis, at her best in front of a moonlit sky. Irving Rapper's direction is suitably grand and cinematographer Sol Polito lights everything with an almost magical touch. It's a movie in which all the elements come together in perfect harmony to give an essentially hackneyed theme the imprint of greatness. SH *DVD*

Bette Davis *Charlotte Vale* • Paul Henreid *Jerry Durrance* • Claude Rains *Dr Jaquith* • Gladys Cooper *Mrs Henry Windle Vale* • Bonita Granville *June Vale* • John Loder *Elliot Livingston* • Ilka Chase *Lisa Vale* • Mary Wickes *Dora Pickford* • Janis Wilson *Tina Durrance* ■ *Dir* Irving Rapper • *Scr* Casey Robinson, from the novel by Olive Higgins Prouty • *Music* Max Steiner

Now You See Me ★★★ 12
Caper 2013 · US · Colour · 110min

This fast-paced drama features a quartet of flashy Las Vegas magicians, including Jesse Eisenberg and Woody Harrelson, who use their elaborate stage illusions as a front for a series of audacious bank robberies. FBI agent Mark Ruffalo enlists the help of magic specialist Morgan Freeman to figure out how the modern-day Robin Hoods pull off their spectacular feats. Old hands Freeman and Michael Caine, as the magicians' moneybags benefactor, bring gravitas to a likeable tale, while Eisenberg and Harrelson add a touch of subversive attitude to a glitzy showbiz world. A sequel is due in 2016. TeS Some violence, swearing, sexual references. *DVD* *Blu-ray* *CS*

Jesse Eisenberg *J Daniel Atlas* • Mark Ruffalo *Dylan Rhodes* • Woody Harrelson *Merritt McKinney* • Morgan Freeman *Thaddeus Bradley* • Michael Caine *Arthur Tressler* • Isla Fisher *Henley Reeves* ■ *Dir* Louis Leterrier • *Scr* Edward Ricourt, Ed Solomon, Boaz Yakin, from a story by Yakin, Ricourt

Now You See Me 2 ★★ 12A
Crime caper 2016 · US · Colour · 129min

The magicians who rob the super-rich return for more digital illusion in this bustling caper sequel. The gang of Jesse Eisenberg, Woody Harrelson and Dave Franco are joined by Lizzy Caplan as the token feisty female, and this time they find themselves tangling with tech-magnate Daniel Radcliffe (trying too hard), while the previous movie's illusionist-debunker Morgan Freeman plots revenge from prison. First-time round, the trickery seemed fresh enough, but now the magic sadly just isn't there. TJ Some violence, swearing.

Jesse Eisenberg *J Daniel Atlas* • Mark Ruffalo *Dylan Rhodes* • Woody Harrelson *Merritt McKinney* • Dave Franco *Jack Wilder* • Daniel Radcliffe *Walter Mabry* • Lizzy Caplan *Lula* • Morgan Freeman *Thaddeus Bradley* • Michael Caine *Arthur Tressler* ■ *Dir* Jon M Chu • *Scr* Ed Solomon, Peter Chiarelli, from characters by Boaz Yakin, Edward Ricourt

Nowhere ★★★ 18
Experimental comedy drama 1997 · US/Fr · Colour · 78min

Gregg Araki is certainly a film-making original, expressing teenage disillusionment through an otherwordly Los Angeles populated by surreal characters, trippy production design (the pop-art decor echoes each teen's inner psyche) and pounding music. This charts a day in the lives of the young, the restless and the really disturbed. The attractive cast is a who's who of teen talent. JC Violence, sex scenes, drug abuse. *DVD*

James Duval *Dark* • Rachel True *Mel* • Nathan Bexton *Montgomery* • Chiara Mastroianni *Kriss* • Debi Mazar *Kozy* • Kathleen Robertson *Lucifer* • Heather Graham *Lilith* • Mena Suvari *Zoe* ■ *Dir/Scr* Gregg Araki

Nowhere Boy ★★★★ 15
Biographical drama 2010 · UK · Colour · 93min

The teenage years of one John Lennon are revealed in this intriguing biopic. In 1950s Liverpool, schoolboy John (played by newcomer Aaron Johnson) is brought up by his stern Aunt Mimi (Kristin Scott Thomas), only to discover that his mother Julia (Anne-Marie Duff) lives nearby with another brood of kids. Persuasive lookalike Johnson holds his own against experienced performers Duff and Scott Thomas (who is as marvellous as ever), while provocative British artist Sam Taylor-Wood takes a surprisingly measured approach in her directorial feature debut. Balancing pop history and evocative period piece, the film is undeniably engrossing and an illuminating addition to the Beatles mythology. TJ Swearing, sex scenes. *DVD* *Blu-ray*

Anne-Marie Duff *Julia Lennon* • Kristin Scott Thomas *Mimi Smith* • Aaron Johnson *John Lennon* • Thomas Brodie Sangster [Thomas Brodie-Sangster] *Paul McCartney* • David Morrissey *Bobby Dykins* • Josh Bolt *Pete* ■ *Dir* Sam Taylor-Wood • *Scr* Matt Greenhalgh • *Cinematographer* Seamus McGarvey

Nowhere in Africa ★★★★ 15
Period drama 2001 · Ger · Colour · 134min

Writer/director Caroline Link has composed a love letter to Africa with this visually stunning and immaculately acted drama. It's the emotional tale of a family of German-Jewish refugees who settle on a remote farm in Kenya in 1938. Against a landscape that can be cruel as well as beautiful, Juliane Köhler and Merab Ninidze and their five-year-old daughter struggle to adjust and survive. Link's drama delivers fresh insight into the Jewish experience of that era for, despite the setting, it's very much a Holocaust story. However, its characters are not victims - they are rounded individuals who provide a striking, and often ironic, portrait of the tenacity of the human spirit. SF English, German, Swahili +subtitles. Swearing, brief nudity. *DVD*

Juliane Köhler *Jettel Redlich* • Merab Ninidze *Walter Redlich* • Sidede Onyulo *Owuor* • Matthias Habich *Süsskind* • Lea Kurka *Regina Redlich, younger* • Karoline Eckertz *Regina Redlich, older* • Gerd Heinz *Max* • Hildegard Schmahl *Ina* ■ *Dir* Caroline Link • *Scr* Caroline Link, from the novel *Nirgendwo in Afrika* by Stefanie Zweig

Nowhere to Go ★★ PG
Crime drama 1958 · UK · BW · 99min

Don't be fooled by the label "Made at Ealing": this is nothing more than a low-budget programme filler. Co-written by director Seth Holt and critic Kenneth Tynan, it is a routine crime drama in which thief George Nader goes into partnership with unscrupulous Bernard Lee. Neither the central round of robberies and escapes nor the finale in the Brecon Beacons are presented with any imagination. Only Maggie Smith, making her film debut, rises above the material. DP *DVD*

George Nader *Paul Gregory* • Maggie Smith *Bridget Howard* • Bernard Lee *Vic Sloane* • Bessie Love *Harriet Jefferson* • Geoffrey Keen *Inspector Scott* • Andrée Melly *Rosa* • Howard Marion-Crawford *Cameron* ■ *Dir* Seth Holt • *Scr* Seth Holt, Kenneth Tynan, from Donald MacKenzie's novel

Nowhere to Hide ★★ 15
Action thriller 1987 · Can · Colour · 90min

This Canadian action thriller boasts some surprisingly good performances, particularly from Amy Madigan as an ex-marine who flees into hiding with her son when crooked defence contractors kill her husband. Michael Ironside also does well as the survivalist who shelters her and helps her fight back. Though made for cinemas, the film has the dark look, tone and slow pacing of a typical, low-budget TV drama. KB

Amy Madigan *Barbara Cutter* • Michael Ironside *Ben* • John Colicos *General Howard* • Daniel Hugh-Kelly *Rob Cutter* • Robin MacEachern *Johnny Cutter* ■ *Dir* Mario Azzopardi • *Scr* Alex Rebar, George Goldsmith, from a story by Alex Rebar

Nowhere to Hide ★★★ 15
Crime thriller 1999 · S Kor · Colour · 96min

Although it looks riotously modern, Lee Myeong-Se's police tale owes as much to Georges Méliès as it does to John Woo. The rain-streaked, neon-tinted vistas lend the complex plot and sardonic voiceover the feel of a latterday *film noir*. But Lee's use of slapstick silhouettes, varied film speeds, caption cards, ironic inserts and the occasional digitised image only serves to emphasise the director's endearingly playful spirit. Park Jung-Hun gives a superbly hard-boiled performance as a world-weary cop enduring endless stakeouts with rookie partner Jang Dong-Keon in pursuit of a killer. DP Korean +subtitles. *DVD*

Park Joong-Hoon *Detective Woo* • Ang Seong-Ki *Chang Sungmin* • Jang Dong-Keon [Jang Dong-gun] *Detective Kim* ■ *Dir/Scr* Lee Myeong-Se

Nowhere to Land ★★ 12
Thriller 2000 · US/Aus · Colour · 87min

Prolific TV director Armand Mastroianni trots out all the clichés in this leaden plane-in-peril thriller. But rather than the usual political terrorist planting a biochemical device onboard a Boeing 747, it's an individual with a more personal axe to grind who creates chaos on the Sydney to LA flight. Given the increased state of airport security post 9/11, many events are hard to swallow, while an overall lack of tension and emotion only highlights the plot's formulaic nature. Ernie Hudson proves a solid diversion as a bomb expert who guides pilot Jack Wagner through the dismantling process, though the otherwise wooden acting and unconvincing finale swiftly return the film to soap opera territory. SF Some violence. *DVD*

Jack Wagner *Captain John Prescott* • Christine Elise *Kim McGee* • James B Sikking *George Eller* • Ernie Hudson *Danny Gorlin* • Mark Lee *Phillip Deacon* • Rachael Blake *Anne Prescott* • Damian Pike *Agent Mike Tanner* ■ *Dir* Armand Mastroianni • *Scr* Matt Dorff

Nowhere to Run ★★ 15
Romantic action adventure 1992 · US · Colour · 90min

Jean-Claude Van Damme comes unstuck when he attempts to show his more sensitive side in this soft-centred thriller. He plays a convict on the run who holes up with a young widow (Rosanna Arquette) and her children. Bad guy Joss Ackland is trying to evict Arquette from her land, but Van Damme comes to her rescue. The fighting sequences are a letdown. JF Swearing, violence, nudity. *DVD*

Jean-Claude Van Damme *Sam* • Rosanna Arquette *Clydie* • Kieran Culkin *Mookie* • Ted Levine *Mr Dunston* • Tiffany Taubman *Bree* • Edward Blatchford *Lonnie* • Anthony Starke *Billy* • Joss Ackland *Franklin Hale* ■ *Dir* Robert Harmon • *Scr* Joe Eszterhas, Leslie Bohem, Randy Feldman

The Nude Bomb ★ PG
Spy spoof 1980 · US · Colour · 89min

This feature-length adaptation of the 1960s TV spy spoof *Get Smart* has agent Maxwell Smart (Don Adams) called in to stop a madman who is threatening to destroy all the clothing in the world. One has to wonder why the film-makers bothered to get the rights to the show, considering Smart here bears little resemblance to the character in the TV series. This plays like a lame, expanded sitcom that's missing its laughter track. KB

Don Adams *Maxwell Smart/Agent 86* • Sylvia Kristel *Agent 34* • Vittorio Gassman *Nino Salvatore Sebastiani/Norman Saint Sauvage* • Rhonda Fleming *Edith Von Secondberg* • Dana Elcar *Chief* ■ *Dir* Clive Donner • *Scr* Arne Sultan, Bill Dana, Leonard Stern, from characters by Mel Brooks, Buck Henry

Nude on the Moon ★ 15

Cult science-fiction drama
1961 · US · Colour · 70min

"You're acting like a schoolboy. Don't forget we're rocket scientists," says an ageing doctor to a multi-millionaire playboy as they lift off in this weird space oddity from bargain-basement cult director Doris Wishman. Their journey ends, as the title suggests, with the discovery of topless models on the Moon. This pitiful production contains Nasa stock footage and is decorated with toy spaceships, funny-coloured tights and star-covered astronaut boots. AJ *DVD*

Marietta *Cathy/Moon Goddess* ■ *Dir/Scr* Doris Wishman

La Nuit de Varennes ★★ 12

Period drama   1983 · Fr · Colour · 144min

In this historical conceit, various notables arrive by coach at Varennes where the fugitive king Louis XVI and Marie Antoinette were captured. Thus Casanova (Marcello Mastroianni), political theorist Tom Paine (Harvey Keitel) and an Austrian countess (Hanna Schygulla) gather to discuss politics, sex, art, history and everything that can be crammed into almost two and a half hours. An excellent supporting cast should delight followers of European cinema, but Ettore Scola's film is neither as witty nor clever as it thinks it is. AT French +subtitles.

Marcello Mastroianni *Casanova* • Hanna Schygulla *Countess Sophie de la Borde* • Jean-Louis Barrault *Nicolas Edme Restif* • Harvey Keitel *Thomas Paine* • Michel Piccoli *King Louis XVI* • Eléonore Hirt *Queen Marie-Antoinette* • Jean-Louis Trintignant *M Sauce* • Jean-Claude Brialy *M Jacob* ■ *Dir* Ettore Scola • *Scr* Ettore Scola, Sergio Amidei

La Nuit du Carrefour ★★★★

Mystery   1932 · Fr · BW · 75min

The first Georges Simenon story to reach the screen is a triumph of location film-making. Eschewing the studio artifice that characterises so many early talkies, Jean Renoir shot this dense mystery in almost permanent shadow and with direct sound to enhance the atmosphere of Inspector Maigret's pursuit of a murderous jewel thief. Pierre Renoir holds centre stage, while Winna Winifried is the addled, but alluring *femme fatale*. Anticipating the look and feel of *film noir*, this is not just a compelling whodunnit, but also a superbly observed portrait of an isolated community. DP French +subtitles.

Pierre Renoir *Inspector Maigret* • Georges Terof *Lucas* • Winna Winifried *Else Andersen* • Georges Koudria *Carl Andersen* • Dignimont *Oscar* • Lucie Vallat *Michelle* • GA Martin *Granjean* ■ *Dir* Jean Renoir • *Scr* Jean Renoir, from the novel by Georges Simenon

Nuit et Brouillard ★★★★★ 15

Documentary 1955 · Fr · Colour and BW · 30min

Exploring his perennial themes of time and memory, Alain Resnais described this documentary as a "warning siren" to those who believed that the horrors of Auschwitz were now consigned to history. Transposing hideous monochrome images of the camp in wartime with prowling takes capturing the melancholic calm that descended in the ensuing decade, the footage is often as unbearable to watch as the crimes are impossible to comprehend. Former deportee Jean Cayrol contributes a commentary that, for all its poignancy, makes several incontrovertible points.

François Truffaut declared this the greatest film ever made. DP French +subtitles. *DVD*
Michel Bouquet *Narrator* ■ *Dir* Alain Resnais • *Scr* Jean Cayrol

La Nuit Fantastique ★★★★

Wartime comedy fantasy
1942 · Fr · BW · 103min

The most widely known of Marcel L'Herbier's sound films was one of the great successes of the French cinema during the occupation. Although this atmospheric comedy fantasy has a dark side, the film catered to a population that needed escapist entertainment. It tells of a student who continually dreams of a woman in white, whom he then meets. He and the woman have a series of fantastic adventures, so that he is still not sure whether he's dreaming or not. Fernand Gravey was soon to join the French Resistance movement, while co-star Micheline Presle continued to work under the Nazi occupation. RB In French.

Fernand Gravey [Fernand Gravet] *Denis* • Micheline Presle *Irène* • Saturnin Fabre *Thalès* • Bernard Blier *Lucien* • Charles Granval *Adalbert* • Jean Parédès *Cadet* • Christiane Néré *Nina* • Michel Vitold *Boris* ■ *Dir* Marcel L'Herbier • *Scr* Louis Chavance, Maurice Henry, Marcel L'Herbier, Henri Jeanson, from a story by Louis Chavance

Les Nuits Fauves ★★★★ 18

Biographical drama   1992 · Fr · Colour · 122min

This brutally honest insight into the mind of an HIV-positive man was written and directed by its bisexual star, Cyril Collard, who succumbed to an Aids-related illness just three days before the film's triumph at the Césars. Also released under its English title *Savage Nights*, this uncompromising picture is made particularly compelling by the credibility of its characters. So what if Collard's actions are reckless, or if teenage waif Romane Bohringer's decision to have unprotected sex with him is incomprehensible? These are the failings and irrationalities of real people. DP French +subtitles. Violence, swearing, sex scenes, drug abuse, nudity.

Cyril Collard *Jean* • Romane Bohringer *Laura* • Carlos Lopez (1) *Samy* • Corine Blue *Laura's mother* • Claude Winter *Jean's mother* • René-Marc Bini *Marc* • Maria Schneider *Noria* ■ *Dir* Cyril Collard • *Scr* Cyril Collard, Jacques Fieschi, from the novel by Cyril Collard

Number One ★★

Drama   1969 · US · Colour · 104min

Seldom have actor and director shown such mutual understanding first time out as Charlton Heston and Tom Gries in the masterly western *Will Penny*. This contemporary version, about an ageing quarterback player with the New Orleans Saints, followed almost immediately, but turned out to be a complete failure. Heston is relatively convincing, albeit no football player, and the setting is interesting, but few scenes really work and the script and direction are slovenly. TS

Charlton Heston *Ron "Cat" Catlan* • Jessica Walter *Julie Catlan* • Bruce Dern *Richie Fowler* • John Randolph *Coach Jim Southerd* • Diana Muldaur *Ann Marley* • GD Spradlin *Dr Tristler* • Richard Elkins *Kelly Williams* ■ *Dir* Tom Gries • *Scr* David Moessinger

Number One ★★ 15

Drama   1984 · UK · Colour · 98min

This British crime drama boasts the presence of two legendary pop stars – Bob Geldof in the lead role and Ian Dury. They put in admirable performances, Geldof as a snooker hustler and Dury as an ineffectual hold-up man. But they and the rest of the cast are let down by wayward direction and an unfocused script, which borrows too blatantly from other films. AJ *DVD*

Bob Geldof *Harry "Flash" Gordon* • Mel Smith *Billy Evans* • Alison Steadman *Doreen* • PH Moriarty *Mike the Throat* • Phil Daniels *Terry the Boxer* • Alfred Molina *Constable Rogers* • Ian Dury *Teddy Bryant* ■ *Dir* Les Blair • *Scr* GF Newman

Number One with a Bullet ★★ 15

Action thriller   1986 · US · Colour · 96min

In this standard action pic, director Jack Smight can do little with the hackneyed cops-versus-drug lord plotline. He does at least manage to wring a few laughs out of the mismatched pairing of Billy Dee Williams, a smooth and urbane cop, and Robert Carradine. Known for his unorthodox police tactics, Carradine is obsessed with bringing down the Mr Big of the Los Angeles drug scene. RS

Robert Carradine *Berzak* • Billy Dee Williams *Hazeltine* • Valerie Bertinelli *Teresa Berzak* • Peter Graves (2) *Captain Ferris* • Doris Roberts *Mrs Berzak* ■ *Dir* Jack Smight • *Scr* Gail Morgan Hickman, Andrew Kurtzman, Rob Riley, James Belushi, from a story by Hickman

Number Seventeen ★★★ U

Crime comedy   1932 · UK · BW · 61min

Anne Grey is the member of a gang of criminals who falls for the gentlemanly detective (John Stuart) who is investigating their nefarious activities, and helps bring her former colleagues to justice. Little-seen and largely forgotten, this is an Alfred Hitchcock film of minor entertainment value but superb technical expertise. It's especially notable for a climactic chase sequence involving a train. RK *DVD*

Leon M Lion *Ben* • Anne Grey *The girl* • John Stuart *Detective* • Garry Marsh *Sheldrake* • Ann Casson *Miss Ackroyd* • Henry Caine *Mr Ackroyd* ■ *Dir* Alfred Hitchcock • *Scr* Alma Reville, Alfred Hitchcock, Rodney Ackland, from a play by J Jefferson Farjeon

The Number 23 ★★ 15

Psychological thriller
2006 · US/Ger · Colour · 93min

From Shakespeare's birth date (23 April 1564) to the time taken for blood to circulate throughout the human body (23 seconds), everything in life connects to the number 23. The so-called "23 enigma" has generated a vast body of literature and now forms the basis of this initially intriguing psychological thriller. Jim Carrey stars as dog-catcher Walter Sparrow, who becomes engrossed in a murder mystery novel given to him by his wife (Virginia Madsen), only to find that the disturbing events it depicts mirror his own past. Director Joel Schumacher neatly disguises the shift-in-reality twist, but visual flair can't disguise the deficiencies of the plot, and as the laughably conventional ending limps into view, *The Number 23* just doesn't add up. AJ Violence, swearing. *DVD* ◁

Jim Carrey *Walter Sparrow/Fingerling* • Virginia Madsen *Agatha Sparrow/Fabrizia* • Logan Lerman *Robin Sparrow* • Danny Huston *Isaac French/Dr Miles Phoenix* • Lynn Collins *Suicide blonde/Mrs Dobkins/Young Fingerling's mother* • Rhona Mitra *Laura Tollins* • Michelle Arthur *Sybil* • Mark Pellegrino *Kyle Flinch* ■ *Dir* Joel Schumacher • *Scr* Fernley Phillips

Number Two ★★

Experimental drama   1975 · Fr · Colour · 88min

Absent from film-making for three years owing to a motorcycle crash, influential French director Jean-Luc Godard returned with this dour tale of an ordinary family coping with the problems and pressures of modern life. However, Godard seems most preoccupied by the husband's impotence and the wife's constipation. The style of the film is striking – Godard shot it all on video and uses a variety of split-screen effects. AT In French.

Sandrine Battistella *Wife* • Pierre Oudrey *Husband* • Alexandre Rignault *Grandpa* • Rachel Stefanopoli *Grandma* • Jean-Luc Godard ■ *Dir* Jean-Luc Godard • *Scr* Anne-Marie Miéville, Jean-Luc Godard

The Numbers Station ★★ 15

Thriller   2013 · UK/US/Bel · Colour · 85min

John Cusack stars as an undercover agent haunted by a botched mission who, to regain his mojo, is assigned to guard a programmer (Malin Ackerman) in this straight-to-DVD guff. When the duo comes

under attack, cue lots of running through dimly lit corridors, but there's very little excitement. And when the film starts to harvest bits of the Bourne saga, you know the game is up. JA Violence, swearing. *DVD* *BL*

John Cusack *Emerson Kent* • Malin Akerman *Katherine* • Liam Cunningham *Grey* • Richard Brake *Max* ■ *Dir* Kasper Barfoed • *Scr* F Scott Frazier • *Cinematographer* Ottar Gudnason

The Nun ★★★ 12A

Period drama   2013 · Fr/Ger/Bel · Colour · 111min

A teenage girl is forced to remain in a convent and finds her faith shaken by hypocrisy in this adaptation of Denis Diderot's infamous, anti-clerical novel. The misfortune of Suzanne (Pauline Etienne) is that her cash-strapped aristocratic parents have exhausted their coffers, so holy orders are the solution. While Jacques Rivette's 1965 version of the same story (*La Religieuse*) was initially suppressed in France, this update is unlikely to cause a stir. It's a generally classy yet dramatically underpowered affair traversing a steady path between respectable costume drama and habit-lifting exploitation. Etienne acquits herself well but is outshone by Isabelle Huppert as a very worldly Mother Superior. TJ French, Latin +subtitles.

Pauline Etienne *Suzanne Simonin* • Isabelle Huppert *Supérieure Saint-Eutrope* • Louise Bourgoin *Supérieure Christine* • Martina Gedeck *Madame Simonin, mère de Suzanne* • Françoise Lebrun *Madame de Moni* ■ *Dir* Guillaume Nicloux • *Scr* Guillaume Nicloux, Jerome Beaujour, from the novel *Memoirs of a Nun* by Denis Diderot

Nuns on the Run ★★★ 15

Comedy   1990 · UK · Colour · 88min

Writer/director Jonathan Lynn, one half of the team behind the scorching wit of *Yes, Minister*, tries to squeeze a whole film from the single joke of Robbie Coltrane and Eric Idle decked out as nuns. There is a natural spark between the two performers that saves many a scene here and, when the genial proceedings are not burdened by the full weight of cliché, they do begin to catch fire. JM Violence. *DVD*

Eric Idle *Brian Hope* • Robbie Coltrane *Charlie McManus* • Camille Coduri *Faith* • Janet Suzman *Sister Superior* • Doris Hare *Sister Mary of the Sacred Heart* • Lila Kaye *Sister Mary of the Annunciation* • Robert Patterson *"Case" Casey* ■ *Dir/Scr* Jonathan Lynn

The Nun's Story ★★★★★ PG

Drama   1959 · US · Colour · 145min

Kathryn C Hulme's popular novel makes a magnificent vehicle for the luminous Audrey Hepburn, battling with her conscience and wondering if she is truly cut out for her calling. Hepburn is a marvel, whether flirting with passion in the Congo (in the guise of Peter Finch, terrific as an agnostic doctor) or discovering that some nuns (Dames Edith Evans and Peggy Ashcroft) are only human after all. This is arguably director Fred Zinnemann's finest movie; it won eight nominations, but no Oscars, in the year of *Ben-Hur*. Unjust, really, as you watch Franz Planer's superb photography, listen to Franz Waxman's haunting score and wonder to what greater heights popular cinema can aspire. TS *DVD*

Audrey Hepburn *Sister Luke/Gabrielle Van Der Mal* • Peter Finch *Dr Fortunati* • Edith Evans *Mother Emmanuel* • Peggy Ashcroft *Mother Mathilde* • Dean Jagger *Dr Van Der Mal* • Mildred Dunnock *Sister Margharita/Mistress of Postulance* • Beatrice Straight *Mother Christophe* • Patricia Collinge *Sister William* • Rosalie Crutchley *Sister Eleanor* • Colleen Dewhurst *Archangel Gabriel* • Lionel Jeffries *Dr Goovaerts* ■ *Dir* Fred Zinnemann • *Scr* Robert Anderson, from the novel by Kathryn C Hulme

Nurse Betty ★★★ 18

Black comedy drama
2000 · US · Colour · 105min

Renée Zellweger excels in director Neil LaBute's adroit blend of comic fantasy and social satire. Yet LaBute's trademark acerbity has been somewhat diluted by the fact that he didn't write the occasionally fanciful script. So, while it's possible to believe that witnessing her husband's brutal murder could send a TV-addicted waitress on an odyssey to romance her hospital soap hero, it takes a sizeable suspension of disbelief to accept that the actor playing that role (Greg Kinnear) would buy into her delusion. Her impact on professional hitman Morgan Freeman is similarly strained. Still, engagingly offbeat and enjoyable. DP Violence, swearing, sex scenes. *DVD*

Morgan Freeman *Charlie* • Renée Zellweger *Betty Sizemore* • Chris Rock *Wesley* • Greg Kinnear *Dr David Ravel/George McCord* • Aaron Eckhart *Del Sizemore* • Tia Texada *Rosa Herrera* • Crispin Glover *Rcy Ostrey* • Pruitt Taylor Vince *Sheriff Eldon Ballard* ■ *Dir* Neil LaBute • *Scr* John C Richards, James Flamberg, from a story by John C Richards

Nurse Edith Cavell ★★ PG
First World War drama 1939 · US · BW · 93min

English producer/director Herbert Wilcox's first Hollywood film is an account of Nurse Edith Cavell, the brave and self-sacrificing heroine of the First World War who smuggled English soldiers out of German-occupied Belgium and was executed as a spy for her pains. Anna Neagle (Wilcox's wife), an actress not noted for her dramatic range, makes do with her natural regal dignity in a film that is sober, competent and dull. RK *DVD*

Anna Neagle *Nurse Edith Cavell* • George Sanders *Captain Heinrichs* • Edna May Oliver *Countess de Mavon* • May Robson *Mme Rappard* • ZaSu Pitts *Mme Moulin* • Sophie Stewart *Sister Watkins* ■ *Dir* Herbert Wilcox • *Scr* Michael Hogan, from his novel

Nurse on Wheels ★★★ U
Comedy 1963 · UK · BW · 82min

Peter Rogers and his wife Betty Box seem to have had an obsession with medical matters. She produced the popular *Doctor* series, while he was responsible for four hospital-based *Carry Ons* and this charming comedy that reunited him with Juliet Mills, who had played a nurse in the previous year's *Twice round the Daffodils*. It has its moments of broad humour, but old-fashioned family fun is to the fore as district nurse Mills encounters a range of eccentrics in a village. DP

Juliet Mills *Joanna Jones* • Ronald Lewis *Henry Edwards* • Joan Sims *Deborah Walcott* • Athene Seyler *Miss Farthingale* • Norman Rossington *George Judd* • Barbara Everest *Nurse Merrick* • Ronald Howard *Dr Harold Golfrey* • Joan Hickson *Mrs Wood* ■ *Dir* Gerald Thomas • *Scr* Norman Hudis, from the novel *Nurse Is a Neighbour* by Joanna Jones

The Nut Job ★★ U
Animated comedy adventure 2014 · Can/S Kor/US · Colour · 85min

A promising set-up and a decent voice cast aren't enough to elevate this animated caper. Self-serving rogue Surly the Squirrel (Will Arnett) is banished from the park by his fellow animals after accidentally destroying their food reserves. Heading into the city, he stumbles upon a nut shop that has enough food to help the entire community survive the impending winter. There are a few amusing sight gags and the animation is pleasing on the eye, but this lacks inspiration, resulting in an unremarkable romp. SC *DVD* Blu-ray 3D CS

Will Arnett *Surly* • Katherine Heigl *Andie* • Brendan Fraser *Grayson* • Liam Neeson *Raccoon* • Stephen Lang *King* • Maya Rudolph *Precious* ■ *Dir* Peter Lepeniotis • *Scr* Lorne Cameron, Peter Lepeniotis, from a story by Daniel Woo

Nutcracker ★★ 18
Drama 1982 · UK · Colour · 96min

When Russian ballerina Finola Hughes defects and joins an international ballet company, she soon realises she is being used by its owner (Joan Collins) as a high-class call girl to local politicians. Meanwhile, photojournalist Paul Nicholas goes to extraordinary lengths to snap a scoop picture of Collins's new star dancer in action. A thin plot full of soap-opera

theatrics and soft-core erotica is played out against intensely cheap sets. AJ

Joan Collins *Mme Carrere* • Carol White *Margaux Lasselle* • Paul Nicholas *Mike McCann* • Finola Hughes *Nadia* • William Franklyn *Sir Arthur Cartwright* ■ *Dir* Anwar Kawadri • *Scr* Raymond Christodoulou

Nutcracker ★ U
Ballet 1986 · US · Colour · 81min

This version of the Christmas classic is performed by the Pacific Northwest Ballet. Despite inspired design by Maurice Sendak and direction by Carroll Ballard, this never transcends its stage origins, regardless of Ballard's attempts to create a fourth wall. Similarly, his overly tricky, close-up shots of dancers' limbs in action give the film the feel of a pop promo. LH

Hugh Bigney *Herr Drosselmeier* • Vanessa Sharp *Young Clara* • Patricia Barker *Dream Clara/Ballerina Doll* • Wade Walthall *Nutcracker* • Maia Rosal *Frau Stahlbaum/Peacock* • Carey Homme *Dr Stahlbaum/Moor* ■ *Dir* Carroll Ballard • *Scr* Maurice Sendak, Kent Stowell, from the ballet by Peter Ilich Tchaikovsky, from the fairy tale *The Nutcracker and the Mouse King* by ETA Hoffman

The Nutcracker in 3D ★ PG
Part-animated musical fantasy 2010 · UK/Hun · Colour · 108min

It's more scary-tale than fairy-tale as director Andrei Konchalovsky re-imagines Tchaikovsky's ballet in disastrously dark and rambling fashion. Ambitious yet woefully ill-conceived, the hideous family musical opens in a beautifully designed 1920s Vienna, where young Elle Fanning receives a magical toy nutcracker for Christmas that turns out to be a boy prince bewitched by the evil Rat Queen (Frances de la Tour) for her military dictator son (John Turturro). With no colour and excitement, the flimsy events feel poorly paced, wasting the starry cast, and leaving it entirely to Tim Rice's blandly modified songs to fake a sense of momentum. SF *DVD* Blu-ray 3D

Elle Fanning *Mary* • Nathan Lane *Uncle Albert* • Frances de la Tour *The Rat Queen/Frau Eva* • John Turturro *The Rat King* • Richard E Grant *Father* • Shirley Henderson *The Nutcracker* ■ *Dir* Andrei Konchalovsky • *Scr* Andrei Konchalovsky, Chris Solimine [Christopher Solimine], from the novel *The Nutcracker and the Mouse King* by ETA Hoffmann

The Nutcracker Prince ★★ U
Animated fantasy 1990 · Can · Colour · 70min

Canada has a proud tradition of ground-breaking animation, but this lowbrow, low-budget offering is something of an embarrassment. The story sees a young girl shrink to the size of her toys to help her model soldiers overcome a tyrannical rodent. Kiefer Sutherland and Peter O'Toole provide effective voiceovers, and there's Tchaikovsky's music on the soundtrack, but the artwork looks shoddy and Paul Schibli's direction is anything but magical. DP

Peter O'Toole *Pantaloon* • Kiefer Sutherland *Nutcracker/Hans* • Megan Follows *Clara* • Michael MacDonald *Mouse King* ■ *Dir* Paul Schibli • *Scr* Patricia Watson, from the fairy tale *The Nutcracker and the Mouse King* by ETA Hoffmann

Nuts ★★★ 18
Drama 1987 · US · Colour · 110min

You can imagine Tom Topor's play about a prostitute proving her sanity so that she can stand trial for manslaughter making for a cracking night at the theatre. That it is marginally less compelling as a film is down to director Martin Ritt's decision to reveal key facts via clumsily staged flashbacks rather than as courtroom testimony, as this considerably diminishes their impact. Even though the outcome is inevitable, this is still an involving drama thanks to the bullish performances of Barbra Streisand as the hooker and Richard Dreyfuss as her attorney. DP

Barbra Streisand *Claudia Draper* • Richard Dreyfuss *Aaron Levinsky* • Maureen Stapleton *Rose Kirk* • Eli Wallach *Dr Herbert A Morrison* • Karl Malden *Arthur Kirk* • Robert Webber *Francis MacMillan* ■ *Dir* Martin Ritt • *Scr* Alvin Sargent, Darryl Ponicsan, Tom Topor, from his play

The Nutty Professor ★★★★ PG
Comedy 1963 · US · Colour · 102min

In spite of almost universal criticism, this immensely accomplished comedy remains Jerry Lewis's best and funniest screen work. It's really "Doctor Jerry and Mister Love" (the film's French title translated), as Lewis plays a nerdish chemistry professor who is hooked on lovely student Stella Stevens. Lewis makes and takes a potion that turns him into Buddy Love, singing lounge lizard par excellence. The witty design and the use of fabulously rich Technicolor are major bonuses, and this clever movie remains extremely funny. TS *DVD*

Jerry Lewis *Professor Julius Kelp/Buddy Love* • Stella Stevens *Stella Purdy* • Del Moore *Dr Hamius R Warfield* • Kathleen Freeman *Millie Lemmon* ■ *Dir* Jerry Lewis • *Scr* Jerry Lewis, Bill Richmond, from a story by Lewis

The Nutty Professor ★★★★ 12
Comedy 1996 · US · Colour · 91min

This reworking of the 1963 Jerry Lewis comedy finds Eddie Murphy back on form as Sherman Klump, a sweet-natured, obese science teacher who perfects a potion that turns him into a svelte, sexy love machine. Of course, the potion wears off at the most unfortunate times, making his attempts at romance with attractive teaching assistant Jada Pinkett a bit of a lottery. Murphy plays the professor to perfection; thanks to the genius of the Oscar-winning make-up and computer graphics departments, he also portrays three generations of his family. Snappily directed, this isn't as daft as the original, but it is an enjoyable laughfest. JB *DVD*

Eddie Murphy *Sherman Klump/Buddy Love* • Jada Pinkett [Jada Pinkett Smith] *Carla Purty* • James Coburn *Harlan Hartley* • Larry Miller *Dean Richmond* • Dave Chappelle *Reggie Warrington* • John Ales *Jason* • Patricia Wilson *Dean's secretary* ■ *Dir* Tom Shadyac • *Scr* David Sheffield, Barry W Blaustein, Tom Shadyac, Steve Oedederk, from the 1963 film

Nutty Professor 2: the Klumps ★★★ 12
Comedy 2000 · US · Colour · 102min

In this sequel to Eddie Murphy's 1996 success, Murphy gets to play rotund scientist Sherman Klump and his corpulent family, including his father at two different ages. His performance is an amazing tour de force, which could be compared to the best work of Alec Guinness and Peter Sellers if it weren't for the fact that half the time he's unintelligible. Klump is desperate to rid himself of his slim, supercool alter ego, Buddy Love, but only manages to regenerate (and mutate) him. Janet Jackson is sweetly effective, playing it straight as Klump's long-suffering girlfriend. DM Sexual references. *DVD*

Eddie Murphy *Professor Sherman Klump/Cletus "Papa" Klump/Young Cletus Klump/Anna "Mama" Klump/Ernie Klump/Grandma Klump/Buddy Love/Lance Perkins* • Janet Jackson *Professor Denise Gaines* • Larry Miller *Dean Richmond* • John Ales *Jason* • Richard Gant *Denise's father* • Anna Maria Horsford *Denise's mother* • Melinda McGraw *Leanne Guilford* • Jamal Mixon *Ernie Klump Jr* • Freda Payne *Claudine* ■ *Dir* Peter Segal • *Scr* Barry W Blaustein, David Sheffield, Paul Weitz, Chris Weitz, from a story by Steve Oedekerk, Blaustein, Sheffield, from characters by Jerry Lewis, Bill Richmond

A Nymphoid Barbarian in Dinosaur Hell ★★ 18
Science-fiction fantasy 1991 · US · Colour · 81min

Even the guys from Troma, who produced this sci-fi fantasy, would be the first to admit it isn't one of their finest hours. The plot outline is as scanty as Linda Corwin's costume, as she endures the nightmare of being the last female alive following a nuclear conflagration. Moreover, it's hard to dispute the claim that it cost a mere $5,000

to shoot somewhere in New England, though the hilarious stop-motion Tromasaurus and the one-eyed "D'ya-think-e-saurus" almost save the day. DP Violence, nudity. *DVD*

Linda Corwin *Lea* • Paul Guzzi *Marn* • Mark Deshaies *Man with No Face* ■ *Dir/Scr* Brett Piper

Nymphomaniac Vol I ★★★★ 18
Erotic drama 2013 · Den/Ger/Fr/Bel/UK · Colour and BW · 112min

Director Lars von Trier's latest provocation completes his so-called "Trilogy of Depression". It charts the life story of Charlotte Gainsbourg's self-loathing sex addict in vivid, annotated flashback, as told to Stellan Skarsgård's bookish bachelor. Sexual frankness threatens to define the viewing experience. More than that, however, *Nymphomaniac* is a picaresque about self-discovery, which strays into extreme Mike Leigh territory when Uma Thurman's wronged wife challenges our promiscuous protagonist. AC *DVD*

Charlotte Gainsbourg *Joe* • Stellan Skarsgård *Seligman* • Stacy Martin *Young Joe* • Shia LaBeouf *Jerome* • Christian Slater *Joe's father* • Uma Thurman *Mrs H* • Hugo Speer *Mr H* ■ *Dir/Scr* Lars von Trier

Nymphomaniac Vol II ★★★★ 18
Erotic drama 2014 · Den/Ger/Fr/Bel/UK · Colour · 118min

The second half of Danish auteur Lars von Trier's explicit sex-addiction tale follows on from *Vol I*, as Stacy Martin's self-diagnosed nymphomaniac has reached a stalemate in her quest for carnal inspiration. She is imprisoned in a strait-laced relationship with Shia LaBeouf, then in middle age (played by a fearless Charlotte Gainsbourg) she descends into a disturbing world of humiliation (typified by Jamie Bell's chilling sadist). The office-based satire gives way to a more conventional thriller storyline, but von Trier holds his nerve, and the four-hour whole emerges as a powerful treatise on the depths of human desire. AC *DVD*

Charlotte Gainsbourg *Joe* • Stellan Skarsgård *Seligman* • Stacy Martin *Young Joe* • Shia LaBeouf *Jerome* • Christian Slater *Joe's father* • Uma Thurman *Mrs H* • Jamie Bell *K* • Willem Dafoe *L* ■ *Dir/Scr* Lars von Trier

N

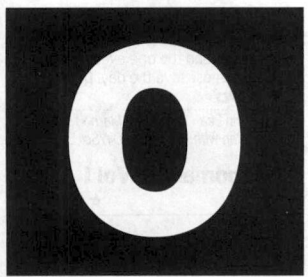

O

★★★★ 🄵
Drama 2001 · US · Colour · 90min

Director Tim Blake Nelson's modern version of Shakespeare's *Othello* is set in a high school in the American South, and the drama twists its themes of vengeance, jealousy and racism into a chilling and timely snapshot of contemporary teenage life. There's no glimmer of hope or salvation here, as black basketball hero Mekhi Phifer staggers like a sleepwalker into an inescapable hell. Set up by his embittered pal (a poisonously good Josh Hartnett), who envies him his sporting prowess and beautiful girlfriend Julia Stiles, Phifer's fall from grace is painfully bleak and downright nasty. SF Violence, swearing, sex scenes, drug abuse, nudity. *DVD*

Mekhi Phifer *Odin James* • Josh Hartnett *Hugo Goulding* • Julia Stiles *Desi Brable* • Martin Sheen *Coach Duke Goulding* • Andrew Keegan *Michael Casio* • Rain Phoenix *Emily* ■ *Dir* Tim Blake Nelson • *Scr* Brad Kaaya, from the play *Othello* by William Shakespeare • *Cinematographer* Russell Lee Fine

O Brother, Where Art Thou?
★★★★ 🄵
Comedy 2000 · US/UK/Fr · Colour · 102min

"Based upon Homer's *Odyssey*" runs the opening title, which – as well as setting the tongue-in-cheek tone of this Coen brothers' comedy – also happens to contain more than an element of truth. Ethan and Joel Coen's eighth collaborative effort concerns the attempts of an escaped convict (a nicely self-mocking George Clooney) to get back to his wife (Holly Hunter) and the picaresque adventures he has on the way. The movie also contrives to encapsulate every con-on-the-run picture one has ever seen, as well as southern period crime dramas. Yet again, the Coens' cinematic alchemy has worked a treat. RB *DVD*

George Clooney *Ulysses Everett McGill* • John Turturro *Pete* • Tim Blake Nelson *Delmar* • Charles Durning *Pappy O'Daniel* • John Goodman *Big Dan Teague* • Michael Badalucco *George Nelson* • Holly Hunter *Penny* ■ *Dir* Joel Coen • *Scr* Ethan Coen, Joel Coen, from the poem *The Odyssey* by Homer • *Producer* Ethan Coen

OC and Stiggs
★★ 🄵
Comedy 1987 · US · Colour · 105min

Before returning to fine, focused form with *The Player*, director Robert Altman barked up several wrong trees in the preceding years. This film was one of them: a meandering, stop-start sprawl, with a tone too blunt for satire. The eponymous characters are a couple of teen clowns who get up to all kinds of merry japes. There are, however, some semi-inspired moments of Altman strangeness. JM *DVD*

Daniel H Jenkins [Daniel Jenkins] *OC Ogilvey* • Neill Barry *Mark Stiggs* • Jane Curtin *Elinore Schwab* • Paul Dooley *Randall Schwab* • Jon Cryer *Randall Schwab Jr* • Laura Urstein *Lenore Schwab* • Victor Ho *Frankie Tang* • Dennis Hopper *Sponson* ■ *Dir* Robert Altman • *Scr* Donald Cantrell, Ted Mann, from a story by Tod Carroll, Mann, from a story in *National Lampoon* magazine

O Henry's Full House
★★★★ 🄤
Portmanteau comedy drama
1952 · US · BW · 117min

This compendium of five short stories by a genius of the form is beautifully adapted, well cast and directed. The most moving tale is *The Last Leaf*, with Anne Baxter as a dying woman saved by self-sacrificing artist Gregory Ratoff. Charles Laughton stars as a tramp trying to get arrested in the cruelly ironic *The Cop and the Anthem*, in which Marilyn Monroe appears as a streetwalker; Dale Robertson is a cop who must arrest his good friend Richard Widmark in the tough-minded *The Clarion Call*; while *The Ransom of Red Chief* has kidnappers offering to pay the parents of the ghastly child they've nabbed to take him back. However, perhaps the most fondly remembered is the painfully tender *Gift of the Magi*, with Jeanne Crain and Farley Granger as the poverty-stricken young couple who each sacrifice a treasured possession to buy the other a Christmas gift. RK

Jeanne Crain *Della* • Farley Granger *Jim* • Sig Rumann [Sig Ruman] *Menkie* • Anne Baxter *Joanna* • Jean Peters *Susan* • Gregory Ratoff *Behrman* • Charles Laughton *Soapy* • Marilyn Monroe *Streetwalker* • Dale Robertson *Barney Woods* • Richard Widmark *Johnny Kernan* • Fred Allen (2) *Sam* • Oscar Levant *Bill* • John Steinbeck *Narrator* ■ *Dir* Henry Hathaway, Henry Koster, Henry King, Howard Hawks, Jean Negulesco • *Scr* Lamar Trotti, Richard L Breen, Ben Roberts, Ivan Goff, Walter Bullock, Nunnally Johnson, from stories by O Henry

O Lucky Man!
★★★ 🄵
Satirical fantasy 1973 · UK · Colour · 169min

This irreligious, updated *Pilgrim's Progress* through society remains a determined attempt to irritate, incite and entertain. The fine cast is led by director Lindsay Anderson's regular collaborator Malcolm McDowell, who plays an everyman adrift in a surreal landscape littered with British character actors such as Ralph Richardson, Rachel Roberts and Arthur Lowe, all playing multiple parts. The title is not so much ironic as downright sarcastic and, despite the jarring clash of symbols, it's a provocative fable not to be missed, even if it is now somewhat dated. Alan Price's energetic score is a bonus. TH Sex scenes. *DVD*

Malcolm McDowell *Mick Travis* • Ralph Richardson *Monty/Sir James Burgess* • Rachel Roberts (1) *Gloria/Mme Paillard/Mrs Richards* • Arthur Lowe *Mr Duff/Charlie Johnson/Dr Munda* • Helen Mirren *Patricia Burgess* • Dandy Nichols *Tea lady/Neighbour* ■ *Dir* Lindsay Anderson • *Scr* David Sherwin, from an idea by Malcolm McDowell • *Music/lyrics* Alan Price

OSS
★★★
Spy drama 1946 · US · BW · 105min

Paramount's resident tough guy Alan Ladd finds himself spying in France during the Second World War in the dark days before D-Day. It's pretty routine action material for the studio, but it's given dignity by the strength of the star's performance. As the movie is so obviously a Ladd vehicle, there are no other stellar names in support; Geraldine Fitzgerald is an attractive though unexciting heroine, and Patric Knowles is as wooden as ever. TS Violence.

Alan Ladd *John Martin* • Geraldine Fitzgerald *Ellen Rogers* • Patric Knowles *Commander Brady* • John Hoyt *Colonel Meister* • Gloria Saunders *Mary "Sparks" Kenny* • Richard Benedict *Bernay* ■ *Dir* Irving Pichel • *Scr* Richard Maibaum

OSS 117: Cairo – Nest of Spies
★★★ 🄵
Spy spoof
2006 · Fr/Bel · Colour and BW · 94min

Before their Oscar triumph with *The Artist*, director Michel Hazanavicius and star Jean Dujardin teamed up for this, the first of two spy spoofs sending up the Bond-like creation of author Jean Bruce. Dujardin is Hubert Bonisseur de La Bath, aka OSS 117, a suave but stupid French agent who is tasked with investigating the disappearance of his former sidekick in the Egyptian capital on the brink of the Suez Crisis. Our chauvinistic, bigoted and clueless hero soon finds himself the target of extremists. Dujardin's deadpan performance is a constant delight, while Hazanavicius demonstrates his affection for the genre. JH French, Arabic +subtitles. *DVD*

Jean Dujardin *OSS 117/Hubert Bonisseur de la Bath* • Philippe Lefebvre (2) *Jack Jefferson* • Bérénice Bejo *Larmina El Akmar Betouche* ■ *Dir* Michel Hazanavicius • *Scr* Jean-Francois Halin, inspired by the OSS 117 series of novels by Jean Bruce

OSS 117: Lost in Rio
★★★★ 🄵
Spy spoof 2009 · Fr · Colour · 100min

Strewn with pratfalls, quips and casual assaults on political correctness, Michel Hazanavicius's parody of the 1950s espionage novels of Jean Bruce is sharp, uproarious and outrageous enough to overcome its minor lulls and flaws. Having survived a nest of spies in Cairo, 1960s spy OSS 117 (Jean Dujardin) finds himself in Brazil tracking a Nazi war criminal (Rüdiger Vogler). Dujardin plays the charismatic and incompetent agent with a swaggering dash that's matched by the excellence of the supporting cast and the impeccable period designs. DP French +subtitles. Swearing, sexual references, drug abuse.

Jean Dujardin *Hubert Bonisseur de La Bath, OSS 117* • Louise Monot *Dolorès Koulechov* • Rüdiger Vogler *Professor Von Zimmel* • Alex Lutz *Heinrich Von Zimmel* • Reem Kherici *Carlotta* • Pierre Bellemare *Lesignac* ■ *Dir* Michel Hazanavicius • *Scr* Jean-François Halin, Michel Hazanavicius, from characters by Jean Bruce

The Oberwald Mystery
★★★
Drama 1980 · It/W Ger · Colour · 128min

Sixteen years after *The Red Desert*, Michelangelo Antonioni and his muse, Monica Vitti, reunited for this flawed but fascinating reworking of Jean Cocteau's courtly melodrama. As the royal widow roused from a decade of mourning by anarchist poet Franco Branciaroli, Vitti is both vulnerable and tragic. However, Antonioni's attempt to fuse Cocteau's escapist flamboyance with his own coolly detached style was ill-conceived. Similarly, his scheme to shoot on video and then transfer the footage to 35mm proved visually unsatisfactory. DP In Italian.

Monica Vitti *The Queen* • Luigi Diberti *Willenstein* • Paolo Bonacelli *Count of Foehn* • Franco Branciaroli *Sebastian* ■ *Dir* Michelangelo Antonioni • *Scr* Michelangelo Antonioni, Tonino Guerra, from the play *The Eagle Has Two Heads* by Jean Cocteau

The Object of Beauty
★★★ 🄵
Comedy drama 1991 · US/UK · Colour · 98min

As the Americans who live on their wits and other people's money, Andie MacDowell and John Malkovich make an unexpectedly good team, with their on-screen limitations actually contributing to the credibility of their characters. Indeed, the insurance scam involving a Henry Moore sculpture rather gets in the way of their bantering, as it shifts the focus on to the deaf-mute maid who has purloined it. This is a pleasing comedy of crooked manners. DP *DVD*

John Malkovich *Jake* • Andie MacDowell *Tina* • Lolita Davidovich *Joan* • Rudi Davis *Jenny* • Joss Ackland *Mr Mercer* • Bill Paterson *Victor Swayle* • Ricci Harnett *Steve* • Peter Riegert *Larry* • Jack Shepherd *Mr Slaughter* • Rosemary Martin *Mrs Doughty* ■ *Dir/Scr* Michael Lindsay-Hogg

The Object of My Affection
★★ 🄵
Romantic comedy 1998 · US · Colour · 106min

Jennifer Aniston tries to escape her *Friends* persona in this uneven romantic comedy, directed by Nicholas Hytner. Aniston plays a girl who gets pregnant by her oafish ex-boyfriend, but decides to ask her gay friend Paul Rudd to help her bring up the child. She falls in love with him, of course, but the resulting mess it makes of both their lives is more sad than humorous, while the ending is contrived. Well-meaning, with some nice performances from co-stars Alan Alda and Nigel Hawthorne, but ultimately unsatisfying. JB Swearing, a sex scene. *DVD*

Jennifer Aniston *Nina Borowski* • Paul Rudd *George Hanson* • John Pankow *Vince McBride* • Alan Alda *Sidney Miller* • Tim Daly [Timothy Daly]

Dr Robert Joley • Nigel Hawthorne *Rodney Fraser* • Allison Janney *Constance Miller* • Amo Gulinello *Paul James* ■ *Dir* Nicholas Hytner • *Scr* Wendy Wasserstein, from the novel by Stephen McCauley

Objective, Burma!
★★★ 🄿🄶
Second World War drama
1945 · US · BW · 135min

Errol Flynn parachutes into the Burmese jungle to destroy a Japanese radio station in this rousing war drama. It went unshown in Britain for seven years because it made no mention of the fact that the British played the major role in Burma. For some reason, action director Raoul Walsh stretches things out for over two hours. But, despite its frequent longueurs, it's exciting stuff, with Flynn bringing all his swashbuckling swagger to his role as the scourge of South East Asia. AT *DVD*

Errol Flynn *Major Nelson* • James Brown (1) *Sergeant Treacy* • William Prince *Lieutenant Jacobs* • George Tobias *Gabby Gordon* • Henry Hull *Mark Williams* • Warner Anderson *Colonel Carter* • John Alvin *Hogan* ■ *Dir* Raoul Walsh • *Scr* Ranald MacDougall, Lester Cole, from a story by Alvah Bessie

Oblivion
★★★ 🄵
Science-fiction action adventure
2013 · US · Colour · 119min

Tom Cruise plays a security repairman who maintains the airborne robot drones that monitor the Earth in 2077, following an interplanetary war. Cruise and communications officer Andrea Riseborough, their memories erased for security reasons, are waiting for a call to rejoin the rest of humankind on a lunar colony. But when he rescues astronaut Olga Kurylenko from a downed spacecraft, Cruise uncovers the dark secrets behind the war. He also encounters Morgan Freeman, who gives a suitably statesmanlike performance as the leader of a rebel force. *Tron Legacy* director Joseph Kosinski delivers a thought-provoking story, packed with edge-of-your-seat action and impressive special effects, although it does borrow too liberally from other well-known sci-fi films. Fortunately, Cruise is good value as a man haunted by snatches of memories of his earlier life. TeS Violence, swearing. *DVD* 🅱

Tom Cruise *Jack* • Andrea Riseborough *Victoria "Vika" Olsen* • Olga Kurylenko *Julia* • Melissa Leo *Sally* • Morgan Freeman *Beech* ■ *Dir* Joseph Kosinski • *Scr* Karl Gajdusek, Michael deBruyn [Michael Arndt], from the comic book by Joseph Kosinski, Arvid Nelson

Oblomov
★★★★ 🄤
Satire 1980 · USSR · Colour · 140min

Covering only half of Ivan Goncharov's sprawling novel, this two-part period piece dissects the dissolute charm of the aristocracy. Transfixed by ennui, corpulent 30-something Oleg Tabakov cannot be roused from his lethargy by a series of idyllic flashbacks prompted by his best friend, Yuri Bogatyrev. But the reformist zeal of Elena Solovei is another matter altogether. Criticised for a lack of incident and its stately pace, Nikita Mikhalkov's film is both intelligently faithful to the spirit of its source and meticulous in its blend of satire and sentimentality. Superbly photographed by Pavel Lebeshev, it's also slyly subversive in its stance on progress. DP In Russian.

Oleg Tabakov *Oblomov* • Yuri Bogatyrev *Stoltz* • Elena Solovei *Olga* ■ *Dir* Nikita Mikhalkov • *Scr* Nikita Mikhalkov, Aleksander Adabashyan, from the novel by Ivan Goncharov

The Oblong Box
★★★ 🄵
Horror 1969 · UK · Colour · 87min

Hitchcock protégé Gordon Hessler took over the direction of this obvious shocker when Michael Reeves committed suicide after planning it as his follow-up to *Witchfinder General*. A deranged and disfigured voodoo victim is buried alive by his brother, Vincent Price, only to return from the grave to wreak gory vengeance. A pervasive aura of evil is summoned up in a well-mounted period piece containing

🄤 SUITABLE FOR ALL 🄤🄲 SUITABLE ESPECIALLY FOR YOUNG CHILDREN (DVD ONLY) 🄿🄶 PARENTAL GUIDANCE 🄸🄸🄰 UNDER 12s TO BE ACCOMPANIED (CINEMA ONLY)

occasional flashes of Hessler's trademark visual flair. Yet, while Price is well used, adding weight to the clichéd dialogue, Christopher Lee in a wig is wasted. AJ

Vincent Price *Julian Markham* • Christopher Lee *Dr Neuhartt* • Alistair Williamson *Sir Edward Markham* • Hilary Dwyer *Elizabeth Markham* • Peter Arne *Samuel Trench* • Harry Baird *N Galo* • Carl Rigg *Mark Norton* • Maxwell Shaw *Tom Hackett* • Michael Balfour *Ruddock* ■ *Dir* Gordon Hessler • *Scr* Lawrence Huntingdon, Christopher Wicking, from the story by Edgar Allan Poe

Observe and Report ★★ 15
Comedy 2009 · US · Colour · 82min

Unlike *Paul Blart: Mall Cop*, which played a similar idea for belly laughs, this mall-based comedy is something of a disturbing oddity. It follows a thuggish, bipolar security guard (played by the usually lovable man-child Seth Rogen) as he wages a one-man war against a flasher who's terrorising his workplace. At first sight, it looks like just another gross-out movie, but turns out to be an unsettling anti-comedy that might have benefited from some restraint, much like its troubled hero. JR *DVD* 🔵

Seth Rogen *Ronnie Barnhardt* • Anna Faris *Brandi* • Ray Liotta *Detective Harrison* • Michael Peña *[Michael Pena] Dennis* • Celia Weston *Mom* • Collette Wolfe *Nell* ■ *Dir/Scr* Jody Hill

Obsessed ★ 12
Thriller 2009 · US · Colour · 103min

Singer Beyoncé Knowles co-produces and stars in this completely witless, sub-*Fatal Attraction* psychological thriller. But as Sharon Charles, the wife of a high-flying executive, she spends much of the film in the background as husband Derek (Idris Elba) grapples with the increasingly blatant sexual advances of a barmy temp (played by an accidentally comic Ali Larter). As this one-dimensional drama unfolds, it becomes increasingly difficult to see what drew Knowles to the project in the first place. SP Violence, swearing. *DVD* 🔵

Idris Elba *Derek Charles* • Ali Larter *Lisa Sheridan* • Beyoncé Knowles *Sharon Charles* • Christine Lahti *Detective Reese* • Bruce McGill *Joe Gage* • Scout Taylor-Compton *Samantha* • Jerry O'Connell *Ben* ■ *Dir* Steve Shill • *Scr* David Loughery

Obsession ★★★ PG
Thriller 1948 · UK · BW · 93min

Blacklisted by the McCarthy witch-hunts for being a communist, director Edward Dmytryk came to Britain and made three films, including this suspenseful "perfect murder" thriller. Robert Newton overacts as the doctor who plans the murder of his wife's American lover. Keeping the man alive and locked in a room, he plans to dissolve him in acid when the police call off the search. AT *DVD*

Robert Newton *Dr Clive Riordan* • Sally Gray *Storm Riordan* • Naunton Wayne *Superintendent Finsbury* • Phil Brown *Bill Kronin* • Olga Lindo *Mrs Humphreys* • Ronald Adam *Clubman* • James Harcourt *Aitkin* ■ *Dir* Edward Dmytryk • *Scr* Alec Coppel, from his novel *A Man about a Dog*

Obsession ★★★ 12
Thriller 1976 · US · Colour · 98min

Director Brian De Palma makes a brave stab at a homage to his idol Alfred Hitchcock with this sexy thriller in which Paul Schrader's screenplay offers more than one nod to *Vertigo*. Further echoes of Hitch are supplied in the Oscar-nominated score by *Psycho* composer Bernard Herrmann. Geneviève Bujold is fetching as Cliff Robertson's dead wife and her double, but John Lithgow in his second movie steals the acting honours as Robertson's suspicious business partner. Nearly, but not quite, as clever as it thinks it is. TS *DVD* 🔵

Cliff Robertson *Michael Courtland* • Geneviève Bujold *Elizabeth Courtland/Sandra Portinari* • John Lithgow *Robert LaSalle* • Sylvia "Kuumba" Williams *Judy* • Wanda Blackman *Amy Courtland* • J Patrick McNamara *Kidnapper* • Stanley J Reyes *Inspector Brie* ■ *Dir* Brian De Palma • *Scr* Paul Schrader, from a story by Brian De Palma, Paul Schrader

The Obsession ★★
Drama 2006 · Can/US · Colour · 88min

A ballet tutor's Lolita-style obsession with a teenage pupil forms the basis of this bland drama. But it takes such a long time for stalker Sebastian Spence to reveal his true nature that there's little tension in anything that unfolds. Instead, director David Winkler fuels the tedium by repeating the same slow-motion sequences of teen victim Elise Gatien dancing, while establishing her newly divorced mum Daphne Zuniga as his focal character. Worse still, Gatien's supposedly outstanding moves are as unconvincing as her shouty acting. SF

Daphne Zuniga *Deborah Matthews* • Elise Gatien *Erika Matthews* • Sebastian Spence *Reed Halton* • Jenny Levine *Linda* • Nels Lennarson *Jason Matthews* • Herbert Beaverstone *Mr Capas* ■ *Dir* David Winkler • *Scr* Christopher Morro

Obvious Child ★★★★ 15
Romantic comedy 2014 · US · Colour · 80min

Gillian Robespierre's debut feature announces her as an original spirit. The superb Jenny Slate plays an ethical-bookstore employee and blowsy amateur stand-up whose extraordinary run of bad luck sees her dumped and ousted from her job in quick succession, before getting pregnant from a one night stand. Writer-director Robespierre's passionately pro-choice film handles its weighty issues deftly, managing to be breezy and hilarious without sacrificing intelligence or empathy. Romantic comedy clichés are eschewed so that a largely bungled romance (with the nevertheless charming Jake Lacy) plays second fiddle to a robust, heartening friendship (with the marvellous Gaby Hoffmann) while the sharp script strikes an entertaining balance between wise polemic, candid confession and toilet humour. EAS Swearing, sexual references. *DVD*

Jenny Slate *Donna Stern* • Jake Lacy *Max* • Gaby Hoffmann *Nellie* • Gabe Liedman *Joey* • Polly Draper *Nancy Stern* • Richard Kind *Jacob Stern* ■ *Dir* Gillian Robespierre • *Scr* Gillian Robespierre, from the 2009 short film by Robespierre, Anna Bean, Karen Maine

Ocean's Eleven ★★★★ PG
Crime caper 1960 · US · Colour · 127min

The story for this great (and critically underrated) caper movie was discovered by Peter Lawford and brought to fellow Rat Rack member Frank Sinatra, who effectively produced the movie. He cast himself as former sergeant Danny Ocean, who calls on his old wartime pals to help him in a raid on Las Vegas. Sleek, audacious and superbly cast, it's directed by veteran Lewis Milestone, who keeps a tight lid on the Rat Pack's antics. The ending, if rather derivative, is still brilliant. TS *DVD*

Frank Sinatra *Danny Ocean* • Dean Martin *Sam Harmon* • Sammy Davis Jr *Josh Howard* • Peter Lawford *Jimmy Foster* • Angie Dickinson *Beatrice Ocean* • Richard Conte *Anthony Bergdorf* • Cesar Romero *Duke Santos* • Patrice Wymore *Adele Ekstrom* • Joey Bishop *"Mushy" O'Conners* • Akim Tamiroff *Spyros Acebos* ■ *Dir* Lewis Milestone • *Scr* Harry Brown, Charles Lederer, from a story by George Clayton Johnson, Jack Golden

Ocean's Eleven ★★★★ 12
Action crime caper 2001 · US/Aus · Colour · 111min

George Clooney and his A-list pals have fun in the Las Vegas sun in this thoroughly enjoyable caper from director Steven Soderbergh. In a loose remake of the same-name movie, a Rat Pack venture of the same name, Clooney comfortably steps into Frank Sinatra's shoes as Danny Ocean, who is fresh out of jail but still sets about putting together an audacious heist with the help of a ten-man crew. His star cronies include Brad Pitt, Matt Damon, Carl Reiner and Don Cheadle, who affects the worst cockney accent you've ever heard. The plan is to hit the vault containing the take from three of the biggest casinos in Vegas, all of which belong to Andy Garcia, the guy who just happens to be dating Ocean's ex-wife Julia Roberts. This is one of those films that's a joy from start to finish, but doesn't strain the brain for a second. JB *DVD* 🔵

George Clooney *Danny Ocean* • Brad Pitt *Rusty Ryan* • Julia Roberts *Tess Ocean* • Matt Damon *Linus Caldwell* • Andy Garcia *Terry Benedict* • Don Cheadle *Basher Tarr* • Bernie Mac *Frank Catton* • Elliott Gould *Reuben Tishkoff* • Carl Reiner *Saul Bloom* • Scott Caan *Turk Malloy* • Casey Affleck *Virgil Malloy* • Qin Shaobo *Yen* ■ *Dir* Steven Soderbergh • *Scr* Ted Griffin, from the 1960 film

Ocean's Twelve ★★ 12
Action crime caper 2004 · US/Aus · Colour · 120min

Steven Soderbergh's *Ocean's Eleven* was a sharp, witty remake of a rather self-indulgent vehicle for Frank Sinatra's Rat Pack. With this sequel, George Clooney, Brad Pitt and company seem to have fallen into the same sort of trap. The lazy, convoluted plot has the smooth criminals hitting the robbery trail in Europe to raise the cash needed to pay back casino boss Andy Garcia. Soderbergh gives the movie a hip surface sheen and there's no denying the chemistry between the starry ensemble cast, but this is contrived and a little too knowing for its own good. JF *DVD* 🔵

George Clooney *Danny Ocean* • Brad Pitt *Rusty Ryan* • Matt Damon *Linus Caldwell* • Catherine Zeta-Jones *Isabel Lahiri* • Andy Garcia *Terry Benedict* • Don Cheadle *Basher Tarr* • Bernie Mac *Frank Catton* • Julia Roberts *Tess Ocean* • Casey Affleck *Virgil Malloy* • Scott Caan *Turk Malloy* • Vincent Cassel *François Toulour* • Eddie Jemison *Livingston Dell* • Carl Reiner *Saul Bloom* • Elliott Gould *Reuben Tishkoff* • Qin Shaobo *Yen* • Eddie Izzard *Roman Nagel* • Robbie Coltrane *Matsui* • Jeroen Krabbé *van der Woude* ■ *Dir* Steven Soderbergh • *Scr* George Nolfi, from characters by George Clayton Johnson, Jack Golden Russell

Ocean's Thirteen ★★ PG
Crime comedy caper 2007 · US · Colour · 117min

Despite returning to Las Vegas where the series began, Steven Soderbergh's second sequel to *Ocean's Eleven* (2001) fails to rediscover the sheer insouciance of its predecessors. George Clooney, Brad Pitt, Matt Damon and the rest of the over-stuffed cast reprise their roles as the charming conmen, this time targeting the hi-tech casino of a Vegas businessman (Al Pacino), who's double-crossed one of their team. The strength of the series was always its breezy enthusiasm, but here there's a chronic lack of fun: Pacino barely gets out of first gear, while Clooney seems to have his mind on other things. Only Ellen Barkin shines in a comic role. At least there won't be an "Ocean's Fourteen". JR English, Spanish +subtitles. *DVD* 🔵

George Clooney *Danny Ocean* • Brad Pitt *Rusty Ryan* • Matt Damon *Linus Caldwell/Lenny Pepperidge* • Andy Garcia *Terry Benedict* • Don Cheadle *Basher Tarr* • Bernie Mac *Frank Catton* • Ellen Barkin *Abigail Sponder* • Al Pacino *Willy Bank* • Casey Affleck *Virgil Malloy* • Scott Caan *Turk Malloy* ■ *Dir* Steven Soderbergh • *Scr* Brian Koppelman, David Levien, from characters by George Clayton Johnson, Jack Golden Russell • *Cinematographer* Peter Andrews [Steven Soderbergh]

The Octagon ★★ 18
Martial arts action 1980 · US · Colour · 98min

With his penchant for martial art butt-kicking and monosyllabic, mahogany-table acting, Chuck Norris was probably the precursor to the likes of Van Damme and Seagal. Here he plays a retired kung fu champ hired as a bodyguard for a wealthy woman against attack by sinister ninja types. As chop-socky movies go, this is better than most, but still devoid of a single brain cell. RS *DVD* 🔵

Chuck Norris *Scott James* • Karen Carlson *Justine* • Lee Van Cleef *McCarn* • Art Hindle *A J* • Carol Bagdasarian *Aura* ■ *Dir* Eric Karson • *Scr* Leigh Chapman, from a story by Paul Aaron, Leigh Chapman

Octane ★★★ 15
Horror 2003 · UK/Lux · Colour · 86min

Embittered divorcee Madeleine Stowe searches for her teenage daughter, lost to a blood-drinking cult who scour motorway service stations for their victims. Laced with sex-and-splatter jolts, this unusual terror tale is a gripping collision of neon-lit car smashes, disorientating close-ups and well-oiled eeriness. Marcus Adams's haunting *danse macabre* exerts a lethal grip even when navigating a few climactic speed bumps. With a great soundtrack from Orbital, it's a canny package of surreal nightmare scenarios. AJ Violence, swearing, drug abuse. *DVD*

Madeleine Stowe *Senga* • Mischa Barton *Nat* • Jonathan Rhys Meyers *The Father* • Norman Reedus *Recovery man* • Bijou Phillips *Backpacker* • Leo Gregory *Joyrider* • Gary Parker *Vacation man* • Amber Batty *Vacation woman* ■ *Dir* Marcus Adams • *Scr* Stephen Volk

October ★★★★ PG
Silent historical epic 1928 · USSR · Colour · 99min

Despite being made to celebrate the tenth anniversary of the overthrow of Kerensky's provisional government, this impersonal tribute to the proletariat found little official or critical favour in the Soviet Union. Bitingly satirical and overtly political, it marked Sergei Eisenstein's most ambitious experiment in intellectual montage. There are some memorable set pieces, such as the assault on the Winter Palace, the raising of the bridge and the toppling of Alexander III's statue, but the obscurity of some of its imagery and the uncomfortable blend of symbolism and realism render it less dramatically unified and emotionally overwhelming than its predecessor, *The Battleship Potemkin*. DP *DVD*

Nikandrof *Lenin* • N Popov *Kerensky* • Boris Livanov *Minister* ■ *Dir* Sergei Eisenstein, Grigori V Aleksandrov • *Scr* Sergei Eisenstein, Grigori Alexandrov • *Cinematographer* Edouard Tissé

The October Man ★★★★ PG
Murder mystery 1947 · UK · BW · 91min

Sturdily scripted from his own novel by Eric Ambler, cannily directed by Roy Baker and atmospherically photographed by Erwin Hillier, this is one of British cinema's best stabs at *film noir*. John Mills gives a highly accomplished performance as the man who, having been responsible for an accidental death, now has to prove to himself and the authorities that he didn't kill fellow boarding-house tenant Kay Walsh. But what really makes this seedy thriller so compelling is the support playing of Joan Greenwood, Joyce Carey and Edward Chapman. Keep an eye out for a six-year-old Juliet Mills, making her third screen appearance. DP

John Mills *Jim Ackland* • Joan Greenwood *Jenny Carden* • Edward Chapman *Peachy* • Kay Walsh *Molly Newman* • Joyce Carey *Mrs Vinton* • Catherine Lacey *Miss Selby* • Adrianne Allen *Joyce Carden* • Felix Aylmer *Dr Martin* • Frederick Piper *Detective Inspector Godby* • Juliet Mills *Child* ■ *Dir* Roy Baker [Roy Ward Baker] • *Scr* Eric Ambler, from his novel

October Sky ★★★★ PG
Drama based on a true story 1999 · US · Colour · 102min

Joe Johnston, director of *Honey, I Shrunk the Kids*, reins himself in with this charming true story of pluck and determination in 1950s West Virginia. Although his dad (Chris Cooper) is superintendent of the town mine, schoolboy Jake Gyllenhaal is determined to avoid a life underground. With Sputnik launching the space age, he gathers a group of friends together to build their own rockets. Encouraged by teacher Laura Dern, the lads hope to enter the state science fair. Droll, touching and engrossing. SR *DVD*

Jake Gyllenhaal *Homer Hickam* • Chris Cooper *John Hickman* • Laura Dern *Miss Riley* • Chris Owen *Quentin* • William Lee Scott *Roy Lee* • Chad Lindberg *O'Dell* ■ *Dir* Joe Johnston • *Scr* Lewis Colick, from the autobiography *Rocket Boys* by Homer Hickam Jr

Octopussy ★★★ PG
Spy adventure 1983 · UK · Colour · 125min

This was the 13th Bond movie and is possibly the most frivolous (and certainly the most careless) to date. The plot meanders as Roger Moore follows Maud Adams and renegade Soviet general Steven

Berkoff across India and Central Europe. All the usual paraphernalia are on view (although the gadgets aren't quite up to Q's customary standard), but director John Glen never quite seems in control, either of the breathless action or the overly glib dialogue. DP Violence. DVD BL

Roger Moore *James Bond* • Maud Adams *Octopussy* • Louis Jourdan *Kamal* • Kristina Wayborn *Magda* • Kabir Bedi *Gobinda* • Steven Berkoff *General Orlov* • David Meyer *One of twins* • Tony Meyer *One of twins* • Vijay Amritraj *Vijay* • Desmond Llewelyn *"Q"* • Robert Brown *"M"* • Walter Gotell *Gogol* • Geoffrey Keen *Minister of Defence* • Lois Maxwell *Miss Moneypenny* ■ *Dir* John Glen • *Scr* George MacDonald Fraser, Richard Maibaum, Michael G Wilson, from the stories *Octopussy* and *The Property of a Lady* by Ian Fleming

Oculus ★★★★ 15
Horror 2013 · US · Colour · 103min

The haunted-mirror scenario gets an impressive workout in writer/director Mike Flanagan's expansion of his award-winning 2005 short. *Doctor Who* star Karen Gillan and Brenton Thwaites work hard at playing disturbed orphaned siblings who endeavour to destroy the antique-looking glass they think killed their parents a decade earlier. Named after its first recorded owner, the Lasser Glass infects the minds of those it mirrors, leading to paranoia, distorted visions and possession. Flanagan mines these genre staples with cool ease, as taut action and floating camerawork extract maximum creepiness and reflective jolts. AJ DVD BL

Karen Gillan *Kaylie Russell* • Katee Sackhoff *Marie Russell* • Brenton Thwaites *Tim Russell* • Rory Cochrane *Alan Russell* ■ *Dir* Mike Flanagan • *Scr* Mike Flanagan, Jeff Howard, from a short film *Oculus: the Man with the Plan* by Flanagan, Jeff Seidman

The Odd Angry Shot ★★★ 15
War drama 1979 · Aus · Colour · 88min

This Vietnam War movie fired off a barrage of controversy in its native Australia, with its story of a group of Aussie professional soldiers, bitterly complaining about a conflict they don't think is any of their business and feeling danger has been foisted on them by politicians. John Hargreaves and Bryan Brown are outstanding, despite having to play stereotypical boozing and brawling comrades, while director Tom Jeffrey catches the claustrophobia of the occasion as much as the violent action. TH Violence, swearing, sex scenes DVD

Graham Kennedy *Harry* • John Hargreaves *Bung* • John Jarratt *Bill* • Bryan Brown *Rogers* • Graeme Blundell *Dawson* • Richard Moir *Medic* • Brandon Burke *Isaacs* • Ian Gilmour *Scott* ■ *Dir* Tom Jeffrey • *Scr* Tom Jeffrey, from a novel by William Nagle

The Odd Couple ★★★★ PG
Comedy 1968 · US · Colour · 101min

Jack Lemmon, devastated by the break-up of his marriage, packs his sinuses and his nervous tics and moves in with happily divorced Walter Matthau. While Lemmon is the finicky housewife (crustless sandwiches, coasters for drinks, nifty hoover technique), Matthau is the arch slob (brimming ashtrays, unmade bed, linguini on the walls), and they inevitably drive each other nuts. Apart from a cringe-making scene with two English girls, Neil Simon's comedy has weathered well, bristling with one-liners timed to perfection by the two leads. DP DVD

Jack Lemmon *Felix Ungar* • Walter Matthau *Oscar Madison* • John Fiedler *Vinnie* • Herb Edelman *Murray* • David Sheiner *Roy* • Larry Haines *Speed* • Monica Evans *Cecily* • Carole Shelley *Gwendolyn* ■ *Dir* Gene Saks • *Scr* Neil Simon, from his play

The Odd Couple II ★★★ 15
Comedy 1998 · US · Colour · 92min

Although it comes 30 years after the original, this belated sequel would have us believe it's really only 17 years since Jack Lemmon and Walter Matthau shared an apartment. The 78-year-old Matthau has retired to Florida to play poker with rich widows, but the impending marriage of his son to Lemmon's daughter brings the bickering pair together again. Scripted by original author Neil Simon, it's rarely more than a contrivance and a pension enhancement for all concerned, but Lemmon and Matthau are still eminently watchable. AT Swearing. DVD

Jack Lemmon *Felix Ungar* • Walter Matthau *Oscar Madison* • Richard Riehle *Detective* • Jonathan Silverman *Brucey Madison* • Lisa Waltz *Hannah Ungar* • Mary Beth Peil *Felice* • Christine Baranski *Thelma* • Jean Smart *Holly* • Barnard Hughes *Beaumont* ■ *Dir* Howard Deutch • *Scr* Neil Simon

Odd Girl Out ★★★
Drama 2005 · US · Colour · 84min

SPYkids star Alexa Vega plays a bullied schoolgirl in this harrowing teen drama. After going from popular clique member to outcast as a result of rivalry over a boy, the naive youngster is subjected to a venomous barrage of verbal and Internet abuse. It's like *Mean Girls* without the humour, as Vega is increasingly pushed over the edge emotionally, despite observant mum Lisa Vidal's endeavours to help her daughter. The film is well acted and largely believable, only coming undone in its excessively simplistic finale. Still, any serious attempt to explore the tough reality of bullying deserves credit, even if some of its self-conscious, stylistic devices undermine its overall message. SF Some swearing.

Alexa Vega *Vanessa Snyder* • Lisa Vidal *Barbara Snyder* • Leah Pipes *Stacey Larson* • Alicia Morton *Tiffany* • Rhoda Griffis *Denise* • Michael Arata *Dave* ■ *Dir* Tom McLoughlin • *Scr* Richard Kletter, from a story by Kletter, Matthew McDuffie, Rachel Simmons

The Odd Job ★★ 15
Comedy 1978 · UK · Colour · 84min

A key member of the *Monty Python* team, Graham Chapman seemed lost without a little help from his friends in his solo ventures. The cast he gathers around him in this off-colour black comedy tries its hardest to tune into the cockeyed humour at which he excelled, but only David Jason, as the hitman hired by the heartbroken Chapman to kill him, and Bill Paterson, as a pompous flatfoot, come close. A one-joke movie. DP

Graham Chapman *Arthur Harris* • David Jason *Odd Job Man* • Diana Quick *Fiona Harris* • Simon Williams *Tony Sloane* • Edward Hardwicke *Inspector Black* • Bill Paterson *Sergeant Mull* • Michael Elphick *Raymonde* • Stewart Harwood *Bernard* ■ *Dir* Peter Medak • *Scr* Graham Chapman, Bernard McKenna, from a TV play by Bernard McKenna

The Odd Life of Timothy Green ★★ U
Fantasy comedy drama 2012 · US · Colour · 100min

This fantasy tale aims for the sort of live-action whimsy that Disney Studios used to specialise in, but it completely misfires. There's too much schmaltz and sentimentality in the story of a childless couple (Jennifer Garner and Joel Edgerton) who find a mud-covered boy in their garden the night after burying a wish-list that describes their dream offspring. A terrific cast makes the most of underwritten roles but this is an uphill struggle. Not so much moving as stomach churning. AJ DVD

Jennifer Garner *Cindy Green* • Joel Edgerton *Jim Green* • CJ Adams *Timothy Green* • Odeya Rush *Joni Jerome* • Shohreh Aghdashloo *Evette Onat* • David Morse *James Green Sr* • M Emmet Walsh *Uncle Bub* ■ *Dir* Peter Hedges • *Scr* Peter Hedges, from a story by Ahmet Zappa

Odd Man Out ★★★★★ PG
Drama 1947 · UK · BW · 111min

This is as agonising a piece of cinema as you are ever likely to see. James Mason gives the performance of a lifetime as an IRA man on the run in the backwaters of Belfast after he is fatally wounded during a robbery. Mason conveys his pain and isolation with consummate skill, but his desperate plight is made unbearable by the masterly direction of Carol Reed and the chillingly atmospheric photography of Robert Krasker – the unforgiving landscape is exploited with outrageous camera angles and photographic distortions to fashion a city that is at once forbiddingly cold and worth dying for. DP DVD BL

James Mason *Johnny* • Robert Newton *Lukey* • Kathleen Ryan *Kathleen* • Robert Beatty *Dennis* • FJ McCormick *Shell* • Kitty Kirwan *Granny* • Fay Compton *Rosie* • Cyril Cusack *Pat* ■ *Dir* Carol Reed • *Scr* FL Green, RC Sherriff, from the novel by FL Green

Odd Thomas ★★ 15
Fantasy comedy thriller 2013 · US · Colour · 92min

A peculiar supernatural thriller, in which a clairvoyant amateur detective (Anton Yelchin) fights to prevent a plague of evil descending on his small town. This quirky tale starts off well, aided by Yelchin's easy on-screen charm, but it's not enough to stop a quick decline as the uneven story progresses. A clunky script, which includes an irritatingly persistent narration, also adds to the feeling that you're watching an episode of a surreal TV show rather than a movie. JL Violence.

Anton Yelchin *Odd Thomas* • Addison Timlin *Stormy Llewellyn* • Willem Dafoe *Chief Wyatt Porter* • Gugu Mbatha-Raw *Viola Peabody* ■ *Dir* Stephen Sommers • *Scr* Stephen Sommers, from Dean R Koontz's novel

Oddball and the Penguins ★★★ U
Adventure based on a true story 2015 · Aus · Colour · 95min

A good-natured but accident-prone dog becomes the unlikely saviour of a group of rare penguins in this immensely likeable tale from Down Under. Taking "inspiration" from 1990s animal crackers like *Babe* and *Beethoven*, the story is slight with some subplots that don't go anywhere, but it has heart in all the right places. The adorable penguins create just enough peril, and it's impossible not to fall in love with the bungling, four-legged star who tries to protect them. JL

Shane Jacobson *Swampy* • Sarah Snook *Emily Marsh* • Alan Tudyk *Bradley Slater* • Coco Jack Gillies *Olivia* ■ *Dir* Stuart McDonald • *Scr* Peter Ivan

Odds against Tomorrow ★★★★ 12
Crime drama 1959 · US · BW · 92min

A terrific heist movie, grimly told and well performed, this has a prescient and tough racist subtext that makes for compulsive viewing. Executive produced by Harry Belafonte and directed by master craftsman Robert Wise, it benefits from a high octane cast, headed by Belafonte himself, with Robert Ryan as the bigoted ex-con at his throat. There's also fine nervy back-up from Shelley Winters as Ryan's wife, Gloria Grahame as his mistress and Ed Begley, as the disgraced ex-cop who has the idea for the robbery. TS DVD

Harry Belafonte *Johnny Ingram* • Robert Ryan *Earl Slater* • Shelley Winters *Lorry* • Ed Begley *Dave Burke* • Gloria Grahame *Helen* • Will Kuluva *Bacco* ■ *Dir* Robert Wise • *Scr* John O Killens [Abraham Polonsky], Nelson Gidding, from the novel by William P McGivern

Ode to Billy Joe ★★★★ 15
Drama 1976 · US · Colour · 101min

The heartache of teenage love has rarely been so sensitively caught as in this romantic tragedy set in a Mississippi backwater, dramatising Bobby Gentry's 1967 hit-song lyric. Robby Benson is Billy Joe McAllister and Glynnis O'Connor the schoolgirl Bobbie Lee Hartley, while the Tallahatchie Bridge looms as the predestined doom. Although the ending is overly sentimental, the achievement of director Max Baer Jr and writer Herman Raucher is to mingle small-town behaviour with small-scale romance and to give a dramatic poignancy to both. TH

Robby Benson *Billy Joe McAllister* • Glynnis O'Connor *Bobbie Lee Hartley* • Joan Hotchkis *Mrs Hartley* • Sandy McPeak *Mr Hartley* • James Best *Dewey Barksdale* ■ *Dir* Max Baer Jr • *Scr* Herman Raucher, from the song by Bobbie Gentry

The Odessa File ★★★ PG
Thriller 1974 · UK · Colour · 123min

A terrific Frederick Forsyth plot and impressive production values make this thriller eminently watchable, even if veteran director Ronald Neame lets the pace drag and the length feels excessive. However, the often undervalued Jon Voight is superb as the journalist tracking down a concentration camp commandant, his quest hindered at every turn by members of the sinister Odessa organisation. There are splendid moments along the way, but Derek Jacobi is wasted and female lead Mary Tamm is inadequate. TS Violence, swearing. DVD

Jon Voight *Peter Miller* • Maximilian Schell *Eduard Roschmann* • Maria Schell *Frau Miller* • Mary Tamm *Sigi* • Derek Jacobi *Klaus Wenzer* • Peter Jeffrey *David Porath* • Klaus Lowitsch [Klaus Löwitsch] *Gustav Mackensen* • Kurt Meisel *Alfred Oster* ■ *Dir* Ronald Neame • *Scr* George Markstein, Kenneth Ross, from the novel by Frederick Forsyth

Odette ★★★ PG
Second World War drama 1950 · UK · BW · 112min

There is an inescapable predictability about wartime exploits movies, even though there is no denying the magnitude of the achievements of people such as Odette Churchill who faced Nazi torture while working for the French Resistance. Director Herbert Wilcox has little new to offer in his depiction of underground activities and pulls his punches during Odette's interrogation by sadistic Gestapo types. Anna Neagle suggests a certain stiffness of the upper lip, but she is not at her best. DP DVD

Anna Neagle *Odette* • Trevor Howard *Captain Peter Churchill* • Marius Goring *Henri* • Peter Ustinov *Arnaud* • Bernard Lee *Jack* • Marie Burke *Mme Glière* • Gilles Quéant *Jacques* • Alfred Shieske *Commandant* • Marianne Waller *Wardress* ■ *Dir* Herbert Wilcox • *Scr* Warren Chetham-Strode, from the book by Jerrard Tickell

The Odyssey ★★★ 12
Fantasy adventure 1997 · Ger/It/US · Colour · 172min

Whittled down from a mini-series, this lavish dramatisation of Homer's epic poem has some breathtaking Mediterranean scenery, including the ruins of Troy that lend unrivalled authenticity to the famous Trojan Horse episode. Armand Assante is suitably heroic as the King of Ithaca, who encountered the Cyclops, the treacherous Eurymachus and the bewitching Circe and Calypso during his 20-year adventure. Andrei Konchalovsky directs with a judicious blend of mythical spectacle and philosophical insight, and expertly handles his stellar cast. DP

Armand Assante *Odysseus* • Greta Scacchi *Penelope* • Isabella Rossellini *Athene* • Bernadette Peters *Circe* • Eric Roberts *Eurymachus* • Irene Papas *Anticlea* • Jeroen Krabbé *King Alcinous* • Geraldine Chaplin *Eurycleia* ■ *Dir* Andrei Konchalovsky • *Scr* Andrei Konchalovsky, Christopher Solimine, from the poem by Homer

Oedipus Rex ★★★ 15
Tragedy 1967 · It · Colour · 100min

Working from his own translation, Pier Paolo Pasolini seeks to emphasise the continued universality of Sophocles's tragedy by bookending the action with episodes set in modern-day Bologna. He also imparts additional atmosphere by staging the play in the dramatic setting of a 15th-century adobe city deep in the Moroccan desert, and by employing a primordially powerful soundtrack. For all its impressive qualities, though, it's a strangely dispassionate picture. DP Italian +subtitles. DVD Blu

Franco Citti *Oedipus* • Silvana Mangano *Jocasta* • Carmelo Bene *Creon* • Julian Beck *Tiresias* • Ninetto Davoli *Messenger* • Pier Paolo Pasolini *High Priest* ■ *Dir* Pier Paolo Pasolini • *Scr* Pier Paolo Pasolini, from the play by Sophocles

Oedipus the King ★★
Tragedy 1967 · UK · Colour · 94min

Neither a full-blooded epic nor an engrossing art house tale, *Oedipus the King* goes to show that even with a decent cast and with Sophocles as your source you can still come a cropper. As Oedipus, Christopher Plummer is far from compelling, despite the fact that he murders his father, marries his mother and then takes out his own eyes. This should be juicy stuff, but it just fails to ignite and even Orson Welles comes across as just the town bore. AT

Christopher Plummer *Oedipus* • Lilli Palmer *Jocasta* • Richard Johnson *Creon* • Orson Welles *Tiresias* • Cyril Cusack *Messenger* • Roger Livesey *Shepherd* • Donald Sutherland *Chorus leader* ■ *Dir* Philip Saville • *Scr* Philip Saville, Michael Luke, from the play by Paul Roche, from the play by Sophocles

Of a Thousand Delights ★★★
Psychological drama 1965 · It · BW · 100min

Luchino Visconti's operatic tale of guilt, betrayal and incest, derived from the Electra myth, is pretty unconvincing. But it boasts fine black-and-white photography by Armando Nannuzzi, and powerful performances from Marie Bell and Claudia Cardinale as a mother and daughter in conflict while commemorating their husband and father respectively, a Jewish scientist killed by the Nazis. RB In Italian.

Claudia Cardinale *Sandra* • Jean Sorel *Gianni* • Michael Craig *Andrew* • Renzo Ricci *Gilardini* ■ *Dir* Luchino Visconti • *Scr* Suso Cecchi D'Amico, Enrico Medioli, Luchino Visconti

Of Freaks and Men ★★★ 18
Period drama 1998 · Rus · BW/Sepia · 88min

Alexei Balabanov's sojourn in the sinful backwaters of 1900s St Petersburg could not be any more different from his bruisingly realistic *Brother*. However, the swaggering disregard for political correctness is again to the fore as widows, virgins and Siamese twins are exploited by immigrant pornographer Sergei Makovetsky. Such shock tactics are not employed to titillate, but to expose the corruption inherent in Russian society throughout the last century. Littered with references to the nation's cinematic heritage, this is an eccentric and enthralling allegory. DF Russian +subtitles.

Sergei Makovetsky *Johan* • Dinara Drukarova *Liza* • Lika Nevolina *Ekaterina Kirillovna* • Viktor Sukhorukov *Victor Ivanovich* ■ *Dir/Scr* Alexei Balabanov

Of Gods and Men ★★★★ 15
Drama 2010 · Fr · Colour · 117min

A terror campaign initiated by Islamic insurgents in 1990s North Africa proves a test of faith for a group of French monks in this drama inspired by actual events. Accepted by their local community in a remote mountain region, the brothers not only provide valuable medical facilities, but have also grown to appreciate their common ground with the beliefs of Islam. Because of this, they feel a strong duty to remain even when a series of killings puts their safety at risk. Far from some pro-Christian tract, this tense and ultimately moving film offers a call for tolerance, and touchingly demonstrates the spiritual rewards of generosity towards our fellow man. An impressive performance from Lambert Wilson as the careworn head of the monastery merely sets the seal on a thought-provoking experience, one that's definitely shaped by the post 9/11 landscape yet is timeless in its humanity. TJ French, Arabic +subtitles. Violence, swearing. DVD Blu

Lambert Wilson *Christian* • Michael Lonsdale [Michel Lonsdale] *Luc* • Olivier Rabourdin *Christophe* • Philippe Laudenbach *Célestin* • Jacques Herlin *Amédée* • Loïc Pichon *Jean-Pierre* ■ *Dir* Xavier Beauvois • *Scr* Xavier Beauvois, Etienne Comar

Of Human Bondage ★★★★ PG
Drama 1934 · US · BW · 82min

In the first, and best, screen version of Somerset Maugham's famous novel, Leslie Howard is sensitive and polished as the gentlemanly artist turned medical student who almost ruins his life over his obsessive infatuation with a vindictive teashop waitress. Bette Davis proves her credentials in this latter role, offering a nuanced portrayal that rises above her cockney accent. There is excellent support, too, and plaudits must go to John Cromwell's tightly controlled and atmospheric direction. RK DVD

Leslie Howard *Philip Carey* • Bette Davis *Mildred Rogers* • Frances Dee *Sally Athelny* • Reginald Owen *Thorpe Athelny* • Reginald Denny *Harry Griffiths* • Kay Johnson *Norah* • Alan Hale *Emil Miller* • Reginald Sheffield *Dunsford* ■ *Dir* John Cromwell • *Scr* Lester Cohen, from the novel by W Somerset Maugham

Of Human Bondage ★★
Drama 1946 · US · BW · 105min

This miscast effort stars Paul Henreid and Eleanor Parker: he too sophisticated and uncomfortably wooden, she doing her best to convince as a cockney. The film is solid and respectable, but ends up dull and unconvincing. For all its intrinsic deficiencies, however, one keeps watching, buoyed by a good supporting cast that includes Alexis Smith and Edmund Gwenn. RK

Eleanor Parker *Mildred Rogers* • Paul Henreid *Philip Carey* • Alexis Smith *Nora Nesbitt* • Edmund Gwenn *Athelny* • Janis Paige *Sally Athelny* • Patric Knowles *Griffiths* • Henry Stephenson *Dr Tyrell* • Marten Lamont *Dunsford* ■ *Dir* Edmund Goulding • *Scr* Catherine Turney, from the novel by W Somerset Maugham

Of Human Bondage ★★
Drama 1964 · UK · BW · 98min

This unnecessary third version of W Somerset Maugham's tale of a doctor besotted with a floozy has both leads so miscast that it took three directors (Henry Hathaway, Bryan Forbes and the credited Ken Hughes) to get something credible on screen. Kim Novak is far too intelligent a person to cope with cockney Mildred's idiocies, and it's anyone's guess what Laurence Harvey thought he was up to. TS

Kim Novak *Mildred Rogers* • Laurence Harvey *Philip Carey* • Robert Morley *Dr Jacobs* • Siobhan McKenna *Norah Nesbitt* • Roger Livesey *Thorpe Athelny* • Jack Hedley *Griffiths* • Nanette Newman *Sally Athelny* ■ *Dir* Ken Hughes • *Scr* Bryan Forbes, from the novel by W Somerset Maugham

Of Human Hearts ★★★ U
Period drama 1938 · US · BW · 103min

This period drama focuses on the conflict between heavily religious paterfamilias Walter Huston, his rebellious son James Stewart who wishes to break away and become a surgeon, and the lad's mother Beulah Bondi (Oscar-nominated), caught in the middle and making sacrifices to help him. Beautifully directed by Clarence Brown, with top-class production values and impeccable acting from a cast that includes stage actor Charles Coburn, virtually a newcomer to films at age 61, and John Carradine as Abraham Lincoln. RK

James Stewart *Jason Wilkins* • Walter Huston *Rev Ethan Wilkins* • Beulah Bondi *Mary Wilkins* • Guy Kibbee *Mr George Ames* • Charles Coburn *Dr Charles Shingle* • John Carradine *President Lincoln* • Ann Rutherford *Annie Hawks* • Charley Grapewin *Jim Meeker* • Leatrice Joy Gilbert *Annie Hawks at age 10* ■ *Dir* Clarence Brown • *Scr* Bradbury Foote, from the novel *Benefits Forgot* by Honoré Morrow

Of Love and Shadows ★ 18
Romantic political drama 1994 · Sp/Arg · Colour · 103min

Antonio Banderas and Jennifer Connelly star as the lovers whose relationship is set against a backdrop of corruption in Chile. Connelly is unconvincing as a naive journalist, unfamiliar with Chile's criminal underbelly. Banderas is a photographer trying to expose her fiancé as a fascist involved in official torture and the corruption at the heart of government. Notable for appalling direction and dialogue, the film jolts from one dysfunctional scene to another. LH

Antonio Banderas *Francisco* • Jennifer Connelly *Irene* • Stefania Sandrelli *Beatriz* • Diego Wallraff *Jose* • Camillo Gallardo *Gustavo* • Patricio Contreras *Mario* ■ *Dir* Betty Kaplan • *Scr* Donald Freed, from the novel by Isabel Allende

Of Mice and Men ★★★★ PG
Drama 1939 · US · BW · 106min

The aptly named Lewis Milestone created a little Hollywood history with this adaptation of John Steinbeck's best-loved novel, by commencing the action before the opening credits. However, its reputation really rests on the astute performances and Aaron Copland's superb score. Burgess Meredith and Lon Chaney Jr excel as the wiry drifter and genial giant wandering the west seeking refuge from the Depression. But every bit as effective is B-western star Bob Steele, who casts off his matinée idol persona to bring genuine menace to the part of the ranch owner's sadistic son, whose inability to control enticing wife Betty Field leads to tragedy. DP DVD

Burgess Meredith *George* • Betty Field *Mae* • Lon Chaney Jr *Lennie* • Charles Bickford *Slim* • Roman Bohnen *Candy* • Bob Steele *Curley* • Noah Beery Jr *Whit* ■ *Dir* Lewis Milestone • *Scr* Eugene Solow, from the novel and play by John Steinbeck • *Music* Aaron Copland

Of Mice and Men ★★★★ PG
Drama 1992 · US · Colour · 106min

Twelve years after they first played George and Lennie on stage at Chicago's Steppenwolf Theater, Gary Sinise and John Malkovich reprised their roles in this sensitive screen adaptation of John Steinbeck's classic novel. Blending tenderness and confusion with temper and power, Malkovich is quite superb as the simple-minded hulk whose titanic strength brings the pair of farmhands untold trouble. On the directorial side, Sinise acquits himself remarkably well, at times even improving on the excellent Lewis Milestone version. DP Violence, swearing. DVD

John Malkovich *Lennie* • Gary Sinise *George* • Ray Walston *Candy* • Casey Siemaszko *Curley* • Sherilyn Fenn *Curley's wife* • John Terry *Slim* • Richard Riehle *Carlson* • Alexis Arquette *Whitt* • Joe Morton *Crooks* • Noble Willingham *The boss* ■ *Dir* Gary Sinise • *Scr* Horton Foote, from the novel and play by John Steinbeck

Of Time and the City ★★★ 12
Historical documentary 2008 · UK · Colour and BW · 73min

Film-maker Terence Davies ruminates on his alienation from God and the Liverpool of his youth in this highly personal documentary that slips between eulogy and onslaught with a waspish wit. Juxtaposing idealised recollections of austere Christmases, day trips to New Brighton and divine visitations to the movies with jaundiced snipes at "Betty Windsor" and the Beatles, Davies delights in his own sentimentality and indignation, as his hushed narration laments the failure of the world to live up to his youthful expectations. But while the intimate reveries recall the brilliance of his earlier autobiographical features, such as *Distant Voices, Still Lives*, the despondent diatribe on the decaying multicultural port that Davies left behind is regrettably dismissive. DP DVD Blu

Terence Davies *Narrator* ■ *Dir/Scr* Terence Davies

Of Unknown Origin ★★★★ 15
Horror 1983 · Can · Colour · 85min

This minor gem insightfully outlines the psychological breakdown of a high-powered business executive, which manifests itself in the form of a larger-than-life rat. Director George Pan Cosmatos wrings every ounce of terror and suspense from this simple premise, as Peter Weller believably fights for his sanity in a battle of wits with the vicious rodent when it moves into his Manhattan brownstone. Seat-edged tension is evoked by giving out horrendous facts concerning the very real threat rats are to our society and through nerve-racking dream sequences, which cleverly trade on universal phobias. AJ Violence, swearing. DVD

Peter Weller *Bart Hughes* • Jennifer Dale *Lorrie Wells* • Lawrence Dane *Eliot Riverton* • Kenneth Welsh *James Hall* • Shannon Tweed *Meg Hughes* • Maury Chaykin *Dan* ■ *Dir* George Pan Cosmatos • *Scr* Brian Taggert, from the novel *The Visitor* by Chauncey G Parker III

Off Beat ★★ PG
Comedy 1986 · US · Colour · 88min

Judge Reinhold – best known as the gormless LA detective in the *Beverly Hills Cop* trilogy – tries (and fails) to be a leading man in this below-average comedy about a librarian who poses as a police officer and ends up falling in love with unsuspecting policewoman Meg Tilly. Worth watching for John Turturro and Harvey Keitel in roles they'd now rather forget. JB DVD

Judge Reinhold *Joe Gower* • Meg Tilly *Rachel Wareham* • Cleavant Derricks *Abe Washington* • Joe Mantegna *Pete Peterson* • Jacques d'Amboise *August* • Amy Wright *Mary Ellen Gruenwald* • John Turturro *Neil Pepper* • Fred Gwynne *Commissioner* • Harvey Keitel *Mickey* ■ *Dir* Michael Dinner • *Scr* Mark Medoff, from a story by Dezso Magyar

Off the Dole ★★
Detective comedy 1935 · UK · BW · 89min

Shot on a shoestring in a primitive Manchester studio, George Formby's second feature for producer John E Blakeley offers an insight into 1930s music-hall humour. But as cinema it's something of a chore, with an often static camera, poor sound and negligible quality control. Thrown out of the queue at the labour exchange, Formby takes over his uncle's detective agency and blunders his way through a number of cases. DP

George Formby *John Willie* • Beryl Formby *Grace, Charm and Ability* • Constance Shotter *Irene* • Dan Young *The Inimitable Dude* • James Plant *Crisp and Debonaire* • Stan Pell *A Most Inoffensive Parson* ■ *Dir* Arthur Mertz • *Scr* John E Blakeley, Arthur Mertz

The Offence ★★★★ 15
Psychological drama 1972 · UK · Colour · 107min

Sean Connery turns in one of his finest performances as a copper on the verge of a nervous breakdown in this blistering psychological drama. The star (fresh from finishing with Bond) is a revelation as a tough cop whose interrogation of a suspected child rapist (Ian Bannen) turns into a destructive game of cat and mouse with brutal consequences. Bannen is excellent, too, but it's Connery who dominates: like Kurtz in *Apocalypse, Now*, his experience of death and horror has so warped his moral compass that his disintegration before our eyes is agonising to behold. JA Violence, swearing. DVD Blu

Sean Connery *Detective Sergeant Johnson* • Trevor Howard *Cartwright* • Vivien Merchant *Maureen Johnson* • Ian Bannen *Baxter* • Derek Newark *Jessard* • John Hallam *Panton* • Peter Bowles *Cameron* ■ *Dir* Sidney Lumet • *Scr* John Hopkins, from his play *This Story of Yours*

Offending Angels ★ 15
Romantic comedy fantasy 2000 · UK · Colour · 89min

Conceived by writer/director Andrew Rajan as a vehicle for actors of ethnic origin (playing roles in which their ethnicity is irrelevant), the film at least has its heart in the right place, but has failed to locate any wit, style or invention. This tale of two greenhorn guardian angels (Susannah Harker and Shaun Parkes), who get a little too involved in the affairs of man, is dull and drawn out. DA *DVD*

Susannah Harker *Paris* • Andrew Lincoln *Sam* • Shaun Parkes *Zeke* • Andrew Rajan *Baggy* • Paula O'Grady *Alison* ■ *Dir* Andrew Rajan • *Scr* Andrew Rajan, Tim Moyler

Office Space ★★★15
Satirical comedy 1999 · US · Colour · 85min

This unconventional satire of work relationships and office politics comes courtesy of Mike Judge, one of the creators of the far from subtle *Beavis and Butt-head*. Jennifer Aniston (as a waitress) and Gary Cole (as a dreary boss) are the familiar faces, and the offbeat jokes range from droll references to singer Michael Bolton to swipes at restaurant etiquette and office technology. Not for all tastes. **JC** Swearing, nudity, sex scenes. *DVD*

Ron Livingston *Peter Gibbons* • Jennifer Aniston *Joanna* • David Herman *Michael Bolton* • Ajay Naidu *Samir* • Gary Cole *Bill Lumbergh* • Diedrich Bader *Lawrence* • John C McGinley *Bob Slydell* ■ *Dir/Scr* Mike Judge

An Officer and a Gentleman ★★★15
Romantic drama 1982 · US · Colour · 119min

Hugely popular in its day and appealing to the incurable romantic in all of us, this is a highly manipulative mixture of "boot camp is good for you" and "every girl loves a uniform." More sophisticated thoughts on human relationships form no part of Taylor Hackford's glossy hymn to overcoming a trailer-park background. Richard Gere looks a treat in his pristine white togs, and gives a performance more wooden than a wardrobe. Not even the combined talents of Debra Winger and Louis Gossett Jr can turn this one into a great movie, but if you're in the mood for a wallow, it's perfect. **SH** Some violence, swearing, sex scenes, nudity. *DVD* *BL*

Richard Gere *Zack Mayo* • Debra Winger *Paula Pokrifki* • David Keith *Sid Worley* • Robert Loggia *Byron Mayo* • Lisa Blount *Lynette Pomeroy* • Lisa Eilbacher *Casey Seeger* • Louis Gossett Jr *Sergeant Emil Foley* • David Caruso *Topper Daniels* • Grace Zabriskie *Esther Pokrifki* ■ *Dir* Taylor Hackford • *Scr* Douglas Day Stewart

The Officers' Ward ★★★★15
Wartime drama 2001 · Fr · Colour · 126min

This is a sensitive yet unflinching examination of human indomitability. At the outset of the First World War, Eric Caravaca is hideously disfigured by a bomb blast to the face and spends the rest of the war in a Parisian hospital where he undergoes reconstructive surgery. The extent of Caravaca's injuries is not revealed for nearly an hour, so the reaction on the faces of the hospital staff is our only source for the severity of his plight. By refusing to capitalise on the visual horror of the officers' injuries, director François Dupeyron lends dignity to their determination and despair. **DP** French +subtitles. Violence, sex scenes. *DVD*

Eric Caravaca *Adrien Fournier* • Denis Podalydès *Henri* • Grégori Derangère *Pierre* • Sabine Azéma *Anaïs* ■ *Dir* François Dupeyron • *Scr* François Dupeyron, from a novel by Marc Dugain

The Official Story ★★★★15
Drama 1985 · Arg · Colour · 113min

The winner of the Oscar for best foreign film, this is the compelling story of a history teacher whose acquiescence in the military regime is shaken when she begins to suspect she has adopted the child of a "disappeared" couple. It's an impressive effort from Luis Puenzo, who made his name directing commercials, that uses Norma Aleandro's credible conversion and the dignified determination of the ever-vigilant women of the Plaza del Mayo to

make its political points. This subtly impassioned drama is both persuasive and uplifting. **DP** Spanish +subtitles. Violence, swearing. *DVD*

Héctor Alterio *Roberto* • Norma Aleandro *Alicia* • Chela Ruiz *Sara* • Chunchuna Villafane *Ana* ■ *Dir* Luis Puenzo • *Scr* Aída Bortnik, Luis Puenzo

Offside ★★★★PG
Comedy drama 2006 · Iran · Colour · 87min

Forthright, funny and fascinating, this film follows a group of young women who disguise themselves as men in order to gain illegal access to a World Cup qualifier football match between Iran and Bahrain in Tehran. As the unmasked girls are apprehended and guarded by a unit of reluctant rural recruits, Jafar Panahi explores a wide range of social issues, while never losing sight of the unifying power of sport – something that proves vital to the exhilarating (if somewhat contrived) dénouement. Superbly played by the non-professional cast, this is an intriguing glimpse at the realities behind the propaganda issued by both Tehran and its western opponents. **DP** Farsi +subtitles. *DVD*

Sima Mobarak Shahi *First girl* • Safar Samandar *Azari soldier* • Shayesteh Irani *Smoking girl* • M Kheyrabadi *Mashadi soldier* • Ida Sadeghi *Girl soccer player* • Golnaz Farmani *Girl with chador* • Mahnaz Zabihi *Soldier girl* ■ *Dir* Jafar Panahi • *Scr* Jafar Panahi, Shadmehr Rastin

Oh Dad, Poor Dad, Mama's Hung You in the Closet and I'm Feelin' So Sad ★
Comedy 1967 · US · Colour · 86min

Rosalind Russell plays the horrendously awful, dominating mother of Robert Morse who is a worthless, emasculated creep. Morse's father, Jonathan Winters, is dead, murdered by Russell and stored in a coffin, but his ghost emerges on occasion to narrate the story. Barbara Harris is a sort of sex maniac who drives Morse so crazy with desire that he turns into Norman Bates. This black comedy about all-American "momism" is very much a product of its time. **AT**

Rosalind Russell *Madame Rosepettle* • Robert Morse *Jonathan* • Barbara Harris *Rosalie* • Hugh Griffith *Commodore Roseabove* • Jonathan Winters *Dad/Narrator* • Lionel Jeffries *Airport commander* ■ *Dir* Richard Quine, Alexander Mackendrick • *Scr* Ian Bernard, Pat McCormick, Herbert Baker, from the play by Arthur L Kopit

Oh, God! ★★★★PG
Comedy 1977 · US · Colour · 93min

This very, very funny original, together with *The Sunshine Boys*, revitalised the career of cigar-chomping veteran comedian George Burns. He plays the Almighty, visiting Earth to seek a messenger to convey to an indifferent world that He is still around, and choosing a supermarket assistant manager for the task (the perfectly cast country singer John Denver). Director Carl Reiner works wonders with this material, which in other hands could have been extremely tasteless. Teri Garr and Ralph Bellamy provide wonderful support, and the whole has a marvellous feel-good quality to it. **TS**

George Burns *God* • John Denver *Jerry Landers* • Teri Garr *Bobbie Landers* • Donald Pleasence *Dr Harmon* • Ralph Bellamy *Sam Raven* • William Daniels (2) *George Summers* ■ *Dir* Carl Reiner • *Scr* Larry Gelbart, from the novel by Avery Corman

Oh God! Book II ★PG
Comedy 1980 · US · Colour · 89min

Directed with cloying sentimentality, this follow-up should have spawned a new aphorism – never work with children or deities. The combination of George Burns growling out street-preacher wisdom and Louanne burbling kiddie banalities is enough to drive saints to sin. This story has God (Burns) ask a troubled schoolgirl to spearhead an advertising campaign to prove He's alive and well. **DP**

George Burns *God* • Suzanne Pleshette *Paula* • David Birney *Don* • Louanne *Tracy* • John Louie *Shingo* • Conrad Janis *Mr Benson* • Dr Joyce Brothers • Wilfrid Hyde White *Judge Miller* ■ *Dir* Gilbert Cates • *Scr* Josh Greenfeld, Hal Goldman, Fred S Fox, Seaman Jacobs, Melissa Miller, from a story by Josh Greenfeld

Oh, God! You Devil ★★15
Comedy 1984 · US · Colour · 91min

This is a third heavenly outing for veteran vaudevillian George Burns, here playing both the Almighty and his Satanic counterpart, the Devil. The *Faust*-like plot reveals a lack of ideas and Ted Wass is not as affable a leading man as John Denver in the first of the series, but Burns is, nevertheless, watchable. **TS** Swearing.

George Burns *God/The Devil* • Ted Wass *Bobby Shelton* • Ron Silver *Gary Frantz* • Roxanne Hart *Wendy Shelton* • Eugene Roche *Charlie Gray* • Robert Desiderio *Billy Wayne* ■ *Dir* Paul Bogart • *Scr* Andrew Bergman

Oh, Men! Oh, Women! ★★★U
Comedy 1957 · US · Colour · 90min

David Niven stars in this slightly farcical comedy but it's successful Broadway actor Tony Randall, making his screen debut, who runs away with the movie. Niven is a psychiatrist about to be married to screwball Barbara Rush. Then he learns that Dan Dailey, the husband of his patient Ginger Rogers, is making a play for his fiancée, a situation topped by another patient (Randall), when he reveals his current amour as the same girl. The movie has its longueurs, but takes enough sideswipes at psychiatrists to provide some fun. **RK**

Ginger Rogers *Mildred Turner* • David Niven *Dr Alan Coles* • Dan Dailey *Arthur Turner* • Barbara Rush *Myra Hagerman* • Tony Randall *Cobbler* ■ *Dir* Nunnally Johnson • *Scr* Nunnally Johnson, from the play by Edward Chodorov (uncredited)

Oh, Mr Porter! ★★★★U
Comedy 1937 · UK · BW · 80min

This is easily the funniest film Will Hay made with his willing stooges Moore Marriott and Graham Moffatt. As the incompetent master of an Irish railway station, Hay is at his blustering best, whether trying to bring the facilities into the 20th century or curtailing the scrounging schemes of his staff. In addition to the endlessly inventive comic quips, there is also plenty of action, as the trio takes on a gang of gunrunners, with the confrontation in the windmill and the final chase (starring Gladstone the steam engine) particularly entertaining. **DP** *DVD*

Will Hay *William Porter* • Moore Marriott *Jeremiah Harbottle* • Graham Moffatt *Albert Brown* • Sebastian Smith *Charles Trimbletow* • Agnes Lauchlan *Mrs Trimbletow* ■ *Dir* Marcel Varnel • *Scr* JOC Orton, Val Guest, Marriott Edgar, from a story by Frank Launder

Oh, Rosalinda!! ★★★★U
Musical 1955 · UK · Colour · 100min

This splendidly original British musical is an update of the Strauss opera *Die Fledermaus*, set in postwar Vienna, though clearly based at Elstree Studios, with a marvellous international cast enjoying itself under co-directors Michael Powell and Emeric Pressburger. Time has been kind to this stylish exercise, which was derided on its first release. Michael Redgrave and Ludmila Tcherina are the stars, with support from Anton Walbrook and Mel Ferrer. **TS**

Michael Redgrave *Colonel Eisenstein* • Ludmila Tcherina *Rosalinda* • Anton Walbrook *Dr Falke* • Mel Ferrer *Captain Westerman* • Dennis Price *Major Frank* • Anthony Quayle *General Orlofsky* ■ *Dir* Michael Powell, Emeric Pressburger • *Scr* Michael Powell, Emeric Pressburger, from the opera *Die Fledermaus* by Johann Strauss

Oh! What a Lovely War ★★★★PG
First World War musical satire 1969 · UK · Colour · 138min

Based on Joan Littlewood's stage production, Richard Attenborough's first film as a director is a stylised, satirical and ultimately moving tribute to the soldiers who answered their country's call and fought in the Great War. An all-star cast performs the original's jingoistic music hall songs, which Attenborough cleverly stages in the Brighton Pavilion and on the old pier. While there was animosity behind the scenes – Len Deighton refused screen credit as the film's writer – this remains a distinctive piece of work and by far the most audacious film Attenborough has ever made. **AT** *DVD*

Dirk Bogarde *Stephen* • Phyllis Calvert *Lady Haig* • Jean-Pierre Cassel *French Colonel* • John Clements *General Von Molke* • John Gielgud *Count Berchtold* • Jack Hawkins *Emperor Franz Joseph* • Kenneth More *Kaiser Wilhelm II* • Laurence Olivier *Field Marshal Sir John French* • Michael Redgrave *General Sir Henry Wilson* • Vanessa Redgrave *Sylvia Pankhurst* • Ralph Richardson *Sir Edward Grey* • Maggie Smith *Music hall star* • Susannah York *Eleanor* • John Mills *Sir Douglas Haig* • Ian Holm *President Poincaré* • Paul Daneman *Tsar Nicholas II* • Joe Melia *Photographer* • Mary Wimbush *Mary Smith* • Wendy Allnutt *Flo Smith* • Corin Redgrave *Bertie Smith* • Maurice Roëves *George Smith* • Angela Thorne *Betty Smith* ■ *Dir* Richard Attenborough • *Scr* Len Deighton (uncredited), from the stage musical, from the play *The Long, Long Trail* by Charles Chilton

Oh, What a Night ★★★15
Romantic comedy 1992 · Can · Colour · 87min

This is a familiar enough rites-of-passage tale: at the end of the 1950s, Corey Haim is a troubled teenager who moves to the country with his father and stepmother and begins an affair with an older woman (Barbara Williams). Although director Eric Till overdoes the golden hued shots of the countryside, he brings perception and a wry sense of humour to the action. Robbie Coltrane pops up as Haim's confidant, and there's a great soundtrack. **JF** Nudity.

Corey Haim *Eric* • Robbie Coltrane *Todd* • Barbara Williams (2) *Vera* • Keir Dullea *Thorvald* • Geneviève Bujold *Eva* ■ *Dir* Eric Till • *Scr* Richard Nielsen

Oh, You Beautiful Doll ★★★U
Musical biography 1949 · US · Colour · 93min

Broadway star, and later one of America's favourite raconteurs, George Jessel achieved some success later in his career as producer of a series of colourful vaudeville-based light musicals at 20th Century-Fox. The alleged biography of little-known popular composer Fred Fisher, this is a treasure trove of popular songs, and a typical example of such glossy star vehicles. Fisher is portrayed by the wonderful character actor SZ "Cuddles" Sakall, whose delightful hamming is always watchable. **TS**

June Haver *Doris Breitenbach* • Mark Stevens *Larry Kelly* • SZ Sakall *Fred Fisher* • Charlotte Greenwood *Anna Breitenbach* • Gale Robbins *Marie Carle* • Jay C Flippen *Lippy Brannigan* • Andrew Tombes *Ted Held* ■ *Dir* John M Stahl • *Scr* Albert Lewis, Arthur Lewis

Ohayo ★★★★U
Comedy drama 1959 · Jpn · BW · 90min

Director Yasujiro Ozu turns a feud between two small boys and their parents into a gently vibrant study of everyday life and a wittily wise treatise on the importance of communication. Shooting in his typically unobtrusive style, Ozu demonstrates again how fully he understands the human condition, as two businessmen face up to their shortcomings, a woman is driven from her home by gossip and a couple hide their true feelings in platitudes. In the midst of this misunderstanding and misery, the boys refuse to speak until their folks accept the westernising influence of television. **DP** Japanese +subtitles. *DVD* *BL*

Koji Shidara *Minoru Hayashi, older brother* • Masahiko Shimazu *Isamu Hayashi, younger brother* • Chishu Ryu *Keitaro Hayashi, father* • Kuniko Miyake *Tamiko Hayashi, mother* • Yoshiko Kuga *Setsuko Arita, aunt* • Keiji Sada *Heichiro Fukui, English teacher* • Haruo Tanaka *Tatsuko* • Haruko Sugimura *Kikue, Tatsuko's wife* ■ *Dir* Yasujiro Ozu • *Scr* Yasujiro Ozu, Kogo Noda

O'Horten ★★★ 12
Comedy drama
2007 · Nor/Ger/Fr/Den · Colour · 86min

Norwegian train driver Odd Horten (Baard Owe) is underwhelmed by the prospect of his retirement until he meets sprightly pensioner Trygve (Espen Skjonberg), whose *joie de vivre* lures Odd into a brave new world of casual burglary, ski jumping, skinny dipping and daredevil driving. Although the film's insights into underdogs having their day and growing old disgracefully are hardly new, this deadpan rite-of-passage tale has the courage of its quirky convictions. For all the hilarity of the vignettes, there's also a melancholy here, helped by Owe's solemn impassivity and subtly reinforced by John Christian Rosenlund's camerawork and John Erik Kaada's score. **DP** Norwegian +subtitles. **DVD**

Baard Owe *Odd Horten* • Espen Skjonberg *Trygve Sissener* • Ghita Norby *Fru Thogersen* • Henny Moan *Svea* • Bjørn Floberg *Flo* • Kai Remlov *Steiner Sissener* ■ *Dir/Scr* Bent Hamer

Oil City Confidential ★★★ 15
Music documentary 2009 · UK · Colour · 111min

After profiling the Sex Pistols (twice), Clash frontman Joe Strummer and the Glastonbury festival in previous documentary features, punk veteran Julien Temple here turns his lens on pub rockers Dr Feelgood, a band that enjoyed fleeting but massive success on the British music scene in the mid-1970s. Using talking-head interviews interspersed with archive footage and clips from a host of crime movies, Temple portrays the band as working-class renegades who unexpectedly rose from Canvey Island outsiders to mainstream chart-toppers with their 1976 live album *Stupidity*. Temple tries his best to make the story lively and interesting, but Dr Feelgood remains an R&B band of limited appeal, and this won't create many new converts. **DW**

Lee Brilleaux • Wilko Johnson • John Martin (2) *John "The Big Figure" Martin* • John B Sparkes *Sparkes, John B "Sparko"* • Christopher Fenwick ■ *Dir* Julien Temple

Oklahoma! ★★★★ U
Musical 1955 · US · Colour · 147min

The film version of the massively influential and, in its day, revolutionary Rodgers and Hammerstein Broadway musical preserves both the magnificent songs and the key Agnes DeMille choreography. Heading the notable cast is the underrated Gordon MacRae as a finely shaded romantic Curly, while Shirley Jones, in her film debut, is superb as Laurey. If Rod Steiger is a shade morose and out of kilter, well, so is his character Jud Fry. Trouble is, director Fred Zinnemann can't quite manage the pizzazz the movie really needs, and messes up the stirring title number. **TS DVD**

Gordon MacRae *Curly* • Shirley Jones *Laurey* • Rod Steiger *Jud Fry* • Gloria Grahame *Ado Annie* • Gene Nelson *Will Parker* • Eddie Albert *Ali Hakim* • James Whitmore *Carnes* • Barbara Lawrence *Gertie* • Jay C Flippen *Skidmore* ■ *Dir* Fred Zinnemann • *Scr* Sonya Levien, William Ludwig, from the musical by Richard Rodgers, Oscar Hammerstein II, from the play *Green Grow the Lilacs* by Lynn Riggs

Oklahoma Crude ★★
Drama 1973 · US · Colour · 112min

If ever a movie ran out of steam it's this one. Sumptuously produced and directed by Stanley Kramer on a high budget, it boasts terrific production values (though weak special effects work) and a fine cast led by Faye Dunaway and George C Scott at their respective ripsnorting bests. But once the oil gushers have gushed there's precious little plot or characterisation left,

only the vicious Jack Palance, who wants Dunaway's oil well. **TS**

George C Scott *Noble "Mase" Mason* • Faye Dunaway *Lena Doyle* • John Mills *Cleon Doyle* • Jack Palance *Hellman* • William Lucking *Marion* • Harvey Jason *Wilcox* ■ *Dir* Stanley Kramer • *Scr* Marc Norman

The Oklahoma Kid ★★★
Western 1939 · US · BW · 77min

Warner Bros achieved hit-and-miss results with its 1930s westerns, often making cowboy versions of its gangster movies. This film is no exception and is no less effective for its unbelievable casting because the outlaw hero is played by none other than New York's own James Cagney, strapping on his six-guns and singing like the best of them. The villain is snarling Humphrey Bogart, and there's a lot of pleasure to be had from watching Bogie and Cagney out west. The plot is that old western stand-by about trying to find out who was responsible for the death of the hero's father. **TS**

James Cagney *Jim Kincaid/"Oklahoma Kid"* • Humphrey Bogart *Whip Kincaid* • Rosemary Lane *Jane Hardwick* • Donald Crisp *Judge Hardwick* • Harvey Stephens *Ned Kincaid* • Hugh Sothern *John Kincaid* • Charles Middleton *Alec Martin* ■ *Dir* Lloyd Bacon • *Scr* Warren Duff, Robert Buckner, Edward E Paramore, from a story by Edward E Paramore, Wally Klein

The Oklahoma Woman ★★
Western 1956 · US · BW · 71min

This was one of four low-budget westerns Roger Corman made for the drive-in market. Richard Denning is the reformed gunfighter who lines up against an old flame, the villainous Peggie Castle, when he falls for nice girl Cathy Downs. Corman assembles his usual eclectic cast but he shows little feel for the genre and the lack of production money doesn't help. **JF**

Richard Denning *Steve Ward* • Peggie Castle *Marie "Oklahoma" Saunders* • Cathy Downs *Susan Grant* • Tudor Owen *Ed Grant* ■ *Dir* Roger Corman • *Scr* Lou Rusoff

The Oklahoman ★★ U
Western 1957 · US · Colour · 79min

This minor western features a too-old Joel McCrea in the lead and next to nothing spent on a wardrobe for leading lady Barbara Hale (Della Street from TV's *Perry Mason*). The screenplay's nothing either, as McCrea befriends an Indian (Michael Pate) and upsets some townies. Director Francis D Lyon was a superb editor but turned into a truly mediocre director. **TS**

Joel McCrea *Dr John Brighton* • Barbara Hale *Anne Barnes* • Brad Dexter *Cass Dobie* • Gloria Talbott *Maria Smith* • Verna Felton *Mrs Waynebrook* • Douglas Dick *Mel Dobie* • Michael Pate *Charlie Smith* ■ *Dir* Francis D Lyon • *Scr* Daniel B Ullman

Old Acquaintance ★★★
Drama 1943 · US · BW · 110min

The great Bette Davis is reteamed here with Miriam Hopkins in a melodrama that sees the two stars battle it out as a pair of childhood friends who become lifelong literary rivals. At the time, art started to imitate life and the resonances are plain to see, and enjoy, on screen. The unsympathetic Hopkins has a tough time holding her own against Davis, but director Vincent Sherman ensures that the scenery chewing is kept to a minimum. **TS**

Bette Davis *Kitty Marlowe* • Miriam Hopkins *Millie Drake* • Gig Young *Rudd Kendall* • John Loder *Preston Drake* • Dolores Moran *Deirdre* • Philip Reed *Lucian Grant* ■ *Dir* Vincent Sherman • *Scr* John Van Druten, Lenore Coffee, from the play by John Van Druten

Old Bill and Son ★★ U
Second World War comedy
1940 · UK · BW · 95min

Envious of son John Mills enlisting in the army, First World War veteran Morland Graham blags his way into the Pioneer Corps and finds himself in France assisting in the capture of a Nazi platoon. With its cast of practised *farceurs*, this flag-waver is

very much of its time. But its behind-the-scenes personnel is pretty remarkable, with Georges Périnal on camera, Vincent Korda responsible for the production design and Charles Crichton on duty in the cutting room. **DP**

Morland Graham *Old Bill Busby* • John Mills *Young Bill Busby* • Mary Clare *Maggie Busby* • Renee Houston *Stella Malloy* • René Ray *Sally* • Gus McNaughton *Alf* • Ronald Shiner *Bert* ■ *Dir* Ian Dalrymple • *Scr* Captain Bruce Bairnsfather [Bruce Bairnsfather], Ian Dalrymple, Arthur Wimperis, from the comic strip *Old Bill* by Bruce Bairnsfather

Old Bones of the River ★★ PG
Comedy 1938 · UK · BW · 86min

This muddled lampoon at the expense of the colonial service completed a decidedly disappointing 1938 for Will Hay. A rather uninspired spoof of the old Edgar Wallace story *Sanders of the River*, this struggles to combine a worthwhile storyline with the endless stream of ancient music-hall gags. However, they are infinitely more preferable to the racist remarks, which are unacceptable today. **DP DVD**

Will Hay *Prof Benjamin Tibbetts* • Moore Marriott *Jerry Harbottle* • Graham Moffatt *Albert* • Robert Adams *Bosambo* • Jack Livesey *Capt Hamilton* • Jack London *M'Bapi* • Wyndham Goldie *Commissioner Sanders* ■ *Dir* Marcel Varnel • *Scr* Marriott Edgar, Val Guest, JOC Orton, from the stories by Edgar Wallace

Old Boy ★★★ 18
Action thriller 2013 · US · Colour · 104min

This fairly faithful remake of Park Chan-wook's acclaimed 2003 Korean thriller stars Josh Brolin as an arrogant, alcoholic advertising executive. Brolin is kidnapped and held in solitary confinement for 20 years, during which time he's framed for murder and his daughter is taken into care. When he's eventually released, he sets out to uncover the motives of his abductors. Director Spike Lee replicates many of the original film's violent set pieces, but never quite delivers the same levels of menace. And while Brolin gives a steely performance, Sharlto Copley veers a little too close to pantomime villainy. **TeS DVD**

Josh Brolin *Joe Doucett* • Elizabeth Olsen *Marie Sebastian* • Samuel L Jackson *Chaney* • Sharlto Copley *Adrian Pryce* • Michael Imperioli *Chucky* • James Ransone *Dr Tom Melby* ■ *Dir* Spike Lee • *Scr* Mark Protosevich, from the 2003 film

Old Boyfriends ★★
Comedy drama 1979 · US · Colour · 102min

It should have worked, but somehow it doesn't. Talia Shire plays a clinical psychologist who, after a botched suicide attempt, goes on the trail of her past relationships. John Belushi and Keith Carradine are just two of the old beaus she meets up with in this lukewarm comedy drama. It marked the feature debut of Joan Tewkesbury, writer of *Nashville*, and was scripted by Paul and Leonard Schrader – which only goes to show that good pedigrees do not always a great movie make. **FL**

Talia Shire *Diane Cruise* • Richard Jordan *Jeff Turrin* • John Belushi *Eric Katz* • Keith Carradine *Wayne Van Til* • John Houseman *Dr Hoffman* • Buck Henry *Art Kopple* • Bethel Leslie *Mrs Van Til* • Joan Hotchkis *Pamela Shaw* ■ *Dir* Joan Tewkesbury • *Scr* Paul Schrader, Leonard Schrader

The Old Curiosity Shop ★★★ U
Period drama 1935 · UK · BW · 92min

Director Thomas Bentley was a former Dickens impersonator on the stage and had already filmed several silent versions of his novels. Here he does a commendable job of condensing the sprawling story of the destitute storekeeper and his granddaughter, Little Nell, who are forced to endure the hardship of the road after being terrorised by a monstrous moneylender, although his direction is occasionally lacklustre. Ben Webster and

Elaine Benson make tolerably troubled Trents, but the film belongs to Hay Petrie, whose Quilp is the embodiment of evil. **DP DVD**

Ben Webster *Grandfather Trent* • Elaine Benson *Nell Trent* • Hay Petrie *Quilp* • Beatrix Thompson *Mrs Quilp* • Gibb McLaughlin *Sampson Brass* • Lily Long *Sally Brass* • Reginald Purdell *Dick Swiveller* • Polly Ward *Marchioness* • James Harcourt *Single gentleman* ■ *Dir* Thomas Bentley • *Scr* Margaret Kennedy, Ralph Neale, from the novel by Charles Dickens

The Old Dark House ★★★★ PG
Classic comedy horror 1932 · US · BW · 69min

This is splendidly ghoulish nonsense, about a group of stranded travellers forced to take refuge from a storm in a sinister house, directed by that master of camp horror, James Whale. Charles Laughton and Boris Karloff are magnificent, and Melvyn Douglas is both suitably suave and puzzled, while the young female lead is Gloria Stuart. The 1963 William Castle version isn't a patch on this marvellous original. **TS DVD**

Boris Karloff *Morgan* • Melvyn Douglas *Roger Penderel* • Charles Laughton *Sir William Porterhouse* • Gloria Stuart *Margaret Waverton* • Lillian Bond *Gladys DuCane* • Ernest Thesiger *Horace Femm* • Eva Moore *Rebecca Femm* • Raymond Massey *Philip Waverton* • Brember Wills *Saul Femm* • John Dudgeon [Elspeth Dudgeon] *Sir Roderick Femm* ■ *Dir* James Whale • *Scr* Benn W Levy, RC Sherriff, from the novel *Benighted* by JB Priestley

The Old Dark House ★★ PG
Comedy horror 1963 · US/UK · Colour · 82min

William Castle forewent cinema audience-participation antics such as "Emergo" and "Coward's Corner" for this fumbling Hammer horror, in which the utterly inept Tom Poston comes to stay at Peter Bull's crumbling family pile. Instead, he concentrates on the macabre tics of such stalwarts as Joyce Grenfell (knitting manically), Robert Morley (perpetually tinkering with firearms) and Mervyn Johns (obsessively building an ark). The overall sloppiness means this soon outstays its welcome. However, with credits drawn by the creator of *The Addams Family*, it has a certain so-bad-it's-fun value. **DP**

Tom Poston *Tom Penderel* • Robert Morley *Roderick Femm* • Janette Scott *Cecily Femm* • Joyce Grenfell *Agatha Femm* • Peter Bull *Casper Femm/Jasper Femm* • Mervyn Johns *Potiphar* • Fenella Fielding *Morgana Femm* • Danny Green *Morgan Femm* ■ *Dir* William Castle • *Scr* Robert Dillon, from the novel *Benighted* by JB Priestley

Old Dogs ★★ PG
Comedy 2009 · US · Colour · 84min

John Travolta reteams with *Wild Hogs* director Walt Becker and shares top billing with Robin Williams for this ramshackle comedy. The stars play two friends and business partners who suddenly end up babysitting a pair of seven-year-old twins, the product of Williams's one-day marriage years before. The sight gags come thick and fast and there are some eye-catching cameos (Bernie Mac appears in his last screen performance), but essentially this comes across as nothing more than a Hollywood in-joke for which "you had to be there". **KK DVD**

John Travolta *Charlie* • Robin Williams *Dan* • Kelly Preston *Vicki* • Seth Green *Craig* • Ella Bleu Travolta *Emily* • Lori Loughlin *Amanda* • Conner Rayburn *Zach* • Matt Dillon *Barry* • Bernie Mac *Jimmy Lunchbox* ■ *Dir* Walt Becker • *Scr* David Diamond, David Weissman

An Old-Fashioned Thanksgiving ★★
Period drama 2008 · US/Can · Colour · 90min

The value of family over money is the homespun message behind this far-fetched period morality tale. Loosely inspired by Louisa May Alcott's classic short story, it sees heroine Tatiana Maslany cause class-centred conflict when she tries to repair the broken relationship between her struggling widowed mother and socialite grandmother (Jacqueline Bisset). Initially creaky dialogue

0

and stilted performances make way for some much-needed vitality, as the arrival of an enjoyably imperious Bisset shakes up both the rural household and the film itself. SF

Jacqueline Bisset *Isabella Caldwell* • Tatiana Maslany *Mathilda Bassett* • Helene Joy *Mary Bassett* • Vivien Endicott-Douglas *Prudence Bassett* • Kristopher Turner *Gad Hopkins* ■ *Dir* Graeme Campbell • *Scr* Shelley Evans, from the short story by Louisa May Alcott

The Old-Fashioned Way
★★★★ U

Comedy   1934 · US · BW · 68min

In one of WC Fields's greatest comedies, based on his own story, he appears as an impecunious impresario heading a travelling vaudeville troupe, outwitting landladies and writ-servers, putting on a full performance of the wheezy vintage melodrama *The Drunkard* and even finding time for his juggling routines. In addition, he conducts a running battle with Baby LeRoy – with the nipper inflicting the most damage. William Beaudine's direction gives it a polished look. AE

WC Fields *The Great McGonigle* • Judith Allen *Betty McGonigle* • Joe Morrison *Wally Livingston* • Jan Duggan *Cleopatra Pepperday* • Nora Cecil *Mrs Wendelschaffer* • Baby LeRoy *Albert Wendelschaffer* • Jack Mulhall *Dick Bronson* • Tammany Young *Marmaduke Gump* ■ *Dir* William Beaudine • *Scr* Garnett Weston, Jack Cunningham, from a story by Charles Bogle [WC Fields]

Old Gringo
★★★ 15

Period drama   1989 · US · Colour · 115min

This adaptation of Carlos Fuentes's acclaimed novel is meticulously staged, played with great conviction and studiously faithful to the psychological and historical complexities of the original. The only problem is that it is just a tad dull. Set in Mexico at the time of Pancho Villa's uprising, it skirts around the political issues and takes the easy way out by concentrating on the romance that develops between Jane Fonda's wayward traveller and Jimmy Smits's revolutionary leader. Gregory Peck steals every scene he's in. DP Swearing. *DVD*

Jane Fonda *Harriet Winslow* • Gregory Peck *Ambrose Bierce* • Jimmy Smits *Arroyo* • Patricio Contreras *Colonel Frutos Garcia* • Jenny Gago *La Garduna* • Jim Metzler *Ron* • Gabriela Roel *La Luna* • Pedro Armendáriz Jr *Pancho Villa* ■ *Dir* Luis Puenzo • *Scr* Aida Bortnik, Luis Puenzo, from the novel *Gringo Viejo* by Carlos Fuentes

Old Joy
★★★★ 15

Drama   2005 · US · Colour · 73min

Making exceptional use of stillness and silence, this is a wryly melancholic study of the passing of traditional concepts of masculinity along with the landscape that forged them. Mark (Daniel London) and Kurt (country singer Will Oldham) were once inseparable slacker buddies. But time has seen Mark acquire responsibilities, while Kurt has drifted even closer to society's margins. On a camping trip in the Oregon backwoods, they try to reminisce about their past, only to find that they have irrevocably changed – making the occasion more of a farewell than a reunion. Director Kelly Reichardt deftly contrasts the chaos and inconsequence of modern urban living with the consoling solitude of the wild outdoors. DP Swearing. *DVD*

Daniel London *Mark* • Will Oldham *Kurt* • Tanya Smith *Tanya* • Keri Moran *Lawnmower* ■ *Dir* Kelly Reichardt • *Scr* Kelly Reichardt, Jonathan Raymond, from a short story by Raymond • *Cinematographer* Peter Sillen • *Editor* Kelly Reichardt

The Old Lady Who Walked in the Sea
★★★ 18

Comedy   1991 · Fr · Colour · 90min

As the haughty con artist seeking to pass on the tricks of her trade, Jeanne Moreau gives a much better performance than this slight comedy really deserves. Although Michel Serrault stooges selflessly as her loyal partner, Moreau is badly let down by

the feebleness of Luc Thuillier, as the beach baby she nominates as her protégé, but she thoroughly merited her César award. DP French +subtitles. Swearing, sex scenes, nudity.

Jeanne Moreau *Lady M* • Michel Serrault *Pompilius* • Luc Thuillier *Lambert* • Géraldine Danon *Noémie* • Marie-Dominique Aumont *Muriel* ■ *Dir* Laurent Heynemann • *Scr* Dominique Roulet, from the novel *La Vieille Qui Marchait dans la Mer* by San Antonio

Old Louisiana
★

Period adventure drama   1938 · US · BW · 63min

Former western hero Tom Keene starred in a series of period adventures made on a shoestring budget, of which this is a particularly poor specimen. Keene stars as an American living in Louisiana when it was still a Spanish colony. An actress called Rita Cansino plays the daughter of the Spanish governor; after she became famous as Rita Hayworth, the film was relaunched as *Louisiana Gal*, giving her top billing. AE

Tom Keene *John Colfax* • Rita Cansino [Rita Hayworth] *Dona Angela Gonzalez* • Will Morgan *Steve* • Robert Fiske *Luke E Gilmore* ■ *Dir* Irvin Willat • *Scr* Mary Ireland, from a story by John T Neville

The Old Maid
★★★★ U

Period drama   1939 · US · BW · 90min

This wonderful slice of melodramatic soap opera froths and crackles with gloriously histrionic performances. This is Bette Davis at her best as an unmarried mother whose unsuspecting daughter prefers the company of Davis's deeply machiavellian sister Miriam Hopkins. Davis and Hopkins spar like a pair of theatrical prizefighters, and the period setting provides the perfect costumes to accompany all the flouncing. Never a dull moment. SH *DVD*

Bette Davis *Charlotte Lovell* • Miriam Hopkins *Delia Lovell Ralston* • George Brent *Clem Spender* • Jane Bryan *Tina* • Donald Crisp *Dr Lanskell* ■ *Dir* Edmund Goulding • *Scr* Casey Robinson, from the play by Zoë Akins [Zoe Akins], from the novel by Edith Wharton

Old Man
★★★★

Period drama   1997 · US · Colour · 98min

This outstanding adaptation of a William Faulkner story was written by Academy Award-winning playwright/screenwriter Horton Foote. In 1928 rural Mississippi, after a disastrous flood, convict Arliss Howard is ordered to take a boat up river to save a pregnant single woman and becomes a reluctant hero while falling in love with the new mother. Howard eloquently captures the simple intelligence of his character; Jeanne Tripplehorn gives an elegant, understated performance, while director John Kent Harrison exhibits great finesse in capturing the natural essence of Faulkner's milieu. A rare TV-movie treat. MC

Jeanne Tripplehorn *Addie* Rebecca Brice • Arliss Howard *JJ Taylor* • Leo Burmester *Plump Convict* • Daro Latiolais *Cajun Man* • Ray McKinnon *Shanty Man with Gun* ■ *Dir* John Kent Harrison • *Scr* Horton Foote, from the short story by William Faulkner

The Old Man and the Sea
★★★ U

Drama   1958 · US · Colour · 86min

Spencer Tracy is Ernest Hemingway's obsessed angler, riding the Caribbean with macho rubbish in his head and a giant marlin on the line. Inconsistent use of back projection and a certain monotony to the fishing sequences are drawbacks, but Tracy is tremendous, capturing the simple humanity and heroism of the central character, and nearly capturing an Oscar as well. Director John Sturges took over the project after Fred Zinnemann had laboured for months on it. AT

Spencer Tracy *Old Man* • Felipe Pazos *Boy* • Harry Bellaver *Martin* ■ *Dir* John Sturges • *Scr* Peter Viertel, from the novella by Ernest Hemingway

The Old Man and the Sea
★★ U

Drama   1990 · UK · Colour · 92min

This is a well-intentioned but mediocre adaptation of Ernest Hemingway's Pulitzer Prize-winning novella about a Cuban fisherman who finally lands a mighty marlin. Anthony Quinn gives a layered performance as the embattled protagonist despite the difficult-to-film subject matter. Quinn's family members populate this remake of the 1958 film, which starred Spencer Tracy (a hard act to follow). MC
DVD

Anthony Quinn *Santiago* • Patricia Clarkson *Mary* • Gary Cole *Tom* • Francesco Quinn *Santiago as a young man* • Valentina Quinn *Angela* • Joe Santos *Innkeeper* ■ *Dir* Jud Taylor • *Scr* Roger Hirson, from the novella by Ernest Hemingway

Old Man Rhythm
★★★ U

Musical comedy   1935 · US · BW · 74min

It's as lightweight as tissue paper but music buffs and film collectors still shouldn't miss this treat, which features a very young Betty Grable, and a rare appearance by the great songwriter Johnny Mercer as a college boy (he's the one on the train, with the southern accent). Watch out, too, for Lucille Ball. The plot, surprisingly, does have some relevance to its title, as George Barbier plays a businessman who goes back to college to keep a stern paternal eye on his playboy son, Charles "Buddy" Rogers, who is way too old for the part. TS

Charles "Buddy" Rogers *Johnny Roberts* • George Barbier *John Roberts Sr* • Barbara Kent *Edith* • Grace Bradley *Marion* • Betty Grable *Sylvia* • Eric Blore *Phillips* • Johnny Mercer *Colonel* • Lucille Ball *College girl* ■ *Dir* Edward Ludwig • *Scr* Sig Herzig, Ernest Pagano, HW Hanemann, from a story by Lewis Gensler, Sidg Herzig, Don Hartman • *Music/lyrics* Johnny Mercer, Lewis Gensler

The Old Man Who Read Love Stories
★★★

Drama   2000 · Fr/Aus/Sp/Neth · Colour · 111min

Reluctantly rousing himself from his passion for penny dreadfuls to hunt a vengeful jaguar, Richard Dreyfuss grows into the role of the lonely widower who has eked out an existence in a small Amazonian village since setting out to colonise the region decades before. Exploring environmental, political and human themes with a deceptive insouciance, Rolf De Heer's primary concern lies with Dreyfuss's evolving relationships with tribal chief Victor Bottenbley, blustering mayor Timothy Spall and itinerant dentist Hugo Weaving and his sensuous mistress, Cathy Tyson. DP

Richard Dreyfuss *Antonio Bolivar* • Timothy Spall *Luis Agalla, mayor* • Hugo Weaving *Rubicondo, dentist* • Cathy Tyson *Josefina* • Victor Bottenbley *Nushino* ■ *Dir* Rolf De Heer • *Scr* Rolf De Heer, from the novel by Luis Sepulveda

The Old Mill
★★★★★ U

Animation   1937 · US · Colour · 9min

This landmark Disney short marked the first use of the multiplane camera, a 14ft-tall construction that enabled several layers of artwork to be filmed simultaneously, giving a greater illusion of depth. Appropriately, the action mirrors the contraption that filmed it, as we are taken through the various stories of a ruined windmill and the wildlife living in it, from the ducks on the pond outside to the sleeping bats in the rafters. When a storm breaks out, the mill begins "working", jeopardising its inhabitants. Winner of the Oscar for best short cartoon, it remains a lyrical mood piece. CLP

■ *Dir* Wilfred Jackson • *Music* Leigh Harline

Old Mother Riley
★★ U

Comedy   1937 · UK · BW · 75min

This is the first of 15 cross-dressing comedies starring Arthur Lucan that ran from 1937 to 1952, although by the last he'd parted acrimoniously from singing sidekick Kitty McShane. The husband-and-wife team

had been playing the Irish washerwoman and her man-mad daughter since the 1920s, but their music-hall schtick always felt thinly spread on screen, despite efforts to vary the setting. Starting out at northern indie, Butchers, the duo were lured to Rank at the height of their fame, only to fade away at Renown. DP

Arthur Lucan *Old Mother Riley* • Kitty McShane *Kitty Riley* • Barbara Everest *Mrs Briggs* • Patrick Ludlow *Edwin Briggs* • J Hubert Leslie *Captain Lawson* • Edith Sharpe *Matilda Lawson* ■ *Dir* Oswald Mitchell • *Scr* Con West, from a story by John Argyle

Old School
★★★ 15

Comedy   2003 · US · Colour · 88min

A well-scripted frat-boy flick with a twist, this tale's so irrepressible that it's hard not to warm to its infantile charms. Luke Wilson, Will Ferrell and Vince Vaughn let it all hang out as bored buddies who try to recapture the fun of their college years by establishing their own off-campus fraternity. While Wilson's dry comic style only really comes to life during the film's bolder set pieces, Vaughn and Ferrell are such natural clowns that they up the tempo whenever they're on screen. SF Swearing, sex scenes, nudity. *DVD* *Blu*

Luke Wilson *Mitch* • Will Ferrell *Frank* • Vince Vaughn *Beanie* • Jeremy Piven *Gordon Pritchard* • Ellen Pompeo *Nicole* • Juliette Lewis *Heidi* • Leah Remini *Lara* • Seann William Scott *Peppers* • Snoop Dogg ■ *Dir* Todd Phillips • *Scr* Todd Phillips, Scot Armstrong, from a story by Court Crandall, Todd Phillips, Scot Armstrong

Old Scores
★★★

Sports drama   1991 · UK/NZ · Colour · 93min

This odd little rugby drama is a well played, if rather preachy, look at the re-match of a Wales–All Blacks game discovered to have been fixed 25 years previously. The players have long since scattered between God, drink and all points in between, but Windsor Davies and Glyn Houston round them up and add some necessary gravitas. Lots of famous rugby faces are also featured. SH

Robert Pugh *Bleddyn Morgan* • Glyn Houston *Aneurin Morgan* • Alison Bruce *Ngaire Morgan* • Clayton Spence *Dai Morgan* • Dafydd Emyr *Owen Llewellyn* • John Francis *David Llewellyn* • Beth Morris *Bronwen Llewellyn* • Windsor Davies *Evan Price* ■ *Dir* Alan Clayton • *Scr* Dean Parker, Greg McGee

An Old Spanish Custom
★★

Comedy   1935 · UK · BW · 61min

Working with British director Adrian Brunel, this comedy was an incongruous flop for Buster Keaton. The star plays a wealthy yachtsman who sails to Spain. While there, he falls under the spell of scheming siren Lupita Tovar. Pretty miserable stuff, especially when one remembers what the stone-faced genius was capable of when he really put his mind to it. TH

Buster Keaton *Leander Proudfoot* • Lupita Tovar *Lupita Malez* • Esme Percy *Jose* • Lyn Harding *Gonzalo Gonzalez* • Webster Booth *Serenader* ■ *Dir* Adrian Brunel • *Scr* Edwin Greenwood

Old Yeller
★★★★ U

Adventure drama   1957 · US · Colour · 80min

This epic about man's best friend will not leave a dry eye in the house. This was Walt Disney's first boy-and-his-dog adventure and remains resolutely the best, largely because of sensitive direction from British-born Robert Stevenson. Dorothy McGuire and Fess Parker make an upstanding and sympathetic Texas couple, and the frontier atmosphere is well re-created, though Tommy Kirk and Kevin Corcoran behave more like 20th- than 19th-century kids. A disappointing sequel, *Savage Sam*, came out in 1963. TS *DVD*

Dorothy McGuire *Katie Coates* • Fess Parker *Jim Coates* • Tommy Kirk *Travis Coates* • Kevin Corcoran *Arliss Coates* • Jeff York *Bud Searcy* • Beverly Washburn *Lisbeth Searcy* • Chuck Connors *Burn Sanderson* ■ *Dir* Robert Stevenson • *Scr* Fred Gipson, William Tunberg, from the novel by Fred Gipson

Oldboy ★★★★ 18

Action thriller 2003 · S Kor · Colour · 114min

Director Park Chan-wook received the Grand Prix at the 2004 Cannes film festival for this mind-bending action thriller. Choi Min-sik plays the happily married father, who is kidnapped and incarcerated for no apparent reason. He's then horrified to discover that his wife has been murdered with himself as the principal suspect. Fifteen years of unexplained Kafka-esque detention follow. Suddenly, he wakes up to find himself free, and gets down to the serious business of vengeance. Some viewers will be repulsed by scenes of self-mutilation; however, this has more to offer than action and violence - it's an imaginative tale of guilt and revenge, with a shocking twist in the tale. BP Korean +subtitles. Violence. **DVD BL**

Choi Min-sik *Oh Dae-su* • Yu Ji-tae *Lee Woo-jin* • Gang Hye-jung *Mido* • Chi Dae-han *No Joo-hwan* • Oh Dal-su *Park Cheol-woong* • Kim Byeong-ok *Chief guard (Mr Han)* ■ *Dir* Park Chan-wook • *Scr* Hwang Jo-yun, Lim Joon-hyung, Park Chan-wook, from a story by Garon Tsuchiya, Nobuaki Minegishi

Oleanna ★★

Drama 1994 · US/UK · Colour · 89min

Exploring the theme of inter-gender power-plays long before Michael Crichton dabbled with it in *Disclosure*, David Mamet's play enraged nearly all who saw it by forcing them to declare exactly where they stood on the subjects of sexual harassment and political correctness. Even though Mamet opts for a straight filmed record of the stage show, the screen version has markedly less impact, because the intensity of the theatrical experience cannot possibly be re-created, in spite of the spirited performances of William H Macy and Debra Eisenstadt. DF Violence, swearing.

William H Macy *John* • Debra Eisenstadt *Carol* ■ *Dir* David Mamet • *Scr* David Mamet, from his play

Oliver! ★★★★ U

Musical 1968 · UK · Colour · 139min

In this immensely popular film version of Lionel Bart's musical, Ron Moody - Oscar-nominated as Fagin - brings a certain magnificence to the role he had created on stage. The film collected six Oscars, including best picture and best director (Carol Reed, a last minute substitute for Lewis Gilbert, who probably would have brought the charm the fable sometimes lacks), and there's no denying that the Academy recognition for sound and art direction is justified. Today, the film works well as a child's introduction to Dickens, while adults can enjoy Shani Wallis's Nancy and Onna White's brisk Broadway choreography. TS **DVD BL**

Ron Moody *Fagin* • Oliver Reed *Bill Sikes* • Mark Lester (2) *Oliver* • Harry Secombe *Mr Bumble* • Shani Wallis *Nancy* • Jack Wild *Artful Dodger* • Hugh Griffith *Magistrate* • Sheila White *Bet* • Joseph O'Conor *Mr Brownlow* • Peggy Mount *Widow Corney* • Leonard Rossiter *Mr Sowerberry* • Hylda Baker *Mrs Sowerberry* ■ *Dir* Carol Reed • *Scr* Vernon Harris, from the musical play by Lionel Bart, from the novel *Oliver Twist* by Charles Dickens • *Cinematographer* Oswald Morris • *Production Designer* John Box

Oliver & Company ★★★ U

Animated drama 1988 · US · Colour · 70min

Disney gives Oliver a new Twist in this animated drama about a cute orphan kittycat who's drafted into a canine pack of streetwise New York pickpockets whose human master, Fagin, is up to his ears in debt to crime kingpin Sykes. It's a nicely told tale that, though a little lacking in Disney's customary charm, is still entertaining. DA **DVD BL**

Joey Lawrence *Oliver* • Bette Midler *Georgette* • Billy Joel *Dodger* • Richard "Cheech" Marin *Tito* • Richard Mulligan *Einstein* • Roscoe Lee Browne *Francis* • Sheryl Lee Ralph *Rita* • Dom DeLuise *Fagin* • Robert Loggia *Sykes* ■ *Dir* George Scribner • *Scr* Jim Cox, Timothy J Disney, James Mangold, suggested by the novel *Oliver Twist* by Charles Dickens

Oliver Sherman ★★ 15

Thriller 2010 · Can · Colour · 79min

In this Canadian chamber drama from writer/director Ryan Redford, an emotionally damaged war veteran (Garret Dillahunt) unexpectedly turns up on the doorstep of the friend (Donal Logue) who once saved his life in the field. A familiar set-up gives way to rather predictable interpersonal tensions, as this sincere, decently acted film struggles to find anything new to say about the psychological damage of war. Redford's compassion is never in doubt and the cast members give all they can, but this is essentially well-meaning stodge. TJ Swearing, brief violence.

Garret Dillahunt *Sherman Oliver* • Molly Parker *Irene Page* • Donal Logue *Franklin Page* • Kaelan Meunier *Jacob Page* • Marc Strange *Raymond Saddler* • Fiona Highet *Joan* ■ *Dir* Ryan Redford • *Scr* Ryan Redford, from the short story *Veterans* by Rachel Ingalls

Oliver the Eighth ★★★ U

Comedy 1934 · US · BW · 26min

Typical Laurel and Hardy high jinks in this short in which the great double act play a pair of barbers who both write to a rich widow who is advertising for a husband. However, Ollie neglects to post Stan's letter, planning to woo the widow by himself. She has, however, already seen off seven husbands and intends Ollie to be her eighth victim. In some territories the prefix "The Private Life of" was added to the title to mirror that of a hugely successful British film of the period, *The Private Life of Henry VIII* (1933). DF

Stan Laurel *Stan* • Oliver Hardy *Ollie* • Mae Busch *Eccentric widow at Box 204J* • Jack Barty *Jitters, the butler* ■ *Dir* Lloyd French

Oliver Twist ★★

Silent drama 1922 · US · BW · 74min

Wonderful lighting and production design, which beautifully evoke Dickensian London, are the saving grace of this otherwise disappointing silent version of the classic novel. Lon Chaney is ineffectual as Fagin, one of his few performances that fails to satisfy. Jackie Coogan, playing the title role, had become a phenomenal success the previous year starring with Chaplin in *The Kid* and this was one of the first films he made under a million-dollar contract with MGM. TV

Jackie Coogan *Oliver Twist* • Lon Chaney *Fagin* • Gladys Brockwell *Nancy Sikes* • George Siegmann *Bill Sikes* • Edouard Trebaol *Artful Dodger* • Lionel Belmore *Mr Brownlow* • Carl Stockdale *Monks* • Eddie Boland *Toby Crackit* ■ *Dir* Frank Lloyd • *Scr* Frank Lloyd, Harry Weil, Walter Anthony (t tles), from the novel by Charles Dickens • *Art Director* Stephen Goosson • *Lighting* Lewis Johnson

Oliver Twist ★★★★★ U

Classic drama 1948 · UK · BW · 110min

David Lean's masterly adaptation of the Dickens novel brims with unforgettable scenes and performances, notably Alec Guinness's Fagin and Robert Newton's genuinely frightening Bill Sikes. From the opening, with Oliver's mother struggling to the workhouse to give birth, to the climax on the roofs of Docklands, the picture brings the novel vividly to life. The movie caused riots in Germany and was initially banned and then heavily cut in America for its alleged anti-Semitism. AT **DVD**

Alec Guinness *Fagin* • Robert Newton *Bill Sikes* • John Howard Davies *Oliver Twist* • Kay Walsh *Nancy* • Anthony Newley *Artful Dodger* • Ralph Truman *Monks* • Francis L Sullivan *Mr Bumble* • Henry Stephenson *Mr Brownlow* • Josephine Stuart *Oliver's mother* • Henry Edwards *Police official* • Diana Dors *Charlotte* • Maurice Denham *Chief of police* ■ *Dir* David Lean • *Scr* David Lean, Stanley Haynes, from the novel by Charles Dickens • *Cinematographer* Guy Green • *Art Director* John Bryan

Oliver Twist ★★★ PG

Period drama 1982 · US · Colour · 98min

Made for American television but released theatrically outside the States, this umpteenth version of Charles Dickens's famous tale poses no threat to David Lean's definitive British version. It does, however, boast a rumbunctious rasping Fagin played by George C Scott. He alone provides positive reason for viewing. However, director Clive Donner also gets value for money out of a slew of British thespians. The screenplay by James Goldman is adult and respectful. Literature the easy way. TS **DVD**

George C Scott *Fagin* • Richard Charles *Oliver Twist* • Tim Curry *Bill Sikes* • Michael Hordern *George Brownlow* • Timothy West *Mr Bumble* • Eileen Atkins *Mrs Mann* • Cherie Lunghi *Nancy* • Oliver Cotton *Monks* • Martin Tempest *Artful Dodger* ■ *Dir* Clive Donner • *Scr* James Goldman, from the novel by Charles Dickens

Oliver Twist ★★★ PG

Period social drama 2005 · Cz Rep/UK/Fr/It · Colour · 124min

There's something just a little too reverent about Roman Polanski's well-crafted take on the Charles Dickens tale. Ronald Harwood's screenplay efficiently fillets the sprawling novel and moves us through the well-known story at a pleasing canter. Prague stands in admirably for the bustling, stinking, crime-ridden streets of 19th-century London and, in general, the performances are adequate. But, despite his affinity for the source material, Polanski never channels the rage at the social conditions of the poor that inspired Dickens, while Ben Kingsley's Fagin is an oddly anaemic creation. AS **DVD**

Ben Kingsley *Fagin* • Barney Clark *Oliver Twist* • Jamie Foreman *Bill Sikes* • Harry Eden *Artful Dodger* • Leanne Rowe *Nancy* • Lewis Chase *Charley Bates* • Edward Hardwicke *Mr Brownlow* • Jeremy Swift *Mr Bumble* • Mark Strong *Toby Crackit* • Frances Cuka *Mrs Bedwin* ■ *Dir* Roman Polanski • *Scr* Ronald Harwood, from the novel by Charles Dickens

Oliver's Ghost ★★

Supernatural comedy drama 2010 · US · Colour · 120min

Patience, understanding and forgiveness are the simple yet valuable messages in this TV movie about an unhappy 11-year-old (Nicholas Stargel) who discovers his new suburban home is haunted by a previous owner (Martin Mull). Initially, the curmudgeonly spook wants to reclaim his house, but, of course, it's not long before boy and ghost have become pals, with the pair helping each other face personal truths. The gently manipulative ending is particularly sweet and moving. SF

Martin Mull *Clive Rutledge* • Rhea Perlman *Eloise* • Nicholas Stargel *Oliver McCaffrey* • Cameron Daddo *Doug McCaffrey* ■ *Dir* David S Cass Sr • *Scr* David Golden

Oliver's Story ★★

Romantic drama 1978 · US · Colour · 90min

The less than successful sequel to schmaltzy *Love Story* has Ryan O'Neal trying to get his life together. The original was a complete one-off which should never have been revisited but even so director John Korty makes a game fist of dealing with the complexities of dating after your loved one's death. O'Neal looks a trifle jaded as well he might (his own personal life was going through several shades of hell at the time) but if you adored the blockbusting first picture you will be fascinated by this. SH

Ryan O'Neal *Oliver Barrett IV* • Candice Bergen *Marcie Bonwit* • Nicola Pagett *Joanna Stone* • Edward Binns *Phil Cavilleri* • Benson Fong *John Hsiang* • Charles Haid *Stephen Simpson* • Kenneth McMillan *James Francis* • Ray Milland *Mr Barrett* • Josef Sommer *Dr Dienhart* • Swoosie Kurtz *Gwen Simpson* ■ *Dir* John Korty • *Scr* Erich Segal, John Korty, from the novel by Erich Segal

Olivia ★★★★

Period psychological drama 1950 · Fr · BW · 91min

The death, in a car accident, of Jacqueline Audry, sister of Colette, robbed cinema of a respected talent. She directs this restrained adaptation of a pseudonymously published novel set in a girls' boarding school towards the end of the 19th century. In 1950, our censor cut ten minutes from it, although the lesbian undertones are just that. The story centres on two sisters, Edwige Feuillère and Simone Simon, who generate suppressed passions and affiliations among their charges. Dated in our permissive age, but still elegant, provocative and beautifully acted. BB French +subtitles.

Edwige Feuillère *Mlle Julie* • Simone Simon *Mlle Cara* • Marie-Claire Olive *Olivia Realey* • Yvonne de Bray *Victoire* • Suzanne Dehelly *Mlle Dubois* ■ *Dir* Jacqueline Audry • *Scr* Colette Audry, Pierre Laroche, from the novel by Olivia

Olivier Olivier ★★★★ 15

Drama 1991 · Fr · Colour · 104min

Anyone who enjoyed *The Return of Martin Guerre* and its Hollywood remake *Sommersby* will find themselves on familiar ground with this puzzling true-life tale of a runaway who returns. Is Grégoire Colin really a long-lost son, or is he, as his older sister Marina Golovine suspects, an impostor? Set in a rural idyll usually associated with innocence, this is both a mystery story and a disturbingly dark dissection of the modern family. Polish director Agnieszka Holland's persistent camera and the totally credible performances make this compelling viewing. DP French +subtitles. **DVD**

François Cluzet *Serge* • Brigitte Roüan *Elisabeth* • Jean-François Stévenin *Druot* • Grégoire Colin *Olivier* • Marina Golovine *Nadine* ■ *Dir/Scr* Agnieszka Holland

Ollie Kepler's Expanding Purple World ★★ 15

Drama 2010 · UK · Colour · 88min

Mental illness in movies is so often depicted glibly, so it's a shame that a film that attempts to explore its paralysing effects with seriousness and sensitivity rather loses its balance. Edward Hogg certainly gives an impressive performance as a web designer who slips beyond mere grief after his girlfriend (Jodie Whittaker) dies suddenly, but because his condition is so internalised, it's hard to feel anything other than bemused concern for him. Writer/director Viv Fongenie works hard, but any claims that this movie is *Donnie Darko* meets *Billy Liar* are well wide of the mark. DP Swearing.

Edward Hogg *Ollie Kepler* • Andrew Knott *Tom Hines* • Jodie Whittaker *Noreen Stokes* • Cathy Tyson *Jackie* ■ *Dir/Scr* Viv Fongenie

Los Olvidados ★★★★★ 12

Crime drama 1950 · Mex · BW · 76min

Luis Buñuel restored his critical reputation with this harsh, almost neorealist, study of street poverty that earned him the best director prize at Cannes in 1951. Shot in only 21 days and brimming with shrewd humanity, this keenly observed film is not without its surreal moments. But for all its political awareness, this is not a blindly liberal portrait of the crime, corruption and intimidation that is part of slum life. Society may be culpable for their plight, but Roberto Cobo and Alfonso Mejía, as the two leaders of a gang of boys who wreak havoc on their home town, are by no means saints. DP Spanish +subtitles. Violence, sexual references. **DVD**

Estela Inda *Mother* • Alfonso Mejía *Pedro* • Roberto Cobo *Jaibo* ■ *Dir* Luis Buñuel • *Scr* Luis Buñuel, Luis Alcoriza • *Cinematographer* Gabriel Figueroa

Olympiad ★★★★

Documentary 1938 · Ger · BW · 225min

After *Triumph of the Will* (1935), the documentary of the Nuremberg Rally, Leni Riefenstahl was commissioned to film the 1936 Berlin Olympics "as a song of praise to the ideals of National Socialism". With over 30 cameramen as well as planes and airships at her disposal, Riefenstahl provided a two-part epic that links the Olympic ideal with that of the Third Reich. But even Riefenstahl couldn't avoid showing the victories of the black American Jesse Owens. Despite the bad taste it

0

leaves in the mouth, one cannot be blind to the exceptional technique and beauty of the film, which many consider one of the greatest documentaries ever made. **RB** In German.

■ *Dir/Scr* Leni Riefenstahl

Olympus Has Fallen ★★★ 15
Action thriller   2013 · US · Colour · 114min

When the White House is infiltrated by terrorists, it's up to Gerard Butler to save the day in this fast-paced, *Die Hard*-influenced thriller. He stars as Mike Banning, a former bodyguard to the US president (Aaron Eckhart) who is being held hostage. Using his inside knowledge of the building, the resourceful Banning wages a one-man war against the bad guys, even as they threaten to disarm America's missile defences. The momentum drops off after the initial, audaciously staged terrorist attack, and Butler isn't quite spot on at delivering the pithy one-liners, but he is solid and capable as the hero who's got what it takes to get the job done. **TeS** English, Korean +subtitles. Violence, swearing. DVD Blu

Gerard Butler *Mike Banning* • Aaron Eckhart *President Benjamin Asher* • Morgan Freeman *Speaker Trumbull* • Angela Bassett *Lynn Jacobs* • Dylan McDermott *Forbes* • Melissa Leo *Secretary of Defense Ruth McMillan* ■ *Dir* Antoine Fuqua • *Scr* Creighton Rothenberger, Katrin Benedikt

Om Shanti Om ★★★ 12
Supernatural romantic drama
2007 · Ind · Colour · 161min

Writer/director Farah Khan (*Main Hoon Na*) reverses the recent Bollywood trend towards action and glamour, with this romantic and colourful supernatural romp. India's leading man Shah Rukh Khan stars here alongside newcomer Deepika Padukone in a story of thwarted passion, violence and rebirth that begins in the 1970s. Khan plays Om, a young artist madly in love with superstar actress Shanti (Padukone) But before their love can flourish, Khan meets with an untimely death – only to return years later determined to expose the truth. With themes of loss and grief delicately handled, this makes for charming viewing. Khan excels as the humorous Om while newcomer Padukone proves she has the acting ability to back up her flawless looks. **OA** Hindi +subtitles.
DVD

Shahrukh Khan [Shah Rukh Khan] *Om Prakash Makhija/Om Kapoor* • Deepika Padukone *Shantipriya/Sandy* • Arjun Rampal *Mukesh Mehra* • Bindu *Kamini* • Shreyas Talpade *Pappau master* • Kirron Kher [Kiron Kher] *Bela Makhija* ■ *Dir* Farah Khan • *Scr* Farah Khan, Mayur Puri, Mushtaq Sheikh

Omar ★★★★ 15
Thriller
2013 · Palestinian Territories · Colour · 98min

Tense relations with Israel form the backdrop of this well-crafted and effective thriller set on the West Bank. The title character, played by Adam Bakri, is a young Palestinian baker whose friends rope him into a plot to kill an Israeli soldier. It becomes clear that someone close to him cannot be trusted. But who is it, and which side are they on? Hany Abu-Assad doesn't offer any easy answers, instead delivering a powerful study of disaffection – one that explains how otherwise ordinary people can be led into committing acts of terror. **DW** In Arabic, Hebrew. DVD Blu

Adam Bakri *Omar* • Leem Lubany *Nadia* • Eyad Hourani *Tarek* • Samer Bisharat *Amjad* ■ *Dir/Scr* Hany Abu-Assad

Omar Khayyam ★★ U
Period adventure   1957 · US · Colour · 100min

There's only a slight inkling in this childish *Arabian Nights* adventure that Omar Khayyam was actually the medieval Persian poet of love and indolence and also a brilliant mathematician and astronomer. First and foremost he's a muscle-flexing, scimitar-swishing Cornel Wilde intent on saving Shah Raymond Massey from murderous foes while hazardously

romancing his leader's beloved Debra Paget. Now so preposterously cute, this romp is watchably camp. **TH**

Cornel Wilde *Omar Khayyam* • Michael Rennie *Hasani* • Debra Paget *Sharain* • John Derek *Prince Malik* • Raymond Massey *Shah of Persia* • Sebastian Cabot *Nizam* • Yma Sumac *Karina* • Margaret Hayes *Zarada* ■ *Dir* William Dieterle • *Scr* Barré Lyndon

Omega Doom ★ 15
Science-fiction thriller
1996 · US · Colour · 80min

Those familiar with director Albert Pyun's movies will not be surprised by the poor quality of this, or the fact it reworks the premise of a better-known film. This time, Pyun borrows from *A Fistful of Dollars*, updating the basic story to a post-apocalyptic future. Rutger Hauer sleepwalks through his role as a mysterious robot who arrives in a ruined amusement park occupied by two robot groups. **KB**

Rutger Hauer *Omega Doom* • Shannon Whirry *Zed* • Tina Cote *Blackheart* • Anna Katarina *Bartender* • Norbert Weisser *The Head* • Jill Pierce *Zinc* • Simon Pollard *Zed Too* • Cynthia Ireland *Ironface* ■ *Dir* Albert Pyun • *Scr* Albert Pyun, Ed Naha, from a story by Albert Pyun

The Omega Man ★★★★ PG
Science-fiction thriller
1971 · US · Colour · 93min

If you're hooked on sci-fi, this weirdly engrossing futuristic tale about the world after a viral apocalypse is for you. The conflict between "normals" (led by Charlton Heston) and light-sensitive mutants (led by Anthony Zerbe) is one of science against superstition, and, while lacking the vampiristic teeth of Richard Matheson's novel, it still has an eerie topicality. **TH** Violence, swearing. DVD Blu

Charlton Heston *Robert Neville* • Anthony Zerbe *Matthias* • Rosalind Cash *Lisa* • Paul Koslo *Dutch* • Lincoln Kilpatrick *Zachary* • Eric Laneuville *Richie* ■ *Dir* Boris Sagal • *Scr* John William Corrington, Joyce H Corrington, from the novel *I Am Legend* by Richard Matheson

The Omen ★★★★ 15
Horror   1976 · US · Colour · 106min

This big-budget horror blockbuster is given class by a distinguished cast and an unsettling atmosphere created by director Richard Donner. Cleverly borrowing a prophecy from the Book of Revelation about Armageddon, scriptwriter David Seltzer fashions a supernatural terror tale of religious epic proportions. When the wife of the American ambassador to Britain has a stillborn child, a baby whose mother died during childbirth is substituted for the dead infant. Five years later, a series of mysterious deaths lead the boy's parents to suspect that their son has supernatural powers. This carries its suspenseful premise with great uneasiness and there are several remarkably imaginative deaths. Three sequels and a remake followed, beginning with *Damien – Omen II* (1978). **AJ** Violence, swearing. DVD Blu

Gregory Peck *Robert Thorn* • Lee Remick *Katherine Thorn* • David Warner *Jennings* • Billie Whitelaw *Mrs Baylock* • Harvey Stephens (2) *Damien* • Leo McKern *Bugenhagen* • Patrick Troughton *Father Brennan* • Martin Benson *Father Spiletto* • Anthony Nichols *Dr Becker* • John Stride *Psychiatrist* ■ *Dir* Richard Donner • *Scr* David Seltzer • *Music* Jerry Goldsmith

The Omen ★★★ 15
Horror thriller   2006 · US · Colour · 105min

Director John Moore seems to have followed the original screenplay of Richard Donner's horror classic to the letter, making only a few cosmetic changes and upping the gore content. Liev Schreiber inherits the Gregory Peck role of American diplomat Robert Thorn, who finds himself in a pickle when he realises that his adopted son Damien is the Antichrist. The classy cast includes Mia Farrow, hamming it up magnificently as Mrs Baylock, Damien's devilish nanny. Competently directed and reasonably enjoyable. **AS** DVD Blu

Liev Schreiber *Robert Thorn* • Julia Stiles *Katherine Thorn* • Mia Farrow *Mrs Baylock* • David Thewlis *Jennings* • Seamus Davey-Fitzpatrick *Damien Thorn* • Michael Gambon *Bugenhagen* • Pete Postlethwaite *Father Brennan* • Nikki Amuka-Bird *Dr Becker* • Reggie Austin *Tom Portman* ■ *Dir* John Moore (3) • *Scr* David Seltzer

Omen III: the Final Conflict ★★ 18
Horror   1980 · US · Colour · 103min

This second sequel to *The Omen* finds Devil-child Damien as US Ambassador to the Court of St James, thus following in father's footsteps. Intending to do a Herod by killing every male child born on a certain day, Damien unleashes a load of special effects, obliging the priests to dust off the seven daggers of Megiddo yet again. The climax is mind-bogglingly silly, but not final enough because there was yet another sequel, *Omen 4: The Awakening*, in 1991. **AT** DVD Blu

Sam Neill *Damien Thorn* • Rossano Brazzi *Father DeCarlo* • Don Gordon *Harvey Dean* • Lisa Harrow *Kate Reynolds* • Barnaby Holm *Peter Reynolds* • Mason Adams *President* • Robert Arden *American Ambassador* ■ *Dir* Graham Baker • *Scr* Andrew Birkin, from characters by Dave Seltzer

On a Clear Day ★★★ 12
Drama   2004 · UK · Colour · 94min

Peter Mullan plays a redundant, middle-aged shipyard worker who decides to swim the English Channel, aided and encouraged by a bunch of misfits who pass for friends. A man of steely determination but few words, he finds training to swim the Channel easier than communicating with his wife (Brenda Blethyn) and grown-up son (Jamie Sives), whose twin drowned in childhood. Despite its formulaic origins, this succeeds largely due to the convincing Mullan. **BP** DVD

Peter Mullan *Frank* • Brenda Blethyn *Joan* • Sean McGinley *Eddie* • Jamie Sives *Rob* • Billy Boyd (1) *Danny* • Ron Cook *Norman* • Jodhi May *Angela* • Benedict Wong *Chan* ■ *Dir* Gaby Dellal • *Scr* Alex Rose

On a Clear Day You Can See Forever ★★★ U
Musical fantasy comedy
1970 · US · Colour · 124min

A great libretto from Alan Jay Lerner is delivered with gusty force by Barbra Streisand as the Brooklyn "goil" who regresses to the 19th century while being hypnotised to stop smoking. Vincente Minnelli could direct these musical heart-twangers with his eyes closed, and it does, indeed, look like he has done just that in some wayward scenes. Yet it is hard to dislike a movie that combines so much talent at full throttle. It is a bit long-winded, but Minnelli's awesome gifts are deployed in full, especially in the glorious opening sequences. **SH** DVD

Barbra Streisand *Daisy Gamble* • Yves Montand *Dr Marc Chabot* • Bob Newhart *Dr Mason Hume* • Larry Blyden *Warren Pratt* • Simon Oakland *Dr Conrad Fuller* • Jack Nicholson *Tad Pringle* • John Richardson *Robert Tentrees* • Pamela Brown *Mrs Fitzherbert* • Irene Handl *Winnie Wainwhisle* • Roy Kinnear *Prince Regent* • Mabel Albertson *Mrs Hatch* • John Le Mesurier *Pelham* ■ *Dir* Vincente Minnelli • *Scr* Alan Jay Lerner, from the musical play by Alan Jay Lerner, Burton Lane

On an Island with You ★★★ U
Musical   1948 · US · Colour · 103min

Former Olympic swimmer Esther Williams proved that not only was she a superb athlete, but with her robust good humour and innate sexiness she was a major musical star. Trouble was, the inevitable swimming sequences placed ridiculous strictures on Esther's plots. Here she plays a movie star, on location in Hawaii, torn between dashing Ricardo Montalban and stalwart Peter Lawford. The production numbers are the thing, though, and, as ever, the use of Technicolor is exquisite. **TS**

Esther Williams *Rosalind Reynolds* • Peter Lawford *Lt Larry Kingslee* • Ricardo Montalban *Ricardo Montez* • Jimmy Durante *Buckley* • Cyd Charisse *Yvonne* • Leon Ames *Commander Harrison* • Kathryn Beaumont *Penelope Peabody* • Dick Simmons *George Blaine* ■ *Dir* Richard Thorpe • *Scr* Dorothy Kingsley, Charles Martin, Hans Wilhelm, from a story by Charles Martin, Hans Wilhelm

On Any Sunday ★★★★
Documentary   1971 · US · Colour · 82min

Steve McQueen's love of motorsport existed off screen as well as in films such as *The Great Escape*. So, it's appropriate there should be so much footage of him in this lyrical documentary that celebrates being on two wheels with no speed limit. There are crashes galore – though not for ace Mert Lawwill – and champion surfer Bruce Brown, who made the fine surfing movie *The Endless Summer*, exhibits his fascination for motorbiking, showing that road-surfing is just as much fun. And there are no Hell's Angels to bother the eye, even if the country-and-western soundtrack irritates the ear. **TH** DVD

Steve McQueen (1) *Steve McQueen* ■ *Dir* Bruce Brown

On Connaît la Chanson ★★★ PG
Musical comedy   1997 · Fr · Colour · 117min

Alain Resnais's enjoyable comedy owes a debt to Dennis Potter, as its characters burst into lip-synched song at the least provocation. Polished, sophisticated, yet occasionally obvious, it will most intrigue those with a sound knowledge of French pop music, as the uninitiated not only miss out on the thrill of hearing familiar tunes, but they are also deprived of any socio-cultural significance they possess. The conceit is undermined by the slightness of the satire into which the tunes are inserted, as various self-obsessed bourgeois types fall prey to their passions. **DP** French +subtitles. DVD

Pierre Arditi *Claude* • Sabine Azéma *Odile Lalande* • Jean-Pierre Bacri *Nicolas* • André Dussollier *Simon* • Agnès Jaoui *Camille Lalande* • Lambert Wilson *Marc Duveyrier* • Jane Birkin *Jane* ■ *Dir* Alain Resnais • *Scr* Agnès Jaoui, Jean-Pierre Bacri

On Dangerous Ground ★★
Crime drama   1951 · US · BW · 82min

Like many a major director, Nicholas Ray often did minor work, but even his lesser movies are of interest. This RKO crime drama has a terrific beginning, with tough cop Robert Ryan leading a manhunt and displaying a totally unsympathetic, even sadistic, temperament. Then he falls for blind Ida Lupino, his world is turned upside down and the movie loses its edge. Nevertheless, the mood is well maintained, boosted by a remarkable score, but it's not nearly grim enough for its subject matter. **TS**

Robert Ryan *Jim Wilson* • Ida Lupino *Mary Malden* • Ward Bond *Walter Brent* • Charles Kemper *Bill Daly* • Anthony Ross *Pete Santos* • Ed Begley *Captain Brawley* ■ *Dir* Nicholas Ray • *Scr* Al Bezzerides, Nicholas Ray, from the novel *Mad with Much Heart* by Gerald Butler • *Music* Bernard Herrmann

On Dangerous Ground ★★★ PG
Thriller   1986 · US · Colour · 91min

If you catch this bizarrely plotted piece of hokum in the right mood, you might find much to enjoy in it. All-American Stephen Collins plays a physicist who takes on an evil industrialist illegally dumping nuclear waste. Filmed by former actor and stunt co-ordinator Chuck Bail, it's not surprising its limited dramatic appeal is significantly broadened by plentiful action and some dazzling aerial sequences. Only the sloppy editing disappoints. **RS**

Stephen Collins *David Lowell* • Janet Julian *Vanessa Pilgrim* • Lance Henriksen *Brook Alistair* • Bo Svenson *Captain* • Victoria Racimo *Rachel* •

U SUITABLE FOR ALL   Uc SUITABLE ESPECIALLY FOR YOUNG CHILDREN (DVD ONLY)   PG PARENTAL GUIDANCE   12A UNDER 12s TO BE ACCOMPANIED (CINEMA ONLY)

Nicholas Pryor *John Pilgrim* ■ *Dir* Chuck Bail • *Scr* Sheila Goldberg, Ovidio G Assonitis, Alfonso Brescia, Steve Luctto

On Deadly Ground ★★★ 15
Action adventure 1994 · US · Colour · 96min

Action star Steven Seagal has always brought a vaguely liberal slant to his no-brain thrillers and his directorial debut is admirably politically correct. It's just a shame that the caring, sharing, eco-friendly message tends to overpower what Seagal does best – kicking the stuffing out of bad guys. Here he's a troubleshooter who goes into battle with oil tycoon Michael Caine who is about to pollute virtually all of Alaska. JF Swearing, violence, nudity. *DVD*

Steven Seagal *Forrest Taft* • Michael Caine *Michael Jennings* • Joan Chen *Masu* • John C McGinley *MacGruder* • R Lee Ermey *Stone* • Shari Shattuck *Liles* • Billy Bob Thornton *Homer Carlton* • Richard Hamilton *Hugh Palmer* ■ *Dir* Steven Seagal • *Scr* Ed Horowitz, Robin U Russin

On Golden Pond ★★★★ PG
Drama 1981 · US · Colour · 104min

Nominated for ten Oscars, this old-fashioned family melodrama won three – best adapted screenplay for Ernest Thompson and, more notably, Katharine Hepburn's fourth award for best actress and Henry Fonda's first as best actor. Considering neither was in the best of health, their performances are remarkable. The quiet authority of their acting is all the more apparent in their scenes with Jane Fonda, who overdoes the angst, particularly when opposite the father with whom she occasionally disagreed in real life. Complementing the subtle shades of performance are cinematographer Billy Williams's superb images, using to dramatic effect the changing light of the countryside in summer. DP *DVD*

Henry Fonda *Norman Thayer Jr* • Katharine Hepburn *Ethel Thayer* • Jane Fonda *Chelsea Thayer Wayne* • Doug McKeon *Billy Ray* • Dabney Coleman *Bill Ray* • William Lanteau *Charlie Martin* • Chris Rydell [Christopher Rydell] *Sumner Todd* ■ *Dir* Mark Rydell • *Scr* Ernest Thompson, from his play

On Her Majesty's Secret Service ★★★★ PG
Spy adventure 1969 · UK · Colour · 142min

If any James Bond yarn is a cult film, it's this one, so divided have fans and critics been over the years. Sean Connery's replacement, George Lazenby, underwhelmed some, but irrespective of his shortcomings the sixth outing for 007 is a magnificent adventure that sees Bond out to stop the evil schemes of bald baddie Blofeld (Telly Savalas). The script throws up superb action sequences and nerve-frazzling suspense. Add Diana Rigg and a classic John Barry score and you have an adventure that's right up there with the best of them. JA Violence. *DVD*

George Lazenby *James Bond* • Diana Rigg *Tracy* • Telly Savalas *Blofeld* • Ilse Steppat *Irma Bunt* • Gabriele Ferzetti *Draco* • Yuri Borienko *Gruenther* • Bernard Horsfall *Campbell* • George Baker *Sir Hilary Bray* • Bernard Lee *"M"* • Lois Maxwell *Miss Moneypenny* • Desmond Llewelyn *"Q"* ■ *Dir* Peter Hunt • *Scr* Richard Maibaum, Simon Raven, from the novel by Ian Fleming

On Moonlight Bay ★★★ U
Period musical comedy
1951 · US · Colour · 91min

Doris Day shines as the tomboyish heroine in this elegantly designed but slight movie that beautifully evokes its early-20th-century setting. She's surrounded by warm-hearted character players such as Mary Wickes and Rosemary DeCamp. Based on stories by Booth Tarkington, this was so popular that the same cast was reunited two years later for an equally perky sequel, *By the Light of the Silvery Moon.* TS

Doris Day *Marjorie Winfield* • Gordon MacRae *William Sherman* • Jack Smith (1) *Hubert Wakeley* • Leon Ames *George Winfield* • Rosemary DeCamp *Mrs Winfield* • Mary Wickes *Stella* • Ellen Corby *Miss Stevens* • Billy Gray *Wesley Winfield* • Jeffrey Stevens *Jim Sherman* ■ *Dir* Roy Del

Ruth • *Scr* Jack Rose, Melville Shavelson, from the novel *Alice Adams* and the story *Penrod* by Booth Tarkington

On My Own ★★★
Drama 1992 · It/Can/Aus · Colour · 97min

Australian actress Judy Davis proves once more that she is one of the most remarkable actresses around in this thoughtful drama from director Antonio Tibaldi. As a schizophrenic whose outbursts and shameless behaviour intrude upon the already troubled life of her adolescent son, she erupts on to the screen and lurches between reason and recklessness with a power that shocks with its intensity. Unfortunately, we get too little of her and the burden of carrying the action falls on Matthew Ferguson as her son. DP Swearing, nudity.

Judy Davis *Mother* • Matthew Ferguson *Simon Henderson* • David McIlwraith *John Henderson* • Jan Rubes *The Colonel* • Michele Melega *Shammas* ■ *Dir* Antonio Tibaldi • *Scr* Antonio Tibaldi, Gill Dennis, John Frizzell

On My Way to the Crusades, I Met a Girl Who... ★
Farce 1967 · It/US · Colour · 110min

Also known as *The Chastity Belt* and left waiting for two years on the shelf, this sex comedy stars Tony Curtis as a Middle Ages knight who keeps gamekeeper's daughter Monica Vitti securely locked up in order to preserve her "reputation". The bawdiness of the story owes something to the success of *Tom Jones*. Curtis remembered it mainly for Vitti's unwillingness to be photographed from any angle except head-on. He's quoted as saying, "She had a big nose and would never turn in profile." AT

Tony Curtis *Guerrando Da Montone* • Monica Vitti *Boccadoro* • Hugh Griffith *Ibn-el-Rascid* • John Richardson *Dragone* ■ *Dir* Pasquale Festa Campanile • *Scr* Luigi Magni, Larry Gelbart, from a story by Ugo Liberatore

On Our Merry Way ★★ U
Portmanteau comedy drama
1948 · US · BW · 107min

This mediocre and unconvincing movie, directed by (among others) the illustrious King Vidor on a bad day, links its several episodic stories by means of a newspaper ad salesman (Burgess Meredith) who dreams of being an investigative journalist. He fibs to his new wife (Paulette Goddard, Meredith's then real-life wife) that he is the reporter responsible for a series of stories and then must make good the lie. The cast does include some notable names, with Henry Fonda and James Stewart teamed as musicians in the best segment, which was directed – uncredited – by John Huston and George Stevens. RK *DVD*

Burgess Meredith *Oliver Pease* • Paulette Goddard *Martha Pease* • Fred MacMurray *Al* • Hugh Herbert *Elisha Hobbs* • James Stewart *Slim* • Dorothy Lamour *Gloria Manners* • Victor Moore *Ashton Carrington* • Eilene Janssen *Peggy Thorndyke* • Henry Fonda *Lank* • William Demarest *Floyd* • Dorothy Ford *Lola* ■ *Dir* King Vidor, Leslie Fenton • *Scr* Laurence Stallings, Lou Breslow, from a story by John O'Hara, Arch Oboler

On Purge Bébé ★★
Farce 1931 · Fr · BW · 62min

Jean Renoir's silent films enjoyed scant success at the box office, so with this first move to sound he needed a commercial success. Adapted from a Georges Feydeau farce, it was shot quickly and was one of the first movies to contain the sound of a flushing toilet. The film, which betrays its stage origins by scarcely moving from its proscenium arch setting, tells the silly story of a porcelain manufacturer who attempts to sell thousands of chamber pots to the French army. It made enough profit for Renoir to move forward into his great period of film-making. BB In French.

Marguerite Pierry *Julie Follavoine* • Jacques Louvigny *M Follavoine* • Sacha Tarride *Toto Follavoine* • Michel Simon *M Chouilloux* •

Fernandel *Truchet* ■ *Dir* Jean Renoir • *Scr* Jean Renoir, Pierre Prévert, from the play by Georges Feydeau

On the Avenue ★★★ U
Musical comedy 1937 · US · BW · 84min

A host of classic Irving Berlin songs cut a swathe through this bright, cliché-free musical like gold in rock. Director Roy Del Ruth was well known for extracting thoughtful, multilayered performances from his stars, and Dick Powell as the showbiz charmer and Madeleine Carroll as the lovestruck uptown lady are both stunning. The movie has much to say on the nature of love and passion, serving it up with enormous verve and incisive wit. SH *DVD*

Dick Powell *Gary Blake* • Madeleine Carroll *Mimi Caraway* • Alice Faye *Mona Merrick* • The Ritz Brothers [Al Ritz] • The Ritz Brothers [Jimmy Ritz] • The Ritz Brothers [Harry Ritz] • George Barbier *Commodore Caraway* • Alan Mowbray *Frederick Sims* • Cora Witherspoon *Aunt Fritz Peters* • Walter Catlett *Jake Dribble* • Douglas Fowley *Eddie Eads* • Joan Davis *Miss Katz* ■ *Dir* Roy Del Ruth • *Scr* Gene Markey, William Conselman

On the Beach ★★ PG
Drama 1959 · US · BW · 128min

An atomic submarine boldly goes where no atomic sub has gone before: to survey a nuclear-wasted Earth. The few survivors suffer from contamination by cliché, a sickness of conversational banality. Stanley Kramer's film of Nevil Shute's bestseller means well, and Gregory Peck, Ava Gardner and Anthony Perkins certainly try their best, but it lacks any apocalyptic excitement to go with its appalling premise. Dreary and solemn. TH *DVD* *Blu*

Gregory Peck *Dwight Towers* • Ava Gardner *Moira Davidson* • Fred Astaire *Julian Osborn* • Anthony Perkins *Peter Holmes* • Donna Anderson *Mary Holmes* • John Tate *Admiral Bridie* • Lola Brooks *Lieutenant Hosgood* ■ *Dir* Stanley Kramer • *Scr* John Paxton, James Lee Barrett, from the novel by Nevil Shute

On the Beat ★★ U
Comedy 1962 · UK · BW · 101min

In this fitfully amusing comedy, Norman Wisdom plays a would-be policeman who is reduced to being a Scotland Yard car park attendant because he's not tall enough to be a bobby. Then it turns out that he's the spitting image of a criminal – you can probably guess the rest. Wisdom is funny enough, and a host of British character actors goes through the motions, but this is pretty simplistic stuff. TS *DVD*

Norman Wisdom *Norman Pitkin/Giulio Napolitani* • Jennifer Jayne *Rosanna* • Raymond Huntley *Sir Ronald Ackroyd* • David Lodge *Superintendent Hobson* • Esma Cannon *Mrs Stammers* • Eric Barker *Doctor* ■ *Dir* Robert Asher • *Scr* Jack Davies, Norman Wisdom, Eddie Leslie

On the Black Hill ★★★ 15
Drama 1987 · UK · Colour · 110min

Adapted from Bruce Chatwin's bestseller, this charming film balances its realism and whimsy with a light hand. Director Andrew Grieve's careful storytelling is rewarded with some lovely performances, notably from Bob Peck and Gemma Jones as a farming couple enduring the hardships and grasping the fleeting joys of life in the Welsh Marches. Mike and Robert Gwilym do well as the twins at the centre of the story, although their acting inexperience shows through during the weightier scenes. DP *DVD*

Mike Gwilym *Benjamin Jones* • Robert Gwilym *Lewis Jones* • Bob Peck *Amos Jones* • Gemma Jones *Mary Jones* • Jack Walters *Sam Jones* • Nesta Harris *Hannah Jones* ■ *Dir* Andrew Grieve • *Scr* Andrew Grieve, from the novel by Bruce Chatwin • *Cinematographer* Thaddeus O'Sullivan

On the Buses ★ PG
Comedy 1971 · UK · Colour · 84min

This spin-off from a popular ITV comedy series was a box-office hit back in 1971. Nostalgia masochists should account for the bulk of those tuning in to this atrocious film, in which women drivers are taken on

at Blakey's depot, much to the frustration of those "lovable" misogynists Reg Varney and Bob Grant. Two further films followed: *Mutiny on the Buses* and *Holiday on the Buses.* DP *DVD*

Reg Varney *Stan Butler* • Doris Hare *Mrs Butler* • Anna Karen *Olive* • Michael Robbins *Arthur* • Stephen Lewis *Inspector Blake* • Bob Grant *Jack* ■ *Dir* Harry Booth • *Scr* Ronald Chesney, Ronald Wolfe

On the Double ★★
Comedy 1961 · UK · Colour · 93min

Danny Kaye plays a dual role as a soldier-mimic and the general he resembles. Most Kaye movies have their moments, and there are a few good laughs, notably a quick-change sequence in which Kaye does a breathtaking set of imitations (including Marlene Dietrich), and Diana Dors perks things up as a German spy, but the script and Melville Shavelson's direction are below par. TV

Danny Kaye *PFC Ernest Williams/Gen Sir Lawrence Mackenzie-Smith* • Dana Wynter *Lady Margaret Mackenzie-Smith* • Wilfrid Hyde White *Colonel Somerset* • Margaret Rutherford *Lady Vivian* • Diana Dors *Sergeant Bridget Stanhope* • Allan Cuthbertson *Captain Patterson* ■ *Dir* Melville Shavelson • *Scr* Jack Rose, Melville Shavelson

On the Fiddle ★★ PG
Comedy 1961 · UK · BW · 96min

Sean Connery was only a year away from becoming an international superstar in *Dr No* when he took the role of a dim-witted gypsy in this hit-and-miss comedy. He plays second fiddle to Alfred Lynch, who stars as a conman inducted into the army. Known in the States as *Operation Snafu*, this was presumably meant to be a minor variation on the Bilko theme. Sadly, it feels like one of those wartime morale boosters featuring a couple of fading music-hall comics. DP *DVD*

Alfred Lynch *Horace Pope* • Sean Connery *Pedlar Pascoe* • Cecil Parker *Group Captain Bascombe* • Stanley Holloway *Mr Cooksley* • Alan King *T/ Sergeant Buzzer* • Eric Barker *Doctor* • Wilfrid Hyde White *Trowbridge* • Kathleen Harrison *Mrs Cooksley* • Eleanor Summerfield *Flora McNaughton* ■ *Dir* Cyril Frankel • *Scr* Harold Buchman, from the novel *Stop at a Winner* by RF Delderfield

On the Line ★★ PG
Romantic comedy 2001 · US · Colour · 82min

It's hard to imagine even the most devoted fans of boy band NSync deriving much pleasure from this crass Chicago romantic comedy. Lance Bass and Joey Fatone star as roommates, but while party animal Fatone wallows in self-indulgence, Bass's bashful ad man covers the Windy City with handbills in a bid to trace Emmanuelle Chriqui, whom he met on the subway but was too tongue-tied to ask out. Neither band member has much screen presence. DP *DVD*

Lance Bass *Kevin Gibbons* • Joey Fatone *Rod* • Emmanuelle Chriqui *Abbey* • G Q *Eric* • James Bulliard *Randy* • Al Green • Tamala Jones *Jackie* • Richie Sambora *Mick Silver* • Jerry Stiller *Nathan* ■ *Dir* Eric Bross • *Scr* Eric Aronson, Paul Stanton

On the Riviera ★★★
Musical comedy 1951 · US · Colour · 88min

Here, Danny Kaye deserts his mentor Samuel Goldwyn for 20th Century-Fox, and a remake of one of the company's main plotlines – the dual identity used by Kaye in *That Night in Rio* and *Folies Bergère.* As both musical star and military hero, Kaye makes the film very much his own, aided by glossy Technicolor and support from his two comely co-stars, Gene Tierney and Corinne Calvet. TS

Danny Kaye *Henri Duran/Jack Martin* • Gene Tierney *Lilli* • Corinne Calvet *Colette* • Marcel Dalio *Philippe Lebrix* • Jean Murat *Periton* • Henri Letondal *Louis Forel* • Clinton Sundberg *Antoine* • Sig Rumann [Sig Ruman] *Gapeaux* • Gwyneth Verdon [Gwen Verdon] *Specialty dancer* ■ *Dir* Walter Lang • *Scr* Valentine Davies, Phoebe Ephron, Henry Ephron, from a play by Rudolph Lothar, Hans Adler

On the Road ★★★ 15

Road movie
2011 · Fr/UK/US/Bra/Can · Colour · 119min

Beautifully shot, handsomely mounted and well cast (Kristen Stewart hits every right note as uncomplicated Marylou), this polished attempt to cram in every Benzedrine-drenched detail of Jack Kerouac's spontaneous cross-country adventures makes for shallow semi-autobiography. It's helped by a classy soundtrack that snapshots the era, but director Walter Salles rarely hits the necessary freewheeling atmosphere to make this strangely flat road trip an absolute must-see for fans of the book or even for the curious. AJ English, French +subtitles. Swearing, sexual references, drug abuse, nudity. *DVD* *BD*
Garrett Hedlund *Dean Moriarty* · Kristen Stewart *Marylou* · Amy Adams *Jane* · Viggo Mortensen *Old Bull Lee* · Kirsten Dunst *Camille* ■ *Dir* Walter Salles · *Scr* José Rivera, from Jack Kerouac's novel

On the Run ★★

Action drama
1983 · Aus · Colour · 101min

Rod Taylor returned to his native Australia for this routine thriller. Playing against type, he turns in a menacing performance as the respected, multilingual farmer who also masquerades as a calculating hitman, nicknamed "The Dingo". Director Mende Brown makes good use of the Sydney conurbation, but the action is derivative and predictable. DP
Paul Winfield *Harry* · Rod Taylor *Payette* · Beau Cox *Paul* ■ *Dir* Mende Brown · *Scr* Michael Fisher

On the Town ★★★★★ U

Classic musical
1949 · US · Colour · 93min

This utterly exhilarating landmark movie musical gave Gene Kelly and choreographer Stanley Donen their directing break. The opening sequence is magnificent, as three sailors on a 24-hour pass (Kelly, Frank Sinatra and Jules Munshin) hail the delights of *New York, New York* in Manhattan itself (it was unusual for MGM to leave its Hollywood lot). There are minor irritations: the substitution of dancers for Sinatra and Munshin in the ballet and a third act that's not as pithy as it should be. But these are quibbles, and the rest is a joy to behold. TS
DVD *BD*
Gene Kelly *Gabey* · Frank Sinatra *Chip* · Vera-Ellen *Ivy Smith* · Jules Munshin *Ozzie* · Betty Garrett *Brunhilde Esterhazy* · Ann Miller *Claire Huddesen* · Florence Bates *Madame Dilyovska* · Alice Pearce *Lucy Shmeeler* · George Meader *Professor* ■ *Dir* Stanley Donen, Gene Kelly · *Scr* Adolph Green, Betty Comden, from the musical play by Adolph Green, Betty Comden, Leonard Bernstein, from the ballet *Fancy Free* by Jerome Robbins · *Cinematographer* Harold Rosson · *Music* Roger Edens, Adolph Green, Betty Comden, Leonard Bernstein

LANDMARK FILM
Method cinema enters the ring big-time with this Oscar-winning crime drama and its realistic depiction of frustration and anger

On the Waterfront ★★★★★ PG

Classic crime drama
1954 · US · BW · 103min

In this seminal classic, Marlon Brando is unforgettable as Terry Malloy – a brooding misfit among the rampant corruption of the New York docks – and was rightly awarded an Oscar for best actor (the youngest ever at the time). On the surface it's a well-crafted drama, but peel away some layers and you'll discover an apologia for informing. Mix in Leonard Bernstein's score, memorable dialogue from Budd Schulberg and great performances from screen newcomers Eva Marie Saint and Rod Steiger – if ever a movie deserved its eight Oscars, it was this one. TS *DVD* *BD*
Marlon Brando *Terry Malloy* · Karl Malden *Father Barry* · Lee J Cobb *Johnny Friendly* · Rod Steiger *Charley Malloy* · Pat Henning *"Kayo" Dugan* · Eva Marie Saint *Edie Doyle* · Leif Erickson *Glover* · James Westerfield *Big Mac* · Marty Balsam [Martin Balsam] *Gillette* · Fred Gwynne *Slim* ■ *Dir* Elia Kazan · *Scr* Budd Schulberg, from a

series of articles by Malcolm Johnson · *Cinematographer* Boris Kaufman · *Music* Leonard Bernstein · *Art Director* Richard Day

On the Yard ★★★ 15

Prison drama
1978 · US · Colour · 96min

A rare return to the style of Warner Bros dramas of the 1930s, this prison-set tale is good at evoking the conflicts and conversation of convicts milling around the vast exercise yard into which they're released for daily recreation. While it's not so good at establishing a story and revealing the character of the four inmates who are at the centre of the narrative, director Raphael D Silver still efficiently summons up the atmosphere of a volatile community. TH
John Heard *Juleson* · Thomas Waites [Thomas G Waites] *Chilly* · Mike Kellin *Red* · Richard Bright *Nunn* · Joe Grifasi *Morris* · Lane Smith *Captain Blake* · Richard Hayes *Stick* ■ *Dir* Raphael D Silver · *Scr* Malcolm Braly, from his novel

On Top of Old Smoky ★★ U

Western
1953 · US · BW · 58min

It's amazing that "Public Cowboy No 1" Gene Autry actually found time to churn out series movies like this one, since by the 1950s his many careers as radio station owner, publishing magnate, composer and recording artist had turned him into one of the hardest working and richest men in America. His fans, though, expected films in which he practised his cowboy code: no hitting anyone smaller than him, no shooting men in the back, no gambling, drinking or smoking and, especially, no kissing. TS
Gene Autry · Smiley Burnette · Gail Davis *Jen Larrabee* · Grandon Rhodes *"Doc" Judson* · Sheila Ryan *Lila Maryland* · Kenne Duncan *McQuaid* ■ *Dir* George Archainbaud · *Scr* Gerald Geraghty, from his story

On Tour ★★★ 15

Comedy drama
2010 · Fr/Ger · Colour · 106min

In actor/director Mathieu Amalric's bawdy comedy drama-cum-road movie, former hotshot TV producer Joachim Zand (played by Amalric) returns to France as the manager of a troupe of ageing American burlesque artists. Touring the coastal towns of Joachim's homeland, the five vivacious ladies ply their trade, content in the fact they are due to perform a grand finale in Paris. But little do they know that not only has their mentor lost the venue, but his past life – friends, enemies, family – has come back to haunt him. Amalric won the best director prize at Cannes with this movie, and his brooding presence is always watchable. JA French, English +subtitles. Swearing, a sex scene, nudity. *DVD*
Mathieu Amalric *Joachim Zand* · Miranda Colclasure *Mimi Le Meaux* · Angela De Lorenzo *Evie Lovelle* · Alexander Craven *Roky Roulette* · Ulysse Klotz *Ulysse* · Anne Benoît *Supermarket cashier* · Julie Ferrier ■ *Dir* Mathieu Amalric · *Scr* Mathieu Amalric, Philippe di Folco, Marcelo Novais Teles, Raphaëlle Valbrune

Once ★★★★ 15

Musical drama
2006 · Ire/US · Colour · 82min

This delightful Irish low-budget musical drama puts a smile on your face and a satisfied spring in your step. It's the tale of two kindred souls (played by Glen Hansard and Marketa Irglova) who meet on the streets of Dublin. He's a busker with his sights set on London and a recording contract; she's an immigrant Czech pianist with a daughter. They discover a mutual love of song and wind up making beautiful music together, both personally and professionally. The stars are clearly capable musicians for real, with Hansard also known for his role as guitarist Outspan Foster in *The Commitments*. The result is a sweet little charmer that shows that a film made for relative peanuts can still pack more of an emotional wallop than a dozen bloated blockbusters. DA Swearing. *DVD* *BD*
Glen Hansard *Guy* · Marketa Irglova *Girl* · Hugh Walsh *Timmy Drummer* · Gerry Hendrick *Lead guitarist* · Alastair Foley *Bassist* · Geoff Minogue

Eamon · Bill Hodnett *Guy's dad* · Danuse Ktrestova *Girl's mother* ■ *Dir/Scr* John Carney · *Cinematographer* Tim Fleming

Once a Jolly Swagman ★★ U

Drama
1948 · UK · BW · 98min

This is an improbably melodramatic tale of love, honour and speedway. Set in the 1930s, it scores with its realistic portrait of track life, but the wheels come off during the studio-bound sequences, in which ex-factory worker Dirk Bogarde is dazzled both by his new-found fame and the radiance of socialite Moira Lister. Bill Owen and Renée Asherson provide dependable support, but Bogarde never gets out of first gear. DP
DVD
Dirk Bogarde *Bill Fox* · Bonar Colleano *Tommy Possey* · Renée Asherson *Pat Gibbon* · Bill Owen *Lag Gibbon* · Cyril Cusack *Duggie Lewis* · Thora Hird *Ma Fox* · James Hayter *Pa Fox* ■ *Dir* Jack Lee (2) · *Scr* Jack Lee, William Rose, Cliff Gordon, from a novel by Montagu Slater

Once a Thief ★★

Crime drama
1965 · US · BW · 106min

This routine cops and robbers melodrama was French star Alain Delon's first American feature and he looks unusually awkward and out of place as an ex-con trying to go straight while being harassed by a vengeful cop and becoming a pawn in his brother's plans for a million-dollar heist. Director Ralph Nelson assembles an able support cast but the strength of his semi-documentary approach and the San Francisco locations are undercut by a cliché-ridden script. RS
Alain Delon *Eddie Pedak* · Ann-Margret *Kristine Pedak* · Van Heflin *Mike Vido* · Jack Palance *Walter Pedak* · John Davis Chandler *James Sargatanas* · Jeff Corey *Lt Kebner* ■ *Dir* Ralph Nelson · *Scr* Zekial Marko, from his novel *Scratch a Thief* · *Music* Lalo Schifrin

Once a Thief ★★★ 15

Romantic action comedy
1991 · HK · Colour · 103min

John Woo remade this five years later for TV, wasn't able to touch this light-hearted caper movie, atypical for him. Beginning in France, three crooks (Chow Yun-Fat, Leslie Cheung, and Cherie Chung), who were raised as thieves after being orphaned in their childhood, plan one last caper to steal a valuable painting. Woo goes for comedy and less violent action in this effort, and the result is alternately charming and hilarious. Those expecting the standard grandiose Woo shoot-outs will be disappointed – until the surprisingly violent climax. KB Cantonese +subtitles. *DVD*
Chow Yun-Fat *Joe* · Leslie Cheung *Jim* · Cherie Chung *Cherie* ■ *Dir* John Woo · *Scr* John Woo, Clifton Ko, Janet Chung

Once Around ★★★ 15

Romantic comedy
1991 · US · Colour · 110min

Some of the best talent Hollywood could muster graces this often affecting story of a repressed little rich girl, the excellent Holly Hunter, who falls madly in love with a garrulous salesman, a rather caricatured performance from Richard Dreyfuss, much to her family's chagrin. The tightly packed, occasionally lyrical script gives each character suitable depth and emotional history, but almost imperceptibly goes off the boil as the movie progresses. Oddly flat. SH Swearing.
Holly Hunter *Renata Bella* · Richard Dreyfuss *Sam Sharpe* · Danny Aiello *Joe Bella* · Gena Rowlands *Marilyn Bella* · Laura San Giacomo *Jan Bella* · Roxanne Hart *Gail Bella* · Danton Stone *Tony Bella* · Tim Guinee *Peter Hedges* ■ *Dir* Lasse Hallström · *Scr* Malia Scotch Marmo, Lasse Hallström

Once before I Die ★★

Second World War drama
1965 · US · Colour · 96min

What on earth is Ursula Andress doing in the middle of the jungle and in the thick of the war in the Philippines? Well, appearing in then husband John Derek's movie is the answer. Viewers may find it difficult to

fathom whether Derek wanted to deck a dull war movie out with glam shots of his wife, or vice versa. Either way, this is a blatant vanity project. AT
Ursula Andress *Alex* · John Derek *Major Bailey* · Rod Lauren *Captain* · Richard Jaeckel *Lt Custer* · Ron Ely *Soldier* ■ *Dir* John Derek · *Scr* Vance Skarstedt, from the story *Quit for the Next* by Anthony March

Once Bitten ★★ 15

Horror comedy
1985 · US · Colour · 88min

This dumb teenage sex comedy has supernatural overtones and very few gags. Countess Lauren Hutton is a 400-year-old vampire looking for virgin blood in Los Angeles. Supplies are short until she picks up a student nerd (future superstar Jim Carrey) who hasn't managed to get his girlfriend Karen Kopins into bed. Cleavon Little as Hutton's gay manservant has some funny moments, but the one-joke premise soon screeches to a halt. AJ *DVD*
Lauren Hutton *Countess* · Jim Carrey *Mark Kendall* · Karen Kopins *Robin Pierce* · Cleavon Little *Sebastian* · Thomas Ballatore *Jamie* ■ *Dir* Howard Storm · *Scr* David Hines, Jeffrey Hause, Jonathan Roberts, from a story by Dimitri Villard

Once in a Lifetime: the Extraordinary Story of the New York Cosmos ★★★ 15

Documentary
2006 · US/UK · Colour and BW · 93min

This well-researched and cleverly presented documentary reveals the amazing story of the New York Cosmos, the superstar soccer squad put together in the 1970s to spark dormant American interest in the sport. Even those unenthusiastic about the beautiful game will find much to enjoy in this anecdote-laden extravaganza from the Oscar-winning producers of *One Day in September*, as the Cosmos legacy to the current state of global soccer is persuasively described by narrator Matt Dillon. Bolstered by terrific match footage and fabulous yarns about the club's notorious heyday, the ace in directors Paul Crowder and John Dower's movie is the authentic sense of period. AJ Nudity.
Matt Dillon *Narrator* · Johan Cruyff · Franz Beckenbauer ■ *Dir* Paul Crowder, John Dower · *Scr* Mark Monroe, from a story by John Dower, Monroe

Once Is Not Enough ★★

Melodrama
1975 · US · Colour · 120min

Adapted from Jacqueline Susann's potboiler novel, this is a forerunner of the *Dallas* and *Dynasty* soap operas, peppered with starry names and an appallingly camp plotline. Kirk Douglas plays a past-it producer and doting dad to Deborah Raffin. He is so keen to keep his darling daughter in the best that money can buy that he marries Alexis Smith – a rich, bisexual woman, who is still involved with her lesbian lover, Melina Mercouri. Brenda Vaccaro won a Golden Globe for her supporting role as a man-mad fashion editor. FL
Kirk Douglas *Mike Wayne* · Alexis Smith *Deidre Milford Granger* · David Janssen *Tom Colt* · George Hamilton *David Milford* · Melina Mercouri *Karla* · Gary Conway *Hugh* · Brenda Vaccaro *Linda* · Deborah Raffin *January Wayne* ■ *Dir* Guy Green · *Scr* Julius J Epstein, from the novel by Jacqueline Susann

Once More, My Darling ★★

Romantic comedy
1949 · US · BW · 92min

Robert Montgomery, past the peak of his stardom, directs himself in this romantic comedy about an actor turned lawyer who is hired by the army to romance lovely young heiress Ann Blyth and find out how she came by some stolen Nazi jewellery. The stars play well together, and Montgomery's direction is competent, but the end result is unconvincing. RK
Robert Montgomery *Collier Laing* · Ann Blyth *Marita Connell* · Lillian Randolph *Mamie the maid* · Jane Cowl *Mrs Laing* · Steven Geray *Kalzac* ■ *Dir* Robert Montgomery · *Scr* Robert Carson, from the story *Come Be My Love* by Robert Carson

Once upon a Crime ★ PG

Comedy 1992 · US · Colour · 90min

The comic genius of John Candy is there for all to see in this dismal crime caper. Only someone of his immense talent could raise a laugh out of material this bad. All around him flounder, particularly Richard Lewis and Sean Young as the couple who become embroiled in a trans-European murder mystery after finding a valuable dachshund. Inept. DP Swearing.

John Candy *Augie Morosco* · James Belushi *Neil Schwary* · Cybill Shepherd *Marilyn Schwary* · Sean Young *Phoebe* · Richard Lewis *Julian Peters* · Ornella Muti *Elena Morosco* · Giancarlo Giannini *Inspector Bonnard* · George Hamilton *Alfonso de la Pena* · Roberto Sbaratto *Detective Toussaint* · Joss Ackland *Hercules Popodopoulos* ■ *Dir* Eugene Levy · *Scr* Charles Shyer, Nancy Meyers, Steve Kluger, from a screenplay (unproduced) by Rodolfo Sonego, Giorgio Arlorio, Stefano Strucchi, Luciano Vincenzoni

Once upon a Dream ★★

Comedy 1948 · UK · BW · 87min

Googie Withers is the attractive wife of army officer Guy Middleton. She conceives a fancy for her husband's former aide Griffith Jones, who comes to work as a servant in their household. When she wakes from a romantic dream about Jones, believing their love affair to be real, all kinds of complications ensue. The actors give their best, but the plot is paper-thin and the now-dated humour is only intermittently amusing. RK

Googie Withers *Mrs Carol Gilbert* · Griffith Jones *Jackson* · Guy Middleton *Major Gilbert* · Betty Lynne *Mlle Louise* · David Horne *Registrar* · Geoffrey Morris *Registrar's clerk* · Maurice Denham *Vicar* · Mona Washbourne *Vicar's wife* · Dora Bryan *Barmaid* ■ *Dir* Ralph Thomas · *Scr* Victor Katona, Patrick Kirwan

Once upon a Forest ★★ U

Musical animated adventure
1992 · US · Colour · 67min

The tone of this politically correct tale is often rather preachy, but the "furlings" who venture out into the big bad world to find the herbs needed to save one of their sickly playmates are cute and courageous, and their encounters with some unthinking humans and menacing machines should keep youngsters on the edge of their seats. Sadly, in common with so many non-Disney cartoons, the standard of the songs is poor and the animation lacks magic. DP DVD

Michael Crawford *Cornelius, the Badger* · Ben Vereen *Phineas* · Ellen Blain *Abigail* · Ben Gregory [Benjamin Gregory] *Edgar* · Paige Gosney *Russell* · Elisabeth Moss *Michelle* ■ *Dir* Charles Grosvenor · *Scr* Mark Young, Kelly Ward, from the story by Rae Lambert

Once upon a Honeymoon ★★ PG

Wartime comedy drama 1942 · US · BW · 114min

This lengthy and astoundingly tasteless comedy drama reveals how little America knew about the Nazis back in the early 1940s. The sequences involving Cary Grant and Ginger Rogers being mistaken for Jews and shipped off to a concentration camp leave a strange taste in the mouth. Director Leo McCarey later disowned the film, but it's well made and contemporary audiences simply accepted what was on screen; time has rendered that impossible. TS

Cary Grant *Pat O'Toole* · Ginger Rogers *Katie O'Hara* · Walter Slezak *Baron Von Luber* · Albert Dekker *LeBlanc* · Albert Basserman *General Borelski* · Ferike Boros *Elsa* · Harry Shannon *Cumberland* ■ *Dir* Leo McCarey · *Scr* Sheridan Gibney, from a story by Sheridan Gibney, Leo McCarey

Once upon a Spy ★★★ PG

Spy adventure 1980 · US · Colour · 91min

Christopher Lee chews the scenery again as a paralysed mad scientist who invents a shrinking machine in a whimsical spy spoof that hits the 007 targets dead on, especially in the Bond theme department. Jimmy Sangster, another Hammer veteran, scripted this glitzy tale of unbelievable

derring-do – or rather don't – in star Ted Danson's case which moves along at a bright and breezy pace, thanks to some engagingly quirky humour. AJ

Ted Danson *Jack Chenault* · Mary Louise Weller *Paige Tannehill* · Christopher Lee *Marcus Valorium* · Eleanor Parker *The Lady* · Leonard Stone *Dr Charlie Webster* ■ *Dir* Ivan Nagy · *Scr* Jimmy Sangster, from a story by Jimmy Sangster, Lemuel Pitkin

Once upon a Texas Train ★★★ U

Western 1988 · US · Colour · 87min

Texas Ranger Richard Widmark and ageing outlaw Willie Nelson discover that youngster Shaun Cassidy is about to disrupt their unlawful business by intercepting some ill-gotten loot in this entertaining TV movie. In addition to the stellar leads, there's a fine supporting cast of western stalwarts. The light-hearted tone might offend western purists, but others will probably enjoy this rollicking entertainment. TS DVD

Willie Nelson *John Henry Lee* · Richard Widmark *Captain Oren Hayes* · Angie Dickinson *Maggie Hayes* · Shaun Cassidy *Cotton* · Chuck Connors *Nash Crawford* · Jack Elam *Jason Fitch* · Ken Curtis *Kelly Sutton* · Royal Dano *Nitro Jones* · Stuart Whitman *George Agnew* ■ *Dir/Scr* Burt Kennedy

Once upon a Time ★★★ U

Comedy 1944 · US · BW · 88min

This amazing piece of whimsy is about impecunious theatre producer Cary Grant promoting a dancing caterpillar. Thanks to the talent of the ever-dependable Grant and the cleverness of the screenplay, it works. Director Alexander Hall was skilled at this kind of fantasy and casts the quizzical James Gleason and Janet Blair, supporting the debonair Grant with some style. Slight and trivial in the extreme, but supremely watchable in its daffy, good-natured way. TS

Cary Grant *Jerry Flynn* · Janet Blair *Jeannie Thompson* · James Gleason *The Moke* · Ted Donaldson *Pinky Thompson* · Howard Freeman *McKenzie* · William Demarest *Brandt* ■ *Dir* Alexander Hall · *Scr* Lewis Meltzer, Oscar Saul, Irving Fineman, from the radio play *My Client Curly* by Norman Corwin, Lucille Fletcher Herrmann

Once upon a Time in America ★★★★★ 18

Epic crime drama 1984 · US · Colour · 251min

Sergio Leone's final film is an extraordinary crime drama that runs for nearly four hours in its full length-version and chronicles the lives of two New York gangsters, played by Robert De Niro and James Woods. Four decades roll past in flashback, underpinned by a great Ennio Morricone score. The plotting is often arbitrary but, unlike *The Godfather*, Leone and his fine actors never try to win our sympathy: these are nasty people and there are two rape scenes, involving Tuesday Weld and Elizabeth McGovern, that may be among the most shocking ever filmed. But just gasp at the scale, at the immaculate period reconstruction and at that incredible opening with its endlessly ringing phone. A resounding flop on its US release, it fared better in Europe, where it was hailed as a masterpiece of 1980s cinema. AT Violence, swearing, nudity. DVD

Robert De Niro *Noodles* · James Woods *Max* · Elizabeth McGovern *Deborah* · Treat Williams *Jimmy O'Donnell* · Tuesday Weld *Carol* · Burt Young *Joe* · Joe Pesci *Frankie* · Danny Aiello *Police chief* · Bill Forsythe [William Forsythe] *Cockeye* ■ *Dir* Sergio Leone · *Scr* Leonardo Benvenuti [Leo Benvenuti], Piero De Bernardi, Enrico Medioli, Franco Arcalli, Franco Ferrini, Sergio Leone, Stuart Kaminsky, from the novel *The Hoods* by Harry Grey · *Cinematographer* Tonino Delli Colli

Once upon a Time in Anatolia ★★★★ 15

Crime drama
2011 · Tur/Bosnia · Colour · 150min

Director Nuri Bilge Ceylan examines the widening fissures in Turkish society in this simmering study of corruption and incompetence. The story sees a small-town police chief take two confessed murderers, a doctor and a prosecutor on a nocturnal trek across inhospitable terrain to find the spot where the killers buried their victim. The performances are as impeccable as Gokhan Tiryaki's cinematography, but it's Ceylan's mastery of composition and pacing that makes this so visually striking and dramatically compelling. DP Turkish +subtitles. Swearing. DVD SD

Muhammet Uzuner *Doctor Cemal* · Yilmaz Erdogan *Commissioner Naci* · Taner Birsel *Prosecutor Nusret* · Ahmet Mumtaz Taylan *Arab Ali, driver* · Firat Tanis *Kenan, suspect* · Ercan Kesal *Mukhtar* ■ *Dir* Nuri Bilge Ceylan · *Scr* Nuri Bilge Ceylan, Ebru Ceylan, Ercan Kesal

Once upon a Time in China ★★★★ 15

Martial arts action drama
1991 · HK · Colour · 128min

Wong Fei-Hung (1847-1924) was one of the undisputed masters of such kung fu techniques as the no-shadow kick and drunken boxing. He was already a cult figure in pulp fiction before his exploits finally reached the screen in the late 1940s. Tsui Hark revitalised the legend with this box-office smash, which itself launched a whole new series of adventures that made a superstar of Jet Li. Notable for its stance against foreign influences, this is an explosive picture, with breakneck action sequences. DP Cantonese +subtitles. DVD

Jet Li *Wong Fei-Hung* · Yuen Biao *Leung Foon* · Jacky Cheung *Buck Teeth Sol* · Rosamund Kwan *Aunt Yee* ■ *Dir* Tsui Hark · *Scr* Tsui Hark, Yuen Kai-Chi, Leung Yiu-Ming

Once upon a Time in China II ★★★ 15

Martial arts action drama
1992 · HK · Colour · 107min

The explosive combination of Tsui Hark and Jet Li as Wong Fei-Hung ensured a sequel to the smash hit and the result is another extravagant action pic. Jet Li bowed out of the third and fourth sequels, but returned triumphantly for the sixth adventure. All of these films (even the non-Li ones) deliver some great cinematic action sequences. DF Cantonese +subtitles. DVD

Jet Li *Wong Fei-Hung* · Rosamund Chi-Lam Kwan [Rosamund Kwan] *Aunt Yee* · Donnie Chi-Tan Yen [Donnie Yen] *Lan* · David Chiang *Luke* · Max Siu Chung Mok [Max Mok] *Leung Fu* ■ *Dir* Tsui Hark · *Scr* Tsui Hark, Hanson Chan [Chan Tin Suen], Cheung Tan

Once upon a Time in Mexico ★★★ 15

Crime action adventure
2003 · US · Colour · 97min

While you can see why director Robert Rodriguez might want to remake his 1992 ultra-low-budget debut *El Mariachi* as *Desperado* (1995) to take advantage of a studio-sized budget, remaking it yet again would seem to indicate that he's stuck in a groove. This third outing again stars Antonio Banderas as the wandering South American minstrel with an arsenal in his guitar case to take on evil drug lords. He's aided this time by an unorthodox CIA agent (Johnny Depp) who's the most entertaining thing in the film, although the action is certainly spectacular. AS English, Spanish +subtitles. Violence, swearing. DVD

Antonio Banderas *El Mariachi* · Salma Hayek *Carolina* · Johnny Depp *Sands* · Mickey Rourke *Billy Chambers* · Eva Mendes *Ajedrez* · Danny Trejo *Cucuy* · Enrique Iglesias *Lorenzo* · Cheech Marin [Richard "Cheech" Marin] *Belini* · Rubén Blades *Jorge* · Willem Dafoe *Barillo* ■ *Dir* Robert Rodriguez · *Scr* Robert Rodriguez, from his characters

Once upon a Time in the Midlands ★★★ 15

Drama 2002 · UK · Colour · 100min

Full of familiar Britpic faces and spaghetti western references, Shane Meadows's third feature opens with promise and panache. However, once petty crook Robert Carlyle arrives in Nottingham to prevent ex-wife Shirley Henderson from marrying garage boss Rhys Ifans, the Leone tone is replaced by a diluted brand of Ken Loach realism, in which quips and slapstick leaven the underlying atmosphere of aggression and despair. Consequently, the story loses momentum and minor characters are marginalised in favour of introspection. DP DVD

Robert Carlyle *Jimmy* · Rhys Ifans *Dek* · Kathy Burke *Carol* · Shirley Henderson *Shirley* · Ricky Tomlinson *Charlie* · Finn Atkins *Marlene* · Vanessa Feltz *Vanessa* · Vic Reeves *Plonko the clown* · Bob Mortimer *Kung fu clown* · Shane Meadows *Bingo caller* ■ *Dir* Shane Meadows · *Scr* Paul Fraser, Shane Meadows

Once upon a Time in the West ★★★★★ 15

Spaghetti western
1968 · It/US · Colour · 158min

In seeking to paint "a fresco on the birth of a great nation", Sergio Leone turned to the Hollywood western, rather than American history, for his inspiration. Set at the time when the dollar replaced the bullet as the currency of the frontier, this is a breathtaking tale of progress, greed and revenge. The story focuses on gunfighter Henry Fonda, who dreams of becoming a tycoon, but who is still prepared to resort to trusted methods to drive widow Claudia Cardinale off the land coveted by a railroad company. Much of the action was improvised around the mood of the score, which Ennio Morricone had composed in advance. No wonder many critics described the film as an operatic masterpiece. DP DVD Blu-ray

Henry Fonda *Frank* · Claudia Cardinale *Jill McBain* · Jason Robards *Cheyenne* · Charles Bronson *Harmonica* · Frank Wolff *Brett McBain* · Gabriele Ferzetti *Morton* · Keenan Wynn *Sheriff* ■ *Dir* Sergio Leone · *Scr* Sergio Leone, Sergio Donati, from a story by Leone, Dario Argento, Bernardo Bertolucci · *Cinematographer* Tonino Delli Colli

Once Were Warriors ★★★★ 18

Drama 1994 · NZ · Colour · 98min

Told in a bold, unflinching manner, director Lee Tamahori's drama grips and fascinates as it lifts the lid on ghetto Maori life. Rena Owen is drainingly moving as the put-upon housewife, pushed physically and mentally to the brink while trying to hold her family together, bearing the brunt of her unemployed husband's drink-fuelled frustrations. Tamahori's bleak film is raw, brutal cinema with a unique voice, showing a people adrift from their cultural roots and trapped in an urban nightmare of cheap housing and gangland controlled precincts. *What Becomes of the Broken Hearted?* was the belated 1999 sequel. AJ Violence, swearing. DVD

Rena Owen *Beth Heke* · Temuera Morrison *Jake Heke* · Mamaengaroa Kerr-Bell *Grace Heke* · Julian Arahanga *Nig Heke* · Taungaroa Emile *Boogie Heke* · Rachael Morris Jr *Polly Heke* · Clifford Curtis [Cliff Curtis] *Bully* ■ *Dir* Lee Tamahori · *Scr* Riwia Brown, from the novel by Alan Duff

Ondine ★★ 12

Fantasy drama 2009 · Ire/US · Colour · 98min

There's drama and intrigue here when an Irish fisherman hauls up a young woman in his net – is she some sort of mythical creature? The sickly young daughter of trawlerman Syracuse (Colin Farrell) certainly thinks so. He's not so sure, but gives the mysterious Ondine (Alicja Bachleda-Curus) a place to stay. Writer/director Neil Jordan takes his time in unravelling this tall tale, benefiting from atmospheric West Cork locations and a warm-hearted turn from Farrell. While it looks classy, however, it just doesn't come off. TJ Some violence, swearing. **DVD**

Colin Farrell (2) *Syracuse* • Alicja Bachleda [Alicja Bachleda-Curus] *Ondine* • Alison Barry *Annie* • Tony Curran *Alex* • Emil Hostina *Vladic* • Dervla Kirwan *Maura* • Stephen Rea *Priest* ■ *Dir/Scr* Neil Jordan

The One ★★★ 15
Science-fiction martial arts adventure
2001 · US · Colour · 83min

Sci-fi action films don't come any more simplistic than this offering from James Wong, who goes all out to deliver an exhilarating, nonstop adrenaline rush. Jet Li gets to battle himself in his portrayal of two martial arts whirlwinds – one, a killer moving between parallel universes in order to murder his alter egos; the other, a Los Angeles police officer who's the last intergalactic double and next intended victim. Jaw-droppingly extreme set pieces punctuate this wildly over-the-top joy ride. SF **DVD**

Jet Li *Gabriel "Gabe" Yulaw/Lawless* • Delroy Lindo *Harry Roedecker/Attendant* • Carla Gugino *Traci "TK" Katherine/Massie Walsh* • Jason Statham *Ethan Funsch* • James Morrison *Aldrich/ "A" World Inmate No 1* • Dylan Bruno *Yates* • Richard Steinmetz *D'Antoni* ■ *Dir* James Wong • *Scr* Glen Morgan, James Wong

One against the Wind
★★★★ PG
War drama based on a true story
1991 · US · Colour · 95min

This excellent wartime drama is based on the real-life exploits of Mary Lindell, a British woman who used her Paris home as a halfway house for Allied soldiers trapped behind enemy lines. This TV movie is tense and emotive, mainly because of the array of talent on display: Judy Davis, one of the greatest and least "starry" actresses around, plays Lindell and brings the same sensivity that she brought to her roles in *A Passage to India* and Woody Allen's *Husbands and Wives*. There is also fine support from Sam Neill, Kate Beckinsale and the always dependable Denholm Elliott in one of his final screen appearances. AT

Judy Davis *Mary Lindell* • Sam Neill *Captain James Leggatt* • Denholm Elliott *Father LeBlanc* • Christien Anholt *Maurice* • Kate Beckinsale *Barbe* • Anthony Higgins *Herman Gruber* ■ *Dir* Larry Elikann • *Scr* Chris Bryant

A One and a Two ★★★★ 15
Drama
1999 · Tai/Jpn · Colour · 173min

Notable for their complex structure, arresting visuals, measured pace and spare dialogue, Edward Yang's films have always provided a humanist insight into the modern urban experience. But rarely has he exhibited such poetry and precision as in this engrossing domestic epic. With his nerve-frazzled wife dabbling in religion and his kids experiencing growing pains, Wu Nianzhen hits a midlife crisis that not only proves the unpredictability of life, but also slyly mirrors Taiwan's political insecurity. The performances are superb. DP Mandarin, English +subtitles. Swearing. **DVD**

Wu Nianzhen *NJ Jian* • Issey Ogata *Ota* • Elaine Jin *Min-Min* • Kelly Lee *Ting Ting* • Jonathan Chang *Yang Yang* • Adrian Lin *Lili* ■ *Dir/Scr* Edward Yang

The One and Only ★★★
Comedy drama
1978 · US · Colour · 97min

Henry Winkler plays a man whose huge ego is only matched by his determination to become an acting star. Convinced he knows better than anyone else, he alienates would-be employers by his insistence on changing lines and suggesting alterations in his roles. However he then does make a success of a wrestler, although his long-suffering wife and her parents are less enamoured with this new career. TV's Fonzie here finds a decent vehicle for his comedic talents and a sparkling script ensures plenty of laughs. DF

Henry Winkler *Andy Schmidt* • Kim Darby *Mary Crawford* • Gene Saks *Sidney Seltzer* • William Daniels (2) *Mr Crawford* • Harold Gould *Hector*

Moses • Polly Holliday *Mrs Crawford* • Herve Villechaize *Milton Miller* • Ed Begley Jr *Arnold the King* ■ *Dir* Carl Reiner • *Scr* Steve Gordon

The One and Only ★★ 15
Romantic comedy 2001 · UK/Fr · Colour · 87min

Having triumphed on the small screen with *Our Friends in the North*, director Simon Cellan Jones and screenwriter Peter Flannery remain on Tyneside for this mirthless romantic comedy. Despite its meticulous contrivances, the storyline refuses to slot together as neatly as the fitted kitchen that the romantically attached Richard Roxburgh installs for pregnant footballer's wife Justine Waddell. Consequently it's hard to summon up much enthusiasm, let alone sympathy, for their plight – both are trapped in loveless marriages and being pushed into parenthood by their respective spouses. DP **DVD**

Richard Roxburgh *Neil* • Justine Waddell *Stevie* • Jonathan Cake *Sonny* • Patsy Kensit *Stella* • Michael Hodgson *Stan* • Aisling O'Sullivan *Jenny* • Angel Thomas *Mgala* ■ *Dir* Simon Cellan Jones • *Scr* Peter Flannery, from the film *Den Eneste Ene* by Kim Fupz Aakeson

The One and Only, Genuine, Original Family Band ★★ U
Period musical drama
1968 · US · Colour · 105min

This Disney family drama is notable only for the fact that it has a young Kurt Russell and Goldie Hawn appearing on screen together for the first time. Set during the 1888 presidential campaign, the film follows the efforts of Walter Brennan to win the right for his family band to perform in the face of both political opposition and domestic discord. The Sherman brothers' songs are of little interest. DP

Walter Brennan *Granpa Bower* • Buddy Ebsen *Calvin Bower* • John Davidson *Joe Carder* • Lesley Ann Warren *Alice Bower* • Janet Blair *Katie Bower* • Kurt Russell *Sidney Bower* • Steve Harmon *Ernie Stubbins* • Goldie Jeanne Hawn [Goldie Hawn] *Giggly girl* ■ *Dir* Michael O'Herlihy • *Scr* Lowell S Hawley, from the autobiography *Nebraska 1888* by Laura Bower Van Nuys

One-Armed Swordsman
★★★
Martial arts action drama
1967 · HK · Colour · 109min

Before Bruce Lee took up the mantle of King of Kung Fu in the 1970s, the biggest star in martial arts cinema was arguably Shanghai-born Wang Yu, thanks to this career-defining swordplay tale. All chiselled cheekbones, Wang is a brooding presence as the prodigal student of a master swordsman, who's forced to consider a farmer's life after the shock loss of an appendage, but returns to his warrior ways. Wang came back in a sequel two years later and continued to excite audiences for years to come in variations on this uniquely one-armed hero. JA Mandarin +subtitles. Violence.

Wang Yu (1) *Fang Kang/One-Armed Swordsman* • Chiao Chiao *Hsiao Man* • Hsin Huang Chung *Wei Hsuan* ■ *Dir* Chang Cheh • *Scr* Chang Cheh, Ni Kuang

[One] Cavale ★★★★ 15
Thriller 2002 · Fr/Bel · Colour · 109min

Writer/director Lucas Belvaux also headlines the first instalment in this laudably ambitious triptych, which succeeds in introducing the recurring characters, and is also a gripping thriller in its own right. As the one-time revolutionary who jumps jail in order to wreak revenge on the man he believes betrayed him, Belvaux becomes increasingly hamstrung by circumstance and the despair he feels at the self-seeking society that emerged as a result of the failure of 1960s radicalism. The work of the entire ensemble cast is impeccable, but Catherine Frot excels as the comrade-turned-teacher whose past loyalties jeopardise her future. Followed by *[Two] Un Couple Epatant*. DP French +subtitles. Swearing, violence, drug abuse. **DVD**

Catherine Frot *Jeanne Rivet* • Lucas Belvaux *Bruno Le Roux* • Dominique Blanc *Agnès Manise* • Ornella Muti *Cécile Costes* • Gilbert Melki *Pascal Manise* • Alexis Tomassian *Banane* ■ *Dir/Scr* Lucas Belvaux

One Chance ★★★ 12
Comedy drama based on a true story
2013 · UK · Colour · 99min

Everyone loves a tale of triumph over adversity and the journey of Paul Potts to fame and fortune via *Britain's Got Talent* is certainly full of adversity. So you can expect heartstrings to be tugged using every trick in the book, as Potts (James Corden) endures bullying at school; belittling by his father; humiliation in front of his idol, Pavarotti; and career-threatening illness. And yet, despite the flagrant abuse of dramatic licence and an inescapably cheesy story arc, the film is still utterly charming and has an effortlessly witty script. Holding it all together is Corden's sincere and comically astute portrayal of a man whose impossible dream did come true. AIS **DVD**

James Corden *Paul Potts* • Alexandra Roach *Julie-Ann "Julz" Cooper* • Julie Walters *Yvonne Potts* • Colm Meaney *Roland Potts* • Mackenzie Crook *Braddon* • Jemima Rooper *Hydrangea* ■ *Dir* David Frankel • *Scr* Justin Zackham

One Crazy Summer ★★ PG
Comedy 1986 · US · Colour · 89min

There are youthful appearances by John Cusack and Demi Moore in this offbeat comedy about a college wannabe who has to learn about love on holiday in Nantucket before he goes off to the educational institution of his choice. It's filmed in a cartoon-style with some fun sight gags, witty dialogue and even a handful of well-integrated animation sequences, but there's little connective tissue. DA

John Cusack *Hoops McCann* • Demi Moore *Cassandra* • Curtis Armstrong *Ack Ack Raymond* • Joel Murray *George Calamari* • Joe Flaherty *General Raymond* • Bobcat Goldthwait *Egg Stork* • Mark Metcalf *Aguilla Beckersted* • William Hickey *Old Man Beckersted* ■ *Dir/Scr* Savage Steve Holland

One Dark Night ★★ 15
Supernatural horror 1982 · US · Colour · 88min

Even by the early 1980s the teens-in-peril scenario was well past its sell-by-date. In her first leading role a young Meg Tilly, sister of Jennifer, is forced to spend the night in a creepy mausoleum as part of a gang initiation test unaware that its recently interned occupant is about to wake up! Director Tom McLoughlin manages to muster not one ounce of tension and the gore count is fatally low. At least the climax is adequately staged. RS

Meg Tilly *Julie* • Robin Evans *Carol* • Leslie Speights *Kitty* • Elizabeth Daily *Leslie* • Adam West *Allan* • Melissa Newman *Olivia* • Donald Hotton *Dockstader* • Kevin Peter Hall *Eddie* ■ *Dir* Tom McLoughlin • *Scr* Tom McLoughlin, Michael Hawes

1 Day ★★ 15
Crime drama 2009 · UK · Colour · 98min

This urban drama about gang rivalries and drug-related violence in Birmingham takes an offbeat twist by having the cast start rapping in the midst of the action. Showcasing non-professionals from the local communities, enterprising director Penny Woolcock traces the tensions caused when a young hustler has only one day to settle a debt with a dealer. Woolcock deserves praise for ambition, but this tumbles awkwardly into some netherworld between streetwise musical and social-conscience crime chronicle. TJ Violence, swearing, sexual references, drug abuse.

Dylan Duffus *Flash* • Ohran Whyte *Pest* • Yohance Watson *Angel* • Tobias Duncan *Evil* ■ *Dir/Scr* Penny Woolcock

One Day ★★★ 12
Romantic comedy drama
2011 · US · Colour · 102min

One Day spans two decades in the life of two friends, played by Anne Hathaway and

Jim Sturgess, and muses on the possibility of something more between them. Adapting the script from this bestselling novel, David Nicholls finds less time for the nostalgia and modern angst that gives the book its epic sweep, and instead produces an impressionistic take on the frustration of missed opportunities. Sturgess does especially well to remain sympathetic even as he wilfully plays the bad boy. His evolution into someone deserving of Hathaway – all sweetness and light – is what finally lends the film some weight. SP Some violence, swearing, brief nudity, drug abuse. **DVD**

Jim Sturgess *Dexter* • Anne Hathaway *Emma* • Patricia Clarkson *Alison Mayhew* • Romola Garai *Sylvie* • Jodie Whittaker *Tilly* • Ken Stott *Steven* ■ *Dir* Lone Scherfig • *Scr* David Nicholls, from his novel

One Day in September
★★★★ 12
Documentary 1999 · UK · Colour · 90min

Controversy has somewhat tarnished the sheen of Kevin Macdonald's Oscar-winning documentary, but it remains a revelatory account of the terrorist atrocity at the 1972 Munich Olympics. Narrated by Michael Douglas and linking news footage, interviews and graphics, this meticulously researched exposé of the hideously bungled German security operation simply beggars belief. Examples of poor communication, military inexpertise and governmental dithering almost overshadow the horror of the Black September action, which left 11 Israeli Olympians, five Palestinians and one policeman dead. A damning indictment of political violence and bureaucratic arrogance. DP

Michael Douglas (1) *Narrator* ■ *Dir* Kevin Macdonald

One Day in the Life of Ivan Denisovich ★★★
Prison drama 1971 · UK/Nor · Colour · 104min

Although meticulously adapted by Ronald Harwood from Alexander Solzhenitsyn's celebrated novel, this co-production only hints at the appalling conditions inside a Soviet labour camp in the late-Stalinist era, and the dignity and ingenuity with which Ivan survived them. Admittedly, it is a difficult novel to film, even when photographed by a genius like Sven Nykvist and interpreted with such intelligence by Tom Courtenay. But director Caspar Wrede has turned it into the wrong sort of ordeal; overwhelmed by the political and literary significance of his material, he has missed both art and life. DP

Tom Courtenay *Ivan Denisovich* • Espen Skjonberg *Tiurin* • James Maxwell *Captain Buinovsky* • Alfred Burke *Alyosha* • Eric Thompson *Tsezar* • John Cording *Pavlo* • Mathew Guinness *Kilgas* ■ *Dir* Caspar Wrede [Casper Wrede] • *Scr* Ronald Harwood, from the novel by Alexander Solzhenitsyn

One Deadly Summer
★★★★ 18
Thriller 1983 · Fr · Colour · 127min

Exploiting her beauty to disarming effect, Isabelle Adjani won a César for her smouldering performance in this deceptively complex thriller. Working from his own novel, Sébastien Japrisot fashions a script that consistently disconcerts the viewer as the narrative focus shifts between Adjani's vengeful temptress and her besotted husband, Alain Souchon. Similarly director Jean Becker refuses to mislead us simply with appearances, as what seems to be a study of provincial boorishness is overtaken by more sinister events. Atmospherically photographed with a roving camera by Etienne Becker, this meticulously paced picture is a tad overlong, but it's undeniably dark, daring and disturbing. DP French +subtitles. **DVD**

Isabelle Adjani *Eliane/Elle* • Alain Souchon *Florimond/Pin Pon* • Suzanne Flon *Cognata* • Jenny Clève *Pin Pon's mother* • Michel Galabru *Gabriel Devigne* • François Cluzet *Mickey* ■ *Dir* Jean Becker • *Scr* Sébastien Japrisot, from his novel

One Direction: This Is Us ★★★🄿🄶

Music documentary 2013 · US · Colour · 88min

Morgan Spurlock, the director of *Super Size Me*, takes a behind-the-scenes look at the teen pop sensation that won worldwide success after coming third in the *X-Factor* TV talent show. It's a standard biography, full of clearly choreographed backstage japes, wide shots of screaming fans, and proud mums hugging their pin-up sons, Niall, Zayn, Liam, Louis and Harry. Ultimately though, it's the high-energy concert sequences that work best, giving a more tangible sense of the frenzy surrounding the band. TeS Some swearing.

🄳🅅🄳 🄱🄻 🄢🄿

Harry Styles *Rio* · Niall Horan · Zayn Malik · Louis Tomlinson · Liam Payne ■ *Dir* Morgan Spurlock

One Eight Seven ★★🄸🄴

Drama 1997 · US · Colour · 114min

Samuel L Jackson's typically intense work is the sole merit of this over-directed, uninvolving school drama. Jackson plays a New York teacher physically and psychologically scarred after a vicious knife assault by a student. He transfers to a new school in Los Angeles to rebuild his life, only to find equally violent conditions. Shot in a distracting MTV style, Jackson's sincere performance is wasted on such clichéd fare. JC Swearing, violence, nudity. 🄳🅅🄳

Samuel L Jackson *Trevor Garfield* · John Heard *Dave Childress* · Kelly Rowan *Ellen Henry* · Clifton González González [Clifton Collins Jr] *Cesar* · Karina Arroyave *Rita* · Jonah Rooney *Stevie Middleton* · Lobo Sebastian *Benny* · Jack Kehler *Hyland* ■ *Dir* Kevin Reynolds · *Scr* Scott Yagemann

One-Eyed Jacks ★★★★🄿🄶

Western 1961 · US · Colour · 141min

This stunning and deeply satisfying western is the only film Marlon Brando directed, but Paramount had reason to regret indulging its star - not only does the movie contain levels of sadism and perversity that made it unique for a Hollywood studio film of the period, but it also failed to recoup its $6 million outlay in the States. In a story that is loosely based on the legend of Billy the Kid and Pat Garrett, Brando seeks revenge on his devious partner Karl Malden. It's a fine, adult work, with the Monterey seascapes (magnificently photographed by Charles Lang Jr) making an unusual setting. Incidentally, Brando took over from Stanley Kubrick, who left to direct *Spartacus*. TS 🄳🅅🄳 🄱🄻

Marlon Brando *Rio* · Karl Malden *Dad Longworth* · Katy Jurado *Maria* · Pina Pellicer *Louisa* · Slim Pickens *Lon* · Ben Johnson (1) *Bob Amory* ■ *Dir* Marlon Brando · *Scr* Guy Trosper, Calder Willingham, from the novel *The Authentic Death of Hendry Jones* by Charles Neider

One False Move ★★★★🄸🄴

Crime drama 1992 · US · Colour · 101min

For a mesmerising slice of modern *film noir*, director Carl Franklin skilfully steers past the usual clichés to deliver a thoughtful, ultimately tragic tale. A trio of criminals sets off on a murderous cross-country journey, fleeing Los Angeles with the takings from a brutal drugs heist. LA cops Jim Metzler and Earl Billings are convinced the criminals will head for the tiny southern town where one of their number (Cynda Williams) used to live, and lie in wait with the naive local cop (the ever excellent Bill Paxton). It's a gripping affair, punctuated with isolated splashes of shocking violence, and is superbly acted. JF Swearing, drug abuse. 🄳🅅🄳

Cynda Williams *Fantasia/Lila* · Bill Paxton *Dale "Hurricane" Dixon* · Billy Bob Thornton *Ray Malcolm* · Jim Metzler *Dud Cole* · Michael Beach *Pluto* · Earl Eillings *McFeely* · Natalie Canerday *Cheryl Ann* · Robert Ginnaven *Charlie* · Robert Anthony Bel *Byron* · Kevin Hunter *Ronnie* ■ *Dir* Carl Franklin · *Scr* Billy Bob Thornton, Tom Epperson

One Fine Day ★★★🄿🄶

Romantic comedy 1996 · US · Colour · 104min

In this warm-hearted but underwritten romantic comedy, George Clooney stars as a newspaper columnist saddled with parental responsibilities when he's forced to look after his five-year-old daughter while his ex-wife is on honeymoon. Into his life comes Michelle Pfeiffer, who's struggling to hold down a job and bring up a child, and the couple reluctantly agree to help each other out - only to find that what can go wrong does. The leads are charming, but they are let down by the uninspired direction of Michael Hoffman. JB 🄳🅅🄳
🄱🄻

Michelle Pfeiffer *Melanie Parker* · George Clooney *Jack Taylor* · Mae Whitman *Maggie Taylor* · Alex D Linz *Sammy Parker* · Charles Durning *Lew* · Jon Robin Baitz *Yates Jr* · Ellen Greene *Elaine Lieberman* · Joe Grifasi *Manny Feldstein* ■ *Dir* Michael Hoffman · *Scr* Terrel Seltzer, Ellen Simon

One Flew over the Cuckoo's Nest ★★★★★🄸🄸

Drama 1975 · US · Colour · 128min

Adapted from Ken Kesey's novel, this film is one of the classic movies of the 1970s, thanks in no small measure to the talents of director Milos Forman, who propelled the comic antics to a horrifyingly poignant finale and resounding critical and commercial success. It became one of the few films to be awarded all the major Oscars, winning for best picture, director, screenplay, actor (Jack Nicholson) and actress (Louise Fletcher). Nicholson's performance as McMurphy, a free spirit at loose in a state mental home, is one of his greatest characterisations, as he stirs up rebellion against the oppressive regime of Fletcher's ward sister. And among the patients are such then almost unknowns as Danny DeVito, Brad Dourif and Christopher Lloyd. TH Violence, swearing 🄳🅅🄳 🄱🄻

Jack Nicholson *Randle P McMurphy* · Louise Fletcher *Nurse Mildred Ratched* · William Redfield *Harding* · Will Sampson *Chief Bromden* · Brad Dourif *Billy Bibbit* · Sydney Lassick *Charlie Cheswick* · Christopher Lloyd *Taber* · Danny DeVito *Martini* · Sherman "Scatman" Crothers [Scatman Crothers] *Turkle* ■ *Dir* Milos Forman · *Scr* Lawrence Hauben, Bo Goldman, from the play by Dale Wasserman, from the novel by Ken Kesey · *Cinematographer* Haskell Wexler

One Foot in Heaven ★★★🄤

Biographical drama 1941 · US · BW · 107min

The illustrious Fredric March is at the centre of this Oscar-nominated, pleasingly old-fashioned movie about William Spence, a Methodist minister who, at the turn of the 20th century, takes his message from parish to parish, and must grapple with the changes in society that conflict with his beliefs. This is a loving, if slighty mawkish, piece, peddling piety but not sanctimoniousness. March is well-supported, while Irving Rapper directs with a nice sense of period. RK

Fredric March *William Spence* · Martha Scott *Hope Morris Spence* · Beulah Bondi *Mrs Lydia Sandow* · Gene Lockhart *Preston Thurston* · Grant Mitchell *Clayton Potter* · Moroni Olsen *Dr John Romer* · Harry Davenport *Elias Samson* · Elisabeth Fraser *Eileen Spence, aged 17* · Frankie Thomas *Hartzell Spence, aged 18* · Laura Hope Crews *Mrs Thurston* ■ *Dir* Irving Rapper · *Scr* Casey Robinson, from the biography by Hartzell Spence

One Foot in Hell ★★★

Western 1960 · US · Colour · 89min

As an argument for America to introduce a National Health Service, this western takes some beating. Alan Ladd is the Civil War soldier whose wife dies in Arizona because he doesn't have the money to buy her medicine. Nevertheless, he becomes sheriff and plots revenge by robbing the bank and killing everyone he can. Giving a novel twist to the western formula, this has some fresh characters and doesn't readily cop out in the end. AT

Alan Ladd *Mitch Barrett* · Don Murray *Dan Keats* · Dan O'Herlihy *Harry Ivers* · Dolores Michaels *Julie Reynolds* · Barry Coe *Stu Christian* · Larry Gates *Doc Seltzer* · Karl Swenson *Sheriff Olson* ■ *Dir* James B Clark · *Scr* Aaron Spelling, Sydney Boehm, from the story by Aaron Spelling

One for the Money ★🄸🄴

Comedy crime thriller 2012 · US · Colour · 87min

A down-on-her-luck New Jersey divorcee tries her hand as a bail-bondswoman in this comedy thriller adapted from the first in the series of Janet Evanovich's popular Stephanie Plum novels. Katherine Heigl proves rather too brittle in the central role of the feisty underdog, however, and although she's nowhere near as likeable as the part demands, the producer/star can't take all the blame for the script's lifeless plotting and clunky one-liners. The end result, unfortunately, is an absolute stinker. TJ Violence, swearing. 🄳🅅🄳 🄱🄻

Katherine Heigl *Stephanie Plum* · John Leguizamo *Jimmy Alpha* · Daniel Sunjata *Ranger* · Jason O'Mara *Joe Morelli* · Debbie Reynolds *Grandma Mazur* · Sherri Shepherd *Lula* ■ *Dir* Julie Anne Robinson · *Scr* Liz Brixius, Karen Ray, Stacy Sherman, from the novel by Janet Evanovich

One for the Road ★🄸🄴

Black comedy 2003 · UK · Colour · 91min

It's hard to think of a more inept outing than writer/director Chris Cooke's feature debut. Stripped of their licenses for drink driving, boy racer Greg Chisholm, cabbie Mark Devenport, salesman Rupert Procter and wealthy entrepreneur Hywel Bennett refuse to take their rehabilitation classes seriously. Few will care about these losers or their miserable lives. DP 🄳🅅🄳

Greg Chisholm [Gregory Chisholm] *Jimmy* · Hywel Bennett *Richard Stevens* · Rupert Procter [Rupert Proctor] *Paul* · Mark Devenport *Mark* · Julie Legrand *Liz* · Micaiah Dring *Eve* · Johnny Phillips [Jonathan Phillips] *Ian* ■ *Dir/Scr* Chris Cooke

One Froggy Evening ★★★★★

Animated comedy 1955 · US · Colour · 7min

The best-known of Chuck Jones's Warner Bros one-shot cartoons (that is, those not featuring a recurring character) tells the story of a construction worker who dreams of riches when he finds a singing-and-dancing frog in the cornerstone of a building he is demolishing. Jones is probably alone among the great Hollywood cartoon directors in being able to tell a moral tale without drawing attention to the fact. The message that one should enjoy art for its own sake is subtly transmitted amid the bittersweet humour. CLP

Bill Roberts *Frog, singing* ■ *Dir* Charles M Jones [Chuck Jones] · *Scr* Michael Maltese

One from the Heart ★★★🄸🄶

Musical romance 1982 · US · Colour · 98min

Francis Ford Coppola famously bankrupted his own studio Zoetrope making this $23 million-budget "musical Valentine" entirely on a sound stage, so its merits were subsumed by the commercial and logistical fiasco it turned into. It tells the simple tale of Frederic Forrest and Teri Garr, who split up and have affairs with a circus performer (Nastassja Kinski) and singing waiter (Raul Julia) while intoxicated by one neon-lit Las Vegas night. The songs, by Tom Waits and Crystal Gayle, are bittersweet gems, and the sets are magnificent. Unfortunately, the human element is dwarfed by the technical achievement. AC 🄳🅅🄳

Frederic Forrest *Hank* · Teri Garr *Frannie* · Nastassja Kinski *Leila* · Raul Julia *Ray* · Lainie Kazan *Maggie* · Harry Dean Stanton *Moe* · Allen Goorwitz [Allen Garfield] *Restaurant owner* ■ *Dir* Francis Ford Coppola · *Scr* Armyan Bernstein, Francis Ford Coppola, from a story by Armyan Bernstein · *Cinematographer* Vittorio Storaro

One Full Moon ★★★🄸🄴

Drama 1991 · UK · Colour · 97min

This poetic exercise in rural realism shifts between the 1950s and the 1920s, as Dyfan Roberts revisits the slate-mining community where he was raised by his mother. The relationship between Betsan Llwyd and young Tudor Roberts is both touching and unfeigned, as they put on a united front against the harshness of their existence and the censoriousness of the local preacher. But the nostalgic humour dissipates after Llwyd is assaulted by a travelling tinker and their grim idyll begins to unravel. DP Welsh +subtitles.

Dyfan Roberts *Man* · Tudor Roberts *Boy* · Betsan Llwyd *Mother* · Delyth Einir *Jini* · Ciaran Huw · Dilwyn Vaughn Thomas *Moi* ■ *Dir* Endaf Emlyn · *Scr* Gwenlyn Parry, Endaf Emlyn, from the novel by Caradog Prichard

One Good Cop ★★★🄸🄴

Drama 1991 · US · Colour · 100min

A smoothly orchestrated movie, veering unapologetically between shameless sentimentality and violent melodrama, is given a gritty reality by Michael Keaton's performance as a decent cop planning to adopt his murdered partner's three children. How he blots his record after robbing a local drug baron is a wrenching tale, skilfully told by writer/director Heywood Gould, whose true-life experiences were the basis of *Cocktail*. AJ Violence, swearing. 🄳🅅🄳

Michael Keaton *Artie Lewis* · Rene Russo *Rita Lewis* · Anthony LaPaglia *Stevie Diroma* · Kevin Conway *Lieutenant Danny Quinn* · Rachel Ticotin *Grace* · Tony Plana *Beniamino* · Benjamin Bratt *Felix* ■ *Dir/Scr* Heywood Gould

One Good Turn ★★★🄤

Comedy 1954 · UK · BW · 90min

This is the cleverly constructed follow-up to Norman Wisdom's smash-hit debut *Trouble in Store*. Arguably the best of his vehicles, it features the bumbling star as a handyman trying to save the orphanage that employs him from collapse. His money-raising schemes are invariably hilarious, while his sequences with leading ladies Joan Rice and Australian zither girl Shirley Abicair are charming. Of course, the film is overly sentimental, but sentiment was part of Wisdom's stock-in-trade, and today we can recognise the rare quality of a true cinematic clown. TS 🄳🅅🄳

Norman Wisdom *Norman* · Joan Rice *Iris* · Shirley Abicair *Mary* · Thora Hird *Cook* · William Russell *Alec* · Richard Caldicot *Bigley* · Marjorie Fender *Tuppeny* ■ *Dir* John Paddy Carstairs · *Scr* Maurice Cowan, John Paddy Carstairs, Ted Willis, from a story by Dorothy Whipple, Sid Colin, Talbot Rothwell

One Good Turn ★★🄸🄴

Thriller 1996 · US · Colour · 88min

There's a whole lot of set-up for very little payoff here. Lenny Von Dohlen is a successful software designer who spots James Remar living as a vagrant on the streets of LA. Since Remar had saved Von Dohlen's life years before when they were in the army together, he offers him a job, and then spends the next hour or so of screen time ignoring glaringly obvious clues that Remar has some insane agenda of his own. Little more than an average psycho-stalker movie. ST

James Remar *Simon* · Suzy Amis *Laura* · Lenny Von Dohlen *Matt* · Richard Minchenberg *John* · Audie England *Kristen* · Rowena Guinness *Kim* · John Savage *Santapietro* ■ *Dir* Tony Randel · *Scr* Jim Piddock

One Heavenly Night ★★🄤

Romantic musical 1931 · US · Colour · 76min

Budapest flower-seller Evelyn Laye is persuaded by musical hall star Lilyan Tashman to take her place in her absence, in which guise Laye finds romance with handsome count John Boles. English star Laye was spirited away from the London stage by Samuel Goldwyn, who had this operetta especially written for her Hollywood debut. She is charming, pretty and graceful, but the film founders on an inadequate script and, when it lost money, Goldwyn dropped his protégée. RK

Evelyn Laye *Lilli* · John Boles *Count Mirko Tibor* · Leon Errol *Otto* · Lilyan Tashman *Fritzi Vyez* · Hugh Cameron *Janos* · Marian Lord [Marion

0

Lord] *Liska* • Lionel Belmore *Zagen* ■ *Dir* George Fitzmaurice • *Scr* Sidney Howard, from a story by Louis Bromfield

One Hour Photo ★★★★ 15
Psychological thriller 2001 · US · Colour · 91min
Robin Williams is hauntingly moving as the supermarket photo processor, whose lonely existence feeds an escalating obsession with a glamorous local family. A simple yet effective reflection on modern society's fixation with so-called flawless lifestyles, it's meticulously composed and tautly executed. Each frame of this unnerving psychological chiller is a visually stunning snapshot of an innocent world distorted by human complexities. Director Mark Romanek draws on his music video background of storytelling through imagery, by applying varying degrees of colour and contrast to reflect the positive and negative emotions on display. SF Swearing, violence, nudity. *DVD* BL
Robin Williams *Seymour "Sy" Parrish* • Connie Nielsen *Nina Yorkin* • Michael Vartan *Will Yorkin* • Gary Cole *Bill Owens* • Eriq La Salle *Detective Van Der Zee* • Dylan Smith *Jakob "Jake" Yorkin* • Erin Daniels *Maya Burson* • Paul Hansen Kim *Yoshi Araki* • *Dir/Scr* Mark Romanek

One Hour with You ★★★
Musical romantic comedy
1932 · US · BW · 78min
Parisian doctor Maurice Chevalier and his wife Jeanette MacDonald are still utterly devoted to each other after three years of marriage. But their harmony is disrupted when her devious, man-eating best friend Genevieve Tobin gets her clutches into Chevalier, and his best friend Charles Ruggles declares his passion for MacDonald. Paramount's master of sophistication, Ernst Lubitsch, remakes his 1924 silent hit, *The Marriage Circle*, beautifully orchestrating an experimental mix of verse, song and soliloquies delivered straight to camera. The result is frothy, sophisticated and risqué. RK
Maurice Chevalier *Dr André Bertier* • Jeanette MacDonald *Colette Bertier* • Genevieve Tobin *Mitzi Olivier* • Charlie Ruggles [Charles Ruggles] *Adolph* • Roland Young *Professor Olivier* • George Barbier *Police commissioner* ■ *Dir* Ernst Lubitsch • *Scr* Samson Raphaelson, from the play *Nur ein Traum, Lustspiel in 3 Akten (Only a Dream)* by Lothar Schmidt [Lothar Goldschmidt] • *Cinematographer* Victor Milner

One Hundred and One Dalmatians ★★★★★ U
Animated comedy adventure
1960 · US · Colour · 76min
From the novel by Dodie Smith, this hardy perennial from Disney rivals the studio's *The Aristocats* for its deft mix of cute talking animals and largely foolish humans. While there's little faulting the draughtsmanship and personality of the Dalmatians, the two-legged foils are vital to the story's dynamic: monstrous, fur-loving villainess Cruella De Vil and her hapless cockney henchmen Horace and Jasper. The "twilight bark" sequence, in which London's dogs communicate in woofs, brings poignancy to what is otherwise a thrilling caper created when the Disney artists were at the height of their powers. AC *DVD* BL
Rod Taylor *Pongo* • Ben Wright (1) *Roger Radcliff* • J Pat O'Malley *Colonel/Jasper Badun* • Cate Bauer *Perdita* • Betty Lou Gerson *Cruella De Vil/Miss Birdwell* • Dave Frankham [David Frankham] *Sergeant Tibs* • Martha Wentworth *Nanny/Queenie/Lucy* • Frederick Worlock *Horace Badun/Inspector Craven* • Lisa Davis *Anita Radcliff* ■ *Dir* Wolfgang Reitherman, Hamilton S Luske [Hamilton Luske], Clyde Geronimi • *Scr* Bill Peet, from the novel by Dodie Smith

101 Dalmatians ★★★ U
Comedy adventure 1996 · US · Colour · 98min
Disney updates its classic animated tale with this live-action version starring a deliciously over-the-top Glenn Close as infamous villain Cruella De Vil, who wants to turn loads of cuddly little dalmatian puppies into a fur coat. Jeff Daniels and Joely Richardson (as the couple trying to stop

her) are slightly more subdued, but enjoyable to watch nonetheless. The only complaint for older viewers (and those sentimental about the original) is that live dogs lack the variety of expression – and the vocals – of their animated counterparts. That said, children will love it. JB *DVD*
Glenn Close *Cruella De Vil* • Jeff Daniels *Roger* • Joely Richardson *Anita* • Joan Plowright *Nanny* • Hugh Laurie *Jasper* • Mark Williams *Horace* • John Shrapnel *Skinner* • Tim McInnerny *Alonzo* • Hugh Fraser *Frederick* ■ *Dir* Stephen Herek • *Scr* John Hughes, from the novel by Dodie Smith

101 Reykjavik ★★★ 18
Comedy
2000 · Ice/Den/Nor/Fr/Ger · Colour · 84min
In this laconic comedy of sexual manners, wastrel Hilmir Snaer Gudnason impregnates both his on-off girlfriend Thrudur Vilhjalmsdottir, and Victoria Abril, the Spanish dance teacher who has just started a lesbian relationship with his newly liberated mother Hanna Maria Karlsdottir. The combination of Abril's hot-blooded sassiness and Gudnason's cool deadpan is highly effective, but what lingers longest are cinematographer Peter Steuger's snow-speckled backstreets. DP Icelandic, English +subtitles. Swearing, sex scenes. *DVD*
Victoria Abril *Lola Milagros* • Hilmir Snaer Gudnason *Hlynur* • Hanna Maria Karlsdottir *Berglind* ■ *Dir* Baltasar Kormakur • *Scr* Baltasar Kormakur, from a novel by Hallgrimur Helgason

112 Weddings ★★★ PG
Documentary 2014 · US/Ger · Colour · 95min
This revealing documentary attempts to put marriage under a microscope by catching up with couples several years after they exchanged vows. The title refers to the number of wedding videos director Doug Block has shot over the last two decades, and here he returns to check on the progress of a handful of his former clients – uncovering candid accounts of struggle, separation, divorce and the occasional happy-ever-after. It's a novel twist on a where-are-they-now theme, veering from the comical to the heartbreaking. But such a random selection, while engrossing, doesn't offer any tangible conclusions about the overall condition of marriage as an institution. TeS Some swearing.
■ *Dir* Doug Block • *Scr* Doug Block, Maeve O'Boyle

127 Hours ★★★★ 15
Drama based on a true story
2011 · US/UK /Aus · Colour · 89min
In 2003 hiker Aron Ralston embarked on a wilderness jaunt in a Utah national park, without informing anyone where he was going. But a freak accident saw him become quite literally stuck between a rock and a hard place – trapped by his forearm between a boulder and a cliff-face. Over the next six days, with no sign of rescue and his water gone, the brutal solution to his ghastly predicament became increasingly clear. Director Danny Boyle re-creates this true story of survival with incredible brio. By using flashbacks, hallucinations and kinetic editing, Boyle transforms a necessarily static situation into a collage in which we get to see a man pondering his imminent demise and discovering whether he has what it takes to save himself. James Franco, who is rapidly emerging as one of the most promising actors of his generation, matches Boyle's technical brilliance with a mesmerising depiction of Ralston's strange internal journey. AS Swearing, gore. *DVD* BL
James Franco *Aron Ralston* • Kate Mara *Kristi* • Amber Tamblyn *Megan* • Clémence Poésy *Rana* • Lizzy Caplan *Sonja* • Treat Williams *Aron's dad* ■ *Dir* Danny Boyle • *Scr* Danny Boyle, Simon Beaufoy, from the book *Between a Rock and a Hard Place* by Aron Ralston

102 Dalmatians ★★★ U
Comedy adventure 2000 · US · Colour · 96min
Glenn Close returns as the villainous Cruella De Vil in this follow-up to Disney's 1996 live-action hit *101 Dalmatians*. This is as much fun as the first film, with the supposedly

reformed fur-lover Cruella released after a spell of incarceration and funding an animal rescue operation. Before you can say "cutesy wootsie puppies", she's got outrageous designer Gérard Depardieu preparing to make an overcoat out of you know who. JB *DVD*
Glenn Close *Cruella De Vil* • Ioan Gruffudd *Kevin* • Alice Evans *Chloe* • Tim McInnerny *Alonzo* • Ian Richardson *Mr Torte* • Gérard Depardieu *Le Pelt* • Eric Idle *Waddlesworth* ■ *Dir* Kevin Lima • *Scr* Kristen Buckley, Brian Regan, Brian Tzudiker, Noni White, from a story by Kristen Buckley, Brian Regan, from the novel *The One Hundred and One Dalmatians* by Dodie Smith • *Costume Designer* Anthony Powell

100 Days before the Command ★★★ 15
Drama 1990 · USSR · Colour · 66min
Completed in 1990 but withheld for four years, Uzbek-born Hussein Erkenov's featurette is as compelling as it is complex. Shot secretly during the last days of Communism, this expressionist, elliptical and quietly subversive study of authority and obedience follows a unit of raw Red Army unit recruits as they are gradually dehumanised by the rigidity of their routine. Adhering to the prescribed socialist-realist style, this is a political, as well as a pacifist tract, which is given poetic power by cinematographer Vladimir Menshikov's astonishing use of light. DP Russian +subtitles. *DVD*
Oleg Vasilkov *Elin* • Vladimir Zamansky *The Unknown Man* • Oleg Khusainov *Angel* ■ *Dir* Hussein Erkenov • *Scr* Yuri Polyakov, Vladimir Kholodov, from a story by Yuri Polyakov

One Hundred Men and a Girl ★★★★ U
Musical 1937 · US · BW · 80min
Deanna Durbin, the devoted daughter of a classical trombonist Adolphe Menjou, seeks the assistance of famous conductor Leopold Stokowski (playing himself) to form an Orchestra of the Unemployed. The result is a quintessential feel-good movie, played with precocious zest by Universal Studios' meal ticket and a splendid supporting cast that includes Mischa Auer and bombastic fat man Eugene Pallette. All one needs in order to enjoy this nonsense is the ability to surrender to its fairy-tale sweetness and enjoy the classical music under Stokowski's baton. RK *DVD*
Deanna Durbin *Patricia "Patsy" Cardwell* • Adolphe Menjou *John Cardwell* • Leopold Stokowski • Alice Brady *Mrs Frost* • Eugene Pallette *John R Frost* • Mischa Auer *Michael Borodoff* • Billy Gilbert *Garage owner* • Alma Kruger *Mrs Tyler* ■ *Dir* Henry Koster • *Scr* Bruce Manning, Charles Kenyon, James Mulhauser

The 100-Year-Old Man Who Climbed out of the Window and Disappeared ★★ 15
Comedy 2013 · Swe · Colour · 109min
Adapted from Jonas Jonasson's hit novel, this Swedish shaggy dog story bears comparison with such sentimental Hollywood fare as *Forrest Gump*, but its uneven tone and thuddingly unfunny historical satire are likely to make it less appealing to English-speaking audiences. Robert Gustafsson does a runner from his nursing home, accidentally picking up a bag full of drug money on the way. As he absconds with the loot, the film flashes back through his life. In the too-frequent flashback sequences Gustafsson comes across as not much more than a tiresome drunk. The film may have been a huge box-office hit in Sweden, but the intended hilarity doesn't translate well. AS Swedish, English, German, Spanish, French, Russian +subtitles. Swearing, some violence, sexual references. *DVD* BL
Robert Gustafsson *Allan Karlsson* • Iwar Wiklander *Julius Jonsson* • David Wiberg *Benny* • Mia Skäringer *Gunilla* • Alan Ford *Pim* ■ *Dir* Felix Herngren • *Scr* Felix Herngren, Hans Ingemansson, from Jonas Jonasson's novel

One in a Million ★★★ U
Romantic musical comedy
1936 · US · BW · 94min
Norwegian ice skating star Sonja Henie's first American film was a smash hit which resulted in a 20th Century-Fox contract and top international screen stardom. Viewed today it is probably her best vehicle; there's a winsome topicality attached to this film, dealing as it did with the pre-war Winter Olympics, where the blonde cutie wins the gold and is schlepped to Madison Square Garden by manager Adolphe Menjou. There she meets likeable Don Ameche. TS
Sonja Henie *Greta Muller* • Adolphe Menjou *Thadeus "Tad" Spencer* • Jean Hersholt *Heinrich Muller* • Ned Sparks *Danny Simpson* • Don Ameche *Bob Harris* • The Ritz Brothers [Al Ritz] *Ritz Brother* • The Ritz Brothers [Jimmy Ritz] *Ritz Brother* • The Ritz Brothers [Harry Ritz] *Ritz Brother* • Arline Judge *Billie Spencer* • Borrah Minevitch *Adolphe* • Dixie Dunbar *Goldie* • Montagu Love *Ratoffsky alias Sir Frederick Brooks* ■ *Dir* Sidney Lanfield • *Scr* Leonard Praskins, Mark Kelly, from a story by Leonard Praskins

One Is a Lonely Number ★★★ 15
Drama 1972 · US · Colour · 93min
Trish Van Devere plays a wife who grapples with the aftermath of divorce, travelling the emotional rollercoaster with the help of Hollywood stalwarts Melvyn Douglas, who plays a lonely shopkeeper, and Janet Leigh, an acerbic president of a group for divorced women. Though a little lightweight at times, it has been treated perhaps more harshly than it deserves. FL
Trish Van Devere *Amy Brower* • Monte Markham *Howard Carpenter* • Janet Leigh *Gert Meredith* • Melvyn Douglas *Joseph Provo* • Jane Elliott *Madge Frazier* ■ *Dir* Mel Stuart • *Scr* David Seltzer, from the story *The Good Humor Man* by Rebecca Morris

One Last Chance ★★ 15
Comedy drama 2003 · UK/Nor · Colour · 92min
In this fitfully amusing caper set in the Scottish Highlands, Jamie Sives is desperate to leave the backwater of Tullybridge and steals a gold nugget that he hopes will finance his father's stay in an old people's home, enabling him to escape. However, his plan to sell the nugget to fence Dougray Scott goes awry, with Sives falling foul of gangster James Cosmo and a decidedly sinister curling club. Ultimately, too many key moments are contrived. DP Swearing. *DVD*
Jamie Sives *Fitz* • Iain Robertson *Nellie* • Kevin McKidd *Seany* • Neve McIntosh *Barbara* • Jimmy Chisholm *Harry* • Ewan Stewart *Fitz's father* • James Cosmo *Big John* • Dougray Scott *Frankie the Fence* ■ *Dir/Scr* Stewart Svaasand

One Life ★★★★
Wildlife documentary 2011 · UK · Colour · 84min
Daniel Craig narrates this fascinating documentary from BBC Earth that depicts in stunning detail the life cycles of the planet's flora and fauna. As well as familiar crowd-pleasers including gorillas, elephants and whales, there's a welcome look at such species as venus flytraps, grasscutter ants and even the strawberry poison arrow frog. Four years in the making, this is simply a staggering achievement, with a standard of photography that continues Britain's excellence in the field of wildlife film-making. DA *DVD* BL
Daniel Craig *Narrator* ■ *Dir/Scr* Michael Gunton, Martha Holmes • *Music* George Fenton

One Little Indian ★★ U
Western comedy drama
1973 · US · Colour · 86min
In this sentimental Disney western, James Garner plays a cavalryman who tries to save the Indians during a massacre and is sentenced to hang. His neck and everyone else's conscience is saved by a white boy who has been brought up by Indians. Aimed firmly at the family audience, it boasts a Jerry Goldsmith score, the familiar backdrops of Utah's deserts and buttes, and

an early appearance by a young Jodie Foster. AT

James Garner *Clint Keyes* • Vera Miles *Doris* • Pat Hingle *Capt Stewart* • Morgan Woodward *Sgt Raines* • John Doucette *Sgt Waller* • Clay O'Brien *Mark* • Robert Pine *Lt Cummins* • Bruce Glover *Schrader* • Jodie Foster *Martha* ■ *Dir* Bernard McEveety • *Scr* Harry Spalding • *Music* Jerry Goldsmith

One Love ★★🔞
Romantic drama 2003 • UK/Nor • Colour • 96min

In this clichéd Jamaica-set romance, Bob Marley's son Ky-mani and songbird Cherine Anderson play a Rastafarian reggae artist and a Pentecostal gospel singer who struggle to overcome their cultural and religious differences after falling for each other at the auditions for a new talent competition. The scenarios are predictable and the supporting characters crudely drawn stereotypes, but the music is exuberant. SF Swearing, violence. *DVD*

Ky-mani Marley *Kassa* • Cherine Anderson *Serena* • Idris Elba *Aaron* • Winston Bell *Selector G* • Winston Stona *Pastor Johnson* • Carl Bradshaw *Obeah Man* • Vas Blackwood *Scarface* ■ *Dir* Don Letts, Rick Elgood • *Scr* Trevor Rhone [Trevor D Rhone], from a story by Yvonne Deutschmann

One Magic Christmas ★★🅄
Fantasy drama 1985 • US • Colour • 85min

One suspects that the intention here was to put a modern slant on the Dickens tale *A Christmas Carol*. But quite how her husband's redundancy, impending homelessness and bankruptcy are supposed to rekindle the Christmas spirit in housewife Mary Steenburgen is anybody's guess. It takes a huge leap of faith for anyone to believe that an angel (Harry Dean Stanton) can do much to rectify the situation, but then, this is Disney. Earnestly played, but far too downbeat for the festive season. DP *DVD*

Mary Steenburgen *Ginnie Grainger* • Gary Basaraba *Jack Grainger* • Elisabeth Harnois *Abbie Grainger* • Arthur Hill *Caleb* • Wayne Robson *Harry Dickens* • Harry Dean Stanton *Gideon* • Jan Rubes *Santa Claus* • Elias Koteas *Eddie* ■ *Dir* Phillip Borsos • *Scr* Thomas Meehan, from a story by Thomas Meehan, Phillip Borsos, Barry Healey

One Man's Way ★★🅄
Biographical drama 1964 • US • BW • 104min

This is a devout biopic about Norman Vincent Peale, a reporter who became one of those aspirational Dale Carnegie-types in American pop culture. Don Murray gives a sympathetically sanitised performance under Denis Sanders's direction. TH

Don Murray *Norman Vincent Peale* • Diana Hyland *Ruth Peale* • William Windom *Rev Clifford Peale* • Virginia Christine *Anna Peale* • Veronica Cartwright *Mary* ■ *Dir* Denis Sanders • *Scr* Eleanore Griffin, John W Bloch, from the biography *Norman Vincent Peale: Minister to Millions* by Arthur Gordon

One Million BC ★★
Prehistoric adventure 1940 • US • BW • 76min

Hal Roach is best known as the producer who teamed Laurel and Hardy. Unfortunately, he got laughs in all the wrong places for this ambitious but ultimately preposterous prehistoric adventure. Yet the film does have a place in cinema history. This owes nothing to the story about the Rock and Shell tribes, to the shoestring special effects, or to the grunting mime of Victor Mature, Carole Landis and Lon Chaney Jr in the principal roles. The claim to fame lies in the uncredited assistance of DW Griffith, the legendary silent director, working on his final picture after a decade in the wilderness. DP

Victor Mature *Tumak* • Carole Landis *Loana* • Lon Chaney Jr *Akhoba* • Conrad Nagel *Archaeologist/Narrator* • John Hubbard *Ohtao* • Robert Kent *Mountain guide* • Mamo Clark *Nupondi* ■ *Dir* Hal Roach, Hal Roach Jr • *Scr* Mickell Novak, George Baker, Joseph Frickert

One Million Years BC ★★★🅿🅖
Adventure 1966 • US/UK • Colour • 96min

Raquel Welch wears a furry bikini and roams the wilderness in this Jurassic lark. Welch has a stunning physique but no dialogue, merely some grunts and a furrowed brow, which is fine as she's not called upon to communicate much beyond fear or desire. Made by Hammer, it's an absolute hoot, as it follows the war between the Rock People and the Shell People, and throws in some wobbly prehistoric monsters, courtesy of effects maestro Ray Harryhausen. AT *DVD*

Raquel Welch *Loana* • John Richardson *Tumak* • Percy Herbert *Sakana* • Robert Brown *Akhoba* • Martine Beswick *Nupondi* • Jean Wladon *Ahot* • Lisa Thomas *Sura* ■ *Dir* Don Chaffey • *Scr* Michael Carreras, from the film *One Million BC* by Mickell Novak, George Baker, Joseph Frickert

One Minute to Zero ★★
War drama 1952 • US • BW • 105min

Robert Mitchum goes into action during the Korean War, here teaming up with Ann Blyth who represents the United Nations and provides the love interest. Their romance comes under strain when Mitchum mows down some innocent refugees but, hey, they soon get together for a syrupy song called *Tell Me Golden Moon*. Despite the pains taken with the battle scenes, this is a pretty dismal job, designed to show how the UN was deep inside Uncle Sam's pocket. AT

Robert Mitchum *Colonel Steve Janowksi* • Ann Blyth *Linda Day* • William Talman *Colonel Parker* • Charles McGraw *Sgt Baker* • Margaret Sheridan *Mary Parker* • Richard Egan *Captain Ralston* ■ *Dir* Tay Garnett • *Scr* Milton Krims, William Wister Haines

One Missed Call ★🔢🔞
Horror thriller 2007 • Jpn/US/Ger/UK • Colour • 169min

Based on Takashi Miike's enjoyably daft Japanese horror movie about a supernatural curse that propagates itself through mobile phone technology, this abysmal Hollywood remake misdials every scare. Uprooting the action to the US, French director Eric Valette struggles with a cast of pretty but wooden actors led by Shannyn Sossamon. She plays a college student whose friends are being murdered in strange circumstances after they receive voicemails of their own impending death throes. When not lazily rehashing Miike's jittery set pieces (including a videotaped exorcism that goes horribly wrong), Valette deploys scares over-familiar from *The Ring* and *The Grudge* to minimal effect. JR *DVD* 🔵

Shannyn Sossamon *Beth Raymond* • Edward Burns *Jack Andrews* • Ana Claudia Talancón *Taylor Anthony* • Ray Wise *Ted Summers* • Azura Skye *Leann Cole* • Johnny Lewis *Brian Sousa* • Jason Beghe *Ray Purvis* ■ *Dir* Eric Valette • *Scr* Andrew Klavan, from the 2003 film by Miwako Daira, from the novel *Chakushin ari* by Yasushi Akimoto

One More Kiss ★★★★🔢
Romantic drama 1999 • UK • Colour • 97min

Director Vadim Jean has taken a difficult subject – terminal illness – and created a beautiful movie that manages to be moving without being too sentimental. It tells the story of single-minded Valerie Edmond, who returns from New York to her home town of Berwick-upon-Tweed to patch things up with her father (James Cosmo) before she dies of cancer. She also meets up with now-married old flame Gerard Butler and becomes friends with fellow cancer patient Danny Nussbaum. Thanks to some sterling performances, particularly from Cosmo, this is an uplifting, rewarding film that, while occasionally harrowing, is also full of gutsy humour. SR Swearing. *DVD*

Gerard Butler *Sam* • James Cosmo *Frank* • Valerie Edmond *Sarah* • Valerie Gogan *Charlotte* • Carl Proctor *Barry* • Danny Nussbaum *Jude* • Dilys Miller *Mary* • Ron Guthrie *Robin* ■ *Dir* Vadim Jean • *Scr* Suzie Halewood

One More River ★★★
Drama 1934 • US • BW • 85min

Looking fearfully dated today, this once prestigious Universal feature is based upon the last novel in John Galsworthy's *The Forsyte Saga*. Despite being directed by the talented expatriate Englishman James Whale, this Hollywood, England, study of a divorce remains relentlessly theatrical, although Diana Wynyard is sublime as the wife accused by Colin Clive of committing adultery with young Frank Lawton. Watch for the screen debut of Jane Wyatt. TS

Diana Wynyard *Clare Corven* • Frank Lawton *Tony Croom* • Mrs Patrick Campbell *Lady Mont* • Jane Wyatt *Dinny Cherrell* • Colin Clive *Sir Gerald Corven* • Reginald Denny *David Dornford* • C Aubrey Smith *General Charwell* • Henry Stephenson *Sir Lawrence Mont* • Lionel Atwill *Brough* • Alan Mowbray *Forsyte* ■ *Dir* James Whale • *Scr* RC Sherriff, from the novel by John Galsworthy

One More Time ★★
Comedy 1970 • UK • Colour • 95min

Salt & Pepper, a lacklustre British-made comedy vehicle for Sinatra clan cronies Sammy Davis Jr and Peter Lawford, rather surprisingly spawned this even weaker sequel, in which the buddies are again Soho club-owners involved in crime. This time Lawford plays identical twin brothers; the death of one leads to attempts on the life of the other in a Scottish castle. Interesting (for a while) is the way director Jerry Lewis, who doesn't appear, transfers his zany persona to Davis and interpolates typical Lewis set-ups and sentimentality. DM

Sammy Davis Jr *Charlie Salt* • Peter Lawford *Chris Pepper/Lord Sydney Pepper* • Maggie Wright *Miss Tomkins* • Leslie Sands *Inspector Crook* • Christopher Lee • Peter Cushing ■ *Dir* Jerry Lewis • *Scr* Michael Pertwee

One Night at McCool's ★★🔢
Black comedy 2001 • US • Colour • 88min

Great cast, good start – shame, then, that this night out begins to flag by early evening. Set in McCool's bar, the film kicks off with the arrival of slinky, red-sheathed *femme fatale* Liv Tyler. She's the sort of woman that men don't so much live for as die for. And guess what? One does. Yet the killing further fuels the passions of besotted barman Matt Dillon, waterholing lawyer Paul Reiser and investigating homicide detective John Goodman. Starting out fine as a black comedy, the film loses its way with a desperate desire to be hip. DA Violence, swearing, sex scenes. *DVD*

Liv Tyler *Jewel Valentine* • Matt Dillon *Randy* • John Goodman *Detective Dehling* • Paul Reiser *Carl Lumpke* • Michael Douglas (1) *Mr Burmeister* • Reba McEntire *Dr Green* • Andrew Silverstein [Andrew Dice Clay] *Utah/Elmo* ■ *Dir* Harald Zwart • *Scr* Stan Seidel

One Night in Turin ★★★🔢
Sports documentary 2010 • UK • Colour • 92min

The Italia 90 World Cup finals revived England's love affair with football. Yet, going into the tournament, few had much faith in either manager Bobby Robson or his under-performing team. However, as James Erskine recalls in this competent documentary, the side survived an indifferent group stage to progress to the semi-finals against West Germany. Erskine doesn't ignore the wider context of the competition, but the emphasis is most firmly on Robson's battles with the media and the emergence of Paul Gascoigne as the tournament's superstar. The narration, delivered by Gary Oldman, is often overwritten, but the movie relives the events with suitable enthusiasm and nostalgia. DP *DVD* *DVD*

Gary Oldman *Narrator* ■ *Dir* James Erskine • *Scr* From the non-fiction book *All Played Out* by Pete Davies

One Night of Love ★★★★🅄
Musical 1934 • US • BW • 83min

This is the hit musical that made a movie star out of the diva Grace Moore, and

brought opera to a wide film-going public. Somewhat mirroring her own career, it tells of an American soprano who studies in Italy and wins fame at the Met. After being turned down by MGM for *The Merry Widow* (1934), because she was considered too fat, Moore slimmed down and was signed with Columbia for this first (and best) of five deliriously silly, well-mounted and tuneful operettas she made for the studio. The director Victor Schertzinger, an accomplished musician, co-wrote the title song. RB

Grace Moore *Mary Barrett* • Tullio Carminati *Giulio Monteverdi* • Lyle Talbot *Bill Houston* • Mona Barrie *Lally* • Jessie Ralph *Angelina* • Luis Alberni *Giovanni* ■ *Dir* Victor Schertzinger • *Scr* SK Lauren, James Gow, Edmund North, from a play by Dorothy Speare, Charles Beahan

One Night Stand ★★🔞
Romantic drama 1997 • US • Colour • 98min

After the superb *Leaving Las Vegas*, director Mike Figgis took a misstep with this annoying drama about 1990s relationships and how one indiscretion can change the course of your life forever. The characters who swap beds and partners (Wesley Snipes, Nastassja Kinski, Kyle MacLachlan and Wen Ming-Na) are all unlikeable and annoying. Only Robert Downey Jr – as Snipes's dying friend – emerges unscathed, delivering a believable performance. JB Violence, swearing, sex scenes. *DVD*

Wesley Snipes *Max Carlyle* • Nastassja Kinski *Karen* • Kyle MacLachlan *Vernon* • Wen Ming-Na [Ming-Na] *Mimi Carlyle* • Robert Downey Jr *Charlie* ■ *Dir/Scr* Mike Figgis

One Night with You ★★🅄
Musical comedy 1948 • UK • BW • 92min

An Italian tenor and movie star, played by Italian tenor and movie star Nino Martini, and an English girl (Patricia Roc) meet on a station. While he rescues her dog from a fight, his bags are stolen, they miss their trains, and experience a night of adventures and mishaps before reaching their destination in Rome and a hearts-and-flowers dénouement. This is occasionally diverting. RK

Nino Martini *Giulio Moris* • Patricia Roc *Mary Santell* • Bonar Colleano *Piero Santellini* • Hugh Wakefield *Santell* • Guy Middleton *Matty* • Stanley Holloway *Tramp* ■ *Dir* Terence Young • *Scr* Caryl Brahms, SJ Simon, from the film *Fuga a Due Voci* by Carlo Ludovico Bragaglia

One Nite in Mongkok ★★★★🔢
Crime thriller 2004 • HK • BW and Colour • 110min

Director Derek Yee's stylish Hong Kong crime thriller combines elements of *film noir*, police procedural and romantic tragedy. Assassin Daniel Wu is imported from rural China to Kowloon's overcrowded Mongkok district to kill a Triad boss, but he also has a more personal mission to fulfil. When the hitman saves tart-with-a-heart Cecilia Cheung from being caught in the crossfire, the pair form an unlikely alliance and are soon being hotly pursued by both gangs and cops. Yee may not be breaking any new ground here, but the high production values, insightful characterisations and swift precision editing make this a highly entertaining ride. AJ Cantonese, Mandarin +subtitles. Violence. *DVD*

Cecilia Cheung *Dan Dan* • Daniel Wu *Roy* • Alex Fong *Inspector Miao* • Anson Leung *Ben* ■ *Dir/Scr* Derek Yee

One of Our Aircraft Is Missing ★★★🅄
Second World War drama 1942 • UK • BW • 102min

This is an exciting enough Second World War adventure, as the crew of a Wellington bomber attempts to evade Nazi patrols and reach home after their plane is shot down over the Netherlands. Directors Michael Powell and Emeric Pressburger are more successful at re-creating the bomber raid and its spectacular crash than they are at capturing an authentic Dutch atmosphere.

0

It's a classic example of the way in which fictional stories were given a documentary style in order to increase their propaganda impact, and the script received an Oscar nomination. However, the film looks rather dated now. DP **DVD**

Godfrey Tearle *Sir George Corbett* • Eric Portman *Tom Earnshaw* • Hugh Williams *Frank Shelley* • Bernard Miles *Geoff Hickman* • Hugh Burden *John Glyn Haggard* • Emrys Jones *Bob Ashley* • Pamela Brown *Els Meertens* • Googie Withers *Jo de Vries* ■ *Dir/Scr* Michael Powell, Emeric Pressburger

One of Our Dinosaurs Is Missing ★★★ U

Period comedy   1975 · US · Colour · 90min

In this offering from Disney, a top-secret formula is hidden by aristocrat Derek Nimmo inside the skeleton of a dinosaur at the Natural History Museum in London. There's not even a sniff of a velociraptor, but there is Peter Ustinov as a Chinese agent and Helen Hayes leading a gang of nannies that even Mary Poppins would be hard-pressed to join. A couple of kung fu fights, a very silly car chase and some wildly over-the-top acting help liven things up. DP **DVD**

Peter Ustinov *Hnup Wan* • Helen Hayes *Hettie* • Clive Revill *Quon* • Derek Nimmo *Lord Southmere* • Joan Sims *Emily* • Bernard Bresslaw *Fan Choy* • Natasha Pyne *Susan* • Roy Kinnear *Superintendent Grubbs* • Joss Ackland *BJ Spence* ■ *Dir* Robert Stevenson • *Scr* Bill Walsh, from the novel *The Great Dinosaur Robbery* by David Forrest

One of Our Spies Is Missing ★★★ U

Spy adventure   1966 · US · Colour · 91min

The Man from UNCLE TV series began as a spoof of James Bond but took off with a life – albeit a mechanical one – of its own. This is one of the classier feature outings, with Robert Vaughn as indomitable Napoleon Solo and David McCallum as impassive Illya Kuryakin in an adventure that lives up to its title and to the series' hallmarks of well-groomed suspense and jingly music. Nostalgia buffs should have a ball with all those bouffant hairdos and the snappy stylised editing. TH

Robert Vaughn (1) *Napoleon Solo* • David McCallum (1) *Illya Kuryakin* • Leo G Carroll *Mr Waverly* • Vera Miles *Madame de Sala* • Maurice Evans *Sir Norman Swickert* • Ann Elder *Joanna Sweet* • Bernard Fox *Jordin* • Dolores Faith *Lorelei Lancer* • Anna Capri [Ahna Capri] *Do Do* • Harry Davis *Alexander Gritsky* • Yvonne Craig *Wanda* ■ *Dir* E Darrell Hallenbeck • *Scr* Howard Rodman, from a story by Henry Slesar

One of the Hollywood Ten ★★

Historical drama   2000 · UK/Sp · Colour · 110min

Fear of the Red Menace prompted Senator Joseph McCarthy and his Hollywood acolytes to organise a blacklist in the early years of the Cold War. Among its victims was politically committed director Herbert Biberman, and his story is related in this impassioned but somewhat strained drama. It doesn't help that neither Jeff Goldblum nor Greta Scacchi is comfortably cast as Biberman and his actress wife, Gale Sondergaard. DP

Jeff Goldblum *Herbert Biberman* • Greta Scacchi *Gale Sondergaard* • Angela Molina *Rosaura Revueltas* • Christopher Fulford *Riffkind* • John Sessions *Paul Jarrico* • Peter Bowles *Jack Warner* • Geraint Wyn Davies *Michael Wilson* • Sean Chapman *Edward Dmytryk* ■ *Dir/Scr* Karl Francis

One of Us ★★★★ U

Drama   1989 · Is · Colour · 110min

This perceptive insight into the Middle East conflict brings home with some force the realisation that, for all the efforts of the politicians, peace depends on the actions of committed men whose convictions and loyalties do not always coincide with the greater good. Sharon Alexander gives an impressive performance as the army investigator who discovers that those suspected of the murder of an Arab are

brothers in arms, his dilemma made all the more credible by the persuasive playing of Alon Aboutboul as the friend he must betray. DP Hebrew +subtitles. Violence, some nudity.

Alon Aboutboul *Yotam* • Sharon Alexander *Rafa* • Dan Toren *Amir* • Dahlia Shimko *Tamar* • Arnon Tzadok *The Colonel* ■ *Dir* Uri Barbash • *Scr* Benny Barbash, from his play

One Potato, Two Potato ★★★

Drama   1964 · US · BW · 89min

This drama could have been quite a hot potato, made at a time of racial unrest in America and telling a story of a mixed romance that leads to marriage. The relationship is treated as utterly normal until the woman's former husband enters the frame, inciting a bitter dispute over the custody of their child. While a starry cast might have paid dividends at the box-office, the unknowns give this liberal film added authenticity, even though the Oscar-nominated script does lapse into sentimentality. AT

Barbara Barrie *Julie Cullen Richards* • Bernie Hamilton *Frank Richards* • Richard Mulligan *Joe Cullen* • Harry Bellaver *Judge Powell* • Marti Mericka *Ellen Mary* ■ *Dir* Larry Peerce • *Scr* Raphael Hayes, Orville H Hampton, from a story by Orville H Hampton

One Rainy Afternoon ★★★ U

Romantic comedy   1936 · US · BW · 80min

This typical 1930s romance bears as much relevance to "real lurv" as Ida Lupino to your average gal. But it works, with a deft combination of slick script, daft idea cleverly executed and wonderful light performances from all concerned. An innocuous kiss causes a major stir in Paris and sets the assembled company on a helter-skelter ride of rearranged lives. Lupino has a luminous screen presence. SH

Francis Lederer *Philippe Martin* • Ida Lupino *Monique Pelerin* • Hugh Herbert *Toto* • Roland Young *Maillot* • Erik Rhodes *Count Alfredo Donstelli* • Joseph Cawthorn *Mr Pelerin* • Countess Liev de Maigret *Yvonne* • Donald Meek *Judge* ■ *Dir* Rowland V Lee • *Scr* Stephen Morehouse Avery, Maurice Hanline, from the film *Monsieur Sans-Gêne* by Emeric Pressburger, from the film by René Pujol

One Romantic Night ★

Romantic drama   1930 · US · BW · 73min

Lillian Gish made her talking picture debut in this stumbling adaptation about a young aristocratic girl being groomed for marriage to a prince. The film, which co-stars a wooden Rod La Rocque, a ridiculously mannered Conrad Nagel and Marie Dressler doing battle with the script, went through three directors – George Fitzmaurice, Harry D'Abbadie D'Arrast and Paul L Stein (the only one credited) – only to emerge as a stilted bore. RK

Lillian Gish *Alexandra* • Rod La Rocque *Prince Albert* • Conrad Nagel *Dr Nicholas Haller* • Marie Dressler *Princess Beatrice* • OP Heggie *Father Benedict* • Albert Conti *Count Lutzen* • Edgar Norton *Col Wunderlich* ■ *Dir* Paul L Stein • *Scr* Melville Baker, from the play *The Swan* by Ferenc Molnar

One Single Night ★★★

Drama   1939 · Swe · BW · 90min

Reunited with Gustaf Molander, the director who had done so much to make her a star in films such as *Intermezzo*, Ingrid Bergman gives a polished performance in this mildly shocking drama of illegitimacy and pre-marital sex. Bergman plays the ward of an aristocrat who has just discovered that he has an illegitimate son who has been raised by circus folk. The problem facing son Edvin Adolphson is whether to opt for romance with the well heeled Bergman or stay true to circus owner Aino Taube. The cross-class themes and the romantic interludes are handled with a sure touch by Molander. DP Swedish +subtitles.

Ingrid Bergman *Eva Beckman* • Edvin Adolphson *Valdemar Moreaux* • Aino Taube *Helga Martenson* • Olof Sandborg *Colonel Magnus Von*

Brede ■ *Dir* Gustaf Molander • *Scr* Gösta Stevens, from the story *En Eneste Natt* by Harald Tandrup

One Special Night ★★★

Seasonal drama   1999 · US · Colour · 87min

A simple premise – a man and a woman are stranded in a snowstorm on Thanksgiving, spend the night learning about each other and form an important friendship – becomes a moving TV movie thanks to the accomplished performances of James Garner and Julie Andrews. This is subtly directed by Roger Young and never descends into the mushiness you might expect from such a plot. The cast is uniformly good, but the real pleasure comes from watching the two leads go through their paces. JB

James Garner *Robert* • Julie Andrews *Catherine* • Patricia Charbonneau *Lori* • Stacy Grant *Jaclyn* • Stewart Bick *Jeff* ■ *Dir* Roger Young • *Scr* Nancey Silvers, from the play *A Winter Visitor* by Jan Hartman

One Spy Too Many ★★ PG

Spy adventure   1966 · US · Colour · 97min

One of a number of features spun-off from the hit TV series *The Man from UNCLE* to be released in the 1960s, this lazy effort comprises situations from previously aired episodes and the result is most unsatisfactory. Robert Vaughn and David McCallum have the film stolen from under their noses by the excellent Rip Torn, who throws restraint to the winds. There are some hilarious dices with death along the way, but it's far too long for a cut-and-paste job. DP **DVD**

Robert Vaughn (1) *Napoleon Solo* • David McCallum (1) *Illya Kuryakin* • Rip Torn *Alexander* • Dorothy Provine *Tracey Alexander* • Leo G Carroll *Mr Waverly* • Yvonne Craig *Maude Waverly* ■ *Dir* Joseph Sargent • *Scr* Dean Hargrove

One Summer Love ★ 15

Romantic drama   1975 · US · Colour · 93min

Also known as *Dragonfly*, this is a stinker under any name. Gilbert Cates directs this worn-out romantic tale about the relationship between a man recently released from a mental asylum and a young woman who works at a cinema. Despite Beau Bridges and Susan Sarandon giving it their all, this never engages, enthrals or amuses at any point in the proceedings. JB

Beau Bridges *Jesse Arlington* • Susan Sarandon *Chloe* • Mildred Dunnock *Mrs Barrow* • Michael B Miller *Gabriel Arlington* • Linda Miller *Willa Arlington* • Martin Burke *Lonnie Arlington* • James Otis *Clifford* • James Noble *Dr Leo Cooper* ■ *Dir* Gilbert Cates • *Scr* N Richard Nash

The One That Got Away ★★★ U

Second World War drama
1957 · UK · BW · 106min

A swaggering Hardy Kruger is excellent as Franz von Werra, the Luftwaffe pilot who not only escaped from several camps in this country, but who also absconded from Canada and crossed America in his bid to rejoin his outfit. Directed at a fair clip by Roy Baker, this true-life tale is more notable for its fair-minded approach than for its thrills, but still delivers the occasional exciting moment. DP **DVD**

Hardy Kruger *Franz von Werra* • Colin Gordon *Army interrogator* • Michael Goodliffe *RAF interrogator* • Terence Alexander *RAF intelligence officer* • Jack Gwillim *Commandant at Grizedale* • Andrew Faulds *Lieutenant at Grizedale* • Alec McCowen *Duty Officer Hucknall* ■ *Dir* Roy Baker [Roy Ward Baker] • *Scr* Howard Clewes, from a book by Kendal Burt, James Leasor

One Third of a Nation ★★★

Drama   1939 · US · BW · 71min

Wealthy New Yorker Leif Erickson helps a young boy who has escaped from a fire in a slum tenement fire and falls in love with the boy's sister. Sylvia Sidney, in her final film under her Paramount contract, stars as the girl; future director Sidney Lumet, in his only screen appearance, is the young boy.

The screenplay was adapted from the controversial Broadway drama produced by the Works Progress Administration Federal Theater Project – part of President Franklin Roosevelt's New Deal – and places more emphasis on the love story than the horrors of slum conditions. It is nevertheless an affecting piece of social commentary. RK

Sylvia Sidney *Mary Rogers* • Leif Erickson *Peter Cortlant* • Myron McCormick *Sam Noon* • Hiram Sherman *Donald Hinchley* • Sidney Lumet *Joey Rogers* ■ *Dir* Dudley Murphy • *Scr* Oliver HP Garrett, Dudley Murphy, from the play by Arthur Arent

One Touch of Venus ★★★ U

Comedy fantasy   1948 · US · BW · 81min

This is the movie where the love goddess herself, Ava Gardner, plays *the* love goddess, Venus, and comes to life for 24 hours on a window dresser's kiss. Gardner is fabulous: sexy, alluring, warm and womanly, and more than a match for feeble, miscast Robert Walker. The direction by William A Seiter isn't up to much, though, and neither are the production values. TS

Ava Gardner *Venus* • Robert Walker *Eddie Hatch* • Dick Haymes *Joe Grant* • Eve Arden *Molly* • Olga San Juan *Gloria* • Tom Conway *Whitfield Savory* ■ *Dir* William A Seiter • *Scr* Harry Kurnitz, Frank Tashlin, from the musical play by Kurt Weill, SJ Perelman, Ogden Nash, from the novel *The Tinted Venus* by F Anstey

One-Trick Pony ★★★ 15

Musical drama   1980 · US · Colour · 98min

Paul Simon stars as a failing rock singer, facing up to an uncertain future after 14 years on the road, in this unusually harsh look at the realities of being a pop performer. Semi-autobiographical in the way it clearly reflects his post Simon and Garfunkel feelings, Simon fans will relish the ten new songs written for his vanity production even if they don't like his caustic screenplay. AJ Swearing, nudity.

Paul Simon *Jonah* • Blair Brown *Marion* • Rip Torn *Walter Fox* • Joan Hackett *Lonnie Fox* • Allen Garfield *Cal Van Damp* • Mare Winningham *Modeena Dandridge* • Michael Pearlman *Matty Levin* • Lou Reed *Steve Kunelian* ■ *Dir* Robert M Young • *Scr* Paul Simon

One True Thing ★★★ 15

Drama   1998 · US · Colour · 122min

Get those hankies out for this family weepie, which earned Meryl Streep an Oscar nomination. She's the cancer-stricken mum whom daughter Renee Zellweger comes home to look after, even though the pair have never got along. Rounding out the family are William Hurt, as Zellweger's revered father, and Tom Everett Scott as her brother, but it is Streep who steals every scene and wrings tears you didn't know you had out of you. Subtly handled by actor-turned-director Carl Franklin. JB **DVD**

Meryl Streep *Kate Gulden* • Renee Zellweger [Renée Zellweger] *Ellen Gulden* • William Hurt *George Gulden* • Tom Everett Scott *Brian Gulden* • Lauren Graham *Jules* • Nicky Katt *Jordan Belzer* • James Eckhouse *District attorney* ■ *Dir* Carl Franklin • *Scr* Karen Croner, from the novel by Anna Quindlen

One, Two, Three ★★★★ U

Political comedy   1961 · US · BW · 104min

If you count the punch lines per minute, this has to be one of the fastest, talkiest comedies ever made. Billy Wilder's satire never lets up and gives James Cagney his finest role for many years. Cagney plays a combustible Coca-Cola executive in West Berlin, desperate to improve sales at any cost, while his boss's visiting daughter falls for a communist named Piffl, played by Horst Buchholz. While some may find Wilder's scattershot approach a trifle obvious – capitalism and communism are both subjected to ridicule – it remains, like *Dr Strangelove*, a key product of the Cold War, when some things were just too serious to take seriously. AT **DVD**

James Cagney *CR MacNamara* • Horst Buchholz *Otto Ludwig Piffl* • Pamela Tiffin *Scarlett Hazeltine* • Arlene Francis *Phyllis MacNamara* • Lilo Pulver [Liselotte Pulver] *Ingeborg* • Howard

St John *Hazeltine* • Hanns Lothar *Schlemmer* • Lois Bolton *Mrs Hazeltine* • Leon Askin *Peripetchikoff* • Peter Capell *Mishkin* • Ralf Wolter *Borodenko* ■ *Dir* Billy Wilder • *Scr* Billy Wilder, IAL Diamond, from the play *Egy, Ketto, Harom* by Ferenc Molnar

1234 ★★★ 15
Drama 2008 · UK · Colour · 78min

This charming low-budget British drama follows the fortunes of the nerdy Stevie (Ian Bonar), who dreams of quitting his despised day job and making a go of things as a singer/guitarist. After meeting the more experienced Billy (Kieran Bew), he finds himself one step closer to achieving his goals. An unexpected romance, however, forces Stevie to choose between success and happiness. Though it makes some wonderful observations about the world of amateur rock, this is where director Giles Borg's feature debut works best: it's more *Gregory's Girl* than *The Commitments*. DW Swearing, drug abuse. *DVD*

Ian Bonar *Stevie* • Lyndsey Marshal *Emily* • Kieran Bew *Billy* • Mathew Baynton *Neil* • Giles Maythan *Richard* • Luke Rutherford *Tony* • Matthew Sim *Mark* ■ *Dir/Scr* Giles Borg

One Way Out ★★ 15
Crime drama 2002 · Can · Colour · 94min

This TV-movie thriller's intriguing premise is frittered away by sloppy writing and injudicious casting. James Belushi is suitably self-absorbed as a cop whose addiction to gambling leaves him in thrall to a pair of club-owning mobsters. But things start to unravel when they suggest that Belushi pay off his debts by helping the hopelessly miscast Jason Bateman bump off his wife. DP Sex scenes, swearing, violence. *DVD*

James Belushi *Harry Woltz* • Angela Featherstone *Gwen Buckley* • Jason Bateman *John Farrow* • Guylaine St-Onge [Guylaine St Onge] *Evans Farrow* • Angelo Tsarouchas *Mickey Russell* ■ *Dir* Allan A Goldstein • *Scr* John Salvati

One Way Passage ★★★★
Romantic drama 1932 · US · BW · 68min

Aboard an ocean liner homeward bound for the United States, William Powell (returning to face a murder charge) and Kay Francis (suffering from an incurable illness) enjoy a necessarily short-lived love affair. Very short, poignantly sweet, and discreetly directed by Tay Garnett, this is the kind of romantic drama redolent of 1930s Hollywood which, at its best, is involving and effective. Enhanced by Frank McHugh and Aline MacMahon as a pair of confidence tricksters, the movie won the Oscar for Robert Lord's original story. RK

William Powell *Dan Hardesty* • Kay Francis *Joan Ames* • Frank McHugh *Skippy* • Aline MacMahon *Betty the countess* • Warren Hymer *Steve Burke* • Frederick Burton *Doctor* ■ *Dir* Tay Garnett • *Scr* Wilson Mizner, Joseph Jackson, from a story by Robert Lord

One Way Pendulum ★★★ U
Comedy 1965 · UK · BW · 85min

While Eric Sykes constructs a model of the Old Bailey in the living room, his son Jonathan Miller teaches his collection of I-Speak-Your-Weight machines to sing. The rest of the family are equally strange in this movie adaptation of NF Simpson's surreal stage play, which climaxes in a do-it-yourself murder trial organised by Sykes. The theatre production was a triumph of bizarre nonsense but the film never quite captures its spirit. DF

Eric Sykes *Mr Groomkirby* • George Cole *Defense Counsel/Friend* • Julia Foster *Sylvia* • Jonathan Miller (1) *Kirby* • Peggy Mount *Mrs Gantry* • Alison Leggatt *Mrs Groomkirby* • Mona Washbourne *Aunt Mildred* ■ *Dir* Peter Yates • *Scr* NF Simpson, from his play

One Week ★★★★ U
Silent comedy 1920 · US · Colour · 17min

Blissful mayhem for Buster Keaton fans as honeymooners Keaton and Sybil Sealey are given a home to assemble, only to watch it go cock-eyed because a rival to Buster has changed the numbers on the home components. The result is a lop-sided structure which gets swept away by an oncoming train. A tad mechanical, but it has some ground-breaking gags, most of which are still used by comedians today. TH

Buster Keaton *Newlywed husband* • Sybil Seeley *Newlywed wife* • Joe Roberts *Piano mover* ■ *Dir/Scr* Buster Keaton, Eddie Cline [Edward Cline]

Onegin ★★ 12
Period romantic drama 1999 · UK/US · Colour · 106min

Ralph Fiennes is directed by his sister Martha in this ponderous adaptation of Pushkin's classic. Fiennes is well cast as Evgeny Onegin, a decadent, dissipated aristocrat who moves to his recently deceased uncle's estate in rural Russia. There he proceeds to devastate the lives of all around him, rejecting the advances of the luscious Liv Tyler and driving bumpkin Toby Stephens into a deadly duel. Though beautifully shot, this desperately needs pace. LH Violence. *DVD*

Ralph Fiennes *Evgeny Onegin* • Liv Tyler *Tatyana Larin* • Toby Stephens *Vladimir Lensky* • Lena Headey *Olga Larin* • Martin Donovan (2) *Prince Nikitin* • Alun Armstrong *Zaretsky* • Harriet Walter *Madame Larina* • Irene Worth *Princess Alina* • Francesca Annis *Katiusha* ■ *Dir* Martha Fiennes • *Scr* Peter Ettedgui, Michael Ignatieff, from the novel *Eugene Onegin* by Alexander Pushkin

The Ones Below ★★ 15
Thriller 2015 · UK · Colour · 82min

Writer and theatre director David Farr's screen debut takes a sledgehammer to a delicate subject in its exploration of pregnancy-related paranoia. Clémence Poésy and Stephen Campbell Moore play soon-to-be parents who are intrigued when a more ostentatious expectant couple (Laura Birn and David Morrissey) move in downstairs. It's fertile territory, and there are uncomfortable truths at its heart, but Farr's handling of the themes is desperately unsubtle, and the performances are compromised by the erratic material. EAS Swearing, a sex scene, nudity. *DVD*

Clémence Poésy *Kate* • David Morrissey *Jon* • Stephen Campbell Moore *Justin* • Laura Birn *Theresa* • Deborah Findlay *Tessa* • Tuyen Do *Doctor* ■ *Dir/Scr* David Farr

Ong-Bak ★★★★ 18
Martial arts action adventure 2003 · Thai · Colour · 103min

Described as "the new Bruce Lee", Thai fighter Tony Jaa makes his movie debut in this back-to-basics martial arts outing that is notable for the total absence of CGI and wirework. Jaa, who does all his own stunts, stars as a country bumpkin sent to Bangkok to retrieve his village's Buddha statue, which has been stolen and handed over to a big-city gangster. What sketchy plot there is matters little since it's the sheer spectacle of Jaa's astonishing muay thai skills that really takes the breath away. Despite the threadbare production values and questionable acting, this game of death is a gleeful throwback to the days when Bruce Lee was the only person wearing a yellow jump suit. JR Thai, English +subtitles. Violence, drug abuse. *DVD*

Tony Jaa *Ting* • Petchthai Wongkamlao *George* • Pumwaree Yodkamol *Muay Lek* • Rungrawee Borrijindakul *Ngek* • Chetwut Wacharakun *Peng* • Wannakit Siriput *Don* • Sukhaaw Phongwilai *Khom Tuan* ■ *Dir* Prachya Pinkaew • *Scr* Suphachai Sittiaumponpan, from a story by Prachya Pinkaew, Panna Rittikrai

Ong-Bak: the Beginning ★★ 15
Martial arts action adventure 2008 · Thai · Colour · 93min

Tony Jaa again demonstrates his phenomenal fighting skills in this adventure set in medieval Thailand about a warrior prince looking for revenge on the evil usurper who killed his family. Famously eschewing a body double or wire-hoisting assistance, Jaa and his lightning Muay Thai moves (his knees and elbows are just as lethal as his fists and feet) make Jet Li and Jackie Chan look like they're wading through treacle. Unfortunately, the film spends far too much time burying a simple story of vengeance under layers of flashbacks, and just doesn't leave enough room for what we really want to see – Jaa unleashed on the bad guys. TJ Thai +subtitles. Violence. *DVD* *Blu*

Tony Jaa *Tien* • Sorapong Chatree *Chernang* • Sarunyu Wongkrachang [Sarunyoo Wongkrachang] *Lord Rajasena* • Nirut Sirijanya *Master Bua* • Santisuk Promsiri *Lord Sihadecho* • Primrata Dej-Udom *Pim* ■ *Dir* Tony Jaa, Panna Rittikrai • *Scr* Ek Lemchuen, Nontakorn Taveesuk, from a story by Tony Jaa, Panna Rittikrai

Onibaba ★★★ 15
Horror 1964 · Jpn · BW · 98min

Set during the 16th-century Japanese civil wars, this cult favourite focuses on the tensions that arise when widow Jitsuko Yoshimura defies mother-in-law Nobuko Otowa by flirting with a neighbour and jeopardising their livelihood – the sale of armour stripped from murdered samurai. This is a frankly erotic and often hysterically acted tale, which director Kaneto Shindo clearly intended as an allegory on the modern world. However, it works best as a disturbing study of ruthless survivalism and supernatural punishment. DP Japanese +subtitles. *DVD*

Nobuko Otowa *Mother* • Jitsuko Yoshimura *Daughter-in-law* • Kei Sato *Hachi, farmer* • Jukichi Uno *Warrior* ■ *Dir/Scr* Kaneto Shindo

The Onion Field ★★★ 18
Police drama 1979 · US · Colour · 121min

Cop-turned-novelist Joseph Wambaugh was so upset by the way *The Choirboys* was turned into a movie, he had complete control over this script based on a real-life case in 1963 when two small-time hoods kidnap two cops and murder one of them in an onion field. As a documentary-style record of police procedure and the fallibility of the legal system, this is a gripping and disturbing movie, powerfully acted by John Savage as the surviving cop who quits the force to become a gardener and by Franklyn Seales and James Woods as the killers. AT

John Savage *Karl Hettinger* • James Woods *Gregory Powell* • Franklyn Seales *Jimmy Smith* • Ted Danson *Ian Campbell* • Priscilla Pointer *Chrissie Campbell* • Ronny Cox *Pierce Brooks* • David Huffman *DA Phil Halpin* • Christopher Lloyd *Jailhouse lawyer* ■ *Dir* Harold Becker • *Scr* Joseph Wambaugh, from his novel

Only Angels Have Wings ★★★★★ U
Action adventure 1939 · US · BW · 115min

This Howard Hawks movie about a civil airline taking mail and freight over the treacherous Andes contains all of producer/director Hawks's key themes and some of his finest sequences, and boasts a splendid cast headed by hard-bitten Cary Grant and chirpy Jean Arthur. They are superbly backed by Rita Hayworth as a vamp and Richard Barthelmess as a disgraced flier. Back in 1939, one of the most memorable years in cinema history, it was overlooked as a simple action adventure, but now it can be recognised as a superb study of grace under pressure. This is great cinema: supremely entertaining, with mature storytelling. TS *DVD* *Blu*

Cary Grant *Geoff Carter* • Jean Arthur *Bonnie Lee* • Richard Barthelmess *Bat McPherson* • Rita Hayworth *Judith McPherson* • Thomas Mitchell *Kid Dabb* • Sig Rumann [Sig Ruman] *Dutchman* • Victor Kilian [Victor Kilian] *Sparks* ■ *Dir* Howard Hawks • *Scr* Jules Furthman, from a story by Howard Hawks

The Only Game in Town ★★★
Drama 1970 · US · Colour · 113min

And that game is love, if you can believe a word of this rather talky story of the love affair between chorus girl Elizabeth Taylor and gambling piano player Warren Beatty. The actors give it all they've got, and director George Stevens, making his last film, convincingly sets up the Las Vegas location as a place of glamour and sleaze, but it never quite involves as it should. TH

Elizabeth Taylor *Fran Walker* • Warren Beatty *Joe Grady* • Charles Braswell *Thomas Lockwood* • Hank Henry *Tony* • Olga Valery *Woman with purple wig* ■ *Dir* George Stevens • *Scr* Frank D Gilroy, from his play

Only God Forgives ★★★★ 18
Crime thriller 2012 · Fr/Den · Colour · 86min

At times agonisingly slow, and punctuated with graphic scenes of violence, the ninth feature film by Nicolas Winding Refn will nevertheless reward those brave enough to stay with its fractured storyline. Ryan Gosling runs a drug-dealing operation from the cover of his Bangkok boxing club. When his psychotic brother is killed in a revenge murder, Gosling comes under pressure from their domineering mother (Kristin Scott Thomas) to kill the man responsible. So begins an artful, nightmarish vision of hell, as Gosling unwittingly summons up a supernatural angel of vengeance in the form of blade-wielding detective Vithaya Pansringarm, who stalks him through the city streets. DW Violence. *DVD* *Blu*

Ryan Gosling *Julian* • Kristin Scott Thomas *Crystal* • Vithaya Pansringarm *Chang* • Rhatha Phongam *Yayaying Mai* ■ *Dir/Scr* Nicolas Winding Refn

Only Human ★★★ 15
Romantic comedy 2004 · Sp/UK/Arg/Por · Colour · 85min

This light and fast-paced comedy centres on a chaotic Jewish household in Madrid into which one of the family's daughters introduces her Palestinian partner. When a tub of frozen soup hurtles from the family's high-rise apartment and strikes a pedestrian, whether or not this is a "murder" that requires covering up elevates the near-slapstick farce. Sure-footed performances and immaculate comic timing make the most of a snappy script, but it gets a little predictable towards the end. KK Spanish +subtitles. Swearing. *DVD*

Norma Aleandro *Gloria Dalinsky* • Guillermo Toledo *Rafi* • María Botto *Tania Dalinsky* • Marián Aguilera *Leni Dalinsky* • Fernando Ramallo *David Dalinsky* • Max Berliner *Dudu Dalinsky* • Alba Molinero *Paula Dalinsky* • Mario Martín *Ernesto Dalinsky* ■ *Dir/Scr* Teresa de Pelegrí, Dominic Harari

Only Lovers Left Alive ★★★ 15
Romantic horror 2013 · US · Colour · 117min

A teasing riff on his own relationship with partner and fellow film-maker Sara Driver, Jim Jarmusch's laconic vision of vampirism is suffused with wry wit and soulful melancholy. Centuries-old Eve (Tilda Swinton) leaves an undead Christopher Marlowe (John Hurt) in Tangier to check on her husband Adam (Tom Hiddleston) in the Detroit garret where he makes dirge-like rock music and despairs of the "zombie" humans who have messed up the world. DP Swearing. *DVD* *Blu*

Tom Hiddleston *Adam* • Tilda Swinton *Eve* • Mia Wasikowska *Ava* • John Hurt *Marlowe* • Anton Yelchin *Ian* • Jeffrey Wright *Dr Watson* ■ *Dir/Scr* Jim Jarmusch

The Only Son ★★★★
Drama 1936 · Jpn · BW · 103min

Having demonstrated an intuitive mastery of silent technique, Yasujiro Ozu proved his sound credentials with this delicate, character-driven entry in the *shomin-geki* genre of lower middle-class dramas that would become his speciality. Chishu Ryu (an Ozu regular) is outstanding as the Tokyo teacher, who borrows a small fortune so he can prove to his doting small-town mother that the sacrifices she made for his education had all been worthwhile. DP Japanese +subtitles.

Choko Iida *Otsune Nonomiya* • Shinichi Himori *Ryosuke, Otsune's son* • Masao Hayama *Ryosuke as a child* • Yoshiko Tsubouchi *Sugiko, Ryosuke's wife* ▪ *Dir* Yasujiro Ozu • *Scr* Tadao Ikeda, Masao Arata, from a story by James Maki [Yasujiro Ozu]

Only the Lonely ★★★ 12

Romantic comedy 1991 · US · Colour · 100min

Chris Columbus directs this understated little gem. It's a sweet, rather old-fashioned comedy about a shy policeman, John Candy, who falls for equally bashful mortician Ally Sheedy, much to the dismay of his overbearing mother, Maureen O'Hara. Although it occasionally lapses into sentimentality, it is sympathetically written and there are winning performances from the two leads. However, the film is all but stolen by O'Hara and Anthony Quinn. JF Swearing. *DVD*

John Candy *Danny Muldoon* • Maureen O'Hara *Rose Muldoon* • Ally Sheedy *Theresa Luna* • Kevin Dunn *Patrick Muldoon* • Milo O'Shea *Doyle Ryan* • Bert Remsen *Spats Shannon* • Anthony Quinn *Nick Acropolis* • James Belushi *Sal Buonarte* • Macaulay Culkin *Billy* ▪ *Dir/Scr* Chris Columbus

Only the Strong ★★ 15

Martial arts action drama
1993 · US · Colour · 92min

An OK action thriller, this has martial-arts hero Mark Dacascos encouraged by his former teacher Geoffrey Lewis to instruct students in how to acquire self-discipline and battle the drug dealers infesting the high-school campus. The gimmick here is that Dacascos is a master of the Brazilian fighting skill *capoeira* – a sort of cross between kung fu and the lambada. Mild violence and samba music make this one an easy-listening no-brainer. AJ Swearing.

Mark Dacascos *Louis Stevens* • Stacey Travis *Dianna* • Geoffrey Lewis *Kerrigan* • Paco Christian Prieto *Silverio* • Todd Susman *Cochran* ▪ *Dir* Sheldon Lettich • *Scr* Sheldon Lettich, Luis Esteban

Only the Valiant ★★ PG

Western 1950 · US · BW · 104min

Gregory Peck plays the cavalry commander whose harsh methods make him less than popular with his men, though everyone pulls together heroically when the Apaches gather at the mountain pass. In this traditional, no-nonsense western, Peck gives a decent role as the martinet, and the supporting cast includes many familiar faces. AT

Gregory Peck *Capt Richard Lance* • Barbara Payton *Cathy Eversham* • Ward Bond *Cpl Timothy Gilchrist* • Gig Young *Lt William Holloway* • Lon Chaney Jr *Trooper Kebussyan* • Neville Brand *Sgt Ben Murdock* • Jeff Corey *Joe Harmony* ▪ *Dir* Gordon Douglas • *Scr* Edmund H North, Harry Brown, from the novel by Charles Marquis Warren

The Only Thrill ★★★ 15

Romantic drama 1997 · US · Colour · 103min

In 1960s small-town America, Diane Keaton and Sam Shepard begin an illicit affair. Shepard, a second-hand shop owner with a comatose wife, is attracted to widow Keaton and, ten years on, the two loners are still as linked to each other as Shepard's wife is to her life-support machine. Both leads are excellent, but director Peter Masterson misses opportunities to deal with illness and is loaded down with an unnecessary subplot involving the parallel relationship between Keaton and Shepard's kids. LH

Diane Keaton *Carol Fitzsimmons* • Sam Shepard *Reece McHenry* • Diane Lane *Katherine Fitzsimmons* • Robert Patrick *Tom McHenry* • Sharon Lawrence *Joleen Quillet* ▪ *Dir* Peter Masterson • *Scr* Larry Ketron, from his play *The Trading Post*

Only Two Can Play ★★★★ PG

Comedy 1961 · UK · BW · 101min

This small-town drama is played out as farce and makes its satirical points with comic deftness. The title is misleading because the players in this story of a would-be adulterous Welsh librarian (Peter Sellers) and his wannabe mistress (Mai Zetterling)

also include Virginia Maskell as his dispirited wife and Richard Attenborough as the poet she flirts with. That the film succeeds is partly down to Sellers's unusually restrained performance, which makes his character more believable. TH

Peter Sellers *John Lewis* • Mai Zetterling *Elizabeth Gruffydd-Williams* • Virginia Maskell *Jean Lewis* • Richard Attenborough *Gareth Probert* • Kenneth Griffith *Ieuan Jenkins* • Maudie Edwards *Mrs Davies* • Frederick Piper *Davies* • Graham Stark *Hyman* • John Arnatt *Bill* • Sheila Manahan *Mrs Jenkins* • John Le Mesurier *Salter* ▪ *Dir* Sidney Gilliat • *Scr* Bryan Forbes, from the novel *That Uncertain Feeling* by Kingsley Amis

Only When I Dance ★★★★ PG

Dance documentary
2008 · UK/Fr/Neth · Colour · 83min

The favelas of Rio de Janeiro are such a hotbed of samba that few would readily associate them with classical ballet. But dance teacher Mariza Estrella has devoted over 35 years to guiding poor but gifted Brazilian students to coveted prizes at both domestic and international competitions. Director Beadie Finzi's focus falls on two young black dancers for whom ballet is a chance of escape from the deprivation that has lured so many of their contemporaries into crime. The film contains some impressive dance scenes – the sequences in which one of the youngsters, Irlan, competes for the prestigious Prix de Lausanne are compelling. DP Portuguese, English +subtitles. *DVD*

Irlan Santos Da Silva • Isabela Coracy Alves Nascimento Santos • Mariza Estrella ▪ *Dir* Beadie Finzi

Only When I Larf ★★★

Comedy 1968 · UK · Colour · 103min

Three confidence tricksters – Richard Attenborough, David Hemmings, Alexandra Stewart – begin plotting against each other. The succession of scams, disguises and surprises is very entertaining and builds to a quadruple-cross (multiple double-crossing was very popular at the time). The production, in several glamorous locations, is amusingly trendy, in Swinging Sixties style, and Attenborough gives one of his most uninhibited comedy performances. DM

Richard Attenborough *Silas* • David Hemmings *Bob* • Alexandra Stewart *Liz* • Nicholas Pennell *Spencer* • Melissa Stribling *Diana* • Terence Alexander *Gee Gee Gray* • Edric Connor *Awana* • Clifton Jones *General Sakut* ▪ *Dir* Basil Dearden • *Scr* John Salmon, from the novel by Len Deighton

Only When I Laugh ★★★ 15

Comedy drama 1981 · US · Colour · 114min

This is a bittersweet Neil Simon comedy about a brilliant but boozy and self-destructive actress (Marsha Mason) striving to strike up a relationship with her teenage daughter (Kristy McNichol). This has fine performances from the two leading ladies, and from support stars James Coco and Joan Hackett, as a failed gay actor and an ageing New York society beauty, respectively. DA

Marsha Mason *Georgia Hines* • Kristy McNichol *Polly* • James Coco *Jimmy Perino* • Joan Hackett *Toby Landau* • David Dukes *David Lowe* ▪ *Dir* Glenn Jordan • *Scr* Neil Simon, from his play *The Gingerbread Lady*

Only Yesterday ★★★★

Romantic drama 1933 · US · BW · 106min

During the First World War, innocent young Margaret Sullavan and a handsome lieutenant John Boles meet at a dance in Virginia and fall in love, but he is shipped to France before they can meet again. Pregnant with his child, she goes to live with her feminist aunt Billie Burke in New York, but when Boles returns he has forgotten her. This is romantic soap opera to be sure but, as directed by genre specialist John M Stahl, of a superior kind. Sullavan, as ever, suffers with poignant dignity. RK

Margaret Sullavan *Mary Lane* • John Boles *James Stanton Emerson* • Edna May Oliver *Leona* • Billie Burke *Julia Warren* • Benita Hume *Phyllis Emerson* • Reginald Denny *Bob* • George Meeker *Dave Reynolds* • Marie Prevost *Amy* ▪ *Dir* John M Stahl • *Scr* William Hurlbut, Arthur Richman, George O'Neill, from the novel *Briefe einer Unbekannten* by Stefan Zweig

Only You ★★★ 15

Romantic comedy 1992 · US · Colour · 87min

This romantic comedy features *St Elmo's Fire* brat-packer Andrew McCarthy as the shy bloke who finds himself lucking out when he falls for two different women – glamorous Kelly Preston and the more sensible, studious Helen Hunt. This is sweetly enjoyable, thanks to a witty script and nice performances from the cast. JB Nudity.

Andrew McCarthy *Clifford Godfrey* • Kelly Preston *Amanda* • Helen Hunt *Claire* ▪ *Dir* Betty Thomas • *Scr* Wayne Allan Rice

Only You ★★★★ PG

Romantic comedy 1994 · US · Colour · 103min

Moonstruck director Norman Jewison successfully mines the same territory with this delicious "Cinderella Italian-style" romantic comedy. Following the prophecy of a childhood Ouija game, Pittsburgh schoolteacher Marisa Tomei runs out on her wedding and goes to Rome to find the man of her dreams. There she meets shoe salesman Robert Downey Jr, who may or may not fit the bill. The pairing of Tomei and Downey Jr works like a charm: both inject scintillating substance into an unashamedly lightweight affair through their winning chemistry. Billy Zane is also on hand to provide a neat twist in the tale, and the lush Italian scenery will have you changing your holiday plans. AJ *DVD*

Marisa Tomei *Faith Corvatch* • Robert Downey Jr *Peter Wright* • Bonnie Hunt *Kate* • Joaquim de Almeida *Giovanni* • Fisher Stevens *Larry* • Billy Zane *The false Damon Bradley* • Adam LeFevre *Damon Bradley* • John Benjamin Hickey *Dwayne* • Siobhan Fallon *Leslie* ▪ *Dir* Norman Jewison • *Scr* Diane Drake

Ooh... You Are Awful ★★ PG

Comedy 1972 · UK · Colour · 92min

No prizes will be handed out for guessing that this is a vehicle for the late Dick Emery. When Emery discovers his dead accountant has left the number of a safety deposit account tattooed to the derrière of several young models, he sets to with gusto. This is a McGill seaside postcard come to boozy, nudge-nudge, wink-wink life, and if that's to your taste then it belts along like a runaway Blackpool tram. SH *DVD*

Dick Emery *Charlie Tully* • Derren Nesbitt *Sid Sabbath* • Ronald Fraser *Reggie Campbell Peek* • Pat Coombs *Libby Niven* • William Franklyn *Arnold Van Cleef* • Cheryl Kennedy *Jo Mason* • Norman Bird *Warder Burke* • Liza Goddard *Liza Missenden Green* ▪ *Dir* Cliff Owen • *Scr* John Warren, John Singer

Opal Dream ★★★

Drama 2005 · Aus/UK · Colour · 82min

Adapted from the novella *Pobby and Dingan* by Ben Rice, this rites-of-passage tale set in a tough Australian mining settlement marks quite a departure for *Full Monty* director Peter Cattaneo. Yet he makes a neat job of this touching story about brotherly love, in which sceptical sibling Ashmol (Christian Byers) sets out to find the two imaginary friends of his ailing nine-year-old sister Kellyanne (Sapphire Boyce), who has been wasting away since their disappearance. However, this means that he has to learn to believe in them himself and then persuade his family and friends that they really exist, too. It's a touch schmaltzy in places and neither child is wholly convincing, but the rugged setting lends the story some gritty authenticity. DP

Sapphire Boyce *Kellyanne Williamson* • Christian Byers *Ashmol Williamson* • Vince Colosimo *Rex Williamson* • Jacqueline McKenzie *Annie Williamson* • Robert Morgan *Sid* • Anna Linarello *Betsy* • Denise Roberts *Vera Dunkley* ▪ *Dir* Peter Cattaneo • *Scr* Peter Cattaneo, Phil Traill, from the novella *Pobby and Dingan* by Ben Rice

Open Hearts ★★★★ 15

Romantic drama 2002 · Den · Colour · 108min

The 28th feature to be shot in adherence to the Dogme aesthetic, this focuses wholly on the raw emotions of doctor Mads Mikkelsen and 20-something cook Sonja Richter. The pair are brought together when Mikkelsen's wife, Paprika Steen, is involved in a road accident that leaves Richter's fiancé, Nikolaj Lie Kaas, paralysed from the neck down. Director Susanne Bier explores the inevitability of their attraction in this intriguing, compelling story, and all the performances are exceptional. DP Danish +subtitles. *DVD*

Sonja Richter *Cecilie* • Nikolaj Lie Kaas *Joachim* • Mads Mikkelsen *Niels* • Paprika Steen *Marie* • Stine Bjerregaard *Stine* • Birthe Neumann *Hanne* • Niels Olsen *Finn* ▪ *Dir* Susanne Bier • *Scr* Anders Thomas Jensen, from a story by Susanne Bier

Open Range ★★★★ 12

Western 2003 · US/UK · Colour · 133min

Actor/director Kevin Costner's western is a beautifully crafted, well-acted example of the genre, that only occasionally lurches a little too close to cliché for comfort. It's set in a fascinating transitional period of frontier history – as the traditional free-ranging cattlemen and their herds were harassed and attacked by settled ranchers – but Costner finds most of the film's interest in the relationships between the main characters. He is impressive as the taciturn Charley, whose Civil War memories haunt him, but it is Robert Duvall's restrained performance as the de facto father to the "family" of travelling cowpokes that is the movie's real powerhouse. AS Violence. *DVD*

Robert Duvall *Boss Spearman* • Kevin Costner *Charley Waite* • Annette Bening *Sue Barlow* • Michael Gambon *Denton Baxter* • Michael Jeter *Percy* • Diego Luna *Button* • James Russo *Sheriff Poole* • Abraham Benrubi *Mose* • Dean McDermott *Doc Barlow* • Kim Coates *Butler* ▪ *Dir* Kevin Costner • *Scr* Craig Storper, from the novel *The Open Range Men* by Lauran Paine

Open Season ★ 18

Action 1974 · US/Sp · Colour · 98min

Three Vietnam vets kidnap a man and a woman, force them to act as servants at the remote cabin, sexually abuse the woman, then hunt them down like game. Full of psychological baloney to justify its story, this exploitation effort makes some cheap shots about American democracy and justice before getting down to the nitty-gritty of gratuitous sex and violence. AT

Peter Fonda *Ken* • Cornelia Sharpe *Nancy* • John Phillip Law *Greg* • Richard Lynch *Art* • Albert Mendoza [Alberto de Mendoza] *Martin* • William Holden (2) *Wolkowski* ▪ *Dir* Peter Collinson • *Scr* David Osborn, Liz Charles-Williams

Open Season ★★★

Comedy satire 1995 · US · Colour · 97min

In a sharp-edged satire on contemporary television, a foul-up in the ratings mistakenly suggests that US viewers are giving dumb dross the thumbs down, and tuning in to shows of culture and intellect instead. Predictably, the very idea puts programmers in a tizz. Robert Wuhl stars, writes and directs, while Rod Taylor, Helen Shaver and Gailard Sartain co-star. A spot-on comedy, this retains its relevance. DA

Robert Wuhl *Stuart Sain* • Rod Taylor *Billy Patrick* • Gailard Sartain *George Plunkett* • Helen Shaver *Rachel Rowen* • Maggie Han *Cary Sain* • Dina Merrill *Doris Hays-Britton* • Saul Rubinek *Eric Schlockmeister* ▪ *Dir/Scr* Robert Wuhl

Open Season ★★★ PG

Animated comedy adventure
2006 · US · Colour · 82min

This boisterous inaugural feature from Sony Pictures Animation won't give Pixar any sleepless nights, but it does have a simplistic appeal. Co-directed by *The Lion King* film-maker Roger Allers, it's a familiar, computer-generated eco-fable in which domesticated grizzly bear Boog (voiced by Martin Lawrence) sees his pampered existence as a mountain-town tourist attraction cut short when he befriends a mischief-making deer (a fantastic Ashton Kutcher). In a hilarious set piece, the duo cause so much mess in a convenience store that Boog eventually ends up released back into the wilderness - three days before hunting season begins. What follows is a predictable lesson about man's destructive effects on nature. SF DVD BD

Martin Lawrence *Boog* • Ashton Kutcher *Elliot* • Debra Messing *Beth* • Gary Sinise *Shaw* • Billy Connolly *McSquizzy* • Jon Favreau *Reilly* • Patrick Warburton *Ian* • Jane Krakowski *Giselle* ■ *Dir* Jill Culton, Anthony Stacchi, Roger Allers • *Scr* Steve Bencich, Ron J Friedman, Nat Mauldin, from a screen story by Jill Culton, Anthony Stacchi, from an original story by Steve Moore, John Carls

Open Season 2 ★★ PG
Animated comedy adventure
2008 · US · Colour · 73min

The sequel to 2006's debut for Sony Pictures Animation sees a slight lifting of the plot from *Toy Story 2* as the woodland creatures head off to rescue Mr Weenie the dachshund. The mix of scatological jokes for the kids (who will love the butt-sniffing) plus mild innuendo for the adults remains familiar, while the animation aims for Looney Tunes levels of madcap mayhem. There's also no Ashton Kutcher and Martin Lawrence in the under-par voice cast. An even more lacklustre cast turned up for a 2010 threequel. SvM DVD BD

Mike Epps *Boog* • Joel McHale *Elliot* • Jane Krakowski *Giselle* • Billy Connolly *McSquizzy* ■ *Dir* Matthew O'Callaghan, Todd Wilderman

Open Season 3 ★★ U
Animated comedy adventure
2010 · US · Colour · 74min

Boog the bear and best mate Elliot the deer learn yet more lessons about friendship and loyalty in this tired and unnecessary cash-in from the co-director of *Cloudy with a Chance of Meatballs 2*. Thin is putting it mildly, as weak scripting and blocky, low-quality animation suck most of the fun out of the irreverent franchise, that here has an aggrieved Boog switching places with a look-alike circus grizzly after feeling let down by his forest pals. SF DVD BD 3D

Matthew J Munn *Boog/Doug* • Matt Taylor *Ian/ Reilly/Buddy/Deni/Elliot* • Melissa Sturm *Giselle/ Ursa* • Karley Scott Collins *Gisela* • Cody Cameron *Mr Weenie/Nate/Distinctive Dog* ■ *Dir* Cody Cameron • *Scr* David I Stern

Open Water ★★★ 15
Thriller
2004 · US · Colour · 76min

Blanchard Ryan and Daniel Travis play a couple who embark on a scuba diving excursion in the Caribbean, only to find themselves stranded in shark-infested waters with no sign of rescue. Shot on digital video, the film gains atmosphere from resembling an amateur undersea documentary; it's simple, short and effective because it leaves everything to the imagination. Anyone frightened of shark attacks can expect a full hands-in-front-of-eyes workout in this nail-biter with a surprising payoff. AJ Swearing. DVD BD

Blanchard Ryan *Susan* • Daniel Travis *Daniel* • Saul Stein *Seth* • Estelle Lau *Estelle* • Michael E Williamson *Davis* • Cristina Zenarro *Linda* • John Charles *Junior* ■ *Dir/Scr* Chris Kentis

Open Your Eyes ★★★★ 15
Psychological thriller 1997 · Sp · Colour · 119min

This is a dazzling second feature from young Spanish film-maker Alejandro Amenábar. As the pampered playboy whose life begins to unravel after a disfiguring car crash, Eduardo Noriega conveys both resentment and vulnerability as he strives to make sense of a relentless sequence of disconcerting events. This delirious treatise on appearance and reality requires total concentration, right through to its dissatisfyingly glib dénouement. Penélope Cruz reprised her role in Cameron Crowe's remake, *Vanilla Sky*, with Tom Cruise in the César role. DP Spanish +subtitles. DVD

Eduardo Noriega (2) *César* • Penélope Cruz *Sofia* • Chete Lera *Antonio* • Fele Martínez *Pelayo* • Najwa Nimri *Nuria* ■ *Dir* Alejandro Amenábar • *Scr* Alejandro Amenábar, Mateo Gil

Opening Night ★★★★ 15
Drama 1977 · US · Colour · 138min

In addition to his own talent and daring as actor/writer/director, John Cassavetes was blessed in his wife and regular collaborator, Gena Rowlands, for whom this is a tour de force. Rowlands is spellbinding as the star experiencing an intense emotional and spiritual crisis before the first performance of her new play. A truthful testament to the self-absorption, fragility and art of actors, it's hard going if you're not keen on Cassavetes's unconventional style. But the acting is suitably riveting, with Cassavetes compelling as Rowlands's leading man, and veteran Joan Blondell in splendid form as her author friend. AME DVD BD

Gena Rowlands *Myrtle Gordon* • John Cassavetes *Maurice Aarons* • Ben Gazzara *Manny Victor* • Joan Blondell *Sarah Goode* • Paul Stewart *David Samuels* • Zohra Lampert *Dorothy Victor* ■ *Dir/Scr* John Cassavetes

Opera ★★★ 18
Horror 1987 · It · Colour · 91min

There's no phantom in Italian horror maestro Dario Argento's masterwork, just a mentally deranged maniac obsessed with ingénue singer Cristina Marsillach as she rehearses Verdi's *Macbeth*. But this aria of savage beauty contains Argento's single most potent and self-revelatory image: Marsillach, forced to watch orchestrated murders, is unable to close her eyes due to needles taped under the lids. Argento's relentless search for the outer limits of hard-core gore doesn't make much sense, but for those of a certain dispositon, it's bravura cinema. AJ In Italian. Violence DVD

Cristina Marsillach *Betty* • Urbano Barberini *Inspector Santini* • Daria Nicolodi *Mira* • Ian Charleson *Marco* ■ *Dir* Dario Argento • *Scr* Dario Argento, Franco Ferrini

Opera do Malandro ★★★★ 15
Musical fantasy 1986 · Bra · Colour · 107min

This is less a stylised snapshot of Brazil on the eve of war than a tribute to the musical extravaganzas of MGM. Directing with visual and visceral panache, Ruy Guerra allows his camera to prowl around Rio's seedy bars and crumbling slums, as small-time racketeer Edson Celulari's plan to corrupt the daughter of his deadly, pro-Nazi rival calamitously backfires. It's sensual, surreal and subversive, and throbs with life. DP Portuguese +subtitles.

Edson Celulari *Max* • Claudia Ohana *Ludmila* • Elba Ramalho *Margot* ■ *Dir* Ruy Guerra • *Scr* Chico Buarque, Orlando Senna, Ruy Guerra, from the play by Chico Buarque

Operation Amsterdam ★★★ U
Second World War drama
1958 · UK · BW · 104min

It might seem like double Dutch these days, but director Michael McCarthy's final film (he died the following year) was convincing enough on its release. A British pseudo-documentary, it's set in 1940 and is about a bunch of spies sent into Holland to recover a hoard of industrial diamonds before the Nazis get to them. Diamond expert Alexander Knox locks grave and concerned, and Peter Finch is dashing and daring. TH

Peter Finch *Jan Smit* • Eva Bartok *Anna* • Tony Britton *Major Dillon* • Alexander Knox *Walter Keyser* • Malcolm Keen *Johann Smit* • Christopher Rhodes *Alex* ■ *Dir* Michael McCarthy • *Scr* Michael McCarthy, John Eldridge, from the book *Adventure in Diamonds* by David E Walker

Operation Bullshine ★★ U
Comedy 1959 · UK · Colour · 83min

It's just feasible that this feeble comedy might have raised a smile in the darkest days of the Second World War, but more than a decade after the event there was

simply no excuse for the tired collection of jokes that aren't worth a smutty snigger. This is a clear case of too much bull and not enough shine. Donald Sinden and Barbara Murray could do this sort of marital misunderstanding material in their sleep, and it's to their credit that they try to give it some pep, as does the splendid supporting cast. DP

Donald Sinden *Lt Gordon Brown* • Barbara Murray *Private Betty Brown* • Carole Lesley *Private Marge White* • Ronald Shiner *Gunner Slocum* • Naunton Wayne *Major Pym* • Dora Bryan *Private Cox* • John Cairney *Gunner Willie Ross* • Fabia Drake *Junior Commander Maddox, ATS* • Joan Rice *Private Finch* • Daniel Massey *Bombardier Palmer* ■ *Dir* Gilbert Gunn • *Scr* Anne Burnaby, Rupert Lang, Gilbert Gunn

Operation CIA ★★★
Spy action thriller 1965 · US · BW · 90min

This nifty spy thriller sees agent Burt Reynolds (in one of his earliest roles) sent to Saigon during the Vietnam conflict to prevent an assassination. Not totally American propaganda, the film maintains a detached stance on the differing values of the goodies and the baddies, while director Christian Nyby keeps it all very lively. TH

Burt Reynolds *Mark Andrews* • Kieu Chinh *Kim-chinh* • Danielle Aubry *Denise, French agent* • John Hoyt *Wells* • Cyril Collick *Withers* • Vic Diaz *Prof Yen* • William Catching *Frank Decker* ■ *Dir* Christian Nyby • *Scr* Peer J Oppenheimer, Bill S Ballinger, from a story by Peer J Oppenheimer

Operation Condor: the Armour of God II ★★★★ 15
Martial arts adventure
1990 · HK · Colour · 102min

Hong Kong superstar Jackie Chan plays an Indiana Jones-style secret agent (codenamed Condor) searching for a stash of Nazi gold in the Sahara. Cue some wonderfully choreographed kung fu fights with militant desert rats, hugely entertaining action-hero parodies and silly slapstick for which Chan has the perfect timing. AJ Cantonese dubbed.

Jackie Chan *Jackie* • Carol Cheng *Ada* • Eva Cobo de Garcia [Eva Cobo] *Elsa* • Shoko Ikeda *Momoko* • Alfredo Brel Sanchez [Aldo Sambrell] *Adolf* ■ *Dir* Jackie Chan • *Scr* Jackie Chan, Edward Tang, Szeto Chuek-Hun, Ken Lowe, John Sheppard, from a story by Barry Wong

Operation Crossbow ★★★ PG
Second World War drama
1965 · It/US/UK · Colour · 111min

The credits are impressive, the plot intriguing and the production values impeccable, but they only add up to an average wartime thriller. In common with many blockbuster writers, Emeric Pressburger and his colleagues were confounded by the dual task of telling a ripping yarn and finding enough to do for a big-name cast. As a result, the mission to replace German V-2 rocket scientists with Allied boffins is often of secondary interest to the stargazing. However, there is plenty of derring-do, although director Michael Anderson struggles to find a workable balance between action and chat. DP English, German +subtitles. DVD

George Peppard *Lieutenant John Curtis* • Sophia Loren *Nora* • Trevor Howard *Professor Lindemann* • John Mills *General Boyd* • Richard Johnson *Duncan Sandys* • Tom Courtenay *Robert Henshaw* • Jeremy Kemp *Phil Bradley* • Anthony Quayle *Bamford* • Lilli Palmer *Frieda* • Paul Henreid *General Ziemann* ■ *Dir* Michael Anderson • *Scr* Richard Imrie [Emeric Pressurger], Derry Quinn, Ray Rigby, from a story by Duilio Coletti, Vittoriano Petrilli

Operation Daybreak ★★★ 15
Second World War thriller
1975 · US/UK/Cz · Colour · 114min

This is a grimly exciting drama about the Czech resistance's plot to kill Reinhard Heydrich, deputy chief of the Gestapo and better known as "Hitler's Hangman". It is drily, if expertly, directed by veteran Lewis Gilbert, and features a motley cast including American Timothy Bottoms and a particularly excellent Anthony Andrews as Czech patriots. Today, when the village of

Lidice, which was razed by the Nazis in reprisal for the assassination, is hardly remembered, its telling is still timely. TS

Timothy Bottoms *Jan Kubis* • Martin Shaw *Karel Curda* • Joss Ackland *Janak* • Nicola Pagett *Anna* • Anthony Andrews *Joseph Gabcik* • Anton Diffring *Reinhard Heydrich* • Diana Coupland *Aunt Marie* • Cyril Shaps *Father Petrek* • Ray Smith *Hajek* • Timothy West *Vaclav* ■ *Dir* Lewis Gilbert • *Scr* Ronald Harwood, from the novel *Seven Men at Daybreak* by Alan Burgess

Operation Delta Force ★★ 15
Action drama 1996 · US · Colour · 89min

Jeff Fahey is the lead in this standard action film, in which he plays the commander of a special military unit that is charged with retrieving a super-virus from Afrikaaner terrorists. The movie is fairly slickly made, but occasionally low-budget touches shine through the gloss: during a shoot-out in a train car, there are four or five people emptying machine guns at each other, yet the interior furnishings never show the slightest damage! ST Violence, swearing. DVD

Jeff Fahey *Lang* • Ernie Hudson *Tipton* • Rob Stewart (1) *Sparks* • Frank Zagarino *McKinney* • Joe Lara *Nash* • Todd Jensen *Hutch* • Hal Holbrook *Henshaw* ■ *Dir* Sam Firstenberg • *Scr* David Sparling

Operation Delta Force II: Mayday ★★ 15
Action thriller 1998 · US · Colour · 103min

This is not only numbingly predictable, but also robotically performed. Hurtling blindly between various unspecified locations, the plot turns around Edgar Allan Poe-quoting villain J Kenneth Campbell's plan to steal a Russian nuclear submarine by hijacking an American liner. But, unfortunately for him, the ship's skipper is Dale Dye, estranged father of Delta Force commander Michael McGrady. Director Yossi Wein stages the action sequences with the finesse of a bulldozer. Three further sequels (to date) followed. DP DVD

Michael McGrady *Captain Skip Long* • Simon Jones [John Simon Jones] *Vickers* • Robert Patteri *McKinney* • Todd Jensen *Lombardi* • Dale Dye *Captain Halsey Long* • Spencer Rochfort *Hutch* ■ *Dir* Yossi Wein • *Scr* David Sparling, from a story by Danny Lerner

Operation Dumbo Drop ★★★ PG
Comedy adventure 1995 · US · Colour · 103min

This amiable family comedy has more than a fair share of surprisingly adult-orientated jokes. Director Simon Wincer's harmless allegory stars Danny Glover and Ray Liotta as the leaders of a group of Green Beret soldiers who promise to deliver an elephant to a Vietnamese village. The problems they face in order to carry out their pledge lead to lots of fun escapades and a winning climax. AJ DVD

Danny Glover *Captain Sam Cahill* • Ray Liotta *Captain Doyle* • Denis Leary *David Poole* • Doug E Doug *Harvey Ashford* • Corin Nemec *Lawrence Farley* • Tcheky Karyo *Goddard* ■ *Dir* Simon Wincer • *Scr* Gene Quintano, Jim Kouf, from a story by Jim Morris

Operation Mad Ball ★★★ U
Comedy 1957 · US · BW · 104min

After his Oscar-winning turn in *Mister Roberts*, Jack Lemmon enlisted in the army for this breakneck comedy. It's set in Normandy in 1945 where the low-ranking soldiers in a military hospital stage a "mad ball" in order to fraternise with the otherwise off-limits nurses. Lemmon is in sparkling form as the "Mr Fixit" and Mickey Rooney's performance will either reduce you to hysterics or set your teeth on edge. Despite the setting, it's really a comedy about American sexual mores in the 1950s. AJ

Jack Lemmon *Private Hogan* • Kathryn Grant *Lieutenant Betty Bixby* • Ernie Kovacs *Captain Paul Locke* • Arthur O'Connell *Colonel Rousch* • Mickey Rooney *Yancy Skibo* • Dick York *Corporal*

Bohun • James Darren *Private Widowskas* ■ *Dir* Richard Quine • *Scr* Arthur Carter, Jed Harris, Blake Edwards, from the play by Arthur Carter

Operation Pacific ★★ U
Second World War drama
1951 · US · BW · 104min

Like most of John Wayne's war pictures, this is gung ho, action-packed and sentimental – the plot takes in homeless children, dewy-eyed nuns, a batch of dud torpedoes and marital difficulties. Wayne, of course, takes everything in his stride, scuppering the Japanese fleet, playing daddy to the youngsters and winning back the hand of Patricia Neal. The navy liked this one so much it held regular screenings at all its bases. AT **DVD**

John Wayne *"Duke" Gifford* • Patricia Neal *Mary Stuart* • Ward Bond *"Pop" Perry* • Scott Forbes *Larry* • Philip Carey *Bob Perry* • Paul Picerni *Jonesy* • William Campbell *Talker* • Kathryn Givney *Commander Steele* • Martin Milner *Caldwell* • Jack Pennick *Chief* ■ *Dir/Scr* George Waggner

Operation Petticoat ★★★★ U
Wartime comedy   1959 · US · Colour · 120min

This wonderfully wacky comedy teams those two great *farceurs* Cary Grant and Tony Curtis in their only movie together. Here Grant is a submarine commander trying to keep his ropey old vessel in the water with the help of wheeler-dealer junior officer Curtis. Complications arise as the sub takes on board a number of unorthodox passengers. Grant is brilliant, with every reaction immaculately timed. Director Blake Edwards ensures no gag is missed, and the whole is a deliciously tasteless joy. TS **DVD**

Cary Grant *Admiral Matt Sherman* • Tony Curtis *Lt Nick Holden* • Joan O'Brien *Lt Dolores Crandall* • Dina Merrill *Lt Barbara Duran* • Gene Evans *Molumphrey* • Arthur O'Connell *Sam Tostin* • Richard Sargent *[Dick Sargent] Stovall* ■ *Dir* Blake Edwards • *Scr* Stanley Shapiro, Maurice Richlin, from a story by Paul King, Joseph Stone

Operation Snatch ★★★
Second World War comedy
1962 · UK · BW · 86min

This enjoyably daft British comedy is inspired by the legend that if the Barbary apes leave Gibraltar, the Rock will leave the British Empire. During the Second World War, Lieutenant Terry-Thomas and his batman (Lionel Jeffries) are sent on a mission to find a breeding specimen to increase the dwindling colony. There are too many stock characters, but this does have several ridiculously funny scenes. DM

Terry-Thomas *Lt "Piggy" Wigg* • George Sanders *Maj Hobson* • Lionel Jeffries *Evans* • Jackie Lane *[Jocelyn Lane] Bianca Tabori* • Lee Montague *Miklos Tabori* • Michael Trubshawe *Colonel Marston* • James Villiers *Lt Keen* • Dinsdale Landen *Capt Whittington* ■ *Dir* Robert Day • *Scr* Alan Hackney, John Warren, Len Heath

Operator 13 ★★★ U
Period war drama   1934 · US · BW · 85min

A vehicle for William Randolph Hearst's actress mistress, Marion Davies, who was much praised for her performance at the time, this is a tale of espionage and romance with a difference. Set during the American Civil War, this has an immensely complicated plot that revolves around actress Davies becoming a Yankee spy in Confederate territory and donning a series of disguises. In the course of the dramatic action, romance rears its head in the shape of enemy scout Gary Cooper. Engaging tosh, expensively filmed, this is strong on Southern atmosphere. RK

Marion Davies *Gail Loveless/Lucille/Operator 13/ Anne Claybourne* • Gary Cooper *Capt Jack Gailliard* • Jean Parker *Eleanor Shackleford* • Katharine Alexander *[Katherine Alexander] Pauline Cushman/Mrs Vale/Operator 27* • Ted Healy *Capt /Doctor Hitchcock* • Russell Hardie *Littledale* ■ *Dir* Richard Boleslavsky *[Richard Boleslawski]* • *Scr* Harvey Thew, Zelda Sears, Eve Greene, from the novel *Secret Service Operator* by Robert W Chambers

Ophélia ★★
Drama   1962 · Fr · BW · 103min

The textual influence may be Shakespeare, but the atmospheric sire of this dramatic curio from Claude Chabrol is clearly Franz Kafka. With Jean Rabier's camera prowling around the shabby grandeur of a murky mansion, the familiar story of the grieving son who becomes convinced that his mother and lecherous uncle were responsible for his father's death is laced with juvenile humour and melodramatic excess. DP French +subtitles.

André Jocelyn *Yvan Lesurf* • Alida Valli *Claudia* • Juliette Mayniel *Lucie* • Claude Cerval *Adrien Lesurf* • Robert Burnier *André Lagrange* • Jean-Louis Maury *Sparkos* ■ *Dir* Claude Chabrol • *Scr* Claude Chabrol, Martial Matthieu [Paul Gégauff]

The Opportunists ★★★ 15
Heist drama   2000 · US/UK · Colour · 89min

Hollywood's favourite psycho Christopher Walken is beautifully understated in this wryly melancholic crime caper about a bunch of small-time crooks. Walken is a former robber, an expert on cracking safes, who is dragged back into the life of crime by his Irish cousin (Peter McDonald) who offers him the opportunity to solve his financial woes. First-time director Myles Connell stages some nifty robbery set pieces, but most of the enjoyment comes from the interplay between the disparate gang of losers. JF

Christopher Walken *Victor Kelly* • Peter McDonald *Michael* • Cyndi Lauper *Sally* • Donal Logue *Pat Duffy* • José Zuniga *Jesus Del Toro* • Vera Farmiga *Miriam* ■ *Dir/Scr* Myles Connell

Opportunity Knocks ★★ 15
Comedy   1990 · US · Colour · 96min

Made two years before he struck paydirt as Garth in *Wayne's World*, Dana Carvey takes the lead in this fumbled comedy of errors. Trotting out the full repertoire of silly voices he made famous on *Saturday Night Live*, Carvey just about carries the story of a conman who wins the confidence of a wealthy family while on the run from a gangster. Robert Loggia contributes some assured support, but it's the script that lets the side down. DP

Dana Carvey *Eddie Farrell* • Robert Loggia *Milt Malkin* • Todd Graff *Lou Pasquino* • Julia Campbell *Annie Malkin* • Milo O'Shea *Max* • James Tolkan *Sal Nichols* ■ *Dir* Donald Petrie • *Scr* Mitchel Katlin, Nat Bernstein

The Opposite of Sex ★★★★ 18
Comedy   1998 · US · Colour · 96min

Former screenwriter Don Roos cuts through the thicket of political correctness with rapier wit and rude humour in his eye-opening feature debut about contemporary sexual values and lifestyles. Christina Ricci is deadly funny as the teenager who steals her gay half-brother's boyfriend so she can have an instant father for the child she's carrying. With Lisa Kudrow from *Friends* also giving a spot-on turn as a self-righteous old maid, Roos's bitchy oddball comedy is hilarious. AJ Violence, swearing. **DVD**

Christina Ricci *Dedee Truitt* • Martin Donovan (2) *Bill Truitt* • Lisa Kudrow *Lucia Dalury* • Lyle Lovett *Sheriff Carl Tippett* • Johnny Galecki *Jason Bock* • William Lee Scott *Randy* ■ *Dir/Scr* Don Roos

The Opposite Sex ★★★
Musical comedy   1956 · US · Colour · 116min

The MGM classic *The Women* featured no men in its cast, but this musical remake makes the mistake of letting them in. Jeff Richards and a young Leslie Nielsen are pretty dreary, appearing opposite Joan Collins, Dolores Gray, Ann Sheridan, Ann Miller and Joan Blondell. Another fly in the ointment is top-billed June Allyson, who seems neither sophisticated nor brittle enough for the shenanigans in Clare Boothe Luce's play. There's good use of early CinemaScope, and the result is sexy, witty and glamorous. TS

June Allyson *Kay Hilliard* • Joan Collins *Crystal Allen* • Dolores Gray *Sylvia Fowler* • Ann Sheridan *Amanda Penrose* • Ann Miller *Gloria Dell* • Leslie Nielsen *Steve Hilliard* • Jeff Richards *Buck Winston* • Agnes Moorehead *Countess Lavaliere* ■ *Dir* David Miller (1) • *Scr* Fay Kanin, Michael Kanin, from the play by Clare Boothe Luce

The Opposite Sex and How to Live with Them ★★ 15
Romantic comedy   1993 · US · Colour · 82min

Courteney Cox plays the daughter of conservative parents who endures a mismatched, up-and-down relationship with Arye Gross. The two leads are fine, but the best performances and lines go to their respective best friends, Julie Brown and Kevin Pollak. Director Matthew Meshekoff attempts to spice up the formula with some raunchy scenes and characters talking directly to the camera. JF

Arye Gross *David* • Courteney Cox *Carrie* • Kevin Pollak *Eli* • Julie Brown *Zoe* • Jack Carter *Rabbi* • Kimber Sissons *Tracy* • Mitchell Ryan *Kenneth Davenport* ■ *Dir* Matthew Meshekoff • *Scr* Noah Stern

The Optimists of Nine Elms ★★★ PG
Drama   1973 · UK · Colour · 106min

This was originally to have been a vehicle for Danny Kaye, but it's hard to see how his energetic style would have been suitable for the part of Sam the busker, who has little to sustain him apart from his music-hall memories and his faithful dog. Resisting the temptation for pathos, Peter Sellers gives a surprisingly sensitive and somewhat overlooked performance. Lionel Bart's songs aren't among his best, but these musings on poverty and community spirit are nicely expressed. DP

Peter Sellers *Sam* • Donna Mullane *Liz* • John Chaffey *Mark* • David Daker *Bob Ellis* • Marjorie Yates *Chrissie Ellis* ■ *Dir* Anthony Simmons • *Scr* Anthony Simmons, Tudor Gates, from the novel by Anthony Simmons

The Oracle ★★ U
Fantasy comedy   1952 · UK · BW · 85min

Gilbert Harding voices the oracle at the bottom of a well in this piffling comedy in which whimsy is heaped on to make up for the absence of genuine humour. Ordinarily, Harding dispenses his wisdom to the inhabitants of a small Irish island. But then journalist Robert Beatty begins using him to predict horse races and other momentous events until the British mainland is reduced to chaos. Celebrated at the time as the rudest man on TV, Harding comes over today as an irascible prig. DP

Robert Beatty *Bob Jefferson* • Joseph Tomelty *Terry Roche* • Michael Medwin *Timothy Blake* • Mervyn Johns *Tom Mitchum* • Virginia McKenna *Shelagh* • Gillian Lind *Jane Bond* • Ursula Howells *Peggy* • Gilbert Harding *Oracle's voice* ■ *Dir* CM Pennington-Richards • *Scr* Patrick Campbell, from the radio play *To Tell You the Truth* by Robert Barr

Orange County ★★★ 12
Comedy   2001 · US · Colour · 78min

In addition to its offbeat observations, quirky sensibilities and marvelous performances, this is also noteworthy for showcasing the second generation Hollywood talents of Colin Hanks (Tom's son), Schuyler Fisk (Sissy Spacek's daughter) and Jake Kasdan (director Lawrence's son). Set in the "perfect" Californian region of the title, where Hanks finds his life changed when a clerical mistake means his brilliant grades are attributed to another student and he has 24 hours to fix the error before Stanford University closes its application ranks. AJ Swearing. **DVD**

Colin Hanks *Shaun Brumder* • Jack Black *Lance* • Catherine O'Hara *Cindy Beugler* • Schuyler Fisk *Ashley* • John Lithgow *Bud Brumder* • Brett Harrison *[Bret Harrison] Lonny Munsack* • Harold Ramis *Don Durkett* • Lily Tomlin *Charlotte Cobb* • Chevy Chase *Principal Harbert* • Kevin Kline *Marcus Skinner* • Ben Stiller *Fireman* ■ *Dir* Jake Kasdan • *Scr* Mike White

The Oranges ★★ 15
Romantic comedy drama
2011 · US · Colour · 86min

This laboured families-in-strife comedy drama doesn't merit the calibre of its stellar line-up. Hugh Laurie, Catherine Keener, Oliver Platt and Allison Janney play best friends and neighbours in a well-to-do New Jersey suburb. They hope that Laurie and Keener's son (Adam Brody) will fall for Platt and Janney's daughter (Leighton Meester) when she comes home for Thanksgiving after a five-year absence. Instead, she begins an affair with Laurie, causing turmoil and threatening marriages. It's all mildly amusing, but you can't help feeling that the superb cast deserves something rather more worthy of their talents. DA Swearing, sexual references. **DVD**

Hugh Laurie *David Walling* • Leighton Meester *Nina Ostroff* • Catherine Keener *Paige Walling* • Allison Janney *Cathy Ostroff* • Oliver Platt *Terry Ostroff* • Adam Brody *Toby Walling* ■ *Dir* Julian Farino • *Scr* Ian Helfer, Jay Reiss

Oranges and Sunshine ★★★ 15
Historical drama
2010 · Aus/UK · Colour · 100min

Director Jim Loach (son of Ken) tells the story of the thousands of "disadvantaged" British kids who were deported without parental knowledge or consent to Australia in the 1940s and 50s. It's a compelling true story of social scandal, and Emily Watson is excellent as social worker Margaret Humphreys who, years later, stumbled on the outrage and was determined to see justice done. This often painful drama makes good, comparative use of locations in sun-bleached Adelaide and the grey East Midlands, and will swell your heart with indignation. AC Swearing. **DVD**

Emily Watson *Margaret Humphreys* • Hugo Weaving *Jack* • David Wenham *Len* • Tara Morice *Pauline* • Stuart Wolfenden *Bill* ■ *Dir* Jim Loach • *Scr* Rona Munro, from the non-fiction book *Empty Cradles* by Margaret Humphreys

Orca... Killer Whale ★★ PG
Action adventure   1977 · US · Colour · 88min

This man-versus-beast tale was an obvious attempt to jump on the *Jaws* bandwagon, but some of the scenes are just laughable. Richard Harris plays the macho hunter who incurs the wrath of a super-intelligent killer whale after he slaughters its pregnant mate. The female cast and some remarkable underwater photography fail to make up for the daft narrative. TH **DVD**

Richard Harris *Captain Nolan* • Charlotte Rampling *Rachel Bedford* • Will Sampson *Umilak* • Bo Derek *Annie* • Keenan Wynn *Novak* • Scott Walker (1) *Swain* • Robert Carradine *Ken* • Peter Hooten *Paul* ■ *Dir* Michael Anderson • *Scr* Luciano Vincenzoni, Sergio Donati

Orchestra Rehearsal ★★★ PG
Drama   1978 · It/Fr/W Ger · Colour · 69min

Prompted by the murder of ex-Prime Minister Aldo Moro, yet also clearly a swipe at the strikers who had disrupted the production of *Amarcord* and *Casanova*, Federico Fellini's microcosmic burlesque on the shortcomings of both anarchy and authoritarianism was originally made for Italian television. Dismissed as a one-gag vignette, it's actually a revealing snapshot of late 1970s attitudes and an unconscious rebellion against the cult of auteurism. DP Italian +subtitles. **DVD**

Balduin Baas *Conductor* • Clara Colosimo *Harpist* • Elisabeth Labi *Pianist* ■ *Dir* Federico Fellini • *Scr* Federico Fellini, Brunello Rondi • *Art Director* Dante Ferretti • *Music* Nino Rota

Orchestra Seats ★★★ 12
Comedy drama   2005 · Fr · Colour · 100min

Directed with easy charm by Danièle Thompson, this bittersweet confection provides some reassuring old-fashioned entertainment. Set on the Avenue Montaigne in Paris, the action revolves around the preparations for a classical concert, an art auction and the opening of a

Feydeau farce. Linking the plot strands is Cécile de France, a waitress who befriends restless pianist Albert Dupontel, frustrated TV actress Valérie Lemercier, stuffy intellectual Christopher Thompson (who also co-wrote the screenplay with his mother), and theatre concierge Dani. The scripting and performances are so polished that it's easy to overlook the contrivances and succumb to the romantic locations, the charmingly optimistic insights into the elusive nature of talent and the galling disparity between achievement and satisfaction. DP French +subtitles. **DVD**

Cécile de France *Jessica* • Valérie Lemercier *Catherine Versen* • Albert Dupontel *Jean-François Lefort* • Claude Brasseur *Jacques Grumberg* • Dani *Claudie* • Christopher Thompson *Frédéric Grumberg* • Laura Morante *Valentine* ■ *Dir* Danièle Thompson • *Scr* Danièle Thompson, Christopher Thompson

Orchestra Wives ★★★PG
Musical 1942 · US · BW · 93min

Life on the road as lived by a touring swing orchestra and, more particularly the musicians' wives, with the new wife (Ann Rutherford) of trumpeter George Montgomery having to cope with the female rivalry and backbiting. The mediocre script and second-rung cast, however, are secondary to the delights of the Mack Gordon-Harry Warren score, the Glenn Miller Orchestra, vocalists Tex Beneke and Marion Hutton and the Modernaires, and dazzling tap-dancing team the Nicholas Brothers. RK

George Montgomery *Bill Abbott* • Ann Rutherford *Connie* • Glenn Miller *Gene Morrison* • Cesar Romero *Sinjin* • Lynn Bari *Jaynie* • Carole Landis *Natalie* • Virginia Gilmore *Elsie* • Jackie Gleason *Beck* • Nicholas Brothers *Specialty* • Tex Beneke • Marion Hutton ■ *Dir* Archie Mayo • *Scr* Karl Tunberg, Darrel Ware, from a story by James Prindle • *Music* Mack Gordon, Harry Warren

The Order ★★15
Action thriller 2001 · US · Colour · 85min

Jean-Claude Van Damme is always consistent. Whatever the storyline, he'll perform the same specific kick-boxing moves and at some stage bare his super-toned chest. So it's no surprise that this tired action thriller incorporates both these trademarks, along with all the requisite chase sequences and explosions. Here he plays an artefacts thief who gets embroiled with a religious cult in Israel after they kidnap his archaeologist father. It's tedious hokum, strewn with one-liners, but die-hard fans will no doubt lap it up. SF Violence, swearing. **DVD**

Jean-Claude Van Damme *Rudy Cafmeyer* • Charlton Heston *Professor Finley* • Brian Thompson *Cyrus* • Ben Cross *Ben Ner* • Sofia Milos *Dalia* • Vernon Dobtcheff *Oscar Cafmeyer* ■ *Dir* Sheldon Lettich • *Scr* Les Weldon, Jean-Claude Van Damme

Order of Death ★★★18
Thriller 1983 · It · Colour · 96min

Harvey Keitel has an early vicious role, with Sex Pistol John Lydon (aka Johnny Rotten) as his sociopathic confessor, in this genre-twisting spaghetti thriller. Lydon shows up at detective Keitel's secret Central Park apartment, paid for by drug dealers' backhanders, and admits he's the serial killer responsible for slaughtering numerous narcotics division cops. Is he telling the truth and what is Keitel going to do now the punk has seen his illicit apartment? A cleverly crafted, homoerotic minuet of strong wills. AJ

Harvey Keitel *Lt Fred O'Connor* • John Lydon *Leo Smith* • Nicole Garcia *Lenore Carvo* • Leonard Mann *Bob Carvo* • Sylvia Sidney *Margaret Smith* ■ *Dir* Roberto Faenza • *Scr* Ennio De Concini, Hugh Fleetwood, Roberto Faenza, from the novel by Fleetwood

Orders Are Orders ★★U
Comedy 1954 · UK · BW · 74min

A play from the 1930s was dug up to provide the basis for this army comedy, which pokes fun at American producers coming to Britain to make cheap science-

fiction movies. The film is chiefly of interest today because of the amount of radio talent involved. Brian Reece, who had just finished a long run as PC49, stars, and up-and-coming Peter Sellers and Tony Hancock lend support, while even Eric Sykes was brought in to pep up the corny old script. DM

Peter Sellers *Private Goffin* • Sidney James *Ed Waggermeyer* • Brian Reece *Capt Harper* • Margot Grahame *Wanda Sinclair* • Raymond Huntley *Col Bellamy* • Tony Hancock *Lt Wilfrid Cartroad* • Clive Morton *Gen Grahame-Fox* • June Thorburn *Veronica Bellamy* • Bill Fraser *Private Slee* • Donald Pleasence *Lance Cpl Martin* • Eric Sykes *Private Waterhouse* ■ *Dir* David Paltenghi • *Scr* Donald Taylor, Eric Sykes, Geoffrey Orme, from the play by Ian Hay, Anthony Armstrong

Orders to Kill ★★★★12
Second World War drama 1958 · UK · BW · 107min

A forgotten gem of the British cinema, this wartime drama sends a French-speaking American bomber pilot, Paul Massie, to Paris to liquidate a double agent. However, when Massie meets his target and finds him to be friendly and mild-mannered, he questions the man's guilt. But orders are orders. After that comes a succession of major ironies and a complex moral argument, tightly directed by Anthony Asquith. AT **DVD**

Eddie Albert *Major MacMahon* • Paul Massie *Gene Summers* • Lillian Gish *Mrs Summers* • James Robertson-Justice *Naval commander* • Irene Worth *Leonie* • Leslie French *Marcel Lafitte* • John Crawford *Kimball* • Lionel Jeffries *Interrogator* ■ *Dir* Anthony Asquith • *Scr* Paul Dehn, George St George, from a story by Donald C Downes

Ordet ★★★★★12
Religious drama 1955 · Den · BW · 119min

Thirty-five years after he first saw Kaj Munk's play, Carl Th Dreyer finally brought this much-cherished project to the screen and won the Golden Lion at Venice. His only feature of the 1950s is filled with sharp contrasts - lively faith and dour dogma, optimism and fatalism, youth and age, cynical sanity and mystical madness - which are further highlighted by the authentic starkness of the Jutland setting and the simplicity of the long mobile takes. This establishes the atmosphere in which a family feud is resolved by a miraculous resurrection. It's simply a masterpiece. DP Danish +subtitles. **DVD**

Henrik Malberg *Morten Borgen* • Emil Hass Christensen *Mikkel Borgen* • Preben Lerdorff Rye *Johannes Borgen* • Cay Kristiansen *Anders Borgen* • Birgitte Federspiel *Inger, Mikkel's wife* ■ *Dir* Carl Th Dreyer • *Scr* Carl Th Dreyer, from the play by Kaj Munk • *Cinematographer* Henning Bendtsen

Ordinary Decent Criminal ★★★15
Crime caper 1999 · UK/Ger/Ire · Colour · 90min

This is a thinly veiled attempt to retell the story of real-life Irish criminal Martin Cahill, the subject of John Boorman's critically acclaimed *The General*. This time Kevin Spacey plays Cahill (here renamed Michael Lynch), the cocky Dublin gangster who spent his days robbing the rich, annoying the police and falling foul of the IRA. However, the man on whom Michael is based would bristle at his transformation into a lovable rogue who likes nothing better than flashing his naked bum at policemen. This is worth seeing for another powerhouse performance from Spacey (dodgy accent notwithstanding). JB **DVD**

Kevin Spacey *Michael Lynch* • Linda Fiorentino *Christine Lynch* • Peter Mullan *Stevie* • Stephen Dillane *Noel Quigley* • Helen Baxendale *Lisa* • David Hayman *Tony Brady* • Patrick Malahide *Commissioner Daly* ■ *Dir* Thaddeus O'Sullivan • *Scr* Gerry Stembridge [Gerard Stembridge]

An Ordinary Execution ★★★12
Drama 2010 · Fr · Colour · 100min

In this austere if somewhat academic drama, first-time director Marc Dugain

draws on his own bestselling novel to speculate on the conspiracy-shrouded demise of Soviet dictator Joseph Stalin. The action centres on the (fictional) secret treatment sessions that an ailing Stalin (André Dussollier) receives from Anna (Marina Hands), a doctor famed for her unconventional healing techniques. With the help of cinematographer Yves Angelo's brooding Kremlin atmosphere, Dugain concentrates on the tensions between Stalin and Anna. The result is a movie that's impeccably played and chillingly compelling. DP French +subtitles. Sexual references, torture descriptions. **DVD**

André Dussollier *Stalin* • Marina Hands *Anna* • Edouard Baer *Vassili* • Denis Podalydès *Concierge* • Tom Novembre *Hospital director* • Grégory Gadebois *Head of department* ■ *Dir* Marc Dugain • *Scr* Marc Dugain, from his novel

Ordinary Magic ★★
Drama 1993 · Can · Colour · 104min

This is notable for the appearance of Paul Anka, pop star from the 1950s and early 1960s. Ryan Reynolds is a 15-year-old boy brought up in India by his social activist parents. He's shipped off to his aunt (Glenne Headly) in Canada after their death. When his aunt is unfairly evicted by a property developer (Anka), he puts into practice everything he has learned in India to right the wrong. An interesting if unsatisfying attempt to portray both alienation and Hindu ideals. FL

Glenne Headly *Charlotte* • Ryan Reynolds *Ganesh/Jeffrey* • David Fox *Father/Warren* • Heath Lamberts *Mayor* • Paul Anka *Joey Dean* ■ *Dir* Giles Walker • *Scr* Jefferson Lewis, from a novel by Malcolm Bosse

Ordinary Miracles ★★
Drama 2005 · US · Colour · 99min

A well-preserved Jaclyn Smith leads a proficient cast in this simple though solid Hallmark drama. She plays a career-orientated judge who learns valuable lessons about family and forgiveness when she takes temporary custody of a troubled 16-year-old foster child (*Desperate Housewives's* Lyndsy Fonseca). The storyline is predictable yet compelling, and benefits from sympathetic characters and convincing performances. But it's Fonseca's ability to capture the loneliness and distress of teenager Sally that really raises the film above its clichés. SF

Jaclyn Smith *Judge Kay Woodbury* • Lyndsy Fonseca *Sally Powell* • Corbin Bernsen *Davis Woodbury* • C Thomas Howell *Jim Powell* • Sarah Aldrich *Miranda Powell* • Erik Eidem *Pete Smalling* ■ *Dir* Michael Switzer • *Scr* Bud Schaetzle

Ordinary People ★★★★15
Drama 1980 · US · Colour · 118min

A critically acclaimed blockbuster in its time, *Ordinary People* won four Oscars, including best film and best director for Robert Redford, stepping behind the camera for the first time. There is one truly great performance from Mary Tyler Moore as the thin, elegant, golfing and social-mixing mother strung tighter than a piano wire, and she is ably assisted by Donald Sutherland and Timothy Hutton, who won a best supporting actor Oscar. There is something very pat about Redford's exposition of the seemingly cosy middle-class family simmering with unconscious angst after the death of a son, but it's still an auspicious directorial debut that stands as one of the first films to deal intelligently with the role of therapy. SH Swearing. **DVD**

Donald Sutherland *Calvin* • Mary Tyler Moore *Beth* • Judd Hirsch *Berger* • Timothy Hutton *Conrad* • M Emmet Walsh *Swimming coach* • Elizabeth McGovern *Jeannine* • Dinah Manoff *Karen* • Fredric Lehne *Lazenby* • James B Sikking *Ray* ■ *Dir* Robert Redford • *Scr* Alvin Sargent, from the novel by Judith Guest

The Organization ★★★★15
Crime drama 1971 · US · Colour · 106min

Sidney Poitier embarks on his third tour of duty as San Francisco homicide cop Virgil Tibbs - first seen in 1967's *In the Heat of the Night* - and there's still life left in his character. This story is neatly linked to the emerging youth culture of the time as Tibbs sets out to smash a drug syndicate with the help of young vigilantes out to get the organisation for what it's done to their family and friends. Director Don Medford keeps this moving in a convincingly tense manner and Poitier doesn't need to play the superhero to still come out on top. TH Violence, swearing. **DVD**

Sidney Poitier *Lieutenant Virgil Tibbs* • Barbara McNair *Valerie Tibbs* • Gerald S O'Loughlin *Lieutenant Jack Pecora* • Sheree North *Gloria Morgan* • Fred Beir *Bob Alford* • Allen Garfield *Benjy* • Bernie Hamilton *Lieutenant Jessop* • Raul Julia *Juan Mendoza* • Ron O'Neal *Joe Peralez* • James A Watson Jr *Stacy Baker* ■ *Dir* Don Medford • *Scr* James R Webb, from characters by John Ball

The Organizer ★★★★
Period drama 1963 · It/Fr/Yug · BW · 126min

In Turin in the 1890s textile workers stage a massive and bitter strike and are organised by a radical intellectual played by Marcello Mastroianni. The government sends in strikebreakers and then the army. Released when Italy was in the grip of industrial action, Mario Monicelli's film, almost a black comedy, aroused considerable controversy. Mastroianni, hiding behind a beard and glasses, gives a superb performance, consolidating his position as Italy's pre-eminent actor. AT Italian +subtitles.

Marcello Mastroianni *Professor Sinigaglia* • Renato Salvatori *Raoul* • Annie Girardot *Niobe* • Gabriella Giorgelli *Adele* • Bernard Blier *Martinetti* ■ *Dir* Mario Monicelli • *Scr* Mario Monicelli, Age, Scarpelli

Orgazmo ★★★18
Comedy 1997 · US · Colour · 88min

The characters may be real-life actors rather than crudely drawn caricatures, but this second full-length feature from the co-creator of *South Park*, Trey Parker, admirably continues to flout all things tasteful, politically correct and sophisticated. Parker also stars as a naive Mormon actor doing the rounds in LA, who finds himself cast as the lead player in a porn movie. Sensitive souls will be outraged by the relentless flow of lavatorial laughs and vulgarity. JF Violence, swearing, sex scenes, nudity. **DVD**

Trey Parker *Joe Young* • Dian Bachar *Ben Chapleski* • Robyn Lynne Raab *Lisa, Joe's fiancée* • Michael Dean Jacobs *Maxxx Orbison* • Ron Jeremy *Clark* • Andrew W Kemler *Rodgers* • David Dunn *A-Cup* • Matt Stone *Dave the lighting guy* ■ *Dir/Scr* Trey Parker

Original Gangstas ★★★18
Crime drama 1996 · US · Colour · 98min

Attention all blaxploitation fanatics! Five 1970s icons - Pam Grier, Fred Williamson, Jim Brown, Ron O'Neal and Richard Roundtree - team up to teach a Gary, Indiana, ghetto gang a tough-guy lesson in veteran B-movie director Larry Cohen's hip, black, badass action update. Exciting and thought-provoking (should fire be fought with fire?), it's both a contemporary morality tale and a nostalgic look back at the *Shaft* and *Foxy Brown* era. AJ

Fred Williamson *John Bookman* • Jim Brown *Jake Trevor* • Pam Grier *Laurie Thompson* • Paul Winfield *Reverend Marshall Dorsey* • Ron O'Neal *Bubba* • Richard Roundtree *Slick* • Isabel Sanford *Gracie Bookman* ■ *Dir* Larry Cohen • *Scr* Aubrey Rattan

The Original Kings of Comedy ★★★★15
Comedy concert 2000 · US · Colour · 111min

This is the least controversial of all director Spike Lee's movies: although the views on race in America are as hard-hitting as those in *Do the Right Thing* or *Bamboozled*, here they are embodied in the words and gestures of four black comedians. Lee's documentary, filmed in Charlotte, North Carolina, uses the quartet's blisteringly hilarious presence as a battering ram to jolt us into laughing at human bigotries. Steve Harvey, DL Hughley, Cedric the Entertainer and Bernie Mac are the wisecracking four, who draw on a vaudeville background that has all but disappeared. TH Swearing.

■ *Dir* Spike Lee • *Cinematographer* Malik Sayeed

Original Sin ★★ 18
Period melodrama 2001 · US/Fr · Colour · 111min

Antonio Banderas and Angelina Jolie star in a corny, cliché-ridden bodice-ripper. Set in late 19th-century Cuba, Banderas plays a wealthy coffee merchant who orders a mail-order bride from the US to bear his children. What he gets is Ms Jolie so it's lust at first sight, but Jolie has a sinister secret agenda, and Banderas soon finds himself embroiled in a cat-and-mouse con game. DA Sex scenes, violence, nudity. 🅳🅥🅳

Antonio Banderas *Luis Antonio Vargas* • Angelina Jolie *Julia Russell/Bonny Castle* • Thomas Jane *Walter Downs/Billy/Mephisto* • Jack Thompson *Alan Jordan* • Gregory Itzin *Colonel Worth* • Allison Mackie *Augusta Jordan* ■ *Dir* Michael Cristofer • *Scr* Michael Cristofer, from the novel *Waltz into Darkness* by Cornell Woolrich

Orion: the Man Who Would Be King ★★★★ 12A
Documentary 2015 · US/UK · Colour · 86min

Orphan Jimmy Ellis was unable to launch a singing career despite having a voice just like Elvis Presley's. But with Elvis's death in 1977, Ellis was persuaded by Sun Records' Shelby Singleton to adopt the persona of a masked character called Orion. As Elvis fans became convinced Orion was the King, things took off. Director Jeanie Finlay delivers a thoughtful, revelatory rock 'n' roll story about a cult phenomenon – this is certainly not a simple fable about an Elvis impersonator on the make. JA Some swearing, sexual references.

■ *Dir* Jeanie Finlay

Orlando ★★★ PG
Historical fantasy
1992 · UK/Rus/Fr/It/Neth · Colour · 89min

Director Sally Potter achieves the near-impossible task of bringing Virginia Woolf's complex tale to the screen in a series of burnished and glittering images. The film tells the story of young nobleman Orlando who lives for 400 years and mysteriously changes into a woman during the 18th century. As the hero/heroine, Tilda Swinton moves passively through the romantic, dramatic and intriguing events that befall Orlando, and there's an excellent supporting cast that includes Quentin Crisp as Elizabeth I. Sometimes puzzling, sometimes boring, but also sumptuous and atmospheric. RK 🅳🅥🅳 🅑🅛

Tilda Swinton *Orlando* • Billy Zane *Shelmerdine* • John Wood (2) *Archduke Harry* • Lothaire Bluteau *The Khan* • Charlotte Valandrey *Sasha* • Heathcote Williams *Nick Greene/Publisher* • Quentin Crisp *Queen Elizabeth I* • Dudley Sutton *King James I* • Thom Hoffman *King William of Orange* • Anna Healy *Euphrosyne* • Simon Russell Beale *Earl of Moray* • Ned Sherrin *Mr Addison* ■ *Dir* Sally Potter • *Scr* Sally Potter, from the novel by Virginia Woolf

Orphan ★★★ 15
Horror thriller
2009 · US/Ger/Fr/Can · Colour · 117min

House of Wax director Jaume Collet-Serra here delivers a stylish shocker that's streaked with morbid playfulness. A couple adopt a nine-year-old girl, but the youngster is not what she seems... Before you can say "Bad Seed", she is playing Russian roulette with her younger, deaf sister, threatening her older brother with emasculation and hammering nuns to death. Will her mother's internet research into "children who kill" make her oblivious husband finally face the truth about their terror tyke? Even an over-extended finale can't entirely dampen this

enjoyably daffy yet suitably sick crowd-pleaser. AJ Violence, swearing. 🅳🅥🅳 🅑🅛

Vera Farmiga *Kate Coleman* • Peter Sarsgaard *John Coleman* • Isabelle Fuhrman *Esther* • CCH Pounder *Sister Abigail* • Karel Roden *Dr Varava* ■ *Dir* Jaume Collet-Serra • *Scr* David Leslie Johnson, from a story by Alex Mace

The Orphanage ★★★ 15
Supernatural horror
2006 · Sp/Fr · Colour · 105min

Spanish director JA Bayona's debut feature is an exceptionally effective and surprisingly moving ghost story. After Laura (Belén Rueda) and her husband Carlos (Fernando Cayo) move into the abandoned orphanage where she grew up, they become concerned for their young adopted son as he develops a plethora of imaginary friends. The appearance of an aged and distinctly suspicious social worker further deepens the atmosphere of mystery and approaching tragedy. Bayona and screenwriter Sergio G Sánchez negotiate the inevitable clichés of the haunted-house genre expertly, while Rueda and Caya give perfectly judged performances as the young couple. AS Spanish +subtitles. 🅳🅥🅳

Belén Rueda *Laura* • Fernando Cayo *Carlos* • Roger Príncep *Simón* • Montserrat Carulla *Benigna* • Geraldine Chaplin *Aurora* • Mabel Rivera *Pilar* ■ *Dir* JA Bayona [Juan Antonio Bayona] • *Scr* Sergio G Sánchez

Orphans ★★★ 15
Drama 1987 · US · Colour · 110min

Albert Finney had played the drunken kidnap victim on stage in 1986 at the Hampstead Theatre Club, received rave reviews and filmed it a year later with Matthew Modine and Kevin Anderson as his kidnappers. Influenced by Harold Pinter, Lyle Kessler's play is a dark fable about domination, and director Alan J Pakula, respecting the source material, eschews the sort of visual flourishes that distinguish his other films. Stagey, but Finney is great. AT Swearing.

Albert Finney *Harold* • Matthew Modine *Treat* • Kevin Anderson *Phillip* • John Kellogg *Barney* • Anthony Heald *Man in park* • Novella Nelson *Mattie* ■ *Dir* Alan J Pakula • *Scr* Lyle Kessler, from his play

Orphans ★★★★ 18
Black comedy drama 1998 · UK · Colour · 97min

Actor Peter Mullan takes a turn behind the camera to write and direct this black comedy drama about four siblings and the long night they experience before burying their dearly departed mum. Star-in-the-making Douglas Henshall is the brother who ends up being stabbed following a bar brawl, while Rosemarie Stevenson – as the sister with cerebral palsy – gets stranded in an alley when her electric wheelchair breaks down. Unusual and quirky stuff indeed, yet Mullan deftly mixes humour with pathos. JB Swearing, violence. 🅳🅥🅳 🅑🅛

Douglas Henshall *Michael Flynn* • Gary Lewis *Thomas Flynn* • Stephen McCole *John Flynn* • Rosemarie Stevenson *Sheila Flynn* • Frank Gallagher *Tanga* • Alex Norton *Hanson* ■ *Dir/Scr* Peter Mullan

Orphans of the Storm ★★★★
Silent period melodrama
1921 · US · BW · 125min

DW Griffith, writing under the name of Gaston de Tolignac, tackled the French Revolution, built a period Paris on 14 acres at his Mamaroneck studios, and had his luminous star, Lillian Gish, and her sister, Dorothy, play the orphaned sisters caught up in the bloody events. The plot, bursting with melodramatic incident, has Lillian, the carer of her blind sister, sent to the guillotine for harbouring her aristocrat lover (the splendid Joseph Schildkraut), only to be saved at the last minute by the intervention of Danton (Monte Blue). Not quite a masterpiece, it's still spectacular and absorbing. RK

Lillian Gish *Henriette Girard* • Dorothy Gish *Louise* • Joseph Schildkraut *Chevalier de Vaudrey* • Frank Losee *Count de Linières* •

Katherine Emmett *Director* • Monte Blue *Danton* ■ *Dir* DW Griffith • *Scr* Marquis Gaston de Tolignac [DW Griffith], from the play *Les Deux Orphelines* by Adolphe Philippe Dennery, Eugène Cormon, adapted by N Hart Jackson, Albert Marshman Palmer

Orphée ★★★★★ PG
Fantasy 1950 · Fr · BW · 90min

Jean Cocteau's updating of the Orpheus myth to post-Liberation Paris is one of the cinema's great artistic masterpieces, a piece of Méliès-like magic that is intensely powerful and moving even at its most bewildering. Jean Marais is the poet who falls in love with Death (Maria Casarès); her assistant, angel François Périer, snatches the poet's wife and forces him to enter the underworld to get her back. The use of images, especially the looking-glass that turns into water, is still daring and – it might be said – rich in gay iconography. In 1960, Cocteau made a sequel, *Le Testament d'Orphée*. AT French +subtitles. 🅳🅥🅳

Jean Marais *Orphée* • François Périer *Heurtebise* • Maria Casarès *Princess* • Marie Déa *Eurydice* • Henri Cremieux *The editor* • Juliette Gréco [Juliette Greco] *Aglaonice* • Roger Blin *The writer* • Edouard Dermithe *Cégeste* • Pierre Bertin *The Inspector* • Jacques Varennes *First Judge* • Jean Cocteau *The voice* ■ *Dir/Scr* Jean Cocteau • *Cinematographer* Nicolas Hayer

Orthodox ★★★ 18
Crime drama 2015 · UK · Colour · 94min

A northern English Jewish community is, unusually, the setting for this dark crime drama. Stephen Graham stars as a struggling butcher who moonlights as an illegal bare-knuckle boxer to provide for his family. However, when the community's shady fixer, Michael Smiley, proposes a job for easy money, a fateful decision turns Graham's life inside out. The frequent change of tone means the film never quite settles, but the chemistry between Graham and Smiley keeps things simmering until their inevitable showdown. DW Violence, swearing 🅳🅥🅳

Stephen Graham *Benjamin* • Michael Smiley *Shannon* • Giacomo Mancini *Daniel* • Rebecca Callard *Alice* ■ *Dir/Scr* David Leon

Osaka Elegy ★★★★★ PG
Drama 1936 · Jpn · BW · 68min

Inspired by the sacrifices made by his own geisha sister, Kenji Mizoguchi's masterly drama marked the beginning of his longtime collaboration with screenwriter Yoshikata Yoda. Scrupulously avoiding sensationalism, it charts the descent into prostitution of a young telephonist, who becomes her boss's mistress in a bid to repay her embezzling father's debts and fund her brother's education. Mizoguchi regular Isuzu Yamada contributes a superb display of abused decency, but it's the director's astute visual sense that gives the picture its power, with the stylised realism of his claustrophobic compositions suggesting the exploitative repression of a corrupt patriarchal society. DP In Japanese. 🅳🅥🅳 🅑🅛

Isuzu Yamada *Ayako Murai* • Seiichi Takegawa *Junzo, Ayako's father* • Chiyoko Okura *Sachiko* • Shinpachiro Asaka *Hiroshi* • Benkei Shiganoya *Sonosuke Asai* • Yoko Umemura *Sumiko* • Kensaku Hara *Susumu Nishimura* • Shizuko Takizawa *Apartment maid* • Eitaro Shindo *Fujino* ■ *Dir* Kenji Mizoguchi • *Scr* Yoshikata Yoda, Kenji Mizoguchi, from the serial *Mieko* by Saburo Okada in the magazine *Shincho*

Osama ★★★★ 12
Drama 2003 · Afg/Jpn/Ire · Colour · 79min

The first feature produced in post-Taliban Afghanistan is a revealing political fairy tale, in which a plucky heroine attempts to challenge a chauvinist tyranny. Director Siddiq Barmak relies on trusted neorealist techniques to tell his tale and draws a moving performance from Marina Golbahari as the 12-year-old forced to disguise herself as a boy to find work after the closure of the hospital in which her war-widowed mother was a doctor. Indeed, the wholly untrained Golbahari exudes uncomprehending trust and innocent

courage, until she is sent to a strict Koranic school where she lives in daily dread of her secret being exposed. DP Afghani +subtitles. 🅳🅥🅳

Marina Golbahari *Osama* • Arif Herati *Espandi* • Zubaida Sahar *Mother* • Khwaja Nader *Mullah* • Hamida Refah *Grandmother* ■ *Dir/Scr* Siddiq Barmak

The Oscar ★★★
Drama 1966 · US · Colour · 120min

Stephen Boyd makes a fair fist of villainy here as actor Frank Fane who has been nominated for an Oscar and sits in the Shrine Auditorium waiting for the envelope to be opened. As he waits the flashback starts, showing how this slimeball walked over countless people and survived a slew of sex scandals to be a major movie star. It's hugely, trashily enjoyable and filled with a lot of in-jokes and bursting with cameos. AT

Stephen Boyd *Frank Fane* • Elke Sommer *Kay Bergdahl* • Milton Berle *Kappy Kapstetter* • Eleanor Parker *Sophie Cantaro* • Joseph Cotten *Kenneth H Regan* • Jill St John *Laurel Scott* • Tony Bennett *Hymie Kelly* • Edie Adams *Trina Yale* • Ernest Borgnine *Barney Yale* • Ed Begley *Grobard* • Walter Brennan *Orrin C Quentin* • Broderick Crawford *Sheriff* • Peter Lawford *Steve Marks* • Edith Head • Bob Hope • Merle Oberon • Frank Sinatra • Nancy Sinatra • Hedda Hopper ■ *Dir* Russell Rouse • *Scr* Harlan Ellison, Russell Rouse, Clarence Greene, from the novel by Richard Sale

Oscar ★★★ PG
Comedy 1991 · US · Colour · 105min

Director John Landis manages a semblance of form with this gangster farce based on a French play. Sylvester Stallone strives a touch too hard for laughs as the mobster whose plans to quit the rackets are confounded by a series of domestic crises and that old standby, the "mixed-up bags" routine. The main interest lies in the sly cameos, with Peter Riegert and Chazz Palminteri the standouts in the supporting cast. DP Some swearing. 🅳🅥🅳

Sylvester Stallone *Angelo "Snaps" Provolone* • Ornella Muti *Sofia Provolone* • Peter Riegert *Aldo* • Vincent Spano *Anthony Rossano* • Marisa Tomei *Lisa Provolone* • Elizabeth Barondes *Theresa* • Kirk Douglas *Eduardo Provolone* • Art LaFleur *Officer Quinn* • Ken Howard *Kirkwood* • Don Ameche *Father Clemente* • Chazz Palminteri *Connie* • Tim Curry *Dr Thornton Poole* ■ *Dir* John Landis • *Scr* Michael Barrie, Jim Mulholland, from the play by Claude Magnier

Oscar and Lucinda ★★ 15
Romantic drama
1997 · US/Aus · Colour · 126min

Adapted from Peter Carey's Booker Prize-winning novel, this story about two Victorian eccentrics with a passion for gambling was never going to be an easy choice to make into a film. Unfortunately, the end result is an irritating and generally incomprehensible art movie. Anglican minister Ralph Fiennes's wagers heiress Cate Blanchett that he can transport a glass chapel across the Australian outback. AT Swearing, violence, sex scenes. 🅳🅥🅳

Ralph Fiennes *Oscar Hopkins/Oscar's great grandson* • Cate Blanchett *Lucinda Leplastrier* • Ciaran Hinds *Reverend Dennis Hasset* • Tom Wilkinson *Hugh Stratton* • Richard Roxburgh *Mr Jeffris* • Clive Russell *Theophilus* ■ *Dir* Gillian Armstrong • *Scr* Laura Jones, from the novel by Peter Carey

Oscar Wilde ★★★
Biographical drama 1959 · UK · BW · 96min

Emboldened by the Government's Wolfenden Report, British film-makers at the turn of the 1960s began to deal frankly with homosexual themes. This modest production, directed by Gregory Ratoff, who died months after the premiere, had its thunder stolen by the more ambitious *The Trials of Oscar Wilde*. Nevertheless it is well worth seeing, with Sir Ralph Richardson and Alexander Knox sparring in a grippingly staged courtroom scene, and Robert Morley, although too old, revealing hidden depths in the title role. DM

U SUITABLE FOR ALL   Uc SUITABLE ESPECIALLY FOR YOUNG CHILDREN (DVD ONLY)   PG PARENTAL GUIDANCE   12A UNDER 12s TO BE ACCOMPANIED (CINEMA ONLY)

Robert Morley *Oscar Wilde* • Phyllis Calvert *Constance Wilde* • John Neville *Lord Alfred Douglas* • Ralph Richardson *Sir Edward Carson* • Dennis Price *Robert Ross* • Alexander Knox *Sir Edward Clarke* • Edward Chapman *Marquis of Queensbury* • Martin Benson *George Alexander* ■ *Dir* Gregory Ratoff • *Scr* Jo Eisinger, from a play by Leslie Stokes, Sewell Stokes

Oslo, August 31st ★★★★ 15
Drama   2011 · Nor/Swe/Der/Ger · Colour · 90min

In director Joachim Trier's second feature (following *Reprise* in 2006) Anders Danielsen Lie (the star of *Reprise*) plays a 30-something writer on the verge of completing a drug rehabilitation programme, who sabotages the job interview that offers him a future and hooks up with old friends in the vague hope one can rouse him out of his suicidal disappointment and isolation. Each encounter exacerbates a growing despair that contrasts with the sights and sounds he witnesses around the city. It all sounds a bit doom-laden, but the gliding camera, shifts in focus and sound, deft editing and eloquent voiceovers enliven this intellectually challenging, compelling and poignant day-in-the-life odyssey. DP Norwegian +subtitles. Swearing, drug abuse. **DVD**

Anders Danielsen Lie *Anders* • Malin Crepin *Malin* • Akel Thanke *Therapist* • Hans Olav Brenner *Thomas* ■ *Dir* Joachim Trier • *Scr* Joachim Trier, Eskil Vogt, from the novel *Le Feu Follet* by Pierre Drieu La Rochelle

Osmosis Jones ★★★ PG
Part-animated comedy   2001 · US · Colour · 91min

Bobby and Peter Farrelly (*There's Something about Mary*) direct an intriguing mix of live-action and inventive animation starring arch slob Bill Murray. He plays a sloppy zoo worker with bad eating habits who becomes infected with a killer cold virus (voiced by Laurence Fishburne) intent on murdering him within 48 hours. Here's where the audience gets to explore Murray's animated innards, "the city of Frank", and meet maverick police corpuscle Osmosis Jones (Chris Rock) and his cold-cure pal Drix (David Hyde Pierce). The puns on bodily functions and fluids are aimed at the young. TH **DVD**

Bill Murray *Frank Detorri* • Chris Rock *Osmosis Jones, "Ozzy"* • Laurence Fishburne *Thrax* • David Hyde Pierce *Drix* • Brandy Norwood [*Brandy*] *Leah* • William Shatner *Mayor Phlegmming* ■ *Dir* Bobby Farrelly, Peter Farrelly • *Scr* Marc Hymar

Ossessione ★★★★ PG
Drama   1942 · It · BW · 134min

A drifter gets a job at a roadside café and has a torrid affair with the owner's wife who then asks her lover to murder her fat, loutish husband. Yes, this is the Italian version of *The Postman Always Rings Twice*, and it marked the directing debut of the Marxist aristocrat, Luchino Visconti. This transposition to the flat marshland of the Po Valley, with its working-class characters, drab settings and base morality, was banned by Mussolini's censors for its depiction of working-class life. The Fascists burned the negative, but Visconti managed to save a print. It was later credited with starting a new movement in Italian cinema called neorealism. AT Italian +subtitles. **DVD**

Clara Calamai *Giovanna* • Massimo Girotti *Gino* • Juan de Landa *The husband* • Elia Marcuzzo *Giuseppe Tavolato, "The Spaniard"* • Dhia Cristani *Anita* • Vittorio Duse *The lorry driver* ■ *Dir* Luchino Visconti • *Scr* Mario Alicata, Antonio Pietrangeli, Gianni Puccini, Giuseppe De Santis, Luchino Visconti, from the novel *The Postman Always Rings Twice* by James M Cain

The Osterman Weekend ★★★ 18
Thriller   1983 · US · Colour · 97min

In Sam Peckinpah's final film, Burt Lancaster is the CIA chief with presidential ambitions, who gets operative John Hurt to persuade TV journalist Rutger Hauer that there are Soviet agents among the guests assembled for a weekend get-together. Video gadgets push the atmosphere of post-Watergate paranoia to breaking point, but the confusion experienced by the characters is nothing compared to the audience's bafflement at the convoluted plot. TH Violence, swearing, brief nudity. **DVD**

Rutger Hauer *John Tanner* • John Hurt *Lawrence Fassett* • Craig T Nelson *Bernard Osterman* • Dennis Hopper *Richard Tremayne* • Chris Sarandon *Joseph Cardone* • Burt Lancaster *Maxwell Danforth* • Meg Foster *Ali Tanner* • Helen Shaver *Virginia Tremayne* ■ *Dir* Sam Peckinpah • *Scr* Ian Sharp, Ian Masters, from the novel by Robert Ludlum

Otello ★★★★ U
Opera   1986 · It · Colour · 117min

Franco Zeffirelli transposes Verdi's classic version of Shakespeare's tragedy into sweeping big-screen melodrama. Placido Domingo is magnificent as the jealous Moor, whose corruption by Iago crucifies his marriage to the gentle Desdemona. Domingo looks relaxed on screen, with Zeffirelli managing to remove the static tendencies of stage-bound singers to make a fluid and compelling film drama. Katia Ricciarelli is a delicate Desdemona, Justino Diaz a demonic Iago and Urbano Barberini a Cassio worthy of arousing crippling infidelity anxiety. One of the best films of opera ever made. LH Italian +subtitles. **DVD**

Placido Domingo *Otello* • Katia Ricciarelli *Desdemona* • Justino Diaz *Iago* • Petra Malakova *Emilia* • Urbano Barberini *Cassio* ■ *Dir* Franco Zeffirelli • *Scr* Franco Zeffirelli, from the libretto by Arrigo Boito for the opera by Giuseppe Verdi

Othello ★★★★★ U
Tragedy   1952 · LS/Fr/Mor/It · Colour · 89min

Orson Welles found filming Shakespeare's tale about the Moor far from straightforward – most disruptively, he had to close production down three times so he could go away and earn the money to continue. But it's testimony to the master film-maker's tremendous talent that he continually turned the many setbacks to his advantage. When the costumes failed to arrive, he improvised one of the movie's finest scenes, the murder in the Turkish bath; and he compensates for the lack of purpose-built sets by making inspired use of the north African architecture to sculpt a world of shadows and treachery. Perhaps the most cinematic Shakespeare adaptation ever. NPF **DVD**

Orson Welles *Othello* • Michael MacLiammoir *Iago* • Suzanne Cloutier *Desdemona* • Robert Coote *Roderigo* • Hilton Edwards *Brabantio* • Michael Laurence (1) *Cassio* • Fay Compton *Emilia* ■ *Dir* Orson Welles • *Scr* Orson Welles, from the play by William Shakespeare

Othello ★★★★ U
Tragedy   1955 · USSR · Colour · 103min

Having striven for 20 years to make this film, Sergei Yutkevitch got his just desserts by being named Best Director at Cannes. Working from a free translation by the novelist Boris Pasternak, and employing a symbolic palette to emphasise the play's physical and temperamental contrasts, Yutkevitch played down the Moor's rage to concentrate on the corruption of his nobility by the scheming Iago. Director-in-waiting Sergei Bondarchuk acquits himself admirably as Othello opposite his future wife, Irina Skobtseva, as the wrongfully accused Desdemona. DP Russian dubbed.

Sergei Bondarchuk *Othello* • Irina Skobtseva *Desdemona* • Andrei Popov *Iago* • Vladimir Soshalsky *Cassio* • E Vesnik *Roderigo* • Antonina Maximova *Emilia* ■ *Dir* Sergei Yutkevitch • *Scr* Sergei Yutkevitch, from a translation by Boris Pasternak of the play by William Shakespeare

Othello ★★★★ U
Tragedy   1965 · UK · Colour · 158min

Stagebound and elegantly lit by cinematographer Geoffrey Unsworth, this is a stunning transfer of Laurence Olivier's legendary National Theatre production to film. While it does not have the cinematic fireworks of Orson Welles's version, it is an indispensable record of Olivier's titanic, vigorously African performance as the Moor of Venice who "loved not wisely but too well". This also has the distinction of being the only Shakespearean film for which all four principals received Oscar nominations (Olivier, Maggie Smith, Frank Finlay and Joyce Redman) and features the screen debut of a young Derek Jacobi. AME **DVD**

Laurence Olivier *Othello* • Maggie Smith *Desdemona* • Frank Finlay *Iago* • Joyce Redman *Emilia* • Derek Jacobi *Cassio* • Robert Lang *Roderigo* • Kenneth Mackintosh *Lodovico* • Anthony Nicholls *Brabantio* • Sheila Reid *Bianca* ■ *Dir* Stuart Burge • *Scr* Margaret Unsworth, from the stage production by John Dexter of the play by William Shakespeare

Othello ★★★ 12
Tragedy   1995 · US/UK · Colour · 118min

Laurence Fishburne follows in the footsteps of Orson Welles and Laurence Olivier. Young, gifted and appropriately black, he plays the title role as a sensual, bald and tattooed soldier, and is joined by Irène Jacob as Desdemona and Kenneth Branagh as a magnificently seething Iago. Shakespeare's tragedy has been hacked roughly in half by director Oliver Parker whose choice of locations is a plus but whose scaling down is generally a minus. AT **DVD**

Laurence Fishburne *Othello* • Irène Jacob *Desdemona* • Kenneth Branagh *Iago* • Nathaniel Parker *Cassio* • Michael Maloney *Roderigo* • Anna Patrick *Emilia* • Nicholas Farrell *Montano* • Indra Ove *Bianca* • Michael Sheen *Lodovico* • André Oumansky *Gratiano* ■ *Dir* Oliver Parker • *Scr* Oliver Parker, from the play by William Shakespeare

The Other ★★★★ 12
Horror   1972 · US · Colour · 96min

A commercial flop, with no stars, too "arty" for popular taste, this highly atmospheric spook drama is much admired by aficionados. It is the only horror film from distinguished director Robert Mulligan, who adds beautiful visual touches to former actor Tom Tryon's screenplay, an adaptation of his own first novel. Set in 1935, the slow-moving but increasingly disturbing tale concerns a ten-year-old boy (a wonderful performance by Chris Udvarnoky) who claims that a series of murders are the work of his dead identical twin. The twins' grandmother is played by noted drama teacher Uta Hagen. Be prepared for a shocking climax. DM Swearing. **DVD** **Blu-ray**

Uta Hagen *Ada* • Chris Udvarnoky *Niles Perry* • Martin Udvarnoky *Holland Perry* • Diana Muldaur *Alexandra Perry* • Norma Connolly *Aunt Vee* • Victor French *Angelini* • Loretta Leversee *Winnie* • Lou Frizzell *Uncle George* • John Ritter *Rider* ■ *Dir* Robert Mulligan • *Scr* Thomas Tryon [Tom Tryon], from his novel

The Other Boleyn Girl ★★ 12
Historical romantic drama   2008 · UK/US · Colour · 110min

Justin Chadwick's adaptation of Philippa Gregory's novel certainly boasts an impressive cast, with Natalie Portman (Anne) and Scarlett Johansson (Mary) playing the Boleyn sisters. Their ambitious father (Mark Rylance) and uncle (David Morrisey) see an opportunity, as King Henry VIII (Eric Bana) becomes frustrated by Katherine of Aragon's failure to produce a surviving male heir. It's the demure Mary who first takes his fancy – much to the chagrin of her sister. Although Mary is presented as the heroine here, she comes across as a simpering idiot and there is little attempt to humanise the scheming Anne. With its crass dialogue and dubious, join-the-dots plotting, this tawdry tale has all the subtlety of an axe. SP Swearing, sex scenes. **DVD** **Blu-ray**

Natalie Portman *Anne Boleyn* • Scarlett Johansson *Mary Boleyn* • Eric Bana *Henry Tudor* • Jim Sturgess *George Boleyn* • Mark Rylance *Sir Thomas Boleyn* • Kristin Scott Thomas *Lady Elizabeth Boleyn* • David Morrissey *The Duke of*

Norfolk • Ana Torrent *Katherine of Aragon* ■ *Dir* Justin Chadwick • *Scr* Peter Morgan (1), from the novel by Philippa Gregory

The Other Guys ★★★ 12
Action comedy   2010 · US · Colour · 103min

This mismatched-cops comedy takes several well-aimed swipes at the action genre, blending knockabout farce with quick-witted humour. Will Ferrell and Mark Wahlberg play deskbound detectives envious of their all-guns-blazing frontline colleagues (played to the hilt by Samuel L Jackson and Dwayne Johnson), who get their chance while investigating a billionaire fraudster's building permit violation. What could have been a bog-standard buddy movie is elevated here by the two terrific leads, and the fine supporting cast also gets the opportunity to show off some comic talent. TeS Some violence, swearing, sexual references. **DVD** **Blu-ray**

Will Ferrell *Allen Gamble* • Mark Wahlberg *Terry Hoitz* • Samuel L Jackson *PK Highsmith* • Dwayne Johnson *Christopher Danson* • Eva Mendes *Dr Sheila Gamble* • Michael Keaton *Captain Gene Mauch* • Lindsay Sloane *Francine* ■ *Dir* Adam McKay • *Scr* Adam McKay, Chris Henchy

The Other Love ★★ PG
Romantic drama   1947 · US · BW · 88min

This larded, treacly plot comes firmly under the heading of Nonsense. Barbara Stanwyck is dying, as only a cinema diva can, but instead of taking the advice of devoted doctor David Niven, she hightails it with charismatic gambler Richard Conte. Niven pines, Conte leers and Stanwyck over-eggs the pudding alarmingly with every twinge. SH

Barbara Stanwyck *Karen Duncan* • David Niven *Dr Anthony Stanton* • Richard Conte *Paul Clermont* • Gilbert Roland *Croupier* • Joan Lorring *Celestine* • Richard Hale *Professor Linnaker* ■ *Dir* Andre De Toth • *Scr* Ladislas Fodor, Harry Brown, from the short story *Beyond* by Erich Maria Remarque

The Other Man ★★ 15
Drama   2008 · UK · Colour · 84min

A mysterious love triangle and the all-star cast of Liam Neeson, Antonio Banderas and Laura Linney can't save this ponderous romantic thriller from mediocrity. Based on a short story by novelist Bernhard Schlink (*The Reader*), it follows software exec Neeson as he uncovers details of an affair between his wife (Linney) and her lover (Banderas). Despite being handsomely shot, its plot proves embarrassingly slight. At its heart is a familiar story about whether we can ever really know those we love, yet it's executed with so little passion it might as well be about car upholstery. JR **DVD**

Liam Neeson *Peter* • Laura Linney *Lisa* • Antonio Banderas *Rafe* • Romola Garai *Abigail* • Craig Parkinson *George* • Paterson Joseph *Ralph* ■ *Dir* Richard Eyre • *Scr* Richard Eyre, Charles Wood, from a short story by Bernhard Schlink

Other Men's Women ★★★★
Melodrama   1931 · US · BW · 69min

Basically a conventional love-triangle story, this early talkie is given tremendous power and resonance by the vigorous direction of William A Wellman and the tight editing that was a trademark of the Warner Bros studio in the 1930s. Enacted in nocturnal, sometimes rainswept settings, it provides riveting viewing. In a typically audacious sequence, James Cagney, playing a minor role in his third film but clearly a star in the making, walks into a dance hall and breaks into an impromptu tap routine. A remarkable moment in an inventive movie. TV

Grant Withers *Bill* • Mary Astor *Lily* • Regis Toomey *Jack* • James Cagney *Ed* • Fred Kohler *Haley* • J Farrell MacDonald *Pegleg* • Joan Blondell *Marie* • Walter Long *Bixby* ■ *Dir* William A Wellman • *Scr* William K Wells, Maude Fulton, from a story by Maude Fulton

0

Other People's Money
★★★ 15

Comedy drama   1991 · US · Colour · 96min

Danny DeVito plays Larry the Liquidator, whose asset-stripping gaze falls upon the old-fashioned New England company run by stubborn Gregory Peck. However, the battle becomes complicated when he falls for the company's lawyer, Penelope Ann Miller, who is leading the fight against him. DeVito is charmingly sleazy, while Peck embodies honourable liberal capitalism. Norman Jewison's direction is smooth and he is well served by cinematographer Haskell Wexler. **JF** Swearing.

Danny DeVito *Lawrence Garfield* • Gregory Peck *Andrew Jorgenson* • Penelope Ann Miller *Kate Sullivan* • Piper Laurie *Bea Sullivan* • Dean Jones *Bill Coles* • RD Call *Arthur* • Mo Gaffney *Harriet* • Bette Henritze *Emma* • Tom Aldredge *Ozzie* ■ *Dir* Norman Jewison • *Scr* Alvin Sargent, from the play by Jerry Sterner

The Other Side of Midnight
★★★ 18

Melodrama   1977 · US · Colour · 158min

Based on a blockbuster novel by Sidney Sheldon, this melodrama runs for nearly three hours, covers the whole of the Second World War and its aftermath, and flits between the continents without pausing for breath. It has the courage of its clichés, so sometimes we laugh as the characters bump into each other across the years, tears and oceans. **AT**

Marie-France Pisier *Noelle Page* • John Beck *Larry Douglas* • Susan Sarandon *Catherine Douglas* • Raf Vallone *Constantin Demeris* • Clu Gulager *Bill Fraser* • Christian Marquand *Armand Gautier* • Michael Lerner *Barbet* ■ *Dir* Charles Jarrott • *Scr* Herman Raucher, Daniel Taradash, from the novel by Sidney Sheldon

The Other Side of Sunday
★★★

Comedy drama   1996 · Nor · Colour · 103min

Nominated for the best foreign film Oscar, this charming drama unassumingly captures the curiosity and contumacy of a strictly raised small-town teenager. But what sets it apart is a take on religion that unmistakeably echoes that of the great Danish film-maker, Carl Th Dreyer. This tragicomic study of repression and rebellion adroitly avoids both melodrama and the clichés of the rites-of-passage picture. But, thanks to Maria Theisen's spirited performance, there is also subtle power in Berit Nesheim's attack on the patriarchal nature of both church and state. **DP** Norwegian +subtitles.

Marie Theisen *Maria* • Bjørn Sundquist *Father* • Sylvia Salvesen *Mother* • Hildegunn Riise *Fru Tunheim* ■ *Dir* Berit Nesheim • *Scr* Berit Nesheim, Lasse Glomm, from the novel *Søndag (Sunday)* by Reidun Nortvedt

The Other Side of the Bed
★★★ 15

Romantic musical comedy
2002 · Sp · Colour · 104min

With Ernesto Alterio cheating on Paz Vega with best pal Guillermo Toledo's girlfriend Natalia Verbeke, the plot of this romantic comedy couldn't be more formulaic. But such is the eloquence of the dialogue, the aptitude of the cast and the action's slick shifts in tone and pace that it's easy to forgive the familiarity. However, it's harder to comprehend the decision to interrupt the farce with a series of second-rate musical numbers. **DP** Spanish +subtitles. Swearing, sex scenes. *DVD*

Ernesto Alterio *Javier* • Paz Vega *Sonia* • Guillermo Toledo *Pedro* • Natalia Verbeke *Paula* • Alberto San Juan *Rafa* • María Esteve *Pilar* • Ramón Barea *Sagaz* • Nathalie Poza *Lucía* ■ *Dir* Emilio Martínez-Lázaro • *Scr* David Serrano

The Other Side of the Door
★★★ 15

Horror   2016 · Ind/UK · Colour · 95min

The Walking Dead's Sarah Wayne Callies is the mum grieving for her son in India where the family antiques business is based, in this respectable nail-biter from the savvy Johannes Roberts. Performing a dark rite to help herself find closure, she unwittingly unleashes the ancient spirit of an evil goddess. This efficient supernatural shocker is at its best when Mumbai's evocative eeriness shines through. However, excellent production values and a *Pet Sematary* vibe mean its shortcomings are easily overlooked. **AJ** Violence.

Sarah Wayne Callies *Maria* • Jeremy Sisto *Michael* • Javier Botet *Myrtu* ■ *Dir* Johannes Roberts • *Scr* Johannes Roberts, Ernst Riera • *Cinematographer* Maxime Alexandre

The Other Side of the Mountain
★★★

Biographical drama   1975 · US · Colour · 99min

This is a superior and heart-wrenching biopic about Jill Kinmont, an Olympic-standard skier whose career was cut short when a fall left her paralysed. Marilyn Hassett makes an impressive film debut as Kinmont, portraying her as a fighter whose gutsiness initially arouses expectations of recovery that were destined to be unfulfilled. The film's modest success prompted a sequel three years later. **DA**

Marilyn Hassett *Jill Kinmont* • Beau Bridges *Dick Buek* • Belinda J Montgomery *Audra-Jo* • Nan Martin *June Kinmont* • William Bryant *Bill Kinmont* • Dabney Coleman *Dave McCoy* ■ *Dir* Larry Peerce • *Scr* David Seltzer, from the biography *A Long Way Up* by EG Valens

The Other Sister
★★ 15

Romantic drama   1999 · US · Colour · 130min

It needs a sure and delicate touch to use a mental disability as a dramatic device; otherwise, it's a tasteless gimmick to move the plot along. Sadly, despite a fine performance from Juliette Lewis, this is both clumsy and manipulative. Lewis is a rich San Francisco teenager fresh out of a mental institution. She wants to be a vet's assistant; despite the approval of father Tom Skerritt, but she has to fight mother Diane Keaton every step of the way. **TH**
DVD

Diane Keaton *Elizabeth* • Juliette Lewis *Carla Tate* • Tom Skerritt *Radley Tate* • Giovanni Ribisi *Danny* • Poppy Montgomery *Caroline* • Sarah Paulson *Heather* • Linda Thorson *Drew* • Joe Flanigan *Jeff* • Juliet Mills *Winnie* ■ *Dir* Garry Marshall • *Scr* Garry Marshall, Bob Brunner, from a story by Alexandra Rose, Blair Richwood

Other Voices, Other Rooms
★★ 12

Period drama   1995 · US/UK · Colour · 98min

British director David Rocksavage made an inauspicious start to his feature career with this achingly dull adaptation of Truman Capote's debut novel. Trotting out all those tired Deep South Gothic clichés, Rocksavage seems uncertain whether to concentrate on atmosphere, plot or character, and ends up fudging all three. David Speck works hard as the teenager sent to live with his suspiciously infirm father. As his disturbed cousins, Anna Thomson is twitchily timid, while Lothaire Bluteau's effete aesthete is embarrassingly melodramatic. **DP**

Lothaire Bluteau *Randolph Skully* • Anna Thomson [Anna Levine] *Amy Skully* • David Speck *Joel Sansom* • April Turner *Zoo* • Frank Taylor *Edward "Ed" R Sansom* ■ *Dir* David Rocksavage • *Scr* Sara Flanigan, David Rocksavage, from the novel by Truman Capote

The Other Woman
★★★ 12

Comedy   2014 · US · Colour · 104min

Cameron Diaz and Leslie Mann team up to bring down love rat Nikolaj Coster-Waldau in this bubbly comedy. Kate Upton proves to be a bit of a gooseberry as the third conspirator, but Mann shines in a slapstick turn as the wronged wife that finds her swinging between grief and rage like a drunken ninja. Director Nick Cassavetes (*The Notebook*) is certainly guilty of dragging out the action and overcooking the finale, but this all makes for good naughty fun, nonetheless. **SP** Swearing, sexual references. *DVD* ⟷

Cameron Diaz *Carly Whitten* • Leslie Mann *Kate King* • Kate Upton *Amber* • Nikolaj Coster-Waldau *Mark King* • Nicki Minaj *Lydia* • Taylor Kinney *Phil* ■ *Dir* Nick Cassavetes • *Scr* Melissa Stack

The Others
★★★ 12

Period horror thriller
2001 · US/Sp · Colour · 99min

Nicole Kidman gives a powerful turn as a highly strung woman living alone in a postwar Jersey mansion with her two light-sensitive children. It's when she engages a trio of new servants that her shadowy home suddenly turns very creepy indeed, as her daughter starts to see "things" and they all experience seemingly supernatural events. Relying on deliberately old-fashioned bumps in the night for suspense, Alejandro Amenábar (in his English-language debut feature) creates a study in terror that relies on presence, atmosphere and mood. **AJ** *DVD* ⓑⓛ

Nicole Kidman *Grace* • Fionnula Flanagan *Mrs Mills* • Christopher Eccleston *Charles* • Alakina Mann *Anne* • James Bentley *Nicholas* • Eric Sykes *Mr Tuttle* • Elaine Cassidy *Lydia* • Renée Asherson *Old lady* ■ *Dir/Scr* Alejandro Amenábar

Otherworld
★★★ 12A

Part-animated adventure
2003 · UK · Colour · 108min

This ambitious animation is based on a collection of Welsh myths, and director Derek Hayes concentrates on four "branches" to recount the tales of King Bendigeidfran's war with Ireland, Rhiannon's domestic woes and Lleu's adventures with his magician uncle, Gwydion. The live-action bookends involving three teenagers are an unfortunate miscalculation. However, once the trio's cartoon selves appear on a floating island, the complex plotlines begin to weave their spell. This occasionally gory fable may lack spectacle, but the folkloric aspects are fascinating. **DP**

Ioan Gruffudd *King Bendigeidfran* • Matthew Rhys *Lleu* • Daniel Evans *Dan* • Jenny Livesy *Rhiannon* • Paul McGann *King Matholwch* • Philip Madoc *Gwydion* • Lisa Palfrey *Arianrhod* • Anton Lesser *Teyrnon* ■ *Dir* Derek Hayes • *Scr* Martin Lamb, Penelope Middleboe, inspired by the Celtic text *Y Mabinogi (The Mabinogion)/Tales of Young Men*

Otley
★★★ PG

Spy spoof   1968 · UK · Colour · 87min

Even when it was released, this London-set Swinging Sixties spy spoof looked old-fashioned. Indeed, without the comic genius of writers Dick Clement and Ian La Frenais, it might have been a disaster. Forget about the labyrinthine plot that is impossible to follow and concentrate instead on the delightful performance of Tom Courtenay as the hapless petty criminal caught up in the slick world of spy Romy Schneider. **DM**

Tom Courtenay *Gerald Arthur Otley* • Romy Schneider *Imogen* • Alan Badel *Hadrian* • James Villiers *Hendrickson* • Leonard Rossiter *Johnston* • Freddie Jones *Proudfoot* • Fiona Lewis *Lin* • James Bolam *Albert* ■ *Dir* Dick Clement • *Scr* Ian La Frenais, Dick Clement, from the novel by Martin Waddell

Ouija
★★ 15

Horror   2014 · US · Colour · 89min

Death via dental floss is a first. But everything else about this contrived seance-gone-wrong saga is strictly by the bloodless horror handbook. It sees close friends uncovering the demonic powers of the titular board game after summoning up the spirit of a recently deceased suicide victim. Lead actress Olivia Cooke (*Bates Motel*) is the one saving grace among the bevy of bland TV stars, where the age-old seance question "Is anybody there?" can equally be aimed at those behind the camera. **AJ**

Olivia Cooke *Laine Morris* • Ana Coto *Sarah Morris* • Daren Kagasoff *Trevor* • Bianca Santos *Isabelle* ■ *Dir* Stiles White • *Scr* Stiles White, Juliet Snowden

Our Betters
★★★★

Comedy   1933 · US · BW · 79min

RKO producer David O Selznick deployed the polished gifts of director George Cukor and actress Constance Bennett for this now dated screen version of W Somerset Maugham's equally dated but far from uninteresting play. An acid and brittle comedy of manners exposing the amorality of the English upper classes, it focuses on an American heiress (Bennett) who marries an English aristocrat (Alan Mowbray), only to realise that her money was what attracted him. Bennett gives a meticulous performance in this sophisticated film. **RK**

Constance Bennett *Lady Pearl Grayston* • Gilbert Roland *Pepi D'Costa* • Anita Louise *Bessie* • Hugh Sinclair *Lord Bleane* • Alan Mowbray *Lord George Grayston* • Grant Mitchell *Thornton Clay* • Charles Starrett *Fleming Harvey* • Phoebe Foster *Princess* ■ *Dir* George Cukor • *Scr* Jane Murfin, Harry Wagstaff Gribble, from the play by W Somerset Maugham

Our Brand Is Crisis
★★★★ 15

Comedy drama based on a true story
2015 · US · Colour · 107min

Originally a vehicle for George Clooney, this fictionalised adaptation of Rachel Boynton's 2005 documentary would have completed an interesting political trilogy after *Goodnight, and Good Luck.* and *The Ides of March.* Featuring Sandra Bullock, it is perhaps a little lighter but no less provocative with the star in fine form as notorious US spin doctor "Calamity" Jane Bodine, who has been lured out of retirement to help a totalitarian right-wing politician win the 2002 elections in Bolivia. As meaty political satire this stands tall in a near-empty field. **DW** Swearing.

Sandra Bullock *"Calamity" Jane Bodine* • Billy Bob Thornton *Pat Candy* • Anthony Mackie *Ben* • Joaquim de Almeida *Castillo* • Ann Dowd *Nell* ■ *Dir* David Gordon Green • *Scr* Peter Straughan, from the 2006 documentary by Rachel Boynton

Our Children
★★★★ 15

Drama based on a true story
2012 · Bel/Fr/Lux/Swi · Colour · 106min

An exceptional performance by Emilie Dequenne dominates this powerful drama inspired by the harrowing case of Brussels mother of five Geneviève Lhermitte. When Moroccan-born Mounir (Tahar Rahim) marries her teacher Murielle (Dequenne), his fiercely protective Belgian benefactor, Dr Pinget (Niels Arestrup), suggests they share his home and soon begins to exercise his control. Director Joachim Lafosse skilfully shows how Murielle's comfortable domestic environment gradually becomes her prison and subtly suggests the reasons why she might be driven to commit her hideous crime. **DP** French, Arabic +subtitles. *DVD* ⓑⓛ

Emilie Dequenne *Murielle* • Tahar Rahim *Mounir* • Niels Arestrup *Dr Pinget* • Baya Belal *Rachida* • Stéphane Bissot *Françoise* ■ *Dir* Joachim Lafosse • *Scr* Joachim Lafosse, Thomas Bidegain, Matthieu Reynaert

Our Daily Bread
★★

Drama   1934 · US · BW · 75min

A young couple (Karen Morley and Tom Keene), victims of the Depression, leave the city for a derelict farm they've inherited. Revisiting the socially conscious territory of *The Crowd*, his 1928 silent masterpiece about the Depression, master director King Vidor picks up the same protagonists (played by different actors), to make a film of admirable and serious intentions, though lacking in pace and clarity. **RK**

Karen Morley *Mary Sims* • Tom Keene *John Sims* • John Qualen *Chris* • Barbara Pepper *Sally* • Addison Richards *Louie* • Harry Holman *Uncle Anthony* ■ *Dir* King Vidor • *Scr* King Vidor, Elizabeth Hill, Joseph L Mankiewicz

Our Dancing Daughters
★★★

Silent romantic drama   1928 · US · BW · 86min

A melodrama reflecting the morals and mores of the jazz age, this is the movie that catapulted Joan Crawford to major stardom. She plays a wild-living, hard-drinking, man-eating socialite who pulls herself out of the fast lane in the nick of time, settling for true love with John Mack Brown. Some of her friends are less fortunate. It's directed with an accurate sense of its milieu by Harry Beaumont, who went on to make several more films with Crawford. RK

Joan Crawford *Diana Medford* • John Mack Brown [Johnny Mack Brown] *Ben Blaine* • Nils Asther *Norman* • Dorothy Sebastian *Beatrice* • Anita Page *Ann* • Kathlyn Williams *Ann's mother* • Edward Nugent *Freddie* • Dorothy Cumming *Diana's mother* ■ *Dir* Harry Beaumont • *Scr* Josephine Lovett, Marion Ainslee (titles), Ruth Cummings (titles), from a story by Josephine Lovett

Our Family Wedding ★ 12

Romantic comedy   2010 · US · Colour · 98min

A Latino woman's decision to marry her black doctor boyfriend prompts consternation when their respective families get wind of the affair in this tepid ensemble comedy. It's certainly promising as an idea – think *Guess Who's Coming to Dinner* meets *Father of the Bride* – but the result's a dire disappointment. *Ugly Betty* star America Ferrara and groom-to-be Lance Gross perform creditably enough, but the sparring between the warring fathers (Carlos Mencia and a sorely miscast Forest Whitaker) proves painful to behold when the script provides only tediously forced confrontations and some pitiful knockabout farce. TJ Sexual references, brief swearing. DVD

Forest Whitaker *Brad Boyd* • America Ferrara *Lucia Ramirez* • Carlos Mencia *Miguel Ramirez* • Regina King *Angela* • Lance Gross *Marcus Boyd* • Shannyn Sossamon *Ashley McPhee* ■ *Dir* Rick Famuyiwa • *Scr* Wayne Conley, Malcolm Spellman, Rick Famuyiwa, from a story by Conley

Our First Christmas ★★

Seasonal drama   2008 · US · Colour · 89min

Julie Warner and Steven Eckholdt play the newlyweds whose planned first Christmas together is jeopardised when their children from previous marriages refuse to embrace new seasonal rituals. Cue an emotional tug of war, predictably followed by a blizzard of life lessons, as shrewd grandpa John Ratzenberger helps to show everyone the error of their actions. Even the feel-good finale is surprisingly underwhelming, despite piling on the sentiment to the max. SF

Julie Warner *Cindy* • John Ratzenberger *Joe* • Steven Eckholdt *Tom* • Katerina Graham *Bernie* ■ *Dir* Armand Mastroianni • *Scr* Edithe Swensen

Our Girl Friday ★★ U

Comedy   1953 · UK · Colour · 79min

This is one of those films that you think you've seen before until you realise that all the oh-so-familiar scenes have come from many different pictures. The story of amorous castaways competing for a single woman makes for a one-joke movie, although George Cole and Robertson Hare are amusing as the no-hopers tilting their caps at Joan Collins's very sexy Sadie. DP

Joan Collins *Sadie* • Kenneth More *Pat* • George Cole *Jimmy Carroll* • Robertson Hare *Gibble* • Hermione Gingold *Spinster* • Walter Fitzgerald *Captain* • Hattie Jacques *Mrs Patch* ■ *Dir/Scr* Noel Langley

Our Guys: Outrage in Glen Ridge ★★★ 15

Crime drama   1999 · US · Colour · 90min

This is an affecting fact-based TV drama with a solid cast, in which a group of affluent high-school jocks sexually assault a mildly mentally disabled 17-year-old girl (Heather Matarazzo). Determined detective Ally Sheedy faces a conspiracy of silence from the community, the school board and the police who are intent on protecting the winning athletes. Matarazzo, although at times unsympathetic, gives a stand-out performance, while Eric Stoltz, as the

prosecutor, invokes moral outrage. MC DVD

Eric Stoltz *Robert Laurino* • Ally Sheedy *Detective Kelly Brooks* • Heather Matarazzo *Leslie Faber* • Sara Botsford *Mrs Faber* • Scott Vickaryous *Paul Archer* ■ *Dir* Guy Ferland • *Scr* Paul Brown, from the book *Our Guys* by Bernard Lefkowitz

Our Hospitality ★★★★★ U

Silent comedy   1923 · US · BW · 65min

Buster Keaton co-directed with John Blystone this feudin' and fussin' masterpiece. He plays William, the last of the McKays, returning to Rockville to inherit his father's estate and falling foul of the vengeful Canfields, whose daughter (Natalie Talmadge) he's fallen in love with. Buster's beloved trains supply a hilarious track of running gags and there is some astonishing stuntwork, all of which Buster did himself. It's one of his few films in which he puts on drag – to escape the Canfields – and there's a sequence with a waterfall that is brilliant in its audacity. Three generations of Keatons are featured, from Joseph the elder to Buster's own son, while the period detail is at once comic and totally accurate. TH DVD

Buster Keaton *William McKay* • Kitty Bradbury *Aunt Mary* • Joseph Keaton [Joe Keaton] *Lem Doolittle, train engineer* • James Duffy *Sam Gardner, train guard* • Natalie Talmadge *Virginia Canfield* • Ralph Bushman *Clayton Canfield* • Buster Keaton Jr *William McKay as a baby* ■ *Dir* Buster Keaton, John Blystone [John G Blystone] • *Scr* Jean Havez, Clyde Bruckman, Joseph Mitchell

Our House ★★ 12

Black comedy   2003 · US · Colour · 85min

This ham-fisted slapstick farce is as much a test of patience for the viewer as elderly Irish neighbour Eileen Essell is for Ben Stiller and Drew Barrymore, who find that their new Brooklyn residence comes with Essell's overbearing upstairs tenant. Soon the dotty pensioner is driving them crazy and Stiller and Barrymore hire hitman James Remar to solve their problem. Even Stiller's genius comic timing can't compensate for the tastelessness or clumsy tone of this wildly uneven film. AJ Swearing. DVD BL

Ben Stiller *Alex Rose* • Drew Barrymore *Nancy Kendricks* • Eileen Essell *Mrs Connelly* • Harvey Fierstein *Kenneth* • Justin Theroux *Coop* • Robert Wisdom *Officer Dan* • James Remar *Chick* • Swoosie Kurtz *Jean* • Wallace Shawn *Herman* ■ *Dir* Danny DeVito • *Scr* Larry Doyle

Our House ★★

Drama   2006 · US · Colour · 110min

Screenwriter Michael Lach based this TV movie on his own experiences of helping the homeless. It's a sentimental saga, but its heart is in the right place. Five-time Emmy winner Doris Roberts stars as Ruth, a Beverly Hills widow who takes an overdose following the death of her husband. However, she's saved by vagrant Billy (Judy Reyes) and the two women strike up an unlikely friendship. Ruth begins to realise that some street people are decent folk facing personal crisis and not drop-outs and spongers and – to the chagrin of her daughter and neighbours – turns her mansion into a hostel. It's highly predictable, but competently done. DP

Doris Roberts *Ruth Galloway* • Judy Reyes *Billy* • Ellen Geer *Rose* • Jim Cody Williams *Tunes* • Stacy Solodkin *Dallas* • EJ Callahan *Max* ■ *Dir* Mark Griffiths • *Scr* Michael Lach

Our Idiot Brother ★★★ 15

Comedy drama   2011 · US · Colour · 86min

This gentle entertainment won few prizes for tight structure but its ensemble playing and Paul Rudd's goofy star turn lift it above the average. Rudd plays a bearded 21st-century refugee from the hippie era who, after doing time, is released into the care of his sisters. There, he unwittingly wreaks havoc on their relationships. The casting suggests a film intended for greater things, but if the whole feels ramshackle and overbearingly quirky, at least the star turns

mean you're never too far away from someone you like. SvM DVD

Paul Rudd *Ned* • Elizabeth Banks *Miranda* • Emily Mortimer *Liz* • Steve Coogan *Dylan* • Zooey Deschanel *Natalie* • Hugh Dancy *Christian* ■ *Dir* Jesse Peretz • *Scr* Evgenia Peretz, David Schisgall

Our Kind of Traitor ★★★ 15

Thriller   2016 · UK · Colour · 107min

What would you do if a mobster asked you for help? In Susanna White's globetrotting spy thriller based on a John le Carré novel, university lecturer Perry (Ewan McGregor) is surprisingly amenable, having discovered that his new friend, Dima (Stellan Skarsgård), launders money for the Russian Mafia and is looking for a way out. The plot does offer mild intrigue throughout as Perry dices with danger, and it receives a lift whenever the focus shifts to dogged MI6 agent Damian Lewis. Unfortunately, though, far too many scenes play out in a predictable manner. SC Violence, swearing, sex scenes, drug abuse, nudity.

Ewan McGregor *Perry* • Naomie Harris *Gail* • Stellan Skarsgård *Dima* • Damian Lewis *Hector* • Jeremy Northam *Aubrey Longrigg* • Mark Gatiss *Billy Matlock* ■ *Dir* Susanna White • *Scr* Hossein Amini, from John le Carré's novel

Our Lady of the Assassins ★★★

Drama   2000 · Col/Sp/Fr · Colour · 98min

Shot on digital video in Colombia, this is a visceral adaptation of Fernando Vallejo's novel about the rapidity with which corruption, brutality and greed can conquer a once proud community. Returning after 30 years in European exile, gay writer German Jaramillo is both appalled by the ruination of his home and determined to impart his memories to teenage hustler Anderson Ballesteros. However, by ensuring that the characters are as vibrant as the locale, Barbet Schroeder avoids any glib solutions. DP Spanish +subtitles.

German Jaramillo *Fernando* • Anderson Ballesteros *Alexis* • Juan David Restrepo *Wilmar* • Manuel Busquets *Alfonso* ■ *Dir* Barbet Schroeder • *Scr* Fernando Vallejo, from his novel *La Virgen de los Sicarios*

Our Lips Are Sealed ★★ PG

Comedy   2000 · US · Colour · 89min

Since striking out from the sitcom *Full House*, Mary-Kate and Ashley Olsen have built up quite a following in the United States. Unable to stay schtum after witnessing a crime, the twins are whisked off to Sydney under the FBI's Witness Protection Programme. But the mobsters soon catch up with them and a modicum of plot threatens to interrupt their shopping and sightseeing. With its patronising depiction of Australia as a land of endless beach parties, this is eminently resistible fluff. DP DVD

Ashley Olsen *Ashley Parker/Abby Turtleby* • Mary-Kate Olsen *Mary Kate Parker/Maddy Turtleby* • Jim Meskimen *Rick Parker/Stanley Turtleby* • Tamara Clatterbuck *Teri Parker/Shirley Turtleby* ■ *Dir* Craig Shapiro • *Scr* Elizabeth Kruger, Craig Shapiro

Our Little Girl ★★ U

Drama   1935 · US · BW · 62min

In this typical Shirley Temple vehicle, the star runs away to the circus while conspiring to reunite her estranged parents (Joel McCrea and Rosemary Ames) by driving the wolf (Lyle Talbot) from the door. Made at the peak of Temple's popularity, this was her weakest film of the period, an under-developed, slow-moving and predictable tale. The star is as charming as ever, particularly in her scenes with Poodles Hanneford as a clown, but this is only for her keenest admirers. TV DVD

Shirley Temple *Molly Middleton* • Rosemary Ames *Elsa Middleton* • Joel McCrea *Dr Donald Middleton* • Lyle Talbot *Rolfe Brent* • Erin O'Brien-Moore *Sarah Boynton* • Poodles Hanneford *Circus performer* ■ *Dir* John S Robertson • *Scr* Stephen Avery, Allen Rivkin, Jack Yellen, from the story *Heaven's Gate* by Florence Leighton Pfalzgraf

Our Little Sister ★★★★ PG

Drama   2015 · Jpn · Colour · 127min

Perhaps Hirokazu Koreeda's most restrained work to date. The story focuses on three sisters who discover they have a stepsister, Suzu, when they attend their father's funeral. On a whim, the trio invite the girl to come and live with them. It's handsomely shot to emphasise the sensual pleasures that Suzu discovers with her sisters: cherry blossom, orchards of greengages, a local mackerel dish, fireworks, little moments the like of which Koreeda builds into an exquisite life-affirming collage. WI Japanese +subtitles.

Haruka Ayase *Sachi* • Masami Nagasawa *Yoshino* • Kaho *Chika* • Suzu Hirose *Suzu Asano* • Ryo Kase *Sakashita* ■ *Dir* Hirokazu Koreeda • *Scr* Hirokazu Koreeda, from the graphic novel *Umimachi Diary* by Akimi Yoshida

Our Man Flint ★★★ PG

Spy spoof   1966 · US · Colour · 102min

The success of Ian Fleming's 007 led to a rash of Bond spoofs in the 1960s, and Derek Flint was one of the better creations. James Coburn stars as the playboy, martial artist and owner of a gadget-packed cigarette lighter boasting 82 uses ("83 if you want to light a cigar") who is recruited by intelligence agency Zowie when scientists threaten to throw the world into meteorological turmoil. The studio-bound locations betray a modest budget, but the panther-like Coburn keeps things moving, throwing himself into the chop-socky action and flashing those pearly whites with glee. JH DVD

James Coburn *Derek Flint* • Lee J Cobb *Cramden* • Gila Golan *Gila* • Edward Mulhare *Malcolm Rodney* • Benson Fong *Dr Schneider* • Shelby Grant *Leslie* • Sigrid Valdis *Anna* • Gianna Serra *Gina* • Helen Funai *Sakito* ■ *Dir* Daniel Mann • *Scr* Hal Fimberg, Ben Starr, from a story by Hal Fimberg

Our Man in Havana ★★★ PG

Comedy drama   1959 · UK · BW · 102min

What a different film this would have been if Graham Greene had been able to overcome his antipathy towards Alfred Hitchcock. Instead, he offered the film rights to his amusing spy spoof to Carol Reed and Hitch went off to make *Psycho*. Reed drew deft performances from his superb cast, with Alec Guinness in fine fettle as the vacuum cleaner salesman-turned-agent. But he seemed uncertain how dark to make the action once the joke took its sinister turn. DP DVD

Alec Guinness *Jim Wormold* • Burl Ives *Doctor Hasselbacher* • Maureen O'Hara *Beatrice Severn* • Ernie Kovacs *Captain Segura* • Noël Coward *Hawthorne* • Ralph Richardson *"C"* • Jo Morrow *Milly Wormold* ■ *Dir* Carol Reed • *Scr* Graham Greene, from his novel

Our Man in Marrakesh ★★ U

Spy spoof   1966 · UK · Colour · 93min

The excellent Tony Randall stars as an American tourist caught up in spy antics in Morocco. The scenery is fabulous and the second-rung supporting cast fun to watch, but the script and production budget would defeat the hardiest director. Still, veteran professionals such as Herbert Lom, Wilfrid Hyde White and Terry-Thomas do what they can with the material, and Klaus Kinski and John Le Mesurier turn up, too. TS

Tony Randall *Andrew Jessel* • Senta Berger *Kyra Stanovy* • Terry-Thomas *El Caid* • Herbert Lom *Narim Casimir* • Wilfrid Hyde White *Arthur Fairbrother* • Grégoire Aslan *Achmed* • John Le Mesurier *George Lillywhite* • Klaus Kinski *Jonquil* ■ *Dir* Don Sharp • *Scr* Peter Yeldham, from a story by Peter Welbeck [Harry Alan Towers]

Our Miss Fred ★★ PG

Second World War comedy   1972 · UK · Colour · 91min

Danny La Rue, Britain's most popular female impersonator during the 1970s, seems terribly constricted in his one major film, an old-fashioned wartime comedy written by distinguished playwright Hugh Leonard. Soldier La Rue is playing a woman on stage in France when the Germans invade. He escapes, wearing his costume, and, somewhat implausibly, remains in drag as he evades the enemy. The photography is quite pretty, which is more than can be said for La Rue, already somewhat matronly. DM *DVD*

Danny La Rue *Fred Wimbush* • Alfred Marks *General Brincker* • Lance Percival *Smallpiece* • Frances de la Tour *Miss Lockhart* ■ *Dir* Bob Kellett • *Scr* Hugh Leonard

Our Modern Maidens ★★
Silent drama 1929 · US · BW · 75min

Capitalising on the success of *Our Dancing Daughters* (1928), MGM again starred Joan Crawford as a socialite in this follow-up romance, which was also released as a talkie. Anita Page returns as well for a second outing, and is joined by Rod La Rocque. But the main focus of the movie was the on-screen love affair between Crawford (dressed by Adrian, as she would be for many years) and Douglas Fairbanks Jr; they were the hot gossip item in Hollywood at the time and would soon be married in real life. RK

Joan Crawford *Billie* • Rod La Rocque *Abbott* • Douglas Fairbanks Jr *Gil* • Anita Page *Kentucky* • Edward Nugent *Reg* • Josephine Dunn *Ginger* ■ *Dir* Jack Conway • *Scr* Josephine Lovett, Marian Ainslee, Ruth Cummings, from a story by Josephine Lovett • *Costume Designer* Adrian

Our Mother's House ★★★
Drama 1967 · UK/US · Colour · 105min

This weird and often chilling horror story is about some children (including a pre-*Oliver!* Mark Lester) who bury their mother's dead body in the garden and carry on as if she were still alive. Then shifty cockney Dirk Bogarde shows up, claiming to be their errant father. Bogarde and director Jack Clayton believed they had failed, but Luchino Visconti thought it was a "beautiful" film and hired Bogarde for *The Damned* and *Death in Venice* on the strength of it. AT

Dirk Bogarde *Charlie Hook* • Margaret Brooks *Elsa Hook* • Pamela Franklin *Diana Hook* • Louis Sheldon Williams *Hubert Hook* • John Gugolka *Dunstan Hook* • Mark Lester (2) *Jiminee Hook* • Sarah Nicholls [Phoebe Nicholls] *Gerty Hook* • Gustav Henry *Willy Hook* ■ *Dir* Jack Clayton • *Scr* Jeremy Brooks, Haya Harareet, from the novel by Julian Gloag

Our Relations ★★★ U
Comedy 1936 · US · BW · 64min

In this masterful double act, Laurel and Hardy turn in four great comic performances for the price of two. Comic mayhem is assured when family men Laurel and Hardy encounter their long lost identical twin brothers, a pair of jolly sailors who are enjoying shore leave. The inevitable mistaken identity occurs and our heroes find themselves up to their armpits in misunderstandings and sophisticated slapstick. Delightful, sometimes hilarious, shenanigans. DF *DVD*

Stan Laurel *Stan/Alfie Laurel* • Oliver Hardy *Ollie/Bert Hardy* • Sidney Toler *Captain of the SS Periwinkle* • Alan Hale *Joe Groagan, waiter* • Daphne Pollard *Mrs Daphne Hardy* • Betty Healy *Mrs Betty Laurel* ■ *Dir* Harry Lachman • *Scr* Richard Connell, Felix Adler, Charles Rogers, Jack Jevne, from the short story *The Money Box* by WW Jacobs

Our Town ★★
Period drama 1940 · US · BW · 87min

This exercise in Hollywood bathos is based on Thornton Wilder's play about a small village in New Hampshire where a boy and girl's childhood friendship leads to adolescent romance, marriage and a tragic ending, which Hollywood tinkered with. An on-screen narrator - local pharmacist Frank Craven - guides us through the town and the 1901, 1904 and 1913 settings, but mostly we have William Holden and Martha Scott as the lovers. This is often like wading through an ocean of the stickiest maple syrup, but the Oscar-nominated music is by Aaron Copland. AT *DVD*

Frank Craven *Mr Morgan, the narrator* • William Holden (2) *George Gibbs* • Martha Scott *Emily Webb* • Fay Bainter *Mrs Gibbs* • Beulah Bondi *Mrs Webb* • Thomas Mitchell *Dr Gibbs* • Guy Kibbee *Editor Webb* ■ *Dir* Sam Wood • *Scr* Thornton Wilder, Frank Craven, Harry Chandlee, from the play by Thornton Wilder • *Music* Aaron Copland

Our Very Own ★★ U
Drama 1950 · US · BW · 88min

Whenever producer Samuel Goldwyn announced a serious drama about a socially significant subject, you could bet your bottom dollar that you were in for a cosy domestic melodrama with just the vaguest whiff of controversy about it. That's certainly what you get here in this underwritten and overplayed saga, in which spoiled teenager Ann Blyth snubs parents Jane Wyatt and Donald Cook on learning she's been adopted. DP

Ann Blyth *Gail* • Jane Wyatt *Lois Macaulay* • Donald Cook *Fred Macaulay* • Farley Granger *Chuck* • Joan Evans *Joan* • Ann Dvorak *Mrs Lynch* • Natalie Wood *Penny* • Gus Schilling *Frank* • Phyllis Kirk *Zaza* • Jessie Grayson *Violet* ■ *Dir* David Miller (1) • *Scr* F Hugh Herbert • *Cinematographer* Lee Garmes

Our Vines Have Tender Grapes ★★★★ U
Drama 1945 · US · BW · 105min

This warm-hearted MGM drama contains a simply superb performance from Edward G Robinson as the Norwegian dad of lovable little Margaret O'Brien, set against a Wisconsin (though largely studio) background. There's not a lot of plot as incident follows incident: the barn burns down, the floods come, there's a quarrel over some roller skates, the circus passes through town... There's a boring romance, too, but don't be put off: this is a movie of great charm, well directed by Roy Rowland. TS

Edward G Robinson *Martinius Jacobson* • Margaret O'Brien *Selma Jacobson* • James Craig *Nels Halverson* • Agnes Moorehead *Bruna Jacobson* • Jackie "Butch" Jenkins *Arnold Hanson* • Morris Carnovsky *Bjorn Bjornson* ■ *Dir* Roy Rowland • *Scr* Dalton Trumbo, from the novel by George Victor Martin

Out for a Kill ★★ 15
Crime action drama 2003 · US · Colour · 86min

Steven Seagal cobbles together elements from *Hard to Kill* and *Out for Justice* in a bullish attempt to give this Indiana Jones clone a kung fu kick. Seagal's archaeologist is framed for smuggling narcotics by a Tong crime lord, but then his wife is murdered and the oaken Seagal reveals that beneath his academic exterior lurks a martial artist. The ending, editing and effects are pretty ropey, but the real letdown is the ham-fisted fight choreography. DP Violence, swearing, drug abuse, nudity. *DVD*

Steven Seagal *Robert Burns* • Corey Johnson *Ed Grey* • Michelle Goh *Tommie Ling* • Kata Dobo *Maya Burns* • Elaine Tan *Luo Yi* • Michael Junior Harvey *King* ■ *Dir* Michael Oblowitz • *Scr* Danny Lerner, Dennis Dimster-Denk

Out for Justice ★★ 18
Action crime drama 1991 · US · Colour · 87min

Steven Seagal gets more dialogue than in all his other movies put together, in this lukewarm attempt to give him a lot more heart and soul. He plays a Brooklyn cop who comes up against old neighbourhood foe William Forsythe, resulting in much retaliatory violence. Frankly, Seagal is no actor and his career has been founded upon his ability to look cool in combat situations, rather than convey the sort of softly spoken sadness he's aiming for here. JC Swearing, violence, drug abuse, nudity. *DVD*

Steven Seagal *Gino Felino* • William Forsythe *Richie Madano* • Jerry Orbach *Detective Ronnie Donziger* • Jo Champa *Vicky Felino* • Sal Richards *Frankie* • Gina Gershon *Patti Madano* ■ *Dir* John Flynn • *Scr* David Lee Henry, Steven Seagal

Out in the Dark ★★★ 15
Romantic drama 2012 · Is/US · Colour · 95min

Following on from films like *Yossi & Jagger*, writer/director Michael Mayer puts a political spin on the problem of being gay in contemporary Israel. It might have been enough for Tel Aviv lawyer Roy (Michael Aloni) and Ramallah student Nimr (Nicholas Jacob) to challenge cultural convention by having a passionate affair. But Mayer overcomplicates matters by having Nimr's brother belong to an Islamic fundamentalist cadre. The switches between love story, melodrama and tense thriller are slightly cumbersome, but the leads are convincing and the restless handheld camerawork enables Mayer to convey the dangers of being different in a tinderbox society. DP Hebrew, Arabic +subtitles.

Nicholas Jacob *Nimr Mashrawi* • Michael Aloni *Roy Schaefer* • Jameel Khoury *Nabil Mashrawi* • Alon Pdut *Gil* ■ *Dir* Michael Mayer (2) • *Scr* Michael Mayer (2), Yael Shafrir

Out of Africa ★★★★ PG
Biographical drama 1985 · US · Colour · 154min

Or "Afreeka" as Meryl Streep would have it, with a bizarre Danish accent that manages to overshadow her entire performance as awkward, free-spirited writer and farmer Karen Blixen. This is a beautifully filmed movie, with director Sydney Pollack propelling the camera across the lush, Kenyan country teeming with all manner of exotic beasts. The other exotic beasts – Streep, Klaus Maria Brandauer as her husband and Robert Redford as her adventurer lover - overact on a level to match the magnificence of the backdrop, but with this cast it is still eminently watchable stuff. What the movie loses in emotional realism it gains in epic audacity. SH *DVD* 🔵

Meryl Streep *Karen* • Robert Redford *Denys Finch Hatton* • Klaus Maria Brandauer *Baron/ Hans* • Michael Kitchen *Berkeley Cole* • Malick Bowens *Farah* • Joseph Thiaka *Kamante* • Stephen Kinyanjui *Kinanjui* • Michael Gough *Lord Delamere* • Suzanna Hamilton *Felicity* • Rachel Kempson *Lady Belfield* ■ *Dir* Sydney Pollack • *Scr* Kurt Luedtke, from the autobiographical books by Isak Dinesen [Karen Blixen], from *Isak Dinesen: the Life of a Storyteller* by Judith Thurman, from *Silence Will Speak* by Errol Trzebinski • *Cinematographer* David Watkin • *Music* John Barry (1)

Out of Darkness ★★★
Biographical drama 1990 · US · Colour · 89min

This clumsy biopic rather dims the brightness of its subject, Albert Schweitzer, musician, intellectual, missionary and Nobel Peace Prize winner, who rejected European acclaim to minister to disease-ridden natives in the African jungle. It's not a whitewash - according to this he ran his deliberately run-down hospital like a tyrant - but its simplistic plot doesn't do the man justice. However, Malcolm McDowell is on top form. TH Some violence, nudity.

Malcolm McDowell *Dr Albert Schweitzer* • Susan Strasberg *Helene Schweitzer* • Andrew Davis Lionel Curtis • Helen Jessop *Amanda Hampton* • John Carson *Horton Herschel* • Henry Cele *Onganga* ■ *Dir* Gray Hofmyer [Gray Hofmeyr] • *Scr* Michel Potts, Patrick Lee

Out of Darkness ★★ 15
Drama 1994 · US · Colour · 87min

Given her impressive performance in the Billie Holliday biopic *Lady Sings the Blues*, it's surprising that soul diva Diana Ross hasn't appeared more on the screen. With this, her TV-movie debut, she gets her chance to sink her teeth into a good meaty role as a woman suffering from schizophrenia, who, after years of being a recluse, is coaxed back into normal society. Sadly, Larry Elikann's direction is a touch on the bland side. JF

Diana Ross *Paulie Cooper* • Ann Weldon *Virginia Cooper* • Beah Richards *Mrs Cooper* • Lindsay Crouse *Kim Donaldson* • Rhonda Stubbins White *Zoe Price* • Carl Lumbly *Addison Haig* ■ *Dir* Larry Elikann • *Scr* Barbara Turner

Out of Reach ★★ 15
Action drama 2004 · US/Pol · Colour · 82min

It's not often that you get to hear characters thinking, but this is just one of the unusual tactics adopted by Hong Kong director Po Chih Leong in this otherwise workaday Steven Seagal vehicle. Seagal plays a retired government agent who corresponds with Polish orphan Ida Nowakowska, a resident at a hostel he helped to establish. When she suddenly disappears, Seagal travels to Poland to investigate. DP Violence, swearing. *DVD*

Steven Seagal *William Lancing* • Ida Nowakowska *Irena Morawska* • Agnieszka Wagner *Kasia Lato* • Matt Schulze *Faisal* • Krzysztof Pieczynski *Ibo* • Robbie Gee *Lewis Morton* • Murat Yilmaz *Azimi* • Nick Brimble *Mister Elgin* ■ *Dir* Po Chih Leong • *Scr* Trevor Miller, James Townsend

Out of Season ★★ 18
Drama 1975 · UK · Colour · 86min

This stagey, moody, ambiguous love triangle, played in and around a holiday hotel in winter, will either intrigue or irritate, depending on one's predilection. The plot, such as it is, consists of the sex/power games played by three people: a middle-aged woman (Vanessa Redgrave), her teenage daughter (Susan George) and an American (Cliff Robertson) who enters their lives 20 years after his affair with the older woman. Director Alan Bridges cleverly teases suspense from the conflict, but the female roles are, by today's standards, sexual stereotypes. DM

Vanessa Redgrave *Ann* • Cliff Robertson *Joe* • Susan George *Joanna* ■ *Dir* Alan Bridges • *Scr* Eric Bercovici, Reuben Bercovich

Out of Sight ★★★★ 15
Romantic crime drama 1998 · US · Colour · 117min

George Clooney and Jennifer Lopez sizzle in director Steven Soderbergh's sexy, sly and snappy crime caper, which neatly combines its 1970s heist-picture roots with sparkling romantic comedy. The Elmore Leonard plot gets a classy screen makeover as the stars on opposite sides of the law fight their instant attraction when robber Clooney escapes from prison and cop Lopez vows to bring him to justice. Using intricate flashbacks and a keen visual style, Soderbergh takes a sharp script and weaves it into an ambitious and accomplished work. AJ Violence, swearing. *DVD* 🔵

George Clooney *Jack Foley* • Jennifer Lopez *Karen Sisco* • Ving Rhames *Buddy Bragg* • Don Cheadle *Maurice (Snoopy) Miller* • Dennis Farina *Marshall Sisco* • Albert Brooks *Richard Ripley* • Michael Keaton *Ray Nicolette* • Samuel L Jackson *Hejira Henry* ■ *Dir* Steven Soderbergh • *Scr* Scott Frank, from the novel by Elmore Leonard

Out of the Blue ★★
Comedy 1947 · US · BW · 84min

Displaying an unexpected flair for comedy, George Brent is a Greenwich Village resident, married to Carole Landis and feuding with his exotic artist neighbour (Turhan Bey). With Landis away, Brent invites interior designer Ann Dvorak in for a drink; already pretty loaded, she passes out. He thinks she's dead and dumps her body on Bey's porch. The plot might signal *film noir*, but what you actually get, under Leigh Jason's direction, is a chaotic mix of black farce, slapstick and screwball comedy. RK

George Brent *Arthur Earthleigh* • Virginia Mayo *Deborah Tyler* • Turhan Bey *David Gelleo* • Ann Dvorak *Olive Jensen* • Carole Landis *Mae Earthleigh* ■ *Dir* Leigh Jason • *Scr* Vera Caspary, Walter Bullock, Edward Eliscu, from a story by Vera Caspary

Out of the Blue ★★ 15
Drama 1980 · US/Can · Colour · 89min

Dysfunctional family relationships are examined in a typically downbeat fashion by director Dennis Hopper. He also plays the ex-con whose return to his put-upon wife (Sharon Farrell) and rebellious teenage daughter (an exceptional Linda Manz) leads to intense conflict and inevitable tragedy. While not a pretty picture, it is one that occasionally resonates with honest emotion. AJ **DVD**

Linda Manz *Cindy "CeBe" Barnes* • Sharon Farrell *Kathy Barnes* • Dennis Hopper *Don Barnes* • Raymond Burr *Dr Brean* ■ *Dir* Dennis Hopper • *Scr* Leonard Yakir, Gary Jules Jouvenat, Brenda Nielson

Out of the Blue ★★★ 15
Drama based on a true story 2006 · NZ · Colour · 98min

Director Robert Sarkies first film was the cheerful black comedy *Scarfies*, a sort of kiwi take on *Shallow Grave*. His second feature, based on the worst case of mass murder in New Zealand's history, is a much darker affair that chillingly details the events leading up to the killing of 13 people in the sleepy seaside village of Aramoana in November 1990. The massacre remains a sensitive subject in New Zealand and Sarkies treats the incident with the respect it deserves. Expat star Karl Urban (*The Bourne Supremacy*) receives top billing as the local bobby, although the film belongs to Matthew Sutherland, who provides a subtle portrait of evil as the disturbed gunman. JF **DVD**

Karl Urban *Nick Harvey* • Matthew Sunderland *David Gray* • Lois Lawn *Helen Dickson* • Simon Ferry *Garry Holder* • Tandi Wright *Julie Anne Bryson* • Paul Glover *Paul Knox* ■ *Dir* Robert Sarkies • *Scr* Robert Sarkies, Graeme Tetley, from the non-fiction book *Aramoana: Twenty Two Hours of Terror* by Bill O'Brien

Out of the Clouds ★★ U
Drama 1954 · UK · Colour · 76min

This was the last and least in the series of compendium dramas made by Ealing Studios by director Basil Dearden and producer Michael Relph. This time, the newly expanded London Airport forms the backdrop for vignettes that put passengers and pilots alike through their clichéd paces. The documentary-style glimpses into the day-to-day running of the airport are fascinating, but the performances are no more than adequate. DP **DVD**

Anthony Steel *Gus Randall* • Robert Beatty *Nick Milbourne* • David Knight *Bill Steiner* • Margo Lorenz *Leah Roche* • James Robertson-Justice *Captain Brent* • Eunice Gayson *Penny Henson* • Isabel Dean *Mrs Malcolm* • Michael Howard *Purvis* • Gordon Harker *Taxi driver* ■ *Dir* Basil Dearden • *Scr* John Eldridge, Michael Relph, Rex Rienits, from the novel *The Springboard* by John Fores

Out of the Dark ★★★ 18
Thriller 1988 · US · Colour · 83min

In an original take on the serial-killer genre, a murderer in a clown mask kills staff members of a phone-sex service one by one. Director Michael Schroeder lays on the visual agony, while Cameron Dye and Lynn Danielson emote strenuously, but the real hysteria comes from actors such as Paul Bartel (a Roger Corman alumnus) and Divine, cast here a police detective! TH

Cameron Dye *Kevin/Bobo* • Karen Black *Ruth* • Lynn Danielson *Kristi* • Karen Witter *Jo Ann* • Starr Andreeff *Camille* • Karen Mayo-Chandler *Barbara* • Bud Cort *Stringer* • Divine *Detective Langella* • Paul Bartel (1) *Motel clerk* • Tab Hunter *Driver* • Lainie Kazan *Hooker Nancy* ■ *Dir* Michael Schroeder • *Scr* Zane W Levitt, J Gregory DeFelice

Out of the Dark ★★ 15
Supernatural horror 2014 · US/Col/Sp · Colour · 89min

Julia Stiles and Scott Speedman play the tormented couple with cause to regret moving to Colombia to run the family business in this haunted-house horror. Everything seems fairly idyllic until supernatural shenanigans put their little girl (Pixie Davies) at the mercy of mysterious masked phantoms. Spanish director Lluís Quílez's first feature certainly looks good (thanks to the Bogota locations) and is not bereft of atmosphere, but it soon begins to lumber along, even when the panicky parents have something to get panicky about. It's a shame because the cast,

including Stephen Rea as Stiles's shifty dad, is a good one. JA English, Spanish +subtitles. Violence. **DVD**

Julia Stiles *Sarah Harriman* • Scott Speedman *Paul Harriman* • Stephen Rea *Jordan* • Pixie Davies *Hannah Harriman* • Vanesa Tamayo *Catalina* ■ *Dir* Lluís Quílez • *Scr* Javier Gullón, Alex Pastor, David Pastor

Out of the Darkness ★★★★
Crime thriller based on a true story 1985 · US · Colour · 96min

A strong central role in this TV movie attracted big name Martin Sheen, and he doesn't let anybody down. He is superb as detective Ed Zigo, who helped to solve the "Son of Sam" murders in the late 1970s, and he is almost matched by stage actor Robert Trebor as the killer. Sheen's son Charlie, later a major star in his own right, makes a brief appearance. NF

Martin Sheen *Ed Zigo* • Hector Elizondo *Father George* • Matt Clark *John Hubbard* • Jennifer Salt *Ann Zigo* • Eddie Egan *Tom Duncan* • Robert Trebor *David Berkowitz* • Charlie Sheen ■ *Dir* Jud Taylor • *Scr* TS Cook

Out of the Fog ★★★
Crime drama 1941 · US · BW · 84min

A Brooklyn tailor and a short-order chef enjoy their little fishing trips around the bay, until a minor league gangster moves in, offering them protection and offering the tailor's daughter something else. More of a character study than a thriller, it spins on a surprising twist and then goes on to become a sentimental tale about exploitation. A good cast, though. AT

John Garfield *Harold Goff* • Ida Lupino *Stella Goodwin* • Thomas Mitchell *Jonah Goodwin* • Eddie Albert *George Watkins* • George Tobias *Gregor Propotkin* • John Qualen *Olaf Johnson* • Aline MacMahon *Florence Goodwin* ■ *Dir* Anatole Litvak • *Scr* Robert Rossen, Jerry Wald, Richard Macaulay, from the play *The Gentle People* by Irwin Shaw

Out of the Furnace ★★★ 15
Thriller 2013 · US/UK · Colour · 111min

Family loyalty counts for everything in this second film from *Crazy Heart* writer/director Scott Cooper. It's set in a fading Pennsylvania steel town where dire economic straits send two brothers down dangerous pathways. Christian Bale is absolutely exceptional as a decent man running out of options when his volatile Iraq-vet sibling (Casey Affleck) gets in too deep with local loan shark Willem Dafoe and badass psycho Woody Harrelson. A strong sense of place and full-on performances keep it watchable, yet it falls short of its 1970s cinematic forbears like *Deliverance* by veering off into a bare-knuckle boxing subplot. See it for Bale, though, who doesn't just play his part, he seems to live it. TJ Violence, swearing, drug abuse. **DVD**

Christian Bale *Russell Baze* • Woody Harrelson *Harlan DeGroat* • Casey Affleck *Rodney Baze Jr* • Forest Whitaker *Wesley Barnes* • Willem Dafoe *John Petty* • Zoë Saldana *Lena Taylor* • Sam Shepard *Gerald "Red" Baze* ■ *Dir* Scott Cooper • *Scr* Scott Cooper, Brad Ingelsby

Out of the Woods ★★
Drama 2005 · US · Colour · 87min

The committed playing of the cast takes some of the mawkishness out of this TV-movie drama. The story starts slowly, as LA lawyer Jason London struggles to cope with his finances and commitment-craving girlfriend, Meredith Salenger. But once he heads into the backwoods to find his eccentric grandfather, things begin to perk up. Ed Asner has a bit of fun as the old-timer who has rejected consumer society and now lives a naturist existence. Unfortunately, director Stephen Bridgewater dilutes this entertaining situation with a needless subplot. DP Violence, swearing.

Edward Asner *Jack Green* • Jason London *Matt Fleming* • Missy Crider *Gwen Blitzer* • Don R Williams *[Don Williams] Mr Fleming* • Mel Harris *Mrs Fleming* • Meredith Salenger *Linda* • Sean Squire *Charles* ■ *Dir* Stephen W Bridgewater [Stephen Bridgewater] • *Scr* Jeffrey Alan [Jeff] Schechter

Out of This World ★★★
Musical 1945 · US · BW · 96min

Bing Crosby is heard but not seen in this amusingly satirical look at fame and pop fans, 1940s-style. Eddie Bracken is the small-town telegram boy who sings like Crosby and is taken to New York by Diana Lynn, the leader of a girls' band. Crosby dubbed the songs, including the enduring title number by Harold Arlen and Johnny Mercer. Crosby's four sons can be seen as part of Bracken's adoring audience. TV

Eddie Bracken *Herbie Fenton* • Veronica Lake *Dorothy Dodge* • Diana Lynn *Betty Miller* • Cass Daley *Fanny the Drummer* • Parkyakarkus *Gus Palukas* • Donald MacBride *JC Crawford* • Bing Crosby ■ *Dir* Hal Walker • *Scr* Walter DeLeon, Arthur Phillips, from stories by Elizabeth Meehan, Sam Coslow

Out of Time ★★ 12
Crime thriller 2003 · US · Colour · 101min

Carl Franklin reunites here with his *Devil in a Blue Dress* star Denzel Washington, but debutant screenwriter Dave Collard's laboured exposition saps any suspense from an already predictable premise. Washington's small-town cop is having an affair with married old flame Sanaa Lathan, for whose medical care he steals a vast sum of confiscated cash. Then he must stay one step ahead of his estranged wife (and fellow detective) Eva Mendes's investigation. Polished, but superficial. DP **DVD**

Denzel Washington *Matt Lee Whitlock* • Eva Mendes *Alex Diaz Whitlock* • Sanaa Lathan *Ann Merai Harrison* • Dean Cain *Chris Harrison* • John Billingsley *Chae* • Robert Baker (2) *Tony Dalton* • Alex Carter *Cabot* • Antoni Corone *Deputy Baste* • Terry Loughlin *Agent Stark* ■ *Dir* Carl Franklin • *Scr* Dave Collard • *Cinematographer* Theo van de Sande

The Out of Towners ★★★★ U
Comedy 1970 · US · Colour · 93min

Playwright Neil Simon blends comedy with pain in his first solo original screenplay, directed by Arthur Hiller. Jack Lemmon stars as the Ohio businessman who decides to combine a job interview in New York with a night on the town in the company of his wife Sandy Dennis. However, their excursion turns into a nightmare as they become increasingly bothered and bewildered by the Big Apple's ruthless manners. Lemmon takes it all with despairing aplomb, but Dennis seems less able to deal with the calamities; one wonders if comedy should be so serious. TH **DVD**

Jack Lemmon *George Kellerman* • Sandy Dennis *Gwen Kellerman* • Milt Kamen *Counterman* • Sandy Baron *TV man* • Anne Meara *Woman in police station* • Robert Nichols *Man in aeroplane* • Ann Prentiss *Airline stewardess* • Ron Carey *Boston cab driver* • Phil Bruns [Philip Bruns] *Officer Meyers* ■ *Dir* Arthur Hiller • *Scr* Neil Simon

The Out-of-Towners ★★ 12
Comedy 1999 · US · Colour · 86min

This listless, pointless remake of Neil Simon's 1970 comedy stars Steve Martin and Goldie Hawn. They play a couple from the sticks who fly to New York for a job interview. No sooner have they left the ground than everything that could possibly go wrong (getting mugged, having their credit cards cancelled and so on), does. The two stars do their best, but they lack the desperation that Jack Lemmon and Sandy Dennis brought to the roles, while John Cleese's Basil Fawlty reprise is embarrassing. JF Swearing. **DVD**

Goldie Hawn *Nancy Clark* • Steve Martin *Henry Clark* • John Cleese *Mr Mersault* • Mark McKinney *Greg* • Oliver Hudson *Alan* • Valerie Perri *Stewardess* • Rudolph Giuliani [Rudy Giuliani] *Mayor* ■ *Dir* Sam Weisman • *Scr* Marc Lawrence, from the 1970 film

Out on a Limb ★ PG
Comedy 1992 · US · Colour · 79min

Turning his back on a $140 million business deal, yuppie Matthew Broderick heads for Buzzsaw, California, to save his sister from

the clutches of a villain, played by Jeffrey Jones. The fact that Jones is a twin confuses things and makes this movie even less watchable than it already is. Indeed, this stinker was barely released. AT Swearing.

Matthew Broderick *Bill Campbell* • Jeffrey Jones *Matt/Peter* • Heidi Kling *Sally* • John C Reilly *Jim Jr* • Marian Mercer *Ann* • Larry Hankin *Darren* • David Margulies *Buchenwald* ■ *Dir* Francis Veber • *Scr* Joshua Goldin, Daniel Goldin

Out on a Limb ★★ 15
Black comedy 2005 · UK · Colour · 99min

When tippling TV chef Felix Limb (Henry Goodman) finally drinks himself out of a cookery show, the worst day of his life is just beginning. He still has a dinner party to prepare, then, to make matters worse, two armed robbers (Neil Stuke and Costa Milton) crash the party, mistaking Limb's house for their intended target. This only moderate comedy is made bearable by Stuke and Goodman's comic timing, and Julianne White makes a real impression as Limb's long-suffering wife. KK Violence, swearing, sex scenes. **DVD**

Henry Goodman *Felix Limb* • Neil Stuke *Simon* • Julianne White *Michelle Limb* • Costa Milton *Vaughn* • Jeremy Crutchley *Ramsey Harrison* • Peter Gevisser *Bruce Ash* • Bo Petersen *Isabella Leach* • Rolanda Marais *Amy Hardcastle* ■ *Dir* Robert Heath • *Scr* Bob McCabe, Rob Churchill

Out West with the Hardys ★★★ U
Comedy drama 1938 · US · BW · 83min

Judge Hardy and family take a vacation on a dude ranch for this fifth in the series. While Lewis Stone gives his legal advice to the ranch owner, daughter Cecilia Parker runs off with the foreman and Mickey Rooney's ego is punctured by 11 year-old ranch temptress Virginia Weidler who steals the show something rotten. It's all quite witty and charming. AT

Lewis Stone *Judge James K Hardy* • Mickey Rooney *Andy Hardy* • Fay Holden *Mrs Emily Hardy* • Cecilia Parker *Marian Hardy* • Ann Rutherford *Polly Benedict* • Sara Haden *Aunt Milly* • Don Castle *Dennis Hunt* • Virginia Weidler *"Jake" Holt* ■ *Dir* George B Seitz • *Scr* Kay Van Riper, Agnes Christine Johnston, William Ludwig, from characters by Aurania Rouverol

Outbreak ★★★★ 15
Thriller 1995 · US · Colour · 122min

In this exciting eco-thriller, Dustin Hoffman plays an army medic who's trying to save the world from a lethal virus imported into America from Africa. You could read this as an Aids allegory, but it also works well as a regular against-the-clock jeopardy thriller with almost mandatory conspiracy cover-up overtones. Director Wolfgang Petersen marshals the effects superbly and there's terrific support from the likes of Morgan Freeman, Kevin Spacey and a nasty Donald Sutherland. TS Violence, swearing. **DVD**

Dustin Hoffman *Col Sam Daniels* • Rene Russo *Dr Roberta "Robby" Keough* • Morgan Freeman *General Billy Ford* • Cuba Gooding Jr *Major Salt* • Kevin Spacey *Major Casey Schuler* • Patrick Dempsey *Jimbo Scott* • Donald Sutherland *General Donald McClintock* ■ *Dir* Wolfgang Petersen • *Scr* Laurence Dworet, Robert Roy Pool

The Outcast ★★ U
Western 1954 · US · Colour · 90min

John Derek stars in one of Republic's better-written westerns of the 1950s, playing a youngster who comes back to claim land stolen by his uncle, portrayed by Jim Davis. The film teeters on bedroom farce at one point when Davis insists on entering the hotel room of his fiancée, Catherine McLeod, while she's sheltering his wounded nephew, but director William Witney, a veteran of Republic serials and B-movies, stages the numerous outdoor action scenes with commendable vigour. AE

John Derek *Jet Cosgrave* • Joan Evans *Judy Polsen* • Jim Davis (1) *Major Cosgrave* • Catherine McLeod *Alice Austin* • Ben Cooper *The Kid* • Taylor Holmes *Andrew Devlin* • Nana Bryant *Mrs*

O

Banner • Slim Pickens *Boone Polsen* ■ *Dir* William Witney • *Scr* John K Butler, Richard Wormser, from a story by Todhunter Ballard

Outcast ★★ 18

Horror 2010 · Ire/UK · Colour · 93min

Television director Colm McCarthy (*Hustle, Spooks*) boldly ventures into unfamiliar realms for his debut feature. *Outcast* tells of the "Sidhe" – shape-shifters of ancient Celtic folklore – but despite this fresh supernatural angle, the mix of arcane ritual magic, bleak social drama and *Terminator* tropes quickly begins to feel muddled. The limitations of the budget are betrayed in the flat presentational style and some suspect casting decisions, and especially in the special-effects department, when the monster rears its cheap, ugly head. AJ Violence, swearing. *DVD*

James Nesbitt *Cathal* • Kate Dickie *Mary* • Niall Bruton *Fergal* • Hanna Stanbridge *Petronella* • James Cosmo *Laird* • Karen Gillan *Ally* • Therese Bradley *Jitta* • Claire Catterson *Susan* ■ *Dir* Colm McCarthy • *Scr* Colm McCarthy, Tom K McCarthy

Outcast of the Islands ★★ PG

Drama 1951 · UK · BW · 95min

Joseph Conrad's bustling, disquieting tale about a self-seeking wastrel's calamitous impact on a group of Far Eastern islands has, sadly, been turned into a loud, disjointed and rather disagreeable picture by Carol Reed. Such is the haphazard nature of the script that incidents come and go at an alarming rate, leaving the usually poised Reed powerless to tie them into a cohesive narrative. The exotic locations are exotic, and Ralph Richardson and Robert Morley give controlled performances. DP *DVD*

Trevor Howard *Willems* • Ralph Richardson *Lingard* • Robert Morley *Almayer* • Kerima *Aissa* • Wendy Hiller *Mrs Almayer* • George Coulouris *Babalatchi* • Betty Ann Davies *Mrs Williams* • Peter Illing *Alagappan* • James Kenney *Ramsey* • Dharma Emmanuel *Ali* ■ *Dir* Carol Reed • *Scr* William Fairchild, from Joseph Conrad's novel

The Outfit ★★★★ 15

Thriller 1973 · US · Colour · 98min

In this brutal but compelling thriller, taken from the novel by Richard Stark (a pseudonym for Donald E Westlake), bank robber Robert Duvall leaves prison determined to find out who murdered his brother; the trail leads to ageing mobster Robert Ryan. Duvall is excellent, and there's a terrific supporting cast. The underrated writer/director John Flynn lets the story unfold in an unflashy way, but stages some marvellous, if extremely violent, set pieces. JF Swearing.

Robert Duvall *Earl Macklin* • Joe Don Baker *Cody* • Robert Ryan *Mailer* • Karen Black *Bett* • Timothy Carey *Jake Menner* • Richard Jaeckel *Chemey* • Sheree North *Buck's wife* • Marie Windsor *Madge Coyle* • Jane Greer *Alma* • Henry Jones *Doctor* • Joanna Cassidy *Rita* • Elisha Cook [Elisha Cook Jr] *Carl* ■ *Dir* John Flynn • *Scr* John Flynn, from the novel by Richard Stark [Donald E Westlake]

Outland ★★ 15

Science-fiction action adventure
1981 · UK · Colour · 104min

It's *High Noon* in outer space as mining colony marshal Sean Connery confronts the pushers peddling lethal drugs to Jupiter moon workers so they'll produce more ore. This bleak dramatisation of final frontier contamination comes complete with *Alien*-inspired decor and smooth direction by Peter Hyams. Hyams, however, sinks this far-flung fantasy with cheap scare tactics, illogical science and B-movie western-style laser gun battles that scupper credibility. AJ Violence, swearing. *DVD*

Sean Connery *O'Niel* • Peter Boyle *Sheppard* • Frances Sternhagen *Lazarus* • James B Sikking *Montone* • Kika Markham *Carol* • Clarke Peters *Ballard* • Steven Berkoff *Sagan* • John Ratzenberger *Tarlow* • Nicholas Barnes *Paul O'Niel* ■ *Dir/Scr* Peter Hyams

Outlander ★★ 15

Science-fiction action adventure
2008 · US · Colour · 110min

In this cheap and cheerful sci-fi thriller, a spaceman named Kainan (Jim Caviezel) crash-lands in Norway during the Viking age, but has unwittingly brought an unwanted guest – a vicious alien predator called the Moorwen. The creature proceeds to terrorise the locals, so Kainan joins forces with the warrior community to stalk and kill it. References to a host of sci-fi classics abound, but the key influence is the epic poem *Beowulf*, and the muddy period setting gives the basic plot an interesting twist. Sadly, the film's limited purse doesn't stretch far enough to create a wholly satisfying fantasy world, but the vibrant young cast, and a grizzled, hammy John Hurt, have a lot of fun, nevertheless. DW English, Old Norse +subtitles. *DVD*

Jim Caviezel *Kainan* • Sophia Myles *Freya* • Jack Huston *Wulfric* • John Hurt *Rothgar* • Ron Perlman *Gunnar* ■ *Dir* Howard McCain • *Scr* Dirk Blackman, Howard McCain

Outlanders ★★ 15

Crime drama 2006 · UK/US · Colour · 98min

Dominic Lees's study of exploited Polish workers in Britain is pitched somewhere between Jerzy Skolimowski's *Moonlighting* (1982) and Ken Loach's *It's a Free World...* (2007). Adam (Jakub Tolak) arrives in London to break the news of their father's death to his older brother Jan (Przemyslaw Sadowski), a building-site fixer who's heavily involved in the trafficking of illegal labour. The siblings' relationship is strained by a death at a construction site and further complicated when Adam falls for a Russian woman (played by Alexis Raben). With Shaun Dingwall hamming it up as a racially insensitive cop, this ultimately feels like a glorified episode of a TV cop show, with a melodramatic climax undermining the carefully wrought authenticity. DP

Jakub Tolak *Adam Jasinski* • Przemyslaw Sadowski *Jan Jasinski* • Shaun Dingwall *DI Cartwright* • Alexis Raben *Anna* • Joe Tucker *Tommy* ■ *Dir* Dominic Lees • *Scr* Jimmy Gardner (2), Dominic Lees

The Outlaw ★★★ U

Western 1943 · US · BW · 112min

"Mean, moody, magnificent" was the advertising tag for this infamous movie, and it didn't refer to the outlaw of the title – Billy the Kid – but to Doc Holliday's delectable mistress, played so memorably here by Howard Hughes's exciting discovery, Jane Russell. Censorship and reshooting led to a three-year release delay for this languorous western, originally directed by the estimable Howard Hawks, which contrives strange fictional relationships between Billy (colourless newcomer Jack Buetel), Pat Garrett (Thomas Mitchell) and Holliday (the superb Walter Huston). Something of a kitsch curio. TS *DVD*

Jack Buetel *Billy the Kid* • Jane Russell *Rio* • Thomas Mitchell *Pat Garrett* • Walter Huston *Doc Holliday* • Mimi Aguglia *Aunt Guadelupe* • Joseph Sawyer [Joe Sawyer] *Woodruff* • Gene Rizzi *Stranger* • Frank Darien *Shorty* ■ *Dir* Howard Hughes • *Scr* Jules Furthman

Outlaw ★★★ 18

Crime action drama 2006 · UK · Colour · 100min

Vigilante justice is the theme of this hard-hitting action drama from *The Football Factory* writer/director Nick Love. A provocative indictment of modern Britain, it explores the devastating effects of violent crime and the apparent inability of the authorities to deal with it. Sean Bean plays a former paratrooper who takes the law into his own hands after returning disillusioned from Iraq. Joining him on his social clean-up mission is a ragtag group of crime victims, including Lennie James's grief-stricken London barrister, disfigured Cambridge student Rupert Friend and an uncharacteristically mild-mannered Danny Dyer. Though his arguments are underdeveloped and frequently naive, Love's vision is heartfelt and powerful, with strong performances adding to the film's overall intensity. SF Swearing, racist references. *DVD* *Blu*

Sean Bean *Danny Bryant* • Danny Dyer *Gene Dekker* • Rupert Friend *Sandy Mardell* • Sean Harris *Simon Hillier* • Lennie James *Cedric Munroe* • Bob Hoskins *Walter Lewis* ■ *Dir/Scr* Nick Love

The Outlaw and His Wife ★★★

Silent drama 1917 · Swe · BW · 73min

This fateful melodrama is set against the seasonal shifts of the Icelandic wilderness. Forced to flee after stealing a sheep to feed his family, 19th-century peasant Victor Sjöström falls for wealthy widow Edith Erastoff and they have a child during an idyllic summer in hiding from the authorities. However, as harsher conditions close in, psychological pressures impinge on the couple's relationship and tragedy ensues. Expertly locating his characters in the landscape that will destroy them, Sjöström brought a new visual and emotional maturity to Swedish cinema, thanks, in no small measure, to Julius Jaenzon's atmospheric photography. DP

Victor Sjöström *Berg-Ejvind* • Edith Erastoff *Halla* • John Ekman *Arnes* • Nils Arehn *Municipal official* ■ *Dir* Victor Sjöström • *Scr* Sam Ask, Victor Sjöström, from the play *Bjaerg-Ejvind og Hans Hustru* by Johan Sigurjönsson

Outlaw Blues ★★★ 15

Comedy drama 1977 · US · Colour · 96min

If you can cope with Peter Fonda singing country and western ditties, then you might just find yourself having a good time with this scattershot mixture of comedy, musical and road movie. Fonda is clearly enjoying himself as a convict who breaks parole to get even with shyster singer James Callahan who has stolen his song. Director Richard T Heffron overdoes the motor mayhem, but does well to keep his cast at full throttle. DP

Peter Fonda *Bobby Ogden* • Susan Saint James *Tina Waters* • John Crawford *Chief Cavenaugh* • James Callahan *Garland Dupree* • Michael Lerner *Hatch* ■ *Dir* Richard T Heffron • *Scr* BWL Norton

The Outlaw Josey Wales

★★★★★ 18

Western 1976 · US · Colour · 135min

Clint Eastwood seized the directorial reins from Phil Kaufman and fashioned this tough, sprawling post-Civil War western epic into something approaching a personal testament. The tale of a wronged farmer bent on revenge consists of more of a series of vignettes and lacks the tightness of structure that so distinguishes the director's later *Unforgiven*. But there's much strength and power derived from the iconographic value of Eastwood the star, with Jerry Fielding's fine score and Chief Dan George's drily humorous Lone Watie also major pluses. TS Violence, some swearing, brief nudity. *DVD*

Clint Eastwood *Josey Wales* • Sondra Locke *Laura Lee* • Chief Dan George *Lone Watie* • Bill McKinney *Terrill* • John Vernon *Fletcher* • Paula Trueman *Grandma Sarah* • Sam Bottoms *Jamie* • Geraldine Keams *Little Moonlight* ■ *Dir* Clint Eastwood • *Scr* Phil Kaufman [Philip Kaufman], Sonia Chernus, from the novel *Gone to Texas* by Forrest Carter

The Outlaws Is Coming

★★★ U

Comedy western 1965 · US · BW · 88min

Hardworking comedy team the Three Stooges appeared in nearly 200 shorts and over 20 feature films in their long career and this western spoof marks their last big-screen appearance together. Loved by millions, loathed by many, the Stooges never strayed far from their comic roots as violent exponents of lightning-paced slapstick. Here those skills are used to good effect in a story of the boys taking on gunslingers and other villains. DF

Moe Howard • Larry Fine • Joe De Rita • Adam West *Kenneth Cabot* • Nancy Kovack *Annie Oakley* • Mort Mills *Trigger Mortis* • Don Lamond *Rance Roden* ■ *Dir* Norman Maurer • *Scr* Elwood Ullman, from a story by Norman Maurer

Outpost ★★ 18

Action horror 2007 · UK · Colour · 86min

In director Steve Barker's bleached-out nightmare, mercenaries raid a barren east European outpost where an underground bunker contains a Nazi gadget that has inadvertently created an unstoppable zombie fighting force. Cue endless creeping through dark tunnels, the soldiers of misfortune continually disbelieving their own eyes, and much pumping of obviously non-effective bullets into sadistic spectres. The film has some well-staged gore and a few suspenseful moments, but much of this territory has been explored by films like *The Keep*, *The Bunker* and *Deathwatch*. AJ *DVD*

Ray Stevenson *DC* • Julian Wadham *Hunt* • Richard Brake *Prior* • Paul Blair *Jordan* • Brett Fancy *Taktarov* • Enoch Frost *Cotter* • Julian Rivett *Voyteche* • Michael Smiley *McKay* ■ *Dir* Steve Barker • *Scr* Rae Brunton

Outpost in Morocco ★★ U

Romantic action adventure
1949 · US · BW · 92min

Filmed in authentic locations with the full co-operation of the French Foreign Legion, this desert adventure is cited as one of the turning points in the career of George Raft. But, it also helped persuade that most underrated of directors, Robert Florey, to consider his options in television, after a string of unworthy B-movie projects. There's nothing special about the plot, except for the fact that it rather daringly explores the idea of interracial romance, as Raft's legionnaire debates whether to slaughter emir Eduard Franz, the father of his beloved, Marie Windsor. DP

George Raft *Captain Paul Gerard* • Marie Windsor *Cara* • Akim Tamiroff *Lieutenant Glysko* • John Litel *Colonel Pascal* • Eduard Franz *Emir of Bel-Rashad* ■ *Dir* Robert Florey • *Scr* Charles Grayson, Paul de Sainte-Colombe, from a story by Joseph N Ermolieff

The Outrage ★★★ 12

Western 1964 · US · BW · 92min

Having successfully remade Akira Kurosawa's *Seven Samurai* as *The Magnificent Seven*, Hollywood turned its sights on the Japanese maestro's earlier classic *Rashomon*, the story of a rape and a murder told by four people with differing perspectives. The story is transposed to the Wild West, with Paul Newman playing the Mexican bandit accused of the crimes, Claire Bloom and Laurence Harvey as the victims, and Edward G Robinson as a conman. It's a starry cast and worth watching for that reason alone, though Martin Ritt's direction labours every point and lacks the intensity of the original film. AT *DVD*

Paul Newman *Juan Carrasco* • Laurence Harvey *Husband* • Claire Bloom *Wife* • Edward G Robinson *Con Man* • William Shatner *Preacher* • Howard Da Silva *Prospector* • Albert Salmi *Sheriff* • Thomas Chalmers *Judge* ■ *Dir* Martin Ritt • *Scr* Michael Kanin, from the TV play *Rashomon* by Michael and Fay Kanin, from the 1950 film *Rashomon*

Outrage ★★

Drama 1993 · Sp/It · Colour · 108min

Francesca Neri's exotic circus performer, an accomplished sharpshooter, hunts down the thugs who gang-raped her. Seasoned director Carlos Saura undermines his powerful message with some gratuitous nudity and by romanticising her pitiless spree in having it viewed through the eyes of besotted journalist Antonio Banderas. The result, while staged with sophistication, is less shocking and provocative than Tony Garnett's similarly themed *Handgun*. DP Spanish +subtitles. Violence, nudity.

Antonio Banderas *Marcos Vallez* • Francesca Neri *Ana* • Walter Vidarte *Manuel* • Eulalia Ramón *Mother* • Chema Manzo *Father* • Archero Manas

---

O

Mario ■ *Dir* Carlos Saura • *Scr* Carlos Saura, Enzo Monteleone, from the story *Spara Che Ti Pasa* by Giorgio Scerbanenco

Outrageous! ★★★
Drama 1977 · Can · Colour · 96min

The hilarious and touching story of overweight Toronto hairdresser Craig Russell, whose dream is to dazzle the world as a top-class female impersonator. His best friend, Hollis McLaren, is a certified schizophrenic who's pregnant. How director Richard Benner shows these misfits sticking two fingers up at society as they liberate their fantasies makes a sympathetic, uncompromising and well-acted feel-good gay movie. A well-rounded view of the way it was in the heady disco days, pre-Aids. A disappointing sequel, *Too Outrageous!*, followed in 1987. AJ

Craig Russell *Robin Turner* • Hollis McLaren *Liza Connors* • Richert Easley *Perry* • Allan Moyle *Martin* • David McIlwraith *Bob* • Gerry Salzberg *Jason* • Andrée Pelletier *Anne* • Helen Shaver *Jo* ■ *Dir* Richard Benner • *Scr* Richard Benner, from the story *Butterfly Ward* by Margaret Gibson

Outrageous Fortune ★★★ 15
Action comedy 1987 · US · Colour · 95min

Bette Midler and Shelley Long team up for this buddy-buddy comedy to play two women from different sides of the tracks who find they have the same two-timing boyfriend (Peter Coyote, in a serious piece of miscasting). Director Arthur Hiller keeps the action and comedy rolling along at a fairly boisterous rate, and he is helped by the assured performances of Midler and Long, who refuse to let the humour lapse for a second. JB Swearing. *DVD*

Bette Midler *Sandy Brozinsky* • Shelley Long *Lauren Ames* • Peter Coyote *Michael Sanchez* • Robert Prosky *Stanislav Korzenowski* • John Schuck *Atkins* • George Carlin *Frank* • Anthony Heald *Weldon* ■ *Dir* Arthur Hiller • *Scr* Leslie Dixon

The Outriders ★★ U
Western 1950 · US · Colour · 93min

In a very average Technicolor western from MGM, a seemingly uninterested Joel McCrea gets involved with Quantrill's Raiders and redhead Arlene Dahl. It's given some distinction by the studio's high production values and excellent location photography; the plot, though, is disappointingly routine. Director Roy Rowland manages an excellent and suspenseful river crossing, but the movie badly needs a grittier lead. TS

Joel McCrea *Will Owen* • Arlene Dahl *Jen Gort* • Barry Sullivan *Jesse Wallace* • Claude Jarman Jr *Roy Gort* • James Whitmore *Clint Priest* • Ramon Novarro *Don Antonio Chaves* • Jeff Corey *Keeley* ■ *Dir* Roy Rowland • *Scr* Irving Ravetch

Outside Bet ★★ 12
Comedy drama 2011 · UK · Colour · 96min

The odds are pretty good that any film featuring Bob Hoskins, Phil Davis, Jenny Agutter and Rita Tushingham won't be a complete donkey. Here, against a backdrop of 1980s union unrest, Hoskins and co play a group of retired or redundant print workers who sink their savings into buying and running a racehorse. The film starts well, but it quickly falls back on repetitive low comedy interspersed with hackneyed high drama. Nonetheless, the quality of the cast makes it worth at least an each-way flutter. DA A sex scene, some swearing, sexual references. *DVD*

Bob Hoskins *Percy "Smudge" Smith* • Philip Davis *Threads* • Jenny Agutter *Shirley Baxter* • Calum MacNab *Mark "Bax" Baxter* • Adam Deacon *Sam the Soleman* • Terry Stone *Jonny Gossamer* • Rita Tushingham *Martha* ■ *Dir* Sacha Bennett • *Scr* Nigel Smith, Sacha Bennett, from the novel *The Mumper* by Mark Baxter, Paolo Hewitt

The Outside Man ★★★
Crime thriller 1973 · Fr/US · Colour · 103min

Director Jacques Deray adds Gallic cool to Californian chic in this meandering thriller, which relies more on character than mystery to sustain its suspense. Hired for a

hit to pay his debts back in France, Jean-Louis Trintignant's mission seems to have gone without a hitch, until he becomes the target of rival assassin, Roy Scheider. The women's roles are somewhat stereotypical, with Ann-Margret as a tart with a heart and Angie Dickinson as the fatal femme. But it's Deray's assured shifts between amateur sleuthing and amoral slaughter that makes this so satisfyingly sordid. DP English, French +subtitles.

Jean-Louis Trintignant *Lucien* • Ann-Margret *Nancy Robson* • Roy Scheider *Lenny* • Angie Dickinson *Jackie* • Georgia Engel *Mrs Barnes* • Felice Orlandi *Anderson* • Talia Shire *Make-up girl* ■ *Dir* Jacques Deray • *Scr* Jean-Claude Carrière, Jacques Deray, Ian McLellan Hunter, from a story by Jacques Deray, Jean-Claude Carrière

Outside Providence ★★ 15
Comedy 1999 · US · Colour · 91min

To say this demonstrates the sensitive side of the Farrelly brothers may be pushing it a little, but it's certainly a lot more tasteful than their usual fare. Set in the 1970s, it stars Shawn Hatosy as a working-class youth whose constant scrapes with the law lead his dad (Alec Baldwin) to pull a few strings to get him sent to an exclusive prep school. Although this doesn't break any new ground, the performances are appealing. JF

Alec Baldwin *Old Man Dunphy* • Shawn Hatosy *Tim Dunphy* • George Wendt *Joey* • Tommy Bone *Jackie Dunphy* • Samantha Lavigne *"Clops"* • Jonathan Brandis *Mousy* • Jesse Leach *Decenz* ■ *Dir* Michael Corrente • *Scr* Peter Farrelly, Michael Corrente, Bobby Farrelly, from a novel by Peter Farrelly

The Outsider ★★★
Biographical drama 1961 · US · BW · 108min

One of the seminal images of the Second World War showed a group of US marines raising the flag at Iwo Jima; it was a photograph first, then a memorial in Washington. This ambitious biography tells the story of Ira Hamilton Hayes, a native American who volunteers for the navy and suffers from racial hostility, yet ends up a part of that famous photograph. After the war he becomes a celebrity, but alcoholism turns his life into a tragedy. A committed performance from Tony Curtis helps glide over the stickier parts of the script, resulting in a moving account of a tragic hero. TS

Tony Curtis *Ira Hamilton Hayes* • James Franciscus *Jim Sorenson* • Gregory Walcott *Sgt Kiley* • Bruce Bennett *General Bridges* • Vivian Nathan *Mrs Nancy Hayes* ■ *Dir* Delbert Mann • *Scr* Stewart Stern

The Outsider ★★★
Political thriller 1979 · US/Neth · Colour · 127min

Irish-American Vietnam vet Craig Wasson is welcomed by the IRA who send him to Belfast, knowing that if he's killed he will become a martyr in America, aiding the organisation's fund-raising. Wasson's journey turns out to be through minefields of cross and double-cross and generations of hate. The whole film is somewhat partisan in its approach – the British security forces are depicted as the oppressors who are not above a little torture, something which got the film a lot of flak on its limited release. But as a thriller, it has tension and some superb location work. Blink and you'll miss Gabriel Byrne's screen debut. AT

Craig Wasson *Michael Flaherty* • Sterling Hayden *Seamus Flaherty* • Patricia Quinn *Siobhan* • Niall O'Brien *Emmet Donovan* • TP McKenna *John Russell* • Niall Tobin *Farmer* • Frank Grimes *Tony Coyle* • Gabriel Byrne ■ *Dir* Tony Luraschi • *Scr* Tony Luraschi, from the novel *The Heritage of Michael Flaherty* by Colin Leinster

The Outsider ★★
Crime drama 1983 · Fr · Colour · 100min

How does Jean-Paul Belmondo keep getting away with it? This would go straight to video anywhere else in the world, but in France the man remains such a phenomenon that this umpteenth action

adventure in the Belmondo canon broke all box-office records. Belmondo plays a maverick cop who invents a gang war to cover up his murderous pursuit of a Paris-Marseille drugs cartel. Director Jacques Deray keeps things brisk, but this is pretty unremarkable. DP French +subtitles.

Jean-Paul Belmondo *Philippe Jordan* • Henry Silva *Sauveur Meccaci* • Claude Brosset *Antonio Baldi* • Carlos Sotto Mayer *Livia Maria Dolores* • Pierre Vernier *Rojinsky* • Tcheky Karyo *Francis Pierron* ■ *Dir* Jacques Deray • *Scr* Jacques Deray, Jean Herman

The Outsider ★★
Western romance 2001 · US · Colour · 119min

This clichéd, Wild West love story benefits from strong casting and attractive scenery, as a young widow (Naomi Watts) risks ostracism from her Amish-type community by taking in a wounded gunslinger (Tim Daly). Romance naturally blossoms, though in a slower more subtle way than most comparable TV movies, which causes Watts a melodramatic crisis of morality and faith. Based on a Penelope Williamson novel, this is handsomely shot and decently acted, making the clunky dialogue less noticeable. SF

Naomi Watts *Rebecca Yoder* • Tim Daly [Timothy Daly] *Johnny Gault* • David Carradine *Doctor Lucas Henry* • Keith Carradine *Noah Weaver* ■ *Dir* Randa Haines • *Scr* Jenny Wingfield, from Penelope Williamson's novel

The Outsiders ★★★ 12
Drama 1983 · US · Colour · 110min

Francis Ford Coppola's re-creation of the sights and sounds of 1960s Tulsa is more than a little ham-fisted, a situation not helped by some stilted dialogue and a ludicrously over-the-top score by his father Carmine. If you think the rivalry between the gangs looks authentic, it was because Coppola pampered the Socs and persecuted the Greasers throughout the shoot so that a genuine resentment built up between them. DP Violence, swearing. *DVD* *SD*

Matt Dillon *Dallas Winston* • Ralph Macchio *Johnny Cade* • C Thomas Howell *Ponyboy Curtis* • Patrick Swayze *Darrel Curtis* • Rob Lowe *Sodapop Curtis* • Emilio Estevez *Two-bit Matthews* • Tom Cruise *Steve Randle* • Glenn Withrow *Tim Shepherd* • Diane Lane *Cherry Valance* • Leif Garrett *Bob Sheldon* • Tom Waits *Buck Merrill* ■ *Dir* Francis Ford Coppola • *Scr* Kathleen Knutsen Rowell, from the novel by SE Hinton

Over Her Dead Body ★★★ 15
Black comedy 1990 · US · Colour · 97min

For some reason, at the tail end of the 1980s, there was a mini-vogue for body-disposal comedies. *Weekend at Bernie's* may be the most recognisable title, but this jet-black comedy is the funniest of the lot – that is, if you like your humour served as macabre as possible. Elizabeth Perkins shines as the woman who accidentally kills her much-hated sister after being caught in bed with the latter's cop husband. How she tries to elude discovery and bury the body gives rise to some very rewarding slapstick and laughter-inducing grossness. AJ Violence, swearing.

Elizabeth Perkins *June* • Judge Reinhold *Harry* • Jeffrey Jones *Floyd* • Maureen Mueller *Enid Purley* • Rhea Perlman *Mavis* • Brion James *Trucker* • Charles Tyner *Man at Indian burial site* • Henry Jones *Old man* • Michael J Pollard *Hotel manager* ■ *Dir* Maurice Phillips • *Scr* AJ Tipping, James Whaley, Maurice Phillips

Over Her Dead Body ★ 12
Romantic comedy fantasy 2008 · US · Colour · 90min

Desperate Housewives star Eva Longoria Parker must have been desperate to take the lead in this pointless supernatural romantic comedy. She plays deceased bride-to-be Kate, who returns as a ghost to haunt psychic Ashley (Lake Bell) who is falling in love with her ex-fiancé Henry (Paul Rudd). The slight story couldn't be more contrived, the performances are flat, the

direction lazy and the slapstick just plain crude. There's nothing worse than a bungled comedy, but this just might be it. AJ Brief swearing, sexual references. *DVD*

Eva Longoria Parker [Eva Longoria] *Kate* • Paul Rudd *Henry* • Lake Bell *Ashley* • Jason Biggs *Dan* • Lindsay Sloane *Chloe* • Stephen Root *Sculptor* ■ *Dir/Scr* Jeff Lowell

Over She Goes ★★★ U
Musical comedy 1937 · UK · BW · 72min

One of the better films featuring British musical comedy star Stanley Lupino, father of actress/director Ida, this was a stage success for him, and the film version manages to transfer all its unsubtleties intact. The hopelessly dated blackmail plot involves three girls quite literally falling for three men, one of whom is the likeable Lupino. TS *DVD*

John Wood (1) *Lord Drewsden* • Claire Luce *Pamela* • Laddie Cliff *Billy Bowler* • Sally Gray *Kitty* • Stanley Lupino *Tommy Teacher* • Gina Malo *Dolly Jordan* • Judy Kelly *Alice Mayhill* • Max Baer *Silas Morner* • Syd Walker *Inspector Giffnock* ■ *Dir* Graham Cutts • *Scr* Elizabeth Meehan, Hugh Brooke, from the play *Over She Goes* by Stanley Lupino

Over the Brooklyn Bridge ★★★ 15
Romantic comedy 1983 · US · Colour · 101min

Elliott Gould is the owner of a Brooklyn nosherie who dreams of running a big-time Manhattan restaurant and is in love with a Catholic girl, played by Margaux Hemingway. This romance irks Gould's traditional Jewish relatives. Though it's set in the 1980s, this is the kind of film that could have been made 50 years earlier. Shelley Winters does her usual schtick as a Jewish momma, but it's Sid Caesar who steals the show – a great movie comeback for the television legend. AT

Elliott Gould *Alby Sherman* • Margaux Hemingway *Elizabeth Anderson* • Sid Caesar *Uncle Benjamin* • Burt Young *Phil Romano* • Shelley Winters *Becky Sherman* • Carol Kane *Cheryl Goodman* ■ *Dir* Menahem Golan • *Scr* Arnold Somkin

Over the Edge ★★★★ 18
Drama 1979 · US · Colour · 90min

This is Matt Dillon's first film – and a humdinger of a debut it is, too. Dillon plays a disaffected teenager in a sterile planned community that is more concerned with attracting big business than it is with providing amenities for its kids. Bored out of their skulls, and fuelled on drugs and drink, the kids start running riot and laying siege to the place. Jonathan Kaplan directs this powerful portrayal of alienated youth, with Dillon excellent in the causeless-rebel. Even the soundtrack is a stunner. DA

Michael Kramer *Carl* • Pamela Ludwig *Cory* • Matt Dillon *Richie* • Vincent Spano *Mark* • Tom Fergus *Claude* • Harry Northup *Doberman* • Andy Romano *Fred Willat* • Ellen Geer *Sandra Willat* ■ *Dir* Jonathan Kaplan • *Scr* Charles Haas, Tim Hunter

Over the Hedge ★★★ U
Animated comedy adventure 2006 · US · Colour · 79min

This seduces you with cute critters, clever dialogue and fast-paced derring-do before predictably imparting a lesson in family values. It's still fun, though, with Bruce Willis leading a stellar voice cast as rascally raccoon RJ. He cons a gullible tribe of animals into gathering food to pay off a debt, but nuts and berries are out, in favour of the cookies and crisps that can be found on a housing development that encroaches on their woodland home. SP *DVD* *CS*

Bruce Willis *RJ* • Garry Shandling *Verne* • Steve Carell *Hammy* • Wanda Sykes *Stella* • William Shatner *Ozzie* • Nick Nolte *Vincent* • Thomas Haden Church *Dwayne* • Allison Janney *Gladys* • Eugene Levy *Lou* ■ *Dir* Tim Johnson, Karey Kirkpatrick • *Scr* Len Blum, Lorne Cameron, David Hoselton, Karey Kirkpatrick, from characters by T Lewis, Michael Fry

Over the Hill ★★★ PG
Drama 1992 · Aus · Colour · 97min

This highly sentimental look at ageing, directed by the other Australian George Miller (not the one who directed *Mad Max*), has Olympia Dukakis setting out on "a journey of personal odyssey" to prove to her selfish, chilly family that she is not, in fact, over the hill. Dukakis, an accomplished, always watchable actress, gives the rather hackneyed material a lift, and watch out for Bill Kerr and Derek Fowlds, who provide polished supporting performances. **SH** Swearing, brief nudity.

Olympia Dukakis *Alma Harris* • Sigrid Thornton *Elizabeth* • Derek Fowlds *Dutch* • Bill Kerr *Maurio* • Steve Bisley *Benedict* • Martin Jacobs *Alan Forbes* ■ *Dir* George Miller (1) • *Scr* Robert Caswell, from the book *Alone in the Australian Wilderness* by Gladys Taylor

Over the Moon ★★ U
Romantic comedy 1937 · UK · Colour · 75min

This was one of two early Technicolor movies set up by Alexander Korda for Merle Oberon – the other was *The Divorce of Lady X* – and her frozen-faced acting does little for the role of a sudden heiress who is helped in squandering her money by Ursula Jeans among others. Rex Harrison, as a village doctor, doesn't help much, either. There's usually a quaint charm about this sort of dated attempt at British sophistication, but it's not much in evidence here.

Merle Oberon *June Benson* • Rex Harrison *Dr Freddie Jarvis* • Ursula Jeans *Lady Millie Parsmill* • Robert Douglas *John Flight* • Louis Borell *Count Pietro d'Altamura* • Zena Dare *Julie Deethorpe* • Peter Haddon *Lord Petcliffe* • Elisabeth Welch *Cabaret singer* ■ *Dir* Thornton Freeland • *Scr* Anthony Pelissier, Alec Coppel, Arthur Wimperis, from a story by Robert E Sherwood, from a story by Lajos Bíró • *Cinematographers* Harry Stradling, Robert Krasker

Over the Top ★★ PG
Drama 1987 · US · Colour · 89min

This tacky action adventure has its roots in that old Wallace Beery classic, *The Champ*. Here, boxing is replaced by arm wrestling, as trucker Sylvester Stallone tries to re-establish a relationship with his military academy-trained son on a make-up or break trek across the States. The grapple scenes are so devoid of thrills that you long to return to the mushy melodramatics. **DP** Violence, swearing. *DVD*

Sylvester Stallone *Lincoln Hawk* • Robert Loggia *Jason Cutler* • Susan Blakely *Christina Hawk* • Rick Zumwalt *Bob "Bull" Hurley* • David Mendenhall *Michael Cutler* • Chris McCarty *Tim Salanger* • Terry Funk *Ruker* ■ *Dir* Menahem Golan • *Scr* Stirling Silliphant, Sylvester Stallone, from a story by Gary Conway, David C Engelbach

Over 21 ★★
Second World War comedy 1945 · US · BW · 104min

Successful writer Irene Dunne and her editor husband Alexander Knox move out of town, where the nearby army base attracts him to go for officer training. He leaves her to cope with wartime domestic difficulties, and his boss Charles Coburn to manage the newspaper without him. This adaptation of actress/writer Ruth Gordon's first play is kept afloat by Dunne's immaculate screen presence, Gordon's wit and Charles Vidor's sharp direction. Yet it remains essentially theatrical, Knox is dull, and the film hasn't much of interest to say. **RK**

Irene Dunne *Paula Wharton* • Alexander Knox *Max Wharton* • Charles Coburn *Robert Gow* • Jeff Donnell *Jan Lupton* • Loren Tindall *Roy Lupton* ■ *Dir* Charles Vidor • *Scr* Sidney Buchman, from the play by Ruth Gordon

Over Your Cities Grass Will Grow ★★★★ U
Documentary 2010 · Fr/Neth/UK · Colour · 100min

Aimed at an adventurous and culturally aware audience, Sophie Fiennes's beautifully shot documentary chronicles a ten-year project by German avant-gardist Anselm Kiefer. Kiefer's studio is a 35-hectare area around a former factory in southern France. His materials include concrete blocks, molten lead, and broken glass and crockery. And his tools include blowtorches and mechanical diggers. The film features scenes of the man at work, but the bulk of it is a hypnotically slow and dialogue-free tour of Kiefer's incredible "world" itself, with its post-apocalyptic artworks, soaring towers and network of tunnels. **DA** In English, French, German. *DVD*

Anselm Kiefer • Klaus Dermutz ■ *Dir* Sophie Fiennes • *Cinematographers* Sophie Fiennes, Remko Schnorr

Overboard ★★★★ PG
Romantic comedy 1987 · US · Colour · 107min

This charming throwback to the screwball comedies of the 1930s is one of the better vehicles designed for Goldie Hawn. She plays the pampered heiress to a fortune, who loses her memory after falling off her luxury yacht. Carpenter Kurt Russell, who had clashed with her earlier, sees the chance for revenge, and convinces her that she is his wife. The chemistry between the two stars (a couple in real life) is complemented by the performances of an experienced support cast. The entire package is slickly directed by Garry Marshall, who juggles the sharp repartee and slapstick with ease. **JF** Swearing. *DVD* *Blu*

Goldie Hawn *Joanna Stayton/Annie* • Kurt Russell *Dean Proffitt* • Edward Herrmann *Grant Stayton III* • Katherine Helmond *Edith Mintz* • Michael Hagerty [Michael G Hagerty] *Billy Pratt* • Roddy McDowall *Andrew* • Jared Rushton *Charlie* • Jeffrey Wiseman *Joey* ■ *Dir* Garry Marshall • *Scr* Leslie Dixon

Overland Stage Raiders ★★ U
Western 1938 · US · BW · 54min

This up-to-date Republic B-western features hold-ups not of stagecoaches but of motor coaches. The gang then rob a plane carrying gold in mid-flight, handing the passengers parachutes and booting them out. Its plot is of serial-like simplicity but it's directed by George Sherman with positive vigour. John Wayne is the upright leader of the "Three Mesquiteers" and the luminous silent star Louise Brooks (in her very last film role) displays a relaxed radiance and good humour. **AE**

John Wayne *Stony Brooke* • Ray "Crash" Corrigan *Tuscon Smith* • Max Terhune *Lullaby Joslin* • Louise Brooks *Beth Hoyt/Beth Vincent* • Anthony Marsh *Ned Hoyt/Ned Vincent* • Ralph Bowman *Bob Whitney* • Gordon Hart *Mullins* ■ *Dir* George Sherman • *Scr* Luci Ward, from a story by Bernard McConville, Edmond Kelso, from characters by William Colt MacDonald

The Overlanders ★★★ U
War drama based on a true story 1946 · UK · BW · 87min

This is a very impressive re-creation of a spectacular event that took place in Australia during the Second World War: the moving to safety of 500,000 head of cattle (reduced in the movie to a mere thousand), made necessary by the prospect of a Japanese invasion of the Northern Territory. This was one of Ealing's first Australian-made movies, and it is mightily effective under the direction of documentary film-maker Harry Watt. Trouble is, Watt also wrote the screenplay, and the clichés come thick and fast. **TS** *DVD*

Chips Rafferty *Dan McAlpine* • John Nugent Hayward *Bill Parsons* • Daphne Campbell *Mary Parsons* • Jean Blue *Mrs Parsons* • Helen Grieve *Helen Parsons* • John Fernside *Corky* ■ *Dir/Scr* Harry Watt

Overlord ★★ 15
Second World War drama 1975 · UK · BW · 83min

Made with the co-operation of the Imperial War Museum, this account of the D-Day landings attempts to convey the grim reality of the soldier's lot by combining newsreel footage with dramatic re-enactments. Unfortunately, too much time was spent rooting out clips and not enough on the script, which is a collection of clichéd ideas and utterances. A bold venture, but poorly executed. **DP** *DVD* *Blu*

Brian Stirner *Tom* • Davyd Harries *Jack* • Nicholas Ball *Arthur* • Julie Neesam *Girl* ■ *Dir* Stuart Cooper • *Scr* Stuart Cooper, Christopher Hudson

Overnight ★★ 15
Documentary 2004 · US · Colour · 81min

Hubris is the name of the game in this slightly unsatisfactory documentary following rock artist and first-time director Troy Duffy as he tries to get his movie, *The Boondock Saints*, off the page and onto the big screen. Duffy reveals himself as an arrogant, foul-mouthed, temperamental egoist, and there's certainly some *Schadenfreude* to be enjoyed as we watch him being screwed over by, among others, Miramax's Harvey Weinstein. However, half way through it's revealed that the film-makers are actually two disenchanted ex-band members and thus are anything but non-partisan. For all their sniggering, Duffy did eventually get his movie made (though the result was awful). **AS** Swearing. *DVD*

Troy Duffy • Taylor Duffy • Mark Wahlberg • Paul Reubens • Willem Dafoe • Billy Connolly • Vincent D'Onofrio *Vincent D'Onofrio* • Harvey Weinstein ■ *Dir/Scr* Tony Montana, Mark Brian Smith

The Overnight ★★★ 15
Comedy 2015 · US · Colour · 78min

Though it deals with many of the same issuesas many Judd Apatow comedies *The Overnight* has more modest ambitions and, at a lean 79 minutes, doesn't overstay its welcome. Adam Scott and Taylor Schilling star as Alex and Emily, a couple who move to LA and meet the ridiculously bohemian Kurt (Jason Schwartzman) while their son is at a children's party. Scott and Schilling are the heart of the piece, but the movie really belongs to the weirdly adorable Schwartzman, who literally lets it all hang out. **DW** Swearing, drug abuse, sex scenes, nudity.

Adam Scott *Alex* • Taylor Schilling *Emily* • Jason Schwartzman *Kurt* • Judith Godrèche *Charlotte* ■ *Dir/Scr* Patrick Brice

Overnight Delivery ★★ 15
Romantic comedy 1997 · US · Colour · 84min

This could be regarded as one of Reese Witherspoon's misfires, though it's an entertaining enough teen romp. Paul Rudd plays a frustrated student who drowns his sorrows with a stripper (Witherspoon) when he discovers that his virginal girlfriend is apparently stepping out with a jock. Having sent compromising "evidence" of his sexual prowess through the post to his girlfriend, he is horrified to discover he was wrong and must intercept the mail. The two leads spark off each other quite nicely, but it's a slight affair. **JF** Swearing.

Reese Witherspoon *Ivy Miller* • Paul Rudd *Wyatt Trips* • Larry Drake *Hal Ipswich* • Christine Taylor *Kimberly* • Tobin Bell *John Dwayne Beezly* ■ *Dir* Jason Bloom • *Scr* Marc Sedaka, Steven L Bloom

An Oversimplification of Her Beauty ★★★ 12A
Part-animated drama documentary 2012 · US · Colour · 84min

Director Terence Nance can't be accused of playing safe with his debut feature. Expanding upon the 2010 short *How Would You Feel?*, he trudges through a variety of tasks while ruminating about his crush on best friend, muse and fellow film-maker Namik Minter. Flitting between flashbacks, animated interludes, speeches to camera, digressions and doodles, Nance compiles what is essentially a cine-scrapbook of his encounters with and emotions for Minter. Some may struggle to warm to this atypical love story but there's no denying Nance has a distinctive voice. **DP** Nudity.

Terence Nance • Namik Minter • Chanelle Pearson • Dexter Jones ■ *Dir/Scr* Terence Nance

Overture to Glory ★★★ U
Musical melodrama 1940 · US · BW · 88min

This was the first US feature made by exiled German director, Max Nosseck. It follows Vilna cantor Moishe Oysher, as he defies the synagogue authorities to find fame in the Warsaw opera, only to lose his voice on hearing of the death of his neglected son and find redemption on the Day of Atonement. With surprisingly lavish production values, this Yiddish film found little favour because of its downbeat ending, despite the superb singing of its star. **DP** Yiddish +subtitles.

Moishe Oysher *Yoel David Strashunsky* • Florence Weiss *Chana Strashunsky* • Lazar Freed *Rabbi* • Helen Beverly *Countess Wanda Mirova* • Jack Mylong *Stanislaw Maniusko* ■ *Dir* Max Nosseck • *Scr* Max Nosseck, Ossip Dymow, Jacob Gladstone, from the legend *The Vilna Balabessel* by Ossip Dymow

Owd Bob ★★★ U
Drama 1938 · UK · BW · 75min

Prepare to shed a tear at this shamelessly sentimental sheepdog drama set in the Lake District. The tale turns on the rift between ageing shepherd Will Fyffe and his new neighbour, John Loder, when the latter's dog – the Owd Bob of the title – upstages Fyffe's prized Black Wull at the local trials. With flavoursome support coming from the likes of Moore Marriott and Graham Moffatt, there's barely room for Margaret Lockwood to make an impression as Loder's love interest. **DP**

Will Fyffe *Adam McAdam* • John Loder *Black Moore* • Margaret Lockwood *Jeannie* • Graham Moffatt *Tammas* • Moore Marriott *Samuel* • Wilfred Walter *Thwaites* ■ *Dir* Robert Stevenson • *Scr* Michael Hogan, JB Williams, from the novel *Bob, Son of Battle* by Alfred Ollivant

The Owl and the Pussycat ★★★ 15
Romantic comedy 1970 · US · Colour · 92min

Barbra Streisand plays against type, as well as actually letting co-star George Segal get a word in edgeways, in this slick adaptation of Bill Manhoff's Broadway hit. She's an eccentric hooker who moves in with bookish neighbour Segal who had her evicted from her own flat in this Neil Simon-esque comedy. Director Herbert Ross and scriptwriter Buck Henry give the raucous original an extra glow of warmth and Streisand and Segal are so good together you wonder why they never did a sequel. **TH** *DVD*

Barbra Streisand *Doris* • George Segal *Felix* • Robert Klein *Barney* • Allen Garfield *Dress shop proprietor* • Roz Kelly *Eleanor* • Jacques Sandulescu *Rapzinsky* • Jack Manning *Mr Weyderhaus* ■ *Dir* Herbert Ross • *Scr* Buck Henry, from the play by Bill Manhoff

Owning Mahowny ★★ 15
Drama based on a true story 2002 · Can/UK · Colour · 100min

As 1980s Canadian bank manager and gambling addict Dan Mahowny, Philip Seymour Hoffman works hard to convince, but his performance suffers under weak direction and a tedious script. The film is too bogged down with the mechanics of his multi-million dollar theft to offer any genuine insights into his motivations and emotions, while an almost unrecognisable Minnie Driver is underused as Mahowny's drippy girlfriend. But the real scandal is John Hurt's poor turn as an Atlantic City casino boss. **SF** *DVD*

Philip Seymour Hoffman *Dan Mahowny* • Minnie Driver *Belinda* • Maury Chaykin *Frank Perlin* • John Hurt *Victor Foss* • Sonja Smits *Dana Selkirk* • Ian Tracey *Detective Ben Lock* • Roger Dunn *Bill Gooden* • Jason Blicker *Dave Quinson* ■ *Dir* Richard Kwietniowski • *Scr* Maurice Chauvet, from the non-fiction book *Stung: the Incredible Obsession of Brian Molony* by Gary Stephen Ross

The Owl ★★
Crime drama   1991 · US · Colour

In this above-average pilot for a series that never saw the light of day, Adrian Paul plays Alex L'Hiboux, a ruthless mercenary-cum-vigilante, also known as "the Owl" because of chronic insomnia brought on by a combination of a medical disorder and recurring nightmares of his wife and daughter's murder. When he's approached by a young girl to find her missing father, the standard revenge plot kicks in. AJ

Adrian Paul *The Owl* • Patricia Charbonneau *Danny Santerre* • Brian Thompson *Norbert* • Erika Flores *Lisa* • Jacques Apollo Bolton *Cool Ice* ■ *Dir* Allan Smithee [Tom Holland (1)] • *Scr* Allan Smithee [Tom Holland], from the novel by Robert Forward

The Ox ★★★ 15
Period drama based on a true story
1991 · Swe · Colour · 88min

Sven Nykvist, best known for his work as a cinematographer with Ingmar Bergman, here directs a heart-rending true-life drama set in 19th-century rural Sweden. Bergman regulars Liv Ullmann, Erland Josephson and Max von Sydow turn in polished support performances, but the action is carried by the excellent Stellan Skarsgård and Ewa Froling as the couple driven to desperate measures to survive a merciless famine. While Nykvist occasionally allows the pace to drop, he maintains an atmosphere worthy of his mentor. DP Swedish +subtitles.

Stellan Skarsgård *Helge* • Ewa Fröling *Elfrida* • Lennart Hjulstrom *Svenning* • Max von Sydow *Pastor* • Liv Ullmann *Maria* • Erland Josephson *Silver* ■ *Dir* Sven Nykvist • *Scr* Sven Nykvist, Lasse Summanen

The Ox-Bow Incident
★★★★★ PG
Western drama   1943 · US · BW · 72min

This celebrated indictment of lynching remains a brave and unorthodox piece of film-making, based on the novel by Walter Van Tilburg Clark and pushed through the studio system by director William A Wellman as a personal project. It is a western only in setting (the exteriors are largely created on studio sound stages) and its grim tale lacks any heroes – Henry Fonda and Henry "Harry" Morgan are passing cattlemen who observe rather than intervene. The lynch mob mentality is tellingly explored, but the letter so beautifully read out by Fonda is far too literate to be the last testament of a humble cowboy. AE *DVD* *Blu-ray*

Henry Fonda *Gil Carter* • Dana Andrews *Donald Martin* • Mary Beth Hughes *Rose Mapen* • Anthony Quinn *The Mexican* • William Eythe *Gerald Tetley* • Henry Morgan [Harry Morgan] *Art Croft* • Jane Darwell *Ma Grier* • Matt Briggs *Judge Daniel Tyler* • Francis Ford *"Dad" Hardwick* ■ *Dir* William A Wellman • *Scr* Lamar Trotti, from the novel by Walter Van Tilburg Clark

Oxford Blues ★★ 12
Drama   1984 · US · Colour · 93min

It's easy to see why this brat-pack version of *A Yank at Oxford* was delayed for two years before being released in the UK. It's familiar teen territory all the way as Rob Lowe finances an Oxford education via gambling, but fails to impress titled debutante Amanda Pays. With the bias towards bland travelogue footage, a major point of interest is noting how many actors in the student bit parts have now become stars. AJ Swearing.

Rob Lowe *Nick D'Angelo* • Ally Sheedy *Rona* • Amanda Pays *Lady Victoria* • Julian Firth *Geordie* • Alan Howard *Simon* • Gail Strickland *Las Vegas Lady* • Michael Gough *Dr Ambrose* • Aubrey Morris *Dr Boggs* • Cary Elwes *Lionel* ■ *Dir/Scr* Robert Boris

The Oxford Murders ★★ 15
Crime thriller
2008 · Sp/UK/Fr · Colour · 103min

Perhaps it'll come as no surprise that this murder mystery set in the university world of Oxford is far too clever for its own good.

John Hurt is the class act here but sadly he phones in his performance as the world-weary maths professor who uses advanced number theories to crack the symbols left by a serial killer. His endless brainstorming sessions with an adoring grad student (a typically wide-eyed Elijah Wood) are about as thrilling to watch as chalk dust being wiped from a blackboard. Also, Spanish writer/director Alex de la Iglesia (who co-adapted the novel by Guillermo Martínez) fails to inject any sense of urgency in the lead-up to the murders, and the finale is especially tedious. This purely intellectual exercise is a neat formula for a crime story, but in the end it adds up to nothing. SP *DVD*

Elijah Wood *Martin* • John Hurt *Arthur Seldom* • Leonor Watling *Lorna* • Julie Cox *Beth* • Burn Gorman *Podorov* • Anna Massey *Mrs Eagleton* • Jim Carter *Inspector Petersen* • Alex Cox *Kalman* ■ *Dir* Alex de la Iglesia • *Scr* Alex de la Iglesia, Jorge Guerricaechevarría, from the novel by Guillermo Martínez

Oxygen ★★★ 18
Psychological crime thriller
1999 · US · Colour · 88min

This thriller doesn't score many points for originality, but it's well staged and has a decent twist. Adrien Brody stars as a psychopath who is obsessed with the feats of Harry Houdini. When he is caught, he plays a high-stakes game of cat and mouse with the police over the whereabouts of a woman he has buried alive. Maura Tierney gives a believable performance as the cop on the case and Brody is everything you'd expect as the killer. ST *DVD*

Maura Tierney *Madeline* • Adrien Brody *Harry* • Terry Kinney *Tim* • Dylan Baker *Jackson* • Paul Calderon *Jessie* • James Naughton *Hannon* ■ *Dir/Scr* Richard Shepard

Oye Lucky! Lucky Oye!
★★ 12
Crime comedy based on a true story
2008 · Ind · Colour · 120min

There's a touch of Steven Spielberg's *Catch Me If You Can* in Bollywood director Dibakar Banerjee's true-story-inspired black comedy. Slickly shot and appealingly playful, it sees infamous Delhi conman and super-thief Lucky Singh (portrayed as an adult by a suitably smooth and confident Abhay Deol) reflecting on his life and career, after finally being nabbed by police. The larcenous charmer's activities are both amusingly colourful and laden with sharp social commentary but the film drags its heels in the second half, while becoming increasingly repetitive and far-fetched. SF Hindi +subtitles. Violence. *DVD*

Abhay Deol *Lucky* • Paresh Rawal *Lucky's father/ Gogi/Dr Handa* • Neetu Chandra *Sonal* • Archana Puran Singh *Mrs Handa* ■ *Dir* Dibakar Banerjee • *Scr* Dibakar Banerjee, Urmi Juvekar, Manu Rishi, from a story by Banerjee, Juvekar

The Oyster Princess ★★★★
Silent romantic drama   1919 · Ger · BW · 65min

Satirising Prussian militarism, American materialism and fadism, and snobbery in general, this was the first comedy that former slapstick clown Ernst Lubitsch felt demonstrated "the Lubitsch touch" of sly sophistication that would become his trademark. Combining visual opulence with narrative intricacy, the tale of the nouveau riche heiress and the impoverished prince, who are matchmade in the pursuit of dynastic and fiscal legitimacy, is packed with mistaken identities, unlikely developments and inspired resolutions. In short, it's a delight. DP

Ossi Oswalda *The Princess, daughter of the Oyster King* • Victor Janson *Quaker, the Oyster King* • Julius Falkenstein *Josef, servant of Nuki* • Harry Liedtke *Prince Nuki* ■ *Dir* Ernst Lubitsch • *Scr* Hans Kräly, Ernst Lubitsch • *Cinematographer* Theodor Sparkuhl

Oz the Great and Powerful
★★★ PG
Fantasy adventure
2013 · US · Colour and BW · 125min

How did charlatan magician Oscar Diggs end up as the Wizard in the Land of Oz? And what caused the Wicked Witch of the West to become so evil? All that and more is skilfully answered in director Sam Raimi's vibrantly colourful flight of fairy-tale fantasy. Following the established yellow brick road pattern, it sees the engaging James Franco whisked from Kansas to Oz by tornado (this monochrome prologue being a particular highlight). The film tries hard to be an original adventure as well as paying tribute to *The Wizard of Oz*, but it lacks the emotional resonance of the 1939 Judy Garland classic. It's good-looking and fun to watch, but it's certainly no *Wicked*. AJ *DVD* *Blu-ray* *3D*

James Franco *Oscar Diggs* • Mila Kunis *Theodora* • Rachel Weisz *Evanora* • Michelle Williams *Annie/Glinda* • Zach Braff *Frank/Finley* • Joey King *Girl in wheelchair/China Girl* • Martin Klebba *Nikko* • Bruce Campbell *Winkie gate keeper* ■ *Dir* Sam Raimi • *Scr* Mitchell Kapner, David Lindsay-Abaire, from the works by L Frank Baum • *Music* Danny Elfman

PCU ★★ 15
Comedy   1994 · US · Colour · 77min

A flawed attempt to revive that 1980s staple, the fraternity house flick, this brings it bang up to date by making political correctness, rather than teachers, the main enemy. The slobbish devotees of the old-style of campus education (drink, sex, pranks and parties) declare war on the caring, liberal face of responsible studenthood. It's a nice idea, but the members of the largely unknown cast don't have the charisma to carry off the antics. JF Swearing.

Jeremy Piven *Droz* • Chris Young *Tom Lawrence* • Megan Ward *Katy* • Jon Favreau *Gutter* • Sarah Trigger *Samantha* • David Spade *Rand McPherson* ■ *Dir* Hart Bochner • *Scr* Adam Leff, Zak Penn

PoW the Escape ★★ 15
War action adventure
1986 · US · Colour · 85min

This is yet another gung ho American Vietnam war movie that attempts to rewrite the history books while also apeing the *Rambo* movies. Shot in the Philippines, it stars David Carradine, who plays a high-ranking Vietcong prisoner determined to lead his comrades to freedom in the last days before the fall of Saigon. Oriental-for-hire Mako plays the camp commandant as if he's been cast as Ming the Merciless. RS

David Carradine *Colonel Jim Cooper* • Charles R Floyd *Sparks* • Mako *Captain Vinh* • Steve James (1) *Jonston* • Phil Brock *Adams* ■ *Dir* Gideon Amir • *Scr* Jeremy Lipp, James Bruner, Malcolm Barbour, John Langley, from a story by Avi Kleinberger, Gideon Amir

PSI Love You ★★ 12
Comedy drama   2007 · US · Colour · 120min

In this second-rate *Truly Madly Deeply*, based on Cecelia Ahern's novel, Hilary Swank and Gerard Butler play lovers Holly and Gerry, who marry after a whirlwind romance. But their happiness is short-lived. He dies of a terminal illness – but not before writing, for posthumous delivery, umpteen letters of guidance. Such advice from beyond the grave is creepy enough, but Gerry's assumption that Holly's every mood and move can be predicted with complete accuracy is somewhat arrogant. It also means that, despite being adapted from a book written by a woman, this ropey if slickly made romantic comedy has an unpleasant chauvinistic overtone. DA *DVD*

Hilary Swank *Holly Kennedy* • Gerard Butler *Gerry Kennedy* • Lisa Kudrow *Denise* • Harry Connick Jr *Daniel* • Gina Gershon *Sharon* • Jeffrey Dean Morgan *William* • Kathy Bates *Patricia* • James Marsters *John* ■ *Dir* Richard LaGravenese • *Scr* Richard LaGravenese, Steven Rogers, from the novel by Cecelia Ahern

PT 109 ★★★ U
Biographical Second World War drama
1963 · US · Colour · 134min

During his war service, John F Kennedy's torpedo boat was blown in half by the Japanese. Towing a wounded shipmate for three miles by swimming with the man's life belt clamped between his teeth, JFK landed on an uninhabited Pacific island and was rescued some days later. Cliff Robertson makes a fine pre-president, though the build-up to the incident is rather slow. But as a piece of hero worship and political propaganda, released just after the Cuban missile crisis, the movie is a fascinating relic from a less cynical age. AT

Cliff Robertson *Lieutenant John F Kennedy* • Ty Hardin *Ensign Leonard J Thom* • James Gregory *Commander CR Ritchie* • Robert Culp *Ensign "Barney" Ross* • Grant Williams *Lieutenant Alvin Cluster* • Lew Gallo *Yeoman Rogers* • Errol John *Benjamin Kevu* • Michael Pate *Lieutenant Reginald Evans* • Robert Blake *"Bucky" Harris* ■ *Dir* Leslie H Martinson • *Scr* Richard L Breen, Howard Sheehan, Vincent X Flaherty, from the non-fiction book *PT 109, John F Kennedy in World War II* by Robert J Donovan

P2 ★★ 18

Horror thriller   2006 · US · Colour · 93min

P2 is a location-bound experiment in terror: what if a beautiful young businesswoman (Rachel Nichols) was taken hostage by a basement car park security guard (Wes Bentley) on a long, lonely Christmas Eve nightshift? And what if he believed that all she really needed was a romantic meal with him (and his vicious Rottweiler)? Frank Khalfoun makes his feature debut as writer/director here, with a screenplay co-written by the duo responsible for the chillingly enthralling *Switchblade Romance*. They have created a rather hysterical, often comic-bookish horror film, which could have been a lot smarter. Still, there are a few shocks as the heroine's options run out and her irrational assailant begins to see his fantasy evening take a turn for the worse. Nichols's performance is above average as the woman in peril who manages to summon up her inner tough girl, but Bentley plays it strictly for laughs. KK
Violence, swearing. DVD Blu

Wes Bentley *Thomas, "Tom"* • Rachel Nichols *Angela Bridges* • Simon Reynolds *Bob Harper* • Philip Akin *Karl* • Stephanie Moore *Lorraine* • Miranda Edwards *Jody* ■ *Dir* Franck Khalfoun • *Scr* Franck Khalfoun, Alexandre Aja, Grègory Levasseur

Pacific Heights ★★★ 15

Thriller   1990 · US · Colour · 98min

Michael Keaton enjoys himself immensely as the tenant from hell, turning the lives of nice yuppie couple Matthew Modine and Melanie Griffith into a nightmare. It's a little hard to summon up much sympathy for a landlord, and it must be said that the story just gets sillier as the film progresses. However, director John Schlesinger is an old hand when it comes to this sort of thing and Keaton delivers a genuinely creepy performance. JF Swearing, violence, nudity.

Melanie Griffith *Patty Palmer* • Matthew Modine *Drake Goodman* • Michael Keaton *Carter Hayes* • Mako *Toshio Watanabe* • Nobu McCarthy *Mira Watanabe* • Laurie Metcalf *Stephanie MacDonald* • Carl Lumbly *Lou Baker* • Dorian Harewood *Dennis Reed* • Tippi Hedren *Florence Peters* ■ *Dir* John Schlesinger • *Scr* Daniel Pyne

Pacific Inferno ★ 15

Second World War adventure
1979 · US/Phil · Colour · 85min

This bottom-of-the-barrel Second World War action hokum was produced by and stars Jim Brown as the leader of a team of captured American Navy divers. They are forced by the Japanese to recover $16 million in silver pesos that General MacArthur dumped in Manila Bay to prevent them falling into enemy hands. RS

Jim Brown *Clyde Preston* • Richard Jaeckel *Dealer* • Tim Brown [Timothy Brown] *Zoe* • Tad Horino *Yamada* • Dindo Fernando *Totoy* • Wilma Reading *Tita* • Rik Van Nutter *Dennis* ■ *Dir/Scr* Rolf Bayer

Pacific Rim ★★★ 12

Science-fiction action adventure
2013 · US · Colour · 125min

Monster aliens emerge to colonise the planet in this cheesy hybrid of *Transformers* and *Godzilla* from director Guillermo del Toro. Earth's resistance, led by Idris Elba, consists of colossal robots operated by two humans sharing a neurological connection. Sadly, there's little romantic chemistry between star-crossed co-pilots Charlie Hunnam and Rinko Kikuchi, while the other peripheral characters are of little interest. But when the gallery of supersized creatures face off against their towering iron giant opponents, this does become an engaging muddle of weird monsters and hardware. AJ DVD Blu

Charlie Hunnam *Raleigh Becket* • Idris Elba *Stacker Pentecost* • Rinko Kikuchi *Mako Mori* • Charlie Day *Dr Newton Geiszler* • Ron Perlman *Hannibal Chau* ■ *Dir* Guillermo del Toro • *Scr* Guillermo del Toro, Travis Beacham, from Beacham's story

The Pacifier ★★ PG

Action comedy   2005 · US · Colour · 91min

Vin Diesel cheekily sends up his tough-guy persona in this uneven comedy. He plays a Navy SEAL who's assigned to protect the five unruly offspring of an assassinated scientist. Diesel camps it up wildly, but is let down by an underdeveloped script and an overall lack of vitality. Director Adam Shankman never achieves a boisterous sense of fun, but in the final third things pick up. SF DVD

Vin Diesel *Shane Wolfe* • Lauren Graham *Principal Claire Fletcher* • Faith Ford *Julie Plummer* • Brittany Snow *Zoe Plummer* • Max Thieriot *Seth Plummer* • Chris Potter *Captain Bill Fawcett* • Morgan York *Lulu Plummer* • Scott Thompson *Director* • Carol Kane *Helga* ■ *Dir* Adam Shankman • *Scr* Thomas Lennon (3), Robert Ben Garant

The Pack ★★★ 15

Horror   1977 · US · Colour · 94min

In this snarlingly effective horror movie, marine biologist Joe Don Baker is sent in to stop a bunch of ferocious dogs raiding and ravaging holidaymakers on a remote island. Although the idea is drawn from Alfred Hitchcock's *The Birds*, this film doesn't have the same terrifying sense of nature arbitrarily fighting back, but it comes across as an intriguing adventure nonetheless. TH

Joe Don Baker *Jerry* • Hope Alexander-Willis *Millie* • Richard B Shull *Hardiman* • RG Armstrong *Cobb* • Ned Wertimer *Walker* • Bibi Besch *Marge* • Delos V Smith Jr *McMinnimee* • Richard O'Brien *Dodge* ■ *Dir* Robert Clouse • *Scr* Robert Clouse, from a novel by Dave Fisher

Pack Up Your Troubles ★★★★★ U

Comedy   1932 · US · BW · 64min

Seldom seen intact since it was made, this Laurel and Hardy delight has gone through the mincing machine of distributors' cuts but still remains one of their best movies for producer Hal Roach. After a disastrous wartime service, Stan and Ollie try to keep their promise to a dying buddy that they would look after his little girl (Jacquie Lyn). The usual ins-and-outs follow as they try to reunite her with her grandparents. It touches the nerves of comedy and pathos with just the right amount of pressure and also has a vivid portrayal of a revenge-crazed army cook by George Marshall, the film's co-director. TH DVD

Stan Laurel *Stan* • Oliver Hardy *Ollie* • Donald Dillaway *Eddie Smith* • Jacquie Lyn *Eddie's baby* • James Finlayson *General* • Mary Carr *Elderly woman* • Rychard Cramer [Richard Cramer] *Uncle Jack* • Grady Sutton *Eddie, the bridegroom* • Billy Gilbert *Mr Hathaway* • Paulette Goddard ■ *Dir* George Marshall, Raymond McCarey [Ray McCarey] • *Scr* HM Walker

Pack Up Your Troubles ★★★ U

Comedy   1939 · US · BW · 75min

This is a very funny vehicle for the comedy team the Ritz Brothers. Jane Withers, the child star who memorably bullied Shirley Temple in *Bright Eyes*, here makes a successful transition to adolescent actress. The brothers play First World War soldiers mistaken for the enemy who escape in a balloon and find themselves actually in Germany. The team are an acquired taste but this is one of their best. TV

The Ritz Brothers [Al Ritz] • The Ritz Brothers [Jimmy Ritz] • The Ritz Brothers [Harry Ritz] • Jane Withers *Colette* • Lynn Bari *Yvonne* • Joseph Schildkraut *Hugo Ludwig* • Stanley Fields *Sergeant "Angel Face" Walker* • Fritz Leiber *Pierre Ferrand* ■ *Dir* H Bruce Humberstone • *Scr* Lou Breslow, Owen Francis, from their story

The Package ★★ 15

Political thriller   1989 · US · Colour · 103min

This post-Cold War thriller comes apart like a package damaged in the post. In fact, "the package" is Tommy Lee Jones, whom sergeant Gene Hackman has to escort to America from Berlin, but the complications and coincidences are so formidable that not even the participants seem to know what's going on. Director Andrew Davis is used to working with action men such as Chuck Norris and Steven Seagal, so perhaps working with Hackman went to his head. TH Swearing. DVD

Gene Hackman *Sgt Johnny Gallagher* • Tommy Lee Jones *Thomas Boyette* • Joanna Cassidy *Lt Col Eileen Gallagher* • John Heard *Col Glen Whitacre* • Kevin Crowley *Walter Henke* • Chelcie Ross *General Thomas Hopkins* • Joe Greco *General Robert Carlson* • Dennis Franz *Milan Delich* • Pam Grier *Ruth Butler* ■ *Dir* Andrew Davis • *Scr* John Bishop, from a story by Dennis Haggerty, John Bishop

The Pact ★★★ 15

Horror mystery thriller
2011 · US · Colour · 85min

If you look hard enough, there's a fair bit to like about this mildly chilling debut from writer/director Nicholas McCarthy. Caity Lotz plays Annie, who returns to her despised family home after the death of her mother only to be greeted by some deeply spooky goings-on. Both her sister and her cousin disappear, and then, in a well-realised early sequence, she is actually flung about the place by a spectral force. Unfortunately, the first half promises more than the second half delivers, but there are enough shocks and twists to maintain the interest. AS Violence, swearing. DVD Blu

Caity Lotz *Annie* • Casper Van Dien *Creek* • Agnes Bruckner *Nicole* • Mark Steger *Charles* • Haley Hudson *Stevie* • Kathleen Rose Perkins *Liz* ■ *Dir/Scr* Nicholas McCarthy

Paddington ★★★★ PG

Comedy   2014 · UK/Fr · Colour · 91min

Although the plot and setting have been updated, the essence of Michael Bond's much-loved character remains in this classy comedy. After a prologue set in darkest Peru, the eponymous young bear (beautifully voiced by Ben Whishaw) moves into the west London household of the Brown family. Although mishaps aplenty soon ensue, Paddington eventually wins their affections. But can they keep him safe from the clutches of a mysterious, stiletto-heeled taxidermist (Nicole Kidman)? While children will break out in fits of giggles over the well-timed slapstick sequences, adults will relish the wink-wink grown-up jokes of this thrillingly, lovingly, deeply British film. LF DVD Blu

Ben Whishaw *Paddington Bear* • Hugh Bonneville *Mr Henry Brown* • Sally Hawkins *Mrs Mary Brown* • Nicole Kidman *Millicent* • Julie Walters *Mrs Bird* • Jim Broadbent *Mr Gruber* • Peter Capaldi *Mr Curry* • Samuel Joslin *Jonathan Brown* • Madeleine Harris *Judy Brown* • Michael Gambon *Uncle Pastuzo* • Imelda Staunton *Aunt Lucy* ■ *Dir* Paul King (2) • *Scr* Paul King (2), from a story by King (2), Hamish McColl, from characters by Michael Bond

Padre Padrone ★★★★ 15

Drama based on a true story
1977 · It · Colour · 108min

Winner of the Palme d'Or at Cannes, brothers Paolo and Vittorio Taviani had their first international success with this portrayal of primitive patriarchal Sardinian life in the late 1940s. It tells of how a peasant father sends his small son to the mountains to look after the sheep all by himself for years. Deprived of company and language, the young man struggles to adapt when he re-enters society. Perhaps if the sibling directors had approached the tale in a more sober and detached manner, the film might have been even more moving. RB Italian +subtitles. DVD Blu

Omero Antonutti *Efisio Ledda, Gavino's father* • Saverio Marconi *Gavino Ledda* • Marcella Michelangeli *Gavino's mother* ■ *Dir* Paolo Taviani, Vittorio Taviani • *Scr* Paolo Taviani,

Vittorio Taviani, from the autobiographical novel *Padre Padrone: l'Educazione di un Pastore* by Gavino Ledda

Page Miss Glory ★★ U

Comedy   1935 · US · BW · 94min

Promoter Pat O'Brien, something of a chancer, sends in a composite photograph of a girl for a beauty contest, wins, and then has to find a real girl to live up to the illustrated ideal. She comes along in the shape of Marion Davies, starring in the first of four pictures at Warner Bros under a deal made by her lover, William Randolph Hearst, for his Cosmopolitan Pictures. Mervyn LeRoy directed this pleasing lightweight comedy in which Davies, a better comedian than straight actress, is fine. RK

Marion Davies *Loretta Dalrymple/"Dawn Glory"* • Pat O'Brien *Dan "Click" Wiley* • Dick Powell *Bingo Nelson* • Mary Astor *Gladys Russell* • Frank McHugh *Ed Olsen* ■ *Dir* Mervyn LeRoy • *Scr* Delmer Daves, Robert Lord, from the play by Joseph Schrank, Philip Dunning

A Page of Madness ★★★★★

Silent melodrama   1926 · Jpn · BW · 60min

Director Teinosuke Kinugasa, who made his name with a series of samurai movies, came across this lost silent masterpiece in his storeroom in the early 1970s, and released it with a music soundtrack. Relying on its eloquent images without the need for intertitles, the film tells of how an elderly man, working in a mental hospital where his wife is confined, hopes to set her free. Kinugasa, who would study with Sergei Eisenstein after this film, displays a remarkable range of cinematic techniques to give the impression of madness, in between the sane flashbacks to the wife's pre-asylum days. RB

Masao Inoue *Custodian* • Yoshie Nakagawa *Wife* • Ayako Iijima *Daughter* ■ *Dir* Teinosuke Kinugasa • *Scr* Yasunari Kawabata, Teinosuke Kinugasa • *Cinematographer* Kohei Sugiyama

Page One: Inside the New York Times ★★

Documentary   2011 · US · Colour · 91min

As the collapse of the UK's *News of the World* in July 2011 proved, the early 21st century has been a time of change and challenge for the newspaper industry. Beginning with the unravelling of the WikiLeaks scandal of 2010, this documentary deals first and foremost with the problems facing the print media in this digital age. The access-all-areas title is something of a cheat, since it never answers any of its own questions as to whether the paper will survive. But there are some interesting insights, most of them courtesy of journalist David Carr, whose gruff manner and astonishing personal story give this scattershot film much-needed focus. DW Swearing, sexual references. DVD

■ *Dir* Andrew Rossi • *Scr* Andrew Rossi, Kate Novack

The Page Turner ★★★★ 15

Psychological thriller   2006 · Fr · Colour · 81min

The influence of French master Claude Chabrol hangs heavy over this psychological suspense movie from writer/director Denis Dercourt, making for pleasurably tense and twisted viewing. As a child, butcher's daughter Mélanie Prouvost blows her audition for music school. Ten years later, the adult Mélanie (played by Déborah François) gets a job first at the law firm of Ariane's husband, then at their home as an au pair and finally as the now-neurotic Ariane's page turner at concerts. Revenge is clearly the ruthless young woman's goal. This is a low-key but genuinely gripping thriller that revels in the trappings of wealth and good taste even as the rich characters are made to suffer. LF French +subtitles. Violence. DVD

Catherine Frot *Ariane Fouchécourt* • Déborah François *Mélanie Prouvost* • Pascal Greggory *Jean Fouchécourt* • Clotilde Mollet *Virginie* • Xavier de Guillebon *Laurent* • Christine Citti *Madame Prouvost* • Jacques Bonnaffé *Monsieur*

P

Prouvost ■ *Dir* Denis Dercourt • *Scr* Denis Dercourt, Jacques Sotty • *Cinematographer* Jérôme Peyrebrune

The Pagemaster ★★U
Part-animated adventure
1994 · US · Colour · 72min

Macaulay Culkin takes refuge in a library during a thunderstorm, turns into a two-dimensional cartoon and is transported into an animated world where classic literature comes to life. Although the homilies "There's no place like home" and "Books are worth reading" are repeated continuously, the dull story and crude animation sabotage any well-intentioned message. AJ

Macaulay Culkin *Richard Tyler* • Ed Begley Jr *Alan Tyler* • Mel Harris *Claire Tyler* • Christopher Lloyd *Mr Dewey/Pagemaster* • Patrick Stewart *Adventure* • Whoopi Goldberg *Fantasy* • Frank Welker *Horror* • Leonard Nimoy *Dr Jekyll/Mr Hyde* ■ *Dir* Joe Johnston, Maurice Hunt • *Scr* David Casci, David Kirschner, Ernie Contreras, from a story by David Casci, David Kirschner

Pagliacci ★★★
Opera
1948 · It · BW · 80min

Fresh from completing his version of *Don Giovanni*, Mario Costa embarked on this Calabrian-set adaptation of Ruggiero Leoncavallo's one-act opera about the lachrymose clown whose act of charity towards a homeless waif is repaid by treachery and heartache. Although the star of the show is, nominally, the celebrated baritone, Tito Gobbi, Costa was more interested in showcasing the talents of his "discovery", Gina Lollobrigida. Even though her singing voice was dubbed, "La Lollo" made sufficient impression to be prised away from her mentor by Lux Films, where stardom beckoned. DP In Italian.

Tito Gobbi *Tonio/Silvio* • Gina Lollobrigida *Nedda* • Onelia Fineschi *Nedda (singing voice)* • Afro Poli *Canio* • Galliano Masini *Canio* ■ *Dir* Mario Costa • *Scr* from the opera by Ruggiero Leoncavallo

Paheli ★★U
Fantasy romance
2005 · Ind · Colour · 133min

In this good-humoured but flimsy fantasy, Rani Mukherji plays the beautiful bride mercilessly abandoned by her smug and conceited businessman husband after a loveless wedding night. A friendly ghost assumes her wayward spouse's identity (Shah Rukh Khan plays both roles) and then attempts to seduce her. Adapted from a classic folk tale, Amol Palekar's film is an unevenly paced affair with its surfeit of ghostly japes and musical interludes. OA Hindi +subtitles. DVD

Shah Rukh Khan *Ghost/Kishen* • Rani Mukherji *Lachhi* • Juhi Chawla *Gajrobai* • Amitabh Bachchan *The shepherd* • Sunil Shetty *Sunderlal* • Anupam Kher *Bhanwarlal* ■ *Dir* Amol Palekar • *Scr* Sandhya Gokhale, from a story by Amol Palekar, from the short story *Duvidha* by Vijaydan Detha

Paid in Full ★★
Drama
1950 · US · BW · 105min

Feeling responsible for the death of her sister's child, a woman who knows pregnancy stands to endanger her own life decides to get pregnant in order to give the sister a replacement baby. As if this isn't enough to contend with, the tormented heroine, played by Lizabeth Scott, is in love with her sister's husband. Oh dear. Efficient enough tear-jerker, but so steeped in bleak and relentless suffering that even the presence of Eve Arden is unable to lift it from the depths. RK

Robert Cummings *Bill Prentice* • Lizabeth Scott *Jane Langley* • Diana Lynn *Nancy Langley* • Eve Arden *Tommy Thompson* • Ray Collins *Dr Fredericks* • Frank McHugh *Ben* ■ *Dir* William Dieterle • *Scr* Robert Blees, Charles Schnee, from a story by Frederic M Loomis

Pain & Gain ★★15
Action comedy
2013 · US · Colour · 124min

This hyperactive caper comedy is the true story of three obsessive Miami body builders who scheme to get rich quick by kidnapping a wealthy gym client and forcing him to sign over all his worldlies. Mark Wahlberg, Dwayne "The Rock" Johnson and Anthony Mackie play the pumped-up musclemen and, admittedly, give it some welly. The mix of cartoonish slapstick and violent mayhem caused some fuss Stateside, where the nastiness of the original crime still resonates, and it makes for uncomfortable, uneasy viewing here, too. DA Violence, swearing, sex scenes, drug abuse. DVD BD

Mark Wahlberg *Daniel Lugo* • Dwayne Johnson *Paul Doyle* • Rebel Wilson *Robin Peck* • Anthony Mackie *Adrian Doorbal* • Ed Harris *Ed Du Bois* • Tony Shalhoub *Victor Kershaw* ■ *Dir* Michael Bay • *Scr* Christopher Markus, Stephen McFeely, from articles by Pete Collins

A Pain in the A...! ★★★★
Crime black comedy
1973 · Fr/It · Colour · 84min

This very funny ebony-hued comedy has Lino Ventura as a hitman trying to carry out a murder contract, constantly hindered by the suicidal Jacques Brel. The contrast between the implacable Ventura and Brel's walking nervous breakdown is a constant source of laughs. Edouard Molinaro directs this adaptation of Francis Veber's stage success, later remade by Billy Wilder as *Buddy Buddy*. This is the original and the best version. TH In French.

Jacques Brel *Pignon* • Lino Ventura *Ralph* • Caroline Cellier *Louise* • Nino Castelnuovo *Bellhop* • Jean-Pierre Darras *Fuchs* ■ *Dir* Edouard Molinaro • *Scr* Edouard Molinaro, Francis Veber, from the play *Le Contrat* by Francis Veber • *Music* Jacques Brel • *Cinematographer* Raoul Coutard

Paint Your Wagon ★★★PG
Musical comedy western
1969 · US · Colour · 153min

Alan Jay Lerner invented a new "adult" plot, quite unnecessarily, for this screen version of his own Broadway show, in which Lee Marvin and Clint Eastwood share Jean Seberg in a *ménage à trois*. Joshua Logan directs with the heaviest of hands, and only Harve Presnell as Rotten Luck Willie emerges with credit but then he does have all the best songs, even though Marvin topped the UK charts with *Wandrin' Star*. Clint uses his own singing voice charmingly, too, and there's some of the finest chorale work (directed by Roger Wagner) ever heard in a film musical. TS DVD

Lee Marvin *Ben Rumson* • Clint Eastwood *Pardner* • Jean Seberg *Elizabeth* • Harve Presnell *Rotten Luck Willie* • Ray Walston *Mad Jack Duncan* • Tom Ligon *Horton Fenty* • Alan Dexter *Parson* • William O'Connell *Horace Tabor* ■ *Dir* Joshua Logan • *Scr* Alan Jay Lerner, Paddy Chayefsky, from the musical play by Alan Jay Lerner, Frederick Loewe • *Cinematographer* William A Fraker

Painted Boats ★★★U
Drama
1945 · UK · BW · 61min

A wartime docudrama highlighting the importance of Britain's canal network. Revolving around the rivalry between a motorised bargee and a horse-pulled traditionalist, this beautifully observed picture devotes time to life on the cut. It recalls 1930s films made according to John Grierson's tenets of creative realism, with a commentary by poet Louis MacNeice and lyrical imagery from Douglas Slocombe. Director Charles Crichton grounds everything so effectively that when the call comes to fight, it really means something. DP DVD

Jenny Laird *Mary Smith* • Robert Griffiths *Ted Stoner* • Bill Blewitt *Pa Smith* • Harry Fowler *Alf Stoner* ■ *Dir* Charles Crichton • *Scr* Stephen Black, Louis MacNeice, Michael McCarthy

The Painted Desert ★★U
Western
1931 · US · BW · 83min

Two miners discover a six-month-old baby in the wilderness, leading to a long and bitter feud. Doubtless very creaky by modern standards, this is well worth seeing for its cast. The heroine is played by Helen Twelvetrees, a beautiful New York-born actress whose career collapsed in 1938, while the hero is played by William Boyd,

four years before he hit paydirt as Hopalong Cassidy. And then there's Clark Gable, in his first speaking role. AT

Bill Boyd [William Boyd (1)] *Bill Holbrook* • Helen Twelvetrees *Mary Ellen Cameron* • William Farnum *Cash Holbrook* • J Farrell MacDonald *Jeff Cameron* • Clark Gable *Rance Brett* ■ *Dir* Howard Higgin • *Scr* Howard Higgin, Tom Buckingham

A Painted House ★★
Coming-of-age drama
2003 · US · Colour · 97min

This underwhelming TV adaptation of John Grisham's coming-of-age tale offers a romanticised view of life in 1950s rural America, as it charts the experiences of the young son of a cotton farmer over one difficult Arkansas summer. As far as the plot goes, the film feels bitty and inconsequential, touching on serious issues from class conflict to murder without depth or emotional impact. SF

Scott Glenn *Eli "Pappy" Chandler* • Melinda Dillon *Gran Chandler* • Robert Sean Leonard *Jesse Chandler* • Arija Bareikis *Kathleen Chandler* • Logan Lerman *Luke Chandler* • Geoffrey Lewis *Mr Spruill* ■ *Dir* Alfonso Arau • *Scr* Patrick Sheane Duncan, from John Grisham's novel

The Painted Smile ★12
Crime drama
1961 · UK · BW · 56min

This dreadfully dull British B-movie makes its brief running time seem like an eternity. From the moment that Liz Fraser's partner-in-crime is murdered, fugitive Kenneth Griffith tries desperately to avoid the finger of suspicion pointing at him. The cast members do what they can with the script, but they clearly received little directorial encouragement. DP DVD

Liz Fraser *Jo Lake* • Kenneth Griffith *Kleinie* • Peter Reynolds *Mark Davies* • Anthony Wickert *Tom* • Craig Douglas *Nightclub singer* • Nanette Newman *Mary* • Ray Smith *Glynn* • David Hemmings *Roy* ■ *Dir* Lance Comfort • *Scr* Pip Baker, Jane Baker, from an idea by Brock Williams

The Painted Veil ★★★
Drama
1934 · US · BW · 84min

Greta Garbo, the newlywed wife of doctor Herbert Marshall, accompanies her husband to China, where his work leads to his frequent absence, and his absence to her affair with married physician George Brent. Several dramatic upheavals follow, including a cholera epidemic. This melodramatic hokum is glitzed up with Cedric Gibbons's oriental sets, Adrian's costumes and William H Daniels's photography, and is given committed direction by Richard Boleslawski; Garbo is at her loveliest in her familiar "noble suffering" mode. RK

Greta Garbo *Katherine Koerber Fane* • Herbert Marshall *Dr Walter Fane* • George Brent *Jack Townsend* • Warner Oland *General Yu* • Jean Hersholt *Prof Koerber* • Beulah Bondi *Frau Koerber* • Katherine Alexander *Mrs Townsend* • Cecilia Parker *Olga* ■ *Dir* Richard Boleslawski • *Scr* John Meehan, Salka Viertel, Edith Fitzgerald, from the novel by W Somerset Maugham • *Cinematographer* William Daniels (1)

The Painted Veil ★★★12
Period romantic drama
2006 · US/Chi · Colour · 119min

W Somerset Maugham's classic novel gets a third movie adaptation in this handsome period romance, in which an adulterous wife gradually finds redemption through her husband's cruel vengeance. Edward Norton plays the earnest English bacteriologist who hastily weds socialite Naomi Watts and relocates her to 1920s Shanghai. However, she begins an affair, prompting him to retaliate by accepting a job in a remote, cholera-ravaged village and forcing her to accompany him. The leads deliver performances that are immaculate yet detached, which dilutes the narrative's potency and feels incongruous among the vivid Chinese landscapes and atmospheric historical detail. Fortunately, events are enlivened by Toby Jones's raffish deputy commissioner, while an award-winning score complements the ravishing

visuals. SF English, Mandarin +subtitles. A sex scene, brief nudity. DVD

Naomi Watts *Kitty Fane* • Edward Norton *Walter Fane* • Liev Schreiber *Charlie Townsend* • Toby Jones *Waddington* • Diana Rigg *Mother Superior* • Anthony Wong Chau-Sang [Anthony Wong (1)] *Colonel Yu* ■ *Dir* John Curran • *Scr* Ron Nyswaner, from the novel by W Somerset Maugham • *Cinematographer* Stuart Dryburgh • *Music* Alexandre Desplat

Painting the Clouds with Sunshine ★★★U
Musical
1951 · US · Colour · 86min

Here Warner Bros reworked its highly successful *Gold Diggers* format, updated to take in Las Vegas and dressed in glowing 1950s Technicolor. Nothing to shout about, but this pleasant film does feature a cast of bright young performers (bland top-billed Dennis Morgan is the exception) entertaining us with recognisable songs and dances in glamorous settings. Worth watching for hoofer Gene Nelson alone, but keep an eye out for George Sanders's brother, the suave Tom Conway. TS

Dennis Morgan *Vince Nichols* • Virginia Mayo *Carol* • Gene Nelson *Ted Lansing* • Lucille Norman *Abby* • Tom Conway *Bennington* • Wallace Ford *Sam Parks* • Tom Dugan (1) *Barney* ■ *Dir* David Butler • *Scr* Harry Clark, Roland Kibbee, Peter Milne, from the play *Gold Diggers of Broadway* by Avery Hopward

A Pair of Briefs ★★
Comedy
1961 · UK · BW · 90min

This tepid comedy falls flat for the simple reason that feuding barristers Michael Craig and Mary Peach just don't click. Not only is the romantic banter very poor, but there is also none of the knowing courtroom comedy that made the Boulting brothers' *Brothers in Law* so enjoyable. James Robertson-Justice contributes some bullish support, but this just isn't funny enough. DP

Michael Craig *Tony Stevens* • Mary Peach *Frances Pilbright* • Brenda de Banzie *Gladys Pudney* • James Robertson-Justice *Justice Hadden* • Roland Culver *Sir John Pilbright* • Liz Fraser *Pearly Girl* • Ron Moody *Sid Pudney* ■ *Dir* Ralph Thomas • *Scr* Nicholas Phipps, from the play *How Say You?* by Harold Brooke, Kay Bannerman

Paisà ★★★PG
Second World War drama
1946 · It · BW · 120min

Following *Rome, Open City*, Roberto Rossellini moved on from the dramas of resistance workers to the Allied invasion of Sicily to the declaration of victory. The film, using entirely unknown and largely non-professional actors, focuses on a series of individual encounters - one between a black American soldier and an Italian urchin, for example - as well as showing the arrest and execution of partisans. Not as good as its predecessor, but the documentary style and flavour make for a realistic, involving, and significant film. RK Italian +subtitles.

Carmela Sazio *Carmela* • Robert Van Loon *Joe* • Alfonsino Pasca *Boy* • Harriet White [Harriet Medin] *Harriet* • Dots Johnson *MP* • William Tubbs *Capt Bill Martin* ■ *Dir* Roberto Rossellini • *Scr* Sergio Amidei, Federico Fellini, Roberto Rossellini, Annalena Limentani (English dialogue), from a story by Klaus Mann

The Pajama Game ★★★★U
Musical
1957 · US · Colour · 96min

Workers' demands for a seven-and-a-half per cent pay rise in a pajama factory is the unlikely subject for this bouncy, infectious musical. However, it provided an exuberant Doris Day with several terrific songs and one of her best roles as the head of the workers' grievance committee who falls in love with the foreman (John Raitt). Co-directors Stanley Donen and George Abbott demonstrated that it was possible to remain true to a stage original, in this case the Broadway hit, while using creative camerawork and editing. RB DVD

Doris Day *Katie "Babe" Williams* • John Raitt *Sid Sorokin* • Carol Haney *Gladys Hotchkiss* • Eddie Foy Jr *Vernon Hines* • Reta Shaw *Mabel* • Barbara Nichols *Poopsie* • Thelma Pelish *Mae* • Jack Straw *Prez* ■ *Dir* George Abbott, Stanley

P

Donen • *Scr* George Abbott, Richard Bissell, from their musical, from the novel *Seven and a Half Cents* by Richard Bissell • *Music/lyrics* Richard Adler, Jerry Ross • *Choreographer* Bob Fosse

Pal Joey ★★★ PG
Musical comedy 1957 · US · Colour · 104min

Frank Sinatra's expert delivery of some great Richard Rodgers/Lorenz Hart songs, which include *The Lady Is a Tramp* and *My Funny Valentine*, more than makes up for the whitewash here of the black-hearted hero from the stage version. Joey is now a crooner, not a hoofer as on stage, and his rapacious greed for bed (on the make for fading star Rita Hayworth, but really loving Kim Novak) and bright lights has been toned down to give it a happy ending. The heel proves to have a soul, which is rather a pity as novelist John O'Hara's original Broadway exposé deserves a more sarcastic treatment. **TH** *DVD*

Frank Sinatra *Joey Evans* • Rita Hayworth *Vera Simpson* • Kim Novak *Linda English* • Barbara Nichols *Gladys* • Bobby Sherwood *Ned Galvin* • Hank Henry *Mike Miggins* • Elizabeth Patterson *Mrs Casey* ■ *Dir* George Sidney (2) • *Scr* Dorothy Kingsley, from the musical play by John O'Hara, Richard Rodgers, Lorenz Hart, from stories in the *New Yorker* magazine by John O'Hara

Pale Rider ★★★ 15
Western 1985 · US · Colour · 110min

This handsome, mystical western is one of director/star Clint Eastwood's more sombre offerings. A small community of prospectors struggles to scrape a living in the shadow of a strip-mining company that is intent on driving them out, by any means necessary. A young girl (Sydney Penny) prays for deliverance from the violence – cue Eastwood's entrance as the enigmatic "Preacher". We are in classic "man with no name" territory here – with added religious symbolism – but despite a reliably good performance from Eastwood and excellent support from Penny and Carrie Snodgress, this takes itself a little too seriously. **TS** Swearing. *DVD* BL

Clint Eastwood *Preacher* • Michael Moriarty *Hull Barret* • Carrie Snodgress *Sarah Wheeler* • Christopher Penn [Chris Penn] *Josh Lahood* • Richard Dysart *Coy Lahood* • Sydney Penny *Megan Wheeler* • Richard Kiel *Club* • Doug McGrath *Spider Conway* ■ *Dir* Clint Eastwood • *Scr* Michael Butler, Dennis Shryack

The Paleface ★★★★★ U
Silent comedy 1921 · US · Colour · 20min

Buster Keaton's movie is in a comedy class of its own, containing gags that have survived through the years. In his quest to catch butterflies, a collector innocently wanders into an Indian encampment and becomes involved in a war between rival tribes with hilarious results. In one great sequence, Keaton is tied to a stake, then uproots it and walks away. In another, he is locked in an embrace with a pretty Indian; a title-card flashes up saying, "Two years later!" When it cuts back, they are still kissing. **TH** *DVD*

Buster Keaton • Joe Roberts *Indian chief* • Virginia Fox *Indian maid* ■ *Dir* Buster Keaton, Eddie Cline [Edward Cline]

The Paleface ★★★ U
Comedy western 1948 · US · Colour · 91min

This is one of Bob Hope's most popular films, in which he plays a correspondence school-qualified dentist meeting up with sharpshooter Jane Russell (as Calamity Jane) out west. Russell proves here that she can handle droll comedy, and Hope provides a lively mix of wisecracks and slapstick. The film has fun spoofing the western genre and includes the Oscar-winning song by Jay Livingston and Ray Evans, *Buttons and Bows*. It was Hope's biggest box-office hit and very entertaining, though the sequel *Son of Paleface* (1952), is even better. **TV**

Bob Hope *"Painless" Peter Potter* • Jane Russell *Calamity Jane* • Robert Armstrong *Terris* • Iris Adrian *Pepper* • Robert Watson [Bobby Watson] *Toby Preston* • Jack Searl [Jackie Searle] *Jasper Martin* • Joseph Vitale *Indian scout* • Charles

Trowbridge *Governor Johnson* ■ *Dir* Norman Z McLeod • *Scr* Edmund Hartmann [Edmund L Hartmann], Frank Tashlin, Jack Rose

Palermo oder Wolfsburg ★★★
Drama 1980 · W Ger/Swi · Colour · 175min

The rough cut of Werner Schroeter's operatic parable reportedly ran for some eight hours. So he clearly trimmed it down drastically before it took the Golden Bear at the Berlin film festival. Yet time still hangs heavy after Nicola Zarbo leaves his impoverished family in Sicily to find work at the Volkswagen factory in Wolfsburg, only to be charged with murder after defending his honour in a knife fight. Considering he had never acted before, Zarbo admirably conveys the resentment of the exploited migrant. But once the trial sequence takes a messianic turn, the story's otherwise impressive realism succumbs to pompous polemic. **DP** In German, Italian.

Nicola Zarbo *Nicola* • Ida Di Benedetto *Giovanna* • Brigitte Tilg *Brigitte Hahn* • Otto Sander *Staatsanwalt* • Magdalena Montezuma *Rechtsanwältin* • Johannes Wacker *Richter* • Antonio Orlando *Antonio* • Calogero Arancio *Nicola's father* ■ *Dir* Werner Schroeter • *Scr* Werner Schroeter, Giuseppe Fava, Klaus Dethloff

Palindromes ★★ 15
Black comedy drama 2004 · US/Fr · Colour · 100min

No one but Todd Solondz's die-hard fans will find this film anything other than dull and distasteful. The episodic story follows Aviva, a 12-year-old girl – played for no discernible reason by eight actors of various ages, race and gender – who embarks on an odyssey intending to become pregnant. Although there is the (very) occasional grim laugh along the way, this fulfils the promise of its title and ends up where it begins – nowhere of any real interest. **AS** *DVD*

Ellen Barkin *Joyce Victor* • Richard Masur *Steve Victor* • Stephen Adly Guirgis *Joe/Earl/Bob* • Debra Monk *Mama Sunshine* • Jennifer Jason Leigh *Aviva* • Sharon Wilkins *Aviva* • Emani Sledge *Aviva* • Valerie Shusterov *Aviva* • Hannah Freiman *Aviva* • Rachel Corr *Aviva* • Will Denton *Aviva* • Shayna Levine *Aviva* ■ *Dir/Scr* Todd Solondz

The Pallbearer ★★ 12
Romantic comedy 1996 · US · Colour · 93min

David Schwimmer gets himself into a pickle when he is asked to be a pallbearer at the funeral of a schoolfriend he doesn't remember by the deceased's mother (Barbara Hershey). You can see the young-man-older-woman seduction coming a mile off, and Schwimmer is so whiny it's hard to imagine that any woman would want him. Only worth enduring for the performances of Gwyneth Paltrow and the talented Michael Rapaport. **JB** Swearing. *DVD*

David Schwimmer *Tom Thompson* • Gwyneth Paltrow *Julie DeMarco* • Michael Rapaport *Brad Schorr* • Toni Collette *Cynthia* • Carol Kane *Tom's Mom* • Bitty Schram *Lauren* • Barbara Hershey *Ruth Abernathy* ■ *Dir* Matt Reeves • *Scr* Jason Katims, Matt Reeves

The Palm Beach Story ★★★★ U
Screwball comedy 1942 · US · BW · 84min

Made by the brilliant writer/director of satirical comedy, Preston Sturges, this stars Claudette Colbert who, by the early 1940s, had become firmly established as Hollywood's queen of romantic comedy. Watching her antics and listening to her way with a witty line in the face of this film's absurdities, it's easy to see why. Teamed with Joel McCrea, Colbert is the young wife who decides that her poverty-stricken husband would be better off without her. So she leaves for Florida to seek a divorce and a rich man. **RK** *DVD*

Claudette Colbert *Gerry Jeffers* • Joel McCrea *Tom Jeffers* • Mary Astor *Princess Centimillia* • Rudy Vallee *JD Hackensacker III* ■ *Dir/Scr* Preston Sturges • *Costume Designer* Irene

Palm Springs Weekend ★★
Comedy drama 1963 · US · Colour · 100min

Various teens follow the spring exodus to Palm Springs, Florida, where grim police chief Andrew Duggan tries to keep order. One of them, Troy Donahue, is interested in Stefanie Powers, who unfortunately for him is the chief's daughter. Fans of TV''s *Lost in Space* will easily spot Will Robinson (Billy Mumy) as Boom Boom. Moderately entertaining. **JG**

Troy Donahue *Jim Munroe* • Connie Stevens *Gail Lewis* • Ty Hardin *Stretch Fortune* • Stefanie Powers *Bunny Dixon* • Robert Conrad *Eric Dean* • Andrew Duggan *Chief Dixon* • Jack Weston *Coach Campbell* • Billy Mumy [Bill Mumy] *Boom Boom* ■ *Dir* Norman Taurog • *Scr* Earl Hamner Jr

Palmer's Pick-Up ★★
Road movie 1999 · US · Colour · 106min

Offered a lot of money to drive a crate to Florida in time for the millennium New Year, LA package delivery duo Robert Carradine and Richard Hillman hit the highway and rub hard shoulders with a gay ex-con, a nymphomaniac trucker (Rosanna Arquette) and an androgynous Mob boss. Disco diva Grace Jones adds a further level of kitsch to another entry from the multi-talented Coppola family. This quirky road movie is the sum of its often camp and hilarious parts rather than an overall long-haul success. **AJ**

Robert Carradine *Bruce Palmer* • Richard Hillman *Pearl* • Patrick Kilpatrick *Bo* • Neil Giuntoli *Mac* • Rosanna Arquette *Dawn* • Alice Ghostley *Mrs Eleanor Palmer* • Grace Jones *Ms Remo* • Piper Laurie *Radio Evangelist* ■ *Dir* Christopher Coppola • *Scr* Christopher Coppola, Nick Johnson

Palmetto ★★ 15
Crime thriller 1998 · US/Ger · Colour · 109min

This update of James Hadley Chase's 1961 novel *Just Another Sucker* to contemporary Florida is fudged and fuzzy. Ex-con Woody Harrelson returns home to the title town to get suckered into a fake kidnapping scam by a dying millionaire's trophy wife, Elisabeth Shue. Although at times an artful blend of atmosphere and sharp dialogue, Schlöndorff's low energy suspense film fails because Harrelson's character is so unsympathetic it's hard to care what happens to him. **AJ** Swearing, sex scenes, violence, nudity.

Woody Harrelson *Harry Barber* • Elisabeth Shue *Rhea Malroux* • Gina Gershon *Nina* • Rolf Hoppe *Felix Malroux* • Michael Rapaport *Donnelly* • Chloë Sevigny *Odette Malroux* • Tom Wright *District Attorney John Renick* • Marc Macaulay *Miles Meadows* ■ *Dir* Volker Schlöndorff • *Scr* E Max Frye, from the novel *Just Another Sucker* by James Hadley Chase

Palmy Days ★★★ U
Musical comedy 1931 · US · BW · 73min

Banjo-eyed comedian Eddie Cantor gets involved with a gang of crooks masquerading as fortune tellers, one of whom is a young George Raft. There's some funny stuff in a bakery involving high-kicking Charlotte Greenwood, but the credited ace choreographer Busby Berkeley was still a fair way from finding the unique style that made him a household name at Warner Bros. Despite the somewhat perfunctory direction, Cantor is genuinely amusing. **TS**

Eddie Cantor *Eddie Simpson* • Charlotte Greenwood *Helen Martin* • Spencer Charters *Ab Clark* • Barbara Weeks *Joan Clark* • George Raft *Joe the Frog* • Paul Page *Steve Clayton* • Harry Woods *Plug Moynihan* ■ *Dir* A Edward Sutherland • *Scr* Morrie Ryskind, Eddie Cantor, from a story by Morrie Ryskind, Keene Thompson, David Freedman, David Freedman, Eddie Cantor

Palo Alto ★★★ 15
Drama 2013 · US · Colour · 95min

Marking the directorial debut of Gia Coppola (granddaughter of Francis Ford, niece of Sofia), this dreamy tale of wasted youth provides a familiar yet authentic portrait of the teenage experience. Emma Roberts is caught between her feelings for

sensitive stoner Jack Kilmer and a crush on her soccer coach, James Franco. These characters aren't particularly interesting, and the film tends to drift away from them as it shifts back and forth. But the performances are appealing, and it's refreshing to see a teen movie where the teenagers actually look and sound like teenagers. **SC** *DVD*

Jack Kilmer *Teddy* • Nat Wolff *Fred* • Emma Roberts *April* • James Franco *Mr B* • Colleen Camp *Sally Grossman* ■ *Dir* Gia Coppola • *Scr* Gia Coppola, from short stories by James Franco

Palooka ★★★★
Comedy 1934 · US · BW · 87min

Hey, youse guys this is the bee's knees! Promoter Knobby Walsh (the great Jimmy Durante) has plucked a comer (hick Stu Erwin) from the streets, and is grooming him for the big fight, only the Palooka doesn't know what's (about to) hit him. Fabulous stuff, with the Schnoz on top form. Heck of a support cast, too. A Joe Palooka series of B-movies followed, with Joe Kirkwood Jr as the chump champ. **TS**

Jimmy Durante *Knobby Walsh* • Lupe Velez *Nina Madero* • Stuart Erwin *Joe Palooka* • Marjorie Rambeau *Mayme Palooka* • Robert Armstrong *Pete Palooka* • Mary Carlisle *Anne* • William Cagney *Al McSwatt* • Thelma Todd *Trixie* • Franklyn Ardell *Doc Wise* ■ *Dir* Benjamin Stoloff [Ben Stoloff] • *Scr* Ben Ryan, Murray Roth, Gertrude Purcell, Jack Jevne, Arthur Kober, from the comic strip by Ham Fisher

Palookaville ★★★★ 15
Comedy crime drama 1995 · US · Colour · 88min

Clever, richly atmospheric and perfectly pitched, Alan Taylor's directorial debut is a low-key delight that's strong on character and packed with sharp, witty dialogue. It's inspired by the works of Italian author Italo Calvino, but the story events are incidental to the superbly nuanced interplay between the uniformly excellent William Forsythe, Vincent Gallo and Adam Trese. They star as dead-end New Jersey buddies who turn to a life of petty crime to ease their boredom, with remarkably unspectacular results. Frances McDormand lends winning support as a hooker. **AJ** *DVD*

Adam Trese *Jerry* • Vincent Gallo *Russ* • William Forsythe *Sid* • Gareth Williams *Ed* • Frances McDormand *June* ■ *Dir* Alan Taylor • *Scr* David Epstein

Le Paltoquet ★★★★ 15
Crime drama 1986 · Fr · Colour · 90min

In this sophisticated surrealist whodunnit, director/writer Michel Deville allows his camera to rove around the bistro run by Jeanne Moreau and Michel Piccoli. The atmospheric visual symbolism complements the sparkling verbal exchanges between inspector Jean Yanne and the card-playing quartet he suspects of murder: journalist Daniel Auteuil, doctor Richard Bohringer, tradesman Philippe Léotard and teacher Claude Piéplu. Fanny Ardant adds support from a hammock in this cerebral delight, with Piccoli also excelling. **DP** French +subtitles. *DVD*

Fanny Ardant *Lotte* • Daniel Auteuil *Journalist* • Richard Bohringer *Doctor* • Philippe Léotard *Tradesman* • Jeanne Moreau *Proprietress* • Michel Piccoli *Paltoquet* • Claude Piéplu *Teacher* ■ *Dir* Michel Deville • *Scr* Michel Deville, from the novel *On A Tué Pendant l'Escale* by Franz-Rudolph Falk

Pan ★★★★ PG
Fantasy comedy adventure 2015 · US/UK/Aus · Colour · 106min

Orphan Peter Pan (Levi Miller) fulfils his flying destiny – defeating the evil pirate Blackbeard (Hugh Jackman) who's holding Neverland to ransom – in this wonderfully oddball prequel to JM Barrie's classic tale. This irreverent delight touches base with all the familiar characters while drawing on a raft of movie inspirations – *Moulin Rouge!*, *Avatar*, *Mad Max*, *Oliver!* to name but a few. The result is an eclectic eye-popper expertly combining the old-fashioned swashbuckler

P

and the modern fantasy adventure. AJ
DVD **Blu-ray**

Levi Miller *Peter Pan* • Hugh Jackman *Blackbeard* • Rooney Mara *Tiger Lily* • Garrett Hedlund *Hook* • Amanda Seyfried *Mary* • Kathy Burke *Mother Barnabas* ■ Dir Joe Wright • Scr Jason Fuchs, from characters by JM Barrie • Music John Powell

Pancho Villa ★★ PG
Western 1971 · Sp · Colour · 87min

Hammy *Kojak* star Telly Savalas might not be ideally cast as Mexico's saviour, yet this is still an interesting example of a Spanish western, set against a background of arid landscapes, with a watchable cast of Hollywood veterans. Director Eugenio Martin has a clever knack for handling train sequences. TS

Telly Savalas *Pancho Villa* • Clint Walker *Scotty* • Anne Francis *Flo* • Chuck Connors *Colonel Wilcox* • Angel Del Pozo *Lieutenant Eager* • José Maria Prada *Luis* ■ Dir Gene Martin [Eugenio Martin] • Scr Julian Halevy [Julian Zimet], from a story by Gene Martin [Eugenio Martin]

Pandaemonium ★★★ 12
Period drama 2000 · UK/US · Colour · 124min

Julien Temple, film biographer of the Sex Pistols, conducts a fascinating, if superficial, study into the ramifications of intellectual curiosity in this archly anachronistic fantasy. Not content with conveying something of the excitement of both radical thought and the hallucinogenic effect of opium, Temple coaxes Linus Roache into playing Samuel Coleridge as an addled dreamer, while John Hannah's William Wordsworth becomes an envious dullard. The warnings about tinkering with nature are worth making, but a greater focus on poetry and personality might have reduced the need for flamboyance. DP **DVD**

John Hannah *William Wordsworth* • Linus Roache *Samuel Coleridge* • Samantha Morton *Sara Coleridge* • Emily Woof *Dorothy Wordsworth* • Emma Fielding *Mary Wordsworth* • Andy Serkis *John Thelwall* • Samuel West *Robert Southey* ■ Dir Julien Temple • Scr Frank Cottrell Boyce

Pandemonium ★ 15
Horror spoof 1982 · US · Colour · 77min

Hard to believe that the numerous comic talents assembled for this shoddy *Friday the 13th* spoof in the *Airplane!* vein barely manage to raise a single smile between them. A Jason-type killer is spearing trainee cheerleaders, and displaced Mountie Tom Smothers and his addled deputy Paul (Pee Wee) Reubens are sent to investigate. Nothing the able director Alfred Sole does with the weak script can generate a laugh. AJ

Tom Smothers *Cooper* • Carol Kane *Candy* • Miles Chapin *Andy* • Debralee Scott *Sandy* • Marc McClure *Randy* • Judge Reinhold *Glenn* • Paul Reubens *Johnson* • Donald O'Connor *Glenn's dad* • Kaye Ballard *Glenn's mum* • Tab Hunter *Blue Grange* • Eve Arden *Warden June* ■ Dir Alfred Sole • Scr Jaime Klein, Richard Whitley

Pandora and the Flying Dutchman ★★★★ PG
Romantic fantasy drama
1950 · UK · Colour · 118min

Albert Lewin was in some ways Hollywood's answer to Michael Powell and Emeric Pressburger, as a maker of weird, exotic and often slightly barmy Technicolor fantasies. This bizarre British-made effort stars the ravishing Ava Gardner as a woman incapable of returning the love of her men, and James Mason as the sailor of legend, condemned to roam the seas for eternity until he meets a woman willing to give up her life for him. Set in Spain, its flights of romantic fantasy are heightened by the work of Powell and Pressburger's regular cinematographer, Jack Cardiff. An acquired taste, perhaps, but Lewin was a genuine maverick talent. AT In In English and Spanish. **DVD** **Blu-ray**

James Mason *Hendrick Van der Zee* • Ava Gardner *Pandora Reynolds* • Nigel Patrick *Stephen Cameron* • Sheila Sim *Janet Fielding* • Harold Warrender *Geoffrey Fielding* • Mario Cabré *Juan Montalvo* • Marius Goring *Reggie*

Demarest • John Laurie *Angus* ■ Dir Albert Lewin • Scr Albert Lewin, from a story by Albert Lewin, suggested by the legend of the Flying Dutchman

Pandora's Box ★★★★★ PG
Silent drama 1929 · Ger · BW · 104min

American-born Louise Brooks is devastating as the *femme fatale* who murders her husband and tangos with a lesbian countess before falling victim herself to Jack the Ripper. Screenwriter Ladislaus Vajda makes a superb job of condensing Frank Wedekind's two Lulu plays, but it's the visual imagination of director GW Pabst that most fully conveys the story's brooding sexual tension and all-pervading atmosphere of latent violence. A masterly mix of expressionism and street realism, this ranks among the masterpieces of German silent cinema. DP **DVD**

Louise Brooks *Lulu* • Fritz Kortner *Dr Peter Schön* • Franz Lederer [Francis Lederer] *Alwa Schön* • Carl Götz *Schigolch* • Alice Roberts *Countess Anna Geschwitz* ■ Dir GW Pabst • Scr Ladislaus Vajda, from *Die Erdgeist/Die Büchse der Pandora* by Frank Wedekind • Cinematographer Günther Krampf

Pandora's Promise ★★★★ 12A
Documentary 2013 · US · Colour · 86min

This provocative documentary makes the case that nuclear energy represents the only genuine choice when it comes to meeting the power requirements of a rapidly expanding global economy in the decades ahead. Director Robert Stone is just one of the committed environmentalists, including British writer Mark Lynas, who line up to admit that they've changed their minds and now endorse the nuclear option. Articulate and defiantly one-sided, it may not change everyone's mind, but anyone who considers themselves an environmentalist should at least expose themselves to its potent arguments. TJ Swearing.

■ Dir/Scr Robert Stone (3)

Pandorum ★ 15
Science-fiction horror
2009 · US/Ger · Colour · 103min

An intergalactic mission starts to go horribly wrong in this dull and often incomprehensible sci-fi shocker from director Christian Alvart (*Antibodies*, *Case 39*). When astronauts Dennis Quaid and Ben Foster awake disorientated from hyper-sleep, with no memory of their assignment, they find themselves at the mercy of fast-moving mutant monsters that have infiltrated their ship. It's essentially *The Descent* in outer space with no real menace or horror, just jerky editing supplying mechanical jolts against a dingy industrial backdrop. AJ Violence, swearing. **DVD** **Blu-ray**

Ben Foster *Bower* • Dennis Quaid *Lieutenant Payton* • Cam Gigandet *Gallo* • Antje Traue *Nadia* • Cung Le *Manh* • Eddie Rouse *Leland* ■ Dir Christian Alvart • Scr Travis Milloy, from a story by Milloy, Christian Alvart

Panic ★★★ 15
Crime drama 2000 · US · Colour · 84min

Henry Bromwell emerges from his TV background to make an impressive feature debut with this assured blend of crime thriller, domestic drama and black comedy. There's a whisp of *Analyze This* about the way covert hitman William H Macy reveals to psychiatrist John Ritter the hold domineering father Donald Sutherland exerts over him. With Tracey Ullman and Neve Campbell competing for Macy's affections, this is adroit and discerningly downbeat. DP **DVD**

William H Macy *Alex* • Donald Sutherland *Michael* • Neve Campbell *Sarah* • Tracey Ullman *Martha* • Barbara Bain *Deidre* • David Dorfman *Sammy* • John Ritter *Josh Parks* ■ Dir/Scr Henry Bromell

Panic Button ★★
Comedy 1964 · US · BW · 90min

Michael Connors is the producer looking to make a flop as a tax write-off who hires forgotten movie star Maurice Chevalier – completely unsuited to the role – to play Romeo, and professional tart Jayne Mansfield as Juliet, for a TV pilot of Shakespeare's play. For good measure, he gets Akim Tamiroff as a director who is only too happy to give him the garbage he wants. Barely released, this is a minor but quite appealing comedy. RK

Maurice Chevalier *Philippe Fontaine* • Jayne Mansfield *Angela* • Michael Connors [Mike Connors] *Frank Pagano* • Eleanor Parker *Louise Harris* • Akim Tamiroff *Pandowski* ■ Dir George Sherman • Scr Hal Biller, from a story by Mort Friedman, Ron Gorton

The Panic in Needle Park ★★★★ 18
Drama 1971 · US · Colour · 103min

Drug abuse movies can be hard to take, but this compelling drama has a superior screenplay (by Joan Didion and her husband John Gregory Dunne) and sensational performances from young Al Pacino and Kitty Winn. He's the cheeky bad boy and she the nice, sweet girl irresistibly drawn to him, and together their youthful dabbling in drugs drags them down into addiction and a harrowing spiral of squalor and loathing. Pacino's electrifying presence here convinced Francis Ford Coppola to fight enormous studio resistance to cast him as Michael Corleone in *The Godfather*. AME **DVD**

Al Pacino *Bobby* • Kitty Winn *Helen* • Alan Vint *Hotchner* • Richard Bright *Hank* • Angie Ortega *Irene* • Marcia Jean Kurtz *Marcie* • Raul Julia *Marco* • Kiel Martin *Chico* • Paul Sorvino *Samuels* ■ Dir Jerry Schatzberg • Scr Joan Didion, John Gregory Dunne, from a novel by James Mills

Panic in the Streets ★★★★ PG
Drama 1950 · US · BW · 92min

This tense drama might have seemed an unusual choice for director Elia Kazan. Yet, given the mood of xenophobia that prevailed in the United States at the time, the storyline – the killing of an illegal immigrant results in a potential plague outbreak – is very much in keeping with Kazan's preoccupation with racism. Richard Widmark gives one of his more restrained performances as the health inspector teaming up with cop Paul Douglas to apprehend the plague-infected murderers, compellingly played by Jack Palance and Zero Mostel. DP **DVD**

Richard Widmark *Clinton Reed* • Paul Douglas *Police Captain Tom Warren* • Barbara Bel Geddes *Nancy Reed* • Walter (Jack) Palance [Jack Palance] *Blackie* • Zero Mostel *Raymond Fitch* • Dan Riss *Neff* ■ Dir Elia Kazan • Scr Richard Murphy, Daniel Fuchs, from the stories *Quarantine* and *Some Like 'Em Cold* by Edna Anhalt, Edward Anholt

Panic in Year Zero ★★★ 15
Science-fiction drama 1962 · US · BW · 88min

Ray Milland directs and stars in this story about a nuclear war and the breakdown of society that follows. Milland's nondescript direction sometimes makes the film even more chilling, as survivors take the law into their own hands and head for the hills, through a traffic jam of surreal proportions. Milland plays the boring, everyday Joe who holds up a store, takes his wife and family to live in a cave and kills the thugs who threaten them. There's a lot going on in this movie, with much to think about. AT **DVD**

Ray Milland *Harry Baldwin* • Jean Hagen *Ann Baldwin* • Frankie Avalon *Rick Baldwin* • Mary Mitchel *Karen Baldwin* • Joan Freeman *Marilyn Hayes* • Richard Garland *Mr Johnson* ■ Dir Ray Milland • Scr Jay Simms, John Morton, from a story by Jay Simms

Panic Room ★★★ 15
Thriller 2002 · US · Colour · 107min

In this dark thriller, David Fincher exploits modern society's home-security paranoia, as a bunker-like safe room becomes a source of escalating horror for mother Jodie Foster and daughter Kristen Stewart, trapped by thieves in their New York brownstone. Though the plot is formulaic, it's ruthlessly executed, with the tension building to claustrophobic levels. However, Fincher seems obsessed with breakneck camera movement and unconventional angles, which means at times his extraordinary visual style gets in the way of the action. SF Violence, swearing. **DVD** **Blu-ray**

Jodie Foster *Meg Altman* • Forest Whitaker *Burnham* • Dwight Yoakam *Raoul* • Jared Leto *Junior* • Kristen Stewart *Sarah Altman* • Ann Magnuson *Lydia Lynch* • Ian Buchanan *Evan Kurlander* • Patrick Bauchau *Stephen Altman* • Nicole Kidman *Stephen's girlfriend on the phone* ■ Dir David Fincher • Scr David Koepp • Cinematographer Darius Khondji

Pan's Labyrinth ★★★★★ 15
Period fantasy horror
2006 · Sp/Mex/US · Colour · 118min

Guillermo del Toro's extraordinarily rich and detailed visual style weaves entrancing metaphorical fantasy horror through political allegory with stunning brilliance. At the end of the Spanish Civil War in 1944, young Ivana Baquero seeks refuge in a mysterious maze to escape the harsh realities of life. There guardian satyr Pan (Doug Jones) sets her three perilous tasks. These mirror her soul-destroying existence and help her to cope with the perversions of innocence that fascism represents in this dark fable for adults. Superbly acted, vividly beautiful and uniquely imaginative, del Toro's mesmerising phantasmagoria soars with an emotional scope that packs a shocking and moving punch. AJ Spanish +subtitles. Swearing, violence. **DVD** **Blu-ray**

Sergi López [Sergi Lopez] *Captain Vidal* • Maribel Verdú *Mercedes* • Ivana Baquero *Ofelia* • Alex Angulo *Doctor* • Doug Jones *Pan* • Ariadna Gil *Carmen* ■ Dir/Scr Guillermo del Toro

Panther ★★★ 15
Political drama 1995 · US · Colour · 124min

The troubled rise of the Black Panther group, from their formation in Oakland, California, to their media hounding by J Edgar Hoover, is put under the spotlight by director Mario Van Peebles in a "factional" account of an important chapter in American race politics. Although densely plotted, the director's use of extreme close-ups and energetic flashy visuals keep the attention riveted. Highly controversial, this is a thought-provoking political drama that works on a number of levels. AJ Violence, swearing, drug abuse.

Kadeem Hardison *Judge* • Bokeem Woodbine *Tyrone* • Joe Don Baker *Brimmer* • Courtney B Vance *Bobby Seale* • Tyrin Turner *Cy* • Marcus Chong *Huey Newton* • Anthony Griffith *Eldridge Cleaver* • Bobby Brown *Rose* ■ Dir Mario Van Peebles • Scr Melvin Van Peebles, from his novel

Papadopoulos & Sons ★★★ 15
Comedy drama 2012 · UK · Colour · 104min

A self-made millionaire is knocked sideways by the financial crisis in this wry comedy drama, the feature debut of writer/director Marcus Markou. The familiar riches-to-rags tale is set apart by Markou's analysis of the immigrant mindset and Stephen Dillane's picture of quiet desperation as Harry Papadopoulos. Ejected from his mansion, Harry is forced to relaunch the fish-and-chip shop he co-owns with estranged brother Spiros (Georges Corraface). A late pitch at pathos isn't convincing, but, otherwise, Markou's use of subtle, observational humour and witty dialogue makes this a fresh and poignant snapshot of ethnic life in London. SP Swearing. **DVD**

Stephen Dillane *Harry Papadopoulos* • Georgia Groome *Katie Papadopoulos* • Ed Stoppard *Rob* • Frank Dillane *James Papadopoulos* • Thomas Underhill *Theo Papadopoulos* ■ *Dir/Scr* Marcus Markou

Paparazzi ★★ 15
Thriller   2004 · US · Colour · 80min

Mel Gibson's ex-hair stylist Paul Abascal directs his debut feature (with Gibson co-producing), a rough-hewn revenge thriller that shows the effects of paparazzi persecution from the point of view of the celebrity. When up-and-coming movie action hero Cole Hauser antagonises unscrupulous snapper Tom Sizemore, he finds that his wife and child are targeted by the photographer and his three sleazy cronies. With the police unable to take action, Hauser decides to take matters into his own hands. Low on quality and virtually morality free, this crass film makes its point with a sledgehammer. KK Violence. **DVD**

Cole Hauser *Bo Laramie* • Robin Tunney *Abby Laramie* • Tom Sizemore *Rex Harper* • Dennis Farina *Detective Burton* • Daniel Baldwin *Wendell Stokes* • Tom Hollander *Leonard Clark* • Kevin Gage *Kevin Rosner* • Blake Bryan *Zach Laramie* • Mel Gibson *Man in waiting room* ■ *Dir* Paul Abascal • *Scr* Forrest Smith

Papa's Delicate Condition ★★★★ U
Period comedy   1963 · US · Colour · 97min

Jackie Gleason has a touch of the staggers which, considering his size, is a risky lurch to be in the way of. It's a totter brought about by too many nips of liquor, an ailment his loving household in their turn-of-the-century Texas small town has to deal with or avoid. Based on memoirs by silent screen star Corinne Griffith and with an Oscar winner of a song (*Call Me Irresponsible*) by James Van Heusen and Sammy Cahn, it's the kind of ode to old-time family values that has gone out of fashion, if not favour. TH

Jackie Gleason *Jack "Papa" Griffith* • Glynis Johns *Ambolyn Griffith* • Charles Ruggles *Grandpa Anthony Ghio* • Laurel Goodwin *Augusta Griffith* • Linda Bruhl *Corinne Griffith* ■ *Dir* George Marshall • *Scr* Jack Rose, from the non-fiction book by Corinne Griffith

The Paper ★★★★ 15
Comedy drama   1994 · US · Colour · 106min

Michael Keaton heads a formidable cast as a city editor on the New York *Sun* in a highly engaging and absorbing look at 24 hours in the life of an ailing tabloid. As Keaton faces another day of decisions, deadlines and compromises both job-wise (he's being head-hunted by rival editor Spalding Gray) and personally (his pregnant wife, Marisa Tomei, is feeling neglected), director Ron Howard deftly ties the numerous story strands together with some vibrantly snappy dialogue. This is very much an ensemble film: Robert Duvall is superb as the editor who has sacrificed his life for the paper, while Glenn Close cleverly shows the difficulties of being a woman with power over men. DP Swearing. **DVD**

Michael Keaton *Henry Hackett* • Glenn Close *Alicia Clark* • Robert Duvall *Bernie White* • Marisa Tomei *Martha Hackett* • Randy Quaid *McDougal* • Jason Robards *Graham Keighley* • Jason Alexander *Marion Sandusky* • Spalding Gray *Paul Bladden* • Catherine O'Hara *Susan* • Lynne Thigpen *Janet* ■ *Dir* Ron Howard • *Scr* David Koepp, Stephen Koepp

The Paper Chase ★★★★ PG
Comedy drama   1973 · US · Colour · 106min

The 71-year-old John Houseman won a best supporting actor Oscar for his unforgettable portrayal of a Harvard law professor in this fine drama from James Bridges. While the central, intellectual duel between Houseman, an absolute stickler for excellence, and Timothy Bottoms as his rather obnoxious student makes for bracing entertainment, Bridges also tosses in some contrived subplots, including a rather gooey romance. Houseman repeated his role in the TV series that followed. AT

Timothy Bottoms *Hart* • Lindsay Wagner *Susan* • John Houseman *Kingsfield* • Graham Beckel *Ford* • Edward Herrmann *Anderson* • Bob Lydiard *O'Connor* • Craig Richard Nelson *Bell* ■ *Dir* James Bridges • *Scr* James Bridges, from the novel *The Paper Chase* by John Jay Osborn Jr

Paper Clips ★★★ U
Documentary   2004 · US · Colour · 83min

Tolerance and diversity are celebrated in this unsophisticated yet well-intentioned documentary. Exploring the way a 1999 American school project to commemorate the Holocaust resulted in a lasting monument to the victims of Hitler's Final Solution, it's a fascinating story if clumsily told. In over-stretched detail, co-directors Elliot Berlin and Joe Fab catalogue how pupils at Whitwell Middle School in Tennessee attempted to visualise the enormity of the Nazis' crimes by collecting one paper clip (a symbol of Second World War Norwegian resistance) for every Jew murdered. SF English, German +subtitles. **DVD**

■ *Dir* Joe Fab, Elliot Berlin • *Scr* Joe Fab • *Cinematographer* Michael Marton

Paper Heart ★★ PG
Documentary comedy drama   2009 · US · Colour · 84min

An over-arching smugness blights this comic investigation into true love, as performance artist Charlyne Yi adopts a faux childlike inability to understand affairs of the heart when she traverses the US to question couples, marriage-industry eccentrics and even bikers about romance. However, she and director Nicholas Jasenovec go off-track, as Yi "falls for" *Juno* star Michael Cera. The precise nature of their relationship has been much debated, but it's an irrelevance beside the superciliousness of the mockumentary conceit and the mediocrity of the pair's acting. DP **DVD** Blu

Charlyne Yi • Michael Cera • Jake Johnson *Nicholas Jasenovec* • Seth Rogen ■ *Dir* Nicholas Jasenovec • *Scr* Charlyne Yi, Nicholas Jasenovec

Paper Hearts ★★★
Drama   1993 · US · Colour · 90min

Sally Kirkland is a good 'ole Southern gal, dutifully married to wandering lothario James Brolin with two grown-up daughters (Renée Estevez and Pamela Gidley) and a patient, biding-his-time cowboy boyfriend (Kris Kristofferson). It's an intelligent, grown-up movie that is both resonant and affecting, if a little pat. FL

Sally Kirkland *Jenny* • James Brolin *Henry* • Kris Kristofferson *Tom* • Pamela Gidley *Samantha* • Laura Johnson *Patsy* • Michael Moore (4) *Bill* • Renée Estevez *Kat* • Mickey Cottrell *Brady* ■ *Dir/Scr* Rod McCall

Paper Lion ★★★
Comedy drama based on a true story
1968 · US · Colour · 107min

This is an engagingly good-tempered "mockumentary" from sports writer George Plimpton's bestseller about his time as quarterback for the Detroit Lions American football team. Technical knowledge of the game is unnecessary because Alan Alda, in his first starring role, interprets for us through his naive, amateurish actions, while Lauren Hutton is a pleasure to watch as Alda's secretary. There are also cameos from middleweight boxing champion Sugar Ray Robinson, and other American sporting heroes. TH Swearing.

Alan Alda *George Plimpton* • Lauren Hutton *Kate* • David Doyle *Oscar* • Ann Turkel *Susan* ■ *Dir* Alex March • *Scr* Lawrence Roman, from the book by George Plimpton

Paper Marriage ★★ 15
Romantic comedy drama
1991 · UK/Pol · Colour · 84min

A Polish woman arrives in Newcastle to marry a British man, but discovers he's decided against it. Reluctant to return to home, she blindly suggests marriage to the astonished Gary Kemp, hoping she can then get to stay in the country. As the down-on-his-luck artist desperately needs money, he

goes along with her indecent proposal. Strong on characterisation and humour, low on plausibility, but shot through with engaging pathos. AJ

Gary Kemp *Aiden Carey* • Joanna Trzepiecinska *Alicja Stralkowska* • Rita Tushingham *Lou* • Richard Hawley *Red* • William Ilkley *Jack* • Gary Whelan *Boss* • Ann Mitchell *Phyllida* • Fred Pearson *Officer Crane* ■ *Dir* Krzysztof Lang • *Scr* Krzysztof Lang, Marek Kreutz, Debbie Horsfield

Paper Mask ★★★ 15
Thriller   1990 · UK · Colour · 99min

The stories you occasionally read in the papers about people who somehow manage to pass themselves off as medics are the inspiration for this dark tale. It stars Paul McGann as the hospital porter-turned-bogus doctor and Amanda Donohoe as the A&E nurse who becomes involved in his deception. Director Christopher Morahan turns in a spookily plausible thriller. PF Some violence, nudity. **DVD**

Paul McGann *Matthew Harris* • Amanda Donohoe *Christine Taylor* • Frederick Treves *Dr Mumford* • Tom Wilkinson *Dr Thorn* • Barbara Leigh-Hunt *Celia Mumford* • Jimmy Yuill *Alec Moran* • Mark Lewis Jones *Dr Lloyd* ■ *Dir* Christopher Morahan • *Scr* John Collee

Paper Moon ★★★★ PG
Period comedy drama   1973 · US · BW · 98min

The wandering star of Peter Bogdanovich's directorial talent brilliantly lights up this cynical charmer of a story – set during the Depression – of a Bible-toting conman (Ryan O'Neal) forming a bizarre partnership with the brattish nine-year-old (real-life daughter Tatum O'Neal) who may or may not be his child. Laszlo Kovacs's outstanding monochromatic photography lends an affectionate sheen to a quest through the Kansas dustbowl in which the girl gradually becomes mother to the man. With this, *Targets*, and *The Last Picture Show*, Bogdanovich looked set to be one of Hollywood's finest but, sadly, he hasn't managed to repeat the excellence of these three movies. TH **DVD** Blu

Ryan O'Neal *Moses Pray* • Tatum O'Neal *Addie Loggins* • Madeline Kahn *Trixie Delight* • John Hillerman *Sheriff Hardin/Jess Hardin* • PJ Johnson *Imogene* • Randy Quaid *Leroy* ■ *Dir* Peter Bogdanovich • *Scr* Alvin Sargent, from the novel *Addie Pray* by Joe David Brown

Paper Planes ★★★ U
Drama   2014 · Aus · Colour · 96min

Ed Oxenbould is the Outback lad who's a whiz at folding and flying paper planes. But his plans to enter regional heats for a world paper plane throwing competition look like being scuppered by grieving dad Sam Worthington, who's been barely functional since the death five months earlier of his wife. No prizes for guessing that paper planes ultimately play a key role in renewed father/son bonding. It's as corny as Kellogg's, but it's worth catching if you and the kids are in the mood for some pleasant Oz escapism. DA **DVD**

Ed Oxenbould *Dylan* • Sam Worthington *Jack* • Deborah Mailman *Maureen* • Nicholas Bakopoulos-Cooke *Jason* ■ *Dir* Robert Connolly • *Scr* Robert Connolly, Steve Worland

Paper Souls ★★★ 12A
Romantic fantasy
2013 · Fr/Lux/Bel · Colour · 97min

Plagued by writer's block since his wife's death five years earlier, novelist Stéphane Guillon now makes a living writing funeral orations. However, he has misgivings when bookshop owner Julie Gayet asks him to commemorate her long-dead husband on her son's eighth birthday. The performances are admirably restrained but, for all its melancholy charm, this never delves deeply enough into issues like loss, loneliness, memory and healing before tying up the loose ends a tad too neatly. DP French +subtitles. Swearing.

Stéphane Guillon *Paul* • Julie Gayet *Emma* • Jonathan Zaccaï *Nathan* • Pierre Richard *Victor* • Jules Rotenberg *Adam* ■ *Dir* Vincent Lannoo • *Scr* François Uzan

Paper Tiger ★★★ PG
Comedy adventure   1974 · UK · Colour · 95min

David Niven was a fine actor, at his best when playing life-cashiered failures, as in *Separate Tables* for which he won an Oscar, and in this otherwise tedious effort. He's the tutor to a Japanese child who finds he has to live up to the Walter Mitty-ish fantasies with which he's entertained the boy when both are kidnapped by terrorists. His performance as a man trying to make up for a loser's lifetime is at once noble and sad, and it lifts this rather leaden idea. TH

David Niven *Walter Bradbury* • Toshiro Mifune *Ambassador Kagoyama* • Hardy Kruger *Muller* • Ando Koichi *Kagoyama* • Ivan Desny *Foreign minister* • Irene Tsu *Talah* • Ronald Fraser *Forster* ■ *Dir* Ken Annakin • *Scr* Jack Davies

Paper Towns ★★★ 12
Romantic road movie
2015 · US · Colour · 109min

The consequences of a nerdy teen's infatuation with the free-spirited girl across the street shape this adaptation of John Green's bestseller. One evening, Cara Delevingne's independent night-owl calls on Nat Wolff's protagonist for help on a revenge spree – and that's the catalyst for her sudden disappearance. Credibility isn't the movie's strongest suit, but there are some insights into the downside of youthful romantic obsession, and Wolff's high-school chums warrant comparison with those of the John Hughes era. TJ Some swearing, sexual references. **DVD** Blu

Nat Wolff *Quentin Jacobsen* • Cara Delevingne *Margo Roth Spiegelman* • Halston Sage *Lacey Pemberton* • Austin Abrams *Ben Starling* ■ *Dir* Jake Schreier • *Scr* Scott Neustadter, Michael H Weber, from John Green's novel

A Paper Wedding ★★★
Drama   1989 · Can · Colour · 90min

Released around the same time as *Green Card*, this Canadian drama also focuses on a marriage of convenience, only without the laughs. Although normally outspoken in his political views, director Michel Brault resists the temptation to soapbox about either the conditions in Chile at the time or the illogicalities of the Canadian immigration system. Consequently, what emerges is a film that argues its case without distracting from the human drama that unfolds when college professor Geneviève Bujold is given just three days to dispose of her married lover and get to know exiled Chilean dissident Manuel Aranguiz. DP French +subtitles.

Geneviève Bujold *Claire* • Manuel Aranguiz *Pablo* • Dorothée Berryman *Annie* • Monique Lepage *Gaby* • Teo Spychalski *Milosh* ■ *Dir* Michel Brault • *Scr* Jefferson Lewis, Andrée Pelletier, with the collaboration of Sylvain Brault

Paperback Hero ★★★ 15
Romantic comedy   1998 · Aus · Colour · 92min

The karaoke love duet should be the nail in any film's coffin. Yet this outback-set romantic comedy survives reasonably intact thanks to the amiable performances of Hugh Jackman, as a handsome trucker who secretly pens period romances, and Claudia Karvan, as the feisty crop-dusting mate he persuades to front his popular novel on a PR campaign so that she can afford to marry the local vet. Pleasing but utterly predictable entertainment. DP **DVD**

Claudia Karvan *Ruby Vale* • Hugh Jackman *Jack Willis* • Angie Milliken *Ziggy Keane* • Andrew S Gilbert *Hamish* • Jeanie Drynan *Suzie* • Bruce Venables *Artie* • Barry Rugless *Mad Pete* • Barry Lea *Policeman* ■ *Dir/Scr* Antony J Bowman

The Paperboy ★ 15
Thriller   2012 · US · Colour · 102min

Ostensibly a steamy crime thriller, this begins in John Grisham territory with Florida slacker Zac Efron teaming up with his high-flying reporter brother (Matthew McConaughey) to investigate the possibly unsafe conviction of local cop killer John Cusack. They are aided by white-trash murder groupie Nicole Kidman, whose arrival signals the film's rapid descent into camp farce. Inept y directed and clumsily acted, *The Paperboy*'s brute, laugh-out-loud awfulness does add some entertainment value. But it is hard to identify anything in this mess that can really, in any way seriously, be described as good. DW **DVD**

Matthew McConaughey *Ward Jansen* • Zac Efron *Jack Jansen* • Nicole Kidman *Charlotte Bless* • David Oyelowo *Yardley Acheman* • Macy Gray *Anita Chester* • John Cusack *Hillary Van Wetter* • Scott Glenn *WW James* ■ *Dir* Lee Daniels • *Scr* Lee Daniels, Pete Dexter, from Dexter's novel

Paperhouse ★★★ 15
Fantasy horror 1988 · UK · Colour · 88min

This is a highly intelligent horror, in which the terror comes from the exploration of the subconscious rather than from banal schlock set pieces. Neglected by busy father Ben Cross and at loggerheads with (miscast) mother Glenne Headly, Charlotte Burke is the 11-year-old who enters a threatening world shaped by her dreams and the drawings in her notebook. Great credit must go to the art designers Frank Walsh and Anne Tilby for turning the childish sketches into disturbing landscapes. DP Swearing. **DVD**

Charlotte Burke *Anna Madden* • Elliott Spiers *Marc* • Glenne Headly *Kate* • Ben Cross *Dad* • Gemma Jones *Dr Sarah Nichols* • Sarah Newbold *Karen* • Samantha Cahill *Sharon* ■ *Dir* Bernard Rose • *Scr* Matthew Jacobs, from the novel *Marianne Dreams* by Catherine Storr

Papillon ★★★★ 15
Biographical prison drama 1973 · US · Colour · 144min

On its original release, the critics had few good words to say about this adaptation of Henri Charrière's autobiographical account of his escape from Devil's Island. But time has looked favourably on *The Shawshank Redemption* of its day, with director Franklin J Schaffner's stately pace and careful development of the forbidding prison atmosphere adding greatly to a harrowing study of confinement and single-mindedness. Steve McQueen plays the convict bent on breaking free and is perhaps a little too enigmatic for his own good. But Dustin Hoffman (as a fretful counterfeiter) produces a splendid depiction of cunning corruption. DP Violence, swearing, nudity. **DVD**

Steve McQueen (1) *Henri Charrière, Papillon* • Dustin Hoffman *Louis Dega* • Victor Jory *Indian Chief* • Don Gordon *Julot* • Anthony Zerbe *Toussaint, Leper Colony Chief* • Robert Deman *Maturette* • Woodrow Parfrey *Clusiot* • Bill Mumy *Lariot* • George Coulouris *Dr Chatal* ■ *Dir* Franklin J Schaffner • *Scr* Dalton Trumbo, Lorenzo Semple Jr, from the novel by Henri Charrière

Paprika ★★★★ 15
Animated science-fiction thriller 2006 · Jpn · Colour · 86min

This surreal *anime* delves into the language of the unconscious and has been cited by Christopher Nolan as an inspiration for his 2010 dream thriller *Inception*. It centres on a revolutionary high-tech device that lets a psychotherapist enter her patients' dreams and analyse their neuroses in situ. But after several of the machines are stolen, the line between reality and dreams begins to blur. It's too labyrinthine for its own good, but the cavalcade of images builds into a visually ravishing cartoon for grown-ups. JR Japanese +subtitles.

Megumi Hayashibara *Paprika/Dr Atsuko Chiba* • Toru Furuya *Kosaku Tokita* • Akio Ohtsuka *Detective Toshimi Konakawa* ■ *Dir* Satoshi Kon • *Scr* Seishi Minakami Satoshi Kon, from Yasutaka Tsutsui's novel

Paracelsus ★★★
Historical drama 1943 · Ger · BW · 107min

This is one of the most controversial films from the great impressionist director GW Pabst. Made for the Nazi regime, and starring the favourite actor of both Pabst and the Third Reich, Werner Krauss, the film transforms its hero, who rescues a city from the plague only to have its inhabitants

turn on him, into a surrogate Führer, a poor-boy-made-good and a genius ahead of his time. Excessively talky, episodic and blatantly tendentious, it has been condemned by some as an example of a great talent reduced to studio hack, but at least one astounding sequence displays the director's celebrated pictorial imagination and flair. TV German +subtitles.

Werner Krauss *Paracelsus* • Mathias Wieman *Ulrich von Hutten* • Harald Kreutzberg *Fliegenbein* • Martin Urtel *Johannes* • Harry Langewisch *Hans Pfefferkorn* • Annelies Reinhold *Renata Pfefferkorn, his daughter* ■ *Dir* GW Pabst • *Scr* Kurt Heuser • *Cinematographer* Herbert Stephan

Parade ★ U
Comedy documentary 1974 · Fr/Swe · Colour · 112min

This Swedish TV co-production filmed in a circus tent in Sweden using video techniques was sadly Jacques Tati's last film. Basically, the film records a series of dismal repetitive provincial circus acts in between Tati's own appearances. As director, Tati attempts to demonstrate his whimsical philosophy that everyone's a clown by showing members of the audience. There are few more depressing experiences in the cinema than watching admired comedians in stuff far below their talent. RB **DVD**

Jacques Tati *Circus performer* ■ *Dir/Scr* Jacques Tati • *Cinematographers* Jean Badal, Gunnar Fischer

The Parade ★★★★ PG
Drama 1984 · US · Colour · 91min

Directed with considerable care by Peter Hunt, this compelling TV drama is set in a small Kansas town on the eve of the annual Fourth of July parade. The story focuses on the impact on three women of the return of a recently released prisoner. Frederic Forrest gives one of his best performances as the returning drifter, inspiring solid work from his co-stars in the process. DP **DVD**

Michael Learned *Rachel Kirby* • Frederic Forrest *Matt Kirby* • Rosanna Arquette *Tilda Kirby* • Maxwell Caulfield *Jeff* • James Olson *Andy Janacek* • Geraldine Page *Sarah* ■ *Dir* Peter H Hunt • *Scr* N Richard Nash, Emily Tracy, from the story by N Richard Nash

The Paradine Case ★★★ U
Crime drama 1947 · US · BW · 114min

This is one of those pictures that no amount of professional polish could save. Producer David O Selznick and director Alfred Hitchcock disagreed over the script, the shooting style and the leads (Hitchcock wanting Laurence Olivier and Greta Garbo for the roles filled by Gregory Peck and Alida Valli, in her US film debut), and the discord shows on screen. Peck looks uncomfortable as the lawyer who jeopardises his career and his marriage to help Valli, who's accused of murdering her husband. Hitchcock is always watchable, but this should have been so much better. DP **DVD**

Gregory Peck *Anthony Keane* • Valli [Alida Valli] *Maddalena Paradine* • Ann Todd *Gay Keane* • Charles Laughton *Lord Horfield* • Charles Coburn *Sir Simon Flaquer* • Ethel Barrymore *Lady Sophie Horfield* • Louis Jourdan *Andre Latour* ■ *Dir* Alfred Hitchcock • *Scr* David O Selznick, Alma Reville, James Bridie, from the novel by Robert Hichens

Paradise ★★★ 12
Drama 1991 · US · Colour · 106min

Melanie Griffith and Don Johnson star in this remake of the French film *Le Grand Chemin*, playing a married couple at war over the loss of a child. Elijah Wood is the ten-year-old from Manhattan who comes to stay with them and makes friends with girl-next-door Thora Birch. It's less lurid and more convincing than its Gallic predecessor, and first-time director Mary Agnes Donoghue shows she can cope with people, not just special effects. Both Johnson and Griffith deliver honest performances. TH Swearing, nudity. **DVD**

Melanie Griffith *Lily Reed* • Don Johnson *Ben Reed* • Elijah Wood *Willard Young* • Thora Birch *Billie Pike* • Sheila McCarthy *Sally Pike* • Eve Gordon *Rosemary Young* • Louise Latham *Catherine Reston Lee* ■ *Dir* Mary Agnes Donoghue • *Scr* Mary Agnes Donoghue, from the film *Le Grand Chemin* by Jean-Loup Hubert

Paradise Alley ★★ 15
Period comedy drama 1978 · US · Colour · 102min

Having scripted *Rocky* and *FIST*, Sylvester Stallone made his debut as a writer/director with this sentimental story of three brothers trying to claw their way out of the poverty trap of Hell's Kitchen in the 1940s. When one brother, Lee Canalito, becomes a successful wrestler, the others climb aboard his bandwagon. Stallone's approach is strong on period atmosphere, but with a tendency to overcook the dialogue. AT **DVD**

Sylvester Stallone *Cosmo Carboni* • Lee Canalito *Victor "Kid Salami" Carboni* • Armand Assante *Lenny Carboni* • Frank McRae *Big Glory* • Anne Archer *Annie O'Sherlock* • Kevin Conway *"Stitch" Mahon* • Terry Funk *"Franky the Thumper"* • Joyce Ingalls *Bunchie* ■ *Dir/Scr* Sylvester Stallone

Paradise Canyon ★★ U
Western 1935 · US · BW · 52min

This is another of John Wayne's many films for poverty row studio Monogram, so like all the others that it's virtually impossible to tell them apart: plenty of scenes of horses galloping across the brush and a few fist fights. Once again stunt specialist Yakima Canutt plays the baddie and the Duke's undercover agent has to call on the help of suspicious locals to bring him to book. DP **DVD**

John Wayne *John Wyatt* • Marion Burns *Linda Carter* • Earle Hodgins *Dr Carter* • Yakima Canutt *Curly Joe Gale* • Reed Howes *Trigger* ■ *Dir* Carl Pierson • *Scr* Lindsley Parsons, Robert Tansey [Robert Emmett], from a story by Lindsley Parsons

Paradise for Three ★★★ U
Comedy 1938 · US · BW · 77min

The delightful Mary Astor sues American millionaire soap-manufacturer Frank Morgan for breach of promise in this romantic comedy. Set in the German Alps on the eve of the Second World War, there are some thoughtful undertones, as Morgan's character tries to assimilate himself with the German people to understand their way of life. Eddie Buzzell directs with a light touch, and the supporting cast includes Edna May Oliver as Morgan's housekeeper. TV

Frank Morgan *Rudolph Tobler/Edward Schultze* • Robert Young (1) *Fritz Hagedorn* • Mary Astor *Mrs Mallebre* • Edna May Oliver *Aunt Julia Kunkel* • Florence Rice *Hilde Tobler* • Reginald Owen *Johann Kesselhut* • Henry Hull *Sepp* ■ *Dir* Edward Buzzell • *Scr* George Oppenheimer, Harry Ruskin, from the novel *Three Men in the Snow* by Erich Kästner

Paradise Grove ★★ 15
Black comedy drama 2003 · UK · Colour · 93min

Retirement-home carer Leyland O'Brien's existence among the Jewish OAPs of Paradise Grove is thrown into utter confusion by the arrival of waif-like beauty Lee Blakemore, who's on the run. Joining O'Brien as he attempts to help his ageing grandfather (Ron Moody) deal with the onset of senility, Blakemore offers proof that there is a life waiting beyond the four walls of "Death's departure lounge". This an uneven blend of Yiddish stereotypes and mawkish sentiment, with only Moody and Rula Lenska hitting the right tone. JR Swearing.

Ron Moody *Izzie Goldberg* • Rula Lenska *Dee Perry* • Lee Blakemore *Kim Wright* • Leyland O'Brien *Keith Perry* • John Cunningham (2) *Dr Norman* • Dorothea Alexander *Mrs Wallenstein* • Leelo Ross *Annie Libowitz* • Georgette Pallard *Carolina* • Andy Lucas *Garrison Moss* ■ *Dir/Scr* Charles Harris

Paradise, Hawaiian Style ★★ U
Musical 1966 · US · Colour · 87min

Elvis Presley struck box-office gold with the massive hit *Blue Hawaii* back in 1961, and the combination of sun, surf, girls and song was too good to let rest. Unfortunately, this time out, the formula looks decidedly shopworn, and this movie formed part of the downward spiral that would eventually destroy the on-screen credibility of the King of rock 'n' roll. Elvis himself reveals a charming persona, but the thin plot and unmemorable songs undermine his efforts. TS **DVD**

Elvis Presley *Rick Richards* • Suzanna Leigh *Judy Hudson* • James Shigeta *Danny Kohana* • Donna Butterworth *Jan Kohana* • Marianna Hill *Lani* • Irene Tsu *Pua* • Linda Wong *Lehua* ■ *Dir* Michael Moore (1) • *Scr* Allan Weiss, Anthony Lawrence, from a story by Allan Weiss

Paradise Lost ★★★ 18
Horror adventure thriller 2006 · US · Colour · 91min

Six tourists backpacking through Brazil get stranded in the jungle after their bus crashes, in this cross between *The Beach* and *Hostel*. A local boy offers to let them stay at his uncle's house (who just happens to be a surgeon), but they soon find that the hospitality comes at a very high price. Things start off bright and breezy, before turning dark and grungy as the overly naive travellers (including Josh Duhamel and Melissa George) slowly recognise the true dangers facing them. There are some sharp shocks and grisly scenes involving skewers, hooks and staple guns, but what grips most here is a breathtaking underwater chase. A savvy twist on the horror staple of brash strangers clashing with an alien culture. AJ English, Portuguese +subtitles. **DVD**

Josh Duhamel *Alex* • Melissa George *Pru* • Olivia Wilde *Bea* • Desmond Askew *Finn* • Beau Garrett *Amy* • Max Brown *Liam* • Agles Steib *Kiko* ■ *Dir* John Stockwell • *Scr* Michael Arlen Ross

Paradise Now ★★★★ 15
Political drama 2005 · Neth/Ger/Fr/Palestinian Territories · Colour · 87min

Director Hany Abu-Assad's Oscar-nominated and sobering drama is combustible and controversial political cinema. Two Palestinian suicide bombers (Kais Nashef and Ali Suliman) are prepared for a mission into Israel. But it all goes horribly wrong and leaves one of the men on the run with immovable explosives strapped to his chest. Both humane and non-partisan sides of the conflict are presented in understandable terms, and further authenticity is supplied by the dusty action actually being filmed on the West Bank. The mindset of those primed to sacrifice their futures for a cause they barely comprehend is chillingly conveyed here. AJ Arabic +subtitles. Swearing. **DVD**

Kais Nashef *Said* • Ali Suliman *Khaled* • Lubna Azabal *Suha* • Amer Hlehel *Jamal* • Hiam Abbass *Said's mother* • Ashraf Barhoum *Abu-Karem* • Mohammad Bustami *Abu-Salim* ■ *Dir* Hany Abu-Assad • *Scr* Hany Abu-Assad, Bero Beyer

Paradisio ★
Spy spoof 1962 · UK · BW and Tinted · 90min

Even though Jacques Henrici does have a blink-and-you'll-miss-it screen credit, no one ever publicly owned up to directing this silly comedy and it's easy to see why. Arthur Howard (brother of the more famous Leslie) struggles as a dotty professor whose discovery of x-ray sunglasses makes him the target for spies and the bane of women everywhere. Downright odd, but nice European locations. DP Nudity.

Arthur Howard (1) *Professor Sims* • Eva Waegner *Lisa Hinkle* ■ *Dir* Jacques Henrici • *Scr* Lawrence Zeitlin, Henri Haile, Jacques Henrici

Paragraph 175 ★★★★
Documentary 1999 · UK/Ger/US · BW and Colour · 76min

This is another fine documentary from the makers of *The Celluloid Closet*, Rob Epstein and Jeffrey Friedman. By the fall of the Berlin Wall, only ten of the tens of thousands of gay men detained by the Nazis were still alive (lesbians were not subjected to such energetic oppression). Recalling the good old days of Weimar decadence and the living hell of the camps, these unassuming survivors piece together a genuinely moving "forgotten history" of the persecution that, like that of Romanies, has not received as much media or historical attention as the Jewish Holocaust. **DP** English, French, German +subtitles.

Rupert Everett *Narrator* ■ *Dir* Rob Epstein, Jeffrey Friedman • *Scr* Sharon Wood

The Parallax View
★★★★★ 15
Thriller   1974 · US · Colour · 97min

Two years before *All the President's Men*, Alan J Pakula directed this potent and startling conspiracy thriller. Investigating a political assassination, reporter Warren Beatty uncovers evidence of a sinister agency called the Parallax Corporation, which recruits its marksmen from the dregs of disillusioned society. With an excellent script, stunning photography, and perfect acting, the story of Beatty's infiltration of the society and his attempt to foil yet another killing is riveting and fascinating. **AJ** Violence, swearing. *DVD*

Warren Beatty *Joe Frady* • Paula Prentiss *Lee Carter* • William Daniels (2) *Austin Tucker* • Walter McGinn *Jack Younger* • Hume Cronyn *Rintels* • Kelly Thordsen *LD* • Chuck Waters *Assassin* • Earl Hindman *Red* ■ *Dir* Alan J Pakula • *Scr* David Giler, Lorenzo Semple Jr, from the novel by Loren Singer • *Cinematographer* Gordon Willis

Paramount on Parade   ★★
Musical revue
1930 · US · BW and Colour · 102min

One of the earliest but not one of the best of a seemingly endless supply of studio revues designed to show off a roster of contract stars. In later years the formula occasionally had some flimsy excuse for a plot attached to it, but this overstuffed ragbag, utilising the services of 11 directors, offers no such distraction. Sometimes tedious, sometimes ill-judged in matching the players to the material, this is nonetheless a collector's piece. **RK**

Jean Arthur • Mischa Auer • Clara Bow • Clive Brook • Nancy Carroll • Ruth Chatterton • Maurice Chevalier • Gary Cooper • Mitzi Green • Helen Kane • Fredric March • Nino Martini • Jack Oakie • Eugene Pallette • William Powell • Lillian Roth • Fay Wray ■ *Dir* Dorothy Arzner, Otto Brower, Edmund Goulding, Victor Heerman, Edwin H Knopf, Rowland V Lee, Ernst Lubitsch, Lothar Mendes, Victor Schertzinger, Edward Sutherland [A Edward Sutherland], Frank Tuttle

Paranoia   ★★ 12
Thriller   2013 · US/Fr · Colour · 101min

Owing a little to Oliver Stone's *Wall Street*, director Robert Luketic's moribund industrial espionage thriller stars Liam Hemsworth (*Hunger Games*) as a whizz-kid programmer who's tempted to sell his soul to pay for his ailing father's healthcare. Gary Oldman is the class act here, playing the corporate shark determined to find out what his former mentor (a scarily bald Harrison Ford) has up his sleeve. True, a movie that features Oldman and Ford (and Richard Dreyfuss) can't be all bad, but the bland leading man and lack of suspense create feelings of inertia rather than paranoia. **JA** Violence, swearing, a sex scene. *DVD*

Liam Hemsworth *Adam Cassidy* • Gary Oldman *Nicolas Wyatt* • Harrison Ford *Jock Goddard* • Amber Heard *Emma Jennings* • Richard Dreyfuss *Frank Cassidy* • Lucas Till *Kevin* ■ *Dir* Robert Luketic • *Scr* Jason Dean Hall, Barry L Levy [Barry Levy], from Joseph Finder's novel

Paranoiac   ★★★ 12
Horror   1963 · UK · BW · 79min

This is one of the best of a cycle of psychological horror films Hammer made in the 1960s. Heiress Janette Scott and her

crazy brother Oliver Reed are confronted by Alexander Davion, who claims to be their long-lost sibling. The plot and the devices (organ played in the middle of the night, car brakes tampered with) now seem very hackneyed. But this was very popular with rebellious teens, and the twist ending is still not easily guessable. **DM** *DVD* *BL*

Janette Scott *Eleanor Ashby* • Oliver Reed *Simon Ashby* • Liliane Brousse *Françoise* • Alexander Davion *Tony Ashby* • Sheila Burrell *Aunt Harriet* • Maurice Denham *John Kossett* • John Bonney *Keith Kossett* ■ *Dir* Freddie Francis • *Scr* Jimmy Sangster

Paranoid Park   ★★★ 15
Drama   2007 · Fr/US · Colour · 80min

In Gus Van Sant's indie drama suburban kid Alex (Gabe Nevins) starts hanging out with skateboarders and drifters in the real-life Portland park of the title, and is drawn into a murder mystery after a security guard is killed. Employing a highly experimental style, Van Sant delivers a disturbingly amoral portrait of American adolescence at its most apathetic. The movie frustrates as a drama but succeeds as a mood piece, as Van Sant re-creates the cocoon-like bubble of his protagonist's hormonal angst. It makes an absorbing, though considerably less controversial, companion piece to the film-maker's Columbine-inspired drama *Elephant*. **JR** *DVD* *BL*

Gabe Nevins *Alex* • Taylor Momsen *Jennifer* • Jake Miller *Jared* • Daniel Liu *Detective Richard Lu* • Lauren McKinney *Macy* • Scott Green *Scratch* • John Mike Burrowes *Security guard* • Grace Carter *Alex's mom* ■ *Dir* Gus Van Sant • *Scr* Gus Van Sant, from the novel by Blake Nelson

Paranormal Activity   ★★★★ 15
Supernatural horror   2007 · US · Colour · 82min

Writer/director Oren Peli's no-budget horror has a simplicity and a heightened sense of reality that creates a surprisingly effective sense of dread. The story is hardly original: a young couple thinks their new home is haunted. Nor is the *Blair Witch/Cloverfield* faux documentary way it's filmed: they set up video surveillance to capture what happens as they sleep. But the increasingly unpredictable and terrifying scares, playing to the most basic of primal fears, is what makes Peli's chiller work its spell. The minimal special effects and absence of music complement the eerie tension. **AJ** *DVD* *BL*

Katie Featherston *Katie* • Micah Sloat *Micah* • Amber Armstrong *Neighbour* • Mark Fredrichs *Psychic* • Ashley Palmer *Girl on internet* ■ *Dir/Scr* Oren Peli

Paranormal Activity 2   ★★ 15
Supernatural horror   2010 · US · Colour · 87min

This semi-prequel to the scary original is not as frightening as the first film. Here the action follows Katie's sister Kristi (Sprague Grayden) as unexplained phenomena occur in her family's California home after the birth of her son. There are a few loud bangs and the odd creepy visual to enliven the mundane surveillance-camera events, but the ominous foreboding and brooding intensity of the original are missing. Momentum does pick up in the final act when the connection between the two films becomes clearer, but this is mainly a calculated rehash. **AJ** Violence, swearing, sexual references. *DVD* *BL*

Sprague Grayden *Kristi* • Brian Boland *Daniel* • Molly Ephraim *Ali* • Katie Featherston *Katie* ■ *Dir* Tod Williams • *Scr* Michael R Perry, from characters by Oren Peli

Paranormal Activity 3   ★★★ 15
Horror   2011 · US · Colour · 80min

Surely wringing the last gasps from its exhausted found-footage premise, *Catfish* co-directors Henry Joost and Ariel Schulman's trip to the things-that-go-bump-in-the-night well is a tedious tease until a massive boost in the mad finale. Like

Paranormal Activity 2, this is also a prequel to the first film, but goes back even further, showing sisters Katie and Kristi traumatised by an "imaginary" playmate in 1988. In terms of location, this episode opens out more than the first two, and the slow-building, low-key creepiness finally explodes with a welcome rattling ingenuity. Joost directed a fourth film in 2012, with a fifth released in 2014. A spin-off was also released in 2014, but this time directed by Christopher Landon. **AJ** Swearing. *DVD* *BL*

Lauren Bittner *Julie* • Chris Smith [Christopher Nicholas Smith] *Dennis* • Katie Featherston *Adult Katie* • Sprague Grayden *Adult Kristi* ■ *Dir* Henry Joost, Ariel Schulman • *Scr* Christopher Landon [Christopher B Landon], from characters by Oren Peli

Paranormal Activity 4   ★★ 15
Horror   2012 · US · Colour · 87min

Doors creak, shadows flicker, cats jump: the laziest sequel yet in the supernatural franchise barely bothers to change the formula at all. After recapping the conclusion of the second film, the story jumps to 2011, when a Nevada family take in the young son of their mysterious new neighbour after she's admitted to hospital. Soon the boy is having a detrimental effect on the family's own six-year-old, talking to an invisible "friend" and awakening malevolent forces. This instalment adds absolutely nothing to the series mythology, but horror fans will at least cling to the *Rosemary's Baby* and *Poltergeist* references when little else is happening on screen for long periods of time. Joost directed a fifth film in 2014, with a spin-off also released in 2014, this time directed by Christopher Landon. **AJ** Swearing.

Kathryn Newton *Alex* • Matt Shively *Ben* • Brady Allen *Robbie* • Aiden Lovekamp *Wyatt* • Katie Featherston *Katie* ■ *Dir* Henry Joost, Ariel Schulman • *Scr* Zack Estrin, from characters by Oren Peli

Paranormal Activity: the Ghost Dimension   ★★ 15
Horror   2015 · US · Colour · 87min

Editor of the found-footage franchise since Part 2, Gregory Plotkin makes his directing debut with chapter six of the varying series. Here the Fleege family is subjected to the familiar terrors hidden in their new home, where they find a vintage video camera and VHS tapes. The most cinematic episode so far sports impressive special effects, but it still leans too hard on unexceptional scare tactics, with the dragged out ending collapsing into conventional ghost whispering and devilish dreariness. **AJ** Some violence, swearing. *sp*

Murray Chris J *Ryan Fleege* • Brit Shaw *Emily* • Dan Gill *Mike* • Ivy George *Leila* ■ *Dir* Gregory Plotkin • *Scr* Jason Pagan, Andrew Stark [Andrew Deutschman], Gavin Heffernan, Andrew Robitel, from characters by Oren Peli

ParaNorman   ★★★★ PG
Animated horror comedy
2012 · US · Colour · 88min

A misunderstood boy sees dead people and learns that his legacy is to break a 300-year-old witch's curse hanging over his New England community, in this delightfully quirky animated horror comedy that treats both genres with respect. Despite the subject matter, things always remain family friendly: kids will love the scary, spooky antics while adults can appreciate the superb stop-motion craftsmanship, clever humour and the look and atmosphere of the classic horror films. The thrilling finale is a terrific blend of heartfelt emotion, surreal visuals and inventive ghostly spectacle. **AJ** *DVD* *BL*

Kodi Smit-McPhee *Norman Babcock* • Tucker Albrizzi *Neil* • Anna Kendrick *Courtney* • Casey Affleck *Mitch* • Christopher Mintz-Plasse *Alvin* • Leslie Mann *Sandra Babcock* • Jeff Garlin *Perry Babcock* • John Goodman *Mr Prenderghast* ■ *Dir* Chris Butler, Sam Fell • *Scr* Chris Butler

Parasite   ★ 18
Science-fiction horror
1982 · US · Colour · 84min

In a post-holocaust future, where paramilitary forces and mutant punks clash, scientist Robert Glaudini creates a parasitic monster that burrows into its victims and eats them from the inside. This is a crummy exploitation movie that wastes the talents of its cast. Its one feature of note is that it cashed in on the early 1980s 3D revival frenzy, but it's junk. **AJ** *3D*

Robert Glaudini *Dr Paul Dean* • Demi Moore *Patricia Welles* • Luca Bercovici *Ricus* • James Davidson *Merchant* • Al Fann *Collins* • Tom Villard *Zeke* • Cherie Currie *Dana* ■ *Dir* Charles Band • *Scr* Michael Shoob, Frank Levering, Alan Adler [Alan J Adler]

Pardes   ★★★ PG
Musical romantic drama
1997 · Ind · Colour · 189min

This culture-clashing masala confirmed Subhash Ghai's status as a major Bollywood crowd pleaser. The common link is Shah Rukh Khan, who is detailed by US-based foster father Amrish Puri to matchmake his decadent son, Apoorva Agnihotri, with his old friend Alok Nath's demure daughter, Mahima Chaudhary. However, in teaching the couple about each other's values, virtues and vices, he ends up forming the third side of an inevitable romantic triangle. Chaudhary impresses in a role originally intended for Madhuri Dixit. **DP** Hindi +subtitles.

Shah Rukh Khan *Arjun* • Apoorva Agnihotri *Rajiv* • Mahima Chaudhary *Kusum Ganga* • Amrish Puri *Kishorilal* • Alok Nath *Suraj Dev* ■ *Dir* Subhash Ghai • *Scr* Subhash Ghai, Javed Siddiqi, from a story by Subhash Ghai

Pardners   ★★ U
Musical western spoof
1956 · US · Colour · 84min

Dean Martin and Jerry Lewis, making a last-ditch stand before splitting up their partnership, star as a ranch foreman and the well-intentioned but inept city greenhorn who helps him fend off a bunch of cattle raiders. Stomping about in buckskins and ten-gallon hats, the pair burlesques every cliché of the western tradition, but the one-dimensional screenplay yields insufficient hilarity. **RK** *DVD*

Dean Martin *Slim Mosely Sr/Slim Mosely Jr* • Jerry Lewis *Wade Kingsley Sr/Wade Kingsley Jr* • Lori Nelson *Carol Kingsley* • Jeff Morrow *Rio* • Jackie Loughery *Dolly Riley* • John Baragrey *Dan Hollis* • Agnes Moorehead *Mrs Kingsley* • Lon Chaney Jr *Whitey* • Lee Van Cleef *Gus* ■ *Dir* Norman Taurog • *Scr* Sidney Sheldon, Jerry David, from the story *Rhythm on the Range* by Marvin J Houser

Pardon Mon Affaire   ★★★
Comedy   1976 · Fr · Colour · 108min

If you think Yves Robert's sex comedy looks familiar, that's probably because it borrows heavily from *The Seven Year Itch* and was remade as *The Woman in Red*. However, neither Tom Ewell nor Gene Wilder can hold a candle to the comic ingenuity of Jean Rochefort, whose deliciously restrained performance atones for the slightness of the story, in which he risks his happy marriage to Danièle Delorme to pursue poster girl Anny Duperey. **DP** French dubbed.

Jean Rochefort *Etienne* • Claude Brasseur *Daniel* • Guy Bedos *Simon* • Victor Lanoux *Bouly* • Danièle Delorme *Marthe* • Anny Duperey *Charlotte* ■ *Dir* Yves Robert • *Scr* Jean-Loup Dabadie, Yves Robert

Pardon My Past   ★★★
Comedy   1945 · US · BW · 88min

While demobbed GI Fred MacMurray is on his way to start a mink farm with his pal William Demarest, he is hauled in by a gambler (Akim Tamiroff) who believes he is Francis Pemberton (also MacMurray), a playboy idler who owes Tamiroff money. MacMurray is appealing in his dual role, trying to deal with the complications that arise before this neat little comedy of mistaken identity resolves itself and he gets the girl (Marguerite Chapman). Director Leslie Fenton keeps an effective grip on the proceedings. RK

Fred MacMurray *Eddie York/Francis Pemberton* • Marguerite Chapman *Joan* • Akim Tamiroff *Jim Arnold* • William Demarest *Chuck Gibson* • Rita Johnson *Mary Pemberton* • Harry Davenport *Grandpa Pemberton* • Douglass Dumbrille *Uncle Wills* ■ *Dir* Leslie Fenton • *Scr* Earl Felton, Karl Kamb, from a story by Patterson McNutt, Harlan Ware

Pardon My Sarong ★★ U
Comedy 1942 · US · BW · 84min

Director Erle C Kenton finds himself cast adrift with comedians Bud Abbott and Lou Costello. Made to cash in on the South Seas bubble of the time – Dorothy Lamour's sarong was much in vogue – the duo are bus drivers who find themselves all at sea with a jewel thief, the sinister Lionel Atwill from Universal's horror stable. TH

Bud Abbott *Algy Shaw* • Lou Costello *Wellington Phlug* • Virginia Bruce *Joan Marshall* • Robert Paige *Tommy Layton* • Lionel Atwill *Dr Varnoff* • Leif Erickson *Whaba* • William Demarest *Detective Kendall* ■ *Dir* Erle C Kenton • *Scr* True Boardman, Nat Perrin, John Grant

Pardon Us ★★★ U
Prison comedy 1931 · US · BW · 64min

In this parody of the 1930 prison melodrama, *The Big House*, Laurel and Hardy play unintentional bootleggers who are imprisoned with two of their old faithfuls: spluttering James Finlayson and two-fisted hard man Walter Long. Some scenes are far from politically correct – the boys don blackface at one point – but Ollie warbles an attractive tenor, while Stan's loose tooth means it's raspberries all round. TH

Stan Laurel *Stan* • Oliver Hardy *Ollie* • June Marlowe *Warden's daughter* • Wilfred Lucas *Warden* • James Finlayson *Instructor* • Walter Long *Tiger* • Stanley J Sandford *Officer LeRoy Shields* ■ *Dir* James Parrott • *Scr* HM Walker • *Cinematographer* Jack Stevens

The Parent Trap ★★★ U
Comedy 1961 · US · Colour · 121min

Hayley Mills stars in a dual role as twins trying to reunite their divorced parents, played by Maureen O'Hara and an undercast, and seemingly uncomfortable, Brian Keith. Like many Disney films of the period, it's overlong, drawn out by the interminable section at a summer camp. But David Swift's direction is adroit – he also guided Mills through the previous year's *Pollyanna* which earned her a special Oscar – and Lucien Ballard's Technicolor photography is particularly fetching. Several sequels followed, and Disney remade the original in 1998. TS *DVD*

Hayley Mills *Sharon/Susan* • Maureen O'Hara *Maggie McKendrick* • Brian Keith *Mitch* • Charlie Ruggles [Charles Ruggles] *Charles McKendrick* • Una Merkel *Verbena* • Leo G Carroll *Rev Mosby* • Joanna Barnes *Vicky Robinson* • Cathleen Nesbitt *Louise McKendrick* ■ *Dir* David Swift • *Scr* David Swift, from the novel *Das Doppelte Lottchen* by Erich Kästner

The Parent Trap ★★★ PG
Comedy drama 1998 · US · Colour · 122min

Freckle-faced Lindsay Lohan is the American youngster who steps into Hayley Mills's shoes for this update of the 1961 original. Lohan plays twins separated not long after birth, one growing up with British wedding-gown designer Natasha Richardson, the other with her ex-husband, American vineyard owner Dennis Quaid. Meeting by chance at an American summer camp, the twins plot to bring their parents back together. Thanks to seamless special effects, it's impossible to tell there aren't really two Lohans, and this sentimental comedy should delight its target audience of young girls. SR *DVD*

Lindsay Lohan *Hallie James/Annie James* • Dennis Quaid *Nick Parker* • Natasha Richardson *Elizabeth James* • Elaine Hendrix *Meredith Blake* • Lisa Ann Walter *Chessy* • Simon Kunz *Martin* ■

Dir Nancy Meyers • *Scr* Nancy Meyers, Charles Shyer, David Swift, from the novel *Das Doppelte Lottchen* by Erich Kästner

Parental Guidance ★★ U
Comedy 2012 · US · Colour · 100min

Billy Crystal and Bette Midler play a couple of kooky old-timers who are asked to babysit their mollycoddled grandchildren. That means the kids are often left to their own devices, providing the perfect opportunity for some old-fashioned slapstick. Crystal and Midler make a charming double-act, with wisecracks aplenty, but they're reined in for a family audience. The story is as much about the strained relationship with their daughter (a frazzled Marisa Tomei) as their grandchildren, and although lessons are inevitably learned by all, it all feels a bit obvious, perfunctory and dated. SP *DVD* *blu* *CS*

Billy Crystal *Artie Decker* • Bette Midler *Diane Decker* • Marisa Tomei *Alice Decker Simmons* • Tom Everett Scott *Phil Simmons* • Bailee Madison *Harper Decker Simmons* • Joshua Rush *Turner Decker Simmons* • Kyle Harrison Breitkopf *Barker Decker Simmons* ■ *Dir* Andy Fickman • *Scr* Lisa Addario, Joe Syracuse

Parenthood ★★★★ 15
Comedy 1989 · US · Colour · 118min

Director Ron Howard's feel-good family ensemble piece just manages to stay the right side of sentimentality, and the result is an affectionate, leisurely comedy about the joys (and otherwise) of bringing up children. Steve Martin grabs the comic honours as the elder son of a family headed by crotchety Jason Robards, although there are fine performances, too, from the rest of the star-studded cast. Howard handles the large number of different story strands adeptly and he makes the most of the sharp script and some neat set pieces. JF Swearing. *DVD* *blu*

Steve Martin *Gil Buckman* • Mary Steenburgen *Karen Buckman* • Dianne Wiest *Helen* • Jason Robards *Frank* • Rick Moranis *Nathan* • Tom Hulce *Larry* • Keanu Reeves *Tod* • Martha Plimpton *Julie* • Harley Kozak [Harley Jane Kozak] *Susan* • Leaf Phoenix [Joaquin Phoenix] *Garry* ■ *Dir* Ron Howard • *Scr* Lowell Ganz, Babaloo Mandel, from a story by Lowell Ganz, Babaloo Mandel, Ron Howard

Parents ★★★★★ 18
Horror comedy 1988 · US · Colour · 78min

If the horsemeat scare didn't put you off eating beef, then Bob Balaban's grim horror comedy certainly will. Could Bryan Madorsky's suburban parents really be the cannibals he thinks they are? Or is he just a disturbed child suffering from juvenile hallucinations brought on by the atom-age anxieties of the Eisenhower 1950s? Set firmly in *Blue Velvet* territory, with a spot-on big band Muzak soundtrack, this disquieting explosion of the nuclear family unit will have you screaming with both laughter and revulsion. AJ Swearing.

Randy Quaid *Nick Laemle* • Mary Beth Hurt *Lily Laemle* • Sandy Dennis *Millie Dew* • Bryan Madorsky *Michael Laemle* • Juno Mills-Cockell *Sheila Zellner* • Kathryn Grody *Miss Baxter* • Deborah Rush *Mrs Zellner* • Graham Jarvis *Mr Zellner* ■ *Dir* Bob Balaban • *Scr* Christopher Hawthorne • *Music* Angelo Badalamenti

Les Parents Terribles ★★★★★
Drama 1948 · Fr · BW · 102min

Making few alterations to his original text, Jean Cocteau proved with this tragicomic tale of dysfunction and sexual frustration that it was possible to adapt a play and be inventively cinematic at the same time. The credits may roll over a stage curtain, the acts may be divided by captions and the action may be confined to two stylised sets, but through judicious use of telephoto lenses, rigid framing and punctilious editing, Cocteau is able to register every twisted emotion and treacherous expression as the skeletons tumble out of the closet and domineering matriarch Yvonne de Bray's world slowly falls apart. This remains one of

---

the finest examples of ensemble excellence in French screen history. DP In French.

Jean Marais *Michel* • Yvonne de Bray *Yvonne* • Gabrielle Dorziat *Aunt Léo* • Marcel André *Georges* • Josette Day *Madeleine* • Jean Cocteau *Narrator* ■ *Dir* Jean Cocteau • *Scr* Jean Cocteau, from his play • *Cinematographer* Michel Kelber

Le Parfum d'Yvonne ★★★ 18
Drama 1994 · Fr · Colour · 85min

Patrice Leconte always manages to create a world in which reality and fantasy happily co-exist. However, here he overdoes the unlikely to the extent that this charming but flimsy study of daydreaming and delusion has too little substance to support its more serious undercurrents. Hippolyte Girardot, in Swiss exile to avoid Algerian War service, and Sandra Majani, as the girl dreaming of movie stardom, are as dull as Jean-Pierre Marielle is camp. DP French +subtitles. Sex scenes, nudity. *DVD*

Jean-Pierre Marielle *René Meinthe* • Hippolyte Girardot *Victor Chmara* • Sandra Majani *Yvonne* • Richard Bohringer *Uncle Roland* • Paul Guers *Daniel Hendrickx* • Corinne Marchand *Tilleuls Patron* • Philippe Magnan *Pulli* ■ *Dir* Patrice Leconte • *Scr* Patrice Leconte, from the novel *Villa Triste* by Patrick Modiano

Parineeta ★★★★ U
Romantic drama 1953 · Ind · BW · 107min

Saratchandra Chatterjee's 1914 novel (which like his later *Devdas* is an Indian classic) has now been filmed five times. But this Bimal Roy adaptation remains the most admired and it's easy to see why. The story is rather convoluted, with Ashok Kumar's father seeking to cheat Meena Kumari's uncle out of his house, only for a neighbour (unaware that Ashok and Meena have wed) to settle the debt in return for Kumari's hand. The staging of the musical numbers and the tone of the romance are suitably restrained, making this an old-fashioned Bollywood delight. DP Hindi +subtitles. *DVD*

Ashok Kumar *Shekhar Rai* • Meena Kumari *Lalita* • Nasir Hussain (I) *Gurcharan Babu* • Ashit Baram [Asitbaran] *Girin Babu* • Badri Prasad *Nabin Rai* ■ *Dir* Bimal Roy • *Scr* Bimal Roy, Vrajendra Gaur, from the novel by Saratchandra Chatterjee

Parineeta ★★★★ 12
Romantic drama 2005 · Ind · Colour · 130min

This well crafted and spectacularly made love story exemplifies the stern determination Indian culture demands of the relationship between men and women. Saif Ali Khan plays the son of an affluent businessman whose deep friendship with neighbour Vidya Balan ignites with the arrival of outsider Sanjay Dutt. The literate script, rich colour schemes and wonderfully energetic song-and-dance set pieces evolve naturally in Pradeep Sarkar's splendid film. Khan brings his usual instinctive grace, but it's newcomer Balan who really catches the eye. OA Hindi +subtitles. *DVD*

Sanjay Dutt *Girish* • Vidya Balan *Lolita* • Raima Sen *Koel* • Saif Ali Khan *Shekhar* • Diya Mirza *Gayatri Tantia* • Sabyasachi Chakraborty *Navin* ■ *Dir* Pradeep Sarkar • *Scr* Vidhu Vinod Chopra, Pradeep Sarkar, from the novel by Sarat Chandra Chattopadhyay [Saratchandra Chatterjee]

Paris ★★★ 15
Romantic comedy drama 2007 · Fr · Colour · 123min

Like a Gallic Robert Altman, Cédric Klapisch populates this warm-hearted and sprawling portrait of the French capital with overlapping lives: Romain Duris plays a nightclub dancer who falls ill and needs a heart transplant, so his sister (Juliette Binoche), a single mother of three, moves in with him. Largely housebound, Duris spies on an attractive neighbour (Mélanie Laurent), while a university professor (Fabrice Luchini) bombards her with amorous text messages. What makes this work is the pace and sweep of the film and its sheer passion for Paris – from the Eiffel Tower to the fish market. It's a very likeable, if hardly ground-breaking, celebration of a great city. BP French +subtitles. Swearing. *DVD*

Juliette Binoche *Elise* • Romain Duris *Pierre* • Fabrice Luchini *Roland Verneuil* • Albert Dupontel *Jean* • François Cluzet *Philippe Verneuil* • Mélanie Laurent *Laetitia* ■ *Dir/Scr* Cédric Klapisch

Paris Blues ★★★★ 12
Romantic drama 1961 · US · BW · 94min

Paul Newman and Sidney Poitier click as footloose, free-spirited American jazzmen on the razzle in Paris, where pretty tourists Joanne Woodward and Diahann Carroll are understandably captivated by the charismatic musicians. The sensational Duke Ellington score provides the film's highlight. This offbeat affair from one of Newman's favourite directors, Martin Ritt, is also one of the most delightful jazz movies ever made. AME Some violence. *DVD*

Paul Newman *Ram Bowen* • Joanne Woodward *Lillian Corning* • Sidney Poitier *Eddie Cook* • Louis Armstrong *Wild Man Moore* • Diahann Carroll *Connie Lampson* • Serge Reggiani *Michel Duvigne* ■ *Dir* Martin Ritt • *Scr* Jack Sher, Irene Kamp, Walter Bernstein, Lulla Adler, from the novel by Harold Flender

Paris by Night ★★★ 15
Drama 1988 · UK · Colour · 99min

Film noir meets allegorical Thatcherite morality as the problems pile up for Conservative Euro MP Charlotte Rampling. Her marriage to alcoholic Michael Gambon is on the rocks and she's convinced she's being blackmailed. While in Paris for political talks, she is surprised by her suspected blackmailer and murders him. Utilising brittle dialogue, wilful obscurity and nightmarish visuals, David Hare conjures up a symbolic and often devastating fable about warped values in the yuppie 1980s. AJ

Charlotte Rampling *Clara Paige* • Michael Gambon *Gerald Paige* • Robert Hardy *Adam Gillvray* • Iain Glen *Wallace Sharp* • Jane Asher *Pauline* • Andrew Ray *Michael Swanton* • Niamh Cusack *Jenny Swanton* ■ *Dir/Scr* David Hare

Paris Calling ★★
Second World War drama 1941 · US · BW · 95min

Elisabeth Bergner's sole stab at a Hollywood career came with this routine wartime melodrama about underground resistance after the Germans capture Paris. She plays the wealthy Parisienne who joins the fight for freedom, with intrepid Randolph Scott as a downed RAF pilot and heinous Basil Rathbone as a French politician turned collaborator. Add Lee J Cobb as the top Nazi, and you have a cast that makes the proceedings just about watchable. AE

Elizabeth Bergner [Elisabeth Bergner] *Marianne* • Randolph Scott *Nick* • Basil Rathbone *Benoit* • Gale Sondergaard *Colette* • Lee J Cobb *Schwabe* ■ *Dir* Edwin L Marin • *Scr* Benjamin Glazer, Charles S Kaufman, from a story by John S Toldy

Paris Holiday ★★ U
Comedy 1958 · US · Colour · 109min

American comedian Bob Hope, while in Paris, buys a French script, unaware that it carries clues to a gang of counterfeiters. They send sexy blonde Anita Ekberg to lure Hope into their clutches, but she falls for him and shoves him into a lunatic asylum from where he is rescued by Fernandel. Wisecracker Hope and France's comic idol, Fernandel, prove an ill-matched pair, and this outing is strictly for committed fans of the two stars. RK

Bob Hope *Robert Leslie Hunter* • Fernandel *Ferndel* • Anita Ekberg *Zara* • Martha Hyer *Ann McCall* • Preston Sturges *Serge Vitry* • André Morell *American Ambassador* • Maurice Teynac *Dr Bernais* ■ *Dir* Gerd Oswald • *Scr* Edmund Beloin, Dean Riesner, from a story by Bob Hope

Paris Honeymoon ★★
Comedy 1939 · US · BW · 83min

Texas millionaire Bing Crosby, complete with ten-gallon hat, falls for countess Shirley Ross, pursues her to Europe, and rents himself a castle. Once installed, he falls in love with a local peasant girl (Franciska Gaal). As insubstantial as

P

---

gossamer, this nonsense, directed by Frank Tuttle with minimum style, includes a handful of forgotten songs and is definitely of interest only to Crosby fans. RK

Bing Crosby *"Lucky" Lawton* • Franciska Gaal *Manya* • Akim Tamiroff *Peter Karloca* • Shirley Ross *Barbara Wayne* • Edward Everett Horton *Ernest Figg* • Ben Blue *Sitska* • Albert Dekker *Drunken peasant* ■ *Dir* Frank Tuttle • *Scr* Frank Butler, Don Hartman, from a story by Angela Sherwood • *Cinematographer* Karl Struss

Paris Is Burning ★★★★ 15

Documentary 1990 · US · Colour · 73min

This brilliantly entertaining documentary peeks into the New York subculture of drag queens and transsexuals centred around "The Ball", a regular event that's part competition, part performance art and part ritual. Director Jennie Livingston's acerbic look at gay society's fringe-dwellers is a rapturous mixture of high spirits (the vogueing dance craze started in its hallowed Harlem venue), camp (the legendary Pepper Labeija living out an outlandish parody of a Hollywood star's life) and pathos (long-time pro Dorian Corey ashamed that the upcoming she-males don't even know who Marlene Dietrich is). AJ *DVD*

■ *Dir* Jennie Livingston

Paris, Je T'Aime ★★★ 15

Portmanteau drama
2006 · Fr/Liechtenstein/Swi · Colour and BW · 115min

Portmanteau pictures are notoriously patchy affairs and this handsome collection of 18 stories by 20 directors is no exception. Each vignette is set in a different arrondissement of Paris and is intended to capture the ambience of the locale. But while directors such as Wes Craven make effective use of their surroundings, others – including Isabelle Coixet, Richard LaGravenase, and Gérard Depardieu and Frédéric Auburtin – offer more intriguing insights into human nature. The most rounded and engaging episodes, however, are Alexander Payne's snapshot of American tourist Margo Martindale's holiday, Alfonso Cuarón's teasing record of Nick Nolte's rendezvous with Ludivine Sagnier, and the Coen brothers' comic account of Steve Buscemi's bruising encounter at the Tuileries Métro station. DP French, English +subtitles. *DVD*

■ *Dir* Bruno Podalydès, Gurinder Chadha, Gus Van Sant, Joel Coen, Ethan Coen, Walter Salles, Daniela Thomas, Christopher Doyle, Isabel Coixet, Nobuhiro Suwa, Sylvain Chomet, Alfonso Cuarón, Olivier Assayas, Oliver Schmitz, Richard LaGravenese, Vincenzo Natali, Wes Craven, Tom Tykwer, Frédéric Auburtin, Gérard Depardieu, Alexander Payne • *Scr* Gurinder Chadha, Gus Van Sant, Joel and Ethan Coen, Walter Salles, Alfonso Cuarón, Wes Craven, Gena Rowlands, Alexander Payne and others, from an original idea by Tristan Carne, from a feature concept by Emmanuel Benbihy

Paris-Manhattan ★★★ 12A

Romantic comedy 2012 · Fr · Colour · 77min

Riffing on everything from *Hannah and Her Sisters* to *Play It Again, Sam*, this comedy is a fun but insubstantial fan letter to Woody Allen. Alice (Alice Taglioni) lives her life according to the wisdom of Woody but because the men she meets never match up to her idol, she is still single, much to the despair of her dysfunctional Jewish family. However, when she has a choice between two admirers - one an Allen fan, the other who isn't, but may understand her better than she thinks - Alice is soon in a quandary. This homage to one of the Hollywood greats has oodles of charm, but if it was an actual Woody Allen film, it would have to go down as a minor work. JF French +subtitles.

Alice Taglioni *Alice* • Patrick Bruel *Victor* • Marine Delterme *Hélène* • Louis-Do de Lencquesaing *Pierre* • Michel Aumont *Father* • Marie-Christine Adam *Mother* • Yannick Soulier *Vincent* • Woody Allen ■ *Dir/Scr* Sophie Lellouche

Paris Nous Appartient ★★★★ 12

Mystery drama 1960 · Fr · BW · 135min

Like many French New Wave film-makers, Jacques Rivette began his career as a critic. Indeed, he was still working for the famous journal *Cahiers du Cinéma* while making this intense conspiracy picture, for which he had to borrow film stock from François Truffaut and a camera from Claude Chabrol. Betty Schneider stars as the Paris student who becomes curious about the suicide of a young Spaniard and decides to investigate. The fact that the action was shot over a two-year period is clearly evident in the inconsistent quality of the performances, but Rivette still crafts a complex and intriguing story. DP French +subtitles. *DVD*

Betty Schneider *Anne Goupil* • Gianni Esposito *Gérard Lenz* • Françoise Prévost *Terry Yordan* • Daniel Crohem *Philip Kaufman* • François Maistre *Pierre Goupil* • Jean-Claude Brialy *Jean-Marc* ■ *Dir* Jacques Rivette • *Scr* Jacques Rivette, Jean Gruault

Paris Qui Dort ★★

Silent fantasy 1923 · Fr · BW · 61min

René Clair's first feature, completed in three weeks, reflected some of the anarchic preoccupations of the surrealist and Dadaist artists with whom Clair associated at the time. The story, which he wrote in one night, tells of a crazed inventor who creates a "sleep ray" that suspends animation throughout Paris. Although the film is full of comic invention and absurdity, it is sometimes too self-consciously in love with its own cleverness, and the cinematic tricks begin to pall. RB

Henri Rollan *Albert* • Madeleine Rodrigue *Woman passenger* • Marcel Vallée *Thief* • Albert Préjean *Pilot* ■ *Dir/Scr* René Clair

Paris, Texas ★★★★★ 12

Drama 1984 · W Ger/Fr · Colour · 138min

Character actor Harry Dean Stanton enjoys a rare leading role in German director Wim Wenders's emotionally charged road movie. The odyssey begins as restless drifter Stanton walks out of the desert after a four-year absence and is reunited with his small son Hunter Carson, who's being cared for by his brother Dean Stockwell. Stanton then sets out to reclaim his family life by seeking out his estranged wife Nastassja Kinski, now a peep-show stripper. There's an urgency to the film, as Wenders brings an outsider's fresh eye to create this massive metaphor about rootless America. TH *DVD* *Blu-ray*

Harry Dean Stanton *Travis Anderson* • Nastassja Kinski *Jane* • Dean Stockwell *Walter R Anderson* • Aurore Clément *Anne Anderson* • Hunter Carson *Hunter Anderson* • Bernhard Wicki *Dr Ulmer* ■ *Dir* Wim Wenders • *Scr* Sam Shepard, from his story adapted by LM Kit Carson

Paris 36 ★★★★

Period drama 2008 · Fr/Ger/Cz Rep · Colour · 120min

Set in a working-class area of Paris in 1936, this tribute to traditional music-hall from *The Chorus* director Christophe Barratier cleverly re-creates the contrasting cultural styles of the era. Vaudevillian Germain (Gérard Jugnot) is determined to win back the son he lost when his marriage collapsed. So when scheming bigwig Galapiat (Bernard-Pierre Donnadieu) attempts to take over the theatre that has been his life, Germain rallies his fellow artistes to keep it out of his clutches. However, things don't run smoothly. While Jean Rabasse's sets, Tom Stern's photography and Reinhardt Wagner's chansons are exemplary, it's Barratier's meticulous direction that prevents the classic Hollywood backstage storyline from descending into kitschy pastiche. DP French +subtitles.

Gérard Jugnot *Germain Pigoil* • Clovis Cornillac *Emile "Milou" Leibovich* • Kad Merad *Jacky Jacquet* • Pierre Richard *Monsieur TSF* • Bernard-Pierre Donnadieu *Galapiat* • Maxence Perrin *Jojo* • Nora Arnezeder *Douce* ■ *Dir* Christophe Barratier • *Scr* Christophe Barratier, Pierre Philippe, Julien Rappeneau, from an idea by Jean-Michel Derenne, Frank Thomas, Reinhardt

Wagner • *Cinematographer* Tom Stern (2) • *Music* Reinhardt Wagner • *Set Designer* Jean Rabasse

Paris Trout ★★★★ 18

Period drama 1991 · US · Colour · 95min

Paris Trout is a person: played by Dennis Hopper, he's a bigoted Deep South storekeeper who murders the young sister of a black man who has reneged on a debt. Appalled wife Barbara Hershey finds herself becoming the target of Hopper's violence and eventually retreats to the arms of lawyer Ed Harris. This pressure cooker of a plot, set in 1949 and adapted by Pete Dexter from his own novel, is tensely directed by Stephen Gyllenhaal. Hopper - crewcut, wild-eyed and utterly horrific - delivers a mesmerising portrayal of a monster who believes he's behaving normally. AT Violence.

Dennis Hopper *Paris Trout* • Barbara Hershey *Hanna Trout* • Ed Harris *Harry Seagraves* • Ray McKinnon *Carl Bonner* • Tina Lifford *Mary Sayers* • Darnita Henry *Rosie Sayers* • Eric Ware *Henry Ray Sayers* • Ronreaco Lee *Chester Sayers* ■ *Dir* Stephen Gyllenhaal • *Scr* Pete Dexter, from his novel

Paris Vu Par... ★★★ 15

Portmanteau drama 1965 · Fr · Colour · 91min

Shot in 16mm and capturing the spontaneity of the *nouvelle vague*, this portmanteau picture is patchy but entertaining. Jean-Daniel Pollet chronicles a nervous man's encounter with a prostitute; an angry wife is too preoccupied to help a potential suicide in Jean Rouch's entry; an American in Paris swaps boyfriends for Jean Douchet; Eric Rohmer puts Jean-Michel Rouzière through the emotional wringer; Jean-Luc Godard has a woman mixing up her billets-doux; and in Claude Chabrol's contribution, a boy is frustrated by his parents' arguing. DP In French.

Nadine Ballot *Odile* • Barbet Schroeder *Jean-Pierre* • Micheline Dax *Prostitute* • Claude Melki *Léon* • Jean-Michel Rouzière *Jean-Marc* • Marcel Gallon *Victim* • Joanna Shimkus *Monica* • Philippe Hiquilly *Roger* • Stéphane Audran *Wife* • Claude Chabrol *Husband* ■ *Dir* Jean Douchet, Jean Rouch, Jean-Daniel Pollet, Eric Rohmer, Jean-Luc Godard, Claude Chabrol • *Scr* Jean Douchet, Georges Keller, Jean Rouch, Jean-Daniel Pollet, Eric Rohmer, Jean-Luc Godard, Claude Chabrol

Paris Was a Woman ★★★

Documentary
1995 · UK/Ger/US · Colour and BW · 77min

This is a compelling documentary about the creative community that haunted Left Bank Paris between the world wars. Using newsreel footage, stills and interviews, Greta Schiller marginalises the literary titans to discuss the likes of troubled novelist Djuna Barnes, photographer Gisele Freud, the tragic artist Romaine Brooks, Sapphic hostess Natalie Barney and essayist Janet Flanner. An inevitable air of nostalgia pervades the memoirs of Gertrude Stein and Alice B Toklas, Colette and Josephine Baker, but Schiller also celebrates the emergence of women as an intellectual force and the advent of their long-overdue social and sexual emancipation. DP *DVD*

Juliet Stevenson *Narrator* ■ *Dir* Greta Schiller • *Scr* from the non-fiction book by Andrea Weiss

Paris When It Sizzles ★★ U

Romantic comedy 1964 · US · Colour · 105min

Gowned in her trademark Givenchy, the irresistible Audrey Hepburn does her best in director Richard Quine's leaden remake of a soufflé-light French comedy in which screenwriter William Holden, facing a deadline, is devoid of inspiration. He enlists the help of his secretary (Hepburn) in acting out possible scenarios, sending the film off into an unsuccessful hotch-potch of genres, periods and fantasy sequences. Hepburn is charming and keeps the nonsense afloat. RK *DVD*

William Holden (2) *Richard Benson* • Audrey Hepburn *Gabrielle Simpson* • Grégoire Aslan *Police inspector* • Raymond Bussières *Gangster* • Christian Duvallex *Maître d'hôtel* • Noël Coward *Alexander Meyerheimer* • Tony Curtis *2nd*

policeman • Marlene Dietrich *Guest star* • Mel Ferrer • Fred Astaire • Frank Sinatra ■ *Dir* Richard Quine • *Scr* George Axelrod, from the film *La Fête à Henriette* by Julien Duvivier, Henri Jeanson

Une Parisienne ★★★ PG

Comedy 1957 · Fr/It · Colour · 81min

This saucy comedy takes every opportunity to show Brigitte Bardot, France's favourite sex kitten, in a state of undress. Yet Michel Boisrond's romantic caper is nowhere near as naughty as it would like to suggest - hence the fact that Bardot's politician's daughter succumbs to a cold rather than the charms of Charles Boyer's aristocratic roué after she decides to take revenge on her philandering husband, Henri Vidal. Bardot proves herself an adept comedienne, but Boisrand's direction lacks the sophistication his mentor, René Clair. DP French +subtitles. *DVD*

Charles Boyer *Prince Charles* • Henri Vidal *Michel* • Brigitte Bardot *Brigitte Laurier* • Noël Roquevert *Herblay* • Madeleine Lebeau *Monique* • Fernand Sardou *Fernand* • André Luguet *Premier Laurier* • Nadia Gray *Queen Greta* ■ *Dir* Michel Boisrond • *Scr* Michel Boisrond, Jean Aurel, Jacques Emmanuel, Annette Wademant

Park Row ★★★★ PG

Period drama 1952 · US · BW · 83min

Hard-boiled director Samuel Fuller returns to the profession that launched him – American big-city journalism - with this belter of a story about rivalry between two ruthless 19th-century newspaper owners. Gene Evans stars as the reporter who sets up his own paper, incurring the wrath of his former boss, played by Mary Welch, who resorts to underhand tactics to ensure he fails. In their dog-eat-dog world, they battle to feed sleaze-hungry readers with all the news that's fit to get away with. TH *DVD*

Gene Evans *Phineas Mitchell* • Mary Welch *Charity Hackett* • Bela Kovacs *Ottmar Mergenthaler* • Herbert Heyes *Josiah Davenport* • Tina Rome *Jenny O'Rourke* • George O'Hanlon *Steve Brodie* ■ *Dir/Scr* Samuel Fuller

Parked ★★★ 15

Drama 2010 · Ire/Fin · Colour · 90min

Very much in the quirky Irish realist tradition of *Adam & Paul* (2004) and *Garage* (2007), Darragh Byrne's feature debut deftly captures the mood of a recession-hit society seeking a little support while searching for some answers. Colm Meaney plays Fred Daly, who returns to Ireland after drifting around England, and takes up residence in a car looking out over Dublin Bay. Screenwriter Ciaran Creagh creates some credible and empathetic characters, while Byrne uses John Conroy's views of the desolate seafront and the suburbs to reinforce the notion of a tempest that can best be ridden out within a community rather than in isolation. DP Violence, swearing, drug abuse.

Colm Meaney *Fred Daly* • Colin Morgan *Cathal O'Regan* • Milka Ahlroth *Jules* • Stuart Graham *George O'Regan* ■ *Dir* Darragh Byrne • *Scr* Ciaran Creagh

Parker ★★★ 15

Crime thriller 2013 · US · Colour · 113min

Jennifer Lopez joins Jason Statham for this entertainingly silly revenge thriller. It's standard Statham stuff, with him playing the eponymous crook who's double-crossed and dumped by his gang mates. Despite being beaten, shot, thrown from a moving car, then shot again, Parker's up and after them within hours. He follows the trail to Florida, where he co-opts the help of a cash-strapped real-estate agent (Lopez), who predictably falls for our hero, despite the fact that he's now wearing a Stetson (don't ask!) and is implausibly posing as a rich Texan. The film has some bone-crunchingly good action sequences, one decent one-liner and it's all daftly watchable. DA Violence, swearing *DVD* *Blu-ray*

Jason Statham *Parker* • Jennifer Lopez *Leslie Rodgers* • Nick Nolte *Hurley* • Michael Chiklis *Melander* • Clifton Collins Jr *Ross* • Wendell

P

Pierce *Carlson* ■ *Dir* Taylor Hackford • *Scr* John J McLaughlin, from the novel *Flashfire* by Richard Stark [Donald E Westlake]

Parkland ★★★★ 15
Drama based on a true story
2013 · US · Colour · 89min

Writer/director Peter Landesman's feature debut is an as-it-happened, on-the-ground reconstruction of events, named after the Dallas hospital to which a dying President John F Kennedy was rushed on 22 November 1963, followed a day later by his assassin, Lee Harvey Oswald. The fidelity to the "lone gunman" theory may irk conspiracy theorists, but in sticking to the facts known on the day and focusing on ordinary people at work, this assured, involving and personal view of history cuts through the myth. From a note-perfect ensemble cast, Marcia Gay Harden and Zac Efron stand out as doughty head nurse and shell-shocked junior doctor in the fraught, gory, politically sensitive ER sequences. AC Swearing. *DVD*

Zac Efron *Dr Charles "Jim" Carrico* • Billy Bob Thornton *Forrest Sorrels* • Paul Giamatti *Abraham Zapruder* • Marcia Gay Harden *Nurse Doris Nelson* • Jeremy Strong *Lee Harvey Oswald* • Colin Hanks *Dr Malcolm Perry* ■ *Dir* Peter Landesman • *Scr* Peter Landesman, from the non-fiction book *Four Days in November* by Vincent Bugliosi • *Music* James Newton Howard

Parlor, Bedroom and Bath ★★
Comedy 1931 · US · BW · 72min

Suffocated by the studio system and uncomfortable with sound, Buster Keaton's spell at MGM became one of the unhappiest and least inspired of his career. Originally a Broadway hit and a popular 1920 silent, this frantic farce was bought specially for Keaton by production chief Irving G Thalberg to make amends after they fell out over the Great Stone Face's talkie debut, *Free and Easy*. A top-notch supporting cast was assembled and Keaton was given a measure of creative freedom, but farce just wasn't his forte. DP

Buster Keaton *Reginald Irving* • Charlotte Greenwood *Polly Hathaway* • Reginald Denny *Jeffery Haywood* • Cliff Edwards *Bellhop* • Dorothy Christy *Angelica Embrey* • Joan Peers *Nita Leslie* • Sally Eilers *Virginia Embrey* ■ *Dir* Edward Sedgwick • *Scr* Richard Schayer, Robert E Hopkins, from the play by Charles W Bell, Mark Swan

Parnell ★★
Biographical drama 1937 · US · BW · 117min

This lavish biopic became known as the worst film Clark Gable ever made and it's true he looks uncomfortable playing the Irish MP whose bid to secure Home Rule was thwarted by his scandalous liaison with a married woman (Myrna Loy). But Gable's star quality still shines through and there's genuine tenderness in his scenes with Loy. The direction lacks personality, too, but this is not the calamity of repute. DP

Clark Gable *Charles Stewart Parnell* • Myrna Loy *Katie O'Shea* • Edna May Oliver *Aunt Ben* • Edmund Gwenn *Campbell* • Alan Marshal *Willie O'Shea* • Donald Crisp *Davitt* • Randolph Churchill *MP* ■ *Dir* John M Stahl • *Scr* John Van Druten, SN Behrman, from Elsie T Schauffler's play

The Parole Officer ★★★ 12
Crime comedy 2001 · UK · Colour · 90min

This light, old-fashioned bank-job comedy in the Ealing vein is a departure for Australian director John Duigan, but a natural step for Steve Coogan, well established on TV as Alan Partridge, Paul and Pauline Calf and others. His parole officer character here is less frenetic and cutting edge than his previous creations, but that also makes him more immediately sympathetic. In a nice set-up, Coogan must convince the only three ex-lags he has successfully put on the straight and narrow (Om Puri, Ben Miller, Steve Waddington) to return to crime and help him steal a videotape from a bank vault and thus clear his name, as he's been framed by bent cop Stephen Dillane. AC *DVD*

Steve Coogan *Simon Garden* • Lena Headey *Emma* • Om Puri *George* • Steven Waddington *Jeff* • Ben Miller *Colin* • Jenny Agutter *Victor's wife* • Stephen Dillane *Inspector Burton* ■ *Dir* John Duigan • *Scr* Steve Coogan, Henry Normal

Une Partie de Campagne ★★★★★ PG
Romantic drama 1936 · Fr · BW · 38min

Based on the Maupassant story, Jean Renoir's short feature is one of the most lyrical pieces of cinema ever produced. Set in 1880, it follows a Parisian family on a Sunday outing that results in a stolen moment of passion and a lifetime of regret. Slyly observing middle-class foibles, the film is exuberantly played and majestically photographed by Claude Renoir and Jean Bourgoin. Abandoned because of incessant rain (with only two scenes left to shoot), the picture was not released until 1946, and even then incomplete, with captions explaining the missing action. DP French +subtitles. *DVD*

Sylvia Bataille *Henriette* • Georges Saint Saens *Henri* • Jeanne Marken [Jane Marken] *Mme Dufour* • Gabriello [André Gabriello] *Monsieur Dufour* • Jacques Borel [Jacques Brunius] *Rudolph* • Paul Temps *Anatole* • Gabrielle Fontan *The Grandmother* • Jean Renoir *Papa Poulin* • Marguerite Renoir *Servant* ■ *Dir* Jean Renoir • *Scr* Jean Renoir, from the story by Guy de Maupassant

Une Partie de Plaisir ★★★ 15
Melodrama 1974 · Fr/It · Colour · 96min

When Paul Gégauff, the screenwriter on many of Claude Chabrol's films, wrote this autobiographical account of the break-up of his marriage, Chabrol persuaded him, his real ex-wife and his daughter to play versions of themselves. Gégauff comes across as a chic poseur, who treats his wife abominably. Chabrol is fascinated and disgusted by his friend's behaviour, and the audience might feel the same, though the exhibitionism of the whole enterprise sometimes outweighs the interest. RB French +subtitles. Violence, swearing, sex scenes. *DVD*

Paul Gégauff *Philippe* • Danièle Gégauff *Esther* • Paula Moore *Sylvia Murdoch* • Michel Valette *Katkof* ■ *Dir* Claude Chabrol • *Scr* Paul Gégauff

Parting Glances ★★★ 15
Drama 1985 · US · Colour · 90min

Set during 24 hours in the Aids-ravaged confines of New York's swanky gay scene, director Bill Sherwood's earnestly tender drama is an old-fashioned love story at heart about two men finishing their relationship because one gets a job transfer abroad. Basically a series of heartfelt farewells to friends and family, this character-driven ensemble piece tells its bittersweet tale with warmth, grace and droll humour. Sherwood himself died of an Aids-related illness in 1990. AJ Swearing. *DVD*

Richard Ganoung *Michael* • Steve Buscemi *Nick* • John Bolger *Robert* • Adam Nathan *Peter* • Kathy Kinney *Joan* • Patrick Tull *Cecil* ■ *Dir/Scr* Bill Sherwood

Parting Shots ★ 12
Black comedy 1998 · UK · Colour · 94min

Michael Winner's serial-killer comedy is excruciatingly awful, with every member of its august cast guilty of a gross error of judgement by agreeing to participate. As a dying man punishing those who've slighted him, singer Chris Rea's totally inadequate performance is made to look even more inept by the smug script. DP Violence.

Chris Rea *Harry Sterndale* • Felicity Kendal *Jill Saunders* • Bob Hoskins *Gerd Layton* • Ben Kingsley *Renzo Locatelli* • Joanna Lumley *Freda* • Oliver Reed *Jamie Campbell-Stewart* • Diana Rigg *Lisa* • John Cleese *Maurice Walpole* • Gareth Hunt *Inspector Bass* • Peter Davison *John* ■ *Dir* Michael Winner • *Scr* Michael Winner, Nick Mead, from a story by Michael Winner

Partisan ★★★ 15
Futuristic thriller 2015 · Aus · Colour · 93min

The first full-length feature from Ariel Kleiman is an eerie coming-of-age tale set mainly on the outskirts of an unnamed city (it was partly shot in Georgia). Vincent Cassel is the seemingly benign head of a commune who is actually training the children to become assassins. But, when a new arrival rebels against the regime, others begin to question their patriarch's actions. Cassel's quietly menacing turn helps compensate for a story that drifts along rather aimlessly, while Kleiman's dreamy visuals mark him out as a talent to watch. JF Gore. *DVD*

Vincent Cassel *Gregori* • Jeremy Chabriel *Alexander* • Florence Mezzara *Susanna* • Viviana Martinez *Sophia* ■ *Dir* Ariel Kleiman • *Scr* Ariel Kleiman, Sarah Cyngler

Partition ★★ 15
Period romantic drama 2006 · Can/US/UK · Colour · 116min

Canadian film-maker Vic Sarin draws upon his Indian heritage for this hackneyed love story set during the last days of the British Raj. In 1947, as partition divides India and Pakistan, a Sikh ex-soldier (Jimi Mistry) rescues a young Muslim refugee (Kristin Kreuk) from a massacre and falls in love with her. Painting the prejudice they face in broad brush strokes, Sarin aims for a timely tale about religious extremism of all stripes. Instead he delivers a soft-focus weepie that falls back on caricatures, postcard scenery and a stirring score. JR *DVD*

Jimi Mistry *Gian Singh* • Kristin Kreuk *Naseem Khan* • Neve Campbell *Margaret Stilwell* • John Light *Walter* • Irrfan Khan [Irfan Khan] *Avtar Singh* • Madhur Jaffrey *Shanti Singh* ■ *Dir* Vic Sarin • *Scr* Vic Sarin, Patricia Finn

Partner ★★★
Drama 1968 · It · Colour · 105min

The fact that Pierre Clémenti speaks French while everyone else converses in Italian rather betrays the fact that Bernardo Bertolucci was totally enthralled with Jean-Luc Godard at this stage of his career. The repressed, middle-class Clémenti adopts a cockily anarchic alter ego in a bid to impress Stefania Sandrelli. Brimming over with political and cinematic ideas, this has an exuberance that compensates for its naivety. DP In French, Italian.

Pierre Clémenti *Jacob I/Jacob II* • Stefania Sandrelli *Clara* • Tina Aumont *Salesgirl* • Sergio Tofano *Petrushka* • Giulio Cesare Castello *Professor Mozzoni* ■ *Dir* Bernardo Bertolucci • *Scr* Bernardo Bertolucci, Gianni Amico, from the novel *The Double* by Fyodor Dostoyevsky

Partner ★★★ PG
Romantic comedy 2007 · Ind · Colour · 136min

In this lavish Bollywood romp from director David Dhawan, Salman Khan stars as successful "love guru" Prem who knows how to make a good first impression and is willing to teach men the ropes - for a price. However, the romantic quarry for Prem's latest client Bhaskar (Govinda) appears to be forever beyond his reach; he's a plump, shy financial adviser who's head over heels in love with his stunningly beautiful and powerful boss (Katrina Kaif). There are plenty of predictable twists and turns, yet *Partner* still works best as a buddy comedy, with Khan and Govinda having a blast with some uncommonly snappy dialogue. But ultimately it's Bollywood veteran Govinda who steals the show with his witty one-liners. OA Hindi +subtitles. *DVD*

Salman Khan *Prem* • Govinda *Bhaskar* • Katrina Kaif *Priya Jaisingh* • Lara Dutta *Naina* • Rajpal Yadav *Chotta Don* ■ *Dir* David Dhawan • *Scr* Sanjay Chhel

Partners ★★ 15
Comedy 1982 · US · Colour · 88min

A twist is given to the stale conventions of the buddy-cop movie when two detectives, one straight (Ryan O'Neal) and one gay (John Hurt), step out on to the streets of Los Angeles. Hurt takes on the role of a gay cop with ease, while O'Neal also pretends to be gay for the sake of the plot which involves a murder in the homosexual community. AT

Ryan O'Neal *Benson* • John Hurt *Kerwin* • Kenneth McMillan *Wilkins* • Robyn Douglass *Jill* • Jay Robinson *Halderstam* ■ *Dir* James Burrows • *Scr* Francis Veber

Partners ★★
Action comedy 2000 · US · Colour · 87min

Joey Travolta makes a tidy job of this odd couple caper, which trades effectively on the physical disparity of its stars. Having stolen a top-secret program, in order to flog it to some Japanese computer pirates, David Paymer finds himself in a shaky alliance with Casper Van Dien, an opportunist thief who ends up acting as his nerdy buddy's bodyguard. Brisk minor league fun. DP

Casper Van Dien *Drifter* • David Paymer *Bob* • Vanessa Angel *Angel* • Jenifer Lewis *Detective* ■ *Dir* Joey Travolta • *Scr* Jeff Ferrell, Timothy Puntillo [Tim Puntillo]

The Party ★★★ PG
Comedy 1968 · US · Colour · 94min

Peter Sellers always had to be kept in check but director Blake Edwards was hardly the one to do it, especially in this straight-up farce that he'd promised Sellers as a diversion from Inspector Clouseau. The result is a one-joke idea in the two-reel style of a silent comedy. Sellers puts on the accent that enraptured Sophia Loren in *The Millionairess* to play a clumsy Indian actor who inadvertently wrecks a Hollywood production. There are some very funny moments, but Sellers, like the character he plays, overstays his welcome. TH *DVD*

Peter Sellers *Hrundi V Bakshi* • Claudine Longet *Michele Monet* • Marge Champion *Rosalind Dunphy* • Sharron Kimberly *Princess Helena* • Denny Miller *Wyoming Bill Kelso* • Gavin Macleod *CS Divot* • Buddy Lester *Davey Kane* • Corinne Cole *Janice Kane* ■ *Dir* Blake Edwards • *Scr* Blake Edwards, Tom Waldman, Frank Waldman, from a story by Blake Edwards

The Party and the Guests ★★★★ U
Political drama 1966 · Cz · BW · 67min

A Kafka-esque portrait of modern Czechoslovakia, packed with resonating contemporary motifs, this sinister study of social conformity and political dissent was a collaboration between director Jan Nemec and his writer/designer wife, Ester Krumbachova. Set in Edenic woodlands, the film follows the pursuit, with savage dogs, of the sole self-determining individualist whose refusal to acquiesce in the system threatens the status quo. Nemec's film was withheld for two years because of government censure. DP Czech +subtitles. *DVD*

Ivan Vyskocil *The Host* • Jan Klusak *Rudolf* • Jiri Nemec *Josef* • Zdenka Skvorecka [Zdena Skvorecka] *Eva* • Pavel Bosek *Frantisek* • Helena Pejskova *Marta* • Karel Mares *Karel* • Jana Pracharova *Wife* • Evald Schorm *Husband* ■ *Dir* Jan Nemec • *Scr* Ester Krumbachova, Jan Nemec, from a short story by Ester Krumbachova

Party Girl ★★★
Drama 1930 · US · BW · 67min

In this society drama about escort services and respectable businessmen, rich client Douglas Fairbanks Jr is blackmailed into marrying one of the girls (Marie Prevost). Even though this rather racy melodrama was made before the puritanical Hays Code came into being, it does try to suggest that the girls only ever dance and drink with their clients. Rather dated but enjoyable stuff, with lovely silent star Prevost, who starved herself to death aged 38, making her sound debut. RB

Douglas Fairbanks Jr *Jay Rountree* • Jeanette Loff *Ellen Powell* • Judith Barrie *Leeda Cather* • Marie Prevost *Diana Hoster* • John St Polis *John Rountree* • Lucien Prival *Paul Nucast* ■ *Dir* Victor Halperin • *Scr* Monte Katterjohn, George Draney, Victor Halperin, from their story, from the novel *Dangerous Business* by Edwin Balmer

Party Girl ★★
Crime drama 1958 · US · Colour · 98min

On the surface, this has everything going for it: a tough and glossy MGM gangster melodrama starring a mature Robert Taylor as a corrupt lawyer and leggy Cyd Charisse, directed by Nicholas Ray. Trouble is, it doesn't quite come off, sabotaged by an over-the-top performance from chief villain Lee J Cobb and an uncertainty of tone, not helped by Charisse's relentlessly non-acting performance and an awkward, subdued Taylor. TS

Robert Taylor (1) *Thomas Farrell* • Cyd Charisse *Vicki Gaye* • Lee J Cobb *Rico Angelo* • John Ireland *Louis Canetto* • Kent Smith *Jeffery Stewart* • Claire Kelly *Genevieve* • Corey Allen *Cookie* ■ *Dir* Nicholas Ray • *Scr* George Wells, from a story by Leo Katcher

Party Monster ★★★ 18
Crime drama based on a true story
2003 · US/Neth · Colour · 94min

Macaulay Culkin returns to the screen after a nine-year absence in this colourful, true-story drama. The former child sensation slaps on glitter and lip gloss to portray late-1980s nightclub promoter Michael Alig. The toast of Manhattan, flamboyant Alig and his Club Kid pals turned dance floors into living art installations, only for drugs, in-fighting and murder to shatter their hedonistic dreams. Having already presented the sensational story in a 1998 documentary, directors Fenton Bailey and Randy Barbato vividly capture the superficial glamour of these Warhol-inspired youngsters. SF *DVD*

Macaulay Culkin *Michael Alig* • Seth Green *James St James* • Chloë Sevigny *Gitsie* • Natasha Lyonne *Brooke* • Wilmer Valderrama *Keoki* • Wilson Cruz *Angel Melendez* • Diana Scarwid *Elke Alig* • Dylan McDermott *Peter Gatien* • Marilyn Manson *Christina* ■ *Dir* Fenton Bailey, Randy Barbato • *Scr* Fenton Bailey, Randy Barbato, from the non-fiction book *Disco Bloodbath* by James St James

Party Party ★ 15
Comedy 1983 · UK · Colour · 93min

This charmless comedy shambles is set around a New Year's Eve celebration, and only early glimpses of now-familiar TV faces make the hard slog worthwhile. Directed by film-school graduate Terry Winsor and co-scripted by *Comic Strip* regular Daniel Peacock (who also stars), this expanded student short will have everyone congregating in the kitchen in double-quick time. AJ *DVD*

Daniel Peacock *Toby* • Karl Howman *Johnny* • Perry Fenwick *Larry* • Sean Chapman *Sam Diggins* • Phoebe Nicholls *Rebecca* • Gary Olsen *Terry* • Clive Mantle *Bobby* • Caroline Quentin *Shirley* ■ *Dir* Terry Winsor • *Scr* Terry Winsor, Daniel Peacock

The Party's Over ★ 12
Drama 1965 · UK · BW · 90min

This bizarre study in necrophilia was shot in 1963 and banned outright by the British film censor. When it was re-edited and then released in 1965, producer Anthony Perry and director Guy Hamilton took their names off the credits. While one admires their integrity, the movie is a real stinker. Set in Chelsea in the Swinging Sixties, it's about the daughter of an American industrialist who falls in with a crowd of beatniks, led by a menacing Oliver Reed. The poor girl goes to the party, ends up dead and is then ravished. AT *DVD* *Blu*

Oliver Reed *Moise* • Clifford David *Carson* • Ann Lynn *Libby* • Catherine Woodville *Nina* • Louise Sorel *Melina* ■ *Dir* Guy Hamilton • *Scr* Marc Behm

Pas sur la Bouche ★★★★ PG
Musical romantic comedy
2003 · Fr/Swi · Colour · 116min

Alain Resnais's remarkable career as a director hits another peak with this delicious adaptation of André Barde's 1925 musical comedy. The farcical plot has Parisian socialite Sabine Azéma trying to prevent her high-principled husband Pierre Arditi from discovering that his new American business partner, Lambert Wilson, is her ex-husband. Enacted on a stylised period set by a cast singing all the songs live, the action could have resembled an up-market amateur operatics production. However, the sparkling musical numbers and the polished performances ensure that Resnais's mischievous satire is wholly cinematic and hugely enjoyable. DP French +subtitles.

Sabine Azéma *Gilberte Valandray* • Isabelle Nanty *Arlette Poumaillac* • Audrey Tautou *Huguette Verberie* • Pierre Arditi *Georges Valandray* • Darry Cowl *Madame Foin* • Jalil Lespert *Charley* • Daniel Prévost *Faradel* • Lambert Wilson *Eric Thomson* ■ *Dir* Alain Resnais • *Scr* From the operetta by André Barde, Maurice Yvain

Pascali's Island ★★★★ 15
Period drama 1988 · UK · Colour · 98min

Helen Mirren is the prime suspect for acting honours in this adaptation of the Barry Unsworth novel about treachery and betrayal. Set in the year 1908, she's the painter torn between bogus archaeologist Charles Dance and spy Ben Kingsley, the Pascali of the title. Her love and loyalty are as divided as Nisi, the Turkish-occupied Greek island, part of the Ottoman empire which is crumbling around them. Pascali's sexual ambiguity is beautifully observed by Ben Kingsley, but it's the observed beauty of Helen Mirren that upstages languid atmospherics and lyrical vistas. TH

Ben Kingsley *Basil Pascali* • Charles Dance *Anthony Bowles* • Helen Mirren *Lydia Neuman* • George Murcell *Herr Gesing* • Sheila Allen *Mrs Marchant* • Nadim Sawalha *Pasha* • TP McKenna *Dr Hogan* • Danielle Allan *Mrs Hogan* ■ *Dir* James Dearden • *Scr* James Dearden, from the novel by Barry Unsworth • *Cinematographer* Roger Deakins

Pasolini ★★★ 18
Biographical drama
2014 · Bel/It/Fr · Colour · 80min

Even cineastes with a knowledge of Pier Paolo Pasolini's life and works are going to struggle with this capriciously intricate account of his final days in November 1975. Director Abel Ferrara intersperses staged extracts from an unfinished novel and an unfilmed allegory with encounters with friends and family members, but neither shed much light on the man. Willem Dafoe bears a marked resemblance to Pasolini and plays him with stately intensity, but Ferrara's flitting between factual and fictional episodes is arbitrary. DP English, Italian, French +subtitles. Violence, swearing, sex scenes, nudity.

Willem Dafoe *Pier Paolo Pasolini* • Riccardo Scamarcio *Ninetto Davoli* • Maria de Medeiros *Laura Betti* ■ *Dir* Abel Ferrara • *Scr* Maurizio Braucci, from an idea by Abel Ferrara, Nicola Tranquilino

The Passage ★
Second World War drama
1978 · UK · Colour · 98min

This ludicrous war movie has Anthony Quinn as a Basque shepherd who guides James Mason and his family to safety over the Pyrenees. Trotting out his usual Zorba act, Quinn's "life force" is exhausting while Malcolm McDowell camps it up as the SS sadist who wears a swastika on his jock strap and treats Michael Lonsdale's fingertips as a gourmet snack. Laughable and repellent. AT

Anthony Quinn *The Basque* • James Mason *Professor John Bergson* • Malcolm McDowell *Captain Von Berkow* • Patricia Neal *Ariel Bergson* • Kay Lenz *Leah Bergson* • Christopher Lee *Head Gypsy* • Michael Lonsdale [Michel Lonsdale] *Renoudot* ■ *Dir* J Lee Thompson • *Scr* Bruce Nicolaysen, from his novel *The Perilous Passage*

Passage Home ★★
Drama 1955 · UK · BW · 102min

Thirty men and one woman sail from South America to London in 1931. Tensions run high among the superstitious crew because of the presence of a woman passenger, played by sultry Diane Cilento. Captain Peter Finch turns to the bottle when she rebuffs him; first mate Anthony Steel saves her from the captain but fancies his chances. Never more than a B-movie, this recycles old material with a modicum of style. AT

Anthony Steel *First Mate Vosper* • Peter Finch *Captain Lucky Ryland* • Diane Cilento *Ruth Elton* • Cyril Cusack *Bohannon* • Geoffrey Keen *Ike* • Hugh Griffith *Pettigrew* • Duncan Lamont *Llewellyn* • Gordon Jackson *Burne* • Bryan Forbes *Shorty* • Patrick McGoohan *McIsaacs* ■ *Dir* Roy Ward Baker • *Scr* William Fairchild, from Richard Armstrong's novel

A Passage to India
★★★★★ PG

Period drama 1984 · UK · Colour · 156min

Nominated for 11 Academy Awards, David Lean's final feature trespasses on territory usually reserved for Merchant Ivory: EM Forster and India. But Lean was the master of the stately epic and, in this lusciously photographed picture, the 75-year-old director showed that none of his powers had waned. Stripping away the sheen of Raj life, he exposes the tensions, prejudices and snobberies of imperialism with a satirical blade every bit as sharp as Forster's. Oscar-winning Peggy Ashcroft garnered the acting headlines, but she is surpassed by Judy Davis as the outsider whose disregard for the rules shatters the calm of this Eden. DP *DVD*

Judy Davis *Adela Quested* • Victor Banerjee *Dr Aziz* • Peggy Ashcroft *Mrs Moore* • James Fox *Richard Fielding* • Nigel Havers *Ronny Heaslop* • Alec Guinness *Professor Godbole* • Richard Wilson (3) *Turton* • Antonia Pemberton *Mrs Turton* • Michael Culver *McBryde* • Art Malik *Mahmoud Ali* • Saeed Jaffrey *Hamidullah* ■ *Dir* David Lean • *Scr* David Lean, from the play by Santha Rama Rau, from the novel by EM Forster • *Cinematographer* Ernest Day

Passage to Marseille
★★★ PG

Second World War drama
1944 · US · BW · 104min

Despite the efforts of the eminently watchable Humphrey Bogart, Sydney Greenstreet, Peter Lorre and Claude Rains, this is tiresome and hard to follow. As the girl in the flashbacks, Michèle Morgan doesn't really register and Bogart is strangely cast as a French journalist leading an escape from a penal colony to join the French Resistance. But director Michael Curtiz does what he can, and he's aided by great camerawork from James Wong Howe and a superb score by Max Steiner. TS

Humphrey Bogart *Matrac* • Claude Rains *Captain Freycinet* • Michèle Morgan *Paula* • Philip Dorn *Renault* • Sydney Greenstreet *Major Duval* • Peter Lorre *Marius* • George Tobias *Petit* • Victor Francen *Captain Patain Malo* • Helmut Dantine *Garou* • John Loder *Manning* ■ *Dir* Michael Curtiz • *Scr* Casey Robinson, Jack Moffitt, from the novel *Men without a Country* by Charles Nordhoff, James Norman Hall

Passchendaele ★ 15
First World War drama
2007 · Can · Colour · 109min

Paul Gross, the former star of TV series *Due South*, overreaches himself here as the star, writer and director of this embarrassing melodrama. Gross plays dashing Sergeant Michael Dunne, who is wounded in a heroic attack and returns to Calgary where he swaggers his way into the lives of nurse Sarah Mann (Caroline Dhavernas) and her brother David (Joe Dinicol). The dialogue is wincingly anachronistic and the performances rarely rise above risible caricature, but it's Gross's direction that makes this so excruciating, with the climactic battle sequences weighed down by trite religious symbolism. DP In English, German. Violence, swearing, sex scenes, nudity, drug abuse. *DVD* *Blu*

Paul Gross *Michael Dunne* • Caroline Dhavernas *Sarah Mann* • Joe Dinicol *David Mann* • Meredith Bailey *Cassie Walker* • Jim Mezon *Randolph Dobson-Hughes* • Michael Greyeyes *Highway* • David Ley *Dr Walker* ■ *Dir/Scr* Paul Gross • *Cinematographer* Gregory Middleton

Passed Away ★★★ 12
Black comedy 1992 · US · Colour · 92min

This entertaining comedy grabs the attention thanks to some exceptional ensemble acting, but in the end settles for schmaltz and neatly tied loose ends. Gathering the members of his clan for their father's funeral, Bob Hoskins is nominally the star of the picture, but his midlife crisis is never as interesting as brother William Petersen's problems, sister Pamela Reed's passion for embalmer Peter Riegert or liberated nun Frances McDormand's deadpan Marxism. Its quip count remains high throughout, but the script runs out of steam too early. DP *DVD*

Bob Hoskins *Johnny Scanlan* • Blair Brown *Amy Scanlan* • Tim Curry *Boyd Pinter* • Frances McDormand *Nora Scanlan* • William Petersen [William I Petersen] *Frank Scanlan* • Pamela Reed *Terry Scanlan* • Peter Riegert *Peter Syracusa* • Maureen Stapleton *Mary Scanlan* • Nancy Travis *Cassie Slocombe* • Jack Warden *Jack Scanlan* ■ *Dir/Scr* Charlie Peters

Passenger ★★★★
Drama 1963 · Pol · BW · 60min

Director Andrzej Munk was partway through his masterpiece when he was killed in a car crash. Yet, although Witold Lesiewicz used a voiceover and an adroit collage of stills to approximate its resolution, its very incompleteness reinforces the powerful message that while the Holocaust may belong to history, its legacy can never be forgotten. Aleksandra Slaska gives a chilling performance as the cruise liner passenger who attempts to reinvent her career as an overseer at Auschwitz following a chance encounter with a survivor she thought long dead. Despite the horror of the camp sequences, there's no bitterness, just aching sadness. DP Polish +subtitles.

Aleksandra Slaska *Liza* • Jan Kreczmar *Walter* • Anna Ciepielewska *Marta* • Irena Malkiewicz *"Ober"* • John Rees *English narrator* ■ *Dir* Andrzej Munk, Witold Lesiewicz • *Scr* Zofia Posmysz-Piasecka, Andrzej Munk

The Passenger ★★★★ 12
Drama 1975 · Fr/It/Sp · Colour · 120min

This typically enigmatic movie from director Michelangelo Antonioni portrays what happens to a burnt-out TV reporter (an excellent Jack Nicholson) who adopts the identity of a dead gunrunner and loses himself in Africa's civil wars. Antonioni's favourite theme of the emptiness of existence is examined here, along with a visual debate about the exploitation of the Third World. There's magnificent location photography of the Sahara and the Gaudi buildings in Barcelona. And like his preceding movies *Blowup* and *Zabriskie Point*, it's a meandering if hypnotically dreamlike experience. AT *DVD*

Jack Nicholson *David Locke* • Maria Schneider *Girl* • Jenny Runacre *Rachel Locke* • Ian Hendry *Martin Knight* • Steven Berkoff *Stephen* • Ambrose Bia *Achebe* ■ *Dir* Michelangelo Antonioni • *Scr* Mark Peploe, Peter Wollen, Michelangelo Antonioni, from a story by Mark Peploe • *Cinematographer* Luciano Tovoli

Passenger 57 ★★★ 15
Action thriller 1992 · US · Colour · 80min

This enjoyable airborne thriller stars Wesley Snipes as a security expert who finds himself on the same aeroplane as British master criminal Bruce Payne, temporarily in police custody. Of course, Payne's henchmen have hitched a ride as well and when they duly free him, it's up to Snipes to save the day. Despite the hand-me-down plot and dialogue, director Kevin Hooks wrings the requisite suspense out of some expertly staged action set pieces. JF Violence, swearing. *DVD*

Wesley Snipes *John Cutter* • Bruce Payne *Charles Rane* • Tom Sizemore *Sly Delvecchio* • Alex Datcher *Marti Slayton* • Bruce Greenwood *Stuart Ramsey* • Robert Hooks *Dwight Henderson* • Elizabeth Hurley *Sabrina Ritchie* ■ *Dir* Kevin Hooks • *Scr* David Loughery, Dan Gordon, from a story by Stewart Raffill, David Gordon

U SUITABLE FOR ALL   Uc SUITABLE ESPECIALLY FOR YOUNG CHILDREN (DVD ONLY)   PG PARENTAL GUIDANCE   12A UNDER 12s TO BE ACCOMPANIED (CINEMA ONLY)

Passengers
Science-fiction adventure   2016 · US · Colour

This is a preview – no prints were available to review as we went to press: A spacecraft on a 120-year mission to transport thousands of people to new colony planet Homestead II suffers a malfunction, resulting in two of the passengers being woken decades early. Jennifer Lawrence and Chris Pratt star as the pair who are now stranded or the ship with only half the mission completed. What fate befalls them we'll have to wait and see – but smart and funny was how director Morten Tyldum described the script. TP

Jennifer Lawrence (2) *Aurora Dunn* · Chris Pratt *Jim Preston* · Michael Sheen *Arthur* · Laurence Fishburne *Gus Mancuso* ■ *Dir* Morten Tyldum · *Scr* Jon Spaihts

The Passing of the Third Floor Back   ★★★ U
Fantasy drama   1935 · UK · BW · 90min

The German-born actor Conrad Veidt, so often cast in sinister roles, had one of the best parts of his career in this allegorical tale of a mysterious stranger who takes a back room in a boarding house run by a greedy landlord and populated by sad inhabitants. The newcomer profoundly affects their lives before disappearing as swiftly as he arrived. It was co-written by Alma Reville, better known as Mrs Alfred Hitchcock, from a play by Jerome K Jerome. Well observed and intriguing. RK

Conrad Veidt *The stranger* · René Ray *Stasia* · Frank Cellier *Wright* · Anna Lee *Vivian Tompkin* · John Turnbull *Major Tompkin* · Cathleen Nesbitt *Mrs Tompkin* ■ *Dir* Berthold Viertel · *Scr* Michael Hogan, Alma Reville, from a play by Jerome K Jerome

A Passion   ★★★★ 12
Drama   1969 · Swe · Colour · 96min

This ranks among Ingmar Bergman's most powerful, personal and pessimistic statements on the human condition. Utilising forbidding island landscape and the recurrence of dreams to emphasise the isolation of the protagonists, Bergman explores the impossibility of escaping from one's past and finding contentment in an irrational and violent society. Hell is definitely other people in this godless place, especially once Liv Ullmann drags Max von Sydow out of his reclusive self-sufficiency and into confrontation with both his neighbours and her ghosts. Released on DVD as *The Passion of Anna*. DP Swedish +subtitles. DVD

Liv Ullmann *Anna Fromm* · Bibi Andersson *Eva Vergerus* · Max von Sydow *Andreas Winkelman* · Erland Josephson *Elis Vergerus* · Erik Hell *Johann Andersson* ■ *Dir/Scr* Ingmar Bergman · *Cinematographer* Sven Nykvist

Passion   ★★ 15
Drama   1982 · Fr/Swi · Colour · 83min

This marks Jean-Luc Godard's semi-return to a more commercial way of movie-making, reuniting him with Raoul Coutard, the man who photographed all the early, epoch-making films, and using big-name stars of the time. Its central story – about a Polish film director and his crew staying in a hotel – is almost lifted from François Truffaut's *Day for Night*, except in Godard's hands it is vague, fragmented and experimental. AT French +subtitles.

Isabelle Huppert *Isabelle* · Hanna Schygulla *Hanna* · Jerzy Radziwilowicz *Jerzy* · Michel Piccoli *Michel* · Laszlo Szabo ■ *Dir/Scr* Jean-Luc Godard · *Cinematographer* Raoul Coutard

Passion   ★★★★
Musical drama   1996 · US · Colour · 114min

This film version of Stephen Sondheim's 1994 Tony Award-winning Broadway musical – itself an adaptation of Iginio Ugo Tarchetti's classic novel *Fosca* – contains all the emotional intimacy and dramatic intensity that made the show such a success. In what's basically a *Beauty and the Beast* fable in reverse, Donna Murphy (re-creating her Tony Award-winning role)

stars as the plain, mortally ill Fosca who falls for handsome officer Jere Shea and eventually melts his heart. The rich score is one of Sondheim's best, the performances are dazzling and anyone expecting the usual static and stilted approach to such stagebound material is in for a surprise. AJ

Jere Shea *Giorgio* · Marin Mazzie *Clara* · Donna Murphy *Fosca* · Gregg Edelman *Colonel Ricci* · Tom Aldredge *Dr Tambourri* · Francis Ruivivar *Lt Torasso* ■ *Dir* James Lapine · *Scr* James Lapine, from the musical by Stephen Sondheim, from the novel *Fosca* by Iginio Ugo Tarchetti

Passion   ★★★ 15
Biographical drama   1999 · Aus/US · Colour · 98min

Following the success of *Shine*, it was inevitable that the early life of another celebrated Australian pianist would reach the screen – especially one who was a devotee of flagellation and was rumoured to have had an incestuous relationship with his mother. Richard Roxburgh turns in an energetic performance as Percy Grainger, the unconventional maestro who wrote *Country Gardens* and took pre-First World War London by storm, while Barbara Hershey valiantly attempts to capture the eccentricity of his syphilitic mother. But this biographical fantasy lacks focus. DP DVD

Richard Roxburgh *Percy Grainger* · Barbara Hershey *Rose Grainger* · Emily Woof *Karen Holten* · Claudia Karvan *Alfhild de Luce* · Simon Burke *Herman Sandby* · Linda Cropper *Mrs Lowery* ■ *Dir* Peter Duncan · *Scr* Don Watson, from the non-fiction book *Percy Grainger* by John Bird, from the play *Percy & Rose* by Rob George

Passion   ★★ 15
Thriller   2012 · Ger/Fr · Colour · 96min

Brian De Palma harks back to the 1980s here, but he can't ignite this remake of director Alain Corneau's last film, *Love Crime*. Rachel McAdams and Noomi Rapace slip into the roles of the backstabbing ad agency boss and her ambitious protégé played by Kristin Scott Thomas and Ludivine Sagnier in the 2010 original. Rapace realises all is not fair in love and corporate war when the manipulative McAdams steals her ideas and then humiliates her, plunging the pair into a wicked web of jealousy, deceit and murder. McAdams is suitably bitchy but can't match the porcelain ice-queen qualities that made Scott Thomas so convincing. JA In English, German. Violence, swearing, sex scenes, brief nudity DVD

Rachel McAdams *Christine Stanford* · Noomi Rapace *Isabelle James* · Karoline Herfurth *Dani* · Paul Anderson (2) *Dirk* ■ *Dir* Brian De Palma · *Scr* Brian De Palma, from the 2010 film *Love Crime*

Passion Fish   ★★★★ 15
Drama   1992 · US · Colour · 129min

Trust writer/director John Sayles to lift a theme that's often used in TV movies and transform it into something finer and richer. Mary McDonnell received an Oscar nomination for her performance as May-Alice, a daytime soap opera star who is paralysed after an accident and returns to her family home in Louisiana. Starting off as a "bitch on wheels" and taking to drink and self-pity, her disability and personality undergo a dramatic change with the help of her companion, played by Alfre Woodard. Sayles judges the tone expertly and creates a striking study of courageous individuals within a small community. AT Substance abuse, swearing.

Mary McDonnell *May-Alice* · Alfre Woodard *Chantelle* · David Strathairn *Rennie* · Vondie Curtis-Hall *Sugar LeDoux* · Angela Bassett *Dawn/Rhonda* · Lenore Banks *Nurse Quick* · William Mahoney *Max* ■ *Dir/Scr* John Sayles

A Passion for Murder   ★★ 18
Thriller   1992 · US/Can · Colour · 87min

Joanna Pacula is an undercover CIA agent who, following the death of her politician lover, ends up going on the run with cab driver Michael Nouri while being pursued by assassin Michael Ironside. Silly stuff indeed,

but worth watching for bug-eyed Ironside, who seems to have made a career for himself playing mesmerising killers, bad guys and mercenaries. JB Swearing, violence, sex scenes, nudity. DVD

Joanna Pacula *Vanessa* · Michael Nouri *Ben Shorr* · Michael Ironside *Quinn* · Lee J Campbell *Sheriff* ■ *Dir* Neill Fearnley · *Scr* Arne Olsen, John Alan Schwartz

Passion in the Desert   ★★★ 12
Period drama   1998 · UK · Colour · 87min

Lavinia Currier's debut feature is clearly a labour of love. Set against the backdrop of Napoleon's Egyptian campaign, it opens as a treatise on man's disrespect for art, as painter Michel Piccoli and his officer escort Ben Daniels lament the wanton destruction of war. However, once circumstances force Daniels into the wilderness, the emphasis shifts to his primeval relationship with the leopardess that teaches him to survive in his breathtaking but treacherous surroundings. Strikingly shot by Russian cinematographer Alexei Rodionov, this is a disconcerting tale. DP Violence, nudity.

Ben Daniels *Augustin Robert* · Michel Piccoli *Jean-Michel Venture de Paradis* · Paul Meston *Grognard* · Kenneth Collard *Officer* · Nadi Odeh *Bedouin bride* ■ *Dir* Lavinia Currier · *Scr* Lavinia Currier, Martin Edmunds, from a novella by Honoré de Balzac

The Passion of Darkly Noon   ★★★ 18
Drama   1995 · UK/Ger · Colour · 100min

Beauty and the Beast meets *Twin Peaks* in an intellectual stalk-and-slasher picture about religion, redemption and repression. Brendan Fraser gives an eerie performance as the titular drifter Darkly Noon, sole survivor of a religious cult, who becomes obsessed with local beauty Ashley Judd. Written and directed by Philip Ridley, this intriguingly warped fairy tale is a challenging, inventive and deeply stylish exploration of forbidden desire. AJ

Brendan Fraser *Darkly Noon* · Ashley Judd *Callie* · Viggo Mortensen *Clay* · Loren Dean *Jude* · Grace Zabriskie *Roxie* · Lou Meyers *Quincey* ■ *Dir/Scr* Philip Ridley

The Passion of Joan of Arc   ★★★★★ PG
Classic silent drama   1928 · Fr · BW · 80min

Based on authentic trial records and drawing on artistic styles from the Renaissance to the avant-garde, Danish director Carl Th Dreyer's film is one of the masterpieces of the silent era. Working with cinematographer Rudolph Maté, Dreyer used all manner of symbolic angles, zooms, tilts and pan shots to capture the dramatic intensity of the action, only for the flow to be interrupted too often by the descriptive captions. In her only screen appearance, Maria Renée Falconetti gives an astonishing performance, filmed almost exclusively in close-up both to convey her personal agony and to contrast her sincerity with the duplicity of her accusers. DP DVD BD

Mlle Falconetti [Maria Renée Falconetti] *Jeanne* · Eugène Silvain *Bishop Pierre Cauchon* · André Berley *Jean d'Estivet* · Maurice Schultz *Nicolas Loyseleur* · Antonin Artaud *Jean Massieu* · Michel Simon *Jean Lemaître* · Jean d'Yd *Guillaume Erard* · Ravet [Louis Ravet] *Jean Beaupère* ■ *Dir* Carl Th Dreyer · *Scr* Carl Th Dreyer, Joseph Delteil, from a novel by Joseph Delteil

Passion of Mind   ★ 12
Romantic fantasy drama   2000 · US · Colour · 100min

Demi Moore clearly believed the challenge of playing a New York literati and a French single mother existing within the same mental space would finally establish her acting credentials. But what on earth possessed *Ma Vie en Rose* director Alain Berliner to embark on such a debacle? An embarrassment. DP

Demi Moore *Marie/Martha Marie "Marty" Talmadge* · Stellan Skarsgård *William Granther* · William Fichtner *Aaron Reilly* · Sinead Cusack

Jessie · Peter Riegert *Dr Peters* · Joss Ackland *Dr Langer* ■ *Dir* Alain Berliner · *Scr* Ron Bass [Ronald Bass], David Field

The Passion of the Christ   ★★★ 18
Religious drama   2004 · US · Colour · 121min

Compelling yet repetitive, shocking yet plodding, Mel Gibson's labour of love charts the last 12 hours of Jesus's life on Earth, from his betrayal by Judas in the Garden of Gethsemane through to the most punishing depiction of the Crucifixion ever mounted. Gibson's commitment to the material is tangible, the much talked about brutality is unflinching and the earthy atmosphere is expertly evoked. But Jim (credited as James) Caviezel's Jesus makes for an impenetrable figure, some of the imagery doesn't quite come off and the narrow focus does little to provide a context to Jesus's teachings and suffering. Gibson subsequently re-released the film as *The Passion: Recut*, deleting six minutes of violence for a new 15 certificate, but the flaws of the original remain. IF Aramaic, Latin +subtitles. Violence. DVD BD

James Caviezel [Jim Caviezel] *Jesus* · Maia Morgenstern *Mary* · Monica Bellucci *Mary Magdalene* · Mattia Sbragia *Caiphas, the High Priest* · Hristo Naumov Shopov *Pontius Pilate* · Claudia Gerini *Claudia Procles, Pilate's wife* · Luca Lionello *Judas Iscariot* · Hristo Jivkov *John* · Francesco De Vito *Peter* · Toni Bertorelli *Annas* · Sergio Rubini *Dismas* ■ *Dir* Mel Gibson · *Scr* Mel Gibson, Benedict Fitzgerald

The Passionate Friends   ★★ PG
Romantic drama   1948 · UK · BW · 86min

This is one of three films made by David Lean with Ann Todd, whom he married in 1949. It's a stuffy melodrama, in which Todd is forced to choose between luxury and love. Her cause is not helped by the script, which buries one of HG Wells's more forgettable novels in a welter of confused flashbacks and clipped platitudes. Todd's haughty manner renders her eminently resistible and she is further disadvantaged by comparison with those astute actors Trevor Howard and Claude Rains. DP

Ann Todd *Mary Justin* · Claude Rains *Howard Justin* · Trevor Howard *Steven Stratton* · Isabel Dean *Pat* · Betty Ann Davies *Miss Layton* ■ *Dir* David Lean · *Scr* Eric Ambler, David Lean, Stanley Haynes, from the novel by HG Wells

The Passionate Plumber   ★
Comedy   1932 · US · BW · 73min

This is one of the last, and worst, comedies of the great Buster Keaton, owing to MGM's poor choice of script and the studio's decision to combine him with the coarser comedy of Jimmy Durante. Directed with all the subtlety of an overflow by Edward Sedgwick, it has Keaton hired by Parisienne Irene Purcell to pose as her *amour* to make Gilbert Roland jealous. Keaton's own personal problems overwhelmed this underwhelming rubbish. TH

Buster Keaton *Elmer E Tuttle* · Jimmy Durante *Julius J McCracken* · Irene Purcell *Patricia Jardine* · Polly Moran *Albine* · Gilbert Roland *Tony Lagorce* ■ *Dir* Edward Sedgwick · *Scr* Laurence E Johnson, Ralph Spence, from the play *Her Cardboard Lover* by Valerie Wyngate, PG Wodehouse, from the play *Dans Sa Candeur Naïve* by Jacques Deval

The Passionate Stranger   ★★ PG
Comedy   1957 · UK · BW and Colour · 93min

This feeble comedy wastes the talent of Margaret Leighton, playing a novelist who bases one of her characters on her chauffeur. Marital complications follow when he misunderstands her motives. Part of the film shows the central characters in real life and the rest dramatises sections of her book, but unfortunately the conceit does not work. BB DVD

Ralph Richardson *Roger Wynter/Sir Clement Hathaway* · Margaret Leighton *Judith Wynter/Leonie* · Patricia Dainton *Emily/Betty* · Carlo Giustini *Carlo/Mario* ■ *Dir* Muriel Box · *Scr* Muriel Box, Sydney Box

P

Passionate Summer ★★ U
Romantic drama 1958 · UK · Colour · 103min

Noted television producer Rudolph Cartier – best known for the *Quatermass* serials – made a rare foray into features with this hothouse Rank melodrama, set in a sweltering Jamaica. Virginia McKenna is the air hostess who lusts after Carl Mohner, while Bill Travers is in love with McKenna but being seduced by wicked Yvonne Mitchell. Travers and McKenna may have been a real-life couple, but they really are the most unconvincing of screen lovers here. **DP**

Virginia McKenna *Judy* • Bill Travers *Douglas Lockwood* • Yvonne Mitchell *Mrs Pawley* • Alexander Knox *Mr Pawley* • Carl Mohner *Louis* • Ellen Barrie *Silvia* • Guy Middleton *Duffield* ■ *Dir* Rudolph Cartier • *Scr* Joan Henry, from the novel *The Shadow and the Peak* by Richard Mason

La Passione ★ 15
Musical fantasy 1996 · UK · Colour · 89min

A young boy's obsession with Ferraris and his hero worship of a German racing driver form the basis of rock star Chris Rea's script for this misfiring drama, set in Yorkshire in the early 1960s. When his idol is killed at Monza, the boy becomes withdrawn and the film resorts to fantasies involving Shirley Bassey. You really want to like this movie, but, like many 1960s sports cars, it looks good and goes wrong a lot. **AT**

Shirley Bassey • Paul Shane *Papa* • Jan Ravens *Mama* • Carmen Silvera *Grandmother* • Gorden Kaye *PC Keecy* • Sean Gallagher *Jo* • Thomas Orange *Young Jo* • Keith Barron *Roy* ■ *Dir* John B Hobbs • *Scr* Chris Rea

Passions ★★
Drama 1984 · US · Colour · 83min

Joanne Woodward puts in another good performance in this TV drama as a widow who discovers that her late husband had another life and a mistress. Lindsay Wagner is the quivering-lipped other woman, but her presence, and Woodward's, still cannot save what is in fact a very predictable "women's" drama. **JB**

Joanne Woodward *Catherine Kennerly* • Lindsay Wagner *Nina Simon* • Richard Crenna *Richard Kennerly* • Mason Adams *Ron Sandler* • Heather Langenkamp *Beth Kennerly* • John Considine *Jack Blaine* • Viveca Lindfors *Lila* ■ *Dir* Sandor Stern • *Scr* Janet Green, Robin Maxwell, Sandor Stern

P Passport to Pimlico ★★★★ U
Comedy 1949 · UK · BW · 81min

The cosiest of the Ealing comedies, this is essentially a one-joke affair that is spun out with masterly skill by that most gifted teller of shaggy-dog stories, TEB Clarke, who received an Oscar nomination for his story and screenplay. Once local historian Margaret Rutherford discovers that Pimlico belongs to the Duchy of Burgundy, the scene could have been set for a sniping satire on the state of postwar England. Clarke and director Henry Cornelius's decision to cock only the gentlest of snooks at such bugbears as rationing and the breakdown of wartime camaraderie is slightly disappointing, but the majority of the situations are ingenious, and the cast is top quality. **DP** *DVD* (Blu-ray)

Stanley Holloway *Arthur Pemberton* • Margaret Rutherford *Professor Hatton-Jones* • Basil Radford *Gregg* • Naunton Wayne *Straker* • Hermione Baddeley *Edie Randall* • John Slater *Frank Huggins* • Betty Warren *Connie Pemberton* • Barbara Murray *Shirley Pemberton* ■ *Dir* Henry Cornelius • *Scr* TEB Clarke

Passport to Shame ★★★
Drama 1958 · UK · BW · 92min

In the late 1950s, the BBFC reluctantly allowed producers to tackle prostitution as long as the films masqueraded as "Awful Warnings". This typical example has poor French waif Odile Versois coming to England and tricked into working for a brothel run by evil Herbert Lom. A cheap, tawdry and fascinating piece of vintage

sexploitation. Way down the cast list, Michael Caine plays a bridegroom. **DM**

Eddie Constantine *Johnny* • Diana Dors *Vicki* • Odile Versois *Malou* • Herbert Lom *Nick* • Brenda de Banzie *Madame* • Robert Brown *Mike* • Elwyn Brook-Jones *Heath* • Cyril Shaps *Willie* • Dennis Shaw [Denis Shaw] *Mac* • Joan Sims *Miriam* • Michael Caine *Bridegroom* ■ *Dir* Alvin Rakoff • *Scr* Patrick Alexander

Passport to Suez ★★
Spy detective drama 1943 · US · BW · 71min

The last of nine Lone Wolf thrillers starring Warren William, this adequate outing presses the suave playboy sleuth into service on behalf of the British government, smashing a German spy ring in Egypt. As his butler and sidekick, Eric Blore figures prominently in the twist and turns of the plot while Ann Savage stands out as a shady war correspondent. This was Hungarian director Andre De Toth's first American assignment and he livens it up with considerable camera movement. **AE**

Warren William *Michael Lanyard aka The Lone Wolf* • Ann Savage *Valerie King* • Eric Blore *Llewellyn Jameson* • Robert Stanford *Donald Jameson* • Sheldon Leonard *Johnny Booth* • Lloyd Bridges *Fritz* ■ *Dir* Andre De Toth • *Scr* John Stone, from a story by Alden Nash, from characters by Louis Joseph Vance

Passport to Treason ★ U
Mystery 1956 · UK · BW · 83min

Western star Rod Cameron should never have packed his passport to play the private eye in this dire British B-feature with its sub-Hitchcockian plot about neo-fascists in London concealing their activities within an organisation for world peace. A better actor than granite-jawed Cameron might have breathed some life into the line-up of hackneyed situations. **AE**

Rod Cameron *Mike O'Kelly* • Lois Maxwell *Diane Boyd* • Clifford Evans *Orlando Sims* • Peter Illing *Giorgio Sacchi* • Marianne Stone *Miss Jones* ■ *Dir* Robert S Baker • *Scr* Norman Hudis, Kenneth R Hayles, from a novel by Manning O'Brine

The Password Is Courage ★★★ U
War drama based on a true story 1962 · UK · BW · 115min

Rather a forgotten film in Dirk Bogarde's canon, this is a fitfully amusing war offering, based on the true-life exploits of one Charles Coward, a cocky PoW who spent his time humiliating his guards and preparing his colleagues for escape. Writer/director Andrew L Stone occasionally pushes too hard for comic effect and Bogarde is hardly perfect casting, but the story of Coward's attempts to reach the Polish Resistance is fascinating. **DP**

Dirk Bogarde *Charles Coward* • Maria Perschy *Irena* • Alfred Lynch *Billy Pope* • Nigel Stock *Cole* • Reginald Beckwith *Unteroffizier* • Richard Marner *Schmidt* • Ed Devereaux *Aussie* ■ *Dir* Andrew L Stone • *Scr* Andrew L Stone, from the biography of Charles Coward by John Castle

The Past ★★★★ 12
Drama 2013 · Fr · Colour · 125min

The first film made by writer/director Asghar Farhadi (*Nader and Simin, a Separation*) outside his native Iran sees Ali Mosaffa return to suburban Paris to finalise his divorce from Bérénice Bejo. The fate of their relationship is far from certain, however, as Bejo's teenage daughter intensely dislikes her pregnant mother's new fiancé (Tahar Rahim). Closely guarded home truths emerge and keep the action moving, but for all its intensity and the excellence of the ensemble, there is less at stake here than in Farhadi's previous films and it feels less compelling. Nonetheless, he delivers some intimate insights into modern family life. **DP** French, Farsi +subtitles. *DVD* (Blu-ray)

Bérénice Bejo *Marie Brisson* • Tahar Rahim *Samir* • Ali Mosaffa *Ahmad* • Pauline Burlet *Lucie* • Elyes Aguis *Fouad* ■ *Dir* Asghar Farhadi • *Scr* Asghar Farhadi, Massoumeh Lahidji

Pastor Hall ★★★★
Second World War drama 1940 · UK · BW · 97min

This highly impressive third feature from the Boulting brothers has been dismissed as a routine wartime flag-waver on the theme of Nazi intolerance. Rather, it is a bold and often stirring tribute to the universal power of faith, courage and personal conviction. The picture is based on the life of the Protestant minister Martin Niemoller who was interned in a concentration camp for failing to preach against either socialism or Judaism. Wilfrid Lawson plays the pastor with great dignity. **DP**

Wilfrid Lawson *Pastor Hall* • Nova Pilbeam *Christine Hall* • Seymour Hicks *General von Grotjahn* • Marius Goring *Fritz Gerte* • Brian Worth *Werner von Grotjahn* • Percy Walsh *Herr Veit* • Hay Petrie *Nazi Pastor* ■ *Dir* Roy Boulting • *Scr* Leslie Arliss, Anna Reiner, Haworth Bromley, John Boulting, Roy Boulting, Miles Malcolm, from a play by Ernest Toller

Pasty Faces ★★ 15
Crime comedy 2000 · UK · Colour · 83min

Originally performed at a local arts centre, this is yet another British crime flick that's directed by a novice who's convinced watching lots of movies equips you for making one. David Paul Baker even has the assurance to star as the wannabe actor who abandons his dead-end Glasgow existence for Hollywood. Everything goes belly up and he agrees to participate in a Vegas casino heist. This threatens to hold its own before collapsing into a crass collection of clichés. **DP** *DVD*

David Baker [David Paul Baker] *Mickey* • Alan McCafferty *Joe* • Gary Cross *Steve* • Martin McGreechin *Bobby* ■ *Dir/Scr* David Baker [David Paul Baker]

Pat and Mike ★★★★ U
Sports romantic comedy 1952 · US · BW · 91min

This is a rollicking vehicle for the wonder team of Katharine Hepburn and Spencer Tracy: she's a sportswoman, he's a rugged, cynical sports promoter. Compared with the divine sophistication of other Tracy/Hepburn films, the Oscar-nominated story and screenplay are weak. Hepburn is born to play the all-round athlete, but Tracy, despite his top billing, distinctly the secondary role, and seems uncomfortable at times. For non-sports fans there are only the stars to watch, but what stars, and how they shine! **TS** *DVD*

Spencer Tracy *Mike Conovan* • Katharine Hepburn *Pat Pemberton* • Aldo Ray *Davie Hucko* • William Ching *Collier Weld* • Charles Buchinski [Charles Bronson] *Hank Tasling* • Sammy White *Barney Grau* • Chuck Connors *Policeman* ■ *Dir* George Cukor • *Scr* Ruth Gordon, Garson Kanin, from their story

Pat Garrett and Billy the Kid ★★★★ 18
Western 1973 · US · Colour · 116min

Despite studio tinkering, this near-masterpiece from director Sam Peckinpah is almost on a par with *The Wild Bunch*. It's a brooding meditation on violence, honour and loyalty in the last days of the Old West, as gunman-turned-sheriff Garrett (James Coburn) races for the past before taking on his one-time partner Billy (Kris Kristofferson). It becomes an elegy for the father-son relationship that figures in so much American literature, as both men try to live up to their legends. **TH** Violence, swearing, nudity. *DVD*

James Coburn *Pat Garrett* • Kris Kristofferson *Billy the Kid* • Bob Dylan *Alias* • Jason Robards *Governor Lew Wallace* • Richard Jaeckel *Sheriff Kip McKinney* • Katy Jurado *Mrs Baker* • Slim Pickens *Sheriff Baker* • Chill Wills *Lemuel* • John Beck *Poe* • Rita Coolidge *Maria* • Jack Elam *Alamosa Bill* • Harry Dean Stanton *Luke* ■ *Dir* Sam Peckinpah • *Scr* Rudolph Wurlitzer • *Music* Bob Dylan

Patagonia ★★★ 15
Road movie 2010 · Arg/UK · Colour · 113min

The Welsh fascination with its Argentine outpost (settled in 1865) recurs in this rather meandering road movie set in the

two countries. In Wales, Marta Lubos's spirited Patagonian eightysomething is on a pilgrimage to the farm where her mother was raised. Meanwhile, in Patagonia with her photographer boyfriend Matthew Gravelle, broody Cardiff girl Nia Roberts takes out her frustration by throwing herself at guide Matthew Rhys. Director Marc Evans makes fine use of cinematographer Robbie Ryan's contrasting images of the parched pampas and lush valleys. And singer Duffy makes her feature debut as a Welsh student. **DP** Welsh, Spanish +subtitles. A sex scene. *DVD* (Blu-ray)

Matthew Rhys *Mateo* • Nia Roberts *Gwen* • Duffy *Sissy* • Nahuel Pérez Biscayart *Alejandro* • Matthew Gravelle *Rhys* • Marta Lubos *Cerys* ■ *Dir* Marc Evans • *Scr* Marc Evans, Laurence Coriat

Patch Adams ★★★ 12
Biographical comedy drama 1998 · US · Colour · 110min

Robin Williams is ideally cast as an irrepressible idealist whose dream of becoming a doctor is threatened by his inability to conform to medical school dictates. Williams's penchant for playing the clowning do-gooder is indulged by director Tom Shadyac, and the pat manipulation of the emotions comes with a high level of saccharin. But anyone who's ever felt aggrieved by impersonal treatment from the medical establishment will enjoy the system-bucking antics. **AME** Swearing, sexual references. *DVD* (Blu-ray)

Robin Williams *Hunter "Patch" Adams* • Daniel London *Truman* • Monica Potter *Carin* • Philip Seymour Hoffman *Mitch* • Bob Gunton *Dean Walcott* • Josef Sommer *Dr Eaton* • Irma P Hall *Joletta* • Frances Lee McCain *Judy* ■ *Dir* Tom Shadyac • *Scr* Steve Oedekerk, from the book *Gesundheit, Good Health Is a Laughing Matter* by Hunter Doherty Adams, Maureen Mylander

A Patch of Blue ★★★
Drama 1965 · US · BW · 105min

Elizabeth Hartman plays a young blind woman and Sidney Poitier is the man she meets in the park who becomes her closest friend in this moving drama. Hartman is remarkably stable despite her tragic history, while Poitier is as solid as Mount Rushmore. The picture lacks any semblance of subtlety: Shelley Winters as Hartman's monstrous mother goes straight for the jugular, and won an Oscar as best supporting actress. **AT**

Sidney Poitier *Gordon Ralfe* • Shelley Winters *Rose-Ann D'Arcy* • Elizabeth Hartman *Selina D'Arcy* • Wallace Ford *Ole Pa* • Ivan Dixon *Mark Ralfe* • Elisabeth Fraser *Sadie* ■ *Dir* Guy Green • *Scr* Guy Green, from the novel *Be Ready with Bells and Drums* by Elizabeth Kata • *Cinematographer* Robert Burks

A Patch of Fog ★★★★
Drama 2015 · UK · Colour

This murky psychological thriller follows two men who are involved in an unusual power struggle. Set in Belfast, it centres on Sandy Duffy (Conleth Hill), a celebrated, well-to-do novelist who has a penchant for shoplifting. One night, he's caught in the act by a lonely security guard named Robert (Stephen Graham), and his comfortable life is turned upside down. The film serves as a terrific showcase for Hill, while Graham ensures his character never feels like a one-dimensional weirdo, in a suspenseful, absorbing tale that offers plenty of tension. **SC**

Conleth Hill *Sandy Duffy* • Lara Pulver *Lucy Walsh* • Stephen Graham *Robert Green* • Ian McIlhinney ■ *Dir* Michael Lennox • *Scr* Michael McCartney, John Cairns

Patema Inverted ★★★ PG
Animated science-fiction adventure 2013 · Jpn · Colour · 98min

Expanding on ideas originally explored in his four-part online series *Patema Inverted: Beginning of the Day*, writer/director Yasuhiro Yoshiura's film is a visually striking fantasy with an ingenious premise. A failed scientific experiment has disrupted gravity, forcing some people to retreat below ground, where they live in fear of falling into the sky. Adventurous subterranean dweller Patema, keen to follow her missing friend Lagos, heads upwards. This starts well, but requires such a suspension of disbelief that it can feel a little forced. But the sense of place is as exemplary as the graphics. DP Japanese +subtitles. **DVD** Blu-ray

Yukiyo Fujii *Patema* • Nobuhiko Okamoto *Age* • Shintaro Ohata *Porta* • Takaya Hashi *Izamura* • Masayuki Kato *Lagos* ■ *Dir/Scr* Yasuhiro Yoshiura

Paternity ★★ 15
Romantic comedy 1981 · US · Colour · 88min

Burt Reynolds plays the middle-aged manager of Madison Square Gardens who decides he wants an heir to carry on his name. Of course he doesn't want the wife to go with it. Beverley D'Angelo is a struggling musician waiting tables, so she is more than happy to play surrogate mother to his progeny. An unlovely subject, with a charmless script FL

Burt Reynolds *Buddy Evans* • Beverly D'Angelo *Maggie Harden* • Norman Fell *Larry* • Paul Dooley *Kurt* • Elizabeth Ashley *Sophia Thatcher* • Lauren Hutton *Jenny Lofton* • Juanita Moore *Celia* • Peter Billingsley *Tad* ■ *Dir* David Steinberg • *Scr* Charlie Peters

Path of Destruction ★
Science-fiction action thriller 2005 · US · Colour · 105min

A cloud of experimental nanobots causes deadly superstorms across America's west coast in this ridiculous sci-fi yarn. Danica McKellar is out of her depth playing the tenacious reporter racing to clear her name after villain David Keith frames her for the catastrophe. Logic and realism are quickly jettisoned in favour of the poorest of special effects and horribly lame dialogue. SF

David Keith *Roy Stark* • Danica McKellar *Katherine Stern* • Chris Pratt *Nathan McCain* • Stephen Furst *Terry* • Franklin Dennis Jones *Col Thomas Miller* • Richard Wharton *Dr Van Owen* ■ *Dir* Stephen Furst • *Scr* Chase Parker

Path to War ★★★★ 15
Historical drama 2002 · US · Colour · 157min

Although made for TV, this final film from director John Frankenheimer is among his most powerful work. A slow-burning look at the political machinery behind America's conflict in Vietnam under Lyndon B Johnson, the feature is brilliantly executed and meticulously detailed. Interweaving original archive footage with believable dramatisation, Frankenheimer turns potentially tedious melodrama into a highly charged and fascinating exploration of arrogance, ignorance and tragedy. Michael Gambon gives an emotional and finely nuanced performance as the guilt-racked president, supported by an electrifying Donald Sutherland as his adviser Clark Clifford. SF Swearing, violence. **DVD**

Michael Gambon *Lyndon Baines Johnson* • Donald Sutherland *Clark Clifford* • Alec Baldwin *Robert McNamara* • Bruce McGill *George Ball* • James Frain *Dick Goodwin* • Felicity Huffman *Ladybird Johnson* • Frederic Forrest *General Earle "Buzz" Wheeler* • John Aylward *Dean Rusk* • Philip Baker Hall *Everett Dirkson* • Tom Skerritt *General Westmoreland* ■ *Dir* John Frankenheimer • *Scr* Daniel Giat

Pather Panchali ★★★★★ U
Drama 1955 · Ind · BW · 119min

Satyajit Ray made his debut as director with this masterpiece of world cinema. Played with restraint by a non-professional cast and influenced by such Italian neorealist features as *Bicycle Thieves*, its story of a young Bengali boy's introduction to the ways of the world is remarkable for its simplicity and humanity. The first in the acclaimed Apu trilogy (*Aparajito* and *The World of Apu* make up the saga), it astounded everyone when it won the Special Jury Prize at Cannes, particularly as it was filmed on weekends and holidays over a four-year period, with Ray having to pawn his wife's jewellery to complete the

shoot. The title translates as *Song of the Road*. DP Bengali +subtitles. **DVD**

Kanu Bannerjee *Harihar, the father* • Karuna Bannerjee *Sarbojaya, the mother* • Subir Bannerjee *Apu* • Runki Bannerjee *Durga, as a child* ■ *Dir* Satyajit Ray • *Scr* Satyajit Ray, from a novel by Bibhutibhusan Bannerjee

Pathfinder ★★★★ 15
Adventure drama 1987 · Fin · Colour · 82min

Described as the very first film to be made in the Lapp language, *Pathfinder* is far more than a curiosity, being a splendid excursion into myth and legend above the Arctic Circle. The first scenes suggest a variant of *Conan*, with a young boy witnessing the massacre of his parents; but instead of growing into a strapping warrior, he remains a boy whose plan for revenge takes us into a morass of betrayal and cunning in which the leading figure is a mythological reindeer. Set against this bleak and grand landscape, Nils Gaup's picture - a rites-of-passage saga - has an intense authenticity and exoticism. AT Lappish +subtitles.

Mikkel Gaup *Aigin* • Ingvald Guttorm *Father* • Ellen Anne Buljo *Mother* • Inger Utsi *Sister* ■ *Dir/Scr* Nils Gaup • *Cinematographer* Erling Thurmann-Andersen

Pathfinder ★★ 15
Period action adventure 2006 · US · Colour · 102min

Set several centuries before Christopher Columbus discovered the Americas, *Pathfinder* centres on the battles between Viking raiders and native Americans. Although technologically inferior, the native villagers do have the help of Ghost (Karl Urban), a Viking child left behind after a previous raid and adopted by the tribe. Now a man, Ghost attempts to defend his new family against the marauding Vikings and prove where his loyalties lie. In this reworking of the 1987 Finnish film, director Marcus Nispel charges headlong into the action, making slick use of frozen lakes, misty forests and cliff-top passes. Yet by giving only cursory attention to plot and character, Nispel hamstrings all his stylish set pieces and delivers an ill-conceived epic that feels more like an extended trailer. JR **DVD** Blu-ray

Karl Urban *Ghost* • Moon Bloodgood *Starfire* • Russell Means *Pathfinder* • Clancy Brown *Gunnar* • Jay Tavare *Blackwing* • Ralf Moeller *Ulfar* • Nathaniel Arcand *Wind in Tree* ■ *Dir* Marcus Nispel • *Scr* Laeta Kalogridis, from the 1987 film by Nils Gaup

Pathology ★★ 18
Horror thriller 2007 · US · Colour · 90min

Medical thrillers often revolve around surgeons with a God complex, but this bleak and unlikeable tale of pathologists gone bad sets a new precedent for flouting the Hippocratic oath. When Ivy League doctor Ted Grey (Milo Ventimiglia from *Heroes*) takes a position in a forensic pathology lab, he's quickly drawn into an amoral clique of interns who have started using their professional abilities to commit random murders. Wallowing in its tailor-made nihilism, *Pathology* lingers over shots of latex chest cavities and dissected cadavers, and mixes in risqué scenes of characters having sex and doing drugs among the dead. Its model is the German thriller *Anatomy*, but, much like the autopsied bodies the film gleefully desecrates, it lacks a heart and a brain. JR Violence, sex scenes. **DVD**

Milo Ventimiglia *Ted Grey* • Michael Weston *Jake Gallo* • Lauren Lee Smith *Juliette Bath* • Dan Callahan *Chip Bentwood* • Alyssa Milano *Gwen Williamson* • John de Lancie *Dr Quentin Morris* ■ *Dir* Marc Schölermann • *Scr* Brian Taylor, Mark Neveldine

Paths of Glory ★★★★★ PG
First World War drama 1957 · US · BW · 86min

Winston Churchill claimed this film came closest to capturing the atmosphere of the First World War and exposing the workings of the military mind. As the general who orders a hopeless attack on a German

position, Adolphe Menjou is a villain not because he is an officer slavishly adhering to the letter of army law, but because he is an arrogant aristocrat, motivated more by fear of the lower classes than by hatred of the enemy. Kirk Douglas and Timothy Carey are outstanding among the troops on the front line, while Stanley Kubrick's relentlessly probing camera offers constant evidence of a film-maker at the height of his powers. DP **DVD** Blu-ray

Kirk Douglas *Colonel Dax* • Ralph Meeker *Corporal Paris* • Adolphe Menjou *General Broulard* • George Macready *General Mireau* • Wayne Morris *Lieutenant Roget* • Richard Anderson *Major Saint-Auban* • Joseph Turkel [Joe Turkel] *Private Pierre Arnaud* • Timothy Carey *Private Ferol* ■ *Dir* Stanley Kubrick • *Scr* Stanley Kubrick, Calder Willingham, Jim Thompson from the novel by Humphrey Cobb • *Cinematographer* Georg Krause

Patience (After Sebald) ★★★★ 12A
Documentary 2011 · UK · Colour and BW · 86min

This exceptional documentary resists the temptation simply to follow in the footsteps of WG Sebald on the Suffolk odyssey that inspired his 1995 masterpiece *The Rings of Saturn*. Instead, it proves to be an essential companion to the sights, ideas and meditations that made the book so compelling. In addition to depicting the coastal landscape in all its moody beauty, director Grant Gee also makes fascinating use of photographs, printed pages and Google maps to form a visual backdrop to the readings provided by Jonathan Pryce and the scholarly but accessible insights of the writers, academics, psychiatrists and critics who have been inspired by the novel and its diverse range of themes. DP

Jonathan Pryce *Narrator* ■ *Dir* Grant Gee

The Patience Stone ★★★★ 15
Drama 2012 · Afg/Fr/Ger · Colour · 102min

Afghan exile Atiq Rahimi teams with veteran screenwriter Jean-Claude Carrière for this adaptation of his own award-winning novel. The story revolves around a confession. But the husband (Hamidreza Javdan) cannot hear a word his wife (Golshifteh Farahani) is saying because he is in a coma after being shot in a petty squabble. Furious at being deserted by his family after a decade of marital servility, the wife vents her frustrations in a series of monologues whose critique of traditional patriarchal Islamic values will provoke more fury than her unchaperoned encounters with a bashful soldier. Farahani is no stranger to controversy and plays her part to perfection. But it's Rahimi's courage as both writer and director that makes this intense and perceptive picture so unflinchingly compelling. DP Farsi +subtitles. Violence.

Golshifteh Farahani *The woman* • Hamidreza Javdan [Hamid Javdan] *The man* • Massi Mrowat *The young soldier* • Hassina Burgan *The aunt* ■ *Dir* Atiq Rahimi • *Scr* Jean-Claude Carrière, Atiq Rahimi, from the novel by Rahimi

Patlabor: the Mobile Police ★★★ PG
Animated adventure 1989 · Jpn · Colour · 98min

With *manga* movies, the emphasis is usually on ultra violence and stunning design, but this is a more cerebral affair. The plot revolves around an attempt by the Tokyo police, assisted by advanced robots, to track down a gang of criminals intent on bringing down the city. There are still the trademark scenes of explosive action, but director Mamoru Oshii takes a more measured approach to the tale. A sequel followed in 1993. JF In Japanese. **DVD**

■ *Dir* Mamoru Oshii • *Scr* Kazunori Ito, from a story by Masami Yuuki

The Patricia Neal Story ★★★★
Drama based on a true story 1981 · US · Colour · 100min

Oscar-winning actress Patricia Neal's recovery from a series of debilitating strokes is detailed here in a well-cast TV movie that benefits immensely from the sensitive playing of Glenda Jackson as Neal and an intelligent script. Although lacking Neal's American ranginess (and accent), Jackson possesses the resolute wilfulness the part needs, and she performs beautifully. Dirk Bogarde, also excellent in his US TV-movie debut, plays celebrated children's novelist Roald Dahl, who was married to Neal at the time of the story. TS

Glenda Jackson *Patricia Neal* • Dirk Bogarde *Roald Dahl* • Ken Kercheval *Dr Charles Carton* • Jane Merrow *Val Eaton* • John Reilly *Barry Farrell* • James Hayden *Martin Sheen* ■ *Dir* Anthony Harvey, Anthony Page • *Scr* Robert Anderson, from the book *Pat and Roald* by Barry Farrell

Patrick ★★★ 15
Horror 1978 · Aus · Colour · 108min

Although it rather loses its way, this deeply disturbing gothic grotesque benefits from the creepy atmosphere director Richard Franklin generates in the hospital ward, where the comatose Robert Thompson develops a passion for nurse Susan Penhaligon that acts as a catalyst for a series of increasingly malevolent telekinetic happenings. Amid the mayhem, there is a delicious performance from ballet maestro Robert Helpmann as a sadistic doctor. DP

Susan Penhaligon *Kathy Jacquard* • Robert Helpmann *Dr Roget* • Rod Mullinar *Ed Jacquard* • Bruce Barry *Dr Brian Wright* • Julia Blake *Matron Cassidy* • Helen Hemingway *Sister Williams* • Robert Thompson *Patrick* ■ *Dir* Richard Franklin • *Scr* Everett De Roche

Patrick the Great ★★ U
Musical comedy 1944 · US · BW · 89min

This breezy musical has the usual corny showbiz setting, but it allows Donald O'Connor and Peggy Ryan to shine in a few pleasant numbers and gives O'Connor the chance to perform some spectacular tap-dancing. The paper-thin plot has O'Connor and his father (a colourless Donald Cook) as rivals for the same part in a Broadway show. Eve Arden, usually relied on to perk up the dullest screenplay, only has a few wisecracks here. RB

Donald O'Connor *Pat Donahue Jr* • Peggy Ryan *Judy Watkins* • Frances Dee *Lynn Andrews* • Donald Cook *Pat Donahue Sr* • Eve Arden *Jean Mathews* • Thomas Gomez *Max Wilson* ■ *Dir* Frank Ryan • *Scr* Dorothy Bennett, Bertram Millhauser, from a story by Jane Hall, Frederick Kohner, Ralph Block

The Patriot
Silent historical drama 1928 · US · BW · 113min

Sadly, no prints exist of this now lost film, in which Emil Jannings is the tyrannical Tsar Paul I, in the grip of dangerous insanity, so his trusted confidante Lewis Stone puts aside loyalty to his ruler in an attempt to save his country. This was the last silent to be directed by Ernst Lubitsch, here departing from his customary romantic comedies; it was also the first film made during his long and sparklingly successful tenure at Paramount. Jannings, a frequent Lubitsch star in Germany, was nearing the end of his Hollywood sojourn, his thick German accent unsuited to the talkies. Stone, Lubitsch and the picture were all nominated for Oscars, but the only winner was Hans Kräly's screenplay. RK

Emil Jannings *Tsar Paul the First* • Lewis Stone *Count Pahlen* • Florence Vidor *Countess Ostermann* • Neil Hamilton *Crown Prince Alexander* • Harry Cording *Stefan* • Vera Voronina *Mlle Lapoukhine* ■ *Dir* Ernst Lubitsch • *Scr* Hans Kräly, Julian Johnson, from the novel *Der Patriot: Drama in 5 Akten* by Alfred Neumann, from its stage adaptation by Ashley Dukes, from the story *Paul I* by Dimitri Merejkowski

P

The Patriot ★ 15
Action drama   1986 · US · Colour · 88min

This apology for a movie is unmitigated rubbish, with dire production levels, a non-plot and an unintentionally camp air. Gregg Henry stars as a burned-out Vietnam vet redeeming his dignity by attempting to save the western world from nuclear annihilation. AJ Violence, nudity.

Gregg Henry *Lieutenant Matt Ryder* · Simone Griffeth *Sean* · Michael J Pollard *Howard* · Jeff Conaway *Mitchell* · Stack Pierce *Atkins* · Leslie Nielsen *Admiral Frazer* ■ *Dir* Frank Harris · *Scr* Andy Ruben, Katt Shea Ruben

The Patriot ★★★ 15
Period war drama   2000 · US · Colour · 157min

Mel Gibson stars in this action drama set during the American War of Independence. Living peacefully in South Carolina, Gibson and his gung-ho son Heath Ledger come out fighting against the British army. The battle scenes are ferociously well-staged, but some may baulk at the almost pantomimic villainy of Jason Isaacs's cruel Colonel Tavington and the historically inaccurate atrocities he is seen to commit. TH Violence, swearing. DVD BL

Mel Gibson *Benjamin Martin* · Heath Ledger *Gabriel Martin* · Joely Richardson *Charlotte Selton* · Tcheky Karyo *Major Jean Villeneuve* · Jason Isaacs *Colonel William Tavington* · Tom Wilkinson *General Cornwallis* · Chris Cooper *Colonel Harry Burwell* ■ *Dir* Roland Emmerich · *Scr* Robert Rodat

Patriot Games ★★★ 15
Thriller   1992 · US · Colour · 111min

Harrison Ford takes over from Alec Baldwin as CIA analyst Jack Ryan in this follow-up to box-office hit *The Hunt for Red October*. Director Phillip Noyce has the now former agency man rescuing peer James Fox from an IRA attack in London and being hounded for his trouble by renegade terrorist Sean Bean. But, apart from one brilliant sequence showing a remote-controlled desert massacre, Noyce's thriller (based on the novel by Tom Clancy) never gets its act together to provide the direct appeal that all good action flicks should have. TH Swearing. DVD BL

Harrison Ford *Jack Ryan* · Anne Archer *Dr Cathy Ryan* · Patrick Bergin *Kevin O'Donnell* · Sean Bean *Sean Miller* · Thora Birch *Sally Ryan* · James Fox *Lord Holmes* · Samuel L Jackson *Robby Jackson* · Polly Walker *Annette* · James Earl Jones *Admiral James Greer* · Richard Harris *Paddy O'Neil* ■ *Dir* Phillip Noyce · *Scr* W Peter Iliff, Donald Stewart, Steve Zaillian, from the novel by Tom Clancy

The Patrol ★★★ 15
War drama   2013 · UK/Mor · Colour · 79min

Tom Petch's directorial debut works hard to convey the lot of the ordinary soldier on duty in Helmand Province in Afghanistan. Petch served in the British army for eight years, and his frontline experience shines through in dialogue that crackles with gritty jargon and slang, as a patrol is left exposed in the desert with confused orders and malfunctioning kit. As invisible Taliban guerrillas make their presence felt, tensions mount, along with a growing sense of disillusion with a war that has long since ceased to be a surgical strike. While the composition of the unit is too conveniently cosmopolitan and some of the performances are stiff, Petch's film reeks of authenticity. DP DVD

Nav Sidhu *Smudge* · Ben Righton *Captain Bill Richardson* · Owain Arthur *Taff* · Nicky Beveney [Nicholas Beveney] *Sergeant "Sol" Campbell* · Daniel Fraser *Lieutenant Johnny Bradshaw* ■ *Dir/Scr* Tom Petch

The Patsy ★★★
Silent comedy   1928 · US · BW · 64min

King Vidor's silent film showcases the not inconsiderable comedic talents of Marion Davies. The unimportant plot concerns the efforts of Davies to overcome her position as the family "patsy" and captivate her sister's boyfriend. The high point has Davies, for no particular reason, doing very funny impersonations of silent stars Mae

Murray, Lillian Gish and the exotic Pola Negri. RK

Marion Davies *Patricia Harrington* · Orville Caldwell *Tony Anderson* · Marie Dressler *Ma Harrington* · Dell Henderson *Pa Harrington* · Lawrence Gray *Billy* · Jane Winton *Grace Harrington* ■ *Dir* King Vidor · *Scr* Agnes Christine Johnston, Ralph Spence (titles), from the play by Barry Connors

The Patsy ★★★ U
Comedy   1964 · US · Colour · 97min

This is a very black premise indeed from Jerry Lewis, whose adulation by French cineastes is sometimes regarded with puzzlement here. Judge for yourself, as co-writer/director Lewis casts star Jerry as the bellboy who stumbles upon a group of desperate showbiz types who have lost their meal ticket and who groom Lewis to replace the noted comedian killed in a plane crash. Tasteless, but also clever and very funny, with a marvellous cast of movie veterans. It may be a one-gag sketch stretched to feature length, but it works for the brilliant Lewis. TS DVD

Jerry Lewis *Stanley Belt* · Ina Balin *Ellen Betz* · Everett Sloane *Caryl Fergusson* · Keenan Wynn *Harry Silver* · Peter Lorre *Morgan Heywood* · John Carradine *Bruce Alden* · Phil Harris *Chic Wymore* · Hans Conried *Dr Mule-rrr* ■ *Dir* Jerry Lewis · *Scr* Jerry Lewis, Bill Richmond

Patterns ★★★
Drama   1956 · US · BW · 83min

This exposé of unethical American big business is a remake of a live television play. In Rod Serling's strong script Van Heflin portrays the new business executive who is being groomed by the machiavellian company head, Everett Sloane, to replace the ageing and likeable Ed Begley. Shooting in New York, director Fielder Cook extracts fine performances from the cast. AE

Van Heflin *Fred Staples* · Everett Sloane *Walter Ramsey* · Ed Begley *William Briggs* · Beatrice Straight *Nancy Staples* · Elizabeth Wilson *Marge Fleming* · Joanna Roos *Miss Lanier* ■ *Dir* Fielder Cook · *Scr* Rod Serling, from his TV play

Patti Rocks ★★★ 18
Comedy   1987 · US · Colour · 83min

Karen Landry is a man-wary Minnesotan who tells her chauvinist boyfriend Chris Mulkey she's pregnant. Unfortunately, Mulkey is married with children and doesn't know how he's going to break it to her. An incisive look at masculine double-standards and hypocrisy, David Burton Morris's fiercely independent feature digs down deep and isn't afraid to get dirty doing it. Tough-talking and adult. AJ

Chris Mulkey *Billy Regis* · John Jenkins *Eddie Hassit* · Karen Landry *Patti Rocks* · David L Turk *Barge worker* · Stephen Yoakam *Bartender* ■ *Dir* David Burton Morris · *Scr* David Burton Morris, Chris Mulkey, John Jenkins, Karen Landry, from characters by Victoria Wozniak in the film *Loose Ends*

Patti Smith: Dream of Life ★★★★
Documentary
2007 · US · BW and Colour · 109min

Made over a period of 11 years, this largely non-linear collection of scenes from Patti Smith's life is an effective portrait of the artist as enigma. On stage, Smith is an intense rocker/poet who launches into furiously articulate tirades when not belting out classics like *Gloria*. Yet away from the limelight she is sweetness personified, whether fussing over her ageing parents or doting on her two children. She and director Steven Sebring conspire to slip in the odd arty moment in tribute to her friend and collaborator Robert Mapplethorpe. But any doubts about the sincerity of Smith's affection for those who helped shape her sensibilities are allayed by her touching regard for late husband Fred "Sonic" Smith's rendition of his unrecorded song *She Walked Home*. DP DVD

Patti Smith · Philip Glass · Sam Shepard · Tom Verlaine · Bob Dylan ■ *Dir* Steven Sebring

Patton ★★★★★ 12
Biographical drama   1970 · US · Colour · 163min

Released while US forces were still in Vietnam, this can be viewed as both a tribute to the indomitability of the fighting man and a satire on the myth of the American hero. The screenplay, by Francis Ford Coppola and Edmund H North, received one of the picture's seven Oscars, while director Franklin J Schaffner took another, thanks to the horrific majesty of the battle sequences. But the bedrock of this biopic is the performance in the title role of George C Scott, who became the first actor in Oscar history to refuse his award. Combining blimpish bluster with moments of monstrous ego and unexpected humanity, Scott makes this unforgettable. DP Swearing. DVD BL

George C Scott *General Patton* · Karl Malden *General Bradley* · Michael Bates *Field Marshal Montgomery* · Frank Latimore *Lt Col Davenport* · Michael Strong *Brig Gen Carver* · Stephen Young *Captain Hansen* · Albert Dumortier *Moroccan minister* · Cary Loftin [Carey Loftin] *General Bradley's driver* ■ *Dir* Franklin J Schaffner · *Scr* Francis Ford Coppola, Edmund H North, from the books *Patton: Ordeal and Triumph* by Ladislas Farago and *A Soldier's Story* by General Omar N Bradley

Patty Hearst ★★ 15
Biographical drama
1988 · US/UK · Colour · 99min

Inspired by Patricia Hearst's autobiography, this was meant to be a bold cinematic experiment to re-create the deprivations and sensations that transformed her from want-for-nothing press heiress into committed terrorist. Yet Paul Schrader's use of darkness, dazzling light and off-screen voices fails to convey the fearful disorientation, and the Symbionese Liberation Army propaganda soon has the attention wandering. DP Violence, swearing, nudity. DVD

Natasha Richardson *Patricia Campbell Hearst* · William Forsythe *Teko* · Ving Rhames *Cinque* · Frances Fisher *Yolanda* · Jodi Long *Wendy Yoshimura* · Olivia Barash *Fahizah* · Dana Delany *Gelina* ■ *Dir* Paul Schrader · *Scr* Nicholas Kazan, from the autobiography *Every Secret Thing* by Patricia Campbell Hearst, Alvin Moscow

Paul ★★★ 15
Science-fiction comedy
2010 · Fr/UK · Colour · 99min

Having lampooned zombie flicks in *Shaun of the Dead* and cop action movies in *Hot Fuzz*, dynamic comedy duo Simon Pegg and Nick Frost tackle science fiction in this amusing culture-clash romp. They play a pair of British comic-book nerds who take a road trip to the Nevada desert in order to see America's most famous UFO sites. Then, lo and behold, they encounter Paul, a little green hitch-hiker - spookily animated in CGI and voiced by Seth Rogen - who's trying to get to his spaceship. Although *Superbad's* Greg Mottola doesn't have the firm directorial grip of the pair's usual collaborator, Edgar Wright, for the most part this is a far-out, funny ride. SP Swearing, drug abuse, sexual references. DVD BL

Simon Pegg *Graeme Willy* · Nick Frost *Clive Gollings* · Seth Rogen *Paul* · Jason Bateman *Special Agent Lorenzo Zoil* · Jane Lynch *Pat Stevens* · Sigourney Weaver *The Big Guy* · Bill Hader *Haggard* · Kristen Wiig *Ruth Buggs* ■ *Dir* Greg Mottola · *Scr* Nick Frost, Simon Pegg

Paul and Michelle ★
Romantic drama   1974 · Fr/UK · Colour · 102min

Lewis Gilbert directs this sequel to his own tale of teenage romance, *Friends* (1971). Yet, in his long career, he never missed his step as badly as this. Every emotion and every romantic interlude rings false, as Sorbonne student Sean Bury seeks to lure Anicée Alvina away from pilot Keir Dullea. The performances are insufferably inept and Claude Renoir's cloying soft-focus photography makes things worse. DP

Anicée Alvina *Michelle Latour* · Sean Bury *Paul Harrison* · Keir Dullea *Garry* · Ronald Lewis *Sir Robert Harrison* · Catherine Allégret *Joanna* ■ *Dir* Lewis Gilbert · *Scr* Angela Huth, Vernon Harris, from a story by Lewis Gilbert

Paul Blart: Mall Cop ★★ PG
Comedy   2009 · US · Colour · 87min

After playing the lovable patsy in *Hitch* and long-running US sitcom *The King of Queens*, Kevin James retains his amiable buffoon character here, as a gauche mall cop with ambitions to be a state trooper. His bumbling exploits are uninspiring to watch until the plot bursts into some sort of life with the arrival of a gang of acrobatic robbers that lays siege to the mall. At least, James provides some fun spoofing action flicks like *Die Hard* by doing a lot of running, jumping and getting stuck in an air vent. Thankfully, the fat gags aren't too cruel and his boundless enthusiasm makes him easy to root for. It's just a shame the film takes so long for his slapstick talents to shine. SP DVD BL

Kevin James *Paul Blart* · Jayma Mays *Amy* · Keir O'Donnell *Veck Sims* · Bobby Cannavale *Commander Kent* · Stephen Rannazzisi *Stuart* · Shirley Knight *Mom* · Raini Rodriguez *Maya Blart* ■ *Dir* Steve Carr · *Scr* Nick Bakay, Kevin James

Paul Blart: Mall Cop 2 ★★ PG
Comedy   2015 · US · Colour · 89min

This inevitable sequel sees kingsize comic Kevin James reprising his hit 2009 role as the amiable buffoon who wanted to be a cop, but who wound up a shopping-centre security guard instead. Having somehow thwarted a sophisticated gang of mall thieves in the undemanding but mildly amusing first film, Blart here attends a security convention in Las Vegas, and once again finds his dubious action skills called on when his daughter disturbs a casino art heist. It's a slow starter, but things pick up slightly with the belated introduction of James's trademark pratfalls and slapstick action. But it's still essentially more of the same, only less so, with comedy that isn't so much telegraphed as sent by second-class post. But, if you liked the first film, you'll almost certainly like this. And if you didn't, you won't. DA DVD BL

Kevin James *Paul Blart* · Raini Rodriguez *Maya* · David Henrie *Lane* · Neal McDonough *Vincent* · Daniella Alonso *Divina* ■ *Dir* Andy Fickman · *Scr* Nick Bakay, Kevin James

Paul Temple Returns ★★ U
Crime mystery   1952 · UK · BW · 68min

It was all change for the last of the Paul Temple pictures produced by Butcher's Film Service - only John Bentley remained from the original cast for this mystery (aka *Bombay Waterfront*). However, Bentley is spiritedly supported by an ensemble that includes Christopher Lee, whose menacing archaeologist holds the key to a string of murders. The plot is short on twists, however, so few will be surprised when the perpetrator is unmasked. DP DVD

John Bentley *Paul Temple* · Patricia Dainton *Steve Temple* · Peter Gawthorne *Sir Graham Forbes* · Christopher Lee *Sir Felix Raybourne* ■ *Dir* Maclean Rogers · *Scr* Francis Durbridge, from his radio play *Paul Temple Intervenes*

Paul Temple's Triumph ★★ U
Crime mystery   1950 · UK · BW · 76min

Once believed lost, Maclean Rogers's adaptation of the Francis Durbridge radio serial *News of Paul Temple* is the most densely plotted of the shoestring quartet made at Nettlefold Studios. It also comes closest to pitching John Bentley into James Bond territory, as he and Dinah Sheridan search for the scientist behind a pioneering nuclear missile shield after he is kidnapped by the shadowy Z organisation. The plot rattles along, and the supporting cast hams it up splendidly. DP DVD

John Bentley *Paul Temple* · Dinah Sheridan *Steve Temple* · Barbara Couper *Mrs Morgan* · Hugh Dempster *Oliver Ffollett* · Jack Livesey *Sir*

P

Graham Forbes ■ *Dir* Maclean Rogers • *Scr* AR Rawlinson, from a radio series by Francis Durbridge

Paulie ★★★ Ⓤ

Comedy adventure 1998 · US · Colour · 87min

Voiced by Jay Mohr, Paulie is a blue-crown conure parrot who lives in the basement of an animal study institute. How he got there and why he's so desperate to find the little girl he helped cure of a stammer form the basis of the story, as told to the building's Russian janitor, Tony Shalhoub. Refreshingly free of gratuitous pyrotechnics and sentimental moralising, this fine-feathered film has longueurs, but mostly flies by. DP **DVD**

Gena Rowlands *Ivy* • Tony Shalhoub *Misha* • Cheech Marin [Richard "Cheech" Marin] *Ignacio* • Bruce Davison *Dr Reingold* • Jay Mohr *Paulie/ Benny* • Trini Alvarado *Adult Marie* • Buddy Hackett *Artie* • Hallie Kate Eisenberg *Marie* ■ *Dir* John Roberts • *Scr* Laurie Craig

Pauline & Paulette ★★★ ᴾᴳ

Comedy drama 2001 · Bel/Neth/Fr · Colour · 74min

Tackling such sensitive issues as age, sibling responsibility and self-sacrifice with a frankness that belies the film's "chocolate-box" visual style, director Lieven Debrauwer's cosily caustic study of relative values is a delight. As the gaudy boutique owner who has to care for an elderly sister – with the mental age of a child – to claim her share of an inheritance, Ann Petersen achieves the perfect blend of kitsch and bitch that makes Dora van der Groen's infantile dottiness seem both harmless and harrowing. With Hilde Duyck's picture-book art direction reinforcing the fairy-tale atmosphere, this is disarmingly droll and endlessly endearing. DP Flemish +subtitles. **DVD**

Ann Petersen *Paulette* • Dora van der Groen *Pauline* • Rosemarie Bergmans *Cécile* • Idwig Stéphane *Albert* • Julienne de Bruyn *Martha* • Camilia Blereau *Butcher's wife* ■ *Dir* Lieven Debrauwer • *Scr* Lieven Debrauwer, Jaak Boon

Pauline at the Beach ★★★★ ⓁⓈ

Comedy drama 1983 · Fr · Colour · 90min

Earning Eric Rohmer the best director prize at Berlin, this was originally conceived in the 1950s, with Brigitte Bardot in the role of the flirtatious divorcee that was eventually taken by Arielle Dombasle. Considerably racier than Rohmer's earlier outings, but just as witty and eloquent, the film is light enough to be blown away on the same sea breeze which fans the flames of holiday lust felt by Dombasle and her cousin, Amanda Langlet, as they dally with a trio of willing men. Sparklingly played and staged with a master's touch. DP French +subtitles. **DVD**

Amanda Langlet *Pauline* • Arielle Dombasle *Marion* • Pascal Greggory *Pierre* • Féodor Atkine *Henry* • Simon de la Brosse *Sylvain* ■ *Dir/Scr* Eric Rohmer • *Cinematographer* Nestor Almendros

Pavee Lackeen: the Traveller Girl ★★★ ⓁⓈ

Drama 2005 · Ire · Colour · 84min

Photographer Perry Ogden makes an impressive directorial debut with this stark but alternately touching and amusing portrait of a traveller family living in a lay-by on the outskirts of Dublin. The episodic action concedes that ten-year-old Winnie Maughan and her mother and sister have a tendency to be their own worst enemies. But they are consistently subjected to prejudice and bureaucratic indifference, and are invariably let down by those who promise to help them. Shot on digital video, the film reinforces the authenticity of the non-professional performances, but Ogden is less persuasive when he imposes some dramatic impetus. DP English +subtitles. **DVD**

Winnie Maughan *Winnie* • Rose Maughan *Mum* • Rosie Maughan *Rosie* • Paddy Maughan *Leroy* • Michael Collins *Uncle Martin* • Helen Joyce *Marie* • Abbie Spallen *Shannon* ■ *Dir* Perry Ogden • *Scr* Perry Ogden, Mark Venner

Paw ★★★

Drama 1959 · Den · Colour · 93min

Denmark received its first Oscar nomination for this popular picture. Working from her own script, director Astrid Henning-Jensen draws on the documentary experience gained in partnership with her husband, Bjarne. There's a pleasing authenticity to this tale of a West Indian orphan billeted on his Danish aunt, and Jimmy Sterman's disillusion with his racist schoolmates is as convincing as his delight in the local wildlife. The drama may be naive in both message and staging, but the intentions are admirable. DP

Jimmy Sterman *Paw* • Edvin Adolphson *Anders Nilsson* • Ninja Tholstrup *Aunt Frieda* • Asbjørn Andersen *Yvonne* ■ *Dir* Astrid Henning-Jensen • *Scr* Astrid Henning-Jensen, Bjarne Henning-Jensen, from the story *Paw, der Indianerjunge* by Torry Gredsted

The Pawnbroker ★★★★★ ⑫

Psychological drama 1965 · US · BW · 110min

Rod Steiger established his credentials as an actor of international standing with this complex psychological portrait of a Holocaust survivor. He's a Jewish refugee in New York who has tried to withdraw from life into the small fortress of the Harlem pawn shop where he works, but is inescapably haunted by his memories of the concentration camp. Director Sidney Lumet treats his material with solemnity and compassion, and the tone is sensitively enhanced by an evocative jazz score from first-time film composer Quincy Jones. AME

Rod Steiger *Sol Nazerman* • Geraldine Fitzgerald *Marilyn Birchfield* • Brock Peters *Rodriguez* • Jaime Sanchez *Jesus Ortiz* • Thelma Oliver *Ortiz's girl* • Marketa Kimbrell *Tessie* • Baruch Lumet *Mendel* ■ *Dir* Sidney Lumet • *Scr* David Friedkin, Morton Fine, from the novel by Edward Lewis Wallant

The Pawnshop ★★★★ Ⓤ

Silent comedy 1916 · US · BW · 20min

One of the first of the dozen short films that Charlie Chaplin made for Mutual, this is a slight, but extremely effective comedy with Chaplin as an assistant in a pawnbroker's shop "where the depressed poor come to try to redeem their pledges". There is some remarkable knockabout as Chaplin battles with his colleague John Rand and abuses his customers, but also more subtle moments such as the sequence in which the star tries to wash dishes by pushing them through a clothes wringer, repeats the process to dry them and then cleans his hands in the same way. For lovers of happy endings, Edna Purviance is there along with the jokes. TH **DVD**

Charles Chaplin *Pawnshop assistant* • Edna Purviance *Pawnbroker* • John Rand *Clerk* • Henry Bergman *Pawnbroker* • Albert Austin *Customer* ■ *Dir/Scr* Charles Chaplin

Paws ★★★★ Ⓤ

Comedy adventure 1997 · UK/Aus · Colour · 80min

This good-natured comedy is about a computer-literate Jack Russell terrier called PC (brilliantly voiced by Billy Connolly) who speaks with the aid of a microchip voice implant. Though the story is standard – a missing fortune, a recently bereaved teenager – director Karl Zwicky whisks the slapstick humour, technical gimmickry, outrageous action and appealing animal whimsy into a subtle soufflé packed with warmth. AJ

Billy Connolly *PC* • Nathan Cavaleri *Zac Feldman* • Emilie François *Samantha Arkwright* • Joe Petruzzi *Stephen Feldman* • Caroline Gillmer *Susie Arkwright* • Rachael Blake *Amy Feldman* ■ *Dir* Karl Zwicky • *Scr* Harry Cripps, from a story by Harry Cripps, from a story by Karl Zwicky, Stephen Dando-Collins

Pay Day ★★★ Ⓤ

Silent comedy 1922 · US · BW · 22min

This was the last of Charlie Chaplin's short films, coming just after *The Kid* (1921) and before his non-starring drama, *A Woman of Paris* (1923). It's about what happens when

a pay check finally arrives in a working-class home and stars Chaplin as a construction worker struggling to avoid the wrath of his nagging wife. There are some inventive sight gags, but also some Dickensian insight, showing the lengths the needy will go to for money. TH

Charles Chaplin *Worker* • Phyllis Allen *His wife* • Mack Swain *The foreman* • Edna Purviance *Foreman's daughter* • Sydney Chaplin [Syd Chaplin] *Friend* ■ *Dir/Scr* Charles Chaplin

Pay It Forward ★★ ⑫

Comedy drama 2000 · US · Colour · 118min

When asked to come up with a way of making the world a better place as part of a class project, schoolboy Haley Joel Osment concocts the notion of carrying out random acts of kindness to strangers, who then pay the favour forward to new beneficiaries rather than back to the giver. This notion brings together the youngster's emotionally scarred, alcoholic mum (Helen Hunt) and physically scarred schoolteacher (Kevin Spacey), both in need of companionship. Reasonable performances in stereotyped roles sustain interest during the early part of film, but the sentimentality may prove hard to stomach. DA **DVD**

Kevin Spacey *Eugene Simonet* • Helen Hunt *Arlene McKinney* • Haley Joel Osment *Trevor McKinney* • Jay Mohr *Chris Chandler* • James Caviezel [Jim Caviezel] *Jerry* • Jon Bon Jovi *Ricky* • Angie Dickinson *Grace* ■ *Dir* Mimi Leder • *Scr* Leslie Dixon, from a novel by Catherine Ryan Hyde

Pay or Die ★★★

Crime drama based on a true story 1960 · US · BW · 111min

From the opening religious ceremony in New York's Little Italy in which the evil force of the "Black Hand" cuts down a girl dressed as an angel, this is a powerful study, based on fact, of a community living in fear. Relishing the opportunity to play a heroic role, Ernest Borgnine gives a vivid and rounded performance as the tough and incorruptible cop who heads a special force to fight the Mafia's secret terror organisation. Director Richard Wilson brings a fresh look to familiar situations helped by a supporting cast of little-known players. AE

Ernest Borgnine *Lt Joseph Petrosino* • Zohra Lampert *Adelina Saulino* • Alan Austin *Johnny Viscardi* • Robert F Simon *Commissioner* • Renata Vanni *Mama Saulino* • Bruno Della Santina *Papa Saulino* ■ *Dir* Richard Wilson (1) • *Scr* Richard Collins, Bertram Millhauser, from the short story *Pay-Off in Sicily* by Burnett Hershey

Payback ★★ ⓁⓈ

Drama 1997 · US · Colour · 83min

In this TV movie, Mary Tyler Moore plays a shop owner who one night witnesses a gang of policemen beat a robbery suspect half to death. Reluctantly, she agrees to testify against them, only to find a campaign of harassment being launched against her entire family. Moore and her former sitcom co-star Edward Asner deliver capable performances but are let down by the plodding direction of Ken Cameron. JF Violence, some swearing. **DVD**

Mary Tyler Moore *Kathryn Stanfill* • Edward Asner *Lt Jack Patkanis* • Fredric Lehne *Sgt Brian Kaleen* • Tobias Andersen *Dean* • Kate Asner *Lisa* ■ *Dir* Ken Cameron • *Scr* Dennis Nemec

Payback ★★★ ⑱

Action crime thriller 1998 · US · Colour · 96min

The source material that provided Lee Marvin with an unforgettable role in *Point Blank* is here recycled for the solid directing debut of *LA Confidential* writer Brian Helgeland (though he refused to re-shoot some scenes and has effectively disowned the result). Mel Gibson stars as violent antihero Porter, a professional thief who seeks revenge when his wife and crime partner double-cross him during a successful hold-up of some Chinese gangsters and leave him for dead. AJ Violence, some swearing, sex scenes. **DVD**
Blu-ray

Mel Gibson *Porter* • Gregg Henry *Val* • Maria Bello *Rosie* • David Paymer *Stegman* • Bill Duke *Detective Hicks* • Deborah Kara Unger *Lynn* • John Glover *Phil* • William Devane *Carter* • Kris Kristofferson *Bronson* • James Coburn *Fairfax* ■ *Dir* Brian Helgeland • *Scr* Brian Helgeland, Terry Hayes, from the novel *The Hunter* by Richard Stark [Donald E Westlake]

Payback Season ★★ ⑮

Drama 2012 · UK · Colour · 91min

Adam Deacon has done far better work (*Kidulthood*, *Adulthood*) than this oddly footie-free football drama. He plays the new hotshot striker for a top-flight club whose council-estate roots come back to haunt him in the shape of the thuggish, bullying leader of his former gang. The main problem with Danny Donnelly's film is its credibility, as it's hard to believe in Deacon as a pro-footballer when you never really see him kick a ball, not even in training. Added to that, the story never really goes anywhere. For Deacon, this may pay his bills but artistically his talent goes untested. DA **DVD** **Blu-ray**

Adam Deacon *Jerome* • Nichola Burley *Lisa* • Leo Gregory *Andy* • David Ajala *Baron* • Anna Popplewell *Izzy* • Geoff Hurst *Adam Avely* ■ *Dir* Danny Donnelly • *Scr* Danny Donnelly, Jenny Fitzpatrick

Paycheck ★★ ⑫

Science-fiction action thriller 2003 · US · Colour · 113min

Electronics genius Ben Affleck undertakes the last in a series of lucrative, top-secret corporate projects that require a memory-wipe on completion. Emerging with no recollection of the three years that have passed, including a relationship with biologist Uma Thurman, he's baffled to discover he's forfeited his pay in favour of an envelope of apparently worthless items. Director John Woo's vision of the future is an uninspiring, under-stylised twist on the present. SF **DVD** **Blu-ray**

Ben Affleck *Michael Jennings* • Aaron Eckhart *Rethrick* • Uma Thurman *Rachel Porter* • Paul Giamatti *Shorty* • Colm Feore *Wolfe* • Joe Morton *Agent Dodge* • Michael C Hall *Agent Klein* ■ *Dir* John Woo • *Scr* Dean Georgaris, from the short story by Philip K Dick

Payday ★★★★

Drama 1972 · US · Colour · 103min

Rip Torn gives the definitive performance of a fading country-and-western star in this magnificently grim but sadly overlooked film that uncompromisingly captures the music business gone sour. Torn – cruel, self-centred and as empty as the bottle he is always holding – has never been better. The film follows his last 36 hours as he ping-pongs from one lowlife honky-tonk bar to another, portraying the booze, the groupies, the hangers-on and the payoffs in a manner as far away from rhinestones and fringes as it is possible to get. FL

Rip Torn *Maury Dann* • Ahna Capri *Mayleen* • Elayne Heilveil *Rosamond* • Michael C Gwynne *Clarence* ■ *Dir* Daryl Duke • *Scr* Don Carpenter

Payment Deferred ★★★

Crime drama 1932 · US · BW · 80min

Charles Laughton is brilliant, despite some pretty hokey dialogue, as a poverty-stricken bank teller, with a wife (Dorothy Peterson) and daughter (Maureen O'Sullivan) to support, who resorts to poisoning his wealthy nephew (a young, almost unrecognisable, Ray Milland). Directed by Lothar Mendes, who perfectly captures the grimly claustrophobic atmosphere of an ugly, constantly rain-drenched suburban house and the bleak lives of its inhabitants, this is a curiously intriguing little piece. RK

Charles Laughton *William Marble* • Neil Hamilton *Gordon Holmes* • Maureen O'Sullivan *Winnie Marble* • Dorothy Peterson *Annie Marble* • Verree Teasdale *Mme Collins* • Ray Milland *James Medland* • Billy Bevan *Hammond* ■ *Dir* Lothar Mendes • *Scr* Ernest Vajda, Claudine West, from the play by Jeffrey Dell

P

Payment on Demand ★★★
Melodrama 1951 · US · BW · 90min

Bette Davis is stunned when husband Barry Sullivan announces he loves Frances Dee and wants a divorce. At first she turns vindictive, until she realises her own contribution to the breakdown of her marriage. Curtis Bernhardt's movie eschews the more obvious clichés of the genre and charts the course of the central relationship in flashback. The first of Davis's films as a freelance following her rupture with Warner Bros after 18 years under contract, it was made before the hugely successful *All About Eve*, but released after. RK

Bette Davis *Joyce Ramsey* • Barry Sullivan *David Ramsey* • Jane Cowl *Mrs Hedges* • Kent Taylor *Robert Townsend* • Betty Lynn *Martha Ramsey* • Frances Dee *Eileen Benson* • Peggie Castle *Diana Ramsey* ■ *Dir* Curtis Bernhardt • *Scr* Bruce Manning, Curtis Bernhardt

Payroll ★★
Crime drama 1961 · UK · BW · 102min

Sidney Hayers is one of the forgotten journeymen of 1960s British cinema. This is a solidly crafted crime story in which the perfect blag begins to unravel as the gang lies low. Michael Craig is on surprisingly good form as the gang leader, but it's Billie Whitelaw, as the widow of a murdered security van guard, who commands centre stage as she risks her own life to snare the culprits. DP

Michael Craig *Johnny Mellors* • Françoise Prévost *Katie Pearson* • Billie Whitelaw *Jackie Parker* • William Lucas *Dennis Pearson* • Kenneth Griffith *Monty* • Tom Bell *Blackie* ■ *Dir* Sidney Hayers • *Scr* George Baxt, from the novel by Derek Bickerton

The Peace Game ★★★
Futuristic satire 1969 · Swe · Colour · 91min

Made four years after the BBC banned his Oscar-winning holocaust masterpiece *The War Game*, Peter Watkins sought to wreak revenge on the Establishment by holding it up to ridicule in this futuristic satire. Comfortably predating the millennial vogue for actuality TV, the premise posits that warfare has been outlawed and that the global hierarchy is now decided by a cynical updating of the ancient gladiatorial games, which are more a means of mass repression than a celebration of national prowess. Cinematographer Peter Suschitzky achieves some memorable images, but Watkins's message is lost in the imprecision of his protest. DP

Arthur Pentelow *British general* • Frederick Danner *British staff officer* • Hans Bendrik *Capt Davidsson* • Daniel Harle *French officer* • Hans Berger *West German officer* • Rosario Gianetti *American officer* ■ *Dir* Peter Watkins • *Scr* Nicholas Gosling, Peter Watkins

Peace, Love & Misunderstanding ★★
Comedy drama 2011 · US · Colour · 96min

Jane Fonda leaps at the chance to grow old disgracefully in this harmless piece of fluff about the value of family and community. Fonda's unwillingness to give up her flower-power lifestyle has estranged her from her uptight lawyer daughter, Catherine Keener. However, the latter swallows her pride and decides to reconnect with Fonda after she learns her husband wants a divorce. Unfortunately, the fine ensemble playing and the leisurely direction don't quite succeed in papering over some cringeworthy hippy clichés. JF Drug references.

Jane Fonda *Grace* • Catherine Keener *Diane* • Jeffrey Dean Morgan *Jude* • Elizabeth Olsen *Zoe* • Chace Crawford *Cole* • Kyle MacLachlan *Mark* ■ *Dir* Bruce Beresford • *Scr* Christina Mengert, Joseph Muszynski

The Peacekeeper ★★★
Action thriller 1997 · Can · Colour · 94min

Any resemblance to the George Clooney/Nicole Kidman vehicle *The Peacemaker* is, of course, completely intentional! Actually, this suspense thriller gives that post-Cold War adventure a good run for its money, as maverick air force major Dolph Lundgren gets in the way of a sinister plot to nuke Washington. An exciting roof-top car chase and an explosive attack on Mount Rushmore make up for the two-dimensional acting from Lundgren in this better-than-average flag-waver. AJ Swearing, violence.

Dolph Lundgren *Major Frank Cross* • Montel Williams *Lt Col Northrop* • Michael Sarrazin *Lt Col Douglas Murphy* • Roy Scheider *President Robert Baker* • Christopher Heyerdahl *Hettinger* ■ *Dir* Frederic Forestier • *Scr* Robert Geoffrion, James H Stewart

Peacemaker ★★★ 18
Science-fiction action thriller 1990 · US · Colour · 90min

Despite an at times quite noticeable low budget this exhilarating sci-fi thriller really delivers the goods for action fans. A well-worn theme for sure – alien cop tracking down alien villain – but the twist comes when they crash-land on Earth and both claim to be the good guy. Cue a virtual nonstop montage of chases, explosions and shoot-outs. Kevin S Tenney keeps you engrossed, while Robert Forster and Lance Edwards as the humanoid and virtually indestructible aliens make it fun guessing who's who. RS

Robert Forster *Yates* • Lance Edwards *Townsend* • Hilary Shepard *Dori Caisson* • Robert Davi *Sergeant Frank Ramos* • Bert Remsen *Doc* • John Denos *Reeger* • Wally Taylor *Moses* ■ *Dir/Scr* Kevin S Tenney

The Peacemaker ★★★ 15
Action thriller 1997 · US · Colour · 118min

George Clooney and Nicole Kidman attempt to save Manhattan from nuclear destruction in this pacey thriller. When a Russian train is blown up to disguise the theft of a nuclear warhead, the stage is set for a nail-biting countdown. Kidman isn't entirely convincing as a government scientist, but Clooney gives a confident lead performance as a Special Forces officer. This failed to ignite at the box office, but action fans will enjoy the explosions, car crashes and shots of the ticking bomb. AT Violence, swearing.

George Clooney *Thomas Devoe* • Nicole Kidman *Julia Kelly* • Armin Mueller-Stahl *Dimitri Vertikoff* • Marcel Iures *Dusan Gavrich* • Alexander Baluev *Alexsander Kodoroff* • Rene Medvesek *Vlado Mirich* • Randall Batinkoff *Ken* ■ *Dir* Mimi Leder • *Scr* Michael Schiffer, from an article by Leslie Cockburn, Andrew Cockburn

Peaches ★★ 15
Comedy 2000 · Ire · Colour · 82min

In Nick Grosso's adaptation of his own 1994 play, peaches are pretty girls and the obsession of likely lads Matthew Rhys, Justin Salinger and Matthew Dunster. Rhys is the focus of attention, discovering that he would actually like his girl "friend", Kelly Reilly, to be rather more than a "chick for chats", but is at a complete loss as to how to woo her. Salinger and Dunster are mere two-dimensional cutouts with a crass *Loaded* mentality and little else. LH

Matthew Rhys *Frank* • Kelly Reilly *Cherry* • Justin Salinger *Johnny* • Sophie Okonedo *Pippa* ■ *Dir* Nick Grosso • *Scr* Nick Grosso, from his play

The Peanut Butter Solution ★★★
Fantasy drama 1985 · Can · Colour · 90min

This is a Roald Dahl-style children's fantasy from Canada, also known as *Michael's Fright*. After losing all his hair, young Mathew Mackay is given a special type of peanut butter which is supposed to help his hair grow back. Unfortunately, he uses too much and is soon rivalling Samson in the long tresses department. A fun tale that will delight most children. JB

Mathew Mackay *Mathew Baskin* • Siluck Saysanasy *Connie* • Alison Podbrey *Suzie* • Michael Hogan (3) *Billy* • Michael Maillot *Signor* ■ *Dir/Scr* Michael Rubbo

The Pearl Button ★★★★ 12A
Documentary 2015 · Fr/Sp/Chil/Swi · Colour and BW · 81min

Chilean director Patricio Guzmán continues his life-long crusade to expose the crimes of General Pinochet in this central section of a trilogy that began with *Nostalgia for the Light* (2010). Survivors from the islands around Tierra del Fuego strive to preserve their culture, and the fate of a teenager lies in the hands of a boat captain. Contrasting sea and sand, buttons and stars, Guzmán laments Chile's failure to protect its resources in this typically astute, potent and beautifully photographed essay. DP Spanish, Kawesqar +subtitles. Distressing scenes.

Patricio Guzmán *Narrator* ■ *Dir/Scr* Patricio Guzmán

Pearl Harbor ★★ 12
Second World War romantic drama 2001 · US · Colour · 175min

The surprise bombing of Pearl Harbor on 7 December 1941 was a major event in US history and who better to capture it on screen than the big-thinking producer/director team of Jerry Bruckheimer and Michael Bay? Perhaps unsurprisingly, the actual attack, which forms the middle act of the film's bloated three hours, is an amazing spectacle. But sheer cinematic power is undermined by our total lack of empathy for any of the cardboard cut-out characters. Weaknesses of plot are only amplified by the film's unwieldy size, while the script is toe-curling. AC Violence, swearing.

Ben Affleck *Rafe McCawley* • Josh Hartnett *Danny Walker* • Kate Beckinsale *Evelyn Johnson* • Cuba Gooding Jr *Doris "Dorie" Miller* • Tom Sizemore *Earl Sistern* • Jon Voight *President Franklin D Roosevelt* • Colm Feore *Admiral Kimmel* • Alec Baldwin *Gen James H Doolittle* • Dan Aykroyd *Captain Thurman* ■ *Dir* Michael Bay • *Scr* Randall Wallace • *Cinematographer* John Schwartzman

Pearl Jam Twenty ★★ 15
Music documentary 2011 · US · Colour and BW · 119min

Director Cameron Crowe (*Jerry Maguire*, *Almost Famous*) first met Pearl Jam founding members Stone Gossard and Jeff Ament in the late 1980s when he was a rock journalist. That makes him perfectly placed to stitch together this exhaustive overview of their formative moments over a 20-year career. Pulling together grainy old camcorder footage, powerful performances and interviews with all the key players, Crowe draws out the outfit's motivations and concerns with the eye of a true aficionado. DC

Chris Cornell • Eddie Vedder • Stone Gossard • Jeff Ament ■ *Dir* Cameron Crowe

The Pearl of Death ★★★ PG
Mystery 1944 · US · BW · 68min

Basil Rathbone and Nigel Bruce did pick 'em! This is the one in which Rondo Hatton creeps out of the crypt of bad dreams as homicidal sidekick to jewel thief Miles Mander. Not only is he encumbered with a zombie-lumbering walk and a nasty ability to break backs, but also an unhealthy obsession with Evelyn Ankers that results in the villain's comeuppance – a nightmare for us, but an elementary deduction for Holmes. TH

Basil Rathbone *Sherlock Holmes* • Nigel Bruce *Dr Watson* • Evelyn Ankers *Naomi Drake* • Dennis Hoey *Inspector Lestrade* • Miles Mander *Giles Conover* • Rondo Hatton *"Creeper"* ■ *Dir* Roy William Neill • *Scr* Bertram Millhauser, from the story *The Adventure of the Six Napoleons* by Sir Arthur Conan Doyle

Pearl of the South Pacific ★★ U
Adventure 1955 · US · Colour · 84min

This piece of tosh is enjoyable if you're unsophisticated, aged under ten, or both. There's a great deal of period charm in the Technicolored tale for fans of both the exotic and of cheesy interior set dressing trying to look like authentic locations, but, although Virginia Mayo is just about adequate, her co-stars, Dennis Morgan and David Farrar, are well past their primes, playing pearl-hunters on an South Sea island. TS

Virginia Mayo *Rita Delaine* • Dennis Morgan *Dan Merrill* • David Farrar *Bully Hayes* • Lance Fuller *George* • Murvyn Vye *Halemano* ■ *Dir* Allan Dwan • *Scr* Talbot Jennings, Jesse Lasky Jr, from a story by Anna Hunger

La Peau Douce ★★★★ PG
Romantic drama 1964 · Fr · BW · 112min

The influence of Alfred Hitchcock is apparent in this darkly comic and wonderfully observed tale of *femmes fatales* and *crimes passionels*. François Truffaut depicts air hostess Françoise Dorléac (Catherine Deneuve's sister) as a blonde ice maiden whose passing fancy for intellectual Jean Desailly has a life-shattering effect. There are also touches of Jean Renoir's humanism and echoes of Jacques Tati's despair at the mechanised world in what was wrongly considered to be a coolly cynical melodrama. It is, in fact, an overlooked gem. DP French +subtitles.

Jean Desailly *Pierre Lachenay* • Françoise Dorléac *Nicole Chomette* • Nelly Benedetti *Franca Lachenay* ■ *Dir* François Truffaut • *Scr* François Truffaut, Jean-Louis Richard

The Pebble and the Penguin ★★ U
Animated fantasy 1995 · US · Colour · 70min

This undistinguished offering from the Don Bluth studio owes little to nature and too much to the kind of clawing sentimentality that spoils so many animated features. The story of Hubie, the shy bird whose hopes of romance are dashed by the dastardly Drake, is further disadvantaged by the poor voiceovers of Martin Short, James Belushi and Tim Curry and Barry Manilow's dreadful songs. DP

Shani Wallis *Narrator* • Martin Short *Hubie* • James Belushi *Rocko* • Tim Curry *Drake* • Annie Golden *Marina* • Scott Bullock *Chubby/Gentoo* ■ *Dir* Don Bluth • *Scr* Rachel Korestsky, Steve Whitestone • *Music* Barry Manilow • *Lyrics* Bruce Sussman

Pecker ★★★ 15
Satirical comedy 1998 · US · Colour · 86min

John Waters movies don't come more sweet and adorable than this portrait of a young and ingenuous Baltimore photographer (a rather low-key Edward Furlong) who becomes an instant "art star" after winning over New York's jaded establishment with his neighbourhood snaps. The scanty story charts Pecker's rise to fame and the subsequent attempts to pluck him from his proletarian backwater. Waters gently – though at times didactically – satirises the vampiric art world as a frame for a comparatively sympathetic picture of his B-list Maryland home town. DO Nudity, sexual references, swearing.

Edward Furlong *Pecker* • Christina Ricci *Shelley* • Bess Armstrong *Dr Klompus* • Mark Joy *Jimmy* • Mary Kay Place *Joyce* • Martha Plimpton *Tina* • Brendan Sexton III *Matt* • Mink Stole *Precinct captain* • Lili Taylor *Rorey* • Patricia Hearst *Lynn Wentworth* • Brigid Berlin [Brigid Polk] *Super market rich lady* ■ *Dir/Scr* John Waters (2)

The Pedestrian ★★★
Drama 1974 · W Ger · Colour · 97min

Austrian-born actor/director Maximilian Schell wrote, directed and starred in this film, influenced by his own experience of fleeing with his family to Switzerland in 1938. Through the story of a wealthy German industrialist – a former Nazi officer, who is exposed in the press – Schell examines the nature of collective guilt and was coolly received in Germany. BB In German.

Gustav Rudolf Sellner *Heinz Alfred Giese* • Ruth Hausmeister *Inge Maria Giese* • Peter Hall *Rudolf Hartmann* • Maximilian Schell *Andreas Giese* • Gila Von Weitershausen *Karin* • Alexander May *Alexander Markowitz* • Peggy Ashcroft *Lady Gray*

• Elisabeth Bergner *Frau Lilienthal* • Lil Dagover *Frau Eschenlohr* • Françoise Rosay *Frau Dechamps* ■ *Dir/Scr* Maximilian Schell

Pee-wee's Big Adventure ★★★ U

Comedy　1985 · US · Colour · 87min

A film built around a cult children's TV character may seem a strange place for Tim Burton to start his feature career, but, actually, it's not that big a leap from Pee-Wee Herman to Edward Scissorhands, Batman or Ed Wood. At the centre of this cartoonish comedy, Paul Reubens is wonderful as the curious little chap whose world falls apart when his precious bicycle is stolen. But some of the gags are spectacularly unfunny and Pee-Wee's nervous prattling can become irritating. A bold attempt to do something dazzlingly original. DP

Paul Reubens *Pee-wee Herman* • Elizabeth Daily *Dottie* • Mark Holton *Francis* • Diane Salinger *Simone* • Judd Omen *Mickey* • Monte Landis *Mario* • Damon Martin *Chip* • Daryl Roach *Chuck* • Alice Nunn *Large Marge* ■ *Dir* Tim Burton • *Scr* Phil Hartman, Paul Reubens, Michael Varhol, from the character created by Paul Reubens

Peeping Tom ★★★★★ 15

Thriller　1960 · UK · Colour · 97min

This infamous thriller was director Michael Powell's first solo project after 20 years of collaboration with Emeric Pressburger. A Freudian nightmare about a film technician (Karlheinz Böhm) who photographs the look of terror in the eyes of the women he kills, it was badly received at the time. Only in recent years has it been recognised, by directors such as Martin Scorsese (who was instrumental in having the film restored and re-released in the late-1970s), as a risk-all masterpiece from one of our greatest film-makers. Maxine Audley and Moira Shearer are among those who encounter the killer's lethal voyeurism, while Powell himself plays the father who created a monster. TH
Violence, sexual situations. DVD BD

Carl Boehm [Karlheinz Böhm] *Mark Lewis* • Moira Shearer *Vivian* • Anna Massey *Helen Stephens* • Maxine Audley *Mrs Stephens* • Esmond Knight *Arthur Baden* • Bartlett Mullins *Mr Peters* • Shirley Anne Field *Diane Ashley* • Michael Goodliffe *Don Jarvis* • Brenda Bruce *Dora* ■ *Dir* Michael Powell • *Scr* Leo Marks • *Cinematographer* Otto Heller

Peg o' My Heart ★★★

Comedy drama　1933 · US · BW · 86min

This charts the travails of the unspoilt, uneducated daughter of a widowed Irish fisherman after she inherits two million pounds. She is wrenched away from her beloved father to lodge with a gruesomely awful family in England, upper class but broke, who are being paid to turn her into a lady. Awash in sentimentality, this combines the poignant, the coyly comical and the melodramatic on the way to its fairy-tale climax. RK

Marion Davies *Peg O'Connell* • Onslow Stevens *Sir Jerry Markham* • J Farrell MacDonald *Pat O'Connell* • Juliette Compton *Ethel Chichester* • Irene Browne *Mrs. Chichester* • Tyrrell Davis *Alaric Chichester* • Alan Mowbray *Capt Christopher Brent* ■ *Dir* Robert Z Leonard • *Scr* Frank R Adams, Frances Marion (adaptation), from J Hartley Manners's play

Peggy Guggenheim: Art Addict ★★★ 15

Documentary　2015 · US/UK · Colour · 95min

Director Lisa Immordino Vreeland's brisk but often frustrating film portrait of the doyenne of modern art patrons puts little emphasis on her subject's torrid love life to concentrate on how she learned about art during her bohemian sojourn in 1920s Paris. Robert De Niro and Marina Abramovic guest among the talking heads, but the majority are arts luvvies whose insights sometimes feel as bland as the archive material Vreeland uses. DP Sexual references. DVD

■ *Dir* Lisa Immordino Vreeland

Peggy Sue Got Married ★★★ 15

Comedy fantasy　1986 · US · Colour · 98min

Francis Ford Coppola's time-travelling fantasy sees the unhappily married Kathleen Turner passing out during her 25th high-school reunion and waking up back in 1960, in the body of her younger self. Her subtle performance beautifully re-creates the traits of teenagehood, and earned an Oscar nomination, while Nicolas Cage (whose performance was originally slated in many quarters) is amazing as the boy she knows will grow up into a slob. It's not Coppola's usual territory, and he overplays the Capra card a little, but he has fashioned a rewarding tale. DP Swearing. DVD

Kathleen Turner *Peggy Sue Bodell* • Nicolas Cage *Charlie Bodell* • Barry Miller *Richard Norvik* • Catherine Hicks *Carol Heath* • Joan Allen *Maddy Nagle* • Kevin J O'Connor *Michael Fitzsimmons* • Barbara Harris *Evelyn Kelcher* • Don Murray *Jack Kelcher* • Maureen O'Sullivan *Elizabeth Alvorg* • Leon Ames *Barney Alvorg* • Helen Hunt *Beth Bodell* • John Carradine *Leo* • Sofia Coppola *Nancy Kelcher* • Jim Carrey *Walter Getz* ■ *Dir* Francis Coppola [Francis Ford Coppola] • *Scr* Jerry Leichtling, Arlene Sarner

Peking Express ★★

Drama　1951 · US · BW · 84min

This is a typical "Red Menace" yarn, with Chinese villains instead of Russian ones. Aboard the train is UN doctor Joseph Cotten, who is going to perform an operation on a anti-communist leader; there's also Cotten's love interest, a priest and a communist apparatchik. The hefty doses of ideological dialogue make for a rather slow journey but things liven up when bandits raid the train and take everyone hostage. AT

Joseph Cotten *Michael Bachlin* • Corinne Calvet *Danielle Grenier* • Edmund Gwenn *Father Joseph Murray* • Marvin Miller *Kwon* • Benson Fong *Wong* ■ *Dir* William Dieterle • *Scr* John Meredyth Lucas, Jules Furthman, from a story by Harry Hervey

Peking Opera Blues ★★★★ 18

Period action adventure
1986 · HK · Colour · 101min

Among the best films made in Hong Kong in the 1980s, this dazzling period adventure will leave you breathless and begging for more. Director Tsui Hark packs so much into the movie that it's hard to know what to praise first – the spectacle, the athleticism, the sprawling storyline, the slapstick or the exhilarating action. Yet there isn't a martial arts hero in sight, as Cherie Chung, Lin Ching Hsia and Sally Yeh take centre stage to challenge the sexist prejudices that survived the republican uprising of 1911. Both brutally balletic and intricately frantic, this will have you cheering out loud. DP Cantonese +subtitles. Violence.

Lin Ching Hsia [Brigitte Lin] *Tsao Wan* • Mark Cheng *Ling Pak Ho* • Sally Yeh • Cherie Chung • Lin Ching Hsia [Brigitte Lin] ■ *Dir* Tsui Hark • *Scr* To Kwok Wai

The Pelican Brief ★★★★ 12

Thriller　1993 · US · Colour · 135min

Julia Roberts stars as the aspiring young legal eagle who stumbles upon a massive conspiracy reaching right to the Oval Office. Her only ally is Denzel Washington, a sceptical reporter who finds himself investigating the scoop of a lifetime. The two leads are fine, but the real coup is the depth of talent in the supporting cast. Sam Shepard and John Heard are among those delivering killer cameos, although all are eclipsed by Robert Culp's witty portrayal of a shifty president. Director Alan J Pakula weaves his way adeptly through the myriad characters and subplots. JF Violence, swearing. DVD BD

Julia Roberts *Darby Shaw* • Denzel Washington *Gray Grantham* • Sam Shepard *Thomas Callahan* • John Heard *Gavin Verheek* • Tony Goldwyn *Fletcher Coal* • James B Sikking *Denton Voyles* • William Atherton *Bob Gminski* • Robert Culp

President • Stanley Tucci *Khamel* • Hume Cronyn *Justice Rosenberg* • John Lithgow *Smith Keen* ■ *Dir* Alan J Pakula • *Scr* Alan J Pakula, from the novel by John Grisham

La Pelle ★★★

Second World War drama
1981 · It/Fr · Colour · 131min

Set during the Allied liberation of Naples in 1943, this adaptation captures the moral collapse and social chaos of a decimated nation. Relating stories both shocking and dolorous, Liliana Cavani refuses to shy away from the city's grinding poverty and the desperate measures to which many resorted to survive. Marcello Mastroianni holds the piece together as a liaison officer, while Burt Lancaster is brusque as the head of the US forces. DP English, Italian, French +subtitles.

Marcello Mastroianni *Curzio Malaparte* • Burt Lancaster *General Mark Cork* • Claudia Cardinale *Princess Consuelo Caracciolo* • Ken Marshall *Jimmy Wren* • Alexandra King *Deborah Wyatt* ■ *Dir* Liliana Cavani • *Scr* Robert Katz, Liliana Cavani, from the memoirs by Curzio Malaparte

Pelle the Conqueror ★★★★ 15

Period drama　1987 · Den/Swe · Colour · 150min

Max von Sydow gives a towering performance as the elderly Swede who emigrates to Denmark in the early 20th century with his son Pelle (played by Pelle Hvenegaard) to seek employment. Hvenegaard is also outstanding as the youngster who must grow up quickly when his father finds work on a farm. Director Bille August's adaptation of the first part of Nobel Prize winner Martin Andersen Nexo's four-volume novel is genuine life-affirming drama. So many strands of conflict are unravelled that it's occasionally hard to keep track, but the power of the acting (von Sydow was Oscar nominated) and the dialogue will keep you gripped. TH Danish +subtitles. DVD

Max von Sydow *Lasse Karlsson* • Pelle Hvenegaard *Pelle Karlsson* • Erik Paaske *Farm manager* • Kristina Tornqvist *Anna* ■ *Dir* Bille August • *Scr* Bille August, from a novel by Martin Andersen Nexo

Pelo Malo ★★★★ 15

Drama
2013 · Ven/Peru/Arg/Ger · Colour · 93min

In this Venezuelan drama, a nine-year-old boy and his widowed mum embark on a battle of wills over straightening his curly hair for a school photo. Junior simply wants to look like the pop singers on TV, but his mother knows that in Caracas's unforgiving public housing such seemingly minor decisions are loaded with cultural significance. With a title that translates as "Bad Hair", the subject might not seem strong enough for an entire feature, yet director Mariana Rondon's approach is intimate and low-key, and the story is genuinely thought-provoking and involving. TJ Spanish +subtitles.

Samuel Lange *Junior* • Samantha Castillo *Marta* • Nelly Ramos *Carmen* • Maria Emilia Sulbaran *Niña* ■ *Dir/Scr* Mariana Rondon

The Penalty ★

Crime drama　1941 · US · BW · 80min

A feeble attempt to resurrect the violent gangster film of the 1930s, this stars burly character actor Edward Arnold as the ruthless and egotistical bank robber whose only soft spot is for his young son, played by Gene Reynolds, whom he grooms for a life of crime. But after the son is exposed to traditional family values on a farm, he turns against his father. Predictable, and Lionel Barrymore grates as the invalid grandfather. AE

Edward Arnold *Martin "Stuff" Nelson* • Lionel Barrymore *"Grandpop" Logan* • Marsha Hunt *Katherine Logan* • Robert Sterling *Edward McCormick* • Gene Reynolds *"Roosty"* • Emma Dunn *"Ma" McCormick* • Veda Ann Borg *Julie* • Phil Silvers ■ *Dir* Harold S Bucquet • *Scr* Harry Ruskin, John C Higgins, from the play by Martin Berkeley

Pendulum ★★★ 15

Detective crime drama
1969 · US · Colour · 97min

George Peppard turns in a tough performance in this above-par thriller as a police captain who becomes a murder suspect when his wife (Jean Seberg) and her lover are murdered. Ostracised by his former colleagues and thrown in prison, he escapes to hunt down the real culprit. JG

George Peppard *Captain Frank Matthews* • Jean Seberg *Adele Matthews* • Richard Kiley *Woodrow Wilson King* • Charles McGraw *Deputy Chief Hildebrand* • Madeleine Sherwood *Mrs Eileen Sanderson* • Robert F Lyons *Paul Martin Sanderson* ■ *Dir* George Schaefer • *Scr* Stanley Niss

Penelope ★★ U

Comedy　1966 · US · Colour · 97min

This glossy comedy has Natalie Wood as the compulsive thief who robs a bank and is then persuaded by her shrink to break into the bank again and put the money back. Heist movies were very big in the mid-1960s and this one certainly has the most gorgeous-looking thief. If only it also had a wittier script, pacier direction and a real leading man to play opposite the vivacious Natalie Wood. AT

Natalie Wood *Penelope Elcott* • Ian Bannen *James B Elcott* • Dick Shawn *Dr Gregory Mannix* • Peter Falk *Lt Bixbee* • Jonathan Winters *Professor Klobb* ■ *Dir* Arthur Hiller • *Scr* George Wells, from the novel by EV Cunningham [Howard Fast]

Penelope ★ U

Fantasy drama　2006 · UK · Colour · 85min

This stilted modern role-reversal take on *Beauty and the Beast* is too bland for adults and too grounded in reality for youngsters. Christina Ricci stars as the eponymous wealthy recluse who was born with a pig snout as the result of a family curse. Down-on-his-luck gambler Max (James McAvoy) is hired to take photos of Penelope's face. But could he turn out to be her Prince Charming? The twists are too predictable, the slapstick farce too broad and the roster of British comics in minor roles(Lenny Henry, Russell Brand, Ronni Ancona) a hollow gimmick. The fact Penelope really isn't that ugly doesn't help, either. AJ DVD

Christina Ricci *Penelope Wilhern* • James McAvoy *Max* • Catherine O'Hara *Jessica Wilhern* • Peter Dinklage *Lemon* • Richard E Grant *Franklin Wilhern* • Reese Witherspoon *Annie* • Simon Woods *Edward Vanderman* • Ronni Ancona *Aunt Wanda* ■ *Dir* Mark Palansky • *Scr* Leslie Caveny

The Penguin Pool Murder ★★★

Comedy mystery　1932 · US · BW · 65min

This marvellous RKO B-movie has sleuthing teacher Hildegarde Withers (played by Edna May Oliver) and cigar-chewing cop Oscar Piper (James Gleason) teaming up to investigate a bizarre death in an aquarium. The experience is mesmerising and the two characters end up contemplating marriage. Stuart Palmer's original stories were spun out into six films from 1932 to 1937, but Oliver only graced the first three – a pity, as it's the stars that make this film so watchable. *Murder on the Blackboard* (1934) followed. TS

Edna May Oliver *Hildegarde Martha Withers* • James Gleason *Inspector Oscar Piper* • Mae Clarke *Gwen Parker* • Robert Armstrong *Barry Costello* • Donald Cook *Philip Seymour* • Clarence Wilson *Bertrand B Hemingway* ■ *Dir* George Archainbaud • *Scr* Willis Goldbeck, from the novel by Stuart Palmer

Penguins of Madagascar ★★★ U

Animated adventure　2014 · US · Colour · 88min

Those scene-stealing penguins from the *Madagascar* movies deservedly get their own spin-off, as they're recruited to thwart the world-takeover plans of a dastardly octopus. The film-makers struggle at times with a generic plot, contrived gags and a tendency to assume frantic is fun. But the

P

penguins (voiced by their animators) are kiddie-friendly cute and there are enough mirthful moments – many splendidly surreal – to make this a trip worth taking. Benedict Cumberbatch and John Malkovich are the guest voices. DA DVD Blu 3D

Tom McGrath *Skipper* • Chris Miller *Kowalski* • Christopher Knights *Private* • Conrad Vernon *Rico* • John Malkovich *Dave* • Benedict Cumberbatch *Classified* ■ *Dir* Eric Darnell, Simon J Smith • *Scr* Michael Colton, Brandon Sawyer, John Aboud, from characters by Tom McGrath, Eric Darnell

The Penitent ★★★ 15
Drama 1988 · US · Colour · 90min

Actor Cliff Osmond turned writer/director with this weird, heavily symbolic tale about an isolated Hispanic village that has an annual religious festival which climaxes with a re-enactment of the Crucifixion. Few survive the ordeal, even though ropes are used instead of nails. The penitent this year is Raul Julia, trapped in a sexless marriage and watching his wife being easily seduced by Armande Assante. AT

Raul Julia *Ramon Guerola* • Armand Assante *Juan Mateo* • Rona Freed *Celia Guerola* • Julie Carmen *Corina* • Lucy Reina *Margarita* ■ *Dir/Scr* Cliff Osmond

Penitentiary ★★★ 15
Blaxploitation prison drama
1979 · US · Colour · 103min

This late entry in the blaxploitation cycle cleverly mixes gritty prison drama with the boxing movie. Leon Isaac Kennedy is the clichéd innocent inmate who puts his fighting skills to good use competing in a prison boxing tournament where victory offers early parole. As written, directed and produced by Jamaa Fanaka, this is a relatively uncompromising look at daily prison life which dumps the usual blaxploitation stereotypes in a bid for more realistic and deeper characterisations. Successful enough to spawn two sequels. RS DVD

Leon Isaac Kennedy *Too Sweet* • Thommy Pollard *Eugene* • Hazel Spears *Linda* • Wilbur "Hi-Fi" White *Sweet Pea* • Gloria Delaney *Inmate* ■ *Dir/Scr* Jamaa Fanaka

Penn & Teller Get Killed ★
Black comedy 1989 · US · Colour · 91min

It's hard to figure out why Arthur Penn would direct a goofball comedy starring two magician comedians who are an acquired taste. There is a plot buried somewhere here – a psychopath sets his sights on assassinating one of the duo during their nationwide tour – but the movie makes excuses to show the pair involved with material better suited to one of their talk-show appearances. KB

Penn Jillette *Penn* • Teller *Teller* • Caitlin Clarke *Carlotta* • Jon Cryer *3rd Frat Boy* • David Patrick Kelly *Fan* • Christopher Durang *Jesus Freak* • Leonardo Cimino *Ernesto* ■ *Dir* Arthur Penn • *Scr* Penn Jillette, Teller

Pennies from Heaven ★★★ U
Musical comedy drama 1936 · US · BW · 77min

This is one of a stream of Depression-era movies that consolidated the star power of crooner Bing Crosby, giving him the chance to warble the title song into posterity and an Oscar nomination. The slight plot and even slighter production values don't really matter, though these days it's hard to take Bing seriously as he befriends an orphaned little girl and wanders through life's incidents with her and her near-dotty grandad, played by the wonderful Donald Meek. TS DVD

Bing Crosby *Larry Poole* • Madge Evans *Susan Sprague* • Edith Fellows *Patsy Smith* • Donald Meek *Gramp Smith* • John Gallaudet *Hart* • Louis Armstrong *Henry* • Tom Dugan (1) *Crowbar* • Nana Bryant *Miss Howard* ■ *Dir* Norman Z McLeod • *Scr* Jo Swerling, from the novel *The Peacock's Feather* by Katherine Leslie Moore

Pennies from Heaven ★★★ 15
Musical romantic drama
1981 · US · Colour · 103min

Dennis Potter's TV serial is given the Hollywood treatment here with Steve Martin. Set in Chicago during the Depression, Martin's frustrating marriage spurs him into a dalliance with schoolteacher Bernadette Peters. The drama is offset and enriched by their happy-go-lucky musical numbers – the most enjoyable feature of the film. The cinematography is rich and slick, the leads engaging and Christopher Walken worth seeing in support. LH

Steve Martin *Arthur Parker* • Bernadette Peters *Eileen* • Christopher Walken *Tom* • Jessica Harper *Joan* • Vernel Bagneris *Accordion man* • John McMartin *Mr Warner* • John Karlen *Detective* • Jay Garner *Banker* ■ *Dir* Herbert Ross • *Scr* Dennis Potter, from his TV serial • *Cinematographer* Gordon Willis

Penny Gold ★★ 12
Thriller 1973 · UK · Colour · 86min

Never trust a twin sister if she looks like Francesca Annis and behaves with such suspicion-inviting self consciousness, especially as her sibling's been found dead. Director Jack Cardiff, taking time off from being one of British cinema's great cameramen, just couldn't come to terms with this thriller about stamp dealing. The film lacks credibility, and the flashback structure would have looked dated even in the 1970s. TH Some violence.

Francesca Annis *Delphi Emerson* • James Booth *Matthews* • Nicky Henson *Roger* • Una Stubbs *Anna* • Joseph O'Conor *Charles Blachford* • Joss Ackland *Jones* • Richard Heffer *Claude Grancourt* • Sue Lloyd *Model* ■ *Dir* Jack Cardiff • *Scr* David Osborne, Liz Charles-Williams

Penny Paradise ★★ U
Comedy 1938 · UK · BW · 69min

A Merseyside tugboat captain wins the football pools, celebrates with an uproarious party, and must cope with a grasping aunt and his daughter's unscrupulous suitor who both hope to profit from his good fortune. A simple and oft-told tale makes for a short and straightforward British film, given an authentic background by director Carol Reed, and beautifully played by Welsh character actor Edmund Gwenn, soon to find Hollywood stardom. RK DVD

Edmund Gwenn *Joe Higgins* • Jimmy O'Dea *Pat* • Betty Driver *Betty Higgins* • Maire O'Neill *Widow Clegg* • Jack Livesey *Bert* • Ethel Coleridge *Aunt Agnes* ■ *Dir* Carol Reed • *Scr* Thomas Thompson, Thomas Browne, WL Meade, from a story by Basil Dean

Penny Points to Paradise ★★ U
Crime comedy 1951 · UK · BW · 68min

This cheap and cheerful curio stars The Goon Show's Harry Secombe, Spike Milligan and Peter Sellers. Although down-to-earth Harry Flakers (Secombe) has had a big win on the pools, he still takes his annual holiday at his favourite Brighton boarding house. While at the seaside he must contend with several individuals who want to get their hands on his fortune. The plot, such as it is, is merely an excuse for the trio to each do their comic turns, while the acting is mannered and the slapstick humour weak, making this one for Goons fans only. LB DVD Blu

Harry Secombe *Harry Flakers* • Alfred Marks *Edward Haynes* • Peter Sellers *The Major/Arnold Fringe* • Paddy O'Neil *Paddie O'Neil* • Christine Russell • Spike Milligan *Spike Donnelly* ■ *Dir* Anthony Young • *Scr* John Ormonde

Penny Princess ★★★ U
Comedy 1952 · UK · Colour · 93min

As a British spoof on the free market – New York girl inherits European principality and invigorates flagging economy – this is so gentle that the satire is scarcely as noticeable as the appearance of a young

Dirk Bogarde as star Yolande Donlan's suitor. But Donlan, the wife of writer/director Val Guest, still puts in an effervescent performance despite the rather lacklustre plot. TH

Yolande Donlan *Lindy Smith* • Dirk Bogarde *Tony Craig* • Edwin Styles *Chancellor/Cobbler* • Reginald Beckwith *Finance minister/Blacksmith* • Kynaston Reeves *Burgomeister/Policeman* ■ *Dir/Scr* Val Guest

Penny Serenade ★★★★ U
Romantic melodrama 1941 · US · BW · 119min

In this heartbreaking melodrama, Irene Dunne looks back over the highs and lows of her marriage to Cary Grant as they prepare to part. It's all expertly controlled by master director George Stevens, but don't watch if the deaths of young children are upsetting to you. Grant gives a lesson in screen acting and was rightly Oscar-nominated for a superb, subtly-shaded portrayal that keeps sentimentality at bay. If you can take it, this is quite a viewing experience. TS DVD Blu

Cary Grant *Roger Adams* • Irene Dunne *Julie Gardiner Adams* • Beulah Bondi *Miss Oliver* • Edgar Buchanan *Applejack* • Ann Doran *Dotty* ■ *Dir* George Stevens • *Scr* Morrie Ryskind, from a story by Martha Cheavens

The Pentagon Wars ★★★★ 15
Comedy 1998 · US · Colour · 103min

This is a wonderfully biting made-for-TV comedy, with the American defence industry as the target, in particular the gravy train responsible for developing new technology. Cary Elwes is the idealistic officer determined to crack down on dodgy practices. Kelsey Grammer is his adversary. Director Richard Benjamin (who also makes a brief cameo) wisely allows the very funny script to take centre stage. JF Some swearing.

Kelsey Grammer *General Partridge* • Cary Elwes *Colonel Burton* • Viola Davis *Fanning* • John C McGinley *Colonel Bock* • Clifton Powell *Sergeant Benjamin Dalton* • Richard Schiff *Smith* • Tom Wright *Major William Sayers* • Richard Benjamin *Casper Weinberger* ■ *Dir* Richard Benjamin • *Scr* Martyn Burke, Jamie Malanowski, from a non-fiction book by James G Burton

Penthouse ★★★
Crime mystery 1933 · US · BW · 88min

When lawyer Phillips Holmes is framed for murder by criminal heavy C Henry Gordon, the crime is solved by respectable lawyer/sleuth Warner Baxter with Myrna Loy co-starring as his helpmate. This Hunt Stromberg production was written by Albert Hackett and Frances Goodrich, who livened the formula up with a good seasoning of wit, directed with excellent judgement for the nuances of comedy drama by WS Van Dyke. RK

Warner Baxter *Jackson Durant* • Myrna Loy *Gertie Waxted* • Charles Butterworth *Layton* • Mae Clarke *Mimi Montagne* • Phillips Holmes *Tom Siddall* • C Henry Gordon *Jim Crelliman* • Martha Sleeper *Sue Leonard* • Nat Pendleton *Tony Grazotti* ■ *Dir* WS Van Dyke • *Scr* Frances Goodrich, Albert Hackett, from the novel by Arthur Somers Roche

The Penthouse ★
Thriller 1967 · UK · Colour · 96min

Married estate agent Terence Morgan and his mistress Suzy Kendall are terrorised in their love nest by Tom and Dick (Tony Beckley and Norman Rodway), a knife-wielding pair of villains – Harry turns up later. After tying up the estate agent, they force him to watch them abuse the girlfriend as well as listen to self-justifying monologues and musings on the sad state of the world. The original stage play was probably more effective; the film version, however, comes across as grim, tasteless and pretentious. JG

Suzy Kendall *Barbara Willason* • Terence Morgan *Bruce Victor* • Tony Beckley *Tom* • Norman Rodway *Dick* • Martine Beswick *Harry* ■ *Dir* Peter Collinson • *Scr* Peter Collinson, from the play *The Meter Man* by C Scott Forbes

The People against O'Hara ★★★
Crime drama 1951 · US · BW · 102min

James Arness may have the title role, but the main interest in this legal potboiler lies in watching longtime buddies Spencer Tracy and Pat O'Brien share the screen for the first time. Unfortunately, their time together is limited, as lawyer Tracy is mostly confined to a courtroom, attempting to disprove DA John Hodiak's murder charge. John Sturges's pacing is often over-deliberate and the jibes made against the judicial system are far from original. DP

Spencer Tracy *James Curtayne* • Pat O'Brien *Vincent Ricks* • Diana Lynn *Ginny Curtayne* • John Hodiak *Louis Barra* • Eduardo Ciannelli *Knuckles Lanzetta* • James Arness *Johnny O'Hara* • Yvette Duguay [Yvette Dugay] *Mrs Lanzetta* • Jay C Flippen *Sven Norson* • Charles Buchinsky [Charles Bronson] *Angelo Korvac* ■ *Dir* John Sturges • *Scr* John Monks Jr, from the novel by Eleazar Lipsky

People I Know ★★ 15
Thriller 2002 · Ger/US · Colour · 94min

Al Pacino's acute overacting as a past-his-prime publicist fails to give this disappointing film heavyweight status. Charting a turbulent 24 hours in the murky world of his ailing New York PR veteran, director Daniel Algrant interweaves various social and political intrigues with limited credibility or conviction. The script's tart dialogue and a terrific supporting turn from Téa Leoni as a drugged-up good-time girl lend the film some minor distinction, but this is decidedly low-voltage drama. JC Swearing, drug abuse, sex scenes. DVD

Al Pacino *Eli Wurman* • Kim Basinger *Victoria Gray* • Téa Leoni *Jilli Hopper* • Ryan O'Neal *Cary Launer* • Richard Schiff *Elliot Sharansky* ■ *Dir* Daniel Algrant • *Scr* Jon Robin Baitz

People like Us ★★★ 12
Comedy drama 2012 · US · Colour · 109min

Real-life events are the inspiration for this forthright drama about a slick salesman (Chris Pine) trying to get in touch with his feelings. Pine goes from annoying to engaging as he handles the news of his estranged father's death, and then has to deal with the revelation that he has a half-sister (Elizabeth Banks), with a claim to the estate. But Banks misinterprets the nature of Pine's interest in her, and co-writer/director Alex Kurtzman makes this development the crux of the story. A few laughs alleviate the tension, but it's the performances, rather than script or direction, that keep the film anchored to some kind of reality. SP Swearing, drug abuse.

Chris Pine *Sam* • Elizabeth Banks (2) *Frankie* • Michelle Pfeiffer *Lillian* • Olivia Wilde *Hannah* • Michael Hall D'Addario *Josh* • Philip Baker Hall *Ike Rafferty* ■ *Dir* Alex Kurtzman • *Scr* Alex Kurtzman, Roberto Orci, Jody Lambert

People on Sunday ★★★★★
Documentary drama 1929 · Ger · BW · 89min

This launched the careers of a number of film-makers who would subsequently make it in Hollywood: the Siodmak brothers (Robert and Curt), Edgar G Ulmer, Billy Wilder and Fred Zinnemann. Predating neorealism by some years, being shot in a free-wheeling style on location with non-professional actors, the film follows 24 hours in the lives of a group of Berliners on a day's outing, among them a bachelor, his married friend, a model and a shopgirl. Still as fresh, romantic and humorous as ever, it allows one to notice the details of everyday life in Berlin in the late 1920s. RB DVD

■ *Dir* Robert Siodmark [Robert Siodmak], Edgar G Ulmer • *Scr* Robert Siodmark, Kurt Siodmark [Curt Siodmak], Billy Wilder, from an idea by Kurt Siodmark [Curt Siodmak] • *Production Assistant* Fred Zinnemann • *Cinematographer* Eugen Schüfftan

The People That Time Forgot ★★ U

Adventure 1977 · UK · Colour · 86min

In this OK sequel to The Land That Time Forgot, missing explorer Doug McClure is traced to an exotic prison on the lost island of Caprona. It's not as trashy as the original Edgar Rice Burroughs adventure, but director Kevin Connor's constipated confection still features ludicrous mechanised dinosaurs and hopeless acting from an interesting cast – John Wayne's son Patrick and Dave Prowse (the original body of Darth Vader). A few shots, composed around celebrated fantasy illustrations, compensate for all the film's shortcomings. AJ DVD

Patrick Wayne Major Ben McBride • Doug McClure Bowen Tyler • Sarah Douglas Lady Charlotte "Charly" • Dana Gillespie Ajor • Thorley Walters Dr Edward Norfolk • Shane Rimmer Hogan • Tony Britton Captain Lawton • David Prowse [Dave Prowse] Executioner ■ Dir Kevin Connor • Scr Patrick Tilley, from the novel by Edgar Rice Burroughs

The People under the Stairs ★★★ 18

Horror 1991 · US · Colour · 97min

Wes Craven was back to nearly his very best with this sly, satirical shocker, a modern-day fable in which the rich are literally feeding off the poor. Young Brandon Adams is the lad from the ghetto who gets trapped in the house owned by mad slum landlords Everett McGill and Wendy Robie, and discovers that he is not the only person to fall victim to the couple. The plot stretches credibility, but McGill and Robie have a ball as the monstrous duo, while Craven keeps the adrenaline pumping. JF Violence, swearing. DVD

Brandon Adams "Fool" • Everett McGill Man • Wendy Robie Woman • AJ Langer Alice • Ving Rhames LeRoy • Sean Whalen Roach • Bill Cobbs Grandpa Booker ■ Dir/Scr Wes Craven

The People vs Dr Kildare ★★

Medical drama 1941 · US · BW · 77min

Moving out of the operating theatre and into the courtroom, MGM's Dr Kildare series was showing signs of exhaustion by this seventh instalment (out of nine). Lew Ayres's James Kildare is sued for gross negligence by Bonita Granville's skating star after an emergency operation leaves her with a paralysed leg. Red Skelton makes the first of two appearances in the series, providing some painful comedy relief as an orderly. AE

Lew Ayres Dr James Kildare • Lionel Barrymore Dr Leonard Gillespie • Laraine Day Mary Lamont • Bonita Granville Frances Marlowe • Alma Kruger Molly Byrd • Red Skelton Vernon Briggs, janitor • Diana Lewis Fay Lennox • Paul Stanton Mr Reynolds ■ Dir Harold S Bucquet • Scr Willis Goldbeck, from a story by Lawrence P Bachmann, Max Brand, from characters by Max Brand

The People vs Larry Flynt ★★★★ 18

Biographical drama 1996 · US · Colour · 124min

America's most notorious and successful pornographer is played with red-blooded bawdiness by Woody Harrelson in this sanitised biopic. Director Milos Forman would have you believe that obscenity is therapy as he charts Larry Flynts rise from the Kentucky backwoods to run a series of strip clubs and publish explicit nude magazines. But his film was entertaining enough to gain him and Harrelson Oscar nominations. The real tour de force comes from Courtney Love as Flynt's stripper wife, Althea Leasure. TH Swearing, sex scenes, drug abuse, nudity. DVD

Woody Harrelson Larry Flynt • Courtney Love Althea Leasure • Edward Norton Isaacman • Brett Harrelson Jimmy Flynt • Donna Hanover Ruth Carter Stapleton • James Cromwell Charles Keating • Crispin Glover Arlo • Vincent Schiavelli Chester ■ Dir Milos Forman • Scr Scott Alexander, Larry Karaszewski

People Will Talk ★★★ U

Comedy drama 1951 · US · BW · 105min

The title is apt indeed: this is one of the talkiest movies Joseph L Mankiewicz ever wrote and directed. On paper, it's a romantic comedy about a doctor (Cary Grant) who treats, then marries already pregnant Jeanne Crain, much to the chagrin of both the academic fraternity and the moral majority. Along the way, Mankiewicz takes pot shots at American sexual morality, tax evasion, the Korean war, the McCarthy witch-hunts and a lot more besides. Though the film is bombastic and visually static, Grant is on top form, while you have to hand it to Mankiewicz for bravery. AT DVD

Cary Grant Dr Noah Praetorius • Jeanne Crain Annabel Higgins • Finlay Currie Shunderson • Hume Cronyn Professor Elwell • Walter Slezak Professor Barker • Sidney Blackmer Arthur Higgins • Margaret Hamilton Miss Pickett ■ Dir Joseph L Mankiewicz • Scr Joseph L Mankiewicz, from the play Dr Praetorius by Curt Goetz

Pepe ★ U

Musical comedy 1960 · US · Colour · 194min

This atrocious all-star mess is led by the unappealing Mexican actor Cantinflas. It starts in Mexico, where Cantinflas plays a stupid ranch foreman whose beloved white stallion is sold to an American film director. The story then moves to Hollywood, where a mind-boggling array of stars drop in for a look, a line, a song or a scene with the befuddled Cantinflas. The joke might have just passed muster at 80 minutes, but the film originally lasted over three hours, stretching the plot and the audience's patience beyond endurance. AT

Cantinflas Pepe • Dan Dailey Ted Holt • Shirley Jones Suzie Murphy • Carlos Montalban Auctioneer • Vicki Trickett Lupita • Matt Mattox Dancer • Hank Henry Manager • Ernie Kovacs Immigration inspector • William Demarest Studio gateman • Joey Bishop • Maurice Chevalier • Charles Coburn • Bing Crosby • Tony Curtis • Bobby Darin • Sammy Davis Jr • Jimmy Durante • Zsa Zsa Gabor • Judy Garland • Greer Garson • Peter Lawford • Janet Leigh • Jack Lemmon • Dean Martin • Kim Novak • André Previn • Debbie Reynolds • Edward G Robinson • Cesar Romero • Frank Sinatra ■ Dir George Sidney (2) • Scr Dorothy Kingsley, Claude Binyon, from a story by Leonard Spigelgass, Sonya Levien

Pépé le Moko ★★★★★ PG

Romantic melodrama 1937 · Fr · BW · 90min

An unmissable French classic, a little bit frayed at the edges this still possesses irresistible Gallic glamour as Jean Gabin's fugitive from justice hangs out in the Algiers Casbah and is only tempted out of his hideaway by romantic love. Photographed like a thriller, with lots of shadows, the film is dominated by Gabin's superb portrayal of the self-sufficient loner – just one look at his sad face, and you know he's haunted by his past and doomed to life as an exile (or worse). A huge hit in France, this influenced a whole range of Hollywood movies, notably Algiers (1938) which was a remake of sorts, and, most famous of all, Casablanca (1942). AT French +subtitles. DVD

Jean Gabin Pépé le Moko • Mireille Balin Gaby Gould • Line Noro Inès • Lucas Gridoux Inspector Slimane • Gabriel Gabrio Carlos • Fernand Charpin Régis ■ Dir Julien Duvivier • Scr Julien Duvivier, Henri Jeanson, Detective Ashelbe [d'Henri La Barthe], Jacques Constant, from a novel by Detective Ashelbe [d'Henri La Barthe] • Cinematographers Jules Krüger, Marc Fossard

Pepi, Luci, Bom... ★★★ 18

Comedy 1980 · Sp · Colour · 77min

The first full-length movie from Spanish director Pedro Almodóvar set the camp/trash/kitsch seal on his future output. Informed by the Andy Warhol pop art, photo romances and John Waters cult movies of his youth, Almodóvar's zany dissection of what constitutes happiness for people living on the edge is a flawed home-movie in which the flaws dictate a surreal style all their own. Featuring a cast of actual investors in the picture, including friends (and future leading ladies) Carmen Maura and Cecilia Roth, it tells the story of how three Madrid girls set up house. AJ Spanish +subtitles. DVD

Carmen Maura Pepi • Félix Rotaeta Policeman • Olvido "Alaska" Gara Bom • Eva Siva Luci • Cecilia Roth • Pedro Almodóvar ■ Dir/Scr Pedro Almodóvar

Peppermint Frappé ★★★

Drama 1967 · Sp · Colour · 94min

Although dedicated to Luis Buñuel, the shadows of Alfred Hitchcock and Michelangelo Antonioni fall just as heavily across this tale of repressed sexuality and physical transformation. The film couches its political message in terms of a Vertigo-like plot, in which a rural physician transforms his comely nurse into the double of his stunning sister-in-law. That Carlos Saura won the best director prize at Berlin is due in no small measure to his future companion, Geraldine Chaplin, who handles the dual role with a panache that has since eluded her. DP Spanish +subtitles.

Geraldine Chaplin Elena/Ana • José Luis Lopez Vazquez Julian • Alfredo Mayo Pablo ■ Dir Carlos Saura • Scr Rafael Azcona, Angelino Fons, Carlos Saura

Perceval le Gallois ★★★★ PG

Period adventure 1978 · Fr/W Ger/It/Swi · Colour · 133min

This adaptation of the 12th-century Arthurian poem by Chrétien de Troyes is an unexpected film from Eric Rohmer, the anatomist of French modern-day sexual relationships. Yet the episodic story about the naive young Welsh knight's quest for the Holy Grail is observed with much ironic wit. Shot completely in the studio against stylised painted sets, it combines the means of cinema and theatre, with medieval music, mime and verse. It takes a while to adjust to the style and language, and the film needs quite a bit of concentration, but many sensual as well as intellectual pleasures can be gained. RB In French.

Fabrice Luchini Perceval • André Dussollier Gauvain • Marie-Christine Barrault Queen Guinevere • Marc Eyraud King Arthur ■ Dir Eric Rohmer • Scr Eric Rohmer, from the poem by Chrétien de Troyes • Cinematographer Nestor Almendros

Percy ★ 15

Sex comedy 1971 · UK · Colour · 97min

Denholm Elliott clearly revels in the opportunity to perform the world's first penis transplant. Sadly, his wonderfully manic turn is the only reason to catch a film whose awfulness has earned it a certain cult kudos. Phallic gags abound as Hywel Bennett seeks the identity of the donor and becomes wrapped up in his complicated love life. No wonder he refused the equally dreadful sequel, Percy's Progress. DP Some swearing, a sex scene, nudity.

Hywel Bennett Edwin Anthony • Denholm Elliott Emmanuel Whitbread • Elke Sommer Helga • Britt Ekland Dorothy Chiltern-Barlow • Cyd Hayman Moira Warrington • Janet Key Hazel • Julia Foster Marilyn ■ Dir Ralph Thomas • Scr Hugh Leonard, Terence Feel, from the novel by Raymond Hitchcock

Percy Jackson & the Lightning Thief ★★★ PG

Fantasy adventure 2010 · Can/US · Colour · 113min

A teenage boy learns he's the son of the Greek god Poseidon and has powers he never knew about in this fantasy adventure, adapted from the first of Rick Riordan's popular novels. It's a delightful notion, but the film gets bogged down in explaining all the legends. Still, the superior effects work provides enough thrilling spectacle to keep the clunky storytelling moving along and diverts attention from Logan Lerman's synthetic performance as the troubled adolescent. TJ Violence. DVD BLU CS

Logan Lerman Percy Jackson • Brandon T Jackson Grover • Alexandra Daddario Annabeth • Sean Bean Zeus • Pierce Brosnan Chiron/Mr Brunner • Steve Coogan Hades, God of the Underworld • Rosario Dawson Persephone • Catherine Keener Sally Jackson • Kevin McKidd Poseidon • Uma Thurman Medusa ■ Dir Chris Columbus • Scr Craig Titley, from the novel by Rick Riordan

Percy Jackson: Sea of Monsters ★★ PG

Fantasy adventure 2013 · US · Colour · 101min

Three years after the first film, the half-human son of sea god Poseidon pops up again, carried on a wave of the novels' popularity. Working from Rick Riordan's bestselling books, director Thor Freudenthal creates a world where Greek deities, humans and demigods coexist. This time, Percy (Logan Lerman) goes on a quest for the Golden Fleece, leading him to the ominous-sounding "Sea of Monsters" (aka the Bermuda Triangle). The story often hits choppy waters and only just about stays afloat. DA Some swearing. DVD BLU

Logan Lerman Percy Jackson • Alexandra Daddario Annabeth Chase • Brandon T Jackson Grover • Jake Abel Luke • Sean Bean Zeus ■ Dir Thor Freudenthal • Scr Marc Guggenheim, from the novel Percy Jackson and the Sea of Monsters by Rick Riordan

Percy's Progress ★ 15

Sex comedy 1974 · UK · Colour · 96min

This sorry sequel to the dire sex comedy Percy was surely the career low of all who participated. There's a certain poetic justice in the fact that this limp effort should be about the entire male population of the world being rendered infertile, although infantile would be a better word to describe the dismal contribution of director Ralph Thomas. DP Swearing, sex scenes.

Leigh Lawson Percy Edward Anthony • Elke Sommer Clarissa • Denholm Elliott Sir Emmanuel Whitbread • Judy Geeson Dr Fairweather • Harry H Corbett Prime minister • Vincent Price Stavos Mammonian • Adrienne Posta Iris • Julie Ege Miss Hanson • Barry Humphries Dr Anderson/Australian TV lady ■ Dir Ralph Thomas • Scr Sid Colin, Ian La Frenais, from a story by Harry H Corbett, from the novel by Raymond Hitchcock

Perdita Durango ★★★ 18

Black comedy road movie 1997 · Sp/Mex/US · Colour · 118min

Rosie Perez gives a flamboyant performance in this insanely violent, amoral black comedy thriller. She teams up with black magic cult leader Javier Bardem to kidnap a couple of young lovers for human sacrifice, then moves on to smuggle a cargo of human foetuses to Las Vegas. Director Alex de la Iglesia sets out to offend just about everybody and pretty much succeeds, but the mix of Latin craziness and ultra-violence is utterly compulsive. JF DVD

Rosie Perez Perdita Durango • Javier Bardem Romeo Dolorosa • Harley Cross Duane • Aimee Graham Estelle • James Gandolfini Dumas • Screamin' Jay Hawkins Adolfo • Carlos Bardem Reggie • Santiago Segura Shorty Dee • Alex Cox Agent Doyle ■ Dir Alex de la Iglesia • Scr Alex de la Iglesia, David Trueba, Jorge Guerricaechevarría, Barry Gifford, from the novel 59 Degrees and Raining: the Story of Perdita Durango by Barry Gifford

The Perez Family ★★ 15

Romantic comedy drama 1995 · US · Colour · 108min

This disappointing romantic comedy stars Marisa Tomei and Alfred Molina as Cubans, mistaken for husband and wife when they arrive in Miami because they have the same surname, who decide to take advantage of the coincidence. Set against the backdrop of a real-life drama (the 1980 Mariel Boatlift of Cuban refugees), this picks up whenever Anjelica Huston (as Molina's wife, who's been waiting for him in Miami for 20 years) is on screen. JB

Marisa Tomei Dottie Perez • Anjelica Huston Carmela Perez • Alfred Molina Juan Raul Perez • Chazz Palminteri Lieutenant John Pirelli • Trini Alvarado Teresa Perez • Celia Cruz Luz Paz • Diego Wallraff Angel Perez • Angela Lanza Flavia ■ Dir Mira Nair • Scr Robin Swicord, from a novel by Christine Bell

P

Perfect ★★ 15
Drama 1985 · US · Colour · 115min

Writing an exposé of the Californian fitness industry to keep busy while chasing a drug story, *Rolling Stone* reporter John Travolta falls in love with Jamie Lee Curtis, the aerobics guru whose club he intends to destroy in his feature. Director James Bridges's air-head film is one of the prime reasons Travolta fell out of favour before his *Pulp Fiction* rediscovery. AJ Swearing, nudity. DVD

John Travolta *Adam Lawrence* • Jamie Lee Curtis *Jessica Wilson* • Jann Wenner *Mark Roth* • Anne De Salvo *Frankie* • Stefan Gierasch *Charlie* • John Napierala *City news editor* • Laraine Newman *Linda* • Marilu Henner *Sally* • Carly Simon ■ *Dir* James Bridges • *Scr* Aaron Latham, James Bridges, from articles in *Rolling Stone* by Aaron Latham

Perfect Alibi ★★ 15
Thriller 1994 · US · Colour · 95min

How perfect can an alibi be if Teri Garr can unravel it with one phone call? Garr plays the nosey friend of Kathleen Quinlan whose doctor husband (Alex McArthur) is having sex with their French au pair (Lydie Denier). Soon people begin to die, and it looks as if the wife is next. The doctor's plan for a perfect crime is so prosaic that the movie seems pointless. ST

Teri Garr *Laney Tolbert* • Hector Elizondo *Detective Ryker* • Alex McArthur *Keith Bauers* • Lydie Denier *Janine* • Kathleen Quinlan *Melanie Bauers* ■ *Dir* Kevin Meyer • *Scr* Kevin Meyer, from the novel *Where's My Mommy Now?* by Rochelle Majer Krich

The Perfect Assistant ★★
Thriller 2008 · US · Colour · 91min

You only need catch the set-up to know exactly where this sluggish TV movie is going. In fact, it's so by-the-numbers, even the irony-laden dialogue is amusingly easy to predict, as gooey-eyed personal assistant Josie Davis becomes psychotically obsessed with marrying her already hitched boss (Chris Potter). The sinister score stands in for any genuine atmosphere and, ultimately, the most entertaining aspect is Davis's agitated performance, which is just crazy enough to keep you watching until the ridiculous climax. SF

Josie Davis *Rachel Parsons* • Chris Potter *David Wescott* • Rachel Hunter *Judith Manion* • Jason Harper *Wally* ■ *Dir* Douglas Jackson • *Scr* Christine Conradt

Perfect Blue ★★★ 18
Animated psychological thriller 1998 · Jpn · Colour · 81min

Clearly influenced by Katsuhiro Otomo, who directed that *anime* classic *Akira*, Satoshi Kon's atmospheric visuals disconcertingly mirror the growing paranoia of Mima, the clean-cut pop star whose drastic image change not only alienates her fans, but also puts her life in danger. Superbly drawn and packed with ambitious visuals, this impressive picture only stumbles in the later stages with a surfeit of dream sequences muddling an already unconvincing ending. DP Japanese dubbed. Violence, swearing, nudity.

Ruby Marlowe • Wendee Lee • Gil Starberry • Lia Sargent • Steve Bulen • James Lyon • Frank Buck • David Lucas [Steven Jay Blum] ■ *Dir* Satoshi Kon • *Scr* Sadayuki Murai, from the novel *Perfect Blue* by Yoshikazu Takeuchi, from characters by Hisashi Eguchi

The Perfect Catch ★★★ PG
Romantic comedy 2005 · Ger/US · Colour · 99min

Farrelly brothers Bobby and Peter here remake *Fever Pitch*, Nick Hornby's autobiographical chronicle of an obsessive sports fan. Moving the action to America, baseball takes the place of football and the Boston Red Sox take over from Arsenal in the affections of the story's protagonist. Jimmy Fallon is the maths teacher with the anorak, while Drew Barrymore is the high-flying executive with whom he strikes up an unlikely romance. The Farrellys rein in their usual excesses, but still produce the laughs,

albeit accompanied by a dose of terminal cuteness. BP DVD

Drew Barrymore *Lindsey* • Jimmy Fallon *Ben* • James B Sikking *Doug Meeks* • JoBeth Williams *Maureen Meeks* • Willie Garson *Kevin* • Jason Spevack *Ben (1980)* • Jack Kehler *Al* • Scott H Severance *Artie* ■ *Dir* Bobby Farrelly, Peter Farrelly • *Scr* Lowell Ganz, Babaloo Mandel, from the non-fiction book *Fever Pitch* by Nick Hornby

A Perfect Couple ★★★
Romantic comedy 1979 · US · Colour · 111min

Director Robert Altman abandons the scattershot technique that made *Nashville* so memorable to concentrate on an intimate, offbeat love story brought about by computer dating. Paul Dooley plays a strait-laced prude intimidated by his oppressive Greek-American family, who is drawn to Marta Heflin, the member of a rock group. Gently awkward dilemmas result in the magic that only a fine director can create. TH

Paul Dooley *Alex Theodopoulos* • Marta Heflin *Sheila Shea* • Titos Vandis *Panos Theodopoulos* • Belita Moreno *Eleousa* • Henry Gibson *Fred Bott* ■ *Dir* Robert Altman • *Scr* Robert Altman, Allan Nicholls

Perfect Creature ★★★ 15
Action horror 2005 · NZ/UK · Colour · 84min

Adhering to the now standard *Underworld*-type plot about centuries-old racial harmonies being rocked, here the balance of power between benign vampires and understanding humans is upset by renegade Leo Gregory, who's turned into the evil bloodsucker of Bram Stoker legend by a genetically mutated virus. Elder vampire statesman Dougray Scott and policewoman Saffron Burrows team up for the damage control job in a dark, gritty neo-Gothic alternative universe. The stunning look and atmospheric production design belie Standring's low budget and are the best assets of this slow moving futuristic Dickensian fantasy. AJ Violence, swearing. DVD

Dougray Scott *Silus* • Leo Gregory *Edgar* • Saffron Burrows *Lilly* • Scott Wills *Jones* • Stuart Wilson *Augustus* ■ *Dir/Scr* Glenn Standring

Perfect Day ★★★★★ U
Comedy 1929 · US · BW · 19min

One of the very best of Laurel and Hardy's short comedies, with an alarming soundtrack – a bell is sounded when Stanley is struck on the head. Edgar Kennedy is the sublimely exasperated uncle with a gouty foot which is being continually attacked by the family dog. Our heroes are off on a picnic with wives Isabelle Keith and Kaye Deslys, but a series of incidents keep the car immovable until the end. Lovingly inventive and as cherishable as the duo themselves. TH DVD

Stan Laurel *Stan* • Oliver Hardy *Ollie* • Edgar Kennedy *Uncle Edgar* • Kay Deslys *Mrs Hardy* • Isabelle Keith *Mrs Laurel* ■ *Dir* James Parrott • *Scr* HM Walker, from a story by Leo McCarey, Hal Roach

A Perfect Day ★★ PG
Fantasy drama 2006 · US · Colour · 87min

The importance of family is hammered home in this contrived fantasy drama. Rob Lowe plays the devoted husband and father who loses sight of his real priorities when his first novel becomes a runaway success. Fortunately, he receives a shock prediction from a mysterious stranger (Christopher Lloyd) to frighten him out of his selfish behaviour. For all its clichés, this imbalanced blend of wish-fulfilment fantasy and simplistic morality tale remains a pleasant diversion. SF DVD

Rob Lowe *Robert Harlan* • Christopher Lloyd *Michael* • Frances Conroy *Camille* • Paget Brewster *Allyson Harlan* • Jude Ciccolella *Chuck* • Rowena King *Heather* ■ *Dir* Peter Levin • *Scr* Joyce Eliason, from the novel by Richard Paul Evans

Perfect Friday ★★★ 12
Crime caper 1970 · UK · Colour · 90min

This sprightly crime caper is hardly the kind of material normally associated with its

director, Peter Hall. Stanley Baker stars as the timid banker who teams up with aristocratic wastrel David Warner and his bored wife Ursula Andress for a raid on his own bank. The raid never completely enthrals us, which is as much down to the script as Hall's discomfort with the genre, for, while the scam is smoothly staged, the suspense seems contrived. DP Swearing, a sex scene, brief nudity. DVD

Ursula Andress *Britt* • Stanley Baker *Mr Graham* • David Warner *Nicholas* • Patience Collier *Nanny* • TP McKenna *Smith* • David Waller *Williams* • Joan Benham *Miss Welsh* ■ *Dir* Peter Hall • *Scr* Anthony Greville-Bell, C Scott Forbes, from a story by C Scott Forbes

The Perfect Furlough ★★
Comedy 1958 · US · Colour · 92min

Tony Curtis and Janet Leigh star in their third film together, and the second Curtis made for director Blake Edwards. It's a sex comedy, with Curtis plucked by lottery from a secret military base in the Arctic and sent to Paris for a little R&R with dream girl Linda Cristal and army shrink Leigh, the idea being that Curtis's tales will raise morale when he gets back to base. This is very much a 1950s movie – glossily made and very coy. AT

Tony Curtis *Corporal Paul Hodges* • Janet Leigh *Lieutenant Vicki Loren* • Linda Cristal *Sandra Roca* • Keenan Wynn *Harvey Franklin* • Elaine Stritch *Liz Baker* • Marcel Dalio *Henri* • Les Tremayne *Colonel Leland* • Jay Novello *René* ■ *Dir* Blake Edwards • *Scr* Stanley Shapiro

The Perfect Gentleman ★★★
Musical comedy drama 1935 · US · BW · 65min

Cicely Courtneidge strikes up an acquaintance with "perfect gentleman" Frank Morgan during a train journey and invites him to her opening night. Matters don't go quite as planned at the theatre, but Morgan comes to the rescue, paving the way for romance. This piece of insubstantial but sweet-natured nonsense was Hollywood's sole attempt (courtesy of MGM) to popularise the British comedian in America. That the attempt was unsuccessful is hardly surprising, since the movie is far too insubstantial. RK

Frank Morgan *Major Horatio Chatteris* • Cicely Courtneidge *April Maye* • Heather Angel *Evelyn* • Herbert Mundin *Hitch* • Una O'Connor *Harriet* • Richard Waring *John Chatteris* • Tim Whelan *Usher* ■ *Dir* Tim Whelan • *Scr* Edward Childs Carpenter, from his unproduced play, from the short story *The Prodigal Father* by Cosmo Hamilton

Perfect Gentlemen ★★★ PG
Comedy thriller 1978 · US · Colour · 91min

A heist movie with an ingenious twist: Lauren Bacall, Sandy Dennis and Lisa Pelikan plan a bank robbery because their husbands are all serving time in jail. They are joined by a cantankerous old biddy (Ruth Gordon) who happens to be a professional safe-cracker. This comedy thriller was directed for TV by former child star Jackie Cooper and was the first produced script by Nora Ephron. She later wrote *When Harry Met Sally* and went on to become a major director with such films as *Sleepless in Seattle*. AT

Lauren Bacall *Lizzie Martin* • Ruth Gordon *Mama Cavagnaro* • Sandy Dennis *Sophie Rosenman* • Lisa Pelikan *Annie Cavagnaro* • Robert Alda *Ed Martin* • Stephen Pearlman *Murray Rosenman* ■ *Dir* Jackie Cooper • *Scr* Nora Ephron

A Perfect Getaway ★★★ 15
Thriller 2009 · US · Colour · 93min

A Hawaiian honeymoon turns into a nightmare in this twisty thriller where newlyweds (Steve Zahn in a rare dramatic role, Milla Jovovich) begin to suspect their hiking companions are ruthless killers. While the film has to reveal its hand eventually and although the secret's not unguessable, writer/director David Twohy entertainingly blends character comedy and escalating tension, and there's a crunching climactic set-to that's delivered with maximum impact. Curiously, the digitally contrived

scenery proves reminiscent of an old-fashioned B-movie, but as B-movies go, the mid-ranking cast clearly raising their game and plenty of sly wit to enjoy, at least it's a good one. TJ Violence, swearing, drug abuse, nudity. DVD Blu

Milla Jovovich *Cydney* • Timothy Olyphant *Nick* • Steve Zahn *Cliff* • Kiele Sanchez *Gina* • Marley Shelton *Cleo* ■ *Dir/Scr* David Twohy

The Perfect Guy ★★★ 15
Thriller 2015 · US · Colour · 95min

Sanaa Lathan is the 30-something professional lobbyist whose biological clock is ticking, causing the break-up of her latest relationship. But when dreamboat Michael Ealy appears in her life, he seems too good to be true – a suspicion which plays out as events shift inexorably from aspirational romance to home-invasion thriller. Ealy makes a decent fist of switching from blue-eyed charmer to IT-savvy psychopath in a movie which moves through its paces, borrowing judiciously from the Hitchcock playbook along the way. A superficial, yet effective time-killer. TJ Violence, sex DVD

Sanaa Lathan *Leah* • Michael Ealy *Carter* • Morris Chestnut *Dave* • L Scott Caldwell *Evelyn* • Charles S Dutton *Roger* • John Getz *Renkin* ■ *Dir* David M Rosenthal • *Scr* Tyger Williams, from a story by Alan B McElroy

The Perfect Husband ★★ PG
Romantic comedy 2003 · US · Colour · 111min

Writer/director Priya Ruth Paul makes her feature debut with this comedy of marital manners that contrasts traditional family values with the bustle of the modern, northern city of Chandigarth. However, the humour surrounding manipulative matriarch Sinia Duggal's refusal to contemplate either asthmatic daughter Rajeshwari Sachdev's liaison with gentlemanly English visitor William Russell or granddaughter Neha Dubey's romance with doctor Parvin Dabas is far too gentle and formulaic. DP English, Hindi +subtitles.

Neha Dubey *Jaya* • Parvin Dabas *Doctor* • Rajeshwari Sachdev *Uma* • William Randall *William* • Sinia Duggal *Badi Mummy* ■ *Dir/Scr* Priya Ruth Paul

The Perfect Man ★ PG
Romantic comedy 2005 · US · Colour · 96min

In this thoroughly dim-witted film, Hilary Duff plays a teen cursed with a frankly certifiable mother (Heather Locklear) who drags her from state to state in search of the mythical "perfect man". Gina Wendkos's asinine, gaseous and often illogical screenplay together with Mark Rosman's insultingly lazy direction render this almost unwatchable. AS DVD

Hilary Duff *Holly Hamilton* • Heather Locklear *Jean Hamilton* • Chris Noth [Christopher Noth] *Ben Cooper* • Mike O'Malley *Lenny Horton* • Ben Feldman *Adam Forrest* • Vanessa Lengies *Amy Pearl* ■ *Dir* Mark Rosman • *Scr* Gina Wendkos, from a story by Michael McQuown, Heather Robinson, Katherine Torpey

The Perfect Marriage ★★
Thriller 2006 · Can · Colour · 91min

Weak scripting and direction turn a tale of murder, deceit and betrayal into a flat snooze-fest, as TV-movie veteran Douglas Jackson delivers another of his forgettable, cookie-cutter thrillers. It doesn't help that the acting's awful too, with lead actress Jamie Luner particularly unconvincing, playing a reinvented, married woman who reverts to her former deadly ways after her past catches up with her – in the shape of ex-lover and crime partner James Wilder. Even the inevitable climactic confrontation proves unsatisfyingly toothless. SF

Jamie Luner *Marianne Danforth/Annie Grayson* • William R Moses *Richard Danforth* • James Wilder *Brent Richter* ■ *Dir* Douglas Jackson • *Scr* Christine Conradt, Kaadi Taylor

The Perfect Murder ★ PG
Murder mystery 1988 · UK/Ind · Colour · 93min

This is a simply dreadful adaptation of one of HRF Keating's Inspector Ghote yarns. Ghote is played by Naseeruddin Shah, a big star in Bombay talkies, who investigates the murder of a man named Perfect (that's the only clever thing in the picture). Madhur Jaffrey and her real-life daughter Sakeena also appear. Produced by the Merchant Ivory stable, it's badly photographed by Walter Lassally and comes across like nothing more than an amateur dramatics production. AT **DVD**

Naseeruddin Shah *Inspector Ghote* • Madhur Jaffrey *Mrs Lal* • Stellan Skarsgård *Axel Svensson* • Dalip Tahil *Dilip Lal* • Dinshaw Daji *Mr Perfect* ■ *Dir* Zafar Hai • *Scr* Zafar Hai, HRF Keating, from a novel by HRF Keating

A Perfect Plan ★★🔞
Romantic comedy   2012 · Fr · Colour · 105min

This contrived but occasionally diverting French romantic comedy stars Diane Kruger as Isabelle, an unadventurous dentist who's about to marry her long-term boyfriend. But all the females in Isabelle's family have a history of first marriages that end badly, so she decides to avoid this trend by quickly marrying and divorcing a random stranger. The stranger is Jean-Yves (Dany Boon), an affable travel writer who forces her out of her routine existence. The story that follows is entirely predictable, but Kruger is impressively game in her first comedic role and Boon provides dorky charm as the love interest. SC French, English, Russian, Swahili, Dutch +subtitles. Swearing, sexual references.

Diane Kruger *Isabelle* • Dany Boon *Jean-Yves* • Alice Pol *Corinne* • Robert Plagnol *Pierre* • Jonathan Cohen *Fatrick* ■ *Dir* Pascal Chaumeil • *Scr* Laurent Zeitoun, Yoann Gromb, Béatrice Fournera, from a story by Philippe Mechelen

Perfect Romance ★★
Romantic comedy   2004 · Can/US · Colour · 90min

Attempts at internet matchmaking go sweetly awry in this undemanding romantic comedy. Kathleen Quinlan is delightful as a meddling mother who secretly finds her divorcee daughter a new suitor on-line (Henry Ian Cusick from TV series *Lost*) – only to fall for the articulate charmer herself. While Lori Heuring as her tomboy-like offspring frequently seems affected, there's real chemistry between Quinlan and Cusick. The increasing warmth and gentleness they share is an easy-going pleasure, and a welcome contrast to the superficiality of the rest of the formulaic film and its characters. SF

Kathleen Quinlan *Tess* • Henry Ian Cusick *Peter Campbell* • Lori Heuring *Jenny Kelley* • Michael Trucco *Miles Healey* • JR Bourne *Rick Meadows* ■ *Dir* Douglas Barr (2) • *Scr* Allison Burnett

The Perfect Score ★★🔞
Comedy   2004 · US/Ger · Colour · 88min

Stressed-out older kids coping with exam pressure might find a little to identify with in this below-par teen comedy, but everyone else would be advised to give this derivative caper movie a miss. A group of high-schoolers desperate to get into university are led by Chris Evans in a plan to steal the question papers for a vital aptitude test. All the stereotypes are present: the jock, the stoner, the brain. What isn't in evidence is any charm. AS Swearing. **DVD**

Erika Christensen *Anna* • Chris Evans *Kyle* • Bryan Greenberg *Matty* • Scarlett Johansson *Francesca* • Darius Miles *Desmond* • Leonardo Nam *Roy* • Tyra Ferrell *Desmond's mother* • Matthew Lillard *Larry* ■ *Dir* Brian Robbins • *Scr* Mark Schwahn, Marc Hyman, Jon Zack, from a story by Marc Hyman, Jon Zack

Perfect Sense ★★🔞
Romantic science-fiction drama   2011 · UK/Den/Ire/Ger/Swe · Colour · 88min

In this unconvincing pandemic drama, Ewan McGregor plays a chef in an upmarket Glasgow restaurant who meets epidemiologist Eva Green while on a break. The fact that he works has brought her into contact with a patient who has lost his sense of smell seems incidental at first. Then McGregor and Green are hit by the ailment. As the virus develops, each sense

in turn is lost, and the film charts the impact on the lovers – and the restaurant. There is little chemistry between the two leads, and the film is too slow to build any dramatic tension. BP Swearing, sex scenes. **DVD**

Ewan McGregor *Michael* • Eva Green *Susan* • Ewen Bremner *James* • Denis Lawson *Boss* • Stephen Dillane *Stephen* • Connie Nielsen ■ *Dir* David Mackenzie • *Scr* Kim Fupz Aakeson

The Perfect Specimen ★★★Ⓤ
Comedy   1937 · US · BW · 99min

Warner Bros gave their resident swashbuckler Errol Flynn a crack at contemporary comedy in this tale of a rich, upper-class young man who has been raised as an over-protected hothouse specimen and kept from any contact with the dangers of reality. Things change when attractive young Joan Blondell crashes her car through his fence and brings love into his life. Flynn, not quite in control of comedy technique, nonetheless is a perfect model of looks and charm and the film, directed by Michael Curtiz, is a pleasing, if not too believable, romantic comedy romp. RK

Errol Flynn *Gerald Beresford Wicks* • Joan Blondell *Mona Carter* • Hugh Herbert *Killigrew Shaw* • Edward Everett Horton *Mr Grattan* • Dick Foran *Jink Carter* • Beverly Roberts *Alicia* • May Robson *Mrs Leona Wicks* • Allen Jenkins *Pinky* ■ *Dir* Michael Curtiz • *Scr* Norman Reilly Raine, Lawrence Riley, Brewster Morse, Fritz Falkenstein, from the novel by Samuel Hopkins Adams

The Perfect Storm ★★★🔞
Action drama based on a true story
2000 · US · Colour · 124min

Based on a true story, this tempestuous drama concerns the *Andrea Gail*, a fishing vessel that, while sailing in the North Atlantic in 1991, was caught up in the 20th century's worst storm. A stubbled George Clooney and a smooth-talking Mark Wahlberg, last seen together in *Three Kings*, head the crew, while director Wolfgang Petersen takes a deep breath and plunges audiences in and out of skyscraper-tall waves. TH Violence, swearing. **DVD**

George Clooney *Captain Billy Tyne* • Mark Wahlberg *Bobby Shatford* • Diane Lane *Christina Cotter* • John C Reilly *Dale "Murph" Murphy* • William Fichtner *David "Sully" Sullivan* • Mary Elizabeth Mastrantonio *Linda Greenlaw* • Karen Allen *Melissa Brown* ■ *Dir* Wolfgang Petersen • *Scr* Bill Wittliff [William D Wittliff], from the non-fiction book *The Perfect Storm* by Sebastian Junger • *Music* James Horner

Perfect Stranger ★★★🔞
Thriller   2007 · US · Colour · 104min

Halle Berry and Bruce Willis take top billing in this tricky little whodunnit that is clunkingly unoriginal but entertainingly trashy nonetheless. Berry plays an investigative reporter who is convinced that Willis's oily ad-agency boss is somehow involved in the internet seduction and subsequent murder of her friend. She goes undercover both on the internet and at the agency in a bid to expose him. Giovanni Ribisi provides his customarily creepy support in a film that boasts more red herrings than a Moscow fishmonger. The first half of the film is fine, but the second half becomes dafter and dafter, as suspects are wheeled out and discarded with hilarious regularity. Still, director James Foley (*Glengarry Glen Ross*) directs with stylish aplomb, and the film is never less than undemandingly watchable. DA Swearing, sexual references. **DVD** **BD**

Halle Berry *Rowena Price* • Bruce Willis *Harrison Hill* • Giovanni Ribisi *Miles Haley* • Gary Dourdan *Cameron* • Jason Antoon *Bill Patel* • Nicki Aycox [Nicki Lynn Aycox] *Grace* ■ *Dir* James Foley • *Scr* Todd Komarnicki, from a story by Jon Bokenkamp

Perfect Strangers ★★★
Drama   1945 · UK · BW · 102min

With the outbreak of the Second World War, a nondescript clerk (Robert Donat) and his dowdy wife (Deborah Kerr), locked in a staid

and indifferent marriage, join the navy and the Wrens respectively. Their separate wartime experiences transform them and their postwar relationship. Adapted from a story by Clemence Dane, and produced and directed by Alexander Korda, this is an interesting, engaging and sympathetic film, guaranteed to please thanks to the presence of its attractive co-stars. RK

Robert Donat *Robert Wilson* • Deborah Kerr *Catherine Wilson* • Glynis Johns *Dizzy Clayton* • Ann Todd *Elena* • Roland Culver *Richard* ■ *Dir* Alexander Korda • *Scr* Clemence Dane, Anthony Pelissier, from a story by Clemence Dane

Perfect Strangers ★★
Romantic drama   1950 · US · BW · 87min

Married Dennis Morgan and divorced Ginger Rogers meet and fall in love while doing jury duty on a love-nest murder case. Sadly, these perfect strangers make for a less than perfect film, which suffers from a woolly script. It aims for romantic comedy in a dramatic setting, but only gets real laughs from Thelma Ritter's splendid performance as a dumb housewife. TH

Ginger Rogers *Terry Scott* • Dennis Morgan *David Campbell* • Thelma Ritter *Lena Fassler* • Margalo Gillmore *Isobel Bradford* • Anthony Ross *Robert Fisher* • Howard Freeman *Timkin* • Alan Reed *Harry Patullo* • Paul Ford *Judge Byron* • Harry Bellaver *Bailiff* ■ *Dir* Bretaigne Windust • *Scr* Edith Sommer, George Oppenheimer, from the play *Ladies and Gentleman* by Ben Hecht, Charles MacArthur, from the play *Twelve in the Box* by Ladislaus Bus-Fekete

Perfect Strangers ★★
Romantic comedy
2004 · UK/US · Colour · 120min

Ad agency hotshots Rob Lowe and Anna Friel find themselves falling in love over the phone in this unconvincing and frequently lazy culture-clash comedy, based on the novel by Robyn Sisman. Swapping jobs temporarily as part of a corporate exchange, slick New Yorker Lowe and chirpy London-dweller Friel are thrown into exaggerated, fish-out-of-water predicaments that only split-screen, transatlantic chats can resolve. But while the caricatured pair have an easy charm on the line together, individually they're undermined by a flimsy narrative that relies on lame and obvious laughs. An escalating subplot involving Lowe's backstabbing female rival finally adds a bit more depth and focus, though sadly that just becomes a convenient device to accelerate the stars' predictable union. SF

Rob Lowe *Lloyd Rockwell* • Anna Friel *Susie Wilding* • Khandi Alexander *Christie Kaplan* • Sarah Alexander *Alix Mason* • Jennifer Baxter *Betsy* ■ *Dir* Robin Shepperd • *Scr* Simon Booker, from Robyn Sisman's novel

The Perfect Teacher ★★
Thriller   2010 · Can · Colour · 90min

There's nothing original – or even very convincing – about this predictable tale of a schoolgirl crush that turns nasty. But thanks to a juicy central performance and enjoyably exaggerated plotting, psycho teen Megan Park's increasingly desperate attempts to seduce her new maths teacher (former *Baywatch* hunk David Charvet) keep you watching. Park quickly establishes her bunny-boiler credentials, but in the last third, the thriller implodes, wasting its twisted build-up with a rushed finale. SF

Megan Park *Devon* • David Charvet *Jim* • Boti Bliss [Boti Ann Bliss] *Rachel* • James McGowan *Reid* • Keeva Lynk *Annique* ■ *Dir* Jim Donovan • *Scr* Christine Conradt, from a story by Gregory Henn

The Perfect Woman ★★★Ⓤ
Comedy   1949 · UK · BW · 83min

Patricia Roc was rarely given the chance to show what she could do in starring roles. When she did get her name above the title, she was invariably given a raw deal when it came to dialogue. This frantic comedy of errors is a case in point, for while she handles the role of a scientist's social-climbing niece who poses as a robot with considerable ease, the choicest lines land in

the laps of co-stars Stanley Holloway and Nigel Patrick. DP

Patricia Roc *Penelope* • Stanley Holloway *Ramshead* • Nigel Patrick *Roger Cavendish* • Miles Malleson *Professor Belmond* • Irene Handl *Mrs Butter* • Pamela Devis *Olga, the robot* ■ *Dir* Bernard Knowles • *Scr* Bernard Knowles, JB Boothroyd, George Black, from the play by Wallace Geoffrey, Basil John Mitchell

A Perfect World ★★★★🔞
Drama   1993 · US · Colour · 132min

It should have been perfect: Clint Eastwood was fresh from Oscar-winning success with *Unforgiven*, while Kevin Costner was challenging his heroic status forged in such hits as *The Bodyguard* by playing a bad guy. As it is, the chemistry isn't quite there and this drama film has to settle for being just very good indeed. Costner is perhaps a little too introspective as the escaped convict who kidnaps a young boy and heads for freedom in Alaska, developing a curious bond with the child en route. Eastwood is the veteran Texas Ranger on his trail, growling his way through some trademark throwaway lines and proving yet again that nobody directs Clint better than Eastwood himself. JF Violence, swearing, sex scenes. **DVD**

Kevin Costner *Butch Haynes* • Clint Eastwood *Red Garnett* • Laura Dern *Sally Gerber* • TJ Lowther *Phillip Perry* • Keith Szarabajka *Terry Pugh* • Leo Burmester *Tom Adler* • Paul Hewitt *Dick Suttle* • Bradley Whitford *Bobby Lee* ■ *Dir* Clint Eastwood • *Scr* John Lee Hancock

Perfectly Normal ★★★🔞
Comedy   1990 · Can · Colour · 101min

This is so eager to please that it nearly sits up and begs, as a hockey-playing brewery worker (Michael Riley) teams up with an aspiring chef (Robbie Coltrane) to open a restaurant that serves up opera as a special addition to the menu. It means well, but it comes across as rather bizarre, though Coltrane gives a good-natured performance. TH Swearing.

Robbie Coltrane *Alonzo Turner* • Michael Riley *Renzo Parachil* • Deborah Duchene *Denise* • Eugene Lipinski *"Hopeless"* • Kenneth Welsh *Charlie Glesby* • Patricia Gage *Mrs Hathaway* • Jack Nichols *Duane Bickle* ■ *Dir* Yves Simoneau • *Scr* Eugene Lipinski, Paul Quarrington, from a story by Eugene Lipinski

Performance ★★★★★🔞
Drama   1970 · UK · Colour · 101min

Warner Bros executives reeled in shock when they first saw it, and the censor reached for the smelling salts. This seminal cult classic still has the power to disturb with its examination of the lifestyles of a masochistic gangster (played by James Fox) and a bisexual pop star (Mick Jagger) as they enter into a drugged-out parallel universe of their own creation. With its fragmented narrative, hallucinatory images and arcane literary references, ranging from Jorge Luis Borges to Harold Pinter, this profound study of sexuality and identity remains a sensibility-shattering masterpiece. AJ Violence, swearing, drug abuse, sex scenes, nudity. **DVD**

James Fox *Chas Devlin* • Mick Jagger *Turner* • Anita Pallenberg *Pherber* • Michèle Breton *Lucy* • Ann Sidney *Dana* • Johnny Shannon *Harry Flowers* • John Bindon *Moody* • Anthony Valentine *Joey Maddocks* ■ *Dir* Nicolas Roeg, Donald Cammell • *Scr* Donald Cammell • *Cinematographer* Nicolas Roeg

Perfume de Violetas ★★★🔞
Drama based on a true story
2001 · Mex/US/Neth · Colour · 88min

The collapse of the family unit, grinding urban poverty and society's indifference to morality are discussed by Maryse Sistach in this fact-based Mexican story that avoids melodramatics. Ximena Ayala poignantly captures the descent from innocence to introspection, as the tomboyish teenager whose stepbrother, Luis Fernando Peña, allows a bus company colleague to rape her in return for a few pesos. She is matched by the waif-like Nancy Gutiérrez, who plays her best friend, but the incessant intrusion of

P

the pop soundtrack tends to debase the authenticity. DP Spanish +subtitles.
Ximena Ayala *Yessica* • Nancy Gutiérrez *Miriam* • Arcelia Ramírez *Alicia* • Maria Rojo *Yessica's mother* • Luis Fernando Peña *Jorge* ■ *Dir* Maryse Sistach • *Scr* José Buil, Maryse Sistach

Perfume of the Cyclone
★★ 18

Thriller 1989 · US/S Afr · Colour · 85min

The only surprising thing about this decidedly underwhelming thriller is that it managed to attract performers of the calibre of Kris Kristofferson and Marisa Berenson. This is one of the lower spots in Kristofferson's patchy career. Growling his lines with little enthusiasm, he plays a Chicago cop who uncovers a white slavery racket while searching an exotic island for his missing daughter. DP Swearing, nudity.
Kris Kristofferson *Stan* • Marisa Berenson *Françoise* • Jeff Meek [Jeffrey Meek] *Adam* • Alla Kurot *Angélique* • Bud T Chud [Gerrit Graham] *Lt France* ■ *Dir* David Irving • *Scr* Patrick Lee

Perfume: the Story of a Murderer
★★★ 15

Period horror 2006 · Fr/Sp/Ger/US · Colour · 132min

Novelist Patrick Süskind's so-called "unfilmable" story of obsession and murder in 18th-century France gets a ravishing big-screen adaptation courtesy of *Run Lola Run* director Tom Tykwer. An offbeat and sensuous adult fairy tale, it revolves around a chilling turn by Ben Whishaw (*Bright Star*) as the Parisian perfumer's apprentice, Jean-Baptiste Grenouille. Born with an exceptional sense of smell, Grenouille becomes monstrously fixated on preserving the aroma of young women – particularly the only daughter of merchant Antoine Richis (a poignant Alan Rickman). The tragic horror that unfolds has a seductive quality reminiscent of German expressionist cinema. But it's the extraordinary visuals and evocative soundtrack that are the movie's greatest strengths. SF Violence, sex scenes, nudity. DVD
Ben Whishaw *Jean-Baptiste Grenouille* • Dustin Hoffman *Giuseppe Baldini* • Alan Rickman *Antoine Richis* • Rachel Hurd-Wood *Laura Richis* • John Hurt *Narrator* • Karoline Herfurth *The Plum Girl* • David Calder *Bishop of Grasse* • Simon Chandler *Mayor of Grasse* ■ *Dir* Tom Tykwer • *Scr* Andrew Birkin, Bernd Eichinger, Tom Tykwer, from the novel by Patrick Süskind

The Perils of Pauline
★★★ U

Comedy adventure 1967 · US · Colour · 98min

The famous 1914 silent cliffhanger serial thrilled cinema audiences and made a star out of action heroine Pearl White. In 1947, a feature film of the same title told White's story, but this 1967 version returns to the original serial for inspiration. Pamela Austin plays Pauline, an orphan who enjoys adventures and escapades on her international travels. Pat Boone is a fellow orphan who pursues her romantically. Terry-Thomas brings an extra dash of class to proceedings, and the whole thing is an enjoyable romp played out to manic piano music from Vic Mizzy. DF
Pat Boone *George* • Terry-Thomas *Sten Martin* • Pamela Austin *Pauline* • Edward Everett Horton *Casper Coleman* • Hamilton Camp *Thorpe* • Doris Packer *Mrs Carruthers* • Kurt Kasznar *Consul General* ■ *Dir* Herbert B Leonard, Joshua Shelley • *Scr* Albert Beich, suggested by the play *The Perils of Pauline; a Drama in One Act* by Charles W Goddard

Period of Adjustment
★★★★ 15

Comedy drama 1962 · US · BW · 103min

Based on one of Tennessee Williams's most light-hearted and accessible plays, this adult comedy drama receives a delightful screen treatment blessed with a superb cast provided by MGM. Everyone looks like the epitome of 1960s glamour, including sexy Jane Fonda and talented Jim Hutton as a pair of newlyweds concerned over the marriage troubles of friends Tony Franciosa and the sublime Lois Nettleton, who has the

film's best moments. The black-and-white photography enhances the sense of period, and many viewers will find this neglected gem deeply satisfying. TS DVD
Tony Franciosa [Anthony Franciosa] *Ralph Baitz* • Jane Fonda *Isabel Haverstick* • Jim Hutton *George Haverstick* • Lois Nettleton *Dorothea Baitz* • John McGiver *Stewart P Mcgill* • Mabel Albertson *Mrs Alice McGill* • Jack Albertson *Desk sergeant* ■ *Dir* George Roy Hill • *Scr* Isobel Lennart, from the play by Tennessee Williams

The Perks of Being a Wallflower
★★★ 12

Coming-of-age romantic drama 2012 · US · Colour · 98min

Stephen Chbosky adapts his own 1990s-set young adult novel here, and focuses on the glorious, and eventually gory, underbelly of late high-school life. But he walks a wobbly line between schmaltz and sincerity. Emma Watson is the sharp and beautiful senior pupil who introduces damaged intellectual Logan Lerman to her camp stepbrother and his social circle. The superb cast, including Paul Rudd as an inspirational teacher, manages to turn this potentially queasy teen drama into something worth watching. KK Some sexual references, drug abuse, swearing. DVD BD
Logan Lerman *Charlie* • Emma Watson *Sam* • Ezra Miller *Patrick* • Mae Whitman *Mary Elizabeth* • Kate Walsh *Mother* • Dylan McDermott *Father* • Paul Rudd *Bill* • Melanie Lynskey *Aunt Helen* • Nina Dobrev *Candace* ■ *Dir* Stephen Chbosky • *Scr* Stephen Chbosky, from his novel

Permanent Midnight
★★★ 18

Biographical drama 1998 · US · Colour · 84min

Ben Stiller makes the most of a meaty role in this gripping drugs drama, set in the Hollywood fast lane. It's based on the autobiography of Jerry Stahl, a writer working in television whose career self-destructed when his heroin addiction overtook his life. Stiller plays him warts and all and at times it's actually hard to work up any sympathy for his descent into drugs hell. There are good supporting turns, and even Elizabeth Hurley acquits herself quite well as the naive producer who ends up in a marriage of convenience with Stiller. JF DVD
Ben Stiller *Jerry Stahl* • Elizabeth Hurley *Sandra* • Janeane Garofalo *Jana* • Maria Bello *Kitty* • Owen Wilson *Nicky* • Lourdes Benedicto *Vola* • Jay Paulson *Phoenix Punk* • Jerry Stahl *Dr Murphy* ■ *Dir* David Veloz • *Scr* David Veloz, from the autobiography by Jerry Stahl

Permanent Record
★★★ 15

Drama 1988 · US · Colour · 88min

An early, and affecting, performance from Keanu Reeves is the sole reason for bothering with this "social issue" movie about what drives teens to suicide. Reeves is the under-achieving best friend of the seemingly perfect pupil (Alan Boyce) who throws himself off a cliff. For what reason is endlessly discussed, although the self-obsessed, angst-ridden traumas of the classmates left behind provide more than enough motive. Only in Reeves's case does such vapid posturing ring heartbreakingly true and appealingly sincere. AJ Swearing.
Alan Boyce *David Sinclair* • Keanu Reeves *Chris Townsend* • Michelle Meyrink *MG* • Jennifer Rubin *Lauren* • Pamela Gidley *Kim* • Michael Elgart *Jake* • Richard Bradford *Leo Verdell* ■ *Dir* Marisa Silver • *Scr* Jarre Fees, Alice Liddle, Larry Ketron

Permanent Vacation
★★★ 12

Drama 1982 · US · Colour · 71min

Jim Jarmusch signed up to the film programme at New York University, where he was tutored by the great film-maker Nicholas Ray. The dying Ray encouraged Jarmusch in the production of his graduation project, *Permanent Vacation*. The spare, quirky Jarmusch style is already in evidence in this slight story about a disillusioned New Yorker who decides his future lies in Europe. Jarmusch regular John Lurie provides both a typically

deadpan performance and a slick score. DP DVD
Chris Parker *Aloysious Parker* • Leila Gastil *Leila* • Maria Duval *Latin girl* • Ruth Bolton *Mother* • Richard Boes *War veteran* • John Lurie *Sax player* ■ *Dir/Scr* Jim Jarmusch

Permission to Kill
★★ 15

Spy thriller 1975 · Austria/UK/US · Colour · 92min

A decade before he was fitted for 007's tuxedo, Timothy Dalton found himself knee-deep in double-dealing in this humdrum spy thriller. However, Dirk Bogarde headlines as a security chief anxious to prevent Third World exile Bekim Fehmiu from returning to lead his oppressed people in a revolution. The film resolutely fails to gather momentum and Ava Gardner looks decidedly uncomfortable as Fehmiu's mistress. DP
Dirk Bogarde *Alan Curtis* • Ava Gardner *Katin Petersen* • Bekim Fehmiu *Alexander Diakim* • Timothy Dalton *Charles Lord* • Nicole Calfan *Melissa Lascade* • Frederic Forrest *Scott Alexander* ■ *Dir* Cyril Frankel • *Scr* Robin Estridge, from a play by Robin Estridge

Perrier's Bounty
★★★ 15

Crime comedy drama 2009 · Ire/UK · Colour · 84min

Cillian Murphy takes on a lighter than usual role in this madcap thriller, playing Michael, a chancer on the run from Dublin gangsters. Brendan Gleeson hams it up as the titular kingpin who puts a price on Michael's head after he fails to pay his debts and is implicated in the murder of a henchman. In fact it's Michael's neurotic neighbour (Jodie Whittaker) who did the deed and she tags along for the getaway, along with Michael's errant father (Jim Broadbent). Ultimately, this doesn't have the emotional resonance of the similarly-themed caper *In Bruges*, but it does keep you smiling. SP Violence, swearing, sexual references, drug abuse. DVD BD
Cillian Murphy *Michael McCrea* • Jim Broadbent *Jim McCrea* • Brendan Gleeson *Darren Perrier* • Jodie Whittaker *Brenda* • Padraic Delaney *Shamie* ■ *Dir* Ian FitzGibbon • *Scr* Mark O'Rowe

Persecution
★★★ 15

Psychological thriller 1974 · UK · Colour · 91min

Lana Turner stars as a rich American widow living in Britain with her oppressed son Ralph Bates, whose dark past is catching up with her. Director Don Chaffey tries hard to make the action sinister and succeeds in promoting a few chills. Adding to the entertainment value is an experienced support cast that includes Trevor Howard. By now, Turner's prolific film career was nearing its end and she only made three more features. TH Violence.
Lana Turner *Carrie Masters* • Ralph Bates *David Masters* • Trevor Howard *Paul Bellamy* • Olga Georges-Picot *Monique Kalfon* ■ *Dir* Don Chaffey • *Scr* Robert B Hutton, Rosemary Wootten, Frederick Warner

Persepolis
★★★★ 12

Animated coming-of-age drama 2007 · Fr/US · BW and Colour · 91min

Adapted from Marjane Satrapi's (autobio)graphic novel of the same name, this animated feature is both a rewarding history lesson and a beautiful rites-of-passage tale. It begins in France, where the grown-up Marjane (Chiara Mastroianni) is about to return to modern-day Iran, and recalls her days as a pre-teen terror, obsessed with Bruce Lee, communism and religion. These are the film's wonder years, as the exile of the Shah brings a momentary glimpse of freedom before strict Islamic law moves in to fill the gap. The remainder of the film deals with Marjane's adolescent fallout, and though these scenes aren't quite as engaging as what has come before, this is still a a stylish, innovative and very moving memoir. Also shown in a subtitled version. DW French dubbed. Violence, brief swearing, drug abuse. DVD BD

Chiara Mastroianni *Marjane, as a teenager and woman* • Catherine Deneuve *Tadji, Marjane's mother* • Sean Penn *Ebi, Marjane's father* • Iggy Pop *Uncle Anouche* • Gena Rowlands *Marjane's grandmother* ■ *Dir* Marjane Satrapi, Vincent Paronnaud • *Scr* Marjane Satrapi, Vincent Paronnaud, from the graphic novel *Persepolis: the Story of an Iranian Childhood* by Satrapi

LANDMARK FILM
This audacious drama advances the idea of film as consciousness, of flickering images as a brain in action

Persona
★★★★★ 15

Drama 1966 · Swe · BW · 79min

Ingmar Bergman devised this ambitious drama while recovering in hospital from debilitating dizziness. Inspired by the physical similarity between Liv Ullmann and Bibi Andersson – playing an actress struck mute and the nurse who treats her – it explores the very nature of art and reality. Everything about this most modern of films is designed to disorientate the viewer – the inclusion of off-screen voices and the paraphernalia of film-making, the sudden melting of the frame, the disjointed structure of the narrative and, finally, the famous melding of Ullmann and Andersson's faces into a single identity. Proclaiming the artist to be both communicator and charlatan, this is audacious, complex and unforgettable. DP Swedish +subtitles. DVD
Bibi Andersson *Alma, the nurse* • Liv Ullmann *Elisabeth Vogler* • Margaretha Krook *Doctor* • Gunnar Björnstrand *Herr Vogler* • Jörgen Lindström *Boy* ■ *Dir/Scr* Ingmar Bergman • *Cinematographer* Sven Nykvist

Personal Affair
★★ U

Crime drama 1953 · UK · BW · 78min

Hollywood beauty Gene Tierney co-stars as the wife of village schoolmaster Leo Genn in this small-scale tale. Teenage pupil Glynis Johns at Genn's school becomes infatuated with him and, after a confrontation with Tierney, disappears. The girl is assumed to be dead and suspicion falls on the luckless schoolmaster. A somewhat overheated and unconvincing drama, this nevertheless illustrates the ease with which relationships in small communities can become damaged by gossip. RK
Gene Tierney *Kay Barlow* • Leo Genn *Stephen Barlow* • Glynis Johns *Barbara Vining* • Pamela Brown *Evelyn* • Walter Fitzgerald *Henry Vining* • Megs Jenkins *Vi Vining* • Thora Hird *Mrs Usher* • Michael Hordern *Headmaster* ■ *Dir* Anthony Pelissier • *Scr* Anthony Pelissier, from the play *A Day's Mischief* by Lesley Storm

Personal Best
★★★ 18

Sports drama 1982 · US · Colour · 122min

Robert Towne was accused of voyeurism for his depiction of Mariel Hemingway and Patrice Donnelly in this lesbian love story played against the backdrop of the Moscow Olympic Games. In his directorial debut, Towne demonstrates a sure visual sense as he not only chronicles the athletes' romance, but also their physical progress under martinet coach Scott Glenn. This is occasionally over-reliant on sporting clichés, but it's still subtle, sensual stuff. DP
Mariel Hemingway *Chris Cahill* • Scott Glenn *Terry Tingloff* • Patrice Donnelly *Tory Skinner* • Kenny Moore *Denny Stites* • Jim Moody *Roscoe Travis* • Kari Gosswiller *Penny Brill* • Jodi Anderson *Nadia "Pooch" Anderson* ■ *Dir/Scr* Robert Towne

Personal Best
★★★ 12A

Sports documentary 2012 · UK · Colour · 89min

This thoughtful documentary portrait joins *Town of Runners* and *The Athlete* on the podium of movies about sporting endeavour released during the year of the London Olympics. Filmed over four years, it follows the fortunes of a quartet of British sprinters as they train, prepare for and dream of Olympic glory. Sam Blair's film (expanding on his 2008 short film *Sprinters*) is not about superstars, though, but dedicated, hardworking athletes. Their trials and tribulations are absorbing to follow, though this may be too unspectacular and intimate for those who like their sport adrenalised and loud. JA Swearing. *DVD*

James Ellington • Jeanette Kwakye • Richard Alleyne • Omardo Anson ■ *Dir* Sam Blair

Personal Property ★★
Comedy   1937 · US · BW · 88min

Starry but feeble, this comedy has Robert Taylor as a London playboy given the job of overseeing a house belonging to a penniless American widow (Jean Harlow). A victim of censorship codes, this inoffensive picture dawdles from one non-event to the next, though the female audiences of the time appreciated the lingering shots of Taylor in the bathtub. AT

Robert Taylor (1) *Raymond Dabney* • Jean Harlow *Crystal Wetherby* • Reginald Owen *Claude Dabney* • Una O'Connor *Clara* • EE Clive *Mr Dabney* • Henrietta Crosman *Mrs Dabney* • Cora Witherspoon *Mrs Burns* ■ *Dir* WS Van Dyke II [WS Van Dyke] • *Scr* Hugh Mills, Ernest Vajda, from the play *The Man in Possession* by HM Harwood

Personal Services ★★★ 18
Comedy   1987 · UK · Colour · 100min

This is a gently witty, if curiously coy, attempt by director Terry Jones to re-create the odd career of "luncheon voucher madam" Cynthia Payne. Julie Walters is a good choice to portray her droll matter-of-factness about the sexual proclivities of a succession of middle-aged men, but in its jolly, almost seaside postcard approach, the movie loses edge and bite. SH Swearing, nudity. *DVD*

Julie Walters *Christine Painter* • Alec McCowen *Wing Commander Morton* • Shirley Stelfox *Shirley* • Danny Schiller *Dolly* • Victoria Hardcastle *Rose* • Tim Woodward *Timms* ■ *Dir* Terry Jones • *Scr* David Leland

Personal Shopper ★★
Psychological thriller   2016 · Fr · Colour

A celebrity personal shopper thinks she's in paranormal contact with her dead brother in this vapid hybrid of suspenseless ghost story, stodgy psychodrama and obvious pop culture satire. Kristen Stewart's second successive alliance with director Olivier Assayas finds the ever-watchable *Twilight* star in Paris tending to the wardrobe needs of a fashionista while trying to access the spirit world. Predictable twists lead to a daft ending and merely underscore the inept strangeness and po-faced inanity Assayas mistakes for style. AJ

Kristen Stewart *Maureen* • Anders Danielsen Lie *Erwin* • Lars Eidinger *Ingo* ■ *Dir/Scr* Olivier Assayas

Personal Velocity ★★★ 15
Portmanteau drama   2001 · US · Colour · 82min

The second feature from Arthur Miller's writer/director daughter Rebecca may lack the froth commonly associated with "chick flicks", but it's most definitely a woman's film. The drama is split into three inter-connected segments, each dealing with a woman who has reached a turning point in her life. Kyra Sedgwick plays the battered wife who's finally had enough, Parker Posey the married book editor suddenly liberated by her career, and a typecast Fairuza Balk is the rebel forced to face adult responsibilities. This is emotionally invigorating, with an articulate script and spirited performances. SF Violence, swearing, sex scenes, nudity. *DVD*

Kyra Sedgwick *Delia Shunt* • Parker Posey *Greta Herskovitz* • Fairuza Balk *Paula* • John Ventimiglia *Narrator* • Ron Leibman *Avram Herskovitz* • Wallace Shawn *Mr Gelb* • David Warshofsky *Kurt Wurtzle* • Leo Fitzpatrick *Mylert* • Tim Guinee *Lee Schneeweiss* • Patti D'Arbanville *Celia* ■ *Dir* Rebecca Miller • *Scr* Rebecca Miller, from her short story collection

Persons Unknown ★★ 18
Thriller   1996 · US · Colour · 94min

Before it turns into a soppy love story, this cynical thriller is a stylish and innovative take on the usual cops-and-robbers scenario. Joe Mantegna plays an ex-cop-turned-security systems rep who has a one-night stand with Kelly Lynch, who uses the

opportunity to steal his files detailing the defences of the local drug dealers. Mantegna then gets involved at a distance, Lynch's handicapped sister (Naomi Watts) arrives to take part in the robbery, and this caper loses its way and slips into bathos. AJ Swearing, violence, sex scenes.

Joe Mantegna *Jim Holland* • Kelly Lynch *Amanda* • JT Walsh *Cake* • Naomi Watts *Molly* • Xander Berkeley *Tosh* • Jon Favreau *Terry* ■ *Dir* George Hickenlooper • *Scr* Craig Smith

Persuasion ★★★★ U
Period romance   1995 · UK/US/Fr · Colour · 102min

Amanda Root glows as gentle Anne Elliot, past her bloom and thoughtlessly put-upon by her horrid, snobbish family when the once-poor suitor she was persuaded to reject returns in the shape of dashing Captain Wentworth (Ciaran Hinds). Now he's rich, socially desirable and eager to find a wife – just as long as she's not Anne. However, the attentions of a caddish admirer revive the resentful hero's interest. This artful adaptation of Jane Austen's most mature love story is beautifully realised by *Notting Hill* director Roger Michell and a class ensemble who never let the superb period detail intrude on the emotional realism. AME *DVD*

Amanda Root *Anne Elliot* • Ciaran Hinds *Captain Wentworth* • Susan Fleetwood *Lady Russell* • Corin Redgrave *Sir Walter Elliot* • Fiona Shaw *Mrs Croft* • John Woodvine *Admiral Croft* • Phoebe Nicholls *Elizabeth Elliot* • Samuel West *Mr Elliot* • Sophie Thompson *Mary Musgrove* • Judy Cornwell *Mrs Musgrove* • Simon Russell Beale *Charles Musgrove* ■ *Dir* Roger Michell • *Scr* Nick Dear, from the novel by Jane Austen

Pet Sematary ★★★ 18
Horror   1989 · US · Colour · 98min

In this morbid but compulsive horror, adapted by Stephen King from his own novel, a young couple (Dale Midkiff and Denise Crosby) discover that corpses buried in the pet cemetery near their new home come back to life. For much of its length, the story, which seems to be yet another re-working of the classic *The Monkey's Paw*, provides only the occasional shudder and is interrupted by awkward flashbacks. But those who stick with it are rewarded with a ghastly climax, cleverly engineered to tweak every raw nerve. A sequel followed in 1992. DM *DVD*

Fred Gwynne *Jud Crandall* • Dale Midkiff *Louis Creed* • Denise Crosby *Rachel Creed* • Brad Greenquist *Victor Pascow* • Michael Lombard *Irwin Goldman* ■ *Dir* Mary Lambert • *Scr* Stephen King, from his novel

Pet Shop ★★ U
Comedy fantasy   1995 · US · Colour · 84min

In the suburb of Cactus Flats, Arizona, a magical pet shop sells pets that are actually fantastic animals in disguise. A Mob family in the witness protection programme ends up with some of the magic animals, with supposedly hilarious consequences ensuing. The characters are so stereotypical and the humour so broad that this low-budget kids' movie will appeal only to unsophisticated youngsters. ST

Terry Kiser *Joe Yeagher* • Leigh Ann Orsi *Dena Yeagher* • Spencer Vrooman *Mike* • Joanne Baron *Marilyn Yeagher* • David Wagner *Charlie Yeagher* ■ *Dir* Hope Perello • *Scr* Mark Goldstein, Greg Suddeth, Brent Friedman, from an idea by Peter Von Sholly

Pétain ★★★★ 15
Historical war drama 1992 · Fr · Colour · 129min

With the scars of the Occupation still running deep, it took director Jean Marboeuf six years to find willing collaborators for this meticulously researched history of the Vichy government. Much of the action takes place inside the infamous Hôtel du Parc, which tends to isolate the population at large from the enormity of the deeds carried out in its name by Pétain and his chief minister, Laval. As the Great War hero-cum-figurehead, Jacques Dufilho turns in a

momentous display of shabby pride and gullible opportunism. DP French +subtitles.

Jacques Dufilho *Philippe Pétain* • Jean Yanne *Laval* • Jean-Pierre Cassel *Hans Roberto* • Jean-Claude Dreyfus *Dumoulin* • Antoinette Moya *Eugénie Pétain* ■ *Dir* Jean Marboeuf • *Scr* Jean-Pierre Marchand, Marc Ferro, Alain Riou, Jean Marboeuf, from a non-fiction book by Marc Ferro

Pete Kelly's Blues ★★★★ PG
Drama   1955 · US · Colour · 91min

This tale of a Kansas City cornet player is one of the most sympathetic and understanding movies about jazz. It's a marvellous one-off, directed by, produced by and starring *Dragnet*'s Jack Webb, who cast his film perfectly: not just moll Janet Leigh and bootlegger Edmond O'Brien, but also Ella Fitzgerald and Peggy Lee, the latter touching and Oscar-nominated for a performance that includes the affecting *Sing a Rainbow*. It's also is superbly designed and photographed in a real CinemaScope, deploying that letterbox frame to its best advantage. The melancholy tone is brilliantly sustained, the attitudes and language resolutely adult. TS

Jack Webb *Pete Kelly* • Janet Leigh *Ivy Conrad* • Edmond O'Brien *Fran McCarg* • Peggy Lee *Rose Hopkins* • Andy Devine *George Tenell* • Lee Marvin *Al Gannaway* • Ella Fitzgerald *Maggie Jackson* ■ *Dir* Jack Webb • *Scr* Richard L Breen

Pete 'n' Tillie ★★★
Romantic comedy   1972 · US · Colour · 100min

"When you're my age, blind dates are a way of life," says Carol Burnett to Walter Matthau at the start of this romantic comedy. Later, they get married and have a son with a terminal disease. Yes, this is unashamedly manipulative, but its saving grace is the acting: Burnett was making a big screen comeback after a decade's absence, and Matthau is a sheer delight as a character who speaks in puns and riddles and lives for practical jokes. As Burnett's matchmaking friend, Geraldine Page won an Oscar nomination, as did the sudsy script. AT

Walter Matthau *Pete* • Carol Burnett *Tillie* • Geraldine Page *Gertrude* • Barry Nelson *Burt* • René Auberjonois *Jimmy* • Lee H Montgomery [Lee Montgomery] *Robbie* ■ *Dir* Martin Ritt • *Scr* Julius J Epstein, from the novella *Witch's Milk* by Peter De Vries

Peter and Pavla ★★★★
Drama   1964 · Cz · BW · 85min

Milos Forman made his feature directorial debut with this story about a store detective pressurised by his parents to succeed in life and love. Making atmospheric use of the Bohemian town of Kolin and coaxing wondrously naturalistic, improvised performances from Ladislav Jakim and Pavla Martinkova, Forman began his perpetual fascination with the outsider with a sympathetic wit that would never desert him. DP Czech +subtitles.

Ladislav Jakim *Peter* • Pavla Martinkova *Pavla* ■ *Dir* Milos Forman • *Scr* Milos Forman, Jaroslav Papousek • *Cinematographer* Jan Nemecek

Peter Ibbetson ★★★★
Romantic fantasy drama 1935 · US · BW · 82min

This Hollywood oddity became a landmark for members of the European surrealist movement in the 1930s, with Gary Cooper and Ann Harding as lovers who communicate their passion in dreams. Off-the-wall casting (Cooper is not very effective) adds to the sense of alienation in this adaptation of George du Maurier's novel and John Nathaniel Raphael's play, while the finale's fulfilment of *l'amour fou* received a rapturous reception from the surrealists. TH In English and French.

Gary Cooper *Peter Ibbetson* • Ann Harding *Mary, Duchess of Towers* • John Halliday *Duke of Towers* • Ida Lupino *Agnes* • Douglass Dumbrille *Colonel Forsythe* • Virginia Weidler *Mimsey (Mary age 6)* • Dickie Moore *Gogo (Peter age 8)* ■ *Dir* Henry Hathaway • *Scr* Vincent Lawrence, Waldemar Young, Constance Collier, John Meehan, Edwin Justus Mayer, from the play by

John Nathaniel Raphael, from the novel by George du Maurier • *Cinematographer* Charles Lang

Peter Pan ★★★★ U
Animated fantasy adventure 1953 · US · Colour · 76min

Although Peter Pan purists disliked Bobby Driscoll's twangy American voice as the leader of JM Barrie's Lost Boys, this is still a well-crafted animated feature from Disney with such great songs by Sammy Cahn and Sammy Fain as *You Can Fly* and *What Makes the Red Man Red?*. The artists based Tinker Bell on Marilyn Monroe, while the ongoing battle between Captain Hook and the crocodile is a delight. TH *DVD* *BL*

Bobby Driscoll *Peter Pan* • Kathryn Beaumont *Wendy* • Hans Conried *Capt Hook/Mr Darling* • Bill Thompson *Mr Smee* • Heather Angel *Mrs Darling* • Paul Collins *Michael Darling* • Tommy Luske *John* • Tom Conway *Narrator* ■ *Dir* Hamilton Luske, Clyde Geronimi, Wilfred Jackson • *Scr* Ted Sears, Bill Peet, Joe Rinaldi, Erdman Penner, Winston Hibler, Milt Banta, Ralph Wright, from the play by JM Barrie

Peter Pan ★★★ PG
Fantasy action adventure 2003 · US/UK/Aus · Colour · 107min

In searching for a mother, Peter (Jeremy Sumpter) very nearly ends up with a wife. It's no wonder that fairy Tinker Bell (Ludivine Sagnier) occasionally throws a tantrum. Peter and Wendy (Rachel Hurd-Wood) trifle with each other's hearts as they tussle with Jason Isaacs's terrifying Captain Hook. PJ Hogan gives this spin on the boy who wouldn't grow up an eye-catching makeover and, despite Sumpter's American accent, retains the essential Englishness of the source text. TH *DVD* *BL*

Jason Isaacs *Captain Hook/Mr Darling* • Jeremy Sumpter *Peter Pan* • Rachel Hurd-Wood *Wendy Darling* • Olivia Williams *Mrs Darling* • Ludivine Sagnier *Tinker Bell* • Richard Briers *Smee* • Lynn Redgrave *Aunt Millicent* • Geoffrey Palmer *Sir Edward Quiller Couch* • Harry Newell *John Darling* • Freddie Popplewell *Michael Darling* ■ *Dir* PJ Hogan • *Scr* PJ Hogan, Michael Goldenberg, from the play by JM Barrie, from the novel *Peter and Wendy* by JM Barrie

Peter's Friends ★★★ 15
Comedy drama   1992 · UK · Colour · 97min

Seeming rather small, smug and insignificant when it first played in the cinema, Kenneth Branagh's engaging ensemble comedy is far more at home (and considerably more enjoyable) on the small screen. The air of "luvviness" still hangs heavy, but Rita Rudner's script succeeds in being sharp and cosy without ever over-straining for effect, and Branagh's handling of his players is impeccable (if only he could get the hang of camera movement). Emma Thompson's performance as the lonely, winsomely twee bachelor girl is a delight. DP Swearing, nudity. *DVD*

Hugh Laurie *Roger* • Imelda Staunton *Mary* • Stephen Fry *Peter* • Emma Thompson *Maggie* • Kenneth Branagh *Andrew* • Alphonsia Emmanuel *Sarah* • Rita Rudner *Carol* • Phyllida Law *Vera* • Alex Lowe *Paul* • Tony Slattery *Brian* ■ *Dir* Kenneth Branagh • *Scr* Martin Bergman, Rita Rudner

Pete's Dragon ★★ U
Part-animated musical fantasy 1977 · US · Colour · 101min

The magic largely left the Disney kingdom in the 1970s and this mix of animation and live action is a long way from the likes of *Toy Story*. Sean Marshall plays the lonely youngster who finds an unlikely friend in the shape of a dragon called Elliott (voiced by Charlie Callas). Despite a stellar cast, the special effects pale alongside the sharper technologies of today, and, sadly, the tunes fail to provide much in the way of compensation. Disney's remake is due in summer 2016. JF *DVD*

Helen Reddy *Nora* • Jim Dale *Dr Terminus* • Sean Marshall *Pete* • Mickey Rooney *Lampie* • Red Buttons *Hoagy* • Shelley Winters *Lena Gogan* • Jean Kean *Miss Taylor* • Jim Backus *Mayor* ■ *Dir* Don Chaffey • *Scr* Malcolm Marmorstein, from a story by SS Field, Seton I Miller

Pete's Dragon ★★★★ PG

Fantasy adventure 2016 · US · Colour · 102min

Disney's 1977 original, about a boy and his guardian dragon, blended live-action humans with a green-and-purple cartoon creature. Forty years on, their thoroughly entertaining re-imagining uses cutting-edge CGI to make dragon Elliot look rather more realistic, yet he pleasingly retains his goofy characteristics. Young Pete is found feral in the woods and his survival remains a mystery until a supportive forest ranger, Bryce Dallas Howard, and her dad, Robert Redford, are introduced to Pete's unusual forest friend. DA

Bryce Dallas Howard *Grace* · Oakes Fegley *Pete* · Robert Redford *Meacham* · Wes Bentley *Jack* ■ *Dir* David Lowery · *Scr* Toby Halbrooks, David Lowery, from the 1977 film

Le Petit Prince A Dit
★★★★ PG

Drama 1992 · Fr/Swi · Colour · 104min

Although its main protagonist has been diagnosed with an inoperable brain tumour, rather than being a mawkish melodrama, Christine Pascal's unconventional road movie is a joyous celebration of life. While her divorced parents, scientist Richard Berry and actress Anémone, wallow in recrimination and self-pity, ten-year-old Marie Kleiber simply gets on with the business of getting the most out of each day, as Berry whisks her away on an Alpine tour that he desperately hopes will forestall the onset of the disease. Demonstrating wondrous maturity, Kleiber is a revelation, and her rapport with Berry is both persuasive and poignant. DP French +subtitles.

Richard Berry *Adam Leibovich* · Anémone *Melanie* · Marie Kleiber *Violette* · Lucie Phan *Lucie* · Mista Préchac *Minerve* ■ *Dir* Christine Pascal · *Scr* Christine Pascal, Robert Boner

Le Petit Soldat ★★★★ 15

Spy drama 1960 · Fr · BW · 84min

Jean-Luc Godard's second feature was a controversial dramatisation of the Algerian civil war that was then tearing France apart. Initially banned by the French government for its violence, the film concerns a secret agent sent to Geneva to assassinate a leading member of the Algerian resistance. Godard shoots it like a gangster thriller, with some disturbing sequences of bathroom torture, and achieves a chilling portrait of colonialism's last gasp. The film's heroine is played by Anna Karina, who became his wife and the star of many of his subsequent films. AT French +subtitles. DVD

Michel Subor *Bruno Forestier* · Anna Karina *Véronica Dreyer* · Henri-Jacques Huet *Jacques* · Paul Beauvais *Paul* · Laszlo Szabo *Laszlo* · Georges de Beauregard *Beauregard* · Jean-Luc Godard *Bystander at railway station* ■ *Dir/Scr* Jean-Luc Godard

La Petite Voleuse ★★★

Drama 1988 · Fr · Colour · 105min

Teenager Charlotte Gainsbourg, abandoned by her mother and living with her aunt and uncle in a small French town, longs for adulthood, freedom and excitement. She looks for it by stealing, working as a maid, losing her virginity to a married man and decamping with a young thief (Simon de la Brosse). Adapted and directed by François Truffaut's one-time assistant Claude Miller. The film is well-cast, well-made, accurately observed and hard to fault. However, those who fail to respond to the deeply irritating and fundamentally uninteresting heroine will find the whole thing utterly tedious. RK French +subtitles.

Charlotte Gainsbourg *Janine Castang* · Didier Bezace *Michel Davenne* · Simon de la Brosse *Raoul* · Raoul Billerey *André Rouleau* · Chantal Banlier *Aunt Léa* ■ *Dir* Claude Miller · *Scr* François Truffaut, Claude de Givray

Petites Coupures ★★ 15

Comedy drama 2002 · Fr/UK · Colour · 91min

Daniel Auteuil struggles valiantly to make an impact as the ageing lothario in this meandering comedy drama of sexual manners. But director Pascal Bonitzer succeeds only in keeping his star shuttling between a variety of transient characters without pausing to let us learn very much about him. This tactic also reduces the performances of wife Emmanuelle Devos and his countless lovers to mere walk-on parts, with only Kristin Scott Thomas registering. Polished but aimlessly superficial. DP French +subtitles. Sex scenes, swearing, violence. DVD

Daniel Auteuil *Bruno* · Kristin Scott Thomas *Béatrice* · Ludivine Sagnier *Nathalie* · Pascale Bussières *Mathilde* · Catherine Mouchot *Anne* · Emmanuelle Devos *Gaëlle* · Jean Yanne *Gérard* ■ *Dir* Pascal Bonitzer · *Scr* Pascal Bonitzer, Emmanuel Salinger · *Cinematographer* William Lubtchansky

Les Petites Vacances
★★★★ 12

Comedy drama 2006 · Fr · Colour · 87min

Best known for her *nouvelle vague* collaborations with Claude Chabrol (*Le Beau Serge*, *Les Bonnes Femmes*), Bernadette Lafont gives one of the best performances of her 50-year career in this disconcerting road movie. Entrusted with her grandchildren during a school holiday, Danièle (Lafont) spirits them across the Swiss border and severs all contact with their parents. As it becomes apparent that she can't keep running, Danièle's demons begin to close in. The schizophrenic manner in which Lafont balances indulgent grandmother with fraying woman recalls Gena Rowlands at her best. But it's 28-year-old director Olivier Peyon's insights into the fears and disillusions of a pensioner that makes this so intriguing. DP French +subtitles. DVD

Bernadette Lafont *Danièle* · Adèle Csech *Marine* · Lucas Franchi *Thomas* · Claire Nadeau *Nicole* · Claude Brasseur *Man at ballroom* · Éric Savin *Eric* · Benjamin Rolland *Stéphane* ■ *Dir* Olivier Peyon · *Scr* Cyril Brody, Olivier Peyon, Gladys Marciano · *Cinematographer* Alexis Kavyrchine

The Petrified Forest
★★★★ PG

Drama 1936 · US · BW · 78min

This studio-bound adaptation of playwright Robert E Sherwood's Broadway success afforded character actor Humphrey Bogart the star-making role of his life as snarling Duke Mantee, the escaped thug who holds a motley group of travellers at bay as hostages. Star Leslie Howard insisted Bogie play the role, and in gratitude Bogart named his daughter "Leslie". Some of Sherwood's moralising may have dated, but there's no denying the power and conviction of the performances as Howard, Bogie and Bette Davis fire up the screen, setting the style and pace for future Warner Bros melodramas. TS DVD

Leslie Howard *Alan Squier* · Bette Davis *Gabrielle Maple* · Genevieve Tobin *Mrs Chisholm* · Dick Foran *Boze Hertzlinger* · Humphrey Bogart *Duke Mantee* · Joseph Sawyer [Joe Sawyer] *Jackie* · Porter Hall *Jason Maple* · Charley Grapewin *Gramp Maple* ■ *Dir* Archie Mayo · *Scr* Charles Kenyon, Delmer Daves, from the play by Robert E Sherwood

Petticoat Pirates ★ U

Comedy 1961 · UK · Colour · 82min

In his third tilt at movie stardom, TV comic Charlie Drake again finds himself up a well-known creek without a script. This time, however, he's only got himself to blame, as he co-wrote this woeful comedy, in which he plays a timid stoker forced to disguise himself as a Wren in order to recover a battleship hijacked by a mutinous all-woman crew. DP

Charlie Drake *Charlie* · Anne Heywood *Anne Stephens* · Cecil Parker *Commander in Chief* · John Turner *Captain Michael Patterson* · Maxine Audley *Superintendent* · Thorley Walters *Lieutenant Jerome Robertson* · Eleanor

Summerfield *Mabel* · Victor Maddern *COC Nixon* ■ *Dir* David MacDonald · *Scr* Lew Schwartz, Charlie Drake, from a story by TJ Morrison

The Petty Girl ★★★

Biographical musical comedy 1950 · US · Colour · 87min

George Petty was a real-life popular mid-20th-century illustrator and this is a light-hearted depiction of Petty's daily rounds, as portrayed here by affable Robert Cummings. The humour's very dated: he's a pin-up artist, whereas co-star Joan Caulfield is a bit of a prude, but it makes for agreeable viewing. The film is stolen by comedians Elsa Lanchester and the inimitable Mary Wickes, and watch closely for a glimpse of Hitchcock's "discovery" Tippi Hedren, a decade before *Marnie*. TS

Robert Cummings *George Petty* · Joan Caulfield *Victoria Braymore* · Elsa Lanchester *Dr Crutcher* · Melville Cooper *Beardsley* · Audrey Long *Connie* · Mary Wickes *Prof Whitman* · Tippi Hedren *Ice box, Petty girl* ■ *Dir* Henry Levin · *Scr* Nat Perrin, from a story by Mary McCarthy

Petulia ★★★★ 15

Drama 1968 · US/UK · Colour · 100min

Few directors embraced the technical trickery of the French New Wave with as much enthusiasm as Richard Lester. But the kind of narrative leap-frogging and camera eccentricity that worked a treat on *A Hard Day's Night* is something of a distraction in this Swinging Sixties story in which freewheeling Julie Christie cheats on volatile husband Richard Chamberlain with divorced surgeon George C Scott. The film has dated just a tad, but Christie and Scott make a surprisingly potent couple. DP DVD

Julie Christie *Petulia Danner* · George C Scott *Archie Bollen* · Richard Chamberlain *David Danner* · Arthur Hill *Barney* · Shirley Knight *Polo* · Pippa Scott *May* · Kathleen Widdoes *Wilma* · Joseph Cotten *Mr Danner* · Austin Pendleton *Intern* · René Auberjonois *Salesman* ■ *Dir* Richard Lester · *Scr* Lawrence B Marcus, from the novel *Me and the Arch-Kook Petulia* by John Haase, adapted by Barbara Turner · *Cinematographer* Nicolas Roeg

Peyton Place ★★★★ 15

Drama 1957 · US · Colour · 150min

This is an excellent rendering of the steamy, sexy small-town novel that was a runaway bestseller for author Grace Metalious. Lana Turner is perfectly cast in this tight, taut film, and she shows what a riveting screen presence she could be, given a passable script. Nothing is crassly overt, but you can feel the tension of people wound-up like coiled springs. To this end, passion tugs at the skirts of hick morality throughout. Fans will enjoy the 1961 sequel, *Return to Peyton Place*. SH DVD

Lana Turner *Constance MacKenzie* · Hope Lange *Selena Cross* · Lee Philips *Michael Rossi* · Lloyd Nolan *Dr Matthew Swain* · Diane Varsi *Allison MacKenzie* · Arthur Kennedy *Lucas Cross* · Russ Tamblyn *Norman Page* ■ *Dir* Mark Robson · *Scr* John Michael Hayes, from the novel by Grace Metalious

Phaedra ★

Drama 1962 · US/Gr/Fr · BW · 115min

Melina Mercouri, the second wife of Greek shipping tycoon Raf Vallone, falls for her husband's son Anthony Perkins. They embark on a steamy affair in Paris, before continuing to the island of Hydra where all is revealed to Vallone. This overheated updating of a classical Greek tragedy by Mercouri's producer/writer/director husband Jules Dassin is risibly awful. RK

Melina Mercouri *Phaedra* · Anthony Perkins *Alexis* · Raf Vallone *Thanos* · Elizabeth Ercy *Ercy* · Olympia Papadouka *Anna* ■ *Dir* Jules Dassin · *Scr* Jules Dassin, Margarita Liberaki, from a story by Margarita Liberaki, from the play *Hippolytus* by Euripides

Phantasm ★★★ 18

Horror 1978 · US · Colour · 84min

A fantasy horror with a science-fiction twist, director Don Coscarelli's lurid chiller is as wildly imaginative as it is totally illogical.

Angus Scrimm impresses as the memorable celluloid demon who sends human victims into another dimension where they become slave dwarves. Don't even ask! Coscarelli's main concern is to shock you senseless while weaving a powerful primal spell. With the unforgettable flying sphere that drills out brains, a macabre fun-house mortuary and cemetery romance, he easily fulfils that aim. AJ Violence, swearing, a sex scene, brief nudity. DVD

A Michael Baldwin *Mike* · Bill Thornbury *Jody Pearson* · Angus Scrimm *Tall Man* · Reggie Bannister *Reggie* · Kathy Lester *Lady in lavender* · Lynn Eastman *Sally* ■ *Dir/Scr* Don Coscarelli

Phantasm II ★★ 18

Horror 1988 · US · Colour · 92min

Director Don Coscarelli waited ten years before making a follow-up to his weirdly different cult classic because he didn't want to be pigeonholed as a horror director. But he ended up merely rehashing the original with an equally gory but far less effective entry that barely carries the story forward. Slickly made, but with all the appeal of an empty crisp packet. Two further sequels completed the series. RS Violence, swearing, a sex scene, nudity. DVD

James LeGros *Mike Pearson* · Reggie Bannister *Reggie* · Angus Scrimm *Tall Man* · Paula Irvine *Liz* · Samantha Phillips *Alchemy* ■ *Dir/Scr* Don Coscarelli

The Phantom ★★★ 12

Action adventure 1996 · US/Aus · Colour · 96min

The equivalent of watching ten episodes of a Saturday matinée serial rolled into one *Die Hard* package, director Simon Wincer's cruise through the comic book pages of Lee Falk's masked avenger story is a retro fantasy adventure. Billy Zane plays the orphaned jungle "ghost" trying to stop master criminal Treat Williams unlocking the magical powers of three legendary skulls. Wincer's gently self-mocking tone makes this pulp-fiction treasure a slice of exotic escapism. AJ DVD

Billy Zane *The Phantom/Kit Walker* · Kristy Swanson *Diana Palmer* · Treat Williams *Xander Drax* · Catherine Zeta-Jones *Sala* · James Remar *Quill* · Cary-Hiroyuki Tagawa *Kabai Sengh* · Bill Smitrovich *Uncle Dave* ■ *Dir* Simon Wincer · *Scr* Jeffrey Boam, from a character created by Lee Falk

The Phantom Carriage
★★★★ U

Silent fantasy drama 1920 · Swe · BW · 107min

Victor Sjöström's eerie adaptation of the novel about the feckless husband whose 11th-hour redemption spares him the onerous duty of soul-taking is one of the key films in the development of expressionist cinema. The sermon on the demon power of drink could have come from a DW Griffith short, but Sjöström's inspired use of superimposition and time frames is infinitely more sophisticated. Indeed, it was a little too ingenious, as he was forced to simplify the structure to make the various flashbacks and visions more accessible for contemporary audiences. DP DVD

Victor Sjöström *David Holm* · Hilda Borgström *Mrs Holm* · Tore Svennberg *Georges* · Astrid Holm *Edit* · Lisa Lundholm *Maria* · Olof As *Driver* ■ *Dir* Victor Sjöström · *Scr* Victor Sjöström, from the novel *Körkarlen* by Selma Lagerlöf

Phantom India ★★★★

Documentary 1968 · Fr · Colour · 378min

In tune with the student rebellion in Paris in 1968, Louis Malle decided to give up fictional films for a while (it was three years, in fact) and embark on a six-month voyage to India to find both himself and the country. It resulted in this TV documentary series in seven 54-minute parts, later shown in theatres. Malle, who narrates, makes it a personal journey, and reveals quite a number of fascinating things about the people and society. The Indian government protested at what they saw as a negative view of their country,

U SUITABLE FOR ALL   Uc SUITABLE ESPECIALLY FOR YOUNG CHILDREN (DVD ONLY)   PG PARENTAL GUIDANCE   12A UNDER 12s TO BE ACCOMPANIED (CINEMA ONLY)

complaining that the director had put too much emphasis on the poverty and overcrowding. RE

Louis Malle *Narrator* ■ *Dir/Scr* Louis Malle • *Cinematographer* Etienne Becker

Phantom Lady ★★★★

Film noir 1944 · US · BW · 86min

This is one of the high points of *film noir*. Based on a Cornell Woolrich novel, it's about businessman Alan Curtis, accused of strangling his wife, and the search for the woman – the phantom lady – who can give him an alibi and save him from the electric chair. Leading the search is Curtis's secretary Ella Raines, a policeman who believes in his innocence and his best friend Franchot Tone. The plot spins into spirals of cross and double-cross, all deliriously decked out by Robert Siodmak with a dizzying array of camera angles, light and shadows. AT

Franchot Tone *Jack Marlow* • Ella Raines *Carol "Kansas" Richman* • Alan Curtis *Scott Henderson* • Aurora Miranda *Estela Monteiro* • Thomas Gomez *Inspector Burgess* • Fay Helm *Ann Terry* • Elisha Cook Jr *Cliff* ■ *Dir* Robert Siodmak • *Scr* Bernard C Schoenfeld, from the novel by William Irish [Cornell Woolrich] • *Cinematographer* Woody Bredell

The Phantom Light ★ U

Thriller 1934 · UK · BW · 76min

This has gained a high reputation among Michael Powell's early films because of its good cast, lurid subject matter, continued availability, and tenuous links to later major works. But Powell is really sunk by the atrocious story, more suited to a Will Hay send-up, as new lighthouse keeper Gordon Harker uncovers a shipwreckers' plot. The director tried hard to create atmosphere with his limited location work at Portmadoc and by some dramatic lighting effects but he achieved far more in some of his other B-pictures of the period. AE

Binnie Hale *Alice Bright* • Gordon Harker *Sam Higgins* • Ian Hunter *Jim Pearce* • Donald Calthrop *David Owen* • Milton Rosmer *Dr Carey* • Reginald Tate *Tom Evans* • Mickey Brantford *Bob Peters* ■ *Dir* Michael Powell • *Scr* J Jefferson Farjeon, Austin Melford, Ralph Smart, from the play *The Haunted Light* by Evadne Price, Joan Roy Byford

Phantom of Death ★★ 18

Horror 1988 · It · Colour · 88min

This marked a welcome return to the Italian horror thriller by director Ruggero Deodato, who was sidetracked by the success of his infamous and controversial *Cannibal Holocaust*. Famous classical pianist Michael York is diagnosed with a rare disease that prematurely ages him and twists his mind to such an extent he doesn't recall committing horrendous murders. A thoughtful production, mainly because York conveys his physical and mental disintegration extremely credibly. AJ Italian dubbed. DVD

Michael York *Robert Domenici* • Donald Pleasence *Inspector Downey* • Edwige Fenech *Hélène Martell* • Mapi Galan *Susanna* • Fabio Sartor *Davide* ■ *Dir* Ruggero Deodato • *Scr* Gigliola Battagnin, Vincenzo Mannino, Gianfranco Clerici

The Phantom of the Opera ★★★★ PG

Classic silent horror
1925 · US · BW Tinted and Colour · 90min

This is the influential classic silent first version of Gaston Leroux's novel about a deformed composer living in the Paris Opera House tunnels, who is obsessed by a young soprano (Mary Philbin). Despite outdated acting techniques and staging, this is a must-see for all cinema buffs, as make-up genius Lon Chaney's Phantom is a Hall of Horror landmark. New prints restore the famous experimental two-colour section, including the awesome "Masque of the Red Death" sequence. AJ DVD BD

Lon Chaney *Erik/The Phantom* • Mary Philbin *Christine Daae* • Norman Kerry *Raoul de Chagny* • Gibson Gowland *Simon* • Snitz Edwards *Florine Papillon* • George B Williams *Monsieur Ricard* • Bruce Covington *Monsieur Moncharmin* ■ *Dir* Rupert Julian • *Scr* Raymond Schrock, Elliott J Clawson, Tom Reed, Frank M McCormack, from the novel *Le Fantôme de l'Opéra* by Gaston Leroux

Phantom of the Opera ★★ PG

Horror 1943 · US · Colour · 88min

Claude Rains plays the Phantom in this remake of the lavish silent film of 1925 that starred Lon Chaney. However, those expecting a horror movie will be disappointed from the outset when Nelson Eddy's name appears in the opening credits. Rains wears the mask and suffers as Eddy and his co-star Susanna Foster sing *Lullaby of the Bells*. Director Arthur Lubin's film won Oscars for its cinematography and art direction, with nominations for its score and sound. AT DVD BD

Nelson Eddy *Anatole Garron* • Susanna Foster *Christine Dubois* • Claude Rains *Enrique Claudin* • Edgar Barrier *Inspector Raoul de Chagny* • Leo Carrillo *Signor Feretti* • Jane Farrar *Biancarolli* ■ *Dir* Arthur Lubin • *Scr* Eric Taylor, Samuel Hoffenstein, from the novel *Le Fantôme de l'Opéra* by Gaston Leroux, adapted by John Jacoby • *Cinematographers* Hal Mohr, W Howard Greene • *Art Directors* Alexander Golitzen, John B Goodman

The Phantom of the Opera ★★★ PG

Horror 1962 · UK · Colour · 80min

Hammer's film of Gaston Leroux's perennially popular story was treated with polite disdain in 1962, when it was released as one half of a double bill. It still appears a minor contribution to the *Phantom* cycle, and a pale shadow of the 1925 Lon Chaney version. The main problem is the casting, with perfectly competent actors playing at too low a key for the operatic passions. Hammer relocated the action from Paris to London and went to town on the art direction, particularly for the subterranean lair – the film's most impressive aspect. DM DVD BD

Herbert Lom *The Phantom* • Heather Sears *Christine Charles* • Thorley Walters *Lattimer* • Michael Gough *Lord Ambrose D'Arcy* • Edward De Souza *Harry Hunter* • Martin Miller *Rossi* ■ *Dir* Terence Fisher • *Scr* Anthony Hinds, from the novel *Le Fantôme de l'Opéra* by Gaston Leroux

The Phantom of the Opera ★ 18

Horror 1989 · US · Colour · 88min

This version of Gaston Leroux's timeless classic finds Robert Englund doing his Freddy Krueger routine and the story reduced to "composer by day, serial killer by night" basics. Coming on strong like a bad British sex farce crossed with junk Hammer horror, the look is heavily gothic, the acting is hilariously mannered and the gore is shakily pizzicato (with the emphasis on the pits). AJ

Robert Englund *Erik Destler, the Phantom* • Jill Schoelen *Christine* • Alex Hyde-White *Richard* • Bill Nighy *Barton* • Stephanie Lawrence *Carlotta* • Peter Clapham *Harrison* • Terence Harvey *Hawking* ■ *Dir* Dwight H Little • *Scr* Duke Sandefur, Gerry O'Hara, from the novel *Le Fantôme de l'Opéra* by Gaston Leroux

The Phantom of the Opera ★★★ 18

Horror 1998 · It · Colour · 99min

Italian horror maestro Dario Argento's postmodern version of the classic Gaston Leroux tale is a typically gory, scary and spectacular *Grand Guignol* epic brimming with his trademark rich visual poetry. Rather than the deformed masked composer of old, however, Julian Sands's telepathic Phantom is a handsome orphan raised by sewer rats who resorts to gruesome murder to put ingénue soprano Christine Daae (a touching performance from Asia Argento) centre stage at the Paris Opera House. Although Sands is weak as the obsessed fiend, Argento takes his enigmatic story down refreshingly different dark alleyways. AJ DVD

Julian Sands *The Phantom* • Asia Argento *Christine Daae* • Andrea Di Stefano *Raoul de Chagny* • Nadia Rinaldi *Carlotta* ■ *Dir* Dario Argento • *Scr* Dario Argento, Gérard Brach

The Phantom of the Opera ★★★ 12

Musical romantic drama
2004 · US/UK · Colour · 135min

Director Joel Schumacher's big-screen take on Andrew Lloyd Webber's hit stage musical is sumptuous to look at and lavishly produced, but suffers from being too faithful, and therefore too flat, an adaptation. An overfamiliarity with the story (disfigured sewer dweller falls for ingénue diva) doesn't help, nor do the colourless leads, but at least Minnie Driver has a laugh as demanding Italian prima donna Carlotta. However, the power and theatrical romance of the show often shines thrillingly through. AJ DVD BD

Gerard Butler *The Phantom* • Emmy Rossum *Christine* • Patrick Wilson *Vicompte Raoul de Chagny* • Miranda Richardson *Madame Giry* • Minnie Driver *Carlotta* • Ciaran Hinds *Richard Firmin* • Simon Callow *Gilles Andre* • Victor McGuire *Piangi* • Jennifer Ellison *Meg Giry* ■ *Dir* Joel Schumacher • *Scr* Joel Schumacher, Andrew Lloyd Webber, from the musical by Andrew Lloyd Webber, from the novel *Le Fantôme de l'Opéra* by Gaston Leroux

Phantom of the Paradise ★★★★ 15

Satirical rock opera 1974 · US · Colour · 87min

Arguably the best musical comedy fantasy on film after *The Rocky Horror Picture Show*, Brian De Palma's funky retelling of the Faust legend via *The Phantom of the Opera* is a savvy satire on the rock industry, delivering plenty of diabolical chills in the process. Paul Williams may be hard to take as the eternally youthful impresario who lusts after Jessica Harper, but Gerrit Graham is superb as the effeminate glam-rocker Beef. This being a De Palma film, the Hitchcock references are in abundance, including the wittiest *Psycho* shower scene send-up ever. AJ Violence, swearing. DVD BD

Paul Williams *Swan* • William Finley *Winslow Leach* • Jessica Harper *Phoenix* • George Memmoli *Philbin* • Gerrit Graham *Beef* ■ *Dir* Brian De Palma • *Scr* Brian De Palma

The Phantom President ★★ U

Musical comedy 1932 · US · BW · 77min

George M Cohan is one of the great legends of American showbusiness. A playwright, screenwriter, stage actor, songwriter, singer and dancer who was worshipped by Broadway and radio audiences, and famously portrayed by James Cagney in *Yankee Doodle Dandy*. Here Cohan plays a singing medicine quack commandeered to impersonate and undermine a presidential candidate. The result was a box office disaster, though it does offer a rare and valuable opportunity to see the legend in action. RK

George M Cohan *Theodore K Blair/Peter "Doc" Varney* • Claudette Colbert *Felicia Hammond* • Jimmy Durante *Curly Cooney* • George Barbier *Jim Ronkton* • Sidney Toler *Prof Aikenhead* • Louise Mackintosh *Sen Sarah Scranton* ■ *Dir* Norman Taurog • *Scr* Walter DeLeon, Harlan Thompson, from the novel by George F Worts • *Music/lyrics* Richard Rodgers, Lorenz Hart, George M Cohan

Phantom Raiders ★★★

Detective drama 1940 · US · BW · 70min

The second of three films (after 1939's *Nick Carter, Master Detective*) made by MGM featuring the private detective created in 1886. All three were updated, given the studio polish that disguised their B-status, and fast-paced enough to overcome fanciful storylines. In this adventure, Walter Pidgeon investigates sabotage in the Panama Canal, and Jacques Tourneur directs efficiently. *Sky Murder*, also 1940, completed the series. TV

Walter Pidgeon *Nick Carter* • Donald Meek *Bartholomew* • Joseph Schildkraut *Al Taurez* • Florence Rice *Cora Barnes* • Nat Pendleton *"Gunboat" Jacklin* • John Carroll *John Ramsell Jr* • Steffi Duna *Dolores* • Cecil Kellaway *Franklin Morris* ■ *Dir* Jacques Tourneur • *Scr* William R Lipman, from a story by Jonathan Latimer

The Phantom Tollbooth ★★★★ U

Part-animated fantasy
1969 · US · Colour · 85min

This is what happens when Bugs Bunny and Daffy Duck let Chuck Jones, their favourite artist, out on his own: he becomes a bit solemn and preachy. By and large an animated story, this has a live start and finish, but in between Jones animates the adventures of a bored boy who passes through a magic tollbooth into a wondrous land where he has to rescue Rhyme and Reason from Ignorance Demons. It's likely to be a bit above the heads of very young children. The rest should enjoy it, especially listening to the superb Mel Blanc, Toonville's greatest ever voice. TH

Butch Patrick *Milo* • Mel Blanc ■ *Dir* Chuck Jones, Abe Levitow, David Monahan • *Scr* Chuck Jones, Sam Rosen, from the book by Norton Juster

Phantoms ★★ 15

Horror 1998 · US · Colour · 92min

In a curiously clunky mix of sci-fi and horror, Rose McGowan and Joanna Going play sisters who return to their isolated home town and discover that virtually everyone has vanished. Ben Affleck is the puzzled local cop, while Peter O'Toole hams it up as a dotty scientist who holds the key to the mystery. However, despite a script from horror maestro Dean R Koontz (adapting his own novel), this fails in the fright department, with too much talk and not enough gore. JF Violence, swearing. DVD

Peter O'Toole *Timothy Flyte* • Joanna Going *Dr Jennifer Pailey* • Rose McGowan *Lisa Pailey* • Ben Affleck *Sheriff Bryce Hammond* • Liev Schreiber *Deputy Stu Wargle* • Clifton Powell *General Leland Copperfield* • Nicky Katt *Deputy Steve Shanning* • Michael DeLorenzo *Soldier Velazquez* • Rick Otto *Scientist Lockland* ■ *Dir* Joe Chappelle • *Scr* Dean R Koontz, from his novel

Phar Lap ★★★★ PG

Drama 1983 · Aus · Colour · 102min

This thoroughbred drama tells the story of the Australian horse that dominated world racing during the 1920s and early 1930s. The film follows the horse's career, up to and including its mysterious death in 1932. En route, it also takes a behind-the-scenes look at the cruel practices then prevalent in racehorse training. Impeccably staged and nicely acted, it survives the sort of turn-off title that could have brought it down within the first furlong. DA

Tom Burlinson *Tommy Woodcock* • Martin Vaughan *Harry Telford* • Judy Morris *Bea Davis* • Celia De Burgh *Vi Telford* • Ron Leibman *Dave Davis* • Vincent Ball *Lachlan McKinnon* ■ *Dir* Simon Wincer • *Scr* David Williamson

Phase IV ★★ PG

Science-fiction thriller
1973 · UK/US · Colour · 79min

This messy eco-upheaval picture was the first feature directed by title sequence maestro Saul Bass, whose work is notable for its animation and stylised use of colour and caption. Here, he fails to conjure up any sense of suspense. The special effects don't improve matters much, nor do the lacklustre performances of Nigel Davenport and Michael Murphy as scientists who discover that a desert ant colony is preparing to take over the planet. DP DVD

Nigel Davenport *Ernest Hubbs* • Michael Murphy *(1) James Lesko* • Lynne Frederick *Kendra* • Alan Gifford *Eldridge* • Robert Henderson *Clete* • Helen Horton *Mrs Eldridge* ■ *Dir* Saul Bass • *Scr* Mayo Simon

P

The Phenix City Story ★★★
Crime drama   1955 · US · BW · 86min

Sensational in its day, this exposé of vice and corruption in an Alabama town was filmed in the wake of the infamous Senator Estes Kefauver investigations into crime across the United States, and expertly directed by Phil Karlson. Co-star Richard Kiley embodies moral uprightness as the returning lawyer, who finds his life dramatically changed by encroaching home-town vice. The movie is brutally unsparing in its depiction of corruption, and the sense of realism is heightened by a non-stellar cast. **TS**

John McIntire *Albert Patterson* • Richard Kiley *John Patterson* • Kathryn Grant *Ellie Rhodes* • Edward Andrews *Rhett Tanner* • Lenka Peterson *Mary Jo Patterson* • Biff McGuire *Fred Gage* • Truman Smith *Ed Gage* ■ *Dir* Phil Karlson • *Scr* Crane Wilbur, Daniel Mainwaring

Phenomenon ★★★ PG
Fantasy drama   1996 · US · Colour · 118min

A strange light in the sky gives small-town mechanic John Travolta paranormal powers in director John Turteltaub's feel-good sci-fi fable. As scientists attempt to evaluate his sudden escalation to genius, Travolta battles against an obvious script to focus all his energies on wooing divorced single mother Kyra Sedgwick. Hidden among the waves of sentiment are some genuinely funny moments, but, for all its well-meaning tear-jerking, this tribute to human potential is less than phenomenal. **AJ** DVD

John Travolta *George Malley* • Kyra Sedgwick *Lace Pennamin* • Forest Whitaker *Nate Pope* • Robert Duvall *Doc* • David Gallagher *Al* • Ashley Buccille *Glory* • Tony Genaro *Tito* ■ *Dir* Jon Turteltaub • *Scr* Gerald DiPego

Phffft! ★★★
Comedy   1954 · US · BW · 88min

This started as an unproduced play by George Axelrod, rewritten for the movies and specifically for Judy Holliday, who was so good as the dumb blonde in *Born Yesterday*. Like *The Seven Year Itch*, it's a comedy of sexual angst, with Holliday divorcing Jack Lemmon and relishing her freedom. She moves in with grouchy bachelor Jack Carson thereby inspiring *The Odd Couple* and starts to canoodle with Kim Novak. It's all very 1950s, stagey and not particularly funny now, though Holliday was one of a kind and is always a pleasure to watch. **AT**

Judy Holliday *Nina Tracy* • Jack Lemmon *Robert Tracy* • Jack Carson *Charlie Nelson* • Kim Novak *Janis* • Luella Gear *Mrs Chapman* • Donald Randolph *Dr Van Kessel* • Donald Curtis *Rick Vidal* ■ *Dir* Mark Robson • *Scr* George Axelrod

Phil Spector ★★★★
Drama based on a true story   2013 · US · Colour · 92min

Basing a film on a cause célèbre murder trial is always going to be tricky and this superb drama from David Mamet caused a furore on its release in the US. Ostensibly about the attempts by Phil Spector's legal team to build a defence case for his trial, at its heart is the growing relationship between Spector (Al Pacino) and his lawyer (Helen Mirren). Mamet's dialogue crackles with wit, while Pacino's spooky resemblance to Spector is all grandiloquence and paranoia in a fright wig. It's got a great soundtrack, too. **DC**

Al Pacino *Phil Spector* • Helen Mirren *Linda Kenney Baden* • Jeffrey Tambor *Bruce Cutler* • Chiwetel Ejiofor *Mock prosecutor* • Rebecca Pidgeon *Dr Fallon* • John Pirruccello *Nick Stavros* ■ *Dir/Scr* David Mamet

Philadelphia ★★★★★ 12
Drama   1993 · US · Colour · 120min

This was the first major Hollywood movie about Aids, and it won Tom Hanks his first best actor Oscar. Hanks plays a gay lawyer who takes his employers to court for sacking him. The company bigwigs claim he was dismissed for incompetence, but Hanks suspects the real reason is his Aids-related illness. His counsel is Denzel Washington, who despises homosexuals but worships fair play, while company boss Jason Robards is a bigot whose intolerance is hidden by bluff camaraderie. Hanks portrays the ravaged, dying lawyer as a disabled everyman whose life has lessons for all of us. His passionate praise for opera is a tour de force of close-up acting. **TH** Swearing. DVD

Tom Hanks *Andrew Beckett* • Denzel Washington *Joe Miller* • Jason Robards *Charles Wheeler* • Mary Steenburgen *Belinda Conine* • Antonio Banderas *Miguel Alvarez* • Ron Vawter *Bob Seidman* • Robert Ridgely *Walter Kenton* • Charles Napier *Judge Garnett* • Lisa Summerour *Lisa Miller* • Joanne Woodward *Sarah Beckett* ■ *Dir* Jonathan Demme • *Scr* Ron Nyswaner

The Philadelphia Experiment ★★★ PG
Science-fiction adventure   1984 · US · Colour · 101min

Michael Paré and Bobby DiCicco play a couple of American sailors from 1943 who are yanked into 1984 when an experiment to render ships invisible to radar backfires. They team up with gung ho Nancy Allen in a bid to get home. The cast delivers their lines with deadpan élan in this enjoyably intriguing slice of sci-fi hokum. The project had been kicking around Hollywood since the late 1970s; by the time it got rolling, Stewart Raffill had replaced original director John Carpenter, who installed himself as executive producer. A belated and decidedly inferior sequel appeared in 1993 starring Brad Johnson. **RS** Some violence DVD

Michael Paré *David Herdeg* • Nancy Allen *Allison Hayes* • Eric Christmas *Dr James Longstreet* • Bobby DiCicco *Jim Parker* • Kene Holliday *Major Clark* • Joe Dorsey *Sheriff Bates* ■ *Dir* Stewart Raffill • *Scr* William Gray, Michael Janover, from a story by Don Jakoby, Wallace Bennett, from the book by William I Moore, Charles Berlitz

The Philadelphia Story ★★★★★ U
Classic romantic comedy   1940 · US · BW · 107min

Fans of the musical remake *High Society* who haven't seen this classic, all-talking, no-dancing original might wish to remedy that. In order to reverse her reputation as "box-office poison" Katharine Hepburn shrewdly bought the rights to the Broadway play (written for her by Philip Barry) in which she had been a hit. With old pal George Cukor as director and a hand-picked cast, this film was a success. In it, her society girl is engaged to John Howard's executive dullard; her ex-husband Cary Grant turns up with information about an imminent press scandal, while a rival publication's reporter (James Stewart) finds his class-war cynicism melting away as he falls for Hepburn. There's more to it than that, but this is romantic comedy at its most sublime. **AC** DVD

Cary Grant *CK Dexter Haven* • Katharine Hepburn *Tracy Samantha Lord* • James Stewart *Macaulay "Mike" Connor* • Ruth Hussey *Elizabeth Imbrie* • John Howard (1) *George Kittredge* • Roland Young *Uncle Willie* • John Halliday *Seth Lord* • Mary Nash *Margaret Lord* • Virginia Weidler *Dinah Lord* • Henry Daniell *Sidney Kidd* ■ *Dir* George Cukor • *Scr* Donald Ogden Stewart, from the play by Philip Barry

Philomena ★★★★ 12
Drama based on a true story   2013 · US/UK/Fr · Colour · 97min

Judi Dench is on sparkling form as the Irishwoman whose child was snatched away by nuns at a time when giving birth out of wedlock was treated as a criminal act. Decades later, journalist Martin Sixsmith represents Philomena's only hope of finding her son (the film is based on his 2009 book). Steve Coogan is suitably irascible as the former BBC correspondent, initially turning his nose up at the idea of pursuing a "human interest story". Director Stephen Frears exploits the odd-couple dynamic to great effect, generating wonderful comic moments amid the tragedy of Philomena's life. You'll laugh and you'll cry, sometimes both at the same time. **SP** Strong language, sexual references. DVD

Judi Dench *Philomena Lee* • Steve Coogan *Martin Sixsmith* • Michelle Fairley *Sally Mitchell* • Barbara Jefford *Sister Hildegarde* • Anna Maxwell Martin *Jane* • Mare Winningham *Mary* • Simone Lahbib *Kate Sixsmith* ■ *Dir* Stephen Frears • *Scr* Steve Coogan, Jeff Pope, from the non-fiction book *The Lost Child of Philomena Lee* by Martin Sixsmith

Phobia ★ 15
Murder mystery   1980 · Can · Colour · 86min

Paul Michael Glaser plays an unorthodox doctor who treats patients suffering from various phobias in eccentric ways. Soon, his patients start getting killed one by one in manners related to their individual phobias. The story is so poor, most viewers will be able to figure out who the killer is even before the first murder occurs. Shoddy. **KB**

Paul Michael Glaser *Dr Peter Ross* • Susan Hogan *Jenny St Clair* • John Colicos *Inspector Barnes* • Alexandra Stewart *Barbara Grey* • Robert O'Ree *Bubba King* • David Bolt *Henry Owen* • David Eisner *Johnny Venuti* • Lisa Langlois *Laura Adams* ■ *Dir* John Huston • *Scr* Lew Lehman, Jimmy Sangster, Peter Bellwood, from a story by Gary Sherman, Ronald Shusett

Phoenix ★★★ 15
Crime thriller   1998 · US · Colour · 102min

Though it's obviously influenced by *Pulp Fiction*, this absorbing crime drama manages to do quite a lot on its own. Ray Liotta gives a commendable performance as a cop addicted to gambling who gets involved in a "foolproof" plan to rob a local loan shark. Liotta's self-destructive behaviour is repulsive yet riveting, especially when interacting with a number of other well-developed characters. **KB** DVD

Ray Liotta *Harry Collins* • Anjelica Huston *Leila* • Anthony LaPaglia *Mike Henshaw* • Daniel Baldwin *James Nutter* • Jeremy Piven *Fred Shuster* • Tom Noonan *Chicago* ■ *Dir* Danny Cannon • *Scr* Eddie Richey

Phoenix ★★★ 12A
Drama   2014 · Ger/Pol · Colour · 98min

Postwar Germany is the setting for a tale of denial and betrayal in this melancholy Holocaust drama originally filmed in 1965 as *Return from the Ashes* with Maximilian Schell and Ingrid Thulin. At the centre of director Christian Petzold's adaptation isNina Hoss as a concentration camp survivor who decides to track down her husband after having facial reconstruction surgery. The plot plays out in a way that is restrained and understated to a fault, with Hoss quietly devastating and there are one or two affecting moments. **SC** German, English +subtitles. Brief swearing. DVD

Nina Hoss *Nelly Lenz* • Ronald Zehrfeld *Johannes Lenz, "Johnny"* • Nina Kunzendorf *Lene Winter* ■ *Dir* Christian Petzold • *Scr* Christian Petzold, Harun Farocki, from the novel *Le Retour des Cendres* by Hubert Monteilhet

Phone ★★★ 15
Horror   2002 · S Kor · Colour · 102min

Those who view the mobile phone as one of the evils of modern life will warm to Ahn Byeong-ki's eerie tale of the journalist whose handset brings her into contact with the malevolent spirit of a dead schoolgirl. Ha Ji-won is suitably spooked by the spate of menacing text messages, but it's Eun Seo-woo who steals the show as the young daughter of a friend who becomes possessed. The influence of *Ring* and *The Exorcist* is a little too apparent, but Ahn still springs a surprise or two. **DP** Korean +subtitles. DVD

Ha Ji-won *Ji-won* • Kim Yu-mi *Ho-jung* • Choi Woo-jae *Chang-hoon* • Choi Ji-yeon *Jin-hie* • Eun Seo-woo *Young-ju* ■ *Dir/Scr* Ahn Byeong-ki

Phone Booth ★★★ 15
Thriller   2002 · US · Colour · 77min

This lean, innovative thriller has a compelling premise, but is too gimmicky to maintain its grip until the end. Colin Farrell plays an arrogant publicist who is trapped in a New York phone booth by an unseen sniper, apparently as retribution for attempting to start an affair with a client (Katie Holmes). The psychological warfare waged on Farrell by "The Caller" – voiced with malevolence by Kiefer Sutherland – carries a suspenseful charge. **JC** Violence, swearing. DVD

Colin Farrell (2) *Stu Shepard* • Kiefer Sutherland *The caller* • Forest Whitaker *Captain Ramey* • Radha Mitchell *Kelly Shepard* • Katie Holmes *Pamela McFadden* • Richard T Jones *Sgt Cole* • Keith Nobbs *Adam* ■ *Dir* Joel Schumacher • *Scr* Larry Cohen

Phone Call from a Stranger ★★★ U
Portmanteau drama   1952 · US · BW · 95min

Portmanteau movies were a fashion in the late 1940s and early 1950s, and this is an excellent example of such multi-chaptered works. A survivor from a plane crash calls the families of the three people with whom he became close on the flight. It's television fodder today, perhaps, but, in the hands of a grade-A 20th Century-Fox team, this is a fine, gripping drama, well acted by Gary Merrill and, especially, Keenan Wynn as the husband of a bedridden Bette Davis, on screen all too briefly. **TS**

Shelley Winters *Binky Gay* • Gary Merrill *David Trask* • Michael Rennie *Dr Fortness* • Keenan Wynn *Eddie Hoke* • Evelyn Varden *Sally Carr* • Warren Stevens *Marty Nelson* • Bette Davis *Marie Hoke* ■ *Dir* Jean Negulesco • *Scr* Nunnally Johnson, from the story by IAR Wylie

Photographing Fairies ★★★ 15
Fantasy drama   1997 · UK · Colour · 101min

Made at the same time as *FairyTale: a True Story* and inspired by the same report of two little girls who took photos of fairies at the bottom of their garden, Nick Willing's film stars Toby Stephens as a professional debunker of photographic forgeries who stumbles upon a genuine supernatural phenomenon. Convinced that the pixies caught on camera by two young sisters will allow him to contact his dead wife, Stephens's investigation brings him into conflict with local pastor Ben Kingsley. Imaginatively shot, Willing's fantasy drama is also rather dour and downbeat. **JF** DVD

Toby Stephens *Charles Castle* • Emily Woof *Linda* • Ben Kingsley *Reverend Templeton* • Frances Barber *Beatrice Templeton* • Phil Davis [Philip Davis] *Roy* • Edward Hardwicke *Sir Arthur Conan Doyle* ■ *Dir* Nick Willing • *Scr* Chris Harrald, Nick Willing, from the book by Steve Szilagyi

Physical Evidence ★★ 15
Thriller   1988 · US · Colour · 95min

Jurassic Park's Michael Crichton directs, in dinosaur-lumbering fashion, this tough courtroom drama in which ex-cop Burt Reynolds is defended by Theresa Russell for a murder he says he didn't commit. Russell's ability to suggest obsession never matches up to her fatal attractiveness, but Reynolds manages a depressive attitude with real effectiveness. It never works up much tension, but it has its moments. **TH** Violence, swearing.

Burt Reynolds *Joe Paris* • Theresa Russell *Jenny Hudson* • Ned Beatty *James Nicks* • Kay Lenz *Deborah Quinn* • Ted McGinley *Kyle* • Tom O'Brien *Matt Farley* • Kenneth Welsh *Harry Norton* ■ *Dir* Michael Crichton • *Scr* Bill Phillips, from a story by Steve Ransohoff, Bill Phillips

Pi ★★★ 15
Psychological science-fiction thriller   1997 · US · BW · 80min

In this original, fascinating thriller, Sean Gullette stars as a reclusive maths genius who becomes obsessed with the notion that everything in the universe can be broken down into mathematics and therefore follows a predictable pattern. This acclaimed feature debut from Darren Aronofsky is filled with complex issues and makes arresting use of disorientating camerawork to depict Gullette's distorted view of the world. **JC** Swearing, violence. DVD

Sean Gullette *Maximillian Cohen* • Mark Margolis *Sol Robeson* • Ben Shenkman *Lenny Meyer* • Pamela Hart (2) *Marcy Dawson* • Stephen Pearlman *Rabbi Cohen* • Samia Shoaib *Devi* ■ *Dir* Darren Aronofsky • *Scr* Darren Aronofsky, from a story by Sean Gullette, Eric Watson, Darren Aronofsky • *Cinematographer* Matthew Libatique

The Pianist ★★★★ 15

Second World War biographical drama
2002 · Fr/Pol/Ger/UK · Colour · 142min

Evoking his own childhood experiences in the Krakow ghetto, Roman Polanski laid some personal ghosts to rest with this poignant Holocaust drama based on the memoirs of survivor Wladyslaw Szpilman, and won an Oscar as best director in the process. Events are seen through the eyes of Szpilman (Adrien Brody), a Jewish concert pianist who escaped the Warsaw Ghetto as deportations to the death camps began, but witnessed its systematic destruction while in hiding. Although Brody never quite gets under Szpilman's skin, his performance remains admirable. By avoiding the simplistic and manipulative clichés of many Holocaust films, Polanski adds a new layer of understanding to the cinematic depictions of the period. SF Violence, swearing. *DVD* *Blu*

Adrien Brody *Wladyslaw Szpilman* • Thomas Kretschmann *Captain Wilm Hosenfeld* • Frank Finlay *Mr Szpilman* • Maureen Lipman *Mrs Szpilman* • Emilia Fox *Dorota* • Ed Stoppard *Henryk Szpilman* • Julia Rayner *Regina Szpilman* • Jessica Kate Meyer *Halina Szpilman* • Ruth Platt *Janina* ■ *Dir* Roman Polanski • *Scr* Ronald Harwood, from the non-fiction book *Death of a City* by Wladyslaw Szpilman

The Piano ★★★★★ 15

Period drama
1993 · Aus · Colour · 120min

Director Jane Campion's superbly staged tale of passion and obsession won her an Oscar for best screenplay. Holly Hunter, who chose to stop speaking at the age of six, communicates through her daughter Anna Paquin, and her piano, which she brings with her to New Zealand when she is sent to marry local landowner Sam Neill. Hunter's new husband can read her hurriedly written notes, but he does not appreciate her music and won't take the trouble to learn either her sign language or the local Maori dialect. The illiterate Harvey Keitel, on the other hand, has fully embraced the customs of his adopted home and, belying his uncouth outward appearance, proves to be much more tender and passionate. There's a masterly score by Michael Nyman and splendid photography from Stuart Dryburgh, and Campion coaxes stupendous performances from Hunter and Paquin, who both won Oscars. DP English, Maori +subtitles. Violence, nudity. *DVD* *Blu*

Holly Hunter *Ada* • Harvey Keitel *Baines* • Sam Neill *Stewart* • Anna Paquin *Flora* • Kerry Walker *Aunt Morag* • Geneviève Lemon *Nessie* • Tungia Baker *Hira* • Ian Mune *Reverend* ■ *Dir/Scr* Jane Campion

A Piano for Mrs Cimino ★★★

Drama
1982 · US · Colour · 100min

This TV movie provided the 74-year-old Bette Davis with another opportunity to demonstrate her vitality and her appetite for scene-stealing. It's hardly a subtle performance, but the story of a widow battling to overturn a court ruling that she's mentally incompetent has a definite feel-good factor. This may be shameless melodrama, but it's also polished, knowingly played and involving. DP

Bette Davis *Esther Cimino* • Penny Fuller *Mrs Polanski* • Alexa Kenin *Karen Cimino* • George Hearn *George Cimino* • Christopher Guest *Philip Ryan* • Keenan Wynn *Barney Fellman* • Leroy Schulz *Harold Cimino* ■ *Dir* George Schaefer • *Scr* John Gay, from the novel by Robert Oliphant

The Piano Teacher ★★★ 18

Drama 2001 · Austria/Fr/Ger · Colour · 125min

Isabelle Huppert plays the middle-aged tutor who lives at home with a possessive mother in spite of her morbid interest in voyeurism and pornography. No surprise then that the relationship she starts with talented but wayward student Benoît Magimel is a dark and disturbing one. Yet, for all its thematic fidelity, Michael Haneke's often overwrought melodrama falters because of the increasing implausibility of the plot and the problems the two leads have with conveying their anguish. DP French +subtitles. *DVD*

Isabelle Huppert *Erika Kohut* • Annie Girardot *Mother* • Benoît Magimel *Walter Klemmer* • Susanne Lothar *Mrs Schober* • Udo Samel *Dr Blonskij* • Anna Sigalevitch *Anna Schober* ■ *Dir* Michael Haneke • *Scr* Michael Haneke, from the novel *Die Klavierspielerin* by Elfriede Jelinek

The Picasso Summer ★★

Surreal drama 1969 · US · Colour · 94min

Astonishingly based on a short story by the great science-fiction writer Ray Bradbury, this is an account of a young couple (Albert Finney and Yvette Mimieux) so addicted to Picasso's works that they wander through France in the hope of meeting him. Sadly for us, it's more of a dutiful trudge than a pleasurable ramble, though the animated sequence is worth staying awake for. TH

Albert Finney *George Smith* • Yvette Mimieux *Alice Smith* • Luis Miguel Dominguin • Theo Marcuse *The Host* • Jim Connell *The Artist* ■ *Dir* Serge Bourguignon, Robert Sallin • *Scr* Douglas Spaulding [Ray Bradbury], Edwin Boyd, from the short story by Ray Bradbury

Piccadilly ★★ PG

Crime melodrama 1929 · UK · BW · 113min

Directed by EA Dupont as a British silent, with sound added the following year, this crime melodrama, atmospherically designed by Alfred Junge, was much admired in its day as a stylish piece of work. Now, though, its old-fashioned acting is more likely to cause giggles. The plot has a nightclub owner (Jameson Thomas) fomenting rivalry between his fiancée (Gilda Gray) and his Chinese mistress (Anna May Wong). When the mistress is murdered, the fiancée is accused. Charles Laughton appears in the supporting cast, as does one Raymond (later Ray) Milland. RK *DVD*

Gilda Gray *Mabel Greenfield* • Jameson Thomas *Valentine Wilmot* • Anna May Wong *Shosho* • King Ho Chang *Jim* • Cyril Ritchard *Victor Smiles* • Hannah Jones *Bessie* • Charles Laughton *Greedy nightclub diner* • Raymond Milland [Ray Milland] ■ *Dir* EA Dupont • *Scr* Arnold Bennett

Piccadilly Incident ★★

Second World War melodrama
1946 · UK · BW · 102min

Anna Neagle and Michael Wilding co-star in this British tale about a Wren and a Royal Marine who meet during an air raid, fall in love and marry, only for her to go missing, presumed dead, after the fall of Singapore. Producer/director Herbert Wilcox teamed his wife Neagle with Wilding for the first time in this emotional drama of love, war and noble sacrifice. Old-fashioned, occasionally laboured and heavily sentimental. RK

Anna Neagle *Diana Fraser* • Michael Wilding *Capt Alan Pearson* • Michael Laurence (1) *Bill Weston* • Frances Mercer *Joan Draper* • Coral Browne *Virginia Pearson* • Reginald Owen *Judge* • Roger Moore ■ *Dir* Herbert Wilcox • *Scr* Nicholas Phipps, from a story by Florence Tranter

Piccadilly Jim ★★★ U

Comedy 1936 · US · BW · 95min

PG Wodehouse's story, previously filmed in 1920, glides through London's clubland and has an American cartoonist, Robert Montgomery, as its hero. The main plot has Montgomery converting the life of his sweetheart's family into a cartoon strip but it's the gallery of secondary characters and MGM's idea of what London Town is like that makes this creaky picture still watchable. Eric Blore plays an English butler to perfection. AT

Robert Montgomery *Jim Crocker/Jim Bayliss* • Frank Morgan *Mr James Crocker/Count Olav Osrio* • Madge Evans *Ann Chester* • Eric Blore *Bayliss* • Billie Burke *Eugenia Willis* • Robert Benchley *Bill Macon* • Ralph Forbes *Lord Freddie Priory* • Cora Witherspoon *Nesta Pett* ■

Dir Robert Z Leonard • *Scr* Charles Brackett, Edwin Knopf, Lynn Starling, Samuel Hoffenstein, from the novel *Piccadilly Jim* by PG Wodehouse as serialised in *The Saturday Evening Post*

Piccadilly Jim ★★ 12

Period romantic comedy
2004 · UK · Colour · 90min

PG Wodehouse's novel gets a third feature film outing in this frivolous but scattershot period farce, adapted by *Gosford Park* screenwriter Julian Fellowes. A tale of class snobbery, one-upmanship and deceit, it stars Sam Rockwell as a 1930s playboy who assumes a virtuous fake identity to impress his dream girl (Frances O'Connor). The ping-pong theatrics that follow are uneven in tone and gratingly overplayed, flattening the occasionally witty banter. Even the visuals lack focus, rendered additionally tedious by deliberately anachronistic styling. SF *DVD*

Sam Rockwell *James Crocker* • Tom Wilkinson *Mr Crocker* • Frances O'Connor *Anne* • Brenda Blethyn *Aunt Nesta* • Hugh Bonneville • Allison Janney *Mrs Crocker* ■ *Dir* John McKay • *Scr* Julian Fellowes, from the novel by PG Wodehouse

Piccadilly Third Stop ★

Crime thriller 1960 · UK · BW · 90min

This is a plodding low-budget thriller, with Terence Morgan playing a London lowlife who dates ambassador's daughter Yoko Tani in order to gain access to the embassy safe. Dennis Price, William Hartnell and Mai Zetterling are among those who obviously needed the work. DP

Terence Morgan *Dominic Colpoys-Owen* • Yoko Tani *Seraphina Yokami* • John Crawford *Joe Pready* • Mai Zetterling *Christine Pready* • William Hartnell *Colonel* • Dennis Price *Edward* ■ *Dir* Wolf Rilla • *Scr* Leigh Vance

Pick a Star ★ U

Musical comedy 1937 · US · BW · 66min

Innocent young hopeful Rosina Lawrence arrives in Hollywood hoping for stardom and, after some disillusion, gets a screen test thanks to Jack Haley. This thoroughly feeble movie was misleadingly presented as a Laurel and Hardy comedy – they appear in only a couple of brief sequences that make for the brightest spots. RK

Patsy Kelly *Nellie Moore* • Jack Haley *Joe Jenkins* • Rosina Lawrence *Cecilia Moore* • Mischa Auer *Rinaldo Lopez* • Stan Laurel *Stan* • Oliver Hardy *Oliver* ■ *Dir* Edward Sedgwick • *Scr* Richard Flournoy, Arthur Vernon Jones, Thomas J Dugan

The Pick-Up Artist ★ 15

Comedy drama 1987 · US · Colour · 77min

A great cast is stymied by half-baked dialogue and a barely-there plot in cult director James Toback's dating disaster. Serial womaniser Robert Downey Jr puts the make on feisty Molly Ringwald and is amazed when she doesn't respond to his chat-up lines. Wise girl! Downey Jr emits none of his future star charisma. AJ Swearing.

Molly Ringwald *Randy Jensen* • Robert Downey Jr *Jack Jericho* • Dennis Hopper *Flash Jensen* • Danny Aiello *Phil* • Mildred Dunnock *Nellie, Jack's grandmother* • Harvey Keitel *Alonzo* • Brian Hamill *Mike* • Vanessa L Williams *Rae* ■ *Dir/Scr* James Toback

Picking Up the Pieces ★ 15

Black comedy 2000 · US · Colour · 91min

This abysmal religious satire consistently misses the easiest of targets and succeeds only in humiliating a stellar cast. Least besmirched is Woody Allen, as a New Mexico butcher who murders shrewish wife Sharon Stone and dismembers her corpse, only to discover her severed hand is being credited with a series of miracles. So far, so unfunny. But with the arrival of Elliott Gould at the head of a Vatican fact-finding commission, the whole sorry mess spirals into irreverent misanthropy. DP *DVD*

Woody Allen *Tex Cowley* • David Schwimmer *Father Leo Jerome* • Maria Grazia Cucinotta *Desi* • Cheech Marin [Richard "Cheech" Marin] *Mayor Machado* • Kiefer Sutherland *Bobo* • Sharon

---

Stone *Candy Cowley* • Elliott Gould *Father LaCage* • Fran Drescher *Sister Frida* • Lou Diamond Phillips *Officer Alfonso* ■ *Dir* Alfonso Arau • *Scr* Bill Wilson

The Pickle ★ 15

Comedy 1993 · US · Colour · 98min

Danny Aiello plays a film director (whose most recent movie is a sci-fi tale about a giant pickle hence the title) desperately in need of a career boost. Unfortunately, despite an interesting supporting cast, this is virtually unwatchable. It fails to find the appropriate tone and generally misfires on all cylinders. TS

Danny Aiello *Harry Stone* • Dyan Cannon *Ellen Stone* • Clotilde Courau *Françoise* • Shelley Winters *Yetta* • Barry Miller *Ronnie Liebowitz* • Jerry Stiller *Phil Hirsch* • Chris Penn *Gregory Stone* • Little Richard *President* • Griffin Dunne *President's man* • Dudley Moore *Planet Cleveland Man* • Donald Trump ■ *Dir/Scr* Paul Mazursky

Pickpocket ★★★★ PG

Crime drama 1959 · Fr · BW · 72min

A mesmeric sequence in which a young thief learns the tricks of the trade from a master pickpocket is the highlight of Robert Bresson's exceptional study of obsession, desperation and guilt. Inspired by Dostoyevsky's *Crime and Punishment*, the film follows a theme used several times by Bresson as lonely individuals lay bare their souls in the midst of personal torment. Martin Lassalle gives a performance of chilling restraint as the possessed "dip", but it is Bresson's control over his cast, the Parisian locations and the austere imagery that makes this extraordinary film so compelling. DP French +subtitles. *DVD*

Martin Lassalle [Martin Lasalle] *Michel* • Marika Green *Jeanne* • Jean Pélégri *Inspector* • Dolly Scal *Michel's mother* • Pierre Leymarie *Jacques* • Kassagi *Accomplice* • Pierre Etaix *Accomplice* • César Gattegno *Detective* ■ *Scr* Robert Bresson • *Cinematographer* Léonce-Henri Burel

Pickup on South Street ★★★ PG

Film noir 1953 · US · BW · 77min

Director Sam Fuller's gritty *film noir* sees petty thief Richard Widmark pocket more than he bargained for when he steals Jean Peters's purse and finds it contains secret documents. The anti-Communist aspects of the story may not resonate quite so well now but the performances have conviction – notably Thelma Ritter as the acid-drop old lady, betraying all and sundry to save up for "a plot and a stone". TH *DVD* *Blu*

Richard Widmark *Skip McCoy* • Jean Peters *Candy* • Thelma Ritter *Moe* • Murvyn Vye *Captain Dan Tiger* • Richard Kiley *Joey* ■ *Dir* Samuel Fuller • *Scr* Samuel Fuller, from a story by Dwight Taylor

The Pickwick Papers ★★★ U

Period comedy 1952 · UK · BW · 104min

Dickens's sprawling, episodic novel has been reined in by writer/director Noel Langley without sacrificing too much of its jaunty good nature. Brimming over with memorable characters, the film is well served by some solid performances from a strong cast. James Hayter is the embodiment of Pickwick, really hitting his stride during the breach of promise trial. Not all the vignettes come off, but Nigel Patrick is bang on form as the disreputable Mr Jingle, and Kathleen Harrison is ever-excellent. DP

James Hayter *Samuel Pickwick* • James Donald *Mr Winkle* • Alexander Gauge *Mr Tupman* • Lionel Murton *Mr Snodgrass* • Nigel Patrick *Mr Jingle* • Kathleen Harrison *Rachael Wardle* • Joyce Grenfell *Mrs Leo Hunter* • Hermione Gingold *Miss Tomkins* • Donald Wolfit *Sergeant Buzfuz* • Hermione Baddeley *Mrs Bardell* • Hattie Jacques *Mrs Nupkins* ■ *Dir* Noel Langley • *Scr* Noel Langley, from the novel by Charles Dickens

Picnic ★★★ U

Drama 1955 · US · Colour · 108min

Adapted by Daniel Taradash from William Inge's Pulitzer Prize-winning play, and directed for maximum cinematic effect by Joshua Logan, *Picnic* earned six Oscar

---

nominations for its daringly frank depiction (by 1950s standards) of the emotional havoc wrought on the women of a rustic Kansas town when a sexy itinerant wanders in to their Labour Day picnic. William Holden (not ideal for the role, but giving a polished performance) is the attractive cat among the pigeons. Enjoyable drama with an edge. RK 𝗗𝗩𝗗

William Holden (2) *Hal Carter* • Rosalind Russell *Rosemary Sydney* • Betty Field *Flo Owens* • Kim Novak *Madge Owens* • Susan Strasberg *Millie Owens* • Cliff Robertson *Alan* ■ *Dir* Joshua Logan • *Scr* Daniel Taradash, from the play by William Inge

LANDMARK FILM
With this mystical period piece, Peter Weir puts Australian cinema on the map

Picnic at Hanging Rock
★★★★ 🄿🄶

Period psychological mystery
1975 · Aus · Colour · 110min

On St Valentine's Day in 1900 a party of schoolgirls enjoys a day at Hanging Rock, a local beauty spot. But something odd is at work: clocks stop at midday and three girls vanish. Dingo dogs, extraterrestrials, kidnappers or what? Director Peter Weir leaves clues hanging in the air like a glistening spider's web, hears celestial choirs and thrumming insects – he hasn't the foggiest, but he adores ambiguity, mysticism and metaphor. This is a very sexy picture, which stares an enigma straight in the eye. There are fine performances, which, with the outstanding location work, add up to a class act. AT 𝗗𝗩𝗗 🄱🄻🄸

Rachel Roberts (1) *Mrs Appleyard* • Dominic Guard *Michael Fitzhubert* • Helen Morse *Dianne de Poitiers* • Jacki Weaver *Minnie* • Vivean Gray *Miss McCraw* • Kirsty Child *Dora Lumley* • Anne Lambert [Anne Louise Lambert] *Miranda* ■ *Dir* Peter Weir • *Scr* Cliff Green, from the novel by Joan Lindsay • *Cinematographer* Russell Boyd

Picture Bride
★★🄸🄸

Period drama
1994 · US · Colour · 94min

Set in 1918, Kayo Hatta's debut feature recalls the old custom of using photographs to arrange marriages between Japanese workers in Hawaii and girls back home. The action captures a sense of period and place in spite of financial restraint. But there are few fresh insights into loveless marriage or the trials facing women in a patriarchal society, as 16-year-old Youki Kudoh attempts to escape the elderly husband who tricked her into emigrating. DP English, Japanese +subtitles.

Youki Kudoh *Riyo* • Akira Takayama *Matsuji* • Tamlyn Tomita *Kana* • Cary-Hiroyuki Tagawa *Kanzaki* • Toshiro Mifune *The Benshi* • Yoko Sugi *Aunt Sode* ■ *Dir* Kayo Hatta • *Scr* Kayo Hatta, Mari Hatta, Kayo Hatta, Mari Hatta, Diane Mei Lin Mark

The Picture of Dorian Gray
★★★★

Period horror drama
1945 · US · BW and Colour · 109min

This big-budget version of Oscar Wilde's only novel was rather a curious venture for a studio that prided itself on its family entertainment. But flamboyant screenwriter/director Albert Lewin turned in a compelling picture that teeters between sophistication and vulgarity. Hurd Hatfield gives a muted performance as Dorian and is thus easily surpassed by Angela Lansbury, who plays the chirpy music-hall singer with whom he falls in lust, and by George Sanders as the languidly witty Lord Henry Wotton. The picture earned supervising art director Cedric Gibbons one of his record 40 Oscar nominations. DP

George Sanders *Lord Henry Wotton* • Hurd Hatfield *Dorian Gray* • Donna Reed *Gladys Hallward* • Angela Lansbury *Sibyl Vane* • Peter Lawford *David Stone* • Lowell Gilmore *Basil Hallward* • Richard Fraser *James Vane* • Douglas Walton *Allen Campbell* ■ *Dir* Albert Lewin • *Scr* Albert Lewin, from the novel *The Picture of Dorian Gray* by Oscar Wilde • *Cinematographer* Harry Stradling

Picture Perfect
★★★ 🄿🄶

Romantic comedy 1997 · US · Colour · 97min

Glenn Gordon Caron directs Jennifer Aniston in this good-natured romantic comedy. Aniston is the single girl who discovers she needs a boyfriend to succeed at work. So she invents a fiancé using a photo of her with a complete stranger taken at a wedding. Of course, it's not long before her bosses want to meet the man (Jay Mohr), so she has to track him down, complicating the secret affair she's having with a corporate sleaze (a fun performance from Kevin Bacon). Preposterous, but sweetly done. JB Swearing. 𝗗𝗩𝗗

Jennifer Aniston *Kate* • Jay Mohr *Nick* • Kevin Bacon *Sam* • Olympia Dukakis *Rita* • Illeana Douglas *Darcy* • Kevin Dunn *Mr Mercer* • Anne Twomey *Sela* • Faith Prince *Mrs Mercer* ■ *Dir* Glenn Gordon Caron • *Scr* Glenn Gordon Caron, Arleen Sorkin, Paul Slansky, from a story by May Quigley, Arleen Sorkin, Paul Slansky

Picture Snatcher
★★★

Crime drama 1933 · US · BW · 74min

Great title for a terrific James Cagney vehicle from that marvellous period at Warner Bros when pace was everything and dialogue just snapped and crackled its way across the screen. Cagney was making five or six movies a year at this time, his cocky optimism at odds with the downbeat reality of everyday living. He is seldom more dynamic than here, playing a whirlwind photographer, based on a true character, who succeeded in getting published a gruesome photo of a murderess being electrocuted. TS

James Cagney *Danny Kean* • Ralph Bellamy *McLean* • Patricia Ellis *Patricia Nolan* • Alice White *Allison* • Ralf Harolde *Jerry* ■ *Dir* Lloyd Bacon • *Scr* Allen Rivkin, PJ Wolfson, Ben Markson, from a story by Danny Ahearn

Pie in the Sky
★★★🄸🄸

Romantic comedy 1995 · US · Colour · 90min

This quirky romantic comedy neatly avoids the usual slushy clichés. Josh Charles plays an offbeat teen, who was conceived during a traffic jam, and now remains obsessed with gridlock. That is, until the girl next door grows up into beautiful dancer Anne Heche. The two leads are charming, although the film is stolen by a typically larger-than-life performance from John Goodman as a wacky eye in the sky traffic reporter. Bryan Gordon's direction is unobtrusive and, even if it fades a little towards the end, there are plenty of funny moments. JF

Josh Charles *Charlie* • Anne Heche *Amy* • John Goodman *Alan Davenport* • Christine Lahti *Ruby* • Christine Ebersole *Mom Dunlap* • Peter Riegert *Dad Dunlap* • Dey Young *Mrs Tarnell* • Bob Balaban *Mr Entamen* • Wil Wheaton *Jack* ■ *Dir/Scr* Bryan Gordon

A Piece of the Action ★★🄸🄸

Comedy 1977 · US · Colour · 129min

The third teaming of Sidney Poitier and Bill Cosby (after *Uptown Saturday Night* and *Let's Do It Again*) continues their comic misadventures as two con artists. This time they avoid a jail sentence by volunteering to work with under-privileged kids. It's a well-intentioned, occasionally funny farce, exploiting the easy charm of the two able leads, but Poitier's direction overemphasises the preachy and saccharine elements. AJ

Sidney Poitier *Manny Durrell* • Bill Cosby *Dave Anderson* • James Earl Jones *Joshua Burke* • Denise Nicholas *Lila French* • Hope Clarke *Sarah Thomas* • Tracy Reed *Nikki McLean* • Titos Vandis *Bruno* ■ *Dir* Sidney Poitier • *Scr* Charles Blackwell, from a story by Timothy March

Pieces
★ 🄸🄸

Horror 1982 · It/Sp · Colour · 81min

Real-life husband-and-wife team Christopher and Lynda Day George must rue the day they agreed to star in this twisted stalk-and-slash flick. George is a cop hunting down a psycho who chops up college girls for body parts to make a grotesque human jigsaw. Is one really to take Spanish director Juan Piquer Simon's

effort seriously, riddled as it is with goofs and inane dialogue? RS

Christopher George *Lieutenant Bracken* • Edmund Purdom *Dean* • Lynda Day George *Mary Riggs* • Paul Smith *Willard* ■ *Dir* Juan Piquer Simon • *Scr* Dick Randall, John Shadow [Aristide Massaccesi]

Pieces of April
★★★🄸🄸

Comedy drama 2002 · US · Colour · 78min

Katie Holmes plays the grunged-up and scowling April Burns, whose shifting moods reach a crescendo when she decides to host a Thanksgiving meal for her estranged family, including her cancer-stricken mother (Patricia Clarkson). Everything that could go wrong invariably does, leading to moments of bittersweet comedy that are as touching as they are amusing. Holmes excels as the black sheep of the Burns clan, but her heartfelt performance is overshadowed by the Oscar-nominated Clarkson, whose brutal honesty and coldness are poignantly exact. SF Swearing, drug abuse. 𝗗𝗩𝗗

Katie Holmes *April Burns* • Patricia Clarkson *Joy Burns* • Derek Luke *Bobby* • Sean Hayes *Wayne* • Oliver Platt *Jim Burns* • Alison Pill *Beth Burns* • John Gallagher Jr *Timmy Burns* • Alice Drummond *Grandma Dottie* • SisQo [Sisqo] *Latrell* ■ *Dir/Scr* Peter Hedges

Pieces of Dreams
★★

Romantic drama 1970 · US · Colour · 99min

Despite touching on controversial subjects that challenged the Catholic Church, this adaptation is too melodramatic for any serious examination of doctrinal issues. Disenchanted with his pastoral role, Robert Forster's inner-city priest has to endure a street gang accusing him of being gay as well as bishop Will Geer and his family badgering him to keep the faith. No wonder he comes to question his vocation after falling for wealthy social worker Lauren Hutton. This is a very human crisis, but director Daniel Haller seems more concerned with sensationalism. DP

Robert Forster *Gregory Lind* • Lauren Hutton *Pamela Gibson* • Will Geer *Bishop* • Ivor Francis *Father Paul Schaeffer* • Richard O'Brien *Mgr Francis Hurley* ■ *Dir* Daniel Haller • *Scr* Roger Hirson, from the novel *The Wine and the Music* by William E Barrett

The Pied Piper
★★★🄤

Second World War drama
1942 · US · BW · 86min

The Pied Piper theme is transferred to the Second World War, with Monty Woolley emotionally allergic to children but forced to lead two of them out of Nazi-occupied France. Woolley gives a fine performance, successfully overturning our belief in his pathological state, and helping what could have been a squeakily saccharine offering become an often intensely moving film, sadly spoilt overall by some very dull patches. SH

Monty Woolley *Howard* • Roddy McDowall *Ronnie Cavanaugh* • Anne Baxter *Nicole Rougeron* • Otto Preminger *Major Diessen* • J Carrol Naish *Aristide Rougeron* • Lester Matthews *Mr Cavanaugh* • Jill Esmond *Mrs Cavanaugh* • Ferike Boros *Madame* ■ *Dir* Irving Pichel • *Scr* Nunnally Johnson, from the novel by Nevil Shute

Pièges
★★★★

Thriller 1939 · Fr · BW · 115min

This was Robert Siodmak's last French-made film before his departure for Hollywood, and it is interesting to see how much this thriller, with its police investigation and seedy characters, prefigures the "night city" movies of his American period. The excellent cast includes Maurice Chevalier as a nightclub owner, with Pierre Renoir (Jean's elder brother) and Erich von Stroheim as prime suspects connected with the disappearance of a number of young women. The film was remade in 1947 by Douglas Sirk as *Lured*. RB In French.

Maurice Chevalier *Robert Fleury* • Erich von Stroheim *Pears* • Pierre Renoir *Brémontière* • Marie Déa *Adrienne* • André Brunot *Ténier* ■ *Dir* Robert Siodmak • *Scr* Jacques Companeez, Ernest Neuville, Simon Gantillon

Pierrepoint
★★★ 🄸🄸

Biographical drama 2005 · UK · Colour · 91min

The story of British hangman Albert Pierrepoint is laid bare in this riveting and thought-provoking biopic. It centres on a magnificent performance from Timothy Spall as the man who executed more than 600 people between 1932 and 1956. Although he strove for professional perfection, his work had a destructive impact on both himself and his disapproving wife (an excellently chilly Juliet Stevenson). Richly detailed yet visually dour, the film explores the profound psychological effects of Pierrepoint's occupation, but overall this is a little too understated and austere. SF 𝗗𝗩𝗗 🄱🄻🄸

Timothy Spall *Albert Pierrepoint* • Juliet Stevenson *Anne Fletcher* • Cavan Clerkin *George Cooper* • Eddie Marsan *Tish* • Christopher Fulford *Charlie Sykes* • Ian Shaw *Percy* • Maggie Ollerenshaw *Mary Pierrepoint* ■ *Dir* Adrian Shergold • *Scr* Jeff Pope, Bob Mills

Pierrot le Fou
★★★★★ 🄸🄸

Drama 1965 · Fr/It · Colour · 105min

"*Pierrot le Fou* isn't really a film," said director Jean-Luc Godard on its release, "It's an attempt at cinema." Although it's based on Lionel White's novel *Obsession*, the action was nearly all improvised as Godard was inspired by the locations en route from Paris to the south of France. Shot in razor- sharp colour by Raoul Coutard, it is a bewildering blend of genres and visual styles, but the overriding atmosphere is one of despair for both runaways Jean-Paul Belmondo and Anna Karina and for the violent world of the mid-1960s. DP French +subtitles. 𝗗𝗩𝗗 🄱🄻🄸

Jean-Paul Belmondo *Ferdinand Griffon, "Pierrot"* • Anna Karina *Marianne Renoir* • Dirk Sanders *Fred, Marianne's brother* • Raymond Devos *Man on pier* • Graziella Galvani *Ferdinand's wife* • Sam Fuller [Samuel Fuller] *Sam Fuller* • Laszlo Szabo *Political exile* • Jean-Pierre Léaud *Young man in cinema* ■ *Dir* Jean-Luc Godard • *Scr* Jean-Luc Godard, from the novel *Obsession* by Lionel White

Pieta
★★🄸🄸

Drama 2012 · S Kor · Colour · 103min

South Korean director Kim Ki-Duk's downbeat tale concerns a loner debt collector (Lee Jung-jin) who uses violence to extract insurance money from those who can't pay their horrendous loan-shark bills. When a woman (Cho Min-soo) arrives at his door claiming to be the long-lost mother who was forced to give him up at birth, he gradually develops feelings for her – and then she disappears. Inspired by Michelangelo's *Pietà* sculpture, this is an extreme moral parable whose meditations on Christian mercy, gangster spirituality and motherly love are about as subtle as a brick. AJ Korean +subtitles.

Cho Min-soo *Mi-Sun* • Lee Jung-jin *Lee Kang-do* • Woo Gi-hong *Hoon-chul* • Kang Eun jin *Myeong-ja* ■ *Dir/Scr* Kim Ki-Duk

A Pigeon Sat on a Branch Reflecting on Existence
★★★★🄸🄸

Comedy drama
2014 · Swe/Ger/Nor/Fr · Colour · 95min

This long-windedly titled film is the last component, after *Songs from the Second Floor* and *You, the Living*, in Swedish director Roy Andersson's trilogy, but don't worry if you haven't seen the first two. There's no ongoing story that links them together – indeed, the films themselves hardly have any story to speak of at all. Instead, Andersson presents a series (37, to be exact) of highly stylised and carefully composed tableaux (the camera never moves) in which everything is in focus like a hyper-realist painting. The best way to enjoy this is to just let it wash over you and embrace the weirdness. LF Swedish, English +subtitles. 𝗗𝗩𝗗 🄱🄻🄸

Nisse Vestblom [Nils Westblom] *Sam* • Holger Andersson *Jonathan* • Charlotta Larsson *waitress* • Viktor Gyllenberg *Charles XII* ■ *Dir/Scr* Roy Andersson

P

The Pigeon That Took Rome ★★
Second World War comedy
1962 · US · BW · 101min

Charlton Heston plays an American army captain smuggled into Rome under the nose of its German occupiers. He makes contact with the partisans - especially Elsa Martinelli - and falls in with a daft spy scheme involving a carrier pigeon. It's all a bit silly, and the American studio interiors make for some ugly joins with the exterior locations. Heston is miscast, though his discomfort proves to be the source of the biggest chuckles. **AT**

Charlton Heston *Capt Paul MacDougall* • Elsa Martinelli *Antonella Massimo* • Harry Guardino *Sgt Joseph Contini* • Salvatore Baccaloni *Ciccio Massimo* • Marietto *Livio Massimo* ■ *Dir* Melville Shavelson • *Scr* Melville Shavelson, from the novel *The Easter Dinner* by Donald Downes

Piggy ★★ 18
Thriller   2012 · UK · Colour · 101min

First-time writer/director Kieron Hawkes's edgy avenging-angel crime drama may be short on novelty, but he does cast a sinister pall over his London backdrop. Martin Compston plays Joe, the disaffected courier who forges a pact with the vicious Piggy (Paul Anderson) to mete out pitiless justice to the quintet who murdered his older brother. There's an unnecessary romantic subplot, and a risible voiceover, but Hawkes sickeningly conveys the manic brutality of the story. It's decidedly unpleasant, ruthlessly competent and dismayingly plausible. **DP** Violence, swearing, drug abuse. *DVD*

Martin Compston *Joe* • Paul Anderson (2) *Piggy* • Neil Maskell *John* • Josh Herdman *Anthony* • Louise Dylan *Claire* • Jumayn Hunter *Frank* ■ *Dir/Scr* Kieron Hawkes

Piglet's Big Movie ★★★ U
Animated adventure 2003 · US · Colour · 71min

A juvenile audience will be enchanted by this animated tribute to the diminutive sidekick from *Winnie the Pooh* – and some adults could find enough here to go along with them. Tiny Piglet (voiced by John Fiedler) is feeling very low because he's far too near the ground. He sets off into the woods, wondering how he can gain height to be able to help his friends. Director Francis Glebas and writer Brian Hohlfeld have created a well-crafted fable, while Carly Simon's songs boost the film's charm and moments of poignancy. **TH** *DVD*

John Fiedler *Piglet* • Jim Cummings *Winnie the Pooh/Tigger* • Andre Stojka *Owl* • Kath Soucie *Kanga* • Nikita Hopkins *Roo* • Peter Cullen *Eeyore* • Ken Sansom *Rabbit* • Tom Wheatley *Christopher Robin* ■ *Dir* Francis Glebas • *Scr* Brian Hohlfeld, inspired by the stories by AA Milne • *Music* Carly Simon

A Pig's Tale ★★ U
Comedy   1994 · US · Colour · 89min

When oddball youngster Joe Flaherty is sent to summer camp, he finds himself sharing a cabin with three other losers. Together they manage to triumph against the odds stacked against them. Juvenile high jinks with the simple message that even misfits can make good. **DF**

Joe Flaherty *Milt* • Graham Sack *Andy* • Mike Damus *Frank* • Andrew Harrison Leeds *Beckerwood* • Lisa Jakub *Tiffany* • Jake Beecham *Swackback* • Jimmy Zepeda *Cruz* ■ *Dir* Paul Tassie • *Scr* Charles Ransom, Scott Sandorf, Todd Richardson

Pigskin Parade ★★★ U
Musical comedy   1936 · US · BW · 92min

This rather silly, if charming, 20th Century-Fox football musical is worth watching today for its cast, including a young Judy Garland in her first feature. Stuart Erwin and Patsy Kelly are the leads in this likeable romp, but keep an eye out for a gauche Tony Martin, Betty Grable a decade before she became Queen of the Fox lot, and don't-blink-or-you'll-miss Alan Ladd, singing with the Yacht Club Boys. **TS**

Stuart Erwin *Amos Dodd* • Patsy Kelly *Bessie Winters* • Jack Haley *"Slug" Winston Winters* • Johnny Downs *Chip Carson* • Betty Grable *Laura Watson* • Arline Judge *Sally Saxon* • Dixie Dunbar *Ginger Jones* • Judy Garland *Sairy Dodd* • Alan Ladd *Student* • Anthony Martin [Tony Martin (1)] *Tommy Barker* ■ *Scr* Harry Tugend, Jack Yellen, William Conselman, from a story by Arthur Sheekman, Nat Perrin, Mark Kelly

Pigsty ★★★ 15
Satirical drama   1969 · It/Fr · Colour · 93min

After great success during the 1960s, Pier Paolo Pasolini's career suffered popular decline with three films, including this satire, paralleling a story of cannibalistic soldier Pierre Clémenti roaming a medieval wasteland, with that of the son (Jean-Pierre Léaud) of a former Nazi industrialist. The latter is more enamoured of the pigs, which finally devour him, than of his fiancée. Pasolini appears little interested in the narrative and more concerned with appalling images that parody his work and that of other directors and attacking the capitalist society he despised while experimenting with language and film form. **BB** Italian +subtitles. *DVD* *Blu-ray*

Pierre Clémenti *Young cannibal* • Jean-Pierre Léaud *Julian Klotz* • Ugo Tognazzi *Herdhitze* • Marco Ferreri *Hans Guenther* ■ *Dir/Scr* Pier Paolo Pasolini

The Pilgrim ★★★ U
Silent comedy   1923 · US · BW · 41min

Charles Chaplin's genius at creating comedy out of desperate situations is well illustrated in this film. He's in hot water as an escaped convict who steals the clothes of a gospel minister and gets roped in to preaching to the congregation of Hell's Hinges, falling for Edna Purviance while bringing a former fellow inmate to justice. Inevitably, the film drew protests from both redneck religionists and the Ku Klux Klan. **TH**

Charlie Chaplin [Charles Chaplin] *The pilgrim* • Edna Purviance *The girl* • Kitty Bradbury *Her mother* • Mack Swain *The deacon* • Loyal Underwood *The elder* • Dinky Dean *The boy* • Mai Wells *his mother* • Sydney Chaplin [Syd Chaplin] *Her husband* • Chuck Reisner [Charles Reisner] *The crook* ■ *Dir* Charles Chaplin • *Scr* Charles Chaplin

Pilgrimage ★★★
Drama   1933 · US · BW · 96min

Cruelly possessive mother Henrietta Crosman, wanting to keep her son from the girl (Marian Nixon) he loves, enlists him in the army, resulting in his death on the Western Front. Nixon bears his son, who is also harshly treated by an even more hardened Crosman - until the woman goes on a pilgrimage to the war graves in France. This is uncharacteristic material for John Ford, but it's beautifully shot and a great showcase for the formidable stage actress Crosman. Its themes and incidents seem overfamiliar now, but it offers depth, sweep and conviction, despite its unrealistic "happy" ending. **RK**

Henrietta Crosman *Hannah Jessop* • Heather Angel *Suzanne* • Norman Foster *Jim Jessop* • Marian Nixon *Mary Saunders* • Maurice Murphy *Gary Worth* • Lucille La Verne *Mrs Hatfield* • Charley Grapewin *Dad Saunders* • Hedda Hopper *Mrs Worth* ■ *Dir* John Ford • *Scr* Philip Klein, Barry Connors, Dudley Nichols, from the story *Gold Star Mother* by IAR Wylie

Pillars of Society ★★
Drama   1935 · Ger · BW · 82min

After 20 years in America, Albrecht Schoenhals returns to his native Norway and a reunion with his former business partner Heinrich George. His presence causes upheaval, as he threatens to reveal dark secrets hiding behind the veneer of respectable society. This German adaptation of Ibsen's play never transcends its stage origins and plays out as a rather static and ponderous melodrama. Director Detlef Sierck, however, does display the touch which would bring him fame as Hollywood's Douglas Sirk. **RK** In German.

Heinrich George *Consul Bernick* • Maria Krahn *Betty, his wife* • Horst Teetzmann *Olaf, his son* • Albrecht Schönhals *Johann Tonnessen* ■ *Dir* Detlef Sierck [Douglas Sirk] • *Scr* Dr Georg C Klaren, Karl Peter Gillman, from the play by Henrik Ibsen

Pillars of the Sky ★★
Western   1956 · US · Colour · 92min

This handsome-looking CinemaScope western stars two of Universal's smouldering contract icons, Jeff Chandler and Dorothy Malone, in a tale with a decidedly sanctimonious tone. Chandler's the cavalry scout who predicts disaster when the army decide to build a fort on Indian land. Director George Marshall does what he can with a weak script, but there's a feeling that no one's heart is in tune with the sentiments expressed. **TS**

Jeff Chandler *First Sergeant Emmett Bell* • Dorothy Malone *Calla Gaxton* • Ward Bond *Doctor Joseph Holden* • Keith Andes *Captain Tom Gaxton* • Lee Marvin *Sergeant Lloyd Carracart* ■ *Dir* George Marshall • *Scr* Sam Rolfe, from the novel *Frontier Fury* by Will Henry [Heck Allen]

The Pillow Book ★★★★ 18
Erotic drama
1995 · Neth/Fr/UK · Colour and BW · 121min

Extraordinary. Ravishing. Preposterous. The usual descriptions of director Peter Greenaway's work can all be applied here in spades. Even more overwrought and over-decorated than his previous films, Greenaway's Hong Kong-set tale of sex and power centres on the fetish of Vivian Wu who enjoys having her flesh written upon, and who takes a dreadful revenge on the homosexual publisher who degraded her father. The split-screen motifs are a wonder to behold but, although it deals with white-hot emotions, the film is as ice-cold as winter. **TH** English, Japanese +subtitles. Violence, sex scenes, drug abuse, nudity. *DVD* *Blu-ray*

Vivian Wu *Nagiko* • Ewan McGregor *Jerome* • Yoshi Oida *Father* • Ken Ogata *Father* • Hideko Yoshida *Aunt/Maid* • Judy Ongg *Mother* • Ken Mitsuishi *Husband* ■ *Dir/Scr* Peter Greenaway

Pillow of Death ★★
Mystery   1945 · US · BW · 66min

This negligible entry in Universal's *Inner Sanctum* series offers Lon Chaney Jr one of its more interesting challenges. As a lawyer unhappily married to Victoria Horne, he's released due to lack of evidence following her murder. However, as he tries to start again with secretary Brenda Joyce, the killings keep occurring and he's haunted by the voice of his dead spouse. Chaney's mournful bewilderment adds a surprisingly affecting human element to the story, but Wallace Fox's direction is short on both suspense. **DP**

Lon Chaney [Lon Chaney Jr] *Wayne Fletcher* • Brenda Joyce *Donna Kincaid* • J Edward Bromberg *Julian Julian* • Rosalind Ivan *Amelia Kincaid* • Clara Blandick *Belle Kincaid* • George Cleveland *Samuel Kincaid* • Victoria Horne *Vivia Fletcher* ■ *Dir* Wallace Fox • *Scr* George Bricker, from a story by Dwight V Babcock

Pillow Talk ★★★★ PG
Romantic comedy   1959 · US · Colour · 98min

This is the first and most entertaining of the series of comedies Doris Day made for Universal Studios that successfully teamed her with the likes of Cary Grant, James Garner and her most popular partner, Rock Hudson. It's ultra-glossy froth, and the smart plot - about Day and Hudson sharing a telephone party line - won an Oscar for best story and screenplay. Hudson displays a flair for adroit humour, but the funniest material goes to Tony Randall (never better) and the acerbic Thelma Ritter (*Rear Window*). **TS** *DVD* *Blu-ray*

Doris Day *Jan Morrow* • Rock Hudson *Brad Allen* • Tony Randall *Jonathan Forbes* • Thelma Ritter *Alma* • Nick Adams *Tony Walters* • Julia Meade *Marie* ■ *Dir* Michael Gordon • *Scr* Stanley Shapiro, Maurice Richlin, from a story by Russell Rouse, Clarence Greene

Pilot #5 ★★
Second World War drama
1943 · US · BW · 70min

Lawyer Franchot Tone is in league with a fascist politician. But then Tone atones for his misjudgment of character by becoming a fighter pilot. Told in a series of flashbacks, this is heavily contrived and rather dully directed by George Sidney, later famous for his musicals. Also famous for musicals was third-billed Gene Kelly, making his second film appearance as Tone's buddy. **AT**

Franchot Tone *Lt George Braynor Collins* • Marsha Hunt *Freddie Andrews* • Gene Kelly *Vito S Alessandro* • Van Johnson *Everett Arnold* • Alan Baxter *Winston Davis* • Dick Simmons *Henry Willoughby Claven* • Peter Lawford *English soldier* • Ava Gardner *Girl* ■ *Dir* George Sidney (2) • *Scr* David Hertz, from his story

Pimp ★ 18
Thriller   2010 · UK · Colour · 87min

A week in the life of a Soho pimp unfolds before the cameras in this faux documentary. With one of his best earners absconding, the prospect of a turf war with the Chinese Triads and a boss (Danny Dyer) running out of patience, the last thing Woody (Robert Cavanah) needs is an apparent snuff video falling into his lap. But that's exactly what happens in this lamentable attempt at faking a peek into the murky corners of the sex industry. Dyer's attempts to channel Al Pacino are grim enough, but the real blame must be laid at the door of director/star/co-writer Cavanah. **TJ** Violence, swearing, sex scenes. *DVD* *Blu-ray*

Danny Dyer *Stanley* • Robert Cavanah *Woody* • Billy Boyd (1) *Chief* • Scarlett Johnson *Lizzy* • Corey Johnson *Axel* • Barbara Nedeljakova *Petra* • Susie Amy *Tammy* • Martin Compston *Zeb* ■ *Dir* Robert Cavanah • *Scr* Robert Cavanah, Jon Kirby, from a story by Kirby

Pimpernel Smith ★★★★ U
Second World War spy drama
1941 · UK · BW · 115min

The screen's greatest Scarlet Pimpernel, Leslie Howard, updates the character to Nazi-occupied Europe in this smashing piece of wartime propaganda. Howard also directs with style, and if the plot is preposterous - archaeologist Howard smuggles refugees out from under the very noses of the Gestapo and then goes back to Berlin to rescue a girl - it awakened the world, and particularly America, to Europe's plight. **TS**

Leslie Howard *Prof Horatio Smith* • Francis Sullivan [Francis L Sullivan] *Gen von Graum* • Mary Morris *Ludmila Koslowski* • Hugh McDermott *David Maxwell* • Raymond Huntley *Marx* • Manning Whiley *Bertie Gregson* • Peter Gawthorne *Sidimir Koslowski* • Allan Jeayes *Dr Beckendorf* • Michael Rennie *Officer at concentration camp* ■ *Dir* Leslie Howard • *Scr* Anatole de Grunwald, Roland Pertwee, Ian Dalrymple, from a story by AG MacDonell, Wolfgang Wilhelm

Pin ★★★★ 18
Psychological thriller
1988 · Can · Colour · 98min

David Hewlett gives the performance of his career as a schizophrenic who develops a symbiotic relationship with a medical mannequin called Pin in this first-rate psychological chiller. The film was written and directed by Sandor Stern, who also penned *The Amityville Horror*, and provides a truly spooky portrayal of a kid teetering on the tightrope between fantasy and reality. **DA**

David Hewlett *Leon* • Cyndy Preston *Ursula* • John Ferguson [John Pyper-Ferguson] *Stan Fraker* • Terry O'Quinn *Dr Linden* • Bronwen Mantel *Mrs Linden* ■ *Dir* Sandor Stern • *Scr* Sandor Stern, from the novel by Andrew Neiderman

A Pin for the Butterfly ★★
Political drama
1994 · UK/Cz Rep · Colour · 113min

Despite the excellent use of Prague locations and superb photography from Ivan Slapeta, this film lets itself down by its

P

confused structure and an ill-chosen but hard-working British cast. Joan Plowright seems to have cornered the market in European matriarchs, yet here her passively benign character is severely underwritten, while Ian Bannen merely reprises *Hope and Glory*'s Grandpa. Most ill-at-ease, though, is Hugh Laurie's subversive uncle. **TS**

Florence Hoath *Marushka* • Imogen Stubbs *Mother* • Hugh Laurie *Uncle* • Ian Bannen *Grandpa* • Ian Hogg *Great Uncle* • Joan Plowright *Grandma* ■ *Dir/Scr* Hannah Kodicek

Pin Up Girl ★★Ⓤ
Musical comedy　　1944 · US · Colour · 79min

In her days at 20th Century-Fox, pin-up queen Betty Grable was usually cushioned with glamorous leading men, zippy tunes and Technicolor to disguise the fact that, in her own words, she "couldn't act, couldn't sing, couldn't dance". She might have also added "didn't matter", for her sheer good-naturedness won the public's heart. Here she's playing a secretary determined to become an entertainer, but this isn't very good. There's little wit, few jokes, no decent songs and hardly any plot. **TS** *DVD*

Betty Grable *Lorry Jones* • John Harvey *Tommy Dooley* • Martha Raye *Marian* • Joe E Brown *Eddie* • Eugene Pallette *Barney Briggs* ■ *Dir* H Bruce Humberstone • *Scr* Robert Ellis, Helen Logan, Earl Baldwin, from a story by Libbie Block

Pina ★★★★Ⓤ
Dance documentary
2011 · Ger/Fr/UK · Colour · 99min

This art house 3D movie is a celebration of the work of German choreographer Pina Bausch, who died in 2009 while preparing the film with writer/director/producer Wim Wenders – he then saw the project to fruition as a memorial. A besotted Wenders takes care to give every breath and footstep of the 40 or so dancers as they re-create four Bausch pieces in the company's home at the Tantztheater Wuppertal. But the work – humorous, torrid, sexual, overwrought and obsessive-compulsive – needs no help to captivate and amaze. **AC** German, English, French, Italian, Spanish, Portuguese, Mandarin +subtitles. Brief nudity. 🔊

■ *Dir/Scr* Wim Wenders • *Choreographer* Pina Bausch • *Music* Thom Hanreich

Pineapple Express ★★★🔞
Action crime comedy
2008 · US · Colour · 107min

Director David Gordon Green cranks up the action for this stoner comedy from the production house of Judd Apatow (*Knocked Up*, *Superbad*). Seth Rogen plays Dale Denton, a process server whose world mostly revolves around smoking marijuana. After his friendly dealer Saul Silver (James Franco) sells Dale some ultra-high quality "Pineapple Express" reefer, the dope ends up being traced back to them in a gangland murder. Soon the buddies are on the run, smashing their mobile phones and trying to avoid being shot by a corrupt cop (Rosie Perez). It's well paced, well thought-out and highly absurd, yet the characters are hard to warm to. It's still a fun ride, though. **KK** *DVD* 🔵

Seth Rogen *Dale Denton* • James Franco *Saul Silver* • Gary Cole *Ted Jones* • Rosie Perez *Carol* • Danny McBride (2) • Amber Heard *Angie* • Bill Hader *Private Miller* • James Remar *General Brat* ■ *Dir* David Gordon Green • *Scr* Seth Rogen, Evan Goldberg, from a story by Judd Apatow, Rogen, Goldberg

Piñero ★★🔞
Biographical drama
2001 · US · Colour and BW · 90min

Born in Puerto Rico, Miguel Piñero endured an abusive upbringing and a spell in jail before finding fame as the Tony-nominated playwright of the semi-autobiographical *Short Eyes*. Yet he succumbed to drug addiction and died derelict in 1988. Benjamin Bratt captures Piñero's pain with affecting power. But director Leon Ichaso confuses the issues with a flashbacking structure, shaky digi-camerawork, and

shifts between monochrome and colour. **DP** Swearing, drug abuse. *DVD*

Benjamin Bratt *Miguel Piñero* • Giancarlo Esposito *Miguel Algarin* • Talisa Soto *Sugar* • Nelson Vasquez *Tito* • Michael Irby *Reinaldo Povod* • Michael Wright *Edgar* • Rita Moreno *Mother* • Jaime Sanchez *Father* • Mandy Patinkin *Joseph Papp* ■ *Dir/Scr* Leon Ichaso

Ping Pong ★★★★⑫
Sports comedy drama
2002 · Jpn · Colour · 113min

Fumihiko Sori's directorial debut is a stylish hybrid of the high-school buddy movie and the sporting underdog melodrama. This tale of two boys whose friendship is tested by their participation in a local table-tennis tournament gets inside the competitive mind while considering the mechanics of friendship. The loyalty that the taciturn Arata shows the grandstanding Yosuke Kubozuka is genuinely touching, yet Sori is just as intrigued by the fierce rivalry between the duo and some posh, shaven-headed poseurs. The matches are filmed with grace and panache. **DP** Japanese +subtitles. Violence. *DVD*

Yosuke Kubozuka *Peco* • Arata *Smile* • Sam Lee *China* • Shido Nakamura [Shidou Nakamura] *Dragon* • Koji Ohkura *Akuma* ■ *Dir* Sori [Fumihiko Sori] • *Scr* Kankuro Kudo, from the comic book by Taiyou Matsumoto

Ping Pong ★★★🔞
Documentary　2012 · UK · Colour · 76min

This introduction to the fiercely competitive world of veterans table tennis proves that age is just a number if you retain a zest for life and the will to win. The primary focus is on Brits Les D'Arcy (89) and Terry Donlon (81), who have both overcome serious health issues to stay at the top of their game. They travel to Inner Mongolia for the world championships, where fellow octogenarians prove equally committed. The actual game coverage is perfunctory and confused, but the doughty spirit of D'Arcy and Donlon shines through, as they keep on defying the odds to play another day. **DP** English, German, Mandarin, Japanese +subtitles.

■ *Dir* Hugh Hartford

Pink Cadillac ★★🔞
Comedy drama　1989 · US · Colour · 115min

This overlong film is one of Clint Eastwood's rare mistakes. Lazily directed by his long-serving associate Buddy Van Horn, it strains for laughs as it follows Eastwood's bounty hunter on the trail of a runaway wife, played by Bernadette Peters. The car looks great, even if it does hide a stash of drugs and another endless subplot, and if you blink you may miss the then unknown Jim Carrey. **AT** Violence, swearing. *DVD*

Clint Eastwood *Tommy Nowak* • Bernadette Peters *Lou Ann McGuinn* • Timothy Carhart *Roy McGuinn* • John Dennis Johnston *Waycross* • Michael Des Barres *Alex* • Geoffrey Lewis *Ricky Z* • William Hickey *Barton* • Frances Fisher *Dinah* • Jim Carrey *Lounge entertainer* ■ *Dir* Buddy Van Horn • *Scr* John Eskow

LANDMARK FILM
Defines bad taste for future generations

Pink Flamingos ★★★★★🔞
Satirical melodrama 1972 · US · Colour · 100min

This is the film that not only defined bad taste, but also unashamedly celebrated it. Cult director John Waters's notorious gross-out has upstart perverts David Lochary and Mink Stole trying to wrest the honour of "Filthiest Person Alive" from the tenacious grip of sleaze superstar Divine. Chicken sex, a singing rectum, artificial insemination, lesbian motherhood and the incomparable Edith Massey are paraded before our appalled eyes in this screamingly funny shocker. Featuring the infamous coda where Divine eats a dog excrement (for real), this unique obscenity is the grandfather of midnight movies. **AJ** Sex scenes, swearing, violence.

Divine *Babs Johnson/Divine* • David Lochary *Raymond Marble* • Mary Vivian Pearce *Cotton* • Mink Stole *Connie Marble* • Danny Mills *Crackers* •

Edith Massey *Mama Edie* • Channing Wilroy *Channing* • Cookie Mueller *Cookie* ■ *Dir/Scr* John Waters (2)

Pink Floyd – The Wall ★★🔞
Musical drama　1982 · UK · Colour · 95min

While undoubtedly lacking in symbolic subtlety – schoolchildren fed into a mincer, the adoration of Bob Geldof's central rock star likened to a Nazi rally, the wall itself (isolation, oppression, yes we get it) – Alan Parker's realisation of Roger Waters' s mega-selling 1979 concept album is not without visual flourish, not least when the pen and ink of Gerald Scarfe is animated into disturbing life. Those who dig the Floyd songs will put up with the pat imagery and Geldof's sleepwalking turn. Unbelievers should walk on by. **AC** *DVD*

Bob Geldof *Pink* • Christine Hargreaves *Pink's mother* • James Laurenson *Pink's father* • Eleanor David *Pink's wife* • Kevin McKeon *Young Pink* • Bob Hoskins *Band manager* • David Bingham *Little Pink* • Jenny Wright *American groupie* ■ *Dir* Alan Parker • *Scr* Roger Waters, from the album by Pink Floyd • *Animator* Gerald Scarfe • *Cinematographer* Peter Biziou

The Pink Jungle ★★★Ⓤ
Crime caper　　1968 · US · Colour · 103min

James Garner plays a fashion photographer who is stranded in the South American jungle with model Eva Renzi when George Kennedy steals their helicopter in his quest to locate a hidden diamond mine. This is a jolly caper that manages to be tense and spoofish at the same time. Garner is his usual charming self, while Kennedy, who plays everything for laughs, is very amusing. **AT**

James Garner *Ben Morris* • Eva Renzi *Alison Duquesne* • George Kennedy *Sammy Ryderbeit* • Nigel Green *Crowley* • Michael Ansara *Raul Ortega* ■ *Dir* Delbert Mann • *Scr* Charles Williams, from the novel *Snake Water* by Alan Williams

Pink Narcissus ★★★★🔞
Experimental erotic fantasy
1971 · US · Colour · 64min

"Seminal" is the only word for this fine and rare example of screen homoerotica. A reinterpretation of the Greek myth of a beautiful youth in love with his own reflection, the film consists of the intercut reveries of a male prostitute, who keeps harsh reality at bay by imagining himself as various romantic characters. The film's meticulously crafted "look" – stagey painted sets and spangly costumes – may now appear plain camp, but it influenced countless other gay film-makers. The sequences were shot on 8mm intermittently and virtually single-handedly from 1965 by photographer James Bidgood. Because Bidgood felt unable to take sole credit, the film was released anonymously. It was passed uncut by the BBFC in 1993, allegedly because examiners had not noticed the ejaculation shot. **DM**

Bobby Kendall • *Editor* Martin Jay Sadoff

The Pink Panther ★★★★🅿🅶
Comedy　　　1963 · US · Colour · 110min

Peter Sellers went into this film as character support and came out a star. David Niven is the ostensible lead in a rather dull setting up of the plot, in which the bumbling Inspector Clouseau is called in to prevent the theft of a precious diamond known as the Pink Panther. But Sellers's dud officer was so scene-stealingly comic that director Blake Edwards inserted new scenes. The rest is hysterical history. See it from the beginning: the cartoon title sequence with its Henry Mancini theme is an in-the-pink joy. Sellers took top billing the following year in *A Shot in the Dark*. **TH** *DVD* 🔵

David Niven *Sir Charles Lytton* • Peter Sellers *Inspector Jacques Clouseau* • Robert Wagner *George Lytton* • Capucine *Simone Clouseau* • Claudia Cardinale *Princess Dala* • Brenda de Banzie *Angela Dunning* • John Le Mesurier

Defence attorney ■ *Dir* Blake Edwards • *Scr* Maurice Richlin, Blake Edwards • *Title Animator* DePatie-Freleng

The Pink Panther ★★🅿🅶
Comedy　　　2006 · US · Colour · 88min

Having already tried to fill Phil Silvers's boots in *Sgt Bilko*, Steve Martin here tackles the equally iconic Inspector Clouseau, a character immortalised by Peter Sellers. Martin does his best and certainly works hard, but this slapstick farce just isn't that funny. The plot sees Clouseau tracking down a fabulous diamond ring and leaving a trail of destruction in his wake. Kevin Kline should have been a riot as Clouseau's long-suffering superior, but his subtle comic skills are wasted on a poor script and over-obvious humour. **DA** *DVD* 🔵

Steve Martin *Inspector Jacques Clouseau* • Kevin Kline *Chief Inspector Dreyfus* • Jean Reno *Gendarme Gilbert Ponton* • Emily Mortimer *Nicole* • Henry Czerny *Yuri* • Kristin Chenoweth *Cherie* • Roger Rees *Larocque* • Beyoncé Knowles *Xania* ■ *Dir* Shawn Levy • *Scr* Len Blum, Steve Martin, from a story by Blum, Michael Saltzman, from characters by Maurice Richlin, Blake Edwards

The Pink Panther 2 ★★🅿🅶
Comedy　　　2009 · US · Colour · 88min

In this second outing for Steve Martin's Inspector Clouseau, the bumbling gendarme gathers an international squad of detectives to find valuable stolen artefacts, including the Pink Panther diamond. An impressive supporting cast – among them John Cleese, Lily Tomlin, Jeremy Irons and Andy Garcia – adds weight to an otherwise slapstick-heavy comic caper that tends to rely on silliness and elaborate set pieces rather than wit or surprise. It's gorgeously filmed, but the traditional Pink Panther cartoon accompanying the opening credits merely brings back memories of Peter Sellers in his pomp and serves as a reminder to how far the series has fallen. **KK** *DVD* 🔵

Steve Martin *Chief Inspector Jacques Clouseau* • Jean Réno [Jean Reno] *Gendarme Gilbert Ponton* • Emily Mortimer *Nicole* • Andy Garcia *Vincenzo* • Alfred Molina *Pepperidge* • Aishwarya Rai Bachchan [Aishwarya Raj] *Sonia* • John Cleese *Chief Inspector Dreyfus* • Lily Tomlin *Mrs Berenger* • Jeremy Irons *Avellaneda* ■ *Dir* Harald Zwart • *Scr* Scott Neustadter, Michael H Weber, Steve Martin, from a story by Neustadter, Weber, from characters by Blake Edwards, Maurice Richlin

The Pink Panther Strikes Again ★★★🅿🅶
Comedy　　　1976 · UK · Colour · 99min

The critics were divided on the fourth entry in Blake Edwards's *Pink Panther* series. Some thought that Chief Inspector Dreyfus's increasingly desperate attempts to bump off the incompetent Clouseau were a riot of bawdy humour and inspired slapstick, while others considered the film to be a repetitive rehash. The box-office evidence suggests that the public voted with the "pro" lobby, but there is a shortage of inspiration here. *Revenge of the Pink Panther* continued the series. **DP** *DVD*

Peter Sellers *Jacques Clouseau* • Herbert Lom *Dreyfus* • Colin Blakely *Alec Drummond* • Leonard Rossiter *Superintendent Quinlan* • Lesley-Anne Down *Olga* • Bert Kwouk [Burt Kwouk] *Cato* • André Maranne *François* ■ *Dir* Blake Edwards • *Scr* Frank Waldman, Blake Edwards

Pink String and Sealing Wax ★★★🅿🅶
Period crime drama 1945 · UK · BW · 85min

Set in Victorian Brighton, this roaring melodrama takes its title from the way in which pharmacists used to wrap parcels containing poison. There's not an ounce of subtlety in either the acting or in Robert Hamer's direction, but the film is none the worse for that, as restraint would have rendered the whole production ridiculous. The villains have all the fun, with Mervyn Johns unexpectedly severe as the tyrannical father, Garry Marsh on career best form as the brutal husband and Googie Withers gloriously wicked as the landlady

Ⓤ SUITABLE FOR ALL　　Ⓤⓔ SUITABLE ESPECIALLY FOR YOUNG CHILDREN (DVD ONLY)　　🅿🅶 PARENTAL GUIDANCE　　12A UNDER 12s TO BE ACCOMPANIED (CINEMA ONLY)

leading timid Gordon Jackson astray. DP
DVD BD

Mervyn Johns *Mr Edward Sutton* • Googie Withers *Pearl Bond* • Gordon Jackson *David Sutton* • Sally Ann Howes *Peggy Sutton* • Mary Merrall *Mrs Ellen Sutton* • Catherine Lacey *Miss Porter* • Garry Marsh *Joe Bond* ■ *Dir* Robert Hamer • *Scr* Diana Morgan, Robert Hamer, from the play by Roland Pertwee

Pinky ★★★
Drama 1949 · US · BW · 101min

This is one of a group of important Hollywood movies that dealt with serious racial issues in the wake of the Second World War. While these films may seem naive and dated to today's audiences, getting them seen and discussed by the general public of the time was little short of miraculous. Here, the white Jeanne Crain gives an affecting performance in the lead, though cast in a role patently requiring a black actress, but the film probably would not have been made otherwise, and Ethel Waters is marvellous as the southern grandmother she visits. Elia Kazan took over the directorial reins from John Ford and the result is extremely moving, despite the unconvincing studio interior sets. TS

Jeanne Crain *Pinky*, Patricia Johnson • Ethel Barrymore *Miss Em* • Ethel Waters *Granny Dysey Johnson* • William Lundigan *Dr Thomas Adams* • Basil Ruysdael *Judge Walker* • Kenny Washington *Dr Canady* ■ *Dir* Elia Kazan • *Scr* Philip Dunne, Dudley Nichols, from the novel *Quality* by Cid Ricketts Sumner

Pinocchio ★★★★★
Classic animated fantasy
1940 · US · Colour · 87min

Some films you think you know well, until you revisit them, and are struck all over again by that sense of wonder that moved you in the first place. This is the case with all of Disney's early feature-length cartoons: they have enthralled us for so long that we take them for granted. There is just such a magic in this tale of the little wooden boy, whose nose grows when he tells a lie and who is instructed to follow his conscience. Jiminy Cricket, Figaro, Geppetto and Monstro the Whale, and even those arch-felons who lead wayward boys to Pleasure Island, have all become a part of 20th-century mythology. The score, which includes the song that became Disney's anthem, *When You Wish upon a Star*, is magnificent, as is the use of early Technicolor. TS DVD BD

Dickie Jones *Pinocchio* • Cliff Edwards *Jiminy Cricket* • Christian Rub *Geppetto* • Evelyn Venable *The Blue Fairy* ■ *Dir* Ben Sharpsteen, Hamilton Luske • *Scr* Ted Sears, Otto Englander, Webb Smith, William Cottrell, Joseph Sabo, Erdman Penner, Aurelius Battaglia, from the novel *The Adventures of Pinocchio* by Carlo Collodi

Pinocchio ★★
Fantasy adventure 2002 · It · Colour · 105min

Despite breaking domestic box office records, Roberto Benigni's adaptation has none of the eccentric charm it might have possessed had he realised a lifetime ambition in undertaking the project with Federico Fellini. Much affection has been lavished on the costumes, music and effects, while Dante Spinotti's photography cleverly marries Tuscan landscapes and studio sets. The supporting cast is both pantomimic and literate, but Benigni is too old for Pinocchio. DP Italian +subtitles.

Roberto Benigni *Pinocchio* • Nicoletta Braschi *Blue Fairy* • Mino Bellei *Medoro* • Carlo Giuffrè *Geppetto* • Peppe Barra *Cricket* ■ *Dir* Roberto Benigni • *Scr* Vincenzo Cerami, Roberto Benigni, from the story by Carlo Collodi

Pioneer ★★★[15]
Conspiracy thriller 2013 · Nor · Colour · 106min

Nordic *noir* takes an interesting turn in this conspiracy drama. In the late 1970s, lucrative oil deposits are found in Norwegian waters, leading to an uneasy collaboration with a sinister US oil company. This atmospheric thriller finds diver Aksel Hennie trying to find out the truth behind the death of his brother while testing the

Americans' experimental breathing equipment. *Headhunters* star Hennie is at his vulnerable best and the deep-sea scenes are exciting and urgent, but the film flounders on land, where the story becomes distractingly convoluted. DW Norwegian, English +subtitles. DVD BD

Aksel Hennie *Petter* • Wes Bentley *Mike* • Stephanie Sigman *Maria* • Jorgen Langhelle *Leif* • Jonathan LaPaglia *Ronald* ■ *Dir* Erik Skjoldbjaerg • *Scr* Nikolaj Frobenius, Hans Gunnarsson, Cathinka Nicolayson, Erik Skjoldbjaerg, Kathrine Valen Zeiner

Pipe Dreams ★★★[U]
Drama 1976 · US · Colour · 89min

Having launched a number of acting careers (including Sylvester Stallone's) in his own co-directing debut *The Lords of Flatbush*, director Stephen Verona focused on a first-time thespian of a different kind for his initial solo venture. Disco diva Gladys Knight acquits herself admirably as a woman who journeys to Alaska to find her husband (Barry Hankerson, to whom she was married in real life) who is working on the pipeline there. The scarcity of women in the frontier town means the only roommate she can find is prostitute Shirley Bain. Slight but sensitively handled. FL

Gladys Knight *Maria Wilson* • Wayne Tippit *Mike Thompson* • Barry Hankerson *Rob Wilson* • Altovise Davis *Lydia* • Bruce French *Duke* • Sylvia Hayes *Sally* ■ *Dir/Scr* Stephen Verona

The Piper's Tune ★★[U]
Period adventure 1962 · UK · BW · 62min

This costume adventure focuses on a gang of children whose attempts to flee the chaos of the Napoleonic Wars are jeopardised by a seemingly kindly doctor. Director Muriel Box valiantly seek to convey the uncertainties of the period, and Frederick Piper shows well as the treacherous spy. But the inexperience of the juveniles, and a lack of finance, fatally undermines their efforts to bring weight and scale to the action. DP

Mavis Ranson *Anna* • Roberta Tovey *Suzy* • Angela White *Maria* • Malcolm Ranson *Thomas* • Brian Wills *Paul* • Graham Wills *Peter* ■ *Dir* Muriel Box • *Scr* Michael Barnes, from a story by Frank Wells

Pippi Longstocking ★★
Adventure 1968 · Swe · Colour · 99min

This adventure for Astrid Lindgren's popular character was successful enough to warrant two sequels by the same team. Pippi is a super-strong, red-haired nine-year-old who leads a wild, independent life with her pet monkey and horse while her ship's captain father is apparently lost at sea. The primitive dubbing may irritate grown-ups, but children will find it cheerful and enjoyable. JG Swedish dubbed.

Inger Nilsson *Pippi Longstocking* • Maria Persson *Annika* • Paer Sundberg *Tommy* • Oellegard Welton *Mother* • Fredrik Ohlsson *Father* • Hans Alfredson *Konrad* • Margot Trooger *Miss Prusselius* • Beppe Wolgers *Captain Longstocking* ■ *Dir* Olle Hellbom • *Scr* Astrid Lindgren

Pippi Longstocking ★★★[U]
Animated musical adventure
1997 · Can/Swe/Ger · Colour · 74min

Astrid Lindgren's perky heroine comes to the big screen in this lively animated adventure, packed with the uplifting values that characterise her original stories. The strongest girl in the world (appropriately voiced at full belt by Melissa Altro) battles an interfering neighbour and a couple of bungling burglars. Though not up to Disney standards, there's enough here to keep little girls amused: animation that's full of colour and vitality, a couple of rousing musical numbers and some appealing animals in tow. JF DVD

Melissa Altro *Pippi Longstocking* • Dave Thomas *Thunder-Karlsson* • Catherine O'Hara *Mrs Prysselius* • Gordon Pinsent *Captain Longstocking* • Carole Pope *The Teacher* • Wayne Robson *Bloom* • Richard Binsley *Mr Nilsson/Dog* • Rick Jones *O'Malley* ■ *Dir* Clive Smith • *Scr* Catharina Stackelberg, from the books by Astrid Lindgren

Piranha ★★★[15]
Horror 1978 · US · Colour · 93min

In this sly, witty cash-in on *Jaws*, director Joe Dante and writer John Sayles dream up a deliriously silly tale about a shoal of killer fish, bred by the army for use in Vietnam, that escapes and munches its way through the waterways of America. Bradford Dillman keeps an admirably straight face as the hero and there are neat supporting turns from Kevin McCarthy, Keenan Wynn, Dick Miller and Barbara Steele. Even at this early stage of his career, Dante embellishes the film with an array of references to other movies, and the laughs and blood flow in equal measure. JF Violence, swearing, nudity. DVD BD

Bradford Dillman *Paul Grogan* • Heather Menzies *Maggie McKeown* • Kevin McCarthy *Dr Robert Hoak* • Keenan Wynn *Jack* • Dick Miller *Buck Gardner* • Barbara Steele *Dr Mengers* ■ *Dir* Joe Dante • *Scr* John Sayles, from a story by Richard Robinson, John Sayles

Piranha II: the Spawning ★[18]
Horror 1981 · Neth · Colour · 90min

In this appalling follow-up to Joe Dante's entertaining original, the performances are amateurish (even a young Lance Henriksen lacks conviction), the direction is leaden and the deadly fish are laughably bargain-basement. It's a bit of a shock to find that this was the feature debut of James Cameron. JC DVD

Tricia O'Neil *Anne Kimbrough* • Steve Marachuk *Tyler* • Lance Henriksen *Steve Kimbrough* • Ricky G Paull *Chris Kimbrough* • Ted Richert *Raoul* • Leslie Graves *Allison* ■ *Dir* James Cameron • *Scr* HA Milton

Piranha ★★★[18]
Horror comedy 2010 · US · Colour · 84min

An underwater earthquake releases prehistoric man-eating fish into an Arizona lake in this average spin on Joe Dante's 1978 *Jaws* knock-off. Aside from the 3D gimmick, there's not much on offer here that the budget original didn't include – comical gore, snappy thrills and in-joke references (Richard Dreyfuss is the pre-credits victim). Christopher Lloyd is a hoot as a mad scientist and Jerry O'Connell is equally over the top, but the rest relies on easy gross-out laughs. AJ Violence, swearing, drug abuse, nudity. DVD BD 3D

Elisabeth Shue *Julie Forester* • Adam Scott *Novak* • Jerry O'Connell *Derrick Jones* • Ving Rhames *Deputy Fallon* • Kelly Brook *Danni* • Christopher Lloyd *Mr Goodman* • Richard Dreyfuss *Matt* • Eli Roth *Wet T-shirt emcee* ■ *Dir* Alexandre Aja • *Scr* Alexandre Aja, Josh Stolberg, Pete Goldfinger, Grégory Levasseur

Piranha 3DD ★[18]
Horror 2011 · US · Colour · 82min

Those pesky prehistoric piranhas migrate from Lake Victoria to the Big Wet Water Park in this crass, gross and witless sequel to the 2010 hit. Misfiring on all cylinders, the film begins with a gaseous cow corpse excreting fish eggs, setting the tone for an insulting, juvenile, soft-core sex-obsessed carnival of splatter. "Welcome to rock bottom", says David Hasselhoff, reduced to badly emulating his role in *Baywatch*. He never spoke a truer word. AJ Gore, nudity. DVD BD 3D CS

Danielle Panabaker *Maddy* • Katrina Bowden *Shelby* • Christopher Lloyd *Mr Goodman* • Ving Rhames *Deputy Fallon* • Gary Busey *Clayton* • David Hasselhoff ■ *Dir* John Gulager • *Scr* Marcus Dunston, Patrick Melton

Piranhaconda ★★[15]
Science-fiction horror
2011 · US · Colour · 82min

Fans of previous monster mash-ups from Roger Corman will probably enjoy yet another tale of a hungry hybrid beastie scoffing its way through an appetising if uncharismatic cast. Here, the crew of a low-budget horror film, a gang of kidnappers and an intrepid scientist (played by token "star" Michael Madsen) are on the menu of a local Hawaiian legend. The B-movie

acting, unconvincing special effects and gratuitous cleavage shots become tiresome after a while, but prolific exploitation director Jim Wynorski does have some beautiful locations and a modicum of Madsen cool to keep proceedings watchable. JA DVD

Michael Madsen *Professor Lovegrove* • Rachel Hunter *Talia* • Shandi Finnessey *Kimmy* • Terri Ivens *Rose* ■ *Dir* Jim Wynorski • *Scr* Mike MacLean, from a concept by J Brad Wilke

The Pirate ★★★★[U]
Musical 1948 · US · Colour · 97min

This picturesque and largely enjoyable MGM musical swashbuckler was a commercial flop in its day but has since picked up a considerable following. Its latter-day popularity stems more from the Cole Porter songs, opulent sets and lavish choreography than from the story about a sheltered young woman who dreams of escape and adventure with a glamorous pirate. Vincente Minnelli directs his wife Judy Garland and Gene Kelly with gusto and panache. PF

Judy Garland *Manuela* • Gene Kelly *Serafin* • Walter Slezak *Don Pedro Vargas* • Gladys Cooper *Aunt Inez* • Reginald Owen *Advocate* • George Zucco *Viceroy* ■ *Dir* Vincente Minnelli • *Scr* Albert Hackett, Frances Goodrich, from the play by SN Behrman

Pirates ★[15]
Adventure 1986 · Fr/Tun · Colour · 113min

Roman Polanski wanted Jack Nicholson to play the lead in what would be a lark, a send-up of Errol Flynn movies and their ilk - a lark, however, that Hollywood wouldn't underwrite. But a dozen years later Polanski found Tunisian backers and shot the picture in the Seychelles with Walter Matthau hiding behind a forest of face-fur, walking on a wooden leg and talking Hollywood-cockney. The waste of money and talent, together with the sub-Python japes, make this a depressing experience. AT

Walter Matthau *Captain Red* • Cris Campion *Jean-Baptiste, "the Frog"* • Damien Thomas *Don Alfonso* • Olu Jacobs *Boumako* • Ferdy Mayne *Captain Linares* • David Kelly *Surgeon* • Charlotte Lewis *Dolores* • Anthony Peck *Spanish officer* • Anthony Dawson *Spanish officer* • Roy Kinnear *Dutch* ■ *Dir* Roman Polanski • *Scr* Gérard Brach, Roman Polanski, John Brownjohn

The Pirates! in an Adventure with Scientists! ★★★★[U]
Animated comedy adventure
2012 · UK/US · Colour · 84min

The rousing good humour of Aardman Animations (home of Wallace & Gromit) catches fire with this tale of derring-do - and don't - on the high seas. Hugh Grant voices Pirate Captain, who sets out to win the coveted Pirate of the Year award against his more impressive rivals, including Black Bellamy (Jeremy Piven) and Cutlass Liz (Salma Hayek). The stop-frame animation work is simply marvellous, the dialogue is crisp, the characters are hugely appealing and the voice work from a heady ensemble cast (David Tennant, Imelda Staunton, Martin Freeman) cannot be faulted. Despite a little sag in the middle, this wonderfully imaginative movie succeeds in being that rare thing: a family film that the whole family will enjoy. KK DVD BD 3D

Hugh Grant *Pirate Captain* • David Tennant *Charles Darwin* • Martin Freeman *Pirate with a scarf* • Imelda Staunton *Queen Victoria* • Brendan Gleeson *Pirate with gout* • Jeremy Piven *Black Bellamy* • Salma Hayek *Cutlass Liz* • Ashley Jensen *Surprisingly curvaceous pirate* ■ *Dir* Peter Lord, Jeff Newitt • *Scr* Gideon Defoe, from his book

The Pirates of Blood River ★★[U]
Swashbuckling adventure
1961 · UK · Colour · 94min

This Hammer swashbuckler is a colourful, action-packed adventure. Kerwin Mathews is a Huguenot who falls into the clutches of pirate king Christopher Lee, a buccaneer

P

complete with eye-patch and hook. There are wenches and scurvy knaves galore, but only tantalising vestiges of the X-rated bloodbath intended, as the film was reduced to U certificate derring-do for the school holidays after long sessions at the censor's office. **DM**

Christopher Lee *LaRoche* • Kerwin Mathews *Jonathan Standing* • Glenn Corbett *Henry* • Marla Landi *Bess* • Oliver Reed *Brocaire* • Andrew Keir *Jason Standing* • Dennis Waterman *Timothy* ■ *Dir* John Gilling • *Scr* John Gilling, John Hunter, from a story by Jimmy Sangster

The Pirates of Penzance
★★★ U

Musical   1983 · US · Colour · 107min

Director Wilford Leach adapted Joseph Papp's famously successful stage production of Gilbert and Sullivan's popular operetta, retaining the original cast plus Angela Lansbury as Ruth. Kevin Kline repeated his rich performance as the Pirate King, with Linda Ronstadt as Mabel and George Rose as "the very model of a model major-general". The familiar and much loved score was pepped up with a contemporary treatment by William Elliott. The high-spirited energy of the cast, however, can't disguise the show's theatrical origins, and the whole enterprise is somewhat dwarfed by the Panavision screen. **RK**

Kevin Kline *Pirate King* • Angela Lansbury *Ruth* • Linda Ronstadt *Mabel Stanley* • George Rose *Major-General Stanley* • Rex Smith *Frederic* • Tony Azito *Sergeant* ■ *Dir* Wilford Leach • *Scr* Wilford Leach, from the operetta by WS Gilbert and Arthur Sullivan

Pirates of Silicon Valley
★★ 12

Biographical drama   1999 · US · Colour · 92min

This TV movie is a considered account of the meteoric rise of the Apple and Microsoft computer empires. Part-sniping, part-admiring, writer/director Martyn Burke's approach is studiously resolute in its refusal to side with either laid-back pioneers Steve Jobs (Noah Wyle) and Steve Wozniak (Joey Slotnick) or ex-Harvard maverick Bill Gates (Anthony Michael Hall). But where this biopic errs is in seeing the eventual showdown as a clash of personalities, rather than business practices. **DP**

Noah Wyle *Steve Jobs* • Anthony Michael Hall *Bill Gates* • Joey Slotnick *Steve Wozniak* • John DiMaggio *Steve Ballmer* • Josh Hopkins *Paul Allen* ■ *Dir* Martyn Burke • *Scr* Martyn Burke, from the non-fiction book *Fire in the Valley* by Paul Freiberger, Michael Swaine

Pirates of the Caribbean: the Curse of the Black Pearl
★★★★ 12

Fantasy action adventure
2003 · US · Colour · 143min

Based on one of Disney's most famous theme-park attractions, this shiver-me-timbers swashbuckler could have been short on plot and long on action. In fact it delivers plenty of both, with brio. This lavish Hollywood voyage into pirate country effortlessly fills its running time as blacksmith Orlando Bloom and governor's daughter Keira Knightley fall foul of cursed buccaneers. The real treasure comes courtesy of Johnny Depp's swaggering, slurring, mascara-wearing rascal Jack Sparrow, a seafaring rock-star type and an irresistible comic hero. Geoffrey Rush also milks his role as an archetypal pirate captain, while some superb special effects reveal the skeletal curse of the Black Pearl's crew under moonlight. **JC** DVD 🔵 CS

Johnny Depp *Capt Jack Sparrow* • Geoffrey Rush *Capt Barbossa* • Orlando Bloom *Will Turner* • Keira Knightley *Elizabeth Swann* • Jack Davenport *Commander Norrington* • Kevin R McNally [Kevin McNally] *Joshamee Gibbs* • Zoë Saldana *Anamaria* • Jonathan Pryce *Governor Weatherby Swann* ■ *Dir* Gore Verbinski • *Scr* Ted Elliott, Terry Rossio, from a story by Ted Elliott, Terry Rossio, Stuart Beattie, Jay Wolpert, from the Disney theme-park ride

Pirates of the Caribbean: Dead Man's Chest
★★★ 12

Fantasy action adventure
2006 · US · Colour · 144min

Johnny Depp's lovable rogue Jack Sparrow returns for more swashbuckling high jinks in this frenetic yet overlong follow-up. Only this time, it's not just Sparrow's neck that's in danger but his very soul, as cunning undead captain Davy Jones (a squid-faced Bill Nighy) tries to recover the ultimate unpaid debt. Never mind that the narrative is meandering or that Orlando Bloom is as uncharismatic as ever, it's the elaborate set pieces and dazzling CGI that make this such no-brainer fun. **SF** DVD 🔵 CS

Johnny Depp *Capt Jack Sparrow* • Orlando Bloom *Will Turner* • Keira Knightley *Elizabeth Swann* • Bill Nighy *Davy Jones* • Stellan Skarsgård *"Bootstrap" Bill* • Jack Davenport *Norrington* • Kevin R McNally [Kevin McNally] *Gibbs* • Naomie Harris *Tia Dalma* • Jonathan Pryce *Governor Weatherby Swann* ■ *Dir* Gore Verbinski • *Scr* Ted Elliott, Terry Rossio, from characters by Elliott, Rossio, Stuart Beattie, Jay Wolpert, from the Disney theme-park ride

Pirates of the Caribbean: at World's End
★★ 12

Fantasy action adventure
2007 · US · Colour · 161min

Shot simultaneously with its predecessor, this bloated third film in the *Pirates of the Caribbean* franchise is a resounding disappointment. The swashbuckling insouciance of the original and the CGI spectacle of its sequel are gone, replaced here by talky plot exposition. At nearly three hours long, and with a notable absence of stand-out set pieces, the dull proceedings are only enlivened by Johnny Depp's louche pirate antihero Captain Jack Sparrow. He's a remarkable comic creation and a joy to watch, yet even his scurrilous charms are unable to illuminate a turgid script that seems more interested in trying to work out the limits of its own mythology than entertaining the audience. The climactic sea battle is brilliantly shot and edited, however, and gives octopus-faced Davy Jones (Bill Nighy) another memorable outing. Elsewhere Rolling Stone Keith Richards – who inspired Depp's larger-than-life performance – has a brief but suitably ironic cameo. A fourth instalment, *On Stranger Tides*, is in production. **JR** DVD 🔵 CS

Johnny Depp *Capt Jack Sparrow* • Geoffrey Rush *Capt Barbossa* • Orlando Bloom *Will Turner* • Keira Knightley *Elizabeth Swann* • Jack Davenport *Norrington* • Bill Nighy *Davy Jones* • Jonathan Pryce *Governor Weatherby Swann* • Chow Yun-Fat *Capt Sao Feng* • Lee Arenberg *Pintel* • Mackenzie Crook *Ragetti* • Stellan Skarsgård *"Bootstrap" Bill* • Keith Richards (2) *Capt Teague* ■ *Dir* Gore Verbinski • *Scr* Ted Elliott, Terry Rossio, from characters by Elliott, Rossio, Stuart Beattie, Jay Wolpert, inspired by the Disney theme-park ride • *Music* Hans Zimmer

Pirates of the Caribbean: on Stranger Tides
★★★ 12

Fantasy action adventure
2011 · US · Colour · 130min

Johnny Depp rides out a rickety plot to keep the franchise afloat in Captain Jack Sparrow's fourth seafaring adventure. This time his wandering eye settles on the womanly shape of Penélope Cruz, playing the daughter of legendary pirate Blackbeard. Ian McShane is a welcome addition as Blackbeard, bringing grizzled charm while committing acts of great evil. As usual, the quest (to find the Fountain of Youth) is long-winded, but thankfully Depp retains the ability to rise above the nonsense with his customary sly humour. **SP** Some violence. DVD 🔵 🔵 CS

Johnny Depp *Capt Jack Sparrow* • Penélope Cruz *Angelica* • Ian McShane *Blackbeard* • Geoffrey Rush *Capt Barbossa* • Stephen Graham *Scrum* • Astrid Bergès-Frisbey *Syrena* • Sam Claflin *Philip Swift* • Kevin R McNally [Kevin McNally] *Joshamee Gibbs* • Keith Richards *Captain Teague* ■ *Dir* Rob Marshall • *Scr* Ted Elliott, Terry Rossio, from the novel *On Stranger*

Tides by Tim Powers, from characters by Elliott, Rossio, Stuart Beattie, Jay Wolpert, from the Disney theme-park ride

Pirates of the Caribbean: Dead Men Tell No Tales

Fantasy action adventure   2017 · US · Colour

This is a preview – no prints were available to review prior to publication: Jack Sparrow sets sail again in this, the fifth instalment in the series. By now, Johnny Depp could do this kohl-eyed, quivery-limbed schtick in his sleep, which might work very well for the perpetually soused Sparrow who this time is on a quest to find Poseidon's trident. Jerry Bruckheimer stays on board as producer, ensuring splashy spectacle, and the new blood includes Javier Bardem playing a ghostly captain seeking vengeance for his brother's murder. **SP**

Johnny Depp *Captain Jack Sparrow* • Geoffrey Rush *Barbossa* • Javier Bardem *Captain Salazar* • Kaya Scodelario *Carina Smyth* ■ *Dir* Espen Sandberg, Joachim Ronning • *Scr* Jeff Nathanson

Pistol Whipped
★★ 15

Action drama   2008 · US · Colour · 95min

This entry in Steven Seagal's nonstop assault on the straight-to-DVD market sees him playing a washed-up ex-cop with a drink problem and gambling debts. His 12-step programme involves being dispatched by Lance Henriksen's government operative to wipe out various bad guys (though, kept largely immobile by his paunch, Seagal takes them out with little more than a scowl). The final shoot-out is set in a graveyard; could Seagal be writing the epitaph to his career? **JR** Violence, swearing. DVD

Steven Seagal *Matt Connor* • Lance Henriksen *The Old Man* • Paul Calderon *Blue* • Mark Elliot Wilson *Steve* • Lydia Jordan *Becky* ■ *Dir* Roel Reiné • *Scr* JD Zeik

Pit and the Pendulum
★★★★ 12

Horror   1961 · US · Colour · 77min

Roger Corman's seminal series of Edgar Allan Poe adaptations ensures that he can never be dismissed as just a purveyor of schlock. This followed the first in the cycle, *The Fall of the House of Usher*, and boasts an intelligent script from Richard Matheson and another fine performance from Vincent Price. He plays the sinister Nicholas Medina, haunted by his father's tortuous past in the days of the Inquisition. Corman creates an effective gothic air and works wonders with his limited budget. **JF** DVD 🔵

Vincent Price *Nicholas Medina* • Barbara Steele *Elizabeth Barnard Medina* • John Kerr *Francis Barnard* • Luana Anders *Catherine Medina* • Antony Carbone *Dr Charles Leon* ■ *Dir* Roger Corman • *Scr* Richard Matheson, from the story by Edgar Allan Poe

The Pit and the Pendulum
★★★ 18

Horror   1991 · US · Colour · 92min

Like the 1961 version, this film pretty much ignores Edgar Allan Poe's original story. The action takes place during the Spanish Inquisition and focuses on Inquisitor-General Torquemada (Lance Henriksen) who, attracted to a baker's wife (Rona De Ricci) accused of witchcraft, makes plans to do away with her husband (Jonathan Fuller). Henriksen hams it up, while director Stuart Gordon gives the torture scenes a gleefully ghoulish edge. **KB** DVD 🔵

Lance Henriksen *Torquemada* • Rona De Ricci *Maria* • Jonathan Fuller *Antonio* • Frances Bay *Esmeralda* • Jeffrey Combs *Francisco* • Oliver Reed *Cardinal* ■ *Dir* Stuart Gordon • *Scr* Dennis Paoli, from the story by Edgar Allan Poe

Pit of Darkness
★ PG

Crime drama   1961 · UK · BW · 78min

William Franklyn had the misfortune to land the lead in this desperate B-feature, as a safe-maker who loses his memory and finds himself implicated in a jewel robbery. With assassination attempts coming thicker and clues, the plot plods along to its predictable

conclusion. In spite of the best efforts of writer/director Lance Comfort and a talented cast, this is awful. **DP** DVD

William Franklyn *Richard Logan* • Moira Redmond *Julie Logan* • Bruno Barnabe *Maxie* • Leonard Sachs *Conrad* • Nigel Green *Jonathan* • Anthony Booth *Ted Mellis* • Nanette Newman *Mary* ■ *Dir* Lance Comfort • *Scr* Lance Comfort, from the novel *To Dusty Death* by Hugh McCutcheon

Pitch Black
★★★★ 15

Science-fiction thriller
1999 · Aus/US · Colour · 103min

It might start out resembling another assembly-line sci-fi saga, but this visually stunning adventure soon becomes as thrilling as it is imaginatively striking. The setting is a world with three suns, where a tri-solar eclipse allows screeching, flesh-hungry creatures to emerge from underground. The motley crew that must traverse this nightmare landscape is led by tough guy Vin Diesel, giving a charismatic performance. With the first half sporting a brilliant desert surrealism and the second loaded with stylised gore, director David Twohy's frightener is a vivid achievement. *The Chronicles of Riddick* is the much less successful sequel. **AJ** DVD 🔵

Radha Mitchell *Fry* • Vin Diesel *Riddick* • Cole Hauser *Johns* • Keith David *Imam* • Lewis Fitz-Gerald *Paris* • Claudia Black *Shazza* ■ *Dir* David Twohy • *Scr* Jim Wheat, Ken Wheat, David Twohy, from a story by Jim Wheat, Ken Wheat • *Cinematographer* David Eggby • *Production Designer* Graham Walker

Pitch Perfect
★★★ 12

Musical comedy   2012 · US · Colour · 107min

This campus comedy is like *Glee* – only bigger, meaner and funnier. Anna Kendrick plays Beca, a would-be DJ who becomes embroiled in the cut-throat world of university *a cappella* singing, pitting her group, the Barden Bellas against male rivals The Treblemakers. It's perfectly obvious where the story is headed, but razor-sharp energy and a terrific script make up for fistfuls of clichés. It's a lightweight confection, but *Pitch Perfect* is great fun while the fat lady (and the skinny one) sings. **KK** Swearing, sexual references. DVD 🔵

Anna Kendrick *Beca* • Skylar Astin *Jesse* • Ben Platt *Benji* • Brittany Snow *Chloe* • Anna Camp *Aubrey* • Elizabeth Banks (2) *Gail* ■ *Dir* Jason Moore • *Scr* Kay Cannon, from the non-fiction book *Pitch Perfect: The Quest for Collegiate A Cappella Glory* by Mickey Rapkin

Pitch Perfect 2
★★★ 12

Musical comedy   2015 · US · Colour · 109min

Who'd have thought that a film about unaccompanied college singing would be such a big hit, but that's exactly what the first *Pitch Perfect* was. So, three years later, here's another one, and it's kind of fun, too, though director Elizabeth Banks (who also plays one of the contest commentators) has to work harder at it than Jason Moore did with the original. Anna Kendrick and Rebel Wilson return, and the film is sassy and smartly written, but waffles badly through the middle hour before rediscovering its mojo in the climax. **DA** Some swearing, sexual references. DVD 🔵

Anna Kendrick *Beca* • Rebel Wilson *Fat Amy* • Hailee Steinfeld *Emily* • Brittany Snow *Chloe* • Skylar Astin *Jesse* • Adam Devine *Bumper* ■ *Dir* Elizabeth Banks (2) • *Scr* Kay Cannon, from a non-fiction book by Mickey Rapkin

Pitch Perfect 3

Comedy   2017 · US · Colour

This is a preview – no prints were available to review as we went to press: With track one and track two hitting high notes at the box office, it was inevitable that producers would return to the format for a third film. But whereas sequels of sequels often see the original cast jump ship to be replaced by lesser names, the front office has scored something of a coup with Anna Kendrick, Rebel Wilson and Brittany Snow all returning for another chorus, while Elizabeth Banks once again directs as well as stars. Let's hope the franchise remains as entertaining to watch as it obviously is to work on. TP

Anna Kendrick *Beca* • Elizabeth Banks (2) *Gail* • Hailee Steinfeld *Emily* • Rebel Wilson *Fat Amy* • Brittany Snow *Chloe* ■ *Dir* Elizabeth Banks (2) • *Scr* Kay Cannon

Pitfall ★★★★

Film noir   1948 · US · BW · 85min

Bored with his perfect wife and son, an insurance agent falls for a charmer with tragic results in this excellent adult drama, which takes *film noir* into the world of middle-class domesticity. Dick Powell is basically honest, but that doesn't stop his momentary philandering leading to deceit and murder. Lizabeth Scott excels as the seductive adventuress, and Raymond Burr is superbly sleazy as the villain of the piece. Andre De Toth maintains a tense pace in a film with a surprisingly modern view of the American Dream turned sour. TV

Dick Powell *John Forbes* • Lizabeth Scott *Mona Stevens* • Jane Wyatt *Sue Forbes* • Raymond Burr *Mack MacDonald* • John Litel *District Attorney* • Byron Barr *Bill Smiley* • Jimmy Hunt *Tommy Forbes* • Ann Doran *Maggie* ■ *Dir* Andre De Toth • *Scr* Karl Kamb, from the novel by Jay Dratler

Pitfall ★★★★ 15

Crime drama   1962 · Jpn · BW · 96min

Hiroshi Teshigahara's debut feature draws on the stylised realism he perfected in his early documentary shorts, while anticipating the existential themes of such later collaborations with screenwriter Kobo Abe as *Woman of the Dunes* (1963) and *The Face of Another* (1966). Exploring the moral bankruptcy of postwar Japanese society and the inexplicability of fate, this strikingly photographed film chronicles the travels of miner Hisashi Igawa and his son Kazuo Miyahara, whose discontent and dishonesty culminate in Igawa's murder by white-suited stranger Kunie Tanaka in a ghost town populated solely by sweetshop clerk Sumie Sasaki. DP Japanese +subtitles. Swearing, sex scenes, violence. *DVD*

Hisashi Igawa *Miner* • Kunie Tanaka *Man in white suit* • Kazuo Miyahara *Son* • Sumie Sasaki *Woman* ■ *Dir* Hiroshi Teshigahara • *Scr* Kobo Abe, from his novel • *Cinematographer* Hiroshi Segawa

Pittsburgh ★★ U

Melodrama   1942 · US · BW · 87min

John Wayne, Marlene Dietrich and Randolph Scott star in this drama about coal mining in Pittsburgh. Wayne and Scott own the mine but operate it differently: Wayne is the ruthless capitalist, while Scott is more concerned with the health and safety of the workforce. Dietrich is sort of in the middle, though the movie isn't much interested in romance. AT

Marlene Dietrich *Josie Winters* • Randolph Scott *Cash Evans* • John Wayne *Pittsburgh "Pitt" Markham* • Frank Craven *Doc Powers* • Louise Allbritton *Shannon Prentiss* ■ *Dir* Lewis Seiler • *Scr* Kenneth Gamet, Tom Reed, John Twist, from a story by George Owen, from Tom Reed

Pixels ★★ 12

Science-fiction action comedy
2015 · US · Colour · 101min

Adam Sandler, Kevin James and Josh Gad play three 1980s arcade geeks tasked with saving the world from invading aliens who are attacking the planet in the form of popular video games from the past. Impressive effects fail to gloss over an inane plot and childish humour, as our heroes scream and quip their way to Earth's salvation. Moments may raise a smirk, but more will draw a groan. JL *DVD* *Blu-ray* *3D*

Adam Sandler *Sam Brenner* • Kevin James *President Will Cooper* • Josh Gad *Ludlow Lamonsoff* • Peter Dinklage *Eddie Plant* • Michelle Monaghan *Lt Col Violet Van Patten* • Sean Bean *Corporal Hill* ■ *Dir* Chris Columbus • *Scr* Tim Herlihy, Timothy Dowling, from a story by Herlihy, from a short film by Patrick Jean

Pixote ★★★★★ 18

Drama   1981 · Bra · Colour · 119min

The knowledge that Fernando Ramos Da Silva was killed in a shoot-out with the police just six years after playing a ten-year-old orphan inexorably drawn into a living hell of prostitution, drugs and murder makes Hector Babenco's ultra-realistic picture of São Paulo streetlife all the more chilling. Da Silva genuinely lives a role that stands as an indictment of us all. Adapted from José Louzeirc's novel, the film focuses on the facts of an appalling situation, without offering glib socio-political solutions. DP Portuguese +subtitles.

Fernando Ramos Da Silva *Pixote* • Marilia Pêra *Sueli* • Jorge Juliao *Lilica* • Gilberto Moura *Dito* • José Nilson Dos Santos *Diego* ■ *Dir* Hector Babenco • *Scr* Hector Babenco, Jorge Duran, from the novel *Infancia dos Mortos* by José Louzeiro

The Place beyond the Pines ★★★★ 15

Crime drama   2012 · US · Colour · 134min

Ryan Gosling stars in this unconventional crime tale as a motorcycle stunt rider who turns to crime in order to raise the son he never knew he had, while the policeman on his tail, Bradley Cooper, has father issues of his own. Writer/director Derek Cianfrance relies a little too much on the film's many twists, but this remains a smart, sprawling and beautifully crafted morality tale that explores the more sensitive side of the male psyche. DW *DVD* *Blu-ray*

Ryan Gosling *Luke* • Bradley Cooper *Avery Cross* • Dane DeHaan *Jason* • Emory Cohen *AJ* • Eva Mendes *Romina* • Ben Mendelsohn *Robin* ■ *Dir* Derek Cianfrance • *Scr* Derek Cianfrance, Ben Coccio, Darius Marder

A Place Called Home ★★

Drama   2004 · US · Colour · 88min

In this flimsy drama, Ann-Margret plays an elderly widow with failing eyesight whose reclusive life is transformed after a drifter and his ten-year-old daughter arrive on her doorstep. Trouble is, the veteran actress is much too glamorous and self-reliant from the outset to seem believable, even if she's agreeable to watch. The rest of the film is just as unconvincing, apart from the sweetly developing relationship between Ann-Margret and the young girl, which provides enough heart to distract from the feature's chief attraction - its ravishing rural scenery. SF

Ann-Margret *Tula Jeeters* • Matthew Settle *Hank Ford* • Hunter Tylo *Billie Jeeters* • Shailene Woodley *California "Cali" Ford* • Gary Sandy *Doctor Douglas "Doc" Hamilton* ■ *Dir* Michael Tuchner • *Scr* JP Martin, from a story by Martin, Frank Q Dobbs

A Place for Annie ★★★★ PG

Drama   1994 · US · Colour · 95min

The year before she gave such an impressive performance as the HIV-positive Robin in *Boys on the Side*, Mary-Louise Parker produced another powerful portrayal of a young woman with Aids in this deeply affecting TV movie. She is admirably supported by Sissy Spacek as the nurse who wants to adopt the HIV-infected baby Parker has abandoned, and by Joan Plowright and S Epatha Merkerson as, respectively, a nanny and a social worker caught up in the case. This is handled with intelligence rather than sensationalism. DP *DVD*

Sissy Spacek *Susan Lansing* • Mary-Louise Parker *Linda Morsten* • Joan Plowright *Dorothy Kilgore* • S Epatha Merkerson *Alice Blakely* • Jack Noseworthy *David Lansing* • David Spielberg *Dr Palmer* ■ *Dir* John Gray • *Scr* Lee Guthrie, Cathleen Young, Nancy Barr

A Place for Lovers ★

Romantic drama   1968 · It/Fr · Colour · 88min

Italy is the setting for this sudsy film in which American divorcee and fashion designer Faye Dunaway falls in love with engineer Marcello Mastroianni. Well, she would, wouldn't she? She did in reality as well, leading to a well-publicised affair with

the archetypal Latin lover. This movie is trash of a fairly low order. AT

Faye Dunaway *Julia* • Marcello Mastroianni *Valerio* • Caroline Mortimer *Maggie* • Karin Engh *Griselda* • Esmeralda Ruspoli ■ *Dir* Vittorio De Sica • *Scr* Vittorio De Sica, Julian Halevy [Julian Zimet], Peter Baldwin, Ennio de Concini, Tonino Guerra, Cesare Zavattini, from a story by Brunello Rondi

A Place in the Sun ★★★★ U

Drama   1951 · US · BW · 116min

Elizabeth Taylor has never looked lovelier, or the young Montgomery Clift more tortured than in this glossy adaptation of Theodore Dreiser's dour novel *An American Tragedy*, previously filmed by Josef von Sternberg. This film won six Oscars, including best director for George Stevens, whose trademark dissolves are most tellingly displayed as ambitious Clift and wealthy Taylor meet for the first time. Trouble is, this tale of love across the tracks has dated badly, and today seems rather drawn out. But Clift and Shelley Winters, as the girl who wants to get rid of, are brilliant, so forget the plot and just revel in what was once Hollywood's idea of classy movie-making. TS

Montgomery Clift *George Eastman* • Elizabeth Taylor *Angela Vickers* • Shelley Winters *Alice Tripp* • Anne Revere *Hannah Eastman* • Raymond Burr *Marlowe* • Herbert Heyes *Charles Eastman* • Keefe Brasselle *Earl Eastman* ■ *Dir* George Stevens • *Scr* Michael Wilson, Harry Brown, from the play *An American Tragedy* by Patrick Kearney, from the novel *An American Tragedy* by Theodore Dreiser • *Cinematographer* William C Mellor • *Costume Designer* Edith Head

A Place of One's Own ★★★ U

Supernatural drama   1944 · UK · BW · 88min

This is a genuinely eerie adaptation of Osbert Sitwell's novel of strange happenings in an English country house. Former cameraman-turned-director Bernard Knowles knows just how to achieve the right spine-chilling touch, cleverly keeping the supernatural themes light in tone. The cast is delightful, with James Mason and Barbara Mullen as the retired homeowners, and lovely Margaret Lockwood as their companion who is the catalyst for the ghostly goings-on. Time has lent this Gainsborough picture a veneer of charm - well worth watching. TS

Margaret Lockwood *Annette* • James Mason *Mr Smedhurst* • Barbara Mullen *Mrs Smedhurst* • Dennis Price *Dr Selbie* • Helen Haye *Mrs Manning-Tuthorn* • Michael Shepley *Major Manning-Tuthorn* • Dulcie Gray *Sarah* ■ *Dir* Bernard Knowles • *Scr* Brock Williams, from the novel by Osbert Sitwell

A Place to Go ★★

Crime drama   1963 · UK · BW · 88min

Michael Sarne goes all mean and moody to unfortunately comic effect as he bids to beat the Bethnal Green blues with an ill-conceived factory heist. Rita Tushingham and Bernard Lee do what they can with a dodgy script, while director Basil Dearden captures something of the flavour of the East End. Lacklustre. DP

Bernard Lee *Matt Flint* • Rita Tushingham *Catherine* • Michael Sarne *Ricky Flint* • Doris Hare *Lil Flint* • Barbara Ferris *Betsy* • John Slater *Jack Ellerman* • David Andrews (1) *Jim* • Roy Kinnear *Bunting* ■ *Dir* Basil Dearden • *Scr* Michael Relph, Clive Exton, from the novel *Bethnal Green* by Michael Fisher

Place Vendôme ★★★ 15

Romantic thriller   1998 · Fr · Colour · 112min

Catherine Deneuve won the best actress prize at Venice for her performance as an alcoholic widow recovering her sense of worth in this mannered thriller from actress-turned-director Nicole Garcia. While her icy detachment and vulnerability are impressive, and Deneuve's attempts to sell the stolen gems left by her husband are not without intrigue, this sparkles all too rarely. DP French +subtitles. Swearing. *DVD*

Catherine Deneuve *Marianne* • Jean-Pierre Bacri *Jean-Pierre* • Emmanuelle Seigner *Nathalie* • Jacques Dutronc *Battistelli* • Bernard Fresson *Vincent Malivert* • François Berléand *Eric Malivert* • Philippe Clévenot *Kleiser* ■ *Dir* Nicole Garcia • *Scr* Nicole Garcia, Jacques Fieschi

Places in the Heart ★★★★ PG

Period drama   1984 · US · Colour · 106min

This beautifully paced and sumptuously shot heart-twanger won Sally Field a best actress Oscar, even if her acceptance speech will go down in the annals of excessive luvviedom. Field is wonderfully moving as the feisty, sorely tried small-town farmer battling the Depression and her emotions, and there's a fine supporting cast that includes John Malkovich, Danny Glover and Amy Madigan. Written and directed by Robert Benton, who won an Oscar for his screenplay, this is a lovingly crafted homage to the community values of his Texas home town. SH *DVD*

Sally Field *Edna Spalding* • Danny Glover *Moze* • John Malkovich *Mr Will* • Lindsay Crouse *Margaret Lomax* • Ed Harris *Wayne Lomax* • Amy Madigan *Viola Kelsey* • Yankton Hatten *Frank Spalding* • Gennie James *Possum Spalding* ■ *Dir/Scr* Robert Benton

The Plague ★★★ 15

Drama   1992 · Fr/UK/Arg/US · Colour · 116min

The reunion of *Kiss of the Spider Woman* stars William Hurt and Raul Julia is something of a disappointment. Adapted from the Albert Camus novel by director Luis Puenzo, it involves a dedicated doctor (Hurt), a French reporter (Sandrine Bonnaire) and a TV cameraman (Jean-Marc Barr) whose lives become entangled during an outbreak of a lethal pestilence in a South American city. The existentialism of the original is lost in this version, which doesn't make up for it with action or tension. TH Swearing, sex scenes, violence. *DVD*

William Hurt *Dr Bernard Rieux* • Sandrine Bonnaire *Martine Rambert* • Jean-Marc Barr *Jean Tarrou* • Robert Duvall *Joseph Grand* • Raul Julia *Cottard* • Lautaro Murua *Father Paneloux* • Victoria Tennant *Alice Rieux* ■ *Dir* Luis Puenzo • *Scr* Luis Puenzo, from the novel *La Peste* by Albert Camus

Plague City: Sars in Toronto ★★

Disaster drama based on a true story
2005 · Can · Colour · 115min

Canadian bureaucracy comes under fire in this fictionalised account of the events of summer 2003, when Toronto suffered a crippling outbreak of severe acute respiratory syndrome (Sars). Following the crisis through the eyes of nurse and young mother Amy (Kari Matchett), the cautionary tale contrasts the heroic work of medical staff tackling the disease with the dangerous damage limitation policies of local government. Initially, the heart wrenching is kept to a minimum, leaving it to the chilling facts about the spread of Sars to make an impact. But as the death toll rises, the screenplay becomes increasingly melodramatic, with cheesy dialogue and wooden acting transforming the tragedy into a soap opera. SF

Kari Matchett *Amy* • Ron White *Dr Royce* • Rick Roberts *Dr Jeremy Neville* • Lannette New *Rosie* • Rahnuma Panthaky *Laura Weston* • Merwin Mondesir *Rob Connell* ■ *Dir* David Wu • *Scr* Collin Friesen

The Plague Dogs ★★★ PG

Animated adventure   1982 · US/UK · Colour · 81min

After *Watership Down*, Martin Rosen went on to adapt another Richard Adams novel, though the film's troubling and downbeat nature possibly explains its comparative lack of success. Two laboratory dogs (voiced by John Hurt and Christopher Benjamin) escape from a British laboratory and seek a canine paradise while trying to avoid recapture. The animation does not reach modern standards, but it's pretty good for the period it was produced and still manages to convey the gritty emotion

P

dictated by the bleak yet absorbing story. KB Some violence and swearing. *DVD*

John Hurt *Snitter* • Christopher Benjamin *Rowf* • James Bolam *The Tod* • Nigel Hawthorne *Dr Robert Boycott* • Warren Mitchell *Tyson/Wag* • Bernard Hepton *Stephen Powell* ▪ *Dir* Martin Rosen • *Scr* Martin Rosen, from the novel by Richard Adams

The Plague of the Zombies ★★★★ 12

Horror 1965 · UK · Colour · 86min

Voodoo rituals in 18th-century Cornwall disguise a savage indictment of the British class system in a superior Hammer horror with a strong plotline. It's John Gilling's best work, and his tight direction and stylish visuals build the tension most effectively. Especially memorable moments include the green-tinted dream sequence, where churchyard corpses are resurrected, and a quite stunning decapitation scene. A vintage bloodcurdler. AJ *DVD*

André Morell *Sir James Forbes* • Diane Clare *Sylvia Forbes* • Brook Williams *Dr Peter Tompson* • Jacqueline Pearce *Alice* • John Carson *Clive Hamilton* • Alexander Davion *Denver* • Michael Ripper *Sergeant Swift* • Marcus Hammond *Martinus* ▪ *Dir* John Gilling • *Scr* Peter Bryan, John Elder [Anthony Hinds]

Plain Clothes ★★★ PG

Comedy thriller 1988 · US · Colour · 93min

Some strong, gritty performances, particularly from George Wendt and Robert Stack, lift this workaday thriller above a script that lumbers along like an old car, accompanied by a man with a flag signalling "twist in the plot ahead". We've been undercover before with a disgruntled cop – in this case, he's posing as a student to clear his brother's name – so there is a strong whiff of familiarity about his quest. But this is still professional movie-making. SH Swearing.

Arliss Howard *Nick Dunbar/Nick Springsteen* • Suzy Amis *Robin Torrence* • George Wendt *Chet Butler* • Diane Ladd *Jane Melway* • Seymour Cassel *Ed Malmburg* • Larry Pine *Dave Hechtor* • Jackie Gayle *Coach Zeffer* • Abe Vigoda *Mr Wiseman* • Robert Stack *Mr Gardner* ▪ *Dir* Martha Coolidge • *Scr* A Scott Frank, from a story by A Scott Frank, Dan Vining

The Plainsman ★★★★ U

Western 1936 · US · BW · 108min

This no-holds-barred spectacle from Cecil B DeMille impressively captures the landscape of the Wild West, teeming with hordes of Sioux and Cheyenne Indians, and merrily ignores historical truths. This western also presents us with a totally fictitious romance between Wild Bill Hickok and Calamity Jane, gloriously glamorised by Gary Cooper and Jean Arthur. The result is a highly enjoyable action epic in true DeMille style. RK *DVD*

Gary Cooper *Wild Bill Hickok* • Jean Arthur *Calamity Jane* • James Ellison *Buffalo Bill Cody* • Charles Bickford *John Latimer* • Porter Hall *Jack McCall* • Helen Burgess *Louisa Cody* • John Miljan *Gen George Armstrong Custer* • Victor Varconi *Painted Horse* • Anthony Quinn *Cheyenne warrior* • Frank McGlynn Sr *Abraham Lincoln* ▪ *Dir* Cecil B DeMille • *Scr* Waldemar Young, Harold Lamb, Lynn Riggs, Grover Jones, from the novel *Wild Bill Hickok, the Prince of the Pioneers* by Frank J Wilstach and from stories by Courtney Ryley Cooper

The Plainsman ★★ U

Western 1966 · US · Colour · 91min

In this pointless remake of Cecil B DeMille's 1936 classic western, a callow Don Murray and a comical Abby Dalton (as Wild Bill Hickok and Calamity Jane) prove no match for the charismatic stars of the original. DeMille's film wasn't noted for its plot, and 30 years on the storyline remains hopelessly old-fashioned and cliché-ridden. Even the colour photography is mediocre. AE

Don Murray *Wild Bill Hickock* • Guy Stockwell *Buffalo Bill Cody* • Abby Dalton *Calamity Jane* • Bradford Dillman *Lieutenant Stiles* • Henry Silva *Crazy Knife* • Leslie Nielsen *Col George A Custer* ▪ *Dir* David Lowell Rich • *Scr* Michael Blankfort, from the 1936 film

Plainsong ★★

Drama 2004 · US · Colour · 120min

This is an earnest and deeply sentimentalised study of a Colorado prairie community. In a quality cast, Aidan Quinn and Rachel Griffiths play the teachers whose private lives become touched by tragedy, but not even a dark turn of events can deflect this TV movie's resolutely upbeat message. DP

Aidan Quinn *Tom Guthrie* • Rachel Griffiths *Maggie Jonas* • America Ferrera *Victoria Roubideaux* • Geoffrey Lewis *Raymond McPheron* • William Andrews *Harold McPheron* • Megan Follows *Ella Guthrie* • Zachery Ty Bryan *Russell Beckman* ▪ *Dir* Richard Pearce • *Scr* Oliver Goldstick, from the novel by Kent Haruf

Le Plaisir ★★★★★ PG

Portmanteau drama 1951 · Fr · BW · 93min

In the second of his four last masterpieces made in France, Max Ophüls approaches these three tales based on stories by Guy de Maupassant in a virtuoso manner. The first one tells of an old man who finds his youth again by wearing a magic mask; the second accompanies a group of prostitutes on a trip to the country; and the third relates how an artist marries his model after she tries to commit suicide. Each episode has memorable sequences, there is splendid period detail, and the wonderful cast includes Jean Gabin, Simone Simon, Danielle Darrieux and Madeleine Renaud as the madam of the brothel. RB

Claude Dauphin *The doctor* • Jean Galland *Ambroise, "The Mask"* • Daniel Gélin *Jean* • Simone Simon *Josephine* • Madeleine Renaud *Mme Tellier* • Jean Gabin *Joseph Rivet* • Danielle Darrieux *Rosa* • Peter Ustinov *Guy de Maupassant* ▪ *Dir* Max Ophüls • *Scr* Max Ophüls, Jacques Natanson, from the stories *The Mask/ The House of Madame Tellier/The Model* by Guy de Maupassant

Plan 9 from Outer Space ★ PG

Science-fiction thriller 1959 · US · BW · 75min

Camp aliens attempt to take over the world by reviving the dead in Ed Wood Jr's science-fiction opus, built around a few minutes of footage Bela Lugosi shot days before he died and often cited as the worst movie ever made. There is some unintentional humour to be had from the way Wood desperately incorporates his shots of Lugosi (and a fake body double) into a mess of stock footage, amateur acting, crude special effects and wobbly sets. Tediously depressing. AJ *DVD*

Gregory Walcott *Jeff Trent* • Bela Lugosi *Ghoul man* • Mona McKinnon *Paula Trent* • Duke Moore *Lieutenant Harper* • Richard Powers [Tom Keene] *Colonel Tom Edwards* • Vampira *Ghoul Woman* • Lyle Talbot *General Roberts* ▪ *Dir/Scr* Edward D Wood Jr

Plan 10 from Outer Space ★★

Science-fiction spoof 1995 · US · Colour · 82min

Why Salt Lake City film-maker Trent Harris would purposely want to invoke the memory of the worst movie ever made is not the only cause of wonderment in this science-fiction spoof. While researching a book about local Mormon history, Stefene Russell finds a plaque that reveals faith founder Brigham Young married an alien queen from the planet Kolob (Karen Black) who's currently plotting a revenge attack on Utah. The chuckles may be few and far between, but good special effects and Black's over-the-top performance add to the eye-rolling bemusement. AJ

Stefene Russell *Lucinda Hall* • Karen Black *Nehor* • Karen Nielson ▪ *Dir/Scr* Trent Harris

Planes ★★★ U

Animated adventure 2013 · UK · Colour · 87min

In what is essentially an airborne *Cars*, a crop duster (Dane Cook) enters the "Wings around the Globe" race... except he's afraid of heights, his veteran coach (Stacy Keach) is a fraud and the other contestants think he's a redneck upstart. Will he conquer his fears? The agile animation will thrill the youngsters, while those older will find the mariachi version of *Love Machine* and gags about Skypads a hoot, as the sweetness and excitement continually builds from a relatively unpromising start. AJ *DVD* *Blu*

Dane Cook *Dusty Crophopper* • Stacy Keach *Skipper Riley* • Brad Garrett *Chug* • Teri Hatcher *Dottie* • Julia Louis-Dreyfus *Rochelle* • Cedric the Entertainer *Leadbottom* • John Cleese *Bulldog* • John Ratzenberger *Harland* ▪ *Dir* Klay Hall • *Scr* Jeffrey M Howard, from a story by John Lasseter

Planes: Fire and Rescue ★★★ U

Animated adventure 2014 · US · Colour · 80min

When his old-fashioned gearbox collapses and a replacement can't be found Dusty Crophopper (voice Dane Cook) fears his racing days are over. So he retrains as a fire-fighter under the instruction of helicopter Blade Ranger (Ed Harris) just as a raging forest fire threatens Piston Peak National Park. Soaring aerial sequences, blazing action and easygoing chuckles are folded into a predictable story, which is slightly better than its predecessor. AJ *DVD* *Blu* *sp* *CS*

Dane Cook *Dusty Crophopper* • Julie Bowen *Dipper* • Ed Harris *Blade Ranger* • Curtis Armstrong *Maru* • John Michael Higgins *Cad* • Hal Holbrook *Mayday* • Anne Meara *Winnie* • Dale Dye *Cabbie* ▪ *Dir* Bobs Gannaway [Roberts Gannaway] • *Scr* Jeffrey M Howard, Bobs Gannaway [Roberts Gannaway], from a story by Howard, Gannaway

Planes, Trains and Automobiles ★★★★ 15

Comedy 1987 · US · Colour · 88min

Steve Martin and John Candy give excellent performances as the not-so-good companions desperately trying to get home for Thanksgiving in this amiable comedy, which sends up the vagaries of the whole American transport system. Written and directed by John Hughes, it occasionally finds it difficult to balance the slapstick with the sentiment, but the cheerfully astute playing by the disaster-prone "little-and-large" leads ensures that the farcical proceedings are always fun to watch. AJ Swearing. *DVD* *Blu* *CS*

Steve Martin *Neal Page* • John Candy *Del Griffith* • Laila Robbins *Susan Page* • Michael McKean *State trooper* • Kevin Bacon *Taxi racer* • Dylan Baker *Owen* • Carol Bruce *Joy* • Olivia Burnette *Marti* ▪ *Dir/Scr* John Hughes

Planet 51 ★★★ U

Animated fantasy adventure 2009 · Sp/UK · Colour · 86min

Chisel-jawed astronaut Chuck Baker (voiced by Dwayne Johnson) lands on what he thinks is an uninhabited planet, only to find it populated by little green men, in this fun animated adventure. What's more, this alien world bears a striking resemblance to 1950s America and its attendant fashions, fears and morals. With the help of some well-meaning alien teens, Chuck has to find his way back to his spaceship before it returns to Earth without him. This sprightly kid-pleaser is full of slapstick set pieces and memorable characters, while more grown-up viewers will find themselves grinning at pastiches of the Cold War paranoia of bygone sci-fi movies. TeS *DVD* *Blu*

Dwayne Johnson *Captain Charles "Chuck" Baker* • Seann William Scott *Skiff* • Jessica Biel *Neera* • Justin Long *Lem* • Gary Oldman *General Grawl* • John Cleese *Professor Kipple* • Freddie Benedict *Eckle* • Alan Marriott *Glar* ▪ *Dir* Jorge Blanco, Javier Abad, Marcos Martinez • *Scr* Joe Stillman

Planet of Blood ★★

Science-fiction horror 1966 · US · Colour · 81min

This largely unmemorable space opera from the Roger Corman stable is distinguished by an eclectic cast and may be viewed today as a precursor to *Alien* with its tale of a US manned space probe rescuing an alien craft that has ditched on the surface of Mars. Unfortunately, the green-skinned female occupant (Florence Marly) turns out to be a galactic vampire.

Filmed in a week for just $65,000, the crude plot was concocted by writer/director Curtis Harrington to fit around cannibalised footage from a big-budget Russian sci-fi movie. RS

Basil Rathbone *Dr Farraday* • John Saxon *Allan* • Dennis Hopper *Paul* • Judi Meredith *Laura* • Florence Marly *Alien queen* ▪ *Dir/Scr* Curtis Harrington

Planet of the Apes ★★★★★ PG

Science-fiction adventure 1967 · US · Colour · 107min

In this seminal sci-fi gem, Charlton Heston stars as the leader of a team of astronauts who crashes on a desolate planet where the apes rule and human beings are the dumb animals. Heston is appropriately square-jawed as the rebellious human, and Roddy McDowall and Kim Hunter shine through the marvellous ape make-up from John Chambers, who received an honorary Oscar for his work. Rod Serling and Michael Wilson provide a sly, clever script that elevates this movie to classic status. Followed by a number of increasingly inferior sequels (beginning with 1969's *Beneath the Planet of the Apes*), plus a rather mundane TV series. Tim Burton remade this in 2001 and an origins film, *Rise of the Planet of the Apes*, was released in 2011. JA Violence. *DVD* *Blu*

Charlton Heston *George Taylor* • Roddy McDowall *Cornelius* • Kim Hunter *Dr Zira* • Maurice Evans *Dr Zaius* • James Whitmore *President of the assembly* • James Daly *Honorious* • Linda Harrison *Nova* • Robert Gunner *Landon* • Lou Wagner *Lucius* ▪ *Dir* Franklin J Schaffner • *Scr* Michael Wilson, Rod Serling, from the novel *La Planète des Singes* by Pierre Boulle

Planet of the Apes ★★★ 12

Science-fiction adventure 2001 · US · Colour · 114min

Tim Burton's "re-imagining" of the 1967 sci-fi classic begins, like the original, with an astronaut (Mark Wahlberg) crash-landing and being captured by apes on horseback. So far, so similar. What's immediately different is the ape make-up. Though John Chambers's 1967 prosthetic work was ground-breaking, multi-Oscar winner Rick Baker has upgraded it in style, so that the actors can truly emote and express through the latex. That's the good news. The bad news is the story: slight and littered with convenience. AC Violence. *DVD* *Blu*

Mark Wahlberg *Captain Leo Davidson* • Tim Roth *Thade* • Helena Bonham Carter *Ari* • Michael Clarke Duncan *Attar* • Paul Giamatti *Limbo* • Estella Warren *Daena* • Cary-Hiroyuki Tagawa *Krull* ▪ *Dir* Tim Burton • *Scr* William Broyles Jr, Lawrence Konner, Mark D Rosenthal [Mark Rosenthal], from the novel *La Planète des Singes* by Pierre Boulle

Planet of the Vampires ★★★ 15

Science fiction 1965 · It/Sp/US · Colour · 83min

Italian horror maestro Mario Bava's only pure science-fiction movie melds the supernatural to space opera with haunting results. Barry Sullivan and Norma Bengell investigate the mysterious planet Aura and discover that its ancient inhabitants are disembodied spirits who await visitors in order to possess them as a means of escaping their dying planet. This is a superb example of how Bava's impressive visual sensibilities disguised a very low budget to depict a convincing alien environment and atmosphere. AJ

Barry Sullivan *Capt Mark Markary* • Norma Bengell *Sanya* • Angel Aranda *Wess* • Evi Marandi *Tiona* • Fernando Villena *Karan* ▪ *Dir* Mario Bava • *Scr* Mario Bava, Alberto Bevilacqua, Callisto Cosulich, Antonio Roman, Rafael J Salvia, Louis M Heyward, Ib Melchior, from a story by Ib Melchior, Renato Pestriniero

Planet Terror ★★ 18

Action horror 2007 · US · Colour · 101min

This homage to the cheap horror flicks of the 1970s has a plot as gossamer thin as those of its cinematic forbears: after an experimental gas is released from a military base, the inhabitants of a small town are transformed into zombies forcing the survivors to battle their way out. The tone hovers uncomfortably between tribute and spoof, but this offering from Robert Rodriguez is neither funny enough to function as a comedy nor scary enough to be taken as a horror movie. Originally intended as one half of the double-bill, *Grindhouse* (Quentin Tarantino directed the other half in the shape of *Death Proof*), it was released in Europe separately after a disastrous US opening. AS Violence, swearing, a sex scene, nudity. DVD ⬇

Rose McGowan *Cherry Darling* • Freddy Rodriguez *Wray* • Michael Biehn *Sheriff Hague* • Jeff Fahey *JT* • Josh Brolin *Block* • Marley Shelton *Dr Dakota Block* • Naveen Andrews *Abby* • Stacy Ferguson *Tammy* • Bruce Willis *Muldoon* • Quentin Tarantino *Rapist* ■ *Dir/Scr* Robert Rodriguez • *Cinematographer* Robert Rodriguez

Planeta Burg ★★★★
Science fiction 1962 · USSR · BW · 74min

It's likely you've seen this Soviet space odyssey without realising it. Roger Corman acquired the rights and hacked off huge chunks for his own B-movies, Curtis Harrington's *Voyage to the Prehistoric Planet* (1965) and *Planet of Blood* (1966). Pavel Klushantsev's film, however, is an original and highly entertaining piece of work, chronicling a three-ship mission to Venus and the encounters of cosmonaut Gennadi Vernov with both the treacherous landscape and various hostile life forms. Colourfully designed and wittily directed, in short, a minor classic. DP In Russian.

Gennadi Vernov *Aloysha* • Vladimir Temelianov *Ilya Vershinin* • Yuri Sarantsev *Scherba* • Georgi Zhonov *Bobrov* • Kyunna Ignatova *Masha* ■ *Dir* Pavel Klushantsev • *Scr* Alexander Kazantsev, Pavel Klushantsev

The Plank ★★★ U
Silent comedy 1967 · UK · Colour · 27min

This joyously inventive "silent" comedy from writer/director Eric Sykes is about the misadventures of two builders delivering wood to a house. Sykes himself is "Smaller workman" to Tommy Cooper's "Larger workman", and, although not all the jokes are completely fresh, the fun is in the effective sound effects, and the spotting of comedy icons such as Jimmy Edwards, Jimmy Tarbuck and Roy Castle in unfamiliar poses. Music hall on the hoof. TH DVD

Tommy Cooper *Larger workman* • Eric Sykes *Smaller workman* • Jimmy Edwards *Policeman* • Roy Castle *Man covered in garbage* • Graham Stark *Amorous van driver* • Stratford Johns *Station sergeant* • Jim Dale *House painter* • Jimmy Tarbuck *Barman* • Hattie Jacques *Woman with rose* • Johnny Speight *Chauffeur* ■ *Dir/Scr* Eric Sykes

The Planter's Wife ★★
Drama 1952 · UK · BW · 91min

She's Claudette Colbert, towards the end of her career, in the middle of a then-topical tale about the "troubles" in Malaya, drifting apart from hubby Jack Hawkins and into the arms of Anthony Steel. Then the rebels attack their plantation and the threat to their lives reunites husband and wife. Interestingly, this picture, intended as a tribute to the courage of the rubber planters and their families, inadvertently ends up as a damning indictment of imperialism. Colbert seems uncomfortable, both in the location work and the ill-matched studio interiors. TS

Claudette Colbert *Liz Frazer* • Jack Hawkins *Jim Frazer* • Anthony Steel *Inspector Hugh Dobson* • Ram Gopal *Nair* • Jeremy Spenser *Mat* • Tom Macaulay *Jack Bushell* ■ *Dir* Ken Annakin • *Scr* Peter Proud, Guy Elmes, from the novel by SC George

Plastic ★★ 15
Action crime drama 2014 · UK · Colour · 97min

This con caper starts well, as a group of hip young credit card fraudsters, led by Ed Speleers and Will Poulter, inadvertently rip off a vicious mobster and are given just two weeks to rustle up two million pounds to

pay off their debt - or else. To this end, they contrive a scam that involves a trip to Miami, a prince, several dodgy disguises, and a good deal of diamonds. There are some half-decent moments, but director Julian Gilbey (*A Lonely Place to Die*) squanders the cast's talents, while the transatlantic sojourn feels like a sly marketing ploy to attract American movie-goers. DA DVD ⬇

Ed Speleers *Sam* • Will Poulter *Fordy* • Alfie Allen *Yatesey* • Sebastian De Souza *Rafa* • Emma Rigby *Frankie* ■ *Dir* Julian Gilbey • *Scr* Julian Gilbey, Will Gilbey [William Gilbey], Chris Howard

Platform ★★★★ 12
Drama 2000 · Chi/HK/Jpn/Fr/Swi · Colour · 148min

Set in Shanxi province in the 1980s, this is an assured if occasionally over-elaborate study of China at its socio-economic crossroads. Filmed in long takes that locate the characters in their slowly changing surroundings, the allegorical action focuses on the Fenyang Peasant Culture Group's tortuous transition into the All-Star Rock and Breakdance Electronic Band, as its style of propagandised pop is surpassed by western imports. However, Jia Zhang Ke is careful to leaven the cultural analysis with human interest, as two young couples seek to persuade their intractable elders to accept their modern approach to romance. DP Mandarin +subtitles. DVD

Wang Hong-wei *Minliang* • Zhao Tao *Ruijuan* • Liang Jing-Dong *Chang Jun* • Yang Tian-Yi *Zhong Pin* ■ *Dir/Scr* Jia Zhang Ke

Platinum Blonde ★★★ U
Comedy 1931 · US · BW · 90min

Jean Harlow is all aglow (and very revealing) in this fast-moving comedy satire. But the real star of the show is leading man Robert Williams (as the reporter who marries debutante Harlow), an inventive, screen-dominating light comedian who tragically died prematurely in the year of this, his greatest hit. The jokes at the expense of high society aren't as funny now, and much of the movie's shooting style has dated badly, but director Frank Capra keeps this zipping along, and the central trio of Harlow, Williams and lovely Loretta Young is a joy to behold. TS

Loretta Young *Gallagher* • Robert Williams (1) *Stew Smith* • Jean Harlow *Anne Schuyler* • Louise Closser Hale *Mrs Schuyler* • Donald Dillaway *Michael Schuyler* • Reginald Owen *Dexter Grayson* ■ *Dir* Frank Capra • *Scr* Jo Swerling, Dorothy Howell, Robert Riskin, from a story by Harry E Chandlee, Douglas W Churchill

Platinum High School ★★
Drama 1960 · US · BW · 93min

Mickey Rooney stars in this partly interesting, partly nonsensically sensationalist drama, directed by Charles Haas. Rooney is the father, estranged from his son by divorce, who arrives at the military academy where his boy has been killed. There, he realises that the establishment is home to delinquent misfits from wealthy families and suspects foul play in his son's death. RK

Mickey Rooney *Steven Conway* • Terry Moore *Jennifer Evans* • Dan Duryea *Major Redfern Kelly* • Yvette Mimieux *Lorinda Nibley* • Conway Twitty *Billy Jack Barnes* • Jimmy Boyd *Bud Starkweather* • Harold Lloyd Jr *Charley Boy Cable* • Richard Jaeckel *Hack Marlow* • Elisha Cook Jr *Harry Nesbitt* ■ *Dir* Charles Haas • *Scr* Robert Smith, from a story by Howard Breslin

Platoon ★★★★★ 15
War drama 1986 · US · Colour · 114min

It took ten years for Oliver Stone to get his script made, but when this film finally reached the screen it became a box-office smash and won four Oscars. Unlike other directors who made major Vietnam movies, Stone has the edge in that he was actually there, as a volunteer who fought for patriotic reasons and got wounded before becoming disillusioned. From the scary opening when the new arrivals are greeted by the sight of body bags bound for home, the movie is an authentically messy tour of

duty through the paddy fields where two Americans (Willem Dafoe and Tom Berenger) are at war with each other and fight for the soul of rookie Charlie Sheen. A modern classic. AT Violence, swearing. DVD ⬇

Tom Berenger *Sergeant Barnes* • Willem Dafoe *Sergeant Elias* • Charlie Sheen *Chris* • Forest Whitaker *Big Harold* • Francesco Quinn *Rhah* • John C McGinley *Sergeant O'Neill* • Richard Edson *Sal* • Kevin Dillon *Bunny* • Reggie Johnson *Junior* • Keith David *King* • Johnny Depp *Lerner* ■ *Dir/Scr* Oliver Stone • *Cinematographer* Robert Richardson

Play ★★★ 15
Romantic drama 2005 · Chi/Arg/Fr · Colour · 101min

Chilean director Alicia Scherson's debut feature cleverly experiments with time frames and locations in an affecting study of near-missing kindred spirits in Santiago. Bored carer Cristina (Viviana Herrera) becomes obsessed with businessman Tristán (Andrés Ulloa), whose life unravels when his wife dumps him. After discovering his stolen briefcase, Cristina begins to follow him, but he remains blissfully unaware of her existence. Scherson captures the vibrancy of urban life, while also highlighting the alienation and melancholy experienced by so many city dwellers. But a playful sense of humour and romance also pervades proceedings, whose intricacy and occasional flights of fancy make this a minor delight. DP Spanish +subtitles. DVD

Viviana Herrera *Cristina* • Andrés Ulloa *Tristán* • Aline Küppenheim *Irene* • Coca Guazzini *Laura* • Jorge Alis *Ricardo* • Francisco Copello *Milos* ■ *Dir/Scr* Alicia Scherson

Play ★★★ 15
Drama based on a true story 2011 · Swe/Den/Fr/Ger/Nor · Colour · 112min

Swedish writer/director Ruben Ostlund's disconcerting feature ponders the links between social inequality and toxic cultural branding, informed by real-life incidents in Gothenburg, where groups of black immigrant teens picked on more affluent middle-class white kids. This is risky film-making, and although Ostlund allows proceedings to run on long after we've grasped his key ideas, the action looks convincingly real and the young cast members are credible throughout. TJ Swedish +subtitles. Swearing, sexual references. DVD

Kevin Vaz *Kevin* • Anas Abdirahman *Anas* • Sebastian Blyckert *Sebastian* • Sebastian Hegmar *Alex* ■ *Dir/Scr* Ruben Ostlund

Play Dead ★ 18
Horror 1981 · US · Colour · 81min

In her post-*Addams Family* years, Yvonne De Carlo lent dignity to a seemingly unending series of completely worthless scripts. This devilish drivel is yet another waste of her inestimable talents. De Carlo makes a satanic pact with a rottweiler to kill off her relatives, all because her late sister married her only true love. Electrocution, strangulation and poisoning are all in the canny canine's canon of carnage, as if anyone cares. Good dog - bad film! AJ

Yvonne De Carlo *Hester* • Stephanie Dunnam *Audrey* • David Cullinane *Jeff* • Glenn Kezer *Otis* • Ron Jackson *Richard* ■ *Dir* Peter Wittman • *Scr* Lothrop W Jordan

Play Dirty ★★ 15
Second World War drama 1969 · UK · Colour · 113min

Co-written by Melvyn Bragg at his least cultured and directed by Andre De Toth at his most action-led, this predictable wartime story of inexperienced officer Michael Caine leading a unit to blow up an enemy fuel dump has its moments - especially when roguish Nigel Davenport is around - but not many. It's another take on Robert Aldrich's *The Dirty Dozen* and, though some of the skirmishes do have an impact, this is not in the same class. TH Violence, swearing, nudity. DVD ⬇

Michael Caine *Captain Douglas* • Nigel Davenport *Cyril Leech* • Nigel Green *Colonel Masters* • Harry Andrews *Brigadier Blore* • Aly Ben Ayed *Sadok* • Vivian Pickles *German nurse* • Bernard Archard *Colonel Homerton* ■ *Dir* Andre De Toth • *Scr* Lotte Colin, Melvyn Bragg, from a story by George Marton

Play It Again, Sam ★★★★ 15
Comedy 1972 · US · Colour · 81min

Adapted by Woody Allen from his own 1969 stage play, this is one of the very few entries on his CV that America's leading film auteur has not directed himself. That task fell to Herbert Ross, who adopts an overcautious approach to the story of film buff Allen's tentative relationship with Diane Keaton, the wife of best pal Tony Roberts. But such is the calibre of the playing and the assurance of the writing that it's almost impossible to resist. The more politically correct may feel their hackles rise from time to time, but the one-liners are among Allen's best and the Bogart allusions are priceless. DP DVD

Woody Allen *Allan Felix* • Diane Keaton *Linda Christie* • Tony Roberts *Dick Christie* • Jerry Lacy *Humphrey Bogart* • Susan Anspach *Nancy Felix* • Jennifer Salt *Sharon* • Joy Bang *Julie* • Viva *Jennifer* ■ *Dir* Herbert Ross • *Scr* Woody Allen, from his play

Play It as It Lays ★★★
Drama 1972 · US · Colour · 98min

Underrated director Frank Perry dissects the Hollywood glitterati in this confident adaptation. The story flashes back from Tuesday Weld's convalescence from a suicide bid. It unflinchingly exposes the dog-eat-dog nature of the fame game, as Weld's model-turned-actress falls back on the friendship of troubled producer Anthony Perkins, after she is dumped by husband Adam Roarke (the minor-league director who discovered her) when his own career takes off. It's pure soap, but there are sharp edges beneath the gloss. DP

Tuesday Weld *Maria Wyeth* • Anthony Perkins *BZ* • Tammy Grimes *Helene* • Adam Roarke *Carter Lang* • Ruth Ford *Carlotta* • Eddie Firestone *Benny Austin* • Diana Ewing *Susannah* • Paul Lambert *Larry Kulik* ■ *Dir* Frank Perry • *Scr* John Gregory Dunne, Joan Didion, from the novel by Joan Didion

Play It Cool ★★ U
Comedy drama 1962 · UK · BW · 78min

This wonderfully nostalgic pre-Beatles teen fest stars Britain's answer to Elvis, Billy Fury, in a genuine pop musical, as the Liverpool rocker who stops Anna Palk from straying off the straight and narrow - as if the plot matters! It's a real period artefact, with guest appearances from the likes of Bobby Vee, and a batch of splendid English veterans like Dennis Price and Richard Wattis along for the ride. It isn't any good, really, but at least it's fun and moves along briskly. TS DVD

Billy Fury *Billy Universe* • Michael Anderson Jr *Alvin* • Dennis Price *Sir Charles Bryant* • Richard Wattis *Nervous man* • Anna Palk *Ann Bryant* ■ *Dir* Michael Winner • *Scr* Jack Henry

Play It to the Bone ★★★ 18
Sports comedy drama 2000 · US · Colour · 123min

Antonio Banderas and Woody Harrelson play second-rate pugilists who get a shot at the big time when they are asked to box each other on the same bill as a Mike Tyson bout. The catch is they have less than 12 hours to get to Vegas, so the two friends hit the road with feisty Lolita Davidovich at the wheel. Too much chat and the aggravating presence of Lucy Liu as a hitch-hiking nymphomaniac make the road trip a long haul, but things pick up during the climactic fisticuffs. NS Swearing, violence, drug abuse, sex scenes, nudity. DVD

Antonio Banderas *Cesar Dominguez* • Woody Harrelson *Vince Boudreau* • Lolita Davidovich *Grace Pasic* • Tom Sizemore *Joe Domino* • Lucy Liu *Lia* • Robert Wagner *Hank Goody* • Richard Masur *Artie* • George Foreman *HBO commentator* • Rod Stewart • Kevin Costner •

James Woods • Drew Carey • Tony Curtis • Wesley Snipes • Natasha Gregson Wagner • Jennifer Tilly ■ *Dir/Scr* Ron Shelton

Play Misty for Me ★★★★ 18

Thriller   1971 · US · Colour · 97min

In Clint Eastwood's fine directorial debut, the star is also totally convincing as a DJ who rejects fan Jessica Walter after a one-night stand, only to discover that she's determined to keep him whatever the cost – 16 years before *Fatal Attraction*. Jealousy is one of the hardest emotions to delineate with any kind of subtlety in cinema, yet Walter is superb as the deranged woman. Eastwood's sideburns and flares lend the movie a period charm today, but its power to grip and chill remains undiminished. Look out for *Dirty Harry* director Don Siegel as Murphy the bartender, and don't watch this one on your own. TS Swearing, drug abuse, brief nudity. *DVD* *BL*

Clint Eastwood *Dave Garver* • Jessica Walter *Evelyn Draper* • Donna Mills *Tobie Williams* • John Larch *Sergeant McCallum* • James McEachin *Al Monte* • Donald Siegel [Don Siegel] *Murphy the bartender* ■ *Dir* Clint Eastwood • *Scr* Jo Heims, Dean Riesner, from a story by Heims • *Cinematographer* Bruce Surtees

Play Up the Band ★★ U

Comedy   1935 · UK · BW · 72min

The subject of many a Stanley Holloway monologue, Sam Small gets his own movie in this jaunty take on the North-South divide at the end of the 1930s. Indeed, director Harry Hughes even finds room for a couple of Holloway's celebrated recitations, as the Heckdyke Steam Wagon Works Prize Brass Band heads to London to compete in a prestigious competition at the Crystal Palace. It's fun in places, but the racist lyrics of the Sweeney Todd song are simply no longer acceptable. DP *DVD*

Stanley Holloway *Sam Small* • Betty Ann Davies *Betty Small* • Leslie Bradley *Jack* • Frank Atkinson *Alf Ramsbottom* ■ *Dir* Harry Hughes • *Scr* Aveling Ginever, from a story by Frank Atkinson

The Playboy of the Western World ★★ PG

Comedy drama   1962 · Ire · Colour · 95min

Brian Desmond Hurst returned to his roots for this authentic version of the Irish play. However, this theatre-bound work has only a strong cast to recommend it over the other screen versions of Synge's garrulous piece. The playboy is a boastful young man who beguiles the inhabitants of a County Mayo village with stories, perhaps real, perhaps fantasy. Gary Raymond has a field day, but for many viewers the main delight will be seeing one of Ireland's greatest actors, Siobhan McKenna, as one of the women who falls for his charm. BB

Siobhan McKenna *Pegeen Mike* • Gary Raymond *Christy Mahon* • Elspeth March *Widow Quin* • Michael O'Briain *Shawn Keogh* • Liam Redmond *Michael James* • Niall MacGinnis *Old Mahon* ■ *Dir* Brian Desmond Hurst • *Scr* Brian Desmond Hurst, from the play by John Millington Synge

The Playboys ★★★ PG

Drama   1992 · UK · Colour · 104min

You wait ages for a film about a single Irish mother who refuses to name the father of her child to turn up, and then, typically, two come along at once. Roddy Doyle's *The Snapper* has the edge over *The Playboys*, although Shane Connaughton cannot be faulted for his part in a script brimming with incident and credible characters. However, a bombastic Albert Finney over-balances the picture in the role of the village policeman, whose jealousy at Robin Wright's romance with Aidan Quinn spills over into violence. DP Violence, swearing.

Albert Finney *Hegarty* • Aidan Quinn *Tom Casey* • Robin Wright *Tara Maguire* • Milo O'Shea *Freddie* • Alan Devlin *Malone* • Niamh Cusack *Brigid* ■ *Dir* Gillies MacKinnon • *Scr* Shane Connaughton, Kerry Crabbe

The Player ★★★★★ 15

Satire   1992 · US · Colour · 119min

From its masterly eight-minute opening crane shot to the final blockbuster pastiche, this swingeing satire is easily the best movie about Tinseltown since *Sunset Blvd.* Director Robert Altman turns the spotlight on the industry hands that feed him and scores a bullseye on each target in Michael Tolkin's deft script. Don't let the galaxy of cameos distract from the gloriously cynical plot and a towering turn from a marvellously oily Tim Robbins. He stars as the high-flying studio executive who is troubled by poison-pen postcards from a discarded scriptwriter, the ambitions of wunderkind Peter Gallagher and the snooping of cop Whoopi Goldberg, who suspects him of murder. This is Hollywood at its worst told by Hollywood at its best. DP Violence, swearing, nudity. *DVD*

Tim Robbins *Griffin Mill* • Greta Scacchi *June Gudmundsdottir* • Fred Ward *Walter Stuckel* • Whoopi Goldberg *Detective Susan Avery* • Peter Gallagher *Larry Levy* • Brion James *Joel Levison* • Cynthia Stevenson *Bonnie Sherow* • Vincent D'Onofrio *David Kahane* • Dean Stockwell *Andy Civella* • Richard E Grant *Tom Oakley* • Sydney Pollack *Dick Mellen* ■ *Dir* Robert Altman • *Scr* Michael Tolkin, from his novel

Players ★★ PG

Romantic drama   1979 · US · Colour · 115min

This charts the rise of a young tennis player who makes it to the Wimbledon final, despite the distractions of a romance with a millionaire's mistress. Dean Paul Martin (Dean's son) stars, with Ali MacGraw as the love interest, in a curate's egg that's very good as a tennis action movie but risibly poor away from the court. But with appearances by Guillermo Vilas, John McEnroe, Ilie Nastase and John Lloyd among others, this is sure to appeal to aficionados of the game. RK

Ali MacGraw *Nicole* • Dean Paul Martin *Chris* • Maximilian Schell *Marco* • Pancho Gonzalez (1) *Pancho* • Steve Guttenberg *Rusty* • Melissa Prophet *Ann* • Guillermo Vilas ■ *Dir* Anthony Harvey • *Scr* Arnold Schulman

The Players ★★ 18

Portmanteau comedy
2012 · Fr · Colour · 103min

After his performance in *The Artist*, Oscar winner Jean Dujardin returns to the sketch comedy format that launched his career for this vulgar, variable and very French anthology about infidelity. The politically incorrect series of tales looks at such subjects as sex addiction, May-December affairs, marriage breakdown and bromance. While many will find the deliberate misogyny rather off-putting, some of the bedroom farce segments do have their sparkling moments. But it must be said that Dujardin often looks like he's having a better time than the viewer in exploring the subject of cheating as a man's right. AJ French, English +subtitles. *DVD*

Jean Dujardin *Fred/Oliver/François/Laurent/James* • Gilles Lellouche *Greg/Nicolas/Bernard/Antoine/Eric* • Alexandra Lamy *Lisa* • Guillaume Canet *Thibault* ■ *Dir* Emmanuelle Bercot, Fred Cavayé, Alexandre Courtès, Jean Dujardin, Michel Hazanavicius, Eric Lartigau, Gilles Lellouche • *Scr* Gilles Lellouche, Jean Dujardin, Nicolas Bedos, Philippe Caverivière, Stéphane Joly

The Players Club ★★★ 18

Crime drama   1998 · US · Colour · 98min

This is an interesting but flawed crime drama, written and directed by rap star/actor Ice Cube (who also pops up in a brief cameo). Newcomer LisaRaye plays an aspiring journalist who takes up stripping to pay her way through college and soon finds herself drawn into the murkier aspects of the business. She delivers a feisty performance, although Bernie Mac steals the show as the motormouth owner of the club where she works. There's an exploitative nature to the whole affair, and both the writing and direction are somewhat erratic. LB Violence, swearing, drug abuse, sex scenes, nudity.

LisaRaye *Diana Armstrong/Diamond* • Monica Calhoun *Ebony* • Bernie Mac *Dollar Bill* • Jamie Foxx *Blue* • Chrystale Wilson *Ronnie* • Adele Givens *Tricks* • AJ Johnson [Anthony Johnson] *Li'l Man* • Ice Cube *Reggie* ■ *Dir/Scr* Ice Cube

Playgirl ★★

Drama   1954 · US · BW · 85min

Old-fashioned melodrama is given a 1950s flavour as a simple Nebraska lass (Colleen Miller) arrives in New York to seek fame and fortune. She rapidly finds herself gracing the cover of *Glitter* magazine, incurring the jealousy of her roommate (Shelley Winters); other undesirable consequences include her descent into the sleazy party scene and her implication in a gangster's murder. Acceptable couch-potato fodder. RK

Shelley Winters *Fran Davis* • Barry Sullivan *Mike Marsh* • Colleen Miller *Phyllis Matthews* • Gregg Palmer *Tom Bradley* • Richard Long *Barron Courtney* • Kent Taylor *Ted Andrews* • Dave Barry *Jonathan* • Philip Van Zandt *Lew Martel* ■ *Dir* Joseph Pevney • *Scr* Robert Blees, from a story by Ray Buffum

Playing Away ★★★ 15

Satire   1986 · UK · Colour · 97min

In Horace Ove's immensely likeable film, Britain's race relations and its imperial hangover are boiled down to a game of cricket, played on a village green between the local side and a team from Brixton. The country lads are confident of victory and are staging the match to raise money for the Third World. The cosy, quaint English movie of the pre-war years has been fondly updated and spiked with razor-sharp social observation. AT *DVD*

Norman Beaton *Willy Boy* • Robert Urquhart *Godfrey* • Helen Lindsay *Marjorie* • Nicholas Farrell *Derek* • Brian Bovell *Stuart* • Suzette Llewellyn *Yvette* ■ *Dir* Horace Ové • *Scr* Caryl Phillips

Playing by Heart ★★★★ 15

Comedy drama   1998 · US · Colour · 116min

This beautifully wrought multi-character love story provides great roles for Sean Connery, Ellen Burstyn and Gena Rowlands, and also puts newer Hollywood hopefuls Ryan Phillippe, Gillian Anderson and Angelina Jolie in the spotlight. Director Willard Carroll's glossy ensemble is engaging and emotionally resonant as it cuts between a multitude of stormy confrontations, intriguing trysts and startling dates, and then neatly ties them all off with a bravura conclusion that's both clever and satisfying. AJ Swearing. *DVD*

Gillian Anderson *Meredith* • Angelina Jolie *Joan* • Madeleine Stowe *Gracie* • Anthony Edwards *Roger* • Ryan Phillippe *Keenan* • Gena Rowlands *Hannah* • Sean Connery *Paul* • Dennis Quaid *Hugh* • Ellen Burstyn *Mildred* • Nastassja Kinski *Melanie* ■ *Dir/Scr* Willard Carroll

Playing for Keeps ★★ 12

Romantic comedy   2012 · US · Colour · 100min

This slick but light-on-laughs romantic comedy stars Gerard Butler as a former star footballer who's reduced to coaching kids in the United States. He's immediately hit on by a bunch of attractive soccer moms but his off-pitch antics threaten his bid to get back together with his ex-wife (Jessica Biel) and son, whose team he's coaching. Butler does his best, yet lacks the requisite charm and comic touch of, say, a George Clooney. But what's even more terrible is the film's portrayal of women – the moms are all giggly, sex-mad or both. And as they're played (badly, as it happens) by such talented actresses as Catherine Zeta-Jones, Uma Thurman and Judy Greer, it's doubly distressing to watch. DA Brief swearing, sexual references. *DVD* *BL*

Gerard Butler *George* • Jessica Biel *Stacie* • Catherine Zeta-Jones *Denise* • Uma Thurman *Patti King* • Dennis Quaid *Carl King* • Judy Greer *Barb* ■ *Dir* Gabriele Muccino • *Scr* Robbie Fox

Playing for Time ★★★★

Drama based on a true story
1980 · US · Colour · 149min

This highly acclaimed and well-acted TV movie is based on the experiences of a

Jewish Holocaust survivor who managed to avoid death by forming an orchestra with fellow captives. Vanessa Redgrave, who caused controversy when she accepted the role owing to her Palestinian sympathies, is as impressive and heartfelt as ever, and she is given memorable support by Jane Alexander and Melanie Mayron. Perhaps too heart-rending for some tastes, this is nonetheless a thought-provoking and moving drama. JB

Vanessa Redgrave *Fania Fenelon* • Jane Alexander *Alma Rose* • Maud Adams *Mala* • Christine Baranski *Olga* • Robin Bartlett *Etalina* • Marisa Berenson *Elzvieta* • Verna Bloom *Paulette* ■ *Dir* Daniel Mann • *Scr* Arthur Miller, from the book by Fania Fenelon

Playing God ★★ 18

Crime thriller   1997 · US · Colour · 93min

Playing against type, David Duchovny stars as a disgraced surgeon with a drug habit who becomes unofficial physician to slimy mobster Timothy Hutton and his gang. Both Hutton and underworld rival Peter Stormare are flamboyantly over the top, and Angelina Jolie supplies the glamour. The plot is ridiculously far-fetched while the direction is slick but a touch erratic. JF Violence, swearing. *DVD*

David Duchovny *Dr Eugene Sands* • Timothy Hutton *Raymond Blossom* • Angelina Jolie *Claire* • Michael Massee *Gage* • Peter Stormare *Vladimir* • Andrew Tiernan *Cyril* ■ *Dir* Andy Wilson • *Scr* Mark Haskell Smith

Playing It Cool ★★ 15

Romantic comedy   2014 · US · Colour · 90min

Chris Evans takes a break from saving the world as Captain America to play a screenwriter struggling to write a romantic comedy because he doesn't believe in love. That all changes when he meets, and falls for, an already attached woman (Michelle Monaghan). Director Justin Reardon's feature debut starts out with the intention of being a smart pastiche of generic romantic movies, but the film's witty satire fades as it then becomes a generic romantic movie. Throw in some surreal adult humour to muddle the tone, and you have a movie that (like its hero) has lost its way. JL Swearing, sex scenes. *DVD*

Chris Evans *Narrator* • Michelle Monaghan *Her* • Aubrey Plaza *Mallory* • Topher Grace *Scott* • Anthony Mackie *Bryan* ■ *Dir* Justin Reardon • *Scr* Chris Shafer, Paul Vicknair

Playmates ★ U

Musical comedy   1941 · US · BW · 95min

The last film made by John Barrymore is a bizarrely awful comedy musical starring Kay Kyser and his band, with the usual Kyser appendages such as comedian Ish Kabibble. The ludicrous plot presents the humiliating spectacle of a self-parodying Barrymore as a washed-up actor trying for a comeback on radio by teaching Shakespeare to Kyser. Adding to the comic chaos (which some might find amusing), is Lupe Velez, once known as the "Mexican Spitfire", exhibiting her particular brand of crude slapstick. RK

John Barrymore • Kay Kyser • Lupe Velez *Carmen Del Toro* • Ginny Simms *Ginny* • May Robson *Grandma* • Patsy Kelly *Lulu Monahan* • Peter Lind Hayes *Peter Lindsey* • Ish Kabibble ■ *Dir* David Butler • *Scr* James V Kern, Arthur Phillips, from a story by Kern, MM Musselman

Playtime ★★★★★ U

Satirical comedy   1967 · Fr · Colour · 114min

It took Jacques Tati close to ten years to realise his greatest achievement, but it left him virtually broke. No wonder. He and his designer Eugène Roman built an ultramodern Paris of steel and glass skyscrapers through which Monsieur Hulot, Tati's marvellous comic creation, continues his battle with mechanical objects. The amiable, bumbling Hulot gets caught up with a group of American tourists, and finds himself at the opening of a nightclub that is far from ready. Ironically, given Tati's technophobe philosophy, his use of stereophonic sound and the 70mm screen has seldom been equalled. Unfortunately,

U SUITABLE FOR ALL   Uc SUITABLE ESPECIALLY FOR YOUNG CHILDREN (DVD ONLY)   PG PARENTAL GUIDANCE   12A UNDER 12s TO BE ACCOMPANIED (CINEMA ONLY)

the film, originally 152 minutes long, has mainly been shown since its first release in versions reduced in time and space. RB **DVD** **BL**

Jacques Tati *Monsieur Hulot* • Rita Maiden *Mr Schultz's companion* • Barbara Dennek *Young tourist* • Jacqueline Lecomte *Her friend* • Valérie Camille *Monsieur Luce's secretary* • France Delahalle *Shopper in department store* • Billy Kearns *Monsieur Schulz* ■ *Dir* Jacques Tati • *Scr* Jacques Tati, Jacques Lagrange, Art Buchwald (English dialogue)

Plaza Suite ★★★ PG
Comedy   1971 · US · Colour · 109min

You get three Walter Matthaus for the price of one here, as he cynically bulldozes his way through three acts of Neil Simon's play about the goings-on in a swanky hotel suite. As nervous comedy, it's best when it's most serious (Maureen Stapleton trying to keep husband Matthau from his mistress). Yet the more slapstick episodes (Hollywood producer trying to bed old flame; bemused father trying to coax bride-to-be daughter out of a locked loo) have their moments, even if the top-of-the-voice humour is sometimes strident. TH

Walter Matthau *Sam Nash/Jesse Kiplinger/Roy Hubley* • Maureen Stapleton *Karen Nash* • Louise Sorel *Miss McCormack* • Barbara Harris *Muriel Tate* • Lee Grant *Norma Hubley* • Jenny Sullivan *Mimsey Hubley* • Tom Carey *Borden Eisler* ■ *Dir* Arthur Hiller • *Scr* Neil Simon, from his play

Pleasantville ★★★★ 12
Fantasy comedy drama
1998 · US · Colour and BW · 119min

Tobey Maguire and Reese Witherspoon play sparring siblings who, while fighting over the TV remote control, get zapped inside Maguire's favourite soap, a 1950s rerun called *Pleasantville*. They find themselves in what is literally a black-and-white world. How the youngsters' progressive attitudes to sex and marriage begin to induce unfamiliar feelings in the show's two-dimensional caricatures forms the basis of this witty and affectionate comedy. And how these new-found emotions are depicted by the gradual encroachment of colour into their monochrome lives is where its brilliance lies. It's a clever concept, although the multiple metaphors do pile up somewhat. DA Swearing. **DVD**

Tobey Maguire *David* • Reese Witherspoon *Jennifer* • Joan Allen *Betty Parker* • William H Macy *George Parker* • Jeff Daniels *Mr Johnson* • JT Walsh *Big Bob* • Don Knotts *TV repairman* ■ *Dir/Scr* Gary Ross

Please Believe Me ★★★ U
Romantic comedy   1950 · US · BW · 86min

Efficient acting by an attractive cast turns this run-of-the-mill and somewhat dated romantic comedy into a pleasant diversion. English rose Deborah Kerr stars as an English rose who inherits a large and profitable ranch. Off she goes to Texas, pursued and wooed by layabout Robert Walker, who sees her as the answer to his gambling debts, and womanising millionaire playboy Peter Lawford, looking for a good time. Lawford's sly, respectable lawyer, Mark Stevens, comes along, too. RK

Deborah Kerr *Alison Kirbe* • Robert Walker *Terence Keath* • Mark Stevens *Matthew Kinston* • Peter Lawford *Jeremy Taylor* • James Whitmore *Vincent Maran* • J Carrol Naish *Lucky Reilly* • Spring Byington *Mrs Milwright* ■ *Dir* Norman Taurog • *Scr* Nathaniel Curtis

Please Don't Eat the Daisies ★★★★ U
Comedy   1960 · US · Colour · 106min

This brash, colourful and fast-moving MGM comedy is based on Jean Kerr's episodic reminiscences about life with hubby, ace Broadway drama critic Walter Kerr. The couple are delightfully played here by Doris Day and the ever-urbane David Niven, who is hilarious in the scenes where he's pursued by panned Broadway actress Janis Paige. Director Charles Walters maintains a fast pace and the stylish use of CinemaScope is exemplary, providing a

clever cinematic contrast as Day and Niven decamp from the city to a country abode. TS **DVD**

Doris Day *Kate Mackay* • David Niven *Larry Mackay* • Janis Paige *Deborah Vaughn* • Spring Byington *Suzie Robinson* • Richard Haydn *Alfred North* • Patsy Kelly *Maggie* ■ *Dir* Charles Walters • *Scr* Isobel Lennart, from the book by Jean Kerr

Please Give ★★★ 15
Comedy drama   2010 · US · Colour · 86min

This thoughtful ensemble piece is like a Woody Allen movie with no real story and a wealth of wayward subplots. Which is actually much better than it sounds; for where Allen's films live or die by the strength of the narrative, this New York–set story very eloquently captures the absurdities and frustrations of modern life. The focus is Kate (Catherine Keener), an antique furniture dealer who runs a business that profits handsomely by buying from the children of dead people. Kate and her husband are waiting for their crabby neighbour to die so they can extend their apartment, a situation that brings them into contact with the old lady's granddaughters (Rebecca Hall and Amanda Peet). Director Nicole Holofcener ably depicts the awkwardness of the ensuing relationships, and is adept at portraying women in a believable way, drawing strong performances from a talented cast. DW Swearing, some sex scenes. **DVD**

Catherine Keener *Kate* • Amanda Peet *Mary* • Oliver Platt *Alex* • Rebecca Hall *Rebecca* • Ann Guilbert *Ann Morgan Guilbert* *Andra* • Sarah Steele *Abby* ■ *Dir/Scr* Nicole Holofcener

Please Sir! ★★ PG
Comedy   1971 · UK · Colour · 97min

Inspired by the Sidney Poitier feature *To Sir with Love*, ITV's often hilarious sitcom ran for four years from 1968. The original class of 5C were all ready to depart for their own series, *The Fenn Street Gang*, when this shambolic film version was made. John Alderton is good as the put-upon form teacher, but the few funny moments belong to Joan Sanderson as the headmaster's formidable assistant. DP **DVD**

John Alderton *Bernard Hedges* • Deryck Guyler *Norman Potter* • Noel Howlett *Mr Cromwell* • Joan Sanderson *Doris Ewell* • Richard Davies (2) *Mr Price* • Erik Chitty *Mr Smith* ■ *Dir* Mark Stuart • *Scr* John Esmonde, Bob Larbey, from their TV series

Please Turn Over ★★★ 12
Comedy   1960 · UK · BW · 84min

Notwithstanding its *Carry On* credentials, this gentle comedy of embarrassment could not be further from the bawdy humour of the celebrated series. Adapted by Norman Hudis, it boasts Leslie Phillips, Joan Sims and Charles Hawtrey among those aghast at the revelations contained in a potboiling novel populated by local luminaries. It's a one-joke affair, but director Gerald Thomas ensures the cast keeps it light and frothy. DP **DVD**

Ted Ray *Edward Halliday* • Jean Kent *Janet Halliday* • Leslie Phillips *Dr Henry Manners* • Joan Sims *Beryl* • Julia Lockwood *Jo Halliday* • Tim Seely *Robert Hughes* • Charles Hawtrey *Jeweller* • Dilys Laye *Millicent Jones* • Lionel Jeffries *Ian Howard* • Joan Hickson *Saleswoman* ■ *Dir* Gerald Thomas • *Scr* Norman Hudis, from the play *Book of the Month* by Basil Thomas

Pleasure at Her Majesty's ★★★★ 12
Concert comedy documentary
1976 · UK · Colour · 71min

This is the first in a long line of celebrity galas featuring major comedy and music stars performing in aid of Amnesty International. Originally screened on TV, then given a theatrical release, this elegantly filmed piece captures the magic of a special night. The Monty Python team dominate the proceedings, but there are wonderful contributions from all the artists involved. This documentary, and the others that followed, provide an invaluable historical (and hysterical) record of many

artists at the peak of their powers. DF **DVD**

John Cleese • Terry Gilliam • Terry Jones • Michael Palin • Graham Chapman • Alan Bennett • Peter Cook • Dudley Moore • John Bird • John Fortune • Eleanor Bron • Tim Brooke-Taylor • Carol Cleveland • Graeme Garden • Barry Humphries ■ *Dir* Roger Graef

The Pleasure Garden ★★★ U
Silent drama   1925 · UK/Ger · BW · 60min

Chorus girl Virginia Valli follows new husband Miles Mander to the Tropics. There, she discovers he's really a psychotic alcoholic who's living with a native woman. Made at the UFA studios in Germany as a co-production between Michael Balcon and Erich Pommer, this is a creaky, unconvincing and sometimes tedious silent melodrama. However, it does mark the solo feature directing debut of Alfred Hitchcock and, for all its shortcomings, reveals in embryo several of the master's stylistic devices. A must for students of his work. RK **DVD**

Virginia Valli *Patsy Brand* • Carmelita Geraghty *Jill Cheyne* • Miles Mander *Levet* • John Stuart *Hugh Fielding* • Nita Naldi *Native girl* ■ *Dir* Alfred J Hitchcock [Alfred Hitchcock] • *Scr* Eliot Stannard, from the novel by Oliver Sandys

The Pleasure Girls ★★ 12
Drama   1965 · UK · BW · 87min

This attempt to show the problems facing a young model in the Swinging Sixties is an exasperating effort from writer/director Gerry O'Hara, who seems to think that incessant references to sexual freedom are enough to sustain a paper-thin story about the ever-changing relationships of Francesca Annis and her flatmates. The script strains every sinew to be gear and fab. DP **DVD** **BL**

Ian McShane *Keith Dexter* • Francesca Annis *Sally Feathers* • Klaus Kinski *Nikko* • Mark Eden *Prinny* • Tony Tanner *Paddy* • Rosemary Nicols *Marion* ■ *Dir/Scr* Gerry O'Hara

The Pleasure of His Company ★★ U
Romantic comedy   1961 · US · Colour · 113min

Fred Astaire brings all his easy, debonair charm but not, alas, his twinkling feet to this, the second non-musical of his long career. The film shows what happens when ageing playboy Astaire, long-separated from his family, turns up for his daughter's wedding. Debbie Reynolds is delighted to see her father again; husband-to-be Tab Hunter is bemused; while Astaire's ex-wife Lilli Palmer, now remarried to Gary Merrill, is none too pleased. RK

Fred Astaire *Biddeford "Pogo" Poole* • Debbie Reynolds *Jessica Poole* • Lilli Palmer *Katharine Dougherty* • Tab Hunter *Roger Henderson* • Gary Merrill *James Dougherty* • Charlie Ruggles [Charles Ruggles] *Mackenzie Savage* • Edith Head *Dress designer* ■ *Dir* George Seaton • *Scr* Samuel Taylor, from the play by Samuel Taylor, Cornelia Otis Skinner • *Costume Designer* Edith Head

The Pleasure Seekers ★★★
Romantic musical   1964 · US · Colour · 106min

A rare example of a successful movie remade by the same director as the original, this is Jean Negulesco's reworking of his own *Three Coins in the Fountain*, this time set in Spain. The cast is exemplary, with sexy Ann-Margret, Pamela Tiffin and Carol Lynley more than a match for their glossy 1950s predecessors. The novelty has worn a bit thin, and Fox's standard "three girls out on the town" plot looks stale, but this fun film is still worth a look. TS

Ann-Margret *Fran Hobson* • Tony Franciosa [Anthony Franciosa] *Emilio Lacaye* • Carol Lynley *Maggie Williams* • Gardner McKay *Pete Stenello* • Pamela Tiffin *Susie Higgins* • Andre Lawrence *Dr Andres Briones* • Gene Tierney *Jane Barton* • Brian Keith *Paul Barton* ■ *Dir* Jean Negulesco • *Scr* Edith Sommer, from the novel *Coins in the Fountain* by John H Secondari

The Pledge ★★★★ 15
Psychological detective drama
2000 · US · Colour · 118min

In this utterly gripping drama, Jack Nicholson plays a detective on the eve of retirement who just can't let go of a case that begins when a young girl's mutilated body is discovered in a remote snowy forest in Nevada. His fellow cops believe simple-minded ex-con Benicio Del Toro committed the crime. But Nicholson's promise to the girl's parents that he would find the actual murderer leads him to conduct his own investigations, which embroil Robin Wright Penn and her young daughter. The pacing may be languid but this is a movie that continually gets under your skin, thanks to Sean Penn's atmospheric direction and the terrific performances. JB Violence, swearing. **DVD**

Jack Nicholson *Jerry Black* • Robin Wright Penn [Robin Wright] *Lori* • Sam Shepard *Eric Pollack* • Aaron Eckhart *Stan Krolak* • Vanessa Redgrave *Annalise Hansen* • Michael O'Keefe *Duane Larsen* • Benicio Del Toro *Toby Jay Wadenah* • Mickey Rourke *Jim Olstad* • Harry Dean Stanton *Floyd Cage* • Helen Mirren *Doctor* ■ *Dir* Sean Penn • *Scr* Jerzy Kromolowski, Mary Olson-Kromolowski, from the novel *Das Versprechen* by Friedrich Dürrenmatt

Plein Soleil ★★★★ PG
Crime drama   1960 · Fr/It · Colour · 112min

This shimmering and suspenseful *film noir* is based on the Patricia Highsmith novel *The Talented Mr Ripley*. You may think that the sunny backdrop would upset the mood of such a sinister tale, but cinematographer Henri Decaë's picture-postcard views are every bit as atmospheric as the gloomiest *film noir* cityscape. Director René Clément makes extensive use of a moving camera to pick up every nuance and detail as the murderous Alain Delon seeks to assume the identity of his well-to-do pal, Maurice Ronet. Stylish, impeccably played and utterly engrossing. DP French +subtitles. **DVD** **BL**

Alain Delon *Tom Ripley* • Marie Laforêt *Marge* • Maurice Ronet *Philippe Greenleaf* • Bill Kearns [Billy Kearns] *Freddy Miles* • Erno Crisa *Inspector Riccordi* • Frank Latimore *O'Brien* ■ *Dir* René Clément • *Scr* René Clément, Paul Gégauff, from the novel *The Talented Mr Ripley* by Patricia Highsmith • *Cinematographer* Henri Decaë

Plenty ★★ 15
Drama   1985 · US · Colour · 119min

David Hare's trenchant, deeply layered stage plays transfer badly to film and *Plenty* is a prime example of how the requisite small nervy performances, here from Meryl Streep, Charles Dance and Sam Neill, appear affected and over-stylised on screen. As always, Hare does have some interesting points to make, but everything is spelt out laboriously with a glum and squeakily pretentious air. SH Violence, swearing. **DVD** **BL**

Meryl Streep *Susan Traherne* • Charles Dance *Raymond Brock* • Tracey Ullman *Alice Park* • John Gielgud *Sir Leonard Darwin* • Sting *Mick* • Ian McKellen *Sir Andrew Charleson* • Sam Neill *Lazar* • Burt Kwouk *Mr Aung* • Lim Pik Sen *Madame Aung* • André Maranne *Villon* ■ *Dir* Fred Schepisi • *Scr* David Hare, from his play

The Plot against Harry ★★★ PG
Comedy   1969 · US · BW · 80min

Finally released 20 years after it was filmed, Michael Roemer's pseudo-*cinéma vérité* comedy was clearly ahead of its time. But, by 1989, its determinedly deadpan style had become such a familiar part of the comic landscape in the films of directors such as Jim Jarmusch that its impact was somewhat reduced. Newly sprung from jail, petty mobster Martin Priest is convinced that life has got it in for him. And a series of incidents, including a car accident that leads him to discover that he is the father of a family he never knew he had, seem to uphold his suspicions. DP

Martin Priest *Harry Plotnick* • Ben Lang *Leo Perlmutter* • Maxine Woods *Kay Skolnik* • Henry Nemo *Max* • Jacques Taylor *Jack* • Jean Leslie

Irene • Ellen Herbert *Mae* • Sandra Kazan *Margie* • Ronald Coralian *Mel Skolnik* • Ruth Roemer *Linda Skolnik* ■ *Dir/Scr* Michael Roemer

Plot for Peace ★★★ 12

Documentary
2013 · S Afr/Congo/US/Moz/Fr/Cub/Ang · Colour and BW · 80min

This probing historical documentary suggests that Jean-Yves Ollivier, a French-Algerian commodities salesman acting on his own initiative, proved a key player in the geopolitical machinations prior to Nelson Mandela's release from prison and the creation of the new South Africa. Known as "Monsieur Jacques" Ollivier was undoubtedly building up his own business interests, yet also committed to promoting engagement with a Pretoria leadership firmly isolated by the international community. Events unfold with all the intrigue of a good political thriller in this fascinating record of the shadowy world behind the headlines. TJ English, French, Portuguese, Afrikaans, Spanish +subtitles. Violence. *DVD*

■ *Dir* Carlos Agulló, Mandy Jacobson • *Scr* Stephen Smith

The Plot Thickens ★★ U

Mystery
1936 · US · BW · 64min

ZaSu Pitts took over the role of RKO's schoolmarm sleuth Hildegarde Withers from Helen Broderick, who herself succeeded Edna May Oliver, and was responsible for this more comedic entry in a most likeable series. Her flustery mode of performance isn't ideal for acutely rational detective Withers, but she's nevertheless fun to watch, paired opposite series regular irascible James Gleason. As the title indicates, this is a particularly complex mystery, full of humour; Pitts and Gleason were to team again for one more film (*40 Naughty Girls*) which was to be the last of the series. TS

James Gleason *Oscar Piper* • ZaSu Pitts *Hildegarde Withers* • Owen Davis Jr *Robert Wilkins* • Louise Latimer *Alice Stevens* • Arthur Aylesworth *Kendall* • Richard Tucker *John Carter* • Paul Fix *Joe* • Barbara Barondess *Marie* ■ *Dir* Ben Holmes • *Scr* Clarence Upson Young, Jack Townley, from a story by Stuart Palmer

The Plot to Kill Hitler ★★★ PG

Historical drama
1990 · US · Colour · 89min

Although this TV movie glamorises the facts and is weak on the hatching of the plot, it's still a fascinating if overfamiliar story, as members of the German high command led by Colonel von Stauffenberg (Brad Davis) try to dispose of the man who had led them to victory but was now in charge of a retreating army. The assassination attempt comes across as muddled both in organisation and execution, even though the film portrays the collaborators as heroic. TH Violence.

Brad Davis *Colonel Claus von Stauffenberg* • Madolyn Smith *Countess Nina von Stauffenberg* • Ian Richardson *General Ludwig Beck* • Michael Byrne *Friedrich Olbright* • Michael Gwilym [Mike Gwilym] *Adolf Hitler* • Helmut Griem *Field Marshal Rommel* ■ *Dir* Lawrence Schiller • *Scr* Steven Elkins

The Plough and the Stars ★★

Drama
1936 · US · BW · 66min

Barbara Stanwyck is magnificently miscast as the loyal wife fearing for the life of her IRA husband, played by the incredibly dreary Preston Foster, and the supporting cast is so authentically Irish that the two leads seem even more at sea. It's truly dispiriting to watch a major Irish play sink into the Hollywood mire, particularly since John Ford should have known better, and the cheap production values and ill-chosen intercut newsreel clips don't help. TS

Barbara Stanwyck *Nora Clitheroe* • Preston Foster *Jack Clitheroe* • Barry Fitzgerald *Fluther Good* • Denis O'Dea *The Young Covey* • Eileen Crowe *Bessie Burgess* • FJ McCormick *Captain*

Brennon • Arthur Shields *Padraic Pearse* ■ *Dir* John Ford • *Scr* Dudley Nichols, from the play by Sean O'Casey

The Ploughman's Lunch ★★★★ 15

Drama
1983 · UK · Colour · 102min

This is a well-observed and thought-provoking drama about the way in which the private life of a BBC radio news producer affects his work. The background detail looks absolutely authentic, and the performances, particularly from Jonathan Pryce as the producer and Charlie Dore as the TV researcher he beds, are excellent. The film is a collaboration between novelist Ian McEwan and director Richard Eyre, who went on to head the National Theatre. Slow-starting, but stay with it. DM

Jonathan Pryce *James Penfield* • Tim Curry *Jeremy Hancock* • Rosemary Harris *Ann Barrington* • Frank Finlay *Matthew Fox* • Charlie Dore *Susan Barrington* ■ *Dir* Richard Eyre • *Scr* Ian McEwan

The Plow That Broke the Plains ★★★★

Documentary
1934 · US · BW · 49min

Sponsored by the United States Resettlement Administration, this piece of New Deal propaganda is usually considered the cornerstone of American documentary film-making. Made on a shoestring, yet filmed with evocative expertise by socialist cinematographers Ralph Steiner, Paul Strand and Leo Hurwitz, ex-critic Pare Lorentz's debut explored the history of the Great Plains and the ecological causes of the Dust Bowl that had made the Depression even more disastrous for the Mid-West's valiant farmers. With a superb score by Virgil Thompson and a rhythmic commentary delivered by Thomas Chalmers, it is emotive, persuasive and powerful, both in its message and its imagery. DP

Thomas Chalmers *Narrator* ■ *Dir/Scr* Pare Lorentz

Plughead Rewired: Circuitry Man II ★ 15

Science-fiction thriller
1994 · US · Colour · 92min

Dennis Christopher, so good in *Breaking Away*, is wasted in a witless sequel that makes his character look even more foolish and aimless than he was in the original. The film feels like a collection of out-takes from the first *Circuitry Man*, even recycling some of its effects. The incomprehensible plot has something to do with Vernon Wells again setting his sights on capturing Jim Metzler. KB *DVD*

Vernon Wells *Plughead* • Deborah Shelton *Kyle* • Jim Metzler *Danner* • Dennis Christopher *Leech* • Nicholas Worth *Rock* • Traci Lords *Norma* ■ *Dir/Scr* Steven Lovy, Robert Lovy

The Plumber ★★★ 12

Black comedy
1979 · Aus · Colour · 74min

An early film from director Peter Weir, this black comedy, made on 16mm in just three weeks for Australian television, this is about a coarse plumber who arrives at a middle-class household. He fixes the pipes, but refuses to budge, acting as a catalyst and provoking some very funny but also some scary responses. Behind it all is the evocation of otherness that Weir explores in all his films. AT

Judy Morris *Jill Cowper* • Robert Coleby *Brian Cowper* • Ivar Kants *Max, The Plumber* • Candy Raymond *Meg* ■ *Dir/Scr* Peter Weir

Plunder Road ★★★ U

Crime thriller
1957 · US · BW · 71min

Veteran players Gene Raymond and Wayne Morris clearly relished the opportunity to star in this cleverly written story of a train hold-up and the robbers' doomed attempts to shift their massive haul of gold ingots. Elisha Cook Jr already knew his loser's part by heart but plays it, as usual, to perfection. Aided by veteran cameraman Ernest Haller, new director Hubert Cornfield makes a

visually exciting picture that squeezes every ounce of suspense from the story. AE

Gene Raymond *Eddie* • Jeanne Cooper *Fran* • Wayne Morris *Commando* • Elisha Cook Jr *Skeets* • Stafford Repp *Roly Adams* • Steven Ritch *Frankie* • Nora Hayden *Hazel* ■ *Dir* Hubert Cornfield • *Scr* Steven Ritch, from a story by Jack Charney, Steven Ritch

The Plunderers ★★ U

Western
1948 · US · Colour · 87min

Joseph Kane was among the most prolific directors of formulaic westerns at Republic Studios, but this is one of his more considered efforts. It's aimed less at the Saturday matinée crowd than at the adherents of the pulp novels. As a result, outlaw Forrest Tucker is a step up from a straightforward black-hatted villain, as army agent Rod Cameron discovers when he infiltrates his gang. That said, the Sioux attack on the fort returns to traditional western values. DP

Rod Cameron *John Druin* • Ilona Massey *Lin Conner* • Adrian Booth [Lorna Gray] *Julie McCabe* • Forrest Tucker *Whit Lacey* • George Cleveland *Sam Borden* • Grant Withers *Tap Lawrence* • Taylor Holmes *Eben Martin* • Paul Fix *Calico* • Francis Ford *Barnaby* ■ *Dir* Joseph Kane • *Scr* Gerald Adams [Gerald Drayson Adams], Gerald Geraghty, from a story by James Edward Grant

Plunkett & Macleane ★★ 15

Period action adventure
1999 · UK · Colour · 97min

Robert Carlyle and Jonny Lee Miller star as the infamous highwaymen who terrorised high society in 18th-century London in this misfiring adventure, which marked the debut feature of Jake (son of Ridley) Scott. Music and design are both deliberately anachronistic in an attempt to make the larcenous odd couple a hip, English *Butch Cassidy and the Sundance Kid* for the 1990s. Liv Tyler, as Macleane's aristocratic groupie, adds a touch of romance, but this is mostly a chaotic jumble of style over substance. AME Violence, swearing. *DVD*

Robert Carlyle *Will Plunkett* • Jonny Lee Miller *James Macleane* • Liv Tyler *Lady Rebecca* • Ken Stott *Chance* • Michael Gambon *Lord Gibson* • Alan Cumming *Lord Rochester* ■ *Dir* Jake Scott • *Scr* Robert Wade, Neal Purvis, Charles McKeown, from a screenplay (unproduced) by Selwyn Roberts

Pluto ★★★★ 15

Thriller
2012 · S Kor · Colour · 107min

This South Korean drama suggests there's a dark truth behind the country's stellar education statistics, as the fight for top marks turns very nasty indeed. Dorky new arrival David Lee is desperate to join the top ten pupils afforded special tuition for university entrance, but academic alpha male June Sung and his privileged cohorts may not accept this working-class interloper so easily. The engrossing storyline switches back and forth between the aftermath of and run-up to a brutal killing, in a bleak, confrontational story that plays like a modern Korean *if...* TJ Korean +subtitles.

David Lee *Kim June* • June Sung *Yujin Taylor* • Cho Sung-ha *Senior detective* • Kim Kkob-bi [Kim Kkobbi] *Jung Su-jin* • Kwon Klm *Han Myung-ho* ■ *Dir/Scr* Shin Su-won

Pluto Nash ★ PG

Science-fiction action comedy
2001 · US/Aus · Colour · 90min

With elaborate special effects substituting for the missing script, director Ron Underwood's alleged sci-fi comedy is a $100 million turkey. An unusually bland Eddie Murphy plays former crook Pluto Nash, who is struggling to keep his moon nightclub from falling under intergalactic Mafia control in 2087. Accompanying Murphy on these lunar-tic rambles is his outdated robot bodyguard (a truly asinine Randy Quaid) and wannabe singer Rosario Dawson. A flop of epic proportions. AJ *DVD*

Eddie Murphy *Pluto Nash* • Randy Quaid *Bruno* • Rosario Dawson *Dina Lake* • Joe Pantoliano *Mogan* • Jay Mohr *Anthony "Tony" Francis* • Luis

Guzman *Felix Laranga* • James Rebhorn *Belcher* • Pam Grier *Flura Nash* • John Cleese *James* ■ *Dir* Ron Underwood • *Scr* Neil Cuthbert

Plymouth Adventure ★★ U

Historical drama
1952 · US · Colour · 104min

Spencer Tracy is the stern skipper of the *Mayflower* as it sets sail for America in 1620. His heavyweight presence is sorely needed in a ponderous rendering of an unwieldy script that is overloaded with history. The special effects, which won an Oscar, and Miklos Rozsa's rousing score are among the few highlights in director Clarence Brown's rather dull depiction of the epic journey. JM

Spencer Tracy *Captain Christopher Jones* • Gene Tierney *Dorothy Bradford* • Van Johnson *John Alden* • Leo Genn *William Bradford* • Dawn Addams *Priscilla Mullins* • Lloyd Bridges *Coppin* • Barry Jones *William Brewster* ■ *Dir* Clarence Brown • *Scr* Helen Deutsch, from a novel by Ernest Gebler

Pocahontas ★★★ U

Animated adventure
1995 · US · Colour · 77min

This is a visually stunning but historically botched re-creation of the legendary romance between native American maiden Pocahontas (Irene Bedard) and captain John Smith (Mel Gibson) in the 17th-century New World. The first Disney animation to deal with a factual subject skilfully communicates both its "love conquers all" and ecological messages, although the greedy governor (David Ogden Stiers) is over the top. Supporting voice actor Christian Bale would later appear in Terrence Malick's superb 2005 live-action rendition of the same story, while Bedard also voiced the sequel three years later. TH *DVD*

Irene Bedard *Pocahontas* • Mel Gibson *John Smith* • Joe Baker *Lon* • Christian Bale *Thomas* • Billy Connolly *Ben* • Linda Hunt *Grandmother Willow* • David Ogden Stiers *Governor Ratcliffe/Wiggins* ■ *Dir* Mike Gabriel, Eric Goldberg • *Scr* Carl Binder, Susannah Grant, Philip LaZebnik

Pocket Money ★★ PG

Western
1972 · US · Colour · 95min

After Martin Ritt pulled out, Paul Newman installed his friend Stuart Rosenberg in the director's chair for this tepid western, but he never comes to grips with Terrence Malick's rambling screenplay. The result is a directionless, if fitfully amusing, tale in which Newman and Lee Marvin try to round up some cattle for shady beef baron Strother Martin. Laszlo Kovacs's photography is so authentic it leaves you with dust in your eyes, but Newman and Marvin look like they're acting in different movies. DP

Paul Newman *Jim Kane* • Lee Marvin *Leonard* • Strother Martin *Garrett* • Christine Belford *Adelita* • Kelly Jean Peters *Wife* • Fred Graham *Herb* • Wayne Rogers *Stretch Russell* • Hector Elizondo *Juan* ■ *Dir* Stuart Rosenberg • *Scr* Terry Malick [Terrence Malick], John Gay, from the novel *Jim Kane* by JPS Brown

Pocketful of Miracles ★★ U

Comedy
1961 · US · Colour · 131min

Frank Capra's remake of his 1933 comedy *Lady for a Day* is a disappointing end to his distinguished career. Damon Runyon's yarn worked during the Depression, but here this tale of class envy and economic inequality now seems dated. It has its sentimental moments, but it's too long, and Bette Davis is badly miscast as the apple-seller transformed into a wealthy socialite by a superstitious gangster (Glenn Ford) and his gang of hoodlums. AT *DVD*

Glenn Ford *Dave the Dude* • Bette Davis *Apple Annie* • Hope Lange *Queenie Martin* • Arthur O'Connell *Count Alfonso Romero* • Peter Falk *Joy Boy* • Thomas Mitchell *Judge Henry G Blake* • Edward Everett Horton *Butler* • Ann-Margret *Louise* • Mike Mazurki *Big Mike* ■ *Dir* Frank Capra • *Scr* Hal Kanter, Harry Tugend, Jimmy Cannon, from the film *Lady for a Day* by Robert Riskin, from the story *Madame La Gimp* by Damon Runyon

A Poem Is a Naked Person
★★★ 15

Music documentary 1974 · US · Colour · 90min

Les Blank's 1974 study of piano maverick Leon Russell spent an eternity on the shelf before finally securing a theatrical release. The film has a ramshackle approach, as Blank seems much less interested in RussellDespite the lack of biographical information and psychological insight, there's spaced-out prattle to spare and an excess of eccentricity. Moreover, there's lots of laid-back music, with Russell doing concert numbers like *A Song for You* and *Yes I Am*, as well as a superb studio version of *Goodnight Irene*. DP

Leon Russell • Jim Franklin • George Jones • Willie Nelson ■ *Dir/Scr* Les Blank

Poetic Justice
★★ 15

Drama 1993 · US · Colour · 104min

After making a big splash with his first film, *Boyz N the Hood*, John Singleton lost his way somewhat with this twee, right-on drama that charts the burgeoning romance between hairdresser and poetess Janet Jackson and postal worker Tupac Shakur as they get to know each other on the road to Oakland. Mawkish and well-intentioned instead of gritty and real, the movie is saved by the acting of the two leads. Incidentally, Maya Angelou wrote the poetry for Jackson's character. AJ Violence, swearing, sex scenes. *DVD*

Janet Jackson *Justice* • Tupac Shakur *Lucky* • Tyra Ferrell *Jessie* • Regina King *Iesha* • Joe Torry *Chicago* • Roger Guenveur Smith *Heywood* • Lori Petty *Penelope* • Billy Zane *Brad* • Khandi Alexander *Simone* • Maya Angelou *Aunt June* ■ *Dir/Scr* John Singleton

Poetry
★★★★ 12

Drama 2010 · S Kor · Colour · 133min

For those who appreciate the world of cinema out there this low-key South Korean drama is a little gem. Actress Yoon Jung-Hee plays a grandmother faced with the twin traumas of Alzheimer's and the involvement of her grandson in the suicide of a schoolmate. The film is long and languid as she takes solace and strength from a poetry class, yet Yoon's nuanced and subtle performance is superb. Allowances must be made or its pace and, at times, for its poetry. But the effort is worthwhile. DA Korean +subtitles. Sexual references, brief swearing, sex scene. *DVD*

Yoon Jung-hee *Yang Mija* • David Lee (2) *Jongwook* • Kim Hira *Mr Kang* • Ahn Nae-Sang *Kibum's father* ■ *Dir/Scr* Lee Chang-Dong [Lee Chang-dong]

Poil de Carotte
★★★★

Drama 1932 · Fr · BW · 80min

Assembled from Jules Renard's novels and one of his plays, this is a glorious remake of the touching rites-of-passage drama director Julien Duvivier first attempted as a silent in 1925. Avoiding the sentimentality that tainted so many Hollywood studies of childhood, this is a resolutely grown-up account of the misery endured by red-headed Robert Lynen at the hands of his uncaring mother, Catherine Fontenay. Beautifully filmed by Armand Thirard, the film acquired added poignancy after Lynen's execution while fighting for the Resistance in 1944. DP French +subtitles.

Harry Baur *M Lepic* • Robert Lynen *François, "Poil de Carotte"* • Catherine Fonteney *Mme Lepic* • Christiane Dor *Annette* • Colette Segall *Young Mathilde* • Louis Gauthier *Godfather* ■ *Dir* Julien Duvivier • *Scr* Julien Duvivier, from the play *Poil de Carotte* by Jules Renard, from the novels *Poil de Carotte/La Bigote* by Jules Renard

Point and Shoot
★★★ 15

Documentary 2014 · US/UK/Den · Colour · 79min

It's difficult not to think of Timothy Treadwell, the tragic subject of Werner Herzog's *Grizzly Man*, while viewing this inconclusive but fascinating film about a young man obsessed with his own image. It follows Matthew VanDyke, a pampered only child whose severe OCD and loathing of his cosseted lifestyle prompts him to take a wildly risky motorcycle trip to the Middle East. Quietly spoken and apparently unremarkable, VanDyke slowly reveals himself as an impossibly naive and confused product of the selfie culture. AS Swearing.

■ *Dir/Scr* Marshall Curry

Point Blank
★★★★★ 18

Thriller 1967 · US · Colour · 87min

British director John Boorman's US directing debut was this grim, violent, virtually metaphysical thriller. It's a gripping and sexy action movie, with a magnificent performance from Lee Marvin as the revenge-seeking Walker, the ultimate lethal weapon, whose insane quest to retrieve Mob money assumes mythical proportions. With the subtle complexity of the storytelling and Philip H Lathrop's brilliant cinematography, the film is a superior and powerful work. AT Violence, swearing.
DVD

Lee Marvin *Walker* • Angie Dickinson *Chris* • Keenan Wynn *Yost* • Carroll O'Connor *Brewster* • Lloyd Bochner *Frederick Carter* • Michael Strong *Stegman* • John Vernon *Mal Reese* • Sharon Acker *Lynne* • James Sikking [James B Sikking] *Hired gun* ■ *Dir* John Boorman • *Scr* Alexander Jacobs, David Newhouse, Rafe Newhouse, from the novel *The Hunter* by Richard Stark [Donald E Westlake] • *Cinematographer* Philip H Lathrop [Philip Lathrop]

Point Blank
★ 18

Action thriller 1997 · US · Colour · 85min

Mickey Rourke's detractors will have a field day when they see the actor hilariously humiliated in this *Die Hard* rip-off. Rourke stars as ex-Texas Ranger who sneaks into a shopping mall that's been taken over by a gang of escaped convicts; the star is only given about 25 lines of dialogue in the entire movie. The film mixes utter sleaze and graphic violence. KB

Mickey Rourke *Rudy Ray* • Kevin Gage *Joe Ray* • Michael Wright *Sonny* • Danny Trejo *Wallace* • Frederic Forrest *Mac Bradford* ■ *Dir* Matt Earl Beesley • *Scr* James Bannon, Cary Solomon, Chuck Konzelman, Daniel Raskov, from a story by Daniel Raskov, Cary Solomon, Chuck Konzelman

Point Blank
★★★★ 15

Thriller 2010 · Fr · Colour · 80min

Violent strangers threaten to kill the pregnant wife of a Paris hospital employee unless he smuggles out an injured patient in this blisteringly exciting crime thriller from Fred Cavayé (*Anything for Her*). Rugged Gilles Lellouche is perfect as the Hitchcockian "Wrong Place, Wrong Time, Wrong Man" whose life spirals out of control as he is drawn into a web of police corruption and murder in high places. Roschdy Zem is also terrific playing the sinister convalescent he's forced to buddy up with, and together the pair are hunted across the city in a series of relentlessly paced, action-packed chase sequences. AJ French +subtitles. Violence, swearing.
DVD +subtitles

Gilles Lellouche *Samuel Pierret* • Roschdy Zem *Hugo Sartet* • Gérard Lanvin *Commandant Werner* • Elena Anaya *Nadia Pierret* • Mireille Perrier *Commandant Fabre* • Claire Perot *Capitaine Susini* ■ *Dir* Fred Cavayé • *Scr* Fred Cavayé, Guillaume Lemans

Point Break
★★★★ 18

Action thriller 1991 · US · Colour · 116min

Kathryn Bigelow shows that the action adventure is not just the preserve of the lads in this silly but hugely enjoyable thriller. Keanu Reeves plays the young FBI agent who unsurprisingly makes a very convincing surfing dude when he goes under cover to infiltrate a gang, headed by Patrick Swayze, suspected of carrying out a string of audacious bank robberies. Try to ignore the mystical claptrap and concentrate instead on Bigelow's stunningly conceived action set pieces, as well as some exhilarating skydiving and surfing scenes. JF Violence, swearing, nudity. *DVD* *Blu*

Patrick Swayze *Bodhi* • Keanu Reeves *Johnny Utah* • Gary Busey *Angelo Pappas* • Lori Petty *Tyler* • John C McGinley *Ben Harp* • James LeGros *Roach* • John Philbin *Nathanial* ■ *Dir* Kathryn Bigelow • *Scr* W Peter Iliff, from a story by Rick King, Iliff

Point Break
★★ 12

Action thriller 2015 · US · Colour · 109min

The 1991 action classic gets an unnecessary upgrade. *Home & Away* regular Luke Bracey replaces Keanu Reeves as Johnny Utah, infiltrating a gang of extreme sports-loving criminals responsible for a spate of elaborate heists. Whereas the original was filled with humour and gung-ho machismo, this *Fast and Furious*-style update is a joyless experience. Without any lighter moments, the criminals' quest to live on the edge becomes a series of (admittedly well-choreographed) stunts sandwiching a predictable plot. JL Some violence, swearing, sex scenes. *DVD* *Blu* *3D*

Luke Bracey *Johnny Utah* • Edgar Ramírez *Bodhi* • Teresa Palmer *Samsara* • Ray Winstone *Angelo Pappas* • Delroy Lindo *Instructor Hall* • Bojesse Christopher *FBI Director* ■ *Dir* Ericson Core • *Scr* Kurt Wimmer, from a story by Wimmer, Rick King, W Peter Iliff, from the 1991 film

The Point Men
★★ 18

Action thriller 2000 · UK/Fr/Lux · Colour · 86min

After overseeing Roger Moore's final two James Bond appearances and Timothy Dalton's only two 007 contributions, the work all but dried up for John Glen in the 1990s. This finds him back in the director's chair, but even he can't bring much fizz to this tame action thriller. Christopher Lambert is the disgraced Israeli secret agent called back into action when members of his old team start getting bumped off by an old adversary, terrorist Vincent Regan. JF
DVD

Christopher Lambert *Tony Eckhardt* • Kerry Fox *Maddy Hope* • Vincent Regan *Amar Kamil* • Cal MacAninch *Horst* • Maryam D'Abo *Francie Koln* ■ *Dir* John Glen • *Scr* Ripley Highsmith, from the novel *The Heat of Ramadan* by Steven Hartov

Poison
★★★ 18

Drama 1990 · US · Colour and BW · 85min

Todd Haynes's feature debut showcases his ability to re-create faithfully eras and film styles. Haynes cleverly interweaves three entirely different stories into a quirky and provocative lesson on sexual and social stereotyping: *Hero*, shot like a 1980s TV documentary, records a community's responses to a missing boy who murdered his father; *Horror* portrays a 1950s B-movie-style tale of a scientist whose sexual libido experiments go hideously wrong; while *Homo* plays with the gritty sensual eroticism of gay cinema with its depiction of a prisoner's cruel obsession with a fellow inmate. SF

Edith Meeks *Felicia Beacon* • Millie White *Millie Sklar* • Buck Smith *Gregory Lazar* • Anne Giotta *Evelyn McAlpert* • Lydia Lafleur *Sylvia Manning* ■ *Dir* Todd Haynes • *Scr* Todd Haynes, from the novels *Our Lady of the Flowers, Miracle of the Roses, Thief's Journal* by Jean Genet

Poison Ivy
★★★ 18

Thriller 1992 · US · Colour · 89min

Drew Barrymore came of age in this alluring tale about a poor girl from the wrong side of the tracks who befriends fellow loner Sara Gilbert and inveigles her way into her wealthy family, with deadly results. There's a touch of music-video style about director Katt Shea Ruben's over-glossy visuals, but she is well-served by the leads, particularly Barrymore, who's a sexy but vulnerable junior *femme fatale*. Look out, too, for Leonardo DiCaprio in one of his earliest roles. JF Violence, swearing, nudity. *DVD*

Sara Gilbert *Sylvie Cooper* • Drew Barrymore *Ivy* • Tom Skerritt *Darryl Cooper* • Cheryl Ladd *Georgie Cooper* • Alan Stock *Bob* • Jeanne Sakata *Isabelle* • Leonardo DiCaprio *Guy* ■ *Dir* Katt Shea Ruben [Katt Shea] • *Scr* Katt Shea Ruben, Andy Ruben, from the story by Melissa Goddard, Peter Morgan (2)

Poison Ivy 2
★ 18

Erotic thriller 1995 · US · Colour · 101min

The connection to the 1992 *Poison Ivy* comes with repressed college student Alyssa Milano finding Drew Barrymore's old diary. After reading it, she is inspired to transform herself into a sexually liberated woman, confusing her boyfriend and generating lust in her professor. After her transformation, the movie doesn't know what to do, with Berkeley's sudden change in character only occurring to facilitate some kind of climax. Jaime Pressly took over the lead for a second sequel in 1997. KB Violence, swearing, sex scenes, nudity. *DVD*

Alyssa Milano *Lily* • Xander Berkeley *Donald Falk* • Johnathon Schaech *Gredin* • Belinda Bauer *Angela Falk* • Camilla Belle *Daphne Falk* ■ *Dir* Anne Goursaud • *Scr* Chloe King

Poison Pen
★★★

Psychological drama 1939 · UK · BW · 79min

Here's an early and powerful working of an intrinsically downbeat subject, as a rash of anonymous letters cause major misery and distress among the inhabitants of an English hamlet. Catherine Lacey's seamstress is wrongly hounded as the likely perpetrator because she's an outsider. Could it possibly be that the saintly spinster sister of the vicar is not all she seems? When she's played by Flora Robson, you have to wonder. AE

Flora Robson *Mary Rider* • Robert Newton *Sam Hurrin* • Ann Todd *Ann Rider* • Geoffrey Toone *David* • Reginald Tate *Rev Rider* • Belle Chrystall *Sucal Hurrin* • Edward Chapman *Len Griffin* • Edward Rigby *Badham* • Catherine Lacey *Connie Fateley* • Wilfrid Hyde White *Postman* ■ *Dir* Paul L Stein • *Scr* Doreen Montgomery, William Freshman, NC Hunter, Esther McCracken, from the play by Richard Llewellyn

Pokémon the First Movie: Mewtwo Strikes Back
★ PG

Animated fantasy adventure 1998 · Jpn · Colour · 72min

The big-screen debut of the cuddly Japanese monsters of trading card, video game and TV fame could hardly have been worse. The movie actually comprises two films, the first being a plotless short (*Pikachu's Vacation*). In the main feature, genetically modified monster Mewtwo goes on the rampage. The climactic battle is boring. Numerous cinema and TV movies have followed and the franchise remains popular. DM Japanese dubbed. *DVD* *CS*

■ *Dir* Kunihiko Yuyama, Michael Haigney • *Scr* English adaptation by Norman J Grossfeld, Michael Haigney, John Touhey, from characters by Satoshi Tajiri • *Chief Animator* Sayuri Ichiishi

Pola X
★★ 18

Drama 1999 · Fr/Ger/Swi · Colour · 128min

Leos Carax's film takes its acronymic name from the French title of Herman Melville's novel *Pierre, or the Ambiguities*; the "X" refers to the fact that there were ten drafts of the screenplay. Guillaume Depardieu plays the carefree son of wealthy widow Catherine Deneuve whose world is changed irrevocably when he meets a young woman (Katerina Golubeva) who claims to be his illegitimate half-sister. With its nihilistic antihero and unfeeling urban landscape, this bleak film is too dull to engage. NS French +subtitles.

Catherine Deneuve *Marie* • Guillaume Depardieu *Pierre Valombreuse* • Katerina Golubeva *Isabelle* • Delphine Chuillot *Lucie de Boisieux* • Laurent Lucas *Thibault* ■ *Dir* Leos Carax • *Scr* Léos Carax, Jean-Pol Fargeau, Lauren Sedofsky, from the novel *Pierre, or the Ambiguities (Pierre, ou les Ambiguités)* by Herman Melville

The Polar Express
★★★ U

Animated fantasy 2004 · US · Colour · 95min

In this animated tale, a sceptical boy finds his belief in Father Christmas restored by an incredible journey to the North Pole on board a magical train. Director Robert

Zemeckis's fantasy adventure is undoubtedly technically impressive, thanks to the introduction of "Performance Capture" - a new type of CGI that transfers the live actions of actors into a digital format. The process enables star Tom Hanks to take on six different roles. However, as a fast-moving life lesson about faith and hope, the film weaves sentimentality and gentle moralising into every scene. SF **DVD** **BL**

Tom Hanks *Hero boy/Father/Conductor/Hobo/Scrooge/Santa Claus* • Michael Jeter *Smokey/Steamer* • Nona Gaye *Hero girl* • Peter Scolari *Lonely boy* • Eddie Deezen *Know-it-all* • Charles Fleischer *Elf General* • Steven Tyler *Elf Lieutenant/Elf singer* • Leslie Zemeckis *Sister Sarah/Mother* • Daryl Sabara *Hero boy* ■ *Dir* Robert Zemeckis • *Scr* Robert Zemeckis, William Broyles Jr, from the illustrated children's book by Chris Van Allsburg

Polar Storm ★

Science-fiction action drama
2009 · US · Colour · 93min

A doomsday scenario becomes the source of unintended humour in this ineffectual, made-for-TV disaster movie. Throwing together the usual mix of bad dialogue, dodgy effects and increasingly ludicrous events, it sees bland astrophysicist Jack Coleman (from TV's *Heroes*) forced to save mankind when a comet near miss causes Earth's magnetic poles to begin reversing. Hilariously for a race-against-time situation, there's neither a sense of urgency nor any realistic emotional responses, and the supposedly poignant climax just falls flat. SF

Jack Coleman *Dr James Mayfield* • Holly Dignard [Holly Elissa Dignard] *Cynthia Mayfield* • Tyler Johnston *Shane Mayfield* ■ *Dir* Paul Ziller • *Scr* Paul Ziller, Jason Bourque

Police ★★★★ 15

Crime thriller   1985 · Fr · Colour · 109min

Sophie Marceau was the wunderkind of French cinema and Maurice Pialat was its most uncompromisingly realistic director, so the off-screen clashes were inevitable, but the tensions are also evident on the screen and they help give this superior crime drama an added charge. The opening sequences, in which bruising cop Gérard Depardieu muscles in on a Tunisian drugs-ring, make for compelling viewing thanks to Pialat's attention to authentic detail, but the erotic duel between Depardieu and the drug-dealing Marceau is less effective, even though sparks certainly fly from this oddly matched pair. Not your average thriller, but a cracking one, nevertheless. DP French +subtitles. Violence, swearing, nudity. **DVD**

Gérard Depardieu *Mangin* • Sophie Marceau *Noria* • Richard Anconina *Lambert* • Pascale Rocard *Marie Vedret* • Sandrine Bonnaire *Lydie* ■ *Dir* Maurice Pialat • *Scr* Maurice Pialat, Catherine Breillat, Sylvie Danton, Jacques Fieschi, from a story by Catherine Breillat

Police Academy ★★★ 15

Comedy   1984 · US · Colour · 92min

It's hard to imagine that, back in 1984, anyone would have thought this would spawn six sequels as well as a cartoon series. However, it struck a chord with audiences around the world and made a star (briefly) out of Steve Guttenberg. While the follow-ups became increasingly puerile as the series went on, the original film produces its fair share of belly laughs. Guttenberg leads a group of oddballs into police training, where they clash with authority but prove themselves in the end. It's crude and juvenile, but fans will be in heaven. JF Swearing, violence, nudity. **DVD** **BL**

Steve Guttenberg *Carey Mahoney* • Kim Cattrall *Karen Thompson* • GW Bailey *Lieutenant Harris* • Bubba Smith *Moses Hightower* • Donovan Scott *Leslie Barbara* • George Gaynes *Commandant Lassard* • Andrew Rubin *George Martin* • David Graf *Tackleberry* • Leslie Easterbrook *Sergeant Callahan* ■ *Dir* Hugh Wilson • *Scr* Neal Israel, Pat Proft, Hugh Wilson, from a story by Israel, Proft

Police Academy 2: Their First Assignment ★ 12

Comedy   1985 · US · Colour · 83min

The international success of the first movie in the *Police Academy* series meant that new director Jerry Paris wasn't going to mess with a winning formula. This time the misfits get the opportunity to cause chaos on the streets, but, while it features many members of the original cast, this is a lazy replay of the original outing, with grossness substituting for any genuine humour. JF Swearing, violence, brief nudity. **DVD** **BL**

Steve Guttenberg *Carey Mahoney* • Bubba Smith *Hightower* • David Graf *Tackleberry* • Michael Winslow *Larvell Jones* • Bruce Mahler *Doug Fackler* • Marion Ramsey *Laverne Hooks* • Colleen Camp *Kirkland* • Howard Hesseman *Pete Lassard* • Art Metrano *Lieutenant Mauser* • Bob Goldthwait [Bobcat Goldthwait] *Zed* ■ *Dir* Jerry Paris • *Scr* Barry Blaustein [Barry W Blaustein], David Sheffield, from characters by Neal Israel, Pat Proft

Police Academy 3: Back in Training ★★ PG

Comedy   1986 · US · Colour · 80min

The title sums up the plot, really, although predictably the lovable losers eventually save the day as rival police academies battle for survival in an era of cutbacks in public spending. It is an improvement of sorts on the first sequel, but by this stage you were either a fan or holding the series up as a prime example of Hollywood puerility. JF Swearing, violence. **DVD** **BL**

Steve Guttenberg *Sergeant Mahoney* • Bubba Smith *Sergeant Hightower* • David Graf *Sergeant Tackleberry* • Michael Winslow *Sergeant Jones* • Marion Ramsey *Sergeant Hooks* • Leslie Easterbrook *Lieutenant Callahan* • Art Metrano *Commandant Mauser* • Bobcat Goldthwait *Cadet Zed* ■ *Dir* Jerry Paris • *Scr* Gene Quintano, from characters by Neal Israel, Pat Proft

Police Academy 4: Citizens on Patrol ★ PG

Comedy   1987 · US · Colour · 87min

This sequel is only worth watching for the opportunity to watch a pre-*Basic Instinct* Sharon Stone stranded down the cast list with the thankless role of star Steve Guttenberg's girlfriend. George Gaynes is the feeble-minded commander who finds himself training an even crazier bunch of recruits when citizens are encouraged to become part-time policemen. JF Swearing. **DVD** **BL**

Steve Guttenberg *Mahoney* • Bubba Smith *Hightower* • Michael Winslow *Jones* • David Graf *Tackleberry* • Sharon Stone *Claire Mattson* • George Gaynes *Commandant Lassard* • Bobcat Goldthwait *Zed* • Leslie Easterbrook *Callahan* ■ *Dir* Jim Drake • *Scr* Gene Quintano, from characters by Neal Israel, Pat Proft

Police Academy 5: Assignment Miami Beach ★ PG

Comedy   1988 · US · Colour · 86min

What could audiences have possibly done to deserve such torture? As this inane series continues, each episode becomes sillier and more slapdash than the last. There's no Steve Guttenberg in this one (he must have read the script), and all you need to know is that the bumbling cops visit Miami for a convention. JB Swearing, violence. **DVD** **BL**

Matt McCoy *Nick* • Janet Jones *Kate Stratton* • George Gaynes *Commandant Lassard* • GW Bailey *Captain Harris* • René Auberjonois *Tony Stark* • Bubba Smith *Moses Hightower* • David Graf *Eugene Tackleberry* • Michael Winslow *Larvelle Jones* • Leslie Easterbrook *Debbie Callahan* ■ *Dir* Alan Myerson • *Scr* Stephen J Curwick, from characters by Neal Israel, Pat Proft

Police Academy 6: City under Siege ★ PG

Comedy   1989 · US · Colour · 79min

Having run out of inventive gags and originality by the final scene of the very first *Police Academy*, the series had overstayed its welcome long before this fifth sequel by stretching a thin premise to breaking point. Aside from the vocal gymnastics of Michael Winslow, this laughter-free zone couldn't even get itself arrested for indecency. AJ Swearing, violence. **DVD** **BL**

Bubba Smith *Hightower* • David Graf *Tackleberry* • Michael Winslow *Jones* • Leslie Easterbrook *Callahan* • Marion Ramsey *Hooks* • Lance Kinsey *Proctor* • Matt McCoy *Nick* • Bruce Mahler *Fackler* ■ *Dir* Peter Bonerz • *Scr* Stephen J Curwick, from characters by Neal Israel, Pat Proft

Police Academy: Mission to Moscow ★ PG

Comedy   1994 · US · Colour · 79min

To mark the tenth anniversary of the series, back came George Gaynes and his crew of cockeyed cops to prove once more the law of diminishing sequels. Christopher Lee can never have been in a more terrifying movie - terrifyingly bad, that is. There isn't a single joke worthy of the name in this humiliating farrago. DP **DVD** **BL**

George Gaynes *Commandant Lassard* • Michael Winslow *Sgt Jones* • David Graf *Sgt Tackleberry* • Leslie Easterbrook *Capt Callahan* • GW Bailey *Capt Harris* • Christopher Lee *Commandant Alexander Rakov* • Ron Perlman *Constantine Konali* ■ *Dir* Alan Metter • *Scr* Randolph Davis, Michele S Chodos, from characters by Neal Israel, Pat Proft

Police, Adjective ★★★★ 12

Crime drama   2009 · Rom · Colour · 109min

Writer/director Corneliu Porumboiu takes a harsh, realist look at post-Communist Romania in this story of a police officer, Cristi (Dragos Bucur), who endures a soul-destroying stakeout, only to then be frustrated by the intricacies of office bureaucracy as he attempts to file his report. However, his problems are only just beginning, as by-the-book Captain Anghelache (Vlad Ivanov) summons him to explain his findings. This concluding section provides a disturbing insight into the cynicism of the legal system and the niceties of language, and Porumboiu's film is proof that a police procedural can be compelling even without the genre's usual maverick sleuthing or combustible action. DP Romanian +subtitles. Drug abuse. **DVD**

Dragos Bucur *Cristi* • Vlad Ivanov *Captain Anghelache* • Irina Saulescu *Anca* • Ion Stoica *Nelu* • Marian Ghenea *Attorney* • Cosmin Selesi *Costi* ■ *Dir/Scr* Corneliu Porumboiu

Police Dog ★★ U

Crime drama   1955 · UK · BW · 74min

This competent quota quickie from Derek Twist is, in all honesty, "mutt ado about nothing". In one of his few movie excursions, Tim Turner plays a bobby who adopts an alsatian stray and has reason to break out the Bonio when it helps him on the trail of his friend's murderer. It's hardly a baffling mystery - even Scooby Doo would have sussed it! DP

Joan Rice *Pat Lewis* • Tim Turner *Frank Mason* • Sandra Dorne *Blonde* • Charles Victor *Sergeant* • Jimmy Gilbert *Ken Lade* • Nora Gordon *Mrs Lewis* • John Le Mesurier *Inspector* ■ *Dir/Scr* Derek Twist

Police Story ★★ 15

Crime drama   1975 · Fr/It · Colour · 107min

Based on a real-life case - which explains the 1940s setting - this efficient thriller stars Alain Delon as a French detective and Jean-Louis Trintignant as his quarry, a psychotic killer and robber. Director Jacques Deray is clearly influenced by the work of Jean-Pierre Melville, and there are also traces of a Gallic *Dirty Harry* in Delon's parallel fight against bureaucratic red tape and liberal policies. This is a routine *policier* that was a big hit at the French box office. AT In French. **DVD**

Alain Delon *Borniche* • Jean-Louis Trintignant *Buisson* • Renato Salvatori *Le Rital* • Maurice Barrier *Bollec* • André Pousse *Le Nus* ■ *Dir* Jacques Deray • *Scr* Deray Alphonse Boudard, from an autobiography by Roger Borniche

Police Story ★★★ 15

Martial arts comedy thriller
1985 · HK · Colour · 95min

Jackie Chan became an international superstar on the back of this fast-paced martial arts comedy thriller, in which he plays a Hong Kong police officer on the trail of drug-dealing gangsters. Chan also directs, providing the action with some spectacular set pieces, the best being a car chase through a shantytown and the shopping mall climax. The lightweight story is merely an excuse to display Chan's death-defying agility and his inventive use of scenery and props. TH Cantonese dubbed. Violence, brief nudity. **DVD**

Jackie Chan *Chan Ka Kui* • Brigitte Lin *Selina Fong* • Maggie Cheung *May* • Yuen Cho *Chu Tao* • Bill Tung *Inspector Wong* ■ *Dir* Jackie Chan • *Scr* Edward Tang

Police Story 2 ★★ 15

Martial arts comedy thriller
1986 · HK · Colour · 101min

Jackie Chan directs, co-writes and stars as the policeman in this chop-socky sequel. Like many Hong Kong action films, its breathless pace cannot prevent it from becoming a drag, and the soundtrack seems to have been recorded in a cardboard box. AT Cantonese dubbed. Violence, brief nudity. **DVD**

Jackie Chan *Kevin Chan* • Maggie Cheung *May* • Bill Tung *Inspector Wong* • Lam Kwok Hung *Superintendent Lee* ■ *Dir* Jackie Chan • *Scr* Edward Tang, Jackie Chan

Police Story III: Supercop ★★★ 15

Martial arts comedy thriller
1992 · HK · Colour · 91min

The best part of this typically lively Jackie Chan outing is the final credit sequence featuring the reckless stunts that failed to make the picture. This is a cracking romp in which Hong Kong cop Chan and Chinese police director Michelle Yeoh team up to infiltrate the gang of a vicious drugs baron. Riotous fun throughout. Michelle Yeoh returned to the role in 1993's *Project S*. DP Cantonese dubbed. Violence, swearing. **DVD**

Jackie Chan *Chen Chia-Chu* • Maggie Cheung *May* • Michelle Yeoh *Inspector Yang* ■ *Dir* Stanley Tong • *Scr* Edward Tang, Filre Ma, Lee Wai Yee

The Polish Bride ★★★★ 15

Romantic drama   1998 · Neth · Colour · 85min

This warmly sympathetic chamber-work certainly puts Dutch-based director Karim Traïdia on the map. It's an acute analysis of an oddball relationship: Jaap Spijkers is a near-bankrupt farmer who gives shelter to Monic Hendrickx, a Polish prostitute on the run from abusing city pimps. She becomes his housekeeper and they form a relationship that turns to love. For all its heartache, this is an engrossing affirmation that's a tonic for the spirit. TH Dutch, German, Polish +subtitles. A sex scene, violence.

Jaap Spijkers *Henk Woldring* • Monic Hendrickx *Anna Krzyzanowska* • Rudi Falkenhagen *Father* • Roef Ragas *Son* • Hakim Traïdia *Postman* ■ *Dir* Karim Traïdia • *Scr* Kees van der Hulst

Polish Wedding ★★ 15

Romantic comedy   1998 · US · Colour · 101min

This tale of a Polish-American family in Detroit works quite well, but fails to stir up much emotion in the audience. Claire Danes is the teenager whose actions send her family into a turmoil - though perhaps they should be more alarmed at the casting. Not only are the leads not Polish; they're not even American! (Gabriel Byrne is Irish, while Lena Olin is a Swede.) They handle the accents well enough, but this is one of those slight films that can best be described as "nice". JB Some swearing. **DVD**

Lena Olin *Jadzia Pzoniak* • Gabriel Byrne *Bolek Pzoniak* • Claire Danes *Hala Pzoniak* • Adam Trese *Russell Schuster* • Mili Avital *Sofie Pzoniak* • Daniel Lapaine *Ziggy Pzoniak* • Rade Serbedzija *Roman* ■ *Dir/Scr* Theresa Connelly

P

Pollock ★★★★ 18
Biographical drama 2000 · US · Colour · 118min

Unfettered passion fuelled tormented American artist Jackson Pollock and, watching this remarkable biopic of his life, it would seem this same fervour possessed actor Ed Harris. Assuming the roles of first-time director, co-producer and star, the often underrated Harris turns an obvious labour of love into a respectable addition to Hollywood's "tortured artist" canon. Harris paints a compelling and passionate portrait of a creative genius consumed by personal demons. Gritty faded visuals and an understated, naturalistic style focus attention on the plot and characterisation. SF Swearing, drug abuse, sex scenes. *DVD*

Ed Harris *Jackson Pollock* • Marcia Gay Harden *Lee Krasner* • Amy Madigan *Peggy Guggenheim* • Jennifer Connelly *Ruth Kligman* • Jeffrey Tambor *Clement Greenberg* • Bud Cort *Howard Putzel* • John Heard *Tony Smith* • Val Kilmer *Willem de Kooning* ■ *Dir* Ed Harris • *Scr* Barbara Turner, Susan J Emshwiller, from the book *Jackson Pollock: an American Saga* by Steven Naifeh, Gregory White Smith

Polly of the Circus ★★ U
Romantic drama 1932 · US · BW · 69min

It took MGM some time to get the measure of their rising star Clark Gable and cast him according to his personality. This romantic drama, a perfect example of studio misjudgment, has Gable playing a man of the cloth who rescues a trapeze artist (a colourless Marion Davies) from physical and moral degradation in the face of disapproval from his bishop (C Aubrey Smith). A thin little film, devoid of sparks, despite Gable's flaming good looks. RK

Marion Davies *Polly Fisher* • Clark Gable *Reverend John Hartley* • C Aubrey Smith *Reverend James Northcott* • Raymond Hatton *Downey* • David Landau *Beef* • Ruth Selwyn *Mitzi* • Ray Milland *Rich young man* ■ *Dir* Alfred Santell • *Scr* Carey Wilson, Laurence Johnson, from the play by Margaret Mayo

Pollyanna ★★★★
Silent drama 1920 · US · BW · 60min

This adaptation of Eleanor H Porter's book is probably Mary Pickford's most sugary confection. "The world's sweetheart" plays an orphan girl whose irresistible good nature converts the hard hearts of Aunt Polly (Katherine Griffith) and her grumpy New England neighours. (Her final, near-fatal illness is schmaltz with a temperature.) Pickford is wonderful, while director Paul Powell catches the mood of the time, and the town, with casual expertise. TH

Mary Pickford *Pollyanna* • Wharton James *Rev Whittier* • Katherine Griffith *Aunt Polly Harrington* • Herbert Prior *Dr Chilton* • William Courtleigh *John Pendleton* • Helen Jerome Eddy *Nancy* • George Berrell *Tom* ■ *Dir* Paul Powell • *Scr* Frances Marion, from the novel by Eleanor H Porter

Pollyanna ★★★★ U
Period drama 1960 · US · Colour · 128min

Considering this was his debut, writer/director David Swift made a splendid job of adapting Eleanor H Porter's 1912 children's classic for the screen. Disney spared no expense in re-creating the look and feel of small-town Vermont, and signed up such top-line performers as Agnes Moorehead, Karl Malden, Adolphe Menjou and Jane Wyman. They play the cheerless citizens whose lives are transformed by effervescent orphan Pollyanna (Hayley Mills) and her bottomless supply of "gladness". Mills won a special Oscar for her spirited performance. If there is a fault, it is that it's a bit too long. DP *DVD*

Hayley Mills *Pollyanna* • Jane Wyman *Aunt Polly Harrington* • Richard Egan *Dr Edmond Chilton* • Karl Malden *Reverend Paul Ford* • Nancy Olson *Nancy Furman* • Adolphe Menjou *Mr Pendergast* • Donald Crisp *Mayor Warren* • Agnes Moorehead *Mrs Snow* ■ *Dir* David Swift • *Scr* David Swift, from the novel by Eleanor H Porter

Poltergeist ★★★★ 15
Horror 1982 · US · Colour · 109min

Evil spirits enter the home of a typical suburban American family through their possessed television set in this spectacular horror film, co-produced and co-written by Steven Spielberg. After a deceptively cute opening, Tobe Hooper gets down to some serious haunting and piles on the thrilling special effects and grisly moments. Hooper's direction may lack its usual edgy personality – apparently over-ruled by Spielberg's script suggestions – but he puts on a dazzling show. AJ Violence, swearing, drug abuse. *DVD* *BL*

JoBeth Williams *Diane Freeling* • Craig T Nelson *Steve Freeling* • Beatrice Straight *Dr Lesh* • Dominique Dunne *Dana Freeling* • Oliver Robbins *Robbie Freeling* • Heather O'Rourke *Carol Anne Freeling* • Michael McManus (1) *Ben Tuthill* • Virginia Kiser *Mrs Tuthill* • Zelda Rubinstein *Tangina Barrons* ■ *Dir* Tobe Hooper • *Scr* Steven Spielberg, Michael Grais, Mark Victor, from a story by Steven Spielberg

Poltergeist ★★★ 15
Horror 2015 · US · Colour · 93min

This "things that go bump in the night" excursion is a decent, sharply written remake of Tobe Hooper's highly rated horror. As with the 1982 original (based on a rare Steven Spielberg story), the setting is an ordinary suburban home beset by something spooky. Sam Rockwell stars as the nerve-wracked dad who calls in Jared Harris's TV ghost hunter when his daughter is abducted by otherworldly entities. It's high on atmosphere, low on tedium and the effects are unnervingly effective. DA *DVD* *BL* *3D*

Sam Rockwell *Eric Bowen* • Rosemarie DeWitt *Amy Bowen* • Jared Harris *Carrigan Burke* • Nicholas Braun *Boyd* ■ *Dir* Gil Kenan • *Scr* David Lindsay-Abaire, from a story by Steven Spielberg [uncredited]

Poltergeist II: the Other Side ★★★ 15
Horror 1986 · US · Colour · 86min

The haunted Freeling family has moved to Arizona, but the evil spirits aren't giving up their pursuit of the family's daughter, Heather O'Rourke. This sequel does little more than recycle the original story, yet there are enough supernatural visitations and grisly surprises to prevent the ghostly goings-on from getting dull. Julian Beck gives a marvellous fire-and-brimstone performance. AJ Violence. *DVD* *BL*

JoBeth Williams *Diane Freeling* • Craig T Nelson *Steve Freeling* • Heather O'Rourke *Carol Anne Freeling* • Oliver Robins *Robbie Freeling* • Zelda Rubinstein *Tangina Barrons* • Will Sampson *Taylor* • Julian Beck *Reverend Henry Kane* • Geraldine Fitzgerald *Gramma Jess* ■ *Dir* Brian Gibson • *Scr* Mark Victor, Michael Grais

Poltergeist III ★ 15
Horror 1988 · US · Colour · 93min

"Enough, stop this stupid sideshow!" says the obnoxious psychiatrist in this repetitious and completely unnecessary second sequel. You'll give voice to the same sentiment long before the end of this dull, lifeless movie. Heather O'Rourke died, at the age of 12, shortly after the film's completion, only adding to the legendary stories about a curse stalking the variable series. AJ Swearing, violence. *DVD* *BL*

Tom Skerritt *Bruce Gardner* • Nancy Allen *Patricia Gardner* • Heather O'Rourke *Carol Anne Freeling* • Zelda Rubinstein *Tangina Barrons* • Lara Flynn Boyle *Donna Gardner* • Kip Wentz *Scott* • Richard Fire *Dr Seaton* ■ *Dir* Gary Sherman • *Scr* Gary Sherman, Brian Taggert

Polyester ★★★★ 18
Satirical melodrama 1981 · US · Colour · 79min

A fabulously vulgar suburban tale of a materially minded housewife with a perverse and ultimately tragic sense of gentility, *Polyester* brought about a long overdue reunion between director John Waters and Divine. Devoid of any conventional artistry while referencing lurid Hollywood melodrama in its satirical take on the lower-middle classes, the film showcases several other Waters regulars and also features resurrected sun-and-surf heart-throb Tab Hunter. Unmissable for anyone interested in the origins of what are now institutionalised obsessions with trash, kitsch and consumerist America, this candy-coloured, "mainstream" landmark arrived in cinemas with scratch-and-sniff Odorama cards. DO

Divine *Francine Fishpaw* • Tab Hunter *Todd Tomorrow* • Edith Massey *Cuddles Kevinsky* • Mink Stole *Sandra Sullivan* • David Samson *Elmer Fishpaw* • Joni Ruth White *La Rue* • Mary Garlington *Lu-Lu Fishpaw* • Cookie Mueller *Betty Lelinski* ■ *Dir/Scr* John Waters (2) • *Costume Designer* Van Smith

Pom Poko ★★ PG
Animated fantasy adventure 1994 · Jpn · Colour · 114min

In another of Studio Ghibli's imaginative eco-fables, raccoon-like creatures from Japanese folklore – known as "tanuki" – fight to save their forest home from urban development. Visual humour initially distracts from the long-winded and preachy storytelling that unfolds, but when the tragedy of events increases, so too does writer/director Isao Takahata's heavy-handed moralising. Though admirably heartfelt, this clogs up an already erratically paced narrative and overshadows many of the feature's more subtle charms. SF Japanese dubbed. *DVD* *BL*

Tress MacNeille *Fireball Oroku* • Clancy Brown *Gonta* • Jonathan Taylor Thomas *Shoukichi* • Maurice LaMarche *The Narrator* • Jillian Bowen *Okiyo* ■ *Dir/Scr* Isao Takahata

POM Wonderful Presents: The Greatest Movie Ever Sold ★★ 12
Documentary 2011 · US · Colour · 83min

Documentarian/activist Morgan Spurlock is still best known for *Super Size Me*, in which he ate nothing but McDonald's food for a month. In this film he attempts to fund his entire movie via product placement – everything in the film (which cost $1.5 million) is up for sale, right down to the jacket he wears on American chat shows to promote it. It's occasionally entertaining watching Spurlock, with disarming honesty, pitch his bizarre idea to bewildered potential corporate partners. But other than the obvious observation that marketing is pervasive, it's difficult to see what his point is. AS Some swearing, sexual references. *DVD*

Morgan Spurlock • Brett Ratner • Ralph Nader • Quentin Tarantino ■ *Dir* Morgan Spurlock • *Scr* Jeremy Chilnick, Morgan Spurlock • *Cinematographer* Daniel Marracino

Pompeii ★★★ 12
Action adventure 2014 · Can/Ger/US · Colour · 100min

Corrupt Roman senator Kiefer Sutherland arrives in Pompeii with plans to nab noblewoman Emily Browning as his wife. Trouble is she's smitten by slave-turned-gladiator Kit Harington. Not that any of this turgid soap in togas matters because its 79 AD and Mount Vesuvius is about to erupt. Director Paul WS Anderson's sword-and-sandal spectacular is pretty nonsensical, from the laughable dialogue and predictable romance to the ludicrous carnage and cheesy acting. But when the volcanic fire and brimstone explodes and the CGI catastrophe runs rampant, this pot-boiler finally provides the thrilling epic destruction you've waited an hour to witness. Complete with tsunami! AJ Some violence, swearing. *DVD* *BL*

Kit Harington *Milo* • Carrie-Anne Moss *Aurelia* • Emily Browning *Cassia* • Jared Harris *Severus* • Kiefer Sutherland *Corvus* ■ *Dir* Paul WS Anderson [Paul Anderson (1)] • *Scr* Janet Scott Batchler, Lee Batchler, Michael Robert Johnson

Ponette ★★★ PG
Drama 1996 · Fr · Colour · 93min

Four-year-old Victoire Thivisol won the best actress prize at Venice for her remarkable work in this exquisite study of loss and the indomitability of innocence. Bruised and confused after surviving the car crash that killed her mother, she has to cope not only with the shocked anger of her father, but also the conflicting advice of her teachers and playmates on the nature of death and the afterlife. However, director Jacques Doillon undermines the authenticity of Thivisol's pain and bewilderment by tacking on a cosy, contrived ending. DP French +subtitles.

Victoire Thivisol *Ponette* • Matiaz Bureau Caton *Matiaz* • Delphine Schiltz *Delphine* • Léopoldine Serre *Ada* • Luckie Royer *Luce* • Carla Ibled *Carla* • Antoine du Merle *Antoine* • Marie Trintignant *Ponette's mother* ■ *Dir/Scr* Jacques Doillon

Pontiac Moon ★★ 12
Comedy drama 1994 · US · Colour · 102min

This cloying drama stars Ted Danson as a rural science teacher who decides to take his son (Ryan Todd) on the road to discover the meaning of life on the eve of the Apollo XI Moon mission. Mary Steenburgen and Cathy Moriarty go along for the mawkish ride. Peter Medak's direction errs on the side of the sentimentally mundane and only the good-natured performances make this journey worth following. AJ

Ted Danson *Washington Bellamy* • Mary Steenburgen *Katherine Bellamy* • Ryan Todd *Andy Bellamy* • Eric Schweig *Ernest Ironplume* • Cathy Moriarty *Lorraine* • Max Gail *Jerome Bellamy* • Lisa Jane Persky *Alicia Frook* ■ *Dir* Peter Medak • *Scr* Finn Taylor, Jeffrey Brown, from an idea by Finn Taylor

Pontius Pilate ★★
Biblical drama 1961 · It/Fr · Colour · 100min

The Crucifixion is replayed from the viewpoint of the Roman procurator whose hand-wringing has earned him a place in the Christian faith. French superstar Jean Marais is directed by Hollywood stalwart Irving Rapper, who went to Europe for this concatenation on Pilate's love affairs. The muddled dubbing makes some of the plot almost impenetrable. TH Italian, French dubbed.

Jean Marais *Pontius Pilate* • Jeanne Crain *Claudia Procula* • Basil Rathbone *Caiaphas* • Leticia Roman *Sarah* • Massimo Serato *Nicodemus* • Riccardo Garrone *Galba* • Livio Lorenzon *Barabbas* • Gianni Garko *Jonathan* • John Drew Barrymore *Jesus/Judas* ■ *Dir* Irving Rapper, Gian Paolo Callegari • *Scr* O Biancolo, Gino DeSantis, Gian Paolo Callegari, from a story by Gino DeSanotis

Pontypool ★★★ 15
Horror thriller 2008 · Can · Colour and BW · 92min

Director Bruce McDonald delivers an inventive take on the zombie movie in this compact and claustrophobic chiller that sees humans infected by the English language itself. As the residents of a sleepy Ontario town fall victim to the aurally received plague, a DJ (Stephen McHattie) and his two colleagues piece together the unfolding story, while broadcasting from their basement radio station. Events ooze with slow-burning suspense; but since the undead chaos occurs predominantly off-screen, viewers are left to imagine the actual carnage. The overall result is a low-budget lesson in the power of words that's elevated further by quick-firing McHattie's seamlessly natural performance. SF English, French +subtitles. Swearing, some violence. *DVD* *BL*

Stephen McHattie *Grant Mazzy* • Lisa Houle *Sydney Briar* • Georgina Reilly *Laurel-Ann Drummond* • Hrant Alianak *Dr John Mendez* • Rick Roberts *Ken Loney* ■ *Dir* Bruce McDonald • *Scr* Tony Burgess, from his novel *Pontypool Changes Everything*

The Pony Express ★★★
Silent western 1925 · US · BW · 110min

This major silent western, directed by James Cruze for Paramount to follow up his smash hit, *The Covered Wagon*, was again about an historical aspect of the Old West. Ricardo Cortez plays the gambler turned pony express rider who carries vital news of the election of President Lincoln to California, thereby linking both sides of the

P

huge country. Although overburdened with plot and subsidiary characters, it does have a spectacular climactic attack by Indians and some vivid villainy from George Bancroft. AE

Ricardo Cortez *Jack Weston* • Betty Compson *Molly Jones* • Ernest Torrence *"Ascension" Jones* • Wallace Beery *"Rhode Island" Red* • George Bancroft *Jack Slade* ■ *Dir* James Cruze • *Scr* Walter Woods, from a novel by Henry James Forman, Walter Woods

Pony Express ★★ U
Western   1953 · US · Colour · 101min

Charlton Heston, always cast in roles where he can lead with his chin, is fuelled by purposeful action, decency and high moral fibre in a western which has all the expected shorthand of the genre. The lightweight plot revolves around the adventures of Heston, as Buffalo Bill Cody, and Forrest Tucker, as Wild Bill Hickok, and the opening of mail routes to California. This is a lumpy stew of lean crackerjack action and rather earnest, talky stretches. JM

Charlton Heston *Buffalo Bill Cody* • Rhonda Fleming *Evelyn* • Jan Sterling *Denny* • Forrest Tucker *Wild Bill Hickok* • Michael Moore (3) *Rance Hastings* • Porter Hall *Bridger* ■ *Dir* Jerry Hopper • *Scr* Charles Marquis Warren, from a story by Frank Gruber

Pony Soldier ★★ U
Western   1952 · US · Colour · 82min

The Mounties certainly had their day in the early 1950s, what with Alan Ladd in *Saskatchewan* and Howard Keel and Ann Blyth in *Rose Marie*, and here's Tyrone Power sent to don the scarlet as MacDonald of the Canadian Mounties (the film's British title). To be honest, Power looks thoroughly bored and ill-at-ease in this lame adventure. TS

Tyrone Power *Duncan MacDonald* • Cameron Mitchell *Konah* • Thomas Gomez *Natayo* • Penny Edwards *Emerald Neeley* • Robert Horton *Jess Calhoun* • Anthony Earl Numkena *Comes Running* • Adeline De Walt Reynolds *White Moon* • Howard Petrie *Inspector Frazer* ■ *Dir* Joseph M Newman • *Scr* John C Higgins, from a story by Garnett Weston in *The Saturday Evening Post*

Ponyo ★★★★ U
Animated fantasy adventure   2008 · Jpn · Colour · 98min

Acclaimed Japanese writer/director Hayao Miyazaki (*Spirited Away*) has crafted another delightful animated fantasy here, a tale about a little fish who dreams of becoming a human girl. The simple story concerns a young boy called Sosuke who lives in a small coastal town and whose relationship with a pretty goldfish he names Ponyo threatens to disrupt the balance of nature. Miyazaki's trademark visual flights of fancy are matched by the eco-minded story, believable characters and unhurried unfolding of the magical events. This serves as a reminder that animated films can be imaginative, enchanting and exciting while still telling a sweet, good-hearted story. LB *DVD* *BLU*

Noah Cyrus [Noah Lindsey Cyrus] *Ponyo* • Cate Blanchett *Gran Mamare* • Matt Damon *Koichi* • Tina Fey *Lisa* • Frankie Jonas *Sosuke* • Cloris Leachman *Noriko* • Liam Neeson *Fujimoto* ■ *Dir* Hayao Miyazaki, John Lasseter, Brad Lewis, Peter Sohn • *Scr* Hayao Miyazaki, adapted by Melissa Mathison

Poodle Springs ★★ 15
Mystery thriller   1998 · US · Colour · 95min

Ageing private eye Philip Marlowe, laconically played by James Caan, gets mixed up with blackmail and murder among the elite 1960s in-crowd in director Bob Rafelson's stilted take on Raymond Chandler. Despite a brave and literate attempt by scriptwriter Tom Stoppard to solve the contradictions of a story which existed only in sketch form at the time of the writer's death, this TV *faux film noir* is a thin stylistic oddity. AJ Swearing, nudity, violence. *DVD*

James Caan *Philip Marlowe* • Dina Meyer *Laura* • David Keith *Larry Victor* • Tom Bower *Arnie Burns* • Julia Campbell *Muffy Blackstone* • Brian

Cox (1) *Clayton Blackstone* • Nia Peeples *Angel* ■ *Dir* Bob Rafelson • *Scr* Tom Stoppard, from the novel by Robert B Parker, Raymond Chandler

Pooh's Heffalump Movie ★★ U
Animated comedy adventure   2005 · US · Colour · 65min

Winnie the Pooh and his pals learn valuable lessons about friendship and diversity in Disney's slight and sugary tale, which is clearly aimed at young children. Believing that a mysterious rumbling noise in the Hundred Acre Wood is the sound of a much-feared Heffalump monster, the grown-up animals set out to catch the creature, leaving a disappointed young Roo behind. The 2-D animation is a bit flat and quaint. SF *DVD*

Jim Cummings *Winnie the Pooh/Tigger* • John Fiedler *Piglet* • Nikita Hopkins *Roo* • Kath Soucie *Kanga* • Ken Sansom *Rabbit* • Peter Cullen *Eeyore* • Brenda Blethyn *Mama Heffalump* • David Ogden Stiers *Narrator* ■ *Dir* Frank Nissen • *Scr* Brian Hohlfeld, Evan Spiliotopoulos, from characters by AA Milne

The Pool ★★★ 12
Comedy drama   2007 · US · Colour · 90min

Writer/director Chris Smith moves a Randy Russell short story from Iowa to Panjim in the Indian state of Goa (and from English to Hindi) for this cross-class love story. Very much a latter-day fairy tale, it has 18-year-old hotel worker Venatesh Chavan building a friendship with Ayesha Mohan, while cleaning the pool of her businessman father. Chavan is an unlikely romantic hero, but Smith avoids clichés and stereotypes by maintaining a discreet distance, and allows the charming action to unfold through to its poignant finale. DP Hindi +subtitles. *DVD*

Venatesh Chavan *Venkatesh* • Jhangir Badshah *Jhangir* • Ayesha Mohan *Ayesha* • Malcolm Faria *Malcolm* ■ *Dir* Chris Smith • *Scr* Chris Smith, Randy Russell, from a short story by Russell

Pool of London ★★ PG
Crime drama   1950 · UK · BW · 81min

The thriller elements may be routine, but the mixed-race romance in this Ealing Studios production broke new ground for British cinema. Set in London's Docklands, it's a smuggling yarn involving a black stevedore, his white girlfriend and plenty of double-crosses before the cops close in. Director Basil Dearden makes the most of his eclectic cast. AT *DVD*

Bonar Colleano *Dan MacDonald* • Susan Shaw *Pat* • Renée Asherson *Sally* • Earl Cameron *Johnny* • Moira Lister *Maisie* • Max Adrian *Vernon* • Joan Dowling *Pamela* • James Robertson-Justice *Trotter* ■ *Dir* Basil Dearden • *Scr* Jack Whittingham, John Eldredge

Poor Cow ★★★ 15
Drama   1967 · UK · Colour · 97min

Ken Loach made his feature debut with this adaptation of Nell Dunn's social realist (if unashamedly sensationalist) novel. The first of several films with working-class themes made by Loach, this isn't a patch on either his TV plays *Up the Junction* and *Cathy Come Home*, or his follow-up feature, *Kes*. This determinedly grim tale centres on the tangled love life of teenager Carol White, who turns to Terence Stamp after her thieving lover John Bindon is sent to prison. But only Queenie Watts impresses as White's prostitute aunt. Watch out for a debuting Malcolm McDowell. DP *DVD* *BLU*

Carol White *Joy* • Terence Stamp *Dave* • John Bindon *Tom* • Kate Williams *Beryl* • Queenie Watts *Aunt Emm* • Geraldine Sherman *Trixie* • James Beckett *Tom's friend* • Billy Murray *Tom's friend* • Malcolm McDowell *Billy* ■ *Dir* Kenneth Loach [Ken Loach] • *Scr* Kenneth Loach, Nell Dunn, the novel by Nell Dunn

Poor Little Rich Girl ★★★ U
Musical comedy   1936 · US · BW · 76min

She's little Shirley Temple, and it's jolly difficult to care when such an obviously talented, bright-and-shiny youngster feels neglected and runs away from the home of her wealthy widower father. She's befriended by blonde Alice Faye and Tin

Man-to-be Jack Haley and turned into a major radio star. Temple was the biggest movie star in the world at this time, and her studio, 20th Century-Fox, was hard-pressed to find suitable vehicles to showcase her talents. It did her proud with this one, and the finale is mesmerising. TS *DVD*

Shirley Temple *Barbara Barry* • Alice Faye *Jerry Dolan* • Gloria Stuart *Margaret Allen* • Jack Haley *Jimmy Dolan* • Michael Whalen *Richard Barry* • Sara Haden *Collins* • Jane Darwell *Woodward* • Billy Gilbert *Waiter* ■ *Dir* Irving Cummings • *Scr* Sam Hellman, Gladys Lehman, Harry Tugend, from stories by Eleanor Gates, Ralph Spence

Pop & Me ★★★ 12
Documentary   1999 · US · Colour · 88min

Brandishing a raw honesty that often leaves the viewer feeling like an intruder, this is a relentlessly revealing insight into father-son relationships around the world. The focus falls on Californian graphic designer Chris Roe, who agrees to help his broker father, Richard, through a midlife crisis by reprising the family's 1979 globe-trotting expedition. Starting with Richard's reunion with the alcoholic father he'd not seen for over 30 years, the trip soon opens up fissures in the Roes' affinities. But while the various international tensions are compelling, the real coup is persuading Julian Lennon to speak so candidly about his Beatle dad. DP

■ *Dir* Chris Roe • *Scr* Chris Roe, Richard Roe, Erik Arnesen, Jesse Negron, Juliann Jannus, Mark Kornweibel

Popcorn ★★ 15
Horror   1991 · US · Colour · 86min

This quirky little movie puts too much on its plate, trying to mix a standard slasher tale with attempts to satirise campy old horror movies. The satire is more successful than the slash, with amusing and on-target homages to William Castle and failed cinematic innovations such as "Smell-O-Vision". The sporadic cuts to these segments are nice breaks in an otherwise predictable opus about a university film class sponsoring an all-night horror festival. KB *DVD*

Jill Schoelen *Maggie* • Tom Villard *Toby* • Dee Wallace Stone *Suzanne* • Derek Rydall *Mark* • Malcolm Danare *Bud* • Elliott Hurst *Leon* ■ *Dir* Mark Herrier • *Scr* Alan Ormsby, from a story by Mitchell Smith

Pope Joan ★★ 15
Period drama   1972 · UK · Colour · 107min

Before he wrote his Oscar-winning script for *Gandhi*, John Briley penned this mythical tale of a woman who disguises herself as a monk and (to cut a long story short) ends up as Pope. The main question is not what it all means, but why Liv Ullmann was such a riveting actress for Ingmar Bergman and such a prissy plum pudding for everyone else. The strong supporting cast pop in and out of the story, while the ninth-century settings are no more than perfunctory. AT

Liv Ullmann *Joan* • Keir Dullea *Dr Stevens* • Maximilian Schell *Adrian* • Olivia de Havilland *Mother Superior* • Lesley-Anne Down *Cecilia* • Trevor Howard *Pope Leo* ■ *Dir* Michael Anderson • *Scr* John Briley

The Pope Must Die ★★★ 15
Comedy   1991 · UK · Colour · 95min

This feature-length outing for the *Comic Strip* team is a little ragged around the edges, but there are enough sharp gags to make it entertaining. Robbie Coltrane plays the simple, rock 'n' roll-loving priest who is mistakenly elected Pope, only to discover a hot-bed of corruption within the Vatican. Coltrane can do this sort of thing in his sleep, and the best performances come from some canny scene-stealers not normally associated with the TV show. JF Violence, swearing, nudity.

Robbie Coltrane *Dave Albinizi* • Beverly D'Angelo *Veronica Dante* • Herbert Lom *Vittorio Corelli* • Alex Rocco *Cardinal Rocco* • Paul Bartel (1) *Monsignor Vitchie* • Balthazar Getty *Joe Don Dante* • William Hootkins *Cardinal Verucci* • Robert Stephens *Carmelengo* • Annette Crosbie

Mother Superior • Steve O'Donnell *Rico* • John Sessions *Dino* ■ *Dir* Peter Richardson • *Scr* Peter Richardson, Pete Richens

The Pope of Greenwich Village ★★★ 15
Crime drama   1984 · US · Colour · 118min

This never once approaches the creatively crazed energy of Martin Scorsese's *Mean Streets*, on whose coat-tails it rather obviously hangs. But what the film lacks in imagination and drive it gains in rich character acting, particularly from those who look as if they've been pushed and pulled by New York life or just spent too long in its gutters. JM Swearing.

Mickey Rourke *Charlie* • Eric Roberts *Paulie* • Daryl Hannah *Diane* • Geraldine Page *Mrs Ritter* • Kenneth McMillan *Barney* • Tony Musante *Pete* • M Emmet Walsh *Burns* • Burt Young *"Bedbug" Eddie* ■ *Dir* Stuart Rosenberg • *Scr* Vincent Patrick, from his novel

Popeye ★★ U
Musical comedy   1980 · US · Colour · 92min

Robert Altman fails spectacularly here, trying to turn the comic strip *Popeye* into a live-action musical comedy. Robin Williams raps inarticulately as the heroic sailorman searching for his long-lost Pappy with the help of Shelley Duvall's witless though seductive Olive Oyl. There are compensations – the brilliantly designed town of Sweethaven and Harry Nilsson's songs, for example – but it's all too manic, jittery and overblown. TH *DVD*

Robin Williams *Popeye* • Shelley Duvall *Olive Oyl* • Ray Walston *Poopdeck Pappy* • Paul L Smith [Paul Smith] *Bluto* • Paul Dooley *Wimpy* • Richard Libertini *Geezil* • Roberta Maxwell *Nana Oyl* • Donald Moffat *Taxman* ■ *Dir* Robert Altman • *Scr* Jules Feiffer, from comic strip characters by EC Segar • *Production Designer* Wolf Kroeger

Poppy ★★★
Drama   1935 · Jpn · BW · 72min

This Kenji Mizoguchi adaptation has been somewhat overlooked. At its core lies the contrasting social attitudes of two women: dutiful daughter Yukichi Iwata, who reluctantly accedes to her betrothal to Daijiro Natsukawa, and older, more liberated English student, Kuniko Miyake. The director abandoned his now customary long takes and adopted a traditional Hollywood narrative approach, with editing, not camera movement, creating the rhythm and significance of the action. DP Japanese +subtitles.

Kuniko Miyake *Fujio Kono* • Ichiro Tsukida *Seizo Ono* • Daijiro Natsukawa *Hajime Munechika* • Kazuyoshi Takeda *Kingo Kono* • Yukichi Iwata *Tomotaka Inoue* • Chiyoko Okura *Sayoko Inoue* ■ *Dir* Kenji Mizoguchi • *Scr* Haruo Takayanagi, Daisuke Ito, from the novel *Gubijinso* by Soseki Natsume • *Cinematographer* Minoru Miki

Poppy ★★★★ U
Comedy   1936 · US · BW · 70min

WC Fields made the role of travelling medicine seller Eustace McGargle his own when he first appeared in Dorothy Donnelly's play back in the early 1920s and in the 1925 silent version, *Sally of the Sawdust*. This film version finds him setting up his stall in a small town where his adopted daughter (Rochelle Hudson) falls in love with the mayor's son. There's more sentimentality than is usual, but the delight of watching him never giving a sucker an even break is still a pleasure. TH *DVD*

WC Fields *Prof Eustace McGargle* • Rochelle Hudson *Poppy* • Richard Cromwell *Billy Farnsworth* • Granville Bates *Mayor Farnsworth* • Catherine Doucet *Countess Maggie Tubbs DePuizzi* ■ *Dir* A Edward Sutherland • *Scr* Waldemar Young, Virginia Van Upp, from the play by Dorothy Donnelly

The Poppy Is Also a Flower ★★ PG
Crime thriller   1966 · US · Colour · 95min

For incurable star-spotters and collectors of 007 trivia, this thriller about two UN agents who go up against the international heroin trade is absolutely unmissable. James Bond author Ian Fleming had the original idea of opening with a shot of a pretty poppy growing in the fields of Iran and following its progress to the ugly streets of Harlem. Among the host of stars, Bond fans will immediately spot Harold Sakata, who played Oddjob in *Goldfinger*. First seen on US TV, then released in European cinemas as *Danger Grows Wild*. DP

EG Marshall *Jones* • Trevor Howard *Lincoln* • Gilbert Roland *Marco* • Rita Hayworth *Monique* • Anthony Quayle *Captain* • Angie Dickinson *Linda Benson* • Yul Brynner *Colonel Salem* • Eli Wallach *Locarno* • Harold Sakata *Martin* • Marcello Mastroianni *Inspector Mosca* • Stephen Boyd *Benson* • Omar Sharif *Dr Rad* • Grace Kelly *Introduction* ■ Dir Terence Young • Scr Jo Eisinger, from an idea by Ian Fleming

Popsy-Pop ★
Crime drama   1970 · Fr · Colour · 88min

This dreary romantic thriller stars Stanley Baker as an incorruptible cop sent to arrest jewel smuggler Claudia Cardinale as she collects another consignment of stones from her double-crossing partner. Unsurprisingly, the couple fall in lust as their bad-tempered cat-and-mouse game grinds along to its predictable conclusion. DP French dubbed.

Stanley Baker *Silva* • Claudia Cardinale *Popsy* • Henri Charrière *Marco* • Georges Aminel *Priest* • Ginette Leclerc *Madame* ■ Dir Jean Herman • Scr Henri Charrière, Jean Herman

Populaire ★★★ 12
Romantic comedy   2012 · Fr · Colour · 106min

A fresh and colourful romantic comedy about typing? Surely some mistake? Au contraire. Director Régis Roinsard makes his debut with this fun period piece set in the 1950s that plays like a cross between *Mad Men* and *The Artist*. Déborah François plays Rose, a small-town girl whose flying fingers take her up in the world when Louis (Romain Duris) spots her talent and enters her in a series of typewriting contests. Love, on the other hand, seems just out of touching distance, as the attractive Louis is a die-hard bachelor who keeps her at arm's length. *Populaire* is not completely predictable, though it does hark back to those sassy, screwball love stories that Hollywood used to churn out in the 1930s. KK French, English, German +subtitles. DVD BD

Romain Duris *Louis Echard* • Déborah François *Rose Pamphyle* • Bérénice Bejo *Marie Taylor* • Shaun Benson *Bob Taylor* • Mélanie Bernier *Annie Leprince-Ringuet* • Miou-Miou *Madeleine Echard* ■ Dir Régis Roinsard • Scr Régis Roinsard, Daniel Presley, Romain Compingt

Porco Rosso ★★★ PG
Animated comedy adventure   1992/2005 · Jpn · Colour · 93min

Spirited Away director Hayao Miyazaki indulges his love for aviation with this visually impressive anime. Evoking the atmosphere of a 1930s Hollywood drama, it charts the exploits of a former First World War pilot who's been turned into a sort of man-pig by a mysterious curse. Scratching a living as a bounty hunter, Porco incurs the wrath of pirates. Miyazaki's animation is rich with a vibrancy that will delight young and old alike, even if the story isn't quite as polished. Also shown in Japanese- and French-language versions. SF Japanese dubbed. DVD

Michael Keaton *Porco Rosso* • David Ogden Stiers *Piccolo* • Kimberly Williams-Paisley [Kimberly Williams] *Fio* • Cary Elwes *Curtis* • Susan Egan *Gina* ■ Dir Hayao Miyazaki • Scr Hayao Miyazaki, with Cindy Davis Hewitt, Donald H Hewitt (English-language version)

Porgy and Bess ★★★
Opera   1959 · US · Colour · 170min

Producer Samuel Goldwyn bowed out at the age of 75 with this film version of the folk opera about crippled Porgy, his girl Bess and the inhabitants of Catfish Row. The familiar music, given Oscar-winning treatment by André Previn and Ken Darby, is gloriously intact. However, despite a starry cast of principals, the result disappoints. Otto Preminger's direction is heavy-handed, the singing not as good as it

should be, and the whole production too lavish to convince as a poignant tale of slum life. RK

Sidney Poitier *Porgy* • Dorothy Dandridge *Bess* • Sammy Davis Jr *Sportin' Life* • Pearl Bailey *Maria* • Brock Peters *Crown* • Leslie Scott *Jake* • Diahann Carroll *Clara* • Ruth Attaway *Serena* ■ Dir Otto Preminger • Scr N Richard Nash, from the opera by George Gershwin, Ira Gershwin, DuBose Heyward, from the stage play by DuBose Heyward, Dorothy Heyward

Pork Chop Hill ★★★★ PG
War drama   1959 · US · BW · 93min

This is the definitive Korean War movie from director Lewis Milestone, who dealt with the Second World War impressively in *A Walk in the Sun* and the First World War unforgettably in the classic *All Quiet on the Western Front*. Bleak and grim, it boasts a superb all-male cast, headed by Gregory Peck at his glummest. Watch out for the young Martin Landau and Harry Dean Stanton (billed here as plain Dean Stanton) amid all the shrapnel. As with Milestone's other war films, the action sequences are terrific. TS DVD BD

Gregory Peck *Lieutenant Clemons* • Harry Guardino *Forstman* • Rip Torn *Lieutenant Russell* • George Peppard *Feaderson* • James Edwards *Corporal Jurgens* • Bob Steele *Kern* • Woody Strode *Franklin* • George Shibata *Lieutenant O'Hashi* • Norman Fell *Sergeant Coleman* • Robert Blake *Velie* • Barry Atwater *Davis* • Martin Landau *Marshall* • Dean Stanton [Harry Dean Stanton] *MacFarland* ■ Dir Lewis Milestone • Scr James R Webb, from a story by General SLA Marshall

Porky's ★★★ 18
Comedy   1981 · Can · Colour · 94min

Set in the 1950s, this crude, crass comedy centres around the elaborate revenge plotted by a group of students on the redneck owner of the local bar-cum-whorehouse, Porky's. Director Bob Clark makes a few misguided nods to serious issues such as anti-Semitism. For the most part, though, he sticks to a seamless mix of vulgar sexual gags and spectacular slapstick, which is most definitely not PC but is often hugely entertaining. JF Swearing, nudity. DVD BD

Dan Monahan *Pee Wee* • Mark Herrier *Billy* • Wyatt Knight *Tommy* • Roger Wilson *Mickey* • Cyril O'Reilly *Tim* • Tony Ganios *Meat* • Kim Cattrall *Honeywell* • Nancy Parsons *Ms Balbricker* • Susan Clark *Cherry Forever* • Chuck Mitchell *Porky* ■ Dir/Scr Bob Clark

Porky's Revenge ★ 18
Comedy   1985 · Can · Colour · 88min

This third entry in the series is easily the worst. The energetic vulgarity of the first two films is replaced here by a leering coarseness – which is ironic, as the first two films were unfairly condemned (by those that hadn't seen them) for containing exactly this sort of crudity. The thin plot revolves around our heroes being forced to throw a basketball match by bar owner Chuck Mitchell. DF

Dan Monahan *Pee Wee* • Wyatt Knight *Tommy* • Tony Ganios *Meat* • Mark Herrier *Billy* • Kaki Hunter *Wendy* • Scott Colomby *Brian* • Nancy Parsons *Ms Balbricker* • Chuck Mitchell *Porky Wallace* ■ Dir James Komack • Scr Ziggy Steinberg, from characters by Bob Clark

The Pornographer ★★★ 18
Psychological drama   2001 · Fr/Can · Colour · 105min

The inspired casting of Jean-Pierre Léaud is the key to this thoughtful examination of the strictures of reputation and the increasing difficulty of making meaningful movies. Léaud turns in a pensive portrayal of dejected disillusionment as the one-time porn director whose debts force him to return to an industry in which tastes have coarsened considerably since his 1970s heyday. The hard-core sex scene graphically symbolises his ambivalence, but director Bertrand Bonello wisely places greater emphasis on Léaud's fractured relationship with his student activist son (Jérémie Rénier). DP French +subtitles. DVD

Jean-Pierre Léaud *Jacques Laurent* • Jérémie Rénier *Joseph* • Dominique Blanc *Jeanne* • Catherine Mouchet *Olivia Rochet* • Thibault de Montalembert *Richard* • André Marcon *Louis* ■ Dir/Scr Bertrand Bonello

Porridge ★★★ PG
Comedy   1979 · UK · Colour · 89min

The original TV series had ended two years earlier and Ronnie Barker had even been *Going Straight* before he was talked back into the role of Norman Fletcher for this movie spin-off. He's excellent and this is one of the best of its kind, thanks to a tightly focused plot from series creators Dick Clement (who also directs) and Ian La Frenais, involving an escape arranged to correspond with an inmates-versus-celebrity football match. Genial, affable fun. AC DVD

Ronnie Barker *Norman Fletcher* • Richard Beckinsale *Lennie Godber* • Fulton Mackay *Mackay* • Brian Wilde *Barrowclough* • Peter Vaughan *"Grouty"* • Julian Holloway *Bainbridge* ■ Dir Dick Clement • Scr Dick Clement, Ian La Frenais, from their TV series

Port of Call ★★★ PG
Drama   1948 · Swe · BW · 93min

Alienated Nine-Christine Jönsson is tormented by her relationship with her destructive mother and the puritanical restraints placed on her by social workers. Recently released from a reformatory, she seeks solace in a love affair with a simple young sailor (Bengt Eklund), who is unable to comprehend her complexities. This interesting early entry from Ingmar Bergman, well-photographed in semi-documentary style on location in the Gothenburg docks, is, as one would expect, downbeat. It's marred by touches of melodrama, but Jönsson's performance is compelling. RK Swedish +subtitles. DVD

Nine-Christine Jönsson *Berit* • Bengt Eklund *Gösta* • Berta Hall *Berit's mother* • Erik Hell *Berit's father* • Mimi Nelson *Gertrud* ■ Dir Ingmar Bergman • Scr Ingmar Bergman, from a story by Olle Länsberg

Port of Escape ★★★
Crime drama   1956 · UK · BW · 75min

The skilled performances of John McCallum and Googie Withers and an atmospheric treatment of the London Docks setting give this modest melodrama a considerable lift. McCallum is the Aussie adventurer who accidentally kills a man while helping his mentally ill American friend (played by Bill Kerr). They commandeer a boat owned by journalist Withers, whose initial hostility gives way to love for the Australian. An obscure director, Anthony Young, lets the pace slacken occasionally, but overall this is an intelligent and offbeat work that deserves to be better known. AE

Googie Withers *Anne Stirling* • John McCallum *Mitchell Gillie* • Bill Kerr *Dinty Missouri* • Joan Hickson *Rosalie Watchett* ■ Dir Tony Young [Anthony Young] • Scr Barbara Harper, Abby Mann, Tony Young [Anthony Young], from the story *Safe Harbour* by Barbara Harper

Port of New York ★★
Crime drama   1949 · US · BW · 81min

The main interest in this minor thriller is the screen debut of Yul Brynner as a New York drug trafficker whose operation is infiltrated by narcotics agents Scott Brady and Richard Rober. Brynner had hair in those days and isn't easily recognisable as the mafioso who smuggles the drugs through the New York docks. Laslo Benedek directs in pseudo-documentary style, revelling in his locations. AT

Scott Brady *Michael "Mickey" Waters* • Richard Rober *Jim Flannery* • KT Stevens *Toni Cardell* • Yul Brynner *Paul Vicola* • Arthur Blake *Dolly Carney* ■ Dir Laslo Benedek • Scr Eugene Ling, Leo Townsend, from a story by Arthur A Ross, Bert Murray

Port of Seven Seas ★★★
Drama   1938 · US · BW · 80min

James Whale inherited this project from William Wyler, although neither was exactly suited to adapt Marcel Pagnol's Marseille

classic, *Fanny*. Delivered to the accompaniment of Franz Waxman's twee score, Preston Sturges's dialogue lacks the easy charm of the original. But Wallace Beery and Frank Morgan grow into the roles of the waterfront bar owner and the widower who agrees to marry his daughter, Maureen O'Hara, after she's left pregnant by her sailor lover. DP

Wallace Beery *Cesar* • Frank Morgan *Panisse* • Maureen O'Sullivan *Madelon* • John Beal *Marius* • Jessie Ralph *Honorine* • Cora Witherspoon *Claudine* • Étienne Girardot *Bruneau* ■ Dir James Whale • Scr Preston Sturges, from the play *Fanny* by Marcel Pagnol, from the books *Marseilles Trilogy* by Marcel Pagnol

Les Portes de la Nuit ★★★★
Drama   1946 · Fr · BW · 106min

The film that marked the end of both the fruitful partnership between director Marcel Carné and screenwriter Jacques Prévert and the sombre, poetic-realist tradition of which they formed an important part. The action focuses on a quartet of doomed lovers and a tramp, who is the personification of Destiny. Pretty gloomy, portentous stuff, but it does have a heady, nocturnal 1940s atmosphere, impressive sets by Alexander Trauner and a haunting theme song, known in English as *Autumn Leaves*. The film, which misjudged the postwar mood, failed miserably at the box office. RB French +subtitles.

Nathalie Nattier *Malou* • Yves Montand *Diego* • Pierre Brasseur *Georges* • Saturnin Fabre *Monsieur Senechal* • Raymond Bussières *Raymond Lecuyer* • Serge Reggiani *Guy* ■ Dir Marcel Carné • Scr Jacques Prévert • *Production Designer* Alexander Trauner [Alexandre Trauner]

Portnoy's Complaint ★ 18
Comedy drama   1972 · US · Colour · 96min

For his directing debut, screenwriter Ernest Lehman chose Philip Roth's scandalous novel about the difficulties of being Jewish and the joys of masturbation. Portnoy (a smirking Richard Benjamin) has been a lonely, repressed child who has grown up playing obsessively with himself. Various prostitutes and fashion models try to help Portnoy in this satire that emerges as a limp, unfunny imitation of *The Graduate*. AT

Richard Benjamin *Alexander Portnoy* • Karen Black *Mary Jane Reid/The Monkey* • Lee Grant *Sophie Portnoy* • Jack Somack *Jack Portnoy* • Renee Lippin *Hannah Portnoy* ■ Dir Ernest Lehman • Scr Ernest Lehman, from the novel by Philip Roth

Portrait from Life ★★
Drama   1948 · UK · BW · 90min

Terence Fisher's film tackles the then thorny topic of rehabilitating Nazi sympathisers within postwar German society. The cast is first rate, with Mai Zetterling particularly good as the amnesiac forced to explore her association with a high-ranking fascist. However, the dramatic demands of a reconciliation with her father and a romance with Robert Beatty soon swamp the infinitely more fascinating background story. DP

Mai Zetterling *Hildegarde* • Robert Beatty *Campbell Reid* • Guy Rolfe *Major Lawrence* • Herbert Lom *Hendlemann* • Patrick Holt *Ferguson* • Arnold Marlé *Professor Menzel* • Thora Hird *Mrs Skinner* ■ Dir Terence Fisher • Scr Muriel Box, Sidney Box, Frank Harvey Jr, from a story by David Evans

Portrait in Black ★★
Murder mystery   1960 · US · Colour · 112min

This is tosh, and don't think producer Ross Hunter didn't know it. Lana Turner stars in a film with a plot so full of holes that it's hard to stop the cast falling through them. But Hunter was shrewd enough to know that if it looked good and was cleverly cast you could get away with murder (almost). Trouble is, Turner is too genteel for the hysterics, and director Michael Gordon has a tough time pulling all the threads together. TS

Lana Turner *Sheila Cabot* • Anthony Quinn *Dr David Rivera* • Sandra Dee *Catherine Cabot* • John Saxon *Blake Richards* • Richard Basehart

Howard Mason • Lloyd Nolan *Matthew Cabot* • Ray Walston *Cob O'Brien* • Virginia Grey *Miss Lee* • Anna May Wong *Tani* • *Dir* Michael Gordon • *Scr* Ivan Goff, Ben Roberts, from their play

The Portrait of a Lady ★★★ 12

Period drama
1996 · NZ/UK/US · Colour and BW · 138min

Nicole Kidman is captivating as Henry James's heroine, an independent American woman seduced into the machinations of Barbara Hershey and her lover John Malkovich. She's caught like a bright bird in their trap, and her loss of spirit is the central tragedy of this beautifully shot tale. Where Stephen Frears's *Dangerous Liaisons* combined sexual games and social climbing with humour, here there's nothing to laugh about – you'll walk away with a troubled brow. LH Brief nudity. *DVD*

Nicole Kidman *Isabel Archer* • John Malkovich *Gilbert Osmond* • Barbara Hershey *Madame Serena Merle* • Mary-Louise Parker *Henrietta Stackpole* • Martin Donovan (2) *Ralph Touchett* • Shelley Winters *Mrs Touchett* • Richard E Grant *Lord Warburton* • Shelley Duvall *Countess Gemini* • Christian Bale *Edward Rosier* • Viggo Mortensen *Caspar Goodwood* • John Gielgud *Mr Touchett* ■ *Dir* Jane Campion • *Scr* Laura Jones, from the novel by Henry James • *Cinematographer* Stuart Dryburgh • *Costume Designer* Janet Patterson

Portrait of Clare ★★ PG

Period drama
1950 · UK · BW · 87min

British director Lance Comfort had a successful early career, but by the time he came to make this flashback frippery, he had rather lost the knack for this kind of "woman's picture", with its all-too-familiar blend of reminiscence, romance and regret. Australian-born actress Margaret Johnston fails to make much impact as she recounts details of her three marriages and her granddaughter. DP *DVD*

Margaret Johnston *Clare Hingston* • Richard Todd *Robert Hart* • Robin Bailey *Dudley Wilburn* • Ronald Howard *Ralph Hingston* • Jeremy Spenser *Steven Hingston* • Marjorie Fielding *Aunt Cathie* ■ *Dir* Lance Comfort • *Scr* Leslie Landau, Adrian Arlington, from the novel by Francis Brett Young

Portrait of Hell ★★★ 12

Action drama
1969 · Jpn · Colour · 95min

This is both a piercing plea for racial tolerance and a nightmarish allegory of life on earth. Obsessed by the afterlife following a bloody military campaign, 14th-century ruler Kinnosuke Nakamura kidnaps Korean beauty Yoko Naito to ensure her artist father completes a heavenly mural. However, as Naito is subjected to pitiless torture, Tatsuya Nakadai abuses his commission to reflect the cruelties of Nakamura's regime. Taking stylistic risks to capture the painting's texture, Shiro Toyoda not only generates a sense of evil, but also afair measure of socio-political indignation. DP Japanese +subtitles. *DVD*

Tatsuya Nakadai *Yoshihide* • Yoko Naito *Yoshika* • Kinnosuke Nakamura *Lord Hosokawa* ■ *Dir* Shiro Toyoda • *Scr* Toshio Yasumi, from a novel by Ryunosuke Akutagawa

Portrait of Jennie ★★★★ U

Romance
1948 · US · BW and Colour · 82min

Produced by David O Selznick as a monument to the beauty of his wife-to-be, Jennifer Jones, this is one of Hollywood's best romantic fantasies. A long opening title sequence ponders eternal questions of life, space and death, and then we meet Joseph Cotten as a struggling artist who falls in love with the mystical Jones. The movie has considerable passion and conviction and Jones is simply gorgeous, while Cotten's innate weakness and vulnerability are perfect for his role. With William Dieterle's stylish direction and composer Dimitri Tiomkin plagiarising Debussy, the movie heads into a surreally romantic world of its own. AT *DVD*

Jennifer Jones *Jennie Appleton* • Joseph Cotten *Eben Adams* • Ethel Barrymore *Miss Spinney* • Cecil Kellaway *Mr Matthews* • David Wayne *Gus O'Toole* • Albert Sharpe *Mr Moore* • Florence Bates *Mrs Jekes* • Lillian Gish *Mother Mary of*

Mercy ■ *Dir* William Dieterle • *Scr* Paul Osborn, Peter Berneis, Leonardo Bercovici, from the novel by Robert Nathan

Portrait of Maria ★★★

Drama
1943 · Mex · BW · 101min

Romanticising the spartan splendour of the Mexican countryside, director Emilio Fernandez and ace cinematographer Gabriel Figueroa came to international attention with this tragic tale of misunderstood motives and patriarchal prejudice. Dolores Del Rio gives a luminous performance as the woman who, like her mother, is stoned by the reactionary inhabitants of pre-revolutionary Xochimilco after they wrongly surmise she has posed nude for painter Alberto Galán. DP Spanish +subtitles.

Dolores Del Rio *Maria Candelaria* • Pedro Armendáriz *Lorenzo Rafael* • Alberto Galán *Pintor* • Margarita Cortés *Lupe* ■ *Dir* Emilio Fernandez • *Scr* Emilio Fernandez, Mauricio Magdaleno

A Portrait of the Artist as a Young Man ★★★★ 15

Drama
1977 · Ire · Colour · 91min

Director Joseph Strick could never match talent to integrity, so his inability to compromise meant that attempts to film modern classics such as this one by James Joyce never lived up to his expectations. This is one of his most successful, with Bosco Hogan as the young Dubliner in an Ireland that is "the sow that eats her farrow", while John Gielgud preaches the famous sermon with the power and eloquence Strick wanted for all his films, but which he seldom achieved. TH Sex scenes. *DVD*

Bosco Hogan *Stephen Dedalus* • TP McKenna *Simon Dedalus* • John Gielgud *Preacher* • Rosaleen Linehan *May Dedalus* • Maureen Potter *Dante* • Cecil Sheehan *Uncle Charles* ■ *Dir* Joseph Strick • *Scr* Judith Rascoe, from the novel by James Joyce

Portraits Chinois ★★★ 15

Drama
1996 · Fr/UK · Colour · 106min

Set among the young Parisian smart set, this is a slight but enjoyable comedy from director Martine Dugowson. At the centre of a web of interweaving plot strands is fashion designer Helena Bonham Carter, whose contentment is threatened by pushy newcomer Romane Bohringer. Everyone in the ensemble gets their moment in the spotlight, although none can match shopaholic underachiever Elsa Zylberstein's gloriously awful cabaret routine. DP French +subtitles. Swearing. *DVD*

Helena Bonham Carter *Ada* • Romane Bohringer *Lise* • Marie Trintignant *Nina* • Elsa Zylberstein *Emma* • Yvan Attal *Yves* • Sergio Castellitto *Guido* • Jean-Claude Brialy *René Sandre* ■ *Dir* Martine Dugowson • *Scr* Martine Dugowson, Peter Chase

The Portuguese Nun ★★★★ PG

Drama
2009 · Por/Fr · Colour · 121min

Eugène Green adopts a minimalist style that is hypnotically beautiful in this intense but often amusingly self-deprecating study of life, love, faith and film. Arriving in Lisbon to shoot an adaptation of an obscure 17th-century novel, a French actress (Leonor Baldaque) comes to question her lifestyle after encounters with a lusty co-star, a lonely aristocrat, a cherubic orphan and a nun who spends her nights deep in prayer. Green lampoons low- and highbrow attitudes to art house cinema, while also exploring the differences between earthly and heavenly goodness. This is potent, passionate and provocative stuff, but it's also irresistibly poetic and unexpectedly playful. DP Portuguese, French +subtitles. *DVD*

Leonor Baldaque *Julie de Hauranne* • Ana Moreira *Irma Joana* • Adrien Michaux *Martin Dautand* • Diogo Dória *D Henrique Cunha Mello de Lencastre* • Francisco Mozos *Vasco* • Eugène Green *Denis Verde* ■ *Dir/Scr* Eugène Green

Poseidon ★★ 12

Disaster movie
2006 · US · Colour · 94min

The original disaster movie, about an ocean liner capsized by a wave and a band of survivors clawing their way up to the hull, relied on huge sets and big stars. Wolfgang Petersen's refit relies on CGI and middling stars. It dispenses with character, asset-strips the plot and flips the ship without delay or backstory, furnishing a succession of exciting, waterlogged set pieces, but lacking any substance. AC *DVD* *BLU*

Josh Lucas *Dylan Johns* • Kurt Russell *Robert Ramsey* • Jacinda Barrett *Maggie James* • Richard Dreyfuss *Richard Nelson* • Emmy Rossum *Jennifer Ramsey* • Mia Maestro *Elena* • Mike Vogel *Christian* • Kevin Dillon *Lucky Larry* • Freddy Rodriguez *Valentin* • Jimmy Bennett *Conor James* • Andre Braugher [André Braugher] *Captain Michael Bradford* ■ *Dir* Wolfgang Petersen • *Scr* Mark Protosevich, from the novel *The Poseidon Adventure* by Paul Gallico

LANDMARK FILM
A box-office smash, this makes the 1970s disaster movie cycle inevitable

The Poseidon Adventure ★★★★ PG

Disaster movie
1972 · US · Colour · 116min

In this memorable calamity-at-sea epic from disaster-movie specialist Irwin Allen, an ocean liner turns turtle under a tidal wave and survivors fight their way to the ship's underside in an attempt to find an exit. The religious aspects of Paul Gallico's source novel get buried under a barrage of set pieces as director Ronald Neame cranks up the suspense and minister Gene Hackman leads a group of uptight passengers to what they hope will be their salvation. There are wonderfully poignant performances, but it's always Hackman's movie – not even the remarkable effects can upstage him. TH *DVD* *BLU*

Gene Hackman *Reverend Frank Scott* • Ernest Borgnine *Mike Rogo* • Red Buttons *James Martin Acres* • Carol Lynley *Nonnie Parry* • Roddy McDowall *Acres* • Stella Stevens *Linda Rogo* • Shelley Winters *Belle Rosen* • Jack Albertson *Manny Rosen* • Leslie Nielsen *Ship's captain* • Pamela Sue Martin *Susan Shelby* ■ *Dir* Ronald Neame • *Scr* Stirling Silliphant, Wendell Mayes, from the novel by Paul Gallico

Positive ID ★★★ 18

Thriller
1986 · US · Colour · 91min

Stephanie Rascoe is a young housewife who discovers she cannot live her life as before following an assault. Instead, she takes on a new identity and proceeds to track down her attacker. This interesting thriller certainly has a different twist-in-the-tale from other movies on the same subject, and Rascoe is a convincing victim-turned-avenger. JB

Stephanie Rascoe *Julie Kenner/Bobbie King* • John Davies [John S Davies] *Don Kenner* • Steve Fromholz *Roy* • Laura Lane *Dana* • Gail Cronauer *Melissa* ■ *Dir/Scr* Andy Anderson

The Positively True Adventures of the Alleged Texas Cheerleader-Murdering Mom ★★★ 15

Comedy drama
1993 · US · Colour · 98min

Director Michael Ritchie has had an erratic career, but here he has created a delightfully sardonic, stranger-than-fiction TV movie. Holly Hunter is the potty mom, who decides the best way to get her daughter on to the cheerleading team is murder. Ritchie exploits the comic potential of the story to the hilt and makes some neat satiric jibes at American family values. Hunter has a ball in the lead role and the talented supporting cast delivers broad comic performances. JF Swearing. *DVD*

Holly Hunter *Wanda Holloway* • Beau Bridges *Terry Harper* • Swoosie Kurtz *Marla Harper* • Matt Frewer *Troy McKinney* • Fred Koehler [Frederick Koehler] *Shane Holloway* ■ *Dir* Michael Ritchie • *Scr* Jane Anderson

Posse ★★★

Western
1975 · US · Colour · 93min

This is a rare assignment behind the cameras for Kirk Douglas, who also stars in this likeably quirky western. Bruce Dern, cast against type, plays a Robin Hood-style bandit being hunted by a marshal (Douglas) who thinks Dern's capture will give his career a boost. Douglas the director takes a no-nonsense approach to the material and draws able performances from a winning support cast. JF

Kirk Douglas *Marshal Howard Nightingale* • Bruce Dern *Jack Strawhorn* • Bo Hopkins *Wesley* • James Stacy *Hellman* • Luke Askew *Krag* • David Canary *Pensteman* ■ *Dir* Kirk Douglas • *Scr* William Roberts, Christopher Knopf, from a story by Christopher Knopf

Posse ★★★ 15

Western
1993 · US · Colour · 105min

Mario Van Peebles's ambitious attempt to fuse the spaghetti western with 1990s black consciousness doesn't always work, but it remains a provocative and entertaining addition to the revitalised genre. Van Peebles himself plays the mean and moody leader of a disparate group of black soldiers, plus token white good guy Stephen Baldwin, who find themselves caught between a cruel, racist sheriff (Richard Jordan) and their psychopathic old colonel (Billy Zane). Van Peebles's flashy, hyperactive direction is sometimes at odds with the genre, as is some of the dialogue, but he succeeds with his astonishingly eclectic cast. Followed by *Los Locos* in 1997. JF Violence, swearing, nudity. *DVD*

Mario Van Peebles *Jessie Lee* • Stephen Baldwin *Little J* • Charles Lane (3) *Weezie* • Tiny Lister [Tom "Tiny" Lister Jr] *Obobo* • Big Daddy Kane *Father Time* • Billy Zane *Colonel Graham* • Blair Underwood *Sheriff Carver* • Melvin Van Peebles *Papa Joe* • Isaac Hayes *Cable* • Woody Strode *Storyteller* ■ *Dir* Mario Van Peebles • *Scr* Sy Richardson, Dario Scardapane

Possessed ★★★

Melodrama
1931 · US · BW · 75min

This MGM melodrama has some hard-edged dialogue and a positively glowing Joan Crawford playing the low-class mistress of aspiring politician Clark Gable. Crawford becomes the most famous courtesan in New York as Gable puts his career on the line in a genuinely witty movie. TS

Joan Crawford *Marian Martin* • Clark Gable *Mark Whitney* • Wallace Ford *Al Mannings* • Richard "Skeets" Gallagher *Wally Stuart* • Frank Conroy *Travers* • Marjorie White *Vernice* ■ *Dir* Clarence Brown • *Scr* Lenore Coffee, from the play *The Mirage* by Edgar Selwyn

Possessed ★★ PG

Melodrama
1947 · US · BW · 103min

In her second movie with the same title, Joan Crawford stars as a guilt-ridden (and overacting) schizophrenic. This begins promisingly, with a dazed and confused Crawford wandering the streets of Los Angeles before being taken to hospital, but then resorts to pretentious psychological waffle. Van Heflin and Raymond Massey have little chance to impress in underwritten roles, but Geraldine Brooks shines as Massey's daughter. TS *DVD*

Joan Crawford *Louise Howell Graham* • Van Heflin *David Sutton* • Raymond Massey *Dean Graham* • Geraldine Brooks *Carol Graham* • Stanley Ridges *Dr Harvey Willard* • John Ridgely *Lieutenant Harker* • Nana Bryant *Pauline Graham* • Moroni Olsen *Dr Ames* ■ *Dir* Curtis Bernhardt • *Scr* Silvia Richards, Ranald MacDougall, from the story *One Man's Secret* by Rita Weiman

Possessed ★ 15

Horror drama
2000 · US · Colour · 105min

Based on the "true story" of modern-day America's only documented exorcism (performed in the 1950s), this is an extraordinarily awful TV horror movie. Timothy Dalton reaches a career low as a Catholic priest with his own personal demons, who's called upon to investigate the case of a cute child who's showing the full signs of possession. JC *DVD*

Timothy Dalton *Father William Bowden* • Henry Czerny *Father Raymond McBride* • Jonathan Malen *Robbie Mannheim* • Christopher Plummer *Archbishop Hume* • Piper Laurie *Aunt Hanna* ■ *Dir* Steven E de Souza • *Scr* Steven E de Souza, Michael Lazarou, from the non-fiction book *Possessed: the True Story of an Exorcism* by Thomas B Allen

Possession ★★ 12
Romantic drama 2002 · US/UK · Colour · 97min

This wispy, time-shifting romance represents a clumsy change of pace for edgy director Neil LaBute. His adaptation of AS Byatt's 1990 Booker Prize-winning novel evokes neither the poetry nor the passion of its source, while Gwyneth Paltrow and LaBute regular Aaron Eckhart phone in their drippy roles as literary sleuths researching the amorous secrets of bisexual Victorian poet Jennifer Ehle and her married lover Jeremy Northam. Low on mystery and emotional engagement, but high on clichés. AJ *DVD*

Gwyneth Paltrow *Maud Bailey* • Aaron Eckhart *Roland Michell* • Jeremy Northam *Randolph Henry Ash* • Jennifer Ehle *Christabel LaMotte* • Lena Headey *Blanche Glover* • Toby Stephens *Dr Fergus Wolfe* • Tom Hickey *Professor Blackadder* • Trevor Eve *Prof Mortimer Cropper* • Tom Hollander *Euan* • Graham Crowden *Sir George Bailey* • Anna Massey *Lady Bailey* ■ *Dir* Neil LaBute • *Scr* David Henry Hwang, Laura Jones, Neil LaBute, from the novel by AS Byatt

The Possession ★★★ 15
Horror thriller 2012 · US · Colour · 89min

When their youngest daughter (Natasha Calis) becomes strangely obsessed with an antique wooden box bought at a yard sale, a divorced couple learns she has become possessed by a dibbuk, a malicious Jewish spirit. Danish director Ole Bornedal has made far better movies (*Nightwatch*) than this Jewish *Exorcist*, based on a "true" story about a haunted wine cabinet sold on ebay. But it's a serviceable shocker given a distinctive cold shimmer and slick style. AJ

Jeffrey Dean Morgan *Clyde Brenek* • Kyra Sedgwick *Stephanie Brenek* • Natasha Calis *Em* • Madison Davenport *Hannah* ■ *Dir* Ole Bornedal • *Scr* Juliet Snowden, Stiles White, from an article by Leslie Gornstein, Kevin Mannis

The Possession of Joel Delaney ★★★ 15
Supernatural horror 1971 · US · Colour · 100min

For some, this occult thriller was superior to *The Exorcist*, but time has not been kind and it now feels ponderously slow while its modishly violent climax seems to belong to another film. Through the eyes of his rich bitch sister Shirley MacLaine, we see the gradual disintegration of Perry King, possessed by the spirit of a Puerto Rican psycho with a penchant for decapitation. The horror is dignified by social comment, although the message is garbled, but the script and performances are strong. DM *DVD*

Shirley MacLaine *Norah Benson* • Perry King *Joel Delaney* • Michael Hordern *Justin Lorenz* • Edmundo Rivera Alvarez *Don Pedro* • Robert Burr *Ted Benson* ■ *Dir* Waris Hussein • *Scr* Matt Robinson, Grimes-Grice [Albert Maltz], from the novel by Ramona Stewart

Possible Worlds ★★★ 15
Science-fiction mystery 2000 · Can · Colour · 88min

A theatrical legend, but yet to convince wholly on film, Québecois Robert Lepage makes his English-language debut with this highly stylised slice of cerebral sci-fi. This adaptation is also an identity drama, a whodunnit and a philosophical romance, so it's easy to lose sight of the complex ideas and intricate scene shifts. Central to the conceit is the murder of Thomas McCamus. But discovering who stole his brain matters less than whether he'll find love – in one of several parallel universes – with the chameleon-like Tilda Swinton. DP *DVD*

Tilda Swinton *Joyce* • Tom McCamus *George Barber* • Sean McCann *Inspector Berkley* • Gabriel Gascon *Kleber/Doctor* • Rick Miller *Williams* ■ *Dir* Robert Lepage • *Scr* John Mighton, from his play

Post Grad ★★ 12
Comedy drama 2009 · US · Colour · 84min

A recent college graduate returns to the bosom of her slightly strange family in this unchallenging comedy drama that seems pre-moulded for 13-year-old girls. After her hopes of a career in publishing don't quite come to fruition, the likeably resilient Ryden (Alexis Bledel, of TV's *Gilmore Girls*) finds herself living back at home and working in her dad's luggage shop. Michael Keaton is solidly endearing as Ryden's goofy dad, and the rest of her eccentric family is well played by the likes of Carol Burnett and Jane Lynch, so the film is never flat-out terrible – just thoroughly bland. TJ Sexual references, brief swearing. *DVD*

Alexis Bledel *Ryden Malby* • Zach Gilford *Adam Davies* • Michael Keaton *Walter Malby* • Jane Lynch *Carmella Malby* • Bobby Coleman *Hunter Malby* • Carol Burnett *Grandma Maureen* • Rodrigo Santoro *David Santiago* • Catherine Reitman *Jessica Bard* ■ *Dir* Vicky Jenson • *Scr* Kelly Fremon

Post Mortem ★★★ 15
Political drama 2010 · Chil/Ger/Mex · Colour · 97min

Director Pablo Larrain reunites with his *Tony Manero* star Alfredo Castro in this drama that centres around Chile's American-backed military coup of 1973, which brought Augusto Pinochet to power. Castro plays a man who works in a morgue, recording the coroner's comments, who strikes up a relationship with a neighbour (Antonia Zegers), the washed-up "star" of a burlesque show. Larrain employs a cold and seemingly detached style, but his way of lingering on certain shots adds to the sinister sense of unease that accompanies this snapshot of history. BP Spanish +subtitles. Sex scenes.

Alfredo Castro *Mario* • Antonia Zegers *Nancy Puelmas* • Jaime Vadell *Dr Castillo* • Amparo Noguera *Sandra* ■ *Dir* Pablo Larraín • *Scr* Pablo Larrain, Mateo Iribarren

Post Tenebras Lux ★★★ 18
Drama 2012 · Mex/Fr/Neth/Ger · Colour · 114min

Neurotic architect Adolfo Jiménez Castro finds his troubled home life contrasts with the daily struggle of his peasant neighbours, in this latest drama from maverick Mexican film-maker Carlos Reygadas (*Silent Light*). Greeted with both critical incomprehension and the best director prize at Cannes last year, the film has divided opinion from the outset, not least because of its provocative collage approach to storytelling, which leaps back and forth in time and space with dizzying freedom. The film does come across as an evidently sincere attempt to create a new kind of cinema, but opinion will certainly vary on whether Reygadas really does offer, as his title suggests, light after darkness. TJ Spanish, English, French +subtitles. Violence, swearing, sex scenes, nudity, drug abuse. *DVD* *SL*

Adolfo Jiménez Castro *Juan* • Nathalia Acevedo *Natalia* • Rut Reygadas *Rut* • Eleazar Reygadas *Eleazar* • Willebaldo Torres *El Siete* ■ *Dir/Scr* Carlos Reygadas

Postcards from America ★★★ 18
Biographical drama 1994 · UK/US · Colour · 87min

This moving and adroitly made feature is based on the life of New York multi-media artist and Aids activist David Wojnarowicz, who died in 1992. Divided into three segments (with the lead shifting between Olmo and Michael Tighe, and James Lyons), the film moves from his abused childhood, through a period of prostitution and petty crime, to an adulthood of audacious creativity, emotional instability and casual sex. This stylised drama is directed by Wojnarowicz's sometime British collaborator Steve McLean. DP Violence, substance abuse.

James Lyons *David Wojnarowicz* • Michael Tighe *Teenage David* • Olmo Tighe *Young David* • Michael Imperioli *The hustler* • Michael Ringer

Father • Maggie Low *Mother* ■ *Dir* Steve McLean • *Scr* Steve McLean, from the books *Close to the Knives* and *Memories That Smell like Gasoline* by David Wojnarowicz

Postcards from the Edge ★★★★ 15
Comedy drama 1990 · US · Colour · 97min

It bears little resemblance to Carrie Fisher's screamingly funny bestselling novel, yet director Mike Nichols's grand tour through "Hollywood Babylon" still emerges as a savage showbiz satire. Meryl Streep is the selfish actress in celebrity detox, who moves back home with her overbearing mother (Shirley MacLaine), in this thinly veiled account of Fisher's own poignant relationship with her real-life mother Debbie Reynolds. Both stars rise to the bitchy one-liner occasion and turn on the glitz, glamour and grit. AJ Swearing, drug abuse. *DVD*

Meryl Streep *Suzanne Vale* • Shirley MacLaine *Doris Mann* • Dennis Quaid *Jack Falkner* • Gene Hackman *Lowell* • Richard Dreyfuss *Dr Frankenthal* • Rob Reiner *Joe Pierce* • Mary Wickes *Grandma* • Conrad Bain *Grandpa* • Annette Bening *Evelyn Ames* • Simon Callow *Simon Asquith* ■ *Dir* Mike Nichols • *Scr* Carrie Fisher, from her novel

The Posters Come from the Wall ★★★★
Documentary 2008 · UK · Colour · 72min

British film-maker Nicholas Abrahams and Turner Prize-winning artist Jeremy Deller celebrate the transformative power of fandom in this affectionate portrait of Depeche Mode followers worldwide. From the Brazilian choirs performing the UK rock band's songs in church to the ardent Russians who mark frontman Dave Gahan's birthday with an annual parade, these entertainingly combined stories of devotion are in turn amusing, poignant and frequently plain astonishing. But the most unexpected aspect is the political impact of the band's music, which has provided a symbol of freedom in restrictive regimes that spans 1980s East Germany to modern-day Iran. Even without the directors' skilful editing and eye for visual detail, the richness of such intimate revelations makes for compelling viewing. SF

■ *Dir* Jeremy Deller, Nick Abrahams

Il Postino ★★★★★★ U
Romantic drama 1994 · It/Fr · Colour · 103min

Massimo Troisi stars as a shy postman on an Italian island whose only port of call is the residence of legendary exiled Chilean poet Pablo Neruda (Philippe Noiret). Too timid to talk to the local beauty (Maria Grazia Cucinotta), the postman turns to his new-found friend for poetic assistance to win her heart. Wonderful contrasting performances from the two stars, beautiful scenery and understated direction from British film-maker Michael Radford give this delightfully different international gem the radiance of a Mediterranean *Local Hero*. In a tragic footnote, Troisi died the day after completing this life-affirming movie. JC Italian +subtitles. *DVD*

Massimo Troisi *Mario* • Philippe Noiret *Pablo Neruda* • Maria Grazia Cucinotta *Beatrice Russo* • Linda Moretti *Donna Rosa* • Renato Scarpa *Telegraph operator* ■ *Dir* Michael Radford • *Scr* Anna Pavignano, Michael Radford, Furio Scarpelli, Giacomo Scarpelli, Massimo Troisi, from a story by Furio Scarpelli, Giacomo Scarpelli, from the novel *Il Postino di Neruda* by Antonio Skarmeta

The Postman ★ 15
Futuristic epic 1997 · US · Colour · 170min

There's more than a touch of vanity about Kevin Costner's overlong futuristic epic. Costing more than $100 million, it has gone down as one of Hollywood's biggest flops, in which Costner drifts across a post-apocalyptic America, claiming to be a postman with 15-year-old mail. A complete dud. AT Violence, swearing, sex scene, nudity. *DVD*

Kevin Costner *The Postman* • Will Patton *Bethlehem* • Larenz Tate *Ford* • Olivia Williams *Abby* • James Russo *Idaho* • Tom Petty *Bridge*

City mayor • Daniel Von Bargen *Sheriff Briscoe* ■ *Dir* Kevin Costner • *Scr* Eric Roth, James Helgeland, from the novel by David Brin

The Postman Always Rings Twice ★★★★★★ PG
Classic film noir 1946 · US · BW · 108min

Sweaty and sensuous, this MGM *film noir* remains utterly electrifying today, thanks to the riveting sexual chemistry between its stars, Lana Turner and John Garfield, and Tay Garnett's tense directorial style. Garnett clearly understood the world of James M Cain's original novel, though he was forced to circumvent certain sections because of the censorship demands of the day. Despite competition from several other movies, notably Luchino Visconti's *Ossessione* and Bob Rafelson's 1981 film, this has proved to be the definitive interpretation of the novel, and the Turner/Garfield coupling undoubtedly the most incandescent – their first meeting remains a classic moment of screen desire. TS *DVD*

Lana Turner *Cora Smith* • John Garfield *Frank Chambers* • Cecil Kellaway *Nick Smith* • Hume Cronyn *Arthur Keats* • Leon Ames *Kyle Sackett* • Audrey Totter *Madge Gorland* ■ *Dir* Tay Garnett • *Scr* Harry Ruskin, Niven Busch, from the novel by James M Cain • *Costume Designer* Irene

The Postman Always Rings Twice ★★★ 18
Crime drama 1981 · US · Colour · 116min

Following James M Cain's novel more closely than was allowed in the classic 1946 version, Bob Rafelson's take on the murderous morality fable opts for explicit action over extra adulterous tension. Despite luminous performances from Depression drifter Jack Nicholson and young wife Jessica Lange as the plotters-in-lust, the loose ends point to a below par effort from Rafelson, and the final result is not up to the standard of his masterly work with Nicholson on *Five Easy Pieces* and *The King of Marvin Gardens*. AJ Violence, swearing, sex scenes. *DVD*

Jack Nicholson *Frank Chambers* • Jessica Lange *Cora Papadakis* • John Colicos *Nick Papadakis* • Christopher Lloyd *Salesman* • Michael Lerner *Katz* • John P Ryan *Kennedy* • Anjelica Huston *Madge* • William Traylor *Sackett* ■ *Dir* Bob Rafelson • *Scr* David Mamet, from the novel by James M Cain

Postman Pat: the Movie ★★★ U
Animated comedy 2013 · UK · Colour · 84min

The long-running *Postman Pat* children's TV series used gentle, stop-motion animation to portray a simple rustic life moving at a snail's pace. But everyone's favourite first-class male gets a fast-paced CGI makeover for his big-screen debut. Pat purists will have kittens at the very thought of our hero swapping Greendale for a world of TV talent shows, celebrities and evil "Patbots" – postie lookalikes that want to take over, if not the world, then at least its postal service. While Pat's souped-up "new look" won't be for everyone, it's actually very well done. Kids will enjoy it, and accompanying grown-ups may crack a smile, too. DA *DVD* *SL*

Stephen Mangan *Postman Pat* • Jim Broadbent *The CEO (Mr Brown)* • Rupert Grint *Josh* • David Tennant *Wilf* • Ronan Keating *Postman Pat (singing voice only)* ■ *Dir* Mike Disa • *Scr* Nicole Dubuc, from a story by Kim Fuller, Annika Bluhm, from characters by John Cunliffe, Ivor Wood

Postman's Knock ★ U
Comedy 1961 · UK · BW · 86min

This is one of two comedies (the other is *Invasion Quartet*) created for Spike Milligan by John Briley and Jack Trevor Story, talented writers not noted for their eccentric humour. Consequently, the brilliant Goon flounders in the conventional, happy-go-lucky tale of a village postman who is transferred to London and comes up against mail robbers and sorting equipment. The supporting cast is, disastrously, funnier than the star. DM

P

Spike Milligan *Harold Petts* • Barbara Shelley *Jean* • John Wood (2) *PC Woods* • Ronald Adam *Fordyce* • Wilfrid Lawson *Postman* • Miles Malleson *Psychiatrist* • Warren Mitchell *Rupert* ■ *Dir* Robert Lynn • *Scr* John Briley, Jack Trevor Story, Spike Milligan, George Barclay [Ronald Kinnoch], from a story by Jack Trevor Story

Postmortem ★★ 18
Crime thriller 1999 · US/UK · Colour · 105min

In terms of personnel, this has to go down as one of the oddest Scottish films in recent years. Director Albert Pyun, best known for his straight-to-video martial arts thrillers, here links up with Hollywood bad boy Charlie Sheen for a moody and surprisingly gritty thriller set in and around Glasgow. Sheen plays a boozy American ex-cop, now writing "true crime" books, who finds himself drawn into the hunt for a serial killer playing mind games with the police. JF Violence, swearing. *DVD*

Charles Sheen [Charlie Sheen] *James McGregor* • Michael Halsey *Inspector Balantine* • Stephen McCole *George Statler* • Gary Lewis *Wallace* ■ *Dir* Albert Pyun • *Scr* John Lowry Lamb, Robert McDonnell

Il Posto ★★★★ U
Comedy drama 1961 · It · BW · 92min

True to his neorealist roots, former documentarist Ermanno Olmi employed a wholly non-professional cast for this vaguely autobiographical insight into the hostile world of work. As the provincial whose delight at finding a job in a Milanese office blinds him to the dehumanising effect of the daily urban grind, the impassive Sandro Panzeri proves himself to be a clown in the Buster Keaton mould as he performs mundane tasks with eager pride in the hope of impressing sympathetic colleague Loredano Detto. Yet it's Olmi's attention to satirical detail and his gentle pacing that make this episodic comedy so engaging. DP Italian +subtitles. *DVD*

Sandro Panzeri *Domenico* • Loredano Detto *Antonietta* ■ *Dir/Scr* Ermanno Olmi

The Pot Carriers ★★★ PG
Comedy drama 1962 · UK · BW · 81min

Part social drama, part knockabout comedy, this is an odd but entertaining account of British prison life in the 1950s. It's based on a 1960 TV play by Mike Watts, who used real-life experience for his story of an old lag (Ronald Fraser, the only member of the TV cast to reprise his role) who befriends new inmate Paul Massie and shows him the ropes. The depiction of prison routine still has an impact. DM *DVD*

Ronald Fraser *Redband* • Paul Massie *James Rainbow* • Carole Lesley *Wendy* • Dennis Price *Smooth Tongue* • Paul Rogers *Governor* ■ *Dir* Peter Graham Scott • *Scr* Mike Watts, TJ Morrison, from the play by Watts

Pot Luck ★★★ 15
Comedy 2002 · Fr/Sp · Colour · 121min

This mischievous study of the national characteristics that stand in the way of genuine European integration is too often sidetracked by melodramatic subplots. Cédric Klapisch manipulates his ensemble cast with great skill, particularly when the cosmopolitan students sharing a Barcelona apartment set to gossiping and squabbling. But the pace begins to flag once attention shifts to Romain Duris's relationships with Parisian girlfriend Audrey Tautou and neglected housewife Judith Godrèche. A sequel, *Russian Dolls* followed in 2005. DP French, Spanish, Catalan, English, Danish +subtitles.

Romain Duris *Xavier* • Judith Godrèche *Anne-Sophie* • Audrey Tautou *Martine* • Cécile de France *Isabelle* • Kelly Reilly *Wendy* • Kevin Bishop *William* • Federico D'Anna *Alessandro* • Barnaby Metschurat *Tobias* • Cristina Brondo *Soledad* • Christian Pagh *Lars* ■ *Dir/Scr* Cédric Klapisch

Pot o' Gold ★★ U
Musical comedy 1941 · US · BW · 85min

James Stewart sings with Horace Heidt and his Orchestra on his uncle Charles Winninger's radio show, while falling for

Mary Gordon's lovely daughter Paulette Goddard. That's all there is to the plot, really, and Stewart later publicly declared this the worst of his films. Viewed today, it has a quaint period charm, though the songs don't exactly light any fires. The title was also the name of a popular long-running radio show featuring bandleader Heidt. TS *DVD*

James Stewart *Jimmy Haskell* • Paulette Goddard *Molly McCorkle* • Charles Winninger *CJ Haskell* • Mary Gordon *Ma McCorkle* • Frank Melton *Jasper* • Jed Prouty *Mr Louderman* • Dick Hogan *Willie McCorkle* ■ *Dir* George Marshall • *Scr* Walter DeLeon, from a story by Monte Brice, Andrew Bennison, Harry Tugend, from an idea by Haydn Roth Evans, Robert Brilmayer

Potiche ★★★ 15
Comedy 2010 · Fr/Bel · Colour · 98min

Set in 1977, this comedy stars Catherine Deneuve as Suzanne, the submissive wife of a tyrannical businessman who believes a woman's place is in the home. When the striking workforce of hubby's umbrella factory take him hostage and he ends up in hospital, Suzanne takes over as boss and creates a happier work environment, with a little help from former union firebrand Gérard Depardieu. Director François Ozon recalls the mild farce of an earlier era of French cinema thanks to the broad, exaggerated performances he elicits, but Deneuve's charming and assured comic presence brings a modicum of subtlety to proceedings. TeS French +subtitles. Sex scenes. *DVD* *Blu*

Catherine Deneuve *Suzanne Pujol* • Gérard Depardieu *Maurice Babin* • Fabrice Luchini *Robert Pujol* • Karin Viard *Nadège* • Judith Godrèche *Joëlle* • Jérémie Rénier *Laurent Pujol* ■ *Dir* François Ozon • *Scr* François Ozon, from the play by Jean-Pierre Gredy, Pierre Barillet

Pourquoi Pas! ★★★
Drama 1977 · Fr · Colour · 93min

Coline Serreau directs this gently subversive utopian tale, in which she inverts the traditional *ménage à trois* by having homemaker Sami Frey, breadwinner Christine Murillo and musician Mario Gonzales take on a fourth member in Nicole Jamet. However, their idiosyncratic idyll is disturbed by the intrusion of police inspector Michel Aumont, whose investigation into an accident results in him having an affair himself. DP French +subtitles.

Sami Frey *Fernand* • Mario Gonzalez *Louis* • Christine Murillo *Alexa* • Nicole Jamet *Sylvie* • Michel Aumont *Inspector* • Alain Salomon *Roger* ■ *Dir/Scr* Coline Serreau

Powaqqatsi ★★★ U
Documentary 1988 · US · Colour · 97min

Having censured the old world order for allowing itself to be enslaved by modern technology in *Koyaanisqatsi*, director Godfrey Reggio condemns it for the merciless manner in which it exploits the Third World in this heartfelt eco-documentary, whose title comes from the Hopi language word for "parasite". As in the original, it is an ambitious collage of images (some stunning, some shocking and some straining to make their point), combined with the futuristic music of Philip Glass. Ultimately it's an unsatisfactory exercise, as Reggio too often states the obvious and settles for gloss when grit might have been more effective. DP *DVD* *Blu*

■ *Dir* Godfrey Reggio • *Scr* Godfrey Reggio, Ken Richards • *Music* Philip Glass

Powder ★★★★ 12
Fantasy drama 1995 · US · Colour · 107min

This extremely moving fantasy drama tells the tale of a teenager whose mother was struck by lightning during labour, giving him a ghostly white appearance, an extraordinary intellect and miraculous powers. Sean Patrick Flanery delivers a wonderfully sympathetic central performance as the young misfit whose unique abilities generate feelings of hostility in the small-minded townsfolk. There's fine

support , too, from Jeff Goldblum, Mary Steenburgen and an unusually expressive Lance Henriksen. Victor Salva's intelligent script and assured direction take some fairly familiar themes to some quite unexpected places. JC Violence, swearing. *DVD*

Mary Steenburgen *Jessie Caldwell* • Sean Patrick Flanery *Jeremy Reed, "Powder"* • Lance Henriksen *Sheriff Barnum* • Jeff Goldblum *Donald Ripley* • Brandon Smith *Duncan* • Bradford Tatum *John Box* • Susan Tyrrell *Maxine* ■ *Dir/Scr* Victor Salva

Powder ★ 15
Black comedy drama 2010 · UK · Colour · 104min

In Kevin Sampson's lacklustre adaptation of his own novel, moping musician Liam Boyle shuns the limelight and disappears to Ibiza while struggling with the juvenile traumas that inspired his music. Despite an eager cast who try to breathe life into sketchily drawn and unsympathetic caricatures, this clumsily structured charade is hampered by pop clichés and dead-end subplots. The feeble tunes were composed by the usually dependable James Walsh (of Starsailor fame). DP

Liam Boyle *Keva McCluskey* • Aneurin Barnard *Miguel* • Alfie Allen *Wheezer* • Ralf Little *Syd* • Oliver Lee *James Love* • Al Weaver *Helmet* ■ *Dir* Mark Elliott • *Scr* Kevin Sampson, from his novel *Powder: an Everyday Story of Rock 'n' Roll Folk*

Powder River ★★ U
Western 1953 · US · Colour · 77min

This taut little western, made with some style, features a top-notch, albeit second-string, cast. Rory Calhoun is on the right side of the law for once, looking for a killer, and Cameron Mitchell is excellent as the doctor who becomes his pal. Corinne Calvet makes a fetching heroine and Penny Edwards also scores as the other woman in the picture. Director Louis King doesn't get in the way. TS

Rory Calhoun *Chino Bullock* • Corinne Calvet *Frenchie* • Cameron Mitchell *Mitch Hardin* • Penny Edwards *Debbie* • Carl Betz *Loney Hogan* • John Dehner *Harvey Logan* ■ *Dir* Louis King • *Scr* Geoffrey Homes [Daniel Mainwaring], from an idea by Sam Hellman, from a novel by Stuart N Lake

Powder Room ★★★ 15
Comedy 2013 · UK · Colour · 86min

A nightclub ladies' toilet over the course of one serious night of clubbing is the setting for this life-in-microcosm comedy. Though it's probably women who will recognise and appreciate the antics on show, director MJ Delaney's debut feature avoids ghettoising itself as female-only viewing by pandering, one suspects, to what men imagine goes on behind closed doors. Sheridan Smith and Jaime Winstone are the star names in an energetic and committed cast. But it's Johnnie Fiori as the powder room's ever-present attendant, who quietly steals the show. She may not have much dialogue, but her disapproving looks speak volumes. DA Swearing, sexual references, drug abuse.

Sheridan Smith *Sam* • Jaime Winstone *Chanel* • Kate Nash *Michelle* • Oona Chaplin *Jess* • Riann Steele *Paige* • Johnnie Fiori *Toilet attendant* ■ *Dir* MJ Delaney • *Scr* Rachel Hirons, from her play *When Women Wee*

The Power ★★
Science-fiction thriller 1968 · US · Colour · 109min

A number of B-league players (George Hamilton, Suzanne Pleshette, Michael Rennie) can't invest much conviction or authority in this science-fiction tale about a group of scientists who discover that one of them can kill by willpower alone. Director Byron Haskin adds some clever touches of menace, but authenticity is sorely lacking. TH

George Hamilton *Jim Tanner* • Suzanne Pleshette *Margery Lansing* • Richard Carlson *NE Van Zandt* • Yvonne De Carlo *Sally Hallson* • Earl Holliman *Talbot Scott* • Gary Merrill *Mark Corlane*

• Michael Rennie *Arthur Nordlund* ■ *Dir* Byron Haskin • *Scr* John Gay, from the novel by Frank M Robinson • *Music* Miklos Rozsa

Power ★★★ 15
Political drama 1986 · US · Colour · 105min

Not quite as sophisticated or as clever as it thinks it is, this political drama nevertheless has much to recommend it, despite cursory reviews at the time from critics who were snobby about its glamorous media-based theme. Newly greying Richard Gere plays a public relations manipulator, heading for a welcome comeuppance, undeterred by warnings from his alcoholic mentor (another of those seemingly effortless performances from the redoubtable Gene Hackman). This is eminently watchable nonsense, smoothly controlled by director Sidney Lumet, though it sank without trace on its cinema release. TS A sex scene, violence, swearing.

Richard Gere *Pete St John* • Julie Christie *Ellen Freeman* • Gene Hackman *Wilfred Buckley* • Kate Capshaw *Sydney Betterman* • Denzel Washington *Arnold Billings* • Michael Learned *Governor Andrea Stannard* • JT Walsh *Jerome Cade* ■ *Dir* Sidney Lumet • *Scr* David Himmelstoin

The Power and the Glory ★★
Drama 1933 · US · BW · 76min

This is the movie that made a massive impact on the young Orson Welles, telling the story of a railway magnate's life in a series of non-chronological flashbacks, with different characters revealing different aspects of the great man himself. Sound familiar? Well, *Citizen Kane* this isn't. William K Howard's direction is turgid in the extreme and Preston Sturges's script is underdeveloped. Historically interesting, but something of an endurance test. TS

Spencer Tracy *Tom Garner* • Colleen Moore *Sally* • Ralph Morgan *Henry* • Helen Vinson *Eve* • Clifford Jones [Philip Trent] *Tom Garner Jr* • Henry Kolker *Mr Borden* ■ *Dir* William K Howard • *Scr* Preston Sturges

The Power and the Prize ★★
Drama 1956 · US · BW · 98min

This drama about the ruthless nature of American big business is relatively weak stuff. Robert Taylor is rather too old to convince as the executive being groomed by Burl Ives's tycoon to be his successor. Elisabeth Mueller is unexciting, but there is sterling support from Mary Astor, Charles Coburn and Cedric Hardwicke. AE

Robert Taylor (1) *Cliff Barton* • Elisabeth Mueller *Miriam Linka* • Burl Ives *George Salt* • Charles Coburn *Guy Eliot* • Cedric Hardwicke *Mr Carew* • Mary Astor *Mrs George Salt* ■ *Dir* Henry Koster • *Scr* Robert Ardrey, from the novel by Howard Swiggett

The Power of One ★★★ 15
Period drama 1991 · US · Colour · 121min

A solid and gritty adaptation of Bryce Courtenay's rites-of-passage novel set in South Africa in the 1930s and 1940s. Stephen Dorff stars as an outsider whose friendship, as a young boy, with tutor Armin Mueller-Stahl and prisoner Morgan Freeman inspires him to fight against racial injustice. Dorff gives a mature performance, but he struggles to carry the action, while his experienced co-stars never put a foot wrong. John G Avildsen handles the boxing scenes with some skill, but his grasp of political discourse and teenage romance is less assured. DP Violence, swearing.

Stephen Dorff *PK, aged 18* • Morgan Freeman *Geel Piet* • Armin Mueller-Stahl *Doc* • John Gielgud *Headmaster St John* • Fay Masterson *Maria Marais* • Daniel Craig *Sergeant Jaapie Botha* ■ *Dir* John G Avildsen • *Scr* Robert Mark Kamen, from Bryce Courtenay's novel

Power Play ★★ 18
Thriller 1978 · Can/UK · Colour · 97min

This is a confused thriller in which an international cast struggles to get to grips with an uninspired script about a power

P

struggle in an unframed country. Peter O'Toole, Donald Pleasence and David Hemmings bring class to the proceedings, but for the most part it is entirely forgettable. JF

Peter O'Toole *Colonel Zeller* • David Hemmings *Colonel Anthony Narriman* • Donald Pleasence *Blair* • Barry Morse *Dr Jean Rousseau* ■ *Dir* Martyn Burke • *Scr* Martyn Burke, from a novel by Edward N Luttwak

Power Play ★★18

Erotic thriller　1998 · US · Colour · 87min

No one can touch Shannon Tweed when it comes to erotic thrillers. Unlike so many of her younger competitors, she's not simply cast for her physical attributes, and here she brings a Cruella De Vil-like glee to her villainy, as she schemes and seduces her way to ill-gotten wealth. Tweed's gold-digging is rooted in the *femme fatale* tradition of *film noir* and she deserves wider recognition. DP

Shannon Tweed *Jacqueline Knight* • Jim Richer *Steve Ganse* • Danielle Ciardi *Candice Alcott* • Bryan Kent *Benjamin Alcott* • Ron McCoy *Max DeLaine* ■ *Dir* Chris Baugh • *Scr* Chris Baugh, Geri Cudia Barger

The Powerpuff Girls ★★★PG

Animated action comedy
2002 · US · Colour · 70min

Short and sweet has always been the strength of Cartoon Network's *Powerpuff Girls*. So it's to the credit of director and original series creator Craig McCracken that he has managed to turn a bite-sized animated format into a convincing feature-length cartoon. He does so by making a prequel to the programme, concentrating on the superhero sisters' origins and how they learnt to use their special powers to crack crime and take on lab-monkey-turned-megalomaniac Mojo Jojo. Brought winningly to life with retro-style animation in ice-cream shades, the bubbly confection is easy on the eye and the mind. SF **DVD**

Catherine Cavadini [Cathy Cavadini] *Blossom* • Tara Strong [Tara Charendoff] *Bubbles* • EG Daily [Elizabeth Daily] *Buttercup* • Roger L Jackson *Mojo Jojo* • Tom Kane *Professor Utonium* • Tom Kenny *Mayor/Narrator* • Jennifer Hale *Ms Keane* ■ *Dir* Craig McCracken • *Scr* Craig McCracken, Charlie Bean, Lauren Faust, Paul Rudish, Don Shank from characters by Craig McCracken

Powwow Highway ★★★15

Road movie　1988 · UK/US · Colour · 87min

A film of great warmth and easy-going morality, this follows two men as they travel to New Mexico in an old Buick – one is a philosophical Cheyenne, the other a fiery activist. In the lead roles unknowns Gary Farmer and A Martinez deliver performances of charm and understanding. A courageous film that deserves to be better known, as does its director, Jonathan Wacks. TS Some violence, swearing.

A Martinez *Buddy Red Bow* • Gary Farmer *Philbert Bono* • Amanda Wyss *Rabbit Layton* • Joanelle Nadine Romero *Bonnie Red Bow* • Sam Vlahos *Chief Joseph* ■ *Dir* Jonathan Wacks • *Scr* Janet Heaney, Jean Stawarz, from the novel by David Seals

Practical Magic ★★12

Romantic black comedy
1998 · US · Colour · 99min

Nicole Kidman and Sandra Bullock star in this uneven romance, playing two sisters who are descended from witches. Kidman is the wilder sibling, while Bullock is the home-loving store owner who falls for Aidan Quinn, the detective who investigates when Kidman's abusive boyfriend disappears. Director Griffin Dunne fails to make either a moving comedy romance or a funny romantic comedy. JB Violence, swearing. **DVD**

Sandra Bullock *Sally Owens* • Nicole Kidman *Gillian Owens* • Stockard Channing *Aunt Frances* • Dianne Wiest *Aunt Jet* • Aidan Quinn *Gary Hallet* • Goran Visnjic *Jimmy Angelov* ■ *Dir* Griffin Dunne • *Scr* Robin Swicord, Akiva Goldsman, Adam Brooks, from the novel by Alice Hoffman

Practically Yours ★★U

Second World War romantic comedy
1944 · US · BW · 89min

Claudette Colbert and Fred MacMurray co-star for the umpteenth time in what proved an unworthy swan song to the sparkling Colbert's 16-year tenure at Paramount. The tale of a young woman who suffers from a vivid and over-romantic imagination and comes to believe she is the fiancée of a supposedly dead fighter pilot, can be summed up in one word: drivel. It's a tribute to the expertise of the stars that parts are perfectly tolerable. RK

Claudette Colbert *Peggy Martin* • Fred MacMurray *Lt SG Daniel Bellamy* • Gil Lamb *Albert Beagell* • Cecil Kellaway *Marvin P Meglin* • Robert Benchley *Judge Oscar Stimson* • Rosemary DeCamp *Ellen Macy* • Yvonne De Carlo *Employee* ■ *Dir* Mitchell Leisen • *Scr* Norman Krasna

Prairie Fever ★★

Western drama　2008 · US · Colour · 80min

In this clichéd western, Kevin Sorbo plays a drunken ex-lawman who's asked to escort three troubled mail-order brides across harsh terrain. These so-called "prairie fever"-afflicted women (among them a showy Dominique Swain) give an unusual slant to an otherwise archetypal mix of characters and events, but frustratingly the plotline only deals superficially with the roots of their anguish. Meanwhile, vindictive villains (including cardsharp Lance Henriksen) clutter up the narrative as it rushes to its wishy-washy conclusion. SF

Kevin Sorbo *Sheriff Preston Biggs* • Lance Henriksen *Monte James* • Dominique Swain *Abigail* • Jamie Anne Allman *Olivia Thibodeaux* • Jillian Armenante *Lettie* • Don Swayze *James* ■ *Dir* Stephen W Bridgewater [Stephen Bridgewater], David S Cass Sr • *Scr* Steven H Berman

A Prairie Home Companion ★★★★PG

Comedy　2006 · US · Colour · 100min

The final film from one of Hollywood's best-loved mavericks, the late Robert Altman, is a gentle, affectionate salute to Garrison Keillor's equally gentle and affectionate radio show. Keillor plays himself, the genial host of a long-running live public radio show that is about to be closed down. Ruthless millionaire Tommy Lee Jones is demolishing the theatre after the final performance. Not a lot actually happens and a sub-plot involving a mysterious woman (Virginia Madsen) is just daft. However, the joy comes from the relaxed interplay between the show's regulars and some great country music performances from the likes of Meryl Streep, Lily Tomlin and John C Reilly. A fine way for Altman to bow out. JF Some swearing, sexual references. **DVD**

Woody Harrelson *Dusty* • Tommy Lee Jones *The Axeman* • Garrison Keillor *GK* • Kevin Kline *Guy Noir* • Lindsay Lohan *Lola Johnson* • Virginia Madsen *Dangerous Woman* • John C Reilly *Lefty* • Maya Rudolph *Molly* • Meryl Streep *Yolanda Johnson* • Lily Tomlin *Rhonda Johnson* ■ *Dir* Robert Altman • *Scr* Garrison Keillor, from a story by Keillor, Ken LaZebnik, from a radio series by Keillor

Praise Marx and Pass the Ammunition ★★★

Political comedy　1968 · UK · Colour · 89min

Do not be deterred by this formidable-looking piece of political propaganda, made for virtually nothing and originally seen by virtually no one. Although it is part agitprop, with lots of facts and figures on social deprivation, it is, as the title suggests, mostly satire and takes amusing swipes at a Swinging Sixties stereotype, the Marxist-Leninist revolutionary with noble ideals and feet of clay. Partly shot during the Paris student riots, it is a fascinating testament to long-lost hopes. DM

John Thaw *Dom* • Edina Ronay *Lucy* • Louis Mahoney *Julius* • Anthony Villaroel *Arthur* • Helen Fleming *Clara* ■ *Dir* Maurice Hatton • *Scr* Maurice Hatton, from an idea by Michael Wood, Maurice Hatton

The Pram ★★★

Drama　1963 · Swe · Colour · 93min

Bo Widerberg's feature debut drew favourable comparisons with Ingmar Bergman, François Truffaut and Jean-Luc Godard. Inger Taube gives a truly Bergmanesque performance as an aimless young girl unable to decide between a dull, dependable friend and a wannabe pop singer. Using many of the tricks associated with the French New Wave, Widerberg draws us into the heart of his tale, while passing astute asides on Swedish society. DP Swedish +subtitles.

Inger Taube *Britt* • Thommy Berggren *Bjorn* • Lars Passgård *Robban* ■ *Dir/Scr* Bo Widerberg

Prancer ★★★U

Fantasy drama　1989 · US · Colour · 98min

In this charming family film, Rebecca Harrell plays a nine-year-old girl, recovering from the death of her mother, who finds an injured reindeer and thinks it belongs to Santa Claus. Unfortunately, her grief-stricken father (Sam Elliott) is struggling to save their farm from the bailiffs, and has little patience with his daughter's attempt to nurse the beast. Sentimental without being mawkish, with the grown-ups given as much character as the children, this is lump-in-the-throat stuff from start to finish. TH **DVD**

Sam Elliott *John Riggs* • Rebecca Harrell *Jessica Riggs* • Cloris Leachman *Mrs McFarland* • Rutanya Alda *Aunt Sarah* ■ *Dir* John Hancock • *Scr* Greg Taylor, from his story • *Music* Maurice Jarre

Prancer Returns ★★U

Christmas fantasy drama
2001 · Can/US · Colour · 86min

It's something of a surprise to see veteran hard man Jack Palance getting into the festive spirit, but he lends a certain credibility to this sequel to the 1989 film. Here, a lonely boy believes that the deer he has found in the forest near his home belongs to Santa and vows to return it to the North Pole. Gavin Fink acquits himself well as the misunderstood misfit, but the sense of magic is missing. DP **DVD**

John Corbett *Tom Sullivan* • Stacy Edwards *Denise Holton* • Michael O'Keefe *Mr Klock* • Gavin Fink *Charlie Holton* • Jack Palance *Old Man Richards* • Robert Clark *Ryan Holton* ■ *Dir* Joshua Butler • *Scr* Greg Taylor

A Prayer for the Dying ★★★15

Crime thriller　1987 · UK · Colour · 103min

Sadly, those involved in this political thriller could never decide what they wanted to make of Jack Higgins's novel about the moral dilemma of a priest unable to shop an IRA terrorist because he has identified himself in the confessional. The end result works relatively well as a fast-paced action adventure, but it is certainly shallow and melodramatic, and Bob Hoskins is hard to take as the priest. As the terrorist, Mickey Rourke was also unpopular, though his Belfast accent isn't at all bad. DM **DVD**

Mickey Rourke *Martin Fallon* • Bob Hoskins *Father Da Costa* • Alan Bates *Jack Meehan* • Liam Neeson *Liam Docherty* • Sammi Davis *Anna* ■ *Dir* Mike Hodges • *Scr* Edmund Ward, Martin Lynch, from the novel by Jack Higgins

Prayer of the Rollerboys ★★15

Futuristic adventure
1990 · US/Jpn · Colour · 90min

In a future where the American economy has failed, Los Angeles is run by a group of rollerblading junior fascists known as the Rollerboys. Standing against them is Corey Haim, a pizza delivery boy who used to be a friend of the Rollerboys' leader, Christopher Collet. Patricia Arquette plays Haim's love interest, and the action scenes are sometimes exciting. All rather silly. ST

Corey Haim *Griffin* • Patricia Arquette *Casey* • Christopher Collet *Gary Lee* • JC Quinn *Jaworski* • Julius Harris *Speedbagger* • Devin Clark *Miltie* • Mark Pellegrino *Bingo* ■ *Dir* Rick King • *Scr* W Peter Iliff

Prayers for Bobby ★★

Biographical drama　2009 · US · Colour · 120min

A dowdy-looking Sigourney Weaver brings class to this tragic true-story drama, playing a 1970s suburban mother who's struggling to reconcile her young son's homosexuality with her devout religious beliefs. But while she and troubled screen offspring Ryan Kelley give strong performances, director Russell Mulcahy incorporates a mess of camera techniques and odd angles more suited to his music video past, and foolishly detracts from the tale's emotional core. SF

Sigourney Weaver *Mary Griffith* • Henry Czerny *Robert Griffith* • Ryan Kelley *Bobby Griffith* • Dan Butler *Reverend Whitsell* • Austin Nichols *Ed Griffith* ■ *Dir* Russell Mulcahy • *Scr* Katie Ford, from the non-fiction book *Prayers for Bobby: a Mother's Coming to Terms with the Suicide of Her Gay Son* by Leroy Aarons

The Preacher's Wife ★★U

Romantic fantasy　1996 · US · Colour · 118min

This 1990s version of *The Bishop's Wife* has Denzel Washington as the angel sent to Earth to restore the wavering faith of pastor Courtney B Vance, as well as save his marriage to gospel-singing Whitney Houston. Unsurprisingly, with diva Houston in the cast, there's lots of singing, leaving Washington and Vance on the sidelines to act as scenery for her musical moments. JB **DVD**

Denzel Washington *Dudley* • Whitney Houston *Julia Biggs* • Courtney B Vance *Henry Biggs* • Gregory Hines *Joe Hamilton* • Jenifer Lewis *Marguerite Coleman* • Loretta Devine *Beverly* ■ *Dir* Penny Marshall • *Scr* Nat Mauldin, Allan Scott, from the film *The Bishop's Wife* by Robert E Sherwood, Leonardo Bercovici, from the novel *In Barleyfields* by Robert Nathan

Preaching to the Perverted ★★18

Sex comedy　1997 · UK · Colour · 99min

The first film to focus on the London fetish scene is an odd mix of traditional British sex comedy and serious message. It starts well with atmospheric, if glamorised scenes in a fetish club run by sexy Guinevere Turner. Thereafter, it doesn't seem to know where to go, and its story of a government man seduced by the depravity he's investigating is very weak. The result will probably shock the easily shocked and disappoint sensation-seekers hoping for something stronger. DM

Guinevere Turner *Tanya Cheex* • Christien Anholt *Peter Emery* • Tom Bell *Henry Harding* • Julie Graham *Eugenie* • Julian Wadham *Prosecuting lawyer* • Georgina Hale *Miss Wilderspin* • Ricky Tomlinson *Fibbin' Gibbins* ■ *Dir/Scr* Stuart Urban

Precious (Base on Nol by Saf) (Based on the Novel "Push" by Sapphire) ★★★★15

Drama　2008 · US · Colour · 105min

Lee Daniels's heartfelt drama tells the story of Clarieece "Precious" Jones (Gabourey Sidibe), a 16-year-old black girl whose life reads like a litany of horrors. She is illiterate and morbidly obese, has been raped and impregnated twice by her father and is systematically abused by her mother (Mo'Nique). But into this chaos comes a glimmer of hope, as a pregnant Precious begins to attend a specialist school and slowly comes to realise her own worth. Daniels draws impressive performances from his cast, including a dressed-down Mariah Carey. But the film's real strengths are the two leads, with Sidibe expressing so much with just a slight smile or a single tear, and Mo'Nique outstanding in a role that could have been cartoonishly monstrous. LB Violence, swearing, sexual abuse references. **DVD** **BD**

Gabourey Sidibe *Clarieece "Precious" Jones* • Mo'Nique *Mary* • Paula Patton *Ms Rain* • Mariah Carey *Ms Weiss* • Sherri Shepherd *Cornrows* • Lenny Kravitz *Nurse John* • Stephanie Andujar *Rita* • Chyna Layne *Rhonda* ■ *Dir* Lee Daniels • *Scr* Geoffrey Fletcher, from the novel *Push* by Sapphire

P

Precious Cargo ★★ 15

Action crime thriller 2016 · Can · Colour · 86min

Don't be fooled that this is a Bruce Willis action yarn, as he merely shuffles through a cameo before exiting. He barely contains his disdain for dialogue that raises laughs for all the wrong reasons, and leaves Mark-Paul Gosselaar and Claire Forlani to carry the burden of cliché that director Max Adams has piled high. Willis is furious with Forlani for cheating him out of his heist proceeds, so she tempts Gosselaar back to protect her and her unborn baby. Adams stages a speedboat race with style, but the shootouts are formulaic. **DP** Violence, swearing, sexual references. **DVD** **BL**

Mark-Paul Gosselaar *Jack* • Claire Forlani *Karen* • Bruce Willis *Eddie* • Daniel Bernhardt *Simon* • Nick Loeb *Andrew* ■ *Dir* Max Adams • *Scr* Paul V Seetachit, Max Adams

Predator ★★★★ 18

Science-fiction action thriller 1987 · US · Colour · 106min

This is one of Arnold Schwarzenegger's most efficient movies: a stripped-down thriller that cheerfully sacrifices characterisation on the altar of exhilarating action and special effects. Schwarzenegger is the leader of an elite special forces team whose jungle mission is thrown into chaos when they are tracked by a lethal alien game-hunter. As with *Aliens*, much of the fun derives from watching a bunch of macho soldiers crack under pressure. Director John McTiernan ensures the tension is kept at snapping point. A fresh sequel has been announced for 2018. **JF** Violence, swearing. **DVD** **BL**

Arnold Schwarzenegger *Major Alan "Dutch" Schaeffer* • Carl Weathers *Dillon* • Elpidia Carrillo *Anna* • Bill Duke *Mac* • Jesse Ventura *Sergeant Blain* • Sonny Landham *Billy* • Kevin Peter Hall *Predator* ■ *Dir* John McTiernan • *Scr* Jim Thomas, John Thomas

Predator 2 ★★★ 15

Science-fiction action thriller 1990 · US · Colour · 103min

In Los Angeles in 1997, Danny Glover is the unorthodox cop who can't work out who or what is murdering the city's gangsters, or why sinister government official Gary Busey is so interested. However, it's not long before he realises that the culprit is far from human. The action sequences are ably staged but it lacks the sweaty, claustrophobic tension of the Arnold Schwarzenegger original. **JF** Swearing, violence. **DVD** **BL**

Danny Glover *Detective Mike Harrigan* • Gary Busey *Peter Keyes* • Rubén Blades *Danny Archuleta* • Maria Conchita Alonso *Leona Cantrell* • Kevin Peter Hall *Predator* • Bill Paxton *Jerry Lambert* ■ *Dir* Stephen Hopkins • *Scr* Jim Thomas, John Thomas

Predators ★★★ 15

Science-fiction action thriller 2010 · US · Colour · 102min

The worst bad guys the Earth has to offer are transported to another planet as prey in director Nimród Antal's back-to-basics reboot of the invisible-alien-hunter franchise. Produced by fan boy Robert Rodriguez (*Sin City*), this human predator vs intergalactic predator battle royale is a serviceably solid sci-fi action thriller. There's not much visual originality, but the atmosphere of menace is well created and maintained, as the group of killers led by a buff Adrien Brody try to work out what's happening. **AJ** **DVD** **BL**

Adrien Brody *Royce* • Topher Grace *Edwin* • Alice Braga *Isabelle* • Walton Goggins *Stans* • Laurence Fishburne *Noland* • Danny Trejo *Cuchillo* ■ *Dir* Nimród Antal • *Scr* Michael Finch, Alex Litvak, Robert Rodriguez

Predestination ★★★ 15

Science-fiction thriller 2014 · Aus · Colour · 93min

Until it spirals out of all logical control, the Spierig Brothers' expansion of sci-fi legend Robert A Heinlein's 1958 short story *All You Zombies* is a thoughtful, if wonky, small-scale epic of retro-futurism. On his final time-travelling assignment to 1975, a temporal agent (Ethan Hawke) must stop the elusive Fizzle Bomber terrorist blowing up Manhattan while recruiting an enigmatic magazine agony aunt (an astonishingly multi-levelled Sarah Snook) into his organisation. The less said about the ornate plot the better. **AJ** Violence, swearing, sex scenes. **DVD** **BL**

Ethan Hawke *The Bartender* • Sarah Snook *The Unmarried Mother* • Noah Taylor *Mr Robertson* • Madeleine West *Mrs Stapleton* • Christopher Kirby *Agent Miles* ■ *Dir* The Spierig Brothers [Michael Spierig], The Spierig Brothers [Peter Spierig] • *Scr* Michael Spierig, Peter Spierig, from the story *All You Zombies* by Robert A Heinlein • *Music* Peter Spierig

Prefontaine ★★

Sports biography 1997 · US · Colour · 106min

For his follow-up to his acclaimed documentary *Hoop Dreams*, writer/director Steve James made this biography of Steve Prefontaine, the Olympic runner who died in a car crash at the tragically young age of 24. Jared Leto does an excellent job impersonating Prefontaine and keeps a straight face while wearing some of the worst hairstyles the 1970s had to offer. R Lee Ermey plays the coach. **ST** Violence, swearing.

Jared Leto *Steve Prefontaine* • R Lee Ermey *Bill Bowerman* • Ed O'Neill *Bill Dellinger* • Breckin Meyer *Pat Tyson* • Lindsay Crouse *Elfriede Prefontaine* ■ *Dir* Steve James (2) • *Scr* Steve James, Eugene Corr

Pregnancy Pact ★★

Drama based on a true story 2010 · US · Colour · 83min

The 2008 case in which a group of high-school girls allegedly made a pact to get pregnant is the inspiration for this TV movie. Clearly trying to offer something that parents and their daughters can watch together, it sees video blogger Thora Birch investigating the reasons for a teenage pregnancy boom. There are strong performances, particularly from Nancy Travis as a conservative-values mum, and some affecting moments, but the attempt to tackle so many points dilutes its overall impact. **SF**

Thora Birch *Sidney Bloom* • Camryn Manheim *Nurse Kim Daly* • Nancy Travis *Lorraine Dougan* • Madisen Beaty *Sara Dougan* ■ *Dir* Rosemary Rodriguez • *Scr* Pamela Davis, Teena Booth

Prehysteria! ★★★ PG

Fantasy 1993 · US · Colour · 80min

In a junior-league *Jurassic Park*, kids hatch a clutch of pygmy-dino eggs and a comic book bad guy tries to force the family to hand them over. The dialogue is surprisingly good for a low-budget movie such as this and the diddly dinos, if not exactly state-of-the-art special effects, are cute and cuddly enough to keep younger kids enthralled. **DA**

Brett Cullen *Frank Taylor* • Colleen Morris *Vicki* • Austin O'Brien *Jerry Taylor* • Tony Longo *Louis* • Stuart Fratkin *Richie* • Stephen Lee *Rico Sarno* ■ *Dir* Charles Band, Albert Band • *Scr* Greg Suddeth, Mark Goldstein, from an idea by Peter Von Sholly

Prelude to a Kiss ★★★ PG

Romantic comedy fantasy 1992 · US · Colour · 98min

In this offbeat, gentle romantic fantasy, Alec Baldwin plays the groom who begins to suspect something is up with new wife Meg Ryan, whose personality change may or may not be connected to the appearance of an elderly stranger at their wedding. This certainly isn't the usual romantic fare from Hollywood, but director Norman René directs the proceedings with subtlety and summons up a charming, if slightly melancholic air, and the performances are first-rate all round. **JF** Swearing. **DVD**

Alec Baldwin *Peter Hoskins* • Meg Ryan *Rita Boyle* • Kathy Bates *Leah Blier* • Ned Beatty *Dr Boyle* • Patty Duke *Mrs Boyle* • Sydney Walker *Julius, the old man* ■ *Dir* Norman René • *Scr* Craig Lucas, from his play

Prelude to Fame ★★ U

Drama 1950 · UK · BW · 88min

Films about classical music have nearly always been box-office poison. This uninspired tale about a child prodigy whose tutor is his only refuge from expectation and exploitation was no exception. Adapted from a minor Aldous Huxley story, the film was directed with little flair by Fergus McDonell, who keeps the focus firmly on the sickly soloist, played rather well by Jeremy Spenser. The film was the last made using the ill-fated Independent Frame method, which aimed to cut costs by using back-projected interior scenery. **DP**

Guy Rolfe *John Morell* • Kathleen Byron *Signora Bondini* • Kathleen Ryan *Catherine Morell* • Jeremy Spenser *Guido* • Rosalie Crutchley *Carlotta* ■ *Dir* Fergus McDonell • *Scr* Robert Westerby, from the story *Young Archimedes* by Aldous Huxley

Prelude to War ★★

Second World War documentary 1943 · US · BW · 53min

This was the first of director Frank Capra's *Why We Fight* series, which was originally intended for military use only. Theatrical release was the subject of prolonged debate, and only came after President Roosevelt's personal approval. There is little historical or social analysis, and this film simply demonises Hitler, which it does quite efficiently through footage, maps and graphics, with an uncredited voiceover by Walter Huston. It was one of four documentaries to win an Oscar in 1943. **AT**

Walter Huston *Narrator* ■ *Dir* Ernst Lubitsch, Major Anatole Litvak [Anatole Litvak], Robert Flaherty • *Scr* Eric Knight, Anthony Veiller, Robert Heller • *Music* Alfred Newman

Premature ★★ 15

Comedy 2014 · US · Colour · 89min

A bad idea gets worse with each repetition in this puerile rehash of *Groundhog Day*. At its centre is John Karna as a preppy type whose early-morning wet dream sends him into an ejaculatory spiral that causes him to endlessly repeat the same day. Little is done with this derivative premise that clearly equates crudity with hilarity. But, while Karna lacks charisma, his co-star Katie Findlay is sweetly supportive and Alan Tudyk cameos amusingly. **DP** In English, French. Swearing, sex

John Karna *Rob Crabbe* • Craig Roberts *Stanley* • Katie Findlay *Gabrielle* • Alan Tudyk *Jack Roth* ■ *Dir* Dan Beers • *Scr* Dan Beers, Mathew Harawitz

The Premature Burial ★★★ 15

Horror 1962 · US · Colour · 77min

Originally not intended as one of Roger Corman's unofficial Edgar Allan Poe series – the reason Ray Milland starred instead of Vincent Price – this moody chiller jettisoned any pretence of a plot for an eerie essay on the terrors of being buried alive. Although somewhat starchily written and slightly static in approach, the B-movie master of the macabre still manages to raise the odd claustrophobic spine-tingle or two thanks to graveyard-loads of gloomy atmosphere. **AJ** **DVD**

Ray Milland *Guy Carrell* • Hazel Court *Emily Gault* • Richard Ney *Miles Archer* • Heather Angel *Kate Carrell* • Alan Napier *Dr Gideon Gault* ■ *Dir* Roger Corman • *Scr* Charles Beaumont, Ray Russell, from the story by Edgar Allan Poe in *Dollar Newspaper* (31 July 1884)

Premium Rush ★★★ 12

Action thriller 2012 · US · Colour · 87min

You don't have to be crazy to be one of New York's 1,500 bicycle messengers, but it helps. Joseph Gordon-Levitt plays super-cyclist Wilee, who tries to outmanoeuvre an amoral cop (Michael Shannon) attempting to get his hands on the valuable parcel the young daredevil has been assigned to deliver. Bright, fun and smoothly logical, the film pivots on believable danger, a delicious bad guy and a solid cast, including Gordon-Levitt, who incurred an injury requiring 31 stitches while doing many of his own stunts. **KK** Some violence, brief swearing. **DVD** **BL**

Joseph Gordon-Levitt *Wilee* • Michael Shannon *Bobby Monday* • Dania Ramirez *Vanessa* • Jamie Chung *Nima* ■ *Dir* David Koepp • *Scr* David Koepp, John Kamps

Premonition ★ 12

Supernatural thriller 2007 · US · Colour · 92min

In this dreadful supernatural thriller Sandra Bullock plays a wife and mother who is told that her husband (Julian McMahon) has died in a car crash. So she's astounded to wake up the next day and find him still alive. It appears that time has somehow come unstuck and she's experiencing the week of his demise in random order. Can she reshuffle the days in order to learn the facts and save his life? It's languidly paced and drearily shot, and Bullock's utterly pedestrian performance matches the sappy imagery and uninspired scares. **AJ** **DVD**

Sandra Bullock *Linda Hanson* • Julian McMahon *Jim Hanson* • Nia Long *Annie* • Kate Nelligan *Joanne* • Amber Valletta *Claire* • Peter Stormare *Dr Norman Roth* ■ *Dir* Mennan Yapo • *Scr* Bill Kelly

Prescription: Murder ★★★★ PG

Detective mystery 1968 · US · Colour · 94min

This superbly scripted thriller marks the small-screen debut of an American TV legend. Peter Falk is now so associated with the role of shambling Los Angeles detective Lt Columbo that it is impossible to believe that anyone else could have played him. However, Thomas Mitchell was Columbo in Richard Levinson and William Link's stage play, and first choice for the TV series was Bing Crosby, who turned it down because it would interfere with his golf. In the event, Falk made the character his own and here the deceptively haphazard way in which he dismantles the master plan of smug, wife-murdering psychiatrist Gene Barry is a delight to watch. **DP** **DVD**

Peter Falk *Lt Columbo* • Gene Barry *Doctor Ray Flemming* • Katherine Justice *Joan Hudson* • Nina Foch *Carol Flemming* • William Windom *Burt Gordon* ■ *Dir* Richard Irving • *Scr* Richard Levinson, William Link, from the play by Richard Levinson, William Link

Presenting Lily Mars ★★ U

Musical comedy 1943 · US · BW · 103min

Stage-struck singer Judy Garland leaves her small Indiana town to follow young Broadway producer Van Heflin to Manhattan. There, despite falling foul of his temperamental star (Marta Eggerth), she eventually finds stardom and romance. This formula musical in the *Cinderella* vein is enlivened by Garland's usual high-calibre performance and a climactic appearance from Tommy Dorsey and his Orchestra. **AJ**

Judy Garland *Lily Mars* • Van Heflin *John Thornway* • Fay Bainter *Mrs Thornway* • Richard Carlson *Owen Vail* • Spring Byington *Mrs Mars* • Marta Eggerth *Isobel Rekay* • Tommy Dorsey ■ *Dir* Norman Taurog • *Scr* Richard Connell, Gladys Lehman, from the novel by Booth Tarkington

The President ★★★

Silent melodrama 1919 · Den · Tinted · 90min

The tale of three women who are abused, impregnated and abandoned by shiftless, socially superior males, Carl Th Dreyer's directorial debut established several traits that would persist throughout his career. The influence of little-known Danish painter Vilhelm Hammershoi is evident in his austere interiors, while his choice of source material began a lifetime of basing his films on works of little literary merit. This narratively sophisticated and compositionally precise melodrama can now be seen in a lustrous, tinted print . **DP**

Halvard Hoff *Karl Victor von Sendlingen, president* • Elith Pio *The president's father* • Carl Meyer *The president's grandfather* • Olga Raphael-Linden *Victorine Lippert, president's daughter* • Betty Kirkebye *Hermine Lippert* ■ *Dir* Carl Th Dreyer • *Scr* Carl Th Dreyer, from the novel by Karl Emil Franzos

The President ★★★ 15
Political drama
2014 · UK/Fr/Ger/Georgia/S Kor · Colour · 118min

Subtlety is at a premium in this allegorical study of dictatorial disdain and revolutionary recrimination. But there's no denying the potency of a story co-scripted by Mohsen Makhmalbaf and his film-making partner, Marziyeh Meshkini. Set in an unnamed country, the action follows a toppled tyrant (Misha Gomiashvili) and young grandson (Dachi Orvelashvili) as they embark upon a Lear-like odyssey disguised as a street musician and his dancing boy. The result is a poignant insight into childlike incomprehension and trust, though, because the political analysis often feels didactic and simplistic, it's less effective as a treatise on the cyclical nature of violence and the state of the modern world. DP Georgian +subtitles. Violence, swearing, sexual references. ■

Misha Gomiashvili *President* · Dachi Orvelashvili *Grandson* · Ia Sukhitashvili *Prostitute* · Guja Burduli *Singer Political Prisoner* ■ *Dir* Mohsen Makhmalbaf · *Scr* Mohsen Makhmalbaf, Marziyeh Meshkini

The President's Analyst ★★★★
Political satire   1967 · US · Colour · 102min

It may seem dated today, but this clever satire was the ultimate hip trip back in the Swinging Sixties, and it is still very, very funny. Talented iconoclast Theodore J Flicker wrote and directed, and profited from the presence of James Coburn in the lead as the suave psychiatrist earmarked for secret service assassination, only to be saved by other agencies interested in the information they assume has passed between the president and his shrink. Coburn leads them all a merry chase, notably causing international havoc during a hilarious sex romp with hippy Jill Banner. TS Some violence. ■

James Coburn *Dr Sidney Schaefer* · Godfrey Cambridge *Don Masters* · Severn Darden *Kropotkin* · Joan Delaney *Nan Butler* · Pat Harrington *Arlington Hewes* · Barry McGuire *Old wrangler* · Jill Banner *Snow White* ■ *Dir/Scr* Theodore J Flicker

The President's Lady ★★★
Biographical drama   1953 · US · BW · 97min

Charlton Heston takes on one of his iconic roles with this neat portrayal of American president Andrew Jackson and the two loves of his life. One, his country, naturally, in all its early 19th-century tumult and the other, luscious Susan Hayward as the woman with a dodgy past he is determined to marry. Based soundly on Irving Stone's novel rather than historical fact, it allows Heston once again to convey the heavy burden of office with an endearing helping of agonising self-doubt. Like Hayward's stays, however, this does creak a bit. SH

Susan Hayward *Rachel Donelson Robards* · Charlton Heston *Andrew Jackson* · John McIntire *Jack Overton* · Fay Bainter *Mrs Donelson* ■ *Dir* Henry Levin · *Scr* John Patrick, from the novel by Irving Stone

The President's Man ★★ 15
Action adventure thriller
2000 · US · Colour · 86min

Action heroes never die, they just get smaller budgets. Not that Chuck Norris was ever in the Schwarzenegger league, despite having a cult following among martial arts aficionados. But the penny-pinching shows in this TV effort, in which Norris plays a veteran Secret Service agent who is forced back into the fray when the wife of the US president is kidnapped by a shady terrorist organisation. DP Violence. DVD

Chuck Norris *Joshua McCord* · Dylan Neal *Deke Slater* · Jennifer Tung *Que* · Ralph Waite *President Matthews* ■ *Dir* Michael Preece, Eric Norris · *Scr* Bob Gookin

The Presidio ★★★ 15
Mystery thriller   1988 · US · Colour · 94min

Director Peter Hyams is an underrated master of the high concept action thriller and this effort boasts his usual strengths and weaknesses. On the downside, the plotting - in which San Francisco cop Mark Harmon is paired with an old enemy, military policeman Sean Connery, to solve a murder mystery - is perfunctory to say the least. However, Hyams distracts attention from that with some humdinger action sequences. Meg Ryan is a feisty love interest. JF Violence, swearing. DVD

Sean Connery *Lt Col Alan Caldwell* · Mark Harmon *Jay Austin* · Meg Ryan *Donna Caldwell* · Jack Warden *Sergeant Major Ross Maclure* · Mark Blum *Arthur Peale* ■ *Dir* Peter Hyams · *Scr* Larry Ferguson

Presque Rien ★★★ 18
Romantic drama   2000 · Fr/Bel · Colour · 93min

Consciously seeking to explore a traumatic train of events in a non-linear fashion, Sébastien Lifshitz provides a perceptive insight into the pain of realising one's sexual identity in this Rohmeresque tale of summer love turned sour. Although he switches time frames to great visual and emotional effect, what is particularly impressive about Lifshitz's direction is the way in which he leaks the snippets of information that link Jérémie Elkaïm's idyllic seaside romance and his desperate attempt to track down his lover, Stéphane Rideau, in the bleakest of midwinters. DP French +subtitles. DVD

Jérémie Elkaïm *Mathieu* · Stéphane Rideau *Cédric* · Marie Matheron *Annick* · Dominique Reymond *Mother* · Laetitia Legrix *Sarah* · Nils Ohlund *Pierre* ■ *Dir* Sébastien Lifshitz · *Scr* Sébastien Lifshitz, Stéphane Bouquet

Press for Time ★ U
Comedy   1966 · UK · Colour · 98min

After headlining in 14 consecutive films, this was Norman Wisdom's last starring role before his impressive supporting performance in American comedy *The Night They Raided Minsky's* in 1968, and a sorry swan song it makes. He is woefully out of form playing a bungling reporter on a local rag in this feeble comedy. DP DVD

Norman Wisdom *Norman Shields/Sir Wilfred Shields/Emily Shields* · Derek Bond *Major Bartlett* · Angela Browne *Eleanor* · Tracey Crisp *Ruby Fairchild* · Noel Dyson *Mrs Corcoran* · Derek Francis *Alderman Corcoran* ■ *Dir* Robert Asher · *Scr* Norman Wisdom, Eddie Leslie, from the novel *Yea Yea Yea* by Angus McGill

Pressure ★★★ 15
Drama   1976 · UK · Colour · 120min

Horace Ové's pioneering feature, which was the first to be released in the United Kingdom by a black director, explores the subject of being black and British. Ové focuses on the limited opportunities offered to young black men in the face of institutional and individual hostility, but he also examines the resentment exhibited by Herbert Norville's own family when he tries to conform. It would be easy to dismiss the film as dated were it not for the fact that little has actually changed. DP DVD

Herbert Norville *Anthony* · Oscar James *Colin* · Frank Singuineau *Lucas* · Lucita Lijertwood *Bopsie* · Sheila Scott-Wilkinson *Sister Louise* · Ed Devereaux *Police inspector* · Norman Beaton *Preacher* ■ *Dir* Horace Ové · *Scr* Horace Ové, Samuel Selvon

Pressure ★★★ 15
Thriller   2015 · UK · Colour · 87min

Director Ron Scalpello's second feature (following his gritty prison flick *Offender*) will have claustrophobes in a cold sweat, as a quartet of divers is trapped underwater in the middle of the Indian Ocean. The scenario is authentically staged, and the cast of Matthew Goode, Danny Huston, Joe Cole (*Peaky Blinders*) and co-writer Alan McKenna give committed performances as they struggle to cheat their fate. It's perfectly watchable, if not quite on a nerve-shredding par with *The Poseidon Adventure* or *The Abyss*. JA Swearing, sexual references, nudity DVD

Danny Huston *Engel* · Matthew Goode *Mitchell* · Joe Cole *Jones* · Alan McKenna *Hurst* ■ *Dir* Ron Scalpello · *Scr* Paul Staheli, Alan McKenna, from a story by Louis Baxter

Pressure Point ★★★★
Drama   1962 · US · BW · 86min

Based on a real-life story, this case history about a black prison psychiatrist and his ongoing confrontations with a fascist, racist inmate was considered very controversial in its day. Sidney Poitier, as the doctor, gives a brilliantly controlled performance while singer Bobby Darin - in one of his rare dramatic appearances - is bellowingly obnoxious as the bigoted prisoner. Director Hubert Cornfield stresses the caged claustrophobia of life inside with casual expertise. TH

Sidney Poitier *Doctor* · Bobby Darin *Patient* · Peter Falk *Young psychiatrist* · Carl Benton Reid *Chief medical officer* ■ *Dir* Hubert Cornfield · *Scr* Hubert Cornfield, S Lee Pogostin, from the story *Destiny's Tot* by Robert Mitchell Lindner in *The Fifty-Minute Hour: a Collection of True Psychoanalytic Tales*

The Prestige ★★★★ 12
Period mystery thriller
2006 · US/UK · Colour · 125min

Christopher Nolan's period drama manages to seem both highly original and slightly old-fashioned. Hugh Jackman and Christian Bale are magicians in Victorian England whose intense rivalry dates back to a time when they were both apprentices and Jackman's wife died after a trick went wrong. Fuelled by professional jealousy and personal hatred, they dedicate their talents to destroying each other. Nolan constructs a fascinating tale that twists and turns at every opportunity, although there is perhaps one twist too many in a slightly overbaked dénouement. But the film is grounded by fine performances all round. BP Violence. DVD BD

Hugh Jackman *Robert Angier* · Christian Bale *Alfred Borden* · Michael Caine *Cutter* · Scarlett Johansson *Olivia* · Piper Perabo *Julia* · Rebecca Hall *Sarah* · Samantha Mahurin *Jess* · David Bowie *Tesla* · Andy Serkis *Alley* · Daniel Davis *Judge* ■ *Dir* Christopher Nolan · *Scr* Christopher and Jonathan Nolan, from the novel by Christopher Priest

Presumed Innocent ★★★★ 18
Thriller   1990 · US · Colour · 121min

Harrison Ford was at the peak of his popularity when he starred in this glossy, highly polished blockbuster, playing a lawyer assigned to untangle the murder of his former mistress. Based on the multi-million-selling novel by Scott Turow, this could have been a great movie, but, despite being a darn good yarn well told, the essential magic is somehow missing. Quite what turns a competent movie into a classic remains the great Hollywood conundrum - the elements are here, but they're too tightly threaded for this to attain true classic status. SH Swearing, violence, sex scenes, nudity. DVD

Harrison Ford *Rozat "Rusty" Sabich* · Brian Dennehy *Raymond Horgan* · Raul Julia *Alejandro "Sandy" Stern* · Bonnie Bedelia *Barbara Sabich* · Paul Winfield *Judge Larren Lyttle* · Greta Scacchi *Carolyn Polhemus* ■ *Dir* Alan J Pakula · *Scr* Frank Pierson, Alan J Pakula, from the novel by Scott Turow

Pret-a-Porter ★★★ 15
Satirical comedy   1994 · US · Colour · 127min

Director Robert Altman was always going to struggle to surpass the sprawling perfection of his episodic drama *Short Cuts*, and when this satirical look at the fashion industry opened the backlash really kicked in. Yes, it does lack the bite and subtlety of Altman's best work, but it's not half as bad as some have made it out to be. Setting the action against the backdrop of the French spring fashion shows, Altman characteristically weaves a bewildering number of subplots through the piece, some of which you care about, some of which you don't. There's also a cast to die for - a fascinating failure, but a star-gazer's delight. JF Swearing, drug abuse, nudity. DVD

Julia Roberts *Anne Eisenhower* · Tim Robbins *Joe Flynn* · Stephen Rea *Milo O'Brannagan* · Lauren Bacall *Slim Chrysler* · Marcello Mastroianni *Sergei/Sergio* · Sophia Loren *Isabella de la Fontaine* · Anouk Aimée *Simone Lowenthal* · Lili Taylor *Fiona Ulrich* · Kim Basinger *Kitty Potter* · Sally Kellerman *Sissy Wanamaker* · Tracey Ullman *Nina Scant* · Linda Hunt *Regina Krumm* · Rupert Everett *Jack Lowenthal* · Forest Whitaker *Cy Bianco* · Richard E Grant *Cort Romney, fashion designer* · Danny Aiello *Major Hamilton, retail buyer* · Teri Garr *Louise Hamilton, Major Hamilton's wife* · Lyle Lovett *Clint Lammeraux, Texas cowboy-boot mogul* ■ *Dir* Robert Altman · *Scr* Robert Altman, Barbara Shulgasser

Pretty Baby ★★★ U
Comedy   1950 · US · BW · 91min

This is an innocuous Warner Bros crowd-pleaser about what a working girl has to resort to in order to get a seat on the subway. Betsy Drake (Mrs Cary Grant at the time) is perky in the lead, and for once Dennis Morgan's bland performance matches his bland role, so no harm done there. Morgan is no match for sophisticated Zachary Scott, who yet again demonstrates why he was nicknamed "The Eyebrow". *Miracle on 34th Street*'s Edmund Gwenn also makes a welcome appearance. TS

Betsy Drake *Patsy Douglas* · Dennis Morgan *Sam Morley* · Zachary Scott *Barry Holmes* · Edmund Gwenn *Cyrus Baxter* ■ *Dir* Bretaigne Windust · *Scr* Everett Freeman, from the book *Gay Deception* by Jules Furthman, John Klorer

Pretty Baby ★★★★ 18
Period drama   1978 · US · Colour · 104min

"Scandal!" yelled the moralists of the time about the under-age sex theme of director Louis Malle's depiction of brothel life in the New Orleans of 1917. It's a cosier treatment than might have been expected, though, with Brooke Shields as the bordello girl awaiting her 12th birthday and the official loss of her virginity. Keith Carradine is the photographer whose candid camera strips the romance from her naive view of life with the women who are the only family she's got. Louis Malle treats the difficult subject with sensitivity. TH DVD

Keith Carradine *EJ Bellocq* · Susan Sarandon *Hattie* · Brooke Shields *Violet* · Frances Faye *Madame Nell Livingston* · Antonio Fargas *Professor, piano player* · Barbara Steele *Josephine* ■ *Dir* Louis Malle · *Scr* Polly Platt, from a story by Polly Platt, Louis Malle, from the book *Storyville, New Orleans: Being an Authentic Account of the Notorious Redlight District* by Al Rose · *Cinematographer* Sven Nykvist

Pretty Bird ★★ 15
Comedy   2008 · US · Colour

Big dreams have messy consequences for Billy Crudup and a highly strung Paul Giamatti in this enjoyably performed if excessively offbeat tale from debuting director Paul Schneider. Crudup's fast-talking fantasist teams up with an equally idealistic mate (David Hornsby) and volatile engineer Giamatti to produce a rocket belt - think James Bond in *Thunderball* - they hope will revolutionise personal transport. It's an intriguing premise, but like the trio's uneasy partnership it quickly crumbles. SF Swearing.

Billy Crudup *Curtis Prentiss* · Paul Giamatti *Rick Honeycutt* · Kristen Wiig *Mandy Riddle* · David Hornsby *Kenny Owenby* ■ *Dir/Scr* Paul Schneider (2)

Pretty in Pink ★★★ 15
Comedy drama   1986 · US · Colour · 92min

Molly Ringwald stars in this Brat Pack take on Cinderella, making a game fist of playing a rebellious teenager from the wrong side of the tracks who meets an up-market designer boy (Andrew McCarthy). Ringwald, all flaming red hair and grungy attire, brings a touch of charisma to the well-worn theme, and she receives sterling support from Harry Dean Stanton as her deadbeat dad. It belts along pleasingly enough, but is too hackneyed to be entirely successful. **SH** Swearing. **DVD**

Molly Ringwald *Andie Walsh* • Andrew McCarthy *Blane McDonough* • James Spader *Steff McKee* • Jon Cryer *Phil "Duckie" Dale* • Harry Dean Stanton *Jack Walsh* • Annie Potts *Iona* • Jim Haynie *Donnelly* ■ *Dir* Howard Deutch • *Scr* John Hughes

Pretty Maids All in a Row ★
Black comedy thriller 1971 · US · Colour · 91min

Roger Vadim made his Hollywood debut with this dire sex satire. It also poses itself as a thriller, starting with a girl found murdered in a high school and suspicion initially falling on a shy, introverted boy. But then Rock Hudson takes the film over, laughingly playing the school counsellor who advises students on their sex lives. Mainly, though, Vadim just wants his cast of starlets to get their clothes off. Tacky and hopelessly dated. **AT**

Rock Hudson *Michael "Tiger" McDrew* • Angie Dickinson *Miss Smith* • Telly Savalas *Capt Sam Surcher* • John David Carson *Ponce de Leon Harper* • Roddy McDowall *Mr Proffer* • Keenan Wynn *Chief John Poldaski* • James Doohan *Follo* • William Campbell *Grady* ■ *Dir* Roger Vadim • *Scr* Gene Roddenberry, from a novel by Francis Pollini • *Music* Lalo Schifrin

Pretty Persuasion ★★★ 18
Black comedy drama 2005 · US · Colour · 104min

Evan Rachel Wood is a poisonously manipulative Beverly Hills student, an aspiring actress who exacts a terrible revenge on her drama teacher Ron Livingston after he sacks her from the school play. Director Marcos Siega's movie can't quite make up its mind what it thinks about the Machiavellian heroine, whose soul is corrupted by her foul-mouthed, racist father (James Woods). But, despite the occasional abrupt shift of tone, this film is stylishly shot, with Wood's performance providing further evidence of her talent. **LF** **DVD**

Evan Rachel Wood *Kimberly Joyce* • Ron Livingston *Percy Anderson* • James Woods *Hank Joyce* • Jane Krakowski *Emily Klein* • Elisabeth Harnois *Brittany Wells* • Selma Blair *Grace Anderson* • Adi Schnall *Randa Azzouni* • Stark Sands *Troy* • Danny Comden *Roger* • Jaime King *Kathy Joyce* ■ *Dir* Marcos Siega • *Scr* Skander Halim

Pretty Poison ★★★ 15
Psychological crime thriller 1968 · US · Colour · 84min

In one of his more subtle variations on his Norman Bates character in *Psycho*, Anthony Perkins plays a young man, just released on parole from reform school, who hooks up with high school cheerleader Tuesday Weld to destroy a polluting factory. Shot on a low budget, and influenced by the French New Wave, Noel Black's first feature remained pretty poisonous at the box office, though it later gained cult status. **RB** **DVD**

Anthony Perkins *Dennis Pitt* • Tuesday Weld *Sue Ann Stepanek* • Beverly Garland *Mrs Stepanek* • John Randolph *Azenauer* • Ken Kercheval *Harry Jackson* ■ *Dir* Noel Black • *Scr* Lorenzo Semple Jr, from the novel *She Let Him Continue* by Stephen Geller

Pretty Polly ★★
Comedy drama 1967 · UK · Colour · 99min

This is a soft-centred adaptation of Noël Coward's harder-edged short story about the transformation from ugly duckling to swan of diffident young Hayley Mills, thanks to the accidental death of her wealthy aunt (Brenda de Banzie) in the swimming pool of a Singapore hotel. Mills is agreeably fresh, and Guy Green's direction of this pleasantly escapist film is helped by some attractive locations, Trevor Howard as Polly's unconventional uncle, and Indian actor Shashi Kapoor as the romantic interest. **RK**

Hayley Mills *Polly Barlow* • Trevor Howard *Robert Hook* • Shashi Kapoor *Amaz* • Brenda de Banzie *Mrs Innes-Hook* • Dick Patterson *Rick Preston* • Patricia Routledge *Miss Gudgeon* ■ *Dir* Guy Green • *Scr* Keith Waterhouse, Willis Hall, from the story *Pretty Polly Barlow* by Noël Coward

Pretty Village Pretty Flame ★★★★ 18
War drama 1996 · Ser · Colour · 123min

Set at the height of the Bosnian conflict, this is the sobering story of how the friendship between a Serb and a Muslim was shattered by civil war. The film was attacked for appearing pro-Serbian, yet, as the Serb's unit is trapped inside the Tito-inspired tunnel that stood for unity and progress, it's clear that no one is immune from blame. Crisply acted and tautly directed, the action is strewn with striking scenes, but nothing can prepare you for the horror of the final image. **DP** Serbo-Croat +subtitles. Violence. **DVD**

Dragan Bjelogrlic *Milan* • Nikola Kojo *Velja Kozic* • Dragan Maksimovic *Petar aka "Professor"* • Velimir Bata Zivojinovic [Bata Zivojinovic] *Gvozden Maksimovic* • Zoran Cvijanovic *"Speedy"* ■ *Dir* Srdjan Dragojevic • *Scr* Vanja Bulic, Srdjan Dragojevic, Nikola Pejakovic, from a war report by Bulic as published in *Duga*

Pretty Woman ★★★★ 15
Romantic comedy 1990 · US · Colour · 114min

Originally meant to be a serious drama (called *$3,000*) about a man buying a prostitute for the night, this turned into a delightful romantic comedy in the hands of Garry Marshall and sent the career of star Julia Roberts into the stratosphere. Co-star Richard Gere didn't do badly either as the tycoon. On screen, they make the "hooker falls for a millionaire in Beverly Hills" Cinderella tale completely plausible, aided by Marshall's glossy direction, the hit-filled soundtrack, a perky script from JF Lawton and hilarious support from Marshall stalwart Hector Elizondo. **JB** Swearing, nudity, a sex scene. **DVD** 🔵

Richard Gere *Edward Lewis* • Julia Roberts *Vivian Ward* • Ralph Bellamy *James Morse* • Laura San Giacomo *Kit De Luca* • Hector Elizondo *Hotel manager* • Jason Alexander *Philip Stuckey* • Alex Hyde-White *David Morse* ■ *Dir* Garry Marshall • *Scr* JF Lawton

Prey ★ 18
Science-fiction horror 1977 · UK · Colour · 77min

An alien in human disguise (Barry Stokes) moves in with a lesbian couple (Sally Faulkner, Glory Annen) to ascertain the protein value of human flesh for a possible invasion. Norman J Warren's uninspired direction makes this already padded mix of madness, cannibalism and sexual titillation. A sluggish, gruelling slog. **AJ** **DVD**

Barry Stokes *Anders* • Sally Faulkner *Josephine* • Glory Annen *Jessica* • Sandy Chinney *Sandy* ■ *Dir* Norman J Warren • *Scr* Max Cuff, from a story by Quinn Donoghue

A Price above Rubies ★★★ 15
Drama 1997 · US/Fr/UK · Colour · 116min

This fierce assault on today's orthodox Jewish community in Brooklyn features a sympathetic performance by Renee Zellweger as a young Hasidic woman locked into a world where rules are laid down by men. As feminist propaganda, the film overdoes the hypocrisy and bigotry; as a portrait of a religious community, it is unconvincing and provides little insight; but, as a fictional tale of repression and liberation, it makes you want to cheer. **TH** Swearing, sex scenes.

Renee Zellweger [Renée Zellweger] *Sonia Horowitz* • Christopher Eccleston *Sender* • Allen Payne *Ramon* • Glenn Fitzgerald *Mendel* • Julianna Margulies *Rachel* • Kim Hunter *Rebbitzn* • John Randolph *Rebbe* ■ *Dir/Scr* Boaz Yakin

The Price of Desire ★★ 12A
Period drama based on a true story 2015 · Fr · Colour · 108min

Irish architect and feminist icon Eileen Gray is a fascinating character, ill-served by this precious biopic from Mary McGuckian. Presuming too much knowledge, she plunges into the art world of 1920s Paris, as Gray (Orla Brady) falls in love under the jaundiced gaze of architectural titan Le Corbusier (Vincent Perez). But rather than

exploring the ideas and emotions of a real woman, McGuckian has her caricatures spout pithy epigrams about life, love and art. There's evocative use of Côte d'Azur locations but key episodes feel rushed. **DP** Brief nudity, sexual references.

Orla Brady *Eileen Gray* • Vincent Perez *Le Corbusier* • Francesco Scianna *Jean Badovici* • Alanis Morissette *Marisa Damia* • Dominique Pinon *Fernand Leger* • David Herlihy *Aristotle Onassis* ■ *Dir/Scr* Mary McGuckian

Price of Glory ★★ 15
Sports drama 2000 · US · Colour · 112min

Had sportswriter Phil Berger based this screenplay on the bouts he'd witnessed rather than the movies he'd seen, this might have been a contender. But with every pug being a caricature and almost every situation (in and out of the ring) being a cliché, it's hard to go the distance with the story of a nearly man living out his dreams through his kids. Jimmy Smits pulls no punches as the father who makes boxing glory his sole priority and Ron Perlman scores points as a seedy promoter. **DP** **DVD**

Jimmy Smits *Arturo Ortega* • Ron Perlman *Nick Everson* • Jon Seda *Sonny Ortega* • Clifton Collins Jr *Jimmy Ortega* • Maria Del Mar *Rita Ortega* ■ *Dir* Carlos Avila • *Scr* Phil Berger

The Price of Passion ★★★ 15
Drama 1988 · US · Colour · 100min

Also known as *The Good Mother*, this is a rather depressing tale about a divorced mother (Diane Keaton) who finds love and sexual fulfilment in the arms of Liam Neeson, only to have her ex-husband sue her for custody of their daughter because he is convinced Neeson is sexually abusing the child. There are good performances and it's an interesting subject, but the result is rather dreary drama. **JB** Swearing, nudity. **DVD**

Diane Keaton *Anna Dunlap* • Liam Neeson *Leo Cutter* • Jason Robards Jr [Jason Robards] *Muth* • Ralph Bellamy *Grandfather* • Teresa Wright *Grandmother* • James Naughton *Brian Dunlap* • Asia Vieira *Molly* • Joe Morton *Frank Williams* ■ *Dir* Leonard Nimoy • *Scr* Michael Bortman, from the novel *The Good Mother* by Sue Miller

Priceless ★★★ 12
Romantic comedy 2006 · Fr · Colour · 101min

Audrey Tautou conjures the spirit of Audrey Hepburn in this frothy French farce that bears more than a passing resemblance to *Breakfast at Tiffany's*. Pierre Salvadori's film harks back to an age when the French Riviera was only for the elite and even gold-diggers had a bit of class. Tautou is the material girl who is determined to snare a wealthy older man, while Gad Elmaleh is the humble barman she beds, after mistaking him for a wealthy hotel guest. He is smitten but she soon dumps him, and his extravagant attempts to win her affections cause him to blow his life's savings, before deciding to do a bit of gold-digging of his own. Tautou is a little too sweet to be entirely convincing as the temptress, but Elmaleh is a deadpan delight as the unlikely gigolo. **JF** French +subtitles. Swearing, sexual references. **DVD**

Audrey Tautou *Irène* • Gad Elmaleh *Jean* • Marie-Christine Adam *Madeleine* • Vernon Dobtcheff *Jacques* • Jacques Spiesser *Gilles* • Annelise Hesme *Agnès* ■ *Dir* Pierre Salvadori • *Scr* Pierre Salvadori, Benoît Graffin

Prick Up Your Ears ★★★★★ 18
Biographical drama 1987 · UK · Colour · 105min

The life of doomed gay British playwright Joe Orton gets a tart, no-holds-barred, sure-handed telling by director Stephen Frears, with Gary Oldman giving a marvellous performance as the promiscuous cheeky chappy. Alan Bennett's wonderful script is full of hilarious one-liners, and is more interesting when focusing on what it meant to be homosexual in the 1960s rather than on Orton's lauded theatrical achievements.

Yet, with Alfred Molina also a joy as his jealous lover, this is still British film-making at its finest. **AJ** Violence, swearing, sex scenes. **DVD**

Gary Oldman *Joe Orton* • Alfred Molina *Kenneth Halliwell* • Vanessa Redgrave *Peggy Ramsay* • Wallace Shawn *John Lahr* • Lindsay Duncan *Anthea Lahr* • Julie Walters *Elsie Orton* • Frances Barber *Leonie Orton* ■ *Dir* Stephen Frears • *Scr* Alan Bennett, from the biography by John Lahr

Pride ★★ PG
Biographical sports drama 2007 · US · Colour · 104min

Clichéd though it may be, this biopic of black swimming coach Jim Ellis manages to inspire, if not exactly entertain, thanks to the bullish performances of Terrence Howard and Bernie Mac. Struggling to get a job in mid-1970s Philadelphia, ex-college swimming star Ellis (Howard) locks horns with caretaker Elston (Mac) when he is sent to decommission a run-down sports facility. A showdown with a drug dealer fleshes out the slender storyline, but it's too deliberate to get you cheering on these genial underdogs. **DP** **DVD**

Terrence Howard *Jim Ellis* • Bernie Mac *Elston* • Kimberly Elise *Sue Davis* • Tom Arnold *Bink* ■ *Dir* Sunu Gonera • *Scr* Kevin Michael Smith, Michael Gozzard, J Mills Goodloe, Norman Vance Jr, from a story by Smith, Gozzard

Pride ★★★★ 15
Comedy drama based on a true story 2014 · UK · Colour · 115min

An unlikely union between the more politically conscious gays and lesbians of London and a depressed mining town in Wales is the subject of this joyous and often riotously funny British comedy. The year is 1984, and prime minister Margaret Thatcher is putting ever more pressure on the striking miners, so gay activist Ben Schnetzer rallies a ragtag group of friends to collect money for the cash-strapped workers. A broad, light and characterful romp, this smuggles in some serious points about unity and togetherness in between the ribald one-liners. **DW** **DVD** 🔵

Bill Nighy *Cliff* • Imelda Staunton *Hefina* • Dominic West *Jonathan* • Paddy Considine *Dai* • Andrew Scott *Gethin* • Joseph Gilgun [Joe Gilgun] *Mike* • Freddie Fox *Jeff* ■ *Dir* Matthew Warchus • *Scr* Stephen Beresford

Pride and Glory ★★★ 15
Crime drama 2007 · US/Ger · Colour · 124min

NYPD blue turns a murky shade of grey in this wintry crime thriller about police corruption and family loyalty. After four officers are gunned down on duty, semi-retired police detective Edward Norton returns to the front line but soon finds himself mired in a conspiracy that involves fellow policemen, including his brother-in-law Colin Farrell. Gavin O'Connor's film proves a competent addition to the cop thriller genre – without being particularly original. That's mainly because Norton and Farrell's good cop/bad cop pairing fails to spark and the screenplay's serious intent doesn't deliver. As a whole, it hovers somewhere between gritty and silly. **JR** **DVD** 🔵

Edward Norton *Ray Tierney* • Colin Farrell (2) *Jimmy Egan* • Noah Emmerich *Francis Tierney Jr* • Jon Voight *Francis Tierney Sr* • Jennifer Ehle *Abby Tierney* • John Ortiz (1) *Ruben Santiago* • Shea Whigham *Kenny Dugan* • Frank Grillo *Eddie Carbone* ■ *Dir* Gavin O'Connor • *Scr* Gavin O'Connor, Joe Carnahan, from a story by Gavin & Gregory O'Connor, Robert Hopes

Pride and Prejudice ★★★★ U
Period romantic drama 1940 · US · BW · 112min

This Jane Austen adaptation, co-scripted by novelist Aldous Huxley, is set half a century in advance of the book's period, to take advantage of more glamorous costumes – a very MGM trick. Greer Garson is a sprightly, lively Elizabeth Bennet, but Laurence Olivier, though dashing and handsome, seems slightly uncomfortable as Darcy. The supporting cast, notably Mary Boland's very funny Mrs Bennet and Maureen O'Sullivan as a very sweet-natured Jane, is utterly superb, and the art direction won an Oscar. TS

Greer Garson *Elizabeth Bennet* • Laurence Olivier *Mr Darcy* • Mary Boland *Mrs Bennet* • Edna May Oliver *Lady Catherine de Bourgh* • Maureen O'Sullivan *Jane Bennet* • Ann Rutherford *Lydia Bennet* • Frieda Inescort *Miss Caroline Bingley* • Edmund Gwenn *Mr Bennet* • Karen Morley *Charlotte Lucas* • Heather Angel *Kitty Bennet* • Marsha Hunt *Mary Bennet* • Bruce Lester *Mr Bingley* ■ *Dir* Robert Z Leonard • *Scr* Aldous Huxley, Jane Murfin, from the play by Helen Jerome, from Jane Austen's novel • *Art Directors* Cedric Gibbons, Paul Groesse • *Costume Designer* Adrian

Pride & Prejudice ★★★★ U

Period romantic drama
2005 · US/UK/Fr · Colour · 121min

Debut director Joe Wright does a beautiful job with his gutsy and less idealised interpretation of Jane Austen's classic novel. Focusing on wit and intellect rather than heaving bosoms, he presents his Regency heroine Elizabeth Bennet (Keira Knightley) as a waspish tomboy, able to tie sullen bachelor Darcy's (Matthew MacFadyen) heart in knots with her spirited ripostes. Knightley is a memorable leading lady, as delightful to watch as her well-shot surroundings, but mournful MacFadyen lacks magnetism. The support cast is strong, too, with Brenda Blethyn and Donald Sutherland particularly exceptional as Lizzie's marriage-obsessed mother and doting father. SF *DVD* *BL*

Keira Knightley *Elizabeth Bennet* • Matthew Macfadyen *Mr Darcy* • Brenda Blethyn *Mrs Bennet* • Donald Sutherland *Mr Bennet* • Tom Hollander *Mr Collins* • Rosamund Pike *Jane Bennet* • Jena Malone *Lydia Bennet* • Judi Dench *Lady Catherine de Bourg* • Penelope Wilton *Mrs Gardiner* • Carey Mulligan *Kitty Bennet* ■ *Dir* Joe Wright • *Scr* Deborah Moggach, from the novel by Jane Austen

Pride and Prejudice and Zombies ★★★★ 15

Period action horror 2015 · US · Colour · 103min

Jane Austen's celebrated classic about Regency social manners and aristocratic romance meets George A Romero-style zombies in this consistently engaging mash-up based on Seth Grahame-Smith's 2009 parody novel. The story remains anchored by Austen's original hero/heroine, but here feisty Elizabeth Bennet (pitch-perfect Lily James) is a martial arts expert, who joins Colonel Darcy (deadpan Sam Riley) in fighting off the zombie menace while figuring out her own conflicted feelings. Director Burr Steer's perversely clever construct is superbly cast while polished production values add enormously to the film's success. AJ Violence. *DVD* *BL* *CS*

Lily James *Elizabeth Bennet* • Sam Riley *Mr Darcy* • Lena Headey *Lady Catherine de Bourgh* • Matt Smith *Parson Collins* • Jack Huston *Mr Wickham* • Douglas Booth *Mr Bingley* • Charles Dance *Mr Bennet* • Sally Phillips *Mrs Bennet* ■ *Dir* Burr Steers • *Scr* Burr Steers, David O Russell, from Seth Grahame-Smith's novel, from characters by Jane Austen • *Cinematographer* Remi Adefarasin

The Pride and the Passion ★★★★ PG

Epic period adventure
1957 · US · Colour · 129min

Much abused in its day, this is a splendidly calculated spectacle, with a priceless, eye-catching cast, though criticism at the time centred on Frank Sinatra's Spanish accent (excellent) and Cary Grant's British prissiness (unavoidable). Flamenco queen Sophia Loren provides the glamour, and the Franz Planer photography is remarkable. No expense was spared by producer/director Stanley Kramer to tell the tale of a guerrilla band dragging a massive cannon across the Iberian Peninsula in 1810 to blow up a French stronghold. Sincere and brutal. TS *DVD*

Cary Grant *Capt Anthony Trumbull* • Frank Sinatra *Miguel* • Sophia Loren *Juana* • Theodore Bikel *General Jouvet* • John Wengraf *Sermaine* •

Jay Novello *Ballinger* • José Nieto *Carlos* ■ *Dir* Stanley Kramer • *Scr* Edna Anhalt, Edward Anhalt, from the novel *The Gun* by CS Forester

The Pride of St Louis ★★★ U

Sports biography 1952 · US · BW · 92min

One of the most likeable baseball biopics, this is the tale of pitcher Dizzy Dean, a witty and talented player elevated to his sport's Hall of Fame. He is expertly played by the versatile Dan Dailey, an often underrated, clever and skilful screen actor who is better remembered for his work in musicals, but who began and ended his screen career in dramas. TS

Dan Dailey *Dizzy Dean* • Joanne Dru *Patricia Nash Dean* • Richard Hylton *Johnny Kendall* • Richard Crenna *Paul Dean* • Hugh Sanders *Horst* • James Brown (3) *Moose* ■ *Dir* Harmon Jones • *Scr* Herman J Mankiewicz, from a story by Guy Trosper

Pride of the Blue Grass ★★ U

Drama 1954 · US · Colour · 70min

Director William Beaudine's career spanned Mary Pickford silents through the television series *Lassie* to such bizarre projects as *Billy the Kid vs Dracula*, and his reputation for efficiency and lack of artistic pretention gained him plenty of work, albeit variable in quality as well as content. This enjoyable, sentimental tale features Lloyd Bridges as a stableman who spots racing potential in a horse owned by Vera Miles. JG

Lloyd Bridges *Jim* • Vera Miles *Linda* • Margaret Sheridan *Helen* • Arthur Shields *Wilson* ■ *Dir* William Beaudine • *Scr* Harold Shumate, from his story

Pride of the Bowery ★★ U

Comedy 1941 · US · BW · 60min

Also known as *Here We Go Again*, this is a sprightly comedy drama that reunites several of the gang that had first appeared on screen as the Dead End Kids, and would later be known as the Bowery Boys. It's pretty standard B-movie fare, with the kids befriending a boxer while staying at a training camp run by a welfare charity. Wise-cracking series regular Leo Gorcey is as rough-and-ready as ever, and he's well served by a cast that includes his brother David. DP

Leo Gorcey *Muggs Maloney* • Bobby Jordan *Danny* • Donald Haines *Skinny* • Carleton Young *Norton* • Kenneth Howell *Al* • David Gorcey *Peewee* • Sunshine Morrison ["Sunshine Sammy" Morrison] *Scruno* ■ *Dir* Joseph H Lewis • *Scr* George Plympton, William Lively, from the story by Steven Clensos

The Pride of the Clan ★★★

Silent drama 1917 · US · BW · 84min

Mary Pickford later admitted her Scottish accent was dreadful, so it's just as well this was a silent. Pickford plays a fisherman's daughter who becomes head of her clan after her father drowns at sea. She and Matt Moore are sweethearts, but their romance is threatened when it turns out he is the son of the countess Kathryn Browne Decker. Maurice Tourneur directs with the kind of conviction that pleased Pickford's legion of fans. TH

Mary Pickford *Marget MacTavish* • Matt Moore *Jamie Campbell* • Warren Cook *Robert, Earl of Dunstable* • Kathryn Browne Decker *Countess of Dunstable* ■ *Dir* Maurice Tourneur • *Scr* Elaine Sterne, Charles E Whittaker

Pride of the Marines ★★

Biographical drama 1945 · US · BW · 119min

John Garfield gives a convincing performance as real-life marine and war hero Al Schmid who is blinded in the battle against Japanese forces at Guadalcanal in 1942 and dreads going home because he "don't want nobody to be a seeing-eye dog for me". Eleanor Parker is the girlfriend he married on the eve of war and Rosemary DeCamp is the nurse who gets him through the crisis. Designed to give comfort and even inspiration to returning war veterans,

it's well meaning and upbeat, but often grossly oversentimental. AT

John Garfield *Al Schmid* • Eleanor Parker *Ruth Hartley* • Dane Clark *Lee Diamond* • John Ridgely *Jim Merchant* • Rosemary DeCamp *Virginia Pfeiffer* • Ann Doran *Ella Merchant* • Warren Douglas *Kebabian* ■ *Dir* Delmer Daves • *Scr* Albert Maltz, Marvin Borowsky, from a story by Roger Butterfield

The Pride of the Yankees ★★★★

Sports biography 1942 · US · BW · 122min

Lou Gehrig played 2,130 consecutive games for the New York Yankees, becoming one of baseball's immortals. Not bad for a tenement kid who only began playing professionally because his mother needed an operation. There's not a lot of sporting action in Sam Wood's movingly inspirational biopic, as the tale concentrates on the romance between Gary Cooper and Teresa Wright, and there's drama aplenty as "Iron Horse" battles the neurological condition that has since become known as Lou Gehrig's disease. Coop gives a typically sympathetic performance. DP

Gary Cooper *Lou Gehrig* • Teresa Wright *Eleanor Gehrig* • Walter Brennan *Sam Blake* • Babe Ruth ■ *Dir* Sam Wood • *Scr* Jo Swerling, Herman J Mankiewicz, from a story by Paul Gallico

Priest ★★★★ 15

Drama 1994 · UK · Colour · 104min

Antonia Bird's timely and compassionate portrait of a gay priest, struggling to live up to his vows is wryly written by *Cracker* creator Jimmy McGovern, and is a biting indictment of a religion that preaches love and forgiveness yet shuns another human for not conforming. A sensitive, if harrowing, tale of lives needlessly destroyed by hypocrisy, it pulls no punches dealing with the subjects of incest and homosexuality, and contains an unforgettably moving finale. Linus Roache gives an amazing performance as the torn cleric. AJ Sex scenes, nudity.

Linus Roache *Father Greg Pilkington* • Tom Wilkinson *Father Matthew Thomas* • Robert Carlyle *Graham* • Cathy Tyson *Maria Kerrigan* • James Ellis *Father Ellerton* • Lesley Sharp *Mrs Unsworth* • Robert Pugh *Mr Unsworth* ■ *Dir* Antonia Bird • *Scr* Jimmy McGovern

Priest ★★ 12

Action horror thriller 2010 · US · Colour · 83min

Loosely based on a cult South Korean graphic novel, director Scott Stewart's blend of gothic horror, sci-fi western and existential drama is a dourly humourless, futuristic farrago. Paul Bettany is the titular man of the cloth who breaks his vows to rescue a relative from the fangs of eyeless ghouls while running afoul of a corrupt theocracy. The mood attempted here is supernatural Sergio Leone with a Vietnam veteran analogy; sadly, the result on screen is a post-apocalypse jumble. At least the bombastic score from Christopher Young (*Hellraiser*) moves things along. AJ Violence, brief swearing. *DVD* *BL* *3D*

Paul Bettany *Priest* • Karl Urban *Black Hat* • Cam Gigandet *Hicks* • Maggie Q *Priestess* • Lily Collins *Lucy Pace* • Stephen Moyer *Aaron Pace* • Christopher Plummer *Monsignor Orelas* • Mädchen Amick *Shannon Pace* ■ *Dir* Scott Stewart • *Scr* Cory Goodman, from the series of graphic novels by Hyung Min-woo • *Music* Christopher Young

Priest of Love ★★ 15

Biographical drama 1981 · UK · Colour · 94min

Christopher Miles directs this biopic of the novelist DH Lawrence, dealing with his early life (in flashback) and the controversy his novels caused in England, bringing about his various exiles - to New Mexico and Provence where he coughs himself to death. The locations are often lavish but the movie feels puny, mainly due to Ian McKellen's pedantic, archly theatrical performance. Janet Suzman plays his German wife and there's a clutch of distracting cameos. AT *DVD*

Ian McKellen *DH Lawrence* • Janet Suzman *Frieda Lawrence* • Ava Gardner *Mabel Dodge Luhan* • Penelope Keith *Honorable Dorothy Brett* • Jorge Rivero *Tony Luhan* • Maurizio Merli *Angelo Ravagli* • John Gielgud *Herbert G Muskett* • Sarah Miles *Actress* ■ *Dir* Christopher Miles • *Scr* Alan Plater, from the book by Harry T Moore

The Priest's Wife ★★

Comedy 1970 · It/Fr · Colour · 103min

It's hard to convey to an Anglo-Saxon audience how controversial this title - *La Moglie del Prete* - would be to Italians. Singer Sophia Loren, therefore, should know better than to try to persuade priest Marcello Mastroianni out of his vows in order to wed and bed her. What sounds like a promising sex comedy turns out to be a wordy bore, and quite an unworthy vehicle for the two stars. The couple have little to do but bicker and argue, and what passes for humour falls very flat indeed. For some perverse artistic reason, director Dino Risi filmed this in deliberately muted colours. TS Italian dubbed.

Sophia Loren *Valeria Billi* • Marcello Mastroianni *Don Mario* • Venantino Venantini *Maurizio* • Jacques Stany *Jimmy Guitar* • Pippo Starnazza *Valeria's father* ■ *Dir* Dino Risi • *Scr* Ruggero Maccari, Bernardino Zapponi, from a story by Maccari, Dino Risi, Zapponi

Primal ★★ 18

Horror 2010 · Aus · Colour · 80min

Backpackers in the outback are turned into cannibal zombie killers in this silly Oz horror about an ancient evil lurking among lost Aborigine cave paintings. Slickly put together, it's a pretty pointless exercise in latex appliances that rolls through all the standard clichés, as its bickering, barely likeable characters are turned, one by one, into monsters. Not a patch on the best Oz horror, like *Wolf Creek*, *Primal's* black-humoured silliness only manages to raise the odd chuckle. *Picnic at Hanging Rock* was never like this... JR Violence, swearing, nudity. *DVD*

Zoe Tuckwell-Smith *Anja* • Wil Traval *Dace* • Krew Boylan *Mel* • Lindsay Farris *Chad* ■ *Dir* Josh Reed • *Scr* Josh Reed, from a story by Nigel Christensen

Primal Fear ★★★★ 18

Courtroom thriller 1996 · US · Colour · 125min

When hotshot lawyer Richard Gere takes on the high-profile case of bewildered altar boy Edward Norton, accused of murdering an archbishop, his cut-and-dried life begins to unravel. Having squared up to state prosecutor Laura Linney, who just happens to be his ex-girlfriend, Gere begins to suspect that still waters run deep in his seemingly angelic client. The movie brims with humour and excitement, while the performances crackle with energy. AJ Swearing, violence, a sex scene. *DVD*

Richard Gere *Martin Vail* • Laura Linney *Janet Venable* • John Mahoney *DA John Shaughnessy* • Alfre Woodard *Judge Miriam Shoat* • Frances McDormand *Dr Molly Arrington* • Edward Norton *Aaron Stampler* • Terry O'Quinn *Assistant DA Bud Yancy* ■ *Dir* Gregory Hoblit • *Scr* Steve Shagan, Ann Biderman, from the novel by William Diehl

Primary Colors ★★★★ 15

Political comedy drama
1998 · US · Colour · 137min

John Travolta is convincing as a womanising senator running for president in this smart and witty satire, written by Elaine May and directed by her frequent partner, Mike Nichols. Adapted from the novel by Joe Klein, it has some great, cynical set pieces while, as the combative wife, Emma Thompson gives as good as she gets. Both leads turn in accomplished performances, but they're almost outshone by Kathy Bates as the future president's lesbian hatchet woman. This is politics with an all-too-human face. TH Swearing. *DVD*

John Travolta *Governor Jack Stanton* • Emma Thompson *Susan Stanton* • Billy Bob Thornton *Richard Jemmons* • Adrian Lester *Henry Burton* • Maura Tierney *Daisy* • Paul Guilfoyle (2) *Howard Ferguson* • Larry Hagman *Governor Fred Picker* • Kathy Bates *Libby Holden* • Diane Ladd *Mamma*

Stanton • Rob Reiner *Izzy Rosenblatt* ■ *Dir* Mike Nichols • *Scr* Elaine May, from the novel *Primary Colors: a Novel of Politics* by Anonymous [Joe Klein]

Primary Suspect ★★ 18
Action thriller   2000 · US · Colour · 91min

This able enough police thriller stars William Baldwin as a cop who goes off the deep end when his wife, a fellow cop, is murdered during a drugs raid that goes wrong. Two years on, he gets the opportunity for a little personal payback, but instead finds himself drawn into a deeper conspiracy. Unremarkable, but the performances are solid. JF *DVD*

William Baldwin *Christian Box* • Brigitte Bako *Nikki* • Lee Majors *Lt Blake* • Vincent Castellanos *Reuben* ■ *Dir* Jeff Celentano • *Scr* MF McDowell

Primates of the Caribbean
★ PG
Animated comedy   2012 · Den · Colour · 72min

This Danish tale of mechanical monkey mayhem misfires thanks to charmless characters and flat animation. Beginning poorly with a limp song, the simple family comedy struggles to add interest during its mercifully short running time, as a simian beach cop tries to stop a fellow primate from taking over his home and stealing his childhood sweetheart. The baddie's weapon is a King Kong-sized giant robot, disguised as a Las Vegas-style casino building – the film's only semi-imaginative idea, and it sadly comes to very little. SF *DVD*

JJ Lewis • Rachael Zinn • Anthony Jenkins • John Littlerocks • Phil Meyers ■ *Dir* Jan Rahbek

Prime ★★★ 12
Romantic comedy   2005 · US · Colour · 101min

Uma Thurman is a 30-something divorcee who falls for the younger Bryan Greenberg. However, the real chemistry is between Thurman and Meryl Streep, her therapist who is also Greenberg's mother. While the lovebirds are unaware of this, Streep tries to reconcile her responsibility to her client with her desire for her son to marry a nice Jewish girl. Thurman and Greenberg aren't entirely convincing as a couple, but writer/director Ben Younger aims to uncover deeper truths about relationships and serves up his conclusions with a wickedly deadpan humour. SP Some swearing. *DVD*

Meryl Streep *Lisa Metzger* • Uma Thurman *Rafi Gardet* • Bryan Greenberg *David Bloomberg* • Jon Abrahams *Morris* • Zak Orth *Randall* • Annie Parisse *Katherine* ■ *Dir/Scr* Ben Younger

Prime Cut ★★★ 18
Crime thriller   1972 · US · Colour · 82min

In director Michael Ritchie's sleazy and irreverent crime thriller, Lee Marvin plays a Chicago Mob enforcer sent to Kansas to teach renegade slaughterhouse owner Gene Hackman a lesson. While the engaging quirkiness initially comes thick and fast, Ritchie is unable to sustain the offbeat style for the duration. However, bloody bursts of violent action and great performances help this skewed movie through its rough patches. Look out for Sissy Spacek in her film debut. AJ Swearing, nudity.

Lee Marvin *Nick Devlin* • Gene Hackman *"Mary Ann"* • Sissy Spacek *Poppy* • Angel Tompkins *Clarabelle* • Gregory Walcott *Weenie* • Bob Wilson *Reaper driver* ■ *Dir* Michael Ritchie • *Scr* Robert Dillon

Prime Evil ★ 18
Horror   1988 · US · Colour · 86min

Notorious horror/porno director Roberta Findlay has had a hand in some of the most controversial and reprehensible exploitation movies in film history. This dire Satanist drama isn't one of them. A 14th-century devil cult grants the Parkman family eternal life, which explains why they're now scouring contemporary New York for victims to sacrifice in the name of Lucifer. Although as tedious and amateurish as usual, this doesn't have the offensive shock value of Findlay's "best" work. AJ

William Beckwith *Thomas Seaton* • Christine Moore *Alexandra Parkman* • Tim Gail *Bill King* • Max Jacobs *George Parkman* ■ *Dir* Roberta Findlay • *Scr* Ed Kelleher, Harriette Vidal

The Prime Gig ★★★★ 15
Crime drama   2000 · US · Colour · 93min

Director Gregory Mosher's "cold calling" features an engrossing script plus the high calibre star trio of Vince Vaughn, Ed Harris and Julia Ormond. Vaughn is perfectly cast as a sceptical high-flyer recruited to an organisation selling shares in land containing gold, run by ex-inside trader Harris. Mosher's thoughtful direction makes great use of extended takes to draw us into the tale, Vaughn and Ormond share genuine screen chemistry and Harris, as ever, dominates every moment of screen time. JC *DVD*

Vince Vaughn *Pendelton "Penny" Wise* • Julia Ormond *Caitlin Carlson* • Ed Harris *Kelly Grant* • Rory Cochrane *Joel* • Wallace Shawn *Gene* • George Wendt *Archie* • Stephen Tobolowsky *Mick* ■ *Dir* Gregory Mosher • *Scr* William Wheeler

The Prime Minister ★★ U
Biographical drama   1940 · UK · BW · 109min

The Victorian novelist and prime minister Benjamin Disraeli once said, "Never complain and never explain" but one wonders if he would have kept quiet after seeing this dull-as-ditchwater biopic. John Gielgud is plummy of tone, supercilious of manner and always convincing as the writer persuaded to run for parliament who ends up running the nation and the Empire. But it's a stodgy history lesson and soapy domestic drama, made primarily to remind audiences embroiled in the second year of war of what they were fighting for. AT

John Gielgud *Benjamin Disraeli* • Diana Wynyard *Mary Anne Wyndham-Lewis* • Will Fyffe *Agitator* • Stephen Murray *William E Gladstone* • Fay Compton *Queen Victoria* ■ *Dir* Thorold Dickinson • *Scr* Brock Williams, Michael Hogan

The Prime of Miss Jean Brodie ★★★★★ 15
Period drama   1969 · UK · Colour · 110min

Although Vanessa Redgrave was a hit in the West End version of Muriel Spark's novel, few would argue that the part of liberated Edinburgh schoolmarm Jean Brodie now belongs solely to Maggie Smith. Never have such politically incorrect opinions been expressed with such disarming charm or been received with such trusting innocence. While Smith thoroughly deserved her Oscar, it is somewhat surprising that Celia Johnson was overlooked for her superb performance as the disapproving headmistress. Robert Stephens and Gordon Jackson are also on form as the men in Smith's life, and Pamela Franklin impresses as the pupil who turns Judas. *Crème de la crème*, indeed. DP Brief nudity.

Maggie Smith *Jean Brodie* • Robert Stephens *Teddy Lloyd* • Pamela Franklin *Sandy* • Gordon Jackson *Gordon Lowther* • Celia Johnson *Miss Mackay* • Diane Grayson *Jenny* • Jane Carr (2) *Mary McGregor* • Shirley Steedman *Monica* ■ *Dir* Ronald Neame • *Scr* Jay Presson Allen, from her play, from the novel by Muriel Spark

Primer ★★ 12
Science-fiction thriller
2004 · US · Colour · 73min

A pretentious headache of a movie, this ultra-low-budget film requires complete concentration. Self-taught film-maker Shane Carruth directs himself in the role of one of two boffins who spend their leisure time conducting scientific experiments. While tinkering with their latest project the duo accidentally discovers that it has time-shift capabilities. Though well shot, with an attractive, over-exposed look, it's undone by the tedious plot and droning dialogue. SF *DVD*

Shane Carruth *Aaron* • David Sullivan (3) *Abe* • Casey Gooden *Robert* • Anand Upadhyaya *Phillip* • Carrie Crawford *Kara* ■ *Dir/Scr* Shane Carruth

Primeval ★★ 15
Horror thriller   2007 · US · Colour · 90min

A man-eating, monster croc is on the loose in this toothless creature feature based on the real-life story of Gustave, Africa's biggest crocodile, and a US news network dispatches a Pulitzer Prize-chasing reporter (Dominic Purcell) and his team to catch the beast. Director Michael Katleman uses his South African locations to paint an insultingly facile portrait of the Third World as the real horror show, as machete-wielding warlords slaughter civilians. Giant reptile and liberal handwringing sometimes collide, but this attempt to blend *Jaws* with *Hotel Rwanda* is misguided one. JR In English, Swahili, French. Violence, swearing. *DVD* *BL*

Dominic Purcell *Tim Manfrey* • Brooke Langton *Aviva Masters* • Orlando Jones *Steven Johnson* • Jürgen Prochnow *Jacob Krieg* • Gideon Emery *Matthew Collins* ■ *Dir* Michael Katleman • *Scr* John D Brancato [John Brancato], Michael Ferris

The Primitives ★★ U
Crime drama   1962 · UK · BW · 69min

The Primitives are four jewel thieves – three men led by one woman – posing as entertainers, who draw upon their skill with disguises in their nefarious schemes. Jan Holden is Cheta, well named as the female cat burglar of the team, who becomes an inconvenient love interest. When they rob a London jewellers, the British police spot the unusual thespian quality of the crime and get on their tails. All pretty incredible, yet watchable. JG

Jan Holden *Cheta* • Bill Edwards *Peter* • Rio Fanning *John* • George Mikell *Claude* • Terence Fallon *Sgt Henry* ■ *Dir* Alfred Travers • *Scr* Alfred Travers, Moris Farhi

Primrose Path ★★★
Melodrama   1940 · US · BW · 92min

Determined to escape from the wrong side of the tracks, where her mother is a woman of easy virtue and her father a drunk, Ginger Rogers finds love and respectability with decent Joel McCrea – until he meets her family, that is. Director Gregory La Cava's film was quite daring within the censorious climate of the time, although it compromises its attempt at dramatic realism with a predictably sentimental, romantic outcome. Interesting, though, thanks to the standard of direction and the convincing cast. RK

Ginger Rogers *Ellie May Adams* • Joel McCrea *Ed Wallace* • Marjorie Rambeau *Mamie Adams* • Henry Travers *Gramp* • Miles Mander *Homer Adams* • Queenie Vassar *Grandma* ■ *Dir* Gregory La Cava • *Scr* Allan Scott, Gregory La Cava, from the play by Robert Buckner, Walter Hart, from the novel *February Hill* by Victoria Lincoln

The Prince & Me ★★ PG
Romantic comedy
2004 · US/Can · Colour · 106min

Julia Stiles plays a hard-working undergraduate whose dreams of becoming a doctor are threatened when she falls for a fellow student (Luke Mably), unaware that he's actually the Crown Prince of Denmark. Director Martha Coolidge creates a modern fairy tale that's as cautionary as it is frothy. The likeable performances from Stiles and Mably give this slushy nonsense a certain warmth. A sequel without Julia Stiles went straight to DVD in 2006, while Luke Mably had departed the series by the third film in 2008. SF *DVD*

Julia Stiles *Paige Morgan* • Luke Mably *Prince Edvard/"Eddie"* • Ben Miller *Soren* • James Fox *King Haarald* • Miranda Richardson *Queen Rosalind* • Alberta Watson *Amy Morgan* • John Bourgeois *Ben Morgan* • Eliza Bennett *Princess Arabella* ■ *Dir* Martha Coolidge • *Scr* Jack Amiel, Michael Begler, Katherine Fugate, from a story by Mark Amin, Katherine Fugate

The Prince and the Pauper ★★★ U
Period adventure   1937 · US · BW · 113min

This Warner Bros version of the much-filmed Mark Twain tale about a street urchin who swaps roles with the young

Prince Edward was billed as an Errol Flynn feature, but Flynn doesn't even appear as swashbuckler Miles Hendon until nearly halfway through. The title youngsters are played by the Mauch twins and it's hard to summon up any interest in their adventures. The things that actually give this movie its verve and style are a fabulous score by Erich Wolfgang Korngold and a wonderful supporting cast. TS

Errol Flynn *Miles Hendon* • Claude Rains *Earl of Hertford* • Henry Stephenson *Duke of Norfolk* • Barton MacLane *John Canty* • Billy Mauch *Tom Canty* • Bobby Mauch *Prince Edward Tudor* • Alan Hale *Captain of the Guard* • Eric Portman *First lord* ■ *Dir* William Keighley • *Scr* Laird Doyle, from the play by Catherine Chisholm Cushing, from the novel by Mark Twain

The Prince and the Pauper ★★★ U
Period adventure   1962 · US · Colour · 93min

This is an entertaining American TV-movie version of Mark Twain's classic story about the humble street urchin who trades places with a lookalike prince. The tale had already been told to more lavish effect on the big screen with Errol Flynn and Claude Rains in 1937, and would be made as an extravagant romp with Oliver Reed and Mark Lester in 1977. Here, Donald Houston and company do well enough, while Disney's stamp provides a minimum quality guarantee. PF

Sean Scully *Edward, Prince of Wales/Tom Canty* • Donald Houston *John Canty* • Niall MacGinnis *Father Andrew* • Jane Asher *Lady Jane Grey* • Laurence Naismith *Lord Hertford* ■ *Dir* Don Chaffey • *Scr* Jack Whittingham, from the novel by Mark Twain

The Prince and the Pauper ★★ PG
Period adventure
1977 · Pan/US · Colour · 115min

Oliver Reed, Charlton Heston and Raquel Welch, following on from the success of Richard Lester's two Musketeers films, don costumes once again for another period romp. No expense was spared on production values and the distinguished cast has a fine time hamming things up. Despite the extravagance, it remains a lifeless affair that isn't helped by an unconvincing lead performance from Mark Lester as the prince who changes places with a beggar. JF *DVD*

Mark Lester (2) *Tom Canty/Prince Edward* • Oliver Reed *Miles Hendon* • Raquel Welch *Lady Edith* • Ernest Borgnine *John Canty* • George C Scott *Ruffler* • Rex Harrison *Duke of Norfolk* • David Hemmings *Hugh Hendon* • Charlton Heston *Henry VIII* • Harry Andrews *Hertford* ■ *Dir* Richard Fleischer • *Scr* George MacDonald Fraser, Berta Dominguez, Pierre Spengler, from the novel by Mark Twain

The Prince and the Showgirl ★★★ PG
Romantic comedy   1957 · UK · Colour · 111min

What should have been an explosive pairing of Hollywood's golden girl, Marilyn Monroe, and England's greatest theatre actor, Laurence Olivier, doesn't quite come off, largely owing to the vapidity of the vehicle chosen: a tired Terence Rattigan play, written for the Queen's coronation and already dated before it hit the West End boards. As you would expect, Monroe sparkles, showing a terrific sense of comic timing in a performance of great skill and beauty. Olivier, who also directed, seems overawed, and hampers himself with a Balkan accent that's a cross between Garbo and Bela Lugosi. But Richard Wattis and especially Sybil Thorndike are splendid. TS *DVD*

Marilyn Monroe *Elsie Marina* • Laurence Olivier *Charles, Prince Regent* • Sybil Thorndike *Queen Dowager* • Richard Wattis *Northbrooke* • Jeremy Spenser *King Nicholas* ■ *Dir* Laurence Olivier • *Scr* Terence Rattigan, from his play *The Sleeping Prince* • *Costume Designer* Beatrice Dawson

Prince Avalanche ★★★ 15
Comedy drama   2012 · US · Colour · 89min

This low-key tale is set in Texas in the late 1980s and focuses on two social misfits as they undertake the tedious job of repainting lines in the middle of desolate rural highways. Alvin (Paul Rudd) is a deep thinker, while his girlfriend's brother, Lance (Emile Hirsch), is more concerned with partying and chasing women. The comedy is delicate and understated, relying mostly on the unspoken failings of both men, with Rudd especially convincing as the would-be intellectual trapped in menial labour to support his young family. TeS Sexual references. DVD

Paul Rudd *Alvin* • Emile Hirsch *Lance* ■ *Dir* David Gordon Green • *Scr* David Gordon Green, from the film *Either Way* by Hafsteinn Gunnar Sigurdsson • *Cinematographer* Tim Orr

Prince Charming ★★ PG

Fairy tale comedy   2001 · US · Colour · 87min

In this zestful update of an old fairy-tale favourite, Sean Maguire plays a libidinous medieval prince who's condemned to spend eternity as a frog (along with his squire, Martin Short) unless he can persuade a fair maiden to kiss and then marry him. The pair provide mischievous fun in their short-lived guise as CGI amphibians in modern-day Manhattan, and the energetic pacing and exuberant performances compensate in part for some of the cheesier moments. SF DVD

Martin Short *Rodney* • Christina Applegate *Kate* • Billy Connolly *Harnish* • Bernadette Peters *Margo*/"*Titania*" • Sean Maguire *Prince John* • Andrea Martin *Serena* • Colin Fox *King Leo* • Marcia Bennett *Queen Isabel* ■ *Dir* Allan Arkush • *Scr* Doug Palau

Prince of Darkness ★★ 18

Horror   1987 · US · Colour · 101min

In what is virtually a supernatural remake of his own *Assault on Precinct 13*, director John Carpenter takes one of his sporadic delves into Nigel Kneale sci-fi/horror territory (he even wrote the script as Martin Quatermass) with tedious results. It's old superstitions versus the computer age in an awkward yarn about a weird container full of green liquid in an LA church that contains pure evil. AJ Violence, swearing. DVD

Donald Pleasence *Priest* • Jameson Parker *Brian* • Victor Wong (2) *Professor Birack* • Lisa Blount *Catherine* • Dennis Dun *Walter* • Susan Blanchard *Kelly* • Alice Cooper *Street people leader* ■ *Dir* John Carpenter • *Scr* Martin Quatermass [John Carpenter]

The Prince of Egypt ★★★★ U

Animated biblical drama   1998 · US · Colour · 94min

DreamWorks's animated interpretation of the story of Moses has a visual grandeur that's almost a match for the best of Disney. From its magical opening sequence, showing the baby Moses's journey down the river, to the visually stunning sections involving the parting of the Red Sea and the plagues – the curse on the first born is particularly disturbing – this makes for epic cinema. A host of Hollywood heavyweights provide emotive vocal contributions, enhanced by Stephen Schwartz's stirring, Broadway-style songs (the moving *When You Believe* earned an Oscar). Some may even see it as religious propaganda, but this is still an astonishing achievement. A direct-to-video sequel, *Joseph: King of Dreams*, followed with the voices of Ben Affleck and Mark Hamill. JC DVD

Val Kilmer *Moses* • Ralph Fiennes *Rameses* • Michelle Pfeiffer *Tzipporah* • Sandra Bullock *Miriam* • Jeff Goldblum *Aaron* • Danny Glover *Jethro* • Patrick Stewart *Pharaoh Seti* • Helen Mirren *The Queen* • Steve Martin *Hotep* • Martin Short *Huy* ■ *Dir* Brenda Chapman, Stephen Hickner, Simon Wells • *Scr* Philip LaZebnik • *Music/lyrics* Stephen Schwartz

Prince of Foxes ★★★

Historical drama   1949 · US · BW · 106min

This is a lavish historical pageant about the wicked Borgias, with Orson Welles giving a magnificently over-ripe performance as the machiavellian Cesare Borgia, and Tyrone Power as his loyal aide. Filmed in Florence,

Siena, Venice and San Gimignano by Oscar-nominated cameraman Leon Shamroy, the picture looks handsome, and Welles has a whale of a time stabbing everyone in the back. AT

Tyrone Power *Andrea Corsini* • Orson Welles *Cesare Borgia* • Wanda Hendrix *Camilla Verano* • Everett Sloane *Mario Belli* • Marina Berti *Angela Borgia* ■ *Dir* Henry King • *Scr* Milton Krims, from the novel by Samuel Shellabarger

Prince of Jutland ★ 15

Historical drama   1994 · Den · Colour · 103min

A basic great cast of British thespians back up Christian Bale in this retelling of Shakespeare's *Hamlet*. More medieval Viking than Danish Royal Court, this is a risible and mucky affair, sticking to the nutshell plot (man murders king, marries queen and father's ghost calls on son to avenge) it flails around mixing poor dialogue, laughable fight sequences and worse cinematography. LH DVD

Christian Bale *Amled* • Helen Mirren *Queen Geruth* • Gabriel Byrne *Fenge* • Kate Beckinsale *Ethel* • Steven Waddington *Ribold* • Brian Cox (1) *Aethelwine, Duke of Lindsey* • Brian Glover *Caedmon* ■ *Dir* Gabriel Axel • *Scr* Gabriel Axel, Erik Kjersgaard, from the book *The Denmark Chronicle* by Saxo Grammaticus

The Prince of Pennsylvania ★ 15

Comedy drama   1988 · US · Colour · 89min

This dreadfully unbelievable small-town movie stars Keanu Reeves as a misunderstood loner, whose father (Fred Ward) harbours dreams of being the King of Pennsylvania. Reeves's problems increase when he discovers his mother Bonnie Bedelia in bed with his father's best friend. He seeks solace in Amy Madigan, on feisty form as the hippy owner of a down-town drive-in. A good cast can't rise above the absurdities of the plot. LH

Keanu Reeves *Rupert Marshetta* • Amy Madigan *Carla Headlee* • Bonnie Bedelia *Pam Marshetta* • Fred Ward *Gary Marshetta* • Jeff Hayenga *Jack Sike* • Jay O Sanders *Trooper Joe* ■ *Dir/Scr* Ron Nyswaner

Prince of Persia: the Sands of Time ★★★ 12

Fantasy action adventure   2010 · US · Colour · 111min

After creating a hit franchise based on a theme-park ride with *Pirates of the Caribbean*, producer Jerry Bruckheimer is obviously hoping to work the same magic with this movie based on a video-game title. The eponymous hero is Dastan (Jake Gyllenhaal), a street urchin adopted by a king, who must fight to clear his name when he's framed as a traitor. This leads Dastan to team up with a no-nonsense princess (Gemma Arterton) to protect a magical dagger from the power-mad Nizam (Ben Kingsley). The film coasts by on its Saturday matinée charms and the likeable leads' love/hate chemistry. However, considering the award-winning game series involves nothing but running and jumping, the action scenes here fall surprisingly flat. JR Some violence. DVD Blu

Jake Gyllenhaal *Prince Dastan* • Ben Kingsley *Nizam* • Gemma Arterton *Princess Tamina* • Alfred Molina *Sheikh Amar* • Toby Kebbell *Garsiv* • Richard Coyle *Tus* ■ *Dir* Mike Newell • *Scr* Carlo Bernard, Doug Miro, Boaz Yakin, from a story by Jordan Mechner, based on his video-game series

Prince of Players ★★★

Biographical drama   1955 · US · Colour · 102min

This is a biopic of the American actor Edwin Booth who achieved a sort of notoriety by being the brother of Abraham Lincoln's assassin, John Wilkes Booth. Richard Burton plays Booth the actor and is at his best in the Bardian clips, starting with the time he played Richard III when his father was too drunk to go on. Marriage and extracts from *Hamlet*, *Othello* and *Romeo and Juliet* follow, building up to the Lincoln assassination and the public demonstrations against all actors that apparently followed. AT

Richard Burton *Edwin Booth* • Maggie McNamara *Mary Devlin* • John Derek *John Wilkes Booth* • Raymond Massey *Junius Brutus Booth* • Charles Bickford *Dave Prescott* • Elizabeth Sellars *Asia* ■ *Dir* Philip Dunne • *Scr* Moss Hart, from the biography by Eleanor Ruggles • *Music* Bernard Herrmann

Prince of the City ★★★ 15

Crime drama based on a true story   1981 · US · Colour · 160min

This movie has a marvellously complex plot about a cop who reveals interdepartmental corruption, yet, sadly, it lacks both a star and an audience-friendly running time. Treat Williams, excellent though he is, doesn't have the power to hold the attention, and, despite sterling support from Jerry Orbach and sinister prosecutor James Tolkan, the film's length diminishes its impact. TS Violence, swearing.

Treat Williams *Daniel Ciello* • Jerry Orbach *Gus Levy* • Richard Foronjy *Joe Marinaro* • Don Billett *Bill Mayo* • Kenny Marino *Dom Bando* • Carmine Caridi *Gino Mascone* ■ *Dir* Sidney Lumet • *Scr* Jay Presson Allen, Sidney Lumet, from a book by Robert Daley

The Prince of Thieves ★★ U

Adventure   1948 · US · Colour · 71min

Rarely has Lincoln Green looked as bilious as in this Cinecolor romp. But then, just about everything in Howard Bretherton's Sherwood adventure is off colour. The action centres on Adele Jurgens's reluctance to marry a suitor selected by her father and Jon Hall's bid to ensure that true love wins out. Hall typifies the film's inadvertent tone, which is compounded by Patricia Morison's anaemic Maid Marian. DP

Jon Hall *Robin Hood* • Patricia Morison *Lady Marian* • Alan Mowbray *Friar Tuck* • Michael Duane *Sir Allan Claire* • HB Warner *Gilbert Head* • Syd Saylor *Will Scarlet* ■ *Dir* Howard Bretherton • *Scr* Charles Schnee, Maurice Tombragel

The Prince of Tides ★★★★ 15

Romantic drama   1991 · US · Colour · 126min

Pat Conroy's epic novel about a dysfunctional southern family is deftly translated to the screen under the subtle direction of Barbra Streisand, who also stars as the New York psychiatrist helping Nick Nolte to come to terms with his twin sister's attempted suicide. Nolte is superb as he wrestles with his family's demons, and Streisand sensibly stays on the sidelines. Jason Gould (Streisand's son from her marriage to Elliott Gould) also features as Streisand's on-screen son. JB Violence, swearing, sex scenes. DVD

Nick Nolte *Tom Wingo* • Barbra Streisand *Susan Lowenstein* • Blythe Danner *Sallie Wingo* • Kate Nelligan *Lila Wingo Newbury* • Jeroen Krabbé *Herbert Woodruff* • Melinda Dillon *Savannah Wingo* • George Carlin *Eddie Detreville* • Jason Gould *Bernard Woodruff* • Brad Sullivan *Henry Wingo* ■ *Dir* Barbra Streisand • *Scr* Pat Conroy, Becky Johnston, from the novel by Pat Conroy

Prince Valiant ★★ U

Period adventure   1954 · US · Colour · 100min

This jovial Arthurian spectacle, based on the comic strip by Harold Foster, is in that strange dialect called Hollywood Archaic, a tongue known to no one except Hollywood executives. James Mason plays Sir Brack, a Knight of the Round Table, and Robert Wagner (in his first leading role) is Valiant, the son of a beleaguered Swedish king who arrives in Camelot seeking assistance in the clanking armour and sword department. Janet Leigh swoons whenever Wagner's around, but goodness knows why, considering his terrible wig. AT DVD Blu

Robert Wagner *Prince Valiant* • Janet Leigh *Princess Aleta* • James Mason *Sir Brack* • Debra Paget *Ilene* • Sterling Hayden *Sir Gawain* • Victor McLaglen *Boltar* • Donald Crisp *King Aguar* • Brian Aherne *King Arthur* ■ *Dir* Henry Hathaway • *Scr* Dudley Nichols, from the comic strip by Harold R Foster

Prince Valiant ★★ PG

Period adventure   1997 · Ger/UK/Ire/US · Colour · 87min

Cod-historical hokum derived from the popular US comic strip, in which King Arthur's sword, Excalibur, is stolen by marauding Vikings. Things go from bad to Norse when the legendary British symbol falls into the hands of an evil Euro king with designs on Arthur's seat. Fortunately, the heroic Prince Valiant rides to the sword's rescue. The obvious cash restraints plus ham-fisted editing relegate the film to definite B-movie status. DA

Stephen Moyer *Prince Valiant* • Katherine Heigl *Princess Ilene* • Thomas Kretschmann *Thagnar* • Edward Fox *King Arthur* • Udo Kier *Sligon* • Joanna Lumley *Morgan Le Fey* • Ron Perlman *Boltar* • Warwick Davis *Pechet* ■ *Dir* Anthony Hickox • *Scr* Michael Frost Beckner, Anthony Hickox, Carsten Lorenz., from a story by Michael Frost Beckner, from the comic strip by Harold R Foster

The Prince Who Was a Thief ★★

Adventure   1951 · US · Colour · 88min

From the days when Tony Curtis was a tousle-haired idol for teenagers, this *Arabian Nights* nonsense showed him at his athletic, if not dramatic, best. He's a royal baby brought up by kindly thieves who then duels his way to his rightful throne. Perhaps most surprising, this fantasy was adapted from a story by Theodore Dreiser. TH

Tony Curtis *Julna* • Piper Laurie *Tina* • Everett Sloane *Yussef* • Betty Garde *Mirna* • Jeff Corey *Mokar* • Peggie Castle *Princess Yasmin* ■ *Dir* Rudolph Maté • *Scr* Gerald Drayson Adams, Aeneas MacKenzie, from a story in the book *Chains* by Theodore Dreiser

Les Princes ★★★ 15

Drama   1982 · Fr · Colour · 99min

This is the first instalment of Tony Gatlif's Romany trilogy, which was completed by *Latcho Drom* (1993) and *Gadjo Dilo* (1997). The villains of the piece are clearly the gendarmes who harass the despised *gitanes*. But Gatlif isn't blind to the problems caused by the patriarchal conservatism that prompts French Romany Gérard Darmon to disown his wife after discovering she's followed a social worker's advice on birth control. Living in squalor with his octogenarian mother and young daughter, he's bitter and unstable, yet he's every bit as authentic as Jacques Loiseleux's gloomy photography. DP French +subtitles.

Gérard Darmon *Nara* • Muse Dalbray *Nara's grandmother* • Dominique Maurin *Petiton* • Hagop Arslanian *Chico* • Tony Gatlif *Leo* • Tony Librizzi *Tony* • Céline Militon *Zorka* • Concha Tavora *Miralda* ■ *Dir/Scr* Tony Gatlif

The Princess and the Frog ★★★ U

Animated fantasy   2009 · US · Colour · 93min

Disney's trumpeted return to hand-drawn animation is set in New Orleans in the Roaring Twenties, where waitress Tiana (Anika Noni Rose) longs to fulfil a lifelong dream of owning a restaurant. But a witch doctor's curse on playboy Prince Naveen (Bruno Campos) transforms him into a frog, and when Tiana agrees to kiss him she too is changed. Notable for featuring Disney's first African-American cartoon lead, in the shape of the ambitious and hard-working Tiana, the film tweaks the original fairy tale and stretches its premise rather thin. But the zany antics of Tiana's creature pals will get the kids laughing, especially trumpet-playing alligator Louis and Cajun firefly Ray. The animation is also impressive, with vibrant fluorescents for the (fun if scary) French Quarter voodoo scenes and a warm richness for the bayou. AJ DVD Blu

Anika Noni Rose *Tiana* • Bruno Campos *Prince Naveen* • Keith David *Dr Facilier* • Jenifer Lewis *Mama Odie* • Jim Cummings *Ray* • Michael-Leon Wooley *Louis* • John Goodman *Eli "Big Daddy" La Bouff* • Oprah Winfrey *Eudora* ■ *Dir* Ron Clements, John Musker • *Scr* Ron Clements, John Musker, Rob Edwards, from a story by

P

Clements, Musker, Greg Erb, Jason Oremland, from the novel *The Frog Princess* by ED Baker • Music Randy Newman

The Princess and the Goblin ★★★ U

Animated fantasy adventure
1992 · UK/Hun · Colour · 78min

This animated feature film will keep most children happy, although even they won't fail to notice that the drawings are way below the standard of Disney features. Princess Irene enlists the help of her magical great-great-grandmother and miner's son Curdi to prevent a tribe of goblins from capturing the royal palace. With their ugly faces, hatred of poetry and jealousy of humans (because people have toes and they don't), the goblins easily steal the show. DP

Joss Ackland *King* • Claire Bloom *Irene's great great grandmother* • Roy Kinnear *Mump* • Sally Ann Marsh *Princess Irene* • Rik Mayall *Froglip* • Peggy Mount *Goblin Queen* • Peter Murray *Curdi* • Victor Spinetti *Glump* ■ *Dir* Jozsef Gemes • *Scr* Robin Lyons, from the fairy tale by George MacDonald

The Princess and the Pirate ★★★ U

Swashbuckling comedy
1944 · US · Colour · 90min

Comedian Bob Hope, in one of his better vehicles, plays the cowardly "Sylvester the Great Man of Seven Faces", an 18th-century variety artist with an aversion to pirates. Hope is surrounded by superb character actors, and there's a hilarious turn from Walter Brennan, who seems to have based his part on Disney's cartoon dwarf Dopey. Virginia Mayo partners Hope ably, especially when they do their vaudeville number in the splendidly art-directed Bucket of Blood Inn. TS

Bob Hope *Sylvester Crosby/The Great Sylvester* • Virginia Mayo *Princess Margaret* • Walter Brennan *Featherhead* • Walter Slezak *La Roche* • Victor McLaglen *The Hook* • Bing Crosby *Commoner* ■ *Dir* David Butler • *Scr* Don Hartman, Melville Shavelson, Everett Freeman, Allen Boretz, Curtis Kenyon, suggested by a story by Sy Bartlett

The Princess & the Warrior ★★★ 15

Drama   2000 · Ger · Colour · 129min

Director Tom Tykwer bravely drops the pace and stuffs this intense romantic drama with mysterious symbolism, muddled motivations and unresolved incidents. Despite referencing numerous art house icons, this is actually a highly personal piece, hence the setting is Tykwer's home town, Wuppertal. But he spends too much time demonstrating his technical virtuosity to involve us in the tortuous relationship between psychiatric nurse Franka Potente and widowed ex-soldier Benno Fürmann. With its shifting tone and wayward plot, this isn't an easy watch. DP German +subtitles. *DVD*

Franka Potente *Sissi* • Benno Fürmann *Bodo* • Joachim Król *Walter* • Lars Rudolph *Steini* • Melchior Beslon *Otto* ■ *Dir/Scr* Tom Tykwer

The Princess Bride ★★★★ PG

Fantasy adventure   1987 · US · Colour · 94min

Rob Reiner has always been careful to avoid typecasting as a director, so following the warm nostalgia of *Stand by Me* he opted for this curious but charming fable. The film opens with Peter Falk reading the story to the young Fred Savage, and this ironic distancing continues throughout the movie. Although the requisite monsters, giants and sword fights are present and correct for the children, Reiner also ensures there are plenty of quiet chuckles for adults, largely thanks to the eclectic cast. A delight for all. JF *DVD* Blu

Cary Elwes *Westley* • Mandy Patinkin *Inigo Montoya* • Chris Sarandon *Prince Humperdinck* • Christopher Guest *Count Rugen* • Wallace Shawn *Vizzini* • André the Giant *Fezzik* • Fred Savage *Grandson* • Robin Wright *Buttercup, the Princess Bride* • Peter Falk *Grandfather* • Peter Cook

Impressive clergyman • Billy Crystal *Miracle Max, the Wizard* • Mel Smith *Albino* ■ *Dir* Rob Reiner • *Scr* William Goldman, from his novel

Princess Caraboo ★★★ PG

Historical romance   1994 · US · Colour · 92min

Is exotic Phoebe Cates a Javanese princess, washed up on the Devon coastline after escaping from pirates? Or is she really a clever con artist using her suspect credentials to infiltrate the parlours and palaces of 19th-century England? Cates exudes the necessary glamour, but it's Jim Broadbent who nets the biggest laughs, while Kevin Kline (Cates's real-life husband) steals every scene he's in. Based on a true slice of history, Michael Austin's satirical fairy tale is disarming fluff with little more substance than a marshmallow. AJ Swearing.

Phoebe Cates *Princess Caraboo* • Jim Broadbent *Mr Worrall* • Wendy Hughes *Mrs Worrall* • Kevin Kline *Frixos* • John Lithgow *Professor Wilkinson* • Stephen Rea *Gutch* • John Sessions *Prince Regent* • Peter Eyre *Lord Apthorpe* ■ *Dir* Michael Austin • *Scr* Michael Austin, John Wells

The Princess Comes Across ★★★

Romantic comedy mystery
1936 · US · BW · 75min

Carole Lombard is perfectly cast in this combination of romantic comedy and comedy detective thriller, set on board a transatlantic passenger ship, and directed with appropriate zip by William K Howard. Lombard stars as a Brooklyn showgirl with aspirations to be another Garbo. To this end, she poses as a Swedish princess during a sea voyage, but falls in love with ship's musician Fred MacMurray. Together they get caught up in trying to solve the murder of a blackmailing fellow passenger. Delightfully screwy nonsense, harmoniously played by the winning star combination. RK

Carole Lombard *Princess Olga/Wanda Nash* • Fred MacMurray *King Joe Mantell* • Douglass Dumbrille *Paul Musko/Detective Lorel* • Alison Skipworth *Lady Gertrude "Gertie" Allwyn* • George Barbier *Capt Nicholls* • William Frawley *Benton* ■ *Dir* William K Howard • *Scr* Walter DeLeon, Francis Martin, Don Hartman, Frank Butler, from a story by Philip MacDonald, from the novel *A Halakabin* by Louis Lucien Rogger [Laszlo Aigner, Louis Aczel]

The Princess Diaries ★★★ U

Comedy   2001 · US · Colour · 110min

Despite the regality of the title, this is a downmarket comedy with its box-office intentions very much aimed at the pre-teen market. Julie Andrews projects her usual sweet-faced radiance as Queen Clarisse Renaldi of Genovia in another variation on the *Pygmalion* story. The Eliza Doolittle character here is San Francisco schoolgirl Anne Hathaway, who's so clumsy that she's always at the mercy of cheerleader bullies. But when the gauche geek finds out she's next in line to the throne of a small European country, she receives a royal makeover from her new-found grandmother. A wish-fulfilling romance, featuring a performance of class from Andrews. TH *DVD*

Julie Andrews *Queen Clarisse Renaldi* • Anne Hathaway *Mia Thermopolis* • Hector Elizondo *Joe* • Heather Matarazzo *Lilly Moscovitz* • Mandy Moore *Lana Thomas* • Caroline Goodall *Mia's mom, Helen* • Robert Schwartzman *Michael Moscovitz* ■ *Dir* Garry Marshall • *Scr* Gina Wendkos, from the novels by Meg Cabot

The Princess Diaries 2: Royal Engagement ★★ U

Romantic comedy   2004 · US · Colour · 108min

After the cheery feel-good charm of his original rags-to-royal-riches fairy tale, director Garry Marshall should have aimed higher than the feel-okay of this barely amusing follow-up. When Anne Hathaway's grandmother (Julie Andrews) steps down from the Genovian throne, the ancient constitution decrees that Hathaway must be married to be crowned queen. The highlight is Andrews singing on screen for

the first time since her 1997 throat surgery. AJ *DVD*

Anne Hathaway *Mia Thermopolis* • Julie Andrews *Queen Clarisse Renaldi* • Hector Elizondo *Joe* • John Rhys-Davies *Viscount Mabrey* • Heather Matarazzo *Lilly Moscovitz* • Chris Pine *Lord Nicholas Devereaux* • Callum Blue *Lord Andrew Jacoby* • Kathleen Marshall *Charlotte Kutaway* ■ *Dir* Garry Marshall • *Scr* Shonda Rhimes, from a story by Gina Wendkos, Shonda Rhimes, from the novel by Meg Cabot

Princess Mononoke ★★★★ PG

Animated action fantasy
1997/2001 · Jpn · Colour · 128min

This boldly surrealistic and starkly experimental cartoon is beautifully drawn, using the inspiration of classic Japanese artwork, and drums home a modern ecological message with a feminist bias. Set in the 14th century, it's a complicated tale of cursed Prince Ashitaka condemned to roam the land looking for a way to lift the malediction that has given him supernatural gifts. AJ Japanese dubbed. *DVD* Blu

Claire Danes *San, the Princess Mononoke* • Minnie Driver *Eboshi* • Gillian Anderson *Moro* • Billy Crudup *Ashitaka* ■ *Dir* Hayao Miyazaki • *Scr* Neil Gaiman, Hayao Miyazaki, from a story by Miyazaki

The Princess of Montpensier ★★★ 15

Historical romantic drama
2010 · Fr/Ger · Colour · 134min

This lavish period epic is set against the backdrop of the 16th-century French Wars of Religion, although director Bertrand Tavernier is more interested here by the personal entanglements of the titular aristocrat (Mélanie Thierry) than the Machiavellian politics of the era. Although a tad too long, there's enough intrigue – both political and romantic – and dashing swordplay to keep everyone happy. JF French +subtitles. Some sex scenes. *DVD* Blu

Mélanie Thierry *Princess Maris de Montpensier* • Lambert Wilson *Comte de Chabannes* • Grégoire Leprince-Ringuet *Prince de Montpensier* • Gaspard Ulliel *Henri de Guise* • Raphaël Personnaz *Duc d'Anjou* • Anatole de Bodinat *Joyeuse* ■ *Dir* Bertrand Tavernier • *Scr* Bertrand Tavernier, François-Olivier Rousseau, Jean Cosmos, from a short story by Madame de La Fayette • *Cinematographer* Bruno de Keyzer

Princess of the Nile ★★ U

Adventure   1954 · US · Colour · 70min

This is one of those costume pantomimes that 20th Century-Fox used to churn out as insurance against box-office failure elsewhere. Debra Paget is the medieval Egyptian princess who moonlights as an exotic dancer, a move that doesn't endear her to nasty Bedouin invader Michael Rennie. Fortunately Jeffrey Hunter comes to her rescue. Colourful nonsense that looks good but doesn't bear close analysis. TH

Debra Paget *Princess Shalimar/Taura the Dancer* • Jeffrey Hunter *Prince Haidi* • Michael Rennie *Rama Khan* • Dona Drake *Mirva* • Wally Cassell *Goghi* • Edgar Barrier *Shaman* • Michael Ansara *Captain Kral* • Jack Elam *Basra* ■ *Dir* Harmon Jones • *Scr* Gerald Drayson Adams

Princess O'Rourke ★★ U

Romantic comedy   1943 · US · BW · 94min

When ace flyer Robert Cummings and princess Olivia de Havilland fall in love with one another, they cause consternation at diplomatic levels which requires the intervention of President Franklin D Roosevelt. Writer/director Norman Krasna's screenplay for this frothy wartime comedy won an Academy Award, and it offers a few good laughs and attractive star performances, but is no more than a pleasant time-waster. RK

Olivia de Havilland *Princess Maria/Mary Williams* • Robert Cummings *Eddie O'Rourke* • Charles Coburn *Uncle* • Jack Carson *Dave* • Jane Wyman *Jean* • Harry Davenport *Supreme court judge* ■ *Dir/Scr* Norman Krasna

The Princess Yang Kwei Fei ★★★ U

Period romantic drama
1955 · Jpn/HK · Colour · 91min

This colourful period drama was only undertaken with the greatest reluctance by director Kenji Mizoguchi. However, such was his consummate professionalism that he overcame artistic misgivings and chronic health problems to fashion a dramatically involving and visually beguiling tale of court intrigue and familial feuding. Machiko Kyo gives a touching display of naivety and self-sacrificing nobility as the servant who marries one of the last Tang emperors of 8th-century China and remains true to his love from beyond the grave. DP In Japanese. *DVD*

Machiko Kyo *Yang Kwei Fei* • Masayuki Mori *Emperor Hsuan-tsung* • So Yamamura *An Lu-shan* • Sakae Ozawa [Eitaro Ozawa] *Yang Kuo-chung* ■ *Dir* Kenji Mizoguchi • *Scr* Yoshikata Yoda, T'ao Chin, Matsutaro Kawaguchi, Masashige Narusawa, from the poem *Ch'ang Hen Ko* by T'ien Pai Lo

The Principal ★★ 18

Drama   1987 · US · Colour · 105min

This adequate reworking of an overfamiliar tale stars James Belushi as a "problem" teacher whose career seems to have reached rock bottom when he is made principal of the worst school in the neighbourhood. His new charges are an unwholesome mixture of delinquents and drug addicts. Belushi is likeable, but Louis Gossett Jr, as the school's tough-nut security chief, takes the acting honours. The mix of comedy and drama is perhaps hard to take. DA *DVD*

James Belushi *Rick Latimer* • Louis Gossett Jr *Jake Phillips* • Rae Dawn Chong *Hilary Orozco* • Michael Wright *Victor Duncan* • JJ Cohen *"White Zac"* • Esai Morales *Raymi Rojas* ■ *Dir* Christopher Cain • *Scr* Frank Deese

The Principles of Lust ★ 18

Drama   2002 · UK · Colour · 104min

Writer/director Penny Woolcock's grimy social melodrama veers between the ludicrous and the obvious with a spectacularly exploitative dreariness. What should jobless drifter Alec Newman do? Stay as househusband to working mum Sienna Guillory and her son? Or join the uninhibited Marc Warren on the road to excess with pub strippers, high-stakes gambling, amphetamine addiction, juvenile bare-knuckle boxing and group sex? AJ Swearing, sex scenes, violence, drug abuse. *DVD*

Alec Newman *Paul* • Marc Warren (1) *Billy* • Sienna Guillory *Juliette* • Lara Clifton *Hole* • Alexander Popplewell *Harry* • Julian Barratt *Phillip* • Gwyne Hollis *Jude* • Kelli Hollis *Lizzie* ■ *Dir* Penny Woolcock • *Scr* Penny Woolcock, from the unpublished novel by Tim Cooke

Prison ★★★ 18

Horror   1987 · US · Colour · 98min

Renny Harlin's classy direction, some startling make-up effects and atmospheric use of jail locations enliven this low-budget horror. This tale of the ghost of a wrongly executed prisoner on a vengeance spree pays unusual attention to its characters – you wouldn't know it was a scary movie for the first half hour – and when the gruesome fireworks begin, they certainly light up the screen. Decent performances from Viggo Mortensen and Lane Smith compensate for the film's unnecessary abundance of prison clichés. JC *DVD*

Lane Smith *Ethan Sharpe* • Viggo Mortensen *Connie Burke* • Chelsea Field *Katherine Walker* • Lincoln Kilpatrick *Cresus* • André De Shields *Sandor* • Steven Little *Rhino* ■ *Dir* Renny Harlin • *Scr* C Courtney Joyner, from a story by Irwin Yablans

The Prisoner ★★★ U

Psychological drama   1955 · UK · BW · 89min

Alec Guinness reprises his stage role in this adaptation of Bridget Boland's play about a Catholic cardinal's encounter with an official from the totalitarian government

P

that has arrested him. Frequently shown in close-up, Guinness superbly conveys the humility, isolation and commitment of a man who is fighting as much for his flock as for his own survival. Yet, the theatrical direction won't do much to persuade those without religious or political convictions to become involved. DP

Alec Guinness *Carcinal* • Jack Hawkins *Interrogator* • Wilfr d Lawson *Cell warder* • Kenneth Griffith *Secretary* • Jeannette Sterke *Girl* • Ronald Lewis *Warder* ■ *Dir* Peter Glenville • *Scr* Bridget Boland, from her play

Prisoner of Honor ★★★★ PG

Historical drama 1991 · US/UK · Colour · 84min

In this made-for-TV dramatisation of the famous Dreyfus case that obsessed France for more than a decade, Richard Dreyfuss stars as French officer Lieutenant Colonel Picquart, who comes to believe that Dreyfus, a Jewish officer languishing on Devil's Island, was wrongly convicted for treason. Co-executive produced by Dreyfuss and directed by Ken Russell, this boasts a splendid cast. AT

Richard Dreyfuss *Lt Col Picquart* • Oliver Reed *General Boisdeffre* • Peter Firth *Major Henry* • Jeremy Kemp *General DePellieux* • Brian Blessed *General Gonse* • Peter Vaughan *General Mercier* • Kenneth Colley *Captain Alfred Dreyfus* ■ *Dir* Ken Russell • *Scr* Ron Hutchinson

The Prisoner of Second Avenue ★★★ PG

Comedy 1974 · US · Colour · 93min

Working from his own play, Neil Simon unusually fails to strike the right balance between wit and pathos in this strained study of midlife crisis. Jack Lemmon pulls out all the stops as the executive who not only has to cope with being sacked after 22 years, but also with the evident delight with which wife Anne Bancroft embraces her new career at the local TV station. Gene Saks provides stiff support as his brother, while Sylvester Stallone pops up as an innocent bystander suspected of theft. DP

Jack Lemmon *Mel* • Anne Bancroft *Edna* • Gene Saks *Harry* • Elizabeth Wilson *Pauline* • Florence Stanley *Pearl* • Maxine Stuart *Belle* • Sylvester Stallone *Youth in park* • F Murray Abraham *Cab driver* • M Emmet Walsh *Doorman* ■ *Dir* Melvin Frank • *Scr* Neil Simon, from his play

The Prisoner of Shark Island ★★★ U

Historical prison drama 1936 · US · BW · 91min

Dr Samuel Mudd, a Maryland physician, was sentenced to life imprisonment on Shark Island for complicity in the assassination of Abraham Lincoln. John Ford's film about this unfortunate man is part adventure and part penal drama, beginning with John Wilkes Booth's visit to the theatre, where he shoots Lincoln and is injured escaping. Mudd treats Booth's leg and gets thrown into jail, where he helps fight an outbreak of yellow fever. The film, scripted by Nunnally Johnson, has a well-measured anger at the injustice and Warner Baxter's performance as the doctor penalised for his dedication to saving life is persuasive. AT DVD

Warner Baxter *Dr Samuel A Mudd* • Gloria Stuart *Mrs Peggy Mudd* • Joyce Kay *Martha Mudd* • Claude Gillingwater *Colonel Dyer* • Douglas Wood *General Ewing* • John Carradine *Sergeant Rankin* ■ *Dir* John Ford • *Scr* Nunnally Johnson

Prisoner of the Mountains ★★★★ 15

War drama 1996 · Rus/Kaz · Colour · 94min

Inspired by a Tolstoy short story, this was the first fictional film to tackle the Chechen conflict. Having been ambushed on patrol, along with battle-scarred sergeant Oleg Menshikov, rookie private Sergei Bodrov Jr falls for Susanna Mekhralieva, the Muslim warlord's daughter, who is nearly tempted by passion to betray her own people. Exhausting combat stereotypes, director Sergei Bodrov reinforces his pacifist plea by unearthing wit and warmth amid the war's brutal ethnic and political realities. DP Russian +subtitles. Swearing, sexual references, violence.

Oleg Menshikov *Sacha Kostylin* • Sergei Bodrov Jr *Ivan "Vania" Zhilin* • Susanna Mekhralieva *Dina* • Dzhemal Sikharulidze *Abdul-Murat* ■ *Dir* Sergei Bodrov • *Scr* Arif Aliev, Sergei Bodrov, Boris Giller, from an idea by Giller, from the short story *Kavkazsky Plennik (Prisoner of the Caucasus)* by Leo Tolstoy • *Cinematographer* Pavel Lebeshev

Prisoner of War ★

War drama 1954 · US · BW · 80min

Ronald Reagan parachutes behind enemy lines into North Korea and – unbelievably – allows himself to be taken prisoner. His mission is dangerous yet silly: he is there to verify reports that the Communists have been treating their prisoners harshly. This is just about as cretinous as Hollywood's "Red Scare" movies ever got. AT

Ronald Reagan *Web Sloane* • Steve Forrest *Corporal Joseph Robert Stanton* • Dewey Martin *Jesse Treadman* • Oscar Homolka *Colonel Nikita Biroshilov* ■ *Dir* Andrew Marton • *Scr* Allen Rivkin

The Prisoner of Zenda ★★★

Silent swashbuckling adventure
1922 · US · BW · 125min

Rex Ingram directs this silent version of the swashbuckler about the English commoner Rudolf Rassendyll (Lewis Stone), forced to impersonate his lookalike, the kidnapped king of the small kingdom of Ruritania. Not as stalwart or convincing as the later 1937 version, but Alice Terry makes an adorable princess and Stone excels in his dual role. TH

Lewis Stone *Rudolf Rassendyll/King Rudolf* • Alice Terry *Princess Flavia* • Robert Edeson *Col Sapt* • Stuart Holmes *Duke "Black" Michael* • Ramon Samaniegos [Ramon Novarro] *Rupert of Hentzau* ■ *Dir* Rex Ingram (1) • *Scr* Mary O'Hara, from the play by Edward E Rose, from the novel by Anthony Hope • *Cinematographer* John F Seitz

The Prisoner of Zenda ★★★★★ U

Swashbuckling adventure
1937 · US · BW · 101min

This is the first sound version of Anthony Hope's famous novel of derring-do in the mythical kingdom of Ruritania. Producer David O Selznick was determined to make a splash and raised a budget of $1.25 million, a more than generous sum at the time. The cast is top drawer, but director John Cromwell was less than happy with his stars, convinced that Ronald Colman didn't know his lines and that Douglas Fairbanks Jr and David Niven were indulging in too many wild nights. Selznick came down in favour of his stars and, with production nearly complete, he removed Cromwell and hired George Cukor to shoot some of the final scenes as well as using WS Van Dyke to do the action sequences, both without credit. There's no evidence of the behind-the-scenes crises, however, as the picture is seamlessly enjoyable, with Colman typically assured in the dual role of king and commoner. But it's Fairbanks Jr's swaggering turn that gives this swashbuckler its five-star status. DP

Ronald Colman *Rudolf Rassendyll/King Rudolf V* • Madeleine Carroll *Princess Flavia* • Douglas Fairbanks Jr *Rupert of Hentzau* • Mary Astor *Antoinette De Mauban* • C Aubrey Smith *Colonel Zapt* • Raymond Massey *Black Michael* • David Niven *Captain Fritz von Tarlenheim* ■ *Dir* John Cromwell • *Scr* John Balderston, Wells Root, Donald Ogden Stewart, from the play by Edward Rose, from the novel by Anthony Hope • *Cinematographer* James Wong Howe • *Editor* James E Newcom • *Art Director* Lyle Wheeler • *Music* Alfred Newman

The Prisoner of Zenda ★★★★ U

Swashbuckling adventure
1952 · US · Colour · 96min

There are those who prefer the popular 1937 Ronald Colman movie, but the Ruritanian romance cried out for this MGM Technicolor treatment, plus the dashing splendour of an experienced cast. Stewart Granger is simply marvellous in the dual central role, born to fence and carouse, and

equally at ease romancing Deborah Kerr. The 1937 score by Alfred Newman is retained, and apparently a Moviola on set ensured that the camera set-ups were also copied. Filmed with panache. TS

Stewart Granger *Rudolf Rassendyll/King Rudolf V* • Deborah Kerr *Princess Flavia* • James Mason *Rupert of Hentzau* • Louis Calhern *Colonel Zapt* • Lewis Stone *Cardinal* ■ *Dir* Richard Thorpe • *Scr* John L Balderston, Noel Langley, Wells Root, Donald Ogden Stewart, from the play by Edward Rose, from the novel by Anthony Hope • *Cinematographer* Joseph Ruttenberg • *Music* Alfred Newman

The Prisoner of Zenda ★★ PG

Comedy adventure 1979 · US · Colour · 103min

This spoof remake of the oft-filmed classic story stars Peter Sellers as a London cabbie who bears an uncanny likeness to Prince Rudolph of Ruritania. Sellers is conned into acting as a decoy for the Prince, whose throne is under threat. The film was plagued by on-set troubles, most reputedly emanating from Sellers's increasingly bizarre behaviour and superstitious nature. On screen these troubles were all too evident. DF

Peter Sellers *Prince Rudolph/Sydney Frewin/Old King* • Lynne Frederick *Princess Flavia* • Lionel Jeffries *General Sapt* • Elke Sommer *Countess* • Simon Williams *Fritz* ■ *Dir* Richard Quine • *Scr* Dick Clement, Ian La Frenais, from the novel by Anthony Hope

Prisoners ★★★★ 15

Crime thriller 2013 · US · Colour · 146min

Hugh Jackman is pushed to the limit in this deeply haunting thriller. He stars as the father of a kidnapped daughter, while Jake Gyllenhaal is the cop who, in his eyes, fails to put away the chief suspect: a young man with learning difficulties, played by Paul Dano. This can be difficult to watch, not only for the vividly portrayed violence, but also because of the disheartening turn of events that leads to other decent people (including Terrence Howard and Viola Davis, whose girl has also gone missing) becoming party to the torture. The tension is almost unbearable, though the plot does spiral off towards the end, but you're kept rooted to your seat throughout. SP Violence, swearing. DVD

Hugh Jackman *Keller Dover* • Jake Gyllenhaal *Detective Loki* • Viola Davis *Nancy Birch* • Maria Bello *Grace Dover* • Terrence Howard *Franklin Birch* • Paul Dano *Alex Jones* ■ *Dir* Denis Villeneuve • *Scr* Aaron Guzikowski • *Cinematographer* Roger A Deakins [Roger Deakins]

Prisoners of the Casbah ★

Romance adventure 1953 · US · Colour · 78min

Gloria Grahame, suitably veiled and gowned in gossamer robes, is a princess who, with her sheik-like suitor, Turhan Bey, hides out in the teeming Casbah to escape the clutches of villain Cesar Romero. This would be good for a laugh if it weren't so wooden and dreary. Threadbare and thoroughly dismal. RK

Gloria Grahame *Princess Nadja* • Cesar Romero *Firouz* • Turhan Bey *Ahmed* • Nestor Paiva *Marouf* ■ *Dir* Richard Bare [Richard L Bare] • *Scr* DeVallon Scott, from a story by William Raynor

Private ★★★★ 15

Drama 2004 · It · Colour · 89min

The Arab-Israeli conflict is distilled into the struggle for control of one house in former documentarian Saverio Costanzo's gripping feature debut. The home of a middle-class Palestinian family in the occupied zone becomes a prison when Israeli soldiers commandeer the building. As the family is penned in the lounge together, tensions between patriarchal schoolteacher Mohammad Bakri and his wife intensify, and the young troops experience misgivings over their commander's aggressive treatment of their "hosts". The even-handed screenplay ensures both sides are represented by multi-dimensional

characters. LF Arabic, Hebrew, English +subtitles. Swearing. DVD

Lior Miller *Commander Ofer* • Mohammad Bakri [Muhamad Bakri] *Mohammad B* • Tomer Russo *Private Eial* • Areen Omari *Samia* • Hend Ayoub *Mariam B* • Karem Emad Hassan Aly *Karem B* ■ *Dir* Saverio Costanzo • *Scr* Camilla Costanzo, Saverio Costanzo, Alessio Cremonini, Sayed Qashua

The Private Affairs of Bel Ami ★★★★

Period drama 1947 · US · BW and Colour · 112min

This is based on a novel by Guy de Maupassant and, in return for cutting out the more sordid aspects of the original story, director Albert Lewin gives it an extraordinary visual exoticism. George Sanders is marvellous as the lecherous rake and Angela Lansbury is the young widow he loves all along. It's weird, melodramatic, delirious, in black and white and suddenly colour, and how Lewin sneaked it around the studio's financial bosses is anyone's guess. AT

George Sanders *Georges Duroy* • Angela Lansbury *Clotilde de Marelle* • Ann Dvorak *Madeleine Forestier* • Frances Dee *Marie de Varenne* • John Carradine *Charles Forestier* ■ *Dir* Albert Lewin • *Scr* Albert Lewin, from the story by Guy de Maupassant

Private Benjamin ★★★ 15

Comedy 1980 · US · Colour · 105min

This high octane tale about a Jewish princess who joins the US Army is basically a one-joke effort, but that joke has Goldie Hawn throwing herself with great gusto into the role of a bewildered spoilt brat who comes good. If only director Howard Zieff had allowed someone else to get a look in - the members of the supporting cast are mere satellites around a perky sun. SH Swearing, sex scenes, brief nudity. DVD

Goldie Hawn *Judy Benjamin* • Eileen Brennan *Captain Doreen Lewis* • Armand Assante *Henri Tremont* • Robert Webber *Colonel Clay Thornbush* • Sam Wanamaker *Teddy Benjamin* • Harry Dean Stanton *Sergeant Jim Ballard* • Albert Brooks *Yale Goodman* ■ *Dir* Howard Zieff • *Scr* Nancy Myers, Charles Shyer, Harvey Miller

Private Confessions ★★★

Period drama 1996 · Swe · Colour · 131min

Ingmar Bergman reunited the key members of his creative family – Liv Ullmann, Sven Nykvist and Max von Sydow – for this concluding episode in the trilogy about his parents that began with *Best Intentions* and *Sunday Children*. Samuel Froler and Pernilla August reprise their roles as the strict pastor and his unhappy wife, whose confession of an affair brings forth several shocking revelations and some long-suppressed emotions. Ullmann directs as inobtrusively as possible to keep Bergman's screenplay to the fore. It's an excruciatingly personal film that dissects human nature with rare skill and honesty. DP Swedish +subtitles.

Pernilla August *Anna* • Max von Sydow *Jacob* • Samuel Froler *Henrik Bergman* • Kristina Adolphson *Maria* • Anita Björk *Karin Akerblom* ■ *Dir* Liv Ullmann • *Scr* Ingmar Bergman • *Cinematographer* Sven Nykvist

A Private Conversation ★★★ PG

Drama 1983 · USSR · Colour · 93min

Also known as *Without Witnesses*, this is a two-hander about a divorced man who pays a surprise visit on his ex-wife at her apartment. Gradually they discuss their life together and the reasons for their separation, though his attempts to seduce her are not entirely successful. Strong performances, the constricted setting and the "real time" structure are major virtues, while the twist at the end is likely to surprise everyone. AT Russian +subtitles.

Irina Kupchenko *Woman* • Mikhail Ulyanov *Man* ■ *Dir* Nikita Mikhalkov • *Scr* Nikita Mikhalkov, Sofia Prokofyeva, Ramiz Fataliyev, from the play *A Talk without Witnesses* by Sofia Prokofyeva

P

The Private Eyes ★★★
Mystery spoof   1980 · US · Colour · 92min

Another outing for comedy duo Tim Conway and Don Knotts who seemed destined to become the Abbott and Costello of the 1970s and 1980s. This time they're lampooning every private eye flick ever made, in a tall story of a murder investigation set in a 250-room English mansion. Huge amounts of slapstick as is usual with the pairing, but there are plenty of good comic sequences. DF

Tim Conway *Dr Tart* • Don Knotts *Inspector Winship* • Trisha Noble *Mistress Phyllis Morley* • Bernard Fox *Justin* • Grace Zabriskie *Nanny* • Irwin Keyes *Jock* • Suzy Mandel *Hilda* ■ *Dir* Lang Elliott • *Scr* Tim Conway, John Myhers

Private Fears in Public Places ★★★★12
Romantic comedy drama
2006 · Fr/It · Colour · 120min

Dividing the action into 50 short scenes, director Alain Resnais has made a cinematic virtue of the theatrical limitations of Alan Ayckbourn's stage study of six people in search of love. Serving as a metaphor for the Parisian protagonists' self-contained lives, the scenes flit between lonely heart Isabelle Carré, her estate agent brother André Dussollier, his bickering clients Laura Morante and Lambert Wilson, and his demure assistant Sabine Azéma. Revisiting such key Resnais themes as memory, time, identity and isolation, this minor gem is formally fascinating, cerebral and compassionate. DP French +subtitles. Brief swearing, sexual references. *DVD*

Sabine Azéma *Charlotte* • André Dussollier *Thierry* • Lambert Wilson *Dan* • Pierre Arditi *Lionel* • Laura Morante *Nicole* • Isabelle Carré *Gaëlle* • Claude Rich *Arthur* ■ *Dir* Alain Resnais • *Scr* Jean-Michel Ribes, from the play by Alan Ayckbourn • *Production Designers* Jacques Saulnier, Solange Zeitoun • *Cinematographer* Eric Gautier

The Private Files of J Edgar Hoover ★★★
Crime drama   1977 · US · Colour · 110min

This lurid, enjoyable exploitation flick from horror maestro Larry Cohen purports to reveal the truth about America's legendary head of the FBI. As Hoover, a closet homosexual cross-dresser, jowly Broderick Crawford is hard to beat, but Dan Dailey is actually even better as Hoover's long-time partner Clyde Tolson. If it all seems a mite unbelievable, only Hoover himself knew the whole truth, and he took it with him to the grave. Scored, surprisingly, by Miklos Rozsa. TS Swearing, violence.

Broderick Crawford *J Edgar Hoover* • José Ferrer *Lionel McCoy* • Michael Parks *Robert F Kennedy* • Ronee Blakley *Carrie DeWitt* • Rip Torn *Dwight Webb* • Celeste Holm *Florence Hollister* • Michael Sacks *Melvin Purvis* • Dan Dailey *Clyde Tolson* ■ *Dir/Scr* Larry Cohen

A Private Function ★★★★15
Comedy   1984 · UK · Colour · 92min

With its gentle, witty portrait of postwar Britain and its sly digs at bourgeois aspirations, this comedy has the stamp of Ealing about it. Scripted by Alan Bennett, it is an often hilarious mixture of well-observed social comedy and sometimes laborious earthy humour, much of the latter being inspired by the bodily functions of a pig being fattened for a feast to celebrate the 1947 royal wedding. Michael Palin does a nice line in mortified meekness, but he is upstaged by Maggie Smith, as his scheming wife, and Liz Smith, whose eccentric antics and ramblings provide some of the highlights. DP Swearing. *DVD*

Michael Palin *Gilbert Chilvers* • Maggie Smith *Joyce Chilvers* • Denholm Elliott *Dr Charles Swaby* • Richard Griffiths *Henry Allardyce* • Tony Haygarth *Bernard Sutcliff* • John Normington *Frank Lockwood* • Pete Postlethwaite *Douglas Nuttal* • Bill Paterson *Maurice Wormold* • Liz Smith *Mother* • Alison Steadman *Mrs Allardyce* • Jim Carter *Inspector Howard Noble* • Reece

Dinsdale *PC Penny* ■ *Dir* Malcolm Mowbray • *Scr* Alan Bennett, from a story by Alan Bennett, Malcolm Mowbray

Private Hell 36 ★★★
Crime drama   1954 · US · BW · 81min

Ida Lupino co-wrote and produced this tense thriller with ex-husband Collier Young, co-starred with then husband Howard Duff, and played her love scenes with Steve Cochran. He's the hard-up cop who pockets some loot so that she will marry him, and Howard Duff is the partner who reluctantly goes along with the lapse. The strong cast performs well under director Don Siegel's confident hand. AE

Ida Lupino *Lilli Marlowe* • Steve Cochran *Cal Bruner* • Howard Duff *Jack Farnham* • Dean Jagger *Captain Michaels* • Dorothy Malone *Francey Farnham* • Bridget Duff *Farnham child* • King Donovan *Burglar* ■ *Dir* Don Siegel • *Scr* Collier Young, Ida Lupino • *Cinematographer* Burnett Guffey

Private Investigations ★★★18
Thriller   1987 · US · Colour · 87min

The film that was meant to make actor Clayton Rohner a star back in 1987 manages to be a watchable if overly complicated thriller, vaguely in the mould of *The Man Who Knew Too Much*. Rohner plays a Los Angeles architect, who is falsely set up as being privy to a Mob secret and finds himself hunted by hired guns as a consequence. Slickly made, it offers some decent performances, especially by the ever reliable Ray Sharkey as a hapless hitman. DA

Clayton Rohner *Joey Bradley* • Ray Sharkey *Ryan* • Paul Le Mat *Detective Wexler* • Talia Balsam *Jenny Fox* • Phil Morris *Eddie Gordon* • Martin Balsam *Cliff Dowling* ■ *Dir* Nigel Dick • *Scr* John Dahl, David W Warfield, from a story by Nigel Dick

Private Life ★★★
Drama   1982 · USSR · Colour · 104min

Yuli Raizman earned himself an Oscar nomination for best foreign film for this wry parable on the growing detachment between the Communist Party and the People. Overlooked for promotion, Mikhail Ulyanov decides to focus on his family, only to discover that his careerism has alienated him from them, too. Laboured in its symbolism and languorous in its pacing, this is, nevertheless, a sincere, if occasionally sentimental, study in disillusion and redemption. The mournful Ulyanov is well supported by Iya Savvina as his wife and Irina Gubanova as his initially sympathetic former secretary. DP Russian dubbed.

Mikhail Ulyanov *Sergei Abrikosov* • Iya Savvina *Natalya Ilyinichna* • Irina Gubanova *Nelly Petrovna* ■ *Dir* Yuli Raizman • *Scr* Anatoly Grebnyev, Yuli Raizman

The Private Life of Don Juan ★★U
Romantic adventure   1934 · UK · BW · 83min

The marks the rather sad end to the soaring, dynamic career of the original swashbuckler, Douglas Fairbanks. Legendary lover Don Juan, now in middle age, returns to Seville, where he discovers that a young man has been impersonating him. It's directed by the inimitable Alexander Korda, but sadly, Fairbanks is well past his swashbuckling prime, but there are still a few moments to savour. SH

Douglas Fairbanks *Don Juan* • Merle Oberon *Antonia* • Binnie Barnes *Rosita* • Joan Gardner *Carmen* • Benita Hume *Dolores* ■ *Dir* Alexander Korda • *Scr* Frederick Lonsdale, Lajos Biró, Arthur Wimperis, from the play *L'Homme à la Rose* by Henri Bataille

The Private Life of Helen of Troy ★★
Silent period drama   1927 · US · BW · 87min

Hardly a serious slice of history, this irreverent dip into Ancient Greece was made during Alexander Korda's Hollywood period. Korda's wife, Maria Corda, stars as Helen, whisked off by Paris (Ricardo

Cortez), away from her husband Menelaus (Lewis Stone). It's essentially just a Flapper Era sex comedy in togas. AT

Maria Corda *Helen* • Lewis Stone *Menelaus* • Ricardo Cortez *Paris* • George Fawcett *Eteoneus* ■ *Dir* Alexander Korda • *Scr* Carey Wilson, from the novel by John Erskine and from the play *The Road to Rome, a Play* by Robert Emmet Sherwood [Robert E Sherwood]

LANDMARK FILM
Charles Laughton's performance ensures this is the first UK production to win an Academy Award

The Private Life of Henry VIII ★★★★U
Biographical drama   1933 · UK · BW · 89min

This superb, sexy, roistering biographical drama about the corpulent and much-married monarch was the British movie that finally cracked the American market. It caused a sensation and started the trend for portraying Henry as a roaring glutton – belching in public and tossing used meat bones over his shoulder – after he was immortalised as such by the great Charles Laughton. His subtle and clever portrayal rightly won him the best actor Oscar at the age of 33, the first time a British actor in a British film had been honoured by the Academy. Director and co-producer Alexander Korda pulls out all the stops, and, although the style looks creaky today, the performances are simply splendid, especially Mrs Laughton, Elsa Lanchester, who is very funny as Anne of Cleves. TS *DVD*

Charles Laughton *Henry VIII* • Robert Donat *Thomas Culpepper* • Elsa Lanchester *Anne of Cleves* • Merle Oberon *Anne Boleyn* • Binnie Barnes *Katherine Howard* • Wendy Barrie *Jane Seymour* • Everley Gregg *Catherine Parr* ■ *Dir* Alexander Korda • *Scr* Lajos Biró, Arthur Wimperis

The Private Life of Sherlock Holmes ★★★★PG
Mystery   1970 · UK · Colour · 120min

Director Billy Wilder gives an affectionate comic spin to the great detective partnership, casting a wondrously theatrical Robert Stephens as Holmes and a bemusedly stolid Colin Blakely as Dr Watson. Always one of Wilder's favourite films, the director was enraged when studio executives insisted on whittling the proposed four stories in the screenplay down to two. *Holmes in Love* (with Genevieve Page), though, is a sight to behold and *The Adventure of the Mini-Submarine*, featuring Queen Victoria, is bizarre and even wistful fun. The Baker Street set by the great Alexander Trauner is a joy of craftsmanship. TH *DVD*

Robert Stephens *Sherlock Holmes* • Colin Blakely *Dr John H Watson* • Irene Handl *Mrs Hudson* • Christopher Lee *Mycroft Holmes* • Tamara Toumanova *Petrova* • Genevieve Page *Gabrielle Valladon* • Clive Revill *Rogozhin* • Catherine Lacey *Old lady* • Stanley Holloway *First gravedigger* • Mollie Maureen *Queen Victoria* ■ *Dir* Billy Wilder • *Scr* Billy Wilder, IAL Diamond, from characters by Sir Arthur Conan Doyle • *Music* Miklos Rozsa

Private Lives ★★★
Romantic comedy   1931 · US · BW · 82min

Norma Shearer and Robert Montgomery star in Noël Coward's most famous and enduring light comedy about divorced couple Amanda and Elyot, who were once "so ridiculously over-in love". They meet again unexpectedly while on their respective honeymoons and run away to start their fiery relationship all over again. Given how deeply English the play is and, with its tight three acts and confined sets, how uncinematic, director Sidney Franklin did quite well by it. It lacks the brilliance of the original, but Shearer is perfect. RK

Norma Shearer *Amanda Chase Prynne* • Robert Montgomery *Elyot Chase* • Reginald Denny *Victor Prynne* • Una Merkel *Sibyl Chase* • Jean Hersholt *Oscar* ■ *Dir* Sidney Franklin • *Scr* Hans Kräly, Richard Schayer, Claudine West, from the play by Noël Coward

The Private Lives of Adam and Eve ★
Comedy fantasy
1959 · US · BW and Colour · 87min

Stranded bus passengers have a collective dream in which they become characters in the biblical story of the Creation. In 1959 this satire was condemned as "blasphemous and sacrilegious" by America's Legion of Decency. Universal was obliged to withdraw the film and re-shoot to make the fantasy less ambiguous. This version was released in 1961, but was not seen in Britain until 1988. The Garden of Eden comedy was revealed to be an extended revue sketch, racy but naive and witless, despite the distinguished names involved. DM

Mickey Rooney *Nick Lewis/Devil* • Mamie Van Doren *Evie Simms/Eve* • Fay Spain *Lil Lewis/Lilith* • Mel Tormé *Hal Sanders* • Marty Milner [Martin Milner] *Ad Simms/Adam* • Cecil Kellaway *Doc Bayles* • Tuesday Weld *Vangie Harper* • Paul Anka *Pinkie Parker* ■ *Dir* Albert Zugsmith, Mickey Rooney • *Scr* Robert Hill, from a story by George Kennett

The Private Lives of Elizabeth and Essex ★★★U
Historical drama   1939 · US · Colour · 102min

This ridiculous piece of pomp and circumstantial evidence stars Bette Davis as Elizabeth I, who's infatuated with the Earl of Essex, played by Errol Flynn. Unfortunately, without a buckle to swash, Flynn seems stranded in the reams of ripe Hollywood dialogue. Yet the stirring Erich Wolfgang Korngold music and lavish sets almost compensate for the film's travesty of history. Davis herself hated doing the picture and didn't enjoy being cast against Flynn – she wanted Laurence Olivier as Essex – though studio head Jack Warner knew that Davis and Flynn were a marriage made in box-office heaven. AT

Bette Davis *Queen Elizabeth I* • Errol Flynn *Robert Devereaux, Earl of Essex* • Olivia de Havilland *Lady Penelope Gray* • Donald Crisp *Francis Bacon* • Alan Hale *Earl of Tyrone* • Vincent Price *Sir Walter Raleigh* ■ *Dir* Michael Curtiz • *Scr* Norman Reilly Raine, Aeneas MacKenzie, from the play *Elizabeth the Queen* by Maxwell Anderson

The Private Lives of Pippa Lee ★★★15
Drama   2009 · US · Colour · 94min

This eccentric yarn stars Robin Wright Penn as Pippa, an increasingly desperate housewife forced to live in a retirement village by her much older husband (Alan Arkin). Her new life provides stark contrast to her wild days as a teenager – played in flashback by bright young thing Blake Lively. Writer/director Rebecca Miller has a similarly contradictory approach, mixing grim tragedy and goofball comedy. The wisecracking Arkin is much livelier than the average OAP and Winona Ryder is also very funny as Pippa's unhinged friend. Ultimately, it's Wright Penn who anchors the story, however, keeping her performance credible even when she's being led astray by a mysterious neighbour (Keanu Reeves) with a tattoo of Jesus on his chest. SP Swearing, sex scenes, drug abuse. *DVD*

Robin Wright Penn [Robin Wright] *Pippa Lee* • Keanu Reeves *Chris Nadeau* • Julianne Moore *Kat* • Alan Arkin *Herb Lee* • Winona Ryder *Sandra Dulles* • Maria Bello *Suky Sarkissian* • Monica Bellucci *Gigi Lee* • Blake Lively *Young Pippa* ■ *Dir* Rebecca Miller • *Scr* Rebecca Miller, from her novel

A Private Matter ★★★★PG
Drama based on a true story
1992 · US · Colour · 88min

Back in the 1960s, Sherri Finkbine presented a children's programme on US TV called *Romper Room*. However, the mother of four made more headlines when she opted for an abortion after discovering that her unborn child had been damaged by the drug thalidomide. Scripted by William Nicholson (of *Shadowlands* fame) and directed with intelligence and sensitivity by

P

Joan Micklin Silver, this intense TV movie explores the storm of media and pressure group controversy that followed her decision. Sissy Spacek excels as Finkbine and Aidan Quinn provides unfussy support as her husband Bob. DP

Sissy Spacek Sherri Finkbine • Aidan Quinn Bob Finkbine • Estelle Parsons Mary Chessen • Sheila McCarthy Diane Callaghan ■ Dir Joan Micklin Silver • Scr William Nicholson

The Private Navy of Sgt O'Farrell ★★U
Second World War comedy
1968 · US · Colour · 92min

Bob Hope was an unabashed Republican whose support for the war in Vietnam and Richard Nixon post-Watergate gave him the reputation of a stolid right-winger. Strange then to find him in this shipshape satire with anti-war undertones, co-produced by his own company, about lost beer and a crazy nurse (Phyllis Diller). JG

Bob Hope Dan O'Farrell • Phyllis Diller Nurse Nellie Krause • Jeffrey Hunter Lt Lyman Jones • Gina Lollobrigida Maria • Mylène Demongeot Gaby • John Myhers Lt Cdr Snavely • Mako Calvin Coolidge Ishimura ■ Dir Frank Tashlin • Scr Frank Tashlin, from a story by John L Greene, Robert M Fresco

Private Parts ★★★★18
Biographical comedy
1997 · US · Colour · 104min

This is an enthralling biopic of American "shock jock" Howard Stern, notorious for his sexually explicit media broadcasts and for his bust-ups with just about everybody. Charting his rise from hopeless DJ to America's most outspoken radio celebrity, this presents Stern (playing himself) as a deeply offensive human being, but it also reveals a softer off-air side, particularly in his relationship with Catherine McCormack. Although obviously toned down, this rude, crude and highly entertaining adaptation of Stern's own book doesn't flinch from re-creating many of his raunchier moments. JC Swearing, nudity, sexual references. DVD

Howard Stern • Robin Quivers • Mary McCormack Alison Stern • Fred Norris • Paul Giamatti Kenny • Gary Dell'Abate • Jackie Martling • Carol Alt Gloria • Ozzy Osbourne • Mia Farrow ■ Dir Betty Thomas • Scr Len Blum, Michael Kalesniko, from the autobiography by Howard Stern

Private Peaceful ★★★12
First World War drama
2012 · UK · Colour · 102min

A less lavish affair than Steven Spielberg's take on Michael Morpurgo's War Horse, this adaptation of another Morpurgo Great War saga stars George MacKay as Tommo Peaceful, who lies awake on a Flanders battlefield and looks back on his and his brother's (Jack O'Connell) life on the Devon estate of colonel Richard Griffiths, their love for the same girl (Alexandra Roach) and their brutal experience of the war and a feud involving gruff sergeant John Lynch. The grime and the grind of the period is expertly re-created and the performances admirable, but the story is rather undermined by khaki cliché and the mawkish insistence of Rachel Portman's score. DP Some violence, swearing. DVD

George MacKay Tommo Peaceful • Jack O'Connell (2) Charlie Peaceful • Alexandra Roach Molly Monks • Frances de la Tour Grandma Wolf • Richard Griffiths The Colonel • John Lynch Sergeant Hanley • Maxine Peake Hazel Peaceful ■ Dir Pat O'Connor • Scr Simon Reade, from Michael Morpurgo's novel

Private Potter ★★U
War drama
1963 · UK · BW · 88min

Tom Courtenay is the eponymous soldier whose inexperience causes him to cry out while on a mission, leading to the death of a colleague. In his defence, Courtenay claims that at the critical moment he had a vision of God. This leads to a debate over whether he should be court martialled, the existence of God and a lot of other weighty issues. Courtenay is utterly convincing, but Ronald

Harwood's script is a sermon few actors could survive. Flashy direction doesn't help matters, either. AT

Tom Courtenay Pte Potter • Mogens Wieth Yannis • Ronald Fraser Doctor • James Maxwell Lt Col Gunyon • Ralph Michael Padre • Brewster Mason Brigadier • Eric Thompson Capt Knowles • John Graham (1) Maj Sims • Frank Finlay Capt Patterson ■ Dir Casper Wrede • Scr Casper Wrede, Ronald Harwood, from the TV play by Ronald Harwood

Private Property ★★★★15
Drama
2006 · Lux/Bel/Fr · Colour · 88min

Tensions simmer beneath the surface of a dysfunctional family in this acutely powerful drama from Belgian writer/director Joachim Lafosse. Isabelle Huppert adds to her catalogue of damaged, vulnerable heroines with Pascale, the divorced mother of grown-up twins Thierry and François (played by real-life brothers Jérémie and Yannick Renier). Dreaming of opening a B&B with new lover Jan (Kris Cuppens), Pascale is confronted with her sons' innate selfishness. Filmed with clinical precision in slow, static takes that belie the tumultuous feelings expressed by the characters, it's an unbearably intimate family portrait set around a claustrophobic, womb-like farmhouse. JR French +subtitles. DVD

Isabelle Huppert Pascale • Jérémie Renier [Jérémie Rénier] Thierry • Yannick Renier François • Kris Cuppens Jan • Patrick Descamps Luc • Raphaëlle Lubansu Anne • Sabine Riche Gerda • Dirk Tuypens Dirk ■ Dir Joachim Lafosse • Scr Joachim Lafosse, François Pirot

Private Resort ★★18
Sex comedy
1985 · US · Colour · 78min

This is a typical 1980s sun, sea and sex movie about the exploits of two friends on the hunt for girls at a Miami resort. The main point of interest in what would otherwise be a forgettable movie is a first starring role for Johnny Depp. Here he plays Jack, who with pal Ben (Rob Morrow from TV's Northern Exposure) seeks simple hedonistic pleasure. Even this early in his career Depp shows promise, demonstrating that most important screen attribute: presence. DF

Rob Morrow Ben • Johnny Depp Jack Marshall • Emily Longstreth Patti • Karyn O'Bryan Dana • Hector Elizondo The Maestro • Dody Goodman Amanda Rawlings ■ Dir George Bowers • Scr Gordon Mitchell, from a story by Mitchell, Ken Segall, Alan Wenkus

The Private War of Major Benson ★★★U
Comedy
1955 · US · Colour · 104min

Charlton Heston knocked off this dated but likeable comedy while on a month-long lay-off during the shooting of DeMille's gargantuan The Ten Commandments. Heston plays a hard-nosed army major, who displeases his superiors and winds up drilling the students at a military school run by nuns. Heston's intense physicality is often the source of the comedy, and the Oscar-nominated screenplay delivers the message that in the postwar era the US military needn't be for tough nuts only. AT

Charlton Heston Major Bernard Benson • Julie Adams Dr Kay Lambert • William Demarest John • Tim Considine Cadet Sergeant Hibler • Sal Mineo Cadet Colonel Dusik ■ Dir Jerry Hopper • Scr William Roberts, Richard Alan Simmons, from a story by Joe Connelly, Bob Mosher

Private Worlds ★★★
Medical drama
1935 · US · BW · 80min

Producer Walter Wanger bought Phyllis Bottome's novel because its setting - a mental hospital - had not been featured in an American film before, but both Fredric March and Warner Baxter turned down the male lead. Wanger then hired Charles Boyer, about to return to his native France after finding little success in Hollywood. The film brought him a huge female following and a reputation as "the great lover", and Claudette Colbert, as the doctor who initially encounters prejudice from Boyer, received an Oscar nomination. TV

Claudette Colbert Dr Jane Everest • Charles Boyer Dr Charles Monet • Joan Bennett Sally MacGregor • Helen Vinson Claire Monet • Joel McCrea Dr Alex MacGregor • Esther Dale The matron • Sam Hinds [Samuel S Hinds] Dr Arnold ■ Dir Gregory La Cava • Scr Lynn Starling, Gregory La Cava, Gladys Unger, from the novel by Phyllis Bottome • Cinematographer Leon Shamroy

Privates on Parade ★★15
Comedy drama
1982 · UK · Colour · 107min

This is a sort of Virgin Soldiers with pretentious knobs on, based on Peter Nichols's play in which a troupe of soldiers put on musical revues in Singapore. The Malay emergency, when communists threatened to topple the British colony, provides the background. In the foreground are John Cleese, Denis Quilley and lots of dodgy racial innuendo. The palm trees are all plastic as the picture was filmed in England, the jokes are a notch above the Carry On level and Cleese is an inch away from a nervous breakdown. Not nearly as funny as it should have been. AT Some violence, swearing. DVD

John Cleese Major Giles Flack • Denis Quilley Captain Terri Dennis • Nicola Pagett Sylvia Morgan • Patrick Pearson Private Steven Flowers ■ Dir Michael Blakemore • Scr Peter Nichols, from his play

Private's Progress ★★★★U
Second World War comedy
1956 · UK · BW · 95min

This pleasing mix of satire and nostalgia was unusual at the time for suggesting that not every tommy who went to fight in the Second World War was a hero. Ian Carmichael is superbly cast as the hapless Stanley Windrush, whose natural ineptitude is seen as a God-given gift by the roguish Richard Attenborough and Dennis Price. Although the Boulting brothers rather lose track of the plot once Carmichael goes after Nazi art treasures, this is still richly entertaining, not least because of the smashing performance of Terry-Thomas. DP DVD

Richard Attenborough Private Cox • Dennis Price Brigadier Bertram Tracepurcel • Terry-Thomas Major Hitchcock • Ian Carmichael Stanley Windrush • Peter Jones Egan • William Hartnell Sergeant Sutton ■ Dir John Boulting • Scr John Boulting, Frank Harvey, from the novel by Alan Hackney

Privilege ★★PG
Satirical drama
1967 · UK · Colour · 98min

Peter Watkins, who made the chilling atomic warning The War Game, directed this uneven satire in which real-life pop star Paul Jones is the rock idol who finds himself manipulated by the Church and the State, who seek to contain the violent instincts of his fans. This entails a change of image that transforms him into a religious leader. It's filled with confidence, but little conviction. Jean Shrimpton, one of the fashion icons of the time, is the singer's girlfriend, but her acting talent doesn't match her looks. TH DVD BD

Paul Jones Steve Shorter • Jean Shrimpton Vanessa Ritchie • Mark London Alvin Kirsch • Max Bacon Julie Jordan • Jeremy Child Martin Crossley ■ Dir Peter Watkins • Scr Norman Bogner, Peter Watkins, from a story by Johnny Speight

Prix de Beauté ★★★
Silent drama
1930 · Fr · BW · 109min

One for Louise Brooks fans, and a perfect showcase for her specialist gifts as a tragic heroine, this was made as a silent in Paris by Italian director Augusto Genina. Disastrously badly dubbed as sound came into fashion, its American release, as Miss Europe, was an understandable failure. In its pure silent version, however, a print of which was rediscovered in Italy and restored, this tale of an ordinary girl of extraordinary beauty, who wins a beauty contest with tragic consequences, is replete with many exquisite images. RK

Louise Brooks Lucienne Garnier • Georges Charlia André • H Bandini Antonin ■ Dir Augusto Genina • Scr René Clair, Georg Wilhelm Pabst

[GW Pabst], Bernard Zimmer, from a story by Augusto Genina, René Clair, Bernard Zimmer, Alessandro de Stefani • Cinematographers Rudolf Maté, Louis Née • Editor Edmond T Gréville

The Prize ★★★
Spy thriller
1963 · US · Colour · 134min

The Nobel prizes are handed out in Stockholm, with Paul Newman winning his for literature and Edward G Robinson getting his for physics. But this is the Cold War, Russia is almost next door, and Newman smells a big fat communist conspiracy. Screenwriter Ernest Lehman wrote Hitchcock's classic chase picture North by Northwest; here he recycles some of those ideas and cares not a jot about plausibility. A bit long perhaps, but this is still an enjoyable romp that displays a healthy cynicism towards international politics and culture. AT

Paul Newman Andrew Craig • Edward G Robinson Dr Max Stratman • Elke Sommer Inger Lisa Andersen • Diane Baker Emily Stratman • Micheline Presle Dr Denise Marceau • Gérard Oury Dr Claude Marceau ■ Dir Mark Robson • Scr Ernest Lehman, from the novel by Irving Wallace

A Prize of Arms ★★★
Crime thriller
1961 · UK · BW · 104min

This clever and exciting caper about the heist of army loot stars Stanley Baker, who was never quite as effective in leading roles as he was playing the supporting villain. Master cameraman and later cult director Nicolas Roeg co-wrote the original story while underrated Cliff Owen took on the directorial duties. The nail-biting climax is very well handled and there's a terrific co-starring performance from Tom Bell. Good reviews at the time didn't help this film's box office takings. TS

Stanley Baker Turpin • Helmut Schmid Swavek • Tom Bell Fenner • David Courtenay Lieutenant Davies • Tom Adams Corporal Glenn • Anthony Bate Sergeant Reeves • Rodney Bewes Private Maynard ■ Dir Cliff Owen • Scr Paul Ryder, from a story by Nicolas Roeg, Kevin Kavanagh

A Prize of Gold ★★
Crime adventure
1955 · UK · Colour · 101min

For reasons never satisfactorily explained, Mai Zetterling wants to take a number of orphaned children from their home in Germany to a new life in South America. Her lover, an American soldier played by Richard Widmark, agrees to help her and decides to steal a load of gold bullion which is being flown from Berlin to London. It's part routine thriller, part soggy melodrama with a lot of winsome kiddies, and Richard Widmark plays a softie! In a word, unconvincing. AT

Richard Widmark Sergeant Joe Lawrence • Mai Zetterling Maria • Nigel Patrick Brian Hammell • George Cole Sergeant Roger Morris • Donald Wolfit Alfie Stratton ■ Dir Mark Robson • Scr Robert Buckner, John Paxton, from the novel by Max Catto

The Prizefighter and the Lady ★★★
Sports romance
1933 · US · BW · 101min

Heavyweight boxing champion Max Baer (displaying enough acting talent to go on to several more films) stars as a fighter who falls for Myrna Loy. He marries her - with the permission of her former lover, gangster Otto Kruger - only to lose her through his own arrogance and womanising. The romantic plot, however, is incidental to the action in the ring, climaxing in a bloody battle with Primo Carnera. WS Van Dyke directed for MGM with his usual pace, enlisting the services of several fighters playing themselves, including Carnera, Jack Dempsey, Jess Willard and Jim Jeffries. RK

Myrna Loy Belle Morgan • Max Baer Steve Morgan • Primo Carnera • Jack Dempsey • Walter Huston "Professor" Edwin J Bennett • Otto Kruger Willie Ryan • Vince Barnett Bugsie • Jess Willard • Jim Jeffries ■ Dir WS Van Dyke • Scr John Lee Mahin, John Meehan, from a story by Frances Marion

Prizzi's Honor ★★★★ 15
Black comedy 1985 · US · Colour · 123min

Director John Huston's penultimate movie sees a return to the type of *film noir* with which he made his name in the 1940s, sent up here as a black comedy. His daughter Anjelica has an Oscar-nominated supporting role and her then-partner Jack Nicholson is the Oscar-nominated lead. He plays a grizzled Mafia hitman who falls for and marries Kathleen Turner's foxy freelance hitwoman. Their loyalties are tested (he works for the powerful East Coast Prizzi family; she, a West Coast operator, does not) and then shattered when each is tasked with bumping off the other. Complex farce ensues under the steady hand of Huston, and it's all irresistibly dark. AC Nudity, swearing, sex, violence. *DVD*

Jack Nicholson *Charley Partanna* • Kathleen Turner *Irene Walker* • Anjelica Huston *Maerose Prizzi* • Robert Loggia *Eduardo Prizzi* • William Hickey *Don Corrado Prizzi* • John Randolph *Angelo "Pop" Partanna* • Lee Richardson *Dominic Prizzi* ■ *Dir* John Huston • *Scr* Richard Condon, Janet Roach, from the novel by Richard Condon

Problem Child ★ PG
Comedy 1990 · US · Colour · 77min

In this dreadful mishmash of a comedy, John Ritter stars as a man who adopts a child so dysfunctional it is a wonder any part of him works at all. Not only is it crude and deeply unfunny, but it also fails to work on the simplest level as an object lesson in giving love and eventually receiving it. There is something offensive about using an unloved and rebellious child as the butt of bad jokes in this way. But, unfortunately, it led to some even more obnoxious sequels. SH Swearing. *DVD*

John Ritter *Ben Healy* • Jack Warden *"Big" Ben Healy Sr* • Michael Oliver *Junior* • Gilbert Gottfried *Mr Peabody* • Amy Yasbeck *Flo Healy* ■ *Dir* Dennis Dugan • *Scr* Scott Alexander, Larry Karaszewski

Problem Child 2 ★ PG
Comedy 1991 · US · Colour · 86min

There are those who like nothing better than a full celluloid cacophony of life's more basic bodily functions and, if you find lavatorial humour a must, you will be well served by this execrable film. Continuing where the original film left off, this was justifiably slated on its release. Amazingly, a further, made-for-TV sequel followed in 1995. SH Swearing, violence. *DVD*

John Ritter *Ben Healy* • Michael Oliver *Junior Healy* • Jack Warden *"Big" Ben Healy* • Laraine Newman *LaWanda Dumore* • Amy Yasbeck *Annie Young* • Ivyann Schwan *Trixie Young* • Gilbert Gottfried *Mr Peabody* • Charlene Tilton *Debbie Claukinski* ■ *Dir* Brian Levant • *Scr* Scott Alexander, Larry Karaszewski

Le Procès de Jeanne d'Arc ★★★★ PG
Drama 1962 · Fr · BW · 61min

Robert Bresson, a master of minimalist technique, returned to the original trial transcripts to give an authentic feel to this remarkable featurette that deservedly won the Special Jury Prize at Cannes. Florence Carrez seems overawed by the part, but this only helps make Joan's torment all the more credible. The deeply moving final shot will live long in the memory. DP French +subtitles. *DVD*

Florence Carrez *Jeanne d'Arc* • Jean-Claude Fourneau *Bishop Cauchon* • Marc Jacquier *Jean Lemaître, Inquisitor* • Roger Honorat *Jean Beaupère* • Jean Gillibert *Jean de Châtillon* • André Régnier *d'Estivet* ■ *Dir/Scr* Robert Bresson

The Prodigal ★★
Biblical drama 1955 · US · Colour · 112min

"Two years in the making!" shrieked the gaudily coloured posters for this very studio-bound MGM epic based on the New Testament tale of the prodigal son, but clearly less than two minutes were spent on the script. Director Richard Thorpe was obviously smitten by having hordes of extras, and, regrettably, lets himself linger, tableau-style. Top-billed Lana Turner, though perfectly typecast, is a shade too old for her predatory role, but is mesmerisingly watchable. TS

Lana Turner *Samarra, high priestess of Astarte* • Edmund Purdom *Micah, high priest of Baal* • Louis Calhern *Nahreeb, high priest of Baal* • Audrey Dalton *Ruth* • James Mitchell *Asham* • Neville Brand *Rhakim* • Walter Hampden *Eli, Micah's father* ■ *Dir* Richard Thorpe • *Scr* Maurice Zimm, Joe Breen Jr, Samuel James Larsen

The Prodigal Son ★★★ 18
Martial arts drama 1983 · HK · Colour · 100min

Yuen Biao and Sammo Hung co-star in this action-packed but nevertheless stylish tale of deception and revenge. With his cheeky grin and flying fists, the irrepressible Yuen is on top form as a disappointed street fighter who joins a Chinese opera company to study under a martial arts master after he discovers that his over-protective father has been rigging all his bouts. The stocky Hung brings a typical touch of good humour. DP Cantonese dubbed. Violence. *DVD*

Sammo Hung *Wong Wah Bo* • Yuen Biao *Leung Jan* • Frankie Chan *Lord Ngai* • Lam Ching Ying *Leung Yee Tai* ■ *Dir* Sammo Hung • *Scr* Samo Hung, Wong Bing Yiu

The Producers ★★★★★ PG
Comedy 1968 · US · Colour · 85min

This triumphantly tasteless affair was Mel Brooks's first feature and it fully deserves its status as a comedy classic. Zero Mostel plays the sweaty, down-on-his-luck Broadway impresario who links up with shy accountant Gene Wilder in a scam to fleece theatrical investors with the worst play of all time: a musical biopic of Adolf Hitler. The two leads are wonderful, as is Dick Shawn as the hippy star who takes the lead role in their production, and, while the gags flow freely throughout, it's the jaw-dropping numbers from *Springtime for Hitler* that cement its place in cinema history. JF *DVD*

Zero Mostel *Max Bialystock* • Gene Wilder *Leo Bloom* • Kenneth Mars *Franz Liebkind* • Estelle Winwood *"Hold me, touch me" old lady* • Renee Taylor *Eva Braun* • Christopher Hewett *Roger De Bris* • Lee Meredith *Ulla* • Andreas Voutsinas *Carmen Giya* • Dick Shawn *Lorenzo St Du Bois* • Josip Elic *Violinist* • Madlyn Cates *Concierge* • John Zoller *Drama critic* • William Hickey *Drunk in theatre bar* ■ *Dir/Scr* Mel Brooks

The Producers ★★ 12
Musical comedy 2005 · US · Colour · 128min

Few movies can have a history as odd as this one's: a 1968 comedy film about a pair of impresarios deliberately making a flop Broadway musical is transformed into a hit Broadway musical before being retransformed into a film musical. Which is a flop. While Mel Brooks's Oscar-winning original was an orgy of exquisitely wrought bad taste, this picture is a bloated and unimaginative remake. Nathan Lane and Matthew Broderick are just about passable as Bialystock and Bloom, but Susan Stroman's direction is flat and the additional songs are far from toe tapping. AS Swearing. *DVD CS*

Nathan Lane *Max Bialystock* • Matthew Broderick *Leo Bloom* • Uma Thurman *Ulla* • Will Ferrell *Franz Liebkind* • Gary Beach *Roger DeBris* • Roger Bart *Carmen Ghia* • Jon Lovitz *Mr Marks* ■ *Dir* Susan Stroman • *Scr* Mel Brooks, Thomas Meehan, from their play, from the 1968 film by Mel Brooks

The Professional ★★★ 15
Thriller 1981 · Fr · Colour · 103min

This is an absorbing thriller, with Jean-Paul Belmondo as a French Secret Service agent sent to assassinate the ruler of a minor African republic. However, a change in his political circumstances prompts the dictator to sue for an alliance. The contract is cancelled, but Belmondo is determined to fulfil his mission, placing him at the top of the French government's hit list. Belmondo's vigour elevates this above the norm. DP French dubbed. Violence, nudity. *DVD*

Jean-Paul Belmondo *Joss Beaumont* • Robert Hossein *Rosen* • Michel Baune *Valera* ■ *Dir* Georges Lautner • *Scr* Georges Lautner, Michel Audiard, from the novel *La Mort d'une Bête à la Peau Fragile* by Patrick Alexander

A Professional Gun ★★★
Spaghetti western 1968 · It/Sp · Colour · 105min

This spaghetti western – with Franco Nero as the professional gun, Tony Musante as a workers' liberator and Jack Palance as a sadistic homosexual – lays on the gallows humour with bloodshot zest. That's because director Sergio Corbucci used to be a gag writer, so it's jokier than most of its kind, even if its jokes are as simple-minded as Nero striking a match on a villain's stubble. TH Some dialogue dubbed.

Franco Nero *Sergei Cowalski* • Tony Musante *Eufemio* • Jack Palance *Ricciolo* • Giovanna Ralli *Columba* • Eduardo Fajardo *Alfonso Garcia* ■ *Dir* Sergio Corbucci • *Scr* Luciano Vincenzoni, Sergio Spina, Sergio Corbucci, from a story by Franco Solinas, Giorgio Arlorio

The Professionals ★★★★ PG
Western 1966 · US · Colour · 112min

Richard Brooks's action western was a box-office smash, repairing the damage that the flop *Lord Jim* had done to his reputation two years before. Burt Lancaster, Lee Marvin, Robert Ryan and Woody Strode are the magnificent four, flawed and fearsome, hired to rescue Claudia Cardinale from the clutches of manic Mexican bandit Jack Palance. Grittily shot in canyon country, bursting with violence and with pit stops for philosophising. AT *DVD* Blu

Burt Lancaster *Bill Dolworth* • Lee Marvin *Henry Rico Farden* • Robert Ryan *Hans Ehrengard* • Jack Palance *Captain Jesus Raza* • Claudia Cardinale *Maria Grant* • Ralph Bellamy *JW Grant* • Woody Strode *Jacob Sharp* • Joe De Santis *Ortega* ■ *Dir* Richard Brooks • *Scr* Richard Brooks, from the novel *A Mule for the Marquesa* by Frank O'Rourke

Profile ★
Crime drama 1954 · UK · BW · 65min

Steel-jawed magazine editor John Bentley is accused of forging a cheque in the name of his publisher, who inconveniently keels over with a heart attack. Meanwhile, the publisher's wife (a totally wasted Kathleen Byron) lusts after Bentley (who's in love with her daughter), but is soon murdered herself. Rubbish? You bet, from Monarch, one of the lowest on the British B-movie totem pole: don't look for style here. TS

John Bentley *Peter Armstrong* • Kathleen Byron *Margot Holland* • Thea Gregory *Susan Holland* • Stuart Lindsell *Aubrey Holland* • Garard Green *Charlie Pearson* ■ *Dir* Francis Searle • *Scr* John Gilling, from a story by John Temple-Smith, Maurice Temple-Smith

The Profound Desire of the Gods ★★★★ 15
Drama 1968 · Jpn · Colour · 173min

Shohei Imamura embraced the Japanese New Wave's genius for controversy in this head-on collision between tradition and progress. There's seemingly no taboo that Imamura is not willing to tackle here, as engineer Kazuo Kitamura arrives on an isolated island to arrange the water supply for a modern sugar refinery only to find himself embroiled in the incest and insanity of Kanjuro Arashi's eccentric family. With a subplot involving a shamanist shrine, this is a scathing study of a society about to implode that's made all the more disconcerting by Imamura's typically uncompromising realism. DP Japanese +subtitles. Sex scenes. *DVD* Blu

Rentaro Mikuni *Nekichi Futori, the chained son* • Choichiro Kawarazaki *Kametaro Futori* • Kazuo Kitamura *Engineer Kariya* • Hideko Okiyama *Toriko Futori, the backward daughter* • Yoshi Kato *Ritsugen Ryu* • Yasuko Matsui *Uma Futori, the priestess daughter* • Kanjuro Arashi *Yamamori Futori, the patriarch* ■ *Dir* Shohei Imamura • *Scr* Shohei Imamura, Keiji Hasebe

Profoundly Normal ★★
Drama based on a true story 2003 · Can · Colour · 96min

In this uplifting TV drama, Kirstie Alley and Delroy Lindo play a real-life couple with learning disabilities who face the challenge of becoming parents. Forced to learn how to live outside an institution, they overcome the opposition of social services and local prejudice. Alley and Lindo are a quality act, so it's watchable – just try to ignore the saccharine moments. SF

Kirstie Alley *Donna Lee Shelby Thornton* • Delroy Lindo *Ricardo Thornton* • Rosemary Dunsmore *Charlotte Johnson* • Kevin Duhaney *Ricky* • Catherine Fitch *Margaret* ■ *Dir* Graeme Clifford • *Scr* Paris Qualles

Progeny ★★★ 18
Science-fiction horror 1998 · US · Colour · 91min

Splatter specialist Brian Yuzna directs this *Outer Limits*-style tale of a pregnancy that might not be of this world. Arnold Vosloo isn't exactly leading man material, but he does convey an escalating sense of paranoia with some gusto, while Lindsay Crouse and Brad Dourif provide solid support. Although Yuzna does occasionally betray his roots with dollops of gore and nudity, this is a far more restrained and atmospheric tale than you might expect. JC Violence, nudity, swearing. *DVD*

Arnold Vosloo *Dr Craig Burton* • Jillian McWhirter *Sherry Burton* • Brad Dourif *Dr Bert Clavell* • Lindsay Crouse *Dr Susan Lamarche* ■ *Dir* Brian Yuzna • *Scr* Aubrey Solomon, from a story by Stuart Gordon, Solomon

The Program ★★ 15
Sports drama 1993 · US · Colour · 107min

American sporting movies rarely translate well for British audiences and this is no exception, despite its fine cast. James Caan plays the hard-bitten coach (with the obligatory soft heart) who is told to transform the fortunes of his struggling college football team. The playing – both the football and the acting – is the best thing about the movie, with the dependable Caan receiving nice support. But director David S Ward can't resist turning out all the usual clichés. DP Swearing, drug abuse, violence.

James Caan *Coach Sam Winters* • Halle Berry *Autumn* • Omar Epps *Darnell Jefferson* • Craig Sheffer *Joe Kane* • Kristy Swanson *Camille* • Abraham Benrubi *Bud-Lite* ■ *Dir* David S Ward • *Scr* Aaron Latham, David S Ward

The Program ★★ 15
Sports drama based on a true story 2015 · Fr/Fr · Colour · 98min

The doping scandal that turned cyclist Lance Armstrong from hero to villain is the focus for director Stephen Frears here, but the man behind the headlines (played by Ben Foster) remains frustratingly remote. His confession on *Oprah* in 2013 abruptly opens the film, before Frears tracks back to see his unlikely transition from day racer to seven-time Tour de France winner. Armstrong comes across as a sort of Frankenstein's monster and his skin is too thick for Frears to get through. Whilethere are hints of a victim complex, his battle with cancer is a mere footnote. SP Swearing, drug abuse. *DVD* Blu

Ben Foster *Lance Armstrong* • Chris O'Dowd *David Walsh* • Guillaume Canet *Dr Michele Ferrari* • Lee Pace *Bill Stapleton* • Dustin Hoffman *Bob Hamman* ■ *Dir* Stephen Frears • *Scr* John Hodge, from the non-fiction book *Seven Deadly Sins: My Pursuit of Lance Armstrong* by David Walsh

Project A ★★★ 12
Martial arts adventure 1983 · HK · Colour · 100min

For those who think kung fu is kung-phooey, a chance to be converted by one of the masters. With an overworked soundtrack – thwack! kapow! crunch! – and fight choreography enough to make you die for, Jackie Chan is a turn-of-the-century coastguard battling pirates. Credibility walks the buccaneers' plank, but the humour-

P

leavened action takes some beating. TH Cantonese dubbed. *DVD*

Jackie Chan *Dragon Ma* • Sammo Hung *Fei* • Yuen Biao *Hung Tin Tze* • Lau Hak Suen *Admiral* ■ *Dir* Jackie Chan • *Scr* Jackie Chan, Edward Tang

Project A: Part II ★★★ 15
Martial arts adventure
1987 · HK · Colour · 101min

Starting and finishing with the sequences of previous picture highlights and hair-raising set piece out-takes that have become a familiar feature of a Jackie Chan sequel, this rattling chop-socky adventure has all the action and slapstick we've come to expect from this unique star. Corrupt cops, spies, revolutionaries and pirates hurtle across the screen as Chan teams with the rebellious Maggie Cheung to confound bent bobby David Lam. DP Cantonese +subtitles. *DVD*

Jackie Chan *Dragon Ma* • Maggie Cheung • David Lam ■ *Dir* Jackie Chan • *Scr* Edward Tang

Project ALF ★★
Science-fiction comedy
1996 · US/Ger · Colour · 95min

Spun off from an 1980s American television series, director Dick Lowry's unassuming sci-fi comedy about an orange, furry and funny extraterrestial – ALF stands for Alien Life Form – is amiable family fare. Here the wisecracking ET has close encounters with the military, who have taken him to a top secret base for analysis. Miguel Ferrer, Ed Begley Jr and Martin Sheen are the well known faces in an otherwise unfamiliar cast. TH

Miguel Ferrer *Dr Dexter Moyers* • William O'Leary *Captain Rick Mulligan* • Jensen Daggett *Major Melissa Hill* • Scott Michael Campbell *Lieutenant Reese* • Ed Begley Jr *Dr Warner* • Martin Sheen *Colonel Millfoil* ■ *Dir* Dick Lowry • *Scr* Tom Patchett, Paul Fusco

Project Almanac ★★★ 12
Science-fiction drama
2014 · US · Colour · 106min

It's a brave time-travel tale that dares to reference *Looper* and *The Terminator*. Director Dean Israelite's found-footage B-movie is nowhere near as noteworthy as either, but it's a pretty fun ride. Brilliant science student Jonny Weston and pals uncover blueprints for a time machine in his inventor father's basement. But as they start to use it they unwittingly change their present with devastating results. Winning humour and top-notch visuals help this to be better than expected. AJ Some swearing, sexual references. *DVD*

Jonny Weston *David Raskin* • Amy Landecker *Kathy Raskin* • Virginia Gardner *Christina Raskin* • Allen Evangelista *Adam Le* • Sam Lerner *Quinn Goldberg* ■ *Dir* Dean Israelite • *Scr* Jason Pagan, Andrew Stark [Andrew Deutschman]

Project Nim ★★★★ 12
Drama documentary
2011 · UK · Colour and BW · 95min

This jaw-dropping documentary examines the real-life 1970s experiment to teach a chimpanzee, Nim, to communicate through sign language by raising and nurturing him like a human child. Director James Marsh (an Oscar winner for *Man on Wire*) charts the heartbreaking and often incredible events without ever veering towards mawkish sentimentality. It's as much a story about human folly and arrogance as it is the traumatic journey of an animal being shunted from pillar to post in the name of science. TeS Swearing, drug abuse. *DVD*

Stephanie LaFarge • Herb Terrace • Jenny Lee • Laura-Ann Petitto • Bob Ingersoll ■ *Dir* James Marsh • *Scr* From the non-fiction book *Nim Chimpsky: The Chimp Who Would Be Human* by Elizabeth Hess • *Cinematographer* Michael Simmonds

Project Wild Thing ★★★ PG
Documentary
2013 · UK · Colour · 82min

Spurred into action by the fact his children spend a mere 4% of their time playing outside, documentary director David Bond

has come up with a well-meaning film charting his efforts to market Nature itself as a brand. But as this amiable everyman discovers, it's just not that simple to sell such a thing to the masses. Urbanisation, parental dread of predators, and health and safety issues also play a large part in our retreat indoors. Bond's heartfelt concern certainly pricks the conscience (particularly if you are a parent), but this could so easily have been a feature on *Newsnight* – and with a lot more bite. JA

David Bond (2) *David Bond* • Susan Greenfield • George Monbiot • Chris Packham • Michael Wolff ■ *Dir* David Bond (2) • *Scr* David Bond (2), Ashley Jones

Project X ★★★ 12
Comedy thriller
1987 · US · Colour · 102min

There is plenty going on in this pleasing piece of monkey business. Matthew Broderick stars as a cocky USAF pilot who is sent to a strategic weapons unit to care for the chimpanzees being used to test flight simulators. However, when he learns that they are being subjected to radiation, he decides to stop the programme before Virgil, an orphan chimp trained in sign language, is strapped into the hot seat. Helen Hunt proves an able accomplice, but Jonathan Kaplan fails to sustain the suspense. DP

Matthew Broderick *Jimmy Garrett* • Helen Hunt *Teresa "Teri" McDonald* • Bill Sadler [William Sadler] *Dr Lynnard Carroll* • Johnny Ray McGhee *Isaac Robertson* • Jonathan Stark *Sergeant "Kreig" Kreiger* • Robin Gammell *Colonel Niles* • Stephen Lang *Watts* ■ *Dir* Jonathan Kaplan • *Scr* Stanley Weiser, from a story by Stanley Weiser, Lawrence Lasker

Project X ★★★ 18
Comedy
2012 · US · Colour · 92min

A trio of misfit high-school students plan the party to end all parties and get themselves noticed in this rude, outrageous and occasionally hilarious comedy. Birthday boy Thomas (Thomas Mann) desperately struggles to contain the festivities and prevent his parents' suburban home from being wrecked by over 1,000 party animals, and director Nima Nourizadeh's "found footage" technique plants the viewer to great effect in the centre of the debauchery and destruction. The film loses its way as the night wears on, but the earlier scenes have plenty of wit and snappy dialogue. TeS Swearing, drug abuse, nudity. *DVD*

Thomas Mann (2) *Thomas* • Jonathan Daniel Brown *JB* • Oliver Cooper *Costa* • Dax Flame *Dax* • Kirby Bliss Blanton *Kirby* • Brady Hender *Everett* ■ *Dir* Nima Nourizadeh • *Scr* Matt Drake, Michael Bacall, from a story by Bacall

The Projectionist ★★★★
Comedy fantasy
1970 · US · Colour · 84min

In an independent, low-budget pearl from writer/director Harry Hurwitz, Chuck McCann is the lonely projectionist whose job leads him into flights of fantasy in which he is transformed into superhero Captain Flash, clashing with archenemy The Bat (Rodney Dangerfield). Film clips from other movies are well used, as McCann's daydreams lead him into adventures with fictional characters from Hollywood classics as well as historical characters. This early effort now enjoys a cult following. TH

Chuck McCann *Projectionist/Captain Flash* • Ina Balin *Girl* • Rodney Dangerfield *Renaldi/The Bat* • Jara Kohout *Candy Man/Scientist* • Harry Hurwitz *Friendly usher* • Robert Staats *TV pitchman* ■ *Dir/Scr* Harry Hurwitz

Prom ★★ U
Comedy
2011 · US · Colour · 103min

Pitched fairly and squarely at young fans of *High School Musical* and *Glee*, this cute but bland story focuses on the romantic dramas of a stereotypical bunch of youngsters (the princess, the jock, the loner, the loser, the weirdo, the geek) preparing for their pre-graduation dance. This is U-certificate Disney, but the trouble is that *Prom* is so wholesome it hurts. Even younger viewers would surely relish a little more raunch. It's hard to hate, however, and parents can

take confidence in the fact that it could never be accused of being a corrupting influence. DA

Aimee Teegarden *Nova Prescott* • Thomas McDonell *Jesse Richter* • DeVaughn Nixon *Tyler Barso* • Danielle Campbell *Simone Daniels* ■ *Dir* Joe Nussbaum • *Scr* Katie Wech

Prom Night ★★★ 18
Horror   1980 · Can/US · Colour · 88min

Jamie Lee Curtis cemented her Scream Queen title with this inventively plotted, (relatively) light on gore, entry in the teenagers-in-jeopardy/stalk-and-slash cycle inaugurated by *Halloween*. Four youngsters cause the death of a fifth in the modishly formula opening prologue, and several years later an axe-wielding killer turns up at the school prom seeking belated revenge. A suspenseful chase sequence through the campus and the surprise identity of the masked maniac lift it above average. Three sequels followed. AJ Violence, swearing, some nudity. *DVD*

Leslie Nielsen *Mr Hammond* • Jamie Lee Curtis *Kim* • Casey Stevens *Nick* • Antoinette Bower *Mrs Hammond* • Eddie Benton [Anne-Marie Martin] *Wendy* • Michael Tough *Alex* • Robert Silverman *Sykes* ■ *Dir* Paul Lynch • *Scr* William Gray, from a story by Robert Guza Jr

Prom Night ★ 15
Horror thriller   2008 · US · Colour · 85min

Three years after her family were brutally slaughtered by deranged teacher Richard Fenton (Johnathon Schaech), distraught teen Donna (Brittany Snow) prepares to attend her senior prom. Naturally, it falls on the day that her homicidal stalker escapes from prison, intent on finishing what he started. Director Nelson McCormick's loose remake of the 1980 horror proves to be lighter on gore, thrills, suspense and sense – taking the soft option at every turn. Who cares how flimsy the plot is, as long as there are beautiful people up on the screen and dance hits on the soundtrack? AJ *DVD*

Brittany Snow *Donna Keppel* • Scott Porter *Bobby* • Jessica Stroup *Claire* • Dana Davis *Lisa* • Collins Pennie *Ronnie* • Kelly Blatz *Michael* • Johnathon Schaech *Richard Fenton* ■ *Dir* Nelson McCormick • *Scr* JS Cardone

La Promesse ★★★★ 15
Drama   1996 · Bel/Fr/Tun/Lux · Colour · 90min

Borrowing its uncompromising style from the British school of realism, this harrowing rites-of-passage story was partly inspired by Dostoyevsky's *The Brothers Karamazov*. Depicting Europe as a soulless capitalist subjecting the underdeveloped world to a new form of slavery, the film focuses on the feud that develops between an apprentice mechanic and his immigrant-trafficking father over how to help the widow of an African worker. Co-directors Luc and Jean-Pierre Dardenne pull no punches in this grimy study of human misery, saving their fiercest body blow for the very end. DP French +subtitles. *DVD*

Jérémie Rénier *Igor* • Olivier Gourmet *Roger* • Assita Ouedraogo *Assita* • Rasmane Ouedraogo *Amidou* ■ *Dir/Scr* Jean-Pierre Dardenne, Luc Dardenne

Prometheus ★★★★ 15
Science-fiction horror
2012 · US · Colour · 118min

Director Ridley Scott's eagerly anticipated return to science fiction, 30 years after *Blade Runner*, shares much of its DNA with *Alien*, his first foray into the genre, though it's more of a precursor than a prequel to that 1979 shocker. In the latter half of the 21st century, a spacecraft with a crew including idealistic archaeologists (Noomi Rapace, Logan Marshall-Green), ruthless star voyagers (Charlize Theron, Idris Elba) and a super-computer android (Michael Fassbender) sets out to find an extraterrestrial race that may hold the key to the origins of man. The thrilling, edge-of-the-seat story is the movie's beating heart, though Scott also explores themes of identity and self-worth that run through films like *Blade Runner*, *Thelma & Louise* and *Gladiator*, and asks profound questions

about creation and mortality. TeS Violence, swearing. *DVD* Blu-ray 3D

Noomi Rapace *Elizabeth Shaw* • Michael Fassbender *David* • Charlize Theron *Meredith Vickers* • Idris Elba *Captain Janek* • Guy Pearce *Peter Weyland* • Logan Marshall-Green *Charlie Holloway* ■ *Dir* Ridley Scott • *Scr* Damon Lindelof, Jon Spaihts, based on elements by Dan O'Bannon, Ronald Shusett

Promise ★★★★
Drama   1986 · US · Colour · 96min

Party animal James Garner promises his dying mother that he will take care of his schizophrenic brother (James Woods) in this award-winning, critically acclaimed and heartfelt drama. Remarkably similar to *Rain Man*, made two years later, this emotional roller coaster ride is no less memorable in all artistic departments. A TV movie gem, beautifully written by Richard Friedenberg and shot entirely on location in Oregon. AJ

James Garner *Bob* • James Woods *DJ* • Piper Laurie *Annie* • Peter Michael Goetz *Stuart* • Michael Alldredge *Gibb* • Alan Rosenberg *Dr Pressman* • Mary Marsh *Mrs Post* ■ *Dir* Glenn Jordan • *Scr* Richard Friedenberg, from a story by Richard Friedenberg, Tennyson Flowers, Kenneth Blackwell

The Promise ★★ 15
Romantic drama
1994 · Ger/Fr/Swi · BW and Colour · 110min

Once one of the most vital forces in New German Cinema, Margarethe von Trotta has been forced into something of a festival backwater of late. The reasons are not hard to identify in this laboured romantic allegory about Germany in the era of the Wall. Initially, there's a certain sweetness about the doomed relationship between young easterners Anian Zollner and Meret Becker. But once she escapes to the West and the couple mature into August Zirner and Corinna Harfouch, the political ironies and cruel coincidences begin to mount up. DP German +subtitles.

Corinna Harfouch *Sophie* • Meret Becker *Sophie, as a young woman* • August Zirner *Konrad* • Anian Zollner *Konrad, as a young man* • Jean-Yves Gautier *Gerard* • Eva Mattes *Barbara* ■ *Dir* Margarethe von Trotta • *Scr* Peter Schneider, Margarethe von Trotta, Felice Laudadio, from an idea by Francesco Laudadio

A Promise ★★ 12A
Romantic drama   2013 · Fr/Bel · Colour · 98min

Patrice Leconte's English-language debut is a tepid adaptation of Stefan Zweig's novella *Journey into the Past*. Opening in Frankfurt in 1912, the film sees steel tycoon Alan Rickman hire engineer Richard Madden, who becomes besotted with the ailing magnate's young wife (Rebecca Hall). The pair then have to fight their feelings as the country drifts towards war. The lack of chemistry between Madden and Hall drains the film of energy and their unrequited longing is often unintentionally amusing. DP Sex scenes.

Rebecca Hall *Lotte Hoffmeister* • Richard Madden *Friedrich Zeitz* • Alan Rickman *Karl Hoffmeister* • Toby Murray *Otto Hoffmeister* • Maggie Steed *Frau Hermann* ■ *Dir* Patrice Leconte • *Scr* Patrice Leconte, Jérôme Tonnerre, from the novel *Journey into the Past* by Stefan Zweig

Promise Her Anything ★
Comedy   1966 · UK · Colour · 96min

The worst movie of Warren Beatty's career cast him as a porno film-maker redeemed by his relationship with next-door neighbour Leslie Caron and her baby son. Tacky and flashily directed, it is set in New York but was shot entirely in London since Beatty was living there with Caron who was unable to leave because of a court order regarding her children. AT

Warren Beatty *Harley Rummel* • Leslie Caron *Michele O'Brien* • Bob Cummings [Robert Cummings] *Dr Peter Brock* • Hermione Gingold *Mrs Luce* • Lionel Stander *Sam* • Keenan Wynn *Angelo Carelli* • Asa Maynor *Rusty* • Michael Bradley *John Thomas* • David Sutherland *Baby's father* ■ *Dir* Arthur Hiller • *Scr* William Peter Blatty, from a story by Arne Sultan, Marvin Worth

Promised a Miracle

★★★★ PG

Drama based on a true story
1988 · US · Colour · 95min

This classy and highly intelligent TV movie takes a great moral conundrum and for once gives it the breadth and vision it deserves. Based on the true story of the Parkers, a deeply religious couple who were accused of manslaughter after refusing medical treatment for their diabetic son, it addresses a subject on which most people will have strong views. But, far from portraying the Parkers as negligent nutters, director Stephen Gyllenhaal extracts two wonderfully complex, compassionate performances from Rosanna Arquette and Judge Reinhold. All concerned acquit themselves exceptionally well. SH

Rosanna Arquette *Alice "Lucky" Parker* • Judge Reinhold *Larry Parker* • Tom Bower *Michael Elliott* • Vonni Ribisi *[Giovanni Ribisi] Wesley Parker* • Robin Pearson Rose *Beth* ■ *Dir* Stephen Gyllenhaal • *Scr* David Hill, from the book *We Let Our Son Die* by Larry Parker, Donald Tanner

Promised Land

★★★ 15

Coming-of-age drama
1988 · US · Colour · 101min

Michael Hoffman marked himself out as a promising young director on the strength of this underrated coming-of-age drama. There is much to enjoy in this accomplished tale of high schoolfriends discovering that adulthood is not quite what they expected. Kiefer Sutherland gives one of his best performances as the drop-out of the group, who hooks up with misunderstood bad girl Meg Ryan. Meanwhile, back home his old chum Jason Gedrick is now a cop with romantic problems of his own. The interweaving stories don't quite gel, but the cinematography is superb and Hoffman succeeds in summoning up an air of quiet melancholy. JF Swearing, nudity.

Jason Gedrick *Davey Hancock* • Tracy Pollan *Mary Daley* • Kiefer Sutherland *Danny Rivers* • Meg Ryan *Bev* • Googy Gress *Baines* • Deborah Richter *Pammie* • Oscar Rowland *Mr Rivers* • Jay Underwood *Circle K Clerk* ■ *Dir/Scr* Michael Hoffman

Promised Land

★★★ 15

Drama
2012 · US/UAE · Colour · 114min

This even-handed fictional tale about an energy corporation buying up farmland is as gently paced as the similarly pitched David-and-Goliath fable *Local Hero*. Matt Damon and Frances McDormand are the slick company reps who come up against local retired engineer Hal Holbrook and charismatic eco-warrior John Krasinski. But the real focus of the story – co-written by Damon and Krasinski – hinges on Damon's crisis of corporate confidence, which is subtly played. The material is deftly handled by director Gus Van Sant, who unashamedly hymns the rolling American landscape, but the narrative would have benefited from having a few more surprises up its plaid sleeve. AC Swearing. DVD BL

Matt Damon *Steve Butler* • John Krasinski *Dustin Noble* • Frances McDormand *Sue Thomason* • Rosemarie DeWitt *Alice* • Scoot McNairy *Jeff Dennon* • Hal Holbrook *Frank Yates* ■ *Dir* Gus Van Sant • *Scr* Matt Damon, John Krasinski, from a story by Dave Eggers • *Music* Danny Elfman

Pronto

★★

Crime comedy thriller
1996 · US · Colour · 100min

Elmore Leonard adaptations tend to be hit-and-miss affairs – and this mediocre comedy crime thriller certainly comes into the latter category. Betraying its TV-movie status in every frame, the tale stars *Columbo* mainstay Peter Falk as a Miami bookmaker who flees to Italy when a Mob boss sets him up for murder. Despite brisk pacing and frequently snappy dialogue, the film is hampered by its flimsy plot and clumsy execution. SF

Peter Falk *Harry Arno* • Glenne Headly *Joyce Patton* • James LeGros *Raylan Givens* • Sergio Castellitto *Tommy "The Zip"* • Walter Olkewicz *Jimmy "Cap" Capatorto* • Glenn Plummer *Robert Gee* • Luis Guzman *Torres* ■ *Dir* Jim McBride • *Scr* Michael Butler, from the novel by Elmore Leonard

Proof

★★★★ 15

Psychological drama 1991 · Aus · Colour · 86min

An astonishing Australian oddity that should have established the reputation of writer/director Jocelyn Moorhouse, but didn't, this is about a blind photographer (that's right) who relies on others to describe his work and who is lusted after by his cleaner. Rejected, she discovers that her employer has become friends with another young man and from this point the triangular eroticism strikes an even more bizarre note. Hugo Weaving, Genevieve Picot and Russell Crowe as the romantically inclined threesome pursue their outlandish course with skill and humour. TH Swearing, nudity. DVD

Hugo Weaving *Martin* • Genevieve Picot *Celia* • Russell Crowe *Andy* • Heather Mitchell *Martin's mother* • Jeffrey Walker *Young Martin* • Belinda Davey *Doctor* ■ *Dir/Scr* Jocelyn Moorhouse

Proof

★★ 12

Psychological drama 2005 · US · Colour · 96min

This heavy-handed adaptation of David Auburn's Pulitzer Prize-winning play follows Gwyneth Paltrow's struggles to come to terms with the death of her mathematical father (Anthony Hopkins) and her own frustrated ambitions in that discipline. As student Jake Gyllenhaal delves into her father's legacy, questions of sanity and authorship arise over a newly discovered document. The story feels static and overly talky, and nothing disguises the staginess of this pretentious psychological whodunnit. AJ Swearing, sex scenes. DVD

Gwyneth Paltrow *Catherine* • Anthony Hopkins *Robert* • Jake Gyllenhaal *Hal* • Hope Davis *Claire* • Gary Houston *Professor Barrow* • Roshan Seth *Professor Bhandari* ■ *Dir* John Madden • *Scr* David Auburn, Rebecca Miller, from the play by David Auburn

Proof of Life

★★★ 15

Action suspense drama
2000 · US/UK · Colour · 129min

Part action movie, part romance and part thriller, Taylor Hackford's efficient kidnap drama is set in a fictional South American country where Meg Ryan's marriage comes under further strain when her engineer husband David Morse is taken hostage by guerrillas. Enter the heroic Russell Crowe, a professional "K&R" (that's kidnap and ransom) man, who agrees to help Ryan. The leads enjoyed a well-publicised romance during filming, but any steaminess apparently ended up on the cutting room floor. JB Swearing, violence. DVD

Meg Ryan *Alice Bowman* • Russell Crowe *Terry Thorne* • David Morse *Peter Bowman* • David Caruso *Dino* • Pamela Reed *Janis Goodman* ■ *Dir* Taylor Hackford • *Scr* Tony Gilroy

Prophecy

★★ 15

Horror 1979 · US · Colour · 97min

One of the earliest of the eco-shockers, this demonstrates the decline of director John Frankenheimer. Doctor Robert Foxworth and his pregnant wife Talia Shire go to investigate a report of mercury poisoning in the Maine backwoods and find themselves battling giant mutants. If only the direction had been as fluid as the mercury. TH

Talia Shire *Maggie* • Robert Foxworth *Rob Vern* • Armand Assante *John Hawks* • Richard Dysart *Isley* • Victoria Racimo *Ramona* • George Clutesi *M'Rai* ■ *Dir* John Frankenheimer • *Scr* David Seltzer

The Prophecy

★★★ 18

Supernatural horror 1994 · US · Colour · 93min

Priest-turned-cop Elias Koteas gets caught up in an earthly battle between renegade angels Christopher Walken and Eric Stoltz in a strangely ambiguous and slightly pretentious horror fantasy. The wildly imaginative premise and poetic development, along with a solid cast that includes Virginia Madsen and Amanda Plummer, make this often compelling, sometimes corny, chiller a bizarre cult item. Lacking the sort of special effects you would expect from such an apocalyptic notion, this was successful enough to spawn two sequels. AJ Violence, swearing. DVD

Christopher Walken *Angel Gabriel* • Elias Koteas *Thomas Dagget* • Eric Stoltz *Angel Simon* • Virginia Madsen *Katherine* • Moriah Shining Dove Snyder *Mary* • Adam Goldberg *Jerry* • Amanda Plummer *Rachael* • Viggo Mortensen *Lucifer* ■ *Dir/Scr* Gregory Widen

The Prophecy II

★★ 18

Supernatural horror 1997 · US · Colour · 79min

Carrying on from the first movie, Christopher Walken's archangel Gabriel, angered that God has favoured humans over his kind, returns to hunt down Jennifer Beals, who is pregnant with the saviour of mankind. But where the original boasted some good, offbeat ideas, this degenerates into just another dumb chase movie. RS Swearing, violence, nudity. DVD

Christopher Walken *Gabriel* • Jennifer Beals *Valerie Rosales* • Brittany Murphy *Izzy* • Russell Wong *Danyael* • William Prael *Rafayel* • Danny Strong *Julian* • Glenn Danzig *Samayel* • Eric Roberts *Michael* ■ *Dir* Greg Spence • *Scr* Matt Greenberg, Greg Spence

The Prophecy 3: the Ascent

★★ 15

Supernatural horror 2000 · US · Colour · 80min

This disappointing climax to the series lacks both narrative ingenuity and visual élan. Returning as the Archangel Gabriel, Christopher Walken isn't given nearly enough to do, as the ambitious Vincent Spano seeks to destroy street preacher Dave Buzzotta (replacing Russell Wong as Danyael, the half-human, half-angel nephilim). It's the unsung Spano who seizes the attention with his quirky display of celestial malevolence. DP DVD

Christopher Walken *Gabriel* • Scott Cleverdon *Pyriel* • Brad Dourif *Zealot* • Vincent Spano *Zophael "Jones"* • Dave Buzzotta *Danyael* ■ *Dir* Patrick Lussier • *Scr* Joel Soisson

A Prophet

★★★★ 18

Prison drama 2009 · Fr/It · Colour · 148min

This relentlessly gripping thriller emphasises the humanity of its characters while in no way flinching from the brutality of criminal life. Tahar Rahim is utterly compelling as Malik, a 19-year-old French-Arab man sent to jail for a petty crime. Behind prison walls, his youth and inexperience leave him open to exploitation, but Malik also uses his time inside to get an education – both academic and criminal. The movie has a grimy, downbeat air that is lightened by some moments of surrealism, but it's Rahim's bold portrait of a man struggling to survive inside without losing his identity that makes this an unforgettable experience. LB French, Arabic, Corsu +subtitles. Violence, swearing, sex scenes, drug abuse. DVD BL

Tahar Rahim *Malik El Djebena* • Niels Arestrup *César Luciani* • Adel Bencherif *Ryad* • Reda Kateb *Jordi the gypsy* • Hichem Yacoubi *Reyeb* • Jean-Philippe Ricci *Vettorri* ■ *Dir* Jacques Audiard • *Scr* Thomas Bidegain, Jacques Audiard, from an original screenplay by Abdel Raouf Dafri, Nicolas Peufaillit, from an idea by Dafri

The Prophet's Game

★★ 18

Thriller 1999 · US · Colour · 103min

The pairing of Dennis Hopper with clean-cut Stephanie Zimbalist is probably the most imaginative thing about this undemanding serial-killer thriller. Hopper is the retired Seattle detective whose past comes back to haunt him with the seeming reappearance of his old nemesis The Prophet – a killer who likes to confess his crimes to the veteran policeman. As the body count mounts, Zimbalist is the only local cop who believes Hopper s story. The two leads are watchable, but it fails to chill the bones. JF DVD

Dennis Hopper *Vincent Swan* • Stephanie Zimbalist *Det Francis Aldobrandi* • Joe Penny *Walter Motter* • Robert Yocum *Alan Joyce* • Sondra Locke *Adele Highsmith* • Shannon Whirry *Barb* • Michael Dorn *Chief Bob Bowman* ■ *Dir* David Worth • *Scr* Carol Chrest

The Proposal

★★★ 18

Crime thriller 2000 · US · Colour · 86min

Nick Moran stars with considerable aplomb in this direct-to-video offering. Credibly suggesting the pressures of his perilous situation, he plays an undercover cop whose sting on mobster Stephen Lang is jeopardised by both the divided loyalties of rookie Jennifer Esposito and the heavy-handed tactics of the FBI. Considering this was his directorial debut, Richard Gale sustains the tension without resort to self-conscious flourish and allows the action to turn on character, not contrivance. DP

Nick Moran *Terry Martin* • Jennifer Esposito *Susan Reese* • Stephen Lang *Simon Bacig* • William B Davis *Agent Frank Gruning* ■ *Dir* Richard Gale • *Scr* Maurice Hurley, Richard Gale

The Proposal

★★★ 12

Romantic comedy 2009 · US · Colour · 103min

Sandra Bullock is a big-shot at a New York publishing house who, to avoid deportation to her native Canada, pressures her assistant (Ryan Reynolds) into marrying her. The hitch comes when officials nose around, forcing them to spend a weekend away with her family. A gentle, predictable plot is fleshed out with strong comic turns from Bullock and Reynolds, who share real chemistry and snappy dialogue. Betty White also shines as the matriarch in a film that's comfortingly similar to the screwball comedies of old. KK Some swearing, sexual references. DVD BL

Sandra Bullock *Margaret Tate* • Ryan Reynolds *Andrew Paxton* • Mary Steenburgen *Grace Paxton* • Craig T Nelson *Joe Paxton* • Betty White *Grandma Annie* • Denis O'Hare *Mr Gilbertson* • Michael Nouri *Chairman Bergen* ■ *Dir* Anne Fletcher • *Scr* Pete Chiarelli

The Proposition

★★★ 18

Period romantic drama
1996 · UK/US · Colour · 92min

This period drama has a plot that sounds like a classic western, but it's actually set in 19th-century Wales around the time of the Napoleonic Wars. Theresa Russell plays a feisty widow who refuses to be forced into a marriage of convenience to local sheriff Richard Lynch, despite her dire financial situation. Instead she opts to save the estate by driving her herd of cattle to market herself – with a little help from Patrick Bergin. It's a strong story, well told, with good use of landscape, and memorable performances from Russell and co-stars Bergin and Lynch. DA

Theresa Russell *Catherine Morgan* • Patrick Bergin *Rhys Williams* • Richard Lynch *Sheriff Williams* ■ *Dir* Strathford Hamilton • *Scr* Paul Matthews

The Proposition

★★★ 12

Romantic crime drama
1998 · US · Colour · 107min

The plot for this crime film set in Boston in the 1930s is more suited to a lurid soap opera than a major movie, but it's saved by the quality of the acting on show. Director Lesli Linka Glatter's overwrought drama centres on impotent lawyer William Hurt, who "hires" Neil Patrick Harris to impregnate his wife Madeleine Stowe. The trouble starts when Harris falls in love with Stowe, and clergyman Kenneth Branagh arrives on the scene to further confuse matters. TH Swearing.

Kenneth Branagh *Father Michael McKinnon* • Madeleine Stowe *Eleanor Barret* • William Hurt *Arthur Barret* • Neil Patrick Harris *Roger Martin* • Robert Loggia *Hannibal Thurman* • Blythe Danner *Syril Danning* • Josef Sommer *Father Dryer* ■ *Dir* Lesli Linka Glatter • *Scr* Rick Ramage

The Proposition ★★★★ 18
Period revenge drama
2004 · Aus/UK · Colour · 99min

John Hillcoat's gritty, grimy and blood-drenched "western" paints a bleak, violent picture of the Australian outback in the 1880s. Guy Pearce plays the middle brother in a troika of violent outlaws who are accused of a heinous crime. When he is captured by British lawman Ray Winstone, Pearce is faced with the invidious proposition of the title: bring in the head of his older brother (Danny Huston) or his younger sibling will hang. Winstone brilliantly demonstrates his twin capacities for sentiment and sudden violence, and there's excellent support from Huston and John Hurt as a crazed bounty hunter. AS Swearing, violence. DVD BD
Guy Pearce *Charlie Burns* · Ray Winstone *Captain Stanley* · Danny Huston *Arthur Burns* · John Hurt *Jellon Lamb* · David Wenham *Eden Fletcher* · Emily Watson *Martha Stanley* · Richard Wilson (4) *Mike Burns* · Noah Taylor *Brian O'Leary* · David Gulpilil *Jacko* ■ *Dir* John Hillcoat · *Scr* Nick Cave

The Proprietor ★★ 12
Drama   1996 · UK/Fr/Tur/US · Colour · 108min

Ismail Merchant's second solo directorial outing is a middlebrow misfire. Pitted with clumsy flashbacks, the story turns around author Jeanne Moreau's memories of her mother, who was murdered by the Nazis, and her hopes for a screen version of her most famous novel. Romances and reunions provide diversions, but the action too often lapses into kitsch and cultural snobbery. DP French, English +subtitles. DVD
Jeanne Moreau *Adrienne Mark* · Sean Young *Virginia Kelly/Sally* · Austin Pendleton *Willy Kunst* · Nell Carter *Milly* · Marc Tissot *Patrice Legendre* · Christopher Cazenove *Elliott Spencer* · Sam Waterston *Harry Bancroft* · Jean-Pierre Aumont *Franz Legendre* ■ *Dir* Ismail Merchant · *Scr* Jean-Marie Besset · George Trow

Prospero's Books ★★★★ 15
Drama   1991 · Neth/Fr/It/UK · Colour · 120min

Historically important both as a record of John Gielgud's celebrated stage rendition of Prospero, and as the first film to be shot entirely in High Definition Video, this visually stunning fantasy is more than just a straightforward adaptation of *The Tempest*. Focusing on the exiled Duke of Milan's beloved 24-volume library, Peter Greenaway overlays multiple images and textual information in a meditation on the processes of thought and artistic creation, with Gielgud's voicing of all Shakespeare's characters. Viewers may find Greenaway's experiments with non-linear narrative challenging, but patience is rewarded. TH
John Gielgud *Prospero* · Michael Clark *Caliban* · Michel Blanc *Alonso* · Erland Josephson *Gonzalo* · Isabelle Pasco *Miranda* · Tom Bell *Antonio* · Kenneth Cranham *Sebastian* · Mark Rylance *Ferdinand* ■ *Dir* Peter Greenaway · *Scr* Peter Greenaway, from the play *The Tempest* by William Shakespeare · *Music* Michael Nyman

The Protector ★★★ 18
Martial arts action drama
1985 · US · Colour · 90min

This was one of Jackie Chan's early American productions, an efficient action movie tinged with 007-style hardware. He plays a tough cop battling bad guys in New York before being sent on assignment with Danny Aiello to Hong Kong to track down a drug kingpin. As usual with Chan movies, the plot and dialogue are forgettable but the all-out action scenes dazzle the eye. RS
Jackie Chan *Billy Wong* · Danny Aiello *Danny Garoni* · Sandy Alexander *Gang leader* · Roy Chiao *Mr Ko* · Victor Arnold *Police Captain* ■ *Dir/Scr* James Glickenhaus

Protégé ★★ 18
Thriller
2007 · HK/Sing/UK/Chi · Colour · 108min

Reminiscent of 2002 Asian hit *Infernal Affairs*, this casts Hong Kong superstar Andy Lau as a drug trafficker looking for a successor to take over his heroin import business. Unfortunately for him, he chooses undercover cop (Daniel Wu) who is working his way up the supply chain in an effort to nab the gang's Thai supplier. Ambitious in its scope, this is simultaneously a competent police thriller, a half-baked exposé of the Golden Triangle's heroin trade and a morally simplistic warning about the dangers of drug abuse. Not all these elements fuse together seamlessly and while Lau's trafficker is nicely drawn, the main focus is on Wu's insipid cop. JR Cantonese, English, Thai +subtitles. DVD
Andy Lau *Lin Quin, "Banker"* · Daniel Wu *Nick* · Zhang Jingchu *Jane* · Louis Koo *Jane's husband* · Anita Yuen *Quin's wife* · Nirut Sirijanya *General Chachai* ■ *Dir/Scr* Derek Yee

Proteus ★★★ 18
Science-fiction horror
1995 · UK · Colour · 92min

This typical monsters-on-the-loose movie is creepy all the way, floundering only slightly in its pacing and acting. A group of inept yuppies-turned-amateur drug-runners stumble upon a seemingly abandoned research rig in mid-ocean. The few people left seem terrified of something, but they never stick around long enough to say what. The dark industrial setting makes for good atmosphere, but it's still just a monster movie. ST Swearing, violence. DVD
Craig Fairbrass *Alex* · Toni Barry *Linda* · William Marsh *Mark* · Jennifer Calvert *Rachel* · Robert Firth *Paul* · Margot Steinberg *Christine* ■ *Dir* Bob Keen · *Scr* John Brosnan, from the novel *Slimer* by Harry Adam Knight [John Brosnan]

Protocol ★★★ PG
Comedy   1984 · US · Colour · 90min

This is hardly A-grade Goldie Hawn, but a charming enough comedy all the same. She plays, unsurprisingly, a dizzy blonde, thrown into the world of intrigue in Washington when she saves the life of a Middle Eastern politician. The engaging cast struggles valiantly with an uneven script from writer Buck Henry, but director Herbert Ross puts sufficient energy into his task to paper over the creative cracks. JF Violence, swearing.
Goldie Hawn *Sunny Davis* · Chris Sarandon *Michael Ransome* · Richard Romanus *Emir of Ohtar* · Andre Gregory *Nawaf Al Kabeer* · Gail Strickland *Mrs St John* · Cliff De Young *Hilley* · Ed Begley Jr *Hassler* ■ *Dir* Herbert Ross · *Scr* Buck Henry, from a story by Charles Shyer, Nancy Meyers, Harvey Miller

The Proud Ones ★★★
Drama   1953 · Fr/Mex · BW · 103min

It's difficult to accept that this simmering Mexican melodrama was adapted from a Jean-Paul Sartre novel. But, while it's deficient in the psychological department, Yves Allégret's tale of damaged souls and redemption through love and sacrifice has many other things going for it, not least the atmospheric photography of Alex Phillips, who captures the stifling desperation of a small coastal town at the height of a meningitis epidemic. Michèle Morgan has rarely combined vulnerability and eroticism to better effect, as the stranded widow who rouses doctor Gérard Philipe from his alcoholic haze. DP French dubbed.
Michèle Morgan *Nellie* · Gérard Philipe *Georges* · Victor Manuel Mendoza *Don Rodrigo* · Carlos Lopez Moctezuma *Doctor* · Michèle Cordoue *Anna* ■ *Dir* Yves Allégret · *Scr* Jean Aurenche, Yves Allégret, from the novel *Typhus* by Jean-Paul Sartre

The Proud Ones ★★★ U
Western   1956 · US · Colour · 94min

Robert Ryan, so good at being bad, was in heroic mould for this minor-league western with some high-impact moments. As a sheriff, hampered by disability but psyching himself up for a showdown with a mixed bag of outlaws, his vulnerability is as credible as his courage. It's his performance that makes this modest suspenseful tale better than average. TH
Robert Ryan *Marshal Cass Silver* · Virginia Mayo *Sally Kane* · Jeffrey Hunter *Thad Anderson* · Robert Middleton *Honest John Barrett* · Walter Brennan *Jake* · Arthur O'Connell *Jim Dexter* ■ *Dir* Robert D Webb · *Scr* Edmund H North, Joseph Petracca, from the novel *The Proud Ones* by Verne Athanas

The Proud Rebel ★★★★ U
Western   1958 · US · Colour · 99min

Alan Ladd's finest achievement from the years following *Shane* carries echoes of that film, particularly in the prominence of a small boy. Ladd plays father to his own son, David, who's mute since witnessing his mother's death in the Civil War. It's about the search for a cure, the boy's beloved dog, Olivia de Havilland's kindly spinster farmer, and an evil brood of sheep farmers that includes a young Harry Dean Stanton. Exquisitely photographed, beautifully acted and directed with quiet mastery by Michael Curtiz. AE
Alan Ladd *John Chandler* · Olivia de Havilland *Linnett Moore* · Dean Jagger *Harry Burleigh* · David Ladd *David Chandler* · Cecil Kellaway *Dr Enos Davis* · James Westerfield *Birm Bates* · Henry Hull *Judge Morley* · Dean Stanton [Harry Dean Stanton] *Jeb Burleigh* ■ *Dir* Michael Curtiz · *Scr* Joseph Petracca, Lillie Hayward, from the story *Journal of Linnett Moore* by James Edward Grant · *Cinematographer* Ted McCord

The Proud Valley ★★ PG
Drama   1940 · UK · BW · 73min

This rather dated parable on the need for community unity in the face of wartime tragedy was one of six films Paul Robeson made in Britain, and it gave him the rare opportunity to escape from typecasting as a tribal African. However, his presence is the only thing not to ring true in this well-crafted tale about a mining disaster in a small Welsh village, as he is more prone to melodrama than the solid supporting cast. DP DVD
Paul Robeson *David Goliath* · Edward Chapman *Dick Parry* · Simon Lack *Emlyn Parry* · Rachel Thomas *Mrs Parry* · Dilys Thomas *Dilys* · Edward Rigby *Bert Rigby* ■ *Dir* Penrose Tennyson [Pen Tennyson] · *Scr* Roland Pertwee, Louis Goulding, Jack Jones, Penrose Tennyson, from a story by Herbert Marshall, Alfredda Brilliant

Providence ★★★★★ 15
Drama   1977 · Fr/Swi · Colour · 102min

Alain Resnais's English-language debut was voted the film of the 1970s by an international panel of film-makers and critics. As ever playing intricate games with time and memory, the director has constructed a typically complex film that leaves you unsure whether the action is a flashback to a real event or a figment of the imagination of dying novelist John Gielgud. Intensifying the illusion, David Mercer's script is a perfect pastiche of the kind of florid dialogue found in purple fiction. Gielgud is outstanding, but Dirk Bogarde and Ellen Burstyn also give fine performances. Wonderful cinema from a true master of the art. DP Swearing.
John Gielgud *Clive Langham* · Dirk Bogarde *Claude Langham* · Ellen Burstyn *Sonia Langham* · David Warner *Kevin Woodford* · Elaine Stritch *Helen Weiner/Molly Langham* · Denis Lawson *Dave Woodford* · Cyril Luckham *Dr Mark Eddington* ■ *Dir* Alain Resnais · *Scr* David Mercer · *Music* Miklos Rozsa

Provoked: a True Story ★★ 15
Drama based on a true story
2006 · UK/Ind · Colour · 113min

This British-Indian co-production purports to tell the true story of systematically abused British Punjabi housewife Kiranjit Ahluwalia (played by Bollywood star and former Miss World Aishwarya Rai), who set light to her husband Deepak (Naveen Andrews from TV's *Lost*) in his bed in 1989 and was sentenced to life for murder. She was eventually freed from prison after a campaign that led to a broader legal interpretation of "provocation" in such cases and a greater understanding of the plight of battered spouses. If only this film did the subject justice. AC In English, Punjabi.
Aishwarya Rai *Kiranjit Ahluwalia* · Naveen Andrews *Deepak Ahluwalia* · Miranda Richardson *Veronica Scott* · Robbie Coltrane *Lord Edward Foster* · Ray Panthaki *Ravi* · Nandita Das *Radha Dalal* ■ *Dir* Jag Mundhra · *Scr* Carl Austin, Rahila Gupta

The Prowler ★★★
Film noir   1951 · US · BW · 92min

While investigating a prowler in the neighbourhood, embittered policeman Van Heflin meets Evelyn Keyes whose sterile husband Emerson Treacy is a night-duty disc jockey. Cop and wife then embark on an affair that leads to murder. A taut, bleak *film noir*, well-handled by director Joseph Losey, and by the cast, notably Van Heflin. RK
Van Heflin *Webb Garwood* · Evelyn Keyes *Susan Gilvray* · John Maxwell *Bud Crocker* · Katherine Warren *Mrs Crocker* · Emerson Treacy *William Gilvray* · Madge Blake *Martha Gilvray* ■ *Dir* Joseph Losey · *Scr* Dalton Trumbo, Hugo Butler, from a story by Robert Thoren, from a story by Hans Wilhelm

Prudence and the Pill ★★ 15
Comedy   1968 · UK · Colour · 88min

David Niven and Deborah Kerr's marriage has degenerated into separate bedrooms and lovers. When their niece Judy Geeson steals her mother Joyce Redman's contraceptive pills, substituting aspirin, and Redman gets pregnant, Niven tries the same trick on Kerr, hoping she'll get pregnant by lover Keith Michell and give him grounds for divorce. Topical at the time with the coming of the pill, this British-made farce was directed by Ronald Neame (taking over from Fielder Cook). The polished expertise of Niven and Kerr more or less holds this witless farrago together. RK
Deborah Kerr *Prudence Hardcastle* · David Niven *Gerald Hardcastle* · Robert Coote *Henry Hardcastle* · Irina Demick *Elizabeth* · Joyce Redman *Grace Hardcastle* · Judy Geeson *Geraldine Hardcastle* · Keith Michell *Dr Alan Hewitt* · Edith Evans *Lady Roberta Bates* ■ *Dir* Fielder Cook, Ronald Neame · *Scr* Hugh Mills, from his novel

Psych 9 ★ 15
Horror thriller
2010 · US/UK/Cz Rep · Colour · 98min

In this would-be horror thriller, Sara Foster plays a disturbed young woman who takes a night-job collating files in a ridiculously creepy abandoned hospital. Friendly shrink Cary Elwes is also on admin duty, and provides some free therapy as he tries to untangle Foster's troubled psyche, while all around a veritable firework display of terrifying phenomena erupts. British-born director Andrew Shortell spoils the promising premise and potentially atmospheric setting of his feature debut with a frenzy of ludicrous plotting and overwrought shock effects. AS
Sara Foster *Roslyn* · Cary Elwes *Dr Clement* · Michael Biehn *Detective Marling* · Gabriel Mann *Cole* · Colleen Camp *Beth* ■ *Dir* Andrew Shortell · *Scr* Lawrence Robinson

Psyche '59 ★★
Drama   1964 · UK · BW · 94min

This is an intriguing though slightly over-the-top melodrama about the blind wife (Patricia Neal) of a businessman, who is forced to see (yes, her illness is psychosomatic) when her sister Samantha Eggar, fresh from a divorce, comes to stay. You've seen it all before, and the cod psychology may be a bit irritating, but the cast is strong and the movie is glossily photographed. JG
Curt Jurgens *Eric Crawford* · Patricia Neal *Allison Crawford* · Samantha Eggar *Robin* · Ian Bannen *Paul* · Beatrix Lehmann *Mrs Crawford* · Elspeth March *Mme Valadier* · Sandra Lee *Susan* ■ *Dir* Alexander Singer · *Scr* Julian Halevy [Julian Zimet], from the novel *Psyché 58* by Françoise des Ligneris

P

Psycho

LANDMARK FILM
The modern horror genre begins with Hitchcock's bold, innovative landmark, also revolutionary in terms of plot and marketing

Psycho ★★★★★ 15
Classic horror thriller 1960 · US · BW · 108min

Containing the most famous montage sequence since *The Battleship Potemkin*, this is easily the most shocking film produced by the "Master of Suspense", yet Alfred Hitchcock always maintained it was a black comedy. Working with a TV crew, he completed the picture for a mere $800,000. But the California Gothic tale of the Bates Motel went on to become his greatest commercial success. The opening segment, involving Janet Leigh and an envelope of stolen cash, is the biggest MacGuffin in Hitchcock's career. His most audacious achievement, however, was in getting us to side with the creepy Anthony Perkins against the authorities, Leigh's lover and sister, and his incessantly shrewish mother. DP *DVD* *Blu-ray*

Anthony Perkins *Norman Bates* · Janet Leigh *Marion Crane* · Vera Miles *Lila Crane* · John Gavin *Sam Loomis* · Martin Balsam *Milton Arbogast* · John McIntire *Sheriff Chambers* · Simon Oakland *Dr Richmond* ■ *Dir* Alfred Hitchcock · *Scr* Joseph Stefano, from the novel by Robert Bloch · *Cinematographer* John L Russell · *Music* Bernard Herrmann · *Editor* George Tomasini

Psycho ★ 15
Horror 1998 · US · Colour · 99min

Gus Van Sant must have been a little mad when he agreed to direct this near word-for-word, scene-for-scene impersonation of Hitchcock's most celebrated movie. It simply doesn't work, because every major character is horribly miscast – Anne Heche plays Marion Crane as a kooky cutie and Vince Vaughn's Norman is an effeminate hunk. The pointlessness of watching a stagey, badly acted replica of one of cinema's true masterpieces cannot be ignored. JC Violence, brief nudity. *DVD*

Vince Vaughn *Norman Bates* · Anne Heche *Marion Crane* · Julianne Moore *Lila Crane* · Viggo Mortensen *Sam Loomis* · William H Macy *Milton Arbogast* · Robert Forster *Dr Simon* · Philip Baker Hall *Sheriff Chambers* · Anne Haney *Mrs Chambers* · Chad Everett *Tom Cassidy* ■ *Dir* Gus Van Sant · *Scr* Joseph Stefano, from the 1960 film

Psycho II ★★★ 18
Horror 1983 · US · Colour · 107min

Two decades after the motel murders, Norman Bates is released from the asylum and returns to the scene of his crimes but has "Mother" come too? Of course, this isn't Hitchcock, but it's a highly credible, nicely creepy and well paced sequel, and Anthony Perkins reprises his most famous role with no visible signs of ennui, and there are several other enjoyable and gritty performances, most notably from original cast member Vera Miles and Dennis Franz. SH Violence, swearing, nudity. *DVD*

Anthony Perkins *Norman Bates* · Vera Miles *Lila Loomis* · Meg Tilly *Mary* · Robert Loggia *Dr Raymond* · Dennis Franz *Toomey* · Hugh Gillin *Sheriff Hunt* · Claudia Bryar *Mrs Spool* ■ *Dir* Richard Franklin · *Scr* Tom Holland, from characters by Robert Bloch

Psycho III ★★ 18
Horror 1986 · US · Colour · 88min

Anthony Perkins stars in and directs a rather mean-spirited second sequel to the Hitchcock classic in which Norman falls in love with a suicidal nun, poignantly played by Diana Scarwid. Filled with overwrought in-jokes (the *Vertigo*-influenced opening), flashbacks to the original film (Janet Leigh's face turning into Scarwid's) and copious blood-letting (the studio added extra gore), Perkins goes for the jugular in a melodramatic way. AJ Swearing, violence. *DVD*

Anthony Perkins *Norman Bates* · Diana Scarwid *Maureen Coyle* · Jeff Fahey *Duane Duke* · Roberta Maxwell *Tracy Venable* · Hugh Gillin *Sheriff Hunt* · Lee Garlington *Myrna* · Robert

Alan Browne *Statler* ■ *Dir* Anthony Perkins · *Scr* Charles Edward Pogue, from characters by Robert Bloch

Psycho IV: the Beginning ★★ 18
Horror 1990 · US · Colour · 92min

The Norman Bates saga came to an end in this sorry made-for-TV finale. It's a shame because the plot at least offers up an intriguing twist: as the now rehabilitated Norman (Anthony Perkins, again excellent) discusses his fears over a radio phone-in, we flash back to the young Norman (played here by *ET*'s Henry Thomas) and his troubled relationship with his mother. However, this is sloppily executed and the climax is just plain silly. JF Violence, nudity. *DVD*

Anthony Perkins *Norman Bates* · Henry Thomas *Young Norman* · Olivia Hussey *Norma Bates* · CCH Pounder *Fran Ambrose* · Warren Frost *Dr Leo Richmond* · Donna Mitchell *Connie Bates* ■ *Dir* Mick Garris · *Scr* Joseph Stefano, from characters by Robert Bloch

Psychomania ★★★
Horror 1972 · UK · Colour · 90min

This British horror cheapie is so ridiculous it works. For much of the time this psychedelic zombie biker frightener is utter drivel, but director Don Sharp throws in some cracking scenes, notably the one in which leader of the gang Nicky Henson rises from the grave, bike and all. Henson has a hoot as the Angel from Hell, and he is superbly supported by Beryl Reid as his devil-worshipping mum and George Sanders as her ghoulish butler. Sanders committed suicide shortly after this film was made. DP

Nicky Henson *Tom Latham* · Beryl Reid *Mrs Latham* · George Sanders *Shadwell* · Mary Larkin *Abby* · Roy Holder *Bertram* · Robert Hardy *Chief Inspector Hesseltine* · Patrick Holt *Sergeant* · Denis Gilmore *Hatchet* ■ *Dir* Don Sharp · *Scr* Arnaud D'Usseau, Julian Halevy [Julian Zimet]

The Psychopath ★
Horror thriller 1966 · UK · Colour · 82min

Hammer's main rival, Amicus, produced some highly original shockers but, despite a screenplay by Robert Bloch, author of *Psycho*, this isn't one of them. Once again, a psychopath murders his enemies one by one, leaving a model of the victim next to each body, and it doesn't take much imagination to work out who the culprit is. There's little atmosphere, and Margaret Johnston overplays to the point of burlesque. DM

Patrick Wymark *Inspector Holloway* · Margaret Johnston *Mrs Von Sturm* · John Standing *Mark Von Sturm* · Alexander Knox *Frank Saville* · Judy Huxtable *Louise Saville* ■ *Dir* Freddie Francis · *Scr* Robert Bloch

P'Tang, Yang, Kipperbang ★★★★ PG
Comedy 1982 · UK · Colour · 76min

This surreal phrase chanted by 14-year-old schoolboys illustrates the gentle, oddball comedy of this story by TV playwright Jack Rosenthal. John Albasiny has a crush on the prettiest girl in class (Abigail Cruttenden) but a host of obstacles are put in the way of his declaration of passion. Directed by Michael Apted, it's a wry and highly comic look at teenage lust with some splendid performances. TH *DVD*

John Albasiny *Alan Duckworth* · Abigail Cruttenden *Ann* · Maurice Dee *Geoffrey* · Alison Steadman *Estelle Land* · Mark Brailsford *Abbo* · Chris Karallis *Shaz* · Frances Ruffelle *Eunice* · Robert Urquhart *Headmaster* ■ *Dir* Michael Apted · *Scr* Jack Rosenthal

Puberty Blues ★★ 15
Drama 1981 · Aus · Colour · 82min

Here two young Aussie women (Nell Schofield and Jad Capelja) try to break into the male bastion of the surfing set, experiencing all the frustrations and rejections that you'd expect. It's sensitively handled, if ultimately a little weak. Not one

of director Bruce Beresford's finest moments by any means. FL

Nell Schofield *Debbie Vickers* · Jad Capelja *Sue Knight* · Geoff Rhoe *Garry* · Tony Hughes *Danny* · Sandy Paul *Tracy* ■ *Dir* Bruce Beresford · *Scr* Margaret Kelly, from the novel by Kathy Lette, Gabrielle Carey

Public Access ★★★★ 18
Thriller 1993 · US · Colour · 85min

Clean-cut Ron Marquette starts a show on public access cable TV in the small town of Brewster. Marquette encourages his viewers to call in and sound off about the problems in their town, stirring up antipathy. But what is his motive for getting people to reveal their grievances? This was Bryan Singer's first feature film as writer/director, and you can already see his propensity for camera tricks and intelligent scripts. Ron Marquette is arresting as the mild-mannered Whiley and probably had an interesting career ahead, but he committed suicide in 1995. ST *DVD*

Ron Marquette *Whiley Pritcher* · Dina Brooks *Rachel* · Burt Williams *Bob Hodges* · Larry Maxwell *Jeff Abernathy* · Charles Kavanaugh *Mayor Breyer* · Brandon Boyce *Kevin Havey* ■ *Dir* Bryan Singer · *Scr* Christopher McQuarrie, Michael Feit Dugan, Bryan Singer

Public Enemies ★★★★ 15
Biographical crime drama 2009 · US · Colour · 134min

Sporting a uniformly strong cast, this epic crime drama from director Michael Mann makes a documentary-style fable out of the infamous moments in the short, sharp career of Depression-era gangster John Dillinger (Johnny Depp). The sumptuous production design and vibrant natural lighting enhance the daring prison break-outs, well-planned bank robberies and doomed romance with hat-check girl Billie Frechette (Marion Cotillard) that lead to a fateful meeting with G-Man Melvin Purvis (Christian Bale) and J Edgar Hoover's fledgeling FBI. Directed with astute flair and fascinatingly detailed, this is freshly conceived myth-making on a grand scale, with the captivating Depp/Cotillard chemistry an added bonus. AJ *DVD* *Blu-ray*

Johnny Depp *John Dillinger* · Christian Bale *Melvin Purvis* · Marion Cotillard *Billie Frechette* · Giovanni Ribisi *Alvin Karpis* · Stephen Dorff *Homer Van Meter* · Billy Crudup *J Edgar Hoover* · David Wenham *Harry "Pete" Pierpont* · Channing Tatum *Pretty Boy Floyd* · Emilie de Ravin *Anna Patzke* · Leelee Sobieski *Polly Hamilton* ■ *Dir* Michael Mann · *Scr* Ronan Bennett, Ann Biderman, Michael Mann, from the non-fiction book *Public Enemies: America's Greatest Crime Wave and the Birth of the FBI, 1933-34* by Brian Burrough

The Public Enemy ★★★★★ PG
Classic crime drama 1931 · US · BW · 80min

This is the film that transformed James Cagney from a sparky song-and-dance man into the world's favourite gangster. But it was not his brutal bootlegging methods, his machine-gun delivery of threats and wisecracks or his ruthless rubbing out of his enemies that secured his tough-guy image, but the shoving of a grapefruit into moll Mae Clarke's face. Cagney makes the most of his chance, giving a performance of raw power. Action expert William A Wellman keeps the story racing along at the speed of a getaway car, setting a style for Warner Bros (fast pace, crackling dialogue, unsentimental scripting and playing) that glamorised the gangster in the 1930s and inadvertently helped pave the way to the Hays Code and film censorship. DP *DVD*

James Cagney *Tom Powers* · Jean Harlow *Gwen Allen* · Edward Woods *Matt Doyle* · Joan Blondell *Mamie* · Beryl Mercer *Ma Powers* · Donald Cook *Mike Powers* · Mae Clarke *Kitty* · Mia Marvin *Jane* · Leslie Fenton *"Nails" Nathan* · Robert Emmett O'Connor *Paddy Ryan* ■ *Dir* William A Wellman · *Scr* Kubec Glasmon, John Bright, Harvey Thew, from the story *Beer and Blood* by John Bright, Kubec Glasmon

Public Enemy ★★★ 18
Action drama 2002 · S Kor · Colour · 138min

A maverick cop and a cold-blooded financier lock horns in this compelling South Korean character study. But director Kang Woo-seok is in no hurry to bring shambolic ex-boxer Seol Gyeong-gu and preening yuppie Lee Seong-jae together, even after the latter murders his parents to prevent them from blowing a deal. Littered with moments of violence and hilarity, this is a no-nonsense exercise in macho posturing and sinister style. A sequel, *Another Public Enemy*, followed in 2005. DP Korean +subtitles. *DVD*

Seol Gyeong-gu *Kang Cheol-gu* · Lee Seong-jae *Jo Kyo-hwan* · Kang Shin-il *Eom Ban-jeong* · Kim Jeong-hak *Detective Kim Hyeong-sa* ■ *Dir* Kang Woo-suk · *Scr* Gaek Seung-jae, Jung Yoon-seup, Kim Hyun-jung, Chae Yoon-suk, from a story by Gu Bon-han

The Public Eye ★★★ 15
Period crime drama 1992 · US · Colour and BW · 94min

Joe Pesci is a 1940s tabloid crime photographer who secretly dreams of being recognised as an artist. When wealthy widow Barbara Hershey offers to help him create a book of his photographs in return for some information, he is pulled into her world which involves a war between opposing Mob families. Although this looks great – dark shadows and moody lighting aplenty – the *film noir* style needs a stronger script, and the final product, clearly inspired by real-life photographer Weegee, is rather tedious. JB Swearing.

Joe Pesci *Leon Bernstein* · Barbara Hershey *Kay Levitz* · Stanley Tucci *Sal Minetto* · Jerry Adler *Arthur Nabler* · Jared Harris *Danny the doorman* · Gerry Becker *Conklin* · Richard Riehle *Officer O'Brien* ■ *Dir/Scr* Howard Franklin · *Cinematographer* Peter Suschitzky

Puckoon ★★★ PG
Period comedy 2002 · Ire/UK/Ger · Colour · 80min

For an hour, this adaptation of Spike Milligan's cult comic novel comes close to capturing the anarchic dexterity of the ex-Goon's matchless wit. The cockamamie characters – whose village is rent asunder by the 1924 border division of Ireland – are brought vividly to life. Yet once writer/director Terence Ryan turns his attention to the increasingly fraught narrative, the offbeat quips and surreal happenstance are replaced by contrived confusions and knockabout farce. It's all enjoyable, but Milligan's sublime, literate lunacy belongs on the page. DP *DVD*

Sean Hughes *Dan Madigan* · Elliott Gould *Dr Goldstein* · Richard Attenborough *Writer/Director* · Daragh O'Malley *Father Rudden* · John Lynch *O'Brien* · Griff Rhys Jones *Colonel Stokes* · Nickolas Grace *Foggerty* · BJ Hogg *Rafferty* ■ *Dir* Terence Ryan · *Scr* Terence Ryan, from the novel by Spike Milligan

Pudsey the Dog: the Movie ★★ U
Comedy 2014 · UK · Colour · 83min

The dancing dog from *Britain's Got Talent* is voiced by David Walliams in a story about a London stray who befriends three city kids and moves with them and their widowed mum to a farm. There, Pudsey helps to thwart boo-hiss baddie John Sessions and learns about being part of a family. Pudsey himself is appealing enough, although something of a one-trick puppy, but this is a cute enough confection for younger kids. DA *DVD*

David Walliams *Pudsey* · Jessica Hynes [Jessica Stevenson] *Gail* · Izzy Meikle-Small *Molly* · Spike White *George* · Malachy Knights *Tommy* · John Sessions *Thorne* · Olivia Colman *Nelly* ■ *Dir* Nick Moore · *Scr* Paul Rose

Puerto Escondido ★★★ 15
Comedy 1992 · It · Colour · 106min

Gabriele Salvatores's follow-up to the Oscar-winning *Mediterraneo* was coolly received by the critics, who couldn't believe that the director capable of such quiet observation could now produce a work of such broad comedy and cack-handedness. However, Diego Abatantuono turns in a splendid performance as the Milan bankteller who is shot during a robbery by deranged police commissioner Renato Carpentieri and hides out in a Mexican backwater to avoid the corrupt copper's wrath. Slow in places, manic in others, but mostly entertaining. DP Italian +subtitles.

Diego Abatantuono *Mario* • Valeria Golino *Anita* • Claudio Bisio *Alex* • Renato Carpentieri *Commissario Viola* • Antonio Catania *Di Gennaro* ■ *Dir* Gabriele Salvatores • *Scr* Enzo Monteleone, Diego Abatantuono, Gabriele Salvatores, from a novel by Pino Cacucci

Puffball ★★ 18

Mystery thriller 2006 · UK/Can/Ire · Colour · 119min

Director Nicolas Roeg's first film in over ten years stars Kelly Reilly as an architect renovating a cottage in rural Ireland. She becomes pregnant and is then targeted by neighbour Miranda Richardson for allegedly "stealing" the baby she was conjuring up for herself with the help of a fertility potion from witchy mother Rita Tushingham. Adapted from Fay Weldon's novel, this is a misfiring, often hysterical melodrama in which the mix of naturalism and clumsy symbolism conspire to make a far-fetched story increasingly preposterous. Reilly copes adequately as the beleaguered expectant mother, but her co-stars overplay at every opportunity, including Donald Sutherland in an eccentric cameo as Reilly's former boss. Even the lush photography is out of kilter with the mood of rustic realism and the frequent "womb cam" images are just plain bizarre. DP

Kelly Reilly *Liffey* • Miranda Richardson *Mabs* • Rita Tushingham *Molly* • Donald Sutherland *Lars* • William Houston *Tucker* • Oscar Pearce *Richard* • Tina Kellegher *Carol* ■ *Dir* Nicolas Roeg • *Scr* Dan Weldon, from the novel by Fay Weldon

The Puffy Chair ★★★ 15

Road movie comedy 2005 · US · Colour · 84min

A reclining lounge chair becomes the catalyst for an escalating series of wryly amusing misadventures in this ultra-low-budget, indie road movie. Marking the feature debut of film-making brothers Jay and Mark Duplass, it's limited in scope yet rich with youthful brio. Mark himself plays the overbearing lead, Josh, who thinks he's found some purpose in his loser life when he embarks on a cross-country drive from New York to Atlanta to pick up the titular chair for his dad's birthday. Along for the ride are his needy girlfriend (Kathryn Aselton) and dippy, neo-hippy brother (a scene-stealing Rhett Wilkins), who together help turn an apparently simple task into an emotional and physical trial. SF *DVD*

Mark Duplass *Josh* • Kathryn Aselton *Emily* • Rhett Wilkins *Rhett* • Julie Fischer *Amber* • Bari Hyman *Motel lady* • Gerald Finnegan *Puffy chair salesman* ■ *Dir* Jay Duplass • *Scr* Mark Duplass, Jay Duplass

Pufnstuf ★★ U

Fantasy 1970 · US · Colour · 94min

This unoriginal, uninspired children's musical features the adventures of a young boy, led by his talking flute to a land where he encounters creatures, including a dragon and several witches. Based on an US TV series, it stars Jack Wild, a bunch of life-size puppets and Martha Raye as the leader of a witches' convention. Highlight of a forgettable score is Mama Cass, another witch, belting out a number called *Different*. RK

Jack Wild *Jimmy* • Billie Hayes *Witchiepoo* • Martha Raye *Boss Witch* • "Mama" Cass Elliot *Witch Hazel* • Billy Barty *Googy Gopher* ■ *Dir* Hollingsworth Morse • *Scr* John Fenton Murray, Si Rose

Pull My Daisy ★★★★

Experimental drama 1959 · US · BW · 27min

Directed by Alfred Leslie and by Robert Frank, this delightful 27-minute short is the only film the Beat writers of the 1950s actually created themselves. Largely a

spontaneous experiment, it hovers around a slim storyline that's based on an incident in the life of Neal Cassady and his wife, when they invited a respectable neighbourhood bishop over for dinner with their unrespectable Beat friends, among them poets Allen Ginsberg, Gregory Corso and artist Larry Rivers. With the daddy of them all, Jack Kerouac, providing voiceover, it offers a fascinating glimpse into the lives of the major Beat writers. RB

Allen Ginsberg *Allen* • Gregory Corso *Gregory* • Peter Orlovsky *Peter* • Larry Rivers *Milo* • Delphine Seyrig *Milo's wife* • David Amram *Mez McGillicuddy* • Jack Kerouac *Narrator* ■ *Dir* Alfred Leslie, Robert Frank • *Scr* Jack Kerouac

Pulp ★★★ 12

Comedy thriller 1972 · UK · Colour · 91min

One of the more interesting teams in the British post-New Wave period was that of the three Michaels - star Caine, writer/director Hodges, producer Klinger - who failed to hit their former *Get Carter* pay dirt with this, their second outing. Nevertheless, the sheer knowing coolness of this bizarre original bears watching. The central theme involving the hiring of a ghostwriter is explored with wit and style, as Hodges deploys his camera cleverly through Maltese locations, and the uncompromising plot makes excellent use of Hollywood icons Mickey Rooney and Lizabeth Scott. TS Violence, swearing. *DVD*

Michael Caine *Mickey King* • Mickey Rooney *Preston Gilbert* • Lionel Stander *Ben Dinuccio* • Lizabeth Scott *Princess Betti Cippola* • Nadia Cassini *Liz Adams* • A. Lettieri *Miller* • Dennis Price *Mysterious Englishman* ■ *Dir/Scr* Michael Hodges [Mike Hodges]

LANDMARK FILM
Tarantino's second feature boosts the US indie scene by combining pop iconography with an art house sensibility

Pulp Fiction ★★★★★ 18

Crime drama 1994 · US · Colour · 154min

While not as abrasive or compelling as *Reservoir Dogs*, Quentin Tarantino's follow-up not only confirmed his genius for writing hard-boiled comic dialogue, but also demonstrated a control over a wealth of characters and crossplots that was simply astonishing for a film-maker still, essentially, in the process of learning his trade. The picture went on to scoop the Palme d'Or at the Cannes film festival and win Oscars for Tarantino and his co-writer Roger Avary. Scorching though the writing is, it needed a high-calibre cast to carry it off. Uma Thurman, Bruce Willis, Maria de Medeiros and Christopher Walken are excellent, but the revitalised John Travolta and the then largely unknown Samuel L Jackson are unforgettable. As much pop as pulp, this is exhilarating and one of the best films of the 1990s. DP Violence, swearing, sex scenes, drug abuse, nudity. *DVD* *Blu*

John Travolta *Vincent Vega* • Samuel L Jackson *Jules Winnfield* • Uma Thurman *Mia Wallace* • Harvey Keitel *The Wolf* • Tim Roth *Pumpkin* • Amanda Plummer *Honey Bunny* • Maria de Medeiros *Fabienne* • Ving Rhames *Marsellus Wallace* • Eric Stoltz *Lance* • Rosanna Arquette *Jody* • Christopher Walken *Captain Koons* • Bruce Willis *Butch Coolidge* • Quentin Tarantino *Jimmie* • Steve Buscemi *Surly Buddy Holly Waiter* • Stephen Hibbert *The Gimp* • Peter Greene *Zed* ■ *Dir* Quentin Tarantino • *Scr* Quentin Tarantino, Roger Avary, from their stories • *Cinematographer* Andrzej Sekula

Pulp: a Film about Life, Death and Supermarkets ★★★ 12

Music documentary 2014 · UK · Colour · 86min

Pulp's final show of their 2012 reunion tour is given an unorthodox spin in this documentary from New Zealand film-maker Florian Habicht. The director complements Jarvis Cocker's songs about the experiences of everyday folk with interviews with the people of Sheffield in an attempt to instil his work with a similar earthy lyricism. The ploy doesn't always work and tends to sideline the band, with little attempt to catalogue Pulp's history in

any depth, but there are some amusing moments. JH Swearing, sexual references.

Jarvis Cocker • Nick Banks • Candida Doyle • Steve Mackey • *Scr* Peter O'Donoghue (2), Florian Habicht, from a concept by Habicht, Jarvis Cocker

Pulse ★★★ 18

Science-fiction horror 1988 · US · Colour · 86min

This quirky little horror tale makes up for what it lacks in blood and gore with a neat line in suspense. Cliff De Young is the puzzled suburbanite who can't work out why all the appliances in the house are beginning to turn on their owners. Writer/director Paul Golding pokes some fun at life in the 'burbs, and makes ingenious use of the rogue electrical machines. JF

Cliff De Young *Bill* • Roxanne Hart *Ellen* • Joey Lawrence *David* • Matthew Lawrence *Stevie* • Charles Tyner *Old man* ■ *Dir/Scr* Paul Golding

Pulse ★ 15

Horror thriller 2006 · US · Colour · 84min

Hollywood remakes of Japanese horror movies - *The Grudge*, *Dark Water* - have met with mixed success, but this atrocious retread of 2001's *Kairo* must be a new low. In a technological advance on *The Ring's* deadly videotape, student Kristen Bell and hacker Ian Somerhalder discover a life-sapping webcam feed that's transporting ghosts back to the land of the living and triggering a suicide epidemic. Co-scripted by Wes Craven (who was initially down to direct), director Jim Sonzero's rehash streamlines the original's narrative obliqueness and renders its atmospheric sense of communication breakdown in the blandest of generic terms. AJ

Kristen Bell *Mattie Webber* • Ian Somerhalder *Dexter McCarthy* • Christina Milian *Isabell Fuentes* • Rick Gonzalez *Stone* • Jonathan Tucker *Josh* • Samm Levine *Tim* • Octavia L Spencer [Octavia Spencer] *Landlady* ■ *Dir* Jim Sonzero • *Scr* Wes Craven, Ray Wright, from the film *Kairo* by Kiyoshi Kurosawa

Pump Up the Volume ★★★ 15

Drama 1990 · US · Colour · 97min

Christian Slater has been involved in some of the more thought-provoking teen movies to venture out of Hollywood and he hardly puts a foot wrong here. He plays a quiet high-school student who metamorphoses into a radio shock jock, enraging the authorities but becoming a cult hero to his fellow students. Director Allan Moyle shows a sensitive feel for adolescent angst, Samantha Mathis is impressive in an early role and the music is a cut above the FM pap that normally inhabits American teen movies. JF Swearing, drug abuse, nudity. *DVD*

Christian Slater *Mark Hunter* • Samantha Mathis *Nora Diniro* • Ellen Greene *Jan Emerson* • Scott Paulin *Brian Hunter* • Cheryl Pollak *Paige* • Andy Romano *Murdock* • Mimi Kennedy *Marta Hunter* ■ *Dir/Scr* Allan Moyle

Pumping Iron ★★★★ 12

Documentary 1976 · US · Colour · 82min

The real centre of attention in this entertaining tour of the body building world is an Austrian man-mountain by the name of Arnold Schwarzenegger, who is aiming to retain his Mr Olympia title. Big Arnie's personality is as overdeveloped as any of the biceps on display here, and whether he's explaining the sexual pleasure he gets from lifting weights or psyching-out an opponent over breakfast, it's clear that you're witnessing a star in the making. And you'll never guess who wins! JC *DVD*

Charles Gaines *Narrator* • Arnold Schwarzenegger • Lou Ferrigno ■ *Dir* George Butler, Robert Fiore • *Scr* George Butler, from the non-fiction book by Charles Gaines, George Butler

Pumping Iron II: the Women ★★★★ PG

Documentary 1984 · US · Colour · 102min

The sequel to the film that made Arnold Schwarzenegger a star, this may be a little more contrived than some fly-on-the-wall documentaries, but it's still hugely entertaining and highly revealing of how so many men view the female form. Concentrating on the 1983 Caesar's Cup contest, director George Butler not only sets out to justify the sport of women's body building, but also proves that most of the competitors can intellectually knock spots off he-men and beauty queens alike. DP

■ *Dir* George Butler • *Scr* Charles Gaines, George Butler, from their book *Pumping Iron II: the Unprecedented Woman*

The Pumpkin Eater ★★★★ 12

Drama 1964 · UK · BW · 105min

This study of a marriage is based on Penelope Mortimer's novel, with Anne Bancroft as the mother of several screaming brats and the wife of adulterous screenwriter husband Peter Finch. She suffers a nervous collapse in Harrods, undergoes psychoanalysis, then a hysterectomy. Bancroft and Finch deliver blockbuster performances and the supporting cast is equally impressive. There's also beautifully modulated direction from Jack Clayton but scriptwriter Harold Pinter's acidulent signature is all over it, for this is so arty and alienating it almost needs subtitles. AT *DVD*

Anne Bancroft *Jo Armitage* • Peter Finch *Jake Armitage* • James Mason *Bob Conway* • Cedric Hardwicke *Mr James, Jo's father* • Richard Johnson *Giles* • Maggie Smith *Philpot* • Eric Porter *Psychiatrist* ■ *Dir* Jack Clayton • *Scr* Harold Pinter, from the novel by Penelope Mortimer

Pumpkinhead ★★★ 18

Horror 1988 · US · Colour · 82min

For his directorial debut Oscar-winning special effects genius Stan Winston stayed on safe ground with this EC Comic inspired dark horror morality tale. Well-cast Lance Henriksen invokes an ancient witch curse to resurrect the demon Pumpkinhead to take vengeance on the vacationing bikers who killed his son. The smoky backwoods ambience and several plot twists paper over some plodding and under-characterised exposition, and the gore murders are of a standard issue nature. But Winston's creature is as awesomely frightening and brilliantly constructed and offers more than enough feral scream-lined chills to thrill along to. The sequel *The Revenge of Pumpkinhead - Blood Wings* followed in 1994. AJ *DVD*

Lance Henriksen *Ed Harley* • Jeff East *Chris* • John DiAquino *Joel* • Kimberly Ross *Kim* • Joel Hoffman *Steve* • Cynthia Bain *Tracy* • Kerry Remsen *Maggie* • Tom Woodruff Jr *Pumpkinhead* ■ *Dir* Stan Winston • *Scr* Mark Patrick Carducci, Gary Gerani, from a story by Mark Patrick Carducci, Stan Winston, Richard C Weinman, from a poem by Ed Justin

The Punch and Judy Man ★★ U

Comedy 1962 · UK · BW · 88min

Cast adrift from his regular scriptwriters Ray Galton and Alan Simpson for the first time in a decade studded with radio and TV triumphs, Tony Hancock comes unstuck in this glum comedy. This tale about a seaside showman driven to distraction by the petty dictates of the local authorities and the social ambitions of his grasping wife (Sylvia Syms) is overwhelmed by moments of unrelieved melancholy. Hancock's lack of finesse allows the despondency to descend into bathos. DP *DVD*

Tony Hancock *Wally Pinner* • Sylvia Syms *Delia Pinner* • Ronald Fraser *Mayor Palmer* • Barbara Murray *Lady Jane Caterham* • John Le Mesurier *Charles the Sandman* • Hugh Lloyd *Edward Cox* •

Mario Fabrizi *Nevil Shanks* ■ *Dir* Jeremy Summers • *Scr* Tony Hancock, Phillip Oakes, from a story by Tony Hancock

Punch-Drunk Love

★★★★ 15

Romantic comedy drama
2002 · US · Colour · 91min

Adam Sandler stars as the head of a bathroom novelties company who collects air-mile coupons in his spare time, is prone to uncontrollable rages and is mercilessly bullied by his seven sisters. In the first five minutes of the movie a car flips over outside his office, an old harmonium is abandoned and Emily Watson appears from nowhere and asks him to look after her car. Then things start to get really strange. Much has been made of lowbrow favourite Sandler teaming up with art house darling Paul Thomas Anderson, but the curious combination works. Sandler handles the movie's moments of slapstick and pathos with equal ease. StH *DVD Blu*

Adam Sandler *Barry Egan* • Emily Watson *Lena Leonard* • Philip Seymour Hoffman *Dean Trumbell* • Luis Guzman *Lance* • Mary Lynn Rajskub *Elizabeth* • Lisa Spector *Susan* • Hazel Mailloux *Rhonda* ■ *Dir/Scr* Paul Thomas Anderson

Punchline

★★★ 15

Comedy drama 1988 · US · Colour · 117min

In this comedy drama set in the world of comedy clubs, Sally Field stars as a New Jersey housewife and mother who longs to tread the boards as a stand-up comedian. Tom Hanks plays the medical school failure and disillusioned entertainer she turns to for help. Director David Seltzer's look at the laughter-makers is slow in places, but both stars are good enough to help make this a thoughtful study as to why professional humour is no joke. TH Swearing. *DVD*

Sally Field *Lilah Krytsick* • Tom Hanks *Steven Gold* • John Goodman *John Krytsick* • Mark Rydell *Romeo* • Kim Greist *Madeline Urie* • Paul Mazursky *Arnold* ■ *Dir/Scr* David Seltzer

The Punisher

★★ 18

Action crime thriller
1989 · US/Aus · Colour · 84min

The Marvel Comics vigilante is brought to the screen in the guise of square-jawed giant Dolph Lundgren. He's no superhero though, merely a leather-clad man on a motorbike avenging the murder of his family by the New York Mob. Lundgren certainly looks every inch the comic-book hero, plus there's better-than-average support from Louis Gossett Jr and Jeroen Krabbé, but the lack of visual style, repetitive action scenes and a lifeless script place this in the second division of comic book adaptations. JC *DVD Blu*

Dolph Lundgren *Frank Castle/The Punisher* • Louis Gossett Jr *Jake Berkowitz* • Jeroen Krabbé *Gianni Franco* • Barry Otto *Shake* • Bryan Marshall *Dino Moretti* • Kim Miyori *Lady Tanaka* ■ *Dir* Mark Goldblatt • *Scr* Robert Mark Kamen, Boaz Yakin, from a story by Boaz Yakin, from the Marvel comicbook character created by Gerry Conway, John Romita Sr, Ross Andru

The Punisher

★★★ 18

Action crime thriller
2004 · US/Ger · Colour · 118min

This more faithful take on Marvel Comic's character obliterates the 1989 Dolph Lundgren version. It's loud, fast and extremely vicious. Tom Jane stars as former FBI special agent Frank Castle, who turns vigilante when his family is gunned down on Florida Mob boss John Travolta's orders. Jane has the cool air of a super-human rock star as he orchestrates the darkest of revenge. There's no let up to the destruction and violence, nor is there any semblance of reality. SF Violence. *DVD Blu*

Tom Jane [Thomas Jane] *Frank Castle/The Punisher* • John Travolta *Howard Saint* • Rebecca Romijn-Stamos *Joan* • Will Patton *Quentin Glass* • Roy Scheider *Frank Castle Sr* • Laura Harring *Livia Saint* • Ben Foster *Spacker Dave* • Samantha Mathis *Maria Castle* • James Carpinello *John Saint/Bobby Saint* • Russell Andrews *Jimmy Weeks* ■ *Dir* Jonathan

Hensleigh • *Scr* Jonathan Hensleigh, Michael France, from the Marvel comic book character created by Gerry Conway, John Romita Sr, Ross Andru

Punisher: War Zone

★★ 18

Action crime thriller
2008 · US/Can/Ger · Colour · 98min

The third attempt to launch the Marvel Comics vigilante hero as a viable franchise is based on the harder-edged *Punisher Max* series. *Rome*'s Ray Stevenson takes over the role of ex-marine Frank Castle, who sets his sights on the ruthless Jigsaw (Dominic West) after the hideously disfigured mob boss causes him to kill an undercover FBI agent. The dialogue is comically bad and the graphic gore vicious and unrelenting, yet director Lexi Alexander (*Green Street*) brings a certain brainless energy to what is quality trash, while Doug Hutchison has a ball playing Jigsaw's deranged brother. AJ Violence, swearing. *DVD Blu*

Ray Stevenson *Frank Castle/The Punisher* • Dominic West *Billy Russoti/Jigsaw* • Julie Benz *Angela Donatelli* • Colin Salmon *Agent Paul Budiansky* • Doug Hutchison *Loony Bin Jim* • Dash Mihok *Martin Soap* • Wayne Knight *Linus Lieberman/"Micro"* ■ *Dir* Lexi Alexander • *Scr* Nick Santora, Art Marcum, Matt Holloway, from the Marvel comic book character created by Gerry Conway, John Romita Sr, Ross Andru

Punishment Park

★★★★ 15

Drama 1971 · US · Colour · 87min

This is the best of the socio-political fantasies made by Peter Watkins, whose controversial films include the futuristic satire *Privilege* and *The War Game*. This drama retains the latter's documentary feel, as draft dodgers who oppose America's military involvement in Indo-China are put in detention camps where they must chose between a long jail sentence or a three-day ordeal in "Punishment Park". Watkins plays the leader of a British documentary film unit observing one group of dissenters as they face fascist terror tactics. Powerful and depressing, this is an outstanding indictment of repression and state bullyboy tactics. AJ Swearing, violence. *DVD Blu*

Jim Bohan *Captain, Sheriff's Department* • Van Daniels *County Sheriff* • Frederick Franklyn *Professor Daly* • Carmen Argenziano *Jay Kaufman* • Stan Armsted *Charles Robbins* • Gladys Golden *Mrs Jergens* • Peter Watkins *Documentarist* ■ *Dir/Scr* Peter Watkins

The Punk

★★ 18

Romantic drama 1993 · UK · Colour · 92min

This punk-induced ode to Romeo and Juliet, set on the streets of Notting Hill, features 1960s star Jess Conrad as the father of a rich girl who falls for a local punk, much to the disgust of parents and the like. Director Michael Sarne turns out something approaching a modern fairy tale. FL Swearing, violence, sex scenes.

Charlie Creed-Miles *David* • Vanessa Hadaway *Rachel* • David Shawyer *David's father* • Jess Conrad *Rachel's father* • Jacqueline Skarvellis *David's mother* • Yolanda Mason *Rachel's stepmother* • Alex Mollo *Stray Cat* ■ *Dir* Mike Sarne [Michael Sarne] • *Scr* Michael Sarne, from the novel by Gideon Sams

The Punk Rock Movie

★★★ 15

Music documentary 1978 · UK · Colour · 79min

An 8mm-blown-up-to-35mm record of the London punk scene just as it was exploding globally to shake up the moribund music world irrevocably . Filmed by Don Letts, the road manager for various Brit-punk bands, this technically haphazard chronicle covers all the bases – tiny hothouse venues, cramped recording studios, road tours, pogo rituals (featuring a young Shane McGowan), razor blade fashions and drug-taking. Filmed mostly at London's Roxy Club, this is a simply presented but valuable history lesson. AJ

■ *Dir* Don Letts

The Punk Singer

★★★ 15

Music documentary 2013 · US · Colour · 81min

Kathleen Hanna was the leading light of the Riot Grrrl scene of the 1990s – a feminist movement that called for women to take their place on the stage. Archive footage reveals Hanna to be a charismatic frontwoman, both with her first band, Bikini Kill, and her later, poppier, group, Le Tigre. But she dropped out of the spotlight in 2005, and the truth about the illness that stopped her in her tracks is revealed here. This is a celebratory portrait of a fascinating subject, but you can't help but think it could have been much more. LB Swearing, sexual references.

Kathleen Hanna • Joan Jett • Adam Horovitz ■ *Dir* Sini Anderson

The Punk Syndrome

★★★

Music documentary 2012 · Fin/Nor/Swe · Colour · 85min

Jukka Karkkainen and J-P Passi's documentary profiles the nihilistic Finnish band Pertti Kurikka's Name Day, whose members rejoice in the fact that they are not like so-called normal people. Guitarist Pertti Kurikka uses music to explore his cerebral palsy and obsessive compulsive behaviour, with his lyrics often being as edgy and amusing as they are poignant and revealing. But Pertti doesn't always see eye to eye with bassist Sami Helle, who, like drummer Toni Valitalo, has Down's syndrome. Amid the tantrums and tensions that arise, manager Kalle Pajamaa tries to heal rifts and book the gigs that earn the group an enthusiastic following. The band dynamic and the music are certainly intriguing, but too many of the interlinking incidents here smack of contrivance. DP Finnish +subtitles.

■ *Dir* Jukka Karkkainen, J-P Passi • *Scr* Jukka Karkkainen, J-P Passi, Sami Jahnukainen

Puppet Master

★★ 18

Horror 1989 · US · Colour · 86min

The first of a long series of horror films about the puppets given life by their creator, William Hickey. Some highly unlikely psychic researchers, including Paul Le Mat, are terrorised in a hotel by the murderous marionettes. Director David Schmoeller, veteran of much low-grade horror, does little with the formulaic script, which is slow to get going, but finally delivers the gory goods. The puppets are cleverly animated by special effects expert David Allen. DM *DVD*

Paul Le Mat *Alex* • Irene Miracle *Dana Hadley* • Matt Roe *Frank* • Kathryn O'Reilly *Clarissa* • Robin Frates *Megan Gallagher* • Merrya Small [Marya Small] *Theresa* • Jimmie F Scaggs *Neil* • William Hickey *Toulon* ■ *Dir* David Schmoeller • *Scr* Joseph G Collodi, from a story by Charles Band, Kenneth J Hall

The Puppet Masters

★★ 15

Science-fiction drama
1994 · US · Colour · 104min

This dumb incarnation of Robert Heinlein's excellent science-fiction short novel takes liberties with the story in such a way that Heinlein might have objected. If you've seen Donald Sutherland's other alien invasion flick, 1978's *Invasion of the Body Snatchers*, you've already got a pretty good idea of what's in store here when there's hidden menace in a meteorite strike in rural Iowa. While technically competent, it offers little in the way of plot. ST *DVD*

Donald Sutherland *Andrew Nivens* • Eric Thal *Sam Nivens* • Julie Warner *Mary Sefton* • Yaphet Kotto *Ressler* • Keith David *Holland* • Will Patton *Graves* • Richard Belzer *Jarvis* • Tom Mason *President Douglas* ■ *Dir* Stuart Orme • *Scr* David S Goyer, Ted Elliot, Terry Rossio, from the novel by Robert A Heinlein

Puppet on a Chain

★★ 15

Thriller 1970 · UK · Colour · 93min

Director Geoffrey Reeve is saddled with Swedish actor Sven-Bertil Taube, whose charmless playing makes involvement in the Alistair MacLean-based-plot almost impossible. However, his performance

serves to make the final speedboat chase along the canals of Amsterdam (a sequence directed by Don Sharp) even more thrilling. DP Violence, some swearing. *DVD*

Sven-Bertil Taube *Paul Sherman* • Barbara Parkins *Maggie* • Alexander Knox *Colonel de Graaf* • Patrick Allen *Inspector Van Gelder* • Vladek Sheybal *Meegeren* • Ania Marson *Astrid Leman* ■ *Dir* Geoffrey Reeve • *Scr* Alistair MacLean, Paul Wheeler, Don Sharp, from the novel by Alistair MacLean

The Puppetmaster

★★★ 15

Biographical drama 1993 · Tai · Colour · 136min

Steeped in the folklore of his beloved Taiwan, this hypnotic account of puppetmaster Li Tianlu's first 36 years features fleeting appearances from Li himself. Taking us from Li's troubled childhood in what was still essentially a feudal society to the liberation of the island from the Japanese at the end of the Second World War, the film is enlivened throughout by some compelling dramatic sequences and several wonderful displays of puppetry. Yet director Hou Hsiao-Hsien's sometimes heavy-handed symbolism and his decision to adopt such a funereal pace occasionally counts against the intrigue of the story. DP Mandarin, Taiwanese, Japanese +subtitles.

Li Tianlu • Lim Giong [Lin Qiang] *Li Tianlu, young adult* • Chen Kuizhong *Li Tianlu, teenager* • Zuo Juwei *Li Tianlu, child* ■ *Dir* Hou Xiaoxian [Hou Hsiao-Hsien] • *Scr* Wu Nianzhen, Zhu Tianwen, from the book *Ximeng Rensheng* by Li Tianlu Li, Hou Xiaoxian [Hou Hsiao-Hsien], Zheng Yumen

The Purchase Price

★★★

Melodrama 1932 · US · BW · 66min

Manhattan torch singer Barbara Stanwyck, eager to escape the clutches of her gangster lover, Lyle Talbot, becomes a mail order bride to North Dakota farmer George Brent. How the couple, especially Stanwyck, cope with adjusting to their unlikely alliance, and the series of dramatic incidents that attends them, is the stuff of this full-blooded melodrama. Director William A Wellman extracts as much humour as possible from clichéd secondary characters, while squeezing some credibility from the bizarre incidents. The sublime Stanwyck rises, as always, above the material. RK

Barbara Stanwyck *Joan Gordon* • George Brent *Jim Gilson* • Lyle Talbot *Ed Fields* • Hardie Albright *Don* • David Landau *Bull McDowell* • Murray Kinnell *Spike Forgan* ■ *Dir* William A Wellman • *Scr* Robert Lord, from the story *The Mud Lark* by Arthur Stringer

Pure

★★★★ 18

Drama 2002 · UK · Colour · 92min

An exceptional performance from Harry Eden, John de Borman's unflinching images of a West Ham housing estate and director Gillies MacKinnon's courageous reclamation of the subject of drug crime from soap sensationalism give this drama a sobering power that recalls a bygone era of British social realism. The despair and degradation of the addict's existence is laid bare by Molly Parker as a widowed mother so dependent on dealer David Wenham that she can no longer care for her young sons. But the real drama lies in ten-year-old Harry Eden's gradual realisation of her plight (which eventually prompts him to try crack himself). Starkly touching and shockingly authentic. DP *DVD*

Molly Parker *Mel* • David Wenham *Lenny* • Harry Eden *Paul* • Geraldine McEwan *Nanna* • Kate Ashfield *Helen* • Gary Lewis *Det Insp French* • Marsha Thomason *Vicki* • Karl Johnson (2) *Granddad* ■ *Dir* Gillies MacKinnon • *Scr* Alison Hume

Pure Country

★★ PG

Drama 1992 · US · Colour · 107min

"Pure Corn" might have been a better title for this slice of country-and-western hokum. Your opinion of this tale of a troubled superstar will depend on your reaction to George Strait. There's no denying he's handy with a tune, but dialogue proves more difficult for him. It's a shame we couldn't spend more time with

U SUITABLE FOR ALL   **Uc** SUITABLE ESPECIALLY FOR YOUNG CHILDREN (DVD ONLY)   **PG** PARENTAL GUIDANCE   **12A** UNDER 12s TO BE ACCOMPANIED (CINEMA ONLY)

his tacky manager, played by Lesley Ann Warren. Rory Calhoun is wasted in an undemanding supporting role. DP

George Strait *Dusty Wyatt Chandler* • Lesley Ann Warren *Lula Rogers* • Isabel Glasser *Harley Tucker* • Kyle Chandler *Buddy Jackson* • John Doe *Earl Blackstock* • Rory Calhoun *Ernest Tucker* • Molly McClure *Grandma Ivy Chandler* ■ *Dir* Christopher Cain • *Scr* Rex McGee

A Pure Formality ★★ 12
Psychological mystery drama
1994 · It/Fr · Colour · 106min

Director Giuseppe Tornatore had a hit with *Cinema Paradiso*, a near hit with *The Legend of 1900* and a big miss here. Gérard Depardieu stars as a famous French writer fleeing from a mysterious gunshot. The movie centres on his interrogation by inspector Roman Polanski in a wet, seedy shed in the middle of a dank forest. These two film giants cannot pull together a ponderous plot and meandering monologues. LH French +subtitles. *DVD*

Gérard Depardieu *Onoff* • Roman Polanski *Inspector* • Sergio Rubini *Andre, the young policeman* • Nicola DiPinto *The captain* • Paolo Lombardi *The warrant officer* • Tano Cimarosa *The old attendant* ■ *Dir* Giuseppe Tornatore • *Scr* Giuseppe Tornatore, Pascal Quignard, from a story by Tornatore

The Pure Hell of St Trinian's ★★ U
Comedy   1960 · UK · BW · 90min

Bereft of Alastair Sim, the third film in the St Trinian's series (that began with *The Belles of St Trinian's*) has its moments, but sadly all too few of them. With the school reduced to smouldering ashes, mysterious child psychologist Cecil Parker takes charge of the tearaways, in league with white-slaving sea captain Sidney James. Woefully short on mayhem, the film spends too much time in the company of eventual castaways Parker and Joyce Grenfell. Followed by *The Great St Trinian's Train Robbery*. DP

Cecil Parker *Professor Canford* • Joyce Grenfell *Sergeant Ruby Gates* • George Cole *Flash Harry* • Thorley Walters *Betters* • Eric Barker *Culpepper-Brown* • Irene Handl *Miss Harker-Packer* • Sidney James *Alphonse O'Reilly* • Dennis Price *Gore-Blackwood* ■ *Dir* Frank Launder • *Scr* Frank Launder, Val Valentine, Sidney Gilliat, from the drawings by Ronald Searle

Pure Luck ★★ PG
Comedy   1991 · US · Colour · 91min

A limp attempt to find life in the corpse of the buddy-buddy movie, this stars Danny Glover as a gumshoe and Martin Short as his idiotic sidekick who go shooting off to Mexico in search of a missing heiress. This lazy wheeze, which abandons any pretence at a decent script at an early stage, relies for the odd outbreak of energy on Short, who is required to shore up the film with a volley of pratfalls. JM Swearing.

Martin Short *Eugene Proctor* • Danny Glover *Raymond Campanella* • Sheila Kelley (1) *Valerie Highsmith* • Sam Wanamaker *Mr Highsmith* • Scott Wilson *Grimes* • Harry Shearer *Monosoff* • Jorge Russek *Inspector Segura* ■ *Dir* Nadia Tass • *Scr* Herschel Weingrod, Timothy Harris

Purely Belter ★★★ 15
Social comedy   2000 · UK · Colour · 98min

This feel-good social comedy from Mark Herman is set in football-mad Newcastle upon Tyne, where cash-strapped Chris Beattie and Greg McLane are two Toon Army tykes desperate to raise the necessary money for season tickets. As the underprivileged but enterprising pair pursue their goal by fair means and foul, Herman fashions some telling social commentary from the slight tale. An amusing script and likeable performances make this an interesting diversion. DA Swearing, drug abuse. *DVD*

Chris Beattie *Gerry McCarten* • Greg McLane *Sewell* • Charlie Hardwick *Mrs McCarten* • Tim Healy *Mr McCarten* • Roy Hudd *Mr Sewell* • Kevin Whately *Mr Caird* • Jody Baldwin *Gemma* • Alan Shearer ■ *Dir* Mark Herman • *Scr* Mark Herman, from the novel *The Season Ticket* by Jonathan Tulloch

Purgatory ★★★ 15
Western   1999 · US · Colour · 90min

This barmy but richly enjoyable western fable stars Eric Roberts as a bank robber who holes up with his gang in a sleepy, weapons-free village south of the border. One of the young gang members (Brad Rowe) realises that this is Purgatory for legends of the West – Billy the Kid (Donnie Wahlberg), Doc Holliday (Randy Quaid), Jesse James (JD Souther) and Wild Bill Hickock (Sam Shepard). But if they take up arms against the newcomers, will they be refused their place in heaven? JF Sexual references, violence, swearing.

Sam Shepard *Sheriff Forest* • Eric Roberts *Blackjack* • Randy Quaid *Doc Woods* • Peter Stormare *Cavin* • Brad Rowe *Sonny* • Donnie Wahlberg *Deputy Glen* • JD Souther *Brooks* ■ *Dir* Uli Edel • *Scr* Gordon Dawson

The Purge ★★★ 15
Futuristic horror thriller
2013 · US · Colour · 81min

Ethan Hawke and Lena Headey play the husband and wife plunged into a long night's journey into day in this absorbing home-invasion thriller. The setting is America in the year 2022, where, for 12 hours every year, any crime is allowed with no interference from the authorities. Hawke is a security salesman and the owner of a luxury home-cum-fortress, so the night promises to pass safely for him and his family. However, a good Samaritan act from his son (Max Burkholder) has them all battling to survive the depraved attentions of a vicious mob of masked murderers. Although it raises political and ethical questions, this is essentially a survival-of-the-fittest tale, which is sustained by convincing lead performances and a memorably scary turn from Rhys Wakefield as the grinning, unnervingly polite leader of the psycho gang. JA *DVD* *Blu-ray*

Ethan Hawke *James Sandin* • Lena Headey *Mary Sandin* • Max Burkholder *Charlie Sandin* • Adelaide Kane *Zoey Sandin* • Edwin Hodge *Bloody stranger* • Rhys Wakefield *Polite stranger* ■ *Dir/Scr* James DeMonaco

The Purge: Anarchy ★★★ 15
Futuristic horror   2014 · US/Fr · Colour · 99min

James DeMonaco returns to expand on the provocative premise for 2013's *The Purge* – that for 12 hours every year, all crime goes without punishment. But whereas the first film was essentially a watchable siege movie (in the mould of *Assault on Precinct 13*), this incident-packed sequel has more in common with the run-for-your-life thrills of *The Warriors* and *Hard Target*. By the end, however, it's evident that an intriguing idea might be stretching itself a little too far. JA Violence, swearing. *DVD* *Blu-ray*

Frank Grillo *Sergeant* • Zach Gilford *Shane* • Kiele Sanchez *Liz* • Michael K Williams [Michael Kenneth Williams] *Carmelo* ■ *Dir* James DeMonaco • *Scr* From characters by James DeMonaco

Puritan ★★★ 12A
Supernatural horror thriller
2004 · UK · Colour · 93min

Nick Moran, the largely forgotten member of the *Lock, Stock*… crew, reveals an unexpected intensity in Hadi Hajaig's supernatural *film noir*. He plays alcoholic paranormalist Simon Puritan, whose resort to rigged séances brings him into contact with *femme fatale* Anne (Georgina Rylance), who needs help dealing with her husband. Despite warnings from an elusive stranger to steer clear of her, Simon embarks on a passionate affair with Anne under the nose of said husband, sinister business guru Eric (David Soul). Told with eerie assurance and secreting its twists with *Sixth Sense*-like dexterity, this is a disconcerting chiller. DP

Nick Moran *Simon Puritan* • Georgina Rylance *Anne* • David Soul *Eric Bridges* • Ralph Brown (2) *Mickey Conway* • Robin Hellier *Dr Miles* • Peter Sullivan *Richard* • Pete Hodge *Jonathan Grey* ■ *Dir/Scr* Hadi Hajaig

The Purple Heart ★★★ PG
Second World War drama
1944 · US · BW · 95min

This unashamed wartime propaganda movie is directed by Lewis Milestone, the man responsible for some of the greatest war films ever. Here, a group of US air force personnel is falsely accused of war atrocities after being captured by the Japanese. When they refuse to admit to the charges, they face a terrible ordeal. This isn't one of Milestone's best, mainly because every character seems such an obvious stereotype, despite the fact that the tragic events depicted are based on fact. TS *DVD*

Dana Andrews *Captn Harvey Ross* • Richard Conte *Lt Angelo Canelli* • Farley Granger *Sgt Howard Clinton* • Kevin O'Shea *Sgt Jan Skvoznik* • Donald Barry *Lt Peter Vincent* ■ *Dir* Lewis Milestone • *Scr* Jerome Cady, from a story by Melville Crossman [Darryl F Zanuck]

Purple Hearts ★★ 15
War drama   1984 · US · Colour · 110min

In this Vietnam romance, former *Charlie's Angel* Cheryl Ladd is the nurse who falls for doctor Ken Wahl during the war, intending to spend the rest of her medical career by his side. It's tosh, of course, but not unenjoyable, with a *Romeo and Juliet*-style series of endings, as you wonder who's been killed, or not. Watch out for former military drill instructor Lee Ermey, appearing in a Vietnam feature three years before *Full Metal Jacket*. TS Swearing.

Ken Wahl *Don Jardian* • Cheryl Ladd *Deborah Solomon* • Stephen Lee *Wizard* • David Harris *Hanes* • Cyril O'Reilly *Zuma* • Lane Smith *Commander Markel* • Lee Ermey [R Lee Ermey] *Gunny* ■ *Dir* Sidney J Furie • *Scr* Rick Natkin, Sidney J Furie

The Purple Mask ★★ PG
Period adventure   1955 · US · Colour · 81min

This Napoleonic frolic stars Tony Curtis in historical mode – that is to say, adding adenoidal timbre and generally camping it up. The plot is some nonsense about Napoleon and those irritating Royalists who keep losing their heads on the guillotine. Curtis sports a mask and waves his rapier at arch rival, Dan O'Herlihy. Angela Lansbury is a milliner whose shop is also a cover for the Resistance, while the love interest is Colleen Miller. AT *DVD*

Tony Curtis *Rene* • Colleen Miller *Laurette* • Gene Barry *Capt Laverne* • Dan O'Herlihy *Brisquet* • Angela Lansbury *Madame Valentine* • George Dolenz *Marcel Cadonal* • John Hoyt *Rochet* ■ *Dir* H Bruce Humberstone • *Scr* Oscar Brodney, from the play *Le Chevalier aux Masques* by Paul Armont, Jean Manoussi, adapted by Charles Latour

The Purple People Eater ★★★ U
Musical fantasy   1988 · US · Colour · 90min

Thirty years after Sheb Wooley had a hit with the song of the title in 1958, this daft little movie attempted to rekindle the spirit of a time when aliens were synonymous with communists and rock 'n' roll was considered the Devil's music. There's something irresistible about seeing Ned Beatty and Shelley Winters playing helpless pensioners, while Neil Patrick Harris co-stars as the lad who brings the eponymous alien to Earth by playing Wooley's hit. DP

Ned Beatty *Grandpa* • Neil Patrick Harris *Billy Johnson* • Shelley Winters *Rita* • Peggy Lipton *Mom* • James Houghton *Dad* • Thora Birch *Molly Johnson* • John Brumfield *Mr Noodle* • Little Richard *Mayor* • Chubby Checker *Singer* ■ *Dir* Linda Shayne • *Scr* Linda Shayne, from the song by Sheb Wooley

The Purple Plain ★★★ PG
Second World War drama
1954 · UK · Colour · 97min

In this romantic adventure, Gregory Peck plays the Canadian Second World War pilot, haunted by the death of his wife, who regains his confidence via a love affair and a bungled combat mission in Burma. Adapted by Eric Ambler from the novel by HE Bates, this is quite a classy production,

directed by Robert Parrish and impressively shot by Geoffrey Unsworth in the jungles of Ceylon. AT *DVD*

Gregory Peck *Squadron Leader Forrester* • Win Min Than *Anna* • Bernard Lee *Dr Harris* • Maurice Denham *Blore* • Brenda de Banzie *Miss McNab* • Ram Gopal *Mr Phang* • Lyndon Brook *Carrington* • Anthony Bushell *Commander Aldridge* • Jack McNaughton *Sergeant Brown* • Harold Siddons *Navigator Williams* ■ *Dir* Robert Parrish • *Scr* Eric Ambler, from the novel by HE Bates

Purple Rain ★★★ 15
Musical drama   1984 · US · Colour · 106min

This is the first and easily the best of pint-sized rock star Prince's forays into film. Breathtakingly egotistical, it follows the adventures of struggling rock singer "The Kid" as he battles to the top, despite the underhand tactics of his rivals. The less said about the lead performances the better, although Morris Day eclipses the star with a charismatic turn. Prince and the Revolution were at the height of their powers and their hits are memorably captured by director Albert Magnoli. A sequel of sorts, *Graffiti Bridge*, followed in 1990. JF Sex scenes.violence, nudity. *DVD* *Blu-ray*

Prince *The Kid* • Apollonia Kotero *Apollonia* • Morris Day *Morris* • Olga Karlatos *Mother* • Clarence Williams III *Father* • Jerome Benton *Jerome* • Billy Sparks *Billy* • Jill Jones *Jill* ■ *Dir* Albert Magnoli • *Scr* Albert Magnoli, William Blinn

The Purple Rose of Cairo ★★★★ PG
Fantasy romantic comedy
1985 · US · Colour and BW · 78min

In Woody Allen's short story *The Kugelmass Episode*, an academic is transported into the bedroom of the literary character Madame Bovary. *The Purple Rose of Cairo* is a film inversion of this idea, with Mia Farrow as a brutalised waitress who wins the heart of a character in her favourite movie (played by Jeff Daniels) who steps out of the screen to court her. Farrow and Daniels are charming and writer/director Allen poignantly recalls the importance of Hollywood dreams to people weighed down by the cares of the 1930s. Technically polished and ingenious. DP *DVD*

Mia Farrow *Cecilia* • Jeff Daniels *Tom Baxter/Gil Shepherd* • Danny Aiello *Monk* • Dianne Wiest *Emma* • Van Johnson *Larry* • Zoe Caldwell *Countess* • John Wood (2) *Jason* • Milo O'Shea *Father Donnelly* ■ *Dir/Scr* Woody Allen • *Cinematographer* Gordon Willis

The Purple Taxi ★★★
Drama   1977 · Fr/It/Ire · Colour · 107min

The multinational producers and cast give this curio a strange cross-cultural edge. The drama centers on several moneyed expats of widely varying backgrounds who cross paths in the west of Ireland after escaping their previous lives. Doctor Fred Astaire drives the purple taxi, millionaire Edward Albert searches for traces of his Irish ancestry, while the sexy wife of a German prince, Charlotte Rampling, tries to seduce a terminally ill patient. Offbeat and watchable. JG

Charlotte Rampling *Sharon* • Philippe Noiret *Philippe* • Agostina Belli *Anne Taubelman* • Peter Ustinov *Taubelman* • Fred Astaire *Dr Scully* • Edward Albert *Jerry* • Mairin O'Sullivan *Colleen* • Jack Watson *Sean* ■ *Dir* Yves Boisset • *Scr* Yves Boisset, Michel Déon, from a novel by Michel Déon

Pursued ★★★★ PG
Western   1947 · US · BW · 101min

Not as well-known as *High Noon*, *The Searchers* or *Red River*, this was one of the first "psychological westerns" and has the same sort of story, theme and flashback structure usually found in the urban *film noir*. Robert Mitchum plays a tortured soul who was adopted as a child, murders his half-brother and then marries his brother's wife. It has the feel of a classical tragedy, with Mitchum superb as the brooding hero who journeys back into his past. Critics have laid all the praise at the door of the director,

P

Raoul Walsh, but it's largely the creation of screenwriter Niven Busch. **AT**

Robert Mitchum *Jeb Rand* • Teresa Wright *Thorley Callum* • Judith Anderson *Mrs Medora Callum* • Dean Jagger *Grant Callum* • Alan Hale *Jake Dingle* • John Rodney *Adam Callum* • Harry Carey Jr *Prentice McComber* ■ *Dir* Raoul Walsh • *Scr* Niven Busch • *Cinematographer* James Wong Howe • *Music* Max Steiner

The Pursuers ★★
Crime thriller   1961 · UK · BW · 63min

The arrest and trial of Adolph Eichmann made the pursuit of Nazi war criminals a fitting topic for thrillers such as this. The plot resembles any fugitive-on-the-run yarn, with the Nazi hiding out in a nightclub singer's flat in London, hunted by a German organisation and unable to flee the country because he's damaged his passport. Never more than a B-movie, it's worth seeing for its treatment of its subject and for the performance of Cyril Shaps. **AT**

Cyril Shaps *Karl Luther* • Francis Matthews *David Nelson* • Susan Denny *Jenny Walmer* • Sheldon Lawrence *Rico* • George Murcell *Freddy* ■ *Dir* Godfrey Grayson • *Scr* Brian Clemens, David Nicholl

The Pursuit of DB Cooper ★★15
Comedy crime drama   1981 · US · Colour · 96min

This thriller begins with Treat Williams jumping out of a plane with a bag containing $200,000. Amazingly, this airborne robbery, with its James Bond-style stunt, really happened and DB Cooper vanished into myth. This is where fiction takes over, conjuring up Cooper's subsequent life and the attempts of a former Green Beret (Robert Duvall) to track him down. Sadly, the picture bungles a nifty idea and it's rarely more than routine. **AT** Violence.

Robert Duvall *Gruen* • Treat Williams *Meade* • Kathryn Harrold *Hannah* • Ed Flanders *Brigadier* • Paul Gleason *Remson* • RG Armstrong *Dempsey* ■ *Dir* Roger Spottiswoode • *Scr* Jeffrey Alan Fiskin, from the book *Free Fall* by JD Reed

The Pursuit of Happiness ★
Drama   1971 · US · Colour · 98min

Robert Mulligan directs this clichéd, hopelessly dated story of a disenchanted hippy who rejects the lifestyle of his affluent Manhattan family. Michael Sarrazin's life goes wrong – he kills someone in an auto accident, goes to jail and then thinks he should escape and hop over the Canadian border. Barbara Hershey is his girlfriend and there's a song, repeated often, by Randy Newman. **AT**

Michael Sarrazin *William Popper* • Barbara Hershey *Jane Kauffman* • Arthur Hill *John Popper* • Ruth White *Mrs Popper* • EG Marshall *Daniel Lawrence* • Robert Klein *Melvin Lasher* • William Devane *Pilot* ■ *Dir* Robert Mulligan • *Scr* Jon Boothe, George L Sherman, from a novel by Thomas Rogers

The Pursuit of Happyness ★★★12
Drama based on a true story   2006 · US · Colour · 112min

Will Smith reins in his customary exuberance to deliver a beautifully understated performance as real-life San Francisco father Chris Gardner, who, in the 1980s, battled against astonishing adversity to achieve his American Dream. When his wife Linda (Thandie Newton) leaves him, Gardner takes custody of their five-year-old child (played by Smith's delightful real-life son, Jaden) and then faces a catalogue of disasters as they become homeless and he tries to pursue a new career. Smith's restraint works wonderfully here and he makes every facial flicker count. The overall message may be a positive one, but it's agonising to watch such a decent man suffer. Ultimately the film is expertly constructed with faultless central turns, but it would have benefited from being more uplifting. **SF** Brief swearing. **DVD** **Blu-ray**

Will Smith *Chris Gardner* • Jaden Christopher Syre Smith [Jaden Smith] *Christopher* • Thandie Newton *Linda* • Brian Howe *Jay Twistle* • James Karen *Martin Frohm* • Dan Castellaneta *Alan Frakesh* • Kurt Fuller *Walter Ribbon* ■ *Dir* Gabriele Muccino • *Scr* Steven Conrad

Pursuit to Algiers ★★U
Mystery   1945 · US · BW · 65min

Basil Rathbone and Nigel Bruce simply cruise through this lacklustre entry in the Universal Sherlock Holmes series, escorting an imperilled prince to his home country on an ocean liner. Holmes looks decidedly sniffy about the whole affair, as if lamenting the poor production values and wafer-thin sets. Watson makes the best of a mediocre job, however, at one point even bursting into song. **TH**

Basil Rathbone *Sherlock Holmes* • Nigel Bruce *Dr John H Watson* • Marjorie Riordan *Sheila Woodbury, singer* • Rosalind Ivan *Agatha Dunham* • Martin Kosleck *Mirko* • John Abbott *Jodri* • Frederick Worlock *Prime Minister* • Morton Lowry *Sanford, ship's steward* ■ *Dir* Roy William Neill • *Scr* Leonard Lee, from characters by Sir Arthur Conan Doyle

Push ★★12
Science-fiction thriller   2009 · US/Can · Colour · 106min

Chris Evans and Dakota Fanning are blessed and cursed with powerful telekinetic and psychic powers in this convoluted thriller from British director Paul McGuigan (*Gangster No 1*). The two find themselves wanted by a shadowy government agency and a deadly underworld gang, and are chased through the seedier streets of Hong Kong, all in pursuit of a suitcase of money and a miracle serum that will help boost their abilities. The special effects are used economically, but the escapist fun is undermined by some pedestrian dialogue, a plot riddled with holes, and a central premise that's been handled with more wit and flair by TV's *Heroes*. **TeS** English, Cantonese +subtitles. **DVD**

Chris Evans *Nick Gant* • Dakota Fanning *Cassie Holmes* • Camilla Belle *Kira Hudson* • Djimon Hounsou *Henry Carver* • Ming-Na *Emily Wu* • Nate Mooney *Pinky Stein* ■ *Dir* Paul McGuigan • *Scr* David Bourla

Pusher ★★★18
Crime drama   1996 · Den · Colour · 105min

Although debuting Danish director Nicolas Winding Refn gives as his references such American indie icons as Quentin Tarantino and Abel Ferrara, the grungy hand-held visuals, improvised dialogue and dark sense of humour mean this feels more like a European art house movie. Always a picture on the move, in keeping with drug dealer Kim Bodnia's occupational ducking and diving, the action becomes increasingly claustrophobic as his options run out. Capturing the predatory nature and paranoia of a hideous existence, this is a sobering, violent drama. **DP** Danish +subtitles. **DVD**

Kim Bodnia *Frank* • Zlatko Buric *Milo* • Laura Drasbaek *Vic* • Slavko Labovic *Radovan* ■ *Dir* Nicolas Winding Refn • *Scr* Nicolas Winding Refn, Jens Dahl

Pusher II ★★★★18
Crime drama   2004 · Den · Colour · 95min

Mads Mikkelsen stars as a terminal screwup, who first appeared as a minor character in writer/director Nicolas Winding Refn's 1996 crime drama, *Pusher*. For most of the movie, shaven-headed Mikkelsen tries unsuccessfully to curry favour with his ruthless gangland dad (Leif Sylvester Petersen), who only has eyes for his younger half-brother. Mikkelsen is superb throughout, but it's Refn's innovative but controlled direction that really shines here as terrifically funny comedy sequences alternate with much darker material. **LF** Danish +subtitles. Violence, swearing, sex scenes, drug abuse. **DVD**

Mads Mikkelsen *Tonny* • Leif Sylvester Petersen *Smeden* • Kurt Nielsen *KusseKurt* • Anne Sorensen *Charlotte* • Oyvind Traberg Hagen *O* • Karsten Schroder *Rode* • Maria Erwolter *Gry* ■ *Dir/Scr* Nicolas Winding Refn

Pusher 3 ★★★18
Crime drama   2005 · Den · Colour · 107min

Nicolas Winding Refn continues his walk on the wild side of Copenhagen life with the third part of his gritty urban crime series. This time the story focuses on Milo (a poignant Zlatko Buric), the now ageing Serbian drug baron from the original *Pusher*. Milo's domestic travails, as he struggles to prepare for his daughter's birthday party, are horrifically contrasted with his own heroin addiction and the catastrophic consequences of a botched ecstasy deal. The vengeful events that unfold are gut-wrenchingly raw, yet laced with the blackest humour that makes even the grimmest scenes palatable. **SF** Serbian, Danish, Albanian +subtitles.

Zlatko Buric *Milo* • Ilyas Agac *Little Mohammed* • Marinela Dekic *Milena* • Kujtim Loki *Luan* • Ramadan Huseini *Rexho* • Slavko Labovic *Radovan* ■ *Dir/Scr* Nicolas Winding Refn

Pusher ★★★18
Crime thriller   2012 · UK · Colour · 85min

A remake of Nicolas Winding Refn's gritty 1996 Danish break-out movie, this vibrant urban update set in post-rave culture East London works surprisingly well, mostly because its antihero Frank (Richard Coyle) is no longer a thick-set blue-collar bruiser but a charming, likeable cocaine dealer who mostly sells drugs to his friends. It's this which makes his descent into hell all the more dramatic. Coyle is by far the standout in a neon-saturated thriller that throbs with a persuasive clubland beat, but the elements around him don't quite match. **DW** Violence, swearing, sexual references, drug abuse, a sex scene. **DVD** **Blu-ray**

Richard Coyle *Frank* • Bronson Webb *Tony* • Agyness Deyn *Flo* • Zlatko Buric *Milo* • Paul Kaye *Fitz* ■ *Dir* Luis Prieto • *Scr* Matthew Read

Pushing Hands ★★★12
Comedy drama   1991 · Tai/US · Colour · 100min

The title of this early gem from director Ang Lee refers to the Oriental t'ai chi exercise during which you keep your balance while unbalancing your opponent. This is an apt metaphor for the narrative about retired martial arts expert Lung Sihung, whose life is turned upside down when he moves in with his son and his American wife in a New York suburb. While not as assured as his later works, Lee's subtle observations are very much worth watching as the older man struggles to fit in with his hostile daughter-in-law (Deb Snyder). **LH** English, Mandarin +subtitles. **DVD**

Lung Sihung *Mr Chu* • Wang Lai *Mrs Chen* • Bo Z Wang *Alex Chu* • Deb Snyder *Martha Chu* • Lee Haan *Jeremy Chu* ■ *Dir* Ang Lee • *Scr* Ang Lee, James Schamus

Pushing Tin ★★★15
Comedy drama   1999 · US · Colour · 123min

This uneven but fascinating comedy drama looks at the air-traffic controllers who guide planes in and out of New York's airspace. Mike Newell's film focuses on two in particular: supercool John Cusack and Zen-like Billy Bob Thornton, who challenges Cusack's claim to be the best controller in town. It's not only Cusack's ego that is bruised by his rivalry with Thornton; their wives (Cate Blanchett and Angelina Jolie) also get caught in the crossfire. Overly dramatic in places, this boasts superb performances from Thornton and Cusack. **JB** Swearing, a sex scene. **DVD**

John Cusack *Nick Falzone* • Billy Bob Thornton *Russell Bell* • Cate Blanchett *Connie Falzone* • Angelina Jolie *Mary Bell* • Jake Weber *Barry Plotkin* ■ *Dir* Mike Newell • *Scr* Glen Charles, Les Charles, from the article *Something's Got to Give* by Darcy Frey

Pushover ★★★
Crime drama   1954 · US · BW · 87min

In a smart and unpredictable thriller, Fred MacMurray is the cop who puts a bank robber's girlfriend (Kim Novak) under surveillance, only to fall in love with her himself. Novak's glamorous and glacial

presence, not to mention the easy-going charm of MacMurray, makes this movie a sort of forerunner to Hitchcock's *Vertigo*. The basic idea was reprised three decades later in the comedy *Stakeout*. **AT**

Fred MacMurray *Paul Sheridan* • Kim Novak *Lona McLane* • Phil Carey [Philip Carey] *Rick McAllister* • Dorothy Malone *Ann* • EG Marshall *Lt Carl Eckstrom* ■ *Dir* Richard Quine • *Scr* Roy Huggins, from a story and novel by Thomas Walsh, from the novel *Rafferty* by William S Ballinger

Puss in Boots ★★★★U
Animated comedy adventure   2011 · US · Colour · 90min

That suave, scene-stealing cat from *Shrek 2* finally gets his own swashbuckling adventure and it couldn't be a more colourful feline fairy tale. Here the dashing Puss (impeccably voiced by Antonio Banderas) finds romance with slinky Kitty Softpaws (Salma Hayek) as they team up with Puss's former partner-in-crime Humpty Dumpty on a quest for a golden goose. This lively romp veers delightfully between *Mother Goose*, *Zorro* and Sergio Leone western, and is lovely to look at, cleverly written and beautifully visualised. The cat puns are rife with almost every image, and while that cute big eyes gag is used quite a few times, it never gets old. **AJ** **DVD** **Blu-ray**

Antonio Banderas *Puss in Boots* • Salma Hayek *Kitty Softpaws* • Zach Galifianakis *Humpty Dumpty* • Billy Bob Thornton *Jack* • Amy Sedaris *Jill* • Walt Dohrn [Walter Dohrn] *Narrator* ■ *Dir* Chris Miller • *Scr* Tom Wheeler, from a story by Brian Lynch, Will Davies, Wheeler

Pussy Riot: a Punk Prayer ★★★18
Documentary   2013 · Rus/UK · Colour · 88min

This provocative documentary is more important for what it says than how it says it. Using home video, talking heads and court footage, director Mike Lerner chronicles the controversy surrounding the well-publicised protest by feminist punk group Pussy Riot in Moscow's iconic Orthodox cathedral in February 2012, ostensibly to rail against Vladimir Putin and his grip on the Russian presidency. This is no objective treatise; it's not difficult to take the side of the outspoken activists, whose eloquence under duress is often inspirational. **JA** Russian, English +subtitles. Swearing, sex scenes, nudity.

Maria Alyokhina • Yekaterina Samutsevich • Nadezhda Tolokonnikova ■ *Dir* Mike Lerner, Maxim Pozdorovkin

The Putin System ★★★12A
Documentary   2007 · Fr · Colour and BW · 97min

This fascinating documentary from director Jean-Michel Carré examines Vladimir Putin's rise from obscure KGB officer to the office of Russian President in March 2000. Former colleagues, dissidents and political analysts describe how the dream of democracy in the post-Soviet era was superseded by Putin's vision of a new, all-powerful Russian empire. Putin's shrewd recognition of "energy as a tool for power", his manipulation of oligarchs like Boris Berezovsky and his ruthless intervention in Chechnya confirm his status as a consummate political operator. Archive footage is effectively used to contrast the pomp of the Kremlin with the bloody realities of recent Russian history – as well as the odd lighter moment. **SS** English, Russian +subtitles.

■ *Dir* Jean-Michel Carré • *Scr* Jean-Michel Carré, Jill Emery

Puzzle of a Downfall Child ★★
Drama   1970 · US · Colour · 104min

A once-famous fashion model (Faye Dunaway), now in a state of disintegration as a result of her less than savoury lifestyle, retires to a beach house. There, she recounts her sordid past (in flashback) to photographer Barry Primus. Former fashion photographer Jerry Schatzberg made his directing debut with this visually excellent movie in which Dunaway, looking stunning, gives a good account of herself. RK *DVD* *Blu-ray*

Faye Dunaway *Lou Andreas Sand* • Barry Primus *Aaron Reinhardt* • Viveca Lindfors *Pauline Galba* • Barry Morse *Dr Calba* • Roy Scheider *Mark* • Ruth Jackson *Barbara Casey* • John Heffernan *Dr Sherman* ■ *Dir* Jerry Schatzberg • *Scr* Adrien Joyce [Carole Eastman], from a story by Jerry Schatzberg, Adrien Joyce [Carole Eastman]

Pyaasa ★★★★ U
Romantic musical drama
1957 · Ind · BW · 133min

This heart-rending masala is a solemn meditation on the impossibility of poetry in a cruel world and it marked a distinct change in tone for actor/director Guru Dutt. From the opening image of a bee being trodden on as it pollinates a flower, the central theme is clear. But VK Murthy's sublime photography and a memorable score by SD Burman and Sahir Ludhianvi elevate this classic tale of romance and disappointment way above formulaic melodrama. DP Hindi +subtitles. *DVD*

Mala Sinha *Meena* • Guru Dutt *Vijay* • Waheeda Rehman *Gulabo* • Rehman *Mr Ghosh* • Johnny Walker *Abdul Sattar* • Leela Misra [Leela Mishra] *Vijay's mother* ■ *Dir* Guru Dutt • *Scr* Abrar Alvi

Pygmalion ★★★★★ U
Comedy
1938 · UK · BW · 91min

This is a superb rendering of George Bernard Shaw's most popular play, for which Shaw himself was awarded a special Academy Award for his contribution (the embassy ball scene) to the screenplay. The film actually won Oscars for the adaptors of the screenplay. Leslie Howard was never better as Henry Higgins (a role Shaw wanted to go to Charles Laughton) and both he and Wendy Hiller (quite brilliant as Eliza Doolittle) were unlucky not to win Oscars themselves. Although Howard took a co-directing credit, Anthony Asquith handled most of the action, acquiring himself an unrivalled reputation for stage adaptation in the process. DP *DVD*

Leslie Howard *Professor Henry Higgins* • Wendy Hiller *Eliza Doolittle* • Wilfrid Lawson *Alfred Doolittle* • Marie Lohr *Mrs Higgins* • Scott Sunderland *Colonel Pickering* • Jean Cadell *Mrs Pearce* • David Tree *Freddy Eynsford-Hill* • Everley Gregg *Mrs Eynsford-Hill* ■ *Dir* Anthony Asquith, Leslie Howard • *Scr* George Bernard Shaw, from his play, adapted by WP Lipscomb, Cecil Lewis, Ian Dalrymple • *Editor* David Lean

The Pyramid ★★ 15
Horror
2014 · US · Colour · 88min

The haunted house movie gets an uninspired Egyptian twist as a team of archaeologists find a three-sided pyramid. Once inside, they become trapped in a complex labyrinth designed to keep whoever enters from ever escaping. Danger lies in the darkness in a cynical movie that makes no bones about its intentions. Once the premise is established and the characters are trapped inside, jump scares, gore and "found footage" genre clichés repeat in a process that may trouble the nerves but not the mind. JL

Ashley Hinshaw *Dr Nora Holden* • Denis O'Hare *Dr Miles Holden* • James Buckley *Fitzie* • Christa Nicola *Sunni* ■ *Dir* Grégory Levasseur • *Scr* Daniel Meersand, Nick Simon

Pyrates ★★ 18
Comedy
1991 · US · Colour · 91min

In this oddity, real-life husband-and-wife leads Kevin Bacon and Kyra Sedgwick play a young couple with a fiery love life, literally – when the pair get together, buildings tend to go up in smoke. It's an unusual concept, with the two stars giving it their best shot, but director Noah Stern doesn't take the original idea anywhere interesting and it's far too self-consciously wacky for its own good. JF Swearing, sex scenes, nudity.

Kevin Bacon *Ari* • Kyra Sedgwick *Sam* • Bruce Martyn Payne [Bruce Payne] *Liam* • Kristin Dattilo *Pia* • Buckley Norris *Dr Weiss* • Deborah Falconer *Rivkah* • David Pressman *Carlton* ■ *Dir/Scr* Noah Stern

A Pyromaniac's Love Story ★★ PG
Romantic comedy
1995 · US · Colour · 90min

Love-starved workers at Armin Mueller-Stahl's bakery try to find romance while dealing with a mystery arsonist in this witless comedy directed by Joshua Brand, the creator of *Northern Exposure*. Each of the game cast wants to be known as the pyromaniac responsible for the fire so they can say their motive was love. Despite some cute turns, this incomprehensible farce raises little heat. AJ *DVD*

William Baldwin *Garet* • John Leguizamo *Sergio* • Sadie Frost *Hattie* • Erika Eleniak *Stephanie* • Michael Lerner *Perry* • Joan Plowright *Mrs Linzer* • Armin Mueller-Stahl *Mr Linzer* • Richard Crenna *Businessman* ■ *Dir* Joshua Brand • *Scr* Morgan Ward

Python ★★ 15
Horror
2000 · US · Colour · 95min

The 130ft snake really should be the star of this 1950s-style horror movie, yet the abysmal effects make this genetically engineered python feel about as terrifying as an earthworm. Still, this horror does have a sense of humour, typified by genre regular Robert Englund's knowing performance as a verbose reptile expert. In fact, it is mainly of note to genre fans for its cast, but if you're watching this for decent shocks or effects, beware. JC *DVD*

Casper Van Dien *Special Agent Bart Parker* • Robert Englund *Dr Anton Rudolph* • Frayne Rosanoff *John Cooper* • Wil Wheaton *Tommy* • Sara Mornell *Theresa* • Chris Owens *Brian Cooper* ■ *Dir* Richard Clabaugh • *Scr* Chris Neal, Gary Hershberger, Paul JM Bogh, from a story by Phillip Roth [Phillip J Roth]

Q & A ★★★ 18
Crime drama
1990 · US · Colour · 126min

Sidney Lumet, who was once described as New York's Charles Dickens, chronicles yet another case of civic corruption and bigotry. Nick Nolte, giving a charismatic performance, stars as a cop who is suspected of killing a drug pusher. Seeking the truth behind the murder is Timothy Hutton, a squeaky-clean assistant district attorney. It is best appreciated now as a showcase for Nolte's explosive talent. AT Violence, swearing, nudity. *DVD*

Nick Nolte *Lieutenant Mike Brennan* • Timothy Hutton *Al Reilly* • Armand Assante *Bobby Texador* • Patrick O'Neal (1) *Kevin Quinn* • Lee Richardson *Leo Bloomenfeld* • Luis Guzman *Luis Valentin* • Charles Dutton [Charles S Dutton] *Sam Chapman* • Jenny Lumet *Nancy Bosch* ■ *Dir* Sidney Lumet • *Scr* Sidney Lumet, from the novel by Edwin Torres

Q Planes ★★★ U
Second World War spy drama
1939 · UK · BW · 78min

Laurence Olivier (as a test pilot) and Ralph Richardson (as a Scotland Yard officer) co-star in this terrific Irving Asher/Alexander Korda produced espionage romp. Richardson is especially good value as the policeman trying to discover why planes are disappearing off the coast of Cornwall and it's rare to find light-heartedness working so well in a British film of the period. DP *DVD*

Laurence Olivier *Tony McVane* • Valerie Hobson *Kay Hammond* • Ralph Richardson *Charles Hammond* • George Curzon *Jenkins* • George Merritt (1) *Barrett* ■ *Dir* Tim Whelan • *Scr* Ian Dalrymple, from a story by Jack Whittingham, Brock Williams, Arthur Wimperis

Q – the Winged Serpent ★★★★ 15
Cult fantasy horror
1982 · US · Colour · 92min

The ancient Aztec god Quetzacoatl, a giant flying serpent-bird, is reincarnated by a Manhattan cult and decapitates New Yorkers from its nest atop the Chrysler Building. As detectives David Carradine and Richard Roundtree try to make sense of the myth, petty crook Michael Moriarty holds the Big Apple to ransom. Larry Cohen's classic B picture is part wonderfully entertaining cop thriller, part old-fashioned monster movie. AJ Violence, swearing, nudity. *DVD*

Michael Moriarty *Jimmy Quinn* • David Carradine *Detective Shepard* • Candy Clark *Joan* • Richard Roundtree *Sgt Powell* • James Dixon *Lt Murray* • Malachy McCourt *Police commissioner* ■ *Dir/Scr* Larry Cohen • *Special Effects* David Allen

Quackser Fortune Has a Cousin in the Bronx ★★★
Comedy drama
1970 · US · Colour · 91min

The dreadful title apart, this is a charming Irish fable with Gene Wilder cast as Quackser Fortune – his duck imitations earn him the nickname – who shovels horse manure for a living, selling it to housewives all over Dublin. A know-all American student, Margot Kidder, distracts him romantically and patronises him intellectually, until the cousin in the Bronx brings about an ironic conclusion. Cameraman Gilbert Taylor turns the city's glistening Georgian buildings and cobbled streets into a tourist agent's dream. AT

Gene Wilder *Quackser Fortune* • Margot Kidder *Zazel Pierce* • Eileen Colgan *Betsy Bourke* • Seamus Ford *Mr Fortune* • May Ollis *Mrs Fortune* • Liz Davis *Kathleen Fortune* ■ *Dir* Waris Hussein • *Scr* Gabriel Walsh

Quadrophenia ★★★★ 18
Social drama
1979 · UK · Colour · 115min

The Who's *My Generation* musical tribute to Mods and Rockers in pre-1960s England is a near-perfect integration of cinematic story and rousing pop. It specifically focuses on the antics of parka-clad Phil Daniels, whose alienation is fuelled by pill-popping, scooter rave-ups and seaside battles in Brighton. Director Franc Roddam evokes the budding Swinging Sixties and the teenage sense of frustration and disillusionment with a lively precision. Sting makes his acting debut in this musical milestone crackling with energy and great performances. AJ Swearing, violence, sex scenes. *DVD* *Blu-ray*

Phil Daniels *Jimmy Michael Cooper* • Leslie Ash *Steph* • Philip Davis *Chalky* • Mark Wingett *Dave* • Sting *Ace Face* • Raymond Winstone [Ray Winstone] *Kevin* • Garry Cooper *Peter* • Toyah Willcox *Monkey* ■ *Dir* Franc Roddam • *Scr* Dave Humphries, Martin Stellman, Franc Roddam

Le Quai des Brumes ★★★★★ PG
Romantic melodrama
1938 · Fr · BW · 87min

As war clouds gathered, French poetic realism grew increasingly pessimistic. None expressed this despondency more poignantly than Marcel Carné and screenwriter Jacques Prévert, who collaborated on this mist-shrouded waterfront tale of doomed romance. Confining the action entirely to the sublime studio sets designed by Alexandre Trauner and evocatively shot by Eugen Schüfftan, Carné was able to control every detail of his meticulous compositions and, thus, make the plight of army deserter Jean Gabin and waif Michèle Morgan all the more allegorically tragic. Pure melancholic magic. DP French +subtitles. *DVD* *Blu-ray*

Jean Gabin *Jean* • Michèle Morgan *Nelly* • Michel Simon *Zabel* • Pierre Brasseur *Lucien* • Robert Le Vigan *Michel Krauss* ■ *Dir* Marcel Carné • *Scr* Jacques Prévert, from the novel by Pierre MacOrlan

Quai des Orfèvres ★★★★ PG
Thriller
1947 · Fr · BW · 102min

The title of this wonderfully atmospheric thriller refers to the French equivalent of Scotland Yard. The story revolves around a seedy music hall, where singer Suzy Delair thinks she has committed a murder for which her husband becomes a suspect. The director Henri-Georges Clouzot portrays a Paris teeming with life and mystery in which he observes human frailty with wit and compassion. Outstanding is Louis Jouvet as a police inspector, part cynic, part sentimentalist. It was Clouzot's first film for four years because his previous picture, *The Raven (Le Corbeau)*, had been accused of being anti-French propaganda. RB French +subtitles. *DVD*

Simone Renant *Dora* • Suzy Delair *Jenny Lamour* • Bernard Blier *Maurice Martineau* • Charles Dullin *Brignon the industrialist* • Louis Jouvet *Inspector Antoine* ■ *Dir* Henri-Georges Clouzot • *Scr* Henri-Georges Clouzot, Jean Ferry, from the novel *Légitime Défense* by Stanislas-André Steeman

Quality Street ★★ U
Comedy drama
1937 · US · BW · 82min

JM Barrie's now hopelessly dated whimsy came to the screen as a vehicle for Katharine Hepburn in a last-ditch – and unsuccessful – attempt by RKO to arrest her box-office decline. She's in love with the dashing Franchot Tone, who goes off to the Napoleonic Wars for several years without declaring his intentions. Amid studio-bound Toytown sets, George Stevens directs at a deadly pace for the first half, and the star's stagey and hysterical performance is more deranged southern belle than genteel Englishwoman. RK

Katharine Hepburn *Phoebe Throssel* • Franchot Tone *Dr Valentine Brown* • Fay Bainter *Susan Throssel* • Eric Blore *Recruiting Sergeant* • Cora Witherspoon *Patty the Maid* • Joan Fontaine *Charlotte Parratt* ■ *Dir* George Stevens • *Scr* Mortimer Offner, Allan Scott, from the play by JM Barrie

Quantez ★★
Western   1957 · US · Colour · 80min

This is distinguished by its location photography and the tough performance of Dorothy Malone. Unfortunately, Malone is paired with an ageing – though still top-billed – Fred MacMurray and callow John Gavin to little advantage in this slow-paced tale about a group journeying to Mexico through Apache territory. TS

Fred MacMurray *Gentry/John Coventry* • Dorothy Malone *Chaney* • James Barton *Minstrel* • Sydney Chaplin *Gato* • John Gavin *Teach* • John Larch *Heller* ■ *Dir* Harry Keller • *Scr* R Wright Campbell, from a story by R Wright Campbell, Anne Edwards

Quantrill's Raiders ★★ U
Western   1958 · US · Colour · 70min

This CinemaScope western programme filler is made interesting not by the presence of star Steve Cochran, but by Leo Gordon as the legendary William Quantrill himself, whom this movie kills off during the raid on an ammunitions dump at Lawrence, Kansas, and not, as actually happened, two years later in Kentucky. The thickset Gordon specialised in villains, and eventually found a natural haven in Europe. Here, as Quantrill, his psychoses are given free rein. TS

Steve Cochran *Westcott* • Diane Brewster *Sue* • Leo Gordon *Quantrill* • Gale Robbins *Kate* • Will Wright *Judge* • Kim Charney *Joel* ■ *Dir* Edward Bernds • *Scr* Polly James

Quantum of Solace ★★★ 12
Spy adventure   2008 · UK/US · Colour · 101min

Daniel Craig's second outing as James Bond had a famously troubled production, which may explain why it fails to deliver on the promise of its predecessor, *Casino Royale*. Picking up events directly after that film's climax, it sees Bond looking for answers after the death of his lover, Vesper Lynd. The trail leads to Quantum, a mysterious organisation that has infiltrated the world's corridors of power and is moving to instigate a regime change in Bolivia. Marc Forster's take on 007 was hit by a writer's strike, and the script suffers as a result, with the paranoid storyline as nonsensical as the Ian Fleming-inspired title. But viewed solely as an action spectacle, there's still plenty of excitement, while Craig's committed performance remains eminently watchable. JH English, Spanish, Italian, French +subtitles. Violence DVD ⬄

Daniel Craig *James Bond* • Olga Kurylenko *Camille* • Mathieu Amalric *Dominic Greene* • Judi Dench *M* • Giancarlo Giannini *Rene Mathis* • Gemma Arterton *Agent Fields* • Jeffrey Wright *Felix Leiter* • Jesper Christensen *Mr White* ■ *Dir* Marc Forster • *Scr* Paul Haggis, Neal Purvis, Robert Wade, from characters by Ian Fleming • *Cinematographer* Roberto Schaefer • *Production Designer* Dennis Gassner • *Music* David Arnold

Quarantine ★★★ 18
Horror   2008 · US · Colour · 85min

Director John Erick Dowdle's instant remake of the 2007 Spanish horror hit *[Rec]* relocates the action to Los Angeles, where a young TV reporter (*Dexter's* Jennifer Carpenter) and her cameraman are on assignment at a fire station. They're called to an emergency at an apartment block, and before long they find themselves recording a bloody nightmare in the now-quarantined building, where a rabies-like infection has taken hold. What raw energy and shock value there is will have more impact for those who haven't already seen *[Rec]* – for those who have, this is a near-pointless exercise. AJ DVD ⬄

Jennifer Carpenter *Angela Vidal* • Jay Hernandez *Jake* • Columbus Short *Danny Wilensky* • Greg Germann *Lawrence* • Steve Harris *Scott Percival* • Dania Ramirez *Sadie* • Rade Sherbedgia [Rade Serbedzija] *Yuri Ivanov*

Johnathon Schaech *George Fletcher* ■ *Dir* John Erick Dowdle • *Scr* John Erick Dowdle, Drew Dowdle, from the 2007 film *[Rec]*

The Quare Fellow ★★★ 15
Drama   1962 · Ire · Colour · 86min

Patrick McGoohan stars in this anti-capital punishment treatise, a gloomily sincere adaptation of Brendan Behan's renowned play. He's the novice prison warder who has his hanging convictions severely shaken after meeting the wife of one "Quare Fellow", Irish slang for a criminal on death row. And they're rattled again when another reprieved murderer takes his own life. The claustrophobic prison atmosphere is expertly conjured up in a well-intentioned, if downbeat, protest movie. AJ

Patrick McGoohan *Thomas Crimmin* • Sylvia Syms *Kathleen* • Walter Macken *Regan* • Dermot Kelly *Donnelly* • Jack Cunningham *Chief warder* • Hilton Edwards *Holy Healy* ■ *Dir* Arthur Dreifuss • *Scr* Arthur Dreifuss, Jacqueline Sundstrom, from the play by Brendan Behan

Quartet ★★★ PG
Portmanteau drama   1948 · UK · BW · 114min

With W Somerset Maugham introducing the four vignettes based on his celebrated short stories, an air of literary portentousness hangs over this portmanteau picture, but, each tale is told with refreshing lightness. In *The Facts of Life*, Jack Watling enjoys the attentions of Monte Carlo gold-digger Mai Zetterling; *The Alien Corn* sees Dirk Bogarde driven to despair by his ambition to become a concert pianist; nerdy inventor George Cole is caught between wife Susan Shaw and hectoring mother, Hermione Baddeley in *The Kite*; while in *The Colonel's Lady*, Cecil Parker frets about the contents of a slim volume of love poems published by his wife, Nora Swinburne. DP

Basil Radford *Henry Garnet* • Jack Watling *Nicky* • Mai Zetterling *Jeanne* • Dirk Bogarde *George Bland* • Honor Blackman *Paula* • George Cole *Herbert Sunbury* • Hermione Baddeley *Beatrice Sunbury* • Susan Shaw *Betty* • Cecil Parker *Colonel Peregrine* • Nora Swinburne *Mrs Peregrine* ■ *Dir* Ralph Smart, Harold French, Arthur Crabtree, Ken Annakin • *Scr* RC Sherriff, from stories by W Somerset Maugham

Quartet ★★★ 18
Period drama   1981 · UK/Fr · Colour · 96min

Based on the novel by Jean Rhys, this is a typically classy piece of film-making from director James Ivory. In 1920s Paris, Isabelle Adjani takes refuge with married couple Alan Bates and Maggie Smith after her husband (Anthony Higgins) is jailed. She eventually submits to the advances of Bates at the expense of his rather sad bullied wife, as the film explores with subtlety an upper-class lifestyle beset with moral corruption. LH DVD

Isabelle Adjani *Marya Zelli* • Anthony Higgins *Stephan Zelli* • Maggie Smith *Lois Heidler* • Alan Bates *HJ Heidler* • Pierre Clémenti *Theo the pornographer* • Daniel Mesguich *Pierre Schlamovitz* ■ *Dir* James Ivory • *Scr* Ruth Prawer Jhabvala, from the novel *Quartet* by Jean Rhys

Quartet ★★★★ 12
Comedy drama   2012 · UK · Colour · 94min

Dustin Hoffman's first film as a director is a treat for the actors involved, and what actors they are: the cast includes Maggie Smith, Tom Courtenay, Pauline Collins and Billy Connolly. Scripted by Ronald Harwood from his play, *Quartet* is a romantic comedy drama about the travails and delights of a handful of aged opera singers living in a stately retirement home. Their relatively content lives are turned upside down when diva Jean Horton (Smith) – the final member of a famous quartet to arrive at the home and also the ex-wife of Reggie (Courtenay) – shows up unannounced. Hoffman has cast his actors in roles that fit them well and they reward him with fine performances. There is nothing startling or challenging about *Quartet*, but it's a delightful film that touches on themes of ageing and the enduring importance of art. KK Swearing. DVD ⬄

Maggie Smith *Jean Horton* • Tom Courtenay *Reggie Paget* • Billy Connolly *Wilf Bond* • Pauline Collins *Cissy Robson* • Michael Gambon *Cedric Livingston* • Sheridan Smith *Dr Lucy Cogan* ■ *Dir* Dustin Hoffman • *Scr* Ronald Harwood, from his play

Quatermass II ★★★★ 12
Science-fiction thriller   1957 · UK · BW · 81min

The second in Hammer's *Quatermass* trilogy is a potent, low-budget rollercoaster ride through government conspiracies and alien invasions, set against the chilling backdrop of postwar new town paranoia. Great writing by Nigel Kneale (based on his original BBC TV serial), superb direction by Val Guest and Gerald Gibbs's stark black-and-white photography make this British classic one of the best science-fiction allegories of the 1950s. AJ DVD

Brian Donlevy *Quatermass* • John Longden *Inspector Lomax* • Sidney James *Jimmy Hall* • Bryan Forbes *Marsh* • William Franklyn *Brand* • Vera Day *Sheila* • Charles Lloyd Pack *Dawson* • Michael Ripper *Ernie* ■ *Dir* Val Guest • *Scr* Val Guest, Nigel Kneale, from the TV serial by Nigel Kneale • *Cinematographer* Gerald Gibbs

Quatermass and the Pit ★★★ 12
Science-fiction thriller   1967 · UK · Colour · 93min

This remains the most popular of the movies taken from Nigel Kneale's acclaimed BBC TV serial. Although the Deluxe Color dissipates some of the atmosphere and mystery, the story of the Martian spaceship uncovered in a London Tube station retains much of its intrigue and sense of disquiet thanks to Roy Ward Baker's careful direction and special effects that never attempt to exceed their technical or budgetary limitations. As well as providing a generous helping of shocks, Kneale's script gives his complex themes and theories plenty of space, and both action and argument are neatly judged. DP DVD ⬄

James Donald *Dr Matthew Roney* • Andrew Keir *Professor Bernard Quatermass* • Barbara Shelley *Barbara Judd* • Julian Glover *Colonel Breen* • Duncan Lamont *Sladden* ■ *Dir* Roy Ward Baker • *Scr* Nigel Kneale, from his TV serial

The Quatermass Conclusion ★★★ 15
Science-fiction thriller   1979 · UK · Colour · 101min

After *Quatermass and the Pit*, the Professor returned to television in a four-part serial that was generally regarded as a failure. This cut-down feature film was released to cinemas abroad and on video in the UK. As author Nigel Kneale correctly observed, the serial was too long and the film too short. Nevertheless, the story, which uses a favourite Kneale theme, the re-emergence of old fears and religions, begins and ends well. Quatermass (a creditable John Mills) discovers that aliens are harvesting humans from places of congregation. DM DVD

John Mills *Professor Bernard Quatermass* • Simon MacCorkindale *Joe Kapp* • Barbara Kellerman *Clare Kapp* • Margaret Tyzack *Annie Morgan* • Brewster Mason *Gurov* ■ *Dir* Piers Haggard • *Scr* Nigel Kneale, from his TV serial.

The Quatermass Xperiment ★★★ PG
Science-fiction thriller   1955 · UK · BW · 78min

Hammer's film of Nigel Kneale's ground-breaking television serial was a huge success, encouraging the studio to concentrate on the production of horror films – in that regard, it can truly be said to have changed the course of British film history. The story, of an astronaut who returns to Earth only to mutate gradually into a vegetable, was subsequently much emulated. Director Val Guest detested the casting of American actor Brian Donlevy, though his portrayal of Quatermass was generally well-received at the time. DM DVD

Brian Donlevy *Professor Bernard Quatermass* • Jack Warner *Inspector Lomax* • Margia Dean *Judith Carroon* • Richard Wordsworth *Victor Carroon* • David King-Wood *Dr Gordon Briscoe* •

Thora Hird *Rosie* • Gordon Jackson *TV producer* • Lionel Jeffries *Blake* ■ *Dir* Val Guest • *Scr* Val Guest, Richard Landau, from the TV serial by Nigel Kneale

Le Quattro Volte ★★★★★ U
Drama   2010 · It/Ger/Swi · Colour · 84min

Taken simply, this is a poetic treatise on the cycle of life that centres on an ailing goatherd and one of his mischievous flock, a felled fir tree and a charcoal kiln. However, Michelangelo Frammartino also shows how the changing seasons in a remote part of Calabria help explain Pythagoras's concepts of transmigration and the indivisibility of matter. It sounds forbidding, but the director draws on his own local knowledge to fashion a study of faith, ritual, nature and folklore that is both profoundly moving and delightfully funny. DP DVD ⬄

Giuseppe Fuda *Old shepherd* • Bruno Timpano *Serra San Bruno charcoal miner* • Nazareno Timpano *Serra San Bruno charcoal miner* ■ *Dir/Scr* Michelangelo Frammartino • *Cinematographer* Andrea Locatelli

Que la Bête Meure ★★★★ 15
Thriller   1969 · Fr/It · Colour · 107min

Adapted from a novel by Nicholas Blake (pseudonym of former poet laureate Cecil Day Lewis), this is one of Claude Chabrol's most accomplished pictures. Starting out as a whodunnit – widower Michel Duchaussoy seeks the hit-and-run driver who killed his son – the film turns into a psychological thriller. Duchaussoy inveigles himself into the culprit's family, only to decide that his planned revenge would be inappropriate. Chabrol mischievously muddies the waters by allowing Jean Yanne to portray the killer as an oaf who, despite alienating his own boy, is somehow grotesquely engaging. DP French +subtitles. DVD

Michel Duchaussoy *Charles Thenier* • Caroline Cellier *Helene Lanson* • Jean Yanne *Paul Decourt* • Anouk Ferjac *Jeanne* • Marc DiNapoli *Philippe Decourt* • Maurice Pialat *Police inspector* ■ *Dir* Claude Chabrol • *Scr* Paul Gegauff, Claude Chabrol, from the novel *The Beast Must Die* by Nicholas Blake [Cecil Day Lewis]

The Queen ★★★★★ 12
Historical drama   2006 · UK/Fr/It · Colour · 98min

Destined to become the apocryphal truth, this poignantly amusing mix of fact and fiction is set after Princess Diana's fatal car crash in 1997 and speculates on the Royal Family's reaction to the tragedy. Superbly scripted by Peter Morgan and deservedly beating a strong field to the best film Bafta, this benefits from director Stephen Frears's clever manipulation of iconic newsreel footage and flawless re-creation, with surprisingly moving results. The acting is exemplary, with Michael Sheen's newly elected Tony Blair spot on, Sylvia Syms a joy as the Queen Mother and James Cromwell hilariously pompous as Prince Philip. But it's Helen Mirren's faultless, Bafta-winning lookalike Queen Elizabeth II, facing the demands of a changing monarchy, that resonates with pure regal brilliance. AJ Brief swearing. DVD ⬄

Helen Mirren *Queen Elizabeth II* • Michael Sheen *Tony Blair* • James Cromwell *Prince Philip* • Sylvia Syms *HM The Queen Mother* • Alex Jennings *Prince Charles* • Mark Bazeley *Alastair Campbell* • Helen McCrory *Cherie Blair* • Paul Barrett *Trevor Rhys Jones* ■ *Dir* Stephen Frears • *Scr* Peter Morgan (1) • *Music* Alexandre Desplat

Queen and Country ★★ 15
Drama   2014 · UK · Colour · 114min

Not quite setting a record for length of time between original film and sequel by the same director, this is John Boorman's follow-up to his much loved 1987 film *Hope and Glory*. Now Bill is a strapping young man with a keen interest in movies, doing his National Service. Not a lot really happens: Bill survives army life and experiences a tepid first love (with a miscast Tamsin Egerton). The acting is uneven, although David Thewlis provides good value in a supporting role. What a shame Boorman chose to portray what is a

---

fairly dull stretch of his life. **LF** Swearing, a sex scene, brief nudity. *DVD*

Callum Turner *Bill Rohan* • David Thewlis *Bradley* • Caleb Landry Jones *Percy* • Vanessa Kirby *Dawn Rohan* • Richard E Grant *Major Cross* • Tamsin Egerton *Ophelia* • Sinead Cusack *Grace Rohan* ■ *Dir/Scr* John Boorman

Queen Bee ★★★ PG

Melodrama 1955 · US · BW · 90min

Joan Crawford virtually breathes fire as the power-crazed woman who marries into an unhappy Southern family and then ruins their lives. Crawford is perfectly cast in her Tennessee Williams-style role and acts up a storm in one fabulous hostess gown after another, while expertly cutting the rest of the cast down to size. An overblown extravaganza much beloved by Crawford fans and lovers of glossy Hollywood melodramas in the grand tradition. **AJ**

Joan Crawford *Eva Phillips* • Barry Sullivan *John Avery Phillips* • Betsy Palmer *Carol Lee Phillips* • John Ireland *Judson Prentiss* • Fay Wray *Sue McKinnon* ■ *Dir* Ranald MacDougall • *Scr* Ranald MacDougall, from the novel by Edna Lee

Queen Christina ★★★★ U

Historical romantic drama 1933 · US · BW · 95min

Greta Garbo stars as a 17th-century queen of Sweden who falls in inappropriate love with the Spanish ambassador sent to deliver a marriage proposal from his king. Garbo is quintessentially Garbo-esque in one of her most famous roles, while John Gilbert, her crony from silent days, is the ambassador, a role he played only at her insistence, after she had failed to warm to Laurence Olivier. The action is better when Garbo is travelling the kingdom dressed as a man than when she is weighed down by the worries of her throne. **PF** *DVD*

Greta Garbo *Queen Christina* • John Gilbert (1) *Don Antonio de la Prada* • Ian Keith *Magnus* • Lewis Stone *Chancellor Oxenstierna* ■ *Dir* Rouben Mamoulian • *Scr* HM Harwood, Salka Viertel, SN Behrman, from a story by Salka Viertel, Margaret Levin • *Cinematographer* William Daniels (1)

Queen Kelly ★★★ PG

Silent romantic melodrama 1928 · US · BW · 99min

Despite Erich von Stroheim's legendary profligacy, Gloria Swanson hired him to direct this silent tale of the waif who is mistreated by both a Teutonic aristocrat and a mad Ruritanian monarch, in the hope he could turn a simmering melodrama into a sophisticated masterpiece. However, on learning her character would inherit a chain of brothels in German East Africa, Swanson pulled the plug and cobbled together a save-face version that included a musical number to cash in on the talkie boom. Von Stroheim evidently forgave her, as together they watch clips from this visual feast in *Sunset Blvd.* **DF**

Gloria Swanson *Patricia Kelly, an orphan* • Walter Byron *Prince "Wild" Wolfram Von Hohenberg Falsenstein* • Seena Owen *Queen Regina V, his cousin and fiancée* • Sidney Bracey *Prince Wolfram's valet* • William von Brincken *Adjutant to Wolfram* ■ *Dir/Scr* Erich von Stroheim • *Cinematographer* Paul Ivano

Queen of Earth ★★★ 15

Psychological thriller 2015 · US · Colour · 89min

This creepy, unconventional psychodrama begins with a break-up. The person being dumped is *Mad Men's* Elisabeth Moss, a fragile, miserable woman who is still reeling from the death of her father. Looking for a change of scenery, she goes to stay with her best friend (Katherine Waterston) at an idyllic, upscale lake house. But, over the next seven days, their conversations include a number of venomous exchanges. A sense of dread hangs over every scene, and overall this is an unnerving if challenging experience. **SC** Swearing. *DVD* *Blu*

Elisabeth Moss *Catherine* • Katherine Waterston *Virginia* • Patrick Fugit *Rich* • Kentucker Audley *James* ■ *Dir/Scr* Alex Ross Perry

Queen of Hearts ★★★★ PG

Drama 1989 · UK · Colour · 107min

In Italy, sometime after the Second World War, Anita Zagaria breaks off her engagement to fierce Vittorio Amandola, and runs off to London with her lover, Joseph Long. But has she seen the last of her ex-fiancé? No chance. In later life, her ten-year-old son tells the whole magical tale. Jon Amiel debuts as director with a smashing mixture of vivid reality and dream-like surrealism. He introduces us to a world where people fly out of towers, where pigs dispense wisdom like Greek oracles, and where espresso machines puff out steam like mechanical dragons. Add terrific period atmosphere, and engaging performances from a largely unknown cast, and you've a terrific piece of offbeat entertainment. **DA**

Vittorio Duse *Nonno* • Joseph Long *Danilo* • Anita Zagaria *Rosa* • Eileen Way *Mama Sibilla* • Vittorio Amandola *Barbariccia* • Jimmy Lambert *Bruno* • Anna Pernicci *Angelica* ■ *Dir* Jon Amiel • *Scr* Tony Grisoni

Queen of Outer Space ★ U

Science-fiction adventure 1958 · US · Colour · 79min

A serious contender for the worst film ever made list, this idiot's would-be sexy sci-fi movie stars Zsa Zsa Gabor, who rescues our astronaut heroes, headed by Eric Fleming, who should have known better than to land on Venus, anyway. The colour gives the film an illusion of expense, but most British prints have faded to pink. **TS**

Zsa Zsa Gabor *Talleah* • Eric Fleming *Patterson* • Laurie Mitchell *Queen Yllana* • Paul Birch *Professor Konrad* • Barbara Darrow *Kaeel* ■ *Dir* Edward Bernds • *Scr* Charles Beaumont, from a story by Ben Hecht

The Queen of Spades ★★★★ PG

Supernatural drama 1948 · UK · BW · 91min

Set in Imperial Russia, this is the definitive film version of Pushkin's short story about an army captain who takes on more than he bargained for when he tries to discover the secret of an old countess's success at cards. Director Thorold Dickinson creates what is generally regarded as his best film: a handsomely mounted and highly atmospheric ghost story which still chills the blood. In her first major film, Edith Evans was heavily made up to add decades to her true age of 50. Sadly, Dickinson directed only two more films before retirement from movie-making. **DM** *DVD*

Anton Walbrook *Herman Savorin* • Edith Evans *Countess Ranevskaya* • Yvonne Mitchell *Lizavetta Ivanova* • Ronald Howard *Andrei* • Mary Jerrold *Old Varvarushka* • Anthony Dawson *Fyodor* ■ *Dir* Thorold Dickinson • *Scr* Rodney Ackland, Arthur Boys, from a short story by Alexander Pushkin • *Cinematographer* Otto Heller • *Music* Georges Auric

Queen of the Damned ★★ 15

Horror 2002 · US/Aus · Colour · 97min

Camp and often silly, this is an adaptation of another Anne Rice novel, and as such is a sort of sequel to 1994's *Interview with the Vampire.* Stuart Townsend takes over from Tom Cruise in the role of the vampire Lestat, here woken from centuries of slumber by the lure of rock music. Fanged temptress Akasha (Aaliyah) wants him to join her in a confused scheme to take over the world. R&B star Aaliyah's performance is rather wooden; sadly, she was killed in a plane crash shortly after the production wrapped. **TH** Violence, swearing. *DVD*

Stuart Townsend *Lestat* • Marguerite Moreau *Jesse Reeves* • Aaliyah *Akasha* • Vincent Perez *Marius* • Paul McGann *David Talbot* • Lena Olin *Maharet* ■ *Dir* Michael Rymer • *Scr* Scott Abbott, Michael Petroni, from the novel *The Vampire Chronicles: Queen of the Damned* by Anne Rice

Queen of the Desert ★★

Biographical drama 2015 · US/Mor · Colour · 128min

The life of adventurer Gertrude Bell is explored in Werner Herzog's drama,

starring Nicole Kidman as the British aristocrat travelling to the furthest reaches of the British Empire. With beautiful camera work and a talented cast, this should have all the makings of a hit in the mould of *Lawrence of Arabia.* Sadly, that promise is ruined by Herzog's overwhelming lack of direction, leaving the elegant Kidman often staring into the sand dunes. A crime given the real life story it draws upon. **JL**

Nicole Kidman *Gertrude Bell* • Robert Pattinson *Col TE Lawrence* • Damian Lewis *Charles Doughty-Wylie* • Holly Earl *Cousin Florence* • Mark Lewis Jones *Frank Lascelles* • Christopher Fulford *Winston Churchill* ■ *Dir/Scr* Werner Herzog • *Cinematographer* Peter Zeitlinger

The Queen of Versailles ★★★★

Documentary 2012 · US/Neth/UK/Den · Colour · 100min

This engrossing documentary charts the rise (and fall, though the term is relative) of US property magnate David Siegel and his wife Jackie, as their hopes of building the most palatial private home in the country come crashing down around them. Having made billions from his time-share business, David falls victim to the 2008 economic crisis. But can shopaholic Jackie rein in her spending? Despite David's troubles, it's the stoic and optimistic Jackie who is the true focus of a film that's in turn both hilarious and heartbreaking. **TeS** Swearing, sexual references. *DVD*

■ *Dir* Lauren Greenfield

The Queen's Guards ★

Drama 1960 · UK · Colour · 110min

"The most inept piece of film-making that I have ever produced or directed," said Michael Powell of this wearisome slice of pomp and circumstance. It's a family drama about two brothers, one of whom dies at Tobruk leaving the other to maintain the family tradition by joining the Guards and fighting for the Empire in some fly-blown Arab state. Raymond Massey plays the father, Daniel Massey the son and it's all jolly well British, a sort of belated reaction to the humiliation of Suez. **AT**

Daniel Massey *John Fellowes* • Robert Stephens *Henry Wynne-Walton* • Raymond Massey *Captain Fellowes* • Ursula Jeans *Mrs Fellowes* • Judith Stott *Ruth Dobbie* ■ *Dir* Michael Powell • *Scr* Roger Milner, from a idea by Simon Harcourt-Smith

Queens Logic ★★★ 15

Comedy drama 1991 · US · Colour · 108min

As in *The Big Chill,* a group of old friends are brought together by a life-changing event – in this case the impending marriage of Ken Olin and Chloe Webb. Gathering for the bachelor party (in Queens, of course) are Joe Mantegna, a fishmonger married to Linda Fiorentino, a gay but celibate John Malkovich and Kevin Bacon, now living in Hollywood. The film provides a gritty and thoroughly watchable group, but is essentially a series of well-written sketches. **LH**

Kevin Bacon *Dennis* • Linda Fiorentino *Carla* • John Malkovich *Eliot* • Joe Mantegna *Al* • Ken Olin *Ray* • Tony Spiridakis *Vinny* • Chloe Webb *Patricia* • Tom Waits *Monte* • Jamie Lee Curtis • Helen Hunt ■ *Dir* Steve Rash • *Scr* Tony Spiridakis, from a story by Joseph W Savino, Tony Spiridakis

Quentin Durward ★★★★ U

Period drama 1955 · US · Colour · 116min

This marvellous romp gave a new lease of life to the mature Robert Taylor and his career. Based on Sir Walter Scott's novel, and clearly an attempt to emulate the success of *Ivanhoe* (same star, same director, same fiery climax), this is deliberately more tongue-in-cheek. Taylor is charmingly witty as the noble Durward, dignified by a moustache and a trimmed beard, and is the only American in a prestige, mainly British cast. The leading lady is Kay Kendall, and she and the fabulous location shooting in the Loire valley are reasons enough to watch. **TS**

Robert Taylor (1) *Quentin Durward* • Kay Kendall *Isabelle Countess of Marcoy* • Robert Morley *King Louis XI* • Alec Clunes *Charles, Duke of Burgundy* • Marius Goring *Count Philip de Creville* • Wilfrid Hyde White *Master Oliver* • Ernest Thesiger *Lord Crawford* • George Cole *Hayraddin* ■ *Dir* Richard Thorpe • *Scr* Robert Ardrey, George Froeschel, from the novel by Sir Walter Scott

Querelle ★★★ 18

Erotic drama 1982 · W Ger/Fr · Colour · 104min

Rainer Werner Fassbinder didn't live to see the release of this long-cherished adaptation of Jean Genet's once-banned novel. By consistently deflecting away from the drama and by having the cast recite lines rather than give performances, Fassbinder was able to explore the cinematic quality of non-action. Moreover, his use of blatantly theatrical sets emphasises the unreality of the events that follow sailor Brad Davis's arrival at Jeanne Moreau's waterfront brothel. It's a despondent wallow in a world full of drugs, murder, alienation and suppressed emotion and is, therefore, more valuable as a final self-portrait than as a work of art. **DP** German +subtitles. *DVD*

Brad Davis *Querelle* • Franco Nero *Lieutenant Seblon* • Jeanne Moreau *Lysiane* • Günther Kaufmann *Nono* • Laurent Malet *Roger Bataille* ■ *Dir* Rainer Werner Fassbinder • *Scr* Rainer Werner Fassbinder, Burkhard Driest, from the novel *Querelle de Brest* by Jean Genet

The Quest ★★★ 18

Martial arts action adventure 1996 · US · Colour · 90min

Jean-Claude Van Damme made his directorial debut with this adventure, and he also stars as a small-time street criminal in 1920s New York who finds himself a stowaway on a ship headed for the South China Sea. Following an attack by pirates, Van Damme meets Roger Moore, and soon the two are scheming to enter Van Damme in the "ultimate fighting match" with its winning prize of a solid gold dragon statue. Remarkably better than his usual films. **ST** Violence, swearing. *DVD*

Jean-Claude Van Damme *Chris Dubois* • Roger Moore *Lord Edgar Dobbs* • James Remar *Maxie Devine* • Janet Gunn *Carrie Newton* ■ *Dir* Jean-Claude Van Damme • *Scr* Steven Klein, Paul Mones, from a story by Frank Dux, Jean-Claude Van Damme

Quest for Fire ★★ 15

Prehistoric drama 1981 · Fr/Can · Colour · 95min

The accepted wisdom is that cavemen movies don't work. Even if you dress them up with anthropological significance, the action will still be limited by the spartan simplicity of the prehistoric lifestyle. To his credit, Jean-Jacques Annaud succeeds in locating the characters within their hostile environment (Canada, Scotland, Iceland and Kenya) and explores the primitive intelligence of the questing Ulams without patronising them or the less civilised Ivakas. But it's still a trying experience. **DP** *DVD* *Blu*

Everett McGill *Naoh* • Ron Perlman *Amoukar* • Nameer El-Kadi *Gaw* • Rae Dawn Chong *Ika* • Gary Schwartz *Rouka* ■ *Dir* Jean-Jacques Annaud • *Scr* Gérard Brach, from the novel *La Guerre du Feu* by JH Rosny Sr

Quest for Love ★★★ PG

Science-fiction drama 1971 · UK · Colour · 87min

Before *Dynasty* became her destiny, Joan Collins made many attempts at acting, including this beguiling British science-fiction idea from *Carry On* producer Peter Rogers and *Doctor in the House* director Ralph Thomas. Tom Bell co-stars as a physicist who, after an explosion, finds himself in an alternative universe where his girlfriend Collins is dying. Bell is believably bemused. And Collins? A moving performance minus the power-shoulders. **TH** *DVD*

Joan Collins *Ottilie* • Tom Bell *Colin Trafford* • Denholm Elliott *Tom Lewis* • Laurence Naismith *Sir Henry Lanstein* • Lyn Ashley *Jennifer* • Juliet Harmer *Geraldine Lambert* • Ray McAnally *Jack*

Q

Kahn ■ *Dir* Ralph Thomas • *Scr* Terence Feely, from the short story *Random Quest* by John Wyndham

Quest for Love ★★★ 15
Drama 1988 · S Afr · Colour · 90min

Helen Nogueira became the first South African woman to direct a feature with this confident combination of political thriller and lesbian love story. Set in the fictional state of Mozania, shortly after black independence, the yacht-board action focuses on a romantic triangle comprising journalist Jana Cilliers, her passionate friend, Sandra Prinsloo, and her flighty lover, Joanna Weinberg. The film is primarily concerned with breaking with the stereotypical depiction of lesbian sensuality, but Cilliers's relationship with terrorist Wayne Bowman (and graphic scenes of torture) reinforce the political dimension. DP

Jana Cilliers *Alex* • Sandra Prinsloo *Dorothy* • Joanna Weinberg *Mabel* • Wayne Bowman *Michael* • Lynn Gaines *Isabella* ■ *Dir* Helen Nogueira • *Scr* Helen Nogueira, from the novel *QED* by Gertrude Stein

A Question of Silence
★★★★ 15
Crime drama 1982 · Neth · Colour · 95min

Without any prior film-making experience, Marleen Gorris received state funding for this highly controversial debut, which posits that patriarchal capitalism exists solely to exploit, repress and abuse women. One of the angriest (yet most lucid and undogmatic) feminist statements ever committed to celluloid, it uses cleverly contrasting flashbacks to chart court psychiatrist Cox Habbema's gradual appreciation of the motives that drove housewife Edda Barends, waitress Nelly Frijda and secretary Henriette Tol to beat to death a smug male boutique owner. This is compelling and provocative cinema. DP Dutch +subtitles.

Edda Barends *Christine M* • Nelly Frijda *Waitress* • Henriette Tol *Secretary* • Cox Habbema *Dr Janine Van Den Bos* • Eddy Brugman *Rudd* ■ *Dir/Scr* Marleen Gorris

Quick ★★ 18
Action crime drama 1993 · US · Colour · 94min

This unremarkable shoot-'em up action filler is notable for the performance of Teri Polo. She outshines the material as a hit woman in Los Angeles who does favours for her corrupt cop boyfriend Jeff Fahey. Things really hot up when she's asked to kidnap a government witness Martin Donovan and a relationship develops between them. It's a plot thinner than a negligee but there is adequate action and snappy dialogue. RS

Jeff Fahey *Muncie* • Teri Polo *Quick* • Robert Davi *Davenport* • Tia Carrere *Janet* • Martin Donovan (2) *Herschel Brewer* ■ *Dir* Rick King • *Scr* Frederick Bailey

The Quick and the Dead
★★★ PG
Western 1987 · US · Colour · 86min

With a spaghetti-style plot and its overtones of *Shane* and *Friendly Persuasion*, this is a superior TV-movie western, that only lets itself down with its uncertain re-creation of the frontier of the 1870s. The story is involving and well told by director Robert Day, but it is the performances that elevate this above the pack. Tom Conti is admirable as the Indian war veteran whose pacifism is put to the test, and Sam Elliott obviously enjoys picking off baddies and smouldering around Conti's wife, played with some vigour by Kate Capshaw. DP

Sam Elliott *Con Vallian* • Tom Conti *Duncan McKaskel* • Kate Capshaw *Susanna McKaskel* • Kenny Morrison *Tom McKaskel* ■ *Dir* Robert Day • *Scr* James Lee Barrett, from a story by Louis L'Amour

The Quick and the Dead
★★★ 15
Western 1995 · US · Colour · 103min

Sharon Stone stars as a mysterious stranger, riding Clint Eastwood-style into a

town called Redemption to take part in a gunfighting competition presided over by the evil Gene Hackman. This homage to the spaghetti western style of Sergio Leone is as daft as they come. Director Sam Raimi smacks his lips in every OTT scene, but today this wacky movie will draw a new audience because it also stars Russell Crowe and Leonardo DiCaprio. AT Violence, swearing, sex scenes. DVD BD

Sharon Stone *Ellen* • Gene Hackman *John Herod* • Russell Crowe *Cort* • Leonardo DiCaprio *Kid* • Tobin Bell *Dog Kelly* • Lance Henriksen *Ace Hanlon* • Gary Sinise *Marshall* ■ *Dir* Sam Raimi • *Scr* Simon Moore

Quick, before It Melts ★★
Comedy 1965 · US · Colour · 97min

Steady Delbert Mann wasn't the best choice for this scattershot adaptation of Philip Benjamin's Cold War comedy. Dispatched to Antarctica to report on American efforts to protect the Pole from communist incursion, timid journalist Robert Morse soon finds himself out of his depth, as he's seduced by Anjanette Comer, falls foul of brass hat James Gregory, is corrupted by womanising photographer George Maharis and can't find a bad word to say about the only Russian he can find, Michael Constantine. Frantic – but unfunny – anarchy. DP

George Maharis *Peter Santelli* • Robert Morse *Oliver Cromwell Cannon* • Anjanette Comer *Tiare Marshall* • James Gregory *Vice admiral* • Michael Constantine *Mikhail Drozhensky* ■ *Dir* Delbert Mann • *Scr* Dale Wasserman, from the novel by Philip Benjamin

Quick Change ★★★ 15
Crime comedy 1990 · US · Colour · 84min

Bill Murray chose an offbeat, small-scale project for his directorial debut, and the result is a warm, slightly melancholic comedy. Murray also stars, playing a reluctant robber who pulls off the perfect bank raid dressed as a clown but who is driven to despair trying to leave the city with partners in crime Geena Davis and Randy Quaid. The three leads are great and there is fine support, too, from Jason Robards Jr as the cop on their trail. The source novel was filmed earlier, in 1985, as *Hold-Up*, starring Jean-Paul Belmondo. JF Swearing, violence.

Bill Murray *Grimm* • Geena Davis *Phyllis* • Randy Quaid *Loomis* • Jason Robards Jr *[Jason Robards]* Chief *Rotzinger* • Dale Grand *Street barker* • Bob Elliott *Bank guard* ■ *Dir* Howard Franklin, Bill Murray • *Scr* Howard Franklin, from the novel by Jay Cronley

Quick, Let's Get Married ★
Comedy 1964 · US · Colour · 100min

The great Ginger Rogers bowed out of films in the 1950s but returned briefly in the 1960s to make two new movies, this one and later a biopic *Harlow*. Rogers features here as the madam of a brothel and this was supposed to be the first of a new string of Rogers comedies produced by her ex-husband William Marshall. No further titles were made and this film itself wasn't released until 1971. DF

Ginger Rogers *Mme Rinaldi* • Ray Milland *Mario Forni* • Barbara Eden *Pia* • Walter Abel *The mute* • Elliott Gould *The mute* • Michael Ansara *Mayor* ■ *Dir* William Dieterle • *Scr* Allan Scott

Quick Millions ★★ U
Crime drama 1931 · US · BW · 61min

Spencer Tracy plays a truck driver who organises a protection racket and becomes a mobster, almost against his will since he really craves respectability. His bodyguard is played by George Raft. Boasting much less action than others of the genre, it is directed by the combative left-winger, Rowland Brown. AT

Spencer Tracy *Daniel J "Bugs" Raymond* • Marguerite Churchill *Dorothy Stone* • John Wray *Kenneth Stone* • George Raft *Jimmy Kirk* ■ *Dir* Rowland Brown • *Scr* Courtney Terrett, Rowland Brown

Quicksand ★★★ PG
Crime drama 1950 · US · BW · 78min

This excellent but forgotten little programme filler features a well-cast Mickey Rooney as a car mechanic who's got the hots for no-good *femme fatale* Jeanne Cagney (James's real-life sister). Rooney is superb, and his demented persona is admirably suited to this underlit half-world. Even better, however, is sleazy Peter Lorre in one of his finer depictions of screen menace as a penny arcade owner. Director Irving Pichel cleverly puts all the elements together to produce an undervalued *film noir*. TS DVD

Mickey Rooney *Dan Brady, auto mechanic* • Jeanne Cagney *Vera Novak, cafe cashier* • Barbara Bates *Helen* • Peter Lorre *Nick Dramoshag, penny arcade owner* • Art Smith *Mackey, garage owner* ■ *Dir* Irving Pichel • *Scr* Robert Smith

Quicksand ★★ 15
Crime thriller 2003 · Fr/UK · Colour · 90min

Michael Keaton stars as a New Yorker investigating shady monetary activity in the south of France in this crime thriller directed by *The Long Good Friday* veteran John Mackenzie. Michael Caine is wasted in a supporting role and, despite some clever moments, the script is poor and the budget too low for the action to make any impact. SuR DVD

Michael Keaton *Martin Raikes* • Michael Caine *Jake Mellows* • Judith Godreche *[Judith Godrèche]* *Lela Forin* • Rade Sherbedgia *[Rade Serbedzija]* *Oleg Butraskaya* • Matthew Marsh *Michel Cote* • Xander Berkeley *Joey Patterson* • Kathleen Wilhoite *Beth Ann* ■ *Dir* John Mackenzie (1) • *Scr* Timothy Prager, from the novel *Boudapesti 3* by Desmond Lowden

Quicksand: No Escape
★★★ PG
Thriller 1992 · US · Colour · 88min

This effective thriller stars Donald Sutherland as a detective hired by an architect's wife who suspects her husband of having an affair. From this conventional opening, the plot spins some clever webs of intrigue, but this TV movie's main attraction is Sutherland, whose character has some of the weird, repressed spookiness of his earlier creation, John Klute. AT

Donald Sutherland *Doc* • Tim Matheson *Scott Reinhardt* • Jay Acovone *Ted Herman* • Timothy Carhart *Charlie* • John Joseph Finn *[John Finn]* • Ken Griffith *Felicity Huffman Joanna Reinhardt* ■ *Dir* Michael Pressman • *Scr* Peter Baloff, Dave Wollert

Quicksilver ★★ 15
Drama 1986 · US · Colour · 101min

The mind boggles at how films like this ever get the money to be made. Imagine the pitch to the studio: "OK, there's this hotshot financial whizzkid who drops out of the Wall Street rat race to become – wait for it – a bicycle messenger. But heh, I see bicycle messengers as America's new cowboys, wheels instead of hoofs, get it? Still not sold? How about roping in your usual 1980s music soundtrack suspects. It could be another *Flashdance* or *Footloose*. Heh, that gives me a great idea, let's cast Kevin Bacon!" "Sounds great kid, here's $7 million, go make it!!!" RS

Kevin Bacon *Jack Casey* • Jami Gertz *Terri* • Paul Rodriguez *Hector Rodriguez* • Rudy Ramos *Gypsy* • Andrew Smith *Gabe Kaplan* • Larry Fishburne *[Laurence Fishburne]* *Voodoo* ■ *Dir* Tom Donnelly *[Thomas Michael Donnelly]* • *Scr* Thomas Michael Donnelly

The Quiet American ★★★ PG
Period political drama 1958 · US · BW · 116min

America's most decorated Second World War soldier was baby-faced Audie Murphy, who carved out a screen career with a gun in his hand, notably in a stream of support westerns, until his tragic death in 1971. Following the filming of his own autobiography *To Hell and Back*, Murphy became a major star for a short while, and was ideally cast as the naive American in this worthy but rather dull adaptation of

Graham Greene's novel about Saigon politics in the pre-Vietnam era. He is well cast, and actually very good, but at the time the critics over-praised co-star Michael Redgrave and, as ever, underrated Murphy. TS DVD

Audie Murphy *The American* • Michael Redgrave *Fowler* • Giorgia Moll *Phuong* • Claude Dauphin *Inspector Vigot* • Kerima *Miss Hei* • Bruce Cabot *Bill Granger* ■ *Dir* Joseph L Mankiewicz • *Scr* Joseph L Mankiewicz, from the novel by Graham Greene

The Quiet American
★★★★ 15
Political drama 2002 · US/Ger · Colour · 96min

Graham Greene's classic 1955 novel – about the political rumblings in Indo-China that would eventually lead to the Vietnam War – gets a faithful, elegant and resonant adaptation in director Philip Noyce's version. A love triangle between disillusioned journalist Michael Caine (a commanding, yet beautifully restrained performance), mysterious American aid worker Brendan Fraser and young Vietnamese woman Do Thi Hai Yen is all the narrative hook Noyce needs to explore assuredly the complex issues surrounding Vietnam's fight for independence from French colonial rule, and make it a powerful and provocative drama. AJ Violence, swearing, drug abuse. DVD BD

Michael Caine *Thomas Fowler* • Brendan Fraser *Alden Pyle* • Do Thi Hai Yen *Phuong* • Rade Sherbedgia *[Rade Serbedzija]* *Inspector Vigot* • Ma Tzi Hinh • Robert Stanton *Joe Tunney* • Holmes Osborne *Bill Granger* ■ *Dir* Phillip Noyce • *Scr* Christopher Hampton, Robert Schenkkan, from the novel by Graham Greene

Quiet Days in Clichy ★★ 18
Biographical comedy 1969 · Den · BW · 99min

The French New Wave meets the Danish skin flick in this wild adaptation of Henry Miller's novel. Badly showing its age, it now stands as a fascinating tribute both to the freewheeling spirit of Miller's sexual odyssey and to the technical excess that was hailed as progressive film-making in the 1960s. Played out to the eccentric folk music of Country Joe McDonald, the amorous adventures of a lusty American in Paris are punctuated by jump cuts, captions, speech bubbles and moments of soft-core sex and actorly incompetence. DP Danish +subtitles. DVD

Paul Valjean *Joey* • Louise White *Surrealist* • Wayne John Rodda *Carl* • Ulla Lemvigh-Mueller *Nys* ■ *Dir* Jens Jørgen Thorsen • *Scr* Jens Jørgen Thorsen, from the novel by Henry Miller

The Quiet Earth ★★★ 15
Science-fiction thriller
1985 · NZ · Colour · 87min

A scientist awakes one morning only to realise he may be the only person left alive on Earth after an experiment goes wrong. It's an intriguing if not altogether original concept. Bruno Lawrence gives a beguiling central performance as someone who is suddenly able to live out his fantasies, to enjoy the empty city without guilt or interference. Shot against stunning Auckland backdrops, the early section develops a strong sense of mystery, but after Lawrence discovers two other survivors, one male, one female, the script follows an all too predictable path. RS DVD

Bruno Lawrence *Zac Hobson* • Alison Routledge *Joanne* • Pete Smith *Api* • Anzac Wallace *Api's mate* • Norman Fletcher *Perrin* • Tom Hyde *Scientist* ■ *Dir* Geoff Murphy • *Scr* Bill Baer, Bruno Lawrence, Sam Pillsbury, from the novel by Craig Harrison

The Quiet Family ★★★ 15
Black comedy thriller
1998 · S Kor · Colour · 98min

Shades of *Arsenic and Old Lace* colour this dark romp. No sooner has the "Misty Lodge" opened its doors than the bodies start to pile up and the garden begins to resemble a cemetery. But there's worse to come when a murderous businessman lures his detested stepmother to the isolated hilltop cottage and the government announces plans for a new road – right past the front gate. This is a wickedly anarchic comedy of errors. DP Korean +subtitles. *DVD*

Choi Min-sik • Mun-hee Na • Park In-hwan • Song Kang-ho ■ Dir/Scr Kim Ji-woon

The Quiet Man ★★★★★ U
Romantic comedy drama
1952 · US · Colour · 124min

John Ford won his fourth best director Oscar for this immenselaus popular chunk of old blarney, much of it shot on location in the west of Ireland. John Wayne is, of course, splendid as the boxer returning to his roots, with feisty Maureen O'Hara more than a match for him. Victor Young's lilting score is also very enjoyable, while Winton Hoch and Archie Stunt's Techincolor photography deservedly won the film a second Oscar. If you're in the right mood, this will make you laugh and cry. TS *DVD* *Blu-ray*

John Wayne *Sean Thornton* • Maureen O'Hara *Mary Kate Danaher* • Barry Fitzgerald *Michaeleen Flynn* • Ward Bond *Father Peter Lonergan* • Victor McLaglen *"Red" Will Danaher* ■ Dir John Ford • Scr Frank S Nugent (uncredited), Richard Llewellyn, from the story by Maurice Walsh • Cinematographer Winton C Hoch • Music Victor Young

The Quiet Ones ★★★ 15
Supernatural horror · 2013 · US · Colour · 93min

In this slow-burring terror tale from the 21st-century incarnation of Hammer Films, a young cameraman (*Hunger Games* star Sam Claflin) joins Oxford professor Jared Harris at a rural mansion to record an experiment to discover what unspeakable force resides within suicidal teenager Olivia Cooke. But is it a poltergeist, demonic possession or something else that ails the girl? Some heart-stopping moments and potent performances, particularly from Cooke, more than compensate for any overfamiliarity with the plot. JA Violence, swearing, brief nudity. *DVD* *Blu-ray*

Jared Harris *Professor Joseph Coupland* • Sam Claflin *Brian McNeil* • Olivia Cooke *Jane Harper* • Erin Richards *Krissi Dalton* ■ Dir John Pogue • Scr Oren Moverman, John Pogue, Craig Rosenberg, from a screenplay (unproduced) by Tom de Ville

Quiet Please, Murder ★★
Detective drama · 1942 · US · BW · 70min

This interesting little programme filler stars the suave George Sanders. He plays a master forger, passing off his imitations as First Folio Shakespeare, in a clever and relatively sophisticated blend of romance and murder. His female co-star is Gail Patrick, who later went on to produce the *Perry Mason* TV series. Virtually unknown director John Larkin doesn't get in the way of some cleverish writing, though budgetary limitations don't help. TS

George Sanders *Fleg* • Gail Patrick *Myra Blandy* • Richard Denning *Hal Mcbyrne* • Lynne Roberts *Kay Ryan* • Sidney Blackmer *Martin Cleaver* ■ Dir John Larkin • Scr John Larkin, from a story by Lawrence G Blochman

Quiet Wedding ★★★
Comedy · 1940 · UK · BW · 80min

Based on a very successful stage play, this delightful British romantic comedy stars a fresh and charming Margaret Lockwood in her pre-*Wicked Lady* days. The escalation of wedding plans, culminating in the arrival of an army of objectionable relatives, overwhelms Lockwood's bride-to-be, causes tension with hapless groom Derek Farr and threatens to scupper their entire relationship. Stylishly directed by Anthony Asquith, the movie benefits from a stand-out cast of supporting players. It was remade as *Happy Is the Bride* in 1957 with Janette Scott and Ian Carmichael. *Quiet Weekend* was the less successful sequel. RK

Margaret Lockwood *Janet Royd* • Derek Farr *Dallas Chaytor* • Marjorie Fielding *Mildred Royd, Janet's mother* AE Matthews *Arthur Royd, Janet's father* • Athene Seyler *Aunt Mary Jarrow* • Jean Cadell *Aunt Florence Bute* • Peggy

Ashcroft *Flower Lisle* ■ Dir Anthony Asquith • Scr Terence Rattigan, Anatole de Grunwald, from the play by Esther McCracken

Quiet Weekend ★★ U
Comedy 1946 · UK · BW · 86min

As anyone familiar with Anthony Asquith's classic comedy of manners *Quiet Wedding* will know, the title of this disappointing sequel is ironic in the extreme. The screenplay lacks the crisp chaos of the original co-written by Terence Rattigan. Consequently, the romantic tangles of Derek Farr and the poaching misadventures of George Thorpe and magistrate Frank Cellier fail to deliver the laughs deserving of such whole-hearted playing. DP *DVD*

Derek Farr *Denys Royd* • Frank Cellier *Adrian Barrasford* • Marjorie Fielding *Mildred Royd* • George Thorpe *Arthur Royd* • Barbara White *Miranda Bute* • Helen Shingler *Rowena Hyde* ■ Dir Harold French • Scr Warwick Ward, Victor Skutezky, Stephen Black, TJ Morrison, from the play by Esther McCracken

The Quiet Woman ★ U
Crime thriller 1950 · UK · BW · 70min

Writer/director John Gilling was a vital cog in the conveyor belt that churned out quota quickie-style films in the 1950s. Jane Hylton stars in this feeble thriller as the woman whose fresh start is threatened when her jailbird ex-husband arrives on her doorstep. Romance and a smuggling subplot can't save the picture from sinking deservedly into the mire. DP

Derek Bond *Duncan Mcleod* • Jane Hylton *Jane Foster* • Dora Bryan *Elsie* • Michael Balfour *Lefty* • Dianne Foster *Helen* ■ Dir John Gilling • Scr John Gilling

Quigley Down Under ★★★ 15
Western 1990 · US · Colour · 114min

In this entertaining attempt to transplant the western genre Down Under, a grizzled Tom Selleck plays a laid-back sharpshooter who rebels against Australian land baron Alan Rickman's plan for a little Aborigine genocide. Director Simon Wincer makes full use of the grand Australian locations. Selleck is likeable enough in the title role, but unwittingly joins the list of Hollywood stars who have been effortlessly upstaged by Rickman, who delivers another wonderfully villainous performance. JF *DVD*

Tom Selleck *Matthew Quigley* • Laura San Giacomo *Crazy Cora* • Alan Rickman *Elliott Marston* • Chris Haywood *Major Ashley Pitt* • Ron Haddrick *Grimmelman* • Tony Bonner *Dobkin* ■ Dir Simon Wincer • Scr John Hill

The Quiller Memorandum ★★★★ PG
Spy thriller 1966 · UK · Colour · 100min

The menace of Harold Pinter's script is marvellously sustained by director Michael Anderson in this espionage thriller, with George Segal giving one of his finest performances as the secret agent investigating a neo-Nazi movement in 1960s Berlin. Alec Guinness and Max von Sydow excel as the British spy chief and his evil Nazi counterpart, and, for once, a woman (Senta Berger) plays a formidable part in an ambiguous role, the true nature of which is only revealed in the final shots. TH *DVD* *Blu-ray*

George Segal *Quiller* • Alec Guinness *Pol* • Max von Sydow *Oktober* • Senta Berger *Inge* • George Sanders *Gibbs* • Robert Helpmann *Weng* ■ Dir Michael Anderson • Scr Harold Pinter, from the novel *The Berlin Memorandum* by Adam Hall [Elleston Trevor]

Quills ★★★★★ 18
Biographical drama
2000 · US/Ger · Colour · 118min

This is either a remarkable testimony to the importance of artistic freedom or the debauched tale of a devilish man: either way it's a considerable cinematic achievement. Geoffrey Rush is perfect as the unrepentant Marquis de Sade, confined to a mental institution and smuggling his "smut" to a publisher care of laundry maid Kate Winslet. When hard-line Michael Caine

is sent to oversee the liberal regime of priest Joaquin Phoenix, de Sade has to use all his ingenuity to continue writing. Director Philip Kaufman's multilayered exploration of cruelty, repression and hypocrisy celebrates de Sade's indomitable spirit, while reminding us of the corruptive power of his imagination. LH Violence, swearing, sex scenes, nudity. *DVD*

Geoffrey Rush *Marquis de Sade* • Kate Winslet *Madeleine* • Joaquin Phoenix *Abbé Coulmier* • Michael Caine *Dr Royer-Collard* • Billie Whitelaw *Madame LeClerc* • Patrick Malahide *Delbène* • Amelia Warner *Simone* • Jane Menelaus *Renée Pelagie* ■ Dir Philip Kaufman • Scr Doug Wright, from his play • Production Designer Martin Childs • Costume Designer Jacqueline West • Set Designer Jill Quertier • Cinematographer Rogier Stoffers

The Quince Tree Sun ★★★★ U
Documentary 1991 · Sp · Colour · 132min

You'll get a whole new angle on the phrase "as interesting as watching paint dry" after seeing this wonderful documentary by the Spanish director Victor Erice. The film focuses on Antonio Lopez's meticulous execution of a painting of the quince tree in his garden. While this provides fascinating insights into the creative process, what is even more compelling is the artist's interaction both with the camera and the numerous visitors who drop in to see him. Best known for the haunting *Spirit of the Beehive*, Erice allows events to dictate the pace and what emerges is a mesmerising portrait. DP Spanish +subtitles.

Antonio López Garcia [Antonio López] ■ Dir Victor Erice • Scr Victor Erice, Antonio López, from an idea by Erice, Antonio López Garcia [López]

Quintet ★★ 15
Science-fiction drama
1979 · US · Colour · 113min

This is one of Robert Altman's more forgettable films, made during a spell when he was out of favour with critics and audiences alike (see also *Popeye*). An uncomfortable looking Paul Newman heads a largely European cast in a slow-moving and pretentious piece of post-apocalyptic sci-fi, about a deadly survival game played out in a deep-frozen future city. Everyone looks cold and watching it has a similar effect on the viewer. DA

Paul Newman *Essex* • Vittorio Gassman *St Christopher* • Fernando Rey *Grigor* • Bibi Andersson *Ambrosia* • Brigitte Fossey *Vivia* • Nina Van Pallandt *Deuca* ■ Dir Robert Altman • Scr Robert Altman, Frank Barhydt, Patricia Resnick, from a story by Lionel Chetwynd, Altman, Resnick

Quiz Show ★★★★ 15
Drama based on a true story
1994 · US · Colour · 127min

Intelligently crafted by director Robert Redford, this is a riveting account of a true-life scandal in 1950s America, in which the winning contestant of the popular *Twenty-One* television game show was exposed as a fraud. Week after week, millions of viewers tuned in to watch a debonair professor (another memorable performance from Ralph Fiennes) flex his intellectual muscles, but it was later revealed he was given the answers in advance by a corrupt network. John Turturro matches Fiennes as the show's deposed champion, while Rob Morrow plays the lawyer investigating the scam. AJ Swearing. *DVD*

John Turturro *Herbie Stempel* • Rob Morrow *Dick Goodwin* • Ralph Fiennes *Charles Van Doren* • Paul Scofield *Mark Van Doren* • David Paymer *Dan Enright* • Hank Azaria *Albert Freedman* ■ Dir Robert Redford • Scr Paul Attanasio, from the book *Remembering America: a Voice from the Sixties* by Richard N Goodwin

Quo Vadis ★★★ PG
Historical epic 1951 · US · Colour · 167min

Long and bloated, Mervyn LeRoy's film shows both the best and worst of depicting religious fervour in the Hollywood epic style. Alongside too-lengthy scenes of po-faced piety involving pallid hero Robert

Taylor and wan Deborah Kerr, there is Peter Ustinov revelling in his role as the Emperor Nero. He pouts, simpers and fiddles while Rome burns, ad-libs to perfection and sends Christians to the lions in some spectacular arena scenes. Superbly cast against him is Leo Genn as Petronius, arbiter of fashion, whose speech before he opens his veins ("Do not mutilate the arts") is a veiled attack on the communist witch-hunts. AT *DVD* *Blu-ray*

Deborah Kerr *Lygia* • Robert Taylor (1) *Marcus Vinicius* • Peter Ustinov *Nero* • Leo Genn *Petronius* • Patricia Laffan *Poppaea* • Finlay Currie *Peter* • Abraham Sofaer *Paul* • Elizabeth Taylor *Christian prisoner* • Sophia Loren *Lygia's slave* • Walter Pidgeon *Narrator* ■ Dir Mervyn LeRoy • Scr John Lee Mahin, Sonya Levien, SN Behrman, from the novel by Henryk Sienkiewicz

R ★★★ 🔞
Prison drama · 2010 · Den · Colour · 95min

Tobias Lindholm and Michael Noer's film debut was shot on a shoestring in Denmark's notorious Horsens State prison and is a rougher, readier cellmate to Jacques Audiard's award-winning *A Prophet*. Johan Phillip Asbaek impresses as the novice inmate determined to crack the system, while Lindholm and Noer refuse to flinch in depicting the cruel lessons learnt in a way that's both convincing and disconcerting. The intrusive camera and clanking sound mix reinforces the sense of claustrophobia. DP Danish +subtitles.

Pilou Asbaek [Johan Phillip Asbaek] *Rune* · Dulfi Al-Jabouri *Rashid* · Roland Moller *Mureren* · Jacob Gredsted *Carsten* ■ Dir/Scr Tobias Lindholm, Michael Noer

R.I.P.D. ★★★ 12
Supernatural crime comedy · 2013 · US · Colour · 91min

This odd couple buddy movie stars Ryan Reynolds as a recently slain policeman sent back to the mortal world by the Rest in Peace Department of the title. He's partnered by Jeff Bridges as the grizzled ghost of a Wild West sheriff, and together they're assigned to round up deceased villains who have also returned to earth to continue their wrongdoings. Director Robert Schwentke attempts to concoct a hybrid of *Men in Black* and *Ghost Busters*, but the script can't match either of those films in terms of gag-count or snappy performances. The saving grace is Bridges as the over-the-top lawman of yore. TeS DVD BLU

Jeff Bridges *Roy Pulsipher* · Ryan Reynolds *Nick Walker* · Kevin Bacon *Bobby Hayes* · Mary-Louise Parker *Proctor* · Stephanie Szostak *Julia Walker* · Mike O'Malley *Elliot* ■ Dir Robert Schwentke · Scr Phil Hay, Matt Manfredi, from a story by David Dobkin, Hay, Manfredi, from the graphic novel by Peter M Lenkov

RKO 281 ★★★★ 15
Period drama based on a true story · 1999 · US · Colour · 83min

When Orson Welles embarked upon his directorial debut, he described RKO as the biggest train set a boy could ever have. However, there was nothing juvenile about project 281, as *Citizen Kane* was to become the most critically lauded film of all time. Its production was anything but untroubled, though, as this stylish TV movie demonstrates. The feuds with co-scenarist Herman J Mankiewicz and media tycoon William Randolph Hearst are fully explored in this splendidly cast drama. DP DVD

Liev Schreiber *Orson Welles* · James Cromwell *William Randolph Hearst* · Melanie Griffith *Marion Davies* · John Malkovich *Herman Mankiewicz* · Brenda Blethyn *Louella Parsons* · Roy Scheider *George Schaefer* · David Suchet *Louis B Mayer* · Fiona Shaw *Hedda Hopper* ■ Dir Benjamin Ross · Scr John Logan, from the original documentary script for *The Battle over Citizen Kane* by Richard Ben Cramer, Thomas Lennon (2)

RPM – Revolutions per Minute ★
Political drama · 1970 · US · Colour · 91min

This woeful effort stars Anthony Quinn as a campus professor, Ann-Margret as his mistress and Gary Lockwood as the student who organises a takeover of the university's administration offices. Stanley Kramer, never the subtlest of directors, gets heavy with empty parallels to the student riots in Chicago and at Kent State University. AT

Anthony Quinn *Perez* · Ann-Margret *Rhoda* · Gary Lockwood *Rossiter* · Paul Winfield *Dempsey* · Graham Jarvis *Thatcher* ■ Dir Stanley Kramer · Scr Erich Segal

R-Point ★★★ 15
Supernatural war horror · 2004 · S Kor · Colour · 107min

South of Saigon lies the strategically important island region, R-Point. That's where a South Korean platoon is sent to investigate mysterious radio transmissions from a supposedly dead squadron in this slow-burning psychological horror. With the Vietnam War making an excellent backdrop to all the atmospheric creepiness, the accent is more on allegory than the gory. Too drawn out and often hilariously overacted, this does benefit from strong, beautifully photographed images and some truly haunting moments. AJ Korean, English +subtitles. DVD

Kam Woo-seong *First Lieutenant Choi Tae-In* · Son Byung-ho *Sergeant Jin* · Oh Tae-kyung *Sergeant Jang* · Park Won-sang *Sergeant Mah* · Lee Seon-gyun ■ Dir/Scr Kong Su-chang

RV ★★ PG
Comedy · 2006 · Ger/US · Colour · 94min

Stressed out executive Robin Williams swaps his planned Hawaiian vacation for an RV (that's recreational vehicle) road trip. He's been ordered to attend a business meeting in Colorado, but the family – who are in the dark about his work commitments – are suitably unimpressed, particularly when they are befriended by a creepily nice clan led by Jeff Daniels. There are a few snappy one-liners here, but director Barry Sonnenfeld seems more interested in staging predictable slapstick set pieces. JF Some sexual references. DVD BLU

Robin Williams *Bob Munro* · Jeff Daniels *Travis Gornicke* · Cheryl Hines *Jamie Munro* · Kristin Chenoweth *Mary Jo Gornicke* · Joanna "JoJo" Levesque *Cassie Munro* · Josh Hutcherson *Carl Munro* · Will Arnett *Tod Mallory* · Hunter Parrish *Earl Gornicke* · Chloe Sonnenfeld *Moon Gornicke* ■ Dir Barry Sonnenfeld · Scr Geoff Rodkey

Raaz ★★★ 15
Horror thriller · 2001 · Ind · Colour · 151min

Bollywood's master of suspense Vikram Bhatt directs this teasing psychological thriller. Supermodel Bipasha Basu shows to advantage as the unhappy wife who hopes to save her marriage by returning to the isolated hill station where she first fell in love. But she becomes increasingly fraught as she starts to believe that the house is haunted. Dino Morea is lumpen as her husband, while Ashutosh Rana chomps the scenery as an eccentric academic, but the movie still exerts a strong grip until its formulaic plotting forces a slipshod resolution. DP Hindi +subtitles. Swearing, violence. DVD

Dino Morea *Aditya* · Bipasha Basu *Sanjana* · Malini Sharma *Malini* · Shruti Ulfat *Priya* · Ashutosh Rana *Professor Agni* · Mink [Mink Singh] *Nisha* ■ Dir Vikram Bhatt · Scr Mahesh Bhatt

Rabbit Fever ★ 18
Comedy · 2005 · UK · Colour · 82min

Women confess their obsession with the "Rabbit" vibrator in this embarrassingly limp British "mockumentary". It could have been a one-joke film if only debut film-maker Ian Denyer had figured out what that one joke is. Instead, he relies on loving close-ups of the big pink pleasure tool and the sound of buzzing from behind locked doors. The director also fails to coax a titter from his random assortment of talking heads – airline head Richard Branson inviting people to join the "Rabbit High Club". Running through this barely coherent patchwork of scenes are the strands of a relationship subplot, but they are as predictable as they are unfunny. SP Sexual references.

Rabbit Hole ★★★★ 12
Drama · 2010 · US · Colour · 87min

The most dramatic event in *Rabbit Hole* has already occurred before the story begins. The Corbetts were a happily married couple with a young son, but their domestic idyll was shattered when the boy was killed in an accident. Becca (Nicole Kidman) and Howie (Aaron Eckhart) attend a therapy group, but find it increasingly difficult to communicate with each other, let alone come to terms with their loss. Both of them embark on clandestine relationships with others, looking for the understanding they cannot find at home. What follows is darkly ironic, and yet in context it seems perfectly natural and is even amusing in places. The performances from Kidman and Eckhart are beautifully judged, while the film is as delicate and as finely nuanced as the characters and relationships it portrays. BP Brief swearing, drug abuse. DVD

Nicole Kidman *Becca Corbett* · Aaron Eckhart *Howie Corbett* · Dianne Wiest *Nat* · Tammy Blanchard *Izzy* · Sandra Oh *Gabby* · Miles Teller *Jason* · Giancarlo Esposito *Auggie* · Jon Tenney *Rick* ■ Dir John Cameron Mitchell · Scr David Lindsay-Abaire, from his play

Rabbit-Proof Fence ★★★ PG
Period drama based on a true story · 2002 · Aus/UK · Colour · 89min

Though rather worthy, director Philip Noyce's superbly photographed fact-based drama is not without impact as it throws light on a shameful period in Australia's past. In 1931, 14-year-old Molly (Evelyn Sampi) is interned by the Australian government as part of its policy to forcibly integrate mixed-race Aborigines into white society. Molly escapes with her younger sister and cousin, and walks the 1,200 miles back home. The children are wonderfully natural, Kenneth Branagh and David Gulpilil are excellent, but Noyce's predictable direction fails to engage us emotionally. AJ DVD

Everlyn Sampi *Molly Craig* · Tianna Sansbury *Daisy Craig* · Laura Monaghan *Gracie Fields* · David Gulpilil *Moodoo* · Kenneth Branagh *Mr AO Neville* · Deborah Mailman *Mavis* · Jason Clarke (2) *Constable Riggs* · Ningali Lawford *Molly's mother* ■ Dir Phillip Noyce · Scr Christine Olsen, from the biography *Follow the Rabbit-Proof Fence* by Doris Pilkington Garimara

Rabbit, Run ★★ 18
Drama · 1970 · US · Colour · 90min

With its open discussion of fellatio and sodomy, Howard B Kreitsek's adaptation of John Updike's novel was one of the most daring dramas to emerge from a Hollywood newly liberated from the Production Code. Director Jack Smight, who was so disgruntled with the final edit that he attempted to have his name removed from the credits, allows James Caan to overdo the self-pity as the washed-up former basketball star who abandons pregnant wife Carrie Snodgress for mistress Anjanette Comer. DP

James Caan *Rabbit Angstrom* · Carrie Snodgress *Janice Angstrom* · Anjanette Comer *Ruth* · Jack Albertson *Marty Tothero* · Arthur Hill *Reverend Jack Eccles* ■ Dir Jack Smight · Scr Howard B Kreitsek, from the novel by John Updike

Rabid ★★★★ 18
Horror · 1976 · Can · Colour · 86min

This is another formative exercise in fear and loathing of the human body from director David Cronenberg, which takes up the themes of his first "mainstream" success, *Shivers*. This time a plague is let loose after accident victim Marilyn Chambers becomes the carrier of a rabid disease that turns people into bloodsuckers. This disturbing film lacks the claustrophobia of *Shivers*, but is a slicker affair, and the spiralling violence still shocks. JF DVD BLU

Marilyn Chambers *Rose* · Frank Moore *Hart Read* · Joe Silver *Murray Cypher* · Howard Ryshpan *Dr Dan Keloid* · Patricia Gage *Dr Roxanne Keloid* · Susan Roman *Mindy Kent* ■ Dir/Scr David Cronenberg

Rabid Grannies ★ 18
Comedy horror · 1989 · Bel · Colour · 88min

This badly-made Belgian splatter movie is both boring and offensive. A waft of smoke from a Satanist turns two wealthy old aunts into slobbering, blood-crazed zombies during their birthday party. The guests are all obvious stereotypes who end up being slaughtered. AJ French dubbed. DVD

Catherine Aymerie *Helen* · Caroline Braekman *Suzie* · Danielle Daven *Elisabeth Remington* · Richard Cotica *Gilbert* · Raymond Lescot *Reverend Father* ■ Dir/Scr Emmanuel Kervyn

Race ★★ PG
Sports drama based on a true story · 2016 · Fr/Ger/Can · Colour · 134min

This workmanlike true-life drama tells the story of Jesse Owens, the athlete who exposed Adolf Hitler's misguided belief in Aryan supremacy at the 1936 Berlin Olympics. Owens (played by Selma's Stephan James) was not only American but black as well, and won four gold medals, much to Hitler's annoyance. It's a great yarn, but this solid if stodgy account is rather tough-going, and takes way too long to cut to the Olympics chase. Good-looking and watchable enough, but there's a better film to be made about the Owens story. DA Some violence, swearing.

Stephan James *Jesse Owens* · Jason Sudeikis *Larry Snyder* · Jeremy Irons *Avery Brundage* · William Hurt *Jeremiah Mahoney* · Carice van Houten *Leni Riefenstahl* ■ Dir Stephen Hopkins · Scr Joe Shrapnel, Anna Waterhouse · Music Rachel Portman

Race for the Yankee Zephyr ★★ PG
Adventure · 1981 · Aus/NZ · Colour · 93min

Actor David Hemmings (*Blowup*) directed this muddled and messy adventure with Donald Pleasence and Ken Wahl competing with George Peppard to recover a fortune from a Second World War plane wreck. It's not just the map to the treasure that gets lost, but also the plot. Lesley Ann Warren is the only guiding star. TH

Donald Pleasence *Gibbie* · George Peppard *Theo Brown* · Ken Wahl *Barney* · Lesley Ann Warren *Sally* · Bruno Lawrence *Barker* · Grant Tilly *Collector* ■ Dir David Hemmings · Scr Everett De Roche

Race for Your Life, Charlie Brown ★★ U
Animation · 1977 · US · Colour · 72min

The *Peanuts* people leave the familiar neighbourhood for a summer camp in this third feature-length outing for Charles M Schulz's enduring creations. As usual, Charlie Brown is the goat all the other kids mock as he fails hopelessly at each activity, with Peppermint Patty adding the kind of scathing encouragement only she can. However, the little round-headed kid finally proves his worth during a white-water raft race. There are plenty of the customarily witty observations on life, but the pace is slack. DP

Duncan Watson *Charlie Brown* · Greg Felton *Schroeder* · Stuart Brotman *Peppermint Patty* · Gail Davis *Sally* · Liam Martin *Linus Van Pelt* ■ Dir Bill Melendez, Phil Roman · Scr Charles M Schulz, from his comic strip

Race the Sun ★★ PG
Comedy · 1996 · US · Colour · 95min

Disadvantaged Hawaiian high school students, inspired by their teacher Halle Berry, build a solar-powered vehicle and enter it into a race across Australia. Along the way they get to prove they aren't quitters, and show up evil corporations and arrogant foreigners. This features a number of young actors who would go on to greater success. ST

Julian Rhind-Tutt *Rupert* · Tara Summers *Ally* · Lisa Barbuscia *Nicky* · Flora Montgomery *Georgia* · Sienna Guillory *Newscaster* · Stefanie Powers *Georgia's mum* · John Standing *Ally's dad* · Sorcha Cusack *Ally's mum* · Tom Conti *Professor Rosenberg* · Germaine Greer · Richard Branson ■ Dir Ian Denyer · Scr Stephen Raphael

Halle Berry *Sandra Beecher* • James Belushi *Frank Machi* • Bill Hunter *Commissioner Hawkes* • Casey Affleck *Daniel Webster* • Eliza Dushku *Cindy Johnson* • Kevin Tighe *Jack Fryman* • Steve Zahn *Hans Fooiman* ■ *Dir* Charles T Kanganis • *Scr* Barry Morrow

Race to Space ★★ PG
Adventure drama based on a true story
2001 · US · Colour · 100min

Although it's rooted in fact, this is a feel-good family melodrama of the most calculatingly saccharine kind. The action revolves around Alex D Linz, the neglected son of widowed, expatriate German rocket scientist James Woods, who finds solace from his troubled home life in a lab monkey named Mac, who is being trained for a pioneering mission. DP *DVD*

James Woods *Wilhelm von Huber* • Annabeth Gish *Donni McGuiness* • Alex D Linz *Billy von Huber* • William Devane *Roger Thornhill* • William Atherton *Ralph Stanton* • Mark Moses *Alan Shepard* • Wesley Mann *Rudolph* • Patrick Richwood *Dieter* ■ *Dir* Sean McNamara • *Scr* Eric Gardner, Steve H Wilson

Race to Witch Mountain ★★★ PG
Science-fiction adventure fantasy
2009 · US · Colour · 94min

Disney reworks 1975's *Escape to Witch Mountain* here, with solid if unspectacular results. Like the original, this adventure pitches two mysterious teenagers (AnnaSophia Robb and Alexander Ludwig) at the heart of the action, though the new film is more upfront about revealing that their weirdly inflected English and supernatural powers derive from the fact that they're extraterrestrials on a mission to save their own distant planet. Dwayne "The Rock" Johnson, as brawny Las Vegas cabbie Jack Bruno, does his best to feign surprise at encountering these interplanetary fugitives. The movie soon settles into an extended chase, which keeps it pacey while offering opportunities for mild fisticuffs and CGI explosions, though it's never more than moderately exciting. TJ *DVD*

Dwayne Johnson *Jack Bruno* • AnnaSophia Robb *Sara* • Alexander Ludwig *Seth* • Carla Gugino *Dr Alex Friedman* • Ciaran Hinds *Burke* • Garry Marshall *Dr Donald Harlan* • Tom Everett Scott *Matheson* ■ *Dir* Andy Fickman • *Scr* Mark Bomback, Matt Lopez, from a story by Lopez, from a novel by Alexander Key

Race with the Devil ★★★ 15
Horror thriller
1975 · US · Colour · 84min

Easy Rider was both a triumph and a millstone for its star and producer, Peter Fonda, who lurched from one rip-off to the next. The bad guys are Satanists from the back of Texas beyond, but this is a studio concoction and the characters are taken straight off the shelf. Director Jack Starrett keeps things moving and Fonda's co-star, Warren Oates, is always worth watching. AT Swearing.

Peter Fonda *Roger* • Warren Oates *Frank* • Loretta Swit *Alice* • Lara Parker *Kelly* • RG Armstrong *Sheriff Taylor* ■ *Dir* Jack Starrett • *Scr* Wes Bishop, Lee Frost

The Racers ★★
Sports drama
1955 · US · Colour · 91min

Set around Europe but shot on the backlot at 20th Century-Fox with an overworked back projection machine, this motor-racing saga stars Kirk Douglas as the reckless driver who trashes his car and kills a dog whose owner, Bella Darvi, falls in love with him and finances his new car. Polish-born Darvi was a compulsive gambler and then the mistress of studio boss Darryl F Zanuck. Mrs Zanuck had her banished from Hollywood, and she later committed suicide. AT

Kirk Douglas *Gino* • Bella Darvi *Nicole* • Gilbert Roland *Dell 'Oro* • Lee J Cobb *Maglio* ■ *Dir* Henry Hathaway • *Scr* Charles Kaufman, from a novel by Hans Ruesch

Rachel and the Stranger ★★★
Romantic western
1948 · US · BW · 92min

This utterly charming quasi-western is distinguished by one of Robert Mitchum's most likeable, deceptively throwaway roles, as the itinerant tracker who momentarily comes between husband and wife William Holden and Loretta Young. Mitchum's vocal talents are given full rein here; indeed, he had a hit record of sorts in the duet he performs with youngster Gary Gray, *Just Like Me*. Sadly, its fame, as so often happens, outlived the film from which it came. TS

Loretta Young *Rachel* • William Holden (2) *Big Davey Harvey* • Robert Mitchum *Jim Fairways* • Gary Gray *Little Davey* • Tom Tully *Parson Jackson* ■ *Dir* Norman Foster • *Scr* Waldo Salt, from the stories *Rachel and Neighbor Sam* by Howard Fast

Rachel Getting Married ★★★ 15
Drama
2008 · US · Colour · 108min

Anne Hathaway plays a believably self-absorbed addict in this lengthy and intense drama. Hathaway's Kym is a bad girl released from rehab in order to attend her sister's wedding. She's been in recovery for years, and socialising nicely was never her strong suit, so when she descends on the celebration old resentments quickly surface. Director Jonathan Demme transforms what initially resembles a mock documentary into an unsettling tale that contains some very powerful scenes, as well as dark humour. Skilfully written by Jenny Lumet (daughter of director Sidney), the story builds to a breathtaking climax in which Kym and her estranged mother (Debra Winger) confront each other, and the result is electrifying. KK *DVD* *Blu*

Anne Hathaway *Kym Buchman* • Rosemarie DeWitt *Rachel Buchman* • Bill Irwin *Paul Buchman* • Tunde Adebimpe *Sidney Williams* • Mather Zickel *Kieran* • Debra Winger *Abby* ■ *Dir* Jonathan Demme • *Scr* Jenny Lumet

The Rachel Papers ★★ 18
Comedy drama
1989 · UK · Colour · 90min

Writer/director Damian Harris is responsible for this misfiring adaptation of Martin Amis's novel. Dexter Fletcher does well enough as the lovesick youngster who keeps a record of former girlfriends to aid future seductions, but the fact that he spends so much time talking directly to camera (in a clumsy bid to reproduce the book's first-person perspective) says a good deal about Harris's uninspired direction. DP Swearing, nudity.

Dexter Fletcher *Charles Highway* • Ione Skye *Rachel Seth-Smith* • Jonathan Pryce *Norman* • James Spader *DeForest* • Bill Paterson *Gordon Highway* • Shirley Anne Field *Mrs Seth-Smith* • Michael Gambon *Dr Knowd* • Amanda De Cadenet *Yvonne* • Aubrey Morris *Sir Herbert* ■ *Dir* Damian Harris • *Scr* Damian Harris, from the novel by Martin Amis

Rachel, Rachel ★★★★
Drama
1968 · US · Colour · 101min

This may have been Paul Newman's directorial debut, but it's the performance of his wife Joanne Woodward that makes it such a moving and memorable drama. As the bashful teacher for whom returning childhood friend James Olson presents the last chance of romance, she brilliantly conveys the timidity born of a frustrated life spent in the service of others. Woodward's quiet power also comes to Newman's rescue when his inexperience allows the tone and tempo to slip. Their daughter Nell Potts plays the young Rachel. DP

Joanne Woodward *Rachel Cameron* • James Olson *Nick Kazlik* • Kate Harrington *Mrs Cameron* • Estelle Parsons *Calla Mackie* • Donald Moffat *Niall Cameron* • Terry Kiser *Preacher* • Nell Potts *Rachel as a child* ■ *Dir* Paul Newman • *Scr* Stewart Stern, from the novel *A Jest of God* by Margaret Laurence

Racing Dreams ★★★
Documentary
2009 · US · Colour · 90min

In following the final five races of the World Karting Association National Championship, Marshall Curry amassed 500 hours of footage. Thankfully, much of the motoring action has been jettisoned so he can concentrate on the off-track experiences of 11-year-old Annabeth Barnes, 12-year-old Josh Hobson and 13-year-old Brandon Warren. The graphic techniques that Curry employs to explain the races are a touch gimmicky, but this is a fascinating introduction to junior petrolheads and their high-octane world. DP *DVD*

■ *Dir* Marshall Curry

Racing for Time ★★
Prison drama
2008 · US · Colour · 86min

Charles S Dutton directs and stars in this formulaic prison drama, about a guard at a Texas juvenile facility who sets up a multiracial track team to help rehabilitate female offenders. While this true story is clearly a heartfelt project for Dutton (who served time in jail as a young man), it doesn't quite make the intended impact thanks to a rushed and unconvincing narrative, and gratuitously gimmicky visuals. The naturalistic performances are the only memorable aspect of the film, with Yaya DaCosta especially impressive. SF

Charles S Dutton *Cleveland "Stack" Stackhouse* • Elizabeth Peña *Flores* • Yaya DaCosta *Vanessa* • Aunjanue Ellis *Officer Baker* ■ *Dir* Charles S Dutton • *Scr* Glenn German, Adam Rodgers

Racing Stripes ★★ U
Part-animated comedy adventure
2004 · US/S Afr · Colour · 97min

Take one unsophisticated *Babe* clone, add a dollop of *Seabiscuit* sentiment, stir in a positive message and you have *Racing Stripes*. Director Frederik Du Chau's comedy uses the trick of live animals with CGI mouths to lip-synch the broad one-liners, but this yarn tries too hard to appeal to all members of the family. Although well served by its human actors and voice cast, this remains a charmless and predictable confection. AJ *DVD*

Bruce Greenwood *Nolan Walsh* • Hayden Panettiere *Channing Walsh* • M Emmet Walsh *Woodzie* • Wendie Malick *Clara Dalrymple* • Frankie Muniz *Stripes* • Mandy Moore *Sandy* • Michael Clarke Duncan *Clydesdale* • Jeff Foxworthy *Reggie* • Joshua Jackson *Trenton's Pride* • Joe Pantoliano *Goose* • Snoop Dogg *Lightning* • Dustin Hoffman *Tucker* • Whoopi Goldberg *Franny* ■ *Dir* Frederik Du Chau • *Scr* David F Schmidt, from a story by David F Schmidt, Steven P Wegner, Kirk DeMicco, Frederik Du Chau

Racing with the Moon ★★★ 15
Second World War romantic drama
1984 · US · Colour · 103min

Considering it was written by Steve Kloves when in his 20s and features such stars in the making as Sean Penn, Elizabeth McGovern and Nicolas Cage, this is a curiously old-fashioned rites-of-passage romance. The atmosphere of a wartime Christmas has been deftly achieved without undue nostalgia by director Richard Benjamin, who artfully masks the story's comparative lack of incident by allowing his cast to explore their characters fully. Slight, but charmingly authentic. DP *DVD*

Sean Penn *Henry "Hopper" Nash* • Elizabeth McGovern *Caddie Winger* • Nicolas Cage *Nicky* • John Karlen *Mr Nash* • Rutanya Alda *Mrs Nash* • Max Showalter *Mr Arthur* ■ *Dir* Richard Benjamin • *Scr* Steven Kloves

The Rack ★★
Drama
1956 · US · BW · 100min

In this early starring role, Paul Newman plays the previously heroic army captain on trial for having collaborated with the enemy while a captive in Korea. This big-screen version of a TV drama by Rod Serling is an intelligent but overlong examination of the Newman character's psychological make-up and what brought him to the breaking point. Unfortunately, Newman's performance is mostly boorish and monotonous. AE

Paul Newman *Capt Edward W Hall Jr* • Wendell Corey *Maj Sam Moulton* • Walter Pidgeon *Col Edward W Hall Sr* • Edmond O'Brien *Lt Col Frank Wasnick* • Lee Marvin *Capt John R Miller* • Cloris Leachman *Caroline* ■ *Dir* Arnold Laven • *Scr* Stewart Stern, from the TV play by Rod Serling

The Racket ★★★
Silent crime drama
1928 · US · BW · 60min

Long unseen, this was a notable entry in the silent gangster cycle of the late 1920s, directed with considerable flair by Lewis Milestone. The film's exposé of crooked cops and politicians was daring for its time and it was widely banned in the United States. There would be more pressure to revive it had the star of the original Broadway play, Edward G Robinson, repeated his role as the big bootlegger; instead the film cast Louis Wolheim. The 1951 remake with Robert Mitchum was updated and conventionalised. AE

Thomas Meighan *Capt McQuigg* • Marie Prevost *Helen Hayes, an entertainer* • Louis Wolheim *Nick Scarsi, bootleg king* • George Stone [George E Stone] *Joe Scarsi* • John Darrow *Ames, a cub reporter* ■ *Dir* Lewis Milestone • *Scr* Harry Behn, Del Andrews, Eddie Adams, Bartlett Cormack, from the play by Bartlett Cormack

The Racket ★★★ PG
Crime drama
1951 · US · BW · 88min

Robert Mitchum plays an honest cop who goes up against gangster Robert Ryan. Despite being made by RKO for peanuts, this tough film has some decent action scenes and car chases, and co-directors John Cromwell and Nicholas Ray lace the rather hackneyed story with a welcome dash of political cynicism. RKO was owned at the time by Howard Hughes and this is a remake of a 1928 film that Hughes produced. AT *DVD*

Robert Mitchum *Captain McQuigg* • Lizabeth Scott *Irene* • Robert Ryan *Nick Scanlon* • William Talman *Johnson* • Ray Collins *Welch* • Joyce MacKenzie *Mary McQuigg* • Robert Hutton *Ames* ■ *Dir* John Cromwell, Nicholas Ray • *Scr* William Wister Haines, WR Burnett, from the play by Bartlett Cormack

Racket Busters ★★
Crime drama
1938 · US · BW · 65min

Humphrey Bogart relishes an early starring role as the racketeer muscling in on the fruit and produce market in this crisp but forgettable Warner Bros crime drama. By contrast, George Brent is duller than usual, miscast as the honest trucker who eventually stands up to Bogart. Allegedly based on the crime-busting exploits of New York district attorney Thomas E Dewey, this is a lesser example of the studio's penchant in the 1930s for headline-based stories. AE

Humphrey Bogart *John Martin* • George Brent *Denny Jordan* • Gloria Dickson *Nora Jordan* • Allen Jenkins *Skeets Wilson* • Walter Abel *Hugh Allison* • Henry O'Neill *Governor* • Penny Singleton *Gladys* ■ *Dir* Lloyd Bacon • *Scr* Robert Rossen, Leonardo Bercovici

Radiator ★★★ 15
Drama
2014 · UK · Colour · 93min

Actor Tom Fisher assumes the name Tom Browne for this touching directorial debut, which is inspired by the relationship between his own parents. It also makes evocative use of their stone cottage in the Lake District. Co-writer Daniel Cerqueira plays Daniel, a son summoned from his not entirely successful life in London to help his mother (Gemma Jones) cope with his aged father (Richard Johnson), who has seemingly given up on life. In his final role, 87-year-old Johnson captures the curmudgeonly confusion of an impotent tyrant, while Jones touchingly conveys the grief of a woman about to lose the man who has made and marred her existence. Filmed for just £140,000, this low-key saga rings true without resorting to melodrama. DP Swearing.

Richard Johnson *Leonard* • Gemma Jones *Maria* • Daniel Cerqueira *Daniel* • Julia Ford *Jean* ■ *Dir* Tom Browne • *Scr* Tom Browne, Daniel Cerqueira

Radio ★🅿🅶

Drama based on a true story
2003 · US · Colour · 104min

This true-life feel-good tale starring Cuba Gooding Jr may be marginally better than his dire *Boat Trip*, but it's still a mawkish slushfest. Set in the South Carolina of the 1970s, Gooding plays – or, rather overplays – "Radio", a mentally disabled kid who's made team mascot by Ed Harris's high-school football coach. Radio's new-found status arouses the hostility of the town's narrow-minded locals, making Harris's mentoring of Gooding problematic. DA
DVD

Cuba Gooding Jr *James Robert "Radio" Kennedy* • Ed Harris *Coach Harold Jones* • Alfre Woodard *Principal Daniels* • S Epatha Merkerson *Maggie Kennedy* • Brent Sexton *Honeycutt* • Chris Mulkey *Frank Clay* • Sarah Drew *Mary Helen Jones* • Riley Smith *Johnny Clay* • Debra Winger *Linda Jones* ■ *Scr* Mike Rich, from the *Sports Illustrated* article "Someone to Lean On" by Gary Smith

Radio Days ★★★★🅿🅶

Period comedy
1987 · US · Colour · 84min

An underrated entry in the Woody Allen canon, this is an intelligent and endlessly delightful examination of childhood and the process of memory. Although it is subtly directed and played to a nicety by a splendid ensemble cast, the film stands and falls on the wit and insight of the script and the minute period detail of the production design, and both Allen and production designer Santo Loquasto deserved more than just Oscar nominations. Cutting effortlessly from the crowded family home in Brooklyn to the empty glamour of Radioland, this celluloid scrapbook is evocative and irresistible. DP Swearing, brief nudity. *DVD*

Mia Farrow *Sally White* • Julie Kavner *Mother* • Michael Tucker *Father* • Seth Green *Little Joe* • Dianne Wiest *Aunt Bea* • Josh Mostel *Uncle Abe* • Danny Aiello *Rocco* • Diane Keaton *New Year's singer* • Woody Allen *Narrator* ■ *Dir/Scr* Woody Allen

Radio Flyer ★★★12

Fantasy drama
1992 · US · Colour · 109min

The importance of belief in the impossible is the central theme of director Richard Donner's difficult yet delicate fantasy about two boys who escape the physical abuse of their stepfather via their toy red wagon, the *Radio Flyer*. Reconciling the children's battered background with their desperate need for release, Donner punctuates his affecting fable with surreal and mystical twists that weave a powerful spell. Well acted by an excellent cast (Tom Hanks is the uncredited narrator). AJ Swearing

Lorraine Bracco *Mary* • John Heard *Daugherty* • Adam Baldwin *The King* • Elijah Wood *Mike* • Joseph Mazzello *Bobby* • Ben Johnson (1) *Geronimo Bill* • Sean Baca *Fisher* • Tom Hanks *Narrator* ■ *Dir* Richard Donner • *Scr* David Mickey Evans

Radio On ★★★18

Road movie
1979 · UK/W Ger · BW · 124min

In this striking British road movie, David Beames plays the disc jockey who drives haphazardly from London to Bristol to find out why his brother died, only to reach a dead end of existential despair. Much influenced by German director Wim Wenders (who acts as associate producer), director Christopher Petit casts a bleak eye over the British countryside, but any attempt to construct a multilayered narrative is undercut by wooden acting. Yet its use of pop music and landscape make this a captivating, if cryptic, experience. TH Swearing *DVD*

David Beames *Robert* • Lisa Kreuzer *Ingrid* • Sandy Ratcliff *Kathy* • Andrew Byatt *Deserter* • Sue Jones-Davies *Girl* • Sting *Just Like Eddie* • Sabina Michael *Aunt* ■ *Dir* Christopher Petit • *Scr* Christopher Petit, Heidi Adolph

Radioland Murders ★★🅿🅶

Period comedy thriller
1994 · US · Colour · 103min

After his success with *The Tall Guy*, comic-turned-director Mel Smith was courted by Hollywood. He ended up with this misfire. Intended as a salute to the golden age of radio, this finds Brian Benben and Mary Stuart Masterson overacting frantically as they attempt to find out who is dispatching the employees of a radio station in 1939 Chicago. An unsuccessful mix of lame gags and stodgy slapstick. JF

Brian Benben *Roger* • Mary Stuart Masterson *Penny Henderson* • Ned Beatty *General Whalen* • George Burns *Milt Lackey* • Scott Michael Campbell *Billy* • Michael McKean *Rick Rochester* • Christopher Lloyd *Zoltan* ■ *Dir* Mel Smith • *Scr* Willard Huyck, Gloria Katz, Ron Osborne, from a story by George Lucas

Radioman ★★★

Documentary
2012 · UK · Colour · 70min

Elderly, bearded former down-and-out Craig Castaldo has a boom box tied around his neck, and cycles around New York film sets, where he is known and loved by the great and the good of Hollywood. Radioman is what they call Craig Castaldo, and he's the subject of this captivating slice-of-life documentary. The affable film fan (with over 100 movie appearances to his name, mainly as a background extra) muses on his alcoholism, homelessness and spell in Belle Vue. But what really comes across here is the amiable eccentric's genuine love of movies and movie-making. JA Swearing.

Radioman [Craig Castaldo] *Craig Castaldo* • George Clooney • Tom Hanks • Matt Damon • Johnny Depp • Jude Law • Eva Mendes • Helen Mirren • Meryl Streep ■ *Dir* Mary Kerr

Raffles ★★★

Romantic crime adventure
1930 · US · BW · 70min

Villainy is all very well if you can carry it off with a smile, smooth out misunderstandings with a mellifluous voice and look as handsome as Ronald Colman does here playing the elusive AJ Raffles. This urbane adaptation makes the toff thief amusingly likeable, a rogue with charm – unless you're his victim, of course. The result is a fascinating curio. TH

Ronald Colman *AJ Raffles* • Kay Francis *Lady Gwen Manders* • Bramwell Fletcher *Bunny Manders* • Frances Dade *Ethel Crowley* • David Torrence *McKenzie* • Alison Skipworth *Lady Kitty Melrose* • Frederick Kerr *Lord Harry Melrose* ■ *Dir* Harry d'Abbadie D'Arrast • *Scr* George Fitzmaurice, Sidney Howard, from the play *Raffles, the Amateur Cracksman* by Ernest William Hornung, Eugene Wiley Presbrey, from the novel *The Amateur Cracksman* by Ernest William Hornung

Raffles ★★★🅄

Romantic crime adventure
1939 · US · BW · 68min

This pleasant but mindless remake by producer Samuel Goldwyn of his 1930 film stars debonair David Niven, who lacks the suave charm of Ronald Colman's incarnation of the famed gentleman thief. Olivia de Havilland is lovely, however, and more than makes up for Niven's over-casual approach. What is truly amazing is that this film is particularly strong on English mores and atmosphere, yet not a frame was shot outside Hollywood. TS

David Niven *AJ Raffles* • Olivia de Havilland *Gwen Manders* • Douglas Walton *Bunny Manders* • Dudley Digges *Inspector McKenzie* • Dame May Whitty *Lady Kitty Melrose* • Lionel Pape *Lord Harry Melrose* ■ *Dir* Sam Wood, William Wyler • *Scr* John Van Druten, Sidney Howard, F Scott Fitzgerald, from the novel *The Amateur Cracksman* by Ernest William Hornung

Rag Tale ★★15

Satirical drama
2005 · UK/Lux/US/Ire · Colour · 118min

Mary McGuckian explores the murky world of tabloid journalism in this frenetic satire. Largely improvised, the film chronicles a week in the life of salacious London newspaper *The Rag*. While the editorial team brainstorms ways to exploit the Royal Family, scandal erupts closer to home following the revelation that editor Rupert Graves is sleeping with deputy editor Jennifer Jason Leigh, who also happens to be the wife of the chairman (Malcolm McDowell). The manically edited hand-held camerawork may distract, but picture excels in its depiction of office politics. SF Swearing, drug abuse. *DVD*

Rupert Graves *Eddy Somerset Taylor* • Jennifer Jason Leigh *Mary Josephine "MJ" Morton* • Lucy Davis *Debbs* • John Sessions *Felix Miles Sty* • Bill Paterson *Tulloch "Lucky" Lloyd* • Sara Stockbridge *Sally May Ponsonby* • Cal Macaninch *Paul "Mac" Macavoy* • David Hayman *Geoff "P3" Randal* • Simon Callow *Cormac "Fat Boy" Rourke* • Malcolm McDowell *Richard "The Chief" Morton* • Kerry Fox *Peach James Taylor* ■ *Dir/Scr* Mary McGuckian

Rage ★★★15

Drama
1966 · US/Mex · Colour · 99min

Glenn Ford is the resident medico at a construction site in the wilds of Mexico. One day he's bitten by his pet dog which turns out to have rabies, so Ford has two days in which to get to a proper hospital and have the serum pumped into him before he starts foaming at the mouth. Instead of rushing, he tends to a pregnant woman who goes into labour; then his jeep breaks down; then Stella Stevens, as a tart with a heart, takes a shower, delaying things still further. AT

Glenn Ford *Reuben* • Stella Stevens *Perla* • David Reynoso *Pancho* • Armando Silvestre *Antonio* • Ariadna Welter *Blanca* • José Elias Moreno *Fortunato* ■ *Dir* Gilberto Gazcon • *Scr* Teddi Sherman, Gilberto Gazcon, Fernando Mendez, from a story by Jesus Velazquez, Guillermo Hernandez, Gilberto Gazcon

Rage ★★15

Drama
1972 · US · Colour · 95min

Rancher George C Scott and his son Nicolas Beauvy are accidentally caught in the spray of what turns out to be a deadly nerve gas. When the boy dies, Scott learns the truth about the chemical and takes revenge by destroying the company where the gas was made. What might have been developed as a provocative social conscience drama emerges as thin and uninteresting melodrama. Actor Scott made his feature directing debut with the film. RK

George C Scott *Dan Logan* • Richard Basehart *Dr Caldwell* • Martin Sheen *Major Holliford* • Barnard Hughes *Dr Spencer* • Nicolas Beauvy *Chris Logan* ■ *Dir* George C Scott • *Scr* Philip Friedman, Dan Kleinman

Rage ★★15

Crime drama
1999 · UK · Colour · 96min

Newton I Aduaka's rites-of-passage debut feature falls into all the familiar traps, as it equates *vérité* camerawork with dramatic realism. But there's an honesty about his attempt to portray the limited options open to mixed-race teenager Fraser Ayres and his mates, Shaun Parkes and John Pickard, as they resort to desperate measures in order to fund their hip-hop recording ambitions. As much about dreams and friendship as gangsta rap and crime, this smacks of authenticity, yet ultimately succumbs to street clichés and violence. DP Swearing, violence, drug abuse *DVD*

Fraser Ayres *Jamie, "Rage"* • Shaun Parkes *Godwin, "G"* • John Pickard *Thomas, "T"* • Shango Baku *Marcus* • Wale Ojo *Pin* ■ *Dir/Scr* Newton I Aduaka

Rage ★15

Revenge thriller
2014 · US/Fr · Colour · 94min

In this mindless revenge movie, Nicolas Cage plays a gangster-gone-legit who reverts back to his criminal ways after learning that his daughter has been kidnapped. The set-up reeks of *Taken*, except in that movie you can't help but root for Liam Neeson's ageing avenger. Here, you begin to feel sorry for the random assortment of scumbags who are despatched with excessive force by Cage, seemingly just to let off a bit of steam. If vigilante movies leave you with a bad taste in the mouth, then you'll need a whole bottle of mouthwash to swallow this dud. JH *DVD*

Nicolas Cage *Paul Maguire* • Rachel Nichols *Vanessa Maguire* • Danny Glover *Detective Peter St John* • Peter Stormare *Francis O'Connell* • Max Ryan *Kane* ■ *Dir* Paco Cabezas • *Scr* Jim Agnew, Sean Keller

Rage at Dawn ★★🅄

Western
1955 · US · Colour · 85min

In a handsome-looking but lethargic western, special agent Randolph Scott goes undercover to trap one of the earliest bands of outlaws, that of the Reno brothers who committed the first train hold-up in 1866. The Renos also have an attractive sister (Mala Powers), which naturally complicates matters for Scott. The rage at dawn refers to the historically accurate conclusion in which a lynch mob plucks the Renos from jail. AE *DVD*

Randolph Scott *James Barlow* • Forrest Tucker *Frank Reno* • Mala Powers *Laura Reno* • J Carrol Naish *Sim Reno* • Edgar Buchanan *Judge Hawkins* • Myron Healey *John Reno* • Richard Garland *Bill Reno* • Denver Pyle *Clint Reno* ■ *Dir* Tim Whelan • *Scr* Horace McCoy, from a story by Frank Gruber

The Rage: Carrie 2 ★18

Horror
1999 · US · Colour · 100min

A belated sequel to Brian De Palma's terrifying masterpiece *Carrie*, this abysmal travesty goes through the same narrative motions as the 1976 classic, even using clips as redundant flashbacks. Yet it repeatedly stomps on the memory of that class Stephen King act with utterly routine direction, tired gore and a complete lack of pathos. AJ *DVD*

Emily Bergl *Rachel Lang* • Jason London *Jesse Ryan* • Dylan Bruno *Mark* • J Smith-Cameron *Barbara Lang* • Zachery Ty Bryan *Eric* • Amy Irving *Sue Snell* ■ *Dir* Katt Shea • *Scr* Rafael Moreu, Howard A Rodman, from characters by Stephen King

A Rage in Harlem ★★★★18

Crime thriller
1991 · UK/US · Colour · 103min

In this stylish, fast-moving and often humorous thriller, Robin Givens looks every inch the sex siren. She arrives in 1950s Harlem with a bag full of stolen gold. As she tries to exchange the booty for cash, various seedy characters get involved in her scheming, as does an innocent undertaker's assistant (played with charm and naivety by the ever-dependable Forest Whitaker). The cast is enjoyable to watch as the twisting tale unfolds, but the squeamish should beware: there is quite a lot of violence. JB Swearing, nudity. *DVD*

Forest Whitaker *Jackson* • Gregory Hines *Goldy* • Robin Givens *Imabelle* • Zakes Mokae *Big Kathy* • Danny Glover *Easy Money* • Badja Djola *Slim* • John Toles-Bey *Jodie* ■ *Dir* Bill Duke • *Scr* John Toles-Bey, Bobby Crawford, from the novel by Chester Himes

Rage in Heaven ★★

Drama
1941 · US · BW · 84min

The English heir to a fortune (Robert Montgomery) returns home to his mother Lucile Watson after an absence in France where, unbeknown to her, he has been in a mental hospital. He marries his mother's social secretary (Ingrid Bergman), but his psychosis soon surfaces in unfounded jealousy of his wife and his friend (George Sanders), leading to violent and melodramatic events. WS Van Dyke directed this overheated nonsense and was unable to rescue Montgomery from an unconvincing parody of a mad Englishman. RK

Robert Montgomery *Philip Monrell* • Ingrid Bergman *Stella Bergen* • George Sanders *Ward Andrews* • Lucile Watson *Mrs Monrell* • Oscar Homolka *Dr Rameau* ■ *Dir* WS Van Dyke • *Scr* Christopher Isherwood, Robert Thoeren, from the novel by James Hilton

The Rage in Placid Lake ★★15

Comedy drama
2002 · Aus/UK · Colour · 86min

Australian teenager Placid Lake (played by musician Ben Lee) is no ordinary rebel. The

🅄 SUITABLE FOR ALL   🅄c SUITABLE ESPECIALLY FOR YOUNG CHILDREN (DVD ONLY)   🅿🅶 PARENTAL GUIDANCE   12A UNDER 12s TO BE ACCOMPANIED (CINEMA ONLY)

bullied son of two ageing hippies, Lee decides to try to fit in with the straight world by getting a job in insurance. Sketching a ruthless corporate world where hearts and souls are swapped for executive perks, this quirky Aussie satire is worthy yet rarely witty. Lee charms in the lead role, yet not even he can make Placid's calculated plans for acceptance seem anything more than a lazy contrivance. JR Swearing, sexual references. *DVD*

Ben Lee *Placid Lake* • Rose Byrne *Gemma Taylor* • Miranda Richardson *Sylvia Lake* • Garry McDonald *Doug Lake* • Christopher Stollery *Joel* • Nicholas Hammond *Bill Taylor* • Francis McMahon *Anton* • Saskia Smith *Jane* ■ *Dir* Tony McNamara • *Scr* Tony McNamara, from his play *The Cafe Latte Kid*

The Rage of Paris ★★★
Romantic comedy 1938 · US · BW · 78min

This amoral, sophisticated romantic comedy was made at Universal as a vehicle for French star Danielle Darrieux, making her Hollywood debut. Directed with a light touch by Henry Koster, the movie has Darrieux as a casino girl who, finding herself unemployed, turns model, and then, with the collusion and encouragement of two friends, gold-digger. These are the bare bones of an intricate plot that involves suspicions of blackmail and an unexpected love affair. The wildly glamorous Darrieux sparkles in this outrageous flim-flam. RK

Danielle Darrieux *Nicole de Cortillon* • Douglas Fairbanks Jr *Jim Trevor* • Mischa Auer *Mike* • Louis Hayward *Bill Jerome Duncan* • Helen Broderick *Gloria Patterson* • Charles Coleman *Rigley* ■ *Dir* Henry Koster • *Scr* Bruce Manning, Felix Jackson, from their story

Raggedy Man ★★★ 15
Drama 1981 · US · Colour · 89min

Sissy Spacek is a wartime divorcee who falls in love with a sailor played by Eric Roberts. This causes problems with her two children as well as the local predatory men, including Sam Shepard. Spacek had just won an Oscar for *Coal Miner's Daughter* and produces another trademark backwoods performance, heavy on the Texan accent and the wistful look. Her real-life husband, former art director Jack Fisk, directs the show with sensitivity, though the violent ending seems misjudged. AT

Sissy Spacek *Nita Longley* • Eric Roberts *Teddy* • Sam Shepard *Bailey* • William Sanderson *Calvin* • Tracey Walter *Arnold* • RG Armstrong *Rigby* • Henry Thomas *Harry* ■ *Dir* Jack Fisk • *Scr* William D Wittliff

The Raggedy Rawney ★★★ 15
Period drama 1987 · UK · Colour · 98min

Much maligned on its original release, Bob Hoskins's directorial debut is undeniably ragged in places, but there is still much to admire in this plea for toleration and peace set in an unidentified war-torn European country at the turn of the century. Once you've accepted the premise that Dexter Fletcher (a deserter who has disguised himself as a woman) could be mistaken for a "rawney", a gypsy with magical powers, then this intriguing venture into the mysterious Romany world has many rewards. DP Violence, swearing, nudity. *DVD*

Bob Hoskins *Darky* • Dexter Fletcher *Tom* • Zoë Nathenson *Jessie* • Zoë Wanamaker *Elle* • Dave Hill *Lamb* • Ian Dury *Weazel* • Ian McNeice *Stanley, the farmer* ■ *Dir* Bob Hoskins • *Scr* Bob Hoskins, Nicole de Wilde

Raging Bull ★★★★★ 18
Biographical sports drama 1980 · US · BW and Colour · 123min

Critics and film-makers are always being asked to reel off their desert island films: this, without question, is one such great. Director Martin Scorsese makes no concession to character likeability as he portrays Jake La Motta's downward slide from arrogant prizefighter to frustrated, hateful dropout. Robert De Niro, who piled on the pounds to play the latter-day La Motta, proves he is the ultimate Method

actor, both utterly convincing in the ring (the brutal fight sequences are spectacularly staged) and as the empty barrel abusing everyone (including his wife, Cathy Moriarty, and brother, Joe Pesci) at home. Scorsese effortlessly fuses top-drawer acting (De Niro rightly won a best actor Oscar for his efforts), pumping narrative drive and blitzkrieg camera technique to deliver a giddy, claustrophobic classic. JM Violence, swearing. *DVD* *BL*

Robert De Niro *Jake La Motta* • Cathy Moriarty *Vickie La Motta* • Joe Pesci *Joey La Motta* • Frank Vincent *Salvy* • Nicholas Colasanto *Tommy Como* • Theresa Saldana *Lenore* • Johnny Barnes *"Sugar" Ray Robinson* ■ *Dir* Martin Scorsese • *Scr* Paul Schrader, Mardik Martin, from the non-fiction book by Jake La Motta, Joseph Carter, Peter Savage • *Editor* Thelma Schoonmaker • *Cinematographer* Michael Chapman

The Raging Moon ★★★ PG
Romantic drama 1970 · UK · Colour · 106min

The suggestion that disabled people might enjoy a sexual relationship was still shocking when this romance in wheelchairs appeared, offering invaluable insight into a previously closed world. Malcolm McDowell is the young buck embittered by his crippling illness until he meets Nanette Newman, who is better adjusted to her fate. Director Bryan Forbes (Newman's husband in real life) tends to overdo everything, particularly the sentimentality, but the leads are sympathetic. DM *DVD* *BL*

Malcolm McDowell *Bruce Pritchard* • Nanette Newman *Jill* • Georgia Brown *Sarah Charles* • Bernard Lee *Uncle Bob* • Gerald Sim *Reverend Corbett* • Michael Flanders *Clarence Marlow* ■ *Dir* Bryan Forbes • *Scr* Bryan Forbes, from the novel by Peter Marshall

The Ragman's Daughter ★★★ 15
Romantic drama 1972 · UK · Colour · 90min

Written by Alan Sillitoe from his own story, this is an intelligent, romantic drama that has unfortunately been tagged with the "kitchen sink" label. It features an ingenious thief (Simon Rouse) who falls for the astonishingly beautiful daughter (Victoria Tennant) of a rich rag-and-bone man. Beautifully acted and stylishly executed, this British independent feature marked the directorial debut of Harold Becker (*Sea of Love*). A little gem. FL

Simon Rouse *Tony Bradmore* • Victoria Tennant *Doris Randall* • Patrick O'Connell *Tony, aged 35* • Leslie Sands *Doris's father* • Rita Howard *Doris's mother* • Brenda Peters *Tony's mother* • Brian Murphy *Tony's father* • Sydney Livingstone *Prison officer* ■ *Dir* Harold Becker • *Scr* Alan Sillitoe, from his story

Ragtime ★★★ 15
Period drama 1981 · US · Colour · 148min

EL Doctorow's novel was a publishing sensation and producer Dino De Laurentiis spent $27 million on re-creating (at Shepperton Studios) New York in 1906. But the novel is almost unfilmable, a chaotic bundle of characters and situations that relies solely on Doctorow's flashy wordplay. However, Milos Forman grabs bits and bobs of plot and relies on dazzling sets and photography. Plus there's James Cagney (back on the screen after a 20-year retirement) and Norman Mailer as Stanford White, the real-life architect murdered by Harry K Thaw (played here by Robert Joy). AT Swearing, nudity.

James Cagney *Police commissioner Waldo* • Brad Dourif *Younger brother* • Moses Gunn *Booker T Washington* • Elizabeth McGovern *Evelyn Nesbit* • Kenneth McMillan *Willie Conklin* • Pat O'Brien *Delmas* • Mandy Patinkin *Tateh* • Norman Mailer *Stanford White* • Robert Joy *Harry K Thaw* ■ *Dir* Milos Forman • *Scr* Michael Weller, from the novel by EL Doctorow

The Raid ★★★ U
Historical war drama 1954 · US · Colour · 82min

This little-known Civil War drama, about a group of escaped Confederate soldiers who lay vengeful siege to a town near the Canadian border, has much to commend it: a tight construction, bursts of action, strong characters and a great cast. The script

plays like an allegory of a wider conflict, while Hugo Fregonese (an Argentinian director who deserved greater public recognition) keeps the tension bubbling. AT

Van Heflin *Major Neal Benton* • Anne Bancroft *Katy Bishop* • Richard Boone *Captain Foster* • Lee Marvin *Lieutenant Keating* • Tommy Rettig *Larry Bishop* • Peter Graves (2) *Captain Dwyer* ■ *Dir* Hugo Fregonese • *Scr* Sydney Boehm, from the story by Francis Cockrell, from the article *Affair at St Albans* by Herbert Ravenal Sass

The Raid ★★★★ 18
Action thriller 2011 · Indonesia/US · Colour · 96min

Most action movies spend some time on plot, character and dialogue. Not *The Raid*, which features nonstop combat from beginning to end. In Jakarta, Rama (Iko Uwais) is part of an elite police squad sent to clean out a 15-storey tower block where the only law is that of crime lord Tama, whose hideout is on the top floor. The officers storm the building and begin to take each level by (impressively brutal) force. But by the time they reach the sixth floor, Tama has turned the tables, leaving the outnumbered cops in a desperate battle for survival. With its claustrophobic atmosphere and inventive scenes of violence, the film is heavily influenced by John Woo, *Die Hard* and John Carpenter's *Assault on Precinct 13*. But Welsh director Gareth Evans has gone a step further, distilling the action movie down to its barest essentials, to intense and immensely satisfying effect. LB Indonesian +subtitles. *DVD* *BL*

Iko Uwais *Rama* • Joe Taslim *Jaka* • Donny Alamsyah *Andi* • Yayan Ruhian *Mad Dog* • Pierre Gruno *Wahyu* ■ *Dir/Scr* Gareth Huw Evans [Gareth Evans]

The Raid 2 ★★★★★ 18
Action thriller 2013 · Indonesia · Colour · 143min

Made in Jakarta by ex-pat Welshman Gareth Evans, 2011's *The Raid* was a first-class fusion of throwback B-movie and bone-cracking martial arts flick, telling the story of a police raid on a mob-run high-rise. This excellent sequel continues the franchise in spirit only, with rookie officer Rama (Iko Uwais) being whisked off within hours of the first film's end and sent under cover to gain the trust of a violent crime family. Though it is more ambitious in scope than the first film, this remains primarily a visceral pulp action movie, and this is where it soars. DW Indonesian, Japanese, English +subtitles. Violence. *DVD* *BL*

Iko Uwais *Rama* • Arifin Putra *Uco* • Tio Pakusadewo *Bangun* • Oka Antara *Eka* ■ *Dir/Scr* Gareth Evans

Raid on Entebbe ★★★ PG
Drama based on a true story 1977 · US · Colour · 120min

This TV movie is the pick of three films about the Israeli commando mission in Uganda in 1976 to save the passengers of a plane hijacked by Palestinian terrorists. Peter Finch, in his last screen role, heads a distinguished cast as Israeli prime minister Yitzhak Rabin, and he's given fine support by Charles Bronson, Martin Balsam and Jack Warden. Director Irvin Kershner doesn't get carried away with the *Boys' Own* heroics and builds the tension nicely to its explosive climax. JF *DVD*

Peter Finch *Yitzhak Rabin* • Martin Balsam *Daniel Cooper* • Horst Buchholz *Wilfrid Boese* • John Saxon *Maj Gen Benny Peled* • Sylvia Sidney *Dora Bloch* • Jack Warden *Lt Gen Mordechai Gur* • Yaphet Kotto *President Idi Amin* • Charles Bronson *Brig Gen Dan Shamron* ■ *Dir* Irvin Kershner • *Scr* Barry Beckerman

Raid on Rommel ★★ 15
Second World War drama 1971 · US · Colour · 93min

It says a lot for Richard Burton that he was able to plumb the depths in dreary Second World War action movies such as this one, about a British officer releasing prisoners to attack Tobruk, without doing any apparent damage to his career. Even the usually dependable director Henry Hathaway

falters in this flawed effort that was originally meant for TV. TH *DVD*

Richard Burton *Captain Foster* • John Colicos *MacKenzie* • Clinton Greyn *Major Tarkington* • Danielle De Metz *Vivi* • Wolfgang Preiss *General Rommel* ■ *Dir* Henry Hathaway • *Scr* Richard Bluel

The Raiders ★★
Western 1952 · US · Colour · 80min

Old California is the location for this creaky revenge western from genre veteran Lesley Selander. Released theatrically as *The Raiders*, it offers very little to keep modern viewers engaged, as gold prospector Richard Conte goes after the land baron's heavies who murdered his wife and stole his claim. The events that follow are hackneyed and unevenly paced, with unconvincing performances that make the expected fisticuffs and gunfights feel particularly flat, despite the rousing accompanying score. Only Viveca Lindfors manages to transcend her two-dimensional role, playing Conte's new love interest and voice of reason with feistiness and charm. But her impact is diluted by a weak final act that ultimately relies on history rather than ingenious plotting for its convenient ending. SF

Richard Conte *Jan Morrell* • Viveca Lindfors *Elena de Ortega* • Barbara Britton *Elizabeth Ainsworth* • Hugh O'Brian *Hank Purvis* ■ *Dir* Lesley Selander • *Scr* Lillie Hayward, Polly James, from a story by Lyn Crost Kennedy

Raiders of the Lost Ark ★★★★★ PG
Period action adventure 1981 · US · Colour · 110min

Executive producer George Lucas and director Steven Spielberg minted fresh excitement from the cliffhanger serials of their youth in this breathless fantasy extravaganza. Archaeologist Indiana Jones (a part that fits Harrison Ford like a glove) searches Egypt for the fabled Ark of the Covenant, and finds himself up to his neck in booby-trapped caves, snake chambers, Nazi spies, religious demons, damsels in distress and even a spot of romance. The brilliantly evocative 1930s-set saga treats all the old clichés as if they've just been newly minted, and adds dazzling special effects to craft a wonderful action yarn that rattles along with wit, invention and the raw spirit of true adventure. No surprise then that one of the four Oscars this fabulous production picked up was for visual effects. Three sequels followed, *Indiana Jones and the Temple of Doom*, *Indiana Jones and the Last Crusade* and *Indiana Jones and the Kingdom of the Crystal Skull*. AJ Violence. *DVD* *BL*

Harrison Ford *Indiana Jones* • Karen Allen *Marion Ravenwood* • Paul Freeman *Bellog* • Ronald Lacey *Toht* • John Rhys-Davies *Sallah* • Denholm Elliott *Brody* • Wolf Kahler *Dietrich* • Anthony Higgins *Gobler* • Alfred Molina *Satipo* • Vic Tablian *Barranca/Monkey man* ■ *Dir* Steven Spielberg • *Scr* Lawrence Kasdan, from a story by George Lucas, Philip Kaufman • *Cinematographer* Douglas Slocombe • *Editor* Michael Kahn • *Music* John Williams • *Special Effects* Richard Edlund, Kit West, Joe Johnston, Bruce Nicholson • *Art Director* Leslie Dilley • *Production Designer* Norman Reynolds

Raiders of the Seven Seas ★★ U
Swashbuckling adventure 1953 · US · Colour · 88min

Red-bearded pirate John Payne commandeers a prison ship and takes on all-comers in this lively swashbuckler filmed in lush Technicolor. The love interest is supplied by Donna Reed who, as is often the way in these by-the-book high-seas adventures, is won over by our dashing hero's charms. TS

John Payne *Barbarossa* • Donna Reed *Alida* • Gerald Mohr *Salcedo* • Lon Chaney Jr *Peg Leg* ■ *Dir* Sidney Salkow • *Scr* John O'Dea, from a story by John O'Dea, Sidney Salkow

R

Railroaded! ★★★
Crime melodrama 1947 · US · BW · 72min

Anthony Mann brings a sure touch to this low-budget crime B-movie. Innocent youngster Ed Kelly is framed for murder by psychopathic professional John Ireland, whose penchant is spraying bullets with perfume before discharging them into his victims. Although formula stuff, it's taut, coolly violent and very tough, particularly in its treatment of female characters. **RK**

John Ireland *Duke Martin* • Sheila Ryan *Rosa Ryan* • Hugh Beaumont *Mickey Ferguson* • Jane Randolph *Clara Calhoun* • Ed Kelly *Steve Ryan* ■ *Dir* Anthony Mann • *Scr* John C Higgins, from a story by Gertrude Walker

The Railrodder ★★★★ U
Comedy 1965 · Can · Colour · 24min

Director Gerald Potterton's short film is a whimsical, poetic farewell to an elderly Buster Keaton. It is in some ways a diminutive view of Keaton's *The General*, in which Keaton makes his way across Canada on a railway trolley. The solo slapstick is sweet-natured, the adoration of the director for his star is obvious and Buster Keaton recalls his silent days by not saying a word, which makes it all the more poignant. **TH** *DVD*

Buster Keaton *The Railrodder* ■ *Dir/Scr* Gerald Potterton

Rails & Ties ★★ 12
Drama 2007 · US · Colour · 96min

The conventions of Hollywood screenwriting demand that when an 11-year-old boy (Miles Heizer) watches his mother commit suicide in front of an oncoming passenger train driven by Tom (Kevin Bacon), the pair's lives must intersect. Escaping from his new foster home, the boy tracks down his mother's killer and demands justice. What he discovers instead is Tom's terminally ill, childless wife (Marcia Gay Harden) who decides to mother him. You can probably join the dots from there to the tearful yet upbeat conclusion of this workmanlike melodrama. **JR** Brief swearing. *DVD*

Kevin Bacon *Tom Stark* • Marcia Gay Harden *Megan Stark* • Miles Heizer *Davey Danner* • Marin Hinkle *Renee* • Eugene Byrd *Otis Higgs* • Laura Ceron *Susan Garcia* ■ *Dir* Alison Eastwood • *Scr* Micky Levy

Rails into Laramie ★★ U
Western 1954 · US · Colour · 81min

This routine western is given distinction by a snarling study in black-hearted villainy by Dan Duryea, who is trying to stop the railroad from reaching Laramie for his own devious purpose. Meanwhile, sexy Mari Blanchard aims to rustle up an all-female jury to put Duryea away. All this would be interesting were it not for the presence of John Payne, past his prime and looking ill-at-ease. **TS**

John Payne *Jefferson Harder* • Mari Blanchard *Lou Carter* • Dan Duryea *Jim Shanessy* • Joyce MacKenzie *Helen Shanessy* • Barton MacLane *Lee Graham* • Lee Van Cleef *Ace Winton* ■ *Dir* Jesse Hibbs • *Scr* DD Beauchamp, Joseph Hoffman

The Railway Children ★★★★★ U
Classic period drama 1970 · UK · Colour · 104min

Directed by Lionel Jeffries, this adaptation of E Nesbit's much loved novel is simply the finest children's film ever made in the UK. Told with quiet intelligence and wry humour, the story follows three Edwardian siblings as they relocate to Yorkshire with their mother (Dinah Sheridan), following their father's wrongful arrest for treason. The set pieces are equally memorable – whether it's the prevention of a train wreck, the rescue of a schoolboy trapped in a tunnel, or the collection of birthday gifts for the proud but kindly stationmaster (winningly played by Bernard Cribbins). Jenny Agutter's magnificent performance stands out, perfectly balancing a child's passion for adventure with a growing sense of responsibility. **DP** *DVD* *Blu*

Jenny Agutter *Bobbie* • Sally Thomsett *Phyllis* • Gary Warren *Peter* • Dinah Sheridan *Mother* • Bernard Cribbins *Perks* • William Mervyn *Old gentleman* • Iain Cuthbertson *Father* • Peter Bromilow *Doctor* ■ *Dir* Lionel Jeffries • *Scr* Lionel Jeffries, from the novel by E Nesbit

The Railway Man ★★★ 15
Biographical drama 2013 · Aus/UK · Colour · 116min

Though it adds an extra hallmark of quality, the casting of Nicole Kidman alongside Colin Firth in this polished biographical drama is rather deceptive, suggesting a love story that never quite materialises. The story begins in 1983, when trainspotter Eric Lomax (Firth) meets future wife Patti (Kidman) en route to Scotland. After they marry, Patti learns that the nerdy ex-soldier is given to horrific nightmares about his past, when he was captured by the Japanese in 1942. When Eric learns that the soldier who once tortured him is still alive, it prompts him to journey east for a confrontation. The flashback structure of the film can't help but make it feel disjointed, but the narrative builds to an unexpected and powerful conclusion. **DW** In English, Japanese. Violence.

Colin Firth *Eric Lomax* • Nicole Kidman *Patti Lomax* • Jeremy Irvine *Young Eric Lomax* • Stellan Skarsgård *Finlay* • Hiroyuki Sanada *Nagase* • Sam Reid *Young Finlay* ■ *Dir* Jonathan Teplitzky • *Scr* Frank Cottrell Boyce, Andy Paterson, from Eric Lomax's autobiography

Rain ★★★ PG
Drama 1932 · US · BW · 93min

Somerset Maugham's tale of a hellfire-and-damnation church missionary's lust for a prostitute who fetches up at a trading post on a rain-drenched South Sea island was a steamy shocker in its day, and has attracted three film versions and three major actresses. Gloria Swanson starred in the silent *Sadie Thompson* (1928), earning a best actress nomination in the first ever Oscars; Rita Hayworth was a Technicolored (and terrific) *Miss Sadie Thompson*, in 1953. Here Joan Crawford, dressed and made-up to kill, gives her considerable all in a much underrated performance. Co-star Walter Huston is hammy, while the screenplay and direction fail to hit the right note. **RK** *DVD*

Joan Crawford *Sadie Thompson* • Walter Huston *Rev Alfred Davidson* • William Gargan *Sgt "Handsome" O'Hara* • Guy Kibbee *Joe Horn* • Walter Catlett *Quartermaster Hal Bates* ■ *Dir* Lewis Milestone • *Scr* Maxwell Anderson, from the play by John Colton, Clemence Randolph, from the short story by W Somerset Maugham

Rain ★★★★ 15
Coming-of-age drama 2001 · NZ/US · Colour · 87min

A haunting, dreamy tale, the debut feature of award-winning New Zealand commercials director Christine Jeffs marks her out as a major talent. A 13-year-old girl (a stunning turn from newcomer Alicia Fulford-Wierzbicki) travels with her younger brother and parents for a traditional sleepy summer holiday by the beach. However, the cracks in their idyllic life soon begin to appear. The marriage of her parents (Sarah Peirse and Alistair Browning) is falling apart, while both mother and daughter find themselves drawn to charismatic photographer Marton Csokas. Jeffs's measured direction, along with the hazy cinematography of John Toon, make the tragic finale compelling. **JF** *DVD*

Alicia Fulford-Wierzbicki *Janey* • Sarah Peirse *Kate* • Marton Csokas *Cady* • Alistair Browning *Ed* • Aaron Murphy *Jim* ■ *Dir* Christine Jeffs • *Scr* Christine Jeffs, from the novel by Kirsty Gunn

Rain Man ★★★★★ 15
Drama 1988 · US · Colour · 128min

While everyone remembers this film about an autistic man as Dustin Hoffman's Oscar-winning triumph, it is equally Tom Cruise's. As a wheeler-dealer living out the 1980s dream, he learns that not only is he out of his father's will (save for a 1949 Buick), he also has an institutionalised elder brother (Hoffman). This is a classic road movie, with the two siblings crossing country to California in the Buick. Hoffman's savant is one of modern cinema's great triumphs: believable, unsentimental, often hilarious. But without Cruise, whose emotional journey runs from confused and impatient to understanding, protective and eventually loving, there is no film. Director Barry Levinson handles the whole thing beautifully. **AC** Swearing. *DVD* *Blu*

Dustin Hoffman *Raymond Babbitt* • Tom Cruise *Charlie Babbitt* • Valeria Golino *Susanna* • Jerry Molen *Dr Bruner* • Jack Murdock *John Mooney* • Michael D Roberts *Vern* ■ *Dir* Barry Levinson • *Scr* Ronald Bass, Barry Morrow, from a story by Barry Morrow

Rain or Shine ★★
Comedy drama 1930 · US · BW · 90min

This very early Frank Capra-directed peek beneath the big top has a trio of clowns (Joe Cook, Dave Chasen and Tom Howard) attempting a lacklustre stab at the hackneyed "tears behind the greasepaint" scenario. The movie's problems stem from an overindulgence in leering acrobats and acres of sawdust at the expense of a plot and characterisation. **SH**

Joe Cook *Smiley* • Louise Fazenda *Frankie* • Joan Peers *Mary* • William Collier Jr *Bud* • Tom Howard *Amos* • David Chasen *Dave* ■ *Dir* Frank Capra • *Scr* Jo Swerling, Dorothy Howell, from the play by James Gleason

The Rain People ★★
Drama 1969 · US · Colour · 101min

This early outing from director Francis Ford Coppola is certainly not without interest today, but its 1960s attitudes have dated badly. Nevertheless, it is fascinating to see James Caan and Robert Duvall at a stage of their careers prior to *The Godfather*, and there's a superb performance from Shirley Knight in the leading role as the neurotic pregnant housewife who takes life on the lam with brain-damaged Caan. Uneven and slackly paced, but a curiosity. **TS** Violence, swearing, brief nudity.

James Caan *Jimmie "Killer" Kilgannon* • Shirley Knight *Natalie Ravenna* • Robert Duvall *Gordon* • Marya Zimmet *Rosalie* • Tom Aldredge *Mr Alfred* • Laurie Crewes *Ellen* ■ *Dir/Scr* Francis Ford Coppola

Rainbow ★★★
Biographical drama 1978 · US · Colour · 97min

Judy Garland fans will love this better-than-average TV movie devoted to the legendary diva's early career. Based on Christopher Finch's acclaimed biography, its main focus is on the formative incidents that would impact on Frances Ethel Gumm's troubled psyche later. From "The Gumm Sisters" to lasting fame in *The Wizard of Oz*, Judy is shown pleasing her driven stage mother (Piper Laurie) and forging a moving relationship with her father (Don Murray) while trying to retain a normal childhood within the MGM studio system. Broadway's *Annie* sensation Andrea McArdle completes the showbiz illusion with terrific renditions of Garland's signature evergreen tunes. **AJ**

Andrea McArdle *Judy Garland* • Don Murray *Frank Gumm* • Michael Parks *Roger Edens* • Rue McClanahan *Ida Koverman* • Nicholas Pryor *Will Gilmore* • Jack Carter *George Jessel* • Donna Pescow *Jinnie Gumm* • Erin Donovan *Janey Gumm* • Martin Balsam *Louis B Mayer* • Piper Laurie *Ethel Gumm* • Moosie Drier *Mickey Rooney* ■ *Dir* Jackie Cooper • *Scr* John McGreevey, from the biography by Christopher Finch

The Rainbow ★★ 15
Period drama 1988 · UK · Colour · 106min

Director Ken Russell takes a further dip after *Women in Love* into the DH Lawrence lucky bag, but to decidedly lacklustre effect. All clichés are alive and thrashing, including monosyllabic but "deeply meaningful" dialogue interspersed with heaving bosoms and frantic copulation by crashing waterfalls. Only Sammi Davis's portrayal of the feisty, no-nonsense Ursula lifts the unleavened load. **SH** Swearing, nudity. *DVD*

Sammi Davis *Ursula Brangwen* • Paul McGann *Anton Skrebensky* • Amanda Donohoe *Winifred Inger* • Christopher Gable *Will Brangwen* • David Hemmings *Uncle Henry* • Glenda Jackson *Anna Brangwen* • Dudley Sutton *MacAllister* • Jim Carter *Mr Harby* ■ *Dir* Ken Russell • *Scr* Ken Russell, Vivian Russell, from the novel by DH Lawrence

Rainbow ★★ PG
Fantasy comedy adventure 1995 · UK/Can · Colour · 94min

Four kids go searching for the end of the rainbow in the second feature directed by Bob Hoskins. Unfortunately, when they find it in New Jersey, one of them takes pieces of gold from the spectrum causing all colour to drain from the real world and a crime wave to break out. One of the first features to be shot on Digital High Definition, the results are not entirely successful. Hoskins doesn't have the light touch such hokum demands as the whimsy he aims for never quite comes into focus. **AJ**

Bob Hoskins *Frank Bailey* • Dan Aykroyd *Sheriff Wyatt Hampton* • Willy Lavendal *Mike* • Saul Rubinek *Sam Cohen* ■ *Dir* Bob Hoskins • *Scr* Ashley Sidaway, Robert Sidaway

Rainbow Bridge ★★ 15
Documentary drama 1971 · US · Colour · 125min

Although it captures the mood of the late 1960s, director Chuck Wein's mixture of hippy fact and impenetrable fiction is a rambling and tedious artefact from the era. Centred around model Pat Hartley making a pilgrimage to the Rainbow Bridge Occult Research Meditation Centre on the Hawaiian island of Maui, this disjointed mess is only worth watching to see Jimi Hendrix play a short concert by the side of the Haleakala volcano three months before his death. **AJ**

■ *Dir/Scr* Chuck Wein

The Rainbow Jacket ★★ PG
Crime drama 1954 · UK · Colour · 96min

Screenwriter TEB Clarke was the brains behind many of the Ealing comedies. Yet he also had a well-developed social conscience, as he proves in this unconvincing racing drama. As the disgraced jockey who saves his protégé from a bribes scandal, Bill Owen has one of his meatiest screen roles. However, this is a workmanlike film, with some suitably downbeat photography from Otto Heller and neat cameos from Sidney James and Wilfrid Hyde White. **DP**

Robert Morley *Lord Logan* • Kay Walsh *Barbara Crain* • Edward Underdown *Geoffrey Tyler* • Bill Owen *Sam Lilley* • Honor Blackman *Monica Tyler* • Wilfrid Hyde White *Lord Stoneleigh* • Sidney James *Harry* ■ *Dir* Basil Dearden • *Scr* TEB Clarke

The Rainbow Thief ★★★
Fantasy 1990 · UK · Colour · 91min

Alexandro Jodorowsky's most ardent fans will enjoy this obscure, whimsical fable about a man and his servant, played by Peter O'Toole and Omar Sharif. O'Toole is the eccentric who lives in the city sewers with Sharif, his servant who scavenges for food. Christopher Lee plays O'Toole's uncle who leaves his fortune to his dogs and his whores. **AT**

Peter O'Toole *Prince Meleagre* • Omar Sharif *Dima* • Christopher Lee *Uncle Rudolf* • Berta Dominguez D *Tiger Lily* ■ *Dir* Alexandro Jodorowsky • *Scr* Berta Dominguez D

Rainbow Warrior ★★★ PG
Historical drama 1992 · US/NZ · Colour · 89min

The true story of the bombing of the Greenpeace vessel *Rainbow Warrior*, whose passive resistance to nuclear testing should have meant peaceful isolation – but didn't. Jon Voight and Sam Neill are the two men who embody the political complexities of the situation as the ship's skipper and the investigating cop respectively. Michael Tuchner directs vividly, but the script should have examined the complicated issues in greater depth. TH

Jon Voight *Peter Willcox* • Sam Neill *Alan Galbraith* • Kerry Fox *Andrea Joyce* • Greg Johnson *Bert White* ▪ *Dir* Michael Tuchner • *Scr* Martin Copeland, Scott Busby

Raining Stones ★★★★15
Comedy drama 1993 · UK · Colour · 86min

The genius of director Ken Loach lies in his ability to point out the comic ironies and absurdities of existence while exposing the prejudices and injustices of working-class life. While a touch uneven, this is one of his most effective films, showing the desperate measures an unemployed man is willing to take in order to raise the cash for his daughter's Communion dress. Bruce Jones occasionally loses his way, but mostly he conveys the stubborn pride and determination of his character with considerable skill. Julie Brown shows up well as his wife, while Ricky Tomlinson steals scenes as his mate. DP Violence, swearing. *DVD*

Bruce Jones *Bob Williams* • Julie Brown *Anne Williams* • Gemma Phoenix *Coleen Williams* • Ricky Tomlinson *Tommy* • Tom Hickey *Father Barry* • Mike Fallor *Jimmy* • Ronnie Ravey *Butcher* ▪ *Dir* Ken Loach • *Scr* Jim Allen

The Rainmaker ★★★
Comedy drama 1956 · US · Colour · 121min

Burt Lancaster only made *Gunfight at the OK Corral* on condition that he star in this period comedy drama. Based on a Broadway play, the story is set in Kansas, 1913, with Lancaster as the conman who promises he will bring an end to a serious drought, while also finding time to charm local spinster Katharine Hepburn. Director Joseph Anthony staged the original play and clearly has a reverential ear for dialogue, but while Lancaster is solid, Hepburn is miscast. AT

Burt Lancaster *Starbuck* • Katharine Hepburn *Lizzie Curry* • Wendell Corey *File* • Lloyd Bridges *Noah Curry* • Earl Holliman *Jim Curry* • Wallace Ford *Sheriff Thomas* ▪ *Dir* Joseph Anthony • *Scr* N Richard Nash, from his play

The Rains Came ★★★
Romantic melodrama 1939 · US · BW · 104min

Torrid stuff from 1939, Hollywood's *annus mirabilis*, and generally overlooked among the welter of great films on display. This is major tosh, set in a very 20th Century-Fox India with classy Myrna Loy chasing a turbaned Tyrone Power, face-darkened by make-up as a Hindu doctor. The flood effects, tame by today's standards, won an Oscar. Author Louis Bromfield's novel was ruthlessly pared by the censorship of the time. TS

Myrna Loy *Lady Edwina Esketh* • Tyrone Power *Major Rama Safti* • George Brent *Tom Ransome* • Brenda Joyce *Fern Simon* • Nigel Bruce *Albert, Lord Esketh* ▪ *Dir* Clarence Brown • *Scr* Philip Dunne, Julien Josephson, from the novel by Louis Bromfield

The Rains of Ranchipur ★★
Romantic drama 1955 · US · Colour · 103min

This widescreen remake of the 1939 movie *The Rains Came* has Richard Burton in ludicrous brown make-up as the Indian doctor Lana Turner decides to seduce. The Oscar-nominated special effects are pathetic by today's standards, while co-stars Fred MacMurray, Joan Caulfield and Michael Rennie look particularly lost, as well they might, for director Jean Negulesco struggles to overcome the underdeveloped subplots. TS

Lana Turner *Edwina Esketh* • Richard Burton *Dr Safti* • Fred MacMurray *Tom Ransome* • Joan Caulfield *Fern Simon* • Michael Rennie *Lord Esketh* • Eugenie Leontovich *Maharani* ▪ *Dir* Jean Negulesco • *Scr* Merle Miller, from the novel *The Rains Came* by Louis Bromfield

Raintree County ★★★★
Period drama 1957 · US · Colour · 166min

MGM's follow-up to its masterpiece *Gone with the Wind* failed to meet with much critical or public approval in its day. Such lack of enthusiasm now seems unfair and

unwarranted, as this is a stunning, complex epic, dealing with issues and themes way ahead of its time. It's superbly cast and benefits from a particularly emotive and evocative vocal from Nat "King" Cole. This is the movie for which Elizabeth Taylor should have got her Oscar, as it contains some of the finest screen work she has ever done. TS

Montgomery Clift *John Wickliff Shawnessy* • Elizabeth Taylor *Susanna Drake* • Eva Marie Saint *Nell Gaither* • Nigel Patrick *Professor Jerusalem Webster Stiles* • Lee Marvin *Orville "Flash" Perkins* • Rod Taylor *Garwood B Jones* • Agnes Moorehead *Ellen Shawnessy* ▪ *Dir* Edward Dmytryk • *Scr* Millard Kaufman, from the novel by Ross Lockridge Jr

Raise the Red Lantern ★★★★★PG
Drama 1991 · Chi · Colour · 119min

Although a lesser film than the stunning *Ju Dou*, this is still one of the jewels of recent Chinese cinema. Once again making exceptional use of bright colour, symbolic compositions, stylised sets and the breathtaking rural landscape, director Zhang Yimou has fashioned a compelling and at times erotic story about the repression of women in 1920s China. Gong Li excels as the teenager who is forced to abandon her studies to become the fourth wife of a nobleman, but He Caifei, as the usurped third wife, matches her throughout their struggle for the right to the red lantern that signifies the master's favour. DP Mandarin +subtitles. Violence.

Gong Li *Songlian* • Ma Jingwu *Chen Zuoqian* • He Caifei *Meishan* • Cao Cuifeng *Zhuoyun* • Jin Shuyuan *Yuru* • Kong Lin *Yan'er* • Ding Weimin *Mother Song* • Cui Zhigang *Doctor Gao* ▪ *Dir* Zhang Yimou • *Scr* Ni Zhen, from the short story by Su Tong

Raise the Titanic ★★PG
Adventure 1980 · US · Colour · 109min

One of Lew Grade's most memorable flops, this adventure cost a fortune, was touted as a major blockbuster and then proceeded to sink faster than the world famous liner. Jason Robards and Richard Jordan are among the actors trying to raise the ship – accompanied by a distinctive score from composer John Barry – while Alec Guinness pops up as a crusty member of the *Titanic*'s original crew. JB Swearing. *DVD* *Blu*

Jason Robards *Admiral James Sandecker* • Richard Jordan *Dirk Pitt* • David Selby *Dr Gene Seagram* • Anne Archer *Dana Archibald* • Alec Guinness *John Bigalow* • M Emmet Walsh *Vinnie Giordino* ▪ *Dir* Jerry Jameson • *Scr* Adam Kennedy, from the novel by Clive Cussler

Raise Your Voice ★★PG
Drama 2004 · US · Colour · 102min

Small-town girl Hilary Duff makes her singing dreams come true in this sprightly but predictable romantic drama. Aimed squarely at pre-teens, it's a feel good romp-cum-life lesson as Duff is forced to conquer her fears and insecurities during a summer at a highly competitive performing arts school in Los Angeles. While older viewers may scoff at the contrived and often cheesy plot, younger girls will respond to its positive messages and frothy atmosphere. SF *DVD*

Hilary Duff *Terri Fletcher* • Oliver James *Jay Corgan* • David Keith *Simon Fletcher* • Rita Wilson *Francis Fletcher* • Rebecca De Mornay *Aunt Nina* • John Corbett *Mr Torvald* • Dana Davis *Denise Gilmore* ▪ *Dir* Sean McNamara • *Scr* Sam Schreiber, from a story by Mitch Rotter

A Raisin in the Sun ★★PG
Drama 1961 · US · BW · 122min

Lorraine Hansberry's play opened on Broadway in 1959 and became a smash hit, showing white audiences what it was like to be black, working-class and living in a Chicago tenement. Within that social framework lies a melodrama of family life, built around a son's struggle to achieve some sort of status and independence away from his dominant mother and sister. For the film version, Daniel Petrie slavishly follows every last syllable of dialogue and

stage direction. Though inherently theatrical, it should be viewed in the context of the developing civil rights movement. AT *DVD*

Sidney Poitier *Walter Lee Younger* • Claudia McNeil *Lena Younger* • Ruby Dee *Ruth Younger* • Diana Sands *Beneatha Younger* • Ivan Dixon *Asagai* • John Fiedler *Mark Lindner* • Louis Gossett [Louis Gossett Jr] *George Murchison* ▪ *Dir* Daniel Petrie • *Scr* Lorraine Hansberry, from her play

Raising a Riot ★★U
Comedy 1955 · UK · Colour · 94min

Left to cope with three unruly children during his wife's absence in Canada, naval officer Kenneth More takes his offspring to his father's converted windmill and institutes a strictly ordered regime. Of course, chaos ensues. An inconsequential comedy, kept moving by the polished More, but old-fashioned and rather flat. RK

Kenneth More *Tony* • Shelagh Fraser *Mary* • Mandy Miller (1) *Anne* • Gary Billings *Peter* • Fusty Bentine *Fusty* • Ronald Squire *Grampy* • Olga Lindo *Aunt Maud* • Michael Bentine *Museum official* ▪ *Dir* Wendy Toye • *Scr* Ian Dalrymple, Hugh Perceval, James Matthews, from the novel by Alfred Toombs

Raising Arizona ★★★★12
Comedy 1987 · US · Colour · 90min

A delirious mix of slapstick, surrealism and sentimentality, this film by Joel and Ethan Coen remains one of their warmest, most complete works. Nicolas Cage and Holly Hunter are the couple who decide to kidnap one of a set of famous Arizona quintuplets when they discover they can't have children, only to find themselves pursued by the lone biker of the apocalypse. Cage and Hunter (in her breakthrough role) are superb, and there are winning supporting performances from John Goodman and William Forsythe as two cons on the run. However, in the end it is the dazzling invention of the Coen brothers that shines through. JF Violence, swearing. *DVD*

Nicolas Cage *Hi McDonnough* • Holly Hunter *Edwina* • Trey Wilson *Nathan Arizona Sr* • John Goodman *Gale* • William Forsythe *Evelle* • Frances McDormand *Dot* ▪ *Dir* Joel Coen • *Scr* Ethan Coen, Joel Coen

Raising Cain ★★★★15
Thriller 1992 · US · Colour · 87min

After the mauling he received for his disastrous adaptation of *The Bonfire of the Vanities*, director Brian De Palma returned to his attempts at reinventing Hitchcock. The result was his best movie in years: a sly, witty thriller in which the tortuous plot takes a back seat to a virtuoso display of cinematic technique. John Lithgow, getting into the grisly, over-the-top spirit of the piece, plays a suspect in a series of kidnappings, Lolita Davidovich is his unfaithful wife, and there's solid support from Steven Bauer, Frances Sternhagen and Gregg Henry. JF Swearing. *DVD* *Blu*

John Lithgow *Carter/Cain/Dr Nix/Josh/Margo* • Lolita Davidovich *Jenny* • Steven Bauer *Jack* • Frances Sternhagen *Dr Waldheim* • Gregg Henry *Lieutenant Terri* • Tom Bower *Sergeant Cally* ▪ *Dir/Scr* Brian De Palma

Raising Helen ★★★PG
Romantic comedy drama 2004 · US · Colour · 114min

Kate Hudson stars as a hip, carefree Manhattan model agency employee who gains an instant family when her sister is killed in a car crash. The three children pose problems enough, but adding to Hudson's woes is her mumsy elder sister Joan Cusack, who resents the fact that the kids were not entrusted to her. Helen Mirren features as Hudson's boss, while John Corbett plays the pastor who's the potential love in her life. The material is saved from slush by spirited performances from Hudson and the reliable Cusack. DA *DVD*

Kate Hudson *Helen Harris* • John Corbett *Pastor Dan Parker* • Joan Cusack *Jenny Portman* • Hector Elizondo *Mickey Massey* • Helen Mirren *Dominique* • Hayden Panettiere *Audrey Davis* • Spencer Breslin *Henry Davis* • Abigail Breslin *Sarah Davis* • Felicity Huffman *Lindsay Davis* ▪

Dir Garry Marshall • *Scr* Jack Amiel, Michael Begler, from a story by Patrick J Clifton, Beth Rigazio

Raising the Wind ★★★U
Comedy 1961 · UK · Colour · 87min

Leslie Phillips stars in this laboured but likeable Gerald Thomas comedy as a penniless music student whose talent for writing pop songs while drunk jeopardises his scholarship at a top classical academy until gruff tutor James Robertson-Justice unexpectedly comes to his rescue. These accomplished funnymen go through their usual paces with aplomb, but the film belongs to the delightful Esma Cannon as a deaf landlady, Kenneth Williams as a toffee-nosed swot and Sidney James as the publisher behind Phillips's predicament. DP

James Robertson-Justice *Sir Benjamin* • Leslie Phillips *Mervyn* • Sidney James *Sid* • Paul Massie *Malcolm* • Kenneth Williams *Harold* • Eric Barker *Morgan Rutherford* • Liz Fraser *Miranda* • Esma Cannon *Mrs Deevens* • Jim Dale *Bass trombone player* ▪ *Dir* Gerald Thomas • *Scr* Bruce Montgomery

Raising Victor Vargas ★★★15
Drama 2002 · US/Fr · Colour · 84min

Director Peter Sollet makes a creditable debut with this tale of first love in New York's Lower East Side. The result of extensive workshopping, the performances of the juvenile cast are touchingly authentic, with Victor Rasuk swaggering in the title role as he disses his siblings and seeks to impress neighbour Judy Marte, who is as much amused as seduced by his tactics. However, the standout is Altagracia Guzman, the grandmother who keeps threatening her charges with social services to keep them in line. The ending's a touch too cute, but the overall tone is one of restrained realism. DP *DVD*

Victor Rasuk *Victor Vargas* • Judy Marte *"Juicy"* • Judy Ramirez • Melonie Diaz *Melonie* • Altagracia Guzman *Grandma* • Silvestre Rasuk *Nino Vargas* • Krystal Rodriguez *Vicki Vargas* • Kevin Rivera *Harold* ▪ *Dir* Peter Sollett • *Scr* Peter Sollett, from a story by Peter Sollett, Eva Vives

Raising Waylon ★★
Romantic comedy drama 2004 · NZ/US · Colour · 120min

In this far-fetched yet clichéd romantic comedy drama, two selfish single people have to learn to work together when they unexpectedly become legal guardians of their deceased friends' nine-year-old son. Poppy Montgomery and Thomas Gibson are hard to warm to as the antagonistic duo, as they bicker and banter their way to a predictable conclusion. But it's Jeremy Bergman's overt cockiness as the eponymous orphan that grates most, reducing both the humour and poignancy of his circumstances. However, a shift to more serious parenting issues finally brings some emotional depth, along with the obligatory - though well-meaning - life lessons. SF

Thomas Gibson *Reg* • Poppy Montgomery *Julia* • Jeremy Bergman *Waylon* • Ross Anderson *Mr Myers* • Catherine Boniface *Tracy* • Susan Brady *Terry Allen* ▪ *Dir* Sam Pillsbury • *Scr* Neena Beber

The Rake's Progress ★★★U
Drama 1945 · UK · BW · 115min

The first film produced by Frank Launder and Sidney Gilliat for their Individual Pictures company is a brisk comedy drama that, if not as elegant and sophisticated as it would have us believe, perfectly suits the debonair style of Rex Harrison. His exploits, first as a student at Oxford and then among the upper reaches of polite society, have a jaunty air and provide a nostalgic glimpse of Britain between the wars. Although some of its feel-good aura has diminished, the film still entertains. DP *DVD*

R

Rex Harrison *Vivian Kenway* • Lilli Palmer *Rikki Krausner* • Godfrey Tearle *Colonel Kenway* • Griffith Jones *Sandy Duncan* ■ *Dir* Sidney Gilliat • *Scr* Frank Launder, Sidney Gilliat, from a story by Val Valentine

Rambling Rose ★★★ 15
Romantic comedy drama
1991 · US · Colour · 106min

This neat, rather eccentric movie shines for a while but ends up being rather aptly named. Laura Dern is very good as the sexually precocious girl with a big heart who arrives to work for a rich Southern family surrounded by 1930s poverty. Director Martha Coolidge does play the "whale I do deeclare" card a mite too often, but the movie is saved from parody by Robert Duvall's performance as the clan's kindly patriarch. Dern and her real-life mother Diane Ladd were both rewarded with Oscar nominations. **SH** *DVD*

Laura Dern *Rose* • Robert Duvall *Daddy Hillyer* • Diane Ladd *Mother Hillyer* • Lukas Haas *Buddy Hillyer* • John Heard *Willcox "Buddy" Hillyer* • Kevin Conway *Doctor Martinson* • Robert Burke *Police Chief Dave Wilkie* • Lisa Jakub *Doll Hillyer* ■ *Dir* Martha Coolidge • *Scr* Calder Willingham, from his novel

Rambo: First Blood, Part II ★★★ 15
Action drama   1985 · US · Colour · 91min

This explosive action sequel to 1982's *First Blood* is entertaining, if implausible. Sylvester Stallone flexes his muscles for some cartoon-like heroics, rescuing American prisoners in Vietnam but discovering that he's considered as expendable as the men he's trying to save. All this might be thought laughable, but it comes across as deadly serious and, therefore, rather scary. **TH** Violence, swearing. *DVD* *Blu*

Sylvester Stallone *John Rambo* • Richard Crenna *Colonel Trautman* • Charles Napier *Marshall Murdock* • Steven Berkoff *Lieutenant Podovsky* • Julia Nickson [Julia Nickson-Soul] *Co Bao* ■ *Dir* George Pan Cosmatos • *Scr* Sylvester Stallone, James Cameron, from a story by Kevin Jarre, from characters by David Morrell

Rambo III ★★ 18
Action drama   1988 · US · Colour · 97min

Sylvester Stallone transforms from slightly confused loner to the Free World's white knight. Reluctantly giving up his blissfully mystic life in Thailand (hilariously parodied in *Hot Shots! Part Deux*) to go on one more mission, he seemingly takes on the entire Soviet army in Afghanistan when his old boss (Richard Crenna) is taken prisoner. There's cartoon action by the bucketful, but the mindless celebration of carnage leaves a nasty taste in the mouth. **JF** Violence, swearing. *DVD* *Blu*

Sylvester Stallone *John Rambo* • Richard Crenna *Colonel Trautman* • Marc de Jonge *Colonel Zaysen* • Kurtwood Smith *Griggs* • Spiros Focas *Masoud* ■ *Dir* Peter MacDonald • *Scr* Sylvester Stallone, Sheldon Lettich, from characters by David Morrell

Rambo ★★ 18
Action drama   2007 · Ger/US · Colour · 87min

Sylvester Stallone dons the red bandana for a fourth time in this belated sequel that was also co-written and directed by the 60-something star. Vietnam veteran John Rambo is sent to civil war-torn Burma to rescue a group of earnest American missionaries who've been kidnapped by government soldiers. Trying to sidestep the embarrassing political legacy of *Rambo III* (where Stallone's one-man army fought alongside the Mujahidin in Afghanistan), this film spends little time setting the scene. The only advancements here are Stallone's age and the use of CGI effects to show limbs being ripped from bodies. Racist, sadistic and completely in thrall to the thundering fire of heavy weapons, it's a leadenly un-ironic nostalgia piece that belongs to another era. **JR** Violence. *DVD* *Blu*

Sylvester Stallone *John Rambo* • Julie Benz *Sarah Miller* • Paul Schulze *Dr Michael Burnett* • Matthew Marsden *School Boy* • Graham McTavish *Lewis* • Tim Kang *En-Joo* • Rey

Gallegos *Diaz* ■ *Dir* Sylvester Stallone • *Scr* Sylvester Stallone, Art Monteristelli, from the character created by David Morrell

Ramona and Beezus ★★★ U
Comedy   2010 · US · Colour · 99min

There's something refreshingly old-fashioned about this film's gimmick-free story, which concentrates on imaginative, good-hearted nine-year-old Ramona (Joey King), and her day-to-day trials and tribulations of home, school, getting on with big sis Beezus (Selena Gomez) and wondering if dad's recent redundancy will mean losing their suburban Portland home. True, it's just a bit overlong for junior attention spans, but Ms King's central performance is cute without being precocious, and there's always former *Sex and the City* heart-throb John Corbett (as the world's loveliest daddy) to keep the mums happy. **TJ** Some swearing. *DVD*

Joey King *Ramona Quimby* • Selena Gomez *Beezus Quimby* • John Corbett *Robert Quimby* • Bridget Moynahan *Dorothy Quimby* • Ginnifer Goodwin *Aunt Bea* • Josh Duhamel *Hobart* • Jason Spevack *Howie Kemp* ■ *Dir* Elizabeth Allen • *Scr* Laurie Craig, Nick Pustay, from novels by Beverly Cleary

Rampage ★★ 18
Crime drama   1987 · US · Colour · 96min

This is a story that actually seems to advocate the application of the death penalty - in some cases. Michael Biehn is a prosecutor who desperately wants to get an obviously psychotic killer (Alex McArthur) into the electric chair. Despite his flair for controversy, director William Friedkin doesn't address the complexities of the issue of legal insanity, which forms the basis of the killer's defence. **ST**

Michael Biehn *Anthony Fraser* • Alex McArthur *Charles Reece* • Nicholas Campbell *Albert Morse* • Deborah Van Valkenburgh *Kate Fraser* ■ *Dir* William Friedkin • *Scr* William Friedkin, from the novel by William P Wood

Rampage ★★★ 15
Documentary   2006 · Aus · Colour · 103min

This is a sequel of sorts to *Soundtrack to War*, George Gittoes's raw, exhilarating documentary about young US soldiers and the music that has driven them while on duty in Iraq. This time, the Australian director zooms in on one of the grunts who featured in the first film, charismatic rapper Elliot Lovett. He lives with his equally talented brothers in an arguably even more dangerous war zone: the tough Miami project of Brown Sub. Gittoes offers a gritty indictment of ghetto life and the senseless waste of the talents - and lives - of young African-Americans, although you can't help feeling that he got a little too close to his subjects. **JF** *DVD*

Elliot Lovett • Marcus Lovett • Denzell Lovett • Swizz Beatz • Fat Joe ■ *Dir* George Gittoes

Rampart ★★★★ 15
Crime drama   2011 · US · Colour · 103min

Oren Moverman's film is adapted from an original screenplay by crime writer James Ellroy (*LA Confidential*) and it captures some of the grit and dynamism of the author's hard-boiled style. Key to its strength is a powerhouse performance by Woody Harrelson as Dave Brown, an LAPD cop who is caught on tape beating an African-American suspect. He begins to feel that he is a scapegoat to distract attention from a scandal that's brewing. As a thriller, *Rampart* can be hard going at times, since it suggests a conspiracy that never really materialises. As a character study, though, it is superb, with Harrelson on top form as the tough, cocky antihero, unaware that he's really at the mercy of his own self-sabotaging demons. **DW** Swearing, sex scenes drug abuse, brief nudity. *DVD* *Blu*

Woody Harrelson *Dave Brown* • Ned Beatty *Hartshorn* • Ben Foster *Terry* • Anne Heche *Catherine* • Ice Cube *Kyle Timkins* • Cynthia Nixon *Barbara* • Sigourney Weaver *Joan Confrey* • Robin Wright *Linda Fentress* ■ *Dir* Oren Moverman • *Scr* Oren Moverman, James Ellroy, from an idea by Ellroy

Ramrod ★★★ PG
Western   1947 · US · BW · 90min

War on the range, as sultry ranch owner Veronica Lake stakes her personal claim to land owned by her weak-willed father Charlie Ruggles, who's selling out to baddie Preston Foster. Joel McCrea's the titular ramrod (or ranch foreman) in this tense and violent western directed by Lake's then husband, the talented Andre De Toth. The stark black-and-white photography, the presence of disenfranchised characters and Lake's *femme fatale*-like portrayal lend this the look of a western *film noir*. **TS** *DVD*

Veronica Lake *Connie Dickason* • Joel McCrea *Dave Nash* • Ian MacDonald *Walt Shipley* • Charles Ruggles *Ben Dickason* • Preston Foster *Frank Ivey* • Arleen Whelan *Rose* • Lloyd Bridges *Red Cates* ■ *Dir* Andre De Toth • *Scr* Jack Moffitt, Graham Baker, Cecile Kramer, from a story by Luke Short

Rams ★★★ 15
Drama   2015 · Ice/Den/Nor/Pol · Colour · 92min

An award winner at Cannes, this Icelandic oddity tells the story of two sheep-rearing rivals who haven't spoken to each other in 40 years - quite a feat considering they're also brothers and neighbours in a remote hinterland. Director Grimur Hakonarson's tragicomic look at a threat to their ancient livelihood is informed by his intimate knowledge of the area. Credible, hilarious and poignant by turns, *Rams* is a keenly detailed, well-paced and entertaining tale heightened by two of Iceland's most respected actors. **KK** Icelandic +subtitles. Swearing. *DVD*

Sigurdur Sigurjonsson *Gummi* • Theodor Juliusson *Kiddi* • Charlotte Boving *Katrin* • Jon Benonysson *Runolfur* • Gunnar Jonsson *Grimur* ■ *Dir/Scr* Grimur Hakonarson

Ran ★★★★★ 12
Epic drama   1985 · Jpn/Fr · Colour · 155min

Having reworked *Macbeth* in *Throne of Blood*, Akira Kurosawa tackled another Shakespearean tragedy, *King Lear*, in this majestic epic, in which a ruler's decision to partition his land between his sons plunges his realm into civil war. There is so much to admire here, but special mention must be made of Kurosawa's genius as a storyteller and his masterly movement of the camera (particularly in the stunning battle sequences), the remarkable performances of Tatsuya Nakadai as the repentant monarch and Mieko Harada as his machiavellian daughter-in-law, and the sumptuous use of colour and period detail by production designers Yoshiro and Shinobu Muraki. A true classic. **DP** Japanese +subtitles. Violence. *DVD* *Blu*

Tatsuya Nakadai *Lord Hidetora* • Akira Terao *Taro* • Jinpachi Nezu *Jiro* • Daisuke Ryu *Saburo* • Mieko Harada *Lady Kaede* • Peter Kyoami *The Fool* • Hisashi Igawa *Kurogane* • Masayuki Yui *Tango* • Yoshiko Miyazaki *Lady Sué* ■ *Dir* Akira Kurosawa • *Scr* Akira Kurosawa, Hideo Oguni, Masato Ide, from the play *King Lear* by William Shakespeare

Rancho Deluxe ★★★ 15
Comedy western   1975 · US · Colour · 89min

This is not so much a modern buddy-buddy western as a younger generation nose-thumbing at the traditions of the range. Jeff Bridges and Sam Waterston star as disdainful young cattle rustlers who rightly end up behind bars but for the wrong reasons. Director Frank Perry's overwrought style is tightly reined in this time to make the most of the humour and the heroes, while cowboy specialist Thomas McGuane's screenplay is a joy. **TH** Swearing, nudity. *DVD*

Jeff Bridges *Jack McKee* • Sam Waterston *Cecil Colson* • Elizabeth Ashley *Cora Brown* • Charlene Dallas *Laura Beige* • Clifton James *John Brown* • Slim Pickens *Henry Beige* • Harry Dean Stanton *Curt* ■ *Dir* Frank Perry • *Scr* Thomas McGuane

Rancho Notorious ★★★ PG
Western   1952 · US · Colour · 85min

This ridiculously over-the-top western has developed quite a cult following. There is pleasure to be had from watching Marlene Dietrich past her prime, running a hole in the wall called "Chuck-a-Luck" and being romanced by louche Mel Ferrer. But director Fritz Lang's hand falls heavy on the proceedings, and the cheap studio settings don't help. The dialogue occasionally sparkles and writer Daniel Taradash knows how to create and embellish a legend. **TS** *DVD*

Marlene Dietrich *Altar Keane* • Arthur Kennedy *Vern Haskell* • Mel Ferrer *Frenchy Fairmont* • Gloria Henry *Beth* • William Frawley *Baldy Gunder* • Jack Elam *Geary* • George Reeves *Wilson* ■ *Dir* Fritz Lang • *Scr* Daniel Taradash, from the story *Gunsight Whitman* by Sylvia Richards

Rancid Aluminium ★ 18
Comedy thriller   1999 · UK · Colour · 87min

James Hawes brings his own cult novel to the screen with unengaging characters and incoherent plotting to match the unappetising title. Rhys Ifans is so preoccupied with his low sperm count and broody girlfriend (Sadie Frost), that he naively allows scheming buddy Joseph Fiennes to embroil him in a deadly partnership with a pair of cartoonish Russian gangsters (Steven Berkoff and Tara FitzGerald). This coarse, cluttered caper has lots of nudity and sex but little will. **AME** Violence, swearing, drug abuse. *DVD*

Joseph Fiennes *Sean Deeny* • Rhys Ifans *Pete Thompson* • Tara FitzGerald *Masha* • Sadie Frost *Sarah* • Steven Berkoff *Mr Kant* • Keith Allen *Dr Jones* • Dani Behr *Charlie* • Andrew Howard *Trevor* ■ *Dir* Ed Thomas • *Scr* James Hawes, from his novel

Random Harvest ★★★★ U
Romance   1942 · US · BW · 126min

This is, rightly, one of the best-loved and best-remembered movies of all time, teaming two of MGM's most romantic stars, Ronald Colman and Greer Garson, in a superb James Hilton story. Genuinely moving under Mervyn LeRoy's masterly direction, and produced with all the wartime gloss MGM could muster, this film regularly seduces generation after cynical generation. If you're not totally hooked when Colman doesn't return to Garson after his trip to Liverpool, you've no soul. This is clever, gracious and superbly satisfying. **TS**

Ronald Colman *Charles Rainier* • Greer Garson *Paula* • Philip Dorn *Dr Jonathan Benet* • Susan Peters *Kitty* • Reginald Owen *Biffer* • Henry Travers *Dr Sims* • Edmund Gwenn *Prime Minister* • Margaret Wycherly *Mrs Deventer* ■ *Dir* Mervyn LeRoy • *Scr* Claudine West, George Froeschel, Arthur Wimperis, from the novel by James Hilton

Random Hearts ★★★ 15
Romantic drama   1999 · US · Colour · 127min

When Washington cop Harrison Ford and Republican congresswoman Kristin Scott Thomas discover that their respective spouses have died in the same plane crash, the couple are drawn together over the realisation that their partners were having an affair. Sydney Pollack directs with real skill, convincingly portraying the emotional complications of middle-aged passion, and is aided by the marvellous performances of Ford and Scott Thomas, though the action sequences often seem out of tune with the romance. **TH** Violence, swearing, a sex scene. *DVD*

Harrison Ford *Dutch Van Den Broeck* • Kristin Scott Thomas *Kay Chandler* • Charles S Dutton *Alcee* • Bonnie Hunt *Wendy Judd* • Dennis Haysbert *Detective George Beaufort* • Sydney Pollack *Carl Broman* • Peter Coyote *Cullen Chandler* • M Emmet Walsh *Bartender at Billy's* ■ *Dir* Sydney Pollack • *Scr* Kurt Luedtke, from the novel by Warren Adler

Randy Rides Alone ★★ U
Western   1934 · US · BW · 52min

One of the more entertaining of John Wayne's Monogram Studio westerns

R

features not only the Duke singing (well, pretending to: he's dubbed by cowboy crooner Smith Ballew) but also starting on a chilling note – Wayne rides into a deserted town and finds a saloon full of dead men. The mystery is quite well sustained for what is no more than a B-western. **TS** *DVD*

John Wayne *Randy Bowers* • Alberta Vaughn *Sally Rogers* • George "Gabby" Hayes *Matt the Mute/Marvin Black* • Yakima Canutt *Spike* • Earl Dwire *Sheriff* ■ *Dir* Harry Fraser • *Scr* Lindsley Parsons, from his story

Rang De Basanti ★★★★ 15
Comedy drama　　2006 · Ind · Colour · 160min

When a young Londoner (Alice Patten) travels to Delhi to make a documentary about India's struggle for independence from the British, she has no idea what impact her film will have on the amateur actors that she hires. Displaying more vitality and genuine passion here than in any big-budget Bollywood extravaganza, director Rakesh Omprakash Mehra deserves great praise for progressing this initially intimate tale of heart-warming romance and camaraderie into an intense and powerfully epic treatise on how corruption and religious bigotry – so rampant in modern India – can turn patriots into killers. **OA** Hindi, English +subtitles. *DVD*

Aamir Khan *DJ/Chandrashekhar Azad* • Siddharth *Karan/Bhagat Singh* • Sharman Joshi *Sukhi/Rajguru* • Kunal Kapoor *Aslam/Ashfaqullah* • Atul Kulkarni *Laxman Pandey/Ramprasad Bismil* • Alice Patten *Sue* • Soha Ali Khan *Sonia/Durga Vohra* ■ *Dir* Rakesh Omprakash Mehra • *Scr* Rakesh Omprakash Mehra, Rensil D'Silva, from a story by Kamlesh Pandey

Rango ★★★ PG
Animated western adventure
2011 · US · Colour · 102min

A word to the wise. The pop-eyed poster may scream "child-friendly", but much of *Rango*'s humour, its angsty introspection and its wealth of western clichés may well go right over younger heads. One thing is for sure, though – this is one weird western. Johnny Depp voices Rango, a self-questioning chameleon who winds up sheriff of a drought-stricken town in a "critterised" Wild West that oddly, and no doubt metaphorically, sits cheek by jowl with a modern-day world of humans, motorways and big cities. It's all technically brilliant, but maybe lacking a little in charm and wit. **DA** *DVD*

Johnny Depp *Rango* • Isla Fisher *Beans* • Abigail Breslin *Priscilla* • Ned Beatty *Mayor* • Alfred Molina *Roadkill* • Bill Nighy *Rattlesnake Jake* • Harry Dean Stanton *Balthazar* • Ray Winstone *Bad Bill* ■ *Dir* Gore Verbinski • *Scr* John Logan, from a story by Gore Verbinski, James Ward Byrkit, Logan

Ransom! ★★★
Crime drama　　1956 · US · BW · 109min

During the 1950s Glenn Ford averaged three films a year. Mainly westerns and thrillers, they gave the stern-faced star angst-ridden roles on both sides of the law. Here he is in trouble as the wealthy father of a boy who has been kidnapped. In a novel idea for the period, he contacts the abductors on television, offering the ransom for their capture and threatening to kill them if they harm his son. Originally made for television, it's the inspiration for Mel Gibson's 1996 film. **BB**

Glenn Ford *David G Stannard* • Donna Reed *Edith Stannard* • Leslie Nielsen *Charlie Telfer* • Juano Hernandez *Jesse Chapman* • Robert Keith (1) *Chief Jim Backett* • Mabel Albertson *Mrs Partridge* ■ *Dir* Alex Segal • *Scr* Cyril Hume, Richard Maibaum

Ransom ★ PG
Action drama　　1975 · UK · Colour · 89min

This lamely directed and badly written drama about international terrorism is a rare dud from Sean Connery. He plays a security chief tackling a ransom demand for a kidnapped British ambassador while also dealing with a hijacked plane. Confusion reigns for most of the time, and that's just among the cast – so the audience will have

virtually no chance of following the plot. **AT** *DVD* *BL*

Sean Connery *Nils Tahlvik* • Ian McShane *Petrie* • Norman Bristow *Captain Denver* • John Cording *Bert* • Robert Harris *Gerald Palmer* • Isabel Dean *Mrs Palmer* ■ *Dir* Casper Wrede • *Scr* Paul Wheeler

Ransom ★★★ 18
Action thriller　　1996 · US · Colour · 116min

In this entertaining remake of a 1956 Glenn Ford thriller, Mel Gibson stars as a maverick tycoon who must decide whether to pay a $2 million ransom for his kidnapped son or take the law into his own hands. There are no prizes for guessing the *Die Hard*-style avenue Gibson takes, but his method of action is an interesting one. The film suffers overall under Ron Howard's unusually starchy direction and Rene Russo is wasted as Gibson's concerned wife, but Gary Sinise gives his villainous role a few wry twists. **AJ** *DVD*

Mel Gibson *Tom Mullen* • Rene Russo *Kate Mullen* • Gary Sinise *Jimmy Shaker* • Brawley Nolte *Sean Mullen* • Delroy Lindo *Agent Lonnie Hawkins* • Lili Taylor *Maris Connor* • Liev Schreiber *Clark Barnes* ■ *Dir* Ron Howard • *Scr* Richard Price, Alexander Ignon, from the 1956 film

Ransom for a Dead Man ★★★ PG
Detective mystery　　1971 · US · Colour · 91min

Four years after he first played Lieutenant Columbo in the TV movie *Prescription: Murder*, Peter Falk reprised the role in this pilot for the long-running TV series (which was released theatrically in the UK). Based on a story by William Link and Richard Levinson, who created the original character, the tale sees the perceptive detective on the trail of a lawyer who has passed off her rich husband's murder as a kidnap plot. Lee Grant was rewarded with an Emmy nomination for her bravura performance as the lawyer, and Falk is typically sly as he seemingly stumbles towards the solution. **DP** *DVD*

Peter Falk *Lieutenant Columbo* • Lee Grant *Leslie Williams* • John Fink *Michael Clarke* • Harold Gould *Carlson* • Patricia Mattick *Margaret Williams* ■ *Dir* Richard Irving • *Scr* Dean Hargrove, from a story by Richard Levinson, William Link

Rapa Nui ★ 12
Drama　　1994 · US · Colour · 102min

The *moai*, the huge stone faces that dominate the landscape of Easter Island, make a hugely tempting topic for a film-maker. How did they get there? Who made them? What purpose did they serve? Kevin Reynolds succumbed to the temptation of the tale, but the result is an insulting concoction. Crass and ridiculous. **DP** Violence, nudity.

Jason Scott Lee *Noro* • Esai Morales *Make* • Sandrine Holt *Ramana* • Emilio Tuki *Hito Messenger* • Gordon Hatfield *Riro* • Faenza Reuben *Heke* ■ *Dir* Kevin Reynolds • *Scr* Tim Rose Price, Kevin Reynolds, from a story by Reynolds

The Rape of Aphrodite ★★★
Drama　　1985 · Cyp · Colour · 150min

This sweeping study of 30 years of the country's turbulent history was one of the first Cypriot films to attract international attention. Costas Timvios stars as a former member of the Greek Cypriot terrorist group EOKA, who dedicates his life to searching for his wife and child who vanished during the 1974 Turkish invasion that resulted in the island being partitioned. It's obviously an emotive story, full of provocative insight, but the director doesn't always keep far enough back from his subject. **DP** Greek +subtitles.

Costas Timvios *Evagoras* • Thalia Argiriou *Aphrodite* • Ilias Aletras *Taxi driver* ■ *Dir/Scr* Andreas Pantzis

The Rape of Richard Beck ★★★★ 18
Drama　　1985 · US · Colour · 91min

Director Karen Arthur has built a reputation for producing powerful films about women who draw on hidden resources to overcome all manner of ailments and abuses. That's why she was the ideal choice for this compelling TV movie in which macho cop Richard Crenna comes to appreciate the hell female sexual assault victims go through when he himself is raped. Crenna won an Emmy for his wonderfully aware performance. **DP** Violence.

Richard Crenna *Richard Beck* • Meredith Baxter Birney [Meredith Baxter] *Barbara McKay* • Pat Hingle *Chappy Beck* • Frances Lee McCain *Caroline Beck* • Cotter Smith *Lieutenant Hugo* • George Dzundza *Blastig* ■ *Dir* Karen Arthur • *Scr* James G Hirsch

Rapid Fire ★★★ 18
Martial arts thriller　　1992 · US · Colour · 91min

Brandon Lee may have lacked the martial arts grace of his father, but there was no denying his charisma, and this serviceable action thriller offered him the opportunity to make the transition from straight-to-video star to a man with genuine box-office appeal. There's not much subtlety involved in this story of a college student who finds himself on the run from villainous Nick Mancuso, but the production values are a notch above the usual B-movie action adventures. **JF** Swearing, sex scenes, nudity. *DVD*

Brandon Lee *Jake Lo* • Powers Boothe *Mace Ryan* • Nick Mancuso *Antonio Serrano* • Raymond J Barry *Agent Stuart* • Kate Hodge *Karla Withers* • Ma Tzi *Kinman Tau* ■ *Dir* Dwight H Little • *Scr* Alan McElroy, from the story by Cindy Cirile, McElroy

Rappin' ★ PG
Drama　　1985 · US · Colour · 88min

In one of the many exploitation films released in the aftermath of the rap, break-dancing and hip-hop explosion, ex-con Mario Van Peebles takes on a crooked property baron who has recruited a gang to bully and evict the tenants from a run-down Pittsburgh ghetto. Van Peebles puts his rhyming skills to good use in this absurdly unrealistic social thriller teeming with offensive action and ludicrous stereotypes. **AJ** *DVD*

Mario Van Peebles *John Hood* • Tasia Valenza *Dixie* • Charles Flohe *Duane* • Leo O'Brien *Allan* • Eriq La Salle *Ice* • Richie Abanes *Richie* ■ *Dir* Joel Silberg • *Scr* Robert Litz, Adam Friedman

Rapt ★★★ 15
Crime drama　　2009 · Fr/Bel · Colour · 120min

Writer/director Lucas Belvaux' brutal yet compelling abduction drama sees tycoon Yvan Attal snatched the day before he is due to visit China with the French president. Attal is kept in isolation (minus a fingertip) and with each hour of incarceration he becomes further convinced that wife Anne Consigny has discovered his reckless double life, while his company's board debates whether he is worth the large ransom demanded by his kidnappers. Depicting Attal's plight in excruciating detail, Belvaux also examines the family's humiliation and the role played by the media in sensationalising the case. **DP** French +subtitles. Violence. *DVD*

Yvan Attal *Stanislas Graff* • Anne Consigny *Françoise Graff* • André Marcon *André Peyrac* • Françoise Fabian *Marjorie* • Alex Descas *Maître Walser* • Michel Voïta *Le Commissaire Paoli* ■ *Dir/Scr* Lucas Belvaux

Rapture ★★★★ 12
Drama　　1965 · US/Fr · BW · 104min

On the windswept Brittany coast, troubled teenager Sylvia Gozzi grows up fast when sailor Dean Stockwell takes refuge in her home, in this seemingly untypical drama from British stalwart John Guillermin. It's an emotive turn from the talented Gozzi and, although the central relationship remains slightly uncomfortable, the storytelling is far from exploitative, Guillermin instead

generating sympathy for the girl overwhelmed by feelings she can barely comprehend. **TJ** In English, French. Some violence.

Melvyn Douglas *Frederick Larbaud* • Patricia Gozzi *Agnes Larbaud* • Dean Stockwell *Joseph* • Gunnel Lindblom *Karen* ■ *Dir* John Guillermin • *Scr* Stanley Mann, from the novel *Rapture in My Rags* by Phyllis Hastings

The Rapture ★★★ 18
Drama　　1991 · US · Colour · 96min

Mimi Rogers reminds us what a fine actress she can be as a bored LA telephone operator and part-time swinger who joins a fundamentalist religious movement that believes the end of the world is nigh. Michael Tolkin makes a striking debut with this admittedly imperfect but also ambitious, challenging and intelligent offering that perfectly captures the conspiratorial creepiness of such zealous religious sects. **RS**

Mimi Rogers *Sharon* • David Duchovny *Randy* • Patrick Bauchau *Vic* • Kimberly Cullum *Mary* • Will Patton *Sheriff Foster* • Terri Hanauer *Paula* ■ *Dir/Scr* Michael Tolkin

The Rare Breed ★★★ U
Western　　1966 · US · Colour · 92min

In this warm-hearted, sprawling western, widow Maureen O'Hara imports a prize Hereford bull to the Old West for breeding purposes. The pleasure's really in watching the languid by-play between O'Hara, lovable drifter James Stewart and rugged cattle baron Brian Keith, and enjoying a supporting cast that looks as if it stepped out of a John Ford movie. Director Andrew V McLaglen brings out the best in his actors, and if it is all a bit jovial and sub-Ford, well, that's no bad thing. **TS** *DVD*

James Stewart *Sam Burnett* • Maureen O'Hara *Martha Price* • Brian Keith *Alexander Bowen* • Juliet Mills *Hilary Price* • Don Galloway *Jamie Bowen* • David Brian *Charles Ellsworth* • Jack Elam *Deke Simons* ■ *Dir* Andrew V McLaglen • *Scr* Ric Hardman

Rare Exports from the Land of the Original Santa Claus ★★★ 15
Action fantasy
2010 · Fin/Nor/Fr/Swe · Colour · 79min

In a feature-length prequel to his two online shorts, Finnish film-maker Jalmari Helander constructs one of the oddest and quirkiest nightmares before Christmas. Lapland legend describes Santa Claus as a horned ancient demon who terrorises children with merciless spanking. So when an American drilling team unearths the mountain tomb of the "Yule Goat", a local boy (Onni Tommila) and a trio of reindeer herders must prevent the festive evil from escaping. Filled with unnerving images (a giant iced Santa) and visually eerie delights, all set against stunning frozen Scandinavian vistas, the overall vibe here is playful fantasy in the *Gremlins* vein. **AJ** Finnish, English +subtitles. Violence, nudity. *DVD* *BL*

Onni Tommila *Pietari* • Jorma Tommila *Rauno, Pietari's father* • Tommi Korpela *Aimo* • Per Christian Ellefsen *Riley* • Peeter Jakobi *Pietari's elf* • Jonathan Hutchings *Greene* ■ *Dir* Jalmari Helander • *Scr* Jalmari Helander, from an idea by Jalmari and Juuso Helander

LANDMARK FILM
Akira Kurosawa experiments with the truth using conflicting flashbacks

Rashomon ★★★★★ 12
Drama　　1950 · Jpn · BW · 87min

Showered with prizes at festivals worldwide, this was the film that introduced western audiences to Japanese cinema. Exploring the relativity of truth, Akira Kurosawa presents four equally credible accounts of the woodland encounter between a wealthy married couple and a bandit that results in the husband's death. The endlessly moving camera, the stylised composition of the shots and the subtly shifting performances enable Kurosawa to challenge the notion that the camera never lies. Machiko Kyo as the wife and Toshiro Mifune as the bandit are superb, but it's Kurosawa's control that makes this exercise in emphasis and atmosphere so mesmerising. Hollywood remade this as *The Outrage* in 1964, starring Paul Newman. DP Japanese +subtitles. DVD BL

Toshiro Mifune *Tajomaru* • Machiko Kyo *Masago* • Masayuki Mori *Takehiro* • Takashi Shimura *Firewood dealer* • Minoru Chiaki *Priest* ■ *Dir* Akira Kurosawa • *Scr* Shinobu Hashimoto, Akira Kurosawa, from the short story *Yabu no Naka* and the novel *Rasho-Mon* by Ryunosuke Akutagawa

Rasputin ★★★★ 15
Biographical drama 1996 · US · Colour · 100min

This Emmy and Golden Globe-winning biopic made for cable by HBO is as far from staid costume television drama as you can get. Alan Rickman is dangerously dynamic as the Mad Monk and spiritual adviser to Russia's royals on the brink of dissolution. He's well matched by Greta Scacchi as Tsarina Alexandra and Ian McKellen as Tsar Nicholas II. This was a huge hit Stateside and while there are historical inaccuracies, it captures the flavour of this often told tale of the enigmatic royals confronting the onset of revolution. LH DVD

Alan Rickman *Rasputin* • Greta Scacchi *Tsarina Alexandra* • Ian McKellen *Tsar Nicholas* • David Warner *Dr Botkin* • John Wood (2) *Stolypin* • James Frain *Prince Yussoupov* ■ *Dir* Uli Edel • *Scr* Peter Pruce

Rasputin and the Empress ★★
Historical drama 1932 · US · BW · 93min

A trio of Barrymores on display: Lionel as the demonic monk, Ethel as the tsarina and John as the nobleman who puts an end to Rasputin's sinister influence. Ethel had not made a picture for 13 years, and, in an effort to please her, Louis B Mayer hired Charles Brabin, who immediately became embroiled in sibling rivalry and John's excessive drinking. After a month of delays, Brabin was replaced by Richard Boleslawski. The resulting overlong stodge caused fireworks at MGM's legal department when surviving members of Russia's aristocracy claimed they were misrepresented in the film. AT

John Barrymore *Prince Paul Chegodieff* • Ethel Barrymore *Empress Alexandra* • Lionel Barrymore *Rasputin* • Ralph Morgan *Emperor Nikolai* • Diana Wynyard *Natasha* • Tad Alexander *Alexis* • C Henry Gordon *Grand Duke Igor* ■ *Dir* Richard Boleslawski • *Scr* Charles MacArthur

Rasputin, the Mad Monk ★★★ 15
Horror 1965 · UK · Colour · 87min

Christopher Lee's commanding presence is splendidly suited to his role here as the lecherous mystic who dominated the Romanov court of pre-revolutionary Russia and carved a debauched path through its ladies-in-waiting. But, although it was an intriguing change of pace for Hammer, with stylish studio regular Barbara Shelley present and correct as a different sort of scream queen, the tale eventually degenerates into wild-eyed hysteria. TH Violence. DVD BL

Christopher Lee *Rasputin* • Barbara Shelley *Sonia* • Richard Pasco *Dr Zargo* • Francis Matthews *Ivan* • Suzan Farmer *Vanessa* • Joss Ackland *Bishop* ■ *Dir* Don Sharp • *Scr* John Elder [Anthony Hinds]

Rat ★★★ PG
Fantasy comedy 2000 · UK/US · Colour · 87min

In this barbed Irish fantasy, Dubliner Pete Postlethwaite metamorphoses into a rodent. Had the focus remained on the socio-political circumstances that wrought this astonishing transformation, the film might have been even sharper. But there's still much to amuse and contemplate, as journalist David Wilmot tempts Imelda Staunton into exploiting her husband's unexpected celebrity. Slight, but mischievously satirical. DP DVD

Imelda Staunton *Conchita Flynn* • Pete Postlethwaite *Hubert Flynn* • David Wilmot *Phelim Spratt* • Frank Kelly *Uncle Matt* • Ed Byrne *Rudolph* • Geoffrey Palmer *Doctor* ■ *Dir* Steve Barron • *Scr* Wesley Burrowes

The Rat Pack ★★★ 15
Biographical drama 1998 · US · Colour · 114min

Ray Liotta as Frank Sinatra, Joe Mantegna as Dean Martin, Don Cheadle as Sammy Davis Jr and Angus MacFadyen as Peter Lawford. You don't really believe it's them until they go on stage at one of JFK's fundraisers and sing *High Hopes* and the movie snaps into gear. The pulse of the era is beautifully evoked in this TV film that explores Sinatra's twin links to the Mob and to Jack and Robert Kennedy. AT Violence, swearing, a sex scene. DVD

Ray Liotta *Frank Sinatra* • Joe Mantegna *Dean Martin* • Don Cheadle *Sammy Davis Jr* • Angus MacFadyen *Peter Lawford* • William L Petersen *John F Kennedy* • Zeljko Ivanek *Bobby Kennedy* • Bobby Slayton *Joey Bishop* ■ *Dir* Rob Cohen • *Scr* Kario Salem

Rat Pfink a Boo Boo ★★ 18
Spoof comedy thriller 1965 · US · BW · 69min

Trash film-maker Ray Dennis Steckler intended this film as a "roughie" (a sexploitation picture with violence) in which hoodlums kidnap the girlfriend (Steckler's real-life wife Carolyn Brandt) of rock singer Vin Saxon (alias real-life rock singer Ron Haydock). This, the first section of the film, is an adequate melodrama. Then, inexplicably, Saxon and his superhero (Titus Moede) turn into comic book superheroes and the plot disentegrates into a desperately unfunny spoof of *Batman*. Famously, the title came about when "Rat Pfink and Boo Boo" was accidentally misspelled. DM

Vin Saxon [Ron Haydock] *Lonnie Lord/Rat Pfink* • Titus Moede *Titus Twimbly/Boo Boo* • Carolyn Brandt *Cee Bee Beaumont* • George Caldwell *Linc* • Mike Kannon *Hammer* • James Bowie *Benjie* ■ *Dir* Ray Dennis Steckler • *Scr* Ronald Haydock, from a story by Ray Dennis Steckler

The Rat Race ★★
Comedy 1960 · US · Colour · 105min

Saxophone player Tony Curtis arrives from the sticks in New York, moves into a run-down tenement boarding house, and tries to make a career in the sleazy nightclub run by Don Rickles. He's just an inch away from crime and a bit closer to Debbie Reynolds, a dance-hall "hostess". This is Hollywood's idea of what a Beat movie should be like; the settings are picturesquely drab and Elmer Bernstein contributes a racy score but Curtis and Reynolds are much too clean-looking to be convincing. AT

Tony Curtis *Peter Hammond Jr* • Debbie Reynolds *Peggy Brown* • Jack Oakie *Mac* • Kay Medford *Soda* • Don Rickles *Nellie* • Joe Bushkin *Frankie* ■ *Dir* Robert Mulligan • *Scr* Garson Kanin, from his play

Rat Race ★★★ 12
Comedy 2001 · US/Can · Colour · 107min

This is an infectiously silly comedy packed with celebrities and gags. John Cleese – complete with the maddest set of dentures ever seen on film – is the billionaire casino owner who decides to give his high-rolling gamblers something unusual to bet on: the outcome of a race from Las Vegas to a locker a few hundred miles away in New Mexico that just happens to contain $2 million. A group of ordinary people are given the chance to get their hands on the loot – the only rule being that whoever gets there first, takes the cash. A fun, old-fashioned chase movie. JB DVD

Whoopi Goldberg *Vera Baker* • John Cleese *Donald Sinclair* • Cuba Gooding Jr *Owen Templeton* • Rowan Atkinson *Enrico Pollini* • Jon Lovitz *Randy Pear* • Kathy Najimy *Beverly Pear* • Amy Smart *Tracy Faucet* ■ *Dir* Jerry Zucker • *Scr* Andy Breckman

Ratatouille ★★★★ U
Animated comedy 2007 · US · Colour · 106min

A country rat (voiced by stand-up comedian Oswalt Patton) with a gift for *haute cuisine*

ends up saving the soup – and the job – of a young garbage boy (voiced by Lou Romano) working at Paris's finest restaurant. A wee bit on the long side at 110 minutes, this fast-moving, wholesome comedy from Pixar nevertheless has some absolutely brilliant comic turns. And the highlight: Peter O'Toole as Atom Ego, the tough bitter restaurant critic, who just happens to look like Will Self. Working with a tight, well-considered script and sensational animation that make you want to go home and cook as well as be nicer to rodents, directors Brad Bird and Jan Pinkava have delivered the best family comedy of the year. KK DVD BL CS

Patton Oswalt *Remy* • Ian Holm *Skinner* • Lou Romano *Linguini* • Brian Dennehy *Django* • John Ratzenberger *Mustafa* • Peter O'Toole *Anton Ego* • Brad Garrett *Auguste Gusteau* • Janeane Garofalo *Colette* • Will Arnett *Horst* • James Remar *LaRousse* ■ *Dir/Scr* Brad Bird

Ratboy ★★ PG
Drama 1986 · US · Colour · 99min

Sondra Locke directs and stars in yet another tale of an exploited misfit. This time it's a half boy, half rat creature (SL Baird) and again we have the archetypal outsider being exposed and promoted as a weird commercial fairground attraction. Plucked from the comfort of his Hollywood rubbish dump into a media circus, Ratboy is "rescued" by Locke, who has her own plans to exploit her protégé. LH

Sondra Locke *Nikki Morrison* • Robert Townsend *Manny* • Christopher Hewett *Acting coach* • Larry Hankin *Jewell* • Sydney Lassick *"Dial-a-Prayer"* • SL Baird *Ratboy* ■ *Dir* Sondra Locke • *Scr* Rob Thompson

Ratcatcher ★★★★ 15
Drama 1999 · UK · Colour · 93min

Lynne Ramsay made her feature debut with this unsentimental portrait of growing up in Glasgow in the 1970s. Achieving a lyrical realism that often recalls Jean Vigo's 1934 classic *L'Atalante*, Ramsay manages to turn a run-down housing estate at the height of a refuse strike into fertile ground for the imagination of 12-year-old William Eadie (giving a remarkably natural performance), as a neglected scallywag forced to bear the burden of accidentally drowning his friend in the canal. Assured and affecting. DP Swearing, nudity. DVD

William Eadie *James* • Tommy Flanagan *Da* • Mandy Matthews *Ma* • Michelle Stewart *Ellen* • Lynne Ramsay Jr *Anne Marie* • Leanne Mullen *Margaret Anne* • John Miller (4) *Kenny* ■ *Dir/Scr* Lynne Ramsay

Ratchet & Clank ★★ U
Animated comedy adventure 2016 · US · Colour · 90min

Based on the video game of the same name, this brash and workmanlike CG spin-off sees wily super-mechanic Ratchet and robot buddy Clank joining the heroic Galactic Rangers to tackle planet-destroying baddy Drek. For those not familiar with gaming, at least the plot references everything from *Stars Wars* to *Guardians of the Galaxy*, though with neither the charm nor quality of those influences. Snappy dialogue and fast pacing keep things lively, but essentially, this is a video game you can't play. DA DVD 3D

James Arnold Taylor *Ratchet* • David Kaye *Clank* • Jim Ward *Captain Qwark* • Rosario Dawson *Elaris* • Paul Giamatti *Chairman Drek* • John Goodman *Grimroth* • Armin Shimerman *Dr Nefarious* • Sylvester Stallone *Victor Von Ion* ■ *Dir* Kevin Munroe, Jerrica Cleland • *Scr* Kevin Munroe, TJ Fixman, Gerry Swallow, from a computer game by Insomniac Games

Rated X ★★ 18
Biographical drama 2000 · US · Colour · 109min

Emilio Estevez's fact-mangling odyssey through the sleazy showbiz excesses of the 1970s has all the class and conviction of a teleplay. Yet, there's a ghoulish fascination in watching him and brother Charlie Sheen portray Jim and Artie Mitchell, the feuding, drug-addled siblings that transformed the

American porn industry with their "sophisticated" soft core. This untidy film leaves you hoping the story will eventually be revisited by a steadier hand. DP DVD

Charlie Sheen *Artie Mitchell* • Emilio Estevez *Jim Mitchell* • Tracy Hutson *Marilyn Chambers* • Megan Ward *Meredith* • Terry O'Quinn *JR Mitchell* • Danielle Brett *Adrienne* • Nicole de Boer *Karen Mitchell* ■ *Dir* Emilio Estevez • *Scr* David Hollander, Anne Meredith, Norman Snider, from the non-fiction book *X-Rated: The Mitchell Brothers, a True Story of Sex, Money and Death* by David McCumber

The Rats ★★★
Drama 1955 · W Ger · BW · 97min

Hollywood exile and *film noir* expert Robert Siodmak returned to his native Germany to make this drama about a refugee from the East who gives her newborn baby to a childless woman from the West. As an allegory, it may now seem exceptionally crude but in 1955, when the still bombed-out Berlin was divided into four militarised zones, it carried enormous weight – indeed, the film won the main prize at the Berlin film festival. AT In German.

Curt Jurgens *Bruno Mechelke* • Maria Schell *Pauline Karka* • Heidemarie Hatheyer *Anna John* • Gustav Knuth *Karl John* ■ *Dir* Robert Siodmak • *Scr* Jochen Huth, from a play by Gerhart Hauptmann

Rattle of a Simple Man ★★ 15
Comedy drama 1964 · UK · BW · 91min

Harry H Corbett strays into Norman Wisdom territory in this disappointing comedy from the husband-and-wife team of Sydney and Muriel Box. In adapting his play for the big screen, Charles Dyer so overdoes the pathos that what few laughs there are seem rather cruel and out of place. As the innocent following his football team to Wembley, Corbett is unconvincingly wide-eyed, although his scenes with prostitute Diane Cilento have a certain sweetness about them. DP DVD

Harry H Corbett *Percy Winthram* • Diane Cilento *Cyrenne* • Thora Hird *Mrs Winthram* • Michael Medwin *Ginger* • Charles Dyer *Chalky* • Hugh Futcher *Ozzie* • Brian Wilde *Fred* ■ *Dir* Muriel Box • *Scr* Charles Dyer, from his play

The Raven ★★★★ 15
Horror 1935 · US · BW · 58min

The second of Universal's horror vehicles to co-star Bela Lugosi and Boris Karloff is an unusually sadistic slice of shock from the Golden Age of *Grand Guignol*. Lugosi plays a crazed surgeon obsessed with the works of Edgar Allan Poe, who builds a dungeon with torture devices inspired by the writer. Karloff is the scarred criminal he promises to fix surgically if he carries out a few murderous tasks. Remarkably scripted, this vintage horror show, combining both the striking imagery and mournfully beautiful poetry of Poe, is brought to startling life by performances of twisted ferocity. AJ DVD

Karloff [Boris Karloff] *Edmond Bateman* • Bela Lugosi *Dr Richard Vollin* • Lester Matthews *Dr Jerry Halden* • Irene Ware *Jean Thatcher* • Samuel S Hinds *Judge Thatcher* ■ *Dir* Louis Friedlander [Lew Landers] • *Scr* David Boehm, from the poem by Edgar Allan Poe

The Raven ★★★★ PG
Mystery thriller 1943 · Fr · BW · 87min

Such was the hostility levelled at this excoriating study of French provincial life that, on the Liberation, Henri-Georges Clouzot was accused of peddling collaborationist propaganda and banned from directing until 1947. Subsequently, this atmospheric thriller, about a poison-pen campaign that exposes the malicious hypocrisy simmering beneath the respectable surface of a tightly knit community, was reclaimed as an indictment of the paranoia that existed under the Nazi occupation. A riveting whodunnit, thanks to exceptional ensemble playing and Clouzot's claustrophobic staging, this was remade in 1950 by Otto Preminger as *The 13th Letter*. DP French +subtitles. DVD

Pierre Fresnay *Dr Germain* • Ginette Leclerc *Denise Saillens* • Pierre Larquey *Vorzet* • Micheline Francey *Laura Vorzet* ■ *Dir* Henri-Georges Clouzot • *Scr* Louis Chavance, Henri-Georges Clouzot

The Raven ★★★★ PG
Comedy horror 1963 · US · Colour · 84min

The most flippant of Roger Corman's Edgar Allan Poe cycle, this is, nevertheless, a minor B-movie classic, and a cast containing Vincent Price, Boris Karloff, Peter Lorre and a young Jack Nicholson alone makes it a must-see. There's also a script littered with throwaway one-liners and some unashamedly home-made special effects that add considerably to the charm of this beautifully pitched gothic romp. As the duelling masters of the black arts, Price and Karloff selflessly send up their screen images, but it's Lorre's performance of tipsy incompetence that endures. DP *DVD*

Vincent Price *Dr Erasmus Craven* • Peter Lorre *Dr Adolphus Bedlo* • Boris Karloff *Dr Scarabus* • Hazel Court *Lenore Craven* • Olive Sturgess *Estelle Craven* • Jack Nicholson *Rexford Bedlo* ■ *Dir* Roger Corman • *Scr* Richard Matheson, from the poem by Edgar Allan Poe in *American Review*

The Raven ★★★ 15
Period thriller 2012 · US/Hun/Sp Colour · 106min

This atmospheric period thriller focuses on a serial killer at large in 19th-century Baltimore. The twist here is that each slaying echoes grisly fictional deaths from the writings of local author Edgar Allan Poe (John Cusack). After being eliminated as a suspect, Poe lends his expertise to the investigation, but is drawn further into the killer's web when his fiancée is taken hostage. The movie starts as an intriguing spin on a standard police procedural yarn, full of vivid references to Poe's celebrated work, but tends to lose momentum and falls back on predictable plot twists. Cusack is eminently watchable as the boozy, perpetually broke Poe, but a touch more suspense would have been welcome. TeS Violence, swearing. *DVD*

John Cusack *Edgar Allan Poe* • Luke Evans *Detective Emmett Fields* • Alice Eve *Emily Hamilton* • Brendan Gleeson *Colonel Hamilton* • Kevin R McNally [Kevin McNally] *Henry Maddox* • Oliver Jackson-Cohen *John Cantrell* • Pam Ferris *Mrs Bradley* • Jimmy Yuill *Captain Eldridge* ■ *Dir* James McTeigue • *Scr* Hannah Shakespeare, Ben Livingston

Ravenous ★★★★ 18
Period black comedy horror 1999 · US/UK · Colour · 96min

Priest director Antonia Bird's stunning mix of gut-spilling gore and *Carry On*-style banter is a shocker that you'll either love for its edgy tone, or absolutely hate because it's so in-your-face. Inspired by the tragic Donner Pass disaster of 1846-7, the film stars Robert Carlyle as a devious maneater, decimating the inhabitants of a mountain outpost to keep human flesh on his winter menu. Bird's highly disturbing and thought-provoking film features a couple of impeccable performances. Carlyle etches the strongest portrait of pure evil since Anthony Hopkins in *The Silence of the Lambs*, while Guy Pearce is equally brilliant as the army captain who tries to stop his bloodthirsty exploits. AJ Swearing. *DVD*

Robert Carlyle *Colqhoun/Ives* • Guy Pearce *Captain John Boyd* • David Arquette *Cleaves* • Jeremy Davies *Private Toffler* • Jeffrey Jones *Colonel Hart* • John Spencer *Gen Slauson* ■ *Dir* Antonia Bird • *Scr* Ted Griffin

Raven's End ★★★
Drama 1963 · Swe · BW · 100min

Lauded at the time for its realism, Bo Widerberg's Oscar-nominated second feature is actually more notable for the economy of its storytelling. Constantly underplaying key events, Widerberg forces us to concentrate on the characters enduring the harsh conditions that existed in Malmö during the 1930s. Thommy Berggren is ingratiatingly feckless as the budding novelist deliberating whether to break for freedom or accept the responsibility to his pregnant girlfriend. But the star turn is Keve Hjelm's drunken, workshy father. DP Swedish +subtitles.

Thommy Berggren *Anders* • Keve Hjelm *Father* • Emy Storm *Mother* • Ingvar Hirdwall *Sixten* • Christina Frambäck *Elsie* ■ *Dir/Scr* Bo Widerberg

A Ravishing Idiot ★★ PG
Spy comedy 1964 · Fr/It · BW · 06/05/2006min

Any espionage comedy in which the female spy's codename is 0038-24-36 is clearly desperate for laughs and Edouard Molinaro's clumsy romp lurches from one unfunnily forced situation to another. Brigitte Bardot stars in this James Bond spoof, but it's not her finest hour. Neither is it Anthony Perkins's - he mugs shamelessly as agrees to steal some Nato naval documents for Soviet spymaster Grégoire Aslan. DP French +subtitles. *DVD*

Brigitte Bardot *Penelope Lightfeather* • Anthony Perkins *Harry Compton/Nicholas Maukouline* • Grégoire Aslan *Bagda* • Jean-Marc Tennberg *Cartwright* • Hélène Dieudonné *Mamie* • Jacques Monod *Surgeon* • André Luguet *Sir Reginald Dumfrey* ■ *Dir* Edouard Molinaro • *Scr* Edouard Molinaro, André Tabet, Georges Tabet, from the novel *Une Ravissante Idiote* by Charles Exbrayat

Raw Deal ★★★★
Film noir 1948 · US · BW · 78min

This smashing, low-budget thriller is photographed by John Alton so as to disguise the lack of money for sets by plunging whole areas of the screen into mysterious, menacing blackness. In and out of these voids stalk and flee some desperate characters - including gangster Dennis O'Keefe on the run from jail and aiming to kill the man who framed him, Raymond Burr. Marsha Hunt is his hostage and Claire Trevor is O'Keefe's girlfriend who helped him escape and who narrates the movie like an ode to the dead. A masterly exercise in atmospherics and tension from Anthony Mann. AJ

Dennis O'Keefe *Joe Sullivan* • Claire Trevor *Pat Regan* • Marsha Hunt *Ann Martin* • John Ireland *Fantail* • Raymond Burr *Rick Coyle* ■ *Dir* Anthony Mann • *Scr* Leopold Atlas, John C Higgins, from a story by Arnold B Armstrong, Audrey Ashley

Raw Deal ★★★ 18
Action thriller 1986 · US · Colour · 101min

This entertaining exercise in crash-bang policing comes from John Irvin, whose only previous action assignment was the less-than-inspiring *Dogs of War*. Fresh from the critically panned *Red Sonja*, Arnold Schwarzenegger was probably keen to get back to the old routine and here stars as an ex-FBI agent who goes undercover to nail a mobster (Sam Wanamaker). The film is populated with stereotypes and Arnie dispatches a great many bad guys with his usual lack of expression - suspend your disbelief and have a ball. DP Violence, swearing. *DVD*

Arnold Schwarzenegger *Mark Kaminski* • Kathryn Harrold *Monique* • Sam Wanamaker *Luigi Patrovita* • Paul Shenar *Rocca* • Robert Davi *Max* ■ *Dir* John Irvin • *Scr* Gary M DeVore, Norman Wexler, from a story by Luciano Vincenzoni, Sergio Donati

Raw Edge ★★★
Western 1956 · US · Colour · 76min

One of those splendid Universal programme fillers produced by *Touch of Evil's* Albert Zugsmith, this time in lurid colour and boasting an equally lurid plot about a gang of ranch hands trying to kill Herbert Rudley so they can lay claim to his wife, Yvonne De Carlo. There's no direction to speak of, but who cares? TS

Rory Calhoun *Tex Kirby* • Yvonne De Carlo *Hannah Montgomery* • Mara Corday *Paca* • Rex Reason *John Randolph* • Herbert Rudley *Gerald Montgomery* ■ *Dir* John Sherwood • *Scr* Harry Essex, Robert Hill, from a story by William Kozlenka, James Benson Nablo

Raw Nerve ★★★ 18
Thriller 1991 · US · Colour · 87min

Hollywood legends often made late career appearances in movies they'd have been well advised to steer clear of. Who can forget Joan Crawford in *Trog*? Glenn Ford, though, star of *The Blackboard Jungle* and *Gilda* fares rather better in this thriller about a racing driver who's having nightmares about a local killer in action. Schlock it may be, but it's superior schlock, made with an understanding of genre conventions. DA *DVD*

Glenn Ford *Captain Gavin* • Jan-Michael Vincent *Lieutenant Ellis* • Sandahl Bergman *Gloria Freeman* • Randall "Tex" Cobb *Blake Garrett* • Traci Lords *Gina Clayton* ■ *Dir* David A Prior • *Scr* David A Prior, Lawrence L Simeone

Raw Wind in Eden ★
Romantic drama 1958 · US · Colour · 93min

Her bathing beauty days at MGM over, Esther Williams ventured into romantic drama at Universal, and found herself as a fashion model who lands up on a remote island when her playboy escort Carlos Thompson's plane crashes. The location allows her to take a dip, while falling in love with island inhabitant Jeff Chandler. Thompson conveniently departs, leaving Esther and Jeff to an affair that was rather more dramatic than this, back in Hollywood when filming was over. RK

Esther Williams *Laura* • Jeff Chandler *Mark Moore/Scott Moorehouse* • Rossana Podesta *Costanza* • Carlos Thompson *Wally Tucker* ■ *Dir* Richard Wilson (1) • *Scr* Richard Wilson, Elizabeth Wilson, from a story by Dan Lundberg, Elizabeth Wilson

Rawhead Rex ★★ 18
Horror 1986 · UK · Colour · 85min

This was only the second Clive Barker script to be filmed and could have dealt a fatal blow to his career. No wonder the horror master practically disowned George Pavlou's movie. Beautifully shot in southern Ireland, the slender tale concerns a village farmer smashing an ancient Celtic monument, thus unleashing an age-old demon who terrorises the country, taking chunks out of people. This low-budget horror is derivative of every bad monster movie you've ever seen, complete with requisite unconvincing rubber-suited creature. RS *DVD*

David Dukes *Howard Hallenbeck* • Kelly Piper *Elaine Hallenbeck* • Ronan Wilmot *Declan O'Brien* • Niall Toibin *Reverend Coot* • Niall O'Brien *Detective Inspector Gissing* • Heinrich von Schellendorf *Rawhead Rex* ■ *Dir* George Pavlou • *Scr* Clive Barker, from his short story

Rawhide ★★★ PG
Western 1951 · US · BW · 83min

Initially evoking the romance of running a stagecoach line, this quickly turns into a superior suspense drama that happens to be set in the Old West, with the outlaws behaving rather like gangsters. Tyrone Power is too mature to play the young stageline trainee who becomes the captive of a hold-up gang, while Susan Hayward, as a passenger mistaken for his wife and imprisoned with him, has more to do at the climax. The villains are well characterised, with Hugh Marlowe as their businesslike leader and Jack Elam as a lecherous henchman. AE *DVD*

Tyrone Power *Tom Owens* • Susan Hayward *Vinnie Holt* • Hugh Marlowe *Zimmerman* • Dean Jagger *Yancy* • Edgar Buchanan *Sam Todd* • Jack Elam *Tevis* • George Tobias *Gratz* ■ *Dir* Henry Hathaway • *Scr* Dudley Nichols

The Rawhide Years ★★
Western 1956 · US · Colour · 84min

Universal used up sets and props from *The Mississippi Gambler* to decorate this vehicle for its young star Tony Curtis. The plot's a bit of a hand-me-down as well, but the supporting cast is good value, particularly Arthur Kennedy. While it's not very good, it is watchable in parts. TS

Tony Curtis *Ben Mathews* • Colleen Miller *Zoe* • Arthur Kennedy *Rick Harper* • William Demarest *Brand Comfort* • William Gargan *Marshal Sommers* • Peter Van Eyck *Andre Boucher* ■ *Dir* Rudolph Maté • *Scr* Earl Felton, Robert Presnell Jr, DD Beauchamp, from the novel by Norman A Fox

Ray ★★★★ 15
Musical biographical drama 2004 · US · Colour · 146min

Sex, drugs and rock 'n' roll (or, in Ray Charles's case, soul, gospel, blues and even a little bit of country) are the basic ingredients for a biopic. Throw in childhood poverty, tragedy, racial prejudice and blindness and you are in danger of producing an indigestible mixture of cliché and sentimentality. Taylor Hackford's movie avoids that trap, with Charles emerging as a hugely original talent (his recordings are used throughout the film) and a sympathetic human being, despite his heroin addiction and serial adultery. This is thanks to the assured script and direction, and to Oscar-winning star Jamie Foxx. BP Drug abuse. *DVD* *Blu-ray*

Jamie Foxx *Ray Charles* • Kerry Washington *Della Bea Robinson* • Regina King *Margie Hendricks* • Clifton Powell *Jeff Brown* • Aunjanue Ellis *Mary Ann Fisher* • Harry Lennix *Joe Adams* • Terrence Dashon Howard [Terrence Howard] *Gossie McKee* • Larenz Tate *Quincy Jones* • Bokeem Woodbine *Fathead Newman* ■ *Dir* Taylor Hackford • *Scr* James L White, from a story by Taylor Hackford, James L White

Ray Harryhausen: Special Effects Titan ★★★★ PG
Documentary 2011 · US · Colour and BW · 93min

This lively and engrossing documentary celebrates the work of special-effects maestro Ray Harryhausen, whose pioneering stop-motion creatures, in such films as *The 7th Voyage of Sinbad* and *Jason and the Argonauts*, have inspired film-makers right up to the present day. As the man himself talks candidly about his craft, this excellent chronicle is interspersed with vintage clips and archive test footage of the beasts during construction. In addition, director Gilles Penso assembles an impressive roll call of A-list directors to pay tribute to the influence Harryhausen had on their own movies - Steven Spielberg describes him as "the father of all we do today in science fiction, fantasy and adventure". TeS

Ray Harryhausen • Peter Jackson • James Cameron • Terry Gilliam • Steven Spielberg ■ *Dir/Scr* Gilles Penso

Razor Blade Smile ★ 18
Erotic action horror 1998 · UK · Colour and BW · 97min

A terminally trendy take on a tired theme, director Jake West's erotic popcorn vampire movie gives trash a bad name. *Femme fatale* Eileen Daly is made immortal in 1850 after a visit from aristocratic vampire Christopher Adamson. In modern London, she becomes a leather cat-suit clad assassin with a coffin full of weapons in her bedroom. Derivative, not even unintentionally funny, and technically inept. AJ Swearing, violence, sex scenes. *DVD*

Eileen Daly *Lilith Silver* • Christopher Adamson *Sir Sethane Blake* • Jonathan Coote *Detective Inspector Ray Price* • Kevin Howarth *Platinum* ■ *Dir/Scr* Jake West

Razorback ★★ 18
Horror 1984 · Aus · Colour · 90min

Partly inspired by the dingo baby case that became the basis of the Meryl Streep drama *A Cry in the Dark*, this black horror tale about a giant wild pig terrorising the Australian outback borrows, too, from *The Texas Chain Saw Massacre* in its depiction of sick and depraved backwoods yokels. Making his directorial debut, Russell Mulcahy dishes up too rich a visual feast for what is a meandering man-against-nature storyline; the creature, when it finally appears, is also a big letdown. RS *DVD*

R

Gregory Harrison *Carl Winters* • Arkie Whiteley *Sarah Cameron* • Bill Kerr *Jake Cullen* • Chris Haywood *Benny Baker* ■ *Dir* Russell Mulcahy • *Scr* Everett DeRoche, from the novel by Peter Brennan

The Razor's Edge ★★★ PG
Drama   1946 · US · BW · 144min

Tyrone Power plays a First World War veteran who, after a tragic love affair in Paris, goes to India for spiritual renewal. Based on W Somerset Maugham's novel (the author himself is played by Herbert Marshall), this big-budget melodrama bursts with incident and was pitched as Power's return to the screen after distinguished war service. Glamorous stars Gene Tierney and Anne Baxter tug on Power's heartstrings. **AT** Swearing.

Tyrone Power *Larry Darrell* • Gene Tierney *Isabel Bradley* • John Payne *Gray Maturin* • Anne Baxter *Sophie MacDonald* • Clifton Webb *Elliott Templeton* • Herbert Marshall *W Somerset Maugham* • Elsa Lanchester *Miss Keith* ■ *Dir* Edmund Goulding • *Scr* Lamar Trotti, from the novel by W Somerset Maugham

The Razor's Edge ★★ 12
Drama   1984 · US · Colour · 123min

Another attempt to film W Somerset Maugham's novel, relating how an American First World War survivor takes stock of his life as those close to him go through historically based personal crises. Comedian Bill Murray thought the *Gump*-like soap opera would open up a whole new dramatic career. Theresa Russell livens things up as a drunken hooker in Paris, but there's little else to enjoy. **AJ** Swearing.

Bill Murray *Larry Darrell* • Theresa Russell *Sophie* • Catherine Hicks *Isabel* • Denholm Elliott *Elliot Templeton* • James Keach *Gray Maturin* • Peter Vaughan *Mackenzie* • Saeed Jaffrey *Raaz* ■ *Dir* John Byrum • *Scr* Bill Murray, John Byrum, from the novel by W Somerset Maugham

Razzle Dazzle: a Journey into Dance ★★★ PG
Comedy   2006 · Aus · Colour · 87min

As with the best mockumentaries, this Australian comedy induces almost as many cringes as it does guffaws. Chronicling the bitchy, egotistical and, at times, downright creepy world of kids' dance competitions, it centres on two dance academies – the reigning champs, run by snooty traditionalist Jane Hall, and the Jazzketeers, whose teacher (Ben Miller) is committed to changing the world through dance. Both are pretty appalling creations, although most of the movie's venom is saved for the pushy showbiz mums, in particular the monstrous Kerry Armstrong. While director Darren Ashton doesn't bring anything particularly new to the genre, his direction is suitably deadpan and he is rewarded with superb performances from his leads. **JF** *DVD*

Kerry Armstrong *Justine* • Ben Miller *Mr Jonathon* • Nadine Garner *Paulette* • Tara Morice *Marianne* • Denise Roberts *Barbara* • Jane Hall *Miss Elizabeth* • Toni Lamond *Sherry Leonard* • Barry Crocker *Donnie Destry* ■ *Dir* Darren Ashton • *Scr* Robin Ince, Carolyn Wilson, from a story by Wilson, Darren Ashton • *Cinematographer* Garry Phillips

Reach for Glory ★★★
Drama   1962 · UK · BW · 86min

This is a strange, haunting study of a family of Second World War evacuees and the young son who feels shamed by his conscientious objector brother and his shanghaied father. Joining up with a local gang of kids, he turns into a fervent nationalist who persecutes the local Jewish immigrant boy, then befriends him, before the ritualistic tragedy that lies ahead. This drama poses some disturbing questions and is well worth seeking out. **AT**

Harry Andrews *Capt Curlew* • Kay Walsh *Mrs Curlew* • Michael Anderson Jr *Lewis Craig* • Oliver Grimm *Mark Stein* • Martin Tomlinson *John Curlew* ■ *Dir* Philip Leacock • *Scr* John Kohn, Jud Kinberg, John Rae, from the novel *The Custard Boys* by John Rae

Reach for the Sky ★★★★ U
Second World War biographical drama
1956 · UK · BW · 130min

While many of Hollywood's tales about heroism during the Second World War were tainted by smug patriotism and unwelcome sentiment, postwar British cinema tended to handle the events of the conflict with fidelity and dignity. This inspiring tale of courage is one of the finest in a proud tradition. Lewis Gilbert masterfully makes the drama as compelling as the action sequences, and Kenneth More gives the performance of his career as Douglas Bader, who overcame the loss of his legs in a pre-war flying accident to become one of the RAF's most decorated heroes. **DP** *DVD*

Kenneth More *Douglas Bader* • Muriel Pavlow *Thelma Bader* • Lyndon Brook *Johnny Sanderson* • Lee Patterson *Stan Turner* • Alexander Knox *Mr Joyce* • Dorothy Alison *Nurse Brace* • Michael Warre *Harry Day* ■ *Dir* Lewis Gilbert • *Scr* Lewis Gilbert, Vernon Harris, from the biography *Story of Douglas Bader* by Paul Brickhill

Reaching for the Moon ★★★ 12
Romantic drama based on a true story
2013 · Bra · Colour · 113min

Bruno Barreto's account of the 15-year lesbian romance between American poet Elizabeth Bishop and Brazilian architect Lota de Macedo Soares is initially compelling. 40-year-old Bishop (Miranda Otto) goes to stay with old chum Mary Morse (Tracy Middendorf) outside Rio De Janeiro. However, Bishop falls for Morse's lover, the vivacious Soares (Gloria Pires), and they form a ménage that somehow endures as Bishop and Morse compete for Soares's emotional and sexual attention. But Barreto chronicles subsequent events, as well as Bishop's alcoholism and Soares's depression, with less finesse than he brings to the love story. Nevertheless, the conclusion has a touching melancholic grace. **DP** English, Portuguese +subtitles. Swearing, sexual references. *DVD*

Miranda Otto *Elizabeth Bishop* • Gloria Pires *Lota de Macedo Soares* • Tracy Middendorf *Mary Morse* • Marcello Airoldi *Carlos Lacerda* • Lola Kirke *Margaret Bennett* • Treat Williams *Robert Lowell* ■ *Dir* Bruno Barreto • *Scr* Matthew Chapman, Julie Sayres, from an unproduced screenplay by Carolina Kotscho, from the novel *Flores Raras e Banalissimas* by Carmen L Oliveira

Read My Lips ★★★ 15
Thriller   2001 · Fr · Colour · 113min

Director Jacques Audiard shrewdly manipulates both sound and audience expectation in this compelling critique of gender politics. However, he then opts for systematic thrills rather than concentrating on the meticulously established psychological intrigue between deaf secretary Emmanuelle Devos and thuggish parolee Vincent Cassel. Her ruthless pursuit of both professional advancement and personal revenge against those who have spurned her is realised in a chilling display of outward humility and simmering self-belief. **DP** French +subtitles. *DVD*

Vincent Cassel *Paul Angeli* • Emmanuelle Devos *Carla Behm* • Olivier Gourmet *Marchand* • Olivia Bonamy *Annie* • Olivier Perrier *Masson* • Bernard Alane *Morel* ■ *Dir* Jacques Audiard • *Scr* Tonino Benacquista, Jacques Audiard

The Reader ★★★ 15
Romantic drama
2008 · US/Ger · Colour · 118min

Director Stephen Daldry and *The Hours* screenwriter David Hare reteam for this sensitively handled adaptation of Bernhard Schlink's novel, which provides a sombre reflection on how the Second World War fractured the German psyche. Oscar-winning Kate Winslet excels in the difficult role of Hanna, a woman whose lack of education drew her into working as a prison guard for the SS. She seeks solace from her guilt in a sexual relationship with fresh-faced teenager Michael (David Kross), who reads to her in bed and is unaware of her past. But her secret years are revealed years after at a public trial, and in his later life Michael (now played by Ralph Fiennes) is the one forced to shoulder the burden of regret and reconciliation. **SP** *DVD* *Blu-ray*

Kate Winslet *Hanna Schmitz* • Ralph Fiennes *Michael Berg* • Lena Olin *Ilana Mather/Rose Mather* • Alexandra Maria Lara *Young Ilana Mather* • Bruno Ganz *Rohl* • David Kross *Young Michael Berg* • Linda Bassett *Ms Brenner* • Volker Bruch *Dieter* ■ *Dir* Stephen Daldry • *Scr* David Hare, from the novel by Bernhard Schlink

The Reading Room ★★
Drama   2005 · US · Colour · 105min

James Earl Jones gives a dignified performance in this heartfelt drama. He plays a wealthy, retired businessman who carries out his wife's dying wish by opening a free reading room in the crime-riddled neighbourhood where he grew up. While the film is keen to touch on gritty issues, the solutions it offers are based more on idealism than reality. Nonetheless, the end result is warm and engaging despite its simplistic nature. **SF** Some violence, brief swearing.

James Earl Jones *William Campbell* • Kathryne Dora Brown *Jillian* • Joanna Cassidy *Diana Weston* • Adam Crosby *Nick* ■ *Dir* Georg Stanford Brown • *Scr* Randy Feldman

Ready to Rumble ★★ 15
Sports comedy   2000 · US · Colour · 101min

David Arquette and Scott Caan play two obsessed wrestling fans who are determined to resurrect the career of their favourite fighter, Jimmy King, when he "loses" his world title after falling out with his manager. This suffers from crass dialogue, limp gags and predictable plot twists. That the film still grows on you is thanks mainly to the endearing performances of the two young leads. However, Oliver Platt (as King) is very obviously too puny to be king of the ring, and his trademark extra-large acting only makes some amends for any physical deficiencies. **JF** Violence, swearing.

David Arquette *Gordie Boggs* • Oliver Platt *Jimmy King* • Scott Caan *Sean Dawkins* • Bill Goldberg • Rose McGowan *Sasha* • Diamond Dallas Page • Martin Landau *Sal* ■ *Dir* Brian Robbins • *Scr* Steven Brill, from World Championship Wrestling characters

The Real Blonde ★★★ 15
Romantic comedy   1997 · US · Colour · 101min

The pursuit of perfection in the shallow world of film, fashion and advertising lies at the core of writer/director Tom DiCillo's bright and breezy showbiz exposé. Matthew Modine is an idealist aspiring actor in his mid-30s, who draws everyone he meets into interlocking morality tales about sexism and image obsession that overlap in increasingly comic and complex ways. A wonderful cast makes the most of the shrewd observations, even though the satire does meander at times. **AJ** Swearing, sex scenes. *DVD*

Matthew Modine *Joe* • Catherine Keener *Mary* • Daryl Hannah *Kelly* • Maxwell Caulfield *Bob* • Elizabeth Berkley *Tina* • Christopher Lloyd *Ernst* • Kathleen Turner *Dee Dee Taylor* • Denis Leary *Doug* • Steve Buscemi *Nick* ■ *Dir/Scr* Tom DiCillo

Real Genius ★★★ 15
Comedy   1985 · US · Colour · 101min

Enjoyable, if at times slightly silly, screwball comedy, moulded by some of the same minds that brought *Police Academy* and *Bachelor Party* to the screen. Val Kilmer plays one of a gang of scientific prodigies holed up in an institute for young boffins. But, while the youngsters are supposed to be expanding technology, and might be exploring the moral responsibilities of the post-nuclear arms race, they are far keener on getting up to fiendish japes in the corridor. No real genius here, but still fun. **PF** *DVD*

Val Kilmer *Chris Knight* • Gabe Jarret *Mitch Taylor* • Michelle Meyrink *Jordan Cochran* • William Atherton *Professor Jerome Hathaway* • Patti D'Arbanville *Sherry Nugil* ■ *Dir* Martha Coolidge • *Scr* Neal Israel, Pat Proft, Peter Torokvei, from a story by Israel, Proft

The Real Glory ★★★ PG
War adventure   1939 · US · BW · 92min

Intended to be a Spanish-American War rerun of the previously successful Gary Cooper/Henry Hathaway collaboration *The Lives of a Bengal Lancer*, this Philippines-based saga stints on nothing, and the action sequences are particularly well staged and suitably bloody. Only an actor of Cooper's integrity could bring off a character so utterly brilliant at problem-solving, and he does so with aplomb. **TS**

Gary Cooper *Dr Bill Canavan* • David Niven *Lt Terrence McCool* • Andrea Leeds *Linda Hartley* • Reginald Owen *Capt Steve Hartley* • Broderick Crawford *Lt Swede Larson* • Kay Johnson *Mabel Manning* ■ *Dir* Henry Hathaway • *Scr* Jo Swerling, Robert R Presnell, from the novel by Charles L Clifford

The Real Howard Spitz ★★★ PG
Comedy   1998 · UK/Can · Colour · 97min

Kelsey Grammer is perfectly cast as a reclusive writer struggling to get his Raymond Chandler-esque pulp novels published in this comic winner. He finds success with his new Crafty Cow children's detective books, but goes to insane lengths to avoid public engagements. Grammer gives an accomplished performance as the curmudgeon with a heart, and the droll script offers amusing dialogue and cynical charm. **JC** *DVD*

Kelsey Grammer *Howard Spitz* • Genevieve Tessier *Samantha* • Joseph Rutten *Lou* • Amanda Donohoe *Laura* • Kay Tremblay *Theodora Winkle* • Cathy Lee Crosby *Librarian* • Gary Levert *Allen* ■ *Dir* Vadim Jean • *Scr* Jurgen Wolff

Real Life ★★★ PG
Satirical comedy   1979 · US · Colour · 88min

In 1973 on US TV, docusoap *An American Family* shocked audiences with its voyeuristic chronicling of the everyday life of an average US family – including on-screen divorce and the revelation that one of the kids was gay. For his directorial debut, Albert Brooks effectively spoofed the series and film documentaries in general. Brooks (as a darker version of himself) is the director filming the lives of an average family just at the point when the family is going into meltdown. Brooks even involved his own relatives in the film to make sure it had an authentic look. A fine debut from an under-appreciated talent. **DF**

Dick Haynes *Councilman Harris* • Albert Brooks • Matthew Tobin *Dr Howard Hill* • JA Preston *Dr Ted Cleary* • Mort Lindsey • Joseph Schaffler *Paul Lowell* • Phyllis Quinn *Donna Stanley* • James Ritz *Jack from Cincinnati* ■ *Dir* Albert Brooks • *Scr* Albert Brooks, Monica Johnson, Harry Shearer

Real Life ★★ PG
Crime drama   1983 · UK · Colour · 88min

In his debut feature, Rupert Everett works hard to convey the whimsicality of the fantasist whose claims that a valuable Rembrandt has been stolen coincide with a genuine attempt on the painting. However, he fails to gel with Cristina Raines as the smarter older woman who not only extricates him from his dilemma, but also helps him make up with exasperated girlfriend, Catherine Rabett. **DP**

Rupert Everett *Tim* • Cristina Raines *Laurel* • Catherine Rabett *Kate* • James Faulkner *Robin* • Isla Blair *Anna* • Norman Beaton *Leon McDonald* • Warren Clarke *Gerry* • Lynsey Baxter *Jackie* ■ *Dir* Francis Megahy • *Scr* Francis Megahy, Bernie Cooper

The Real McCoy ★★ 15
Crime thriller   1993 · US · Colour · 100min

Kim Basinger stars as a reformed thief who is forced back into crime in this fair comic thriller. To make matters worse, Basinger is also saddled with a klutzy partner played by Val Kilmer. Mulcahy's cinematic eye for detail is on vivid show once more but the handsome stars have little to do except pose in front of his eye-popping electric backdrops. **AJ** Some swearing. *DVD*

R

Kim Basinger *Karen McCoy* • Val Kilmer *JT Barker* • Terence Stamp *Jack Schmidt* • Gailard Sartain *Gary Buckner* • Zach English *Patrick* • Raynor Scheine *Baker* • Deborah Hobart *Cheryl Sweeney* • Pamela Stubbart *Kelly* ■ *Dir* Russell Mulcahy • *Scr* William Davies, William Osborne

Real Men ★★ 15

Spy comedy   1987 · US · Colour · 82min

James Belushi is the hotshot CIA agent, John Ritter is the shy insurance clerk he's forced to recruit as a courier. It's that mismatched-buddy/fish-out-of-water concept again, which can work so well but all too often falls decidedly flat. Despite some moments of inventive farce, this spy comedy belongs in the latter category as it fails to gel under Dennis Feldman's overactive direction. AJ

James Belushi *Nick Pirandello* • John Ritter *Bob Wilson* • Barbara Barrie *Mom* • Bill Morey *Cunard* • Iva Andersen *Dolly* • Gail Berle *Sherry* ■ *Dir/Scr* Dennis Feldman

The Real St Nick ★★

Seasonal romantic comedy
2012 · US · Colour · 85min

A mysterious young man (Callard Harris) who believes he's Santa Claus after getting knocked unconscious brings Christmas magic to a California hospital in this quirky festive romp from *Wayne's World* director Penelope Spheeris. Pretty psychiatrist Torrey DeVitto figures he's delusional, but naturally falls hard for him nonetheless, while variously troubled patients in the children's and mental health wings are transformed by his infectious energy. The result is a reality-light TV movie that's familiar yet fun. SF

Torrey DeVitto *Kate* • Callard Harris *Nick* • Matt Felker *Spaulding Tyler* • Kenneth Choi *Jack/RP McMurphy* ■ *Dir* Penelope Spheeris • *Scr* Steven Palmer Peterson, from a story by Stephanie Rennie

Real Steel ★★ 12

Science-fiction action drama
2011 · US · Colour · 121min

This uneasy mix of hi-tech sci-fi adventure and redemptive family drama stars Hugh Jackman as Charlie Kenton, a down-at-heel former boxer in a not-too-distant future where robot boxing has become the world's biggest sport. Struggling to find a new lean, mean fighting machine to take on his robot rivals and clear his debts, Charlie instead finds himself saddled with the young son he abandoned at birth. Director Shawn Levy stages a handful of electrifying fight scenes, although there's nothing particularly ground-breaking in terms of the special effects, with the robots coming across as little more than polite, lower-league Transformers. TeS Some violence, swearing. *DVD* *Blu-ray*

Hugh Jackman *Charlie Kenton* • Dakota Goyo *Max Kenton* • Evangeline Lilly *Bailey Tallet* • Anthony Mackie *Finn* • Kevin Durand *Ricky* • Phil LaMarr *ESPN boxing commentator* ■ *Dir* Shawn Levy • *Scr* John Gatins, from a story by Dan Gilroy, Jeremy Leven, from the short story *Steel* by Richard Matheson

Real Women Have Curves ★★★ 12

Comedy drama   2002 · US · Colour · 82min

Newcomer America Ferrera is impressive as the headstrong Ana, a Mexican-American high-school graduate who constantly challenges tradition after her overbearing mother (a ripely humorous Lupe Ontiveros) forces her to give up dreams of college for a job at her sister's dress-making factory. Essentially a warm and sassy chick flick infused with world cinema sensibilities, the film hits back at preconceived notions of class, race and beauty. SF *DVD*

Lupe Ontiveros *Carmen* • America Ferrera *Ana* • Ingrid Oliu *Estela* • George Lopez *Mr Guzman* • Brian Sites *Jimmy* • Soledad St Hilaire *Pancha* • Lourdes Perez *Rosali* • Jorge Cervera Jr *Raul* ■ *Dir* Patricia Cardoso • *Scr* George Lavoo, Josefina Lopez, from the play by Josefina Lopez

Reality ★★★ 15

Comedy drama   2012 · It/Fr · Colour · 116min

Gomorrah director Matteo Garrone's swipe at celebrity culture sees Neapolitan fish seller Aniello Arena become convinced that he has made such an impression on the casting directors of the Italian version of *Big Brother* that they have followed him from Rome to test his suitability for the reality TV show. He becomes so gripped by delusions of grandeur that his wife (Loredana Simioli) and pious pal (Nando Paone) struggle to save him. Arena is plausibly naive as the starstruck wannabe, but Garrone's critique of Italy's current cultural vapidity is too indulgently affectionate and lacks both originality and bite. DP Italian +subtitles. *DVD*

Aniello Arena *Luciano* • Loredana Simioli *Maria* • Nando Paone *Michele* • Nello Iorio *Massimone* • Nunzia Schiano *Aunt Nunzia* ■ *Dir* Matteo Garrone • *Scr* Ugo Chiti, Maurizio Braucci, Matteo Garrone, Massimo Gaudioso, from a story by Garrone, Gaudioso • *Cinematographer* Marco Onorato • *Music* Alexandre Desplat

Reality Bites ★★★ 12

Comedy drama   1994 · US · Colour · 94min

Ben Stiller made his directorial debut with this Generation X comedy, which wouldn't know reality if it jogged its arm during a showy but superficial hand-held camera movement. Strip away the attitude and you'll find an old-fashioned romantic comedy, in which Winona Ryder can't make up her mind between geek Stiller and tuned-in drop-out Ethan Hawke. For all its faults, this still has moments of hip charm. DP Some swearing, drug abuse. *DVD*

Winona Ryder *Lelaina Pierce* • Ethan Hawke *Troy Dyer* • Janeane Garofalo *Vickie Miner* • Steve Zahn *Sammy Gray* • Ben Stiller *Michael Grates* • Swoosie Kurtz *Charlane McGregor* • Harry O'Reilly *Wes McGregor* • Susan Norfleet *Helen Anne Pierce* • Joe Don Baker *Tom Pierce* • Renee Zellweger [Renée Zellweger] *Tami* ■ *Dir* Ben Stiller • *Scr* Helen Childress

Re-Animator ★★★★ 18

Black comedy horror   1985 · US · Colour · 85min

This ground-breaking horror black comedy reintroduced HP Lovecraft to a new generation, and set a new level as to how far on-screen outrageousness could go. It also introduced cult star Jeffrey Combs, excellent as the funny and scary borderline-mad medical student working on a formula that brings the dead back to life. However, the dead don't come back in either tip-top or co-operative shape. First-time director Stuart Gordon constantly pushes the limits with the gory antics, but also shows an absurd side to such sequences. Followed in 1990 by *Bride of Re-Animator*. KB Violence, sex scenes. *DVD* *Blu-ray*

Jeffrey Combs *Herbert West* • Bruce Abbott *Dan Cain* • Barbara Crampton *Megan Halsey* • Robert Sampson *Dean Halsey* • David Gale *Dr Carl Hill* • Gerry Black *Mace* • Peter Kent *Melvin, the Re-animated* ■ *Dir* Stuart Gordon • *Scr* Dennis Paoli, William J Norris, Stuart Gordon, from the story *Herbert West - the Re-Animator* by HP Lovecraft

Reap the Wild Wind ★★★ PG

Adventure   1942 · US · Colour · 118min

This lurid melodrama seems to take an interminable amount of time to reach its famous Oscar-winning climax with a giant squid unless, of course, you happen to care whether it's John Wayne or a miscast Ray Milland that ends up with southern belle Paulette Goddard. If that little bit of romance isn't enough for Mills and Boon fans, there's another involving Susan Hayward and Robert Preston. The beginning and end are spectacular, but this maritime vessel does get very watery amidships. TS

John Wayne *Captain Jack Stuart* • Ray Milland *Stephen Tolliver* • Paulette Goddard *Loxi Claiborne* • Raymond Massey *King Cutler* • Robert Preston *Dan Cutler* • Lynne Overman *Captain Phillip Philpott* • Susan Hayward *Drusilla Alston* ■ *Dir* Cecil B DeMille • *Scr* Alan LeMay, Charles Bennett, Jesse Lasky Jr, Jeanie Macpherson (uncredited), from a story by

Thelma Strabel • *Special Effects* Gordon Jennings, Faricot Edouart, William L Pereira, Louis Mesenkop

The Reaping ★★★ 15

Supernatural horror thriller
2006 · US · Colour · 95min

When a bayou backwater is afflicted by what appear to be the ten Old Testament plagues, locals call on the services of academic Hilary Swank, who specialises in debunking miracles. She searches for a rational explanation while the terrified residents bay for the blood of a young girl (AnnaSophia Robb) they believe to be possessed by Satan. The setting and feeling of suspense are neatly established as director Stephen Hopkins's shocker builds an enjoyably moody and mysterious atmosphere. But the moment the recycled plot reveals its debt to other faith-based horrors - *Rosemary's Baby* and *The Wicker Man* in particular - all creepy menace is lost in the pile-up of scares and clichés about reality versus illusion. AJ *DVD* *Blu-ray*

Hilary Swank *Katherine Winter* • David Morrissey *Doug Blackwell* • AnnaSophia Robb *Loren McConnell* • Idris Elba *Ben* • Stephen Rea *Father Costigan* • William Ragsdale *Sheriff Cade* • John McConnell *Mayor Brooks* ■ *Dir* Stephen Hopkins • *Scr* Carey W Hayes [Carey Hayes], Chad Hayes, from a story by Brian Rousso

Rear Window ★★★★★ PG

Classic thriller   1954 · US · Colour · 109min

Like his earlier *Rope*, this masterpiece from director Alfred Hitchcock began as a technical stunt: Hitchcock wondered if he could make a film on just one set, from one single vantage point. James Stewart plays a photojournalist with a broken leg and a high society girlfriend, Grace Kelly. Confined to his apartment, he whiles away the time gazing out of the window through his telephoto lens and becomes convinced that a neighbour opposite (Raymond Burr) has murdered his wife and chopped her into disposable pieces. Hitchcock's "stunt" became a classic study of voyeurism - all those windows, shaped like movie screens, each containing a mini-drama of their own - and the tension builds brilliantly, complemented by the sexy repartee between Stewart and Kelly, and the cynical humour provided by nurse Thelma Ritter. An extraordinary achievement. AT *DVD* *Blu-ray*

James Stewart *LB "Jeff" Jeffries* • Grace Kelly *Lisa Carol Fremont* • Wendell Corey *Detective Thomas J Doyle* • Thelma Ritter *Stella* • Raymond Burr *Lars Thorwald* • Judith Evelyn *Miss Lonely Hearts* • David Seville [Ross Bagdasarian] *Songwriter* • Georgine Darcy *Miss Torso* • Sara Berner *Woman on fire escape* ■ *Dir* Alfred Hitchcock • *Scr* John Michael Hayes, from the short story *It Had to Be Murder* by Cornell Woolrich • *Cinematographer* Robert Burks

Rear Window ★★★ PG

Thriller   1998 · US · Colour · 85min

It takes a brave man to remake one of Alfred Hitchcock's finest films, and director Jeff Bleckner was always going to be on a hiding to nothing with this made-for-TV update. This does score, however, with the presence of Christopher Reeve in the lead role of a wheelchair-using architect. Reeve's own condition adds an extra dimension to the role, as does the range of hi-tech equipment at his disposal. JF Violence, swearing. *DVD*

Christopher Reeve *Jason Kemp* • Daryl Hannah *Claudia Henderson* • Robert Forster *Detective Charlie Moore* • Ruben Santiago-Hudson *Antonio* ■ *Dir* Jeff Bleckner • *Scr* Larry Gross, Eric Overmyer, from a short story by Cornell Woolrich

A Reason to Live, a Reason to Die ★★★

Spaghetti western
1972 · Sp/It/Fr/W Ger · Colour · 89min

James Coburn followed up his role in Sergio Leone's *A Fistful of Dynamite* with this less artful but equally watchable spaghetti western. The central conceit pretty much follows that of *The Dirty Dozen*, with Coburn's disgraced Union officer

assembling a ragtag band of desperadoes to join him on a death-or-glory mission. There's plenty of action to be had as Coburn and his gang attempt to retake the fort that he surrendered under duress, while the final confrontation is surprising for its sheer poignancy - especially given the machine-gun bloodbath that precedes it. JH

James Coburn *Col Pembroke* • Telly Savalas *Maj Ward* • Bud Spencer *Eli Sampson* ■ *Dir* Tonino Valerii • *Scr* Tonino Valerii, Ernesto Gastaldi

Reasonable Doubt ★★ 15

Crime thriller   2014 · Ger/Can · Colour · 90min

Dominic Cooper lacks the everyman quality needed to carry this *noir*-like thriller, in which he plays a cocky hotshot Chicago lawyer whose ethics are tested to the extreme when he kills a pedestrian while driving drunk and then flees the scene. But that's not the overriding problem with the film. British director Peter Howitt serves up a meaty moral dilemma and, for Cooper, this should be the precursor to fleshing out a more complex character. Unfortunately, the rules of the game change halfway through and the plot is twisted beyond the realms of credibility. SP Violence, swearing. *DVD* *Blu-ray*

Dominic Cooper *Mitch Brockden* • Samuel L Jackson *Clinton Davis* • Gloria Reuben *Det Blake Kanon* • Ryan Robbins *Jimmy Logan* ■ *Dir* Peter P Croudins [Peter Howitt] • *Scr* Peter A Dowling

A Reasonable Man ★★

Courtroom drama
1999 · Fr/S Afr · Colour · 103min

In Gavin Hood's directorial debut set in post-apartheid South Africa, he also stars as a lawyer defending Kwazulu herd boy Loyiso Gxwala, who insists he bludgeoned a baby to death because it was possessed by evil spirits. Disappointingly, in the courtroom battle that ensues before judge Nigel Hawthorne, Gxwala's belief in traditional "tikoloshe" matters less than Hood's memories of his tour of duty in Angola. DP

Gavin Hood *Sean Raine* • Nigel Hawthorne *Judge Wendon* • Janine Eyssler *Jennifer Raine* • Vusi Kunene *Prosecutor Linde* • Loyiso Gxwala *Sipho Mbombela* ■ *Dir/Scr* Gavin Hood

Rebecca ★★★★★ PG

Classic romantic thriller
1940 · US · BW · 130min

Director Alfred Hitchcock's first Hollywood film is a sumptuous and suspenseful adaptation of Daphne du Maurier's romantic novel, produced by David O Selznick, immaculately played and rightly awarded the Oscar for best picture. That Laurence Olivier as Maxim de Winter is superb goes without saying, but it's mousey Joan Fontaine who is a revelation as the second Mrs de Winter. Lovers of lesbian subtexts will have a field day with Judith Anderson's sinister housekeeper, Mrs Danvers, as Hitchcock circumvents the censors who forced plot changes to accommodate the Hays Code. TS *DVD*

Laurence Olivier *Maxim de Winter* • Joan Fontaine *Mrs de Winter* • George Sanders *Jack Favell* • Judith Anderson *Mrs Danvers* • Nigel Bruce *Major Giles Lacy* • Reginald Denny *Frank Crawley* • C Aubrey Smith *Colonel Julyan* • Gladys Cooper *Beatrice Lacy* • Florence Bates *Mrs Edythe Van Hopper* • Melville Cooper *Coroner* • Leo G Carroll *Dr Baker* • Leonard Carey *Ben* ■ *Dir* Alfred Hitchcock • *Scr* Robert E Sherwood, Joan Harrison, Philip MacDonald, Michael Hogan, Barbara Keon, from the novel by Daphne du Maurier • *Cinematographer* George Barnes • *Editor* Hal C Kern • *Art Director* Lyle Wheeler • *Music* Franz Waxman

Rebecca of Sunnybrook Farm ★★★

Silent drama   1917 · US · BW · 78min

The first screen adaptation of the novel and play by Kate Douglas Wiggin stars "America's Sweetheart" Mary Pickford in one of the most famous of her perennial little girl roles. This silent version of the tale of Rebecca, who is sent away to live with stern aunts, displays Pickford at her sympathetic, amusing best, as she matures from childish rebellion to young adulthood and romance under Marshall Neilan's direction. RK

Mary Pickford *Rebecca Randall* • Eugene O'Brien (1) *Adam Ladd* • Helen Jerome Eddy *Hannah Randall* • Charles Ogle *Mr Cobb* • Marjorie Daw *Emma Jane Perkins* • ZaSu Pitts ■ *Dir* Marshall Neilan • *Scr* Frances Marion, from the play by Kate Douglas Wiggin, Charlotte Thompson, from the novel by Kate Douglas Wiggin

Rebecca of Sunnybrook Farm ★★ U

Musical comedy   1938 · US · BW · 77min

Unable to get Shirley Temple a break in radio, her stepfather deposits her down on the farm to live with her rigid, puritanical, anti-show biz aunt, Helen Westley. Fate intervenes when new neighbour Randolph Scott who, entranced by the child, also turns out to be a radio executive. The classic tale was totally remodelled as a vehicle for the all-singing, all-dancing moppet, a veteran at 10. RK DVD

Shirley Temple *Rebecca Winstead* • Randolph Scott *Anthony Kent* • Jack Haley *Orville Smithers* • Gloria Stuart *Gwen Warren* • Phyllis Brooks *Lola Lee* • Helen Westley *Aunt Miranda Wilkins* • Slim Summerville *Homer Busby* • Bill Robinson *Aloysius* ■ *Dir* Allan Dwan • *Scr* Karl Tunberg, from the novel by Kate Douglas Wiggin

Rebecca's Daughters ★★★ 15

Historical comedy   1991 · UK/Ger · Colour · 92min

Based on a screenplay by Dylan Thomas, this is inspired by the somewhat surreal events of the 1840s Rebecca Riots in which the Welsh poor, fed up with toll charges and taxes, and starving while the English landowners were getting fat, began rioting, disguised as women. Each leader was known as Rebecca and followers were "her daughters", a reference from Genesis. Peter O'Toole hams it up as the drunken Lord Sarn and Paul Rhys is Anthony Raine, a liberal from the landowning class, who incites the rioters. FL

Paul Rhys *Anthony Raine* • Joely Richardson *Rhiannon* • Peter O'Toole *Lord Sarn* • Dafydd Hywel *Rhodri* • Sue Roderick *Sarah Hughes* • Simon Dormandy *Captain Marsden* • Clive Merrison *Sir Henry* • Keith Allen *Davy* ■ *Dir* Karl Francis • *Scr* Guy Jenkin, from a screenplay (unproduced) by Dylan Thomas

The Rebel ★★★ U

Comedy   1960 · UK · Colour · 100min

Tony Hancock's first star vehicle is no masterpiece, but it is a fascinating misfire. Written by regular collaborators Ray Galton and Alan Simpson, the film has all the touches that made *Hancock's Half-Hour* so popular, although they seem a little strained over the course of a feature-length film. Happier in suburbia using landlady Irene Handl as a model for "Aphrodite by the Waterhole" than he is fooling the pretentious Parisians of the Left Bank, Hancock is his usual deluded, pompous self, while George Sanders's suave shiftiness is as watchable as ever. DP DVD

Tony Hancock *Anthony Hancock* • George Sanders *Sir Charles Brouard* • Paul Massie *Paul* • Margit Saad *Margot Carreras* • Grégoire Aslan *Aristotle Carreras* • Dennis Price *Jim Smith* • Irene Handl *Mrs Crevatte* • John Le Mesurier *Office manager* • Liz Fraser *Waitress* ■ *Dir* Robert Day • *Scr* Ray Galton, Alan Simpson, from the story by Galton, Simpson, Tony Hancock

Rebel ★★ 15

Thriller drama   1973 · US · Colour · 80min

Sylvester E Stallone, as he is credited here, takes his first leading screen role in this conspiracy thriller about a group of anti-war hippies who are infiltrated by an FBI *agent provocateur* and encouraged to blow up a New York skyscraper. This straightforward paranoia drama gives few kudos to America's political institutions. Contains violence and bad haircuts. JG

Anthony Page *Tommy* • Sylvester E Stallone [Sylvester Stallone] *Jerry* • Vickey Lancaster *Estelle* • Dennis Tate *Ray* • Barbara Lee Govan *Marlena* ■ *Dir* Robert Allen Schnitzer • *Scr* Robert Allen Schnitzer, Larry Beinhart

Rebel ★★ 15

Period musical drama   1985 · Aus · Colour · 89min

This wildly ill-conceived curiosity from Australia is an obscure must for Matt Dillon fans, although he seems understandably ill at ease in a musical drama set in the Second World War. Dillon's a troubled American GI who goes AWOL in Sydney and hides out with nightclub singer Debbie Byrne, who has a dance routine for every melodramatic development. Lots of flashy production numbers fail utterly to evoke the right era or further the scanty plot. AME

Matt Dillon *Rebel* • Debbie Byrne *Kathy* • Bryan Brown *Tiger* • Bill Hunter *Browning* • Ray Barrett *Bubbles* • Julie Nihill *Joycie* • John O'May *Bernie* • Kim Deacon *Hazel* ■ *Dir* Michael Jenkins • *Scr* Michael Jenkins, Bob Herbert, from the play *No Names ... No Packdrill* by Herbert

Rebel Rousers ★★ 15

Drama   1967 · US · Colour · 73min

This is a low-budget trough, but most of the young hopefuls have become today's stars. Here's Bruce Dern and Diane Ladd the year after they had daughter Laura, and here's Dean Stanton before he added the Harry. The nominal lead is Cameron Mitchell, and the truly tasteless plot involves a drag race organised to offer Mitchell's pregnant girlfriend to the champion dragster. The release of this movie was delayed until after Nicholson had scored in *Easy Rider*. TS Some violence, swearing. DVD

Cameron Mitchell *Paul Collier* • Jack Nicholson *"Bunny"* • Bruce Dern *JJ"* • Diane Ladd *Karen* • Dean Stanton [Harry Dean Stanton] *Randolph Halverson* ■ *Dir* Martin B Cohen • *Scr* Abe Polsky, Michael Kars, Martin B Cohen

LANDMARK FILM
Thanks to this quintessential teen rebellion movie and his early death, James Dean becomes a poster boy for adolescent angst

Rebel without a Cause ★★★★★ PG

Classic drama   1955 · US · Colour · 106min

The theme of the teenager as an alienated victim of family and society has never been done better. James Dean gives a superb performance as a frustrated youth from a well-to-do family, who rebels against his weak father and shrewish mother with such delinquent behaviour as boozing, knife-fighting and rock rod hots in hazardous games of "chicken". Natalie Wood and Sal Mineo also stand out in an excellent, youthful cast that's wonderfully controlled by director Nicholas Ray, but it's Dean who remains most memorable, and his heartfelt portrayal epitomised his tragically short career. TH DVD

James Dean (1) *Jim* • Natalie Wood *Judy* • Jim Backus *Jim's father* • Ann Doran *Jim's mother* • William Hopper *Judy's father* • Rochelle Hudson *Judy's mother* • Corey Allen *Buzz* • Sal Mineo *Plato* • Dennis Hopper *Goon* ■ *Dir* Nicholas Ray • *Scr* Stewart Stern, from the story *The Blind Run* by Robert M [Mitchell] Lindner, adapted by Irving Shulman

Rebellion ★★★★

Period action drama   1967 · Jpn · BW · 120min

Rivalling any of Akira Kurosawa's more famous samurai dramas, *Rebellion* stars the great Toshiro Mifune as a dishonoured samurai searching for revenge. In fact, it's the usual samurai stuff, given hardly any new twists, and seemingly influenced by Sergio Leone's *Dollars* films. But what is remarkable is Masaki Kobayashi's magnificent evocation of a vanished era in Japanese history and his stunning images, shot in the traditional black-and-white Scope format. Mifune's intensity is something to marvel at. AT Japanese +subtitles.

Toshiro Mifune *Isaburo Sasahara* • Go Kato *Yogoro Sasahara* • Tatsuoshi Ebara *Bunzo Sasahara* • Michiko Otsuka *Suga Sasahara* • Yoko

Tsukasa *Ichi Sasahara* ■ *Dir* Masaki Kobayashi • *Scr* Shinobu Hashimoto, from the story *Hairyo Zuma Shimatsu Yori* by Yasuhiko Takiguchi • *Cinematographer* Kazuo Yamada

Rebellion ★★★ 15

Action drama based on a true story   2011 · Fr · Colour · 134min

Writer/director Mathieu Kassovitz has struggled to recapture the edgy acuity of his early feature *La Haine* (1995), but this reconstruction of a contentious moment in recent French history exudes conviction and outrage. When Kanak separatists take hostages on the Pacific island of Ouvéa in 1988, Captain Philippe Legorjus (Kassovitz) of the elite GIGN anti-terrorist squad is dispatched to New Caledonia to negotiate with the group's leader, Alphonse Dianou (Iabe Lapacas). This is an undoubtedly well-intentioned piece, but Kassovitz's evident sympathies deprive the narrative of balance and tension, and too many secondary characters are crudely drawn ciphers. DP French +subtitles. Violence, swearing. DVD

Mathieu Kassovitz *Capitaine du GIGN Philippe Legorjus* • Iabe Lapacas *Alphonse Dianou* • Malik Zidi *JP Perrot* • Alexandre Steiger *Jean Bianconi* • Daniel Martin *Bernard Pons* • Philippe Torreton *Christian Prouteau* ■ *Dir* Mathieu Kassovitz • *Scr* Mathieu Kassovitz, Benoît Jaubert, Pierre Geller, Serge Frydman, from the non-fiction book *La Morale et l'Action* by Philippe Legorjus

Rebels of the Neon God ★★★★

Drama   1992 · Tai/HK · Colour · 106min

Establishing what would come to be trademark preoccupations with water, confined spaces and disaffected youth, Taiwanese minimalist Tsai Ming-liang presents a dispiriting yet often amusing insight into inner-city ennui in this hugely impressive debut. A homoerotic charge crackles throughout the drama, as college dropout Lee Kang-sheng is caught between admiration and revenge when he starts stalking Chen Chao-jung, the petty crook who smashed the wing-mirror on his father's taxi. Tsai explores the human cost of the techno era with a compassion that's matched only by his idiosyncratic wit. Forms a triology with 1996's *Vive l'Amour* and 1997's *The River*. DP Mandarin, Hokkien +subtitles.

Chen Chao-jung *Ah-Tze* • Wang Yu-wen *Ah-Kuei* • Lee Kang-sheng *Hsiao-Kang* • Jen Ch'ang-pin *Ah-Bing* ■ *Dir/Scr* Tsai Ming-liang

Rebound ★★ PG

Sports comedy   2005 · US · Colour · 83min

Martin Lawrence provides the only real surprise in this by-the-numbers family comedy. He gives an uncharacteristically restrained performance as a disgraced college basketball coach who attempts to restore his reputation by training a team of losers at his old school. Slapstick and sight gags dominate, as the stereotypical misfits demonstrate their on-court liabilities, while playful visuals add to the knockabout atmosphere. Naturally, social zeros soon transform into heroes, but this cosy turnaround can't disguise the rushed plotting. SF Some violence. DVD

Martin Lawrence *Roy McCormick/Preacher Don* • Wendy Raquel Robinson *Jeanie Ellis* • Breckin Meyer *Tim Fink* • Horatio Sanz *Mr Newirth* • Oren Williams *Keith Ellis* • Megan Mullally *Principal Walsh* ■ *Dir* Steve Carr • *Scr* Jon Lucas, Scott Moore, from a story by William Wolff, Ed Decter, John J Strauss

The Rebound ★★★ 15

Romantic comedy   2009 · US · Colour · 90min

A recently divorced mum falls for a college graduate 15 years her junior in this glossy romantic comedy. Since the leading lady's played by Catherine Zeta-Jones, it's hard to imagine her character ever wanting for male company, but the point of her growing attraction to 20-something Justin Bartha (the groom from *The Hangover*) is that he's just... nice. Bart Freundlich's movie is not side-splittingly funny, or emotionally trenchant, but Zeta-Jones and Bartha are

both decidedly charming. TJ Swearing, sexual references, drug abuse. DVD BL

Catherine Zeta-Jones *Sandy* • Justin Bartha *Aram Finklestein* • Andrew Cherry *Frank Jr age seven* • Kelly Gould *Sadie age nine* • Sam Robards *Frank* • Art Garfunkel *Harry Finklestein* • Jake Cherry *Frank Jr* ■ *Dir/Scr* Bart Freundlich

[Rec] ★★★★ 18

Horror   2007 · Sp · Colour · 75min

The crew of a Spanish TV reality show, accompanying Barcelona firemen on a routine call to an apartment block, records the sudden outbreak of a rabid virus in this well-sustained and often terrifying shocker. With the exits sealed off, they continue taping the unfolding pseudo-zombie nightmare in a frenetic, shaky-cam style, complete with creepy night-vision footage, startling jumps and out-of-focus menace. Matter-of-fact performances and the absence of soundtrack music add extra realism, before a breathtaking swerve into unexpected territory. Writer/directors Jaume Balagueró and Paco Plaza pool their wayward cult horror talents to work the *Blair Witch* faux-documentary aesthetic to perfection. AJ Spanish +subtitles. DVD BL

Manuela Velasco *Angela* • Ferran Terraza *Manu* • Manuel Bronchud *Grandfather* • María Teresa Ortega *Grandmother* • Vicente Gil *Older policeman* • Claudia Silva *Jennifer* • Pablo Rosso *Marcos* • Martha Carbonell *Señora Izquierdo* ■ *Dir* Jaume Balagueró, Paco Plaza • *Scr* Jaume Balagueró, Luis A Berdejo [Luis Berdejo], Paco Plaza

[Rec]² ★★★ 18

Horror thriller   2009 · Sp · Colour · 81min

This real-time sequel begins the moment its predecessor ends, as a four-man Spanish SWAT team escorts a doctor into the quarantined Barcelona apartment block to procure a sample of the deadly virus that's turning everyone into rabid zombies. A shoulder-cam provides shaky subjective visuals as co-writer/directors Jaume Balagueró and Paco Plaza shift the documentary-like scenario into weirder territory spring-loaded with sudden jolts. While it's more of the same to some degree, it can't be classed a lazy sequel owing to the directors' firm grasp of their material and some major surprises that lurk in the final act. AJ Spanish +subtitles. Violence, swearing. DVD BL

Manuela Velasco *Angela Vidal* • Pablo Rosso *Rosso* • Ferran Terraza *Manu* • Ariel Casas *Larra* • David Vert *Alex* ■ *Dir* Jaume Balagueró, Paco Plaza • *Scr* Jaume Balagueró, Paco Plaza, Manu Díez

[Rec]³ Génesis ★★★★ 18

Horror thriller   2012 · Sp · Colour · 76min

In this third film in the jolting Spanish zombie franchise, all hell breaks loose during wedding celebrations at a swanky Barcelona mansion. Separated from each other, the newlyweds endure the rabid madness using chainsaws and food blenders, only to reunite for a nasty shock twist. Initially filmed in hand-held style, the shooting shifts to conventional mode for the gruesome gore, but there's a lighter tone to the whole affair and an overall romantic sweetness that lends a refreshing fairy-tale feel to the grim action. AJ In Spanish. Violence, swearing. DVD BL

Leticia Dolera *Clara* • Diego Martin *Koldo* • Javier Botet *Nina Medeiros* • Carla Nieto *Rebeca Vinas* ■ *Dir* Paco Plaza • *Scr* Paco Plaza, Luiso Berdejo

[REC] 4: Apocalypse ★★★ 18

Horror   2014 · Sp · Colour · 91min

Saved from the original block of flats infested by slavering rage monsters, Manuela Velasco wakes up in a tanker-cum-laboratory with shady scientist types pawing over her to discover the source of the virus. And there's little time to look for safety or answers, as a thunderous storm is about to break. The found-footage immediacy and nonstop tension of earlier *[Rec]* flicks are sadly lacking, but the shipboard location delivers claustrophobic shivers and provides nooks and crannies for drooling ghouls to pounce from. JA Spanish +subtitles. Violence. *DVD*

Manuela Velasco *Angela Vidal* • Paco Manzanedo *Guzman* • Ismael Fritschi *Nic* • Héctor Colomé *Dr Ricarte* ■ *Dir* Jaume Balagueró • *Scr* Jaume Balagueró, Manu Díez

Recess: School's Out ★★★ U
Animated comedy 2001 · US · Colour · 79min

This is yet another big-screen spin-off from a popular children's TV animation. The premise is simple enough: young TJ Detweiler and chums take to the playground to save their school (and the world's weather system) from dastardly forces who plan to put an end to their six weeks of freedom. Brightly if basically cartooned, the film's real plus point is subject matter that kids everywhere can identify with. Parents will have fun spotting the starry voice talents, while hyperactive six-to-nine-year-olds will be entertained. DA *DVD*

Ricky D'Shon Collins *Vince* • Jason Davis *Mikey* • Ashley Johnson *Gretchen* • Andy Lawrence *TJ* • Courtland Mead *Gus* • Pamela Segall *Spinelli* • Dabney Coleman *Principal Prickly* • Robert Goulet *Mikey* • Melissa Joan Hart *Becky* • Peter MacNicol *Fenwick* • James Woods *Benedict* • Dan Castellaneta *First guard* • Robert Stack *Superintendent* ■ *Dir* Chuck Sheetz • *Scr* Jonathan Greenberg, from a story by Joe Ansolabehere, Paul Germain, Jonathan Greenberg

Recipe for Murder ★★
Detective murder mystery
2001 · UK/Can/US · Colour · 88min

Gary Basaraba comes across as more like a mobster than a chief medical examiner in this bland and flimsily plotted murder mystery. Delivering his clunky dialogue with an amusingly broad New York accent, he investigates the apparent accidental death of his actress goddaughter (Anne Openshaw). The end result resembles a poorly written TV pilot, with echoes of *Quincy, ME* and *Diagnosis Murder*, but with none of their narrative appeal. SF

Gary Basaraba *Murray Maguire* • Larissa Laskin *Corinne Riggs* • Anne Openshaw *Leona Spencer* ■ *Dir* Vic Sarin • *Scr* Joe Wiesenfeld

Reckless ★★★
Romantic musical 1935 · US · BW · 96min

This wildly unbelievable MGM vehicle for blonde bombshell Jean Harlow was reportedly based on the notorious shooting scandal involving real-life torch singer Libby Holman. Harlow plays a Broadway actress and she's ably backed up by Franchot Tone (their third film together) and suave, debonair William Powell, who actually fell for Harlow off-screen and left flowers on her grave for many years after her death in 1937. Glossy and contrived, but very watchable. TS

Jean Harlow *Mona Leslie* • William Powell *Ned Riley* • Franchot Tone *Bob Harrison* • May Robson *Granny* • Ted Healy *Smiley* • Nat Pendleton *Blossom* • Robert Light *Paul Mercer* • Rosalind Russell *Josephine* • Henry Stephenson *Harrison* • Louise Henry *Louise* ■ *Dir* Victor Fleming • *Scr* PJ Wolfson, from the story *A Woman Called Cheap* by Oliver Jeffries [David O Selznick], Victor Fleming

Reckless ★★★ 18
Romantic comedy drama
1984 · US · Colour · 89min

James Foley was extremely fortunate to get ace German cinematographer Michael Ballhaus to light his debut feature, as he gives an otherwise routine tale of teen rebellion a rough edge that is noticeably lacking from newcomer Chris Columbus's script. Every romantic cliché is in place, as squeaky clean suburban cheerleader Daryl Hannah dumps her meathead beau after she's paired at a charity dance with bad boy footballer Aidan Quinn. The 1980s attitudes and raunchy sex scenes haven't worn well, but nostalgia nuts will love the soundtrack. DP

Aidan Quinn *Johnny Rourke* • Daryl Hannah *Tracey Prescott* • Kenneth McMillan *John Rourke Sr* • Cliff De Young *Phil Barton* • Lois Smith *Mrs Prescott* • Adam Baldwin *Randy Daniels* • Dan Hedaya *Peter Daniels* • Jennifer Grey *Cathy Bennario* ■ *Dir* James Foley • *Scr* Chris Columbus • *Cinematographer* Michael Ballhaus

Reckless ★★
Black comedy thriller 1995 · US · Colour · 91min

This strange, nightmarish comedy thriller stars Mia Farrow, suitably gauche and naive, as a woman who discovers her husband has hired a hitman to knock her off on Christmas Eve. Escaping into the snow, Farrow begins a bizarre journey and has a series of encounters in which no one is what they seem. All a bit too *Twilight Zone* in the final analysis. LH

Mia Farrow *Rachel* • Scott Glenn *Lloyd* • Mary-Louise Parker *Pooty* • Tony Goldwyn *Tom* • Eileen Brennan *Sister Margaret* • Giancarlo Esposito *Game show host* • Stephen Dorff *Tom Jr* ■ *Dir* Norman René • *Scr* Craig Lucas, from his play

Reckless Kelly ★★ PG
Comedy 1993 · Aus · Colour · 76min

The spirit of Aussie outlaw Ned Kelly is alive and well and dwelling in director/star Yahoo Serious in this frantic and not particularly funny crime comedy. It begins well, as Yahoo's island idyll is threatened by evil banker Hugo Weaving and his explosive sidekick, Alexei Sayle. But, from the moment he arrives in the US intent on robbing banks to save his home, the gags begin to fall flat. DP Violence, swearing.

Yahoo Serious *Reckless Kelly* • Melora Hardin *Robin Banks* • Alexei Sayle *Major Wimp* • Hugo Weaving *Sir John* • Kathleen Freeman *Mrs Delance* • John Pinette *Sam Delance* • Bob Maza *Dan Kelly* ■ *Dir* Yahoo Serious • *Scr* Yahoo Serious, Warwick Ross, Lulu Serious, David Roach

The Reckless Moment ★★★ 12
Thriller 1949 · US · BW · 78min

Short, sharp and to the point, this pitches anxious mother Joan Bennett against James Mason after her gauche daughter Geraldine Brooks has an affair with older married man Shepperd Strudwick. Paying less attention than usual to set detail and ornate camera movement, ultra-sophisticated German director Max Ophüls directs with a cool detachment. But, while this allows Bennett to suffer and scheme without the histrionics of a Joan Crawford, it prevents Mason from trying out any new tricks as a blackmailing cad. DP *DVD*

James Mason *Martin Donnelly* • Joan Bennett *Lucia Harper* • Geraldine Brooks *Beatrice Harper* • Henry O'Neill *Mr Harper* • Shepperd Strudwick *Ted Darby* ■ *Dir* Max Opuls [Max Ophüls] • *Scr* Henry Garson, Robert W Soderberg, Mel Dinelli, Robert E Kent, from the novel *The Blank Wall* by Elisabeth Sanxay Holding

The Reckoning ★★★
Drama 1969 · UK · Colour · 111min

A tough but troubled businessman is forced to deal with the chip on his shoulder when he learns his father is dying. Returning to Liverpool and his roots, he decides to take revenge on the teenager who attacked his father. An adult drama about class in Britain, it's held together with a muscular performance from Nicol Williamson as the dislikeable hero. JG

Nicol Williamson *Michael Marler* • Ann Bell *Rosemary Marler* • Lilita De Barros *Maria* • Tom Kempinski *Brunzy* ■ *Dir* Jack Gold • *Scr* John McGrath, from the play *The Harp That Once* by Patrick Hall

The Reckoning ★★★ 15
Period murder mystery
2001 · UK/Sp · Colour · 105min

This medieval murder-mystery play follows a troupe of travelling players who drop their religious repertoire to expose the corruption hiding under the Church's righteous protection. Paul Bettany, playing a young priest on the run from an adulterous past, joins a group of itinerant

actors led by Willem Dafoe. Arriving in a town where Elvira Minguez has been sentenced to death for the murder of a young boy, the company decides to tell the story of the killing in the form of a production for the local townsfolk. Director Paul McGuigan maintains a mood as dark as the plague-ridden times, but lapses into theatricality. TH Violence, sex scenes. *DVD*

Willem Dafoe *Martin* • Paul Bettany *Nicholas* • Gina McKee *Sarah* • Brian Cox (1) *Tobias* • Ewen Bremner *Simon Damian* • Vincent Cassel *Robert de Guise* • Simon McBurney *Stephen* • Tom Hardy *Straw* • Elvira Minguez *Martha* ■ *Dir* Paul McGuigan • *Scr* Mark Mills, from the novel *Morality Play* by Barry Unsworth

Recollections of the Yellow House ★★★ 18
Drama 1989 · Por · Colour · 122min

Strewn with references to silent classics such as *Greed*, *The Cabinet of Dr Caligari* and *Nosferatu*, this is a frustrating, yet persistently fascinating study on self-obsession and misery. Exercising rigid control over both the *mise-en-scène* and his elliptical storyline, writer/director João César Monteiro turns in a seedily antiheroic performance, as the academic whose growing sense of dissatisfaction with life in general and his desolate Lisbon boarding house in particular results in an assault that sees him consigned to an asylum. This is often as funny as it is despondent. DP Portuguese +subtitles.

João César Monteiro *Joao De Deus* • Manuela De Freitas *Dona Violeta* • Sabina Sacchi *Mimi* • Teresa Calado *Menina Julieta* • Ruy Furtado *Señor Armando* • Henrique Viana *Police Captain* ■ *Dir/Scr* João César Monteiro

Reconstruction ★★★ 12
Romantic mystery drama
2003 · Den /Swe/Ger · Colour · 87min

Danish director Christoffer Boe explores the relationship between cinema and literature in this teasingly slight *film noir*-like mystery. Tempted into a fling with novelist Krister Henriksson's glamorous wife, photographer Nikolaj Lie Kaas awakes in a seemingly alternative universe, where neither friends nor family know him and he suspects he's being manipulated by a higher force. Playing fast and loose with the rules of storytelling, Boe delights in misleading the viewer, a conceit made easier by the fact that both the women in Kaas's life are played by the bewitching Maria Bonnevie. DP Danish +subtitles. Swearing. *DVD*

Nikolaj Lie Kaas *Alex David* • Maria Bonnevie *Aimee Holm/Simone* • Krister Henriksson *August Holm* • Nicolas Bro *Leo Sand* • Peter Steen *Mel David* • Ida Dwinger *Monica* ■ *Dir* Christoffer Boe • *Scr* Christoffer Boe, Mogens Rukov

Record of a Tenement Gentleman ★★★★ PG
Drama 1947 · Jpn · BW · 71min

Recalling the visual style and emotional tone of pre-War Japanese social cinema, Yasujiro Ozu's delicate character drama combines unsentimental nostalgia and contemporary comment to poignant effect. Self-contained widow Choko Iida slowly becomes fond of abandoned, bed-wetting urchin Hohi Aoki, whose tenacious desire to belong awakens Iida's suppressed maternal instincts. Cleverly using camera angles to create a sense of place and parallel motifs to unify the action, Ozu reveals his directorial genius. DP Japanese +subtitles. *DVD*

Chishu Ryu *Tashiro, the fortune teller* • Choko Iida *Otane* • Takeshi Sakamoto *Kihachi* • Eitaro Ozawa *Kohei's father* ■ *Dir* Yasujiro Ozu • *Scr* Yasujiro Ozu, Tadao Ikeda

Recount ★★★★
Documentary drama 2008 · US · Colour · 115min

This is a surprisingly compelling dramatisation of the uncertain weeks after the 2000 US presidential election (George W Bush versus Al Gore), when the final result depended on a series of ballot recounts in Florida. Kevin Spacey leads the

cast as the Democrats' legal adviser, and Tom Wilkinson and John Hurt provide gravitas as party grandees. Laura Dern's Golden Globe-winning turn as the self-serving Secretary of State for Florida (who became a laughing stock) lifts the tone from earnest reconstruction to something more outrageous, with a nifty script and consistently winning performances manage to introduce genuine tension and intrigue to an episode whose outcome is all-too-well known. AC

Kevin Spacey *Ron Klain* • Bob Balaban *Ben Ginsberg* • Ed Begley Jr *David Boies* • Laura Dern *Katherine Harris* • John Hurt *Warren Christopher* • Denis Leary *Michael Whouley* • Bruce McGill *Mac Stipanovich* • Tom Wilkinson *James Baker* ■ *Dir* Jay Roach • *Scr* Danny Strong

The Recruit ★★ 12
Spy thriller 2002 · US · Colour · 110min

Al Pacino gives another gruff, seen-it-all performance here, as a veteran CIA agent who recruits cocksure computer whizz kid Colin Farrell. The same could be said about the plot of this thriller from director Roger Donaldson. Most of the action takes place in "The Farm", a CIA training facility where would-be agents are taught hi-tech espionage and survival skills, and where Farrell meets and falls for enigmatic rival Bridget Moynahan. Predictable. AJ Violence, swearing, sex scenes. *DVD* *Blu*

Al Pacino *Walter Burke* • Colin Farrell (2) *James Clayton* • Bridget Moynahan *Layla* • Gabriel Macht *Zack* • Karl Pruner *Dennis Slayne* • Eugene Lipinski *Husky man* ■ *Dir* Roger Donaldson • *Scr* Roger Towne, Kurt Wimmer, Mitch Glazer

Red ★★ 12
Action comedy 2010 · US · Colour · 106min

This tongue-in-cheek espionage affair stars Bruce Willis as a retired CIA operative whose knowledge of previous covert activities makes him a security risk. Having found a potential soulmate in Mary-Louise Parker, Willis is looking forward to the next chapter in his life – until that future is interrupted by gun-toting assailants. Time then to assemble the old gang: Morgan Freeman (stuck in an old folks' home), John Malkovich (a loopy survivalist), Helen Mirren (now doing occasional assassinations for fun) and Brian Cox (still working for Russian intelligence). As they reunite to fend off the baddies all seems set for a jaunty spy caper, whereupon the movie simply runs out of inspiration, threading together perfunctory shoot-outs, middling wisecracks and predictable twists. TJ *DVD* *Blu*

Bruce Willis *Frank Moses* • Morgan Freeman *Joe Matheson* • John Malkovich *Marvin Boggs* • Helen Mirren *Victoria* • Karl Urban *William Cooper* • Mary-Louise Parker *Sarah Ross* • Richard Dreyfuss *Alexander Dunning* ■ *Dir* Robert Schwentke • *Scr* Erich Hoeber, Jon Hoeber, from the graphic novel by Warren Ellis, Cully Hamner

Red 2 ★★★ 12
Action comedy 2013 · US · Colour · 110min

More antiquated, globetrotting nonsense fuels this OAP spy mix for a slightly better espionage thriller sequel. This time Bruce Willis calls on his ageing secret agent buddies to track down a nuclear device invented by Cold War-era weapons genius Anthony Hopkins, whose mental instability poses a threat to world peace. Like before, the winning rapport between the stars is the film's best asset, and Helen Mirren in gunplay slo-mo still hits the spot. But it's newcomer Lee Byung-hun as a contract killer on Willis's trail who makes the best impression as a choreographed fighting whirlwind. AJ Violence, swearing. *DVD* *Blu*

Bruce Willis *Frank Moses* • John Malkovich *Marvin Boggs* • Mary-Louise Parker *Sarah Ross* • Anthony Hopkins *Edward Bailey* • Helen Mirren *Victoria* • Catherine Zeta-Jones *Katja* • David Thewlis *The Frog* ■ *Dir* Dean Parisot • *Scr* Erich and Jon Hoeber, from a graphic novel by Warren Ellis (writer), Cully Hamner (artist)

R

The Red and the White
★★★ 12

Historical war drama
1967 · Hun/USSR · BW · 87min

Made to celebrate the 50th anniversary of the Bolshevik Revolution, this is ostensibly a tribute to the Hungarian volunteers who fought with the Red Army against the pro-Tsarist Whites. But Miklos Jancso clearly has an ironic agenda. Employing lateral tracking shots and meticulously composed widescreen images of the sweeping plains, he suggests the changing fortunes of the two armies and the enormity of the stakes for which they were fighting. DP In Hungarian. **DVD**

Jozsef Madaras *Hungarian commander* · Tibor Molnar *Andras* · Andras Kozak *Laszlo* · Jacint Juhasz *Istvan* ■ *Dir* Miklos Jancso · *Scr* Georgiy Mdivani, Gyula Hernadi, Miklos Jancso

Red and White
★★ 15

War drama
2009 · Indonesia · Colour · 111min

This first entry in a proposed *Freedom Trilogy* is a provocative account of the Indonesian Republican Army's resistance to the Van Mook offensive, launched by the Dutch in the summer of 1947. Adopting the *Full Metal Jacket* template, screenwriters Conor and Rob Allyn split the action into boot camp and combat sequences to ensure we're always rooting for a rookie band of brothers against their barbaric colonial oppressors. The training montages are standard issue, but director Yadi Sugandi makes solid use of the jungle setting, although his unwaveringly patriotic perspective reduces the characterisation to coarse stereotypes. DP Indonesian, Dutch +subtitles. Violence. **DVD**

Lukman Sardi *Amir* · Darius Sinathrya *Marius* · Donny Alamsyah *Tomas* · T Rifnu Wikana *Dayan* · Rahayu Saraswati *Senja* ■ *Dir* Yadi Sugandi · *Scr* Conor Allyn, Rob Allyn

The Red Badge of Courage
★★★★ U

War drama
1951 · US · BW · 66min

Apart from the brilliance of individual scenes, John Huston's American Civil War epic is also famous for having been butchered by the studio. Audie Murphy, America's most decorated soldier in the Second World War, plays the young recruit who is given a baptism of fire and emerges a hero, his experiences on the battlefield captured in some remarkable documentary-style, black-and-white photography. Although a shadow of the film Huston intended (James Whitmore's narration fills in the gaps created by MGM's scissor-happy editors), this is still a powerful study of the waste of war. AT **DVD**

Audie Murphy *Henry Fleming, the youth* · Bill Mauldin *Tom Wilson, the loud soldier* · Douglas Dick *Lieutenant* · Royal Dano *Tattered soldier* · John Dierkes *Jim Conlin, the tall soldier* · Arthur Hunnicutt *Bill Porter* · Andy Devine *Talkative soldier* · James Whitmore *Narrator* ■ *Dir* John Huston · *Scr* John Huston, from the novel by Stephen Crane, adapted by Albert Band · *Cinematographer* Harold Rosson

Red Ball Express
★★★ U

Second World War drama
1952 · US · BW · 83min

Alfred Hitchcock's favourite screenwriter of the 1950s, John Michael Hayes was perhaps an odd choice to pen a war picture. But he manages to inject enough tension into this routine story about the problems facing a transportation unit as it accompanies General Patton on his push to Paris. By giving sergeant Alex Nicol a chip on his shoulder and corporal Sidney Poitier a sense of racial injustice, he makes unit leader Jeff Chandler seem a very human hero. Intriguing and underrated. DP

Jeff Chandler *Lieutenant Chick Campbell* · Alex Nicol *Sergeant Ernest Kalleck* · Charles Drake *Private Ronald Partridge* · Judith Braun *Joyce McClellan* · Hugh O'Brian *Private Wilson* · Jacqueline Duval *Antoinette DuBois* · Sidney Poitier *Corporal Andrew Robertson* ■ *Dir* Budd Boetticher · *Scr* John Michael Hayes, from the story by Marcel Klauber, Billy Grady Jr

The Red Balloon
★★★★ U

Fantasy
1956 · Fr · Colour · 33min

The first dialogue-less film to receive an Oscar nomination for its screenplay since the silent era (it went on to win), Albert Lamorisse's simple fable about the unique friendship between a lonely boy and a vibrant red balloon remains one of the most enchanting children's films ever made. Responding with adorable naturalism to his father's direction, Pascal Lamorisse seems lost in awe at the mischievous balloon's ingenuity as it follows him across Paris and into his classroom. The triumph of loyalty and love over envy and cruelty is a weighty message for such a slight tale, but Lamorisse carries it off magnificently with a joyous balloon-filled finale. DP **DVD BD**

Pascal Lamorisse *Little boy* · Sabine Lamorisse *Little girl* ■ *Dir/Scr* Albert Lamorisse

The Red Baron
★★ 12

First World War biographical drama
2008 · Ger · Colour · 101min

Top Gun meets *Brideshead Revisited* in this lavish but wayward biopic of First World War flying ace Manfred von Richthofen. Matthias Schweighöfer plays the man dubbed the Red Baron, with Joseph Fiennes as his nemesis, Canadian pilot Roy Brown. Their encounters touch on issues of honour, but writer/director Nikolai Muellerschoen loses interest in the concept that these dashing young airmen are "sportsmen not butchers" as soon as Von Richthofen falls for nurse Käte Otersdorf (Lena Headey). Meanwhile, confusing combat choreography and an overreliance on CGI prevent the dogfight sequences from soaring. DP Violence. **DVD BD**

Matthias Schweighöfer *Manfred von Richthofen, "The Red Baron"* · Lena Headey *Käte Otersdorf* · Til Schweiger *Werner Voss* · Joseph Fiennes *Captain Roy Brown* · Volker Bruch *Lothar von Richthofen* · Steffen Schroeder *Lieutenant Bodenschatz* ■ *Dir/Scr* Nikolai Muellerschoen [Nikolai Müllerschön]

Red Beard
★★★★ 15

Period drama
1965 · Jpn · BW · 172min

The plot is simple: an ageing doctor (Toshiro Mifune) persuades his younger, rather feckless assistant to dedicate himself to work among the disadvantaged in 19th-century Japan. But what (almost) justifies the film's three-hour running time is Akira Kurosawa's wider interest in Japan's transition from its feudal past to its future as a modern industrialised society. Perhaps too slow for modern tastes, and too obscure for western audiences, it's a major work from a major director. AT Japanese +subtitles. **DVD**

Toshiro Mifune *Doctor Kyojo "Akahige" Niide* · Yuzo Kayama *Doctor Noboru Yasumoto* · Yoshio Tsuchiya *Doctor Handayu Mori* · Tatsuyoshi Ehara *Genzo Tsugawa* ■ *Dir* Akira Kurosawa · *Scr* Akira Kurosawa, Ryuzo Kikushima, Hideo Oguni, Masato Ide, from the novel *Akahige Shinryo Tan* by Shugoro Yamamoto

The Red Beret
★★★ PG

Second World War drama
1953 · UK · Colour · 84min

Wags recall that a trench was dug at Shepperton for the action sequences, but the diminutive Alan Ladd was too small to use it. However, the star puts in an excellent performance as a guilt-racked American who joins the famous parachute battalion. An interesting note for film historians: this rip-roaring film comes from the same team responsible for the first Bond movie, *Dr No*, nine years later. TS **DVD**

Alan Ladd *Canada MacKendrick* · Leo Genn *Major Snow* · Susan Stephen *Penny Gardner* · Harry Andrews *RSM* · Donald Houston *Taffy* · Anthony Bushell *General Whiting* · Stanley Baker *Breton* ■ *Dir* Terence Young · *Scr* Richard Maibaum, Frank S Nugent, from the book by Hilary St George Saunders, adapted by Sy Bartlett

Red Canyon
★★★ U

Western
1949 · US · Colour · 82min

In this charming western based on Zane Grey's novel *Wildfire*, former radio actor

Howard Duff plays a drifter trying to tame a wild stallion, who falls for Ann Blyth, daughter of horse breeder George Brent. Blyth is particularly good, and there's an interesting supporting cast of western veterans such as Edgar Buchanan and Chill Wills, plus a youthful Lloyd Bridges. The Utah locations are beautifully shot by cinematographer Irving Glassberg. TS

Ann Blyth *Lucy Bostell* · Howard Duff *Lin Slone/Cordt* · George Brent *Mathew Boatel* · Edgar Buchanan *Jonah Johnson* · John McIntire *Floyd Cordt* · Chill Wills *Brackton* · Jane Darwell *Aunt Jane* · Lloyd Bridges *Virgil Cordt* ■ *Dir* George Sherman · *Scr* Maurice Geraghty, from the novel *Wildfire* by Zane Grey

The Red Circle
★★★★ PG

Thriller
1970 · Fr/It · Colour · 136min

Before he began writing *The Red Circle*, Jean-Pierre Melville made a list of his favourite thriller situations and came up with 19, noting that the only film to use them all was *The Asphalt Jungle*. Thus *The Red Circle* is a sort of condensation of all thrillers, with the sort of fully developed characters, ambiguities, betrayals, tense scenes and intricate plotting one expects from the best of them. It's about a robbery, of course, near the Ritz in Paris, immaculately performed by some of France's top male stars. Avoid seeing the English-dubbed version, which is cut by some 45 minutes; the four stars are for the original. AT French +subtitles. **DVD BD**

Alain Delon *Corey* · Yves Montand *Jansen* · Bourvil *Inspector Mattei* · Gian Maria Volonté *Vogel* · André Eykan *Rico* · François Périer *Santi* ■ *Dir/Scr* Jean-Pierre Melville

Red Cliff
★★★★ 15

Historical action drama
2008 · Chi/Jpn/Tai/S Kor/US · Colour · 141min

John Woo's first project to be shot in mainland China is a lavish spectacular that re-creates a famous battle of the Han era (208 AD, to be precise), when the clash of three great armies was to shape the course of Chinese history. It's hard not to be impressed by Woo's blend of widescreen pageantry and up-close martial arts skills, even if the action does rather marginalise a strong cast that includes Tony Leung and charismatic co-star Takeshi Kaneshiro. It's undeniably a long haul, but there's enough derring-do and epic sweep here to carry the audience along regardless. TJ Mandarin +subtitles. **DVD BD**

Tony Leung (2) *Zhou Yu* · Takeshi Kaneshiro *Kongming, "Zhuge Liang"* · Zhang Fengyi *Prime Minister Cao Cao* · Chang Chen *Sun Quan* · Zhao Wei *Sun Shang Xiang* · Hu Jun *Zhao Yun* ■ *Dir* John Woo · *Scr* John Woo, Khan Chan, Cheng Kuo, Sheng Heyu, from the novel *Romance of the Three Kingdoms* by Luo Guanzhong

Red Corner
★★ 15

Courtroom thriller
1997 · US · Colour · 117min

In this courtroom thriller set in Beijing, something of the terror of being trapped in the machinery of a foreign legal system comes across, as Richard Gere's smarmy American TV executive finds himself relying on a Chinese female lawyer, Bai Ling, to defend him on a fraudulent murder charge. Yet, for all its Zen idealism, the film lacks tension and focus. DP English, Mandarin +subtitles. A sex scene, violence, swearing. **DVD**

Richard Gere *Jack Moore* · Bai Ling *Shen Yuelin* · Bradley Whitford *Bob Ghery* · Byron Mann *Lin Dan* · Peter Donat *David McAndrews* · Robert Stanton *Ed Pratt* ■ *Dir* Jon Avnet · *Scr* Robert King

The Red Dance
★★★★

Romantic drama
1928 · US · BW · 103min

The influence of European art films affected even no-nonsense action directors such as Raoul Walsh, whose control of this excursion into the Russian Revolution – starring Charles Farrell and Dolores Del Rio – makes it a joy to look at. Camerawork is by Charles Clark and John Marta, with art direction by Ben Carrie, and the story and action are incidental to the visuals, making it remarkable entertainment for its time. TH

Charles Farrell (1) *The Grand Duke Eugen* · Dolores Del Rio *Tasia* · Ivan Linow *Ivan Petroff* · Boris Charsky *Agitator* · Dorothy Revier *Princess Varvara* · Andrés De Segurola *General Tanaroff* · Demetrius Alexis *Rasputin* ■ *Dir* Raoul Walsh · *Scr* James Ashmore Creelman, Pierre Collings (adaptation), Philip Klein (adaptation), from a story by Eleanor Browne, from the novel *The Red Dancer of Moscow* by Henry Leyford Gates

The Red Danube
★★

Period drama
1949 · US · BW · 118min

American army officers Walter Pidgeon and Peter Lawford, stationed in Allied-occupied Vienna after the Second World War, are involved in the repatriation of Russians as a result of which, it is implied, they will suffer the cruel retribution of the Communist state. Janet Leigh is a ballerina loved by Lawford and Ethel Barrymore is a nun. Directed by George Sidney, this heavy-handed drama cashes in on the anti-Red climate of the times. Despite a large cast of authentic Europeans, it's ineffectual and unpersuasive. RK

Walter Pidgeon *Colonel Michael "Jokey" Nicobar* · Ethel Barrymore *Mother Superior* · Peter Lawford *Major John "Twingo" McPhimister* · Angela Lansbury *Audrey Quail* · Janet Leigh *Maria Buhlen* · Louis Calhern *Colonel Piniev* · Francis L Sullivan *Colonel Humphrey "Blinker" Omicron* ■ *Dir* George Sidney (2) · *Scr* Gina Kaus, Arthur Wimperis, from the novel *Vespers in Vienna* by Bruce Marshall

Red Dawn
★★ 15

Action drama
1984 · US · Colour · 109min

A small band of American teenagers wages guerrilla warfare against Russian and Cuban troops staging an invasion of their small town in a ludicrously gung-ho fantasy. Some of Hollywood's finest struggle with the highly unconvincing dialogue to justify the bombastic militarism, and the result is a scrambled action adventure smothered by political insensitivity. AJ Violence, swearing.

Patrick Swayze *Jed* · C Thomas Howell *Robert* · Lea Thompson *Erica* · Charlie Sheen *Matt* · Darren Dalton *Daryl* · Jennifer Grey *Toni* · Brad Savage *Danny* · Doug Toby *Aardvark* · Ben Johnson (1) *Mason* · Harry Dean Stanton *Mr Eckert* · Powers Boothe *Andy* ■ *Dir* John Milius · *Scr* John Milius, Kevin Reynolds, from the novel by Reynolds

Red Dawn
★★ 12

Action drama
2012 · US · Colour · 89min

Way back in 1984, when John Milius first made this trashy tale of teen resistance to an invasion of the US, his choice of bad guys was the Russians (and their Cuban allies). There was still a Cold War on, after all. Almost 30 years on, this slick but unimaginative remake is implausibly forced to replace Russia as aggressor with rogue-state North Korea. The story sees US marine Chris Hemsworth (Thor) and a ragtag bunch of patriotic teens stand between the invading Koreans and their occupation plans. It's all as daft as a brush, of course, but suspend your disbelief and you'll find enough whizz-bang action to sustain interest. DA Violence, swearing. **DVD BD**

Chris Hemsworth *Jed Eckert* · Josh Peck *Matt Eckert* · Josh Hutcherson *Robert Kitner* · Adrianne Palicki *Toni Walsh* · Will Yun Lee *Captain Cho* · Jeffrey Dean Morgan *Tanner* ■ *Dir* Dan Bradley · *Scr* Carl Ellsworth, Jeremy Passmore, from the 1984 film

Red Desert
★★ 15

Drama
1964 · Fr/It · Colour · 111min

Here, Michelangelo Antonioni has almost exhausted his theme of urban alienation and simply rehashes it in colour, taking his symbolism to artistic extremes as streets are repainted and a room changes hue. The story, though, is opaque – Monica Vitti plays a manic depressive who sleeps with her husband's friend (Richard Harris). Vitti is, as ever, convincingly neurotic, but Harris is totally miscast, dubbed and barely a presence. Most viewers will regard this as pretentious twaddle, no matter how beautiful the photography. AT Italian +subtitles. Sexual references. **DVD BD**

U SUITABLE FOR ALL   Uc SUITABLE ESPECIALLY FOR YOUNG CHILDREN (DVD ONLY)   PG PARENTAL GUIDANCE   12A UNDER 12s TO BE ACCOMPANIED (CINEMA ONLY)

R

Monica Vitti *Giuliana* • Richard Harris *Corrado Zeller* • Carlo Chionetti *Ugo* • Xenia Valderi *Linda* • Rita Renoir *Emilia* • Lili Rheims *Workman's wife* • Aldo Grotti *Max* • Valerio Bartoleschi *Valerio, Giuliana's son* ■ *Dir* Michelangelo Antonioni • *Scr* Michelangelo Antonioni, Tonino Guerra, from a story by Antonioni, Guerra • *Cinematographer* Carlo Di Palma

Red Dog ★★★ PG

Comedy drama   2011 · Aus/US · Colour · 88min

This feel-good snaggy-dog story was a smash Down Under, scooping best film at the Aussie equivalent of the Baftas. Based on the bestseller by Louis de Bernières, *Red Dog* is the touching but endearingly quirky tale of a scruffy kelpie who appears seemingly out of nowhere and is adopted by bus driver Josh Lucas (*Sweet Home Alabama*) and the inhabitants of a remote mining community in the 1970s. Kriv Stenders's whizz-bang direction helps paper over the somewhat episodic plotting and he is well served by a talented ensemble cast – although it's the marvellously expressive canine star Koko who steals the show. JF Swearing. *DVD*

Josh Lucas *John* • Rachael Taylor *Nancy* • John Batchelor *Peeto* • Noah Taylor *Jack* • Keisha Castle-Hughes *Rose* • Luke Ford *Tom* ■ *Dir* Kriv Stenders • *Scr* Daniel Taplitz, from the novel by Louis de Bernières

The Red Dragon ★★

Mystery   1945 · US · BW · 64min

Sidney Toler's 18th Charlie Chan series outing was also the seventh to be released by Poverty Row studio Monogram, after it took over the franchise from 20th Century-Fox. By now the cases were becoming mundane affairs and, although Toler is suitably inscrutable as Earl Derr Biggers's sleuth, Benson Fong's Tommy Chan is nowhere near as effective as Keye Luke's "Number One Son". Moreover, Fortunio Bonanova is given too little to do as the police inspector left in Chan's wake as he searches for stolen plans. DP

Sidney Toler *Charlie Chan* • Fortunio Bonanova *Inspector Luis Carvero* • Benson Fong *Tommy Chan* • Robert E Keane *[Robert Emmett Keane]* • Alfred Wyans • Willie Best *Chattanooga Brown* • Carol Hughes (1) *Marguerite Fontan* ■ *Dir* Phil Rosen • *Scr* George Callahan, from his story, from characters by Earl Derr Biggers

Red Dragon ★★★ 15

Thriller   2002 · US/Ger · Colour · 119min

In this remake of Michael Mann's revered *Manhunter* (the first version of Thomas Harris's novel *Red Dragon* filmed in 1986), ex-FBI agent Edward Norton investigates a series of killings committed by a tattooed Ralph Fiennes, known only as "The Tooth Fairy". To get inside the killer's head, Norton has to consult his archenemy – and the man he put behind bars – Dr Hannibal Lecter (Anthony Hopkins). Closer to *The Silence of the Lambs* than *Hannibal* in tone and tension, this is a classier, less campy outing for the gourmet doctor, who is well matched in the psycho stakes by Fiennes's killer. TH Violence, swearing, nudity. *DVD*

Anthony Hopkins *Dr Hannibal Lecter* • Edward Norton *Will Graham* • Ralph Fiennes *Francis Dolarhyde* • Harvey Keitel *Jack Crawford* • Emily Watson *Reba* • Mary-Louise Parker *Molly Graham* • Philip Seymour Hoffman *Freddy Lounds* • Anthony Heald *Dr Chilton* • Frankie Faison *Barney* • Lalo Schifrin *Conductor* • Ellen Burstyn *Grandmother Dolarhyde* ■ *Dir* Brett Ratner • *Scr* Ted Tally, from the novel by Thomas Harris

Red Dust ★★★★ PG

Romantic drama   1932 · US · BW · 79min

Love in a hot climate is the theme of this melodrama, directed by Victor Fleming, which today risks looking clichéd, if not over-the-top. The film was a hit in its time, thanks not just to Fleming's direction, but also to sultry stylish performances of Clark Gable, as the macho boss of a rubber plantation in the tropics, and Jean Harlow and Mary Astor as the two very different women in his life. John Ford directed the 1953 re-make, *Mogambo*. PF

Clark Gable *Dennis Carson* • Jean Harlow *Vantine* • Mary Astor *Barbara Willis* • Gene Raymond *Gary Willis* • Donald Crisp *Guidon* • Tully Marshall *McQuarg* • Forrester Harvey *Limey* ■ *Dir* Victor Fleming • *Scr* John Mahin, from the play by Wilson Collison

Red Dust ★★★ 15

Drama   2004 · UK/S Afr · Colour · 106min

The continuing injustices of post-apartheid South Africa are laid bare in this impressive feature debut from British director Tom Hooper. The handsomely-shot drama offers a fictionalised account of the country's real-life legal amnesty system that enabled soldiers and policemen to be officially absolved of apartheid-era crimes. Assisted by tenacious lawyer Hilary Swank, Chiwetel Ejiofor's ANC politician confronts his torturer (Jamie Bartlett) 14 years after his ordeal, and his performance gives the story genuine emotional impact. SF Swearing, violence. *DVD*

Hilary Swank *Sarah Barcant* • Chiwetel Ejiofor *Alex Mpondo* • Jamie Bartlett *Dirk Hendricks* • Marius Weyers *Ben Hoffman* • Ian Roberts (1) *Piet Muller* ■ *Dir* Tom Hooper • *Scr* Troy Kennedy Martin, from the novel by Gillian Slovo

Red Eye ★★★ 12

Suspense thriller   2005 · US · Colour · 81min

Rachel McAdams finds terror at 30,000 feet in this airborne thriller in which hardly a plane journey cliché is left unexploited. Nervous flyer McAdams discovers she's the key element in a political assassination plot engineered by fellow passenger Cillian Murphy. Though hitman Murphy informs her that her father Brian Cox's life is at stake, the quick-thinking heroine does everything she can to avoid co-operating with his demands. The predictable action is efficiently taut in this absurd but deliciously entertaining ride. SF Violence, swearing. *DVD*

Rachel McAdams *Lisa Reisert* • Cillian Murphy *Jackson Rippner* • Brian Cox (1) *Dad* • Jayma Mays *Cynthia* • Jack Scalia *Charles Keefe* • Robert Pine *Bob Taylor* ■ *Dir* Wes Craven • *Scr* Carl Ellsworth, from a story by Ellsworth, Dan Foos

Red Firecracker, Green Firecracker ★★★ 15

Romantic drama   1993 · HK/Chi · Colour · 111min

The story of an artist's forbidden love for the female head of a firework manufacturing family is right out of the ordinary. In a country where women are permitted to have only one child, this study of repressed sexuality takes on a whole new meaning. However, Da Ying's cumbersome screenplay and Ning Jing's unsubtle portrayal of the cross-dressing heiress undermine the beauty of He Ping's direction and the irrepressible performance of Wu Gang. DP Cantonese +subtitles. Nudity.

Ning Jing *Chun Zhi* • Wu Gang *Niu Bao, painter* • Zhao Xiaorui *Mr Mann* • Gai Yang *Mr Zhao* • Xu Zhengyun *Mr Xu* ■ *Dir* He Ping • *Scr* Ying Da, Feng Jicai

Red Garters ★★★ U

Western musical comedy   1954 · US · Colour · 90min

Set in the fictional town of Paradise Lost, the action revolves around sharp-shooting cowboy Guy Mitchell out to avenge his brother's death, sassy saloon singer Rosemary Clooney and lawyer Jack Carson on whom her sights are set. The neither-here-nor-there plot, unremarkable script and hit-free score undermine an adventurously styled production (the art direction was Oscar-nominated), lively performances and some genuinely funny upending of every heroic western cliché in the book. RK

Rosemary Clooney *Calaveras Kate* • Jack Carson *Jason Carberry* • Guy Mitchell *Reb Randall* • Pat Crowley *Susana Martinez De La Cruz* • Joanne Gilbert *Sheila Winthrop* • Gene Barry *Rafael Moreno* ■ *Dir* George Marshall • *Scr* Michael Fessier

Red-Headed Woman ★★★

Romantic drama   1932 · US · BW · 79min

Infamously banned by the British censors at the time of its release, audiences here didn't have sight of this raunchy little opus until its TV bow some decades ago, and only then realised what all the fuss was about. This is a torrid tale that positively glorifies husband-stealing, and the electric Jean Harlow leaves no doubt where her sympathies lie. There's a sexual candour in the telling that provoked the pro-censorship lobby, but it's that startling erotic charge that makes this movie so electrifyingly watchable today. Look out for a young Charles Boyer, impressive as Harlow's uniformed chauffeur. TS

Jean Harlow *Lil Andrews* • Chester Morris *Bill Legendre Jr* • Lewis Stone *William Legendre Sr* • Leila Hyams *Irene Legendre* • Una Merkel *Sally* • Henry Stephenson *Gaersate* • May Robson *Aunt Jane* • Charles Boyer *Albert* • Harvey Clark *Uncle Fred* ■ *Dir* Jack Conway • *Scr* Anita Loos, from the novel by Katherine Brush

Red Heat ★★★ 18

Action thriller   1988 · US · Colour · 99min

This routine thriller from director Walter Hill offered Arnold Schwarzenegger one of his more interesting action roles before he became a superstar. Playing a stony, monosyllabic Soviet cop poses no real acting problems for the big man, and in James Belushi he has an agreeably foul-mouthed foil, as the pair team up to hunt for an escaped Russian drug dealer. Hill stages a series of entertainingly violent and increasingly silly set pieces. JF Violence, swearing, a sex scene, nudity. *DVD* *BL*

Arnold Schwarzenegger *Captain Ivan Danko* • James Belushi *Det Sgt Art Ridzik* • Peter Boyle *Lou Donnelly* • Ed O'Ross *Viktor Rostavili* • Larry Fishburne *[Laurence Fishburne] Lieutenant Stobbs* • Gina Gershon *Catherine Manzetti* ■ *Dir* Walter Hill • *Scr* Harry Kleiner, Walter Hill, from a story by Troy Kennedy Martin, Hill

Red Hill ★★★ 15

Crime thriller   2010 · Aus · Colour · 93min

One-time *Home and Away* star Ryan Kwanten is better known these days for his role in *True Blood*, but this cracking little thriller finds him back in his Australian homeland. He plays Shane Cooper, an inexperienced city cop who transfers to the sleepy rural town of the title to provide a less stressful environment for his pregnant wife (Claire van der Boom). Unfortunately for Cooper, his arrival coincides with the escape from prison of murderer Jimmy Conway (Tom E Lewis), a former Red Hill resident who is intent on exacting revenge on the community. Patrick Hughes's lean, muscular direction ensures it plays out like a modern-day western, and Kwanten makes for a likeable hero, although Steve Bisley steals the show as the hard-bitten police chief Old Bill. JF Violence, swearing. *DVD* *BL*

Ryan Kwanten *Shane Cooper* • Steve Bisley *Old Bill* • Tom E Lewis *[Tommy Lewis] Jimmy Conway* • Claire van der Boom *Alice Cooper* • Christopher Davis *Slim* • Kevin Harrington *Barlow* ■ *Dir/Scr* Patrick Hughes (2)

The Red House ★★★

Mystery thriller   1947 · US · BW · 100min

A splendid thriller with grand passions and Freudian undertones, this has grown in reputation. Now often described as *noir*, it is closer in style to the psychological horror of the 1960s. Edward G Robinson has a meaty role as the tormented, crippled farmer, who warns juveniles Allene Roberts and Lon McCallister to keep away from the Red House, and hires hunky Rory Calhoun to make sure they do. There are longueurs during the build-up to the awful truth, but compensation is provided by the beautiful Sierra Nevada locations and Miklos Rozsa's score. DM

Edward G Robinson *Pete Morgan* • Lon McCallister *Nath Storm* • Judith Anderson *Ellen Morgan* • Allene Roberts *Meg Morgan* • Julie London *Tibby* • Rory Calhoun *Teller* ■ *Dir* Delmer Daves • *Scr* Delmar Daves, from the novel by George Agnew Chamberlain

Red Light ★★

Crime drama   1949 · US · BW · 83min

This turgid crime drama from director Roy Del Ruth is not helped by the low-key performance of its star, the past-his-prime George Raft, here playing a businessman searching (seemingly interminably) for the killer of his army chaplain brother. What sexy Virginia Mayo sees in the gloomy Raft is a mystery known only to the casting department. It's redeemed only by its black-and-white photography and some sterling support. TS

George Raft *John Torno* • Virginia Mayo *Carla North* • Raymond Burr *Nick Cherney* • Gene Lockhart *Warni Hazard* • Barton MacLane *Strecker* • William "Bill" Phillips *Ryan* ■ *Dir* Roy Del Ruth • *Scr* George Callahan • *Cinematographer* Bert Glennon

Red Lights ★★★★ 15

Thriller   2003 · Fr · Colour · 101min

Once again a Georges Simenon story provides exceptional cinematic material, as Cédric Kahn combines sly comedy with controlled suspense in this revisionist road movie. Alternating between resentment, penitence and distraction, Jean-Pierre Darroussin is outstanding as the everyman made to pay an extreme price for the uncharacteristic lapse in judgement that prompts wife Carole Bouquet to storm off in the middle of a cross-country car journey and promptly disappear. Tense, mischievous and darkly optimistic. DP French +subtitles. Swearing, violence. *DVD*

Jean-Pierre Darroussin *Antoine Dunan* • Carole Bouquet *Hélène* • Vincent Deniard *Man on the run* • Charline Paul *Waitress* • Jean-Pierre Gos *Inspector Levet* ■ *Dir* Cédric Kahn • *Scr* Cédric Kahn, Laurence Ferreira Barbosa, Gilles Marchand, from the novel *Feux Rouges* by Georges Simenon

Red Lights ★★ 15

Supernatural thriller   2012 · Sp/US · Colour · 109min

Robert de Niro is the headline act in this murky thriller, playing a blind psychic. But writer/director Rodrigo Cortés (*Buried*) keeps him in the background, and also squanders the talents of Cillian Murphy's sceptical paranormal investigator, and his mentor, Sigourney Weaver. Unfortunately, the more Murphy digs, the deeper we get into a hole where nothing makes sense. Cortes holds back information for a last-minute twist and the preposterous climax falls utterly flat. SP Violence, swearing. *DVD* *BL*

Cillian Murphy *Tom Buckley* • Sigourney Weaver *Margaret Matheson* • Robert De Niro *Simon Silver* • Toby Jones *Shackleton* • Joely Richardson *Monica Handsen* • Elizabeth Olsen *Sally Owen* ■ *Dir/Scr* Rodrigo Cortés

Red Line 7000 ★★

Action drama   1965 · US · Colour · 110min

Director Howard Hawks returns to territory that he'd first tackled in 1932's *The Crowd Roars*, but somehow this racetrack movie doesn't quite measure up. The Technicolor is particularly fine, with that Paramount gloss much in evidence, but new boy James Caan is a woeful lead, and the process shots are poor, making the whole look rather like an Elvis Presley movie with fewer songs. TS

James Caan *Mike Marsh* • Laura Devon *Julie Kazarian* • Gail Hire *Holly MacGregor* • Charlene Holt *Lindy Bonaparte* • John Robert Crawford *Ned Arp* • Marianna Hill *Gabrielle Queneau* • James Ward *Dan McCall* • George Takei *Kato* ■ *Dir* Howard Hawks • *Scr* George Kirgo, from a story by Howard Hawks • *Cinematographer* Milton Krasner

Red Mist ★ 18

Horror   2008 · UK · Colour · 85min

In his 2007 slasher movie *Shrooms*, Irish director Paddy Breathnach showed us what happens when the drugs don't work. He's at it again here as a group of obnoxious medical students accidentally put a hospital janitor (Andrew Lee Potts) in a coma then inject him with an experimental drug in the hope of reviving him. Arielle Kebbel plays

R

the student who watches in horror as her human guinea pig uses out of body experiences to murder those who did him wrong. Although presenting itself in the po-faced vein of medical thrillers like *Flatliners* and *Pathology*, this quickly descends into nonsense, as the atrocious screenplay and numerous plot holes take their toll. JR DVD BL

Arielle Kebbel *Catherine* • Sarah Carter *Kim* • Stephen Dillane *Dr Harris* • Andrew Lee Potts *Kenneth* • Katie McGrath *Harriet* • Martin Compston *Sean* ■ *Dir* Paddy Breathnach • *Scr* Spence Wright

Red Mountain ★★
Western 1951 · US · Colour · 84min

This is one of those Civil War dramas transposed to the Wild West, where the scenery is more dramatic and where the Indians turn the dilemma of the Confederates and the Unionists into a "trilemma". Alan Ladd, a Confederate captain, kills a man, and another Southerner, Arthur Kennedy, gets blamed, but is saved from a lynch mob. Meanwhile, John Ireland has abandoned "The Cause" and is organising Indians and mercenaries for a war of his own. There's a decent moral, bright-as-a-button Technicolor and a rousing finale. AT

Alan Ladd *Captain Brett Sherwood* • Lizabeth Scott *Chris* • Arthur Kennedy *Lane Waldron* • John Ireland *Quantrell* • Jeff Corey *Skee* • James Bell *Dr Terry* • Bert Freed *Randall* ■ *Dir* William Dieterle • *Scr* John Meredyth Lucas, George Slavin, George W George, from a story by Slavin

Red Planet ★★12
Science-fiction action horror
2000 · US/Aus · Colour · 102min

It's 2050 and Val Kilmer, Tom Sizemore, Carrie-Anne Moss and a hammier-than-ever Terence Stamp are sent to investigate when long-range efforts to make Mars habitable run into problems. Vital equipment is damaged in a crash-landing and the survivors are forced to depend on one another to survive in the inhospitable terrain. Director Antony Hoffman's feel-bad fantasy can't be faulted technically, but the plot lacks dramatic drive. AJ Violence, swearing, brief nudity. DVD

Val Kilmer *Gallagher* • Tom Sizemore *Burchenal* • Carrie-Anne Moss *Kate Bowman* • Benjamin Bratt *Santen* • Simon Baker (2) *Pettengil* • Terence Stamp *Chantilas* ■ *Dir* Antony Hoffman • *Scr* Chuck Pfarrer, Jonathan Lemkin, from a story by Pfarrer • *Cinematographer* Peter Suschitzky

Red Planet Mars ★★U
Science-fiction drama 1952 · US · BW · 87min

One of the oddest science-fiction movies ever made and worth sitting through every unwatchable preachy moment and ludicrous plot twist just to feel your jaw drop at various junctures. Could utopian Mars really be ruled by God? It's really a Nazi plot, run by Soviet agents, to destroy the world's economy. What can Earth do? Easy. Draft religious revolutionaries into Russia to overthrow the Communist government. This slice of po-faced seriousness is sci-fi's most explicit anti-Communist tract. AJ

Peter Graves (2) *Chris Cronyn* • Andrea King *Linda Cronyn* • Orley Lindgren *Steward Cronyn* • Bayard Veiller *Roger Cronyn* • Walter Sande *Admiral Carey* • Marvin Miller *Arjenian* • Herbert Berghof *Franz Calder* • Willis Bouchey *President* ■ *Dir* Harry Horner • *Scr* Anthony Veiller, John L Balderson, from the play *Red Planet* by Balderson, John Hoare

The Red Pony ★★PG
Drama 1949 · US · Colour · 84min

John Steinbeck's tale of a boy and his horse is an awkward blend of children's picture and social realist drama, and it isn't really good enough in either department. However, while Myrna Loy seems miscast as the boy's mum, Robert Mitchum is impressive as the ranch hand. The most impressive thing here is the fine "outdoor" score by Aaron Copland, who also wrote the music for Milestone's earlier Steinbeck adaptation, *Of Mice and Men*. AT DVD

Robert Mitchum *Billy Buck* • Myrna Loy *Alice Tiflin* • Louis Calhern *Grandpa* • Shepperd Strudwick *Fred Tiflin* • Peter Miles *Tom Tiflin* • Beau Bridges *Beau* • Margaret Hamilton *Teacher* ■ *Dir* Lewis Milestone • *Scr* John Steinbeck, from his story

Red Riding Hood ★★12
Supernatural horror 2011 · US · Colour · 96min

Twilight director Catherine Hardwicke's tween-friendly take on the folk legend veers between soapy romance and pantomime camp. Amanda Seyfried stars as the red-cloaked virgin torn between hunky suitors Shiloh Fernandez and Max Irons (son of Jeremy), while her snowy forest village comes under CGI werewolf attack. It's pretty to look at, yet the dialogue and performances are pretty banal. *The Company of Wolves* did it so much better. AJ Some violence. DVD BL

Amanda Seyfried *Valerie* • Gary Oldman *Father Solomon* • Billy Burke *Cesaire* • Shiloh Fernandez *Peter* • Max Irons *Henry* • Virginia Madsen *Suzette* • Lukas Haas *Father Auguste* • Julie Christie *Grandmother* ■ *Dir* Catherine Hardwicke • *Scr* David Leslie Johnson [David Johnson] • *Cinematographer* Mandy Walker

Red River ★★★★★U
Classic western 1948 · US · BW · 127min

This magnificent cattle-driving western is one of the greatest achievements of American cinema. Basing his film on co-screenwriter Borden Chase's novel, producer/director Howard Hawks created a rich masterpiece. Hawks is aided by arguably John Wayne's finest performance (as cattle boss Tom Dunson), and he's matched by young Montgomery Clift (as Dunson's ward). This is Hollywood film-making at its highest level, with music (Dimitri Tiomkin) and photography (Russell Harlan) that enhances and embellishes the text, it's not to be missed. Inexplicably remade as a TV movie in 1988. TS DVD BL

John Wayne *Thomas Dunson* • Montgomery Clift *Matthew Garth* • Joanne Dru *Tess Millay* • Walter Brennan *Groot Nadine* • Coleen Gray *Fen* • John Ireland *Cherry Valance* • Noah Beery Jr *Buster McGee* • Harry Carey Sr [Harry Carey] *Mr Melville* • Harry Carey Jr *Dan Latimer* • Shelley Winters *Dance-hall girl* ■ *Dir* Howard Hawks • *Scr* Borden Chase, Charles Schnee, from the novel *The Chisholm Trail* by Chase

Red River Range ★★U
Western 1938 · US · BW · 55min

This "Three Mesquiteers" B-western starring John Wayne takes less than an hour to trot out its modern-day story of the trio (Wayne, Ray Corrigan, Max Terhune) catching highly organised cattle rustlers. Veteran comedian Polly Moran takes a supporting role. AE

John Wayne *Stony Brooke* • Ray "Crash" Corrigan *Tucson Smith* • Max Terhune *Lullaby Joslin* • Polly Moran *Mrs Maxwell* • Lorna Gray *Jane Mason* • Kirby Grant *Tex Reilly* ■ *Dir* George Sherman • *Scr* Luci Ward, Stanley Roberts, Betty Burbridge, from a story by Luci Ward, from characters by William Colt MacDonald

Red Road ★★★18
Drama 2006 · UK/Den · Colour · 109min

The dangers of "Big Brother" society are explored through one woman's obsession in this dark, redemptive drama from writer/director Andrea Arnold (Oscar winner for the 2003 short *Wasp*). In her first big screen role, Kate Dickie (BBC TV's *Tinsel Town*) excels as Glaswegian CCTV operator Jackie, who develops a mysterious fixation on ex-con Clyde (a compellingly feral Tony Curran) after capturing him on her street surveillance monitors. Slow burning yet grittily atmospheric, this Cannes prizewinner is the inaugural segment of an experimental trilogy devised by Danish filmmakers Lone Scherfig and Anders Thomas Jensen that utilises the same characters and actors but with different directors. Though its melodramatic finale strains credibility, the picture remains provocative and gripping. SF Swearing, sex scenes. DVD BL

Kate Dickie *Jackie* • Tony Curran *Clyde* • Martin Compston *Stevie* • Natalie Press *April* • Paul Higgins *Avery* • Andy Armour *Alfred* ■ *Dir* Andrea Arnold • *Scr* Andrea Arnold, from characters by Lone Scherfig, Anders Thomas Jensen

Red Rock West ★★★★15
Black comedy thriller 1992 · US · Colour · 94min

The Last Seduction was the film that finally made people stand up and take notice of director John Dahl, but this *film noir* thriller is almost its equal. Nicolas Cage is the hapless drifter who is mistaken for a hitman by JT Walsh and is sent to murder Walsh's wife Lara Flynn Boyle. Things go from bad to worse when the real assassin (the demonic Dennis Hopper) turns up. The plot twists and turns deliciously, and Dahl's direction strikes a deft balance between knowing humour and genuine suspense. JF Violence, swearing. DVD

Nicolas Cage *Michael Williams* • Lara Flynn Boyle *Suzanne Brown* • Dennis Hopper *Lyle* • JT Walsh *Wayne Brown* • Craig Reay *Jim* • Vance Johnson *Mr Johnson* ■ *Dir* John Dahl • *Scr* John Dahl, Rick Dahl

Red Salute ★★U
Romantic comedy 1935 · US · BW · 79min

General's daughter Barbara Stanwyck falls for a communist and her father sends her to Mexico, where she meets a young soldier. Ensuing complications have them both on the run. Made when the radical movement in American universities was strong, this is basically a road comedy, with the spoiled daughter having to see the error of her leftist enthusiasms. At its premiere, students picketed and critics either condemned it as propaganda or felt it burlesqued the "American Way". Discounting the politics, it's diverting enough, with a particularly disarming performance by Stanwyck. TV

Barbara Stanwyck *Drue Van Allen* • Robert Young (1) *Jeff* • Hardie Albright *Leonard Arner* • Ruth Donnelly *Mrs Edith Rooney* • Cliff Edwards *PJ Rooney* • Gordon Jones *Lefty* • Paul Stanton *Louis Martin* ■ *Dir* Sidney Lanfield • *Scr* Humphrey Pearson, Manuel Seff, from a story by Pearson

Red Sands ★★18
Action horror 2009 · US · Colour · 85min

There's too much talk and not enough action in *Dead Birds* director Alex Turner's second wartime horror. Slow and predictable, it sees bored US soldiers in Afghanistan inadvertently unleash something demonic by destroying an ancient statue. But although Turner puts great energy into depicting the tedium of military life, he neglects to make even the story's supernatural elements exciting. SF Violence, swearing.

Shane West *Specialist Jeff Keller* • JK Simmons *Lieutenant Colonel Arson* • Leonard Roberts *Staff Sergeant Marcus Howston* • Aldis Hodge *Trevor Anderson* • Callum Blue *Gregory Wilcox* ■ *Dir* Alex Turner (1) • *Scr* Simon Barrett

Red Scorpion ★15
Action adventure 1989 · US · Colour · 102min

Dolph Lundgren stars in this awful action adventure as a Soviet agent who is sent to a warring African state to take out a resistance leader. Inexplicably, this was a big hit on video, perhaps because there's loads of mindless mass destruction, but the script and the performances make Rambo look positively Wildean. Lundgren didn't return for the 1995 sequel. JF DVD BL

Dolph Lundgren *Lt Nikolai* • M Emmet Walsh *Dewey Ferguson* • Al White *Kallunda* • TP McKenna *General Vortek* • Carmen Argenziano *Zayas* • Alex Colon *Mendez* • Brion James *Krasnov* ■ *Dir* Joseph Zito • *Scr* Arne Olsen, from a story by Robert Abramoff, Jack Abramoff

The Red Shoes ★★★★★U
Romantic dance drama
1948 · UK · Colour · 127min

In her film debut, Moira Shearer stars as the ballerina whose life is torn between a career with a manipulative impresario (Anton Walbrook) and marriage to a young composer (Marius Goring). This is arguably the best-loved dance film of all time, enabling the team of Michael Powell and Emeric Pressburger to ponder the power and nature of the subject matter with some extravagant, exuberant dance sequences and a riot of Oscar-winning Technicolor designs. Shearer and Walbrook give impeccable portrayals of innocence and tragedy at the service of art. AT DVD BL

Anton Walbrook *Boris Lermontov* • Moira Shearer *Victoria Page* • Marius Goring *Julian Craster* • Léonide Massine *Grischa Ljubov* • Robert Helpmann *Ivan Boleslawsky* • Albert Basserman *Sergei Ratov* • Esmond Knight *Livy* • Ludmilla Tcherina *Irina Boronskaja* ■ *Dir* Michael Powell, Emeric Pressburger • *Scr* Michael Powell, Emeric Pressburger, Keith Winter • *Cinematographer* Jack Cardiff • *Editor* Reginald Mills • *Music* Brian Easdale • *Art Directors* Hein Heckroth, Arthur Lawson • *Choreographer* Robert Helpmann

The Red Shoes ★★★15
Horror 2005 · S Kor · Colour · 103min

The Hans Christian Andersen fable is given a distinctive Korean makeover as, after discovering her husband's infidelity, a mother moves into a Seoul slum with her ballerina daughter and finds a pair of cursed shoes (actually a shade of pink) on the subway that proceed to cause death, disaster and major foot severing to anyone wearing them. Although dancing on familiar ground, the deaths are coolly inventive, the scares plentiful and the neo-Gothic fairy-tale atmosphere (the blood-red snow a stylish highpoint) well maintained. Contrived it may be, but this is still pleasingly fast-paced and skilfully graceful. AJ In Korean. Violence. DVD

Kim Hye-su *Seon-jae* • Park Yeon-ah *Tae-su* • Go Su-heui *Mi-heui* ■ *Dir* Kim Yong-gyun • *Scr* Ma Sang-ryeol

Red Skies of Montana ★★
Adventure drama 1952 · US · Colour · 89min

Richard Widmark and Richard Boone just about make this old-time action adventure worth watching. Both charismatic tough guys, they play firefighters in the Rockies who parachute into forest fires and either hose them down or create corridors over which the flames can't jump. You can't do this for an entire movie so various subplots are trumped up, with Widmark haunted by the death of a colleague while his wife (Constance Smith) gazes lovingly at him. AT

Richard Widmark *Cliff Mason* • Constance Smith *Peg* • Jeffrey Hunter *Ed Miller* • Richard Boone *Dryer* • Warren Stevens *Steve* • James Griffith *Boise* • Joe Sawyer *Pop Miller* • Charles Buchinsky [Charles Bronson] *Neff* ■ *Dir* Joseph M Newman • *Scr* Harry Kleiner, from a story by Art Cohn

Red Sky at Morning ★★
Drama 1971 · US · Colour · 112min

Left to his own devices in a strange New Mexico town, Richard Thomas struggles to come to terms with mother Claire Bloom's despairing fling after his father Richard Crenna is killed while serving with the navy. In contrast to this domestic bombast, James Goldstone tackles both Thomas's friendship with Desi Arnaz Jr and his hesitant romance with Catherine Burns with an overweening sensitivity that's punctuated only by monstrously unsubtle symbolism. Vilmos Zsigmond's photography threatens to capture life, but not often enough. DP

Richard Thomas *Josh Arnold* • Catherine Burns *Marcia Davidson* • Desi Arnaz Jr *Steenie Moreno* • Richard Crenna *Frank Arnold* • Claire Bloom *Ann Arnold* • John Colicos *Jimbob Buel* • Harry Guardino *Romeo Bonino* ■ *Dir* James Goldstone • *Scr* Marguerite Roberts, from the novel by Richard Bradford

Red Sonja ★★15
Fantasy adventure 1985 · US · Colour · 84min

Brigitte Nielsen stars as a leather-bikini-clad warrior who aims to avenge the death of her family by confronting wicked queen Sandahl Bergman. But it's Arnold Schwarzenegger who is the real star here, showing off his bulging biceps while trying to retain his dignity in a loincloth as the grunting hero who helps her. This is a sword-and-sorcery adventure for those who like their action fast, their dialogue ropey and their acting filled with more ham than a butcher's shop. JB Violence, brief nudity DVD Blu

Brigitte Nielsen *Red Sonja* • Arnold Schwarzenegger *Kalidor* • Sandahl Bergman *Queen Gedren* • Paul Smith *Falkon* • Ernie Reyes Jr *Prince Tarn* • Ronald Lacey *Ikol* ■ *Dir* Richard Fleischer • *Scr* Clive Exton, George MacDonald Fraser, from the character created by Robert E Howard

Red Sorghum ★★★★★ 15

Period drama   1987 · Chi · Colour · 88min

Having made his name as a cinematographer on such pictures as Chen Kaige's *Yellow Earth*, Zhang Yimou established himself as one of the most important Chinese film-makers with this, his directorial debut. The start of his collaboration with then-partner Gong Li and the winner of the Golden Bear at Berlin, *Red Sorghum* has a visual bravura that has since become Zhang's trademark, making majestic use of colour and setting the scene with stunning long-shots of buildings or breathtaking landscapes. He is also a natural storyteller, switching with great skill from the cosiness of a simple family drama to the brutality of a heroic resistance struggle. A true modern classic. DP Mandarin +subtitles. Violence. DVD

Gong Li *Nine, "my grandma"* • Jiang Wen *Yu, "my grandpa"* • Teng Rujun *Liu Luohan* • Liu Ji Douguan *"my dad"* • Qian Ming *Nine's father* • Ji Chunhua *Bandit Sanpao* • Zhai Chunhua *Hu Er* ■ *Dir* Zhang Yimou • *Scr* Chen Jianyu, Zhu Wei, Mo Yan, from the short stories by Mo

The Red Squirrel ★★★★ 18

Comedy drama   1993 · Sp · Colour · 109min

Exploring such sundry themes as identity and memory, female intuition, male boorishness and Basque nationalism, this is a typically inventive and beguiling outing from director Julio Medem. The frantic pace and dazzling technique complement the endlessly diverging train of events that follows suicidal musician Nancho Novo's chance encounter with runaway amnesiac Emma Suarez. Unconventionally comic, yet deftly passionate in its themes, this virtuoso picture not only benefits from storming lead performances, but also from inspired character turns. DP Spanish +subtitles. Violence, sex scenes, swearing. DVD

Nancho Novo *Jota* • Emma Suarez *Lisa* • Maria Barranco *Carmen* • Carmelo Gomez *Felix* ■ *Dir/Scr* Julio Medem

Red State ★★ 18

Horror thriller   2011 · US · Colour · 84min

Three horny teenage boys answer an online sex advert and find themselves in the clutches of an extreme fundamentalist religious group in director Kevin Smith's uneasy mix of horror movie, action thriller and social commentary. Undermined by misplaced humour and Smith's manic determination to hammer home his political leanings, the finale is an over-familiar anti-climactic mess. Although characterisation is minimal, Michael Parks makes an incredibly strong impression as the frightening pastor on a murderous mission. AJ Violence, swearing, sexual references. DVD Blu

Michael Parks *Abin Cooper* • John Goodman *Joseph Keenan* • Melissa Leo *Sara* • Kyle Gallner *Jarod* • Michael Angarano *Travis* ■ *Dir/Scr* Kevin Smith (2)

Red Sun ★★★ 15

Western   1971 · Fr/It/Sp · Colour · 109min

Toshiro Mifune teams up with gunslinger Charles Bronson to recover a golden, ceremonial sword, stolen by black-clad Alain Delon from the Japanese Ambassador to the US. Ursula Andress and Capucine add glamour to a yarn that's always entertaining and full of heavily stylised violence. Because the spaghetti western owed its origins to the samurai movie, this is a clever example of fusion cinema, but it

lacks cultural insights and wit. AT DVD Blu

Charles Bronson *Link* • Toshiro Mifune *Kuroda – samurai bodyguard* • Alain Delon *Gauche* • Ursula Andress *Cristina* • Capucine *Pepita* • Satoshi Nakamura *Ambassador* ■ *Dir* Terence Young • *Scr* Laird Koenig, Denne Bart Petitclerc, William Roberts, Lawrence Roman, from a story by Koenig

Red Sundown ★★★ U

Western   1956 · US · Colour · 81min

A terrific Universal co-feature, this western stars the excellent Rory Calhoun as a former gunslinger strapping on his guns one more time to thwart an evil cattle baron. Not terribly original but given zest by understanding director Jack Arnold and produced by exploitation king Albert Zugsmith of *Touch of Evil* fame. Martha Hyer gives a fine performance as a frontier woman, and veterans Dean Jagger and Robert Middleton lend supporting class. TS

Rory Calhoun *Alec Longmire* • Martha Hyer *Caroline Murphy* • Dean Jagger *Sheriff Jade Murphy* • Robert Middleton *Rufus Henshaw* • Grant Williams *Chet Swann* • Lita Baron *Maria* • James Millican *Purvis* ■ *Dir* Jack Arnold • *Scr* Martin Berkeley, from the novel *Black Trail* by Lewis B Patten

Red Surf ★ 18

Crime drama   1990 · US · Colour · 98min

This relentlessly predictable, dumber-than-average thriller has some interest value because it stars Hollywood heart-throb George Clooney in an early role. He plays a surfer dude who deals drugs to make ends meet. Deciding to make one last big score, Clooney and best friend Doug Savant involve Doug McKeon in the plan. But when he gets arrested, he names the local drug kingpin, who seeks revenge for the betrayal. A hokey, derivative exercise. AJ

George Clooney *Remar* • Doug Savant *Attila* • Gene Simmons *Doc* • Dedee Pfeiffer *Rebecca* • Rick Najera *Calavera* • Philip McKeon *True Blue* ■ *Dir* H Gordon Boos • *Scr* Vincent Robert, from a story by Brian Gamble, Jason Hoffs, Vincent Robert

Red Tails ★★★ 12

Second World War action adventure   2012 · US · Colour · 119min

This action-packed movie inspired by real-life events tells the story of the Second World War's first all-black fighter squadron, known as the Tuskegee Airmen. Stationed in Italy, but restricted to picking off the remnants of German ground forces because military top brass believe the "negro" is unsuited for aerial combat, the fliers (overseen by major Cuba Gooding Jr) campaign for the chance to engage the Luftwaffe. Director Anthony Hemingway weaves a powerful civil rights message into an otherwise tracitional wartime yarn of conflict and camaraderie. The acting and dialogue may veer (perhaps intentionally) towards the stiff-upper-lip clichés of vintage fighter ace films, but executive producer George Lucas brings a healthy dose of his *Star Wars* magic to the CGI of the spectacular aerial sequences. TeS DVD Blu

Cuba Gooding Jr *Major Emmanuel Stance* • David Oyelowo *Joe "Lightning" Little* • Terrence Howard *Colonel AJ Bullard* • Nate Parker *Marty "Easy" Julian* • Ne-Yo *Andrew "Smokey" Salem* • Michael B Jordan *Maurice Wilson* • *Scr* John Ridley, Aaron McGruder, from a story by Ridley, based in part on the non-fiction book *Red Tails, Black Wings: The Men of America's Black Air Force* by John B Holway

Red Team ★★ 18

Crime thriller   1999 · Can · Colour · 90min

It's a nifty premise – a serial killer who specialises in murdering fellow serial killers. But sadly director Jeremy Haft fails to make the most of the opportunity and the result is routine police thriller. Patrick Muldoon and Cathy Moriarty are the FBI agents who have a crisis of conscience when they cotton on to the fact that someone else is doing their job for them – and that the killer may actually be one of their own. JF DVD

Patrick Muldoon *Jason Chandler* • Cathy Moriarty *Agent Stephanie Dobson* • Tim Thomerson *William Heywood* • Fred Ward *Randall Brooks* • C Thomas Howell *JB Gaines* ■ *Dir* Jeremy Haft • *Scr* Alexander Metcalf

The Red Tent ★★★ U

Historical adventure   1969 · It/USSR · Colour · 120min

This ran at over four hours in Russia but was half that length in Europe and the United States. The movie deals with the dramatic rescue in 1928 of an Italian expedition to the Arctic. Playing the leader of the expedition, Peter Finch had to endure the entire 16-month shoot – a near record – while Sean Connery's role, as Roald Amundsen, was added later in the hope of boosting the film's box-office appeal. As a survivalist epic, it has its moments and the authentic locations are often spectacular. Finch, too, is always excellent and there's an Ennio Morricone score as a bonus. AT Some dialogue dubbed.

Sean Connery *Roald Amundsen* • Claudia Cardinale *Nurse Valeria* • Hardy Kruger *Aviator Lundborg* • Peter Finch *General Umberto Nobile* • Massimo Girotti *Romagna, rescue coordinator* • Luigi Vannucchi *Captain Zappi* • Mario Adorf *Biagi, radio operator* • Edward Marzevic *Finn Malmgren, meteorologist* ■ *Dir* Mikhail K Kalatozov [Mikhail Kalatozov] • *Scr* Ennio De Concini, Richard L Adams, Robert Bolt (uncredited)

The Red Violin ★★★ 15

Drama   1998 · Can/It/UK · Colour · 121min

Spanning 300 years, three continents and five languages, François Girard's musical chain letter looks and sounds superb. But, with locale and narrative carrying more weight than character, it's difficult to identify with any of the temporary owners of the violin, dyed red with the blood of the maker's dead family. Cursed by its maker's obsessive pursuit of perfection, the instrument passes on down the centuries, bringing ill-fortune to Austrian child prodigy Christoph Koncz, English virtuoso Jason Flemyng and Chinese student Sylvia Chang, although, intriguingly, we're left unsure whether crooked antiquarian Samuel L Jackson will suffer the same fate. DP Some sex scenes. DVD

Samuel L Jackson *Charles Morritz* • Greta Scacchi *Victoria Byrd* • Eva Marie Bryer *Sara* • Jason Flemyng *Frederick Pope* • Sylvia Chang *Xiang Pei* • Colm Feore *Auctioneer* • Carlo Cecchi *Nicolo Bussotti* ■ *Dir* François Girard • *Scr* François Girard, Don McKellar

Red White & Blue ★★★ 18

Horror thriller   2010 · UK/US · Colour · 99min

Restraint pays dividends for British writer/director Simon Rumley in this devastating and demanding revenge tragedy set in Austin, Texas. A low-budget tale of broken lives and misguided retribution, Rumley's slow-burner is driven by superbly nuanced performances, with Amanda Fuller's emotionally scarred nymphomaniac gradually forming a relationship with a mysterious Iraq War veteran (an unforgettable Noah Taylor). But a shift from dark character study to more traditional exploitation territory might alienate some and limit the thriller's appeal. SF Violence, sex scenes, nudity.

Amanda Fuller *Erica* • Noah Taylor *Nate* • Marc Senter *Franki* • Jon Michael Davis *Ed* • Nick Ashy Holden *Alvin* • Patrick Crovo *Carl* ■ *Dir/Scr* Simon Rumley

Redacted ★★ 15

War drama   2007 · US/Can · Colour · 86min

This sincere but extremely uneven anti-war statement from veteran director Brian De Palma bears some similarity to his acclaimed 1989 Vietnam film *Casualties of War*, in which a group of American soldiers rape and kill a Vietnamese girl. Here, in a story based on an actual incident, the servicemen are stationed in Iraq and gang rape and kill an Iraqi girl. Sadly, other comparisons with the director's previous film are mostly unfavourable. De Palma's decision to tell the story through a collage of digital video supposedly shot by the

soldiers, as well as staged CCTV footage and internet news stories, is ingenious – after all, this is the first war to be recorded and then posted on the internet by the people fighting it. But his choice of working with unknown and nonprofessional actors, together with his typical lack of emotional attachment, take the edge off what is undeniably a gruelling story. AS In English, French, Arabic. DVD

Izzy Diaz *Angel Salazar* • Daniel Stuart Sherman *BB Rush* • Patrick Carroll *Reno Flake* • Mike Figueroa *Sgt Jim Vazques* • Ty Jones *Master Sgt Sweet* • Rob Devaney *Lawyer McCoy* ■ *Dir/Scr* Brian De Palma

Redbelt ★★★★ 15

Action thriller   2007 · US · Colour · 95min

Pulitzer Prize-winning playwright David Mamet puts the audience in a chokehold with this tightly coiled thriller about honour, ethics and martial arts. The movie rests on a standout performance from Chiwetel Ejiofor, who plays an LA jujitsu instructor asked to put aside his principles of self-defence and compete in a championship bout. He refuses until events involving his ambitious wife (Alice Braga) and a deceitful Hollywood action star (Tim Allen) force him into a corner. Full of Mamet's usual narrative bluffs and feints (not to mention appearances by his regular actors Joe Mantegna and Ricky Jay), *Redbelt* updates the classic 1940s boxing movie. JR DVD Blu

Chiwetel Ejiofor *Mike Terry* • Emily Mortimer *Laura Black* • Alice Braga *Sondra Terry* • Tim Allen *Chet Frank* • Joe Mantegna *Jerry Weiss* • Rodrigo Santoro *Bruno Silva* • Max Martini *Joe Collins* • David Paymer *Richie* ■ *Dir/Scr* David Mamet

Redemption of the Ghost ★★

Drama   2000 · US · Colour · 111min

A couple of young children befriend a fugitive from justice in this well-meaning TV movie. But it isn't in the same class as *Whistle down the Wind* or *The Spirit of the Beehive*. Gene Bicknell plays the escaped embezzler who is inspired by the trust of the children whose barn he is using as a hideout. Diane Ladd plays the siblings' aunt and Alexandra Paul their mother, but no one emerges from this with much credit. Indeed, there's something distastefully misogynistic about the movie's demonising of Rachel Hunter, who plays the wife whose social ambitions prompted Bicknell to take the cash. DP

Diane Ladd *Aunt Helen* • John Savage *Sheriff Burns* • Alexandra Paul *Audrey Powell* • Rachel Hunter *Gloria* • Gene Bicknell *Witt Hampton* • Scott Terra *Jack* ■ *Dir* Richard Friedman • *Scr* Gene Bicknell, Darrel Campbell

The Redhead and the Cowboy ★★★

Wartime western   1950 · US · BW · 82min

A strong trio of leading players – Glenn Ford, Rhonda Fleming and Edmond O'Brien – make this plot-heavy Civil War story watchable, although the title cries out for Technicolor. Fleming is the redheaded messenger for the South, O'Brien the undercover Union officer on her trail, and Ford the cowboy she mistakes for a contact. The film only falls apart when Alan Reed as a renegade Confederate officer starts chewing up the scenery. AE

Glenn Ford *Gil Kyle* • Edmond O'Brien *Dunn Jeffers* • Rhonda Fleming *Candace Bronson* • Alan Reed *Lamartine* • Morris Ankrum *Sheriff* ■ *Dir* Leslie Fenton • *Scr* Jonathan Latimer, Liam O'Brien, from a story by Charles Marquis Warren

The Redhead from Wyoming ★★★ PG

Western adventure   1953 · US · Colour · 77min

If ever anybody deserved to be filmed in colour, it was green-eyed, red-headed Irish beauty Maureen O'Hara, whose Hollywood career was as historic as it was colourful. Besides doing terrific work for John Ford, she invariably starred in swashbucklers and westerns that perfectly showcased her

R

talents. In this movie, she falls for a sheriff while supposedly taking care of a rancher. The story is pure fluff, of course, but when O'Hara's on the screen the weaknesses in the plot aren't important. TS **DVD**

Maureen O'Hara *Kate Maxwell* • Alex Nicol *Stan Blaine* • William Bishop *Jim Averell* • Robert Strauss *"Knuckles" Hogan* • Alexander Scourby *Reece Duncan* • Jack Kelly *Sandy* • Jeanne Cooper *Myra* ■ *Dir* Lee Sholem • *Scr* Polly James, Herb Meadow, from the story by James

Reds
★★★★★ 15
Epic biographical drama
1981 · US · Colour · 187min

It took Warren Beatty's ferocious energy to even attempt this chronicle of the Russian Revolution, focused through a radical love affair, and come up with a final product that is close to the project's original intentions. In telling the story of American journalist John Reed – who wrote *Ten Days That Shook the World*, regarded by many as the definitive account of the revolution – and his on-off romance with left-wing activist Louise Bryant (Diane Keaton), Beatty surrounded himself with massive talent: British writer Trevor Griffiths, cinematographer Vittorio Storaro, composer Stephen Sondheim, the great editor Dede Allen and a scene-stealing Jack Nicholson as playwright Eugene O'Neill. Beatty won a well-deserved Oscar for best direction. TH Swearing. **DVD**

Warren Beatty *John Reed* • Diane Keaton *Louise Bryant* • Jack Nicholson *Eugene O'Neill* • Edward Herrmann *Max Eastman* • Jerzy Kosinski *Grigory Zinoviev* • Maureen Stapleton *Emma Goldman* • Gene Hackman *Pete Van Wherry* • Paul Sorvino *Louis Fraina* • Nicolas Coster *Paul Trullinger* • M Emmet Walsh *Speaker at Liberal club* • Ian Wolfe *Mr Partlow* • Bessie Love *Mrs Partlow* ■ *Dir* Warren Beatty • *Scr* Warren Beatty, Trevor Griffiths

The Reef
★★ U
Animated adventure
2006 · US/S Kor · Colour · 77min

After Pixar's *Finding Nemo* and DreamWorks's *Shark Tale*, this latest aquatic animated adventure proves to be a bit of a letdown. The story centres on Pi (voiced by Freddie Prinze Jr), a cute little fish who's left alone when his parents fall foul of a trawler's nets, and then heads for the Reef to live with his Aunt Pearl. There, he has to compete with bully boy shark Troy (Donal Logue) for the affections of the lovely Cordelia (Evan Rachel Wood), the fish of his dreams. The CGI animation – co-produced by Korean studios Digiart and FX Digital – is fairly bright and breezy, and will doubtless appeal to younger viewers who can't get enough of the deep-sea likes of *Nemo*. But others may feel that they have seen it all before, and usually rather better done. DA **DVD**

Freddie Prinze Jr *Pi* • Rob Schneider *Nerissa* • Evan Rachel Wood *Cordelia* • Donal Logue *Troy* • Andy Dick *Dylan/Curious Shark* • Fran Drescher *Pearl* • John Rhys-Davies *Thornton* • Lee Ermey [R Lee Ermey] *Jack* ■ *Dir* Howard Baker, John Fox, Kyung Ho Lee • *Scr* Scott Clevenger, from a story by Anurag Mehta, Timothy Peternel

The Reef
★★★ 15
Horror thriller based on a true story
2010 · Aus · Colour · 84min

This Australian thriller breaks no new ground. Or, maybe more accurately, treads no new water. When a bunch of attractive guys and gals take a sailboat out to sea, all is fine... for a time. Things begin to go wrong when the yacht capsizes and the crew is forced to choose between staying with the sinking hull or striking out for the safety of a distant reef. A circling great white shark makes their choice more complicated. Andrew Traucki's follow-up to killer-croc movie *Black Water* is nicely filmed and has a particularly effective use of sound. It's no *Jaws*, but *The Reef* still makes for a very decent addition to the roster of watery creature features. DA **DVD**

Damian Walshe-Howling *Luke* • Zoe Naylor *Kate* • Adrienne Pickering *Suzie* • Gyton Grantley *Matt* • Kieran Darcy-Smith *Warren* ■ *Dir/Scr* Andrew Traucki

Reefer and the Model
★★★ 15
Comedy thriller
1988 · UK · Colour · 89min

This spiky, acerbic tale of a small-time criminal and his involvement with a junkie "model", veers alarmingly at times between winsome charm and outré violence. It wins out in the end through sheer bravura of characterisation as director Joe Comerford cuts to the core of his cast's motivations. London's underbelly is exposed in all its visceral glory and the narrative occasionally roves all over the shop, but it's worth sticking with this unusually energetic thriller that contains just enough cutting wit and dark humour. SH

Ian McElhinney *Reefer* • Carol Scanlan *Teresa, the model* • Eve Watkinson *Reefer's mother* • Sean Lawlor *Spider* • Ray McBride *Badger* • Birdy Sweeney *"Instant Photo"* ■ *Dir/Scr* Joe Comerford

Reefer Madness
★★ 15
Cult drama
1936 · US · BW · 68min

Initially released as *The Burning Question* and later retitled *Tell Your Children*, this exploitation classic emerged from decades of obscurity to become a campus classic in the early 1970s. In this hilariously misinformed exposé of the perils of smoking dope, exhortation comes a poor second to sensationalism, as Dave O'Brien tempts his classmates into toking on the weed. DP Drug abuse. **DVD**

Dorothy Short *Mary Lane* • Kenneth Craig *Bill Harper* • Lillian Miles *Blanche* • Dave O'Brien *Ralph Wiley* • Thelma White *Mae Colman* • Carleton Young *Jack Perry* • Warren McCollum *Jimmy Lane* ■ *Dir* Louis Gasnier • *Scr* Arthur Hoerl and Paul Franklin, from an original story by Lawrence Meade

Reeker
★★★ 15
Horror
2005 · US · Colour · 87min

Old-school horror conventions get a creepy contemporary spin in this innovative thrill ride from writer/director Dave Payne. It focuses on five student travelling companions who fall victim to a deadly, decaying creature after becoming stranded in a mysteriously deserted motel in the Californian desert. What sounds on paper like one big celluloid cliché, in Payne's hands feels surprisingly fresh, smart and fun. SF Violence, swearing. **DVD**

Devon Gummersall *Jack* • Derek Richardson *Nelson* • Tina Illman *Gretchen* • Scott Whyte *Trip* • Arielle Kebbel *Cookie* • Eric Mabius *Radford* • Michael Ironside *Henry* ■ *Dir/Scr* Dave Payne

The Referees
★★★ 15
Documentary
2009 · Bel · Colour · 80min

The lives of football referees and linesmen have always been a bit of a mystery, but this fine, no-frills documentary provides some long-overdue insight. Filmed at Euro 2008, it lifts the lid on the on- and off-field experiences of some of the world's top football officials, including England's own Howard Webb. We see how referee Webb copes when a debatable decision leads to internet death-threats. It's all fascinating stuff, and it may make you realise that refs and linesmen have a mighty tough job to do. DA Swearing.

■ *Dir* Yves Hinant, Eric Cardot, Delphine Lehericey

The Reflecting Skin
★★ 15
Drama
1990 · UK · Colour · 95min

The directorial debut of Philip Ridley is a wilfully perverse affair centred on a child (Jeremy Cooper) whose confused perceptions of the adults and events in his 1950s American farming community make for a disturbing vision of childhood. Cooper's cruellest fantasies are fixed on reclusive widow Lindsay Duncan, whose liaison with the boy's hero-brother (Viggo Mortensen) inspires the child to connive at her ruin. Heavy portents and deep symbolism abound to absurd effect. AME Nudity. **DVD**

Viggo Mortensen *Cameron* • Lindsay Duncan *Dolphin Blue* • Jeremy Cooper *Seth* • Sheila Moore *Ruth* • Duncan Fraser *Luke* ■ *Dir/Scr* Philip Ridley • *Cinematographer* Dick Pope

A Reflection of Fear
★★★★ 18
Horror
1973 · US · Colour · 85min

This weird thriller was very unpopular in its day but its unnervingly sinister atmosphere will repay another look. Strange teenager Sondra Locke lives with her mother Mary Ure, her grandmother Signe Hasso and her dolls. Then, when her absentee father (Robert Shaw, Ure's husband in real life) appears out of the blue, she goes completely off the rails, and the film leads to a truly mind-boggling ending. Primarily a cinematographer, William A Fraker ensures everything looks great and creates chills by never quite revealing the menace. Performances are also strong, especially from the ethereal-looking Locke. DM

Robert Shaw *Michael* • Sally Kellerman *Anne* • Mary Ure *Katherine* • Sondra Locke *Marguerite* • Signe Hasso *Julia* • Mitchell Ryan *Inspector McKenna* ■ *Dir* William A Fraker • *Scr* Edward Hume, Lewis John Carlino, from the novel *Go to Thy Deathbed* by Stanton Forbes

Reflections in a Golden Eye
★★★ 15
Drama
1967 · US · Colour · 104min

Carson McCullers's steamy novel is brought to the screen by director John Huston with Elizabeth Taylor as the army wife, unhappily married to latent homosexual major Marlon Brando and having an affair with Brando's superior, Brian Keith. Cameraman Aldo Tonti uses some interesting angles and colour combinations, but it's overblown and unintentionally funny. Buffs will note that shots of Brando in uniform were used later in *Apocalypse Now* to show the young Colonel Kurtz. AT Swearing.

Elizabeth Taylor *Leonora Penderton* • Marlon Brando *Maj Weldon Penderton* • Brian Keith *Lt Col Morris Langdon* • Julie Harris (2) *Alison Langdon* • Zorro David *Anacleto* • Gordon Mitchell (1) *Stables sergeant* • Irvin Dugan *Captain Weincheck* • Fay Sparks *Susie* • Robert Forster *Private Williams* • Douglas Stark *Dr Burgess* ■ *Dir* John Huston • *Scr* Chapman Mortimer, Gladys Hill, from the novel by Carson McCullers

Reflections on a Crime
★★★
Psychological drama
1994 · US · Colour · 94min

Although he will always be remembered for cult low-budget B-movies, Roger Corman sometimes took a chance on artier fare, such as this intriguing movie. Mimi Rogers puts in a mesmerising performance as a woman on death row for the murder of her husband, who reluctantly reveals her story in flashback to prison guard Billy Zane. It's too talky for its own good, but director/writer Jon Purdy still delivers some chilling insights into domestic hell. JF Violence, swearing, nudity.

Mimi Rogers *Regina* • Billy Zane *Colin* • John Terry *James* • Kurt Fuller *Howard* • Lee Garlington *Tina* • Nancy Fish *Ellen* ■ *Dir/Scr* Jon Purdy

Reform School Girl
★ 12
Prison crime drama
1957 · US · BW · 70min

In this trashy exploitation picture aimed at the youth market, Gloria Castillo is the kind of well-developed teenager who has only to iron a dress in her underwear to be propositioned by her uncle. Sent to reform school after refusing to squeal on her car-thief boyfriend, she is victimised and almost murdered before settling down to a more wholesome future. AE **DVD**

Gloria Castillo *Donna Price* • Edward Byrnes [Edd Byrnes] *Vince* • Ross Ford *David Lindsay* • Ralph Reed *Jackie* • Yvette Vickers *Roxy* • Helen Wallace *Mrs Trimble* • Donna Jo Gribble *Cathy* • Luana Anders *Josie* • Sally Kellerman *Girl* ■ *Dir/Scr* Edward Bernds

Reform School Girls
★★ 18
Prison spoof
1986 · US · Colour · 90min

Director Tom DeSimone had a string of enjoyably trashy pictures including porn to

his credit, before making this "women behind bars" spoof. Youngster Linda Carol is sent to a harsh reform school where she has to deal with the usual unsympathetic female warden and a lesbian gang leader, played by one-time rock singer Wendy O Williams. Amusing and campy in spots, with plenty of nudity and gratuitous underwear. JG

Sybil Danning *Sutter* • Wendy O Williams *Charlie* • Linda Carol *Jenny* • Pat Ast *Edna* • Charlotte McGinnis *Dr Norton* • Sherri Stoner *Lisa* • Denise Gordy *Claudie* • Laurie Schwartz *Nicky* ■ *Dir/Scr* Tom DeSimone

The Refuge
★★★ 15
Drama
2009 · Fr · Colour · 88min

An air of melancholy pervades this heartfelt but not always convincing film, which sees Isabelle Carré hide away on the coast while recovering from heroin addiction and awaiting the birth of her overdosed boyfriend's baby. However, she is forced to confront her suppressed feelings when the deceased's brother comes to stay. Handsomely photographed, this is a doggedly undramatic character study that gains poignancy during an unexpected dénouement. DP French +subtitles. Swearing, drug abuse.

Isabelle Carré *Mousse* • Louis-Ronan Choisy *Paul* • Pierre Louis-Calixte *Serge* • Melvil Poupaud *Louis* ■ *Dir* François Ozon • *Scr* François Ozon, Mathieu Hippeau • *Cinematographer* Mathias Raaflaub

Regarding Henry
★★★ 15
Drama
1991 · US · Colour · 102min

What looked like a sure-fire winner on paper – ruthless high-flying lawyer Harrison Ford fights back from brain injury and becomes a better person in the process – in fact emerged as a rather cold, lacklustre affair. Ford was simply the wrong choice for the role, and director Mike Nichols invests the action with too much gloss and polish. Annette Bening looks lovely and gives one of the film's better performances, but from the start it's hard to sympathise with the family and their plight. However, this is still compulsively watchable thanks to the star power on board. SH Some swearing. **DVD**

Harrison Ford *Henry Turner* • Annette Bening *Sarah Turner* • Bill Nunn *Bradley* • Mikki Allen *Rachel Turner* • Donald Moffat *Charlie* • Aida Linares *Rosella* • Elizabeth Wilson *Jessica* • Robin Bartlett *Phyllis* • Bruce Altman *Bruce* • Rebecca Miller *Linda Palmer* ■ *Dir* Mike Nichols • *Scr* Jeffrey Abrams

Regeneration
★★★★
Silent drama
1915 · US · BW · 74min

Bowery hoodlum Owen Kildare published his memoir *My Mamie Rose: the Story of My Regeneration* in 1903 and a play duly followed. Writing with half-brother Carl Harbaugh, Raoul Walsh changed some names and tinkered with the odd fact to produce this vivid crime movie that also provides an invaluable portrait of inner-city slum life in America. Rockliffe Fellowes and Anna Q Nilsson are aptly teamed as the orphan-gone-bad and the selfless socialite whose happiness is thwarted by Harbaugh's crusading DA. The story is affecting, the acting functional, but the images achieved by Walsh and cameraman Georges Benoit are indelible. DP

Rockliffe Fellowes *Owen Conway* • Anna Q Nilsson *Marie Deering* • William Sheer *Skinny* • Carl Harbaugh *District Attorney Ames* • James A Marcus *Jim Conway* • Maggie Weston *Maggie Conway* ■ *Dir* RA Walsh [Raoul Walsh] • *Scr* RA Walsh [Raoul Walsh], Carl Harbaugh, from the play by Owen Kildare, Walter Hackett, from the memoir *My Mamie Rose: the Story of My Regeneration* by Owen Kildare

Regeneration
★★★★ 15
First World War drama
1997 · UK/Can · Colour · 108min

Four shell-shocked men help each other come to terms with their shared horrific First World War experiences in director Gillies MacKinnon's compelling, if sometimes highly romanticised, adaptation of the first book in Pat Barker's trilogy. How they cope in a military psychiatric hospital –

Siegfried Sassoon and Wilfred Owen (James Wilby and Stuart Bunce) wrote their most famous poetry in such institutions to exorcise their feelings – makes for a grim, intelligent drama suffused with haunting and harrowing images, none more so than the opening aerial shot of no-man's-land strewn with the casualties of war. AJ Swearing, nudity. *DVD*

Jonathan Pryce Dr William Rivers • James Wilby Siegfried Sassoon • Jonny Lee Miller Billy Prior • Stuart Bunce Wilfred Owen • Tanya Allen Sarah • David Hayman Dr Bryce • Dougray Scott Robert Graves • John Neville Dr Yealland ■ Dir Gillies MacKinnon • Scr Allan Scott, from the novel by Pat Barker

Regina ★★★
Psychological drama
1982 · Fr/It · Colour · 95min

Ava Gardner is the mother who dominates her husband (Anthony Quinn) and son (Ray Sharkey) to such an extent that, when the boy wants to marry, mum refuses, then takes to her bed with a psychosomatic illness. This rarely seen performance by Ava Gardner is one of her very best and director Jean-Yves Prate has contrived an atmosphere as morbid as the central character herself. TH

Ava Gardner Mother • Anthony Quinn Father • Anna Karina Daughter • Ray Sharkey Son ■ Dir Jean-Yves Prate • Scr from the play by Pierre Rey

LANDMARK FILM
A satirical attack on French high society in decline, notable for its deep-focus photography and its human insight

La Règle du Jeu ★★★★★ PG
Comedy drama
1939 · Fr · BW · 101min

This complex comedy of manners from director Jean Renoir was such a box-office turkey on its first release in 1939 that it was not allowed out again at its original length until the late 1950s. It was then promptly acclaimed as a masterpiece, going on a few years later to selection by an international poll of critics as the third greatest film of all time. Focusing on an up-market country house party, the film is a sophisticated, poignant and often funny study of social mores and the games people play. Renoir stars, directs and co-writes. PF French +subtitles. *DVD*

Marcel Dalio Robert la Chesnaye • Nora Gregor Christine • Jean Renoir Octave • Roland Toutain Jurieu • Mila Parély Geneviève de Marras • Paulette Dubost Lisette • Carette [Julien Carette] Marceau • Gaston Modot Schumacher ■ Dir/Scr Jean Renoir

Regression ★★ 15
Thriller
2015 · Sp/Can · Colour · 101min

While this has the hallmarks of a superior effort, it rarely rises above the satanic thriller pack. A teenage girl (Emma Watson) has accused her father (David Dencik) of abuse. As the detective in charge (Ethan Hawke) probes further, he seems to uncover a diabolical conspiracy. The film's nightmarish imagery impresses, building genuine suspense in places, but the story is slight, and the ending fizzles out into something pretty forgettable. EAS Swearing, sex scenes.

Ethan Hawke Bruce Kenner • Emma Watson Angela Gray • David Thewlis Kenneth Raines • Lothaire Bluteau Reverend Beaumont • David Dencik John Gray ■ Dir/Scr Alejandro Amenábar

Regular Lovers ★★★ 18
Period drama
2005 · Fr · BW · 184min

Having been a key member of the avant-garde Zanzibar group of film-makers at the time of the May 1968 Paris riots, Philippe Garrel is well placed to reconstruct the events that brought down De Gaulle in this epic study of poetic passion and political commitment. Louis Garrel plays a student whose drift towards the barricades is inspired more by fashion consciousness than revolutionary zeal. Indeed, he would rather be sleeping with free spirit Clotilde Hesme or smoking opium with affluent drop-out Julien Lucas than engaging with angrier young men. Intriguing, but rarely

revealing or compelling. DP French +subtitles. *DVD*

Louis Garrel François Dervieux • Clotilde Hesme Lilie • Julien Lucas Antoine • Mathieu Genet Nicolas • Marc Barbé ■ Dir Philippe Garrel • Scr Philippe Garrel, Arlette Langmann, Marc Cholodenko

Reign of Assassins ★★★ 15
Martial arts action adventure
2010 · Chi · Colour · 103min

A female warrior attempts to leave her killing days behind in this polished but overblown Chinese period swordplay adventure. There's an exhilarating showdown involving flaming blades, bending swords, flying needles and lots of Crouching Tiger-style rooftop scurrying. It's a shame that the story descends into a series of unlikely twists, but it's gamely played, with Barbie Hsu a delight as a psychopathic nymph, and the experienced Michelle Yeoh bringing a much-needed steadying presence to proceedings. JH Mandarin +subtitles. Violence, brief nudity.

Michelle Yeoh Zeng Jing • Jung Woo-Sung [Jung Woo-sung] Jiang Ah-Sheng • Wang Xueqi The Wheel King • Barbie Hsu Turquoise ■ Dir/Scr Su Chao-Pin

Reign of Fire ★★ 12
Futuristic fantasy adventure
2001 · US/UK/Ire · Colour · 97min

If it weren't for the dragons, this far-fetched fantasy would have drowned in its own mediocrity. A skeletal, anticlimactic mess from Rob Bowman, it relies totally on its mythological flying fire-breathers to carry the film. These scaly monsters have overrun the world after London Underground workers inadvertently unleashed a slumbering ancestor. The performances range from hammy (Christian Bale) to simply wooden (Gerard Butler). SF Violence, swearing. *DVD*

Christian Bale Quinn Abercromby • Matthew McConaughey Denton Van Zan • Izabella Scorupco Alex Jensen • Gerard Butler Dave Creedy • Scott James Moutter Jared Wilke • David Kennedy Eddie Stax • Alexander Siddig Ajay • Ned Dennehy Barlow ■ Dir Rob Bowman • Scr Gregg Chabot, Kevin Peterka, Matt Greenberg, from a story by Chabot, Peterka

Reign of Terror ★★★★
Historical drama
1949 · US · BW · 89min

A visually exhilarating, ingeniously-plotted political thriller about Robespierre's plot to become dictator after the French Revolution, this even extracts passable performances from usually limp Robert Cummings and insipid but beautiful Arlene Dahl in the starring roles. Richard Basehart makes a superbly malevolent Robespierre and supporting actor Arnold Moss has his finest moment as a sly opportunist. The machiavellian intrigue unfolds in vivid film noir style as the powerful team of director Anthony Mann and cameraman John Alton is joined by the great art director William Cameron Menzies (taking credit only as the producer). The imagery conveys the terror and uncertainty of the period, while the pace overrides the script's contrivances. Heady stuff indeed. AE

Robert Cummings Charles D'Aubigny • Richard Basehart Maximilien Robespierre • Richard Hart François Barras • Arlene Dahl Madelon • Arnold Moss Police chief Fouché • Norman Lloyd Tallien • Charles McGraw Sergeant • Beulah Bondi Grandma ■ Dir Anthony Mann • Scr Philip Yordan, Aeneas MacKenzie, from a story by Yordan, MacKenzie

Reign over Me ★★★ 15
Drama
2007 · US · Colour · 119min

After Punch-Drunk Love and Spanglish, Adam Sandler further enhanced his reputation as a serious actor with this post-9/11 drama. Sandler plays Charlie, a man who has dropped off the radar after the loss of his wife and daughters in one of the hijacked jets. Five years later, Alan (Don Cheadle), his former college roommate, unexpectedly runs across him in the street in New York, and, aghast at Charlie's decline, re-establishes a relationship with him. Reign over Me is contrived and it lacks

zip. But the acting, by a cast that also includes Donald Sutherland and Liv Tyler, is top drawer. This may well prove to be the film that does for Sandler what Eternal Sunshine of the Spotless Mind did for Jim Carrey. DA *DVD* BD

Adam Sandler Charlie Fineman • Don Cheadle Alan Johnson • Jada Pinkett Smith Janeane Johnson • Liv Tyler Angela Oakhurst • Saffron Burrows Donna Remar • Donald Sutherland Judge Raines • Robert Klein Jonathan Timpleman • Melinda Dillon Ginger Timpleman ■ Dir/Scr Mike Binder

Reincarnated ★★★ 18
Music documentary 2013 · US · Colour · 96min

Rap superstar Snoop Dogg heads to Jamaica to make a reggae album in this candid documentary, simultaneously embarking on a spiritual journey that sees him adopt a new performing name, Snoop Lion. Forsaking the violence that informed much of his earlier music, Snoop embraces a new message of peace and love as he immerses himself in Rastafarian culture. Music journalist-turned-director Andy Capper portrays his subject as a man seeking redemption, scarred by his criminal past and mourning the deaths of close friends, and the film strikes an impressive balance between serious concerns and several hilarious episodes – usually involving Snoop and Jamaica's bountiful crops of marijuana. TeS

Snoop Dogg ■ Dir Andy Capper

The Reincarnation of Peter Proud ★★★ 18
Horror mystery 1975 · US · Colour · 101min

Slated in its time, this has become almost a cult movie since. Director J Lee Thompson treated Max Ehrlich's adaptation of his own novel with a seriousness it didn't deserve, but his approach worked. Michael Sarrazin is the history professor who dreams his way back to the past and makes some discoveries about previous lives and loves. The plot never gets it together, but the mood and atmosphere are spot-on. TH

Michael Sarrazin Peter Proud • Jennifer O'Neill Ann Curtis • Margot Kidder Marcia Curtis • Cornelia Sharpe Nora Hayes • Paul Hecht Dr Samuel Goodman • Norman Burton Dr Frederick Spear ■ Dir J Lee Thompson • Scr Max Ehrlich, from his novel

La Reine Margot ★★
Historical drama 1954 · Fr/It · Colour · 103min

Catherine de Medici (Françoise Rosay) rules France through her son, Charles IX (Robert Porte), and hopes to avoid civil war between the Protestants and the Catholics by arranging a marriage between her daughter Margot (Jeanne Moreau) and a handsome count. Dumas's novel was originally adapted by Abel Gance, the director of the legendary silent epic Napoléon, but the film that finally emerged was much more of a bodice-ripper and it suffered cuts for the American and British markets. AT In French.

Jeanne Moreau Marguerite de Valois, Queen Margot • Françoise Rosay Catherine de Medici • Armando Francioli Joseph Peyrac de la Mole • Robert Porte Charles IX • Henri Génès Annibal de Coconas • André Versini Henri de Navarre ■ Dir Jean Dréville • Scr Abel Gance, from the novel by Alexandre Dumas

La Reine Margot ★★★ 18
Historical drama
1994 · Fr/Ger/It · Colour · 155min

One of the dangers of historical film-making is that there is so much information available that the pace becomes fatally slow. Patrice Chéreau avoids this by taking the events described in the novel by Alexandre Dumas at such a furious lick, that the action becomes incomprehensible unless you pay keen attention. Isabelle Adjani won her fourth César as the Catholic Marguerite de Valois, who was married by her scheming mother Catherine de Médici (a César-winning Virna Lisi) to the Protestant leader Henri de Navarre (Daniel Auteuil). The illicit romance with Vincent Perez is deadly dull, but Jean-Hugues

Anglade is outstanding as the deranged Charles IX. DP French +subtitles. Violence, sex scenes, nudity. *DVD*

Isabelle Adjani Marguerite de Valois (Margot) • Daniel Auteuil Henri de Navarre • Jean-Hugues Anglade Charles IX • Vincent Perez La Môle • Virna Lisi Catherine de Médici • Dominique Blanc Henriette de Nevers ■ Dir Patrice Chéreau • Scr Danièle Thompson, Patrice Chéreau, from the novel by Alexandre Dumas

The Reivers ★★★★ PG
Period comedy drama
1969 · US · Colour · 106min

Steve McQueen is well cast here as the ne'er-do-well guiding youngster Mitch Vogel through the minefield of adolescence in early 20th-century Mississippi. McQueen plays a hired hand working for Vogel's grandfather, Will Geer, who makes use of his employer's new car to take the lad on an adventure that includes a brothel and a racetrack. Mark Rydell directs with a gentle pace, while Burgess Meredith tightens it all up as narrator. There's also a scene-stealing, Oscar-nominated performance by Rupert Crosse. TH *DVD*

Steve McQueen (1) Boon Hogganbeck • Sharon Farrell Corrie • Will Geer Boss McCaslin • Michael Constantine Mr Binford • Rupert Crosse Ned McCaslin • Mitch Vogel Lucius McCaslin • Lonny Chapman Maury McCaslin • Juano Hernandez Uncle Possum • Clifton James Butch Lovemaiden • Ruth White Miss Reba • Dub Taylor Dr Peabody • Diane Ladd Phoebe • Burgess Meredith Narrator ■ Dir Mark Rydell • Scr Irving Ravetch, Harriet Frank Jr, from the novel by William Faulkner

The Rejuvenator ★★★ 18
Horror 1988 · US · Colour · 84min

Ageing actress Jessica Dublin is financing demented doctor John Mackay's experiments in eternal youth. When he finally creates a serum from human brains to make her young again, she pretends to be her actress niece in order to revive her film career. But sex makes her mutate into a giant-headed monster with huge claws, which she uses to decapitate victims before eating their brains. Well made and oddly affecting, this is also oppressively creepy. AJ

Vivian Lanko Elizabeth Warren/Monster • John MacKay Dr Gregory Ashton • James Hogue Wilhelm • Katell Pleven Dr Stella Stone • Marcus Powell Dr Germaine • Jessica Dublin Ruth Warren ■ Dir Brian Thomas Jones • Scr Simon Nuchtern, Brian Thomas Jones, from a story by Nuchtern

Relative Stranger ★★
Drama 2009 · US · Colour · 88min

ER's Eriq La Salle learns about the importance of family in this syrupy but solid melodrama. He plays a struggling former American football star who reluctantly returns home following his father's death, to face the kin he deserted six years previously. The stormy conflict that ensues is milked for maximum impact. However, it's the quality performances that carry events, making the emotions on show feel honest even when the plot is at its most contrived and predictable. SF

Eriq La Salle Walter Clemons • Michael Michele Charlotte Clemons • Michael Beach James Clemons • Dana Davis Denise Clemons • Sherri Saum Nicole Tate • Cicely Tyson Pearl ■ Dir Charles Burnett • Scr Eric Haywood

Relative Values ★★★ PG
Satirical comedy 2000 · UK · Colour · 85min

Julie Andrews makes a big-screen comeback in Eric Styles's brittle adaptation of Noël Coward's comedy. Unflappable countess Andrews uses all her feminine wiles to prevent her son Edward Atterton from marrying glamorous Hollywood starlet Jeanne Tripplehorn, who is, in fact, the sister of Andrews's personal maid Sophie Thompson, and arrives with her hell-raising boyfriend William Baldwin in hot pursuit. Styles can't make Coward's creaky characters breathe on film, but Colin Firth and Stephen Fry play supporting roles with élan, while Andrews never puts a foot wrong. NS *DVD*

Julie Andrews *Felicity* • Sophie Thompson *Moxie* • Edward Atterton *Nigel* • Jeanne Tripplehorn *Miranda* • William Baldwin *Don Lucas* • Colin Firth *Peter* • Stephen Fry *Crestwell* ■ *Dir* Eric Styles • *Scr* Paul Rattigan, Michael Walker, from the play by Noël Coward

Relax... It's Just Sex ★★ 18
Comedy 1998 · US · Colour · 105min

The emphasis in this comedy of sexual manners is on same sex relationships, but the action is spiced up by the intervention of straight characters whose tangles add to the overall tone of insecurity and confusion. Notwithstanding the verbosity of the script, Jennifer Tilly is boisterously maternal as the cement keeping the disparate acquaintances together and she's well supported by veterans Seymour Cassel, Paul Winfield and Susan Tyrrell. However, the sitcomedic mood is undermined by a brutal male rape scene. DP *DVD*

Mitchell Anderson *Vincey Sauris* • Jennifer Tilly *Tara Ricotto* • Cynda Williams *Sarina Classer* • Seymour Cassel *Emile Pillsbury* • Susan Tyrrell *Alicia Pillsbury* • Serena Scott Thomas *Megan Pillsbury* • Paul Winfield *Auntie Mahalia* • Lori Petty *Robin Moon* ■ *Dir/Scr* PJ Castellaneta

Release ★ 15
Drama 2010 · UK · Colour · 87min

A young priest serving a prison sentence must come to terms with his past crimes and his homosexuality in this low-budget British drama. It all proves a bit too much for directors Darren Flaxstone and Christian Martin to take on board, since the thuddingly sincere dialogue, one-dimensional characterisation and occasionally wobbly performances turn their sincere intentions into the stuff of cheesy melodrama. There's no little ambition here, but the overwrought storyline and dismally pokey surroundings end up being more reminiscent of *Prisoner: Cell Block H*. TJ Violence, swearing, sex scenes. *DVD*

Daniel Brocklebank *Father Jack Gillie* • Garry Summers *Martin* • Bernie Hodges *Max* • Wayne Virgo *Rook* ■ *Dir/Scr* Darren Flaxstone, Christian Martin

Relentless ★★★
Western 1948 · US · Colour · 92min

Robert Young enjoys an offbeat role as an intelligent cowboy while desert settings in gorgeous Technicolor and a more realistic than usual storyline turn this into an above average western. Wrongly accused of murder, Young stays one jump ahead of a sheriff's posse as he attempts to clear himself with the aid of Marguerite Chapman's travelling saleswoman. That inveterate scene stealer, Akim Tamiroff, upstages surly Barton MacLane in the villainy department. AE

Robert Young (1) *Nick Buckley* • Marguerite Chapman *Luella Purdy* • Willard Parker *Jeff Moyer* • Akim Tamiroff *Joe Faringo* • Barton MacLane *Tex Brandow* • Mike Mazurki *Jake* • Robert Barrat *Ed Simpson* ■ *Dir* George Sherman • *Scr* Winston Miller, from the story *Three Were Thoroughbreds* by Kenneth Perkins

Relentless ★★ 18
Thriller 1989 · US · Colour · 88min

This spawned three sequels and no one can quite understand why. Judd Nelson turns in the greatest performance of his career so far as a serial killer who makes Jack the Ripper seem a dilettante. Apart from Nelson acting his socks off, this is a very ho hum effort which is only passable fare if you're in an undemanding mood. *Relentless 2: Dead On* followed in 1991. SH *DVD*

Judd Nelson *Buck Taylor* • Robert Loggia *Bill Malloy* • Leo Rossi *Sam Dietz* • Meg Foster *Carol Dietz* • Patrick O'Bryan *Todd Arthur* • Ken Lerner *Arthur* • Mindy Seger *Francine* • Angel Tompkins *Carmen* • Beau Starr *Ike Taylor* • Harriet Hall *Angela Taylor* ■ *Dir* William Lustig • *Scr* Jack TD Robinson [Phil Alden Robinson]

The Relic ★★★ 15
Horror 1996 · US · Colour · 105min

Director Peter Hyams pulls out all the stops in this unpretentious, super-slick gothic horror. An ancient Amazonian beast is creeping around Chicago's natural history museum on the night of a gala opening party. Can feisty scientist Penelope Ann Miller or detective Tom Sizemore overcome their fears to battle the blood-lusting demon of superstition? Hardly earth-shattering, a glossy veneer on the time-worn clichés and harum-scarum jolts keep the suspense simmering. AJ *DVD* 🔵

Penelope Ann Miller *Dr Margo Green* • Tom Sizemore *Lt Vince D'Agosta* • Linda Hunt *Dr Ann Cuthbert* • James Whitmore *Dr Albert Frock* • Clayton Rohner *Detective Hollingsworth* ■ *Dir* Peter Hyams • *Scr* Amy Holden Jones, John Raffo, Rick Jaffa, Amanda Silver, from the novel by Douglas Preston, Lincoln Child

La Religieuse ★★★★
Religious drama 1965 · Fr · Colour · 139min

Jacques Rivette's austere allegory was, initially, banned in France for its anti-clerical content. Rejected by her family, Anna Karina is forced to take the veil, only to be subjected to deprivations and beatings by mother superior, Micheline Presle, and then sexually harassed by the lesbian head (Liselotte Pulver) of her new convent. Not even the priest (Francisco Rabal) who rescues her acts out of pure motives. However, this visually rigorous film is more about freedom of conscience than the severity or hypocrisy of religious celibacy and proves as provocative as it's tragic. DP French +subtitles.

Anna Karina *Suzanne Simonin* • Liselotte Pulver *Mme de Chelles* • Micheline Presle *Mme de Moni* • Christine Lenier *Mme Simonin* • Francine Bergé *Sister St Christine* • Francisco Rabal *Dom Morel* ■ *Dir* Jacques Rivette • *Scr* Jacques Rivette, Jean Gruault, from the novel *Memoirs of a Nun* by Denis Diderot

Religulous ★★ 15
Documentary 2008 · US · Colour · 96min

In this inflammatory attack on the extremes of faith, American funnyman and atheist Bill Maher travels around the world interviewing Christians, Jews and Muslims and confronting their beliefs. Rather than offering debate, though, his hectoring, aggressive (and only occasionally funny) interviews are simply interested in ridicule. It's something made all the easier by choosing crackpots as his targets – from a Miami preacher who believes he's the Second Coming, to a born-again Christian who used to be a Satanist priest. The comedian's attack-dog manner ultimately gives the film a mean-spirited edge and makes him look like an arrogant bully who's as rigid in his scepticism as his targets are in their faith. JR English, Spanish, Arabic +subtitles. *DVD*

Bill Maher ■ *Dir* Larry Charles

The Reluctant Debutante ★★★ U
Comedy 1958 · US · Colour · 95min

This soft-centred dig at the London "season" was outmoded the moment it was made. A not very convincing change was the casting of two American teen idols, Sandra Dee, in the title role, and John Saxon, as her drum-playing sweetheart. Thankfully, Dee's father and stepmother were played delightfully by Rex Harrison and Kay Kendall. The nicely designed film was shot in Paris, because Harrison couldn't enter England for tax reasons. RB

Rex Harrison *Jimmy Broadbent* • Kay Kendall *Sheila Broadbent* • John Saxon *David Parkson* • Sandra Dee *Jane Broadbent* • Angela Lansbury *Mabel Claremont* • Peter Myers *David Fenner* • Diane Clare *Clarissa Claremont* ■ *Dir* Vincente Minnelli • *Scr* William Douglas Home, from his play

The Reluctant Dragon ★★ U
Documentary 1941 · US · BW and Colour · 73min

American humorist Robert Benchley fronts this documentary about the Walt Disney studios, which takes its name from the 25-minute short that concludes the picture. Never more than a blatant plug for the studio, it encouraged the trade paper *Variety* to opine: "Dr Goebbels couldn't do a better propaganda job to show the workers in Disney's pen-and-ink factory as a happy and contented lot." In fact, the workers were on strike when the film was released in 1941. The demonstrations of the then up-to-date techniques, though, should interest fans and historians of animation. AT

Robert Benchley • Nana Bryant *Mrs Benchley* • Buddy Pepper *Guide* • Frances Gifford *Doris* • Walt Disney ■ *Dir* Alfred Werker, Hamilton Luske, Jim Handley, Ford Beebe, Erwin Verity, Jasper Blystone • *Scr* Ted Sears, Al Perkins, Larry Clemmons, Bill Cottrell

The Reluctant Fundamentalist ★★★ 15
Drama 2012 · US/UK/Qatar · Colour · 130min

Though a few liberties have been taken with Mohsin Hamid's novel, this study of modern-day racial tensions is admirably faithful to the spirit of its source. Riz Ahmed is splendid as Changez, a Pakistani man from a good family who moves to the West to chase the American Dream, only to find his hopes for the future dashed in the Islamophobic backlash to the events of 9/11. Told in flashback – with Changez now a teacher in Lahore, accused of radicalising his students – Mira Nair's thoughtful, provocative drama makes some very interesting points about how society and the media can combine to create history's monsters. DW Swearing, some violence, a sex scene.

Riz Ahmed [Rizwan Ahmed] *Changez* • Kate Hudson *Erica* • Liev Schreiber *Bobby Lincoln* • Kiefer Sutherland *Jim Cross* • Om Puri *Abu* • Shabana Azmi *Ammi* ■ *Dir* Mira Nair • *Scr* William Wheeler, from a story by Mohsin Hamid, Ami Boghani, from Hamid's novel

The Reluctant Saint ★★ U
Biographical drama 1962 · US/It · BW · 114min

Maximilian Schell stars in this portrait of St Joseph of Cupertino. Considered to be an idiot by his village, the future Franciscan brother apparently entered a monastery as protection from the outside world and then studied successfully – despite lacking a formal education – to become a priest. Director Edward Dmytryk's earnest chronicle follows his progress until his declaration of sainthood, as the result of his exemplary life. This movie was a case of good intentions overwhelming the material. BB

Maximilian Schell *Giuseppe Desa* • Ricardo Montalban *Father Raspi* • Lea Padovani *Francesca Desa* • Akim Tamiroff *Bishop Durso* • Harold Goldblatt *Father Giovanni* ■ *Dir* Edward Dmytryk • *Scr* John Fante, Joseph Petracca

The Reluctant Widow ★★ U
Period drama 1950 · UK · BW · 82min

Romance, espionage and villainy during the Napoleonic Wars unfold at an English country estate inherited by former governess Jean Kent on the death of her wealthy husband. The widow finds herself surrounded by French spies and British traitors, all after some vital documents secreted in the house, but she foils them all. A good-looking but rather muddled and unsatisfactory adaptation of a novel by Georgette Heyer, this entertains in fits and starts. RK

Jean Kent *Elinor* • Peter Hammond *Eustace Cheviot* • Guy Rolfe *Lord Carlyon* • Paul Dupuis *Lord Nivelle* • Kathleen Byron *Mme de Chevreaux* ■ *Dir* Bernard Knowles • *Scr* JB Boothroyd, Gordon Wellesley, from the novel by Georgette Heyer

Remainder ★★★★ 15
Drama 2015 · UK/Ger · Colour · 102min

A young man (Tom Sturridge) is involved in a freak accident and is left with severe memory loss, for which his lawyer secures him £8.5 million. Using this money, he re-enacts a series of half-remembered experiences that might be linked to his past. Though Sturridge creates an unsympathetic character, he's compellingly watchable as a cold, obsessive perfectionist who is unusually particular when it comes to the details. For those who don't mind unusual films, this moody psychological thriller offers an intoxicating experience. SC Violence, swearing, sexual references.

Tom Sturridge *Tom* • Cush Jumbo *Catherine* • Ed Speleers *Greg* • Arsher Ali *Naz* • Shaun Prendergast *DI Merril* ■ *Dir* Omer Fast • *Scr* Omer Fast, from Tom K McCarthy's novel

The Remaining ★★★ 15
Horror thriller 2014 · US · Colour · 88min

Trumpets blow and the wrath of God unleashes the four horsemen of the apocalypse in a religious-themed horror movie aimed at devout Christian audiences. When close knit friends get together for the wedding of Alexa Vega (*SpyKids*), they witness the Rapture instead of the expected nuptials. They then have to face a series of catastrophic events while nocturnal creatures they have only heard about in sermons cause epic mayhem to create a new world order. The film downplays the preachiness, and ensures that the striking nightmare visuals are ace, and it's all performed with surprising conviction. AJ

Alexa Vega *Skylar* • Shaun Sipos *Jack* • Johnny Pacar *Tommy* • Italia Ricci *Allison* • Bryan Dechart *Dan* • Liz E Morgan *Sam* ■ *Dir* Casey La Scala • *Scr* Casey La Scala, Chris Dowling

The Remains of the Day ★★★★★ U
Period drama 1993 · UK/US · Colour · 128min

This impeccable adaptation of Kazuo Ishiguro's Booker Prize-winning novel stars Anthony Hopkins as the emotionally repressed butler and Emma Thompson as the housekeeper he possibly loves. Framed in flashbacks, the story is an English twist on Jean Renoir's classic *La Règle du Jeu*, a broad view of a narrow class of aristocrats on the verge of self-destruction. Co-starring James Fox as a fascistic English lord and Christopher Reeve as an American diplomat (the past and present owners of Darlington Hall), it is as much a study in power and politics as it is Hopkins's blinkered view of the world from behind the gleaming silver salvers. The 1930s and 1940s settings are immaculately staged, and James Ivory's direction is alive to every nuance and chink of the sherry glasses. AT *DVD* 🔵

Anthony Hopkins *Stevens* • Emma Thompson *Miss Kenton* • James Fox *Lord Darlington* • Christopher Reeve *Lewis* • Peter Vaughan *Father* • Hugh Grant *Cardinal* • Michael Lonsdale [Michel Lonsdale] *Dupont D'Ivry* • Tim Pigott-Smith *Benn* • John Haycraft *Auctioneer* • Caroline Hunt *Landlady* • Paula Jacobs *Mrs Mortimer* • Ben Chaplin *Charlie* • Steve Dibben *George* ■ *Dir* James Ivory • *Scr* Ruth Prawer Jhabvala, from the novel by Kazuo Ishiguro

Remains to Be Seen ★★
Comedy mystery 1953 · US · BW · 88min

Van Johnson, drum-playing manager of a Park Avenue block, finds a wealthy tenant mysteriously dead in his apartment. His discovery leads to romance with the corpse's niece, band-singer June Allyson, en route to which the pair outwit the evil, scheming Angela Lansbury. Despite a pretty silly, unconvincing plot, this romantic comedy mystery moves along good-naturedly and comes to life with stars duetting a couple of lively numbers and Dorothy Dandridge (as herself) singing *Taking a Chance on Love*. RK

June Allyson *Jody Revere* • Van Johnson *Waldo Williams* • Louis Calhern *Benjamin Goodwin* • Angela Lansbury *Valeska Chauvel* • John Beal *Dr Glenson* • Dorothy Dandridge ■ *Dir* Don Weis • *Scr* Sidney Sheldon, from the play by Howard Lindsay, Russel Crouse

The Remarkable Mr Pennypacker ★★★ U
Period comedy 1959 · US · Colour · 87min

Clifton Webb is the son of sausage manufacturer Charles Coburn, for whom he works, and married to Dorothy McGuire in 1890s Harrisburg, Pennsylvania. Forced to spend much time at his father's Philadelphia plant, lonely Webb takes a second wife, happily runs two families and fathers a total of 17 children before the truth is revealed. Scripted by Walter Reisch from a successful play and directed by Henry Levin, this is a good-natured, nicely observed period comedy, to which the polished and very "correct" Webb is ideally suited. **RK**

Clifton Webb *Pa Pennypacker* • Dorothy McGuire *Ma Pennypacker* • Charles Coburn *Grampa* • Jill St John *Kate Pennypacker* • Ron Ely *Wilbur Fielding* • Ray Stricklyn *Horace Pennypacker III* • David Nelson (1) *Henry Pennypacker* ■ *Dir* Henry Levin • *Scr* Walter Reisch, from the play by Liam O'Brien

Rembrandt ★★★ U
Biographical drama   1936 · UK · BW · 83min

One of the prestige productions that brought dignity to the British film industry, this distinguished film stars Charles Laughton in a remarkably affecting performance. His tendency to ham is brought under control by Alexander Korda, whose brother Vincent provides some well-designed studio sets, quaintly converting Denham's sound stages to Rembrandt van Rijn's Amsterdam. A rare screen performance from Gertrude Lawrence reveals why this great lady of the stage wasn't loved by the movie camera. **TS**

Charles Laughton *Rembrandt Van Rijn* • Gertrude Lawrence *Geertje Dirx* • Elsa Lanchester *Hendrickje Stoffels* • Edward Chapman *Fabrizius* • Walter Hudd *Banning Cocq* • Roger Livesey *Beggar Saul* • John Bryning *Titus Van Rijn* • Allan Jeayes *Dr Tulp* ■ *Dir* Alexander Korda • *Scr* Carl Zuckmayer, Lajos Biró, June Head, Arthur Wimperis • *Cinematographer* Georges Périnal • *Art Director* Vincent Korda

Remember? ★
Romantic comedy   1939 · US · BW · 83min

Lew Ayres introduces his fiancée Greer Garson to his best friend Robert Taylor over lunch, whereupon friend sweeps her away and marries her, setting in train a series of events encompassing everything from divorce to amnesia-inducing potions. This must surely be one of the most witless comedies ever dreamed up. **RK**

Robert Taylor (1 *Jeff Holland* • Greer Garson *Linda Bronson* • Lew Ayres *Sky Ames* • Billie Burke *Mrs Bronson* • Reginald Owen *Mr Bronson* • George Barbier *Mr McIntyre* • Henry Travers *Judge Milliken* • Richard Carle *Mr Piper* ■ *Dir* Norman Z McLeod • *Scr* Corey Ford, Norman Z McLeod

Remember ★★
Thriller   2015 · Can/Ger · Colour · 95min

The sad decline of Atom Egoyan continues with this melodramatic travesty. Clearly, he thought he was combining Costa-Gavras's *Music Box* with Christopher Nolan's *Memento*. But the chasmic holes in the plot undermine elderly Christopher Plummer's bid to follow the clues provided by wheelchair-bound Auschwitz survivor Martin Landau and track down the block commander responsible for countless deaths. Plummer brings a bemused vulnerability to his role, but it all becomes increasingly implausible. **DP** In English, German.

Christopher Plummer *Zev* • Martin Landau *Max* • Bruno Ganz *Rudy Kurlander 1* • Jürgen Prochnow *Rudy Kurlander 4* • Heinz Lieven *Rudy Kurlander 2* • Henry Czerny *Charles* ■ *Dir* Atom Egoyan • *Scr* Benjamin August

Remember Last Night? ★★★
Comedy mystery   1935 · US · BW · 76min

Universal assigned their star horror movie director James Whale and a first-rate cast, headed by Robert Young, Constance Cummings and Edward Arnold, to this offbeat comedy thriller, in which a group of socialites wake up with hangovers after a party, to find that one of their number has been murdered. A witty, sophisticated and suspenseful puzzler, the film combines, and parodies, a number of styles and genres to fascinating (if occasionally confusing) effect. **RK**

Edward Arnold *Danny Harrison* • Robert Young (1) *Tony Milburn* • Constance Cummings *Carlotta, his wife* • George Meeker *Vic Huling* • Sally Eilers *Bette, his wife* • Reginald Denny *Jack Whitridge* • Louise Henry *Penny, his wife* • Gregory Ratoff *Faronea* • Robert Armstrong *Fred Flannagan* •

Monroe Owsley *Billy Arliss* ■ *Dir* James Whale • *Scr* Harry Clork, Doris Malloy, Dan Totheroh, Murray Roth, from the novel *Hangover Murders* by Adam Hobhouse

Remember Me? ★ PG
Comedy   1996 · UK · Colour · 77min

Although the producers claimed this as a latter-day Ealing comedy, it's actually a single-pace, single-joke farce that leaves an expert cast floundering amid a myriad of clumsy plot contrivances. Yet Michael Frayn's tired script is only part of the problem, as Nick Hurran's direction is rendered even more leaden by the painfully slow editing. **DP**

Robert Lindsay *Jamie* • Rik Mayall *Ian* • Imelda Staunton *Lorna* • Brenda Blethyn *Shirley* • James Fleet *Donald* • Haydn Gwynne *Jamie's wife* ■ *Dir* Nick Hurran • *Scr* Michael Frayn

Remember Me ★★ 12
Romantic drama   2010 · US · Colour · 107min

Twilight's Robert Pattinson reprises his mean and moody act here, playing an all-too-human, angry young man rebelling against his wealthy father (Pierce Brosnan) in the wake of his brother's suicide. *Lost's* Emilie de Ravin plays the girl who might save Tyler from himself, except that the pair seem to drag each other down into a self-indulgent whirl of despair. Brosnan's performance is more intriguing as he reveals emotional depth behind a smug veneer. Alas, the finale is not only shamelessly manipulative but vaguely distasteful. **SP** Violence, swearing, sex scenes. **DVD** **Blu-ray**

Robert Pattinson *Tyler Hawkins* • Pierce Brosnan *Charles Hawkins* • Chris Cooper *Neil Craig* • Lena Olin *Diane Hirsch* • Ruby Jerins *Caroline Hawkins* ■ *Dir* Allen Coulter • *Scr* Will Fetters

Remember My Name ★★★
Drama   1978 · US · Colour · 93min

Written and directed by Alan Rudolph and produced by his mentor Robert Altman, this is a film full of fine moments, but, because of Rudolph's tendency to over-complicate, those moments ultimately add up to an unsatisfying whole. Returning from prison to make life hell for ex-husband Anthony Perkins, Geraldine Chaplin gives a scorching performance, but even she gets bogged down in the subplots involving shopkeeper Jeff Goldblum and landlord Moses Gunn. **DP** Swearing.

Geraldine Chaplin *Emily* • Anthony Perkins *Neil Curry* • Berry Berenson *Barbara Curry* • Moses Gunn *Pike* • Jeff Goldblum *Mr Nudd* • Timothy Thomerson [Tim Thomerson] *Jeff* • Alfre Woodard *Rita* • Marilyn Coleman *Teresa* ■ *Dir/Scr* Alan Rudolph

Remember the Day ★★★ U
Drama   1941 · US · BW · 86min

What usually brought a tear to the eye of tough studio boss Darryl F Zanuck invariably worked with audiences worldwide, and this small-town soap opera is no exception. Claudette Colbert is cast against type as a schoolteacher who, in flashback, tells of her influence on a particular pupil, who grows up to be a presidential candidate. Meanwhile, Colbert falls for dull-but-worthy sports master John Payne. It's all professionally done and, if you like this sort of thing and can enjoy Colbert in a rare straight role, a fair slice of entertainment. **TS**

Claudette Colbert *Nora Trinell* • John Payne *Dan Hopkins* • John Shepperd [Shepperd Strudwick] *Dewey Roberts* • Ann E Todd *Kate Hill* • Douglas Croft *Dewey as a boy* • Jane Seymour (1) *Mrs Roberts* ■ *Dir* Henry King • *Scr* Tess Slesinger, Frank Davis, Allan Scott, from the play by Philo Higley, Philip Dunning

Remember the Night ★★★★
Romantic comedy drama
1940 · US · BW · 94min

Barbara Stanwyck and Fred MacMurray, both at the top of their form and perfect foils for one another, co-star in this romantic comedy, written by Preston Sturges and directed by Mitchell Leisen. The

---

action concerns a shoplifter (Stanwyck) whose trial is delayed by the Christmas holiday, leaving her somewhat adrift. Sympathetic, assistant district attorney MacMurray takes pity on her and brings her to his family's country home for Christmas. An absolute delight, combining warmth and charm with a little sentimentality and humour. **RK**

Barbara Stanwyck *Lee Leander* • Fred MacMurray *John Sargent* • Beulah Bondi *Mrs Sargent* • Elizabeth Patterson *Aunt Emma* • Willard Robertson *Francis X O'Leary* • Sterling Holloway *Willie* • Charles Waldron *Judge – New York* • Paul Guilfoyle (1) *District attorney* ■ *Dir* Mitchell Leisen • *Scr* Preston Sturges

Remember the Titans ★★★ PG
Sports drama based on a true story
2000 · US · Colour · 108min

Denzel Washington tackles the potentially explosive combination of football and racial desegregation in 1970s America. When two Virginia high schools are combined, Washington supersedes his white counterpart Will Patton as head coach of the Titans football team. This causes friction between them and among the players, as they try to overcome hostility and prejudice in the pursuit of sporting glory. Washington gives a typically solid performance, but it's Patton who steals the show. **DA** **DVD**

Denzel Washington *Coach Herman Boone* • Will Patton *Coach Bill Yoast* • Wood Harris *Julius "Big Ju" Campbell* • Ryan Hurst *Gerry Bertier* • Donald Adeosun Faison [Donald Faison] *Petey Jones* • Ethan Suplee *Lewis Lastik* ■ *Dir* Boaz Yakin • *Scr* Gregory Allen Howard

Remo – Unarmed and Dangerous ★★★ 15
Action adventure   1985 · US · Colour · 110min

This solid, unpretentious little action thriller is notable mainly for the presence of Joel Grey, the Oscar-winning MC of *Cabaret*, making a rare return to the big screen. The Remo of the title is Fred Ward, a no-nonsense policeman who is transformed into a super agent by a wise old Oriental (Grey). Director Guy Hamilton would have preferred to have the same sort of budgets that were afforded him for his Bond movies, but he still keeps the action roaring along. **JF** **DVD** **Blu-ray**

Fred Ward *Remo Williams* • Joel Grey *Chiun* • Wilford Brimley *Harold Smith* • JA Preston *Conn MacCleary* • George Coe *General Scott Watson* • Charles Cioffi *George S Grove* • Kate Mulgrew *Major Rayner Fleming* ■ *Dir* Guy Hamilton • *Scr* Christopher Wood, from characters in The *Destroyer* series by Richard Sapir, Warren Murphy

Remote Control ★★ 15
Science-fiction comedy
1988 · US · Colour and BW · 84min

Kevin Dillon is good as a video-store clerk who stumbles into an alien conspiracy involving a video release of a cheesy 1950s movie called *Remote Control*. Viewers of the tape are hypnotised into committing violent psychotic acts. The black-and-white movie-within-a-movie is amusing, but although this is ostensibly a sci-fi comedy, the entire enterprise is frequently stuck awkwardly between being funny and being serious. **KB**

Kevin Dillon *Cosmo* • Deborah Goodrich *Belinda* • Jennifer Tilly *Allegra* • Christopher Wynne *Georgie* • Frank Beddor *Victor* • Kaaren Lee *Patricia* • Bert Remsen *Bill Denver* ■ *Dir/Scr* Jeff Lieberman

Renaissance ★★★ 15
Animated science-fiction thriller
2006 · Lux/Fr/UK · BW and Colour · 100min

Renaissance has somewhat misleadingly been compared to *Sin City* because it pays tribute to classic film noir and is shot in black and white. But the sensibility of the film is much closer to recent Japanese anime, combining futurism, breathtaking backgrounds and stiff human figures, and conveying a vaguely anti-corporate message. Daniel Craig provides the voice (in

---

this English-language version) for detective Karas, who is investigating the disappearance of a top scientist (Romola Garai), and in the process befriends her sister (Catherine McCormack). The animation is spectacular to look at, but it's dispiriting that the script isn't a little bit more original or interesting. **LF** French dubbed. **DVD**

Daniel Craig *Barthélemy Karas* • Catherine McCormack *Bislane Tasuiev* • Romola Garai *Ilona Tasuiev* • Ian Holm *Dr Jonas Muller* • Kevork Malikyan *Nusrat Farfella* • Jonathan Pryce *Paul Dellenbach* • Robert Dauney *Barthélemy Karas* ■ *Dir* Christian Volckman • *Scr* Matthieu Delaporte, Alexandre De La Patellière, Alexandre De La Patellière, Patrick Raynal, Jean Bernard Pouy, from a story by Delaporte, De La Patellière

Renaissance Man ★★ 12
Comedy   1994 · US · Colour · 122min

Penny Marshall directs this misconceived high-concept movie, which just about gets by on the quality of its cast. Danny DeVito, as the unemployed advertising executive called up to teach English to stroppy army recruits, does his best to counteract the sentimentality that keeps rising to the surface, and he is ably supported by some top-line players. Ultimately, however, the film is just too nice for its own good. **JF** Some swearing. **DVD**

Danny DeVito *Bill Rago* • Gregory Hines *Sergeant Cass* • Cliff Robertson *Colonel James* • James Remar *Captain Murdoch* • Lillo Brancato Jr [Lillo Brancato] *Donnie Benitez* • Stacey Dash *Miranda Myers* • Kadeem Hardison *Jamaal Montgomery* • Richard T Jones *Jackson Leroy* • Khalil Kain *Roosevelt Hobbs* • Marky Mark [Mark Wahlberg] *Tommy Lee Haywood* • Ed Begley Jr *Jack Markin* ■ *Dir* Penny Marshall • *Scr* Jim Burnstein

Rendez-vous ★★★ 15
Erotic drama   1985 · Fr · Colour · 79min

Former critic and film teacher André Téchiné has certainly practised what he once preached, having emerged as one of the more highly regarded French directors of the past three decades. This is an atmospheric, backstage drama in which Juliette Binoche plays a girl from the provinces who wants to become a star. She goes to Paris and decides that one way to success and home comfort is to sleep with the young men she meets. But when she gets a part in a production of *Romeo and Juliet*, it is director Jean-Louis Trintignant, an older man, who becomes her salvation. Far from profound, but seldom boring. **BB** French +subtitles. **DVD**

Juliette Binoche *Nina Larrieu* • Lambert Wilson *Quentin* • Wadeck Stanczak *Paulot* • Jean-Louis Trintignant *Scrutzler* • Dominique Lavanant *Gertrude* ■ *Dir* André Téchiné • *Scr* André Téchiné, Olivier Assayas

Les Rendez-vous d'Anna ★★★
Drama   1978 · Fr/Bel/W Ger · Colour · 127min

Made by Belgian film director Chantal Akerman, this follows the meanderings of Anna (Aurore Clément), a young Belgian film director as she travels to several European cities to publicise her latest film. The autobiographical element makes it an uncomfortable film to watch, especially in the long scene when she admits to her mother that she is in love with a woman. Some may find Akerman's minimalist cinema coolly captures the modern malaise, while others might suffer from a sense of malaise while watching it. **RB** French +subtitles.

Aurore Clément *Anna Silver* • Helmut Griem *Heinrich* • Magali Noël *Ida* • Lea Massari *Anna's mother* ■ *Dir/Scr* Chantal Akerman

Les Rendez-vous de Paris ★★★★ PG
Portmanteau romantic drama
1995 · Fr · Colour · 94min

Alighting on his favourite themes of pursuit and evasion, Eric Rohmer fashions three bittersweet vignettes in this fond tribute to capricious youth and the hidden beauties of Paris. As narcissistic as they are garrulous, each protagonist is a choice Rohmer

R

---

archetype – whether it's the girl trying to catch her boyfriend in his infidelity in *The Seven O'Clock Rendezvous*, the student toying with an affair, while summoning the courage to break her engagement, in *The Benches of Paris*, or the artist in *Mother and Child, 1907*, who is gently rebuffed by a recently married woman. Minor perhaps, but still irresistible. **DP** French +subtitles.

Clara Bellar *Esther* • Antoine Basler *Horace* • Aurore Rauscher *Him* • Serge Renko *Him* • Michaël Kraft *Painter* • Bénédicte Loyen *Young woman* ■ *Dir/Scr* Eric Rohmer

Rendezvous ★★★ Ⓤ
Spy comedy   1935 · US · BW · 94min

Puzzle expert William Powell, aching to see frontline action in France during the First World War, is reluctantly seconded to the American war ministry as a code-breaker to rescue a critical situation. He finds himself involved with a spy-ring and the assistant secretary of war's glamorous but dizzy niece (Rosalind Russell). An unusual, even daring, mixture of light – almost screwball – romantic comedy and espionage thriller, this features polished performances and atmospheric, well-judged direction from William K Howard. **RK**

William Powell *Lt Bill Gordon/Anson Meridan* • Rosalind Russell *Joel Carter* • Binnie Barnes *Olivia Karloff* • Lionel Atwill *Maj Charles Brennan* • Cesar Romero *Capt Nikki Nikolajeff* • Samuel S Hinds *John Carter, Assistant Secretary of War* ■ *Dir* William K Howard • *Scr* Bella Spewack, Samuel Spewack, PJ Wolfson, George Oppenheimer, from the novel *American Black Chamber* by Herbert O Yardley

Rendezvous with Annie ★★★
Wartime romantic comedy
1946 · US · BW · 89min

American director Allan Dwan notched up over 400 feature credits in a career that spanned from Douglas Fairbanks's silent epics to RKO co-features in the 1950s. This long-forgotten gem is frantic, fast and extremely entertaining especially for its glimpses of a very Hollywood England, as likeable GI Eddie Albert goes AWOL to check up on his stateside wife. Jolly good fun. **TS**

Eddie Albert *Cpl Jeffrey Dolan* • Faye Marlowe *Annie Dolan* • Gail Patrick *Dolores Starr* • Philip Reed *Lt Avery* • C Aubrey Smith *Sir Archibald Clyde* ■ *Dir* Allan Dwan • *Scr* Richard Sale, Mary Loos

Rendition ★★★ ⑮
Political thriller   2007 · US · Colour · 117min

Oscar-winning South African director Gavin Hood (*Tsotsi*) makes his American debut with this politically charged thriller about "extraordinary rendition" – the US government practice of seizing suspected terrorists, and whisking them abroad for detention in secret prisons. Egyptian-American Omar Metwally is circumstantially linked to a terrorist group, and renditioned for interrogation. As his determined, pregnant wife Reese Witherspoon presses for answers in the US, another chance of rescue lies with CIA analyst Jake Gyllenhaal, who undergoes a crisis of conscience after Metwally's torture. The surfeit of characters (the ensemble cast also includes Meryl Streep as a cold-hearted CIA superior) clutters up the plot, with each given too little screen time, while a needless split time frame is an added irritant. Nevertheless, this is a worthy Hollywood calling card for the director. **DA** *DVD* *Blu*

Jake Gyllenhaal *Douglas Freeman* • Reese Witherspoon *Isabella Fields El-Ibrahimi* • Alan Arkin *Senator Hawkins* • Peter Sarsgaard *Alan Smith* • Meryl Streep *Corrinne Whitman* • Omar Metwally *Anwar El-Ibrahimi* • Igal Naor *Abasi Fawal* • Zineb Oukach *Fatima Fawal* ■ *Dir* Gavin Hood • *Scr* Kelley Sane • *Cinematographer* Dion Beebe

The Rendlesham UFO Incident ★★⑮
Science-fiction horror thriller
2014 · UK · Colour · 83min

Inspired by what's alleged to have been a genuine alien encounter from back in 1980, this routine found-footage thriller depicts three present-day metal detectorists experiencing weird goings-on around the site of the earlier event (an RAF base adjacent to the Rendlesham Forest in Suffolk). The film has the standard wonky camerawork and takes an age to get going, but things perk up a bit in the second half with some half-decent sonic and visual effects. **DA** Swearing.

Danny Shayler *Jake* • Abbie Salt *Sally* • Robert Curtis *Gus* ■ *Dir* Daniel Simpson • *Scr* Daniel Simpson, Adam Preston

Renegade ★★★
Spaghetti western   1987 · It · Colour

This amiable latter day western gets off to an amusing start as Terence Hill (a drifter who makes a living by repeatedly selling a horse with a homing instinct) hits the road with Ross Hill, the young son of a jailed buddy. Their encounters with truckers, bikers, flirts and a crooked knife thrower are all good value, but the picture falls away when villainous Robert Vaughn comes on the scene to steal the boy's farm in order to build a base for his drug business. **DP** Some dialogue dubbed.

Terence Hill *"Renegade"* • Robert Vaughn (1) *Tycoon* • Ross Hill • Norman Bowler • Beatrice Palme • Donald Hodson • Cyros Elias ■ *Dir* EB Clucher [Enzo Barboni] • *Scr* Marco Tullio Barboni, Mario Girotti [Terence Hill], Sergio Donati

Renegade Justice ★⑱
Action drama   2007 · US · Colour · 92min

After a string of dire Euro-thrillers, this sees the increasingly irrelevant Steven Seagal returning to his urban action roots on his home turf. Seagal plays (inevitably) a lethal stranger who arrives in LA to discover the truth about the death of his policeman son (Cory Hart), the apparent victim of a drive-by shooting. But the change of scene and scenery provides no measurable increase in quality – it's another lacklustre effort, sunk by a predictable script and a lazy performance by the star. **JF** *DVD*

Steven Seagal *Simon Ballister* • Eddie Griffin *Armand Tucker* • Carmen Serano *Alice Park* • Cory Hart *Max Ballister* • Liezl Carstens *Linda* • Kirk BR Woller *Detective Frank Shaw* • Danny Trejo *El Chivo* ■ *Dir* Don E FauntLeRoy • *Scr* Gil Fuentes, Gilmar Fortis II

Renegades ★★★
Adventure   1930 · US · BW · 90min

Warner Baxter stars as an officer who leads a small group of Foreign Legionnaires against a band of warlike heathens in the desert and becomes a hero. Lots of blood and thunder, famous horror-star-to-be Bela Lugosi as The Marabout and the distracting, and disruptive, presence of female spy Myrna Loy contribute to a respectable early sound entry in the "exotic heroic adventure melodrama" genre. The movie, directed by Victor Fleming, does, however, suffer from a narrative confusion. **RK**

Warner Baxter *Deucalion* • Myrna Loy *Eleanore* • Noah Beery Sr [Noah Beery] *Machwurth* • Gregory Gaye *Vologuine* • George Cooper (1) *Bilox* • C Henry Gordon *Capt Mordiconi* • Colin Chase *Sgt Maj Olson* • Bela Lugosi *The Marabout* • Victor Jory *Young officer* ■ *Dir* Victor Fleming • *Scr* Jules Furthman, from the novel *Le Renégat* by André Armandy

Renegades ★★⑱
Action thriller   1989 · US · Colour · 101min

This mindless, if energetic, thriller would have benefited considerably from a decent script. As it is, the endless action only serves to highlight that a single, scrawny idea is being stretched to breaking point, and the attempts at "serious" dialogue between the set pieces are just embarrassing. Kiefer Sutherland and Lou

Diamond Phillips were better employed in *Young Guns*. **JM** Swearing, violence.

Kiefer Sutherland *Buster* • Lou Diamond Phillips *Hank* • Jami Gertz *Barbara* • Rob Knepper [Robert Knepper] *Marino* • Bill Smitrovich *Finch* • Floyd Westerman [Floyd Red Crow Westerman] *Red Crow* • Joe Griffin *Matt* ■ *Dir* Jack Sholder • *Scr* David Rich

Reno 911!: Miami ★⑮
Comedy   2007 · US · Colour · 80min

The spirit of *Police Academy* lives on in this ridiculously titled comedy. It's based on an American TV series that spoofs reality show *Cops*, and follows the (highly fictionalised) adventures of the Reno sheriff's department in mock-documentary style. Here, in the tradition of spin-off features, the officers are uprooted from their home town and unleashed on Miami, where a bio-attack has left the city's police force quarantined. A rude, but rarely funny, string of skits ensues as the hapless law enforcers struggle to keep a lid on Miami's crime figures. Aside from some pointlessly brief celebrity cameos (The Rock, Danny DeVito) this aims its sights low, with leering nudity, drug references and some borderline homophobic jokes about sexual orientation. **JR** *DVD* ⒸⓈ

Carlos Alazraqui *Deputy James Garcia* • Mary Birdsong *Deputy Cherisha Kimball* • Robert Ben Garant *Deputy Travis Junior* • Kerry Kenney-Silver *Deputy Trudy Wiegel* • Thomas Lennon (3) *Lieutenant Jim Dangle* • Wendi McLendon-Covey *Deputy Clementine Johnson* ■ *Dir* Robert Ben Garant • *Scr* Robert Ben Garant, Thomas Lennon (3), Kerry Kenney-Silver

Renoir ★★★⑫
Period drama   2012 · Fr · Colour · 107min

Gilles Bourdos's exquisitely photographed drama is set during 1915 at the Côte d'Azur retreat of ageing Impressionist artist Pierre-Auguste Renoir (played by Michel Bouquet). The arthritic Renoir finds fresh inspiration in young Andrée Heuschling (Christa Theret), whose beauty and passion for cinema soon beguile the artist's convalescing soldier son, Jean. The imagery is majestic, and Theret stands out as the deceptively ambitious muse, but the movie's languid pacing and lack of sustained drama frustrate as much as fascinate. **DP** French, Italian +subtitles. Swearing, a sex scene, nudity. *DVD*

Michel Bouquet *Pierre-Auguste Renoir* • Christa Theret *Andrée Heuschling, "Dedée"* • Vincent Rottiers *Jean Renoir* • Thomas Doret *Coco Renoir* • Romane Bohringer *Gabrielle* ■ *Dir* Gilles Bourdos • *Scr* Gilles Bourdos, Jérôme Tonnerre, Michel Spinosa, from the non-fiction book *Le Tableau Amoureux* by Jacques Renoir • *Music* Alexandre Desplat

Rent ★★★⑫
Musical drama   2005 · US · Colour · 129min

Jonathan Larson's hit musical makes a slightly less than fabulous transition from stage to screen in this adaptation by director Chris Columbus. Loosely based on *La Bohème* and set in New York's East Village at the tail end of the 1980s, it has a bunch of young bohemians variously battling Aids, attempting to establish artsy careers and falling in and out of love. The songs are of variable quality but are all energetically performed by a likeable young cast. **AS** Swearing. *DVD* *Blu*

Adam Pascal *Roger Davis* • Rosario Dawson *Mimi Marquez* • Taye Diggs *Benjamin Coffin III* • Wilson Jermaine Heredia *Angel Dumott Schunard* • Jesse L Martin *Tom Collins* • Idina Menzel *Maureen Johnson* • Anthony Rapp *Mark Cohen* • Tracie Thoms *Joanne Jefferson* ■ *Dir* Chris Columbus • *Scr* Stephen Chbosky, from the musical by Jonathan Larson

Rent-a-Cop ★★⑮
Action comedy   1988 · US · Colour · 92min

This lacklustre thriller was the second teaming of stars Burt Reynolds and Liza Minnelli (remember *Lucky Lady*?). Reynolds is an ex-cop with a seriously visible rotten toupee, and Minnelli's a flashy call girl working for ace madam Dionne Warwick.

Say goodbye to credibility right there. **TS** Swearing, violence.

Burt Reynolds *Tony Church* • Liza Minnelli *Della Roberts* • James Remar *Dancer* • Richard Masur *Roger* • Dionne Warwick *Beth* • Bernie Casey *Lemar* • Robby Benson *Pitts* • John Stanton *Alexander* ■ *Dir* Jerry London • *Scr* Dennis Shryack, Michael Blodgett

Rent-a-Kid ★★★ Ⓤ
Comedy   1992 · Can · Colour · 85min

This is a children's film that doesn't patronise its audience by resorting to slapstick for its comedy or sentimentality for its message. Leslie Nielsen crops up in a showy cameo as the father of an orphanage owner, who rents out three children, unwilling to have their family broken up, to a couple who can't decide whether parenting is for them. Although the antiques shop subplot and the final resolution are a tad corny, the scenes in which the couple try to please the threesome are good fun. **DP**

Leslie Nielsen *Harry* • Christopher Lloyd *Lawrence Kady* • Matt McCoy *Russ Syracuse* • Sherry Miller *Val Syracuse* • Tabitha Lupien *Molly Ward* • Amos Crawley *Brandon Ward* • Cody Jones *Kyle Ward* • Tony Rosato *Cliff Haber* ■ *Dir* Fred Gerber • *Scr* Paul Bernbaum

Rentadick ★ ⑫
Comedy   1972 · UK · Colour · 89min

This woeful private eye spoof started out as a project for *Monty Python* team members John Cleese and Graham Chapman, who wrote the original screenplay, but then disowned the film and had their names removed from the credits. John Wells and John Fortune were drafted in as replacements, but couldn't avert a disaster. **DP**

James Booth *Hamilton* • Richard Briers *Gannet* • Julie Ege *Utta* • Ronald Fraser *Upton* • Donald Sinden *Armitage* • Kenneth Cope *West* • John Wells *Owltruss* • Richard Beckinsale *Hobbs* • Michael Bentine *Hussein* • Derek Griffiths *Henson* • Spike Milligan *Customs Officer* • Penelope Keith *Madge* ■ *Dir* Jim Clark • *Scr* John Wells, John Fortune • *Producer* Ned Sherrin

Repeat Performance ★★★
Crime drama   1947 · US · BW · 92min

Playing like an old *Twilight Zone* episode, this literary adaptation offers a brisk and straightforward telling of its time-travel narrative in which Joan Leslie's Broadway actress mysteriously gets to relive the year leading up to her fatal shooting of alcoholic husband Louis Hayward. Sparky dialogue and stylish visuals add to the tale's appeal, and help keep the simple events absorbing until the neat, twist finale. A TV-movie remake, *Turn Back the Clock*, followed in 1989, featuring a cameo by Leslie. **SF**

Louis Hayward *Barney Page* • Joan Leslie *Sheila Page* • Virginia Field *Paula Costello* • Tom Conway *John Friday* • Richard Basehart *William Williams* ■ *Dir* Alfred Werker • *Scr* Walter Bullock, from William O'Farrell's novel

Repentance ★★★★⑫
Political drama   1984 · USSR · Colour · 150min

Not filmed for three years after it was written and then not released for another three after its completion, this was the first Soviet feature to be openly critical of Stalin and is one of the most daring films ever made in the former USSR. Ostensibly a black comedy about the repeated exhumation of the mayor of a small Georgian town, it is a defiant assault on revisionist history, that shows, through a series of harrowing flashbacks, that the crimes of the past cannot simply be buried and forgotten. Exceptionally played and unflinchingly directed. **DP** Georgian +subtitles. Some violence, swearing, brief nudity.

Avtandil Makharadze *Varlam Aravidze/Abel Aravidze* • Zeinab Botsvadze *Keti Barateli* • Ia Ninidze *Guliko Aravidze* • Merab Ninidze *Tornike Aravidze* • Ketevan Abuladze *Nino Barateli* • Edisher Giorgobiani *Sandro Barateli* ■ *Dir* Tengiz Abuladze • *Scr* Nana Janelidze, Tengiz Abuladze, Rezo Kveselava

The Replacement Killers
★★★ 18

Action thriller 1998 · US · Colour · 83min

Forget the fact there's no plot whatsoever and focus on the high-energy action and you'll enjoy this dumb and noisy thriller in which Hong Kong superstar Chow Yun-Fat made his American debut. When he refuses to assassinate an assigned target Stateside, conscientious hitman Chow puts his family in danger back in China. Fiery Mira Sorvino is the expert passport forger who helps him out. Don't think, just thrill to the wild gunplay and slick stunts. AJ Violence, swearing. *DVD* BD

Mira Sorvino *Meg Coburn* • Chow Yun-Fat *John Lee* • Michael Rooker *Stan "Zeedo" Zedkov* • Kenneth Tsang *Terence Wei* • Jürgen Prochnow *Michael Kogan* • Til Schweiger *Ryker* • Danny Trejo *Collins* ■ *Dir* Antoine Fuqua • *Scr* Ken Sanzel

The Replacements
★★ 15

Sports comedy based on a true story 2000 · US · Colour · 113min

This stale and hackneyed sports comedy about a bunch of has-beens and no-hopers replacing striking professional American football players has quite an impressive cast for its type. While it has some funny touches, all the characters are purely one-dimensional, with even Gene Hackman failing to achieve anything with his veteran coach role. JC *DVD*

Keanu Reeves *Shane Falco* • Gene Hackman *Jimmy McGinty* • Brooke Langton *Annabelle Farrell* • Orlando Jones *Clifford Franklin* • Jon Favreau *Daniel Bateman* • Jack Warden *Edward O'Neil* • Rhys Ifans *Nigel "The Leg" Gruff* ■ *Dir* Howard Deutch • *Scr* Vince McKewin

Replicant
★★ 18

Science-fiction action thriller 2001 · US · Colour · 95min

Jean-Claude Van Damme gets a dual role, again, as serial killer and his confused clone in a perfunctory thriller. While it has the makings of a departure for the "Muscles from Brussels", with his sympathetic, naive good guy used and abused by both his villainous "brother" and cop Michael Rooker, his awkwardness sits uncomfortably with his kick-boxing prowess. JC Violence, swearing, a sex scene, nudity *DVD*

Jean-Claude Van Damme *The Torch/Replicant* • Michael Rooker *Jake Riley* • Catherine Dent *Angie* • Ian Robison *Stan Reisman* ■ *Dir* Ringo Lam • *Scr* Lawrence Riggins, Les Weldon

Repo Chick
★★ 15

Crime comedy 2009 · US · Colour · 88min

Maverick writer/director Alex Cox retreads the themes of his cult classic *Repo Man* in a daft and intentionally garish social satire that features some familiar faces from the 1984 movie. Filmed against green screen and set in an economically crippled Los Angeles of the future, this dandy-coloured show-off quickly unravels by trying to be ultra-quirky and camp, as a clichéd, Paris Hilton-esque socialite (Jaclyn Jonet) becomes a repossession agent after being disinherited for her wild ways. The disappointing absence of bling set makes Cox's predictable pot shots at celebrity culture, capitalism and financial greed seem hollow and lazy, but the energetic cast throw themselves into their characters with gusto. SF Swearing. *DVD*

Jaclyn Jonet *Repo Chick* • Miguel Sandoval *Arizona Gray* • Del Zamora *Lorenzo* • Alex Feldman *Marco* • Chloe Webb *Sister Duncan* • Xander Berkeley *Aldrich de la Chasse* • Rosanna Arquette *Lola* ■ *Dir/Scr* Alex Cox

Repo Man
★★★★ 18

Science-fiction thriller 1984 · US · Colour · 88min

Despite poor reviews on its initial release, Alex Cox's darkly satirical swipe at American urban low life mutated into one of the 1980s greatest cult movies. Emilio Estevez plays a novice car repossession man in Los Angeles, learning the tricks of the trade from veteran Harry Dean Stanton,

and coming into contact with aliens and drug pushers. The film is a winning blend of sci-fi, social commentary and *film noir*, with lots of quotable dialogue. The characters exist on the fringes of society and it's a world that's beautifully captured by Wim Wenders's regular cinematographer Robby Müller. RS Violence, swearing. *DVD* BD

Emilio Estevez *Otto* • Harry Dean Stanton *Bud* • Tracey Walter *Miller* • Olivia Barash *Leila* • Sy Richardson *Lite* • Susan Barnes *Agent Rogersz* • Fox Harris *J Frank Parnell* • Tom Finnegan *Oly* • Del Zamora *Lagarto* • Eddie Velez *Napo* ■ *Dir/Scr* Alex Cox

Repo Men
★★ 18

Science-fiction action thriller 2010 · US/Can · Colour · 114min

This futuristic thriller is set in a world where hi-tech artificial organs are all the rage, but come at a deadly price. Jude Law and Forest Whitaker play top repo men – essentially bailiffs-cum-surgeons – sent to hunt down those who can't keep up their payments and take back the replacement parts on the spot. But when Law is given a new heart, he begins to question the morality of the sinister corporation that employs him. Director Miguel Sapochnik's dystopian setting allows for some broad swipes at a runaway consumer culture and the nature of healthcare and scientific progress. But the chase sequences never have enough momentum, Law is a fairly unconvincing renegade hero and there's too much emphasis on blood-soaked violence at the expense of both plot and character development. TeS Violence. *DVD* BD

Jude Law *Remy* • Forest Whitaker *Jake Freivald* • Liev Schreiber *Frank* • Alice Braga *Beth* • Carice van Houten *Carol* • Yvette Nicole Brown *Rhodesia* ■ *Dir* Miguel Sapochnik • *Scr* Eric Garcia, Garrett Lerner, from the novel *The Repossession Mambo* by Garcia

Report to the Commissioner
★★★ 15

Crime drama 1975 · US · Colour · 108min

Michael Moriarty stars as the idealistic rookie detective involved in the killing of an undercover cop, then embroiled in a vast cover-up. A solid script and some crisp action sequences, including a shoot-out in the Saks department store, make this depiction of police corruption eminently watchable, though most eyes now will be on Richard Gere, making his screen debut as a pimp. AT

Michael Moriarty *Beauregard "Bo" Lockley* • Yaphet Kotto *Richard "Crunch" Blackstone* • Susan Blakely *Party Butler* • Hector Elizondo *Captain d'Angelo* • Tony King *Thomas "Stick" Henderson* • Michael McGuire *Lt Hanson* • William Devane *Assistant District Attorney Jackson* • Richard Gere *Billy* ■ *Dir* Milton Katselas • *Scr* Abby Mann, Ernest Tidyman, from the novel by James Mills

Repossessed
★ 15

Horror spoof 1990 · US · Colour · 80min

It must have seemed a good idea at the time. Give *The Exorcist* the *Airplane!* treatment, get Linda Blair to reprise her infamous head-turning/pea-soup-vomit role, cast *The Naked Gun's* Leslie Nielsen as Max von Sydow and wait for the laughs to come thick and fast. Sadly, they come thin and slow in this lame-brained, mistimed fiasco. AJ Swearing. *DVD*

Linda Blair *Nancy Aglet* • Leslie Nielsen *Father Jedidiah Mayii* • Ned Beatty *Ernest Weller* • Anthony Starke *Father Luke Brophy* • Thom J Sharp *Braydon Aglet* • Lana Schwab *Fanny Weller* ■ *Dir/Scr* Bob Logan

Reprise
★★★ 15

Drama 2006 · Nor/Swe · Colour · 106min

This debut feature from Norwegian director Joachim Trier is a determinedly chic treatise on art, ambition, women and friendship, but his fascination with structure and style distracts him from the scrambled lives of his characters. The film opens with a slick voiceover sequence that posits what might have happened had childhood buddies Anders Danielsen Lie and Espen

Klouman Hoiner both published their first novels. However, a fragmentary approach to the rest of the story serves only to distance us from action that is largely devoid of genuine emotion. It's a confident, laudably controlled and occasionally witty picture, but it also feels rather self-conscious. DP Norwegian +subtitles. *DVD*

Anders Danielsen Lie *Phillip* • Espen Klouman Hoiner *Erik* • Viktoria Winge *Kari* • Silje Hagen *Lillian* • Sigmund Saeverud *Sten Egil Dahl* • Henrik Elvestad *Henning* ■ *Dir* Joachim Trier • *Scr* Joachim Trier, Eskil Vogt

The Reptile
★★★ 15

Horror 1966 · UK · Colour · 86min

Hysteria hits a 19th-century Cornish village when murder victims turn up with fang marks on their necks. Could sultry Jacqueline Pearce be the victim of a Malayan curse, doomed to writhe the night away? This splendidly spooky vintage Hammer horror features an endearingly 1950s-style monster, remarkably atmospheric art direction and taut, stylish direction by John Gilling. AJ *DVD* BD

Noel Willman *Dr Franklyn* • Jennifer Daniel *Valerie* • Ray Barrett *Harry* • Jacqueline Pearce *Anna* • Michael Ripper *Tom Bailey* • John Laurie *Mad Peter* • Marne Maitland *Malay* • David Baron *Charles Spalding* • Charles Lloyd Pack *Vicar* • Harold Goldblatt *Solicitor* ■ *Dir* John Gilling • *Scr* John Elder [Anthony Hinds]

Repulsion
★★★★★ 18

Psychological thriller 1965 · UK · BW · 100min

Director Roman Polanski takes us on a deeply disturbing, hallucinatory trip into Catherine Deneuve's mental breakdown in this British psychological thriller, his first film in English. As Swinging London parties in the background, repressed Belgian manicurist Deneuve unsheathes her claws with deadly results. There are shades of Buñuel and Cocteau, but Polanski puts his personal stamp on the violent visuals (the killing of a boyfriend and landlord) and the terrifying soundtrack (the buzzing of flies, a slashing knife). TH Violence. *DVD*

Catherine Deneuve *Carol Ledoux* • Ian Hendry *Michael* • John Fraser *Colin* • Patrick Wymark *Landlord* • Yvonne Furneaux *Helen Ledoux* • Renee Houston *Miss Balch* • Roman Polanski *Spoons player* ■ *Dir* Roman Polanski • *Scr* Roman Polanski, Gérard Brach, David Stone • *Cinematographer* Gilbert Taylor

Requiem
★★

Fantasy drama 1998 · Swi/Fr/Por · Colour · 100min

Alain Tanner uses Lisbon as a stifling backdrop to this slow-moving treatise on memory and regret. The film is intended as a tribute to the Portuguese author Fernando Pessoa, who puts in a guest appearance as one of the mysterious characters Francis Frappat encounters while awaiting a meeting with a ghost from his past. A pall of impossible sophistication hangs over the piece, which wears its intellectual credentials on its sleeve. DP French +subtitles.

Francis Frappat *Paul* • André Marcon *Pierre* ■ *Dir* Alain Tanner • *Scr* Bernard Comment, Alain Tanner, from a novel by Antonio Tabucchi

Requiem
★★★★ 12

Psychological drama 2006 · Ger · Colour · 88min

This study of a supposed demonic possession is markedly less sensationalist than *The Exorcism of Emily Rose*, although based on the same events. Sandra Hüller deservedly won best actress at the Berlin film festival for her performance as the naive, epileptic Catholic girl whose introduction to permissiveness at university results in a breakdown and a belief that she's being tested by evil. But director Hans-Christian Schmid is less concerned with the reasons behind her plight, instead examining the parental indecision, church arrogance and medical incompetence that exacerbate her condition. Consequently, the action is all the more disconcerting and credible. DP German +subtitles. Distressing scenes. *DVD*

Sandra Hüller *Michaela Klingler* • Burghart Klaussner *Karl Klingler* • Imogen Kogge *Marianne Klingler* • Friederike Adolph *Helga Klingler* • Anna Blomeier *Hanna Imhof* • Nicholas Reinke *Stefan Weiser* • Walter Schmidinger *Gerhard Landauer* ■ *Dir* Hans-Christian Schmid • *Scr* Bernd Lange

Requiem for a Dream
★★★★ 18

Drama 2000 · US · Colour · 96min

Junk TV shows, diet pills and Class A drugs are the life blood of these doomed characters: Ellen Burstyn plays the widowed mother hooked on game shows and sweet foods; her heroin addict son Jared Leto and his friend Marlon Wayans pawn the TV for drugs money, while Leto's girlfriend Jennifer Connelly degrades herself at stag parties. Making stylish use of the split-screen technique, huge close-ups and exaggerated sound effects, Darren Aronofsky depicts the highs and lows of drug-taking to chilling effect. TH Swearing, violence, sex scenes, drug abuse. *DVD* BD

Ellen Burstyn *Sara Goldfarb* • Jared Leto *Harry Goldfarb* • Jennifer Connelly *Marion Silver* • Marlon Wayans *Tyrone C Love* • Christopher McDonald *Tappy Tibbons* • Louise Lasser *Ada* • Keith David *Little John* ■ *Dir* Darren Aronofsky • *Scr* Hubert Selby Jr, Darren Aronofsky, from a novel by Hubert Selby Jr

Requiem for a Heavyweight
★★★ PG

Sports drama 1962 · US · BW · 81min

Based on an American live TV production written by Rod Serling, this stars Anthony Quinn as an over-the-hill boxer. He has to continue fighting, risking permanent blindness, in order to pay off debts to the Mafia run up by his manager Jackie Gleason, while Mickey Rooney is his devoted trainer. In the ring (and on the moral message front), this is a bloody, brutal big-hitter of a movie and Quinn gives a committed performance. AT *DVD*

Anthony Quinn *Mountain Rivera* • Jackie Gleason *Maish Rennick* • Mickey Rooney *Army* • Julie Harris (2) *Grace Miller* • Stanley Adams *Perelli* • Madame Spivy *Ma Greeny* • Herbie Faye *Bartender* • Jack Dempsey • Cassius Clay [Muhammad Ali] *Ring opponent* ■ *Dir* Ralph Nelson • *Scr* Rob Serling, from his TV play

Requiem for Dominic
★★★

Historical political thriller 1990 · Austria · Colour · 88min

Set in Ceausescu's Romania on the eve of the 1989 revolution, this intelligent film from Austria follows exile Felix Mitterer, in his quest to prove that his childhood friend August Schmölzer was not responsible for the murder of 80 factory workers in the town of Timisoara. Director Robert Dornhelm based his film on the experiences of his own friend, Dominic Paraschiv, a member of the notorious Securitate who was branded "the Butcher of Timisoara". Making studied use of news footage and fictional material, he has fashioned an engrossing, violent, political thriller. DP German +subtitles.

Felix Mitterer *Paul Weiss* • August Schmolzer *Dominic Paraschiv* • Viktoria Schubert *Clara* • Angelica Schutz *Codrata Paraschiv* • Antonia Rados *Antonia* ■ *Dir* Robert Dornhelm • *Scr* Michael Kohlmeier, Felix Mitterer

The Rescue
★★ PG

Action adventure 1988 · US · Colour · 92min

In this daft adventure, Kevin Dillon (younger brother of the more successful Matt) stars as one of a group of teenagers who mount a rescue mission when they discover the US government is ignoring the plight of their fathers – senior officers from the US Navy's elite SEALs outfit who have been captured behind enemy lines in North Korea. JB Swearing, violence.

Kevin Dillon *JJ Merrill* • Christina Harnos [Christine Harnos] *Adrian Phillips* • Marc Price *Max Rothman* • Ned Vaughn *Shawn Howard* • Ian Giatti *Bobby Howard* • Charles Haid *Commander Howard* • Edward Albert *Commander Merrill* ■ *Dir* Ferdinand Fairfax • *Scr* Jim Thomas, John Thomas

R

Rescue Dawn ★★★ 12

Action drama based on a true story
2006 · US/Lux · Colour · 120min

Writer/director Werner Herzog (*Grizzly Man*, *Fitzcarraldo*) revisits the inspiring true story he first explored in his 1997 documentary *Little Dieter Needs to Fly*. A stripped-down dramatisation of bravery against the odds, it stars a skeletal Christian Bale as German-American fighter pilot Dieter Dengler, who was shot down and captured in Laos during the Vietnam War. But while Bale's effortless portrayal of crazed fortitude fuels the picture, it's his character's poignant relationship with despairing fellow PoW Duane (Steve Zahn, playing brilliantly against type) that provides its depth. Nonetheless, the film is Herzog's least original work – courting mainstream audiences with a solid, yet distinctly well-worn, narrative style. SF In English, Vietnamese. *DVD* Blu

Christian Bale *Dieter Dengler* · Steve Zahn *Duane* · Jeremy Davies *Gene* · Zach Grenier *Squad leader* · Galen Yuen *YC* · Abhijati "Muek" Jusakul *Phisit* · Chaiyan "Lek" Chunsuttiwat *Procet* · Teerawat "Ka-Ge" Mulvilai *Little Hitler* ■ *Dir/Scr* Werner Herzog

Rescue Me ★★ 15

Action comedy 1991 · US · Colour · 94min

In this silly spoof of the action adventure genre, Stephen Dorff is a high-school nerd who suffers from unrequited love for teen-queen Ami Dolenz. Obsessed with cameras (Dorff is a collector of vintage cameras in real life), he takes pictures of Dolenz just as she is being kidnapped instead of rescuing her. He teams up with hard man Michael Dudikoff (taking the mickey out of his screen persona) to rescue his fair maiden. FL

Michael Dudikoff *Daniel "Mac" MacDonald* · Stephen Dorff *Fraser Sweeney* · Ami Dolenz *Ginny Grafton* · Peter DeLuise *Rowdy* · William Lucking *Kurt* · Dee Wallace Stone *Sarah Sweeney* · Liz Torres *Carney* · Danny Nucci *Todd* ■ *Dir* Arthur Allan Seidelman · *Scr* Mike Snyder

The Rescuers ★★★★ U

Animated adventure 1977 · US · Colour · 75min

A thoroughly delightful Disney cartoon, this is about the all-mouse Rescue Aid Society and bids by its leading lights, Bernard and Miss Bianca, to free a little girl held hostage by hiss-boo baddie Madam Medusa. Bob Newhart, Eva Gabor and George C Scott are among the voice artists in a well-told tale with memorable characters. This was one of the animated features that indicated a return to form by Disney after a lengthy spell of cartoon mediocrity. DA *DVD* Blu

Bob Newhart *Bernard* · Eva Gabor *Miss Bianca* · Michelle Stacy *Penny* · Geraldine Page *Madame Medusa* · Joe Flynn *Mr Snoops* ■ *Dir* Wolfgang Reitherman, John Lounsbery, Milt Kahl, Art Stevens · *Scr* Larry Clemmons, Ken Anderson, Vance Gerry, David Michener, Burny Mattinson, Frank Thomas, Fred Lucky, Ted Berman, Dick Sebast, from the books *The Rescuers* and *Miss Bianca* by Margery Sharp

The Rescuers Down Under ★★★ U

Animated adventure 1990 · US · Colour · 80min

This acceptable enough Disney animation is a sequel that came such a long time after *The Rescuers* (1977) that it could be forgiven for having lost the plot, because introductions to the "rescue mice" Miss Bianca and Bernard had to be made all over again. This time they're called to Australia to help a boy and golden eagle in danger from a fearsome trapper. It's likeable enough and the crocodile-snapping climax is exciting stuff. Bob Newhart and Eva Gabor are great as the voices of Bernard and Bianca. TH *DVD*

Bob Newhart *Bernard* · Eva Gabor *Miss Bianca* · John Candy *Wilbur* · George C Scott *Percival McLeach* · *Dir* Hendel Butoy, Mike Gabriel · *Scr* Jim Cox, Karey Kirkpatrick, Byron Simpson, Joe Ranft, from the characters by Margery Sharp

Reservoir Dogs ★★★★★ 18

Crime drama 1991 · US · Colour · 94min

"Robbery, blood, violence, torture all in the comfort of your own home". The film that many consider the most influential of the 1990s was shot in just five weeks on a tight $1.2 million budget. Its runaway success came as something of a surprise even to its debuting writer/director Quentin Tarantino, who was hoping for a cult hit rather than a phenomenon that would inspire countless wannabes. Working wonders with Tarantino's pacey, attitude-laced dialogue, the ensemble cast is uniformly excellent, with Michael Madsen's sadistic, ear-slashing Mr Blonde and Steve Buscemi's exasperated Mr Pink particularly outstanding. Brash, abrasive and unrelenting. DP Violence, swearing. *DVD* Blu

Harvey Keitel *Mr White (Larry)* · Tim Roth *Mr Orange (Freddy)* · Michael Madsen *Mr Blonde (Vic Vega)* · Chris Penn *Nice Guy Eddie* · Steve Buscemi *Mr Pink* · Lawrence Tierney *Joe Cabot* · Randy Brooks *Holdaway* · Kirk Baltz *Marvin Nash* · Eddie Bunker [Edward Bunker] *Mr Blue* · Quentin Tarantino *Mr Brown* ■ *Dir/Scr* Quentin Tarantino · *Cinematographer* Andrzej Sekula

The Resident ★★ 15

Horror thriller 2010 · UK/US · Colour · 87min

This listless stalker shocker from the reborn Hammer Films was touted as a return to the woman-in-peril psycho-thrillers of the company's 1960s heyday. In fact, it's more reminiscent of an episode from the House of Horror's many misbegotten TV series. Hilary Swank stars as the ER doctor who moves into a surprisingly cheap, spacious Brooklyn apartment and begins a flirtation with amenable landlord Jeffrey Dean Morgan. But she soon gets the feeling that she's being watched... AJ Violence, swearing. *DVD* Blu

Hilary Swank *Dr Juliet Devereau* · Jeffrey Dean Morgan *Max* · Christopher Lee *August* · Lee Pace *Jack* · Aunjanue Ellis *Sydney* ■ *Dir* Antti J Jokinen [Antti Jokinen] · *Scr* Antti J Jokinen, Robert Orr

Resident Evil ★★★ 15

Science-fiction action horror
2002 · Ger/UK/Fr · Colour · 96min

Paul Anderson makes amends for his lacklustre *Mortal Kombat* with another video game adaptation. A single-minded tale of genetic research facility workers accidentally turned into ravenous zombies, it's a relentless throat-grabber. Milla Jovovich and a team of commandos move through progressively more dangerous levels to wipe out the undead. There's no enduring substance here, but the nerve-jangling score, co-composed by shock rocker Marilyn Manson, gives it an extra frenetic edge. SF *DVD* Blu

Milla Jovovich *Alice* · Michelle Rodriguez *Rain* · Eric Mabius *Matt* · James Purefoy *Spence* · Martin Crewes *Kaplan* · Colin Salmon *One* ■ *Dir* Paul WS Anderson [Paul Anderson (1)] · *Scr* Paul WS Anderson [Paul Anderson], from a story by Alan McElroy, Anderson, from the video game

Resident Evil: Apocalypse ★ 15

Science-fiction action horror
2004 · US/Can/UK/Fr · Colour · 89min

First-timer Alexander Witt picks up the directorial reins from Paul Anderson for this limp sequel. Continuing from where the original left off, it sees the zombies break out from the Umbrella Corporation's underground research facility to wreak havoc on the quarantined city above. Though once again written by Anderson, the film lacks his visual flair and breakneck pacing, resulting in an uninspired shoot-'em-up. SF Swearing, violence. *DVD* Blu

Milla Jovovich *Alice* · Sienna Guillory *Jill Valentine* · Oded Fehr *Carlos Olivera* · Thomas Kretschmann *Major Cain* · Jared Harris *Dr Charles Ashford* · Mike Epps *LJ* · Sandrine Holt *Terri Morales* · Sophie Vavasseur *Angie Ashford* ■ *Dir* Alexander Witt · *Scr* Paul WS Anderson [Paul Anderson]

Resident Evil: Extinction ★★ 15

Science-fiction action horror
2007 · Ger/Fr/UK/US · Colour · 90min

This third instalment in the game-derived undead horror franchise finds the biogenetically enhanced Alice (Milla Jovovich) joining up with an uninfected armoured convoy (led by *Heroes*' Ali Larter) to fight off yet more hordes of zombies and keep one step ahead of the megalomaniacal Dr Isaacs (Iain Glen), who's after her DNA. *Highlander* director Russell Mulcahy has a keen eye for epic visuals, but rampant CGI means the splatter, zombies and mutant crow flocks only register as remote cartoon chills. The acting is by rote, too, with Glen's Shakespearean delivery seemingly from a different movie. A further sequel, *Degeneration*, went straight to DVD in 2008, while *Afterlife* rebooted the franchise at the cinema in 2010. AJ *DVD* Blu

Milla Jovovich *Alice* · Oded Fehr *Carlos Olivera* · Ali Larter *Claire Redfield* · Iain Glen *Dr Isaacs* · Mike Epps *LJ* · Spencer Locke *K-Mart* · Ashanti *Betty* · Matthew Marsden *Slater* · Jason O'Mara *Albert Wesker* · Christopher Egan *Mikey* ■ *Dir* Russell Mulcahy · *Scr* Paul WS Anderson, based on characters from the Capcom computer game *Resident Evil*

Resident Evil: Afterlife ★★ 15

Science-fiction thriller
2010 · UK/Ger/US · Colour · 96min

Back at the helm of the video game-based franchise he inaugurated, director Paul WS Anderson puts the *zzzz* in zombies with this fourth, mind-numbing instalment. If anyone remains interested, *Afterlife* picks up where *Extinction* left off, with Alice (Milla Jovovich) rescuing the few T-virus survivors left in a Los Angeles under siege from the living dead. It's visually impressive, with plenty of glossy, X-box-influenced action. But it still only adds up to a lame, by-the-numbers horror. AJ Violence, swearing. *DVD* Blu 3D 3DS

Milla Jovovich *Alice* · Ali Larter *Claire Redfield* · Wentworth Miller *Chris Redfield* · Shawn Roberts *Albert Wesker* · Kim Coates *Bennett* ■ *Dir* Paul WS Anderson [Paul Anderson (1)] · *Scr* Paul WS Anderson, from characters from the Capcom computer game *Resident Evil*

Resident Evil: Retribution ★★ 15

Science-fiction horror
2012 · US/Ger · Colour · 91min

Paul WS Anderson seems stuck on repeat in this glossy yet tedious fifth instalment in the video game-based franchise. The writer/director swaps coherent narrative for an unimaginative procession of explosions, gunfire and gore, as zombie-slaying heroine Alice (Milla Jovovich) races to escape from an underground research facility, encountering figures from her past (including an amusing Michelle Rodriguez) along the way. Despite plenty of set-piece battles, it's all about as engaging as looking over the shoulder of someone playing on their Xbox. SF Violence, some swearing. *DVD* Blu 3D

Milla Jovovich *Alice* · Sienna Guillory *Jill Valentine* · Michelle Rodriguez *Rain Ocampo* · Kevin Durand *Barry Burton* ■ *Dir* Paul WS Anderson [Paul Anderson (1)] · *Scr* Paul WS Anderson, from the computer game by Capcom

Resident Evil: the Final Chapter

Science-fiction horror
2017 · Ger/Aus/Fr/Can · Colour

This is a preview – no prints were available to review as we went to press: There's a touch of "getting the gang back together" for the last of the franchise that's delivered five movies thus far in an unhurried 15 years. Paul WS Anderson is again at the helm and Milla Jovovich returns as zombie-terminator-in-chief, with faces from previous outings - Iain Glen, Ali Larter and Li Bingbing - lending familiarity. This final chapter (we hope) promises a return to the

Hive, subterranean scene of much of the first movie's shoot-'em-up action. SvM

Milla Jovovich *Alice* · Ali Larter *Claire Redfield* · Ruby Rose *Abigail* · Iain Glen *Dr Alexander Isaacs* ■ *Dir/Scr* Paul WS Anderson [Paul Anderson (1)]

Resistance ★★ PG

Wartime drama 2011 · UK · Colour · 87min

In a remote Welsh valley, a bunch of farmers' wives wake to find their menfolk gone. But where, and why? The women have no more idea than do the valley's small force of occupying Germans (in this alternate reality, the D-Day landings have failed). As a harsh Welsh winter sets in, an uneasy, mutually self-serving truce is forged. And gradually the valley becomes an oasis away from war for both sides. *Resistance* never quite fulfils the promise of its premise, and skirts and skims its issues rather than tackling them, but it's rendered watchable by an interesting basic idea, decent production values and a strong cast. DA *DVD* Blu

Andrea Riseborough *Sarah* · Tom Wlaschiha *Captain Albrecht Wolfram* · Michael Sheen *Tommy Atkins* · Alexander Doetsch *Steiner* · Stanislav Ianevski *Bernhardt* · Iwan Rheon *George* · Kimberley Nixon *Bethan Evans* ■ *Dir* Amit Gupta · *Scr* Amit Gupta, Owen Sheers, from the novel by Sheers

Respiro ★★★ 12

Drama 2002 · It/Fr · Colour · 91min

Unable to cope with wife Valeria Golino's mood swings, Vincenzo Amato bows to communal pressure and agrees to have her committed to an institution on the mainland. However, Golino is protected in her beach hideaway by teenage son Francesco Casisa, who admires her free spirit, even though he doesn't understand it. By contrasting the island of Lampedusa's natural beauty with its inhabitants' struggle to survive, Emanuele Crialese's drama avoids rose-tinted realism and focuses on landscape and character. DP Italian +subtitles. *DVD*

Valeria Golino *Grazia* · Vincenzo Amato *Pietro* · Francesco Casisa *Pasquale* · Veronica D'Agostino *Marinella* · Filippo Pucillo *Filippo* · Emma Loffredo *Nonna* · Elio Germano *Pier-Luigi* ■ *Dir/Scr* Emanuele Crialese · *Cinematographer* Fabio Zamarion

Resting Place ★★★★ PG

Drama 1986 · US · Colour · 98min

Tautly scripted by Walter Halsey Davis and impeccably paced by director John Korty, this is one of the best TV movies ever made in America. Combining the themes of racial prejudice and military cover-up, this engrossing drama shuttles back and forth between Georgia and Vietnam as army officer John Lithgow seeks to discover why a black war hero has been denied burial in his home-town cemetery. Morgan Freeman and CCH Pounder also excel as the boy's proud parents. DP *DVD*

John Lithgow *Major Kendall Laird* · Morgan Freeman *Luther Johnson* · Richard Bradford *General Willard P Hauer* · CCH Pounder *Ada Johnson* · GD Spradlin *Sam Jennings* · Frances Sternhagen *Mrs Eudora McAlister* · M Emmet Walsh *Sarge* ■ *Dir* John Korty · *Scr* Walter Halsey Davis

Restless ★★ PG

Drama 2011 · US · Colour · 87min

The shadow of 1972 black comedy *Harold and Maude* hangs over this quirky, melancholy drama in which two radically different characters meet and become lovers after gatecrashing a funeral. *Jane Eyre*'s Mia Wasikowska plays a perky teen with a tumour, into whose orbit comes Henry Hopper (son and the spitting image of Dennis), an introspective loner whose best friend is the ghost of a Japanese airman. It could have worked, but its winsome tone and earnest delivery leave it stuck in a dreary limbo. DW *DVD*

Henry Hopper *Enoch Brae* · Mia Wasikowska *Annabel Cotton* · Schuyler Fisk *Elizabeth Cotton* · Jane Adams (2) *Mabel Tell* ■ *Dir* Gus Van Sant · *Scr* Jason Lew · *Music* Danny Elfman

U SUITABLE FOR ALL Uc SUITABLE ESPECIALLY FOR YOUNG CHILDREN (DVD ONLY) PG PARENTAL GUIDANCE 12A UNDER 12s TO BE ACCOMPANIED (CINEMA ONLY)

The Restless Breed ★★PG
Western   1957 · US · Colour · 77min

This is veteran director Allan Dwan's last western, a cripplingly low-budgeted colour B-movie starring deadpan Scott Brady in a routine tale, as a lawyer trying to unmask his father's killer, helped by a stalwart cast which includes a pre-stardom Anne Bancroft and Jim Davis. TS *DVD*

Scott Brady *Mitch Baker* • Anne Bancroft *Angelita* • Jay C Flippen *Marshal Steve Evans* • Rhys Williams *Reverend Simmons* • Jim Davis (1) *Ed Newton* • Leo Gordon *Cherokee* ■ *Dir* Allan Dwan • *Scr* Steven Fisher

Restless Natives ★★PG
Comedy   1985 · UK · Colour · 85min

Two Scottish lads become modern-day Robin Hoods, robbing tourists and giving the proceeds to the poor. Soon they are local, then international, heroes. The trouble is that much of the comedy is a parody of the work of the then-popular Scottish director Bill Forsyth, and jokes that were considered feeble in their day now seem even more obscure. A treat, however, for lovers of the Scottish countryside, and an effective career spur for director Michael Hoffman, who went on to make more sophisticated comedies in Hollywood. DM *DVD*

Joe Mullaney *Ronnie* • Vincent Friell *Will* • Ned Beatty *Bender* • Robert Urquhart *Det Insp Baird* • Teri Lally *Margot* • Bernard Hill *Will's Father* • Mel Smith *Pyle* • Bryar Forbes *Man in Car* • Nanette Newman *Woman in Car* ■ *Dir* Michael Hoffman • *Scr* Ninian Dunnet • *Music* Stuart Adamson

The Restless Years ★★
Drama   1958 · US · Colour · 85min

Family traumas abound in a conservative suburban community where Teresa Wright's major goal in life is to protect her teenage daughter Sandra Dee from the knowledge and stigma of illegitimacy, while John Saxon's young life is complicated by the reappearance of his long-absent failure of a father, James Whitmore. As a vehicle for teen stars when teen culture was on the way up, this outmoded drama of small-town life was a curious choice. RK

John Saxon *Will Henderson* • Sandra Dee *Melinda Grant* • Teresa Wright *Elizabeth Grant* • James Whitmore *Ed Henderson* • Luana Patten *Polly Fisher* • Margaret Lindsay *Dorothy Henderson* • Virginia Grey *Miss Robson* • Alan Baxter *Alex Fisher* ■ *Dir* Helmut Kautner [Helmut Käutner] • *Scr* Edward Anhalt, from the play *Teach Me How to Cry* by Patricia Joudry

Restoration ★★★★15
Period drama   1995 · US · Colour · 112min

Michael Hoffman's adaptation of Rose Tremain's novel is a period movie that treats the past as something very, very strange. Filmed at Forde Abbey and other historic sites, the Oscar-winning design is astonishing. The court of Charles II resembles Nero's and the picture subversively suggests that the foppish king lit the Great Fire of London to purge the plague and build a new capital. The casting is as weird as the settings: Sam Neill as the cholic King; Robert Downey Jr as a womanising medic; Hugh Grant as a splendidly pompous artist; but what on earth is Meg Ryan doing as a traumatised patient? A flawed picture with flashes of crazy brilliance. AT Nudity.

Robert Downey Jr *Robert Merivel* • Sam Neill *King Charles II* • David Thewlis *John Pearce* • Polly Walker *Celia* • Meg Ryan *Katherine* • Ian McKellen *Will Gates* • Hugh Grant *Finn* • Ian McDiarmid *Ambrose* ■ *Dir* Michael Hoffman • *Scr* Rupert Walters, from Rose Tremain's novel

Restrepo ★★★15
War documentary   2010 · US · Colour · 93min

Mixing interviews and handheld footage filmed by Sebastian Junger (author of *The Perfect Storm*) and the late photojournalist Tim Hetherington (a casualty of the conflict), this is a compelling and deeply disconcerting insight into the war in Afghanistan. Dispatched to the country's Korengal valley in May 2007, soldiers of the 173rd Airborne Brigade soon realise the futility of their mission against the Taliban in an area described by CNN as "the most dangerous place in the world". Deservedly taking the documentary prize at Sundance, this details a conflict that seems to have no purpose other than to scar those caught up in it. DP Swearing.

■ *Dir* Tim Hetherington, Sebastian Junger • *Cinematographers* Tim Hetherington, Sebastian Junger

Results ★★★★15
Comedy drama   2015 · US · Colour · 104min

Personal trainer Cobie Smulders has a job getting wealthy slob Kevin Corrigan into shape in this serio-comic offering. Corrigan soon falls for his new instructor, but the brittle Smulders - like her uptight boss, Guy Pearce - is no paragon of contentment. Mischievously puncturing the myth that physical fitness brings happiness, the film at times meanders because it refuses to fall back on romcom formulae. Instead, its charm is a matter of getting to know and understand the marvellous cast, Corrigan's "podgy and mellow" vibe playing sweetly against the hints of vulnerability displayed by the buffed-up Pearce and Smulders. TJ *DVD*

Guy Pearce *Trevor* • Cobie Smulders *Kat* • Kevin Corrigan *Danny* • Brooklyn Decker *Erin* • Anthony Michael Hall *Grigory* • Constance Zimmer *Mandy* ■ *Dir/Scr* Andrew Bujalski

Resurrected ★★★★15
Drama   1989 · UK · Colour · 88min

This is a sombre, unsettling account of a soldier who goes AWOL in the Falklands War and returns to his North Country village, with cruelly ironic consequences. Directed by former documentarist Paul Greengrass (the *Bourne* trilogy), it depicts the combat in First World War terms, but with the political complexity of a Vietnam. He imbues the story with a wealth of religious imagery - walking on water, cruciform poses, resurrection - while examining a flagging nation's regeneration and the attendant jingoism. AT *DVD*

David Thewlis *Kevin Deakin* • Tom Bell *Mr Deakin* • Rita Tushingham *Mrs Deakin* • Rudi Davies *Julie* • Michael Pollitt *Gregory Deakin* • William Hoyland *Capt Sinclair* • Ewan Stewart *Cpl Byker* • Christopher Fulford *Slaven* • David Lonsdale *Hibbert* • Peter Gunn *Bonner* ■ *Dir* Paul Greengrass • *Scr* Martin Allen

Resurrecting the Champ ★★★12
Drama based on a true story
2007 · US · Colour · 107min

Very loosely based on a true story, this has Josh Hartnett as a struggling sports reporter who stumbles on a career-making story in the shape of a former boxing champion now living on the streets. Samuel L Jackson gives a tricksy but engaging performance as the pugilist who has taken too many blows to the head, while Hartnett is adequate but no more as the struggling writer. The film's strength is in its plot, which performs an unexpected reversal after a deceptively pedestrian first act, and there are a couple of entertaining performances, one from Alan Alda as a hard-nosed sports editor and another from Teri Hatcher as a TV producer. However, a lack of urgency in the direction and an excess of sentimentality at the end undermines more than a little of what has gone before. AS *DVD*

Samuel L Jackson *Champ* • Josh Hartnett *Erik* • Kathryn Morris *Joyce* • Alan Alda *Metz* • Teri Hatcher *Andrea Flak* • David Paymer *Whitley* ■ *Dir* Rod Lurie • *Scr* Michael Bortman, Allison Burnett • *Cinematographer* Adam Kane

Resurrection ★★★15
Fantasy drama   1980 · US · Colour · 98min

After nearly dying in a car crash, Ellen Burstyn glimpses the "Gates of Heaven" and becomes endowed with healing powers. Is she Christ reborn? That's what neurotic preacher's son Sam Shepard thinks, leading to a provocative and tear-jerking climax. Superb scripting, a terrific cast and Daniel Petrie's heartfelt direction make this rural tale of faith and spirituality a rewarding experience. Burstyn is a revelation as the modest woman who soon realises how much of a burden her "gift" truly is. An underrated moral fantasy. AJ *DVD*

Ellen Burstyn *Edna McCauley* • Sam Shepard *Cal Carpenter* • Richard Farnsworth *Esco* • Roberts Blossom *John Harper* • Clifford David *George* • Pamela Payton-Wright *Margaret* ■ *Dir* Daniel Petrie • *Scr* Lewis John Carlino

Resurrection ★★
Thriller   1999 · US · Colour · 108min

Christopher Lambert stars in this serviceable thriller, in which a religious fanatic spends Lent constructing a corpse to host what he believes will be Christ's resurrection. There's a half-hearted attempt at saying something significant about the modern world, but the emphasis is firmly on action and the various dismemberments. Cinematographer Jonathan Freeman achieves some nice visual effects through the rain and Russell Mulcahy directs with bravado. DP

Christopher Lambert *John Prudhomme* • Rick Fox *Detective Scholfield* • James Kidnie *Walter Chibley* • Leland Orser *Detective Andrew Hollingworth* ■ *Dir* Russell Mulcahy • *Scr* Brad Mirman, from a story by Brad Mirman, Christopher Lambert

Resurrection Man ★★★18
Political crime drama 1997 · UK · Colour · 97min

With the Troubles in Northern Ireland providing a background, this thriller effectively creates an atmosphere of warfare and shows how the situation can affect - and even apparently excuse - the actions of psychopathic killer Stuart Townsend, who leads a gang of Loyalists on a killing spree. Director Marc Evans favours the bloody and the obvious, over defining events and motives, but this is still an engrossing account of humankind's inhumanity. TH Violence, swearing, sex scenes. *DVD*

Stuart Townsend *Victor Kelly* • Geraldine O'Rawe *Heather Graham* • James Nesbitt *Ryan* • John Hannah *Darkie Larche* • Brenda Fricker *Dorcas Kelly* • James Ellis *Ivor Coppinger* • Sean McGinley *Sammy McLure* • Derek Thompson *Herbie Ferguson* ■ *Dir* Marc Evans • *Scr* Eoin McNamee, from his novel

Retreat ★★★15
Psychological thriller 2011 · UK · Colour · 86min

If only it didn't take itself so seriously, this moody, well-played British thriller could attract a bigger audience for its chilly game of cat and mouse, set against an all-too-credible apocalypse scenario. Cillian Murphy and Thandie Newton play a married couple who head to a remote island to patch up their lives after a miscarriage, but matters take an unnerving turn with the arrival of a mysterious soldier (Jamie Bell). The stranger tells them a story about the outside world that beggars belief and the stakes are just too high for the couple to ignore. This dilemma motors the film through a gripping mid-section, but fans of horror might find the machinations too dry, while admirers of upscale drama should brace themselves for a grim and bloody climax. DW *DVD* *BD*

Cillian Murphy *Martin* • Thandie Newton *Kate* • Jamie Bell *Jack* ■ *Dir* Carl Tibbetts • *Scr* Carl Tibbetts, Janice Hallett

Retreat, Hell! ★★
War drama   1952 · US · BW · 94min

Cult B-movie director Joseph H Lewis turns in a conventional combat movie, set during the Korean War. All the clichés are firmly in place: the training routines, the heroic commanding officer; the platoon leader worried about the wife and kids he has left behind; the frayed nerves; and the camaraderie of the men as they are picked off by communist snipers. Made while the Korean War was actually being fought, this was shot on a low budget and is a patch on later films with the same theme. AT

Frank Lovejoy *Steve Corbett* • Richard Carlson *Paul Hansen* • Rusty Tamblyn [Russ Tamblyn] *Jimmy McDermid* • Anita Louise *Ruth Hansen* ■ *Dir* Joseph H Lewis • *Scr* Milton Sperling, Ted Sherdeman

The Return ★★★★12
Drama   2003 · Rus · Colour · 105min

Director Andrey Zvyagintsev's debut feature is an enigmatic rite-of-passage drama, in which brothers Vladimir Garin and Ivan Dobronravov are taken on a fishing trip when their missing father (Konstantin Lavronenko) returns to his home in northern Russia after many unexplained years away. Lavronenko tries gruffly to re-establish a relationship with his sons, but their tense journey to a remote island has an ulterior motive, and attempted bonding quickly turns to paranoia and violence. Atmospheric, meditative and drained of warmth by cinematographer Mikhail Kritchman's blue palette, this chilly film refuses to colour in the blanks where backstory might be, and the result is a stunningly beautiful puzzle that brilliantly captures the boys' confusion. AC Russian +subtitles. *DVD*

Vladimir Garin *Andrey* • Ivan Dobronravov *Ivan* • Konstantin Lavronenko *Father* • Natalia Vdovina *Mother* ■ *Dir* Andrey Zvyagintsev • *Scr* Alexander Novototsky, Vladimir Moiseenko

The Return ★★15
Supernatural thriller 2006 · US · Colour · 81min

Travelling sales rep Sarah Michelle Gellar is haunted by nightmarish visions of a woman's unsolved murder in this American debut of British director Asif Kapadia (*The Warrior*). The film's disorientating supernatural element doesn't kick in until far too late, and so comes across as an afterthought. Stylish bleached-out cinematography exploits the desolate Texas locations well, and Sam Shepard does fine work as Gellar's estranged father. But most viewers will find themselves two steps ahead as the mystery unfolds, and there aren't enough sudden shocks for horror fans. AJ Violence, disturbing scenes. *DVD* *BD*

Sarah Michelle Gellar *Joanna Mills* • Peter O'Brien (2) *Terry Stahl* • Adam Scott *Kurt* • Kate Beahan *Michelle* • Sam Shepard *Ed Mills* ■ *Dir* Asif Kapadia • *Scr* Adam Sussman • *Cinematographer* Roman Osin

Return ★★★15
Drama   2011 · US · Colour · 98min

Artist-turned-director Liza Johnson's considered debut is the downbeat story of an Ohio reservist who struggles to settle back into her old life on returning from action overseas. Kelli (Linda Cardellini) discovers that her husband (Michael Shannon) has been unfaithful, impulsively quits her warehouse job, and must undergo counselling with a maverick Vietnam veteran (*Mad Men's* John Slattery) after being charged with drunk driving. Johnson avoids much of the melodrama that marred Brit Brian Welsh's 2010 civvy street drama *In Our Name*, but things become slightly soapy as Kelli's fitness to raise her daughters and return to the frontline are called into question. Some may find the scenario humdrum and the denouement strained, but Johnson's narrative control is as assured as her keen visual sense. DP

Linda Cardellini *Kelli* • Michael Shannon *Mike* • John Slattery *Bud* • Talia Balsam *Julie* • Paul Sparks *Ed* ■ *Dir/Scr* Liza Johnson

Return from the Ashes ★★★
Crime thriller   1965 · UK/US · BW · 103min

In an extraordinary picture from British director J Lee Thompson, a Jewish woman (Ingrid Thulin) returns to Paris from the Dachau concentration camp with her face and mind deeply scarred, so she has plastic surgery. Her husband Maximilian Schell, a chess master, is now in love with her stepdaughter and at first believes Thulin is a "double" whom he can exploit for compensation money. This bizarre tale at times plumbs depths of awfulness yet rises to the giddiest heights of melodrama. AT

Maximilian Schell *Stanislaus Pilgrin* • Samantha Eggar *Fabienne* • Ingrid Thulin *Dr Michele Wolf* • Herbert Lom *Dr Charles Bovard* • Talitha Pol *Claudine* ■ *Dir* J Lee Thompson • *Scr* Julius J Epstein, from the novel *Le Retour des Cendres* by Hubert Monteilhet

Return from the River Kwai
★★ 15

Second World War action adventure
1988 · UK · Colour · 97min

There's no link between this and David Lean's 1957 classic film, and it doesn't come close in terms of acting or direction, but is still a tough, grim action movie. Set two years after Alec Guinness's bridge-building antics, this recounts with a certain level of realism prisoner of war life in the Far East during the closing months of the war. NF Violence, swearing **DVD**

Edward Fox *Benford* • Denholm Elliott *Colonel Grayson* • Chris Penn *Crawford* • George Takei *Tanaka* • Timothy Bottoms *Miller* • Richard Graham (2) *Perry* ■ *Dir* Andrew V McLaglen • *Scr* Sargon Tamimi, Paul Mayersberg

Return from Witch Mountain
★★★ U

Science-fiction adventure
1978 · US · Colour · 89min

Bette Davis is in her element here, giving a scene-stealing performance as henchwoman to Christopher Lee's mad scientist. Lee is seeking world domination by gaining control of two extraterrestrial kids, who possess all kinds of strange powers (telekinesis, anti-gravity, cute expressions). A sequel to *Escape to Witch Mountain*, it's a Disney fantasy in which the usual blandness has been spiked with an interesting touch of colour, courtesy of the film's legendary star. TH **DVD**

Bette Davis *Letha Wedge* • Christopher Lee *Dr Victor Gannon* • Kim Richards *Tia Malone* • Ike Eisenmann *Tony Malone* • Jack Soo *Mr Yokomoto* • Anthony James *Sickle* • Dick Bakalyan [Richard Bakalyan] *Eddie* • Ward Costello *Mr Clearcole* • Christian Juttner *Dazzler* • Poindexter *Crusher* • Brad Savage *Muscles* • Jeffrey Jacquet *Rocky* • Stu Gilliam *Dolan* ■ *Dir* John Hough • *Scr* Malcolm Marmorstein, from characters by Alexander Key

The Return of a Man Called Horse
★★★ 15

Western
1976 · US · Colour · 120min

This sequel – just as good as the original – has Richard Harris as the peer-turned-native, travelling from England to right the wrongs done to his adoptive Sioux tribe. Sadomasochistic rituals such as the Sun Vow ceremony usually result in near-skinning alive, but director Irvin Kershner keeps it relevant to the story, while Gale Sondergaard, everyone's favourite female villain, breathes vengeful fire. Followed in 1983 by *Triumphs of a Man Called Horse*. TH **DVD**

Richard Harris *John Morgan* • Gale Sondergaard *Elk Woman* • Geoffrey Lewis *Zenas Morro* • Bill Lucking [William Lucking] *Tom Gryce* • Jorge Luke *Running Bull* • Claudio Brook *Chemin D'Fer* • Enrique Lucero *Raven* • Jorge Russek *Blacksmith* • Ana De Sade *Moonstar* • Pedro Damien *Standing Bear* ■ *Dir* Irvin Kershner • *Scr* Jack DeWitt, from characters by Dorothy M Johnson

Return of a Stranger
★★

Crime drama
1937 · UK · BW · 63min

In this creaky melodrama, a scientist disfigured in an explosion returns to London to clear his name, identify a killer and reclaim his girl. The plot is now a cliché, of course, but this remains mesmerisingly watchable because of its period production values and the sheer gall of the finale. Griffith Jones and Rosalyn Boulter are the lacklustre, but remarkably well-spoken leads. TS

Griffith Jones *James Martin* • Rosalyn Boulter *Carol* • Ellis Jeffreys *Lady Wall* • Athole Stewart *Sir Patrick Wall* • Cecil Ramage *John Forbes* • Constance Godridge *Esme* • Sylvia Marriott *Mary*

• James Harcourt *Johnson* ■ *Dir* Victor Hanbury • *Scr* Akos Tolnay, Reginald Long, from a play by Rudolph Lothar

The Return of Bulldog Drummond
★

Detective mystery adventure
1934 · UK · BW · 74min

Based on a real Guards officer (Gerald Fairlie), the character of Bulldog Drummond was conceived by Fairlie's friend "Sapper" or, more correctly, HC McNeile and subsequently developed in novels and films. Drummond is a precursor to many sleuths and gentlemanly detectives. He enjoyed various incarnations including the urbane Jack Buchanan, but here Ralph Richardson takes the part. Neither the role, nor the film, involving the kidnapping of Drummond's wife (Ann Todd) by a secret society, proved worthy of the great actor. BB

Ralph Richardson *Hugh Drummond* • Ann Todd *Phyllis Drummond* • Francis L Sullivan *Carl Peterson* • Claud Allister *Algy Longworth* • H Saxon-Snell *Zadowa* • Spencer Trevor *Sir Bryan Johnstone* • Charles Mortimer *Inspector McIver* ■ *Dir* Walter Summers • *Scr* Walter Summers, from the novel *The Black Gang* by HC "Sapper" McNeile

The Return of Captain Invincible
★★ PG

Spoof adventure
1983 · Aus · Colour · 87min

This intermittently enjoyable comic book spoof stars Alan Arkin as a down-and-out, alcoholic superhero dragged from his retirement to save the world one last time. Christopher Lee rises to the occasion as an evil megalomaniac in a cheaply-made Australian comedy fantasy, peppered with songs by *Rocky Horror Show* creator Richard O'Brien. Director Philippe Mora tries hard to combine all genres, but the film doesn't quite have the courage of his convictions. AJ

Alan Arkin *Captain Invincible* • Christopher Lee *Mr Midnight* • Michael Pate *US President* • Graham Kennedy *Australian PM* • Kate Fitzpatrick *Patty Patria* ■ *Dir* Philippe Mora • *Scr* Steven E de Souza, Andrew Gaty

The Return of Count Yorga
★★★

Horror
1971 · US · Colour · 96min

Robert Quarry dons the black cape once more in this polished picture that is superior to the original *The Loves of Count Iorga, Vampire*, the sexploitation movie that became a cult horror flick. This time he's developed a passion for Mariette Hartley, the daughter of the principal of the orphanage close to his Los Angeles home. But before he can have his wicked way with her he has to overcome her dogged boyfriend Roger Perry. Everything's been done a dozen times before, but Bob Kelljan conjures up a few chills and Quarry turns on the menacing charm with some skill. DP

Robert Quarry *Count Yorga* • Mariette Hartley *Cynthia Nelson* • Roger Perry *Dr David Baldwin* • Yvonne Wilder *Jennifer* • Tom Toner *Reverend Thomas* ■ *Dir* Bob Kelljan • *Scr* Bob Kelljan, Yvonne Wilder

The Return of Dr Fu Manchu
★★

Mystery thriller
1930 · US · BW · 73min

Swedish character actor Warner Oland stars as Sax Rohmer's insidious Chinese villain, struggling with Scotland Yard's Nayland Smith for world domination. In this slow but atmospheric film, the Oriental madman, having used a secret drug that induces catalepsy to fake his death, comes back to get revenge on those responsible for killing his wife and son in the Boxer Rebellion. Oland shines in the star role, one he made his own before becoming the screen's most popular Charlie Chan. AJ

Warner Oland *Dr Fu Manchu* • Neil Hamilton *Dr Jack Petrie* • Jean Arthur *Lila Eltham* ■ *Dir* Rowland V Lee • *Scr* Florence Ryerson, Lloyd Corrigan, from the novel by Sax Rohmer

The Return of Dr X
★★

Horror mystery
1939 · US · BW · 62min

With Humphrey Bogart in a clichéd role as a murderous monster, this is a conventional account of a vampire terrorising a city. An attempt by Warner Bros to appeal to horror fans, it's notable for the inclusion of many members of the studio's acting B-league, including Dennis Morgan and Rosemary Lane. Only two years later, Bogart became a major star – and wisely steered clear of horror films for the rest of his career. TH

Humphrey Bogart *Marshall Quesne/Dr Maurice J Xavier* • Rosemary Lane *Joan Vance* • Wayne Morris *Walter Barnett* • Dennis Morgan *Michael Rhodes* • John Litel *Dr Francis Flegg* • Lya Lys *Angela Merrova* • Huntz Hall *Pinky* ■ *Dir* Vincent Sherman • *Scr* Lee Katz, from the story *The Doctor's Secret* by William J Makin

The Return of Dracula
★★

Horror
1958 · US · BW and Colour · 77min

Dracula turns up in California masquerading as a refugee Transylvanian artist and starts his nasty nocturnal habits among the homely community. Released in the same year as Hammer's *Dracula*, this modern gothic thriller lost out in the vampire sweepstakes for being drearily highbrow in comparison. But undead Francis Lederer turning into a wolf, a bat and a curl of mist (hence the loony British retitling *The Fantastic Disappearing Man*) plus other nifty camera tricks, lift it above the average B-movie rut. Mainly for devotees who will find the more intelligent use of horror clichés a surprising bonus. AJ

Francis Lederer *Bellac* • Norma Eberhardt *Rachel* • Ray Stricklyn *Tim* • Jimmy Baird *Mickey* • Greta Granstedt *Cora* • Virginia Vincent *Jennie* • John Wengraf *Merriman* • Gage Clark [Gage Clarke] *Reverend* • John McNamara *Sheriff Bicknell* ■ *Dir* Paul Landres • *Scr* Pat Fielder

The Return of Frank James
★★ U

Western
1940 · US · Colour · 88min

Henry Fonda had played Frank to Tyrone Power's Jesse in the superb *Jesse James*, and in this disappointing follow-up he spends all his time searching for brothers Charles and, in particular, Bob Ford (John Carradine), the "dirty little coward" who shot his own brother. But, unfortunately, Fonda has neither benefit of a decent script nor a sympathetic director, as Austrian émigré Fritz Lang makes heavy going of this lightweight material, dragging the pace to the point of boredom. Notable mainly for the movie debut of the beautiful Gene Tierney. TS **DVD**

Henry Fonda *Frank James/Ben Woodson* • Gene Tierney *Eleanor Stone* • Jackie Cooper *Clem/Tom Grayson* • Henry Hull *Major Rufus Cobb* • John Carradine *Bob Ford* • Charles Tannen *Charles Ford* • J Edward Bromberg *Runyon* • Donald Meek *McCoy* ■ *Dir* Fritz Lang • *Scr* Sam Hellman

The Return of Godzilla
★★ PG

Monster horror
1984 · Jpn · Colour · 87min

After a decade in hibernation, the King of the Monsters returned as the villain to cause an international Cold War incident after trashing a Soviet submarine. Russia and America want the outsized nuisance destroyed, and Tokyo is nearly razed to the ground for the umpteenth time. Raymond Burr pops up as an intrepid reporter, just as he did in the original 1954 movie, in footage added for western markets. Elsewhere, it's business as usual – thin plot, inane dialogue, daft dubbing and cheap special effects. AJ A Japanese language film +both dubbed and subtitled versions.

Raymond Burr *Steve Martin* • Keiju Kobayashi *Prime Minister Mitamura* • Ken Tanaka *Goro Maki* • Yasuko Sawaguchi *Naoko Okumura* • Shin Takuma *Hiroshi Okumura* • Eitaro Ozawa *Finance Minister Kanzaki* • Taketoshi Naito *Chief Cabinet Secretary Takegami* • Nobuo Kaneko *Home Affairs Minister Isomura* ■ *Dir* Kohji Hashimoto, RJ Kizer • *Scr* Shuichi Nagahara, Lisa Tomei, from a story by Tomoyuki Tanaka

The Return of Ironside
★★ PG

Crime drama
1993 · US · Colour · 88min

In this belated TV-movie spin-off from the popular 1970s cop show, stone-faced ex-police chief Robert Ironside comes out of retirement to lend his powers of deduction to a particularly puzzling murder case. Most of the old gang are present and correct – Don Galloway, Barbara Anderson, Elizabeth Baur and Don Mitchell all reprise their original roles – so fans of the series may be intrigued to see how they have fared. However, plotwise this is pretty flimsy stuff. JF

Raymond Burr *Robert T Ironside* • Don Galloway *Ed Brown* • Barbara Anderson *Eve Whitfield* • Don Mitchell *Mark Sanger* • Elizabeth Baur *Fran Belding* • Dana Wynter *Katherine Ironside* ■ *Dir* Gary Nelson • *Scr* Rob Hedden, William Read Woodfield, from characters by Collier Young

The Return of Josey Wales
★ 15

Western
1986 · US · Colour · 87min

Josey's back! But this time he ain't Clint Eastwood – so who cares? Josey is now played by Michael Parks. This sequel is mainly just a series of shoot-outs. Parks also directs and he filmed it in Mexico with an eye to the Latino market – much of the dialogue is in Spanish and the styling is reminiscent of those paella westerns of the 1970s. AT English, Spanish +subtitles.

Michael Parks *Josey Wales* • Rafael Campos *Chato* • Bob Magruder *Ten Spot* • Paco Vela *Paco* • Everett Sifuentes *Escobedo* • Charlie McCoy *Charlie* ■ *Dir* Michael Parks • *Scr* Forrest Carter, RO Taylor, from the novel *Vengeance Trail of Josey Wales* by Forrest Carter

The Return of Martin Guerre
★★★★ 15

Historical drama
1982 · Fr · Colour · 106min

Infinitely superior to its Hollywood remake, *Sommersby*, Daniel Vigne's suspenseful riddle of identity is a fascinating study of the blind faith, superstition and prejudice that governed most rural communities in the mid-16th century. Gérard Depardieu typically imposes himself on proceedings as the farmer who returns a changed man after nine years at war. But just how changed is he? The winner of a César for its screenplay, this highly literate film benefits from some meticulous historical research and a sensitive performance from Nathalie Baye as the unquestioning wife. DP French +subtitles. **DVD**

Gérard Depardieu *Martin Guerre* • Bernard-Pierre Donnadieu *Martin Guerre* • Nathalie Baye *Bertrande de Rols* • Roger Planchon *Jean de Caros* • Maurice Jacquemont *Judge Rieux* • Isabelle Sadoyan *Catherine Boere* ■ *Dir* Daniel Vigne • *Scr* Daniel Vigne, Jean-Claude Carrière

The Return of Mr Moto
★

Detective drama
1965 · UK · BW · 68min

More than a quarter of a century after Peter Lorre made the last of his eight films as John Philip Marquand's Oriental sleuth, Fox released this bizarre coda to the series. Henry Silva took the title role, but assumed a Japanese disguise only to conclude the case. Stationed in London to protect petroleum magnate Gordon Tanner, Silva's Interpol agent is soon on the trail of Martin Wyldeck, a former Nazi who plans world domination. Crude and ineptly played. DP

Henry Silva *Mr Moto* • Terence Longdon *Jonathan Westering* • Suzanne Lloyd *Maxine Powell* • Marne Maitland *Wasir Hussein* • Martin Wyldeck *Dargo* ■ *Dir* Ernest Morris • *Scr* Fred Eggers, from a story by Randall Hood, from the character created by John Phillip Marquand

The Return of October
★★

Comedy drama
1948 · US · Colour · 89min

October's a racehorse, but he's also the reincarnation of Terry Moore's Uncle Willie – or so she believes in this whimsical comedy bolstered by Technicolor and an ingratiating performance by Glenn Ford, as the professor of psychology who writes a book about the girl's strange belief. Director

U SUITABLE FOR ALL **Uc** SUITABLE ESPECIALLY FOR YOUNG CHILDREN (DVD ONLY) **PG** PARENTAL GUIDANCE **12A** UNDER 12s TO BE ACCOMPANIED (CINEMA ONLY)

Joseph H Lewis shows some talent for comedy, but seems happiest shooting the racetrack sequences - although the races themselves are stock shots from 1938's *Kentucky*. AE

Glenn Ford *Prof Bentley Bassett Jr* • Terry Moore *Terry Ramsey* • Albert Sharpe *Vince, the Tout* • James Gleason *Uncle Willie* • Dame May Whitty *Aunt Martha* • Henry O'Neill *President Hotchkiss* ■ Dir Joseph H Lewis • Scr Melvin Frank, Norman Panama, from a story by Connie Lee, Karen De Wolf

The Return of Peter Grimm ★★★
Fantasy 1935 · US · BW · 81min

The theme of returning from the dead to see how the living are coping has always fascinated dramatists, and this adaptation has Lionel Barrymore as a crusty millionaire allowed after his death to see what a mess he made of things. Though the film suffers from an uncertain tone, with director George Nichols Jr not sure how seriously to treat the story, the performances are strong and the tale's premise remains intriguing and involving. TV

Lionel Barrymore *Peter Grimm* • Helen Mack *Catherine* • Edward Ellis *Dr Andrew MacPherson* • Donald Meek *Mr Batholomew* • George Breakston *William Van Dam* • Allen Vincent *Frederik* • James Bush *James* ■ Dir George Nichols Jr • Scr Francis Edwards Faragoh, from the play by David Belasco

Return of Sabata ★★ 15
Spaghetti western 1971 · W Ger/It/Fr · Colour · 101min

For the last in the light-hearted spaghetti western trilogy trouper Lee Van Cleef returns as the sharp-shooting bounty hunter with more gadgets up his sleeve than James Bond. Now working as a sideshow attraction, Sabata's travelling circus pulls into Hobsonville where he takes on pious villain Giampiero Albertini, who is greedily imposing crippling taxes on the defenceless townspeople. Despite occasional flashes of inspiration, this entry is strictly a routine romp. AJ Italian dubbed. Violence, nudity. DVD

Lee Van Cleef *Sabata* • Reiner Schöne *Clyde* • Giampiero Albertini *McIntock* • Pedro Sanchez [Ignazio Spalla] *Bronco* • Annabella Incontrera *Maggie* • Jacqueline Alexandre *Jackie* • Nick Jordan [Aldo Canti] *Angel* ■ Dir Frank Kramer [Gianfranco Parolini] • Scr Gianfranco Parolini, Renato Izzo

The Return of Swamp Thing ★★ 15
Spoof science-fiction thriller 1989 · US · Colour · 83min

Louis Jourdan returns as evil genius Dr Arcane, back in melodramatic Dr Moreau mode, and still gene-splitting to halt the ageing process. Soap queen Heather Locklear is his stepdaughter searching for the truth behind her mother's death, but how and why she falls for Swampy has to be seen to be believed. It's a moss-eaten slice of splat-stick packed with laboured in-jokes (Jourdan's pet parrot is called "Gigi"). AJ

Louis Jourdan *Dr Anton Arcane* • Heather Locklear *Abby Arcane* • Sarah Douglas *Dr Lana Zurrell* • Dick Durock *Swamp Thing* • Ace Mask *Dr Rochelle* • Joey Sagal *Gunn* ■ Dir Jim Wynorski • Scr Derek Spencer, Grant Morris, from the DC Comics character

Return of the Bad Men ★★
Western 1948 · US · BW · 90min

Cram enough famous western outlaws into one film to keep the action crowd happy and you don't have to worry too much about plot or characterisation. Here, the Youngers, the Daltons, Wild Bill Doolin and Billy the Kid are all spoiling for a fight, but the real villainy comes from Robert Ryan's vicious Sundance Kid, and the only man who can stop him is Randolph Scott's marshal. AE

Randolph Scott *Vance* • Robert Ryan *Sundance Kid* • Anne Jeffreys *Cheyenne* • George "Gabby" Hayes *John Pettit* • Jacqueline White *Madge Allen* • Steve Brodie *Cole Younger* • Richard

Powers [Tom Keene] *Jim Younger* • Robert Bray *John Younger* • Lex Barker *Emmett Dalton* • Walter Reed *Bob Dalton* • Michael Harvey *Grat Dalton* • Dean White *Billy the Kid* • Robert Armstrong *Wild Bill Doolin* ■ Dir Ray Enright • Scr Charles O'Neal, Jack Natteford, Luci Ward, from a story by Jack Natteford, Luci Ward

The Return of the Cisco Kid ★★★ U
Western 1939 · US · BW · 70min

Matinée idol Warner Baxter stars as author O Henry's dashing Mexican hero for the third time her. He received the first talkie best actor Oscar for the role in the 1929 film *In Old Arizona*, and did well commercially in the absurdly heroic 1931 sequel *The Cisco Kid*. But this time, eight long years later, Baxter's drinking, a substandard director and a makeshift plot make for a disappointing outing, which proved to be Baxter's last as the Kid. This led to a movie series, starring Cesar Romero (beginning with *The Cisco Kid and the Lady*). TS

Warner Baxter *Cisco Kid* • Lynn Bari *Ann Carver* • Cesar Romero *Lopez* • Henry Hull *Colonel Jonathan Bixby* • Kane Richmond *Alan Davis* • C Henry Gordon *Mexican Captain* • Robert Barrat *Sheriff McNally* ■ Dir Herbert I Leeds • Scr Milton Sperling, from the characters by O Henry

Return of the Fly ★★ 15
Horror 1959 · US · BW · 76min

The sequel to the original 1958 horror hit is a more standard B-movie retelling of the same story, with Brett Halsey playing Al Hedison's son, repeating his father's teleportation tinkering with similarly disastrous results. Thankfully Vincent Price is back, and goes a long way towards keeping things buzzing along. Director Edward Bernds sadly stresses plot gimmicks at the expense of an involving story. *Curse of the Fly* completed the trilogy. AJ DVD

Vincent Price *François Delambre* • Brett Halsey *Phillipe Delambre* • David Frankham *Alan Hinds* • John Sutton *Inspector Charas* • Dan Seymour *Max Berthold* • Dan elle De Metz *Cecile Bonnard* ■ Dir Edward Bernds • Scr Edward Bernds, from a story by George Langelaan

Return of the Killer Tomatoes ★ 15
Horror comedy 1988 · US · Colour · 94min

As *Attack of the Killer Tomatoes* was a big video rental (solely because of its catchy title), a belated sequel was commissioned and it is even worse. Professor Gangrene (John Astin) turns a tomato into a sexy babe by playing music at it and plans to take over the world with a bevy of similarly exposed red fruits. John DeBello's charmless wonder is only notable for an early appearance by future heart-throb George Clooney. AJ DVD

Anthony Starke *Chad* • Karen Mistal *Tara* • George Clooney *Matt* • Steve Lundquist *Igor* • John Astin *Professor Gangrene* ■ Dir John DeBello • Scr Constantine Dillon, John DeBello, John Stephen Peace [Steve Peace]

Return of the Living Dead ★★★ 18
Comedy horror 1984 · US · Colour · 86min

This enjoyable horror comedy marked the directorial debut of long-time sci-fi scribe Dan O'Bannon. This semi-sequel to George A Romero's 1963 cult classic *Night of the Living Dead* is like an EC comic come alive, in that it'll make you laugh and squirm - often at the same time. "They're back. They're hungry. And they're not vegetarian," blared the poster. O'Bannon cleverly makes the zombies the real stars of this movie and, unlike the Romero variety, these can speak, though they're mostly limited to spouting, "Brains, more brains!" A must for horror fans. RS DVD

Clu Gulager *Burt* • James Karen *Frank* • Don Calfa *Ernie* • Thom Mathews *Freddy* • Beverly Randolph *Tina* • John Philbin *Chuck* • Jewel Shepard *Casey* • Dir Dan O'Bannon • Scr Dan O'Bannon, from a story by Judy Ricci, John Russo, Russell Streiner

Return of the Living Dead Part II ★★ 18
Comedy horror 1988 · US · Colour · 85min

The emphasis here is on humour at the expense of horror - most of it, it must be said, unintentional. Once again small-town America is overrun by brain-eating zombies, the by-products of toxic waste from bacteriological warfare, which has seeped into a local graveyard with familiar results. And it's up to the usual motley crew of teens to sort it out. Predictable, dull and repetitive. RS DVD

James Karen *Ed* • Thom Mathews *Joey* • Dana Ashbrook *Tom Essex* • Marsha Dietlein *Lucy Wilson* • Philip Bruns *Doc Mandel* • Michael Kenworthy *Jesse Wilson* • Suzanne Snyder *Brenda* • Thor Van Lingen *Billy* • Jason Hogan *Johnny* ■ Dir/Scr Ken Wiederhorn

Return of the Living Dead III ★★★ 18
Horror 1993 · US · Colour · 92min

After the risible *Return of the Living Dead Part II*, the series got back on track with this splatter fest from Brian Yuzna. Dispensing with the spoof elements of its predecessors, this is a darker and surprisingly intelligent mix of gore, special effects and tragic romance. J Trevor Edmond is the lovelorn teen who uses the zombie gas that caused such chaos in the earlier movies to resurrect his girlfriend, after she is killed in a motorcycle accident, with predictable results. RS DVD

Mindy Clarke [Melinda Clarke] *Julie* • J Trevor Edmond *Curt Reynolds* • Kent McCord *Colonel John Reynolds* • Basil Wallace *Riverman* ■ Dir Brian Yuzna • Scr Jon Penney

The Return of the Musketeers ★★ PG
Swashbuckling comedy adventure 1989 · UK/Fr/Sp · Colour · 101min

Fifteen years after the success of his sparkling version of Alexandre Dumas's swashbuckling favourite, Richard Lester reunited the musketeers in this bid to save Charles I of England from the executioner's axe. Roy Kinnear's tragic death following a riding accident obviously sapped everyone's enthusiasm for the project. The Dumas book, on which the story is based, inspired the marginally more successful Bertrand Tavernier 1994 film *D'Artagnan's Daughter*. DP Violence.

Michael York *D'Artagnan* • Oliver Reed *Athos* • Frank Finlay *Porthos* • C Thomas Howell *Raoul* • Kim Cattrall *Justine* • Geraldine Chaplin *Queen Anne* • Roy Kinnear *Planchet* • Christopher Lee *Rochefort* • Philippe Noiret *Cardinal Mazarin* • Richard Chamberlain *Aramis* ■ Dir Richard Lester • Scr George MacDonald Fraser, from the novel *Vingt Ans Après* by Alexandre Dumas

The Return of the Pink Panther ★★★ PG
Comedy 1974 · UK · Colour · 107min

With his career flagging, Peter Sellers repeatedly returned to his Inspector Clouseau role, and everyone should be thankful. This is Blake Edwards and Sellers working together at their best, producing memorable moments of film comedy. Clouseau's attempts to woo Catherine Schell with his Bogart-style chat-up lines had even his co-star in fits of laughter, which they thankfully kept on screen. Not as good as the first, but still great fun. Followed by *The Pink Panther Strikes Again* in 1976. NF DVD BLU

Peter Sellers *Inspector Clouseau* • Christopher Plummer *Sir Charles Litton* • Catherine Schell *Claudine* • Herbert Lom *Chief Inspector Dreyfus* • Peter Arne *Colonel Sharki* • Peter Jeffrey *General Wadafi* • Grégoire Aslan *Chief of Lugash Police* • David Lodge *Mac* • Graham Stark *Pepi* • Eric Pohlmann *Fat man* • André Maranne *François* • Burt Kwouk *Cato* ■ Dir Blake Edwards • Scr Frank Waldman, Blake Edwards, from a character created by Blake Edwards, Maurice Richlin

The Return of the Scarlet Pimpernel ★★ U
Period adventure 1937 · UK · BW · 74min

Leslie Howard had such a hit with *The Scarlet Pimpernel* in 1934 that Alexander Korda immediately ordered a sequel - for far less than the budget of the original. After Howard turned the part down to play in a little something called *Gone with the Wind*, the role of Sir Percy Blakeney went to Barry K Barnes, a stage actor who made his screen debut. Being a Korda production, it looks handsome, but that's the best one can say. AT

Barry K Barnes *Sir Percy Blakeney/The Scarlet Pimpernel* • Sophie Stewart *Marguerite Blakeney* • Margaretta Scott *Theresa Cabarrus* • James Mason *Jean Tallien* • Francis Lister *Chauvelin* • Anthony Bushell *Sir Andrew Ffoulkes* • Patrick Barr *Lord Hastings* • David Tree *Lord Harry Denning* • Henry Oscar *Maximilien de Robespierre* ■ Dir Hans Schwartz [Hanns Schwarz] • Scr Lajos Bíró, Arthur Wimperis, Adrian Brunel, from the novel by Baroness Orczy

Return of the Secaucus Seven ★★★★ 15
Drama 1980 · US · Colour · 104min

John Sayles's directing debut was shot for a mere $60,000 and deals with the reunion of seven friends, all of whom were part of the student protest movement of the 1960s and are now definitely older, richer and perhaps wiser. There's a teacher, a singer, a doctor and so on and they talk, attend a play, talk some more, have sex, get arrested and go their separate ways. It has the density of a novel and the non-starry cast is simply marvellous, each creating a real character, yet none making too big a show of it. This is a real ensemble piece that is often regarded as superior to the very similar, big-budgeted *The Big Chill*. AT DVD

Bruce MacDonald (1) *Mike* • Adam LeFevre *JT* • Gordon Clapp *Chip* • Karen Trott *Maura* • David Strathairn *Ron* • Marisa Smith *Carol* • Carolyn Brooks *Meg* • John Sayles *Howie* ■ Dir/Scr John Sayles

Return of the Seven ★★★ PG
Western 1966 · US/Sp · Colour · 90min

Only Yul Brynner actually returns for this sequel to *The Magnificent Seven*. Of the newcomers, trusty tough guys Warren Oates and Claude Akins alone cut the mustard as Brynner and his band attempt to liberate a Mexican village from the slavery imposed by a megalomaniac father, grieving for his dead son. Director Burt Kennedy could always be depended upon to grind out robust westerns, but Larry Cohen's derivative script gives him too little to get his teeth into. Another sequel, *Guns of the Magnificent Seven* followed in 1969. DP DVD

Yul Brynner *Chris* • Robert Fuller *Vin* • Julian Mateos *Chico* • Warren Oates *Colbee* • Jordan Christopher *Manuel* • Claude Akins *Frank* • Virgilio Teixeira *Luis* • Emilio Fernandez *Lorca* • Rudy Acosta [Rodolfo Acosta] *Lopez* • Elisa Montés *Petra* • Fernando Rey *Priest* ■ Dir Burt Kennedy • Scr Larry Cohen

The Return of the Soldier ★★★ PG
Period drama 1982 · UK · Colour · 98min

Alan Bates is in the trenches, leaving wife, Julie Christie emotionally frozen in limbo and cousin, Ann-Margret worried sick and heaving with desire for him. Then Bates returns - shell-shocked and an amnesiac, he may as well be dead. Instead he runs off with an old flame - dour Glenda Jackson, nursing a big social chip on her shoulder. This is an impeccably mounted costume drama in which every class division and every unsaid emotion knows its place. AT

Alan Bates *Captain Chris Baldry* • Ann-Margret *Jenny* • Glenda Jackson *Margaret Grey* • Julie Christie *Kitty Baldry* • Jeremy Kemp *Frank* • Edward De Souza *Edward* • Frank Finlay *William Grey* • Ian Holm *Dr Anderson* • Pauline Quirke *Girl searching in hospital* • Kevin Whately *Hostile soldier's mate* ■ Dir Alan Bridges • Scr Hugh Whitemore, from a novel by Rebecca West

R

The Return of the Vampire
★

Second World War horror
1943 · US · BW · 68min

Playing a vampire for the first time since *Dracula* in 1931, Bela Lugosi is Armand Tesla (because Universal wouldn't let Columbia use its copyright name), a bloodsucker revived when a German bomb hits a cemetery during the Blitz. Our ill-humoured hero is then doomed to wander around foggy wartime London with a werewolf minion in tow to execute an aimless revenge plot. Crude and cornball. AJ

Bela Lugosi *Armand Tesla/Dr Hugo Bruckner* • Frieda Inescort *Lady Jane Ainsley* • Nina Foch *Nicki Saunders* • Miles Mander *Sir Frederick Fleet* • Roland Varno *John Ainsley* ■ *Dir* Lew Landers • *Scr* Griffin Jay, Randall Faye, from an idea by Kurt Neumann

Return to Glennascaul
★★★ U

Supernatural drama
1951 · US · Colour and BW · 22min

Orson Welles was in the middle of his interminable *Othello* shoot when he cameoed in this diverting Irish ghost story, as a favour to writer/director Hilton Edwards, whom he'd known since their days at Dublin's Gate Theatre. However, the brunt of the action is carried by Michael Laurence, who relates the LeFanu-style tale of his midnight encounter with a long-deceased mother and daughter. Views of the isolated house, both in its baroque cosiness and its eerie desolation, are stylishly achieved. DP *DVD*

Orson Welles • Michael Laurence (1) *Sean Merriman* • Sheila Richards *Mrs Campbell* • Helena Hughes *Lucy Campbell* ■ *Dir/Scr* Hilton Edwards

Return to Homs
★★★★ 15

Documentary
2013 · Egy/Ger/Swe/Jpn/Swi/Can/Leb/Neth/ Den/Nor · Colour · 93min

This harrowing account of the rearguard action fought in the Syrian city of Homs against the forces of President Assad was made for just $300,000 and filmed over three years from August 2011. Director Talal Derki faced considerable hardship and danger in amassing over 300 hours of footage, which had to be smuggled out of the country. Derki profiles 24-year-old media activist Ossama al-Homsi, who's desperate to alert the wider world to the shocking assault upon "the capital of the revolution". He is greatly assisted by 19-year-old Basset, who has become one of the country's most wanted dissidents because of his raw genius for rallying supporter. The scenes of devastation and the despondency of ordinary people trapped in a nightmare are almost unbearable to watch. DP Arabic +subtitles.

Abdul Basset Saroot ■ *Dir/Scr* Talal Derki

Return to Horror High
★ 18

Horror spoof
1986 · US · Colour · 90min

A sleazy film company sets up production of a splatter movie on campus at Crippen High, a school haunted by memories of a past massacre. Naturally, an unknown psycho begins decimating the has-been cast in director Bill Froehlich's messy film-within-a-film scenario. This cheap spoof exploiter is now famous for an *ER* doctor's movie debut – Doug Ross aka George Clooney, who's on screen just long enough for someone to tell him he's going to be a big star, one day. AJ *DVD*

Lori Lethin *Callie* • Brendan Hughes *Steven Blake* • Alex Rocco *Barry Sleerik* • Vince Edwards *Richard Birnbaum* • George Clooney *Oliver* ■ *Dir* Bill Froehlich • *Scr* Bill Froehlich, Mark Lisson, Dana Escalante, Greg H Sims

Return to Macon County
★★ 15

Drama
1975 · US · Colour · 85min

This disappointing follow-up to the cult hit *Macon County Line*, is distinguished only by the casting of Nick Nolte and Don Johnson

in early roles. This is really a sequel in name and setting only. Where the original focused on the horrors and violence of backwoods America, this goes down the *American Graffiti* route of a jukebox-friendly soundtrack for a tale of teen sex and hot-rod racing. Nolte and Johnson spend most of the movie picking up girls, driving fast and being chased by a vengeful cop. RS

Nick Nolte *Bo Hollinger* • Don Johnson *Harley McKay* • Robin Mattson *Junell* • Eugene Daniels *Tom* • Matt Greene *Pete* • Devon Ericson *Betty* • Ron Prather *Steve* • Robert Viharo *Sergeant Whittaker* ■ *Dir/Scr* Richard Compton

Return to Me
★★ PG

Romantic comedy drama
2000 · US · Colour · 111min

Recently widowed architect David Duchovny falls in love with waitress Minnie Driver. The catch is that she got his late wife's heart in a transplant. It's a rather grisly premise for an otherwise lightweight affair. The Chicago locations are well used, and a colourful cast deftly hints at the city's broad ethnic mix. Duchovny, however, is a dour leading man, while Driver is strangely subdued. NS *DVD*

David Duchovny *Bob Rueland* • Minnie Driver *Grace Briggs* • Carroll O'Connor *Marty O'Reilly* • Robert Loggia *Angelo Pardipillo* • Bonnie Hunt *Megan Dayton* • David Alan Grier *Charlie Johnson* • Joely Richardson *Elizabeth Rueland* • Eddie Jones *Emmett McFadden* • James Belushi *Joe Dayton* ■ *Dir* Bonnie Hunt • *Scr* Bonnie Hunt, Don Lake, from a story by Hunt, Lake, Andrew Stern, Samantha Goodman

Return to Never Land
★★★ U

Animated musical adventure
2002 · US · Colour · 69min

Disney's recycling of JM Barrie's main themes from their classic animated feature *Peter Pan* is surprisingly effective, although the animation is occasionally a little flat and the snatches of new songs are rather unnecessary. Now married with two children of her own, Wendy Darling has never stopped believing in "The Boy Who Would Never Grow Up". Her daughter Jane has no time for such piffle, until she's kidnapped by Captain Hook. Cleverly set during the Blitz, this is a heartfelt paean to childhood innocence and the power of imagination. AJ *DVD*

Harriet Owen *Jane/Young Wendy* • Blayne Weaver *Peter Pan* • Corey Burton *Captain Hook* • Jeff Bennett *Smee/Pirates* • Kath Soucie *Wendy* • Roger Rees *Edward* ■ *Dir* Robin Budd • *Scr* Temple Mathews, from characters by JM Barrie

Return to Oz
★★★ PG

Fantasy
1985 · US · Colour · 105min

Disney recaptures the dark side of L Frank Baum's *Oz* stories in this exciting sequel to the 1939 classic. Fairuza Balk is wonderful as Dorothy, who ends up back in a ruined Oz facing the evil Nome King and Princess Mombi with her friends Pumpkinhead, Tik Tok the clockwork man and a talking chicken. Sombre in tone it may be, but director Walter Murch's non-musical is imaginative and hugely appealing. The colourful special effects, including Will Vinton's Claymation process that animates the rock faces, are impressive. AJ *DVD*

Fairuza Balk *Dorothy Gale* • Nicol Williamson *Dr Worley/Nome King* • Jean Marsh *Nurse Wilson/ Princess Mombi* • Piper Laurie *Aunt Em* • Matt Clark *Uncle Henry* • Michael Sundin *Tik Tok* • Sean Barrett (2) *Tik Tok* • Stewart Larange *Jack Pumpkinhead* • Brian Henson *Jack Pumpkinhead* • Steve Norrington *Gump* • Justin Case *Scarecrow* ■ *Dir* Walter Murch • *Scr* Walter Murch, Gill Dennis, from the books by L Frank Baum • *Cinematographer* David Watkin • *Art Director* Norman Reynolds

Return to Paradise
★★

Romance
1953 · US · Colour · 100min

Gary Cooper, pursuing a peaceable devil-may-care beachcombing existence on a South Seas paradise, has a love affair with island girl Roberta Haynes and clashes with puritanical missionary Barry Jones. Haynes dies in childbirth and Cooper leaves, only to return during the Second World War when

he meets his now grown-up daughter. The film beguiles with its authentic atmosphere and flavour, but is too erratic to be fully satisfying. RK

Gary Cooper *Mr Morgan* • Roberta Haynes *Maeva* • Barry Jones *Pastor Corbett* • Moira MacDonald *Turia* • John Hudson (1) *Harry Faber* ■ *Dir* Mark Robson • *Scr* Charles Kaufman, from the short story *Mr Morgan* by James A Michener • *Cinematographer* Winton C Hoch

Return to Paradise
★★★★ 15

Drama
1998 · US · Colour · 107min

Would you let a friend die in a Malaysian prison for an offence you committed? That's the dilemma facing Vince Vaughn and David Conrad when lawyer Anne Heche tells them Joaquin Phoenix will hang unless they go back to Asia and serve their part of his prison sentence. Director Joseph Ruben weaves a wrenching tragedy out of the awesome predicament, mining every ounce of indignation and empathy. Acted with anguished conviction, Ruben's crisis-of-conscience thriller doesn't take any easy options and the result casts a singularly provocative spell. AJ Swearing, drug abuse, violence. *DVD*

Vince Vaughn *Sheriff* • Anne Heche *Beth* • Joaquin Phoenix *Lewis* • David Conrad *Tony* • Vera Farmiga *Kerrie* • Nick Sandow *Ravitch* • Jada Pinkett Smith *MJ Major* • Ming Lee *Mr Chandran* ■ *Dir* Joseph Ruben • *Scr* Wesley Strick, Bruce Robinson

Return to Peyton Place
★★★

Drama
1961 · US · Colour · 121min

A sequel to the hit 1957 feature film *Peyton Place*, this offers the same sensational mix as before and needs little comment for devotees of its predecessor, the original bestselling novel, or the long-running TV soap. Carol Lynley provokes outrage in her home town when she publishes her first novel, a thinly veiled exposé of the town's inhabitants. Utterly predictable, glossy tosh, this showcases the then relative newcomer Tuesday Weld and has a stand-out performance from Mary Astor. RK

Carol Lynley *Allison MacKenzie* • Jeff Chandler *Lewis Jackman* • Eleanor Parker *Connie Rossi* • Mary Astor *Roberta Carter* • Robert Sterling *Mike Rossi* • Luciana Paluzzi *Raffaella Carter* • Tuesday Weld *Selena Cross* • Brett Halsey *Ted Carter* ■ *Dir* José Ferrer • *Scr* Ronald Alexander, from the novel by Grace Metalious

A Return to Salem's Lot
★★★ 18

Horror
1987 · US · Colour · 96min

In this genuine treat for undead cultists, Larry Cohen pitches his tone a long way from the original Stephen King book for a loose semi-sequel. Michael Moriarty plays an anthropologist arriving, with son Ricky Addison Reed, in the infamous title locale to take over an inherited farmhouse, only to find the vampire population want him to set down their venerable history for posterity. Watch for veteran director Samuel Fuller, who steals the show as a single-minded vampire hunter. AJ

Michael Moriarty *Joe Weber – Dad* • Richard Addison Reed *Jeremy Weber* • Andrew Duggan *Judge Axel* • Samuel Fuller *Dr Van Meer* • June Havoc *Aunt Clara* • Ronee Blakley *Sally* • Evelyn Keyes *Mrs Axel* ■ *Dir* Larry Cohen • *Scr* Larry Cohen, James Dixon, from a story by Larry Cohen, from the novel *Salem's Lot* by Stephen King

Return to Sender
★★ 18

Thriller
2015 · US · Colour · 91min

Those familiar with *Gone Girl* will experience a sense of déjà vu while watching this derivative thriller, which sees nurse Rosamund Pike methodically plotting revenge on the man who raped her. Although nowhere near her Oscar-nominated role, Pike does hold the picture together with enigmatic steeliness, as she hides from her father (Nick Nolte) what she really has in store for her assailant (Shiloh Fernandez). The camera prowls menacingly through the interiors, but the writers seem

too content with their improbable conceit to bother with back story or character arcs. DP *DVD* *BD*

Rosamund Pike *Miranda Wells* • Nick Nolte *Miranda's father* • Shiloh Fernandez *William Finn* ■ *Dir* Fouad Mikati • *Scr* Patricia Beauchamp, Joe Gossett

Return to Snowy River
★★

Adventure
1988 · Aus · Colour · 110min

Brian Dennehy steals the limelight in a role first played in 1982 by Kirk Douglas in this below-par sequel to *The Man from Snowy River*, the tale of feuding Australian ranchers. Tom Burlinson, who left Snowy River to make his fortune, now wants to come back to his former girlfriend. Burlinson and Sigrid Thornton reprise the roles they played better in George Miller's original film, but the spectacular scenery is some compensation for an unfocused story with and underdeveloped characters. SG

Tom Burlinson *Jim Craig* • Sigrid Thornton *Jessica Harrison* • Brian Dennehy *Harrison* • Nicholas Eadie *Alistair Patton* • Mark Hembrow *Seb* • Bryan Marshall *Hawker* ■ *Dir* Geoff Burrowes • *Scr* John Dixon, Geoff Burrowes

Return to the Blue Lagoon
★ 15

Romantic adventure
1991 · US · Colour · 97min

While 1980's *The Blue Lagoon* had a certain grimly humorous value, this sequel lacks even that, as Brian Krause, playing the son of Brooke Shields's character from the original, and Milla Jovovich experience puberty and nudity on a deserted island. Contains bad acting, an appalling script and some of the most unconvincing love scenes ever committed to film. JB *DVD*

Milla Jovovich *Lilli* • Brian Krause *Richard* • Lisa Pelikan *Sarah Hargrave* • Courtney Phillips *Young Lilli* • Garette Patrick Ratliff *Young Richard* ■ *Dir* William A Graham • *Scr* Leslie Stevens, from the novel *The Garden of God* by Henry de Vere Stacpoole

Return to Treasure Island
★★ U

Adventure
1954 · US · Colour · 75min

In this desperate updating of Robert Louis Stevenson's classic adventure, pirate descendant Dawn Addams is joined in her bid to find Captain Flint's treasure by archaeology student Tab Hunter (a feeble forerunner of Indiana Jones), who relies on a little brawn to outwit bogus professor Porter Hal. It's meagre fare. DP

Tab Hunter *Clive Stone* • Dawn Addams *Jamesina Hawkins* • Porter Hall *Maximillian Harris* • James Seay *Felix Newman* • Harry Lauter *Parker* • William Cottrell *Cookie* • Henry Rowland *Williams* • Lane Chandler *Cardigan* ■ *Dir* EA Dupont • *Scr* Aubrey Wisberg, Jack Pollexfen, from their story

Return to Yesterday
★★ U

Drama
1940 · UK · BW · 69min

English actor Clive Brook, who enjoyed some success in Hollywood, stars in this British film about an English actor who has found success in Hollywood. Yearning for the simplicity of his past, however, he buys his way into a season with a humble British rep company. Directed by Robert Stevenson, a pacifist who publicised his resentment of British film-makers escaping the war by fleeing to Hollywood, this is a mediocre and technically inadequate film. RK

Clive Brook *Robert Maine* • Anna Lee *Carol Sands* • Dame May Whitty *Mrs Truscott* • Hartley Power *Regan* • Milton Rosmer *Sambourne* • David Tree *Peter Thropp, playwright* • Olga Lindo *Grace Sambourne* ■ *Dir* Robert Stevenson • *Scr* Robert Stevenson, Margaret Kennedy, Roland Pertwee, Angus MacPhail, from the play *Goodness How Sad!* by Robert Morley

Returning Lily
★★

Romantic drama
2003 · US · Colour · 95min

Beautiful scenery and an attentive local hunk make this simplistic, Hawaii-set relationship drama easy on both the eye and the brain. Under-appreciated wife and mum Virginia Madsen quickly falls for the island's many charms – including the aforementioned Jason Momoa (star of the 2011 *Conan* remake) – when she honours her late surrogate mother's wish to have her ashes returned to her Kauai birthplace. Naturally, Madsen's reflective character unlocks her true self in the process, but pragmatism prevails, resulting in a contrived yet bittersweet finale. SF

Virginia Madsen *Emma Burke* • Lainie Kazan *Julia* • Jason Momoa *Kala* • Andrew McFarlane *Mike* • Brooke Harman [Brooke Harmon] *Jamie* ■ *Dir* Maggie Greenwald • *Scr* Vivienne Radkoff

Reuben, Reuben ★★★ 15

Comedy   1983 · US · Colour · 95min

Tom Conti was Oscar-nominated for his tour de force as an impossible, alcoholic, womanising, flamboyantly verbose Scottish poet – a character shamelessly but affectionately inspired by Welsh icon Dylan Thomas and Ireland's Brendan Behan – who trades on his fading literary celebrity to scrounge off the generous hospitality of thrilled female admirers in a sleepy American university town. Inspiration to pull himself together comes in the shape of winsome young student Kelly McGillis (in her screen debut). The old-fashioned but witty script and charming performances give this lightweight throwback appeal. AME

Tom Conti *Gowan McGland* • Kelly McGillis *Geneva Spofford* • Roberts Blossom *Frank Spofford* • Cynthia Harris *Bobby Springer* • E Katherine Kerr *Lucille Haxby* • Joel Fabiani *Dr Haxby* • Lois Smith *Mare Spofford* ■ *Dir* Robert Ellis Miller • *Scr* Julius J Epstein, from a novel by Peter DeVries, from the play *Spofford* by Herman Shumlin

Reunion ★★★ 15

Historical drama
1989 · Fr/W Ger/UK · Colour · 105min

Samuel West and Christien Anholt give mature performances and Jason Robards turns in a dignified cameo in this thought-provoking drama, about the interracial implications of Hitler's rise to power and the pain of coming to terms with the past. But it's the behind-the-camera credits that make this co-production so fascinating. Jerry Schatzberg directs steadily from a Harold Pinter script, while the stylish sets were created by the veteran Alexandre Trauner, who had designed some of the most famous French films during his 60-year career. DP

Jason Robards *Henry Strauss* • Christien Anholt *Hans Strauss* • Samuel West *Konradin Von Lohenburg* • Françoise Fabian *Countess Grafin Von Lohenburg* • Maureen Kerwin *Lisa, Henry's daughter* ■ *Dir* Jerry Schatzberg • *Scr* Harold Pinter, from a novel by Fred Uhlman

The Reunion ★★★ 15

Drama   2013 · Swe · Colour · 90min

This Swedish docudrama is a strange but beguiling beast. In the first half of the film, writer/director/leading lady Anna Odell dramatises what might have happened had she attended her school's 20-year class reunion, and the home truths she might have told about her schooldays. Then, in a twist that puts a completely different perspective on things, she tracks down the school bullies, shows them the dramatised reunion, and gives them the right of reply. The movie will undoubtedly resonate with anyone for whom schooldays weren't the happiest days of their lives. DA Swedish +subtitles. Swearing. *DVD* *Blu-ray*

Anna Odell • Anders Berg *Anders* • Robert Fransson *Robban* • Sandra Andreis *Louise* ■ *Dir/Scr* Anna Odell

Reunion at Fairborough ★★★

Romantic drama   1985 · US · Colour · 110min

Over a quarter of a century after they made *Heaven Knows, Mr Allison*, Robert Mitchum and Deborah Kerr teamed up for the fourth time in this burnished tale of reunions and revelations. Originally made for American television but also given a cinema release, Herbert Wise's verbose melodrama centres on ex-GI Mitchum's return to the village

where he'd been based during the war to discover that he not only fathered Kerr's child, but is also now a grandfather. Tony Imi's photography romanticises the rural locations, but the key is the rapport of the leads. DP

Robert Mitchum *Carl Hostrup* • Deborah Kerr *Sally Wells* • Red Buttons *Jiggs Quealy* • Judi Trott *Sheila* • Barry Morse *Dr "Ski" Barsky* • Shane Rimmer *Joe Szyluk* ■ *Dir* Herbert Wise • *Scr* Albert Ruben

Reunion in France ★★★★ U

Second World War romantic drama
1942 · US · BW · 99min

Joan Crawford stars as a vain, thoughtless, wealthy French woman, interested only in her lover Philip Dorn and her wardrobe, who undergoes a transformation after the Nazi occupation of France. Believing that wealthy industrialist Dorn is a high-level collaborator, she develops a new awareness and a sense of patriotism, which is further fuelled by her accidental involvement with American airman John Wayne who is fleeing the Gestapo. Directed with a European sensibility and a hard edge by Jules Dassin, this underrated war drama is – despite some mawkish moments, mainly involving Wayne, and the odd lapse into melodrama – interesting, taut and compelling. RK

Joan Crawford *Michele de la Becque* • John Wayne *Pat Talbot* • Philip Dorn *Robert Cortot* • Reginald Owen *Schultz/Pinkum* • Albert Basserman *Gen Hugo Schroeder* • John Carradine *Ulrich Windler* • Ava Gardner *Marie, salesgirl* ■ *Dir* Jules Dassin • *Scr* Jan Lustig, Marvin Borowsky, Marc Connelly, Charles Hoffman, from a story by Ladislaus Bus-Fekete

Reunion in Vienna ★★

Romantic comedy   1933 · US · BW · 97min

Former lovers Diana Wynyard and John Barrymore meet after ten years, at a monarchists' party in Vienna. Wynard is now married to a famous psychoanalyst (Frank Morgan), while Barrymore, the dethroned Hapsburg archduke, is now a taxi driver. He is determined to rekindle the flame: she is equally determined to resist. This is a largely tedious conversation piece, with Barrymore charmless and hammy for two-thirds of the action. Wynyard, however, is wonderful, as are the sets and clothes. RK

John Barrymore *Rudolf* • Diana Wynyard *Elena* • Frank Morgan *Anton* • Henry Travers *Father Krug* • May Robson *Frau Lucher* • Eduardo Ciannelli *Poffy* • Una Merkel *Isle* ■ *Dir* Sidney Franklin • *Scr* Ernest Vajda, Claudine Westt, from the play by Robert E Sherwood

Reuniting the Rubins ★★ PG

Comedy drama   2010 · UK · Colour · 98min

First-time director Yoav Factor strives for a rollicking Jewish comedy here, but merely produces a mediocre sitcom with too many preachy subplots. He is well served, however, by Timothy Spall as the retired lawyer who postpones a cruise to reunite his bickering children for ailing grandma Honor Blackman. Everyone eventually comes together, although not before such issues as globalisation, human rights and family ties are given an airing. Yet, for all its sentimentality, this is at least amiably amusing. DP

Timothy Spall *Lenny Rubins* • Rhona Mitra *Andie Rubins* • James Callis *Danny Rubins* • Honor Blackman *Gran Rubins* • Blake Harrison *Nick* • Hugh O'Conor *Yona Rubins* ■ *Dir/Scr* Yoav Factor

Revanche ★★★★ 15

Crime thriller   2008 · Austria · Colour · 116min

Director Götz Spielmann's riveting Oscar-nominated study of desire, isolation, guilt and redemption bears the influence of both Robert Bresson and Michael Haneke. The simmering, Oscar-nominated blend of film noir-style thriller and morality play sees Hannes Thanheiser as an ageing man whose blissful existence in a small Austrian town is shattered by the arrival of his grandson (Johannes Krisch), who is there to rob the town's bank. DP German, Russian

+subtitles. Violence, swearing, sex scenes. *DVD*

Johannes Krisch *Alex* • Ursula Strauss *Susanne* • Andreas Lust *Robert* • Irina Potapenko *Tamara* • Hannes Thanheiser *Old man* • Hanno Pöschl *Konecy* ■ *Dir/Scr* Götz Spielmann

Reveille with Beverly ★★★ U

Musical   1943 · US · BW · 77min

One of many B-movies churned out by super-hoofer Ann Miller during her career with Columbia, this light-hearted musical was based on the life and career of a real-life female disc jockey. Miller is fabulous, bringing her customary warm-heartedness and tap-dancing skills to this insubstantial film. Watch for Frank Sinatra, Duke Ellington and Count Basie, and the Mills Brothers, too. A collector's item. TS

Ann Miller *Beverly Ross* • William Wright *Barry Lang* • Dick Purcell *Andy Adams* • Franklin Pangborn *Vernon Lewis* • Tim Ryan *Mr Kennedy* • Larry Parks *Eddie Ross* • Adele Mara *Evelyn Ross* • Frank Sinatra ■ *Dir* Charles Barton • *Scr* Howard J Green, Jack Henley, Albert Duffy

Revelation ★★ 15

Supernatural horror thriller
2001 · UK · Colour · 106min

No one could accuse writer/director Stuart Urban's complex quest movie of not having ideas or ambition but, unfortunately, this saunter across Europe in search of a valuable relic is too ponderous and repetitious to appeal. Bland James D'Arcy and Natasha Wightman follow the trail of the "Loculus", an ancient box also sought by demonic immortal Udo Kier. There are moments of visual panache, but this is dull. JC *DVD*

James D'Arcy *Jake Martel* • Natasha Wightman *Mira* • Terence Stamp *Magnus Martel* • Udo Kier *The Grand Master* • Derek Jacobi *The Librarian* • Liam Cunningham *Father Ray Connolly* • Celia Imrie *Harriet Martel* • Ron Moody *Sir Isaac Newton* ■ *Dir* Stuart Urban • *Scr* Stuart Urban, from an idea by Frank Falco

The Revenant ★★★★★ 15

Historical adventure 2015 · US · Colour · 149min

Director Alejandro González Iñárritu's follow-up to his Oscar winner *Birdman* is another astonishing piece of film-making. An epic true story of revenge and redemption, it stars a shaggy Leonardo DiCaprio as a frontiersman who's mauled by a grizzly – a scene breathtaking in its savagery – and then left for dead by Tom Hardy's fur trapper. Here's a movie where the elements ooze from every shot, and DiCaprio matches it by baring his wounds and his soul in an Oscar-winning performance of agonising honesty and intense emotion. JA Violence *Blu-ray*

Leonardo DiCaprio *Hugh Glass* • Tom Hardy *John Fitzgerald* • Domhnall Gleeson *Captain Henry* • Will Poulter *Jim Bridger* • Forrest Goodluck *Hawk* • Lukas Haas *Jones* • Brendan Fletcher *Fryman* ■ *Dir* Alejandro G Iñárritu [Alejandro González Iñárritu] • *Scr* Alejandro G Iñárritu, Mark L Smith, from Michael Punke's novel • *Cinematographer* Emmanuel Lubezki • *Music* Ryuichi Sakamoto • *Production Designer* Jack Fisk • *Editor* Stephen Mirrione • *Music* Alva Noto

Revenge ★★ 18

Thriller   1990 · US · Colour · 118min

This daft drama has retired navy pilot Kevin Costner going down to Mexico to visit old friend Anthony Quinn, only to incur the latter's wrath when he goes off with his wife, Madeleine Stowe. It all gets exceedingly silly, and overacting abounds as Costner and Stowe flee the understandably irate Quinn. Laboriously directed by the normally fluent action aficionado Tony Scott. JB Swearing, violence, sex scenes.

Kevin Costner *Cochran* • Anthony Quinn *Tiburon Mendez* • Madeleine Stowe *Miryea* • Tomas Milian *Cesar* • Joaquin Martinez *Mauro* • James Gammon *Texan* • Jesse Corti *Medero* • Sally Kirkland *Rock star* ■ *Dir* Tony Scott • *Scr* Jim Harrison, Jeffrey Fiskin, from the novella by Jim Harrison

Revenge: a Love Story ★★★ 18

Crime thriller   2010 · HK · Colour · 90min

Hong Kong director Wong Ching-Po's twisted, though surprisingly moving, tale of love and lost innocence opens with the gruesome slaying of two pregnant women and their partners, followed by the swift capture of the culprit, Chan Kit (Juno Mak). Viewer sympathies are then uncomfortably turned on their head, as flashbacks reveal the terrible events that transformed a tender, rural boy into a killer. Mak is impressively convincing in his emotional pain, but it's Kit's one-dimensional schoolgirl sweetheart Cheung Wing (Sola Aoi) who suffers most, enduring a horrific gang rape that's pivotal yet exploitative. When the tragedy inevitably escalates, you may find yourself rooting for Kit's mission, which makes the moralistic double ending particularly powerful. SF Cantonese +subtitles. Violence. *DVD*

Juno Mak *Chan Kit* • Sola Aoi *Cheung Wing* • Chin Siu-hou *Jeff* • Tony Ho Wah Chiu [Tony Ho] *Kwok Wah* ■ *Dir* Wong Ching-Po • *Scr* Wong Ching-Po, Leung Lai-Yin, from a story by Juno Mak

The Revenge of Frankenstein ★★★ 15

Horror   1958 · UK · Colour · 86min

Hammer's first sequel to *The Curse of Frankenstein*, has the baron rescued from execution, changing his name to Dr Stein and continuing his body-part experiments in a charity hospital. The usual first-rate performances, excellent production values and gothic atmosphere are permeated by a macabre sense of humour in this superior spine-chiller, crisply directed by Terence Fisher. The second sequel was the slightly disappointing *Evil of Frankenstein*. AJ *DVD*

Peter Cushing *Dr Victor Stein* • Francis Matthews *Dr Hans Kleve* • Eunice Gayson *Margaret* • Michael Gwynn *Karl* • John Welsh *Bergman* • Lionel Jeffries *Fritz* • Oscar Quitak *Karl* • Richard Wordsworth *Patient* • Charles Lloyd Pack *President* ■ *Dir* Terence Fisher • *Scr* Jimmy Sangster, H Hurford Janes, from characters by Mary Shelley

The Revenge of Pumpkinhead – Blood Wings ★★★ 18

Horror   1994 · US · Colour · 83min

The engaging return of the monster from *Pumpkinhead* dispenses with the previous story elements to create a mystery. This time, small-town sheriff Andrew Robinson must deduce the monster's reasons for picking particular victims. Pumpkinhead is used to good effect, although no explanation is given as to why a thunderstorm follows the monster wherever he goes. Look out for amusing bit-part turns by American presidential sibling Roger Clinton and Soleil Moon Frye. ST

Andrew Robinson *Sean Braddock* • Ami Dolenz *Jenny Braddock* • J Trevor Edmond *Danny Dixon* • Mark McCracken *Creature* • Gloria Hendry *Delilah Pettibone* • Alexander Polinsky *Paul* • Soleil Moon Frye *Marcie* • Roger Clinton *Mister Bubba* ■ *Dir* Jeff Burr • *Scr* Steve Mitchell, Craig W Van Sickle

Revenge of the Bridesmaids ★★

Comedy   2010 · US · Colour · 95min

Revenge comes watered down but watchable in this undemanding comedy that sees two 20-somethings try to sabotage their ex-friend's wedding for betraying a mutual pal. A feisty Raven-Symoné and Joanna Garcia have a natural chemistry as the loyal mates whose increasingly far-fetched attempts at payback cause headaches for the southern belle bride and her stereotypically controlling mother. Some amusing dialogue and a big dollop of romance keep the tone light and frothy. SF

R

Raven-Symoné *Abigail Scanlon* • Joanna Garcia *Parker Wald* • Beth Broderick *Olivia McNabb* • David Clayton Rogers *Lt Henry Kent* ■ *Dir* James Hayman • *Scr* David Kendall, Bob Young, Stephanie Phillips, Mark Amato

Revenge of the Creature

★★★ PG

Horror 1955 · US · BW · 78min

Almost as enjoyable as the original, director Jack Arnold's follow-up to *Creature from the Black Lagoon* has the "Gill-Man" (Ricou Browning) recaptured and taken to a sea-world park in Florida. There, ichthyologists John Agar and Lori Nelson try to teach him to speak, before the primeval monster goes on the rampage and drags Nelson back to his Everglades hideaway. Look out for Clint Eastwood, in his first screen role, playing a laboratory technician. Though this was made in 3D like the original, very few saw it projected that way after its initial release. A disappointing second sequel, *The Creature Walks among Us*, followed in 1956. **AJ** *DVD*

John Agar *Clete Ferguson* • Lori Nelson *Helen Dobson* • John Bromfield *Joe Hayes* • Robert B Williams *George Johnson* • Nestor Paiva *Lucas* • Grandon Rhodes *Foster* • Dave Willock *Gibson* • Charles Cane *Captain of Police* • Clint Eastwood *Lab technician* • Ricou Browning *Gill-Man* ■ *Dir* Jack Arnold • *Scr* Martin Berkeley, from a story by William Alland

Revenge of the Electric Car

★★

Documentary 2011 · US · Colour · 90min

Revisiting themes explored in his 2006 film *Who Killed the Electric Car?*, Chris Paine seems to have lost the animus that drove his diatribe against the American automotive industry. Largely ignoring industrial intrigue and public indifference, he concentrates on four key players in the race to produce a viable electric vehicle. But appearances by Arnold Schwarzenegger and Danny DeVito make this Tim Robbins-narrated study feel more like a celebrity reality show than a hard-hitting documentary. **DP** *DVD*

Tim Robbins *Narrator* ■ *Dir* Chris Paine • *Scr* Chris Paine, PG Morgan

Revenge of the Green Dragons

★★ 15

Crime drama based on a true story
2013 · HK/US · Colour · 94min

Martin Scorsese's *Gangs of New York* is updated to the 1980s and given an Asian spin in this often brutal drama from Hong Kong. Scorsese takes an executive producer credit (payback, perhaps, for him reworking Lau's *Infernal Affairs* as *The Departed*), but the film exhibits none of the master's skill as it charts how two Chinese kids are recruited into a gang after arriving in the US. Ray Liotta is also criminally underused as the agent trying to smash their operation. **JH** English, Cantonese +subtitles. Violence, swearing, sex scenes, nudity. *DVD*

Justin Chon *Sonny* • Kevin Wu *Steven* • Harry Shum Jr *Paul* • Eugenia Yuan *Snake Head Mama* ■ *Dir* Andrew Lau, Andrew Loo • *Scr* Michael Di Giacomo, Andrew Loo

Revenge of the Middle-Aged Woman

★★★

Drama 2004 · US · Colour · 90min

Female empowerment brings far more effective revenge than knee-jerk vindictiveness in this light-hearted drama. Adapted from Elizabeth Buchan's bestselling novel - only with the action smoothly transposed from London to LA - it centres on a likeable performance from Christine Lahti as the editor whose perfect life abruptly implodes when she loses both her husband and her job to her younger assistant. Though the mood is uneven, the dignity of Lahti's character and the positive messages that she sends out keep the film firmly on track. **SF**

Christine Lahti *Rose* • Brian Kerwin *Nathan Lloyd* • Bryan Brown *Hal Thorne* • Abby Brammell *Mindy* • Caroline Aaron *Madeleine* • Maggie Lawson *Rachel* ■ *Dir* Sheldon Larry • *Scr* Nancy Silvers, from the novel by Elizabeth Buchan

Revenge of the Nerds

★ 15

Comedy 1984 · US · Colour · 86min

In this puerile campus comedy, Anthony Edwards is one of the nerds of the title who decide to fight back against the bullying jocks at school. Amazingly, this dire mix of lavatorial humour and tasteless slapstick spawned three sequels. **JF** Swearing, nudity. *DVD*

Robert Carradine *Lewis* • Anthony Edwards *Gilbert* • Timothy Busfield *Poindexter* • Andrew Cassese *Wormser* • Curtis Armstrong *"Booger"* • Larry B Scott *Lamar* • Brian Tochi *Takashi* • Julie Montgomery *Betty Childs* • Michelle Meyrink *Judy* • Ted McGinley *Stan Gable* ■ *Dir* Jeff Kanew • *Scr* Steve Zacharias, Jeff Buhai, from a story by Tim Metcalfe, Miguel Tejada-Flores, Steve Zacharias, Jeff Buhai

Revenge of the Pink Panther

★★★ PG

Comedy 1978 · US · Colour · 94min

There are so many comedy turns hanging from a slender plotline in this immoderate helping of Inspector Clouseau that it tends to sag in places. But there are still plenty of laughs to be had as Clouseau goes on the trail of drug smugglers. Peter Sellers is well supported by Dyan Cannon, as a drug dealer's girlfriend, and by Burt Kwouk, as the valet. This may lack coherence, but if you accept it as just a vehicle for Sellers's comic genius you won't be disappointed. The depressing *Trail of the Pink Panther* concluded Sellers's Clouseau series. **TH** *DVD*

Peter Sellers *Chief Inspector Clouseau* • Herbert Lom *Chief Inspector Dreyfus* • Dyan Cannon *Simone Legree* • Robert Webber *Philippe Douvier* • Burt Kwouk *Cato* • Paul Stewart *Scallini* • Robert Loggia *Marchione* • Graham Stark *Dr Auguste Balls* • André Maranne *François* • Sue Lloyd *Claude Russo* ■ *Dir* Blake Edwards • *Scr* Frank Waldman, Ron Clark, Blake Edwards, from a story by Blake Edwards

The Revengers' Comedies

★★★

Black comedy 1997 · UK/Fr · Colour · 86min

Alfred Hitchcock's *Strangers on a Train* receives another reworking in this adept amalgamation of two Alan Ayckbourn plays. Meeting on Tower Bridge, Sam Neill and Helena Bonham Carter agree to abandon thoughts of suicide and do away with the other's chief tormentor instead. However, he soon discovers his co-conspirator's true nature after he becomes besotted with his intended victim, Kristin Scott Thomas. The main asset of this unfairly overlooked Britpic is its stellar cast, but Malcolm Mowbray's direction lacks subtlety. **DP** Contain violence, swearing.

Sam Neill *Henry Bell* • Helena Bonham Carter *Karen Knightly* • Kristin Scott Thomas *Imogen Staxton-Billing* • Rupert Graves *Oliver Knightly* • Martin Clunes *Anthony Staxton-Billing* • Steve Coogan *Bruce Tick* • Jim Wood (2) *Colonel Marcus* • Liz Smith *Winnie* ■ *Dir* Malcolm Mowbray • *Scr* Malcolm Mowbray, from two plays by Alan Ayckbourn

Revengers Tragedy

★ 15

Black comedy 2002 · US · Colour · 105min

Director Alex Cox makes a bid to become Britain's answer to Baz Luhrmann with this interpretation of Thomas Middleton's 17th-century play about family, loyalty and vengeance. Christopher Eccleston returns to his home city after a ten-year absence to avenge the murder of his wife, killed on their wedding day by dastardly duke Derek Jacobi. Eccleston displays a wry wit and gleeful dementia, but he is drowned out by a glut of hammy supporting performances. Cox adds to the mess with a profusion of flashy camera techniques and clichéd imagery. **SF** *DVD*

Christopher Eccleston *Vindici* • Eddie Izzard *Lussurioso* • Derek Jacobi *Duke* • Diana Quick *Duchess* • Carla Henry *Castiza* • Andrew Schofield *Carlo* • Anthony Booth *Lord Antonio* •

Margi Clarke *Hannah* • Sophie Dahl *Imogen* ■ *Dir* Alex Cox • *Scr* Frank Cottrell Boyce, from the play by Thomas Middleton

Reverb

★★ 15

Horror 2006 · UK/US · Colour · 88min

In this demon-track chiller, a pop star (Leo Gregory) in need of a hit allows himself to be holed up overnight in a London recording studio with his girlfriend (Eva Birthistle). He soon becomes obsessed with *Blood Sounds*, a 1960s tune that he hears on the radio and downloads to sample. But the rocker behind the song had a sinister history so when a session is planned in a secret studio packed with antiquated recording equipment, horrific consequences ensue. Simon Dennis's photography is fitfully atmospheric and there's some slick stunt editing here, but the cast are unable to inject much interest - let alone scares - into the proceedings. **DP**

Leo Gregory *Alex* • Eva Birthistle *Maddy* • Luke de Woolfson *Dan* • Margo Stilley *Nicky* • Stephen Lord *Wurzel* • Neil Newbon *Mark Griffin* ■ *Dir/Scr* Eitan Arrusi

Reversal of Fortune

★★★★ 15

Biographical drama 1990 · US · Colour · 106min

Jeremy Irons won an Oscar for his portrayal of millionaire Claus von Bulow, who was found guilty of the attempted murder of his wife Sunny (Glenn Close), but acquitted on appeal. Even though there's no surprise about the outcome, this is a thoroughly absorbing and beautifully scripted drama, with events leading to the trial told in flashback and Close's comatose character bringing us up to date by a clever narration. Director Barbet Schroeder shoots with a documentary eye and gives the picture a sense of irony, a quality enhanced by Irons's superb performance as the haughty European aristocrat defended by a Jewish lawyer. **AT** Violence, swearing. *DVD*

Jeremy Irons *Claus von Bulow* • Glenn Close *Martha "Sunny" von Bulow* • Ron Silver *Alan Dershowitz* • Annabella Sciorra *Sarah* • Uta Hagen *Maria* • Fisher Stevens *David Marriott* • Jack Gilpin *Peter Macintosh* • Christine Baranski *Andrea Reynolds* • Stephen Mailer *Elon Dershowitz* • Christine Dunford *Ellen* ■ *Dir* Barbet Schroeder • *Scr* Nicholas Kazan, from the book by Alan Dershowitz

Reverse Angle

★★

Thriller 2008 · Can · Colour · 86min

Poor scripting renders an unrealistic tale of corporate conspiracy and murder both boring and silly, as success-hungry TV journalist Emmanuelle Vaugier finds herself on the run from hitmen after losing her memory in an accident. Unaware of who she is and why she's being pursued, the baffled beauty races to piece together past events via flashbacks that make the cliché-packed film feel badly paced and bitty. **SF**

Emmanuelle Vaugier *Eve Preston* • Anthony Lemke *Harry Griggs* • Al Goulem [Alain Goulem] *Black* • David Patrick Green *Murray* ■ *Dir* Philippe Gagnon • *Scr* Peter Vanderwall

The Revolt of Mamie Stover

★★★

Drama 1956 · US · Colour · 86min

It's a great title for a strictly B-grade melodrama, dressed up with A-movie trappings by 20th Century-Fox, including filming on location in exotic Hawaii. But there's no disguising the fact that this movie really belongs to an earlier decade. Jane Russell is, to be kind, a little past her prime as a dancer in a Honolulu nightclub. Joan Leslie looks slightly weary, and Richard Egan, a leading man once touted as the new Clark Gable proves to be all brawn and little else. **TS**

Jane Russell *Mamie Stover* • Richard Egan *Jim* • Joan Leslie *Annalea* • Agnes Moorehead *Bertha Parchman* • Jorja Curtright *Jackie* • Michael Pate *Harry Adkins* • Richard Coogan *Eldon Sumac* ■ *Dir* Raoul Walsh • *Scr* Sydney Boehm, from the novel by William Bradford Huie

Revolution

★★★ 12

Historical war drama
1985 · UK/Nor · Colour · 121min

Hugh Hudson's look at the American War of Independence was a famous mega-flop, sealing the fate of the already over-extended Goldcrest production house. It is the story of a father and son, and the way history intrudes on their relationship. On the plus side: the battle scenes, brilliantly filmed with a hand-held camera; a remarkable portrayal of a sadistic English officer by a deeply in period Donald Sutherland; and clever art direction which turns King's Lynn into New York. On the debit side is Al Pacino's ludicrous performance and laughable accent. **AT** Some violence, swearing. *DVD* BD

Al Pacino *Tom Dobb* • Nastassja Kinski *Daisy McConnahay* • Donald Sutherland *Sergeant Major Peasy* • Joan Plowright *Mrs McConnahay* • Dave King *Mr McConnahay* • Steven Berkoff *Sergeant Jones* • Annie Lennox *Liberty Woman* • Dexter Fletcher *Ned Dobb* • Sid Owen *Young Ned* • John Wells *Corty* • Richard O'Brien *Lord Hampton* ■ *Dir* Hugh Hudson • *Scr* Robert Dillon

The Revolutionary

★★★

Political drama 1970 · UK/US · Colour · 101min

A compelling portrayal by Jon Voight of a political subversive makes this worth the effort of watching. He moves from handing out revolutionary leaflets at college to an attempted assassination, in a moral tale that's too one-track for its own good, but which poses hard questions for would-be revolutionaries who might become terrorists. Writer Hans Koningsberger and director Paul Williams highlight the way that anything can be excused by strongly held belief. **TH**

Jon Voight *A* • Jennifer Salt *Helen Peret* • Seymour Cassel *Leonard* • Robert Duvall *Despard* • Collin Wilcox-Horne *Anne* • Lionel Murton *Professor* ■ *Dir* Paul Williams • *Scr* Hans Koningsberger, from the novel by Hans Koningsberger

Revolutionary Road

★★★ 15

Period drama 2008 · US/UK · Colour · 114min

Leonardo DiCaprio and Kate Winslet captured all the idealism of first love in *Titanic*, but this adaptation of Richard Yates's acclaimed novel finds them playing characters a little older and a lot more jaded. Frank and April Wheeler are a married couple struggling to reconcile their youthful dreams of "what could have been" with the humdrum reality of life in 1950s suburbia. Director Sam Mendes (Winslet's real-life husband), exposed the rot behind those white picket fences in the Oscar-winning *American Beauty*, but here there is much less humour, with extramarital affairs and an unwanted pregnancy compounding the Wheelers' misery. The dialogue often feels a bit stagey, but Winslet and DiCaprio manage to get beyond the bluster and the self-indulgence of their roles to prove that, however special we think we are, we all share the same heartaches. **SP** Swearing, sex scenes, nudity. *DVD* BD

Leonardo DiCaprio *Frank Wheeler* • Kate Winslet *April Wheeler* • Kathy Bates *Mrs Helen Givings* • Kathryn Hahn *Milly Campbell* • Michael Shannon *John Givings* • Zoe Kazan *Maureen Grube* • Dylan Clark Marshall *Campbell son* ■ *Dir* Sam Mendes • *Scr* Justin Haythe, from the novel by Richard Yates • *Cinematographer* Roger Deakins

Revolver

★★ 15

Crime drama 2005 · Fr/UK · Colour · 110min

Guy Ritchie (with a little help from Luc Besson) concocts an eye-catching if intellectually overblown game of criminal cat-and-mouse. Jason Statham stars as a gangster who vows vengeance after a prison stint covering for his weirdly monikered boss (enthusiastically overplayed by Ray Liotta). What unfolds here is a pretentious and repetitive substitute for a coherent plot. **KK** Violence, swearing, drug abuse, nudity. *DVD* BD

Jason Statham *Jake Green* • Ray Liotta *Dorothy Macha* • Vincent Pastore *Zack* • André Benjamin *Avi* • Mark Strong *Sorter* • Terence Maynard *French Paul* • Francesca Annis *Lily Walker* •

Andrew Howard *Billy* • Anjela Lauren Smith *Doreen* ■ *Dir* Guy Ritchie • *Scr* Guy Ritchie, adapted by Luc Besson

The Revolving Doors
★★★ **U**

Drama   1988 · Can/Fr · Colour · 101min

This absorbing drama shows that the coming of sound to cinema meant the end of a unique form of entertainment, the silent movie, complete with its atmospheric piano accompaniment. As the pianist who leaves the dream palaces to find fame in the jazz joints of New York, Monique Spaziani gives an engaging performance. Francis Mankiewicz directs neatly and there's a solid performance from French actress Miou-Miou. DP French +subtitles.

Monique Spaziani *Céleste Beaumont* • Gabriel Arcand *Blaudelle* • Miou-Miou *Lauda* • Jacques Penot *Pierre Blaudelle* • François Méthé *Antoine* • Françoise Faucher *Simone Blaudelle* ■ *Dir* Francis Mankiewicz • *Scr* Jacques Savoie

The Reward
★★★

Western   1965 · US · Colour · 90min

This slow, elegiac contemporary western is one of the most interesting failures. A motley cast, headed by glum import Max von Sydow, spends a lot of time sitting around in the desert, very slowly motivated by greed to seek a bigger share of the title pay-out. It's not uninteresting, and is intelligently cast, but French director Serge Bourguignon is well out of his *métier*, and the result, though fascinating, is not enjoyable. TS

Max von Sydow *Scott Swanson* • Yvette Mimieux *Sylvia* • Efrem Zimbalist Jr *Frank Bryant* • Gilbert Roland *Captain Carbajal* • Emilio Fernandez *Sargento Lopez* • Henry Silva *Joaquin* • Rafael Lopez *Indian Boy* ■ *Dir* Serge Bourguignon • *Scr* Serge Bourguignon, Oscar Millard, from the novel by Michael Barrett

The Rewrite
★★★ **12**

Romantic comedy   2014 · US · Colour · 102min

Hugh Grant reteams with *Music and Lyrics* writer/director Marc Lawrence for a story about a washed-up Hollywood screenwriter forced to take a teaching post at a provincial university. Grant intends to coast his way through, but single-mum student Marisa Tomei may be about to change his perspective. No-one does likeably shambolic cynicism quite so well as Grant, and Tomei proves an adorably spiky foil in this easy-going charmer in which deftly tailored banter and evident chemistry prevail over predictable plotting. TJ **DVD** **SD**

Hugh Grant *Keith Michaels* • Marisa Tomei *Holly Carpenter* • Allison Janney *Mary Weldon* • JK Simmons *Dr Harold Lerner* • Chris Elliott *Jim* • Bella Heathcote *Karen* ■ *Dir/Scr* Marc Lawrence (2)

Rhapsody
★★★ **U**

Romantic drama   1954 · US · Colour · 115min

Beautiful heiress Elizabeth Taylor is in love with classical violinist Vittorio Gassman, but leaves him - via a broken-hearted suicide attempt when he puts ambition first - for concert pianist John Ericson, who makes her his priority. There's much flitting back and forth between the two men and across Europe, before the final fade. An essentially hollow and old-fashioned romantic soap opera, this is given a cultural gloss by the outpouring of music. Taylor is good and at her loveliest, and the location photography in Technicolor and CinemaScope is eye-catching. RK

Elizabeth Taylor *Louise Durant* • Vittorio Gassman *Paul Bronte* • John Ericson *James Guest* • Louis Calhern *Nicholas Durant* • Michael Chekhov *Professor Schuman* • Barbara Bates *Effie Cahill* • Richard Hageman *Bruno Furst* • Richard Lupino *Otto Krafft* • Stuart Whitman *Dove* ■ *Dir* Charles Vidor • *Scr* Fay Kanin, Michael Kanin, Ruth Goetz, Augustus Goetz, from the novel *Maurice Guest* by Henry Handel Richardson • *Cinematographer* Robert Planck

Rhapsody in August
★★ **U**

Drama   1990 · Jpn · Colour · 93min

This is comfortably the worst film made by the late Akira Kurosawa during his 50-year

career. There is a certain charm in the interaction between Sachiko Murase and the four grandchildren who spend the summer with her, but the storyline is weak and Richard Gere looks distinctly out of place. DP Japanese +subtitles. **DVD**

Sachiko Murase *Kane* • Hisashi Igawa *Tadao* • Narumi Kayashima *Machiko* • Tomoko Ohtakara *Tami* • Mitsunori Isaki *Shinjiro* • Toshie Negishi *Yoshie* • Richard Gere *Clark* ■ *Dir* Akira Kurosawa • *Scr* Akira Kurosawa, from the novel *Nabe-no-Naka* by Kiyoko Murata

Rhapsody in Blue
★★★ **U**

Biographical drama   1945 · US · BW · 139min

This splendid tosh, purporting to be the life story of composer George Gershwin, is actually an enjoyable epic that embraces every single cliché of the Lower East Side, Jewish-kid-makes-good, rags-to-riches saga, and almost brings it off. Robert Alda lacks star power as Gershwin, and Herbert Rudley is undercast as his brother Ira, but there's a wealth of fabulous support, including Al Jolson as himself and the great Oscar Levant, who performs both *Concerto in F* and *Rhapsody in Blue*. TS

Robert Alda *George Gershwin* • Joan Leslie *Julie Adams* • Alexis Smith *Christine Gilbert* • Charles Coburn *Max Dreyfus* • Julie Bishop *Lee Gershwin* • Albert Basserman *Professor Frank* • Morris Carnovsky *Poppa Gershwin* • Rosemary DeCamp *Momma Gershwin* • Anne Brown *Bess* • Herbert Rudley *Ira Gershwin* ■ *Dir* Irving Rapper • *Scr* Howard Koch, Elliott Paul, from a story by Sonya Levien

Rhinestone
★★ **PG**

Comedy   1984 · US · Colour · 106min

Sylvester Stallone does have the knack for comedy, albeit in a light form. However, he frequently lacks the ability to judge if a script is good, especially if he's involved in its writing. Country star Dolly Parton takes a bet on whether she can turn cab driver Stallone into a country singer and the results, as far as both the wager and their interest in each other are concerned, are as expected, but not funny. KB

Sylvester Stallone *Nick* • Dolly Parton *Jake* • Richard Farnsworth *Noah* • Ron Leibman *Freddie* • Tim Thomerson *Barnett* • Steven Apostlee Peck *Father* ■ *Dir* Bob Clark • *Scr* Phil Alden Robinson, Sylvester Stallone, from the story by Phil Alden Robinson, from the song *Rhinestone Cowboy* by Larry Weiss

Rhino!
★★

Adventure   1964 · US · Colour · 91min

Unlike other big game adventures, this one at least has the benefit of a conservationist message, as Hunter Harry Guardino and scientist Robert Culp go in search of a pair of white rhino that are threatened with extinction. Director Ivan Tors makes the most of his South African locations and the majestic wildlife, but his handling of the dramatic sequences is often uncertain. DP

Harry Guardino *Alec Burnett* • Shirley Eaton *Edith Arleigh* • Robert Culp *Dr Jim Hanlon* • Harry Mekela *Jopo* • George Lane Haragay ■ *Dir* Ivan Tors • *Scr* Art Arthur, Arthur Weiss, from a story by Art Arthur

Rhinoceros
★★★ **PG**

Surreal comedy   1974 · US · Colour · 99min

The allegorical material of Eugène Ionesco's absurdist play *Rhinoceros* has always been seen as self-defeating, and actors as distinguished as Laurence Olivier and Orson Welles, among others, have fallen foul of it. Here, the leads from *The Producers*, Zero Mostel and Gene Wilder, are reunited under the iconoclastic direction of Tom O'Horgan, and the result, though fascinating, is very much an acquired taste. TS **DVD**

Zero Mostel *John* • Gene Wilder *Stanley* • Karen Black *Daisy* • Robert Weil *Carl* • Joe Silver *Norman* • Marilyn Chris *Mrs Bingham* ■ *Dir* Tom O'Horgan • *Scr* Julian Barry, from the play by Eugène Ionesco

Rhodes of Africa
★★★

Biographical adventure   1936 · UK · BW · 89min

Walter Huston stars as Cecil John Rhodes in a superior, literate and informative biopic, much of it shot on location. While the film

waters down Rhodes's ruthless streak and is a little stolid and worthy in tone, it does do justice to the story of the diamond magnate, visionary, empire-builder and politician, who endowed the famed Rhodes scholarship scheme and died at the age of 49. Huston is excellent playing one of the most significant figures in an eventful era of Southern African history, and there's a good supporting cast. RK

Walter Huston *Cecil Rhodes* • Oscar Homolka *Kruger* • Basil Sydney *Jameson* • Frank Cellier *Barney Barnato* • Peggy Ashcroft *Anna Carpenter* • Renee De Vaux *Mrs Kruger* • Bernard Lee *Cartwright* ■ *Dir* Berthold Viertel • *Scr* Leslie Arliss, Michael Barringer, Miles Malleson, from the book *Rhodes* by Sarah Gertrude Millin

Rhubarb
★★★ **PG**

Comedy   1951 · US · BW · 94min

Rhubarb is a fiery alley cat who inherits a baseball team. Although he brings the team luck, he poses a triple headache for Ray Milland, the marketing man charged with caring for the new manager/mascot, for not only does Rhubarb insist on living on his own terms, but Milland's girlfriend Jan Sterling is allergic to him and a jilted benefactor is out to prove in the courts that he is an impostor. It's slight and silly, but there are plenty of laughs. DP

Ray Milland *Eric Yeager* • Jan Sterling *Polly Sickles* • Gene Lockhart *Thaddeus J Banner* • William Frawley *Len Sickles* • Elsie Holmes *Myra Banner* • Taylor Holmes *P Duncan Munk* ■ *Dir* Arthur Lubin • *Scr* Dorothy Reid, Francis Cockrell, David Stern, from the novel by H Allen Smith

Rhythm on the Range
★★ **U**

Western musical comedy
1936 · US · BW · 84min

Bing Crosby is the star of this musical western romance in which he sings a song to a mightily large Hereford bull, as well as winning the hand of a rebellious heiress Frances Farmer. The movie's main interest now, and extraordinary box-office success then, is down to motor-mouthed comedian and songstress Martha Raye, who makes her screen debut and delivers an all-stops-out rendition of *Mr Paganini*. RK **DVD**

Bing Crosby *Jeff Larrabee* • Frances Farmer *Doris Halloway* • Bob Burns (2) *Buck* • Martha Raye *Emma Mazda* • Samuel S Hinds *Robert Halloway* • Lucille Webster Gleason *Penelope "Penny" Ryland* • Warren Hymer *Big Brain* ■ *Dir* Norman Taurog • *Scr* John C Moffitt, Sidney Salkow, Walter DeLeon, Francis Martin, from a story by Mervin J Houser

Rhythm on the River
★★★ **U**

Musical drama   1940 · US · BW · 90min

With Bing Crosby and Mary Martin as the leads and a screenplay co-written by Billy Wilder, it's no surprise that this amiable musical was a great hit on release. The third star is Basil Rathbone, taking time off from being Sherlock Holmes to play a composer who finds inspiration lacking and employs Bing and Mary to ghost write his work. They realise that they would be better off writing for themselves, only to discover that without the composer's name their talent is unacknowledged. BB **DVD**

Bing Crosby *Bob Summers* • Mary Martin *Cherry Lane* • Basil Rathbone *Oliver Courtney* • Oscar Levant *Charlie Starbuck* • Oscar Shaw *Charlie Goodrich* • Charley Grapewin *Uncle Caleb* • Lillian Cornell *Millie Starling* • William Frawley *Westlake* ■ *Dir* Victor Schertzinger • *Scr* Dwight Taylor, from a story by Billy Wilder, Jacques Thery • *Music Director* Victor Young

Rhythm Serenade
★★ **U**

Romantic musical   1943 · UK · BW · 83min

During the Second World War, a schoolteacher does her bit for the war effort by opening a nursery school next door to a munitions factory so that the children's mothers can work. Directed by Gordon Wellesley for the British arm of Columbia, this sentimental and unremarkable film combines patriotic flag-waving with romance, some humour and a

few songs, as a vehicle for "Forces' Sweetheart" Vera Lynn. RK **DVD**

Vera Lynn *Ann Martin* • Peter Murray Hill *John Drover* • Julien Mitchell *Mr Jimson* • Charles Victor *Mr Martin* • Jimmy Jewel *Jimmy Martin* • Ben Warriss *Ben Martin* • Irene Handl *Mrs Crumbling* • Jimmy Clitheroe *Joey* ■ *Dir* Gordon Wellesley • *Scr* Marjorie Deans, Basil Woon, Margaret Kennedy, Edward Dryhurst, from a story by Marjorie Deans

Rice People
★★★ **PG**

Drama   1994 · Camb/Fr/Swi/Ger · Colour · 129min

Cambodian director Rithy Panh - an exile in France since the genocidal regime of Pol Pot came to power in 1975 - returns to his roots and builds an entire film around a rice harvest. It's a harvest beset by nature's adversity and human nightmare - the father has visions of the Khmer Rouge and then a thorn infects his foot while the mother is menaced by a cobra. It's a bit of a slog at two hours, but connoisseurs of movies from the developing world should still find plenty to admire here. AT Khmer +subtitles.

Peng Phan *Yim Om, mother* • Mom Soth *Vong Poeuv, father* • Chhim Naline *Sakha, eldest daughter* ■ *Dir* Rithy Panh • *Scr* Rithy Panh, Eve Deboise, from a novel by Shahnon Ahmad

Rich and Famous
★★ **18**

Comedy drama   1981 · US · Colour · 111min

The last film from director George Cukor is a disappointingly ho-hum remake of 1943's *Old Acquaintance*. Jacqueline Bisset and Candice Bergen step into roles Bette Davis and Miriam Hopkins made their own, as childhood friends who become rivals in their writing careers and love. Playing spot the celeb is more entertaining than their tiresome jealous, bitchy confrontations or Bisset's crisis with a younger lover. Teenaged Meg Ryan, cute as a button, makes her film debut as Bergen's daughter. AME

Jacqueline Bisset *Liz Hamilton* • Candice Bergen *Merry Noel Blake* • David Selby *Doug Blake* • Hart Bochner *Chris Adams* • Steven Hill *Jules Levi* • Meg Ryan *Debby, aged 18* • Matt Lattanzi *Jim* ■ *Dir* George Cukor • *Scr* Gerald Ayres, from the play *Old Acquaintance* by John Van Druten

Rich and Strange
★★ **U**

Comedy drama   1932 · UK · BW · 79min

Alfred Hitchcock made this curious, often rather cruel and tiresome comedy when his career was in the doldrums. Henry Kendall and Joan Barry (too sophisticated for their roles) star as the young married couple who spend an inheritance on a world cruise during which their relationship comes under strain, particularly when they become shipwrecked in the Far East. Hitchcock's stylistic touches provide the main interest of the film today but even they are rather exaggerated for such slight subject matter. AE **DVD**

Henry Kendall *Fred Hill* • Joan Barry *Emily Hill* • Percy Marmont *Commander Gordon* • Betty Amann *Princess* ■ *Dir* Alfred Hitchcock • *Scr* Val Valentine, Alma Reville, Alfred Hitchcock, from a novel by Dale Collins

The Rich Are Always with Us
★★★★

Romance   1932 · US · BW · 71min

The brilliant Broadway actress Ruth Chatterton is at the centre of this tale about an unusual and inordinately wealthy society hostess who resists the overtures of handsome young novelist George Brent - until she discovers her husband's infidelity. Meanwhile, a very young Bette Davis sets her sights on Brent; the actor would later become her future and frequent co-star. Polished acting, surprise twists and a dialogue studded with archly witty gems make this period piece entertaining from start to finish - a sophisticated reflection of a bygone world, with a satirical thrust and a bittersweet edge. RK

Ruth Chatterton *Caroline Grannard* • George Brent *Julian Tierney* • Adrienne Dore *Allison Adair* • Bette Davis *Malbro* • John Miljan *Greg*

R

Grannard ■ *Dir* Alfred E Green • *Scr* Austin Parker, from the novel by Mrs Arthur Somers Roche [E Petit]

Rich Kids ★★★
Comedy drama   1979 · US · Colour · 96min

At the centre of the picture is 12-year-old Trini Alvarado, who gradually comes to realise that her parents are about to get divorced; her friend Jeremy Levy, who has already gone through the process, has an endless stream of advice for her on how to deal with the impending split. A rather heavy-handed message movie, this features good performances all round but it's never quite the film it could have been. DF

Trini Alvarado *Franny Philips* • Jeremy Levy *Jamie Harris* • Kathryn Walker *Madeline Philips* • John Lithgow *Paul Philips* • Terry Kiser *Ralph Harris* • David Selby *Steve Sloan* • Roberta Maxwell *Barbara Peterfreund* • Paul Dooley *Simon Peterfreund* ■ *Dir* Robert M Young • *Scr* Judith Ross

The Rich Man's Wife ★★🔞
Mystery thriller   1996 · US · Colour · 90min

Halle Berry is convincing as an unhappily married woman, whose flippant asides to a man she meets in a bar (Peter Greene) result in said man murdering her husband. Berry becomes a key suspect – she is after all, the black widow of a white man. But, all is not as it seems and, despite strong acting and a tight script, the balloon bursts all over the place at the end. DP Swearing, sexual references, violence. DVD

Halle Berry *Jane Potenza* • Christopher McDonald *Tony Potenza* • Clive Owen *Jake Golden* • Peter Greene *Cole Wilson* • Charles Hallahan *Dan Fredricks* • Frankie Faison *Ron Lewis* • *Dir/Scr* Amy Holden Jones

Rich, Young and Pretty ★★★U
Musical   1951 · US · Colour · 94min

This sweet soufflé of an MGM musical was produced by musical supremo Joe Pasternak. It stars Jane Powell as a Texan girl whose sophisticated mother (Danielle Darrieux) fled the ranch for the delights of Europe many years earlier. Powell's father (Wendell Corey) takes her on a trip to Paris where she sees the sights, parties, falls in love with Mr Right (crooner Vic Damone, in his film debut) and meets up with her mother. It's full of fun, romantic innocence and vintage songs. RK

Jane Powell *Elizabeth Rogers* • Danielle Darrieux *Marie Devarone* • Wendell Corey *Jim Stauton Rogers* • Vic Damone *Andre Milan* • Fernando Lamas *Paul Sarnac* • Marcel Dalio *Claude Duval* • Una Merkel *Glynnie* ■ *Dir* Norman Taurog • *Scr* Dorothy Cooper, Sidney Sheldon, from a story by Dorothy Cooper

Richard Pryor: Live in Concert ★★★🔞
Comedy concert   1979 · US · Colour · 78min

This is the first and best of comic Richard Pryor's stand-up movies, filmed in front of a live audience in Long Beach, California, in 1979, and the electrifying atmosphere is more rock concert than comedy club. Freed from the constraints of the TV censors, Pryor lets rip with a torrent of scatological observations that, as ever, draw on aspects of his turbulent private life, from the punishments meted out by his strict father ("Go stand in the middle of the street while I start the car") to his own well-publicised brushes with the law. His relaxed, foul-mouthed approach has the audience in fits – and allows him to skip effortlessly from dirty joke to spot-on mimicry to scalpel-sharp dissection of the taboos surrounding race and sex in the US. KG DVD

Richard Pryor ■ *Dir* Jeff Margolis

Richard Pryor: Live on the Sunset Strip ★★★🔞
Comedy concert   1982 · US · Colour · 77min

Richard Pryor can be an acquired taste, and his concert films are variable, but on form there are few more astute comedians. In this, culled from two one-man shows at the Hollywood Palladium, he is in subdued mood. The Mafia, his drug abuse and his trip to Africa are among the diverse subjects covered, and he even picks up on some of the sick humour directed at his own accident, when he set himself alight while on a cocaine binge. Honest and funny. JG

Richard Pryor ■ *Dir* Joe Layton • *Scr* Richard Pryor

Richard III ★★★★U
Historical drama   1955 · UK · Colour · 150min

After turning *Henry V* into wartime propaganda and *Hamlet* into *film noir* on the battlements, Laurence Olivier made *Richard III* as outright melodrama. Olivier's stage portrayal of Richard was legendary and the film serves principally as a record of that triumph and as such less of a movie than its two predecessors. Olivier's hunchback scowls and lurches around the sets like Charles Laughton's Quasimodo. While Ralph Richardson, John Gielgud and Claire Bloom give performances of great distinction and emotion, Olivier's is more a display of cold technique. AT DVD BL

Laurence Olivier *Richard III* • Ralph Richardson *Buckingham* • Claire Bloom *Lady Anne* • John Gielgud *Clarence* • Cedric Hardwicke *King Edward IV* • Mary Kerridge *Queen Elizabeth* • Pamela Brown *Jane Shore* • Alec Clunes *Hastings* • Stanley Baker *Henry Tudor* • Michael Gough *Dighton* ■ *Dir* Laurence Olivier • *Scr* Alan Dent, Laurence Olivier, Colley Cibber, David Garrick, from the play by William Shakespeare • *Production Designer* Roger Furse [Roger K Furse] • *Art Director* Carmen Dillon • *Cinematographer* Otto Heller

Richard III ★★★★15
Historical drama   1995 · UK/US · Colour · 99min

Ian McKellen authoritatively revisits one of the greatest roles in the English language in Richard Loncraine's daring, flashy reworking of the acclaimed National Theatre production, in which Richard was styled as a 1930s fascist dictator. The excellent cast includes Maggie Smith and Kristin Scott Thomas's drug-addicted Lady Anne, with Annette Bening and a scene-stealing Robert Downey Jr, as an American arriviste queen and her brother. Although the artifice is dispassionately cold, the splashy nods to modern cinema-goers' frame of reference do pep up the appeal without condescension or gutting the text. AME Violence, sex scenes. DVD

Ian McKellen *Richard III* • Annette Bening *Queen Elizabeth* • Robert Downey Jr *Earl Rivers* • Nigel Hawthorne *Clarence* • Maggie Smith *Duchess of York* • Jim Broadbent *Duke of Buckingham* • Kristin Scott Thomas *Lady Anne* ■ *Dir* Richard Loncraine • *Scr* Ian McKellen, Richard Loncraine, from the stage production by Richard Eyre of the play by William Shakespeare

The Richest Girl in the World ★★★
Romantic comedy   1934 · US · BW · 74min

Desperate to find true romance and be loved for herself rather than her money, heiress Miriam Hopkins, whom nobody can recognise since there are no pictures of her and few are privileged to meet her, swaps identities with her best-friend-cum-secretary Fay Wray to test the worth of Joel McCrea. Henry Stephenson and Reginald Denny join the conspiracy under William A Seiter's direction of the Oscar-nominated screenplay. Sweetly sparkling, with Hopkins on delightful form. RK

Miriam Hopkins *Dorothy Hunter* • Joel McCrea *Tony Travers* • Fay Wray *Sylvia Lockwood* • Henry Stephenson *John Connors* • Reginald Denny *Phillip Lockwood* • Beryl Mercer *Marie* • George Meeker *Donald* ■ *Dir* William A Seiter • *Scr* Norman Krasna, Leona D'Ambry, from a story by Norman Krasna

Richie Rich ★★🅿🅶
Comedy   1994 · US · Colour · 90min

Based on the US comic strip, this features Macaulay Culkin as a boy who has unlimited wealth but longs for a normal life. His wish is granted when he takes up with a ragbag gang of kids to foil nasty John Larroquette, who is trying to cheat Culkin out of his fortune. All the usual clichés are present and correct, with Jonathan Hyde as the obligatory British butler. Children will lap up the juvenile slapstick. A straight-to-video sequel, *Richie Rich's Christmas Wish*, followed in 1998, minus Culkin. JF DVD

Macaulay Culkin *Richie Rich* • John Larroquette *Van Dough* • Edward Herrmann *Mr Rich* • Christine Ebersole *Mrs Rich* • Jonathan Hyde *Cadbury* • Michael McShane [Micheal McShane] *Professor Keenbean* ■ *Dir* Donald Petrie • *Scr* Tom S Parker, Jim Jennewein, from a story by Neil Tolkin, from the Harvey Comics characters

Ricki and the Flash ★★★12
Comedy drama   2015 · US · Colour · 97min

Despite financial and marital pressures, failed rock star Ricki (Meryl Streep) lives to please the regulars at a California club at night while slaving by day in a soulless health food store. But one call from her ex-husband (Kevin Kline) and she's back tending to her surly daughter (Streep's own daughter Mamie Gummer). Jonathan Demme's spare direction concentrates a bit too much on several well-wrought tunes sung by Streep, but despite whiffs of vanity project, she of course convinces as the singer with attitude. KK Swearing, sexual/drug references.

Meryl Streep *Ricki* • Kevin Kline *Pete* • Mamie Gummer *Julie* • Sebastian Stan *Joshua* • Ben Platt *Daniel* ■ *Dir* Jonathan Demme • *Scr* Diablo Cody

Ricochet ★★★18
Action crime drama   1991 · US · Colour · 97min

This enjoyable, totally over-the-top action thriller has Denzel Washington's cop being systematically persecuted by John Lithgow's deranged killer, whom he had arrested years earlier in front of enraptured TV viewers. Director Russell Mulcahy keeps the energy levels high and the camera just about active enough to disguise the ridiculousness of the story. Lithgow shows why he is one of modern cinema's premier psycho performers, but Washington's acting skills are somewhat wasted. JC Violence. DVD

Denzel Washington *Nick Styles* • John Lithgow *Earl Talbot Blake* • Ice-T *Odessa* • Kevin Pollak *Larry Doyle* • Lindsay Wagner *Priscilla Brimleigh* • Victoria Dillard *Alice* ■ *Dir* Russell Mulcahy • *Scr* Steven E de Souza, from the story by Fred Dekker, Menno Meyjes

Riddick ★★★15
Science-fiction thriller   2013 · US · Colour · 113min

From start to finish, this adventure is completely ridiculous (no pun intended), but Vin Diesel is charismatic and fun to watch in his signature antihero role as the growling convict left for dead on a sun-scorched planet. There's a digital army of alien predators to fight off in a set-up reminiscent of *Pitch Black* – and that's not the only link to the original film. It's far better than the first sequel, *The Chronicles of Riddick*, with ferocious monsters, slasher-style gore and cheesy one-liners, and writer/director David Twohy enhances the kinetic action with an impressive array of cosmic visuals. AJ Violence, swearing, nudity. DVD BL

Vin Diesel *Riddick* • Jordi Molla [Jordi Mollà] *Santana* • Matt Nable *Boss Johns* • Katee Sackhoff *Dahl* • Karl Urban *Vaako* • Bokeem Woodbine *Moss* ■ *Dir* David Twohy • *Scr* David Twohy, from characters by Jim & Ken Wheat

The Riddle of the Sands ★★★U
Action adventure   1978 · UK · Colour · 98min

Despite the riotous action contained in the original Erskine Childers adventure classic, this brave attempt to pin down the novel's narrative never quite succeeds, because it's too reverent for its own good. Michael York and Simon MacCorkindale are the yachtsmen discovering a fiendish pre-emptive strike against England by the Germans, way ahead of the First World War. Tony Maylam's direction strives to make the most of authentic locations, but the glossiness of the production makes it unconvincing. TH English, German +subtitles. DVD

Michael York *Charles Carruthers* • Jenny Agutter *Clara* • Simon MacCorkindale *Arthur Davies* • Alan Badel *Dollmann* • Jurgen Andersen *Commander Von Brüning* • Michael Sheard *Böhme* ■ *Dir* Tony Maylam • *Scr* Tony Maylam, John Bailey (3), from the novel by Erskine Childers

Ride ★★15
Comedy road movie   1998 · US · Colour · 80min

This cheap and cheerful hip-hop comedy thriller was made by the team behind *House Party*. Melissa DeSouza plays an aspiring film-maker who gets a job with a top music promo director and is given the task of chaperoning a rap group on their way from New York to Miami. Unbeknown to her, one of the number has stolen money from a local gangster, prompting a cross-country chase. Loud and brash, with a pumping hip-hop soundtrack. JF

Malik Yoba *Poppa* • Melissa De Sousa *Leta* • John Witherspoon *Roscoe* • Fredro Starr *Geronimo* • Cedric the Entertainer *Bo* • Snoop Doggy Dogg [Snoop Dogg] *Mente* • Julia Garrison *Blacke* • Guy Torry *Indigo* • Dr Dre *Eight* ■ *Dir/Scr* Millicent Shelton

Ride a Crooked Trail ★★★U
Western   1958 · US · Colour · 87min

The series of westerns made by Universal starring baby-faced war hero Audie Murphy was extremely variable in quality, but it nevertheless made Murphy a household name. This is one of the better examples, using a basic mistaken identity plot, with bank robber Murphy being mistaken for a marshal. Director Jesse Hibbs keeps things moving along and there's also a marvellous supporting cast, including a pre-stardom Walter Matthau as a drunken judge. TS

Audie Murphy *Joe Maybe* • Gia Scala *Tessa Milotte* • Walter Matthau *Judge Kyle* • Henry Silva *Sam Teeler* • Joanna Moore *Little Brandy* • Eddie Little [Eddie Little Sky] *Jimmy* • Mary Field *Mrs Curtis* • Leo Gordon *Sam Mason* • Mort Mills *Pecos* ■ *Dir* Jesse Hibbs • *Scr* Borden Chase, from a story by George Bruce

Ride a Wild Pony ★★★U
Period drama   1976 · US · Colour · 85min

This is a highly moralistic and sentimental tale of love and jealousy adapted from the James Aldridge novel. Set in 18th-century Australia, Robert Bettles plays a poor farm schoolboy battling over the ownership of a prize horse with the rich, but polio-stricken, Eva Griffith. This typical Disney fare is directed with compassion by Don Chaffey. AJ

Robert Bettles *Scott Pirie* • Eva Griffith *Josie Ellison* • Alfred Bell *Angus Pirie* • Melissa Jaffer *Angus' Wife* • Michael Craig *James Ellison* • Lorraine Bayly *Mrs Ellison* • Graham Rouse *Bluey Waters* ■ *Dir* Don Chaffey • *Scr* Rosemary Anne Sisson, from the novel *A Sporting Proposition* by James Aldridge

Ride Along ★★12
Action comedy   2014 · US · Colour · 95min

If you're in the mood for some undemanding action, this routine buddy cop caper offers some cheap laughs. Stand-up comic Kevin Hart plays a wimpish school security guard and wannabe police detective. His other big ambition is to marry Tika Sumpter, but first he has to get the blessing of her hardace cop brother (Ice Cube). Ice insists that Hart ride along on a nightmare shift to hunt down vicious criminal Laurence Fishburne. It's watchable enough, but it wasn't the huge hit in the UK that it was in America. Inevitably, a sequel is due in 2016. DA Violence, swearing, sexual references. DVD BL

Ice Cube *James Payton* • Kevin Hart *Ben Barber* • John Leguizamo *Santiago* • Bruce McGill *Lt Brooks* • Tika Sumpter *Angela Payton* • Laurence Fishburne *Omar* ■ *Dir* Tim Story • *Scr* Greg Coolidge, Jason Mantzoukas, Phil Hay, Matt Manfredi, from a story by Coolidge

Ride Along 2 ★★ 12

Action comedy 2016 · US · Colour · 97min

In this sequel to the surprise 2014 hit, Ice Cube's grizzled detective takes his soon-to-be brother-in-law (Kevin Hart) - now a rookie cop - to Miami on the hunt for a drugs kingpin. If it all sounds familiar, that's because it is. Aside from a couple of amusing action scenes and a limp romantic intrigue for Ice (in the shape of Olivia Munn), this follow-up stays astonishingly close to the first film's plot, with the talented leads left scrambling to put together something new. All but the most devoted Kevin Hart fans will feel slightly cheated. JL Violence, sexual references, drug abuse. DVD Blu-ray

Ice Cube *James Peyton* • Kevin Hart *Ben Barber* • Tika Sumpter *Angela Payton* • Benjamin Bratt *Antonio Pope* • Olivia Munn *Maya Cruz* ■ *Dir* Tim Story • *Scr* Phil Hay, Matt Manfredi

Ride beyond Vengeance ★★★

Western 1966 · US · Colour · 100min

A bartender tells a census taker a local story from the 1880s: as he returns to a wife he hasn't seen for 11 years, hunter Chuck Connors is mistaken for a rustler, sadistically branded and robbed. When he's rescued by the real rustler, he plans his revenge. A tough, brutal western, featuring a number of TV stalwarts. JG

James MacArthur *Delahay, the census taker* • Arthur O'Connell *Narrator* • Ruth Warrick *Aunt Gussie* • Chuck Connors *Jonas Trapp* • Michael Rennie *Brooks Durham* • Kathryn Hays *Jessie* • Joan Blondell *Mrs Lavender* • Gloria Grahame *Bonnie Shelley* • Gary Merrill *Dub Stokes* • Bill Bixby *Johnsy Boy Hood* ■ *Dir* Bernard McEveety • *Scr* Andrew J Fenady, from the novel *The Night of the Tiger* by Al Dewlen

Ride Clear of Diablo ★★ U

Western 1954 · US · Colour · 80min

Audie Murphy is up against a crooked sheriff and a corrupt lawyer as he seeks revenge for the murder of his rancher father and kid brother. Susan Cabot plays the nice girl, while Abbe Lane is the far more interesting saloon singer. Dan Duryea's rich performance as a likeable badman steals the film from the ever stolid Murphy. AE

Audie Murphy *Clay O'Mara* • Dan Duryea *Whitey Kincade* • Susan Cabot *Laurie* • Abbe Lane *Kate* • Russell Johnson *Ringer* • Paul Birch *Sheriff Kenyon* • Jack Elam *Tim* ■ *Dir* Jesse Hibbs • *Scr* George Zuckerman, DD Beauchamp, from a story by Ellis Marcus

Ride 'Em Cowboy ★★★★ U

Musical comedy 1942 · US · BW · 85min

Among the very best Abbott and Costello vehicles, made when the team's routines were still fresh and funny, this is given top-flight treatment by their studio, with some great music providing strong support in between the team's antics, including Ella Fitzgerald singing her hit version of *A Tisket, a Tasket*. The Don Raye and Gene DePaul songs include the classic *I'll Remember April* given class-A treatment with a lovely choral arrangement backing the singer Dick Foran. TV

Bud Abbott *Duke* • Lou Costello *Willoughby* • Anne Gwynne *Anne Shaw* • Samuel S Hinds *Sam Shaw* • Dick Foran *Bronco Bob Mitchell* • Richard Lane *Peter Conway* • Ella Fitzgerald *Ruby* • Dorothy Dandridge ■ *Dir* Arthur Lubin • *Scr* True Boardman, John Grant, Harold Shumate, from a story by Edmund L Hartmann

Ride Him, Cowboy ★★ U

Western 1932 · US · BW · 56min

The first of six B-westerns, largely based on old Ken Maynard silents, that a young John Wayne made for Warner Bros in the early 1930s. This cost the same as a mere two-reeler, but doesn't look it. The plot gives prominence to the white horse, Duke, with whom Wayne shares top billing. The steed is framed by the villains and sentenced to death for violent behaviour until Wayne comes to its rescue. AE

John Wayne *John Drury* • Ruth Hall *Ruth Gaunt* • Henry B Walthall *John Gaunt* • Otis Harlan *Judge Jones* ■ *Dir* Fred Allen (1) • *Scr* Scott Mason, from a story by Kenneth Perkins, from the novel by Kenneth Perkins

Ride Lonesome ★★★★ 12

Western 1959 · US · Colour · 69min

Director Budd Boetticher and executive producer and star Randolph Scott made a short cycle of fine westerns, unequalled in their classic simplicity and under-appreciated on their first release. This is one of the best. The finely tuned Burt Kennedy screenplay wastes not a moment as craggy-featured bounty hunter Scott goes after a young killer (the giggling James Best), ostensibly for the cash reward, but really to flush out his brother, the snarling Lee Van Cleef. Fine western stuff, with brilliantly taut, terse dialogue. Watch out for James Coburn's movie debut. TS DVD

Randolph Scott *Ben Brigade* • Karen Steele *Carrie Lane* • Pernell Roberts *Sam Boone* • James Best *Billy John* • Lee Van Cleef *Frank* • James Coburn *Wid* • Dyke Johnson *Charlie* • Boyd Stockman *Indian chief* ■ *Dir* Budd Boetticher • *Scr* Burt Kennedy

Ride, Rise, Roar ★★★ 15

Music documentary 2010 · US · Colour · 83min

David Byrne helped reinvent the rock concert movie with 1984's *Stop Making Sense* and once again invites cameras to eavesdrop on his preparations to stage a show in support of his 2008 collaboration with Brian Eno, *Everything That Happens Will Happen Today*. On this occasion, Byrne also involves several award-winning choreographers, who interpret key tracks from the album as well as Talking Heads hits. The lengthy interview segments tend to spoil the flow of the piece, but Byrne remains an enigmatic presence. TeS Some swearing. DVD Blu-ray

David Byrne • Brian Eno ■ *Dir* David Hillman Curtis

Ride the High Country ★★★★ PG

Western 1962 · US · Colour · 90min

Director Sam Peckinpah proved his magisterial talent with this, his second movie (and many think his finest), a gentle requiem to the Old West co-starring two icons of the genre, sturdy Joel McCrea and craggy Randolph Scott (in his last role). The casting provides constant delights as the two veterans bicker and cuss their way through a plot about a gold shipment, and should it be stolen or not. The action is superbly photographed by the great Lucien Ballard in eye-filling CinemaScope and Metrocolor, and there are marvellous supporting performances. There's also a knockout vignette from Edgar Buchanan as a drunken judge. A deeply satisfying, mature movie. TS DVD

Randolph Scott *Gil Westrum* • Joel McCrea *Steve Judd* • Mariette Hartley *Elsa Knudsen* • Ronald Starr *Heck Longtree* • RG Armstrong *Joshua Knudsen* • Edgar Buchanan *Judge Tolliver* • John Anderson *Elder Hammond* • LQ Jones *Sylvus Hammond* • Warren Oates *Henry Hammond* • James Drury *Billy Hammond* • John Davis Chandler *Jimmy Hammond* ■ *Scr* NB Stone Jr • *Scr* Sam Peckinpah

Ride the Wild Surf ★★ U

Comedy drama 1964 · US · Colour · 101min

This colourful and exuberant teen movie is about three beach-bum pals who head to Hawaii for the surfing. However, though all three find romance, their new girlfriends (including Barbara Eden of *I Dream of Jeannie* fame) try to persuade them to change their ways. The characters are as flat as their surfboards, but the film is fun and well made, and the surfing sequences are watchable. JG

Fabian *Jody Wallis* • Shelley Fabares *Brie Matthews* • Tab Hunter *Steamer Lane* • Barbara Eden *Augie Poole* • Peter Brown *Chase Colton* ■ *Dir* Don Taylor • *Scr* Jo Napoleon, Art Napoleon

The Ride to Hangman's Tree ★★★ U

Western 1967 · US · Colour · 89min

This is an evocative title for a minor Universal western, utilising the studio's contract players and existing sets. It isn't bad, with Jack Lord (a year before he hit the TV big time with *Hawaii Five-O*) and the ever-excellent James Farentino and Don Galloway playing a trio of outlaws vaguely reminiscent of those cowboy stars whose adventures enthralled young audiences at the Saturday morning pictures. This begins with a cleverly directed and well-staged robbery; stick with it, it's fun. TS

Jack Lord *Guy Russell* • James Farentino *Matt Stone* • Don Galloway *Nevada Jones* • Melodie Johnson *Lillie Malone* • Richard Anderson *Steve Carlson* • Robert Yuro *Jeff Scott* • Ed Peck *Sheriff Stewart* • Paul Reed *Corbett* ■ *Dir* Alan Rafkin • *Scr* Luci Ward, Jack Natteford, William Bowers, from a story by Luci Ward, Jack Natteford

Ride, Vaquero! ★★ U

Western 1953 · US · Colour · 90min

This poorly written western arouses interest from MGM's offbeat casting of the three stars: Robert Taylor, as the quiet but deadly right-hand man of a Mexican bandit; Howard Keel, in a non-singing role as a foolhardy rancher; and Ava Gardner, as the rancher's virtuous wife. Only Anthony Quinn, playing the flamboyant, egotistical Mexican bandit chief who attacks the American ranchers invading his domain, seems cast to type - and he walks away with the picture. AE

Robert Taylor *Rio* • Ava Gardner *Cordelia Cameron* • Howard Keel *King Cameron* • Anthony Quinn *Jose Esqueda* • Kurt Kasznar *Father Antonio* • Ted De Corsia *Sheriff Parker* • Charlita *Singer* • Jack Elam *Barton* ■ *Dir* John Farrow • *Scr* Frank Fenton, John Farrow

Ride with the Devil ★★★★★ 15

Period war drama 1999 · US · Colour · 132min

Director Ang Lee turns in another handsome, moving and unmissable piece of cinema, this time set against the backdrop of the American Civil War. Skeet Ulrich and Tobey Maguire are two members of the "Bushwackers" - southern guerrillas who secretly ambush Yankee platoons along the Missouri backroads. When they have to hide out for the winter, the pair and two fellow irregulars - one an ex-slave - hole up in a cave cut out of a hill, where they are sent food and water by a beautiful young widow (singer Jewel). It's an epic yet intimate portrait of relationships and war, boasting superb performances from the cast and a compelling script by writer/producer James Schamus. JB Violence. DVD

Skeet Ulrich *Jack Bull Chiles* • Tobey Maguire *Jacob Friedel Roedel, "Dutchman"* • Jewel *Sue Lee Shelley* • Jeffrey Wright *Daniel Holt* • Simon Baker (1) *George Clyde* • Jonathan Rhys Meyers *Pitt Mackeson* • James Caviezel [Jim Caviezel] *Black John* • Tom Guiry *Riley Crawford* • Tom Wilkinson *Orton Brown* ■ *Dir* Ang Lee • *Scr* James Schamus, from the novel *Woe to Live On* by Daniel Woodrell

Rider on the Rain ★★★ 18

Thriller 1970 · Fr/It · Colour · 113min

Marlène Jobert kills the man who rapes her and then tries to cover it up, but she's thwarted by Charles Bronson, who starts sniffing around while keeping his identity a mystery. A solid piece of work from veteran director René Clément, who orchestrates subplots galore, this is a sharp portrait of life in a French seaside town, with echoes of Hitchcock in its concern with the burden of guilt. AT French dubbed. DVD

Marlène Jobert *Mellie* • Charles Bronson *Colonel Harry Dobbs* • Jean Gaven *Inspector Toussaint* • Corinne Marchand *Tania* • Jill Ireland *Nicole* • Annie Cordy *Juliette* ■ *Dir* René Clément • *Scr* Sébastien Japrisot, Lorenzo Ventavoli

Riders in the Sky ★★ U

Western 1949 · US · BW · 69min

One of an interminable series of Gene Autry programme fillers, this film allows the singing cowboy to break into the hit song *Ghost Riders in the Sky*. The plot, grafted on to the song, is the usual one about freeing someone framed for murder, but the structure is interesting for this type of production-line fare: a flashback within a flashback that's certainly original and quite amusing. TS

Gene Autry • Gloria Henry *Ann Lawson* • Pat Buttram *Chuckwalla Jones* • Mary Beth Hughes *Julie Steward* • Robert Livingston *Rock McCleary* • Steve Darrell *Ralph Lawson* • Alan Hale Jr *Marshal Riggs* ■ *Dir* John English • *Scr* Gerald Geraghty, from a story by Herbert A Woodbury

Riders of Destiny ★★ U

Western 1933 · US · BW · 49min

Historically important, and prophetically titled, this is the first of a dozen or so B-westerns made by John Wayne for Monogram Pictures under producer Paul Malvern's Lone Star trademark. Here Wayne plays "Singin' Sandy", a government agent sent a-hunting villains, who (are you ready for this?) sings as he guns them down. The villain of the piece is played by stuntman Yakima Canutt, and this is a movie where, to establish the character's black heart, he actually kicks a dog on his entrance. This style of baddie was therefore known as a "dog heavy", and was a popular cliché in westerns. TS DVD

John Wayne *Singin' Sandy Saunders* • Cecilia Parker *Fay Denton* • George Hayes [George "Gabby" Hayes] *Sheriff Denton* • Forrest Taylor *Kincaid* • Lafe McKee *Sheriff* • Fern Emmett *Farm woman* • Yakima Canutt ■ *Dir* Robert North Bradbury [Robert N Bradbury] • *Scr* Robert NorthBradbury

Riders of the Purple Sage ★★★★

Silent western 1925 · US · BW · 56min

Tom Mix, the most famous cowboy-star of his time, rides tall in the saddle for this engrossing yarn, from the novel by western writer Zane Grey. Texas Ranger Mix pursues his sister (Beatrice Burnham) and niece, who have been kidnapped by the evil Warner Oland. Lots of fine "head 'em off at the pass" stuff. The definitive version of this much filmed novel. TH

Tom Mix *Jim Lassiter* • Beatrice Burnham *Millie Erne* • Arthur Morrison *Frank Erne* • Seesel Ann Johnson *Bess Erne as a child* • Warner Oland *Lew Walters/Judge Dyer* • Fred Kohler *Metzger* ■ *Dir* Lynn Reynolds • *Scr* Edfrid Bingham, from the novel by Zane Grey

Riders of the Purple Sage ★★

Western 1931 · US · BW · 58min

Zane Grey's huge popularity as a western novelist made his name the principal selling point of Fox's third filming of his first bestseller, dating from 1912. Early in his career as a series cowboy star, George O'Brien follows Tom Mix as the laconic westerner, seeking the man who killed his sister. Superbly photographed by George Schneiderman and - except for stilted dialogue sequences - briskly directed by Hamilton MacFadden. AE

George O'Brien *Lassiter* • Marguerite Churchill *Jane Witheroteen* • Noah Beery *Judge Dyer* • Yvonne Pelletier *Bess* • James Todd *Venters* • Stanley Fields *Oldring* • Lester Dorr *Judkins* • Shirley Nails *Fay* • Frank McGlynn Sr *Jeff Tull* ■ *Dir* Hamilton MacFadden • *Scr* John F Goodrich, Philip Klein, Barry Connors, from the novel by Zane Grey

Riders of the Purple Sage ★★ U

Western 1941 · US · BW · 65min

Here it's poker-faced George Montgomery who's wrestling with the multiple twists and turns of the complex plot, though Zane Grey's story has been simplified this time around. The bleak, nihilistic ending still works, proving quite a startling climax to

R

what is basically an ordinary 20th Century-Fox B-western. **TS**

George Montgomery *Jim Lassiter* • Mary Howard *Jane Withersteen* • Robert Barrat *Judge Frank Dyer* • Lynne Roberts *Bess* • Kane Richmond *Adam Dyer* • Patsy Patterson *Fay Larkin* • Richard Lane *Steve Oldring* • Oscar O'Shea *Noah Judkins* • James Gillette *Venters* • Frank McGrath *Pete* • LeRoy Mason *Jerry Card* ■ *Dir* James Tinling • *Scr* William Bruckner, Robert Metzler, from the novel by Zane Grey

Riders of the Storm ★★ 15
Satirical comedy   1986 · UK · Colour · 100min

Some Vietnam veterans start up a pirate radio station to hound right-wing senators in this limp satire on American politics. All the offbeat elements are present and correct – weirdo duo Dennis Hopper and Michael J Pollard doing their "wacky" thing, the presidential candidate etched as a full-blown drag queen, the station situated inside an old B-52 bomber – but the whole enterprise doesn't gel or elicit much laughter. **AJ**

Dennis Hopper *Captain* • Michael J Pollard *Doc* • Eugene Lipinski *Ace* • James Aubrey *Claude* • Al Matthews *Ben* • William Armstrong *Jerry* • Nigel Pegram *Sen Willa Westinghouse* • Michael Ho *Minh* • Josie Lawrence *Guerillette* • Ozzy Osbourne *Himself* ■ *Dir* Maurice Phillips • *Scr* Scott Roberts

Riders of the Whistling Pines ★★ U
Western   1949 · US · BW · 69min

There aren't many films in which tussock moths prove pivotal to the plot. But, then again, westerns involving airplane finales are pretty rare, too. Hero Gene Autry is blamed for the murder of a forest ranger and accused of poisoning cattle by crooked lumber tycoon Douglas Dumbrille. He even has time for a dalliance with Patricia White. **DP** *DVD*

Gene Autry • Patricia White [Patricia Barry] *Helen Carter* • Jimmy Lloyd *Joe Lucas* • Douglas Dumbrille [Douglass Dumbrille] *Henry Mitchell* • Damian O'Flynn *Bill Wright* • Clayton Moore *Pete* • Harry Cheshire *Dr Daniel Chadwick* • Leon Weaver *Abner Weaver* ■ *Dir* John English • *Scr* Jack Townley

Ridicule ★★★★ 15
Historical drama   1996 · Fr · Colour · 97min

Winner of four Césars and the Bafta for best foreign language film, Patrice Leconte's insight into life at Louis XVI's Versailles sends an icy chill through the cosy corridors of the costume picture. The rapiers in Remi Waterhouse's script may not be tipped with venom, but there's enough sophistication in the repartee to produce a slyly credible vision of a world founded solely on ambition and indolence. Entering this mausoleum of mordant wit, Charles Berling's country Jekyll turns courtly Hyde, as he seeks to outwit influential black widow Fanny Ardant and her provocative priest, Bernard Giraudeau. An acute, acerbic delight. **DP** French +subtitles. Violence, sex scenes, nudity. *DVD*

Charles Berling *Ponceludon de Malavoy* • Jean Rochefort *Marquis de Bellegrade* • Fanny Ardant *Madame de Blayac* • Judith Godrèche *Mathilde de Bellegarde* • Bernard Giraudeau *L'Abbé de Vilecourt* • Bernard Dhéran *Monsieur de Montalieri* ■ *Dir* Patrice Leconte • *Scr* Remi Waterhouse, Michel Fessler, Eric Vicaut

Riding Alone for Thousands of Miles ★★★★ PG
Drama   2005 · HK/Chi/Jpn · Colour · 105min

Taking a break from martial arts epics, Zhang Yimou adopts a more personal style for this meticulous, small-scale road movie. Determined to heal a breach with his dying son by completing his documentary about Chinese folk opera, Japanese fisherman Ken Takakura goes in search of singer Li Jiamin, only to find him in jail and unwilling to sing until he is reunited with his young son, Yang Zhenbo. Adeptly shifting between picaresque drama, bureaucratic satire and culture clash comedy, Zhang directs with a compassion and restraint that makes this

utterly irresistible. **DP** Mandarin, Japanese +subtitles. *DVD*

Ken Takakura *Gou-ichi Takata* • Shinobu Terajima *Rie Takata* • Kiichi Nakai *Ken-ichi Takata* • Li Jiamin • Qiu Lin *Lingo* ■ *Dir* Zhang Yimou • *Scr* Zou Jingzhi, from a story by Jingzhi, Zhang Yimou, Wang Bin

Riding Giants ★★★★ 12
Documentary   2004 · US/Fr · Colour · 97min

This second excellent documentary feature from ex-skateboard star Stacy Peralta (*Dogtown and Z-Boys* charted the development of vertical skateboarding) examines the development of big-wave surfing from its origins in Hawaii in the 1950s through to the new style of jet-ski assisted surfing that gives adrenaline junkies access to what were impossibly huge waves only a few years ago. Peralta uses archive footage and personal reminiscences to chart the development of the sport, and he's aided by top-notch editing as well as a cracking soundtrack. Peralta's obvious passion for his subject matter gives this superb documentary its abundant energy. **AS** *DVD*

■ *Dir* Stacy Peralta • *Scr* Stacy Peralta, Sam George • *Cinematographer* Peter Pilafian

Riding High ★★ U
Musical western   1943 · US · Colour · 88min

Crooner Dick Powell is out west, as the owner of a silver mine that's not paying. Enter burlesque queen Dorothy Lamour who does her act at a dude ranch, run by shrieking singer Cass Daley, to help Powell and his partner – the whiny Victor Moore – pay off the mortgage on the mine. Pretty forgettable, with unmemorable songs. Released as *Melody Inn* in the UK. **RB**

Dorothy Lamour *Ann Castle* • Dick Powell *Steve Baird* • Victor Moore *Mortimer J Slocum* • Gil Lamb *Bob "Foggy" Day* • Cass Daley *Tess Connors* • Bill Goodwin *Chuck Stuart* • Rod Cameron *Sam Welch* ■ *Dir* George Marshall • *Scr* Walter DeLeon, Arthur Phillips, Art Arthur, from the play *Ready Money* by James Montgomery

Riding High ★★★
Musical comedy   1950 · US · BW · 112min

Director Frank Capra remakes his 1934 hit *Broadway Bill* as a Bing Crosby vehicle, incorporating stock footage from the original – watch closely! – and even recasting some of the same actors. The result is charming and the slight plot changes are an improvement (the hero is now engaged to the heroine, not married to her), but it lacks the feeling of sheer goodwill of the original. The added songs though, don't hurt the narrative and Crosby's real-life affection for horse racing is clearly evident. **TS**

Bing Crosby *Dan Brooks* • Coleen Gray *Alice Higgins* • Charles Bickford *JL Higgins* • William Demarest *Happy McGuire* • Frances Gifford *Margaret Higgins* • Raymond Walburn *Professor Pettigrew* • James Gleason *Racing Secretary* • Ward Bond *Lee* • Clarence Muse *Whitey* • Percy Kilbride *Pop Jones* ■ *Dir* Frank Capra • *Scr* Robert Riskin, Nelville Shavelson, Jack Rose, from the story *Broadway Bill* by Mark Hellinger

Riding in Cars with Boys ★★★ 12
Biographical comedy drama
2001 · US · Colour · 125min

Drew Barrymore ages from teenager to 30-something – she manages 15 but 35 is less convincing - in this drama based on the memoirs of underage mother Beverly Donofrio. As Beverly, Barrymore has a baby while still at school, marries the dim-witted but well-meaning father (a superb performance from Steve Zahn) and regrets that all hopes of going to college and having a writing career are now lost to her. Barrymore's likeable performance makes this enjoyable. **JB** Swearing. *DVD*

Drew Barrymore *Beverly Donofrio* • Steve Zahn *Ray Hasek* • Brittany Murphy *Fay Forrester* • Adam Garcia *Jason, aged 20* • Lorraine Bracco *Mrs Donofrio* • James Woods *Mr Donofrio* • Sara Gilbert *Tina* • Rosie Perez *Shirley* ■ *Dir* Penny Marshall • *Scr* Morgan Upton Ward, from the autobiography by Beverly Donofrio

Riding Shotgun ★★ U
Western   1954 · US · Colour · 74min

Throughout the 1950s, western fans were well-served by colour programme fillers, invariably featuring either baby-faced Audie Murphy or craggy Randolph Scott. Eventually Scott managed to fashion his co-features into a remarkable series of westerns, the Ranown cycle. Prior to that, however, Randy rode a tall saddle, invariably directed by Warners hack-of-all-trades, the one-eyed Andre De Toth, of whose work this is a prime example. The plot is the usual one of Scott attempting to clear his name. Nothing spectacular, but still undemanding entertainment. **TS**

Randolph Scott *Larry Delong* • Wayne Morris *Tub Murphy* • Joan Weldon *Orissa Flynn* • Joe Sawyer *Tom Biggert* • James Millican *Dan Maraday* • Charles Buchinski [Charles Bronson] *Pinto* ■ *Dir* Andre De Toth • *Scr* Tom Blackburn, from the story *Riding Solo* by Kenneth Perkins

Rien Ne Va Plus ★★★★ 15
Comedy thriller   1997 · Fr/Swi · Colour · 101min

Claude Chabrol's 50th movie is a smashing comedy thriller about a pair of con artists, played by Isabelle Huppert and Michel Serrault. Criss-crossing France in search of victims, Huppert and Serrault are exuberant partners in crime, who nearly come unstuck when Huppert sets her sights on a business executive with a suitcase bursting with Mob money. The mood swings wonderfully from comedy to romance to occasionally shocking violence. **AT** French +subtitles. *DVD*

Isabelle Huppert *Elisabeth/"Betty"* • Michel Serrault *Victor* • François Cluzet *Maurice Biagini* • Jean-François Balmer *Monsieur K* • Jackie Berroyer *Robert Châtillon* • Thomas Chabrol *Hotel Waldhaus bellboy* ■ *Dir/Scr* Claude Chabrol

Rien sur Robert ★★★ 18
Comedy drama   1998 · Fr · Colour · 106min

Hamstrung by highbrow pomposity and crippling self-doubt, trapped within a circle of friends vying to become his severest critic, Fabrice Luchini gives a wonderful performance of bourgeois neuroticism in this assured satire from writer/director Pascal Bonitzer. Lacing Rohmer-esque discourses with wisecracks Woody Allen would be proud of, the literate screenplay is seized upon by an excellent cast. It's just a shame the picture loses momentum as it approaches its disappointingly flat finale. **DP** French +subtitles.

Fabrice Luchini *Didier Temple* • Sandrine Kiberlain *Juliette Sauvage* • Valentina Cervi *Aurélie Coquille* • Michel Piccoli *Lord Ariel Chatwick-West* • Bernadette Lafont *Madame Sauvage* • Laurent Lucas *Jérôme Sauveur* ■ *Dir/Scr* Pascal Bonitzer

Riff-Raff ★★
Adventure   1947 · US · BW · 80min

Cinematographer Ted Tetzlaff turned full-time director with this dynamic thriller down Panama way. This is more a comedy adventure than a suspense mystery, with shamus Pat O'Brien and the murderous Walter Slezak going hell for leather to find a map revealing the site of untapped oil reserves. With Percy Kilbride chipping in as a wisecracking cabbie and Anne Jeffreys providing sultry duplicity as a nightclub chanteuse, it's brisk, brash entertainment. **DP**

Pat O'Brien *Dan Hammer* • Walter Slezak *Molinar* • Anne Jeffreys *Maxine* • Percy Kilbride *Pop* • Jerome Cowan *Walter Gredson* • George Givot *Rues* • Jason Robards [Jason Robards Sr] *Dominguez* ■ *Dir* Ted Tetzlaff • *Scr* Martin Rackin

Riff-Raff ★★★★ 15
Drama   1991 · UK · Colour · 95min

Ken Loach's film about life on a London building site gave Robert Carlyle his first shot at stardom, which he seized with both hands. Working from a script by Bill Jesse, who died before the film was finished, this exploration of a gang of ethnically diverse labourers as they work on a closed-down hospital, is lighter in mood than many

Loach movies, though Carlyle's romantic dalliance with Emer McCourt never quite convinces. It also features one of Ricky Tomlinson's first screen performances. **TH** *DVD*

Robert Carlyle *Stevie* • Emer McCourt *Susan* • Jimmy Coleman *Shem* • George Moss *Mo* • Ricky Tomlinson *Larry* • David Finch *Kevin* ■ *Dir* Ken Loach • *Scr* Bill Jesse

Riffraff ★★★
Drama   1936 · US · BW · 94min

This is an MGM major feature about a pair of fisherfolk who end up on the wrong side of the law. At any other studio this would be a potboiler, but here it earns its place in posterity thanks to luminous star performances from blonde bombshell Jean Harlow (disguised in a brown wig) and her likeable co-star, dependable Spencer Tracy. Their scenes together reveal an easy camaraderie that's very pleasant to watch, a sort of "hey we know the plot's not up to much but we're having a good time anyway" quality which gives the movie a distinction that rises above J Walter Ruben's pallid direction and an uneasiness of tone. **TS**

Jean Harlow *Hattie* • Spencer Tracy *Dutch Miller* • Joseph Calleia *Nick Appopolis* • Una Merkel *Lil* • Mickey Rooney *Jimmy* • Victor Kilian *Flytrap* • J Farrell MacDonald *Brains* • Roger Imhof *Pops* • Baby Jane "Juanita" Quigley [Juanita Quigley] *Rosie* ■ *Dir* J Walter Ruben • *Scr* Frances Marion, HW Hanemann, Anita Loos, from a story by Marion

Rififi ★★★★ 12
Classic crime caper   1955 · Fr · BW · 113min

Little did Jules Dassin know, as he sent Jean Servais and his gang into a Rue de Rivoli jewellery store, that he was giving birth to that ever-popular subgenre, the caper movie. However, no one since has matched the tension and cinematic mastery of the near 30-minute robbery sequence, which is executed in the minutest detail and without resort to dialogue or ambient score. The change of pace, as rival mobster Marcel Lupovici moves in for an undeserved cut, is also neatly accomplished. But there's precious little happening beneath the dazzling surface. Incidentally, that's Dassin playing César, under the pseudonym, Perlo Vita. **DP** French +subtitles. *DVD* *BL*

Jean Servais *Tony le Stephanois* • Carl Mohner *Jo le Suedois* • Robert Manuel *Mario* • Perlo Vita [Jules Dassin] *César* • Marie Sabouret *Mado* • Janine Darcey *Louise* • Claude Sylvain *Ida* • Marcel Lupovici *Pierre Grutter* • Magali Noël *Viviane* ■ *Dir* Jules Dassin • *Scr* Jules Dassin, René Wheeler, Auguste Le Breton, from a novel by Auguste Le Breton • *Production Designer* Trauner [Alexandre Trauner]

Right at Your Door ★★★ 15
Thriller   2006 · US · Colour · 91min

A normal day turns into a nightmare in this low-key but disturbing thriller that gnaws at all our deepest fears in a post 9/11 world. The setting is a quiet suburban home in Los Angeles, where self-employed Brad (Rory Cochrane of *CSI: Miami* fame) is seeing Lexi (Mary McCormack) off to work. But the deployment of several "dirty" bombs across the city shatters the calm, wreaking havoc in the streets and filling the air with toxic ash. Debut writer/director Chris Gorak doesn't rely on special effects here - events are seen (and heard) from the perspective of the two protagonists and, after a tense half hour, subtly shift gear to become an ingenious study of survivalism. **DW** Swearing. *DVD*

Mary McCormack *Lexi* • Rory Cochrane *Brad* • Tony Perez *Alvaro* • Scotty Noyd Jr *Timmy* • Jon Huertas *Rick* • Max Kasch *Corporal Marshall* ■ *Dir/Scr* Chris Gorak

Right Bank, Left Bank ★★
Drama   1984 · Fr · Colour · 105min

A much-amended, yet still muddled script and inexact casting undermine this lightweight melodrama. Divorced publicist Nathalie Baye (who has just quit her job because of sexual harassment) slowly comes to trust smooth media lawyer

Gérard Depardieu as he regains his principles through her influence. DP French dubbed.

Gérard Depardieu *Paul Senanques* • Nathalie Baye *Sacha Vernakis* • Bernard Fresson *President* • Charlotte De Turckheim *Catherine* • Robert Bruce (2) *Bobby* • Marcel Bozonnet *Michel Monblanc* ■ *Dir* Philippe Labro • *Scr* Philippe Labro, Françoise Labro

Right Cross ★★★ U
Sports drama   1950 · US · BW · 89min

Mexican Ricardo Montalban has a chip on his shoulder about his racial origins, but faces a real problem when injury to his hand prevents him from boxing. There's a love triangle involving Montalban, June Allyson and sports writer Dick Powell, and Lionel Barrymore features as the fight manager. The movie does capture the flavour of the boxing world, but the introduction of a racial theme seems to be an attempt to provide depth to an otherwise unremarkable plot. Look out for the brief, unbilled appearance of Marilyn Monroe. RK

June Allyson *Pat O'Malley* • Dick Powell *Rick Gavery* • Ricardo Montalban *Johnny Monterez* • Lionel Barrymore *Sean O'Malley* • Teresa Celli *Marian Monterez* • Barry Kelley *Allan Goff* • Tom Powers *Robert Balford* • Marilyn Monroe *Blonde* ■ *Dir* John Sturges • *Scr* Charles Schnee

The Right Stuff ★★★★ 15
Drama based on a true story
1983 · US · Colour · 184min

Tom Wolfe's bestseller about the training of the first American astronauts here becomes an exhilarating, sprawling, Oscar-winning chronicle of the race to put a man into space. The point of director Philip Kaufman's visually dazzling epic is to ally the early test pilots, such as Chuck Yeager (stoically played by Sam Shepard), who clearly have the "right stuff" for the job, with the pioneering heroes of the Old West. Borrowing a great deal from the work of maverick director John Ford in terms of mythological scope and story structuring, Kaufman's historical drama is a great tribute to the space race. It's packed with terrific performances, thought-provoking satire, nail-biting aerial scenes and emotional resonance. AJ DVD

Sam Shepard *Chuck Yeager* • Scott Glenn *Alan Shepard* • Ed Harris *John Glenn* • Dennis Quaid *Gordon Cooper* • Fred Ward *Gus Grissom* • Barbara Hershey *Glennis Yeager* • Kim Stanley *Pancho Barnes* • Veronica Cartwright *Betty Grissom* • Pamela Reed *Trudy Cooper* • Lance Henriksen *Walter Schirra* • Donald Moffat *Lyndon B Johnson* ■ *Dir* Philip Kaufman • *Scr* Philip Kaufman, from the book by Tom Wolfe • *Cinematographer* Caleb Deschanel • *Music* Bill Conti

Righteous Kill ★★ 15
Crime thriller   2008 · US/UK · Colour · 96min

Al Pacino and Robert De Niro share the screen for only the second time, but unlike their explosive pairing in Michael Mann's *Heat* in 1995, this thriller finds them on the same side, playing New York cops assigned to investigate a series of vigilante killings. Director Jon Avnet misses an opportunity by, ironically, giving Pacino and De Niro too much screen time together; past evidence suggests they create more sparks as adversaries. SP DVD Blu

Robert De Niro *Detective Tom "Turk" Cowan* • Al Pacino *Detective David "Rooster" Fisk* • Curtis Jackson [Curtis "50 Cent" Jackson] *Spider* • Carla Gugino *Karen Corelli* • John Leguizamo *Detective Perez* • Donnie Wahlberg *Detective Riley* • Brian Dennehy *Lieutenant Hingis* • Dan Futterman *Aaron Ziedler* ■ *Dir* Jon Avnet • *Scr* Russell Gewirtz • *Cinematographer* Denis Lenoir

Rigoletto ★★★ U
Opera   1946 · It · BW · 104min

Inspired by Victor Hugo's play, *Le Roi S'Amuse*, Verdi's opera is adapted with reverence by veteran director Carmine Gallone. Celebrated baritone Tito Gobbi stars as Rigoletto, the acerbic crookbacked jester of the dilettante Duke of Mantua who, labouring under the curse of an abused count, unknowingly participates in the kidnapping of his own daughter, Gilda. The decor is undeniably theatrical, but the music and the performances (with Lina Pagliughi voicing Marcella Govini's Gilda) are admirable. DP In Italian.

Tito Gobbi *Rigoletto* • Mario Filippeschi *Duke of Mantua* • Marcella Govoni *Gilda* • Anna Maria Canali *Maddalena* • Giulio Neri *Sparafucile* • Marcello Giorda *Monterone* ■ *Dir* Carmine Gallone • *Scr* from the opera by Giuseppe Verdi

Rigor Mortis ★★ 18
Action horror   2013 · HK · Colour · 102min

A washed-up film star moves into a crumbling Hong Kong residential block only to discover it's populated by the restless spirits of deceased former residents in this horror offering from first-time director Juno Mak. Veteran Anthony Chan (who also featured in *Mr Vampire*) steals the show as an old-school vampire-hunter now running a basement restaurant, but the film keeps us waiting far too long before unleashing the flying ghouls in the final reel, and director Mak shows little skill in timing the would-be scary bits. TJ Cantonese +subtitles.

Chin Siu-hou • Kara Wai [Kara Hui] *Yeung Feng* • Nina Paw [Paw Hee Ching] *Auntie Mui* • Anthony "Friend" Chan [Anthony Chan] *Yau* • Lo Hoi-pang *Uncle Yin* ■ *Dir* Juno Mak • *Scr* Philip Yung, Jill Leung [Leung Lai-Yin], Juno Mak

The Ring ★★★ U
Silent drama   1927 · UK · BW · 85min

Alfred Hitchcock's silent concerns a champion fairground boxer (Carl Brisson), the girl he loves (Lilian Hall-Davies), and the Australian fighter (Ian Hunter) who almost tempts her away. On the surface, a routine drama, but watch it closely and it reveals the psychological undertow, signalled in carefully chosen images, that are the hallmarks of the Master's later films. The very word ring, for example, alludes not only to the men's occupation, but the circular artefacts of the fairground (the tents, the carousel), the bracelet Hunter gives the girl, the wedding ring Brisson places on her finger, and the circular journey of the protagonists. RK DVD

Carl Brisson *Jack Sander* • Lillian Hall-Davis *Nelly* • Ian Hunter *Bob Corby* ■ *Dir* Alfred Hitchcock • *Scr* Alfred Hitchcock, Alma Reville, from a story by Alfred Hitchcock

The Ring ★★★ U
Drama   1952 · US · BW · 79min

This little-known but interesting drama about racial discrimination concerns a young Mexican-American who tries to earn the respect of whites by succeeding as a prizefighter. The film is refreshingly small scale, the story sensibly rather than sensationally resolved with an excellent script by Irving Shulman and careful direction by Kurt Neumann, which develops a documentary-like atmosphere. AE

Gerald Mohr *Pete* • Rita Moreno *Lucy* • Lalo Rios *Tommy* • Robert Arthur (1) *Billy Smith* • Robert Osterloh *Freddy* • Martin Garralaga *Vidal* • Jack Elam *Harry Jackson* ■ *Dir* Kurt Neumann • *Scr* Irving Shulman, from the novel *Cry Tough* by Irving Shulman

LANDMARK FILM
Offers the key spine-tingling moment in contemporary horror – ghostly Sadako crawling out of a TV screen

Ring ★★★★ 15
Horror   1997 · Jpn · Colour · 91min

Author Koji Suzuki's bestseller about a cursed video tape that kills all who watch it has spawned franchises in both its native Japan and Hollywood. Director Hideo Nakata was the first to adapt the source material and structures his film like a diary, as a female journalist (Nanako Matsushima) investigates what caused the sudden deaths of her niece and friends. The plot resembles an old-fashioned detective story, but its emphasis on the paranormal recalls both David Cronenberg's brand of body horror and *The X-Files*. Artfully mixing footage formats to achieve a visual texture commensurate with both the tone of the story and Kinji Kawai's eerie score, Nakata inexorably builds the suspense right up to the chilling climax. DP Japanese +subtitles. Violence. DVD

Nanako Matsushima *Reiko Asakawa* • Miki Nakatani *Mai Takano* • Hiroyuki Sanada *Ryuji Takayama* • Yuko Takeuchi *Tomoko Oishi* • Hitomi Sato *Masami Kurahashi* ■ *Dir* Hideo Nakata • *Scr* Hiroshi Takahashi, from the novel by Koji Suzuki

The Ring ★★★ 15
Horror thriller   2002 · US · Colour · 110min

The words "Hollywood remake" may fill film fans with dread but director Gore Verbinski's version of Hideo Nakata's Japanese horror classic is a surprisingly good effort that retains much of the unnerving, creepy atmosphere of the original. An unlabelled videotape is in circulation, bringing death after seven days to anyone who watches it. One of its victims is the niece of journalist Naomi Watts, who decides to uncover the source of the tape and find out if the "curse" is real. AS DVD

Naomi Watts *Rachel Keller* • Martin Henderson *Noah* • David Dorfman *Aidan* • Brian Cox (1) *Richard Morgan* • Jane Alexander *Dr Grasnik* • Lindsay Frost *Ruth* ■ *Dir* Gore Verbinski • *Scr* Ehren Kruger, from the 1997 film, from the novel by Koji Suzuki

Ring 2 ★★ 12
Horror   1998 · Jpn · Colour · 95min

Hideo Nakata's *Ring* (1997) has acquired something of a cult status in Japan, where it also achieved record box-office grosses. Pop star Miki Nakatani returns for this less critically admired sequel, which spends too much time tying up its predecessor's loose ends and not enough developing its own storyline. The cursed video cassette is still causing mayhem, but the strict linearity of the narrative removes much of the unease that made the original so chilling. Followed by *Ring 0* in 2000. DP Japanese +subtitles. DVD

Miki Nakatani *Mai Takano* • Rikiya Otaka *Yoichi Asakawa* • Nanako Matsushima *Reiko Asakawa* • Hitomi Sato *Masami Kurahashi* • Kenjiro Ishimaru *Omuta* • Kyoko Fukada *Kanae Sawaguchi* • Hiroyuki Sanada *Ryuji Takayama* ■ *Dir* Hideo Nakata • *Scr* Koji Suzuki, Hiroshi Takahashi, from the *Ring* series of novels by Koji Suzuki

The Ring Two ★★ 15
Horror thriller   2004 · US · Colour · 104min

In Hideo Nakata's sequel to the US remake of his Japanese horror, Naomi Watts and her son have moved from Seattle to Oregon to escape the nightmare of the cursed videotape, but the vengeful ghost of Samara follows. Bearing no relation to the convoluted Japanese sequel *Ring 2*, and dropping its urban legend hook far too quickly, this illogical and long-winded story ends up as a soggy mess, despite Nakata's elegantly choreographed shocks. The next instalment, *Rings*, is due in early 2016. AJ DVD

Naomi Watts *Rachel Keller* • Simon Baker (1) *Max Rourke* • David Dorfman *Aidan Keller* • Elizabeth Perkins *Dr Emma Temple* • Gary Cole *Martin Savide* • Sissy Spacek *Evelyn* • Ryan Merriman *Jake* • Emily VanCamp *Emily* ■ *Dir* Hideo Nakata • *Scr* Ehren Kruger, from the *Ring* series of novels by Koji Suzuki

Ring 0 ★★★ 15
Horror   2000 · Jpn · Colour and BW · 98min

It doesn't match the clever conceit, haunting atmosphere or visual chill of *Ring* but director Norio Tsuruta's second sequel to that Japanese horror sensation is far better than *Ring 2*. This spookily atmospheric, if confusing, episode charts the reasons why the demon Sadako now terrorises Tokyo teens' videotapes. The slow-building suspense does test the patience at times. AJ Japanese +subtitles. DVD

Yukie Nakama *Sadako Yamamura* • Seiichi Tanabe *Hiroshi Toyama* • Yoshiko Tanaka *Akiko Miyaji* • Atsuko Takahata *Kaoru Arima* • Kumiko Asou *Etsuko Tachihara* • Takeshi Wakamatsu *Shigemori Isamu* ■ *Dir* Norio Tsuruta • *Scr* Hiroshi Takahashi, from the short story *Lemon Heart* by Koji Suzuki

Ring of Bright Water ★★★ U
Drama   1969 · UK · Colour · 102min

Born Free stars Bill Travers and Virginia McKenna yet again allow themselves to be upstaged by an adorable creature in this delightful adaptation of Gavin Maxwell's bestseller. While Mij the otter hasn't the majestic presence of Elsa the lioness, he'll still win the hearts of children with his mischievous escapades, whether careering around a cramped city-flat, splashing in his private swimming tank or romping in the snow. There's even room for a few tears. DP DVD

Bill Travers *Graham Merrill* • Virginia McKenna *Mary MacKenzie* • Peter Jeffrey *Colin Clifford* • Roddy McMillan *Bus driver* • Jameson Clark *Storekeeper* • Jean Taylor-Smith *Sarah Chambers* • Helena Gloag *Flora Elrich* ■ *Dir* Jack Couffer • *Scr* Jack Couffer, Bill Travers, from the book by Gavin Maxwell

Ring of Fire ★★★
Action adventure   1961 · US · Colour · 90min

David Janssen stars as an Oregon deputy sheriff who arrests and is then kidnapped by three juvenile delinquents. While the plot's twists and turns take some believing, the pace is fast enough and the action spectacular enough to make such considerations redundant. Directed, produced, written and edited by Andrew and Virginia Stone, a husband-and-wife team whose work still awaits critical "rediscovery", the picture has the old-fashioned virtues of a gutsy adventure. AT

David Janssen *Sergeant Steve Walsh* • Joyce Taylor *Bobbie Adams* • Frank Gorshin *Frank Henderson* • Joel Marston *Deputy Pringle* • James Johnson *Roy Anderson* • Ron Myron *Sheriff Niles* ■ *Dir/Scr* Andrew L Stone

Ring of Fire ★★ 18
Martial arts drama   1991 · US · Colour · 92min

Don "The Dragon" Wilson plays Johnny Wu, a young medical intern with great martial arts skills who falls in love with a Caucasian woman (Maria Ford), to the disapproval of her friends. After all the fights are done, will these star-crossed lovers be together? Good-natured and endearing. ST DVD

Don "The Dragon" Wilson *Johnny Wu* • Eric Lee Kwong • Dale Edmund Jacoby *Brad* • Steven Vincent Leigh *Terry* • Maria Ford *Julie* ■ *Dir* Richard W Munchkin • *Scr* Richard W Munchkin, Jake Jacobs

Ring of Spies ★★★ PG
Spy drama based on a true story
1963 · UK · BW · 86min

Throughout his career, Frank Launder proved himself to be just as capable of turning out a nail-biting thriller as he was of crafting a chortle-worthy comedy. For once, separated from his usual partner Sidney Gilliatt (although the latter's brother Leslie acted as producer), Launder and co-writer Peter Barnes capably retell the story of the Portland spy ring, whose activities prompted "Reds under the bed" scare stories in the popular press. The docudramatic style rather undermines director Robert Tronson's attempts to build suspense. DP DVD

Bernard Lee *Henry Houghton* • William Sylvester *Gordon Lonsdale* • Margaret Tyzack *Elizabeth Gee* • David Kossoff *Peter Kroger* • Nancy Nevinson *Helen Kroger* • Thorley Walters *Commander Winters* • Gillian Lewis *Marjorie Shaw* • Brian Nissen *Lieutenant Downes* ■ *Dir* Robert Tronson • *Scr* Frank Launder, Peter Barnes

Ring of Steel ★★ 15
Martial arts action   1994 · US · Colour · 89min

A disgraced fencing champion joins an illegal swordfighting club – the Ring of Steel. Lots of fights follow and the champion finds out that the Ring exacts a price from its combatants that's too high to pay. The plot is simple and fairly compelling, even if much of the acting is sub-par. A touch of surrealism is added to the proceedings by the casting of beefy Joe Don Baker as the man who runs the whole show. ST DVD

Joe Don Baker *Man in Black* • Carol Alt *Tanya* • Robert Chapin *Alex Freyer* • Darlene Vogel *Elena* • Gary Kasper *Jack* • Jim Pirri *Brian* ■ *Dir* David Frost • *Scr* Robert Chapin

The Ringer ★★ 12
Sports comedy 2005 · US · Colour · 90min

A politically incorrect comedy set at the Special Olympics, this stars *Jackass* alumnus Johnny Knoxville, playing an able-bodied guy with a sudden need for cash. His amoral gambler uncle (Brian Cox) suggests that he pose as a mentally disabled athlete to win at the Special Olympics and clean up at the bookies. The film offers a surprisingly tender portrait of the mentally disabled, but perhaps a fear of causing offence, combined with weak direction and Knoxville's style of physical comedy, prevent this from being funnier than it is. LF *Swearing.* DVD

Johnny Knoxville *Steve Barker* • Brian Cox (1) *Gary Barker* • Katherine Heigl *Lynn Sheridan* • Jed Rees *Glen* • Bill Chott *Thomas* • Edward Barbanell *Billy* • Leonard Earl Howze *Mark* • Geoffrey Arend *Winston* ■ *Dir* Barry W Blaustein • *Scr* Ricky Blitt

Ringmaster ★ 18
Comedy 1998 · US · Colour · 86min

In this contrived and uninvolving comedy, Jerry Springer plays a talk-show host Jerry Farrelly, a cool observer of the lowlifes who appear as his guests. But everything rings hollow in this thinly disguised *Jerry Springer Show*, from the bed-hopping antics of Molly Hagan's trailer-trash family to Wendy Raquel Robinson's problems with shiftless boyfriend Michael Jai White. DP DVD

Jerry Springer *Jerry Farrelly* • Jaime Pressly *Angel Zorzak* • William McNamara *Troy Davenport* • Molly Hagan *Connie Zorzak* • John Capodice *Mel Riley* • Wendy Raquel Robinson *Starletta* • Michael Jai White *Demond* ■ *Dir* Neil Abramson • *Scr* Jon Bernstein

Rings on Her Fingers ★★★ U
Comedy 1942 · US · BW · 86min

After the popular and critical success of *The Lady Eve*, Henry Fonda's portrayal of naivety was used again as the springboard for a wily female's confidence trick, only this time beautiful Gene Tierney is the fleecer who falls for her victim. There's a regrettable coldness about the Fonda/Tierney partnership, but Laird Cregar and Spring Byington are very watchable as Tierney's crooked partners, and the movie is funny and absorbing in its first half. Unfortunately, it runs out of steam as Tierney reforms her ways. TS

Henry Fonda *John Wheeler* • Gene Tierney *Susan Miller* • Laird Cregar *Warren* • John Shepperd [Shepperd Strudwick] *Tod Fenwick* • Spring Byington *Mrs Maybelle Worthington* • Frank Orth *Kellogg* • Henry Stephenson *Colonel Prentice* ■ *Dir* Rouben Mamoulian • *Scr* Ken Englund, from a story by Robert Pirosh, Joseph Schrank

The Rink ★★★★ U
Silent action comedy 1916 · US · BW · 20min

In his eighth short for Mutual, Charles Chaplin plays both waiter and skater in this celebration of the roller-skating craze that swept Europe and America during the late 19th and early 20th centuries. At once victim and dominant force, he evades heavy Eric Campbell to win the hand of Edna Purviance with a ferocious cascade of pratfalls and near-miss pirouettes. This typically hilarious piece of sophisticated slapstick was based on a routine dating back to his vaudeville days with Fred Karno. TH DVD

Charles Chaplin *A waiter, posing as Sir Cecil Seltzer* • Edna Purviance *The girl* • James T Kelley *Her father* • Eric Campbell *Mr Stout* ■ *Dir/Scr* Charles Chaplin

Rio ★★★★ U
Animated comedy adventure 2011 · US · Colour · 91min

As irresistible as the samba and bossa nova rhythms that pulsate throughout, this sunny animation from the *Ice Age* team is a vibrantly colourful and hugely enjoyable eye-catcher. Jesse Eisenberg voices Blu, a rare but neurotic pet macaw with a fear of flying, who's taken back to Rio from Minnesota to mate with the last female of his species, feisty Jewel (Anne Hathaway). Brazilian director Carlos Saldanha ensures his flock of engaging characters (including a villainous cockatoo and a constantly drooling bulldog) soar from Busby Berkeley-style beginning to spectacular carnival finale. There are the usual life lessons to be learned, but under Saldanha's light touch they seamlessly blend with all the airborne action and riotous musical interludes. AJ DVD Blu SD

Jesse Eisenberg *Blu* • Anne Hathaway *Jewel* • Rodrigo Santoro *Tulio* • Leslie Mann *Linda* • Will i am *Pedro* • Jamie Foxx *Nico* • Jake T Austin *Fernando* • Jemaine Clement *Nigel* ■ *Dir* Carlos Saldanha • *Scr* Don Rhymer, Joshua Sternin, Jeffrey Ventimilia, Sam Harper, from a story by Carlos Saldanha, Earl Richey Jones, Todd Jones

Rio 2 ★★★ U
Animated comedy adventure 2014 · US · Colour · 96min

In a more-is-less sequel overflowing with songs and slapstick, Jewel (voiced by Anne Hathaway), who's thrilled not to be endangered any more after her exploits in *Rio*, convinces her city slicker beau Blu (Jesse Eisenberg) to rediscover their rainforest roots when a flock of blue macaws is discovered deep in the Amazon. As the birds try to defend their habitat against illegal loggers, it's the same mix of colourfully frantic action, sharp sight gags and catchy musical numbers. AJ *In English, Portuguese.* DVD SD SP

Jesse Eisenberg *Blu* • Anne Hathaway *Jewel* • Jemaine Clement *Nigel* • Will i am *Pedro* • Jamie Foxx *Nico* • Bruno Mars *Roberto* ■ *Dir* Carlos Saldanha • *Scr* Don Rhymer, Carlos Kotkin, Jenny Bicks, Yoni Brenner, from a story by Carlos Saldanha, from Saldanha's characters

Rio Bravo ★★★★★ PG
Western 1958 · US · Colour · 135min

Underrated at the time of its release, this majestically paced western is one of the finest achievements of the genre, and stands as a career-best for many of its participants, while its length and simplistic plot mask a work of depth and artistry. Originally intended by director Howard Hawks as a riposte to the liberal *High Noon*, the quality and class of this movie owe little to what had gone before, save some dialogue lifted from Hawks's earlier *To Have and Have Not*. This is a definitive study of male camaraderie, particularly in the wordless opening sequence as John Wayne attempts to preserve the drunken Dean Martin's dignity. The casting is perfect and the sense of fun contagious. Superb Technicolor photography and a Dimitri Tiomkin score provide the icing on a very impressive cake. TS DVD Blu

John Wayne *John T Chance* • Dean Martin *Dude* • Ricky Nelson *Colorado Ryan* • Angie Dickinson *Feathers* • Walter Brennan *Stumpy* • Ward Bond *Pat Wheeler* • John Russell *Nathan Burdette* ■ *Dir* Howard Hawks • *Scr* Jules Furthman, Leigh Brackett, from a story by Barbara Hawks McCampbell • *Cinematographer* Russell Harlan

Rio Breaks ★★★ 12A
Documentary 2009 · US · Colour · 84min

As Justin Mitchell reveals in this affectionate but always clear-sighted documentary, riding the waves offers a credible route out of poverty for Rio de Janeiro teenagers. The sun-kissed footage of the kids seizing the opportunity to escape from the hardships of their home lives may not be particularly spectacular, but their stories are laced with poignancy. DP *Portuguese, English +subtitles. Brief swearing, drug references.* ■ *Dir* Justin Mitchell • *Scr* Justin Mitchell, Vince Medeiros

Rio Conchos ★★
Western 1964 · US · Colour · 106min

This is a violent near remake (uncredited) of *The Comancheros*, a reasonable hit for 20th Century-Fox in 1961, sadly this time without John Wayne, though Richard Boone is a sturdy, if stolid, substitute. It is competently handled by director Gordon Douglas, and is interesting for the feature film debut of American football star Jim Brown. TS

Richard Boone *Lassiter* • Stuart Whitman *Captain Haven* • Tony Franciosa [Anthony Franciosa] *Rodriguez* • Wende Wagner *Sally* • Edmond O'Brien *Colonel Theron Pardee* • Warner Anderson *Colonel Wagner* • Jim Brown *Sgt Ben Franklyn* ■ *Dir* Gordon Douglas • *Scr* Joseph Landon, Clair Huffaker, from the novel *Guns of the Rio Conchos* by Huffaker

Rio Grande ★★★★★ U
Western 1950 · US · BW · 104min

This great western - the third film in John Ford's cavalry trilogy, following *Fort Apache* and *She Wore a Yellow Ribbon* - tells the story of a daring off-the-record solution to Indian raids from across the border. It also features a powerful romantic relationship between John Wayne and Maureen O'Hara as the fort commander and his long-separated wife. O'Hara was the strongest leading lady Wayne ever had and almost his match in stubborn pride (they co-starred in four more films). Here, she re-enters Wayne's life seeking to protect their son (Claude Jarman Jr), a private sent out west to serve under him. Once again, Ford creates a stirring picture of the Old West - if this wasn't the way it was, it's the way it should have been. AE DVD

John Wayne *Lt Colonel Yorke* • Maureen O'Hara *Mrs Yorke* • Ben Johnson (1) *Trooper Tyree* • Claude Jarman Jr *Trooper Jeff Yorke* • Harry Carey Jr *Trooper Boone* • Chill Wills *Dr Wilkins* • J Carrol Naish *General Sheridan* • Victor McLaglen *Quincannon* ■ *Dir* John Ford • *Scr* James Kevin McGuinness

Rio Lobo ★★★ PG
Western 1970 · US · Colour · 109min

It may be a mite saddle-weary, but John Wayne's last film with director Howard Hawks has a wonderful sense of western occasion, together with a sardonic humour that lights up a listless story. Jorge Rivero and Robert's son, Chris Mitchum, play the Confederate looters snatching Union gold, and Wayne is the colonel trying to find the traitor who's feeding information to the robbers. Meanwhile, wild-eyed Jack Elam looks askance at the whole business. Its leisurely, but the characters and circumstance make a real impression. TH DVD Blu

John Wayne *Colonel Cord McNally* • Jennifer O'Neill *Shasta Delaney* • Jack Elam *Phillips* • Chris Mitchum [Christopher Mitchum] *Sergeant Tuscarora* • Jorge Rivero *Captain Pierre Cordona* • Victor French *Ketcham* ■ *Dir* Howard Hawks • *Scr* Leigh Brackett, Burton Wohl, from a story by Burton Wohl

Rio Rita ★★★
Musical revue 1929 · US · BW and Colour · 140min

Little more than canned theatre, with a static camera filming the spectacular Ziegfeld show of the 1920s, this early film musical, which took 24 days to shoot, is, nevertheless, of historical interest. The slim plot has dashing John Boles as a Texas ranger on the trail of a notorious bandit. He loves Bebe Daniels, in the title role, but boy loses girl (temporarily), when he suspects her brother of being the outlaw. Tiresome Bert Wheeler and Robert Woolsey provide what is called "comic relief". The numbers are good and the finale is in pleasing two-strip Technicolor. RB

Georges Renavent *Gen Ravinoff* • Eva Rosita *Carmen* • Bebe Daniels *Rita Ferguson* • John Boles *Capt Jim Stewart* • Don Alvarado *Roberto Ferguson* • Dorothy Lee *Dolly* • Bert Wheeler *Chick* • Robert Woolsey *Lovett* ■ *Dir* Luther Reed • *Scr* Luther Reed, Russell Mack, from the musical by Guy Bolton, Fred Thompson

Rio Rita ★★ U
Wartime musical comedy 1942 · US · BW · 90min

MGM borrowed Abbott and Costello from Universal and placed them in this remake of the 1929 film. The updated version, featuring Nazis and saboteurs, was a bit of an odd fish and didn't serve Abbott and Costello too well - the pair find themselves squeezing their comedy routines in between the love story of John Carroll and Kathryn Grayson. Predictably the film's best moments come when the comedy duo do their stuff. DF

Bud Abbott *Doc* • Lou Costello *Wishy* • Kathryn Grayson *Rita Winslow* • John Carroll *Ricardo Montera* • Patricia Dane *Lucille Brunswick* • Tom Conway *Maurice Craindall* ■ *Dir* S Sylvan Simon • *Scr* Richard Connell, Gladys Lehman, John Grant

Riot ★★
Prison drama 1969 · US · Colour · 96min

Produced by master of schlock William Castle, this jailhouse drama was filmed inside Arizona State Prison, with the real warden and real prisoners appearing as extras. While the warden's away, Gene Hackman leads a revolt and takes over the prison's isolation wing, holding several guards hostage. Jim Brown is a prisoner who thinks Hackman has made a big mistake. Strong performances from the leads and a half-decent script place this film a notch above similar exploitation fare. AT

Jim Brown *Cully Briston* • Gene Hackman *Red Fletcher* • Ben Carruthers *Surefoot* • Mike Kellin *Bugsy* • Gerald S O'Loughlin *Grossman* ■ *Dir* Buzz Kulik • *Scr* James Poe, from the novel *The Riot* by Frank Elli

The Riot Club ★★★ 15
Drama 2014 · UK · Colour · 107min

Privilege and peer pressure amid the dreaming spires of Oxford set the tone for this drama about university students who are members of the elite boys' club of the title. New recruits Max Irons and Sam Claflin are ushered into the club's world of debauchery, but the excesses get out of hand after one particularly wild behind-closed-doors dinner. Director Lone Scherfig (*An Education*) paints on a broader canvas than that of screenwriter Laura Wade's original claustrophobic stage play, *Posh*. Consequently, the action takes a while to get into gear and the film's examination of wealth and class is less tightly focused. TeS DVD Blu

Sam Claflin *Alistair* • Max Irons *Miles* • Douglas Booth *Harry* • Jessica Brown Findlay *Rachel* • Holliday Grainger *Lauren* • Freddie Fox *James* • Tom Hollander *Jeremy* • Natalie Dormer *Charlie* ■ *Dir* Lone Scherfig • *Scr* Laura Wade, from her play *Posh*

Riot in Cell Block 11 ★★★★ 15
Prison drama 1954 · US · BW · 80min

Don Siegel emerged as more than just a Hollywood journeyman director with this hard-hitting, realistic prison picture, which presents a credible account of the riot and the conditions that caused it. Warden Emile Meyer could be accused of being overly sympathetic to the inmates' demands and Frank Faylen is far too dogmatic as the uncompromising senator. But, otherwise, the characters ring true, with Neville Brand's ringleader-turned-scapegoat particularly well realised. Russell Harlan's brooding photography heightens both the tension and the realism, and this remains a powerful indictment of the penal system. DP *Violence.*

Neville Brand *Dunn* • Emile Meyer *Warden* • Frank Faylen *Haskell* • Leo Gordon *Carnie* • Robert Osterloh *Colonel* • Paul Frees *Monroe* • Don Keefer *Reporter* • Alvy Moore *Gator* • Dabbs Greer *Schuyler* • Whit Bissell *Snader* ■ *Dir* Don Siegel • *Scr* Richard Collins

The Ripening Seed ★★★★
Romantic drama 1953 · Fr · BW · 110min

Condemned by the Catholic Church and banned in various parts of the world, this adaptation of Colette's erotic novel may have seemed daring back in 1953. But today it stands simply as a delicate - and often touching - account of a young man's initiation into the delights of physical love. Under Claude Autant-Lara's watchful eye, Pierre-Michel Beck is suitably bashful as the 16-year-old, who exploits a seaside holiday to spare his childhood sweetheart (Nicole Berger) the humiliation of untutored lovemaking. However, it's Edwige Feuillère's exquisite performance, as the ethereal woman in white, that gives the film its soul. DP French +subtitles.

Nicole Berger *Ann* • Pierre-Michel Beck *Phil* • Edwige Feuillère *Madame Dalleray* ■ *Dir* Claude Autant-Lara • *Scr* Pierre Bost, Jean Aurenche, Claude Autant-Lara, from the novel by Colette

Ripley's Game ★★★ 15
Crime thriller
2002 · It/UK/US · Colour · 105min

John Malkovich portrays charming sociopath Tom Ripley in this languid adaptation of the Patricia Highsmith novel. Ripley is now living a cultured, comfortable life in Italy, procuring rare art for collectors by rather dubious methods. When a boorish British associate (Ray Winstone, in an undemanding performance) asks him to bump off a troublesome rival, Malkovich sets himself a diverting challenge: to recruit terminally ill picture-framer Dougray Scott to be the assassin. Despite Malkovich's silky smooth performance, the film doesn't completely succeed owing to implausible plotting and ineffectual direction. JC DVD

John Malkovich *Tom Ripley* • Dougray Scott *Jonathan Trevanny* • Ray Winstone *Reeves* • Lena Headey *Sarah Trevanny* • Chiara Caselli *Luisa Ripley* ■ *Dir* Liliana Cavani • *Scr* Charles McKeown, Liliana Cavani, from the novel by Patricia Highsmith

Riptide ★★★
Romantic drama   1934 · US · BW · 92min

The unusual meeting of British aristocrat Herbert Marshall and Park Avenue party girl with a past Norma Shearer leads to an idyllic love affair then marriage and a child. However, when the wife is caught up in a scandal in Cannes, through the drunken antics of an old flame (Robert Montgomery), the husband is consumed with jealousy and wants a divorce. The film is an intriguing, but sometimes uneasy, mix of romance, farce, arch comedy of manners and moral dilemma. Shearer carries it off superbly, Montgomery (as so often) irritates. Very 1930s. RK

Norma Shearer *Lady Mary Rexford* • Robert Montgomery *Tommy Trent* • Herbert Marshall *Lord Philip Rexford* • Mrs Patrick Campbell *Lady Hetty Riversleigh* • Richard "Skeets" Gallagher *Erskine* • Ralph Forbes *David Fenwick* • Lilyan Tashman *Sylvia* • Arthur Jarrett *Percy* ■ *Dir/Scr* Edmund Goulding

The Rise ★★★ 15
Crime thriller   2012 · UK · Colour · 104min

First-time writer/director Rowan Athale delivers a British crime thriller with a twist: the gangsters here aren't cunning cockneys but callow northerners. Our hero is ex-con Harvey (Luke Treadaway), who we first see bloodied, back in a cell and being interrogated by world-weary detective Timothy Spall. A series of flashbacks shows why this young pretender and his endearingly half-hearted partners-in-crime (*Misfits* star Iwan Rheon, Gerard Kearns and Matthew Lewis), dared to take on the local drug lord (a typically menacing Neil Maskell). The end result is a slick, satisfying debut. CW Violence, swearing, drug abuse. DVD

Luke Treadaway *Harvey* • Iwan Rheon *Dempsey* • Gerard Kearns *Charlie* • Matthew Lewis *Dodd* • Timothy Spall *DI West* • Vanessa Kirby *Nicola* ■ *Dir/Scr* Rowan Athale • *Cinematographer* Stuart Bentley

The Rise and Fall of Legs Diamond ★★★★ PG
Biographical crime drama
1960 · US · BW · 97min

This is a sharply observed and crisply photographed attempt by Warner Bros to revive its gangster cycle. Budd Boetticher, better known for his Randolph Scott westerns, does a terrific job of directing the ice-cold Ray Danton in the leading role, and of sustaining a thoroughly amoral atmosphere on a tight schedule and a very low budget. The black-and-white

cinematography by Lucien Ballard is also a major plus. Watch out for an early appearance by Warren Oates and a glimpse of Dyan Cannon. TS

Ray Danton *Jack "Legs" Diamond* • Karen Steele *Alice Shiffer* • Elaine Stewart *Monica Drake* • Jesse White *Leo Bremer* • Simon Oakland *Lieutenant Moody* • Robert Lowery *Arnold Rothstein* • Judson Pratt *Fats Walsh* • Warren Oates *Eddie Diamond* • Dyan Cannon *Dixie* ■ *Dir* Budd Boetticher • *Scr* Joseph Landon • *Cinematographer* Lucien Ballard

The Rise and Rise of Michael Rimmer ★★ 15
Satirical political comedy
1970 · UK · Colour · 98min

Having played a minor role in Kevin Billington's debut feature, *Interlude*, John Cleese reteamed with the director for this patchy political satire. In addition to co-starring, Cleese and fellow Python, Graham Chapman contributed to the script, which charts the meteoric rise of efficiency expert Peter Cook, who bluffs his way into high office. Although the gags gradually fall flat, there are several scathing swipes at the British character and the nature of power. DP DVD

Peter Cook *Michael Rimmer* • Denholm Elliott *Peter Niss* • Ronald Fraser *Tom Hutchinson* • Arthur Lowe *Ferret* • Vanessa Howard *Patricia Cartwright* • George A Cooper (2) *Blackett* • Graham Crowden *Bishop of Cowley* • Harold Pinter *Steven Hench* • James Cossins *Crodder* • Richard Pearson (1) *Wilting* • Ronnie Corbett *Interviewer* • Dennis Price *Fairburn* • John Cleese *Pumer* • Julian Glover *Col Moffat* ■ *Dir* Kevin Billington • *Scr* Peter Cook, John Cleese, Graham Chapman, Kevin Billington

The Rise of Catherine the Great ★★ U
Historical drama   1934 · UK · BW · 84min

British-based movie mogul Alexander Korda produced this historical saga, hoping it would repeat the transatlantic success of *The Private Life of Henry VIII*. But it's all rather stuffy and lacks the humour of the previous year's royal romp. The director is Paul Czinner, whose wife, Elisabeth Bergner, plays the Tsarina rather glumly, and Douglas Fairbanks Jr is the rakish Grand Duke who quickly goes off his troika. AT

Elisabeth Bergner *Catherine II* • Douglas Fairbanks Jr *Grand Duke Peter* • Flora Robson *Empress Elizabeth* • Gerald du Maurier *Lecocq* • Irene Vanbrugh *Princess Anhalt-Zerbst* • Griffith Jones *Grigory Orlov* ■ *Dir* Paul Czinner • *Scr* Marjorie Deans, Arthur Wimperis, from the play *The Czarina* by Lajos Biró, Melchior Lengyel

Rise of the Footsoldier ★ 18
Crime thriller   2006 · UK · Colour · 114min

Like *Essex Boys* (2000), this British thriller focuses on the real-life Rettendon Range Rover murders. Based on the memoirs of Carlton Leach (played by Ricci Harnett), a former football hooligan turned Essex villain, it charts his violent rise from the terraces to the underworld like a latter-day take on the 1930s gangster movie. But where the old Warner Bros pictures had a moral, this is an empty piece of Neanderthal posturing that revels in gratuitous violence. Aimed at male viewers looking for a testosterone fix, it's thoroughly depressing not only in its brutality but also in its gloating attempt to deify its thuggish antihero. The supporting cast includes familiar faces like former *EastEnders* Craig Fairbrass and Billy Murray, none of whom brings any sense of realism or credibility to the belligerent bravado. JR DVD

Ricci Harnett *Carlton Leach* • Craig Fairbrass *Pat Tate* • Roland Manookian *Craig Rolfe* • Terry Stone *Tony Tucker* • Coralie Rose *Denny* ■ *Dir* Julian Gilbey • *Scr* Julian Gilbey, William Gilbey

Rise of the Guardians ★★★★ PG
Animated adventure   2012 · US · Colour · 97min

This beautifully rendered and energetic revisionist fairy tale is destined to become definitive holiday entertainment for all the

family. A sort of child-friendly *Avengers Assemble* that focuses on iconic figures from childhood, it sees Jack Frost (voiced by Chris Pine) get serious when chosen to join a tattooed Santa Claus (Alec Baldwin), a confrontational Easter Bunny (Hugh Jackman), a flirty Tooth Fairy (Isla Fisher) and the Sandman to overthrow bogeyman Pitch (Jude Law), who's trying to get the children of the world to stop believing in them. It's a classic good v evil saga, revived through a vivid old-fashioned storybook aesthetic with an impressive and often breathtaking sense of scope and scale. AJ
DVD Blu-ray 3D

Chris Pine *Jack Frost* • Alec Baldwin *North* • Jude Law *Pitch* • Isla Fisher *Tooth* • Hugh Jackman *Bunny* ■ *Dir* Peter Ramsey • *Scr* David Lindsay-Abaire, from William Joyce's illustrated children's book *The Guardians of Childhood*

Rise of the Planet of the Apes ★★★★ 12
Science-fiction action adventure
2011 · US · Colour · 100min

This fresh look at an enduring franchise focuses on one chimpanzee, Caesar (a combination of Andy Serkis and CGI), taken into the home of scientist James Franco after his Alzheimer's experiments are shut down. Caesar's intelligence multiplies as he continues to receive the drug, but a violent attack results in him being impounded with apes of normal brain power, where he begins to plot his escape. The thrilling story is occasionally let down by clunky dialogue and hammy acting (John Lithgow, Brian Cox), but they're minor niggles when held against the breathtaking action sequences, most notably a pitched battle on San Francisco's Golden Gate Bridge. TeS DVD Blu-ray

James Franco *Will Rodman* • Freida Pinto *Caroline Aranha* • John Lithgow *Charles Rodman* • Brian Cox (1) *John Landon* • David Oyelowo *Steven Jacobs* • Tom Felton *Dodge Landon* • Andy Serkis *Caesar* ■ *Dir* Rupert Wyatt • *Scr* Rick Jaffa, Amanda Silver, Jamie Moss, from the novel *Planet of the Apes* by Pierre Boulle • *Cinematographer* Andrew Lesnie

The Rise to Power of Louis XIV ★★★★ U
Historical drama   1966 · Fr · BW · 94min

Roberto Rossellini explores the intrigues of Louis XIV's court, without once threatening to turn this docudrama into a stylised history lesson. Employing tracks and zooms to animate the elaborate tableaux, he reveals how the Sun King tamed his treacherous nobility and turned the uncertainties of his regency into a regal dictatorship based at Versailles. This engrossing film (which was originally made for TV) is the perfect riposte to those who denounce costume dramas for their empty spectacle. DP French +subtitles.

Jean-Marie Patte *Louis XIV* • Raymond Jourdan *Colbert* • Silvagni *Cardinal Mazarin* • Katharina Renn *Anne of Austria* • Dominique Vincent *Mme du Plessis* • Pierre Barrat *Fouquet* ■ *Dir* Roberto Rossellini • *Scr* Jean Gruault, Philippe Erlanger

Risen ★★ 12
Biographical sports drama
2010 · UK · Colour · 121min

This pedestrian biopic tells the story of Howard Winstone, Welsh boxing legend and featherweight champion of the world. Stuart Brennan stars as the popular pugilist, a miner's son who battles adversity in and out of the ring. Neil Jones's film tells Winstone's story with soft-focus intimacy, but the re-creation of the 1960s backdrop on a tight budget sadly never allows the director to unleash the epic sweep this against-the-odds yarn really requires. Brennan's subdued performance in the lead role finds little traction in the domestic scenes with Grainne Joughin as Winstone's long-suffering wife, while the brutal fight scenes – full contact bouts inventively shot with cameras attached to boxers' gloves and bodies – offer little compensation for the arid drama. JR

Stuart Brennan *Howard Winstone* • John Noble *Eddie Thomas* • Shane Richie *Mike Barrett* • Erik Morales *Vicente Saldivar* • Grainne Joughin *Benita Winstone* • Helen Griffin *Katie Winstone* ■ *Dir* Neil Jones • *Scr* Neil Jones, Stuart Brennan

Risen ★★ 12A
Biblical drama   2016 · US · Colour · 107min

Joseph Fiennes, Tom Felton and Peter Firth go Roman in an earnest biblical drama that proves, more than anything else, that Hollywood believes there's a market in faith films – *The Passion of the Christ* having set a blockbusting precedent. Fiennes and Felton play officers ordered to look into the disappearance of Christ's body after the Crucifixion. Director Kevin Reynolds applies a glossy finish that elevates the film, but this otherwise clunky offering is aimed squarely at the American Bible Belt, so don't expect any questions raised. DA
DVD Blu-ray

Joseph Fiennes *Clavius* • Tom Felton *Lucius* • Peter Firth *Pontius Pilate* • María Botto *Mary Magdalene* • Cliff Curtis *Yeshua/Jesus* ■ *Dir* Kevin Reynolds • *Scr* Paul Aiello, Kevin Reynolds

Rising Damp ★★ PG
Comedy   1980 · UK · Colour · 94min

The impish touch of Richard Beckinsale is sorely missed from this ill-advised movie version of the much-loved TV sitcom. Eric Chappell, who wrote the series and the original stage play about Rigsby the scheming landlord, overwrites to compensate, and the film suffers from too many padded scenes and too few hilarious situations, despite star turns from Leonard Rossiter and Frances de la Tour as hapless Rigsby and the sophisticated object of his unrequited love, Miss Jones. AC DVD

Leonard Rossiter *Rigsby* • Frances de la Tour *Miss Jones* • Don Warrington *Philip* • Christopher Strauli *John* • Denholm Elliott *Seymour* • Carrie Jones *Sandra* • Glynn Edwards *Cooper* • John Cater *Bert* ■ *Dir* Joe McGrath [Joseph McGrath] • *Scr* Eric Chappell, from his TV series

The Rising of the Moon ★★
Comedy drama   1957 · Ire · BW · 81min

A minor late offering from John Ford, this anthology of three stories was made in Ireland, scene of his own ancestral roots. More a collection of sketches, paying largely comic but occasionally poignant homage to a vanishing way of life, the movie is played with uninhibited gusto by an A-list of Irish actors. Dated, and too whimsical for an era when both Irish history and its cinematic treatment have moved on, the film still evokes a strong sense of place and culture. RK

Tyrone Power *Introduction* • Cyril Cusack *Inspector Michael Dillon* • Noel Purcell *Dan O'Flaherty the old man* • Jack MacGowran *Mickey J, the poteen maker* • Jimmy O'Dea *Porter* • Tony Quinn *Station master* • Paul Farrell *Engine driver* • Denis O'Dea *The police sergeant* • Eileen Crowe *His wife* ■ *Dir* John Ford • *Scr* Frank S Nugent, from the following three sources: the short story *The Majesty of the Law* by Frank O'Connor, the play *A Minute's Wait* by Martin J McHugh, the play by Lady Augusta Gregory

Rising Sun ★★★ 18
Thriller   1993 · US · Colour · 124min

Michael Crichton's novel caused a stir for its portrait of Japan as a tentacular monster, devouring every American corporation in its path. Sean Connery brings his inimitable presence to the cop investigating a politically sensitive murder in the offices of a Japanese company in Los Angeles. Connery's sidekick is played by Wesley Snipes, and there's quirky character support from Harvey Keitel. Often exciting, occasionally brutal and kinky, but still a bit of a letdown. AT Violence, swearing, sex scenes, nudity. DVD Blu-ray

Sean Connery *John Connor* • Wesley Snipes *Web Smith* • Harvey Keitel *Tom Graham* • Cary-Hiroyuki Tagawa *Eddie Sakamura* • Kevin Anderson *Bob Richmond* • Mako *Yoshida-San* • Ray Wise *Senator John Morton* • Stan Egi *Ishihara* • Stan Shaw *Phillips* • Tia Carrere *Jingo Asakuma* • Steve Buscemi *Willy "The Weasel"*

R

Wilhelm ▪ *Dir* Philip Kaufman • *Scr* Philip Kaufman, Michael Crichton, Michael Backes, from the novel by Crichton

Risk ★★★ 18

Crime drama 2000 · Aus · Colour · 89min

Director Allan White adds a little dark humour and saucy seduction to this thriller, giving it a distinctly *noirish* feel. The insurance scam is sketchily outlined and the breakneck chase finale feels tacked on, but Tom Long again impresses (after *The Dish*) as another eager milquetoast, only here he rapidly develops a backbone, as he counters the corrupt schemes of boss Bryan Brown and his shady lawyer lover, Claudia Karvan. DP *DVD*

Bryan Brown *John Kreisky* • Tom Long *Ben Madigan* • Claudia Karvan *Louise Roncoli* • Jason Clarke (2) *Chris* ▪ *Dir* Alan White • *Scr* John Armstrong, Steve Wright, from the short story *The Adjuster* by Tracy Kidder

Risky Business ★★★★ 18

Comedy 1983 · US · Colour · 94min

Tom Cruise stars as the teenager who turns his parents' home into a brothel after an encounter with Rebecca De Mornay's entrepreneurial hooker. Paul Brickman has honed a sharp satire on American go-getting here, as Cruise – parents away, with the use of their Porsche – starts making money out of his sexually frustrated friends. The danger comes when a killer-pimp arrives on the scene ("never muck with a man's business"); that's when this comedy of embarrassment becomes a near-tragedy of class collisions. TH Swearing, sex scenes. *DVD*

Tom Cruise *Joel Goodson* • Rebecca De Mornay *Lana* • Joe Pantoliano *Guido* • Richard Masur *Rutherford* • Bronson Pinchot *Barry* • Curtis Armstrong *Miles* • Nicholas Pryor *Joel's father* • Janet Carroll *Joel's mother* • Shera Danese *Vicki* • Raphael Sbarge *Glenn* ▪ *Dir/Scr* Paul Brickman

Rita, Sue and Bob Too ★★★★ 18

Comedy 1986 · UK · Colour · 88min

Adapted by Andrea Dunbar from two of her controversial plays, this tale of an affair between a married man and two teenage girls caused a right old rumpus on its release. Although much of the shock value has been diluted by seeing so much of the same on our weekly soaps nowadays, this is still a film to make you squirm as you find yourself unable to decide who is being exploited, where the blame lies and how to respond to jokes that are uproariously funny despite their political incorrectness. It is to the credit of Michelle Holmes, Siobhan Finneran and George Costigan that they pitch their performances so perfectly. DP Swearing, sex scenes. *DVD*

Siobhan Finneran *Rita* • Michelle Holmes *Sue* • George Costigan *Bob* • Lesley Sharp *Michelle* • Willie Ross *Sue's father* • Patti Nicholls *Sue's mother* ▪ *Dir* Alan Clarke • *Scr* Andrea Dunbar, from her plays *The Arbour* and *Rita, Sue and Bob Too*

The Rite ★★★★ 15

Drama 1969 · Swe · BW · 72min

Initially made for television, but awarded a cinema release, this intense drama subjects a self-contained community (in this case an acting troupe) to the pressures of the real world. When their show is banned because of an allegedly obscene sketch, Gunnar Björnstrand, Ingrid Thulin and Anders Ek are given a humiliating grilling by the aptly named judge, Erik Hell, whose inquisition not only exposes their own artistic and personal insecurities, but also his own hypocrisy. Stiflingly photographed by Sven Nykvist and unconditionally played, this is Bergman at his most self-denigratingly pessimistic. DP Swedish +subtitles. *DVD*

Ingrid Thulin *Thea Winkelmann* • Anders Ek *Albert Emanuel Sebastian Fischer* • Gunnar Björnstrand *Hans Winkelmann* • Erik Hell *Judge Abramson* • Ingmar Bergman *Clergyman* ▪ *Dir/Scr* Ingmar Bergman

The Rite ★★★★ 15

Supernatural thriller based on a true story
2011 · US · Colour · 108min

This fascinating and frightening supernatural thriller is loosely based on a real-life account of an American priest who studied to be an exorcist in Rome. When seminary student Michael Kovak (capable newcomer Colin O'Donoghue) is sent to work as apprentice to the renowned Father Lucas (a captivating Anthony Hopkins), the cleric is forced to question his scepticism as a troubling case regarding a pregnant teenager forces him to challenge everything he believes. Director Mikael Hafstrom's visual subtlety, brooding menace and deft jolts go a long way in revitalising the old *Exorcist* formula in what is an effective mix of surprising fact and hard-edged fiction. AJ *DVD* *Blu*

Anthony Hopkins *Father Lucas* • Colin O'Donoghue *Michael Kovak* • Alice Braga *Angeline* • Toby Jones *Father Matthew* • Ciaran Hinds *Father Xavier* • Rutger Hauer *Istvan Kovak* • Maria Grazia Cucinotta *Aunt Andria* • Marta Gastini *Rosaria* ▪ *Dir* Mikael Hafstrom • *Scr* Michael Petroni, from the non-fiction book *The Rite: the Making of a Modern Exorcist* by Matt Baglio

Rites of Passage ★★★

Drama 1999 · US · Colour · 95min

Dean Stockwell takes an associate producer credit as well as the lead in this explosive look at familial bonding and male pride. Retreating to a mountain cabin to repair his relationship with his son Robert Keith, Stockwell finds himself having to confront his other son's homosexuality (a powerful performance by Jason Behr). Very much written as an actors' showcase, this has the intensity and constraint of a stage play. DP Swearing, violence.

Jason Behr *Cambell Farraday* • Dean Stockwell *Del Farraday* • James Remar *Frank Dabbo* • Robert Glen Keith *DJ Farraday* • Jaimz Woolvett *Red Tenney* ▪ *Dir/Scr* Victor Salva

The Ritz ★★ 15

Comedy 1976 · US · Colour · 86min

Richard Lester directs this tasteless camp comedy in which straight Jack Weston takes refuge in a New York gay bath-house. Hiding from his gangster father-in-law (George Coulouris) and brother-in-law (Jerry Stiller), Weston encounters Rita Moreno, who is superb as a talentless singer entertaining the patrons. Terrence McNally's script keeps the clichés flowing. TH Violence, swearing.

Jack Weston *Gaetano Proclo* • Rita Moreno *Googie Gomez* • Jerry Stiller *Carmine Vespucci* • Kaye Ballard *Vivian Proclo* • F Murray Abraham *Chris* • Paul B Price *Claude* • Treat Williams *Michael Brick* • John Everson *Tiger* ▪ *Dir* Richard Lester • *Scr* Terrence McNally, from the play by Terrence McNally

Rivals ★★★ 15

Crime drama 2007 · Fr/Bel · Colour · 107min

The garish 1970s decor, dodgy fashions and tacky tunes occasionally threaten to swamp Jacques Maillot's fact-based Lyon crime saga. However, Guillaume Canet and François Cluzet are sufficiently compelling as brothers on opposite sides of the law to keep the kitsch at bay. Vowing to go straight after a stretch for murder, older sibling Gabriel (Cluzet) is helped out by cop François (Canet), who gives him a room and finds him a job. But the uneasy relationship between the pair is soon under further strain, as François's career is jeopardised by Gabriel's antics. Although the style shifts from moments of high-octane thrills – the *Bullitt*-like car chase – to police procedural, this works best as an intimate character study. DP In French.

Guillaume Canet *François* • François Cluzet *Gabriel* • Marie Denarnaud *Nathalie* • Olivier Perrier *Henri* • Carole Franck *Monique* • Hélène Foubert *Colette* ▪ *Dir* Jacques Maillot • *Scr* Jacques Maillot, Eric Veniard, from the autobiography *Deux frères, flic & truand* by Bruno Papet, Michel Papet

The River ★★★★★★ U

Documentary 1937 · US · BW · 31min

Much more cinematically accomplished than its rough-and-ready predecessor, *The Plow That Broke the Plains* (1934), Pare Lorentz's second keystone documentary was sponsored by the Tennessee Valley Authority to expound the significance of its conservation policies. Following a prologue recalling Walt Whitman's poetry, Lorentz charts the history and ecological importance of the Mississippi and its tributaries, with an audiovisual harmony that compensates for its sentimental New Deal liberalism. With clips from *Come and Get It* (1936) and *Show Boat* (1936) juxtaposed with montage sequences, it was widely admired, although Walt Disney vetoed its Oscar nomination; however, it won the Best Documentary at Venice. DP

Thomas Chalmers *Narrator* ▪ *Dir/Scr* Pare Lorentz • *Music* Virgil Thomson

The River ★★★ U

Romantic drama 1951 · US/Ind · Colour · 99min

After his creatively stifling years in Hollywood, the celebrated French director Jean Renoir ventured into Technicolor for the first time to film Rumer Godden's semi-autobiographical novel in India. The focus is on the adolescent longings of Patricia Walters, the eldest daughter of an English family, and her friends, sophisticated Adrienne Corri and Eurasian Radha, all hankering after a handsome, embittered American pilot Thomas E Breen, who has lost a leg in the war. Exquisitely photographed by Claude Renoir, it's more travelogue than narrative entertainment. RK *DVD*

Nora Swinburne *Mother* • Esmond Knight *Father* • Arthur Shields *Mr John* • Thomas E Breen *Captain John* • Suprova Mukerjee *Nan* • Patricia Walters *Harriet* • Radha *Melanie* • Adrienne Corri *Valerie* ▪ *Dir* Jean Renoir • *Scr* Rumer Godden, Jean Renoir, from the novel by Godden

The River ★★ 15

Drama 1984 · US · Colour · 118min

Rural couple Mel Gibson and Sissy Spacek battle against nature and the machinations of a local landowner (Scott Glenn) in Mark Rydell's well shot, but fairly inconsequential drama. Besides the pretty scenery, the film is chiefly of interest for a pre-super stardom Gibson. He offers a strong performance, but is hampered by a superficial script that gives the protagonists an unlikely "love rivals" backstory. JC Violence, swearing, brief nudity. *DVD*

Mel Gibson *Tom Garvey* • Sissy Spacek *Mae Garvey* • Scott Glenn *Joe Wade* • Billy Green Bush *Harve Stanley* • Shane Bailey *Lewis Garvey* • Becky Jo Lynch *Beth Garvey* • James Tolkan *Simpson* • Jack Starrett *Swick* • Barry Primus *Roy* • Amy Rydell *Betty Gaumer* ▪ *Dir* Mark Rydell • *Scr* Robert Dillon, Julian Barry, from a story by Robert Dillon

The River ★★★★ 18

Drama 1997 · Tai · Colour · 113min

This is an alarming study of familial dysfunction in Taiwan. When Li Kangsheng contracts a mysterious neck ailment, after working as an extra for film-maker (Ann Hui), neither of his parents can break their routine to tend to him – father Miao Tien frequents gay saunas, while mother Lu Xialin panders to a lover who pirates porn videos. Tsai Ming-liang shoots the almost wordless action in lingering long takes, which make the final incidence of incest all the more shocking. DP In Mandarin. Sex scenes.

Miao Tien *Father* • Li Kangsheng *The boy* • Lu Xiaolin *Mother* • Ann Hui *Film director* • Chen Xiangqi *The boy's girlfriend* • Chen Zhaorong *Young man at sauna* • Lu Shiao-Lin *Mother's lover* ▪ *Dir* Tsai Ming-liang • *Scr* Tsai Ming-Liang, Yang Pi-Ying, Tsai Yi-Chun

River ★★★ 15

Thriller 2015 · Can/Laos · Colour · 83min

Rossif Sutherland, son of Donald, half-brother to Kiefer, plays a man on the run, a stranger in a strange land, in a Canadian/Laotian co-production that covers much distance and embraces several languages in its lean, mean sub-90 minute running time. Sutherland plays an American surgeon working in Laos. Vacationing up-country, he intervenes in an assault on a local girl, inadvertently kills her attacker, and finds himself a fugitive. The film rattles along, and a sweatily impressive Rossif proves that talent runs deep in the Sutherland family. DA In English, French, Lao, Thai. Violence, swearing. *DVD*

Rossif Sutherland *John Lake* • Douangmany Soliphanh *Douangmany* • Sara Botsford *Dr Stephanie Novella* ▪ *Dir/Scr* Jamie M Dagg

The River and Death ★★★

Drama 1954 · Mex · BW · 90min

Considering the author of the source novel for this soap-operatic plains western was Luis Buñuel's longtime friend, career diplomat Miguel Alvarez Acosta, this was a surprisingly disharmonious project. The main bone of contention was Buñuel's open contempt for the key idea that higher education was the panacea to the ills of this intemperate, macho society. Denied the chance to alter the ending, Buñuel had to content himself with sly digs at the duplicity of the Catholic Church and the ignorance of the peasant nobility. DP Spanish +subtitles.

Columba Dominguez *Mercedes* • Miguel Torruco *Felipe Anguiano* • Joaquin Cordero *Gerardo Anguiano* • Jaime Fernandez *Romulo Menchaca* • Victor Alcocer *Polo Menchaca* ▪ *Dir* Luis Buñuel • *Scr* Luis Buñuel, Luis Alcoriza, from the novel *Muro Blanco en Roca Negra* by Miguel Alvarez Acosta

River Beat ★★ U

Crime drama 1954 · UK · BW · 70min

Hollywood's Phyllis Kirk gives a dash of much needed class to this minor British thriller. She plays the radio operator on an American freighter docked in the Thames, who's caught with diamonds hidden in her cigarettes. It helps in such circumstances to have an inspector in the river police for a boyfriend. Leading cinematographer Guy Green switched over to direction for the first time and proved he could do a reasonably efficient job. AE

Phyllis Kirk *Judy Roberts* • John Bentley *Inspector Dan Barker* • Robert Ayres *Captain Watford* • Glyn Houston *Charlie Williamson* • Leonard White *Sergeant Mcleod* • Ewan Roberts *Customs Officer Blake* • Harold Ayer *Al Gordon* • Charles Lloyd Pack *Hendrick* ▪ *Dir* Guy Green • *Scr* Rex Rienits

River of Death ★ 15

Action adventure 1989 · US · Colour · 97min

Adventurer Michael Dudikoff travels up the "river of death" in search of a woman and a Nazi scientist. Accompanying him on his quest is a toupee-wearing Donald Pleasence and a bunch of other people who all have their own agendas. This extremely violent and unpleasant action film, includes too many of the modern jungle movie clichés and the ending is particularly pointless. ST

Michael Dudikoff *John Hamilton* • Robert Vaughn (1) *Wolfgang Manteuffel* • Donald Pleasence *Heinrich Spaatz* • Herbert Lom *Colonel Ricardo Diaz* • LQ Jones *Hiller* • Sarah Maur-Thorp *Anna Blakesley* ▪ *Dir* Steve Carver • *Scr* Andrew Deutsch, Edward Simpson, from the novel by Alistair MacLean

River of Grass ★★★★

Drama 1994 · US · Colour · 81min

Housewife Lisa Bowman abandons her family to go on the lam with wastrel Larry Fessenden after they think they've killed a man. However, all attempts to become a latterday Bonnie and Clyde are confounded by their incompetence. Partly a lament for her decaying childhood home and partly a stark denunciation of the way rural Florida had been allowed to decline, Kelly Reichardt's quirky and clever directorial debut is a melancholic riposte to the kind of rip-roaring road movie produced in the wake of *Thelma & Louise* (1991). DP

Lisa Bowman *Cozy* • Larry Fessenden *Lee* ▪ *Dir* Kelly Reichardt • *Scr* Kelly Reichardt, from a story by Jesse Hartman, Reichardt

River of No Return ★★★ PG

Western   1954 · US · Colour · 87min

Robert Mitchum mumbles away to Marilyn Monroe and shows what a great job two stars can do with a creaking script and poor dialogue. This is an "event" movie, in that we do not really believe in Mitchum and Monroe cast adrift in the glorious scenery of the Canadian Rockies, but we enjoy seeing them do it. In his only western, Otto Preminger directs with enough sense to let the actors shine within the confines of a far-fetched adventure tale. SH *DVD*

Robert Mitchum *Matt Calder* • Marilyn Monroe *Kay Weston* • Rory Calhoun *Harry Weston* • Tommy Rettig *Mark Calder* • Murvyn Vye *Dave Colby* • Douglas Spencer *Sam Benson* • Ed Hinton *Gambler* ■ *Dir* Otto Preminger • *Scr* Frank Fenton, from a story by Louis Lantz

River Queen ★★ 15

Period drama   2005 · NZ/UK · Colour · 109min

Kiwi director Vincent Ward's first film since *What Dreams May Come* was a troubled production and, sadly, that discord is plain to see on screen. Set during the New Zealand land wars of the 1860s, this stars Samantha Morton as an Irish settler whose young son is taken from her by his Maori relatives to be raised in their culture. When she finds the boy again after seven long years, he has no intention of leaving what he regards as his rightful home. The local stars, such as Cliff Curtis and Temuera Morrison, fare the best, although Morton is as intense as ever. But while competently acted and visually stunning, the film is incoherently plotted and there's a rushed feel to it all. JF In English, Maori. *DVD*

Samantha Morton *Sarah* • Kiefer Sutherland *Doyle* • Cliff Curtis *Wiremu* • Temuera Morrison *Te Kai Po* • Anton Lesser *Baine* • David Rawiri Pene *Boy* • Stephen Rea *Francis* ■ *Dir* Vincent Ward • *Scr* Vincent Ward, Toa Fraser, from a story by Ward • *Cinematographer* Alun Bollinger

The River Rat ★★★ 15

Drama   1984 · US · Colour · 88min

In this drama set in the eerie swamps of Mississippi, Tommy Lee Jones plays an ex-con who meets his teenage daughter (Martha Plimpton) for the first time after serving a long prison sentence for murder. Determined to go straight, Jones's plans unravel when his parole officer, Brian Dennehy, turns nasty. Jones is well cast as the returning father and Plimpton gives a good account of herself in her first major role. AT Violence, swearing.

Tommy Lee Jones *Billy* • Martha Plimpton *Jonsy* • Brian Dennehy *Doc* • Shawn Smith *Wexel* • Nancy Lea Owen *Vadie* • Norman Bennett *Sheriff Cal* • Frank Tony *Poley* • Angie Bolling *Joyce* ■ *Dir/Scr* Tom Rickman

A River Runs through It ★★★★ PG

Period drama   1992 · US · Colour · 118min

This shows us how to fly-fish and live in a state of grace, harmoniously with the land and water. Set in Montana in the early part of the 20th century, the story focuses on the relationships between stern Presbyterian clergyman Tom Skerritt and his two sons, Craig Sheffer and Brad Pitt, who grow increasingly apart aside from their common love of fly-fishing. Philippe Rousselot's exquisite photography deservedly won an Oscar. AT Swearing, nudity. *DVD*

Craig Sheffer *Norman Maclean* • Brad Pitt *Paul Maclean* • Tom Skerritt *Reverend Maclean* • Brenda Blethyn *Mrs Maclean* • Emily Lloyd *Jessie Burns* • Edie McClurg *Mrs Burns* • Stephen Shellen *Neal Burns* ■ *Dir* Robert Redford • *Scr* Richard Friedenberg, from the novella by Norman Maclean■

The River Wild ★★★★ 12

Adventure thriller   1994 · US · Colour · 106min

This excellent adventure thriller has Meryl Streep and family white-water rafting. Their enjoyable break soon turns into a nightmare when armed robbers, Kevin Bacon and John C Reilly, hitch a ride on the raft with $25C,000 of stolen loot. Directed by Curtis Hanson, this is a real rollercoaster ride, filled with hair-raising action scenes (shot in Montana and Oregon) and some equally tense moments on the river bank. The incredible action and Streep's performance more than compensate for any shortcomings. AT Swearing, violence, brief nudity. *DVD* BD

Meryl Streep *Gail Hartman* • Joseph Mazzello *Roarke Hartman* • David Strathairn *Tom Hartman* • Kevin Bacon *Wade* • John C Reilly *Terry* • William Lucking *Frank* • Benjamin Bratt *Ranger Johnny* ■ *Dir* Curtis Hanson • *Scr* Denis O'Neill

The Riverman ★★★ 15

Crime thriller based on a true story   2004 · US · Colour · 86min

In this surprisingly well-made TV-movie thriller, Bruce Greenwood stars as criminologist Dr Bob Keppel who was enlisted by baffled police to help identify the prolific "Green River Killer" in the mid-1980s. What makes this true story so intriguing is that Keppel used interviews with notorious serial killer Ted Bundy to help him in his investigations. Bundy was on death row at the time and, as played by the excellent Cary Elwes, is an unnerving Hannibal Lecter-like presence throughout the movie. JA *DVD*

Bruce Greenwood *Robert Keppel* • Cary Elwes *Ted Bundy* • Kathleen Quinlan *Sande Keppel* • Sam Jaeger *Dave Reichert* ■ *Dir* Bill Eagles • *Scr* Tom Towler, from the non-fiction book *The Riverman: Ted Bundy and I Hunt for the Green River Killer* by Robert D Keppel, William J Birnes

The River's Edge ★★★

Adventure thriller   1957 · US · Colour · 87min

What looks at first glance like a routine action film actually has some surprisingly ironic twists up its sleeve and conveys a rather bleak moral message. Ray Milland is a bank robber on the run who forces Anthony Quinn and his wife, Debra Paget, to guide him and his stolen dollars across the mountainous border to Mexico. An avalanche, the pouting Paget and sundry other inconveniences hinder their progress. Although Milland is slightly miscast, Quinn delivers his usual ethnic exuberance. AT

Ray Milland *Nardo Denning* • Anthony Quinn *Ben Cameron* • Debra Paget *Meg Cameron* • Harry Carey Jr *Chet* • Chubby Johnson *Whiskers* • Byron Foulger *Barry* ■ *Dir* Allan Dwan • *Scr* Harold Jacob Smith. James Leicester, from the story *The Highest Mountain* by Smith

River's Edge ★★★★ 18

Drama   1987 · US · Colour · 95min

This is the chilling chronicle of the differing reactions of a group of teenagers when a friend shows them the body of the girl he murdered. A vivid study of alienation and moral vacuity, Tim Hunter's confident direction underlines the bleakness of the sorry tale, based on a true incident. Keanu Reeves scores as the decent guy who doesn't think the killing should go unpunished, but the stand-out performance comes from Crispin Glover as the speed-freak friend of the killer whose own sorry life is given pathetic meaning by the slaying. AJ *DVD* BD

Crispin Glover *Layne* • Keanu Reeves *Matt* • Ione Skye *Clarissa* • Daniel Roebuck *Samson "John" Tollette* • Dennis Hopper *Feck* • Joshua Miller [Joshua John Miller] *Tim* • Josh Richman *Tony* ■ *Dir* Tim Hunter • *Scr* Neal Jimenez

The Road ★★★★ 15

Futuristic drama   2009 · US · Colour · 106min

Although Hollywood often treats spectacular destruction as entertainment, this adaptation of the Pulitzer Prize-winning novel by Cormac McCarthy is soberingly serious. In an ashen post-apocalyptic landscape, a man and his son make a perilous journey across America searching for better prospects. Viggo Mortensen might be just a bit too rugged as the careworn dad, but Kodi Smit-McPhee's performance as the vulnerable boy is deeply touching, without a hint of child-actor precocity. TJ Violence, swearing, nudity. *DVD* BD

Viggo Mortensen *Man* • Kodi Smit-McPhee *Boy* • Charlize Theron *Woman* • Robert Duvall *Ely, old man* • Guy Pearce *Veteran* • Michael Kenneth Williams *Thief* ■ *Dir* John Hillcoat • *Scr* Joe Penhall, from the novel by Cormac McCarthy

Road ★★★ PG

Sports documentary   2014 · UK/Ire · Colour · 102min

The thrills and perils of motorcycle road racing are laid bare in this affectionate profile of the Dunlop dynasty. Narrated by Liam Neeson, the film's viewpoint shifts between the careers of Joey and Robert Dunlop from Ballymoney in Northern Ireland and the latter's sons, William and Michael, who have continued the family tradition. Co-directors Michael Hewitt and Diarmuid Lavery pack the picture with archive material and even split the screen at one point to compare footage of Robert and Michael riding, but it's the contribution of Joey and Robert's grieving mother and the latter's widow that hits home hardest. DP *DVD* BD

Liam Neeson *Narrator* ■ *Dir/Scr* Michael Hewitt, Diarmuid Lavery

The Road: a Story of Life and Death ★★★ PG

Documentary   2012 · UK/Ire · Colour · 78min

Striving to show how individuals fare in a melting-pot community, documentary-maker Marc Isaacs follows the A5 from Holyhead to Cricklewood to offer an insight into the lives of a variety of characters. Each has a fascinating tale to tell, but Isaacs doesn't afford them equal screen time, so a couple of potentially intriguing stories are neglected. However, his focus on retired labourer Billy and 95-year-old Jewish lady Peggy (who fled from the Nazis in 1938) is understandable, as her recollections of leaving Austria and subsequent unhappy marriage contrast so poignantly with his alcoholic struggle to replace the camaraderie he had known while working in the construction industry. DP

■ *Dir* Marc Isaacs • *Scr* Marc Isaacs, Iqbal Ahmed

The Road Builder ★★★

Psychological horror   1971 · UK · Colour · 100min

The script for this subtle British psycho-thriller was written by famous children's author Roald Dahl. Handsome Nicholas Clay (making his film debut) is a serial killer who buries his victims under a road construction site. How the homicidal handyman sexually manipulates frustrated spinster Patricia Neal (Dahl's then wife) and fools her blind mother Pamela Brown is the thrust of this obsessively dark look at the demented grotesquerie lurking beneath suburban normality. AJ

Patricia Neal *Maura Prince* • Pamela Brown *Mrs Prince* • Nicholas Clay *Billy Jarvis* • Jean Anderson *Mrs McMurtrey* • Graham Crowden *Mr Bolton* • Yootha Joyce *Mrs Palafax* • Peter Sallis *Rev Palafox* ■ *Dir* Alastair Reid • *Scr* Roald Dahl, from the novel *Nest in a Falling Tree* by Joy Crowley

Road Games ★★ 15

Thriller   1981 · Aus · Colour · 96min

Stacy Keach plays a truck driver who picks up hitch-hiker Jamie Lee Curtis during a journey across the Australian outback. When she later disappears, Keach becomes the prime suspect. The classic themes of Hitchcock are here: an innocent man on the run, people placed in danger and an emphasis on suspense over violence. However, the paucity of action makes it hard for director Richard Franklin to maintain the tension. KB Violence, swearing.

Stacy Keach *Patrick Quid* • Jamie Lee Curtis *Pamela Rushworth/"Hitch"* • Marion Edward Madeleine *"Sunny" Day/Frita Frugal* • Grant Page *"Smith or Jones"* • Thaddeus Smith *Abbott* • Stephen Millichamp *Costello* ■ *Dir* Richard Franklin • *Scr* Everett DeRoche

The Road Home ★ 15

Drama   1989 · US · Colour · 111min

Hugh Hudson directs this story of teenage angst, starring Beastie Boy Adam Horovitz as an institutionalised youth and Donald Sutherland as his shrink. Set in Los Angeles, it tries hard to mirror *Rebel without a Cause*, but fails dismally in all departments. The clichéd script, wooden performances and contrived ending are dispiriting to watch. AT Swearing, nudity, violence.

Donald Sutherland *Dr Charles Loftis* • Adam Horovitz *Tim Doolan* • Amy Locane *Cheryl Anderson* • Don Bloomfield *Andy Doolan* • Celia Weston *Felicia Marks* • Graham Beckel *Richard Doolan* • Patricia Richardson *Mrs Anderson* • Ron Frazier *Barton Marks* ■ *Dir* Hugh Hudson • *Scr* Michael Weller

The Road Home ★★★

Adventure   1995 · US · Colour · 90min

Two sons of Irish immigrants are orphaned and then separated when the younger brother is adopted. The older brother absconds with his sibling and together they make for the one place they imagine they can be together – Boys Town. This never strays far from the established stereotypes you usually find in this kind of movie but it's still touching. In an ironic bit of casting, Mickey Rooney, who as a teenager appeared in the most famous film version of *Boys Town*, appears in this TV movie. ST

Danny Aiello *Duke* • Will Estes *Michael* • Kris Kristofferson *Davis* • Keegan Macintosh *John* • Sheila Patterson *Sister Elizabeth* • Mickey Rooney *Father Flanagan* • Dee Wallace Stone *Mrs Bastian* ■ *Dir* Dean Hamilton • *Scr* Keith O'Leary

The Road Home ★★★★ U

Period drama   1999 · Chi · Colour and BW · 85min

Prompted by a son returning for his father's funeral, this is ostensibly a touching love story shot through with painstaking attention to the detail of everyday life in a 1950s rural community. But Zhang Yimou also extols virtues forgotten in modern consumerist China, such as loyalty, faith and permanence, which is why he shoots the present-day book ends in sombre monochrome and the romance between the teenage Zhang Ziyi and the village's new teacher, Zheng Hao, in vibrantly warm colour. Lyrical and nostalgic, but shrewd. DP Mandarin +subtitles. *DVD*

Zhang Ziyi *Zhao Di as a young woman* • Sun Honglei *Luo Yusheng* • Zheng Hao *Luo Changyu* • Zhao Yuelin *Zhao Di, elderly* • Li Bin (1) *Grandmother* ■ *Dir* Zhang Yimou • *Scr* Bao Shi, from his novel *Remembrance*

Road House ★★★

Crime melodrama   1948 · US · BW · 94min

Blues singer Ida Lupino gets a job at Richard Widmark's joint, but ill-advisedly falls for his general manager, Cornel Wilde. Lupino plays the floozy to perfection, her unsmoked cigarettes burning lines in the piano, as she plays and sings her tragic ballads. As the rejected lover, Widmark gives one of his trademark psycho performances. Not one of the great *film noirs*, but still a very gripping movie. AT

Ida Lupino *Lily Stevens* • Cornel Wilde *Pete Morgan* • Celeste Holm *Susie Smith* • Richard Widmark *Jefty Robbins* • OZ Whitehead *Arthur* • Robert Karnes *Mike* • George Beranger *Lefty* ■ *Dir* Jean Negulesco • *Scr* Edward Chodorov, from a story by Margaret Gruen, Oscar Saul

Road House ★★★ 18

Action drama   1989 · US · Colour · 109min

This gloriously brainless, modern-day western is a treat from start to finish and possibly the only time that a bouncer will ever get the full Hollywood hero treatment. Patrick Swayze, with a commendable straight face, plays the softly spoken doorman who brings order and just a little karma to the unruly Double Deuce bar, which is under threat from unsavoury characters and local hoodlums. Kelly Lynch plays the token love interest, but the best roles go to Sam Elliott, as Swayze's old buddy, and Ben Gazzara, as the villain of

R

the piece. JF Swearing, violence, sex scenes, drug abuse, nudity. **DVD**

Patrick Swayze *Dalton* • Kelly Lynch *Dr Elizabeth "Doc" Clay* • Sam Elliott *Wade Garrett* • Ben Gazzara *Brad Wesley* • Marshall Teague *Jimmy* • Julie Michaels *Denise* • Red West *Red Webster* • "Sunshine" Parker [Sunshine Parker] *Emmet* • Jeff Healey *Cody* • Kevin Tighe *Tilghman* ■ *Dir* Rowdy Herrington • *Scr* David Lee Henry, Hilary Henkin, from a story by David Lee Henry

Road House 2 ★★15

Action drama 2006 · US · Colour · 82min

Fans of the thumping 1989 modern-day western starring Patrick Swayze will be mightily disappointed by this turgid follow-up. Here, Johnathon Schaech takes on the muscular tough-guy mantle, as a DEA agent and son of Swayze's enigmatic bouncer character from the original. However, where the Swayze film was good dumb fun with well-choreographed fight scenes and some pithy one-liners, this belated sequel just delivers forgettable shoot-em-ups, unconvincing brawls and a seen-it-all-before plot. JA Violence, swearing, drug abuse, sex scenes, nudity. **DVD**

Johnathon Schaech *Shane Tanner* • Ellen Hollman *Beau* • Richard Norton *Victor Cross* • Will Patton *Nate Tanner* • Jake Busey *Wild Bill* ■ *Dir* Scott Ziehl • *Scr* Johnathon Schaech, Richard Chizmar, Miles Chapman. from a story by Chapman, from characters by David Lee Henry

Road Kill ★★★15

Road movie thriller 2001 · US · Colour · 93min

College kid Paul Walker is on a road trip to pick up pal Leelee Sobieski, after taking a detour to bail his reckless brother (Steve Zahn) out of jail. Unfortunately, a late night prank with their CB radio gets the brothers on the wrong side of an unseen trucker, and it's not long before the boys realise they're being chased by the clearly unhinged driver. This is a nicely paced and suspenseful teen movie, with a smart script and solid performances. JB **DVD**

Steve Zahn *Fuller Thomas* • Paul Walker *Lewis Thomas* • Leelee Sobieski *Venna* • Jessica Bowman *Charlotte* • Stuart Stone *Danny* • Basil Wallace *Car salesman* ■ *Dir* John Dahl • *Scr* Clay Tarver, JJ Abrams [Jeffrey Abrams]

Road Show ★★★U

Comedy 1941 · US · BW · 87min

Millionaire John Hubbard, committed to a lunatic asylum by a vengeful woman, becomes friendly with fellow inmate Adolphe Menjou, who is the inventor of a camera that takes no pictures. Together, they escape and join a carnival owned by Carole Landis, where Hubbard becomes a lion tamer and the carnival runs into riotous (in both senses of the word) trouble. Zany, manic, broad farce. RK

Adolphe Menjou *Col Carleton Carraway* • Carole Landis *Penguin Moore* • John Hubbard *Drogo Gaines* • Charles Butterworth *Harry Whitman* • Patsy Kelly *Jinx* • George E Stone *Indian* • Margaret Roach *Priscilla* ■ *Dir* Gordon Douglas • *Scr* Arnold Belgard, Harry Langdon, Mickell Novak, from the novel by Eric Hatch

Road to Bali ★★★U

Musical comedy 1952 · US · Colour · 90min

A wonderfully wacky and surreal entry in Paramount's *Road* series, this was the penultimate of the seven made and the only one in colour. Alongside Bing Crosby, Bob Hope and Dorothy Lamour (whose camaraderie was by now honed to perfection), there are a variety of star cameos and a number of enjoyable special effects, from materialisation by a snake charmer's flute to volcanic eruption, all done with a warmth missing from today's digital wizardry. TS **DVD**

Bob Hope *Harold Gridley* • Bing Crosby *George Cochran* • Dorothy Lamour *Lalah* • Murvyn Vye *Ken Arok* • Peter Coe *Gung* • Ralph Moody *Bhoma Da* ■ *Dir* Hal Walker • *Scr* Frank Butler, Hal Kanter, William Morrow, from a story by Frank Butler, Harry Tugend

The Road to Corinth ★★12

Crime thriller 1967 · Fr/Gr/It · Colour · 96min

Claude Chabrol was in playful, commercial mood with a thriller made just before his greatest period. Jean Seberg plays the wife of a Nato security officer who is killed. Accused of his murder, she sets out to prove her innocence. Some wonderful Greek locations (and Chabrol in a small role) help the caper along. Though hardly a serious movie, this deserved better than the dubbing and various cuts that led to alternate versions appearing and its silly American title, *Who's Got the Black Box?* BB French dubbed. **DVD**

Jean Seberg *Shanny* • Maurice Ronet *Dex* • Christian Marquand *Robert Ford* • Michel Bouquet *Sharps* • Claude Chabrol *Alcibiades* ■ *Dir* Claude Chabrol • *Scr* Claude Brûlé, Daniel Boulanger, from the novel *La Route de Corinthe* by Claude Rank

The Road to Denver ★U

Western 1955 · US · Colour · 90min

No wonder John Payne looks more morose than ever – he's reduced to playing in a Republic western and his part requires him to be upstaged by his younger brother's wild behaviour, when he's not stationed at a sink washing dishes. Skip Homeier is convincingly hot-headed as the youngster, but the direction is tepid and the script dull. AE

John Payne *Bill Mayhew* • Skip Homeier *Sam Mayhew* • Mona Freeman *Elizabeth Sutton* • Lee J Cobb *Jim Donovan* • Ray Middleton *John Sutton* • Andy Clyde *Whipsaw* • Lee Van Cleef *Pecos Larry* ■ *Dir* Joseph Kane • *Scr* Horace McCoy, Allen Rivkin, from the novel *Man from Texas* by Bill Gulick

The Road to El Dorado ★★★U

Animated adventure 2000 · US · Colour · 85min

The third animated feature from DreamWorks – following *Antz* and *The Prince of Egypt* – features Kevin Kline and Kenneth Branagh, voicing a duo of rascally 16th-century Spaniards who stumble on the fabled South American city of gold. Mistaken for gods, the two must fake divinity long enough to run off with the loot, but evil High Priest Armand Assante has other ideas. The film starts and finishes strongly, and boasts at least two terrific action set pieces, while the talky in-between sequences drag on. DA **DVD**

Elton John *Narrator* • Kevin Kline *Tulio* • Kenneth Branagh *Miguel* • Rosie Perez *Chel* • Armand Assante *Tzekel-Kan* • Edward James Olmos *Chief* • Jim Cummings *Cortes* • Frank Welker *Altivo* • Tobin Bell *Zaragoza* ■ *Dir* Eric "Bibo" Bergeron, Don Paul • *Scr* Ted Elliott, Terry Rossio • *Music* Elton John • *Lyrics* Tim Rice

The Road to Galveston ★★★PG

Drama based on a true story 1996 · US · Colour · 89min

Cicely Tyson stars as a Texas widow who, suffering from the loss of her husband's income, saves her farm by turning it into a nursing home for three women with Alzheimer's disease. Deciding to fulfil a lifelong dream, she takes the women on a drive to Galveston to see the ocean. With a strong ensemble cast of actresses, including Piper Laurie, this TV drama provides the perfect showcase for Tyson's talents. MC

Cicely Tyson *Jordan Roosevelt* • Piper Laurie *Wanda Kirkman* • Tess Harper *Julia Archer* • James McDaniel *Marcus Roosevelt* • Starletta DuPois *Sally McGowan* • Penny Johnson *Laney Roosevelt* ■ *Dir* Michael Toshiyuki Uno • *Scr* Tony Lee

The Road to Glory ★★PG

First World War drama 1936 · US · BW · 97min

Howard Hawks recycles ideas from another of his films, *The Dawn Patrol*, changing the focus from the war in the air, to the war in the trenches. And that wasn't the only instance of recycling. Fox studio boss Darryl F Zanuck had bought a 1932 French movie, *Les Croix des Bois*, but decided not to release it in the US. Instead Zanuck took all

the battle footage from the French movie and got Hawks to graft a plot onto it and glue Hollywood actors around it. AT **DVD**

Fredric March *Lt Michel Denet* • Warner Baxter *Capt Paul Laroche* • Lionel Barrymore *Papa Laroche* • June Lang *Monique* • Gregory Ratoff *Bouffiou* • Victor Kilian *Regnier* • Paul Stanton *Relief Captain* • John Qualen *Duflous* ■ *Dir* Howard Hawks • *Scr* Joel Sayre, William Faulkner, from the film *Les Croix des Bois* by Raymond Bernard, André Lang, from the novel by Roland Dorgelès

The Road to Guantanamo ★★★15

Drama documentary 2006 · UK · Colour · 91min

This film is not the even-handed trial the "Tipton Three" were denied during their time at the USA's "extra-legal" detention centres at Guantanamo Bay, Cuba. It is a personal account of events, told partly to camera, partly dramatised. In October 2001, British citizens Shafiq Rasul, Asif Iqbal and Ruhal Ahmed left their homes in the Midlands to attend Asif's wedding in Pakistan, took a side trip to Afghanistan and were eventually imprisoned, interrogated and tortured as suspected members of al-Qaeda, spending around 25 months in "Gitmo". They were never charged. As documentary cinema, it is far from perfect and better suited to the small screen. As an impassioned, thought-provoking piece of political film-making, however, it is unmissable. AR English, Arabic, Urdu +subtitles. Swearing. **DVD**

Rizwan Ahmed *Shafiq Rasul* • Arfan Usman *Asif Iqbal* • Farhad Harun *Ruhal Ahmed* ■ *Dir* Michael Winterbottom, Mat Whitecross

The Road to Hong Kong ★★U

Musical comedy 1962 · US/UK · BW · 87min

Bing Crosby and Bob Hope reteamed ten years after *Road to Bali* for the seventh and last in a once fabulously funny series. Sadly, by now the spark had gone from the relationship and the English locations and parsimonious filming in black and white make the movie look shabby. Worse is the graceless demoting of Dorothy Lamour to "guest star" and the co-starring role being taken by an ill-suited Joan Collins. There's super work from some distinguished supporting players – especially Peter Sellers – but this is neither funny nor attractive. TS **DVD**

Bing Crosby *Harry Turner* • Bob Hope *Chester Babcock* • Joan Collins *Diane* • Dorothy Lamour • Robert Morley *The Leader* • Walter Gotell *Dr Zorbb* • Roger Delgado *Jhinnah* • Felix Aylmer *Grand Lama* • Peter Madden *Lama* • Peter Sellers • Frank Sinatra • Dean Martin • David Niven • Zsa Zsa Gabor ■ *Dir* Norman Panama • *Scr* Norman Panama, Melvin Frank

The Road to Mandalay ★★★

Silent melodrama 1926 · US · BW · 75min

Lon Chaney, the master of disguise, created a grotesque white cataract in his eye with the skin of an eggshell to play the villainous Chinese owner of a Singapore dive. The evil character has sent his daughter Lois Moran to a convent in Mandalay and kidnaps her sweetheart Owen Moore. As eerily atmospheric as the other collaborations between Chaney (another riveting performance) and director Tod Browning, who shared the star's taste for the macabre, it is by today's standards, an overripe melodrama and strictly non-PC. RB

Lon Chaney *Singapore Joe* • Lois Moran *Joe's daughter* • Owen Moore *The Admiral* • Henry B Walthall *Father James* ■ *Dir* Tod Browning • *Scr* Elliott Clawson, Joe Farnham [Joseph Farnham], from a story by Tod Browning, Herman Mankiewicz [Herman J Mankiewicz]

Road to Morocco ★★★★U

Musical comedy 1942 · US · BW · 78min

"Like Webster's Dictionary, we're Morocco-bound,", sing Bob Hope and Bing Crosby in arguably one of the best – and certainly the funniest – of their zany *Road* series for Paramount. There's much to cherish here: Dorothy Lamour and *Moonlight Becomes You*; Anthony Quinn as a villainous Arab;

the delectable Dona Drake as a slave girl and the talking camels. These comedies may have dated – and certainly they remain unfashionable – but for sheer inventiveness and innate good humour they're hard to beat. In these postmodern times, they're simply full of surreal cinematic in-jokes. TS **DVD**

Bing Crosby *Jeff Peters* • Bob Hope *Orville "Turkey" Jackson* • Dorothy Lamour *Princess Shalmar* • Anthony Quinn *Mullay Kasim* • Dona Drake *Mihirmah* • Mikhail Rasumny *Ahmed Fey* • Vladimir Sokoloff *Hyder Khan* ■ *Dir* David Butler • *Scr* Frank Butler, Don Hartman

Road to Perdition ★★★★15

Period crime drama 2002 · US · Colour · 112min

Director Sam Mendes here follows up his superlative Oscar winner *American Beauty* with another riveting, intelligent drama imbued with lyrical imagery. Set during the Depression era, it features Tom Hanks as a feared hitman working for Irish-American Mob boss Paul Newman, who regards him as a son. Professional and familial loyalties become blurred when Hanks's own family is targeted, forcing him to take to the road with his eldest son, as he embarks on a systematic course of revenge against his betrayers. This evocative gangster movie boasts superb photography, production design and score, which utterly transport the audience back to moody 1930s Chicago. JC Violence, swearing. **DVD** **BL**

Tom Hanks *Michael Sullivan* • Paul Newman *John Rooney* • Jude Law *Maguire* • Jennifer Jason Leigh *Annie Sullivan* • Tyler Hoechlin *Michael Sullivan Jr* • Stanley Tucci *Frank Nitti* • Daniel Craig *Connor Rooney* • Liam Aiken *Peter Sullivan* ■ *Dir* Sam Mendes • *Scr* David Self, from the graphic novel by Max Allan Collins, Richard Piers Rayner • *Cinematographer* Conrad L Hall [Conrad Hall] • *Music* Thomas Newman • *Production Designer* Dennis Gassner • *Set Designer* Nancy Haigh

Road to Rio ★★★★U

Musical comedy 1947 · US · BW · 100min

The fifth of the seven *Road* movies was also one of the best, even though the formula remained much as before: entertainers Bing Crosby and Bob Hope, on the run, fall for Dorothy Lamour, become rivals for her love and land in hot water. This time, Dorothy is being hypnotised by her guardian (the delightfully wicked Gale Sondergaard) so that she'll marry the guardian's brother, who is after Dorothy's estate. "I find myself saying things and I don't know why I say them," says Dot. "Why don't you just run for Congress," Hope quips. Added attractions are the Andrew Sisters singing *You Don't Have to Know the Language* with Bing, and the zany Wiere Brothers doing their famous hat routine. RB **DVD**

Bing Crosby *"Scat" Sweeney* • Bob Hope *"Hot Lips" Barton* • Dorothy Lamour *Lucia Maria de Andrade* • Gale Sondergaard *Catherine Vail* • Frank Faylen *Trigger* • Joseph Vitale *Tony* • Frank Puglia *Rodrigues* • Nestor Paiva *Cardoso* ■ *Dir* Norman Z McLeod • *Scr* Edmund Beloin, Jack Rose

Road to Ruin ★★15

Romantic comedy 1992 · US/Fr · Colour · 90min

Peter Weller rather improbably stars in this Parisian frippery. The city looks glorious, thanks to cinematographer Jean-Yves LeMener, but Erick Anjou's script is right out of the bottom drawer, taking ludicrous turns to prove to Weller's wealthy exile that model Carey Lowell loves him for more than his money. There's little spark between them and, as the elaborate scams come thick and fast, you're left wondering how anyone so harebrained came to be so rich. DP Swearing, sex scenes.

Peter Weller *Jack Sloan* • Carey Lowell *Jessie Taylor* • Michel Duchaussoy *Julien Boulet* • Rebecca Pauly *Arabella* • Sylvie Laguna *Sarah* • Takashi Kawahara *Toshi* ■ *Dir* Charlotte Brandstrom • *Scr* Erick Anjou, from the story by Richard Gitelson, Eric Freiser

Road to Singapore ★★★U

Musical comedy 1940 · US · BW · 81min

Not the best of the *Road* series, but the first, originally intended as a vehicle for a sarong-clad Dorothy Lamour. Several other stars were mooted, notably Jack Oakie with a number of partners, but eventually crooner Bing Crosby and comedian Bob Hope were recruited to team with Lamour in a script which, by then, was nearly ten years old. The public loved the resultant comedy and seeming ad-libs, although the tone of the series (Bing and Bob moon over Lamour, or money, or both) wasn't really established until the second, *Road to Zanzibar*. TS **DVD**

Bing Crosby *Josh Mallon* • Bob Hope *Ace Lannigan* • Dorothy Lamour *Mima* • Charles Coburn *Joshua Mallon IV* • Judith Barrett *Gloria Wycott* • Anthony Quinn *Caesar* • Jerry Colonna *Achilles Bombanassa* • Johnny Arthur *Timothy Willow* • Pierre Watkin *Morgan Wycott* ■ *Dir* Victor Schertzinger • *Scr* Don Hartman, Frank Butler, from a story by Harry Hervey

Road to Utopia ★★★★ PG
Musical comedy 1945 · US · BW · 85min

Sadly, they really don't make them like this any more. Released 20 months after it was completed, this is among the best of a much loved series, with Bing Crosby and Bob Hope as down-at-heel entertainers posing as hardened prospectors in order to get their hands on a Klondike gold map. Told as an elongated flashback and blessed with a mocking commentary by Robert Benchley, the film contains a wealth of insider gags that were a trademark of these freewheeling comedies. This comes complete with the obligatory squabble over Dorothy Lamour, talking animals and other larks. DP **DVD**

Bing Crosby *Duke Johnson* • Bob Hope *Chester Hooton* • Dorothy Lamour *Sal Van Hoyden* • Hillary Brooke *Kate* • Douglass Dumbrille *Ace Larson* • Jack LaRue *Lebec* • Robert Barrat *Sperry* • Robert Benchley *Narrator* ■ *Dir* Hal Walker • *Scr* Norman Panama, Melvin Frank

The Road to Wellville ★★ 18
Period black comedy 1994 · US · Colour · 114min

Director Alan Parker comes unstuck with this tasteless farce about early 20th century health habits. Anthony Hopkins is all wavering accent and buckteeth as Dr John Harvey Kellogg (yes, he of cornflakes fame), who ran a notorious sanatorium in Battle Creek, Michigan, where idle rich Americans flocked to have enemas, salt scrubs, yogurt therapy and bowel inspections. Matthew Broderick turns up with chronic constipation, his sexually frustrated wife Bridget Fonda in tow, to indulge in numerous *Carry On*-style shenanigans. AJ Swearing, sex scenes, nudity. **DVD**

Anthony Hopkins *Dr John Harvey Kellogg* • Bridget Fonda *Eleanor Lightbody* • Matthew Broderick *Will Lightbody* • John Cusack *Charles Ossining* • Dana Carvey *George Kellogg* • Michael Lerner *Goodloe Bender* • Colm Meaney *Dr Lionel Badger* • John Neville *Endymion Hart-Jones* • Lara Flynn Boyle *Ida Muntz* • Traci Lind *Nurse Irene Graves* ■ *Dir* Alan Parker • *Scr* Alan Parker, from the novel by T Coraghessan Boyle

The Road to Yesterday ★★★
Silent romantic drama 1925 · US · BW · 136min

For this lively reincarnation fantasy, spectacle-specialist Cecil B DeMille transports two unhappily-married modern-day couples into the past to teach them a lesson for the future. Unconscious following a train crash, the crotchety quartet find themselves trapped in 16th century England, where their bigotry and unkindness backfire horribly. DeMille proves once again what a crowd-pleaser he is with this agreeable slice of hokum. TH

Joseph Schildkraut *Kenneth Paulton* • Jetta Goudal *Malena Paulton* • Vera Reynolds *Beth Tyrell* • William Boyd (1) *Jack Moreland* ■ *Dir* Cecil B De Mille [Cecil B DeMille] • *Scr* Beulah Marie Dix, Jeanie Macpherson, from a story by Beulah Marie Dix, from the play by Evelyn Greenleaf Sutherland

Road to Zanzibar ★★★ PG
Musical comedy 1941 · US · BW · 87min

The first two *Road* pictures (this is the second after *Singapore*) seem somewhat

disappointing now in light of the wonderful three that followed (Morocco, Utopia and Rio), but this still has Bob Hope, Bing Crosby and Dorothy Lamour, some zany gags and some catchy tunes, so it more than gets by. Bing and Bob are carnival performers, on the run from a gangster to whom they sold a phoney diamond mine, and their ensuing trek through the jungle with Lamour and Una Merkel cues some great satire on jungle pictures. TV **DVD**

Bob Hope *"Fearless" Frazier* • Bing Crosby *Chuck Reardon* • Dorothy Lamour *Donna Latour* • Una Merkel *Julia Quimby* • Eric Blore *Charles Kimble* ■ *Dir* Victor Schertzinger • *Scr* Frank Butler, Don Hartman, from the story *Find Colonel Fawcett* by Hartman, Sy Bartlett

Road Trip ★★ 15
Comedy 2000 · US · Colour · 89min

There are some raunchy and hilarious moments as student Breckin Meyer races from New York to Texas with his friends to avert a disaster that could ruin his relationship with his girlfriend, but the movie is still a jumbled mess. Several redundant subplots keep diverting attention from the central story, and the characters come across as stereotypes, sharing the same "wild college guy" persona. The exception is Tom Green, whose insane character is hilarious. KB **DVD**

Breckin Meyer *Josh* • Seann William Scott *EL* • Amy Smart *Beth* • Paulo Costanzo *Rubin* • DJ Qualls *Kyle* • Rachel Blanchard *Tiffany* ■ *Dir* Todd Phillips • *Scr* Todd Phillips, Scot Armstrong

Roadblock ★★★
Crime thriller 1951 · US · BW · 73min

Playing against type, square-jawed Charles McGraw gives a surprisingly layered performance in this claustrophobic *film noir*. McGraw is a hard-working insurance investigator, who becomes involved in a million-dollar mail robbery in order to finance new wife Joan Dixon's expensive tastes. Cinematographer Nicholas Musuraca's dank cityscapes give the film both its atmosphere and its sense of middle-class malaise. DP

Charles McGraw *Joe Peters* • Joan Dixon *Diane* • Lowell Gilmore *Kendall Webb* • Louis Jean Heydt *Harry Miller* • Milburn Stone *Egan* • Joseph Crehan *Thompson* • Joe Forte *Brissard* ■ *Dir* Harold Daniels • *Scr* Steve Fisher, George Bricker, from a story by Richard Landau, Geoffrey Holmes

Roadflower ★★★ 18
Thriller 1994 · US · Colour · 85min

This intriguing action thriller boasts a high quality, if eclectic, cast. Christopher Lambert is the head of a family driving across the Nevada desert who find themselves locked in combat with a gang of psychos led by Craig Sheffer. Lambert is a tad unconvincing as the humble businessman, but there are unlikely, if solid, supporting performances. JF Violence, swearing.

Christopher Lambert *Jack* • Craig Sheffer *Cliff* • David Arquette *Bobby* • Joseph Gordon-Levitt *Richie* • Adrienne Shelly *Red* • Michelle Forbes *Helen* • Josh Brolin *Tom* • Christopher McDonald *Glen* • Alexandra Lee *Ashley* ■ *Dir* Deran Sarafian • *Scr* Tedi Sarafian

The Roadhouse Murder ★★★
Crime drama 1932 · US · BW · 71min

This terrific idea for a movie has journalist Eric Linden deciding to incriminate himself as a killer for a series of newspaper articles, only to find that it's not that easy to extricate himself from the morass of his own making. B-feature stuff, of course, but co-written by real-life journalist Gene Fowler who brings plenty of life and colour to the proceedings. Linden is an acceptably harassed hero and Dorothy Jordan a fine hapless heroine. TS

Eric Linden *Chick Brian* • Dorothy Jordan *Mary Agnew* • Bruce Cabot *Fred Dykes* • Phyllis Clare *Louise Rand* ■ *Dir* J Walter Ruben • *Scr* J Walter

Ruben, Gene Fowler, from the play *Lame Dog Inn* by Ladislaus Bus-Fekete, from a novel by Maurice Level

Roadie ★★ 12
Music comedy 1980 · US · Colour · 102min

The biggest novelty in this movie is the inspired casting of pop melodramatist Meat Loaf as a wide-eyed innocent lost in the corruptible world of rock 'n' roll. Meat Loaf brings an engaging credibility to the role of a Texas mechanic-turned-roadie, who strikes up an unlikely friendship with a groupie who's been saving herself for Alice Cooper. Robert Altman protégé Alan Rudolph punctuates this straightforward tale with tiresome bar-room brawls and noisy knockabout comic moments made bearable only by the celebrity cameos. RS **DVD**

Meat Loaf *Travis W Redfish* • Kaki Hunter *Lola Bouilliabase* • Art Carney *Corpus C Redfish* • Gailard Sartain *BB Muldoon* • Don Cornelius *Mohammed Johnson* • Rhonda Bates *Alice Poo* • Richard Marion *George* • Sonny Davis [Sonny Carl Davis] *Bird* • Joe Spano *Ace* ■ *Dir* Alan Rudolph • *Scr* Big Boy Medlin, Michael Ventura, from a story by Big Boy Medlin, Michael Ventura, Zalman King, Alan Rudolph

Roadracers ★★ PG
Action drama 1958 · US · BW · 73min

Journeyman Arthur Swerdloff unfussily directs this car-racing action film for American International Pictures, the byword for exploitation cinema in the 1950s. Hot-rodder Joel Lawrence is forced to pursue his ambitions in Europe after his father bans him from the track for causing a death through reckless driving. However, he's soon back stateside to take on Skip Ward to secure both grand prix glory and his true love. DP **DVD**

Joel Lawrence *Rob* • Marian Collier *Liz* • Skip Ward *Greg* • Sally Fraser *Joanie* • Mason Alan Dinehart [Alan Dinehart III] *Kit* • Irene Windust *Alice* • John Shay *Harry* ■ *Dir* Arthur Swerdloff • *Scr* Stanley Kallis, Edward J Lakso

Roadracers ★★ 15
Drama 1994 · US · Colour · 89min

Made as part of a series of TV remakes of teen B-movies from the 1950s, Robert Rodriguez keeps his tongue firmly in his cheek as he recounts the story of cool singer David Arquette, who finds himself caught between a tough gang leader and a cruel detective. It's a tad indulgent and the film's kitsch appeal begins to fade, but it's enthusiastically played and Rodriguez never lets the pace slacken. JF Swearing.

David Arquette *Dude Delaney* • Salma Hayek *Donna* • John Hawkes *Nixer* • Jason Wiles *Teddy* • William Sadler *Sarge* • O'Neal Compton *J T* ■ *Dir* Robert Rodriguez • *Scr* Robert Rodriguez, Tommy Nix

Roads to Koktebel ★★★★ 12
Drama 2003 · Rus · Colour · 102min

Lovingly photographed by Shandor Berkeshi, the feature debut of co-directors Boris Khlebnikov and Alexei Popogrebsky is a cross between a folkloric road movie and a post-Communist critique of a once proud nation's struggle to come to terms with the realities of freedom. Aviation engineer Igor Chernevich and son Gleb Puskepalis journey south to the Crimea. An eccentric encounter with a drunken hermit and a romantic interlude with a kindly doctor punctuate their journey. But it's the father-son relationship that proves most intriguing, especially once the 11-year-old Puskepalis begins to appreciate that promises are made to be broken. Measured and evocative. DP Russian +subtitles. **DVD**

Igor Chernevich *Father* • Gleb Puskepalis *Boy* • Agrippina Steklova *Doctor* • Alexander Ilyin *Truck driver* • Vladimir Kucherenko *Dacha owner* ■ *Dir/Scr* Boris Khlebnikov, Alexei Popogrebsky

Roads to the South ★★
Political drama 1978 · Fr/Sp · Colour · 100min

This downbeat drama about the growing disillusionment of an old-style socialist comes across as an old man's lament for past times and missed opportunities.

Originally intended for the small screen, Joseph Losey's film has touching moments, particularly when Yves Montand and his young lover, Miou-Miou, head back to Spain on the death of Franco. But, mostly, it's an interminably polemical picture, which offers few historical or contemporary insights. DP French +subtitles.

Yves Montand *Larrea* • Miou-Miou *Julia* • France Lambiotte *Eve* • Laurent Malet *Laurent* ■ *Dir* Joseph Losey • *Scr* Joseph Losey, Patricia Losey, Jorge Semprun

Roadside Prophets ★★★ 15
Road movie comedy drama 1992 · US · Colour · 92min

This ultra-hip road movie has many of the leading roles acted out by cutting-edge rock, rap and folk musicians. John Doe, of LA punk band X, and Beastie Boy rapper Adam Horovitz play bikers who hit the highway to deliver a dead friend's ashes for scattering in a remote Nevada town. En route, they encounter deadbeats, philosophers, fighters and loose women. Highly rated by US critics, this doesn't push quite the same buttons in the UK. DA

John Doe *Joe Mosely* • Adam Horovitz *Sam* • Arlo Guthrie *Harvey* • David Carradine *Othello Jones* • John Cusack *Caspar* • David Anthony Marshall *Dave Coleman* • Don Cheadle *Happy Days manager* • Timothy Leary *Salvadore* ■ *Dir* Abbe Wool • *Scr* Abbe Wool, from an idea by David Swinson

Roar ★★★ PG
Adventure 1981 · US · Colour · 96min

The title refers to the lions who star in this sadly self-conscious travelogue featuring wild animals and film-maker Noel Marshall. He's a biological researcher who sends for his family – including his real-life then-wife Tippi Hedren – to come stay at his ranch in the African Bush. That's about all, apart from the yelps of delight from the young humans as they communicate with the oh-so-friendly beasts. TH

Noel Marshall *Hank* • Tippi Hedren *Madeleine* • John Marshall *John* • Jerry Marshall *Jerry* • Melanie Griffith *Melanie* • Kyalo Mativo *Mativo* • Frank Tom *Frank* ■ *Dir/Scr* Noel Marshall • Cinematographer Jan De Bont

The Roaring Twenties ★★★★ PG
Crime drama 1939 · US · BW · 101min

Despite its plentiful shoot-outs, this is not so much a gangster movie but a morality story about a First World War veteran who tries to go straight, then yields to the lure of bootlegging and other crimes. James Cagney is on terrific form as the good guy turned bad and Humphrey Bogart is a vicious hoodlum. Raoul Walsh skilfully creates a convincing Prohibition world of smoky speakeasies and gleaming black cars parked in dark alleys, a world of endless opportunity and rampant corruption, though the script is a typical Warner Bros blend of slang and sermon. AT **DVD**

James Cagney *Eddie Bartlett* • Humphrey Bogart *George Hally* • Jeffrey Lynn *Lloyd Hart* • Priscilla Lane *Jean Sherman* • Gladys George *Panama Smith* • Frank McHugh *Danny Green* ■ *Dir* Raoul Walsh • *Scr* Jerry Wald, Richard Macaulay, Robert Rossen, from a story by Mark Hellinger

Rob Roy ★★★★ 15
Historical adventure 1995 · US · Colour · 132min

Mel Gibson may have grabbed the Oscar glory for *Braveheart*, but this rip-snorting early 18th-century tartan romp is a lot more fun. Liam Neeson plays the principled Robert MacGregor, who becomes the reluctant rebel Rob Roy when his money is stolen and his wife (Jessica Lange) is raped by evil English aristocrat Tim Roth. Neeson is suitably heroic, but Roth is a diabolical delight, and he's matched by fellow villains John Hurt and Brian Cox. Scottish-born director Michael Caton-Jones makes striking use of the rugged locations and stages the action sequences with robust glee. Terrific stuff. JF Violence, swearing. **DVD Blu-ray**

R

Liam Neeson *Robert MacGregor* • Jessica Lange *Mary of Comar* • John Hurt *Marquis of Montrose* • Tim Roth *Archie Cunningham* • Eric Stoltz *McDonald* • Andrew Keir *Argyll* • Brian Cox (1) *Killearn* • Brian McCardie *Alasdair* • Gilbert Martin *Guthrie* • Vicki Masson *Betty* ■ *Dir* Michael Caton-Jones • *Scr* Alan Sharp

Rob Roy, the Highland Rogue ★★ U

Historical adventure
1953 · UK/US · Colour · 81min

Heavy on starch and lacing, this stiff biographical account of the 18th-century Scots clansman is a reminder of the days when Disney would travel to these shores, re-write a bit of history, and provide work for half the British film industry. Richard Todd and Glynis Johns head a cast which also includes anyone who was anyone in 1950s British cinema. **DA**

Richard Todd *Rob Roy MacGregor* • Glynis Johns *Helen Mary MacGregor* • James Robertson-Justice *Duke of Argyll* • Michael Gough *Duke of Montrose* • Jean Taylor-Smith *Lady Glengyll* • Geoffrey Keen *Killearn* • Finlay Currie *Hamish MacPherson* • Archie Duncan *Dougal MacGregor* ■ *Dir* Harold French • *Scr* Lawrence E Watkin

Robbery ★★★ PG

Crime drama   1967 · UK · Colour · 109min

Following the Great Train Robbery of 1963, several film projects were announced, but this is the only British production to have got off the ground. It never fulfils the promise of its opening car chase, during which one vehicle mows down a policeman and a procession of schoolchildren. Thereafter, the plotting and execution of the robbery seems rather trite, and the fictitious characters are not half as colourful as the real-life Ronnie Biggs and company. But there is more action towards the end, enough to impress Hollywood, who summoned Peter Yates to direct *Bullitt*. **DM**
DVD ■

Stanley Baker *Paul Clifton* • Joanna Pettet *Kate Clifton* • James Booth *Inspector Langdon* • Frank Finlay *Robinson* • Barry Foster *Frank* • William Marlowe *Dave* ■ *Dir* Peter Yates • *Scr* Edward Boyd, Peter Yates, George Markstein, from a story by Gerald Wilson

Robbery under Arms ★★ U

Crime adventure   1957 · US · Colour · 99min

This screen-telling of Rolf Boldrewood's popular tale about bushranger Captain Starlight is saved only by Peter Finch in the lead and the panoramic photography of Harry Waxman. Away from the savage beauty of the Australian wilderness, former documentary film-maker Jack Lee drains all the drama from the round of robberies, escapes and betrayals that engulf brothers, David McCallum and Ronald Lewis. **DP**

Peter Finch *Captain Starlight* • Ronald Lewis *Dick Marston* • David McCallum (1) *Jim Marston* • Maureen Swanson *Kate Morrison* • Laurence Naismith *Ben Marston* • Jill Ireland *Jean* • Jean Anderson *Ma* ■ *Dir* Jack Lee • *Scr* WP Lipscomb, Alexander Baron, from the novel by Rolf Boldrewood

LANDMARK FILM
This first film released in CinemaScope successfully wins back audiences lost to TV

The Robe ★★★ U

Religious drama   1953 · US · Colour · 133min

Best known as the first film to be released in CinemaScope, this is a plodding, pious epic, with Richard Burton as the Roman officer who wins Christ's robe in a game of dice during the Crucifixion. The torn and bloody garment works its magic and, before long, Burton and Jean Simmons are hauled before the crazed Roman emperor Caligula. It's awkwardly directed by Henry Koster and scripted as if by a committee anxious not to offend any race or creed. But there are compensations: Burton is handsome in a Roman garb and Jay Robinson makes an unforgettably melodramatic Caligula. Victor Mature starred in the sequel, *Demetrius and the Gladiators*. **AT** **DVD**

Richard Burton *Marcellus Gallio* • Jean Simmons *Diana* • Victor Mature *Demetrius* • Michael Rennie *Peter* • Jay Robinson *Caligula* • Dean Jagger

Justus • Torin Thatcher *Senator Gallio* • Richard Boone *Pilate* • Betta St John *Miriam* • Ernest Thesiger *Emperor Tiberius* ■ *Dir* Henry Koster • *Scr* Albert Maltz (uncredited), Philip Dunne, from the novel by Lloyd C Douglas, adapted by Gina Kaus • *Costume Designers* Charles LeMaire, Emile Santiago • *Cinematographer* Leon Shamroy

Robert Altman's Jazz '34: Remembrances of Kansas City Swing ★★★★

Music documentary   1996 · US · Colour · 72min

Director Robert Altman's 1996 film, *Kansas City* – a jazz-tinged melodrama about a corrupt politician and a gangster – was notable if only for some remarkable 1930s music as arranged by the innovative John Cale. This documentary is the offspring of that movie, featuring sessions recorded on the set of the earlier film. With *Jazz '34's* pumping, grinding blues all set to elevate the spirits, it's a shame that Altman hadn't done a better job on the original move. **TH**

Harry Belafonte *Narrator* ■ *Dir* Robert Altman • *Production Designer* Stephen Altman

Robert et Robert ★★★

Comedy drama   1978 · Fr · Colour · 106min

Often dismissed for promoting style over content, Claude Lelouch is still capable of producing hugely entertaining films. While this odd couple comedy may not have anything resounding to say about the modern French male, it's still full of good-natured humour and spirited performances. The pairing of Charles Denner and Jacques Villeret, as the eponymous bachelors who embark on a series of comic misadventures, is inspired, with the former's outgoing cabbie contrasting splendidly with the latter's timid everyman. **DP** French +subtitles.

Charles Denner *Robert Goldman* • Jacques Villeret *Robert Villiers* • Jean-Claude Brialy *Manager* • Germaine Montero *Madame Goldman* • Régine *Madame Villiers* • Macha Méril *Agathe* ■ *Dir/Scr* Claude Lelouch

Roberta ★★★ U

Musical romantic comedy
1935 · US · BW · 102min

Fred Astaire, Gingers Rogers and Jerome Kern's ravishing 18-carat score are the attractions of this otherwise quite silly musical, adapted from the Broadway show. The plot, such as it is, has he-man footballer Randolph Scott inheriting a chic, Paris fashion house. Designer Irene Dunne (who renders *Smoke Gets in Your Eyes* most touchingly) falls for him. But it's the musical numbers performed by Fred and Ginger on the verge of mega-stardom that has kept the film alive. The rich cornucopia of ballads also includes the Oscar-nominated and enduring *Lovely to Look At* from which the 1952 remake took its name. **RK**

Irene Dunne *Princess Stephanie* • Fred Astaire *Huck Haines* • Ginger Rogers *Comtesse "Tanka" Scharwenka aka Lizzie Gatz* • Randolph Scott *John Kent* • Helen Westley *Roberta aka Minnie* • Victor Varconi *Prince Ladislaw* • Claire Dodd *Sophie Teale* • Luis Alberni *Alexander Petrovich Moskovitch Voyda* • Lucille Ball *Model* ■ *Dir* William A Seiter • *Scr* Jane Murfin, Sam Mintz, Allan Scott, from the musical by Jerome Kern, Otto Harbach, from the novel *Gowns by Roberta* by Alice Duer Miller

Roberto Succo ★★★★ 15

Crime drama based on a true story
2000 · Fr/Swi · Colour · 119min

The young man who murdered his parents while still a teenager and later embarked on a random killing spree in southern France during the 1980s is shown in a harsh light, but this compelling adaptation refrains from total condemnation of its protagonist. Making exemplary use of the often hostile terrain and its small-town locales, director Cédric Kahn's only misjudgment is in lingering on detective Patrick Dell'Isola's manhunt when the main fascination lies in the psychological instability of the mercurial Stefano Cassetti (an utterly mesmerising performance) and his fumbling relationship with his adoring teenage lover, Isild le Besco. **DP** French, Italian +subtitles. Violence, swearing. **DVD**

Stefano Cassetti *"Kurt"/Roberto Succo* • Isild Le Besco *Léa* • Patrick Dell'Isola *Major Thomas* • Vincent Deneriaz *Denis* • Aymeric Chauffert *Delaunay* ■ *Dir* Cédric Kahn • *Scr* Cédric Kahn, from the non-fiction book *Je Te Tu - Histoire Vrai de Roberto Succo* by Pascale Froment

Robin and Marian ★★★★ PG

Adventure   1976 · UK · Colour · 102min

An older and disillusioned Robin Hood returns from the Crusades to find Sherwood empty of outlaws, Marian in a nunnery and the Sheriff of Nottingham still fiddling the books. James Goldman's script has a wonderful way with satire and myth-mongering, while Richard Lester has the sharpest eye for historical detail. Audrey Hepburn was lured out of retirement to play Marian and she is exquisite, but it's Sean Connery's gruff, greybeard performance that ennobles rather than dominates the picture. Great support, too, from Robert Shaw's Sheriff and Ronnie Barker's perfectly judged "heavy relief" as Friar Tuck. What a pity this gorgeous, masterly elegy for a vanished age of chivalry flopped at the box-office. **AT** **DVD**

Sean Connery *Robin Hood* • Audrey Hepburn *Maid Marian* • Robert Shaw *Sheriff of Nottingham* • Richard Harris *King Richard* • Nicol Williamson *Little John* • Denholm Elliott *Will Scarlett* • Kenneth Haigh *Sir Ranulf* • Ronnie Barker *Friar Tuck* • Ian Holm *King John* • Bill Maynard *Mercadier* • Esmond Knight *Old defender* ■ *Dir* Richard Lester • *Scr* James Goldman • *Cinematographer* David Watkin

Robin and the 7 Hoods ★★★★ U

Musical comedy   1964 · US · Colour · 117min

This musical crime comedy from veteran director Gordon Douglas was the final fling of Frank Sinatra's Rat Pack. It's Robin Hood in Prohibition-era Chicago, with gangsters battling for control of the city. Sinatra introduces *My Kind of Town (Chicago Is ...)*, Bing Crosby and Dean Martin join him in *Style*, and Peter Falk, Barbara Rush (as Marian) and Edward G Robinson, no less, decorate the fringes. Funny, irreverent and very enjoyable, this movie is a warm-hearted treat. **TS** [symbol]

Frank Sinatra *Robbo* • Dean Martin *Little John* • Sammy Davis Jr *Will* • Bing Crosby *Allen A Dale* • Peter Falk *Guy Gisborne* • Barbara Rush *Marian* • Edward G Robinson *Big Jim* • Victor Buono *Sheriff Potts* • Hank Henry *Six Seconds* • Allen Jenkins *Vermin* • Jack LaRue *Tomatoes* ■ *Dir* Gordon Douglas • *Scr* David R Schwartz, from his story

Robin Hood ★★★★ PG

Silent romantic adventure
1922 · US · BW · 117min

This is one of the showiest (and slowest) of all the epics starring action man of the silents Douglas Fairbanks. The crowds are imaginatively handled by director Allan Dwan, with Fairbanks as the ever-grinning Robin, swashbuckling his way around Sherwood Forest at the behest of Enid Bennett's Maid Marian. And while Wallace Beery weighs in heavily as Richard the Lion-Hearted, it's Sam De Grasse as Prince John who gives the film's best performance. **TH** **DVD**

Douglas Fairbanks *The Earl of Huntington/Robin Hood* • Wallace Beery *Richard the Lion-Hearted* • Sam De Grasse *Prince John* • Enid Bennett *Lady Marian Fitzwalter* • Paul Dickey *Sir Guy of Gisbourne* • William Lowery *The High Sheriff of Nottingham* • Roy Coulson *The King's Jester* • Willard Louis *Friar Tuck* • Alan Hale *Little John* ■ *Dir* Allan Dwan • *Scr* Lotta Woods, from a story by Elton Thomas [Douglas Fairbanks] • *Costume Designer* Mitchell Leisen

Robin Hood ★★★★ U

Animated adventure   1973 · US · Colour · 82min

This Disney cartoon may not have the heart or the memorable songs of the studio's classics, but the result is still a pleasant and entertaining diversion for children. Here, it's Robin Hood and his Merry Men-agerie, as all the legendary Nottingham characters have been drawn as animals in a delightful

retelling of the "rob from the rich, give to the poor" Sherwood Forest tale. Villainous Prince John (voiced by Peter Ustinov) and slimy Sir Hiss (Terry-Thomas) provide the funniest moments, while the archery contest-turned-American football match is an action highlight. **AJ** **DVD** **Blu**

Brian Bedford *Robin Hood* • Phil Harris *Little John* • Monica Evans *Maid Marian* • Peter Ustinov *Prince John* • Terry-Thomas *Sir Hiss* • Andy Devine *Friar Tuck* ■ *Dir* Wolfgang Reitherman • *Scr* Larry Clemmons, from a story and characters by Ken Anderson

Robin Hood ★★★★ PG

Adventure   1990 · UK/US · Colour · 99min

This version of the classic tale had the misfortune to come out around the same time as Kevin Costner's epic and unsurprisingly was overshadowed by that Hollywood blockbuster. It's a shame because this, in many ways, is a better film. Patrick Bergin sparkles in the title role, doing battle with an enjoyable trio of baddies (Jeroen Krabbé, Jurgen Prochnow and Edward Fox), while Uma Thurman makes for a rather sympathetic Maid Marian. Director John Irvin authentically re-creates the murky medieval milieu, while staging some grand action sequences and rousing swordfights. **JF** Some violence.

Patrick Bergin *Robert Hode/"Robin Hood"* • Uma Thurman *Maid Marian* • Jürgen Prochnow *Sir Miles Folcanet* • Edward Fox *Prince John* • Jeroen Krabbé *Baron Daguerre* • Owen Teale *Will Redding "Will Scarlett"* • David Morrissey *Little John* • Alex Norton *Harry* • Gabrielle Reidy *Lily* • Jeff Nuttall *Friar Tuck* ■ *Dir* John Irvin • *Scr* Mark Allen Smith, John McGrath

Robin Hood ★★★ 12

Adventure   2010 · US/Jpn · Colour · 134min

Ridley Scott's retelling of the Robin Hood legend quickly plunges into the heat of battle, as Richard the Lionheart (Danny Huston) carves his route back from Jerusalem through France. Clarity is achieved once archer Robin Longstride (Russell Crowe, reuniting with his *Gladiator* director) assumes the guise of Robin of Loxley in order to return to an oppressed England. Scott presents a politically complex vision of the tale that boasts tremendous strengths – fine battle scenes, a strongly realised interpretation of events and a commanding lead performance. But the weak spots – a distracting romance with Cate Blanchett's Marion, the purposeless scenes of mead-quaffing and folk dancing – diminish the overall effect, leaving it a valiant try rather than an unqualified success. **AR** English, French +subtitles. Violence, sexual references. **DVD** **Blu**

Russell Crowe *Robin Longstride* • Cate Blanchett *Lady Marion Loxley* • Max von Sydow *Sir Walter Loxley* • William Hurt *William Marshall* • Mark Strong *Sir Godfrey* • Oscar Isaac *Prince John* • Danny Huston *King Richard the Lionheart* • Eileen Atkins *Eleanor of Aquitaine* • Mark Addy *Friar Tuck* • Matthew Macfadyen *Sheriff of Nottingham* ■ *Dir* Ridley Scott • *Scr* Brian Helgeland, from a story by Helgeland, Ethan Reiff, Cyrus Voris • *Cinematographer* John Mathieson

Robin Hood: Men in Tights ★★ PG

Comedy   1993 · US · Colour · 99min

While it's sad that Mel Brooks has hung up his megaphone, there's a certain sense of merciful release, as his last pictures veered from poor to downright awful. This Sherwood spoof has the occasional flash of vintage Brooks and wonderfully po-faced performances from Cary Elwes as Robin and Amy Yasbeck as Marian. On the down side are Roger Rees's ghastly Sheriff of Rottingham, the untidy structure and the fact that the bawdy gags are more notable for their antiquity than their quality. **DP** Swearing. **DVD**

Cary Elwes *Robin Hood* • Richard Lewis *Prince John* • Roger Rees *Sheriff of Rottingham* • Amy Yasbeck *Marian* • Mark Blankfield *Blinkin* • Dave Chappelle *Ahchoo* • Isaac Hayes *Asneeze* • Megan Cavanagh *Broomhilde* • Eric Allan Kramer *Little John* • Matthew Poretta *Will Scarlet O'Hara* • Tracey Ullman *Latrine* • Patrick Stewart *King*

Richard • Dom DeLuise Don Giovanni • Mel Brooks Rabbi Tuckman ■ Dir Mel Brooks • Scr Mel Brooks, Evan Chandler, J David Shapiro, from a story by J David Shapiro, Evan Chandler

The Robin Hood of El Dorado ★★★

Biographical drama   1936 • US • BW • 85min

Spurred by the success of Viva Villa!, its biopic of Pancho Villa, MGM turned out this vigorous account of the life and death in early California of another legendary figure, Joaquin Murrieta. He is depicted as the peaceful farmer who is branded a bandit, after avenging the death of his wife at the hands of four gringos. Former Cisco Kid Warner Baxter takes the role and William A Wellman's typically uneven direction veers from hard-hitting action, to poetic lyricism and sheer sentimentality. AE

Warner Baxter Joaquin Murrieta • Ann Loring Juanita de la Cuesta • Bruce Cabot Bill Warren • Margo Rosita • J Carrol Naish Three fingered Jack • Edgar Kennedy Sheriff Judd • Dir William A Wellman • Scr William A Wellman, Joseph Calleia, Melvin Levy, from a novel by Walter Noble

Robin Hood: Prince of Thieves ★★★★🅟🅖

Action adventure   1991 • US • Colour • 148min

Buckles are truly swashed and derring-do effectively done in Kevin Reynolds's 12th-century adventure, which simply sets out to entertain handsomely and does so with a great deal of dash, flash and panache. Alan Rickman is a joy to behold as the panto-styled Sheriff of Nottingham, while Morgan Freeman's cultured Moor (Robin's early saviour) is a commanding, if unlikely, medieval presence. Kevin Costner is more "Indiana Hood" than the Locksley lad of yore in this popcorn epic of romp and circumstance. Director Reynolds deserves the most praise for disguising such overfamiliar events with imaginative staging and a roving camera. AJ Swearing, violence, brief nudity. 🅳🅥🅳 🅑

Kevin Costner Robin of Locksley/Robin Hood • Mary Elizabeth Mastrantonio Maid Marian • Alan Rickman Sheriff of Nottingham • Morgan Freeman Azeem • Christian Slater Will Scarlett • Geraldine McEwan Mortianna • Micheal McShane Friar Tuck • Brian Blessed Lord Locksley • Michael Wincott Guy of Gisborne • Nick Brimble Little John • Soo Drouet Fanny • Sean Connery King Richard ■ Dir Kevin Reynolds • Scr Pen Densham, John Watson, from a story by Pen Densham

Robinson Crusoe ★★★🅟🅖

Animated comedy adventure
2015 • Bel/Fr/UK/US • Colour • 90min

Very loosely based on Daniel Defoe's castaway classic, this rather classy and fast-paced children's animated adventure takes a very different tack in its retelling of the story. It's told from the points of view of the animals on the island Crusoe gets washed up on - especially a parrot, whose mouthy musings provide the movie's voiceover. Excellent Euro-animation somewhat eclipses the standard, stop-start storyline, but some action sequences are well worth the wait and watch. Some of the darker, more intense sequences may challenge more sensitive young souls, however. DA 🅢🅟

Doug Stone Aynsley • Colin Metzger Carmello • Michael Sorich Cecil • Yuri Lowenthal Robinson Crusoe ■ Dir Vincent Kesteloot • Scr Lee Christopher, Domonic Paris, Graham Welldon, from the novel The Life and Adventures of Robinson Crusoe by Daniel Defoe

Robinson Crusoe on Mars ★★★★🅤

Science-fiction drama
1964 • US • Colour • 105min

Once you get passed the ridiculous title this is a wholly satisfactory and intelligent slice of pulp sci-fi from Byron Haskin, director of The War of the Worlds. Shot in the bleak hostility of California's Death Valley, this is an innovative retelling of the classic Defoe tale, centering on astronaut Paul Mantee's survival challenges following a crash-

landing that leaves him stranded on the red planet. Haskin wisely bypasses flashy effects to concentrate on the human element, notably the growing relationship between Mantee and the alien he rescues from a slave ship. RS 🅳🅥🅳 🅑

Paul Mantee Cmdr Christopher "Kit" Draper • Vic Lundin Friday • Adam West Col Dan McReady ■ Dir Byron Haskin • Scr John C Higgins, Ib Melchior, from the novel The Life and Strange Surprising Adventures of Robinson Crusoe by Daniel Defoe • Cinematographer Winton C Hoch • Special Effects Lawrence W Butler

Robinson in Space ★★★★🅟🅖

Documentary drama   1997 • UK • Colour • 78min

Patrick Keiller was inspired to make this follow-up to 1994's London by the closure of the old Morris Motors works in Oxford. Visiting factories and ports the length and breadth of the country, he seeks to gauge the impact of 18-years of Tory rule on Britain's traditional manufacturing industries and assess how far we have become a service economy. Complete with a voiceover from Paul Scofield that blends socio-economic data, literary references and the quirky opinions of his fictional companion, Robinson, the film has more of a political agenda than its predecessor, but is every bit as compelling. DP 🅳🅥🅳

Paul Scofield Narrator ■ Dir/Scr Patrick Keiller

Robinson in Ruins ★★★★🅤

Documentary   2010 • UK • Colour • 101min

The third film in Patrick Keiller's series (following 1994's London and 1997's Robinson in Space) is another odyssey around Britain. Vanessa Redgrave takes over narrating duties from the late Paul Scofield here, but the director's passion for anecdote and fact is every bit as impeccably researched and visually compelling as in the first two films. This time Robinson's activities are confined to Oxfordshire and Berkshire as the financial crisis worsens during 2008. By pausing periodically to take in the work of nature, Keiller finds melancholic magic in the discarded domestic and industrial edifices of a landscape that has much to tell us - if only we're prepared to look and listen. DP

Vanessa Redgrave Narrator ■ Dir/Scr Patrick Keiller

RoboCop ★★★★★🔟🅰

Satirical science-fiction thriller
1987 • US • Colour • 98min

Hi-tech meets High Noon in Dutch director Paul Verhoeven's deft science-fiction masterpiece, which delivers on both violent action and satirical fronts. Peter Weller gives a great mime performance as the Detroit cop of the near future, resurrected as a cyborg, who goes head-hunting the sadistic gang responsible for his plight as his human memory begins to return. But it's Verhoeven's scabrous dissection of American social issues, trashy sitcom culture and corporate greed that makes this a subversive and thought-provoking edge-of-the-seat epic. AJ Swearing, drug abuse, brief nudity. 🅳🅥🅳 🅑

Peter Weller Murphy/RoboCop • Nancy Allen Officer Anne Lewis • Daniel O'Herlihy [Dan O'Herlihy] Old man • Ronny Cox Dick Jones • Kurtwood Smith Clarence Boddicker • Miguel Ferrer Robert Morton • Robert DoQui Sergeant Reed • Ray Wise Leon ■ Dir Paul Verhoeven • Scr Edward Neumeier, Michael Miner

RoboCop 2 ★★★🔟🅰

Science-fiction thriller
1990 • US • Colour • 111min

Peter Weller returns as the cyborg policeman patrolling the mean streets of Detroit. Daniel O'Herlihy, ostensibly the good tycoon from the first film, becomes the bad guy this time around, teaming up with psycho Tom Noonan to destroy his company's creation. It's once again a spectacularly violent affair and the satirical news items still provide a chuckle or two, but it lacks the original's gloriously black excess. JF Swearing. 🅳🅥🅳 🅑

Peter Weller RoboCop • Nancy Allen Officer Anne Lewis • Belinda Bauer Dr Juliette Faxx • Daniel O'Herlihy [Dan O'Herlihy] Old man • Tom Noonan Cain • Gabriel Damon Hob • Willard Pugh Mayor Kuzak • Stephen Lee Duffy ■ Dir Irvin Kershner • Scr Frank Miller, Walon Green, from a story by Frank Miller, from characters by Edward Neumeier, Michael Miner

RoboCop 3 ★★★🔟🄴

Science-fiction thriller
1993 • US • Colour • 104min

Robert Burke replaces Peter Weller as the unstoppable cyborg cop in this more comedy driven, and far less violent, futuristic fantasy from director Fred Dekker. The mechanised flatfoot this time defends the downtrodden homeless when an amoral Japanese magnate decides to clean up downtown Detroit in order to build a luxury apartment complex. Well directed and written with a firm eye on the family TV series the concept eventually became. AJ Violence, swearing. 🅳🅥🅳 🅑

Robert John Burke [Robert Burke] RoboCop/Alex J Murphy • Nancy Allen Officer Anne Lewis • Rip Torn Merritt W Morton, CEO • John Castle Paul McDaggett • Jill Hennessy Dr Marie Lazarus • CCH Pounder Bertha • Mako Kanemitsu ■ Dir Fred Dekker • Scr Frank Miller, Fred Dekker, from a story by Miller, from characters by Edward Neumeier, Michael Miner

RoboCop ★★★★🔟🄰

Science-fiction action thriller
2014 • US • Colour • 112min

Brazilian director José Padilha brings visceral grit and propulsive punch to this slick reboot of the 1987 sci-fi masterpiece. Joel Kinnaman confidently steps into Peter Weller's formidable shoes as the Detroit cop-turned-cyborg who, once customised by scientist Gary Oldman, targets both the villains responsible for his murder and the corrupt corporation that created him. Tweaked into a political and philosophical treatise, the film is less satirical and subversive than the original. But, smartly updated with sleek CGI, night-vision trickery and video game-style visuals, this is a must for action fans. AJ Some violence, brief swearing. 🅳🅥🅳 🅑

Joel Kinnaman Alex Murphy/RoboCop • Gary Oldman Dr Dennett Norton • Michael Keaton Raymond Sellars • Samuel L Jackson Pat Novak • Abbie Cornish Clara Murphy ■ Dir José Padilha • Scr Joshua Zetumer, from characters by Michael Miner, Edward Neumeier

Robot & Frank ★★★★🔟🄰

Science-fiction comedy drama
2012 • US • Colour • 85min

This futuristic buddy movie is an irresistible charmer and a genuine pleasure to watch. Frank Langella gives a magnificent performance as the cranky, retired cat burglar slipping into dementia whose grown-up children give him a robot carer to improve his quality of life. But the still wily jewel thief soon convinces the ever-calm droid to become his partner in crime and commit one last heist for old time's sake. Springing poignant twists en route to its bittersweet ending, this engaging character study accents compassion and humour above any major use of special effects. The low-tech robot is winningly played by Rachael Ma and voiced by Peter Sarsgaard, while director Jake Schreier hits just the right tone between laughter and emotion in his heartfelt feature debut. AJ Swearing. 🅳🅥🅳 🅑

Frank Langella Frank • James Marsden Hunter • Liv Tyler Madison • Peter Sarsgaard Robot • Susan Sarandon Jennifer • Jeremy Strong Jake ■ Dir Jake Schreier • Scr Christopher D Ford

Robot Jox ★★🔟🄴

Science-fiction action
1989 • US • Colour • 80min

In a post-nuclear world of banished warfare, nations settle scores with one another via televised games, in which representative heroes battle it out while inside hulking, transformer-like robots. The fascinating premise is sadly let down by a scrawny budget and script to match. While the robot

miniature work is effective, the rest of the film has a cheap look. RS

Gary Graham Achilles • Anne-Marie Johnson Athena • Paul Koslo Alexander • Robert Sampson Commissioner Jameson • Danny Kamekona Doctor Matsumoto • Hilary Mason Professor Laplace • Michael Alldredge Tex Conway ■ Dir Stuart Gordon • Scr Joe Haldeman, from a story by Stuart Gordon

Robot Monster ★🅤

Science fiction   1953 • US • BW • 62min

After Plan 9 from Outer Space, this is the best known bad movie in the science-fiction genre. The last six human survivors in existence struggle against the dreaded Ro-Man (a man dressed in a gorilla suit and a plastic diving helmet), whose race has destroyed the planet with their "calcinator ray". Made for next-to-nothing in four days, and padded out with bizarre stock footage montages, this legendary trash masterpiece is hilariously threadbare. AJ 🅢🅟

George Nader Roy • Claudia Barrett Alice • Selena Royle Mother • Gregory Moffett Johnny • John Mylong Professor • Pamela Paulson Carla • George Barrows Ro-Man ■ Dir Phil Tucker • Scr Wyott Ordung

Robot Overlords ★★🔟🄲

Science-fiction action adventure
2014 • UK • Colour • 86min

Alien robots have conquered Earth, forcing humanity to wear transmitters that vaporise anyone straying from home. Affable hero Callan McAuliffe learns how to short circuit the implants, breaks the lethal curfew and sets off to find his missing father who heads the resistance. The scale of the film is more Doctor Who than Transformers, with the British seaside setting only emphasising the quaintness of what is essentially a predictable elongated chase sequence with very little tension. AJ Sexual references. 🅳🅥🅳 🅑

Ben Kingsley Robin Smythe • Gillian Anderson Kate • Callan McAuliffe Sean Flynn • Ella Hunt Alex • James Tarpey Nathan • Steven Mackintosh Danny • Geraldine James Monique ■ Dir Jon Wright • Scr Jon Wright, Mark Stay

Robot Wars ★🅟🅖

Science-fiction western
1993 • US • Colour • 69min

This dire, futuristic tale may be set in 2041, but it's got the production values of 1970. The stop-frame animation of the giant robot vehicles is passable, but the acting and dialogue ("You're way too negative. You're a walking minus sign.") is beyond bad. Don Michael Paul's Han Solo-esque robot pilot barely has a pulse. Chuck in some of the shoddiest back projection work ever seen and you have a film of considerable awfulness. JC

Don Michael Paul Captain Drake • Barbara Crampton Dr Leda Fannon • James Staley Stumpy ■ Dir Albert Band • Scr Jackson Barr, from an idea by Charles Band

Robots ★★★🅤

Animated comedy adventure
2005 • US • Colour • 86min

This visually inventive romp through a world populated entirely by robots uses inspired computer animation to revitalise a familiar story. Leading an eclectic voice cast, Ewan McGregor gives boyish charm to an idealistic small-town robot who journeys to the big city to make his fortune as an inventor. While the comedy is both light and mischievous, some in-jokes and references will be too obscure for younger viewers. SF 🅳🅥🅳

Ewan McGregor Rodney Copperbottom • Halle Berry Cappy • Robin Williams Fender • Greg Kinnear Phineas T Ratchet • Mel Brooks Bigweld • Drew Carey Crank • Jim Broadbent Madame Gasket • Amanda Bynes Piper • Jennifer Coolidge Aunt Fanny • Stanley Tucci Herb Copperbottom • Dianne Wiest Mrs Copperbottom ■ Dir Chris Wedge, Carlos Saldanha • Scr David Lindsay-Abaire, Lowell Ganz, Babaloo Mandel, from a story by Ron Mita, Jim McClain, David Lindsay-Abaire

R

Rocco and His Brothers ★★★ 15

Drama 1960 · Fr/It · BW · 170min

A grimly naturalistic subject – peasant family from southern Italy moves to the corrupting urban jungle of Milan – gets the grand operatic treatment from Luchino Visconti, whose initial restraint should have been maintained throughout. Instead, he goes for empty flourishes of over-the-top despair with which Alain Delon seems somewhat uncomfortable. This may be a long haul, but is certainly worth seeing for Renato Salvatori as the brutish elder brother and the accomplished black-and-white photography of Giuseppe Rotunno. TH Italian +subtitles. DVD

Alain Delon *Rocco Parondi* · Renato Salvatori *Simone Parondi* · Annie Girardot *Nadia* · Katina Paxinou *Rosaria Parondi* · Roger Hanin *Morini* · Paolo Stoppa *Boxing impresario* · Suzy Delair *Luisa* · Claudia Cardinale *Ginetta* ■ *Dir* Luchino Visconti · *Scr* Luchino Visconti, Vasco Pratolini, Suso Cecchi D'Amico, Pasquale Festa Campanile, Massimo Franciosa, Enrico Medioli, Claude Brulé, from a story by Luchino Visconti, Vasco Pratolini, Suso Cecchi D'Amico, from the novel *I Segretti di Milano: il Ponte della Ghisolfa* by Giovanni Testori

Rocinante ★★ PG

Political drama 1986 · UK · Colour · 92min

After a meaningful conversation about film narrative with an ex-projectionist, recluse John Hurt leaves the derelict cinema where he has been hiding out and hitches a ride to Dartmoor in a truck named Rocinante (a reference to Don Quixote's horse). On his aimless quest he meets political activist Maureen Douglass who, inspired by the 1984 miners' strike, is intent on industrial sabotage. The resulting blend of road movie, British folklore and the Don Quixote myth is a slice of pretentious art. AJ

John Hurt *Bill* · Maureen Douglass *Jess* · Ian Dury *Jester* · Carol Gillies *Molly* · Jimmy Jewel *Projectionist* ■ *Dir/Scr* Ann Guedes, Eduardo Guedes

The Rock ★★★★ 15

Action thriller 1996 · US · Colour · 130min

The setting is Alcatraz, which has been taken over by disenchanted general Ed Harris and his crack team of marines, who are threatening to launch deadly poison-gas rockets to contaminate San Francisco. In desperation, the FBI pairs chemical warfare expert Nicolas Cage with jailed former SAS man Sean Connery, who – as the only man to ever escape from the notorious island prison – is seen as their best option to break in. Director Michael Bay's boyish enthusiasm for outlandish stunts and carefree destruction is contagious and even the most cynical of viewers will find it difficult not to feel rushes of adrenaline. JF Violence, swearing, a sex scene. DVD

Sean Connery *John Patrick Mason* · Nicolas Cage *Stanley Goodspeed* · Ed Harris *General Francis X Hummel* · John Spencer *FBI Director Womack* · David Morse *Major Tom Baxter* · William Forsythe *Ernest Paxton* · Michael Biehn *Commander Anderson* · Vanessa Marcil *Carla Pestalozzi* · John C McGinley *Marine Captain Hendrix* ■ *Dir* Michael Bay · *Scr* David Weisberg, Mark Rosner, Douglas S Cook, from a story by David Weisberg, Douglas S Cook

Rock-a-Bye Baby ★★ U

Comedy 1958 · US · Colour · 99min

A famous movie star (Marilyn Maxwell), whose marriage has been kept secret in order to preserve her glamorous image, gives birth to triplets, another event that needs hushing up, and turns to a lifelong besotted fan, a bachelor, to take care of the infant trio. He is Jerry Lewis, pursuing his post-Dean Martin, solo career and calling on his full repertoire of frenzied lunacy. The effect, without Martin as foil, is akin to being hit on the head with a sandbag, but Lewis addicts should be happy with that. RK DVD

Jerry Lewis *Clayton Poole* · Marilyn Maxwell *Carla Naples* · Connie Stevens *Sandy Naples* · Reginald Gardiner *Harold Herman* · Baccaloni [Salvatore Baccaloni] *Salvatore Naples* · Hans Conried *Mr Wright* · Isobel Elsom *Mrs Van Cleve* ·

James Gleason *Dr Simkins* ■ *Dir* Frank Tashlin · *Scr* Frank Tashlin, from the play *The Miracle of Morgan's Creek* by Preston Sturges

Rock All Night ★★ PG

Crime drama 1957 · US · BW · 62min

Fresh from a supporting role in Corman's *Not of This Earth*, Dick Miller landed the lead in this trashy teen crime drama, about a couple of killers who besiege the Cloud Nine rock 'n' roll club. For once playing the good guy, Miller is great value as the nerdy barman who saves the day. The Platters, in their original line-up with Tony Williams and Zola Taylor and at the height of their fame, make the screen sizzle, despite the economy of footage used to film them. A real curio, shot in under a week. DP DVD

Dick Miller *Shorty* · Abby Dalton *Julie* · Robin Morse *Al* · Richard H Cutting *Steve* · Bruno VeSota *Charley* · Chris Alcaide *Angie* ■ *Dir* Roger Corman · *Scr* Charles B Griffith, from the story by David P Harmon

Rock around the Clock ★★★ U

Musical 1956 · US · BW · 74min

In this low-budget movie, disc jockey Alan Freed discovers a rock band in a village in the faraway hills and promotes them in New York. And that would be that, except for the fact that the band is Bill Haley and His Comets, and this little film is now history for the effect they produced on teen audiences worldwide and on the music business. Boasting an abundance of hits, including Haley's *See You Later, Alligator*, this rock-pop fest features numerous other artists, including The Platters. RK

Bill Haley · Alan Freed · Johnny Johnston *Steve Hollis* · Alix Talton *Corinne* · Lisa Gaye *Lisa Johns* · John Archer *Mike Dennis* ■ *Dir* Fred F Sears · *Scr* Robert E Kent, James B Gordon

Rock Hudson's Home Movies ★★★

Documentary 1992 · US · Colour · 63min

This is a smart and sassy probe into the uneasy synthesis of homosexuality and the Hollywood star system. Director Mark Rappaport's camp delight features a Rock Hudson lookalike who takes the viewer on a *That's Entertainment*-style journey of cleverly edited film clips from the heart-throb's life, hilariously underlining their gay connotations. Although tinged with a melancholic sadness over the matinée idol's subsequent Aids-related death in 1985, Rappaport's take on Hudson is a decidedly militant version of the ageing closeted star's persona. AJ

Eric Farr *Rock Hudson* ■ *Dir/Scr* Mark Rappaport

Rock 'n' Roll High School ★★★ 15

Musical comedy 1979 · US · Colour · 87min

A punk homage to the high-school rock 'n' roll films of the 1950s and 1960s, this trails cult credits like a pair of ripped bondage pants. Roger Corman is the executive producer, Joe Dante co-wrote the story with director Allan Arkush and The Ramones appear live and contribute to the score. There is an excuse of a teenage romance plot but the meat has PJ Soles, a Ramones fan, at war with rock-hating high-school principal Mary Woronov. A brilliant soundtrack, a great deal of ludicrous comic book humour and an explosive ending make this head and shoulders above all other teenage music films, including the miserable 1991 follow-up. FL DVD

PJ Soles *Riff Randell* · Vincent Van Patten *Tom Roberts* · Clint Howard *Eaglebauer* · Dey Young *Kate Rambeau* · Mary Woronov *Evelyn Togar* · Dick Miller *Police Chief Klein* · Paul Bartel (1) *Mr McGree* ■ *Dir* Allan Arkush · *Scr* Richard Whitley, Russ Dvonch, Joseph McBride, from a story by Allan Arkush, Joe Dante

Rock of Ages ★★ 12

Musical romantic comedy 2012 · US · Colour · 118min

Based on the stage musical of the same name, Adam Shankman's lightweight 1980s-set confection focuses on a young couple (Julianne Hough and Diego Boneta) pursuing their rock star dreams at a down-on-its-luck nightclub on Hollywood's famed Sunset Strip. To a backdrop of rock hits of the day, the lovers' ambitions are thwarted by puritanical campaigners and the arrival of booze-addled superstar Stacee Jaxx (Tom Cruise). Alec Baldwin exercises his impressive comedy chops as the scruffy club owner, and there's good work from Catherine Zeta-Jones as a politician's wife, but overall the film teeters, close to collapse, on its stacked heels. TeS Sexual references, some swearing. DVD

Julianne Hough *Sherrie Christian* · Diego Boneta *Drew Boley* · Tom Cruise *Stacee Jaxx* · Russell Brand *Lonnie* · Alec Baldwin *Dennis Dupree* · Paul Giamatti *Paul Gill* · Catherine Zeta-Jones *Patricia Whitmore* ■ *Dir* Adam Shankman · *Scr* Chris D'Arienzo, Allan Loeb, Justin Theroux, from the musical book *Rock of Ages* by D'Arienzo

Rock, Pretty Baby ★★ U

Musical 1956 · US · BW · 89min

This was made strictly for a teenage audience at the time, and is still likely to appeal mostly to those who were growing up in the 1950s, though fans of the era's music (shockingly radical at the time but amazingly tame-sounding now) will appreciate seeing the stars of the day performing their hits. The slight plot has John Saxon as the leader of a high-school band, intent on winning a major contest against the wishes of his father. TV

Sal Mineo *Angelo Barrato* · John Saxon *Jimmy Daley* · Luana Patten *Joan Wright* · Edward C Platt [Edward Platt] *Thomas Daley Sr* · Fay Wray *Beth Daley* · Rod McKuen *"Ox" Bentley* · John Wilder *"Fingers" Porter* · Alan Reed Jr *"Sax" Lewis* ■ *Dir* Richard Bartlett · *Scr* Herbert Margolis, William Raynor · *Music* Henry Mancini

Rock, Rock, Rock! ★★ U

Musical 1956 · US · BW · 85min

This cheap quickie is very much a period piece for aficionados. Featuring the man who actually coined the phrase "rock 'n' roll", Alan Freed, the wafer-thin plot hinges on whether teenager Tuesday Weld (songs dubbed by Connie Francis) will get the prom dress of her dreams, set against the backdrop of America's latest novelty craze. Production values? Plot? Acting? It didn't matter then, Daddy-O, and it still doesn't. TS DVD

Tuesday Weld *Dori* · Jacqueline Kerr *Gloria* · Ivy Schulman *Baby* · Fran Manfred *Arabella* · Jack Collins *Father* · Carol Moss *Mother* · Eleanor Swayne *Miss Silky* · Lester Mack *Mr Bimble* · Bert Conway *Mr Barker* ■ *Dir* Will Price · *Scr* Milton Subotsky, from a story by Milton Subotsky, Phyllis Coe

Rock School ★★★ 15

Music documentary 2004 · US · Colour · 89min

This documentary focuses on a year in the life of Philadelphia guitarist-turned-rock-music-teacher Paul Green. Director Don Argott's film shows the larger-than-life Green using a volatile combination of foul-mouthed abuse and gentle encouragement to school his pupils. Their efforts climax in a very creditable performance of some complex rock music at a Frank Zappa festival in Germany. Stylistically, this isn't the most sparkling of documentaries, and there's a lack of backstory about the monstrous Green and his methods. But the kids are compulsively watchable, as is their terrifying teacher, so you'll probably be able to forgive any shortcomings. DA Swearing. DVD

■ *Dir* Don Argott

Rock Star ★★★ 15

Comedy drama based on a true story 2001 · US · Colour · 101min

This rags-to-riches morality lesson is little more than a leather-pants clad *Cinderella*. Inspired by the real-life story of rock group Judas Priest, it centres on tribute band vocalist Mark Wahlberg who learns life's harshest truths when he joins his rock heroes as their new lead singer. Coloured acid-bright with a series of boisterous vignettes plucked from documented rock

history, the film is a wild and often hilarious trip, with a romantic soft centre. The pervasive old-school metal soundtrack is intoxicating enough to help distract from Jennifer Aniston's miscasting as the rock chick girlfriend. SF DVD

Mark Wahlberg *Chris Cole* · Jennifer Aniston *Emily Poule* · Dominic West *Kirk Cuddy* · Timothy Spall *Mats* · Timothy Olyphant *Rob Malcolm* · Dagmara Dominczyk *Tania* · Jason Flemyng *Bobby Beers* ■ *Dir* Stephen Herek · *Scr* John Stockwell

Rock the House ★★

Drama 2011 · US · Colour · 120min

A strained father-daughter relationship is transformed via the power of rock 'n' roll in this by-the-numbers family drama. Jack Coleman (from TV's *Heroes*) wades through the clichés as a workaholic lawyer who conveniently starts to reconnect with introverted teen Cassi Thomson when he reforms his old garage band. But flimsy scripting and unconvincing performances make the pair's contrived journey to reconciliation a predictable and largely unrewarding watch. SF

Jack Coleman *Max Peterson* · Cassi Thomson *Karen Peterson* · Clare Carey *Jesse* · Helen Slater *Diane Peterson* · Andy Milder *Ronny* ■ *Dir* Ernie Barbarash · *Scr* Joe Woolf

Rock the Kasbah ★★ 15

Music comedy 2015 · US · Colour · 106min

Director Barry Levinson and Bill Murray team up for the first time in something of a comedy misfire. Murray plays a road manager for old 70s rock acts, who hears an angel-voiced Pashtun woman singing in Afghanistan – and decides to confront religious traditions and get her on the nation's TV talent show. Similar real-life events were covered in 2008 documentary *Afghan Star*, but in this clunky frolic the liberation of Afghan womanhood plays second string to Murray's redemption. TJ In English, Arabic. Swearing. DVD

Bill Murray *Richie Lanz* · Bruce Willis *Bombay Brian* · Kate Hudson *Merci* · Zooey Deschanel *Ronnie* · Scott Caan *Jake* · Kelly Lynch *Sylvia* ■ *Dir* Barry Levinson · *Scr* Mitch Glazer

Rockabye ★

Drama 1932 · US · BW · 66min

The overwrought tale of an actress who has clawed her way to the top, only to torment herself over her children and sacrifice her lover, this catastrophe stars the stylish and restrained Constance Bennett in a role to which she is totally unsuited. George Fitzmaurice, a veteran of several silents, was wheeled in to direct, and Phillips Holmes was cast as Bennett's leading man. The resulting film was so awful that Joel McCrea was bundled in to replace Holmes and George Cukor called in to direct a slew of retakes. RK

Constance Bennett *Judy Carroll* · Joel McCrea *Jacobs "Jake" Van Riker Pell* · Paul Lukas *Antoine "Tony" de Sola* · Jobyna Howland *"Snooks" Carroll* · Walter Pidgeon *Commissioner Al Howard* · Clara Blandick *Brida* ■ *Dir* George Cukor, George Fitzmaurice · *Scr* Jane Murfin, Kubec Glasmon, from the play by Lucia Bonder, from the short story *Our Judy* by Lucia Bonder

The Rocker ★★★ 12

Comedy 2008 · US · Colour · 97min

There are undertones of Jack Black's *The School of Rock* in this comedy about a washed-up drummer (Rainn Wilson) who joins his nephew's band. Fortunately, what the film lacks in originality, it makes up for in charm and off-the-wall humour. The balance of gags and heartfelt moments is ably handled by British director Peter Cattaneo (*The Full Monty*), and Wilson also deserves credit, graduating from comedy sidekick (in the US version of *The Office*) to carry this film with a winning blend of cynicism and exuberance. SP Sexual references. DVD

Rainn Wilson *Robert "Fish" Fishman* · Christina Applegate *Kim* · Teddy Geiger *Curtis Wood* · Josh Gad *Matt Gadman* · Emma Stone *Amelia* · Jeff Garlin *Stan* · Howard Hesseman *Gator* ■

U SUITABLE FOR ALL Ua SUITABLE ESPECIALLY FOR YOUNG CHILDREN (DVD ONLY) PG PARENTAL GUIDANCE 12A UNDER 12s TO BE ACCOMPANIED (CINEMA ONLY)

Dir Peter Cattaneo • *Scr* Maya Forbes, Wally Wolodarsky [Wallace Wolodarsky], from a story by Ryan Jaffe

Rockers ★★★ 15
Action comedy 1978 · Jam · Colour · 99min

This story of a young Rastafarian trying to drum his way into the music business may well have a see-through story, but it's also high on fruitcake whimsy and meandering charm. Even though the film invites the audience into a world of Rasta ritual and peer-group activity, it always does so with plenty of nimbleness, wit and grace. A relevant and classy soundtrack is provided by the Mighty Diamonds, Peter Tosh et al. JM *DVD*

Leroy Wallace *Horsemouth* • Richard Hall *Dirty Harry* • Monica Craig *Madgie* • Marjorie Norman *Sunshine* • Jacob Miller *Jakes* • Gregory Isaacs *Jah Tooth* • Winston Rodney *Burning Spear* ■ *Dir/Scr* Theodoros Bafaloukos

Rocket Gibraltar ★★★ PG
Drama 1988 · US · Colour · 94min

A family gathers on Long Island to celebrate the 77th birthday of its patriarch, Burt Lancaster. There are the customary resentments and jealousies to exercise and/or exorcise. In this case, the only daughter is a sex addict, while the sons are a faded baseball pitcher and a dried-up, stand-up comedian. Grandpa Lancaster is a former blacklisted writer and general egghead. This offers exceptional future-star spotting: Bill Pullman, Kevin Spacey and even Macaulay Culkin in his screen debut. AT

Burt Lancaster *Levi Rockwell* • Suzy Amis *Aggie Rockwell* • Patricia Clarkson *Rose Black* • Frances Conroy *Ruby Hanson* • Sinead Cusack *Amanda "Billi" Rockwell* • John Glover *Rolo Rockwell* • Bill Pullman *Crow Black* • Kevin Spacey *Dwayne Hanson* • Macaulay Culkin *Cy Blue Black* ■ *Dir* Daniel Petrie • *Scr* Amos Poe

The Rocket Man ★★ U
Science fiction 1954 · US · Colour · 79min

For a film written by the celebrated and notorious satirist Lenny Bruce, and featuring the same Klaatu robot costume from *The Day the Earth Stood Still*, this is nothing more than a minor message comedy. A spaceman gives orphan George Winslow a ray gun which, when fired at human targets, makes them tell the truth. AJ

Charles Coburn *Mayor Ed Johnson* • Spring Byington *Justice Amelia Brown* • George Winslow *Timmy* • Anne Francis *June Brown* • John Agar *Tom Baxter* • Emory Parnell *Big Bill Watkins* ■ *Dir* Oscar Rudolph • *Scr* Lenny Bruce, Jack Henley, from a story by George W George, George F Slavin

The Rocket Post ★★ 12
Comedy drama based on a true story
2003 · UK · Colour · 107min

Set in the 1930s, this whimsical comedy tells the story of Gerhard Zucher (Ulrich Thomsen), a German scientist who's been sent to a Hebridean island to test the potential of mail-carrying rockets. The premise has some basis in historical fact, but that can't help this flatly unfunny film as it turns into a lifeless love story involving Zucher and a local lass (Shauna MacDonald). The humour is fitful at best, with a series of questionable Scottish stereotypes doing no one any favours, but the spectacular scenery will doubtless give the Western Isles' tourist industry a welcome boost. JR

Ulrich Thomsen *Gerhard Zucher* • Shauna Macdonald *Catherine MacKay* • Gary Lewis *Jimmy Roach* • Kevin McKidd *Thomas McKinnon* • Patrick Malahide *Charles Ilford* • Eddie Marsan *Heinz Dombrowsky* • *Dir* Stephen Whittaker (1) • *Scr* James MacInnes, William Morrissey • *Cinematographer* Richard Greatrex

Rocket Science ★★★★ 15
Comedy drama 2007 · US · Colour · 97min

"The geek shall inherit the Earth" is a mantra familiar from Hollywood films – particularly those set in high schools. Refreshingly, the raging hormones here are tempered with sweetness and emotion in documentarist Jeffrey Blitz's first fictional feature. Stuttering schoolboy Reece Daniel Thompson vows to make the debating team in order to impress Anna Kendrick, an ultra-assured bluestocking whose ruthless ambition recalls *Election*. Blitz captures the agonising adolescent need to belong, while also poking fun at the competitive edge that seems to infect all aspects of American society. Thompson is touchingly intelligent as the outsider determined to overcome his limitations, but Kendrick steals the picture. DP Swearing, some sexual references. *DVD*

Reece Daniel Thompson *Hal Hefner* • Anna Kendrick *Ginny Ryerson* • [Nicholas D'Agosto] *Ben Wekselbaum* • Vincent Piazza *Hefner, Earl* • Margo Martindale *Coach Lumbly* • Aaron Yoo *Heston* • Josh Kay *Lewis Garrles* ■ *Dir/Scr* Jeffrey Blitz

Rocketeer ★★★★ PG
Fantasy adventure 1991 · US · Colour · 104min

Based on a cult graphic novel blending Second World War adventure and superhero thrills, director Joe Johnston's vastly entertaining swashbuckler will jet-propel you back to your most cherished childhood fantasies. This brilliant ode to those corny 1930s movie serials has an added Art Deco sheen that enhances the sophisticated nostalgia. Starring Bill Campbell, it also benefits from Timothy Dalton's hissably slimy Nazi agent, masquerading as a devil-may-care, Errol Flynn-inspired matinée idol. AJ Violence. *DVD*

Bill Campbell *Cliff Secord* • Alan Arkin *Peevy* • Jennifer Connelly *Jenny* • Timothy Dalton *Neville Sinclair* • Paul Sorvino *Eddie Valentine* • Terry O'Quinn *Howard Hughes* • Ed Lauter *Fitch* • James Handy *Wooly* • Tiny Ron *Lothar* ■ *Dir* Joe Johnston • *Scr* Danny Bilson, Paul DeMeo, from a story by Bilson, DeMeo, William Dear, from the graphic novel by Dave Stevens

Rocketman ★★★ PG
Science-fiction comedy
1997 · US · Colour · 89min

Computer genius Harland Williams finally gets his chance to be an astronaut. Unfortunately, he's a bit too eccentric for his Nasa colleagues, who are treated to a touch more slapstick chaos than they'd bargained for. This goofy comedy is really a vehicle for the antics of Williams, but credit must be given to William Sadler, who does a slow burn while the star inadvertently spoils his dreams. ST *DVD* *CS*

Harland Williams *Fred Z Randall* • Jessica Lundy *Mission Specialist Julie Ford* • William Sadler *Commdr "Wild Bill" Overbeck* • Jeffrey DeMunn *Chief Flight Director Paul Wick* • James Pickens Jr *Ben Stevens* • Beau Bridges *Bud Nesbitt* • Shelley Duvall *Mrs Randall* ■ *Dir* Stuart Gillard • *Scr* Craig Mazin, Greg Erb, from a story by Oren Aviv

Rockets Galore ★★ U
Comedy 1958 · UK · Colour · 91min

Made a decade after Ealing's classic comedy *Whisky Galore!*, this sequel (albeit adapted from another novel by Compton Mackenzie) was on a hiding to nothing, for no matter how good it might be, it would never be favourably compared with its predecessor. In the event, it is an undeniably feeble follow-up, with only a handful of the original Todday islanders remaining, and the story of their battle to prevent the construction of a missile base lacking both charm and satirical bite. DP

Jeannie Carson *Janet MacLeod* • Donald Sinden *Hugh Mander* • Roland Culver *Captain Waggett* • Noel Purcell *Father James McAllister* • Ian Hunter *Air Commodore Watchorn* • Duncan Macrae *Duncan Ban* • Gordon Jackson *George Campbell* • Ronnie Corbett *Drooby* ■ *Dir* Michael Relph • *Scr* Monja Danischewsky, from the novel by Compton Mackenzie

The Rockford Files ★★★ PG
Crime mystery 1974 · US · Colour · 95min

Spawning more than 100 episodes, the *Rockford* series was devised for *Maverick* star James Garner. Garner later won an Emmy for his portrayal of the private investigator whose wrongful detention in San Quentin prompted him to plump for cases the police had abandoned. In this pilot for the first series, subtitled *Backlash of a Hunter*, Lindsay Wagner wants to trace the killer of her hobo father. As with many pilots, there's a certain amount of scene-setting involved, but Garner's self-depreciating style is fully formed. Both ex-cellmate Stuart Margolin and Joe Santos returned for the series proper, though Noah Beery would replace Robert Donley as Garner's opinionated father. DP

James Garner *Jim Rockford* • Lindsay Wagner *Sara Butler* • Robert Donley *Joseph Rockford* • William Smith *Jerry Grimes* ■ *Dir* Richard T Heffron • *Scr* Stephen J Cannell, John Thomas James [Roy Huggins] ■

The Rocking Horse Winner ★★★★ PG
Drama 1949 · UK · BW · 87min

This is a largely unsung, but terrific British feature based on a story by DH Lawrence about a young boy with the gift of picking racetrack winners. The imaginative story leaves plenty of space for director Anthony Pelissier's aptitude for surprise and emotional complexity. He elicits measured, insightful performances from John Mills and Valerie Hobson, and wrings the last ounce of pathos from an intriguing, thought-provoking tale. A film that has always been a favourite among critics and deserves wider recognition. SH

Valerie Hobson *Hester Grahame* • John Howard Davies *Paul Grahame* • Ronald Squire *Oscar Cresswell* • John Mills *Bassett* • Hugh Sinclair *Richard Grahame* • Charles Goldner *Mr Tsaldouris* • Susan Richards *Nannie* • Cyril Smith *Bailiff* ■ *Dir* Anthony Pelissier • *Scr* Anthony Pelissier, from the story by DH Lawrence

RocknRolla ★★★ 15
Crime drama
2008 · UK/US/Fr · Colour · 109min

After an infamous flop with ex-wife Madonna (*Swept Away*) and a futile stab at intellectual credibility (*Revolver*), Guy Ritchie returns to the familiar world of comic crime capers here. With a higher calibre cast of known talents and rising stars, it's another shaggy dog tale of the kind with which he made his name in *Lock, Stock ... and Snatch*. Gerard Butler plays One Two, a low-ranking criminal who finds himself in hock to vicious hoodlum Lenny Cole (Tom Wilkinson) after a property deal goes wrong. To pay him back, One Two and sidekick Mumbles (Idris Elba) connive to sting a super-rich Russian, little realising that Cole has his own deal going with the oligarch. The stage is set for a tough-guy showdown, but sadly Ritchie sacrifices the bleaker side of things in favour of laddish camaraderie. Still, his visual energy makes up the shortfall, and a subplot involving a scheming junkie pop star (Toby Kebbell) is one of his most twisted and inspired yet. DW Violence, swearing, drug abuse. *DVD* *Blu-ray*

Gerard Butler *One Two* • Tom Wilkinson *Lenny Cole* • Thandie Newton *Stella* • Mark Strong *Archy* • Idris Elba *Mumbles* • Jeremy Piven *Roman* • Chris "Ludacris" Bridges *Mickey* • Gemma Arterton *June* • *Dir/Scr* Guy Ritchie

Rockshow ★★★
Concert movie 1979 · US · Colour · 133min

Paul McCartney spreads his Wings with a filmed concert tour featuring his first post-Beatles band. The line-up includes wife Linda, ex-Moody Blues man Denny Laine and former Thunderclap Newman sidekick Jimmy McCullough. The filming is simple and straightforward (no director is credited). Originally recorded in Dolby stereo, it's best seen in cinemas or on a decent home system. A rarity. DA

• *Cinematographer* Jack Priestly • *Editors* Robin Clarke, Paul Stein

Rocky ★★★★ PG
Sports drama 1976 · US · Colour · 114min

Dusting down the classic Hollywood story of the little man winning big, this triple-Oscar-winning boxing drama is shot through with genuine impassioned commitment, born of the fact that Sylvester Stallone realised that this was his best shot at stardom. The notion, then, of success hanging by a thread unites both the character of boxer Rocky Balboa and of Stallone himself. Sly is highly convincing as a mumbling Philadelphia no-hoper who is makes the most of his opportunities and ends up having a crack at the heavyweight champion of the world, Apollo Creed (Carl Weathers, by way of Muhammad Ali). Sly also wrote the script and was rewarded with an Oscar nomination. JM Violence, swearing. *DVD* *Blu-ray*

Sylvester Stallone *Rocky Balboa* • Talia Shire *Adrian* • Burt Young *Paulie* • Carl Weathers *Apollo Creed* • Burgess Meredith *Mickey* • Thayer David *Jergens* • Joe Spinell *Gazzo* • Joe Frazier • *Dir* John G Avildsen • *Scr* Sylvester Stallone • *Editor* Richard Halsey • *Music* Bill Conti

Rocky II ★★★ PG
Sports drama 1979 · US · Colour · 114min

Sylvester Stallone, as writer, director and star, took his cue from those B pictures set in the inner city where decency and success were able to triumph in the midst of adversity. Taking a clutch of simple ideas and comic-strip characters, he creates a giddy whirlwind of sentiment and fisticuffs. Having gone the distance with the heavyweight champ in the first bout, and now married to the love of his life (Talia Shire), Stallone is contemplating a return to the ring. The big-fight finale is executed with skill, passion and glee. JM *DVD* *Blu-ray*

Sylvester Stallone *Rocky Balboa* • Talia Shire *Adrian* • Burt Young *Paulie* • Carl Weathers *Apollo Creed* • Burgess Meredith *Mickey* • Tony Burton *Apollo's trainer* • Joe Spinell *Gazzo* • Sylvia Meals *Mary Anne Creed* ■ *Dir/Scr* Sylvester Stallone

Rocky III ★★ PG
Sports drama 1982 · US · Colour · 95min

By now the formula was starting to look stale, although more sequels were to follow this tired effort. The opponent here is Mr T, who takes Sylvester Stallone's championship crown; Rocky then battles to reclaim it. The story is predictable and it all goes a little fast outside the ring. JF Violence, swearing. *DVD* *Blu-ray*

Sylvester Stallone *Rocky Balboa* • Carl Weathers *Apollo Creed* • Mr T *Clubber Lang* • Talia Shire *Adrian Balboa* • Burt Young *Paulie* • Burgess Meredith *Mickey* • Ian Fried (1) *Rocky Jr* • Hulk Hogan *Thunderlips* ■ *Dir/Scr* Sylvester Stallone

Rocky IV ★★ PG
Sports drama 1985 · US · Colour · 87min

Sylvester Stallone returns to the *Rocky* road with decidedly less success than before. Nobody boxes clever in this lazy third sequel, also directed by Stallone, which introduced Dolph Lundgren to the movie world, though Brigitte Nielsen easily outstrips Lundgren in the stone-faced acting stakes. It's impossible not to root for his climactic victory, but the mawkish montages accompanied by blaring music are no substitute for plot. AJ Swearing. *DVD* *Blu-ray*

Sylvester Stallone *Rocky Balboa* • Talia Shire *Adrian Balboa* • Burt Young *Paulie* • Carl Weathers *Apollo Creed* • Dolph Lundgren *Drago* • Brigitte Nielsen *Ludmilla* • Tony Burton *Duke* • Michael Pataki *Nicoli Koloff* • James Brown (2) *Godfather of Soul* ■ *Dir/Scr* Sylvester Stallone

Rocky V ★★ PG
Sports drama 1990 · US · Colour · 99min

Despite John G Avildsen being back as director (he did the first *Rocky*, with Stallone himself directing the intervening rounds), the emotional clout of the original has now given way to simple gestures and acting-by-numbers. It would be impossible to surprise with such a prescriptive format, and the only real spark comes courtesy of Sly's own offspring (Sage Stallone) as his screen son. JM Violence, swearing. DVD

Sylvester Stallone *Rocky Balboa* • Talia Shire *Adrian Balboa* • Burt Young *Paulie* • Sage Stallone *Rocky Jr* • Burgess Meredith *Mickey* • Tommy Morrison *Tommy Gunn* • Richard Gant *George Washington Duke* • Tony Burton *Tony* ■ *Dir* John G Avildsen • *Scr* Sylvester Stallone

Rocky Balboa ★★★ 12

Sports drama 2006 · US · Colour · 97min

Sixty-year-old Sylvester Stallone (who writes, directs and stars) offers an affectionate sixth take on the iconic character that launched his career back in 1976. The washed-up boxer is back on the streets of Philadelphia, surveying his life as a widower. Tear-jerking clichés eventually give way to the main event, as Rocky is tempted out of retirement to exorcise his demons in an exhibition bout against the current champ. Hokey and appallingly sentimental, *Rocky Balboa* should be risible. Yet, as Bill Conti's timeless score gathers on the soundtrack and Stallone rolls with the punches, this old warhorse proves it's still a contender. A further sequel, *Creed*, is due in late 2015. JR DVD

Sylvester Stallone *Rocky Balboa* • Burt Young *Paulie* • Milo Ventimiglia *Robert Balboa Jr* • Antonio Tarver *Mason "The Line" Dixon* • Geraldine Hughes *Marie* • Tony Burton *Duke* • Mike Tyson • Talia Shire *Adrian* ■ *Dir* Sylvester Stallone • *Scr* Sylvester Stallone, from characters by Stallone • *Music* Bill Conti

The Rocky Horror Picture Show ★★★★ 15

Cult musical satire 1975 · UK · Colour · 95min

This witty and wickedly naughty Queen Mother of cult movies is a campy, vampy, kinky musical send-up of old horror flicks. Revealing what happens when strait-laced Brad and Janet get stranded at the weird castle of Frank N Furter (Tim Curry, wringing every ounce of deranged humour from his glam-rock role in a landmark performance), it cleverly satirises *Frankenstein*, haunted-house mysteries, science-fiction clichés and *Carry On* sexual identity confusion. Sadly, the formula didn't work for the now-forgotten follow-up film, *Shock Treatment* (1981). AJ Swearing, nudity. DVD

Tim Curry *Dr Frank N Furter* • Susan Sarandon *Janet Weiss* • Barry Bostwick *Brad Majors* • Richard O'Brien *Riff Raff* • Patricia Quinn *Magenta* • Little Nell [Nell Campbell] *Columbia* • Jonathan Adams *Dr Everett V Scott* • Peter Hinwood *Rocky Horror* • Meat Loaf *Eddie* • Charles Gray *The Criminologist* • Christopher Biggins *Transylvanian* ■ *Dir* Jim Sharman • *Scr* Jim Sharman, Richard O'Brien, from the musical by O'Brien • *Music Director* Richard Hartley • *Costume Designers* Richard Pointing, Gillian Dods

Rocky Marciano ★★

Sports biography 1999 · US · Colour · 100min

This biography traces the rise of the legendary boxer who never lost a professional fight. Jon Favreau in the title role does a decent job as the son determined to escape the fate suffered by his immigrant labourer father. With perseverance and raw power he soon becomes a contender. Director Charles Winkler continues in the sports tradition of his father, Irwin, who produced the classic *Rocky*. The strong cast enlivens this TV movie, which is less than a knockout. MC

Jon Favreau *Rocky Marciano* • Judd Hirsch *Al Weill* • Penelope Ann Miller *Barbara* • Tony LoBianco *Frankie Carbo* • Duane Davis *Joe Louis* ■ *Dir* Charles Winkler • *Scr* Larry Golin, Charles Winkler, Dick Beebe

Rocky Mountain ★★ U

Western 1950 · US · BW · 82min

This was really the last of Errol Flynn's mainstream Hollywood movies, and it received a lot of publicity at the time as Flynn married his leading lady, Patrice Wymore, just after shooting ended. It's a

western, with Flynn as a Confederate leader trying to forge an alliance with outlaws in California. Indians soon scupper that plan. AT

Errol Flynn *Lafe Barstow* • Patrice Wymore *Johanna Carter* • Scott Forbes *Lt Rickey* • Guinn "Big Boy" Williams *Pap Dennison* • Dick Jones [Dickie Jones] *Jim Wheat* • Howard Petrie *Cole Smith* • Slim Pickens *Plank* ■ *Dir* William Keighley • *Scr* Alan LeMay, Winston Miller, from the story by LeMay

The Rocky Road to Dublin ★★★★ 12

Documentary 1968 · Ire · BW and Colour · 99min

This portrait of Ireland as a young republic caused such a storm that it was suppressed for many years. With *nouvelle vague* cinematographer Raoul Coutard providing hand-held, *cinéma vérité* immediacy, *The Guardian* reporter Peter Lennon exposes the crippling conservatism of Irish society by echoing novelist Sean O'Faolain's contention that the revolutionaries of 1916 and the Catholic Church had conspired to form a nation of "urbanised peasants", who lacked the intellectual and moral courage to break bonds as repressive as those imposed by the British. A sad and angry film, but not without its moments of wit and warmth. DP DVD

■ *Dir* Peter Lennon

Rodan ★★★

Science-fiction thriller 1956 · Jpn · Colour · 82min

Two years after Ishiro Honda launched the "creature feature" with *Godzilla*, he moved into colour production with this all-action tale of the Cretaceous pterodactyl, which was hatched in a coal mine and gains its powers from consuming giant dragonflies. The atomic theme is once more to the fore, with the seismic shocks created by Rodan's supersonic speeds capable of reducing cities to rubble. But there's also a tragic element, as Rodan seeks to protect its brooding mate from prying scientists. DP Japanese dubbed.

Kenji Sahara *Shigeru* • Yumi Shirakawa *Kiyo* • David Duncan *Narrator* ■ *Dir* Ishiro Honda [Inoshiro Honda] • *Scr* Takeshi Kimura, Takeo Murata, from a story by Takashi Kuronuma • *Special Effects* Eiji Tsuburaya

Rodgers & Hammerstein's Cinderella ★★★ U

Musical fantasy 1997 · US · Colour · 84min

This fanciful, multiracial remake of the 1957 and 1965 TV musicals has a lovely score from Broadway's incomparable songwriting team. Superstar Whitney Houston plays the Fairy Godmother, with singer/actress Brandy Norwood donning a glass slipper for the title role. Under director Robert Iscove's skilful handling, the talented cast sings and dances with just enough gusto, turning this timeless fairy tale with its evil stepmother, odious stepsisters and dashing prince into a delightful family film. MC

Brandy *Cinderella* • Whitney Houston *The Fairy Godmother* • Jason Alexander *Lionel* • Victor Garber *King* • Whoopi Goldberg *Queen Constantina* • Bernadette Peters *Wicked Stepmother* • Veanne Cox *Stepsister* • Natalie Desselle *Stepsister* • Paolo Montalban *Prince* ■ *Dir* Robert Iscove • *Scr* Robert L Freedman, Oscar Hammerstein II, Richard Rodgers, from the story *Cendrillon, ou la Petite Pantoufle de Verre* by Charles Perrault

Roe vs Wade ★★★★

Drama 1989 · US · Colour · 92min

This Emmy-winning TV film tackles the heated subject of abortion rights in the United States. Academy Award winner Holly Hunter stars as Ellen "Jane Roe" Russell, the destitute unwed mother at the centre of the historic Supreme Court case, with Amy Madigan as her novice attorney. Complex layered performances highlight this ground-breaking film, which deservedly provided Hunter with an Emmy. The script manages to promote a balanced point of view, while the sensitive direction by Gregory Hoblit

further enhances this excellent TV drama. MC

Holly Hunter *Ellen Russell aka Jane Roe* • Amy Madigan *Sarah Weddington* • James Gammon *Jimmy Russell* • Terry O'Quinn *Jay Floyd* • Dion Anderson *Bob Flowers* • Kathy Bates *Jessie* • Micole Mercurio *Ida Russell* • Chris Mulkey *Ron Weddington* • Annabella Price *Linda Coffey* • Stephen Tobolowsky *Daryl Horwood* ■ *Dir* Gregory Hoblit • *Scr* Alison Cross

Roger & Me ★★★★★ 15

Satirical documentary 1989 · US · Colour · 86min

This is a glorious "one off", refusing to fit neatly into any celluloid category, which considerably irked some nit-picking critics at the time. A wonderfully intrusive Michael Moore spent three years roaming his Michigan home town after General Motors chairman, Roger Smith, announced his cold-hearted plan to close down operations, thus decimating its working population. Moore's keen eye for truthful quirky detail shines through via the vivid cast of characters with whom we become instantly involved. Roger deserves everything he gets – with interest – and Moore supplies it with a compelling mixture of impish nerve and investigative flair. SH DVD

Michael Moore (2) *Michael Moore* • Roger Smith • Ronald Reagan • Bob Eubanks • Pat Boone ■ *Dir/Scr* Michael Moore

Roger Dodger ★★★★ 15

Black comedy drama 2002 · US · Colour · 101min

Campbell Scott's sharp-tongued advertising copywriter isn't easy to like. Intelligent and attractive, yet cynical and manipulative, he gets a kick out of dispensing his blunt wisdom to unguarded women in Manhattan bars. What begins as a sardonic one-man show receives an original, irresistible twist as Scott's sweet, naive teenage nephew (newcomer Jesse Eisenberg) shows up in town, calling on uncle's supposed skills with the opposite sex to help lose his virginity. The scenes in which Eisenberg's boyish charm wins over out-of-his-league Elizabeth Berkley and Jennifer Beals (both terrific), are beautifully done. An elegantly filmed and impressively performed debut from writer/director Dylan Kidd. JC Swearing, sex scenes. DVD

Campbell Scott *Roger Swanson* • Jesse Eisenberg *Nick* • Isabella Rossellini *Joyce* • Elizabeth Berkley *Andrea* • Jennifer Beals *Sophie* • Ben Shenkman *Donovan* • Mina Badie *Donna* ■ *Dir/Scr* Dylan Kidd

RoGoPaG ★★ PG

Portmanteau drama 1962 · It/Fr · Colour · 117min

This contemporary critique is one of the least satisfying of the 1960s portmanteau pictures. Roberto Rossellini's *Virginity* is the dull tale of a passenger's obsession with an air hostess. Anticipating the futuristic *Alphaville*, Jean-Luc Godard's *The New World* chronicles a doomed post-apocalyptic romance, while Pier Paolo Pasolini received a four-month suspended sentence for defamation for *Cream Cheese*, in which an actor in Orson Welles's religious epic dies on the cross during an orgiastic shoot. The weakest episode, however, is *The Range-Grown Chicken*, Ugo Gregoretti's take on aggressive marketing. DP Italian +subtitles. DVD

Rosanna Schiaffino *Anna Maria* • Bruce Balaban *Joe* • Alexandra Stewart *Alexandra* • Jean-Marc Bory *Narrator* • Jean-Luc Godard *Pill-popping pedestrian* • Orson Welles *The Director* • Mario Cipriani *Stracci* • Laura Betti *The Star* • Ugo Tognazzi *Togni* • Lisa Gastoni *His wife* ■ *Dir/Scr* Roberto Rossellini, Jean-Luc Godard, Pier Paolo Pasolini, Ugo Gregoretti

Rogue ★★★ 15

Horror thriller 2007 · Aus/US · Colour · 95min

In the 1970s, Australia's Finnis River was menaced by a five-metre saltwater crocodile who made headlines after attacking a series of fishing boats. This outback horror thriller takes the facts and embellishes them into an entertaining creature feature in which a boat-load of

tourists are chased and chomped by a reptilian Jaws. Director Greg McLean lets the tension build with admirable skill. JR Violence, swearing. DVD BD

Radha Mitchell *Kate Ryan* • Michael Vartan *Pete McKell* • Sam Worthington *Neil* • John Jarratt *Russell* • Stephen Curry *Simon* • Heather Mitchell *Elizabeth* • Mia Wasikowska *Sherry* ■ *Dir/Scr* Greg McLean

Rogue Cop ★★★

Crime drama 1954 · US · BW · 92min

Robert Taylor plays a cop on the take from the Mob, led by George Raft. But following the murder of his brother and fellow cop, Taylor sees the error of his ways and goes after Raft and his murderous henchmen. The script is at its sharpest when dealing with Taylor's moral quagmire: is he avenging his brother, redeeming himself or on a suicide mission? Director Roy Rowland maintains a sprint throughout and offers the usual barrage of *film noir* shadows and doom-laden ambience. AT

Robert Taylor (1) *Christopher Kelvaney* • Janet Leigh *Karen Stephanson* • George Raft *Dan Beaumonte* • Steve Forrest *Eddie Kelvaney* • Anne Francis *Nancy Corlane* ■ *Dir* Roy Rowland • *Scr* Sydney Boehm, from a novel by William P McGivern

Rogue One: a Star Wars Story

Science-fiction adventure 2016 · US · Colour

This is a preview – no prints were available to review as we went to press: While we wait for the follow-up to JJ Abrams's remarkable 2015 reboot, this spin-off should provide a decent distraction for fans eager for another entry point into the *Star Wars* galaxy. Set directly before the events of *Episode IV*, the film follows the rebel mission to steal the Death Star plans that R2D2 carried in the original movie. Darth Vader is set to make an appearance, and so too is Governor Tarkin – as played by Peter Cushing. Harking back to his Hammer heyday, the late actor is to be resurrected via CGI. BnB sp

Felicity Jones *Jyn Erso* • Ben Mendelsohn *Director Orson Krennic* • Diego Luna *Captain Cassian Andor* • Forest Whitaker *Saw Gerrera* • Mads Mikkelsen *Galen Erso* ■ *Dir* Gareth Edwards • *Scr* Chris Weitz, from a story by John Knoll, Gary Whitta, from characters by George Lucas • *Music* Alexandre Desplat

The Rogue Song

Musical romance 1930 · US · Colour · 115min

One of the things the Hollywood studios did in the early years of sound was sign as many Broadway actors or singers as they could. One of MGM's catches was Lawrence Tibbett, star of the New York Met and described as one of the world's greatest baritones. *The Rogue Song* (sadly, no prints exist of this lost film) was his Oscar-nominated debut, an operatic showcase about a Russian bandit who kidnaps a princess. Apparently the public flocked to see this all-talking, all-singing, all-Technicolor concoction, lured by the voice of Tibbett and by Laurel and Hardy who provided some laughs between arias and plotting. AT

Lawrence Tibbett *Yegor* • Catherine Dale Owen *Princess Vera* • Judith Vosselli *Countess Tatiana* • Nance O'Neil *Princess Alexandra* • Stan Laurel *Ali-Bek* • Oliver Hardy *Murza-Bek* • Florence Lake *Nadja* • Lionel Belmore *Ossman* ■ *Dir* Lionel Barrymore • *Scr* Frances Marion, John Colton, from the operetta *Gypsy Love* by Franz Lehár, AM Willner, Robert Bodansky

Rogue Trader ★★ 15

Biographical drama 1998 · UK/US · Colour · 97min

You'd think the true story of how Watford wide boy Nick Leeson brought about the collapse of Barings Merchant Bank, one of the oldest financial institutions in the City, would make a cracking movie brimming with personal intrigues and trader insights. Sadly, under James Dearden's lacklustre direction, the tabloid tale is reduced to the level of a bland TV movie with its futures-market setting and bewildering jargon making it obscure and uninteresting. AJ Swearing, nudity. **DVD**

Ewan McGregor *Nick Leeson* • Anna Friel *Lisa Leeson* • Yves Beneyton *Pierre Beaumarchais* • Betsy Brantley *Brenda Granger* • Caroline Langrishe *Ash Lewis* • Nigel Lindsay *Ron Baker* • Tim McInnerny *Tony Hawes* • Irene Ng *Bonnie Lee* ■ *Dir* James Dearden • *Scr* James Dearden, from the non-fiction book by Nick Leeson, Edward Whitley

Rogues of Sherwood Forest ★★ U
Swashbuckling adventure
1950 · US · Colour · 79min

Those men in Lincoln-green tights are at it again, this time with John Derek as Robin Hood's son, battling to get anti-democratic villain George Macready to sign the Magna Carta. It's another example of how Hollywood used to rewrite history, though the meagre script couldn't plump out its entertainment with much value. TH

John Derek *Robin, Earl of Huntingdon* • Diana Lynn *Lady Marianne* • George Macready *King John* • Alan Hale *Little John* • Paul Cavanagh *Sir Giles* • Lowell Gilmore *Count of Flanders* • Billy House *Friar Tuck* • Lester Matthews *Alan-a-Dale* ■ *Dir* Gordon Douglas • *Scr* George Bruce, from a story by Ralph Bettinson

Le Roi Danse ★★★ 15
Historical drama
2000 · Fr/Ger/Bel · Colour · 113min

Director Gérard Corbiau's use of authentic period trappings and glorious music has more than mere aesthetic purpose, as it echoes the Sun King's inspirational exploitation of opulence to dazzle his potentially troublesome courtiers into submission. However, the focus is on the latent sexual tension between the young Louis (Benoît Magimel) and his free-spirited court composer, Lully (Boris Terral). Devised with the help of fellow courtier Molière (Tcheky Karyo), the Baroque masques are stunningly staged but tip the tone too far towards kitsch. DP French +subtitles.

Benoît Magimel *Louis XIV* • Boris Terral *Jean-Baptiste Lully* • Tcheky Karyo *Molière* • Colette Emmanuelle *Queen Mother, Anne of Austria* • Cécile Bois *Madeleine* • Claire Keim *Julie* • Johan Leysen *Cambert* • Idwig Stéphane *Conti* ■ *Dir* Gérard Corbiau • *Scr* Eve de Castro, Andrée Corbiau, Gérard Corbiau, Didier Decoin, from the novel *Lully ou le Musicien du Soleil* by Philippe Beaussant

Role Models ★★★★ 15
Comedy
2008 · US/Ger · Colour · 96min

This step-up from the usual crude teen comedy elevates its smutty set pieces and filth-ridden dialogue with strong performances and likeable characters. After crashing his truck in a fit of pique, energy-drink salesman Paul Rudd and his cohort Seann William Scott are sentenced to 150 hours community service mentoring difficult youngsters. Scott's initiation of streetwise Bobb'e J Thompson into the ways of the party animal is funny. However, the real pleasure is in Rudd's relationship with fantasy-obsessed nerd Christopher Mintz-Plasse, which gets much comedy mileage from satirising the murky world of role-playing games. Where this unexpectedly entertaining movie really scores, though, is in its tweaks to the standard formula: while the life lessons and character arcs are inevitable, the journey proves both admirably restrained and winning. IF **DVD BD**

Paul Rudd *Danny* • Seann William Scott *Wheeler* • Christopher Mintz-Plasse *Augie* • Jane Lynch *Sweeny* • Bobb'e J Thompson *Ronnie* • Elizabeth Banks *Beth* ■ *Dir* David Wain • *Scr* Paul Rudd, David Wain, Ken Marino, Timothy Dowling, from a story by Dowling, William Blake Herron

Rollerball ★★★ 15
Futuristic action drama
1975 · US · Colour · 119min

In the Big Business-run world of 2018, anti-social activity and political unrest are kept in check by the gladiatorial spectator sport Rollerball, a lethal mix of hockey, roller derby, motorbike racing and gang warfare.

But when loner champion James Caan bucks the system (one requiring the eventual violent death of its star players), after a ten-year display of provocative individual heroism, cynical corporate patriarch John Houseman attempts to kill him by changing the rules. Although the Rollerball sequences are excitingly staged, director Norman Jewison's over-inflated fable is dull when it leaves the arena. AJ Violence, brief nudity. **DVD BD**

James Caan *Jonathan E* • John Houseman *Bartholomew* • Maud Adams *Ella* • John Beck *Moonpie* • Moses Gunn *Cletus* • Pamela Hensley *Mackie* • Barbara Trentham *Daphne* • Ralph Richardson *Librarian* ■ *Dir* Norman Jewison • *Scr* William Harrison, from his story *Rollerball Murders*

Rollerball ★ 15
Futuristic drama
2001 · US/Ger/Jpn · Colour · 94min

Turgid, spiritless and excitement free, this remake is like an optical lobotomy. Magnifying the original's weaknesses to excruciating levels, it compounds its brain-numbing banality with wooden performances, risible dialogue and an emotionally bankrupt plot. Chris Klein lacks charisma as the sporting hotshot who uncovers global conspiracy, while Rebecca Romijn-Stamos is just an athletic clothes horse. SF Violence, swearing. **DVD BD**

Chris Klein *Jonathan Cross* • Jean Reno *Petrovich* • LL Cool J *Marcus Ridley* • Rebecca Romijn-Stamos *Aurora* • Naveen Andrews *Sanjay* • Oleg Taktarov *Denekin* • David Hemblen *Serokin* ■ *Dir* John McTiernan • *Scr* Larry Ferguson, John Pogue, from the 1975 film by William Harrison

Rollercoaster ★★★ PG
Disaster movie
1977 · US · Colour · 113min

Universal Studios, cleverly promoting its studio tour while knocking rival attractions, came up with this disaster movie in which a terrorist (Timothy Bottoms) targets popular theme parks, planting bombs on the giant rides of the title. The strain of tracking him down prevents George Segal's safety inspector from quitting smoking and makes Richard Widmark twitch uncontrollably. One of the better 1970s disaster movies, this was originally released in Sensurround, a short-lived process that made cinema seats shake at appropriate moments. AT Violence, swearing.

George Segal *Harry Calder* • Richard Widmark *Hoyt* • Timothy Bottoms *Young man* • Henry Fonda *Simon Davenport* • Harry Guardino *Keefer* • Susan Strasberg *Fran* • Helen Hunt *Tracy Calder* • Dorothy Tristan *Helen* • Harry Davis *Benny* • Stephen Pearlman *Lyons* ■ *Dir* James Goldstone • *Scr* Richard Levinson, William Link, from a story by Sanford Sheldon, Richard Levinson, William Link

Rollin with the Nines ★★★ 15
Crime drama
2005 · UK · Colour · 96min

This British urban drama is a gangsta movie with plenty of grit. After her brother (Simon Webbe) is killed in a drive-by slaying and she herself is raped by the murderer, south London girl Naomi Taylor decides to get both revenge and riches by forming a new drug-dealing crew. Some of the acting is pretty amateur, and the dialogue may occasionally sound like leftover lines from *The Bill*, but these are forgivable infractions in what is largely an exciting, slickly made and convincing slab of hard-boiled fiction. LF Swearing, violence. **DVD**

Vas Blackwood *Finny* • Robbie Gee *Pushy* • Naomi Taylor *Hope* • Roffem Morgan *Rage* • Terry Stone *Detective Andy White* • Billy Murray *David Brumby* • Simon Webbe *Too Fine* • Jason Flemyng *Captain Fleming* ■ *Dir* Julian Gilbey • *Scr* Julian Gilbey, William Gilbey

The Rolling Stones Rock and Roll Circus ★★
Concert movie
1995 · UK · Colour · 65min

Intended for American television, but vetoed by Mick Jagger, this legendary 1968 concert, set in a circus tent, surfaced on bootleg video in 1995. Ringmaster Jagger

cracks the whip under the big-top set, as the Rolling Stones perform several songs in costume and John Lennon and Yoko On, Jethro Tull, the Who, Marianne Faithfull, Eric Clapton and Taj Mahal also do turns. Accompanied by a full orchestra and assorted animal and juggling acts, the psychedelic melange also features Lennon leading an all-star jam of *Yer Blues*. AJ

■ *Dir* Michael Lindsay-Hogg

Rolling Thunder ★★★ 18
Drama
1977 · US · Colour · 95min

William Devane impresses here as a haunted Vietnam vet struggling to adjust to civilian life – and the fact his wife is in love with another man. Seemingly in the tradition of films like *The Deer Hunter* (released the following year), this drama then abruptly plunges into *Death Wish* territory when an encounter with thieves leaves him crippled and with vengeance on his mind. Devane oozes danger as the stoic military man and he gets great support from a pre-stardom Tommy Lee Jones as a visibly traumatised colleague, who startlingly only cheers up when combat beckons in the suitably violent climax. JA Swearing, violence, nudity. **DVD BD**

William Devane *Major Charles Rane* • Tommy Lee Jones *Johnny Vohden* • Linda Haynes *Linda Forchet* • Lisa Richards *Janet* • Dabney Coleman *Maxwell* • James Best *Texan* • Luke Askew *Automatic Slim* ■ *Dir* John Flynn • *Scr* Paul Schrader, Heywood Gould, from a story by Schrader

Rollover ★★★ 15
Thriller
1981 · US · Colour · 110min

In director Alan J Pakula's political thriller set in the world of high finance, Jane Fonda plays the film-star widow of a murdered tycoon who's confronted with the news that the Arab world is threatening to withhold monetary reserves, thus putting the global economy at risk. Distracting from the financial elements of the plot is a romance with Kris Kristofferson, and Pakula never quite manages to totally convince that monetary mayhem is on the cards. Nevertheless, this is a bold if flawed attempt to show how the international money markets control our lives. TH Violence, swearing. **DVD**

Jane Fonda *Lee Winters* • Kris Kristofferson *Hub Smith* • Hume Cronyn *Maxwell Emery* • Josef Sommer *Roy Lefcourt* • Bob Gunton *Sal Naftari* • Macon McCalman *Mr Fewster* • Ron Frazier *Gil Hovey* ■ *Dir* Alan J Pakula • *Scr* David Shaber, from a story by David Shaber, Howard Kohn, David Weir

Roman Holiday ★★★★★ U
Romantic comedy
1953 · US · BW · 113min

This sublime film rightly secured a best actress Oscar for Audrey Hepburn (in a role originally intended for Jean Simmons) and resulted in both Hepburn and Rome (not to mention motor scooters) becoming the epitome of postwar chic. It's a charming love story about a princess who falls for a reporter (Gregory Peck) during an official visit to the Eternal City. The script was written by the uncredited, blacklisted Dalton Trumbo (a fact not revealed for almost 40 years after the film was made) and deals in some depth with issues of personal freedom close to his heart, though the setting and characters distance the tale far from the communist witch-hunts in America. Immaculately directed by William Wyler, and written and played with style and grace, this is a film to treasure. TS **DVD**

Audrey Hepburn *Princess Anne* • Gregory Peck *Joe Bradley* • Eddie Albert *Irving Radovich* • Hartley Power *Mr Hennessy* • Margaret Rawlings *Countess Vereberg* • Harcourt Williams *Ambassador* • Laura Solari *Mr Hennessy's secretary* • Tullio Carminati *General Provno* • Paolo Carlini *Mario Delani* ■ *Dir* William Wyler • *Scr* Ian McLellan Hunter, John Dighton, from a story by Hunter (front for Dalton Trumbo) • *Costume Designer* Edith Head • *Cinematographers* Henri Alekan, Franz Planer • *Music* Georges Auric

Roman Polanski: Wanted and Desired ★★★
Documentary
2008 · US · Colour · 100min

Tragedy and sensation have dogged director Roman Polanski all his life. A Holocaust survivor whose wife Sharon Tate was brutally killed by Charles Manson's "family", Polanski was almost destroyed by a trial in 1977 in which he admitted unlawful sex with a minor. The film is strong on legal detail, but too narrow in its focus. MB

Roman Polanski • Douglas Cather • Roger Gunson • Mia Farrow ■ *Dir* Marina Zenovich • *Scr* Joe Bini, PG [Peter G] Morgan, Marina Zenovich

Roman Scandals ★★★ PG
Musical comedy
1933 · US · BW · 87min

Producer Samuel Goldwyn's six Eddie Cantor vehicles were great fun, and here, Cantor falls asleep and finds himself back in pre-censorship ancient Rome. Naked Goldwyn Girls in long blond wigs besport themselves in a wonderfully lewd Busby Berkeley production number. Cantor is an acquired taste, but he's very amusing as food-taster to emperor Edward Arnold. TS

Eddie Cantor *Eddie* • Ruth Etting *Olga* • Gloria Stuart *Princess Sylvia* • David Manners *Josephus* • Verree Teasdale *Empress Agrippa* • Edward Arnold *Emperor Valerius* • Alan Mowbray *Major-Domo* ■ *Dir* Frank Tuttle • *Scr* William Anthony McGuire, George Oppenheimer, Arthur Sheekman, Nat Perrin, from a story by George S Kaufman, Robert E Sherwood

The Roman Spring of Mrs Stone ★★★ 12
Drama
1961 · US/UK · Colour · 99min

Making her penultimate screen appearance, Vivien Leigh is superbly cast as a fading beauty who uses her wealth to lure the young lover who will make her life worthwhile. Warren Beatty, in his second film, is equally impressive as her conquest, while Lotte Lenya thoroughly merited her Oscar nomination as a calculating matchmaker. But this adaptation of Tennessee Williams's one and only novel is somewhat bungled by the precious dialogue and the plodding direction. DP **DVD**

Vivien Leigh *Karen Stone* • Warren Beatty *Pablo di Leo* • Lotte Lenya *Contessa Magda Terribili-Gonzales* • Coral Browne *Meg* • Jill St John *Bingham* • Jeremy Spenser *Young man* • Stella Bonheur *Mrs Jamison-Walker* • Josephine Brown *Lucia* • Cleo Laine *Singer* ■ *Dir* Jose Quintero • *Scr* Gavin Lambert, Jan Read, from the novel by Tennessee Williams

Romance ★★
Romantic drama
1930 · US · BW · 62min

Bishop Gavin Gordon relives in flashback his ill-fated love affair with opera star Greta Garbo, who is the mistress of rich businessman Lewis Stone. The amazing idea of making Garbo an operatic soprano – Italian to boot - boggles the imagination; added to which the film's plot is flimsy and uninteresting. But the usual rules of judgement don't apply to Garbo movies, beyond recognising that some are better than others. This is worse than several, but the Oscar-nominated star transcends the material. RK

Greta Garbo *Rita Cavallini* • Lewis Stone *Cornelius Van Tuyl* • Gavin Gordon *Tom Armstrong* • Elliott Nugent *Harry* • Florence Lake *Susan Van Tuyl* • Clara Blandick *Miss Armstrong* ■ *Dir* Clarence Brown • *Scr* Bess Meredyth, Edwin Justus Mayer, from the play *Signora Cavallini* by Edward Sheldon • *Cinematographer* William Daniels (1)

Romance ★★ 18
Psychological drama
1998 · Fr · Colour · 94min

A woman's sexuality is explored in gynaecological detail in Catherine Breillat's boundary-pushing drama. It's a dull, emotionless movie in which Caroline Ducey isn't getting "the full monty" from her man. So she wanders aimlessly from one bed to another, having pretentious, penetrative thoughts. Supposedly a feminist tale, Breillat's frank film reveals little (apart from Ducey's flesh) and seems to be saying that

R

sex between men and women is passionless and mechanical. JC French +subtitles. Nudity, sex scenes. *DVD*

Caroline Ducey *Marie* • Sagamore Stevenin *Paul* • François Berléand *Robert* • Rocco Siffredi *Paolo* • Reza Habouhossein *Man in the stairs* • Ashley Wanninger *Ashley* • Emma Colberti *Charlotte* • Fabien de Jomaron *Claude* ■ *Dir* Catherine Breillat • *Scr* Catherine Breillat, Severine Siaut

Romance & Cigarettes ★★15

Musical comedy romance
2004 · US/UK · Colour · 106min

John Turturro's feature uses a flimsy tale of marital infidelity as a unifying device for elaborate song-and-dance sequences. In the movie's best performance, Kate Winslet plays gutter-mouthed temptress whose steamy liaisons with James Gandolfini's New York construction worker send his wife Susan Sarandon on the warpath. Reality and fantasy blur as the outlandish characters combine sex-themed banter with hit-and-miss musical outbursts. By concentrating on eccentricity instead of plot, this unfocused picture often feels contrived and self-indulgent. SF Swearing, sex scenes. *DVD*

James Gandolfini *Nick Murder* • Susan Sarandon *Kitty Kane* • Kate Winslet *Tula* • Steve Buscemi *Angelo* • Bobby Cannavale *Fryburg* • Mandy Moore *Baby* • Mary-Louise Parker *Constance* • Aida Turturro *Rosebud* • Christopher Walken *Cousin Bo* • Eddie Izzard *Gene Vincent* ■ *Dir/Scr* John Turturro

Romance in Manhattan ★★★U

Drama
1934 · US · BW · 76min

Ginger Rogers was desperately anxious to prove that she wasn't just Fred Astaire's screen dance partner, and in 1934 made seven features, only one of which co-starred the great Fred. This little gem has Ginger opposite debonair foreign import Francis Lederer. Ironically, he's an illegal alien who's helped by our Ginger, playing a soubrette from the chorus line. Director Stephen Roberts treats this lightweight nonsense with respect, ensuring a polished and charming romantic movie. TS

Ginger Rogers *Sylvia Dennis* • Francis Lederer *Karel Novak* • Arthur Hohl *Attorney* • Jimmy Butler *Frank Dennis* ■ *Dir* Stephen Roberts • *Scr* Jane Murfin, Edward Kaufman, from a story by Norman Krasna, Don Hartman

Romance of a Horse Thief ★★PG

Period comedy drama
1971 · US/Yug · Colour · 93min

This movie gave French-based English actress Jane Birkin one of her first starring roles, as a Jewish woman who returns from education in France to urge her Polish peasant community to fight back against their Cossack oppressors, led by Yul Brynner. This is a well-meaning but at times plodding drama. PF

Yul Brynner *Stoloff* • Eli Wallach *Kifke* • Jane Birkin *Naomi* • Oliver Tobias *Zanvill Kradnik* • Lainie Kazan *Estusha* • David Opatoshu *Schloime Kradnik* • Serge Gainsbourg *Sigmund* ■ *Dir* Abraham Polonsky • *Scr* David Opatoshu, from a story by Joseph Opatoshu

The Romance of Astrea and Celadon ★★★12A

Fantasy romantic drama
2007 · Fr/It/Sp · Colour · 109min

Octogenarian auteur Eric Rohmer ties up a defiantly idiosyncratic career with this apparently final feature – a languid pastoral romance, adapted from Honoré d'Urfé's 17th-century novel *L'Astrée*. Set in an imaginary fifth-century Gaul, partly populated by nymphs and druids, it's a handsome curiosity tracing the turbulent relationship between chivalric shepherd Celadon (Andy Gillet) and obstinate shepherdess Astrea (Stéphanie Crayencour). Rohmer presents a trademark ode to young love and fidelity that's highly stylised yet beautifully in tune with nature. The stodgy dialogue and effusive

philosophising may alienate some viewers, but it's admirable to see a film-maker who's kept his unique sensibilities bravely resisting cinematic trends. SF French +subtitles.

Andy Gillet *Celadon* • Stéphanie Crayencour *Astrea* • Cécile Cassel *Leonide* • Véronique Reymond *Galathee* ■ *Dir* Eric Rohmer • *Scr* Eric Rohmer, from the novel *L'Astrée* by Honoré D'Urfé

A Romance of the Redwoods ★★

Silent western
1917 · US · BW · 90min

In the same year that she played the title child in *Rebecca of Sunnybrook Farm*, Mary Pickford scored a success in this early Cecil B DeMille western, filmed on location in California's redwood country and set against a background of the 1849 gold rush. Pickford is a young woman who, having lost her father in an Indian attack, falls in love with outlaw Elliott Dexter and saves him from the full force of the law by pretending to be pregnant by him. RK

Mary Pickford *Jenny Lawrence* • Elliott Dexter *"Black" Brown* • Charles Ogle *Jim Lyn* • Tully Marshall *Sam Sparks* • Raymond Hatton *Dick Roland* • Walter Long *Sheriff* • William Hall *John Lawrence* ■ *Dir* Cecil B DeMille • *Scr* Jeanie Macpherson, Cecil B DeMille

Romance on the High Seas ★★★

Romantic musical
1948 · US · Colour · 98min

The sudden withdrawal of Betty Hutton (who had herself replaced Judy Garland) is the most significant thing about this breezy Warners musical, as it gave big band singer Doris Day the chance to take her first featured role. The stars of this Caribbean cruise confection were supposed to be Jack Carson and Janis Paige, but time hangs heavy between Day's all-too-brief appearances. Versatile though he was, director Michael Curtiz was never totally comfortable with the musical genre, which explains why Busby Berkeley was brought back to handle the dance routines. DP

Jack Carson *Peter Virgil* • Janis Paige *Elvira Kent* • Don DeFore *Michael Kent* • Doris Day *Georgia Garrett* • Oscar Levant *Oscar Farrar* • Fortunio Bonanova *Plinio* • Eric Blore *Ship's doctor* ■ *Dir* Michael Curtiz • *Scr* Julius J Epstein, Philip G Epstein, IAL Diamond, from the story *Romance in High C* by S Pondal Rios, Carlos A Olivari

Romancing the Stone ★★★★12

Adventure comedy
1984 · US · Colour · 101min

In this cracker of a rollercoaster ride, director Robert Zemeckis spices up a deliberately old-fashioned matinée adventure with tongue-in-cheek gags, unpredictably clever touches and top-of-the-range action. Kathleen Turner gives an exhilarating performance as the New York novelist who forsakes her cosy Manhattan lifestyle to rescue her sister in the jungles of Colombia. Turner dazzles in a role that proved a career turning point, and there's a wonderful chemistry between her and world-weary co-star Michael Douglas. Followed in 1985 by *The Jewel of the Nile*. AJ Swearing, violence. *DVD* *BD*

Michael Douglas (1) *Jack Colton* • Kathleen Turner *Joan Wilder* • Danny DeVito *Ralph* • Zack Norman *Ira* • Alfonso Arau *Juan* • Manuel Ojeda *Zolo* • Holland Taylor *Gloria* • Mary Ellen Trainor *Elaine* ■ *Dir* Robert Zemeckis • *Scr* Diane Thomas

Romanoff and Juliet ★★★U

Comedy
1961 · US · Colour · 102min

Written and directed by Peter Ustinov from his stage play, this is one of those wish-fulfilling fables which blunts its Cold War satire with queasy romanticism. The Americans and Russians are being held to atomic ransom by the tiny nation of Concordia, ruled over by Ustinov. But, while vocal warfare goes on, the kids of the US and Soviet ambassadors (Sandra Dee and John Gavin) fall in love. Charming, but simplistic. TH

Peter Ustinov *The General* • Sandra Dee *Juliet Moulsworth* • John Gavin *Igor Romanoff* • Akim Tamiroff *Vadim Romanoff* • Alix Talton *Beulah Moulsworth* • John Phillips (1) *Hooper Moulsworth* • Tamara Shayne *Evdokia Romanoff* ■ *Dir* Peter Ustinov • *Scr* Peter Ustinov, from the play by Peter Ustinov

The Romantic Age ★

Romantic comedy
1949 · UK · BW · 93min

Schoolgirl Mai Zetterling, feeling put down by her friend's father Hugh Williams, takes revenge by seducing him, but he eventually manages to extricate himself and hold on to his wife and family. The stars of this British film, directed by Edmond T Greville, must really have been desperate for work in 1949. This combination of prurience and coyness is an embarrassment. RK

Mai Zetterling *Arlette* • Hugh Williams *Arnold Dickson* • Margot Grahame *Helen Dickson* • Petula Clark *Julie Dickson* • Carol Marsh *Patricia* • Raymond Lovell *Hedges* • Paul Dupuis *Henri Sinclair* • Margaret Barton *Bessie* • Adrienne Corri *Nora* • Jean Anderson ■ *Dir* Edmond T Gréville • *Scr* Edward Dryhurst, Peggy Barwell, from the novel *Lycee des Jeunes Filles* by Serge Weber

Romantic Comedy ★★15

Comedy
1983 · US · Colour · 97min

Two Broadway playwrights, Dudley Moore and Mary Steenburgen, enjoy a fruitful professional partnership. Their working relationship keeps threatening to teeter over the edge into romance, except that it's never the right time. Each marries someone else, but that doesn't stop them wondering what might have been. A weak script and storyline contributed to Moore's rapid post-*Arthur* (1981) decline. FL

Dudley Moore *Jason Carmichael* • Mary Steenburgen *Phoebe Craddock* • Frances Sternhagen *Blanche* • Janet Eilber *Allison St James* • Robyn Douglass *Kate Mallory* • Ron Leibman *Leo* ■ *Dir* Arthur Hiller • *Scr* Bernard Slade, from his play

The Romantic Englishwoman ★★15

Comedy drama
1975 · UK/Fr · Colour · 111min

Thomas Wiseman wrote the preposterous novel on which this is based, and here he tries to make sense of it with the help of co-scriptwriter Tom Stoppard and director Joseph Losey. They don't succeed. Glenda Jackson goes on an emotional bender with drug-dealer Helmut Berger at Baden-Baden, and husband Michael Caine amazingly invites him to their English country home. The result is high-falutin', puddle-shallow soap opera giving itself airs. TH Swearing, sex scenes, nudity.

Glenda Jackson *Elizabeth Fielding* • Michael Caine *Lewis Fielding* • Helmut Berger *Thomas* • Marcus Richardson *David Fielding* • Kate Nelligan *Isabel* • Michael Lonsdale [Michel Lonsdale] *Swan* • Nathalie Delon *Miranda* ■ *Dir* Joseph Losey • *Scr* Tom Stoppard, Thomas Wiseman, from the novel by Wiseman

Romantics Anonymous ★★★★12

Romantic comedy
2010 · Fr/Bel · Colour · 74min

This delightfully off-the-wall comedy follows two emotionally challenged misfits as they stumble along the path to true love. Angélique (Isabelle Carré) tries to overcome her crippling shyness at a support group for lonely hearts, the "Romantics Anonymous" of the title. She meets the potential man of her dreams when she finds work at a struggling chocolate factory run by the equally awkward Jean-René (Benoît Poelvoorde). Will their mutual love of confectionery help them find their way to future happiness? Director Jean-Pierre Améris's quirky film is a wonderful blend of the comic and the cringe-making that should appeal to viewers charmed by the likes of *Amélie*. Poelvoorde plays the nervous buffoon to perfection, with Carré's clumsiness and wide-eyed innocence an ideal complement – a sweet pairing you'll be rooting for from the start. TeS French +subtitles. *DVD*

Benoît Poelvoorde *Jean-René* • Isabelle Carré *Angélique Delange* • Lorella Cravotta *Magda* • Lise Lamétrie *Suzanne* • Swann Arlaud *Antoine* • Pierre Niney *Ludo* ■ *Dir* Jean-Pierre Améris • *Scr* Jean-Pierre Améris, Philippe Blasband

Romanzo Criminale ★★★15

Period crime drama
2005 · It/UK/Fr/US · Colour · 147min

The smart-mouthed camaraderie of *GoodFellas* combines with the epic quality of *The Godfather* in this blisteringly violent Italian crime drama. Adapted from Giancarlo De Cataldo's fact-based bestseller, the movie tells the story of three childhood friends who reunite as adults in 1970s Rome to brutally conquer the world of organised crime. Although there are traces of the work of Martin Scorsese and Francis Ford Coppola in every handsomely shot frame, the film boasts a uniquely vicious intensity thanks to meticulous period detail, an energetic soundtrack and terrific ensemble performances. SF Italian +subtitles. *DVD*

Kim Rossi Stuart *Freddo/"Ice"* • Anna Mouglalis *Patrizia* • Pierfrancesco Favino *Libanese/"Lebanese"* • Claudio Santamaria *Dandi/"Dandy"* • Stefano Accorsi *Scialoja* • Riccardo Scamarcio *Nero/"Black"* • Jasmine Trinca *Roberta* ■ *Dir* Michele Placido • *Scr* Stefano Rulli, Sandro Petraglia, Giancarlo De Cataldo, from a story by Rulli, Petraglia, De Cataldo, from the novel by De Cataldo

Rome Adventure ★★★

Romantic drama
1962 · US · Colour · 118min

Back in the 1960s, teenage heart-throbs Troy Donahue and Suzanne Pleshette had their every move detailed in America's fan magazines. In this lush and soapy tale they are co-stars, though they did not marry until 1964. Librarian Pleshette is vacationing in Rome and can't choose between callow architect Donahue, and sophisticated roué Rossano Brazzi. Angie Dickinson gets all the best lines as Donahue's other woman, Max Steiner contributes one of his most romantic later scores, and director Delmer Daves knows just how far to go with his material. TS

Troy Donahue *Don Porter* • Angie Dickinson *Lyda* • Rossano Brazzi *Roberto Orlandi* • Suzanne Pleshette *Prudence Bell* • Constance Ford *Daisy* • Al Hirt *Al* • Chad Everett *Young man* ■ *Dir* Delmer Daves • *Scr* Delmer Daves, from the novel by Irving Fineman

Rome Express ★★★★U

Crime drama
1932 · UK · BW · 86min

This wonderfully entertaining Gaumont-British melodrama features a rich variety of passengers (including an art thief, double-crossed accomplices, an American film star, a philanthropist, adulterous lovers and a French police inspector) on a train journey between Paris and Rome. This set the pattern for dozens of later pictures using the same confined setting. The splendid cast includes Conrad Veidt in his first British film. Walter Forde directed it on the cramped sound stages of Shepherd's Bush, cleverly maintaining a sense of continual movement and foreign atmosphere. AE *BD*

Esther Ralston *Asta Marvelle* • Conrad Veidt *Zurta* • Hugh Williams *Tony* • Donald Calthrop *Poole* • Joan Barry *Mrs Maxted* • Harold Huth *Grant* • Gordon Harker *Tom Bishop* • Eliot Makeham *Mills* • Cedric Hardwicke *Alistair McBane* ■ *Dir* Walter Forde • *Scr* Clifford Grey, Sidney Gilliat, Frank Vosper, Ralph Stock, from the story by Clifford Grey

LANDMARK FILM
This neorealist portrait of resistance fighters on the streets of Italy's capital brings a new grit to European film-making

Rome, Open City ★★★★★12

Second World War drama
1945 · It · BW · 101min

Roberto Rossellini came to international prominence with this emotive resistance drama, which formed part of a wartime trilogy that was completed by *Paisà* (1946) and *Germany, Year Zero* (1947). Based on actual events, it's set during the last days of the Nazi occupation of Rome and was shot on location using fragments of

R

painstakingly spliced film negative and still photographer's stock. It's a landmark of neorealist cinema, despite the melodramatic storyline, montage structure and star performances (from Aldo Fabrizi and Anna Magnani at the head of a primarily non-professional cast) that somewhat undermine the social commitment, visual authenticity and technical rigour demanded by the movement's intellectual founder, Cesare Zavattini. **DP** Italian +subtitles. Some violence. **DVD**

Anna Magnani *Pina* • Aldo Fabrizi *Don Pietro Pellegrini* • Marcello Pagliero *Giorgio Manfredi, aka Luigi Ferraris* • Maria Michi *Marina Mari* • Harry Feist *Maj Bergmann* ■ *Dir* Roberto Rossellini • *Scr* Sergio Amidei, Federico Fellini, Roberto Rossellini, from a story by Sergio Amidei, Alberto Consiglio

Romeo and Juliet ★★★★ U
Romantic tragedy   1936 · US · BW · 124min

This is Shakespeare as a star vehicle for Norma Shearer and the too-mature Leslie Howard as the doomed lovers. Made at the instigation of MGM boss Irving Thalberg, the film contains hugely enjoyable performances from studio regulars Basil Rathbone and Edna May Oliver, plus a breathtaking, scenery-chewing turn from John Barrymore as Mercutio. George Cukor directs with a reverent eye for the text and period detail, and it's all worth seeing as a superb example of Hollywood studio kitsch. **TH**

Norma Shearer *Juliet* • Leslie Howard *Romeo* • John Barrymore *Mercutio* • Basil Rathbone *Tybalt* • Edna May Oliver *Nurse* • C Aubrey Smith *Lord Capulet* ■ *Dir* George Cukor • *Scr* Talbot Jennings, from the play by William Shakespeare

Romeo and Juliet ★★★★ U
Romantic tragedy   1954 · UK/It · Colour · 141min

This adaptation of Shakespeare's tragedy of star-crossed lovers tends to be forgotten in the shuffle between George Cukor's all-star 1930s version, Franco Zeffirelli's exquisite 1968 film and Baz Luhrmann's exciting modern take. But Renato Castellani's classically elegant production, beautifully shot on location in Italy with jewel-bright design inspired by Renaissance paintings, did win the Golden Lion at the Venice film festival and can boast attractive, textbook performances. **AME**

Laurence Harvey *Romeo* • Susan Shentall *Juliet* • Flora Robson *Nurse* • Mervyn Johns *Friar Laurence* • Bill Travers *Benvolio* • Enzo Fiermonte *Tybalt* • Aldo Zollo *Mercutio* • Giovanni Rota *Prince* • John Gielgud *Chorus* ■ *Dir* Renato Castellani • *Scr* Renato Castellani, from the play by William Shakespeare

Romeo and Juliet ★★★ U
Ballet   1966 · UK · Colour · 127min

This filmed performance of the Kenneth MacMillan-choreographed ballet that acts, if nothing else, as archive footage of the greatest dance partnership of the last century. Although Margot Fonteyn was 46 at the time, hardly appropriate for the 14-year-old Juliet, her astonishing technicality and musical sense soon overcome any credibility gap. Rudolf Nureyev was always at his best with Fonteyn and their chemistry is almost captured in this stage-bound production. With the stately and beautiful score by Prokofiev, the ballet is enjoyable even for non-balletomanes. **FL**

Rudolf Nureyev *Romeo* • Margot Fonteyn *Juliet* • David Blair (2) *Mercutio* • Desmond Doyle *Tybalt* • Anthony Dowell *Benvolio* • Derek Rencher *Paris* • Michael Somes *Lord Capulet* • Julia Farron *Lady Capulet* ■ *Dir* Paul Czinner • *Scr* from the ballet by Sergei Prokofiev, from the play by William Shakespeare • *Choreographer* Kenneth MacMillan

Romeo and Juliet ★★★ PG
Romantic tragedy
1968 · UK/It · Colour · 132min

Franco Zeffirelli's bold adaptation was notorious for jettisoning almost half the text and its chaste use of nudity, but it's tame indeed beside Baz Luhrmann's scintillating update in *William Shakespeare's Romeo + Juliet*. Olivia Hussey and Leonard

Whiting might have met the age criteria required to play Verona's star-crossed lovers, but neither can hold a candle to their latter-day counterparts, Leonardo DiCaprio and Claire Danes. They're bailed out, to some extent, by the support playing of John McEnery, Michael York and Milo O'Shea, as well as by Pasquelino De Santis's Oscar-winning photography. **DP** **DVD**

Leonard Whiting *Romeo* • Olivia Hussey *Juliet* • Michael York *Tybalt* • Milo O'Shea *Friar Laurence* • John McEnery *Mercutio* • Pat Heywood *Nurse* • Laurence Olivier *Narrator* • Natasha Parry *Lady Capulet* ■ *Dir* Franco Zeffirelli • *Scr* Franco Zeffirelli, from the play by William Shakespeare, adapted by Franco Brusati, Masolino D'Amico

Romeo & Juliet ★★ PG
Romantic tragedy
2012 · UK/US · Colour · 113min

Shakespeare's classic tale of star-crossed lovers from feuding families is given a new treatment from director Carlo Carlei, this time with *Downton Abbey*'s Julian Fellowes putting his own spin on the script. Of the young leads, Douglas Booth makes a decent Romeo, but Hailee Steinfeld has a tendency to rush her lines. The experienced supporting players seem and sound more comfortable with the dialogue, and the glossy Italian locations make it easy on the eye but the movie as a whole remains a decidedly unremarkable affair, not a patch on Franco Zeffirelli's 1968 adaptation or Baz Luhrmann's contemporary urban revamp from 1996. **DA** Some violence. **DVD**

Douglas Booth *Romeo* • Hailee Steinfeld *Juliet* • Ed Westwick *Tybalt* • Christian Cooke *Mercutio* • Paul Giamatti *Friar Laurence* • Damian Lewis *Lord Capulet* • Natascha McElhone *Lady Capulet* • Stellan Skarsgård *Prince Escalus of Verona* ■ *Dir* Carlo Carlei • *Scr* Julian Fellowes, from Shakespeare's play

Romeo Is Bleeding ★★★★ 18
Thriller   1992 · US · Colour · 104min

This deliriously bonkers black comedy thriller makes little sense but is powered along by some wonderfully over-the-top performances and a sheer disregard for anything approaching good taste. Gary Oldman is the corrupt cop whose life falls apart completely when he encounters deranged Lena Olin. Don't worry too much about the niceties of the plot, just sit back and enjoy Olin's whirlwind performance as the *femme fatale* from hell. Oldman is equally good and there are fine turns from an exceptional supporting cast. The *film noir* and comic elements don't always gel, but director Peter Medak ensures that it's always an exhilarating ride. **JF** Violence, swearing, sex scenes, nudity. **DVD**

Gary Oldman *Jack Grimaldi* • Lena Olin *Mona Demarkov* • Annabella Sciorra *Natalie Grimaldi* • Juliette Lewis *Sheri* • Roy Scheider *Don Falcone* • Michael Wincott *Sal* • Ron Perlman *Jack's attorney* • Dennis Farina *Nick Gazzara* • David Proval *Scully* • Will Patton *Martie Cuchinski* ■ *Dir* Peter Medak • *Scr* Hilary Henkin

Romeo Must Die ★★ 15
Romantic action drama
2000 · US · Colour · 109min

Jet Li takes his first starring role in a US movie, as an ex-cop convict who flees to America to avenge the death of his brother and gets entangled in a Mob war. During his investigation, he continually mixes with the daughter (played by singer Aaliyah) of the rival gang's head thug. Even for an American movie, the martial arts sequences are very badly choreographed, and there is far more hip-hop music and lingo than either plot or action. **KB** **DVD**

Jet Li *Han Sing* • Aaliyah *Trish O'Day* • Isaiah Washington *Mac* • Russell Wong *Kai* • DM X *Silk* • Delroy Lindo *Isaak O'Day* • Henry O *Ch'u Sing* • DB Woodside *Colin* • Anthony Anderson *Maurice* ■ *Dir* Andrzej Bartkowiak • *Scr* Eric Bernt, John Jarrell, Jerrold E Brown, from a story by Mitchell Kapner

Romero ★★★ 15
Political biographical drama
1989 · US · Colour · 100min

This is a powerful biopic of Oscar Romero, the El Salvadoran archbishop who, during the late 1970s, voiced the Catholic Church's opposition to his country's ruling repressive regime, and was subsequently assassinated for his outspokenness. The first film ever funded by officials of the US Roman Catholic Church, this is very much a message movie, but its tendency towards heavy-handedness is offset by an understated and dignified performance by Raul Julia. **DA**

Raul Julia *Archbishop Oscar Romero* • Richard Jordan *Father Rutilio Grande* • Ana Alicia *Arista Zalada* • Eddie Velez *Lieutenant Columa* • Alejandro Bracho *Father Alfonso Osuna* • Tony Plana *Father Manuel Morantes* • Harold Gould *Francisco Galedo* • Lucy Reina *Lucia* ■ *Dir* John Duigan • *Scr* John Sacret Young

Romper Stomper ★★★ 18
Drama   1992 · Aus · Colour · 88min

Russell Crowe stars as the leader of a racist gang that preys on Australia's immigrant population in writer/director Geoffrey Wright's unsettling portrait of neo-Nazi thugs. Unflinching in its depiction of the lifestyle of the protagonists, the film caused a *Clockwork Orange*-style controversy Down Under when it was released. Much of the film's power comes from the bruising, raw performances of Crowe, best friend Daniel Pollock and lover Jacqueline McKenzie. Although some may find the violent subject matter a major turn-off, Wright's stylised camerawork and pacey editing make this more than just an exercise in screen brutality. **JC** **DVD**

Russell Crowe *Hando* • Daniel Pollock *Davey* • Jacqueline McKenzie *Gabe* • Alex Scott (2) *Martin* • Leigh Russell *Sonny Jim* • Daniel Wyllie [Dan Wyllie] *Cackles* • James McKenna *Bubs* ■ *Dir/Scr* Geoffrey Wright

Romuald et Juliette ★★★ PG
Romantic comedy   1989 · Fr · Colour · 106min

This cultured romantic comedy features Daniel Auteuil as a yoghurt-company boss who's framed for a food-poisoning scandal, and finds that the only person who can help him, commercially and emotionally, is his company's black cleaning lady (Firmine Richard). Directed with skill and style by Coline Serreau and played with aplomb by the two leads, this is lightweight French film-making at its most likeable best. **DA** French +subtitles. **DVD**

Daniel Auteuil *Romuald* • Firmine Richard *Juliette Bonaventure* • Pierre Vernier *Blache* • Maxime Leroux *Cloquet* • Gilles Privat *Paulin* • Muriel Combeau *Nicole* • Catherine Salviat *Françoise* ■ *Dir/Scr* Coline Serreau

Romulus and the Sabines ★★
Historical adventure   1961 · It/Fr/Yug · Colour

The sword-and-sandal Euro-epics of the 1950s and 60s (often featuring legendary heroes like Hercules, Maciste and Samson) tended to import American beefcake like Steve Reeves or former Tarzan Gordon Scott to play the muscular hero. So it's curious to find a callow young Roger Moore, just before TV fame as the Saint and a decade before superstardom as James Bond, striding around in a natty line of tunics as the eponymous founder of Rome. He's the main attraction of this meandering adventure... despite some nice scenery and hordes of scantily dressed starlets. **JA** Italian dubbed.

Roger Moore *Romulus* • Mylène Demongeot *Rea* • Scilla Gabel *Dusia* • Jean Marais *Mars* • Rosanna Schiaffino *Venus* ■ *Dir* Richard Pottier • *Scr* Edoardo Anton, Carlo Infascelli, Stephen Garrett, Frank Gregory, from a story by Anton, Infascelli

Romy and Michele's High School Reunion ★★★ 15
Comedy   1997 · US · Colour · 88min

This fun comedy stars Mira Sorvino and Lisa Kudrow as the two dim-witted, down-on-their-luck blondes of the title, who

pretend they are high-powered businesswomen at their high school reunion to impress those ex-school mates who once made fun of them. It's a simple enough premise that is enlivened by two infectious performances from the leads as well as slick support from Janeane Garofalo and Alan Cumming. A TV movie prequel followed in 2005. **JB** Swearing, sexual references. **DVD**

Mira Sorvino *Romy* • Lisa Kudrow *Michele* • Janeane Garofalo *Heather* • Alan Cumming *Sandy Frink* • Julia Campbell *Christie* • Mia Cottet *Cheryl* • Kristin Bauer *Kelly* • Elaine Hendrix *Lisa* • Vincent Ventresca *Billy* • Justin Theroux *Cowboy* ■ *Dir* David Mirkin • *Scr* Robin Schiff

Ronaldo ★★ PG
Sports documentary   2015 · UK · Colour · 88min

Cristiano Ronaldo is a phenomenal footballer, but this frequently cringe-inducing profile by Anthony Wonke aims to make him seem like a demi-god. Though he has won silverware at Sporting Lisbon, Manchester United and Real Madrid, this portrait offers no concrete analysis of Ronaldo's talent, development or contribution to club and country, and no sense that he owes it to anyone apart from himself. As an insight into the man and his achievements, this is a vanity project that misses a unique opportunity. **DP** **DVD** **BL**

David Morrissey *Narrrator* ■ *Dir* Anthony Wonke

La Ronde ★★★★★ PG
Drama   1950 · Fr · BW · 88min

The Arthur Schnitzler play on which this is based was a metaphor for the spread of venereal disease. However, director Max Ophüls buried this message beneath a surface elegance and sophistication that characterised his 1950s style. From the dazzling opening sequence, in which master of ceremonies Anton Walbrook flits between studio sets to start this carousel of careless caresses, Ophüls keeps his prying camera on the move in time to the waltz music of Oscar Straus. Each tryst is played to perfection by the remarkable cast. **DP** French +subtitles. **DVD** **BL**

Anton Walbrook *Storyteller* • Simone Signoret *Leocadie, the prostitute* • Serge Reggiani *Franz, the soldier* • Simone Simon *Marie, the maid* • Daniel Gélin *Alfred, the young man* • Danielle Darrieux *Emma Breitkopf, the wife* • Fernand Gravey [Fernand Gravet] *Charles, Emma's husband* ■ *Dir* Max Ophüls • *Scr* Jacques Natanson, Max Ophüls, from the play *Reigen* by Arthur Schnitzler

La Ronde ★★
Drama   1964 · Fr/It · Colour · 110min

The first of the four films Jane Fonda made with one-time husband Roger Vadim, this suffers in every aspect comparison with Max Ophüls's 1950 version. Switching the action to Paris on the eve of the Great War, Vadim makes stylish use of Henri Decaë's widescreen imagery, but the screenplay is surprisingly coarse considering it was written by playwright Jean Anouilh, while many of the cast misread their characters. **DP** In French.

Marie Dubois *Prostitute* • Claude Giraud *Soldier* • Anna Karina *Maid* • Valérie Lagrange *Maid's friend* • Jean-Claude Brialy *Young man* • Jane Fonda *Married woman* • Maurice Ronet *Husband* • Catherine Spaak *Midinette* • Francine Bergé *Maximilienne de Poussy* ■ *Dir* Roger Vadim • *Scr* Jean Anoilh, from the play *Reigen* by Arthur Schnitzler

Ronin ★★★★ 15
Action thriller   1998 · US · Colour · 116min

Resembling a 1970s European espionage caper in atmosphere and style, director John Frankenheimer's deliberately retro thriller bounds along at a cracking pace. In an engrossing action adventure with a sobering political slant, Robert De Niro travels to Paris to join an international gang of criminals (including the always watchable Jean Reno) who have been hired by Irish revolutionary Natascha McElhone to steal an important suitcase. No excuse is missed for a frenzied car chase in the *Bullitt*

R

tradition, or the chance to add a menacing hard edge to the deliciously convoluted plot. AJ Violence, swearing. DVD Blu

Robert De Niro *Sam* • Jean Reno *Vincent* • Natascha McElhone *Deirdre* • Stellan Skarsgård *Gregor* • Sean Bean *Spence* • Skipp Sudduth *Larry* • Michael Lonsdale [Michel Lonsdale] *Jean-Pierre* • Jan Triska *Dapper gent* • Jonathan Pryce *Seamus* ■ *Dir* John Frankenheimer • *Scr* JD Zeik, Richard Weisz [David Mamet], from a story by JD Zeik

Rookery Nook ★★

Farce   1930 · UK · BW · 107min

This, probably the most famous Aldwych farce, was the second to be filmed, but the first talkie. British audiences originally found it thrilling to hear favourite comedians speaking on screen but this appeal has dimmed considerably. Director/star Tom Walls is a lifeless actor and doesn't seem to have considered re-takes important: three fluffed lines are kept in. Walls's regular partner Ralph Lynn is much more fun in his perennial silly-ass role, here a meek husband who gives lovely runaway Winifred Shotter a room in his country house and then has to explain her presence to his family. DM

Tom Walls *Clive Popkiss* • Ralph Lynn *Gerald Popkiss* • Winifred Shotter *Rhoda Marley* • Robertson Hare *Harold Twine* • Mary Brough *Mrs Leverett* • Ethel Coleridge *Mrs Twine* • Griffith Humphreys *Mr Putz* • Doreen Bendix *Poppy Dickey* • Margot Grahame *Clara Popkiss* ■ *Dir* Tom Walls • *Scr* Ben Travers, WP Lipscomb, from Travers's play

The Rookie ★★ 18

Action thriller   1990 · US · Colour · 115min

As both a talented director and actor, Clint Eastwood manages to maintain a spirit of lethargic cynicism when working on formula fare such as this all-action buddy movie. For fans, there's plenty of Clint as a firecracker cop, here part of a double act with Charlie Sheen, but Clint the director makes little effort to freshen up plot, character or car chase. JM Swearing, violence, sex scenes. Blu

Clint Eastwood *Nick Pulovski* • Charlie Sheen *David Ackerman* • Raul Julia *Strom* • Sonia Braga *Liesl* • Tom Skerritt *Eugene Ackerman* • Lara Flynn Boyle *Sarah* • Pepe Serna *Lieutenant Ray Garcia* ■ *Dir* Clint Eastwood • *Scr* Boaz Yakin, Scott Spiegel

The Rookie ★★★ U

Sports drama based on a true story
2002 · US · Colour · 122min

This true story is hampered by some signposted plot developments and undernourished characters. However, it does contain a poignant performance by Dennis Quaid as Jimmy Morris, a former pro-baseball player who pledges to try out again for the major leagues if the school team he coaches makes the play-offs. Rachel Griffiths offers stoic support in the clichéd role of his supportive wife. However, this is a bit too long and has too many dull stretches for what aspires to be a feel-good family film. TH DVD Blu

Dennis Quaid *Jimmy Morris* • Rachel Griffiths *Lorri Morris* • Jay Hernandez *Joaquin "Wack" Campos* • Beth Grant *Olline, Jimmy's mother* • Angus T Jones *Hunter* • Brian Cox (1) *James Morris Sr* • Rick Gonzalez *Rudy Bonilla* • Chad Lindberg *Joe David West* ■ *Dir* John Lee Hancock • *Scr* Mike Rich

Rookie of the Year ★★★ PG

Sports comedy   1993 · US · Colour · 99min

With a few honourable exceptions (*Bull Durham* and *Major League* among them), the British have never really warmed to baseball movies and this one slipped by virtually unnoticed in the UK. It's a slight but affectionate family comedy that follows the adventures of a youngster (Thomas Ian Nicholas) who, after breaking his arm, becomes a wonder pitcher. Director Daniel Stern plays down the cute aspects of the story, while Nicholas is helped by sterling support from Gary Busey, Dan Hedaya and Stern himself. JF DVD

Thomas Ian Nicholas *Henry Rowengartner* • Gary Busey *Chet Steadman* • Albert Hall *Martinella* • Amy Morton *Mary Rowengartner* • Dan Hedaya *Larry "Fish" Fisher* • Bruce Altman *Jack Bradfield* • Eddie Bracken *Bob Carson* ■ *Dir* Daniel Stern • *Scr* Sam Harper

Room ★★★★ 15

Drama   2015 · Can/Ire · Colour · 112min

Emma Donoghue skilfully adapts her own acclaimed novel *Room*, a claustrophobic thriller inspired by the case of Josef Fritzl, the Austrian man who incarcerated his daughter in a basement for 24 years and systematically raped and impregnated her. Both book and film avoid lurid true-crime trappings by telling their fictional story from the innocent point of view of five-year-old Jack (preternaturally assured newcomer Jacob Tremblay), born into the cramped captivity he shares with his mother (a career-minting Brie Larson), abducted seven years ago. Directed with tactile, close-up empathy by Lenny Abrahamson (*Frank*), *Room* is a moving, heartbreaking portrait of the mother-son bond. AC Swearing. DVD Blu

Brie Larson *Ma* • Jacob Tremblay *Jack* • William H Macy *Grandpa Robert* • Sean Bridgers *Old Nick* • Joan Allen *Nancy* • Tom McCamus *Leo* ■ *Dir* Lenny Abrahamson • *Scr* Emma Donoghue, from her novel *Room* • *Cinematographer* Danny Cohen

A Room and a Half or a Sentimental Journey Back Home ★★★★ 12A

Biographical drama
2009 · Rus · Colour · 129min

Poet and nobel laureate Joseph Brodsky was exiled from the Soviet Union in 1972 and never returned, dying in his New York apartment in 1996. However, film-maker Andrey Khrzhanovsky uses an imagined homecoming to spark memories of the poet's youth in this highly stylised and impeccably judged biopic. This fictional Brodsky finds wonderment in everything and Khrzhanovsky juxtaposes extracts from his verses with animated interludes to convey the poet's questing mind. This is a beautifully produced, historically astute and hugely affecting movie. DP Russian +subtitles. Brief swearing. DVD

Grigoriy Dityatkovskiy *Joseph Brodsky* • Alisa Freyndlikh *Mother* • Sergei Yursky *Father* • Artem Smola *Young Brodsky* • Evgeniy Ogandzhanyan *Brodsky in childhood* ■ *Dir* Andrey Khrzhanovsky • *Scr* Yuriy Arabov, Andrey Khrzhanovsky

Room at the Top ★★★★★ 15

Drama   1958 · UK · BW · 112min

This gritty, trenchant film burst upon the late 1950s and stirred a hornet's nest of controversy for its treatment of sex as passionate rather than a merely procreative exercise. Laurence Harvey is at his slit-eyed, manipulative, lizard-like best as the ambitious antihero, with Simone Signoret glorious and sexy as his ill-fated mistress. For once, the North is portrayed as a shade more complicated than previous "flat cap and whippet" outings had shown, in a movie which perfectly captures the gradual demise of Victorian morality and traditional class culture. Seven years later Harvey returned in *Life at the Top*. SH DVD

Laurence Harvey *Joe Lampton* • Simone Signoret *Alice Aisgill* • Heather Sears *Susan Brown* • Donald Wolfit *Mr Brown* • Ambrosine Philpotts *Mrs Brown* • Donald Houston *Charles Soames* • Raymond Huntley *Mr Hoylake* • John Westbrook *Jack Wales* • Allan Cuthbertson *George Aisgill* • Mary Peach *June Samson* • Hermione Baddeley *Elspeth* ■ *Dir* Jack Clayton • *Scr* Neil Paterson, from the novel by John Braine

Room for One More ★★★ U

Comedy drama   1952 · US · BW · 94min

Cary Grant brings much-needed charm to this peculiar comedy drama, in which his then real-life wife Betsy Drake plays his spouse, a woman with a compulsive need to adopt. It's somewhat surprisingly based on a true story and is quite watchable, especially when Grant is pitted against that

formidable child actor, the deadpan George "Foghorn" Winslow. TS

Cary Grant *"Poppy" Rose* • Betsy Drake *Anna Rose* • Lurene Tuttle *Miss Kenyon* • Randy Stuart *Mrs Foreman* • John Ridgely *Harry Foreman* • Irving Bacon *Mayor* • Mary Lou Treen [Mary Treen] *Mrs Roberts* • Hayden Rorke *Doctor* • Iris Mann *Jane* • George "Foghorn" Winslow [George Winslow] *Teensie* • Clifford Tatum Jr *Jimmy-John* • Gay Gordon *Trot* • Malcolm Cassell *Tim* ■ *Dir* Norman Taurog • *Scr* Jack Rose, Melville Shavelson, from the autobiography by Anna Perrott Rose

A Room for Romeo Brass ★★★★ 15

Comedy drama   1999 · UK/Can · Colour · 86min

This is a risky, difficult and very impressive little movie about two 12-year-old mates – the spirited Andrew Shim and the sickly Ben Marshall – who are befriended by likeable, albeit peculiar, loner Paddy Considine. Beginning as an earthy but light-hearted study of adolescent friendship, the film takes a sharp turn into quite shocking drama once Considine reveals his darker side. Although the sudden shift in tone won't please everyone, this honest and unsentimental movie offers many insights into the weirdness of human relationships. JC Swearing. DVD

Andrew Shim *Romeo Brass* • Ben Marshall *Gavin "Knock Knock" Woolley* • Paddy Considine *Morell* • Frank Harper *Joseph Brass* • Julia Ford *Sandra Woolley* • James Higgins *Bill Woolley* • Vicky McClure *Ladine Brass* • Ladene Hall *Carol Brass* • Bob Hoskins *Steven Laws* • Shane Meadows *Fish and chip shop man* ■ *Dir* Shane Meadows • *Scr* Paul Fraser, Shane Meadows

Room Service ★★ U

Comedy   1938 · US · BW · 75min

This oddity in the careers of the Marx Brothers sees a little of their well-established humour applied to a hit Broadway farce. The anarchic personalities of Groucho, Harpo and Chico are fatally weakened by being tied to a situation comedy plot and Groucho is the only brother with a real part, as a penniless Broadway producer trying to put on a new play. There are some inspired moments, but far too few of them. AE DVD

Groucho Marx *Gordon Miller* • Chico Marx *Harry Binelli* • Harpo Marx *Faker Englund* • Lucille Ball *Christine Marlowe* • Ann Miller *Hilda Manney* ■ *Dir* William A Seiter • *Scr* Morrie Ryskind, Glenn Tryon, Philip Loeb, from a play by Allan Boretz, John Murray

Room to Let ★★

Crime thriller   1949 · UK · Colour · 65min

Hammer Films took a step towards its future speciality with this early B-feature from a radio play by mystery writer Margery Allingham. Is Valentine Dyall's creepy Victorian lodger a missing mental patient or possibly even Jack the Ripper? Jimmy Hanley headlines the cast playing a reporter, while Constance Smith, as his girlfriend and landlady's daughter. Modest, but enjoyable. AE

Jimmy Hanley *Curley Minter* • Valentine Dyall *Dr Fell* • Christine Silver *Mrs Musgrave* • Merle Tottenham *Alice* • Charles Hawtrey *Mike Atkinson* • Constance Smith *Molly Musgrave* ■ *Dir* Godfrey Grayson • *Scr* John Gilling, Godfrey Grayson, from the radio play by Margery Allingham

Room to Rent ★★★ 15

Comedy drama   2000 · UK/Fr · Colour · 91min

Directed by an Anglophile Egyptian, this British film stars the French-born Moroccan Saïd Taghmaoui as a student from Egypt struggling to become a successful screenwriter before the expiry of his visa. Essentially a series of encounters with characters Taghmaoui meets as he flits in and out of a succession of rented London rooms, this combination of drama, comedy and tinges of the fantastical does not really gel. However, vibrant performances and the realistic location shooting just about shade things in its favour. DA DVD

Saïd Taghmaoui *Ali* • Juliette Lewis *Linda* • Rupert Graves *Mark* • Anna Massey *Sarah Stevenson* • Karim Belkhadra *Ahmed* ■ *Dir/Scr* Khaled El Hagar

Room 237: Being an Inquiry into The Shining in 9 Parts ★★ 15

Documentary
2012 · US · BW and Colour · 102min

Stanley Kubrick's classic and, initially at least, much underrated, horror film *The Shining* might appear to be the topic of this documentary curio, but its real subject is cinematic obsession. Composed for the most part of slowed down, speeded up and occasionally annotated clips of Jack Torrance and his stricken family, it explores a handful of theories about the "true meaning" of the 1980 film. They range from the barely credible to the truly whacked-out. It's harmless fun at first, but soon becomes vaguely tiresome. AS Violence, nudity. DVD

■ *Dir* Rodney Ascher

A Room with a View ★★★★ PG

Period drama   1985 · UK · Colour · 111min

This is the first of the Merchant Ivory adaptations of EM Forster. While *Howards End* was the one that scooped the major international awards, this is, in many ways, a more more influential picture, as it confirmed the marketability of the "heritage" film that was, until recently, this country's most profitable movie export. Everything about the production proclaims its class: Ruth Prawer Jhabvala's script is witty and erudite, Tony Pierce-Roberts's images of Florence and the English countryside are breathtaking and the performances are of masterclass quality. There are longueurs, but the air of Edwardian charm is irresistible. DP Nudity. DVD Blu

Maggie Smith *Charlotte Bartlett* • Helena Bonham Carter *Lucy Honeychurch* • Denholm Elliott *Mr Emerson* • Julian Sands *George Emerson* • Daniel Day-Lewis *Cecil Vyse* • Simon Callow *Reverend Arthur Beebe* • Judi Dench *Miss Eleanor Lavish* • Rosemary Leach *Mrs Honeychurch* • Rupert Graves *Freddy Honeychurch* ■ *Dir* James Ivory • *Scr* Ruth Prawer Jhabvala, from the novel by EM Forster

The Roommate ★ 15

Psychological thriller 2011 · US · Colour · 87min

First-year student Minka Kelly discovers the sinister truth behind roommate Leighton Meester's overprotective behaviour in this lame and derivative psychological thriller. Having played its hand early on, the movie then has nowhere to go but spin out the action highlights of Meester's aberrant behaviour. It plays like a very pale shadow of Bridget Fonda and Jennifer Jason Leigh's trashy-but-chilling set-to in *Single White Female*. Billy Zane's toe-curlingly awful turn as a preening design professor turns out to be the main entertainment value on display. TJ DVD Blu

Minka Kelly *Sara Matthews* • Leighton Meester *Rebecca* • Cam Gigandet *Stephen* • Aly Michalka [Alyson Michalka] *Tracy* • Frances Fisher *Rebecca's mom* • Billy Zane *Professor Roberts* ■ *Dir* Christian E Christiansen • *Scr* Sonny Mallhi

Roommates ★★ 12

Comedy drama   1995 · US · Colour · 104min

Peter Falk stars as an elderly baker who adopts his grandson to prevent him from being sent to an orphanage. With the help of Oscar-nominated make-up, the film chronicles their relationship over the next three decades. They come to blows when little Michael, played by DB Sweeney, is an adult and studying medicine. Grandad, now over a hundred, is at odds with Sweeney's Chinese roommates and girlfriend Julianne Moore. Daft and overlong, this twaddle is bearable if only for the conviction of Falk's performance. LH

Peter Falk *Rocky* • DB Sweeney *Michael Holczek* • Julianne Moore *Beth* • Ellen Burstyn *Judith* • Jan Rubes *Bolek Krupa* ■ *Dir* Peter Yates • *Scr* Max

U SUITABLE FOR ALL   Uc SUITABLE ESPECIALLY FOR YOUNG CHILDREN (DVD ONLY)   PG PARENTAL GUIDANCE   12A UNDER 12s TO BE ACCOMPANIED (CINEMA ONLY)

R

Apple, Stephen Metcalfe, from the autobiography *Roommates: My Grandfather's Story* by Max Apple

Rooney ★★★ U
Comedy　　1958 · UK · BW · 84min

Ah, the blarney overflows in this very Pinewood version of Catherine Cookson's novel of an Irish dustman in love. Liverpool-born John Gregson makes a likeable stab at the title role, but sadly lacks grit alongside the more authentic Marie Kean, Jack MacGowran, Noel Purcell, Liam Redmond and bedridden Barry Fitzgerald. And if they're all a little too much for you, then so be it, but the result is really quite charming. TS **DVD**

John Gregson *James Ignatius Rooney* • Muriel Pavlow *Maire Hogan* • Barry Fitzgerald *Grandfather* • June Thorburn *Doreen O'Flynn* • Noel Purcell *Tim Hennessy* • Marie Kean *Mrs O'Flynn* • Liam Redmond *Mr Doolan* • Jack MacGowran *Joe O'Connor* ■ *Dir* George Pollock • *Scr* Patrick Kirwan, from the novel by Catherine Cookson

The Roost ★ 18
Horror　　2005 · US · Colour and BW · 80min

Four teenage friends are involved in a car accident en route to a Halloween wedding and seek help at an apparently deserted farm, only to fall prey to ravenous bats whose bites turn their victims into bloodsuckers. Although deliberately envisaged as a throwback to the cheap, straight-to-video titles of the 1980s, Ti West's gimmicky picture re-creates all the negatives and none of the charm of the B-movie "creature feature". SF Swearing, violence.

Tom Noonan *The Horror Host* • Wil Horneff *Elliott* • Karl Jacob *Trevor* • Vanessa Horneff *Allison* • Sean Reid *Brian* • John Speredakos *Officer Mitchell* • Richard Little *Elvin* • Barbara Wilhide *May* ■ *Dir/Scr* Ti West

Rooster Cogburn ★★★ U
Western　　1975 · US · Colour · 102min

This is a memorable collaboration between John Wayne and Katharine Hepburn, with Wayne reprising his Oscar-winning role from *True Grit* and Hepburn playing the same kind of spinster she portrayed in *The African Queen*. Here, Hepburn is the missionary who tames the truculence of one-eyed Wayne as they search for her father's killers. The performances are wonderful, but the film relies too much on its elderly stars and is fatally flawed by Stuart Millar's sluggish direction. However, it remains eminently watchable, as great stars go through their paces. TH **DVD** 🔵

John Wayne *Rooster Cogburn* • Katharine Hepburn *Eula Goodnight* • Anthony Zerbe *Breed* • Richard Jordan *Hawk* • John McIntire *Judge Parker* • Richard Romancito *Wolf* • Strother Martin *McCoy* ■ *Dir* Stuart Millar • *Scr* Martin Julien, from the character created by Charles Portis in his novel *True Grit*

The Root of All Evil ★★ U
Drama　　1946 · UK · BW · 104min

Attempting to break from her wholesome image, Phyllis Calvert here found herself in a role much more suited to her *Man in Grey* co-star, Margaret Lockwood. Her transformation from fresh-faced farm girl to scheming oil tycoon, by way of a breach of promise suit against fiancé Hubert Gregg, is totally implausible, and the harder she tries to be wicked, the more ludicrous the action becomes. DP

Phyllis Calvert *Jeckie Farnish* • Michael Rennie *Charles Mortimer* • John McCallum *Joe Bartle* • Brefni O'Rorke *Mr Farnish* • Arthur Young (1) *George Grice* • Hubert Gregg *Albert Grice* • Pat Hicks *Lucy Grice* ■ *Dir* Brock Williams • *Scr* Brock Williams, from the novel by JS Fletcher

The Roots of Heaven ★★
Drama　　1958 · US · Colour · 131min

Seven years after *The African Queen*, John Huston travelled to French Equatorial Africa for another gruelling location shoot. With Errol Flynn and Trevor Howard in the cast, it was a boozy set, and the movie rather lurches along. Howard is in Africa to save

the elephant from ivory poachers. Flynn supports Howard's campaign, as does TV reporter Orson Welles. It's sadly muddled and Flynn looks raddled. AT **DVD** 🔵

Errol Flynn *Major Forsythe* • Juliette Greco *Minna* • Trevor Howard *Morel* • Eddie Albert *Abe Fields* • Orson Welles *Cy Sedgewick* • Paul Lukas *Saint Denis* • Herbert Lom *Orsini* • Grégoire Aslan *Habib* ■ *Dir* John Huston • *Scr* Romain Gary, Patrick Leigh-Fermor, from the novel by Romain Gary

Rope ★★★ PG
Thriller　　1948 · US · Colour · 76min

This thriller from Alfred Hitchcock is more intriguing today for its use of continuous long takes. The plot sees two homosexual student murderers (Farley Granger and John Dall) giving a party in a posh New York apartment for academic James Stewart and relatives of the young victim, whose body is present in a trunk from which they serve the drinks. Curiously devoid of suspense, the film is more an intriguing cerebral exercise, more famous as an experiment in technique, than as a characteristic Hitchcockian entertainment. Based on the real-life Leopold and Loeb case, it remains historically interesting, but nowadays disappoints. RK **DVD** 🔵

James Stewart *Rupert Cadell* • John Dall *John Brandon* • Farley Granger *Phillip Morgan* • Sir Cedric Hardwicke *(Cedric Hardwicke) Mr Kentley* • Joan Chandler *Janet Walker* • Constance Collier *Mrs Atwater* • Edith Evanson *Mrs Wilson* ■ *Dir* Alfred Hitchcock • *Scr* Arthur Laurents, Hume Cronyn, Ben Hecht (uncredited), from the play by Patrick Hamilton

Rope of Sand ★★
Adventure drama　　1949 · US · BW · 104min

In an improbable Hollywood version of South Africa, heroic big-game hunter Burt Lancaster foils the nefarious activities of gem seekers and rescues the lady caught in the complicated plot. Directed by William Dieterle with Claude Rains as a suave schemer, Paul Henreid a chilling sadist and Peter Lorre a whining opportunist on the edge of things, this gathering of half the cast of *Casablanca*, plus French actress Corinne Calvet making a less than persuasive Hollywood debut, is a nonsensical adventure. RK

Burt Lancaster *Mike Davis* • Paul Henreid *Commandant Paul Vogel* • Claude Rains *Arthur Fred Martingale* • Peter Lorre *Toady* • Corinne Calvet *Suzanne Renaud* • Sam Jaffe *Dr Francis "Doc" Hunter* • John Bromfield *Thompson, guard* ■ *Dir* William Dieterle • *Scr* Walter Doniger, John Paxton, from a story by Walter Doniger

Rosa Luxemburg ★★★★ PG
Biographical drama
1986 · W Ger · Colour · 123min

Despite her surname, Rosa Luxemburg was actually born in Poland, resident in Germany and widely considered one of the most dangerous women of her age: a revolutionary, internationalist, pacifist, Jew and troublemaker and probably vegetarian to boot. Award-winning actress Barbara Sukowa was rightly rewarded for for portraying her in this praised German film. An intelligent biopic, of historical, personal and dramatic interest. PF German +subtitles.

Barbara Sukowa *Rosa Luxemburg* • Daniel Olbrychski *Leo Jogiches* • Otto Sander *Karl Liebknecht* • Adelheid Arndt *Luise Kautsky* • Jürgen Holtz *Karl Kautsky* ■ *Dir/Scr* Margarethe von Trotta

Rosalie ★★ U
Musical comedy　　1937 · US · BW · 124min

Nelson Eddy teams with tap-dancer Eleanor Powell in this crass and kitschy cross between operetta and college musical. Nelson is a West Point cadet in love with Powell, playing Princess Rosalie of Romanza, who is studying at Vassar The best song in the so-so Cole Porter score is *In the Still of the Night*, while the gigantic title number (hated by its composer) had Powell in a frothy tutu and a cast of thousands. RB

Nelson Eddy *Dick Thorpe* • Eleanor Powell *Rosalie* • Ray Bolger *Bill Delroy* • Frank Morgan *King* • Ilona Massey *Brenda* • Edna May Oliver *Queen* • Billy Gilbert *Oloff* • Reginald Owen *Chancellor* • William Demarest *Army's coach* ■ *Dir* WS Van Dyke • *Scr* William Anthony McGuire, from the musical by William Anthony McGuire, by Guy Bolton

Rosalie Goes Shopping ★★★ 15
Comedy　　1989 · W Ger · Colour · 89min

Critics at the time considered German director Percy Adlon's follow-up to the cult favourite *Bagdad Café* to have been something of a disappointment. Yet, in many ways, this is a more assured piece of film-making, largely because Adlon's grasp of modern American mores was much firmer. This is a stinging satire on the consumerist boom that occurred during the Reagan presidency, when acquisition made life worthwhile and payment was an inconvenience. Adlon regular Marianne Sägebrecht gives a beguiling performance as the shopaholic of the title, while Brad Davis provides solid support as her crop-dusting husband. DP Swearing.

Marianne Sägebrecht *Rosalie Greenspace* • Brad Davis *Ray Greenspace, "Liebling"* • Judge Reinhold *Priest* • Erika Blumberger *Rosalie's mum* • Willy Harlander *Rosalie's dad* ■ *Dir* Percy Adlon • *Scr* Percy Adlon, Eleonore Adlon, Christopher Doherty

The Rosary Murders ★★★ 15
Murder mystery　　1987 · US · Colour · 100min

The sometimes mildly threatening Donald Sutherland makes an unlikely Detroit priest, but his fine, controlled performance in this dark, unsettling film lifts its rather plodding pace. Sutherland is the recipient of every priest's occupational nightmare, the serial killer who picks his church to confess in. We witness a neat tussle of conscience, as victims are felled like ninepins for most of the film. One of those promising efforts which starts out at a decent lick but ends up running out of steam and ideas. SH Violence, swearing. **DVD**

Donald Sutherland *Father Bob Koesler* • Charles Durning *Father Ted Nabors* • Josef Sommer *Lieutenant Walt Koznicki* • Belinda Bauer *Pat Lennon* • James Murtaugh *Javison* ■ *Dir* Fred Walton • *Scr* Elmore Leonard, Fred Walton, from the novel by William X Kienzle

The Rose ★★ 15
Musical drama　　1979 · US · Colour · 128min

Trapped by the usual conventions of rock-star biopics – drugs, booze and blues – Bette Midler, playing a singer loosely based on Janis Joplin, is only really effective during her raunchy concert numbers. For the rest of the film she's at the mercy of a script as ridiculous as the hairstyles. Alan Bates gives a skilful performance that makes him a ruthless manager a plausible man, but Midler just muddles through. TH Swearing, nudity. **DVD**

Bette Midler *Rose* • Alan Bates *Rudge* • Frederic Forrest *Dyer* • Harry Dean Stanton *Billy Ray* • Barry Primus *Dennis* • David Keith *Mal* ■ *Dir* Mark Rydell • *Scr* Bo Goldman, William Kerby, Michael Cimino, from the story by Kerby

The Rose Garden ★★ 15
Courtroom drama based on a true story
1989 · W Ger/US · Colour · 108min

Winner of the best foreign film Oscar for his 1986 movie *The Assault*, Dutch director Fons Rademakers returned to the subject of the Second World War with this study of memory and guilt. Set in modern-day Germany, the story of Maximilian Schell's prosecution for attacking the former commandant of the concentration camp where his sister died eschews sentimentality. However, it also mistakes slowness for sincerity and spends too much time exploring lawyer Liv Ullmann's relationship with her estranged husband, Peter Fonda. DP

Liv Ullmann *Gabriele Schlueter-Freund* • Maximilian Schell *Aaron Reichenbach* • Peter Fonda *Herbert Schlueter* • Jan Niklas *George Paessler* • Katarina Lena Muller *Tina* ■ *Dir* Fons Rademakers • *Scr* Paul Hengge

Rose Marie ★★★★ U
Musical romantic comedy　　1936 · US · Colour · 110min

The phenomenally successful 1930s musicals of "America's Sweethearts" Jeanette MacDonald and Nelson Eddy creak mightily now, but there is still abundant fun in this loose adaptation of the popular operetta combined here with a manhunt melodrama. Opera singer MacDonald falls in love with Canadian Mountie Nelson while trying to shield her ne'er-do-well fugitive kid brother James Stewart from the lawman's dogged pursuit. Watch for a brief appearance by David Niven as MacDonald's would-be suitor. AME **DVD**

Jeanette MacDonald *Marie de Flor* • Nelson Eddy *Sgt Bruce* • James Stewart *John Flower* • Reginald Owen *Myerson* • George Regas *Boniface* • Robert Greig *Cafe manager* • Una O'Connor *Anna* • James Conlin *Jimmy Conlin* *Joe, the piano player* • Lucien Littlefield *Storekeeper* • Mary Anita Loos *Corn Queen* • David Niven *Teddy* ■ *Dir* WS Van Dyke II [WS Van Dyke] • *Scr* Frances Goodrich, Albert Hackett, Alice Duer Miller, from the operetta by Otto A Harbach [Otto Harbach], Oscar Hammerstein II, Rudolf Friml, Herbert Stothart

Rose Marie ★★★ U
Musical romantic comedy　　1954 · US · Colour · 99min

MGM's remake of its phenomenally successful 1936 vehicle for Jeanette MacDonald and Nelson Eddy is the first colour CinemaScope musical and takes advantage of locations in the Canadian Rockies, but is nowhere near as beguiling as its predecessor. It stars Ann Blyth, Howard Keel as the Mountie, "Latin Lover" Fernando Lamas as an unlikely fur trapper, and Joan Taylor as the daughter of a tribal chief and a new character in the reworked plot of the operetta. RK

Ann Blyth *Rose Marie Lemaitre* • Howard Keel *Mike Malone* • Fernando Lamas *James Severn Duval* • Bert Lahr *Barney McCorkle* • Marjorie Main *Lady Jane Dunstock* • Joan Taylor *Wanda* ■ *Dir* Mervyn LeRoy • *Scr* Ronald Millar, George Froeschel, from the operetta by Otto A Harbach [Otto Harbach], Oscar Hammerstein II, Rudolf Friml, Herbert Stothart • *Choreographer* Busby Berkeley

Rose of Cimarron ★★ U
Western　　1952 · US · Colour · 72min

Mala Powers is an orphan brought up by native Americans who is seeking revenge for the death of her parents. Powers's co-star is Jack Buetel, but it's up to western veterans such as Jim Davis, Bill Williams and old hand Bob Steele to keep this production on its feet. Incidentally, this was published as a one-off comic book in the 1950s with a knockout cover: mint copies are now much prized by collectors. TS

Jack Buetel *Marshal Hollister* • Mala Powers *Rose of Cimarron* • Bill Williams *George Newcomb* • Jim Davis (1) *Willie Whitewater* • Dick Curtis *Clem Dawley* • Tom Monroe *Mike Finch* • William Phipps *Jeb Dawley* • Bob Steele *Rio* ■ *Dir* Harry Keller • *Scr* Maurice Geraghty

Rose of Washington Square ★★★
Musical　　1939 · US · BW · 86min

Alice Faye plays Rose in a very thinly disguised biopic of Ziegfeld headliner Fanny Brice, later more memorably incarnated by Barbra Streisand in the show and movie *Funny Girl* (and its sequel). Here, Faye falls for handsome but no-good, and severely underwritten, gambler Tyrone Power, and is inspired by him to sing Brice's theme song *My Man*. But the real treat of the movie is the appearance of the great Al Jolson, who sings a batch of his own hits. TS

Tyrone Power *Bart Clinton* • Alice Faye *Rose Sargent* • Al Jolson *Ted Cotter* • William Frawley *Harry Long* • Joyce Compton *Peggy* • Hobart Cavanaugh *Whitey Boone* • Moroni Olsen *Buck*

R

Russell ■ *Dir* Gregory Ratoff • *Scr* Nunnally Johnson, from a story by John Larkin, Jerry Horwin

The Rose Tattoo ★★★
Drama 1955 · US · BW · 116min

Anna Magnani goes wild with desire for Burt Lancaster who has a tattoo on his chest like that of her virile dead husband. Magnani's daughter, who sets a sailor's pulse racing, adds another layer of smouldering compost to this already earthy tale. Tennessee Williams wrote the play for Magnani but she chickened out of doing it on stage; however on film, she carted off an Oscar, a Bafta and a New York Film Critics Circle award, though a more over-the-top performance would be hard to find. AT

Anna Magnani *Serafina Delle Rose* • Burt Lancaster *Alvaro Mangiacavallo* • Marisa Pavan *Rosa Delle Rose* • Ben Cooper *Jack Hunter* • Virginia Grey *Estelle Hohengarten* • Jo Van Fleet *Bessie* ■ *Dir* Daniel Mann • *Scr* Tennessee Williams, Hal Kanter, from the play by Tennessee Williams

Roseanna McCoy ★★★PG
Romantic drama 1949 · US · BW · 84min

The bucolic Ozark mountain feuds between rival family factions have barely been touched on in cinema, and neither this movie nor the later *Lolly Madonna War* really conveyed what internecine warfare over moonshine and sex must've really been like. Producer Samuel Goldwyn used the famous Hatfield-McCoy feud to feature his young contract stars Farley Granger and Joan Evans, but the two leads look far too urbane. TS

Farley Granger *Johnse Hatfield* • Joan Evans *Roseanna McCoy* • Charles Bickford *Devil Anse Hatfield* • Raymond Massey *Old Randall McCoy* • Richard Basehart *Mounts Hatfield* ■ *Dir* Irving Reis • *Scr* John Collier, from the novel by Alberta Hannum

Roseanna's Grave ★★★12
Romantic comedy 1996 · US/UK · Colour · 93min

The delightful Jean Reno stars in this spry comedy as a bistro proprietor whose beloved, dying wife Roseanna (Mercedes Ruehl) has her weak heart set on being buried in the village churchyard, next to their daughter. The problem is there are only a few plots left, so Reno embarks on a frantic mission to secure a cemetery space by rescuing the ailing and concealing inconvenient corpses. Reno and Ruehl give heart-warming performances in this lightweight, genial lark. AME Swearing, some sex scenes.

Jean Reno *Marcello Beatto* • Mercedes Ruehl *Roseanna Beatto* • Polly Walker *Cecilia* • Mark Frankel *Antonio* • Trevor Peacock *Iaccoponi* • Fay Ripley *Francesca* ■ *Dir* Paul Weiland • *Scr* Saul Turteltaub

Les Roseaux Sauvages ★★★★15
Drama 1994 · Fr · Colour · 109min

For all its shimmering images of the beautiful French countryside and its painstaking attention to period detail, this magnificent rites-of-passage drama tackles such complex themes as war, class, sexuality, the age gap and civic responsibility with an intelligence and a naturalism that one has come to expect of director André Téchiné. Rather than delivering a rose-tinted lament for the lost innocence of youth, he takes the emotions, opinions and confusions of teenagers seriously and is rewarded with exceptional performances from his cast. DP French +subtitles.

Frédéric Gorny *Henri* • Gaël Morel *François* • Elodie Bouchez *Maïté* • Stéphane Rideau *Serge* • Michèle Moretti *Madame Alvarez* • Laurent Groulout *The photographer* • Jacques Nolot *Monsieur Morelli* ■ *Dir* André Téchiné • *Scr* André Téchiné, Gilles Taurand, Olivier Massart

Rosebud ★★15
Political action thriller 1975 · US · Colour · 121min

This is a depressing bloom, indeed, from director Otto Preminger in which PLO terrorists kidnap five women who are holidaying aboard a yacht. Intercutting between the women's plight and what's being done to help them slows the idea down to stasis, despite the efforts of CIA agent Peter O'Toole, Richard Attenborough and Adrienne Corri to salvage it. TH Violence, swearing. DVD

Peter O'Toole *Larry Martin* • Richard Attenborough *Sloat* • Cliff Gorman *Hamlekh* • Claude Dauphin *Fargeau* • John V Lindsay *United States Senator Donovan* • Peter Lawford *Lord Carter* • Raf Vallone *George Nikolaos* • Adrienne Corri *Lady Carter* ■ *Dir* Otto Preminger • *Scr* Erik Lee Preminger, from a novel by Joan Hemingway, Paul Bonnecarrere

Roseland ★★★★PG
Dance drama 1977 · US · Colour · 103min

Merchant Ivory's American films are less celebrated than their famously lovely English and Indian literary adaptations, but the American James Ivory is also at his least cosy exploring his homeland. This bittersweet collection of tales set in New York's Roseland ballroom sees a marvellous ensemble of lonely hearts trip the light fantastic reminiscing about life and love. Making one of her rare screen appearances after a premature 1959 retirement, Teresa Wright is moving as the widow with a new lease of life after striking up a dance partnership with Lou Jacobi. Christopher Walken (a trained dancer early in his career) makes an oily impression as a dancehall predator. AME DVD

Teresa Wright *May* • Lou Jacobi *Stan* • Don DeNatale *Master of Ceremonies* • Louise Kirtland *Ruby* • Hetty Galen *Red-haired lady* • Geraldine Chaplin *Marilyn* • Christopher Walken *Russel* • Lilia Skala *Rosa* ■ *Dir* James Ivory • *Scr* Ruth Prawer Jhabvala • *Executive Producer* Ismail Merchant

Roselyne and the Lions ★★★PG
Drama 1989 · Fr · Colour · 113min

It's hard to fathom exactly what director Jean-Jacques Beineix was up to with this too-leisurely parable on the theme of creation and the ever-present spectre of death. As the couple whose desire to tame lions leads to passion, Pasco and Gérard Sandoz look good enough, and the hours of off-screen training they put in with the big cats fully pays off. But the tensions that arise once Pasco is encouraged by a lustful German circus owner are nowhere near as interesting as the manoeuvres of the opening scenes in the Marseille zoo. DP French +subtitles.

Isabelle Pasco *Roselyne* • Gérard Sandoz *Thierry* • Philippe Clevenot *Bracquard* • Günter Meisner *Klint* • Wolf Harnisch *Koenig* • Gabriel Monnet *Frazier* • Jacques Le Carpentier *Markovitch* ■ *Dir* Jean-Jacques Beineix • *Scr* Jean-Jacques Beineix, Jacques Forgeas

Rosemary's Baby ★★★★★18
Classic horror 1968 · US · Colour · 131min

Ira Levin's bestseller about Antichrist cultism in Manhattan is impeccably and faithfully brought to the screen by director Roman Polanski in this genuinely horrifying chiller that quietly builds unbearable tension. Mia Farrow is the perfect satanic foil in a supernatural classic of conspiratorial evil meshed with apocalyptic revelations, and Ruth Gordon won a deserved Oscar for her busy-body portrayal of eccentric menace. It's one of the most powerful films ever made about Devil worship because Polanski winds up the paranoia with spooky atmospherics and morbid humour. AJ Nudity. DVD

Mia Farrow *Rosemary Woodhouse* • John Cassavetes *Guy Woodhouse* • Ruth Gordon *Minnie Castevet* • Sidney Blackmer *Roman Castevet* • Maurice Evans *Hutch* • Ralph Bellamy *Dr Sapirstein* • Tony Curtis *Donald Baumgart* ■ *Dir* Roman Polanski • *Scr* Roman Polanski, from the novel by Ira Levin

Rosemont ★★★
Drama 2015 · US · Colour · 93min

A blizzard throws four mismatched souls together in this contrived but big-hearted yuletide tale from *Beverly Hills Cop* writer-turned-director Daniel Petrie Jr. Sweet though never schmaltzy, it's elevated by quality performances and lots of cast chemistry, as heavily pregnant Ayla Kell and kindly stranger Brendan Michael Coughlin end up stranded at a defunct lodge. Everything's all very obvious yet nicely handled, with agreeable resolutions, a cutely far-fetched twist and a feel-good finale. SF

Brad Dourif *Abe* • Ayla Kell *Lisa* • Michael Gross *Dr Molina* • Grace Zabriskie *Josephine* ■ *Dir* Daniel Petrie Jr • *Scr* Bill Rebane

Rosencrantz and Guildenstern Are Dead ★★★PG
Comedy 1990 · Colour · 112min

Tom Stoppard's screen version of his own hit play, beginning with a splendid long shot of Rosencrantz and Guildenstern making their way to Elsinore, has largely been dismissed by the critics, who disapproved both of his opening out what had been a delightful theatrical experience and his audacity in penning new material. They were also pretty scathing of the performances by Gary Oldman and Tim Roth. Yet, combining verbal dexterity with precise slapstick timing, they capture the bewilderment of these two *Hamlet* also-rans with disarming charm. Richard Dreyfuss as the Player and Ian Richardson as Polonius also score. DP DVD Blu

Gary Oldman *Rosencrantz* • Tim Roth *Guildenstern* • Richard Dreyfuss *Player* • Joanna Roth *Ophelia* • Iain Glen *Prince Hamlet* • Donald Sumpter *King Claudius* • Joanna Miles *Queen Gertrude* • Ian Richardson *Polonius* ■ *Dir/Scr* Tom Stoppard

Rosetta ★★★15
Drama 1999 · Bel/Fr · Colour · 90min

Inspired by Kafka and booed on winning the Palme d'Or at Cannes, Luc and Jean-Pierre Dardenne's starkly realistic insight into life on the lowest rung makes for difficult viewing. However, as the debuting Emilie Dequenne clings to the soul-destroying routine she hopes will land the job she needs for self-esteem as much as pay, the film begins to grip. Spurning both the optimism of American "trailer trash" pictures and the politicking of British social realism, this film makes no commercial concessions and is all the better for it. DP French +subtitles.

Emilie Dequenne *Rosetta* • Fabrizio Rongione *Riquet* • Anne Yernaux *Rosetta's mother* • Olivier Gourmet *Boss* ■ *Dir/Scr* Luc Dardenne, Jean-Pierre Dardenne

Rosewater ★★★★15
Drama based on a true story 2014 · US · Colour · 98min

In 2009, a London-based, Iranian-born journalist named Maziar Bahari was wrongly accused of being a spy, and was placed in solitary confinement for 118 days, during which time he was subjected to various forms of torture. The ordeal he suffered is dramatised in this satirical, thought-provoking political drama, which depicts a battle of wills between Bahari (played by Gael García Bernal) and an ignorant, brutish interrogator (Kim Bodnia). The scenes between the two are slightly repetitive in nature, but Bernal is highly likeable as the compliant reporter, while Bodnia manages to humanise his thuggish captor. In addition, writer/director Jon Stewart (making his debut as a film-maker) captures the absurdity of the situation in a way that is both sobering and surprisingly humorous. SC Violence, swearing. DVD Blu

Gael García Bernal *Maziar Bahari* • Kim Bodnia *Rosewater* • Claire Foy *Paola* • Dimitri Leonidas *Davood* • Shohreh Aghdashloo *Moloojoon* • Golshifteh Farahani *Maryam* • Haluk Bilginer

Baba Akbar ■ *Dir* Jon Stewart • *Scr* Jon Stewart, from the non-fiction book *Then They Came for Me: a Family's Story of Love, Captivity, and Survival* by Maziar Bahari, Aimee Molloy

Rosewood ★★★18
Period drama based on a true story 1997 · US · Colour · 136min

This powerful historical drama from director John Singleton re-creates with shocking intensity a 1920s atrocity that was hushed up until a journalist came across the story by chance in the early 1980s. A false charge of rape leads to the annihilation of a black settlement by a mob of Florida rednecks in 1923. Singleton reconstructs the incident with care, but the intervention of Ving Rhames's fictional First World War hero and the unconvincing repentance of adulterous Jon Voight undermine this otherwise noble attempt. DP

Jon Voight *John Wright* • Ving Rhames *Mann* • Don Cheadle *Sylvester Carrier* • Bruce McGill *Duke Purdy* • Loren Dean *James Taylor* • Esther Rolle *Aunt Sarah* • Elise Neal *Scrappie* ■ *Dir* John Singleton • *Scr* Gregory Poirier

Rosie! ★U
Comedy drama 1967 · US · Colour · 97min

The grasping daughters of a wealthy, off-the-wall widow with an overdeveloped penchant for spending her money, have her committed to a spartan "rest home" in order to curb her extravagance. Rosalind Russell, giving her considerable all as a cut-price version of Auntie Mame, is unable to rescue this unspeakable rubbish adapted from a failed Broadway play by Ruth Gordon. RK

Rosalind Russell *Rosie Lord* • Sandra Dee *Daphne* • Brian Aherne *Oliver Stevenson* • Audrey Meadows *Mildred* • James Farentino *David* • Vanessa Brown *Edith* • Leslie Nielsen *Cabot* • Margaret Hamilton *Mae* ■ *Dir* David Lowell Rich • *Scr* Samuel Taylor, from the play *A Very Rich Woman* by Ruth Gordon, from the play *Les Joies de la Famille* by Philippe Hériat

Rosie Dixon: Night Nurse ★18
Sex comedy 1978 · UK · Colour · 84min

It should give you some idea of the mire into which the British film industry had plunged itself during the 1970s when you read such names as Beryl Reid, John Le Mesurier and Liz Fraser on the cast list of this bawdy hospital comedy. Debbie Ash (sister of Leslie) suffers countless indignities in the title role, but it's Arthur Askey who stoops the lowest, as he resorts to pinching uniformed bottoms to get the cheapest of laughs. DP

Beryl Reid *Matron* • John Le Mesurier *Sir Archibald MacGregor* • Debbie Ash *Rosie Dixon* • Arthur Askey *Mr Arkwright* • Liz Fraser *Mrs Dixon* • John Junkin *Mr Dixon* ■ *Dir* Justin Cartwright • *Scr* Justin Cartwright, Christopher Wood

Rosie the Riveter ★★U
Wartime comedy 1944 · US · BW · 74min

A wartime tribute to the women working in the factories (retitled *In Rosie's Room* in the UK, where few knew what a riveter was), this B-movie is best remembered for its popular title tune. Jane Frazee plays Rosie, who has to share an apartment with three other factory workers (two of them men) due to the housing shortage. TV

Jane Frazee *Rosalind "Rosie" Warren* • Frank Albertson *Charlie Doran* • Vera Vague [Barbara Jo Allen] *Vera Watson* • Frank Jenks *Kelly Kennedy* • Maude Eburne *Grandma Quill* • Lloyd Corrigan *Clem Prouty* ■ *Dir* Joseph Santley • *Scr* Jack Townley, Aleen Leslie, from the story *Room for Two* by Dorothy Curnow Handley

Rosita ★★
Silent period romance 1923 · US · BW · 85min

King of Spain Holbrook Blinn wants guitar-strumming dancing girl Mary Pickford for his mistress, but she loves dashing nobleman George Walsh (director Raoul Walsh's brother) who is under sentence of death for treason. This romantic period melodrama, set in 18th-century Toledo, marked Pickford's failed bid to transform herself from America's "Little Mary" into a tempestuous romantic star. More importantly, it marked the Hollywood debut of director Ernst Lubitsch, whom Pickford imported from Germany for the occasion. They didn't hit it off and the film was completed amid a multitude of disagreements. **RK**

Mary Pickford *Rosita* • Holbrook Blinn *The King* • Irene Rich *The Queen* • George Walsh *Don Diego* • Charles Belcher *The Prime Minister* ■ *Dir* Ernst Lubitsch • *Scr* Edward Knoblock, from a story by Norbert Falk, Hans Kräly, from the play *Don César de Bazan* by Adolphe Philippe Dennery, Philippe François Pinel

Roswell ★★★★ 12
Science-fiction drama
1994 · US · Colour and BW · 87min

The year is 1947, and Kyle MacLachlan is the military intelligence officer who begins investigating what appears to be the crash-landing of a flying saucer and starts to suspect a cover-up. MacLachlan is convincing as the officer, there are neat supporting turns in this TV movie from Martin Sheen and country singer Dwight Yoakam. Director Jeremy Kagan summons up a gripping air of paranoia. **JF** *DVD*

Kyle MacLachlan *Major Jesse Marcel* • Martin Sheen *Townsend* • Dwight Yoakam *Mac Brazel* • Xander Berkeley *Sherman Carson* • Bob Gunton *Frank Joyce* • Kim Greist *Vy Marcel* • Peter MacNicol *Lewis Rickett* ■ *Dir* Jeremy Kagan [Jeremy Paul Kagan] • *Scr* Arthur Kopit, from a story by Paul Davids, Jeremy Kagan [Jeremy Paul Kagan], from the book *UFO Crash at Roswell* by Donald R Schmitt, Steven Poster

Rothschild's Violin ★★★ U
Biographical drama
1996 · Fr/Swi/Fin/Hun · Colour · 101min

Argentinian-born director Edgardo Cozarinsky explores the theme of state intervention in the arts in this astute re-creation of a little-known episode in Stalinist history. The composer Shostakovich sought to make a stand by performing the unfinished opera of his disciple Benjamin Fleischmann, a Jew who had died in the siege of Leningrad. Cozarinsky first combines archive footage and re-enacted material to explore Soviet classical music in the 1930s, before presenting a full performance of *Le Violon de Rothschild* and a scathing assessment of Stalin's rule. Difficult, but rewarding. **DP** Russian +subtitles.

Sergei Makovetsky *Dmitri Shostakovich* • Dainius Kazlauskus *Benjamin Fleischmann* • Miklos B Szekely *Bronia* • Mari Torocsik *Marfa* • Sandor Zsoter *Rothschild* • Ferenc Javori *Chakhkes* ■ *Dir/Scr* Edgardo Cozarinsky

Rotten to the Core ★★
Crime comedy
1965 · UK · BW · 89min

Everywhere you looked during the early 1960s, there was a comic criminal mastermind planning an audacious raid that was doomed to failure because his gang were paid-up members of Dolts Anonymous. Anton Rodgers is the great brain here, posing as a top-ranking general in order to rob an army camp. Charlotte Rampling is slinkily amusing as the moll, but what her laughs there are come from Eric Sykes. Fitfully funny. **DP**

Eric Sykes *Hunt* • Ian Bannen *Vine* • Dudley Sutton *Jelly* • Kenneth Griffith *Lenny* • James Beckett *Scapa* • Avis Bunnage *Countess* • Anton Rodgers *Duke* • Charlotte Rampling *Sara* • Victor Maddern *Anxious* ■ *Dir* John Boulting • *Scr* John Warren, Len Heath, Jeffrey Dell, Roy Boulting, from their story, from an idea by Warren, Heath

La Roue ★★★★★
Silent tragedy
1923 · Fr · BW · 303min

Even before he made *Napoléon* (1927), Abel Gance was considered the Griffith of France; or seeing this masterpiece, Jean Cocteau opined: "There is cinema before and after *La Roue* as there is painting before and after Picasso." The story concerns the suffering of railway engineer Séverin-Mars and his violin-making son Gabriel de Gravone over the marriage of adopted family member Ivy Close to ageing inspector Pierre Magnier. Shot on location

over 16 months and originally running some nine hours, it was eventually released by Pathé at just 144 minutes. Yet, even in truncated form the audacious blend of realism and romanticism achieved by superbly-controlled accelerated and associative montage is clearly evident. A restored 303-minute version was completed by Marie Epstein in 1980. **DP** With French titles, English translation. *DVD*

Séverin-Mars *Sisif* • Gabriel de Gravone *Elie* • Pierre Magnier *Jacques de Hersan, the engineer* • Ivy Close *Norma* • Georges Terof *Mâchefer* ■ *Dir/Scr* Abel Gance

Rouge ★★★★ 15
Supernatural romance
1987 · HK · Colour · 92min

This ghost story-cum-satire oozes quality, from the sublime photography of Bill Wong to the outstanding performance of Anita Mui as the troubled spirit of a 1930s courtesan, condemned to wander the streets of Hong Kong until she meets the lover with whom she entered into a suicide pact. Perfectly re-creating the decadent elegance of the 1930s and gently mocking the consumerism of the 1980s, Stanley Kwan tells his story (co-adapted by Li Bihua from her own novel) with a lightness of touch few modern directors can rival. **DP** Cantonese +subtitles. Drug abuse.

Anita Mui *Fleur* • Leslie Cheung *Chan Chen-Pang* • Alex Man *Yuen* • Emily Chu *Ah Chor* • Irene Wan *Suk-Yin* ■ *Dir* Stanley Kwan • *Scr* Li Bihua, Qiu-Dai Anping, from the novel by Li

Rouge Baiser ★★★ 15
Drama based on a true story
1985 · Fr · Colour · 108min

With its faithful re-creation of the atmosphere of Parisian jazz clubs in the early 1950s, its perceptive insights into the emotional and intellectual naivety of teenagers, and its inch-perfect performances, this neatly observed film should have been a joy. Charlotte Valandrey plays her heart out as the 15-year-old Communist whose world comes tumbling down with the onset of romance and disturbing news from inside Stalin's empire. But director Véra Belmont spoils it all with an overindulgence in flashy camerawork. **DP** French +subtitles.

Charlotte Valandrey *Nadia* • Lambert Wilson *Stéphane* • Marthe Keller *Bronka* • Günter Lamprecht *Herschel* • Laurent Terzieff *Moische* ■ *Dir* Véra Belmont • *Scr* Véra Belmont, Guy Konopnicki, David Milhaud

Le Rouge et le Noir ★★★
Period romantic drama
1954 · Fr · Colour · 153min

Gérard Philipe plays the Stendahl antihero in this pictorialist adaptation of the 1830 novel. Claude Autant-Lara was frequently accused by such critics as François Truffaut for producing *cinéma du papa* or traditionalist narratives that were more literary than filmic. Certainly, for all the surface sheen, a paucity of visual imagination was expended on this tale of the young man who seduces his way up the socio-political ladder, and there's little of the book's biting irony. **DP** French +subtitles.

Gérard Philipe *Julien Sorel* • Danielle Darrieux *Mme Louise de Renal* • Antonella Lualdi *Mathilde de la Mole* • Jean Martinelli *M de Renal* • Antoine Balpêtré *Abbé Pirard* • Anna-Maria Sandri *Elisa* • Jean Mercure *Marquis de la Mole* • André Brunot *Abbé Chelan* ■ *Dir* Claude Autant-Lara • *Scr* Jean Aurenche, Pierre Bost, from the novel by Stendhal

The Rough and the Smooth ★★
Erotic thriller
1959 · UK · BW · 99min

Hollywood director Robert Siodmak, a *film noir* specialist, brought his talents to Britain for this thriller that trades on its steamy sex scenes. Tony Britton stars as an archeologist who has a fling with shady lady Nadja Tiller, who plays secretary to rich and ugly William Bendix. A trademark hammy Donald Wolfit represents the gutter press, to which the sordid story is leaked. It's

intended to show the corruption that lies at the heart of the British establishment. **AT**

Nadja Tiller *Ila Hansen* • Tony Britton *Mike Thompson* • William Bendix *Reg Barker* • Natasha Parry *Margaret Goreham* • Norman Wooland *David Fraser* • Donald Wolfit *Lord Drewell* • Tony Wright *Jack* • Adrienne Corri *Jane Buller* • Joyce Carey *Mrs Thompson* ■ *Dir* Robert Siodmak • *Scr* Audrey Erskine-Lindop, Dudley Leslie, from the novel *The Rough and the Smooth* by Robin Maugham

Rough Cut ★★★ PG
Crime comedy
1980 · US · Colour · 106min

Burt Reynolds does his Cary Grant impersonation in a stylish caper comedy where even the criminals have a touch of class. It's a mellow throwback to those elegant light entertainments of the 1950s, and director Don Siegel injects irony and droll humour into a breezy script that gives charming gentleman burglar Reynolds every opportunity to shine. Rather an atypical movie from action man Siegel who was, in fact, fired and rehired during filming. **AJ** Swearing.

Burt Reynolds *Jack Rhodes* • Lesley-Anne Down *Gillian Bromley* • David Niven *Chief Inspector Cyril Willis* • Timothy West *Nigel Lawton* • Patrick Magee *Ernst Mueller* • Al Matthews *Ferguson* • Susan Littler *Sheila* • Joss Ackland *Inspector Vanderveld* • Isabel Dean *Mrs Willis* ■ *Dir* Don Siegel • *Scr* Francis Burns [Larry Gelbart], from the novel *Touch the Lion's Paw* by Derek Lambert

Rough Diamonds ★★ PG
Romantic comedy 1994 · Aus · Colour · 84min

Angie Milliken leaves her successful lawyer husband and takes to the Australian outback road with her daughter to find herself. What she finds instead is cattleman Jason Donovan struggling to make ends meet on the ranch he inherited from his parents. Will his prize bull win the cash jackpot in the Brisbane championship and solve his financial problems? Prize bull indeed, but harmless enough even though the script is devoid of humour or character development. **AJ**

Jason Donovan *Mike Tyrrell* • Angie Milliken *Chrissie Bright* • Peter Phelps *Dozer Brennan* • Max Cullen *Magistrate Roy* • Haley Toomey *Sam Tyrrell* • Jocelyn Gabriel *Lisa Bright* • Kit Taylor *Les Finnigan* ■ *Dir* Donald Crombie • *Scr* Donald Crombie, Christopher Lee

Rough Magic ★★ 12
Fantasy road movie romance
1995 · Fr/UK · Colour · 100min

Director Clare Peploe wrestles with a mix of genres in the quirky tale of magician's assistant and runaway bride Bridget Fonda, who flees 1950s LA for Mexico, pursued by various men including cynical detective Russell Crowe hired by her peeved millionaire fiancé. En route she discovers her genuine magical powers. It's an oddball road movie, gumshoe romance and fantasy of magic realism whose clumsy peculiarity doesn't best serve its engaging stars. **AME** Swearing, violence.

Bridget Fonda *Myra Shumway* • Russell Crowe *Alex Ross* • Kenneth Mars *Magician* • DW Moffett *Cliff Wyatt* • Jim Broadbent *Doc Ansell* • Paul Rodriguez *Diego* ■ *Dir* Clare Peploe • *Scr* Clare Peploe, William Brookfield, Robert Mundy, from the novel *Miss Shumway Waves a Wand* by James Hadley Chase

Rough Night in Jericho ★★ 12
Western 1967 · US · Colour · 99min

Surprisingly violent (for its day), this Universal western stars an unlikely Dean Martin as the baddie who owns the town of the title and is bent on owning Jean Simmons's stagecoach line and tying up the territory. Ex-marshal George Peppard ain't gonna let him, though. Although expertly directed by Arnold Laven, both Martin and Peppard look far too urbane for this kind of savage western, and there's really little to recommend here. **TS** Violence.

Dean Martin *Alex Flood* • George Peppard *Dolan* • Jean Simmons *Molly Lang* • John McIntire *Ben Hickman* • Slim Pickens *Yarbrough* • Don Galloway *Jace* • Brad Weston *Torrey* ■

Dir Arnold Laven • *Scr* Sydney Boehm, Marvin H Albert, from the novel *The Man in Black* by Marvin H Albert

Rough Shoot ★★★ U
Spy thriller 1952 · UK · BW · 86min

A postwar lull in Joel McCrea's career found him relegated, as happened to most ageing male stars, to co-feature westerns. He still found time, however, to make this interesting thriller in England, based on a Geoffrey Household spy story scripted by Eric Ambler. It actually has one of the oldest western plots: the hero believes that he has killed someone accidentally. The English period setting affords much pleasure today, with a cast of West End veterans offering sterling support. **TS**

Joel McCrea *Lt Col Robert Taine* • Evelyn Keyes *Cecily Taine* • Herbert Lom *Peter Sandorski* • Marius Goring *Hiart* • Roland Culver *Randall* • Frank Lawton *Richard Hassingham* • Patricia Laffan *Magda Hassingham* ■ *Dir* Robert Parrish • *Scr* Eric Ambler, from the novel by Geoffrey Household

Roughly Speaking ★★★
Biographical drama 1945 · US · BW · 117min

This likeable, sprawling account of the life of the engagingly eccentric Louise Randall Pierson, an early exponent of women's lib, covers 40 years of her life in episodic fashion. There are many fine moments here, but Warner Bros possibly erred in allowing Pierson to adapt her own autobiography, for she was by all accounts reluctant to leave anything out. Giving great performances are Rosalind Russell, loaded with grit as the determined wife and mother, and Jack Carson, as her quixotic husband obsessed with get-rich-quick schemes. Michael Curtiz directs, and there's a charming score by Max Steiner. **TV**

Rosalind Russell *Louise Randall* • Jack Carson *Harold Pierson* • Robert Hutton *John, aged 20-28* • Jean Sullivan *Louise Jr, aged 18-26* • Donald Woods *Rodney Crane* • Alan Hale *Mr Morton* • Andrea King *Barbara, aged 21-29* • Ann Doran *Alice Abbott* ■ *Dir* Michael Curtiz • *Scr* Louise Randall Pierson, from her autobiography

Roughshod ★★★
Western 1949 · US · BW · 88min

A likeable western made with unusual care and intelligence, this is also a curiously modest, small-scale undertaking, which failed to make a star out of its leading man, Robert Sterling. With the help of kid brother Claude Jarman Jr, Sterling directs a herd of thoroughbred horses, rescues a troupe of saloon girls, and has a run-in with three vicious outlaws. Gloria Grahame plays the leading floozie with her customary panache while John Ireland makes for a mean killer. **AE**

Robert Sterling *Clay Phillips* • Gloria Grahame *Mary Wells* • John Ireland *Lednov* • Claude Jarman Jr *Steve Phillips* • Jeff Donnell *Elaine Wyatt* • Myrna Dell *Helen Carter* • Martha Hyer *Marcia* • George Cooper (2) *Jim Clayton* • Jeff Corey *Jed Graham* ■ *Dir* Mark Robson • *Scr* Geoffrey Homes [Daniel Mainwaring], Hugo Butler, from a story by Peter Viertel

Roujin Z ★★★★ 15
Animated thriller 1991 · Jpn · Colour · 80min

Written by Katsuhiro Otomo, who made perhaps the best-known *manga* movie, *Akira*, this animated feature concentrates more on character than on the futuristic concepts and designer violence that tends to dominate the genre. Translating roughly as "Old Man Z", this is primarily a "people versus the powers that be" picture, with a student nurse siding with the elderly when they discover that a luxury bed experiment is the front for more sinister activities. However, it's also a mischievously romantic ghost story and an ironic study of male-female hegemony, while for action fans there's a storming finale. **DP** Japanese dubbed. *Blu-ray*

■ *Dir* Hiroyuki Kitakubo • *Scr* Katsuhiro Otomo, from his story

R

Round Ireland with a Fridge... a True Story ★★★ PG

Comedy based on a true story
2010 · UK · Colour · 88min

Replacing Brendan Fraser at the eleventh hour, Tony Hawks makes a decent stab at playing himself in this genial adaptation of his own bestseller. Having bet a friend that he can hitch-hike around Ireland with a fridge, he quickly discovers the folly of his enterprise. But when toiletries salesman Sean Hughes arranges a live feed to Ed Byrne's radio show, Hawks becomes a celebrity. It's more a string of vignettes than a complex narrative, but there are plenty of laughs and neatly judged cameos along the way. DP *DVD*

Tony Hawks *Tony* • Valerie O'Connor *Roisin Mulvaney* • Ed Byrne *Dylan Daley* • Sean Hughes *Brendan* • Josie Lawrence *Sandra* ■ *Dir* Ed Bye • *Scr* Tony Hawks, from his non-fiction book

'Round Midnight ★★★★ 15

Musical drama 1986 · US/Fr · Colour · 125min

According to cinematic formula, when they're not living in poverty until the world finally tunes in on their unique style, jazz musicians are on the skids, playing great music through a drug or booze-induced haze. Bertrand Tavernier's superb film is of this school, but has none of the glib clichés of the Hollywood jazz movie. This is a harrowing and truthful study of talent suffocating under the pressures of creativity. Film debutant and jazz veteran Dexter Gordon earned an Oscar nomination for his remarkable performance, while Herbie Hancock's Oscar-winning soundtrack will send shivers down your spine. DP Swearing.

Dexter Gordon *Dale Turner* • François Cluzet *Francis Borier* • Gabrielle Haker *Bérangère* • Sandra Reaves-Phillips *Buttercup* • Lonette McKee *Darcey Leigh* • Christine Pascal *Sylvie* • Herbie Hancock *Eddie Wayne* ■ *Dir* Bertrand Tavernier • *Scr* Bertrand Tavernier, David Rayfiel, based on incidents in the lives of Francis Paudras, Bud Powell

Round Trip to Heaven ★★ 15

Comedy adventure 1992 · US · Colour · 92min

Corey Feldman and Zach Galligan play two lazy chums who get into all sorts of trouble when they borrow a Rolls-Royce belonging to villain Ray Sharkey for a weekend break. There's a lot of mindless slapstick and the usual obsession with beer and babes, none of which raises more than the occasional chuckle. JF

Corey Feldman *Larry* • Ray Sharkey *Stoneface* • Zach Galligan *Steve* • Julie McCullough *Lucille* • Rowanne Brewer *April* • Lloyd Battista *Mike* • Joey Travolta *Ed* • Shuki Levy *2nd Man* ■ *Dir* Alan Roberts • *Scr* Shuki Levy, Winston Richards

The Round-Up ★★★★★ 15

Historical drama 1966 · Hun · BW · 86min

Set during the 1848 revolution against Hapsburg imperialism, Miklos Jancso's depiction of the mechanics of power and the vulnerability underlying even the most heroic resistance have powerful contemporary resonance. Just as no concession is made by the sadistic police to the peasants trapped inside an isolated stockade, so none is made to the viewer, who is presented with geometrical arrangements of oppressors and victims instead of tangible heroes and villains. The rebels' refusal to surrender testifies to the indomitability of the human spirit, but the film's chilling conclusion is that totalitarianism can be ruthlessly effective. DP Hungarian +subtitles. *DVD*

Janos Görbe *Janos Gajdor* • Tibor Molnar *Kabai* • Istvan Avar *1st interrogator* • Lajos Oze *2nd interrogator* ■ *Dir* Miklos Jancso • *Scr* Gyula Hernádi

The Round Up ★★★ 12A

Historical wartime drama 2010 · Fr/Ger/Hun · Colour and BW · 125min

Viewers may struggle to hold back the tears for this poignant, true-life drama. Set in Paris in 1942, director Rose Bosch's often harrowing account details how 13,000 Jewish citizens, including 4,000 children, were rounded up by the Nazis and their French collaborators and sent to death camps in Poland. Jean Reno and Melanie Laurent (*Inglourious Basterds*) take top billing as a Jewish medic and the Gentile nurse that assists him. But it's the youngsters that the film focuses on, and they are the true stars. Occasionally, the movie flirts with crassness and sometimes it tugs a touch too blatantly at the heartstrings. But, by and large, this is a well-made and moving portrayal of man's inhumanity to man, woman and child. DA French, German, Yiddish +subtitles. Some violence, swearing. *DVD* *BL*

Jean Reno *Dr David Sheinbaum* • Mélanie Laurent *Annette Monod* • Gad Elmaleh *Schmuel Weismann* • Raphaëlle Agogué *Sura Weismann* • Sylvie Testud *Bella Zygler* • Anne Brochet *Dina Traube* • Hugo Leverdez *Joseph Weismann* • Udo Schenk *Adolf Hitler* ■ *Dir/Scr* Rose Bosch [Roselyne Bosch]

The Rounders ★★★

Comedy western 1965 · US · Colour · 84min

This amiable comedy western pairs two of the screen's most watchable veterans, Glenn Ford and Henry Fonda, with a determined horse. The film is basically a series of incidents, affectionately directed by cowboy specialist Burt Kennedy and featuring a nice line in very 1960s risqué humour. In the UK this went out as a co-feature but, although MGM did little to promote it, the movie proved to be a nice little earner for the studio. No great surprises, but very pleasant viewing. TS Some swearing.

Glenn Ford *Ben Jones* • Henry Fonda *Howdy Lewis* • Sue Anne Langdon [Sue Ane Langdon] *Mary* • Hope Holiday *Sister* • Chill Wills *Jim Ed Love* • Edgar Buchanan *Vince Moore* • Kathleen Freeman *Agatha Moore* • Joan Freeman *Meg Moore* • Denver Pyle *Bull* • Barton MacLane *Tanner* ■ *Dir* Burt Kennedy • *Scr* Burt Kennedy, from the novel by Max Evans

Rounders ★★★ 15

Drama 1998 · US · Colour · 115min

Matt Damon plays a legal student-turned-poker player who, after losing his life savings, promises his girlfriend (Gretchen Mol) he'll give up the game. But the lure of the tables proves strong when a friend and fellow gambler (Edward Norton) comes out of jail with a pressing need to pay off a debt. Damon and Norton give accomplished performances, and director John Dahl imbues this with a downbeat atmosphere that atones for the sketchily drawn characters and familiar plot. TH Swearing, violence, a sex scene. *DVD* *BL*

Matt Damon *Mike McDermott* • Edward Norton *Worm* • John Turturro *Joey Knish* • Gretchen Mol *Jo* • Famke Janssen *Petra* • John Malkovich *Teddy KGB* • Martin Landau *Abe Petrovsky* • Josh Mostel *Zagosh* ■ *Dir* John Dahl • *Scr* David Levien, Brian Koppelman

Roustabout ★★★ U

Musical 1964 · US · Colour · 95min

Elvis films are unashamed fluff, containing songs and girls with curiously pointed breasts. This sticks firmly to tradition with Elvis playing the role of a mean, moody general handyman, embittered orphan and karate expert with a very large motorcycle. Barbara Stanwyck plays the fairground owner as if on autopilot, and this time the perky boobs belong to Joan Freeman as her deeply smitten daughter. Very daft, very immature and great fun. SH *DVD*

Elvis Presley *Charlie Rogers* • Barbara Stanwyck *Maggie Morgan* • Joan Freeman *Cathy Lean* • Leif Erickson *Joe Lean* • Sue Ann Langdon [Sue Ane Langdon] *Madame Mijanou* • Pat Buttram *Harry Carver* • Raquel Welch • *Dir* John Rich • *Scr* Paul Nathan, Anthony Lawrence, Allan Weiss, from a story by Allan Weiss

Route Irish ★★★ 15

Thriller 2010 · UK/Fr/Bel/It/Sp · Colour · 104min

Ken Loach can never be accused of ducking issues, and this Iraq-based exposé of exploitative greed and racist arrogance is a case in point. Delving into the reason why his friend Frankie (John Bishop) died on the titular road from Baghdad airport to the Green Zone, ex-soldier Fergus (Mark Womack) discovers a conspiracy concocted by the private security firm for which they both worked. The themes couldn't be more pressing or contentious, but subplots involving Bishop's widow (Andrea Lowe), a blinded squaddie (Craig Lundberg) and an Iraqi musician (Talib Rasool) are sketchy, while Paul Laverty's melodramatic script is far less controlled than when Chris Menges's steely photography. DP In French, Arabic. Violence, swearing. *DVD* *BL*

Mark Womack *Fergus* • Andrea Lowe *Rachel* • John Bishop (4) *Frankie* • Geoff Bell *Walker* • Jack Fortune *Haynes* • Talib Rasool *Harim* • Craig Lundberg *Craig* ■ *Dir* Ken Loach • *Scr* Paul Laverty • *Cinematographer* Chris Menges

The Rover ★★

Period war drama 1967 · It · Colour · 103min

This slow adventure, based on Joseph Conrad's minor novel, finds Anthony Quinn as a piratical rebel in the Napoleonic Wars. He is drawn to a mentally ill young woman, but she is fond of an officer in the French navy. Not lively enough in the action sequences and not intelligent enough in the dialogue, but it's unusual enough to be watchable. Directed by Shanghai-born British director Terence Young between his hits *Thunderball* and *Wait until Dark*. JG

Anthony Quinn *Peyrol* • Rosanna Schiaffino *Arlette* • Rita Hayworth *Aunt Caterina* • Richard Johnson *Real* • Ivo Garrani *Scevola* ■ *Dir* Terence Young • *Scr* Luciano Vincenzoni, Jo Eisinger, from the novel by Joseph Conrad

The Rover ★★★★ 15

Futuristic action drama 2014 · Aus · Colour · 98min

A caption places this story in "Australia. Ten years after the collapse". It's a husk of a society, stripped of morality, with sun-bleached landscapes home to emotionally ravaged characters. There are no heroes or villains, only survivors. After his car is stolen, the suicidally determined Guy Pearce teams up with Robert Pattinson, the wounded brother of one of the thieves, to track it down. There are echoes of *Mad Max* and Cormac McCarthy's *The Road* in this beautifully shot dystopian western and, like *Animal Kingdom*, the film is excruciatingly intense and prone to explosions of violence. EAS Violence, swearing. *DVD* *BL*

Guy Pearce *Eric* • Robert Pattinson *Rey* • Scoot McNairy *Henry* • David Field *Archie* • Tawanda Manyimo *Caleb* • Nash Edgerton *Town soldier* • Gillian Jones *Grandma* ■ *Dir* David Michôd • *Scr* David Michôd, from a story by Joel Edgerton, Michôd

A Row of Crows ★★ 15

Thriller 1991 · US · Colour · 98min

It's mismatched policemen again in this tough mystery thriller, as big city cop Steven Bauer gets sent to Arizona to team up with local sheriff John Beck. As they squabble about various police matters, they have to try to solve the murder of a young woman who is found decapitated in the desert. Fairly standard crime fare, boasting a ropey script and an unusual role for Katharine Ross as a hard-drinking coroner. JB Sex scenes, swearing, violence, nudity.

John Beck *Kyle Shipp* • Katharine Ross *Grace Hines* • Mia Sara *Elise Shipp* • Steven Bauer *Paul McGraw* • Dedee Pfeiffer *Donna* • John Diehl *Wayne Paris* ■ *Dir/Scr* JS Cardone

Roxanne ★★★★ PG

Romantic comedy 1987 · US · Colour · 102min

Nimbly adapted by star Steve Martin (for which he won the American Writers' Guild prize) from the celebrated Edmond Rostand play *Cyrano de Bergerac*, this is romantic comedy as it used to be, with Martin playing the nasally gifted fire chief who falls for stargazer Daryl Hannah. It's remarkably faithful to the original, cleverly transplanting the action from 17th-century Paris to present-day, small-town America, and imbuing the sensitive Martin with considerable duelling skills. From the moment he swashbuckles with a tennis racket, it's clear Martin is on peak form, particularly during the hilarious nose-jokes sequence. DP *DVD*

Steve Martin *CD Bales* • Daryl Hannah *Roxanne Kowalski* • Rick Rossovich *Chris* • Shelley Duvall *Dixie* • John Kapelos *Chuck* • Fred Willard *Mayor Deebs* • Max Alexander *Dean* • Michael J Pollard *Andy* ■ *Dir* Fred Schepisi • *Scr* Steve Martin, from the play *Cyrano de Bergerac* by Edmond Rostand

Roxie Hart ★★★★

Crime comedy 1942 · US · BW · 74min

Ginger Rogers is terrifically hard-boiled and funny in this film based on Maurine Watkins's famous play *Chicago*. There's a crackling script, a magnificent picture-stealing performance from Adolphe Menjou and some super by-play from the supporting cast. Rogers simply scintillates as the on-trial heroine of the title, and, if William A Wellman's direction isn't quite spot-on, or if George Montgomery is a colourless leading man, it doesn't really matter. A minor classic. TS

Ginger Rogers *Roxie Hart* • Adolphe Menjou *Billy Flynn* • George Montgomery *Homer Howard* • Lynne Overman *Jake Callahan* • Nigel Bruce *E Clay Benham* • Phil Silvers *Babe* • Sara Allgood *Mrs Morton* • William Frawley *O'Malley* • Spring Byington *Mary Sunshine* ■ *Dir* William Wellman [William A Wellman] • *Scr* Nunnally Johnson, from the play *Chicago* by Maurine Watkins

A Royal Affair ★★★ 15

Historical romantic drama 2012 · Den/Swe/Cz Rep/Ger · Colour · 132min

Romance and reform are entwined in this conventional but classy tale of court scandal in 18th-century Denmark. The British-born Caroline Mathilde (Swedish actress Alicia Vikander) is married off to the mad King Christian of Denmark (an award-winning performance by Mikkel Boe Folsgaard), but falls for her free-thinking German doctor Johann Struensee (*Casino Royale* baddie Mads Mikkelsen). The tale resonates courtesy of fine scripting, excellent acting, and solid if somewhat leisurely direction. Fans of quality costume drama should love it. DA Danish, English, German, French +subtitles. Swearing, sexual references, a sex scene, brief nudity. *DVD* *BL*

Mads Mikkelsen *Johann Friedrich Struensee* • Mikkel Folsgaard *Christian VII* • Alicia Vikander *Caroline Mathilde* • David Dencik *Ove Hoegh-Guldberg* • Trine Dyrholm *Juliane Marie* • William Johnk Nielsen [William Johnk Juels Nielsen] *Frederik VI* ■ *Dir* Nikolaj Arcel • *Scr* Nikolaj Arcel, Rasmus Heisterberg, from the novel *Prinsesse af Blodet* by Bodil Steensen-Leth

Royal Affairs in Versailles ★★★

Historical drama 1953 · Fr · Colour · 152min

In its day, this was one of the most lavish and expensive French films ever made, a three-hour, all-star evocation of the reigns of three men named Louis - XIV, XV and XVI - and their little cottage outside Paris called Versailles. The director, Sacha Guitry - an alleged Nazi collaborator - himself plays Louis XIV and gets the lion's share of scenes, supported by a gallery of French stars who perform with a lot of pomp and pompadour. AT French +subtitles.

Claudette Colbert *Madame de Montespan* • Sacha Guitry *Louis XIV* • Orson Welles *Benjamin Franklin* • Jean-Pierre Aumont *Cardinal de Rohan* • Edith Piaf *Woman of the People* • Gérard Philipe *D'Artagnan* • Micheline Presle *Madame du Pompadour* • Jean Marais *Louis XV* • Gilbert Boka *Louis XVI* • Brigitte Bardot *Mademoiselle de Rosille* ■ *Dir/Scr* Sacha Guitry

The Royal Family of Broadway ★★ U
Comedy 1930 · US · BW · 106min

Said to be loosely modelled on the Barrymore dynasty, this once relevant attempt at some kind of satirical comedy is now largely a monumental bore. Fredric March was Oscar-nominated for his performance as the wayward matinée idol son of dowager trouper Henrietta Crosman, but that honour should have gone to Ina Claire as his actress sister who, like her own daughter, is briefly torn between career and personal happiness. Although intermittently amusing, it's painfully stagey and slow. RK

Ina Claire *Julia Cavendish* · Fredric March *Tony Cavendish* · Mary Brian *Gwen Cavendish* · Henrietta Crosman *Fanny Cavendish* · Charles Starrett *Perry Stewart* · Arnold Korff *Oscar Wolff* ■ *Dir* George Cukor, Cyril Gardner · *Scr* Herman Mankiewicz, Gertrude Purcell, from the play by George S Kaufman, Edna Ferber

Royal Flash ★★ 15
Period comedy adventure 1975 · UK · Colour · 97min

Author George MacDonald Fraser's series of novels featuring a grown-up Harry Flashman, the bully from *Tom Brown's Schooldays*, were fun, but the character doesn't survive the transition to film. As Flashman, Malcolm McDowell lacks the necessary public school veneer and, despite effective support from the likes of Alan Bates (who would have been better cast in the lead role) and Oliver Reed (ditto), it's really hard to care what happens to him. TS

Malcolm McDowell *Captain Harry Flashman* · Alan Bates *Rud. von Starnberg* · Florinda Bolkan *Lola Montez* · Oliver Reed *Otto von Bismarck* · Britt Ekland *Duchess Irma of Strakenz* · Lionel Jeffries *Kraftstein* · Tom Bell *de Gautet* · Joss Ackland *Sapten* · Christopher Cazenove *Eric Hansen* · Roy Kinnear *Old roué* · Alastair Sim *Mr Greig* · Michael Hordern *Headmaster* ■ *Dir* Richard Lester · *Scr* George MacDonald Fraser, from his novel

The Royal Hunt of the Sun ★★★ U
Historical drama 1969 · UK/US · Colour · 121min

Peter Shaffer's play is made over into a duet for two egos as Spanish conquistador Pizarro (Robert Shaw) embarks on his South American trek to conquer the Inca god-king, Atahualpa (Christopher Plummer) for the gold he thinks the Incas have. Directed by Irving Lerner, this is surprisingly stagey and static although the acting is powerful. TH

Robert Shaw *Francisco Pizarro* · Christopher Plummer *Atahualpa* · Nigel Davenport *Hernando De Soto* · Leonard Whiting *Young Martin* · Michael Craig *Estete* · Andrew Keir *Valverde* · James Donald *King Carlos V* ■ *Dir* Irving Lerner · *Scr* Philip Yordan, from the play by Peter Shaffer

A Royal Night Out ★★★ 12
Romantic thriller 2015 · UK · Colour · 92min

The future queen has her first and last hedonistic hurrah in this fanciful concoction from *Becoming Jane* director Julian Jarrold. It follows the two British princesses, sensible Elizabeth (Canadian actress Sarah Gadon) and giddy, pinwheeling Margaret (Bel Powley) as they take to the heaving streets of London to celebrate VE Day amongst the masses. The concept – supposedly based on a kernel of truth – feels desperately stretched, and, seen through the eyes of the curious, alienated Elizabeth, the populace is rendered as bizarrely quaint. But it's grounded by canny casting and heartfelt performances. EAS Swearing, sexual references. DVD BD

Sarah Gadon *Princess Elizabeth* · Bel Powley *Princess Margaret* · Jack Reynor *Jack* · Rupert Everett *King George* · Emily Watson *Queen Elizabeth* · Jack Laskey *Lieutenant Pryce* ■ *Dir* Julian Jarrold · *Scr* Trevor De Silva, Kevin Hood

A Royal Scandal ★★ U
Period comedy 1945 · US · Colour · 89min

Young soldier William Eythe, passionately loyal to Catherine the Great (Tallulah Bankhead), arrives at court as her self-appointed protector, but finds himself dangerously out of his depth when the empress falls for his charms. A sporadically entertaining but silly and antediluvian period comedy, produced by Ernst Lubitsch but directed by Otto Preminger without any of the sophisticated Lubitsch touches it badly needs. Released as *Czarina* in the UK. RK DVD

Tallulah Bankhead *Tsarina Catherine the Great* · Charles Coburn *Chancellor Nicolai Ilyitch* · Anne Baxter *Countess Anna Jaschikoff* · William Eythe *Lt Alexei Chernoff* · Vincent Price *Marquis de Fleury* · Mischa Auer *Captain Sukov* · Sig Ruman *General Ronsky* ■ *Dir* Otto Preminger · *Scr* Edwin Justis Mayer, Bruno Frank, from the play *The Czarina* by Lajos Biró, Melchior Lengyel

The Royal Tenenbaums ★★★★★ 15
Comedy drama 2001 · US · Colour · 105min

Produced and directed by the hugely talented Wes Anderson, this is about a gifted, but dysfunctional, New York family that is reunited when estranged patriarch Gene Hackman feigns terminal illness. An ambitiously original ensemble comedy, it is related in an episodic, storybook format with off-screen narration from Alec Baldwin. This stylised presentation suggests that the interlocking subplots involving the various Tenenbaums will be resolved in a detached fashion, without warmth or the audience's empathy. That is not so. As the narrative builds, the atmosphere thaws and something like poetry unfolds. Immaculately written and brilliantly performed, this extraordinary fable restores one's faith in American cinema. AC DVD

Gene Hackman *Royal Tenenbaum* · Anjelica Huston *Etheline Tenenbaum* · Ben Stiller *Chas Tenenbaum* · Gwyneth Paltrow *Margot Tenenbaum* · Owen Wilson *Eli Cash* · Bill Murray *Raleigh St Clair* · Danny Glover *Henry Sherman* · Luke Wilson *Richie Tenenbaum* · Alec Baldwin *Narrator* ■ *Dir* Wes Anderson · *Scr* Wes Anderson, Owen Wilson

Royal Wedding ★★★ U
Musical comedy 1951 · US · Colour · 89min

Here's a totally delightful oddity: a topical MGM musical, timed to chime in with the wedding of then Princess Elizabeth and Prince Philip, and actually incorporating library footage. Stanley Donen makes the most of his solo directing debut, despite an over-dependence on English stereotypes and fake fog. Donen has the benefit of the great Fred Astaire in the leading role, who furnishes the director with the movie's highlight, an incredible routine in which he dances effortlessly up the walls and on the ceiling of his room. TS DVD

Fred Astaire *Tom Bowen* · Jane Powell *Ellen Bowen* · Peter Lawford *Lord John Brindale* · Sarah Churchill *Anne Ashmond* · Keenan Wynn *Irving Klinger/Eagar Klinger* · Albert Sharpe *James Ashmond* ■ *Dir* Stanley Donen · *Scr* Alan Jay Lerner

Rubber ★★★ 15
Black comedy horror 2010 · Fr · Colour · 78min

On the face of it, the plot of this cult-movie-in-the-making would appear to be pure B-movie fodder – an old car tyre out in the Californian desert suddenly gains sentience and psychic powers that allow it to exterminate anything that gets in the way. But this absurd, tongue-in-cheek tale from writer/director Quentin Dupieux is strikingly photographed, sharply edited and has more to it than low-budget gore (even if it does owe a significant debt to the splatter effects of David Cronenberg's *Scanners*). With the action occurring in front of an oddball bunch of spectators (whose fate is just as relevant as what happens to the vulcanised rubber villain), this has more in common with David Lynch and Luis Buñuel than your average monster-on-the-rampage flick. JA Violence, swearing. DVD BD

Stephen Spine la *Lieutenant Chad* · Jack Plotnick *Accountant* · Wings Hauser *Man in wheelchair* · Roxane Mesquida *Sheila* ■ *Dir/Scr* Quentin Dupieux · *Music* Mr Oizo [Quentin Dupieux]

Rubin & Ed ★★★
Road movie comedy drama 1991 · UK · Colour · 82min

This unconventional road movie features one of cinema's oddest characters, Rubin Farr (Crispin Glover), a recluse who spends most of his life in a motel room mourning the loss of his cat, whose body lies frozen in the icebox. Glover meets up with salesman Howard Hesseman, who is trying to bring in clients for an upcoming sales seminar. He agrees to accompany Hesseman to the seminar, but only if the two journey via the desert, where Rubin can bury his beloved cat. Of course things start to go haywire once they hit the road. Decidedly odd but with a certain twisted appeal. DF

Crispin Glover *Rubin Farr* · Howard Hesseman *Ed Tuttle* · Karen Black *Rula* · Michael Greene *Mr Busta* · Brittney Lewis *Poster girl* ■ *Dir/Scr* Trent Harris

Ruby ★★ 15
Horror 1977 · US · Colour · 163min

Piper Laurie plays an ex-torch singer, now owner of a drive-in movie theatre, whose deaf-mute daughter seems to be linked to a series of mystifying and chilling deaths. It's mainly a mindless muddle, partly owing to a story cobbled together from chiller clichés and also to director Curtis Harrington's replacement during production by Stephanie Rothman. However, Laurie still manages to hold the 1950s-set bijou blood bath together by the sheer force of her acting ability. AJ Violence.

Piper Laurie *Ruby Claire* · Stuart Whitman *Vince Kemper* · Roger Davis *Doc Keller* · Janit Baldwin *Leslie Claire* · Crystin Sinclaire *Lila June* · Paul Kent *Louie* · Len Lesser *Barney* ■ *Dir* Curtis Harrington, Stephanie Rothman · *Scr* George Edwards, Barry Schneider, from a story by Steve Krantz

Ruby ★★★★ 15
Crime drama 1992 · US · Colour · 105min

Danny Aiello, one of America's best big-screen brooders, leaps at the complexity of Jack Ruby, the man who shot alleged Kennedy assassin Lee Harvey Oswald, and so creates maximum energy from Ruby's insecurity, arrogance and morose, haunted nature. John Mackenzie sensibly skews his film in the direction of a character piece, which helps it transcend the largely fictionalised and sometimes fuzzy plot. This is an interesting take on events, made as it was just before the 30th anniversary of Kennedy's death. JM Violence, swearing.

Danny Aiello *Jack Ruby* · Sherilyn Fenn *Sheryl Ann Dujean/"Candy Cane"* · Frank Orsatti (2) *Action Jackson* · Jeffrey Nordling *Hank* · Jane Hamilton *Telephone Trixie* · Maurice Bernard Diego · Joe Cortese *Louie Vitali* · Marc Lawrence (1) *Santos Alicante* · Arliss Howard *Maxwell* · David Duchovny *Officer Tippit* ■ *Dir* John Mackenzie (1) · *Scr* Stephen Davis, from his play *Love Field*

Ruby and Rata ★★★
Comedy drama 1990 · NZ · Colour · 111min

Yvonne Lawley and Vanessa Rare turn in spirited performances as, respectively, the elderly Auckland suburbanite and the Maori dole scrounger whose feud takes an unexpected turn thanks to Rare's tearaway son, Lee Mete-Kingi. Originally conceived by director Gaylene Preston as a TV series, the film suffers slightly from some underdrawn secondary characters. However, it doesn't hold back in its consideration of such topics as middle-class snobbery, the iniquities of the social security system and anti-Maori prejudice. DP Swearing.

Yvonne Lawley *Ruby* · Vanessa Rare *Rata* · Lee Mete-kingi *Willie* · Simon Barnett *Buckle* ■ *Dir* Gaylene Preston · *Scr* Graeme Tetley

Ruby Blue ★★ 15
Drama 2007 · UK · Colour · 107min

Clearly striving to be a *Kes* for the chav generation, director Jan Dunn's seaside saga owes much to Ken Loach, as it seeks to pack in as many hot social issues as possible. Everything from paedophilia, juvenile delinquency and neglectful parenting to illiteracy, homophobia and booze culture is dragged into a storyline that centres on pigeon-fancying widower Bob Hoskins and his friendships with French train driver Josiane Balasko, waif next-door Jessica Stewart and reformed bad lad Jody Latham. However, the action is frequently allowed to slide into soap operatics and a surfeit of secondary characters are too broadly played to be credible. Nevertheless, Hoskins copes admirably and Dunn makes effective use of her Margate and Ramsgate locations. DP

Bob Hoskins *Jack* · Josiane Balasko *Stephanie* · Jody Latham *Ian* · Josef Altin *Frankie* · Jessica Stewart *Florrie* · Shannon Tomkinson *Stacey* · Sean Wilton *Dick* · Ashley McGuire *Debbie* ■ *Dir/Scr* Jan Dunn

Ruby Cairo ★★ 15
Mystery 1992 · US/Jpn · Colour · 105min

Director Graeme Clifford seems convinced that all he has to do to keep us on the edge of our seats is to whisk Andie MacDowell across three continents in search of the clues that will explain the disappearance of errant husband Viggo Mortensen. This is never a dull film, with MacDowell conveying both vulnerability and tenacity, but you can't quite believe in her love for either naughty Morty or hunky charity worker Liam Neeson. DP Swearing, nudity.

Andie MacDowell *Bessie Faro* · Liam Neeson *Fergus Lamb* · Jack Thompson *Ed* · Viggo Mortensen *Johnny* · Paul Spencer *Young Johnny* · Chad Power *Niles Faro* · Monica Mikala *Alexandria Faro* ■ *Dir* Graeme Clifford · *Scr* Robert Dillon, Michael Thomas, from a story by Robert Dillon

Ruby Gentry ★★★ PG
Melodrama 1952 · US · BW · 82min

This steamy southern melodrama has Jennifer Jones on seductive form, setting her cap at Charlton Heston and marrying Karl Malden to spite him. Unintentionally hilarious or totally turgid depending on your point of view, but Jones is amazingly sexy, clad in the clingiest of jeans, while Heston looks more perplexed than enamoured. For lovers of Hollywood at its most baroque, this is a real one-off. TS

Jennifer Jones *Ruby Gentry* · Charlton Heston *Boake Tackman* · Karl Malden *Jim Gentry* · Tom Tully *Jud Corey* · Bernard Phillips *Dr Saul Manfred* · James Anderson (2) *Jewel Corey* · Josephine Hutchinson *Letitia Gentry* ■ *Dir* King Vidor · *Scr* Sylvia Richards, from a story by Arthyr Fitz-Richard

Ruby in Paradise ★★★ 15
Drama 1993 · US · Colour · 114min

This gentle, if at times bordering on the comatose, little elegy to finding oneself stars Ashley Judd in a debut performance of engaging clarity. Writer/director Victor Nunez does a sterling job with a tiny budget, neatly blending Judd's home territory of Tennessee with the laid-back freedoms of her chosen Florida beach community without resorting to either redneck or post-hippy clichés. As usual with such small American independent movies, this suffered from lack of marketing and undeservedly disappeared without trace. SH Swearing, sex scenes, nudity.

Ashley Judd *Ruby Lee Gissing* · Todd Field *Mike McCaslin* · Bentley Mitchum *Ricky Chambers* · Allison Dean *Rochelle Bridges* · Dorothy Lyman *Mildred Chambers* · Betsy Douds *Debrah Ann* · Felicia Hernandez *Persefina* ■ *Dir/Scr* Victor Nunez

Ruby Sparks ★★★ 15
Romantic fantasy comedy 2012 · US · Colour · 99min

The makers of *Little Miss Sunshine* experiment with some light melancholy in this fascinating fantasy. Paul Dano stars as creatively frustrated writer Calvin Weir-Fields, whose dream woman (played by Dano's real-life girlfriend Zoe Kazan) suddenly comes to life in his kitchen. A spirit of mischief – personified in small roles by Steve Coogan, Antonio Banderas and Annette Bening – helps to temper the angst of Dano's performance, but at crucial moments the balance tips too far one way

R

or the other. On the whole, however, the movie, like the perfect romantic heroine, is full of charm. SP Swearing, sexual references, drug abuse. **DVD** **BL**

Paul Dano *Calvin Weir-Fields* • Zoe Kazan *Ruby Sparks* • Annette Bening *Gertrude* • Antonio Banderas *Mort* • Steve Coogan *Langdon Tharp* ■ *Dir* Jonathan Dayton, Valerie Faris • *Scr* Zoe Kazan

Rude Awakening ★★ 15
Comedy   1989 · US · Colour · 96min

In one of a series of Rip Van Winkle comedies made in recent years, Eric Roberts and Cheech Marin haven't exactly been sleeping between the 1960s and the 1980s – they've been living in a South American commune. When they return to America, they discover life has moved on and – shock, horror– their former pals are yuppies. Nice idea, but this is silly rather than comical, and the jokes are hammered home far too hard. JB Some swearing.

Eric Roberts *Fred* • Richard "Cheech" Marin *Hesus* • Petra Hagerty *Julie* • Robert Carradine *Sammy* • Buck Henry *Lloyd* • Louise Lasser *Ronnie* • Cindy Williams *June* • Cliff De Young *Brubaker* ■ *Dir* Aaron Russo, David Greenwalt • *Scr* Neil Levy, Richard LaGravenese, from a story by Neil Levy

Rude Boy ★★ 18
Music documentary drama
1980 · UK · Colour · 132min

A muddled blend of documentary footage and part-improvised, part-scripted scenes, this concert drama revolves around the trials and tribulations of sex shop salesman Ray Gange employed by the Clash as their roadie in Scotland around the time of their second album *Give 'Em Enough Rope*. The well-staged performances make this anti-establishment comic book more memorable than it deserves to be. AJ **DVD**

Ray Gange *Ray* • John Green [Johnny Green (2)] *Road manager* ■ *Dir* Jack Hazan, David Mingay • *Scr* Jack Hazan, David Mingay, Ray Gange

Rudo y Cursi ★★★ 15
Comedy   2008 · US/Mex · Colour · 97min

Diego Luna and Gael García Bernal are reunited for the first time since *Y Tu Mamá También* in this lively but lightweight football comedy, playing squabbling siblings Rudo and Cursi who sign up for rival Mexico City teams. Director Carlos Cuarón goes for belly laughs rather than subtlety, tackling such issues as Mexico's crushing socio-economic woes with a mixture of cliché, caricature and chauvinism. It entertains with energy and macho comic swagger, but leaves one with the feeling that Cuarón's tone is too flippant if he was intending this as satire. DP Spanish +subtitles. **DVD**

Gael García Bernal *Tato "Cursi" Verdusco* • Diego Luna *Beto "Rudo" Verdusco* • Guillermo Francella *Darío "Batuta" Vidali* • Dolores Heredia *Elvira* • Adriana Paz *Toña* • Jessica Mas *Maya Vega* • Salvador Zerboni *Jorge W* • Tania Esmeralda Aguilar *Nadia* ■ *Dir/Scr* Carlos Cuarón

Rudolph the Red-Nosed Reindeer ★★ U
Animated seasonal fantasy
1998 · US · Colour · 83min

Don't expect the excruciating ditties in this otherwise harmless cartoon to go down in folklore. There are seven altogether and they disrupt a storyline that already struggles for momentum, as Rudolph's run of misfortunes culminates in his confrontation with evil ice-queen Stormella (Whoopi Goldberg). John Goodman provides a jovial voice as Santa, but cameos from Eric Idle and Bob Newhart are less successful. DP **DVD**

John Goodman *Santa Claus* • Whoopi Goldberg *Stormella, the Evil Ice Queen* • Debbie Reynolds *Mrs Claus* • Bob Newhart *Leonard the Polar Bear* • Richard Simmons *Boone* • Eric Idle *Slyly the Fox* ■ *Dir* Bill Kowalchuk • *Scr* Michael Aschner

Rudy ★★ PG
Sports biography   1993 · US · Colour · 109min

Director David Anspaugh made his name with the gritty basketball drama *Hoosiers*,

and he's back battling for the underdog in this less than convincing American football feature that's based on a true story. Sean Astin plays the pint-sized gridiron fanatic who is determined to play for a college team, despite the lack of encouragement. Astin is adequate, but this is both overly sentimental and unintentionally funny. JF Swearing.

Sean Astin *Rudy* • Jon Favreau *D-Bob* • Ned Beatty *Daniel* • Greta Lind *Mary* • Scott Benjaminson *Frank* • Mary Ann Thebus *Betty* • Charles S Dutton *Fortune* • Lili Taylor *Sherry* ■ *Dir* David Anspaugh • *Scr* Angelo Pizzo

Rue Cases Nègres ★★★★ PG
Period drama   1983 · Fr · Colour · 101min

Euzhan Palcy's feature debut is remarkable for her total immersion in its environment and her complete understanding of its characters. Set in a 1930s Martinique shantytown abutting a French-run sugar cane plantation, this is no mere rites-of-passage picture, but an affirmation of the vital part love plays in childhood, even in the midst of oppression and poverty. Winner of the best actress prize at Venice, Darling Legitimus is superb as the proud woman who sacrifices everything for her grandson's education. DP French +subtitles.

Garry Cadenat *Jose* • Darling Legitimus *M'Man Tine* • Douta Seck *Medouze* • Joby Bernabe *Monsieur Saint-Louis* • Francisco Charles *Le Gereur* ■ *Dir* Euzhan Palcy • *Scr* Euzhan Palcy, from the novel by Joseph Zobel

Ruggles of Red Gap ★★★
Silent comedy   1923 · US · BW · 89min

This earlier version of the classic comedy known best for its 1935 outing features Edward Everett Horton as the quintessential British valet whose services are won in a game of poker but who is then whisked away from Europe to the Wild Western town of Red Gap, where he's introduced to the locals as a colonel. Horton is wonderfully funny here, with James Cruze directing the story adapted from Henry Leon Wilson's novel. Bob Hope was to star in yet another version, *Fancy Pants* (1950). TH

Edward Horton [Edward Everett Horton] *"Colonel" Ruggles* • Ernest Torrence *Cousin Egbert Floud* • Lois Wilson *Kate Kenner* • Fritzi Ridgeway *Emily Judson* • Charles Ogle *Jeff Tuttle* • Louise Dresser *Mrs Effie Floud* • Anna Lehr *Mrs Belknap-Jackson* • Thomas Holding *Earl of Brinstead* ■ *Dir* James Cruze • *Scr* Walter Woods, Anthony Coldeway, from the novel by Harry Leon Wilson

Ruggles of Red Gap ★★★★★ U
Comedy   1935 · US · BW · 90min

Charles Laughton is Ruggles, an English butler of impeccable credentials and phlegmatic rectitude, who is sold by his titled employer Roland Young to a visiting American couple at the insistence of the pretentious wife Mary Boland. He is taken out west charged with, among other things, making a gentleman out of his employer's husband (Charlie Ruggles). Once there, events take a surprising turn. A brilliant, hilarious and fondly satirical look at Anglo-American relations and culture gaps, faultlessly directed by Leo McCarey with Laughton in masterly form – magnificently suffering the vulgarities that offend his dignity while slowly learning to profit from another way of life and even falling in love (with ZaSu Pitts). Nobody else could have played it, and the Oscar-nominated film itself could never have emerged with such perfection in any other era. RK **DVD** **BL**

Charles Laughton *Colonel Marmaduke "Bill" Ruggles* • Mary Boland *Effie Floud* • Charlie Ruggles [Charles Ruggles] *Egbert "Sourdough" Floud* • ZaSu Pitts *Mrs Prunella Judson* • Roland Young *Earl of Burnstead* • Leila Hyams *Nell Kenner* • Maude Eburne *"Ma" Pettingill* • Lucien Littlefield *Charles Belknap-Jackson* ■ *Dir* Leo McCarey • *Scr* Walter DeLeon, Harlan Thompson, Humphrey Pearson, from the novel by Harry Leon Wilson

Rugrats Go Wild ★★ U
Animated comedy adventure
2003 · US · Colour · 77min

Nickelodeon's decision to marry together *Rugrats* and *The Wild Thornberrys* proves a qualified success. The cartoon romp is a fast-moving carnival of primary colours, in which the vacationing Rugrats are stranded on an apparently deserted island, unaware that the Thornberry clan are shooting a nature documentary there. The absence of a plot exposes the film's lame humour and nauseating songs. SF **DVD**

Bruce Willis *Spike the Dog* • Chrissie Hynde *Siri the Leopard* • Nancy Cartwright *Chuckie Finster* • Kath Soucie *Philip Deville/Lillian Deville/Betty Deville* • Cheryl Chase *Angelica Pickles* • EG Daily [Elizabeth Daily] *Tommy Pickles* • Tara Strong [Tara Charendoff] *Dil Pickles* • Melanie Chartoff *Didi Pickles* ■ *Dir* Norton Virgien, John Eng • *Scr* Kate Boutilier, from characters by Arlene Klasky, Gabor Csupo, Paul German, Steve Pepoon, David Silverman, Stephen Sustarsic

Rugrats in Paris: the Movie ★★★ U
Animated comedy adventure
2000 · US/Ger · Colour · 75min

This sequel takes TV's adventurous babies to Paris. They invade a Japanese-owned amusement park, where one of the robot movie monsters is malfunctioning. Susan Sarandon supplies the voice of the park's manager, Coco La Bouche, a careerist whose promotion prospects depend on her ability to acquire a ready-made family. Children will enjoy the thrills and spills, all viewed through the Rugrats' eyes. DM **DVD**

EG Daily [Elizabeth Daily] *Tommy Pickles* • Tara Charendoff *Dil Pickles* • Cheryl Chase *Angelica Pickles* • Christine Cavanaugh *Chuckie Finster* • Cree Summer *Susie Carmichael* • Kath Soucie *Philip Deville/Lillian Deville/Betty Deville* • Michael Bell *Drew Pickles/Chas Finster* • Tress MacNeille *Charlotte Pickles* • Casey Kasem *Wedding DJ* • Debbie Reynolds *Lulu Pickles* ■ *Dir* Stig Bergqvist, Paul Demeyer • *Scr* Kate Boutilier, Jill Gorey, Barbara Herndon, J David Stern, David N Weiss, from characters by Arlene Klasky, Gabor Csupo, Paul Germain

The Rugrats Movie ★★★ U
Animated comedy adventure
1998 · US · Colour · 76min

Nickelodeon TV favourites the Rugrats get their own movie in this fun feature-length adventure. Whoopi Goldberg, Tim Curry and David Spade are among the celebrities lending their voices, as cute toddler Tommy Pickles persuades his pals to help him return his newborn brother, Dil, to the hospital so that he can have his parents all to himself again. Of course, their journey doesn't go as planned, and the group end up in a scary forest. There are messages about bravery and friendship here, but they're woven into the fun in a way that won't spoil the enjoyment. JB **DVD** **CS**

EG Daily [Elizabeth Daily] *Tommy Pickles* • Christine Cavanaugh *Chuckie Finster* • Kath Soucie *Philip Deville/Lillian Deville/Betty Deville* • Melanie Chartoff *Didi Pickles/Minka* • Phil Proctor [Philip Proctor] *Howard Deville/Igor* • Cree Summer *Susie Carmichael* • Busta Rhymes *Reptar Wagon* • Iggy Pop *Newborn baby* • Tim Curry *Rex Pester* • Whoopi Goldberg *Ranger Margaret* • David Spade *Ranger Frank* ■ *Dir* Norton Virgien, Igor Kovalyov • *Scr* J David Stern, David N Weiss, from characters by Arlene Klasky, Gabor Csupo, Paul Germain

The Ruins ★★★ 18
Horror thriller
2008 · Aus/US/Ger · Colour · 86min

Five tourists visit a Mayan temple and are confronted by ancient vegetation with a taste for blood in this polished adaptation of Scott Smith's bestseller. Director Carter Smith's film doesn't quite replicate the book's tension, but he has still produced an unpretentious and effectively staged horror thriller. While integral to the plot, the deadly vines are subtly used, never becoming B-movie laughable, and the increasing stress is well played by a cast that includes Jena Malone and *X-Men*'s Shawn Ashmore. The catalogue of graphic amputations and self-

mutilations are gruesomely convincing, but it's the chilling plight of the tourists that makes this rooted nightmare such a satisfying shocker. AJ Violence, swearing, sexual references, nudity. **DVD**

Jonathan Tucker *Jeff* • Jena Malone *Amy* • Shawn Ashmore *Eric* • Laura Ramsey *Stacy* ■ *Dir* Carter Smith • *Scr* Scott B Smith, from his novel

Rulers of the Sea ★★★ U
Historical drama   1939 · US · BW · 96min

Glasgow-born Frank Lloyd, a master craftsman who directed the Academy Award-winning *Mutiny on the Bounty* in 1935, returned to the world of ships to make this excellent, reasonably exciting adventure about the building and maiden voyage of the first steamship. Genuine Scotsman Will Fyffe made a rare excursion into Hollywood, while another import – England's Margaret Lockwood, not yet the nation's favourite wicked lady – was paired with Douglas Fairbanks Jr to supply the romantic subplot that leavens the action. A young, unknown Alan Ladd is in the cast. RK

Douglas Fairbanks Jr *Gillespie* • Margaret Lockwood *Mary Shaw* • Will Fyffe *John Shaw* • George Bancroft *James Oliver* • Montagu Love *Malcolm Grant* • Vaughan Glaser *Junius Smith* • David Torrence *Donald Fenton* • Lester Matthews *Lieutenant Commander Roberts* • Alan Ladd *Colin Farrell* ■ *Dir* Frank Lloyd • *Scr* Talbot Jennings, Frank Cavett, Richard Collins

Rules Don't Apply ★★★
Romantic comedy drama   2016 · US · Colour

This is a preview – no prints were available to review as we went to press: Of the four movies Warren Beatty has directed so far, three won Oscars (and *Bulworth* was nominated). So anticipation is high for Beatty's first feature in 15 years. Beatty stars, too, as Howard Hughes, the endlessly fascinating billionaire who used his wealth to buy a film studio, design the world's largest wooden plane, break global flying records and buy TWA airlines. But prior to him turning raddled recluse, this puts emphasis on an affair Hughes had later in life. SvM

Alden Ehrenreich *Frank Forbes* • Lily Collins *Marla Mabrey* • Warren Beatty *Howard Hughes* • Candice Bergen *Nadine Henley* • Martin Sheen *Noah Dietrich* • Alec Baldwin *Bob Maheu* • Matthew Broderick *Levar Mathis* ■ *Dir/Scr* Warren Beatty • *Cinematographer* Caleb Deschanel

The Rules of Attraction ★★ 18
Romantic thriller
2002 · US/Ger · Colour · 106min

A superficial interpretation of Bret Easton Ellis's cult novel, this is an arrogant combination of social satire and 1980s teen comedy. The film centres on three New England college students: drug-dealing waster James Van Der Beek, bisexual party boy Ian Somerhalder and the virginal Shannyn Sossamon. The stereotypical trio flounder through a devil's playground of sex, drugs and violence. Despite an impertinent edge, this falls down by trying too hard to be hip. SF **DVD** **BL**

James Van Der Beek *Sean Bateman* • Shannyn Sossamon *Lauren Hynde* • Ian Somerhalder *Paul Denton* • Jessica Biel *Lara* • Kip Pardue *Victor* • Thomas Ian Nicholas *Mitchell* • Kate Bosworth *Kelly* • Fred Savage *Marc* • Eric Stoltz *Mr Lance Lawson* • Faye Dunaway *Mrs Denton* • Swoosie Kurtz *Mrs Jared* ■ *Dir* Roger Avary • *Scr* Roger Avary, from the novel by Bret Easton Ellis

Rules of Engagement ★★ 15
Courtroom drama   2000 · US · Colour · 122min

William Friedkin's courtroom melodrama revolves around colonel Samuel L Jackson's decision to fire on a crowd of Arabs storming the US embassy in Yemen. Tommy Lee Jones reluctantly defends him at his court martial, knowing only too well that Jackson has a tendency to buckle under pressure. A terrific cast is wasted as the two leads duke it out with tough prosecution attorney Guy Pearce. Alas, the film is scuppered by unsavoury stereotypes and a Vietnam flashback that suggests the stars have not aged a day in 30 years. NS Violence, swearing. *DVD*

Tommy Lee Jones *Col Hays Hodges* • Samuel L Jackson *Col Terry Childers* • Guy Pearce *Maj Mark Biggs* • Bruce Greenwood *National Security Adviser William Sokal* • Blair Underwood *Captain Lee* • Philip Baker Hall *Gen H Lawrence Hodges* • Anne Archer *Mrs Mourain* • Ben Kingsley *Ambassador Mourain* ■ *Dir* William Friedkin • *Scr* Stephen Gaghan, from a story by James Webb

Rules of Obsession ★★
Erotic thriller 1994 · US · Colour · 93min

In this predictable thriller, Scott Bakula plays a psychiatrist whose best friend (John Getz) returns from a cruise with a new wife (Bakula's real-life wife, Chelsea Field). When she starts acting strangely, Getz asks Bakula to talk to her about her problems, but the doctor finds himself seduced by his patient's charms. Then Getz turns up dead. Only one tiny twist interrupts the pat progress of this routine offering. ST

Scott Bakula *Dr David Lawson* • Chelsea Field *Diana Chamberlain* • Sheila Kelley (1) *Beth* • John Getz *Jerry Chamberlain* ■ *Dir* Rick King • *Scr* William Delligan

The Ruling Class ★★★
Black comedy 1972 · UK · Colour · 153min

A black-hearted assault on British social institutions and the class system, this boasts moments of cruel comedy and real anger thanks to Peter Medak's inspired direction of Peter Barnes's play. Peter O'Toole stars as the madman who inherits the title of the Earl of Gurney. His relatives – played by a flurry of great character actors – then bury their snouts in the trough of expected riches, but O'Toole fools them all: he switches from being Jesus Christ to Jack the Ripper. The film is dated in its approach, though it still has the power to shock. TH Swearing, nudity. *DVD*

Peter O'Toole *Jack* • Alastair Sim *Bishop Lampton* • Arthur Lowe *Tucker* • Harry Andrews *13th Earl of Gurney* • Coral Browne *Lady Claire Gurney* • Michael Bryant *Dr Herder* • Nigel Green *McKyle* • William Mervyn *Sir Charles Gurney* • Carolyn Seymour *Grace Shelley* • James Villiers *Dinsdale Gurney* • Hugh Burden *Matthew Peake* • Graham Crowden *Truscott* • Kay Walsh *Mrs Piggot-Jones* Patsy Byrne *Mrs Treadwell* ■ *Dir* Peter Medak • *Scr* Peter Barnes, from his play

The Rum Diary ★★★
Comedy drama 2011 · US · Colour · 114min

The misadventures of Johnny Depp's boozy journalist in Puerto Rico circa 1960 constitute this return to the screen for writer/director Bruce Robinson, long revered for *Withnail & I*. As marks his serio-comic story based on Hunter S Thompson's novel, in which Depp shambles his way through mischief-making episodes towards a deeper appreciation of the corruption despoiling his paradisal surroundings. Robinson explores a madcap array of hacks and hangers-on (Aaron Eckhart is deliciously slimy as a property wheeler-dealer), and if the end result doesn't quite manage to stir up the indignation he obviously intends, it's still a creditable and very likeable offering. TJ In English, and Spanish with English subtitles. *DVD*

Johnny Depp *Paul Kemp* • Aaron Eckhart *Sanderson* • Michael Rispoli *Bob Sala* • Amber Heard *Chenault* • Richard Jenkins *Lotterman* • Giovanni Ribisi *Moberg* ■ *Dir* Bruce Robinson • *Scr* Bruce Robinson, from the novel by Hunter S Thompson · *Costume Designer* Colleen Atwood

Rumba ★★
Romance 1935 · US · BW · 70min

A moneyed New York society girl meets a Broadway dancer as a result of a duplicated lottery ticket, falls for him and, predictably, steps in to the big number of his new show when his regular partner lets him down. Paramount's shamelessly recycled version of the previous year's hugely successful *Bolero*, once again starring George Raft and Carole Lombard, lacks both the novelty and

the enjoyable melodramatics of its predecessor. RK

George Raft *Joe Martin* • Carole Lombard *Diane Harrison* • Lynne Overman *Flash* • Margo *Carmelita* • Gail Patrick *Patsy* • Iris Adrian *Goldie Allen* • Clara Lou Sheridan [Ann Sheridan] *Dance girl* ■ *Dir* Marion Gering • *Scr* Howard J Green, Harry Ruskin, Frank Partos, from an idea by Guy Endore, Seena Owen

Rumba ★★★ PG
Comedy 2008 · Fr/Bel · Colour · 76min

Candy-coloured and almost silent, this quirky fusion of M Hulot and Mr Bean follows two married, Latin-dance obsessed schoolteachers who meet with comedic tragedy after a dance competition. They battle amputation, disability, amnesia and fire with strangely contained emotions that are funny in themselves. Although some gags are overplayed, the upbeat tone highlights the potentially gloomy story's spare, light feeling. Carried mostly by the chemistry and physical grace of its lead characters, this curio is a marvellous showcase for their elegant, near-wordless exchanges. KK French +subtitles.

Dominique Abel *Dom* • Fiona Gordon *Fiona* • Phillipe Martz *Gérard* ■ *Dir/Scr* Dominique Abel, Fiona Gordon, Bruno Romy

Rumble Fish ★★★★
Drama 1983 · US · BW and Colour · 90min

In the second of Francis Ford Coppola's youth problem pictures adapted from SE Hinton's popular novels, Matt Dillon stars as a vulnerable teenager who idolises his elder brother, Mickey Rourke, a former gang leader. Unlike Coppola's more conventional *The Outsiders*, this alienated teen allegory finds him pulling out all the stylistic stops. The drama is extremely mannered, and the symbolism a mite overdone, but it's a visually startling knockout, brilliantly filmed in moody black and white with some dashes of colour. AJ Swearing. *DVD* *BL*

Matt Dillon *Rusty-James* • Mickey Rourke *Motorcycle Boy* • Diane Lane *Patty* • Dennis Hopper *Father* • Diana Scarwid *Cassandra* • Vincent Spano *Steve* • Nicolas Cage *Smokey* • Christopher Penn [Chris Penn] *BJ Jackson* • Larry Fishburne [Laurence Fishburne] *Midget* • Tom Waits *Benny* ■ *Dir* Francis Ford Coppola • *Scr* SE Hinton, Francis Ford Coppola, from the novel by SE Hinton · *Cinematographer* Stephen H Burum · *Music* Stewart Copeland

Rumble in the Bronx ★★★
Martial arts crime drama 1996 · HK/US · Colour · 85min

Clumsily dubbed and with Vancouver standing in for New York, this is a typical Jackie Chan outing, as he joins his uncle and the new owner of his market stall in seeing off a gang of doltish villains. Anita Mui and Françoise Yip are big stars back in Hong Kong, but they are given little room for manoeuvre in this lightweight adventure. As ever, there's plenty of thrilling action, but as always Chan invests his set pieces with an element of balletic humour. DP Cantonese dubbed. Violence, swearing. *DVD* *BL*

Jackie Chan *Keung* • Anita Mui *Elaine* • Bill Tung *Uncle Bill* • Françoise Yip *Nancy* ■ *Dir* Stanley Tong • *Scr* Edward Tang, from a story by Stanley Tong

Rumor Has It... ★★ 12
Comedy drama 2005 · US · Colour · 92min

What if a young woman discovered that her family was the template for *The Graduate*? In one of the many ludicrous twists that shape director Rob Reiner's movie, the now middle-aged inspiration for stuttering geek played by Dustin Hoffman in the 1967 classic is smooth-talking stud Kevin Costner. He charms Jennifer Aniston, the soon-to-be-wed granddaughter of Shirley MacLaine (the "real" Mrs Robinson). It's a vomit-inducing concept that isn't helped by a dizzying plot that blurs the boundaries between fact and fiction. SP *DVD* *BL*

Jennifer Aniston *Sarah Huttinger* • Kevin Costner *Beau Burroughs* • Shirley MacLaine *Katharine Richelieu* • Mark Ruffalo *Jeff Daly* • Richard

Jenkins *Earl Huttinger* • Christopher McDonald *Roger McManus* • Steve Sandvoss *Scott* • Mena Suvari *Annie Huttinger* • Kathy Bates *Katharine's friend* ■ *Dir* Rob Reiner • *Scr* TM Griffin [Ted Griffin]

A Rumor of Angels ★★
Drama 2000 · US · Colour · 106min

Director Peter O'Fallon's follow-up to his underrated black comedy *Suicide Kings* is a sentimental and far-fetched story about a boy struggling to come to terms with his mother's death. While on vacation at a summer beach house, young Trevor Morgan rebels against his distant father Ray Liotta and unsympathetic stepmother Catherine McCormack by hanging out with dotty local recluse Vanessa Redgrave. LH

Vanessa Redgrave *Maddy Bennett* • Ray Liotta *Nathan Neubauer* • Catherine McCormack *Mary Neubauer* • Trevor Morgan *James Neubauer* • Ron Livingston *Uncle Charlie* ■ *Dir* Peter O'Fallon • *Scr* Peter O'Fallon, Jamie Horton, James Eric, from the novel *Thy Son Liveth: Messages from a Soldier to His Mother* by Grace Duffie Boylan

Rumpelstiltskin ★ U
Fantasy 1986 · US · Colour · 80min

The bad news is that this dire film based on the Brothers Grimm story was intended as the first of a series of such adaptations aimed at children. The good news is that others in the dozen or so mooted failed to materialise. Both the adaptation and direction by David Irving are undernourished and he has tried to compensate by over-the-top performances from an international cast (it was filmed in Israel) who flail around in search of a style. BB

Amy Irving *Katie* • Clive Revill *King Mezzer* • Billy Barty *Rumpelstiltskin* • Priscilla Pointer *Queen Grizelda* • Robert Symonds *Victor, Katie's father* • John Moulder-Brown *Prince* ■ *Dir* David Irving • *Scr* David Irving, from the fairy tale by Wilhelm Grimm, Jacob Grimm

Run ★★ 15
Action thriller 1991 · US · Colour · 87min

Patrick Dempsey is a young college student who inadvertently incurs the wrath of a small-town crime lord and then spends the rest of the film running from assorted hitmen and bent policemen. Director Geoff Burrowes appears to be aiming for some sort of cross between a crime thriller and a yuppie-in-peril drama but the end result is convincing as neither, even though he does engineer some slick action sequences. JF Violence.

Patrick Dempsey *Charlie Farrow* • Kelly Preston *Karen Landers* • Ken Pogue *Matt Halloran* • Alan C Peterson *Denny Halloran* • James Kidnie *Sammy* • Sean McCann *Marv* ■ *Dir* Geoff Burrowes • *Scr* Dennis Shryack, Michael Blodgett

Run All Night ★★★ 15
Action thriller 2015 · US · Colour · 109min

Liam Neeson stars in this edgy thriller as a retired hitman who has one night to save his son from being killed by his former boss. Those fearing another *Taken* will be surprised to see a somewhat different twist on the "geriaction" formula. Some well-crafted action keeps the pace up, while an interesting visual style underlines the plot's claustrophobic feel. While it may not stray too far from familiar territory, this is a fast and entertaining example of just why its star's action rebirth has been so successful. JL Violence, swearing, drug abuse. *DVD*

Liam Neeson *Jimmy Conlon* • Joel Kinnaman *Mike Conlon* • Ed Harris *Shawn Maguire* • Vincent D'Onofrio *Detective John Harding* • Nick Nolte *Eddie Conlon* ■ *Dir* Jaume Collet-Serra • *Scr* Brad Ingelsby

Run and Jump ★★★ 15
Drama 2013 · Ire/Ger/US · Colour · 105min

Director Steph Green and co-writer Ailbhe Keogan make auspicious debuts with this discreet study of the effects of a debilitating illness on both a man and his family. The developing bond between wife Maxine Peake and neuropsychologist Will Forte is nicely judged, but subplots involving

teenage son Brendan Morris's burgeoning sexuality and the resentment Peake endures from her suspicious in-laws are less persuasive. Nonetheless, the performances are admirable, while Green makes intelligent use of the contrasts between softly lit interiors and the lush countryside. DP Swearing, sex scenes, drug abuse.

Maxine Peake *Vanetia Casey* • Will Forte *Ted Fielding* • Edward MacLiam *Conor Casey* • Sharon Horgan *Tara* • Brendan Morris *Lenny* ■ *Dir* Steph Green • *Scr* Ailbhe Keogan, Steph Green

Run Fatboy Run ★★★ 12
Comedy 2007 · UK · Colour · 96min

Simon Pegg squeezes into some very small shorts for this cheeky romance directed by David Schwimmer (with whom he co-starred in *Big Nothing*). As titular "fat boy" Dennis, Pegg looks doomed to failure when he signs up for a marathon to prove his love to former flame Libby (Thandie Newton). She's tough to please though, which is understandable as Dennis left her pregnant at the altar five years earlier. Schwimmer gets plenty of comedy mileage out of Dennis's shortcomings - including the inevitable locker-room scene where he cops an eyeful of Libby's hunky new fiancé (Hank Azaria) in the buff. A few of the gags are obvious and lazy, but overall there's a good balance of laughs and emotion. The last leg of his journey (a race across London), while a bit contrived, will surely raise some hearty cheers. SP *DVD* *BL*

Simon Pegg *Dennis Doyle* • Thandie Newton *Libby* • Dylan Moran *Gordon* • Hank Azaria *Whit* • Matthew Fenton *Jake* • Harish Patel *Mr Ghoshdashtidar* • India de Beaufort *Maya* ■ *Dir* David Schwimmer • *Scr* Michael Ian Black, Simon Pegg, from a story by Black

Run for Cover ★★★ U
Western 1955 · US · Colour · 92min

This wistful, almost elegiac western from director Nicholas Ray pits an ageing Jimmy Cagney against youthful John Derek. The themes are those of a thousand traditional cowboy films - old man teaches young pup new tricks, young pup goes to the bad - but it's handled so sensitively that one forgets its hackneyed origins. Cagney is understated and effective, Derek holds his own and a fine supporting cast provides sound ballast. SH

James Cagney *Mat Dow* • Viveca Lindfors *Helga Swenson* • John Derek *Davey Bishop* • Jean Hersholt *Mr Swenson* • Grant Withers *Gentry* • Jack Lambert *Larsen* • Ernest Borgnine *Morgan* • Ray Teal *Sheriff* ■ *Dir* Nicholas Ray • *Scr* Winston Miller, from a story by Harriet Frank Jr, Irving Ravetch

Run for the Sun ★★
Adventure thriller 1956 · US · Colour · 99min

In yet another remake of *The Most Dangerous Game*, disillusioned author Richard Widmark and journalist Jane Greer are the human prey hunted down in the jungle by Nazis Trevor Howard and Peter Van Eyck. British director Roy Boulting - making one of his few Hollywood films - piles on the tension with a skilful hand, but this is fairly negligible compensation. TH

Richard Widmark *Mike Latimer* • Trevor Howard *Browne* • Jane Greer *Katy Connors* • Peter Van Eyck *Van Anders* • Carlos Henning *Jan* ■ *Dir* Roy Boulting • *Scr* Dudley Nichols, Roy Boulting, from the story *The Most Dangerous Game* by Richard Connell

A Run for Your Money ★★ U
Comedy 1949 · UK · BW · 83min

Directed by Charles Frend, this is one of the weakest comedies produced by Ealing Studios. Chronicling the misadventures of Welsh miners Donald Houston and Meredith Edwards after they win a day out in London, it is nothing more than a string of cheap jokes at the expense of the naive boys from the Valleys lost in the urban jungle. More galling than the patronising humour is the waste of Alec Guinness as their guide. DP

R

Donald Houston *Dai Jones* • Moira Lister *Jo* • Alec Guinness *Whimple* • Meredith Edwards *Twm Jones* • Hugh Griffith *Huw Price* • Clive Morton *Editor* • Leslie Perrins *Barney* • Joyce Grenfell *Mrs Pargiter* ■ *Dir* Charles Frend • *Scr* Charles Frend, Leslie Norman, Richard Hughes, Diana Morgan, from a story by Clifford Evans

Run for Your Wife ★★ 12A

Farce 2013 · UK · Colour · 93min

Ray Cooney's "adult comedy" about a bigamous cabbie was a huge stage hit back in the 1980s. Unfortunately, there's no irony or retro self-awareness about this adaptation, which is played as if the last 30 years simply haven't happened. Danny Dyer stars as the man whose double life begins to unravel when he acts the hero one night, and Denise Van Outen and Sarah Harding play his oblivious wives. In support is a veritable who's-who (and often who's-that?) of ageing British stage and screen stars, from Rolf Harris to Judi Dench. Essentially, this frantic farce is one for nostalgia lovers, who rue the passing of simpler, cornier and less-PC times. **DA**

Danny Dyer *John Smith* • Denise Van Outen *Michelle Smith* • Sarah Harding *Stephanie Smith* • Neil Morrissey *Gary Gardner* • Christopher Biggins *Bobby Franklin* • Lionel Blair *Cyril* • Judi Dench *Bag lady* • Cliff Richard *Busker* • Rolf Harris *Busker* • June Whitfield ■ *Dir* Ray Cooney, John Luton • *Scr* Ray Cooney, from his play

Run Lola Run ★★★★ 15

Crime drama 1998 · Ger · Colour · 80min

This breathtakingly enjoyable German film is faster than a speeding bullet, with a mind-boggling pace that seizes audiences by the scruff of the neck and forces them along with ruthless momentum. Franka Potente receives a phone call from boyfriend Moritz Bleibtreu, who's left the money he owes the Mob on the subway. If it's not delivered, he'll be killed. Can she either find the loot or scrounge it in the time he has left? Director Tom Tykwer pushes cinema to superhuman limits – jump cuts and replays, colour turning to monochrome, action sped to a blur. Not so much a movie as an obstacle course. **TH** Blu-ray +subtitles. Swearing, violence. DVD

Franka Potente *Lola* • Moritz Bleibtreu *Manni* • Herbert Knaup *Lola's father* • Armin Rohde *Mr Schuster* • Ludger Pistor *Herr Meier* • Suzanne von Borsody *Frau Jäger* • Sebastian Schipper *Mike* • Heino Ferch *Ronnie* ■ *Dir/Scr* Tom Tykwer

Run of the Arrow ★★★★ PG

Western 1957 · US · Colour · 81min

This was Rod Steiger's least favourite film because he didn't get on with director Samuel Fuller, but the personality clash sparked one of his greatest performances. He plays the bigoted southerner who, after the American Civil War, joins the Sioux tribe as a way of getting back at the Yankees. Surviving the torturous initiation rite, he manages to reveal the macho ethic at its most dangerous, while at the same time investing an unlikeable character with a certain naive dignity. **TH** DVD

Rod Steiger *O'Meara* • Sarita Montiel *Yellow Moccasin* • Brian Keith *Captain Clark* • Ralph Meeker *Lieutenant Driscoll* • Jay C Flippen *Walking Coyote* • Charles Bronson *Blue Buffalo* • Olive Carey *Mrs O'Meara* ■ *Dir/Scr* Samuel Fuller

The Run of the Country ★★★ 15

Drama 1995 · Ire · Colour · 104min

Albert Finney gives a towering performance as an Irish policeman trying to cope with his wayward son Matt Keeslar in director Peter Yates's moving drama. Unfortunately, the film's glowing portrayal of the Irish countryside rather softens the rites-of-passage roots of the drama, in which Keeslar is taught a few hard lessons in life when he falls for Victoria Smurfit, a girl from north of the border. Politics rarely intrude, with Yates more content to explore how a mundane existence in rural Ireland effects the young. It's beautiful to look at, but too nice for its own good. **TH**

Albert Finney *Father* • Matt Keeslar *Danny* • Victoria Smurfit *Annagh* • Anthony Brophy *Prunty* • David Kelly *Father Gaynor* • Dearbhla Molloy *Mother* ■ *Dir* Peter Yates • *Scr* Shane Connaughton, from his novel

Run Silent Run Deep ★★★★ U

Second World War drama 1958 · US · BW · 88min

One of the best submarine movies, this is a terse, brilliantly directed study in revenge, as commander Clark Gable returns to the dreaded Bongo Straits where he had previously lost a sub and his men. Of course, second-in-command Burt Lancaster isn't happy, feeling that he should be in charge, and his reticence and the resentfulness of the crew make for fine drama in a confined space. The opening, pre-title sequence of this film is a classic example of movie storytelling. Even if you don't like the genre, this film merits watching for its star power alone. **TS** DVD

Clark Gable *Commander Richardson* • Burt Lancaster *Lieutenant Jim Bledsoe* • Jack Warden *Mueller* • Brad Dexter *Cartwright* • Don Rickles *Ruby* • Nick Cravat *Russo* ■ *Dir* Robert Wise • *Scr* John Gay, from a novel by Commander Edward L Beach

Run the Wild Fields ★★★

Second World War drama 2000 · US · Colour · 101min

The American Home Front comes to slow-burning life in this credible Second World War drama, adapted from his own play by Rodney Patrick Vaccaro. With her husband missing in action, Joanne Whalley has let the North Carolina family farm run down while waiting against hope for his return. But the lives of Whalley and her ten-year-old daughter (played by *SPYkids* star Alexa Vega) change after she offers sanctuary to pacifist-turned-itinerant Sean Patrick Flanery. Debutant Paul A Kaufman admirably conveys something of the struggle of keeping the home fires burning, though there is an unfortunate, if inevitable, drift towards melodrama. **DP**

Joanne Whalley *Ruby Miller* • Sean Patrick Flanery *Tom Walker* • Cotter Smith *Silas Green* • Alexa Vega *Opal "Pug" Miller* • Bill Lake *Sheriff Bob* • Christine Brubaker *Teacher* • Bradley Reid *Sammy Carlin* ■ *Dir* Paul A Kaufman • *Scr* Rodney Vaccaro [Rodney Patrick Vaccaro], from his play *And the Home of the Brave*

Run Wild, Run Free ★★★

Drama 1969 · UK · Colour · 94min

This rural fable owes much to the earthy evocation of the wild beauty of Dartmoor. Complete with a tense finale and directed with old-fashioned care by Richard C Sarafian, the story of the timid boy whose love of a free-spirited horse brings him out of his shell should appeal to more discriminating youngsters. Mark Lester has few problems looking vulnerable, while John Mills provides seasoned support as the retired colonel who provides the affection denied by parents Sylvia Syms and Gordon Jackson. **DP**

John Mills *The Moorman* • Gordon Jackson *Mr Ransome* • Sylvia Syms *Mrs Ransome* • Mark Lester (2) *Philip Ransome* • Bernard Miles *Reg* • Fiona Fullerton *Diana* ■ *Dir* Richard C Sarafian • *Scr* David Rook, from the novel *The White Colt* by David Rook • *Cinematographer* Wilkie Cooper

Runaway Bride ★★★ PG

Romantic comedy 1999 · US · Colour · 116min

Julia Roberts, Richard Gere and their *Pretty Woman* director Garry Marshall reunite for this predictable but well-played romantic comedy. Roberts is the small-town girl who has left a trio of heartbroken men at the altar, while Gere is the cynical columnist keen to see if she will actually go through with it on her fourth attempt. Of course, you'll have worked out the ending before you reach the last line of this review. However, thanks to Roberts's deft comedic touch, a zippy script and some nice support, this is a sweet romance that will warm the cockles of wedding fanatics everywhere. **JB** Swearing. DVD CS

Julia Roberts *Maggie Carpenter* • Richard Gere *Ike Graham* • Joan Cusack *Peggy* • Hector Elizondo *Fisher* • Rita Wilson *Ellie* • Paul Dooley *Walter* • Christopher Meloni *Coach Bob* • Reg Rogers *George* • Laurie Metcalf *Mrs Trout* ■ *Dir* Garry Marshall • *Scr* Josann McGibbon, Sara Parriott

The Runaway Bus ★★ U

Comedy thriller 1954 · UK · BW · 76min

This comedy thriller proved the ideal debut vehicle for Frankie Howerd. Never totally at home on film, he wisely follows Bob Hope's lead in combining cowardice and wisecracks as he substitutes for the driver of an airport shuttle bus, blissfully unaware that on this foggy night he has a stash of stolen gold on board. However, he is roundly upstaged by both that expert scene-stealer Margaret Rutherford and the underrated Belinda Lee. **DP**

Frankie Howerd *Percy Lamb* • Margaret Rutherford *Cynthia Beeston* • Petula Clark *Lee Nichols* • George Coulouris *Edward Schroeder* • Belinda Lee *Janie Grey* • Reginald Beckwith *Collector* ■ *Dir/Scr* Val Guest

Runaway Car ★★ PG

Action comedy based on a true story 1997 · US · Colour · 90min

In this TV movie, Judge Reinhold delivers another study in bumbling ineptitude, playing a computer programmer trapped in the passenger seat – along with a skateboarder and a young baby – when goofy nurse Nina Siemaszko's accelerator gets stuck. Luckily, Leon (in the shape of a highway patrolman) is there to save the day. Although the tale is supposedly inspired by a true incident, it doesn't really add up. **SuR** DVD

Judge Reinhold *Ed Lauter* • Nina Siemaszko *Jenny Todd* • Brian Hooks *Dexter "Dex" Strang* • Leon *Isaiah Beaufort* • Paul Eiding • Glenn Morshower • Alec Murdock *Dr Mason* • *Scr* Paul F Edwards

Runaway Jury ★★★ 12

Courtroom thriller 2003 · US · Colour · 122min

A New Orleans woman files a suit against the gun industry (the tobacco conglomerates in John Grisham's original source novel) after her husband is murdered during a madman's shooting spree. Unfortunately for the widow and her idealistic lawyer Dustin Hoffman, the firearms lobby has hired ruthless "jury consultant" Gene Hackman to ensure the people chosen are predisposed to the "right" verdict. Into the mix comes John Cusack as a juror who is not at all what he seems. Well-crafted entertainment, despite the odd implausible plot point and simplistic central message. **JA** DVD Blu-ray

John Cusack *Nick Easter* • Gene Hackman *Rankin Fitch* • Dustin Hoffman *Wendall Rohr* • Rachel Weisz *Marlee* • Bruce Davison *Durwood Cable* • Bruce McGill *Judge Harkin* • Jeremy Piven *Lawrence Green* • Nick Searcy *Doyle* • Jennifer Beals *Vanessa Lembeck* ■ *Dir* Gary Fleder • *Scr* Brian Koppelman, David Levien, Rick Cleveland, Matthew Chapman, from the novel by John Grisham

Runaway Train ★★★★ 15

Action adventure 1985 · US · Colour · 106min

This is a fast-paced thriller based on a screenplay co-written by celebrated Japanese director Akira Kurosawa, which takes it a notch above the average action film. Escaping convicts Jon Voight and Eric Roberts have far more depth than your typical gung-ho hero – both landed Oscar nominations, as did Henry Richardson, whose dynamic editing gives Andrei Konchalovsky's superior direction the breakneck pace that will keep you on the edge of your seat. **DP** Swearing, violence. DVD Blu-ray

Jon Voight *Manny* • Eric Roberts *Buck* • Rebecca De Mornay *Sara* • Kyle T Heffner *Frank Barstow* • John P Ryan *Ranken* • TK Carter *Dave Prince* • Kenneth McMillan *Eddie MacDonald* ■ *Dir* Andrei Konchalovsky • *Scr* Djordje Milicevic, Paul Zindel, Edward Bunker, from a screenplay (unproduced) by Akira Kurosawa, Ryuzo Kikushima, Hideo Oguni

The Runaways ★★★ 15

Biographical music drama 2010 · US · Colour · 96min

Twilight's Kristen Stewart gets even moodier here as the teenage Joan Jett, lead guitarist for 1970s all-girl rock band the Runaways. Sex and drugs are, naturally, integral to this true tale, but it's anchored by the intense friendship between Jett and lead singer Cherie Currie (on whose book the film is based). It's a wild coming-out party for former child star Dakota Fanning, who plays Currie like a juvenile Madonna. As a sob story, this can feel too self-pitying, but the high-wattage pairing of Stewart and Fanning keeps it together. **SP** Swearing, sex scenes, drug abuse. DVD

Kristen Stewart *Joan Jett* • Dakota Fanning *Cherie Currie* • Scout Taylor-Compton *Lita Ford* • Alia Shawkat *Robin* • Tatum O'Neal *Cherie's mom* • Michael Shannon *Kim Fowley* ■ *Dir* Floria Sigismondi • *Scr* Floria Sigismondi

The Runner ★★★★ PG

Drama 1984 · Iran · Colour · 86min

Amir Naderi's film furthers the Iranian cinematic tradition of viewing the world through the eyes of disadvantaged children. Living alone in an abandoned boat in the port of Abadan, Majid Nirumand struggles to compete with the bigger lads in the scramble for redeemable bottles carried on the tide. While this neorealist study of post-revolutionary conditions could have been hopelessly pessimistic, Naderi invests it with startling exhilaration through the joyful thrill this waif derives from running. **DP** Farsi +subtitles.

Majid Nirumand *Amiro* • A Gholamzadeh *Uncle Gholam* • Musa Torkizadeh *Musa* • Reza Ramezani *Ramezan* ■ *Dir* Amir Naderi • *Scr* Amir Naderi, Behruz Gharibpur

The Runner ★★★ 15

Crime drama 1999 · US · Colour · 89min

Ron Eldard is the Las Vegas loser who becomes a runner for gangster John Goodman. Eldard places bets all over the neon city, falling in love with cocktail waitress Courteney Cox and buying her an engagement ring with Goodman's money. There are some fairly macabre twists in store and Goodman is superbly menacing as the man who has reduced everything to a matter of chance. Cox is alluring in a low-rent sort of way, but the weakness is Eldard who hasn't got the required charisma. **AT** DVD

Ron Eldard *Edward Harrington* • Courteney Cox *Karina* • Bokeem Woodbine *477* • John Goodman *Deep Throat* • Joe Mantegna *Rocco* • David Arquette *Bartender* ■ *Dir* Ron Moler • *Scr* Anthony E Zuiker

The Runner ★★ 15

Drama 2015 · US · Colour · 86min

The sausage machine that is Nicolas Cage cranks out another movie. It's no *Joe*, Cage's best in a bad run. But it is a decent drama of fall and redemption that spares us the supernatural schtick that Cage so often saddles himself with. He plays Pryce, a Louisiana congressman whose fight on behalf of claimants seeking compensation for the 2010 BP oil spill in the Gulf of Mexico is starting to earn him national notice. Given the emotive real-life backdrop, *The Runner* leaves one a little cold – it's only watchable rather than gripping. **DA** Swearing, sex scenes.

Nicolas Cage *Colin Pryce* • Sarah Paulson *Kate Haber* • Connie Nielsen *Deborah Pryce* • Peter Fonda *Rayne Pryce* • Wendell Pierce *Frank Legrand* ■ *Dir/Scr* Austin Stark

Runner Runner ★★ 15

Crime thriller 2013 · US · Colour · 87min

Justin Timberlake takes the lead in a thriller that's fast-moving but still manages to feel sluggish. He plays a maths whizz, who uses gambling to pay his way through college, and then lands a job with online mogul Ivan Block (Ben Affleck). What follows is a tired old story of a young achiever who gets in over his head in a reckless pursuit of cash. Affleck is on autopilot as the corrupt boss,

U SUITABLE FOR ALL   Uc SUITABLE ESPECIALLY FOR YOUNG CHILDREN (DVD ONLY)   PG PARENTAL GUIDANCE   12A UNDER 12s TO BE ACCOMPANIED (CINEMA ONLY)

R

while Gemma Arterton is treated like set dressing as the two men's love interest. Far from anyone walking away a winner, all the players here seem to have been dealt an empty hand. SP English, Spanish +subtitles. Violence, swearing, a sex scene. **DVD** **BL**

Justin Timberlake *Richie Furst* • Ben Affleck *Ivan Block* • Gemma Arterton *Rebecca Shafran* • Anthony Mackie *Agent Shavers* • Oliver Cooper *Andrew Cronin* ■ *Dir* Brad Furman • *Scr* Brian Koppelman, David Levien • *Cinematographer* Mauro Fiore

The Runner Stumbles ★
Drama   1979 · US · Colour · 88min

Stanley Kramer is Hollywood's big game hunter. He tracks down the weightiest issues of the day and turns them into corny melodramas. This one stars Dick Van Dyke, of all people, as a priest accused in the 1920s of killing a nun he lusted after. There is hardly a line, let alone a scene, that rings true as Kramer bludgeons us with a new moral dilemma every minute. AT

Dick Van Dyke *Father Rivard* • Kathleen Quinlan *Sister Rita* • Maureen Stapleton *Mrs Shandig* • Ray Bolger *Monsignor Nicholson* • Tammy Grimes *Erna* • Beau Bridges *Toby* ■ *Dir* Stanley Kramer • *Scr* Milan Stitt, from a play by Milan Stitt

Runners ★★★ 15
Drama   1983 · UK · Colour · 102min

With his teenage daughter on the missing list for two years, James Fox refuses to accept that she's dead and sets out on a journey to London to find her. He meets Jane Asher, the member of a support group who has lost her son, and his search turns from a contemporary social issue drama into a fully blown cryptic thriller. Idiosyncratically written by Stephen Poliakoff, directed with an accent on documentary realism by Charles Sturridge and well performed by the sympathetic Fox, this drama engages the attention. AJ

Kate Hardie *Rachel* • James Fox *Tom* • Jane Asher *Helen* • Eileen O'Brien *Gillian* • Ruti Simon *Lucy* • *Dir* Charles Sturridge • *Scr* Stephen Poliakoff

Running ★★ PG
Drama   1979 · Can · Colour · 101min

Michael Douglas is an unemployed father of two who tries to sort out all of his domestic problems by bidding to join the Olympic marathon team. Not really illustrative of Douglas's subsequent career, this is an obvious attempt to cash in on the running craze of the late 1970s, but fails to get off the starting blocks. NF **DVD**

Michael Douglas (1) *Michael Andropolis* • Susan Anspach *Janet Andropolis* • Lawrence Dane *Coach Walker* • Eugene Levy *Richard Rosenberg* • Charles Shamata *[Chuck Shamata] Howard Grant* ■ *Dir/Scr* Steven Hilliard Stern

Running Cool ★★ 18
Action drama   1993 · US · Colour · 101min

This uninspired low-budget movie tells the predictable story of a pair of bikers who get caught up in a battle against an evil property magnate (Paul Gleason). Andrew Divoff is the nominal star, while Dedee Pfeiffer pops up in a supporting role. It's written and directed by exploitation specialists Ferd and Beverly Sebastian. JF Violence, swearing, brief nudity.

Andrew Divoff *Bone* • Tracy Sebastian *Blue Hogg* • Dedee Pfeiffer *Michele* • Paul Gleason *Calvin Hogg* • Arlen Dean Snyder *Sheriff* ■ *Dir/Scr* Beverly Sebastian, Ferd Sebastian

Running Free ★★★ U
Period drama   1999 · US · Colour · 80min

This equine collaboration between producer Jean-Jacques Annaud, director Sergei Bodrov and the screenwriter of *The Black Stallion*, Jeanne Rosenberg, promised much. But the decision to employ Lukas Haas to articulate the thoughts of Lucky, the colt who survives copper mines, the Namibian wilderness and the rivalry of an older horse to lead his herd to safety at the height of the First World War, doesn't work.

A shame, as the cast, animals and scenery are first-rate. DP **DVD**

Chase Moore *Young Richard* • Jan Decleir *Boss Man* • Arie Verveen *Adult Richard* • Maria Geelbooi *Nyka* • Lukas Haas *Narrator (Lucky)* • *Dir* Sergei Bodrov • *Scr* Jeanne Rosenberg, from a story by Jeanne Rosenberg, Jean-Jacques Annaud

The Running, Jumping and Standing Still Film ★★★ U
Silent comedy   1959 · UK · Sepia · 11min

Having worked with ex-Goons Peter Sellers and Spike Milligan on three TV series, Richard Lester was the perfect choice to direct this anarchic short, which marked his cinematic debut. Shot in two days for just £700, using Sellers's new 16mm camera, it boasts such bizarre images as a field receiving a good scrubbing, a man playing a record on a tree stump and Graham Stark getting carried away by his kite before being punched on the nose by Leo McKern wearing a single boxing glove. Nominated for an Oscar, it lost out to Jacques-Yves Cousteau's *The Golden Fish*. DP **DVD**

Peter Sellers • Spike Milligan • Leo McKern • Graham Stark • Mario Fabrizi • David Lodge • Bruce Lacey ■ *Dir* Dick Lester [Richard Lester] • *Scr* Peter Sellers, Spike Milligan, Mario Fabrizi, Dick Lester [Richard Lester]

The Running Man ★★★★
Crime drama   1963 · UK · Colour · 108min

This is one of those cinematic sleights of hand that only exceptional film-makers can hope to pull off. Armed with a clever script by John Mortimer (of Rumpole fame), director Carol Reed turns a thoroughly run-of-the-mill potboiler into a hugely entertaining three-handed thriller thanks to his unerring ability to conjure up atmosphere, the striking photography of Robert Krasker and the canny performances of his splendid cast. Laurence Harvey is gleefully extravagant as a cocky conman, Alan Bates doggedly decent as the insurance assessor on his trail, and Lee Remick beguiling as the "widow" caught between them. DP

Laurence Harvey *Rex Black* • Lee Remick *Stella Black* • Alan Bates *Stephen Maddox* • Felix Aylmer *Parson* • Eleanor Summerfield *Hilda Tanner* • Allan Cuthbertson *Jenkins* • Harold Goldblatt *Tom Webster* ■ *Dir* Carol Reed • *Scr* John Mortimer, from the novel *The Ballad of the Running Man* by Shelley Smith

The Running Man ★★★ 18
Science-fiction action thriller   1987 · US · Colour · 96min

Given TV's increasingly desperate search for new programme formats, this futuristic blockbuster about a game show where a pumped-up audience bays for the blood of convicts on a lethal combat course isn't so far-fetched. Arnold Schwarzenegger is the former police helicopter pilot who is forced into the game of death when he rebels against his totalitarian superiors. Schwarzenegger gets to do what he does best - destroying baddies with a quip - and director Paul Michael Glaser handles the action sequences with panache. JF Swearing, violence. **DVD**

Arnold Schwarzenegger *Ben Richards* • Maria Conchita Alonso *Amber Mendez* • Yaphet Kotto *Laughlin* • Jim Brown *Fireball* • Jesse Ventura *Captain Freedom* • Erland Van Lidth *Dynamo* • Marvin J McIntyre *Weiss* • Gus Rethwisch *Buzzsaw* • Richard Dawson *Damon Killian* ■ *Dir* Paul Michael Glaser • *Scr* Steven E DeSouza, from the novel *The Running Man* by Richard Bachman [Stephen King]

Running on Empty ★★★★ 15
Drama   1988 · US · Colour · 111min

This interesting twist on the effect the 1960s really had on America is also a sad reminder of the late River Phoenix's talents as an actor. He plays Danny, a teenager who leads an unusual life - he and his parents (Judd Hirsch and Christine Lahti) have been on the run from the FBI for 17 years since the couple bombed a university research centre, blinding a janitor in the blast. But now Phoenix wants a more

settled existence, and the film focuses on the family's attempts to keep together. Director Sidney Lumet keeps the drama subtle instead of dissolving into mush. JB Swearing, drug abuse. **DVD**

Christine Lahti *Annie Pope* • River Phoenix *Danny Pope* • Judd Hirsch *Arthur Pope* • Martha Plimpton *Lorna Phillips* • Jonas Abry *Harry Pope* • Ed Crowley *Mr Phillips* • LM Kit Carson *Gus Winant* ■ *Dir* Sidney Lumet • *Scr* Naomi Foner

Running Out of Luck ★ 18
Music drama   1985 · UK · Colour · 86min

An obscure musical drama, directed by Julien Temple and made to accompany a Mick Jagger album, it's basically a feature-length music video with a bizarre plot filling in the gaps between songs. It begins with Jagger, partner Jerry Hall and Dennis Hopper filming a music video in Rio, but the shoot breaks up and somehow Jagger finds himself being beaten up by transvestites and forced into sex slavery on a banana plantation with Rae Dawn Chong. It may sound intriguing, but it's not. DA

Mick Jagger • Jerry Hall • Dennis Hopper *Video director* • Rae Dawn Chong *Slave girl* • Jim Broadbent ■ *Dir* Julien Temple • *Scr* Julien Temple, Mick Jagger

Running Scared ★★★ 15
Action comedy thriller   1986 · US · Colour · 102min

This enjoyable buddy-buddy cop thriller was comic Billy Crystal's breakthrough movie. Both he and Gregory Hines play streetwise Chicago cops, firing wisecracks like bullets, who've decided to retire to Florida. The only problem is they have to work out a month's notice and underworld boss Jimmy Smits is determined to rub them out. Hines and Crystal make an endearing screen partnership although their stream of funny one-liners and the set piece spectacles director Peter Hyams is noted for sit uneasily with the gritty look of the production. RS Violence, swearing, nudity. **DVD**

Billy Crystal *Danny Costanzo* • Gregory Hines *Ray Hughes* • Steve Bauer [Steven Bauer] *Frank* • Darlanne Fluegel *Anna Costanzo* • Joe Pantoliano *Snake* • Dan Hedaya *Capt Logan* • Jimmy Smits *Julio Gonzales* ■ *Dir* Peter Hyams • *Scr* Gary DeVore, Jimmy Huston, from a story by Gary DeVore

Running Scared ★★ 18
Crime thriller   2005 · US · Colour · 116min

Brutally violent, over-stylised to distraction and overdone to a laughable degree, director Wayne Kramer's follow-up to *The Cooler* is an unrelenting and intensely off-putting journey through urban moral depravity. Low-level gangster Paul Walker has been ordered by his bosses to dispose of a gun that was used to kill a dirty cop. But when his son's best friend (Cameron Bright) steals it to shoot his abusive stepfather and then goes on the run, Walker has just one night to retrieve the weapon. AJ Violence, swearing. **DVD**

Paul Walker *Joey Gazelle* • Cameron Bright *Oleg Yugorsky* • Alex Neuberger *Nicky Gazelle* • Vera Farmiga *Teresa Gazelle* • Johnny Messner *Tommy "Tombs" Perello* • Michael Cudlitz *Sal "Gummy Bear" Franzone* • Chazz Palminteri *Detective Rydell* ■ *Dir/Scr* Wayne Kramer

Running Wild ★★★ U
Drama   1973 · US · Colour · 96min

Set in charming and beautiful scenery, this pleasant family drama concerns a news photographer whose horror at the treatment of wild mustangs inspires an exposé. Classy Dina Merrill makes a welcome big-screen return in the pivotal leading role, while gritty veterans Lloyd Bridges, Gilbert Roland, and RG Armstrong give her staunch company. This is a strong and intelligently written piece with its heart in the right place. TS

Lloyd Bridges *Jeff Methune* • Dina Merrill *Whit Colby* • Pat Hingle *Quentin Hogue* • Morgan Woodward *Crug Crider* • Gilbert Roland *Chief Tomacito* • Fred Betts *Cap Methune* • RG Armstrong *Bull* ■ *Dir/Scr* Robert McCahon

Running Wild ★★
Drama documentary   1992 · US · Colour · 98min

Having dedicated 12 years of his life to making a wildlife documentary about an endangered female cat on the Londolozi game reserve, it seems odd that African naturalist and film-maker John Varty should choose to add a fictional element to its sequel. Viewers will be far more interested in the fate of her orphaned cubs, than in the Tinseltown subplot involving producer Martin Sheen, film-maker Brooke Shields and her obstructive colleague David Keith. Unfortunately for the actors, the focus on the leopards makes the movie business seem all the more redundant. DP

Brooke Shields *Christine Shaye* • Martin Sheen *Dan Walker* • David Keith *Jack Hutton* • Renée Estevez *Aimee* • John Varty ■ *Dir* Duncan McLachlan • *Scr* Duncan McLachlan, Andrea Buck, John Varty

Running with Scissors ★★★ 15
Biographical black comedy drama   2006 · US · Colour · 116min

This mordantly amusing tale of family dysfunction from the creator of TV's *Nip/Tuck* is so outrageous that it's hard to believe it's based on a real-life memoir. Charting the 1970s upbringing of US writer Augusten Burroughs (who appears as himself in the closing titles), the highly stylised movie is a patchwork of his formative childhood experiences, held together by juicily idiosyncratic performances. Joseph Cross is sweetly engaging as the adolescent Augusten, who struggles with identity issues after his wannabe-poet mother (Annette Bening) sends him to live with her madcap psychiatrist (Brian Cox). It's only in the downbeat final third that the narrative's overall lack of structure becomes apparent, though fortunately the dialogue retains its enjoyable sharpness amid the gloom. SF **DVD**

Annette Bening *Deirdre Burroughs* • Brian Cox (1) *Dr Finch* • Joseph Fiennes *Neil Bookman* • Evan Rachel Wood *Natalie Finch* • Alec Baldwin *Norman Burroughs* • Joseph Cross *Augusten Burroughs* • Jill Clayburgh *Agnes Finch* • Gwyneth Paltrow *Hope Finch* ■ *Dir* Ryan Murphy • *Scr* Ryan Murphy, from the autobiography *Running with Scissors: A Memoir* by Augusten Burroughs

La Rupture ★★★★ 18
Thriller   1970 · Fr/It/Bel · Colour · 119min

Part of Claude Chabrol's absorbing "Hélène cycle" of films, featuring his wife, the seductive Stéphane Audran, this is another of the director's attacks on the bourgeois family. Here, Audran is less scheming than usual as a woman fighting to gain custody of her child from her drug addict husband and nasty father-in-law. Chabrol's terse and suspenseful style works to great advantage in this neat thriller. The excellent cast includes Jean-Pierre Cassel as a seedy detective and, as the father-in-law, Chabrol favourite Michel Bouquet. RB French +subtitles. **DVD**

Jean-Pierre Cassel *Paul* • Stéphane Audran *Hélène* • Annie Cordy *Mme Pinelli* • Michel Bouquet *Ludovic Regnier* ■ *Dir* Claude Chabrol • *Scr* Claude Chabrol, from the novel *The Balloon Man* by Charlotte Armstrong

Rush ★★★ 18
Thriller   1991 · US · Colour · 115min

It's rare these days to hear Eric Clapton music that smacks of commitment. And yet it's his sensitive soundtrack that contributes to the intensity of a movie that successfully captures the unnerving world of the drug addict. Debut director Lili Fini Zanuck sustains the right air of stifling claustrophobia, while Jennifer Jason Leigh and Jason Patric, as two narcotics cops who get hooked, go on their downward spiral with a great deal of force. JM Violence, swearing, drug abuse. **DVD**

Jason Patric *Jim Raynor* • Jennifer Jason Leigh *Kristen Cates* • Sam Elliott *Larry Dodd* • Max Perlich *Walker* • Gregg Allman *William Gaines* •

Tony Frank *Police Chief Nettle* • William Sadler *Monroe* ■ *Dir* Lili Fini Zanuck • *Scr* Pete Dexter, from the book by Kim Wozencraft

Rush ★★★★ 15
Motor racing drama based on a true story
2013 · US/Ger/UK · Colour · 117min

There's a real Cavalier-versus- Roundhead thrust to Ron Howard's zippy biopic about the rivalry between two 1970s Formula 1 drivers, ladies' man and boozer James Hunt (Chris Hemsworth) and nerdy bucktoothed tactician Niki Lauda (Daniel Brühl). The film's dramatic pivot is the 1976 German Grand Prix, when Lauda's car crashed and burned, forcing a three-race lay-off while he was brought back from the dead and allowing Hunt his shot at the World Championship. Howard captures the characters of the two drivers, helped by near-perfect performances, while Peter Morgan's screenplay is faithful to the facts but doesn't get bogged down in the technical minutiae or sentimentality of the story. Thoughtful and informative, this doesn't forget to be thrilling. **SvM** English, German, Italian +subtitles. Violence, swearing, sex scenes, nudity. **DVD** **BD**

Daniel Brühl *Niki Lauda* • Chris Hemsworth *James Hunt* • Olivia Wilde *Suzy Miller* • Alexandra Maria Lara *Marlene Lauda* • Pierfrancesco Favino *Clay Regazzoni* • Christian McKay *Alexander Hesketh* • Alistair Petrie *Stirling Moss* ■ *Dir* Ron Howard • *Scr* Peter Morgan (1)

Rush: Beyond the Lighted Stage ★★★ 15
Music documentary 2010 · Can · Colour · 107min

With album sales of over 40 million, Rush can be counted alongside the Beatles and the Rolling Stones as one of the most successful bands on the planet. Yet the Canadian trio remains essentially a cult band. Directors Scot McFadyen and Sam Dunn vow to find out why in this standard issue rockumentary, but they quickly get distracted by the engaging personalities of the band's members, whose friendship fascinates more than their ever-changing brand of progressive rock. The survey of their 40-year career, from high-school strummers to stadium superstars, is dotted with testimonies from fans like Gene Simmons (of Kiss) and Jack Black. **DP** Swearing.

Geddy Lee • Alex Lifeson • Neil Peart • Gene Simmons • Jack Black • Trent Reznor ■ *Dir* Sam Dunn, Scot McFadyen

Rush Hour ★★★★ 12
Martial arts action comedy
1998 · US · Colour · 93min

Hong Kong action superstar Jackie Chan teams up with loudmouth American comedian Chris Tucker for this blockbuster thriller. It's essentially an east-meets-west buddy movie about two cops trying to solve an international kidnapping, but director Brett Ratner allows plenty of time for character development between the spectacular set pieces, and Chan and Tucker's inspired double act elevates it above the norm. Equally adept at comic martial arts, Chaplinesque displays and near-superhuman stunts, Chan has never been more engaging. **AJ** Swearing, violence, drug abuse. **DVD** **BD**

Jackie Chan *Detective Inspector Lee* • Chris Tucker *Detective James Carter* • Tom Wilkinson *Griffin/Juntao* • Chris Penn *Clive* • Elizabeth Peña *Tania Johnson* • Rex Linn *Agent Whitney* • Philip Baker Hall *Captain Diel* ■ *Dir* Brett Ratner • *Scr* Ross LaManna, Jim Kouf, from a story by Ross LaManna

Rush Hour 2 ★★★ 12
Martial arts action comedy
2001 · US · Colour · 86min

Pint-sized action star Jackie Chan reteams with motormouth Chris Tucker for this sequel. It's the same hit formula, only this time the two chalk-and-cheese cops find themselves in Hong Kong battling a murderous Triad gang, but with the added spice that head man John Lone was involved in the death of Jackie's dad. There's also the opportunity to see

Crouching Tiger, Hidden Dragon star Zhang Ziyi make her American debut as Lone's beautiful but deadly henchwoman. **DA** Violence, swearing. **DVD** **BD**

Jackie Chan *Detective James Carter* • Chris Tucker *Detective James Carter* • John Lone *Ricky Tan* • Zhang Ziyi *Hu Li* • Roselyn Sanchez *Agent Isabella Molina* • Alan King *Steven Reign* ■ *Dir* Brett Ratner • *Scr* Jeff Nathanson, from characters by Ross LaManna

Rush Hour 3 ★★ 12
Martial arts action comedy
2007 · US · Colour · 87min

Jackie Chan and Chris Tucker reprise their comic martial arts partnership in this under-par second sequel. Dispatched to Paris in search of Triad gangs, the mismatched cops find themselves surrounded by crass French stereotypes and unlikely supporting turns from Max von Sydow and Roman Polanski. Lumbered with a script that's not half as witty as its predecessors, director Brett Ratner unsuccessfully tries to distract us from the lulls with a Parisian car chase, scantily clad showgirls and the world's tallest martial artist. As ever, Tucker's rat-a-tat quips are great fun, but the end-credit out-takes prove what many will have already suspected - this was more amusing to make than it is to watch. **JR** English, Cantonese +subtitles. Violence, swearing, nudity. **DVD** **BD**

Jackie Chan *Chief Inspector Lee* • Chris Tucker *Detective James Carter* • Max von Sydow *Varden Reynard* • Yvan Attal *George* • Vinnie Jones • Noémie Lenoir *Genevieve* • Roman Polanski *Detective Jacques Revi* ■ *Dir* Brett Ratner • *Scr* Jeff Nathanson, from characters by Ross LaManna

Rush to Judgment ★★★
Documentary 1967 · US · BW · 98min

This more thought-provoking than polemical documentary about the assassination of John F Kennedy and its aftermath, is not only of interest to conspiracy buffs. Using witness interviews and footage, the Warren Commission's lone assassin conclusions are challenged and the conspiracy theory of Mark Lane's landmark article is presented. Director Emile de Antonio made several interesting documentaries on aspects of American politics. **JG**

Mark Lane (1) *Narrator* ■ *Dir* Emile de Antonio • *Scr* Mark Lane, from his article *Rush to Judgement: a Critique of the Warren Commission Inquiry into the Murder of President John F Kennedy, Officer JD Tippit and Lee Harvey Oswald*

Rushmore ★★★★ 15
Black comedy drama 1998 · US · Colour · 89min

Director Wes Anderson and his co-writer Owen Wilson - who first caught the eye with their low-budget debut *Bottle Rocket* - score again with this unusual black comedy, which centres around an extremely unconventional teen hero. Jason Schwartzman plays one of the least popular pupils at Rushmore Academy, who nonetheless runs just about every club and school activity in a megalomaniacal effort to further himself. Schwartzman gives a superbly nerdy performance, but Bill Murray - playing a depressed millionaire - steals every scene in this quirky, edgy and very funny tale of an outsider who just might end up leading all those who laugh at him. **JB** Swearing. **DVD**

Jason Schwartzman *Max Fischer* • Bill Murray *Herman Blume* • Olivia Williams *Rosemary Cross* • Brian Cox (1) *Dr Guggenheim* • Seymour Cassel *Bert Fischer* • Mason Gamble *Dirk Calloway* • Owen Wilson *Edward Applebee* ■ *Dir* Wes Anderson • *Scr* Wes Anderson, Owen Wilson

The Russia House ★★★★ 15
Spy drama 1990 · US · Colour · 117min

Adapted from Tom Stoppard from John le Carré's novel, this espionage thriller is a class act in every respect, not least in its clever use of authentic Russian locations. Sean Connery is a tweedy, irascible British publisher and reluctant spy who goes to Russia to check out the truth behind a potentially explosive manuscript. Michelle

Pfeiffer is his contact and her moving performance is simply astonishing, with a wholly convincing accent that never comes across as studied. It's a tense, often puzzling picture, subtly directed by Fred Schepisi and with a great supporting cast. **AT** Swearing. **DVD**

Sean Connery *Barley Blair* • Michelle Pfeiffer *Katya* • Roy Scheider *Russell* • James Fox *Ned* • John Mahoney *Brady* • Klaus Maria Brandauer *Savelev/"Dante"* • Ken Russell *Walter* • JT Walsh *Quinn* • Michael Kitchen *Clive* • David Threlfall *Wicklow* • Martin Clunes *Brock* • Ian McNeice *Merrydew* ■ *Dir* Fred Schepisi • *Scr* Tom Stoppard, from the novel by John le Carré

Russian Ark ★★★★★ U
Experimental drama
2002 · Rus/Ger/Jpn/Can/Fin/Den · Colour · 95min

This compelling compendium of historical incident and cultural ideas will thrill anyone with a passion for film. The manner in which director Aleksandr Sokurov has choreographed Tilman Büttner's single-take Steadicam waltz around St Petersburg's Hermitage Museum is pure cinematic poetry. This ingenuity is matched by the variety of rhythms the action accomplishes, as the HDV camera hurries between rooms or mingles with revellers at a court ball, pauses to consider the symbolism of a Van Dyck painting or observe the cosy domesticity of Tsar Nicholas II taking tea with his family. A masterclass in content and form. **DP** Russian +subtitles. **DVD**

Sergei Dreiden [Sergei Dontsov] *Marquis de Custine, the stranger* • Maria Kuznetsova *Catherine the Great* • Leonid Mozgovoy *Spy* • David Giorgobiani *Orbeli* • Alexander Chaban *Boris Piotrovsky* • Maxim Sergeyev *Peter the Great* ■ *Dir* Aleksandr Sokurov • *Scr* Anatoly Nikiforov, Aleksandr Sokurov, Boris Khaimsky, Svetlana Proskurina

Russian Dolls ★★★ 15
Romantic comedy
2005 · Fr/UK · Colour · 129min

This sequel to *Pot Luck* reunites much of the original multinational cast for this pleasing, if slight, Euro concoction. Set five years on from the first film, this finds the inhabitants of the shared apartment reuniting for the unlikely St Petersburg wedding of Kevin Bishop to a Russian ballerina. However, most of the story is told in flashback and focuses on the complicated relationships of would-be writer Romain Duris with ex-girlfriend Audrey Tautou, his old flatmate Kelly Reilly and supermodel Lucy Gordon. **JF** French, English, Russian +subtitles. Swearing, drug abuse, sex scenes.

Romain Duris *Xavier* • Kelly Reilly *Wendy* • Audrey Tautou *Martine* • Cécile de France *Isabelle Wauquaire* • Kevin Bishop *William* • Evguenya Obraztsova *Natalia nicknamed Natacha* • Irene Montalà *Neus* • Gary Love *Edward* • Lucy Gordon *Celia Shelton* ■ *Dir/Scr* Cédric Klapisch

The Russian Woodpecker ★★★
Documentary 2015 · US/Ukr · Colour · 80min

A corking conspiracy lies at the heart of Chad Gracia's debut documentary. According to Ukrainian artist Fedor Alexandrovich, the 1986 Chernobyl disaster was caused by a Kremlin bureaucrat hoping that a meltdown at the nuclear plant would distract from the fact that the nearby Duga radar system had been a colossal failure. From the conversations Alexandrovich has with Soviet loyalists, something decidedly dodgy was going on. But, while he never quite makes his case, Alexandrovich does reveal the extent to which the accident has shaped both his psyche and his art, while also leaving traces of strontium in his body. **DP** In English, Russian.

■ *Dir/Scr* Chad Gracia

The Russians Are Coming, the Russians Are Coming ★★★★ U
Comedy 1966 · US · Colour · 120min

Norman Jewison's comedy - an Oscar nominee for best picture - now seems

funnier than ever and survives, along with Stanley Kubrick's *Dr Strangelove*, as a key artefact of the Cold War era. The story is simple: Russian Alan Arkin grounds his submarine on the American coast, goes ashore for help and panic ensues. It's a little long and there's some rather sticky moralising as well, but these are minor flaws when set beside the general level of comic invention. **AT** **DVD**

Carl Reiner *Walt Whittaker* • Eva Marie Saint *Elspeth Whittaker* • Alan Arkin *Rozanov* • Brian Keith *Link Mattocks* • Jonathan Winters *Norman Jonas* • Theodore Bikel *Russian captain* • Paul Ford *Fendall Hawkins* ■ *Dir* Norman Jewison • *Scr* William Rose, from the novel *The Off-Islanders* by Nathaniel Benchley

Russkies ★★ PG
Comedy drama 1987 · US · Colour · 94min

Back in the days when he was still known as Leaf, Joaquin Phoenix plays a Florida youngster whose gang stumbles across stranded Russian sailor Whip Hubley and decides to shelter him from the authorities. Predictable grown-up interference and adolescent heroism become increasingly contrived and saccharine as this well-intentioned but clunky rite-of-passage picture proceeds. **DP** Violence, swearing. **DVD**

Whip Hubley *Mischa* • Leaf Phoenix [Joaquin Phoenix] *Danny* • Peter Billingsley *Adam* • Stefan DeSalle *Jason* • Susan Walters *Diane* • Patrick Kilpatrick *Raimy* • Vic Polizos *Sulock* • Summer Phoenix *Candi* ■ *Dir* Rick Rosenthal • *Scr* Michael Nankin, Alan Jay Glueckman, Sheldon Lettich, from a story by Alan Jay Glueckman, Sheldon Lettich

Rust and Bone ★★★ 15
Romantic drama 2012 · Fr/Bel · Colour · 117min

Writer/director Jacques Audiard's next film after award-winning prison parable *A Prophet* re-examines themes of love and disability from his 2001 drama *Read My Lips*. Stephanie (Marion Cotillard) is invalided into social exile after a terrifyingly staged accident at the marine park where she trains killer whales and finds herself indebted and gradually attracted to Ali, a bare-knuckle fighter and reluctant single father. Shot in often blinding natural sunlight and hyper-real close-up, the film powerfully fixates on the fallibility of flesh, exposed in frank sex, rolling surf and backstreet violence, and in Cotillard's ingeniously portrayed broken body. But two powerful performances and an excruciatingly detailed vision cannot atone for the disappointingly conventional third act. **AC** In French. **DVD** **BD**

Marion Cotillard *Stéphanie* • Matthias Schoenaerts *Ali* • Armand Verdure *Sam* • Céline Sallette *Louise* ■ *Dir* Jacques Audiard • *Scr* Jacques Audiard, Thomas Bidegain, from the short story *De Rouille et d'Os* by Craig Davidson

Rustler's Rhapsody ★★★ PG
Western spoof 1985 · US · Colour · 84min

In a fun spoof of the popular "singing cowboy" films of the 1930s, 1940s and 1950s, Tom Berenger plays the cowboy crooner, and has the hunky good looks to carry it off. The parody suffers, though, from the fact that the singing cowboy genre never took itself too seriously in the first place, and that anyone under 50 will have probably never seen one. **DA**

Tom Berenger *Rex O'Herlihan* • Marilu Henner *Miss Tracy* • GW Bailey *Peter* • Fernando Rey *Railroad colonel* • Andy Griffith *Colonel Ticonderoga* ■ *Dir/Scr* Hugh Wilson

Ruth & Alex ★★ 12
Drama 2014 · US · Colour · 88min

In this drama of 70-something lifestyle dilemmas and the New York property market, elderly couple Morgan Freeman and Diane Keaton contemplate selling the Brooklyn apartment they've lived in for over 40 years. As the film's original US title - 5 Flights Up - suggests, the stairs may soon get too much for them, but without any clear idea where to go next, an ailing beloved mongrel to contend with and the pull of some many memories, they're in a quandary. Typically amenable performances from the leads make all this watchable up to a point, but the material is decidedly stretched out over feature length. TJ Some swearing. *DVD*

Morgan Freeman *Alex Carver* • Diane Keaton *Ruth* • Cynthia Nixon *Niece* • Claire van der Boom *Young Ruth* • Korey Jackson *Young Alex* • Carrie Preston *Miriam Carswell* ■ *Dir* Richard Loncraine • *Scr* Charlie Peters, from the novel *5 Flights Up* by Jill Ciment

Ruthless ★★★ PG
Drama 1948 · US · BW · 100min

This splendid chunk of Hollywood B-movie tosh stars Zachary Scott as the man who ruins everyone in his path. Dames he two-times, men he just destroys. Better enjoyed as cheap junk than taken seriously, it was directed by cult maestro Edgar G Ulmer, a man who knew how to stretch a budget and a schedule. The screenplay is somewhat clumsy, but the cast here is better than expected. TS *DVD*

Zachary Scott *Horace Woodruff Vendig* • Louis Hayward *Vic Lambdin* • Diana Lynn *Martha Burnside/Mallory Flagg* • Sydney Greenstreet *Buck Mansfield* • Lucille Bremer *Christa Mansfield* • Martha Vickers *Susan Dunne* • Raymond Burr *Peter Vendig* ■ *Dir* Edgar G Ulmer • *Scr* Alvah Bessie (uncredited), SK Lauren, Gordon Kahn, from the novel *Prelude to Night* by Dayton Stoddart

Ruthless People ★★★★ 15
Comedy 1986 · US · Colour · 90min

Airplane! partners Jim Abrahams, Jerry Zucker and David Zucker teamed up again for this fun comedy about a pair of bumbling kidnappers - Helen Slater and Judge Reinhold - who snatch wealthy Bette Midler, to discover that her husband Danny DeVito doesn't want her back. The movie twists and turns as a whole host of other people get involved. DeVito and Midler are superb in their roles as the greedy philanderer and his overbearing other half. JB Swearing, nudity. *DVD*

Danny DeVito *Sam Stone* • Bette Midler *Barbara Stone* • Judge Reinhold *Ken Kessler* • Helen Slater *Sandy Kessler* • Anita Morris *Carol* • Bill Pullman *Earl* • William G Schilling *Police commissioner* • Art Evans *Lieutenant Bender* • Clarence Felder *Lieutenant Walters* ■ *Dir* Jim Abrahams, David Zucker, Jerry Zucker • *Scr* Dale Launer

The Rutles – All You Need Is Cash ★★★★ 15
Spoof music documentary
1978 · UK/US · Colour · 70min

The career of this mop-topped Liverpudlian band echoes that of a rather more famous quartet, in a witty documentary parody of the Fab Four's career. The brainchild of stars Eric Idle (who writes, co-directs and narrates) and Neil Innes (responsible for music, lyrics and a killer John Lennon impersonation), this cleverly incorporates multiple film stocks and varied musical re-creations to send-up the iconic rise of the Beatles. There's inspired fake newsreel footage, interviews with both invented and real celebrities, elaborate movie clips and brilliantly imitated live performances, using Innes's spot-on pastiches of classic tracks. JC *DVD*

Eric Idle *Dirk McQuickley/Narrator/Stanley Krammerhead III Jr* • Neil Innes *Ron Nasty* • John Halsey *Barry Wom* • Ricky Fataar *Stig O'Hara* • Michael Palin *Eric Manchester* • Bianca Jagger *Martini McQuickley* • George Harrison *The interviewer* • John Belushi *Ron Decline* ■ *Dir* Eric Idle, Gary Weis • *Scr* Eric Idle

Ryan's Daughter ★★★★★ 15
Romantic epic 1970 · UK · Colour · 186min

Released five years after *Doctor Zhivago*, this romantic epic from David Lean was not so much roasted by the critics as incinerated. The story of a dreamy girl who marries a stolid village teacher and then has an affair with a shell-shocked British officer, it began as a script from Flaubert's *Madame Bovary* that Robert Bolt had written for his wife, Sarah Miles. Set in a bleak Irish village in 1916, it co-stars a courageously cast Robert Mitchum as the teacher. Stories

about the year-long making of the picture have duly entered movie legend; as an overblown romance it has no equal and now looks like a masterwork. Freddie Young's Oscar-winning images of the wild Dingle Peninsula need to be seen on the big screen. AT A sex scene, brief nudity. *DVD*

Robert Mitchum *Charles Shaughnessy* • Sarah Miles *Rosy* • Trevor Howard *Father Collins* • John Mills *Michael* • Christopher Jones *Major Randolph Doryan* • Leo McKern *Thomas Ryan* • Barry Foster *Tim O'Leary* • Arthur O'Sullivan *Mr McCardle* • Marie Kean *Mrs McCardle* • Evin Crowley *Moureen* ■ *Dir* David Lean • *Scr* Robert Bolt • *Music* Maurice Jarre

SFW ★★★ 18
Satirical drama 1994 · US · Colour · 95min

It's beginning to show its age, but this satirical drama remains a topical dissection of the American fascination with the cult of the non-celebrity. Stephen Dorff is the angry young man who is among a group taken hostage by camcorder-wielding anarchists. They force the networks to broadcast their tapes, but it's the rebellious Dorff who soon becomes the star attraction, making him, unwillingly, the hottest thing on TV. There's good support from a pre-fame Reese Witherspoon and Jake Busey. JF Violence, swearing, nudity. *DVD*

Stephen Dorff *Cliff Spab* • Reese Witherspoon *Wendy Pfister* • Jake Busey *Morrow Streeter* • Joey Lauren Adams *Monica Dice* • Pamela Gidley *Janet Streeter* ■ *Dir* Jefery Levy • *Scr* Jefery Levy, Danny Rubin, from the novel by Andrew Wellman

SLC Punk! ★★★ 15
Comedy drama 1999 · US · Colour · 97min

As Salt Lake's only hard-core punks, Matthew Lillard and Michael Goorjian have a go at rednecks, posing cultists and the all-pervading influence of Mormonism. How can you be an anarchist, though, when you have good grades, ambitious parents and a social conscience? The stomping soundtrack and some archly designed threads can't forestall the inevitable triumph of conventionality. DP Swearing, violence, drug abuse.

Matthew Lillard *Stevo* • Michael Goorjian *Bob* • Annabeth Gish *Trish* • Jennifer Lien *Sandy* • Christopher McDonald *Father* • Devon Sawa *Sean* • Jason Segel *Mike* • Summer Phoenix *Brandy* ■ *Dir/Scr* James Merendino

SOB ★★★
Comedy 1981 · US · Colour · 121min

This attack on Hollywood values is one of the crudest satires ever made at the expense of Tinseltown, as Richard Mulligan, playing a director, decides to turn his art-movie stinker into a soft-porn success, with screen-wife Julie Andrews in the leading role. As the showbiz in-fighting gets worse, it's obvious that Blake Edwards is paying off old, rancorous scores, but such personal venom slows down the pace and the point. TH Swearing, nudity.

Julie Andrews *Sally Miles* • William Holden (2) *Tim Culley* • Richard Mulligan *Felix Farmer* • Larry Hagman *Dick Benson* • Robert Loggia *Herb Maskowitz* • Stuart Margolin *Gary Murdock* • Marisa Berenson *Mavis* • Robert Preston *Dr Irving Finegarten* • Craig Stevens *Willard Gaylin* • Loretta Swit *Polly Reed* • Robert Vaughn (1) *David Blackman* • Robert Webber *Ben Coogan* • Shelley Winters *Eva Brown* • Jennifer Edwards *Lila* • Rosanna Arquette *Babs* ■ *Dir/Scr* Blake Edwards

SOS Pacific ★★★ PG
Action drama 1959 · UK · BW · 87min

The secret of a good disaster movie is to ensure that the victims hardly have chance to draw breath after one crisis, before another follows hot on its heels. In this Rank adventure, a plane crash-lands on an island, only for the survivors to discover that it is the site for an imminent atomic test. Director Guy Green sustains the suspense well, helped in no small measure by a solid ensemble cast. DP

Eddie Constantine *Mark Reisener* • Pier Angeli *Teresa* • Richard Attenborough *Whitey* • John Gregson *Jack Bennett* • Eva Bartok *Maria* • Jean Anderson *Miss Shaw* ■ *Dir* Guy Green • *Scr* Robert Westerby, from a story by Gilbert Travers

SOS Titanic ★★ PG
Historical disaster drama
1979 · US · Colour · 97min

Originally made for American TV, but released in cinemas in the UK, this detailed account of the famous shipping disaster combines fact and fiction as uneasily as it mixes its Anglo-American cast. Director William Hale's grip on the drama is tenuous, and the result is rather low key and cheap looking. Still, Helen Mirren, Ian Holm, Harry Andrews, David Warner, David Janssen and Susan Saint James suffer nobly. TS *DVD*

David Janssen *John Jacob Astor* • Cloris Leachman *Molly Brown* • Susan Saint James *Leigh Goodwin* • David Warner *Laurence Beesley* • Ian Holm *J Bruce Ismay* • Helen Mirren *May Sloan* • Harry Andrews *Captain Edward J Smith* • Beverly Ross *Madeline Astor* • Ed Bishop *Henry Harris* ■ *Dir* William Hale • *Scr* James Costigan

S21: the Khmer Rouge Killing Machine ★★★
Documentary 2003 · Fr · Colour · 101min

Cambodian artist Vann Nath was one of only three of the 17,000 prisoners detained at the notorious Tuol Sleng interrogation centre to survive their ordeal. The pain is evident in his work. But his courage remains undiminished, as he returns to the former school buildings to confront the Khmer Rouge guards who carried out Pol Pot's hideous policy of genocide. The re-enactment of the daily routines and the inspection of the jail's ghoulishly detailed records are chilling. But director Rithy Panh's unflinching focus may feel a little narrow to those unfamiliar with the historical background to the Killing Fields. DP Khmer +subtitles.

■ *Dir* Rithy Panh

Saadia ★★ U
Drama 1953 · US · Colour · 87min

Albert Lewin was assistant to Irving Thalberg during the great years of MGM. A former critic for the *Jewish Tribune*, he was an intelligent, literate man, who latterly directed six interesting features, including *The Picture of Dorian Gray*, which grew increasingly mediocre as he chased his special muse – *Saadia* was the penultimate, and by far the most preposterous. Mysticism and religiosity obscure a simple Moroccan love story, as Cornel Wilde and Mel Ferrer slug it out for love of dancer Rita Gam. TS

Cornel Wilde *Si Lahssen* • Mel Ferrer *Henrik* • Rita Gam *Saadia* • Michel Simon *Bou Rezza* • Cyril Cusack *Khadir* • Wanda Rotha *Fatima* • Marcel Poncin *Moha* • Anthony Marlowe *Captain Sabert* ■ *Dir* Albert Lewin • *Scr* Albert Lewin, from the novel *Echeck au Destin* by Francis D'Autheville

Saajan ★★★ U
Romantic drama 1991 · Ind · Colour · 173min

Salman Khan, the hunky pin-up of both India's gay community and the nation's teenage girls, stars here as a playboy on one side of a love triangle in Lawrence D'Souza's amiable Bollywood romance. But, unusually for a masala *ménage à trois*, he and impoverished poet Sanjay Dutt appear more than willing to see each other's merits and leave poor old Madhuri Dixit feeling rather neglected. DP Punjabi +subtitles. *DVD*

Salman Khan *Akash* • Sanjay Dutt *Aman/Sagar* • Madhuri Dixit *Pooja* ■ *Dir* Lawrence D'Souza • *Scr* Reema Rakeshnath

Saathiya ★★★ 12
Romantic drama 2002 · Ind · Colour · 134min

With composer AR Rahman and lyricist Gulzar collaborating on the score and Shah Rukh Khan lending stellar support, Mani Ratnam's longtime assistant Shaad Ali established his solo credentials here. Rani Mukerji stars as the dedicated Mumbai medical student whose life is transformed when she falls for fellow commuter Vivek Oberoi. But, no sooner are they married than capricious fate tears them apart and a heart-tugging journey begins. Polished. DP Hindi +subtitles.

Vivek Oberoi *Aditya Sehgal* • Rani Mukerji [Rani Mukherji] *Suhani Sharma* • Sandhya Mridul *Dina, Suhani's sister* • Tanuja *Shobhana, Suhani's mother* • Sharat Saxena *Chandraprakash, Suhani's father* • Satish Shah *Om, Aditya's father* ■ *Dir* Shaad Ali • *Scr* Mani Ratnam

Sabata ★★★ 12
Spaghetti western 1969 · It · Colour · 102min

Having established his spaghetti credentials with *Sartana* (1968), Gianfranco Parolini embarked on a trilogy of violent westerns directed under the pseudonym Frank Kramer. Lee Van Cleef is dangerously deadpan as the gunman who becomes the target of Franco Ressel, after he realises the corrupt town elder was behind a daring raid on a shipment of army gold. Packed with gimmicky gadgetry and eccentric set pieces, this is superior to both *Adios, Sabata* (in which Yul Brynner replaced Van Cleef in the title role) and *The Return of Sabata*. DP Italian dubbed. *DVD*

Lee Van Cleef *Sabata* • William Berger *Banjo* • Pedro Sanchez [Ignazio Spalla] *Carrincha* • Nick Jordan [Aldo Canti] *Indio* • Franco Ressel *Stengel* • Anthony Gradwell [Antonio Gradoli] *Ferguson* • Linda Veras *Jane* ■ *Dir* Frank Kramer [Gianfranco Parolini] • *Scr* Gianfranco Parolini, Renato Izzo

Sabotage ★★★★ PG
Mystery thriller 1936 · UK · BW · 75min

There was no such thing as accepted behaviour for suspense master Alfred Hitchcock, and his nonconformity was never more apparent than in the unnerving scene from this movie in which a small boy (Desmond Tester) carries a time-bomb aboard a bus. Movie-goers suddenly had to confront the unexpected (a Hitchcock trademark) in this adaptation of Joseph Conrad's novel *The Secret Agent*, in which terrorist Oscar Homolka uses his marriage to Sylvia Sidney and his business as a cinema owner as front for his subversive activities. TH *DVD* ⑂

Sylvia Sidney *Sylvia Verloc* • Oscar Homolka *Carl Verloc* • John Loder *Sergeant Ted Spencer* • Desmond Tester *Steve* • Joyce Barbour *Renee* • Matthew Boulton *Superintendent Talbot* ■ *Dir* Alfred Hitchcock • *Scr* Charles Bennett, Ian Hay, Alma Reville, Helen Simpson and EVH Emmett, from the novel *The Secret Agent* by Joseph Conrad

Sabotage ★★ 15
Crime thriller 2013 · US · Colour · 104min

A renegade squad of drug enforcement agents led by Arnold Schwarzenegger find themselves in bloody battle with the cartel they were tasked to bring down in this convoluted shoot-'em-up. As double-crosses come to light, members of Arnie's team are targeted one by one, each killing more grisly than the next. Director and co-writer David Ayer blurs the lines between goodies and baddies, and the focus here is firmly on blood splatter and broken bones - rarely has Arnie been surrounded by so many flimsy stereotypes. TeS Violence, swearing, sexual references, drug abuse, brief nudity. *DVD* ⑂

Arnold Schwarzenegger *John "Breacher" Wharton* • Sam Worthington *James "Monster" Murray* • Olivia Williams *Caroline Brentwood* • Terrence Howard *Julius "Sugar" Edmonds* • Joe Manganiello *Joe "Grinder" Phillips* ■ *Dir* David Ayer • *Scr* Skip Woods, David Ayer

Saboteur ★★★★ PG
Spy thriller 1942 · US · BW · 104min

Dorothy Parker contributed to the screenplay of this cracking Hitchcock thriller, which cleverly served the dual purpose of warning Americans against Fifth Columnists and providing much needed escapism. Although Hitch was unhappy with the stars chosen for him by Universal (Robert Cummings and Priscilla Lane), he clearly enjoyed hurtling them around deserts, ghost towns and luxury mansions. The Statue of Liberty finale is the film's

best known set piece, but the encounter with a circus troupe and the Radio City Music Hall shoot-out are bang on the money. DP *DVD* ⑂

Robert Cummings *Barry Kane* • Priscilla Lane *Patricia Martin* • Otto Kruger *Charles Tobin* • Alan Baxter *Freeman* • Clem Bevans *Neilson* • Norman Lloyd *Frank Fry* • Alma Kruger *Mrs Henrietta Sutton* ■ *Dir* Alfred Hitchcock • *Scr* Peter Viertel, Joan Harrison, Dorothy Parker

Sabrina ★★★★★ U
Romantic comedy 1954 · US · BW · 108min

Ignore the critics who say this is one of Billy Wilder's minor works. It is a major movie, a masterpiece of romantic comedy. This a Cinderella story about a chauffeur's daughter (Audrey Hepburn) and two brothers, Humphrey Bogart as the workaholic zillionaire and William Holden as the playboy. Because Hepburn's infatuation with Holden is unwittingly wrecking a business deal, Bogart decides to divert her - with predictable results. For a film that is so funny, so sophisticated and so technically accomplished, it comes as a surprise to learn that the production was a difficult one. The performances are impeccable, with Hepburn radiant and Holden showing real star quality and Bogart perfectly cast against his tough-guy image so that his entry into a new age of innocence is all the more moving. AT

Humphrey Bogart *Linus Larrabee* • Audrey Hepburn *Sabrina Fairchild* • William Holden (2) *David Larrabee* • Walter Hampden *Oliver Larrabee* • John Williams *Thomas Fairchild* • Martha Hyer *Elizabeth Tyson* • Joan Vohs *Gretchen Van Horn* • Marcel Dalio *Baron* • Marcel Hillaire *The professor* • Nella Walker *Maude Larrabee* ■ *Dir* Billy Wilder • *Scr* Billy Wilder, Samuel Taylor, Ernest Lehman, from the play by Samuel Taylor • *Costume Designer* Edith Head

Sabrina ★★★ PG
Romantic comedy 1995 · US · Colour · 121min

Sydney Pollack must have known before he embarked on this remake of Billy Wilder's 1954 comedy classic, that the ghosts of Humphrey Bogart, Audrey Hepburn and William Holden would be hovering over his production. Yet, with canny casting and some subtle updating, he succeeded in coming up with a charming variation on this Cinderella story, in which the chauffeur's daughter romances the billionaire boss. Julia Ormond and Harrison Ford take a while to settle into their roles, unlike Greg Kinnear, who gives a vibrant debut performance as Ford's brattish brother. Pollack achieves a sparkle to match the picture's polish. DP *DVD*

Harrison Ford *Linus Larrabee* • Julia Ormond *Sabrina Fairchild* • Greg Kinnear *David Larrabee* • Nancy Marchand *Maude Larrabee* • John Wood (2) *Fairchild* • Richard Crenna *Patrick Tyson* • Angie Dickinson *Ingrid Tyson* • Lauren Holly *Elizabeth Tyson* ■ *Dir* Sydney Pollack • *Scr* Barbara Benedek, David Rayfiel, from the 1954 film, from the play by Samuel Taylor

The Sacrament ★★★ 15
Horror thriller 2013 · US · Colour · 95min

Director Ti West's slow-burning tale recalls a real-life atrocity that shook the world in the late 1970s. Reporters Joe Swanberg and AJ Bowen visit a remote compound in South America to investigate a spiritual paradise set up by a religious leader known as "Father" (a charismatic Gene Jones). On the face of it, the inhabitants appear content but after an unnerving interview with the man, it becomes apparent that there's more to the place than meets the eye. Characterisation is pretty perfunctory, but West's use of the notorious 1978 Jonestown massacre as a template will chill anyone who remembers it, and the film remains tense and involving throughout. JA Violence, swearing.

Joe Swanberg *Jake* • AJ Bowen *Sam* • Gene Jones (1) *Father* • Kentucker Audley *Patrick* • Amy Seimetz *Caroline* ■ *Dir/Scr* Ti West

Sacred Flesh ★ 18
Erotic drama 2000 · UK · Colour · 72min

Three years after he finally lost his long struggle to reverse the BBFC's decision to

withhold video certification from his film, *Visions of Ecstasy*, on the grounds of blasphemy, Nigel Wingrove returns with another assault on the taboos surrounding the depiction of Christianity on screen. Many will proclaim this as a courageous affirmation of free speech, but it's nothing more than porn in wimples, posing as a treatise on the mental, physical and spiritual dangers of chastity. DP *DVD*

Sally Tremaine *Sister Elizabeth, the Mother Superior* • Moyna Cope *The Abbess* • Simon Hill *Father Henry, The Abbott* • Kristina Bill *Mary Magdalene* • Rachel Taggart *Catechism* • Eileen Daly *Repression* • Daisy Weston *Sister Brigitte* ■ *Dir/Scr* Nigel Wingrove

The Sacrifice ★★★★ PG
Drama 1986 · Fr/Swe · Colour and BW · 142min

With its location (Faro), themes (alienation, faith and death), cinematographer (Sven Nykvist) and star (Erland Josephson) all primarily associated with Ingmar Bergman, his influence is all-pervasive throughout Andrei Tarkovsky's final film. But the Soviet visionary's tormented lyricism is also very much in evidence, both as he suggests the horror of nuclear war through retired intellectual Josephson's desperate, Faustian reaction to the terrible news broadcast, and as he presents the possibility of redemption, through the intercession of mystical mailman Allan Edwall. DP Swedish +subtitles. *DVD* ⑂

Erland Josephson *Alexander* • Susan Fleetwood *Adelaide* • Allan Edwall *Otto* • Sven Wollter *Victor* ■ *Dir/Scr* Andrei Tarkovsky

Sacrificed Youth ★★★★ PG
Drama 1985 · Chi · Colour · 95min

Having waited 20 years from film school graduation to directing her first feature, Zhang Nuanxin emerged as a key member of the Fourth Generation directors. Although Chinese cinema was changing rapidly, this partly autobiographical tale of a city girl's rural re-education owes much to the post-revolutionary humanist tradition, as Li Fengxu learns more about life from the people around her than from political dictates. Sent to a collective farm in Yunnan during the Cultural Revolution, Li's medical student also matures as a woman, giving the film a subtle eroticism. DP Mandarin +subtitles.

Li Fengxu • Yu Da • Feng Yuanzheng ■ *Dir* Zhang Nuanxin • *Scr* Zhang Nuanxin, from the novel *You Yige Meilide Difang (There Was a Beautiful Place)* by Zhang Manling

Sacro GRA ★★★ 15
Documentary 2013 · It/Fr · Colour · 91min

This portrait of the Grande Raccordo Anulare, the ring road that is to Rome what the M25 is to London, was the first documentary to win the prestigious Golden Lion at the Venice film festival. Given this garlanded reputation, Gianfranco Rosi's film is a surprisingly modest affair, content to flit around between various local characters and capture their daily lot. Luckily, they're a fascinating bunch, as Rosi's agenda-free approach affords his subjects heart-warming dignity without telling us how to judge them. TJ Italian +subtitles. *DVD*

■ *Dir* Gianfranco Rosi • *Scr* From a idea by Nicolo Bassetti

The Sad Horse ★★★ U
Adventure drama 1959 · US · Colour · 77min

A late entry in the seemingly unending series of 20th Century-Fox family films about a boy/girl and his/her horse/dog which included *Kentucky* and *My Friend Flicka*, this story (filmed on location) benefits from sympathetic direction of former Fox film editor James B Clark. Alan Ladd's son David plays the leading role here, and firm support comes from the ever-reliable Chill Wills, sturdy Rex Reason and Patrice Wymore. TS

David Ladd *Jackie Connors* • Chill Wills *Captain Connors* • Rex Reason *Bill MacDonald* • Patrice Wymore *Leslie MacDonald* • Gregg Palmer *Bart Connors* • Leslie Bradley *Jonas* ■ *Dir* James B Clark • *Scr* Charles Hoffman, from a story by Zoe Akins

Sad Inheritance ★★★ 15
Drama 1993 · US · Colour · 89min

After spending the 1980s locked in courtroom battles in TV's *LA Law* , Susan Dey trades in her squeaky-clean image to play a cocaine addict. Her premature baby has been taken away and she faces a desperate struggle to clean up her act and get the child back. Strong stuff, with both Dey and co-star Piper Laurie giving it all they've got in this often powerful, but ultimately clichéd TV drama. JB

Susan Dey *Christina Kinsey* • Piper Laurie *Margaret Kinsey* • Lorraine Toussaint *Florence Crenshaw* • DW Moffett *Gabriel* • Kathleen York *Terry* ■ *Dir* Rod Hardy • *Scr* Janet Heaney, Matthew Eisen

The Sad Sack ★★★ U
Comedy 1957 · US · BW · 98min

After making 17 films with Dean Martin, Jerry Lewis took his unique brand of comedy schtick with him and went solo in 1957. In this effort, surrounded by a notable supporting cast that includes Peter Lorre, Jerry inflicts his screwy antics on the armed forces. He plays an unwilling army recruit with a photographic memory who, in addition to the predictable disasters that befall a misfit, gets himself caught up with spies and an Arab conspiracy. Only fitfully funny, but under veteran director George Marshall's direction, there's enough here to keep Lewis addicts happy. RK

Jerry Lewis *Bixby* • David Wayne *Dolan* • Phyllis Kirk *Major Shelton* • Peter Lorre *Abdul* • Joe Mantell *Private Stan Wenaslawsky* • Gene Evans *Sergeant Pulley* • George Dolenz *Ali Mustapha* ■ *Dir* George Marshall • *Scr* Edmund Beloin, Nate Monaster

The Saddest Music in the World ★★★ 15
Fantasy musical drama 2003 · Can · BW and Colour · 96min

Cult director Guy Maddin's love affair with German expressionist styling continues in this beguiling musical drama set in snowbound Winnipeg during the Great Depression. Beautifully shot in black and white with occasional flashes of colour, the dream-like film blends fantasy and reality into an atmospheric whole. In a wonderfully eccentric turn, a sternly enigmatic Isabella Rossellini plays a double amputee and brewery owner who launches a contest to find the world's most melancholy melody. What follows is a surreal carnival of love, betrayal and revenge. SF Violence, sex scenes. *DVD*

Isabella Rossellini *Lady Helen Port-Huntly* • Mark McKinney *Chester Kent* • Maria de Medeiros *Narcissa* • David Fox *Fyodor Kent* • Ross McMillan *Roderick Kent/Gavrillo the Great* • Louis Negin *Blind seer* • Darcy Fehr *Teddy* ■ *Dir* Guy Maddin • *Scr* Guy Maddin, George Toles, from the screenplay (unproduced) by Kazuo Ishiguro

Saddle the Wind ★★★
Western 1958 · US · Colour · 84min

Robert Taylor (Hollywood professional) and John Cassavetes (New York king of improvisation) star here as a rancher and no-good brother, heading for their last showdown. The clash of acting styles makes for some decently intriguing drama, directed with flair by Robert Parrish, but this is a film with added rarity value because it's the only western to have been written by *The Twilight Zone's* Rod Serling, early television's greatest fantasist. TH

Robert Taylor (1) *Steve Sinclair* • Julie London *Joan Blake* • John Cassavetes *Tony Sinclair* • Donald Crisp *Mr Deneen* • Charles McGraw *Larry Venables* • Royal Dano *Clay Ellison* ■ *Dir* Robert Parrish • *Scr* Rod Serling, from a story by Thomas Thompson

Saddle Tramp ★★★ U
Western 1950 · US · Colour · 76min

This engaging western stars the laconic Joel McCrea as a cowboy who takes care of four orphaned children, trying to keep them a secret from his child-hating boss. Made as a family film, but director Hugo Fregonese keeps the sentimentality in check. The

Technicolor location photography by Charles Boyle is particularly attractive, and Wanda Hendrix (Mrs Audie Murphy at the time) makes a perky heroine. Very appealing. TS

Joel McCrea *Chuck Conner* • Wanda Hendrix *Della* • John Russell *Rocky* • John McIntire *Jess Higgins* • Jeanette Nolan *Ma Higgins* • Russell Simpson *Pop* • Ed Begley *Mr Hartnagle* ■ *Dir* Hugo Fregonese • *Scr* Harold Shumate

Sadgati ★★★ PG
Drama 1981 · Ind · Colour · 45min

This short rural drama from India's most respected director, Satyajit Ray, tells the simple, but cruel story of a high-caste bully who forces a low-caste labourer to work to his death. It is one of Ray's most politically militant films, not only attacking the prejudices of the caste system, but also protesting about the hardships faced by the sub-continent's poorest people. Om Puri gives a performance of great strength and dignity as the repressed bonded labourer, and the final scene is heart-rending. DP Hindi +subtitles. DVD

Om Puri *Dukhi* • Smita Patil *Dukhi's wife* • Mohan Agashe *Brahmin* ■ *Dir/Scr* Satyajit Ray

Sadie McKee ★★
Melodrama 1934 · US · BW · 90min

This typical rags-to-riches melodrama stars Joan Crawford, playing a maid on a romantic rollercoaster ride as she tries to climb the social ladder. Crawford virtually carries this entertaining Cinderella saga single-handedly through star charisma alone - only Edward Arnold's performance as her drunken husband survives Crawford's bid to obliterate her co-stars from the spotlight. AJ

Joan Crawford *Sadie McKee* • Gene Raymond *Tommy Wallace* • Franchot Tone *Michael Alderson* • Esther Ralston *Dolly* • Edward Arnold *Jack Brennon* ■ *Dir* Clarence Brown • *Scr* John Meehan, from the story *Pretty Sadie McKee* by Vina Delmar

Sadie Thompson ★★★
Silent drama 1928 · US · BW · 90min

This silent version of W Somerset Maugham's *Rain*, about a prostitute marooned on a South Seas island where she is almost destroyed by a reforming religious zealot, whose attraction to her undoes him in the end, is the first and most interesting of three attempts to film it (see 1932's *Rain* and 1953's *Miss Sadie Thompson*). Directed by Raoul Walsh, it stars Gloria Swanson (who produced it) and Lionel Barrymore, and it's worth sitting through the now tedious, somewhat heavy-handed first half-hour for the powerful melodrama that follows. Claustrophobic and atmospheric, with Barrymore frightening and Swanson mesmerising. RK

Gloria Swanson *Sadie Thompson* • Lionel Barrymore *Alfred Atkinson* • Raoul Walsh *Sgt Tim O'Hara* • Blanche Frederici *Mrs Atkinson* • Charles Lane (1) *Dr McPhail* • Florence Midgely *Mrs McPhail* • Will Stanton *Quartermaster Bates* ■ *Dir* Raoul Walsh • *Scr* Raoul Walsh, C Gardner Sullivan (titles), from the play *Rain; a Play in Three Acts* by John Colton, Clemence Randolph, from the short story *Rain* by W Somerset Maugham

Safari ★★★
Action adventure 1956 · US · Colour · 90min

This is a marvellously batty African adventure romp from Warwick Films, photographed, to its credit, on genuine locations and in CinemaScope. There's a real sense of the terror of the Mau Maus - *Simba* and *Something of Value* were the only other mainstream features to deal with this subject. Victor Mature plays the hero and Janet Leigh is at her most beguiling, whether terrorised by snakes or taking a bath in the jungle. *Dr No* director Terence Young is very good at this sort of thing, and it shows. TS

Victor Mature *Ken Duffield* • Janet Leigh *Linda Latham* • John Justin *Brian Sinden* • Roland Culver *Sir Vincent Brampton* • Orlando Martins *Jerusalem* ■ *Dir* Terence Young • *Scr* Anthony Veiller, from a story by Robert Buckner

[Safe] ★★★★ 15
Drama 1995 · US · Colour · 118min

This claustrophobic study of a dysfunctional Californian housewife who becomes allergic to the chemical by-products of the 20th century casts an eerie spell with its hypnotic camerawork and unusual soundtrack. From cult director Todd Haynes, it's a modern-day psychological horror story that's made even more harrowing by the intense and impressive performance of Julianne Moore as a woman personally and medically devastated by her surroundings. AJ Swearing, nudity. DVD

Julianne Moore *Carol White* • Xander Berkeley *Greg White* • Peter Friedman *Peter Dunning* • Kate McGregor-Stewart *Claire* • Mary Carver *Nell* • Susan Norman *Linda* • Steven Gilborn *Dr Hubbard* • Ronnie Farer *Barbara* • James LeGros *Chris* ■ *Dir/Scr* Todd Haynes

Safe ★★★ 15
Action thriller 2011 · US · Colour · 90min

This slick, over-the-top action thrillers stars Jason Statham as cage fighter Luke Wright, whose life is torn apart when he incurs the wrath of the Russian mafia. Living on the streets, he saves the life of 12-year-old maths genius Mei (Catherine Chan), who has been smuggled into the US by the Triads. So now he's pitted against the Russians and the Chinese - oh, and corrupt New York cops, too. There's something solid and old-fashioned about *Safe*, with its grainy cinematography and depiction of a sleazy New York, and the typically deadpan Statham showcases his impressive martial arts skills in between some incredibly violent, well-choreographed shoot-outs. LB English, Mandarin, Russian +subtitles. Violence, swearing. DVD

Jason Statham *Luke Wright* • Catherine Chan *Mei* • Robert John Burke [Robert Burke] *Captain Wolf* • Reggie Lee *Yac Chang* • Anson Mount *Alex Rosen* • James Hong *Han Jaio* • Chris Sarandon *Mayor Tremello* ■ *Dir/Scr* Boaz Yakin

Safe Harbor ★★
Drama based on a true story 2009 · US · Colour · 120min

Treat Williams and Nancy Travis add class and heart to this simplistic true-life tale. The stars play a retired, childless couple who get thrust into the challenges of parenthood when a judge friend asks them to temporarily accommodate a group of delinquent teenage boys on board their houseboat. Well cast in the redemptive drama's only really convincing roles, the charmingly natural pair exude compassion and fairness, as their surly screen charges' troublemaking kicks off a predictable but affecting narrative arc. Uplifting moral messages about self-worth and second chances intensify the film's increasing emotional pull. They also temper the unreality of events in which every supporting character is a stereotype and problems are overcome almost as quickly as they arise. SF

Treat Williams *Doug Smith* • Nancy Travis *Robbie Smith* • Reiley McClendon *Luke* • Charlie McDermott *David Porter* ■ *Dir* Jerry Jameson • *Scr* Josef Anderson

Safe Haven ★★ 12
Romantic drama 2013 · US · Colour · 110min

Director Lasse Hallström followed his adaptation of *Salmon Fishing in the Yemen* with this solidly acted but daftly plotted romance based on the novel by Nicholas Sparks. Julianne Hough stars as Katie, a "person of interest" in a crime case, who flees Boston and the cop obsessively hunting her. She holes up in a sleepy coastal town where, predictably, she falls for a hunky widower-with-kids (Josh Duhamel). But Katie's bubble of bliss is eventually burst when the policeman - so sweatily psychotic that you wouldn't be surprised if he had "nutjob" tattooed on his forehead - manages to hunt her down. The film is over-egged, overlong, and boasts a final plot twist that may convince on the

page, but fails to do so on screen. DA Some violence and swearing. DVD Blu

Julianne Hough *Katie Feldman/Erin Tierney* • Josh Duhamel *Alex Wheatley* • David Lyons *Kevin Tierney* • Cobie Smulders *Jo* • Noah Lomax *Josh* • Mimi Kirkland *Lexie* ■ *Dir* Lasse Hallström • *Scr* Dana Stevens, Gage Lansky, from Nicholas Sparks's novel

Safe House ★★★ 15
Action thriller 2012 · US/S Afr · Colour · 110min

In this taut thriller, a CIA rookie (Ryan Reynolds) sees his world turned upside down when enigmatic rogue agent Tobin Frost (Denzel Washington) is delivered to the safe house he mans in Cape Town. Before Frost can be interrogated, the bolt hole is attacked, forcing the pair on the run. Reynolds plays the initially out-of-his-depth younger operative with a mixture of fear and feistiness, while Washington is the epitome of detached cool as the bad guy. Director Daniel Espinosa occasionally gets bogged down in plot complexities, but is more confident with a series of white-knuckle chases and shoot-outs. TeS Violence, swearing. DVD Blu

Ryan Reynolds *Matt Weston* • Denzel Washington *Tobin Frost* • Vera Farmiga *Catherine Linklater* • Brendan Gleeson *David Barlow* • Liam Cunningham *Alec Wade* • Robert Patrick *Daniel Kiefer* • Sam Shepard *Harlan Whitford* • *Scr* Daniel Guggenheim

Safe Men ★★ 15
Crime comedy 1998 · US · Colour · 84min

Yet another comedy based around the cobweb-covered "incompetent guys mistaken for experienced criminals" premise. This one is given a lift by two very watchable leads in Steve Zahn and Sam Rockwell and an enjoyably caricatured supporting cast which includes Michael Lerner and Harvey Fierstein as OTT Jewish gangsters. It's a shame then that the material is so run-of-the-mill as this pair of dumb, fifth-rate musicians find themselves forced into cracking a safe. The plot is paper thin, as is the humour. JC Swearing.

Sam Rockwell *Samuel* • Steve Zahn *Eddie* • Mark Ruffalo *Frank* • Josh Pais *Mitchell* • Paul Giamatti *Veal Chop* • Michael Schmidt *Bernie Jr* • Christina Kirk *Hannah* • Raymond Serra *Barber* • Harvey Fierstein *Good Stuff Leo* • Michael Lerner *Big Fat Bernie Gayle* ■ *Dir/Scr* John Hamburg

Safe Passage ★★ 15
Drama 1994 · US · Colour · 93min

Susan Sarandon gives yet another stunning performance, here playing a frustrated mother of seven boys who struggles to cope with her husband Sam Shepard's bouts of seemingly psychosomatic blindness. Sadly, Sarandon's portrayal is the only thing worth noting in director Robert Allan Ackerman's bland drama. The formula is stale and predictable. LH

Susan Sarandon *Mag Singer* • Sam Shepard *Patrick Singer* • Robert Sean Leonard *Alfred Singer* • Nick Stahl *Simon Singer* • Jason London *Gideon Singer* • Marcia Gay Harden *Cynthia* • Matt Keeslar *Percival Singer* • Sean Astin *Izzy Singer* ■ *Dir* Robert Allan Ackerman • *Scr* Deena Goldstone, from the novel by Ellyn Bache

A Safe Place ★★ PG
Experimental fantasy drama 1971 · US · Colour · 94min

This fantasy is wildly incoherent or poetically experimental, depending on your tastes. Tuesday Weld plays a vulnerable woman who escapes the pressures of New York life into a dream world, courtesy of a magician (Orson Welles). There's a low-budget feel to this, director Henry Jaglom's first release, and indeed it was filmed at his parent's flat, with the cast largely made up of his pals. However, it gives the impression of having been a labour of love. Jack Nicholson is good value as Weld's old lover. JG

Tuesday Weld *Susan/Noah* • Orson Welles *Magician* • Jack Nicholson *Mitch* • Phil Proctor [Philip Proctor] *Fred* • Gwen Welles *Bari* • Dov Lawrence *Dov* • Fanny Birkenmaier *Maid* ■ *Dir/Scr* Henry Jaglom

The Safecracker ★★ U
Second World War thriller 1958 · UK · BW · 96min

Ray Milland directs himself in this lightly entertaining Second World War drama, playing the criminal whose digital dexterity comes in useful to the Allies as he's persuaded to join a Commando unit and prise open a Nazi safe in a Belgian castle. At times, it's rather too apt to recall better movies, but it does, in its own modest way, foreshadow *The Dirty Dozen*. AE

Ray Milland *Colley Dawson* • Barry Jones *Bennett Carfield* • Jeannette Sterke *Irene* • Ernest Clark *Major Adbury* • Melissa Stribling *Angela* • Victor Maddern *Morris* • Cyril Raymond *Inspector Frankham* • Barbara Everest *Mrs Dawson* ■ *Dir* Ray Milland • *Scr* Paul Monash, from the book *The Willie Gordon Story* by Rhys Davies, Bruce Thomas

Safety Last ★★★★★ U
Classic silent comedy 1923 · US · BW · 73min

The film that best illustrates the thrill-comedy of Harold Lloyd with his climactic clock-hanging bravado. Lloyd is the country boy who suggests a high-rise climber as a publicity stunt for the big city store that employs him, and then finds he has to substitute for the original daredevil. No wonder Mildred Davis loves him. As a feature-length expansion of his remarkable acrobatic skills displayed in earlier shorts, it's a movie chock full of incidents to make audiences laugh - and gasp. TH

Harold Lloyd *Boy* • Mildred Davis *Girl* • Bill Strother *Pal* • Noah Young *Law* • Westcott B Clarke *Floorwalker* ■ *Dir* Fred C Newmeyer, Sam Taylor • *Scr* Hal Roach, Tim Whelan, Sam Taylor

Safety Not Guaranteed ★★★★ 15
Comedy 2012 · US · Colour · 81min

You can't travel through time on a shoestring budget but, with his feature debut, director Colin Trevorrow has a lot of fun trying. The film revolves around small-town supermarket worker Kenneth (Mark Duplass), who advertises for a time travel companion and sparks the curiosity of three journalists. Though it has all the mystery of a sci-fi caper, Kenneth remains an enigma, and the question mark over his relationship with sultry, cynical intern Aubrey Plaza provides the suspense. The finale may raise eyebrows, but this is an experience you'll want to relive. SP DVD Blu

Aubrey Plaza *Darius Britt* • Mark Duplass *Ken Calloway* • Jake M Johnson [Jake Johnson] *Jeff Schwensen* • Karan Soni *Arnau* • Kristen Bell *Belinda St Sing* ■ *Dir* Colin Trevorrow • *Scr* Derek Connolly

The Safety of Objects ★★ 15
Drama 2001 · US/UK · Colour · 115min

Like Robert Altman's *Short Cuts*, writer/director Rose Troche's film is based on disparate short stories that have been cleverly woven into a cohesive whole. There, sadly, the similarities end. As four neighbouring families go about the everyday business of their misery and pain, a tragedy from the past awaits its big flashback. Despite a fair cast, the film never takes flight, remaining a string of overfamiliar vignettes that are too neatly resolved. AC DVD

Glenn Close *Esther Gold* • Dermot Mulroney *Jim Train* • Patricia Clarkson *Annette Jennings* • Joshua Jackson *Paul Gold* • Moira Kelly *Susan Train* • Robert Klein *Howard Gold* • Timothy Olyphant *Randy* • Mary Kay Place *Helen Christianson* • Kristen Stewart *Sam Jennings* ■ *Dir* Rose Troche • *Scr* Rose Troche, from stories by AM Homes

The Saga of Anatahan ★★★★
Drama based on a true story 1953 · Jpn · BW · 91min

In Josef von Sternberg's curious final film, the director shows what can be done with a simple studio set and lighting. Narrated by Sternberg himself, it tells the true story of a group of Japanese merchant seamen shipwrecked on the island of Anahatan in

S

1944 who believed, seven years after the war had ended, that Japan was still fighting. Von Sternberg, who was the cinematographer as well, shot the film on a sound stage in a Japanese studio, using synthetic sets made of cellophane and papier maché, sprayed with aluminium paint, making it look as artificial as possible. The acting of the cast, consisting of members of the Kabuki theatre, add to the stylisation of the whole picture. RB In Japanese, English.

Akemi Negishi Keiko, the "Queen Bee" • Tadashi Suganuma Kusakabe, the "Husband" • Josef von Sternberg Narrator ■ Dir Josef von Sternberg • Scr Josef von Sternberg, from the story Anatahan by Michiro Maruyama and an article in Life magazine

The Saga of Hemp Brown ★★★ U
Western   1958 · US · Colour · 77min

In this underrated Universal western, Rory Calhoun stars as a disgraced cavalry officer seeking to clear his name with the help of medicine man Fortunio Bonanova. Behind the camera is actor-turned-director Richard Carlson, best known for battling with 3D monsters in movies such as Creature from the Black Lagoon. Calhoun's co-star is cult favourite Beverly Garland, and if this is nothing special, it is competently done. TS

Rory Calhoun Hemp Brown • Beverly Garland Mona Langley • John Larch Jed Givens • Russell Johnson Hook • Fortunio Bonanova Serge Bolanos, medicine man • Allan "Rocky" Lane [Allan Lane] Sheriff • Morris Ankrum Bo Slauter ■ Dir Richard Carlson • Scr Bob Williams, from a story by Bernard Girard

Sagebrush Trail ★★ U
Western   1934 · US · BW · 53min

This is John Wayne's second Monogram Studios western, and is really only of interest to B-western fans: the plot's average, the direction plods and the cast is unremarkable. What really brings it to life are the stunts, planned and carried out by the incredible Yakima Canutt. Watch out for Canutt doubling for Wayne and hiding underwater. TS DVD

John Wayne John Brant • Nancy Shubert Sally Blake • Lane Chandler Bob Jones • Yakima Canutt Ed Walsh ■ Dir Armand Schaefer • Scr Lindsley Parsons

Sahara ★★★ PG
Second World War action adventure
1943 · US · BW · 93min

Humphrey Bogart spent most of the war years playing loners in civilian clothes, who stuck their necks out for no one until Lauren Bacall or Ingrid Bergman forced him to take sides. It is something of a surprise, then, to find him here as a resourceful army sergeant, leading a bunch of no-hopers across the desert in a dilapidated tank, dodging Nazis as they search for water. Directed by Zoltan Korda, co-written by John Howard Lawson (later blacklisted in the communist witch-hunt), shot by Rudolph Maté and scored by Miklos Rozsa, there's solid talent behind the camera and a lot of derring-do in front of it. AT DVD

Humphrey Bogart Sergeant Joe Gunn • Bruce Bennett Waco Hoyt • Lloyd Bridges Fred Clarkson • Rex Ingram (2) Sergeant Tambul • J Carrol Naish Giuseppe • Dan Duryea Jimmy Doyle • Richard Nugent Captain Jason Halliday ■ Dir Zoltan Korda • Scr John Howard Lawson, Zoltan Korda, James O'Hanlon, from a story by Philip MacDonald

Sahara ★ PG
Adventure   1983 · US · Colour · 106min

After her father dies, flapper Brooke Shields disguises herself as a man and takes his place in the 1920s trans-Sahara automobile race, somehow ending up as the wife of dashing desert sheik Lambert Wilson. This pathetic bodice-ripper tries to emulate the atmosphere and heated eroticism of Rudolph Valentino silent epics, but ends up as a badly plotted and shoddily produced Mills and Boon, setting a new low standard for period romances. AJ

Brooke Shields Dale Gordon • Lambert Wilson Jaffar • John Rhys-Davies Rasoul • Horst Buchholz Von Glessing • Perry Lang Andy • Cliff Potts String • John Mills Cambridge ■ Dir Andrew V McLaglen • Scr James R Silke, from a story by Menahem Golan

Sahara ★★★ 12
Action adventure
2005 · US/Sp/Ger · Colour · 118min

Matthew McConaughey stars as author Clive Cussler's creation Dirk Pitt, an adventurer and salvage expert who stumbles upon evidence that a long-lost American Civil War battleship may have ended up in the desert in West Africa. Along for the ride are sidekick Steve Zahn and Penélope Cruz as a World Health Organisation doctor. The plot is convoluted and at times incomprehensible, but the action sequences are impressive, the locations and villains suitably exotic, and the whole thing remains good fun. BP Violence. DVD ⬛

Matthew McConaughey Dirk Pitt • Steve Zahn Al Giordino • Penélope Cruz Dr Eva Rojas • Lambert Wilson Yves Massarde • Glynn Turman Dr Frank Hopper • Delroy Lindo Carl • William H Macy Admiral Sandecker • Rainn Wilson Rudi Gunn • Patrick Malahide Ambassador Polidori ■ Dir Breck Eisner • Scr Thomas Dean Donnelly, Joshua Oppenheimer, John C Richards, James V Hart from the novel by Clive Cussler

Saigon ★★
Drama   1948 · US · BW · 94min

Ex-army pilot Alan Ladd washes up in Saigon with one healthy buddy and another, terminally ill, but not knowing he's got a month left to live. The three guys go out on the town – but without that song – and rope Veronica Lake into joining them on a caper that goes more than slightly wrong. This sort of malarkey lives or dies on the charm of its stars and Ladd and Lake were never in the Bogart–Bacall league. Saigon appears on the back projection screen while the foreground is pure studio backlot. AT

Alan Ladd Maj Larry Briggs • Veronica Lake Susan Cleaver • Douglas Dick Capt Mike Perry • Wally Cassell Sgt Pete Rocco • Luther Adler Lt Keon ■ Dir Leslie Fenton • Scr PJ Wolfson, Arthur Sheekman, from a story by Julian Zimet

Saigon ★★★ 18
Action thriller   1988 · US · Colour · 97min

Despite its pretensions, this is no more than a variant of Lethal Weapon's "white cop, black cop" formula transposed to Apocalypse Now territory. Willem Dafoe and Gregory Hines are gripping as army cops tracking down a serial killer – who may or may not be military top brass – among the sleazy back alleys of Saigon circa 1968. It's undeniably well crafted, with much macho posturing, and debut director Christopher Crowe offers plenty of twists and turns amid the well-staged action scenes. RS

Willem Dafoe Buck McGriff • Gregory Hines Albaby Perkins • Fred Ward Dix • Amanda Pays Nicole • Scott Glenn Colonel Armstrong • Lim Kay Tong Lime Green • Keith David Maurice ■ Dir Christopher Crowe • Scr Christopher Crowe, Jack Thibeau

Sailing Along ★ U
Romantic musical   1938 · UK · BW · 90min

One of the many substandard – not to say dire – films in which the adored British musical comedy star Jessie Matthews found herself during the 1930s. Directed (and co-written) by her then husband, actor Sonnie Hale, it finds Matthews as a female barge with aspirations to become a stage star, while her co-worker Barry Mackay dreams of being a financier. RK

Jessie Matthews Kay Martin • Barry Mackay Steve Barnes • Jack Whiting Dicky Randall • Roland Young Anthony Gulliver • Noel Madison Windy • Frank Pettingell Skipper Barnes • Alastair Sim Sylvester ■ Dir Sonnie Hale • Scr Lesser Samuels, Sonnie Hale, from a story by Selwyn Jepson

Sailor Beware ★★ U
Comedy   1951 · US · BW · 99min

The fifth film pairing of Dean Martin and Jerry Lewis is easily one of their worst. You are either a fan or you can't bear to be in the same room as the duo who took American showbiz by storm in the late 1940s. Putting the comic style to one side, what really makes this hard to take are the smug references to their fame, as the boys do a stint in the navy. Minor consolations are an uncredited guest appearance by Betty Hutton and a blink-and-miss bit for James Dean. DP DVD

Jerry Lewis Melvin Jones • Dean Martin Al Crowthers • Corinne Calvet Guest Star • Marion Marshall Hilda Jones • Robert Strauss Lardoski • Vincent Edwards [Vince Edwards] Blayden • Leif Erickson Commander Lane • James Dean (1) Sailor • Dan Willis Sailor • Betty Hutton ■ Dir Hal Walker • Scr James Allardice, Martin Rackin, Elwood Ullman (adaptation), from the play by Kenyon Nicholson, Charles Robinson (1)

Sailor Beware! ★★ U
Comedy   1956 · UK · BW · 77min

This politically incorrect comedy established Peggy Mount in the booming shrew persona that was to make her such a hit in television series such as George and the Dragon. Here she terrorises hubby Cyril Smith and prospective son-in-law Ronald Lewis on the eve of daughter Shirley Eaton's wedding. However, while Mount dominates the proceedings, the peerless Esma Cannon steals every scene. DP DVD

Peggy Mount Emma Hornett • Cyril Smith Henry Hornett • Shirley Eaton Shirley Hornett • Ronald Lewis Albert Tufnell • Esma Cannon Edie Hornett • Joy Webster Daphne • Gordon Jackson Carnoustie Bligh • Thora Hird Mrs Lack • Geoffrey Keen Reverend Purefoy • Jack MacGowran Toddy • Michael Caine ■ Dir Gordon Parry • Scr Philip King, Falkland L Cary

The Sailor from Gibraltar ★
Romantic drama   1967 · UK · BW · 90min

One of the two grandiose flops Tony Richardson made with Jeanne Moreau (the other being 1966's Mademoiselle), of whom he was much enamoured at the time. Based on a Marguerite Duras novel, adapted by Christopher Isherwood, it's an insufferably arty exercise in alienation with Ian Bannen as the bored office clerk who has an affair with the La Moreau, who sails around exotic Arabian ports, consorting and philosophising with the likes of Orson Welles. Movies come no more pretentious than this. AT

Jeanne Moreau Anna • Ian Bannen Alan • Vanessa Redgrave Sheila • Orson Welles Louis of Mozambique • Zia Mohyeddin Noori • Hugh Griffith Llewellyn • Umberto Orsini Postcard vendor ■ Dir Tony Richardson • Scr Christopher Isherwood, Don Magner, Tony Richardson, from the novel Le Marin de Gibraltar by Marguerite Duras

A Sailor-Made Man ★★★★ U
Silent comedy   1921 · US · BW · 36min

Yet another Harold Lloyd movie, in which he's the bespectacled wimp who redeems himself by an unexpected show of guts and bravery. Here, he's a wealthy playboy who's told to get a job by the father of the girl (Mildred Davis) he loves – so he joins the Navy. Initially the enemy of tough crew mate Noah Young, they soon become best friends and team-up to save Davis from the lecherous intentions of a maharajah. An entertaining swimming pool dip and a marriage proposal via semaphore contribute towards a very enjoyable Lloyd outing. TH

Harold Lloyd The Boy • Mildred Davis The Girl • Noah Young Rough-House O'Rafferty • Dick Sutherland Maharajah ■ Dir Fred C Newmeyer • Scr Hal Roach, Sam Taylor, HM Walker (titles), Jean Havez

Sailor of the King ★★★ PG
Second World War drama
1953 · UK · BW · 79min

Originally released in the UK as Single-Handed, this is a rather good second screen

version of author CS Forester's novel Brown on Resolution (the earlier one being the weakish 1935 film Forever England starring John Mills). Hollywood heart-throb Jeffrey Hunter is impressive as the courageous Brown, descended from a long line of seafarers, his unlikely parents being Michael Rennie and Wendy Hiller. TS DVD ⬛

Jeffrey Hunter Seaman Andrew Brown • Michael Rennie Captain Richard Saville • Wendy Hiller Lucinda Bentley • Bernard Lee Petty Officer Wheatley • Peter Van Eyck Kapitan von Falk • Victor Maddern Signalman Earnshaw ■ Dir Roy Boulting • Scr Valentine Davies, from the novel Brown on Resolution by CS Forester

The Sailor Takes a Wife ★★
Comedy   1945 · US · BW · 90min

June Allyson and Robert Walker star in this lightweight version of Chester Erskine's play. Director Richard Whorf makes the most of the limited laughs that follow the whirlwind courtship, leaving our newlyweds with nothing but illusions to be shattered. Discharged from the navy, Walker struggles to make an impact on anyone other than Audrey Totter, whose ditzy vamping enlivens the proceedings. DP

Robert Walker John • June Allyson Mary • Hume Cronyn Freddie • Audrey Totter Lisa • Eddie "Rochester" Anderson Harry • Reginald Owen Mr Amboy • Gerald Oliver Smith Butler ■ Dir Richard Whorf • Scr Chester Erskine, Anne Morrison Chapin, Whitfield Cook, from Erskine's play

The Sailor Who Fell from Grace with the Sea ★★★ 18
Drama   1976 · UK · Colour · 100min

This is a weird, sometimes disturbing, sometimes downright laughable adaptation of a novel by the Japanese writer Yukio Mishima – who formed his own right-wing army, committed ritual suicide and became the subject of the brilliant Paul Schrader biopic, Mishima. This story is about a sensual widow whose teenage son is a member of a strange secret society. Experts felt that the core elements of Mishima's novel went AWOL in the transition from Japan to England, but there's no denying the strangeness of the story, the sexually charged atmosphere or the power of Sarah Miles's emotionally naked performance. AT

Sarah Miles Anne Osborne • Kris Kristofferson Jim Cameron • Jonathan Kahn Jonathan Osborne • Margo Cunningham Mrs Palmer ■ Dir Lewis John Carlino • Scr Lewis John Carlino, from the novel by Yukio Mishima

Sailors Three ★★ U
Comedy   1940 · UK · BW · 83min

Who on earth thought that wisecracking Tommy Trinder, silly ass Claude Hulbert and smoothie Michael Wilding would make a winning comedy team? Frankly, even the Ritz Brothers were funnier. Yet, as with most flag-waving pictures made during the Second World War, the aim was to raise morale and not make masterpieces. In that light, this is an effective enough piece of nonsense from Ealing, with our trio of tars taking on the Nazi navy after a boozy shore leave in a South American port. A follow-up film, Fiddlers Three, appeared in 1944. DP

Tommy Trinder Tommy Taylor • Claude Hulbert Admiral • Michael Wilding Johnny • Carla Lehmann Jane • Jeanne de Casalis Mrs Pilkington • James Hayter Hans • Henry Hewitt Professor Pilkington ■ Dir Walter Forde • Scr Angus MacPhail, John Dighton, Austin Melford

The Saint ★ 12
Action thriller   1997 · US · Colour · 111min

This empty, lumbering spectacular turns author Leslie Charteris's gallant law-breaker into a cat-burgling James Bond clone. Both Val Kilmer, in the title role, and Elisabeth Shue are miscast in a mundane tale about a Russian billionaire who's trying to discover a way to glean energy from tap water. Director Phillip Noyce's misjudged fiasco is sloppily plotted, unexciting and laughable. AJ Violence, swearing. DVD

S

Val Kilmer *Simon Templar* • Elisabeth Shue *Dr Emma Russell* • Rade Serbedzija *Ivan Tretiak* • Valery Nikolaev *Ilya Tretiak* • Henry Goodman *Dr Lev Botvin* • Alun Armstrong *Chief Inspector Teal* ■ *Dir* Phillip Noyce • *Scr* Jonathan Hensleigh, Wesley Strick, from a story by Jonathan Hensleigh, from the character created by Leslie Charteris

St Elmo's Fire ★★★ 15
Drama 1985 · US · Colour · 103min

A Brat Pack movie that most of the cast would probably like to forget, this is now a great example of the excesses of the 1980s. Ally Sheedy, Emilio Estevez, Rob Lowe, Andrew McCarthy and Judd Nelson – all of whose careers have never been the same again – are the college pals trying to make their way in the world while wrestling with problems such as drug abuse, a teenage marriage, unrequited love and hidden sexuality. It's glossy and glib like so much else from the decade it represents, but it's also a fascinating record of that generation. JB Swearing, drug abuse. **DVD** **Blu**

Emilio Estevez *Kirby* • Rob Lowe *Billy* • Demi Moore *Jules* • Andrew McCarthy *Kevin* • Judd Nelson *Alec* • Ally Sheedy *Leslie* • Mare Winningham *Wendy* • Martin Balsam *Mr Beamish* • Andie MacDowell *Dale Biberman* ■ *Dir* Joel Schumacher • *Scr* Joel Schumacher, Carl Kurlander

St George's Day ★★★ 18
Crime thriller 2012 · UK · Colour · 110min

This British crime thriller doesn't break any new ground, but it treads familiar turf with some skill. Frank Harper slips smoothly into the director's chair after playing tough guys in films like *Lock, Stock...* and *The Football Factory*), and clearly knows the genre. He also has the budget to use some exotic locations in a tale about two cousins (Harper and Craig Fairbrass) who fall foul of the Russian mafia when a drugs shipment goes awry. Overall, it's a slick production, the leads have good chemistry, and Charles Dance pops up to add a touch of class. DA Violence, swearing, sexual references, drug abuse, nudity. **DVD** **Blu**

Craig Fairbrass *Ray Collishaw* • Frank Harper *Micky Mannock* • Vincent Regan *Albert Ball* • Charles Dance *Treachard* • Dexter Fletcher *Levi* • Sean Pertwee *Proctor* ■ *Dir* Frank Harper • *Scr* Frank Harper, Urs Buehler

The Saint in London ★★★ PG
Crime adventure 1939 · UK/US · BW · 72min

Mention the name Simon Templar nowadays and many will think of Roger Moore, some Ian Ogilvy, and a few Val Kilmer. But the finest Saint of them all was undoubtedly George Sanders, who inherited the role from Louis Hayward in 1939. This tale has our hero pitted against a ruthless counterfeit gang with only dizzy deb Sally Gray in his corner. This was Sanders's second outing as the debonair detective and a rattlingly good yarn it is, too. DP

George Sanders *Simon Templar "The Saint "* • Sally Gray *Penelope Parker* • David Burns *Dugan* • Gordon McLeod *Inspector Teal* • Henry Oscar *Bruno Lang* • Ralph Truman *Kussella* ■ *Dir* John Paddy Carstairs • *Scr* Lynn Root, Frank Fenton, from the novel *The Million Pound Day* by Leslie Charteris

The Saint in New York ★★ PG
Crime adventure 1938 · US · BW · 72min

The first film in RKO's low-budget nine-film series has Louis Hayward perfectly cast as the haloed hero. Subsequent Saints were George Sanders and Hugh Sinclair, but Hayward returned for the last film *The Saint's Girl Friday* made in 1954; the next time the Saint appeared on screen was in the guise of smoothie Roger Moore in the 1960s TV series. However, no other adaptation followed Charteris's source material as closely as this one, which has the Robin Hood of modern crime fighting the New York underworld. TS

Louis Hayward *Simon Templar "The Saint"* • Sig Rumann [Sig Ruman] *Hutch Rellin* • Kay Sutton *Fay Edwards* • Jonathan Hale *Inspector Fernack* • Jack Carson *Red Jenks* • Paul Guilfoyle (1) *Hymie*

Fanro ■ *Dir* Ben Holmes • *Scr* Charles Kaufman, Mortimer Offner, from the novel by Leslie Charteris

The Saint in Palm Springs ★★★
Crime adventure 1941 · US · BW · 65min

George Sanders bade farewell to the role of Simon Templar after this, his fifth outing as Leslie Charteris's suave troubleshooter. There's a pronounced end-of-term feel to the story, in which Sanders crosses swords with a gang intent on preventing him from delivering some rare stamps to their rightful owner. It's not as dull as Sanders's weary expression would have you believe, with director Jack Hively (handling his third Templar adventure) keeping the action brisk, and there is a surprisingly high body count for what was supposed to be a pretty light-hearted series. DP

George Sanders *Simon Templar "The Saint"* • Wendy Barrie *Elna* • Paul Guilfoyle (1) *Pearly Gates* • Jonathan Hale *Fernack* • Linda Hayes *Margaret Forbes* ■ *Dir* Jack Hively • *Scr* Jerry Cady [Jerome Cady], from a story by Leslie Charteris

St Ives ★★ 15
Thriller 1976 · US · Colour · 90min

This rather silly, if glossy, thriller stars an improbable Charles Bronson as a writer who gets drawn into the search for some stolen ledgers. Veteran director J Lee Thompson ensures that it all moves along at a reasonable pace and looks technically proficient. Jacqueline Bisset has nothing to do but look lovely, but keep a sharp eye out for Jeff Goldblum and Robert Englund in early roles. TS

Charles Bronson *Raymond St Ives* • John Houseman *Abner Procane* • Jacqueline Bisset *Janet Whistler* • Maximilian Schell *Dr John Constable* • Harry Guardino *Detective Deal* • Elisha Cook [Elisha Cook Jr] *Eddie the bell boy* • Daniel J Travanti *Johnny Parisi* • Robert Englund *Hood* • Mark Thomas *Hood* • Jeff Goldblum *Hood* ■ *Dir* J Lee Thompson • *Scr* Barry Beckerman, from the novel *The Procane Chronicle* by Oliver Bleeck

Saint Jack ★★★
Drama 1979 · US · Colour · 115min

One of director Peter Bogdanovich's least known movies, based on Paul Theroux's novel, this drama is an effective character study of American Ben Gazzara (in fine form), a well-educated Korean War hero who pimps and wheeler-deals throughout Singapore in the early 1970s. Needing a big cash injection, he accepts an offer to secretly photograph a visiting senator (George Lazenby) with a male prostitute. But will his sense of moral decency actually allow him to carry out the scheme? An evocative and whimsical portrait of sleazy Singapore during the Vietnam era. AJ

Ben Gazzara *Jack Flowers* • Denholm Elliott *William Leigh* • James Villiers *Frogget* • Joss Ackland *Yardley* • Rodney Bewes *Smale* • Mark Kingston *Yates* • Peter Bogdanovich *Eddie Schuman* • George Lazenby *Senator* ■ *Dir* Peter Bogdanovich • *Scr* Howard Sackler, Paul Theroux, Peter Bogdanovich, from the novel by Paul Theroux

Saint Joan ★★★ U
Historical drama 1957 · US · BW · 110min

This is one of Hollywood's celebrated disasters, panned by the critics at the time and seen by almost no one. Loosely based on George Bernard Shaw's play, the script is by none other than Graham Greene and, instead of hiring a major star, director Otto Preminger took a huge gamble with a then unknown young actress called Jean Seberg, who was the right age to play France's great heroine. "Poor Jean Seberg wasn't up to it," said Greene later. "Anyway, I got a few laughs that were not in Bernard Shaw; at least I can claim that." Flops are rarely as fascinating as this one. AT

Jean Seberg *Joan* • Richard Todd *Dunois* • Anton Walbrook *Cauchon, Bishop of Beauvais* • John Gielgud *Earl of Warwick* • Felix Aylmer *Inquisitor* • Harry Andrews *John de Stogumber* • Barry Jones *De Courcelles* • Finlay Currie *Archbishop of Rheims*

Bernard Miles *Master executioner* ■ *Dir* Otto Preminger • *Scr* Graham Greene, from the play by George Bernard Shaw

Saint Laurent ★★★
Biographical drama 2014 · Fr · Colour · 135min

After Yves Saint Laurent's death in 2008, does the world really need two biopics of the influential fashion designer? Whether we do or not, we now have them, and it's surprising how similar they are, despite only one having his estate's approval. This one, Saint Laurent minus the Yves, is the rogue production, with Gaspard Ulliel making a beguiling and sympathetic Saint Laurent, but the storytelling is often annoyingly experimental. Still, the period detail is extraordinary, and there's a cracking soundtrack. DW In French.

Gaspard Ulliel *Yves Saint Laurent* • Jérémie Renier *Pierre Bergé* • Louis Garrel *Jacques de Bascher* • Léa Seydoux *Loulou de la Falaise* • Amira Casar *Anne-Marie Munoz* ■ *Dir* Bertrand Bonello • *Scr* Bertrand Bonello, Thomas Bidegain

St Louis Blues ★★ U
Musical biography 1958 · US · BW · 95min

Nat King Cole stars as the legendary and influential blues composer WC Handy in this disappointing biopic, which deals with Handy's pursuit of his calling in the face of his Bible-punching father's disapproval, and his relationships with the two women in his life (Eartha Kitt, Ruby Dee). The movie is a sadly wasted opportunity, unimaginatively directed and dramatically dull, with Cole woodenly unconvincing. There is compensation, however, in a cast that includes Pearl Bailey, Mahalia Jackson, Cab Calloway and, as herself, Ella Fitzgerald. RK

Nat King Cole *WC Handy* • Eartha Kitt *Gogo Germaine* • Pearl Bailey *Aunt Hagar* • Cab Calloway *Blade* • Ella Fitzgerald • Mahalia Jackson *Bessie May* • Ruby Dee *Elizabeth* ■ *Dir* Allen Reisner • *Scr* Robert Smith, Ted Sherdeman

St Martin's Lane ★★★
Melodrama 1938 · UK · BW · 86min

This prestigious British melodrama was meticulously designed – to the extent that the extras who formed the theatre queues were cast in descending order of height. Yet, for all this preparation, the film was mauled by the critics and flopped at the box office. There's no denying it's a sentimental tale, but it presents a fascinating portrait of theatre land and, while Vivien Leigh overdoes it as the waif yearning for stardom, Charles Laughton is superb as the busker who supports her. DP

Charles Laughton *Charles Saggers* • Vivien Leigh *Libby* • Rex Harrison *Harley Prentiss* • Larry Adler *Constantine* • Tyrone Guthrie *Gentry* • Gus McNaughton *Arthur Smith* • Bart Cormack *Strang* ■ *Dir* Tim Whelan • *Scr* Clemence Dane, from her story

The Saint Meets the Tiger ★
Crime adventure 1943 · US/UK · BW · 78min

After a two-year gap, RKO continued its wildly inconsistent Saint series with this feeble story of smuggled ingots and worthless gold-mine shares. Hugh Sinclair is simply dreadful as Simon Templar in this cheapskate mystery directed by Paul Stein. DP

Hugh Sinclair *Simon Templar "The Saint"* • Jean Gillie *Pat Holmes* • Gordon McLeod *Inspector Teal/Professor Kahn* • Clifford Evans *Tidmarsh* • Wylie Watson *Horace* ■ *Dir* Paul Stein [Paul L Stein] • *Scr* Leslie Arliss, Wolfgang Wilhelm, James Seymour, from the novel *Meet the Tiger* by Leslie Charteris

The Saint of Fort Washington ★★ 15
Drama 1993 · US · Colour · 99min

A well-meaning, but self-conscious social drama, this tackles the rather unfashionable (well, for Hollywood at least) subject of homelessness. Matt Dillon is the mentally disabled young man who finds himself on the streets; salvation comes in the shape of Vietnam veteran Danny Glover. The two leads deliver moving performances, and the

good support cast includes Ving Rhames and Nina Siemaszko. JF Violence.

Danny Glover *Jerry* • Matt Dillon *Matthew* • Rick Aviles *Rosario* • Nina Siemaszko *Tamsen* • Ving Rhames *Little Leroy* • Joe Seneca *Spits* • Robert Beatty Jr *Ex-pharmacist* ■ *Dir* Tim Hunter • *Scr* Lyle Kessler

Saint Ralph ★★★
Period sports drama 2004 · Can · Colour · 98min

Canadian Catholic schoolboy Adam Butcher becomes convinced that winning the 1954 Boston Marathon will be the heavenly miracle needed to jolt his mother from a coma. Ever-dependable Campbell Scott anchors any straining credibility with a dignified performance as the priest trying to discourage this unrealistic goal who gets caught up in Butcher's steely resolve. Writer/director Michael McGowan's coming-of-age saga doles out the usual clichés but leavens them with a light touch, a great sense of period nostalgia, choice sight gags and universally-felt ironies concerning nascent sexuality. AJ

Adam Butcher *Ralph Walker* • Campbell Scott *Father George Hibbert* • Gordon Pinsent *Father Fitzpatrick* • Jennifer Tilly *Nurse Alice* • Shauna MacDonald *Emma* • Tamara Hope *Claire Collins* ■ *Dir/Scr* Michael McGowan

The Saint Strikes Back ★★★
Crime adventure 1939 · US · BW · 64min

Super-suave George Sanders stepped into the shoes of Simon Templar for this sprightly mystery. Here, Sanders takes on the San Francisco underworld in order to prove the innocence of Wendy Barrie's cop father. Jonathan Hale also joins the series in the recurring role of Inspector Fernack, who starts every case by putting Templar at the top of the list of suspects. Briskly directed by John Farrow, the film boasts atmospheric sets by Van Nest Polglase, who designed the Astaire/Rogers musicals as well as *Citizen Kane*. DP

George Sanders *Simon Templar "The Saint"* • Wendy Barrie *Valerie Travers* • Jonathan Hale *Henry Fernack* • Jerome Cowan *Cullis* • Neil Hamilton *Allan Breck* • Barry Fitzgerald *Zipper Dyson* • Robert Elliott *Webster* ■ *Dir* John Farrow • *Scr* John Twist, from the novel *Angels of Doom* by Leslie Charteris

The Saint Takes Over ★★★
Crime adventure 1940 · US · BW · 69min

RKO had to borrow George Sanders back from 20th Century-Fox for this entry in the ever-popular *Saint* series. Scripted by Frank Fenton and Lynn Root, it was the first not to be based on a Leslie Charteris story, but the tale of racetrack hoods who implicate Inspector Fernack (Jonathan Hale) in their race-rigging scam is packed with incident and taken at a fair gallop by director Jack Hively. Paul Guilfoyle makes his debut as Simon Templar's light-fingered assistant. DP

George Sanders *Simon Templar "The Saint"* • Wendy Barrie *Ruth* • Jonathan Hale *Inspector Henry Fernack* • Paul Guilfoyle (1) *Clarence "Pearly" Gates* • Morgan Conway *Sam Reese* • Robert Emmett Keane *Leo Sloan* • Cyrus W Kendall [Cy Kendall] *Max Bremer* • James Burke *Mike* ■ *Dir* Jack Hively • *Scr* Lynn Root, Frank Fenton, from characters by Leslie Charteris

St Trinian's ★★★ 12
Comedy 2007 · UK · Colour · 96min

Cartoonist Ronald Searle's most famous creation – the chaotic girls' boarding school that gave rise to the series of hit films in the 1950s and 60s – makes a surprisingly successful comeback here. Directors Oliver Parker and Barnaby Thompson have updated the school for modern audiences, blending dorms and jolly hockey sticks with more contemporary youth culture. Talulah Riley plays Annabelle, the new girl who leads the St Trinian's girls on a mission to save the establishment from closure. Rupert Everett plays both her father and, like Alastair Sim in the original movies, the dotty headmistress, Miss Fritton. The sketch-like comedy works better than the overall story, but it's lively fun for teenagers. The sequel, *Legend of Fritton's Gold*, is released in December 2009. JR **DVD** **BL**

Rupert Everett *Miss Fritton/Carnaby Fritton* • Colin Firth *Geoffrey Thwaites* • Lena Headey *Miss Dickinson* • Jodie Whittaker *Beverly* • Talulah Riley *Annabelle* • Gemma Arterton *Kelly* • Russell Brand *Flash Harry* • Mischa Barton *JJ French* • Anna Chancellor *Miss Bagstock* • Celia Imrie *Matron* • Stephen Fry • Toby Jones *Bursar* ■ *Dir* Oliver Parker, Barnaby Thompson • *Scr* Piers Ashworth, Nick Moorcroft, from the cartoons by Ronald Searle

St Trinian's 2: the Legend of Fritton's Gold ★ PG
Comedy 2009 · UK · Colour · 100min

Those unruly schoolgirl sirens hunt for pirate treasure but end up searching for laughs instead in this very sloppy sequel to the 2007 revamp. Sagging under the weight of too much plot, this sub-*Carry On* romp wearily coasts along on the lines of a rudimentary old-school farce rather than anything resembling wit. Rupert Everett's parody of Camilla Parker-Bowles feels stale this time around, though nothing's quite as disappointing as the depressingly camp villain played by David Tennant – though he does sum up the lacklustre proceedings with the line "Oh, this is interminable". AJ **DVD** **BL**

Rupert Everett *Miss Fritton/Captain Fritton/Fortnum Fritton* • Colin Firth *Geoffrey Thwaites* • David Tennant *Sir Piers Pomfrey* • Talulah Riley *Annabelle* • Gemma Arterton *Kelly* • Jodie Whittaker *Beverley* • Toby Jones *Bursar* • Celia Imrie *Matron* ■ *Dir* Oliver Parker, Barnaby Thompson • *Scr* Piers Ashworth, Nick Moorcroft, from cartoons by Ronald Searle

The St Valentine's Day Massacre ★★★ 15
Crime drama 1967 · US · Colour · 95min

The most authentic documentary-style account – complete with narration giving precise time and location details – of the Chicago gang wars between crime lords Al Capone (Jason Robards) and Bugs Moran (Ralph Meeker), that led to the infamous 1929 massacre. Offbeat casting, lots of bloody action and cult director Roger Corman working for a major studio – and with a decent budget for the first time – make for a compelling and always fascinating throwback to the quick-fire gangster movies of the 1930s. AJ Violence, swearing. **DVD**

Jason Robards *Al Capone* • George Segal *Peter Gusenberg* • Ralph Meeker *George "Bugsy" Moran* • Jean Hale *Myrtle Nelson* • Clint Ritchie *"Machinegun Jack" McGurn* • Frank Silvera *Nicholas Sorello* • Joseph Campanella *Al Weinshank* • Bruce Dern *John May* • Jack Nicholson *Gino* ■ *Dir* Roger Corman • *Scr* Howard Browne

St Vincent ★★★★ 12
Comedy 2014 · US · Colour · 98min

A film about the friendship between a boy and his curmudgeonly Vietnam War vet neighbour might initially set the schmaltz alarms ringing, but this is a keenly observed comedy, its sentimentality liberally laced with top-drawer laughs. Bill Murray stars as Vincent, at first reluctant to keep an eye on single mum Melissa McCarthy's 12-year-old son, but he quickly grows into his role as a hard-drinking, foul-mouthed mentor. Writer/director Theodore Melfi sets up a series of events that brilliantly illustrate Murray's talents in his best role in years. TeS Swearing **DVD** **BL**

Bill Murray *Vincent* • Melissa McCarthy *Maggie* • Naomi Watts *Daka* • Chris O'Dowd *Brother Geraghty* • Terrence Howard *Zucko* ■ *Dir/Scr* Theodore Melfi

The Saint's Double Trouble ★★
Crime adventure 1940 · US · BW · 67min

Perhaps the least accomplished film in RKO's popular B series, this entry, nevertheless, has the added bonus of George Sanders pursuing himself, as he plays both Simon Templar and a criminal

mastermind called "The Boss". The scene in which Templar, posing as his criminal double, meets "The Boss" impersonating Templar, is a classic example of back-projected trickery. The film also has the distinction of being one of Bela Lugosi's final bids to prove he was capable of more than just horror, but here, his Egyptian smuggler makes little impact. DP

George Sanders *Simon Templar "The Saint "/" The Boss"* • Helene Whitney *Anne* • Jonathan Hale *Fernack* • Bela Lugosi *Partner* ■ *Dir* Jack Hively • *Scr* Ben Holmes, from a story by Leslie Charteris

The Saint's Vacation ★★
Crime adventure 1941 · US/UK · BW · 78min

Hugh Sinclair assumed the role of Simon Templar for this tame thriller, made in Britain by RKO. Although co-scripted by Leslie Charteris from his own story, it's hardly a mystery, with Sinclair racing ruthless Nazi agents to a musical box that contains a vital code. Switzerland has never looked quite so much like a series of hurriedly built studio sets. DP

Hugh Sinclair *Simon Templar " The Saint"* • Sally Gray *Mary Langdon* • Arthur Macrae *Monty Hayward* • Cecil Parker *Rudolph Hauser* • Leueen MacGrath *Valerie* • Gordon McLeod *Inspector Teal* • John Warwick *Gregory* • Ivor Barnard *Emil* • Manning Whiley *Marko* • Felix Aylmer *Charles Leighton* ■ *Dir* Leslie Fenton • *Scr* Jeffry Dell, Leslie Charteris, from the novel *Getaway* by Leslie Charteris

La Saison des Hommes ★★★ 12
Drama 2000 · Fr/Tun · Colour · 122min

Contrasting the experiences of neglected carpet weaver Rabiaa Ben Abdallah and those of her 20-something daughters Ghalia Ben Ali and Hend Sabri, Moufida Tlatli's second feature makes few structural or thematic advances on her 1994 directorial debut, *The Silences of the Palace*. Yet again the action skips between time frames and imposing environments to demonstrate the lowly status of women, while her predilection for lengthy, leisurely takes serves to emphasise the isolation and frustration they endure. DP Arabic, French +subtitles.

Rabiaa Ben Abdallah *Aicha* • Sabah Bouzouita *Zeineb* • Ghalia Ben Ali *Meriem* • Hend Sabri *Emna* ■ *Dir* Moufida Tlatli • *Scr* Moufida Tlatli, Nouri Bouzid

Salaam Bombay! ★★★★ 15
Drama 1988 · Ind/Fr/UK · Colour · 109min

Dickensian in its empathy with the poor, uncompromising in its realism and ambitious in both scope and technique, Mira Nair's debut feature is one of the most arresting studies of street life ever made. Shot on location after numerous workshops had drawn together a cast made up mostly of homeless kids, the tale of a runaway's assimilation into the dangerous world of petty crime, drugs and prostitution draws on Nair's documentary experience. But it also demonstrates her skill in coaxing a performance of disarming naturalism from Shafiq Syed as the 11-year-old whose indomitable spirit prevents the film from becoming too painful or sentimental. DP Hindi +subtitles. Sex scenes, violence, swearing. **DVD**

Shafiq Syed *Krishna /Chaipau* • Raghubir Yadav [Raghuvir Yadav] *Chillum* • Aneeta Kanwar *Rekha* • Nana Patekar *Baba* • Hansa Vithal *Manju* ■ *Dir* Mira Nair • *Scr* Sooni Taraporevala, from a story by Mira Nair, Sooni Taraporevala

Salaam E Ishq ★★★★ 12
Romantic drama 2007 · Ind · Colour · 200min

This Bollywood spin on Richard Curtis's *Love Actually* skilfully weaves together half a dozen stories, and imbues the idealistic tales of broken hearts and romantic aspirations with enough infectious optimism to sweep the viewer up. At just under four hours, it's undoubtably a long haul but there's enough genuine charm to make it a hugely enjoyable experience. OA Hindi +subtitles. **DVD**

Salman Khan *Rahul* • Priyanka Chopra *Kkamini* • Anil Kapoor *Vinay* • Juhi Chawla *Seema* • Govinda *Raju* ■ *Dir* Nikhil Advani • *Scr* Suresh Nair, Saurabh Shukla, from a story by Nikhil Advani

The Salamander ★ 15
Thriller 1981 · US/It /UK · Colour · 97min

Morris West's novel becomes a heavy-handed drama about a failed right-wing coup in Italy, with Franco Nero as a spy and Anthony Quinn as a millionaire businessman, who also hunts down war criminals. First time director Peter Zinner (whose editing of *The Deer Hunter* won him an Oscar) gets bogged down in plot and then wastes time on travelogue material, reducing the impressive cast to bystanders. AT

Anthony Quinn *Bruno Manzini* • Franco Nero *Dante Matucci* • Martin Balsam *Stefanelli* • Sybil Danning *Lili Anders* • Christopher Lee *Director Baldassare* • Claudia Cardinale *Elena* • Cleavon Little *Major Malinowski* • Eli Wallach *Leporello* ■ *Dir* Peter Zinner • *Scr* Robert Katz, from the novel by Morris West

Salem Falls ★★
Crime drama 2011 · US/Can · Colour · 89min

In a stripped-back take on *The Crucible*-inspired novel by Jodi Picoult, a former teacher (James Van Der Beek) arrives in the titular small town and is immediately targeted by a schoolgirl (AJ Michalka), who uses spell-casting to try to force his affection. But despite her unrealistically portrayed magic, Van Der Beek only has eyes for a diner owner (Sarah Sanguin Carter). Accusations are made and dark truths revealed in the usual watered-down, TV-movie fashion before a confusingly scripted final twist. SF

James Van Der Beek *Jack McBradden* • Sarah Sanguin Carter [Sarah Carter] *Addie Peabody* • AJ Michalka [Amanda Michalka] *Gillian Duncan* • Rick Roberts *Amos Duncan* ■ *Dir* Bradley Walsh • *Scr* Craig Bolotin, Teena Booth, from Jodi Picoult's novel

Salem's Lot ★★★ 15
Horror 1979 · US · Colour · 105min

More blood and stronger horror was added to the spooky theatrical version of the truncated television mini-series based on Stephen King's bestseller. Novelist David Soul moves to the New England town troubled by vampirism after mysterious James Mason moves into the sinister house on the hill. Director Tobe Hooper plunders *Psycho* and *Nosferatu* to good effect in a brisk bloodsucker saga featuring the very creepy looking Reggie Nalder as the undead nemesis. Larry Cohen directed the 1987 sequel, *A Return to Salem's Lot*. AJ **DVD**

David Soul *Ben Mears* • James Mason *Richard K Straker* • Bonnie Bedelia *Susan Norton* • Lance Kerwin *Mark Petrie* • Lew Ayres *Jason Burke* • Ed Flanders *Dr Bill Norton* • Geoffrey Lewis *Mike Ryerson* • Kenneth McMillan *Parkins Gillespie* • Reggie Nalder *Kurt Barlow* ■ *Dir* Tobe Hooper • *Scr* Paul Monash, from the novel by Stephen King

Salinger ★★★
Documentary 2013 · US · Colour and BW · 129min

As JD Salinger was arguably the most reclusive author of modern times, it's not surprising to discover that this is pretty much reliant on third parties and scratchy archive footage. Although clearly a fan himself, director Shane Salerno doesn't shy away from the darker aspects of Salinger's personality. Ultimately, the film never really gets to the bottom of why Salinger spent almost half of his adult life living in secrecy, but he has delivered a thoughtful portrait of a troubled genius. JF

Philip Seymour Hoffman • Edward Norton • John Cusack • Martin Sheen • Tom Wolfe • Gore Vidal • Danny DeVito • Judd Apatow ■ *Dir* Shane Salerno • *Scr* Shane Salerno, from the non-fiction book *Salinger: a Biography* by Paul Alexander

Sallah ★★★ U
Comedy 1964 · Is · BW · 104min

In 1948, Topol, his wife and seven children arrive in Israel – only to be housed in a transit camp rather than the roomy flat they were expecting. Needing £1,000 to jump the queue and secure the flat, he throws himself into a number of dodgy schemes to raise the money. Warm-hearted satire with Topol playing Sallah like an early, Jewish version of *Minder's* "Arfur" Daley. Perhaps a bit overburdened with local colour and characters, but still a pleasant enough time-passer. DF

Chaim Topol [Topol] *Sallah Shabati* • Geula Noni *Habbubah Shabati* • Gila Almagor *Bathsheva Sosialit* • Arik Einstein *Ziggi* • Shraga Friedman *Neuman* ■ *Dir* Ephraim Kishon • *Scr* Ephraim Kishon, from a story by Ephraim Kishon

Sally in Our Alley ★ PG
Romantic musical drama 1931 · UK · BW · 70min

Of interest only to historians or those addicted to "Our Gracie", this worse-than-mediocre film made Gracie Fields a star and gave her her lifelong signature song, *Sally*. Directed by Maurice Elvey and co-starring Ian Hunter, the plot has Gracie as a teashop entertainer who believes her boyfriend has been killed in the war. Of course he hasn't been. RK **DVD**

Gracie Fields *Sally Winch* • Ian Hunter *George Miles* • Florence Desmond *Florrie Small* • Ivor Barnard *Tod Small* • Fred Groves *Alf Cope* ■ *Dir* Maurice Elvey • *Scr* Miles Malleson, Alma Reville, Archie Pitt, from the play *The Likes of 'Er* by Charles McEvoy

Sally, Irene and Mary ★★
Silent comedy drama 1925 · US · BW · 58min

Edmund Goulding directs this tale of the salutary experiences of three chorus girls on the make. Constance Bennett is the most worldly of the trio; cheerful Sally O'Neil wisely relinquishes the bright lights in favour of her beau; and Joan Crawford comes to a horrible end. This film version of a stage musical inevitably lost much in its transfer to the silent screen and offers little of interest now, apart from its leading ladies. RK

Constance Bennett *Sally* • Joan Crawford *Irene* • Sally O'Neil *Mary* • William Haines *Jimmy Dugan* ■ *Dir* Edmund Goulding • *Scr* Edmund Goulding, from the play by Edward Dowling, Cyrus Wood

Sally, Irene and Mary ★★★ U
Musical comedy 1938 · US · BW · 85min

Borrowing the title, but nothing else of an early stage musical, this stars Alice Faye and her then husband Tony Martin. It's movie jam-packed with plot, action, songs, and a cast that includes Jimmy Durante, Fred Allen, Gregory Ratoff and, as a middle-aged moneybags widow with her sights set on Martin, Louise Hovick – better known as stripper Gypsy Rose Lee. This genial nonsense begin with three girls (Faye, Joan Davis, Marjorie Weaver), working as manicurists while looking for a break into showbiz . RK

Alice Faye *Sally Day* • Tony Martin (1) *Tommy Reynolds* • Fred Allen (2) *Gabriel "Gabby" Green* • Jimmy Durante *Jefferson Twitchell* • Gregory Ratoff *Baron Zorka* • Joan Davis *Irene Keene* • Marjorie Weaver *Mary Stevens* • Louise Hovick [Gypsy Rose Lee] *Joyce Taylor* ■ *Dir* William A Seiter • *Scr* Harry Tugend, Jack Yellen, from a story by Karl Tunberg, Don Ettinger, from the play by Edward Dowling, Cyrus Wood

Sally of the Sawdust ★★ U
Silent comedy 1925 · US · BW · 86min

After the death of her mother, who was disowned for marrying a circus performer, Carol Dempster is raised by juggler and conman WC Fields. When she's grown up, Fields decides to find her grandparents, and sets a multiplicity of complications into motion. Adapted from the play *Poppy*, under which title it was remade in 1936 with Fields again starring, this was the only feature-length comedy made by DW Griffith. RK **DVD**

S

Carol Dempster *Sally* • WC Fields *Prof Eustace P McGargle* • Alfred Lunt *Peyton Lennox* ■ *Dir* DW Griffith • *Scr* Forrest Halsey, from the play *Poppy* by Dorothy Donnelly

Salmon Fishing in the Yemen ★★★ 12
Romantic drama   2011 · UK · Colour · 102min

Fans of Paul Torday's bestselling novel may find Ewan McGregor a curious choice for the part of fisheries scientist Dr Alfred Jones, an officious man who mocks the plans of a wealthy Arab (Amr Waked) to create a salmon run in the Yemeni desert. Emily Blunt plays an executive assistant to the sheikh, and she and McGregor enjoy a cosy rapport. Lasse Hallström's film isn't wholly convincing, but the *Chocolat* director has an affinity with off-kilter love stories, while Kristin Scott Thomas gives a funny turn as the Prime Minister's spin doctor. The result is a sweet, warm and witty romance. SP *Swearing, sexual references.* DVD

Ewan McGregor *Dr Alfred "Fred" Jones* • Emily Blunt *Harriet Chetwode-Talbot* • Kristin Scott Thomas *Patricia Maxwell* • Amr Waked *Sheikh Muhammed* • Tom Mison *Captain Robert Mayers* • Rachael Stirling *Mary Jones* • Catherine Steadman *Ashley* ■ *Dir* Lasse Hallström • *Scr* Simon Beaufoy, from the novel by Paul Torday

Salmonberries ★★ 15
Drama   1991 · Ger · Colour · 90min

Deprived of star Marianne Sägebrecht after a trio of pictures, Percy Adlon seemed to lose his way with this story set in the frozen wastes of Alaska and the newly unified Berlin. Ultimately, it's an optimistic film about the true nature of love and coming to terms with the past, but from its confused opening this is hard to engage with, for all the efforts of kd lang as an Inuit trying to conceal her sexual identity and Rosel Zech as the shy German unsure how best to love her. Some moving moments, but lacking in pace. DP *Swearing, nudity.*

kd lang *Kotzebue* • Rosel Zech *Roswitha* • Chuck Connors *Bingo Chuck* • Jane Lind *Noayak* • Oscar Kawagley *Butch* • Wolfgang Steinberg *Albert* ■ *Dir* Percy Adlon • *Scr* Percy Adlon, Felix O Adlon

Salo, or the 120 Days of Sodom ★★★★ 18
Political drama   1975 · It/Fr · Colour · 111min

Relocating the Marquis de Sade's infamous novel to wartime Italy, this film has become synonymous with sexual deviance and bestial violence. Yet, the soon-to-be-murdered Pier Paolo Pasolini had loftier ambitions than simply shocking the complacent who thought his work obscene. Each of the libertines committing the unspeakably heinous acts represents a social pillar that had delivered the nation into the hands of the Fascists – the law, the merchants, the aristocracy and the church. By depicting their crimes from a distance and by cutting away at the most distasteful moments, he reveals the culpability of the viewer for their passive reponse to the barbarism. Devastating. DP *Italian +subtitles. Graphic violence, sex scenes.* DVD

Paolo Bonacelli *The Duke* • Giorgio Cataldi *The Bishop* • Uberto Paulo Quintavalle *Chief Magistrate* • Caterina Boratto *Signora Castelli* • Hélène Surgère *Signora Vaccari* ■ *Dir* Pier Paolo Pasolini • *Scr* Pier Paolo Pasolini, Sergio Citti, from the novel *Les 120 Journées de Sodome* by the Marquis de Sade

Salome ★★
Silent drama   1922 · US · BW · 38min

Hailed as America's first art film, silent movie star Alla Nazimova lost a personal fortune producing this extravagant version of Oscar Wilde's controversial play, which re-created Aubrey Beardsley's sumptuous text illustrations for the screen. Nazimova plays the lead in this ornate, if stagey, reading of the biblical story of King Herod and his unbridled passion for his adolescent stepdaughter Salome, who demands the head of her own lust object Jokanaan (John the Baptist), in return for the Dance of the Seven Veils. All the sets and costumes were

designed by the future Mrs Rudolph Valentino, Natacha Rambova, and the entire cast and crew were allegedly homosexual in homage to Wilde. AJ

Nazimova [Alla Nazimova] *Salome* • Rose Dione *Herodias* • Mitchell Lewis *Herod* • Nigel de Brulier *Jokaanan* ■ *Dir* Charles Bryant • *Scr* Peter M Winters [Natacha Rambova], from the play by Oscar Wilde

Salome ★★★ PG
Biblical drama   1953 · US · Colour · 98min

This superbly cast tosh from Columbia is directed at a deathly pace by veteran William Dieterle, and given credence only by Alan Badel's sincere portrayal of John the Baptist. But credence isn't what this film's about. You watch it for the stars; the dashing Stewart Granger, flexing his armoured torso for the benefit of ravishing Rita Hayworth, while Charles Laughton chews the scenery as Herod. TS

Rita Hayworth *Princess Salome* • Stewart Granger *Commander Claudius* • Charles Laughton *King Herod* • Judith Anderson *Queen Herodias* • Sir Cedric Hardwicke [Cedric Hardwicke] *Caesar Tiberius* • Alan Badel *John the Baptist* • Basil Sydney *Pontius Pilate* ■ *Dir* William Dieterle • *Scr* Harry Kleiner, from a story by Jesse L Lasky Jr [Jesse Lasky Jr], from a story by Harry Kleiner

Salomé ★★★ 15
Drama   2013 · US · Colour · 80min

He's quite the one for his obsessions, is Al Pacino. Last time, it was Shakespeare's *Richard III*, which resulted in his documentary *Looking for Richard*. This time, it's *Salomé*, Wilde's play about the Judean princess who danced for King Herod, and demanded the head of John the Baptist in return. Estelle Parsons's no-frills 2006 stage performance has Jessica Chastain as a suitably seductive Salomé; Pacino himself plays Herod, over-acting as only Al can; and Kevin Anderson is an all-suffering Baptist. An intense experience, it's all the more so for being filmed up close and personal. DA DVD

Al Pacino *King Herod* • Jessica Chastain *Salomé* • Kevin Anderson *John the Baptist/Jokanaan* • Roxanne Hart *Herodias* ■ *Dir* Al Pacino • *Scr* Al Pacino, from Oscar Wilde's play

Salome, Where She Danced ★★
Wartime spy melodrama   1945 · US · BW · 90min

The sultry Yvonne De Carlo is Salome, a Viennese dancer who teams up with American newsman Rod Cameron during the Franco-Prussian war to out-manoeuvre Bismarck's lot. Forced to flee Europe, she ends up in an Arizona desert town and then San Francisco, attracting adulation and becoming involved in several adventures along the way. This period melodrama has a script that is so bad and acting that's so variable as to make it absolutely hilarious. Indeed, more than half a century after it was made, it has acquired a certain cult status. RK

Yvonne De Carlo *Salome/Anna Maria* • Rod Cameron *Jim Steed* • David Bruce *Cleve "Stagecoach" Blunt* • Walter Slezak *Colonel Ivan Dimitrioff* • Albert Dekker *Count Erik Von Bohlen* • Marjorie Rambeau *Madam Europe* ■ *Dir* Charles Lamont • *Scr* Laurence Stallings, from a story by Michael J Phillips

Salome's Last Dance ★ 18
Drama   1988 · UK · Colour · 85min

Ken Russell's career continued to slide downwards with this execrable re-working of Oscar Wilde's banned play, as an end of the pier show acted by some of his pals. The whole grossly over-the-top farrago shrieks excess and truly abominable acting, particularly from Russell himself, who bounces around the small enclosed set as a leering, ruddy-faced photographer. Worth watching only for Stratford Johns's ability to invest a tiresome Herod with a wry, mischievous air. SH *Swearing, nudity.*

Glenda Jackson *Herodias/Lady Alice* • Stratford Johns *Herod/Alfred Taylor* • Nickolas Grace *Oscar Wilde* • Douglas Hodge *Lord Alfred Douglas/John the Baptist* • Imogen Millais-Scott

Salome/Rose • Denis Ull *Tigellenus/Chilvers* • Ken Russell *Kenneth* ■ *Dir* Ken Russell • *Scr* Ken Russell, from the play *Salomé* by Oscar Wilde

Salon Kitty ★★ 18
Erotic period drama   1976 · It/W Ger · Colour · 133min

In independent director Giovanni Tinto Brass's trashy tale of fascist decadence in Berlin in 1939, young women are trained to entertain Nazi officers with degrading perversions in the famous high-class brothel of the title. A wild mix of graphic sex, fetishistic art direction, heavy-handed political statements and gore, this spawned a rash of nasty Nazi exploitation flicks. AJ *Italian +subtitles.* DVD

Helmut Berger *Captain Helmut Wallenberg* • Ingrid Thulin *Kitty Kellermann* • Teresa Ann Savoy *Margherita* • Bekim Fehmiu *Captain Hans Reiter* ■ *Dir* Giovanni Tinto Brass [Tinto Brass] • *Scr* Ennio De Concini, Maria Pia Fusco, Giovanni Tinto Brass

Saloon Bar ★★★
Crime mystery   1940 · UK · BW · 75min

Gordon Harker was a familiar face in British thrillers during the 1930s, his mournful expression and throaty cockney accent enabled him to play characters on either side of the law. In this engaging Ealing whodunnit, he has a fine old time as a bookie playing detective in his local. Director Walter Forde makes effective use of the claustrophobic set to build tension, and he is well served by an efficient cast of suspects. DP

Gordon Harker *Joe Harris* • Elizabeth Allan *Queenie* • Mervyn Johns *Wickers* • Joyce Barbour *Sally* • Anna Konstam *Ivy* • Cyril Raymond *Harry Small* • Judy Campbell *Doris* • Al Millen *Fred* • Norman Pierce *Bill Hoskins* • Alec Clunes *Eddie Graves* ■ *Dir* Walter Forde • *Scr* Angus MacPhail, John Dighton, from a play by Frank Harvey Jr

Salt ★★ 12
Action thriller   2010 · US · Colour · 95min

CIA superspy Evelyn Salt (Angelina Jolie) finds her reputation in tatters when a Russian defector accuses her of being a Soviet plant in this action-driven espionage thriller with more than a hint of Cold War paranoia. The movie does its best to keep us in suspense, delivering car chases, punch-ups and explosions at frequent intervals. Though Angelina's star-power is never in doubt, she fails to convince and this ends up pacey and empty in equal measures. TJ *English, Russian +subtitles.* DVD

Angelina Jolie *Evelyn Salt* • Liev Schreiber *Theodore "Ted" Winter* • Chiwetel Ejiofor *Peabody* • Daniel Olbrychski *Oleg Vassily Orlov* • August Diehl *Mike Krause* • André Braugher *Secretary of Defense* ■ *Dir* Phillip Noyce • *Scr* Kurt Wimmer

Salt & Pepper ★★★
Comedy caper   1968 · UK · Colour · 102min

Sinatra clan members, Sammy Davis Jr and Peter Lawford came to Britain to make this amiable, though strictly routine, comedy crime caper. They play Soho club-owners involved in a series of murders that turn out to be part of an international conspiracy. The attempt to jump on the "Swinging London" bandwagon, pathetic at the time, now has high camp value and some of the lines are still funny. Although loathed by the press and eventually released as a second-feature, it produced a sequel (*One More Time*) in 1970. DM

Sammy Davis Jr *Charles Salt* • Peter Lawford *Christopher Pepper* • Michael Bates *Inspector Crabbe* • Ilona Rodgers *Marianne Renaud* • John Le Mesurier *Colonel Woodstock* • Graham Stark *Sergeant Walters* • Ernest Clark *Colonel Balsom* • Jeanne Roland *Mai Ling* ■ *Dir* Richard Donner • *Scr* Michael Pertwee

The Salt of Life ★★★ 12
Comedy   2011 · It · Colour · 85min

Lampooning himself and, just possibly, former Italian prime minister Silvio Berlusconi, Gianni Di Gregorio's second feature will disconcert some with its take on

the fantasies of the ageing male. Yet this gentle comedy of sexual manners is knowingly charming in its insights into lively minds and depreciating bodies, as every attempted seduction by Di Gregorio's wistful 60-something misfires and he is forced to accept his wooing days are over. A spiritedly played social satire that will raise the odd indulgent smile. DP *Italian +subtitles.* DVD

Gianni Di Gregorio *Gianni* • Valeria De Franciscis Bendoni [Valeria De Franciscis] *Mother* • Alfonso Santagata *Alfonso* • Elisabetta Piccolomini *Gianni's wife* ■ *Dir* Gianni Di Gregorio • *Scr* Gianni Di Gregorio, Valerio Attanasio

Salt of the Earth ★★★★★★
Drama   1954 · US · BW · 94min

Probably the most left-wing movie ever made in America, this represents an extraordinary act of defiance against McCarthyism and the Hollywood blacklist. Its subject is a miners' strike, but the picture opens a Pandora's box of themes, ranging from immigrant workers, racism, the rights of women and the way that America's postwar economic boom passes these people by. Director Herbert J Biberman, producer Paul Jarrico, Oscar-winning writer Michael Wilson, composer Sol Kaplan and actor Will Geer were all blacklisted at the time and the film, financed by the Miners Union, was subject to constant FBI harassment and barely shown in cinemas. A riveting milestone in the political history of cinema. JG

Rosaura Revueltas *Esperanza Quintero* • Juan Chacon *Ramon Quintero* • Will Geer *Sheriff* • David Wolfe *Barton* • Melvin Williams *Hartwell* • David Sarvis *Alexander* • Henrietta Williams *Teresa Vidal* ■ *Dir* Herbert J Biberman • *Scr* Michael Wilson

The Salt of the Earth ★★★ 12A
Documentary   2014 · Fr/It/Bra · Colour and BW · 109min

This evocative, Oscar-nominated documentary pays tribute to Brazilian photographer Sebastiao Salgado, who has been travelling around the world for the last 40 years, documenting the devastating effects of starvation, poverty, war, displacement and genocide. The film is filled with his photographic work, accompanied by detailed commentary from the man himself. But we learn very little about his working methods and the film occasionally feels like an extended slideshow. That said, it is extremely moving in places and some of the images are genuinely breathtaking. SC *In English, French, Portuguese.* DVD

Sebastiao Salgado • Wim Wenders ■ *Dir* Juliano Ribeiro Salgado, Wim Wenders • *Scr* Juliano Ribeiro Salgado, Wim Wenders, David Rosier

Salt on Our Skin ★★ 18
Romantic drama   1992 · Ger/Can/Fr · Colour · 106min

This tale of attracting opposites provides Greta Scacchi with another opportunity to indulge in a little steamy romance. As the globetrotting feminist whose principles founder on the rippling torso of Scottish fisherman Vincent D'Onofrio, she is a touch too glamorous to convince. But then nothing about Andrew Birkin's drama is credible. DP

Greta Scacchi *George* • Vincent D'Onofrio *Gavin* • Anaïs Jeanneret *Frederique* • Claudine Auger *George's mother* • Rolf Illig *George's father* • Shirley Henderson *Mary* • Charles Berling *Roger* ■ *Dir* Andrew Birkin • *Scr* Bee Gilbert, from the novel *Les Vaisseaux du Coeur* by Benoîte Groult

The Salton Sea ★★★ 18
Crime thriller   2002 · US · Colour · 99min

A rock star-styled Val Kilmer plays it hip as a lowlife pretender hunting for his wife's killers in this eccentric and atmospheric crime thriller. Shot like a frenetic *film noir* within the murky world of LA's crystal meth users, it marks director DJ Caruso's first non-TV feature. Kilmer is on top form as the jazz player masquerading as an addict,

S

while Vincent D'Onofrio steals the show as a big-time dealer whose own habit has worn away his nose. Sophisticated yet irreverent, intelligent yet bizarre, this is left-field viewing with a seriously cool veneer. **SF** Violence, swearing, drug abuse, sex scenes. **DVD**

Val Kilmer *Danny/Tom* • Vincent D'Onofrio *Pooh-Bear* • Adam Goldberg *Kujo* • Luis Guzman *Quincy* • Doug Hutchison *Morgan* • Anthony LaPaglia *Garcetti* • Glenn Plummer *Bobby* ■ *Dir* DJ Caruso • *Scr* Tony Gayton

Saltwater ★★★ 15

Comedy drama
1999 · Ire/UK/Sp · Colour · 95min

Conor McPherson's feature debut is a darkly comic study of the internal strains threatening a tightly knit family in an isolated Irish seaside town. Young Laurence Kinlan gets involved with a dangerous new friend, while potential brother-in-law Conor Mullen has sexual and intellectual problems at the college where he teaches. But the focus falls primarily on café-owner Brian Cox's eldest son, Peter McDonald, who resorts to robbery to repay his father's debt to local loan shark Brendan Gleeson. The narrative is somewhat disjointed, but it's solidly made and played. **DP** Violence, swearing.

Peter McDonald *Frank Beneventi* • Brian Cox (1) *George Beneventi* • Conor Mullen *Dr Raymond Sullivan* • Laurence Kinlan *Joe Beneventi* • Brendan Gleeson *"Simple" Simon McCurdie* ■ *Dir/Scr* Conor McPherson

Salty O'Rourke ★★★★

Sports comedy drama 1945 · US · BW · 97min

Alan Ladd is on top form as a likeable heel in this brightly written racetrack story. A gambler in debt to gangsters, Ladd recruits an obnoxious but talented young jockey, convincingly played by Stanley Clements, to ride a vital race for him. Ladd then has to charm Gail Russell's schoolteacher into tolerating the youth's classroom insolence, as expulsion would bar him from racing. It's a delight from start to finish, thanks to Walsh's polished direction, excellent casting and - most particularly - the original screenplay by Milton Holmes, which gained an Academy Award nomination. **AE**

Alan Ladd *Salty O'Rourke* • Gail Russell *Barbara Brooks* • William Demarest *Smitty* • Stanley "Stash" Clements [Stanley Clements] *Johnny Cates* • Bruce Cabot *Doc Baxter* • Spring Byington *Mrs Brooks* • Rex Williams *The Babe* • Darryl Hickman *Sneezer* ■ *Dir* Raoul Walsh • *Scr* Milton Holmes

Saludos Amigos ★★★ U

Animation 1943 · US · Colour · 40min

Produced to support the United States' "Good Neighbour" policy towards Latin America and to prevent its nations from allying with the Axis powers during the Second World War, *Saludos Amigos* and its 1944 companion *The Three Caballeros* are among the least seen Disney films. While perhaps better propaganda than entertainment, this short feature still has plenty to enjoy. Donald Duck's tour of Peru includes a hilarious meeting with a pesky llama, while Goofy comes a cropper on the pampas. **DP**

■ *Dir* Bill Roberts, Jack Kinney, Hamilton Luske, Wilfred Jackson

Salut Cousin! ★★★ 15

Comedy drama
1996 · Fr/Bel/Alg/Lux · Colour · 102min

Returning to France after a sojourn in his native Algeria, Merzak Allouache opted for a droll approach in relating this sly variation on the town-and-country-mouse theme. In Paris to pick up some clothing, rag-trade gofer Gad Elmaleh accepts the hospitality of his cousin Mess Hattou, who has adapted to the Parisian lifestyle in a way that both shocks and intrigues Elmaleh. An accessible character comedy. **DP** French +subtitles. Swearing, nudity.

Gad Elmaleh *Alilo* • Mess Hattou *Mokrane "Mok" Bensalem* • Magaly Berdy *Fatoumata* • Ann-Gisel Glass *Laurence* • Jean Benguigui *Maurice* ■ *Dir* Merzak Allouache • *Scr* Merzak Allouache, Caroline Thivel

Salute ★★★ PG

Sports documentary
2008 · Aus/US · Colour · 88min

This worthy documentary has the inside story on one of the most iconic political moments in sport: the black power salute of African-American athletes Tommie Smith and John Carlos on the medal podium at the 1968 Mexico Olympics. The movie takes the viewpoint of silver medallist Peter Norman, the white Australian who stood alongside them – director Matt Norman is his nephew. The movie is sometimes repetitive, and lacking in archive footage, but the impact of the moment is well worth documenting. **KK** **DVD**

Chris Kirby [Christopher Kirby] *Narrator* ■ *Dir/Scr* Matt Norman

The Salute of the Jugger ★★ 18

Science-fiction action adventure
1989 · US/Aus · Colour · 91min

Rutger Hauer stars as a veteran player of a savage future sport that combines rugby, basketball and gratuitous violence, who's reduced to leading a ragbag outfit of semi-pros from village to village to take on all comers. That is, until ambitious apprentice Joan Chen spurs him towards a return to the big city. Trite and dull. **RS** Violence, swearing, nudity.

Rutger Hauer *Sallow* • Joan Chen *Kidda* • Vincent D'Onofrio [Vincent D'Onofrio] *Young Gar* • Delroy Lindo *Mbulu* • Anna Katarina *Big Cimber* • Gandhi MacIntyre *Gandhi* • Justin Monju *Dog Boy* • Max Fairchild *Gonzo* • Hugh Keays-Byrne *Lord Vile* ■ *Dir/Scr* David Peoples [David Webb Peoples]

Salvador ★★★★ 18

Biographical war drama
1986 · US · Colour · 116min

In his third feature, director Oliver Stone showed us what he was made of with this indignant, frenetic, politically candid drama. Instead of reflecting the brutality and CIA-supported chaos of the guerrilla war in Central America by making his protagonist the film's moral compass, Stone throws in a cynical, drug-taking, burnt-out foreign correspondent (James Woods), in search of Hunter S Thompson-like kicks with his DJ sidekick James Belushi. It is through Woods, as the scales fall from his eyes and he marries a local girl (Elpidia Carrillo) in order to get her out of the country, that we come to appreciate what's happening. **AC** Violence, drug abuse, swearing, nudity. **DVD**

James Woods *Richard Boyle* • James Belushi *Dr Rock* • Michael Murphy (1) *Ambassador Thomas Kelly* • John Savage *John Cassady* • Elpidia Carrillo *Maria* • Tony Plana *Major Max* • Colby Chester *Jack Morgan* • Cynthia Gibb *Cathy Moore* ■ *Dir* Oliver Stone • *Scr* Oliver Stone, Richard Boyle

Salvage ★★★ 18

Horror thriller 2009 · UK · Colour · 75min

Director Lawrence Gough's home-invasion horror is a smartly budgeted and often scary chiller. A timely air of paranoia is brought to a nightmare scenario involving the contents of a shipwrecked storage container that causes havoc in a sleepy cul-de-sac community on the Wirral. Filmed on the old *Brookside* set, Gough's feature debut is extremely well cast. Neve McIntosh and Shaun Dooley give terrific performances as the mismatched blind-date couple dealing with an extraordinary situation right on their doorstep. McIntosh's attempts to locate her estranged daughter (Linzey Cocker) in the ensuing mayhem drives the main plot, which sustains its gory tension and intrigue right up to the climactic revelation. **AJ** Violence, swearing. **DVD**

Neve McIntosh *Beth* • Shaun Dooley *Kieran* • Linzey Cocker *Jodie* • Dean Andrews *Clive* • Kevin Harvey *Lance Corporal Akede* • Trevor

Hancock *The Savage* ■ *Dir* Lawrence Gough • *Scr* Colin O'Donnell, based on a story by O'Donnell, Lawrence Gough, Alan Pattison

The Salvation ★★★★ 15

Western
2014 · Den/UK/S Afr/Swe/Belg · Colour · 91min

A good man is forced to rack up an impressive body count in this stylish, handsomely shot neo-western.The man in question is Mads Mikkelsen, a peaceful Danish settler whose wife and son are brutally murdered by a couple of drunken outlaws. The story that follows is relatively simplistic, but the villains (including former footie star Eric Cantona) are hateful enough that you can't help but root for their demise, while Mikkelsen is typically magnetic as the steely former soldier. In addition, this gripping revenge thriller is shot against striking landscapes, with the outskirts of South Africa doubling as the American frontier. **SC** In English, Danish. Violence. **DVD** **BL**

Mads Mikkelsen *Jon* • Eva Green *Madelaine, "Princess"* • Jeffrey Dean Morgan *Delarue* • Mikael Persbrandt *Peter* • Michael Raymond-James *Paul* • Alexander Arnold *Voichek* ■ *Dir* Kristian Levring • *Scr* Anders Thomas Jensen, Kristian Levring

Salvation Boulevard ★★ 15

Satirical comedy 2011 · US · Colour · 92min

Greg Kinnear stars here as dopey Carl, who used to be a pot-smoking, womanising Grateful Dead fan, until he met the charismatic Pastor Dan (Pierce Brosnan). But when this poor soul witnesses the clergyman committing a murder, he becomes the fall guy. Though it boasts an eye-catching cast, this helter-skelter comedy quickly unravels into tiresome farce. There are a few moments of warmth, such as Marisa Tomei's appearance as a "Deadhead" security guard who helps Carl rediscover himself, but overall this is a slapdash satire on the Bible Belt that fails to make a lasting impression. **JR** **DVD**

Pierce Brosnan *Dan Day* • Jennifer Connelly *Gwen Vandermeer* • Ed Harris *Dr Paul Blaylock* • Greg Kinnear *Carl Vandermeer* • Marisa Tomei *Honey Foster* ■ *Dir* George Ratliff • *Scr* George Ratliff, Doug Max Stone, from Larry Beinhart's novel

The Salvation Hunters ★★★★

Silent drama 1925 · US · BW · 85min

Though often ponderous and pretentious – "Our aim has been to photograph thought" – this dockyard drama was a remarkable first film by Josef von Sternberg, who produced, directed, wrote and edited. Shot rapidly in actual locations, with a cast and crew of semi-amateurs, it deals with the world of waterfront derelicts in a detached and stylised way. Sternberg got Charles Chaplin, Mary Pickford and Douglas Fairbanks to watch it, they bought it for more than it cost to make (a paltry $6000) and released it through United Artists, although it was more prestigious than profitable. **RB**

George K Arthur *The boy* • Georgia Hale *The girl* • Bruce Guerin *The child* ■ *Dir/Scr* Josef von Sternberg

Salvatore Giuliano ★★★★ 12

Historical crime drama 1961 · It · BW · 123min

Francesco Rosi won the best director prize at Berlin for this documentary-style account of the rise and fall of the eponymous mobster, who was gunned down by disillusioned members of his own gang in Sicily in 1950. Just as the cast comprises a mixture of full-time and non-professional performers, so the elliptical narrative style is a combination of flashbacks, reconstructions and interviews seeking to explore the influence of a corrupt, violent and deeply divided homeland on this self-styled Robin Hood. **DP** In Italian. **DVD** **BL**

Frank Wolff *Gaspare Pisciotta* • Salvo Randone *President of Viterbo Assize Court* • Federico Zardi *Pisciotta's Defense Counsel* • Pietro

Cammarata *Salvatore Giuliano* ■ *Dir* Francesco Rosi • *Scr* Francesco Rosi, Suso Cecchi D'Amico, Enzo Provenzale, Franco Solinas

Salvo ★★★ 12

Crime drama 2013 · It/Fr · Colour · 105min

Expanded from their 2009 short *Rita*, Italian co-directors Fabio Grassadonia and Antonio Piazza revisit the conventions of the Sicilian crime picture, as a Palermo hitman falls for his partially-sighted hostage. Shades of William Wyler's *The Collector* colour the action, as Salvo (Saleh Bakri) kidnaps Rita (Sara Serraiocco) after breaking into her brother's house to exact revenge for an assassination attempt. While the plot twists and turns, the agile camerawork and sensorial sound design enhance the Hitchcockian feel. **DP** Italian +subtitles. Swearing, some violence. **DVD** **BL**

Saleh Bakri *Salvo* • Sara Serraiocco *Rita* • Mario Pupella *Boss* ■ *Dir/Scr* Fabio Grassadonia, Antonio Piazza

Sam Whiskey ★★

Comedy western 1969 · US · Colour · 96min

Amiability covers a multitude of sins, as Burt Reynolds narrows his eyes and widens his smile to try to distract us from this misfiring story about a gambler hired to recover loot from a Colorado river. The movie surrounds him with a trio of western icons (Clint Walker, Ossie Davis and Angie Dickinson) in an effort to beef up the thin tale, but all it succeeds in being is, well, amiable. **TH**

Burt Reynolds *Sam Whiskey* • Angie Dickinson *Laura Breckenridge* • Clint Walker *OW Bandy* • Ossie Davis *Jed Hooker* • Rick Davis *Fat Henry Hobson* ■ *Dir* Arnold Laven • *Scr* William W Norton, from his story

Samaritan Girl ★★★★ 15

Comedy drama 2004 · S Kor · Colour · 96min

South Korean writer/director *provocateur* Kim Ki-Duk provides another piercing insight into contemporary attitudes in this riveting three-act drama. The first segment sees Gwak Ji-min loyally supporting classmate Seo Min-jung, as she works as a prostitute to raise funds for a European holiday. But when Seo is hospitalised, Gwak seeks out her clients to return their money - unaware that her cop father (Lee Eol) is tracking her every misguided move. Resisting the easy soft-core option, Kim devotes more time to the girls' tender friendship than their sexual misdemeanours. He subtly shifts gear from teen pic to quirky comedy to tense domestic morality play, giving the film its fascination and power. **DP** Korean +subtitles. Violence. **DVD**

Lee Eol *Yeong-gi* • Gwak Ji-min *Yeo-jin* • Seo Min-jung *Jae-yeong* • Gweon Hyeon-min *Censor seller No 1* • Oh Yong *Musician* • Lee Jeong-gil *Lucky guy* ■ *Dir/Scr* Kim Ki-Duk

Samba ★★★★ 15

Comedy drama 2014 · Fr · Colour · 118min

Omar Sy, the breakout star of French hit *Untouchable*, reteams with the film's directors Olivier Nakache and Eric Toledano for this vivid look at modern Parisian life. As Senegalese chef Samba, his struggles for legal residency end in a detention centre. However, he soon attracts the attention of a volunteer (Charlotte Gainsbourg) who's using her time there to recover from executive burnout and helps him to get out. It's a film that ricochets between opportunity, hope and despair, but Nakache and Toledano maintain a light touch as they use this engaging and believable tale to tackle the serious issue of stress across immigration, social services and the corporate boardroom. **KK** In French.

Omar Sy *Samba* • Charlotte Gainsbourg *Alice* • Tahar Rahim *Wilson* • Izïa Higelin *Manu* • Issaka Sawadogo *Jonas* ■ *Dir* Olivier Nakache, Eric Toledano • *Scr* Olivier Nakache, Eric Toledano, Delphine & Muriel Coulin, from the novel *Samba pour la France* by Delphine Coulin

S

U SUITABLE FOR ALL   Uc SUITABLE ESPECIALLY FOR YOUNG CHILDREN (DVD ONLY)   PG PARENTAL GUIDANCE   12A UNDER 12s TO BE ACCOMPANIED (CINEMA ONLY)

Samba Traore ★★★ U
Drama 1992 Burkina Faso · Colour · 85min

Tracing the misfortunes that befall a decent man when he is prompted by poverty to steal money to open a bar in his home village, this is a remarkable merger of the African social drama and the Hollywood genre film by the Burkinabe director Idrissa Ouedraogo. Anxious to create a picture with an indigenous setting and a universal theme, Ouedraogo has produced what amounts to the first sub-Saharan *film noir*, even though it retains the brilliant outdoor lighting typical of most of the region's films. DP Bambara +subtitles.

Bakary Sangare *Samba* · Mariam Kaba *Saratou* · Abdoulaye Komboudri *Salif* · Irene Tassembedo *Binta* ■ *Dir* Idrissa Ouedraogo · *Scr* Idrissa Ouedraogo, Jacques Arhex, Santiago Amigorena

Same Time, Next Year ★★★★ 15
Romantic comedy drama 1978 · US · Colour 113min

This cosy apologia for adultery has all you'd expect from a smash Broadway play brought faithfully to the screen. It tells the story of a married (not to each other) couple who meet every year until the silver anniversary of their coupling, to revive their first, fine, careless rapture. Alan Alda and Ellen Burstyn give superb performances under the sensitive direction by Robert Mulligan; affection and sentimentality are in glorious abundance, but there are few insights into the emotional trauma involved in such a relationship. TH Swearing.

Ellen Burstyn *Doris* · Alan Alda *George* · Ivan Bonar *Chalmers* · Bernie Kuby *Waiter* · Cosmo Sardo *Second waiter* · David Northcutt *First pilot* ■ *Dir* Robert Mulligan · *Scr* Bernard Slade, from his play

Sammy and Rosie Get Laid ★★ 18
Drama 1987 · UK · Colour · 96min

In this follow-up to *My Beautiful Laundrette*, a retired Pakistani government torturer (Shashi Kapoor) comes to England to stay with his son (Ayub Khan Din) and daughter-in-law (Frances Barber), and anti-Thatcher messages get spelled out in riots and sexual promiscuity. Well-acted, but the characters are totally unsympathetic, except for Claire Bloom as the old man's former mistress. TH

Frances Barber *Rosie Hobbs* · Ayub Khan Din [Ayub Khan Din] *Sammy* · Shashi Kapoor *Rafi Rahman* · Claire Bloom *Alice* · Roland Gift *Danny/Victoria* · Wendy Gazelle *Anna* · Suzette Llewellyn *Vivia* · Meera Syal *Rani* ■ *Dir* Stephen Frears · *Scr* Hanif Kureishi

Sammy Going South ★★★ PG
Period adventure 1963 · UK · Colour · 114min

Coming between *Mandy* and *A High Wind in Jamaica*, this is the weakest of Alexander Mackendrick's bittersweet trio of films in which the foibles of the adult world are exposed to the gaze of an artless child. Ten-year-old Fergus McClelland heads for South Africa after he is orphaned during the Suez crisis, but the film's episodic structure prevents it from picking up pace. However, McClelland is a likeable lad and his scenes with wizened diamond smuggler Edward G Robinson are of a very high order. DP *DVD*

Edward G Robinson *Cocky Wainwright* · Fergus McClelland *Sammy* · Harry H Corbett *Lem* · Paul Stassino *Spyros Dracondopolous* · Zia Mohyeddin *Syrian* · Zena Walker *Aunt Jane* ■ *Dir* Alexander Mackendrick · *Scr* Denis Cannan, from the novel by WH Canaway

Sammy's Great Escape ★★★ U
Animated adventure 2012 · Bel · Colour · 93min

Aimed fairly and squarely at younger kids, this Belgian cartoon adventure is a sequel of sorts to 2010's *A Turtle's Tale*. Fast, fun and cutely done, it tells the tale of two turtles who wind up stuck inside a Dubai aquarium and have to pool resources with

their fish-mates to escape. Accompanying adults may enjoy the nods to prison, war and mobster movies, and a soundtrack that includes *Rock Lobster* by the B-52s. Despite the U certificate, there are some scenes here that may scare more-sensitive little souls. DA *DVD* *BL*

Wesley Johnny *Sammy* · Isabelle Fuhrman *Shelly* · Carlos McCullers II *Ray* · Joe Thomas (2) *Lulu the lobster* ■ *Dir* Vincent Kesteloot, Ben Stassen · *Scr* Domonic Paris, from a story by Paris, Ben Stassen

Le Samouraï ★★★★★ PG
Thriller 1967 · Fr/It · Colour · 100min

Alain Delon excels in this ultra-stylish study of the ultimate professional. The way in which director Jean-Pierre Melville sets up hitman Delon's next job is mesmerising, attending to each part of the preparation with the detailed eye of a true craftsman. Yet, as in every good *film noir*, there is a *femme fatale* waiting in the shadows to tempt the hero away from his purpose, and Cathy Rosier is about as chic as an angel of doom could be. Almost devoid of dialogue, the film owes everything to the subtlety of the acting, the sinister beauty of Henri Decaë's photography and the intricacy of Melville's direction. DP French +subtitles.

Alain Delon *Jeff Costello* · François Périer *Inspector* · Nathalie Delon *Jane Lagrange* · Cathy Rosier *Valerie* ■ *Dir* Jean-Pierre Melville · *Scr* Jean-Pierre Melville, from the novel *The Ronin* by Joan McLeod

Sam's Son ★★★ 15
Biographical drama 1984 · US · Colour · 107min

Michael Landon is no stranger to sentiment, but he reins in the schmaltz in this neglected drama that is as much a tribute to his stern father, as an account of his own transformation from high school athlete to Hollywood hopeful. In addition to writing and directing, Landon also appears in a cameo as the returning prodigal, leaving Timothy Patrick Murphy to impress as the young Gene Orowitz (Landon's real surname) and real-life couple Eli Wallach and Anne Jackson to steal the picture as his parents. DP Swearing.

Eli Wallach *Sam Orowitz* · Anne Jackson *Harriet* · Timothy Patrick Murphy *Gene* · Hallie Todd *Cathy Stanton* · Alan Hayes *Robert Woods* · Jonna Lee *Bonnie Barnes* · Michael Landon *Gene Orman* · Howard Witt *Cy Mart'n* ■ *Dir/Scr* Michael Landon

Sam's Song ★ 15
Drama 1969 · US · Colour · 83min

In 1980, Cannon Films tried to cash in on Robert De Niro's fame by re-releasing an obscure 1969 independent movie, in which he stars as a film editor spending the weekend on Long Island. Although it was a total flop, Cannon still thought it had commercial value and reworked the De Niro footage into a newly shot film. In the re-edited version, flashbacks show De Niro getting killed while editing a porno movie. Ten years later his ex-con brother Anthony Charnota searches for his murderer. A dull disaster. AJ *DVD*

Robert De Niro *Sam* · Jennifer Warren *Erica* · Jared Mickey *Andrew* · Terrayne Crawford *Carol* · Martin Kelley *Mitch* · Phyllis Black *Marge* · Viva *Girl with the hourglass* · Anthony Charnota *Vito* ■ *Dir* John Shade [Jordan Leondopoulos], John C Broderick

Samson and Delilah ★★★ U
Biblical epic 1949 · US · Colour · 122min

Scooping Oscars for its sets and costumes, this epic prompted veteran American critic Pauline Kael to suggest that Cecil B DeMille considered God to be his co-director. Victor Mature stars as the biblical hero, while Hedy Lamarr brings a gorgeous woodenness to the role of the Philistine whose jealousy over Samson's fondness for Angela Lansbury leads to treachery. The fight with the lion is so lousy it's brilliant, while the oily villainy of George Sanders provides the only acting highlight. DP

Victor Mature *Samson* · Hedy Lamarr *Delilah* · George Sanders *Saran of Gaza* · Angela Lansbury *Semadar* · Henry Wilcoxon *Ahtur* · Olive Deering *Miriam* · Fay Holden *Hazelelponit* ·

Julia Faye *Hisham* · Russell Tamblyn [Russ Tamblyn] *Saul* ■ *Dir* Cecil B DeMille · *Scr* Vladimir Jabotinsky, Harold Lamb, Jesse L Lasky Jr [Jesse Lasky Jr], Frederic M Frank, from the book *Judge and Fool* by Vladimir Jabotinsky · *Costume Designers* Edith Head, Dorothy Jeakins, Elois Jenssen, Gile Steele, Gwen Wakeling

Samson & Delilah ★★★ 15
Romantic drama 2009 · Aus · Colour · 100min

The Australian establishment's ghettoisation of the indigenous population is exposed with stern realism and wry humour in this uncompromising drama. Trapped in a dead-end existence on an Aboriginal settlement, teenager Delilah (Marissa Gibson) devotes herself to caring for her ageing grandmother, whose traditional artworks are bought for a pittance by a white gallery owner in nearby Alice Springs. When Delilah is blamed by the elders for her relative's death, she flees to the city with mute neighbour Samson (Rowan McNamara), who has had a vicious falling out with his older brother. The non-professional leads are exceptional, but the misery is at times unremitting. DP Aboriginal +subtitles. *DVD* *BL*

Rowan McNamara *Samson* · Marissa Gibson *Delilah* · Mitjili Gibson *Nana* · Scott Thornton *Gonzo* · Matthew "MG" Gibson *Samson's brother* · Peter Bartlett *Store manager* ■ *Dir* Warwick Thornton · *Scr* Warwick Thornton, Beck Cole · *Cinematographer* Warwick Thornton

Samurai ★★★ PG
Period action adventure 1954 · Jpn · Colour · 300min

Hiroshi Inagaki was no stranger to the *Meiji-mono*, or historical drama, and he sought to recapture the purity of the genre with this mammoth trilogy. It opens by exploring the humble origins and reckless youth of Musashi Miyamoto, the 17th-century peasant who rose to become the finest swordsman of his generation. Depicting the samurai's rigorous training and explaining the significance of the bushido code, the film was initially released in the US with narration from William Holden. The three films (which won the Honorary Oscar for best foreign film) possess an elegiac quality that atones for their lack of authenticity. DP Japanese +subtitles. *DVD* *BL*

Toshiro Mifune *Takeso/Miyamoto Musashi* · Kaoru Yachigusa *Otsu* · Rentaro Mikuni *Matahachi* · William Holden (2) *Narrator* ■ *Dir* Hiroshi Inagaki · *Scr* Tokuhei Wakao, Hiroshi Inagaki, Hideji Hojo, from the novel *Miyamoto Musashi* by Eiji Yoshikawa

San Andreas ★★★ 12
Disaster action thriller 2015 · US · Colour · 109min

This adrenaline-assisted blockbuster employs state-of-the-art digital artistry to plonk us amid the collapsing buildings of what boffin Paul Giamatti notes is "the largest magnitude quake in recorded history". The vast thrill ride's emotional focus is LA fire department helicopter pilot Dwayne "The Rock" Johnson, who is intent on saving his estranged wife, Carla Gugino, and their daughter, Alexandra Daddario. Nothing is subtle, and the script treads an indistinct line between sincere and ironic, but *San Andreas* is directed with a creditable sense of visual crescendo and Johnson, a human edifice, is more than equal to the preposterous destruction. AC *DVD* *BL* *3D*

Dwayne Johnson *Ray* · Carla Gugino *Emma* · Alexandra Daddario *Blake* · Ioan Gruffudd *Daniel* · Hugo Johnstone-Burt *Ben* · Paul Giamatti *Lawrence Hayes* · Archie Panjabi *Serena* · Colton Haynes *Joby* ■ *Dir* Brad Peyton · *Scr* Allan Loeb, Carlton Cuse, Carey Hayes, Chad Hayes, Andre Fabrizio, Jeremy Passmore

San Antonio ★★ PG
Western 1945 · US · Colour · 104min

This bloated Errol Flynn western boasts lovely Technicolor and the high production values of a big-budget Warner Bros feature, but lacks a decent script. Alexis Smith co-stars as the dance hall singer working for villain Paul Kelly, while Flynn sports some fancy outfits including holsters specially

designed to give him a lightning-fast draw. The climactic shoot-out is worth catching. AE

Errol Flynn *Clay Hardin* · Alexis Smith *Jeanne Starr* · SZ Sakall *Sacha Bozic* · Victor Francen *Legare* · Florence Bates *Henrietta* ■ *Dir* David Butler · *Scr* Alan LeMay, WR Burnett

San Demetrio London ★★★ PG
Second World War drama 1943 · UK · BW · 93min

Thanks to a fine ensemble cast and the authenticity of the action, this Second World War drama about an oil tanker struggling to cross the Atlantic after being attacked by a German battleship not only did its bit in boosting Britain's morale, but also played a key role in the evolution of Ealing Studios. Based on a true story, it served as an allegory for the nation's fortunes since 1939 – the ship may have been damaged, but its gallant crew successfully salvaged it and brought it into port ready to fight another day. Although Charles Frend is credited as sole director, he was indisposed for much of the production and co-writer/producer Robert Hamer actually called the shots. DP *DVD*

Walter Fitzgerald *Chief Engineer Charles Pollard* · Ralph Michael *Second Officer Hawkins* · Frederick Piper *Bosun WE Fletcher* · Gordon Jackson *John Jamieson* · Mervyn Johns *Greaser John Boyle* · Robert Beatty *"Yank" Preston* ■ *Dir* Charles Frend · *Scr* Robert Hamer, Charles Frend, from a story by F Tennyson Jesse

San Francisco ★★★★ U
Disaster movie 1936 · US · BW · 110min

MGM's classic disaster epic is driven by sheer star power. Clark Gable's cynical saloon keeper, Jeanette MacDonald's showgirl and Spencer Tracy's priest battle for one another's souls until San Francisco gets clobbered by the earthquake of 1906. The quake, itself a magnificent testimony to the studio's special effects department, remains one of the most elaborate and exciting action sequences ever filmed, and it's well worth enduring the 90-minute wait while the three heroes squabble over love and life. AT

Clark Gable *Blackie Norton* · Jeanette MacDonald *Mary Blake* · Spencer Tracy *Father Tim Mullin* · Jack Holt *Jack Burley* · Jessie Ralph *Maisie Burley* · Ted Healy *Mat* · Shirley Ross *Trixie* ■ *Dir* WS Van Dyke II [WS Van Dyke] · *Scr* Anita Loos, Erich von Stroheim (uncredited), from a story by Robert Hopkins · *Special Effects* A Arnold Gillespie, James Basevi

The San Francisco Story ★★
Drama 1952 · US · BW · 79min

Hunky Joel McCrea, plays a miner who opposes corrupt politician Sidney Blackmer's plans to take over the city and the state of California. It all ends with a preposterous duel on horseback, by which time the point of dispute isn't political morality, but the fairly blatant charms of Yvonne De Carlo. There's a lot of rough-house stuff, and every interior set is so overdressed it makes San Francisco in the 1850s look like a bordello. AT

Joel McCrea *Rick Nelson* · Yvonne De Carlo *Adelaide McCall* · Sidney Blackmer *Andrew Cain* · Richard Erdman *Shorty* · Florence Bates *Sadie* · Onslow Stevens *Jim Martin* · John Raven *Lessing* ■ *Dir* Robert Parrish · *Scr* DD Beauchamp, from the novel *Vigilante* by Richard Summers

San Quentin ★★★
Prison drama 1937 · US · BW · 71min

This highly enjoyable Warner Bros prison melodrama – with absolutely no redeeming social significance – revolves around Humphrey Bogart as a hardened young hoodlum who goes inside. His sister (Ann Sheridan) is dating the fair-minded new captain of the prison yard. O'Brien is the nominal star of the picture, but broody Bogart and perky young Sheridan are the centre of interest. AE

Pat O'Brien *Capt Stephen Jameson* • Humphrey Bogart *Joe "Red" Kennedy* • Ann Sheridan *May Kennedy* • Barton MacLane *Lt Druggin* • Joseph Sawyer *[Joe Sawyer] "Sailor Boy" Hansen* • Veda Ann Borg *Helen* • James Robbins *Mickey Callahan* • Joseph King (1) *Warden Taylor* ■ *Dir* Lloyd Bacon • *Scr* Peter Milne, Humphrey Cobb, from a story by Robert Tasker, John Bright

Sanctimony ★★ 18
Detective thriller
2000 · US/Ger · Colour · 82min

American Psycho revisited – without the style, satire or savage wit. Casper Van Dien is the arrogant, egotistical financial wizard who becomes the prime suspect in the hunt for the Monkey Maker, a serial killer who has cops Michael Paré and Jennifer Rubin baffled. Writer/director Uwe Boll serves up the occasional jolting image but no real shocks, while the psychological mind games never ring true. JF ⅅⅤⅅ

Casper Van Dien *Tom Gerrick* • Michael Paré *Detective Jim Renart* • Eric Roberts *Lieutenant Mann* • Catherine Oxenberg *Susan Renart* • Jennifer Rubin *Dorothy Smith* ■ *Dir/Scr* Uwe Boll

Sanctuary ★★
Melodrama   1961 · US · BW · 89min

This is high drama in the Greek tradition reduced to swamp melodrama in the Tennessee Williams tradition, though the source is William Faulkner's novel of the same title. Directed by Tony Richardson and starring Lee Remick, it concerns a Mississippi governor's daughter who is raped by a bootlegger. She goes to live in a New Orleans brothel with him and her black maid Odetta which, of course, leads to several tragedies. An opaque, turgid and unsuccessful attempt to bring Faulkner to the screen. RK

Lee Remick *Temple Drake* • Yves Montand *Candy Man* • Bradford Dillman *Gowan Stevens* • Harry Townes *Ira Bobbitt* • Odetta *Nancy Mannigoe* • Howard St John *Governor* ■ *Dir* Tony Richardson • *Scr* James Poe, from the play *Requiem for a Nun* by Ruth Ford, from the novels *Sanctuary* and *Requiem for a Nun* by William Faulkner

Sanctuary ★★ 18
Action thriller   1997 · US · Colour · 99min

This is what happens when you take the retired assassin premise of *The Long Kiss Goodnight* and replace the amnesiac housewife with a hunky clergyman. It may sound far-fetched, but Tibor Takacs is no mug when it comes to action, so there are plenty of shoot-outs and explosions to occupy Mark Dacascos and Jaimz Woolvett. Basic, but crudely effective. DP Swearing, violence, sex scenes. ⅅⅤⅅ

Mark Dacascos *Luke Kovak* • Kylie Travis *Rachel Malcolm* • Jaimz Woolvett *Dominic Grace* • Alan Scarfe *William Dyson* • Monika Schnarre *Colette Fortier* • Nigel Bennett *Senator Stephen Macguire* ■ *Dir* Tibor Takacs • *Scr* Michael Stokes

Sanctum ★★★ 15
Action adventure
2010 · US/Aus · Colour · 104min

Imagine a *National Geographic* take on *The Descent* (minus the nasty creatures) and the result would be director Alister Grierson's unsettling survival saga. A team of underwater explorers endures increasing, unexpected dangers after becoming trapped in Papua New Guinea's Esa'ala cave system after a cyclone hits. It's a scenario that was experienced for real by co-writer Andrew Wight, and the claustrophobic thrills and vertigo-inducing gasps come thick and fast. It is let down slightly by the tritely scripted scenes between the driven Frank (Richard Roxburgh) and his rebellious son (Rhys Wakefield). However, it's the locations, eerie sets, special effects and marine photography that count here, and all are impressively spectacular. AJ ⅅⅤⅅ Ⓑ🄳
Richard Roxburgh *Frank McGuire* • Rhys Wakefield *Josh McGuire* • Alice Parkinson *Victoria* • Dan Wyllie *Crazy George* • Ioan

Gruffudd *Carl Hurley* • Allison Cratchley *Judes* ■ *Dir* Alister Grierson • *Scr* John Garvin, Andrew Wight

The Sand Pebbles ★★★ 15
War drama   1966 · US · Colour · 174min

Set on a US gunboat patrolling the Yangtze River in 1926, this blend of action and melodrama was something of a surprise hit in its day, earning itself no fewer than eight Oscar nominations (although it won none). Part of the reason for its success can be found in its thinly veiled apology for American intervention in Vietnam, but there are some more enduring plus points, too. Steve McQueen and Richard Attenborough both turn in pleasing performances and Joseph MacDonald's cinematography is outstanding. DP ⅅⅤⅅ

Steve McQueen (1) *Jake Holman* • Richard Attenborough *Frenchy Burgoyne* • Richard Crenna *Captain Collins* • Candice Bergen *Shirley Eckert* • Marayat Andriane *Maily* • Mako *Po-Han* • Larry Gates *Jameson* • Charles Robinson [Charles Knox Robinson] *Ensign Bordelles* ■ *Dir* Robert Wise • *Scr* Robert W Anderson, from the novel by Richard McKenna

Sanders of the River ★★★ U
Adventure   1935 · UK · BW · 87min

A famous title in its day, this Alexander Korda production looks patronising and imperialistic to modern eyes. The titular Sanders (Leslie Banks), is a police commissioner in colonial Nigeria, but the real interest here is the performance of the great African-American bass Paul Robeson, as the escaped convict Bosambo (the film's American title), and the "native" chants which greatly enhanced the film's popularity and lead to an infinite number of Robeson impressions in the music halls. The movie still impresses, but it's really best viewed as a fascinating historic document. TS ⅅⅤⅅ

Leslie Banks *RG Sanders* • Paul Robeson *Bosambo* • Nina Mae McKinney *Lilongo* • Robert Cochran *Tibbets* • Martin Walker *Ferguson* • Richard Grey *Hamilton* • Tony Wane *King Mofolaba* ■ *Dir* Zoltan Korda • *Scr* Lajos Biró, Jeffrey Dell, from the stories by Edgar Wallace

The Sandlot ★★★ PG
Comedy adventure   1993 · US · Colour · 96min

An adult does occasionally intrude upon the world of baseball, lifeguards and savage dogs described in this pleasing rites-of-passage picture. However, this enchanted summer really belongs to the kids, in particular Tom Guiry, the pre-teen who makes Charlie Brown look like Babe Ruth. Although the games on the sandlot provide the focus, this isn't just another sports movie. It's about self-discovery and learning how to deal with life. DP ⅅⅤⅅ

Tom Guiry *Scotty Smalls* • Mike Vitar *Benjamin Franklin Rodriguez* • Patrick Renna *Hamilton "Ham" Porter* • Chauncey Leopardi *Michael "Squints" Palledorous* • Marty York *Alan "Yeah-Yeah" McClennan* • Brandon Adams *Kenny DeNunez* • Denis Leary *Bill* • Karen Allen *Mom* • James Earl Jones *Mr Mertle* ■ *Dir* David Mickey Evans • *Scr* David Mickey Evans, Robert Gunter

Sandokan the Great ★★ PG
Adventure   1963 · Fr/It/Sp · Colour · 108min

This sturdy adventure is set in Victorian Borneo. When British forces begin wiping out East Indian villagers, a band of rebels led by warrior Sandokan take on the colonists, kidnapping the commander's niece. Steve Reeves doesn't get to flash as much musculature as in his sword-and-sandal epics, but he makes an athletic lead and there are enough colourful action sequences to hold the interest. Reeves returned for the 1964 sequel *The Pirates of Malaysia*, and Ray Danton took over for the same year's *Sandokan Fights Back* and *Sandokan against the Leopard of Sarawak*. JG Italian dubbed. ⅅⅤⅅ

Steve Reeves *Sandokan* • Geneviève Grad *Mary Ann* • Andrea Bosic *Yanez* • Maurice Poli *Giro Batol* • Rik Battaglia *Sambigliong* ■ *Dir* Umberto Lenzi • *Scr* Umberto Lenzi, Fulvio Gicca, Victor A Catena, from the novel *Le Tigri di Mompracem* by Emilio Salgari

The Sandpiper ★ 15
Romantic drama   1965 · US · Colour · 112min

This truly terrible movie was made by the great Vincente Minnelli. It's a full-blown example of the Elizabeth Taylor/Richard Burton vehicle, and as mindless and inept as it comes. Of course, its sheer awfulness and desperate pretension create a numbing watchability: you have been warned. The California coastline at Big Sur and Charles Bronson emerge with some credit, but Eva Marie Saint is totally wasted. TS

Richard Burton *Dr Edward Hewitt* • Elizabeth Taylor *Laura Reynolds* • Eva Marie Saint *Claire Hewitt* • Charles Bronson *Cos Erickson* • Peter O'Toole ■ *Dir* Vincente Minnelli • *Scr* Dalton Trumbo, Michael Wilson, Irene Kamp, Louis Kamp, from a story by Martin Ransohoff

Sands of Iwo Jima ★★★ PG
Second World War drama
1949 · US · BW · 105min

John Wayne leads his marines to hell and back and they love him for it, every bloodsoaked, heroic foot of the way. Apparently, Kirk Douglas was in line for the role, but, according to the film's producer, Wayne wanted the role so badly "he could taste it." If you believe Wayne's son, though, the Duke worried about the script and only relented when war veterans lobbied him to play the part. The result was a gung-ho classic, made on the cheap, often risible, but it's still eminently watchable and the Duke nabbed his first Oscar nomination to boot. AT ⅅⅤⅅ

John Wayne *Sergeant Stryker* • John Agar *Private Peter Conway* • Forrest Tucker *Corporal Al Thomas* • Adele Mara *Allison Bromley* • Wally Cassell *Private Benny Ragazzi* • James Brown (1) *Private Charlie Bass* • Richard Webb *Private Shipley* ■ *Dir* Allan Dwan • *Scr* Harry Brown, Edward James Grant, from a story by Harry Brown

Sands of the Desert ★ U
Comedy   1960 · UK · Colour · 88min

Poor old Charlie Drake. To call his flirtation with film fame an unmitigated disaster, would be understating the extent to which he failed to translate his stage, radio and TV success to the big screen. Director John Paddy Carstairs also co-wrote this silly story in which travel agent Drake sets out to uncover the saboteur at a holiday camp. Better than his other efforts, but that's not saying much. DP

Charlie Drake *Charlie Sands* • Peter Arne *Sheikh El Jabez* • Sarah Branch *Janet Brown* • Raymond Huntley *Bossom* • Peter Illing *Sheikh Ibrahim* • Harold Kasket *Abdullah* • Marne Maitland *Sheikh's advisor* • Neil McCarthy *Hassan* ■ *Dir* John Paddy Carstairs • *Scr* John Paddy Carstairs, Charlie Drake, from a story by Robert Hall, Anne Burnaby, Stafford Byrne

Sands of the Kalahari ★★★
Action drama   1965 · UK · Colour · 119min

The team behind *Zulu* converges upon South Africa for another gritty adventure. It's a well-cast survival picture, in which a charter plane is grounded by a plague of locusts, leaving the United Nations of passengers to bicker, rape, kill and generally abuse each other in the desert. It's an allegory showing how, given half a chance, humans will regress to ape-like behaviour, with Stuart Whitman taking on the role of the prime primate. It's not in the class of Endfield's previous epic, but it has a raw intensity all of its own thanks to some excellent performances and imposing locations. AT

Stuart Whitman *O'Brien* • Stanley Baker *Bain* • Susannah York *Grace Monckton* • Harry Andrews *Grimmelman* • Theodore Bikel *Dr Bondarahkai* • Nigel Davenport *Sturdevant* • Barry Lowe *Detjens* ■ *Dir* Cy Endfield • *Scr* Cy Endfield, from the novel by William Mulvihill

The Sandwich Man ★★ U
Comedy   1966 · UK · Colour · 91min

Known as the Goon that got away, and as the genius behind *Potty Time*, Michael Bentine was yet another British comedian who failed to repeat his TV and/or radio success on the big screen. This virtually

silent comedy was politely considered "ahead of its time" on its release, but, over 30 years later, this euphemism for "not very good" still applies. The cast is all-star, but the film's few pleasures come from Bentine's often inspired mime as he wanders the streets of London with his sandwich board. DP

Michael Bentine *Horace Quilby* • Dora Bryan *Mrs de Vere* • Harry H Corbett *Stage doorkeeper* • Bernard Cribbins *Photographer* • Diana Dors *Billingsgate woman* • Ian Hendry *Motorcyle cop* • Stanley Holloway *Gardener* • Wilfrid Hyde White *Lord Uffingham* • Michael Medwin *Sewer man* • Ron Moody *Coach* • Anna Quayle *Billingsgate woman* • Terry-Thomas *Scoutmaster* • Norman Wisdom *Father O'Malley* • Suzy Kendall *Sue* • Alfie Bass *Yachtsman* • John Le Mesurier *Sandwich man* • Peter Jones *Escapologist* • Warren Mitchell *Gypsy Syd* ■ *Dir* Robert Hartford-Davis • *Scr* Robert Hartford-Davis, Michael Bentine

Sangam ★★★ U
Melodrama   1964 · Ind · Colour · 213min

This sprawling tale of star-crossed love and heroic sacrifice was Raj Kapoor's first colour film and is one of the earliest Bollywood pictures to utilise European locations. It has a decidedly homoerotic tone as Kapoor and his socially superior buddy, Rajendra Kumar, become involved in a tug-of-war for the affections of Vyjayanthimala, though she is the one finding it difficult to pierce their long-standing exclusivity. Surprisingly suggestive in its approach to sex, yet also subtly insistent in its avowal that women get a raw deal in Indian society, this tragic melodrama also has more than its share of memorable musical routines. DP Hindi +subtitles.

Raj Kapoor *Sunder* • Rajendra Kumar *Gopal* • Vyjayanthimala *Radha* ■ *Dir* Raj Kapoor • *Scr* Inder Raj

Sanjuro ★★★ 12
Period action drama   1962 · Jpn · BW · 91min

Following the success of *Yojimbo*, Akira Kurosawa was persuaded to make a further adventure featuring the self-seeking samurai who uses his own guile and the efforts of others to achieve his ends. Toshiro Mifune returns as Sanjuro, who joins forces with a band of eager warriors to rescue a kidnapped landowner. Until the final eruption of violence, Kurosawa plays the film for laughs, sending up the conventions of the *jidai-geki* (or period costume drama) with an unerring eye, while Mifune bestrides the action with gleeful gravitas. DP Japanese +subtitles. ⅅⅤⅅ Ⓑ

Toshiro Mifune *Sanjuro* • Tatsuya Nakadai *Muroto* • Takashi Shimura *Kurofuji* • Yuzo Kayama *Iori Izaka* • Reiko Dan *Koiso, the Chamberlain's daughter* • Masao Shimizu *Kikui* ■ *Dir* Akira Kurosawa • *Scr* Ryuzo Kikushima, Akira Kurosawa, Hideo Oguni, from the short story *Hibi Heian* by Shugoro Yamamoto

Sans Soleil ★★★★ 15
Documentary   1982 · Fr · Colour · 99min

Still most widely known for his sci-fi short *La Jetée*, Chris Marker emerged in the 1960s as a key practitioner of the *cinéma vérité* documentary style. This is tantamount to a postcard from "a life", as Marker tries to convey his impressions and recollections of cultures as far afield as Africa, Iceland and Japan. Exploiting what was then the latest in video and imaging technology, the film is an exhilarating collage of sights and sounds. Unlike many documentarists, Marker doesn't force his views upon you, but, like a good guide, draws your attention to what you might otherwise have missed. DP ⅅⅤⅅ

Alexandra Stewart *English narration* ■ *Dir/Scr* Chris Marker

Sanshiro Sugata ★★★ PG
Adventure drama   1943 · Jpn · BW · 75min

This intriguing work is the first film directed by the legendary Japanese director Akira Kurosawa, who went on to international fame with *The Seven Samurai*. Made in the latter part of the war, when he was in his early 30s, it was inevitably influenced by

---

U SUITABLE FOR ALL   **Uc** SUITABLE ESPECIALLY FOR YOUNG CHILDREN (DVD ONLY)   **PG** PARENTAL GUIDANCE   **12A** UNDER 12s TO BE ACCOMPANIED (CINEMA ONLY)

S

the authorities, which may have accounted for its economical and straightforward storytelling. This concerns Sugata, who in the late 19th century develops the art of Judo, showing its superiority over the martial art of Ju-Jitsu. There was a second part to the story made a couple of years later. BB Japanese +subtitles. *DVD*

Susumu Fujita *Sanshiro Sugata* • Denjiro Okochi *Shogoro Yano* • Takashi Shimura *Hansuke Murai* • Yukiko Todoroki *Sayo, his daughter* ■ *Dir* Akira Kurosawa • *Scr* Akira Kurosawa, from the novel *Sugata Sanshiro* by Tsuneo Tomita

Sansho the Bailiff ★★★★★ PG
Epic period drama 1954 · Jpn · BW · 208min

One of the masterworks of Japanese cinema, this powerful, poignant period drama discusses tyranny, liberalism and the psychological differences between the sexes. Reworking a traditional folk tale, Kenji Mizoguchi considers how someone can be driven to barbarism simply to survive, with kidnap victim Yoshiaki Hanayagi's collusion with the barbarous bailiff, Eitaro Shindo, contrasting sharply with the idealism that condemned his father to exile, his mother to prostitution and his sister to death, while contriving his escape. Shooting primarily in long takes from a fluid camera, Mizoguchi conveys a sense of intimacy through flashbacks and the performances of his superlative cast. DP Japanese +subtitles. *DVD*

Kinuyo Tanaka *Tamaki* • Yoshiaki Hanayagi *Zushio* • Kyoko Kagawa *Anju* • Masao Shimizu *Tairano no Masauji* • Eitaro Shindo *Sansho Dayu* • Akitake Kono *Taro* • Ryosuke Kagawa *Ritsushi Kumotake* ■ *Dir* Kenji Mizoguchi • *Scr* Yahiro Fuji, Yoshikata Yoda, from a famous legend as related by Ogai Mori in the magazine *Chuo Koron* • *Cinematographer* Kazuo Miyagawa

Santa Claus ★★ U
Seasonal comedy
1985 · UK/US · Colour · 104min

Dudley Moore plays the elf who loses his job with Santa and decides to sell his former employer's secrets to evil toy manufacturer John Lithgow in this rather daft family comedy. It boasts a great opening, but gets bogged down with infantile humour, a silly script and plot twists that a five-year-old would find insulting. JB *DVD* Blu-ray

Dudley Moore *Patch* • John Lithgow *BZ* • David Huddleston *Claus* • Burgess Meredith *Ancient elf* • Judy Cornwell *Anya* • Jeffrey Kramer *Towzer* • Christian Fitzpatrick *Joe* ■ *Dir* Jeannot Szwarc • *Scr* David Newman, from a story by David Newman, Leslie Newman

The Santa Clause ★★★ U
Fantasy comedy 1994 · US · Colour · 93min

Tim Allen gets off rather lightly in this engaging yuletide comedy, and his feature debut brims over with good ideas. The only trouble is, they are all stocking-fillers when what the action really needs is a couple of huge gift-wrapped set pieces. However, as the sceptic bound by the Claus clause, the *Home Improvement* star slips from Scrooge into Santa with some skill and amiability. DP *DVD*

Tim Allen *Scott Calvin* • Judge Reinhold *Neal* • Wendy Crewson *Laura* • Eric Lloyd *Charlie* • David Krumholtz *Bernard* • Larry Brandenburg *Detective Nunzio* ■ *Dir* John Pasquin • *Scr* Leo Benvenuti, Steve Rudnick

The Santa Clause 2 ★★ U
Seasonal fantasy comedy
2002 · US · Colour · 100min

This lacklustre sequel to the amiable 1994 film is a sugary confection of festive clichés, half-baked jokes and blatant product placement - the celluloid equivalent of an expensively wrapped box filled with junk. Superficially the film has its charm, thanks largely to a likeable performance from Tim Allen, who now has to bag the perfect Mrs Claus or lose his job. SF *DVD*

Tim Allen *Scott Calvin/Santa/Toy Santa* • Elizabeth Mitchell *Carol Newman* • David Krumholtz *Bernard* • Eric Lloyd *Charlie Calvin* • Judge Reinhold *Neil Miller* • Wendy Crewson *Laura Miller* • Spencer Breslin *Curtis* • Liliana Mumy *Lucy Miller* • Kevin Pollak *Cupid* ■ *Dir* Michael Lembeck • *Scr* Don Rhymer, Cinco

---

Paul, Ken Daurio, Ed Decter, John Strauss, from a story by Leo Benvenuti, Steve Rudnick, from their characters

The Santa Clause 3: the Escape Clause ★★★ U
Seasonal fantasy comedy
2006 · US · Colour · 88min

A jealous Jack Frost causes chaos at the North Pole in this third instalment of the jovial festive franchise. With Tim Allen amiably filling out the Father Christmas suit once again, it's a more substantial family romp than returning director Michael Lembeck's *The Santa Clause 2*. Unsurprisingly for a yuletide flick, there's still enough sugary sentiment to rot teeth, but the welcome addition of Martin Short's mischief-making Frost gives the comedy a cheeky zing that both adults and kids will enjoy. SF *DVD* Blu-ray

Tim Allen *Santa Claus/Scott Calvin* • Elizabeth Mitchell *Mrs Claus/Carol Calvin* • Judge Reinhold *Neil Miller* • Wendy Crewson *Laura Miller* • Eric Lloyd *Charlie Calvin* • Martin Short *Jack Frost* • Spencer Breslin *Curt's* • Ann-Margret *Sylvia Newman* • Alan Arkin *Bud Newman* • Liliana Mumy *Lucy Miller* ■ *Dir* Michael Lembeck • *Scr* Ed Decter, John J Strauss, from characters by Leo Benvenuti, Steve Rudnick

Santa Fe ★★ U
Western 1951 · US · Colour · 86min

Made virtually back-to-back with *Man in the Saddle* (same year, star, producer and writer), this is a much more routine western. This time Confederate soldier Randolph Scott is involved in unseemly sibling rivalry at the end of the Civil War, as his brothers turn against him when he decides to work for the railroad of the title. Irving Pichel's colourless direction and Janis Carter's uninspiring leading lady don't help this overfamiliar tale. TS

Randolph Scott *Britt Canfield* • Janis Carter *Judith Chandler* • Jerome Courtland *Terry Canfield* • Peter M Thompson *Tom Canfield* • John Archer *Clint Canfield* • Warner Anderson *Dave Baxter* ■ *Dir* Irving Pichel • *Scr* Kenneth Gamet, from a story by Louis Stevens, from the novel by James Marshall

Santa Fe Passage ★★ U
Western 1955 · US · Colour · 90min

This average second-division western is given moderate interest by its trio of stars, well past their primes but still able to hold the attention. John Payne plays an ostracised wagon-train scout battling former B-hero Rod Cameron (here cast against type) for the hand of mixed-race Faith Domergue. TS

John Payne *Kirby Randolph* • Faith Domergue *Aurelie St Clair* • Rod Cameron *Jess Griswold* • Slim Pickens *Sam Beekman* • Irene Tedrow *Ptewaquin* • George Keymas *Satank* ■ *Dir* William Witney • *Scr* Lillie Hayward, from a short story by Clay Fisher [Heck Allen]

Santa Fe Trail ★★ U
Period action adventure
1940 · US · BW · 109min

One of the weakest of the Errol Flynn/Olivia de Havilland series at Warners, this rambling saga concerns the attempts of future Civil War cavalryman Flynn to nail the great abolitionist John Brown (a ranting Raymond Massey). As history, this is wild fiction, even for Hollywood, and, despite a watchable supporting cast including Ronald Reagan as George Armstrong Custer, there's precious little going on here. TS *DVD*

Errol Flynn *Jeb Stuart* • Olivia de Havilland *Kit Carson Halliday* • Raymond Massey *John Brown* • Ronald Reagan *George Armstrong Custer* • Alan Hale *Tex Bell* • Guinn "Big Boy" Williams *Windy Brody* • Van Heflin *Rader* ■ *Dir* Michael Curtiz • *Scr* Robert Buckner

Santa Sangre ★★★ 18
Surreal horror drama
1989 · It/Mex · Colour · 117min

Alexandro Jodorowsky's cross-cultural collage of ideas and images borrows freely from Freud, Fellini and Ferrara, de Milo, Marceau and Psycho. Using the circus as a

---

microcosm, Jodorowsky combines the sacred and the psychedelic, the psychological and the symbolic, as a magician (played variously by the director's sons, Adan and Axel) goes on a murderous rampage to avenge the aerialist mother whose arms were severed by the knife-throwing husband she caught *in flagrante delicto* with the tattooed lady. DP *DVD* Blu-ray

Axel Jodorowsky *Fenix* • Blanca Guerra *Concha* • Guy Stockwell *Orgo* • Thelma Tixou *Tattooed woman* • Sabrina Dennison *Alma* • Adan Jodorowsky *Young Fenix* ■ *Dir* Alexandro Jodorowsky • *Scr* Robert Leoni, Claudio Argento, from a story by Roberto Leoni, Alexandro Jodorowsky

Santa Who? ★★ U
Seasonal comedy 2000 · US · Colour · 88min

Leslie Nielsen plays Santa Claus with pantomimic brio in this cheerful Disney made-for-TV film. Blown off course by turbulence, he crashes his sleigh into Scrooge-like TV reporter Steven Eckholdt's car and suffers amnesia. However, it takes young Max Morrow to realise the implications of Santa's condition and the race to save the festivities begins. It's awash with sentimentality, but William Dear doesn't let it descend into mush. DP *DVD*

Leslie Nielsen *Santa Claus* • Steven Eckholdt *Peter Albright* • Robyn Lively *Claire Dreyer* • Max Morrow *Zack* • Tommy Davidson *Max* ■ *Dir* William Dear • *Scr* Debra Frank, Steve L Hayes, from a story by Chad Hoffman, Robert Schwartz

Santee ★★★ 15
Western 1973 · US · Colour · 86min

Glenn Ford is a bounty hunter, long embittered by the memory of his son who was gunned down by a gang he hunts still. In a twist of fate he becomes the surrogate father to another boy - whose father he has killed - and still the ironies pile upon Ford, turning him into a figure from Greek tragedy. While this does not even approach the westerns that Anthony Mann made with James Stewart, its similar classical references and tormented hero make for an immensely satisfying drama. AT

Glenn Ford *Santee* • Michael Burns *Jody* • Dana Wynter *Valerie* • Jay Silverheels *John Crow* • Harry Townes *Sheriff Carter* • John Larch *Banner* • Robert Wilke [Robert J Wilke] *Deake* ■ *Dir* Gary Nelson • *Scr* Tom Blackburn, from a story by Brand Bell

Santiago ★★★
Adventure drama 1956 · US · Colour · 91min

A cracking script by Martin Rackin and John Twist goes some way to redeeming this period bunkum about gunrunners Alan Ladd and Lloyd Nolan paddle-boating rifles to Cuban revolutionaries fighting Spanish oppression. Gordon Douglas's dull direction backs it all into Cliché Corner, but the writing quite often forces a way out. TH

Alan Ladd *Cash Adams* • Rossana Podesta *Isabella* • Lloyd Nolan *Clay Pike* • Chill Wills *Sidewheel* • Paul Fix *Trasker* • LQ Jones *Digger* ■ *Dir* Gordon Douglas • *Scr* Martin Rackin, John Twist, from the novel *The Great Courage* by Martin Rackin

Los Santos Inocentes ★★★★
Drama 1984 · Sp · Colour · 108min

Although centred on the brutalised existence of one particular peasant family, this epic commentary reflects life in Franco's Spain during the 1960s in broad political terms. The protagonists are a couple, burdened with a mentally handicapped child and backbreaking work, whose only hope is that their older children might escape the feudal system binding them to uncaring landowners. Superbly photographed against imposing landscapes, this compassionate work deserves a wide audience. BB Spanish +subtitles.

Alfredo Landa *Paco* • Francisco Rabal *Azarias* • Terele Pávez *Regula* • Belen Ballesteros *Nieves* • Juan Sachez *Quirce* • Juan Diego *Master Ivan* • Agustín González *Don Pedro* ■ *Dir* Mario Camus

---

• *Scr* Mario Camus, Antonio Larreta, Manuel Matji, from the novel by Miguel Delibes • *Cinematographer* Hans Burmann

The Saphead ★★★ U
Silent comedy 1920 · US · BW · 76min

Buster Keaton's first feature was for Metro who, having lost Fatty Arbuckle, didn't quite know what to do with Buster, so installed him in a Fatty-prepared vehicle. Buster plays the naive son of a rich father, devoted to his father's ward (Carol Holloway). Determined to be "bad", in fact his goodness ensures that he takes the blame for another stockbroker's error. A bit of a letdown for fans, but the character was the basis for many of his later creations. TH *DVD*

Buster Keaton *Bertie Van Alstyne* • William H Crane *Nicholas Van Alstyne* • Irving Cummings *Mark Turner* • Carol Holloway *Rose Turner* • Beulah Booker *Agnes Gates* ■ *Dir* Herbert Blaché • *Scr* June Mathis, from the play *The New Henrietta* by Winchell Smith, Victor Mapes, Bronson Howard

Sapphire ★★★ PG
Murder mystery 1959 · UK · Colour · 87min

A young woman's murder leaves many questions unanswered in this intriguing detective tale. The relatively innovative racial element - the victim is a young black woman who has been passing as white - adds to the historical interest, and gives the search for the murderer a wider resonance. This vividly shot movie may seem dated in its treatment of racism and bigotry, but this was challenging material at the time and it went on to scoop the Bafta for Best British Film. JA *DVD*

Nigel Patrick *Detective Superintendent Hazard* • Michael Craig *Detective Inspector Learoyd* • Yvonne Mitchell *Mildred* • Paul Massie *David Harris* • Bernard Miles *Mr Harris* • Olga Lindo *Mrs Harris* • Earl Cameron *Dr Robbins* • Gordon Heath *Paul Slade* ■ *Dir* Basil Dearden • *Scr* Janet Green, Lukas Heller

The Sapphires ★★★★ PG
Comedy drama based on a true story
2012 · Aus · Colour · 99min

Four Aboriginal teens overcome significant obstacles in 1968 Australia to pursue their girl group dreams in this hugely engaging sleeper hit from Cannes 2012. Things start really happening when talent show chancer Chris O'Dowd (in a scene-stealing performance) agrees to be their manager and takes them on a tour of Vietnam to entertain the US troops. Sparkling with heart-felt humour, terrific performances from all four girls and a hit-packed soul soundtrack, this is a model feel-good movie that's destined for awards attention. AJ *DVD*

Chris O'Dowd *Dave* • Deborah Mailman *Gail* • Jessica Mauboy *Julie* • Shari Sebbens *Kay* • Miranda Tapsell *Cynthia* ■ *Dir* Wayne Blair • *Scr* Tony Briggs, Keith Thompson, from Briggs's play

Saps at Sea ★★ U
Comedy 1940 · US · BW · 57min

This inconsistent comedy was Laurel and Hardy's last film for Hal Roach, and the first of the highly derivative features with which they saw out their distinguished careers. Driven bonkers by honking horns at work, Ollie is prescribed a tranquil sea voyage, during which he and Stan are shanghaied by a fugitive killer. The opening sections are fast and furious, but the action becomes becalmed the moment the boys are afloat. DP

Stan Laurel *Stan* • Oliver Hardy *Ollie* • James Finlayson *Dr JH Finlayson* • Ben Turpin *Mixed-up plumber* • Rychard Cramer *[Richard Cramer]* • Nick Grainger • Charlie Hall *Apartment desk clerk* ■ *Dir* Gordon Douglas • *Scr* Charles Rogers, Felix Adler, Gil Pratt [Gilbert W Pratt], Harry Langdon, from their story

Saraband ★★★ 15
Relationship drama
2003 · Swe/Den/Nor/It/Fin/Ger/Austria · Colour · 107min

Ingmar Bergman closed one of cinema's most significant careers with this sequel to

---

S

Scenes from a Marriage (1973). Divided into ten bookended chapters, this made-for-TV film starts off focusing on Liv Ullmann's long-overdue reunion with ex-husband Erland Josephson. But it soon shifts to the tensions between Josephson's son from an earlier marriage, Börje Ahlstedt, and his teenage cellist granddaughter, Julia Dufvenius. Shooting in high-definition video, the auteur reins in his camera, not only to avoid exposing the obviously theatrical backdrops, but also to emphasise the powerful performances of a cast that makes the occasionally stilted dialogue seem sharp and wounding. DP Swedish +subtitles. Violence. **DVD**

Liv Ullmann *Marianne* • Erland Josephson *Johan* • Börje Ahlstedt *Henrik* • Julia Dufvenius *Karin* • Gunnel Fred *Martha* ■ *Dir/Scr* Ingmar Bergman

Saraband for Dead Lovers ★★★ U

Period romantic drama
1948 · UK · Colour · 92min

Audiences wanted colour, upholstery and royalty in the postwar era, and this sumptuous British movie about a claim to the Hanoverian throne of England has all the ingredients. Joan Greenwood plays the king's wife, but she fancies Stewart Granger, a Swedish count of indifferent pedigree and accent, who was previously involved with Flora Robson, who goes into a fit of jealous rage. It's a shame that Basil Dearden and Michael Relph directed it with straight faces, but no one, thankfully, could suppress Greenwood in full flounce. AT
DVD

Stewart Granger *Count Philip Konigsmark* • Joan Greenwood *Sophie Dorothea* • Françoise Rosay *Electress Sophie* • Flora Robson *Countess Platen* • Frederick Valk *Elector Ernest Augustus* • Peter Bull *Prince George-Louis* • Anthony Quayle *Durer* • Megs Jenkins *Frau Busche* • Michael Gough *Prince Charles* ■ *Dir* Basil Dearden, Michael Relph • *Scr* John Dighton, Alexander Mackendrick, from the novel by Helen Simpson

Sarafina! ★★★ 15

Musical drama
1992 · S Afr/US/UK/Fr · Colour · 111min

Based on the anti-apartheid Broadway musical, this traces the transformation of a schoolgirl in the South African townships of the 1970s from innocent teenage dreamer to political activist. In her school there is only one teacher (Whoopi Goldberg) who refuses to toe the white-endorsed party line and pays a terrible price for her courage. The upbeat musical numbers are invigorating but seem sometimes at odds with the theme. Miriam Makeba, the singer/ actress and *grande dame* of the anti-apartheid movement is in a supporting role. DA

Whoopi Goldberg *Mary Masombuka* • Leleti Khumalo *Sarafina* • Miriam Makeba *Angelina* • John Kani *School principal* • Dumisani Dlamini *Crocodile* ■ *Dir* Darrell James Roodt • *Scr* William Nicholson, Mbongeni Ngema, from the musical by Mbongeni Ngema • *Music* Stanley Meyers

The Saragossa Manuscript ★★★★★ 15

Fantasy drama
1964 · Pol · BW · 175min

This is a complex and exhilarating film that ranks among the most remarkable achievements of 1960s European cinema. Beginning in the Peninsular War, the action shifts, via the pages of a gloriously illustrated tome, to a dazzling compendium of interweaving stories. Zbigniew Cybulski's Walloon guardsman meets with two Muslim princesses, a hermit, a possessed lunatic, a cabalist, a rationalist philosopher, a gypsy and an Inquisitor. Played to the haunting strains of Krzysztof Penderecki's score, this is a highly stylised, darkly surreal exploration of such themes as the capriciousness of nature, authority and, above all, love. DP Polish +subtitles.

Zbigniew Cybulski *Capt Alfons van Worden* • Kazimierz Opalinski *Hermit* • Iga Cembrzynska *Princess Emina* • Joanna Jedryka *Princess Zibelda* • Slawomir Linder *van Worden's father* • Miroslawa Lombardo *van Worden's mother* ■

Dir Wojciech Has • *Scr* Tadeusz Kwiatkowski, from the novel *Manuscrit Trouvé à Saragosse* by Jan Potocki

Sarah and Son ★★★

Drama
1930 · US · BW · 86min

Following her success in *Madame X* as a mother deprived of her child as punishment for her infidelity, Ruth Chatterton returned in this tear-sodden variation on the theme. Here, she is a woman wronged by her cad of a husband who sells their baby to a wealthy couple. The rest of the film is spent with Chatterton as she searches for her lost son while managing to become an opera star. Directed with requisite feeling by Dorothy Arzner, and well-played by the polished Chatteron and Fredric March, it is predictable but effective. RK

Ruth Chatterton *Sarah Storm* • Fredric March *Howard Vanning* • Fuller Mellish Jr *Jim Gray* • Gilbert Emery *John Ashmore* • Doris Lloyd *Mrs Ashmore* • William Stack *Cyril Belloc* • Philippe De Lacy *Bobby* ■ *Dir* Dorothy Arzner • *Scr* Zoe Akins, from a novel by Timothy Shea

Sarah Silverman: Jesus Is Magic ★★★ 15

Comedy concert   2005 · US · Colour · 69min

Sarah Silverman is a Jewish-American comedian and star of her own hit sitcom, who became an internet sensation with a song about doing rude things with Matt Damon. This concert movie is a good introduction to her edgy brand of humour, interspersing stand-up footage with sketches and, more memorably, songs. Silverman's schtick is the juxtaposition between her innocent good looks and the utter filth that comes out of her mouth. And while her attempts to expose hypocrisy by saying the unsayable are more hit than miss, if you're easily offended this is definitely not for you. LB **DVD**

Sarah Silverman ■ *Dir* Liam Lynch • *Scr* Sarah Silverman

Sarah's Key ★★★★ 12

Drama   2010 · Fr · Colour · 98min

Kristin Scott Thomas is superb as a journalist who is preparing an article on the notorious Vel' d'Hiv Roundup of 1942, when thousands of Jews were arrested by French police and transported to camps. To her horror, she learns that her own husband's family appear to be implicated in the shameful episode, with their old home holding a dark secret involving a young Jewish girl (Mélusine Mayance). Director Gilles Paquet-Brenner subtly contrasts Scott Thomas's modern-day investigation with the tragic wartime experiences of Mayance's title character to show how one innocent mistake can resonate across time. JF French, English, Italian, German +subtitles. **DVD** **BluRay**

Kristin Scott Thomas *Julia Jarmond* • Mélusine Mayance *Sarah Starzynski* • Niels Arestrup *Jules Dufaure* • Frédéric Pierrot *Bertrand Tezac* • Aidan Quinn *William Rainsferd* ■ *Dir* Gilles Paquet-Brenner • *Scr* Gilles Paquet-Brenner, Serge Joncour, from the novel by Tatiana De Rosnay

Saratoga ★★★

Comedy   1937 · US · BW · 92min

This robust racetrack romance had its back broken by the tragic and untimely death (during filming) of its star, blonde bombshell Jean Harlow. Her demise cast a pall over the production and resulted in the movie being finished by the necessary use of a none-too-clever double (stand-in Mary Dees) in certain scenes, voice-matched and photographed back-to-camera. It's one of those intelligently crafted, glossy movies from MGM's golden era, with Clark Gable at his most dashing and Lionel Barrymore at his most crusty. Harlow sparkles, sadly for the last time. TS

Jean Harlow *Carol Clayton* • Clark Gable *Duke Bradley* • Lionel Barrymore *Grandpa Clayton* • Walter Pidgeon *Hartley Madison* • Frank Morgan *Jesse Kiffmeyer* • Una Merkel *Fritzi O'Malley* • Cliff Edwards *Tip O'Brien* ■ *Dir* Jack Conway • *Scr* Anita Loos, Robert Hopkins

---

Saratoga Trunk ★★

Melodrama   1945 · US · BW · 135min

This lavish film of Edna Ferber's novel reunites Ingrid Bergman, Gary Cooper, and Sam Wood, the stars and director of *For Whom the Bell Tolls*. Bergman plays a half-Creole beauty, resentful of her illegitimacy, and Cooper is a gambler who fancies her while she sets her sights on a tycoon. Among the embarrassments is Oscar nominee Flora Robson as a maid, blacked up like Hattie McDaniel. AT

Gary Cooper *Colonel Clint Maroon* • Ingrid Bergman *Clio Dulaine* • Flora Robson *Angelique Buiton* • Jerry Austin *Cupidon* • John Warburton *Bartholomew Van Steed* • Florence Bates *Mrs Coventry Bellop* ■ *Dir* Sam Wood • *Scr* Casey Robinson, from the novel by Edna Ferber

Sarkar ★★★★ 15

Political crime drama
2005 · Ind · Colour · 123min

Talented film-maker Ram Gopal Varma's power-packed narrative strikes plenty of universal chords. Amitabh Bachchan plays the head of the embattled Nagare clan, which is caught up in a bloody gang war. His quest to keep his family name respectable is thwarted when he is jailed and his youngest son (played by Amitabh's real-life son Abhishek) is sucked into a life of murder and violence. Loosely inspired by Francis Ford Coppola's masterful *The Godfather*, this razor-sharp drama crackles with intelligence. OA Hindi +subtitles. Violence. **DVD**

Amitabh Bachchan *Subhash Nagare* • Abhishek Bachchan *Shankar Nagare* • Kay Kay Menon *Vishnu Nagare* ■ *Dir/Scr* Ram Gopal Varma

Sarkar Raj ★★★ 12A

Political crime drama
2008 · Ind · Colour · 124min

Director Ram Gopal Varma's sequel to 2005's critically acclaimed Bollywood hit *Sarkar* is an unsettling and slow-burning drama. Amitabh Bachchan again plays Subhash, the patriarch of the wealthy and influential Nagare family, and his son Abhishek returns as Shankar, the favoured son. Aishwarya Rai (Abhishek's real-life wife) also appears, as the CEO of an international company looking to build India's biggest ever power plant – a plan that proves controversial. The younger Bachchan has some fine moments here, and Amitabh is frequently electrifying. Only Rai lets the side down, with her embarrassing performance. OA Hindi +subtitles.

Amitabh Bachchan *Subhash Nagare "Sarkar"* • Abhishek Bachchan *Shankar Nagare* • Aishwarya Rai *Anita Rajan* • Supriya Pathak *Pushpa Nagre* • Tanisha *Avantika Nagre* • Dilip Prabhavalkar *Rao Saab* ■ *Dir* Ram Gopal Varma • *Scr* Ram Gopal Varma, Prashant Pandey

Sarraouina ★★★★ 15

Historical drama
1986 · Fr/Burkina Faso · Colour · 121min

Both a celebration of African culture and a warning against perpetuating the divisions that delivered much of the continent into European rule, Med Hondo's epic account of the battles waged by Sarraounia (Ai Keta), the 19th-century warrior queen of the Aznas, is both inspiring and impressively cinematic. While Guy Famechon's photography conveys the enormity of the Lugu region, Hondo concentrates on the personal problems besetting Kéta's resistance to a local tribe and the marauding French. A landmark in Third World Cinema. DP French +subtitles.

Ai Keta *Sarraounia* • Jean-Roger Milo *Captain Voulet* • Féodor Atkine *Captain Chanoine* • Didier Sauvegrain *Doctor Henric* ■ *Dir* Med Hondo • *Scr* Med Hondo, Abdul War

Sartana ★★★ 15

Spaghetti western   1968 · It · Colour · 91min

A no-nonsense spaghetti western from Gianfranco Parolini, directing under the name of Frank Kramer. John Garko is the eponymous gunfighter who stirs things up for his own ends after a town's leading

---

citizens concoct an elaborate insurance scam. Parolini has a firm grasp of the conventions of the genre, switching between passages of terse dialogue and outbursts of stylised violence with some aplomb. Garko looks the part, but he is occasionally found wanting in the acting department and is easily outshone by co-stars Klaus Kinski and William Berger. Garko and Kinski were reteamed the following year for an unremarkable sequel. DP Italian dubbed.

John Garko [Gianni Garko] *Sartana* • Klaus Kinsky [Klaus Kinski] *Morgan* • William Berger *Lasky* ■ *Dir* Frank Kramer [Gianfranco Parolini]

Saskatchewan ★★ U

Western   1954 · US · Colour · 87min

An underrated actor, Alan Ladd seemed content to make formula pictures rather than stretch himself. His first western after the memorable *Shane* was this routine story of cavalry versus Indians – only this time the troops are Mounties and the location is Canada. Ladd's the Indian-raised officer who defies his superior officer to deal with hostile Sioux crossing the border. Shelley Winters is thrown in as the woman prisoner of Hugh O'Brian's marshal. The uninvolved direction of veteran Raoul Walsh doesn't help. AE

Alan Ladd *Sergeant O'Rourke* • Shelley Winters *Grace Markey* • J Carrol Naish *Batoche* • Hugh O'Brian *Marshal Smith* • Robert Douglas *Inspector Benton* • Jay Silverheels *Cajou* ■ *Dir* Raoul Walsh • *Scr* Gil Doud

Sasquatch ★ U

Adventure   1978 · US · Colour · 101min

Of all the monsters that cinema has unleashed, Bigfoot, supposed inhabitant of the North American forests, seems to be one of the most benign. He's even more harmless in this semi-documentary about an expedition that goes in search of the creature. Some blurred photos are supposed to strike a chill, but they are risible – as is the film. TH

George Lauris *Chuck Evans* • Steve Boergadine *Hank Parshall* • Jim Bradford *Barney Snipe* • Ken Kenzle *Josh Bigsby* • William Emmons *Dr Paul Markham* • Joe Morello *Techka Blackhawk* ■ *Dir* Ed Ragozzini • *Scr* Edward H Hawkins, from a story by Ronald B Olson

The Satan Bug ★★★ PG

Science-fiction thriller
1965 · US · Colour · 109min

Compared to the more straightforward heroics of other Alistair MacLean hits such as *The Guns of Navarone* and *Where Eagles Dare*, this is an altogether more subtle affair, with George Maharis searching for the madman who is threatening to unleash a deadly virus. There's a solid supporting cast, and director John Sturges never lets the suspense slip for a minute. JF

George Maharis *Lee Barrett* • Richard Basehart *Dr Hoffman/Ainsley* • Anne Francis *Ann* • Dana Andrews *The General* • Edward Asner *Veretti* • Frank Sutton *Donald* • John Larkin *Michaelson* ■ *Dir* John Sturges • *Scr* James Clavell, Edward Anhalt, from the novel by Ian Stuart [Alistair MacLean]

Satan in High Heels ★★ 18

Thriller   1962 · US · BW · 89min

Great title, shame about the movie! Burlesque dancer Meg Myles robs her junkie boyfriend, heads for New York and becomes a cabaret club owner's mistress, in a typical exploitation item that features very little strip but lots of tease. Aside from a stand-out sequence where Myles sings *More Deadly Than the Male* wearing full leather and brandishing a riding crop, this is strictly routine trash. AJ Violence, sex scenes, nudity. **DVD**

Meg Myles *Stacey Kane* • Grayson Hall *Pepe* • Mike Keene *Arnold Kenyon* • Robert Yuro *Laurence Kenyon* • Sabrina (1) *Sabrina* • Nolia Chapman *Felice* • Earl Hammond *Rudy* • Del Tenney *Paul* ■ *Dir* Jerald Intrator • *Scr* John T Chapman [John Chapman], from a story by Harold Bennett, John T Chapman [John Chapman]

U SUITABLE FOR ALL   Uc SUITABLE ESPECIALLY FOR YOUNG CHILDREN (DVD ONLY)   PG PARENTAL GUIDANCE   12A UNDER 12s TO BE ACCOMPANIED (CINEMA ONLY)

S

Satan Met a Lady ★
Crime comedy drama 1936 · US · BW · 75min

A reworked version of Dashiell Hammett's *The Maltese Falcon*, this was clearly intended as a sophisticated spoof but emerged as a clumsy, unfunny bore. There is some interest to be had in identifying the worked-over characters and plot points – several questionable characters are after an ancient ivory horn filled with jewels – but that's about it. Bette Davis regarded the movie as one of the low points in her career. RK

Bette Davis *Valerie Purvis* • Warren William *Ted Shayne* • Alison Skipworth *Mme Barabbas* • Arthur Treacher *Anthony Travers* • Winifred Shaw *Astrid Ames* • Marie Wilson *Murgatroyd* • Porter Hall *Mr Ames* • Maynard Holmes *Kenneth* ■ *Dir* William Dieterle • *Scr* Brown Holmes, from the novel *The Maltese Falcon* by Dashiell Hammett

Satan Never Sleeps ★★
Period drama 1962 · US/UK · Colour · 126min

This Catholics v Communists saga is a cross between *The Left Hand of God* and director Leo McCarey's own Oscar-winning whimsy *Going My Way*. With British scenery approximating the Chinese landscape, the film has a rugged look in keeping with its often brutal subject matter. Too much time is spent setting the scene, and not enough on the dramatic events that overwhelm the mission run by the William Holden and Clifton Webb. Devout and dour. DP

William Holden (2) *Father O'Banion* • Clifton Webb *Father Boward* • France Nuyen *Siu Lan* • Athene Seyler *Sister Agnes* • Martin Benson *Kuznietsky* • Edith Sharpe *Sister Theresa* • Burt Kwouk *Ah Wang* ■ *Dir* Leo McCarey • *Scr* Claude Binyon, Leo McCarey, from the novel *Satan Never Sleeps* by Pearl S Buck

The Satanic Rites of Dracula ★★ 18
Horror 1973 · UK · Colour · 83min

Christopher Lee gives a disappointing final appearance as Dracula, masquerading as a mysterious Howard Hughes-style business mogul, plotting to control the world with a vampire virus. It's lacking in Hammer's usual gothic flavour and detail, and Alan Gibson's careless direction proved to be the final nail in the Dracula coffin, despite the indefatigable Peter Cushing performing his usual miracle as a descendant of the original Van Helsing, with Joanna Lumley as his daughter. AJ Nudity.

Christopher Lee *Count Dracula* • Peter Cushing *Van Helsing* • Michael Coles *Inspector Murray* • William Franklyn *Torrence* • Freddie Jones *Professor Keeley* • Joanna Lumley *Jessica* • Richard Vernon *Mathews* • Patrick Barr *Lord Carradine* ■ *Dir* Alan Gibson • *Scr* Don Houghton, from the character created by Bram Stoker

Satan's Brew ★★★ 18
Black comedy 1976 · W Ger · Colour · 106min

Rainer Werner Fassbinder is at his most scathingly anti-bourgeois in this portrayal of a worthless world. His pessimistic conclusion is that all relationships are based on power and that sadomasochism, blind fealty and financial gain have replaced emotion. Playing the burned-out poet capable only of expressing himself in acts of cruelty or self-loathing, Kurt Raab exhibits no redeeming features as a character Fassbinder clearly invests with autobiographical disgust. Fassbinder makes no concessions towards the viewer, who is left to experience either anger or guilt. DP German +subtitles. Swearing, sex scenes, drug abuse.

Kurt Raab *Walter Kranz* • Margit Carstensen *Andrée* • Helen Vita *Luise Kranz* • Volker Spengler *Ernst* • Ingrid Caven *Lilly* • Marquard Bohm *Rolf* • Ulli Lommel *Lauf* ■ *Dir/Scr* Rainer Werner Fassbinder

Satan's Slave ★★★ 18
Horror 1976 · UK · Colour · 83min

Director Norman J Warren lays on the nudity and gore in this obscure, lurid tale of devil worship and ancestral evil. Candace

Glendenning plays the girl coming up to her 20th birthday, whose visit to her eccentric uncle (played by Michael Gough) coincides with the violent death of her parents and an attempt to resurrect a witch. Cinematographer Les Young's intense use of colour is matched by Gough's gregarious performance, but Warren overindulges in horror clichés and garish set pieces. DP **DVD**

Michael Gough *Alexander Yorke* • Candace Glendenning *Catherine Yorke* • Martin Potter *Stephen Yorke* • Barbara Kellerman *Frances* • Michael Craze *John* • James Bree *Malcolm Yorke* • Celia Hewitt *Elizabeth Yorke* • David McGillivray *Priest* ■ *Dir* Norman J Warren • *Scr* David McGillivray

Satellite in the Sky ★★ U
Science-fiction adventure 1956 · UK · Colour · 84min

This full-throttled, but hopelessly inadequate space opera stars Kieron Moore as the commander of an orbital mission to test a tritonium bomb. Lois Maxwell displays none of Miss Moneypenny's sang-froid as a stowed-away pacifist reporter. But no one stands a chance of making much impression alongside Donald Wolfit's risibly bombastic inventor. DP

Kieron Moore *Cmdr Michael Haydon* • Lois Maxwell *Kim Hamilton* • Donald Wolfit *Prof Merrity* • Bryan Forbes *Jimmy Wheeler* • Jimmy Hanley *Larry* • Thea Gregory *Barbara Noble* ■ *Dir* Paul Dickson • *Scr* Edith Dell, John Mather, JT McIntosh

Satisfaction ★★ 12
Drama 1988 · US · Colour · 89min

Justine Bateman, Julia Roberts, Trini Alvarado and Britta Phillips are the four girls in a rock band who spend the summer playing music at a resort and trying to find eligible men. Club owner Liam Neeson is the older man Bateman falls for in this mediocre teenage tale, notable mainly for a cameo from Blondie singer Debbie Harry, and a chance to see a pre-stardom Roberts and Neeson. You know it's time these girls had their instruments confiscated when you hear Bateman's rendition of (I Can't Get No) *Satisfaction*. JB **DVD**

Justine Bateman *Jennie Lee* • Liam Neeson *Martin Falcon* • Julia Roberts *Daryle Shane* • Trini Alvarado *May "Mooch" Stark* • Britta Phillips *Billy Swan* • Scott Coffey *Nickie Longo* • Deborah Harry *Tina* ■ *Dir* Joan Freeman • *Scr* Charles Purpura

Saturday Night and Sunday Morning ★★★★★ PG
Classic drama 1960 · UK · BW · 85min

Arthur Seaton was the only "kitchen sink" hero to accept that, while life was nasty, brutish and short, you had to make the best of it. And there was no one better to convey that complex mix of cynicism, laddishness and resignation than Albert Finney. Both he and Rachel Roberts won British Film Academy awards, while the film itself took the best British picture honour. Author Alan Sillitoe draws on his own experiences of factory life that are given a truly authentic ring by director Karel Reisz. For the first time, the working classes were treated with respect, not condescension. Finney's belligerence towards authority is as convincing as his touching tenderness towards the married woman (Roberts) he seduces, and, while he may not always live by his words – "What I want is a good time. The rest is all propaganda" – the film's affirmation that he can never really be beaten survives. DP **DVD** **BD**

Albert Finney *Arthur Seaton* • Shirley Anne Field *Doreen Gretton* • Rachel Roberts (1) *Brenda* • Hylda Baker *Aunt Ada* • Norman Rossington *Bert* • Bryan Pringle *Jack* • Robert Cawdron *Robboe* ■ *Dir* Karel Reisz • *Scr* Alan Sillitoe, from his novel

Saturday Night Fever ★★★★★ 18
Dance drama 1977 · US · Colour · 114min

John Travolta's role here as Tony Manero, the Brooklyn shop assistant who becomes king of the New York disco scene, turned him from a B-list TV actor into, for a time,

the hottest movie star in the world and a pop culture icon. Party-poopers may find the whole thing a cringeworthy period piece and a reminder that the 1970s really were the naffest decade. But most will sit back and enjoy the snazzy dancing (much of it with co-star Karen Lynn Gorney), the memorable soundtrack and the all-round, high energy entertainment. By contrast, the 1983 sequel, *Staying Alive*, is a near career-low for Travolta. PF Violence, sex scenes, swearing, nudity. **DVD** **BD**

John Travolta *Tony Manero* • Karen Lynn Gorney *Stephanie* • Barry Miller *Bobby C* • Joseph Cali *Joey* • Paul Pape *Double J* • Donna Pescow *Annette* • Bruce Ornstein *Gus* • Julie Bovasso *Flo* ■ *Dir* John Badham • *Scr* Norman Wexler, from the article *Tribal Rites of the New Saturday Night* by Nik Cohn • *Choreographer* Lester Wilson

The Saturday Night Kid ★★
Romantic comedy 1929 · US · BW · 62min

With her scandalous off-screen antics escalating, Paramount's megastar Clara Bow would soon receive her exit visa from the studio. But she survived the transition to sound and here she is a department store assistant. Jean Arthur, playing Clara's sister, is the bigger vamp of the two and both girls have their sights set on James Hall. The script offers some snappy one-liners as well as the attraction of the leading ladies. Future sex symbol Jean Harlow has a bit part. RK

Clara Bow *Mayme* • James Hall *Bill* • Jean Arthur *Janie* • Charles Sellon *Lem Woodruff* • Ethel Wales *Ma Woodruff* • Frank Ross *Ken* • Edna May Oliver *Miss Streeter* • Jean Harlow *Hazel* ■ *Dir* A Edward Sutherland • *Scr* Lloyd Corrigan, Ethel Doherty, Edward E Paramore Jr, from the play *Love 'em and Leave 'em* by George Abbott, John VA Weaver

Saturday Night Out ★★★ 12
Adventure 1963 · UK · BW · 92min

This gritty, low-budget, black-and-white exploitation film was very daring in its day but wouldn't cause a stir now. The plot is negligible: five merchant seamen and their passenger spend a long day's leave in London, but it's the location charm and period cast that keep the movie watchable today. The nominal stars are the lovely sweet-faced Heather Sears and that venerable old grouch Bernard Lee (James Bond's "M"). Francesca Annis and Colin Campbell also impress. TS

Heather Sears *Penny* • Bernard Lee *George Hudson* • Erika Remberg *Wanda* • Francesca Annis *Jean* • John Bonney *Lee* • Colin Campbell *Jamie* • Nigel Green *Paddy* • Vera Day *Arlene* • Freddie Mills *Joe* • David Lodge *Arthur* ■ *Dir* Robert Hartford-Davis • *Scr* Donald Ford, Derek Ford

Saturday the 14th ★ 15
Spoof horror 1981 · US · Colour · 72min

Despite its title, this childish parody is more a monster-movie spoof than a send-up of slasher movies. Richard Benjamin and Paula Prentiss move into a haunted house where their son Kevin Brando opens an ancient book and a horde of monsters, aliens and vampires pop out eager to take up residence. There are some flashes of humour – a *Creature from the Black Lagoon* in the bubble bath – but for the most part this is a crudely produced rag-bag of sketches. AJ

Richard Benjamin *John* • Paula Prentiss *Mary* • Severn Darden *Van Helsing* • Jeffrey Tambor *Waldemar* • Kari Michaelsen *Debbie* • Kevin Brando *Billy* • Rosemary DeCamp *Aunt Lucille* ■ *Dir* Howard R Cohen • *Scr* Howard R Cohen, from a story by Jeff Begun

Saturday the 14th Strikes Back ★ PG
Spoof horror 1988 · US · Colour · 75min

Director Howard R Cohen clearly didn't learn from the mistakes of his original substandard spoof as this sequel is an even more pitiful parody. This time husband and wife Avery Schreiber and Patty McCormack move into a haunted house built over the entrance to Hell which cracks open and unleashes yet another surfeit of monsters,

vampires and werewolves. Footage lifted from bad Roger Corman B-movies replaces the arch-satire of the first movie but with the same poor result. AJ

Jason Presson *Eddie Baxter* • Ray Walston *Gramps* • Avery Schreiber *Frank* • Patty McCormack *Kate* • Julianne McNamara *Linda* • Rhonda Aldrich *Alice* • Daniel Will-Harris *Bert* ■ *Dir/Scr* Howard R Cohen

Saturday's Children ★★★
Drama 1940 · US · BW · 101min

Young inventor John Garfield meets obstacles to his plans and dreams: marriage to ambitious Anne Shirley and the devastating effects of the Depression. Directed by Vincent Sherman with an excellent cast that includes Claude Rains, this was Garfield's successful bid to break out of the slum boy/crime movie mould. Its social concerns are clear but, like the era it explores, the movie is downbeat and depressing. RK

John Garfield *Rimes Rosson* • Anne Shirley *Bobby Halevy* • Claude Rains *Mr Halevy* • Lee Patrick *Florrie Sands* • George Tobias *Herbie Smith* • Roscoe Karns *Willie Sands* • Dennie Moore *Gertrude Mills* ■ *Dir* Vincent Sherman • *Scr* Julius J Epstein, Philip G Epstein, from the play by Maxwell Anderson

Saturn 3 ★★ 15
Science-fiction thriller 1980 · UK · Colour · 83min

Kirk Douglas and Farrah Fawcett live an idyllic Adam and Eve existence in a synthetic food-making factory on Titan, Saturn's largest moon. Then along comes snake Harvey Keitel, a psychopath on the run from Earth, and his equally disturbed robot Hector. It was directed for two weeks by *Star Wars/Superman* production designer John Barry before Stanley Donen took over, but no amount of hardware and fantastic sets can improve the mass of contrivance. AJ **DVD**

Farrah Fawcett *Alex* • Kirk Douglas *Adam* • Harvey Keitel *Benson* • Douglas Lambert *Captain James* • Ed Bishop *Harding* ■ *Dir* Stanley Donen • *Scr* Martin Amis, from a story by John Barry

Satyricon ★★★★ 18
Historical fantasy drama 1969 · Fr/It · Colour · 124min

Federico Fellini received an Oscar nomination for best director for this deliriously surreal moving fresco of ancient Rome. This is *La Dolce Vita* out of Petronius by way of Pasolini and DeMille, with the antics of Nero's empire being used to comment on contemporary godlessness. The adventures of squabbling hedonists Martin Potter and Hiram Keller don't matter a fig beside the debauchery and depravity, which for all their seeming excess are not that divorced from historical reality. Over-indulgence, indiscipline and sexual immaturity are the usual accusations hurled at this hellish vision, but few film-makers would have had the courage to make it. DP Italian +subtitles. **DVD** **BD**

Martin Potter *Encolpius* • Hiram Keller *Ascyltus* • Salvo Randone *Eumolpus* • Max Born *Giton* • Fanfulla *Vernacchio* • Mario Romagnoli *Trimalchio* • Capucine *Tryphaena* • Alain Cuny *Lichas* ■ *Dir* Federico Fellini • *Scr* Federico Fellini, Bernardino Zapponi, Brunello Rondi, from the novel by Gaius Petronius

Sausage Party ★★★ 15
Animated comedy 2016 · US · Colour · 88min

Billed in the US as the first R-rated feature-length animation, this resolutely ribald tale is set in a supermarket where a horny hotdog (Seth Rogen) and a pretty bun (Kristen Wiig) dream of being together in a utopia they believe lies beyond the sliding doors. There are flashes of inspiration like the New York bagel (Edward Norton) channelling Woody Allen. But the concept is stretched thin and the heavy use of foul language can feel like a substitute for wit at times. But if you like your jokes raw and saucy, this hits the spot. SP Swearing, sexual references.

Seth Rogen *Frank* • Kristen Wiig *Brenda* • Edward Norton *Sammy Bagel Jr* • Nick Kroll *Douche* • David Krumholtz *Vash* • Salma Hayek *Theresa Taco* • Michael Cera *Barry* • James Franco *Toast* • Jonah Hill *Carl* ■ *Dir* Greg Tiernan, Conrad Vernon • *Scr* Seth Rogen, Evan Goldberg, Kyle Hunter, Ariel Shaffir, from a story by Rogen, Goldberg

The Savage ★★ U
Western   1953 · US · Colour · 94min

Charlton Heston was the sole star of his fourth Hollywood film. He makes a sturdy job of portraying the white man raised by the Sioux who becomes an army scout, trusted by neither side. As conflict threatens, he has to decide where his loyalties lie. Blandly directed by George Marshall, the western is far too long and the way the Heston character is handled at the end smacks of box-office compromise. AE

Charlton Heston *Warbonnet/Jim Ahern* • Susan Morrow *Tally Hathersall* • Peter Hanson *Lt Weston Hathersall* • Joan Taylor *Luta* • Richard Rober *Capt Arnold Vaugant* ■ *Dir* George Marshall • *Scr* Sydney Boehm, from the novel *The Renegade* by LL Foreman

Savage Dawn ★ 18
Action drama   1985 · US · Colour · 98min

It's an unwritten rule among film critics that movies with titles that start with the word "savage" are invariably awful. *Savage Dawn* confirms it beyond any reasonable doubt. Ploughing the same furrow as a thousand other B-movies, it's the violent, foul-mouthed tale of a biker gang that takes over a small desert town. DA

George Kennedy *Tick Rand* • Richard Lynch *Reverend Romano* • Karen Black *Rachel* • Lance Henriksen *Ben Stryker* • Claudia Udy *Kate Rand* • Bill Forsythe [William Forsythe] *Pigiron* • Leo Gordon *Sheriff* ■ *Dir* Simon Nuchtern • *Scr* William P Milling

Savage Grace ★★★ 15
Drama based on a true story   2007 · Sp/Fr/US · Colour · 93min

Swoon director Tom Kalin's belated second feature is another lurid true story of the rich and deeply dysfunctional. At its core is the unnaturally close and ultimately tragic relationship between brittle American socialite Barbara Daly Baekeland (an impressive Julianne Moore) and her louche son Tony (played as an adult by a well-cast Eddie Redmayne). Beginning in New York in 1946, Tony narrates the story of his mother's miserable marriage to plastics heir Brookes Baekeland (Stephen Dillane) over the next two decades. There's barely a let-up in the procession of social and sexual humiliations that haunts these three unhappy figures, as the tone veers between black comedy, melodrama and moments of genuine pathos. But it is Moore's brave performance that anchors this fascinating yet sometimes frustratingly superficial story. SS English, French, Spanish +subtitles. *DVD*

Julianne Moore *Barbara Baekeland* • Stephen Dillane *Brooks Baekeland* • Eddie Redmayne *Tony Baekeland* • Hugh Dancy *Sam Green* • Anne Reid *Nini Daly* • Elena Anaya *Blanca* • Barney Clark *Tony as a child* ■ *Dir* Tom Kalin • *Scr* Howard A Rodman, from the non-fiction book by Natalie Robins, Stephen ML Aronson

The Savage Innocents ★★ 12
Adventure drama   1960 · It /Fr/UK · Colour · 109min

What started out as a sort of *Nanook of the North*-style look at Inuit culture, with Anthony Quinn in fur and full ethnic mode, was apparently plagued by production problems. These included Peter O'Toole's Mountie sporting his original nose but not his original voice, which was dubbed against the actor's wishes. Quinn makes a creditable attempt at portraying the harsh Inuit lifestyle - hunting, fishing, watching polar bears - but even he can't save this oddity from director Nicholas Ray. AT *DVD*

Anthony Quinn *Inuk* • Yoko Tani *Asiak* • Marie Yang *Powtee* • Peter O'Toole *First Trooper* • Carlo Giustini *Second Trooper* • Kaida Horiuchi

Imina ■ *Dir* Nicholas Ray • *Scr* Nicholas Ray, Hans Ruesch, Franco Solinas, from the novel *Top of the World* by Hans Ruesch

The Savage Is Loose ★
Adventure drama   1974 · US · Colour · 115min

Directed, produced by and starring George C Scott, this is a tale of incest between mother and son after they've been stranded on a desert island with father for some years. Trish Van Devere (Scott's then wife) and John David Carson feature in a story that plumbs the shallows rather ineptly and does Scott's reputation no good. TH

George C Scott *John* • Trish Van Devere *Maida* • John David Carson *David* • Lee H Montgomery [Lee Montgomery] *Young David* ■ *Dir* George C Scott • *Scr* Max Ehrlich, Frank De Felitta

Savage Islands ★★ PG
Swashbuckling adventure   1983 · US/NZ · Colour · 95min

This has to be a low point in the rollercoaster career of Tommy Lee Jones, who didn't get real recognition until his award-winning turn as the US marshal hunting Harrison Ford in *The Fugitive*. Belonging to the bygone age of Saturday morning pictures, this bloodless romp has Jones as a crusty rogue helping missionary Michael O'Keefe to rescue fiancée Jenny Seagrove from the pirates who've kidnapped her. It's a case of all buckle and no swash. DA

Tommy Lee Jones *Captain "Bully" Hayes* • Michael O'Keefe *Nathaniel Williamson* • Jenny Seagrove *Sophie* • Max Phipps *Ben Pease* • Grant Tilly *Count Von Rittenberg* • Peter Rowley *Louis Beck* • Bill Johnson (2) *Reverend Williamson* ■ *Dir* Ferdinand Fairfax • *Scr* John Hughes, David Odell, from a screenplay (unproduced) by David Odell and a story by Lloyd Phillips

Savage Messiah ★★★
Romantic drama   1972 · UK · Colour · 96min

After the excesses of *The Music Lovers* and *The Devils*, director Ken Russell handled the platonic love affair between sculptor Henri Gaudier and his muse Sophie Brzeska, with pleasing restraint (apart from a couple of unnecessary song and dance numbers). Set in Paris and London prior to the First World War, Dorothy Tutin and newcomer Scott Antony give superb, impassioned performances as the seemingly ill-matched couple. DM

Dorothy Tutin *Sophie Brzeska* • Scott Antony *Henri Gaudier-Brzeska* • Helen Mirren *Gosh Smith-Boyle* • Lindsay Kemp *Angus Corky* • Peter Vaughan *Louvre attendant* • Michael Gough *Mons Gaudier* ■ *Dir* Ken Russell • *Scr* Christopher Logue, from a book by HS Ede • *Production Designer* Derek Jarman

Savage Streets ★★ 18
Action drama   1984 · US · Colour · 80min

Following her appearance in *The Exorcist*, Linda Blair made a career out of trashy exploitation flicks. She stars as a typical LA girl who turns into "Charles Bronson in a dress" when her deaf mute sister is raped by a gang of lowlife punks. Linda leads her all-girl gang against those responsible, armed with such niceties as bear traps and a crossbow. Blair's not bad, but she is swamped by the vulgar dialogue and gratuitous violence. RS

Linda Blair *Brenda* • John Vernon *Principal Underwood* • Robert Dryer *Jake* • Johnny Venocur *Vince* • Sal Landi *Fargo* • Scott Mayer *Red* ■ *Dir* Danny Steinmann • *Scr* Norman Yonemoto, Danny Steinmann

Savaged ★★★ 18
Supernatural revenge horror   2013 · US · Colour · 90min

Grittily shot, with a bleached-out look that accentuates the nastiness of events, this ambitious horror sees deaf girl Amanda Adrienne raped and murdered by a racist gang after she intervenes in their tradition of killing native Americans. But things turn novel when the local shaman tries to reanimate her, only for the vengeful spirit of an Apache chief to inhabit her body. Redneck clichés and some horribly

offensive language ensure you really root for the rapidly decaying Adrienne in the far-fetched retribution. SF Violence, swearing. *DVD*

Amanda Adrienne *Zoe* • Joseph Runningfox *Grey Wolf* ■ *Dir/Scr* Michael S Ojeda

Savages ★★ 15
Satirical comedy   1972 · US · Colour, Sepia and BW · 101min

James Ivory returned to his native America for this heavy-handed Buñuelian parable on the thin line between savagery and sophistication. The arch nature of the enterprise - in which human-sacrificing primitives are guided by a croquet ball into a country manor, where they briefly assume the trappings of gentility - is only emphasised by Walter Lassally's decision to photograph the Mud People's progression and inevitable regression in monochrome, sepia and lavish colour. DP *DVD*

Lewis J Stadlen *Julian Branch* • Anne Francine *Carlotta* • Thayer David *Otto Nurder* • Susan Blakely *Cecily* • Russ Thacker *Andrew* • Salome Jens *Emily Penning* • Margaret Brewster *Lady Cora* • Neil Fitzgerald *Sir Harry* ■ *Dir* James Ivory • *Scr* James Ivory, Michael O'Donoghue, George Swift Trow, from an idea by James Ivory

The Savages ★★★ 15
Comedy drama   2007 · US · Colour · 109min

The Savages of the title, siblings Wendy (an Oscar-nominated Laura Linney) and Jon (Philip Seymour Hoffman), are anything but uncivilised. Both are typically middle class and each is undergoing a mild midlife crisis: he is a college professor struggling with a book, while she is a wannabe playwright locked in an unsatisfactory affair with a married man. The pair are reluctantly reunited by the need to find their estranged father a new care home, and ghosts from their past almost emerge. The performances are a quiet delight, with Hoffman predictably fine as the rumpled academic who just wants to return to the sanctuary of his office. Director Tamara Jenkins's screenplay finds odd flashes of humour in the inevitably depressing situation, but this is a little too downbeat for its own good. AS *DVD*

Laura Linney *Wendy Savage* • Philip Seymour Hoffman *Jon Savage* • Philip Bosco *Lenny Savage* • Peter Friedman *Larry* • David Zayas *Eduardo* • Gbenga Akinnagbe *Jimmy* • Cara Seymour *Kasia* • Tonye Patano *Ms Robinson* ■ *Dir/Scr* Tamara Jenkins

Savages ★★★ 18
Crime drama   2012 · US · Colour · 129min

Oliver Stone's brassy and very bloody adaptation of Don Winslow's novel follows California dope dealers Aaron Johnson and Taylor Kitsch, whose hedonistic lifestyle includes sharing a girlfriend, Blake Lively. Lively has little more to do than play the victim after being snatched by Mexican crime lord Salma Hayek. In essence, *Savages* is a love story, but the three-way dynamic just seems frivolous and the finale is horribly overblown, especially as Lively's character is too slight to warrant so much gunplay. The thrills here may be many, but they are also cheap. SP English, Spanish +subtitles. Violence, swearing, drug abuse, brief nudity. *DVD* *BL*

Taylor Kitsch *Chon* • Blake Lively *O* • Aaron Johnson *Ben* • John Travolta *Dennis* • Salma Hayek *Elena* • Trevor Donovan *Matt* ■ *Dir* Oliver Stone • *Scr* Shane Salerno, Don Winslow, Oliver Stone, from Winslow's novel

Savannah Smiles ★★ PG
Comedy drama   1982 · US · Colour · 99min

Bridgette Andersen runs away from her uncaring politician father and makes the mistake of hiding in the car of two not-so-bright crooks. The duo decide to hold her to ransom, but gradually become more like surrogate parents than opportunistic kidnappers as the police close in. Written by co-star Mark Miller, this winsome comedy thriller throws some fresh comic twists into the plot to stop it becoming too mechanical and manipulative. AJ

Mark Miller *Alvie* • Donovan Scott *Boots* • Bridgette Andersen *Savannah Driscoll* • Peter Graves (2) *Harland Dobbs* • Chris Robinson *Richard Driscoll* • Michael Parks *Lt Savage* • Barbara Stanger *Joan Driscoll* ■ *Dir* Pierre DeMoro • *Scr* Mark Miller

Save the Green Planet! ★★★ 18
Science-fiction comedy drama   2003 · S Kor · Colour · 117min

Although it adopts a magpie approach to its visuals and plumps for a plot twist that undoes much of its early good work, Jang Jun-hwan's ambitious debut is still a crafty combination of offbeat comedy, B-movie sci-fi and macabre thriller. Shin Ha-gyun excels as the movie-mad crank whose conviction that Earth is about to be invaded by aliens from Andromeda prompts him to kidnap industrial tycoon Baek Yun-shik. But, as eccentric cop Lee Jae-yong begins to investigate the abduction, an alternative motive for Shin's actions emerges and the tone becomes sombre. DP Korean +subtitles. Violence. *DVD*

Shin Ha-gyun *Lee Byeong-Gu* • Baek Yun-shik *Kang Man-Shik* • Hwang Jeong-min *Su-ni* • Lee Jae-yong *Inspector Choo* • Lee Ju-hyeon *Inspector Kim* ■ *Dir/Scr* Jang Jun-hwan

Save the Last Dance ★★★ 12
Dance drama   2000 · US · Colour · 108min

Julia Stiles is the aspiring ballerina who gives up her ambitions after her beloved mother dies in a car crash while speeding to an important audition. She goes to live with her estranged jazz musician father on Chicago's depressed South Side, where she finds herself part of the minority in a mainly black school, coping with racial slurs when she starts dating model student Sean Patrick Thomas. With its optimistic view of ghetto life, this is fantasy melodrama pure and simple. AJ Swearing, violence. *DVD*

Julia Stiles *Sara Johnson* • Sean Patrick Thomas *Derek* • Kerry Washington *Chenille* • Fredro Starr *Malakai* • Terry Kinney *Roy* • Bianca Lawson *Nikki* ■ *Dir* Thomas Carter • *Scr* Duane Adler, Cheryl Edwards, from a story by Duane Adler

Save the Tiger ★★★ 15
Drama   1973 · US · Colour · 96min

Jack Lemmon stars as a struggling Los Angeles garment manufacturer who contemplates burning down his factory in order to claim the insurance and pay off his debts. This drama about the consumer rat race is bludgeoning rather than hard-hitting, and Lemmon's role is very much in the tradition of Arthur Miller's Willy Loman in *Death of a Salesman*. Though it won Lemmon a best actor Oscar, he has given far better performances in his career. AT Swearing. *DVD*

Jack Lemmon *Harry Stoner* • Jack Gilford *Phil Greene* • Laurie Heineman *Myra* • Norman Burton *Fred Mirrell* • Patricia Smith *Janet Stoner* • Thayer David *Charlie Robbins* • William Hansen *Meyer* ■ *Dir* John G Avildsen • *Scr* Steve Shagan

Saving Grace ★★ PG
Comedy drama   1985 · US · Colour · 106min

The essential decency of Tom Conti just about holds this fragile fable together. As a Pope who slips out of the Vatican to minister to people who truly need him, he wrinkles his brow and smiles sadly with a concern that convinces in a situation that doesn't. Director Robert M Young shoots the southern Italian countryside with the glossy eye of a postcard photographer, while Joaquin Montana's script is overly dependent on easy solutions and glib platitudes. For all its good intentions, this is more of a penance than a pleasure. DP

Tom Conti *Pope Leo XIV* • Fernando Rey *Cardinal Stefano Biondi* • Erland Josephson *Monsignor Francesco Ghezzi* • Giancarlo Giannini *Abalardi* • Donald Hewlett *Monsignor Colin McGee* • Edward James Olmos *Ciolino* ■ *Dir* Robert M Young • *Scr* Joaquin Montana, from the novel by Celia Gittelson

Saving Grace ★★ PG
Comedy   2000 · UK · Colour · 88min

Brenda Blethyn's the eponymous Grace, a recently widowed housewife whose late husband has left her with a mountain of debts to pay. The only way to keep her beautiful Cornish mansion is to grow marijuana with the aid of her Scottish handyman, Craig Ferguson. The screenplay is more juvenile than risqué and makes tittering pot-shots at the expense of characterisation and plot. NS DVD

Brenda Blethyn *Grace* • Craig Ferguson *Matthew* • Martin Clunes *Dr Bamford* • Tcheky Karyo *Jacques* • Jamie Foreman *China* • Bill Bailey (2) *Vince* • Valerie Edmond *Nicky* • Diana Quick *Honey* • Leslie Phillips *Vicar* ■ *Dir* Nigel Cole • *Scr* Craig Ferguson, Mark Crowdy, from a story by Mark Crowdy

Saving Mr Banks ★★★★★ PG
Drama based on a true story
2013 · US/UK/Aus · Colour · 120min

How did Walt Disney (Tom Hanks) finally convince author PL Travers (Emma Thompson) that her Mary Poppins character was safe in his hands after years of stubborn refusal? This hugely entertaining comedy drama reveals that the cantankerous Travers hated cartoons, musicals and Dick Van Dyke, though evocative flashbacks to her childhood reveal the motives for fiercely protecting her character. Her continual interference caused enormous problems with the creative team, but this cultural clash proves sharply witty and poignant under John Lee Hancock's spot-on direction. It's a superlative confection of Hollywood dream and backstage legend, dominated by Thompson's stunningly eccentric performance. AJ DVD

Emma Thompson *PL Travers, Pamela* • Tom Hanks *Walt Disney* • Colin Farrell (2) *Travers Goff* • Paul Giamatti *Ralph* • Jason Schwartzman *Richard M Sherman* • BJ Novak *Robert B Sherman* • Ruth Wilson *Margaret Goff* • Victoria Summer *Julie Andrews* • Kathy Baker *Tommie* ■ *Dir* John Lee Hancock • *Scr* Kelly Marcel, Sue Smith • *Cinematographer* John Schwartzman • *Music* Thomas Newman • *Costume Designer* Daniel Orlandi

Saving Private Ryan ★★★★ 15
Second World War drama
1998 · US · Colour · 162min

With this Oscar-winning attempt to reshape the past through fiction, Steven Spielberg comes closer than ever before to depicting historical truth. The action opens brutally with a wrenching re-creation of the Second World War D-Day landing on Omaha beach. Spielberg and cinematographer Janusz Kaminski succeed in capturing the terrifying and bewildering chaos of the encounter. Yet, away from the fighting, this occasionally lapses into combat picture cliché, but this is still well-meaning, strongly acted and slickly mounted. DP Violence, language, horror. DVD

Tom Hanks *Captain Miller* • Tom Sizemore *Sergeant Horvath* • Edward Burns *Private Reiben* • Barry Pepper *Private Jackson* • Adam Goldberg *Private Mellish* • Vin Diesel *Private Caparzo* • Giovanni Ribisi *T/4 Medic Wade* • Jeremy Davies *Corporal Upham* • Matt Damon *Private Ryan* • Ted Danson *Captain Hamill* • Kathleen Byron *Old Mrs Ryan* ■ *Dir* Steven Spielberg • *Scr* Robert Rodat • *Editor* Michael Kahn

Saving Santa ★★ U
Animated musical comedy
2013 · UK · Colour · 80min

This animated Brit-voiced bauble may lack the clout and quality of, say, Disney's *Frozen*, but it's still a cute festive watch for younger kids. Martin Freeman voices Bernard, an inventor elf whose latest gizmo inadvertently disrupts Santa's North Pole HQ cloaking device, leaving the place open to rival nasty Nevill (Tim Curry). It's down to Bernard to make amends, by using Santa's time globe. Parents should be prepared for probing questions about temporal paradoxes. DA BLU 3D

Martin Freeman *Bernard* • Tim Curry *Nevill Baddington* • Tim Conway *Santa* • Joan Collins *Vera Baddington* • Ashley Tisdale *Shiny* • Pam Ferris *Mrs Claus* ■ *Dir* Leon Joosen, Aaron Seelman • *Scr* Ricky Roxburgh, from a story by Tony Nottage

Savior ★★★★ 18
War drama   1997 · US · Colour · 99min

This Yugoslavian-set tale of cruelty still carries a haunting and shocking impact. Mercenary Dennis Quaid joins the Foreign Legion after his wife and child are killed by Islamic terrorists. While fighting on the Serbian side against the Muslims, circumstances throw him together with a pregnant rape victim and he begins to regain his humanity in the face of Bosnian atrocities. Serbian director Peter Antonijevic draws on his personal experiences to devastating effect and comes up with a grim, but poignant film of rare emotional depth. AJ Swearing, violence. DVD

Dennis Quaid *Joshua Rose/Guy* • Nastassja Kinski *Maria Rose* • Stellan Skarsgård *Peter* • Natasa Ninkovic *Vera* • Pascal Rollin *Paris Priest* ■ *Dir* Peter Antonijevic • *Scr* Robert Orr • *Producer* Oliver Stone

Saw ★★★★ 18
Horror thriller   2004 · US · Colour · 98min

This well-acted thriller chillingly questions how far an individual will go to stay alive. Leigh Whannell (who also wrote the screenplay) and Cary Elwes become the latest playthings of a game-obsessed psychopath, finding themselves chained to opposite walls in a crumbling, subterranean bathroom, with no recollection of how they got there. With its jerky, grainy cinematography and nerve-jangling industrial soundtrack, the film is more disturbing than terrifying. However, just when you think you've got it sussed, the movie throws in some audacious twists. SF Violence, swearing. DVD BLU

Cary Elwes *Dr Lawrence Gordon* • Leigh Whannell *Adam* • Danny Glover *Detective David Tapp* • Monica Potter *Alison Gordon* • Dina Meyer *Kerry* • Tobin Bell *John* • Michael Emerson *Zep Hindle* ■ *Dir* James Wan • *Scr* Leigh Whannell, from a story by James Wan, Leigh Whannell

Saw II ★★★★ 18
Horror thriller   2005 · US · Colour · 88min

Darren Lynn Bousman's sequel is just as deliciously twisted, fiendishly clever and gruesomely gory as the 2004 life-or-death-game movie. Eight people imprisoned in a booby-trapped slum by Jigsaw (a remarkable Tobin Bell) must discover their association to each other and the antidote to a poison gas that's gradually killing them. Once more it's the imaginatively brutal torture contraptions and diabolical demises that delight and disturb. AJ DVD BLU

Tobin Bell *Jigsaw* • Shawnee Smith *Amanda* • Donnie Wahlberg *Eric Matthews* • Erik Knudsen *Daniel Matthews* • Franky G *Xavier* • Glenn Plummer *Jonas* • Beverley Mitchell *Laura* ■ *Dir* Darren Lynn Bousman • *Scr* Darren Lynn Bousman, Leigh Whannell

Saw III ★★ 18
Horror thriller   2006 · US · Colour · 109min

The parade of bloody mutilation continues with ever more outlandish torture machines in this second slash at the *Saw* franchise from director Darren Lynn Bousman. Now aided by an apprentice, games master Jigsaw (Tobin Bell) offers doctor Bahar Soomekh freedom if she can ease his dying pain for as long as it takes another of his pawns (Angus Macfadyen) to survive his cruel machinations. The flashback-within-flashback framework is just confusing, while the sick violence and horrific gore is ramped up to such extreme levels that it becomes funny rather than scary. Overlong and over-the-top, the once exciting gimmick has now been done to death. AJ DVD BLU

Tobin Bell *Jigsaw* • Shawnee Smith *Amanda* • Angus Macfadyen *Jeff* • Bahar Soomekh *Lynn* • Dina Meyer *Kerry* • Barry Flatman *Judge Halden* ■ *Dir* Darren Lynn Bousman • *Scr* Leigh Whannell, from a story by Whannell, James Wan

Saw IV ★★★ 18
Horror thriller   2007 · US · Colour · 91min

Sadistic serial killer Jigsaw (Tobin Bell) may be dead but the game isn't over: a tape-recorded message found in his stomach draws Detective Hoffman (Costas Mandylor) and SWAT Commander Rigg (Lyriq Bent) into a fiendishly convoluted race to save yet more torture victims. Rejuvenating the series after the lacklustre *Saw III*, the rasping and icily emotionless Bell casts a sinister shadow over the proceedings as the character's origins are revealed in labyrinthine flashbacks. It's *Grand Guignol* splatter that's awash with viscera, yet the real horror lies in the film-makers' nihilistic take on human frailty and their apparent sympathy for Jigsaw's reactionary moralism. Scary. JR DVD BLU

Tobin Bell *Jigsaw* • Costas Mandylor *Hoffman* • Scott Patterson *Agent Strahm* • Betsy Russell *Jill* • Lyriq Bent *Rigg* • Justin Louis *Art* • Donnie Wahlberg *Eric Matthews* • Angus MacFadyen *Jeff* • Shawnee Smith *Amanda* ■ *Dir* Darren Lynn Bousman • *Scr* Patrick Melton, Marcus Dunstan, from a story by Melton, Dunstan, Thomas Fenton

Saw V ★★ 18
Horror thriller   2008 · US/Can · Colour · 91min

The scariness has vanished along with the grisly booby-trap inventiveness in the fifth entry of the continuing splatter franchise. The main concerns of this convoluted episode from first-time director David Hackl are why Jigsaw (the ever-compelling Tobin Bell) is mentoring a new murder-game protégé, and how FBI profiler Scott Patterson attempts to unmask this latest acolyte. Meanwhile, five people are trapped in torture chambers to cloak the obvious twist ending. Flashbacks within flashbacks, reused footage from all the previous movies and constant camera movement to give hints of style, produce little of substance, except as a prelude to *Saw VI*. AJ Violence. DVD BLU

Tobin Bell *Jigsaw/John Kramer* • Costas Mandylor *Hoffman* • Scott Patterson *Agent Strahm* • Meagan Good *Luba* • Betsy Russell *Jill* • Mark Rolston *Erickson* • Julie Benz *Brit* ■ *Dir* David Hackl • *Scr* Patrick Melton, Marcus Dunstan

Saw VI ★★★ 18
Horror thriller   2009 · Can/US/UK/Aus · Colour · 87min

In a grisly and canny horror for recession-blighted times, uncaring bankers and medical insurers play their part in this, the directorial debut of series editor Kevin Greutert. Delving further into the grand "conundrum of carnage" of malevolent puppet master Jigsaw, the sixth instalment sees questions answered, mysteries solved and motives laid bare as Jigsaw's latest accomplice puts six more pawns through their death-device paces. With ingenuity and poignancy injected back into the devilishly suspenseful fun, the revitalised fear franchise finds its footing once more. AJ Violence DVD BLU CS

Costas Mandylor *Hoffman* • Mark Rolston *Erickson* • Betsy Russell *Jill* • Tobin Bell *Jigsaw/John* • Shawnee Smith *Amanda* • Peter Outerbridge *William* ■ *Dir* Kevin Greutert • *Scr* Marcus Dunstan, Patrick Melton

Saw: the Final Chapter ★★★★ 18
Horror   2010 · Can/US · Colour · 90min

Saw VI director Kevin Greutert nimbly navigates between two story strands here for maximum gory thrills and swift-paced suspense. As detective Costas Mandylor hunts down police-protected Betsy Russell for betraying him, bogus Jigsaw survivor Sean Patrick Flanery is put to the test in shock scenarios borrowed from sources such as *A Man Called Horse*. The chills run on turbo drive right through to the greatest hits flashback finale, but the 3D adds little to the experience. AJ Violence. DVD BLU 3D

Tobin Bell *Jigsaw/John* • Costas Mandylor *Hoffman* • Betsy Russell *Jill* • Sean Patrick Flanery *Bobby* • Cary Elwes *Dr Gordon* ■ *Dir* Kevin Greutert • *Scr* Marcus Dunstan, Patrick Melton

Sawdust and Tinsel ★★★★ 12
Drama   1953 · Swe · BW · 88min

This symbolic circus drama is now recognised as a landmark in Ingmar Bergman's film career. While the narrative seems similarly fractured (with its bleached out flashback to clown Anders Ek's humiliation before a platoon of mocking soldiers and a Freudian dream sequence), there is an artistic unity about this tale of ageing ringmaster, Ake Grönberg, whose encounter with the love he deserted, almost costs him the love of his mistress, Harriet Andersson. DP Swedish +subtitles. DVD

Harriet Andersson *Anne* • Ake Grönberg *Albert Johansson* • Hakke Ekman *Frans* • Anders Ek *Frost* • Annika Tretow *Agda, Albert's wife* ■ *Dir/Scr* Ingmar Bergman • *Cinematographers* Sven Nykvist, Bladh Hilding

The Saxon Charm ★★★
Drama   1948 · US · BW · 88min

Stage producer Robert Montgomery, an arrogant, amoral egomaniac and bully, causes misery to all who come into his orbit – particularly writer John Payne, whose play he is preparing to stage, Payne's wife Susan Hayward, his own girlfriend Audrey Totter and wealthy backer Harry Von Zell. Reputedly based on Broadway's notoriously unpleasant Jed Harris, this is interesting niche-market stuff for backstage aficionados; it carries an alarming ring of truth, but it's lacking in edge. RK

Robert Montgomery *Matt Saxon* • Susan Hayward *Janet Busch* • John Payne *Eric Busch* • Audrey Totter *Alma Wragg* • Henry Morgan [Harry Morgan] *Hermy* • Harry Von Zell *Zack Humber* • Cara Williams *Dolly Humber* • Chill Wills *Captain Chatham* • Heather Angel *Vivian Saxon* ■ *Dir* Claude Binyon • *Scr* Claude Binyon, from the novel by Frederic Wakeman

Say Anything... ★★★ 15
Comedy drama   1989 · US · Colour · 96min

Not deemed worthy of a UK cinema release, this little gem from Cameron Crowe is a cleverly formatted teenage romance in which nothing is quite as it seems. John Cusack stars as an underachieving student who falls for Ione Skye, "Miss Priss", the brain of the class, but meets opposition from her divorced dad (John Mahoney). TS Swearing. DVD

John Cusack *Lloyd Dobler* • Ione Skye *Diane Court* • John Mahoney *James Court* • Lili Taylor *Corey Flood* • Amy Brooks *D C* • Pamela Segall *Rebecca* • Jason Gould *Mike Cameron* • Bebe Neuwirth *Mrs Evans* • Eric Stoltz *Vahlere* ■ *Dir/Scr* Cameron Crowe

Say Hello to Yesterday ★ PG
Comedy   1971 · UK · Colour · 91min

The beautiful and witty Jean Simmons is the only reason to watch this dreadful, Swinging Sixties effort. Simmons plays a bored housewife from the stockbroker belt who takes the train to London and is hounded by a young dropout (Leonard Whiting). This is *Brief Encounter* in the style of *Blowup*, taking a tourist's-eye view of London before settling down to its chaste sex scene and Antonioni-esque finale of cold alienation. AT DVD

Jean Simmons *Woman* • Leonard Whiting *Boy* • Evelyn Laye *Woman's mother* • John Lee (1) *Woman's husband* • Jack Woolgar *Boy's father* • Constance Chapman *Boy's mother* • Gwen Nelson *Char* ■ *Dir* Alvin Rakoff • *Scr* Alvin Rakoff, Peter King, from a story by Ray Mathew, Alvin Rakoff

Say It Isn't So ★ 15
Romantic comedy   2001 · US · Colour · 91min

The Farrelly brothers, though only producers here, have finally gone too far. This is a gratuitously graphic and unwelcome addition to the type of crude comedy that has been so successful for them in recent years. Chris Klein and Heather Graham, both misused here, play a pair of lovers whose affair is halted by speculation that they are brother and sister. This goes so far beyond decency that it's not even funny. LH Swearing. DVD

Chris Klein *Gilbert "Gilly" Noble* • Heather Graham *Josephine "Jo" Wingfield* • Orlando Jones *Dig McCaffey* • Sally Field *Valdine Wingfield* • Richard Jenkins *Walter Wingfield* • John Rothman *Larry Falwell* • Jack Plotnick *Leon Pitofsky* ■ *Dir* JB Rogers [James B Rogers] • *Scr* Peter Gaulke, Gerry Swallow

Say It with Songs ★★
Musical drama 1929 · US · BW · 95min

Soon after the sound-breaking *The Jazz Singer*, Al Jolson embarked on this miscalculated musical drama, co-written by Darryl F Zanuck. Jolson plays a radio singer imprisoned for manslaughter and yearning for his wife and small boy. It's obvious lump-in-the-throat stuff but almost ends up as a joke with the song *Little Pal* trying to be another *Sonny Boy*. TH

Al Jolson *Joe Lane* • Davey Lee *Little Pal* • Marian Nixon *Katherine Lane* • Fred Kohler *Joe's cellmate* • Holmes Herbert *Dr Robert Merrill* • John Bowers *Surgeon* ■ *Dir* Lloyd Bacon • *Scr* Joseph Jackson, from a story by Darryl F Zanuck, Harvey Gates

Say One for Me ★★ U
Musical comedy 1959 · US · BW · 119min

As his film career faded, ageing crooner Bing Crosby here plays a cleric in charge of a Broadway church for showbiz folk. Alas, this overlong and thinly-scripted affair bears no comparison with Crosby's earlier hits playing a priest, and Frank Tashlin was the wrong man to direct. Debbie Reynolds, like Crosby, has to struggle with both the script and weak musical material, as well as a colourless romantic partner in Robert Wagner. TV

Bing Crosby *Father Conroy* • Debbie Reynolds *Holly LaMaise* • Robert Wagner *Tony Vincent* • Ray Walston *Phil Stanley* • Les Tremayne *Harry LaMaise* • Connie Gilchrist *Mary Manning* • Frank McHugh *Jim Dugan* ■ *Dir* Frank Tashlin • *Scr* Robert O'Brien

Say When ★★★ 15
Comedy drama 2014 · US · Colour · 94min

The problems of a directionless, well-to-do daddy's girl are made palatable by the casting of Keira Knightley in this melancholy but rather traditional indie comedy. Unlikely as it sounds, there's a refreshing intimacy to the pairing of Knightley with Chloë Grace Moretz that charms, as she hides out at the younger girl's home while pretending to attend a life-management seminar. But when the formula kicks in – Knightley meets Moretz's diffident but dishy single dad – all nuance goes out the window. DW *DVD*

Keira Knightley *Megan* • Chloë Grace Moretz *Annika* • Sam Rockwell *Craig* • Ellie Kemper *Allison* • Gretchen Mol *Bethany* ■ *Dir* Lynn Shelton • *Scr* Andrea Seigel

Sayonara ★★★ PG
Drama 1957 · US · Colour · 141min

Marlon Brando's electric acting, not to mention sturdy contributions from Miyoshi Umeki and Red Buttons (both of whom scooped Oscars), forms an almost other-worldly contrast to the travelogue blandness of Joshua Logan's direction. With Brando capably holding centre screen as the Korean War soldier in Japan, and in love, Logan's scenic tendencies are occasionally interrupted by some proper art direction, the quality of which also merited an Oscar. The lovely theme song by Irving Berlin is haunting. JM *DVD*

Marlon Brando *Major Lloyd "Ace" Gruver* • Ricardo Montalban *Nakamura* • Red Buttons *Joe Kelly* • Patricia Owens *Eileen Webster* • Martha Scott *Mrs Webster* • James Garner *Captain Mike Bailey* • Miyoshi Umeki *Katsumi* ■ *Dir* Joshua Logan • *Scr* Paul Osborn, from the novel by James A Michener • *Art Director* Ted Haworth • *Set Designer* Robert Priestley

Scalawag ★
Adventure 1973 · US/It · Colour · 92min

For his first film as a director, Kirk Douglas chose to remodel *Treasure Island* as a landlocked yarn. Set in Mexico, Douglas is the one-legged pirate, trying to get his hands on treasure hidden by his former

colleagues. Mark Lester is the cute kid who brings out his paternal qualities, and Danny DeVito has a small part. It's a catastrophe. AT

Kirk Douglas *Peg* • Mark Lester (2) *Jamie* • Neville Brand *Brimstone/Mudhook* • Lesley-Anne Down *Lucy-Ann* • Don Stroud *Velvet* • Danny DeVito *Flyspeck* • Mel Blanc *Barfly the parrot* ■ *Dir* Kirk Douglas • *Scr* Albert Maltz, Sid Fleischman, from the story by Robert Louis Stevenson

The Scalphunters ★★★ PG
Comedy western 1968 · US · Colour · 99min

Released at the height of civil rights awareness in America, this is an intelligent and highly enjoyable western. If director Sydney Pollack presses home his points about racial tolerance with a heavy hand, he nevertheless coaxes spirited performances from his big-name cast. Trapper Burt Lancaster and runaway slave Ossie Davis play off each other to good effect, but the real sparks fly when scalphunter Telly Savalas and his mistress Shelley Winters are on the screen. DP *DVD*

Burt Lancaster *Joe Bass* • Shelley Winters *Kate* • Telly Savalas *Jim Howie* • Ossie Davis *Joseph Winfield Lee* • Armando Silvestre *Two Crows* • Dan Vadis *Yuma* • Dabney Coleman *Jed* ■ *Dir* Sydney Pollack • *Scr* William Norton, from his story

The Scamp ★★
Drama 1957 · UK · BW · 88min

Having made his name in the Australian-set drama *Smiley*, contemporary critics had high hopes for ten-year-old Colin Petersen. He tries hard in this well intentioned story of a delinquent given a second chance, but he never convinces either as the urchin son of alcoholic music-hall actor Terence Morgan or as the confused kid cajoled by teacher Richard Attenborough and his wife Dorothy Alison. Attenborough overdoes the bourgeois benevolence. DP

Richard Attenborough *Stephen Leigh* • Colin Petersen *Tod Dawson* • Dorothy Alison *Barbara Leigh* • Terence Morgan *Mike Dawson* • Jill Adams *Julie Dawson* • Maureen Delaney *Mrs Perryman* • Margaretta Scott *Mrs Blundell* • David Franks *Eddie* ■ *Dir* Wolf Rilla • *Scr* Wolf Rilla, from the play *Uncertain Joy* by Charlotte Hastings

Scandal ★★★ PG
Drama 1950 · Jpn · BW · 104min

Akira Kurosawa's 11th feature was based on a true story that he heard in a bar. Lamenting the encroachment of Western culture and the growing Japanese obsession with tabloid sensationalism, Kurosawa approaches his story with crusading zeal. But the unshaded characterisation is a little dissuasive, with Toshiro Mifune's artist too conveniently failing to detect the weaknesses in corrupt lawyer Takashi Shimura's personality before engaging him to argue a defamation case against scandal rag editor, Eitaro Ozawa, after he's wrongly accused of an illicit dalliance with a popular female singer. Intense, engaging, but melodramatic. DP Japanese +subtitles. *DVD*

Toshiro Mifune *Ichiro Aoye* • Yoshiko Yamaguchi [Shirley Yamaguchi] *Miyako Saigo* • Takashi Shimura *Hiruta* • Yoko Katsuragi *Masako* • Noriko Sengoku *Sumie* • Sakae Ozawa [Eitaro Ozawa] *Hori* ■ *Dir* Akira Kurosawa • *Scr* Akira Kurosawa, Ryuzo Kikushima

Scandal ★★★ 18
Drama based on a true story 1988 · UK · Colour · 110min

This is a by-the-numbers reconstruction of the Profumo affair, a scandal that contributed to the downfall of the Conservative government in 1964. Joanne Whalley-Kilmer makes a fine Christine Keeler and John Hurt a suitably shallow Stephen Ward. But it's Bridget Fonda who steals the show with her spot-on impersonation of Mandy Rice-Davies. Rather tame in the sleaze department, despite all the hype over the "orgy" scenes, but the Swinging Sixties era is neatly

evoked. AJ Violence, swearing, sex scenes, nudity. *DVD*

John Hurt *Stephen Ward* • Joanne Whalley-Kilmer [Joanne Whalley] *Christine Keeler* • Bridget Fonda *Mandy Rice-Davies* • Ian McKellen *John Profumo* • Leslie Phillips *Lord Astor* • Britt Ekland *Mariella Novotny* • Daniel Massey *Mervyn Griffith-Jones* • Roland Gift *Johnnie Edgecombe* • Jean Alexander *Mrs Keeler* • Jeroen Krabbé *Eugene Ivanov* ■ *Dir* Michael Caton-Jones • *Scr* Michael Thomas, from the book *Nothing But* by Christine Keeler, Sandy Fawkes; the book *Mandy* by Mandy Rice-Davies, Shirley Flack; the book *Stephen Ward Speaks* by Warwick Charlton; the book *The Profumo Affair: a Summing Up* by Judge Sparrow; and the book *Scandal '63* by Clive Irving, Ron Hall, Jeremy Wallington

Scandal at Scourie ★★ U
Drama 1953 · US · Colour · 89min

Walter Pidgeon, leading political, business and religious light of the Protestant community at Scourie – a small town in Canada – reluctantly allows his childless wife Greer Garson to adopt a little girl from a Catholic orphanage that has burnt down. The nuns extract a promise that the child (Donna Corcoran) will be raised a Catholic, and the situation is used as ammunition by Pidgeon's political rivals to discredit him. Directed by Jean Negulesco, this over-plotted, simplistic, anti-bigotry morality tale was the last outing for the once potent Pidgeon-Garson partnership. RK

Greer Garson *Mrs Patrick J McChesney* • Walter Pidgeon *Patrick J McChesney* • Donna Corcoran *Patsy* • Agnes Moorehead *Sister Josephine* • Arthur Shields *Father Reilly* ■ *Dir* Jean Negulesco • *Scr* Norman Corwin, Leonard Spigelgass, Karl Tunberg, from a story by Mary McSherry

Scandalous ★ 15
Comedy thriller 1983 · US · Colour · 88min

As a TV reporter up to his neck in murder, Robert Hays shows flashes of the talent that made him such a hit in the *Airplane!* spoofs, but he doesn't stand a chance with a script so utterly bereft of ideas. John Gielgud does little for his reputation as a master of disguise, but what's most scandalous is that this unfunny mess was shot by cinematographer Jack Cardiff. DP Nudity, swearing.

Robert Hays *Frank Swedlin* • John Gielgud *Uncle Willie* • Pamela Stephenson *Fiona Maxwell Sayle* • M Emmet Walsh *Simon Reynolds* • Nancy Wood *Lindsay Manning* • Conover Kennard *Francine Swedlin* ■ *Dir* Rob Cohen • *Scr* Rob Cohen, John Byrum, from a story by Larry and Rob Cohen, Byrum

Scandalous John ★★★ U
Comedy western 1971 · US · Colour · 109min

This nice nostalgia piece stars grizzled Brian Keith, excellent as an eccentric rancher who is wild about the west. He is touchingly trying to keep to cowboy ways in a world that's long since consigned them to history, and even cattle-drives a single steer. Predictably, his engaging pottiness brings him into conflict with the authorities. Elegiac and moving, with more than a few laughs. DA

Brian Keith *John McCanless* • Alfonso Arau *Paco Martinez* • Michele Carey *Amanda McCanless* • Rick Lenz *Jimmy Whittaker* • Harry Morgan *Sheriff Pippin* • Simon Oakland *Barton Whittaker* • John Ritter *Wendell* ■ *Dir* Robert Butler • *Scr* Bill Walsh, Don DaGradi, from a book by Richard Gardner

Scanner Cop ★★★ 18
Science-fiction horror 1994 · US · Colour · 90min

The fourth entry in the *Scanners* series gets a boost with its change in locale (moving from Canada to LA) and introduces a new psychic hero, who happens to be a police officer. Scanner cop Daniel Quinn is on the trail of bad guy Richard Lynch, a scientist with a grudge against policemen. Lynch is fun as usual, hypnotising innocent people into killing cops in his usual hammy fashion, and the whole movie is executed with zip. A further sequel was released in 1995. KB

Daniel Quinn *Samuel Staziak* • Darlanne Fluegel *Dr Joan Alden* • Richard Lynch *Glock* • Hilary Shepard *Zena* • Richard Grove *Commander Peter Harrigan* ■ *Dir* Pierre David • *Scr* George Saunders, John Bryant

A Scanner Darkly ★★★ 15
Animated science-fiction drama 2006 · US · Colour · 96min

The School of Rock director Richard Linklater uses the process of interpolated rotoscoping, which he pioneered in *Waking Life* (2001), to bring Philip K Dick's tale of a surveillance-crazy near-future to life. The process paints over live footage to create animated action – a technique that certainly isn't new, but which Linklater has manipulated to create his own distinctive visual style. Here, Keanu Reeves is an undercover narcotics officer whose disguise tool – a scramble suit – enables him to take on a new identity and infiltrate a drugs ring. This is a better, more commercial film than the rather wordy *Waking Life*, and technically it is stunning. But you can't help wondering whether fans of Reeves and Robert Downey Jr might not prefer to see the actors themselves rather than their animated equivalents. DA *DVD* *SL*

Keanu Reeves *Bob Arctor/"Fred"* • Robert Downey Jr *James "Jim" Barris* • Woody Harrelson *Ernie Luckman* • Winona Ryder *Donna Hawthorne* • Rory Cochrane *Charles Freck* • Mitch Baker *Brown Bear Lodge host* • Steven Chester Prince *Cop* ■ *Dir* Richard Linklater • *Scr* Richard Linklater, from the novel by Philip K Dick

Scanners ★★★★ 18
Science-fiction horror 1980 · Can · Colour · 98min

Evil Michael Ironside and derelict Stephen Lack are the leaders of two rival groups of telepaths in David Cronenberg's modern horror classic that seamlessly blends the genres of science fiction and conspiracy thriller into an exhilarating ride. The stunning set pieces, such as the exploding heads, and the final apocalyptic battle in particular will delight genre fans. JF *DVD*

Stephen Lack *Cameron Vale* • Jennifer O'Neill *Kim Obrist* • Patrick McGoohan *Dr Paul Ruth* • Lawrence Dane *Braedon Keller* • Charles Shamata [Chuck Shamata] *Gaudi* • Adam Ludwig *Arno Crostic* • Michael Ironside *Darryl Revok* • Victor Desy *Dr Gatineau* ■ *Dir/Scr* David Cronenberg

Scanners II: The New Order ★★ 18
Science-fiction horror 1991 · Can · Colour · 104min

This lacks the thought-provoking script of Cronenberg's original *Scanners*, opting for a more conventional and exploitable story. David Hewlett is the naive "scanner" recruited by police chief Yvan Ponton on the pretext of helping out the city. Director Christian Duguay (in his movie debut) brings more style and a much slicker look to the movie, and never allows the pacing to falter for long. KB Violence. *DVD* *SL*

David Hewlett *David Kellum* • Deborah Raffin *Julie Vale* • Yvan Ponton *Commander John Forrester* • Isabelle Mejias *Alice Leonardo* • Tom Butler *Doctor Morse* • Raoul Trujillo *Drak* • Vlasta Vrana *Lieutenant Gelson* ■ *Dir* Christian Duguay • *Scr* BJ Nelson, from characters by David Cronenberg

Scanners III: the Takeover ★★★ 18
Science-fiction horror 1992 · Can/US · Colour · 99min

The second sequel finds Liliana Komorowska experimenting with a new mind-blowing drug. The result is a serious personality change from sweet young thing to psychotic megalomaniac with an ability to scan through TV airwaves and sway the masses to her ruthless power trip. The only person in her way is brother Steve Parrish who returns from a sojourn in a monastery to give her a piece of his own expanding mind. Director Christian Duguay handles the more knockabout action with flair and wit. AJ *DVD* *SL*

Liliana Komorowska *Helena Monet* • Valerie Valois *Joyce Stone* • Steve Parrish *Alexa Monet* • Colin Fox *Dr Elton Monet* ▪ *Dir* Christian Duguay • *Scr* BJ Nelson, Rene Malo, David Preston, Julie Richard, from characters by David Cronenberg

The Scapegoat ★★
Crime mystery   1959 · UK · BW · 119min
Robert Hamer and Alec Guinness made one of the blackest, greatest comedies of all time - *Kind Hearts and Coronets* - but they can't quite repeat that magic here. Guinness restricts his talents to just two roles - the French count who wants to murder his wife and his double, the meek English teacher who might be tricked into doing it. A hammy Bette Davis plays his mother and Irene Worth is the inconvenient spouse. Co-scripted by Gore Vidal, it's fitfully amusing. **AT**

Alec Guinness *Jacques De Gue/John Barrett* • Bette Davis *Countess* • Nicole Maurey *Bella* • Irene Worth *Françoise De Gue* • Pamela Brown *Blanche* • Annabel Bartlett *Marie-Noël* • Geoffrey Keen *Gaston* ▪ *Dir* Robert Hamer • *Scr* Gore Vidal, Robert Hamer, from the novel by Daphne du Maurier

The Scar ★★★
Drama   1976 · Pol · Colour · 101min
Krzysztof Kieslowski's debut feature was the first of only two pictures not to be based on an original idea. Yet, ironically, the Polish maestro blamed himself for adding characters and situations to the story uncovered by journalist and co-scenarist Romuald Karas. His documentary background stood him in good stead, however, as minor government official Franciszek Pieczka's brushes with both the locals whose rural community is destroyed by the construction of a factory and the Party bigwigs dissatisfied with his management style has an ominous ring of authenticity. Intriguing, but occasionally heavy handed. **DP** Polish +subtitles. **DVD**

Franciszek Pieczka *Stefan Bednarz* • Mariusz Dmochowski • Jerzy Stuhr *Bednarz's assistant* • Jan Skotnicki • Stanislaw Igar *Minister* • Stanislaw Michalski ▪ *Dir* Krzysztof Kieslowski • *Scr* Krzysztof Kieslowski, Romuald Karas

Scar ★★★
Horror thriller   2007 · Can · Colour · 78min
In Jed Weintrob's smartly written, fast-paced and very gory horror, Angela Bettis plays a woman returning to the small town where 16 years earlier she escaped the clutches of a sadistic undertaker, killing him in the process. But no sooner has she arrived than a series of brutal copycat killings begins. This is the first horror to be shot in high-definition 3-D, so that the frequent gruesome scenes appear all the more horrendous. Bettis turns in a committed performance and the twisting narrative adds a level of genuine suspense, making this more than just a case of *Hostel* meets *Prom Night*. **AJ DVD**

Angela Bettis *Joan Burrows* • Kirby Bliss Blanton *Olympia Burrows* • Devon Graye *Paul Watts* • Ben Cotton *Ernie Bishop* • Christopher Titus *Jeff* • Brittney Wilson *Young Joan Burrows* • Monika Mar-Lee *Sandra* • Brandon Jay McLaren *Howard* • Carey Feehan *Brian* • Al Sapienza *Delgado* ▪ *Dir* Jed Weintrob · *Scr* Zack Ford

Scaramouche ★★★★
Silent swashbuckling romance   1923 · US · BW · 124min
Lavishly produced by Metro, which later became MGM, this adaptation of Rafael Sabatini's novel is more an historical pageant than a true swashbuckler. Director Rex Ingram spent months researching the French Revolutionary period so that every detail - from palace to periwig - was as authentic as possible. Yet, while he was keen to ground the adventure in political fact, he was also aware of the spectacular possibilities in law-student-turned-circus-clown Ramon Novarro's feud with pitiless aristocrat Lewis Stone, and the romantic intensity of the heroic swordsman's passion for Alice Terry. The result is a film of rare grace and panache. **DP**

Ramon Novarro *André Moreau/Scaramouche* • Alice Terry *Aline de Kercadiou* • Lewis Stone *Marquis de la Tour d'Azyr* • Lloyd Ingraham *Quintin de Kercadiou* • Julia Swayne Gordon *Countess Thérèse de Plougastel* ▪ *Dir* Rex Ingram (1) · *Scr* Willis Goldbeck, from the novel *Scaramouche; a Romance of the French Revolution* by Rafael Sabatini

Scaramouche ★★★★ U
Swashbuckling adventure   1952 · US · Colour · 114min
Rafael Sabatini's rousing adventure was first filmed in 1923 by the master of the silent swashbuckler, Rex Ingram. This colourful version has been pared down to the bone by its writers, so that only the feuding, flirting and fencing remain of the classic novel's vivacious and complex portrait of Revolutionary France. Stewart Granger exudes charm in his scenes with Janet Leigh and cuts a dash as the mysterious swordsman on the trail of arrogant aristocrat Mel Ferrer. The final duel has the distinction of being the longest in movie history. **DP**

Stewart Granger *Andre Moreau/Scaramouche* • Eleanor Parker *Lenore* • Janet Leigh *Aline de Gavrillac* • Mel Ferrer *Noel, Marquis de Maynes* • Henry Wilcoxon *Chevalier de Chambrillaine* • Nina Foch *Marie Antoinette* • Richard Anderson *Philippe de Valmorin* • Robert Coote *Gaston Binet* ▪ *Dir* George Sidney (2) • *Scr* Ronald Millar, George Froeschel, from the novel *Scaramouche: a Romance of the French Revolution* by Rafael Sabatini

The Scarecrow ★★★★
Silent comedy   1920 · US · BW · 17min
After comedian Fatty Arbuckle's scandal, Buster Keaton took on many of his projects and this was one of the first silent movies for Buster Keaton Productions. The film is filled with sight gags, concentrating on the domestic set-up enjoyed by him and Joe Roberts: a gramophone converts into a stove, all table items are lowered on strings and the table itself - with plates attached - is hung up for washing. As the caption proclaims: "What is home without a mother?!" **TH**

Buster Keaton • Sybil Seely • Joe Keaton *Her father* • Joe Roberts *Rival* • Eddie Cline [Edward Cline] *Truck driver* ▪ *Dir/Scr* Buster Keaton, Eddie Cline [Edward Cline]

Scarecrow ★★★ 18
Road movie drama   1973 · US · Colour · 107min
Ex-con Gene Hackman and drifter Al Pacino hook up in California and travel east together, with the latter hoping to reconcile with the wife and child he abandoned in Detroit. On the journey they meet numerous other social misfits who regale them with various life lessons. This arty road movie can't quite harmonise its bleak realism with its glossy Hollywood approach to suffering, but both leads are excellent, even if Pacino - in an underwritten role - can't match Hackman. The film won the Palme d'Or at the 1973 Cannes festival. **AJ**

Gene Hackman *Max* • Al Pacino *Lion* • Dorothy Tristan *Coley* • Ann Wedgeworth *Frenchy* • Richard Lynch *Riley* • Eileen Brennan *Darlene* • Penny Allen [Penelope Allen] *Annie* • Richard Hackman *Mickey* ▪ *Dir* Jerry Schatzberg • *Scr* Garry Michael White

Scared Stiff ★★★ U
Musical comedy   1953 · US · BW · 107min
Comic teams always get around to a haunted house vehicle and this is the one from Dean Martin and Jerry Lewis. It's a remake of *The Ghost Breakers*, one of Bob Hope's funniest films, and though not as good as the earlier version, it is entertaining fare from the dynamic duo with veteran director George Marshall neatly providing genuine chills with the laughter. Brazilian bombshell Carmen Miranda makes her final film appearance, cueing an impersonation by Jerry Lewis, which is not very good. **TV**

Dean Martin *Larry Todd* • Jerry Lewis *Myron Mertz* • Lizabeth Scott *Mary Carroll* • Carmen Miranda *Carmelita Castina* • George Dolenz *Mr Cortega* • Dorothy Malone *Rosie* • William Ching *Tony Warren* • Paul Marion *Carriso Twins* • Jack Lambert *Zombi* • Bob Hope • Bing Crosby ▪

Dir George Marshall • *Scr* Herbert Baker, Walter DeLeon, Ed Simmons, Norman Lear, from the play *Ghost Breakers* by Paul Dickey, Charles W Goddard

Scared to Death ★★ U
Horror   1947 · US · Colour · 67min
Bela Lugosi made his sole credited appearance in colour in this low-budget chiller. It opens intriguingly, with Molly Lamont's voiceover explaining how she came to be lying on a mortuary slab. But once she begins discussing how Lugosi's hypnotist threatened to expose the past misdeeds of her father-in-law - the ever-malevolent George Zucco), the action veers between tepid haunted house antics and the misjudged comic interventions of dumbbell detective Nat Pendleton and dizzy blonde Joyce Compton. **DP DVD**

Bela Lugosi *Professor Leonide* • George Zucco *Dr Josef Van Ee* • Nat Pendleton *Bill "Bull" Raymond* • Molly Lamont *Laura Van Ee* • Joyce Compton *Jane* • Douglas Fowley *Terry Lee* • Angelo Rossitto *Indigo* • Roland Varno *Ward Van Ee* ▪ *Dir* Christy Cabanne • *Scr* Walter Abbott

The Scarf ★★★
Thriller   1951 · US · BW · 93min
This features John Ireland as the man on the run from an insane asylum who can't remember whether or not he strangled a woman with a scarf. The ever-watchable Mercedes McCambridge plays a singing waitress with a very similar scarf; Emlyn Williams appears as the doctor with some very odd mannerisms; and James Barton portrays a tiresome turkey-farming philosopher. Director EA Dupont indulges in some ripe expressionistic effects, while the screenplay comfortingly demonstrates that psychiatrists can be even crazier than their patients. **AE**

John Ireland *John Barrington* • Mercedes McCambridge *Connie Carter* • Emlyn Williams *David Dunbar* • James Barton *Ezra Thompson* • Lloyd Gough *Dr Gordon* ▪ *Dir* EA Dupont • *Scr* EA Dupont, from a story by IG Goldsmith, EA Rolfe, from the novel by Robert Bloch

LANDMARK FILM
The gangster film comes of age with Howard Hawks's ferociously unglamorous but influential mobster chronicle

Scarface ★★★★★ PG
Crime drama   1932 · US · BW · 89min
This is one of the great gangster movies of the 1930s. Producer Howard Hughes told director Howard Hawks to make it "as realistic, as exciting, as grisly as possible". Hawks happily obliged, though Hollywood's moral watchdog, the Hays Office, later insisted the ending was softened and a subtitle was added - *Shame of the Nation*. The story is a thinly disguised biography of Al Capone, with Paul Muni as a monster who lusts after his own sister, Ann Dvorak, yet whose business acumen embodies the American Dream. It's filled with moments that define the gangster genre - terrific shoot-outs, psychotic characters and George Raft spinning a coin. *Scarface* remains a bracingly violent and subversive tragicomedy that says crime pays. **AT**

Paul Muni *Tony Camonte* • Ann Dvorak *Cesca Camonte* • Karen Morley *Poppy* • Osgood Perkins *Johnny Lovo* • C Henry Gordon *Inspector Guarino* • George Raft *Guino Rinaldo* • Vince Barnett *Angelo* • Boris Karloff *Gaffney* • Howard Hawks *Man on bed* ▪ *Dir* Howard Hawks • *Scr* Ben Hecht, Seton I Miller, John Lee Mahin, WR Burnett, Fred Pasley, from the novel by Armitage Trail

Scarface ★★★★ 18
Crime drama   1983 · US · Colour · 162min
Director Brian De Palma's scorching update of Howard Hawks's 1932 classic relocates events to Miami and follows the rapid rise and violent fall of a Cuban refugee turned cocaine-smuggling kingpin. Al Pacino is the ruthless criminal pursuing the American Dream, and he gets top support from Michelle Pfeiffer as his wife, Steven Bauer as his partner in crime and Mary Elizabeth Mastrantonio as his sister. The sharp, if expletive-ridden, dialogue contained in Oliver Stone's script and the vivid

cinematography of John A Alonzo help make De Palma's urban shocker a modern-day classic. **AJ** Violence, swearing, sex scenes, nudity. **DVD Blu**

Al Pacino *Tony Montana* • Steven Bauer *Manny Ray* • Michelle Pfeiffer *Elvira* • Mary Elizabeth Mastrantonio *Gina* • Robert Loggia *Frank Lopez* • Miriam Colon *Mama Montana* • F Murray Abraham *Omar* ▪ *Dir* Brian De Palma • *Scr* Oliver Stone, from the 1932 film

The Scarlet and the Black ★★★★ PG
Second World War drama   1983 · US/It · Colour · 137min
Gregory Peck made his TV-movie debut in this true story of wartime hide-and-seek. Although it's far too long, it is certainly one of the more impressive efforts made for the small screen. In addition to a cameo from John Gielgud as Pope Pius XII, the film boasts photography by Giuseppe Rotunno and a score by the great Ennio Morricone. Peck's character is a sort of Oskar Schindler in vestments, who gives sanctuary to Jews and other persecuted peoples prior to smuggling them to safety. Christopher Plummer is suitably villainous as the Nazi who can't pin down the elusive priest. **DP DVD**

Gregory Peck *Monsignor Hugh O'Flaherty* • Christopher Plummer *Colonel Herbert Kappler* • John Gielgud *Pope Pius XII* • Raf Vallone *Father Vittorio* • Kenneth Colley *Captain Hirsch* ▪ *Dir* Jerry London • *Scr* David Butler, from the non-fiction book *The Scarlet Pimpernel of the Vatican* by JP Gallagher

Scarlet Angel ★★★ U
Period adventure   1952 · US · Colour · 80min
Saloon girl Yvonne De Carlo, displaced by the Civil War, takes off for San Francisco. There she masquerades as the widow of a wealthy society type and cons her way into the social register. Everything goes swimmingly and her future prospects are looking good until her past re-enters in the shape of hunky Rock Hudson. With a storyline more redolent of films of the 1930s or early 1940s, this romantic adventure is nonetheless well put together and very enjoyable. **RK**

Yvonne De Carlo *Roxy McClanahan* • Rock Hudson *Frank Truscott* • Richard Denning *Malcolm Bradley* • Bodil Miller *Linda Caldwell* • Amanda Blake *Susan Bradley* • Henry O'Neill *Morgan Caldwell* ▪ *Dir* Sidney Salkow • *Scr* Oscar Brodney

The Scarlet Blade ★★ PG
Swashbuckling drama   1963 · UK · Colour · 79min
Oliver Reed is on form here as a renegade swordsman with an eye for the ladies in this period drama from Hammer set during the English Civil War. Swordfights abound as sadistic Cromwellian colonel Lionel Jeffries discovers his daughter has Royalist sympathies. **TH DVD**

Lionel Jeffries *Colonel Judd* • Oliver Reed *Sylvester* • Jack Hedley *Edward* • June Thorburn *Clare* • Michael Ripper *Pablo* • Harold Goldblatt *Jacob* ▪ *Dir/Scr* John Gilling

The Scarlet Claw ★★★★ PG
Mystery   1944 · US · BW · 73min
Here's the greatest of all Sherlocks (Basil Rathbone) and the most bumbling of all Watsons (Nigel Bruce) in possibly the best of the Universal Studios series, with the pair in Canada investigating ghostly and ghastly murders. The underrated Roy William Neill causes consternation with some memorably uneasy visuals: a dead woman's hand clutching a bell-rope, a luminous "monster" stalking Holmes across a marsh and the fog that just avalanches down. **TH DVD**

Basil Rathbone *Sherlock Holmes* • Nigel Bruce *Dr John H Watson* • Gerald Hamer *Potts* • Paul Cavanagh *Lord William Penrose* • Arthur Hohl *Emile Journet* • Kay Harding *Marie Journet* ▪ *Dir* Roy William Neill • *Scr* Roy William Neill, Edmund L Hartmann, from a story by Paul Gangelin, Brenda Weisberg, from characters by Sir Arthur Conan Doyle

S

The Scarlet Clue ★★ PG
Mystery   1945 · US · BW · 62min

The fifth Charlie Chan mystery produced by the Poverty Row Studio, Monogram, is a lively affair that sees Sidney Toler on the track of the sinister boss who ordered the assassination of an Axis spy intent on stealing government radar plans. Much of the action takes place in a building that not only houses a research laboratory, but also a radio station that conveniently employs the majority of the suspects. As ever, director Phil Rosen allows Mantan Moreland a comedy spot. DP *DVD*

Sidney Toler *Charlie Chan* · Benson Fong *Tommy Chan* · Mantan Moreland *Birmingham Brown* · Helen Devereaux *Diane Hall* · Robert E Homans [Robert Homans] *Captain Flynn* · Virginia Brissac *Mrs Marsh* · Jack Norton *Willie Rand* ■ *Dir* Phil Rosen · *Scr* George Callahan, from characters by Earl Derr Biggers

Scarlet Dawn ★★
Period drama   1932 · US · BW · 58min

The dawn here is the colour of the Russian Revolution. In the thick of it is Douglas Fairbanks Jr, an aristocrat from St Petersburg who has no truck with Lenin and instead runs off to Constantinople with Nancy Carroll. He marries her, leaves her for one of his own class and then returns. Made when Hollywood was just discovering that movies could talk and that Fairbanks Jr had charm aplenty but somewhat less talent. AT

Douglas Fairbanks Jr *Baron Nikiti Krasnoff* · Nancy Carroll *Tanyusha* · Lilyan Tashman *Vera Zimina* · Guy Kibbee *Murphy* · Sheila Terry *Marjorie Murphy* · Earle Fox *Boris* · Ivan Linow *Ivan* ■ *Dir* William Dieterle · *Scr* Niven Busch, Edwin Gelsey, Douglas Fairbanks Jr, from the novel *Revolt* by Mary McCall Jr

The Scarlet Empress ★★★★★ 12
Historical drama   1934 · US · BW · 98min

This is more fun than you could ever imagine, more suggestive than you'd thought possible, even in those days prior to the imposition of the Hays Production Code. Director Josef von Sternberg fills the screen with typically lustrous images and staggeringly rich art direction. This movie, which does have its detractors, was influential on Russian director Sergei Eisenstein. More than just a vehicle for the marvellous Marlene Dietrich, the film conveys a real sense of the lusts and intrigues of the court of Catherine the Great. TS

Marlene Dietrich *Sophia Frederica, Catherine II* · Gerald Fielding *Lieutenant Dmitri* · John Lodge *Count Alexei* · Sam Jaffe *Grand Duke Peter* · Louise Dresser *Empress Elizabeth* · C Aubrey Smith *Prince August* · Gavin Gordon *Gregory Orloff* · Ruthelma Stevens *Countess Elisabeth* · Hans von Twardowski *Ivan Shuvolov* ■ *Dir* Josef von Sternberg · *Scr* Manuel Komroff, from a diary of Catherine II · *Cinematographer* Bert Glennon · *Costume Designer* Travis Banton · *Set Designers* Hans Dreier, Peter Ballbusch, Richard Kollorsz

The Scarlet Letter ★★★★
Silent drama   1926 · US · BW · 80min

Lillian Gish gives here what many regard as her finest performance. The fifth screen version of Nathaniel Hawthorne's novel, this is by far the finest adaptation of any era. With Hendrik Sartov's photography bringing a painterly austerity to the already puritanical setting, Hester Prynne's adultery with Pastor Dimmesdale assumes a social enormity that is often disregarded by those concentrating on the story's human aspects. Yet director Victor Sjöström is not blind to the tragedy of the couple's disgrace, as he locates beauty and sensitivity amid the bigotry. DP

Lillian Gish *Hester Prynne* · Lars Hanson *The Reverend Arthur Dimmesdale* · Henry B Walthall *Roger Prynne* · Karl Dane *Giles* · William H Tooker *The governor* · Marcelle Corday *Mistress Hibbins* ■ *Dir* Victor Seastrom [Victor Sjöström] · *Scr* Frances Marion, from the novel by Nathaniel Hawthorne

The Scarlet Letter ★★ 15
Period drama   1995 · US · Colour · 129min

In this absurd version of Nathaniel Hawthorne's classic novel, Demi Moore gives a confused performance as the 17th-century wife who has an affair and is ostracised by the community. Gary Oldman is ludicrously over the top as the preacher with whom Moore has a fling, while Robert Duvall, as her cuckolded husband, gives a performance that is out of place with the period. TH Violence, sex scenes, nudity. *DVD*

Demi Moore *Hester Prynne* · Gary Oldman *Arthur Dimmesdale* · Robert Duvall *Roger Prynne* · Lisa Joliff-Andoh *Mituba* · Edward Hardwick [Edward Hardwicke] *John Bellingham* · Robert Prosky *Horace Stonehall* · Roy Dotrice *Thomas Cheever* · Joan Plowright *Harriet Hibbons* · Jodhi May *Pearl* ■ *Dir* Roland Joffé · *Scr* Douglas Day Stewart, from the novel by Nathaniel Hawthorne

The Scarlet Pimpernel ★★★ U
Period adventure   1934 · UK · BW · 93min

Leslie Howard stars as Sir Percy Blakeney, master of disguise, outwitting Raymond Massey's evil Chauvelin during the French Revolution and fooling his wife, Merle Oberon, who thinks he's just a boorish fop. Its chief virtues are Howard's portrait of strength masquerading as superciliousness and some lavish production design. But it seems rather creaky nowadays, mainly because of the stagey direction from Harold Young. It was a big success in its day, though, and Howard played the role again in the updated 1941 sequel, *Pimpernel Smith*. AT *DVD*

Leslie Howard *Sir Percy Blakeney/The Scarlet Pimpernel* · Merle Oberon *Lady Marguerite Blakeney, formerly Marguerite St Just* · Raymond Massey *Chauvelin* · Nigel Bruce *Prince of Wales (HRH the Prince Regent)* · Bramwell Fletcher *Priest* · Anthony Bushell *Sir Andrew Ffoulkes* · Joan Gardner *Suzanne de Tournay* · Walter Rilla *Armand St Just* ■ *Dir* Harold Young · *Scr* SN Behrman, Robert Sherwood [Robert E Sherwood], Arthur Wimperis, Lajos Biró, from the novel by Baroness Orczy · *Production Designer* Vincent Korda

The Scarlet Pimpernel ★★★★ PG
Period adventure   1982 · UK/US · Colour · 135min

In this superior TV movie, director Clive Donner makes the most of the period plushness to fashion a lively swashbuckler that's true to the spirit of the novels of Baroness Orczy. Anthony Andrews is on form as Sir Percy Blakeney, the foppish English noble who risks all to rescue French aristocrats from the guillotine during the Reign of Terror. Jane Seymour also surpasses herself as the neglected Lady Marguerite, while Ian McKellen has a ripe old time as the villainous Chauvelin. DP *DVD*

Anthony Andrews *Sir Percy Blakeney/The Scarlet Pimpernel* · Jane Seymour (2) *Marguerite St Just* · Ian McKellen *Paul Chauvelin* · James Villiers *Baron de Batz* · Eleanor David *Louise Lenjean* · Malcolm Jamieson *Armand St Just* · Julian Fellowes *Prince Regent* ■ *Dir* Clive Donner · *Scr* William Bast, from the novel by Baroness Orczy

Scarlet Street ★★★ PG
Film noir   1945 · US · BW · 97min

In this effective *noir* drama directed by Fritz Lang, Edward G Robinson stars (brilliantly) as a diffident cashier with a termagant wife (Rosalind Ivan) and limited means, whose only pleasure is painting in his spare time. He falls in love with Joan Bennett who, under the sway of her sadistic boyfriend Dan Duryea, leads him into a tangle of deceptions, embezzlement and murder. The movie is grim, downbeat and well played, with some imaginative and unusual plot developments and an audacious ending. The script, though, does strain credibility at times. RK *DVD*

Edward G Robinson *Christopher Cross* · Joan Bennett *Kitty March* · Dan Duryea *Johnny Prince* · Margaret Lindsay *Millie* · Rosalind Ivan *Adele*

Cross · Jess Barker *Janeway* · Arthur Loft *Dellarowe* ■ *Dir* Fritz Lang · *Scr* Dudley Nichols, from the novel *La Chienne* by Georges de la Fouchardière, from the play *La Chienne* by Georges de la Fouchardière, André Mouëzy-Eon

Scarlet Thread ★★ PG
Crime thriller   1951 · UK · BW · 75min

In one of his early leading roles, Laurence Harvey (working with *Alfie* director Lewis Gilbert) gives this downbeat British crime drama some modest interest. Harvey is convincingly unpleasant as the skirt-chasing spiv and petty criminal with a sleazy charm, who panics and kills a bystander during a jewel robbery. But the twist in the tale is more implausible than ironic. AE

Kathleen Byron *Josephine* · Laurence Harvey *Freddie* · Sydney Tafler *Marcon* · Arthur Hill *Shaw* · Dora Bryan *Maggie* · Eliot Makeham *Jason* ■ *Dir* Lewis Gilbert · *Scr* AR Rawlinson, from the play by Rawlinson, Moie Charles

The Scarlet Tunic ★★★ 12
Period drama   1997 · UK · Colour · 88min

Minimally budgeted, this British period drama concerns the ill-starred romance between a rich man's daughter and a foreign mercenary who's about to set off to fight Napoleon. The melodramatic crunch comes when the soldier has to do a *High Noon* and choose between love and duty. Emma Fielding and Jean-Marc Barr play the lovers while Simon Callow chews the scenery as Barr's brutal military commander. DA Violence. *DVD*

Jean-Marc Barr *Sergeant Matthaus Singer* · Emma Fielding *Frances Elizabeth Groves* · Simon Callow *Captain John Fairfax* · Jack Shepherd *Dr Edward Groves* · John Sessions *Humphrey Gould* ■ *Dir* Stuart St Paul · *Scr* Stuart St Paul, Mark Jenkins, Colin Clements, from the story *The Melancholy Hussar* by Thomas Hardy

Scarred City ★★ 18
Action thriller   1998 · US · Colour · 92min

This unexceptional action thriller boasts a cast that doesn't deserve the film's video-dustbin status. Stephen Baldwin stars as a cop facing investigation after killing some criminal suspects in rather dubious circumstances. Police lieutenant Chazz Palminteri offers him a way out with his very secret squad, although it soon transpires that this force takes neither prisoners nor witnesses. JF Violence, swearing, nudity. *DVD*

Stephen Baldwin *John Trace* · Chazz Palminteri *Lieutenant Laine Devon* · Tia Carrere *Candy* · Michael Rispoli *Sam Bandusky* · Gary Dourdan *Sergeant Creedy* · Bray Poor *Zero* ■ *Dir/Scr* Ken Sanzel

The Scars of Dracula ★★★ 15
Horror   1970 · UK · Colour · 91min

Christopher Lee considered this his weakest *Dracula* sequel, but Hammer horror fans like it because the Count has more screen time here than in any other episode. There's also a dark fairy-tale atmosphere achieved by director Roy Ward Baker as Dracula tries sinking his fangs into naive Transylvanian travellers Dennis Waterman and Jenny Hanley. Propping up the formula vampire tale are a memorable death-by-lightning climax, and more blood, sadism and rubber bats than ever before. AJ *DVD*

Christopher Lee *Count Dracula* · Dennis Waterman *Simon Carlson* · Christopher Matthews *Paul Carlson* · Jenny Hanley *Sarah Framsen* · Patrick Troughton *Klove* · Michael Gwynn *Priest* · Wendy Hamilton *Julie* · Anouska Hempel *Tania* ■ *Dir* Roy Ward Baker · *Scr* John Elder [Anthony Hinds], from characters by Bram Stoker

Scary Movie ★★★ 18
Horror spoof   2000 · US · Colour · 88min

Director Keenen Ivory Wayans lampoons 1990s teenage horror movies, which seems a bit of a redundant exercise when you consider that *Scream* was itself a dig at the horror genre. Luckily, Wayans and family (among the writers are his brothers Shawn and Marlon, who also star) get some good laughs in along the way. The film includes

in-jokes and send-ups, plus a superb spoof of *The Matrix* that will have fans chuckling in the aisles. Instantly forgettable, but fun. JB Swearing, violence, drug abuse, sex scenes. *DVD* *Blu-ray* *CS*

Anna Faris *Cindy Campbell* · Shannon Elizabeth *Buffy Gilmore* · Regina Hall *Brenda Meeks* · Jon Abrahams *Bobby Prinze* · Lochlyn Munro *Greg Phillippe* · Shawn Wayans *Ray Jones* · Marlon Wayans *Shorty Meeks* · Carmen Electra *Drew Decker* ■ *Dir* Keenen Ivory Wayans · *Scr* Shawn Wayans, Marlon Wayans, Buddy Johnson, Phil Beauman, Jason Friedberg, Aaron Seltzer

Scary Movie 2 ★ 18
Horror spoof   2001 · US · Colour · 78min

It wasn't a classic or particularly well made but at least *Scary Movie* was good for a few honest *Scream*-inspired laughs.This uninspired sequel is barely competent on any technical or artistic level. Once past the opening where *The Exorcist* is amusingly sent up by James Woods in a cameo appearance as a priest (a role originally earmarked for Marlon Brando), it descends rapidly into a shoddy satire. AJ *DVD* *Blu-ray*

Shawn Wayans *Ray Jones* · Marlon Wayans *Shorty Meeks* · Anna Faris *Cindy Campbell* · Regina Hall *Brenda Meeks* · Chris Masterson *Buddy* · Kathleen Robertson *Theo* · James Woods *Father McFeely* · Tim Curry *Professor Oldman* · Veronica Cartwright *Mrs Voorhees, Megan's mother* ■ *Dir* Keenen Ivory Wayans · *Scr* Marlon Wayans, Shawn Wayans, Craig Wayans, Alyson Fouse, Greg Grabianski, Dave Polsky, Michael Anthony Snowden, from characters by Marlon Wayans, Shawn Wayans, Buddy Johnson, Phil Beauman, Jason Friedberg, Aaron Seltzer

Scary Movie 3 ★★ 15
Horror spoof   2003 · US · Colour · 80min

David Zucker directs this third entry in the horror-spoof franchise, which, though not as good as the original, is certainly an improvement on the second. This time around, television reporter Anna Faris investigates a planned alien invasion of a farm owned by Charlie Sheen, while a mysterious tape kills all who watch it. All kinds of references are dragged kicking and screaming into the bedraggled plot, but this is not as funny as it thinks it is. There are some inspired moments, however, and Leslie Nielsen is always a joy. TH *DVD* *Blu-ray*

Anna Faris *Cindy Campbell* · Anthony Anderson *Mahalik* · Leslie Nielsen *President Harris* · Camryn Manheim *Trooper Champlin* · Simon Rex *George* · George Carlin *The Architect* · Queen Latifah *The Oracle* · Charlie Sheen *Tom* ■ *Dir* David Zucker · *Scr* Craig Mazin, Pat Proft, from characters by Marlon Wayans, Shawn Wayans, Buddy Johnson, Phil Beauman, Jason Friedberg, Aaron Seltzer

Scary Movie 4 ★ 15
Horror spoof   2006 · US · Colour · 85min

Anna Faris gamely plays the naive, accident-prone Cindy Campbell for the fourth time, in a fatigued franchise that is still recycling the most ancient slapstick and toilet gags. Witless, obvious and completely devoid of anything remotely funny, even the most undemanding audience will find little to laugh at in this unwatchable dud. AJ Swearing. *DVD* *Blu-ray*

Anna Faris *Cindy Campbell* · Regina Hall *Brenda Meeks* · Simon Rex *George* · Leslie Nielsen *President Harris* · Craig Bierko *Tom Ryan* · Carmen Electra *Holly* · Conchita Campbell *Rachel Ryan* · Shaquille O'Neal · Cloris Leachman *Mrs Norris* · Michael Madsen *Oliver* · Bill Pullman *Henry Hale* · Charlie Sheen *Tom Logan* ■ *Dir* David Zucker · *Scr* Jim Abrahams, Craig Mazin

Scary Movie V ★ 15
Horror spoof   2013 · US · Colour · 82min

Not scary, and barely even a movie, this slung-together barrage of genre send-ups hits rock bottom the moment Charlie Sheen and Lindsay Lohan open the sorry show trashing their tabloid reputations in an embarrassing *Paranormal Activity* spoof. From then on the modern ghost story *Mama* takes the most heat. Director Malcolm Lee and writers David Zucker and Pat Proft seem clueless as to what's funny, so throw in everything from tasteless

S

bulimia and pregnancy gags to a surreal *Fifty Shades of Grey* skit. That really is as good as it gets. AJ **DVD** **BLU**

Ashley Tisdale *Jody* • Simon Rex *Dan* • Erica Ash *Kendra* • Katrina Bowden *Natalie* • Heather Locklear *Barbara* ■ *Dir* Malcolm D Lee • *Scr* Pat Proft, David Zucker

A Scene at the Sea ★★★ U
Sports drama   1991 · Jpn · Colour · 96min

This entertaining surfing odyssey marks a change of pace for Takeshi Kitano. The story revolves around a deaf garbage collector (Kuroco Maki) who finds a discarded surfboard and, after reconditioning it, battles to conquer the waves. Kitano's proclivity for slapstick is very much in evidence: Maki repeatedly comes a cropper as he masters the basic skills of surfing and then competes in local championships before the supportive gaze of his deaf girlfriend, Hiroko Oshima. DP Japanese +subtitles. **DVD**

Kurodo Maki *Shigeru* • Hiroko Oshima *Takako* • Sabu Kawahara *Tamukai, garbage truck driver* • Toshizo Fujiwara *Nakajima, owner of surfing goods shops* ■ *Dir/Scr* Takeshi Kitano

Scene of the Crime ★★
Crime drama   1949 · US · BW · 94min

Van Johnson is Los Angeles detective, Mike Conovan, investigating the murder of one of his colleagues. Part of the late 1940s fad for documentary realism and police procedure, the movie spends much time depicting our hero's dogged, dedicated work as well as his blissfully ordinary home life with Arlene Dahl. But a movie about routine inevitably becomes routine. AT

Van Johnson *Mike Conovan* • Gloria De Haven [Gloria DeHaven] *Lili* • Tom Drake *CC Gordon* • Arlene Dahl *Gloria Conovan* • Leon Ames *Captain AC Forster* • John McIntire *Fred Piper* • Norman Lloyd *Sleeper* • Donald Woods *Herkimer* ■ *Dir* Roy Rowland • *Scr* Charles Schnee, from the story *Smashing the Bookie Gang Marauders* by John Bartlow Martin

The Scene of the Crime ★★★
Thriller   1986 · Fr · Colour · 90min

Catherine Deneuve heads a quality cast in this fine French thriller from director André Téchiné. The action takes place over an eventful four-day period, in which a run-in between a 13-year-old boy and two escaped convicts leads to murder, and to the forging of an unlikely alliance between the killer and the boy's mother. DA French +subtitles.

Catherine Deneuve *Lili* • Danielle Darrieux *Grandmother* • Nicolas Giraudi *Thomas* • Wadeck Stanczak *Martin* • Victor Lanoux *Maurice* • Jean Bousquet *Grandfather* ■ *Dir* André Téchiné • *Scr* André Téchiné, Pascal Bonitzer, Olivier Assayas

Scenes from a Mall ★★★ 15
Comedy   1991 · US · Colour · 83min

The notion of Woody Allen and Bette Midler playing a smugly successful couple whose marriage begins to crumble as they go shopping must have brought a big smile to the faces of the producers. Unfortunately, director Paul Mazursky reduces the satirical potential to a torrent of words. Woody's lines, unsurprisingly the best, are not matched by the dialogue or performance of the too-loud Midler, and the added irony of a marriage teetering at Christmas is too corny. But despite the leaden weight of the script, there are some fine moments. JM Swearing.

Bette Midler *Deborah Fifer* • Woody Allen *Nick Fifer* • Bill Irwin *Mime* • Daren Firestone *Sam* • Rebecca Nickels *Jennifer* • Paul Mazursky *Dr Hans Clava* ■ *Dir* Paul Mazursky • *Scr* Paul Mazursky, Roger L Simon

Scenes from a Marriage ★★★★ 15
Drama   1973 · Swe · Colour · 162min

Originally a six-part TV series, this was edited for feature release by writer/director Ingmar Bergman. Mostly shot in tight close-ups to enhance the tensions between the protagonists, this is not easy viewing: some of the insights seem too blatant for a film-maker of Bergman's intellect to be bothered with. However, when the rambling gives way to fierce infighting and wounding insults, the film exerts a much firmer grip. Liv Ullmann as the betrayed wife, Erland Josephson as the philandering husband and Bibi Andersson as the other woman are all quite superb. DP Swedish +subtitles. **DVD**

Liv Ullmann *Marianne* • Erland Josephson *Johan* • Bibi Andersson *Katarina* • Jan Malmsjö *Peter* • Anita Wall *Interviewer* ■ *Dir/Scr* Ingmar Bergman

Scenes from the Class Struggle In Beverly Hills ★★★★ 18
Comedy   1989 · UK · Colour · 99min

Jacqueline Bisset gets a juicy role as a recently widowed soap star who invites her neighbour and her son to stay while their house is being fumigated. Joining them is a hilarious mix of the rich and famous that reaches across sexual and racial divides, and into areas such as body fascism, freak diets and weird sex. A guest spot is reserved for Paul Mazursky, director of both *Bob & Carol & Ted & Alice* and *Down and Out in Beverly Hills*, touchstones for director Paul Bartel's subversive brand of humour that sets out to offend almost everyone. AT **DVD**

Jacqueline Bisset *Clare Lipkin* • Ray Sharkey *Frank* • Robert Beltran *Juan* • Mary Woronov *Lisabeth Hepburn-Saravian* • Ed Begley Jr *Peter* • Wallace Shawn *Howard Saravian* • Arnetia Walker *To-bel* • Paul Mazursky *Sidney Lipkin* ■ *Dir* Paul Bartel (1) • *Scr* Bruce Wagner, from a story by Paul Bartel, Bruce Wagner

Scenes of a Sexual Nature ★★★ 15
Romantic comedy drama   2006 · UK · Colour · 88min

Ewan McGregor and Sophie Okonedo are part of an ensemble cast in this multi-stranded tale of Londoners indulging in relationship angst (and a bit of something else) on Hampstead Heath. Sexually-charged interactions add to the heat of a summer afternoon, but first-time director Ed Blum spares us the graphic details and instead focuses on the characters' emotional dysfunctions. Scenes work best when aiming for laughs, like Tom Hardy striving to be a cockney Casanova or Gina McKee in stilted conversation with Hugh Bonneville during a blind date. At other times, Blum shoots for a melancholy tone but there isn't enough time to really feel for any of the characters. Yet overall there's a free and easy ambience about the film that proves quite seductive. SP Swearing, sexual references. **DVD**

Ewan McGregor *Billy* • Sophie Okonedo *Anna* • Adrian Lester *Pete* • Gina McKee *Julia* • Andrew Lincoln *Jamie* • Catherine Tate *Sara* • Mark Strong *Louis* • Eileen Atkins *Iris* • Holly Aird *Molly* ■ *Dir* Ed Blum • *Scr* Aschlin Ditta

Scent of a Woman ★★★
Comedy drama   1974 · It · Colour · 103min

Dino Risi's adaptation boasts a show-stopping performance from Vittorio Gassman. He won the best actor prize at Cannes for his portrayal of the blind army captain with a stubborn streak to match his simmering sense of resentment. However, that's where the similarities end, as Gassman journeys from Turin to Naples to enter into a suicide pact with a soldier disfigured in the accident that disabled him. There's sly humour in his relationship with rookie escort Alessandro Momo, but the romantic reunion with Agostina Belli is cringingly sentimental. DP In Italian.

Vittorio Gassman *Fausto Ciccio* • Agostina Belli *Sara* • Moira Orfei *Mirka* • Franco Ricci *Raffaele* • Elena Veronese *Michelina* ■ *Dir* Dino Risi • *Scr* Ruggero Maccari, Dino Risi, from the novel *Il Buio e il Miele* by Giovanni Arpino

Scent of a Woman ★★★★ 15
Drama   1992 · US · Colour · 149min

This lengthy melodrama is kept vibrantly alive and out of the clutches of sickly sentimentality by a towering Oscar-winning performance from Al Pacino. He plays the blind ex-soldier who heads for New York to sample once more life's little luxuries over the Thanksgiving weekend. As his unworldly teenage escort, Chris O'Donnell is quietly impressive, but it's Pacino's picture, whether tangoing with Gabrielle Anwar or berating O'Donnell's schoolmates or barking his famous "hoo-ha" cough. DP Swearing, sex scenes. **DVD** **BLU**

Al Pacino *Lt Col Frank Slade* • Chris O'Donnell *Charlie Simms* • James Rebhorn *Mr Trask* • Gabrielle Anwar *Donna* • Philip S Hoffman [Philip Seymour Hoffman] *George Willis Jr* • Richard Venture *WR Slade* • Bradley Whitford *Randy* ■ *Dir* Martin Brest • *Scr* Bo Goldman, suggested by a character from *Profuma di Donna (Scent of a Woman)* by Ruggero Maccari, Dino Risi, from the novel *Il Buio e il Miele* by Giovanni Arpino

The Scent of Green Papaya ★★★★★ U
Period drama   1993 · Fr · Colour · 99min

Set in pre-Vietnam War Saigon, this is the leisurely, minutely observed and thoroughly involving story of a servant girl and the relationships she develops with her employers and a handsome family friend. The opening segment is quite captivating, thanks to the guileless performance of Man San Lu as the ten-year-old maid, but the intensity of the drama as it moves into the 1960s compensates for the mannered innocence of Tran Nu Yen-Khe as the older Mui. A delightful study, it won director Tran Anh Hung the Caméra d'Or at Cannes for best debut feature. DP Vietnamese +subtitles. **DVD**

Tran Nu Yen-Khe *Mui, aged 20* • Lu Man San *Mui, aged 10* • Truong Thi Loc *Mother* • Nguyen Anh Hoa *Old Thi* • Vuong Hoa Hoi *Khuyen* • Tran Ngoc Trung *Father* ■ *Dir/Scr* Tran Anh Hung

Scent of Mystery ★★ U
Mystery   1960 · US · Colour · 132min

This is the only film ever shot in "Smell-O-Vision" – a process that squirted appropriate odours at the audience. Denholm Elliott wanders through Spain and finds he has to protect Beverly Bentley who's being menaced by such classy heavies as Peter Lorre and Paul Lukas. Produced by the American showman Mike Todd, who liked gimmicks, the smellier the better. Not exactly a stinker, but nearly. TH

Denholm Elliott *Oliver Larker* • Beverly Bentley *The Decoy Sally* • Peter Lorre *Smiley, chauffeur* • Paul Lukas *Baron Saradin* • Diana Dors *Winifred Jordan* • Liam Redmond *Johnny Gin, derelict* • Elizabeth Taylor *The Real Sally Kennedy* ■ *Dir* Jack Cardiff • *Scr* William Rose, from a story by Kelley Roos

Schindler's List ★★★★★ 15
War drama based on a true story
1993 · US · BW and Colour · 187min

Steven Spielberg's outstanding Holocaust drama won seven Oscars and tells the story of Second World War entrepreneur Oskar Schindler (played by Liam Neeson), whose operation to supply the German war effort led him to be the unexpected saviour of more than 1,000 Jewish factory workers in Poland. Spielberg uses stark, brutal realism to put over his powerful points, and the stunning black-and-white photography and gritty hand-held camera footage give it a potent documentary style. Ralph Fiennes invokes an awesome mixture of revulsion and sympathy as the inhuman Nazi commandant, and Neeson matches him with a heartfelt performance. Ben Kingsley is also superb as Schindler's Jewish accountant and conscience. AJ Violence, swearing, sex scenes, nudity. **DVD** **BLU**

Liam Neeson *Oskar Schindler* • Ben Kingsley *Itzhak Stern* • Ralph Fiennes *Amon Goeth* • Caroline Goodall *Emilie Schindler* • Jonathan Sagalle *Poldek Pfefferberg* • Embeth Davidtz *Helen Hirsch* • Andrzej Seweryn *Julian Scherner* ■ *Dir* Steven Spielberg • *Scr* Steven Zaillian, from the novel *Schindler's Ark* by Thomas Keneally • *Cinematographer* Janusz Kaminski • *Music* John Williams • *Editor* Michael Kahn

Schizo ★★ 18
Horror   1976 · UK · Colour · 103min

This tepid gore thriller exhibits little of the down-and-dirty histrionic style that built director Pete Walker's cult appeal. Ice skating star Lynne Frederick has the days before her marriage disturbed by the attentions of a brutal assassin provoked to kill by memories of earlier matricide. One slashed psychiatrist, a mutilated medium, one hacked-up housekeeper and a *Psycho* shower scene rip-off later, the maniac's obvious identity is revealed. AJ

Lynne Frederick *Samantha* • John Leyton *Alan Falconer* • Stephanie Beacham *Beth* • John Fraser *Leonard Hawthorne* • Jack Watson *William Haskin* • Queenie Watts *Mrs Wallace* ■ *Dir* Pete Walker • *Scr* David McGillivray

Schizopolis ★★ 15
Experimental comedy drama
1996 · US · Colour · 92min

An inspired surrealist swipe at the American mainstream or a vanity project gone off the rails? The answer lies somewhere in between these verdicts on Steven Soderbergh's ambitious satire on language, identity, fidelity, advertising, self-help and dentistry. Writer/director Soderbergh also stars as a speech writer, whose wife (Betsy Brantley) is having an affair with a dentist (also played by Soderbergh). Mixing the absurd with the autobiographical, this is a riot of ideas but not enough of them come off. DP **DVD**

Steven Soderbergh *Fletcher Munson/Dr Jeffrey Korchek* • Betsy Brantley *Mrs Munson/Attractive woman No 2* • David Jensen (2) *Elmo Oxygen* • Eddie Jemison *Nameless Numberheadman* • Scott Allen *Right hand man* • Mike Malone *T Azimuth Schwitters* ■ *Dir/Scr* Steven Soderbergh

Schlock ★
Science-fiction horror spoof
1971 · US · Colour · 77min

Director John Landis donned an ape suit in his debut as a director. The monkey-suited title character – a thawed prehistoric missing link – runs amok in a small town, and leaves a trail of banana skins in his murderous wake. Nothing more than a poor excuse to lampoon Kubrick's *2001*, this is a game, but lame, student effort. Future Oscar winner Rick Baker designed the hairy costume. AJ

John Landis *The Schlockthropus* • Saul Kahan *Detective/Sgt Wino* • Joseph Piantadosi *Prof Shlibovitz* • Eliza Garrett *Mindy Binerman* • Eric Allison *Joe Puzman* • Enrica Blankey *Mrs Binerman* ■ *Dir/Scr* John Landis

School Daze ★★ 18
Musical comedy   1988 · US · Colour · 120min

In attempting to present campus life as a microcosm of African-American society, Spike Lee succeeds in raising many points without reaching any conclusions. He attacks the conventions of college life without exploring any alternatives and takes pot shots at sexism, racism and the age and class divides without steadying his aim. Laurence Fishburne gives a steady performance, but, overall, this is a disjointed and disappointing satire. DP Swearing, nudity.

Larry Fishburne [Laurence Fishburne] *Vaughn "Dap" Dunlap* • Giancarlo Esposito *Julian "Big Brother Almighty" Eaves* • Tisha Campbell *Jane Toussaint* • Kyme *Rachel Meadows* • Joe Seneca *President McPherson* • Ellen Holly *Odrie McPherson* • Art Evans *Cedar Cloud* • Ossie Davis *Coach Odom* • Bill Nunn *Grady* • Branford Marsalis *Jordan* • Spike Lee *Half-Pint* • Samuel L Jackson ■ *Dir/Scr* Spike Lee

School for Postmen ★★★★
Comedy   1947 · Fr · BW · 18min

Returning behind the camera for the first time since the mid-1930s, Jacques Tati here tried out the routines that would form the core of his feature debut, *Jour de Fête*. A winner on the festival circuit, this hilarious short introduces the character of François, the work-shy postman, as well as containing two scenes – a hilarious tutorial and an eccentric dance – which didn't make the

S

feature. Bearing the influence of Max Linder, Buster Keaton and Charlie Chaplin, the film showcases the athletic slapstick style honed over many years in the French music hall, but it also demonstrates an innate understanding of the cinematic medium. DP In French.

Jacques Tati *Postman* • Paul Demange *Head Postman* ■ Dir/Scr Jacques Tati

School for Scoundrels ★★★ U

Comedy   1960 · UK · BW · 90min

Based on Stephen Potter's popular one-upmanship books, this hit-and-miss comedy passes muster thanks to the willing performances of Ian Carmichael and Terry-Thomas. There are some amusing moments as Carmichael learns how to "confound a bounder" under the tutelage of Alastair Sim, but director Robert Hamer handles the subtle humour with a heavy hand and can't quite knit the various sketches into a convincing whole. DP DVD BL

Ian Carmichael *Henry Palfrey* • Terry-Thomas *Raymond Delauney* • Alastair Sim *Stephen Potter* • Janette Scott *April Smith* • Dennis Price *Dunstan Dorchester* • Peter Jones *Dudley Dorchester* • Edward Chapman *Gloatbridge* • John Le Mesurier *Head waiter* • Irene Handl *Mrs Stringer* • Hattie Jacques *First instructress* ■ Dir Robert Hamer • Scr Hal E Chester, Patricia Moyes, Peter Ustinov, from the books by Stephen Potter

School for Scoundrels ★★ 12

Comedy   2006 · US · Colour · 103min

Hollywood remakes of vintage British comedies are bound to meet with a mixed reception – the Coen brothers take on *The Ladykillers* being a recent example. But *Starsky & Hutch* director Todd Phillips may ruffle fewer feathers here, as he revisits an enjoyable but less revered chapter in cinema history. Billy Bob Thornton combines both the Alastair Sim and Terry-Thomas roles from the 1960 original, playing the tough-nut tutor of a self-assertion course that claims to turn zeroes into heroes. Jon Heder (*Napoleon Dynamite*) steps into Ian Carmichael's shoes, as a meek parking attendant who wants to romance the girl of his dreams. It's all mildly engaging and occasionally amusing – much like the original, in fact, which was fun but no classic. DA DVD

Billy Bob Thornton *Dr P* • Jon Heder *Roger* • Jacinda Barrett *Amanda* • Michael Clarke Duncan *Lesher* • Luis Guzman *Sergeant Moorehead* • David Cross (2) *Ian* • Horatio Sanz *Diego* • Sarah Silverman *Becky* ■ Dir Todd Phillips • Scr Todd Phillips, Scot Armstrong, from the 1960 film

School for Secrets ★★★

Wartime drama   1946 · UK · BW · 107min

After the war the RAF and the Ministry of Defence wanted to boast about their invention of radar and the job of producing, directing and writing the account went to the 25-year-old Peter Ustinov. Ralph Richardson plays the boffin and there are some half-hearted action scenes and mini-melodramas to flesh out the reams of technospeak. Ustinov's refusal to make a blatant back-slapper suffuses the film with both a distorted attitude to heroism and a cartoonish wit. AT

Ralph Richardson *Prof Heatherville* • Richard Attenborough *Jack Arnold* • Raymond Huntley *Prof Laxton-Jones* • John Laurie *Dr McVitie* • Ernest Jay *Dr Dainty* • David Tomlinson *Mr Watlington* • Finlay Currie *Sir Duncan Wilson Wills* • Norman Webb *Dr Wainwright* • Michael Hordern *Lt Cdr Lowther* • Alvar Liddell *BBC announcer* ■ Dir/Scr Peter Ustinov

The School of Rock ★★★★ PG

Musical comedy
2003 · US/Ger · Colour · 104min

Jack Black is outstanding as an unemployed rock guitarist who passes himself off as a supply teacher and enlightens the pupils of a posh private school with the joys of rock and roll. Joan Cusack provides excellent comic support as the school's headmistress who is twitchily uptight but by no means

unsympathetic. Director Richard Linklater deftly avoids the saccharine schmaltz that can easily ruin these kind of films and he extracts natural performances from his precocious young cast. Expertly crafted escapism and a great family movie. AS
DVD CS

Jack Black *Dewey Finn* • Joan Cusack *Principal Rosalie Mullins* • Mike White *Ned Schneebly* • Sarah Silverman *Patty Di Marco* • Joey Gaydos Jr *Zack* • Maryam Hassan *Tomika* • Miranda Cosgrove *Summer* • Kevin Clark *Freddy* ■ Dir Richard Linklater • Scr Mike White

School Spirit ★ 15

Comedy   1985 · US · Colour · 86min

Tom Nolan is a dislikeably sex-mad high school kid who is killed in a car crash, but returns in spirit form for one last day of trying to get it on with the girls. Postmortem powers give him a ghost of a chance. Far less haunting than Nolan is, the film mixes slapstick and sexism to unfunny and unpleasant effect. DA

Tom Nolan *Billy Batson* • Elizabeth Foxx *Judy Hightower* • Roberta Collins *Mrs Grimshaw* • John Finnegan *Pinky Batson* • Larry Linville *President Grimshaw* ■ Dir Alan Holleb • Scr Geoffrey Baere

School Ties ★★★ PG

Drama   1992 · US · Colour · 102min

Although responsible and challenging, *School Ties* isn't just a sermon sugared by the forceful presence of Chris O'Donnell, Matt Damon and Brendan Fraser. The film is a mix of *Gentleman's Agreement* and the code-of-honour subplot of *Scent of a Woman*, as aspiring American footballer Fraser hides his Judaism to ensure that he succeeds at an exclusive school where racist remarks are part of polite conversation. Not all the pitfalls are avoided, but the performances are impressive. DP Some swearing, brief nudity.
DVD

Brendan Fraser *David Greene* • Matt Damon *Charlie Dillon* • Chris O'Donnell *Chris Reece* • Randall Batinkoff *Rip Van Kelt* • Andrew Lowery *McGivern* • Cole Hauser *Jack Connors* • Ben Affleck *Chesty Smith* • Anthony Rapp *McGoo* • Amy Locane *Sally Wheeler* • Kevin Tighe *Coach McDevitt* • Ed Lauter *Alan Greene* ■ Dir Robert Mandel • Scr Dick Wolf, Darryl Ponicsan, from a story by Dick Wolf

The Science of Sleep ★★ 15

Fantasy comedy drama
2005 · Fr · Colour · 102min

Less accessible than his *Eternal Sunshine of the Spotless Mind*, Michel Gondry's pretentious sci-fi vanity production is an overly whimsical, infantile affair. Gael García Bernal plays a graphic artist who returns to Paris after his father's death. Will he ever realise his neighbour Charlotte Gainsbourg is the soulmate he's been searching for? Or will he continually dream he's the host of a one-man TV chat show starring a swirling melting pot of his desires? With its makeshift "Blue Peter"-style special effects, the juvenile approach soon wears thin and the whole self-indulgent mess is a waste of Bernal and Gainsbourg's charms. The "one second time machine" is the single clever laugh. AJ English, French, Spanish +subtitles. Swearing, sexual references.
DVD

Gael García Bernal *Stéphane Miroux* • Charlotte Gainsbourg *Stéphanie* • Alain Chabat *Guy* • Miou-Miou *Christine Miroux* • Pierre Vaneck *Monsieur Pouchet* • Emma de Caunes *Zoë* • Aurélia Petit *Martine* ■ Dir/Scr Michel Gondry

Scissors ★★ 18

Psychological thriller   1991 · US · Colour · 90min

Sharon Stone stars in this little known thriller as a sexually traumatised woman suffering from nightmares and illusions which are in fact a bold plot to drive her insane. Stone gives the part her all and there's creepy support from Steve Railsback in a dual role as her neighbour and his disabled brother. But the leaden direction stifles the life out of what could have been a decent little thriller. RS Violence, swearing, nudity.

Sharon Stone *Angie* • Steve Railsback *Alex/Cole* • Ronny Cox *Dr Carter* • Michelle Phillips *Ann* • Vicki Frederick *Nancy* • Leonard Rogel *Red Beard* ■ Dir Frank De Felitta • Scr Frank De Felitta, from a story by Joyce Selznick

Scooby-Doo ★★ PG

Mystery comedy adventure
2002 · US · Colour · 82min

Hanna-Barbera's much loved teen sleuths make their live-action debut in director Raja Gosnell's colourful but misjudged rendition of the popular cartoon series. It attempts to please knowing adults who remember the TV series from their youth with coded drug references and postmodernism, while delivering gags along the lines of a flatulence duel to satisfy otherwise baffled kids. James Gunn's screenplay stays true to the cartoon, but the CGI Scooby is so charmless he sucks the life out of the film. SF DVD BL

Freddie Prinze Jr *Fred Jones* • Sarah Michelle Gellar *Daphne Blake* • Matthew Lillard *Norville "Shaggy" Rogers* • Linda Cardellini *Velma Dinkley* • Rowan Atkinson *Emile Mondavarious* • Miguel A Nunez Jr *Voodoo maestro* • Isla Fisher *Mary Jane* • Steven Grives *N'Goo Tuana* • Neil Fanning *Scooby-Doo* ■ Dir Raja Gosnell • Scr James Gunn (2), from a story by James Gunn, Craig Titley, from characters by William Hanna, Joseph Barbera

Scooby-Doo 2: Monsters Unleashed ★★★ PG

Mystery comedy adventure
2004 · US · Colour · 88min

The cast and director of 2002's disappointing live-action version of the popular cartoon series reunite for this superior sequel. Sensibly focusing on Mystery Inc's most popular duo – Shaggy and Scooby – the film follows the newly disgraced team as they try to unmask a villain whose monster machine is re-creating all their classic foes. Although some of the effects are ropey, the decision to up the excitement levels with multiple spooky creatures is a prudent one. The enjoyable visual overload makes it easier to ignore the insubstantial plot, but the CGI Scooby still doesn't work. SF DVD BL

Freddie Prinze Jr *Fred Jones* • Sarah Michelle Gellar *Daphne Blake* • Matthew Lillard *Norville "Shaggy" Rogers* • Linda Cardellini *Velma Dinkley* • Seth Green *Patrick Wisely* • Peter Boyle *Jeremiah "Old Man" Wickles* • Tim Blake Nelson *Dr Jonathan Jacobo* • Alicia Silverstone *Heather Jasper-Howe* • Neil Fanning *Scooby-Doo* ■ Dir Raja Gosnell • Scr James Gunn (2), from characters by William Hanna, Joseph Barbera

Scoop ★★ 12

Romantic comedy
2006 · US/UK · Colour · 91min

Woody Allen's second film to be shot in London actually begins in the afterlife, where deceased journalist Ian McShane discovers the identity of a murderer who is terrorising the capital. His ghost appears to American journalism student Scarlett Johansson, who is helping magician Allen with a vanishing act, and gives her the killer's name. Johansson and Allen join forces on a trail that leads them to Hugh Jackman, at which point this clumsy but amiable farce lurches into straight thriller territory and Allen loses all control of the already wayward plot. Sadly, the climax wouldn't even pass muster in a made-for-TV murder mystery. DW DVD

Woody Allen *Sid Waterman* • Hugh Jackman *Peter Lyman* • Scarlett Johansson *Sondra Pransky* • Ian McShane *Joe Strombel* • Charles Dance *Mr Malcolm* • Fenella Woolgar *Jane Cook* ■ Dir/Scr Woody Allen

Scorched ★ 12

Crime comedy   2002 · US/UK · Colour · 90min

There's nothing worse than watching a talented cast mugging frantically to wring laughs out of leaden material. Unless, of course, it's watching John Cleese gnawing the scenery in a bid to recapture past glories. He plays a self-made millionaire whose loot is deposited in the Californian bank that disgruntled employees Alicia Silverstone, Woody Harrelson and Paulo

Costanzo all decide to rob over the same weekend. Directed without a shred of comic finesse or timing. DP Swearing. DVD

Alicia Silverstone *Sheila* • Woody Harrelson *Jason "Woods" Valley* • John Cleese *Charles Merchant* • Rachael Leigh Cook *Shmally* • Paulo Costanzo *Stuart "Stu" Stein* • David Krumholtz *Max Stein* • Joshua Leonard *Rick* ■ Dir Gavin Grazer • Scr Joe Wein, from a story by Joe Wein, Max Wein

Scorchers ★ 18

Drama   1991 · US · Colour · 77min

Talk about a misnomer! But, then, talk is all they ever do in this dismal stage-to-screen transfer. An unusually strong cast, including Faye Dunaway and James Earl Jones, rants and raves to little effect in a philosophical tale of sex and southern girl Emily Lloyd who would rather hide under the bed than be in it on her wedding night. She plays Splendid and her name is the only thing that is in a tepid Tennessee Williams inspired, high-decibel shouting match barely held together by globs of blue bayou mysticism. AJ Swearing, sex scenes.

Faye Dunaway *Thais* • Denholm Elliott *Howler* • Emily Lloyd *Splendid* • James Earl Jones *Bear* • Jennifer Tilly *Talbot* • James Wilder *Dolan* • Anthony Geary *Preacher* • Leland Crooke *Jumper* • Luke Perry *Ray Ray* ■ Dir David Beaird • Scr David Beaird, from his play

The Score ★★★ 15

Crime thriller   2001 · US/Ger · Colour · 118min

Arguably the three finest screen actors of their respective generations – Marlon Brando, Robert De Niro and Edward Norton – combine to flesh out what might have been a bog-standard one-last-job heist movie were it not for two things: one, it's set in Montreal (and not the familiar, over-used cities of Chicago or LA); two, hardly any computer hardware is on display when the attempted heist of a priceless sceptre from Montreal's Customs House takes place. Brando is bizarrely compelling, De Niro is stoic, operating here in a low gear, while Norton walks away with the film as an arrogant young turk. AC Swearing. DVD BL

Robert De Niro *Nick Wells* • Edward Norton *Jack "Jackie" Teller/Brian* • Angela Bassett *Diane* • Marlon Brando *Max Baron* • Gary Farmer *Burt* • Jamie Harrold *Steven* • Paul Soles *Danny* ■ Dir Frank Oz • Scr Kario Salem, Lem Dobbs, Scott Marshall Smith, from a story by Daniel E Taylor, Kario Salem

Scorpio ★★★ 15

Spy thriller   1973 · US · Colour · 109min

All the ingredients are here for a presentable thriller – treachery, murder, intrigue and a handful of foreign locations – but a garbled script and Michael Winner's rather slipshod direction undoes much of the good work put in by his admirable cast. As the CIA agent suspected of having double standards, Burt Lancaster combines the fear of the fugitive with toughness and resourcefulness. Alain Delon does a solid job of blending duty and doubt. DP DVD

Burt Lancaster *Cross* • Alain Delon *Laurier* • Paul Scofield *Zharkov* • John Colicos *McLeod* • Gayle Hunnicutt *Susan* • JD Cannon *Filchock* ■ Dir Michael Winner • Scr David W Rintels, Gerald Wilson, from a story by David W Rintels

Scorpio Rising ★★★★ 18

Erotic parody   1963 · US · Colour · 27min

One of the most famous American underground films and a seminal force in gay cinema, Kenneth Anger's orgiastic study of leather bike boys, was banned as obscene in places as far apart as California and Belgium. Anger injects black humour into the homoeroticism, such as intercutting the action with sequences of Marlon Brando in *The Wild One* and of Christ from Cecil B DeMille's religious epic *King of Kings*. There's also Nazi symbolism, occultism and 13 rock songs on the soundtrack. Tasteless, self-indulgent and juvenile at times, the brilliantly-edited film still has some fascination. RB

Bruce Byron *Scorpio* • Johnny Sapienza *Taurus* • Frank Carifi *Leo* • Bill Dorfman *The Back* • John Palone *Pin* • Ernie Allo *Joker* ■ *Dir/Scr* Kenneth Anger

The Scorpion King ★★★ 12
Action adventure fantasy
2002 · US/Ger · Colour · 87min

Director Chuck Russell's spin-off from *The Mummy Returns* is entertaining, escapist hokum. The plot is hardly original: an evil warlord (Steven Brand), who has conquered and enslaved half the tribes in the desert, is opposed by The Rock (in an imposing, star-making performance), who unites the remaining warring factions and leads them against the common oppressor. There might not be much sense or depth amid the noisy, not terribly gory, violence, but the spirited action makes for an unpretentious adventure. A sequel directed by Russell Mulcahy, *Rise of a Warrior*, was released in 2008, but without The Rock. AJ DVD Blu

The Rock [Dwayne Johnson] *Mathayus, the Scorpion King* • Michael Clarke Duncan *Balthazar* • Steven Brand *Memnon* • Kelly Hu *Cassandra* • Bernard Hill *Philos* • Grant Heslov *Arpid* • Peter Facinelli *Prince Takmet* ■ *Dir* Chuck Russell • *Scr* Stephen Sommers, Will Osborne [William Osborne], David Hayter, from a story by Stephen Sommers, Jonathan Hales

Scorpion Spring ★★★ 18
Road movie thriller 1995 · US · Colour · 85min

Quentin Tarantino has a lot to answer for. His slick genre pastiches have inspired a whole slew of imitations of his imitations. Here's one of the better ones: a sweaty Tex-Mex border yarn about a cross-country driver who's daft enough to give a ride to a couple of drug runners. Though ultimately it lacks a genuine sting in its tale, the plot is twisty and violent enough to hold the interest. DA Drug abuse, violence, swearing. DVD

Alfred Molina *Denis Brabant* • Patrick McGaw *Zac Cross* • Esai Morales *Astor* • Angel Aviles *Nadia* • Rubén Blades *Sam Zaragosa* • Kevin Tighe *Rawley Gill* • Matthew McConaughey *El Rojo* ■ *Dir/Scr* Brian Cox (2)

Scotland Yard Mystery ★★★ 12
Mystery 1933 · UK · BW · 71min

At the heart of this macabre mixture of medicine and malice aforethought is Home Office pathologist George Curzon, who defrauds an insurance company out of a small fortune by sending several of its wealthiest clients into a zomboid trance. Considering the budgetary contraints, this is quite an atmospheric little chiller, with Curzon's ingenuity only being matched by the arrogance and greed that plays right into inspector Gerald du Maurier's hands. DP DVD

Gerald du Maurier *Inspector Stanton* • George Curzon *Dr Masters* • Belle Chrystall *Mary Stanton* • Grete Natzier *Irene* • Leslie Perrins *John* ■ *Dir* Thomas Bentley • *Scr* Frank Miller, from the play by Wallace Geoffrey

Scott Joplin ★★
Musical biography 1977 · US · Colour · 96min

Motown produced this biopic of another great black musical star, after the success of *Lady Sings the Blues* which also starred Billy Dee Williams. Shot quickly as a TV movie, it was given a limited theatrical release. It traces the career of the ragtime pianist who created a nationwide craze from his struggle for recognition to his death. Great performances and terrific music do not always a great movie make, but it's not a bad shot. FL

Billy Dee Williams *Scott Joplin* • Clifton Davis *Louis Chauvin* • Margaret Avery (2) *Belle Joplin* • Eubie Blake *Will Williams* • Godfrey Cambridge *Tom Turpin* • Seymour Cassel *Dr Jaelki* ■ *Dir* Jeremy Paul Kagan • *Scr* Christopher Knopf

Scott of the Antarctic ★★★★ U
Historical adventure drama
1948 · UK · Colour · 105min

This is a documentary-like account of the ill-fated British expedition to the South Pole

that ended in 1912. Although sticking closely to Scott's journal, it plays down his probable errors of judgement in order to concentrate on his reckless courage and the unswerving loyalty of his men. Using many of the team's actual possessions to increase the authenticity, the cast is only rarely allowed to demonstrate the humanity behind the stiff upper lips. John Mills is splendidly British in the title role, although he nearly came a cropper when he fell through the snow while filming in the Alps. DP DVD

John Mills *Captain Scott* • Derek Bond *Captain Oates* • Harold Warrender *Dr Wilson* • Diana Churchill *Kathleen Scott* • Anne Firth *Oriana Wilson* • Reginald Beckwith *Lieutenant Bowers* • James Robertson-Justice *Taffy Evans* • Kenneth More *Teddy Evans* ■ *Dir* Charles Frend • *Scr* Ivor Montagu, Walter Meade, Mary Hayley Bell • *Music* Ralph Vaughan Williams

Scott Pilgrim vs the World ★★★ 12
Romantic action comedy
2010 · US/UK/Jpn · Colour · 112min

Shaun of the Dead director Edgar Wright makes his Hollywood feature debut with this wacky tale of youth angst based on a series of graphic novels. It plays like a surreal video game, as Scott (Michael Cera doing his bumbling hero routine) does battle with the seven evil exes of Ramona Flowers (Mary Elizabeth Winstead) in order to win her heart. The visuals are wildly inventive and there's no doubting Wright's flair for comedy, but the series of showdowns does become repetitive. SP DVD Blu

Michael Cera *Scott Pilgrim* • Mary Elizabeth Winstead *Ramona Flowers* • Ellen Wong *Knives Chau* • Kieran Culkin *Wallace Wells* • Alison Pill *Kim Pine* • Anna Kendrick *Stacey Pilgrim* • Jason Schwartzman *Gideon Graves "G-Man"* • Mark Webber *Stephen Stills* • Brandon Routh *Todd Ingram* • Chris Evans *Lucas Lee* ■ *Dir* Edgar Wright • *Scr* Edgar Wright, Michael Bacall, from the graphic novel series by Brian Lee O'Malley

Scott Walker: 30 Century Man ★★★ 12
Music documentary
2006 · US/UK · Colour · 95min

This terrific documentary explores the life of reclusive musical genius Scott Walker, from American teen idol fame as Scott Engel through Swinging Sixties British stardom in the Walker Brothers to global cult composer of avant-garde solo albums. It's a must-see for fans of the enigmatic performer, who has granted director Stephen Kijak unprecedented access to his very private world. There's a clearly difficult interview with the aloof and nervous singer, who maddeningly alludes to his alcoholism and mysterious love life without going into any real detail. But that's part of what makes him a legend and this long overdue portrait is a well-illustrated celebration of the myth, the man and his enduring magic. AJ DVD Blu

Scott Walker (2) *Scott Walker* • David Bowie • Jarvis Cocker • Damon Albarn • Brian Eno • Johnny Marr • Sting • Lulu • Sara Kestelman *Narrator* ■ *Dir* Stephen Kijak

The Scoundrel ★★★
Drama 1935 · US · BW · 73min

Noël Coward considered this to be his screen debut, though he had appeared briefly in DW Griffith's *Hearts of the World* in 1918. Written and directed jointly by Ben Hecht and Charles MacArthur, this is a fantasy about a publisher who comes back from the dead bearing a bunch of seaweed that he claims will guarantee him true love. Coward liked the idea and was also lured by the promise that his co-star would be Helen Hayes, but she dropped out at the last minute and was replaced by Julie Haydon. AT

Noël Coward *Anthony Mallare* • Julie Haydon *Cora Moore* • Stanley Ridges *Paul Decker* • Rosita Moreno *Carlotta* • Martha Sleeper *Julia Vivian* • Hope Williams *Maggie* • Ernest Cossart *Jimmy Clay* • Ben Hecht *Flophouse bum* • Charles MacArthur *Flophouse bum* • Burgess Meredith ■ *Dir* Ben Hecht, Charles MacArthur • *Scr* Ben Hecht, Charles MacArthur, from their story

The Scout ★★★★ 12
Sports comedy drama
1994 · US · Colour · 97min

Albert Brooks is excellent as a struggling talent scout for big-league baseball teams, and Brendan Fraser is likeable as ever as an unsigned super-pitcher whom Brooks discovers on a scouting trip down Mexico way. Trouble is, Fraser gets "moundfright", and can't pitch straight when crowds are watching. So Brooks turns for help to psychiatrist Dianne Wiest. Very engaging and watchable. DA

Albert Brooks *Al Percolo* • Brendan Fraser *Steve Nebraska* • Dianne Wiest *Doctor Aaron* • Anne Twomey *Jennifer* • Lane Smith *Ron Wilson* • Michael Rapaport *Tommy Lacy* ■ *Dir* Michael Ritchie • *Scr* Andrew Bergman, Albert Brooks, Monica Johnson, from an article by Roger Angell

The Scouting Book for Boys ★★★ 15
Thriller 2009 · UK · Colour · 88min

There are two halves to this promising, low-budget British feature: the first is a bittersweet tale of young friendships and unrequited love; the second is a violent slice of lurid psychodrama. Set in a Norfolk caravan park, it stars Thomas Turgoose (*This Is England*) and Holliday Grainger as David and Emily, two lifelong friends whose future together is threatened when Emily's estranged father reveals plans to take his daughter away. Director Tom Harper's feature debut develops into a wistful and atmospheric drama, with superb performances from Turgoose and especially Grainger. But a strong stomach may be needed for the climax, in which all the story's subtleties are blown away. DW Violence, swearing, sexual references, brief nudity. DVD

Steven Mackintosh *Kertzer* • Thomas Turgoose *David* • Rafe Spall *Steve* • Susan Lynch *Sharon* • Holliday Grainger *Emily* • Tony Maudsley *Jim* ■ *Dir* Tom Harper (3) • *Scr* Jack Thorne

Scouts Guide to the Zombie Apocalypse ★★★ 15
Comedy horror 2015 · US · Colour · 92min

In a bonkers zombie flick, Tye Sheridan and Logan Miller play two sexually frustrated teens who remain scouts only out of obligation to their enthusiastic friend (Joey Morgan). But when their troop's leader (*Anchorman*'s David Koechner, having a ball) becomes the walking dead, along with most of their small American town, these trained survivors come into their own. It's an inherently funny concept, and if the film lacks bite and panache, it's still true to the spirit of its predecessors. EAS Violence, sex references, swearing

Tye Sheridan *Ben* • Logan Miller *Carter* • Joey Morgan *Augie* • Halston Sage *Kendall* ■ *Dir* Christopher Landon (2) • *Scr* Emi Mochizuki, Carrie Evans, Lona Williams

Scram! ★★★★ U
Comedy 1932 · US · BW · 20min

A title that could only be appplied to Laurel and Hardy, whose disreputable appearance ensures they are ordered out of town because they might spoil the town's chances of winning a civic prize. However, several adventures later, they find a judge's wife on their side and it all ends in a lengthy laughfest. The small-town hypocrisy is never punctured as it should be, but the mythic laughmakers are at their most endearing in this short from producer Hal Roach. TH DVD

Stan Laurel *Stanley* • Oliver Hardy *Oliver* • Arthur Housman *Drunk* • Vivien Oakland *Mrs Beaumont* • Richard Cramer *Judge Beaumont* ■ *Dir* Ray McCarey • *Scr* HM Walker

Scratch ★★★ 15
Music documentary 2001 · US · Colour · 87min

Following a survey of the Seattle grunge scene, Doug Pray fixes his aim on the art of DJing in this episodic but energetic documentary. Having explored the differences between rap and hip-hop and charted the latter's history from the 1970s,

Pray concentrates on the turntable techniques – and such unsung labours as digging through mounds of obscure vinyl for samples – that make today's DJs more like musical visionaries than record collections for hire. Encounters with genuine characters such as Jazzy Jay and Qbert punctuate the plentiful performance footage. DP Swearing. DVD

■ *Dir* Doug Pray • *Cinematographer* Robert Bennett • *Editor* Doug Pray

Scream ★★★★★ 18
Black comedy horror
1996 · US · Colour · 106min

The 1990s horror revival started here, with director Wes Craven's intelligent reinvention of the slasher genre. Gleefully exploring the relationship between gore movies and their core audience, while paying clever homage to such key titles as *Halloween* and *Friday the 13th*, the elaborate script subversively keeps things scary even when sinister events are at their funniest. A sick maniac on the loose in a small suburban town murdering anyone who gets horror trivia questions wrong is all Craven needs to expose the genre's knee-jerk devices in this terrific shocker that has gasps galore and a genuinely surprising dénouement. AJ Swearing, violence. DVD Blu

Neve Campbell *Sidney Prescott* • Courteney Cox *Gale Weathers* • David Arquette *Deputy Dwight "Dewey" Riley* • Skeet Ulrich *Billy Loomis* • Drew Barrymore *Casey Becker* • Matthew Lillard *Stuart* • Liev Schreiber *Cotton Weary* • Jamie Kennedy *Randy* • Rose McGowan *Tatum Riley* • Lawrence Hecht *Mr Prescott* • Linda Blair *Obnoxious reporter* • Henry Winkler *Principal Himbry* • Wes Craven *Fred, the janitor* ■ *Dir* Wes Craven • *Scr* Kevin Williamson

Scream 2 ★★★ 18
Horror comedy 1997 · US · Colour · 115min

The body count increases in this easily digestible sequel from director Wes Craven. But the scare factor is considerably diluted in this reheated outing that picks up on events two years after the notorious Woodsboro murders. Although the movie once again cleverly twists the genre rules, it lacks the satirical originality of the first recursive nightmare and coasts on the shrewd achievements of the far superior first film. AJ Violence, swearing DVD Blu

David Arquette *Dwight "Dewey" Riley* • Neve Campbell *Sidney Prescott* • Courteney Cox *Gale Weathers* • Sarah Michelle Gellar *Casey "Cici" Cooper* • Jamie Kennedy *Randy Meeks* • Laurie Metcalf *Debbie Salt* • Elise Neal *Hallie* • Jerry O'Connell *Derek* • Jada Pinkett [Jada Pinkett Smith] *Maureen Evans* • Omar Epps *Phil Stevens* • Liev Schreiber *Cotton Weary* • David Warner *Gus Gold* ■ *Dir* Wes Craven • *Scr* Kevin Williamson

Scream 3 ★★ 18
Horror comedy 1999 · US · Colour · 111min

The *Scream* franchise falters with this unconvincing wrap-up to the original trilogy. The surviving cast members of the previous episodes now merely going through the expected self-referential motions. Despite a reasonably surprising ending, the film runs out of steam and becomes exactly what the first *Scream* so smartly sent up. AJ Sex scenes, violence, swearing. DVD Blu

David Arquette *Dwight "Dewey" Riley* • Neve Campbell *Sidney Prescott* • Courteney Cox Arquette [Courteney Cox] *Gale Weathers* • Patrick Dempsey *Mark Kincaid* • Parker Posey *Jennifer Jolie* • Scott Foley *Roman Bridger* • Lance Henriksen *John Milton* • Matt Keeslar *Tom Prinze* • Jenny McCarthy *Sarah Darling* • Liev Schreiber *Cotton Weary* • Carrie Fisher *Bianca* • Kevin Smith (2) *Silent Bob* • Roger L Jackson *"The Voice"* • Roger Corman *Studio executive* ■ *Dir* Wes Craven • *Scr* Ehren Kruger, from characters by Kevin Williamson

Scre4m ★★ 15
Horror 2011 · US · Colour · 106min

After a 12-year break, Neve Campbell's perpetual survivor is now on a tour to promote her book in this fourth instalment in the *Scream* franchise. This, of course, brings her back to suburban Woodsboro,

S

where Courteney Cox's reporter and David Arquette's sheriff still reside. And, as expected, a new generation of photogenic high schoolers - Emma Roberts, Hayden Panettiere - get sucked into the latest killing spree by a masked psycho, the mystery of whose identity props up a saggy, repetitive plot. Beyond more blood, coarser language and references to internet fame, this fails to convert cleverness into on-screen originality or daring. AC Violence, swearing, gore. DVD SD

Neve Campbell *Sidney Prescott* • Courteney Cox *Gale Weathers-Riley* • David Arquette *Sheriff Dewey Riley* • Emma Roberts *Jill Roberts* • Hayden Panettiere *Kirby Reed* • Mary McDonnell *Aunt Kate* • Rory Culkin *Charlie Walker* • Nico Tortorella *Trevor Sheldon* • Kristen Bell *Chloe* • Anna Paquin *Rachel* ■ *Dir* Wes Craven • *Scr* Kevin Williamson, from characters by Williamson

Scream and Scream Again
★★★ 18

Science-fiction horror mystery
1969 · UK · Colour · 90min

This highly regarded, but confusing, sci-fi horror tale is tinged with political allegory. Vincent Price is a scientist creating an artificial super-race via gruesome transplant surgery for a foreign fascist power. Peter Cushing is an ex-Nazi and Christopher Lee a British agent in veteran genre director Gordon Hessler's imaginative blood-curdler, but the three leads' highly publicised (at the time) teaming is a cheat, as they have virtually no scenes together. Price lends dignity and class to some credible chills. AJ Violence, swearing, nudity.

Vincent Price *Dr Browning* • Christopher Lee *Fremont* • Peter Cushing *Major Benedek Heinrich* • Judy Huxtable *Sylvia* • Alfred Marks *Superintendent Bellaver* • Anthony Newlands *Ludwig* • Peter Sallis *Schweitz* • David Lodge *Det Insp Strickland* ■ *Dir* Gordon Hessler • *Scr* Christopher Wicking, from the novel *The Disorientated Man* by Peter Saxon

Scream of Stone
★★★ 15

Drama
1991 · Can/Ger/Fr · Colour · 102min

The "mountain film" has been a key German genre since the silent era, but Werner Herzog's film lacks the dramatic drive to match its stunning photography. It's as if he's dissipated his trademark intensity by dividing the obsession that motivates nearly all his protagonists between two characters, mountaineer Vittorio Mezzogiorno and indoor climbing champion, Stefan Glowacz, whose race to scale El Toro in Patagonia (sponsored by TV reporter Donald Sutherland) is intensified by a rivalry for the affections of Mathilda May. DP DVD

Mathilda May *Katharina* • Vittorio Mezzogiorno *Roccia* • Stefan Glowacz *Martin* • Donald Sutherland *Ivan* • Brad Dourif *"Fingerless"* ■ *Dir* Werner Herzog • *Scr* Hans-Ulrich Klenner, Walter Saxer, Robert Geoffrion, from an idea by Reinhold Messner • *Cinematographer* Rainer Klausmann

Screamers
★★ 18

Science-fiction thriller
1995 · Can/US/Jpn · Colour · 103min

This dingy adaptation of a Philip K Dick short story is only a moderate success. Peter Weller plays the soldier brokering peace with his futuristic enemies, who comes up against the eponymous deadly defence units, which have evolved into increasingly sophisticated adversaries. Although there are decently mounted action sequences and the post-nuclear production design is nicely realised, there are too many lulls. JC DVD

Peter Weller *Colonel Hendricksson* • Andy Lauer [Andrew Lauer] *Ace* • Roy Dupuis *Becker* • Charles Powell *Ross* • Jennifer Rubin *Jessica* • Ron White *Elbarak* ■ *Dir* Christian Duguay • *Scr* Dan O'Bannon, Miguel Tejada-Flores, from the short story *Second Variety* by Philip K Dick

A Screaming Man
★★★★ PG

Drama
2010 · Fr/Bel/Chad/Cameroon/Burkina Faso/Neth · Colour · 91min

Civil war rips through the African republic of Chad and a former swimming champion now working as a hotel pool attendant has to face up to his own personal crises, in this drama from director Mahamat-Saleh Haroun. As the country's political situation worsens, "Champ", as everyone calls Youssouf Djaoro's protagonist Adam, proves so obsessed by his workplace status that his responsibilities towards his family seem less of a priority. The chastening events that then occur effectively illuminate the destructive side of masculine pride - an issue Haroun suggests runs from top to bottom in many African societies. The director's style is certainly deliberate, but the gradual build-up of events is undeniably thought-provoking, played out in images of stark beauty as Adam's personal odyssey reaches a powerful and moving conclusion. TJ French, Arabic +subtitles. Brief images of dead bodies.

Youssouf Djaoro *Adam* • Diouc Koma [Dioucounda Koma] *Abdel* • Emile Abossolo M'Bo *Chief of District* • Hadjé Fatimé N'Goua *Mariam* • Marius Yelolo *David* • Djénéba Koné *Djénéba* ■ *Dir/Scr* Mahamat-Saleh Haroun

Screaming Mimi
★★

Thriller
1958 · US · BW · 77min

This would-be lurid and sexy thriller, filmed in gritty black and white and directed by Gerd Oswald, falls far short of expectation. A tortuous and virtually incomprehensible plot, and an almost unwatchable hero played by an expressionless Phil Carey are the main culprits. Anita Ekberg is splendidly awful as an assault victim, and there's a palpable sexual tension whenever she's on screen. For 1950s freaks, fans of the bizarre and anyone interested in that late *film noir* style when all the streets were wet ones. TS

Anita Ekberg *Virginia Wilson* • Phil Carey [Philip Carey] *Bill Sweeney* • Gypsy Rose Lee *Joann Mapes* • Harry Townes *Dr Greenwood* • Linda Cherney *Ketti* • Romney Brent *Charlie Wilson* • Alan Gifford *Captain Bline* ■ *Dir* Gerd Oswald • *Scr* Robert Blees, from the book by Frederic Brown

Screw Loose
★ 12

Comedy
1999 · It · Colour · 84min

Mel Brooks co-stars as a colourful mental patient sought as the final wish of a dying man, in a dreadful, near plotless comedy. Italian star/producer/director Ezio Greggio carries out his duties on both sides of the camera with staggering ineptness, not aided by the unmistakeable feeling that the cast are making this up as they go along, not least a manic, unbridled Brooks. Excruciating. JC DVD

Ezio Greggio *Bernardo Puccini* • Mel Brooks *Jake Gordon* • Julie Condra *Dr Barbara Collier* • Gianfranco Barra *Guido Puccini* • Randi Ingerman *Sofia* • John Karlsen *Dr Caputo* ■ *Dir* Ezio Greggio • *Scr* Rudy DeLuca, Steve Haberman

Screwballs
★ 18

Comedy
1983 · US/Can · Colour · 76min

Five high school students on detention blame the school's last remaining virgin, Purity Busch, for their predicament, and plan revenge by contriving to see her ample breasts. This is a leering, juvenile slice of limp titillation that spawned an equally naff sequel. DF DVD

Peter Keleghan *Rick McKay* • Lynda Speciale *Purity Busch* • Alan Deveau *Howie Bates* • Kent Deuters *Brent Van Dusen III* • Jason Warren *Melvin Jerkovski* • Linda Shayne *Bootsie Goodhead* ■ *Dir* Rafal Zielinski • *Scr* Linda Shayne, Jim Wynorski

Screwed
★ 15

Comedy
2000 · US · Colour · 78min

Scott Alexander and Larry Karaszewski fell flat on their faces in directing this black comedy, which owes more to the Farrellys than Milos Forman. Norm MacDonald gives a totally lackadaisical performance as the aggrieved factotum whose bid to kidnap his uppity employer's dog goes predictably wrong. DP DVD

Norm MacDonald *Willard Fillmore* • Dave Chappelle *Rusty P Hayes* • Danny DeVito *Grover Cleaver* • Elaine Stritch *Miss Crock* • Daniel Benzali *Detective Tom Dewey* • Sherman Hemsley *Chip Oswald* ■ *Dir/Scr* Scott Alexander, Larry Karaszewski

Screwed
★★★ 18

Prison drama based on a true story
2011 · UK · Colour · 105min

This gritty British drama leaves no punch unpulled nor cliché unmined in its portrayal of life in a maximum security prison. Straight and bent "screws", good and bad cons, beatings, drug abuse... it's all here, as a war-traumatised ex-squaddie (James D'Arcy) joins the prison service, only to discover corruption and violence so endemic that it's tough to tell on which side of the bars the real bad guys are. Noel Clarke shines as a cocky prisoner, and the film's best scenes are those in which he goes eyeball to eyeball with D'Arcy's greenhorn guard. Too often, though, rather than sticking tightly to this testosterone-fuelled twosome, the film meanders off down the highways and byways of prison life. DA Swearing. DVD SD

James D'Arcy *Sam* • Noel Clarke *Truman* • Frank Harper *Deano* • Kate Magowan *Danielle* • Jamie Foreman *Rumpole* • Doug Allen *Steadman* ■ *Dir* Reg Traviss • *Scr* Colin Butts, Ronnie Thompson, from the non-fiction book *Screwed: the Truth about Life as a Prison Officer* by Thompson

Scrooge
★★ U

Fantasy drama
1935 · US · BW · 77min

Seymour Hicks plays the old curmudgeon and Donald Calthrop is Bob Cratchit in the first talking version of Dickens's *A Christmas Carol*. Viewers who expect something deeply sentimental and technically creaky will not be disappointed but it should not really be compared to the classic Alastair Sim version of 1951. AT

Seymour Hicks *Ebenezer Scrooge* • Donald Calthrop *Bob Cratchit* • Robert Cochran *Fred* • Mary Glynne *Belle* • Garry Marsh *Belle's husband* • Oscar Asche *Spirit of Christmas Present* • Marie Ney *Spirit of Christmas Past* • CV France *Spirit of Christmas Future* ■ *Dir* Henry Edwards • *Scr* Seymour Hicks, H Fowler Mear, from the story *A Christmas Carol* by Charles Dickens

Scrooge
★★★★★ U

Classic period drama
1951 · UK · BW · 86min

Released in the US under Dickens's original title, *A Christmas Carol*, this is easily the best screen version of the much loved yuletide tale. Alastair Sim is impeccable as the miser who comes to see the error of his ways through the promptings of the spirits of Christmas Past, Present and Future. Michael Hordern makes a splendid Jacob Marley and Mervyn Johns a humble Bob Cratchit, while George Cole does well as the younger, carefree Scrooge. Beautifully designed by Ralph Brinton and directed with finesse by Brian Desmond Hurst, this is not to be missed. DP DVD

Alastair Sim *Scrooge* • Kathleen Harrison *Mrs Dilber* • Mervyn Johns *Bob Cratchit* • Hermione Baddeley *Mrs Cratchit* • Michael Hordern *Jacob Marley* • George Cole *Scrooge as young man* • John Charlesworth *Peter Cratchit* • Glynn Dearman *Tiny Tim* • Francis De Wolff *Spirit of Christmas Present* • Rona Anderson *Alice* • Carol Marsh *Fan, Scrooge's sister* • Jack Warner *Mr Jorkins* • Brian Worth *Fred, Scrooge's nephew* • Hattie Jacques *Mrs Fezziwig* • Patrick Macnee *Young Marley* ■ *Dir* Brian Desmond-Hurst [Brian Desmond Hurst] • *Scr* Noel Langley, from the story *A Christmas Carol* by Charles Dickens

Scrooge
★★ U

Musical
1970 · UK · Colour · 108min

This adaptation of the Dickens tale stars an overly made-up Albert Finney, who gives the impression he'd be happier somewhere other than on the palpably phoney Shepperton sets. Only Alec Guinness really registers, and director Ronald Neame oversees matters with the heaviest of hands. There is some compensation in watching fine twilight-year performances from Dame Edith Evans and Kenneth More. SD

Albert Finney *Ebenezer Scrooge* • Alec Guinness *Jacob Marley's Ghost* • Edith Evans *Ghost of Christmas Past* • Kenneth More *Ghost of Christmas Present* • Michael Medwin *Scrooge's nephew* • Laurence Naismith *Fezziwig* • David Collings *Bob Cratchit* • Anton Rodgers *Tom Jenkins* • Suzanne Neve *Isabel* • Roy Kinnear *Portly gentleman* • Gordon Jackson *Nephew's friend* ■ *Dir* Ronald Neame • *Scr* Leslie Bricusse, from the story *A Christmas Carol* by Charles Dickens • *Music/lyrics* Leslie Bricusse

Scrooged
★★★ 12

Seasonal comedy
1988 · US · Colour · 100min

For the opening quarter, this is a joyously black Christmas treat with Bill Murray at his sour-faced best as a monstrous TV executive preparing for the festive break by sacking staff, planning a season of violence and ordering mini antlers to be stapled on the heads of mice. But it's is not long before sentimentality starts seeping in, as Murray is shown what a heel he is by unconventional ghosts John Forsythe, Carol Kane and David Johansen. A missed opportunity, but some of the gags still hit the mark. JF Swearing. DVD SD

Bill Murray *Frank Cross* • Karen Allen *Claire Phillips* • John Forsythe *Lew Hayward* • Bobcat Goldthwait *Eliot Loudermilk* • Robert Mitchum *Preston Rhinelander* • Carol Kane *Ghost of Christmas Present* • John Glover *Brice Cummings* • David Johansen *Ghost of Christmas Past* • Alfre Woodard *Grace Cooley* ■ *Dir* Richard Donner • *Scr* Mitch Glazer, Michael O'Donoghue, from the story *A Christmas Carol* by Charles Dickens

Scrubbers
★★★ 15

Drama
1982 · UK · Colour · 88min

Bursting at the seams with all manner of GBH and blaspheming, director Mai Zetterling's moderately successful attempt at showing the gritty and depressing underbelly of life in a girls' borstal and beyond was highly controversial. Utilising inventive moody camerawork and incisive editing, Zetterling does well in portraying the problems facing her two main protagonists, who emote like fury in realistic performances, but this is dreadfully depressing. SH Some violence, swearing. DVD

Amanda York *Carol* • Chrissie Cotterill *Annetta* • Elizabeth Edmonds *Kathleen* • Pam Ingram *Eddie* • Debbie Bishop *Doreen* • Dana Gillespie *Budd* • Camille Davis *Sharon* • Amanda Symonds *Mac* • Kathy Burke *Glennis* • Robbie Coltrane • Pam St Clement ■ *Dir* Mai Zetterling • *Scr* Mai Zetterling, Roy Minton, Jeremy Watt

Scum
★★★★ 18

Prison drama
1979 · UK · Colour · 96min

Originally written for the BBC's *Play for Today* series, Roy Minton's stark, bruising drama about conditions inside a juvenile detention centre was banned by the BBC in 1978. Minton persuaded director Alan Clarke to make a cinema version on a shoestring budget the following year. He presents an uncompromising picture of borstal life, made all the more shocking by Clarke's docudramatic approach, with the scenes of sexual and physical violence still having the power to revolt and arouse anger. DP Violence, swearing. DVD

Ray Winstone *Carlin* • Mick Ford *Archer* • John Judd *Sands* • Phil Daniels *Richards* • John Blundell *Banks* • Ray Burdis *Eckersly* • Julian Firth *Davis* • Alrick Riley *Angel* ■ *Dir* Alan Clarke • *Scr* Roy Minton

The Sea
★★ 12

Drama
2013 · Ire/UK · Colour · 86min

Recently widowed Ciarán Hinds revisits the seaside stamping ground of his adolescence in this adaptation of John Banville's novel. It's a lumpy affair that proves a disappointing reminder that great literature doesn't necessarily make great cinema. Poor Hinds is left lumbering around a curiously deserted coastal community to pass the time between flashbacks, since it's in his teenage years and the recent past where the action really happens. So though the cast (which also includes Sinéad Cusack and Charlotte Rampling) can't be faulted, by the time the film's key threads eventually knit together, the effect is both predictable and underwhelming. TJ Some violence, swearing. *DVD*

Ciarán Hinds [Ciaran Hinds] *Max Morden* • Charlotte Rampling *Miss Vavasour* • Natascha McElhone *Connie Grace* • Rufus Sewell *Carlo Grace* • Bonnie Wright *Rose* • Sinéad Cusack [Sinead Cusack] *Anna Morden* ■ *Dir* Stephen Brown (2) • *Scr* John Banville, from his novel

The Sea Chase ★★★ U
Second World War adventure
1955 · US · Colour · 112min

John Wayne stars as a German sea captain in this Second World War adventure. However, the real villain of the piece is first mate Lyle Bettger, whose murder of some defenceless fishermen prompts British naval officer David Farrar to pursue Wayne's freighter across the Pacific. Director John Farrow adopts a no-nonsense approach, but Wayne's dalliance with sultry passenger Lana Turner slows up the action. However, the rivalry between the Duke and Farrar gives the picture extra edge. DP

John Wayne *Captain Karl Ehrlich* • Lana Turner *Elsa Keller* • David Farrar *Commander Napier* • Lyle Bettger *Kirchner* • Tab Hunter *Cadet Wesser* • James Arness *Schlieter* • Richard Davalos *Cadet Walter Stemme* ■ *Dir* John Farrow • *Scr* James Warner Bellah, John Twist, from the novel by Andrew Geer

Sea Devils ★★ U
Period adventure 1952 · UK/US · Colour · 86min

One-eyed, macho action maestro Raoul Walsh directs this routine seafaring yarn. The svelte Yvonne De Carlo plays a spy for George III who slips into France to try to uncover Napoleon's invasion plans. Rock Hudson, sporting designer stubble, is a smuggler from Guernsey who, after being duped by her, becomes a patriotic hero. Filmed in the Channel Islands and Brittany, the picture often looks good, but still falls well below Walsh's usually high standards. AT *DVD*

Yvonne De Carlo *Drouette* • Rock Hudson *Gilliatt* • Maxwell Reed *Rantaine* • Denis O'Dea *Lethierry* • Michael Goodliffe *Ragan* • Bryan Forbes *Willie* • Jacques Brunius *Fouche* • Gérard Oury *Napoleon* ■ *Dir* Raoul Walsh • *Scr* Borden Chase, from the novel *The Toilers of the Sea* by Victor Hugo

Sea Fury ★★★
Adventure 1958 · UK · BW · 94min

After the success of *Hell Drivers*, star Stanley Baker and writer/director Cy Endfield teamed up again for this modest but strangely effective action movie set in Spain. Baker plays a drifter who gets a job aboard Victor McLaglen's salvage vessel. The pair end up competing for local siren Luciana Paluzzi. A study in macho posturing, failing sexuality and the virility of the weather, this heady brew also features an early role for Robert Shaw. AT *DVD*

Stanley Baker *Abel Hewson* • Victor McLaglen *Captain Bellew* • Luciana Paluzzi *Josita* • Grégoire Aslan *Fernando* • David Oxley *Blanco* • Robert Shaw *Gorman* • Dermot Walsh *Kelso* • Barry Foster *Vincent* ■ *Dir* C Raker Endfield [Cy Endfield] • *Scr* C Raker Endfield [Cy Endfield], John Kruse

The Sea Gull ★★★
Drama 1968 · UK · Colour · 141min

This is a solid if unsensational version of the Chekhov play about life, loves and hates on a 19th-century Russian estate. Director Sidney Lumet clearly likes filming plays: he'd done *Long Day's Journey into Night* six years earlier, and would later make *Equus*. But it's the cast that really catches the eye here: a veritable who's who of 1960s British cinema. DA

James Mason *Trigorin* • Vanessa Redgrave *Nina* • Simone Signoret *Arkadina* • David Warner *Konstantin* • Harry Andrews *Sorin* • Ronald Radd *Shamraev* • Eileen Herlie *Polina* • Kathleen Widdoes *Masha* • Denholm Elliott *Dorn* ■ *Dir* Sidney Lumet • *Scr* Moura Budberg, from the play by Anton Chekhov

The Sea Hawk ★★★★
Silent swashbuckling adventure
1924 · US · BW · 129min

Rivalling anything produced by Douglas Fairbanks, this thrilling adventure sweeps from Georgian England to the Algerian bazaar in pursuit of baronet Milton Sills as he seeks revenge on his treacherous half-brother Wallace MacDonald. Frank Lloyd is most heavily indebted to art director Stephen Goosson, whose sets for everything from a country manor to a desert palace, a Spanish galleon to a Moorish pirate ship give the action a splendour to match its zest. The performances are also top notch, with Sills's clean-cut hero complemented by Enid Bennett's chaste beloved and Wallace Beery's scowling villain. DP

Milton Sills *Sir Oliver Tressilian, the Sea Hawk* • Enid Bennett *Rosamund Godolphin* • Lloyd Hughes *Master Lionel Tressilian* • Wallace MacDonald *Master Peter Godolphin* • Marc MacDermott *Sir John Killigrew* • Wallace Beery *Jasper Leigh, a freebooter* ■ *Dir* Frank Lloyd • *Scr* JG Hawks, Walter Anthony, from a novel by Rafael Sabatini

The Sea Hawk ★★★★ U
Classic swashbuckling adventure
1940 · US · BW · 121min

This rip-roaring adventure yarn was made at lavish expense, and, as they say, it all shows up there on the screen. Directed by Michael Curtiz, who was soon to make *Casablanca*, and starring Errol Flynn in his swashbuckling prime, it's stronger in its scenes of derring-do and Spanish galleons on the high seas than it is when detailing the political intrigue at the court of Elizabeth I. But, all in all, it even improves on the rousing 1924 silent movie of the same name, of which it is a remake – and that's praise indeed. PF

Errol Flynn *Captain Geoffrey Thorpe* • Claude Rains *Don Jose Alvarez de Cordoba* • Brenda Marshall *Doña Maria Alvarez de Cordoba* • Donald Crisp *Sir John Burleson* • Flora Robson *Queen Elizabeth I* • Alan Hale *Carl Pitt* • Henry Daniell *Lord Wolfingham* • Una O'Connor *Martha, Miss Latham* ■ *Dir* Michael Curtiz • *Scr* Seton I Miller, Howard Koch

The Sea Inside ★★★★★ PG
Biographical drama
2004 · Sp/Fr/It · Colour · 120min

The controversial and emotive subject of euthanasia presents film-makers with ample opportunities to pile on the melodrama and manipulate the audience. Fortunately, Spanish director Alejandro Amenábar keeps this true-story drama funny and free of sentiment, while never sacrificing emotional integrity. Javier Bardem gives an amazing performance as quadriplegic Ramón Sampedro, who became famous in 1990s Spain for waging a one-man war against religious leaders, family members and the authorities for the right to die with dignity. It's clear where Amenábar's sympathies lie, but he presents both sides of the complex argument and his heartfelt human drama is all the better for this balanced view. Enormously touching and relevant. AJ Spanish +subtitles. *DVD*

Javier Bardem *Ramón Sampedro* • Belén Rueda *Julia* • Lola Dueñas *Rosa* • Mabel Rivera *Manuela* • Celso Bugallo *José* • Clara Segura *Gené* • Joan Dalmau *Joaquín* ■ *Dir* Alejandro Amenábar • *Scr* Alejandro Amenábar, Mateo Gil

The Sea Is Watching ★★★ 15
Romantic drama
2002 · Jpn · BW and Colour · 114min

Underrated director Kei Kumai assumed control of this tale set in a 19th-century brothel on the death of Akira Kurosawa. An air of what might have been under Kurosawa's direction hangs heavy over the story of geisha Nagiko Tohno's encounters with disreputable samurai Hidetaka Yoshioka and Masatoshi Nagase. While Kumai ably re-creates the atmosphere within Tokyo's infamous Okabasho district and conceives some affecting monochrome flashbacks to Nagase's childhood, he's

saddled with parallel plots that are only resolved by a dismayingly gauche contrivance. DP Japanese +subtitles. Sex scenes, nudity. *DVD*

Misa Shimizu *Kikuno* • Nagiko Tohno *Oshin* • Masatoshi Nagase *Ryosuke* • Hidetaka Yoshioka *Fusanosuke* • Eiji Okuda *Ginji* • Renji Ishibashi *Zenbei* • Michiko Kawai *Osono* • Miho Tsumiki *Okichi* ■ *Dir* Kei Kumai • *Scr* Akira Kurosawa, from short stories by Shugoro Yamamoto

The Sea of Grass ★★
Western 1947 · US · BW · 123min

This New Mexico-set western wasn't one of the more interesting vehicles for the stellar partnership of Katharine Hepburn and Spencer Tracy. Tracy is the steely cattle rancher who becomes increasingly ruthless in his efforts to protect his livelihood from the influx of homesteaders. Hepburn is his wife, who finds herself driven into the arms of Melvyn Douglas. Despite the high-powered cast, director Elia Kazan fails to engender any interest. AJ

Spencer Tracy *Col Jim Brewton* • Katharine Hepburn *Lutie Cameron* • Melvyn Douglas *Brice Chamberlain* • Robert Walker *Brock Brewton* • Phyllis Thaxter *Sara Beth Brewton* • Edgar Buchanan *Jeff* • Harry Carey *Doc Reid* • Ruth Nelson *Selina Hall* ■ *Dir* Elia Kazan • *Scr* Marguerite Roberts, Vincent Lawrence, from the novel by Conrad Richter

Sea of Love ★★★★ 18
Erotic thriller 1989 · US · Colour · 108min

There's a real sexual charge to this tough thriller, with New York cop Al Pacino and chief murder suspect Ellen Barkin conveying a highly plausible erotic tension. It's a rather lurid story about Manhattan men being killed after advertising in the lonely hearts columns, with a screenplay by Richard Price that's as serrated as a dozen *Jagged Edges*. The film is effectively directed by Harold Becker, who gives it an air of realism that only adds to the suspense. The title record (playing at the scene of each murder) is a bit of an irrelevance, but is still a treat to listen to. TH Nudity, sex scenes. *DVD* *Blu-ray*

Al Pacino *Frank Keller* • Ellen Barkin *Helen* • John Goodman *Sherman Touhey* • Michael Rooker *Terry* • Lorraine Bracco *Denise* • William Hickey *Frank Keller Sr* • Richard Jenkins *Gruber* • Paul Calderon *Serafino* ■ *Dir* Harold Becker • *Scr* Richard Price

Sea of Sand ★★ U
Second World War action adventure
1958 · UK · BW · 94min

Guy Green was a leading British cameraman who, when he became a director, rather lost his way. Here, a desert patrol of British stalwarts (Richard Attenborough, John Gregson, Michael Craig) is sent behind enemy lines to blow up an Axis fuel dump before the battle of El Alamein. Green handles the macho elements with credibility, but the sentimentality that finally consigned him to directing weepies proves to be an irritating distraction. TH *DVD*

Richard Attenborough *Trooper Brody* • John Gregson *Captain Williams* • Michael Craig *Captain Cotton* • Vincent Ball *Sergeant Nesbitt* • Percy Herbert *Trooper White* • Barry Foster *Corporal Matheson* • Ray McAnally *Sergeant Hardy* ■ *Dir* Guy Green • *Scr* Robert Westerby, from a story by Sean Fielding

The Sea of Trees
Drama 2015 · US · Colour · 110min

Booed by critics at Cannes, this undeniably handsome, star-laden stab at prestige awards bait takes a little while to show its hand but when it does, it's really quite mesmerising in its dreadfulness. Matthew McConaughey stars as a physics teacher who is buying a one-way ticket to Japan where he intends to kill himself. For a time, it seems this will be another of director Gus Van Sant's slick, knowing forays into classic Hollywood melodrama, but sadly not. Instead, it reveals itself as silly, supernatural guff. DW

Matthew McConaughey *Arthur Brennan* • Naomi Watts *Joan Brennan* • Ken Watanabe *Takumi Nakamura* • Jordan Gavaris ■ *Dir* Gus Van Sant • *Scr* Chris Sparling

The Sea Shall Not Have Them ★★ U
Second World War adventure
1954 · UK · BW · 91min

Lewis Gilbert fails to generate much excitement with this stiff wartime tale of pluck and endurance, about a plane-load of heroes pitching into the briny. The calamities are utterly predictable, and there is no palpable tension between the castaways (clichés to a man). Each member of the stellar cast is seemingly more preoccupied with holding his own in such august company than contributing to the ensemble effort. DP

Michael Redgrave *Air Commodore Waltby* • Dirk Bogarde *Flight Sergeant Mackay* • Anthony Steel *Flying Officer Treherne* • Nigel Patrick *Flight Sergeant Slingsby* • Bonar Colleano *Sergeant Kirby* • Jack Watling *Flying Officer Harding* ■ *Dir* Lewis Gilbert • *Scr* Lewis Gilbert, Vernon Harris, from the novel by John Harris

The Sea Wall ★★★ 12A
Drama 2008 · Fr/Bel/Camb · Colour · 116min

Isabelle Huppert's performance dominates Rithy Panh's meticulously staged but rarely compelling adaptation of Marguerite Duras's semi-autobiographical novel. Huppert plays a civil servant's widow in 1930s Indochina who has to compromise her principles to keep her lands out of the clutches of corrupt French bureaucrats and scheming Asian tycoons. Panh's documentary background enables him and cinematographer Pierre Milon to evoke a palpable sense of time and place. But he allows the drama to sprawl and draws rather laboured comparisons between Huppert's relationships with her offspring and the imperial power's declining control of the indigenous population. DP In French. Swearing, sex scenes, nudity.

Isabelle Huppert *Mother* • Gaspard Ulliel *Joseph* • Astrid Bergès-Frisbey *Suzanne* • Randal Douc *Monsieur Jo* • Duong Vanthon *Corporal* ■ *Dir* Rithy Panh • *Scr* Michel Fessler, Rithy Panh, from the novel by Marguerite Duras • *Cinematographer* Pierre Milon

Sea Wife ★★ PG
Second World War romantic adventure
1957 · UK · Colour · 81min

This doesn't quite come off, mainly owing to a change of directors mid-production. Richard Burton, Joan Collins, Basil Sydney and Cy Grant play the only survivors of a ship wrecked off the coast of Singapore during the evacuation in 1942. Director Bob McNaught – he took over from Roberto Rossellini – makes a fair job of it, but the characters are predictable types and not even a shark attack can enliven the lifeboat scenes. DP

Joan Collins *Sea Wife* • Richard Burton *Biscuit* • Basil Sydney *Bulldog* • Cy Grant *Number four* • Ronald Squire *Teddy* • Harold Goodwin (2) *Daily Telegraph clerk* • Joan Hickson *Scribe* ■ *Dir* Bob McNaught • *Scr* George K Burke, from the novel *Sea Wyf and Biscuit* by JM Scott

The Sea Wolf ★★★★ PG
Adventure drama 1941 · US · BW · 84min

This exciting nautical melodrama from director Michael Curtiz is based on the classic Jack London tale. Edward G Robinson is terrific as the tormented skipper, trading intellectual barbs with rescued novelist Alexander Knox. John Garfield and Ida Lupino are both wasted in relatively minor roles, and their shipboard romance takes clear second place to the captain's fiendish desire to break the spirits of his crew members. TS

Edward G Robinson *Wolf Larsen* • John Garfield *George Leach* • Ida Lupino *Ruth Webster* • Alexander Knox *Humphrey van Weyden* • Gene Lockhart *Dr Louie Prescott* • Barry Fitzgerald *Cooky* • Stanley Ridges *Johnson* ■ *Dir* Michael Curtiz • *Scr* Robert Rossen, from the novel by Jack London

The Sea Wolf ★ PG
Adventure drama 1993 · US · Colour · 89min

An all-star cast sinks like a lead anchor in this torpid retelling of Jack London's classic novel. In 1890, San Francisco aristocrat

S

Christopher Reeve is shipwrecked and rescued by a brutal and sadistic sea captain (Charles Bronson) who presses him into service aboard his schooner. Reeve and the wooden Bronson are without chemistry and, along with the uninspired direction, drown in this leaky made-for-cable effort. MC

Charles Bronson *Captain Wolf Larsen* • Catherine Mary Stewart *Flaxen Brewster* • Christopher Reeve *Humphrey Van Weyden* • Len Cariou *Doc Picard* • Marc Singer *Johnson* • Clive Revill *Cookie* ■ *Dir* Michael Anderson • *Scr* Andrew J Fenady, from Jack London's novel

The Sea Wolves ★★ PG

Second World War drama
1980 · UK/US/Swi · Colour · 115min

Starring a trio of venerable old sea dogs, the exploits are headed up by Gregory Peck, attempting a most ill-advised English accent, which is especially disturbing when pitched, literally, alongside Roger Moore and David Niven, with whom he once stormed the cliffs at Navarone. This tosh is directed with some verve by Andrew V McLaglen, but there's little point in pretending this has any real merit. It's not boring, though, for all sorts of strange reasons. TS

Gregory Peck *Lt Col Lewis Pugh* • David Niven *Colonel Bill Grice* • Roger Moore *Captain Gavin Stewart* • Trevor Howard *Jack Cartwright* • Barbara Kellerman *Mrs Cromwell* • Patrick Macnee *Major "Yogi" Crossley* • Patrick Allen *Colin Mackenzie* ■ *Dir* Andrew V McLaglen • *Scr* Reginald Rose, from the novel *Boarding Party* by James Leasor

Seabiscuit ★★★ PG

Period drama based on a true story
2003 · US · Colour · 134min

Three broken men came together to own (Jeff Bridges), train (Chris Cooper) and ride (Tobey Maguire) a no-hoper racehorse named Seabiscuit, turning him into an inspirational winner that lifted the spirits of Depression-era America. Gary Ross may be unsubtle in his direction at times but the emotional core of this heart-warming story remains true and the races are grippingly executed. The three leads give superb performances, as does William H Macy, who, as the track announcer, provides some much-needed comic relief in this overly sentimental, yet thoroughly absorbing drama. AJ *DVD*

Tobey Maguire *Johnny "Red" Pollard* • Jeff Bridges *Charles Howard* • Chris Cooper *Tom Smith* • Elizabeth Banks (2) *Marcela Howard* • Gary Stevens *George "The Iceman" Woolf* • William H Macy *"Tick-Tock" McGlaughlin* • Kingston DuCoeur *Sam* • Eddie Jones *Samuel Riddle* • Ed Lauter *Charles Strub* • David McCullough *Narrator* ■ *Dir* Gary Ross • *Scr* Gary Ross, from the non-fiction book *Seabiscuit: an American Legend* by Laura Hillenbrand

Seachd: the Inaccessible Pinnacle ★★★ PG

Fantasy drama
2007 · UK · Colour · 87min

Old traditions die hard in this warm Scottish drama spoken almost entirely in Scottish Gaelic. Young Angus (Padruig Moireasdan) is struggling to come to terms with the tragic death of his parents, and his grandad (Aonghas Padruig Caimbeul) is forever spinning yarns about days of yore for the boy's benefit. These ancient legends are filled with magic, intrigue, and a good dose of humour, as in the dubious tale of a man called MacDonald who opened the world's first chip shop. For the most part, the mix of domestic drama and fantastical folklore works well, but Angus's grief doesn't come across as powerfully as it should when he returns as a man to the mountaintop where mum and dad perished. Even if writer/director Simon Miller doesn't quite scale the heights he aims for, there's a cosy, fairy-tale feel to this story. SP Scottish Gaelic, English +subtitles. *DVD*

Aonghas Padruig Caimbeul *Grandfather* • Padruig Moireasdan *Angus* • Crisdean Domhnallach *Donnchadh* • Winnie Brook Young *Mary* • Dolina MacLennan *Grandmother* • Colla Domhnallach *Angus, aged 20* • Daibhidh Walker

Archie ■ *Dir* Simon Miller • *Scr* Joanne Cockwell, Iain Finlay MacLeod, Aonghas Macneacail, Simon Miller, Ishbel T MacDonald

The Seafarers ★★

Documentary 1953 · US · Colour · 29min

Having failed to make much impact with his feature debut, *Fear and Desire* (1952), Stanley Kubrick undertook this promotional short for the Seafarers International Union in order to bankroll *Killer's Kiss* (1954). Answering an advertisement, Kubrick was very much a director for hire, but he was obviously keen to experiment with colour for the first time and indulges himself with one trademark tracking shot in capturing a bustling scene in a cafeteria. Very much a means to an end, this was such a minor work that it was scarcely seen until its rediscovery in 1973. DP *DVD* ◁▷

Don Hollenbeck *Narrator* ■ *Dir* Stanley Kubrick • *Scr* Will Chasen

Seagulls over Sorrento ★★★ U

Second World War drama
1954 · UK · BW · 91min

One of the stranger products of the Cold War, this stage hit was "opened out" considerably by the Boultings for this film version. In a weird bit of casting, Gene Kelly plays an American navy scientist working on torpedo research on a Scottish island. The British boffins have already blown themselves to bits when the Yanks arrive, thus sparking a lot of transatlantic rivalry and resentment. An enjoyable and often quirky drama about the "Special Relationship". AT

Gene Kelly *Lieutenant Bradville, USN* • John Justin *Lieutenant Wharton* • Bernard Lee *Lofty Turner* • Jeff Richards *Butch Clelland, USN* • Sidney James *Charlie Badger* • Patric Doonan *PO Herbert* ■ *Dir* John Boulting, Roy Boulting • *Scr* Frank Harvey, Roy Boulting, from the play by Hugh Hastings

Sealed Cargo ★★ U

Second World War drama
1951 · US · BW · 89min

Dana Andrews plays a Newfoundland fisherman who comes across a sailing ship with its hold full of guns, bombs and torpedoes. Manned by Nazis in disguise, led by the urbane but miscast Claude Rains, it's actually the mother ship for a German U-boat invasion of the USA. RKO gave Andrews sideburns and Carla Balenda as his leading lady, neither of which makes this film any more convincing. TS

Dana Andrews *Pat Bannon* • Claude Rains *Skalder* • Carla Balenda *Margaret McLean* • Philip Dorn *Conrad* • Onslow Stevens *McLean* • Skip Homeier *Steve* • Eric Feldary *Holger* ■ *Dir* Alfred Werker • *Scr* Dale Van Every, Oliver HP Garrett, Roy Huggins, from the novel *The Gaunt Woman* by Edmund Gilligan

Seance on a Wet Afternoon ★★★ PG

Drama 1964 · UK · BW · 111min

Kim Stanley gives a compelling, Oscar-nominated performance as an unbalanced medium in this engrossing and imaginative drama. She orders her brow-beaten husband Richard Attenborough to kidnap a wealthy industrialist's daughter so she can enhance her reputation as a spiritualist by "finding" the youngster. The tension screws are chillingly turned when Attenborough realises his wife will go to any lengths to achieve celebrity status. Director Bryan Forbes skilfully conjures up suspenseful uncertainty as the ghastly implications of Stanley's plan unfold. AJ *DVD*

Kim Stanley *Myra Savage* • Richard Attenborough *Billy Savage* • Mark Eden *Charles Clayton* • Nanette Newman *Mrs Clayton* • Judith Donner *Amanda Clayton* • Patrick Magee *Supt Walsh* • Gerald Sim *Sergeant Beedle* ■ *Dir* Bryan Forbes • *Scr* Bryan Forbes, from the novel by Mark McShane

The Search ★★★★ U

Drama 1948 · US · BW · 103min

Although Montgomery Clift had already made his first movie *Red River*, protracted delays kept that film off the screen until after *The Search* had premiered, giving movie-goers their first sight of the actor who was the forerunner of the Method style of acting. This semi-documentary won an Oscar for best motion picture story, but Clift largely improvised his own dialogue for his portrayal of a soldier in postwar Germany, who befriends a nine-year-old homeless boy. Clift gives a casual, unaffected performance, and Ivan Jandl, as the boy, was awarded a special juvenile Oscar. TS

Montgomery Clift *Ralph "Steve" Stevenson* • Aline MacMahon *Mrs Murray* • Wendell Corey *Jerry Fisher* • Jarmila Novotna *Mrs Hanna Malik* • Mary Patton *Mrs Fisher* • Ewart G Morrison *Mr Crookes* • William Rogers *Tom Fisher* • Ivan Jandl *Karel Malik* ■ *Dir* Fred Zinnemann • *Scr* Richard Schweizer, David Wechsler, Paul Jarrico

Search and Destroy ★★ 18

Black comedy drama 1995 · US · Colour · 87min

This hopelessly misconceived would-be black comedy was the disappointing debut feature from controversial New York visual artist David Salle. Griffin Dunne stars as a Florida film producer, his business and private life down the tubes, whose last throw of the dice is putting together a film deal with kooky TV guru Dennis Hopper. Salle has assembled a dream cast that only partially redeems this poorly directed film, which relies too heavily on its weird assortment of characters and events to sustain the thin narrative. RS Swearing, nudity, sexual references, some violence.

Griffin Dunne *Martin Mirkheim* • Illeana Douglas *Marie Davenport* • Christopher Walken *Kim Ulander* • Dennis Hopper *Dr Luther Waxling* • John Turturro *Ron* • Rosanna Arquette *Lauren Mirkheim* • Ethan Hawke *Roger* • Martin Scorsese *The accountant* ■ *Dir* David Salle • *Scr* Michael Almereyda, from the play by Howard Korder

Search for Danger ★★

Detective mystery 1949 · US · BW · 66min

The Falcon's 16th and last assignment is a double-murder mystery, with the suave sleuth in pursuit of the gambler who's left Albert Dekker and Ben Welden out of pocket to the tune of $100,000. His task is not made easier, however, by the devious distraction provided by Myrna Dell. Considering he was making his third appearance as Michael Waring, professional magician John Calvert still looks uncomfortable, and it was perhaps as well that he handed over to Charles McGraw for the ensuing TV series. DP

John Calvert *The Falcon/Michael Waring* • Albert Dekker *Kirk* • Myrna Dell *Wilma Rogers* • Ben Welden *Gregory* • Douglas Fowley *Inspector* • Michael Mark *Perry* ■ *Dir* Jack Bernhard • *Scr* Don Martin, from a story by Jerome Epstein, from the character created by Michael Arlen

The Search for John Gissing ★★★

Comedy 2001 · US · Colour · 91min

Moments of inspired situation comedy are swamped by a growing desperation to sustain the madcap momentum in this increasingly contrived office farce. Arriving in London to assume his new post, American executive Mike Binder is sabotaged at every turn by Alan Rickman, the man he's been hired to replace. Rickman's genius for teetering on the brink of excess enables him to steal the show from Binder, who is also frequently upstaged by long-suffering wife, Janeane Garofalo. Fun, but wildly inconsistent. DP

Mike Binder *Matthew Barnes* • Janeane Garofalo *Linda Barnes* • Alan Rickman *John Gissing* • Juliet Stevenson *Gwyneth Moore* ■ *Dir/Scr* Mike Binder

The Search for Signs of Intelligent Life in the Universe ★★★

Comedy drama 1991 · US · Colour · 114min

This is the filmed version of comedian-turned-movie star Lily Tomlin's hit one-woman Broadway show. The bare stage is transformed with colourful sets to reflect the history of each individual, purposely breaking the seamless stand-up illusion. All of Tomlin's familiar characters do a turn, including Lyn, who's going through a midlife crisis. It's a sustained monologue by Lyn – where all her 1960s hippy and feminist revolutionary dreams are catalogued with despair – which ends this engrossing record of Tomlin's talent. AJ

Lily Tomlin ■ *Dir* John Bailey (2) • *Scr* Jane Wagner, from her play

Search Party ★★ 15

Comedy 2014 · US · Colour · 93min

This adult comedy sees two 30-somethings race from LA to Mexico to find their missing friend. Co-writer/director Scot Armstrong, who scripted *Road Trip* and *The Hangover: Part II*, aims at the same audience with this caper that follows likeable stars TJ Miller and Adam Pally who encounter organ harvesters, the police and a psychotic drugs baron en route. Ultimately, charm is not enough to gloss over the clichéd story. JL In English, Spanish. Swearing, sexual references, drug abuse, brief nudity.

TJ Miller *Jason* • Adam Pally *Evan* • Thomas Middleditch *Nardo* • Jason Mantzoukas *The Amazing Hugo* • Krysten Ritter *Christy* • JB Smoove *Berk* ■ *Dir* Scot Armstrong • *Scr* Scot Armstrong, Mike Gagerman, Andrew Waller

The Searchers ★★★★★ U

Classic western 1956 · US · Colour · 113min

Like Monument Valley, where it was filmed, John Ford's masterpiece western of revenge and reconciliation is massive and unmissable. It touches the heart of racist darkness and cleanses itself in the process. As John Wayne's Ethan sets out to kill both the "redskin" butcher of his brother's family and the abducted niece who, in his eyes, has turned native, his five-year quest becomes a search for his own soul. Jeffrey Hunter is the conscience along for the ride, but it's the complexity of Ethan – as the antihero being redeemed – that reveals him as a rootless pioneer, forever framed in the doorways of family homesteads of which he can never become part. TH *DVD* ◁▷

John Wayne *Ethan Edwards* • Jeffrey Hunter *Martin Pawley* • Vera Miles *Laurie Jorgensen* • Ward Bond *Sam Clayton* • Natalie Wood *Debbie Edwards* • John Qualen *Lars Jorgensen* • Olive Carey *Mrs Jorgensen* • Henry Brandon *Chief Scar* • Ken Curtis *Charlie McCorry* • Harry Carey Jr *Brad Jorgensen* ■ *Dir* John Ford • *Scr* Frank S Nugent, from the novel by Alan LeMay • *Cinematographer* Winton C Hoch

Searchers 2.0 ★★★

Comedy road movie 2007 · US · Colour · 96min

Alex Cox provides some revisionist insight into the mythology of the Hollywood western in this fond, funny road movie. Making stunning use of its Midwest locations, this homage to exploitation cinema follows one-time child actors Del Zamora and Ed Pansullo as they travel to Monument Valley with the latter's spirited daughter (Jaclyn Jonet) to confront Sy Richardson, a prolific pulp screenwriter who once subjected them to a whipping on the set of a low-budget western. Full of knowing digs at contemporary political attitudes and the pedantry of film buffs, it's an offbeat delight. DP

Del Zamora *Mel Torres* • Jaclyn Jonet *Delilah Torres* • Ed Pansullo *Fred Fletcher* • Sy Richardson *Fritz Frobisher* • Alex Cox *Bob* • Leonard Maltin *Film critic* • Roger Corman *Producer* ■ *Dir/Scr* Alex Cox

Searching for Sugar Man ★★★ 12

Documentary 2011 · UK/Swe · Colour · 82min

Detroit musician Sixto Rodriguez, a Dylanesque psych-folkie with a social conscience, released two albums in the early 1970s, but he soon faded into obscurity in the US. However, as Malik Bendjelloul's intriguing mix of detective drama and fairy tale reveals, his anti-establishment songs struck a chord in Apartheid-era South Africa. Cult status, with tales of a rock 'n' roll death followed. But further digging by two South Africans revealed a different story. The story is an incredible one, but it's a shame that the man at its centre is such a vague, fleeting presence. JH Brief swearing. **DVD** **Blu**

■ *Dir* Malik Bendjelloul

The Searching Wind ★★★
Drama   1946 · US · BW · 107min

This is a high-toned - in both content and production - exploration of political and ideological issues as represented by an American career diplomat (Robert Young) of vacillating opinions. Set in the 1930s, with the spectre of war hovering over it, the screenplay was written by Lillian Hellman from her own Broadway play, and is directed with gravity by William Dieterle. It's well-played by Young and an excellent cast, but the literate material is more suited to its stage origins. RK

Robert Young (1) *Alex Hazen* • Sylvia Sidney *Cassie Bowman* • Ann Richards *Emily Hazen* • Dudley Digges *Moses* • Albert Basserman *Count Von Stammer* • Dan Seymour *Torrone* • Douglas Dick *Sam* ■ *Dir* William Dieterle • *Scr* Lillian Hellman, from her play

The Seashell and the Clergyman ★★★★
Silent experimental classic
1928 · Fr · BW · 29min

Although dismissed by the Surrealist group at the time, this is generally accepted as the first Surrealist film. The cryptic scenario was written by Antonin Artaud, but the avant-garde theorist, writer and actor, who had intended to direct it and play the lead, later repudiated it - perhaps because it was directed by a woman. Germaine Dulac brought her technical skill to bear on the plotless film which shows, by automatic association, the dreams of a frustrated and celibate clergyman. This is an interesting, but fruitless attempt at "pure cinema", free from the influence of literature, the theatre and other visual arts. RB

Alex Allin *The clergyman* • Génica Athanasiou *The woman* ■ *Dir* Germaine Dulac • *Scr* Antonin Artaud

Season of Dreams ★ PG
Drama   1987 · US · Colour · 90min

This disappointing coming-of-age drama milks the golden hues of rural America for all their worth but sinks under an uninvolving script. Megan Follows plays the troubled young teenager, but not even the presence of such charismatic performers as Christine Lahti, Frederic Forrest, Jason Gedrick and Peter Coyote can rescue this dud. JF Swearing.

Christine Lahti *Kathleen Morgan* • Frederic Forrest *Buster McGuire* • Megan Follows *Anna Mae Morgan* • Jason Gedrick *Gary Connaloe* • Peter Coyote *Photographer* ■ *Dir* Martin Rosen • *Scr* Victoria Jenkins

Season of Passion ★★★
Romantic drama   1960 · Aus · BW · 94min

This willing Australian melodrama slowly creeps under the skin thanks to the fascinating contrasts in the acting styles of its star quartet. John Mills and Ernest Borgnine are cleverly cast as chalk-and-cheese sugar cane cutters in Sydney for their annual holiday, while Anne Baxter and Angela Lansbury are their feisty sheilas who refuse to tolerate their rough-and-ready notions of romance any longer. Director Leslie Norman showcases the performances, but occasionally lets the authentic Aussie atmosphere slip. DP

Ernest Borgnine *Roo* • John Mills *Barney* • Anne Baxter *Olive* • Angela Lansbury *Pearl* • Vincent Ball *Dowd* • Ethel Gabriel *Emma* • Janette Craig *Bubba* ■ *Dir* Leslie Norman • *Scr* John Dighton, from the play *Summer of the Seventeenth Doll* by Ray Lawler

Season of the Witch ★★ 18
Horror   1972 · US · Colour · 104min

Between his classic *Night of the Living Dead* and its sequel, *Dawn of the Dead*, cult director George A Romero experimented with feminist fright in this tedious horror, in which bored suburban housewife Jan White dabbles in black magic, casting a spell that will lead to murder. Apart from some mildly interesting dream sequences, this dated and slow psychological study is unexcitingly presented and for Romero completists only. AJ

Jan White *Joan* • Ray Laine *Gregg* • Ann Muffly *Shirley* • Joedda McClain *Nikki* • Bill Thunhurst *Jack* • Virginia Greenwald *Marion* ■ *Dir/Scr* George A Romero

Season of the Witch ★★ 15
Period action horror   2010 · US · Colour · 90min

Director Dominic Sena's muddled medieval drama can't decide whether it's a supernatural action movie or a dark demonic horror. Crusaders-with-a-conscience Nicolas Cage and Ron Perlman return home from a lengthy quest to find Europe in the grip of the Black Death. They are then charged by a pustule-faced cardinal (Christopher Lee) to transport a witch (Claire Foy) to a remote monastery where an ancient ritual will hopefully end the plague. While the embattled knights face many dangers en route, none creates much excitement or empathy. Despite some terrific locations, this ho-hum 14th-century history lesson remains routine and unconvincing right through to its all-hell-breaks-loose CGI-heavy finale. AJ Violence. **DVD** **Blu**

Nicolas Cage *Behmen* • Ron Perlman *Felson* • Stephen Campbell Moore *Debelzaq* • Claire Foy *The Girl* • Stephen Graham *Hagamar* • Ulrich Thomsen *Eckhart* • Robert Sheehan *Kay* • Christopher Lee *Cardinal D'Ambroise* ■ *Dir* Dominic Sena • *Scr* Bragi Schut

The Seasoning House ★★★★ 18
Horror thriller   2012 · UK · Colour · 89min

British special make-up/prosthetics genius Paul Hyett (*The Descent, The Woman in Black*) makes his directorial debut with this economically savvy and highly effective suspense shocker. In a makeshift Balkan brothel, deaf mute Angel (a dazzling Rosie Day) cares for the drugged sex slaves coerced into satisfying the needs of mercenaries on leave. When the men responsible for slaughtering her entire family arrive to indulge their twisted appetites, Angel takes brutal revenge. The horror is harrowing, the splatter murders startling and the claustrophobia strongly evoked. Sean Pertwee and Kevin Howarth make great villains, and look out for a cameo by *The Descent* director Neil Marshall. AJ Violence, swearing, drug abuse. **DVD** **Blu**

Rosie Day *Angel* • Sean Pertwee *Goran* • Kevin Howarth *Viktor* • Anna Walton *Violeta* • Jemma Powell *Alexa* • David Lemberg *Dimitri* ■ *Dir* Paul Hyett • *Scr* Paul Hyett, Conal Palmer, Adrian Rigelsford, from an idea by Helen Solomon

Seasons of the Heart ★★
Drama   1994 · US · Colour · 120min

It's such a shame that mainstream Hollywood is so ageist, as Carol Burnett, George Segal and Malcolm McDowell demonstrate here what they might do if they were offered a good story. Unfortunately, this is nothing more than a sentimental melodrama, in which Burnett's self-absorbed book publisher is forced to reappraise her priorities when she has to care for her young grandson. Still, director Lee Grant does manage some credible moments of moving intimacy. DP

Carol Burnett *Vivian Levinson* • George Segal *Ezra Goldstine* • Malcolm McDowell *Alfred McGuinnis* • Eric Lloyd *David* • Jill Teed *Ellen* ■ *Dir* Lee Grant • *Scr* Robbyn Burger

Sebastian ★★★
Comedy thriller   1968 · UK · Colour · 99min

This semi-spoof of Swinging Sixties spy stories ends up packing so much plot into the final third that its careful characterisation and smart satire go out of the window. The tensions within John Gielgud's eavesdropping unit are far more intriguing than spymaster Ronald Fraser's attempts to compromise codebuster Dirk Bogarde, and the cast seems more at ease with the knowing humour and hushed tones of this opening segment than it does with the blaring muzak and trippy dreams of the finale. DP

Dirk Bogarde *Sebastian* • Susannah York *Becky Howard* • Lilli Palmer *Elsa Shahn* • John Gielgud *Head of Intelligence* • Janet Munro *Carol* • Margaret Johnston *Miss Elliott* • Nigel Davenport *General Phillips* • Ronald Fraser *Toby* • Donald Sutherland *American* • Alan Freeman *TV disc jockey* ■ *Dir* David Greene • *Scr* Gerald Vaughan-Hughes, from a story by Leo Marks • *Music* Jerry Goldsmith

Sebastiane ★★ 18
Historical drama   1976 · UK · Colour · 81min

Sebastiane was a favourite at the court of Roman Emperor Diocletian and Derek Jarman's explicit biopic details his death at the hands of fellow soldiers while in naked exile. Shot on a semi-improvisational basis, with a largely non-professional cast, Jarman explores with frank honesty why Renaissance artists found this gay hero to be the perfect vehicle to depict homoeroticism in their paintings. A must for gay viewers, but others may find it rather a hard slog. AJ Latin +subtitles.

Leonardo Treviglio *Sebastiane* • Barney James *Severus* • Neil Kennedy *Max* • Richard Warwick *Justin* • Donald Dunham *Claudius* • Ken Hicks *Adrian* ■ *Dir* Derek Jarman, Paul Humfress • *Scr* Derek Jarman, James Waley, Jack Welch (Latin translation)

Second Best ★★★ 12
Drama   1993 · US · Colour · 100min

This largely overlooked drama perfectly illustrates the genius for restraint that is the basis of William Hurt's acting talent. As the shy Welsh postmaster who decides to adopt a son, he brilliantly exposes the mixed emotions of a lonely, self-contained 40-something trying to break with the habits of a lifetime and start anew. Director Chris Menges nearly loses control in the scenes featuring Miles's disturbed dad, Keith Allen, but mostly gets the tone right. DP Some violence, swearing

William Hurt *Graham* • John Hurt *Uncle Turpin* • Chris Cleary Miles *James* • Nathan Yapp *Jimmy* • Keith Allen *John* • Jane Horrocks *Debbie* • Prunella Scales *Margery* ■ *Dir* Chris Menges • *Scr* David Cook, from his novel

The Second Best Exotic Marigold Hotel ★★★★ PG
Comedy drama   2015 · US/UK · Colour · 117min

Another irresistible swirl of heart-warming life lessons, funny valentines and intoxicating local Indian colour, this captivating sequel is a worthy companion piece to the 2011 crowd-pleaser. Here, Dev Patel's dreams of expansion get in the way of his marriage plans while the cream of British acting aristocracy (Bill Nighy, Maggie Smith, Judi Dench) navigate their own romantic complications with effortless chemistry. Newcomers Richard Gere and Tamsin Greig add their own brand of infectious charm to the winning formula, but returning director John Madden and writer Ol Parker make sure not to rock the mature fairy tale boat. AJ **DVD** **Blu**

Judi Dench *Evelyn Greenslade* • Maggie Smith *Muriel Donnelly* • Bill Nighy *Douglas Ainslie* • Richard Gere *Guy* • Celia Imrie *Madge Hardcastle* • Penelope Wilton *Jean Ainslie* • Dev Patel *Sonny Kapoor* • Tamsin Greig *Lavinia* ■ *Dir* John Madden • *Scr* Ol Parker

Second Chance ★★★
Romantic crime drama
1953 · US · Colour · 82min

Originally shown in 3D, this relies on the potency of its star power, as laconic boxer Robert Mitchum falls for lovely gangster's moll Linda Darnell, who is on the run from killer Jack Palance. Director Rudolph Maté keeps this moving along, and the Mexican scenery is striking. This is very much a product of RKO under its new boss Howard Hughes, featuring good-looking stars in exotic locations. TS **3D**

Robert Mitchum *Russ Lambert* • Linda Darnell *Clare Shepperd* • Jack Palance *Cappy Gordon* ■ *Dir* Rudolph Maté • *Scr* Oscar Millard, Sydney Boehm, DM Marshman Jr, from a story by DM Marshman Jr

Second Chance ★★★
Drama   1976 · Fr · Colour · 99min

Charged as an accessory to murder, a young woman gives birth to a baby while in prison. Freed many years later, she is reunited with her teenage son, who falls in love with her friend from prison, while she herself finds happiness with the boy's teacher. This glossy, glamorised and superficial melodrama was written and directed by Claude Lelouch, and is undemanding viewing for the romantically minded. RK French +subtitles.

Catherine Deneuve *Catherine Berger* • Anouk Aimée *Sarah Gordon* • Charles Denner *Lawyer* • Francis Huster *Patrick* • Niels Arestrup *Henri Lano* • Colette Baudot *Lucienne Lano* • Jean-Jacques Briot *Simon Berger* ■ *Dir/Scr* Claude Lelouch • *Music* Francis Lai

A Second Chance ★★★ 15
Drama   2014 · Den · Colour · 101min

Game of Thrones star Nikolaj Coster-Waldau is the saving grace of this Danish melodrama, playing a policeman who feels forced to act when he claps eyes on a badly neglected baby. Director and genre specialist Susanne Bier (*Open Hearts*) resorts to awkward early plot machinations, perhaps as a necessary contrivance to cue questions that provide the meat and bones of the story. And the second half of the film is certainly thought-provoking and tense, as the kidnapper is enlisted to investigate his own crime. SP Danish, Swedish +subtitles. Violence, swearing, drug abuse.

Nikolaj Coster-Waldau *Andreas* • Maria Bonnevie *Anna* • Ulrich Thomsen *Simon* • Nikolaj Lie Kaas *Tristan* • Lykke May Andersen *Sanne* • Thomas Bo Larsen *Klaus* ■ *Dir* Susanne Bier • *Scr* Anders Thomas Jensen

Second Chorus ★★★ U
Musical comedy   1940 · US · BW · 81min

Playing an undergraduate at the age of 41, Fred Astaire considered this the worst film he ever made. But an off-form Fred is still worth watching, even though his dancing style is undeniably cramped by Paulette Goddard, who is the subject of his romantic rivalry with Burgess Meredith. Goddard (then Mrs Charlie Chaplin) married Meredith in 1942. Artie Shaw earned an Oscar nomination for best score and shared another with Johnny Mercer for the song *Love of My Life*. DP **DVD**

Fred Astaire *Danny O'Neill* • Paulette Goddard *Ellen Miller* • Burgess Meredith *Hank Taylor* • Charles Butterworth *Mr Chisholm* • Frank Melton *Stu* ■ *Dir* HC Potter • *Scr* Frank Cavett, Elaine Ryan, Johnny Mercer, Ian McLellan Hunter, from a story by Frank Cavett

Second Coming ★★★★ 15
Drama   2014 · UK · Colour · 100min

This homegrown drama charts the simmering tensions in a suburban household, where wife and mother Nadine Marshall is keeping her pregnancy secret, because sexual relations have long since cooled with husband Idris Elba. But if he's not the father, who is? The title certainly drops a hint, but playwright Debbie Tucker Green's first feature eschews a Christian interpretation of these confounding events, preferring to unfold a story where the everyday and the spiritual are entwined. The events are slightly too drawn-out, and Marshall's guarded protagonist is less appealing than Elba's loving yet tormented hubby, but overall this is a British film of rare ambition and imagination. TJ Swearing. **DVD**

Nadine Marshall *Jackie* • Idris Elba *Mark* • Kai Francis-Lewis *JJ* • Sharlene Whyte *Bernie* • Llewella Gideon *Jackie's mum* • Larrington Walker *Jackie's dad* ■ *Dir/Scr* Debbie Tucker Green

S

The Second Coming of Suzanne ★ 15

Fantasy drama 1974 · US · Colour · 85min

In this pretentious blip in his early career, Richard Dreyfuss plays a frustrated film-maker obsessed with the idea that Christ was a woman. He tries to film his vision, with Sondra Locke as the sex-swapped Messiah. The film was reportedly inspired by the lyrics of the Leonard Cohen song, *Suzanne*, which features on the soundtrack. It's every bit as bad as it sounds. DA *DVD*

Sondra Locke *Suzanne* • Paul Sand *Artist* • Jared Martin *Film-maker* • Richard Dreyfuss *Clavius* • Gene Barry *TV commentator* ■ *Dir/Scr* Michael Barry

Second Fiddle ★★★ U

Musical comedy 1939 · US · BW · 86min

You'd be forgiven if you couldn't tell one Sonja Henie vehicle from the next, but this is the one with the Irving Berlin score, where Tyrone Power plays the Hollywoodite who starts off promoting a romance for La Henie, but ends up falling for her himself. The 20th Century-Fox production values are all high gloss, and the ever-professional director Sidney Lanfield keeps the fluffy proceedings running smoothly. Also on hand, for nostalgia buffs, are the delightful Rudy Vallee and Edna May Oliver. TS

Sonja Henie *Trudi Hovland* • Tyrone Power *Jimmy Sutton* • Rudy Vallee *Roger Maxwell* • Edna May Oliver *Aunt Phoebe Hovland* • Mary Healy *Jean Varick* • Lyle Talbot *Willie Hogger* • Alan Dinehart *George "Whit" Whitney* ■ *Dir* Sidney Lanfield • *Scr* Harry Tugend, from a story by George Bradshaw • *Music/lyrics* Irving Berlin

Second Generation ★★ 15

Comedy thriller 1999 · UK · Colour · 80min

Shot on digital video amid the disparate Asian communities of London's East End, Shane O'Sullivan's ambitious feature is a misfiring comedy thriller which suffers from an uncertainty of tone and some amateur-dramatics acting. Shigetomo Yutani and pop star Hanayo are more willing than able as the hapless Japanese detective and the runaway Hong Kong bride he's sent to track down. But, at least there's an honesty about their work that is surprisingly lacking from Saeed Jaffrey's pantomimic turn. DP English, Hindi, Japanese +subtitles.

Hanayo *Lili* • Shigetomo Yutani *Go* • Nitin Chandra Ganatra *Jamal* • Adrian Pang *Jimmy* • Saeed Jaffrey *Saeed Mian* ■ *Dir/Scr* Shane O'Sullivan

Second in Command ★★ 15

Action thriller 2006 · US/Rom · Colour · 87min

The Muscles from Brussels heads to the Balkans in this lean siege thriller about a group of US personnel trapped inside an embassy during a Communist coup. Former kick-boxing champ Jean-Claude Van Damme is getting a bit too old for the high-kicks that made him famous, so resorts to plenty of gunplay as his ex-SEAL leads an outnumbered band of US marines. It's heavy on tension and internal division and director Simon Fellows keeps the pacing brisk and the bullets flying, but the martial artist's acting is as wooden as ever. JR *DVD*

Jean-Claude Van Damme *Sam Keenan* • Julie Cox *Michelle Whitman* • William Tapley *Frank Gaines* • Alan Mckenna [Alan McKenna] *Captain John Baldwin* • Razaaq Adoti *G Sgt Earl "Gunny" Darnell* • Velibor Topic *Anton Tavarov* ■ *Dir* Simon Fellows • *Scr* Jonathan Bowers, David Corley, Jayson Rothwell, from a story by Bowers, Corley, Milt Bearden

The Second Jungle Book ★★ PG

Adventure 1997 · US · Colour · 85min

Loosely based on the Rudyard Kipling original, and most definitely nothing to do with Disney, this live-action family film has jungle boy Mowgli and bear-friend Baloo driven deep into the interior by the unwanted attentions of a talent scout for PT Barnum's circus. There, they stumble on a lost city whose sole inhabitant is deranged British soldier Roddy McDowall. This offers some fun for kids, but the animal sequences look like they've been spliced in from another film altogether. DA *DVD*

Jamie Williams *Mowgli* • William Campbell [Bill Campbell] *Harrison* • Roddy McDowall *King Murphy* • David Paul Francis *Chuchundra* • Dyrk Ashton *Karait* • Cornelia Hayes O'Herlihy *Emily Reece* ■ *Dir* Duncan McLachlan • *Scr* Matthew Horton, Bayard Johnson, from the books by Rudyard Kipling

Second Serve ★★★★ 15

Biographical drama 1986 · US · Colour · 90min

On paper it has all the signs of a tacky hagiography, but a towering performance from Vanessa Redgrave and a taut, insightful script make this a TV movie of unusual depth and sensitivity. The true story of transsexual surgeon-turned-tennis star Renee Richards is adapted by director Anthony Page into an intriguing, multilayered look at the agonies and resourcefulness of a truly extraordinary personality. Redgrave plays both Richards's male and female personae wonderfully. SH

Vanessa Redgrave *Richard Radley/Renee Richards* • Martin Balsam *Dr Stone* • William Russ *Josh* • Alice Krige *Gwen* • Kerrie Keane *Meriam* ■ *Dir* Anthony Page • *Scr* Stephanie Liss, Gavin Lambert, from the autobiography by Renee Richards, John Ames

Second Skin ★★★ 18

Romantic drama 2000 · Sp · Colour · 104min

The evergreen eternal triangle plot is given a modern twist in director Gerardo Vera's absurdly gripping Spanish melodrama. Jordi Molla is apparently happily married to Ariadna Gil, but his discovery of a hotel bill in his pocket leads to accusations of an affair with another woman. The truth is, he's having a relationship with another man, Javier Bardem. That's really the starting point for Vera's study in fluctuating sexuality, as Molla struggles to come to terms with his double life and Gil with the reality of her failed marriage. AJ Spanish +subtitles. Swearing, sex scenes.

Javier Bardem *Diego* • Jordi Mollà *Alberto Garcia* • Ariadna Gil *Elena* • Cecilia Roth *Eva* • Javier Albala *Rafael* • Adrian Sac *Manuel* ■ *Dir* Gerardo Vera • *Scr* Angeles Gonzalez-Sinde, from an idea by Gerardo Vera

The Second Time Around ★★ U

Comedy western 1961 · US · Colour · 98min

Debbie Reynolds stars as a young widow from the east who moves to an Arizona frontier town to start life afresh. Unfazed by the culture shock, she labours in the mud as a humble ranch-hand (for the always admirable Thelma Ritter) before becoming sheriff and ridding the town of its lawless elements. The spirited Reynolds is the attraction of this innocuous but pleasant movie, which can't decide whether it's a western, a comedy, a romance or a drama. RK

Debbie Reynolds *Lucretia Rogers* • Steve Forrest *Dan Jones* • Andy Griffith *Pat Collins* • Juliet Prowse *Rena* • Thelma Ritter *Aggie* • Ken Scott (1) *Sheriff John Yoss* • Isobel Elsom *Mrs Rogers* ■ *Dir* Vincent Sherman • *Scr* Oscar Saul, Cecil Dan Hansen, from the novel *Star in the West* by Richard Emery Roberts

The Second Victory ★★ 15

Period action drama 1986 · UK · Colour · 98min

Adapted from his own novel by Morris West, this drama is set in Austria shortly after the Second World War. Anthony Andrews is the bold soldier in pursuit of the sniper who shot and killed his sergeant. From there on in, it's strictly action fare, with Andrews looking ill-at-ease, having to tote a gun and look vengeful at the same time. Nice scenery, though. JB

Anthony Andrews *Major Hanlon* • Max von Sydow *Dr Huber* • Helmut Griem *Karl Fischer* • Mario Adorf *Dr Sepp Kunzli* • Birgit Doll *Anna Kunzli* • Wolfgang Reichmann *Max Holzinger* • Renée Soutendijk *Traudi Holzinger* • Immy Schell *Liesl Holzinger* ■ *Dir* Gerald Thomas • *Scr* Morris West, from his novel

The Second Woman ★★

Thriller 1951 · US · BW · 91min

This minor melodrama explains why Robert Young's architect suffers from blackouts and memory loss and is driven to attempt suicide. More usually it's a female who is being victimised in the psychological thrillers of this period, but here it's girlfriend Betsy Drake who exposes the villain who is out to deprive Young of his sanity. The best feature is the photography by Hal Mohr, which aims at a *film noir* moodiness. AE

Robert Young (1) *Jeff Cohalan* • Betsy Drake *Ellen Foster* • John Sutton *Keith Ferris* • Henry O'Neill *Ben Sheppard* • Florence Bates *Amelia Foster* • Morris Carnovsky *Dr Hartley* ■ *Dir* James V Kern • *Scr* Robert Smith, Mort Briskin

Secondhand Lions ★★★ 12

Period comedy drama 2003 · US · Colour · 104min

Haley Joel Osment plays a teenager who is sent to stay with his yarn-spinning great-uncles (Michael Caine and Robert Duvall), two cranky old men who, rumour has it, have a legendary stash of loot hidden on their remote Texas homestead. Caine and Duvall succeed in creating a sense of mystery and mischief, but this is unfortunately dissipated each time director Tim McCanlies flashes back to their all-action past. The comedy is corny and the suspense is rarely sustained, but this is still good fun. DP Violence. *DVD*

Michael Caine *Garth McCann* • Robert Duvall *Hubbard "Hub" McCann* • Haley Joel Osment *Walter* • Kyra Sedgwick *Mae* • Nicky Katt *Stan* • Emmanuelle Vaugier *Princess Jasmine* • Christian Kane *Young Hub* • Kevin Haberer *Young Garth* ■ *Dir/Scr* Tim McCanlies

Seconds ★★★★

Cult science-fiction thriller 1966 · US · BW · 105min

Dealing with the uncomfortable subject of spiritual rebirth, this brilliant social science-fiction movie from seminal director John Frankenheimer was years ahead of its time in both theme and style. The frightening premise is intensified by cameraman James Wong Howe's use of stark black-and-white photography and distorting fish-eye lenses. Underrated star Rock Hudson gives one of his best performances as the deeply disturbed recipient of life-changing plastic surgery that gives him a new, younger body. TS *DVD* *Blu*

Rock Hudson *Antiochus "Tony" Wilson* • Salome Jens *Nora Marcus* • John Randolph *Arthur Hamilton* • Will Geer *Old man* • Jeff Corey *Mr Ruby* • Richard Anderson *Dr Innes* ■ *Dir* John Frankenheimer • *Scr* Lewis John Carlino, from the novel by David Ely

Le Secret ★★★ 18

Drama 2000 · Fr · Colour · 104min

Having co-scripted Erick Zonca's acclaimed drama, *The Dream Life of Angels*, Virginie Wagon reunited with the talented Frenchman for her directorial debut. Anne Coësens is creditably vulnerable as the married encyclopedia saleswoman who disregards husband Michel Bompoil's suggestion of a second child to indulge in a fling with American dancer Tony Todd. A caustic wit complements the psychological intensity and graphic sexuality in this very adult film, and only the cosy ending feels forced. DP French, English +subtitles.

Anne Coësens *Marie* • Michel Bompoil *François* • Tony Todd *Bill* • Quentin Rossi *Paul* ■ *Dir* Virginie Wagon • *Scr* Virginie Wagon, Erick Zonca

A Secret ★★★★ 15

Drama 2007 · Fr/Ger · Colour and BW · 102min

Claude Miller's tightly controlled adaptation of Philippe Grimbert's fact-based novel follows the events that shaped a Jewish family's destiny over five decades. Opening in Paris in 1985, the story cuts from adult François (Mathieu Amalric) as he searches for his missing father to the 1950s as the sickly young François (Valentin Vigourt) tries to cope with disappointing parents (Patrick Bruel and Cécile de France). The action then moves to the 1930s, when Bruel became obsessed with his statuesque sister-in-law on the day he married homebody Ludivine Sagnier. Superbly played by a fine ensemble cast, this is both a tense historical thriller and a melodrama about an illicit romance, with the period detail reinforcing the sense of shifting morality wrought by the Nazi occupation of France and the indelible legacy of the Holocaust. DP In French. *DVD*

Cécile de France *Tania* • Patrick Bruel *Maxime Nathan Grinberg* • Ludivine Sagnier *Hannah Golda Sim Grinberg* • Julie Depardieu *Louise* • Mathieu Amalric *François Grimbert, aged 37* • Yves Verhoeven *Guillaume* • Yves Jacques *Le Commandant Béraud* • Valentin Vigourt *François Grimbert, aged 14* ■ *Dir* Claude Miller • *Scr* Claude Miller, from the novel by Philippe Grimbert

Secret Admirer ★ 15

Comedy 1985 · US · Colour · 93min

An unsigned love letter leads the unwary into a repulsive comedy of errors that verges on the insulting to both teenagers and adults alike. Fred Ward and Dee Wallace Stone do what they can as the parents and C Thomas Howell and Lori Loughlin try to elevate it above the level of farcical teen-sex comedy but ultimately fail. FL

C Thomas Howell *Michael Ryan* • Lori Loughlin *Toni* • Kelly Preston *Deborah Anne Fimple* • Dee Wallace Stone *Connie Ryan* • Cliff De Young *George Ryan* • Fred Ward *Lou Fimple* • Leigh Taylor-Young *Elizabeth Fimple* • Casey Siemaszko *Roger Despard* ■ *Dir* David Greenwalt • *Scr* Jim Kouf, David Greenwalt

The Secret Adventures of Tom Thumb ★★ 12

Animated fantasy 1993 · UK · Colour · 57min

You won't be taking the kids to this adult animated version of the Grimm tale. Into a surreal landscape of mutants and insects is born poor Tom. His parents fail to protect him from kidnappers who conduct a series of bizarre medical experiments on our hero. Escaping, Tom befriends a giant who inadvertently kills him, releasing him into an afterlife that is not harps, clouds and angels. Director Dave Borthwick's ten-minute short has been expanded into a full length feature but not everyone will enjoy his nightmarish vision. LH

Nick Upton *Pa Thumb* • Deborah Collard *Ma Thumb* • Frank Passingham *Man/Giant* • John Schofield *Man/Giant* ■ *Dir/Scr* Dave Borthwick

A Secret Affair ★★ 12

Romantic drama 1999 · US · Colour · 84min

Arriving in Venice on business, bride-to-be Janine Turner falls under the city's spell in this mediocre romantic TV drama. There's nothing new in the voyage of self-discovery that Turner's would-be artist takes after meeting Paudge Behan's Irish TV reporter. Director Bobby Roth leaves a talented supporting cast fumbling in the background. DP *DVD*

Janine Turner *Vanessa Stewart* • Paudge Behan *Bill Fitzgerald* • Fionnula Flanagan *Drucilla Fitzgerald* • Robert Mailhouse *Stephen Rocken* • Gia Carides *Mimi* ■ *Dir* Bobby Roth • *Scr* Carole Real, from the novel by Barbara Taylor Bradford

Secret Agent ★★★★ U

Spy thriller 1936 · UK · BW · 82min

John Gielgud might not be everyone's ideal Hitchcock hero, and critics were quick to point out his lack of derring-do, but he acquits himself admirably in this engaging thriller. A script based on a play that was itself adapted from a clutch of Somerset Maugham's *Ashenden* stories was bound to have more than its fair share of loose ends, but such is the committed playing, and the director's genius for generating suspense out of ordinary situations and locations, that they scarcely seem to matter. DP *DVD*

John Gielgud *Edgar Brodie/Richard Ashenden* • Madeleine Carroll *Elsa Carrington* • Peter Lorre *The General* • Robert Young (1) *Robert Marvin* • Percy Marmont *Caypor* • Florence Kahn *Mrs Caypor* • Lilli Palmer *Lilli* ■ *Dir* Alfred Hitchcock • *Scr* Charles Bennett, Ian Hay, Jesse Lasky Jr,

Alma Reville, from the play by Campbell Dixon, from the *Ashender* stories by W Somerset Maugham

The Secret Agent ★★12
Period spy thriller
1996 · US/UK · Colour · 90min

This slow-moving adaptation of Joseph Conrad's spy tale stars Bob Hoskins as an anarchist living in London at the end of the 19th century who becomes involved in a terrorist attack on the Greenwich Observatory. There's a good performance from Patricia Arquette and an accomplished supporting cast, but Christopher Hampton adheres too slavishly to Conrad's text and the film never really gets off the ground. JB Swearing, violence.

Bob Hoskins *Adolph Verloc* · Patricia Arquette *Winnie Verloc* · Gérard Depardieu *Tom "Alexander" Ossipon* · Jim Broadbent *Chief Inspector Heat* · Christian Bale *Stevie Verloc* · Eddie Izzard *Vladimir* · Elizabeth Spriggs *Winnie's mother* · Peter Vaughan *The driver* · Robin Williams *The professor* ■ *Dir* Christopher Hampton · *Scr* Christopher Hampton, from the novel by Joseph Conrad

The Secret Agent Club ★PG
Action comedy
1995 · US · Colour · 86min

Secret agent Hulk Hogan is kidnapped by arms dealers and spends most of the movie under sedation. His young son gets his friends to help track him down, dodging bullets and killers while having a jolly good time. Reprehensible for its attitude towards violence while children are present, this also contains blatant racist stereotypes. It's a pity the audience couldn't be as unconscious as Hogan was throughout this travesty. KB *DVD*

Hulk Hogan *Ray* · Lesley-Anne Down *Eve* · Barry Bostwick *Vincent Scarletti* · Mathew McCurley *Jeremy* · Edward Albert *Max* · Richard Moll *Wrecks* · Lyman Ward *SHADOW General* · Jack Nance *Doc* ■ *Dir* John Murlowski · *Scr* Rory Johnston

Secret Ballot ★★★★U
Satirical comedy
2001 · It/Iran/Can/Swi/Neth · Colour · 100min

Arriving on an isolated Iranian island, the zealous, chador-clad Nassim Abdi is ferried around by sceptical soldier Cyrus Abidi in a bid to persuade locals to vote in a presidential election. Exploring everything from military inertia and rural ignorance to political idealism and the changing role of women, this is a deliciously absurdist satire on a country where remoteness and indifference are as much a hindrance to reform as doctrine and tradition. Babak Payami reinforces his gently mocking message through the cautious byplay between his non-professional leads. DP Farsi +subtitles. *DVD*

Nassim Abdi *Girl* · Cyrus Abidi *Soldier* ■ *Dir* Babak Payami · *Scr* Babek Payami, inspired by the short film *Testing Democracy* by Mohsen Makhmalbaf

Secret beyond the Door ★★PG
Thriller melodrama
1948 · US · BW · 94min

A woman marries an architect whose house contains his painstaking re-creations of rooms in which brutal murders were committed. Furthermore, there's a first wife she never knew about and a jealous secretary. Director Fritz Lang's third collaboration with Joan Bennett, this is visually accomplished, but Michael Redgrave lacks any romantic appeal as the architect. The complicated flashback structure and a climax that combines lurid melodrama with Freudian explanations make this heavy going and pretentious. AE *DVD*

Joan Bennett *Celia Lamphere* · Michael Redgrave *Mark Lamphere* · Anne Revere *Caroline Lamphere* · Barbara O'Neil *Miss Robey* · Natalie Schafer *Edith Potter* · Paul Cavanagh *Rick Barrett* ■ *Dir* Fritz Lang · *Scr* Silvia Richards, from the story *Museum Piece No.13* by Rufus King

The Secret Bride ★
Political drama
1934 · US · BW · 76min

Attorney general Warren William and governor's daughter Barbara Stanwyck marry in secret but, about to break the happy news to her father, they learn that he is to be impeached for taking a bribe. A nonsensical farrago involving political corruption, murder and a frame-up, typical of the kind of rubbish the peerless Stanwyck was so often forced to endure. Even she can't rise above the comically bad dialogue. RK

Barbara Stanwyck *Ruth Vincent* · Warren William *Robert Sheldon* · Glenda Farrell *Hazel Normandie* · Grant Mitchell *Willie Martin* · Arthur Byron *Gov Vincent* · Henry O'Neill *Jim Lansdale* · Douglass Dumbrille *Dave Bredeen* ■ *Dir* William Dieterle · *Scr* Tom Buckingham, F Hugh Herbert, Mary McCall Jr, from a play by Leonard Ide

Secret Ceremony ★★15
Drama
1968 · UK/US · Colour · 104min

This moody mistaken-identity melodrama quickly becomes a macabre muddle of daft sexual psychosis and suspect psychology when nympho Mia Farrow adopts prostitute Elizabeth Taylor as her surrogate mother after a meeting on a London bus. The return of Farrow's stepfather Robert Mitchum provides this meandering morsel of Swinging Sixties gothic with a suitably off-the-wall climax. Bitter, twisted and pretentious. AJ *DVD*

Elizabeth Taylor *Leonora* · Mia Farrow *Cenci* · Robert Mitchum *Albert* · Peggy Ashcroft *Hannah* · Pamela Brown *Hilda* · Michael Strong *Dr Walter Stevens* · Robert Douglas *Sir Alex Gordon* ■ *Dir* Joseph Losey · *Scr* George Tabori, from the short story *Ceremonia Secreta* by Marco Denevi

Secret Command ★★
Second World War spy drama
1944 · US · BW · 81min

Pat O'Brien is a naval intelligence agent who goes undercover to prevent a Nazi sabotage operation. Chester Morris runs the shipyard under threat, and since he happens to be O'Brien's brother, he's understandably bewildered by O'Brien's sudden arrival with a wife and two children in tow. In fact, the FBI have drafted in another agent, Carole Landis, to play O'Brien's imaginary wife. You can guess what happens to them in between all the fist fights and propaganda. AT

Pat O'Brien *Sam Gallagher* · Carole Landis *Jill McCann* · Chester Morris *Jeff Gallagher* · Ruth Warrick *Lea Damaron* · Barton MacLane *Red Kelly* · Tom Tully *Brownell* · Wallace Ford *Miller* ■ *Dir* A Edward Sutherland · *Scr* Roy Chanslor, from the story *The Saboteurs* by John Hawkins, Ward Hawkins

Secret Defense ★★★PG
Mystery drama
1997 · Fr/Swi/It · Colour · 166min

Jacques Rivette continues his career-long preoccupation with the nature of real-screen time and the concept of plot as conspiracy in this surely, but still intriguing anti-thriller. Investigating the murder of her father, scientist Sandrine Bonnaire becomes embroiled in a cover-up of her own after an accidental shooting. With a subplot involving the mysterious death of Bonnaire's sister (Laure Marsac, who also plays the woman Bonnaire kills), this is more a study of motives, methods and responses than a tension-packed nail-biter, but it still exercises a slow-burning fascination. DP French +subtitles. Violence, swearing. *DVD*

Sandrine Bonnaire *Sylvie Rousseau* · Jerzy Radziwilowicz *Walser* · Laure Marsac *Véronique Lukachevski/Ludivine Lukachevski* · Grégoire Colin *Paul Rousseau* ■ *Dir* Jacques Rivette · *Scr* Jacques Rivette, Pascal Bonitzer, Emmanuelle Cuau

Secret Friends ★★★15
Fantasy drama
1991 · UK/US · Colour · 93min

Dennis Potter was one of Britain's greatest TV playwrights, but this directorial debut – an adaptation of his novel, *Ticket to Ride* – is an embittered mess about sex and the violent impulses that drive his hero Alan Bates to amnesia and beyond, with Gina Bellman as the sexual catalyst. Compelling enough, but the love-making is sleazy and the intercutting flashbacks make an already muddled narrative even more murky. TH

Alan Bates *John* · Gina Bellman *Helen* · Frances Barber *Angela* · Tony Doyle *Martin* · Joanna David *Kate* · Colin Jeavons *Vicar* ■ *Dir* Dennis Potter · *Scr* Dennis Potter, from his novel *Ticket to Ride*

The Secret Garden ★★★U
Drama
1949 · US · BW and Colour · 88min

This solid adaptation of Frances Hodgson Burnett's delightful children's classic is mounted on a lavish scale. Margaret O'Brien makes a spirited Mary Lennox, the orphan whose mischievous optimism brightens up life at her morbid uncle's mansion, and Elsa Lanchester is typically splendid as the kindly maid. Unfortunately, Gladys Cooper overdoes the tyranny as the housekeeper and Herbert Marshall is a damp squib as the uncle. DP

Margaret O'Brien *Mary Lennox* · Herbert Marshall *Archibald Craven* · Dean Stockwell *Colin Craven* · Gladys Cooper *Mrs Medlock* · Elsa Lanchester *Martha* · Brian Roper *Dickon* · Reginald Owen *Ben Weatherstaff* ■ *Dir* Fred M Wilcox · *Scr* Robert Ardrey, from the novel by Frances Hodgson Burnett

The Secret Garden ★★★
Drama
1987 · US · Colour · 100min

Fine performances and an opulent production distinguish this TV film of Frances Hodgson Burnett's classic children's novel. In Victorian England, a spoiled little orphan girl (Gennie James), now living with her nasty uncle, stumbles upon an enchanted garden on their eerie estate, which transforms her life and those of the people around her. Alan Grint's perceptive direction and veteran British stage actors Derek Jacobi and Michael Hordern fill this timeless tale with warmth, humour and wonder. MC

Gennie James *Mary Lennox* · Michael Hordern *Ben* · Billie Whitelaw *Mrs Medlock* · Derek Jacobi *Archibald Craven* · Jadrien Steele *Colin Craven* · Barret Oliver *Dickon Sowerby* · Colin Firth *Adult Colin* · Julian Glover *Col McGraw* · Lucy Gutteridge *Mrs Lennox* ■ *Dir* Alan Grint · *Scr* Blanche Hanalis, from the novel by Frances Hodgson Burnett

The Secret Garden ★★★★U
Period drama
1993 · US · Colour · 97min

Frances Hodgson Burnett's enchanting children's classic is given a new lease of life in this imaginative adaptation by Polish filmmaker Agnieszka Holland. Always a skilled director of children, she draws a spirited performance out of Kate Maberly as the orphan who sweeps away the cobwebs from Misselthwaite Manor. Scripted by Caroline Thompson – who wrote *Edward Scissorhands* – the film retains the gothic atmosphere of the book and looks amazing, thanks to Roger Deakins's photography. Stealing the show is Maggie Smith as the beastly housekeeper. DP *DVD*

Kate Maberly *Mary Lennox* · Heydon Prowse *Colin Craven* · Andrew Knott *Dickon* · Maggie Smith *Mrs Medlock* · Laura Crossley *Martha* · John Lynch *Lord Craven* · Walter Sparrow *Ben Weatherstaff* · Irène Jacob *Mary's mother/Lilas Craven* ■ *Dir* Agnieszka Holland · *Scr* Caroline Thompson, from the novel by Frances Hodgson Burnett

The Secret Heart ★★
Drama
1946 · US · BW · 96min

Widowed by the suicide of the alcoholic husband she married and in spite of loving another man (Walter Pidgeon), Claudette Colbert has devotedly cared for her stepchildren. Now she faces problems with her psychologically traumatised stepdaughter June Allyson. Robert Z Leonard directs this attempt to make a serious domestic drama out of a soap opera, but the material stubbornly refuses to budge. RK

Claudette Colbert *Lee Addams* · Walter Pidgeon *Chris Matthews* · June Allyson *Penny Addams* · Lionel Barrymore *Dr Rossiger* · Robert Sterling *Chase Addams Jr* · Marshall Thompson *Brandon Reynolds* · Elizabeth Patterson *Mrs Stover* · Richard Derr *Larry Addams Sr* ■ *Dir* Robert Z Leonard · *Scr* Whitfield Cook, Anne Morrison Chapin, Rose Franken, from a story by Franken, William Brown Meloney

Secret Honor ★★★★15
Biographical political drama
1984 · US · Colour · 86min

Maverick director Robert Altman's stunning portrayal of a drunken President Richard Milhous Nixon features Philip Baker Hall as Tricky Dicky. Set after his ignominious resignation, he rants and raves about his contemporaries in his White House study, comparing his "secret honour with his public shame". Altman's prowling camera keeps this one-character drama cinematic and on its toes, and ensures that the man's insane, bigoted mediocrity has a certain vivid poignancy. TH

Philip Baker Hall *Richard M Nixon* ■ *Dir* Robert Altman · *Scr* Donald Freed, Arnold M Stone, from the play *Secret Honor, The Last Will and Testament of Richard M Nixon* by Donald Freed

The Secret in Their Eyes ★★★★18
Crime mystery
2009 · Sp/Arg · Colour · 124min

A decades old brutal murder rape case still haunts a retired court investigator in Argentina's 2010 Oscar winner for best foreign language film. But perusing the facts again as the basis for a novel, he unlocks memories and emotions many hoped would remain buried. Not only a taut thriller with a hackle-raising, twisted moral climax, this polished adaptation of Eduardo Sacheri's bestseller is also a tale of unrequited love and a damning indictment of the country's past military junta. A brilliantly staged chase scene through a Buenos Aires stadium during a soccer match is a suspense highlight in an intelligently touching spellbinder made with skilful panache. AJ Spanish +subtitles. Violence, nudity. *DVD*

Ricardo Darín [Ricardo Darin] *Benjamín Espósito* · Soledad Villamil *Irene Menéndez Hastings* · Pablo Rago *Ricardo Morales* · Javier Godino *Isidoro Gómez* · Carla Quevedo *Liliana Coloto* ■ *Dir* Juan José Campanella [Juan José Campanella] · *Scr* Juan José Campanella, Eduardo Sacheri, from the novel by Sacheri

Secret in Their Eyes ★★15
Crime mystery
2015 · US · Colour · 102min

This sombre thriller concerns a group of FBI investigators whose lives are torn apart by a brutal murder. Set in Los Angeles, the story follows a former agent (Chiwetel Ejiofor) as he returns to inform his ex-colleague (Julia Roberts) that he has finally found the suspect they were chasing 13 years before – the man who raped and murdered her daughter. What follows isn't as gripping as it should be, but the whole thing is elevated by a superb ensemble cast, with Ejiofor providing excellent work as a man who is haunted by his past. SC Violence, sexual references. *DVD* *Blu-ray*

Chiwetel Ejiofor *Ray* · Julia Roberts *Jess* · Nicole Kidman *Claire* · Dean Norris *Bumpy* · Michael Kelly (2) *Siefert* ■ *Dir* Billy Ray · *Scr* Billy Ray, from the novel *La Pregunta de Sus Ojos* by Eduardo Sacheri

The Secret Invasion ★★★PG
Second World War action drama
1964 · US · Colour · 93min

Cult director Roger Corman's snappily-paced adventure bears a similarity to *The Dirty Dozen*, but lacks the powerhouse cast. British Intelligence officer Stewart Granger leads five hardened criminals into Dubrovnik during the Second World War to rescue an Italian general from the Nazis. Although cheaply produced, the cast wrings every ounce of conviction from a routine script. AJ

Stewart Granger *Maj Richard Mace* · Raf Vallone *Roberto Rocca* · Mickey Rooney *Terence Scanlon* · Edd Byrnes *Simon Fell* · Henry Silva *John Durrell* · Mia Massini [Spela Rozin] *Mila* · William Campbell *Jean Saval* ■ *Dir* Roger Corman · *Scr* R Wright Campbell

S

The Secret Laughter of Women ★★ 15

Romantic comedy
1998 · UK/Can · Colour · 95min

There's little love and even less humour in this stiffly staged Riviera story of a Nigerian single mother's encounter with an exiled English writer of comic books. Nia Long struggles to suppress her American accent as the former, while Colin Firth mistakes monotone for laconicism as the latter. Even less well-defined is the ex-pat community that tries to force Long into marrying Ariyon Bakare. DP

Colin Firth *Matthew Field* • Nia Long *Nimi Da Silva, "Big Eyes"* • Dan Lett *John* • Joke Silva *Nene* • Ariyon Bakare *Reverend Fola* ■ *Dir* Peter Schwabach • *Scr* OO Sagay

The Secret Life of Bees ★★★ 12

Period adventure drama
2008 · US · Colour · 105min

Growing up is hard to do for 14-year-old Lily Owens, who is haunted by the memory of her late mother. In an inspired piece of casting, Dakota Fanning plays the role with the unsettling knowingness that made her a child star. Lily's growing pains aren't helped by her tyrannical father (Paul Bettany), but it's not long before Lily runs away with the family housekeeper Rosaleen (Jennifer Hudson). She finds lodging with three black bee-keeping sisters, in what is an almost impossibly quirky set-up for the Deep South in the 1960s. Queen Latifah plays the eldest and wisest sister, while Sophie Okonedo and Alicia Keys play her younger siblings. Like the rank and file of bees, everyone has their place here and they work towards an end product that is sweet, but best enjoyed by children. SP

Dakota Fanning *Lily Owens* • Queen Latifah *August Boatwright* • Jennifer Hudson *Rosaleen Daise* • Alicia Keys *June Boatwright* • Sophie Okonedo *May Boatwright* • Paul Bettany *T Ray Owens* ■ *Dir* Gina Prince-Bythewood • *Scr* Gina Prince-Bythewood, from the novel by Sue Monk Kidd

The Secret Life of Marilyn Monroe ★★

Biographical drama 2015 · US · Colour · 165min

Actresses have been attempting to play the real Marilyn Monroe since Norma Jeane Mortenson first tried in the late 1940s. Kelli Garner contributes a fine impersonation to this adaptation of J Randy Taraborrelli's gossipy 2009 biography. Yet, while all the familiar anecdotes are capably retold by screenwriter Stephen Kronish and director Laurie Collyer, they offer few genuine insights into Monroe's fraught relationship with her paranoid schizophrenic mother and too many facts have been simplified for dramatic purposes. DP

Kelli Garner *Marilyn Monroe* • Susan Sarandon *Gladys Monroe Mortenson* • Emily Watson *Grace McKee* • Jack Noseworthy *Alan DeShields* • Jeffrey Dean Morgan *Joe DiMaggio* • Stephen Bogaert *Arthur Miller* ■ *Dir* Laurie Collyer • *Scr* Stephen Kronish, from J Randy Taraborrelli's non-fiction book

The Secret Life of Pets ★★★ U

Animated comedy adventure
2016 · US · Colour · 90min

There's lots of furry fun to be had in this familiar canine caper, despite the plot being overpopulated with too many crazy characters. The latest comic frolic from the team responsible for *Despicable Me* finds a self-obsessed terrier (voiced by Louis CK) forced to share his Manhattan home with a rescue mongrel (Eric Stonestreet). The adventure that follows is stylishly realised but is too indebted to other animation hits. Neat references to the likes of *Grease* and *Some Like It Hot* help the humour hit the spot, however. AJ

Louis CK *Max* • Eric Stonestreet *Duke* • Kevin Hart *Snowball* • Jenny Slate *Gidget* • Ellie Kemper *Katie* • Albert Brooks *Tiberius* ■ *Dir* Chris Renaud • *Scr* Ken Daurio, Brian Lynch, Cinco Paul

The Secret Life of Walter Mitty ★★★★ U

Comedy 1947 · US · Colour · 105min

James Thurber's short story becomes a marvellous Technicolored cavalcade for Danny Kaye, who plays both the daydreaming Mitty and the amazingly heroic characters of his fantasies. Kaye's on top form here, as a surgeon performing a near-impossible operation, an ace gunslinger (the "Perth Amboy Kid") and a pernickety RAF pilot, among others. The energetic star is not so popular today, but this is generally acknowledged to be his finest screen performance and is certainly his most endearing. There's marvellous support from the great Boris Karloff as a homicidal psychiatrist. Ben Stiller's remake is due in December 2013, and will also star Kristen Wiig and Shirley MacLaine. TS

Danny Kaye *Walter Mitty* • Virginia Mayo *Rosalind van Hoorn* • Boris Karloff *Dr Hugo Hollingshead* • Fay Bainter *Mrs Mitty* • Ann Rutherford *Gertrude Griswold* • Thurston Hall *Bruce Pierce* • Konstantin Shayne *Peter van Hoorn* • Florence Bates *Mrs Griswold* • Gordon Jones *Tubby Wadsworth* • Reginald Denny *RAF colonel* ■ *Dir* Norman Z McLeod • *Scr* Ken Englund, Everett Freeman, from James Thurber's short story

The Secret Life of Walter Mitty ★★★ PG

Romantic fantasy adventure
2013 · US · Colour · 109min

Director/star Ben Stiller's glossy adaptation of James Thurber's short story is a far cry from the beloved 1947 musical comedy starring Danny Kaye. Stiller's Mitty remains a man who vividly daydreams about adventure while trying to hold on to a dreary job. Only here he works for *Life* magazine so when redundancy looms, he decides to go in search of globetrotting photographer Sean McConnell (played by Sean Penn, taking the mickey out of himself again). Beautifully shot and incredibly ambitious, the film demonstrates Stiller is well on the way to proving himself as a serious director. KK Swearing, sexual references, some violence. DVD Blu

Ben Stiller *Walter Mitty* • Kristen Wiig *Cheryl* • Shirley MacLaine *Edna Mitty* • Adam Scott *Ted Hendricks* • Sean Penn *Sean O'Connell* ■ *Dir* Ben Stiller • *Scr* Steve Conrad, from a story by Conrad, from the short story by James Thurber

The Secret Lives of Dentists ★★★★ 15

Fantasy comedy drama
2003 · US · Colour · 99min

Director Alan Rudolph, for so long the nearly-man of American independent cinema, makes a welcome return to form with this bleakly funny adaptation. Dentist Campbell Scott (terrific) is having a mental meltdown after becoming convinced his wife (and fellow dentist) Hope Davis is having an affair. Working from a wry, yet acidic script by Craig Lucas, Rudolph beautifully juxtaposes the banalities of domestic life with increasingly bizarre fantasy sequences, most of them revolving around caustic patient Denis Leary, who becomes Scott's imaginary alter-ego. JF DVD

Campbell Scott *David Hurst* • Denis Leary *Slater* • Hope Davis *Dana Hurst* • Robin Tunney *Laura* • Peter Samuel *Larry* • Jon Patrick Walker *Mark* • Gianna Beleno *Lizzie Hurst* • Lydia Jordan *Stephanie Hurst* • Cassidy Hinkle *Leah Hurst* ■ *Dir* Alan Rudolph • *Scr* Craig Lucas, from the novella *The Age of Grief* by Jane Smiley

Secret Mission ★★ U

Second World War spy drama
1942 · UK · BW · 89min

It's hard to see how this flag-waver could have raised anyone's spirits during the darkest days of the Second World War. There's a modicum of excitement in the attempt by Michael Wilding, Hugh Williams and Roland Culver, along with their French guide James Mason, to glean information about Nazi invasion plans. But the comic subplot involving Wilding and his French wife, and the romance that develops between Williams and Mason's sister (Carla Lehmann), are embarrassing. Unremarkable. DP

Hugh Williams *Peter Garnett* • Carla Lehmann *Michele de Carnot* • James Mason *Raoul de Carnot* • Roland Culver *Red Gowan* • Michael Wilding *Nobby Clark* • Nancy Price *Violette* • Herbert Lom *Medical officer* • Stewart Granger *Sub-lieutenant Jackson* ■ *Dir* Harold French • *Scr* Anatole de Grunwald, Basil Bartlett, from a story by Shaun Terence Young [Terence Young]

The Secret of Convict Lake ★★★

Western 1951 · US · BW · 83min

In this routine melodrama set in 19th-century California, escaped prisoners take over a town populated just by women, while the menfolk are away prospecting. The studio boosted the hackneyed plot by putting in top-class players such as Glenn Ford, Gene Tierney, Ethel Barrymore and Zachary Scott, and their presence helps make the rather predictable scenario much more enjoyable. TH

Glenn Ford *Canfield* • Gene Tierney *Marcia Stoddard* • Ethel Barrymore *Granny* • Zachary Scott *Greer* • Ann Dvorak *Rachel* • Barbara Bates *Barbara Purcell* • Cyril Cusack *Limey* ■ *Dir* Michael Gordon • *Scr* Oscar Saul, Victor Trivas, from a story by Anna Hunger, Jack Pollexfen

The Secret of Dr Kildare ★★★

Medical drama 1939 · US · BW · 84min

The relationship between Lew Ayres's idealistic young Dr Kildare and Lionel Barrymore's curmudgeonly old Dr Gillespie was beginning to mature in the third of MGM's popular series. Kildare, concerned for Gillespie's health, tries to get his superior to take a holiday. At the same time, he cures a woman with psychosomatic blindness. All the regulars are on hand, including nurse Mary Lamont (Laraine Day), who provides Kildare with some romance. RB

Lew Ayres *Dr James Kildare* • Lionel Barrymore *Dr Leonard Gillespie* • Lionel Atwill *Paul Messenger* • Laraine Day *Mary Lamont* • Helen Gilbert *Nancy Messenger* • Nat Pendleton *Joe Wayman* • Samuel S Hinds *Dr Stephen Kildare* ■ *Dir* Harold Bucquet [Harold S Bucquet] • *Scr* Willis Goldbeck, Harry Ruskin, from the story by Max Brand

The Secret of Kells ★★★ PG

Animated fantasy
2009 · Fr/Bel/Ire · Colour · 75min

Director Tomm Moore's Oscar-nominated Dark Ages saga tells the story of Brendan, a 12-year-old novice monk, who ventures into the forest to find the materials that the newly arrived Brother Aidan requires to complete his illuminated manuscript of the Gospels. However, with a Norse attack threatened and the fearsome god Crom Cruach to confound, Brendan requires the help of a faerie named Aisling. Combining Celtic design, retro-style animation and the majesty of the *Book of Kells*, this visually ambitious feature boldly mixes Irish mythology and Christian lore. But, while this is a handsome picture that laudably avoids patronising its audience, it's not always as child-friendly as it might be. DP DVD Blu

Brendan Gleeson *Abbot Cellach* • Evan McGuire *Brendan* • Christen Mooney *Aisling* • Mick Lally *Brother Aidan* • Michael McGrath *Adult Brendan* • Paul Tylak [Paul Tylack] *Brother Assoua* ■ *Dir* Tomm Moore, Nora Twomey • *Scr* Fabrice Ziolkowski, from a story by Tomm Moore

The Secret of Madame Blanche ★★★

Period melodrama 1933 · US · BW · 78min

Respectable musical actress Irene Dunne is swept off her feet by Phillips Holmes, a charming but weak upper class idler. She marries him and falls pregnant, but when his cruel and rigid father Lionel Atwill refuses to acknowledge the union, Holmes kills himself. She is stranded in France with her newborn son, whose grandfather steals the baby away. An 18-carat weepie, this is a wonderful wallow, though Dunne – enchanting as the young woman – is less successful as middle-aged "Madame Blanche". RK

Irene Dunne *Sally Sanders St John/Madame Blanche* • Lionel Atwill *Aubrey St John* • Phillips Holmes *Leonard St John* • Una Merkel *Ella* • Douglas Walton *Leonard St John Jr* ■ *Dir* Charles Brabin • *Scr* Frances Goodrich, Albert Hackett, from the play *The Lady* by Martin Brown

The Secret of Moonacre ★★★ U

Fantasy adventure
2008 · Fr/Hun/UK/US/Aus/Cay · Colour · 99min

When Maria (*The Golden Compass's* Dakota Blue Richards) is orphaned, she is forced to leave her London home to live with her reclusive uncle (Ioan Gruffudd) on the rambling Moonacre estate. An inlaid book tells of the legend of the moon princess (of the De Noir clan), her love for Sir Wrolf Merryweather, and the subsequent feud over the precious moon pearls between the De Noir and Merryweather families. This loose adaptation of Elizabeth Goudge's *The Little White Horse* is lovingly designed with exquisite costumes and lavish sets. But with the exception of Richards's strong central performance and Juliet Stevenson's comic turn as governess Mrs Heliotrope, the main characters often seem stifled by their surroundings. Despite its failings, though, this is still well worth watching – if only for the incredible engineering involved in making Maria's dresses. SuR DVD Blu

Dakota Blue Richards *Maria Merryweather* • Ioan Gruffudd *Sir Benjamin/Sir Wrolf Merryweather* • Tim Curry *Coeur de Noir/Sir William De Noir* • Natascha McElhone *Loveday/The Moon Princess* • Juliet Stevenson *Mrs Heliotrope* ■ *Dir* Gabor Csupo • *Scr* Graham Alborough, Lucy Shuttleworth, from the novel *The Little White Horse* by Elizabeth Goudge

The Secret of My Success ★★

Black comedy 1965 · UK · Colour · 107min

Yet another in the seemingly endless parade of lacklustre British comedies, this features James Booth as a naive, garrulous mother's boy who starts the film as a PC and ends up unwittingly helping to overthrow a foreign dictator, becoming a hero in the process. The film owes much to Voltaire's *Candide* but it's just not very funny, though Booth is worth watching, and Lionel Jeffries gets to play four roles. JG

James Booth *Arthur Tate* • Shirley Jones *Marigold Marado* • Stella Stevens *Violet Lawson* • Honor Blackman *Baroness von Lukenberg* • Lionel Jeffries *Inspector Hobart/Baron von Lukenberg/President Esteda/Earl of Aldershot* • Amy Dolby *Mrs Tate* ■ *Dir/Scr* Andrew L Stone

The Secret of My Success ★★★ PG

Comedy 1987 · US · Colour · 105min

In another tailor-made role, Michael J Fox plays a mailroom boy who tries to make his way to the top by spending half his day impersonating an executive. Lots of pratfalls ensue, and Fox is reasonably engaging as he runs around frantically trying to keep up the charade. Margaret Whitton, as the scheming boss's wife, steals the show, however, and makes this rather basic comedy worth watching. JB DVD Blu

Michael J Fox *Brantley Foster* • Helen Slater *Christy Wills* • Richard Jordan *Howard Prescott* • Margaret Whitton *Vera Prescott* • John Pankow *Fred Melrose* • Christopher Murney *Barney Rattigan* • Gerry Bamman *Art Thomas* • Mercedes Ruehl *Sheila* ■ *Dir* Herbert Ross • *Scr* Jim Cash, Jack Epps, AJ Carothers, from a story by AJ Carothers

The Secret of NIMH ★★★ U

Animated fantasy 1982 · US · Colour · 78min

Animator Don Bluth rebelled against the mighty Mouse and set out to remind a then-struggling Disney about the glory days of animation. He largely succeeded (the sentimentality that would cloud his *An American Tail* and *The Land before Time* is the only drawback) with this story of a proud mouse who strikes up an unlikely friendship with the rat branch of Mensa. The animation is lovingly rendered and there is a pedigree cast providing voices. JF **DVD**

Derek Jacobi *Nicodemus* • Elizabeth Hartman *Mrs Brisby* • Arthur Malet *Mr Ages* • Dom DeLuise *Jeremy* • Hermione Baddeley *Auntie Shrew* • John Carradine *Great Owl* • Peter Strauss *Justin* • Paul Shenar *Jenner* • Shannen Doherty *Teresa* ■ *Dir* Don Bluth • *Scr* John Pomeroy, Gary Goldman, Don Bluth, Will Finn, from the novel *Mrs Frisby and the Rats of NIMH* by Robert C O'Brien

The Secret of NIMH II: Timmy to the Rescue ★ U

Animated adventure 1998 · US · Colour · 65min

This made-for-video sequel to animator Don Bluth's one good movie makes his other wretched efforts look like masterpieces. The screenplay here freely ignores or alters key characters and events from the previous movie in this tale of now grown-up mouse Timmy traveling to Thorn Valley to save his furry friends from the returning menace of NIMH. This is blighted by poor animation and art design, plus a grim tone. JF **DVD**

Dom DeLuise *Jeremy* • Andrew Ducote *Timmy, aged 10* • Eric Idle *Martin* • Harvey Korman *Floyd* • Ralph Macchio *Timmy, aged 19* • Peter MacNicol *Narrator* ■ *Dir* Dick Sebast • *Scr* Sam Graham, Chris Hubbell, from characters by Robert C O'Brien

The Secret of Roan Inish ★★★★ PG

Period fantasy 1993 · US · Colour · 97min

This is a gem of a film from talented writer/director John Sayles. Without sentiment and accompanied by stunning cinematography from veteran Haskell Wexler, Sayles spins a tale of ten-year-old Fiona living in 1940s Ireland who believes her family are descendants from selkies: half-seal, half-human creatures from the island of Roan Inish. While staying with her grandparents near the now-deserted island, the youngster starts to uncover her true heritage. The result is a mythical and magical film that will entrance young and old. LH

Jeni Courtney *Fiona Coneelly* • Mick Lally *Hugh Coneelly, Fiona's Grandfather* • Eileen Colgan *Tess Coneelly, Fiona's Grandmother* • Richard Sheridan *Eamon* • John Lynch *Tadhg Coneelly* • Cillian Byrne *Jamie* • Susan Lynch *Selkie* ■ *Dir* John Sayles • *Scr* John Sayles, from the novel *The Secret of the Ron Mor Skerry* by Rosalie K Fry

The Secret of Santa Vittoria ★★★★

Second World War comedy 1969 · US · Colour · 139min

This underrated film is based on a supposedly true incident during the Second World War, when the population of a small village in the Italian hills hid its stocks of wine to prevent them from falling into the hands of the Germans. Producer/director Stanley Kramer has crafted an irresistible game of cat and mouse as town drunk-cum-mayor Anthony Quinn and Nazi officer Hardy Kruger try to outsmart each other. Quinn and fiery Anna Magnani make a dynamic duo and you'll be hard pressed to choose between tears and cheers. DP

Anthony Quinn *Italo Bombolini* • Anna Magnani *Rosa Bombolini* • Virna Lisi *Caterina Malatesta* • Hardy Kruger *Sepp Von Prum, German Commander* • Sergio Franchi *Tufa* ■ *Dir* Stanley Kramer • *Scr* William Rose, Ben Maddow, from the novel by Robert Crichton

Secret of the Incas ★★★ U

Adventure 1954 · US · Colour · 104min

Charlton Heston and Thomas Mitchell play the rivals engaged in a perilous search for a fabled Inca icon in this adventure yarn from director Jerry Hopper. There's romance and Cold War intrigue, so fashionable in

1954, but what distinguishes the film are the location shots of the fabled Inca city of Machu Picchu, which sits swathed in Andean clouds. AT

Charlton Heston *Harry Steele* • Nicole Maurey *Elena Antonescu* • Robert Young (1) *Dr Stanley Moorehead* • Thomas Mitchell *Ed Morgan* • Glenda Farrell *Jane Winston* • William Henry *Phillip Lang* ■ *Dir* Jerry Hopper • *Scr* Ranald MacDougall, Sydney Boehm, from the story *Legend of the Incas* by Sydney Boehm

The Secret of the Loch ★★ U

Comedy adventure 1934 · UK · BW · 72min

Primarily of interest today because it was edited by the 26-year-old David Lean, this is not only one of the first British talkies to attempt location shooting, but it's also among this country's earliest creature features. Co-scripted by Hitchcock collaborator Charles Bennett, the story is pretty predictable, as Seymour Hicks is prepared to risk his own sanity to prove the existence of a Diplodocus at the bottom of Loch Ness. There's some fine underwater photography, but the monster is underwhelming. DP **DVD**

Seymour Hicks *Professor Heggie* • Nancy O'Neil *Angela Heggie* • Gibson Gowland *Angus* • Frederick Peisley *Jimmy Andrews* ■ *Dir* Milton Rosmer • *Scr* Charles Bennett, Billie Bristow, loosely based on the story *The Lost World* by Sir Arthur Conan Doyle

The Secret of the Purple Reef ★ U

Murder mystery 1960 · US · Colour · 79min

An early role for Peter Falk and the screen debut of Richard Chamberlain may be the sole reasons to watch this seaborne schlock. The plot has Jeff Richards and brother Chamberlain looking into the death of another brother who went down in his fishing sloop in the Caribbean. The weather is good, the acting less so, the script scrapes the bottom, and there are any number of suspects. AT

Jeff Richards *Mark Christopher* • Margia Dean *Rue Amboy* • Peter Falk *Tom Weber* • Richard Chamberlain *Dean Christopher* • Robert Earle *Tobias* • Terence DeMarney *Ashby* ■ *Dir* William Witney • *Scr* Harold Yablonsky [Yabo Yablonsky], Gene Corman, from a serial in *The Saturday Evening Post* by Dorothy Cottrell

The Secret Partner ★★★

Crime drama 1961 · UK · BW · 91min

In this implausible but ingenious British thriller, a hooded man forces a dentist to drug a shipping executive during an appointment so that he will reveal the combination of his company's strongroom. It remains watchable thanks to some skilful characterisation and the strong performances of Stewart Granger as the executive, Norman Bird as the dentist and Bernard Lee as the dogged, chain-smoking policeman. AE

Stewart Granger *John Brent* • Haya Harareet *Nicole Brent* • Bernard Lee *Det Supt Hanbury* • Hugh Burden *Charles Standish* • Lee Montague *Det Inspector Henderson* • Norman Bird *Ralph Beldon, dentist* ■ *Dir* Basil Dearden • *Scr* David Pursall, Jack Seddon

The Secret People ★ PG

Crime drama 1951 · UK · BW · 90min

Given carte blanche by Ealing Studios, director Thorold Dickinson set out to make a polemical film about the ethics of political assassination, and encouraged the young Lindsay Anderson to write a book documenting its production. Sadly, the result was a wordy, pretentious and boring picture, too coldly characterised, too unspecific in detail, too cerebral by far. Its sole interest lies in Audrey Hepburn, in one of her earliest roles. AE **DVD**

Valentina Cortesa [Valentina Cortese] *Maria Brentano* • Serge Reggiani *Louis* • Charles Goldner *Anselmo* • Audrey Hepburn *Nora Brentano* • Angela Foulkes *Nora as a child* • Megs Jenkins *Penny* • Irene Worth *Miss Jackson* • Reginald Tate *Inspector Eliot* • Bob Monkhouse

Barber ■ *Dir* Thorold Dickinson • *Scr* Thorold Dickinson, Wolfgang Wilhelm, Christianna Brand, from a story by Dickinson, Joyce Carey

The Secret Policeman's Ball ★★★★ 15

Comedy concert 1980 · UK · Colour · 91min

This recording of the comedy fundraiser for Amnesty International enjoyed a theatrical release (in a much longer form) following its TV screening. A brilliant cast of comedians and performers (including John Cleese, Peter Cook, Clive James, Rowan Atkinson, Billy Connolly, Pete Townshend), and some wonderful sketches provide guaranteed entertainment. This features wonderful moments from some of the most popular comedians of the last 35 years. DF **DVD**

■ *Dir* Roger Graef

The Secret Policeman's Other Ball ★★★ 15

Comedy concert 1982 · UK · Colour · 90min

Combining footage from benefits staged in aid of Amnesty International, this movie is more a souvenir than great cinema. Directors Roger Graef and Julien Temple's video images are murky and jerky, and while they work for such memorable musical slots as Sting's *Message in a Bottle* and the blues teaming of guitar legends Eric Clapton and Jeff Beck, they distract from the comedy without conveying any audience excitement. However, Alan Bennett and John Fortune's dialogue, the Pythons' immortal "Four Yorkshiremen" sketch and the End of the World routine featuring Peter Cook and Rowan Atkinson, all survive the edgy camerawork. DP **DVD**

■ *Dir* Julien Temple, Roger Graef

The Secret Policeman's Third Ball ★★★ 15

Comedy concert 1987 · UK · Colour · 86min

The fourth charity bash – before the three Balls there was *Pleasure at Her Majesty's* – was performed over four evenings at the London Palladium in March 1987. Regulars such as Alan Bennett, Rowan Atkinson and Billy Connolly are notable absentees, though John Cleese strides on to receive an award from Stephen Fry and Hugh Laurie. Lenny Henry plays a clapped out blues singer, Ben Elton outstays his welcome and there are songs by the likes of Bob Geldof, Duran Duran and Peter Gabriel. Ruby Wax sends herself up and *Spitting Image* contributes a scabrous dialogue between Larry Olivier and Johnny Gielgud. Blessings, as they say, are mixed. AT **DVD**

■ *Dir* Kevin O'Neill

The Secret Rapture ★★★★ 15

Drama 1993 · UK · Colour · 96min

Writer David Hare can veer from nuance to crassness in one giddy swoop. Here, for once, he has merged the personal and the political without letting us see too much of the join. Set on the cusp of the shark-toothed 1980s and the more introspective 1990s, this tale of sisterly rivalry is shot through with fine acting, particularly from Juliet Stevenson and Penelope Wilton as the sisters, Joanne Whalley-Kilmer as the stepmother and Neil Pearson as the boyfriend. JM

Juliet Stevenson *Isobel Coleridge* • Joanne Whalley-Kilmer [Joanne Whalley] *Katherine Coleridge* • Penelope Wilton *Marion French* • Neil Pearson *Patrick Steadman* • Alan Howard *Tom French* • Robert Stephens *Max Lopert* • Hilton McRae *Norman* • Robert Glenister *Jeremy* ■ *Dir* Howard Davies • *Scr* David Hare, from his play

A Secret Sin ★★ 15

Period drama 1997 · US · Colour · 120min

Set in the 1950s, this family melodrama appears dated, despite the up-to-the-minute casting of Vince Vaughn, Ashley Judd and Paul Rudd. Kate Capshaw stars as a sultry widow who spends her spare time bedding her farm hands to the detriment of her emotionally damaged son Jeremy Davies.

Drifter Vaughn appears in town and soon becomes involved with Judd; there are dark secrets to be revealed on the way to a suitably dramatic climax. The gothic tone and certain masterful moments transform it from bad to not uninteresting. LH

Kate Capshaw *Delilah Ashford Potts* • Jessica Capshaw *Patsy* • Vince Vaughn *Clay Hewitt* • Ashley Judd *Kitty* • Jeremy Davies *Flyboy* • Daniel Meyer *Joel* • Paul Rudd *Earl* ■ *Dir/Scr* John Patrick Kelley

The Secret Six ★★

Crime drama 1931 · US · BW · 74min

Bootlegger Wallace Beery rises to gangland supremo, only to be brought down by a six-man consortium of influential men, with a little help from newspaperman Clark Gable (in a supporting role). Slow to start, this is a serviceable, though superficially characterised, gangster movie. George Hill directed, with Lewis Stone excellent as a crooked attorney and, in small but key parts, John Mack Brown and Jean Harlow. RK

Wallace Beery *Louis Scorpio* • Lewis Stone *Richard Newton* • John Mack Brown [Johnny Mack Brown] *Hank Rogers* • Jean Harlow *Anne Courtland* • Marjorie Rambeau *Peaches* • Paul Hurst *Nick Mizoski the Gouger* • Clark Gable *Carl Luckner* • Ralph Bellamy *Johnny Franks* ■ *Dir* George W Hill [George Hill] • *Scr* Frances Marion, from her story

Secret Things ★★★ 18

Satirical erotic drama 2002 · Fr · Colour · 112min

Although Marilyn Monroe, Betty Grable and Lauren Bacall shared Coralie Revel and Sabrina Seyvecou's gold-digging aspirations, they never resorted to these lusty tactics in *How to Marry a Millionaire*. As the exotic dancer and naive barmaid whose plan of attack includes frequent bouts of graphic coupling, Revel and Seyvecou give courageous displays of naked ambition, while also exhibiting a delicious sense of fun. Writer/director Jean-Claude Brisseau also stays just the right side of exploitation by making men the target of his most barbed satire, although he also has justified pops at class, consumerism and the corporate mentality. DP French +subtitles.

Sabrina Seyvecou *Sandrine* • Coralie Revel *Nathalie* • Roger Mirmont *Delacroix* • Fabrice Deville *Christophe* • Blandine Bury *Charlotte* • Olivier Soler *Cadene* ■ *Dir/Scr* Jean-Claude Brisseau

The Secret War of Harry Frigg ★★★ U

Second World War comedy 1967 · US · Colour · 109min

Paul Newman was never fully convincing as a comedian, though he makes a fair stab at it here, as a deadbeat private whose one gift is the ability to escape from military prisons. Given the temporary rank of full general, he is sent to Italy to engineer the escape of five Allied generals, who are enjoying their imprisonment in a lavish villa owned by Countess Sylva Koscina. This is a jolly jape, lifted by some lovely turns from the supporting cast, notably John Williams as one of the two terribly English generals. AT

Paul Newman *Harry Frigg* • Sylva Koscina *Countess di Montefiore* • Andrew Duggan *General Armstrong* • Tom Bosley *General Pennypacker* • John Williams *General Mayhew* • Charles Gray *General Cox-Roberts* ■ *Dir* Jack Smight • *Scr* Peter Stone, Frank Tarloff, from a story by Frank Tarloff

The Secret Ways ★★★

Spy thriller 1961 · US · BW · 111min

The always watchable Richard Widmark stars as an American soldier-of-fortune helping a noted Hungarian intellectual and anti-communist escape from behind the Iron Curtain. The tone in this Cold War drama wavers between realism and satire, the result of a dispute between Widmark and director Phil Karlson, who wanted to do it tongue in cheek. AT

S

Richard Widmark *Michael Reynolds* • Sonja Ziemann *Julia* • Charles Regnier *The Count* • Walter Rilla *Jancsi* • Howard Vernon *Colonel Hidas* • Senta Berger *Elsa* • Heinz Moog *Minister Sakenov* ∎ *Dir* Phil Karlson • *Scr* Jean Hazlewood, from a novel by Alistair MacLean

Secret Wedding ★★★★
Romantic political drama
1989 · Arg/Neth/Can · Colour · 95min
Argentinian director Alejandro Agresti provides a fascinating insight into the problems facing the "disappeared", imprisoned under the junta, and now released back into society with the restoration of democracy. From the moment we find him naked on the streets of Buenos Aires, Tito Haas dominates the action, whether coming to terms with the years he has lost, attempting to win back the love of Mirtha Busnelli, or coping with the suspicions of his new neighbours. Ricardo Rodriguez's photography is superb, complementing the unusual camera angles favoured by Agresti. DP Spanish +subtitles.
Tito Haas *Fermin Garcia* • Mirtha Busnelli *Tota* • Sergio Poves Campos *Pipi* • Nathan Pinzon *Priest* • Floria Bloise *Dona Patricia* • Elio Marchi *Leandro* ∎ *Dir/Scr* Alejandro Agresti

Secret Window ★★★ 12
Suspense thriller   2004 · US · Colour · 91min
Movie history is littered with poor attempts to exploit literary cash cow Stephen King, and this lacklustre psychological thriller joins them. Johnny Depp stars as a successful author whose writer's block is nothing compared to the hell that he encounters when menacing stranger John Turturro accuses him of plagiarism. While Depp's emotional seesawing and Turturro's furrow-browed intensity are entertaining in themselves, director David Koepp signposts all the twists. SF Violence. DVD BL
Johnny Depp *Mort Rainey* • John Turturro *John Shooter* • Maria Bello *Amy Rainey* • Timothy Hutton *Ted Milner* • Charles S Dutton *Ken Karsch* • Len Cariou *Sheriff Dave Newsome* ∎ *Dir* David Koepp • *Scr* David Koepp, from the novella *Secret Window, Secret Garden* by Stephen King

Secretariat ★★ U
Sports drama   2010 · US · Colour · 117min
The racehorse Secretariat became part of US sporting history in the 1970s thanks to winning America's Triple Crown. Even so, the thrills and spills of horse racing are downplayed as director Randall Wallace aims for something wholesome and uplifting in this tepid re-creation of events. What we're left with instead is the cold though good-looking true-life story of Penny Chenery (Diane Lane), a wealthy housewife who overcame naysayers and financial worries to promote her father's champion colt. John Malkovich provides welcome comedy relief as the flamboyant trainer and Nelsan Ellis supplies the much-needed emotional centre with his portrayal of the horse's groom. KK Some swearing. DVD BL
Diane Lane *Penny Chenery* • John Malkovich *Lucien Laurin* • Scott Glenn *Chris Chenery* • James Cromwell *Ogden Phipps* • Dylan Walsh *Jack Tweedy* • Fred Dalton Thompson *Bull Hancock* • Kevin Connolly *Bill Nack* • AJ Michalka [Amanda Michalka] *Kate Chenery* ∎ *Dir* Randall Wallace • *Scr* Mike Rich, from the book *Secretariat: the Making of a Champion* by William Nack

Secretary ★★★ 18
Comedy drama   2001 · US · Colour · 106min
Love stories don't come much more bizarre than this strangely touching tale of a sadomasochistic relationship. Maggie Gyllenhaal plays a troubled young woman recently released from a mental hospital, whose obsessive self-harming is a concern to friends and parents alike. Taking a job at a legal firm, Gyllenhaal comes under the control of her boss (James Spader), who has extremely unorthodox attitudes to office discipline. Both leads are excellent, but the (relatively tame) sadomasochistic scenes may be too much for more sensitive viewers. AS Swearing, sex scenes, nudity. DVD BL

James Spader *E Edward Grey* • Maggie Gyllenhaal *Lee Holloway* • Jeremy Davies *Peter* • Patrick Bauchau *Dr Twardon* • Stephen McHattie *Burt Holloway* • Oz Perkins *Jonathan* • Jessica Tuck *Tricia O'Connor* • Amy Locane *Theresa Holloway* • Lesley Ann Warren *Joan Holloway* ∎ *Dir* Steven Shainberg • *Scr* Erin Cressida Wilson, from the short story in the collection *Bad Behavior* by Mary Gaitskill

Secrets ★
Period drama   1933 · US · BW · 84min
This was Mary Pickford's last film and made for an ignominious end to her long career as "America's Sweetheart". Pickford cast herself as a pioneering woman bravely enduring hardships and tragedy – and nobly standing by her philandering husband through 50 years of marriage. Leslie Howard, not surprisingly, is uncharacteristically ill at ease as the wayward spouse in a creaky melodrama that had already passed its sell-by date in the 1930s. RK
Mary Pickford *Mary Marlowe/Mary Carlton* • Leslie Howard *John Carlton* • C Aubrey Smith *Mr William Marlowe* • Blanche Frederici *Mrs Martha Marlowe* • Doris Lloyd *Susan Channing* • Herbert Evans *Lord Hurley* • Ned Sparks *"Sunshine"* ∎ *Dir* Frank Borzage • *Scr* Frances Marion, Salisbury Field, Leonard Praskins, from the play by Rudolf Besier

Secrets & Lies ★★★★★ 15
Drama   1995 · UK · Colour · 141min
Acclaimed director Mike Leigh finally scored a resounding box-office hit with this bittersweet snoop into the nooks and crannies of family life. The winner of the Palme d'Or at Cannes, this is a return to the familiar battleground of suburbia, but without the caricature that occasionally undermines Leigh's razor-sharp social observation. The teasing statements on the original poster best sum up the film's labyrinthine relationships: "Roxanne drives her mother crazy. Maurice never speaks to his niece. Monica can't talk to her husband. Hortense has never met her mother. Cynthia has a shock for her family." But even the secrets and lies themselves are of less significance than how the different characters respond to the revelations. DP Swearing. DVD BL
Timothy Spall *Maurice* • Brenda Blethyn *Cynthia* • Marianne Jean-Baptiste *Hortense* • Phyllis Logan *Monica* • Claire Rushbrook *Roxanne* • Elizabeth Berrington *Jane* • Michele Austin *Dionne* • Lee Ross *Paul* • Lesley Manville *Social worker* • Ron Cook *Stuart* ∎ *Dir/Scr* Mike Leigh

Secrets d'Alcove ★★★
Portmanteau comedy   1954 · Fr/It · BW · 110min
A bed links this amusing collection of short stories, told by a trio of diplomats and their chauffeur. In Henri Decoin's *Le Billet de Logement* Richard Todd parachutes into occupied France and helps Jeanne Moreau deliver a baby; Vittorio De Sica has to spend a night with professional co-respondent Dawn Addams in Gianni Franciolini's *Le Divorce*; the mysteries of the night haunt trucker Marcel Mouloudji when he stops to help the stranded François Périer in Ralph Habib's *Riviera-Express*, while Martine Carol seeks verification of the bed's historical importance in Jean Delannoy's *Le Lit de la Pompadour*. DP English, French +subtitles.
Jeanne Moreau *Mother* • Richard Todd *Soldier* • Martine Carol *Agnes* • Bernard Blier *President* • François Périer *Alfred* • Vittorio De Sica *Bob* • Dawn Addams *Janet* • Mouloudji [Marcel Mouloudji] *Ricky* ∎ *Dir* Henri Decoin, Jean Delannoy, Ralph Habib, Gianni Franciolini • *Scr* Maurice Auberge, Jean Delannoy, Roland Laudenbach, Sergio Amidei, Antoine Blondin, Janet Wolf, Jacques Fano, Niccolo Theodoli, Paul Andreota, Richard Todd

Secrets in the Walls ★★
Horror thriller   2010 · US · Colour · 89min
New house renovations kick off a distressing chain of events for frantic divorcée Jeri Ryan and her two daughters in this derivative ghost story. But though the increasingly far-fetched film hasn't got a single original idea – borrowing liberally from the likes of *Stir of Echoes* and The

Haunting in Connecticut – competent acting and a creepy atmosphere keep things watchable, as a female spectre gradually homes in on eldest child Kay Panabaker. Being a TV movie, the supernatural activity is well watered-down, consisting largely of loud noises and repetitive jump scares; while the narrative focus remains on the family issues these disturbances exacerbate and create. It's these emotion-centred aspects that hold the feature together, particularly in its silly and contrived dénouement. SF
Jeri Ryan *Rachel Easton* • Marianne Jean-Baptiste *Belle* • Kay Panabaker *Lizzie Easton* • Peyton Roi List [Peyton List] *Molly Easton* • Ian Kahn *Marty* ∎ *Dir* Christopher Leitch • *Scr* William Penick, Christopher D Sey

Secrets of a Soul ★★★★
Silent psychological drama
1926 · Ger · BW · 56min
Co-scripted with two of Freud's associates, Hans Neumann and Colin Ross, this was something of a departure for GW Pabst, who was better known for street realism than pure silent expressionism. However, there's no denying the technical ingenuity behind the symbolic dreams experienced by chemistry professor Werner Krauss, as he wrestles with the combined effects of his own sexual inadequacy and his jealous response to wife Ruth Weyher's infatuation with cousin Jack Trevor. Predominantly shot in the camera, the multiple superimpositions have lost none of their potency, although Freud, apparently, wasn't impressed. DP
Werner Krauss *Martin Fellman* • Ruth Weyher *Fellman's wife* • Ilka Grüning *Mother* • Jack Trevor *Erich* • Pawel Pawlow *Dr Charles Orth* ∎ *Dir* GW Pabst • *Scr* Colin Ross, Hans Neumann • *Cinematographers* Guido Seeber, Curt Oertel, Walter Robert Lach

Secrets of an Undercover Wife ★★
Crime drama   2007 · Can · Colour · 92min
In an unconvincing thriller, Shawnee Smith (from the *Saw* franchise) plays a newlywed who goes undercover to prove her husband is innocent of embezzlement and murder. The trouble is, the woman's do-it-yourself detective work isn't very interesting, as she takes an entry-level admin job and then quickly cosies up to the company's villainous CEO (Michael Woods). This bland and predictable narrative is matched by Smith's underwhelming performance. SF
Shawnee Smith *Lisa* • Michael Woods *Michael* • Veena Sood *Frances Bracken* • Brenda Campbell *Valerie Ross* • Linda Ko *Ada Chan* ∎ *Dir* George Mendeluk • *Scr* Keith Shaw, George Mendeluk

Secrets of the Heart ★★★ 12
Fantasy drama   1997 · Sp/Fr/Por · Colour · 104min
Admirers of Victor Erice's *The Spirit of the Beehive* will be intrigued by this Oscar-nominated tale of childhood innocence and the lure of the unknown. Set in the Basque country around Pamplona in the 1960s, the film doesn't overplay its allegorical hand, even though the symbolism of the abandoned house, with its locked rooms and buried secrets, is pretty blatant. Instead, Montxo Armendáriz focuses on the curiosity and incomprehension of nine-year-old Andoni Erburu, who is more interested in rumours that whispering ghosts inhabit the basement than in the relationship between his widowed mother and his uncle. DP Spanish +subtitles. DVD
Andoni Erburu *Javi* • Javier Zabalza • Carmelo Gomez *Uncle* • Maria Charo Lopez *Aunt* • Silvia Munt *Mother* • Vicky Peña *Aunt Rosa* ∎ *Dir/Scr* Montxo Armendáriz

The Sect ★★★ 18
Horror   1991 · It · Colour · 111min
Fans of spaghetti shockers will lap up this offering from Dario Argento acolyte Michele Soavi who established himself as a horror stylist in his own right with this highly atmospheric fantasy about a coven of devil worshippers carrying out ritualistic

killings in modern-day Frankfurt. It's less a story than a succession of surreal and bravura set pieces; Soavi holds back on the gore (for the most part) emphasising suspense instead and succeeds in coming up with a good deal of genuine frights. He wrings good performances from Kelly Leigh Curtis as a schoolteacher caught up in the murders and from Herbert Lom as the cult leader. RS Italian dubbed.
Kelly Leigh Curtis [Kelly Curtis] *Miriam* • Herbert Lom *Gran Vecchio* • Maria Angela Giordano *Kathryn* • Tomas Arana *Damon* • Erica Sinisi *Sara* • Donald O'Brien *Jonathan* • Michel Hans Adatte *Franz* ∎ *Dir* Michele Soavi • *Scr* Dario Argento, Giovanni Romoli, Michele Soavi, from a story by Dario Argento, Giovanni Romoli, Michele Soavi

Secuestro Express ★★★ 18
Crime thriller   2004 · Ven · Colour · 83min
Jonathan Jakubowicz's belligerent drama centres on the spate of quickie kidnappings – in which moderate ransoms are demanded to tight deadlines – that have become a sinister part of the Venezuelan class conflict. But rather than forcing us to identify with either affluent abductees Mia Maestro and Jean Paul Leroux or lowlife perpetrators Carlos Julio Molina, Pedro Perez and Carlos Madera, the screenplay blurs the lines so that it's never totally clear who is the real victim. Jakubowicz makes tense and atmospheric use of his nocturnal Caracas locations. DP Spanish +subtitles.
Mia Maestro *Carla* • Carlos Julio Molina *Trece* • Pedro Perez *Budu* • Carlos Madera *Niga* • Jean Paul Leroux *Martin* • Rubén Blades *Sergio* ∎ *Dir/Scr* Jonathan Jakubowicz

Seduced and Abandoned ★★★ 15
Documentary   2013 · US · Colour · 94min
Film buffs will enjoy this shop-talking trawl backstage at the Cannes film festival. Alec Baldwin and writer/director James Toback corner stars in hotel rooms and hanging out with bigwigs on yachts, in an increasingly desperate effort to finance their new project, a sexual odyssey inspired by Bernardo Bertolucci's *Last Tango in Paris*, but set against the backdrop of the Iraq War. Although Toback doesn't address his own "bankability", both he and Baldwin do retain a sense of humour as they find themselves gradually unseated by the Cannes merry-go-round. SP Swearing, sex scenes. DVD
Alec Baldwin • James Toback • Ryan Gosling • Jessica Chastain • Martin Scorsese ∎ *Dir/Scr* James Toback

The Seduction of Joe Tynan ★★★ 15
Political drama   1979 · US · Colour · 102min
You always get the feeling with this portrait of American political life that it has more than a ring of truth about it. Unfortunately, the echo has a hollowness that undermines the satire. Alan Alda's performance is superior to his script, capturing the glib, Kennedy-like charm that can still win votes, and Meryl Streep is convincing as a ruthless lawyer. However, some of the Senate scenes seem far-fetched, while the melodramatic finale is a shoddy way to end an otherwise well-constructed drama. DP Swearing, brief nudity.
Alan Alda *Joe Tynan* • Barbara Harris *Ellie Tynan* • Meryl Streep *Karen Traynor* • Rip Torn *Senator Hugh Kittner* • Melvyn Douglas *Senator Birney* • Charles Kimbrough *Francis* • Carrie Nye *Althena Kittner* ∎ *Dir* Jerry Schatzberg • *Scr* Alan Alda

The Seduction of Mimi ★★★
Satire   1972 · It · Colour · 92min
Remade in 1977 as the Richard Pryor vehicle *Which Way Is Up?* (1977), Lina Wertmuller's third collaboration with actor Giancarlo Giannini earned her best director kudos at Cannes. A study in sexual hypocrisy and political expediency, it stars Giannini as Mimi, a Sicilian labourer who manages to alienate both the Mob and the communists, lose his wife and his mistress, and impregnate the spouse of the man who cuckolded him. Wertmuller is scarcely more

sympathetic in her depiction of the female characters. DP Italian dubbed.

Giancarlo Giannini *Mimi* • Mariangela Melato *Fiore* • Agostina Belli *Rosalia* • Elena Fiore *Amelia* • Turi Ferro *Tricarico* • Luigi Diberti *Pippino* ■ *Dir/Scr* Lina Wertmuller

See How They Fall ★★★★ 18

Drama   1993 · Fr · Colour · 95min

The inspiration for this frankly homoerotic crime drama is hard-boiled French *film noir* as practised by director Jacques Audiard's screenwriter father, Michel. Stripping down motives to loyalty and survival, the story follows two distinct avenues, which, through the supremely controlled, convoluted structure, eventually coincide with explosive consequences. Ageing conman Jean-Louis Trintignant and reckless rookie Mathieu Kassovitz encounter Jean Yanne, a travelling salesman whose life has fallen apart through his obsessive crusade to avenge the death of the undercover cop to whom he'd become attached. DP French +subtitles. Swearing, violence, sex scenes.

Jean-Louis Trintignant *Marx* • Jean Yanne *Simon* • Mathieu Kassovitz *Johnny* • Bulle Ogier *Louise* • Christine Pascal *Sandrine* • Yvon Back *Mickey* ■ *Dir* Jacques Audiard • *Scr* Alain Le Henry, Jacques Audiard, from the novel *Triangle* by Teri White

See No Evil, Hear No Evil
★ 15

Comedy   1989 · US · Colour · 97min

This dreadful comedy stars Gene Wilder and Richard Pryor in their third movie together, and it manages to waste both men's ability. Their characters are deaf and blind respectively and the movie hinges on a series of appalling jokes and unoriginal situations, wrapped around a makeshift murder plot. Boring and deeply offensive. SH Violence, swearing. *DVD*

Gene Wilder *Dave Lyons* • Richard Pryor *Wally Karew* • Joan Severance *Eve* • Kevin Spacey *Kirgo* • Alan North *Captain Braddock* • Anthony Zerbe *Sutherland* • Louis Giambalvo *Gatlin* • Kirsten Childs *Adele* ■ *Dir* Arthur Hiller • *Scr* Earl Barret, Arne Sultan, Eliot Wald, Andrew Kurtzman, Gene Wilder, from a story by Earl Barret, Arne Sultan, Marvin Worth

See Spot Run ★★★ PG

Comedy   2001 · US/Aus · Colour · 93min

This tells the tale of an FBI supermutt who teams up with a postman to thwart an attempt by the Mob on the dog's life. Toss into the mix a cute little kid and two hitmen, and it all sounds like the recipe for a right dog's dinner. The film has its fair share of boring sequences and third-rate scatological humour, yet David Arquette gives an enthusiastic performance as the postman, and there are some nice supporting performances. DA *DVD*

David Arquette *Gordon* • Michael Clarke Duncan *Agent Murdoch* • Leslie Bibb *Stephanie* • Joe Viterelli *Gino* • Angus T Jones *James* • Steven R Schirripa [Steve Schirripa] *Arliss* • Paul Sorvino *Sonny* ■ *Dir* John Whitesell • *Scr* George Gallo, Gregory Poirier, Danny Baron, Chris Faber, from a story by Andrew Deane, Michael Alexander Miller, George Gallo

See You in the Morning
★★ 15

Romantic drama   1989 · US · Colour · 113min

This is one of those intense relationship dramas in which everyone behaves like an adult – including the children. Jeff Bridges keeps the film on the rails, as a psychiatrist who spends so much time analysing his motives it's a wonder he's got any time left for living. Lukas Haas and Drew Barrymore are very subdued as Bridges's stepchildren, but they are certainly more interesting than their mother (Alice Krige). DP

Jeff Bridges *Larry Livingston* • Alice Krige *Beth Goodwin* • Farrah Fawcett *Jo Livingston* • Drew Barrymore *Cathy Goodwin* • Lukas Haas *Petey Goodwin* • David Dukes *Peter Goodwin* • Frances Sternhagen *Neenie* • George Hearn *Martin* ■ *Dir/Scr* Alan J Pakula

Seed of Chucky ★★★ 15

Horror spoof   2004 · US · Colour · 82min

Screenwriter Don Mancini, who created killer doll Chucky, makes his directorial feature debut with this, the fifth entry in the franchise. Here, Chucky (voiced, as always, by Brad Dourif) and his bride, Tiffany (breathlessly vocalised by Jennifer Tilly), are brought back to life by their gender-bending offspring Glen/Glenda (Billy Boyd) on the set of the Hollywood film chronicling their murderous exploits. The terrible toys then attempt to transfer their souls into the movie's director (real-life rapper Redman) and Tiffany's favourite star, Jennifer Tilly (playing herself). Technically terrific, fitfully funny. Curse of Chucky followed in 2013. AJ *DVD*

Jennifer Tilly *Jennifer Tilly/Tiffany* • Brad Dourif *Chucky* • Billy Boyd (1) *Glen/Glenda* • Redman • Hannah Spearritt *Joan* • John Waters (2) *Pete Peters* • Keith-Lee Castle *Psychs* • Jason Flemyng *Santa* ■ *Dir* Don Mancini • *Scr* Don Mancini, from his characters

Seeing Double ★★ PG

Musical comedy   2003 · UK/Sp · Colour · 87min

Chirpy British pop stars S Club sought to exploit their popularity with pre-teen audiences with this shameful but effective mass-marketing exercise. Wooden, unimaginative and with the feel of an extended pop promo, this nutrient-free nonsense makes *Spice World* look like an epic. It features not one, but two S Clubs, after an evil celebrity-obsessed scientist decides to clone Rachel Stevens (now more famous for her stint on *Strictly Come Dancing*), *Primeval's* Hannah Spearritt and the gang and send the doppelgangers on a world tour. SF *DVD*

Bradley McIntosh *Bradley* • Rachel Stevens *Rachel* • Hannah Spearritt *Hannah* • Jo O'Meara *Jo* • Tina Barrett *Tina* • Jon Lee *Jon* • Joseph Adams *Alistair, the manager* • David Gant *Victor, the clonemaster* • Gareth Gates *Clone Gareth Gates* ■ *Dir* Nigel Dick • *Scr* Kim Fuller, Paul Alexander

The Seekers ★★

Period adventure   1954 · UK · Colour · 90min

This costume adventure from director Ken Annakin is set in 19th-century New Zealand and boasts striking photography by Geoffrey Unsworth. The major influence on this story of colonial expansion at the expense of the Maoris is undoubtedly the Hollywood western and, consequently, it is hardly the most enlightened interpretation of the colonial spirit ever committed to film. Jack Hawkins cuts a dash as the leader of the expedition, however. DP

Jack Hawkins *Philip Wayne* • Glynis Johns *Marion Southey* • Noel Purcell *Paddy Clarke* • Inia Te Wiata *Hongi Tepe* • Kenneth Williams *Peter Wishart* • Laya Raki *Moana* ■ *Dir* Ken Annakin • *Scr* William Fairchild, from John Gutherie's novel

Seeking a Friend for the End of the World ★★★★ 15

Science-fiction romantic comedy 2011 · US · Colour · 97min

Intelligence and subtle wit inform this heartfelt look at unlikely romance blossoming in the shadow of Earth's obliteration by a giant asteroid. As the final countdown begins, the ensuing chaos throws together Steve Carell, who wants to track down his long-lost love, and neighbour Keira Knightley who's trying to reach her faraway family. Both actors put in immensely appealing performances that explore the pain, value and delight of humanity, while director Lorene Scafaria adeptly balances the humour and pathos, wringing genuine laughter and emotion from her slyly etched but ominous backdrop. AJ Swearing. *DVD* *Blu-ray*

Steve Carell *Dodge* • Keira Knightley *Penny* • Adam Brody *Owen* • Gillian Jacobs *Katie* • Melanie Lynskey *Karen* • William Petersen [William L Petersen] *Trucker* ■ *Dir/Scr* Lorene Scafaria

Seems like Old Times ★★ PG

Screwball comedy   1980 · US · Colour · 97min

Despite the presence of stars Goldie Hawn, Chevy Chase and Charles Grodin, plus a screenplay by Neil Simon, this tribute to the heyday of screwball comedy falls as flat as a pancake under the leaden hand of Jay Sandrich, making his film-directing debut. Some sharp lines pass muster, but the plot is limp and witless, while the ending is spectacularly pointless. TS Swearing. *DVD*

Goldie Hawn *Glenda* • Chevy Chase *Nick* • Charles Grodin *Ira* • Robert Guillaume *Fred* • Harold Gould *Judge* • George Grizzard *Governor* • Yvonne Wilder *Aurora* • TK Carter *Chester* ■ *Dir* Jay Sandrich • *Scr* Neil Simon

Seizure ★★★

Horror   1974 · US · Colour · 94min

For a long time after he hit the Hollywood big time, Oliver Stone refused to acknowledge this low-budget horror movie as his directorial debut. If it was bad, one could understand it. But it isn't. In fact, it's an unusually gripping gem starring ex-*Dark Shadows* vampire Jonathan Frid as a demented writer dreaming up three characters (Queen of Evil Martine Beswick, evil dwarf Herve Villechaize and towering Henry Baker) who spring to life to do his murderous bidding. Gory and scary, this is easily recognisable as a talented debut. AJ

Jonathan Frid *Edmund Blackstone* • Martine Beswick *Queen of Evil* • Joseph Sirola *Charlie* • Christina Pickles *Nicole Blackstone* • Herve Villechaize *The Spider* • Anne Meacham *Eunice* • Roger De Koven *Serge* • Troy Donahue *Mark* • Henry Baker [Henry Judd Baker] *Jackal* ■ *Dir* Oliver Stone • *Scr* Edward Mann, Oliver Stone

Selena ★★★ PG

Biographical musical drama 1997 · US · Colour · 122min

Virtually unknown outside the Latino community, Selena Quintanilla was a major figure in Tejano music until, on the very brink of her crossover into mainstream pop charts, she was murdered by the president of her fan club. This glossy biography centres on her relationship with her father (Edward James Olmos) and her determination to hit the big time. It's the perfect vehicle for Jennifer Lopez, who was nominated for a Golden Globe. FL *DVD*

Jennifer Lopez *Selena Quintanilla* • Edward James Olmos *Abraham Quintanilla* • Jon Seda *Chris Perez* • Jackie Guerra *Suzette Quintanilla* • Constance Marie *Marcela Quintanilla* • Jacob Vargas *Abie* ■ *Dir/Scr* Gregory Nava

A Self-Made Hero ★★★★ 15

Drama   1995 · Fr · Colour · 101min

Brilliantly exploiting the confusion precipitated by the liberation of France in the Second World War, this fascinating film from director Jacques Audiard ventures into the "forbidden" territory of Nazi collaboration. Mathieu Kassovitz plays the son of a collaborator who so credibly reinvents his past that he is invited to join a crack war-crimes unit. Kassovitz gives a nerve-end portrayal of an opportunist whose survival depends on deception, while Audiard's direction slyly captures the chilling postwar atmosphere. DP French +subtitles. Swearing.

Mathieu Kassovitz *Young Albert Dehousse* • Anouk Grinberg *Servane* • Sandrine Kiberlain *Yvette* • Albert Dupontel *Dionnet* • Jean-Louis Trintignant *Old Albert Dehousse* ■ *Dir* Jacques Audiard • *Scr* Jacques Audiard, Alain Le Henry, from the novel *Un Héros Très Discret* by Jean-François Deniau

The Selfish Giant ★★★ 15

Drama   2013 · UK · Colour · 86min

Two Yorkshire school friends tangle with an unscrupulous local scrap dealer in order to help their cash-strapped families in this cautionary fable. Nominally based on the Oscar Wilde story, it's a tale of childhood innocence in straitened circumstances that harks back to Ken Loach's *Kes*. But this second feature from promising director Clio Barnard (*The Arbor*) isn't on the same level as its distinguished 1969 predecessor. Although Barnard extracts magical

performances from non-professional leads Conner Chapman and Shaun Thomas, the story's outcome is predictable and the portrait of crushing social inequity often falls prey to broad "grim up north" cliché. TJ Swearing. *DVD* *Blu-ray*

Conner Chapman *Arbor* • Sean Gilder *Fenton* • Shaun Thomas *Swifty* • Sean Gilder *Chris Kane, "Kitten"* • Rebecca Manley Michelle *"Shelly" Fenton* • Siobhan Finneran *Mrs Swift* ■ *Dir* Clio Barnard • *Scr* Clio Barnard, inspired by Oscar Wilde's short story

Self/Less ★★ 12

Science-fiction thriller 2015 · US · Colour · 112min

This dark take on immortality follows dying businessman Damian Hale (Ben Kingsley), who transfers his consciousness to a younger body (Ryan Reynolds) in order to cheat death. But the questions raised by the story (the price of immortality, the nature of consciousness) serve only as building blocks for fight scenes and car chases. Throw in a very predictable ending and the result is a film that, while watchable, makes little use of its stars or premise. JL Violence, swearing, a sex scene. *DVD*

Ryan Reynolds *Young Damian* • Natalie Martinez *Madeline* • Matthew Goode *Albright* • Victor Garber *Martin* • Derek Luke *Anton* • Michelle Dockery *Claire* • Ben Kingsley *Damian Hale* ■ *Dir* Tarsem Singh • *Scr* David & Alex Pastor

The Sellout ★★ 15

Spy drama   1975 · UK/It · Colour · 96min

Before his premature death in 1980, British director Peter Collinson achieved a certain notoriety with a ragbag of action adventures like this one, set and filmed in Israel. It's not surprising to find Oliver Reed and Gayle Hunnicutt on hand, since they tended to prop up international co-productions on attractive locations, but sad to see Richard Widmark slumming it. This would-be thriller about spies brings credit to no one, and the film's pace is leaden. TS

Richard Widmark *Sam Lucas* • Oliver Reed *Gabriel Lee* • Gayle Hunnicutt *Deborah* • Sam Wanamaker *Sickles* • Vladek Sheybal *The Dutchman* • Ori Levy *Major Benjamin* • Assaf Dayan [Assi Dayan] *Lieutenant Elan* • Shmuel Rodensky *Zafron* ■ *Dir* Peter Collinson • *Scr* Murray Smith, Judson Kinberg, from a story by Murray Smith • *Cinematographer* Arthur Ibbetson

Selma ★★★★ 12

Historical drama based on a true story 2014 · UK/US · Colour · 122min

This sweepingly staged history lesson avoids the episodic pitfalls of the biopic by focusing on a single flashpoint in the life of Dr Martin Luther King: the three marches he led in 1965 from Selma in Alabama to the state capital, Montgomery, demanding equal voting rights for blacks. British actor David Oyelowo gives a career-defining performance: stirring and full-blooded in public oratory, fallible in private. If Tim Roth's segregationist Governor Wallace tips into panto, the overall sense of righteous, non-violent anger is palpable. AC Violence, swearing, racist language. *DVD* *Blu-ray*

David Oyelowo *Martin Luther King Jr* • Tom Wilkinson *President Lyndon B Johnson* • Carmen Ejogo *Coretta Scott King* • Giovanni Ribisi *Lee C White* • Alessandro Nivola *John Doar* • Cuba Gooding Jr *Fred Gray* • Tim Roth *George Wallace* • Oprah Winfrey *Annie Lee Cooper* • Common *James Bevel* ■ *Dir* Ava DuVernay • *Scr* Paul Webb

Semi-Pro ★★ 15

Sports comedy   2008 · US · Colour · 87min

Will Ferrell stars in yet another sports spoof here (following *Talladega Nights: the Ballad of Ricky Bobby* and *Blades of Glory*), this one set in the mid-1970s. He plays Jackie Moon, the bubble-permed owner/player/coach of a lowly basketball team who is desperate for them to join the National Basketball Association. However, the already flimsy plot falls to the wayside as this sprawling comedy focuses instead on star names (Ferrell, Woody Harrelson, André Benjamin) and a barrel load of hit-

S

and-miss gags. **KK** Swearing, sexual references. *DVD Blu*

Will Ferrell *Jackie Moon* • Woody Harrelson *Monix* • André Benjamin *Clarence* • Maura Tierney *Lynn* • Andrew Daly *Dick Pepperfield* • Andy Richter *Bobby Dee* ▪ *Dir* Kent Alterman • *Scr* Scot Armstrong

Semi-Tough ★★★ 15
Sports comedy 1977 · US · Colour · 103min

Good-natured and often very funny, this is set around the world of American football. Burt Reynolds is the star player who finds himself competing with team-mate and good pal Kris Kristofferson for the attentions of Jill Clayburgh, whose dad owns the team. Reynolds and Kristofferson exude an easy-going charm and there is some expert comic support from the likes of Richard Masur and Robert Preston. **JF** Swearing.

Burt Reynolds *Billy Clyde Puckett* • Kris Kristofferson *Marvin "Shake" Tiller* • Jill Clayburgh *Barbara Jane Bookman* • Robert Preston *Big Ed Bookman* • Bert Convy *Friedrich Bismark* • Roger E Mosley *Puddin* • Lotte Lenya *Clara Pelf* • Richard Masur *Phillip Hooper* • Carl Weathers *Dreamer Tatum* • Brian Dennehy *TJ Lambert* • Ron Silver *Vlada* ▪ *Dir* Michael Ritchie • *Scr* Walter Bernstein, from the novel by Dan Jenkins

Seminole ★★ U
Western 1953 · US · Colour · 86min

This otherwise effective western from Universal Studios is hobbled by a combination of earnestness and a weak leading performance from Rock Hudson as a cavalry officer who finds that his good intentions cannot prevent a conflict with the Seminole Indians. It's beautifully filmed (with Technicolor photography by Russell Metty) and has a striking turn from Hugh O'Brian, but a stronger script would have helped. **TS**

Rock Hudson *Lieutenant Lance Caldwell* • Barbara Hale *Revere Muldoon* • Anthony Quinn *Osceola/John Powell* • Richard Carlson *Major Harlan Degan* • Hugh O'Brian *Kajeck* • Russell Johnson *Lieutenant Hamilton* • Lee Marvin *Sergeant Magruder* ▪ *Dir* Budd Boetticher • *Scr* Charles K Peck Jr

The Senator Was Indiscreet ★★★ U
Comedy 1947 · US · BW · 81min

This interesting satire on Capitol Hill stars a very tongue-in-cheek William Powell as the senator with an interest in more than just the latest crop sharers' bill. This Universal comedy is unusual for its time, in that it pokes very obvious fun at political institutions when other movies were considerably less direct. Inexplicably, this was the only directorial outing for playwright George S Kaufman, who acquits himself well. Perhaps his brand of no-holds-barred satire was a little too strong for 1940s Hollywood. **SH**

William Powell *Senator Melvin G Ashton* • Ella Raines *Poppy McNaughton* • Peter Lind Hayes *Lew Gibson* • Arleen Whelan *Valerie Shepherd* • Ray Collins *Houlihan* • Allen Jenkins *Farrell* • Charles D Brown *Dinty* • Hans Conried *Waiter* • Myrna Loy *Mrs Ashton* ▪ *Dir* George S Kaufman • *Scr* Charles MacArthur, from a story by Edwin Lanham

Send Me No Flowers ★★★★ U
Romantic black comedy 1964 · US · Colour · 95min

Riotously funny or extraordinarily tasteless, depending on your point of view, this stars Rock Hudson as a hypochondriac who's convinced he's dying. Doris Day is his put-upon wife and Tony Randall the friend who takes the news of Hudson's impending demise badly. This is sophisticated stuff, the last of the Day/Hudson collaborations, and it's shot through with a mordant wit that may chime better with today's audience than it did with movie-goers back in the 1960s. Hudson was invariably underrated as a performer, but here he's excellent, lending grace to a difficult role and imbuing his

character with sly, winning humour. **TS** *DVD*

Rock Hudson *George Kimball* • Doris Day *Judy Kimball* • Tony Randall *Arnold Nash* • Paul Lynde *Mr Akins* • Hal March *Winston Burr* • Edward Andrews *Dr Ralph Morrissey* • Patricia Barry *Linda Bullard* • Clint Walker *Bert Power* ▪ *Dir* Norman Jewison • *Scr* Julius J Epstein, from the play by Norman Barasch, Carroll Moore

The Sender ★★★ 18
Science-fiction thriller 1982 · UK · Colour · 87min

Former art director Roger Christian's directorial debut was this piece of metaphysical sci-fi, in which psychiatrist Kathryn Harrold pieces together the bizarre circumstances of amnesiac Zeljko Ivanek's condition. At times extremely disturbing, and regularly punctuated by set pieces highlighting Nick Allder's special effects, this mystery keeps one constantly alert and on the edge of one's seat. Too bad about the many loose ends. **DM**

Kathryn Harrold *Gail Farmer* • Zeljko Ivanek *Sender* • Shirley Knight *Jerolyn* • Paul Freeman *Dr Denman* • Sean Hewitt *Messiah* • Harry Ditson *Dr Hirsch* • Olivier Pierre *Dr Erskine* • Marsha A Hunt *Nurse Jo* ▪ *Dir* Roger Christian • *Scr* Thomas Baum

Senior Prom ★★ U
Musical 1958 · US · BW · 81min

Passing itself off as a campus musical, the college girl-meets-boy-then meets-another-boy wisp of a plotline serves only as an excuse for stringing together 20 unmemorable musical numbers. Five of the songs spotlight the girl at the centre (Jill Corey). The boys between whom Corey's affections travel - if anyone cares - are rich Tom Laughlin (who picked up some fame in the 1970s for *Billy Jack*) and penniless Paul Hampton. **RK**

Jill Corey *Gay Sherridan* • Paul Hampton *Tom Harper* • Jimmie Komach *Dog* • Barbara Bostock *Flip* • Tom Laughlin *Carter Breed III* • Frieda Inescort *Mrs Sherridan* • Selene Walters *Caroline* • Marvin Miller *Narrator* • Louis Prima • Keely Smith • Ed Sullivan • Mitch Miller • Connee Boswell • Bob Crosby ▪ *Dir* David Lowell Rich • *Scr* Hal Hackady

Senna ★★★★★
Motor racing documentary 2010 · UK · Colour · 105min

In the years leading up to his tragic death at the San Marino Grand Prix in 1994, Ayrton Senna established himself as one of Formula One's most brilliant and controversial drivers. A three-times world champion, the volatile Brazilian was a hero in his homeland, and his ruthlessness behind the wheel, not to mention his spiky challenges to the politics of the racing world, grabbed headlines. Director Asif Kapadia's powerful and engrossing documentary, wholly assembled from thrilling archive footage with new voiceovers from several leading F1 figures, paints a portrait of a determined and deeply spiritual man. His notorious clashes with archrival Alain Prost give the chronological telling of the story added bite, resulting in a fascinating biography that will appeal to more than just fans of fast cars. **TeS** Some swearing. *DVD Blu*

▪ *Dir* Asif Kapadia • *Scr* Manish Pandey

Sensations ★★★ U
Musical 1944 · US · BW · 85min

This is one of those of those musicals with a mouthwatering cast list that promises much more than it delivers. Director Andrew Stone also produced and co-wrote the script so must take most of the blame. Top-billed Eleanor Powell had been MGM's brightest dancing star, but was freelancing when she made this modest affair. She could still dance up a storm and her numbers are the best things in the movie. Her efforts to obtain publicity make up the wispy plot, welcome relief from which is provided by the guest spot of WC Fields (in his last film appearance). **TV**

Eleanor Powell *Ginny Walker* • Dennis O'Keefe *Junior Crane* • C Aubrey Smith *Dan Lindsay* • Eugene Pallette *Gus Crane* • Mimi Forsythe *Julia Westcott* • Lyle Talbot *Randall* • Hubert Castle *The Great Gustafson* • WC Fields ▪ *Dir* Andrew L Stone • *Scr* Dorothy Bennett, Andrew L Stone, from a story by Frederick Jackson, Andrew L Stone

Sense and Sensibility ★★★★★ U
Period romantic drama 1995 · US · Colour · 130min

The decision to hire Taiwan's Ang Lee to direct this adaptation of Jane Austen's first novel was truly inspired. Avoiding the chocolate-box visuals that cheapen so many British costume dramas, Lee brings a refreshing period realism to this tale of two sisters that allows Emma Thompson's respectful Oscar-winning script to flourish. Kate Winslet's spirited Marianne stands out from a solid display of ensemble acting, but the mystery remains why Lee, who became the first director to win Berlin's Golden Bear twice, was not among the film's seven Oscar nominations. **DP** *DVD Blu*

Emma Thompson *Elinor Dashwood* • Kate Winslet *Marianne Dashwood* • Alan Rickman *Colonel Brandon* • Hugh Grant *Edward Ferrars* • Greg Wise *John Willoughby* • Gemma Jones *Mrs Dashwood* • Imogen Stubbs *Lucy Steele* • Elizabeth Spriggs *Mrs Jennings* • Tom Wilkinson *Mr Dashwood* • Harriet Walter *Fanny Dashwood* • James Fleet *John Dashwood* • Emilie François *Margaret Dashwood* • Robert Hardy *Sir John Middleton* • Imelda Staunton *Charlotte Palmer* • Hugh Laurie *Mr Palmer* ▪ *Dir* Ang Lee • *Scr* Emma Thompson, from the novel by Jane Austen

A Sense of Loss ★★
Documentary 1972 · US/Swi · Colour · 135min

Marcel Ophüls's fatally flawed investigation into the Troubles in Northern Ireland was considered sufficiently inflammatory by the BBC for them to ban it. However, such is the evident bias in his assessment of the situation that it has precious little value, either as reportage or propaganda. His presentation of key Protestant apologists such as Ian Paisley is so dismissive that, rather than exposing the prejudice in their polemic, he succeeds only in ridiculing them, thus making the pronouncements of the Republican cause seem wholly acceptable. **DP**

▪ *Dir* Marcel Ophüls

Senseless ★ 15
Comedy 1998 · US · Colour · 89min

This poor man's imitation of a Jim Carrey movie is weak on all fronts. Marlon Wayans stars as a student so desperate to get a junior analyst's job that he agrees to take a sense-enhancing potion. Inevitably this lends him super senses that soon spiral out of control. Not worth the eyestrain. **LH** Swearing, nudity.

Marlon Wayans *Darryl Witherspoon* • Matthew Lillard *Tim LaFlour* • Rip Torn *Randall Tyson* • David Spade *Scott Thorpe* • Brad Dourif *Dr Wheedon* ▪ *Dir* Penelope Spheeris • *Scr* Greg Erb, Craig Mazin • *Music* Yello

Senso ★★★ PG
Period drama 1954 · It · Colour · 116min

This full-blown melodrama from Luchino Visconti is about an Italian countess, trapped in a sexless marriage, falling in love with a dashing Austrian cavalry officer who is invading Italy. As usual with Visconti, there is a welter of baroque effects and an acute sense of history, as the countess betrays her country and her social class for the sake of passion. **AT** Italian dubbed. *DVD*

Alida Valli *Contessa Livia Serpieri* • Farley Granger *Lieut Franz Mahler* • Massimo Girotti *Marquis Roberto Ussoni* • Heinz Moog *Count Serpieri* • Rina Morelli *Laura* ▪ *Dir* Luchino Visconti • *Scr* Luchino Visconti, Suso Cecchi D'Amico, Giorgio Prosperi, Carlo Alianello, Giorgio Bassani, from the *Senso: Nuove Storielle Vane* by Camillo Boito

Sentimental Journey ★★ U
Melodrama 1946 · US · BW · 94min

A stage actress (Maureen O'Hara) with a heart condition adopts an orphan child so that, if she succumbs, her husband, John Payne, won't be left alone. Weepies don't come much weepier than this offering, which is crassly manipulative and the sort of emotional rollercoaster that American audiences responded to immediately after the Second World War. There have been two remakes: with Lauren Bacall in 1958 as *The Gift of Love* and a 1984 TV-movie. **AT**

John Payne *Bill* • Maureen O'Hara *Julie* • William Bendix *Donnelly* • Cedric Hardwicke *Dr Miller* • Glenn Langan *Judson* • Mischa Auer *Lawrence Ayres* ▪ *Dir* Walter Lang • *Scr* Samuel Hoffenstein, Elizabeth Reinhardt, from a story by Nelia Gardner White

The Sentinel ★★ 18
Horror 1977 · US · Colour · 87min

Michael Winner is one of our most frequently disparaged directors, and it isn't difficult to see why on the evidence of this risible attempt to jump on *The Exorcist's* demonic band wagon. Cristina Raines moves into a stately old Brooklyn mansion, is menaced by ghastly apparitions and finds the place is built over a gateway to hell. Even those disposed to find Winner's direction enjoyably trashy - as opposed to clumsy and sensationalist - will be shocked by his decision to use genuinely handicapped people in one scene. **RS**

Chris Sarandon *Michael Lerman* • Cristina Raines *Alison Parker* • Martin Balsam *Professor* • John Carradine *Father Halliran* • José Ferrer *Robed figure* • Ava Gardner *Miss Logan* • Arthur Kennedy *Franchino* • Burgess Meredith *Chazen* • Eli Wallach *Gatz* • Christopher Walken *Rizzo* • Jerry Orbach *Director* • Beverly D'Angelo *Sandra* • Tom Berenger *Man at end* • Jeff Goldblum *Jack* ▪ *Dir* Michael Winner • *Scr* Michael Winner, Jeffrey Konvitz, from the novel by Jeffrey Konvitz

The Sentinel ★★ 12
Thriller 2006 · US · Colour · 103min

Disgraced Secret Service operative Michael Douglas races to foil an inside conspiracy to assassinate the US president in this slickly shot but soulless political thriller from *SWAT* director Clark Johnson. A tension-free hotch-potch of clichés, transparent twists and plain implausibilities, this acts as though the TV drama *24* never happened. Douglas seems past his prime as the respected veteran branded a traitorous mole following a colleague's murder, although it's the scandalous reason behind his failed lie-detector test - involving limp First Lady Kim Basinger - that strains credibility the most. Thank heavens, then, for Kiefer Sutherland, who adds acid intensity to an otherwise routine plot. **SF** *DVD Blu*

Michael Douglas (1) *Pete Garrison* • Kiefer Sutherland *David Breckinridge* • Eva Longoria *Jill Marin* • Martin Donovan *William Montrose* • Ritchie Coster *The Handler* • Kim Basinger *First Lady Sarah Ballentine* • Blair Brown *National Security Adviser* • David Rasche *President John Ballentine* ▪ *Dir* Clark Johnson • *Scr* George Nolfi, from the novel by Gerald Petievich

Separado! ★★★ 12
Music documentary 2010 · UK · Colour · 89min

You don't have to be Welsh to appreciate *Separado!* ... but it helps. Part documentary, part road movie, part music video and part one man's search for his roots, the film chronicles a bid by Gruff Rhys, lead singer with Welsh rock group Super Furry Animals, to track down descendants of kinfolk who, in the 1800s, fled religious and cultural repression in Wales to found a utopian "New Cambria" in South America. Rhys proves an engaging tour guide and performer, but this is too personal, both in terms of subject matter and tricksy visual style, to appeal to all tastes. **DA** English, Welsh, Spanish, Portuguese +subtitles. *DVD*

Gruff Rhys ▪ *Dir* Dylan Goch • *Music* Gruff Rhys

U SUITABLE FOR ALL   **Uc** SUITABLE ESPECIALLY FOR YOUNG CHILDREN (DVD ONLY)   **PG** PARENTAL GUIDANCE   **12A** UNDER 12s TO BE ACCOMPANIED (CINEMA ONLY)

Separate Lies ★★★ 15
Psychological drama
2004 · UK/US · Colour · 81min

Gosford Park screenwriter Julian Fellowes makes his directorial debut with this peculiarly restrained tale of love, lies and loyalty. It's an engaging yet implausible melodrama in which a tragic death sets off a devastating chain of events. Tom Wilkinson and Emily Watson play bourgeois Londoners whose seemingly idyllic marriage is torn apart following a hit-and-run incident near their country retreat. The film is handsomely shot and boasts assured performances from its two leads, but it suffers from excessive politeness. **SF** Swearing. **DVD**

Emily Watson *Anne Manning* · Tom Wilkinson *James Manning* · Rupert Everett *Bill Bule* · Linda Bassett *Maggie* · David Harewood *Inspector Marshall* · John Neville *Lord Rawston* · Hermione Norris *Priscilla* ■ *Dir* Julian Fellowes · *Scr* Julian Fellowes, from the novel *A Way Through the Wood* by Nigel Balchin

Separate Lives ★ 18
Thriller
1995 · US · Colour · 97min

James Belushi and Linda Hamilton are consigned to B-movie hell in a limp psychological thriller from David Madden. Belushi plays a former detective who is persuaded by his college lecturer (Hamilton) to watch her for signs of a murderous multiple personality. Tedious, predictable and awful. **JB** Violence, sex scenes, swearing. **DVD**

James Belushi *Tom Beckwith* · Linda Hamilton *Lauren Porter/Lena* · Vera Miles *Dr Ruth Goldin* · Elisabeth Moss *Ronnie Beckwith* · Drew Snyder *Robert Porter* · Mark Lindsay Chapman *Keno Sykes* · Marc Poppel *Detective Joe Gallo* ■ *Dir* David Madden · *Scr* Steven Pressfield

Separate Tables ★★★★ PG
Drama
1958 · US · BW · 95min

David Niven won an Oscar as the retired "major" whose libido gets the better of him in this wonderfully cast version of Terence Rattigan's play. Wendy Hiller is the proprietor of a Bournemouth boarding house, presiding over a small group of paying guests whose neuroses start to unravel. Deborah Kerr's mother-dominated mousiness is too insistent, but Burt Lancaster's Hemingwayesque turn is great fun and Rita Hayworth, as his ex-wife, is marvellously convincing as a woman who knows that time and her beauty are running out. Delbert Mann's film is both moving and entertaining. There was a TV remake in 1983 starring Julie Christie and Alan Bates. **TH** **DVD**

Rita Hayworth *Ann Shankland* · Deborah Kerr *Sibyl Railton-Bell* · David Niven *Major Pollock* · Burt Lancaster *John Malcolm* · Wendy Hiller *Miss Pat Cooper* · Gladys Cooper *Mrs Railton-Bell* · Cathleen Nesbitt *Lady Matheson* · Rod Taylor *Charles* ■ *Dir* Delbert Mann · *Scr* Terence Rattigan, John Gay, from the play by Terence Rattigan

Separate Tables ★★★ PG
Drama
1983 · US · Colour · 113min

Julie Christie teamed with director John Schlesinger for the fourth time (to date) for this TV-movie version of the celebrated Terence Rattigan play. She's far too beautiful for the role of the mousey Sibyl, but her hesitant performance just about stands comparison with Deborah Kerr's. Alan Bates is a touch too ebullient in the role that earned David Niven an Oscar, but it's clear the couple enjoy working together. Interestingly, Schlesinger retains the "Table by the Window" and the "Table Number Seven" structure of the play. **DP**

Julie Christie *Anne Shankland/Sybil Railton-Bell* · Alan Bates *John Malcolm/Major Pollock* · Claire Bloom *Miss Cooper* · Irene Worth *Mrs Railton-Bell* · Sylvia Barter *Lady Matheson* · Bernard Archard *Mr Fowler* · Liz Smith *Miss Meachum* · Kathy Staff *Mabel* · Brian Deacon *Charles Stratton* ■ *Dir* John Schlesinger · *Scr* Terence Rattigan, from his play

La Séparation ★★★ PG
Drama
1994 · Fr · Colour · 84min

Although a masterclass in actorly restraint, the agonisingly slow deterioration of Isabelle Huppert and Daniel Auteuil's relationship makes for painful viewing. But siding with Auteuil's character, director Christian Vincent makes Huppert's Anne seem unnecessarily callous and allows Auteuil to become increasingly pathetic. The political subtext, on how radicals conform with time, is much more engaging than the detached melodrama. DP French +subtitles. **DVD**

Isabelle Huppert *Anne* · Daniel Auteuil *Pierre* · Jérôme Deschamps *Victor* · Karin Viard *Claire* · Laurence Lerel *Laurence* · Louis Vincent *Loulou* · Nina Morato *Marie* ■ *Dir* Christian Vincent · *Scr* Christian Vincent, Dan Franck, from the novel by Dan Franck

September ★★★★ PG
Drama
1987 · US · Colour · 171min

Woody Allen's autumnal film has a story straight out of Chekhov, as relationships fray between intellectuals in a Vermont mansion and Mia Farrow, Denholm Elliott, Dianne Wiest and Sam Waterston vent their frustrations on each other. One of Allen's "serious" pieces, without his angst-prone presence, this was originally filmed with Maureen O'Sullivan (Farrow's real-life mother), Sam Shepard and Charles Durning. Allen was so unsure about its balance that he largely re-shot it and was forced to find alternative actors because of the cast's other commitments. The result is stylish and beautifully shot. **TH** **DVD**

Denholm Elliott *Howard* · Dianne Wiest *Stephanie* · Mia Farrow *Lane* · Elaine Stritch *Diane* · Sam Waterston *Peter* · Jack Warden *Lloyd* · Ira Wheeler *Mr Raines* · Jane Cecil *Mrs Raines* ■ *Dir/Scr* Woody Allen · *Cinematographer* Carlo Di Palma

September Affair ★★★
Romantic drama
1950 · US · BW · 105min

Set in various Italian locations, this soapy romance might have been more appealing in colour. What it does have, however, are two likeable leads in Joseph Cotten and Joan Fontaine and Kurt Weill's *September Song*, sung by Walter Huston on the soundtrack. The contrived plot has Fontaine, a concert pianist, and wealthy married Cotton falling in love when they miss their plane back to the USA. The plane crashes and they are listed among the dead. Now they can start a new life together. Or can they? Thankfully William Dieterle's direction avoids oversentimentality. **RB**

Joan Fontaine *Manina Stuart* · Joseph Cotten *David Lawrence* · Françoise Rosay *Maria Salvatini* · Jessica Tandy *Catherine Lawrence* · Robert Arthur (1) *David Lawrence Jr* · James Lydon *Johnny Wilson* ■ *Dir* William Dieterle · *Scr* Robert Thoeren, from a story by Fritz Rotter · *Music* Victor Young

The September Issue ★★★★ 12
Documentary
2009 · US · Colour · 86min

RJ Cutler's real-life portrait of the world of American *Vogue* and its English-born editor Anna Wintour (reputedly the inspiration for Miranda Priestly in *The Devil Wears Prada*) resists the temptation to go for cheap laughs, opting instead for something more incisive and highly entertaining. There are no prima-donna blow-ups – Wintour is famously icy – and the tension is all the more memorable for being understated, particularly when it involves long-time lieutenant Grace Coddington, the only person who stands up to Wintour. What the film lacks is the dissident voice of outsiders and the many who have come and gone on *Vogue*, because, in Coddington's words, they "couldn't take the heartbreak". **BP** **DVD**

Anna Wintour ■ *Dir* RJ Cutler · *Cinematographer* Bob Richman [Robert Richman]

September 30, 1955 ★★★
Drama
1977 · US · Colour · 107min

The title is the date on which James Dean crashed his Porsche and turned himself into a legend. This film's hero, Richard Thomas, is a Dean-obsessed student in Arkansas, who hears the news of his idol's death and with other students stages an elaborate pagan-style ceremony which ends in a terrible accident. Moodily shot by Gordon Willis and scored by veteran Leonard Rosenman, this is an effective meditation on the power of celebrity and its impact on youth culture. **AT**

Richard Thomas *Jimmy J* · Susan Tyrrell *Melba Lou* · Deborah Benson *Charlotte* · Lisa Blount *Billie Jean* · Tom Hulce *Hanley* · Dennis Quaid *Frank* · Dennis Christopher *Eugene* ■ *Dir/Scr* James Bridges

Seraphim Falls ★★★ 15
Western drama
2006 · US · Colour · 107min

Pierce Brosnan hightails it across mountains, rivers and desert pursued by a vengeful Liam Neeson in this mean and moody western. Both men are Civil War veterans, but though peace has been declared, there's still a score to settle. Writer/director David Von Ancken doesn't reveal their history till very late, focusing instead on the primal struggle of man against man. The opening half hour runs on pure adrenaline with only snatches of dialogue between breaths in an imposing landscape just as unforgiving as the leads. Midway, however, the chase does get a little wearying, and there's a strange shift into metaphysical territory towards the end. It's not a convincing outcome, but the power of the film is in the blood, sweat and tears shed along the way. **SP** Violence, swearing. **DVD**

Liam Neeson *Carver* · Pierce Brosnan *Gideon* · Anjelica Huston *Madame Louise* · Michael Wincott *Hayes* · Robert Baker *Pope* · Ed Lauter *Parsons* · Tom Noonan *Minister/Abraham* · Kevin J O'Connor *Henry* ■ *Dir* David Von Ancken · *Scr* David Von Ancken, Abby Everett Jaques · *Cinematographer* John Toll

Séraphine ★★★★ PG
Biographical period drama
2008 · Fr/Bel · Colour · 126min

The winner of seven Césars, this fact-based period drama is an exceptional and exquisitely photographed depiction of artistic taste, social snobbery and transient celebrity. Yolande Moreau stars as unsung painter Séraphine Louis, who is dismissed as a simple drudge by her neighbours in the French town of Senlis in the years prior to the First World War. However, her humble existence is soon transformed when she meets German art expert Wilhelm Uhde (Ulrich Tukur), who recognises her as an artist of primitive genius. Moreau (who picked up the best actress award) excels as the eccentric skivvy whose unprepossessing appearance and erratic temperament belie a sensitivity that is rooted in a simple religious faith. **DP** French, German +subtitles. Brief nudity.

Yolande Moreau *Séraphine Louis, "Séraphine de Senlis"* · Ulrich Tukur *Wilhelm Uhde* · Anne Bennent *Anne-Marie Uhde* · Geneviève Mnich *Mme Duphot* ■ *Dir* Martin Provost · *Scr* Marc Abdelnour, Martin Provost

A Serbian Film ★★ 18
Horror
2010 · Ser · Colour · 95min

According to director Srdjan Spasojevic, this story of a washed up porn star lured out of retirement by a psychotic film-maker provides the set-up for a treatise on Serbia's troubled history of war, rape and genocide. But its parade of rape, necrophilia and paedophilia involving newborns feels more like a blatant attempt to create lucrative tabloid controversy than a deconstruction of the politics of fascism. Ironically, the graphic content is less offensive than the depressingly puerile way Spasojevic handles it. At least we're likely to be spared a Hollywood remake. **JR** In Serbian. Violence, sex scenes. **DVD**

September 30, 1955 — right column continues

Srdjan Todorovic *Milos* · Sergej Trifunovic *Vukmir* · Jelena Gavrilovic *Maria* · Katarina Zutic *Lajla* ■ *Dir* Srdjan Spasojevic · *Scr* Aleksandar Radivojevic, Srdjan Spasojevic

Serena ★★★ U
Crime drama
1962 · UK · BW · 62min

Rising well above the usual quota-quickie standards, this entertaining little whodunnit shoehorns about two hours of plot into its short running time. Directed at a fair lick by Peter Maxwell, it revolves around the complicated sex life of smoothie artist Emrys Jones, who wants to leave his wife for his model mistress. When the body of an unknown woman is found in a country cottage, inspector Patrick Holt is called in to investigate. **DP**

Patrick Holt *Inspector Gregory* · Emrys Jones *Howard Rogers* · Honor Blackman *Ann Rogers* · Bruce Beeby *Sergeant Conway* · John Horsley *Mr Fisher* · Robert Perceval *Bank manager* ■ *Dir* Peter Maxwell · *Scr* Edward Abraham, Reginald Hearne, from a story by Edward Abraham, Valerie Abraham

Serena ★★★ 15
Period drama
2013 · US/Cz Rep · Colour · 105min

Following *Silver Linings Playbook* and *American Hustle*, Bradley Cooper and Jennifer Lawrence reunite for a Depression-era drama. After a whirlwind courtship, Lawrence joins husband Cooper in North Carolina and becomes a driving force in his timber business. Unfortunately, a child he has had with an employee haunts their relationship. The whole story feels abbreviate, with Sean Harris, Rhys Ifans and Toby Jones squandered in roles that do little more than advance the plot. Elegant but underdeveloped, *Serena* feels like the bare bones of a magnificent tragedy. Still, there are enough flashes of the film it might have been to make it worth watching. **EAS** **DVD** **Blu**

Jennifer Lawrence (2) *Serena Pemberton* · Bradley Cooper *George Pemberton* · Rhys Ifans *Galloway* · Toby Jones *Sheriff McDowell* · Sean Harris *Campbell* ■ *Dir* Susanne Bier · *Scr* Christopher Kyle, from Ron Rash's novel

Serenade ★★★★ U
Musical drama
1956 · US · Colour · 121min

This film version of James M Cain's steamy novel about a singer who has a homosexual relationship with his patron seems an unlikely vehicle for Hollywood's top tenor Mario Lanza. Even with the book's plot substantially changed (the patron is now a woman), this is compulsive viewing thanks to director Anthony Mann's skill, the urbane villainy of Vincent Price and the sheer soap-opera pleasure of watching cool Joan Fontaine and sultry Sarita Montiel vie for Lanza. The Warner Bros production values are top-notch, but it's a bit long. **TS**

Mario Lanza *Damon Vincenti* · Joan Fontaine *Kendall Hale* · Sarita Montiel *Juana Montes* · Vincent Price *Charles Winthrop* · Joseph Calleia *Maestro Marcatello* · Harry Bellaver *Monte* · Vince Edwards *Marco Roselli* ■ *Dir* Anthony Mann · *Scr* Ivan Goff, Ben Roberts, John Twist, from the novel by James M Cain

Serendipity ★★★ PG
Romantic comedy
2001 · US · Colour · 87min

John Cusack and Kate Beckinsale are the two Christmas shoppers who meet in Bloomingdales. In spite of both being involved with other people, they share a couple of hot chocolates and then, on her insistence, leave the chance that they could make a cute twosome to the fickle hands of fate. Years later, when they're about to go down the aisle with their respective partners, they try to find each other to see if it was really true love. Cusack's winning performance saves this sweet (if occasionally sickly) romantic whimsy. **JB** **DVD** **Blu**

John Cusack *Jonathan Trager* · Kate Beckinsale *Sara Thomas* · Molly Shannon *Eve* · Jeremy Piven *Dean Kansky* · John Corbett *Lars Hammond* · Bridget Moynahan *Halley Buchanan* · Eugene Levy *Bloomingdale's salesman* ■ *Dir* Peter Chelsom · *Scr* Marc Klein

S

Serenity ★★★★ 15
Science-fiction action adventure
2005 · US · Colour · 114min

The sci-fi television series *Firefly* was cancelled mid-run in 2002, but acquired such a fervent cult following that writer/director Joss Whedon was able to revive it for the big screen. Nathan Fillion, commander of the spaceship *Serenity*, is a maverick adventurer in the tradition of Han Solo, eking out a living in the galactic equivalent of the Wild West. The action begins when a doctor (Sean Maher) rescues his sister (Summer Glau) from a top-secret base, where the authorities have been trying to exploit her psychic powers. The film boasts all the thrills and excitement of the early *Star Wars* movies, while making some incisive points about governments that want to impose their views on everyone. BP Violence. *DVD* *BL*
Nathan Fillion *Captain Malcolm "Mal" Reynolds* · Alan Tudyk *Wash* · Adam Baldwin *Jayne* · Summer Glau *River* · Chiwetel Ejiofor *The Operative* · Gina Torres *Zoe* · Morena Baccarin *Inara* · Jewel Staite *Kaylee* · Sean Maher *Simon* ■ *Dir* Joss Whedon · *Scr* Joss Whedon, from his TV series

The Sergeant ★★★
Drama 1968 · US · Colour and BW · 108min

Rod Steiger boldly goes where few actors have dared to go, even in the liberated Swinging Sixties, by portraying a homosexual character. As a US Army sergeant serving in postwar Paris he finds a love object in young private John Phillip Law, though it takes a long time for him to realise why the hands-off relationship means so much to him. John Flynn directs with ponderous seriousness, but Steiger is believably vulnerable as the man caught up in a system that won't allow him to reveal his sexuality. TH
Rod Steiger *Master Sergeant Albert Callan* · John Phillip Law *Private Tom Swanson* · Ludmila Mikael *Solange* · Frank Latimore *Captain Loring* · Elliott Sullivan *Pop Henneken* · Ronald Rubin *Corporal Cowley* · Phillip Roye *Aldous Brown* ■ *Dir* John Flynn · *Scr* Dennis Murphy, from his novel

Sgt Bilko ★★ PG
Comedy 1996 · US · Colour · 90min

Steve Martin must have known the comparisons with Phil Silvers were not going to be favourable when he took on this tepid spin-off, but he combines some of Silvers's character with his own comic personality. Andy Breckman's script is strongest in its double-talk, but the plot – about a top-secret hover-tank – is less than involving and the feud between Martin and Phil Hartman is overcooked. Mediocre, but not a total disaster. DP Swearing. *DVD*
Steve Martin *Master Sgt Ernest G Bilko* · Dan Aykroyd *Colonel Hall* · Phil Hartman *Major Thorn* · Glenne Headly *Rita Robbins* · Daryl Mitchell *Wally Holbrook* · Max Casella *Dino Paparelli* · Eric Edwards *Duane Doberman* · Dan Ferro *Tony Morales* ■ *Dir* Jonathan Lynn · *Scr* Andy Breckman, from the TV series *The Phil Silvers Show* by Nat Hiken

Sergeant Deadhead ★★ U
Musical comedy 1965 · US · Colour · 88min

One-time pop star Frankie Avalon plays a dual role in this watchable, if rowdy, musical comedy. Sergeant OK Deadhead is the kind of nervous, Jerry Lewis-style klutz the US Air Force doesn't need when it's about to launch a top-secret rocket. Deadhead is accidentally blasted off into space with a chimpanzee and, on his return, temporarily becomes a crazed rebel. Buster Keaton, in one of his final movies, supplies some quieter visual humour as a mad electrician. JG
Frankie Avalon *Sgt OK Deadhead/Sgt Donovan* · Deborah Walley *Col Lucy Turner* · Fred Clark *Gen Rufus Fogg* · Cesar Romero *Adm Stoneham* · Gale Gordon *Capt Weiskopf* · Harvey Lembeck *Pte McEvoy* · John Ashley *Pte Filroy* · Buster Keaton *Pte Blinken* ■ *Dir* Norman Taurog · *Scr* Louis M Heyward

Sgt Kabukiman NYPD ★★★ 18
Action comedy adventure
1991 · US/Jpn · Colour · 100min

Gleefully disregarding trifles such as quality and taste, Troma has produced some of the most delirious B-movies of recent times. However, none can rival the silliness of this comic book caper. Doltish cop Rick Gianasi is possessed by the spirit of a kabuki actor and masters the heat-seeking chopsticks and suffocating sushi rolls that will prevent the Evil One from taking over the world. DP *DVD*
Rick Gianasi *Harry Griswold/Sergeant Kabukiman* · Susan Byun *Lotus* · Bill Weeden *Reginald Stuart* · Thomas Crnkovich *Rembrandt* · Larry Robinson *Reverend Snipes* · Noble Lee Lester *Captain Bender* · Brick Bronsky *Jughead* ■ *Dir* Lloyd Kaufman, Michael Herz · *Scr* Lloyd Kaufman, Andrew Osborne, Jeffrey W Sass

Sergeant Madden ★★★
Drama 1939 · US · BW · 82min

Josef von Sternberg, under contract to MGM to make two films, was forced to take on this Wallace Beery vehicle after being removed from *I Take This Woman* with Hedy Lamarr. The director was not happy, either with the screenplay or his pug-ugly star ("beyond direction"), with whom he had many a row. However, this crime melodrama about a moral Irish cop (Beery) whose son (Alan Curtis) goes wrong is far better than expected given the circumstances, owing to the visually advanced Sternberg's careful control, with Beery not allowed to stray into characteristically maudlin mode. Made between Sternberg's run of Dietrich-starring masterworks and his 1941 return to greatness (*The Shanghai Gesture*), it's a relatively minor film that is nevertheless very watchable. RB
Wallace Beery *Shaun Madden* · Tom Brown *Al Boylan Jr* · Alan Curtis *Dennis Madden* · Laraine Day *Eileen Daly* · Fay Holden *Mary Madden* · Marc Lawrence (1) *"Piggy" Ceders* · Marion Martin *Charlotte* · David Gorcey *"Punchy"* ■ *Dir* Josef von Sternberg · *Scr* Wells Root, from the story *A Gun in His Hand* by William A Ullman Jr

Sgt Pepper's Lonely Hearts Club Band ★★ PG
Musical 1978 · US · Colour · 106min

This is a daft attempt to conceptualise the classic Beatles album by linking its songs via a contrived connective storyline. Some sequences are OK, but others are embarrassing. Some interest resides in its pick 'n' mix cast of musicians and actors. Musicians include The Bee Gees, soul band Earth Wind & Fire, and 1970s pin-up Peter Frampton. Actors in the cast include Steve Martin, George Burns, Donald Pleasence and Frankie Howerd. DA
Peter Frampton (2) *Billy Shears* · Barry Gibb *Mark Henderson* · Robin Gibb *Dave Henderson* · Maurice Gibb *Bob Henderson* · Frankie Howerd *Mr Mustard* · Paul Nicholas *Dougie Shears* · George Burns *Mr Kite* · Donald Pleasence *BD Brockhurst* · Steve Martin *Dr Maxwell Edison* · Alice Cooper *Father Sun* · Billy Preston *Sgt Pepper* ■ *Dir* Michael Schultz · *Scr* Henry Edwards

Sergeant Rutledge ★★★ PG
Western drama 1960 · US · Colour · 106min

John Ford directs this rather static courtroom drama about a black cavalry sergeant accused of rape and murder. Daring in its time, it's still powerful today. Woody Strode gets the role of a lifetime as Rutledge, and the sequence where he sings *Captain Buffalo* (the film's original title) and crosses the River Pecos was one of the most significant in Hollywood's treatment of blacks in cinema to that date. Carleton Young is also impressive, but nominal stars Jeffrey Hunter and Constance Towers are inadequate. TS
Jeffrey Hunter *Lt Thomas Cantrell* · Woody Strode *Sgt Braxton Rutledge* · Constance Towers *Mary Beecher* · Willis Bouchey *Colonel Fosgate* · Billie Burke *Mrs Fosgate* · Carleton Young *Captain Shattuck* · Judson Pratt *Lieutenant*

Mulqueen · Juano Hernandez *Sgt Skidmore* ■ *Dir* John Ford · *Scr* Willis Goldbeck, James Warner Bellah, from the novel *Captain Buffalo* by James Warner Bellah

Sergeant Ryker ★★ PG
Courtroom drama 1968 · US · Colour · 82min

Military prosecutor Bradford Dillman is persuaded that bitter, convicted traitor Lee Marvin, who is awaiting execution, may not have received a fair hearing, and he agrees to a retrial. As it was originally an extended TV play and not intended as a film, the courtroom drama jars occasionally, but the intelligent writing and supporting cast make it worth watching. JG *DVD*
Lee Marvin *Sergeant Paul Ryker* · Bradford Dillman *Captain David Young* · Vera Miles *Ann Ryker* · Peter Graves (2) *Major Whitaker* · Lloyd Nolan *General Amos Bailey* · Norman Fell *Sergeant Max Winkler* · Walter Brooke *Colonel Arthur Merriam* ■ *Dir* Buzz Kulik · *Scr* Seeleg Lester, William D Gordon, from a story by Seeleg Lester

Sergeant York ★★★★ U
Biographical war drama 1941 · US · BW · 128min

Nominated for 11 Oscars and winning Gary Cooper his first best actor statuette, this is a model of biopic making. As decent and determined as ever, Cooper is a Tennessee backwoodsman who swears off violence after lightning strikes his rifle during a land dispute, only to become a national hero after single-handedly killing 20 Germans and capturing 132 more during a First World War offensive. Director Howard Hawks handles the action sequences with customary confidence, but he also creates several fully fledged supporting characters, who are convincingly played by Joan Leslie and Oscar nominees Walter Brennan and Margaret Wycherly. DP
Gary Cooper *Alvin C York* · Walter Brennan *Pastor Rosier Pile* · Joan Leslie *Gracie Williams* · George Tobias *"Pusher" Ross* · Stanley Ridges *Major Buxton* · Margaret Wycherly *Mother York* · Ward Bond *Ike Botkin* ■ *Dir* Howard Hawks · *Scr* Abem Finkel, Harry Chandlee, Howard Koch, John Huston, from the *War Diary of Sergeant York* by Alvin C York and edited by Sam K Cowan, and the biographies *Sergeant York and His People* by Sam K Cowan and *Sergeant York – Last of the Long Hunters* by Tom Skeyhill · *Cinematographers* Sol Polito, Arthur Edeson · *Music* Max Steiner

Sergeants 3 ★★★ U
Western comedy 1962 · US · Colour · 112min

Following on from *Ocean's Eleven*, this rambunctious on-screen get-together of the "Rat Pack" – Frank Sinatra, Dean Martin, Peter Lawford, Sammy Davis Jr, Joey Bishop – finds the first three as brawling cavalry officers out to repulse marauding Indians, which they succeed in doing with the help of bugle-blowing ex-slave Davis. Directed by John Sturges from a WR Burnett script that transposes *Gunga Din* to the American west and spoofs that film's heroics, this romp only entertains in parts. RK
Frank Sinatra *1st Sergeant Mike Merry* · Dean Martin *Sgt Chip Deal* · Sammy Davis Jr *Jonah Williams* · Peter Lawford *Sgt Larry Barrett* · Joey Bishop *Sgt Major Roger Boswell* · Henry Silva *Mountain Hawk* · Ruta Lee *Amelia Parent* · Buddy Lester *Willie Sharpknife* ■ *Dir* John Sturges · *Scr* WR Burnett

Serial ★★★ 18
Satirical comedy 1980 · US · Colour · 88min

Christopher Lee plays a gay Hell's Angel in an underrated satire about the worst excesses in 1970s America. Bizarre religious cults, ludicrous fashions, absurd self-help groups, marital fidelity and love affairs with poodle-parlour workers all come under the social mores microscope, in a scattershot spoof. Lee rises to the occasion and the rest of the eclectic cast – including Tuesday Weld, Martin Mull and Sally Kellerman – make their oddball moments count. AJ
Martin Mull *Harvey* · Tuesday Weld *Kate* · Jennifer McAlister *Joan* · Sam Chew Jr *Bill* · Sally Kellerman *Martha* · Anthony Battaglia *Stokeley* · Nita Talbot *Angela* · Bill Macy *Sam* ·

Christopher Lee *Luckman/Skull* · Pamela Bellwood *Carol* ■ *Dir* Bill Persky · *Scr* Rich Eustis, Michael Elias, from the novel by Cyra McFadden

Serial Mom ★★★ 18
Black comedy 1994 · US · Colour · 89min

Kathleen Turner is the archetypal cheerful mother – until someone disrupts her orderly life. Then she turns into the homicidal housewife from hell. Didn't rewind your videotape? Wearing white shoes after Labour Day? Watch out! Cult director John Waters's darkly funny look at the murderer-as-celebrity phenomenon trashes American family values and sends up splatter movies, mining each target for maximum screwball outrage. While not as perverse as some of Waters's previous bad-taste epics, this "Doris Day goes *Psycho*" comedy still retains its trademark shocking edge. AJ Violence, swearing, sex scenes. *DVD* *BL*
Kathleen Turner *Beverly Sutphin, Mom* · Sam Waterston *Eugene Sutphin, Dad* · Ricki Lake *Misty Sutphin* · Matthew Lillard *Chip Sutphin* · Scott Wesley Morgan *Detective Pike* · Walt MacPherson *Detective Gracey* · Justin Whalin *Scotty* · Patricia Dunnock *Birdie* · Lonnie Horsey *Carl* · Mink Stole *Dottie Hinkle* · Mary Jo Catlett *Rosemary Ackerman* · Traci Lords *Carl's date* · Suzanne Somers · Patricia Hearst *Juror No 8* · Mary Vivian Pearce *Book buyer* ■ *Dir/Scr* John Waters (2)

Series 7: the Contenders ★★ 18
Satire 2001 · US · Colour · 87min

First-time writer/director Daniel Minahan began developing this low-budget, no-star project – a game show in which contestants must kill the others to win – at Sundance in 1997, so there's a degree of prescience (or luck) about the timing, as reality TV shows proliferate. Presented in *vérité* style as edited segments of a TV show (*The Contenders*), this is a one-idea film, whose central gimmick soon palls. It's hard to care about any of the promising characters in such an unreal format. AC *DVD*
Brooke Smith *Dawn* · Marylouise Burke *Connie* · Glenn Fitzgerald *Jeff* · Michael Kaycheck *Tony* · Richard Venture *Franklin* · Merritt Wever *Lindsay* · Donna Hanover *Sheila* · Angelina Phillips *Doria* ■ *Dir/Scr* Daniel Minahan

Serious Charge ★★★ PG
Drama 1959 · UK · BW · 95min

Anthony Quayle plays a former army vicar who arrives in a new town (an early Milton Keynes) to run a youth club. Sarah Churchill throws herself at him but Quayle prefers football. Then a local teddy boy accuses Quayle of sexual assault. The movie is especially good at subverting British movie decorum – people exchanging mild gossip over cups of tea – by focusing on the sterility of life in the New Britain of purpose-built towns. All this, plus Cliff Richard making his screen debut. AT
Anthony Quayle *Howard Phillips* · Sarah Churchill *Hester Peters* · Andrew Ray *Larry Thompson* · Irene Browne *Mrs Phillips* · Percy Herbert *Mr Thompson* · Noel Howlett *Mr Peters* · Cliff Richard *Curley Thompson* ■ *Dir* Terence Young · *Scr* Mickey Delamar, Guy Elmes, from the play by Philip King

A Serious Man ★★★★ 15
Black comedy drama
2009 · US/UK/Fr · Colour · 101min

A physics professor in 1960s Minneapolis turns to a series of rabbis for advice when his life starts falling apart at the seams in this thoughtful comedy from the Coen brothers. Michael Stuhlbarg heads an excellent cast refreshingly free of Hollywood heavy-hitters as Larry, who has just learned that his wife (Sari Lennick) wants a divorce. Rigorously controlled, perhaps at the expense of a little emotional light and shade, this is one of the Coens' subtlest films. Expect smiles, grimaces, a slightly furrowed brow, and, finally, a feeling of satisfaction that here is one film whose circuitous storytelling and off-beat wit is worth sticking with. TJ Swearing, sex scenes, nudity, drug abuse. *DVD* *BL*

S

Michael Stuhlbarg *Larry Gopnik* • Richard Kind *Uncle Arthur* • Fred Melamed *Sy Ableman* • Sari Lennick *Judith Gopnik* • Adam Arkin *Divorce lawyer* • Aaron Wolff *Danny Gopnik* • Jessica McManus *Sarah Gopnik* ■ *Dir/Scr* Ethan Coen, Joel Coen • *Cinematographer* Roger Deakins

The Serpent ★★
Spy drama 1972 · Fr/It/W Ger · Colour · 121min

As well as an outstanding cast, this boasts exemplary technical credits, with Claude Renoir behind the camera and Ennio Morricone composing the score. Alas, it turns out to be a distinctly muted cloak-and-dagger affair. Yul Brynner is a top Russian diplomat whose defection to the west is complicated by a series of deaths. The whole production is given a glossy look by director Henri Verneuil and his set pieces display a fine eye for detail, but the overly complicated story never grips the viewer. RS

Yul Brynner *Vlassov* • Henry Fonda *Allan Davies* • Dirk Bogarde *Philip Boyle* • Philippe Noiret *Lucien Berthon* • Michel Bouquet *Tavel* • Farley Granger *Computer chief* • Virna Lisi *Annabel Lee* ■ *Dir* Henri Verneuil • *Scr* Henri Verneuil, Gilles Perrault, Tom Rowe, from the novel *Le Suicide* by Pierre Nord

Le Serpent ★★★ 15
Thriller 2006 · Fr · Colour · 121min

Director Eric Barbier's violent tale of manipulation, paranoia and retribution has a compelling *film noir* atmosphere and dark attitude. The shattered life of wealthy photographer Vincent (Yvan Attal) falls apart further when former classmate Plender (Clovis Cornillac) manoeuvres him into a web of blackmail and murder. With no one believing he's the target of a ruthless vendetta motivated by past misdeeds, Vincent's only chance to save himself is to find Plender's weakness – and very surprising it turns out to be. Attal convincingly essays a man with nothing left to lose, while Cornillac's disquietingly controlled rage provides a tense undercurrent whenever Barbier relaxes the suspense. The plot doesn't bear close scrutiny, but the fast pace, stylish direction and lead performances manage to paper over the cracks. AJ French +subtitles.

Clovis Cornillac *Plender* • Yvan Attal *Vincent* • Pierre Richard *Cendras* • Simon Abkarian *Sam* • Jean-Claude Bouillon *Max* • Veronika Varga *Catherine* ■ *Dir* Eric Barbier • *Scr* Eric Barbier, from the novel *Plender* by Ted Lewis

The Serpent and the Rainbow ★★★ 18
Horror 1987 · US · Colour · 98min

Inspired by Wade Davis's non-fiction account of scouring Haiti for authentic "zombie powder" on behalf of a pharmaceutical company wanting to market a new anaesthetic, director Wes Craven turns his intriguing quest into nothing more than a high-tone fright flick. However, while paying scant attention to the role politics' terror plays in some parts of the West Indies, this is well appointed in the creepy atmosphere department, veering from chilling fact to hallucinatory horror via Craven's sure-handed shock tableaux. AJ Violence, swearing. *DVD*

Bill Pullman *Dennis Alan* • Cathy Tyson *Dr Marielle Duchamp* • Zakes Mokae *Dargent Peytraud* • Paul Winfield *Lucien Celine* • Brent Jennings *Mozart* • Conrad Roberts *Christophe* • Badja Djola *Gaston* • Theresa Merritt *Simone* • Michael Gough *Schoonbacher* ■ *Dir* Wes Craven • *Scr* Richard Maxwell, AR Simoun, from the non-fiction book by Wade Davis

Serpent of the Nile ★ U
Historical drama 1953 · US · Colour · 81min

If Perry Mason's your idea of Mark Antony, this risible historical drama is for you. For, verily, Raymond Burr plays the noble Roman, with red-headed Rhonda Fleming as Queen Cleopatra, seducing him and heading for a suicide pact. Made on a budget that would only have paid for a day's linguini lunches on the Burton/Taylor *Cleopatra*, this effort from director William Castle is lamentable. AT

Rhonda Fleming *Cleopatra* • William Lundigan *Lucilius* • Raymond Burr *Mark Antony* • Jean Byron *Charmion* • Michael Ansara *Florus* ■ *Dir* William Castle • *Scr* Robert E Kent

The Serpent's Egg ★★★ 18
Drama 1977 · W Ger/US · Colour · 114min

The critics have been unkind to this film, attacking it for its noise, its depiction of pain and prejudice and its echoes of the portrait of Germany painted in *Cabaret*. Admittedly, this is one of Ingmar Bergman's lesser pictures – he wasn't used to working in English, his knowledge of the period was somewhat limited and he was still nursing the hurt caused by his brush with the Swedish inland revenue that had driven him into temporary exile. But, occasionally, this bold experiment in style throws up some striking images that capture the mix of decadence and danger of life in the Weimar Republic. DP Some violence, swearing. *DVD*

Liv Ullmann *Manuela Rosenberg* • David Carradine *Abel Roserberg* • Gert Fröbe *Inspector Bauer* • Heinz Bennent *Doctor Hans Vergerus* • James Whitmore *Priest* • Toni Berger *Mr Rosenberg* • Christian Berkel *Student* ■ *Dir/Scr* Ingmar Bergman

The Serpent's Kiss ★ 15
Period mystery 1997 · Fr/Ger/UK · Colour · 105min

Given Ewan McGregor's popularity, it's a sure sign of a bad movie that this sank into obscurity. McGregor plays a landscape architect hired by wealthy Pete Postlethwaite to design a garden for his wife (Greta Scacchi). Not surprisingly, McGregor becomes embroiled in a plot by scheming Richard E Grant to bankrupt Postlethwaite. LH *DVD*

Greta Scacchi *Juliana* • Ewan McGregor *Meneer Chrome* • Pete Postlethwaite *Thomas Smithers* • Richard E Grant *James Fitzmaurice* • Carmen Chaplin *Thea* ■ *Dir* Philippe Rousselot • *Scr* Tim Rose Price

Serpico ★★★★ 18
Police thriller based on a true story 1973 · US · Colour · 124min

Al Pacino gives an outstanding, Oscar-nominated performance as real-life cop Frank Serpico, who helped expose corruption in the New York Police Department in the early 1970s. Director Sidney Lumet shows in fascinating detail how hush-money and bribes were a way of life for Serpico's colleagues and how the idealistic young officer refused to toe the line. After years of watching partners take backhanders, Serpico agreed to testify against a fellow officer and became a marked man. Even though Lumet revisited similar territory, he never found a better purveyor of idealism than Pacino. TH In English, Italian. Violence, swearing, nudity, drug abuse. *DVD* ☐

Al Pacino *Frank Serpico* • John Randolph *Sidney Green* • Jack Kehoe *Tom Keough* • Biff McGuire *McClain* • Barbara Eda-Young *Laurie* • Cornelia Sharpe *Leslie* • Tony Roberts *Bob Blair* • John Medici *Pasquale* ■ *Dir* Sidney Lumet • *Scr* Waldo Salt, Norman Wexler, from the book by Peter Maas

The Servant ★★★★ 15
Drama 1963 · UK · BW · 110min

This claustrophobic tale of envy and manipulation sees James Fox descend from a champagne lifestyle into a decadent dependence upon his servant, Dirk Bogarde. The snarling story is handled with great insight by director Joseph Losey, who had keenly studied the British class system since being exiled from Hollywood in 1951 during the Communist witch-hunt. Sarah Miles and Wendy Craig impress as the women caught in the powerplay, but this is essentially a two-hander, with Fox admirable as a latter-day Sebastian Flyte and Bogarde (finally nailing his matinée reputation) chilling as the mercenary valet. DP *DVD* ☐

Dirk Bogarde *Hugo Barrett* • Sarah Miles *Vera* • Wendy Craig *Susan* • James Fox *Tony* • Catherine Lacey *Lady Mounset* • Richard Vernon *Lord Mounset* • Ann Firbank *Society woman* • Harold Pinter *Society man* ■ *Dir* Joseph Losey •

Scr Harold Pinter, from the novel by Robin Maugham • *Cinematographer* Douglas Slocombe • *Music* John Dankworth

Serving Sara ★★ 12
Comedy 2002 · US/Ger · Colour · 95min

Elizabeth Hurley plays the British trophy wife of Bruce Campbell's unfaithful Texan millionaire. When she receives divorce papers from acerbic process server Matthew Perry, Hurley sets out for financial revenge. Though Perry can't seem to escape his *Friends* persona, his strong chemistry with Hurley and the story's gentle absurdity keep proceedings buoyant. The leads may not be excellent actors, but they are fun to watch, and – like the film itself – don't take themselves too seriously. SF *DVD*

Matthew Perry *Joe Tyler* • Elizabeth Hurley *Sara Moore* • Bruce Campbell *Gordon Moore* • Amy Adams *Kate* • Vincent Pastore *Tony* • Cedric "The Entertainer" [Cedric the Entertainer] *Ray Harris* • Terry Crews *Vernon* • Jerry Stiller *Milton the cop* ■ *Dir* Reginald Hudlin • *Scr* Jay Scherick, David Ronn

Session 9 ★★★★ 15
Horror thriller 2001 · US · Colour · 95min

Brilliantly scripted, atmospherically chilling and seat-edged suspenseful right up to its masterful shock ending, this hard-hitting psychological horror concerns a group of workers hired to clear an abandoned insane asylum of asbestos in one week. As the crew, all harbouring dark secrets of their own, is drawn deeper into the mysteries surrounding the imposing building, the gruelling pressures mount to complete their assignment. Evocatively shot on High Definition Digital Video and graced by superb ensemble performances, director Brad Anderson's cautionary tale of psyche-infection is a stunning success on every character-driven, grimly realistic and spine-tingling front. AJ *DVD*

David Caruso *Phil* • Stephen Gevedon *Mike* • Paul Guilfoyle (2) *Bill Griggs* • Josh Lucas *Hank* • Peter Mullan *Gordon Fleming* • Brendan Sexton III *Jeff* ■ *Dir* Brad Anderson • *Scr* Brad Anderson, Stephen Gevedon

The Sessions ★★★ 15
Comedy drama based on a true story 2012 · US · Colour · 90min

Writer and poet Mark O'Brien drew on his own sexual awakening to write the article on which this comedy drama is based. But what makes this rite of passage so different is that Mark (played here by John Hawkes) is severely disabled, and, at 38, fears he will never lose his virginity. Helen Hunt gives a totally assured performance – often naked – as the sex surrogate Mark engages, but her character's businesslike approach to sex isn't exactly conducive to romance. Instead it's Hawkes's portrayal, in all its wit, intelligence and childlike naivety, that really captures the heart. SP Swearing, sexual references, sex scenes, nudity. *DVD* ☐

John Hawkes *Mark O'Brien* • Helen Hunt *Cheryl Cohen Greene* • William H Macy *Father Brendan* • Moon Bloodgood *Vera* • Annika Marks *Amanda* • W Earl Brown *Rod* ■ *Dir* Ben Lewin • *Scr* Ben Lewin, from the article *On Seeing a Sex Surrogate* by Mark O'Brien

Set Fire to the Stars ★★ 15
Drama 2014 · UK · BW · 96min

This semi-biographical drama chronicles a week in the life of revered poet Dylan Thomas (Celyn Jones), following him as he embarks on a turbulent tour of performed readings in the United States during the early 1950s. Helping to organise the tour is John Malcolm Brinnin (Elijah Wood), a buttoned-up academic who spends most of his time attempting to keep Thomas out of trouble. *Set Fire to the Stars* benefits from crisp monochrome cinematography and two solid lead performances, but the end result feels somewhat flat, and it's difficult to see who the film will appeal to. SC Swearing, sexual references.

Elijah Wood *John Malcolm Brinnin* • Celyn Jones *Dylan Thomas* • Maimie McCoy *Rosie* • Richard Brake *Mr Unlucky* • Shirley Henderson *Shirley* ■ *Dir* Andy Goddard • *Scr* Andy Goddard, Celyn Jones

Set It Off ★★★ 18
Action crime drama 1996 · US · Colour · 117min

Four down-on-their-luck African-American women from Los Angeles band together to pull off a string of bank robberies. The subplots are numerous, resulting in romance, statements about ghetto life and thrilling bullet-strewn action scenes being crammed together, yet they still manage to grab the attention. Jada Pinkett does well in the lead, but it's Queen Latifah who has the acting ability and personality to stand out, though Blair Underwood gives a nice supporting performance. KB *DVD*

Jada Pinkett [Jada Pinkett Smith] *Stony* • Queen Latifah *Cleo* • Vivica A Fox *Frankie* • Kimberly Elise *Tisean* • John C McGinley *Detective Strode* • Blair Underwood *Keith* • Dr Dre *Black Sam* ■ *Dir* F Gary Gray • *Scr* Kate Lanier, Takashi Bufford, from a story by Takashi Bufford

Set the Thames on Fire ★★ 15
Black comedy fantasy 2015 · UK · Colour · 83min

Ben Charles Edwards's potentially cult debut feature is set in a flooded future London. It follows the barely compelling perambulations of a pianist and an aspiring sailor as they criss-cross the waterlogged and seemingly isolated city to encounter such eccentrics as an uncouth Gerard Mcdermott, a perverse Noel Fielding and a lascivious Sadie Frost. The leads struggle against their scene-stealing support stars, but James Hatt's production design and Sergio Delgado's cinematography really are exceptional. DP

Noel Fielding *Dickie* • Sadie Frost *Mrs Hortense* • Sally Phillips *Colette* • Max Bennett *Sal* ■ *Dir* Ben Charles Edwards • *Scr* Al Joshua

The Set-Up ★★★★ PG
Sports drama 1949 · US · BW · 68min

This bruising boxing drama is a knockout production from the great days of RKO studios. It was among the first to show the crippling confrontation between good and evil in the ring, when an over-the-hill boxer is sold out by his manager, and then has to face the consequences of his gangster connections. The usually villainous Robert Ryan is wonderful and plausibly decent as the fighter, though Audrey Totter as his wife is miscast. Director Robert Wise controversially depicts the ringside audience as sadists lusting for blood. And there is plenty of it, as Milton Krasner's camera darts around in a flurry of action to create boxing scenes of brain-jarring ferocity. TH

Robert Ryan *Bill "Stoker" Thompson* • Audrey Totter *Julie* • George Tobias *Tiny* • Alan Baxter *Little Boy* • Wallace Ford *Gus* • Percy Helton *Red* ■ *Dir* Robert Wise • *Scr* Art Cohn, from a poem by Joseph Moncure March

The Set Up ★★★★ 18
Thriller 1995 · US · Colour · 89min

This superior TV movie benefits from a tightly plotted story and a stellar cast led by Billy Zane and featuring thriller icon James Coburn. Zane gives a dogged performance as a cat burglar whose plans to go straight are waylaid by ex-con James Russo, who threatens to kill Zane's girlfriend unless he dismantles the security system he has installed at Coburn's bank. The boxing scene is strong meat, but stick with it because the finale is a belter. DP Violence, sex scenes.

Billy Zane *Charlie Thorpe* • Mia Sara *Gina Sands* • James Russo *Kliff* • James Coburn *Jeremiah Cole* • Louis Mandylor *Pauly* • Tiny "Zeus" Lister [Tom "Tiny" Lister Jr] *Leon* • Mark Rolston *Ray Harris* • Margaret Avery (2) *Olivia Dubois* ■ *Dir* Strathford Hamilton • *Scr* Michael Thoma, from the book *My Laugh Comes Last* by James Hadley Chase

S

Set Up ★ 15
Action crime drama 2011 · US · Colour · 81min

From the production company of Curtis "50 Cent" Jackson comes this embarrassing revenge thriller starring Bruce Willis and Jackson himself. After a diamond heist goes wrong, Jackson must track down the man who betrayed him, with the help of mob boss Willis – on screen for less than ten minutes. Needless to say, Jackson can't act and is barely audible, taking the whole thing incredibly seriously, which jars with the film's ill-fated attempts at dark humour and results in a severely confused tone. DnM *DVD* *Blu-ray*

Curtis "50 Cent" Jackson *Sonny* • Ryan Phillippe *Vincent Long* • Bruce Willis *Biggs* • Rory Markham *Markus* • Jenna Dewan *Mia* ■ *Dir* Mike Gunther • *Scr* Mike Gunther, Mike Behrman

Seul contre Tous ★★★★ 18
Drama 1998 · Fr · Colour · 88min

Setting out to rouse the lethargic cinema establishment, Gaspar Noé succeeds in turning a barrage of shocking images, abrasive captions and jarring sounds into a grotesquely credible portrait of furious misery that enervates and repels in equal measure. Whether spouting self-pitying, misanthropic bile or assaulting his pregnant mistress and handicapped daughter, butcher Philippe Nahon (in an alarmingly courageous performance) still commands our pity, as a victim of poverty, injustice and his own twisted logic. DP French +subtitles. Violence, sex scenes, swearing.

Philippe Nahon *The butcher* • Blandine Lenoir *His daughter, Cynthia* • Frankye Pain *His mistress* • Martine Audrain *Mother-in-law* ■ *Dir/Scr* Gaspar Noé

Seve ★★★ PG
Drama documentary
2014 · UK/Sp · Colour · 124min

Cleverly blending interviews and archive footage with dramatised reconstructions, this fine Anglo-Spanish biopic tells the remarkable rags-to-riches tale of Severiano Ballesteros, the poor Spanish farmer's son who became one of golf's greatest players. Released three years after his death at the age of 54, this story of the five-time Major winner and Ryder Cup captain will primarily appeal to golf fans and admirers of sublime sporting talent. Clocking in at two hours, it's a bit of a long haul, but as a whole it's a fittingly emotional and inspirational docudrama. DA Spanish, English +subtitles. Brief swearing. *DVD* *Blu-ray*

José Luis Gutiérrez *Severiano Ballesteros* ■ *Dir* John-Paul Davidson • *Scr* Tom Hodgson

Seven ★★★ 18
Action comedy 1979 · US · Colour · 96min

Director Andy Sidaris carved out a niche for himself making enjoyable low-budget action films destined for video, rather than big-screen exposure. This is such a film. Veteran hunk William Smith stars as the leader of a seven-strong team of experts assembled by a government agent to combat a syndicate of seven gangsters planning mayhem in Hawaii. That's the cue for lots of fisticuffs, gunplay and female flesh. DF

William Smith *Drew* • Barbara Leigh *Alexa* • Guich Koock *Cowboy* • Art Metrano *Kinsella* • Martin Kove *Skip* • Richard LePore *Professor* ■ *Dir* Andy Sidaris • *Scr* William Driskill, Robert Baird, from a story by Andy Sidaris

Se7en ★★★★★ 18
Crime thriller 1995 · US · Colour · 126min

Director David Fincher's brilliant postmodern crime thriller is a grim and disturbing tale about a vicious serial killer. Intelligently scripted by Andrew Kevin Walker, it is a work of extraordinary style, power and narrative daring. It also boasts fine performances from Morgan Freeman as a disillusioned detective on the brink of retirement and Brad Pitt as his enthusiastic replacement. With only seven days left on the job, Freeman finds himself drawn to a puzzling case of a psychopath who murders his victims in a gruesome manner to atone for the sins he deems them to have committed. Draining his landscapes of colour, and setting all the tense action against rain-washed streets and underlit interiors, Fincher evokes a nightmarish atmosphere. AJ Swearing, violence. *DVD* *Blu-ray*

Brad Pitt *Detective David Mills* • Morgan Freeman *Lieutenant William Somerset* • Gwyneth Paltrow *Tracy Mills* • Richard Roundtree *Talbot* • John C McGinley *California* • R Lee Ermey *Police captain* • Kevin Spacey *John Doe* • Daniel Zacapa *Detective Taylor* ■ *Dir* David Fincher • *Scr* Andrew Kevin Walker • *Cinematographer* Darius Khondji

Seven Angry Men ★★ U
Historical drama 1955 · US · BW · 91min

Raymond Massey takes centre stage as the fanatical abolitionist John Brown. The verbose script by Daniel B Ullman and the heavy-handed direction by Charles Marquis Warren concentrate on Brown's increasingly savage campaign in Kansas to abolish slavery, culminating in his attack on Harper's Ferry. Jeffrey Hunter, as one of Brown's six sons, conducts a romance with Debra Paget in a subplot that's an uninspired attempt to appeal to younger audiences. AE

Raymond Massey *John Brown* • Debra Paget *Elizabeth* • Jeffrey Hunter *Owen* • Larry Pennell *Oliver* • Leo Gordon *White* • John Smith *Frederick* • James Best *Jason* • Dennis Weaver *John Jr* • Guy Williams *Salmon* ■ *Dir* Charles Marquis Warren • *Scr* Daniel B Ullman

Seven Beauties ★★★★ 18
Satirical war drama 1976 · It · Colour · 111min

This really is a film with something to offend everyone. A sizzling satire on the political naivety and military incompetence of the Italian male, it also passes scathing comment on such sensitive issues as obesity, female emancipation, the Mafia and concentration camps. Not all of the jokes come off. But Lina Wertmuller, who received Oscar nominations for both her writing and direction, takes events at a ferocious pace and gets a superb performance from her regular collaborator Giancarlo Giannini, who is the everyman struggling to survive the war and feed his indolent family. DP Italian +subtitles. Violence, sex scenes.

Giancarlo Giannini *Pasqualino Settebellezze* • Fernando Rey *Pedro* • Shirley Stoler *Hilde* • Elena Fiore *Concetta* • Piero Di Iorio *Francesco* ■ *Dir/Scr* Lina Wertmuller

Seven Brides for Seven Brothers ★★★★★ U
Musical 1954 · US · Colour · 97min

Rightly a sensational commercial success in its day, especially in Britain, this joyous romp remains one of the freshest and most satisfying of movie musicals. A screen original, it was fashioned by director Stanley Donen and choreographer Michael Kidd into an exciting, heart-warming and technically accomplished (though perhaps a shade politically incorrect) musical. Jane Powell stars as Oregan rancher Howard Keel's new wife, who's horrified to discover that she also has to look after his six unruly brothers. The early use of CinemaScope is as exquisite as the beautifully stylised MGM interiors. Cleverly cast, the movie gains strength from the two leading performances. TS *DVD*

Howard Keel *Adam Pontipee* • Jane Powell *Milly* • Russ Tamblyn *Gideon* • Jeff Richards *Benjamin* • Tommy Rall *Frank* • Marc Platt *Daniel* • Matt Mattox *Caleb* • Jacques d'Amboise *Ephraim* • Howard Petrie *Pete Perkins* ■ *Dir* Stanley Donen • *Scr* Albert Hackett, Frances Goodrich, Dorothy Kingsley, from the story *The Sobbin' Women* by Stephen Vincent Benet • *Music/lyrics* Gene de Paul, Johnny Mercer • *Cinematographer* George Folsey • *Music Directors* Adolph Deutsch, Saul Chaplin

Seven Chances ★★★ U
Silent farce 1925 · US · BW and Colour · 56min

Made immediately after three Keaton masterpieces, culminating with *The Navigator*, this enjoyable comedy has been somewhat neglected, partly because the highlight is in the last reel. Buster plays his usual doleful character who discovers that he has been left seven million dollars, provided he marries within the day. There are soon plenty of hopefuls and the climax of the film finds him pursued first by would-be brides and then by an avalanche of rocks. BB *DVD*

Buster Keaton *Jimmie Shannon* • Ruth Dwyer *Mary Jones* • T Roy Barnes *Billy Meekin, Jimmie's partner* • Snitz Edwards *Lawyer* • Frankie Raymond *Mary's mother* • Jules Cowles *Hired hand* • Jean Arthur *Miss Jones, switchboard operator at country club* • Erwin Connelly *Clergyman* • Jean Havez *Man on the landing* ■ *Dir* Buster Keaton • *Scr* Jean Havez, Clyde Bruckman, Joseph Mitchell, from the play *Seven Chances: a Comedy in Three Acts* by Roi Cooper Megrue

7 Days in Havana ★★★ 15
Portmanteau drama
2012 · Fr/Sp · Colour · 123min

Seven days, seven stories, seven international film-makers: such is the formula for this portmanteau drama, which captures the seething nightlife, vintage cars and variable living conditions in the Cuban capital. While the overall picture won't change anyone's perceptions of Havana, it's still a highly colourful and intriguing setting, though, inevitably, some stories come off better than others. The two strongest segments feature visiting film-makers playing themselves: Palestinian Elia Suleiman and Serbian Emir Kusturica. TJ Spanish, English +subtitles. Swearing, a sex scene, nudity. *DVD*

Josh Hutcherson *Teddy Atkins* • Emir Kusturica • Elia Suleiman *ES* • Cristella Herrera *Yamilslaidi* • Mirta Ibarra *Mirta* ■ *Dir* Laurent Cantet, Benicio Del Toro, Julio Medem, Gaspar Noé, Elia Suleiman, Juan Carlos Tabío, Pablo Trapero • *Scr* Leonardo Padura

Seven Days in May ★★★★ U
Political thriller 1964 · US · BW · 113min

This outlandish conspiracy thriller is made credible thanks to its outstanding cast that includes Burt Lancaster, Fredric March, Kirk Douglas and Ava Gardner. It follows the machinations of a military group that is trying to topple the US president (March) because he has signed a nuclear disarmament treaty with the Soviet Union. Director John Frankenheimer uses all the mechanical tricks of the surveillance trade – TV monitors, hidden cameras and electronic devices – to suggest the omnipresent miltary machine, but it's the magnificent performances of the stars that keep you watching. TH

Burt Lancaster *General James M Scott* • Kirk Douglas *Colonel Martin "Jiggs" Casey* • Fredric March *President Jordan Lyman* • Ava Gardner *Eleanor Holbrook* • Edmond O'Brien *Senator Raymond Clark* • Martin Balsam *Paul Girard* • George Macready *Christopher Todd* • Whit Bissell *Senator Prentice* • Hugh Marlowe *Harold McPherson* ■ *Dir* John Frankenheimer • *Scr* Rod Serling, from the novel by Fletcher Knebel, Charles Waldo Bailey II

Seven Days' Leave ★★★ U
Wartime musical comedy
1942 · US · BW · 87min

This endearing RKO romp effectively teams a pre-*I Love Lucy* Lucille Ball and handsome hunk Victor Mature, both of whom seem to be having a jolly good time and manage to convey that pleasure to the audience. The plot's a clunker, with army private Mature inheriting $100,000 if he can marry socialite Ball. There's fun and frolics along the way, plus some terrific music from top bands. TS

Victor Mature *Johnny Grey* • Lucille Ball *Terry* • Harold Peary *Great Gildersleeve* • Mapy Cortes *Mapy* • Ginny Simms *Ginny* • Marcy McGuire *Mickey* • Peter Lind Hayes *Jackson* • Walter Reed *Ralph Bell* • Wallace Ford *Sergeant Mead* ■ *Dir* Tim Whelan • *Scr* William Bowers, Ralph Spence, Curtis Kenyon, Kenneth Earl

7 Days to Live ★ 15
Supernatural horror 2000 · Ger · Colour · 92min

This very dull haunted house of shamelessly derivative horrors is directed by Sebastian Niemann as if he were in a coma. Struggling novelist Sean Pertwee and his freaked-out wife Amanda Plummer move to a secluded country home to get over the death of their son. Eerie things start happening, but you won't stick around long enough to find out the answers. Not terrifying, just terrible. AJ

Amanda Plummer *Ellen Shaw* • Sean Pertwee *Martin Shaw* • Nick Brimble *Carl Farrell* • Amanda Walker *Elizabeth Farrell* • Gina Bellman *Claudia* • Eddie Cooper *Tommy Shaw* ■ *Dir* Sebastian Niemann • *Scr* Dirk Ahner

Seven Days to Noon ★★★★ PG
Thriller 1950 · UK · BW · 92min

Doomsday movies were everywhere in the early 1950s, as the Cold War chill began to bite. This is the finest British contribution to that subgenre. Although the threat of an atomic explosion in London makes for compelling viewing, the true power of the picture comes from a magnificent performance by Barry Jones as the professor driven to suicidal despair by the misappropriation of his work. Thanks to Jones and cinematographer Gilbert Taylor's eerie images of the capital, this Boulting brothers film maintains an unbearable tension. DP *DVD*

Barry Jones *Professor Willingdon* • Olive Sloane *Goldie* • André Morell *Superintendent Folland* • Sheila Manahan *Ann Willingdon* • Hugh Cross *Stephen Lane* • Joan Hickson *Mrs Peckett* ■ *Dir* John Boulting, Roy Boulting • *Scr* Roy Boulting, Frank Harvey, from a story by Paul Dehn, James Bernard

The Seven Deadly Sins ★★★
Portmanteau drama 1952 · Fr/It · BW · 155min

Gérard Philipe introduces each of these tales with more charm than they really merit. The main interest in these modern parables – five of them in French and two in Italian – is how much they reveal about the attitude to sex in the early 1950s. Inevitably there are a few duds in the collection, with the best being Roberto Rossellini's *Envy*, based on a story by Colette, about a woman becoming more attached to her cat than her husband. Yves Allégret's *Lust* effectively reveals the difference between puppy and adult love, and Carlo Rim's *Gluttony* tells how a piece of cheese comes between a man and a woman. RB In French, Italian.

Eduardo De Filippo *Eduardo* • Jacqueline Plessis *Laziness* • Frank Villard *Ravila* • Francette Vernillat *Chantel* • Gérard Philipe *Master of Ceremonies* • Noël-Noël *The Director* • Michèle Morgan *Anne-Marie* ■ *Dir* Eduardo De Filippo, Jean Dréville, Yves Allégret, Roberto Rossellini, Carlo Rim, Claude Autant-Lara, Georges Lacombe • *Scr* Charles Spaak, Carlo Rim, Pierre Bost, Jean Aurenche, Roberto Rossellini, Carlo Rim, Pierre Bost, Jean Aurenche, Claude Autant-Lara, Pierre Bost, Jean Aurenche

The Seven Deadly Sins ★★★
Portmanteau drama 1961 · Fr/It · BW · 115min

It must have seemed a good idea at the time to get several of the New Wave French directors to give their slant on the seven deadly sins. But the result is a hit-and-miss affair, as with so many portmanteau films, with a mixture of good, average and awful. Among the better episodes are Philipe de Broca's *Gluttony*, Roger Vadim's *Pride*, Jacques Demy's *Lust*, and Jean-Luc Godard's *Sloth* – about a film star (Eddie Constantine) who is too lazy to have sex even when offered to him on a plate. The other three sins were committed by Claude Chabrol (*Greed*), Edouard Molinaro (*Envy*) and Sylvain Dhomme (*Anger*). RB French +subtitles.

Danièle Barraud *Suzon* • Jacques Charrier *Antoine* • Nicole Mirel *Starlet* • Eddie Constantine *Eddie* • Micheline Presle *Mother* • Jean-Louis Trintignant *Paul* • Michèle Girardon *La maîtrese* •

Marcelle Arnold *The wife* • Georges Wilson *Valentin* • Perrette Pradier *TV announcer* • Marie-José Nat *Young wife* ■ *Dir* Claude Chabrol, Edouard Molinaro, Jean-Luc Godard, Jacques Demy, Roger Vadim, Philippe de Broca, Sylvain Dhomme • *Scr* Félicien Marceau, Claude Chabrol, Claude Mauriac, Jean-Luc Godard, Roger Peyrefitte, Jacques Demy, Félicien Marceau, Daniel Boulanger, Eugène Ionesco

711 Ocean Drive ★★

Crime drama   1950 · US · BW · 101min

This features Edmond O'Brien as a telephone engineer lured into organised crime by the Mob. At first he just fixes the phone lines that link the racetracks, but then he gets a taste for power and starts cutting people off at the neck. It's a little moral tale, which says that crime doesn't pay – except that the Mob are still in control after the spectacular climax on the Hoover Dam. AT

Edmond O'Brien *Mal Granger* • Joanne Dru *Gail Mason* • Donald Porter [Don Porter] *Larry Mason* • Sammy White *Chippie Evans* • Dorothy Patrick *Trudy Maxwell* • Barry Kelley *Vince Walters* • Otto Kruger *Carl Stephans* ■ *Dir* Joseph M Newman • *Scr* Richard English, Frances Swan

7 Faces of Dr Lao ★★★ U

Fantasy western drama
1963 · US · Colour · 99min

This odd, almost surrealistic, fantasy western hit a nerve at the time and became a major success, largely because of the mesmerising performance of Tony Randall, who plays the eponymous doctor and no less than six other roles. It tells the tale of a strange travelling circus, which arrives in town to put the fear of God into the locals and teach them a few of life's lessons along the way. What distinguishes this intriguing movie is the glorious make-up, which won William Tuttle an Oscar. SH

Tony Randall *Dr Lao/Merlin the Magician/Medusa/Apollonius of Tyana/Pan/The Abominable Snowman/Giant Serpent* • Arthur O'Connell *Clint Stark* • John Ericson *Ed Cunningham* • Barbara Eden *Angela Benedict* • Kevin Tate *Mike Benedict* • Noah Beery Jr *Tim Mitchell* • Lee Patrick *Mrs Howard T Cassan* ■ *Dir* George Pal • *Scr* Charles Beaumont, from the novel *The Circus of Dr Lao* by Charles G Finney

Seven Hills of Rome ★★ U

Musical   1957 · US · Colour · 103min

Tenor Mario Lanza's insatiable appetite coupled with appalling manners made him hard both to cast and to like. Although his robust voice was undeniably attractive, his screen persona became awkward and contrived. Here, under the expert directorial hand of Roy Rowland, his performance is a little more mellow – but when those lungs open, nothing seems able to contain him. This film is really for fans only. TS

Mario Lanza *Marc Revere* • Renato Rascel *Pepe Bonelli* • Marisa Allasio *Rafaella Marini* • Peggie Castle *Carol Ralston* • Clelia Matania *Beatrice* • Rossella Como *Anita* • Amos Davoli *Carlo* • Guido Celano *Luigi* ■ *Dir* Roy Rowland • *Scr* Art Cohn, Giorgio Prosperi, from a story by Giuseppi Amato

Seven Hours to Judgment ★★★ 15

Thriller   1988 · US · Colour · 89min

Beau Bridges directs and stars in this revenge thriller, playing a judge who's forced to acquit a gang of killer thugs on a technicality. The victim's husband (Ron Leibman) blames Beau, kidnaps the judge's wife and forces him to run the gauntlet through the gang's tough home turf. The direction is a bit twitchy and Beau is far too baby-faced to be credible in a role that requires a lot more visual gravitas. This is a solid and watchable, if preposterous, action thriller. DA

Beau Bridges *John Eden* • Ron Leibman *David Reardon* • Julianne Phillips *Lisa Eden* • Tiny Ron Taylor [Tiny Ron] *Ira* • Al Freeman Jr *Danny Larwin* • Reggie Johnson *Chino* ■ *Dir* Beau Bridges • *Scr* Walter Davis, Elliot Stephens, from a story by Davis

Seven Little Foys ★★★ U

Musical biography   1955 · US · Colour · 92min

In one of his straighter roles, Bob Hope plays real-life comedian Eddie Foy who, after the early death of his wife, trained his seven children to join him in his vaudeville act. The trouble is that Hope's character is hard to like, and the musical routines are lacklustre, apart from one memorable sequence featuring guest star James Cagney. Reprising his portrayal of George M Cohan from *Yankee Doodle Dandy*, Cagney joins Hope in a song-and-soft-shoe routine to two Cohan favourites, momentarily lifting the film into a classier category. TV DVD

Eddie Foy Jr *Narrator* • Bob Hope *Eddie Foy* • Milly Vitale *Madeleine Morando* • George Tobias *Barney Green* • Angela Clarke *Clara* • Herbert Heyes *Judge* • James Cagney *George M Cohan* ■ *Dir* Melville Shavelson • *Scr* Melville Shavelson, Jack Rose

Seven Men from Now ★★★★ U

Western   1956 · US · Colour · 74min

John Wayne's production company made this modestly budgeted Randolph Scott western and it turned out so well that the Duke wished he'd starred in it himself. Burt Kennedy's lean script has Scott grimly tracking down the seven men who killed his wife during a hold-up, with Lee Marvin's gunman following close behind hoping to grab the loot they've hidden. Wayne gave his former co-star Gail Russell the female lead. Director Budd Boetticher makes terrific use of outdoor settings. AE DVD

Randolph Scott *Ben Stride* • Gail Russell *Annie Greer* • Lee Marvin *Masters* • Walter Reed *John Greer* • John Larch *Pate Bodeen* • Donald Barry *Clete* ■ *Dir* Budd Boetticher • *Scr* Burt Kennedy, from his story • *Cinematographer* William H Clothier [William Clothier]

Seven Miles from Alcatraz ★★★

Second World War spy drama
1942 · US · BW · 62min

As befits someone with Edward Dmytryk's political convictions (he was later one of the Hollywood Ten), he invests this wartime flag-waver with plenty of anti-Nazi fervour. However, the decision of escaped convicts James Craig and Frank Jenks to sacrifice their liberty for the greater good is anything but patriotic propaganda. Indeed, there's a decidedly cynical aspect to Craig's initial refusal to help imprisoned lighthouse keeper George Cleveland warn the San Francisco authorities of an imminent U-boat attack. His change of heart might have been more persuasive had it not been partly inspired by his interest in Cleveland's daughter, Bonita Granville. DP

James Craig *Champ Larkin* • Bonita Granville *Anne Porter* • Frank Jenks *Jimbo* • Cliff Edwards *Stormy* • George Cleveland *Captain Porter* ■ *Dir* Edward Dmytryk • *Scr* Joseph Krumgold, from the unpublished story *Sou'West Pass* by John D Klorer

Seven Minutes ★★★★ 15

Second World War thriller
1989 · W Ger · Colour · 91min

This is an intelligent, auspicious directorial debut from Klaus Maria Brandauer, who also stars as a determined, methodical would-be assassin of Adolf Hitler. Brandauer's strong, impressive performance overlays a thriller that intrigues and grips in equal measure. The cast is excellent, with the always watchable Brian Dennehy chilling but understated as a Gestapo chief. Celebrated cinematographer Lajos Koltai gives the film a suitably dense, atmospheric air. SH

Klaus Maria Brandauer *Elser* • Rebecca Miller *Anneliese* • Brian Dennehy *Wagner* • Nigel Le Vaillant *Mayer* • Maggie O'Neill *Berta* • Roger Ashton-Griffiths *Watchman* ■ *Dir* Klaus Maria Brandauer • *Scr* Stephen Sheppard, from his novel *The Artisan*

Seven Nights in Japan ★ PG

Romantic drama   1976 · UK/Fr · Colour · 99min

Michael York looks far less embarrassed than he should be, as the British prince who evades his bodyguards to indulge in a spot of romance with tour guide Hidemi Aoki. As toffs such as James Villiers and Charles Gray fret patriotically, we are treated to cinematographer Henri Decaë's postcard vistas and the delirious efforts of York and Aoki to look besotted. DP

Michael York *Prince George* • Hidemi Aoki *Somi* • Charles Gray *Ambassador Hollander* • Ann Lonnberg *Jane Hollander* • Eléonore Hirt *Mrs Hollander* • James Villiers *Finn* ■ *Dir* Lewis Gilbert • *Scr* Christopher Wood

Seven Pounds ★★ 12

Drama   2008 · US · Colour · 117min

Following their collaboration on *The Pursuit of Happyness* in 2006, director Gabriele Muccino and Will Smith make a more strenuous lunge at our heartstrings with this unusual, overwrought drama. There's not a glimmer of the cheeky smile that has made Smith a box-office king; instead he reveals his serious side as Ben Thomas, a taxman on a quest for atonement for a past incident. The precise nature of Smith's mission is only gradually unveiled and that, along with the chemistry of its stars, is what ultimately may hold the interest for some. SP DVD Blu

Will Smith *Ben Thomas* • Rosario Dawson *Emily Posa* • Woody Harrelson *Ezra Turner* • Barry Pepper *Dan* • Michael Ealy *Ben's brother* • Elpidia Carrillo *Connie Tepos* • Bill Smitrovich *George Ristuccia* • Tim Kelleher *Stewart Goodman* ■ *Dir* Gabriele Muccino • *Scr* Grant Nieporte

Seven Psychopaths ★★★ 15

Black comedy drama
2012 · UK/US · Colour · 105min

Writer/director Martin McDonagh follows up his hitmen-on-holiday caper *In Bruges* with another darkly comic, dysfunctional-male buddy movie, this time set in Los Angeles. The story centres on Colin Farrell's boozy Irish screenwriter, who's struggling for ideas for his next project, "Seven Psychopaths". Inspiration soon comes calling when the dog-napping scam run by his dodgy best pal Sam Rockwell and partner Christopher Walken backfires after they swipe the prized pooch of crime boss Woody Harrelson. With its LA setting, narrative digressions and wisecrack-tempered violence, this has a certain *Pulp Fiction* flavour to it, and a charismatic performance by a rheumy-eyed Walken also gives it heart. JH Violence, swearing, sexual references, drug abuse, nudity. DVD Blu

Colin Farrell (2) *Marty* • Woody Harrelson *Charlie* • Sam Rockwell *Billy* • Christopher Walken *Hans* • Abbie Cornish *Kaya* • Olga Kurylenko *Angela* • Tom Waits *Zachariah* ■ *Dir/Scr* Martin McDonagh

Seven Samurai ★★★★★ PG

Classic action drama   1954 · Jpn · BW · 190min

One of the undisputed masterpieces of world cinema, Akira Kurosawa's epic was inspired by the westerns of John Ford and had the compliment repaid with John Sturges's classic reworking, *The Magnificent Seven*. In the 17th century, Japanese villagers hire samurai warriors to defend their property from an annual raid by ruthless bandits. The film is a mesmerising combination of historical detail, spectacular action and poignant humanism. It has been described as "a tapestry of motion", with the final battle standing out for its audacious use of moving camera, telephoto lenses, varied film speeds and precision editing. Takashi Shimura and Toshiro Mifune are the pick of an excellent cast, but it's the director's genius that leaves an impression. DP Japanese +subtitles. Violence. DVD Blu

Takashi Shimura *Kambei* • Toshiro Mifune *Kikuchiyo* • Yoshio Inaba *Gorobei* • Seiji Miyaguchi *Kyuzo* • Minoru Chiaki *Heihachi* • Daisuke Kato *Shichiroji* • Isao Kimura *Katsushiro* • Kamatari Fujiwara *Manzo* ■ *Dir* Akira Kurosawa •

Scr Akira Kurosawa, Shinobu Hashimoto, Hideo Oguni • *Cinematographer* Asakasu Nakai • *Editor* Akira Kurosawa

Seven Seas to Calais ★★★ U

Swashbuckling adventure
1962 · It/US · Colour · 101min

Swashbucklers don't come more buckled than this, with Rod Taylor chasing Spanish treasure as Sir Francis Drake. Keith Michell and Irene Worth articulate the "prithee-avast" language with clarity, but director Rudolph Maté, who had made some great *films noirs*, was in decline, and this movie follows that downhill trend in lacking tension and credibility. TH

Rod Taylor *Sir Francis Drake* • Keith Michell *Malcolm Marsh* • Irene Worth *Queen Elizabeth I* • Anthony Dawson *Burleigh* • Basil Dignam *Walsingham* • Mario Girotti [Terence Hill] *Babington* ■ *Dir* Rudolph Maté, Primo Zeglio • *Scr* Filippo Sanjust, George St George, Lindsay Galloway

7 Seconds ★★ 15

Action crime thriller
2005 · US/UK · Colour · 91min

It's like an A-Z of straight-to-DVD, clichés, as professional thief Wesley Snipes falls foul of eastern European gangsters after accidentally nabbing a priceless painting during a botched heist in Romania. With most of his crew killed and his girlfriend kidnapped, the former special ops man ends up in a pace-slowing alliance with a feisty Nato military cop (a miscast Tamzin Outhwaite) to mount a rescue mission. Fans of adrenaline-rush excess will enjoy the frenetic first third, but the remainder of the film is rather dull and sluggish until the shoot-out climax. SF DVD

Wesley Snipes *Jack Tuliver* • Tamzin Outhwaite *Kelly Anders* • Dhobi Oparei [Deobia Oparei] *Spanky* ■ *Dir* Simon Fellows *Scr* Martin Wheeler

Seven Sinners ★★★

Detective drama   1936 · UK · BW · 69min

This brisk British mystery was something of a transatlantic affair, with Edmund Lowe and Constance Cummings lending some Hollywood zing to Michael Balcon's typically efficient production. It doesn't take long to work out who's behind a series of train smashes or what their motive might be, but director Albert de Courville is as much concerned with the banter between Lowe's cocky American detective and Cummings's sassy insurance investigator as he is with the crimes. DP

Edmund Lowe *Harwood* • Constance Cummings *Caryl Fenton* • Thomy Bourdelle *Paul Turbe* • Henry Oscar *Axel Hoyte* • Felix Aylmer *Sir Charles Webber* ■ *Dir* Albert de Courville • *Scr* L du Garde Peach, Sidney Gilliat, Frank Launder, Austin Melford, from the play *The Wrecker* by Arnold Ridley, Bernard Merivale

Seven Sinners ★★★ PG

Drama   1940 · US · BW · 82min

Marlene Dietrich is a sultry cabaret singer who arrives on a South Sea island to perform at the Seven Sinners Café. There, her erotic presence inflames every man in sight and captures the heart of navy lieutenant John Wayne. He wants to marry her, but she's wise enough to know that's a bad idea. Dietrich, giving a knowing, self-mocking parody of a Shanghai Lil stereotype, sings (if that's the right word) three numbers and inflames a climactic bar-room brawl in this rumbustious nonsense. RK DVD

Marlene Dietrich *Bijou Blanche* • John Wayne *Lieutenant Dan Brent* • Broderick Crawford *"Little Ned"*, *Edward Patrick Finnegan* • Mischa Auer *Sasha* • Albert Dekker *Dr Martin* • Billy Gilbert *Tony* • Oscar Homolka *Antro* • Anna Lee *Dorothy Henderson* • Reginald Denny *Captain Church* • Samuel S Hinds *Governor* ■ *Dir* Tay Garnett • *Scr* John Meehan, Harry Tugend, from a story by Ladislaus Fodor [Ladislas Fodor], Laslo Vadnay

S

Seven Swords ★★15

Period martial arts drama
2005 · HK/Chi/S Kor · Colour · 134min

A plodding mess of romance, treachery and lacklustre combat, this action fantasy unfolds in 17th-century China where an edict outlawing martial arts puts a remote village in jeopardy. Earmarked for slaughter, the residents' only hope of survival lies with warriors known as "The Seven Swords". One-time genre maestro Tsui Hark unwisely favours a naturalistic approach, with sparse and bland fight sequences made even less dynamic by muddy visuals and sluggish editing. SF Mandarin +subtitles. Violence.
DVD

Donnie Yen *Chu Zhaonan/The Dragon Sword* · Leon Lai *Yang Yunchong/The Transcience Sword* · Charlie Young *Wu Yuanyin/The Heaven's Fall Sword* · Sun Honglei *General Fire-Wind* · Lu Yi Han *Zhibang/The Deity Sword* · Kim So-yeon *Luzhu, "Green Pearl"* · Lau Kar-Leung *Fu Qingzhu/The Unlearned Sword* · Zhang Jingchu *Liu Yufang, "Fang"* ■ *Dir* Tsui Hark, Cheung Chi-sing, Chun Tin-nam, from the novel *Seven Swordsmen from Mount Tian (Qijian xia tianshan)* by Liang Yu-sheng

Seven Thieves ★★★

Crime drama
1960 · US · BW · 101min

Three Hollywood veterans – star Edward G Robinson, producer/writer Sydney Boehm and director Henry Hathaway – try to breathe life into a caper plot that itself had seen better days. Edward G does manage to add a certain validity to the story of an ageing criminal planning a last assault on a Monte Carlo casino and his acting meshes surprisingly well with that of comparative newcomer and Method actor Rod Steiger. TH

Edward G Robinson *Theo Wilkins* · Rod Steiger *Paul Mason* · Joan Collins *Melanie* · Eli Wallach *Poncho* · Michael Dante *Louis* · Alexander Scourby *Raymond Le May* · Berry Kroeger *Hugo Baumer* ■ *Dir* Henry Hathaway · *Scr* Sydney Boehm, from the novel *Lions at the Kill* by Max Catto

Seven Thunders ★★PG

Wartime drama
1957 · UK · BW · 96min

James Robertson-Justice plays a French physician, ostensibly helping escaped PoWs including Stephen Boyd, who in reality is mass-poisoning refugees for their money and goods. Sadly, Robertson-Justice is like a whale out of water away from his much loved Sir Lancelot in the light-hearted *Doctor* movies. Based on a real-life killer, the character he plays here was more fully realised in the 1990 French film *Docteur Petiot*, which had Michel Serrault playing the title role to chilling effect. TH *DVD*

Stephen Boyd *Dave* · James Robertson-Justice *Dr Martout* · Kathleen Harrison *Madame Abou* · Tony Wright *Jim* · Anna Gaylor *Lise* · Eugene Deckers *Emile Blanchard* · Rosalie Crutchley *Therese Blanchard* · Katherine Kath *Madame Parfait* ■ *Dir* Hugo Fregonese · *Scr* John Baines, from the novel by Rupert Croft-Cooke

The Seven-Ups ★★★15

Police drama
1973 · US · Colour · 98min

The nerve-scraping car-chase in this fast-moving New York police thriller is quite the equal of those pacey pile-ups in *Bullitt* and *The French Connection*. It's not surprising, really, as the producer of those movies, Philip D'Antoni, directs here. Roy Scheider stars as an undercover cop in an unorthodox unit, whose chief informant uses Scheider's criminal lists for his own purposes. It's one of those movies in which you can't tell the good guys from the bad guys, and character development is given the elbow in favour of violent action. TH Some violence, swearing. ∿

Roy Scheider *Buddy Manucci* · Tony LoBianco *Vito Lucia* · Larry Haines *Max Kalish* · Ken Kercheval *Ansel* · Richard Lynch *Moon* · Victor Arnold *Barili* · Jerry Leon *Mingo* · Bill Hickman *Bo* · Lou Polan *Coltello* ■ *Dir* Philip D'Antoni · *Scr* Albert Ruben, Alexander Jacobs, from a story by Sonny Grosso

Seven Waves Away ★★★

Drama
1957 · UK · BW · 99min

Also known as *Abandon Ship!*, this drama has Tyrone Power in charge of a lifeboat filled to the gunwhales with people who survive the sinking of a liner in the South Atlantic. Power decides that the injured and helpless must be thrown overboard and this makes him a hero until a rescue ship appears, when everyone feels guilty at what has happened. Like Hitchcock's earlier *Lifeboat*, it's set entirely at sea, with moral problems floating like flotsam among the cast of familiar British stalwarts. AT

Tyrone Power *Alec Holmes* · Mai Zetterling *Julie* · Lloyd Nolan *Frank Kelly* · Stephen Boyd *Will McKinley* · Moira Lister *Edith Middleton* · James Hayter *"Cookie" Morrow* · Marie Lohr *Mrs Knudson* · Noel Willman *Aubrey Clark* · Gordon Jackson *John Merritt* · Clive Morton *Maj Gen Barrington* · Laurence Naismith *Captain Darrow* · John Stratton *"Sparks" Clary* · Victor Maddern *Willie Hawkins* ■ *Dir/Scr* Richard Sale

Seven Ways from Sundown ★★★U

Western
1960 · US · Colour · 86min

In this satisfying western, Audie Murphy stars as a Texas Ranger bringing in a killer, played by the ever-excellent Barry Sullivan, who gives Murphy more than a run for his money in the acting stakes. There's a nice wryness running through this feature, with a cast of western veterans to lend credibility. Although Murphy would continue filming big-screen westerns, this was his last one of any real merit. TS

Audie Murphy *Seven Jones* · Barry Sullivan *Jim Flood* · Venetia Stevenson *Joy Karrington* · John McIntire *Sergeant Hennessey* · Kenneth Tobey *Lieutenant Herly* · Mary Field *Ma Kerrington* · Ken Lynch *Graves* · Suzanne Lloyd *Lucinda* ■ *Dir* Harry Keller · *Scr* Clair Huffaker, from his novel

7 Women ★★★★

Period drama
1966 · US · Colour · 86min

The last movie from great American director John Ford is, as one might expect, a transplanted western. It's set in Manchuria in 1935, where a group of remarkably resolute women missionaries are threatened by the local Mongolian warlord (a cleverly cast Mike Mazurki). Ford has the benefit of a superb cast, headed by Anne Bancroft as a cynical physician who ends up risking everything to protect the mission. This may seem unlikely Ford material on the surface, but the old maestro certainly makes it his own. TS

Anne Bancroft *Dr Cartwright* · Sue Lyon *Emma Clark* · Margaret Leighton *Agatha Andrews* · Flora Robson *Miss Binns* · Mildred Dunnock *Jane Argent* · Betty Field *Florrie Pether* · Anna Lee *Mrs Russell* · Eddie Albert *Charles Pether* · Mike Mazurki *Tunga Khan* · Woody Strode *Lean warrior* ■ *Dir* John Ford · *Scr* Janet Green, John McCormick, from the novel *Chinese Finale* by Norah Lofts

The Seven Year Itch ★★★★PG

Comedy
1955 · US · Colour · 100min

One of the great moments from this film, when Marilyn Monroe lets the updraft from a subway ventilation shaft lift her skirt, has passed into movie legend; true cineastes will delight in noting that the sequence is divided into two horizontal cuts, since the film was one of Fox's early CinemaScope productions, and director Billy Wilder made it all look so seamless. In the more prudish 1950s this film was very risqué indeed, the title giving a catchphrase to the nation and a new insight into marriage. The film is still very funny, and beautifully played by Monroe and Tom Ewell. Make allowances for the period and enjoy yourself. TS *DVD* ∿

Marilyn Monroe *The Girl* · Tom Ewell *Richard Sherman* · Evelyn Keyes *Helen Sherman* · Sonny Tufts *Tom McKenzie* · Robert Strauss *Mr Kruhulik* · Oskar Homolka [Oscar Homolka] *Dr Brubaker* · Marguerite Chapman *Miss Morris* · Victor Moore *Plumber* ■ *Dir* Billy Wilder · *Scr* Billy Wilder, George Axelrod, from the play by George Axelrod · *Cinematographer* Milton Krasner · *Music* Alfred Newman

Seven Years in Tibet ★★★PG

Biographical adventure drama
1997 · US/UK · Colour · 130min

Jean-Jacques Annaud's magnificently photographed Dalai Lama drama is strong on visual appeal and spiritual ambience, but makes one fatal error – the miscasting of Brad Pitt as real-life Austrian mountaineer Heinrich Harrer, whose eventful life was capped by a lengthy stay in Tibet. Pitt's catalogue model looks and ropey Teutonic accent undermine the whole movie. David Thewlis, however, is excellent as his climbing partner, as is Annaud's feeling for period and place. JC *DVD*

Brad Pitt *Heinrich Harrer* · David Thewlis *Peter Aufschnaiter* · BD Wong *Ngawang Jigme* · Mako *Kungo Tsarong* · Danny Denzongpa *Regent* · Victor Wong (2) *Chinese "Amban"* ■ *Dir* Jean-Jacques Annaud · *Scr* Becky Johnston, from the memoirs of Heinrich Harrer · *Music* John Williams · *Cinematographer* Robert Fraisse

17 Again ★★12

Comedy
2009 · US · Colour · 97min

Aimed squarely at the teen market, this body-switch comedy stars *High School Musical* heart-throb Zac Efron. Mike O'Donnell (Matthew Perry) is a walking disappointment, overlooked for promotion, ignored by his teenage kids and thrown out by wife Scarlett (Leslie Mann). But some hokily convenient business with a magic janitor on a bridge transforms him back into his 17-year-old self (Efron), and he re-enrols at high school. The scenarios that ensue are predictable and undynamic, and while Efron has charm, Perry is all-too-briefly on screen, so it's down to nerdy best friend Ned (Thomas Lennon) to supply offbeat comic substance. And, despite one shoehorned-in opportunity, Efron fans might miss his singing and dancing. AC Some swearing, sexual references. *DVD* ∿

Matthew Perry *Mike O'Donnell as an adult* · Zac Efron *Mike O'Donnell, aged 17* · Leslie Mann *Scarlett O'Donnell as an adult* · Thomas Lennon (3) *Ned Gold* · Michelle Trachtenberg *Maggie* · Allison Miller *Scarlett, aged 17* · Tyler Steelman *Ned, aged 17* · Katerina Graham *Jaime* ■ *Dir* Burr Steers · *Scr* Jason Filardi

Seventeen and Missing ★★

Mystery thriller
2006 · Can · Colour · 90min

The subject of this thriller may be a parent's worst nightmare, but there's surprisingly little drama in this ineffectual, made-for-television abduction tale. Psychic mum Dedee Pfeiffer (Michelle's sister) uses her spooky second sight to help find her missing daughter after the stroppy teen disappears following a party. Only Pfeiffer's horror movie-styled visions bring a jolt of colour, enlivening her character's otherwise dull detective work. SF

Dedee Pfeiffer *Emilie Janzen* · Matthew Harrison (2) *Richard Janzen* · Tegan Moss *Lori Janzen* · Brett Dier *Kevin Janzen* · Victor Ayala *Martin Vetter* ■ *Dir* Paul Schneider (1) · *Scr* Kraig Wenham

7th Cavalry ★★★U

Western
1956 · US · Colour · 76min

Randolph Scott played a key role in the emergence of the psychological western in the late 1950s, in which motives mattered more than action. This disjointed picture does manage to combine excitement and emotion, as Scott seeks to disprove a charge of cowardice by leading a cavalry detail to reclaim the dead after the Battle of the Little Bighorn. The skirmishes are solidly staged by B-movie specialist Joseph H Lewis. DP *DVD*

Randolph Scott *Captain Tom Benson* · Barbara Hale *Martha Kellogg* · Jay C Flippen *Sergeant Bates* · Jeanette Nolan *Mrs Reynolds* · Frank Faylen *Krugger* · Leo Gordon *Vogel* · Denver Pyle *Dixon* · Harry Carey Jr *Corporal Morrison* · Michael Pate *Captain Benteen* ■ *Dir* Joseph H Lewis · *Scr* Peter Packer, from a story by Glendon F Swarthout

The Seventh Coin ★★

Mystery thriller
1993 · US · Colour · 92min

On holiday in old Jerusalem, American teenager Alexandra Powers hangs out with an Arab boy who steals a precious coin that once belonged to King Herod. Soon the duo are being pursued by dotty Peter O'Toole, who believes that he is the reincarnation of the ancient monarch and the coin is his. This is a mild-mannered family thriller, high on lush visuals, but low on basic action and adventure trappings. O'Toole is hilariously OTT. AJ

Peter O'Toole *Emil Saber* · Alexandra Powers *Ronnie Segal* · Navin Chowdhry *Salim Zouabi* · John Rhys-Davies *Captain Galil* · Ally Walker *Lisa* ■ *Dir* Dror Soref · *Scr* Dror Soref, Michael Lewis

The Seventh Continent ★★★★18

Surreal drama
1989 · Austria · Colour · 103min

Echoes of Robert Bresson, Chantal Akerman and Rainer Werner Fassbinder reverberate through Michael Haneke's stark but deeply affecting study of the antiseptic inertia blighting modern Austria. The ritualistic, almost robotic existence endured by Dieter Berner and Birgit Doll is briefly disturbed by the punishment meted out to daughter Leni Tanzer after she feigns blindness – but now the balance of their lives has irrevocably changed. Haneke's use of repetition and fragmentation, coupled with his rigorous pacing, makes this a dispiriting, yet relentlessly provocative experience. DP German +subtitles. *DVD*

Dieter Berner *Georg* · Birgit Doll *Anna* · Leni Tanzer *Eva* · Udo Samel *Alexander* ■ *Dir/Scr* Michael Haneke

The Seventh Cross ★★★

Drama
1944 · US · BW · 111min

Seven inmates escape from a concentration camp in pre-Second World War Germany, but only one (Spencer Tracy), against all the odds, evades capture and execution. This is a gripping story that evokes the poisonous atmosphere of threat and terror and the dangers and difficulties for the Resistance in Nazi Germany. Directed with full command by Austrian émigré Fred Zinnemann and played by Tracy as you would expect, there's also excellent support from the Oscar-nominated Hume Cronyn. RK

Spencer Tracy *George Heisler* · Signe Hasso *Toni* · Hume Cronyn *Paul Roeder* · Jessica Tandy *Liesel Roeder* · Agnes Moorehead *Mme Marelli* · Herbert Rudley *Franz Marnet* ■ *Dir* Fred Zinnemann · *Scr* Helen Deutsch, from the novel *Das Siebte Kreuz* by Anna Seghers

The 7th Dawn ★

Drama
1964 · UK · Colour · 125min

This dismal melodrama stars William Holden as an engineer who finds himself at odds with a former comrade in post-Second World War Malaya. Lewis Gilbert directs the film at a funereal pace and it's packed with clichéd characters who pompously spout political platitudes and entangle themselves in shabby love affairs. DP

William Holden (2) *Ferris* · Susannah York *Candace* · Capucine *Dhana* · Tetsuro Tamba *Ng* · Michael Goodliffe *Trumphey* · Allan Cuthbertson *Cavendish* · Maurice Denham *Tarlton* · Beulah Quo *Ah Ming* ■ *Dir* Lewis Gilbert · *Scr* Karl Tunberg, from the novel *The Durian Tree* by Michael Koen

The Seventh Dimension ★★★15

Supernatural thriller
2009 · UK · Colour · 91min

This conspiracy-laced cyber chiller overcomes an unlikely premise to deliver some solid supernatural entertainment. Student Lucy Evans and best friend Kelly Adams stumble upon an attempt by computer "hacktivist" Jonathan Rhodes and his girlfriend Calita Rainford to break into the Vatican's online vaults. Hidden there, so they believe, is the prophetic Bible Code that will open the gateway to unimagined dimensions of existence. The committed performances ease the plot past its less plausible moments. DP

Kelly Adams *Sarah* • Jonathan Rhodes *Declan* • Lucy Evans *Zoe* • Calita Rainford *Kendra* • David Horton *Malcolm* ■ *Dir/Scr* Brad Watson

The Seventh Fire ★★★ 15
Documentary 2015 · US · Colour · 75min

According to the "seven fires prophecy", the young braves of the Ojibwe nation will rise to defend its culture by restoring its core values. However, it quickly becomes clear in this documentary by Jack Pettibone Riccobono that they are more wrapped up in the trappings and temptations of modern life than native American tradition. Details are frustratingly sketchy in this well-meaning attempt to expose the plight of indigenous peoples in the States, but it paints a depressing picture of life on the fringes of US society. DP Swearing, drug abuse.

■ *Dir* Jack Pettibone Riccobono

7th Heaven ★★★★ PG
Silent romantic drama 1927 · US · BW · 113min

Poor, lonely, and religious Parisian sewer worker Charles Farrell takes in Janet Gaynor off the streets. They fall in love and marry, he is sent to the the First World War battlefront, and she, hearing that he has been killed, loses her faith in God. This classic tear-jerker is an effective drama about love triumphing over adversity and still has the power to draw tears. With its impressive battle scenes and atmospheric production, the film featured large in the first ever Academy Awards, winning Oscars for Frank Borzage, Gaynor, and Benjamin Glazer's script. RK DVD

Janet Gaynor *Diane* • Charles Farrell (1) *Chico* • Ben Bard *Colone Brissac* • David Butler *Gobin* • Marie Mosquini *Mme Gobin* • Albert Gran *Boul* ■ *Dir* Frank Borzage • *Scr* Benjamin Glazer, Katherine Hilliker (titles), HH Caldwell (titles), from the play by Austin Strong

Seventh Heaven ★★★
Romantic drama 1937 · US · BW · 102min

This serviceable remake of the 1927 silent film tells of the love affair, tested by war and tragedy, between a Parisian sewer worker (James Stewart) and a homeless girl. Gale Sondergaard plays the heartless sister who throws Simone Simon onto the streets, while Hollywood's resident screen medic Jean Hersholt exchanges his stethoscope for a priest's dog-collar. Reworked in certain areas (the hero starts out as an atheist, the heroine is a prostitute), it dilutes the sugar quotient of the original, but fails to achieve its dream-like poignancy. RK

Simone Simon *Liane* • James Stewart *Chico* • Gale Sondergaard *Nana* • Gregory Ratoff *Boul* • Jean Hersholt *Father Chevillon* • J Edward Bromberg *Aristide* • *Scr* Melville Baker, from the play by Austin Strong

The Seventh Seal ★★★★★ PG
Period drama 1957 · Swe · BW · 92min

This is an undoubted masterpiece of world cinema. It tells of a crusader knight (Max von Sydow) who refuses to accompany Death (Bengt Ekerot) until he has found a flicker of hope in a world stricken by plague, corruption and fear. While this is a personal film, in which Ingmar Bergman (the son of the chaplain of the Swedish royal family) resolves his own doubts about the existence of God, its conclusions will leave even the most cynical filled with optimism. DP Swedish +subtitles. DVD Blu-ray

Max von Sydow *Antonius Block, the knight* • Gunnar Björnstrand *Jons, Block's squire* • Bengt Ekerot *Death* • Nils Poppe *Jof* • Bibi Andersson *Mia* ■ *Dir* Ingmar Bergman • *Scr* Ingmar Bergman, from his play *Tramalning (Wood Painting)*

The Seventh Sign ★★ 15
Supernatural horror thriller 1988 · US · Colour · 96min

Demi Moore is given the opportunity to save the world, but as blood rains from the sky and earthquakes shake cities, Demi is more worried about her pregnancy. Yet, as a weirdo reads Hebrew in her garage and CNN broadcasts apocalyptic bulletins on the hour, having the baby and saving humanity become synonymous. Moore is good but the movie is a mess. LH DVD

Demi Moore *Abby Quinn* • Jürgen Prochnow *David the Boarder* • Michael Biehn *Russell Quinn* • Peter Friedman *Father Lucci* • Manny Jacobs *Avi* • John Taylor (2) *Jimmy* • John Heard *Reverend* ■ *Dir* Carl Schultz • *Scr* WW Wicket, George Kaplan

Seventh Son ★★ 12
Supernatural fantasy adventure 2014 · US/Chi · Colour · 97min

A notable adventure mainly for the fact that it boasts two Oscar winners in leading roles, Julianne Moore playing a wicked witch and Jeff Bridges as her old nemesis. There are some eye-catching set pieces, but it's unclear whether this is intended to be a family blockbuster, a tween-friendly fantasy or something a little darker for the grown-ups, which means the end result is a bit of a mish-mash. JF Violence, swearing. DVD 3D

Jeff Bridges *Master John Gregory* • Ben Barnes *Tom Ward* • Julianne Moore *Mother Malkin* • Alicia Vikander *Alice* • Olivia Williams *Mam Ward* • Kit Harington *Mr Bradley* ■ *Dir* Sergei Bodrov • *Scr* Charles Leavitt, Steven Knight, from a story by Matt Greenberg, from the novel *The Spook's Apprentice* by Joseph Delaney

The Seventh Veil ★★★ PG
Melodrama 1945 · US · BW · 89min

The Oscar-winning screenplay for this all-stops-out melodrama was written by the husband-and-wife team of Sydney and Muriel Box. But there's no escaping the fact that, for all its aspirations to musical and psychological gravity, this is nothing more than home-cured ham. Ann Todd is at her drippiest as a persecuted pianist whose love/hate relationship with crippled guardian James Mason is founded on romantic clichés that first appeared in Victorian penny-dreadfuls. Nonetheless, it's still irresistible entertainment, done with style. DP

James Mason *Nicholas* • Ann Todd *Francesca Cunningham* • Herbert Lom *Dr Larson* • Hugh McDermott *Peter Gay* • Albert Lieven *Maxwell Leyden* • Yvonne Owen *Susan Brook* • David Horne *Dr Kendal* ■ *Dir* Compton Bennett • *Scr* Sydney Box, Muriel Box

The Seventh Victim ★★
Horror 1943 · US · BW · 70min

The directing debut of former editor Mark Robson is an underwritten but atmospheric and creepy tale about a sect of Satanists who live in deepest Greenwich Village. Tom Conway is a pallid lead, out-performed by Kim Hunter, who screams on cue with considerable conviction. If the main set looks vaguely familiar, it's because it was originally built the previous year for Orson Welles's *The Magnificent Ambersons*. AT

Kim Hunter *Mary Gibson* • Tom Conway *Dr Louis Judd* • Jean Brooks *Jacqueline Gibson* • Isabel Jewell *Frances Fallon* • Evelyn Brent *Natalie Cortez* • Erford Gage *Jason Hoag* • Ben Bard *Brun* • Hugh Beaumont *Gregory Ward* ■ *Dir* Mark Robson • *Scr* DeWitt Bodeen, Charles O'Neal • *Cinematographer* Nicholas Musuraca

The 7th Voyage of Sinbad ★★★★ U
Fantasy adventure 1958 · US · Colour · 84min

The first Sinbad adventure saga from stop-motion genius Ray Harryhausen is still the best. Sokurah the Magician (Torin Thatcher) demands that Sinbad (Kerwin Matthews) find a magic lamp that is being guarded by an ingenious gallery of monsters – brought to fabulous life by Harryhausen's expertise and Bernard Herrmann's rousing score. A 30-foot-tall Cyclops, a two-headed bird, a fire-breathing dragon and a warrior skeleton combine with swashbuckling spectacle and thrilling escapism under Nathan Juran's sure-handed direction. The result is a fantastic family favourite. Followed by *The Golden Voyage of Sinbad*. AJ DVD

Kerwin Mathews *Captain Sinbad* • Kathryn Grant *Princess Parisa* • Richard Eyer *Barroni the Genie* • Torin Thatcher *Sokurah the Magician* • Alec Mango *Caliph* • Danny Green *Karim* • Harold Kasket *Sultan* ■ *Dir* Nathan Juran • *Scr* Kenneth Kolb

'71 ★★★★ 15
Thriller 2014 · UK · Colour · 99min

Set in 1971 during the Troubles in Northern Ireland, this superbly crafted thriller captures the confusion, bigotry and riven loyalties of the conflict. Young Private Jack O'Connell is dispatched to support the RUC as they search for guns in the Catholic Falls Road when a riot kicks off. O'Connell is separated from his unit and must make his way back to safety, navigating between the warring factions. An extraordinarily tense adventure story that recalls *Escape from New York* as much as *Bloody Sunday*. LF Violence, swearing. DVD Blu-ray

Jack O'Connell (2) *Gary Hook* • Paul Anderson (2) *Sergeant Leslie Lewis* • Richard Dormer *Eamon* • Sean Harris *Captain Sandy Browning* • Barry Keoghan *Sean Bannon* • Martin McCann *Paul Haggerty* ■ *Dir* Yann Demange • *Scr* Gregory Burke

71 Fragments of a Chronology of Chance ★★★ 12
Experimental drama 1994 · Austria/Ger · Colour · 95min

As its title suggests, this is a masterly mosaic of a movie, in which a combination of fate and caprice causes the lives of disparate Viennese citizens to be touched by tragedy. Flashing back from a teenage student's seemingly unprovoked Christmas Eve gun rampage, the film assembles various story snippets that are linked together by the desperate pleadings of a homeless Romanian refugee. It's the kind of controlled, cerebral affair we've now come to expect from Michael Haneke. Compelling, if cool and calculating. DP DVD

Gabriel Cosmin Urdes *Romanian boy* • Lukas Miko *Max, student* • Otto Grünmandl *Tomek, old man* • Anne Bennett *Inge Brunner* • Udo Samel *Paul Brunner* ■ *Dir/Scr* Michael Haneke

Severance ★★★ 15
Comedy horror 2006 · UK/Ger · Colour · 91min

Following his terror-on-the-tube-tale, *Creep*, British film-maker Christopher Smith here goes above ground and delivers a skilful blend of comedy and horror. Pitched somewhere between TV's *The Office* and British horror *Dog Soldiers*, this follows a group of armaments firm employees on a team-building weekend in rural Hungary. Lost in the woods, it's not long before the talented ensemble cast, headed by *Human Traffic*'s Danny Dyer, are caught up in something much more deadly than paintball games. Smith effectively switches between crowd-pleasing comedy and genuine suspense as he stages a series of gory deaths. Some might argue this is merely a disposable B-movie, but others will be won over. JR Violence, swearing, drug abuse DVD

Danny Dyer *Steve* • Laura Harris *Maggie* • Tim McInnerny *Richard* • Toby Stephens *Harris* • Claudie Blakley *Jill* • Andy Nyman *Gordon* • Matthew Baker *Noseferatu* ■ *Dir* Christopher Smith • *Scr* Christopher Smith, James Moran, from a story by Moran

A Severed Head ★★★
Black comedy 1970 · UK · Colour · 99min

Though not a patch on Iris Murdoch's 1961 novel, nor its subsequent stage adaptation, this is still an amusing, sophisticated comedy which, in its highly polished way, recalls Ross Hunter's Hollywood films of the 1950s and 1960s. Screenwriter Frederic Raphael was obviously writing about people he knew – academics and posh folk indulging in a mad charade of partner-swapping. In his first screen lead, Ian Holm is the harassed wine merchant juggling a wife and mistresses. DM

Lee Remick *Antonia Lynch-Gibbon* • Richard Attenborough *Palmer Anderson, psychiatrist* • Ian Holm *Martin Lynch-Gibbon, wine merchant* • Claire Bloom *Honor Klein* • Jennie Linden *Georgie Hands* • Clive Revill *Alexander Lynch-Gibbon* • Ann Firbank *Rosemary Lynch-Gibbon* ■ *Dir* Dick Clement • *Scr* Frederic Raphael, from the play by Iris Murdoch, JB Priestley, from the novel by Iris Murdoch

Sex & Drugs & Rock & Roll ★★★ 15
Musical biographical drama 2009 · UK · Colour · 110min

Andy Serkis stars as singer/songwriter Ian Dury in director Mat Whitecross's engaging but overly frenetic biopic. Using the framework of a live gig by Dury and the Blockheads, an abstract portrait of the post-punk poet unfolds. There are flashbacks to his polio-stricken childhood, and the relationships with those he loved: his wife (Olivia Williams), girlfriend (Naomie Harris) and son (Bill Milner). The busy mythologising hews close to the usual price-of-fame biographical clichés, but the top-notch performances give viewers *Reasons to Be Cheerful* – Milner is terrific and Serkis is the tour de force at the film's centre. AJ Swearing, sex scenes, drug abuse DVD Blu-ray

Andy Serkis *Ian Dury* • Bill Milner *Baxter Dury* • Naomie Harris *Denise Roudette* • Tom Hughes *Chaz Jankel* • Olivia Williams *Betty* • Ray Winstone *Bill Dury* • Toby Jones *Hargreaves* ■ *Dir* Mat Whitecross • *Scr* Paul Viragh • *Music* Chaz Jankel

Sex and Lies in Sin City ★★
Crime drama based on a true story 2008 · US · Colour · 95min

Conjecture abounds in this patchy TV dramatisation of the controversy surrounding the 1998 death of drug-addicted Las Vegas casino owner Ted Binion. In a flashback-heavy narrative, Matthew Modine creates an emotionally complex Binion, as director Peter Medak tries to put together the pieces that led to the alleged homicide. But the frequent moving backwards and forwards in time merely makes an already underdeveloped script feel even less cohesive. SF

Matthew Modine *Ted Binion* • Mena Suvari *Sandy Murphy* • Johnathon Schaech *Rick Tabish* • Marcia Gay Harden *Becky* • Mark Sivertsen *Jay Green* ■ *Dir* Peter Medak • *Scr* Teena Booth, from the novel *Murder in Sin City* by Jeff German

Sex and Lucia ★★★ 18
Drama 2001 · Sp/Fr · Colour · 122min

Exploring such perennial themes as identity, coincidence and sexual psychology, this has all the visual bravura and narrative complexity one would expect of writer/director Julio Medem. There's technical assurance and dramatic intensity to spare as the fractured storyline subtly reveals how waitress Paz Vega (the eponymous Lucia), scuba-diver Daniel Freire and nanny Elena Anaya are all bound into novelist Tristan Ulloa's tortuous existence. It's chic and seductive, but its fascination lies solely on the surface. DP Spanish +subtitles. DVD

Paz Vega *Lucia* • Tristan Ulloa *Lorenzo* • Najwa Nimri *Elena* • Daniel Freire *Carlos/Antonio* • Elena Anaya *Belen* ■ *Dir/Scr* Julio Medem

Sex and the City: the Movie ★★★ 15
Romantic comedy 2008 · US · Colour · 139min

Ten years after meeting "Mr Big", New York "sexpert" Carrie Bradshaw (Sarah Jessica Parker) finally gets closure on her dating dilemmas in this big-screen spin-off from the iconic TV show. As ever, Parker brims with infectious whimsy; doubly so when Big (Chris Noth) pops the question. There's rather too much cooing over dresses and shoes for half-an-hour afterwards, but then Carrie and her gal pals are forced to reassess life's priorities. It's the ups and downs between friends that resonate more than the love story, and although some gags veer into *American Pie* territory, there is plenty of dry humour, too – Kim Cattrall is especially wicked as saucy Samantha. SP Swearing, sex scenes. DVD Blu-ray

Sarah Jessica Parker *Carrie Bradshaw* • Kim Cattrall *Samantha Jones* • Cynthia Nixon *Miranda Hobbes* • Kristin Davis *Charlotte York Goldenblatt* • Chris Noth [*Christopher King*] *Mr Big* • Jennifer Hudson *Louise* • Jason Lewis *Jerry "Smith" Jerrod* • Evan Handler *Harry Goldenblatt* • David Eigenberg *Steve Brady* • Willie Garson *Stanford Blatch* ■ *Dir/Scr* Michael Patrick King

Sex and the City 2 ★★15

Romantic comedy   2010 · US · Colour · 140min

Sarah Jessica Parker slips back into those designer heels to play columnist Carrie Bradshaw in this second spin-off from the TV series. After settling down with Mr Big (Chris Noth), she ponders the vagaries of marriage, but writer/director Michael Patrick King is just as hazy as her on the subject. His answer is to create a distraction with a holiday to a first-class resort in Abu Dhabi, where the "girls" totter over sand dunes, sip cocktails and giggle at crude jokes. As usual, it's Kim Cattrall doing the trash talk, but it feels lazy and patronising in this context when she comes up against religious conservatism and a plot as scanty as her own wardrobe. SP *DVD* SL

Sarah Jessica Parker *Carrie Bradshaw* • Kim Cattrall *Samantha Jones* • Cynthia Nixon *Miranda Hobbes* • Kristin Davis *Charlotte York-Goldenblatt* • Chris Noth [*Christopher Noth*] *Mr Big* • David Eigenberg *Steve Brady* • Evan Handler *Harry Goldenblatt* • Jason Lewis *Smith Jerrod* ■ *Dir/Scr* Michael Patrick King

Sex and the Other Man ★★★

Comedy   1995 · US · Colour · 89min

In this blackish comedy, Ron Eldard, suffering from impotence, is shocked when he catches his girlfriend Kari Wuhrer in bed with her boss Stanley Tucci. But this scene has a positive affect on Eldard's libido, and he and Wuhrer then hold Tucci captive while they work out their sexual frustrations. This off-centre farce is lifted by a brilliant performance by Tucci. DF

Ron Eldard *Billy* • Stanley Tucci *Arthur* • Kari Wuhrer *Jessica* ■ *Dir* Karl Slovin • *Scr* Karl Slovin, from the play *Captive* by Paul Weitz

Sex and the Single Girl ★★★

Satirical comedy   1964 · US · Colour · 119min

Tony Curtis and Natalie Wood make an attractive couple in this comedy, which was regarded as very risqué in 1964. It's based on an enormous bestseller by Helen Gurley Brown, the legendary editor of *Cosmopolitan*. Warner's paid a reputed $200,000 for the rights, then realised it didn't have a story, so Joseph Heller (*Catch-22*), wrote the script as a satire on sex therapy in general and Brown's book in particular. Wood played Miss Brown as a virginal sexologist and Curtis as the journalist who interviews her, posing as a man with deep sexual problems, which leads to a lot of in-jokes. AT

Tony Curtis *Bob Weston* • Natalie Wood *Dr Helen Brown* • Henry Fonda *Frank Broderick* • Lauren Bacall *Sylvia Broderick* • Mel Ferrer *Rudy DeMeyer* • Fran Jeffries *Gretchen* • Leslie Parrish *Susan* • Edward Everett Horton *The Chief* • Larry Storch *Motorcycle cop* ■ *Dir* Richard Quine • *Scr* Joseph Heller, David R Schwartz, from the story by Joseph Hoffman, from the book by Helen Gurley Brown

Sex Drive ★15

Comedy   2008 · US/UK · Colour · 104min

This interminable gross-out teen flick aspires to both the raunchy, good-natured smuttiness of the *American Pie* films and the deft sentiment of classic adolescent road movie *The Sure Thing*, but fails on both counts. Ian (Josh Zuckerman) is a sexually frustrated 18-year-old who embarks on a road trip to meet the enticingly named Ms Tasty, an internet date who promises to relieve him of his virginity. Also along for the ride are his best friend Lance (Clark Duke) and Felicia (Amanda Crew), who, inevitably, turns out to be the "real" object of Ian's affections. The characters are unattractive and the jokes

are few and far between and rarely as funny as they think they are. AS *DVD* SL

Josh Zuckerman *Ian Lafferty* • James Marsden *Rex* • Seth Green *Ezekial* • Katrina Bowden *Ms Tasty* • Amanda Crew *Felicia* • Clark Duke *Lance* • Alice Greczyn *Mary* ■ *Dir* Sean Anders • *Scr* Sean Anders, John Morris (2), from the novel *All the Way* by Andy Behrens

Sex, Drugs, Rock & Roll ★★★

Satirical comedy   1991 · US · Colour · 96min

Filmed at Boston's Wilbur Theatre, this record of comic performance artist Eric Bogosian's hit Broadway one-man show is directed to hilarious perfection by John McNaughton. Bogosian offers up an assortment of unpleasant characters to laugh at uncontrollably, including a drug-addled youth remembering a debauched stag night, an entertainment lawyer driven by success, and an ageing English rock star about to play a benefit concert for Amazon Indians. Often surreal, always outrageous and very funny. AJ

Eric Bogosian • *Dir* John McNaughton • *Scr* Eric Bogosian

Sex Is Comedy ★★★18

Comedy drama   2002 · Fr · Colour · 90min

Catherine Breillat's intriguing satire considers the problems a woman faces not only in directing a sex scene, but also in imposing her authority upon a largely male crew. Anne Parillaud adeptly conveys the doubts and frustrations of the auteur struggling to secure the co-operation of arrogant, yet insecure actor Grégoire Colin in coupling convincingly with teenage co-star Roxane Mesquida for their ironically titled movie, *Intimate Scenes*. But while Breillat frequently captures the political import of the various on-set tensions and alliances, some of Parillaud's artistic pronouncements ring luvvily hollow. DP French +subtitles. *DVD*

Anne Parillaud *Jeanne* • Grégoire Colin *The actor* • Roxane Mesquida *The actress* • Ashley Wanninger *Léo* • Dominique Colladant *Willy* ■ *Dir/Scr* Catherine Breillat

sex, lies, and videotape ★★★★18

Drama   1989 · US · Colour · 95min

The winner of the Palme d'Or at Cannes, Steven Soderbergh's debut feature was made for just $1.2 million. Although it took an uncompromisingly adult approach to sex, it wasn't explicit nudity (of which there is none) that made this intelligent film so controversial, but the intimacy of the drama and the frankness of the dialogue. Peter Gallagher is a lawyer having an affair with his sister-in-law (Laura San Giacomo), who has always resented the prissiness of her perfect sibling (Andie MacDowell). However, we never really discover anything about James Spader, the long-lost friend who forces the other three to re-examine their motives and desires. It's this ambiguity that makes Spader's character the most fascinating of the quartet. DP Swearing, sex scenes. *DVD*

James Spader *Graham Dalton* • Andie MacDowell *Ann Millaney* • Peter Gallagher *John Millaney* • Laura San Giacomo *Cynthia Bishop* • Ron Vawter *Therapist* • Steven Brill *Barfly* ■ *Dir/Scr* Steven Soderbergh

Sex Lives of the Potato Men ★18

Comedy   2003 · UK · Colour · 79min

The title more or less tells the whole story of this thoroughly British "smutfest", as Johnny Vegas and Mackenzie Crook play Brummie potato deliverers whose amorous adventures could be summed up as soft-paw corn "comedy". Andy Humphries's film is less a coherent whole than a loosely connected series of sketches. Unfunny and unambitious. DA Swearing. *DVD*

Johnny Vegas *Dave* • Mackenzie Crook *Ferris* • Mark Gatiss *Jeremy* • Dominic Coleman *Tolly* • Julia Davis *Shelley* • Lucy Davis *Ruth* • Kate Robbins (2) *Joan* • Nicolas Tennant *Phil* ■ *Dir/Scr* Andy Humphries

The Sex Monster ★★15

Sex comedy   1998 · US · Colour · 93min

Writer/director Mike Binder plays a wealthy Californian who wants to spice up his sex life and talks his wife (Mariel Hemingway) into a threesome with another woman. Although initially reluctant to satisfy this clichéd male fantasy, Hemingway finds herself increasingly intrigued by lesbianism, and before long Binder has unleashed a bisexual monster on the LA swingers scene. An amiable, if unsophisticated, farce. AJ *DVD*

Mariel Hemingway *Laura Barnes* • Mike Binder *Marty* • Renee Humphrey *Didi* • Missy Crider *Diva* ■ *Dir/Scr* Mike Binder

Sex Tape ★★15

Comedy   2014 · US · Colour · 90min

Apart from the attention-grabbing title, there isn't much to this comedy. Cameron Diaz and Jason Segel had good chemistry in *Bad Teacher* and reunite to play a couple with kids trying to rediscover that old magic under the bedclothes. They capture their efforts on video and, inevitably, the footage gets out. Despite the swearing, the gags are surprisingly timid and the excruciating moments you would expect them to have to deal with never happen, making this a big fat tease of a movie. SP Swearing, sex scenes, drug abuse, brief nudity. *DVD* SL

Cameron Diaz *Annie* • Jason Segel *Jay* • Rob Corddry *Robby* • Ellie Kemper *Tess* • Rob Lowe *Hank* • Jack Black *Owner of YouPorn* ■ *Dir* Jake Kasdan • *Scr* Kate Angelo, Jason Segel, Nicholas Stoller

Sex: the Annabel Chong Story ★★★18

Documentary   1999 · US · Colour · 85min

Grace Quek, the Singaporean student who re-created herself as porn queen Annabel Chong, may believe she set a world record for having sexual intercourse in the name of feminism. However, as Gough Lewis's documentary discloses, it was just another act of self-loathing by a fiercely intelligent but deeply confused innocent abroad in a world of frauds and exploiters. With on-screen acts of self-mutilation undermining the hard-core antics and aggressive psychobabble, this is a film that prompts one to question both the director's motives and those of his convent-educated star. DP *DVD*

■ *Dir* Gough Lewis

Sextette ★★PG

Musical comedy   1978 · US · Colour · 84min

They don't come any stranger than this too-late vehicle for the octogenarian (and virtually embalmed) Mae West. The musical exists in its own inspired limboland, where salaciousness and dated vulgarity ineptly combine to render it mesmerisingly, appallingly, watchable. Interspersed with what attempts to pass for a plot, the movie is padded with some bizarre London locations. The cast is truly astonishing: you'll shudder for their collective embarrassment. TS

Mae West *Marlo Manners* • Timothy Dalton *Sir Michael Barrington* • Dom DeLuise *Dan Turner* • Tony Curtis *Alexei Karansky* • Ringo Starr *Laslo Karolny* • George Hamilton *Vance* • Alice Cooper *Waiter* • Rona Barrett • Keith Moon *Dress designer* • George Raft ■ *Dir* Ken Hughes • *Scr* Herbert Baker, from the play by Mae West

Sexton Blake and the Hooded Terror ★★

Crime drama   1938 · UK/US · BW · 68min

Unlike so many other suave English sleuths, Sexton Blake has never really come to life on the big screen. Tod Slaughter is admittedly below par as the master crook, but the film's failure lies squarely at the door of George Curzon in the title role. He lacks the looks and charm that Ronald Colman brought to the role, while AR Rawlinson's script lacks the zip of Hal Meredith's original story. This is considered the best of the three films in which Curzon starred as Blake. Two more films, in the

1940s, also featured the sleuth (played then by David Farrar). AT

George Curzon *Sexton Blake* • Tod Slaughter *Michael Larron* • Greta Gynt *Mademoiselle Julie* • Charles Oliver *Max Fleming* • Tony Sympson *Tinker* • Marie Wright *Mrs Bardell* ■ *Dir* George King • *Scr* AR Rawlinson, from the novel by Pierre Quiroule, from the character created by Hal Meredith [Harry Blyth]

The Sexual Life of the Belgians 1950-1978 ★★★18

Satirical comedy drama   1994 · Bel · Colour · 78min

Prior to this semi-autobiographical satire, director Jan Bucquoy's greatest claim to fame was as the curator of Belgium's National Museum of Underpants. Whether his intention was to chart his own voyage of sexual discovery or expose every guilty secret in Belgian culture, Bucquoy only partially fulfils his ambitions. In spite of a bravura performance by Jean-Henri Compère as the director's alter ego, the personal side of the story too often finds itself suffocating under the bedclothes or wallowing in the bottom of a glass. The social observations, however, are often very amusing. DP Flemish +subtitles. Swearing.

Jean-Henri Compère *Jan Bucquoy* • No Francq *Jan as a child* • Isabelle Legros *Noella Bucquoy* • Sophie Schneider *Thérèse* • Pascale Binneri *Ariane Bucquoy* • Michele Shor *Aunt Martha* ■ *Dir/Scr* Jan Bucquoy

Sexy Beast ★★★★18

Crime drama   2000 · UK/Sp/US · Colour · 84min

Ray Winstone is in relatively restrained mode as a retired crook, now living the life of Riley on the Costa del Crime. He's content to play second fiddle to a terrifying and transfixing performance from Ben Kingsley as the psychopathic hardman sent to "persuade" him back to Blighty for one last job. Debuting director Jonathan Glazer made his name in advertising – he was the man behind the "Swimmer" and "Surfer" Guinness commercials – and his visual flair is evident here. The idyllic Spanish settings nicely counterpoint the growing sense of menace as cat-and-mouse games spiral toward an inevitable act of violence. DA Swearing. *DVD* SL

Ray Winstone *Gary "Gal" Dove* • Ben Kingsley *Don "Malky" Logan* • Ian McShane *Teddy Bass* • Amanda Redman *DeeDee* • Cavan Kendall *Aitch* • Julianne White *Jackie* • James Fox *Harry* ■ *Dir* Jonathan Glazer • *Scr* Louis Mellis, David Scinto

Shack Out on 101 ★★★

Drama   1955 · US · BW · 80min

Lee Marvin delivers the stand-out performance in this Cold War melodrama centred around a remote roadside café near a top-secret research station. Marvin relishes the part of the dim-witted cook who's not all that he seems. Frank Lovejoy plays the nuclear scientist who romances Terry Moore's waitress and is apparently willing to sell secrets to the other side. Directed on a low budget by Edward Dein, it's an unconventional picture that holds the interest. AE

Terry Moore *Kotty, the waitress* • Frank Lovejoy *Professor* • Keenan Wynn *George* • Lee Marvin *Slob, the cook* • Whit Bissell *Eddie* • Jess Barker *Artie* • Donald Murphy *Pepe* • Frank De Kova *Dillon* ■ *Dir* Edward Dein • *Scr* Edward Dein, Mildred Dein

Shadey ★15

Black comedy   1985 · UK · Colour · 102min

The idea is a good one – a clairvoyant, who can transfer his precognitions to film, is exploited by big business and British Intelligence – and the production values are glossy. But the treatment is a mystifying mishmash of transsexualism, incest, insanity and ESP. Described as black comedy, it is indulgent in the extreme. DM

Antony Sher *Oliver Shadey* • Patrick Macnee *Sir Cyril Landau* • Leslie Ash *Carol Landau* • Bernard Hepton *Capt Amies* • Katherine Helmond *Lady*

Landau • Larry Lamb *Dick Darnley* • Billie Whitelaw *Dr Cloud* ■ *Dir* Philip Saville • *Scr* Snoo Wilson

The Shadow ★★★

Psychological murder mystery
1956 · Pol · BW · 95min

This thriller was something of a change of pace for Jerzy Kawalerowicz and announced him as a versatile and highly individual talent. Set during and immediately after the Second World War, the film is comprised of three separate episodes which are linked by a mysterious villain, who first acts as a Nazi informer and then as an anti-Communist saboteur. An already involved political scenario is further complicated by the enigmatic editing. DP Polish +subtitles.

Zygmunt Kestowicz *Dr Knyszyn* • Adolf Chronicki *Karbowski, security officer* • Emil Karewicz *Jasiczka, his colleague* • Tadeusz Jurasz *Mikula, a young miner* • Ignacy Machowski *Shadow* ■ *Dir* Jerzy Kawalerowicz • *Scr* Aleksander Scibor-Rylski, from his stories

The Shadow ★★★ 12

Action adventure 1994 · US · Colour · 102min

"Who knows what evil lurks in the hearts of men?" Alec Baldwin does, here playing both wealthy socialite Lamont Cranston and his mysterious alter ego, the Shadow, who uses psychic powers to render himself invisible at will. The famous 1930s pulp crime-fighter takes on a descendant of Genghis Khan who's out to conquer the world in director Russell Mulcahy's comic-strip fantasy. It's stuffed with fun clichés of the genre, but the flashy production values rather overshadow the performances, while the plot rarely grips. AJ Swearing, violence. DVD 🔵

Alec Baldwin *Lamont Cranston/The Shadow* • John Lone *Shiwan Khan* • Penelope Ann Miller *Margo Lane* • Peter Boyle *Moe Shrevnitz* • Ian McKellen *Reinhardt Lane* • Tim Curry *Farley Claymore* • Jonathan Winters *Wainwright Barth* • Sab Shimono *Dr Tam* ■ *Dir* Russell Mulcahy • *Scr* David Koepp, from the characters by Walter Gibson

Shadow ★★★ 18

Horror 2009 · It · Colour · 74min

After a tour of duty in Iraq, American soldier James Muxworthy heads to Europe for a mountain biking holiday. But he falls foul of two thuggish hunters (Chris Coppola and Ottaviano Blitch) after rescuing fellow biker Karina Testa from their harassment. In making their escape, they stray into woodland depths that harbour a hideous secret. Writer/director Federico Zampaglione has trouble shifting focus from the forest pursuit to the pitiless torture sequences, while the performances are also patchy. But the mood of menace is admirably maintained, and Zampaglione makes his point about humanity's potential for evil without undue preachiness. DP Violence, swearing. DVD

Jake Muxworthy *David* • Karina Testa *Angeline* • Nuot Arquint *Mortis* • Chris Coppola *Buck* • Ottaviano Blitch *Fred* ■ *Dir* Federico Zampaglione • *Scr* Federico Zampaglione, Domenico Zampaglione, Giacomo Gensini

The Shadow Box ★★★ 15

Drama 1980 · US · Colour · 103min

Co-produced by his daughter Susan, and starring his wife, Joanne Woodward, this was Paul Newman's TV-movie debut as a director. Set in a clinic for the terminally sick, it takes an age to develop, not helped by Newman's insistence on long takes of talking heads. However, the drama intensifies as the relationship between Woodward, ex-husband Christopher Plummer and his gay lover (Ben Masters) draws to its tragic conclusion. The most impressive work comes from Melinda Dillon, as the dutiful daughter trying to make mother Sylvia Sidney's last days more bearable. DP DVD

Joanne Woodward *Beverly* • Christopher Plummer *Brian* • Valerie Harper *Maggie* • James Broderick *Joe* • Sylvia Sidney *Felicity Thomas* •

Melinda Dillon *Agnes* • Ben Masters *Mark* ■ *Dir* Paul Newman • *Scr* Michael Cristofer, from his play

Shadow Conspiracy ★★★ 15

Political action thriller 1996 · US · Colour · 93min

An A-minus cast makes a good fist of this conspiracy thriller that is never less than gripping. Charlie Sheen is a presidential adviser whose life is on the line when he stumbles upon a top-level White House plot. Linda Hamilton is the political journalist in peril who teams up with Sheen, while Donald Sutherland is a high-ranking official whose motives may not be as pure as they seem. One set piece follows another at a cracking pace as Sheen is hunted by a merciless killer intent on silencing him before he can blow the whistle. JF Violence, swearing. DVD

Charlie Sheen *Bobby Bishop* • Linda Hamilton *Amanda Givens* • Donald Sutherland *Conrad* • Stephen Lang *The Agent* • Sam Waterston *The President* • Ben Gazzara *Vice President Saxon* • Nicholas Turturro *Grasso* • Theodore Bikel *Professor Pochenko* • Gore Vidal *Congressman Page* ■ *Dir* George Pan Cosmatos • *Scr* Adi Hasak, Ric Gibbs

Shadow Dancer ★★★★ 15

Thriller 2012 · UK/Ire/Fr · Colour · 97min

Set during the Irish Troubles in the 1990s, this is impressive in its portrayal of a conflict involving people – on all sides – who are both ordinary and utterly cold-blooded. Andrea Riseborough (a powerful performance) is sent to plant a bomb, but is picked up by MI5 and given a choice: go to jail for 25 years or become an informer. The ever-present possibility of discovery makes for a tense thriller (written by former ITN Ireland correspondent Tom Bradby), though there are one or two scenes that stretch credibility. BP DVD 🔵

Andrea Riseborough *Collette McVeigh* • Clive Owen *Mac* • Gillian Anderson *Kate Fletcher* • Aidan Gillen *Gerry McVeigh* • Domhnall Gleeson *Connor McVeigh* ■ *Dir* James Marsh • *Scr* Tom Bradby, from his novel

Shadow Hours ★★★ 18

Drama 2000 · US · Colour · 87min

A pair of first-rate performances from Balthazar Getty and Peter Weller fuel Isaac H Heaton's snappy urban *noir*. Getty is a recovering drug addict and alcoholic driven to distraction by his night time service station job. Rich, unconventional writer Weller takes him under his wing, but an initially invigorating tour of hedonistic night-spots begins to takes its toll. Sharp direction and energetic music add further atmosphere, but there is a major flaw, with a significant murder subplot that's never resolved satisfactorily. JC DVD

Balthazar Getty *Michael Holloway* • Peter Weller *Stuart Chappell* • Rebecca Gayheart *Chloe Holloway* • Peter Greene *Det Steve Adrianson* • Frederic Forrest *Sean* • Brad Dourif *Roland Montague* • Michael Dorn *Det Thomas Greenwood* • Corin Nemec *Vincent* ■ *Dir/Scr* Isaac H Eaton

Shadow Makers ★★ PG

Drama 1989 · US · Colour · 121min

While it's enjoyable to have Paul Newman as a nastily punctilious army officer, this account of the secret project that developed the first American atom bomb never detonates into real drama. There is conflict between the by-the-book soldiers and off-the-wall scientists, and also among the scientists themselves but, despite a quality cast, the story comes to life only when there's the threat of illness on the base. TH DVD

Paul Newman *General Leslie R Groves* • Dwight Schultz *J Robert Oppenheimer* • Bonnie Bedelia *Kitty Oppenheimer* • John Cusack *Michael Merriman* • Laura Dern *Kathleen Robinson* • Ron Frazier *Peer de Silva* • John C McGinley *Richard Schoenfield* • Natasha Richardson *Jean Tatlock* ■ *Dir* Roland Joffé • *Scr* Roland Joffé, Bruce Robinson, from a story by Bruce Robinson

Shadow Man ★ 15

Action drama 2006 · US/UK/Rom · Colour · 91min

An out-of-shape Steven Seagal mumbles his way through yet another woeful action drama, in which he plays an ex-CIA agent trying to rescue his kidnapped young daughter after he's embroiled in a conspiracy involving a deadly virus. The biggest mystery here is how the producers managed to persuade Imelda Staunton on board. It's not Seagal's weakest film, but it certainly comes close. SF Violence, swearing, nudity, drug abuse. DVD

Steven Seagal *Jack Foster* • Eva Pope *Anya* • Imelda Staunton *Ambassador Cochran* • Vincent Riotta *Harry* • Michael Elwyn *George* ■ *Dir* Michael Keusch • *Scr* Steven Collins, Joe Halpin, Steven Seagal

Shadow of a Doubt ★★★★★ PG

Classic thriller 1942 · US · BW · 103min

Early on in Alfred Hitchcock's personal favourite of his own movies, a train, belching out a cloud of ominous black smoke, pulls into Santa Rosa, California. Joseph Cotten has arrived and is met by his adoring niece, Teresa Wright. Both are called "Charlie". She is pumpkin-pie innocence; but is he really a suave killer, wanted back east for relieving widows of their wealth and their lives? Although Hitchcock blurs the line between good and evil, the two Charlies are inevitably pitched against each other, as suspicion increases and the police start nosing around. The movie may lack the show-off set pieces that Hitchcock turned into his trademark, yet its tension never falters. AT DVD 🔵

Teresa Wright *Young Charlie Newton* • Joseph Cotten *Uncle Charlie Oakley/Mr Spencer/Mr Otis* • Macdonald Carey *Jack Graham* • Henry Travers *Joseph Newton* • Patricia Collinge *Emma Spencer Oakley Newton* • Hume Cronyn *Herbie Hawkins* • Wallace Ford *Fred Saunders* • Edna May Wonacott *Ann Newton* ■ *Dir* Alfred Hitchcock • *Scr* Thornton Wilder, Sally Benson, Alma Reville, from a story by Gordon McDonell

Shadow of a Man ★★

Crime drama 1954 · UK · BW · 69min

Thanks to Geoffrey Faithfull's seedy seaside cinematography, this British crime drama has more atmosphere than most of the period. When Bill Nagy is found dead after a nightclub brawl, novelist Paul Carpenter refuses to believe that his friend died from heart failure. Carpenter isn't the most winning of heroes, but Michael McCarthy directs steadily and comes up with a truly original solution. DP

Paul Carpenter *Gene Landers* • Rona Anderson *Linda Bryant* • Jane Griffiths *Carol Seaton* • Tony Quinn *Inspector Gates* • Bill Nagy *Paul Bryant* ■ *Dir* Michael McCarthy • *Scr* Paul Erickson

Shadow of Doubt ★ 15

Courtroom thriller 1998 · US · Colour · 106min

In this highly contrived courtroom drama, Melanie Griffith is the attorney defending a rap star against murder charges from prosecutor and ex-lover Tom Berenger. The proceedings are so jam-packed with wild plot twists, subplots, and unnecessary details that it comes close to being entertaining in its badness. KB DVD

Melanie Griffith *Kitt Devereux* • Tom Berenger *Jack Campioni* • Huey Lewis *Al Gordon* • Nina Foch *Sylvia Saxon* • Kimberley Kates *Bridget* • Wade Dominguez *Bobby Medina* ■ *Dir* Randal Kleiser • *Scr* Myra Byrnes, Raymond DeFelitta

Shadow of Fear ★★ U

Spy drama 1963 · UK · BW · 60min

Paul Maxwell stars in this risible thriller from the Butcher's B-movie factory. When he agrees to deliver a secret message, Maxwell and his girlfriend get caught up in an effort to catch enemy agents operating in Britain. Ernest Morris directs with little enthusiasm, but this does benefit from South Coast locations. DP

Paul Maxwell *Bill Martin* • Clare Owen *Barbara* • Anita West *Ruth* • Alan Tilvern *Warner* • John Arnatt *Sharp* • Eric Pohlmann *Spiroulos* •

Reginald Marsh *Oliver* ■ *Dir* Ernest Morris • *Scr* Ronald Liles, James O'Connolly, from the novel *Decoy Be Damned* by TF Fotherby

The Shadow of the Cat ★★ 12

Horror 1961 · UK · BW · 75min

Hammer removed their credit from director John Gilling's bizarre curiosity for legal quota reasons. But this tale of a manic moggy exacting a terrible revenge on those who conspired to kill its mistress is only a serviceable melodrama at best, despite the addition of House of Horror heroine Barbara Shelley. Notable for the way Gilling shows the deaths of the terrified murderers through the eyes of the feline, but not much else. AJ DVD

André Morell *Walter Venable* • Barbara Shelley *Beth Venable* • William Lucas *Jacob* • Freda Jackson *Clara* • Conrad Phillips *Michael Latimer* ■ *Dir* John Gilling • *Scr* George Baxt

Shadow of the Thin Man ★★ U

Detective comedy 1941 · US · BW · 92min

While Nick and Nora Charles (William Powell and Myrna Loy), now the proud parents of a baby son, are at the races, a jockey is murdered. Nick gets involved when a reporter is also bumped off. By this fourth entry in the popular series, quality was on the decline, with the original sharp wit lessened by injections of broader comedy and more convoluted plotting, but Powell and Loy's polish is undimmed. The series continued with *The Thin Man Goes Home*. RK DVD

William Powell *Nick* • Myrna Loy *Nora* • Barry Nelson *Paul* • Donna Reed *Molly* • Sam Levene *Lieutenant Abrams* • Alan Baxter *"Whitey" Barrow* ■ *Dir* Major WS Van Dyke II [WS Van Dyke] • *Scr* Irving Brecher, Harry Kurnitz, from a story by Harry Kurnitz, from characters by Dashiell Hammett

Shadow of the Vampire ★★★ 15

Horror 2000 · UK/US/Lux · BW and Colour · 87min

John Malkovich and Willem Dafoe gleefully sink their teeth into a couple of juicy roles in director E Elias Merhige's film about German expressionist director FW Murnau. Malkovich plays Murnau in this curiously comic reconstruction of the making of his classic vampire film *Nosferatu, a Symphony of Horrors* (1922). Eschewing historical accuracy, the film portrays the director as a fanatic, who hires a real bloodsucker (Dafoe) to portray the vampire. This starts promisingly but has fewer grand ideas up its sleeve than it thinks. TH Violence, swearing, drug abuse, brief nudity. DVD

John Malkovich *FW Murnau* • Willem Dafoe *Max Schreck, Count Orlok* • Cary Elwes *Fritz Arno Wagner, cameraman* • Aden Gillett *Henrick Galeen, the screenwriter* • Eddie Izzard *Gustav von Wangerheim, Hutter* • Udo Kier *Albin Grau, producer/art director* • Catherine McCormack *Greta Schröder, Ellen* ■ *Dir* E Elias Merhige • *Scr* Steven Katz

Shadow of the Wolf ★★ 15

Period drama 1992 · Can/Fr · Colour · 107min

This costly wilderness epic about the conflict between the Inuit and encroaching whites in the Arctic of the 1930s proves to be an insipid watch. Lou Diamond Phillips stars as a young Inuit hunter banished from his tribe only to be hunted down for murder by Donald Sutherland's cop. Director Jacques Dorfmann allows his narrative to become convoluted and cluttered with mystical mumbo jumbo, though there are some moments of pictorial beauty, courtesy of Oscar-winning cinematographer Billy Williams. RS

Lou Diamond Phillips *Agaguk* • Toshiro Mifune *Ramook* • Jennifer Tilly *Iriook* • Donald Sutherland *Henderson* • Bernard-Pierre Donnadieu *Brown* • Qalingo Tookalak *Tulugak* • Harry Hill (1) *McTavish* ■ *Dir* Jacques Dorfmann • *Scr* Rudy Wurlitzer, Evan Jones, from the novel *Agaguk* by Yves Theriault

S

Shadow on the Mesa ★★
Western   2013 · US · Colour · 87min

In this bland and clichéd made-for-TV western, Wes Brown broods handsomely as a laconic and vengeful bounty hunter who goes in search of his long-lost father (Kevin Sorbo) following his mother's murder, escalating a violent land feud. With events weakly executed, key plot points are just thrown away, making the film's main body seem like a mere filler in preparation for the equally ineffective climactic showdown. Consequently, while the story brims with tragedy, it lacks emotional impact, despite Sorbo's strong efforts to convey his character's feelings. SF

Wes Brown *Wes Rawlins* • Kevin Sorbo *Ray Eastman* • Gail O'Grady *Mona Eastman* ▪ Dir David S Cass Sr • Scr Lee Martin

Shadow Run ★★ 15
Heist thriller   1998 · US · Colour · 91min

Michael Caine is a ruthless bank robber, recruited by dodgy toff James Fox to rob a top-secret van transporting the paper used to produce British currency from a sleepy country town. However, complications ensue when his actions draw the attention of a young schoolboy. There's plenty of familiar TV faces on show, but it's let down badly by diffident direction. JF *DVD*

Michael Caine *Haskell* • Kenneth Colley *Larcombe* • James Fox *Landon Higgins* • Leslie Grantham *Liney* • Christopher Cazenove *Melchior* • Tim Healy *Daltry* ▪ Dir Geoffrey Reeve • Scr Desmond Lowden

Shadowlands ★★★★★★ U
Romantic biographical drama
1993 · UK/US · Colour · 125min

This intimate drama remains one of director Richard Attenborough's best pictures to date. It charts the tragic love affair between the author CS Lewis and American poet Joy Gresham. Anthony Hopkins and Debra Winger give performances that you dream about but rarely see, and the tone is set by Winger's entrance into Oxford's Randolph Hotel: "Anyone here named Loowis?" she rasps, upsetting the decorum of academe and rattling Hopkins's tea cup. Thereafter, Hopkins's life as an emotionally frigid bachelor is transformed. With its immaculate 1950s setting, the film creates a totally convincing world and Attenborough gets beneath the skin of his characters as never before. Be warned: you'll cry. AT *DVD*

Anthony Hopkins *CS "Jack" Lewis* • Debra Winger *Joy Gresham* • John Wood (2) *Christopher Riley* • Edward Hardwicke *Warnie Lewis* • Joseph Mazzello *Douglas Gresham* • Julian Fellowes *Desmond Arding* • Roddy Maude-Roxby *Arnold Dopliss* • Michael Denison *Harry Harrington* • Peter Firth *Doctor Craig* ▪ Dir Richard Attenborough • Scr William Nicholson, from his play

Shadows ★★★ PG
Drama   1959 · US · BW · 77min

This format-breaking social drama was the first film from actor-turned-director John Cassavetes. It's the mainly improvised story of three black siblings – Lelia Goldoni, Ben Carruthers and Hugh Hurd – who are making their way in Manhattan. Goldoni, who passes for white, begins a love affair with a white man, which gives Cassavetes plenty of scope for interracial discussion (unusual in the 1960s), while jazz trumpeter Hurd finds life full of sour notes. Cassavetes's style of ad-lib acting and situations became a benchmark for future independent film-making. TH *DVD* *Blu-ray*

Hugh Hurd *Hugh* • Lelia Goldoni *Lelia* • Ben Carruthers *Ben* • Anthony Ray *Tony* • Dennis Sallas *Dennis* • Tom Allen *Tom* • David Pokitillow *David* ▪ Dir John Cassavetes • Music Charlie Mingus

Shadows and Fog ★★★ 15
Period comedy drama   1991 · US · BW · 81min

Reworking his 1972 one-act play *Death*, Woody Allen originally intended this esoteric drama to be a homage to German expressionism. However, he opted for a look owing more to Universal's pre-war horror movies and, thus, deprived of already slight premise of some visual power. As the nobody who is co-opted into the search for a strangler in an eastern European town, Allen is typically twitchy amid a galaxy of guest stars. Short on humour, perhaps, but this curio is laced with ideas that took on a new relevance when news broke of his split with Mia Farrow. DP Some violence. *DVD*

Woody Allen *Kleinman* • Mia Farrow *Irmy* • John Malkovich *Clown* • Madonna *Marie* • Donald Pleasence *Doctor* • Kathy Bates *Prostitute* • Jodie Foster *Prostitute* • Lily Tomlin *Prostitute* • John Cusack *Student Jack* • Julie Kavner *Alma* ▪ Dir/Scr Woody Allen • Music Kurt Weill

Shadows in the Sun ★★ 12A
Drama   2008 · UK · Colour · 81min

Director David Rocksavage's 1960s-set melodrama is a handsome but dramatically anaemic tale of family tensions. A whiff of danger pervades proceedings, like the smoke from the cannabis that loner Joe (Jamie Dornan) provides for widow Hannah (Jean Simmons) to help her cope with both the pain of a long illness and her isolation in a large house on the East Anglian coast. Her visiting son Robert (James Wilby) makes his reservations clear about Joe, but the stranger casts a very different spell over Robert's teenage daughter (Ophelia Lovibond) and her younger brother (Toby Marlow). Milton Kam's camerawork revels in the Norfolk landscapes, but too many incidents smack of metaphor rather than real life. DP

Jean Simmons *Hannah* • James Wilby *Robert* • Jamie Dornan *Joe* • Ophelia Lovibond *Kate* • Toby Marlow *Sam* ▪ Dir David Rocksavage • Scr David Rocksavage, Margaret Glover

Shadows of Our Forgotten Ancestors ★★★★★ 12
Drama   1964 · USSR · Colour and BW · 91min

A radical departure from his previous films, Sergei Paradjanov's masterpiece sought to challenge accepted notions of narrative and visual representation. This expressionist variation on the Tristan and Isolde theme is not just cinematically subversive, but also politically contentious, through its bold assertion of Ukrainian heritage. Nothing can be taken at face value in this psychologically dense exercise in deconstruction. The hallucinatory affects achieved through camera movement, lens manipulation and cutting, the brilliant "dramaturgy of colour" and the disorientating use of sound all ran counter to existing norms in Soviet art and made its director a marked man. DP Russian +subtitles. *DVD*

Ivan Mikolaychuk *Ivan* • Larisa Kadochnikova *Marichka* • Tatyana Bestayeva *Palagna* • Spartak Bagashvili *Yurko the Sorcerer* ▪ Dir Sergei Paradjanov • Scr Sergey Paradzhanov, Ivan Chendey, from the novelette *Tini Zabutykh Predkiv* by Mikhaylo Mikhaylovich Kotsyubinsky

Shadows of the Peacock ★★
Drama   1987 · Aus · Colour · 92min

Before decamping for Hollywood, Australian director Phillip Noyce signed off with this uneven drama. Wendy Hughes is the mother trying to rebuild her life after discovering her husband has been cheating on her and finding romance in Thailand with John Lone. It looks glorious and is well played by the cast, although the suspicion remains that there is less going on here than meets the eye. JF

Wendy Hughes *Maria McEvoy* • John Lone *Raka* • Steven Jacobs [Steve Jacobs] *George McEvoy* • Peta Toppano *Judy* ▪ Dir Phillip Noyce • Scr Jan Sharp, Anne Brooksbank

Shadowzone ★★★ 18
Science-fiction horror
1990 · US · Colour · 88min

In this intriguing and competent low-budget shocker, a team of scientists working in an isolated underground complex investigates the mysteries of dreams and long-term sleep but accidentally unleashes a shape-shifting monster from another dimension.

An *Alien* rip-off it may be, but writer/director JS Cardone heightens the sense of foreboding inherent within the claustrophobic situation and pumps up the suspense. RS *DVD*

Louise Fletcher *Dr Erhardt* • Miguel A Nunez Jr *Wiley* • David Beecroft *Captain Hickock* • Lu Leonard *Mrs Cutter* • James Hong *Dr Van Fleet* • Shawn Weatherly *Dr Kidwell* • Frederick Flynn *Tommy Shivers* ▪ Dir/Scr JS Cardone

Shaft ★★★ 15
Blaxploitation crime thriller
1971 · US · Colour · 100min

The film that firmly established the blaxploitation genre in the early 1970s is nothing more than an urban ghetto, James Bond-style thriller. But ex-male model Richard Roundtree brings a casual charm to the vicious proceedings as the private dick ("a sex machine to all the chicks") enlisted to find a Harlem racketeer's kidnapped daughter, and director Gordon Parks gives it a fast and furious style. Isaac Hayes won an Oscar for the landmark theme song that laid down the ground rules for all the funky, satin-sheet sounds that followed. AJ Violence, swearing, nudity. *DVD*

Richard Roundtree *John Shaft* • Moses Gunn *Bumpy Jonas* • Charles Cioffi *Lieutenant Vic Androzzi* • Christopher St John *Ben Buford* • Gwenn Mitchell *Ellie Moore* • Lawrence Pressman *Sergeant Tom Hannon* • Victor Arnold *Charlie* • Sherri Brewer *Marcy* ▪ Dir Gordon Parks • Scr Ernest Tidyman, John DF Black, from the novel by Ernest Tidyman

Shaft ★★★★ 18
Crime thriller   2000 · US/Ger · Colour · 95min

Samuel L Jackson has the necessary presence to carry off John Singleton's slick homage to the icon of 1970s blaxploitation. This Shaft is the nephew of the original (Richard Roundtree), and he's one mad, mean mother, especially when wealthy creep Christian Bale gets away with a brutal, racially motivated murder. Jeffrey Wright is brilliant as his drugs lord adversary, while Isaac Hayes's Oscar-winning theme song once again gets the pulse pumping for some maliciously funny twists and heavy violence. AME Violence, swearing, some nudity. *DVD*

Samuel L Jackson *John Shaft* • Vanessa Williams [Vanessa L Williams] *Carmen Vasquez* • Jeffrey Wright *Peoples Hernandez* • Christian Bale *Walter Wade Jr* • Busta Rhymes *Rasaan* • Dan Hedaya *Jack Roselli* • Toni Collette *Diane Palmieri* • Richard Roundtree *Uncle John Shaft* ▪ Dir John Singleton • Scr Richard Price, John Singleton, Shane Salerno, from a story by John Singleton, Shane Salerno, from the 1971 film

Shaft in Africa ★★★ 18
Blaxploitation thriller
1973 · US · Colour · 107min

Richard Roundtree's portrayal of the supercool black private eye is still, in this sequel, the film's most persuasive quality. With a screenplay by Stirling Silliphant, this tale has Shaft lured out of his ghetto domain to break Frank Finlay's slave-smuggling racket. The film gets across its message with some cracking dialogue and bursts of violent skulduggery, with British director John Guillermin showing an eye for sadistic detail. TH Nudity, violence, swearing. *DVD*

Richard Roundtree *John Shaft* • Frank Finlay *Amafi* • Vonetta McGee *Aleme* • Neda Arneric *Jazar* • Debebe Eshetu *Wassa* • Cy Grant *Emir Ramila* • Spiros Focas *Sassari* ▪ Dir John Guillermin • Scr Stirling Silliphant, from the characters by Ernest Tidyman

Shaft's Big Score! ★★★ 15
Blaxploitation thriller
1972 · US · Colour · 100min

Richard Roundtree and Moses Gunn return in the sequel to the huge blockbuster *Shaft*, which kicked off the early 1970s blaxploitation craze. This time the private eye hero acts more like a hip James Bond than a retro Sam Spade, in a routine social conscience tale that finds him avenging the murder of a friend while retrieving money stolen by warring gangsters. It's not as tightly directed by Gordon Parks as the first

movie, but the New York harbour ending is memorably exciting. AJ *DVD*

Richard Roundtree *John Shaft* • Moses Gunn *Bumpy Jonas* • Drew Bundini Brown *Willy* • Joseph Mascolo *Gus Mascola* • Kathy Imrie *Rita* • Wally Taylor *Kelly* • Julius W Harris [Julius Harris] *Captain Bollin* • Rosalind Miles *Arna Asby* ▪ Dir Gordon Parks • Scr Ernest Tidyman, from his characters

Shag ★★★ 15
Comedy   1988 · UK/US · Colour · 95min

This unfortunately titled (it's a dance) youth movie is directed by former continuity girl Zelda Barron. The film features an attractive American cast plus Britain's own Shirley Anne Field, but nobody has anything significant to do. Phoebe Cates is on the verge of matrimony, and her buddies decide to throw her one last fling at Myrtle Beach. Since it's 1963 and the Yanks have yet to discover the Beatles and the Pill, not much happens. Slight and undemanding, but fun in places. TS Swearing.

Phoebe Cates *Carson McBride* • Scott Coffey *Chip Guillyard* • Bridget Fonda *Melaina Buller* • Annabeth Gish *Caroline "Pudge" Carmichael* • Page Hannah *Luanne Clatterbuck* • Robert Rusler *Buzz Ravenel* • Tyrone Power Jr *Harley Ralston* • Shirley Anne Field *Mrs Clatterbuck* ▪ Dir Zelda Barron • Scr Robin Swicord, Lanier Laney, Terry Sweeney, from a story by Lanier Laney, Terry Sweeney

The Shaggy DA ★★★ U
Comedy   1976 · US · Colour · 87min

The belated follow-up to Disney's 1959 hit, *The Shaggy Dog*, finds lawyer Dean Jones turning into a pooch at the slightest provocation. Unfortunately, this peculiar canine condition occurs just as he's up for election as district attorney against the unscrupulous Keenan Wynn. Notable for a juicy scene involving some cherry pies and an ingenious break-out from the dog pound, this is one of those rare occasions when the sequel is superior to the original. DP

Dean Jones *Wilby Daniels* • Suzanne Pleshette *Betty Daniels* • Keenan Wynn *District Attorney John Slade* • Tim Conway *Tim* • Jo Anne Worley *Katrinka Muggelberg* • Dick Van Patten *Raymond* ▪ Dir Robert Stevenson • Scr Don Tait, from the novel *The Hound of Florence* by Felix Salten

The Shaggy Dog ★★★ U
Fantasy comedy   1959 · US · BW · 97min

This was the first of Disney's contemporary slapstick fantasies and typifies the generally reviled genre. It was a big success and led to a belated sequel (1976's *The Shaggy DA*). With his usual aplomb, Fred MacMurray plays the troubled paterfamilias whose son turns into a sheepdog, while Jean Hagen has a thankless role as mom. Disney regulars Annette Funicello and Tommy Kirk head the support cast, but today's audience might be disappointed with this tale. TS

Fred MacMurray *Wilson Daniels* • Jean Hagen *Frieda Daniels* • Tommy Kirk *Wilby Daniels* • Annette Funicello *Allison D'Allessio* • Tim Considine *Buzz Miller* • Kevin Corcoran *Moochie Daniels* • Cecil Kellaway *Professor Plumcutt* • Alexander Scourby *Doctor Mikhail Andrassy* ▪ Dir Charles Barton • Scr Bill Walsh, Lillie Hayward, from the novel *The Hound of Florence* by Felix Salten

The Shaggy Dog ★★★ U
Fantasy comedy   2006 · US · Colour · 94min

Workaholic dad Tim Allen finds himself turning into a dog in this sprightly slapstick fantasy. A reworking of the 1976 Disney film *The Shaggy DA* (a sequel to the studio's 1959 hit), this is an endearingly daft caper aimed largely at the under-10s. Allen is hilarious as a pooch-hating lawyer who is bitten by a 300-year-old mutt that's been dognapped by a shady pharmaceutical conglomerate. Only the grumpiest of viewers will fail to chuckle at Allen's resulting canine metamorphosis. SF *DVD*

Tim Allen *Dave Douglas* • Robert Downey Jr *Dr Kozak* • Kristin Davis *Rebecca Douglas* • Craig Kilborn *Justin* • Zena Grey *Carly Douglas* • Spencer Breslin *Josh Douglas* • Jane Curtin *Judge Whittaker* • Shawn Pyfrom *Trey* • Danny Glover *DA Ken Hollister* ▪ Dir Brian Robbins • Scr

S

The Wibberleys [Cormac Wibberly, Marianne Wibberly], Geoff Rodkey, Jack Amiel, Michael Begler, from the 1959 film *The Shaggy Dog* by Bill Walsh, Lillie Hayward, from the 1976 film *The Shaggy DA* by Don Tait

Shaheed ★★★

Political melodrama   1948 · Ind · BW · 164min

Set in the final days of the Raj, this outspoken drama focuses on the tensions placed on the already strained relationship between a mandarin in the imperial civil service and his freedom fighter son, when the latter is charged with a political killing. Director Ramesh Saigal tackles the thorny subject of divided loyalties with restraint, considering that he had been forced to abandon his native Punjab the previous year after it became part of Pakistan. Intelligent performances from Dilip Kumar and Chandra Mohan ensure the action never descends into melodrama. DP Urdu, Hindi +subtitles.

Dilip Kumar *Ram* · Kamini Kaushal · Chandra Mohan ■ *Dir* Ramesh Saigal · *Scr* Ramesh Saigal, Qamar Jalalabadi, from a story by Ramesh Saigal

Shake Hands with the Devil ★★★

Political drama   1959 · Ire/US · BW · 110min

A distinguished cast of British and Irish actors, plus American Don Murray, bolster James Cagney in this somewhat grim and melodramatic but well-made mix of politics, romance, and violence. Cagney is a professor of medicine in 1921 Dublin, whose respectability is a cover for his IRA activities. When his student Murray, an Irish-American, is beaten up by British officers, a vengeful Cagney abducts the daughter (Dana Wynter) of a British functionary. A provocative, if undeveloped proposition. RK

James Cagney *Sean Lenihan* · Don Murray *Kerry O'Shea* · Dana Wynter *Jennifer Curtis* · Glynis Johns *Kitty Brady* · Michael Redgrave *The General* · Sybil Thorndike *Lady Fitzhugh* · Cyril Cusack *Chris Noonan* · Marianne Benet *Mary Madigan* ■ *Dir* Michael Anderson · *Scr* Ben Roberts, Marian Thompson, Ivan Goff, from the novel by Rearden Conner

Shake, Rattle and Rock! ★★★ PG

Drama   1957 · US · BW · 75min

This is quintessential viewing for rock 'n' roll fans and a key film of its era. Plotwise it's the usual stuff about a town's parents at odds with the new music craze. What makes it worth watching is the music. Highlights include the legendary Joe Turner performing *Lipstick, Powder and Paint* and the great Fats Domino belting out *I'm in Love Again* and the fabulous *Ain't That a Shame*. The cast is headed by Touch Connors, who as Mike Connors achieved stardom in the TV series *Mannix*. TS DVD

Touch Connors [Mike Connors] *Garry Nelson* · Lisa Gaye *June* · Sterling Holloway *Axe* · Margaret Dumont *Georgianna* · Douglass Dumbrille *Eustace* ■ *Dir* Edward L Cahn · *Scr* Lou Rusoff

Shake, Rattle and Rock ★★★ PG

Period drama   1994 · US · Colour · 79min

Part of a series of TV remakes of 1950s B-movies, this is a slight but affectionate take on that old staple, the teen musical. Howie Mandel has a ball as a rebel with a cause allowing teenagers to get down to the rock 'n' roll music hated by their conservative elders. The eclectic cast includes Renee Zellweger, Roger Corman regular Dick Miller, singer Ruth Brown and cult icon Mary Woronov. Director Allan Arkush keeps his tongue firmly in his cheek and conjures up the atmosphere of cheerful irreverence. JF Some swearing.

Renee Zellweger [Renée Zellweger] *Susan Doyle* · Patricia Childress *Cookie* · Max Perlich *Tony* · Howie Mandel *Danny Klay* · Latanyia Baldwin *Sireena Cooper* · Mary Woronov *Joyce* · Stephen Furst *Frank* · Dick Miller *Officer Miller* · Ruth Brown *Ella* · PJ Soles *Evelyn* ■ *Dir* Allan Arkush · *Scr* Trish Soodik

The Shakedown ★★

Crime drama   1959 · UK · BW · 91min

Terence Morgan plays a photographer with an eye for extortion in this film that sets out to shock with sleazy settings and sensationalist suggestions of nudity. However, few of the misdemeanours from this period piece would raise even a blush today. Director John Lemont forgets to concentrate on the storyline, which grinds to its inevitable conclusion. DP

Terence Morgan *Augie Cortona* · Hazel Court *Mildred* · Donald Pleasence *Jessel* · Bill Owen *Spettigue* · Robert Beatty *Inspector Jarvis* · Harry H Corbett *Gollar* · Gene Anderson *Zena* · Eddie Byrne *George* ■ *Dir* John Lemont · *Scr* John Lemont, Leigh Vance

Shakes the Clown ★★ 18

Comedy   1991 · US · Colour · 82min

Stand-up comedian Bobcat Goldthwait exploits the sinister side of the classic circus clown, writing, directing and starring in this bizarre, harsh fantasy. Set in the mythical town of Palukaville, Goldthwait is the eponymous Shakes, an alcoholic clown and regular barfly. When his boss, the clown dispatcher, is found murdered Shakes is the prime suspect. In the end, this is more funny peculiar than funny ha-ha. DF Swearing, drug abuse.

Bobcat Goldthwait *Shakes the Clown* · Julie Brown *Judy* · Bruce Baum *Ty the Rodeo Clown* · Blake Clark *Stenchy the Clown* · Paul Dooley *Owen Cheese* · Marty Fromage [Robin Williams] *Mime Jerry* · Florence Henderson *The Unknown Woman* · Tom Kenny *Binky the Clown* · Sydney Lassick *Peppy the Clown* · Adam Sandler *Dink the Clown* ■ *Dir/Scr* Bobcat Goldthwait

Shakespeare in Love ★★★★★★ 15

Period romantic comedy   1998 · US · Colour · 118min

Taking the writing process behind Shakespeare's *Romeo and Juliet* as its inspiration, John Madden's film combines contemporary humour with a convincing 16th-century setting. Young Will (Joseph Fiennes) falls for the soon-to-be-married Viola (Gwyneth Paltrow) and casts her, disguised as a boy, as his Romeo. As their love affair unfolds, so does the play in a film that is passionate, intelligent and hysterically funny by turns. Fiennes and Paltrow are supported by an outstanding cast, while Judi Dench delivers an Oscar-winning portrayal of Elizabeth I, making fine use of Marc Norman and Tom Stoppard's Oscar-winning script. LH Sex scenes. DVD ⍰

Gwyneth Paltrow *Viola De Lesseps* · Joseph Fiennes *Will Shakespeare* · Colin Firth *Lord Wessex* · Geoffrey Rush *Philip Henslowe* · Judi Dench *Queen Elizabeth* · Tom Wilkinson *Hugh Fennyman* · Ben Affleck *Ned Alleyn* · Simon Callow *Tilney, Master of the Revels* · Jim Carter *Ralph Bashford* · Martin Clunes *Richard Burbage* · Imelda Staunton *Nurse* · Rupert Everett *Christopher Marlowe* ■ *Dir* John Madden · *Scr* Marc Norman, Tom Stoppard · *Cinematographer* Richard Greatrex · *Costume Designer* Sandy Powell · *Art Directors* Martin Childs, Jill Quertier · *Music* Stephen Warbeck

Shakespeare Wallah ★★★ PG

Romantic drama   1965 · Ind · BW · 122min

With its gentle pacing and keen eye for atmospheric detail, anyone seeing this delightful film for the first time could be forgiven for thinking it had been directed by Satyajit Ray. But while he provided both the score and the cinematographer (Subrata Mitra), this tale of strolling players was, in fact, the second collaboration between Merchant Ivory and screenwriter Ruth Prawer Jhabvala. Based on their own experiences performing the Bard around the subcontinent, Geoffrey and Felicity Kendal effortlessly avoid condescension, while Shashi Kapoor is dashing as Felicity's culture-crossed lover. But no one stands a chance alongside Madhur Jaffrey's hilarious Bollywood bitch. DP DVD

Shashi Kapoor *Sanju* · Felicity Kendal *Lizzie Buckingham* · Madhur Jaffrey *Manjula* · Geoffrey Kendal *Tony Buckingham* · Laura Liddell *Carla*

Buckingham · Utpal Dutt *The Maharajah* ■ *Dir* James Ivory · *Scr* Ruth Prawer Jhabvala, James Ivory · *Producer* Ismail Merchant

The Shakiest Gun in the West ★★ U

Comedy western   1967 · US · Colour · 100min

Don Knotts steps into the shoes first worn by Bob Hope in this feeble reworking of that classic comedy western *The Paleface*. Never one to underplay when some shameless mugging will do, the ever-nervous Knotts overcooks every gag. However, this story of the dentist mistaken for a gunfighter isn't entirely as painful as root-canal surgery. DP

Don Knotts *Jesse W Haywood* · Barbara Rhoades *Penelope Cushings* · Jackie Coogan *Matthew Basch* · Don "Red" Barry [Donald Barry] *Reverend Zachary Grant* · Ruth McDevitt *Olive* · Frank McGrath *Mr Remington* ■ *Dir* Alan Rafkin · *Scr* Jim Fritzell, Everett Greenbaum, from the film *The Paleface* by Frank Tashlin, Edmund Hartmann [Edmund L Hartmann]

Shakti – the Power ★★★ 15

Musical drama   2002 · Ind · Colour · 174min

The Sally Field vehicle, *Not without My Daughter*, is the inspiration for Krishna Vamsi's tale of clashing cultures, which calls into question the validity of including musical numbers in even the most politically charged Bollywood features. Granted, rising superstar Aishwarya Rai excels in her dance routine and Shah Rukh Khan makes an impact with his heroic cameo appearance. But the songs undoubtedly distract from Karishma Kapoor's plight, as she seeks to return to California with her young son after discovering, while on a visit to India, that husband Sanjay Kapoor's family is involved in terrorism. DP Hindi +subtitles. DVD

Karishma Kapoor *Nandini* · Nana Patekar *Narsimha* · Sanjay Kapoor *Shekhar* · Shah Rukh Khan *Guide* · Deepti Naval *Narsimha's wife* · Aishwarya Rai ■ *Dir/Scr* Krishna Vamsi

Shalako ★★ PG

Western   1968 · UK · Colour · 112min

Sean Connery and Brigitte Bardot are screen icons well adrift out west in this would-be epic western, though geographically they are not so far from their respective manors since it was filmed entirely in Spain. Despite director Edward Dmytryk in the saddle, this is a slow-moving, high-camp fiasco. Connery (playing a cowboy) and Bardot (an aristocrat) are not alone in being oddly cast, as British actors Jack Hawkins and Eric Sykes also look like fish out of water. TS DVD

Sean Connery *Shalako* · Brigitte Bardot *Countess Irina Lazaar* · Stephen Boyd *Bosky Fulton* · Jack Hawkins *Sir Charles Daggett* · Peter Van Eyck *Frederick von Hallstatt* · Honor Blackman *Lady Julia Daggett* · Woody Strode *Chato* · Eric Sykes *Mako* · Alexander Knox *Henry Clarke* · Valerie French *Elena Clarke* ■ *Dir* Edward Dmytryk · *Scr* JJ Griffith, Hal Hopper, Scot Finch, from a story by Clarke Reynolds, from the novel by Louis L'Amour

Shall We Dance ★★★ U

Musical comedy   1937 · US · BW · 103min

This is the Fred Astaire/Ginger Rogers movie about him chasing her across the Atlantic. He's a Russian ballet dancer and there's a chorus of cardboard Ginger cut-outs at the finale. It's a far cry from the sophisticated *Top Hat*, but never mind: forget the daftness and enjoy the wonderful George and Ira Gershwin score, with the now-classic standards including *Let's Call the Whole Thing Off* and *They Can't Take That Away from Me*. TS DVD

Fred Astaire *Petrov/Pete Peters* · Ginger Rogers *Linda Keene* · Edward Everett Horton *Jeffrey Baird* · Eric Blore *Cecil Flintridge* · Jerome Cowan *Arthur Miller* · Ketti Gallian *Lady Tarrington* ■ *Dir* Mark Sandrich · *Scr* Allan Scott, Ernest Pagano, PJ Wolfson, from the story *Watch Your Step* by Lee Loeb, Harold Buchman

Shall We Dance? ★★★★ PG

Romantic comedy drama   1995 · Jpn · Colour · 114min

Koji Yakusho exudes a salaryman dignity worthy of Chishu Ryu in this acute study of social embarrassment, Japanese style. Having established the tyranny of national reserve, Masayuki Suo presents Tamiyo Kusakari's ballroom dancing studio as a foreign sanctuary, in which inhibition succumbs to the illicit sensuality and liberating grace of the rhythm. Making a delicious contrast to the timid Yakusho and the melancholic Kusakari (who once lost a big competition in Blackpool) is Naoto Takenaka, the office nobody who is transformed into a rumba monster by his macho wig and tight duds. DP Japanese +subtitles. DVD

Koji Yakusho *Shohei Sugiyama* · Tamiyo Kusakari *Mai Kishikawa* · Naoto Takenaka *Tomio Aoki* · Eriko Watanabe *Toyoko Takahashi* ■ *Dir/Scr* Masayuki Suo

Shall We Dance ★★ 12

Romantic comedy drama   2004 · US/Can · Colour · 102min

In westernising Masayuki Suo's 1995 dance-floor delight, this insipid remake loses the warmth and wry social observation that gave the original its appeal. To his credit, Richard Gere makes a charming lead, playing a jaded Chicago lawyer who secretly takes ballroom dancing lessons. Unfortunately, the casting of Jennifer Lopez as his dance instructor is where the film falls down. Her miserable demeanour is a real downer in a tale that's meant to be light and frothy. SF Swearing. DVD ⍰

Richard Gere *John Clark* · Jennifer Lopez *Paulina* · Susan Sarandon *Beverly Clark* · Stanley Tucci *Link Peterson* · Bobby Cannavale *Chic* · Lisa Ann Walter *Bobbie* · Omar Miller [Omar Benson Miller] *Vern* · Richard Jenkins *Devine* ■ *Dir* Peter Chelsom · *Scr* Audrey Wells, from the film by Masayuki Suo

Shallow Grave ★★★★★ 18

Black comedy drama   1994 · UK · Colour · 88min

This incredibly slick and inventive and, at times, gruesome thriller, owes a great deal to the Coen brothers' *Blood Simple*. It starts with a dead body and a stash of money lying in a huge flat. The deceased man's flatmates decide to dismember and dispose of the corpse. Things go slightly haywire after that. Director Danny Boyle's picture bursts with energy and springs some deliciously macabre surprises. Especially brilliant are the use of the cavernous flat and city locations and the performances from Kerry Fox, Christopher Eccleston and Ewan McGregor who are all outwardly ordinary, inwardly strange. Deservedly a box-office smash everywhere, it gave a much-needed shot in the arm to a British film industry preoccupied by Jane Austen. AT Violence, swearing, nudity. DVD ⍰

Kerry Fox *Juliet Miller* · Christopher Eccleston *David Stephens* · Ewan McGregor *Alex Law* · Ken Stott *Detective Inspector McCall* · Keith Allen *Hugo* · Colin McCredie *Cameron* ■ *Dir* Danny Boyle · *Scr* John Hodge

Shallow Hal ★★★ 12

Romantic comedy   2001 · US/Ger · Colour · 109min

Gwyneth Paltrow dons a fat suit in this comedy from the Farrelly Brothers. Prepare to be mildly offended (and intermittently amused) as Jack Black plays a man who only goes for the most attractive of gals, which in his mind means the slender, supermodel type. That is until he's hypnotised by motivational speaker Tony Robbins into only seeing a woman's inner beauty. Black then finds himself falling for sweet-natured but hefty Paltrow. Surprisingly tame, this is more romance than comedy. JB Swearing. DVD ⍰

Jack Black *Hal Larson* · Gwyneth Paltrow *Rosemary Shanahan* · Jason Alexander *Mauricio* · Joe Viterelli *Steve Shanahan* · Rene Kirby *Walt* · Bruce McGill *Reverend Larson* · Tony Robbins ■ *Dir* Bobby Farrelly, Peter Farrelly · *Scr* Sean Moynihan, Bobby Farrelly, Peter Farrelly

S

The Shallows ★★★ 15

Thriller 2016 · US · Colour · 86min

A cleverly constructed treat for aquaphobes, this fun B-movie adds enough potent scares to the *Jaws* handbook to not come across as a lazy Spielberg rip-off. Blake Lively is adequate as the college dropout on a sentimental surfing journey to her late mother's favourite beach when she's attacked by a Great White Shark and ping-pongs between a rotting whale carcass, a rock island and a buoy in an effort to prevent herself being eaten. Shrewd tension and submerged suspense help this find inspired new ways to terrorise. AJ

Blake Lively *Nancy* • Brett Cullen *Father* • Oscar Jaenada *Carlos* ■ *Dir* Jaume Collet-Serra • *Scr* Anthony Jaswinski

Shame ★★★★ 15

Drama 1987 · Aus · Colour · 89min

Released in the same year as the more sensationalised *The Accused*, this is a more down-to-earth, responsible and raw look at the subject of gang rape. Deborra-Lee Furness is the barrister whose bike breaks down in the Australian outback, where she meets rape victim Simone Buchanan. Standing up against the male-led community who believe the girl asked for it, the lawyer takes on her case, battling not only the criminal who must be brought to justice but the prejudices of the town. Excellent, restrained performances turn this into a powerful piece of cinema. Remade in 1992 as an American TV movie, followed by a sequel, starring Amanda Donohoe. JB

Deborra-Lee Furness *Asta Cadell* • Tony Barry *Tim Curtis* • Simone Buchanan *Lizzie Curtis* • Gillian Jones *Tina Farrel* • Peter Aanensen *Sergeant Wal Cuddy* • Margaret Ford *Norma Curtis* ■ *Dir* Steve Jodrell • *Scr* Beverly Blankenship, Michael Brindley

Shame ★★★★ 12

Drama 1968 · Swe · BW · 98min

Apolitical concert violinists Max von Sydow and Liv Ullmann take refuge on a remote island but are dragged back into society when civil war soldiers arrive in huge numbers. As loyalties shift around a corrupt, quisling colonel (Gunnar Björnstrand), Ullmann's strength and tenderness come to the fore, while von Sydow turns into a selfish, treacherous coward. Rigorously played and staged as a hideously realistic nightmare, this is a chilling vision of a world without beauty, trust or love. DP Swedish +subtitles. *DVD*

Liv Ullmann *Eva Rosenberg* • Max von Sydow *Jan Rosenberg* • Gunnar Björnstrand *Colonel Jacobi* • Sigge Furst *Filip* • Birgitta Valberg *Mrs Jacobi* ■ *Dir/Scr* Ingmar Bergman

Shame ★★★

Crime drama 1992 · US · Colour · 96min

No bad deed goes unpunished in this woman's revenge drama. After female lawyer Amanda Donohoe's motorcycle breaks down in a small out-of-the-way town, she befriends teenage rape victim Fairuza Balk. When the girl files charges against her attacker, the whole angry town comes after them both. This frank and brutal TV movie boasts an excellent script based on the 1987 Australian original. MC

Amanda Donohoe *Diana Cadell* • Fairuza Balk *Lizzie Curtis* • Dean Stockwell *Tim Curtis* • Shelley Owens *Lorna* • Dan Gauthier *Danny* ■ *Dir* Dan Lerner • *Scr* Rebecca Soladay, from the 1987 film

Shame ★★★ 18

Drama 2011 · UK · Colour · 96min

Following their acclaimed collaboration on 2008 award winner *Hunger*, Michael Fassbender and director Steve McQueen come together again for this account of a man's obsession with all things carnal. Brandon (Fassbender) is a high-flying New Yorker whose real interests are sex and self-loathing. But when his sister (Carey Mulligan) turns up unexpectedly, complications are introduced into his life. *Shame* is powerfully acted and well directed, the Big Apple has never looked as

harsh and unforgiving, and fans of Michael Fassbender's naked body will find much to enjoy. But, given that everything Brandon does is entirely consensual, it's never explained why he should be ashamed. *Bloody Miserable and Deeply Bored* might have been a better title. AS Violence, drug abuse, sex scenes, nudity, sexual references. *DVD Blu*

Michael Fassbender *Brandon* • Carey Mulligan *Sissy* • James Badge Dale *David* • Nicole Beharie *Marianne* • Mari-Ange Ramirez *Alexa* • Lucy Walters *Woman on subway train* ■ *Dir* Steve McQueen (2) • *Scr* Steve McQueen, Abi Morgan

The Shamer's Daughter ★★★★ 12A

Fantasy adventure 2015 · Den · Colour · 96min

This Nordic medieval fantasy centres on a young girl with an unusual ability - she can see every shameful act a person's committed from their eyes. As the title suggests, she inherited the ability from her mother, and the pair must use their gift to save a murder suspect. From here, the story is littered with fantastical elements - dragons, witchcraft, potions - and as it's intended as the first in a series, the ending doesn't provide much closure. For the most part, though, this is solid, impressively realised entertainment. SC In Danish. Violence.

Rebecca Emilie Sattrup *Dina* • Petra Maria Scott Nielsen *Rosa* • Peter Plaugborg *Drakan* • Maria Bonnevie *Melussina* • Soren Malling *Weapon master* ■ *Dir* Kenneth Kainz • *Scr* Anders Thomas Jensen, from Lene Kaaberbol's novel

Shampoo ★★★ 18

Comedy 1975 · US · Colour · 105min

This one-time *succès de scandale* grossed more than $60 million at the box office in its day. While it is delightfully amoral, producer, co-writer and star Warren Beatty never quite pulls his themes together. Nevertheless, there are striking moments, not least of which is Julie Christie's now classic appearance at a memorable dinner table. The model for the crimper was as widely believed to be Jon Peters, but was actually Jay Sebring, who was killed in the Sharon Tate massacre. TS Swearing, nudity. *DVD*

Warren Beatty *George Roundy* • Julie Christie *Jackie Shawn* • Goldie Hawn *Jill* • Lee Grant *Felicia Carr* • Jack Warden *Lester Carr* • Tony Bill *Johnny Pope* • Carrie Fisher *Lorna Carr* • Jay Robinson *Norman* ■ *Dir* Hal Ashby • *Scr* Warren Beatty, Robert Towne

The Shamrock Conspiracy ★★

Detective thriller 1995 · US · Colour · 100min

Edward Woodward stars as a recently retired Scotland Yard detective who travels to New York to make peace with his estranged daughter Elizabeth Hurley and ends up on the trail of a serial killer with her cop boyfriend Jeffrey Nordling. Woodward and Nordling spark nicely as the mismatched partners, uncovering IRA conspiracies and NYPD corruption as they pursue their quarry. But veteran director James Frawley struggles to maintain the momentum in this TV movie, and the end result is somewhat tedious. A second film, *Harrison: Cry in the City*, followed in 1996. DP

Edward Woodward *Edward "Teddy" Harrison* • Elizabeth Hurley *Cecilia Harrison* • Jeffrey Nordling *Frank Jeffries* • Kim Coates *Sean Nolan* • Daniel Von Bargen *Sternhardt* ■ *Dir* James Frawley • *Scr* Michael Gleason

Shamus ★★★ 18

Comedy thriller 1973 · US · Colour · 94min

Violent (by 1970s standards), fast-moving, if not very original, this Burt Reynolds vehicle is stylishly directed on New York locations by thriller specialist Buzz Kulik. Reynolds is well cast here as the tough-as-nails Brooklyn private eye who gets called in by a tycoon to find some stolen diamonds. There's some terrific character work along the way and Dyan Cannon is particularly fine as the moll. TS Swearing.

Marlene Dietrich *Shanghai Lily* • Clive Brook *Captain Donald "Doc" Harvey* • Anna May Wong *Hui Fei* • Warner Oland *Henry Chang* • Eugene

Burt Reynolds *Shamus McCoy* • Dyan Cannon *Alexis Montaigne* • John Ryan [John P Ryan] *Colonel Hardcore* • Joe Santos *Lieutenant Promuto* • Giorgio Tozzi *Il Dottore* • Ron Weyland *EJ Hume* • Larry Block *Springy* ■ *Dir* Buzz Kulik • *Scr* Barry Beckerman

Shane ★★★★★ PG

Classic western 1953 · US · Colour · 113min

A marvellous distillation of all that is fine about Hollywood cinema, this is a revelation, sweeping you up via magnificent editing and Loyal Griggs's Technicolor photography into a tale of a man, a woman and, especially, a boy, whose lives are changed by the man dressed in buckskin who rides on to their farm. Alan Ladd gives the performance of a lifetime in the title role, and the rest of the cast is also impeccable, notably Jean Arthur as the married woman whose relationship with Shane is subtly understated. Victor Young's majestic main theme lingers long after the movie is over. Directed by the great George Stevens, this is one of the finest American motion pictures, brilliantly constructed and beautifully filmed. TS *DVD Blu*

Alan Ladd *Shane* • Jean Arthur *Marion Starrett* • Van Heflin *Joe Starrett* • Brandon de Wilde *Joey Starrett* • Jack Palance *Wilson* • Ben Johnson (1) *Chris* • Edgar Buchanan *Lewis* • Emile Meyer *Ryker* • Elisha Cook Jr *Torrey* • Douglas Spencer *Mr Shipstead* • John Dierkes *Morgan* • Ellen Corby *Mrs Torrey* ■ *Dir* George Stevens • *Scr* AB Guthrie Jr, Jack Sher, from the novel by Jack Schaefer • *Cinematographer* Loyal Griggs

The Shanghai Cobra ★★ PG

Mystery 1945 · US · BW · 62min

Cobra venom in a jukebox proves the key to this case of a murdered banker. But before Sidney Toler can nab a killer he first encountered a decade earlier, he must first risk the nation's radium supply. Phil Karlson brings an effective *noirish* feel to proceedings that had increasingly become sidetracked by the antics of Mantan Moreland's chauffeur and "Number Three Son", Benson Fong. Addison Richards and Arthur Loft lend better than usual support. DP *DVD*

Sidney Toler *Charlie Chan* • Mantan Moreland *Birmingham Brown* • Benson Fong *Tommy Chan* • James Cardwell *Ned Stewart* • Joan Barclay *Paula* • Addison Richards *John Adams/Jan Van Horn* • Arthur Loft *Bradford Harris* ■ *Dir* Phil Karlson • *Scr* George Callahan, George Wallace Sayre, from a story by Callahan, from characters by Earl Derr Biggers

Shanghai Dreams ★★★ 15

Drama 2005 · Chi/HK · Colour · 121min

Wang Xiaoshuai provides a sobering study of a China caught between the Cultural Revolution and the consumerist leap forward in this low-key drama. Set in the isolated south in 1983, the story chronicles teenager Gao Yuanyuan's rebellious response to her father Yan Anlian's decision to quit their declining industrial community and return to his Shanghai home. DP Mandarin, Shanghainese +subtitles.

Gao Yuanyuan *Wu Qinghong* • Li Bin *Fan Honggen* • Yan Anlian *Wu Zemin, Qinghong's father* • Tang Yang *Meifen, Qinghong's mother* • Wang Xueyang *Xiaozhen* ■ *Dir* Wang Xiaoshuai • *Scr* Wang Xiaoshuai, Lao Ni

Shanghai Express ★★★★ PG

Romantic drama 1932 · US · BW · 78min

The fourth collaboration between Marlene Dietrich and director Josef von Sternberg, this arch melodrama divides audiences. Fans love its exotic lighting (cinematographer Lee Garmes won an Oscar) and its clever, intimate use of confined space; detractors laugh at its high camp histrionics and its ludicrous (but stylish) plot and satirically ridiculous dialogue. This 1930s hokum is immensely enjoyable, as notorious hooker Dietrich is reunited with her former true love Clive Brook (characteristically wooden but well cast) aboard the titular train that's hijacked by brigand Warner Oland. TS

Pallette *Sam Salt* • Lawrence Grant *Reverend Carmichael* • Louise Closser Hale *Mrs Haggerty* • Gustav von Seyffertitz *Eric Baum* • Emile Chautard *Major Lenard* ■ *Dir* Josef von Sternberg • *Scr* Jules Furthman, from a story by Harry Hervey

The Shanghai Gesture ★★★★★ PG

Melodrama 1941 · US · BW · 98min

Gene Tierney is at her loveliest as the spoilt rich girl who, using an alias, enters a Shanghai casino and is seduced by its "incredibly evil" atmosphere, unaware that her entrepreneur dad (Walter Huston) is intent on closing down the iniquitous establishment, domain of the glacial "Mother" Gin Sling (Ona Munson in a series of lacquered, Medusa-like wigs). Director Josef von Sternberg was forced to sanitise his adaptation of John Colton's stage play, but his vision suggestively offers more than the salacious detail he was forced to cut from the script. The film's masterful use of musical rhythms, stylised dialogue and close-ups makes it a high point from the studio age. And her face a mask revealing more than it conceals - the bitterness of lost illusion - Munson creates one of cinema's most sympathetic monsters. DO *DVD*

Gene Tierney *Victoria Charteris/Poppy Smith* • Walter Huston *Sir Guy Charteris* • Victor Mature *Doctor Omar* • Ona Munson *"Mother" Gin Sling* • Phyllis Brooks *Dixie Pomeroy, the chorus girl* • Albert Basserman *Commissioner* • Maria Ouspenskaya *Amah* • Eric Blore *Caesar Hawkins, the bookkeeper* • Mike Mazurki *Coolie* • Marcel Dalio *Master of the spinning wheel* ■ *Dir* Josef von Sternberg • *Scr* Josef von Sternberg, Geza Herczeg, Jules Furthman, Kurt Vollmoeller, from the play by John Colton • *Cinematographer* Paul Ivano

Shanghai Knights ★★★ 12

Period action comedy 2002 · US · Colour · 109min

Jackie Chan's Chinese sheriff and Owen Wilson's slacker outlaw reteam and relocate to what is meant to be Victorian London (actually Prague) for this spry sequel to the immensely successful action comedy *Shanghai Noon*. After a brisk intro involving the theft of an Imperial seal and the murder of Chan's father, the action slows a little so they can plod through some unimaginative gags about the English. However, Chan's action sequences are as spectacularly inventive and meticulously choreographed as ever. AS Swearing, some violence *DVD*

Jackie Chan *Chon Wang* • Owen Wilson *Roy O'Bannon* • Aaron Johnson *Charlie* • Thomas Fisher [Tom Fisher] *Artie Doyle* • Aidan Gillen *Lord Rathbone* • Fann Wong *Chon Lin* • Donnie Yen *Wu Chan* ■ *Dir* David Dobkin • *Scr* Alfred Gough, Miles Millar, from their characters

Shanghai Madness ★★

Adventure 1933 · US · BW · 64min

Adrift in Shanghai after being dishonorably dismissed from the US Navy, former lieutenant Spencer Tracy finds work on a boat carrying guns to the Mandarin government. This ship is also transporting stowaway Fay Wray whose life Tracy saved ashore and who has taken a fancy to him. The boat is attacked by Communists, allowing Tracy the requisite heroics to rescue his reputation. An undemanding but efficient formula adventure. RK

Spencer Tracy *Lt Pat Jackson* • Fay Wray *Wildeth Christie* • Ralph Morgan *Li Po Chang* • Eugene Pallette *Capt Lobo Lornegan* • Herbert Mundin *Third Officer Jones* • Reginald Mason *William Christie* • Arthur Hoyt *Van Emery* ■ *Dir* John Blystone [John G Blystone] • *Scr* Austin Parker, from the short story by Frederick Hazlitt Brennan

Shanghai Noon ★★★ 12

Action comedy western 2000 · US · Colour · 105min

Visually authentic and deliciously anachronistic, this period western from martial arts maestro Jackie Chan is a hugely enjoyable combination of buddy comedy and adventure. Sent to the States to rescue kidnapped princess Lucy Liu, Chan's Imperial Palace guard hooks up with outlaw Owen Wilson, who proves to be his equal in the fish-out-of-water stakes. Using antlers, sheriff's badges and horseshoes to prise himself out of a tight corner, Chan is pure slapstick poetry in motion: falling off horses, getting drunk and confusing slave-owning louse Roger Yuan and corrupt sheriff Xander Berkeley. DP **DVD** **BL**

Jackie Chan *Chon Wang* • Owen Wilson *Roy O'Bannon* • Lucy Liu *Princess Pei Pei* • Brandon Merrill *Indian wife* • Roger Yuan *Lo Fong* • Xander Berkeley *Van Clee* • Walton Goggins *Wallace* • Jason Connery *Andrews* ■ *Dir* Tom Dey • *Scr* Miles Millar, Alfred Gough

Shanghai Surprise ★ 15
Period adventure   1986 · UK · Colour · 92min

Madonna is ludicrously miscast here, playing a peroxide-blonde missionary looking for stolen opium in pre-Second World War China (to put to good use in hospitals, of course). Her then husband Sean Penn is OK as the rogue salesman she hires to help her acquire the vast stash. Otherwise, director Jim Goddard's heavy-handed and over-inflated screwball adventure is desperately seeking laughs at every vulgar turn and is woefully short of the madcap antics that go to define the genre. A witless embarrassment. AJ Swearing, nudity. **DVD**

Sean Penn *Glendon Wasey* • Madonna *Gloria Tatlock* • Paul Freeman *Walter Faraday* • Richard Griffiths *Willie Tuttle* • Philip Sayer *Justin Kronk* • Clyde Kusatsu *Joe Go* • Lim Kay Tong *Mei Gan* • Sonserai Lee *China Doll* • Michael Aldridge *Mr Burns* • George Harrison *Night club singer* ■ *Dir* Jim Goddard • *Scr* John Kohn, Robert Bentley, from the novel *Faraday's Flowers* by Tony Kenrick

Shanghai Triad ★★★ 15
Crime drama   1995 · HK/Fr · Colour · 103min

Longtime companions Gong Li and Zhang Yimou parted during the production of this, their seventh collaboration. As a result, perhaps, this is their least effective picture, with the plot allowed to ramble when swift, atmospheric strokes would have heightened the tension. But the stunning beauty of both Li and director Zhang's imagery give this an allure. In particular, the teasing sensuality of Li's musical numbers and the sudden realisation that her gangster lover has discovered her deceptions are unforgettable. DP Mandarin +subtitles.

Gong Li *Xiao Jinbao, "Jewel"* • Wang Xiaowing *Shuisheng* • Li Baotian *Gangster* • Li Xuejian *Uncle Liu* ■ *Dir* Zhang Yimou • *Scr* Bi Feiyu, from the novel *Men Gu [Gang Law]* by Li Xiao

Shank ★ 15
Futuristic action thriller
2010 · UK · Colour · 90min

This dystopian urban thriller is set in a lawless London in 2015 with youth gangs now fighting over scarce food supplies rather than drugs. It's also one of the dullest gang flicks to ever see the light of day. Newcomer Kedar Williams-Stirling does well enough as Junior, fleet-footed lookout for the Paper Chaserz crew, headed by his tough-guy elder brother Rager. The Paper Chaserz's anti-violence stance comes under pressure after a vicious attack by a rival outfit, and what follows is a lot of musical interludes, computer animation, and traipsing around sundry council estates – but little in the way of a connecting plot or action highlights. TJ **DVD** **BL**

Michael Socha *Craze* • Kaya Scodelario *Tasha* • Ashley "Bashy" Thomas *Rager* • Kedar Williams-Stirling *Junior* • Colin Salmon *Boogie* • Robbie Gee *Beano* • Jan Uddin *Sweet Boy* ■ *Dir* Mo Ali • *Scr* Paul Van Carter

Shannon's Deal ★★★★
Drama   1989 · US · Colour · 95min

Writer/director John Sayles generally adds flavour to even his smallest characters and creates the power of suggestion through dialogue. Writing for director Lewis Teague, Sayles transforms what could so easily have

been a trawl through inanity and cliché into a work of edgy, dramatic clout. He takes the gumshoe genre and puts his own spin on events, and lifts it considerably. The insinuating, unnerving score by Wynton Marsalis for this TV pilot perfectly matches the psychology of the key character. JM

Jamey Sheridan *Jack Shannon* • Elizabeth Peña *Lucy Acosta* • Jenny Lewis *Neala Shannon* • Miguel Ferrer *Todd Snyder* • Stefan Gierasch *Klaus* ■ *Dir* Lewis Teague • *Scr* John Sayles

Shaolin ★★★ 15
Period martial arts drama
2011 · HK/Chi · Colour · 125min

Andy Lau (*House of Flying Daggers*) stars in this engaging action epic as a proud, paranoid and power-mad general whose warring ways result in an unbearable personal tragedy. Redemption comes, but only after he learns to atone for his past in the surroundings of the Shaolin Temple, where a humble cook (Jackie Chan, in a modest but pleasing role) takes him under his wing. Lau's spiritual journey is interspersed with lively subplots and plenty of action spectacle. It's just a shame about the overblown finale. JH Mandarin +subtitles. **DVD** **BL**

Andy Lau *Hou Chieh* • Nicholas Tse *Tsao Man* • Bingbing Fan *Madam Hou* • Jackie Chan *Wudao* ■ *Dir* Benny Chan • *Scr* Cheung Chi-kwong, Chan Wang Qiuyu, Zhang Tan Kam-cheong, from an original screenplay by Alan Yuen

Shaolin Soccer ★★★ 12
Sports action comedy
2001 · HK/Chi/US · Colour · 85min

Stephen Chow turns to football in this cartoonish underdog comedy, which broke box-office records in his native Hong Kong. The action centres on the efforts of Ng Man Tat's disgraced, disabled ex-pro teaming with Chow's Shaolin monk to coach a side capable of defeating Patrick Tse's team of ruthless overachievers. The action is everything here, although Chow also tosses in some ingenious effects, the odd movie parody and several throwaway in-jokes. The result is fast, furious fun. DP Cantonese dubbed. **DVD** **BL**

Stephen Chow *Sing* • Vicki Zhao [Zhao Wei] *Mui* • Ng Man Tat *Golden Leg Fung* • Patrick Tse *Hung* • Wong Yat Fei *Iron Head* ■ *Dir* Stephen Chow • *Scr* Stephen Chow, Tsang Kan-Cheung

The Shape of Things ★★ 15
Drama   2003 · US/Fr/UK · Colour · 92min

Misanthropy and psychological violence have been Neil LaBute's stock in trade ever since his impressive debut, *In the Company of Men*. This serves up yet another helping of the formula, but sadly the result is not so much shocking as silly. Paul Rudd plays a geeky student given a makeover by his radical artist girlfriend Rachel Weisz, but her intentions are not what they seem. The mind games that ensue drag in Rudd's friends Gretchen Mol and Frederick Weller and expose tensions in their relationship. The theatricality of the dialogue is a distraction from the implausible plot. AS **DVD**

Gretchen Mol *Jenny* • Paul Rudd *Adam* • Rachel Weisz *Evelyn* • Frederick Weller *Philip* ■ *Dir* Neil LaBute • *Scr* Neil LaBute, from his play

Shark! ★ 15
Action drama   1969 · US/Mex · Colour · 88min

This watery tale about underwater treasure cast barely a ripple, except for a public row between the producers and director Sam Fuller who wanted his name removed from the credits, claiming the film had been re-edited against his will. Fuller's army of fans accepted this, over-looking the fact that in 1967 Fuller was reduced to making dime-budget stuff in Mexico to pay the rent. The movie spent three years on the shelf only seeing the light of day when Burt Reynolds became a major box-office draw. AT **DVD**

Burt Reynolds *Caine* • Barry Sullivan *Mallare* • Arthur Kennedy *Doc* • Silvia Pinal *Anna* • Enrique Lucero *Barok* ■ *Dir* Samuel Fuller • *Scr* Samuel Fuller, John Kinsgbridge, from the novel *His Bones Are Coral* by Victor Canning

Shark Attack ★★★ 15
Horror thriller   1999 · US · Colour · 91min

Investigating a series of shark attacks, marine biologist Casper Van Dien discovers something fishy in the waters off the coast of Africa. This video fodder is a very long way from the expertly created suspense of its ultimate inspiration, *Jaws*. But, for a B picture, it is ambitious – fast moving, packed with spectacular shark effects and shot on rarely seen, picturesque South African locations. It spawned two sequels. DM **DVD**

Casper Van Dien *Steven McKray* • Ernie Hudson *Laurence Rhodes* • Bentley Mitchum *Dr Miles Craven* • Jennifer McShane [Jenny McShane] *Corinne DeSantis* • Tony Caprari *Mani* ■ *Dir* Bob Misiorowski • *Scr* Scott Devine, William Hooke

Shark Night 3D ★ 15
Horror thriller   2011 · US · Colour · 86min

Just when you thought it was safe to watch another *Jaws* rip-off, along comes this dumb B-movie that lacks bite in every department. Aping the Spielberg classic from the start – except for the funny, scary, thrilling parts – this misconceived effort sees rednecks stock a picturesque Louisiana lake with sharks fitted with belly cameras to stream live-attack carnage to the internet. David R Ellis clearly learnt nothing from directing cheesy exploitation movie *Snakes on a Plane*, as this is contrived to the point of blankness. AJ Violence. **DVD** **BL** **3D**

Sara Paxton *Sara* • Dustin Milligan *Nick LaDuca* • Katharine McPhee *Beth* • Donal Logue *Sheriff Greg Sabin* • Chris Carmack *Dennis* ■ *Dir* David R Ellis • *Scr* Will Hayes, Jesse Studenberg

Shark Tale ★★★ U
Animated comedy adventure
2004 · US · Colour · 86min

A thinly disguised morality lesson, this family comedy from DreamWorks tells the tale of a celebrity-obsessed fish (voiced by Will Smith) who masquerades as a shark-killing hero with the aid of a vegetarian great white (Jack Black). The film is kept buoyant by irreverent humour and some adult-friendly movie skits. The sea life looks rather charmless, but the voice casting shows more imagination, with Robert De Niro's mafioso shark and Martin Scorsese's crooked puffer fish both memorable. SF **DVD**

Will Smith *Oscar* • Robert De Niro *Don Lino* • Renée Zellweger *Angie* • Jack Black *Lenny* • Angelina Jolie *Lola* • Martin Scorsese *Sykes* • Peter Falk *Don Brizzi* • Michael Imperioli *Frankie* ■ *Dir* Eric "Bibo" Bergeron, Vicky Jenson, Rob Letterman • *Scr* Michael J Wilson, Rob Letterman

Sharknado ★ 15
Science-fiction horror
2013 · US · Colour · 88min

Sharks are scooped up out of the ocean and launched by tornados onto the streets of LA in this straight-to-TV schlocker. This film shouldn't have worked. The idea probably shouldn't even have made it off the back of a beer mat. But it was seized upon in social media circles because it is, of course, so bad it's good. ED **DVD**

Tara Reid *April* • Ian Ziering *Fin* • John Heard *George* • Cassie Scerbo *Nova* ■ *Dir* Anthony C Ferrante • *Scr* Thunder Levin

Sharknado 2: the Second One ★★ 15
Science-fiction horror
2014 · US · Colour · 91min

After a first film that went viral on social media, a shark-infested sequel was inevitable. But in a New York-set tale with all manner of film in-jokes and celebrity cameos (Robert Hays, Kelly Osbourne), this is a rather more polished affair. Sadly, the central performances from Ian Ziering and Tara Reid don't live up to the hype. *Sharknado 3: Oh Hell No!* premiered in 2015, and the series is now on its fourth instalment. SuR **DVD** **BL** **CS**

Ian Ziering *Fin* • Tara Reid *April* • Vivica A Fox *Skye* • Mark McGrath *Martin* • Kari Wuhrer *Ellen* ■ *Dir* Anthony C Ferrante • *Scr* Thunder Levin

Shark's Treasure ★★ PG
Adventure   1975 · US · Colour · 91min

For all its trendy references to *Jaws*, this feels like a relic of those deadly dull deep-sea diving movies of the 1950s. Apart from the odd shark, the camera only has eyes for Cornel Wilde, which is hardly surprising, considering he also wrote and directed this hokum about a man who sacrifices his beloved boat in the hope of finding buried treasure. Yaphet Kotto provides burly support and Al Giddings's underwater photography is fine. DP

Cornel Wilde *Jim* • Yaphet Kotto *Ben* • John Neilson *Ron* • Cliff Osmond *Lobo* • David Canary *Larry* ■ *Dir/Scr* Cornel Wilde

Sharkwater ★★★ PG
Wildlife documentary
2006 · Can · Colour · 85min

Wildlife photographer Rob Stewart's unlikely love letter attempts to rehabilitate sharks – among the most feared creatures on earth. He sets out to demonstrate why our terror is driving the species to extinction. Pointing out that elephants kill more people than sharks, Stewart uses stunning images to show the beautiful side of these maligned creatures. Less persuasive is his ill-prepared tirade against the global finning industry, as he falls foul of the Taiwanese mafia and gets arrested by the Costa Rican police. All of this detracts from the film's succinctly ironic point: the shark population has declined by 90 per cent over the last 30 years, making it clear that man is the ocean's most dangerous predator. JR **DVD** **BL**

■ *Dir/Scr* Rob Stewart (2)

Sharky's Machine ★★★ 18
Crime thriller   1981 · US · Colour · 116min

As both director and star, Burt Reynolds proves just a bit too ambitious. His vice cop on the tail of some nasties is not only packed with bull-necked aggression but also has a sensitive interest in woodcarving, while his direction similarly moves abruptly from the overbearing to the light'n'easy and back again. Neither character nor situation is built up enough to obscure the crude joins. However, Burt-the-director has a nifty way with the action set pieces, in which Burt-the-star is at his best. JM Violence, swearing.

Burt Reynolds *Sharky* • Vittorio Gassman *Victor* • Brian Keith *Papa* • Charles Durning *Friscoe* • Earl Holliman *Hotchkins* • Bernie Casey *Arch* • Henry Silva *Billy Score* • Richard Libertini *Nosh* • Rachel Ward *Dominoe* ■ *Dir* Burt Reynolds • *Scr* Gerald Di Pego, from the novel by William Diehl

Sharpay's Fabulous Adventure ★★ U
Musical comedy drama
2011 · US · Colour · 85min

A year after her graduation in *High School Musical: Senior Year*, Sharpay Evans (Ashley Tisdale) is still looking for a direction in life. She jumps at the chance of an audition in New York, but her carefully laid plans come unstuck when her rented flat falls through and the role is not what she was led to believe. To anyone who's seen *Legally Blonde*, much of the action will seem familiar, even down to the pink-themed pad. However, the script is entertaining in places and co-star Bradley Steven Perry (*Good Luck Charlie*) is well cast as her brattish competition. Just don't expect much from the insipid romance. SuR **DVD**

Ashley Tisdale *Sharpay Evans* • Austin Butler *Peyton Leverett* • Cameron Goodman *Amber Lee Adams* • Bradley Steven Perry *Roger Elliston* ■ *Dir* Michael Lembeck • *Scr* Robert Horn, from characters by Peter Barsocchini

S

Shatter ★

Martial arts action thriller
1974 · UK · Colour · 90min

When Hammer's horror movies started to bomb at the box-office, the studio forged a short-lived partnership with Hong Kong studios and made kung fu action films, though they stopped short of calling the company Hammer and Tongs. What everyone failed to appreciate was that while Bruce Lee could invade the west, the traffic was one-way. AT

Stuart Whitman *Shatter* · Peter Cushing *Rattwood* · Ti Lung *Tai Pah* · Anton Diffring *Hans Leber* · Yemi Ajibade *M'Goya* · Huang Pei-Chi *Bodyguard* ■ *Dir* Michael Carreras, Monte Hellman · *Scr* Don Houghton

Shattered ★★★ 15

Thriller 1991 · US · Colour · 93min

Modern directors show no sign of losing their desire to pay their respects to Alfred Hitchcock, and this intriguing thriller from Wolfgang Petersen succeeds better than most. Tom Berenger wakes up after a horrific car accident with amnesia and attempts to put his life back together again with the help of a private detective (Bob Hoskins); Greta Scacchi is the *femme fatale* who may or may not be trying to kill him. There's a very neat twist at the end, but there are so many bluffs and double bluffs it is exhausting to follow. JF Swearing, violence, nudity.

Tom Berenger *Dan Merrick* · Bob Hoskins *Gus Klein* · Greta Scacchi *Judith Merrick* · Joanne Whalley-Kilmer [Joanne Whalley] *Jenny Scott* · Corbin Bernsen *Jeb Scott* · Debi A Monahan *Nancy Mercer* ■ *Dir* Wolfgang Petersen · *Scr* Wolfgang Petersen, from the novel *The Plastic Nightmare* by Richard Neely

Shattered Glass ★★★ 12

Drama based on a true story
2003 · US/Can · Colour · 89min

Hubris is at the heart of this true story about a high-flying young magazine journalist whose scoops turn out to be figments of his imagination. Hayden Christensen is excellent as a wheedling star reporter who manipulates his colleagues into helping him with his writing and defending him against his unpopular but rigorous editor, played with equal skill by Peter Sarsgaard. Debut director Billy Ray keeps the story rattling along and support is uniformly good, particularly from Steve Zahn and Hank Azaria. If there is a flaw, it's the screenplay's failure to provide any real explanation for Glass's motives. AS Swearing. *DVD*

Hayden Christensen *Stephen Glass* · Peter Sarsgaard *Charles "Chuck" Lane* · Chloë Sevigny *Caitlin Avey* · Rosario Dawson *Andy Fox* · Melanie Lynskey *Amy Brand* · Steve Zahn *Adam Penenberg* · Hank Azaria *Michael "Mike" Kelly* ■ *Dir* Billy Ray · *Scr* Billy Ray, from the *Vanity Fair* article by Buzz Bissinger

Shattered Image ★★ 18

Thriller mystery 1998 · US · Colour · 98min

Schizophrenic after a brutal rape, hit woman Anne Parillaud finds herself drifting in and out of reality. The action flips between Seattle and Jamaica and as fantasy begins to take hold, Parillaud must decide what's real: Is she a pitiless revenge-killer of men, or a happy wife on holiday with new husband William Baldwin? Then again, maybe she's a bit of both. A solidly made psychodrama that just about keeps you watching. Director Raúl Ruiz's first American film. DA

William Baldwin *Brian* · Anne Parillaud *Jessie* · Lisanne Falk *Paula/Laura* · Graham Greene (2) *Conrad/Mike* · Bulle Ogier *Mrs Ford* ■ *Dir* Raúl Ruiz · *Scr* Duane Poole

Shattered Silence ★★

Drama 2012 · US · Colour

Devastated single mum Liz Vassey tries to uncover why her pretty teen daughter suddenly committed suicide in this ripped-from-the-headlines TV movie about cyber-bullying and the dangers of "sexting" (the texting of sexually provocative material). *CSI* star Vassey's sense of desperation and

sadness is contagious, but what starts out as a thought-provoking and generally realistic drama, degenerates into a kind of mystery thriller that becomes increasingly far-fetched. SF

Liz Vassey *Rachel Van Cleve* · Jenn Proske *Dina Van Cleve* · Ryan Kelley *Mark Carey* · Kelli Goss *Skylar Reid* ■ *Dir* John Stimpson · *Scr* John Stimpson, Marcy Holland

Shaun of the Dead ★★★★★ 15

Comedy horror
2004 · UK/US/Fr · Colour · 95min

Just as Shaun (Simon Pegg) tries to get his aimless life back on track, London becomes Zombie Central as the dead rise to eat the living. If you liked Pegg and director Edgar Wright's cult series *Spaced*, you'll enjoy this deadpan blend of undergraduate humour and hardcore horror. Shaun's mates are all played by familiar TV faces – Nick Frost, Lucy Davis and Dylan Moran. But the real stars are his mum, Penelope Wilton, and stepdad, Bill Nighy. The first film in Pegg/Wright/Frost's Cornetto Trilogy, this was followed by *Hot Fuzz* and *The World's End*. AJ Violence, swearing. *DVD* *BL*

Simon Pegg *Shaun* · Kate Ashfield *Liz* · Nick Frost *Ed* · Dylan Moran *David* · Lucy Davis *Dianne* · Penelope Wilton *Barbara* · Bill Nighy *Philip* · Jessica Stevenson *Yvonne* ■ *Dir* Edgar Wright · *Scr* Edgar Wright, Simon Pegg

Shaun the Sheep Movie ★★★★ U

Animated comedy adventure
2015 · UK/Fr · Colour · 81min

Mossy Bottom Farm's mischief-maker bounds onto the big screen in this fun-packed yarn. Shaun and the rest of the flock devise a cunning "counting sheep" ruse to make the Farmer fall asleep on the job so they can escape the farm's daily grind. However, the plan backfires and Bitzer the dog, Shaun and friends mount a daring search-and-rescue mission, prompting plenty of japes and scrapes. While many of the jokes may not be particularly new, they are timed to perfection and beautifully conveyed – and no sheep pun goes unfleeced, either. This is Aardman at its most delightful, ingenious and hilarious. JH *DVD* *CG*

Justin Fletcher *Shaun/Timmy* · John Sparkes *The Farmer/Bitzer* · Omid Djalili *Trumper* · Richard Webber *Shirley* · Kate Harbour *Timmy's Mum/Meryl* · Tim Hands *Slip* · Nick Park · Stanley Unwin *Bus station and hospital announcer* ■ *Dir/Scr* Mark Burton, Richard Starzack

The Shawshank Redemption ★★★★★ 15

Prison drama 1994 · US · Colour · 136min

Re-released on its tenth anniversary, this deeply moving version of a Stephen King story from first-time director Frank Darabont is one of the best adaptations of the novelist's work. Tim Robbins plays a Maine banker sent to Shawshank State Prison for murdering his wife and her lover. Regularly brutalised by the inmates and the penal system in general, his existence improves when he befriends fellow lifer and prison fixer Morgan Freeman. Under Darabont's inspired direction, Robbins and Freeman both rise to the challenge of portraying world-weary dignity against the odds, while the severity of the prison system is underlined in the poignant performance of James Whitmore as a veteran convict trying to make it on parole, but ill-equipped to do so. AJ Violence, swearing, nudity. *DVD* *BL*

Tim Robbins *Andy Dufresne* · Morgan Freeman *Ellis Boyd "Red" Redding* · Bob Gunton *Warden Norton* · William Sadler *Heywood* · Clancy Brown *Captain Hadley* · Gil Bellows *Tommy* · Mark Rolston *Bogs Diamond* · James Whitmore *Brooks Hatlen* ■ *Dir* Frank Darabont · *Scr* Frank Darabont, from the short story *Rita Hayworth and Shawshank Redemption* by Stephen King

She ★★

Fantasy adventure 1935 · US · BW · 94min

The first talkie verison of H Rider Haggard's romantic adventure about the explorer

lured by a woman who, having bathed in the Flame of Life, becomes immortal, provides only short-lived interest. Randolph Scott is a grim-jawed explorer, Helen Gahagan a rather muted siren and the story is transferred from Africa to the Arctic Circle. The result is dialogue and acting as frozen as the setting. TH

Helen Gahagan *Hash-A-Mo-Tep, "She"* · Randolph Scott *Leo Vincey* · Helen Mack *Tanya Dugmore* · Nigel Bruce *Archibald Holly* · Gustav von Seyffertitz *Prime Minister Billali* · Samuel S Hinds *John Vincey* · Noble Johnson *Amahagger chief* · Lumsden Hare *Dugmore* ■ *Dir* Irving Pichel, Lansing C Holden · *Scr* Ruth Rose, Dudley Nichols, from the novel by H Rider Haggard

She ★★★ U

Fantasy adventure 1965 · UK · Colour · 101min

Swiss-born Ursula Andress acquits herself better than you might expect in this adaptation of H Rider Haggard's much-filmed fantasy. Indeed, she looks in great shape for a 2,000-year-old queen of a lost kingdom, who is still yearning for the embrace of a lover she killed centuries ago. The jungle backdrops are easily matched by Andress's own brand of exotic beauty and, while there's plenty to criticise, there's also much to enjoy. *The Vengeance of She* followed three years later, minus Andress. PF *DVD*

Ursula Andress *Ayesha* · John Richardson *Leo Vincey* · Peter Cushing *Major Horace Holly* · Bernard Cribbins *Job* · Rosenda Monteros *Ustane* · Christopher Lee *Billali* ■ *Dir* Robert Day · *Scr* David T Chantler, from the novel by H Rider Haggard

She, a Chinese ★★ 18

Social drama
2009 · UK/Fr/Ger · Colour · 98min

In this low-key drama, a young woman stifled by life in rural China tries to make a new start for herself in London. But the lot of a lonely, frightened illegal immigrant hardly seems to leave 20-something Li Mei (Huang Lu) better off. As a Chinese expat who's forged a name for herself in Europe through her novels and documentaries, the film's writer/director Xiaolu Guo obviously knows her subject, though making an effective drama out of the material here has proven a bit of a challenge. The taciturn way the character comes across and Huang Lu's minimalist performance rather keep the viewer on the outside. It's an intriguing journey, but one that demands too much patience from the audience. TJ Mandarin, English +subtitles. *DVD*

Huang Lu *Li Mei* · Wey Yi Bo *Spikey* · Geoffrey Hutchings *Mr Hunt* · Chris Ryman *Rachid* ■ *Dir/Scr* Xiaolu Guo

The She Beast ★★★

Horror 1965 · UK/It · Colour · 75min

Cult director Michael Reeves made his feature debut with this painfully cheap shocker that nevertheless revealed the powerful use of horrific imagery he would harness to perfection in his masterpiece, *Witchfinder General*. Honeymooners Barbara Steele and Ian Ogilvy visit modern-day Transylvania, only to crash their car in the lake where vengeful witch Vardella was tortured to death in the 18th century. Steele transforms into the decrepit hag and goes on a murder spree in this amalgam of stark terror and facile humour. AJ Some Italian dubbed.

Barbara Steele *Veronica/Vardella* · Ian Ogilvy *Philip* · John Karlsen *Count von Helsing* ■ *Dir* Michael Reeves · *Scr* Michael Byron

The She-Creature ★★ 12

Cult horror 1956 · US · BW · 74min

Chester Morris hypnotises sexy Marla English back to prehistoric times, and has her reptilian alter ego materialise in the present to help him and money-grabbing promoter Tom Conway con the police. He predicts a murder and the scaly, large-breasted amphibian carries it out. One of those bonkers 1950s sci-fi quickies that are so awful they become irresistibly compelling. Incidentally, the monster is an impressive work of trash art. AJ *DVD*

Chester Morris *Carlo Lombardi* · Marla English *Andrea* · Tom Conway *Timothy Chappel* · Cathy Downs *Dorothy* · Lance Fuller *Ted Erickson* ■ *Dir* Edward L Cahn · *Scr* Lou Rusoff, from his play

She Creature ★★ 15

Period horror 2001 · US · Colour · 85min

This first in a new series of "Creature Feature" TV remakes from Stan Winston's effects studio is a strange choice, given that Edward L Cahn's 1956 sci-fi quickie isn't exactly held in the highest regard. It's set in the early 20th century, with Rufus Sewell as the owner of a fake freak show who stumbles across the existence of a genuine mermaid and tries to use her to make his fortune. Decent production values and cast fail to compensate for a stagnant script that takes itself far too seriously, while the gore and nudity don't sit easily with the period feel. JC *DVD*

Rufus Sewell *Angus Shaw* · Carla Gugino *Lillian* · Jim Piddock *Capt Dunn* · Reno Wilson *Bailey* · Mark Aiken *Gifford* · Fintan McKeown *Shelly* ■ *Dir/Scr* Sebastian Gutierrez

She Dances Alone ★★★

Documentary drama
1981 · US/Austria · Colour · 87min

This intriguing blend of fact and fiction has Bud Cort as a director trying to make an objective documentary about the legendary dancer Nijinsky. Unfortunately he's blocked at every turn by Nijinsky's daughter, Kyra. Well over 60 years old at the time, Kyra is a huge presence in the film in every sense, and it is as much about her strong-willed desire to make her own career with the burden/blessing of such a famous father as it is about the great man himself. To blur the edges even further, Max von Sydow plays himself and is the voice reading Nijinsky's diary. FL

Max von Sydow *Voice of Nijinsky* · Jon Bradshaw *Narrator* · Bud Cort *Director* · Patrick Dupond *Dancer* ■ *Dir* Robert Dornhelm · *Scr* Paul Davids, from an idea by Robert Dornhelm

She-Devil ★★ 15

Comedy 1989 · US · Colour · 95min

Fay Weldon's dark, acerbic tale of rejection and revenge receives the full Hollywood treatment, reducing its saturnine charm to frothy candyfloss. The whole farrago is hopelessly miscast with a wet and vapid Meryl Streep as the vamp novelist, a cardboard cutout Ed Begley Jr as the errant husband she snares, and, most disappointing of all, Roseanne Barr as a curiously weak and woolly She-Devil. Watching this makes you appreciate once more the celebrated BBC TV adaptation. SH Swearing, sex scenes, brief nudity. *DVD*

Meryl Streep *Mary Fisher* · Roseanne Barr *Ruth Patchett* · Ed Begley Jr *Bob Patchett* · Linda Hunt *Nurse Hooper* · Sylvia Miles *Francine Fisher* · Elisebeth Peters *Nicolette Patchett* · Bryan Larkin (1) *Andy Patchett* · Robin Leach ■ *Dir* Susan Seidelman · *Scr* Barry Strugatz, Mark R Burns, from the novel *The Life and Loves of a She-Devil* by Fay Weldon

She-Devils on Wheels ★★ 18

Action thriller 1968 · US · Colour · 79min

After *Blood Feast*, this tawdry tale of chopper chicks on the rampage is splatter pioneer Herschell Gordon Lewis's most popular drive-in exploiter. The domineering Man-Eaters battle a bunch of male hot-rodders for use of the abandoned airport runway where they hold their weekly Harley races. Ritual humiliation, decapitation, kidnap, torture and the hilarious "stud-line" – the race winner gets to choose which man to sexually abuse – are the main focus of Lewis's Hells Angels in high heels plodder. AJ *DVD*

Betty Connell *Queen* · Pat Poston *Whitey* · Nancy Lee Noble *Honey-Pot* · Christie Wagner *Karen* · Rodney Bedell *Ted* · Ruby Tuesday *Terry* ■ *Dir* Herschell Gordon Lewis · *Scr* Louise Downe

U SUITABLE FOR ALL   Uc SUITABLE ESPECIALLY FOR YOUNG CHILDREN (DVD ONLY)   PG PARENTAL GUIDANCE   12A UNDER 12s TO BE ACCOMPANIED (CINEMA ONLY)

She Done Him Wrong
★★★★ PG

Comedy   1933 · US · BW · 62min

This is probably the classic Mae West movie and a perfect opportunity to make the acquaintance of "the finest woman that ever walked the streets". The truly outrageous West is today mainly regarded as a camp icon. The predatory creature known as Lady Lou in this opus was once West's infamous "Diamond Lil" in her own play, but the requirements of both national and local censors caused the modification of nickname and dialogue for the movie. Young Cary Grant is the person she asks to "come up sometime and see me", a phrase that is now well established as part of cinema iconography. TS **DVD**

Mae West *Lady Lou* · Cary Grant *Captain Cummings* · Owen Moore *Chick Clark* · Gilbert Roland *Serge Starieff* · Noah Beery Sr [Noah Beery] *Gus Jordan* · David Landau *Dan Flynn* ■ *Dir* Lowell Sherman · *Scr* Mae West, Harvey Thew, John Bright, from the play *Diamond Lil* by Mae West

She Freak
★ 18

Cult horror   1967 · US · Colour · 104min

Director Byron Mabe lets this redneck freak tale slip from promising camp trash into complete ineptitude. While the story – an ambitious greasy spoon waitress marries the owner of a seedy side show with gruesome results – is not without its moments, you can see the money drain away from the micro-budget as this grade Z flick staggers to its rip-off climax. AJ Violence, sex scenes. **DVD**

Claire Brennen *Jade Cochran* · Lee Raymond *Blackie Fleming* · Lynn Courtney *Pat Mullins* · Bill McKinney *Steve S* John · Van Teen *Babcock* · Felix Silla *Shortie* ■ *Dir* Byron Mabe · *Scr* David F Friedman

She Hate Me
★★ 15

Comedy drama   2004 · US/Fr · Colour · 132min

Director Spike Lee's messy comedy drama is excruciatingly clichéd and so unconventionally constructed that it plays like a handful of genre movies all competing for supremacy. Suave Anthony Mackie goes into unofficial business by impregnating rich lesbians after being sacked as a whistle-blower from a corporation pushing a defective Aids vaccine. There are some very funny moments, but the feature's increasing ludicrousness and Lee's insistence on pandering to crude male fantasies undermine any serious messages. SF Swearing, sex scenes. **DVD**

Anthony Mackie *John Henry "Jack" Armstrong* · Kerry Washington *Fatima Goodrich* · Ellen Barkin *Margo Chadwick* · Monica Bellucci *Simona Bonasera* · Jim Brown *Geronimo Armstrong* · Ossie Davis *Judge Buchanan* · Brian Dennehy *Chairman Church* · Woody Harrelson *Leland Powell* · Bai Ling *Oni* · John Turturro *Don Angelo Bonasera* · Chiwetel Ejiofor *Frank Wills* ■ *Dir* Spike Lee · *Scr* Michael Genet, Spike Lee, from a story by Michael Genet

She Loves Me Not
★★★

Musical comedy   1934 · US · BW · 80min

Showgirl Miriam Hopkins, fleeing from mobsters, hides out in a boys' college in this enjoyable early musical starring Bing Crosby. Though Hopkins is basically miscast as a burlesque queen, the complications as she is forced to masquerade as a male are fun, and Crosby oozes affable charm. Kitty Carlisle has her best screen role, and gets to introduce with Crosby *Love in Bloom*, which reached number one in the hit parade. TV

Bing Crosby *Paul Lawton* · Miriam Hopkins *Curly Flagg* · Kitty Carlisle *Midge Mercer* · Edward Nugent *Buzz Jones* · Henry Stephenson *Dean Mercer* · Warren Hymer *Mugg Schnitzel* · Lynne Overman *Gus McNeal* ■ *Dir* Elliott Nugent · *Scr* Benjamin Glazer, from the play by Lindsay Howard, from the novel by Edward Hope

She Married Her Boss
★★★ U

Screwball comedy   1935 · US · BW · 88min

Claudette Colbert shines under the deft and witty direction of Gregory La Cava, with a screenplay by Columbia's arch-sophisticate Sidney Buchman. Melvyn Douglas is the titular "boss", and Colbert has to cope with his awful daughter (Edith Fellows) and his drama queen of a sister (Katherine Alexander). The movie is genuinely funny but runs out of comedic steam towards the end. Nevertheless, there are some wonderful performances, most notably Raymond Walburn as a squiffy butler. TS

Claudette Colbert *Julia Scott* · Michael Bartlett *Lonnie Rogers* · Melvyn Douglas *Richard Barclay* · Raymond Walburn *Franklin* · Jean Dixon *Martha* · Katherine Alexander *Gertrude* · Edith Fellows *Annabel* ■ *Dir* Gregory La Cava · *Scr* Sidney Buchman, from the story by Thyra Samter Winslow

She-Monkeys
★★★ 12A

Drama   2011 · Swe/Den · Colour · 83min

Jealousy, competitiveness and burgeoning sexuality push two teenage girls into a complex power struggle in this slow-moving yet provocative coming-of-age drama. An impressive calling card for first-time director Lisa Aschan, this Swedish film sees control freak Emma (Mathilda Paradeiser) form a challenging friendship with a self-assured fellow gymnast (Linda Molin). The pair's increasingly intense feelings are mirrored in Emma's seven-year-old sister Sara (Isabella Lindquist), who grapples with a crush on her babysitting cousin in scenes that progress from darkly amusing to deeply uncomfortable. But while raging female hormones govern the narrative, the feature and its performances remain pleasingly low-key, focusing on gestures and facial expressions rather than dialogue or action. SF Swedish +subtitles.

Mathilda Paradeiser *Emma* · Linda Molin *Cassandra* · Isabella Lindquist *Sara* · Sergej Merkusjev *Ivan* · Adam Lundgren *Jens* ■ *Dir* Lisa Aschan · *Scr* Josefine Adolfsson, Lisa Aschan

She Wore a Yellow Ribbon
★★★★★ PG

Western   1949 · US · Colour · 99min

This first-class cavalry western from director John Ford contains some of John Wayne's finest screen moments. Wayne is marvellously in character as retiring commander Nathan Brittles, who acts on his own to prevent an American Indian war. It's a performance that even those vehemently anti-Wayne, and all he stood for, feel forced to admire. This is one of the great Technicolor movies, justly winning an Oscar for cinematography that expertly captures Ford's favourite Monument Valley locations. There's also a stirring, majestic soundtrack and a mighty fine supporting cast. This is a deeply satisfying work by one of cinema's greatest film-makers. TS **DVD**

John Wayne *Captain Brittles* · Joanne Dru *Olivia Dandridge* · John Agar *Lieutenant Cohill* · Ben Johnson (1) *Tyree* · Harry Carey Jr *Lieutenant Pennell* · Victor McLaglen *Sergeant Quincannon* · Mildred Natwick *Mrs Allshard* · Arthur Shields *Dr O'Laughlin* · Harry Woods *Toucey Rynders* ■ *Dir* John Ford · *Scr* Frank Nugent, Laurence Stallings, from the stories *War Party* and *The Big Hunt* by James Warner Bellah · *Cinematographer* Winton Hoch [Winton C Hoch]

Sheena
★★ 15

Romantic adventure   1984 · US/UK · Colour · 111min

Tanya Roberts is hopelessly miscast as the orphan raised by African natives in this lacklustre adaptation of the 1930s jungle woman comic strip. Roberts learns how to talk to animals and use mystical powers to protect her people against political intrigue and an intrusive newsreel crew. John Guillermin directs the colourful adventure yarn with a straight face and completely avoids the campy tone such exotica cries out for. AJ

Tanya Roberts *Sheena* · Ted Wass *Vic Casey* · Donovan Scott *Fletcher* · Elizabeth of Toro *Shaman* · France Zobda *Countess Zanda* · Trevor Thomas *Prince Otwani* · Clifton Jones *King Jabalani* ■ *Dir* John Guillermin · *Scr* David Newman, Lorenzo Semple Jr · *Music* Richard Hartley

The Sheep Has Five Legs
★★★

Comedy   1954 · Fr · BW · 107min

Seizing the opportunity to demonstrate his genius for comic characterisation, Fernandel takes on six roles in this engaging family album, compiled by Henri Verneuil. In addition to playing the disapproving vitner father, he also essays the five sons, who are reunited on their 40th birthday. The vignettes involving the prissy beautician and the Parisian agony aunt are unremarkable, but Fernandel excels as the hypochondriac window cleaner feuding with a grasping undertaker, the old salt reduced to betting on flies landing on sugar lumps, and the priest weary of being reminded he resembles Don Camillo (a part the star made famous). DP French +subtitles.

Fernandel *Papa Saint Forget* · Delmont [Edouard Delmont] *Dr Bollene* · Louis De Funès *Pilate, the undertaker* ■ *Dir* Henri Verneuil · *Scr* Albert Valentin

The Sheepman
★★★★ U

Comedy western   1958 · US · Colour · 85min

Directed with wit and style by veteran George Marshall, this wonderful Glenn Ford comedy western co-stars a splendidly raucous and unusually sympathetic Shirley MacLaine. The opening is a real humdinger and sets the style for the rest of the movie, as Ford's milk-drinking sheep farmer picks a fight with local character Mickey Shaughnessy, proving that he's not a man to trifle with. This is a reminder that Ford was not only Hollywood's most popular star of this period, but one of America's finest. TS

Glenn Ford *Jason Sweet* · Shirley MacLaine *Dell Payton* · Leslie Nielsen *Johnny Bledsoe* · Mickey Shaughnessy *Jumbo McCall* · Edgar Buchanan *Milt Masters* · Willis Bouchey *Mr Payton* · Pernell Roberts *Choctaw* · Slim Pickens *Marshal* ■ *Dir* George Marshall · *Scr* William Bowers, James Edward Grant, William Roberts, from a story by James Edward Grant

The Sheik
★★★★ PG

Silent adventure melodrama
1921 · US · BW · 86min

Rudolph Valentino achieved iconic status with his performance as the dashing Ahmed Ben Hassan in this overheated desert melodrama. Female fans swooned as he delivered Agnes Ayres from the clutches of the lascivious Walter Long, while their dates looked on in disbelief at his effete heroics and impassioned wooing. There were even those who demanded the film should be banned for its dubious morality and acceptance of miscegenation. Yet, for all its surface glamour and romantic abandon, the story hurtles towards a rather traditional conclusion. DP **DVD**

Agnes Ayres *Diana Mayo* · Rudolph Valentino *Sheik Ahmed Ben Hassan* · Adolphe Menjou *Raoul de Saint Hubert* · Walter Long *Omair* · Lucien Littlefield *Gaston* ■ *Dir* George Melford · *Scr* Monte M Katterjohn, from the novel by Edith Maude Hull

Sheitan
★★ 18

Horror   2006 · Fr · Colour · 87min

There are overtones of both *Deliverance* and *The Hills Have Eyes* in this occasionally unnerving horror outing from debuting director Kim Chapiron. Three oversexed clubbers and their barmaid friend are invited to an out-of-the-way country mansion by enigmatic beauty Eve (Roxane Mesquida) at Christmas. Tales of satanic impregnation and a group of inbred locals add to the unsettling nature of the tale, which certainly has its creepy moments. However, the unsympathetic male protagonists mean you really don't care about their welfare when the going gets gory. JA French +subtitles. **DVD**

Vincent Cassel *Joseph* · Olivier Barthelemy [Olivier Barthélémy] *Bart* · Roxane Mesquida *Eve* · Nico Le Phat Tan *Thai* · Ladj Ly *Ladj* · Leila Bekhti *Yasmine* · Monica Bellucci *La belle vampiresse* ■ *Dir* Kim Chapiron · *Scr* Kim Chapiron, Christian Chapiron

Shelf Life
★★★

Comedy drama   1993 · US · Colour · 83min

On the day President Kennedy is assassinated, a suburban 1960s family retreat to their bomb shelter and stay there for 30 years. When their parents die of food poisoning, the three children resort to acting out scenes from their favourite TV shows to stay sane. Based on their play, the stars – Jim Turner, O-Lan Jones and Andrea Stein – wrote the script that was filmed on one claustrophobic set by cult director Paul Bartel. Much surreal fun is had when the trio indulge in cultural rituals based upon the famous sitcoms of the era. AJ

Andrea Stein *Pam/Mrs St Cloud* · O-Lan Jones *Tina* · Jim Turner *Scotty/Mr St Cloud* · Paul Bartel (1) *Various Apparitions* ■ *Dir* Paul Bartel (1) · *Scr* Jim Turner, O-Lan Jones, Andrea Stein, from their play

Shell
★★ 15

Drama   2012 · UK/Ger · Colour · 87min

Writer/director Scott Graham's film examines a father and daughter's austere existence running a petrol station on a remote road in the Highlands of Scotland. Chloe Pirrie delivers a sensitive, spirited performance as the teenage Shell, but the way the film uses her uncomplicated bond with her epileptic dad (Joseph Mawle, battling with a difficult role) seems like glib dramatic gloss on an unpalatable situation. Graham has an eye for an elegant composition and is able to construct a distinctive sense of place, but he clearly needs to work harder on the basics of putting a plot together. TJ **DVD** **BLU**

Chloe Pirrie *Shell* · Joseph Mawle *Pete* · Michael Smiley *Hugh* · Iain De Caestecker *Adam* · Paul Hickey [Paul Thomas Hickey] *Robert* ■ *Dir/Scr* Scott Graham

She'll Be Wearing Pink Pyjamas
★★ 15

Comedy drama   1984 · UK · Colour · 86min

All talk and no trousers, pyjama or otherwise, in this tiresome natter-fest about a bunch of women who go on a wilderness survival course as part of a company "bonding" scheme. Julie Walters stars and, as always, gives it her all. But neither she nor the supporting girls are particularly well served by the tedious dialogue and aimless plotting. The awful title doesn't help. DA **DVD**

Julie Walters *Fran* · Anthony Higgins *Tom* · Jane Evers *Catherine* · Janet Henfrey *Lucy* · Paula Jacobs *Doreen* · Penelope Nice *Ann* · Maureen O'Brien *Joan* · Alyson Spiro *Anita* ■ *Dir* John Goldschmidt · *Scr* Eva Hardy

She'll Have to Go
★★ U

Comedy   1961 · UK · BW · 86min

Known in the States as *Maid for Murder*, this mediocre comedy was something of a family affair. The Asher brothers co-produced the picture, with Robert also directing and his younger sibling, Jack, as cinematographer. They might have been better off having a crack at the script, too, as John Waterhouse's adaptation is so slipshod that not even Hattie Jacques can bring it to life. But most sympathy goes to Jean-Luc Godard's then wife Anna Karina, who looks lost fighting off gold-digging brothers Bob Monkhouse and Alfred Marks. DP **DVD**

Bob Monkhouse *Francis Oberon* · Alfred Marks *Douglas Oberon* · Hattie Jacques *Miss Richards* · Anna Karina *Toni* · Dennis Lotis *Gilbert* · Graham Stark *Arnold* · Clive Dunn *Chemist* ■ *Dir* Robert Asher · *Scr* John Waterhouse, from the play *We Must Kill Toni* by Ian Stuart Black

Shelter
★ 15

Horror thriller   2008 · US · Colour · 107min

A psychologist who's built her career debunking the notion of multiple-

S

personality disorders finds herself stumped by a unique patient in this incoherent horror puzzler. Julianne Moore furrows her brow and looks deeply concerned as the doctor, while Jonathan Rhys Meyers plays it wide-eyed as the man who mysteriously switches into the personae of a string of murder victims. But their efforts are squandered on this flimsy farrago that wastes their time and ours. TJ DVD SD

Julianne Moore *Dr Cara Jessup* • Jonathan Rhys Meyers *David Bernburg/Adam Saber/Wesley Crite* • Frances Conroy *Mrs Bernburg* • Jeffrey DeMunn *Dr Harding* ■ *Dir* Marlind & Stein [Mans Marlind], Marlind & Stein [Bjorn Stein] • *Scr* Michael Cooney

Shelter ★★★ 18
Drama   2014 · US · Colour · 101min

This well-intentioned drama follows two homeless people as they cope with life on the streets of New York. A compassionate immigrant who earns money as a street drummer encounters an emaciated heroin addict who begs for spare change with a sign that says "I used to be someone". The two of them become friends, and writer/director Paul Bettany (yes, that Paul Bettany) ensures that their path is paved with unpleasant obstacles. It's fairly grim, but it is surprisingly romantic in places and does enough to keep you engaged. SC DVD

Jennifer Connelly *Hannah* • Anthony Mackie *Tahir* • Scott Johnsen *Terry* • Alok Tewari *Abdul* • Rob Morgan *Franklin* ■ *Dir/Scr* Paul Bettany

The Sheltering Sky ★★★ 18
Drama   1990 · UK/It · Colour · 132min

Bernardo Bertolucci directs this immensely ambitious film of Paul Bowles's strange, mystical, metaphysical novel. The tale concerns an American married couple (John Malkovich and Debra Winger) and a friend (Campbell Scott) touring North Africa in 1947 in search of the mystery that is the desert. Filmed in arduous conditions in Algeria and Niger, the movie tries to be bookish and introspective yet full of vast landscapes. Despite Winger's committed, intensely physical performance, it remains a rather soulless and aloof experience. AT Swearing, violence, sex scenes, nudity. DVD

Debra Winger *Kit Moresby* • John Malkovich *Port Moresby* • Campbell Scott *George Tunner* • Jill Bennett *Mrs Lyle* • Timothy Spall *Eric Lyle* • Eric Vu-An *Belqassim* • Paul Bowles *Narrator* ■ *Dir* Bernardo Bertolucci • *Scr* Mark Peploe, Bernardo Bertolucci, from the novel by Paul Bowles • *Cinematographer* Vittorio Storaro

Shenandoah ★★★★ PG
Western   1965 · US · Colour · 100min

This marvellous and moving late western features a superb performance from James Stewart as a widower trying to ignore the Civil War until the tide of history washes over his whole family. Unusually, the deliberate sentimentality does work, and the scene in which Stewart offers a moving soliloquy beside his wife's grave was so popular that it was released on record. Director Andrew V McLaglen achieves a real sense of scale here, and the supporting cast, including many veterans from John Ford's repertory company, is well chosen. TS DVD

James Stewart *Charlie Anderson* • Doug McClure *Sam* • Glenn Corbett *Jacob* • Patrick Wayne *James* • Phillip Alford *Boy* • Katharine Ross *Ann* • Rosemary Forsyth *Jennie* • Charles Robinson [Charles Knox Robinson] *Nathan* • George Kennedy *Colonel Fairchild* ■ *Dir* Andrew V McLaglen • *Scr* James Lee Barrett

The Shepherd ★★ 15
Action thriller   2008 · US · Colour · 90min

Any film that stars Jean-Claude Van Damme busting heads while his pet rabbit watches can't be all bad. Released just before *JCVD* reworked Van Damme's on-screen persona, this strictly conventional action thriller sees the star tracking down drug-trafficking bad guys. The silly plot detracts from the real meat of the movie, the well-choreographed fight sequences

and shoot-outs. British actor Scott Adkins provides solid support as Van Damme's chief adversary, his martial arts prowess something of a surprise for anyone who remembers him from *Holby City*. JR Violence, swearing, sexual references, nudity. DVD

Jean-Claude Van Damme *Jack Robideaux* • Scott Adkins *Karp* • Stephen Lord *Meyers* • Gary McDonald *Billy Pawnell* • Natalie J Robb *Captain Ramona Garcia* ■ *Dir* Isaac Florentine • *Scr* Cade Courtley, Joe Gayton

The Shepherd of the Hills ★★★ PG
Adventure   1941 · US · Colour · 93min

The heavyweight presence of John Wayne helps make this one of the best adaptations of Harold Bell Wright's Missouri-set novel. Wayne stars as the young moonshiner who blames his absent father for the death of his mother and spends his days plotting revenge. Betty Field plays the girl who won't marry Wayne while he's consumed with hate. Director Henry Hathaway just stands back and lets the splendid cast get on with it. JA DVD

John Wayne *Young Matt Matthews* • Betty Field *Sammy Lane* • Harry Carey *Daniel Howitt* • Beulah Bondi *Aunt Mollie* • James Barton *Old Matt* • Samuel S Hinds *Andy Beeler* • Marjorie Main *Granny Becky* • Ward Bond *Wash Gibbs* ■ *Dir* Henry Hathaway • *Scr* Grover Jones, Stuart Anthony, from the novel by Harold Bell Wright

Shepherd on the Rock ★★ PG
Drama   1995 · Can · Colour · 95min

Bernard Hill stars as a Scottish shepherd who takes on a cabal of shiftless property developers. But Bob Keen's film is less interested in environmental issues than the "us and them" tension of the similarly themed *Local Hero*, as Hill's pastoral principles frustrate the ambitions of his neighbours. The scenery's sublime, the performances polished, but the plot is a touch too predictable. DP Some violence

Bernard Hill *Tam Ferrier* • John Bowles *Ewan* • Betsy Brantley *Jean* • Doug Bradley *James Culzean* • Mark McKenna *Andy Murray* • Oliver Parker *Simon McIntyre* ■ *Dir* Bob Keen

The Sheriff of Fractured Jaw ★★★★ U
Comedy western   1958 · UK · Colour · 103min

This is the first western shot in Spain, its standing set later used for Sergio Leone's *Dollars* trilogy. The title role in this super spoof is played by British actor Kenneth More at his most diffident, and the director is the great Raoul Walsh, who films in the grand tradition of the genre. Jayne Mansfield, the 1950s sex symbol, provides the love interest and there's a touching musical interlude in which she croons *In the Valley of Love*, dubbed by Connie Francis. The film's soundtrack is especially witty, and there's an entertaining Anglo-American supporting cast. TS

Kenneth More *Jonathan Tibbs* • Jayne Mansfield *Kate* • Henry Hull *Mayor Masters* • William Campbell *Keno* • Bruce Cabot *Jack* • Robert Morley *Uncle Lucius* • Ronald Squire *Toynbee* • David Horne *James* ■ *Dir* Raoul Walsh • *Scr* Arthur Dales [Howard Dimsdale], from a short story by Jacob Hay • *Music* Robert Farnon

Sheriff of Sage Valley ★★ U
Western   1942 · US · BW · 55min

Buster Crabbe was an Olympic swimmer who played hero figures Tarzan, Flash Gordon and Buck Rogers in series and serials throughout the 1930s that are still recalled with affectionate nostalgia today. But Crabbe was no actor, and he soon became a leading man in B-westerns, of which this is a typical example: skimpy-on-plot but action-packed. TS

Buster Crabbe [Larry "Buster" Crabbe] *Billy The Kid/Kansas Ed* • Al St John *Fuzzy Jones* • Tex O'Brien *Jeff* • Maxine Leslie *Janet* ■ *Dir* Sherman Scott [Sam Newfield] • *Scr* George W Sayre, Milton Raison

Sherlock Holmes ★★★
Mystery   1932 · US · BW · 62min

Call it "the Case of the Clueless Sleuth". Before Basil Rathbone put his definitive imprint on Conan Doyle's famous private detective, matinée idol Clive Brook was a refined and far too discreet Holmes, with Reginald Owen as a very ineffectual Dr Watson. The film loses a lot of gaslight appeal as Chicago gangsters, brought in by the monstrous Moriarty, invade a bewildered London. Holmes's nemesis is given such a wonderfully OTT presence by Ernest Torrence that, in the end, you almost hope he'll win. TH

Clive Brook *Sherlock Holmes* • Ernest Torrence *Professor Moriarty* • Reginald Owen *Dr Watson* • Miriam Jordan *Alice Faulkner* • Howard Leeds *Little Billy* • Alan Mowbray *Gore-King* ■ *Dir* William K Howard • *Scr* Bertram Milhauser, from a play by William Gillette, from stories by Sir Arthur Conan Doyle

Sherlock Holmes ★★★★ 12
Period mystery thriller
2009 · Ger/US/Aus · Colour · 123min

Stuffy period mystery this is not, as director Guy Ritchie approaches his take on Baker Street's finest in the manner of *Lethal Weapon*. Though this may rankle with fans of the original Conan Doyle stories, Robert Downey Jr at least brings his undisputed charisma to bear in his portrayal of the legendary detective. As Watson, Jude Law stands firm in the pair's ongoing verbal sparring match, and the two leads share a mischievous chemistry. A typically sinister Mark Strong impresses, too, as back-from-the-dead villain Lord Blackwood, and the views of Victorian London are as seductive as the leads, though there's little time to look between all the fights and explosions. SP Violence. DVD Blu

Robert Downey Jr *Sherlock Holmes* • Jude Law *Dr John Watson* • Rachel McAdams *Irene Adler* • Mark Strong *Lord Blackwood* • Eddie Marsan *Inspector Lestrade* • Kelly Reilly *Mary Morstan* • William Hope *John Standish* • James Fox *Sir Thomas Rotheram* • Geraldine James *Mrs Hudson* ■ *Dir* Guy Ritchie • *Scr* Michael Robert Johnson, Simon Kinberg, Anthony Peckham, from a story by Lionel Wigram, Johnson, from characters by Sir Arthur Conan Doyle • *Cinematographer* Philippe Rousselot • *Production Designers* Sarah Greenwood, Katie Spencer

Sherlock Holmes: a Game of Shadows ★★★ 12
Period mystery thriller
2011 · US · Colour · 123min

Robert Downey Jr adopts the mantle of Britain's most famous fictional detective once again, although, as in his previous outing, it is more comic book than Conan Doyle. His Holmes is as physical as he is cerebral and the film relies heavily on Downey Jr's natural charm and comic timing. It is 1891 and Holmes and Dr Watson (Jude Law) are required to travel across western Europe to stop the evil genius Professor Moriarty (Jared Harris) from starting the First World War early. The sets are spectacular and many of the characterisations highly entertaining, though the actual detective work is visualised in fast-forward as if it were an MTV video and the whole thing is half an hour too long. BP Violence, brief nudity. DVD Blu

Robert Downey Jr *Sherlock Holmes* • Jude Law *Dr John Watson* • Jared Harris *Professor James Moriarty* • Rachel McAdams *Irene Adler* • Stephen Fry *Mycroft Holmes* • Eddie Marsan *Inspector Lestrade* • Geraldine James *Mrs Hudson* ■ *Dir* Guy Ritchie • *Scr* Kieran Mulroney, Michele Mulroney, from characters by Sir Arthur Conan Doyle • *Music* Hans Zimmer

Sherlock Holmes and the Deadly Necklace ★ 12
Mystery   1962 · W Ger/Fr/It · BW · 82min

Hammer stars Christopher Lee and Thorley Walters and acclaimed Hammer director Terence Fisher, went to Germany to make this Holmes adventure. The plot of this badly edited hotch-potch of clichéd nonsense revolves around Professor

Moriarty's theft of a priceless necklace. Both English and German versions were released, but Lee disowned the whole unpalatable affair because his Holmes was abysmally dubbed in both with high-pitched, nasal vocals. A dreadful disaster. AJ DVD

Christopher Lee *Sherlock Holmes* • Thorley Walters *Dr Watson* • Senta Berger *Ellen Blackburn* • Hans Söhnker *Professor Moriarty* • Hans Nielsen *Inspector Cooper* • Ivan Desny *Paul King* • Leon Askin *Chauffeur Charles* • Wolfgang Lukschy *Peter Blackburn* ■ *Dir* Terence Fisher, Frank Winterstein • *Scr* Curt Siodmak, from the story *The Valley of Fear* by Sir Arthur Conan Doyle

Sherlock Holmes and the Secret Weapon ★★★ PG
Mystery   1942 · US · BW · 68min

The Nazis stood no chance once they knew they were up against the Allies' own secret weapon, Basil Rathbone as Holmes, ably assisted as always by Nigel Bruce as Dr Watson. This modernised, morale-boosting story draws only a fraction of the plot from Sir Arthur Conan Doyle's source story *The Dancing Men*, as Holmes and Watson search for a unique bombsight. As the baleful Moriarty, Lionel Atwill walks the corridors of glower with real malevolence. TH DVD

Basil Rathbone *Sherlock Holmes* • Nigel Bruce *Dr Watson* • Kaaren Verne *Charlotte Eberli* • Lionel Atwill *Professor Moriarty* • William Post Jr *Dr Franz Tobel* • Dennis Hoey *Inspector Lestrade* ■ *Dir* Roy William Neill • *Scr* Edward T Lowe, Scott Darling, Edmund L Hartmann, from the story *The Dancing Men* by Sir Arthur Conan Doyle

Sherlock Holmes and the Spider Woman ★★★ U
Mystery   1944 · US · BW · 59min

The serene elegance of Basil Rathbone as Holmes is just a tad ruffled when he's set up in a shooting gallery by the great Gale Sondergaard – as vicious a foe as Holmes has faced in a film as effective as any in the series. The only fly, or flaw, in the web is that Nigel Bruce's Dr Watson is at his most boringly bumbling. TH DVD

Basil Rathbone *Sherlock Holmes* • Nigel Bruce *Dr Watson* • Gale Sondergaard *Andrea Spedding* • Dennis Hoey *Inspector Lestrade* • Vernon Downing *Norman Locke* • Alec Craig *Radlik* • Arthur Hohl *Adam Gilflower* ■ *Dir* Roy William Neill • *Scr* Bertram Millhauser, from the story *The Sign of the Four* by Sir Arthur Conan Doyle

Sherlock Holmes and the Voice of Terror ★★ U
Mystery   1942 · US · BW · 62min

This was the first of Universal's 11-film series featuring Basil Rathbone and Nigel Bruce as the slender sleuth and his rotund sidekick, though the two actors had already played the roles in two films for 20th Century-Fox. The wartime plot is simplistic, with Holmes searching for the traitor in the government who is supplying a Nazi broadcaster with information. Laborious. TH DVD

Basil Rathbone *Sherlock Holmes* • Nigel Bruce *Dr Watson* • Evelyn Ankers *Kitty* • Reginald Denny *Sir Evan Barham* • Montagu Love *General Jerome Lawford* • Henry Daniell *Anthony Lloyd* • Thomas Gomez *RF Meade* ■ *Dir* John Rawlins • *Scr* Lynn Riggs, John Bright, Robert Andrews, from the story *His Last Bow* by Sir Arthur Conan Doyle

Sherlock Holmes Faces Death ★★★ U
Mystery   1943 · US · BW · 65min

In one of the best of the Basil Rathbone/Nigel Bruce movies, a clock strikes 13 and murder comes in triplicate. For once Dr Watson is the plot's prime mover, in charge of an army officers' convalescent home at Musgrave Manor where shell-shocked patients are the cover for misdeeds in a hidden cellar. It's one of the most old-fashioned of the series, which explains the craftsmanlike grip it exerts. TH DVD

Basil Rathbone *Sherlock Holmes* • Nigel Bruce *Dr Watson* • Dennis Hoey *Inspector Lestrade* • Arthur Margetson *Dr Sexton* • Hillary Brooke *Sally Musgrave* • Halliwell Hobbes *Brunton, the butler* • Minna Phillips *Mrs Howells* ■ *Dir* Roy

William Neill • *Scr* Bertram Millhauser, from the story *The Musgrave Ritual* by Sir Arthur Conan Doyle

Sherlock Holmes in New York ★★★ U

Mystery 1976 · US · Colour · 98min

Roger Moore as Sherlock Holmes, Patrick Macnee as Dr Watson and John Huston as Professor Moriarty enliven this TV movie outing for Conan Doyle's inimitable hero, which involves Huston messing with the world's gold supply. Having already created one of the modern cinema's great villains – Noah Cross in *Chinatown* – Huston slips into Moriarty's wardrobe with ease and dominates this enjoyable movie. AT *DVD*

Roger Moore *Sherlock Holmes* • John Huston *Professor James Moriarty* • Patrick Macnee *Dr John Watson* • Gig Young *Mortimer McGraw* • Charlotte Rampling *Irene Adler* • David Huddleston *Inspector Lafferty* • Signe Hasso *Fraulein Reichenbach* • Jackie Coogan *Hotel Haymarket proprietor* ■ *Dir* Boris Sagal • *Scr* Alvin Sapinsley, from characters by Sir Arthur Conan Doyle

Sherlock Holmes in Washington ★★ U

Mystery 1943 · US · BW · 68min

Sherlock Holmes (Basil Rathbone) smokes a cigarette while Dr Watson (Nigel Bruce) puffs on his pipe in the first of the series not connected, however tenuously, to a story by Arthur Conan Doyle. A weakish update of the character, Holmes is after a microfilm passed to the wrong stranger on a train and a prime target for nasty Nazis. Holmes gets to quote Winston Churchill and waxes paternal about democracy. TH *DVD*

Basil Rathbone *Sherlock Holmes* • Nigel Bruce *Dr Watson* • Marjorie Lord *Nancy Partridge* • Henry Daniell *William Easter* • George Zucco *Stanley* • John Archer *Lt Peter Merriam* • Gavin Muir *Bart Lang* ■ *Dir* Roy William Neill • *Scr* Bertram Millhauser, Lynn Riggs, from a story by Bertram Millhauser, from characters by Sir Arthur Conan Doyle

Sherlock Holmes Returns ★★

Mystery thriller 1993 · US · Colour

This routine TV-movie mystery thriller has the great sleuth awakening from suspended animation for an adventure in the modern world. In this instance, Holmes (played by a dapper Anthony Higgins) has to tackle the descendants of his old adversary Moriarty, as he heads to 1994 Baker Street in San Francisco to lock horns with James Moriarty Booth (played by Ken Pogue). DP

Anthony Higgins *Sherlock Holmes* • Debrah Farentino *Amy Winslow* • Mark Adair-Rios *Zapper* • Ken Pogue *James Moriarty Booth* • Joy Coghill *Mrs Hudson* • Jorge Vargas *Slick* ■ *Dir* Kenneth Johnson • *Scr* Kenneth Johnson, from the character created by Sir Arthur Conan Doyle

Sherlock Junior ★★★★★ U

Silent comedy 1924 · US · BW · 41min

This is one of Buster Keaton's finest comedies, certainly his most inventive and technically audacious. He plays an amateur detective and cinema projectionist who dreams himself into the movie he is showing and, hopefully, into the arms of the girl he loves. As early as 1924 Keaton recognised the cinema's role as escapism in society, and constructed an entire film about it (although the early sequences were directed by Roscoe Arbuckle). The result is richly romantic and oddly educational: audiences were shown all the tricks of the trade, notably editing, back projection and other special effects. But mostly it works as a brilliant comedy, full of the clever bits of business and ambitious stunts one associates with Keaton. AT *DVD*

Buster Keaton *Projectionist* • Kathryn McGuire *His fiancée* • Joseph Keaton [Joe Keaton] *Her father* • Ward Crane *Rival* • Erwin Connelly *Handyman/butler* ■ *Dir* Buster Keaton • *Scr* Clyde Bruckman, Jean Havez, Joseph Mitchell

Sherpa ★★★★ 15

Documentary 2015 · Aus/Nep · Colour · 96min

Combining stunning vistas with intimate insights, Jennifer Peedom's compelling account of life on Mount Everest is an astute appreciation of the Sherpa existence and their value to a $350 million business that often takes them for granted. As filming commenced, an avalanche above base camp claimed the lives of 16 Sherpas. The documentary is a moving record of how the guides, many of them veterans, were forced to reappraise their attitudes to the economic, spiritual and security aspects of their livelihood. DP English, Nepali +subtitles. Swearing.

■ *Dir/Scr* Jennifer Peedom

Sherrybaby ★★★ 15

Drama 2006 · US · Colour · 91min

Maggie Gyllenhaal thrills in this objective yet sympathetic tale, as Sherry Swanson, a 20-something ex-con who tries to reclaim her life and the love of her young daughter. Writer/director Laurie Collyer doesn't flinch from showing the ugly side of her struggle, as Sherry tries to buy her little girl's affections, takes abuse from her parole officer and trades sexual favours for the chance of a good job. Disappointment hangs heavily over the action, with the lure of drugs and disturbing shadows from Sherry's past ever present. Ultimately, the film pivots on the question of what a mother will do for the love of her child. Gyllenhaal's performance is both spectacular and naturalistic – and as a result this is much more watchable than the harrowing subject matter may suggest. KK Swearing, drug abuse. *DVD*

Maggie Gyllenhaal *Sherry Swanson* • Brad William Henke *Bobby Swanson* • Danny Trejo *Dean Walker* • Giancarlo Esposito *Parole Officer Hernandez* • Ryan Simpkins *Alexis Parks* • Bridget Barkan *Lynette Swanson* • Sam Bottoms *Bob Swanson Sr* ■ *Dir/Scr* Laurie Collyer

She's All That ★★★ 12

Romantic comedy 1999 · US · Colour · 95min

This preposterous but fun comedy has Rachael Leigh Cook as the gawky teen who gets a makeover from popular soccer star Freddie Prinze Jr. He's made a secret bet with his pals that he can turn even the most unlikely girl in their high school into a prom queen. Both the leads are enjoyable, but equally worth catching are the supporting stars, especially Matthew Lillard as an egotistical oaf, Anna Paquin as Prinze's sister and Kieran Culkin as Cook's gutsy younger brother. JB Swearing. *DVD*

Freddie Prinze Jr *Zack Siler* • Rachael Leigh Cook *Laney Boggs* • Matthew Lillard *Brock Hudson* • Paul Walker *Dean Sampson* • Jodi Lyn O'Keefe *Taylor Vaughan* • Kevin Pollak *Wayne Boggs* • Kieran Culkin *Simon Boggs* • Anna Paquin *Mackenzie Siler* ■ *Dir* Robert Iscove • *Scr* R Lee Fleming Jr

She's Funny That Way ★★ 12

Comedy 2014 · US/Ger · Colour · 89min

Veteran writer/director Peter Bogdanovich looks to the screwball comedies of the 1930s and 40s for inspiration in the tale of rising starlet Izzy (Imogen Poots) and neurotic director Albert (Owen Wilson) who makes the mistake of bedding her. In fact the story is scattered much wider and spread a lot thinner than that, to include a great cast – Kathryn Hahn, Rhys Ifans and Jennifer Aniston – that's given witty dialogue but whose characters are too roughly drawn. Viewers are more likely to find this funny in the sense of strange. SP Swearing, sexual references.

Owen Wilson *Arnold Albertson* • Imogen Poots *Isabella Patterson/"Izzy"/"Glowstick"* • Jennifer Aniston *Jane Claremont* • Kathryn Hahn *Delta Simmons* • Will Forte *Joshua Fleet* • Rhys Ifans *Seth Gilbert* ■ *Dir* Peter Bogdanovich • *Scr* Peter Bogdanovich, Louise Stratten

She's Gotta Have It ★★★★ 18

Comedy drama 1986 · US · BW and Colour · 80min

Spike Lee's directorial debut hasn't lost any of its vitality over the years and remains his most genuinely entertaining work, refreshingly free of much of the political rhetoric which occasionally overcomes his other projects. Tracy Camila Johns is the strong willed young woman who not only has to have it, but also refuses to be tied down to one of three suitors out to tame her. Lee has plenty of fun deflating the macho egos on parade, grabbing many of the best lines for himself as the irritatingly persistent Mars Blackmon. Vividly shot in black and white apart from one lovely colour sequence at the end. JF Swearing, nudity. *DVD*

Tracy Camila Johns *Nola Darling* • Tommy Redmond Hicks *Jamie Overstreet* • John Canada Terrell *Greer Childs* • Spike Lee *Mars Blackmon* • Raye Dowell *Opal Gilstrap* • Joie Lee *Clorinda Bradford* • Epatha Merkinson [S Epatha Merkerson] *Dr Jamison* • Bill Lee *Sonny Darling* ■ *Dir/Scr* Spike Lee • *Cinematographer* Ernest Dickerson [Ernest R Dickerson]

She's Having a Baby ★★ 15

Comedy 1988 · US · Colour · 101min

This rather humdrum look at young love turning into disgruntled parenthood stars a highly believable Kevin Bacon and a less rooted-in-reality Elizabeth McGovern. There are some neat jokes about bulges, nappies and loss of freedom, and Bacon's terror at the impending event is palpable. But the movie fails to break any new ground and there is a familiar ring to every hackneyed scenario. SH Swearing. *DVD*

Kevin Bacon *Jefferson "Jake" Briggs* • Elizabeth McGovern *Kristy Briggs* • Alec Baldwin *Davis McDonald* • Isabel Lorca *Fantasy girl* • William Windom *Russ Bainbridge* ■ *Dir/Scr* John Hughes

She's out of My League ★★★ 15

Romantic comedy 2008 · US · Colour · 100min

In this oddball romantic comedy from British director Jim Field Smith, Jay Baruchel stars as airport security worker Kirk Kettner, a lanky geek with a good heart who's taken advantage of by his family and his ex-girlfriend. Guided by a motley gaggle of protective friends, Kirk is urged to pursue gorgeous career woman Molly McCleish (Alice Eve) after an incident at the airport. What ensues is more than your average Judd Apatow comedy, even if the film has many recognisable genre hallmarks. Seamless ensemble playing from a solid supporting cast elevates this to the kind of home-town tale in which Jimmy Stewart wouldn't look amiss. KK Swearing, sexual references, nudity. *DVD*

Jay Baruchel *Kirk Kettner* • Krysten Ritter *Patty* • Mike Vogel *Jack* • Lindsay Sloane *Marnie* • Alice Eve *Molly McCleish* • Jasika Nicole *Wendy* • Jessica St Clair *Debbie* ■ *Dir* Jim Field Smith • *Scr* Sean Anders, John Morris

She's So Lovely ★★★ 15

Romantic drama 1997 · US · Colour · 92min

At one time Nick Cassavetes looked as if he would be just another actor with a more famous relative. However, he has successfully reinvented himself as a director and, although the influences of his independent film-maker father John are clear to see, this affectingly offbeat drama stands up in its own right. Sean Penn is a mentally troubled young man who is locked away in a psychiatric hospital. Ten years later he is released and sets out to find his wife (Robin Wright Penn) who has divorced him and married John Travolta. It's a slight tale, but the performances are finely judged. JF Swearing, violence. *DVD*

Sean Penn *Eddie* • Robin Wright *Maureen* • John Travolta *Joey* • Harry Dean Stanton *Shorty* • Debi Mazar *Georgie* • Gena Rowlands *Miss Green* • James Gandolfini *Kiefer* ■ *Dir* Nick Cassavetes • *Scr* John Cassavetes

She's the Man ★★★ 12

Romantic comedy 2006 · US · Colour · 105min

This fast-paced and irreverent teen screwball update of Shakespeare's *Twelfth Night* provides a hilarious platform for Amanda Bynes. When the girls' football team at her school is cancelled, soccer-mad Viola (Bynes) takes the place of her twin brother Sebastian at his school in order to join the boys' team. But a male makeover can't disguise the fact that she is soon attracted to her new room-mate, Duke (Channing Tatum). It may not be caustically witty, intellectual or worthy, but it's still a decent enough romp that has plenty of fun with the genders – and Bynes is a gem to watch. KK Swearing. *DVD*

Amanda Bynes *Viola Hastings* • Channing Tatum *Duke* • Laura Ramsey *Olivia* • Vinnie Jones *Coach Dinklage* • Julie Hagerty *Daphne* • David Cross (2) *Principal Gold* • Jonathan Sadowski *Paul* • Robert Hoffman *Justin* ■ *Dir* Andy Fickman • *Scr* Ewan Leslie, Karen McCullah Lutz, Kirsten Smith, from a story by Leslie

She's the One ★★ 15

Romantic comedy 1996 · US · Colour · 92min

Two brothers, Edward Burns and Mike McGlone, banter about love and marriage: one still smarts from an ex-fiancée's infidelity, the other happily plays away from his wife without conscience. John Mahoney stars as their father, with Cameron Diaz and Jennifer Aniston as the women in question. Witty and well observed by Burns, both directing and starring, the problem is that though it's instantly entertaining, it's also instantly forgettable. LH Swearing, sexual references. *DVD*

Jennifer Aniston *Renee* • Edward Burns *Mickey Fitzpatrick* • Cameron Diaz *Heather* • Mike McGlone *Francis Fitzpatrick* • Maxine Bahns *Hope* • John Mahoney *Mr Fitzpatrick* ■ *Dir/Scr* Edward Burns

She's Working Her Way through College ★★★ U

Musical comedy 1952 · US · Colour · 101min

This is an attractive Warner Bros musical version of James Thurber and Elliott Nugent's stage play *The Male Animal*, filmed previously in 1942 with Henry Fonda. Here Ronald Reagan is the college professor who makes a stand for freedom of expression, and it's not often that you get to see a future US president watching voluptuous Virginia Mayo perform saucy dance routines! The generally underrated Mayo is super as the showgirl determined to improve her mind, and there's nice back-up from hoofer Gene Nelson. TS

Virginia Mayo *Angela Gardner/"Hot Garters Gertie"* • Ronald Reagan *John Palmer* • Gene Nelson *Don Weston* • Don DeFore *Shep Slade* • Phyllis Thaxter *Helen Palmer* • Patrice Wymore *Ivy Williams* • Roland Winters *Fred Copeland* ■ *Dir* H Bruce Humberstone • *Scr* Peter Milne, from the play *The Male Animal* by James Thurber, Elliott Nugent

Shifty ★★★★ 15

Crime drama 2008 · UK · Colour · 85min

Shifty is a welcome antidote to a long line of British urban dramas that veer dangerously close to celebrating the youth culture of drugs and violence they portray. In the title role, Riz Ahmed (*Four Lions*, *Ill Manors*) isn't just a drug dealing thug, but a bright, warm character who has strayed into a life of crime rather than choosing it. His sense of alienation relates to his friendship with Chris (Daniel Mays), a seemingly well-adjusted young man who returns to their suburban stomping ground after four years away. Debuting writer/director Eran Creevy resists the usual flashiness associated with the genre to keep the focus squarely on the actors, and it's that lightness of touch that makes the story so poignant. SP *DVD*

Riz Ahmed [Rizwan Ahmed] *Shifty* • Daniel Mays *Chris* • Jason Flemyng *Glen* • Nitin Ganatra *Rez* • Jay Simpson *Trevor* • Francesca Annis *Valerie* ■ *Dir/Scr* Eran Creevy

S

Shiloh ★★★★ U

Drama 1996 · US · Colour · 86min

In a first-rate family entertainment, a boy befriends a hunting dog that's being cruelly treated by its owner, a neighbouring farmer. The boy's dad reckons it's the neighbour's business, and that he shouldn't get involved. But, convinced by a kindly shopkeeper that a boy's gotta do what a boy's gotta do, the kid takes the paw into his own hands and fights doggedly to become the beagle's new owner. Refreshingly unsentimental and impeccably acted, *Shiloh* is a minor treat for kids and grown-ups alike. A sequel followed in 1999. DA *DVD*

Michael Moriarty *Ray Preston* • Rod Steiger *Doc Wallace* • Blake Heron *Marty Preston* • Scott Wilson *Judd Travers* • Bonnie Bartlett *Mrs Wallace* • Ann Dowd *Louise Preston* ■ *Dir* Dale Rosenbloom • *Scr* Dale Rosenbloom, from a novel by Phyllis Reynolds Naylor

Shine ★★★★★ 12

Biographical drama 1996 · Aus/UK · Colour · 101min

Although reservations have been expressed about the accuracy of the "facts" in this film based on the life of gifted but deeply troubled Australian pianist David Helfgott, the resulting drama is still an exhilarating and uplifting screen experience. While it was Geoffrey Rush who took many of the plaudits, including the best actor Oscar, it's the acumen of Scott Hicks that prevents this often harrowing story from turning into a melodramatic mush. From the over-looked Noah Taylor as the young Helfgott, Googie Withers as the writer who launched Helfgott's career through to Lynn Redgrave as the future wife who saved him, the performances are of an extraordinary quality, with an astonishing screen debut from stage star Rush. DP Swearing, brief nudity. *DVD*

Geoffrey Rush *David as an adult* • Armin Mueller-Stahl *Peter* • Noah Taylor *David as an adolescent* • Lynn Redgrave *Gillian* • John Gielgud *Cecil Parkes* • Googie Withers *Katharine Susannah Prichard* • Sonia Todd *Sylvia* ■ *Dir* Scott Hicks • *Scr* Jan Sardi, from a story by Scott Hicks

Shine a Light ★★★ 12

Music documentary 2007 · US/Can · BW and Colour · 117min

Martin Scorsese's mammoth documentary follows the two-night residency of the Rolling Stones at New York's Beacon Theatre during the 2006 *A Bigger Bang* tour. Multiple cameras capture the band's raw energy on-stage and special guests Jack White, Christina Aguilera and Buddy Guy help the Stones belt out an eclectic set. There are some frustratingly fleeting interludes that show Scorsese coping with the logistical nightmare of a vast touring machine and handpicked archive footage to illustrate the group's 46-year history. *Shine a Light* doesn't match the insight of Scorsese's Bob Dylan documentary *No Direction Home*, which makes it likely that only hardcore Stones fans will find any lasting *Satisfaction* here. JR Brief swearing, drug references. *DVD* *Blu*

Mick Jagger • Keith Richards (2) *Keith Richards* • Charlie Watts • Ronnie Wood [Ron Wood] *Ronnie Wood* • Christina Aguilera • Bill Clinton • Martin Scorsese • Hillary Rodham Clinton [Hillary Clinton] *Hillary Clinton* ■ *Dir* Martin Scorsese • *Cinematographer* Robert Richardson

Shine On, Harvest Moon ★★ U

Western 1938 · US · BW · 55min

This is an early Roy Rogers western, made when Rogers was beginning a challenge to Gene Autry's popularity that would culminate in 1942 when Autry joined up and Rogers officially became "King of the Cowboys". Veteran western director Joseph Kane made dozens of these B-movies with both Autry and Rogers, and knew how to keep the action swift and the running time short. TV

Roy Rogers *Roy* • Mary Hart [Lynne Roberts] *Claire* • Stanley Andrews *Jackson* • William Farnum *Brower* ■ *Dir* Joseph Kane • *Scr* Jack Natteford

Shine On, Harvest Moon ★★★ U

Musical biography 1944 · US · BW and Colour · 112min

This is a lively vehicle for sexy and talented "Oomph Girl" Ann Sheridan. She plays Broadway star Nora Bayes in one of those Warner Bros biopics that owes little to the truth but includes a load of period songs. Dennis Morgan is terrific as songwriter Jack Norworth – also Nora's husband – and there are telling contributions from Warners regulars SZ "Cuddles" Sakall and Jack Carson. If you want the sordid truth about the Bayes/Norworth vaudeville-to-Broadway affair, this isn't the place to look, but it's still a jolly enjoyable movie. TS

Ann Sheridan *Nora Bayes* • Dennis Morgan *Jack Norworth* • Jack Carson *The Great Georgetti* • Irene Manning *Blanche Mallory* • SZ Sakall *Poppa Karl* ■ *Dir* David Butler • *Scr* Sam Hellman, Richard Weil, Francis Swan, James Kern, from the story by Richard Weil

Shiner ★★★ 18

Crime drama 2000 · UK · Colour · 95min

This is so nearly a gem from the punch-drunk British gangster genre. Michael Caine is in cracking form as a small-time boxing promoter, pinning his ego on one big fight involving his son "Golden Boy" (Matthew Marsden) and an American rival. Yet all around him is rotten and while he blinds himself to betrayals from his daughter Frances Barber and others in his coterie, the police are closing in on the illegal prizefighting scene. Director John Irvin has shot the film through with a steely grey dampness, but this is small-screen subject matter. LH *DVD*

Michael Caine *Billy "Shiner" Simpson* • Martin Landau *Frank Spedding* • Frances Barber *Georgie* • Frank Harper *Stoney* • Andy Serkis *Mel* • Claire Rushbrook *Ruth* • Danny Webb *Karl* ■ *Dir* John Irvin • *Scr* Scott Cherry

The Shining ★★★★★ 15

Horror 1980 · US/UK · Colour · 114min

Stanley Kubrick's superb adaptation of Stephen King's horror novel stars Jack Nicholson, Shelley Duvall and young Danny Lloyd as the family that is invited to look after a remote mountain hotel when it's closed for the winter. It's not long before Nicholson becomes unhinged as a series of apparitions, hallucinations and time-warps begins to affect his sanity. Trust Kubrick to be different: this horror film chills rather than shocks, works by stealth and provides nothing but eerie discomfort. Filmed on an amazing set built at Elstree using a gliding Steadicam throughout, the movie boasts a technique that's as overpowering as Nicholson's performance, which is both hammy and deeply disturbing. An extended version was released in 2012. AT Violence, swearing, nudity. *DVD* *Blu*

Jack Nicholson *Jack Torrance* • Shelley Duvall *Wendy Torrance* • Danny Lloyd *Danny* • Scatman Crothers *Dick Halloran* • Barry Nelson *Ullman* • Philip Stone *Grady* • Joe Turkel *Lloyd* • Anne Jackson *Doctor* ■ *Dir* Stanley Kubrick • *Scr* Stanley Kubrick, Diane Johnson, from the novel by Stephen King • *Cinematographer* John Alcott • *Music* Wendy Carlos

The Shining Hour ★★★

Drama 1938 · US · BW · 76min

Ultra-wealthy landowner Melvyn Douglas, ignoring the disapproval of his brother Robert Young and his possessive, embittered sister Fay Bainter, marries nightclub dancer with a past Joan Crawford. Emotional havoc is unleashed as Young, adored by his wife Margaret Sullavan, falls for his sister-in-law. Director Frank Borzage's film is highly entertaining, marked by committed performances, lots of atmosphere and a luminous portrayal from Sullavan. RK

Joan Crawford *Olivia Riley* • Margaret Sullavan *Judy Linden* • Robert Young (1) *David Linden* • Melvyn Douglas *Henry Linden* • Fay Bainter *Hannah Linden* • Allyn Joslyn *Roger Franklin* • Hattie McDaniel *Belvedere* ■ *Dir* Frank Borzage • *Scr* Jane Murfin, Ogden Nash, from the play by Keith Winters

Shining Through ★★ 15

Second World War spy drama 1992 · US · Colour · 127min

This should have won the award for the "most hilarious miscasting in a movie ever". Melanie Griffith stars as the half-Jewish, German-speaking American who goes to work for US agent Michael Douglas and volunteers to risk her life by going to Berlin to spy on debonair Nazi Liam Neeson. There's some tension as Griffith runs the risk of being caught, but the 1990s dialogue, ludicrous plot twists and Griffith spoil the film. JB Sex scenes, violence, swearing. *DVD*

Michael Douglas (1) *Ed Leland* • Melanie Griffith *Linda Voss* • Liam Neeson *Franze-Otto Dietrich* • Joely Richardson *Margrete Von Eberstien* • John Gielgud *Konrad Friedrichs, "Sunflower"* • Francis Guinan *Andrew Berringer* • Stanley Beard *Linda's father* • Sylvia Syms *Linda's mother* ■ *Dir* David Seltzer • *Scr* David Seltzer, from the novel by Susan Isaacs • *Cinematographer* Jan De Bont

Shinjuku Incident ★★★ 18

Action drama 2009 · HK · Colour · 114min

An impressive Jackie Chan has sadness etched into his face in this gritty but convoluted tale of inter-racial gang rivalry in 1990s Japan. Playing a more dramatic role than usual, he stars as an idealistic Chinese worker who arrives illegally in Tokyo to seek a better future and his missing fiancée, only to be caught up in the city's criminal underworld. While veteran Hong Kong director Derek Yee deserves credit for his ambition and visual flair, his film unfortunately gets drowned in detail. SF Cantonese, Mandarin, Japanese, English +subtitles. Violence. *DVD* *Blu*

Jackie Chan *Steelhead* • Xu Jing Lei [Xu Jinglei] *Xiu Xiu* • Daniel Wu *Jie* • Masaya Kato *Eguchi* ■ *Dir* Derek Yee • *Scr* Derek Yee, Chun Tin-nam

Ship Ahoy ★★★ U

Musical comedy 1942 · US · BW · 94min

Forget the silly story of this spy spoof, which culminates in dancer Eleanor Powell sending a Morse code message in taps, and enjoy her sensational dancing, including one of her greatest routines – a breathtaking ship-board tap dance. The first-rate songs include the plaintive *Poor You*, sung by a skinny vocalist with Tommy Dorsey's orchestra – Frank Sinatra. Comics Red Skelton and Bert Lahr are among others contributing to the above-average entertainment quotient. TV

Eleanor Powell *Tallulah Winters* • Red Skelton *Merton K Kibble* • Bert Lahr *Skip Owens* • Virginia O'Brien *Fran Evans* • William Post Jr *HU Bennett* • James Cross *Stump* • Eddie Hartman *Stumpy* • Frank Sinatra ■ *Dir* Edward N Buzzell [Edward Buzzell] • *Scr* Harry Clork, Harry Kurnitz, Irving Brecher, from a story by Matt Brooks, Bradford Ropes, Bert Kalmar

Ship of Fools ★★★ 12

Drama 1965 · US · BW · 143min

This big, bloated and often boring drama marked the final screen appearance of Vivien Leigh. The story concerns a group of refugees – exiles, Jews, aristocrats, and oddballs – who leave Mexico for Germany in 1933, just as Hitler was lying in wait for them. It's a giant allegory that takes itself very seriously indeed. Leigh's performance as a lonely divorcee is absolutely riveting to watch, and there's an amazing supporting cast. AT *DVD*

Vivien Leigh *Mary Treadwell* • Simone Signoret *La Condesa* • José Ferrer *Rieber* • Lee Marvin *Tenny* • Oskar Werner *Dr Schumann* • Elizabeth Ashley *Jenny* • George Segal *David* • José Greco *Pepe* • Werner Klemperer *Lieutenant Heebner* ■ *Dir* Stanley Kramer • *Scr* Abby Mann, from the novel by Katherine Anne Porter • *Cinematographer* Ernest Laszlo • *Art Directors* Robert Clatworthy, Joseph Kish

The Ship of Lost Men ★★★

Silent drama 1929 · Ger · BW · 121min

This is the last silent movie made by Marlene Dietrich before *The Blue Angel* sent her star soaring. The future Hollywood legend plays an heiress who crash-lands during a transatlantic flight and is secretly picked up by a good doctor (British Robin Irvine) and a gentle cook (Vladimir Sokoloff). Although contrived at times, the characters are convincing, the plot is skilfully developed and director Maurice Tourneur's striking visuals and moody atmosphere keep the high seas adventure on an even keel. AJ

Fritz Kortner *Captain Fernando Vela* • Marlene Dietrich *Ethel Marley* • Gaston Modot *Morain* • Robin Irvine *William Cheyne* • Vladimir Sokoloff *Grischa* ■ *Dir* Maurice Tourneur • *Scr* Maurice Tourneur, from the novel by Franzos Keremen

The Ship That Died of Shame ★★ PG

Drama 1955 · UK · BW · 88min

This is one of the more peculiar civvy street pictures made in the decade after the war. It lurches uncomfortably between comedy, social drama and thriller as it follows the fortunes of the washed-up crew of a motor torpedo boat, who recondition the old tub and turn to smuggling because Britain no longer has anything to offer its one-time heroes. Richard Attenborough is the star of the show, but the uncertainty of tone finally gets the better of him. DP

Richard Attenborough *Hoskins* • George Baker *Bill* • Bill Owen *Birdie* • Virginia McKenna *Helen* • Roland Culver *Fordyce* • Bernard Lee *Customs officer* • Ralph Truman *Sir Richard* ■ *Dir* Michael Relph, Basil Dearden • *Scr* Michael Relph, Basil Dearden, John Whiting, from the novel by Nicholas Monsarrat

A Ship to India ★★★

Drama 1947 · Swe · BW · 98min

Set on the Stockholm waterfront, Ingmar Bergman's third feature begins with a happy ending, from which the action flashes back to chronicle the rivalry between captain Holger Lowenadler (whose dreams of seeing the world have been dashed by incipient blindness) and his hunchbacked son, Birger Malmsten, for the affections of dance-hall waif Gertrud Fridh. The structure allows the intensity to wane and the handling is decidedly melodramatic. DP Swedish +subtitles.

Holger Lowenadler *Captain Alexander Blom* • Anna Lindahl *His wife* • Birger Malmsten *Johannes* • Gertrud Fridh *Sally* • Naemi Briese *Selma* • Hjordis Petterson *Sofie* ■ *Dir* Ingmar Bergman • *Scr* Ingmar Bergman, from the play *Skepp till India land* by Martin Söderhjelm

Shipmates Forever ★★ U

Musical 1935 · US · BW · 111min

Continuing the string of Dick Powell–Ruby Keeler musicals that had served them so wonderfully well with *42nd Street*, *Gold Diggers of 1933*, *Footlight Parade* and *Dames*, Warner Bros came up with this slender tale about an admiral's son who would rather be a song and dance man than join the Navy. However, without Busby Berkeley on hand to lift the wafer-thin plot and entirely forgettable score, this is no more than inoffensively nondescript entertainment. RK

Dick Powell *Richard John Melville III* • Ruby Keeler *June Blackburn* • Lewis Stone *Admiral Melville* • Ross Alexander (1) *Sparks Brown* • Dick Foran *Gifford* ■ *Dir* Frank Borzage • *Scr* Delmer Daves, from a story by Delmer Daves

The Shipping News ★★★ 15

Drama 2001 · US · Colour · 106min

The icy mists, haunting sounds and shadows of the Newfoundland shores imbue this movie with a bleak sadness that the intriguing storyline and strong performances fail to dispel. A miscast Kevin Spacey stars as a dull, uninspired man who is seduced into marriage and fatherhood by the sluttish Cate Blanchett, then deserted and widowed in short order. Aunt Judi Dench invites him and his daughter to return with her to the family home in a Newfoundland fishing village. There he lands a job writing the shipping news on the local paper and begins a tentative love affair with widow Julianne Moore. LH *DVD*

Kevin Spacey *Quoyle* • Julianne Moore *Wavey Prowse* • Judi Dench *Agnis Hamm* • Cate Blanchett *Petal Bear* • Pete Postlethwaite *Tert Card* • Scott Glenn *Jack Buggit* • Rhys Ifans *Beaufield Nutbeem* • Gordon Pinsent *Billy Pretty* • Jason Behr *Denris Buggit* ■ *Dir* Lasse Hallström • *Scr* Robert Nelson Jacobs, from the novel by E Annie Proulx

Ships with Wings ★
Second World War action drama
1942 • UK • BW • 105min

An hour could easily be cut from this endless flag-waver designed to glorify the aircraft carrier *Ark Royal* and the men of the Fleet Air Arm. No one doubts their bravery, but did they really deserve this awful mess of soap opera and derring-do? John Clements is the hero who almost turns himself into a kamikaze pilot, his suicidal tactics reportedly worrying Churchill who wanted the film shelved. AT

John Clements *Lt Dick Stacey* • Leslie Banks *Admiral Wetherby* • Jane Baxter *Celia Wetherby* • Ann Todd *Kay Gordon* • Basil Sydney *Captain Fairfax* • Edward Chapman *Papadopulous* • Michael Wilding *Lt Grant* ■ *Dir* Sergei Nolbandov • *Scr* Patrick Kirwan, Austin Melford, Diana Morgan, Sergei Nolbandov

Shipwrecked ★★★ U
Period adventure 1990 • US • Colour • 89min

Scandinavian cinema has an international reputation for children's films, a renown recognised by the Disney studio, who hired Norwegian Nils Gaup to make this lively action tale. There are calm waters to wade through between the swashbuckling, but Gabriel Byrne shivers the odd timber as the pirate captain and Stian Smestad impresses as the cabin boy embarking on the adventure of a lifetime. DP

Stian Smestad *Haakon Haakonsen* • Gabriel Byrne *Lieutenant Merrick* • Louisa Haigh *Mary* • Trond Peter Stamso Munch *Jens* • Bjorn Sundquist *Mr Haakonsen* • Eva Von Hanno *Mrs Haakonsen* • Kjell Stormoen *Captain Madsen* ■ *Dir* Nils Gaup • *Scr* Nils Gaup, Bob Foss, Greg Dinner, Nick Thiel, from the novel *Haakon Haakonsen* by OV Falck-Ytter

Shipyard Sally ★★★ U
Comedy drama 1939 • UK • BW • 79min

Gracie Fields bade farewell to British cinema with this clarion call for the rights of the working class. Considering the international situation, a film that dared to criticise Westminster for leaving Clydeside shipyards idle and poked open fun at our self-satisfied system of government was rather bold. However, it all ends on a note of rousing patrictism, as Gracie's barmaid returns from impersonating a major American star in London in time to belt out *Land of Hope and Glory*. Another song, *Wish Me Luck As You Wave Me Goodbye* became an embarkation favourite during the Second World War. DP

Gracie Fields *Sally Fitzgerald* • Sydney Howard *Major Fitzgerald* • Morton Selten *Lord Randall* • Norma Varden *Lady Patricia* • Oliver Wakefield *Forsyth* • Tucker McGuire *Linda Marsh* ■ *Dir* Monty Banks • *Scr* Don Ettinger, Karl Tunberg, from a story by Gracie Fields, Tom Geraghty, Val Valentine

The Shiralee ★★★ PG
Adventure drama 1957 • UK • BW • 94min

One of several features Ealing Studios made in Australia, *The Shiralee* stars genuine Aussie Peter Finch as a poacher who finds his wife shacked up with another man. Consequently, he leaves for a life on the road with his daughter, who becomes his shiralee - an aboriginal word for "burden". The result is a captivating double-act between Finch and the bright-as-a-button Dana Wilson as each of them realises they have a lot to learn. The location photography is incredible, though attempts to inject some humour with

cameos from Sid James and Tessie O'Shea backfire. AT

Peter Finch *Jim Macauley* • Elizabeth Sellars *Marge Macauley* • Dana Wilson *Buster Macauley* • Rosemary Harris *Lily Parker* • Tessie O'Shea *Bella* • Sidney James *Luke* • George Rose *Donny* ■ *Dir* Leslie Norman • *Scr* Leslie Norman, Neil Paterson, from the novel by D'Arcy Niland • *Cinematographer* Paul Beeson

The Shiralee ★★★★
Adventure drama 1986 • Aus • Colour • 120min

The edited feature film version of the top-rated Australian television mini-series loses a few subplots but still remains an emotionally moving look at father-daughter relationships. Bryan Brown is a swagman, odd-jobbing his way through 1940s Australia looking for permanent work, who gets landed with his daughter Rebecca Smart when he returns to Adelaide and finds his boozy, unfaithful wife romancing the town bookie. On the road the two bond through illness, separation and the final hurdle of his wife's threat to get Smart back. High-class comfort viewing, superbly acted. AJ

Bryan Brown *Macauley* • Noni Hazlehurst *Lily* • Rebecca Smart *Buster* • Lewis Fitz-Gerald *Tony* • Lorna Lesley *Marge* • Ned Manning *Jim* ■ *Dir* George Ogilvie • *Scr* Tony Morphett, from the novel by D'Arcy Niland

Shiri ★★★ 18
Romantic action thriller
1999 • S Kor • Colour • 120min

Director Kang Je-gyu's no-holds-barred blockbuster slickly combines political intrigue and explosive action. The identity of the terrorist co-ordinating an audacious bid to assassinate the leaders of the North and South Korean states at a football match is never in doubt. But what is impressive is the way that Kang finds time to explore security agent Han Suk-kyu's emotions during a breakneck race against the clock. Generic film-making perhaps, but executed with intelligence and panache. DP Korean +subtitles. *DVD*

Han Suk-kyu *Ryu Jung-won* • Choi Min-sik *Park Mu-young* • Song Kang-ho *Lee Jung-gil* • Kim Yun-jin *Lee Myung-hyun/Hee* • Yun Ju-sang *Ko Jung-suk* ■ *Dir* Kang Je-gyu • *Scr* Park Je-hyun, Paek Woon-hak, Jeon Yoon-soo, from a story by Kang Je-gyu

Shirin ★★★★ PG
Drama 2008 • Iran • Colour • 90min

Influential Iranian artist and film-maker Abbas Kiarostami turns the tables on the cinema-goer in this strange, powerful experimental drama. What we see are the faces, reactions and emotions of 113 actresses (including Juliette Binoche) as they apparently watch an adaptation of a fable about the rivalry between a Persian prince and a sculptor for an Armenian princess. In fact, the actresses were looking at three dots on a piece of paper - the director asked them to imagine their own love stories. What concerns Kiarostami here is the art of screen acting, the perceptiveness of the camera and film's potential to manipulate emotion. The result is both engrossing and disconcerting. DP Farsi +subtitles.

Golshifteh Farahani • Taraneh Alidoosti • Juliette Binoche • Niki Karimi ■ *Dir* Abbas Kiarostami • *Scr* Mohammad Rahmanian, from the story *Khosrow and Shirin* by Farrideh Golbou, from the poem *The Story of Khosrow and Shirin* by Hakim Nezami Ganjavi

Shirley Valentine ★★★★ 15
Comedy 1989 • US/UK • Colour • 104min

This is the movie that gladdened a generation of women's hearts and brought cinema stardom to Pauline Collins at an age when actresses are often resigned to sitcom suburbia. Collins's performance as the long-suffering housewife who decamps to a Greek island and Tom Conti is quite sublime and carefully crafted. Director Lewis Gilbert manages to retain the best of Willy Russell's theatrical devices - Collins talking to the kitchen wall, for instance - while opening out the action to embrace a

big-screen atmosphere. The supporting cast, particularly Bernard Hill as Collins's Neanderthal husband, is equally convincing, with only the hammy Conti striking a momentary false note. SR Swearing, nudity. *DVD*

Pauline Collins *Shirley Valentine* • Tom Conti *Costas Caldes* • Julia McKenzie *Gillian* • Alison Steadman *Jane* • Joanna Lumley *Marjorie* • Sylvia Syms *Headmistress* • Bernard Hill *Joe Bradshaw* • George Costigan *Dougie* ■ *Dir* Lewis Gilbert • *Scr* Willy Russell, from his play

Shiver of the Vampires ★★ 18
Horror 1970 • Fr • Colour • 94min

French director Jean Rollin is the latest eccentric personality to be lionised by exploitation genre fans. His banal poverty row output from the early 1970s is now considered chic thanks to its up-front sexual content and hallucinatory visuals streaked with eerie sadism. This honeymooners-meet-hippy-vampires saga verges on boredom, but ranks as one of his better efforts, occasionally throwing up the odd surreal image and macabre moment of delirium. AJ French +subtitles. Violence, nudity. *DVD*

Dominique *Isolde* • Sandra Julien • Jean-Marie Durand • Nicole Nancel • Michel Delahaye ■ *Dir/Scr* Jean Rollin

Shivers ★★★★ 18
Horror 1975 • Can • Colour • 84min

David Cronenberg's first "important" horror film may now look crude, but the obsessions that would colour his later works are already apparent. The story is centred around a vaguely futuristic block of flats where a parasite is gradually working its way through the occupants, transforming them into sex-obsessed zombies. It's not exactly subtle, but Cronenberg delights in some stomach-churning imagery and the stark, chilling design would later be revisited in films such as *Dead Ringers* and *The Fly*. JF Swearing, violence. *DVD*

Paul Hampton *Roger St Luc* • Joe Silver *Rollo Linsky* • Lynn Lowry *Forsythe* • Allan Migicovsky *Nicholas Tudor* • Susan Petrie *Janine Tudor* • Barbara Steele *Betts* ■ *Dir/Scr* David Cronenberg

Shoah ★★★★★
Documentary 1985 • Fr • Colour • 565min

Claude Lanzmann spent over a decade shooting the 350 hours of interviews and location footage - he purposely did not use archive material - that were distilled into this cinematic monument to those who perished in the death camps and ghettos of the Second World War. Several decades on, the ruins of Auschwitz, Chelmno and the rest still induce revulsion, as do the remorseless recollections of the Polish peasants who remain tainted with the hatred that made the Holocaust possible. Yet this is also a testament to the survivors who refused to let their spirit be broken by the daily horrors. Putting a face on inhuman misery, this remarkable achievement demonstrates film's unique power. DP French +subtitles. *DVD*

■ *Dir* Claude Lanzmann

Shock Corridor ★★★★ 15
Psychological drama
1963 • US • BW and Colour • 95min

The characters talk in slogans, the idea verges on the outrageous, but Sam Fuller's direction barrels us through discrepancies in this film's plot with a gut-punching style that flattens objections. Journalist Peter Breck has himself committed to a mental hospital to find a killer and discovers more than he bargained for. Pitting himself against many ideas of good taste, Fuller creates a film with the grip of a straitjacket. TH *DVD*

Peter Breck *Johnny Barrett* • Constance Towers *Cathy* • Gene Evans *Boden* • James Best *Stuart* • Harry Rhodes [Hari Rhodes] *Trent* • Larry Tucker *Pagliacci* • William Zuckert *Swanee* • Philip Ahn *Dr Fong* ■ *Dir* Samuel Fuller • *Scr* Samuel Fuller, from his treatment

A Shock to the System ★★★ 15
Black comedy 1990 • US • Colour • 84min

This adaptation of one of novelist Simon Brett's superb tales lacks forceful direction, but Michael Caine gives a terrific performance as the cold-blooded advertising executive who realises that he can get away with anything, even murder, in his ruthless climb to the top. There are a few fair swipes at some obvious targets. TS Swearing. *DVD*

Michael Caine *Graham Marshall* • Elizabeth McGovern *Stella Anderson* • Peter Riegert *Robert Benham* • Swoosie Kurtz *Leslie Marshall* • Will Patton *Lieutenant Laker* • Jenny Wright *Melanie O'Connor* • Samuel L Jackson *Ulysses* ■ *Dir* Jan Egleson • *Scr* Andrew Klavan, from the novel by Simon Brett

Shock Treatment ★★★ 15
Horror 1973 • Fr/It • Colour • 83min

A short sequence of Alain Delon and Annie Girardot frolicking stark naked gained this film a notoriety that detracted from its value as a Frankensteinian chiller. Girardot has checked into a clifftop clinic to rebuild her self-esteem after a fractured love affair. However, following a friend's death, she deduces the source of Delon's miraculous rejuvenation treatment. With its sinister antiseptic interiors, satirical undercurrent and twist ending, Alain Jessua's third feature is much more than mere exploitation fodder. DP French dubbed. *DVD*

Alain Delon *Dr Devilers* • Annie Girardot *Hélène Masson* • Michel Duchaussoy *Dr Bernard* • Robert Hirsch *Gérôme Savignat* ■ *Dir/Scr* Alain Jessua

Shock Waves ★★★ 15
Horror drama 1975 • US • Colour • 85min

Survivors of a shipwreck are washed up on a tropical island where fugitive Gestapo officer Peter Cushing is busy reanimating drowned Nazi soldiers to form a zombie army. Relying more on atmosphere and tension than gore or jolts, Ken Wiederhorn's directorial debut is an eerie cult favourite featuring a fine performance from Cushing as evil personified. The sub-aqueous undead marching along the ocean floor in jackboots is one of the creepiest sequences in this Florida-shot independent. AJ

Peter Cushing *Scar, SS Commander* • John Carradine *Captain Ben* • Brooke Adams *Rose* • Fred Buch *Chuck* • Jack Davidson *Norman* • Luke Halpin *Keith* • DJ Sidney *Beverly* • Don Stout *Dobbs* ■ *Dir* Ken Wiederhorn • *Scr* John Harrison, Ken Wiederhorn

Shocker ★ 18
Horror thriller 1989 • US • Colour • 104min

This dud from Wes Craven charts the murderous exploits of an electrocuted maniac television repair man who can appear wherever someone switches on a set. Confusing, tedious and far too long, it's a shame such a neat concept was wasted by Craven in his worst movie. AJ *DVD*

Michael Murphy (1) *Lt Don Parker* • Peter Berg *Jonathan Parker* • Mitch Pileggi *Horace Pinker* • Cami Cooper [Camille Cooper] *Alison* • Heather Langenkamp *Victim* • Richard Brooks (2) *Rhino* ■ *Dir/Scr* Wes Craven

The Shocking Miss Pilgrim ★★★ U
Musical 1947 • US • Colour • 84min

This was a rare box-office dud in Betty Grable's series of hit movies for 20th Century-Fox. Today, though, this looks like courageous casting on Fox's part, with Grable as a feisty suffragette in strait-laced 19th-century Boston, and there's a Gershwin brothers score to enjoy as well. Particularly pleasing is co-star Dick Haymes, whose mastery of the romantic ballad does not prevent him having fun with Grable during the up-tempo numbers. Despite all that, a horde of fans wrote in pleading for Grable to get back to the garish flicks that made her name. TS

S

Betty Grable *Cynthia Pilgrim* • Dick Haymes *John Pritchard* • Anne Revere *Alice Pritchard* • Allyn Joslyn *Leander Woolsey* • Gene Lockhart *Saxon* • Elizabeth Patterson *Catherine Dennison* ■ *Dir* George Seaton • *Scr* George Seaton, from the story by Ernest Maas, Frederica Maas

Shockproof ★★★

Film noir   1949 · US · BW · 79min

This deliciously tense *film noir* has parole officer Cornel Wilde drawn into the tangled past of ex-convict Patricia Knight. Unfortunately, director Douglas Sirk's initial pace and stylishness run out of steam, and the dénouement can only be described as a cop-out. However, although the final destination is a disappointment, you can still luxuriate in the journey. SR

Cornel Wilde *Griff Marat* • Patricia Knight *Jenny Marsh* • John Baragrey *Harry Wesson* • Esther Minciotti *Mrs Marat* • Howard St John *Sam Brooks* • Russell Collins *Frederick Bauer* • Charles Bates *Tommy Marat* ■ *Dir* Douglas Sirk • *Scr* Helen Deutsch, Samuel Fuller

The Shoes of the Fisherman ★★★ U

Drama   1968 · US · Colour · 146min

Anthony Quinn, in one of his best performances, plays a Russian priest, a political prisoner for many years, who is suddenly elected to be Pope at a time of superpower instability. Director Michael Anderson and screenwriters John Patrick and James Kennaway make a decent fist of translating Morris West's bestseller, even if there is a tendency towards awe at Vatican bureaucracy when it should be inspecting it for story interest. A celebrity cast adds to the gravitas, but Quinn is the reason to view. TH

Anthony Quinn *Kiril Lakota* • Laurence Olivier *Piotr Ilyich Kamenev* • Oskar Werner *Father David Telemond* • David Janssen *George Faber* • Barbara Jefford *Dr Ruth Faber* • Leo McKern *Cardinal Leone* • Vittorio De Sica *Cardinal Rinaldi* • John Gielgud *Elder Pope* • Clive Revill *Vucovich* ■ *Dir* Michael Anderson • *Scr* John Patrick, James Kennaway, from the novel by Morris West

Shoeshine ★★★★★ 12

Drama   1946 · It · BW · 90min

The recipient of the first best foreign film Oscar (albeit honorary), Vittorio De Sica's unblinking and, at the time, controversial) portrait of postwar Italian society has none of the sentimentality that would coat his other neorealist classics, *Bicycle Thieves* and *Umberto D*. Co-scripted by the movement's co-founder, Cesare Zavattini, the fall from innocence of street scamps Rinaldo Smordoni and Franco Interlenghi is clearly allegorical. But, even bearing in mind the prominence of their longed-for white horse, the symbolism is as unforced as the performances. DP Italian +subtitles. DVD

Rinaldo Smordoni *Giuseppe* • Franco Interlenghi *Pasquale* • Aniello Mele *Raffaele* • Bruno Ortensi *Arcangeli* • Pacifico Astrologo *Vittorio* ■ *Dir* Vittorio De Sica • *Scr* Cesare Zavattini, Sergio Amidei, Adolfo Franci, Cesare Giulio Viola, Vittorio De Sica

Shogun Assassin ★★★ 18

Martial arts action adventure
1980 · US/Jpn · Colour · 81min

Movies don't come any bloodier than this claret-hued samurai tale, which sees a revenge-seeking assassin wandering medieval Japan with his infant son, whom he pushes in a weaponised baby buggy. The extreme, exaggerated violence (limbs are lopped off, bodies butchered and heads cleaved in two) meant the picture was branded a video nasty in the UK, although it was never banned. Its reputation as an exploitation classic was confirmed when Quentin Tarantino borrowed its blood-gushing style for his *Kill Bill* saga, even featuring *Shogun Assassin* in one scene as a child's choice for bedtime viewing. JH Japanese dubbed. DVD

Tomisaburo Wakayama *Lone Wolf* • Lamont Johnson *Lone Wolf* • Kayo Matsuo *Supreme Ninja* • Sandra Bernhard *Supreme Ninja* • Minoru Ohki [Minoru Oki] *Master of Death* ■ *Dir* Robert

Houston, Kenji Misumi • *Scr* Robert Houston, Goseki Kojima, Kazuo Koike, from a manga by Koike

Shogun Warrior ★★★ PG

Period action adventure
1991 · Jpn · Colour · 101min

Boasting a fine cast and some rousing action, it's hard to see why this period adventure went straight to video in America. Sho Kosugi (best known for the *Enter the Ninja* movies) stars as a 17th-century samurai who leaves behind the ravages of a Japanese civil war only to find himself plunged into a rebellion against the Spanish king (Christopher Lee). This is swashbuckling entertainment, martial arts style. DP Violence, brief nudity. DVD

Sho Kosugi *Mayeda* • David Essex *Don Pedro* • Kane Kosugi *Yorimune* • Christopher Lee *King Philip* • Polly Walker *Cecilia* • Norman Lloyd *Father Vasco* • Ronald Pickup *Captain Crawford* • John Rhys-Davies *El Zaidan* • Toshiro Mifune *Lord Akugawa Ieyasu* ■ *Dir* Gordon Hessler • *Scr* Nelson Gidding, from the story by Nelson Gidding, Sho Kosugi

Sholay ★★★★ PG

Adventure   1975 · Ind · Colour · 198min

In making what is considered to be a classic of Indian cinema, director Ramesh Sippy combines elements of Bollywood music, comedy and romance with the spaghetti western genre, creating a technically lauded, as well as massively popular, adventure movie. Told as a couple of extended flashbacks that lead to an all-action finale, the story concerns the rivalry between Amjad Khan's fabled bandit and Sanjeev Kumar, a courageous former policeman, who hires Amitabh Bachchan and Dharmendra to avenge his murdered family. The performances are impressive, especially that of Khan. DP Hindi +subtitles. DVD

Sanjeev Kumar *Thakur Baldev Singh* • Dharmendra *Veeru* • Amitabh Bachchan *Jaidev* • Amjad Khan *Gabbar Singh* ■ *Dir* Ramesh Sippy • *Scr* Salim-Javed, from his story

Shoot 'Em Up ★★★ 18

Action thriller   2007 · US · Colour · 82min

Hollywood has often plagiarised John Woo's highly stylised gunfight choreography, but this audacious effort may be the first film to try and teach the master some new tricks. Writer/director Michael Davis's gun-obsessed thriller opens with a pregnant woman giving birth during a firefight and never lets up. Clive Owen heads the cast as mysterious, carrot-munching hero Smith, who's roped into saving the newborn child from an army of assassins, led by Paul Giamatti's preening bad guy Hertz. Cartoonish dialogue and ugly production values detract from the film's ballistic set pieces: a skydiving gun battle; a sex scene during a shoot-out; and an ingenious moment as Smith becomes a marksman puppeteer, slaying dozens of bad guys using guns on strings. It's fun but terminally adolescent, and unfortunately runs out of ideas long before it runs out of bullets. JR Violence, swearing, sex scenes, nudity. DVD

Clive Owen *Smith* • Monica Bellucci *Donna "DQ" Quintano* • Paul Giamatti *Hertz* • Stephen McHattie *Hammerson* • Greg Bryk *Lone man* • Daniel Pilon *Senator Rutledge* ■ *Dir/Scr* Michael Davis (3)

Shoot Out ★★

Western   1971 · US · Colour · 94min

Henry Hathaway goes to the Rocky Mountains with Gregory Peck for this disappointing revenge western. Peck plays the "good" bad guy, a bank robber who comes out of jail swearing vengeance on the partner who betrayed him. The violence is of the fashionable, post-*Wild Bunch* school, with all the blood but none of the resonance. AT Swearing.

Gregory Peck *Clay Lomax* • Pat Quinn [Patricia Quinn] *Juliana Farrell* • Robert F Lyons *Bobby Jay* • Susan Tyrrell *Alma* • Jeff Corey *Trooper* • James Gregory *Sam Foley* • Rita Gam *Emma* •

Dawn Lyn *Decky* • Pepe Serna *Pepe* ■ *Dir* Henry Hathaway • *Scr* Marguerite Roberts, from the book *The Lone Cowboy* by Will James

Shoot-Out at Medicine Bend ★★ U

Western   1957 · US · BW · 86min

A standard Randolph Scott revenge western is given a fresh suit of clothes as three ex-soldiers dress up and talk like Quakers to bring about the downfall of James Craig's ruthless town boss. Scott leads the trio and James Garner, working his way toward stardom, plays one of Randy's two sidekicks. On the other hand, Angie Dickinson can do little with the undemanding role of Scott's gal. AE

Randolph Scott *Cap Devlin* • James Craig *Clark* • Angie Dickinson *Priscilla* • Dani Crayne *Nell* • James Garner *Maitland* ■ *Dir* Richard L Bare • *Scr* John Tucker Battle, DD Beauchamp

Shoot the Moon ★★★★ 15

Drama   1982 · US · Colour · 118min

In this alarming story of marital collapse, Albert Finney – demonstrating what accomplished screen acting credentials he has – plays a writer parting from housebound wife Diane Keaton and their four children. Creating a character more sympathetic than you'd expect, you can almost hear the ticking timebomb of his enraged personality and, although the photography does Keaton no favours, she is less quirky than in her Woody Allen pictures. One of Alan Parker's most interesting essays in intimate drama, it has an uneven, but literate, script by Bo Goldman. TH Violence, swearing, nudity.

Albert Finney *George Dunlap* • Diane Keaton *Faith Dunlap* • Peter Weller *Frank Henderson* • Karen Allen *Sandy* • Dana Hill *Sherry* • Viveka Davis *Jill* • Tracey Gold *Marianne* ■ *Dir* Alan Parker • *Scr* Bo Goldman

Shoot the Pianist ★★★★★ 12

Crime drama   1960 · Fr · BW · 67min

Coming between *The 400 Blows* and *Jules et Jim*, this is François Truffaut's forgotten masterpiece. It is a knowing homage to Hollywood *films noirs*, with Charles Aznavour excelling as the pianist whose descent from the classical stage to a seedy Parisian bar culminates in his involvement with some unforgiving gangsters. A grab bag of fond memories, both cinematic and personal, this is Truffaut at his most exuberant, with the stylistic flourishes of the *nouvelle vague* enhancing the romantic melancholy of this tragicomic tale. Endlessly inventive and bustling with life. DP French +subtitles. Violence, swearing, nudity. DVD

Charles Aznavour *Charlie Kohler/Edouard Saroyan* • Marie Dubois *Léna* • Nicole Berger *Thérésa* • Michèle Mercier *Clarisse* • Albert Rémy *Chico Saroyan* • Jacques Aslanian *Richard Saroyan* • Richard Kanayan *Fido Saroyan* • Claude Mansard *Momo* ■ *Dir* François Truffaut • *Scr* François Truffaut, Marcel Moussy, from the novel *Down There* by David Goodis • *Cinematographer* Raoul Coutard

The Shooter ★★ 18

Thriller   1994 · US/UK/Sp/Cz Rep · Colour · 100min

The unmistakeable whiff of a Euro-pudding hangs over this fairly dim addition to the Dolph Lundgren canon. Playing a US marshal, Lundgren finds himself mixed up in all sorts of intrigue when he hunts for a glamorous hitwoman (Maruschka Detmers) at a major Cuban/American summit in Prague. The film fails because of the needlessly complicated plotting. JF Swearing, violence.

Dolph Lundgren *Michael Dane* • Maruschka Detmers *Simone Rosset* • Assumpta Serna *Marta* • John Ashton *Alex Reed* • Gavan O'Herlihy *Dick Powell* ■ *Dir* Ted Kotcheff • *Scr* Billy Ray, Meg Thayer, from a story by Yves Andre Martin

Shooter ★★★ 15

Action thriller   2007 · US · Colour · 120min

A kind of *First Blood* for the George W Bush era, *Shooter* is a conspiracy thriller-cum-action movie that's not afraid to wear its

politics on its sleeve. When disillusioned former marine sharpshooter Bob Lee Swagger (Mark Wahlberg) agrees to help the US government capture a sniper who's planning to kill the president, the scene is set for a *Day of the Jackal*-style confrontation. Wahlberg excels in this frantic action movie, his chisel-jawed features perfect for the veteran who has taken his war home with him. It's hardly *The Parallax View*, yet it hammers home its anger over the corruption of America's political elite with unerring accuracy. JR
DVD BL

Mark Wahlberg *Bob Lee Swagger* • Michael Peña [Michael Pena] *Nick Memphis* • Danny Glover *Colonel Isaac Johnson* • Kate Mara *Sarah Fenn* • Elias Koteas *Jack Payne* • Rhona Mitra *Alourdes Galindo* • Jonathan Walker *Louis Dobbler* • Tate Donovan *Russ Turner* ■ *Dir* Antoine Fuqua • *Scr* Jonathan Lemkin, from the novel *Point of Impact* by Stephen Hunter (2)

Shooters ★★ 18

Crime drama   2000 · Neth/US/UK · Colour · 91min

Surely you've heard the one about the ex-con who tries to go straight but ends up getting dragged into a dodgy deal by his loose cannon of a pal? Of course, the underworld's seedy opportunism and latent violence underpin the action. Things might have improved had directors Colin Teague and Glenn Durfort focused on honour and responsibility instead of packing in the double-crosses, but it's unlikely. DP DVD

Adrian Dunbar *Max Bell* • Andrew Howard *J* • Louis Dempsey *Gilly* • Gerard Butler *Jackie Junior* • Jason Hughes *Charlie Franklin* • Matthew Rhys *Eddie* • Ioan Gruffudd *Freddy Guns* ■ *Dir* Glenn Durfort, Colin Teague • *Scr* Gary Young, Howard Andrew, Louis Dempsey

The Shooting ★★★ PG

Western   1967 · US · Colour · 77min

This weird, legendary western's existentialism and minimalism are as much the result of having no budget as they are the philosophical inclinations of its director, Monte Hellman, and its star, Jack Nicholson. Nicholson plays a grinning hired killer involved with bounty hunters and a mysterious woman in a journey into the real or imaginary past, set against the empty Utah deserts. It's a puzzle picture that's either intentionally metaphorical or just ineptly made. Hellman and Nicholson made a second western, *Ride in the Whirlwind*, on the same trip. AT

Jack Nicholson *Billy Spear* • Millie Perkins *Woman* • Warren Oates *Willett Gashade* • Will Hutchins *Coley* • BJ Merholz *Leland Drum* ■ *Dir* Monte Hellman • *Scr* Adrien Joyce [Carole Eastman]

Shooting Dogs ★★ 15

Drama based on a true story
2005 · UK/Ger/Fr · Colour · 110min

Like the Oscar-nominated *Hotel Rwanda*, Michael Caton-Jones's film attempts to address the Rwandan genocide. In April 1994, a world-weary British priest (John Hurt) and an idealistic young teacher (Hugh Dancy) are caught up in inter-tribal violence and stuck in a school compound with hundreds of refugees. The film is well-intentioned but turns the atrocity into a story about the plight of two Englishmen abroad. BP Swearing, violence. DVD

John Hurt *Father Christopher* • Hugh Dancy *Joe Connor* • Dominique Horwitz *Captain Delon* • Louis Mahoney *Sibomana* • Nicola Walker *Rachel* • Steve Toussaint *Roland* • David Gyasi *François* • Susan Nalwoga *Edda* ■ *Dir* Michael Caton-Jones • *Scr* David Wolstencroft, from a story by Richard Alwyn, David Belton

Shooting Elizabeth ★★ 15

Black comedy   1992 · Fr · Colour · 91min

This is an eminently resistible black comedy. Even if nagging wife Mimi Rogers had been grotesquely shrewish, it would have been difficult to snigger along with Jeff Goldblum's inept attempts to dispose of her on a second honeymoon, but the details of their relationship are actually too black for the unsubtle comic elements to work smoothly. Rogers retains her poise in a thankless role, but Goldblum flounders hopelessly in this increasingly distasteful farce. DP

Jeff Goldblum *Harold Pigeon* • Mimi Rogers *Elizabeth Pigeon* • Burt Kwouk *Father Chu/Mad Mountaineer* • Juan Echanove *Detective* ■ *Dir* Baz Taylor • *Scr* Robbie Fox

Shooting Fish ★★★ 12
Romantic comedy 1997 · UK · Colour · 107min

Director Stefan Schwartz's daft, yet endearing, romantic comedy sees two friends – American Dan Futterman and Briton Stuart Townsend – trying to pull off a series of money-making scams. From selling bogus voice-recognition computers to nonexistent loft insulation, the boys are doing well until mutual love interest Kate Beckinsale sets them at odds. This is an Ealing comedy-style caper in a contemporary setting with both a high cuteness factor and some imaginative gags. LH Swearing. *DVD*

Dan Futterman *Dylan* • Stuart Townsend *Jez* • Kate Beckinsale *Georgie* • Nickolas Grace *Mr Stratton-Luce* • Claire Cox *Floss* • Ralph Ineson *Mr Ray* • Dominic Mafham *Roger* • Peter Capaldi *Mr Gilzean* • Annette Crosbie *Mrs Cummins* ■ *Dir* Stefan Schwartz • *Scr* Stefan Schwartz, Richard Holmes

Shooting for Socrates ★★ PG
Sports comedy drama 2014 · UK · Colour · 91min

In 1986, the Northern Ireland football team brought hope to the nation when they qualified for the World Cup. Travelling to Mexico, they prepared for the first round of fixtures, which included a historic, David and Goliath-type match against the mighty Brazil. The squad's journey is loosely re-created in this modest sporting drama, with co-writer/director James Erskine charting a path from the qualifying campaign to the big game. Unfortunately, though, there's no sense of occasion – you never feel like you're watching a real World Cup – and there are too many sequences that don't ring true. SC *DVD*

John Hannah *Billy Bingham* • Conleth Hill *Jackie Fullerton* • Richard Dormer *Arthur* • Nico Mirallegro *David Campbell* • Ciaran McMenamin *Sammy McIlroy* ■ *Dir* James Erskine • *Scr* James Erskine, Marie Jones

Shooting Magpies ★★★ 15
Social drama 2005 · UK · Colour · 79min

This uncompromising insight into the consequences of drug abuse reinforces the reputation for fact-based, workshop drama that the Amber Collective first forged in 1968. When teenage junkie Sanchez Coulson kills himself, ex-youth worker Barry Gough and single mum Emma Dowson become embroiled in father Brian Hogg's quest for revenge against the local dealers. Discussing everything from unemployment and addiction to theft and harness racing with stark authenticity, this is made all the persuasively harrowing by the cast's gritty restraint. DP Swearing, drug abuse.

Emma Dowson *Emma* • Barry Gough *Barry* • Callum Gough *Jackson Callum* • Jade Bell *Jade* ■ *Dir* Amber Production Team • *Scr* Amber Production Team

The Shooting Party ★★★★ 15
Period drama 1984 · UK · Colour · 92min

On target with regard to upper-class attitudes just prior to the First World War, James Mason's penultimate feature film casts him as the aristocratic organiser of a weekend shoot at his country mansion, where class exploitation and numerous infidelities are also on the menu. Similar to Renoir's *La Règle du Jeu* in its theme of a disintegrating social order, it has a cast to die for; this has acting class in abundance. TH Some swearing, brief nudity. *DVD*

James Mason *Sir Randolph Nettleby* • Edward Fox *Lord Gilbert Hartlip* • Dorothy Tutin *Lady Minnie Nettleby* • John Gielgud *Cornelius Cardew* • Gordon Jackson *Tom Harker* • Cheryl Campbell *Lady Aline Hartlip* • Robert Hardy *Lord Bob Lilburn* • Rupert Frazer *Lionel Stephens* • Judi

Bowker *Lady Olivier Lilburn* ■ *Dir* Alan Bridges • *Scr* Julian Bond, from the novel by Isabel Colegate

Shooting the Moon ★★★★
Drama 1998 · It · Colour · 90min

Rome emerges as a soulless city in Francesca Archibugi's unflinching yet warm-hearted study of brotherly love and innocent determination. Niccolo Senni carries the film as the teenage son of heroin-addict Valeria Golina, who so distrusts the adults around him that when his half-sister accidentally pricks herself on one of their mother's needles, he assumes the responsibility of having her Aids-tested. Francesca di Giovanni is also impressively natural as his toddling co-star, which speaks volumes for Archibugi's unforced yet eminently sympathetic direction. DP In Italian.

Valeria Golino *Silvia* • Sergio Rubini *Massimo* • Stefano Dionisi *Roberto* • Niccolo Senni *Siddharta* • Francesca di Giovanni *Domitilla* ■ *Dir/Scr* Francesca Archibugi

The Shootist ★★★★ PG
Western 1976 · US · Colour · 94min

This was John Wayne's last movie and it turned out to be a fitting tribute to a great talent. Director Don Siegel was not a man to dwell on the maudlin, and this fine western plays like a *Shane* for the 1970s. The Duke stars as a retired gunfighter dying of cancer, with Ron Howard as the wide-eyed innocent to Wayne's Alan Ladd. There's also superb support from the likes of James Stewart, Lauren Bacall and, especially, the under-used Hugh O'Brian. The opening titles form a touching montage to an outstanding career; how often does a star of Wayne's magnitude leave the stage with such dignity? TS Violence, swearing. *DVD*

John Wayne *John Bernard Books* • Lauren Bacall *Bond Rogers* • James Stewart *Dr Hostetler* • Ron Howard *Gillom Rogers* • Richard Boone *Sweeney* • Hugh O'Brian *Pulford* • Bill McKinney *Cobb* • Harry Morgan *Marshell Thibido* • John Carradine *Beckum* • Sheree North *Serepta* ■ *Dir* Don Siegel • *Scr* Miles Hood Swarthout, Scott Hale, from the novel by Glendon Swarthout

The Shop around the Corner ★★★★ U
Romantic comedy drama 1940 · US · BW · 98min

Based on Nikolaus Laszlo's play *Parfumerie*, this is a truly wonderful film, deftly directed by the great Ernst Lubitsch and containing a delightful performance by Margaret Sullavan, full of grace and warmth. The plot, about pen pals who fall in love after realising they work together, is paper-thin, but charm is there in abundance, and the young James Stewart is a portrait in perfection. Judy Garland starred in the 1949 musical remake, *In the Good Old Summertime*, and it was also remade in 1998 as *You've Got Mail*, with Tom Hanks and Meg Ryan. TS

James Stewart *Alfred Kralik* • Margaret Sullavan *Klara Novak* • Frank Morgan *Hugo Matuschek* • Joseph Schildkraut *Ferencz Vadas* • Sara Haden *Flora* • Felix Bressart *Pirovitch* • William Tracy *Pepi Katona* • Inez Courtney *Ilona* ■ *Dir* Ernst Lubitsch • *Scr* Samson Raphaelson, from the play *Parfumerie* by Nikolaus Laszlo

The Shop at Sly Corner ★★★
Crime drama 1946 · UK · BW · 94min

This is a splendid showcase for that master of malevolence, Oscar Homolka. With an accent thicker than his eyebrows, he is suitably shifty as an antiques dealer who not only trades in stolen goods but is also a fugitive from Devil's Island. However, he is occasionally in serious danger of having the picture filched from under his nose by Kenneth Griffith, who is revoltingly effective as a blackmailer who threatens to ruin the musical career of Homolka's daughter. DP

Oscar Homolka *Descius Heiss* • Derek Farr *Robert Graham* • Muriel Pavlow *Margaret Heiss* • Kenneth Griffith *Archie Fellowes* • Manning Whiley *Corder Morris* • Kathleen Harrison *Mrs*

Catt • Garry Marsh *Major Elliot* ■ *Dir* George King • *Scr* Katherine Strueby, from a play by Edward Percy

The Shop on the High Street ★★★★ 15
Second World War drama 1965 · Cz · BW · 119min

Winner of the 1965 Oscar for best foreign film, Czech writer/director Jan Kadar's intimate portrait of two simple people destroyed by the Nazi occupation is exquisitely sensitive, brilliantly played and utterly heartbreaking. Ida Kaminska gives a miraculous performance as an old Jewish woman who owns a little button shop where a humble carpenter (a superb Jozef Kroner) is appointed "Aryan comptroller" by the occupiers. He discovers that Kaminska's stock of buttons is depleted almost to nothing, and that she's totally deaf and quite unaware of the war. His growing affection for her leads Kroner into muddled efforts to protect her, with tragic results for both of them. RK Czech +subtitles. *DVD*

Ida Kaminska *Rozalie Lautmannova* • Jozef Kroner *Tono Brtko* • Frantisek Zvarik *Markus Kolkocky* • Hana Slivkova *Evelyna Brtkova* ■ *Dir* Jan Kadar, Elmar Klos • *Scr* Jan Kadár, Elmar Klos

Shopgirl ★★★ 15
Romantic comedy drama 2005 · US/UK · Colour · 102min

Steve Martin delivers one of his finest performances in years in this bittersweet film adapted from his novella. A radiant Claire Danes is the Beverly Hills department store assistant, who is swept off her feet by Martin's wealthy entrepreneur. This attentive sophisticate is the apparent opposite of her other on/off suitor, slacker oddball Jason Schwartzman, and gives her all she could dream of – except, heartbreakingly, the one thing she really needs. This is wry and poignant, yet despite its emotional astuteness, the storyline remains flimsy. SF *DVD*

Claire Danes *Mirabelle Buttersfield* • Steve Martin *Ray Porter* • Jason Schwartzman *Jeremy* • Bridgette Wilson-Sampras [Bridgette Wilson] *Lisa Cramer* • Sam Bottoms *Dan Buttersfield* • Frances Conroy *Catherine Buttersfield* • Rebecca Pidgeon *Christie Richards* • Samantha Shelton *Loki* ■ *Dir* Anand Tucker • *Scr* Steve Martin, from his novella

Shopping ★★★ 15
Drama 1993 · UK · Colour · 102min

Paul Anderson's first feature is a slick, superficial exercise that doesn't quite reach the heights of the Hollywood blockbusters to which he aspires, but is still a riveting ride. Jude Law is the adrenaline freak who, along with Sadie Frost, gets his kicks by joyriding and ram raiding. His nihilistic lifestyle is threatened by the forces of law and order and rival rider Sean Pertwee, who views Law's hobby as a profession. The two leads are unconvincing, but Pertwee excels as the villain. JF Violence, swearing. *DVD*

Sadie Frost *Jo* • Jude Law *Billy* • Sean Pertwee *Tommy* • Fraser James *Be Bop* • Sean Bean *Venning* • Marianne Faithfull *Bev* • Jonathan Pryce *Conway* • Danny Newman *Monkey* ■ *Dir/Scr* Paul Anderson (1)

Shopworn ★★
Melodrama 1932 · US · BW · 68min

The plot is as shopworn as Barbara Stanwyck's notorious showgirl in this perfunctory melodrama. She starts out as a waitress loved by a college student. Framed on morals charges by his wealthy, disapproving mother, she is sent to reform school. Heavy censorship trimmed the details of her subsequent rise in showbusiness, but Stanwyck's terrific performance makes it enjoyable. AE

Barbara Stanwyck *Kitty Lane* • Regis Toomey *Dave Livingston* • ZaSu Pitts *Dot* • Lucien Littlefield *Fred* ■ *Dir* Nicholas Grinde [Nick Grinde] • *Scr* Jo Swerling, Robert Riskin, from a story by Sarah Y Mason

The Shopworn Angel ★★★
Silent romantic drama 1928 · US · BW · 82min

Innocent young Texan Gary Cooper, about to be shipped off to France with the army, meets showgirl Nancy Carroll. To the displeasure of her wealthy lover (Paul Lukas), she befriends the young man, who falls passionately in love with her. A superior romantic drama, this is still worth watching, though it's now understandably superceded by the better-known 1938 remake. The coming of sound allowed Carroll to burst effectively into song at the end of this silent version. RK

Nancy Carroll *Daisy Heath* • Gary Cooper *William Tyler* • Paul Lukas *Bailey* • Emmett King *The chaplain* • Mildred Washington *Daisy's maid* • Roscoe Karns *Dance director* ■ *Dir* Richard Wallace • *Scr* Howard Estabrook, Albert Shelby Le Vino, Tom Miranda (titles), from the story *Private Pettigrew's Girl* by Dana Burnet

The Shopworn Angel ★★★★
Wartime romantic drama 1938 · US · BW · 84min

Benefiting from sound, technical advance and dream casting, this triumphantly successful remake offers the always magical pairing of James Stewart and Margaret Sullavan. With his youthful, gawky attractiveness, Stewart is perfect as the naive and idealistic soldier in love, while Sullavan is exemplary as the self-centred, kept showgirl whose hard-boiled exterior hides a soft heart buried by life's knocks. The stars are marvellous in their scenes together, resolutely unsentimental and extracting every shred of truth from the tale. RK

Margaret Sullavan *Daisy Heath* • James Stewart *Bill Pettigrew* • Walter Pidgeon *Sam Bailey* • Nat Pendleton *Dice* • Hattie McDaniel *Martha the maid* • Charley Grapewin *Wilson the caretaker* • Charles D Brown *Mr Gonigle the stage manager* ■ *Dir* HC Potter • *Scr* Waldo Salt, from the short story *Private Pettigrew's Girl* by Dana Burnet

Short Circuit ★★★ PG
Fantasy comedy 1986 · US · Colour · 94min

Youngsters will love this hip spoof on hardware movies, in which a government robot called Number Five gets struck by lightning, goes AWOL and takes on hilarious human characteristics. As Steve Guttenberg's goofy inventor tries to locate his missing model, the cute cyborg befriends vegetarian animal lover Ally Sheedy and has a series of misadventures. John Badham directs with the lightest of touches, and funny moments include the runaway robot's mimicry of John Wayne, the Three Stooges and John Travolta. AJ Swearing. *DVD* *BL*

Ally Sheedy *Stephanie Speck* • Steve Guttenberg *Newton Crosby* • Fisher Stevens *Ben Jabituya* • Austin Pendleton *Howard Marner* • GW Bailey *Skroeder* • Brian McNamara *Frank* • Tim Blaney *Number Five* ■ *Dir* John Badham • *Scr* SS Wilson, Brent Maddock

Short Circuit 2 ★★ PG
Fantasy comedy 1988 · US · Colour · 105min

This sequel about the former military robot Number Five, now Johnny Five, has several moments of humour, but too many minutes of tedium as it wonders whether to be social satire or pratfall parody. Fisher Stevens returns as the Indian co-inventor of the robot, and again his clichéd character is infuriating. TH *DVD*

Fisher Stevens *Ben Jahrvi* • Michael McKean *Fred Ritter* • Cynthia Gibb *Sandy Banatoni* • Jack Weston *Oscar Baldwin* • Dee McCafferty *Saunders* • David Hemblen *Jones* • Don Lake *Manic Mike* ■ *Dir* Kenneth Johnson • *Scr* SS Wilson, Brent Maddock

Short Cut to Hell ★
Crime drama 1957 · US · BW · 89min

Look in vain for any sign of the vitality you'd expect from the directing debut of James Cagney. He himself appears only in a very brief prologue to introduce two newcomers, Robert Ivers and Georgann Johnson, as the stars of this updated remake of *This Gun for Hire*. In 1942 it did

S

wonders for the careers of Alan Ladd and Veronica Lake, but not here. AE

Robert Ivers *Kyle* • William Bishop *Stan* • Georgann Johnson *Glory Hamilton* • Jacques Aubuchon *Bahrwell* • Peter Baldwin *Adams* • Yvette Vickers *Daisy* • Murvyn Vye *Nichols* ■ *Dir* James Cagney • *Scr* Ted Berkman, Raphael Blau, from the film *This Gun for Hire* by Albert Maltz, WR Burnett, from the novel *A Gun for Sale* by Graham Greene

Short Cuts ★★★★★ 18

Drama 1993 · US · Colour · 187min

Admirers of Raymond Carver, whose stories inspired *Short Cuts*, were less than impressed by Robert Altman's reworking and interweaving of his tales into this tapestry of southern Californian mores. But, for those less wedded to or ignorant of the originals, this is a superbly controlled piece of film-making that invites comparison with Altman's own *Nashville*. The only discordant note is provided by the sole non-Carver story, involving jazz singer Annie Ross and her daughter Lori Singer. The rest, however, are engaging in their own right and spellbinding when taken as a whole. In a brilliant ensemble cast, Lily Tomlin, Tim Robbins, Jennifer Jason Leigh and Andie MacDowell give the stand-out performances, but the real star is Altman. AC Violence, swearing, sex scenes, nudity. *DVD*

Andie MacDowell *Ann Finnigan* • Bruce Davison *Howard Finnigan* • Jack Lemmon *Paul Finnigan* • Julianne Moore *Marian Wyman* • Matthew Modine *Dr Ralph Wyman* • Anne Archer *Claire Kane* • Fred Ward *Stuart Kane* • Jennifer Jason Leigh *Lois Kaiser* • Chris Penn *Jerry Kaiser* • Robert Downey *Bill Bush* • Madeleine Stowe *Sherri Shepard* • Tim Robbins *Gene Shepard* • Lily Tomlin *Doreen Piggot* • Tom Waits *Earl Piggot* • Peter Gallagher *Stormy Weathers* • Frances McDormand *Betty Weathers* • Annie Ross *Tess Trainer* • Lori Singer *Zoe Trainer* ■ *Dir* Robert Altman • *Scr* Robert Altman, Frank Barhydt, from stories by Raymond Carver

A Short Film about Killing ★★★★★ 18

Crime drama 1988 · Pol · Colour · 84min

This harrowing drama from Krzysztof Kieslowski was originally part of a series of television films about the Ten Commandments called *Dekalog*. Expanded to feature length for release in cinemas, it won the Special Jury Prize at Cannes. Powerful in its emotional clout precisely because of its subdued, matter-of-fact approach, this judgement on murder (be it illegal or state-sanctioned) concerns a youth who kills a cab driver and must face the inevitable consequences. Kieslowski, arguably Poland's greatest contemporary director, was a true master of narrative construction, and many of his thoughtful compositions linger long in the memory. JM Polish +subtitles. *DVD*

Miroslaw Baka *Yatzek* • Krzysztof Globisz *Lawyer* • Jan Tesarz *Taxi driver* ■ *Dir* Krzysztof Kieslowski • *Scr* Krzysztof Kieslowski, Krzysztof Piesiewicz

A Short Film about Love ★★★ 15

Drama 1988 · Pol · Colour · 83min

From its bitingly ironic title to its downbeat conclusion, this is one of the most damning pictures of modern city life ever made. Expanding on the seventh part of the *Dekalog* series he made for TV, director Krzysztof Kieslowski revisits the themes of obsession and voyeurism touched on by Alfred Hitchcock in *Rear Window* and Michael Powell in *Peeping Tom*. But his main preoccupation here is with the impossibility of love and the breakdown of community. Impressive and provocative. DP Polish +subtitles. Sex scenes, nudity. *DVD*

Grazyna Szapolowska *Magda* • Olaf Lubaszenko *Tomek* • Stefania Iwinska *Gospodyni* • Piotr Machalica *Roman* • Artur Barcis *Mlody Mezczyzna* ■ *Dir* Krzysztof Kieslowski • *Scr* Krzysztof Kieslowski, Krzysztof Piesiewicz

The Short Night of the Glass Dolls ★★★★

Thriller 1971 · It/W Ger/Yug · Colour · 92min

Aldo Lado creates a minor masterpiece with this superbly controlled tale of paranoia and political persecution. Complete with a haunting score by Ennio Morricone, it makes eerie use of the grey beauty of Prague to chronicle to the abstract, but increasingly terrifying recollections of Jean Sorel, an American journalist whose search for missing lover Barbara Bach leaves him cataleptic in the city morgue. Ingrid Thulin and Mario Adorf provide superior support, but it's Lado's rejuvenation of such tired symbolism as impaled butterflies that make this so chillingly memorable. DP Italian dubbed.

Jean Sorel *Gregory Moore* • Ingrid Thulin *Jessica* • Mario Adorf *Jacques* • Barbara Bach *Mira* ■ *Dir/Scr* Aldo Lado

Short Term 12 ★★★★ 15

Drama 2013 · US · Colour · 92min

This slice-of-life drama set in a Californian care home for adolescents reveals the daily challenges facing troubled residents and staff with urgent problems of their own. Inspired by the personal experiences of writer/director Destin Daniel Cretton, it suggests that carers with unresolved issues often have compelling personal reasons to work in this sector. Thoughtful and engrossing, the result is a film of rich characterisation and strong central performances. Now and again, it's a tad contrived, yet there's a generosity of spirit in the storytelling, and the sudden switches from comic misadventure to aching tragedy feel warranted when each new day brings a fresh crisis. TJ Swearing. *DVD*

Brie Larson *Grace* • John Gallagher Jr *Mason* • Kaitlyn Dever *Jayden* • Keith Stanfield *Marcus* ■ *Dir/Scr* Destin Daniel Cretton

Short Time ★★★ 15

Comedy drama 1990 · US · Colour · 93min

This offers rare leading role for that accomplished comedy actor Dabney Coleman. He plays a cop on the verge of retirement who discovers that not only is he dying, but that the insurers will pay out only if he dies in the line of duty. To the astonishment of partner Matt Frewer, Coleman is then transformed into the craziest risk-taking policeman since Mel Gibson. It's an intriguing concept and Coleman milks it for all it is worth, but director Gregg Champion doesn't look entirely comfortable juggling the action and comedy. JF Violence, swearing. *DVD*

Dabney Coleman *Burt Simpson* • Matt Frewer *Ernie Dills* • Teri Garr *Carolyn Simpson* • Barry Corbin *Captain* • Joe Pantoliano *Scalese* • Xander Berkeley *Stark* ■ *Dir* Gregg Champion • *Scr* John Blumenthal, Michael Berry

Shortbus ★★★ 18

Sex drama 2006 · US · Colour · 97min

Following *Hedwig and the Angry Inch*, the movie adaptation of his own stage musical about a rock star with a botched sex-change, New York-based director John Cameron Mitchell serves up a similarly perverse slice of life on the wild side in *Shortbus*. Linking multiple storylines, the film begins with a gay couple seeking relationship guidance from sex therapist Sofia (Sook-Yin Lee). In the course of the session, Sofia realises some tough truths about herself, principally that she has never had an orgasm. She then journeys deep into the city's hedonistic nightlife to find herself, discovering acceptance at a sex club called Shortbus. DW *DVD*

Sook-Yin Lee *Sofia* • Paul Dawson *James* • Lindsay Beamish *Severin* • PJ DeBoy *Jamie* • Raphael Barker *Rob* • Peter Stickles *Caleb* • Jay Brannan *Ceth* ■ *Dir/Scr* John Cameron Mitchell

Shorts ★★ PG

Fantasy adventure 2009 · US/UAE · Colour · 85min

Bullied schoolboy Jimmy Bennett finds a rainbow-coloured "wishing rock" and proceeds to cause havoc in his

neighbourhood, where all the local people (including his parents, Leslie Mann and Jon Cryer) work for sinister business magnate James Spader. The fragmented structure (the film consists of five jumbled episodes, or shorts) may be confusing for some youngsters and Rodriguez too obviously follows the whims of his own imagination, irrespective of the effect on the action. But strong performances from Cryer and Mann and a quirky relationship between Bennett and Spader's daughter, Jolie Vanier, provide sufficient amusement to keep you watching. SuR *DVD* *BD*

Jon Cryer *Dad Thompson* • William H Macy *Dr Noseworthy* • Leslie Mann *Mom Thompson* • James Spader *Mr Black* • Jimmy Bennett *Toe Thompson* • Kat Dennings *Stacey Thompson* • Jake Short *Nose Noseworthy* • Jolie Vanier *Helvetica Black* ■ *Dir/Scr* Robert Rodriguez

A Shot at Glory ★★ 15

Sports drama 2000 · US · Colour · 110min

What with all the sectarian rivalry, family feuding and boardroom machinations, it's a wonder there's any room left at all for football in this mid-table misfire. Robert Duvall plays the manager of a Scottish club struggling to survive in the lower divisions until new American owner Michael Keaton decides to bring in a star forward, played by real-life footballer Ally McCoist. But his on-going battle with ex-son-in-law and wasted talent McCoist soon become tiresome; much of the problem lies with the falsity of the action sequences. DP *DVD*

Robert Duvall *Gordon McLeod* • Michael Keaton *Peter Cameron* • Ally McCoist *Jackie McQuillan* • Libby Langdon • Brian Cox (1) *Martin Smith* ■ *Dir* Michael Corrente • *Scr* Denis O'Neill

Shot in Bombay ★★★

Documentary 2007 · UK · Colour · 96min

All film-makers are up against it, but none more so than Apoorva Lakhia. Following two flops, his current hope dramatises a real-life shoot-out between police and gangsters. The problem is that the lead – Bollywood megastar Sanjay Dutt – faces jail for his part in the 1993 Bombay bomb blasts. This records the final, chaotic days of filming between court appearances, as Lakhia leaps around, playing every role and yelling "mind-blowing!" (unlucky choice of words) as each scene wraps. Just as captivating are the colourful profiles of those entangled in this stranger-than-fiction tale, including the Mob don unhappy about having his dirty underwear aired on the silver screen. CW

■ *Dir* Liz Mermin

A Shot in the Dark ★★★★ PG

Comedy mystery 1964 · US · Colour · 98min

This was the movie in which Peter Sellers first headed the cast as Clouseau (after stealing every scene from nominal stars David Niven and Capucine in *The Pink Panther* the year before). He mingles accents and mangles motives with his usual skill, producing some of the most hilarious moments in the series. The self-righteous buffoon investigates a murder at a millionaire's Paris apartment, with suave George Sanders as the wealthy resident and saucy chambermaid Elke Sommer the prime suspect. Ten years later he returned to the role in *The Return of the Pink Panther*. TH *DVD*

Peter Sellers *Inspector Jacques Clouseau* • Elke Sommer *Maria Gambrelli* • George Sanders *Benjamin Ballon* • Herbert Lom *Chief Inspector Charles Dreyfus* • Tracy Reed *Dominique Ballon* • Graham Stark *Hercule Lajoy* • Bert Kwouk [Burt Kwouk] *Kato* ■ *Dir* Blake Edwards • *Scr* Blake Edwards, William Peter Blatty, from the plays *A Shot in the Dark* by Harry Kurnitz and *L'Idiote* by Marcel Achard

Shotgun Stories ★★★★ 12

Revenge drama 2007 · US · Colour · 86min

A feud between two sets of Arkansas half-brothers spills over into violence in this simmering, low-budget drama from writer/director Jeff Nichols. Drawing on themes of revenge familiar from the western genre and many literary sources, it begins with

Son Hayes (Michael Shannon) and brothers Boy (Douglas Ligon) and Kid (Barlow Jacobs) turning up at their estranged father's funeral, where Son offends the dead man's new family. Their half-siblings – led by Michael Abbott Jr – demand an apology, but it's not long before the dispute escalates into bloodshed. Adroitly balancing southern caricature with authenticity, Nichols keeps as much violence as possible off-screen, concentrating instead on the inarticulate fury of these two clans. Evocatively photographed by Adam Stone, this frequently recalls the measured melodramas of David Gordon Green (*George Washington*), who co-produces here. DP *DVD*

Michael Shannon *Son Hayes* • Douglas Ligon *Boy Hayes* • Barlow Jacobs *Kid Hayes* • Michael Abbott Jr *Cleaman Hayes* • Travis Smith *Mark Hayes* • Lynnsee Provence *Stephen Hayes* • David Rhodes *John Hayes* • Natalie Canerday *Nicole* ■ *Dir/Scr* Jeff Nichols • *Cinematographer* Adam Stone

Shoulder Arms ★★★ U

Silent comedy drama 1918 · US · BW · 29min

Charles Chaplin's genius at creating comedy out of desperate situations is well illustrated in this short film. But he also drew howls of protests for daring to make fun of conditions for men in the trenches of the First World War. He co-stars with vermin, a sniper, flooding rain, mud and fear, proving that he could laugh in the face of the most horrifying extremes. TH

Charles Chaplin *Recruit* • Edna Purviance *French girl* • Sydney Chaplin [Syd Chaplin] *The American sergeant/The Kaiser* • Loyal Underwood *Short German officer* ■ *Dir/Scr* Charles Chaplin

The Shout ★★★ 15

Horror drama 1978 · UK · Colour · 82min

Robert Graves's weird story becomes a weird movie, directed by Polish émigré Jerzy Skolimowski and starring Alan Bates as the mysterious interloper who claims to have murdered his family in Australia and is the custodian of various aboriginal curses. Chief of these is the ability to shout so loudly that it can kill. John Hurt and Susannah York are among those reaching for their earplugs. AT Swearing. *DVD* *BD*

Alan Bates *Charles Crossley* • Susannah York *Rachel Fielding* • John Hurt *Anthony Fielding* • Robert Stephens *Chief medical officer* • Tim Curry *Robert* • Julian Hough *Vicar* • Carol Drinkwater *Cobbler's wife* • Nick Stringer *Cobbler* ■ *Dir* Jerzy Skolimowski • *Scr* Jerzy Skolimowski, Michael Austin, from a story by Robert Graves

Shout ★★ 15

Drama 1991 · US · Colour · 197min

Until his rebirth as the master of cool in *Pulp Fiction*, John Travolta was sunk by embarrassments such as this. He plays a music teacher at a tough school who just loves rock 'n' roll (what a surprise) and, on the run himself, reaches out naturally to rebel pupil James Walters. Lumpy direction of the first order is enlivened by occasional unexpected charm. JM Some swearing.

John Travolta *Jack Cabe* • James Walters [Jamie Walters] *Jesse Tucker* • Heather Graham *Sara Benedict* • Richard Jordan *Eugene Benedict* • Linda Fiorentino *Molly* ■ *Dir* Jeffrey Hornaday • *Scr* Joe Gayton, from his story

Shout at the Devil ★★ 15

Action adventure 1976 · UK · Colour · 114min

Mixing the rough (Lee Marvin) with the smooth (Roger Moore) wasn't such a good idea, even if their oddball partnership was supposed to be for king and country in the First World War. Based on the Wilbur Smith novel, the tale follows the undynamic duo as they set out to sabotage a German cruiser berthed in an East African delta. Lots of action, but, as neither hero is very likeable, you really don't care. TH Violence, swearing, brief nudity. *DVD* *BD*

Lee Marvin *Flynn* • Roger Moore *Sebastian Oldsmith* • Barbara Parkins *Rosa* • Ian Holm *Mohammed* • Rene Kolldehoff [Reinhard Kolldehoff] *Commissioner Fleischer* • Maurice Denham *Mr Smythe* • Jean Kent *Mrs Smythe* •

George Coulouris *El Keb* ■ *Dir* Peter Hunt • *Scr* Wilbur Smith, Stanley Price, Alastair Reid, from the novel by Wilbur Smith

The Shouting Men ★★15
Comedy drama 2009 · UK · Colour · 91min

Now, here's a novelty - a film about football that isn't obsessed with hooligans. Actually, it does feature one thug, but he's just one of a varied bunch of Gillingham fans who head north when their lowly club is drawn away to mighty Newcastle United in an FA Cup tie. The characters are a little formulaic, and there's too much lazy reliance on toilet humour, but this remains a watchable little comedy drama. DA Swearing, sexual references.

Craig Fairbrass *Tony* • Warren Llambias *Rod* • Matt Daniel-Baker *Terry* • Dudley Sutton *Charlie* • Tony Denham *Micky* ■ *Dir* Steve Kelly • *Scr* Matt Daniel-Baker, Warren Llambias

Show Boat ★★★★★U
Musical 1936 · US · BW · 114min

Arguably the finest creation of the Broadway musical theatre, this Jerome Kern/Oscar Hammerstein II stage masterpiece has been blessed by two equally fine talkie versions. This one is aided by a screenplay from Hammerstein himself, and by the appearances of the great bass Paul Robeson as Joe, who gets to sing *Ol' Man River* and torch singer Helen Morgan. Irene Dunne is fine, strutting and cakewalking as though to the manner born, but Allan Jones is nowhere near as dashing as Howard Keel in the 1951 Technicolor remake. However, there's little to choose between the versions: both are splendid and well worthy of their superb source material. TS

Irene Dunne *Magnolia Hawks* • Allan Jones *Gaylord Ravenal* • Charles Winninger *Captain Andy Hawks* • Helen Westley *Parthy Hawks* • Paul Robeson *Joe* • Helen Morgan (1) *Julie* • Donald Cook *Steve* • Sammy White *Frank Schultz* • Queenie Smith *Ellie* ■ *Dir* James Whale • *Scr* Oscar Hammerstein II, from the musical by Oscar Hammerstein II, Jerome Kern, from the novel by Edna Ferber

Show Boat ★★★★★U
Musical 1951 · US · Colour · 103min

A magnificent musical achievement, and unquestionably one of the finest MGM Technicolor features, this triumph from producer Arthur Freed and director George Sidney is supremely satisfying. The cast couldn't be bettered, with Ava Gardner hitting a career high as Julie LaVerne, never more moving than in the scene where she's left on the river bank to the strains of William Warfield singing *Ol' Man River*. The show was, and is, Broadway at its peak, and here the Kern-Hammerstein score receives a definitive rendering. The plot, with its themes of miscegenation and compulsive gambling, is adult, while the opening sequence of the show boat's arrival is a superb marriage of music, style and colour. TS

Kathryn Grayson *Magnolia Hawks* • Ava Gardner *Julie LaVerne* • Howard Keel *Gaylord Ravenal* • Joe E Brown *Captain Andy Hawks* • Marge Champion *Ellie May Shipley* • Gower Champion *Frank Schultz* • Robert Sterling *Stephen Baker* • Agnes Moorehead *Parthy Hawks* • William Warfield *Joe* ■ *Dir* George Sidney (2) • *Scr* John Lee Mahin (uncredited), George Wells, Jack McGowan, from the musical by Oscar Hammerstein II, Jerome Kern, from the novel by Edna Ferber

Show Business ★★★U
Musical 1944 · US · BW · 92min

After 35 years in showbusiness, saucer-eyed comedian Eddie Cantor decided to produce a film based on his early days in vaudeville. The result was a cliché-packed musical, beginning in 1914, about the ups and downs of two contrasting couples - hoofer George Murphy and singer Constance Moore (almost broken up by vamp Nancy Kelly), and Cantor and the tiresomely madcap Joan Davis. But there are a lot of good old tunes, including *It Had To Be You*, and Cantor favourites such as *Making Whoopee*. RB

Eddie Cantor *Eddie Martin* • Joan Davis *Joan Mason* • George Murphy *George Doane* • Nancy Kelly *Nancy Gaye* • Constance Moore *Constance Ford* • Don Douglas *Charles Lucas* ■ *Dir* Edwin L Marin • *Scr* Joseph Quillan, Dorothy Bennett, Irving Elinson, from a story by Bert Granet

The Show Goes On ★★U
Musical 1937 · UK · BW · 85min

Gracie Fields has the dubious distinction here of starring in a film *à clef* about her own rise to showbiz fame. As the chorus girl who becomes the darling of the music halls, Gracie shows occasional flashes of her unique Lancastrian charm. But director Basil Dean stifles her exuberance by saddling her with some woefully unsuitable material. The backstage details ring false, while the film has a shoddiness that would have been unthinkable in Hollywood. DP
DVD

Gracie Fields *Sally Scowcroft* • Owen Nares *Martin Fraser* • John Stuart *Mack* • Horace Hodges *Sam Bishop* • Edward Rigby *Mr Scowcroft* • Amy Veness *Mrs Scowcroft* ■ *Dir* Basil Dean • *Scr* Austin Melford, Anthony Kimmins, EG Valentine, from a story by Basil Dean

Show Me Love ★★★15
Comedy drama 1998 · Swe · Colour · 85min

A colossal hit in its native Sweden, this charming rite-of-passage picture marks the feature debut of acclaimed poet and short film-maker, Lukas Moodysson. However, its treatment of alienated adolescence, provincial ennui and sexual confusion is every bit as superficial as the numerous American indies that have tackled the subject of lesbian first love. Rebecca Liljeberg's performance as the 15-year-old outsider who falls for school stunner Alexandra Dahlström brims with anti-parental resentment and repressed longing. Alas, such perspicacity is absent from the depiction of more peripheral characters. DP Swedish +subtitles. *DVD*

Alexandra Dahlström *Elin* • Rebecca Liljeberg *Agnes* • Erica Carlson *Jessica* • Mathias Rust *Johan Hult* ■ *Dir/Scr* Lukas Moodysson

A Show of Force ★★15
Political thriller 1990 · US · Colour · 88min

This movie from Brazilian director Bruno Barreto is loosely based on a supposedly true event, when some Puerto Rican student activists were shot as terrorists during an action instigated by a renegade FBI agent. Unfortunately, Barreto's film takes a potentially interesting and controversial subject and turns it into a rather tedious and violent political thriller. JB

Amy Irving *Kate Melendez* • Andy Garcia *Luis Angel Mora* • Robert Duvall *Howard* • Lou Diamond Phillips *Jesus Fuentes* • Kevin Spacey *Frank Curtin* • Erik Estrada *Machado* • Juan Fernandez *Captain Correa* ■ *Dir* Bruno Barreto • *Scr* Evan Jones, John Strong, from the non-fiction book *Murder under Two Flags* by Anne Nelson

The Show of Shows ★★★
Musical revue 1929 · US · BW · 128min

This is an early, technically primitive forerunner of the studio star-parade revues that would remain in the repertoire over the next 15 years, filmed entirely as a stage show and compèred by languid, quirky, deadpan comedian Frank Fay. Basically an experimental PR exercise to showcase Warner Bros contract artists, it demonstrates how rapidly and radically tastes in humour, music and performing styles change. On the one hand a lengthy exercise in indescribable tedium, which only the dedicated will endure; on the other hand, a unique and fascinating social-historical document. RK

Frank Fay *Master of ceremonies/Mexican general* • William Courtenay *The Minister* • HB Warner *The Victim* • Hobart Bosworth *The Executioner* • Myrna Loy *Floradora girl/Chinese fantasy girl* • Douglas Fairbanks Jr *Ambrose* • John Barrymore *Duke of Gloucester* ■ *Dir* John G Adolfi • *Scr* Frank Fay, J Keirn Brennan

The Show of Shows ★★★12A
Documentary 2014 · Ice/UK · Colour and BW · 76min

Given that moving pictures started out as a fairground curiosity, it's perhaps not surprising that film-makers have always been fascinated by carnival and circus folk. Culled from the University of Sheffield's National Fairground Archive, the footage selected by Icelandic director Benedikt Erlingsson also takes in freak shows, cabarets, music halls and seaside attractions to present a nostalgic but considered tribute to an almost extinct lifestyle. Some of the it makes uncomfortable viewing, but Erlingsson doesn't shy away from the more contentious aspects of big-top life. DP Some nudity.

■ *Dir* Benedikt Erlingsson • *Music* Georg Holm, Orri Pall Dyrason

Show People ★★★★★U
Silent satirical comedy 1928 · US · BW · 84min

Here's a wonderful chance to see Marion Davies, the mistress of billionaire William Randolph Hearst and the model for Susan Alexander in *Citizen Kane*. How Orson Welles wronged her! In truth, she was an intelligent comedian, here playing a young Hollywood hopeful who graduates from Keystone Kops to a Gloria Swanson-style *femme fatale*. Hearst didn't want to entrust any old director with Marion, so chose his friend, King Vidor, who makes an appearance in the film-within-a-film at the end. TH

Marion Davies *Peggy Pepper* • William Haines *Billy Boone* • Dell Henderson *Colonel Pepper* • Paul Ralli *André* • Charles Chaplin • Douglas Fairbanks ■ *Dir* King Vidor • *Scr* Wanda Tuchock, Agnes Christine Johnston, Laurence Stallings, Ralph Spence

Showdown ★★★
Western 1963 · US · BW · 78min

Baby-faced Audie Murphy and bluff Charles Drake star as escaped convicts who become involved in a robbery. There's a marvellous supporting cast of western regulars, and director RG Springsteen tells the tale tersely and tautly. Unusually for a Murphy western, it's in black and white. TS

Audie Murphy *Chris Foster* • Kathleen Crowley *Estelle* • Charles Drake *Bert Pickett* • Harold J Stone *Lavalle* • Skip Homeier *Calson* • LQ Jones *Foray* • Strother Martin *Charlie Reeder* ■ *Dir* RG Springsteen • *Scr* Bronson Howitzer

Showdown ★★PG
Western comedy 1973 · US · Colour · 94min

This unremarkable western stars Rock Hudson as a sheriff and Dean Martin as a train robber. Both were the closest of childhood friends until Hudson went into crime and married Martin's sweetheart, Susan Clark, who has to stand referee while these two movie stars slug it out and reach a compromise. There are times when the script scratches around for a classical allusion, though mostly it's a matter of furrowed brows, running sweat and New Mexican vistas. AT

Dean Martin *Billy* • Rock Hudson *Chuck* • Susan Clark *Kate* • Donald Moffat *Art Williams* • John McLiam *PJ Wilson* • Charles Baca *Martinez* • Jackson D Kane *Clem* • Ben Zeller *Perry Williams* • Ed Begley Jr *Pook* ■ *Dir* George Seaton • *Scr* Theodore Taylor, from a story by Hank Fine

Showdown at Abilene ★★
Western 1956 · US · Colour · 80min

Jock Mahoney is no more than adequate playing the American Civil War veteran who refuses to carry a gun as sheriff of Abilene. Much better is Lyle Bettger, who gives a typically intense performance as the one-armed cattle king who has taken Mahoney's girl (Martha Hyer) and wants him dead. Producer Howard Christie liked the story so much he remade it 11 years later as *Gunfight in Abilene*. AE

Jock Mahoney *Jim Trask* • Martha Hyer *Peggy Bigelow* • Lyle Bettger *Dave Mosely* • David Janssen *Verne Ward* • Grant Williams *Chip*

Tomlin • Ted De Corsia *Dan Claudius* ■ *Dir* Charles Haas • *Scr* Bernie Giler, from the novel *Gun Shy* by Clarence Upson Young

Showdown at Boot Hill ★★★
Western 1958 · US · BW · 71min

Charles Bronson plays a US marshal who rides into a strange town, kills the man he has been pursuing, and is then thwarted by the local residents who regarded the deceased as a respectable citizen. Denied his bounty money, Bronson turns all moody and reflective, pondering the ethics of his line of work. Within the conventions of the B-western, this develops into a fairly complex character study, using the townspeople with imagination. AT

Charles Bronson *Luke Welsh* • Robert Hutton *Sloane* • John Carradine *Doc Weber* • Carole Mathews *Jill* • Paul Maxey *Judge* • Thomas Browne Henry *Con Maynor* • Fintan Meyler *Sally* ■ *Dir* Gene Fowler Jr • *Scr* Louis Vittes

Showdown in Little Tokyo ★★18
Martial arts action adventure 1991 · US · Colour · 75min

This brainless martial arts kickabout teams Dolph Lundgren with a pre-*Crow* Brandon Lee as cops hunting down a vicious yakuza gang operating in Los Angeles. Mark L Lester packs in enough shoot-outs and fights to keep undemanding fans of the genre happy, while Tia Carrere crops up as a singer in the gangster's nightclub. But the best thing about this movie is the short running time. RS Violence, swearing, drug abuse, a sex scene, nudity. *DVD*

Dolph Lundgren *Detective Chris Kenner* • Brandon Lee *Johnny Murata* • Cary-Hiroyuki Tagawa *Yoshida* • Tia Carrere *Minako Okeya* • Toshishiro Obata *Sato* • Philip Tan *Tanaka* ■ *Dir* Mark L Lester • *Scr* Stephen Glantz, Caliope Brattlestreet

Shower ★★★12
Comedy drama 1999 · Chi · Colour · 90min

Zhang Yang is among China's most contentious indie directors. However, he's in a less abrasive mood with this obvious but amiable allegory, in which the nation's current obsession with consumerism is symbolised by the imminent closure of a traditional Beijing bath-house to make way for a soulless shopping mall. City slicker Pu Quanxin's gradual conversion to his father and slow-witted brother's viewpoint hardly makes for incisive politicking. Yet Zhang treats us to a gallery of engaging elderly eccentrics who drink, gamble and gossip their days away. DP Mandarin +subtitles. *DVD*

Xu Zhu *Mr Liu* • Pu Quanxin *Liu Daming* • Wu Jiang *Liu Erming* ■ *Dir* Zhang Yang • *Scr* Zhang Yang, Liu Fendou, Huo Xin, Diao Yinan, Cai Xiangjun

Showgirls ★18
Erotic drama 1995 · US · Colour · 125min

According to director Paul Verhoeven, his controversial and much-reviled showbiz exposé is an incisive look at sleazy Las Vegas life. To almost everyone else, it was a posh sexploitation flick charting the rise of small-town girl Elizabeth Berkley from tawdry lap dancer to famed topless revue headliner. Practically nothing works in this tacky sashay through unerotic burlesque. AJ Violence, swearing, drug abuse, sex scenes, nudity. *DVD*

Elizabeth Berkley *Nomi Malone* • Kyle MacLachlan *Zack Carey* • Gina Gershon *Cristal Connors* • Glenn Plummer *James Smith* • Robert Davi *Al Torres* • Alan Rachins *Tony Moss* ■ *Dir* Paul Verhoeven • *Scr* Joe Eszterhas

Showtime ★★12
Action comedy 2002 · US/Aus · Colour · 91min

The pairing of Robert De Niro and Eddie Murphy probably looked better on paper than it proves to be on screen in this so-so action comedy. De Niro is typically tough and taciturn as a serious undercover cop while Murphy's motor-mouthed persona suits his ambitious patrolman with thespian aspirations. The comedy kicks in when the

S

chalk-and-cheese duo are teamed up by a TV producer (an underused Rene Russo) for a new reality cop show. An action subplot, involving the hunt for an illegal supergun, serves simply to bridge the funny bits. DA Violence, swearing. DVD

Robert De Niro *Mitch Preston* • Eddie Murphy *Trey Sellars* • Rene Russo *Chase Renzi* • Frankie R Faison [Frankie Faison] *Captain Winship* • William Shatner • Rachel Harris [Rachael Harris] *Teacher* ■ *Dir* Tom Dey • *Scr* Keith Sharon, Alfred Gough, Miles Millar, from a story by Jorge Saralegui

Shree 420 ★★★★ U
Romantic musical drama
1955 · Ind · BW · 163min

Having charmed audiences with his Chaplin-like performance in *Awara* (1951), Raj Kapoor portrayed another everyman in this provocative study of the corrosive nature of city life. Arriving in Bombay from the country, idealistic graduate Kapoor finds work in a laundry and falls for a humble teacher, played by his regular love interest, Nargis, but he's soon led astray. This uncompromising study of Nehru's India laments the growing divide between rich and poor, but it also makes for engrossing entertainment. DP Hindi +subtitles.

Nargis *Vidya Omkarnath Shastri* • Nadira *Maya* • Raj Kapoor *Ranbir Raj/Raj Kumar of Pipli* • Nemo *Seth Sonachand Dharmanand* ■ *Dir* Raj Kapoor • *Scr* KA Abbas, VP Sathe, from a story by Abbas

LANDMARK FILM
This intelligent computer animation breaks all the rules by putting the names of its all-star voice cast above the title

Shrek ★★★★ U
Animated fantasy comedy
2001 · US · Colour · 86min

This is an irreverent, occasionally scatological fairy tale with state-of-the-art computer-generated images that almost steal a march on *Toy Story*. Shrek is an ugly, antisocial green ogre (variable Scottish accent by Mike Myers), who must rescue a human princess (Cameron Diaz) in order to appease evil Lord Farquaad (John Lithgow) and rid his swamp of an infestation of traditional fairy-tale characters. The animators achieve a startling level of reality but it's the characters who carry what is a slight beauty-and-the-beast story. Eddie Murphy's Donkey steals the show. Children will love it, while adults can enjoy the action-movie homages and Disney-mocking. AC DVD ♙

Mike Myers *Shrek/Blind mouse* • Eddie Murphy *Donkey* • Cameron Diaz *Princess Fiona* • John Lithgow *Lord Farquaad* • Vincent Cassel *Monsieur Hood* • Peter Dennis *Ogre hunter* • Kathleen Freeman *Old woman* ■ *Dir* Andrew Adamson, Vicky Jenson • *Scr* Ted Elliott, Terry Rossio, Joe Stillman, Roger SH Schulman, from a book by William Steig

Shrek 2 ★★★★ U
Animated fantasy comedy
2004 · US · Colour · 88min

This welcome follow-up is every bit as cute, clever and funny as the original. The sequel picks up after the marriage of Shrek (voiced by Mike Myers) and Fiona (Cameron Diaz), and follows their trip to her homeland of Far Far Away. If Fiona's parents, King Harold (John Cleese) and Queen Lillian (Julie Andrews), are shocked to discover she's an ogre, that's nothing compared to Harold's reaction to her new husband. The king wants Fiona to marry the foppish Prince Charming (Rupert Everett), so he hires assassin Puss-in-Boots (marvellously voiced by Antonio Banderas) to kill her new son-in-law. The parodies, pop references and Hollywood send-ups are hilarious, as is Eddie Murphy. AJ DVD ♙

Mike Myers *Shrek* • Eddie Murphy *Donkey* • Cameron Diaz *Princess Fiona* • Julie Andrews *Queen Lillian* • Antonio Banderas *Puss-in-Boots* • John Cleese *King Harold* • Rupert Everett *Prince Charming* • Jennifer Saunders *Fairy Godmother* ■ *Dir* Andrew Adamson, Kelly Asbury, Conrad Vernon • *Scr* Andrew Adamson, Joe Stillman, J David Stern, David N Weiss, from a story by Andrew Adamson, from a book by William Steig

Shrek the Third ★★★ U
Animated fantasy comedy
2007 · US · Colour · 88min

Packed with fairy-tale send-ups and warm humanity, the first two instalments of *Shrek* were an absolute delight for young and old alike. The third outing shows signs of franchise fatigue as it struggles with a half-baked storyline in which the grumpy green ogre (voiced by Mike Myers) searches for an heir to the throne of Far Far Away. The breathtakingly innovative wit of the earlier films may be lacking, yet there's still plenty here to enjoy, from Eddie Murphy and Antonio Banderas's manic double act as Donkey and Puss and some sly, Once upon a Time in-jokes. JR DVD ♙

Mike Myers *Shrek* • Eddie Murphy *Donkey* • Cameron Diaz *Princess Fiona* • Antonio Banderas *Puss-in-Boots* • Julie Andrews *Queen Lillian* • John Cleese *King Harold* • Rupert Everett *Prince Charming* • Justin Timberlake *Artie* • Ian McShane *Captain Hook* ■ *Dir* Chris Miller, Raman Hui • *Scr* Jeffrey Price, Peter S Seaman, Chris Miller, Aron Warner, from a story by Andrew Adamson, from characters by William Steig

Shrek Forever After ★★★ U
Animated fantasy comedy
2010 · US · Colour · 89min

The fourth *Shrek* movie, and the first in 3D, has the not-so-jolly green ogre (voiced by Mike Myers), Princess Fiona (Cameron Diaz) and their three icky, burping babies living in apparent familial bliss. So far, so dull, and Shrek makes a deal with trickster Rumpelstiltskin to return him to his villager-scaring roots for one day. However, a dystopian, *It's a Wonderful Life*-style alternative universe is the cleverly conceived result. The story's themes of responsibility and regret are notably grown-up, and a mangy Donkey (Eddie Murphy) and gone-to-seed Puss (Antonio Banderas) shoulder all the laughs. It's a neat enough way of closing the book – and one hopes it is closed now. AC DVD ♙

Mike Myers *Shrek* • Eddie Murphy *Donkey* • Cameron Diaz *Princess Fiona* • Antonio Banderas *Puss-in-Boots* • Julie Andrews *Queen* • John Cleese *King Harold* • Jon Hamm *Brogan* • Jane Lynch *Gretched* • Ian McShane *Captain Hook* • Maya Rudolph *Rapunzel* • Justin Timberlake *Artie* • Eric Idle *Merlin* ■ *Dir* Mike Mitchell • *Scr* Josh Klausner, Darren Lemke, from characters by William Steig

Shriek If You Know What I Did Last Friday the 13th
★ 15

Horror parody   2000 · US · Colour · 82min

Spoofing a spoof is a risky business, if only because the jokes are already third-hand before the cameras start to roll. This straight-to-video, threadbare rattlebag of slapstick, skit and smut chronicles the crimes of yet another high school serial killer by way of an excuse for tossing in gags about every element of American juvenilia. Infantile in the extreme. DP DVD ⒸⓈ

Julie Benz *Barbara* • Harley Cross *Dawson* • Tom Arnold *Doughy* • Tiffani-Amber Thiessen *Hagitha Utslay* • Majandra Delfino *Martina* • Danny Strong *Boner* • Coolio *Principal* ■ *Dir* John Blanchard • *Scr* Sue Bailey, Joe Nelms

Shrink ★★ 15
Drama   2009 · US · Colour · 100min

Kevin Spacey stars as psychiatrist Henry Carter in this *Crash*-style, multi-stranded modern-day redemption story. A widower with a chronic drug problem, Carter is plugged into the Hollywood A-list, treating two fading celebrities (Saffron Burrows and an uncredited Robin Williams) and a neurotic high-powered agent in his exclusive clinic. At his father's request, Carter begins to treat a poor black girl, Jemma (Keke Palmer), whose mother has committed suicide, a situation that mirrors his own experience. Spacey gives it his best shot, but the movie is whiney, self-righteous tosh with characters whose paths barely cross. DW Swearing, drug abuse, sexual references.

Kevin Spacey *Henry Carter* • Robin Williams *Jack* • Saffron Burrows *Kate* • Keke Palmer *Jemma* • Dallas Roberts *Patrick* • Mark Webber *Jeremy* • Robert Loggia *Dr Robert Carter* ■ *Dir* Jonas Pate • *Scr* Thomas Moffett, from a story by Henry Rearden

The Shrink Is In ★★ 15
Romantic comedy   2000 · US · Colour · 86min

Executively produced by its star Courteney Cox, this misguided goofball comedy also features an equally wasted performance from her real-life husband David Arquette. Although Arquette's eccentricity has a certain wacky charm, Cox is annoying as an anxiety-ridden travel writer masquerading as a psychiatrist to win over her dream man. Director Richard Benjamin confuses slapstick with stupidity at every turn. SF Swearing, drug abuse. DVD

Courteney Cox *Samantha Crumb* • David Arquette *Henry Crumb* • David James Elliott *Michael* • Carol Kane *Dr Louise Rosenberg* • Kimberley Davies *Isabelle* • Viola Davis *Robin* ■ *Dir* Richard Benjamin • *Scr* Joanna Johnson, from a story by Alison Balian

Shrooms ★★★ 18
Horror   2006 · UK/Ire/Den · Colour · 87min

Five American students holiday in rural Ireland where their friend Jake (Jack Huston, grandson of director John) assures them that the magic mushrooms are the most powerful going. Tara (Lindsey Haun) ingests a particularly potent fungus just as her friends start getting brutally slain – seemingly by shadowy urban legend the Black Brother. Can she separate stark reality from psychedelic fantasy in order to survive? Paddy Breathnach uses some Asian horror-influenced trickery, and it's all beautifully photographed in high acid style, which allows for a few unusual scares. The performances are accomplished – particularly Huston, and Sean McGinley and Don Wycherley as a pair of backwoodsmen – and this gives the film a credibility beyond its genre. AJ DVD ♙

Lindsey Haun *Tara* • Jack Huston *Jake* • Max Kasch *Troy* • Maya Hazen *Lisa* • Alice Greczyn *Holly* • Don Wycherley *Ernie* • Sean McGinley *Bernie* • Robert Hoffman *Bluto* ■ *Dir* Paddy Breathnach • *Scr* Pearse Elliott

Shun Li and the Poet
★★★ 15

Drama   2011 · It/Fr · Colour · 97min

Documentarist Andrea Segre makes an accomplished transition to fiction with this slight but affecting drama that focuses upon the human rather than the political side of the immigrant experience. Shun Li (Zhao Tao) works in a Rome textile factory and longs to be reunited with her eight-year-old son. After being forced to transfer to the sleepy Venetian lagoon port of Chioggia, she finds a soul mate in ageing Slavic fisherman Bepi (Rade Sherbedgia). Segre conveys the mood of this shabby backwater and cinematographer Luca Bigazzi superbly captures the canals and alleyways of the Italian locations, while Zhao and Sherbedgia exude an affectionate, melancholy dependency. DP Italian, Mandarin +subtitles. Swearing, sexual references, some violence.

Zhao Tao *Shun Li* • Rade Sherbedgia [Rade Serbedzija] *Bepi, "the Poet"* • Marco Paolini *Coppe* • Roberto Citran *Lawyer* • Giuseppe Battiston *Devis* ■ *Dir* Andrea Segre • *Scr* Marco Pettenello, Andrea Segre, from a story by Segre

Shut Up! ★★★ 12A
Crime comedy   2003 · Fr/It · Colour · 86min

As the inept crook with a terrifying gift for taking things literally, Gérard Depardieu clearly revels in his unlikely liaison with Jean Reno's murderously stoic cellmate, who is frustrating both detective Richard Berry and prison psychologist André Dussollier in their efforts to track down the loot stolen from crime kingpin Jean-Pierre Malo. But while the character comedy is consistently amusing, Veber's scenario relies too heavily on cumbrous contrivance and strained slapstick. DP French +subtitles.

Gérard Depardieu *Quentin* • Jean Reno *Ruby* • Leonor Varela *Katia/Sandra* • André Dussollier *Prison psychiatrist* • Jean-Pierre Malo *Vogel* • Richard Berry *Vernet* • Jean-Michel Noirey *Lambert* • Laurent Gamelon *Mauricet* • Aurélien Recoing *Rocco* ■ *Dir* Francis Veber • *Scr* Francis Veber, from an idea by Serge Frydman

Shut Up & Sing: Dixie Chicks ★★★★ 15
Music documentary   2006 · US · Colour · 87min

During the run up to the invasion of Iraq in 2003, Dixie Chicks lead singer Natalie Maines made headlines after an off-the-cuff jibe against President Bush at a London concert. In the United States, the backlash against their "unpatriotic" remarks was instantaneous: CDs were burnt, death threats were issued and their album sales plummeted. This glossy documentary, directed by Oscar winner Barbara Kopple and Cecilia Peck, captures the likeable trio as they deal with the fallout of opposing the war. Suffused with a warmly affectionate glow and scored by the band's provocatively unrepentant comeback album *Taking the Long Way*, it's an inspiring lesson in putting principles over profit. JR DVD

Natalie Maines • Emily Robison • Martie Maguire • Rick Rubin • Simon Renshaw ■ *Dir* Barbara Kopple, Cecilia Peck • *Cinematographers* Christine Burrill, Joan Churchill, Gary Griffin, Luis Lopez, Seth Gordon

Shutter ★ 15
Horror thriller   2008 · US · Colour · 85min

Upscale photographer Joshua Jackson is on assignment in Japan when he and his new wife are involved in a car accident caused by a spooky figure on the road. Jackson subsequently finds his pictures marred by weird streaks of light – could it be the work of unhappy spirits from beyond the grave? This bland American "refreshment" of the 2004 Thai horror evokes yawns rather than scares as director Masayuki Ochiai moves the already over-exposed plot further towards its obvious precedents, *The Ring* and *The Grudge*. AJ

Joshua Jackson *Benjamin Shaw* • Rachael Taylor *Jane Shaw* • Megumi Okina *Megumi* • David Denman *Bruno* • John Hensley *Adam* • Maya Hazen *Seiko* • James Kyson Lee *Ritsuo* • Adrienne Pickering *Megan* ■ *Dir* Masayuki Ochiai • *Scr* Luke Dawson, from the 2004 film

Shutter Island ★★★ 15
Mystery thriller   2009 · US · Colour · 132min

Leonardo DiCaprio's fourth collaboration with director Martin Scorsese finds him playing a marshal investigating the disappearance of a patient at an isolated mental asylum. This 1950s-set puzzle movie has a psychodrama twist in the tale that some may see coming, but there is still fun to be had as Scorsese weaves his operatic thrills in the gothic surroundings. It may be overlong and overly explained, but *Shutter Island* weaves an impressive and gripping spell. AJ Violence, swearing, nudity. DVD ♙

Leonardo DiCaprio *Teddy Daniels* • Mark Ruffalo *Chuck Aule* • Ben Kingsley *Dr Cawley* • Michelle Williams *Dolores* • Emily Mortimer *Rachel 1* • Patricia Clarkson *Rachel 2* • Max von Sydow *Dr Naehring* • Jackie Earle Haley *George Noyce* ■ *Dir* Martin Scorsese • *Scr* Laeta Kalogridis, from the novel by Dennis Lehane • *Cinematographer* Robert Richardson • *Editor* Thelma Schoonmaker

The Shuttered Room ★★★
Horror   1967 · UK · Colour · 99min

This superior tale of the supernatural was based on a short story by August Derleth and HP Lovecraft. Twenty years after she was driven away from her childhood home by a series of sinister happenings, Carol Lynley returns with her new husband, Gig Young. But the old mill is as daunting as ever and deliriously malevolent cousin Oliver Reed and his gang of New England delinquents are far from the ideal welcoming committee. David Greene leaks the secret of the room at the top of the stairs early on, but he still conveys a sense of evil. DP

Gig Young *Mike Kelton* • Carol Lynley *Susannah Kelton* • Oliver Reed *Ethan* • Flora Robson *Aunt Agatha* • William Devlin *Zebulon Whateley* • Bernard Kay *Tait* ■ *Dir* David Greene • *Scr* DB Ledrov, Nathaniel Tanchuk, from a story by HP Lovecraft, August Derleth

Shy People ★★★ 15
Drama   1987 · US · Colour · 114min

Russian director Andrei Konchalovsky succeeds in coming up with an intriguing, if flawed, variation on the swamp melodrama. Jill Clayburgh is the snooty New Yorker who sets out on a *Roots*-style journey to the bayous, sulky teenage daughter Martha Plimpton in tow, to locate some long-lost relatives, headed up by Barbara Hershey. The ensuing culture clash is a tad predictable, but Konchalovsky does well in invoking a spooky gothic atmosphere. JF
Jill Clayburgh *Diana* • Barbara Hershey *Ruth* • Martha Plimpton *Grace* • Merritt Butrick *Mike* • John Philbin *Tommy* • Don Swayze *Mark* • Pruitt Taylor Vince *Paul* Mare Winningham *Candy* ■ *Dir* Andrei Konchalovsky • *Scr* Gérard Brach, Andrei Konchalovsky, Marjorie David, from a story by Andrei Konchalovsky • *Cinematographer* Chris Menges

Siam Sunset ★★★ 15
Comedy road movie
1999 · Aus/UK · Colour · 91min

A distraught widower's quest to create the perfect paint colour takes him on a wild adventure through the Australian outback in John Polson's quirky road movie. Linus Roache is dogged by disaster – his wife was killed by a refrigerator unit that fell from a passing jumbo – and catastrophes occur wherever he goes. Salvation comes in the shape of Danielle Cormack, a free-spirited young woman who's as accident-prone as he is. While there are laughs aplenty, the movie's biggest achievement is to make us really care about these bizarre characters and their off-kilter universe. NS
Linus Roache *Perry* • Danielle Cormack *Grace* • Ian Bliss *Martin* • Roy Billing *Bill* • Alan Brough *Stuart* • Rebecca Hobbs *Jane* • Terry Kenwrick *Arthur* ■ *Dir* John Polson • *Scr* Max Dann, Andrew Knight

Siberia ★★★ 18
Black comedy
1998 · Neth/Fr · EW and Colour · 83min

This bouncy Dutch black comedy set in Amsterdam is about two friends and flatmates who seduce female backpackers of all nationalities and keep a page from their passport as a memento. Driven by a soundtrack by techno band Junkie XL, this immoral low-budget game of sexual rivalry is full of free-spirited, bed-hopping zeal and has a couple of winning actors in Hugo Metsers and Roeland Fernhout. When Vlatca Simac shows up as the spunky, enigmatic Lara, a dark and dirty *ménage à trois* ensues, but the film retains its cynical anti-romantic stance to the very end. JC
Dutch, English +subtitles.
Hugo Metsers *Hugo* • Roeland Fernhout *Goof* • Nicole Eggert *Kristy* • Vlatca Simac *Lara* • Johnny Lion *Freddy* ■ *Dir* Robert Jan Westdijk • *Scr* Jos Driesser, Robert Jan Westdijk

Sibiriada ★★★
Epic drama
1979 · USSR · Colour · 275min

Running over four hours and covering events from the Tsarist era to the middle of the Cold War, Andrei Konchalovsky's powerfully played, panoramic epic is tantamount to the Soviet *Birth of a Nation*. There are also echoes of *Gone with the Wind* and *Giant*, as family feuds, thwarted romances and industrial conflicts dominate the action. Melodrama holds sway, as the oil prospecting son of a humble peasant accompanies his father to the scene of both his humiliation and his lost love. Imposing, but obtuse. DP Russian +subtitles.
Nikita Mikhalkov *Alexei* • Vitaly Solomin *Nikolai* • Lyudmila Gurchenko *Taia* • Sergei Shakurov *Spiridou* • Natalya Andreichenko [Natasha Andreichenko] *Anastassia* • Yevgeni Petrov *Yerofei* ■ *Dir* Andrei Mikhalkov-Konchalovsky [Andrei Konchalovsky] • *Scr* Valentin Yezhov, Andrei Mikhalkov-Konchalovsky [Andrei Konchalovsky]

Sibling Rivalry ★★★ 15
Black comedy   1990 · US · Colour · 83min

This movie contains a highly ingenious plotline, with some subtle twists and turns that are negotiated skilfully by the likes of Kirstie Alley and Carrie Fisher. They are supported by several familiar American TV faces, who throw themselves wholesale into the frantic, vulgar action with varying degrees of success. It's all pulled together by the stylish direction of Carl Reiner, but the result still disappoints. SH Swearing, sex scenes. *DVD*
Kirstie Alley *Marjorie Turner* • Bill Pullman *Nick Meany* • Jami Gertz *Jeanine* • Carrie Fisher *Iris Turner-Hunter* • Scott Bakula *Harry Turner* • Sam Elliott *Charles Turner Jr* • Ed O'Neill *Wilbur Meany* • Frances Sternhagen *Rose Turner* ■ *Dir* Carl Reiner • *Scr* Martha Goldhirsh

Sicario ★★★★★ 15
Action crime thriller   2015 · US · Colour · 116min

The unofficial war zone that is the North American-Mexican border is the setting for this gripping thriller, which deals with the diminishing returns of the US government's war on drugs. Emily Blunt stars as a high achieving FBI agent who co-ordinates Swat missions in the state of Arizona. She's approached by a special ops team and, now out of her comfort zone, she must try to orientate herself in a world of bloodshed and duplicity. The sense of paranoia is brilliantly conveyed in this savagely compelling action drama. DW In English, Spanish. Violence, swearing. *DVD* *BL*
Emily Blunt *Kate Macer* • Benicio Del Toro *Alejandro* • Josh Brolin *Matt Graver* • Jon Bernthal *Ted* • Jeffrey Donovan *Steve Forsing* ■ *Dir* Denis Villeneuve • *Scr* Taylor Sheridan • *Cinematographer* Roger Deakins

The Sicilian ★★ 18
Crime drama   1987 · US · Colour · 109min

This is a plodding and sententious account of the postwar Sicilian rebel Salvatore Giuliano, whose mania for independence from Italy inspired him to a career of murder and pillage. Christopher Lambert stars as a remarkably uncharismatic Giuliano, who nonetheless charms his way into the hearts of the Sicilian people and even the Mafia (in the person of the sinister Joss Ackland). Director Michael Cimino lets the action swing between huge messy gunfights and tedious moralising. SuR Swearing, violence, nudity. *DVD*
Christopher Lambert *Salvatore Giuliano* • John Turturro *Aspanu Pisciotta* • Terence Stamp *Prince Borsa* • Joss Ackland *Don Masino Croce* • Richard Bauer *Professor Hector Adonis* • Ray McAnally *Minister Trezza* ■ *Dir* Michael Cimino • *Scr* Steve Shagan, from the novel by Mario Puzo

The Sicilian Clan ★★★ 15
Crime drama   1969 · Fr · Colour · 113min

The teaming of charismatic threesome – Alain Delon, Jean Gabin and Lino Ventura – alone guarantees this film's success at the box office in France and abroad. Delon is a Mafia hitman, sprung from jail by godfather Gabin who's planning a heist to steal some jewellery. Ventura is the dogged cop on the case. It's an old-fashioned thriller, expertly made and boasting a score by Ennio Morricone. AT In French. *DVD*
Jean Gabin *Vittoric Manalese* • Alain Delon *Roger Sartet* • Lino Ventura *Inspector Le Goff* • Irina Demick *Jeanne Manalese* • Amedeo Nazzari *Tony Nicosia* ■ *Dir* Henri Verneuil • *Scr* Henri Verneuil, José Giovanni, Pierre Pelegri, from the novel *Le Clan des Siciliens* by Auguste Le Breton

The Sicilians ★★ U
Crime thriller   1964 · UK · BW · 69min

Known for his brisk approach to shooting and his no-nonsense style, Ernest Morris was able to make even the flimsiest of crime thrillers watchable, including this one about a dancer and a diplomat who search for a mafioso's kidnapped son. Robert Hutton is the imported Hollywood has-been and, even though he was never more than a second division star, he is streets ahead of this material. DP

Robert Hutton *Calvin Adams* • Reginald Marsh *Inspector Webb* • Ursula Howells *Madame Perrault* • Alex Scott (1) *Henri Perrault* • Susan Denny *Carole Linden* • Robert Ayres *Angelo di Marco* • Eric Pohlmann *Inspector Bressin* • Patricia Hayes *Passenger* • Warren Mitchell *O'Leary* ■ *Dir* Ernest Morris • *Scr* Ronald Liles, Reginald Hearne

Sick: the Life and Death of Bob Flanagan, Supermasochist ★★★★ 18
Documentary   1997 · US · Colour · 85min

This is an excruciatingly painful documentary about the extraordinary life and dying days of Californian comedian and performance artist Bob Flanagan, who used his own sexual masochism as a means of articulating the suffering caused by cystic fibrosis. His partner, Sheree Rose, at first objected to the intrusion of director Kirby Dick's camera into their private practices, but came to terms with it as Flanagan approached death. The result, though not for the squeamish, is sad and very moving. TH *DVD*
Bob Flanagan • Sheree Rose • *Dir* Kirby Dick

Sicko ★★★★ 12
Documentary   2007 · US · Colour · 118min

After the ferocious *Fahrenheit 9/11*, Michael Moore's surprise encore is this thoughtful, somewhat idealistic critique of the US healthcare system. At two hours, it's a little long and repetitive, with countless casualty-room nightmares boiling down to insurance company penny-pinching. The European leg seems rosy by comparison, with Moore treating the NHS and its French counterpart as a sort of public health Shangri-La. But even those not shocked by the differences can't fail to be astonished by the final 20 minutes, in which Moore takes ailing 9/11 heroes to Guantanamo to get the care they must pay exorbitant prices for at home but is given free to Al Qaeda convicts. His methods may be questionable, but Moore certainly knows how to push buttons: his government's and ours. DW Brief swearing. *DVD*
Michael Moore (2) *Michael Moore* • George W Bush • Reggie Cervantes • John Graham • Richard Nixon • Tony Benn ■ *Dir/Scr* Michael Moore (2) • *Cinematographer* Christoph Vitt

Sid and Nancy ★★★★ 18
Biographical drama   1986 · UK · Colour · 108min

This punk love story is an authentic, uncompromising insight into the obsession of Sid Vicious, who played bass guitar for the Sex Pistols, with drug addict groupie Nancy Spungen, and their inexorable descent into death. It brilliantly recaptures the rage, cynicism and self-destructiveness of the late 1970s punk scene, while never setting up the rock 'n' roll lifestyle as a blissful idyll. Alex Cox directs with an eye for the age and its absurdities, mixing gritty realism with moments of charming romance and black comedy. Gary Oldman and Chloe Webb are outstanding as the lovers. DP Violence, swearing, sex scenes, drug abuse, nudity. *DVD* *BL*
Gary Oldman *Sid Vicious* • Chloe Webb *Nancy Spungen* • Andrew Schofield *Johnny Rotten* • David Hayman *Malcolm McLaren* • Debby Bishop [Debbie Bishop] *Phoebe* • Tony London *Steve* • Courtney Love *Gretchen* ■ *Dir* Alex Cox • *Scr* Alex Cox, Abbe Wool

Siddhartha ★★
Drama   1972 · US · Colour · 89min

Herman Hesse's 1922 novel is brought to the screen with the reverence of a true devotee by American writer/director Conrad Rooks. However, such is the unquestioning dogmatism of the screenplay, the lushness of Sven Nykvist's Indian landscapes and the stylised earnestness of Bollywood icon Shashi Kapoor in the title role that instead of a moving journey to spiritual enlightenment, this comes across as a glossy promo for Buddhism, in which self-discovery is trampled under foot by clumsy symbolism.

An airless adaptation of an obdurate text. DP
Shashi Kapoor *Siddhartha* • Simi Garewal *Kamala* • Romesh Sharma *Govinda* • Pincho Kapoor *Kamaswami* • Zul Vellani *Vasudeva* ■ *Dir* Conrad Rooks • *Scr* Conrad Rooks, from the novel by Hermann Hesse

Side by Side ★★
Comedy   1975 · UK · Colour · 83min

Who'll win the only nightclub licence in town? Old-timer Terry-Thomas at the Golden Nugget, or those groovy new kids on the block at Sound City? Glam rockers Mud and the Rubettes are joined by 1970s sensations Kenny, Fox and Stephanie De Sykes for this candyfloss movie directed by none other than Bruce Beresford, of *Driving Miss Daisy* fame. Barry Humphries also appears in what must rank as one of the strangest musical comedies. AJ
Barry Humphries *Rodney* • Terry-Thomas *Max Nugget* • Stephanie De Sykes *Julia* • Billy Boyle *Gary* • Dave Mount *Flip* • Frank Thornton *Inspector Crumb* ■ *Dir* Bruce Beresford • *Scr* Garry Chambers, Ron Inkpen, Peter James, Bruce Beresford

Side by Side ★★★★ 15
Documentary   2012 · US · Colour · 98min

As digital technology increasingly takes the place of traditional film cameras on movie shoots, this illuminating documentary lines up proponents on both sides to discuss the impact of the power of the pixel. Keanu Reeves (who also co-produced) is on hand to chat with the absolute best directors in the business – James Cameron and Martin Scorsese on going digital, and Christopher Nolan championing traditional methods. Thanks to a host of choice clips, this is both even-handed and surprisingly accessible. TJ *DVD*
Keanu Reeves • Martin Scorsese • James Cameron • David Lynch • David Fincher • Christopher Nolan • Danny Boyle • Lars von Trier ■ *Dir/Scr* Christopher Kenneally

Side Effects ★★★ 15
Psychological thriller   2013 · US · Colour · 101min

Director Steven Soderbergh's hypnotic thriller stars Jude Law as the doctor treating depressive Rooney Mara, whose Wall Street trader husband (Channing Tatum) has recently been in prison for insider dealing. Mara's behaviour becomes increasingly erratic under the medication prescribed to her by Law on the advice of a fellow doctor (Catherine Zeta-Jones), but when events take a more tragic turn, Law cannot accept that he, too, might be at fault. Soderbergh highlights the flaws of psychiatry and the fatal self-absorption of the doctor/patient relationship in an intelligently crafted story, which is briskly paced and highly suspenseful – until a crude and puerile payoff in the third act. A tease, on many levels. SP Violence, swearing, sex scenes, nudity. *DVD* *BL*
Jude Law *Dr Jonathan Banks* • Rooney Mara *Emily Taylor* • Catherine Zeta-Jones *Dr Victoria Siebert* • Channing Tatum *Martin Taylor* • Vinessa Shaw *Deidre Banks* • David Costabile *Carl Millbank* ■ *Dir* Steven Soderbergh • *Scr* Scott Z Burns • *Cinematographer* Peter Andrews [Steven Soderbergh]

Side Street ★★★
Thriller   1950 · US · BW · 82min

This is an absolutely first-rate MGM co-feature, one of those super programme fillers that's not quite a main feature, but far above the average B-movie. The studio's customary production gloss and intelligence is here provided by masterly director Anthony Mann, not long before he hit his stride as one of the finest ever western directors. The film is a virtual *film noir* about a postman (Farley Granger) whose solitary act of theft changes the shape of his life forever. TS
Farley Granger *Joe Norson* • Cathy O'Donnell *Ellen Norson* • James Craig *Georgie Garsell* • Paul Kelly (1) *Captain Walter Anderson* • Edmon Ryan *Victor Backett* • Paul Harvey *Emil Lorrison* • Jean

Hagen *Harriet Sinton* • Charles McGraw *Stanley Simon* ■ *Dir* Anthony Mann • *Scr* Sydney Boehm, from his story

Side Streets ★★ 15
Drama   1998 · US · Colour · 130min

Director/co-writer Tony Gerber's debut depicts New York as a city of self-contained immigrant conclaves that only interact through necessity. While this makes an important sociological point, it doesn't help the structure of this meandering collection of short cuts. Of the five stories, the tragedy of faded Bollywood star Shashi Kapoor has the most heart, while fashion wannabe Valeria Golino's encounter with the pinball of fate offers both satire and slapstick. **DP** Swearing, sex scenes.

Valeria Golino *Sylvie Otti* • Shashi Kapoor *Vikram Raj* • Leon Errol Boyce • Art Malik *Bipin Raj* • Shabana Azmi *Chandra Raj* • Mirjana Jokovic *Elena Iscovescu* • Miho Nikaido *Yuki Shimamura* ■ *Dir* Tony Gerber • *Scr* Lynn Nottage, Tony Gerber • *Executive Producer* Ismail Merchant

Sidewalk Stories ★★★★ 15
Silent drama   1989 · US · BW · 100min

Written, directed, produced by and starring Charles Lane, this remarkable tribute to the art of Charlie Chaplin is virtually without dialogue. As a struggling Greenwich Village artist, Lane pays his debt to the Little Tramp in a knockabout scene that recalls a dozen stand-offs between Chaplin and bushy-browed Eric Campbell. In keeping with the homage there's pathos as well as slapstick, as Lane takes in an abandoned child (played by his own daughter, Nicole Alysia). Rarely has the modern city looked less sinister than in Bill Dill's stylish black-and-white images, while Marc Marder's score is almost a character in itself. **DP** Nudity.

Charles Lane (3) *Artist* • Nicole Alysia *Child* • Sandye Wilson *Young woman* • Darnell Williams *Father* • Trula Hoosier *Mother* • George Riddick *Street partner* • Tom Hoover *Portrait artist* ■ *Dir/Scr* Charles Lane (3)

Sidewalks of New York ★★★ 15
Romantic comedy   2000 · US · Colour · 103min

Writer/director/actor Edward Burns tries to emulate Woody Allen with this romantic comedy that doubles as an ode to the city of New York. It follows the interrelated romantic liaisons of six individuals. Stanley Tucci is suitably sleazy as the philandering husband having a relationship with Brittany Murphy while his wife Heather Graham considers a romance of her own with a TV producer (played by Burns himself). Charming in places, this never quite gels into a captivating story. **JB** *DVD*

Edward Burns *Tommy* • Rosario Dawson *Maria* • Dennis Farina *Carpo* • Heather Graham *Annie* • David Krumholtz *Ben* • Brittany Murphy *Ashley* • Stanley Tucci *Griffin* ■ *Dir/Scr* Edward Burns

Sideways ★★★★★ 15
Romantic comedy drama   2004 · US · Colour · 121min

Director Alexander Payne's dissection of American social mores is his finest movie to date. Middle-aged mates Paul Giamatti and Thomas Haden Church take a trip to California's wine country to celebrate the latter's upcoming wedding. But Giamatti's wine-tasting plans get sidelined by Church's desperation for a last fling and his attempts to set his friend up with an equally grape-savvy waitress (Virginia Madsen). Thanks to astonishing performances from Giamatti (a rumpled bundle of nervous self-loathing), Church (a deliciously deadpan but fading Casanova) and the Oscar-nominated Madsen, Payne's richly rewarding comedy is of the best vintage. It takes oblique glances at the buddy flick and road movie by skewering both with poignancy, truth and wit to give a fresh vitality to each well-worn genre. **AJ** Swearing, sex scenes. *DVD* Blu

Paul Giamatti *Miles Raymond* • Thomas Haden Church *Jack Lopate* • Virginia Madsen *Maya* • Sandra Oh *Stephanie* • Marylouise Burke *Miles's mother* • Jessica Hecht *Victoria* • Missy Doty

Cammi • MC Gainey *Cammi's husband* ■ *Dir* Alexander Payne • *Scr* Alexander Payne, Jim Taylor, from the novel by Rex Pickett

The Siege ★★ 15
Political action thriller
1998 · US · Colour · 111min

Denzel Washington and Annette Bening play rival agents in this muddled thriller that can't decide whether it's a message movie or an action adventure. Islamic terrorists are attacking New York and different Government agencies are competing to deal with the violent outbreak. Listlessly directed by Edward Zwick and understated in key plot areas, this routine potboiler lacks suspense. **AJ** Swearing, violence. *DVD* Blu

Denzel Washington *Anthony "Hub" Hubbard* • Annette Bening *Elise Kraft/Sharon Bridger* • Bruce Willis *General William Devereaux* • Tony Shalhoub *Frank Haddad* • Sami Bouajila *Samir Nazhde* • Ahmed Ben Larby *Sheik Ahmed Bin Talal* ■ *Dir* Edward Zwick • *Scr* Lawrence Wright, Menno Meyjes, Edward Zwick, from a story by Lawrence Wright

The Siege at Red River ★★★ U
Western   1954 · US · Colour · 85min

This is a routine programme filler from producer Leonard Goldstein, who cleverly hijacked the colour climax of an earlier western (1944's *Buffalo Bill*) and used it virtually intact in this movie, inserting new close-ups of his principal players. The cast is headed by the ever interesting, and once hugely popular, Van Johnson. Director Rudolph Maté keeps the film moving, and the 1950s Technicolor, along with the appearance of Joanne Dru make it still worth watching today. **TS**

Van Johnson *Jim Farraday* • Joanne Dru *Nora Curtis* • Richard Boone *Brett Manning* • Milburn Stone *Benjy* • Jeff Morrow *Frank Kelso* • Craig Hill *Lieutenant Braden* ■ *Dir* Rudolph Maté • *Scr* Sydney Boehm, from a story by J Robert Bren, Gladys Atwater

The Siege of Sidney Street ★★
Historical drama   1960 · UK · BW · 93min

Alfred Hitchcock drew on this famous piece of Edwardian history for *The Man Who Knew Too Much*, but this reconstruction sticks a mite closer to the facts. The East End locale looks rather thrown together and the early scenes get bogged down in background information. But once the Russian anarchists have barricaded themselves in, the action begins to come to life. Donald Sinden plods along as the inspector on the trail of Peter Wyngarde and his compatriots, Kieron Moore and Leonard Sachs. **DP**

Peter Wyngarde *Peter the Painter* • Donald Sinden *Inspector John Mannering* • Nicole Berger *Sara* • Kieron Moore *Yoska* • Godfrey Quigley *Blakey* • Angela Newman *Nina* • TP McKenna *Lapidos* • Leonard Sachs *Svaars* ■ *Dir* Robert S Baker, Monty Berman • *Scr* Jimmy Sangster, Alexander Baron, from a story by Jimmy Sangster

The Siege of the Saxons ★★ U
Period adventure   1963 · UK · Colour · 85min

Second-rate British thespians clank around in chain mail while women blush demurely in this Arthurian tosh. The sword Excalibur is still the weapon of choice, sought after by outlaw hero Ronald Lewis, the wooden Mark Dignam as King Arthur himself, and Jerome Willis as a villain with a dodgy leg. Chief damsel is Janette Scott, the daughter of Thora Hird and a leading British starlet of the day. Several knights short of a round table. **AT**

Ronald Lewis *Robert Marshall* • Janette Scott *Katherine* • Ronald Howard *Edmund of Cornwall* • Mark Dignam *King Arthur* • John Laurie *Merlin* • Jerome Willis *Limping man* • Richard Clarke (3) *Saxon Prince* • Charles Lloyd Pack *Doctor* ■ *Dir* Nathan Juran • *Scr* Jud Kinberg, John Kohn

Sierra ★★ U
Western   1950 · US · Colour · 82min

Audie Murphy, America's most decorated war hero, was just settling into his western stride when he starred in this Technicolor remake of a forgotten 1938 film called *Forbidden Valley*. Murphy accompanies his wrongly accused father (Dean Jagger) into hiding. Despite the work of decent director Alfred E Green, the result was still routine. **TS**

Wanda Hendrix *Riley Martin* • Audie Murphy *Ring Hassard* • Burl Ives *Lonesome* • Dean Jagger *Jeff Hassard* • Richard Rober *Big Matt* • Anthony Curtis [Tony Curtis] *Brent Coulter* • James Arness *Little Sam* ■ *Dir* Alfred E Green • *Scr* Edna Anhalt, Milton Gunzberg, from the novel *Mountains Are My Kingdom* by Stuart Hardy

Sierra Passage ★★★
Western   1950 · US · BW · 81min

This gritty Monogram sagebrusher centres on the vengeful quest of 1860s minstrel show sharpshooter Wayne Morris, who as a boy witnessed the murder of his rancher father. Mentors Lloyd Corrigan and Roland Winters hope chanteuse Lola Albright will refocus his mind, but a showdown with outlaw gambler Alan Hale Jr is inevitable. Tautly directed and slickly photographed, this may not be the most original picture, but Morris's brooding obsession gives the action a psychological depth that is unusual for a B-western. **DP**

Wayne Morris *Johnny Yorke* • Lola Albright *Ann Walker* • Lloyd Corrigan *Thaddeus "Thad" Kring* • Alan Hale Jr *Yance Carter* ■ *Dir* Frank McDonald • *Scr* Tom W Blackburn, Sam Roeca, from a story by Warren D Wandberg [Warren Douglas]

Siesta ★ 18
Psychological drama   1987 · US · Colour · 92min

An interesting cast flounders in a plotless scenario which lands (with skydiver Ellen Barkin!) in steamy Spain. There, Barkin's murder and rape fantasies entwine as ineffectually as a soft-porn movie while the film explores her sexual history. One is left feeling conned by an array of stars all purporting to be in something far more interesting than this actually is. **LH**

Ellen Barkin *Claire* • Gabriel Byrne *Augustine* • Julian Sands *Kit* • Isabella Rossellini *Marie* • Martin Sheen *Del* • Alexei Sayle *Cabbie* • Grace Jones *Conchita* • Jodie Foster *Nancy* • Anastassia Stakis *Desdra* ■ *Dir* Mary Lambert • *Scr* Patricia Louisianna Knop, from the novel by Patrice Chaplin • *Music* Miles Davis

Sightseers ★★★★★ 15
Black comedy   2012 · UK · Colour · 84min

Indecently funny, delightfully eccentric and far bloodier than you'll be expecting, this wholly British road movie explores the same terrain as Mike Leigh's *Nuts in May* but goes to a far darker place. A Midlands couple embark on a caravanning holiday that's an erotic odyssey for her and a tourist trip for him, but when other holiday-makers don't follow the country code, it suddenly turns into a killing spree. Director Ben Wheatley's wicked sense of humour keep things playfully sick and effortlessly entertaining. **AJ** Violence, swearing, drug abuse, sex scenes. *DVD* Blu

Alice Lowe *Tina* • Steve Oram *Chris* • Eileen Davies *Carol* • Richard Glover *Martin* • Monica Dolan *Janice* • Jonathan Aris *Ian* ■ *Dir* Ben Wheatley • *Scr* Alice Lowe, Steve Oram, Amy Jump • *Cinematographer* Laurie Rose

Sign o' the Times ★★ 15
Music concert   1987 · US · Colour · 81min

Prince's filmed treatment of his 1987 European concert tour has short scenes filmed in his Paisley Park studios linking together the live tracks, which were shot in Rotterdam. His Royal Purpleness androgynously bumps and grinds his way through one limp MTV-inspired sexual fantasy after another, all of which run the gaudy gamut between laughable machismo and arch feminism. Sheena Easton and Sheila E puncture his posing with their nifty

musical contributions, but this isn't in the same class as *Purple Rain*. **AJ** Swearing.
■ *Dir* Prince

The Sign of Four ★★★ U
Mystery   1932 · UK · BW · 73min

The first sound adaptation of Sir Arthur Conan Doyle's second novel marked Arthur Wontner's third outing as Sherlock Holmes. Much of the focus of this version falls on Watson's obsession with a young woman who has recently been sent some pearls that were part of an Indian treasure trove discovered by her murdered father. Ian Hunter invests the good doctor's fascination with Isla Bevan with precisely the right blend of well-mannered attentiveness and stiff military dignity. **DP** *DVD*

Arthur Wontner *Sherlock Holmes* • Isla Bevan *Mary Morstan* • Ian Hunter *Dr Watson* • Gilbert Davis *Athelney Jones* • Graham Soutten *Jonathan Small* ■ *Dir* Rowland V Lee, Graham Cutts • *Scr* WP Lipscomb, from the novel *The Sign of Four* by Sir Arthur Conan Doyle

The Sign of Four ★★★ PG
Mystery   1983 · UK/US · Colour · 92min

Ian Richardson gives a sly performance as Sherlock Holmes in director Desmond Davis's entertaining version of Conan Doyle's novel. Davis invests the material with a keen sense of atmosphere and mystery as Holmes is called in to investigate events at Pondicherry Lodge, and soon finds himself embroiled in a case of murder and betrayal. By choosing to focus on Holmes's brusqueness and his insufferable vanity rather than his powers of deduction, Davis brings a fresh slant to the genre. **DP** *DVD*

Ian Richardson *Sherlock Holmes* • David Healy *Dr Watson* • Thorley Walters *Major John Sholto* • Terence Rigby *Inspector Layton* • Joe Melia *Jonathan Small* • Cherie Lunghi *Mary Morstan* • Clive Merrison *Bartholomew Sholto* ■ *Dir* Desmond Davis • *Scr* Charles Pogue, from the novel by Sir Arthur Conan Doyle

The Sign of Leo ★★★★ PG
Drama   1959 · Fr · BW · 98min

Eric Rohmer was the editor of the influential French film magazine *Cahiers du Cinéma* when he made his first feature in 1956, which was only released three years later. It told of a 40-year-old American in Paris, borrowing money on the expectation of an inheritance. However, when it is not forthcoming, he becomes a tramp begging outside cafés. The film, which gives little indication as to the direction Rohmer was to take, is an insightful portrait of a good-natured but hopelessly irresponsible man slowly disintegrating in the face of reality. **RB** French +subtitles.

Jess Hahn *Pierre Wesselrin* • Van Doude *Jean-Francois Santeuil* • Michèle Girardon *Dominique* • Jean Le Poulain *The clochard* • Stéphane Audran *Concierge at Hotel de Seine* • Jean-Luc Godard *Man listening to gramophone at party* ■ *Dir/Scr* Eric Rohmer

The Sign of the Cross ★★★★
Historical epic   1932 · US · BW · 118min

Anyone unsure why Cecil B DeMille's name is synonymous with epic showmanship must see this. The territory is familiar: ancient Rome under the rule of the deranged, debauched Nero (Charles Laughton) and his wife Poppaea (Claudette Colbert), and the hunting down of Christians to throw to the lions. The narrative is pegged to a doomed love between Nero's chief prefect (Fredric March) and a young Christian convert (Elissa Landi), but this is secondary to the opulence, decadence, and graphic cruelty of the climactic sequences in the gladiatorial arena. **RK**

Fredric March *Marcus Superbus* • Elissa Landi *Mercia* • Claudette Colbert *Empress Poppaea* • Charles Laughton *Emperor Nero* • Ian Keith *Tigellinus* • Vivian Tobin *Dacia* • Harry Beresford *Flavius* • Ferdinand Gottschalk *Glabrio* ■ *Dir* Cecil

U SUITABLE FOR ALL   Uc SUITABLE ESPECIALLY FOR YOUNG CHILDREN (DVD ONLY)   PG PARENTAL GUIDANCE   12A UNDER 12s TO BE ACCOMPANIED (CINEMA ONLY)

B DeMille • *Scr* Waldemar Young, Sidney Buchman, from the play by Wilson Barrett • *Cinematographer* Karl Struss

Sign of the Pagan ★★★ U
Historical epic 1954 • US • Colour • 92min

Jack Palance has a whale of a time playing the ferocious Attila, king of the Huns. His bold attempt to sack Rome is only halted by a welter of plot contrivances, but Jeff Chandler's centurion seems no real match for the ruthless barbarian. Lustily staged by director Douglas Sirk and strikingly photographed in early CinemaScope by Russell Metty, this is that rarity, an epic with a short running time. AE

Jeff Chandler *Marcian* • Jack Palance *Attila* • Ludmilla Tcherina *Princess Pulcheria* • Rita Gam *Kubra* • Jeff Morrow *Paulinus* • George Dolenz *Theodosius* • Eduard Franz *Astrologer* • Allison Hayes *Ildico* ■ *Dir* Douglas Sirk • *Scr* Oscar Brodney, Barre Lyndon, from a story by Oscar Brodney

The Signal ★★★ 18
Horror 2007 • US • Colour • 99min

A strange signal jams the world's TVs, radios and telephones. Worse than non-communication, the pulse turns people into rampaging killers, but it's hard to tell the difference between those affected and those to trust. That's the interesting premise of this Sundance *28 Days Later...* clone told in three interconnected sections by three different directors. The main focus concerns emotionally stressed Anessa Ramsey leaving her controlling husband for her perfect lover during the bloody mayhem. A potent commentary on electronic dependence and the ease with which homicidal impulses might be excused in the advent of social breakdown, this unusual sci-fi horror mixes a bizarre amateur art house atmosphere with skull-smashing gore to strikingly odd effect. AJ
DVD *Blu-ray*

AJ Bowen • Anessa Ramsey • Justin Welborn • Scott Poythress • Sahr Ngaujah • Cheri Christian ■ *Dir/Scr* David Bruckner, Dan Bush, Jacob Gentry

The Signal ★★★ 15
Science-fiction drama
2014 • US • Colour • 93min

Although this ingenious sci-fi horror hybrid never quite delivers a story as dazzling as its visuals, its ambitions set it apart in an age of carbon-copy superhero movies. Starting slowly in the guise of an innocuous road movie, it finds three tech-savvy students – Nic (Brenton Thwaites), his girlfriend Haley (Olivia Cooke) and best friend Jonah (Beau Knapp) – taking a detour from a cross-country jaunt to follow a mysterious signal that they think will lead them to a computer hacker. But events take a sinister turn. What promises to be a cerebral *Matrix*-style spectacular comes sadly unstuck with an overcomplicated finale. DW *DVD*

Brenton Thwaites *Nic Eastman* • Olivia Cooke *Haley Peterson* • Beau Knapp *Jonah Breck* • Lin Shaye *Mirabelle* • Laurence Fishburne *Dr Wallace Damon* ■ *Dir* William Eubank • *Scr* William & Carlyle Eubank, David Frigerio, from a story by William Eubank, Frigerio

La Signora di Tutti ★★★ PG
Drama 1934 • It • BW • 85min

Made during the nomadic phase of his career, Max Ophüls's sole Italian venture bears the slight influence of the glossy "white telephone" pictures then dominating the local industry. However, this is very much an Ophüls picture, giving early glimpses of the structural fragmentation and visual fluidity that characterises his best work. Told in a series of flashbacks, as actress Ise Miranda undergoes surgery following a suicide attempt, this melodrama reveals the price she has paid for her brush with fame. DP Italian +subtitles. *DVD*

Isa Miranda *Gabriela Murge, "Gaby Doriot"* • Memo Benassi *Leonardo Nanni* • Tatiana Pawlova *Alma Nanni* • Federico Benfer *Roberto Nanni* • Nelly Corradi *Anna* ■ *Dir* Max Ophüls • *Scr* Max Ophüls, Hans Wilhelm, Curt Alexander, from a novel by Salvator Gotta

La Signora senza Camelie ★★★ PG
Drama 1953 • It • BW • 101min

Michelangelo Antonioni's third feature continues to explore the alienating effects of modern society in what was originally conceived as a vehicle for Gina Lollobrigida. Instead, Lucia Bosé shoulders the burden of a faintly improbable storyline, in which her naive shopgirl is transformed into a starlet, only for her to be destroyed through a combination of limited ability, media pressure and the self-seeking ambition of her producer husband, Andrea Checchi, who pushes her into a doomed Joan of Arc project. DP In Italian. *DVD* *Blu-ray*

Lucia Bosé *Clara Manni* • Gino Cervi *Ercole "Ercolino" Bora* • Andrea Checchi *Gianni Franchi* • Ivan Desny *Nardo Rusconi* • Alain Cuny *Lodi* • Enrico Glori *Albonetti, the director* ■ *Dir* Michelangelo Antonioni • *Scr* Michelangelo Antonioni, Suso Cecchi D'Amico, Francesco Maselli, Pier Maria Pasinetti, from a story by Michelangelo Antonioni

Signpost to Murder ★★
Thriller 1964 • US • BW • 77min

This is a well-acted but relentlessly stagey opus, made by MGM in black and white when they still felt the need to produce co-features, and based on a one-set West End play of no particular distinction. Joanne Woodward makes it watchable, and Irish-born Edward Mulhare surfaces in one of his few screen roles. TS

Joanne Woodward *Molly Thomas* • Stuart Whitman *Alex Forrester* • Edward Mulhare *Dr Mark Fleming* • Joyce Worsley *Mrs Barnes* • Leslie Denison *Supt Bickley* ■ *Dir* George Englund • *Scr* Sally Benson, from the play by Monte Doyle

Signs ★★★ 12
Science-fiction fantasy thriller
2002 • US • Colour • 102min

Writer/director M Night Shyamalan here once again deals with extraordinary events from an intimate perspective. Mel Gibson's Pennsylvanian farmer (a former minister who's lost his faith) discovers crop circles in his wheat field, leading him to believe that an alien invasion is imminent. Credible performances from Gibson and Joaquin Phoenix, as his brother, combine with a spooky ambience and some very effective, old-fashioned jolts to lead us into what should have been an enthralling final act. However, mawkish sentimentality and creaky flashbacks blunt the suspense. JC
DVD *Blu-ray*

Mel Gibson *Graham Hess* • Joaquin Phoenix *Merrill Hess* • Cherry Jones *Officer Caroline Paski* • Rory Culkin *Morgan Hess* • Abigail Breslin *Bo Hess* • Patricia Kalember *Colleen Hess* ■ M Night Shyamalan *Ray Reddy* ■ *Dir/Scr* M Night Shyamalan

Signs of Life ★★★
Second World War drama
1968 • W Ger • BW • 91min

Inspired by an event that occurred during the Seven Years' War, Werner Herzog's feature debut incorporates many of the themes that would preoccupy him throughout his career. Peter Brogle is impressively distracted as the Nazi trooper detailed to guard an arms dump on the Greek island of Kos with his wife and two comrades. Using the hostile landscape to explore his psychological state, Herzog contrives a brooding study of an outsider whose sanity ebbs away as isolation, paranoia and the pressures of combat close in on him. Never wholly convincing, but disturbing. DP German +subtitles.

Peter Brogle *Stroszek* • Wolfgang Reichmann *Meinhard* • Athina Zacharopoulou *Nora* • Wolfgang von Ungern-Sternberg *Becker* • Wolfgang Stumpf *Captain* • Henry van Lyck *Lieutenant* • Julie Pinheiro *Gypsy* ■ *Dir/Scr* Werner Herzog

The Silence ★★★★ 15
Drama 1963 • Swe • BW • 91min

The early work of Swedish director Ingmar Bergman is very much an acquired taste, and this enigmatic contemplation on loneliness and obsessive desire is one of his most obscure passion plays. It symbolically explores the bleak lives of two sisters as they embark on individual odysseys to find emotional warmth and tenderness. The overt sexuality caused censorship problems at the time, but now it's hard to see what all the fuss was about. AJ Swedish +subtitles.
DVD

Ingrid Thulin *Ester* • Gunnel Lindblom *Anna* • Jörgen Lindström *Johan* • Håken Jahnberg *Hotel waiter* ■ *Dir/Scr* Ingmar Bergman

The Silence ★★★ 15
Crime drama 2010 • Ger • Colour • 118min

Twenty three years after the unsolved murder of a schoolgirl in a wheat field, another young victim goes missing, in this German thriller that surveys the course of justice from various angles. Occasional lapses in credibility notwithstanding, it's still tense and unsettling fare that treads delicately through difficult territory. It also features a deeply unnerving performance from Danish actor Ulrich Thomsen as a seemingly jovial caretaker concealing the darkest of impulses. TJ German +subtitles.
DVD

Ulrich Thomsen *Peer Sommer* • Wotan Wilke Möhring *Timo Friedrich* • Katrin Sass *Elena Lange* • Burghart Klaussner *Krischan Mittich* ■ *Dir* Baran bo Odar • *Scr* Baran bo Odar, from the novel *Silence* by Jan Costin Wagner

Silence ★★★★ PG
Drama 2012 • Ire/Ger • Colour • 87min

An intriguing hybrid of fiction, documentary and poetic evocation, this story follows a sound recordist on assignment to capture ambient backgrounds. Irish director Pat Collins ventures to the rugged west of the country for ruminative sequences in which we simply listen to the remote landscapes. Eoghan Mac Giolla Bhride (also the co-writer) plays the recordist, who journeys into an Ireland of Gaelic-speakers, half-abandoned islands, remote communities and their songs. Atmospheric and evocative, these sounds and sights will reward patient viewers, particularly those who enjoyed similarly subdued art-house fare like *Sleep Furiously* or *Le Quattro Volte*. TJ

Eoghan Mac Giolla Bhride *Eoghan* • Hilary O'Shaughnessy *Girlfriend* • Andrew Bennett *Barman* • Jens K Müller *Himself* ■ *Dir* Pat Collins (2) • *Scr* Pat Collins, Sharon Whooley, Eoghan Mac Giolla Bhride

Le Silence de la Mer ★★★★★ U
Drama 1947 • Fr • BW • 83min

Filmed using non-union labour and without the rights to Jean Vercors's clandestine tribute to the Resistance, Jean-Pierre Melville's debut feature is a masterclass in nuance and gesture. Employing camera angles derived from Carl Th Dreyer, Melville is able to convey the impact on a patriotically silent uncle and niece of the cultured nostalgia and political idealism espoused by a convalescing Nazi officer, whose essential decency has been blunted by indoctrination. Howard Vernon delivers the monologues to perfection, but the dramatic power comes from the heroic stoicism of Jean-Marie Robain and Nicole Stéphane. DP In French. *DVD* *Blu-ray*

Howard Vernon *Werner von Ebrennac* • Nicole Stéphane *Niece* • Ami Aaroé *Werner's fiancée* • Jean-Marie Robain *Uncle* ■ *Dir* Jean-Pierre Melville • *Scr* Jean-Pierre Melville, from the novel by Jean Vercors

The Silence of Lorna ★★★★ 15
Drama 2008 • Fr/It/Bel/Ger • Colour • 100min

This austere but astute drama from Jean-Pierre and Luc Dardenne is set amid the transient underclass of the Belgian city of Liège. Albanian immigrant Arta Dobroshi has married junkie Jérémie Renier in order to get her residency papers. But now the sinister Fabrizio Rongieni wants Renier dead so Dobroshi can wed a fugitive Russian gangster. As their relationship becomes increasingly complicated, there's a touching naivety about Dobroshi's desperate attempts to feign spousal abuse and secure the divorce that will spare his life. The Dardennes have often been compared to Robert Bresson, and here they allude to more spiritual concerns than in their previous works. But their heroine's road to redemption proves to be excruciatingly rocky. DP French +subtitles.
DVD

Arta Dobroshi *Lorna* • Jérémie Renier [Jérémie Rénier] *Claudy Moreau* • Fabrizio Rongione *Fabio* • Alban Ukaj *Sokol* • Morgan Marinne *Spirou* • Olivier Gourmet *Inspector* • Anton Yakovlev *Andrei* ■ *Dir/Scr* Jean-Pierre Dardenne, Luc Dardenne

The Silence of the Hams ★ 15
Spoof horror 1993 • It/US • Colour • 78min

Possibly the worst film spoof ever made and it's not hard to identify the guilty party: step forward one Ezio Greggio, who not only gets top billing but also wrote, directed and produced this tripe. Character names such as Jo Dee Fostar and Dr Animal Cannibal Pizza illustrate the supposed target, but more tellingly demonstrate the crass level of the humour. JF

Ezio Greggio *Antonio Motel* • Dom DeLuise *Dr Animal Cannibal Pizza* • Billy Zane *Jo Dee Fostar* • Joanna Pacula *Lily* • Charlene Tilton *Jane* • Martin Balsam *Detective Balsam* • Shelley Winters *The mother* • Phyllis Diller *Old secretary* ■ *Dir/Scr* Ezio Greggio

The Silence of the Lambs ★★★★★ 18
Psychological thriller 1991 • US • Colour • 113min

This multi-Oscar-winning classic, adapted from Thomas Harris's bestseller, is responsible for giving cinematic serial killers a better image. So what if Hannibal Lecter was an incarcerated cannibal? Portrayed by the masterful Anthony Hopkins, he enthralled cinema audiences. Hopkins won an Oscar for his performance, as did Jodie Foster for her role as fledgling FBI agent Clarice Starling, who is drawn into a disturbingly close relationship with Lecter as she hunts for serial killer "Buffalo Bill". With a track record for directing quirky comedies, director Jonathan Demme made a seemingly effortless switch to terror, summoning up a magnificent air of gothic gloom. This modern masterpiece was followed by the disappointing sequel, *Hannibal* (2001), and a more successful prequel, *Red Dragon* (2002). JF Violence, swearing, nudity. *DVD* *Blu-ray*

Jodie Foster *Clarice Starling* • Anthony Hopkins *Dr Hannibal Lecter* • Scott Glenn *Jack Crawford* • Ted Levine *Jame Gumb* • Anthony Heald *Dr Frederick Chilton* • Kasi Lemmons *Ardelia Mapp* • Chris Isaak *Swat commander* ■ *Dir* Jonathan Demme • *Scr* Ted Tally, from the novel by Thomas Harris

S

Silence of the North ★★ PG
Historical adventure 1981 • Can • Colour • 89min

Based on a true story, this woman-and-wilderness drama from documentary film-maker Allan King zeroes in on the trials and tribulations that befall a trapper, his soon-to-be-widowed wife and their family in the Canadian wilds in 1919. Ellen Burstyn stars as Olive Fredrickson, who raises her family alone and in harsh conditions before succumbing to a second marriage. The scenery is stunning. FL

Ellen Burstyn *Olive Fredrickson* • Tom Skerritt *Walter Reamer* • Gordon Pinsent *John Fredrickson* • Jennifer McKinney *Little Olive* • Donna Dobrijevic *Vala Reamer* • Jeff Banks *Lewis Reamer* ■ *Dir* Allan King • *Scr* Patricia Knop, from a non-fiction book by Ben East, Olive Fredrickson

Silence... We're Rolling ★★★
Musical comedy 2001 • Egy/Fr • Colour • 102min

Combining – and even lampooning – elements from Bollywood musicals and Hollywood screwball comedies, this represents a change of pace for veteran

Egyptian director Youssef Chahine. Yet he still manages to slip a few comments about prejudice into the story of movie icon Latifa's seduction by Ahmed Wafik's smooth-operating wannabe. The mix of styles in the studio sequences is inspired, but the subplots are overly strained. DP Arabic +subtitles.

Latifa *Malak* • Ahmed Bedir *Alphi* • Ahmed Wafik *Lamei* • Magda Al Khattib *Grandmother* ■ *Dir/Scr* Youssef Chahine

The Silencer ★★ 18
Action thriller 1999 · Can · Colour · 92min

Video star Michael Dudikoff, who can usually give Chuck Norris a run for his money in the woodenness stakes, gives something close to a performance in this OK-ish crime thriller. Dudikoff is the hitman who takes Brennan Elliott under his wing, without realising that he is in fact an undercover government agent. The performances are adequate and there are a few nice plot twists, but it's not ground-breaking. JF DVD

Michael Dudikoff *Quinn Simmons* • Brennan Elliott *Jason Black/Jason Wells* • Terence Kelly *Neal* • Peter LaCroix *Rodeski* • Gabrielle Miller *Jill Martin* ■ *Dir* Robert Lee • *Scr* John A Curtis

The Silencers ★★★ PG
Action comedy 1966 · US · Colour · 97min

A quintessential 1960s spy spoof, this is the first (and best) of four colourful Matt Helm features, with debonair Dean Martin cleverly cast as the womanising smoothie. The attitudes may have dated, but the women continue to delight, especially Stella Stevens as a divine klutz. Also making an impact are former Miss Israel Daliah Lavi and one-time MGM siren Cyd Charisse, whose title song is a highlight. If you care, the plot's about Helm trying to divert a Chinese-aimed missile to avoid global warfare. *Murderers' Row* was the next outing for Martin's spy. TS DVD

Dean Martin *Matt Helm* • Stella Stevens *Gail* • Daliah Lavi *Tina Batori* • Victor Buono *Tung-Tze* • Arthur O'Connell *Wigman* • Robert Webber *Sam Gunther* • James Gregory *MacDonald* • Cyd Charisse *Sarita* ■ *Dir* Phil Karlson • *Scr* Oscar Saul, from the novels *The Silencers* and *Death of a Citizen* by Donald Hamilton • *Music* Elmer Bernstein

The Silences of the Palace ★★★★ 12
Drama 1994 · Fr/Tun · Colour · 123min

Moufida Tlatli's directorial debut is a slow, multilayered drama set during the reign of Tunisia's last king, Sidi Ali. Life within his palace is so cloistered that the mounting protests against royal collaboration with the French barely intrude upon the life of a young servant girl, whose talent for music sparks a bitter rivalry between her mother and the king's barren wife. Well served by a fine ensemble cast, Tlatli superbly contrasts the shabby grandeur of the palace and the rigid protocol of a decaying system with the young girl's innocent beauty and the subtle simplicity of the music. DP Arabic +subtitles.

Ahmel Hedhili *Khedija* • Hend Sabri *Young Alia* • Najia Ouerghi *Khalti Hadda* • Ghalia Lacroix *Adult Alia* ■ *Dir/Scr* Moufida Tlatli

The Silent Army ★★ 15
Drama 2008 · Neth · Colour · 89min

There have been better films about child soldiers – *Johnny Mad Dog*, for one. But this is a decent addition to the genre, despite its inclination towards *Die Hard*-style action silliness towards the close. The setting is some unspecified East African country, where nine-year-old Thomas's best friend Abu is seized by the rebel supporters of a tinpot would-be dictator. The movie is competently made, but the decent and disturbing build-up is marred by a melodramatic climax. A pity. DA Dutch, English, Swahili, French +subtitles. Violence. DVD

Marco Borsato *Eduard Zuiderwijk* • Abby Mukiibi Nkaaga *Michel Obeke* • Andrew Kintu *Abu* • Thekla Reuten *Valérie* • Peter Van den Begin *François Lama* ■ *Dir/Scr* Jean van de Velde

Silent Assassins ★ 18
Action 1988 · US · Colour · 88min

A group of hired killers eccentric enough to be at home in a *Batman* comic book kidnap a scientist who has invented some sort of biological weapon. The only person who can rescue him is Sam Jones, a standard issue cop on the edge whose partners were, of course, victims of these same assassins. Even by action movie standards, this scrapes the bottom of the barrel. ST DVD

Sam J Jones [Sam Jones] *Sam Kettle* • Linda Blair *Sara* • Jun Chong *Jun Kim* • Phillip Rhee *Bernard* • Bill Erwin *Dr London* • Gustav Vintas *Kendrick* • Mako Oyama ■ *Dir* Doo-yong Lee, Scott Thomas • *Scr* Will Gates, Ada Lin, from a story by John Bruner

The Silent Bell ★★★
Period drama 1944 · US · Colour · 69min

In one of the least known of Val Lewton's low-budget productions for RKO, Simone Simon plays a common laundress in an adaptation of two Guy de Maupassant stories. Set during the Prussian invasion of France in the 1870s (paralleling the Nazi occupation of France during the Second World War), the story enables Simon to display real patriotism that shames her aristocratic fellow passengers on a coach journey. AE

Simone Simon *Elizabeth Rousset* • John Emery *Jean Cornudet* • Kurt Kreuger *Lt von Eyrick, "Mademoiselle Fifi"* • Alan Napier *Count de Breville* • Helen Freeman *Countess de Breville* • Jason Robards [Jason Robards Sr] *Wine wholesaler* ■ *Dir* Robert Wise • *Scr* Josef Mischel, Peter Ruric, from the short stories *Mademoiselle Fifi* and *Boule de Suif* by Guy de Maupassant

Silent Conflict ★★ U
Western 1948 · US · BW · 61min

The long-running Hopalong Cassidy series was on its last legs when William Boyd saddled up once more to help a chum who had been hypnotised into a life of crime. Despite the presence of regulars Andy Clyde and Rand Brooks, this entry is long on talk and low on action. JF

William Boyd (1) *Hopalong Cassidy* • Andy Clyde *California Carlson* • Rand Brooks *Lucky Jenkins* • Virginia Belmont *Rene Richards* • Earle Hodgins *Doc Richards* • James Harrison *Speed Blaney* • Forbes Murray *Randall* ■ *Dir* George Archainbaud • *Scr* Charles Belden, from characters by Clarence E Mulford

Silent Dust ★ PG
Drama 1948 · UK · BW · 78min

Adapted by Michael Pertwee from the play he co-wrote with his father Roland, this is supposed to be a provocative treatise on the nature of heroism, but is nothing more than a mawkish drama with a shamelessly sentimental performance by Stephen Murray, whose rose-tinted image of his son is tarnished by the truth. DP DVD

Sally Gray *Angela Rawley* • Stephen Murray *Robert Rawley* • Derek Farr *Maxwell Oliver* • Nigel Patrick *Simon Rawley* • Beatrice Campbell *Joan Rawley* ■ *Dir* Lance Comfort • *Scr* Michael Pertwee, from the play *The Paragon* by Michael Pertwee, Roland Pertwee • *Music* Georges Auric

The Silent Enemy ★★★ PG
Second World War biographical drama
1958 · UK · BW · 107min

This distinguished British war film celebrates the exploits of celebrated Royal Navy frogman Lt Lionel "Buster" Crabb, played here by Laurence Harvey, whose explosive temperament is a perfect match for the volatile character he plays. The underwater shooting is well done, and the plot has more excitement than many fictional tales. The saga is shot through with a rich vein of humour, and at writer/director William Fairchild. TS DVD

Laurence Harvey *Lieutenant Lionel Crabb* • Dawn Addams *Third Officer Jill Masters* • Michael Craig *Leading Seaman Knowles* • John Clements *The Admiral* • Sidney James *Chief Petty Officer Thorpe* • Alec McCowen *Able Seaman Morgan* • Nigel Stock *Able Seaman Fraser* ■ *Dir* William Fairchild • *Scr* William Fairchild, from Marshall Pugh's non-fiction book *Commander Crabb*

Silent Fall ★★★ 15
Psychological thriller 1994 · US · Colour · 96min

Director Bruce Beresford is one of Hollywood's safer pairs of hands and he hardly misses a beat with this absorbing, if somewhat predictable thriller. Richard Dreyfuss is the retired child psychologist called in to help unlock the memory of an autistic child who holds the key to the murder of his parents. Ben Faulkner is movingly believable as the boy and Dreyfuss is as dependable as ever, even though John Lithgow and JT Walsh steal every scene they're in. Look out for for a charismatic debut from Liv Tyler. JF Violence, swearing.

Richard Dreyfuss *Jake Rainer* • Linda Hamilton *Karen Rainer* • John Lithgow *Doctor Harlinger* • JT Walsh *Sheriff Mitch Rivers* • Ben Faulkner *Tim Warden* • Liv Tyler *Sylvie Warden* ■ *Dir* Bruce Beresford • *Scr* Akiva Goldsman

The Silent Flute ★★★ 18
Martial arts fantasy adventure
1978 · US · Colour · 91min

Based on a story Bruce Lee was writing (with James Coburn) before his death, director Richard Moore's beguiling mystical martial arts fantasy tells of arena fighter Jeff Cooper and his quest for the Book of Enlightenment. A series of trials with bizarre opponents stands between him and its Keeper, Christopher Lee. On his travels (through exquisite Israeli locations) he keeps chancing on a blind man (David Carradine, in one of four roles) who plays a silent flute and teaches him the meaning of life. Although Cooper is a weak protagonist, this Oriental fable has a haunting musical score and is too interesting to dismiss. AJ

David Carradine *Blind man/Jungar/Death/ Changsha* • Jeff Cooper *Cord* • Roddy McDowall *White Robe* • Eli Wallach *Man in oil* • Christopher Lee *Zetan* • Erica Creer *Tara* ■ *Dir* Richard Moore • *Scr* Stirling Silliphant, Stanley Mann, from a story by Bruce Lee, James Coburn, Stirling Silliphant

Silent Grace ★★★ 15
Prison drama based on a true story
2001 · Ire/UK · Colour · 86min

Set against the backdrop of the IRA's dirty protest and the hunger strikes of the early 1980s, Maeve Murphy's feature debut efficiently conveys the determination of those women incarcerated within Armagh prison who actively supported their brothers in arms. The rapport between loudmouthed joyrider Cathleen Bradley and Orla Brady's charismatic activist is established rather too conveniently, but the convincing performances command attention. DP Swearing.

Orla Brady *Eileen* • Cathleen Bradley *Aine* • Cara Seymour *Margaret* • Dawn Bradfield *Geraldine* • Conor Mullen *Cunningham* • Robert Newman (2) *Father McGarry* • Patrick Bergin *Peter, IRA man* ■ *Dir* Maeve Murphy • *Scr* Maeve Murphy, from the play *Now and at the Hour of Our Death* by Maeve Murphy, theatre company Trouble and Strife

Silent Hill ★★ 15
Horror thriller 2006 · Jpn/US/Fr · Colour · 120min

The video game *Silent Hill*, with its strange atmosphere, spooky imagery and deliberately slow pace, entranced the world's joypad jockeys on its release in 1999. But this film adaptation seems to have learned little from the success of the game. The plot sees a young mother (Radha Mitchell) fleeing with her sick child to the mysterious, deserted town of Silent Hill, to prevent the girl from being placed in an institution. The film's look is satisfyingly weird, but we're treated to the usual repetitive jolts and threadbare effects. A sequel hit cinemas in 2012. AS Swearing, violence. DVD

Radha Mitchell *Rose Da Silva* • Sean Bean *Christopher Da Silva* • Laurie Holden *Cybil Bennet* • Deborah Kara Unger *Dahlia Gillespie* • Kim Coates *Officer Gucci* • Tanya Allen *Anna* • Alice Krige *Cristabella* • Jodelle Ferland *Sharon Da Silva/Alessa Gillespie* ■ *Dir* Christophe Gans • *Scr*

Roger Avary, from a story by Christophe Gans, Nicolas Boukhrief, from the computer game series by Konami

Silent Hill: Revelation ★ 15
Horror thriller 2012 · Fr/US · Colour · 90min

Confusion and boredom reign in this belated sequel to the 2006 original, which was based on the popular video game. The now-grown girl from the first film (played here by Adelaide Clemens) is forced to return to the haunted title town after cult emissaries kidnap father Sean Bean. This is dismal stuff: convoluted jargon related to the game, hosts of deformed monsters, awkward cameos and endless exposition scenes fatally clog up what little narrative logic exists. AJ Violence, swearing. DVD Blu

Adelaide Clemens *Heather Mason/Alessa* • Kit Harington *Vincent Carter* • Sean Bean *Harry Mason/Christopher Da Silva* • Carrie-Anne Moss *Claudia Wolf* • Radha Mitchell *Rose Da Silva* • Malcolm McDowell *Leonard Wolf* ■ *Dir/Scr* Michael J Bassett

The Silent House ★★ 15
Horror 2011 · Urug/Fr · Colour · 82min

Despite boasting three distinct gimmicks in its spare running time – takes place in real time, shot in a single take and on a digital camera – *The Silent House* promises more than it actually delivers. The story is simple enough: a young woman (Florencia Colucci) is fixing up an old country house with her father, but when night falls things take a turn for the creepy. What follows is an effective enough haunted-house movie that makes good use of darkness. But this low-budget Uruguayan chiller is never terrifying, and, worse, it ends with a silly twist that's much more likely to raise eyebrows than goosebumps. DW Spanish +subtitles. Violence. DVD Blu

Florencia Colucci *Laura* • Abel Tripaldi *Néstor* • Gustavo Alonso *Wilson* • María Paz Salazar *Girl* ■ *Dir* Gustavo Hernández • *Scr* Oscar Estévez, from a story by Gustavo Hernández, Gustavo Rojo

Silent House ★★ 15
Horror 2011 · US/Fr · Colour · 81min

Open Water co-directors Chris Kentis and Laura Lau's remake of the 2011 Uruguayan horror borrows from Alfred Hitchcock's *Rope* technique – ten elongated takes give a real-time feel to Elizabeth Olsen's renovating of the family holiday home while fending off mysterious entities. But as much of the running time is taken up with her roaming through dark rooms, the directors have a hard time sustaining the tempo and the creepy atmosphere. AJ Violence, swearing. DVD Blu

Elizabeth Olsen *Sarah* • Adam Trese *John* • Eric Sheffer Stevens *Peter* • Julia Taylor Ross *Sophia* ■ *Dir* Chris Kentis, Laura Lau • *Scr* Laura Lau, from the 2011 film

Silent Light ★★★ 15
Drama 2007 · Mex/Fr/Neth · Colour · 130min

This sombre tale about the clash between religious duty and carnal desire was shot on location in Chihuahua, Mexico, among the Mennonite community. One of their number is Johan (Cornelio Wall Fehr), whose illicit affair with Marianne (Maria Pankratz) is pushing his family towards crisis. As interested in the stately pace of life among the separatist Mennonites as in Johan's understated crisis of conscience, Mexican film-maker Carlos Reygadas (*Battle in Heaven*) lets the drama inch forward at a funereal pace. There are some beautiful moments, not least of all its opening, time-lapse shot of dawn gradually breaking, but the film's pacing and overbearing stillness ultimately proves rather alienating. JR German, French, Spanish +subtitles. DVD

Cornelio Wall Fehr *Johan* • Miriam Toews *Esther* • Maria Pankratz *Marianne* • Peter Wall *Father* • Elisabeth Fehr *Mother* • Jacobo Klassen *Zacarias* ■ *Dir/Scr* Carlos Reygadas

U SUITABLE FOR ALL   Uc SUITABLE ESPECIALLY FOR YOUNG CHILDREN (DVD ONLY)   PG PARENTAL GUIDANCE   12A UNDER 12s TO BE ACCOMPANIED (CINEMA ONLY)

Silent Movie ★★★ PG
Comedy　1976 · US · Colour · 87min

In a (virtually) dialogue-free movie, Mel Brooks plays film director Mel Funn who plans to make a modern-day silent movie in an attempt to save ailing film corporation Big Picture Studios. Aided by Marty Feldman and Dom DeLuise, Brooks sets out to shoot his masterpiece and on the way runs into a number of well-known movie faces in cameo roles. There's some well-honed slapstick and a number of fair gags, but the film is more of a Brooks comedy than a homage to the silent era. DF **DVD**

Mel Brooks *Mel Funn* • Marty Feldman *Marty Eggs* • Dom DeLuise *Dom Bell* • Bernadette Peters *Vilma Kaplan* • Sid Caesar *Studio Chief* • Harold Gould *Engulf* • Ron Carey *Devour* • *Dir* Mel Brooks • *Scr* Mel Brooks, Ron Clark, Rudy DeLuca, Barry Levinson, by Ron Clark

Silent Night, Deadly Night
★★ 18
Horror　1984 · US · Colour · 81min

This routine stalk-and-slasher movie gained notoriety when American parents protested about the effect that portraying Father Christmas as a mad murderer would have on children. Billy sees his parents slain at Christmas by someone dressed as Santa. Not surprisingly, he grows up hating the festive season. Working in a department store, he's forced into a Santa outfit by his boss and goes on a homicidal rampage. Shallow and depressing. Four sequels followed. AJ

Lilyan Chauvin *Mother Superior* • Gilmer McCormick *Sister Margaret* • Toni Nero *Pamela* • Robert Brian Wilson *Billy, aged 18* • *Dir* Charles E Sellier Jr • *Scr* Michael Hickey, from a story by Paul Caimi

The Silent One ★★★
Spy thriller　1973 · Fr/It · Colour · 117min

Nobody did the chase thriller better than Alfred Hitchcock and on the evidence of this stylish, suspenseful espionage story, Claude Pinoteau had clearly been taking notes. From the moment Soviet nuclear scientist Lino Ventura is revealed to be a kidnapped Frenchman, nothing can be taken for granted, apart from the excellence of the star whose mournful response to freedom is very much that of a spy coming in from the cold with the greatest reluctance. Both intelligent and entertaining. DP French dubbed.

Lino Ventura *Tibère* • Lea Massari *Maria* • Suzanne Flon *Jeanne* • Leo Genn *Man from MI5* • Robert Hardy *MI5 assistant* • *Dir* Claude Pinoteau • *Scr* Jean-Loup Dabadie, Claude Pinoteau, from the novel *Drôle de Pistolet* by Francis Ryck

The Silent Partner ★★★
Crime caper　1978 · Can · Colour · 105min

This thriller boasts a sort of retro 1960s cast and an ingenious script by Curtis Hanson, who later won an Oscar for his adaptation of *LA Confidential*. It's about a bank, which is robbed by Christopher Plummer dressed as Santa Claus, though part of his potential haul is stolen by devious bank clerk Elliott Gould. Both the male leads are in fine fettle but Susannah York has too little to do. It sounds like a comedy but the tone is actually quite dark with some casual violence. AT

Susannah York *Julie Carver* • Christopher Plummer *Harry Reikle* • Elliott Gould *Miles Cullen* • Celine Lomez *Elaine* • Michael Kirby *Charles Packard* • Ken Pogue *Detective Willard* • John Candy *Simonsen* • *Dir* Daryl Duke • *Scr* Curtis Hanson, from the novel *Think of a Number* by Anders Bodelsen

The Silent Passenger ★★ PG
Crime drama　1935 · UK · BW · 70min

Despite being popularly played by Ian Carmichael and Edward Petherbridge on television, Lord Peter Wimsey has failed to make much cinematic impact. Sadly, Peter Haddon seems to be under the impression that he's playing Bertie Wooster masquerading as an amateur sleuth. However, Donald Wolfit makes a splendidly malevolent villain, as he tries to frame innocent passenger John Loder for the murder of the man who had been blackmailing his wife, and the train-board setting suits director Reginald Denham's sedate style. DP **DVD**

Peter Haddon *Lord Peter Wimsey* • John Loder *John Ryder* • Mary Newland *Mollie Ryder* • Austin Trevor *Inspector Parker* • Donald Wolfit *Henry Camberley* • *Dir* Reginald Denham • *Scr* Basil Mason, from an original story by Dorothy L Sayers

Silent Rage ★ 18
Action drama　1982 · US · Colour · 95min

Chuck Norris doesn't say much in his movies, which is just as well given scripts like this one. As a former karate champion turned actor he lets his feet do the talking. Here we discover him in one of those ubiquitous small Texas towns that seem to have, and need, sheriffs like Chuck, especially when an axe killer (Brian Libby) he's already dealt with is back in town. Norris looks bemused in a preposterously silly film which is less fun than it should be. BB

Chuck Norris *Dan Stevens* • Ron Silver *Dr Tom Halman* • Steven Keats *Dr Philip Spires* • Toni Kalem *Alison Halman* • William Finley *Dr Paul Vaughn* • Brian Libby *John Kirby* • Stephen Furst *Charlie* • *Dir* Michael Miller (2) • *Scr* Joseph Fraley

Silent Running ★★★★ U
Science-fiction drama　1971 · US · Colour · 85min

Special-effects ace Douglas Trumbull (of *2001* fame) turned director with this ecologically based thriller about the last of Earth's plant-life preserved on the *Valley Forge* spaceship, lovingly cared for by space ranger Bruce Dern and his three cute "drone" robots. Dern mutinies when orders arrive to destroy the precious cargo. Although the film may seem rather hippy-influenced now (those syrupy Joan Baez ballads), Trumbull's gentle direction highlights a sensitive performance by Dern. Imaginative and much admired. AJ **DVD Blu-ray**

Bruce Dern *Freeman Lowell* • Cliff Potts *Wolf* • Ron Rifkin *Barker* • Jesse Vint *Keenan* • *Dir* Douglas Trumbull • *Scr* Deric Washburn, Mike Cimino, Steve Bocho

Silent Scream ★★ 15
Biographical drama　1989 · UK · Colour · 81min

Extremely powerful in parts, director David Hayman's heartfelt biographical drama, based on the life of convicted murderer Larry Winters, is very much a mixed blessing. Iain Glen gives a marvellous performance as the manic-depressive Winters, jailed for killing a barman, recalling his life while under the influence of drugs in prison. But Hayman drenches his potent polemic in an earnest and inappropriately fractured style. AJ Swearing, drug abuse. **DVD**

Iain Glen *Larry Winters* • Paul Samson *Jimmy* • Andrew Barr *Shuggie* • Kenneth Glenaan *Rab* • Steve Hotchkiss *Mo* • John Murtagh *Ken Murray* • Robert Carlyle *Big Woodsy* • *Dir* David Hayman • *Scr* Bill Beech, Jane Beech, from the life and writings of Larry Winters

The Silent Storm ★★ 15
Romantic drama　2014 · UK · Colour · 102min

In this modest 1950s-set drama, stern minister Damian Lewis resolves to stay on a depopulated Scottish island with long-suffering spouse Andrea Riseborough. However, unexpected company is provided when a youth offender is unloaded on the couple. Hellfire lectures from one side are matched by a nudge into love-triangle territory on the other. Events move sluggishly and Lewis chews the scenery, while Riseborough wrestles with an odd Scandi-Scots accent. A turgid choral score only makes matters worse. TJ Sex scenes.

Andrea Riseborough *Aislin* • Damian Lewis *Balor* • Ross Anderson *Fionn* • Kate Dickie *Mrs McKinnon* • John Sessions *Mr Smith* • *Dir/Scr* Corinna McFarlane • *Cinematographer* Ed Rutherford

The Silent Touch ★★★ 15
Romantic comedy　1992 · UK/Pol/Den · Colour · 91min

A complex display of frustrated creativity, simmering fury and manipulative cunning from Max von Sydow dominates this intense study of the sacrifices art demands of life. Roused from his reclusive ennui by Polish musicologist Lothaire Bluteau, von Sydow's exiled composer battles the bottle, physical pain and his emotional demons to complete his masterpiece, a snatch of which had lingered elusively in the mind of his mystical visitor. This turbulent relationship is delineated with care by director Krzysztof Zanussi. DP

Max von Sydow *Henry Kesdi* • Lothaire Bluteau *Stefan Bugajski* • Sarah Miles *Helena Kesdi* • Sofie Grabol *Annette Berg* • Aleksander Bardini *Professor Jerzy Kern* • *Dir* Krzysztof Zanussi • *Scr* Peter Morgan (1), Mark Wadlow, from a story by Krzysztof Zanussi, Edward Zebrowski

Silent Trigger ★★ 18
Action thriller　1996 · UK/Can · Colour · 89min

Dolph Lundgren and Gina Bellman play a pair of hired killers, waiting in an eerie building for their next target, in a sleep-inducing thriller. This is considered one of Lundgren's better outings, but the competition isn't that stiff. Here his role isn't mere beefcake but demands emotional depth, but he's still guilty of delivering dialogue like a foreign exchange student. RS Violence, swearing, drug abuse, nudity. **DVD**

Dolph Lundgren *Shooter* • Gina Bellman *Spotter* • Conrad Dunn *Supervisor* • Christopher Heyerdahl *O'Hara* • Emma Stevens *Target woman* • *Dir* Russell Mulcahy • *Scr* Sergio Altieri

Silk ★★ 15
Period romantic drama　2007 · Can/Fr/It/UK/Jpn · Colour · 103min

In this yawn-inducingly slow period drama, Keira Knightley plays a 19th-century newlywed whose husband (Michael Pitt), a buyer of silkworms, becomes obsessed by a concubine during his trading trips to Japan. This is star-crossed romance, but Mills & Boon style - dreamy rather than steamy. Knightley looks suitably wistful and there is a mildly pleasing twist in the tail, but it's so sluggishly played that watching worms make silk would probably be more stimulating. The film at least lives up to its title in two respects: it's lovely to look at and is easier to see through than sit through. DA In English, Japanese. **DVD**

Keira Knightley *Hélène Joncour* • Michael Pitt *Hervé Joncour* • Koji Yakusho *Hara Jubei* • Alfred Molina *Baldabiou* • Mark Rendall *Ludovic Berbek* • *Dir* François Girard • *Scr* François Girard, Michael Golding, from the novel by Alessandro Baricco

Silk Stockings ★★★ U
Musical comedy　1957 · US · Colour · 112min

A musical remake of *Ninotchka* with a Cole Porter score might have seemed a good idea at the time, but this MGM CinemaScope special is more than a little heavy-handed under the arthritic direction of veteran Rouben Mamoulian. Nevertheless, the splendid cast and choreography keep it all eminently watchable, even if the anti-Russian jokes and the anti-rock 'n' roll number leave a sour taste in the mouth. The commissars, headed by Peter Lorre, are funny, but it lacks the sparkle of MGM's best. TS

Fred Astaire *Steve Canfield* • Cyd Charisse *Ninotchka* • Janis Paige *Peggy Dainton* • Peter Lorre *Ivanov* • Jules Munshin *Bibinski* • Joseph Buloff *Ivanov* • George Tobias *Commissar Vassili Markovich* • *Dir* Rouben Mamoulian • *Scr* Leonard Gershe, Leonard Spigelgass, Harry Kurnitz, from the musical by George S Kaufman, Leueen McGrath [Leueen MacGrath], Abe Burrows, from the film *Ninotchka* by Charles Brackett, Billy Wilder, Walter Reisch, from a story by Melchior Lengyel • *Choreographer* Hermes Pan

Silkwood ★★★★ 15
Biographical drama　1983 · US · Colour · 125min

This moving film is based on a true story about a female nuclear power plant worker who died under mysterious circumstances on her way to a meeting with the press, at which she intended to show them proof of improprieties at her workplace. Meryl Streep is charismatic and convincing in the lead and there's strong support from Cher and Kurt Russell. But despite the interesting premise, particularly topical at the time of its release, the movie is let down by a lack of tension and director Mike Nichols's tendency to digress into the romantic subplot. Thought-provoking and still relevant. LH **DVD**

Meryl Streep *Karen Silkwood* • Kurt Russell *Drew Stephens* • Cher *Dolly Pelliker* • Craig T Nelson *Winston* • Diana Scarwid *Angela* • Fred Ward *Morgan* • Ron Silver *Paul Stone* • *Dir* Mike Nichols • *Scr* Nora Ephron, Alice Arlen

Silver Bears ★ PG
Comedy crime caper　1977 · US · Colour · 107min

Michael Caine has made some odd choices in his career, but none as peculiar as this caper in which he sets up a bank in Switzerland for gangster Martin Balsam and becomes involved in a scam involving an Iranian silver mine. There's an elegant cast (Louis Jourdan, Cybill Shepherd, Stéphane Audran), but hardly any sympathetic characters. TH

Michael Caine *Doc Fletcher* • Cybill Shepherd *Debbie Luckman* • Louis Jourdan *Prince di Siracusa* • Stéphane Audran *Shireen Firdausi* • David Warner *Agha Firdausi* • Martin Balsam *Joe Fiore* • Jay Leno *Albert Fiore* • Joss Ackland *Henry Foreman* • Tom Smothers *Donald Luckman* • *Dir* Ivan Passer • *Scr* Peter Stone, from the novel by Paul E Erdman

The Silver Brumby ★★★★ U
Adventure　1992 · Aus · Colour · 91min

Less sentimental than most family films, this will transfix those teenagers who are obsessed with all things equine. Shooting both the landscape and the fabulous horses with a genuine passion, director John Tatoulis forgoes the easy rites-of-passage clichés as Ami Daemion learns the lessons contained in her mother Caroline Goodall's book about a white stallion, the "brumby" of the title. Russell Crowe cuts a dash as the cattleman intent on possessing the beast. DP

Caroline Goodall *Elyne* • Russell Crowe *The man* • Ami Daemion [Amiel Daemion] *Indy* • *Dir* John Tatoulis • *Scr* Elyne Mitchell, John Tatoulis, Jon Stephens, from the novel by Elyne Mitchell

Silver Bullet ★★ 18
Horror thriller　1985 · US · Colour · 90min

Scripted by Stephen King from his own story *Cycle of the Werewolf*, this half-hearted horror is a tired sheep in werewolf's clothing. Disabled Corey Haim (his wheelchair is the silver bullet of the title) knows there's a werewolf on the prowl in his small town and convinces his sister (Megan Follows) and their alcoholic uncle (Gary Busey) to help him unmask its human identity. First-time director Daniel Attias draws credible performances from his able cast but the irony-rich murders draw more laughter than terror. AJ **DVD**

Gary Busey *Uncle Red* • Corey Haim *Marty Coslaw* • Megan Follows *Jane Coslaw* • Everett McGill *Reverend Lowe* • Terry O'Quinn *Sheriff Joe Haller* • Lawrence Tierney *Owen Knopfler* • *Dir* Daniel Attias • *Scr* Stephen King, from his story *Cycle of the Werewolf*

The Silver Chalice ★★ U
Religious drama　1954 · US · Colour · 143min

This biblical epic focuses on a Greek slave, freed from bondage to design and make a chalice to hold the silver cup used at the Last Supper, this was the film that launched the career of Paul Newman. Unfortunately, the underdeveloped script gave him no chance to display his considerable acting gifts. Despite William V Skall's Oscar-nominated CinemaScope photography, which made the most of the visual

S

spectacle, and Franz Waxman's sweeping score (also nominated), the dreary writing and Victor Saville's lifeless direction make for a movie that's too long by half. RK

Virginia Mayo *Helena* • Pier Angeli *Deborra* • Jack Palance *Simon* • Paul Newman *Basil* • Walter Hampden *Joseph* • Joseph Wiseman *Mijamin* • Alexander Scourby *Luke* • Lorne Greene *Peter* • Natalie Wood *Helena as a child* ■ *Dir* Victor Saville • *Scr* Lesser Samuels, from the novel by Thomas B Costain

Silver City ★★☆ 🅵
Political satire 2004 · US · Colour · 122min

Dickie Pilager (Chris Cooper) is the tongue-tied, "user-friendly" candidate for Colorado governor (bearing more than a passing resemblance to George W Bush). His family's links with corporate mogul Kris Kristofferson, plus dodgy land deals, environmental damage and illegal workers all drive what is actually an old-fashioned detective story. Disappointingly, Cooper fades into the background as Danny Huston's down-at-heel investigator risks all to join the corrupt dots. In the end, John Sayles's liberal indignation hobbles this baggy and moralising political satire. AC Swearing. *DVD*

Chris Cooper *Richard "Dickie" Pilager* • Richard Dreyfuss *Chuck Raven* • Daryl Hannah *Maddy Pilager* • Maria Bello *Nora Allardyce* • Danny Huston *Danny O'Brien* • Thora Birch *Karen Cross* • Tim Roth *Mitch Paine* • Michael Murphy (1) *Senator Judd Pilager* • Mary Kay Place *Grace Seymour* ■ *Dir/Scr* John Sayles

The Silver Cord ★★★
Drama 1933 · US · BW · 75min

Although this adaptation of a play by Sidney Howard retains the style, atmosphere, small cast of characters and theatrical speeches that betray its origins, it is nonetheless one of the most frightening and powerful studies of poisonously destructive mother-love you are likely to see. Laura Hope Crews delivers something of a tour de force as the selfish, manipulative and unhealthily possessive mother of two adult sons, bent on destroying the engagement of one (Eric Linden) and the marriage of the other (Joel McCrea). Irene Dunne delivers a shining performance. RK

Irene Dunne *Christina Phelps* • Joel McCrea *David Phelps* • Frances Dee *Hester Phelps* • Eric Linden *Robert Phelps* • Laura Hope Crews *Mrs Phelps* • Helen Cromwell *Delia* ■ *Dir* John Cromwell • *Scr* Jane Murfin, from the play by Sidney Howard

The Silver Darlings ★★🅿🅶
Period drama 1947 · UK · BW · 81min

The silver darlings are the herrings that provide a precarious living for the fishermen of the Hebrides in the mid-19th century. This Scottish enterprise was a work of love, made over a two-year span by writer/director Clarence Elder in collaboration with actor and associate director Clifford Evans. A pity, then, that the location footage overwhelms the narrative and is too often back-projected behind actors in the studio. Evans's Welsh accent and Helen Shingler's English one are a hindrance to cultivating an authentic tone. AE *DVD*

Clifford Evans *Roddy* • Helen Shingler *Catrine* • Carl Bernard *Angus* • Norman Shelley *Hendry* • Jean Shepherd [Jean Shepeard] *Mrs Hendry* • Simon Lack *Don* • Norman Williams *Tormad* • Phyllis Morris *Tormad's mother* ■ *Dir* Clarence Elder, Clifford Evans • *Scr* Clarence Elder, from a novel by Neil M Gunn

Silver Dream Racer ★★🅵
Action drama 1980 · UK · Colour · 106min

Whatever happened to David Essex? Here he is, near the end of his heyday, racing motorbikes, dressing in leather, trying to be James Dean and keeping Brylcreem in business. He wrote the music, too. The plot kicks in when Essex is given the mean machine of the title, a space-age ride designed to leave American ace rider Beau Bridges on the starting grid. A vanity project from beginning to end. AT *DVD*

David Essex *Nick Freeman* • Beau Bridges *Bruce McBride* • Cristina Raines *Julie Prince* • Clarke Peters *Cider Jones* • Harry H Corbett *Wiggins* • Diane Keen *Tina* • Lee Montague *Jack Freeman* ■ *Dir/Scr* David Wickes

The Silver Fleet ★★★🆄
Second World War drama 1943 · UK · BW · 84min

This British wartime flag-waver boasts the magic names of Michael Powell and Emeric Pressburger, but they were only producers - it was actually written and directed by Vernon Sewell and Gordon Wellesley. Their influence may well account for the too-stately progress of the tale, in which shipping engineer Ralph Richardson poses as a traitor in Nazi-occupied Holland in order to destroy the U-boat he's just had built. Richardson is convincing, as is the story once it gets going. TH *DVD*

Ralph Richardson *Jaap Van Leyden* • Googie Withers *Helene Van Leyden* • Esmond Knight *Von Schiller* • Beresford Egan *Krampf* • Frederick Burtwell *Captain Muller* • Willem Akkerman *Willem Van Leyden* • Dorothy Gordon *Janni Peters* • Charles Victor *Bastiaan Peters* ■ *Dir/Scr* Vernon Campbell Sewell [Vernon Sewell], Gordon Wellesley

Silver Linings Playbook ★★★★🅵
Romantic comedy drama 2012 · US · Colour · 117min

This beguilingly offbeat love story was adapted by idiosyncratic director David O Russell from the debut novel by Matthew Quick. Bradley Cooper gives a career-changing performance as Pat, a bipolar divorcé returning to his larger-than-life suburban Philadelphia family after a spell in a mental health clinic. After a chance meeting, he partners up with Jennifer Lawrence's fellow neurotic to train hard for a dance competition that promises to prove therapeutic for them both. This is a genuinely unusual, bittersweet romance that also boasts some terrific choreography. AC Violence, swearing, sexual references. *DVD* 🅱🅻🆄

Bradley Cooper *Pat* • Jennifer Lawrence (2) *Tiffany* • Robert De Niro *Pat Sr* • Jacki Weaver *Dolores* • Chris Tucker *Danny* • Anupam Kher *Dr Cliff Patel* • Julia Stiles *Veronica* ■ *Dir* David O Russell • *Scr* David O Russell, from Matthew Quick's novel • *Editors* Jay Cassidy, Crispin Struthers

Silver Lode ★★★
Western 1954 · US · Colour · 80min

John Payne is accused of murder on his wedding day and has to go on the run from a posse led by Dan Duryea. Many critics regard this tale as an allegory about the political witch-hunts of the time. Tightly directed by Allan Dwan and nicely photographed by John Alton, this is one of many RKO productions that belies its dime budget, producing some distinctive sequences, even though Payne makes for a rather colourless hero. AT

John Payne *Dan Ballard* • Lizabeth Scott *Rose Evans* • Dan Duryea *McCarty* • Dolores Moran *Dolly* • Emile Meyer *Sheriff Woolley* • Robert Warwick *Judge Cranston* • John Hudson (1) *Mitch Evans* • Harry Carey Jr *Johnson* ■ *Dir* Allan Dwan • *Scr* Karen De Wolfe

Silver River ★★★🆄
Western 1948 · US · BW · 104min

After *Gentleman Jim* and *They Died with Their Boots On*, director Raoul Walsh and Errol Flynn renewed their parnership in this run-of-the-mill Warner Bros western, not even considered worthy of shooting in colour. Still, movie fans today will find much to enjoy, since the film shows the Hollywood system in fine fettle. Flynn's the former soldier turned gambler who'll stop at nothing to win the affection of Ann Sheridan. TS

Errol Flynn *Capt Mike McComb* • Ann Sheridan *Georgia Moore* • Thomas Mitchell *John Plato Beck* • Bruce Bennett *Stanley Moore* • Tom D'Andrea *Pistol Porter* • Barton MacLane *Banjo Sweeney* • Monte Blue *Buck Chevigee* • Jonathan

Hale *Maj Spencer* ■ *Dir* Raoul Walsh • *Scr* Stephen Longstreet, Harriet Frank Jr, from a novel by Stephen Longstreet

Silver Streak ★★★★🅿🅶
Comedy thriller 1976 · US · Colour · 108min

Gene Wilder and Richard Pryor star in a spectacular comedy thriller set aboard the Los Angeles-Chicago *Silver Streak* train. Publisher Wilder witnesses a murder and thief Pryor helps to hide him as Patrick McGoohan and his gang of villains close in. It harks back to those British thrillers of the 1930s, with some screwball antics and Jill Clayburgh thrown in for good measure. With such an endearing trio of characters, it makes you wonder why there wasn't a sequel, though it paved the way for Wilder and Pryor's 1980 collaboration, *Stir Crazy*. TH *DVD*

Gene Wilder *George Caldwell* • Jill Clayburgh *Hilly Burns* • Richard Pryor *Grover Muldoon* • Patrick McGoohan *Roger Devereau* • Ned Beatty *Sweet* • Clifton James *Sheriff Chauncey* • Ray Walston *Mr Whiney* • Richard Kiel *Reace* • Scatman Crothers *Ralston* ■ *Dir* Arthur Hiller • *Scr* Colin Higgins

Silverado ★★★★🅿🅶
Western 1985 · US · Colour · 127min

Billed as the movie that was going to revive the ailing western, this film merely performed a little resuscitation before Clint Eastwood's *Unforgiven* proved there was life in the old genre yet. Just as Steven Spielberg plundered the Saturday serial for his Indiana Jones yarns, so this rousing tale rustles ideas from virtually every B-western ever made. While this makes for an invigorating adventure, it's also rather untidy. Nevertheless, Kevin Kline, Kevin Costner, Danny Glover and Scott Glenn make attractive heroes, Brian Dennehy is a hissable villain and John Cleese enjoys his cameo as an English lawman. DP Some swearing. *DVD* 🅱🅻🆄

Kevin Kline *Paden* • Scott Glenn *Emmett* • Kevin Costner *Jake* • John Cleese *Sheriff Langston* • Brian Dennehy *Cobb* • Danny Glover *Mal* • Jeff Goldblum *Slick* • Linda Hunt *Stella* • Rosanna Arquette *Hannah* ■ *Dir* Lawrence Kasdan • *Scr* Lawrence Kasdan, Mark Kasdan

Simba ★★
Drama 1955 · UK · Colour · 99min

Simba is the Swahili word for lion, though this is no wildlife adventure frolic. It's a drama about the Mau Mau troubles in Kenya, but it reduces a complex political crisis to a feeble love story and colonial posturings on the verandah, while a back-projected Africa wobbles in the distance. Dirk Bogarde was then in his matinee idol period, while Donald Sinden and Virginia McKenna are pretty lightweight in support. AT

Dirk Bogarde *Alan Howard* • Donald Sinden *Inspector Tom Drummond* • Virginia McKenna *Mary Crawford* • Basil Sydney *Mr Crawford* • Marie Ney *Mrs Crawford* • Joseph Tomelty *Dr Hughes* ■ *Dir* Brian Desmond Hurst • *Scr* John Baines, Robin Estridge, from a novel by Anthony Perry

The Simian Line ★★
Supernatural romantic drama 2000 · US · Colour · 106min

With whispered voiceovers constantly striving to impart psychological depth to scenes of banal domesticity, this ensemble drama takes itself so seriously that it feels like an intrusion to look in on such self-obsession. It all starts when crazed clairvoyant Tyne Daly senses the ghostly presence of William Hurt and Samantha Mathis at the Halloween party thrown by Lynn Redgrave and toyboy lover Harry Connick Jr. It's verbose, precious and dripping with faux significance. DP

Harry Connick Jr *Rick* • Cindy Crawford *Sandra* • Tyne Daly *Arnita* • William Hurt *Edward* • Monica Keena *Marta* • Samantha Mathis *Mae* • Lynn Redgrave *Katharine* • Jamey Sheridan *Paul* • Eric Stoltz *Sam* • Dylan Bruno *Billy* ■ *Dir* Linda Yellen • *Scr* Gisela Bernice [Linda Yellen and the cast], from a story by Yellen, Michael Leeds

Simon ★★🅿🅶
Comedy 1980 · US · Colour · 93min

This half-baked satirical comedy from Woody Allen associate Marshall Brickman (the pair shared *Annie Hall*'s best screenplay Oscar) is too clever by half. In truth, it's not funny where it's meant to be, and tiresomely long. But there's some compensation in Alan Arkin's strong central performance as a professor of psychology who's brainwashed into thinking he's an alien, and clever support from an eccentric cast. TS Swearing.

Alan Arkin *Simon Mendelssohn* • Madeline Kahn *Cynthia* • Austin Pendleton *Becker* • Judy Graubart *Lisa* • Wallace Shawn *Van Dongen* • Max Wright *Hundertwasser* • Fred Gwynne *Korey* • Adolph Green *Commune leader* ■ *Dir/Scr* Marshall Brickman

Simon and Laura ★★
Comedy 1955 · UK · Colour · 90min

Simon and Laura (Peter Finch and Kay Kendall) are a husband-and-wife acting team, publicly celebrated, privately bankrupt and one step from the divorce court. But the BBC, no less, comes to the rescue, offering them a series in which they play a happily married couple. Oh, the irony. Directed by Muriel Box, this starts out as a brisk satire on celebrity, emancipation and cinema's enemy, television. It goes soft by the end, of course, and now looks terribly dated. AT

Peter Finch *Simon Foster* • Kay Kendall *Laura Foster* • Muriel Pavlow *Janet Honeyman* • Hubert Gregg *Bertie Burton* • Maurice Denham *Wilson* • Ian Carmichael *David Prentice* • Richard Wattis *Controller* • Thora Hird *Jessie* ■ *Dir* Muriel Box • *Scr* Peter Blackmore, from the play by Alan Melville

Simon Birch ★★★🅿🅶
Drama 1998 · US · Colour · 109min

This sentimental drama is set in a Norman Rockwell-esque small town in the 1950s and 60s, and tells of the friendship between the illegitimate, pre-adolescent Joseph Mazzello and Ian Michael Smith, a dwarf with an answer for everything and a question for everyone. The story, narrated by Jim Carrey, describes how the boys cope with their disadvantages and what they hope for in the future. The action is predictable, but the acting makes it worthwhile. TH *DVD*

Ian Michael Smith *Simon Birch* • Joseph Mazzello *Joe Wentworth* • Ashley Judd *Rebecca Wentworth* • Oliver Platt *Ben Goodrich* • David Strathairn *Reverend Russell* • Dana Ivey *Grandmother Wentworth* ■ *Dir* Mark Steven Johnson • *Scr* Mark Steven Johnson, from the novel *A Prayer for Owen Meany* by John Irving

Simon Killer ★★★★🔞
Drama 2012 · US/Fr · Colour · 101min

This stark American indie delivers exactly what its title promises: a character study about the banality of evil. It's scored with chirpy Europop, and shot in a loose, freewheeling style that suggests a fair amount of improvisation. Brady Corbet plays Simon, a recent graduate who goes to Paris in the aftermath of a break-up. Lonely and friendless, Simon happens on a local sex club, where he becomes fascinated by one of the girls, Victoria (Mati Diop). Those expecting easy answers may be disappointed by what happens, but *Simon Killer* perhaps works best as a post-modern *Talented Mr Ripley*, with Corbet vulnerable and chilling as the kind of unfathomable psychopath that could be plucked from the headlines on any given day. DW English, French +subtitles. Violence, swearing, drug abuse, sex scenes, nudity. *DVD* 🅱🅻🆄

Brady Corbet *Simon* • Mati Diop *Victoria* • Constance Rousseau *Marianne* • Lila Salet *Sophie* • Solo René ■ *Dir* Antonio Campos • *Scr* Antonio Campos, Brady Corbet, Mati Diop

Simon Magus ★🅿🅶
Romantic fantasy 1998 · UK/Ger/It/Fr · Colour · 106min

Opening with a pseudo-silent movie view of 19th-century Silesia, Ben Hopkins's feature debut quickly descends into costume melodramatics as he loses control of both his multinational cast and his folkloric tale of progress, prejudice and superstition. As the titular village outcast who's convinced he's in the thrall of Satan, Noah Taylor partially conveys the incomprehending resentment that prompts him to spy for anti-Semitic aristocrat, Sean McGinley. DP

Noah Taylor *Simor* • Stuart Townsend *Dovid* • Embeth Davidtz *Leah* • Sean McGinley *Hase* • Rutger Hauer *Squire* • Ian Holm *Sirius* ■ *Dir/Scr* Ben Hopkins

Simon of the Desert ★★★ 12
Religious drama   1965 · Mex · BW · 43min

Winner of the special jury prize at the Venice film festival in 1965, this is one of Luis Buñuel's least strident assaults on Roman Catholicism. How much this was influenced by a consciously playful mood or by having to make do when funds dried up after only 25 days (hence its short running time) is open to conjecture. Based loosely on the story of the 5th-century saint, Simeon Stylites, the film is packed with ribald comments on the improbability of miracles, the hypocrisy of the faithful and the impossibility of holiness. Stylishly photographed, it's a minor film from a master. DP Spanish +subtitles.

Claudio Brook *Simon* • Silvia Pinal *The Devil* • Hortensia Santoveña *Simon's mother* • Jesus Fernandez *Goatherd* • Enrique Alvarez Felix *Brother Matias* ■ *Dir* Luis Buñuel • *Scr* Luis Buñuel, Julio Alejandro • *Cinematographer* Gabriel Figueroa

Simon Sez ★ 12
Action comedy adventure
1999 · Bel/Ger · Colour · 81min

The producer of *Double Team* (1997) didn't learn his lesson with the casting of basketball pro Dennis Rodman in that movie, casting him again in this action comedy that actually seems to be an unofficial sequel. Except for being in one of the most unintentionally funny sex scenes ever filmed, Rodman actually looks good when compared to his sidekick Dane Cook, who comes across as Jim Carrey on cocaine. KB DVD

Dennis Rodman *Simon* • Dane Cook *Nick* • Natalia Cigliuti *Claire* • Filip Nicolic *Michael* • John Pinette *Macro* ■ *Dir* Kevin Elders • *Scr* Andrew Miller, Andrew Lowery, from a story by Moshe Diamant, Rudy Cohen

Simon, Simon ★★ U
Comedy   1970 · UK · Colour · 30min

Unsung character actor Graham Stark made his debut as the writer and director of this fond, if laboured tribute to the silent slapstick style of the Keystone Kops. Comedy stars crop up in cameo roles, as does movie star Michael Caine. But the main focus falls on the rivalry between Stark's council workman and fireman Norman Rossington, as they woo typist Julia Foster. The mugging mime and the excessive crane shots soon become wearisome, but it's still fun. DP DVD

Graham Stark *First workman* • John Junkin *Second workman* • Julia Foster *Typist* • Norman Rossington *Fireman* • Peter Sellers • Michael Caine • Eric Morecambe • Ernie Wise • Bob Monkhouse *Photographer* • Bernie Winters ■ *Dir/Scr* Graham Stark

S1M0NE ★★ PG
Satirical comedy drama
2002 · US · Colour · 112min

This interesting failure from Andrew Niccol is about a computer-generated film star. She's the creation of director Al Pacino, who's fired from a film after his prima donna star walks off set. He "re-versions" the movie, replacing his leading lady with a virtual woman, a computer programme called S1M0Ne, billed as "Simone". Nobody twigs that she's not for real and Simone becomes an international phenomenon. The idea doesn't work on screen because Simone is clearly a pixelated mannequin and it's hard to believe that anyone would be fooled. StH DVD CS

Al Pacino *Viktor Taransky* • Catherine Keener *Elaine Christian* • Pruitt Taylor Vince *Max Sayer* • Jay Mohr *Hal Sinclair* • Jason Schwartzman

Milton • Winona Ryder *Nicola Anders* • Stanley Anderson *Frank Brand* • Simone [Rachel Roberts (2)] *Simone* ■ *Dir/Scr* Andrew Niccol

Simpatico ★★ 15
Drama   1999 · US/Fr · Colour · 101min

A great cast and impeccable credentials add up to nothing much in this awkward drama, the first film of stage director Matthew Warchus. The story revolves around millionaire racehorse owner Jeff Bridges, who answers an SOS from former friend Nick Nolte. The alcoholic Nolte has a precarious hold over Bridges: they used to fix races together, a scam that ended in the ruin of course official Albert Finney. Both men are still in love with Sharon Stone, but her appearance seems merely gratuitous. TH DVD

Nick Nolte *Vincent "Vinnie" T Webb* • Jeff Bridges *Lyle Carter* • Sharon Stone *Rosie Carter* • Catherine Keener *Cecilia Ponz* • Albert Finney *Simms* ■ *Dir* Matthew Warchus • *Scr* Matthew Warchus, David Nicholls, from a play by Sam Shepard

A Simple Life ★★★★ PG
Drama   2011 · HK · Colour · 113min

Director Ann Hui's touching portrait of old age owes its armfuls of awards to an unforgettable central performance by veteran actress Deannie Ip. With naturalism and dignity, she plays the devoted servant of a large family who retires after suffering a stroke. And Andy Lau's jet-setting film-producer son places her in a nursing home, and repays her devotion with regular visits. Though it's overlong, the clichés of old people's homes are deftly avoided, and a dose of humour sugars the pill of encroaching melancholy. AC Cantonese, English, Mandarin +subtitles. DVD BD

Andy Lau *Roger* • Deanie Ip *Ah Tao* ■ *Dir* Ann Hui

The Simple Life of Noah Dearborn ★★★
Drama   1999 · US · Colour · 87min

Screen icon Sidney Poitier makes a rare small-screen appearance in this TV tale of quiet determination and inner strength. An elderly small-town craftsman/farmer refuses to sell his land to a greedy developer, who then tries to get his psychiatrist girlfriend (Mary Louise Parker) to declare the man mentally incompetent. An observant screenplay, sensitive direction and compelling performances paint a vivid picture of innocent dignity under siege. MC

Sidney Poitier *Noah Dearborn* • Dianne Wiest *Sarah McClellan* • Mary-Louise Parker *Valerie Crane* • George Newbern *Christian Nelson* • Bernie Casey *Silas* ■ *Dir* Gregg Champion • *Scr* Sterling Anderson

Simple Men ★★★★ 15
Comedy drama   1992 · US/UK · Colour · 100min

This is one of the most accessible of writer/director Hal Hartley's oddball accounts of his slightly-skewed world. This begins mid-robbery and then follows a white-collar crook Robert Burke and his younger brother William Sage as they search for their father, a former baseball star and suspected bomber who's been on the run for years. Along the way there's a fight between a nun and a cop, romantic interludes and and musings on the meaning of life. The usual Hartley repertory company respond as to a puppeteer's twitch. TH DVD BD

Robert Burke *Bill McCabe* • William Sage [Bill Sage] *Dennis McCabe* • Karen Sillas *Kate* • Elina Lowensohn *Elina* • Martin Donovan (2) *Martin* • Chris Cooke *Vic* ■ *Dir/Scr* Hal Hartley

The Simple-Minded Murderer ★★★★
Drama   1982 · Swe · Colour · 107min

Winning international awards for writer/director Hans Alfredson and star Stellan Skarsgård, this is a chilling period piece with a slow-burning fuse. Alfredson, who co-stars, gives a performance of terrifying brutality as the vicious landowner whose persecution of Skarsgård's village idiot ends

in inevitable tragedy. With its persuasive evocation of rural life in the 1930s and its perceptive insights into the prejudices of enclosed communities, this is a disturbing film that is all the more effective for its sedate pacing and restrained playing. DP Swedish +subtitles.

Stellan Skarsgård *The Idiot* • Hans Alfredson *Hoglund* • Maria Johansson *Anna* • Per Myrberg *Andersson* • Lena-Pia Bernhardsson *Mrs Andersson* ■ *Dir* Hans Alfredson • *Scr* Hans Alfredson, from his novel *En ond man*

A Simple Plan ★★★★ 15
Thriller
1998 · US/UK/Jpn/Ger/Fr · Colour · 116min

Shallow Grave meets *Fargo* in director Sam Raimi's change-of-pace thriller about the corrupting influence of greed. Three men find a crashed plane in thick snow containing over $4 million and hesitantly decide to split the loot once they are sure they won't be suspected. Of course, everything that could go wrong does. In this grim fairy tale, Raimi comes up with a poetic suspense film that delves unassumingly into the cryptic regions of human nature, and the uneasy mood is underscored by two marvellous performances from Bill Paxton and Billy Bob Thornton as the two brothers in the pledge triangle. AJ Violence, swearing. DVD

Bill Paxton *Hank Mitchell* • Billy Bob Thornton *Jacob Mitchell* • Bridget Fonda *Sarah Mitchell* • Gary Cole *Baxter* • Brent Briscoe *Lou* • Becky Ann Baker *Nancy* • Chelcie Ross *Carl* • Jack Walsh *Tom Butler* ■ *Dir* Sam Raimi • *Scr* Scott B Smith, from his novel

A Simple Twist of Fate ★★★ PG
Drama   1994 · US · Colour · 101min

Steve Martin likes to have an audience on his side, and nowhere is that more evident than in this personally-scripted drama, updated from George Eliot's *Silas Marner*. Martin plays a reclusive cabinet-maker who "adopts" the illegitimate toddler of local magnate Gabriel Byrne when the child's mother dies in the snow near his isolated home. The Victorian poignancy of the tale still grips, even in modern-day dress, but Martin unfortunately comes across as a bit of a wimp. Still very watchable, however. TH DVD

Steve Martin *Michael McMann* • Gabriel Byrne *John Newland* • Laura Linney *Nancy Newland* • Catherine O'Hara *Mrs Simon* • Alana Austin *Mathilda McCann aged ten* • Alyssa Austin *Mathilda McCann aged five* • Stephen Baldwin *Tanny Newland* • Byron Jennings *Keating* ■ *Dir* Gillies MacKinnon • *Scr* Steve Martin, from the novel *Silas Marner* by George Eliot

A Simple Wish ★★★ U
Fantasy comedy   1997 · US · Colour · 85min

Martin Short stars as a fumbling fairy godmother who gets into all sorts of trouble when he tries to grant little Mara Wilson's wish that her actor dad (Robert Pastorelli) finally finds success. More interesting, though, is the conflict the fairy godmothers (including Teri Garr and Ruby Dee) are facing against struck-off fairy-turned-witch Kathleen Turner, who chews up the scenery and spits it out in a deliciously evil turn. It's gets a bit flabby towards the middle, but still a fun family romp. JB DVD BD

Martin Short *Murray* • Kathleen Turner *Claudia* • Mara Wilson *Anabel* • Robert Pastorelli *Oliver* • Amanda Plummer *Boots* • Francis Capra *Charlie Greening* • Ruby Dee *Hortense* • Teri Garr *Rena* ■ *Dir* Michael Ritchie • *Scr* Jeff Rothberg

Simply Irresistible ★ PG
Supernatural romantic comedy
1999 · US · Colour · 91min

Sarah Michelle Gellar stars as the mediocre chef of a small New York bistro who suddenly discovers she can magically make wonderful food that affects people's emotions. Sean Patrick Flanery plays the Manhattan businessman who offers her a culinary opportunity and possible romance. Unfortunately, the pair have no chemistry whatsoever, and this is virtually

unwatchable. JB Sexual references, swearing.

Sarah Michelle Gellar *Amanda Shelton* • Sean Patrick Flanery *Tom Bartlett* • Patricia Clarkson *Lois McNally* • Dylan Baker *Jonathan Bendel* • Christopher Durang *Gene O'Reilly* • Larry Gilliard Jr *Nolan Traynor* • Betty Buckley *Aunt Stella* ■ *Dir* Mark Tarlov • *Scr* Judith Roberts

The Simpsons Movie ★★★★ PG
Animated comedy   2007 · US · Colour · 83min

Twenty years after their first appearance on *The Tracey Ullman Show*, America's favourite dysfunctional cartoon family finally makes it on to the big screen. Cheekily described by creator Matt Groening as Homer's Odyssey, this is certainly epic, with 11 writers, a team of South Korean animators and a plot that follows Homer from Springfield to Alaska and back again after he accidentally causes an environmental disaster in his home town (D'oh!). The script is glorious in its ambition, tackling everything from low-brow slapstick to inventive visual gags and barbed political comment (an ill-informed President Arnold Schwarzenegger declaring "I was elected to lead, not to read"). The rich relentlessness of the jokes demands at least two viewings and re-establishes *The Simpsons* as the jewel in the crown of American animation. JR Brief swearing, violence. DVD BD CS

Dan Castellaneta *Homer Simpson/Krusty the Clown* • Julie Kavner *Marge Simpson* • Nancy Cartwright *Bart Simpson* • Yeardley Smith *Lisa Simpson* • Hank Azaria *Moe/Apu/Sea Captain* • Harry Shearer *Seymour Skinner/Ned Flanders / Lenny Leonard/Dr Hibbert* • Kelsey Grammer *Sideshow Bob* • Joe Mantegna *Fat Tony* ■ *Dir* David Silverman • *Scr* James L Brooks, Matt Groening, Al Jean, Ian Maxtone-Graham, George Meyer, David Mirkin, Mike Reiss, Mike Scully, Matt Selman, John Swartzwelder, Jon Vitti, from characters by Groening

Sin ★★ 15
Romantic drama   1972 · US · Colour · 86min

Raquel Welch, looking stunning (of course), gets involved in some serious passion, Mills and Boon style, in a case of forbidden love on a Mediterranean island, which you just know is going to end in tears. Never mind, because both the scenery and Miss Welch look beautiful. An incredibly daft drama from director George Pan Cosmatos. JB Violence, sex scenes, nudity. DVD

Raquel Welch *Elena* • Richard Johnson *Orestes* • Frank Wolff *Hector* • Flora Robson *Antigone* • Jack Hawkins *Father Nicholas* ■ *Dir/Scr* George Pan Cosmatos

Sin City ★★★★ 18
Crime drama
2005 · US · BW and Colour · 118min

Frank Miller's neo-*noir* comic book comes to spectacular life here, meticulously re-creating three interlinked stories. In each segment, cops, criminals and *femmes fatales* collide in love, lust or gory conflict. Bruce Willis brings poignancy as the disgraced ex-cop shielding dancer Jessica Alba, while tough private eye Clive Owen's brutal clash with rival suitor Benicio Del Toro adds a streak of gallows humour. However, Mickey Rourke steals the show, playing a soft-hearted ex-con out to avenge his sweetheart's murder. Stylistically, the movie is a masterpiece, with its astonishing visuals papering over a repetitive plot and some corny dialogue. This is not for every taste, but genre fans will be blown away. SF Violence. DVD BD

Mickey Rourke *Marv* • Bruce Willis *Hartigan* • Clive Owen *Dwight* • Jessica Alba *Nancy Callahan* • Benicio Del Toro *Jackie Boy* • Brittany Murphy *Shellie* • Elijah Wood *Kevin* • Rosario Dawson *Gail* • Carla Gugino *Lucille* • Josh Hartnett *The Man* • Michael Madsen *Bob* • Jaime King *Goldie/Wendy* • Nick Stahl *Roark Jr/Yellow Bastard* • Powers Boothe *Senator Roark* • Rutger Hauer *Cardinal Roark* ■ *Dir* Frank Miller, Robert Rodriguez • *Scr* Robert Rodriguez, Frank Miller, from the *Sin City* graphic novel stories *The Hard Goodbye*, *The Big Fat Kill*, *That Yellow Bastard* by Frank Miller

Sin City: a Dame to Kill For
★★★ 15

Action crime thriller
2014 · US · BW and Colour · 98min

Enough time has elapsed for this belated sequel to feel as fresh, hard-edged and visually stylish as the original 2005 neo-*noir* comic-book adaptation. Continuations and new stories criss-cross, featuring square-jawed bruiser Mickey Rourke, toxic *femme fatale* Eva Green, cocky gambler Joseph Gordon-Levitt and stripper Jessica Alba, who wants vengeance for cop Bruce Willis's death. Once again it's all elegantly rendered in dazzling, textured monochrome sharpened by key colour splashes. Played stark and straight by the stellar cast, it conveys the essence of co-director Frank Miller's art better than ever. AJ Violence, swearing, sex scenes, drug abuse, nudity.
DVD Blu-ray 3D

Josh Brolin *Dwight McCarthy* • Eva Green *Ava Lord* • Bruce Willis *John Hartigan* • Mickey Rourke *Marv* • Joseph Gordon-Levitt *Johnny* • Rosario Dawson *Gail* • Jessica Alba *Nancy Callahan* • Powers Boothe *Senator Roark* • Ray Liotta *Joey* • Dennis Haysbert *Manute* • Lady Gaga *Bertha* ■ *Dir* Frank Miller, Robert Rodriguez • *Scr* Frank Miller, from graphic novels by Miller • *Cinematographer* Robert Rodriguez

The Sin Eater
★★ 15

Horror thriller   2002 · US/Ger · Colour · 98min

This religious farrago suffers from a terminal case of farcical script. Brian Helgeland has constructed what might be called a *roman policier* about young priest Heath Ledger who's sent to Rome with Shannyn Sossamon to investigate the suspicious death of his mentor. The film's candle-lit goings on, familiar religious trappings and diabolical dialogue diminish the occasional moments of ecclesiastical high thinking. TH Swearing, violence. DVD

Heath Ledger *Father Alex Bernier* • Shannyn Sossamon *Mara Sinclair* • Benno Fürmann *William Eden* • Mark Addy *Father Thomas Garrett* • Peter Weller *Cardinal Driscoll* • Francesco Carnelutti *Father Dominic* • Mattia Sbragia *Apathetic Bishop* ■ *Dir/Scr* Brian Helgeland

Sin Nombre
★★★ 15

Social drama
2009 · US/Mex/UK · Colour · 91min

Desperation brings a Mexican gang member and a poverty-stricken Honduran girl into a tragic alliance in writer/director Cary Joji Fukunaga's confident feature debut. Marrying violent social drama with a romance-tinged road movie, the Sundance winner explores the plight of illegal Central American immigrants struggling to reach the US. Fukunaga is undoubtedly talented, and the film is packed with memorable images, but its narrative is less impressive. SF Spanish +subtitles. Violence, swearing, sex scenes, nudity. DVD Blu-ray

Edgar Flores *Willy/El Casper* • Paulina Gaitán *Sayra* • Kristyan Ferrer *El Smiley* • Tenoch Huerta Mejía *Lil' Mago* • Diana Garcia *Martha Marlene* ■ *Dir/Scr* Cary Joji Fukunaga [Cary Fukunaga]

The Sin of Madelon Claudet
★★★★

Drama   1931 · US · BW · 74min

Broadway legend Helen Hayes, who walked off with an Oscar for her performance as the unfortunate heroine, plays an innocent French country girl who elopes to Paris with an American artist, is deserted and left pregnant. How she sacrifices herself for the child who thinks she's dead (shades of is the stuff of an archetypal fine-handkerchief weepie. Lewis Stone is splendid as Madelon's protector-lover, while Jean Hersholt is the mentor of her "orphan" son. RK

Helen Hayes *Madelon Claudet* • Lewis Stone *Carlo Boretti* • Neil Hamilton *Larry* • Robert Young (1) *Dr Jacques Claudet* • Cliff Edwards *Victor* • Jean Hersholt *Dr Dulac* • Marie Prevost *Rosalie* • Alan Hale *Claudet* ■ *Dir* Edgar Selwyn • *Scr* Charles MacArthur, Ben Hecht (uncredited), from the play *The Lullaby* by Edward Knoblock

The Sin of Nora Moran
★★★

Murder mystery melodrama
1933 · US · BW · 67min

This sentimental melodrama stars Zita Johann as a poor orphaned girl who gets into a terrible fix after a romantic entanglement with an ambitious politician. The film was one of many that disappeared, but in 2000 it was rediscovered, restored and hailed as "maybe the best Hollywood B-movie of the 1930s". Its appeal lies in the non-linear construction – there's even a flashback within a flashback – and that treatment does increase our curiosity, but it's debatable whether this really is the best of its kind. DM

Zita Johann *Nora Moran* • Alan Dinehart *DA John Grant* • Paul Cavanagh *Governor Dick Crawford* ■ *Dir* Phil Goldstone, Howard Christy • *Scr* Frances Hyland, from a play by Willis Maxwell Goodhue

Sin Town
★★

Western   1942 · US · BW · 73min

An average little western is kept moving at a rate of knots by an unsung hero of the studio system, director Ray Enright. There's a certain gritty realism in the script, Broderick Crawford is good, but it's the ever elegant Constance Bennett who sweeps up the acting honours. The film packs a surprising amount into its short running time, but sadly little that is above programme filler standard. TS

Constance Bennett *Kye Allen* • Broderick Crawford *Dude McNair* • Anne Gwynne *Laura Kirby* • Patric Knowles *Wade Crowell* • Andy Devine *Judge Eustace Vale* • Leo Carrillo *Angelo Colina* • Ward Bond *Rock Delaney* ■ *Dir* Ray Enright • *Scr* W Scott Darling, Gerald Geraghty, Richard Brooks

Sinbad and the Eye of the Tiger
★★★ U

Fantasy adventure
1977 · UK/US · Colour · 112min

This is not up to the previous two *Sinbad* adventures from the Ray Harryhausen fantasy factory: it's too long and Patrick Wayne is a charisma-free hero. Special effects wizard Harryhausen enhances the romantic exotica with his distinctive brand of visual thrills. It all helps to pass the time away agreeably with the frothy *Arabian Nights* nonsense standing in for the plot. AJ DVD

Patrick Wayne *Sinbad* • Taryn Power *Dione* • Jane Seymour (2) *Princess Farah* • Margaret Whiting *Zenobia* • Patrick Troughton *Melanthius* • Kurt Christian *Rafi* • Nadim Sawalha *Hassan* ■ *Dir* Sam Wanamaker • *Scr* Beverley Cross, from a story by Beverley Cross, Ray Harryhausen

Sinbad: Legend of the Seven Seas
★★★ U

Animated comedy adventure
2003 · US · Colour · 81min

This enjoyable mix of swashbuckling action and *Arabian Nights*-style fantasy demonstrates that there's still plenty of mileage in good old-fashioned storytelling. Scallywag Sinbad (voiced by Brad Pitt) and his crew try to retrieve the powerful Book of Peace from conniving goddess Eris (a fabulously sinister Michelle Pfeiffer). Although some of the animation, like the plotline, is a tad basic, the stops are pulled out for the set pieces. Catherine Zeta-Jones's stowaway is strong and sassy. SF DVD

Brad Pitt *Sinbad* • Catherine Zeta-Jones *Marina* • Michelle Pfeiffer *Eris* • Joseph Fiennes *Proteus* • Dennis Haysbert *Kale* • Timothy West *King Dymas* • Adriano Giannini *Rat* ■ *Dir* Tim Johnson, Patrick Gilmore • *Scr* John Logan

Sinbad the Sailor
★★★ U

Swashbuckling adventure
1947 · US · Colour · 111min

In this splendid Technicolor romp, Douglas Fairbanks Jr ably follows in the dashing footsteps of his father. He stars as the swashbuckling hero who searches for hidden treasure and falls for Maureen O'Hara. The costumes lack flair (as does the plot), and the whole thing's very juvenile, but there's no denying the film's sense of *joie de vivre*. The right tone is defined from the opening: this is great fun. TS DVD

Douglas Fairbanks Jr *Sinbad* • Maureen O'Hara *Shireen* • Walter Slezak *Melik* • Anthony Quinn *Emir* • George Tobias *Abbu* • Jane Greer *Pirouze* • Mike Mazurki *Yusuf* ■ *Dir* Richard Wallace • *Scr* John Twist, from a story by John Twist, George Worthing [George Worthing Yates]

Since Otar Left
★★★★ 15

Drama   2003 · Fr/Bel · Colour · 98min

Julie Bertuccelli's debut feature is a moving study of family loyalty amid societal decay. With Tbilisi facing economic meltdown, nonagenarian Esther Gorintin heads to Paris with her daughter (Nino Khomassouridze) and grandchild (Dinara Droukarova), unaware that her beloved work-away son Otar has been killed. Although afflicted by arthritis, Gorintin is anything but an object of pity, whether she's feistily championing Georgia's Soviet past or facing the truth about her son's fate. Gorintin is superbly supported by her co-stars, as well as an intelligent screenplay and sensitive direction. DP French, Georgian, Russian +subtitles. Swearing. DVD

Esther Gorintin *Eka* • Nino Khomassouridze *Marina* • Dinara Droukarova *Ada* • Temour Kalandadze *Tenguiz* • Roussoudan Bolkvadze *Roussiko* • Sacha Sarichvili *Alexo* • Douta Skhirtladze *Niko* • Mzia Eristavi *Dora* ■ *Dir* Julie Bertuccelli • *Scr* Julie Bertuccelli, Bernard Renucci, Roger Bohbot

Since You Went Away
★★★ U

Wartime drama   1944 · US · BW · 163min

Everything is absolutely certain in this vision of wartime middle-class America. Claudette Colbert waits faithfully, keeping the home fires burning, while husband Neil Hamilton (his only appearance in the film is in a photograph) and family friend Joseph Cotten are off saving everyone from Hitler. Marriage is wonderful, children are dreamboats and democracy rules OK. It's all syrupy nonsense, but the wonderful cast (the brilliant Agnes Moorehead is noteworthy) makes it very watchable. SH

Claudette Colbert *Anne Hilton* • Jennifer Jones *Jane Hilton* • Shirley Temple *Bridget Hilton* • Joseph Cotten *Lieutenant Anthony Willett* • Monty Woolley *Colonel Smollett* • Robert Walker *Corporal William G Smollett II* • Lionel Barrymore *Clergyman* • Hattie McDaniel *Fidelia* • Agnes Moorehead *Emily Hawkins* ■ *Dir* John Cromwell • *Scr* David O Selznick, Margaret Buell Wilder, from the novel *Together* by Margaret Buell Wilder

Since You've Been Gone
★★ 15

Comedy   1998 · US · Colour · 91min

Philip Rayburn Smith plays a doctor who attends his high-school reunion, despite the humiliation he suffered on graduation day. Once there, he begins to understand that his former classmates are far more troubled than he is. The largely talented cast in this TV movie is overshadowed by a juvenile plot and silly innuendo, but David Schwimmer directs effectively. ST

Philip Rayburn Smith *Kevin MacEldowney* • Lara Flynn Boyle *Grace Williams* • Joey Slotnick *Zane Levy* • Teri Hatcher *Maria Goldstein* • David Schwimmer *Robert S Levin* ■ *Dir* David Schwimmer • *Scr* Jeff Steinberg

Sincerely Yours
★ U

Drama   1955 · US · Colour · 120min

This is an ill-judged, ineptly updated and ludicrous remake of *The Man Who Played God*, the unusual, fantastical and rather powerful 1932 melodrama. Liberace takes the role of a concert pianist who goes deaf, learns to lip-read and anonymously helps people in trouble on whose conversations he "eavesdrops" through binoculars. Absolutely awful. RK

Liberace *Anthony Warrin* • Joanne Dru *Marion Moore* • Dorothy Malone *Linda Curtis* • Alex Nicol *Howard Ferguson* • William Demarest *Sam Dunne* • Lori Nelson *Sarah Cosgrove* • Lurene Tuttle *Mrs McGinley* • Richard Eyer *Alvie Hunt* ■ *Dir* Gordon Douglas • *Scr* Irving Wallace, from the play *The Man Who Played God* by Jules Eckert Goodman

Sinful Davey
★★

Period comedy adventure
1969 · UK · Colour · 94min

John Hurt is Scot Davey Haggart, who deserts the British army and, like his father before him, becomes a highwayman, always just an inch away from the hangman's noose. John Huston included this extremely lightweight and modestly enjoyable romp among his failures. Filmed in Ireland, where Huston owned an estate for many years, it boasts some nice camerawork by Freddie Young, a cute performance by Pamela Franklin and the fleeting screen debut of the director's daughter, Anjelica. AT

John Hurt *Davey Haggart* • Pamela Franklin *Annie* • Nigel Davenport *Constable Richardson* • Ronald Fraser *MacNab* • Robert Morley *Duke of Argyll* • Maxine Audley *Duchess of Argyll* • Fionnuala Flanagan [Fionnula Flanagan] *Penelope* • Anjelica Huston ■ *Dir* John Huston • *Scr* James R Webb, from the autobiography *The Life of David Haggart* by David Haggart

Sing
★★★ 15

Musical romance   1989 · US · Colour · 94min

This teen romance is as corny as Kansas in August, September *and* October, but it's so sweet and disingenuous it's hard to dislike it, however clichéd. Richard Baskin's musical drama is set in a Brooklyn high school where the students take part in an annual "Sing" contest. Participating bad boy Peter Dobson and nice Jewish girl Jessica Steen share a certain talent for each other, while empathetic teacher Lorraine Bracco must shield the kids from the nasty education authorities, who want to shut the school down. DA

Lorraine Bracco *Miss Lombardo* • Peter Dobson *Dominic* • Jessica Steen *Hannah* • Louise Lasser *Rosie* • George DiCenzo *Mr Marowitz* • Patti LaBelle *Mrs DeVere* • Susan Peretz *Mrs Tucci* • Laurnea Wilkerson *Zena* ■ *Dir* Richard Baskin • *Scr* Dean Pitchford

Sing

Animated comedy musical   2016 · US · Colour

This is a preview – no prints were available to review as we went to press: Matthew McConaughey lends his dulcet Texan tones to a koala who, rather conveniently, lives in California not Australia. But there's a good array of accents in this animated comedy, with our very own Taron Egerton (*Eddie the Eagle*) voicing a gorilla, alongside John C Reilly's sheep, Reese Witherspoon's pig and Scarlett Johansson doing a punk rocker porcupine. They come together in a bit to help said koala save his theatre. SP

Scarlett Johansson *Ash* • Taron Egerton *Johnny* • Matthew McConaughey *Buster Moon* • Reese Witherspoon *Rosita* • Seth MacFarlane *Mike* ■ *Dir/Scr* Garth Jennings

Sing and Like It
★★★

Comedy   1934 · US · BW · 72min

Echoes of *Citizen Kane* and *Bullets over Broadway* reverberate around this enjoyable romp, which amusingly merges the gangster movie and the backstage musical. Unable to concentrate on blowing a safe when he hears a mawkish ditty about a mother's love, mobster Nat Pendleton vows to make ZaSu Pitts a star, even though she can't sing a note. Briskly played by a fine cast and directed with plenty of pep by William A Seiter, this is a rediscovered treat. DP

ZaSu Pitts *Annie Snodgrass* • Nat Pendleton *T Fenimore "Fenny" Sylvester* • Edward Everett Horton *Adam Frink* • Pert Kelton *Ruby* • Ned Sparks *Toots McGuire* ■ *Dir* William A Seiter • *Scr* Marion Dix, Laird Doyle, from the story *So You Won't Sing, Eh?* by Aben Kandel

Sing as We Go ★★★ U
Musical comedy   1934 · UK · BW · 74min

Gracie Fields is the life and soul of this dated but spirited musical comedy, as she makes for the bright lights of Blackpool after the small-town mill that she works in is forced to close. JB Priestley's source story may not be one of his most original or complex, but Gracie's attempts to hold down a variety of seaside jobs and her encounter with benevolent tycoon Lawrence Grossmith are both amusing and politically astute. DP

Gracie Fields *Grace Platt* • John Loder *Hugh Phillips* • Dorothy Hyson *Phyllis Logan* • Stanley Holloway *Policeman* • Frank Pettingell *Murgatroyd Platt* • Lawrence Grossmith *Sir William Upton* • Morris Harvey *Cowboy* • Arthur Sinclair (1) *Maestro* ■ *Dir* Basil Dean · *Scr* Gordon Wellesley, from a story by JB Priestley

Sing, Baby, Sing ★★★★
Musical comedy   1936 · US · BW · 87min

This fast-moving musical comedy set Alice Faye on the road to becoming 20th Century-Fox's top singing star. Appearing with a softened, more alluring hairstyle, Faye is a nightclub singer who attracts the attentions of a drunken Shakespearean actor. Adolphe Menjou is hilarious in this role, which is obviously based on that great tippler John Barrymore. The film marked the debut of the Ritz Brothers, who have a few funny moments. The singer with the band is Tony Martin, recently married to Alice Faye, who sings the Oscar-nominated song *When Did You Leave Heaven*. RB

Alice Faye *Joan Warren* • Adolphe Menjou *Bruce Farraday* • Gregory Ratoff *Nicky* • Ted Healy *Al Craven* • Patsy Kelly *Fitz* • Montagu Love *Robert Wilson* • The Ritz Brothers [Al Ritz] • The Ritz Brothers [Jimmy Ritz] • The Ritz Brothers [Harry Ritz] ■ *Dir* Sidney Lanfield · *Scr* Milton Sperling, Jack Yellen, Harry Tugend, from a story by Milton Sperling, Jack Yellen

Sing, Boy, Sing ★★
Musical drama   1958 · US · BW · 90min

Tommy Sands, singing idol of the rock 'n' roll era, had a chequered career, but his screen debut in this adaptation of a television play was impressive and promised better things. The story has teen idol Sands being manipulated by a ruthless manager (Edmond O'Brien) while being torn between his love of pop music and his obligation to succeed his grandfather as a preacher. The tale has too much angst and too little originality to be more than mildly entertaining. TV

Tommy Sands *Virgil Walker* • Lili Gentle *Leora Easton* • Edmond O'Brien *Joseph Sharkey* • John McIntire *Reverend Walker* • Nick Adams *CK Judd* • Diane Jergens *Pat* • Josephine Hutchinson *Caroline Walker* • Jerry Paris *Fisher* ■ *Dir* Henry Ephron · *Scr* Claude Binyon, from the TV play *The Singin' Idol* by Paul Monash

Sing Street ★★★★ 12
Musical drama
2015 · Ire/US/UK · Colour · 101min

Sing Street is quite simply one of the nicest films you'll see in a long time. It's written and directed by the impressive John Carney, and follows a lovestruck 15-year-old schoolboy as he woos a slightly older girl and grabs the opportunity to appear in a music video with his band. Carney draws terrific performances from his musically talented young cast, and adds welcome shades of darkness to the film's innate fantasy-tinged fluffiness. The songs, all written specially for the film, are pretty good, too. An absolute delight. DA Swearing, drug abuse, sexual references.

Ferdia Walsh-Peelo *Conor, "Cosmo"* • Lucy Boynton *Raphina* • Aidan Gillen *Robert* • Maria Doyle Kennedy *Penny* • Jack Reynor *Brendan* ■ *Dir* John Carney · *Scr* John Carney, from a story by Carney, Simon Carmody

Sing Your Song ★★★★★
Documentary   2011 · US · Colour · 104min

The life of singer, actor and political activist Harry Belafonte contains enough material for three documentaries, but this joyful and inspiring portrait couldn't be bettered. As a Grammy-award-winning singer, he crossed colour lines and used his fame to promote folk and roots music. As an actor, he studied with Marlon Brando and starred in the ground-breaking all-black 1954 musical *Carmen Jones*. But it is as an activist that Belafonte will leave his legacy. The incredible archive footage gathered by director Susanne Rostock is impressive enough – including a bullish Belafonte bending a nervous JFK's ear – but what stays longest in the mind is the conscience and spirit of a man whose fierce sense of justice has stood firm through decades of political and social change. DW Some violence, swearing. DVD BD

Harry Belafonte ■ *Dir* Susanne Rostock

Singapore ★★
Adventure drama   1947 · US · BW · 79min

Pearl-smuggling sailor Fred MacMurray returns to Singapore after the Second World War to retrieve a valuable bag of pearls he left hidden in his hotel room. In flashback, he relives his romance with Ava Gardner, apparently killed in the Japanese invasion which coincided with their wedding. Back in present time, he discovers her alive but suffering total amnesia and married to wealthy Roland Culver. This nonsensical escapism is really quite entertaining. RK

Fred MacMurray *Matt Gordon* • Ava Gardner *Linda* • Roland Culver *Michael Van Leyden* • Richard Haydn *Chief Inspector Hewitt* • Thomas Gomez *Mr Mauritus* • Spring Byington *Mrs Bellows* • Porter Hall *Mr Bellows* • George Lloyd *Sascha Barda* ■ *Dir* John Brahm · *Scr* Seton I Miller, Robert Thoeren, from a story by Seton I Miller

The Singer ★★★★ 12
Romantic drama
2006 · Fr/Bel · Colour · 108min

Director Xavier Giannoli captures the kitsch charm of a disappearing form of French entertainment in this dextrous, but never condescending snapshot of provincial life. Gérard Depardieu plays ageing singer Alain Moreau, who works the dance-hall circuit of central France. He meets single mother Marion (Cécile de France) and their courtship is played out with a credible hesitancy that's borne out of the difference in their ages and a reluctance to make another romantic mistake. Alain's pursuit of Marion also reveals the insecurity behind his stage façade and his reputation as a womaniser, which is reinforced by his reliance on manager and ex-wife Michèle (Christine Citti). Depardieu revels in delivering his songs, but he avoids the clichés of the washed-up *chanteur*. A bittersweet, understated gem. DP French +subtitles. DVD

Gérard Depardieu *Alain Moreau* • Cécile de France *Marion* • Mathieu Amalric *Bruno* • Christine Citti *Michèle* • Patrick Pineau *Daniel* • Alain Chanone *Philippe Mariani* • Christophe ■ *Dir/Scr* Xavier Giannoli

The Singer Not the Song ★★ U
Western   1960 · UK · Colour · 132min

With Dirk Bogarde strutting around a small Mexican town in the tightest black leather trousers the censors would allow and John Mills spouting Catholic dogma in an abominable Irish accent, this all has the makings of a cult classic. Sadly, the story is so dull that your mind is soon numbed by the actorly excesses of the stars. Director Roy Ward Baker doesn't help matters with his leaden pacing and over-deliberate staging. DP

Dirk Bogarde *Anacleto* • John Mills *Father Keogh* • Mylène Demongeot *Locha* • Laurence Naismith *Old uncle* • John Bentley *Chief of police* • Leslie French *Father Gomez* • Eric Pohlmann *Presidente* ■ *Dir* Roy Ward Baker · *Scr* Nigel Balchin, from the novel by Audrey Erskine Lindop

Invariably voted the finest musical of all time, this marks the genre's artistic peak, at the same time paying homage to its roots

Singin' in the Rain ★★★★★ U
Classic musical   1952 · US · Colour · 99min

Never, in the whole history of the American cinema, has such a collection of talents come together at the peak of their abilities to generate such an enjoyable and clever movie. Not only is this utterly irrepressible, but the story also beautifully evokes the excitement of making motion pictures, while Gene Kelly's joyous rendition of the title song stands as a lasting tribute to a star at his peak. For those who don't know, this is an affectionate parody of the days when sound came to Hollywood in the wake of *The Jazz Singer*, and every incident wittily referred to in Betty Comden and Adolph Green's sparkling screenplay actually happened. TS DVD BD

Gene Kelly *Don Lockwood* • Debbie Reynolds *Kathy Selden* • Donald O'Connor *Cosmo Brown* • Jean Hagen *Lina Lamont* • Millard Mitchell *RF Simpson* • Rita Moreno *Zelda Zanders* • Douglas Fowley *Roscoe Dexter* • Cyd Charisse *Dancer* ■ *Dir* Gene Kelly, Stanley Donen · *Scr* Adolph Green, Betty Comden · *Cinematographer* Harold Rosson · *Music/lyrics* Nacio Herb Brown · *Music Director* Lennie Hayton

The Singing Detective ★★ 15
Period musical drama
2003 · US · Colour · 104min

Dennis Potter's excellent 1980s amalgam of psychological drama, detective thriller and musical fantasy gets hung, drawn and quartered by this ill-advised Hollywood remake. Replacing Michael Gambon as the bitter, psoriasis-afflicted writer, Robert Downey Jr overplays every scene. Truncating the key childhood flashback scenes into almost nothing, the film is more interested in sterile musical numbers and sleazy *film noir* fragments. Aside from some striking, if theatrical, lighting, the only plus point is Mel Gibson's cameo as Downey Jr's psychiatrist. JC DVD

Robert Downey Jr *Dan Dark* • Robin Wright Penn [Robin Wright] *Nicola/Nina/Blonde* • Jeremy Northam *Mark Binney* • Katie Holmes *Nurse Mills* • Carla Gugino *Betty Dark/Hooker* • Adrien Brody *First hood* • Jon Polito *Second hood* • Mel Gibson *Dr Gibbon* ■ *Dir* Keith Gordon · *Scr* Dennis Potter, from his TV series

The Singing Fool ★★
Musical drama   1928 · US · BW · 105min

Al Jolson's follow-up to *The Jazz Singer*, was even more popular and was Hollywood's most financially successful sound film until *Gone with the Wind* in 1939. Its blatant assault on the tear ducts and Jolson's performance take a lot of swallowing now, and its appeal rests purely on its important place in Hollywood history. Jolson plays a singer/composer who loses his wife and small son, the demise of the latter prompting the film's most famous sequence, as Jolson sings *Sonny Boy*. TV

Al Jolson *Al Stone* • Betty Bronson *Grace* • Josephine Dunn *Molly Winton* • Reed Howes *John Perry* • Edward Martindel *Louis Marcus* • Arthur Housman *Blackie Joe* • Davey Lee *Sonny Boy* ■ *Dir* Lloyd Bacon · *Scr* Joseph Jackson, C Graham Baker, from a story by Leslie S Barrows

The Singing Kid ★★★ U
Musical comedy   1936 · US · BW · 85min

If ever a musical was saved by its songs, this is it. Though Al Jolson had been the saviour of Warner Bros when he starred in *The Jazz Singer*, the studio was happy to terminate his contract by the time this film was released. Tastes had changed and Jolson's extrovert style was going out of fashion. Mundane scripts like this one did not help, with Jolson a stage star who loses his voice and goes to the country to convalesce. Fortunately, the songs by Harold Arlen and EY Harburg crop up often enough to provide some adrenaline. TV

Al Jolson *Al Jackson* • Allen Jenkins *Joe Eddy* • Lyle Talbot *Bob Carey* • William B Davidson *Barney Hammond* • Frank Mitchell *Dope* • Edward Keane *Potter* • Sybil Jason *Sybil Haines* • Edward

Everett Horton *Davenport Rogers* ■ *Dir* William Keighley · *Scr* Warren Duff, Pat C Flick, from a story by Robert Lord

The Singing Nun ★★ U
Musical drama   1966 · US · Colour · 96min

Audiences in the mid-1960s must have had sweet teeth for this mawkish musical biopic to be a box-office success. Piously pert Debbie Reynolds plays Soeur Sourire, the guitar-strumming Belgian nun who composed the song *Dominique*, written for a motherless boy, which ended up as an international hit. Greer Garson pours more syrup over it as the Mother Prioress. Schmaltzy. RB

Debbie Reynolds *Sister Ann* • Ricardo Montalban *Father Clementi* • Greer Garson *Mother Prioress* • Agnes Moorehead *Sister Cluny* • Chad Everett *Robert Gerarde* • Katharine Ross *Nicole Arlien* • Juanita Moore *Sister Mary* • Ed Sullivan ■ *Dir* Henry Koster · *Scr* Sally Benson, John Furia Jr, from a story by John Furia Jr

The Singing, Ringing Tree ★★★ U
Fantasy   1957 · E Ger · Colour · 71min

This unassuming fairy tale has captivated three generations. First seen on British television in 1964 (when it was shown in three parts on the BBC series *Tales from Europe*), this colourful fantasy was later rediscovered by London's National Film Theatre, where it became one of the audience's favourite films. The simple story is about a prince who sets out to find the eponymous tree to win the love of a beautiful but arrogant princess. Although slow-paced by modern standards, it is shot on large sets and has the charm of a picture book come to life. DM German +subtitles. DVD

Christel Bodenstein *Thousand-Beauty/Princess* • Charles Hans Vogt *King* • Eckart Dux *Prince/Bear* • Richard Krüger *Dwarf* • Dorothea Thiessing *Nurse* • Fredy Barten *Minister* ■ *Dir* Francesco Stefani · *Scr* Francesco Stefani, Anne Geelhaar, inspired by episodes in stories collected by Jacob Grimm, Wilhelm Grimm

The Singing Sheriff ★★ U
Comedy western   1944 · US · BW · 62min

Intended as a satire on westerns, this works better today as a vehicle for bandleader Bob Crosby (brother of Bing) playing a Broadway cowboy finding himself out in the real Wild West. Much of the spoofing is heavy-handed, but some of it does work and it's all good-natured stuff with Crosby a likeable lead. TS

Bob Crosby *Bob Richards* • Fay McKenzie *Caroline* • Fuzzy Knight *Lefty* • Samuel S Hinds *Seth* • Edward Norris *Vance* ■ *Dir* Leslie Goodwins · *Scr* Henry Blankfort, Eugene Conrad, from a story by John Grey

A Single Man ★★★★ 12
Drama   2009 · US · Colour and BW · 96min

Colin Firth's strength is his ordinariness and he uses it here to great effect in fashion designer Tom Ford's assured directorial debut. He plays the eponymous single man, an English academic living in 1960s Los Angeles, who's struggling to come to terms with the death of his gay partner (Matthew Goode) at a time when attitudes were very different from what they are today. Will the attempts of a male student (Nicholas Hoult) to break through his reserve or an evening spent with boozy best friend Charley (Julianne Moore) persuade Firth that life is still worth living? Ford alludes mischievously to Hitchcock, which adds to the drama and turmoil within Firth's beautifully realised character. BP English, Spanish +subtitles. Nudity, some swearing. DVD BD

Colin Firth *George* • Julianne Moore *Charley* • Nicholas Hoult *Kenny* • Matthew Goode *Jim* • Jon Kortajarena *Carlos* • Paulette Lamori *Alva* • Ryan Simpkins *Jennifer* • Ginnifer Goodwin *Mrs Strunk* ■ *Dir* Tom Ford · *Scr* Tom Ford, David Scearce, from the novel by Christopher Isherwood · *Music* Abel Korzeniowski

S

Single Room Furnished ★★
Drama   1968 · US · Colour · 93min

Like *Game of Death*, this is a salvage job, cobbled together after the death of its star. Her career on the skids, Jayne Mansfield met and married Italian stage director Matteo Ottaviano, later known as Matt Cimber. He found a play about the occupant of a single room, a young woman picked up and dropped by a succession of men, and developed it as a vehicle for his wife. Halfway through shooting, she flounced off the set and was killed in a car crash. Cimber had the script re-written, shot a framing story with new characters, and further padded the running time by adding a prologue in which journalist Walter Winchell pays tribute to Mansfield. Depressingly cheap and tawdry. DM

Jayne Mansfield *Johnnie/Mae/Eilene* · Dorothy Keller *Flo* · Fabian Dean *Charley* · Billy M Greene *Pop* · Terri Messina *Maria Adamo* ■ *Dir* Matteo Ottaviano [Matt Cimber] · *Scr* Michael Musto

Single Santa Seeks Mrs Claus ★★ PG
Comedy drama   2004 · US · Colour · 85min

With Father Christmas contemplating retirement, the time has come for his heir to assume control. But in this affable yuletide romantic comedy, he can't take the reins until he's found himself a wife. Steve Guttenberg may not be everyone's first choice for Santa Jr. Yet he's ably supported by Crystal Bernard as the stressed-out single mother whose son sends a letter to the North Pole requesting a new dad. Of course it's corny, but it delivers everything the title promises. The sequel, *Meet the Santas*, was completed a year later. DP *DVD*

Steve Guttenberg *Nick* · Crystal Bernard *Beth* · Dominic Scott Kay *Jake* · Armin Shimerman *Ernest* · Wendy Braun *Amy* · Sebastian Tillinger *Hennesy* · Mackenzie Fitzgerald *Jocelyn* ■ *Dir* Harvey Frost · *Scr* Pamela Wallace

The Single Standard ★★★
Silent romantic drama   1929 · US · BW · 73min

Greta Garbo's last film with Nils Asther presents her in the familiar mix of convention-defying free spirit and penitent coming to her senses. She plays a San Francisco socialite who jaunts off on a yacht for an affair with Asther, a macho sailor-turned-artist. When he has second thoughts, she returns home to find herself a social outcast. Soft-edged stuff, directed with almost puritan discretion by John S Robertson. RK

Greta Garbo *Arden Stuart* · Nils Asther *Packy Cannon* · John Mack Brown [Johnny Mack Brown] *Tommy Hewlett* · Dorothy Sebastian *Mercedes* · Lane Chandler *Ding Stuart* · Robert Castle *Anthony Kendall* ■ *Dir* John S Robertson · *Scr* Josephine Lovett, from a story by Adela Rogers St Johns

Single White Female ★★★★ 18
Thriller   1992 · US · Colour · 103min

Jennifer Jason Leigh plays the lodger from hell who makes nice Bridget Fonda's life a misery in this ludicrous but hugely enjoyable thriller from director Barbet Schroeder. Based on John Lutz's novel, it has Fonda as a chic Manhattanite looking for a roommate, and Leigh as the shy, frumpy "perfect" candidate. That is, until she starts dressing like Fonda and tries to steal her boyfriend. Yes, you may be able to guess the end from the first five minutes, but that doesn't make this any less enthralling. JB Violence, swearing, sex scenes, nudity. *DVD*

Bridget Fonda *Allison Jones* · Jennifer Jason Leigh *Hedra Carlson* · Steven Weber *Sam Rawson* · Peter Friedman *Graham Knox* · Stephen Tobolowsky *Mitchell Myerson* · Frances Bay *Elderly neighbour* ■ *Dir* Barbet Schroeder · *Scr* Don Roos, from the novel *SWF Seeks Same* by John Lutz

Singles ★★★★ 15
Romantic comedy   1992 · US · Colour · 95min

Former rock journalist Cameron Crowe directs this interesting, wonderfully funny look at love among Seattle's 20-somethings. Matt Dillon is the self-centred grunge rocker in love with Bridget Fonda, while Campbell Scott and Kyra Sedgwick are the couple too scared of commitment because of past experiences. They head an exemplary cast involved in the sort of dating rituals that recall the acerbic wit of early Woody Allen, but appealingly countered with a touching sweetness. AJ Swearing, sex scenes. *DVD*

Bridget Fonda *Janet Livermore* · Campbell Scott *Steve Dunne* · Kyra Sedgwick *Linda Powell* · Sheila Kelley (1) *Debbie Hunt* · Jim True *David Bailey* · Matt Dillon *Cliff Poncier* · Bill Pullman *Dr Jamison* · James LeGros *Andy* ■ *Dir/Scr* Cameron Crowe

Sinister ★★★★ 15
Horror   2012 · US · Colour · 105min

An intense atmosphere of dread and sudden jolts from the darkness fill this compelling, disturbing supernatural shocker – a skilful blend of old-school, haunted-house horror and in-vogue found-footage fear. Struggling true-crime writer Ethan Hawke researches his latest book by moving his family into the actual home where brutal murders took place. There he discovers some home movies containing possible evidence that something unnatural may be responsible for a string of unexplained deaths. Hawke anchors events superbly as the agonised author whose deteriorating state of mind threatens everything he holds dear. A sequel is due in autumn 2015. AJ Violence. *DVD* ⬛

Ethan Hawke *Ellison* · Vincent D'Onofrio *Professor Jonas* · Juliet Rylance *Tracy* · Fred Dalton Thompson *Sheriff* · James Ransone *Deputy* ■ *Dir* Scott Derrickson · *Scr* Scott Derrickson, Robert C Cargill

Sinister 2 ★★ 15
Horror   2015 · US · Colour · 92min

In this superficial sequel to the original subtle horror tale, ex-deputy James Ransone chases the demon Bughuul to another haunted house, this one inhabited by abused Shannyn Sossamon and her twin sons, who are falling prey to the madness conjured up by the boogieman from old film footage of ghostly children. Director Ciaran Foy has an assertive visual style, and the atmosphere is sufficiently gloomy, but the scares are scarce and the uneven tone makes the whole movie creak. AJ Violence, swearing. *DVD* ⬛

Shannyn Sossamon *Courtney* · James Ransone *So & So* · Robert Daniel Sloan *Dylan Collins* · Dartanian Sloan *Zach Collins* · Lea Coco *Clint Collins* ■ *Dir* Ciaran Foy · *Scr* C Robert Cargill, Scott Derrickson

Sink the Bismarck! ★★★★ U
Second World War drama
1960 · UK · BW · 93min

The postwar British film industry relied heavily on "now the story can be told" accounts of engagements that helped turn the Second World War in favour of the Allies. Too many were smug action adventures that devalued the true heroism of the exploits they depicted, but this fine film fully captures the tensions, dangers and complexities of battle by concentrating on the unsung back-room planners as much as on the combatants themselves. DP *DVD*

Kenneth More *Captain Jonathan Shepard* · Dana Wynter *Anne Davis* · Carl Mohner *Captain Lindemann* · Laurence Naismith *First Sea Lord* · Geoffrey Keen *ACNS* · Karel Stepanek *Admiral Lutjens* · Michael Hordern *Commander on King George V* · Maurice Denham *Commander Richards* ■ *Dir* Lewis Gilbert · *Scr* Edmund H North, from the non-fiction book by CS Forester

Sinners in Paradise ★
Drama   1938 · US · BW · 64min

Scraping the bottom of the barrel of stories about strangers thrown together by unusual and unfortunate circumstances, this is the plane crash version. Here the passengers are stranded on a remote tropical island, seemingly deserted until escaped convict John Boles shows himself. Happily, it only takes 64 minutes for their dreary skeletons to come rattling out of the cupboard. RK

Madge Evans *Anne Wesson* · John Boles *Jim Taylor* · Bruce Cabot *Robert Malone/"The Torpedo"* · Marion Martin *Iris Compton* · Gene Lockhart *Senator Corey* · Charlotte Wynters *Thelma Chase/Doris Bailey* ■ *Dir* James Whale · *Scr* Lester Cole, Harold Buckley, Louis Stevens, from the story *Half Way to Shanghai* by Harold Buckley

Sinners in Silk ★★★
Silent romantic fantasy   1924 · US · BW · 68min

Louis B Mayer personally produced this high-society melodrama, which was given a whisper of sensationalism by its incestuous undertone. Little attention is paid to the scientific process by which Jean Hersholt relieves ageing roué Adolphe Menjou of 20 years. Instead, director Hobart Henley concentrates on the fact that Menjou and his dashing son, Conrad Nagel, are in competition for the affections of the ravishing Eleanor Boardman. The sudden resolution leaves all sorts of unsatisfactory loose ends, but it's expertly performed. DP

Adolphe Menjou *Arthur Merrill* · Eleanor Boardman *Penelope Stevens* · Conrad Nagel *Brock Farley* · Jean Hersholt *Dr Eustace* · Edward Connelly *Bates* · Jerome Patrick *Jerry Hall* · Hedda Hopper *Mrs Stevens* ■ *Dir* Hobart Henley · *Scr* Carey Wilson, from a story by Benjamin Glazer

Sinners in the Sun ★★
Romance   1932 · US · BW · 60min

Dress-shop model Carole Lombard and mechanic Chester Morris, madly in love, part after a difference of opinion about their planned marriage. She becomes the kept mistress of wealthy Walter Byron; he graduates from chauffeur to husband of rich socialite Adrienne Ames. Paramount's sophisticated house style is only celluloid deep, a surface cover for a clichéd and simplistic demonstration that money doesn't buy happiness. RK

Carole Lombard *Doris Blake* · Chester Morris *Jimmie Martin* · Adrienne Ames *Claire Kinkaid* · Alison Skipworth *Mrs Blake* · Cary Grant *Ridgeway* · Walter Byron *Eric Nelson* · Rita La Roy *Lil* ■ *Dir* Alexander Hall · *Scr* Waldemar Young, Samuel Hoffenstein, Vincent Lawrence, from the short story *The Beachcomber* by Mildred Cram

The Sins of Rachel Cade ★★★
Wartime melodrama   1960 · US · Colour · 122min

Warner Bros cut a melodramatic swathe through the late 1950s and 1960s with a series of star-studded colourful dramas, tackling "adult" themes and featuring their contract players. Here, missionary nurse Angie Dickinson sweats it out with Peter Finch in the Belgian Congo, while Roger Moore looks on in lust. Director Gordon Douglas understands the quintessential trashiness of the material and does well by it. TS

Angie Dickinson *Rachel Cade* · Peter Finch *Colonel Henri Derode* · Roger Moore *Paul Wilton* · Errol John *Kulu, Rachel's assistant* · Woody Strode *Muwango* · Juano Hernandez *Kalanumu* · Scatman Crothers *Musinga* ■ *Dir* Gordon Douglas · *Scr* Edward Anhalt, from the novel *Rachel Cade* by Charles E Mercer

Sioux City ★★ 15
Mystery thriller   1994 · US · Colour · 101min

Lou Diamond Phillips decided – after starring in a number of movies – that he wanted to direct. He also takes the lead as the Sioux, who has been adopted by an affluent Jewish couple and become a busy doctor in Beverly Hills. He then discovers that his real mother has died mysteriously.

His search for his identity parallels a crime story that lapses into melodrama. This is well intentioned but somewhat less than gripping. BB *DVD*

Lou Diamond Phillips *Jesse Rainfeather Goldman* · Ralph Waite *Chief Drew McDermott* · Melinda Dillon *Leah Goldman* · Salli Richardson *Jolene Buckley* · Adam Roarke *Blake Goldman* · Tantoo Cardinal *Dawn Rainfeather* ■ *Dir* Lou Diamond Phillips · *Scr* L Virginia Browne

Sir Billi ★ U
Animated comedy adventure
2012 · UK · Colour · 75min

Sir Sean Connery breaks his retirement here to voice a skateboarding vet, in a strange, charmless kids' film that follows the hunt for an escaped beaver in a Highlands where animals talk. Alan Cumming, Ruby Wax and Miriam Margolyes also contribute their vocal talents, and Dame Shirley Bassey sings the title song, but all this talent is largely wasted by husband-and-wife creative team Sascha and Tessa Hartmann. It's incoherently plotted, with unremarkable dialogue – even some injudicious James Bond jokes fall, clunkily, on stony ground. DA *DVD*

Sean Connery *Sir Billi* · Alan Cumming *Gordon the Goat* · Miriam Margolyes *Lady Chantal McToff* · Alex Norton *Baron McToff* · Ruby Wax *Patti Turner* · Valentina Hartmann *Bessie Boo* ■ *Dir* Sascha Hartmann · *Scr* Tessa Hartmann

Sirens ★★ 15
Erotic comedy
1994 · Aus/UK/Ger · Colour · 90min

Hugh Grant stars as a prudish clergyman whose first task in his new Australian parish is to prevent bohemian artist Sam Neill from exhibiting both his models and his portraits of them. Director John Duigan contents himself with a few gentle barbs and elegant bons mots, but rather loses his way once Grant's less inhibited wife, Tara FitzGerald, joins Elle Macpherson and her fellow poseurs. DP Swearing, sex scenes, nudity. *DVD*

Hugh Grant *Anthony Campion* · Tara FitzGerald *Estella Campion* · Sam Neill *Norman Lindsay* · Elle Macpherson *Sheela* · Portia de Rossi *Giddy* · Kate Fischer *Pru* · Pamela Rabe *Rose Lindsay* ■ *Dir/Scr* John Duigan

Sirocco ★★★ PG
Spy drama   1951 · US · BW · 94min

This pretty blatant imitation of *Casablanca* was made by Humphrey Bogart's own production company, Santana. Set in Syria in the 1920s, this was by his own admission not one of Bogart's best pictures, but it's still a moodily gripping yarn about gunrunners, political commitment and various other intrigues. What it sadly lacks is a decent heroine though Lee J Cobb is excellent. AT *DVD*

Humphrey Bogart *Harry Smith* · Marta Toren *Violette* · Lee J Cobb *Colonel Feroud* · Everett Sloane *General LaSalle* · Gerald Mohr *Major Leon* · Zero Mostel *Balukjian* · Nick Dennis *Nasir Aboud* ■ *Dir* Curtis Bernhardt · *Scr* Al Bezzerides, Hans Jacoby, from the novel *Coup de Grace* by Joseph Kessel

Sister ★★★ 15
Drama   2012 · Fr/Swi · Colour · 93min

Ursula Meier devised this slice of Alpine realism especially for Kacey Mottet Klein, who made such an impression in her 2008 directorial debut, *Home*. Klein is outstanding as a 12-year-old who steals skiing equipment from well-to-do visitors at a Swiss resort so he can remain with his older sister (Léa Seydoux) in an unprepossessing apartment block in the valley. Although the story struggles to recover from a melodramatic twist concerning their relationship, such is the focus on the contrasting lifestyles of the haves and have-nots that this remains as intriguing and poignant as Meier's fine first film. DP French, English +subtitles. *DVD*

Léa Seydoux *Louise* · Kacey Mottet Klein *Simon* · Martin Compston *Mike* · Gillian Anderson *English lady* ■ *Dir* Ursula Meier · *Scr* Ursula Meier, Antoine Jaccoud, Gilles Taurand

Sister Act ★★★★ PG
Comedy 1992 · US · Colour · 96min

Ghost may have won Whoopi Goldberg an Oscar, but it was his comedy that turned her into a huge Hollywood star. Goldberg plays a Reno lounge singer who witnesses lover Harvey Keitel killing a man, so she accepts a police offer of protection that entails hiding out in a convent. That's about it for plot, while the remainder of the movie follows our heroine as she tries to bring the nuns and Maggie Smith's strict Mother Superior into the 20th century. Relying on some great songs and a superb cast (including Kathy Najimy as sunny Sister Mary Patrick), this gets past the slight story to become a hugely enjoyable movie. JB Some swearing. *DVD* *BL*

Whoopi Goldberg *Deloris Van Cartier* · Maggie Smith *Mother Superior* · Kathy Najimy *Sister Mary Patrick* · Wendy Makkena *Sister Mary Robert* · Mary Wickes *Sister Mary Lazarus* · Harvey Keitel *Vince LaRocca* · Bill Nunn *Eddie Souther* · Robert Miranda *Joey* ■ *Dir* Emile Ardolino · *Scr* Joseph Howard

Sister Act 2: Back in the Habit ★★★ PG
Comedy 1993 · US · Colour · 102min

Las Vegas cabaret singer Whoopi Goldberg dons her Sister Mary Clarence habit again to teach music to a bad-attitude class at a run-down high school in this OK sequel. Goldberg delivers the good-education/family-values/follow-your-dream messages with likeable charm, even if the familiar concept is treated in a heavy-handed fashion. Still, the musical sequences are lively and Maggie Smith gives sterling support. AJ *DVD*

Whoopi Goldberg *Deloris Van Cartier/Sister Mary Clarence* · Kathy Najimy *Sister Mary Patrick* · Barnard Hughes *Father Maurice* · Mary Wickes *Sister Mary Lazarus* · James Coburn *Mr Crisp* · Michael Jeter *Father Ignatius* · Wendy Makkena *Sister Mary Robert* · Maggie Smith *Mother Superior* · Lauryn Hill *Rita Watson* · Jennifer Love Hewitt *Margaret* ■ *Dir* Bill Duke · *Scr* James Orr, Jim Cruickshank, Judi Ann Mason, from characters by Joseph Howard

Sister Kenny ★★★★
Biographical drama 1946 · US · BW · 116min

In this engrossing biographical drama, Rosalind Russel stars as Australian nurse Elizabeth Kenny, who fought the medical establishment to gain acceptance for her pioneering work with polio sufferers. In possibly her finest film performance, the Oscar-nominated Russell totally eschews the maudlin and banal to give a moving portrayal of a woman compelled to battle a feared and potentially fatal disease. Russell dominates the screen and aficionados of the star will probably be able to quote much of the film's dialogue. SH

Rosalind Russell *Elizabeth Kenny* · Alexander Knox *Dr McDonnell* · Dean Jagger *Kevin Connors* · Philip Merivale *Dr Brack* · Beulah Bondi *Mary Kenny* · Charles Dingle *Michael Kenny* ■ *Dir* Dudley Nichols · *Scr* Dudley Nichols, Alexander Knox, Mary McCarthy, Milton Gunzburg (uncredited), from the autobiography *And They Shall Walk* by Elizabeth Kenny, Martha Ostenso

Sister My Sister ★★★ 15
Historical crime drama 1994 · UK · Colour · 85min

In 1933, two French maids murdered their employer and her daughter. This brutal act gave rise to Jean Genet's classic play *The Maids* and, decades later, also inspired American playwright Wendy Kesselman to write *My Sister in This House* on which director Nancy Meckler based this strange but haunting little oddity. Joely Richardson and Jodhi May are the pair who allow their repressions to surface when in the service of Julie Walters. Tautly directed by Meckler, this sinister portrait of corrupted innocence and sisterly love beyond the norm is quite a chilling curiosity. AJ Violence, sex scenes.

Julie Walters *Madame Danzard* · Joely Richardson *Christine* · Jodhi May *Lea* · Sophie Thursfield *Isabelle Danzard* · Amelda Brown

Visitor · Lucita Pope *Visitor* · Kate Gartside *Sister Veronica* ■ *Dir* Nancy Meckler · *Scr* Wendy Kesselman, from her play *My Sister in This House*

Sisterhood ★★ 15
Comedy 2008 · UK/NZ · Colour · 88min

In this long-lost sibling romp, uncouth New Zealand sheep farmer Shirley (Emily Corcoran) comes to London to find snooty half-sister Catherine (Isabelle Defaut). The two women then try to claw back the inheritance that their conman father Jack (Nicholas Ball) swindled from their respective mothers. Writer/star Corcoran proves adept at physical comedy, but her screenplay is less accomplished. There's more to wince at than smile about as the 30-somethings career around London after DNA samples to prove their identity and that of their father. DP

Emily Corcoran *Shirley Zachary* · Isabelle Defaut *Catherine St John-Burke* · Nicholas Ball *Jack McClarky* · Maria Charles *Ethel Bainbridge* · Graham McTavish *Martin* · Paul Gregory (2) *Sir Jack Crawford* ■ *Dir* Richard Wellings-Thomas · *Scr* Emily Corcoran

The Sisterhood of the Traveling Pants ★★★ PG
Comedy drama 2005 · US · Colour · 113min

A shared pair of thrift-shop jeans becomes a powerful friendship talisman for four teenage girls in this feel-good film. With the young women retaining the jeans for a week each, the clothing acts as a spiritual linking device between their very different experiences during their first summer apart. Unfortunately, while director Ken Kwapis expertly weaves together the storylines, he gives greater weight to the least interesting strands. Alexis Bledel's Greek holiday romance and the boy-chasing Blake Lively are clichéd and flimsy. Where the film excels is in America Ferrera and Amber Tamblyn's raw and poignant segments. SF *DVD*

Amber Tamblyn *Tibby* · America Ferrera *Carmen* · Blake Lively *Bridget* · Alexis Bledel *Lena* · Bradley Whitford *Al* · Nancy Travis *Lydia Rodman* · Rachel Ticotin *Carmen's mother* · Jenna Boyd *Bailey* ■ *Dir* Ken Kwapis · *Scr* Delia Ephron, Elizabeth Chandler, from the novel by Ann Brashares

The Sisterhood of the Traveling Pants 2 ★★ 12
Comedy drama 2008 · US · Colour · 114min

Growing pains are once again alleviated by a pair of miracle jeans in this sequel based on Ann Brashares's novel. The mystical power assigned to denim is not nearly as dubious as the trite dilemmas faced by the four girls of the sisterhood, who are now of college age. Three, including America Ferrera (star of TV's *Ugly Betty*), are pursued by boys so impossibly good-looking and sensitive that it's hard to sympathise with their neuroses. Their various storylines eventually entwine on a Greek island in an unlikely quest to find the lost jeans – which probably walked away in disbelief. SP *DVD*

Amber Tamblyn *Tibby* · America Ferrera *Carmen* · Blake Lively *Bridget* · Alexis Bledel *Lena* · Rachel Nichols *Julia* · Tom Wisdom *Ian* ■ *Dir* Sanaa Hamri · *Scr* Elizabeth Chandler, from the series of novels by Ann Brashares

The Sisters ★★★
Period drama 1938 · US · BW · 98min

Sisters be damned! This costume drama is all about how far poor Bette Davis can fall after she's abandoned by drunken husband Errol Flynn. Admittedly, director Anatole Litvak drops in on Anita Louise and Jane Bryan from time to time to see how they're getting along, but Davis dominates the action, whether eloping with sports reporter Flynn, surviving the San Francisco earthquake or flitting around an Oakland bordello. Orry-Kelly's costumes are a delight and Max Steiner's soundtrack neatly captures the feel of the period and the melodramatics of the plot. DP

Bette Davis *Louise Elliott* · Errol Flynn *Frank Medlin* · Anita Louise *Helen Elliott* · Jane Bryan *Grace Elliott* · Ian Hunter *William Benson* · Henry Travers *Ned Elliott* · Beulah Bondi *Rose Elliott*

Susan Hayward *Telephone operator* ■ *Dir* Anatole Litvak · *Scr* Milton Krims, from the novel by Myron Brinig

Sisters ★★★★ 15
Psychological thriller 1973 · US · Colour · 92min

The first foray into fully-fledged fright by director Brian De Palma is a masterful Hitch-cocktail of the sinister and the satirical. De Palma established his flashy style in this well-choreographed shocker about journalist Jennifer Salt who's compelled to investigate when she witnesses her neighbour Margot Kidder appear to commit murder. To some extent a modified version of *Psycho* dealing with duality and psychosis in an insightful way, this is a well-tuned slice of cinematic frenzy complete with red herrings, a fantasy sequence and split-screen suspense. AJ *DVD* *BL*

Margot Kidder *Danielle Breton* · Jennifer Salt *Grace Collier* · Charles Durning *Larch* · William Finley *Emil Breton* · Lisle Wilson *Phillip Woode* · Barnard Hughes *Mr McLennen* · Mary Davenport *Mrs Collier* ■ *Dir* Brian De Palma · *Scr* Louisa Rose, Brian De Palma, from a story by Brian De Palma

Sisters ★★★ 15
Comedy 2015 · US · Colour · 112min

Having honed their craft on *Saturday Night Live* and as co-hosts of the Golden Globes, the double act of Tina Fey and Amy Poehler gets a well-deserved big screen showcase. They are called back to their childhood home to sort out their belongings before their house is sold. That's the cue for throwing a party like it's 1989. There isn't much of a story – aside from Poehler's aim to bed the hunk down the road and Fey's attempts to keep a priggish Maya Rudolph from crashing the scene – but putting a feminine touch to the standard frat-house formula lends a certain edge. SP Swearing, sexual references, drug abuse. *DVD* *BL*

Amy Poehler *Maura Ellis* · Tina Fey *Kate Ellis* · Maya Rudolph *Brinda* · John Leguizamo *Dave* · Madison Davenport *Haley* ■ *Dir* Jason Moore · *Scr* Paula Pell

Sisters in Law ★★★ 12
Documentary 2005 · Cameroon/UK · Colour · 101min

Award-winning documentarist Kim Longinotto (co-directing with Florence Ayisi) follows the formula of her superb *Divorce Iranian Style* (1998) in this uplifting insight into the Cameroonian justice system. Kumba Town lawyer Madame Ngassa dominates proceedings, as she successfully prosecutes the aunt who has been abusing six-year-old Manka, the neighbour who raped the adolescent Sonita and the strict Muslim husband who repeatedly beat his wife Amina. The fact that the latter was the first conviction of its kind in 17 years suggests that this rigidly patriarchal society is finally acknowledging women rights. But, even though the film avoids depicting failed cases, it's clear that such victories remain a rarity. DP *DVD*

Vera Ngassa ■ *Dir* Kim Longinotto, Florence Ayisi

Sisters of the Gion
★★★★★ U
Drama 1936 · Jpn · BW · 66min

Two Japanese geisha sisters differ in their outlook: the elder (Yoko Umemura) subscribes to tradition, while the younger (Isuzu Yamada) embraces a more modern view of life. Both come to grief at the hands of men, one physically abused by a jealous ex-lover, the other deserted by the man she has loved. A masterpiece from Kenji Mizoguchi, one of the truly great directors in world cinema, this restrained, beautifully composed film, replete with gentle sadness and a touch of humour, well demonstrates the film-maker's empathy with women, and his implied critique of society's treatment of them. RK In Japanese. *DVD* *BL*

Isuzu Yamada *Omocha* · Yoko Umemura *Umekichi* · Benkei Shiganoya *Shinbee Furusawa* · Eitaro Shindo *Kudo* · Taizo Fukami *Kimura* · Fumio Okura *Jurakudo, the antiques dealer* ■

Dir Kenji Mizoguchi · *Scr* Yoshikata Yoda, Kenji Mizoguchi, from the novel *Yama* by Alexandr Ivanovich Kuprin

Sisters, or the Balance of Happiness ★★★★ 15
Drama 1979 · W Ger · Colour · 95min

Margarethe von Trotta considered this study of sibling misunderstanding to be a "soul painting", in which the personalities of the protagonists took priority over the political climate that created them. However, the fact that mollycoddling elder sister Jutta Lampe is an efficient secretary and Gudrun Gabriel a depressive biology student suggests that a pronounced socio-feminist view still runs through the piece. With the *mise en scène* taking on symbolic significance, this is both cinematically accomplished and psychologically intriguing. DP German +subtitles.

Jutta Lampe *Maria* · Gudrun Gabriel *Anna* · Jessica Früh *Miriam* · Konstantin Wecker *Robert* · Rainer Delventhal *Maurice* ■ *Dir* Margarethe von Trotta · *Scr* Margarethe von Trotta, Luisa Francia, Martje Grohmann, from the story *Traumprotokolle* by Wolfgang Bachler

A Sister's Secret ★★
Psychological thriller 2009 · US/Can · Colour · 96min

Compassionate businesswoman Alexandra Paul falls foul of her ex-boyfriend's vengeful sister in this ham-fisted thriller. Blamed for the man's suicide, she finds her attempts to save her family's struggling paper mill continually undermined by the meddling of cartoonishly unhinged employee Cynthia Preston. Trouble is, Preston's absurd choice of industrial sabotage as her method of payback is dull to watch and totally unconvincing. Poor editing and some dreadful dialogue add to the shoddiness. SF *DVD*

Alexandra Paul *Katherine* · Cynthia Preston *Jane* · Paul Whitney *Jim* · Deborah Grover *Florence* · Ron Gabriel *Uncle Tony* ■ *Dir* Anthony Lefresne · *Scr* Sean Parker, Bruce Jensen, Christine Conradt

Sitcom ★★★★ 18
Comedy horror fantasy 1997 · Fr · Colour · 80min

François Ozon's send-up of soap opera conventions is raunchy, kitsch and hilariously funny. In this John Waters-tilted farcical fantasy, a bourgeois family's existence is disrupted when the head of the household brings home a pet rat. How this outsider's evil influence causes them all to jettison their sexual inhibitions and embark on a round robin of escalating perversion is ultra camp and very cutting edge. AJ French +subtitles. Sex scenes. *DVD*

Evelyne Dandry *Hélène, the mother* · François Marthouret *Jean, the father* · Marina de Van *Sophie, the daughter* · Adrien de Van *Nicolas, the son* · Stéphane Rideau *David* ■ *Dir/Scr* François Ozon

The Sitter ★★
Thriller 2007 · US · Colour · 90min

The hackneyed psycho-nanny tale gets another re-tread courtesy of this join-the-dots thriller from *Highlander* director Russell Mulcahy. Mariana Klaveno plays a live-in babysitter whose twisted past violently resurfaces after she becomes obsessed with the head of the family (William R Moses). Klaveno is well-cast, but the ludicrous dialogue and pedestrian execution only highlight the feature's overall tackiness, while a weak finale offers an unsatisfactory payoff. SF

Gail O'Grady *Meghan* · Mariana Klaveno *Abby* · William R Moses *Carter* · Madison Davenport *Casey Eastman* · Tristan Lake Leabu *Max* ■ *Dir* Russell Mulcahy · *Scr* Stephen Niver

The Sitter ★★ 15
Comedy 2011 · US · Colour · 77min

Jonah Hill (*Superbad*) is typecast again as a gormless slacker in this lazy comedy. He plays Noah, who is persuaded to babysit his mother's friend's three children. But he's summoned from the sofa by his girlfriend (Ari Graynor), who promises a wild night of passion as long as he brings along some Class A drugs, prompting him to put his base needs above the children's safety. The mix of crude humour and innocent schoolboy pranks falls flat, and even Hill looks unsure, while the kids don't gel with him or each other. SP Swearing, sexual references. *DVD* *BL*

Jonah Hill *Noah Griffith* • Sam Rockwell *Karl* • Ari Graynor *Marisa Lewis* • JB Smoove *Julio* ■ *Dir* David Gordon Green • *Scr* Brian Gatewood, Alessandro Tanaka

Sitting Bull ★ U
Western　　　1954 · US · Colour · 105min

Superficially spectacular, this independent production relied on early use of CinemaScope and on hordes of Mexican extras to fill its wide screen. Something went wrong with the colour, however, while the routine story takes forever to unfold. There's Douglas Kennedy as the usual glory-seeking Custer, Dale Robertson is the honest cavalry major trying to bring about lasting peace, and J Carrol Naish is the dignified Chief Sitting Bull. AE

Dale Robertson *Parrish* • Mary Murphy (1) *Kathy* • J Carrol Naish *Sitting Bull* • Iron Eyes Cody *Crazy Horse* • John Litel *General Howell* • Bill Hopper *Wentworth* • Douglas Kennedy *Colonel Custer* ■ *Dir* Sidney Salkow • *Scr* Jack DeWitt, Sidney Salkow

Sitting Ducks ★★★★
Comedy caper　　1979 · US · Colour · 87min

Michael Emil and Zack Norman rip off a cool $724,000 from their mobster bosses and flee New York. The pair find themselves hitting the road and en route they pick up genial gas-station attendant Richard Romanus and two girls, Patrice Townsend and Irene Forrest. An enjoyable mix of oddball comedy and romance follows. The sadly underrated Henry Jaglom, a great exponent of improvisation, hits pay dirt here with a thoughtful, constantly amusing road movie. DF

Michael Emil *Simon* • Zack Norman *Sidney* • Patrice Townsend *Jenny* • Irene Forrest *Leona* • Richard Romanus *Moose* • Henry Jaglom *Jenny's friend* ■ *Dir/Scr* Henry Jaglom

Sitting in Limbo ★★★ 15
Drama　　　　1986 · Can · Colour · 38min

This is a well-intentioned drama about the limited opportunities available to African-American teenagers living in Montreal. Aiming for a hard-hitting but freewheeling realism, director John N Smith casts engaging non-professionals Fabian Gibbs and Pat Dillon in the leading roles and uses rough-and-ready, documentary-style camera techniques to capture the transient joys and incessant despairs of their hand-to-mouth existence. DP Swearing.

Pat Dillon *Pat* • Fabian Gibbs *Fabian* • Sylvie Clarke *Sylvie* • Debbie Grant *Debbie* • Compton McLean *John* ■ *Dir* John N Smith • *Scr* John N Smith, David Wilson

Sitting Pretty ★★★
Musical comedy drama　1933 · US · BW · 80min

Jack Oakie and Jack Haley, an aspiring Tin Pan Alley songwriting team, are advised by their music publisher and their rehearsal pianist – Mack Gordon and Harry Revel respectively, who also composed the movie's song score – to try their luck in Hollywood. Which they do, finding fame, fortune and lunch-room waitress Ginger Rogers. "Cheerful" is the word for this musical, zippily played and directed by Harry Joe Brown from a script co-written by humorist SJ Perelman that offers some nice Hollywood-satirising-Hollywood comedy. RK

Jack Oakie *Chick Parker* • Jack Haley *Pete Pendleton* • Ginger Rogers *Dorothy* • Gregory Ratoff *Tannenbaum* • Thelma Todd *Gloria Duval* • Lew Cody *Jules Clark* • Harry Revel *Pianist* • Mack Gordon *Song publisher* ■ *Dir* Harry Joe Brown • *Scr* Jack McGowan, SJ Perelman, Lou Breslow, from a story by Harry Stoddard, suggested Nina Wilcox Putnam

Sitting Pretty ★★★ U
Comedy　　　　1948 · US · BW · 84min

Clifton Webb stars in this popular comedy hit as the self-centred, pompous Mr Belvedere. Webb takes a job as a babysitter to Hummingbird Hill parents Robert Young and Maureen O'Hara, and the memorable scene where the toddler pours porridge over Webb's head was not only used as the film's poster motif, but also became part of the cultural imagery of postwar America. Two sequels, *Mr Belvedere Goes to College* (1949) and *Mr Belvedere Rings the Bell* (1951), followed. TS

Robert Young (1) *Harry* • Clifton Webb *Lynn Belvedere* • Maureen O'Hara *Tacey* • Richard Haydn *Mr Appleton* • Louise Allbritton *Edna Philby* • Randy Stuart *Peggy* • Ed Begley *Hammond* • Larry Olsen *Larry* ■ *Dir* Walter Lang • *Scr* F Hugh Herbert, from the novel *Belvedere* by Gwen Davenport

Sitting Target ★★★ 18
Crime thriller　1972 · US/UK · Colour · 90min

Oliver Reed gets to brutalise and barnstorm as a convicted murderer who escapes from jail in order to bump off his wife, Jill St John – she's been putting herself about a bit and now has some other man's bun in the oven. A splendid supporting cast of TV familiars and peculiars make this a juicy and none too subtle excursion into the underworld. AT

Oliver Reed *Harry Lomart* • Jill St John *Pat Lomart* • Ian McShane *Birdy Williams* • Edward Woodward *Inspector Milton* • Frank Finlay *Marty Gold* • Freddie Jones *MacNeil* • Jill Townsend *Maureen* ■ *Dir* Douglas Hickox • *Scr* Alexander Jacobs, from a novel by Laurence Henderson

Situation Hopeless – but Not Serious ★★★
Second World War comedy
1965 · US · BW · 97min

This maverick, oddball film version of actor Robert Shaw's novel is about two Allied airmen who think they are taking refuge but are actually imprisoned in a comfortable cellar for seven years by a meek little shop assistant. It's mildly allegorical, faintly satirical and almost funny. A nearly movie, then, but worth seeing for Alec Guinness's performance as Herr Frick, whose demure exterior conceals a card-carrying Nazi on the verge of emotional meltdown. At times, Guinness makes the movie seem like an Ealing comedy with an umlaut. Notable for an early appearance by Robert Redford as one of the unwitting kidnap victims. AT

Alec Guinness *Herr Wilhelm Frick* • Michael Connors [Mike Connors] *Lucky Finder* • Robert Redford *Hank Wilson* • Anita Hoefer *Edeltraud* • Mady Rahl *Lissie* • Paul Dahlke *Herr Neusel* • Frank Wolff *QM Master Sergeant* • John Briley *Sergeant* ■ *Dir* Gottfried Reinhardt • *Scr* Silvia Reinhardt, Jan Lustig, from the novel *The Hiding Place* by Robert Shaw

Six Black Horses ★★
Western　　　　1962 · US · Colour · 80min

Originally intended for Randolph Scott, this ended up as a vehicle for baby-faced cowboy star Audie Murphy. It's good to see snarling Dan Duryea in his element, and the plot – determined Joan O'Brien hires Murphy and Duryea to apprehend her husband's killer – is unusually seasoned with humour. TS

Audie Murphy *Ben Lane* • Dan Duryea *Frank Jesse* • Joan O'Brien *Kelly* • George Wallace [George D Wallace] *Boone* • Roy Barcroft *Mustanger* • Phil Chambers *Undertaker* ■ *Dir* Harry Keller • *Scr* Burt Kennedy

Six Bridges to Cross ★★★
Crime drama　　　1955 · US · BW · 95min

Sal Mineo made his screen debut here playing a juvenile delinquent and recidivist who grows into a criminal big shot, despite the best efforts of kindly cop George Nader. As the years pass by, Mineo metamorphoses into Tony Curtis (spot the join) who carries the movie across its various moral hurdles. Inspired by Boston's notorious Brinks Robbery of 1950, the film

was scripted by noted crime scenarist Sydney Boehm. AT

Tony Curtis *Jerry Florea* • Julie Adams *Ellen Gallagher* • George Nader *Edward Gallagher* • Jay C Flippen *Vincent Concannon* • Ken Clark *Sanborn* • Sal Mineo *Jerry as a boy* ■ *Dir* Joseph Pevney • *Scr* Sydney Boehm, from the story *They Stole $2,000,000 and Got Away With It* by Joseph F Dinneen

Six Bullets ★★★ 15
Action thriller　　2012 · US · Colour · 109min

There are shades of *Taken* in this gritty and thought-provoking kidnap tale, as guilt-ridden ex-mercenary Jean-Claude Van Damme helps an implausibly hands-on US couple rescue their teenager from Eastern European sex traffickers. Re-united with his *Assassination Games* director Ernie Barbarash, the ageing star impresses, combining solid dramatic skills with his still-slick action moves. But it's his rarely seen emotional depth that really lifts this DVD feature above clichéd and far-fetched plotting. SF Violence, swearing, sexual references. *DVD*

Jean-Claude Van Damme *Samson Gaul* • Joe Flanigan *Andrew Fayden* • Anna-Louise Plowman *Monica Fayden* • Charlotte Beaumont *Becky Fayden* ■ *Dir* Ernie Barbarash • *Scr* Chad & Evan Law

Six Cylinder Love ★★ U
Comedy　　　　1931 · US · BW · 72min

Newly married Sidney Fox and Lorin Raker cause a stir with the purchase of an expensive new car. How they sort themselves out when they have a crash and incur thousands of dollars worth of damage passes for a plot in this inconsequential comedy. The movie is interesting only in reminding us that cars were once considered a privilege and for the chance to see that future great star Spencer Tracy as a car salesman. RK

Spencer Tracy *Donroy* • Sidney Fox *Marilyn Sterling* • Edward Everett Horton *Monty Winston* • Lorin Raker *Gilbert Sterling* • William Collier Sr *Richard Burton* • Una Merkel *Margaret Rogers* • Bert Roach *Harold Rogers* • Ruth Warren *Mrs Burton* ■ *Dir* Thornton Freeland • *Scr* William Conselman, Norman Houston, from the play by William Anthony McGuire • *Cinematographer* Ernest Palmer

Six Days Seven Nights ★★★ 12
Romantic comedy adventure
1998 · US · Colour · 97min

This adventure comedy stars Anne Heche as a New York fashion magazine journalist who sets out on a romantic island trip with her fiancé (David Schwimmer) but ends up stranded on an even more remote island with drunken local pilot Harrison Ford. Unfortunately, director Ivan Reitman decides that pirates and ludicrous plot twists are more intriguing than exploring the far more interesting chemistry between the two leads. Enjoyable, thanks to the stars' attractive screen presence, but it could have been so much better. JB Swearing, sexual references, some violence. *DVD*

Harrison Ford *Quinn Harris* • Anne Heche *Robin Monroe* • David Schwimmer *Frank Martin* • Jacqueline Obradors *Angelica* • Temuera Morrison *Jager* • Allison Janney *Marjorie* • Amy Sedaris *Robin's secretary* ■ *Dir* Ivan Reitman • *Scr* Michael Browning

Six Days, Six Nights ★★
Drama　　　　1994 · Fr/UK · Colour · 90min

The naturalistic style and keen, witty social insights for which Diane Kurys is renowned are notably absent from this disappointing outing. Indeed, there's a distinct shortage of tension and sexual ambiguity in this otherwise carefully constructed tale of female rivalry, as Béatrice Dalle abandons her family in a bid to destroy artist Anne Parillaud's romance with Patric Aurignac. An intriguing premise, undermined by the slack scripting and inconsistent acting. DP French +subtitles. Violence, sex scenes, nudity.

Anne Parillaud *Alice* • Béatrice Dalle *Elsa* • Patric Aurignac *Franck* • Bernard Verley *Sanders* • Alain Chabat *Thomas* ■ *Dir* Diane Kurys • *Scr* Diane Kurys, Antoine Lacomblez • *Music* Michael Nyman

Six Degrees of Separation ★★★★ 15
Drama　　　　1993 · US · Colour · 108min

In this bourgeois satire, Will Smith displays the talents that were to elevate him to the superstar stratosphere. As the young man who talks his way into the rich New York household of liberal-minded art dealer Donald Sutherland and his wife Stockard Channing by purporting to be the friend of their student children, Smith is as busy as a gadfly. Fred Schepisi's direction is too safe for a real sarcastic sting, but Smith's performance shines above these limitations, transcending the too-glib spelling-out of the gulf between integrity and hypocrisy. TH Swearing, nudity. *DVD*

Stockard Channing *Ouisa Kittredge* • Will Smith *Paul* • Donald Sutherland *Flan Kittredge* • Ian McKellen *Geoffrey* • Mary Beth Hurt *Kitty* • Bruce Davison *Larkin* • Richard Masur *Doctor Fine* • Anthony Michael Hall *Trent* • Heather Graham *Elizabeth* ■ *Dir* Fred Schepisi • *Scr* John Guare, from his play

6.5 Special ★★ U
Musical　　　　1958 · UK · BW · 78min

Here's the film version of one of BBC TV's much loved nostalgic teenfests, a programme that grew out of the need to fill the Saturday slot between children's telly and early evening viewing. It was hosted by Josephine Douglas and Pete Murray, both on hand here, and became a key showcase for British pop music in the pre-Beatles era. Ignore the wisp of a plot about two girls taking the titular train to London to crash showbiz; this is a real period treat. TS

Josephine Douglas • Pete Murray ■ *Dir* Alfred Shaughnessy • *Scr* Norman Hudis

The Six Million Dollar Man ★★★ U
Science-fiction adventure
1973 · US · Colour · 70min

This is the appealing feature-length pilot for the popular series that ran for 102 episodes during its five-year history. Lee Majors headlines as the pilot who receives a bionic makeover after crashing an experimental plane, with Martin Balsam as the scientist surgeon who rebuilds him and Darren McGavin as his operations chief. The exploration of Majors's emotions is sophisticated handled by director Richard Irving, making this a cut above the usual pilot. DP

Lee Majors *Colonel Steve Austin* • Barbara Anderson *Jean Manners* • Martin Balsam *Dr Rudy Wells* • Darren McGavin *Oliver Spencer* • Dorothy Green *Mrs McKay* ■ *Dir* Richard Irving • *Scr* Henri Simoun [Howard Rodman], from the novel *Cyborg* by Martin Caidin

Six of a Kind ★★★★
Comedy　　　　1934 · US · BW · 62min

Director Leo McCarey was a whizz where comedy was concerned and triumphed whether the theme was slapstick, screwball or, as in this case, sheer anarchy. Here he has a dream comedy cast, and an unruly Great Dane, fizzing together on a crazy car trip. WC Fields and Alison Skipworth appear late in the film but still manage to steal it from the other two double acts, Charles Ruggles and Mary Boland, and George Burns and Gracie Allen. Fields gets to perform his famous "billiards" routine, a masterpiece in itself. DF

Charles Ruggles *J Pinkham Whinney* • Mary Boland *Flora Whinney* • WC Fields *Sheriff "Honest" John Hoxley* • George Burns *George* • Gracie Allen *Gracie Devore* • Alison Skipworth *Mrs K Rumford* ■ *Dir* Leo McCarey • *Scr* Walter DeLeon, Harry Ruskin, from a story by Keene Thompson, Douglas MacLean

Six Pack ★★
Action comedy　　1982 · US · Colour · 107min

After proving his worth as an actor in a number of TV roles (most famously *The*

Gambler), Kenny Rogers made his big-screen debut in this middle-of-the-road tale of an ex-stock car driver and six orphaned youngsters. The car-crazy kids help Rogers in his attempts to make a comeback in the sport. **DF**

Kenny Rogers *Brewster Baker* • Diane Lane *Breezy* • Erin Gray *Lilah* • Barry Corbin *Sheriff* • Terry Kiser *Terk* • Bob Hannah *Diddler* ■ *Dir* Daniel Petrie • *Scr* Mike Marvin, Alex Matter

633 Squadron ★★★ PG
Second World War action drama
1964 · UK/US · Colour · 93min

This film suffers in comparison with that other tribute to the Royal Air Force, *The Dam Busters*. The mission is less audacious, the casting is less precise (Cliff Robertson as an American in the RAF and George Chakiris as a Norwegian Resistance fighter) and the theme tune is far harder to sing along to. The flying sequences are more thrilling (particularly the Scottish Highlands training exercises), but they cannot compensate for the dullness of the Norwegian-set scenes. **DP** *DVD*

Cliff Robertson *Wing Commander Roy Grant* • George Chakiris *Lieutenant Erik Bergman* • Maria Perschy *Hilde Bergman* • Harry Andrews *Air Marshal Davis* • Donald Houston *Wing Commander Tom Barrett* • Michael Goodliffe *Squadron Leader Bill Adams* ■ *Dir* Walter E Grauman (*Walter Grauman*) • *Scr* James Clavell, Howard Koch, from the novel by Frederick E Smith

Six Ways to Sunday ★★★ 18
Drama 1997 · US · Colour · 97min

This bleak, bitter and very brutal American drama went straight to video in Britain, but deserved better. Norman Reedus plays a sociopathic teenager with an unhealthily close relationship with his mother (an almost unrecognisable Deborah Harry), who gets involved with mobsters impressed with his capacity of violence. Finely performed by the eclectic cast and directed with seedy style by Adam Bernstein. **JF** Swearing, nudity, violence. *DVD*

Norman Reedus *Harry Odum* • Deborah Harry *Kate Odum* • Elina Lowensohn *Iris* • Adrien Brody *Arnie Finklestein* • Isaac Hayes *Bill Bennet* • Jerry Adler *Louis Varga* • Peter Appel *Abie "The Bug" Pinkwise* ■ *Dir* Adam Bernstein • *Scr* Adam Bernstein, Marc Gerald, from the novel *Portrait of a Young Man Drowning* by Charles Perry

Six Weeks ★ PG
Drama 1982 · US · Colour · 107min

The cancer-stricken daughter of Mary Tyler Moore melts the heart of Congressional candidate Dudley Moore, who helps the girl win a role in a ballet. At this point, you'll be either blubbing helplessly or sneering at the crass contrivances of the plot. Are we being too heartless and cynical? A manipulative monstrosity. **AT**

Dudley Moore *Patrick Dalton* • Mary Tyler Moore *Charlotte Dreyfus* • Katherine Healy *Nicole Dreyfus* • Shannon Wilcox *Peg Dalton* • Bill Calvert *Jeff Dalton* • John Harkins *Arnold Stillman* • Joe Regalbuto *Bob Crowther* ■ *Dir* Tony Bill • *Scr* David Seltzer, from a novel by Fred Mustard Stewart • *Music* Dudley Moore

Sixteen ★★★ 15
Drama 2013 · UK · Colour · 79min

In writer/director Rob Brown's promising debut feature a schoolboy refugee (and former Congolese child soldier) is torn between taking a stand or keeping quiet after he witnesses a vicious murder by a fellow pupil. Roger Jean Nsengiyumva (*Africa United*) gives an assured, mature performance as Jumah, a walking powder keg of hurt, anger and confusion, and it's his journey towards either redemption or deadly retaliation that's at the heart of an absorbing if underdeveloped urban drama. But it's an excellent showcase for bright, young talent like Nsengiyumva and Rosie Day, who plays the girlfriend painfully trying to understand what makes her brooding beau tick. **JA** Violence, swearing.

Roger Jean Nsengiyumva [Roger Nsengiyumva] *Jumah* • Rachael Stirling *Laura* • Rosie Day *Chloe* • Fady Elsayed *Josh* ■ *Dir/Scr* Rob Brown (2)

16 Blocks ★★★ 12
Action crime thriller 2006 · US · Colour · 97min

Sharply scripted and solidly performed, Richard Donner's redemptive urban action thriller centres on the mismatched relationship between Bruce Willis's laconic, alcoholic cop and the motormouth criminal (Mos Def) he's assigned to transport from the lock-up to the courthouse. But a routine 16-block ride turns into a fight for survival when corrupt fellow officers (headed by a terrifically callous David Morse) try to execute the prisoner to prevent him from testifying against them. Though the story is simplistic and predictable, its emphasis on fully fleshed-out characters is emotionally rewarding. **SF** Swearing, violence. *DVD*

Bruce Willis *Jack Mosley* • Mos Def *Eddie Bunker* • David Morse *Frank Nugent* • Jenna Stern *Diane Mosley* • Casey Sander *Captain Gruber* • Cylk Cozart *Jimmy Mulvey* • David Zayas *Robert Torres* • Robert Rack *Jerry Shue* ■ *Dir* Richard Donner • *Scr* Richard Wenk

Sixteen Candles ★★★ 15
Comedy drama 1984 · US · Colour · 88min

John Hughes made his directorial debut as the master of the teen pic with this sharp comedy, which not only has a keen ear for the idiom of teenspeak, but also a genuine sympathy with its various geeks, jocks, seniors and girls next door. Molly Ringwald is the personification of the sulky, sweet 16-year-old whose birthday goes from bad to worse as her parents forget the occasion and the school pest begins showing off her underwear to his classmates. Beaming through his braces, Anthony Michael Hall is nigh-on perfect as the nerd trying too hard to impress. **DP** Swearing, nudity. *DVD*

Molly Ringwald *Samantha* • Justin Henry *Mike Baker* • Michael Schoeffling *Jake* • Haviland Morris *Caroline* • Gedde Watanabe *Long Duk Dong* • Anthony Michael Hall *Ted, the geek* • John Cusack *Bryce* • Joan Cusack *First geek girl* ■ *Dir/Scr* John Hughes

16 Years of Alcohol ★★★ 18
Social drama 2003 · UK · Colour · 100min

Richard Jobson's debut feature draws inspiration from both a semi-autobiographical novel and *A Clockwork Orange*. Kevin McKidd and his little gang of sociopaths even cress like the droogs in Kubrick's film. McKidd has grown up in a world where life revolves largely around the pub and drinking. As a youth he develops problems not just with alcohol but also with violence, and attempts to change his ways after meeting art student Susan Lynch. Jobson's film teeters on pretentiousness at times, but is rescued by a towering performance from McKidd and a surprisingly assured visual style. **BP** Swearing. *DVD*

Kevin McKidd *Frankie Mac* • Laura Fraser *Helen* • Susan Lynch *Mary* • Stuart Sinclair Blyth *Miller* • Jim Carter *Director* • Ewen Bremner *Jake* ■ *Dir* Richard Jobson • *Scr* Richard Jobson, from his novel

The 6th Day ★★★★ 15
Science-fiction action thriller 2000 · US/Can · Colour · 118min

Director Roger Spottiswoode's futuristic thriller is fast-paced fare, and provides another satisfying slice of science-fiction action for star Arnold Schwarzenegger. When ex-fighter pilot Schwarzenegger discovers he has been illegally cloned, he embarks on a turbo-charged mission to get his identity back and expose the corrupt organisation behind the experiment. Even if the plot doesn't bear close scrutiny, the movie packs some surprise twists and builds to a chilling climax. **AJ** Violence, swearing, brief nudity. *DVD* *Blu*

Arnold Schwarzenegger *Adam Gibson* • Michael Rapaport *Hank Morgan* • Tony Goldwyn *Michael Drucker* • Michael Rooker *Robert Marshall* • Sarah Wynter *Talia Elsworth* • Rod Rowland [Rodney Rowland] *Wiley* • Terry Crews *Vincent* • Ken Pogue *Speaker Day* • Colin Cunningham *Tripp* • Robert Duvall *Dr Griffin Weir* ■ *Dir* Roger Spottiswoode • *Scr* Cormac Wibberley, Marianne Wibberley

Sixth Happiness ★★★ 12
Biographical drama 1997 · UK · Colour · 94min

Firdaus Kanga not only wrote the screenplay for this moving drama from his autobiographical novel, but he also turns in a riveting performance in this extraordinary account of what it's like being gay, Parsee and disabled in 1970s Bombay. With the endless bounty of suicides, betrayals and doomed relationships going on around him, it almost seems as though being born with osteoporosis is the least of Kanga's problems. The film suffers slightly from the fussy direction, but remains a brave attempt to convey courage. **DP** Nudity. *DVD*

Firdaus Kanga *Brit Kotwal* • Souad Faress *Sera Kotwal* • Khodus Wadia *Sam Kotwal* • Nina Wadia *Dolly Kotwal* • Ahsen Bhatti *Cyrus* ■ *Dir* Waris Hussein • *Scr* Firdaus Kanga, from his autobiography *Trying to Grow*

The 6th Man ★★ 12
Supernatural sports comedy 1997 · US · Colour · 103min

Judging from its first half-hour, this could be a touching drama about two brothers with hoop dreams. When the older brother dies, the younger one is lost without him. Lost, that is, until older bro shows up as a ghost with a wacky sense of humour and a drive to win the college basketball championships. Unless you're a huge fan of poltergeist comedy or basketball, this Marlon Wayans vehicle probably won't score too many points. **ST** Swearing. *DVD*

Marlon Wayans *Kenny Tyler* • Kadeem Hardison *Antoine Tyler* • David Paymer *Coach Pederson* • Michael Michele *RC St John* • Kevin Dunn *Mikulski* ■ *Dir* Randall Miller • *Scr* Christopher Reed, Cynthia Carle

The Sixth Sense ★★★★★ 15
Supernatural drama 1999 · US · Colour · 102min

M Night Shyamalan has fashioned a modern classic here, a chilly, intelligent, emotional ghost story that relies not on gore and knifeplay for its many shocks but on glimpses of an afterlife that's anything but angels and harps. Bruce Willis is it quiet and reflective as the child psychologist attempting to get inside the head of Haley Joel Osment, who sees dead people. Toni Collette is equally convincing as the boy's troubled mum and, though the film's initial impact hinged on chatter about its knockout twist ending, in truth it's the controlled pace of the direction and the simplicity of the storytelling that make it so watchable. **AC** Violence, swearing. *DVD* *Blu*

Bruce Willis *Malcolm Crowe* • Haley Joel Osment *Cole Sear* • Toni Collette *Lynn Sear* • Olivia Williams *Anna Crowe* • Donnie Wahlberg *Vincent Gray* • Glenn Fitzgerald *Sean* • Mischa Barton *Kyra Collins* • Trevor Morgan *Tommy Tammisimo* • M Night Shyamalan *Doctor Hill* ■ *Dir/Scr* M Night Shyamalan

Sixty Glorious Years ★★★ U
Historical drama 1938 · UK · Colour · 91min

Following the success of *Victoria the Great* starring his wife Anna Neagle, producer/director Herbert Wilcox continued the saga up to and including Victoria's death. Peopled with a cast of dignified upper-crust actors such as C Aubrey Smith and Felix Aylmer, the film has Neagle presiding regally, and sometimes touchingly, over events personal, political and public – among them her wedding to Albert (Anton Walbrook), the opening of the Great Exhibition, Albert's death and the Diamond Jubilee. **RK**

Anna Neagle *Queen Victoria* • Anton Walbrook *Prince Albert* • C Aubrey Smith *Duke of Wellington* • Walter Rilla *Prince Ernst* • Charles Carson *Sir Robert Peel* • Felix Aylmer *Lord Palmerston* ■ *Dir* Herbert Wilcox • *Scr* Charles de Grandcourt, Miles Malleson, Robert Vansittart

61* ★★★
Sports drama based on a true story 2001 · US · Colour · 129min

Billy Crystal's passion for baseball informs every frame of this sporting biopic, which recalls the summer of 1961 when New York Yankees team-mates Mickey Mantle and Roger Maris went head to head to break Babe Ruth's home run record. With Haskell Wexler's crisp photography helping him avoid overt nostalgia and Hank Steinberg's teleplay providing him with a rousing, intelligent drama, Crystal adroitly combines diamond action with character study. **DP**

Thomas Jane *Mickey Mantle* • Barry Pepper *Roger Maris* • Anthony Michael Hall *Whitey Ford* • Richard Masur *Milt Kahn* • Bruce McGill *Ralph Houk* ■ *Dir* Billy Crystal • *Scr* Hank Steinberg

Sixty Six ★★★ 12
Period coming-of-age comedy drama 2006 · UK · Colour · 89min

It's 1966 and England is hosting the World Cup finals. It's also the year that 12-year-old Bernie celebrates his bar mitzvah. But guess what? The final match and Bernie's big celebration both fall on the same day. And, as England's hopes of taking the trophy rise, so the scale of Bernie's bar mitzvah falls. Gregg Sulkin makes a likeable lead as Bernie and Eddie Marsan gives a solid performance as his dad, but the real revelation in this engaging coming-of-age comedy is Helena Bonham Carter, who's nicely cast as an ordinary wife and mother. **DA** *DVD*

Eddie Marsan *Manny Reuben* • Helena Bonham Carter *Esther Reuben* • Stephen Rea *Dr Barrie* • Catherine Tate *Aunty Lila* • Peter Serafinowicz *Uncle Jimmy* • Gregg Sulkin *Bernie Reuben* • Ben Newton *Alvie Reuben* ■ *Dir* Paul Weiland • *Scr* Bridget O'Connor, Peter Straughan

Sizzle Beach, USA ★ 18
Sex comedy 1974 · US · Colour · 83min

The history of this creaky soft-core sexploitation movie is of far more interest than the story it tries to tell. The film details the sexual adventures of a trio of girls who share a Malibu beach house. One of their conquests is Kevin Costner (making his screen debut). Years later this appearance returned to haunt him when the schlock horror film company Troma acquired the rights and cheekily touted it round the Cannes film festival as Costner's latest flick. **DF** *DVD*

Terry Congie *Janice* • Leslie Brander *Sheryl* • Roselyn Royce *Dit* • Kevin Costner *John Logan, horse trainer* ■ *Dir* Richard Brander • *Scr* Craig Kusaba

Skateland ★★ 12
Drama 2010 · US · Colour · 96min

A Texan teenager finds himself at a crossroads in his life in this coming-of-age tale set during the early 1980s. Shiloh Fernandez plays Ritchie Wheeler, a talented writer wasting his life away at the local roller disco, whose family and friendships begin to fall apart over the course of an eventful summer. Although the film is dedicated to that master of teen angst John Hughes, this lacks the youthful verve of his iconic 1980s oeuvre, and is often as sluggish as the long, hot days it presents. **JH** Violence, swearing, drug abuse.

Shiloh Fernandez *Ritchie Wheeler* • Ashley Greene *Michelle Burkham* • Heath Freeman *Brent Burkham* • Brett Cullen *David Wheeler* • Melinda McGraw *Debbie Wheeler* ■ *Dir* Anthony Burns • *Scr* Anthony Burns, Brandon Freeman, Heath Freeman

Skatetown, USA ★★
Comedy 1979 · US · Colour · 98min

The first to hop on the minor roller-disco bandwagon that pulled up at the fag end of the 1970s, this brainless little comedy has good guy Greg Bradford in a roller-skating dance duel with bullying nasty Patrick Swayze. A period curiosity at best, it features not only Patrick Swayze's movie debut but also a roll call of fading American TV stars. Further down the cast list is

Playboy playmate Dorothy Stratten, who appeared in a tiny handful of films before her murder in 1980. FL

Scott Baio *Richie* • Flip Wilson *Harvey Ross* • Ron Palillo *Frankey* • Ruth Buzzi *Elvira* • Greg Bradford *Stan* • Patrick Swayze *Ace* • Dorothy Stratten *Girl who orders pizza* ■ *Dir* William A Levey • *Scr* Nick Castle

The Skeleton Key ★★★ 15
Supernatural thriller 2005 · US · Colour · 99min

A decrepit Louisiana mansion holds terrifying secrets in this flimsy yet effective slice of southern gothic horror. Kate Hudson plays a live-in nurse who's hired by elderly Gena Rowlands to look after her ailing husband (an under-used John Hurt). But after discovering a hidden attic room crammed with hoodoo paraphernalia, the inquisitive carer soon realises that all is not what it seems in the foreboding house. It's weakly plotted, but atmospheric, with good performances and a dark and exciting finale. SF *DVD* *BL*

Kate Hudson *Caroline* • Gena Rowlands *Violet* • John Hurt *Ben* • Peter Sarsgaard *Luke* • Joy Bryant *Jill* ■ *Dir* Iain Softley • *Scr* Ehren Kruger

The Skeleton Twins ★★★★ 15
Drama 2014 · US · Colour · 88min

While the presence of comedic actors Kristen Wiig and Bill Hader suggests a light-hearted gag-fest, *The Skeleton Twins* is best described as a bittersweet dramedy. There are plenty of laughs throughout, but the tone is melancholy and the film goes to some dark places as estranged siblings are reunited after the latter's failed suicide attempt and the two of them struggle to repair their fractured relationship. Both Wiig and Hader provide highly impressive dramatic performances, while Luke Wilson is consistently amusing as Wiig's relentlessly positive husband. SC Swearing, sexual references, drug abuse. *DVD* *BL* *CS*

Bill Hader *Milo Dean* • Kristen Wiig *Maggie Dean* • Luke Wilson *Lance* • Ty Burrell *Rich* • Boyd Holbrook *Billy* • Joanna Gleason *Judy* ■ *Dir* Craig Johnson • *Scr* Mark Heyman, Craig Johnson • *Cinematographer* Reed Morano

Skeletons ★★★ 15
Thriller 1996 · US · Colour · 86min

After a heart attack, journalist Ron Silver and his family move out to the country for a year of rest and relaxation, and are welcomed by the surprisingly friendly small-town residents, but when Silver starts investigating the case surrounding a local resident accused of murder, the town's mood turns ugly. The big revelation at the end, while a little unlikely, is still reasonably believable, and much of the credit for the movie's success goes to the cast for their excellent performances. KB Violence, swearing. *DVD*

Ron Silver *Peter Crane* • Christopher Plummer *Reverend Carlyle* • Dee Wallace Stone *Heather Crane* • Kyle Howard *Zach Crane* • James Coburn *Frank Jove* • Arlene Golonka *Melanie Jove* ■ *Dir* David DeCoteau • *Scr* Joshua Michael Stern

Skeletons ★★ 15
Comedy 2010 · UK · Colour · 93min

This micro-budget fantasy comedy drama imagines the literal removal of personal skeletons from your closet. Ed Gaughan and Andrew Buckley play the oddballs who don goggles, point their sensors at a wardrobe and pull past misdemeanours into the open. (Or something to that effect, the film leaves much to the imagination.) Sadly, we're too often left to contemplate the film's oddity instead of its emotional conflicts and, while ambitious, it doesn't quite come off. TJ Swearing. *DVD*

Ed Gaughan *Davis* • Andrew Buckley *Bennett* • Jason Isaacs *The Colonel* • Paprika Steen *Jane* • Tuppence Middleton *Rebecca* • Josef Whitfield *Jo-Jo* ■ *Dir/Scr* Nick Whitfield

Sket ★★ 15
Crime drama 2011 · UK · Colour · 79min

British boy gang films are two a penny. British girl gang films, like this, are much, much rarer. Made in collaboration with a South London charity that supports young women affected by gang culture, *Sket* tells a gritty tale of violence and vengeance among rival girl gangs and their criminal cohorts on a London housing estate. The plot doesn't amount to much, and a big finale is fluffed. But there's an authenticity about the dialogue that also extends to the acting. That's except for an underwhelming performance from, ironically, the film's only "name", Ashley Walters (*Bullet Boy*), as a viciously crooked and manipulative club owner. This film definitely belongs to the girls and, despite its faults, is a fairly involving drama. DA *DVD* *BL*

Lily Loveless *Hannah* • Riann Steele *Shaks* • Aimee Kelly *Kayla* • Emma Hartley-Miller *Danielle* • Adelayo Adedayo *Kerry* • Ashley Walters *Trey* ■ *Dir/Scr* Nirpal Bhogal

Sketches of Frank Gehry ★★★ 12
Documentary 2006 · US/Ger · Colour · 83min

Architect Frank Gehry is best known for the Guggenheim Museum in Bilbao and the Walt Disney Concert Hall in Los Angeles. But for much of his career he specialised in private residences and functional public spaces. In his first documentary, Gehry's long-time friend Sydney Pollack seeks to understand this transformation and the role played in it by therapist Milton Wexler, who persuaded Gehry to divorce his first wife and trust his artistic instincts. There's a pleasing intimacy to the interviews, with the insights into Gehry's working methods being particularly revealing. But the gushings of famous faces like Dennis Hopper, Bob Geldof and Julian Schnabel turn this into something of a eulogy. DP Brief swearing. *DVD*

Frank Gehry • Michael Ovitz • Dennis Hopper • Bob Geldof • Julian Schnabel • Michael Eisner ■ *Dir* Sydney Pollack • *Cinematographers* George Tiffin, Claudio Rocha, Marcus Birsel

Ski Party ★★ U
Musical comedy 1965 · US · Colour · 79min

This amiable, if vastly inferior take on *Some Like it Hot*, is set in a ski resort where college chums Frankie Avalon and Dwayne Hickman do what any red-blooded American males would do on discovering their girlfriends fancy another man – dress up in drag. Predictably, the cross-dressed students then become the focus for male interest. James Brown performs his classic *I Got You (I Feel Good)*, probably the best thing here. JG

Frankie Avalon *Todd Armstrong/Jane* • Dwayne Hickman *Craig Gamble/Nora* • Deborah Walley *Linda Hughes* • Yvonne Craig *Barbara Norris* • Robert Q Lewis *Donald Pevney* • Bobbi Shaw *Nita* • Lesley Gore • Annette Funicello ■ *Dir* Alan Rafkin • *Scr* Robert Kaufman

Skidoo ★
Comedy 1968 · US · Colour · 97min

A rack of top-line comedy stars, not to mention a good score by Harry Nilsson, is wasted in this bizarre and unfunny satire. Reformed gangster Jackie Gleason is bullied out of retirement by gang boss "God" (Groucho Marx, in his final picture) for an unwanted job: to get sent to jail, murder Mickey Rooney, then escape. But within those walls he discovers the alleged joys of LSD. Among the most misguided movies ever made. JG

Jackie Gleason *Tony Banks* • Carol Channing *Flo Banks* • Frankie Avalon *Angie* • Fred Clark *Tower Guard* • Michael Constantine *Leech* • Frank Gorshin *Man* • John Phillip Law *Stash* • Peter Lawford *Senator* • Burgess Meredith *Warden* • George Raft *Captain Garbaldo* • Mickey Rooney *"Blue Chips" Packard* • Groucho Marx *"God"* ■ *Dir* Otto Preminger • *Scr* Doran William Cannon, Elliott Baker (uncredited), Stanley Ralph Ross (uncredited), from a story by Erik Kirkland

Skin ★★★ 12
Biographical drama 2008 · UK/S Afr/Cay · Colour · 102min

Based on a true story, this charts the almost unthinkably dramatic life of Sandra Laing (Sophie Okonedo), a dark-skinned girl born to white parents in apartheid South Africa. Not considered "different" until she is abused at a whites-only girls' school, her staunch father Abraham Laing (Sam Neill) goes to court to prove his daughter's white heritage in the days before DNA testing. Neill and Alice Krige as Laing's mother turn in solid performances, but it is Okonedo's calm, careful work that wrings emotion from the quietly told tale, giving dignity to Sandra's sensational life story. KK Violence, some swearing *DVD*

Sophie Okonedo *Sandra Laing* • Sam Neill *Abraham Laing* • Alice Krige *Sannie Laing* • Tony Kgoroge *Petrus Zwane* • Ella Ramangwane *Young Sandra* ■ *Dir* Anthony Fabian • *Scr* Helen Crawley, Jessie Keyt, Helena Kriel, from a screen story by Anthony Fabian

Skin Deep ★ 18
Comedy 1989 · US · Colour · 96min

This is a deeply unappealing sex comedy from Blake Edwards. John Ritter is the womaniser attempting to win back his ex-wife but finding old habits die hard. The fact that its most memorable gag involves fluorescent condoms is an indication of the level of the humour. As infantile as his *Pink Panther* movies but not nearly as funny. JF Swearing.

John Ritter *Zach Hutton* • Vincent Gardenia *Barney* • Alyson Reed *Alex Hutton* • Joel Brooks *Jake* • Chelsea Field *Amy* • Peter Donat *Sparky* • Don Gordon *Curt* ■ *Dir/Scr* Blake Edwards

The Skin Game ★★
Drama 1931 · UK · BW · 88min

Alfred Hitchcock enjoyed the challenge of the seemingly theatrical confines of restricted space, creating works of extraordinary fluidity. But the actual theatre pieces which dominated his early British career defeated even his genius and this adaptation of Galsworthy's London success is inevitably dated. It concerns a wealthy family, the Hillcrests, dominated by the aristocratic mother (Helen Haye in the film's best performance) which is at loggerheads with a neighbouring builder who wants to replace farms with factories. BB

Phyllis Konstam *Chloe Hornblower* • Edmund Gwenn *Mr Hornblower* • John Longden *Charles Hornblower* • Frank Lawton *Rolf Hornblower* • CV France *Mr Hillcrest* • Jill Esmond *Jill Hillcrest* • Edward Chapman *Dawker* • Helen Haye *Mrs Hillcrest* ■ *Dir* Alfred Hitchcock • *Scr* Alfred Hitchcock, Alma Reville, from the play by John Galsworthy

Skin Game ★★★ PG
Comedy western 1971 · US · Colour · 97min

This enjoyable comedy western teams James Garner and Lou Gossett as conmen in the years before the Civil War. Their scam is an ingenious and contentious one: Garner poses as a slave trader who sells Gossett for big bucks, only for Gossett to escape and rejoin Garner at the next town where someone else is cheated. Garner trades heavily on his *Maverick* persona, Gossett skilfully transforms himself from a free man to a "Stepin Fetchit" menial, and Ed Asner impresses as a slave dealer. AT

James Garner *Quincy* • Lou Gossett [Louis Gossett Jr] *Jason* • Susan Clark *Ginger* • Brenda Sykes *Naomi* • Edward Asner *Plunkett* • Andrew Duggan *Calloway* • Henry Jones *Sam* ■ *Dir* Paul Bogart • *Scr* Pierre Marton [Peter Stone]

The Skin I Live In ★★★★ 15
Drama 2011 · Sp · Colour · 115min

Spanish maestro Pedro Almodóvar offers his own distinctive take on "mad doctor" horror flicks with this story that follows obsessive scientist Antonio Banderas's illicit efforts to perfect synthetic human skin. Behind closed doors in his exquisite country house, the sultry Elena Anaya remains a prisoner clad in a mysterious all-over body suit. Euro-horror aficionados will trace echoes of Georges Franju's surreal shocker *Eyes without a Face* as events unfold, but what's remarkable is how Almodóvar turns the seemingly familiar material to his own ends, as his twisted plot continues to engross and surprise. TJ Spanish +subtitles. Violence, swearing, sex scenes, nudity. *DVD* *BL*

Antonio Banderas *Robert Ledgard* • Elena Anaya *Vera* • Marisa Paredes *Marilia* • Jan Cornet *Vicente* • Blanca Suárez *Norma* • Roberto Alamo *Zeca* ■ *Dir* Pedro Almodóvar • *Scr* Pedro Almodóvar, from the novel *Tarantula* by Thierry Jonquet

Skin of Man, Heart of Beast ★★★
Drama 1999 · Fr · Colour · 96min

An atmosphere of latent violence pervades this uncompromising study of domestic disaffection. Set in southern France, the small-town scenario centres on the tensions between returning prodigal Bernard Blancan, his wastrel younger brother Pascal Cervo and older sibling Serge Riaboukine, a short-fused cop on a break from his duties. But what makes Hélène Angel's debut feature so unpredictable – and occasionally melodramatic – is that Angel views events through the eyes of Riaboukine's alienated adolescent daughter, Virginie Guinand, and her trusting little sister, Cathy Hinderchied. DP French +subtitles. Violence, swearing.

Serge Riaboukine *Francky Pujol* • Bernard Blancan *Coco Pujol* • Maaike Jansen *Marthe* • Pascal Cervo *Alex Pujol* • Jean-Louis Richard *Tac Tac* • Guilaine Londez *Annie* • Cathy Hinderchied *Aurélie Pujol* • Virginie Guinand *Christelle Pujol* ■ *Dir* Hélène Angel • *Scr* Hélène Angel, Agnes de Sacy, Jean-Claude Janer

Skinwalkers ★★ 15
Action horror 2006 · Can/Ger/US · Colour · 88min

There's absolutely no bite in *Jason X* director Jim Isaac's slimly plotted and extremely underwhelming tale of two warring werewolf packs and a boy who holds their future in his hands. A bland and virtually bloodless bore, it revolves around Rhona Mitra and her almost 13-year-old son being protected from their evil counterparts who want the boy dead. What little teeth-and-claw action there is, is so badly lit that you can't see it properly anyway – probably a blessing, given how poor the effects and creature make-up actually are. SF Violence, nudity. *DVD*

Jason Behr *Varek* • Elias Koteas *Jonas* • Rhona Mitra *Rachel* • Kim Coates *Zo* ■ *Dir* James Isaac • *Scr* James DeMonaco, James Roday, Todd Harthan

Skippy ★★★ U
Comedy drama 1931 · US · BW · 85min

Drawing its idea from a comic strip, this wholesome, successful entertainment for all the family recounts the tale of how two youngsters (Jackie Cooper, Robert Coogan) set about earning enough money to buy their mutt back from the neighbourhood dog-catcher. Co-written by Joseph L Mankiewicz and Norman Z McLeod, this simple little movie garnered Oscar nominations for story, script and Cooper, and won Taurog the director's statuette. RK

Jackie Cooper *Skippy Skinner* • Robert Coogan *Sooky* • Mitzi Green *Eloise* • Jackie Searl [Jackie Searle] *Sidney* • Willard Robertson *Dr Herbert Skinner* • Enid Bennett *Mrs Ellen Skinner* • David Haines *Harley Nubbins* • Helen Jerome Eddy *Mrs Wayne* ■ *Dir* Norman Taurog • *Scr* Joseph L Mankiewicz, Norman McLeod [Norman Z McLeod], Don Marquis, Sam Mintz, from the comic strip and novel by Percy Crosby

Skirts Ahoy! ★★★ U
Musical 1952 · US · Colour · 109min

It's three girls rather than boys in the navy for a change in this musical which puts Esther Williams, Vivian Blaine and Joan Evans into uniform . Evans is not really happy with song and dance (she replaced Sally Forrest, reputedly because Forrest's hair colour was too similar to Williams) and Blaine, fresh from her Broadway triumph in *Guys and Dolls*, is not given enough opportunity, but the film is pleasant escapist fare. TV

Esther Williams *Whitney Young* • Joan Evans *Mary Kate Yarbrough* • Vivian Blaine *Una Yancy* • Barry Sullivan *Lt Cmdr Paul Elcott* • Keefe

Brasselle *Dick Halson* • Billy Eckstine • Dean Miller *Archie O'Conovan* • Debbie Reynolds • Bobby Van ■ *Dir* Sidney Lanfield • *Scr* Isobel Lennart

Skokie ★★★★ PG
Drama based on a true story
1981 · US · Colour · 120min

Head and shoulders above the majority of fact-based television dramas, this award-winning reconstruction of the stand-off between the citizens of Skokie, Illinois, and a gang of militant neo-Nazis is a sobering reminder that anti-Semitism did not end with the defeat of Hitler. In his only TV movie, Danny Kaye gives a genuinely moving performance as the Holocaust survivor refusing to be intimidated by the bully boys. But then everyone in this stellar cast is totally credible, including acting guru Lee Strasberg in what proved to be his last role. DP **DVD**

Danny Kaye *Max Feldman* • John Rubinstein *Herb Lewisohn* • Carl Reiner *Abbot Rosen* • Kim Hunter *Bertha Feldman* • Eli Wallach *Bert Silverman* • Lee Strasberg *Morton Weisman* • Brian Dennehy *Chief Arthur Buchanan* • George Dzundza *Frank Callin* ■ *Dir* Herbert Wise • *Scr* Ernest Kinoy

The Skull ★★ 12
Horror
1965 · UK · Colour · 82min

Horror stars Peter Cushing and Christopher Lee are strongly cast in Freddie Francis's disappointing adaptation of Robert Bloch's story about the strange properties of the Marquis de Sade's skull. There are some good moments and impressive special effects, though, while Francis's direction has panache. AJ **DVD**

Peter Cushing *Professor Christopher Maitland* • Patrick Wymark *Marco* • Christopher Lee *Sir Matthew Phillips* • Jill Bennett *Jane Maitland* • Nigel Green *Inspector Wilson* • Michael Gough *Auctioneer* • George Coulouris *Dr Londe* • Patrick Magee *Police doctor* ■ *Dir* Freddie Francis • *Scr* Milton Subotsky, from the story *The Skull of the Marquis de Sade* by Robert Bloch

Skullduggery ★★
Adventure
1969 · US · Colour · 105min

Burt Reynolds managed to rise above unworthy material with a good-natured charm and skill in the early days of his film career, and this weak adventure is a good example of that ability. Reynolds plays an adventurer who accompanies archaeologist Susan Clark to New Guinea. There they discover a tribe that could be a clue to human evolution, but evil scientist Paul Hubschmid forces them to take their find to the courts. TH

Burt Reynolds *Doug Temple* • Susan Clark *Dr Sybil Greame* • Roger C Carmel *Otto Kreps* • Paul Hubschmid *Vancruysen* • Chips Rafferty *Father "Pop" Dillingham* • Alexander Knox *Buffington* • Pat Suzuki *Topazia* • Edward Fox *Bruce Spofford* • Wilfrid Hyde White *Eaton* ■ *Dir* Gordon Douglas, Richard Wilson (1) • *Scr* Nelson Gidding, from the novel *Les Animaux Denaturés (You Shall Know Them)* by Vercours [Jean Marcel Brewer]

The Skulls ★★★ 15
Thriller
2000 · US · Colour · 102min

Joshua Jackson stars in this preposterous but entertaining thriller about a college secret society called the Skulls, which counts politicians and rich businessmen among its alumni and offers them flash benefits. Jackson plays a non-wealthy student who is given the opportunity to join. Shortly after his initiation his best friend (who's been investigating the group) suspiciously commits suicide, leaving Jackson to choose between his jet set pals or Doing The Right Thing. An initially tense set-up gets increasingly daft, but Jackson holds your interest. Two sequels followed. JB **DVD**

Joshua Jackson *Luke McNamara* • Paul Walker *Caleb Mandrake* • Hill Harper *Will Beckford* • Leslie Bibb *Chloe* • Christopher McDonald *Martin Lombard* • Steve Harris *Detective Sparrow* • William Petersen [William L Petersen] *Senator Ames Levitt* • Craig T Nelson *Litten Mandrake* ■ *Dir* Rob Cohen • *Scr* John Pogue

The Sky above, the Mud below ★★★
Documentary
1960 · Bel/Fr/Neth · Colour · 90min

Considering it only had the official Rome Olympics film as competition, it was no surprise that Pierre-Dominique Gaisseau's ethnographical exercise won the feature documentary Oscar. Although it could now be accused of patronising its subjects, this study of life in Dutch New Guinea, as seen during a seven-month Franco-Dutch expedition, at least provides a valuable record of tribal customs - cannibalism, headhunting and so on - and the region's flora and fauna. A version with English-language narration also exists. DP In French.

William Peacock *Narrator* ■ *Dir/Scr* Pierre-Dominique Gaisseau • *Cinematographer* Gilbert Sarthre

Sky Captain and the World of Tomorrow ★★★ PG
Science-fiction action adventure
2004 · US/UK/It · Colour · 102min

Writer/director Kerry Conran uses the latest digital technology to create a hymn to the heroes of cliffhanger serials. In some curiously imprecise era, people work in skyscrapers, ride in airships, and only one man can save the world when leading scientists start disappearing and cities are attacked by enormous robots - Jude Law, aka Sky Captain, accompanied by erstwhile girlfriend and ace reporter Gwyneth Paltrow. What is most impressive is the way in which Conran has created the future as it was perceived back in the 1930s. However, despite being breathtakingly clever, this lacks warmth and charm. BP **DVD**

Jude Law *Joe "Sky Captain" Sullivan* • Gwyneth Paltrow *Polly Perkins* • Angelina Jolie *Franky Cook* • Giovanni Ribisi *Dex* • Michael Gambon *Editor Morris Paley* • Bai Ling *Mysterious Woman* • Omid Djalili *Kaji* ■ *Dir/Scr* Kerry Conran

Sky High ★★★★ PG
Fantasy comedy adventure
2005 · US · Colour · 95min

This futuristic high-school romp gives the trials and tribulations of adolescence a playful comic book-style spin. Michael Angarano stars as the son of revered superheroes Kurt Russell and Kelly Preston, who's sent off to the literally Sky High secret academy to hone his powers. But what his parents don't realise is that his special skills haven't yet emerged, which leads to him being bullied when he's downgraded to "sidekick" status. Boisterously entertaining, with some inspired casting. SF **DVD**

Kurt Russell *Steve Stronghold/The Commander* • Kelly Preston *Josie Stronghold/Jetstream* • Michael Angarano *Will Stronghold* • Danielle Panabaker *Layla* • Kevin Heffernan *Ron Wilson* • Lynda Carter *Principal Powers* • Bruce Campbell *Coach Boomer* • Clor s Leachman *Nurse Spex* ■ *Dir* Mike Mitchell • *Scr* Paul Hernandez, Bob Schooley [Robert Schooley], Mark McCorkle

Sky Murder ★
Second World War detective drama
1940 · US · BW · 72min

Nick Carter, one of the 20th century's earliest pulp fiction detectives and the focus of some early French silent movies, finally made it to the American screen in 1939 with *Nick Carter, Master Detective*. However, only two more movies followed before the series died and this last instalment explains why. The plot concerns killer spies and a millionaire, but the action quotient is almost nil. RK

Walter Pidgeon *Nick Carter* • Donald Meek *Bartholomew* • Karen Verne [Kaaren Verne] *Pat Evens* • Edward Ashley *Cortland Grand* • Joyce Compton *Christina Cross* • Tom Conway *Andrew Hendon* • George Lessey *Senator Monroe* • Dorothy Tree *Kathe* ■ *Dir* George B Seitz • *Scr* William R Lipman

Sky Pirates ★★ PG
Science-fiction adventure
1986 · Aus · Colour · 83min

John Hargreaves does his best as the pilot flying into a time warp in this Australian attempt to recapture the excitement and adventure of the old Saturday morning serials. The secret of remaking old B-movies for modern audiences is to apply A-movie polish and production values, but this effort struggles to rise above C-movie standards. PF

John Hargreaves *Flight Lieutenant Harris* • Meredith Phillips *Melanie Mitchell* • Max Phipps *Squadron Leader Savage* • Bill Hunter *O'Reilly* • Simon Chilvers *Reverend Kenneth Mitchell* • Alex Scott (2) *General Hackett* ■ *Dir* Colin Eggleston • *Scr* John Lamond

Sky West and Crooked ★★★
Romantic drama
1965 · UK · Colour · 105min

John Mills's sole assignment behind the camera is something of a family affair: it was co-scripted by his novelist wife, Mary Hayley Bell, and stars their daughter Hayley Mills. Intended to help Hayley distance herself from her kiddie roles at Disney, the film is a variation on DH Lawrence's *The Virgin and the Gypsy*, with Hayley's slightly touched teen falling for romantic Romany Ian McShane. It's all somewhat melodramatic, but Mills Sr directs with a steady hand. DP

Hayley Mills *Brydie White* • Ian McShane *Roibin* • Laurence Naismith *Edwin Dacres* • Geoffrey Bayldon *Reverend Philip Moss* • Annette Crosbie *Mrs White* • Norman Bird *Cheeseman* ■ *Dir* John Mills • *Scr* Mary Hayley Bell, John Prebble, from a story by Mary Hayley Bell

Skyfall ★★★★★ 12
Spy adventure
2012 · US/UK · Colour · 137min

Daniel Craig begins his third 007 outing all washed-up, having been left for dead after a mission backfires. When national security is compromised, it's a battered and booze-soaked Bond that reports back for duty, casting serious doubts on his fitness for the job. *American Beauty* director Sam Mendes ably delivers on the thrills, but perhaps the biggest stunt he pulls off is creating a convincing human drama - centred on the complex relationship between Judi Dench's M and Bond - to ground the all-important action. It's Javier Bardem as the campy, (almost too) Hannibal Lecter-like villain, who gets all the best lines, though. The sheer class of the production is also felt in Roger Deakins's polished cinematography, Adele's emotionally charged theme song and a beautifully judged appearance by that ultimate Bond accessory, the original Aston Martin DB5. JH Violence, swearing. **DVD** **Blu-ray**

Daniel Craig *James Bond* • Judi Dench *M* • Javier Bardem *Silva* • Ralph Fiennes *Gareth Mallory* • Naomie Harris *Eve* • Bérénice Lim Marlohe [Bérénice Marlohe] *Severine* • Ben Whishaw *Q* • Albert Finney *Kincade* • Helen McCrory *Clair Dowar* ■ *Dir* Sam Mendes • *Scr* Neal Purvis, Robert Wade, John Logan, from characters by Ian Fleming [uncredited] • *Cinematographer* Roger Deakins • *Music* Thomas Newman • *Editor* Stuart Baird

Skyjacked ★★★ PG
Disaster movie
1972 · US · Colour · 96min

Before he made the mother of all disaster movies, *The Towering Inferno*, John Guillermin worked out with this aerial jeopardy epic which cashed in on the rash of terrorist hijackings as well as the box-office success of *Airport*. Charlton Heston is the stoical pilot, Yvette Mimieux the plucky stewardess, and James Brolin the unhinged hijacker who orders Heston to head for Moscow. Passengers either stay calm or go bonkers, the Russians launch their jet fighters and Heston worries about running out of gas. AT

Charlton Heston *Captain O'Hara* • Yvette Mimieux *Angela Thacher* • James Brolin *Jerome K Weber* • Claude Akins *Sgt Ben Puzo* • Jeanne Crain *Mrs Shaw* • Susan Dey *Elly Brewster* • Roosevelt Grier [Rosey Grier] *Gary Brown* • Walter Pidgeon *Senator Arne Lindner* ■ *Dir* John Guillermin • *Scr* Stanley R Greenberg, from the novel *Hijacked* by David Harper

Skylark ★★
Comedy
1941 · US · BW · 94min

After five years of marriage to Ray Milland, Claudette Colbert is fed up with her wifely role as second fiddle to her husband's career. When charming Brian Aherne appears on the scene, he offers just the diversion she's seeking. This is a standard comedy of the period, played with style and given the Paramount studio gloss. Profiting from the attractive stars, it amuses but is nothing special. RK

Claudette Colbert *Lydia Kenyon* • Ray Milland *Tony Kenyon* • Brian Aherne *Jim Blake* • Binnie Barnes *Myrtle Vantine* • Walter Abel *George Gore* • Grant Mitchell *Frederick Vantine* ■ *Dir* Mark Sandrich • *Scr* Zion Myers, Allan Scott, from the play and novel by Samson Raphaelson

Skyline ★★★ 15
Science-fiction thriller
2010 · US · Colour · 88min

There isn't an original idea in the Brothers Strause's sci-fi thriller, but once the ace special effects and full-on monster mania take prominence over the soap opera plot, it does become weirdly fascinating. The action is set entirely in and around an LA penthouse after a boozy birthday party, from where the waking revellers witness the unfolding horror after alien craft descend on the city. There's explosive action and a touch of George Romero horror as events move towards a freaky belly-of-the-beast climax, by which time this peculiar hybrid has mutated into enjoyably bizarre high camp. AJ Violence. **DVD** **Blu-ray**

Eric Balfour *Jarrod* • Scottie Thompson *Elaine* • Brittany Daniel *Candice* • David Zayas *Oliver* • Donald Faison *Terry* • Crystal Reed *Denise* ■ *Dir* The Brothers Strause [Colin Strause], The Brothers Strause [Greg Strause] • *Scr* Joshua Cordes, Liam O'Donnell

Skyrunners ★★
Science-fiction adventure
2009 · US · Colour

A blend of high-school comedy and eco-friendly sci-fi fantasy, this bitty and unevenly paced Disney adventure isn't sure what it really wants to be. Aimed at tweens - and likely to appeal more to boys than girls - the TV movie sees Joey Pollari's wimpy 14-year-old develop superhuman powers after he and his older brother (Kelly Blatz) encounter an alien spaceship. But flimsy fun soon descends into lameness, when the siblings are caught up in an extraterrestrial invasion plan. A rushed climax leaves the audience seriously short-changed. SF

Joey Pollari *Tyler Burns* • Kelly Blatz *Nick Burns* • Conrad Coates *Agent Armstrong* • Jacqueline MacInnes Wood *Julie Gunn* ■ *Dir* Ralph Hemecker • *Scr* Richard C Okie

The Sky's the Limit ★★ U
Musical comedy
1943 · US · BW · 89min

The most forgettable - and largely forgotten - of Fred Astaire's musicals pairs him with Joan Leslie in a wafer-thin romance about a flying hero (Astaire) on leave in New York where, to escape adulation, he pretends to be an idle civilian. Leslie is the news photographer more interested in the war effort than his attempts to woo her. The movie yielded a couple of great songs, including *One for My Baby*, and the dance routines staged by the star aren't bad. RK **DVD**

Fred Astaire *Fred Atwell* • Joan Leslie *Joan Manion* • Robert Benchley *Phil Harriman* • Robert Ryan *Reginald Fenton* • Elizabeth Patterson *Mrs Fisher* • Eric Blore *Jasper* • Marjorie Gateson *Canteen lady* • Peter Lawford *Naval commander* ■ *Dir* Edward H Griffith • *Scr* Frank Fenton, Lynn Root, from their story *A Handful of Heaven*

Skyscraper Souls ★★★
Melodrama
1932 · US · BW · 80min

Working to the same formula as that year's major hit *Grand Hotel*, MGM came up with a New York skyscraper as the location for a group of characters whose personal dramas are interconnected by their location. At the centre of the action is Warren William as the owner of the building and a man as

S

uncompromising with women as he is in his ruthless business deals. The colourful Gregory Ratoff, later to become a leading director, and future scourge of the stars Hedda Hopper are among the supporting cast. Decent entertainment, despite a melodramatic climax. RK

Warren William *David Dwight* • Maureen O'Sullivan *Lynn Harding* • Gregory Ratoff *Vinmont* • Anita Page *Jenny LeGrande* • Verree Teasdale *Sarah Dennis* • Norman Foster *Tom* • Jean Hersholt *Jake Sorenson* • Hedda Hopper *Ella Dwight* ■ *Dir* Edgar Selwyn • *Scr* C Gardner Sullivan, Elmer Harris, from the novel *Skyscraper* by Faith Baldwin

The Slab Boys ★★★ 15
Drama 1997 · UK · Colour · 97min

John Byrne's love of 1950s rock 'n' roll shone through his superb TV series *Tutti Frutti* and it also forms a musical background to this flawed but quirkily entertaining drama. Based on two of Byrne's plays, it's a coming-of-age tale about three young lads employed in a carpet factory who dream of escape from their bleak working-class surroundings. Byrne draws out fine performances from a largely unknown cast and lovingly evokes the era. The superb soundtrack mixes Little Richard and Chuck Berry with Scottish contemporary artists Edwyn Collins and the Proclaimers. JF

Robin Laing *Phil McCann* • Russell Barr *George "Spanky" Farrell* • Bill Gardiner *Hector McKenzie* • Louise Berry *Lucille Bentley* • Julie Wilson Nimmo *Bernadette Rooney* • Duncan Ross *Alan Downie* • Tom Watson *Willie Curry* • Anna Massey *Miss Elsie Walkinshaw* ■ *Dir* John Byrne • *Scr* John Byrne, from his plays *The Slab Boys* and *Cuttin' a Rug*

Slacker ★★★★ 15
Cult comedy 1989 · US · Colour · 96min

Director Richard Linklater made his name with this offbeat, low-budget effort, whose title was taken up by the bored 20-somethings of 1990s America. There's no plot to speak of, with Linklater instead taking a rather hazy ramble through the lives of a large number of eccentrics living in Austin, Texas. It's an occasionally over-indulgent affair, but the natural performances and dizzying number of barmy conspiracy theories and philosophies win you over in the end. JF Swearing.
DVD

Richard Linklater *Should have stayed at the bus station* • Rudy Basquez *Taxi driver* • Jean Caffeine *Roadkill* • Jan Hockey *Jogger* • Stephan Hockey *Running late* • Mark James (1) *Hit-and-run son* ■ *Dir/Scr* Richard Linklater

Slackers ★★★ 15
Comedy 2001 · US · Colour · 83min

This agreeable campus comedy is given an injection of quirky humour by the brilliant Jason Schwartzman (*Rushmore*) who adds another eccentric nerd to his CV. He plays a creepy obsessive who uncovers evidence that three "slackers" – Devon Sawa, Michael Maronna and Jason Segel – have lied and cheated their way through the education system. To stop him blowing the whistle, Sawa agrees to set him up with brainy beauty Jaime King. This wants to have its *American Pie* and eat it, aiming to be both crudely offensive and sweetly soft-centred. JC Swearing, sex scenes. *DVD*

Devon Sawa *Dave* • Jason Schwartzman *Ethan* • Jaime King *Angela* • Jason Segel *Sam* • Michael Maronna *Jeff* • Mamie Van Doren *Mrs Van Graaf* • Leigh Taylor-Young *Valerie Patton* • Cameron Diaz ■ *Dir* Dewey Nicks • *Scr* David H Steinberg

Slackistan ★★★
Drama 2010 · Pak · Colour · 85min

Owing much to Richard Linklater's *Slacker*, director Hammad Khan's confident debut presents an Islamabad that bears little resemblance to the headline image of an embattled city. His depiction of a Pakistani capital scarcely preoccupied with Islam or the Taliban is as fascinating as his insights into a privileged, westernised generation of Islooites (the term for locals) that is barely aware of the poverty in the next neighbourhood, let alone the nation's

precarious position between two very different worlds. The pacing is somewhat languid, the script often ponderous and the performances are mixed, but this knowing drama is undoubtedly a laudable effort. DP

Shahbaz Shigri *Hasan* • Aisha Linnea Akhtar *Aisha* • Ali Rehman Khan *Sheryar* • Shahana Khan Khalil *Zara* • Osman Khalid Butt *Saad* ■ *Dir* Hammad Khan • *Scr* Hammad Khan, Shandana Ayub

Slade in Flame ★★★ PG
Musical drama 1974 · UK · Colour · 86min

The usual rags-to-riches-to-bitching rock 'n' roll saga is given a gritty, thoughtful and far more realistic patina by director Richard Loncraine. After forming the group Flame circa 1967 and having a monster hit, the band members suffer managerial manipulation and financial fraud before acrimoniously breaking up in this somber account of the downsides to the music industry. This is well written, well made and well performed by Slade and Tom Conti. AJ

Noddy Holder *Stoker* • Jim Lea *Paul* • Dave Hill *Barry* • Don Powell *Charlie* • Tom Conti *Seymour* ■ *Dir* Richard Loncraine • *Scr* Andrew Birkin

Slam ★★★ 15
Prison drama 1998 · US · Colour · 99min

This unusual film about the redemptive power of poetry has a small-time drug dealer discovering his true calling courtesy of an arts course he signs up for while in prison. Back on the outside, he becomes a leading light of Washington's black rap-poetry scene. Preachy but powerful, the film makes extensive use of hand-held cameras to give it a genuine feel of the real. Performances are in-your-face and convincing, but the subject matter won't appeal to all tastes. DA Swearing, a sex scene.

Saul Williams *Ray Joshua* • Bonz Malone *Hopha* • Sonja Sohn *Lauren Bell* • Beau Sia *Jimmy Huang* • Lawrence Wilson *Big Mike* • Andre Taylor *China* ■ *Dir* Marc Levin • *Scr* Marc Levin, Richard Stratton, Saul Williams, Sonja Sohn, Bonz Malone, from a story by Marc Levin, Richard Stratton

Slam Dance ★★★ 15
Thriller 1987 · US · Colour · 95min

Director Wayne Wang shows his versatility with this intriguing excursion into the thriller genre. Tom Hulce is the harassed cartoonist who finds himself suspected of murder after a brief liaison with Virginia Madsen. Wang cleverly uses the device of Hulce being hounded by both cops and the violent Don Opper to invoke a disturbing atmosphere of individual paranoia and general psychosis. There are many delicious surprises and red herrings are scattered around like confetti. SH Swearing.

Tom Hulce *CC Drood* • Mary Elizabeth Mastrantonio *Helen Drood* • Adam Ant *Jim Campbell* • Don Opper *Buddy* • John Doe *Gilbert* • Harry Dean Stanton *Detective Smiley* • Robert Beltran *Frank* • Virginia Madsen *Yolanda Caldwell* • Millie Perkins *Bobby Nye* ■ *Dir* Wayne Wang • *Scr* Don Opper

Slam Dunk Ernest ★ U
Comedy 1995 · US · Colour · 92min

The consistently unfunny Jim Varney returns as Ernest P Worrell in another edition in the film series about the madcap adventures of a trouble-prone simpleton. When the dumber than dumb Ernest comes into possession of a pair of magic basketball shoes, he and his work colleagues come up against the professionals of the game. Puerile humour is interspersed with the usual lashings of childish slapstick and sentimentality. JF

Jim Varney *Ernest P Worrell* • Kareem Abdul-Jabbar *Archangel* • Jay Brazeau *Mr Moloch* ■ *Dir* John Cherry [John R Cherry III] • *Scr* John R Cherry III, Daniel Butler

Slap Her, She's French! ★★ 12
Comedy 2001 · Ger/US/UK · Colour · 87min

A cultural exchange visit descends into a teen twist on *Single White Female* in this Texas-set comedy. And the movie's magpie nature doesn't end with that little lift, as director Melanie Mayron was clearly taking copious notes while watching *Legally Blonde* as well. Yet, despite its derivative nature, this still comes across as an entertaining farce thanks to Jane McGregor's vivacious turn as the shallow overachiever whose life is sabotaged by French gamine Piper Perabo. DP *DVD*

Piper Perabo *Genevieve LePlouff* • Jane McGregor *Starla Grady* • Trent Ford *Ed Mitchell* • Michael McKean *Monsieur Duke* • Julie White *Bootsie Grady* • Brandon Smith *Arnie Grady* • Jesse James *Randolph Grady* • Nicki Aycox [Nicki Lynn Aycox] *Tanner Jennings* ■ *Dir* Melanie Mayron • *Scr* Damon Lamar, Robert Lee King

Slap Shot ★★★ 18
Comedy drama 1977 · US · Colour · 117min

Paul Newman is reunited with his *Butch Cassidy* director George Roy Hill for this sharp, satirical look at unethical tactics in professional ice hockey. Fashioned as a series of deliberately crude epithets by scriptwriter Nancy Dowd, the film follows the fortunes of a minor-league team that is encouraged to play dirty to win by ambitious coach Newman. Unfortunately, the relentless violence and profanity that provide the film with its great strength are usually toned down in TV versions, with much of the locker-room language removed. A belated, made-for-video sequel followed in 2002. TS *DVD*

Paul Newman *Reggie Dunlop* • Strother Martin *Joe McGrath* • Michael Ontkean *Ned Braden* • Jennifer Warren *Francine Dunlop* • Lindsay Crouse *Lily Braden* • Jerry Houser *"Killer" Carlson* • Andrew Duncan *Jim Carr* ■ *Dir* George Roy Hill • *Scr* Nancy Dowd

Slattery's Hurricane ★★★
Disaster drama 1949 · US · BW · 83min

Pilot Richard Widmark's post-Second World War career has included flying for a front company for the Mob and an affair with the boss's girlfriend, Veronica Lake. Various complications result in Widmark taking old mate John Russell's place on a dangerous assignment into the eye of a hurricane. This forgettable drama, told in flashback, is not to be taken seriously, but the storm-tossed aerial sequences are entertaining. RK

Richard Widmark *Willard Francis Slattery* • Linda Darnell *Aggie Hobson* • Veronica Lake *Dolores Greeves* • John Russell *Lt FJ "Hobby" Hobson* • Gary Merrill *Comdr ET Kramer* • Walter Kingsford *RJ Milne* ■ *Dir* Andre De Toth • *Scr* Herman Wouk, Richard Murphy, from a story by Herman Wouk

Slaughter on Tenth Avenue ★★★
Crime drama 1957 · US · BW · 102min

Three years after *On the Waterfront*, this formula movie discovered the waterfront racket all over again. Craftily directed by Arnold Laven, it has assistant District Attorney Richard Egan at war with the crime around the docks, and finding true love with longshoreman's widow Jan Sterling. Dan Duryea is the heavy. TH

Richard Egan *William Keating* • Jan Sterling *Madge Pitts* • Dan Duryea *John Jacob Masters* • Julie Adams *Dee* • Walter Matthau *Al Dahlke* • Charles McGraw *Lieutenant Anthony Vosnick* ■ *Dir* Arnold Laven • *Scr* Lawrence Roman, from the memoirs *The Man Who Rocked the Boat* by William J Keating, Richard Carter

Slaughterhouse ★ 18
Comedy horror 1987 · US · Colour · 79min

This features a graphic opening montage of farmyard pigs being killed for real. The tired plot concerns local authorities about to foreclose on the rural homestead-cum-slaughterhouse of Don Barrett and his hog-loving son Joe Barton. Psycho Barton axes anyone who tries to evict them including the usual bunch of witless teens using the

property to shoot a low-budget horror movie. Julianne Moore made her feature debut in the 1988 sequel. AJ

Joe Barton *Buddy* • Don Barrett *Lester Bacon* • Sherry Bendorf *Liz Borden* • William Houck *Sheriff* • Jeffrey Grossi *Buzz* ■ *Dir/Scr* Rick Roessler

Slaughterhouse-Five ★★★★ 15
Science-fiction satire 1972 · US · Colour · 99min

Kurt Vonnegut's science-fiction masterpiece is done marvellous justice in director George Roy Hill's wildly complex, truly bizarre and poignant commentary on the absurdity of human existence. In this postmodern *Pilgrim's Progress*, Michael Sacks is Billy Pilgrim, a man "unstuck in time" who constantly leaves the present to either return to the past, when he was a PoW in Dresden, or flit to the future, where his existence with half-naked actress Valerie Perrine is viewed under glass by aliens. A wry, intelligent and thought-provoking parable with a surreal quality. AJ *DVD*

Michael Sacks *Billy Pilgrim* • Ron Leibman *Paul Lazzaro* • Eugene Roche *Derby* • Sharon Gans *Valencia* • Valerie Perrine *Montana Wildhack* • Roberts Blossom *Wild Bob Cody* • Sorrell Booke *Lionel Merble* • Kevin Conway *Weary* ■ *Dir* George Roy Hill • *Scr* Stephen Geller, from the novel by Kurt Vonnegut Jr

Slaughter's Big Rip-Off ★★★
Blaxploitation crime drama 1973 · US · Colour · 90min

Black Vietnam vet/urban warrior Jim Brown returns to avenge the murder of his mother and father by gangsters, led this time around by Ed McMahon. Jim Brown goes in for a lot of violent confrontations but is really too good for this blaxploitation fix. A hint of humour would have helped. TH

Jim Brown *Slaughter* • Ed McMahon *Duncan* • Brock Peters *Reynolds* • Don Stroud *Kirk* • Gloria Hendry *Marcia* • Richard Williams *Joe Creole* • Judy Brown [Judith Brown] *Norji* ■ *Dir* Gordon Douglas • *Scr* Charles Johnson, from a character created by Don Williams

Slave Girl ★ U
Period comedy adventure 1947 · US · Colour · 79min

A less than charismatic George Brent stars as an American diplomat who is sent off to Tripoli to buy back a group of sailors held hostage by a cruel potentate. En route, the ransom money is stolen and exotic dancing girl Yvonne De Carlo is saved by Brent from a dreadful fate. With its miscasting, ridiculous plot and hackneyed slapstick jokes, the movie falls flat on its face. RK

Yvonne De Carlo *Francesca* • George Brent *Matt Claibourne/Pierre* • Broderick Crawford *Chips Jackson* • Albert Dekker *Pasha* • Lois Collier *Aleta* • Andy Devine *Ben* • Arthur Treacher *Thomas "Liverpool" Griswald* ■ *Dir* Charles Lamont • *Scr* Michael Fessier, Ernest Pagano

A Slave of Love ★★★
Period drama 1976 · USSR · Colour · 92min

Such is the status of silent Soviet cinema that it's easy to overlook the sophistication of film-making in the late-Tsarist era. Unsurprisingly, Nikita Mikhalkov is only able to pay passing tribute to those forgotten masters in this bitingly satirical drama, in which a cash-strapped unit shooting in Odessa gradually becomes aware of the Bolshevik Revolution. The story sees haughty diva Elena Solovei rally to the cause after the death of cameraman-lover Rodion Nakhapetov, who's been secretly filming propaganda footage of White Guard atrocities. DP Russian +subtitles.

Elena Solovei *Olga Voznesenskaya* • Rodion Nakhapetov *Victor Pototsky* • Aleksandr Kalyagin *Kalyagin* • Oleg Basilashvili *Yuzhakov* • Konstantin Grigoryev *Fedotov* ■ *Dir* Nikita Mikhalkov • *Scr* Friedrich Gorenstein, Andrei Mikhalkov-Konchalovsky [Andrei Konchalovsky]

Slave Ship ★★★
Adventure   1937 · US · BW · 90min

Warner Baxter should really have known better than to buy a "blood ship" called the *Albatross*, for no sooner has he sworn to cease slave trading than he has a mutiny on his hands. Wallace Beery plays his trademark soft-centred sourpuss with typical gusto, and he's ably supported by George Sanders as the chief mutineer and Mickey Rooney as a cheeky cabin boy. But the soggy performance of Baxter as the Captain Bligh of the piece makes it almost impossible for director Tay Garnett to keep the wind in the sails of this otherwise boisterous picture. DP

Warner Baxter *Jim Lovett* • Wallace Beery *Jack Thompson* • Elizabeth Allan *Nancy Marlowe* • Mickey Rooney *Swifty* • George Sanders *Lefty* • Jane Darwell *Mrs Marlowe* • Joseph Schildkraut *Danelo* ■ *Dir* Tay Garnett • *Scr* Sam Hellman, Lamar Trotti, Gladys Lehman, from a story by William Faulkner, from the novel *The Last Slaver* by George S King

Slavers ★ 18
Period drama   1977 · W Ger · Colour · 94min

In this bloody, repellent mess, Trevor Howard and Ray Milland are slumming, playing Victoria-era slave traders. Howard owns the trading post, while Milland is browned-up as a shifty Arab, Hassan, who shoots his slaves as target practice (which doesn't make very sound economic sense). Britt Ekland introduces some love interest, while Zimbabwe (then Rhodesia) provides the scenery. AT

Trevor Howard *Alec MacKenzie* • Ron Ely *Steven Hamilton* • Britt Ekland *Anna von Erken* • Jürgen Goslar *Max von Euken* • Ray Milland *Hassan* • Don Jack Rousseau *Mazu* • Helen Morgan (2) *Malika* ■ *Dir* Jürgen Goslar • *Scr* Henry Morrisson, Nathaniel Kohn, Marcia MacDonald

Slaves ★★★
Drama   1969 · US · Colour · 105min

Herbert J Biberman, the blacklisted director of *Salt of the Earth* (1954), had to wait 15 years for his next film, a study of slavery. Ossie Davis plays the hero who is sold to Stephen Boyd, a Mississippi landowner who keeps a black mistress, played by singer Dionne Warwick in her screen debut. While Davis and Warwick are fairly conventional archetypes, Boyd has the best material, playing a satisfyingly complex character – brutal yet haunted by a religious upbringing which draws him to the Christian-motivated Davis. The director's wife Gale Sondergaard – herself both an Oscar winner and a blacklist victim – appears in the New Orleans sequence. It was her first film since 1949. AT

Stephen Boyd *Nathan MacKay* • Dionne Warwick *Cassy* • Ossie Davis *Luke* • Robert Kya-Hill *Jericho* • Barbara Ann Teer *Esther* • Marilyn Clark *Mrs Bennett* • Gale Sondergaard *New Orleans lady* ■ *Dir* Herbert J Biberman • *Scr* Herbert J Biberman, John O Killens, Alida Sherman

Slaves of New York ★★ 15
Comedy drama   1989 · US · Colour · 119min

The genteel style of James Ivory and Ismail Merchant sits uneasily on a series of interrelated short stories about middle-class 30-somethings in a district of New York. The abiding relationship is that between kooky hat designer Bernadette Peters and self-centred artist Adam Coleman Howard, but that's as doomed to fail as the rest of the characters. TH Swearing, sex scenes, nudity.

Bernadette Peters *Eleanor* • Chris Sarandon *Victor Okrent* • Mary Beth Hurt *Ginger Booth* • Madeleine Potter *Daria* • Adam Coleman Howard *Stash Stotz* • Nick Corri *Marley Mantello* • Mercedes Ruehl *Samantha* • Steve Buscemi *Wilfredo* • Tama Janowitz *Abby* • Anthony LaPaglia *Henry* • Stanley Tucci *Darryl* ■ *Dir* James Ivory • *Scr* Tama Janowitz, from her stories • *Producer* Ismail Merchant

sleep furiously ★★★★ U
Documentary   2007 · UK · Colour · 94min

Shot over several months in the mid-Welsh hill-farming village of Trefeurig, this is an intimate study of a way of life that had scarcely changed for centuries until the intrusion of social mobility, new technology and modern methods of farming. However, it's the remote community's most frequent visitor who binds it together, as mobile librarian John Jones not only keeps the lonely informed of the latest gossip, but also provides a link to the wider world. With Aphex Twin's atmospheric score heightening both the sense of place and pace of existence, this is a compelling dissertation on human and physical geography, and an invaluable record of passing practices, sights and sounds. It's also an utterly charming piece of film-making. DP English, Welsh +subtitles.

■ *Dir* Gideon Koppel • *Music* Aphex Twin

Sleep, My Love ★★★ PG
Psychological melodrama   1948 · US · BW · 92min

Shades of that old favourite *Gaslight* haunt this psycho-melodrama, which pairs one-time romantic comedy team Claudette Colbert and Don Ameche. Colbert is the wealthy wife of Ameche, for once swapping his debonair persona to play the impassive, cold husband systematically sending Colbert mad so he can inherit her money and marry siren Hazel Brooks. Robert Cummings is the hero figure in a plot too familiar for surprises, but still somewhat suspenseful. RK

Claudette Colbert *Alison Courtland* • Robert Cummings *Bruce Elcott* • Don Ameche *Richard Courtland* • Rita Johnson *Barby* • George Coulouris *Charles Vernay* • Queenie Smith *Mrs Vernay* • Ralph Morgan *Dr Rhinehart* • Keye Luke *Jimmie* • Raymond Burr *Lt Strake* • Hazel Brooks *Daphne* ■ *Dir* Douglas Sirk • *Scr* St Clair McKelway, Leo Rosten, Cyril Endfield [Cy Endfield], Decla Dunning, from a novel by Leo Rosten

Sleep Tight ★★★★ 15
Horror thriller   2011 · Sp · Colour · 100min

One of the most unique psycho-thrillers in years centres on Spanish star Luis Tosar, who delivers a sensationally disturbing performance as César, a Barcelona janitor fixated with the new tenant at an upscale apartment block. Director Jaume Balaguero co-directed *[Rec]*, and the setting here is similar, but there's also a nod to the work of Roman Polanski in a provocative and intense tale of obsession. The unusually plotted chills and a series of twists that spiral into chaos put Balagueró's creep-fest on the Hitchcockian side of dread. It's dark and unsettling, and the gradual build-up of suspense is of such a startling calibre that it will have you biting your nails to the quick. AJ Spanish +subtitles. Violence, swearing, a sex scene, nudity.

Luis Tosar *César* • Marta Etura *Clara* • Alberto San Juan *Marcos* • Petra Martínez *Señora Verónica* • Iris Almeida Molina *Ursula* ■ *Dir* Jaume Balaguero • *Scr* Alberto Marini

Sleep with Me ★★★ 18
Romantic comedy   1994 · US · Colour · 82min

Suggested by Eric Stoltz and director Rory Kelly, this is a fascinating experiment in film-making. Six writers each penned a different episode; if the end result is a little uneven, the shifts in tone give the picture vibrance and variety. Though the narrative focus is on the twists and trysts involving Stoltz, Meg Tilly and Craig Sheffer, it's the incidentals that stand out, notably Quentin Tarantino's wonderful party piece and Adrienne Shelly's unerring talent for social gaffs. Hilarious when it hits the mark, but never less than amiable. DP Swearing, sex scenes, nudity.

Eric Stoltz *Joseph* • Meg Tilly *Sarah* • Craig Sheffer *Frank* • Todd Field *Duane* • Susan Traylor *Deborah* • Dean Cameron *Leo* • Quentin Tarantino *Sid* • Adrienne Shelly *Pamela* ■ *Dir* Rory Kelly • *Scr* Duane Dell'Amico, Roger Hedden, Neal Jimenez, Joe Keenan, Rory Kelly, Michael Steinberg

Sleeper ★★★★ PG
Science-fiction comedy   1973 · US · Colour · 83min

In this silly but often hilarious comedy, Woody Allen is a jazz musician who comes round from what he thinks was a minor operation only to discover that he has been in cryogenic suspension for 200 years. What follows is partly inspired by *1984* (Allen gets involved with revolutionaries opposing the totalitarian government), but is mainly a homage to great screen comedians of the past. The sight gags (particularly Allen disguised as a robot) include some of the funniest things Allen has ever done. There is also a rich quota of brilliantly witty lines throughout, with Diane Keaton making a fine foil. DM Swearing.

DVD

Woody Allen *Miles Monroe* • Diane Keaton *Luna Schlosser* • John Beck *Erno Windt* • Marya Small *Dr Nero* • Bartlett Robinson *Dr Orva* • Mary Gregory *Dr Melik* • Chris Forbes *Rainer Krebs* ■ *Dir* Woody Allen • *Scr* Woody Allen, Marshall Brickman

Sleepers ★★★ 18
Drama   1996 · US · Colour · 140min

With its powerhouse cast and an A-list director, this is long and exudes importance and integrity. So why does it come across as bogus? Though based on an autobiography, the plot mechanism and its moral stance – that violent revenge is fully justified – is not totally believable. The story concerns four teenagers who are brought up by a priest. When a foolish prank causes a near-fatal accident, the youths are sent to jail where they are repeatedly abused by the guards. Years later, they plot revenge. Director Barry Levinson vividly evokes the hothouse atmosphere of New York's Hell's Kitchen. AT Violence, swearing. DVD

Kevin Bacon *Sean Nokes* • Robert De Niro *Father Bobby* • Dustin Hoffman *Danny Snyder* • Jason Patric *Lorenzo "Shakes" Carcarterra* • Brad Pitt *Michael* • Billy Crudup *Tommy* • Ron Eldard *John Carol Martinez* • Vittorio Gassman *King Benny* • Minnie Driver ■ *Dir* Barry Levinson • *Scr* Barry Levinson, from the autobiography by Lorenzo Carcaterra

Sleeping Beauty ★★★★ U
Animated fantasy   1959 · US · Colour · 71min

Based on Charles Perrault's enduring fairy tale, this was Disney's most expensive cartoon to date, costing $6 million and taking ten years to make. It was an ambitious project that made use of the latest technology, and the score, based on Tchaikovsky's ballet, was Oscar-nominated. Technical wizardry apart, it's the supporting characters that make the difference, in this case the trio of plump guardians Flora, Fauna and Merryweather, and Maleficent the wicked fairy. The battle royal between Maleficent and Prince Phillip is one of Disney's best climaxes. That said, it barely made its money back at the box office in 1959, but has since been re-evaluated by successive audiences. AC DVD

Mary Costa *Princess Aurora* • Bill Shirley *Prince Phillip* • Verna Felton *Flora* • Vera Vague [Barbara Jo Allen] *Fauna* • Barbara Luddy *Merryweather* • Eleanor Audley *Maleficent* • Taylor Holmes *King Stefan* • Bill Thompson *King Hubert* • Candy Candido *Goons* ■ *Dir* Clyde Geronimi, Eric Larson, Wolfgang Reitherman, Les Clark • *Scr* Erdman Penner, from the fairy tale by Charles Perrault

Sleeping Beauty ★★★ 18
Drama   2011 · Aus · Colour · 111min

The erotic dream worlds of David Lynch receive a feminist spin in this often baffling but still strangely absorbing Australian fantasy. When student Lucy (Emily Browning) replies to a newspaper advert to boost her income, it soon transpires that what looks to be a waitressing job is really a gateway to something much more perverse. In exchange for money, Lucy allows herself to be drugged to the point of oblivion as a succession of men pay to spend the night with her. Lucy's curiosity about what happens in this lost time does finally get the better of her, but it's perhaps to the detriment of this initially haunting and often explicit riddle of a film that she does indeed find out. DW DVD Blu

Emily Browning *Lucy* • Rachael Blake *Clara* • Ewen Leslie *Birdmann* • Peter Carroll *Man 1* • Chris Haywood *Man 2* • Hugh Keays-Byrne *Man 3* ■ *Dir/Scr* Julia Leigh

The Sleeping Car Murders ★★★
Crime thriller   1965 · Fr · BW · 91min

After years assisting René Clair and Jacques Demy, the Greek-born film-maker Constantin Costa-Gavras finally made his feature debut with this teasing whodunnit. The members of the all-star cast fall like flies as police inspector Yves Montand tries to discover who killed a woman on the Marseille-Paris express. In addition to a grotesquely lecherous Michel Piccoli, the limelight is hogged by Simone Signoret, whose daughter Catherine Allégret also appears. Costa-Gavras takes the picture at a fast pace and keeps the clues well hidden. DP French +subtitles.

Yves Montand *Inspector Grazzi* • Simone Signoret *Eliane Darrès* • Pierre Mondy *Commissioner* • Catherine Allégret *Bambi* • Pascale Roberts *Georgette Thomas* • Michel Piccoli *Cabourg* • Jean-Louis Trintignant *Eric* ■ *Dir* Costa-Gavras • *Scr* Costa-Gavras, Sébastien Japrisot, from the novel *Compartiment Tueurs* by Sébastien Japrisot

Sleeping Car to Trieste ★★ PG
Spy drama   1948 · UK · BW · 91min

While 1932's *Rome Express* was a sleek, fast-moving turbo of a crime drama, this unnecessary remake is something of a branch-line diesel that director John Paddy Carstairs insists on stopping at every country halt. The story remains basically the same as before, with Albert Lieven and Jean Kent as thieves in pursuit of a diary packed with state secrets, which passes from one shifty passenger to another. Comparisons are inevitable, if slightly unfair, but none of the cast improves on the original characterisations. DP

Jean Kent *Valya* • Albert Lieven *Zurta* • Derrick de Marney *George Grant* • Paul Dupuis *Jolif* • Rona Anderson *Joan Maxted* • David Tomlinson *Tom Bishop* • Finlay Currie *Alastair MacBain* ■ *Dir* John Paddy Carstairs • *Scr* Allan MacKinnon, from the story *Rome Express* by Clifford Grey

The Sleeping City ★★★
Crime drama   1950 · US · BW · 83min

Critics at the time thought this documentary-style thriller was heavily derived from the 1948 drama *The Naked City*. Set in a New York hospital, it weaves together several strands of narrative and the deaths of two interns who have been stealing drugs to pay off gambling debts. George Sherman's film was one of the earliest Hollywood movies to confront the drug problem and it doesn't stint on the grim details. AT

Richard Conte *Fred Rowan* • Coleen Gray *Ann Sebastian* • Peggy Dow *Kathy Hall* • John Alexander (1) *Inspector Gordon* • Alex Nicol *Dr Bob Anderson* • Richard Taber *Pop Ware* ■ *Dir* George Sherman • *Scr* Jo Eisinger

Sleeping Dogs Lie. ★★★ 18
Black comedy romance   2006 · US · Colour · 86min

The perils of total honesty in a relationship lie at the core of this hilariously tasteless sex comedy from former stand-up comic Bobcat Goldthwait. For when Melinda Page Hamilton finally reveals to her insistent fiancé the beastly sexual indiscretion she committed in college, the fallout is epic and her life spins out of control. It's cheaply and cheerfully made, but the amateurish visuals don't detract from the rich seam of humour that's effortlessly mined by a game cast. In a fearless performance, Hamilton plays every emotion from embarrassment to panic with a delightfully quick wit. The film increases in warmth and sweetness as it nears its unsurprising climax. AJ DVD

S

Melinda Page Hamilton *Amy* • Bryce Johnson *John* • Geoff Pierson *Dad* • Colby French *Ed* • Jack Plotnick *Dougie* • Bonita Friedericy *Mom* ■ *Dir/Scr* Bobcat Goldthwait

The Sleeping Tiger ★★★★ U

Crime drama   1954 · UK · BW · 85min

This highly charged melodrama was made in England by Hollywood blacklistees, director Joseph Losey (hiding behind the name of the film's actual producer, Victor Hanbury) and co-writer Carl Foreman (under the alias Derek Frye). An important film, it brought together for the first time one of British cinema's most accomplished pairings in director Losey and star Dirk Bogarde, who would create a stunning body of work. Losey seemed able to tap Bogarde's smouldering sexual and social ambivalence, and his scenes here with Alexis Smith are electric. The plot, about a psychiatrist taking a known criminal into his home, is reminiscent of Hollywood at its battiest. TS *DVD*

Dirk Bogarde *Frank Clements* • Alexis Smith *Glenda Esmond* • Alexander Knox *Dr Clive Esmond* • Hugh Griffith *Inspector Simmons* • Patricia McCarron *Sally* • Maxine Audley *Carol* • Glyn Houston *Bailey* • Harry Towb *Harry* • Billie Whitelaw *Receptionist* ■ *Dir* Victor Hanbury [Joseph Losey] • *Scr* Derek Frye [Harold Buchman, Carl Foreman], from the novel by Maurice Moiseiwitsch

Sleeping with Other People

★★★ 15

Romantic comedy   2015 · US · Colour · 101min

In this salty slant on *When Harry Met Sally...* writer/director Leslye Headland offers her own unapologetically filthy, reliably funny take on whether men and women can be just good friends. Alison Brie and Jason Sudeikis play pals who lose their virginity to each other at university and reconnect a decade later in a sex addiction group, keeping things strictly platonic, of course. If the story eventually surrenders to convention, this is still a refreshingly adult, often rule-breaking romantic comedy. EAS Swearing, sex scenes. *DVD*

Jason Sudeikis *Jake* • Alison Brie *Lainey* • Adam Scott *Matthew* • Jason Mantzoukas *Xander* • Natasha Lyonne *Kara* ■ *Dir/Scr* Leslye Headland

Sleeping with the Enemy

★★★ 15

Thriller   1991 · US · Colour · 94min

Julia Roberts is the abused spouse who stages her own death to escape her marriage from hell with Patrick Bergin. She begins her life anew and meets nice Kevin Anderson but her crazed husband is never far behind. This was Roberts's bid for grittier material and she acquits herself well, while Bergin relishes his role as the bad guy. Director Joseph Ruben manages some chilling sequences. JF Violence, sex scenes, swearing. *DVD* *Blu*

Julia Roberts *Laura Burney/Sara Waters* • Patrick Bergin *Martin Burney* • Kevin Anderson *Ben Woodward* • Elizabeth Lawrence *Chloe* • Kyle Secor *Fleishman* • Claudette Nevins *Dr Rissner* • Tony Abatemarco *Locke* • Marita Geraghty *Julie* ■ *Dir* Joseph Ruben • *Scr* Ronald Bass, from the novel by Nancy Price

Sleepless in Seattle

★★★★ PG

Romantic comedy   1993 · US · Colour · 100min

Nora Ephron, the writer of *When Harry Met Sally...*, came up trumps again as co-writer and director of this gloriously old-fashioned tale. Tom Hanks, recently widowed, moves to a new home in Seattle where he just grieves and grieves. His young son (Ross Malinger), concerned over his dad's state of mind, calls a radio phone-in and when Hanks himself goes on air, he pours his heart out. Meg Ryan, a Baltimore journalist who hears the broadcast, recognises a kindred lonely heart and starts tracking Hanks down. For nearly two hours, Ephron keeps her marvellous stars apart, a potentially dangerous tactic that works superbly. AT *DVD*

Tom Hanks *Sam Baldwin* • Meg Ryan *Annie Reed* • Ross Malinger *Jonah Baldwin* • Rosie O'Donnell *Becky* • Rob Reiner *Jay* • Bill Pullman *Walter* • Rita Wilson *Suzy* • Victor Garber *Greg* • David Hyde Pierce *Dennis Reed* ■ *Dir* Nora Ephron • *Scr* Nora Ephron, David S Ward, Jeff Arch, from a story by Jeff Arch

Sleepover ★ PG

Comedy   2004 · US/Can · Colour · 85min

Flatulence jokes, grating stereotypes and an avalanche of female neuroses feature in this unappealing adolescent comedy. In a sadly wasted performance, Alexa Vega (*SPYkids*) plays an uncool 14-year-old, whose sleepover is turned on its head when the trendiest girls in school challenge her and her guests to a risky scavenger hunt. Lazily scripted and shoddily executed. SF *DVD*

Alexa Vega *Julie* • Mika Boorem *Hannah* • Jane Lynch *Gabby* • Sam Huntington *Ren* • Sara Paxton *Staci* • Brie Larson *Liz* • Scout Taylor-Compton *Farrah* • Sean Faris *Steve* ■ *Dir* Joe Nussbaum • *Scr* Elisa Bell

Sleepstalker ★★ 18

Horror   1995 · US · Colour · 102min

A serial killer whose calling card is pouring sand in his victims' eyes is sent to the gas chamber and ritually resurrected as a demon by the evil Preacher (Michael D Roberts) and his albino acolytes. The Sandman must then kill journalist Jay Underwood, who is investigating Los Angeles street gangs, to avoid eternal torment. This has good special effects work, but the often tiresomely conventional plot gets in the way. AJ Violence, swearing. *DVD*

Jay Underwood *Griffin Davis* • Kathryn Morris *Megan* • Michael Harris (2) *The Sandman* • Michael D Roberts *Rev Jonas, preacher* ■ *Dir* Turi Meyer • *Scr* Turi Meyer, Al Septien

Sleepwalkers ★ 18

Fantasy horror   1992 · US · Colour · 85min

Hailed as the first Stephen King story expressly written for the screen, this minor horror entry revolves around the gory small-town exploits of shape-shifting, incestuous, psychic vampires. Director Mick Garris tries to inject life into the pathetic script by gyrating the camera, adding some neat computer-generated transformations and flashily accenting what little action there is, but the material is poor and underdeveloped. AJ *DVD*

Brian Krause *Charles Brady* • Mädchen Amick *Tanya Robertson* • Alice Krige *Mary Brady* • Jim Haynie *Sheriff Ira* • Cindy Pickett *Mrs Robertson* • Ron Perlman *Captain Soames* • John Landis *Lab technician* • Joe Dante *Lab assistant* • Stephen King *Cemetery caretaker* • Clive Barker *Forensic technician* • Tobe Hooper *Forensic technician* ■ *Dir* Mick Garris • *Scr* Stephen King

Sleepy Hollow ★★★★ 15

Gothic horror fantasy   1999 · US · Colour · 100min

An alchemic combination of visual splendour, dreamy bloodthirstiness and sly humour, this supernatural gothic whodunnit is another beautifully crafted offering from eccentric maestro Tim Burton. With a cast milking every sinister nuance, his clever revision of Washington Irving's timeless tale of terror enlists the classic retro look of Hammer's golden horror era to great effect. Johnny Depp, sporting a clipped English accent, is brilliant as radical-thinking police constable Ichabod Crane, sent to the small Dutch community of Sleepy Hollow to investigate three mysterious beheadings the locals are blaming on the ghost of the legendary Headless Horseman. AJ *DVD* *Blu*

Johnny Depp *Ichabod Crane* • Christina Ricci *Katrina Van Tassel* • Miranda Richardson *Lady Van Tassel/Crone* • Michael Gambon *Baltus Van Tassel* • Casper Van Dien *Brom Van Brunt* • Jeffrey Jones *Reverend Steenwyck* • Richard Griffiths *Magistrate Philipse* • Christopher Walken *Hessian Horseman* ■ *Dir* Tim Burton • *Scr* Andrew Kevin Walker, from a story by Kevin Yagher, Andrew Kevin Walker, from the story *The Legend of Sleepy Hollow* by Washington

Irving • *Cinematographer* Emmanuel Lubezki • *Production Designer* Rick Heinrichs • *Set Decorator* Peter Young

The Slender Thread ★★★

Drama   1965 · US · BW · 98min

Sidney Poitier stars in this tense little thriller as a volunteer social worker trying to locate Anne Bancroft who's taken a drugs overdose. Based upon an actual incident, what led this wife and mother to take such desperate steps is told in flashback. In his feature debut, director Sydney Pollack concentrates on the telephoned interchange between the two principals, and the suspense that the conversation generates keeps this race against time engrossing. TH

Sidney Poitier *Alan Newell* • Anne Bancroft *Inga Dyson* • Telly Savalas *Dr Coburn* • Steven Hill *Mark Dyson* • Indus Arthur *Marion* • Greg Jarvis *Chris Dyson* • Edward Asner *Det Judd Ridley* • Dabney Coleman *Charlie* ■ *Dir* Sydney Pollack • *Scr* Stirling Silliphant, from the story *Decision To Die* in *Life* magazine by Shana Alexander

Sleuth ★★★★ 15

Mystery   1972 · UK · Colour · 134min

Both leading players in this mystery were nominated for the best actor Oscar. Neither Michael Caine nor Laurence Olivier won, but they surely had their reward in the fun they had in making this engrossing sleight of hand from playwright Anthony Shaffer. As theatrical duplicity inevitably packs more of a punch than its cinematic counterpart, the impact of the elaborate role-playing is weakened by its translation to the screen. However, the corkscrew plot and the delicious hamming of the leads ensure that it still remains a thundering good watch. DP Some swearing, sexual references. *DVD*

Laurence Olivier *Andrew Wyke* • Michael Caine *Milo Tindle* ■ *Dir* Joseph L Mankiewicz • *Scr* Anthony Shaffer, from his play

Sleuth ★ 15

Mystery   2007 · US/UK · Colour · 84min

Director Joseph L Mankiewicz's 1972 adaptation of Anthony Shaffer's stage play about a cuckolded writer battling with his wife's lover starred Laurence Olivier and Michael Caine. Thirty-five years later, Caine takes over the Olivier role as the vengeful scribe and Jude Law plays the young actor and his opponent in the psychological games that ensue. Both would have been well advised not to have bothered. Kenneth Branagh's uncertain direction is partly to blame, as he never finds a satisfactory tone for the piece. But the chief offender is screenwriter Harold Pinter, whose leaden, misjudged screenplay has none of the sense of mischievous glee that animated the earlier screen version. AS *DVD*

Michael Caine *Andrew Wyke* • Jude Law *Milo Tindle* • Harold Pinter *Man on TV* ■ *Dir* Kenneth Branagh • *Scr* Harold Pinter, from the play by Anthony Shaffer

Sliding Doors ★★★ 15

Romantic fantasy comedy
1997 · UK/US · Colour · 94min

If you could live your life again, would you do it differently? In this lightweight British comedy directed by Peter Howitt, Gwyneth Paltrow plays out two different scenarios after she misses/doesn't miss a Tube train home. In one reality she finds out her boyfriend is a two-timing louse, so she leaves him and gets a cute new haircut. In her parallel world the hair is long and boring – very much like her life. Paltrow handles her English accent with ease, and she gets some nice support from John Hannah and John Lynch, but the movie never quite gels. JB Swearing. *DVD*

Gwyneth Paltrow *Helen* • John Hannah *James* • John Lynch *Gerry* • Jeanne Tripplehorn *Lydia* • Zara Turner *Anna* • Douglas McFerran *Russell* • Paul Brightwell *Clive* • Nina Young *Claudia* • Virginia McKenna *James's mother* ■ *Dir/Scr* Peter Howitt

A Slight Case of Murder ★★★ U

Crime comedy   1938 · US · BW · 86min

This terrific fast-paced Warner Bros movie provides a knockout role for Edward G Robinson as the bootlegging hood left high and dry at the end of Prohibition. Robinson hogs the picture, though there's a very funny climax during which four corpses have all the best moments. This was based on a popular Broadway play by Damon Runyon and Howard Lindsay, and the theatrical structure does show through at times, but the marvellous cast doesn't let you dwell on it for a second. The studio remade this in 1952 as *Stop! You're Killing Me*. TS

Edward G Robinson *Remy Marko* • Jane Bryan *Mary Marko* • Willard Parker *Dick Whitewood* • Ruth Donnelly *Nora Marko* • Allen Jenkins *Mike* • John Litel *Post* • Eric Stanley Ritter • Margaret Hamilton *Mrs Cagle* ■ *Dir* Lloyd Bacon • *Scr* Earl Baldwin, Joseph Schrank, from the play by Damon Runyon, Howard Lindsay

A Slight Case of Murder ★★★ 15

Detective comedy thriller
1999 · US · Colour · 89min

William H Macy stars as a film critic seeking to conceal his involvement in the accidental death of his lover. Having tailored the tale (as co-writer) to his own strengths, Macy turns in a splendidly astute performace. Shifting from speeches to camera to lectures on the conventions of *film noir*, he manipulates everyone around him, including blackmailing private eye James Cromwell and cop Adam Arkin. Occasionally glib and self-satisfied, this TV movie is never anything less than intriguing and entertaining. DP

William H Macy *Terry Thorpe* • Adam Arkin *Det Fred Stapelli* • Felicity Huffman *Kit Wannamaker* • James Cromwell *John Edgerson* • Julia Campbell *Patricia Stapelli* ■ *Dir* Steven Schachter • *Scr* William H Macy, Steven Schachter, from a novel by Donald E Westlake

Slightly Dangerous ★★ U

Comedy   1943 · US · BW · 94min

At this point in her career, Lana Turner had already successfully co-starred with Clark Gable and Robert Taylor, and could afford to relax in this tosh about a waitress who lies about her origins. MGM was preparing the definitive waitress movie for Turner, but in the end it was Judy Garland who made *The Harvey Girls*, leaving Turner to find notoriety with *The Postman Always Rings Twice*. TS

Lana Turner *Peggy Evans/Carol Burden/Narrator* • Robert Young (1) *Bob Stuart* • Walter Brennan *Cornelius Burden* • Dame May Whitty *Baba* • Eugene Pallette *Durstin* • Alan Mowbray *English gentleman* • Florence Bates *Mrs Roanoke-Brooke* • Howard Freeman *Mr Quill* ■ *Dir* Wesley Ruggles • *Scr* Charles Lederer, George Oppenheimer, from a story by Ian McLellan Hunter, Aileen Hamilton

Slightly French ★★

Musical comedy   1949 · US · BW · 80min

In this take on *Pygmalion*, a Brooklyn hoochy-cooch dancer (Dorothy Lamour) is given a crash-course in conduct by film director Don Ameche, who digs himself out of a hole by passing her off as a quality French actress. Smoothly directed by Douglas Sirk and played with pleasing nonchalance by the stars, it's a slightly good idea, slightly amusing, and bears a slight resemblance to *Let's Fall in Love* (1934) – hardly surprising, since it's a makeover of that film's story. RK

Dorothy Lamour *Mary O'Leary/Rochelle Olivier* • Don Ameche *John Gayle* • Janis Carter *Louisa Gayle* • Willard Parker *Douglas Hyde* • Adele Jergens *Yvonne La Tour* • Jeanne Manet *Nicolette* ■ *Dir* Douglas Sirk • *Scr* Karen De Wolf, from a story by Herbert Fields

Slightly Honorable ★★

Mystery   1939 · US · BW · 85min

Suspected of murder, lawyer Pat O'Brien determines to track down the real killer. He

S

eventually does so with the help of Broderick Crawford and uncovers the villainy of corrupt politician Edward Arnold. Heavily populated with corpses, suspects and jokes – several of them delivered by ace wisecracker Eve Arden – this comedy thriller veers uncertainly between laughter and suspense, with the former winning to the detriment of the latter. Tay Garnett directs, with a large cast of supporting players. RK

Pat O'Brien *John Webb* • Edward Arnold *Vincent Cushing* • Broderick Crawford *Russ Sampson* • Ruth Terry *Ann Seymour* • Claire Dodd *Alma Brehmer* ■ *Dir* Tay Garnett • *Scr* Ken Englund, John Hunter Lay, Robert Tallman, from the novel *Send Another Coffin* by Frank G Presnell

Slightly Scarlet ★★★
Crime drama 1956 · US · Colour · 92min

In the dying days of RKO following Howard Hughes's ownership, producer Benedict Bogeaus mounted a series of westerns and melodramas using up leftover sets and contract artists, glossily directed by the talented veteran Allan Dwan. This is one of the better examples, a crime drama about a guy (John Payne) involved with a pair of redheaded sisters (Rhonda Fleming and Arlene Dahl), hence the title. The corruption of power theme is well handled, and Dahl is terrific as the slightly sozzled sister. TS

John Payne *Ben Grace* • Rhonda Fleming *June Lyons* • Arlene Dahl *Dorothy Lyons* • Kent Taylor *Frank Jansen* • Ted De Corsia *Sol Caspar* • Lance Fuller *Gauss* • Buddy Baer *Lenhardt* ■ *Dir* Allan Dwan • *Scr* Robert Blees, from the novel *Love's Lovely Counterfeit* by James M Cain

Slim ★★★
Drama 1937 · US · BW · 86min

A young Henry Fonda is a farm boy who realises his dream of becoming an electric lineman when hardened expert Pat O'Brien makes him his protégé (later his partner) and exposes him to the addiction of a dangerous and wandering life on the pylons. Ray Enright directs this tightly made movie that holds the attention, despite a beginning that plays like a propaganda film for linemen. RK

Pat O'Brien *Red Blayd* • Henry Fonda *Slim* • Margaret Lindsay *Cally* • Stuart Erwin *Stumpy* • J Farrell MacDonald *Pop Traver* • Jane Wyman *Stumpy's girlfriend* ■ *Dir* Ray Enright • *Scr* William Wister Haines, from his novel

Sling Blade ★★★★ 15
Drama 1995 · US · Colour · 129min

This shockingly moving drama brought debutant director Billy Bob Thornton to international attention. In addition to winning an Oscar for his screenplay, he also drew a best actor nomination for his mesmerising performance as the hesitant, seemingly harmless handyman who befriends a lonely boy on being released from the secure hospital where he'd been held for 25 years after murdering his mother and her beau. With unseen sparks flying around an emotional powder keg, this is darkly comic, superbly acted and utterly compelling. DP Violence, swearing. *DVD* 🔵

Billy Bob Thornton *Karl Childers* • Dwight Yoakam *Doyle Hargraves* • JT Walsh *Charles Bushman* • John Ritter *Vaughan Cunningham* • Lucas Black *Frank Wheatley* • Natalie Canerday *Linda Wheatley* • James Hampton *Jerry Woolridge* • Jim Jarmusch *Dairy Queen boy* ■ *Dir/Scr* Billy Bob Thornton

The Slingshot ★★★ 12
Biographical drama 1993 · Swe · Colour · 98min

Touching upon such topics as sex, sibling rivalry, poverty, royalty and anti-Semitism, this evocation of growing up in 1920s Stockholm is an incredibly busy film. Stellan Skarsgård contributes some uncompromising support and Jesper Salen looks suitably put-upon as the incomprehending son of a lame socialist and the punchbag brother of an aspiring boxer. But Ake Sandgren's episodic approach to his fact-based material means that the action never really gains momentum. DP Swedish +subtitles.

Jesper Salen *Roland Schutt* • Stellan Skarsgård *Fritiof Schutt* • Basia Frydman *Zipa Schutt* • Niclas Olund *Bertil Schutt* ■ *Dir* Ake Sandgren • *Scr* Ake Sandgren, from the novel by Roland Schütt

The Slipper and the Rose ★★ U
Musical fantasy 1976 · UK · Colour · 136min

The story of Cinderella doesn't quite gel in this lavish British musical that has neither the magic nor the songs to turn it into the extravaganza that director Bryan Forbes obviously had in mind. Gemma Craven has the voice but not the allure to give Cinders a fairy-tale sheen, and Richard Chamberlain looks a little long in the tooth to play the prince. Edith Evans and Kenneth More steal scenes with ease. DP *DVD*

Richard Chamberlain *Prince* • Gemma Craven *Cinderella* • Annette Crosbie *Fairy Godmother* • Edith Evans *Dowager Queen* • Christopher Gable *John* • Michael Hordern *King* • Margaret Lockwood *Stepmother* • Kenneth More *Lord Chamberlain* ■ *Dir* Bryan Forbes • *Scr* Bryan Forbes, Robert B Sherman, Richard M Sherman

Slippery When Wet ★★★
Documentary 1958 · US · Colour · 43min

Having been impressed by an 8mm short that Bruce Brown shot while stationed on a submarine in Hawaii, Californian surfboard salesman Dale Velzy presented the 20-year-old lifeguard with $5,000 to make a full-length surfing movie. Armed with a 16mm camera and 50 reels of film, Brown flew five buddies to Oahu to launch a career that was to do as much for riding the waves as the Beach Boys. While Brown's self-edited footage is unquestionably rough-and-ready, it still has that endless summer feel. DP *DVD*

■ *Dir* Bruce Brown

Slipstream ★★ PG
Science-fiction adventure 1989 · US/UK · Colour · 87min

The forgotten man of *Star Wars*, Mark Hamill, attempted to get his career airborne again with a return to the sci-fi genre. However, this muddled affair barely got off the ground itself. The concept – a post-apocalyptic world where the favoured form of transportation is the glider – has potential, but director Steven Lisberger never makes up his mind whether this is an escapist fantasy or a more cerebral affair. JF

Mark Hamill *Tasker* • Bob Peck *Byron* • Bill Paxton *Matt Owen* • Kitty Aldridge *Belitski* • Tony Allen *Bartender* • Susan Leong *Abigail* • F Murray Abraham *Cornelius* • Ben Kingsley *Avatar* ■ *Dir* Steven Lisberger • *Scr* Tony Kayden, Charles Pogue, Steven Lisberger, from a story by Bill Bauer

Slither ★★★ 15
Comedy thriller 1973 · US · Colour · 92min

Easy Rider, *Vanishing Point* and *Two-Lane Blacktop* started a vogue for counterculture road movies. *Slither* took it to extremes, a comedy thriller that has the frenetic absurdity of a *Roadrunner* cartoon and a stash of stolen loot as the reason for it all. MGM, wanting out of its cosy middle-American image, hired the combustible James Caan and surrounded him with oddball characters from the likes of Peter Boyle and Sally Kellerman. Played largely deadpan and set in mobile home parks and bingo parlours, it's a charming mess. AT

James Caan *Dick Kanipsia* • Peter Boyle *Barry Fenaka* • Sally Kellerman *Kitty Kopetzky* • Louise Lasser *Mary Fenaka* • Allen Garfield *Vincent J Palmer* • Richard B Shull *Harry Moss* ■ *Dir* Howard Zieff • *Scr* WD Richter

Slither ★★★ 15
Science-fiction horror comedy 2006 · US/Can · Colour · 91min

Smalltown bigshot Michael Rooker is infected by an outer space parasite in this homage to the outrageous splatter and surreal prosthetics of 1980s horror. Soon, he is transformed into a squid-like monster whose spawn of giant slugs worm their way inside any human host. But his wife

Elizabeth Banks and lovesick local cop Nathan Fillion have other ideas. This amiably retro gore extravaganza is full of in-jokes, wisecracks and ironic dialogue. AJ Violence, swearing. *DVD* CS

Nathan Fillion *Bill Pardy* • Elizabeth Banks (2) *Starla Grant* • Michael Rooker *Grant Grant* • Gregg Henry *Jack MacReady* • Tania Saulnier *Kylie Strutemyer* • Brenda James *Brenda Gutierrez* • Don Thompson *Wally* • Jennifer Copping *Margaret* ■ *Dir/Scr* James Gunn (2)

Sliver ★★★ 18
Erotic thriller 1993 · US · Colour · 103min

Sharon Stone consolidated her reputation as Hollywood's hottest sex symbol in another steamy thriller from the pen of Joe Eszterhas, who also scripted her breakthrough hit *Basic Instinct*. Stone is the rather unlikely book editor who moves into an apartment block where the tenants have a worrying habit of moving to the morgue rather than new residences. She's then pursued by two of her neighbours, the oafish author Tom Berenger and the mysterious William Baldwin, either one of whom could be a murderer or a voyeur. Director Phillip Noyce cranks up the tension, and there are some pretty raunchy sex scenes. JF *DVD*

Sharon Stone *Carly Norris* • William Baldwin *Zeke Hawkins* • Tom Berenger *Jack Lansford* • Polly Walker *Vida Jordan* • Colleen Camp *Judy* • Amanda Foreman *Samantha* • Martin Landau *Alex* • CCH Pounder *Lieutenant Victoria Hendrix* ■ *Dir* Phillip Noyce • *Scr* Joe Eszterhas, from the novel by Ira Levin

Slow Burn ★★ 15
Thriller 2003 · US · Colour · 88min

Nothing is what it seems in this implausible mess of corruption and deceit. Ray Liotta's ambitious district attorney struggles to unravel the truth when his assistant and lover (Jolene Blalock) kills a man she claims was assaulting her. Consequently, screenwriter and debut director Wayne Beach unleashes a bewildering welter of revelations without anything meaty to substantiate them. But the biggest weakness is the ludicrous neo-*noir* dialogue, which brings unintended laughs at inopportune moments. SF Swearing, sex scenes, violence. *DVD*

Ray Liotta *Ford Cole* • James Todd Smith aka LL Cool J [LL Cool J] *Luther Pinks* • Mekhi Phifer *Issac Duparde* • Jolene Blalock *Nora Timmer* • Bruce McGill *Godfrey* • Chiwetel Ejiofor *Ty Trippin* • Taye Diggs *Jeffrey Sykes* ■ *Dir* Wayne Beach • *Scr* Wayne Beach, from a story by Beach, Anthony Walton

Slow Dancing in the Big City ★
Drama 1978 · US · Colour · 110min

Journalist Paul Sorvino falls in love with ballerina Anne Ditchburn while performing his Good Samaritan act on an eight-year-old street urchin. Connoisseurs of the soap-opera-as-social-tract won't be surprised to learn that Ditchburn's dancing days are numbered and that the kid has a drug problem. The tear-jerking bathos gets piled on in ever increasing measures until the absolutely breathtaking ending. You have been warned. AJ

Paul Sorvino *Lou Friedlander* • Anne Ditchburn *Sarah Gantz* • Nicolas Coster *David Fillmore* • Anita Dangler *Franny* • Thaao Penghlis *Christopher* • Linda Selman *Barbara Bass* ■ *Dir* John G Avildsen • *Scr* Barra Grant

Slow Motion ★★★ 18
Drama 1980 · Fr/Swi · Colour · 84min

This was Jean-Luc Godard's first bona fide movie for ten years, the previous decade having been dedicated to increasingly impoverished and experimental video, documentary and TV work. There is nod to the autobiographical – a character who's a washed-up film-maker called Godard – but it's also about the director's pet themes of prostitution, exploitation and cultural politics. No Godard movie is ever conventional, and this one isn't either, but the presence of major stars is oddly reassuring and shows the respect Godard

enjoys among the French film community. AT French +subtitles. *DVD*

Isabelle Huppert *Isabelle Rivière* • Jacques Dutronc *Paul Godard* • Nathalie Baye *Denise Rimbaud* • Anna Baldaccini *Isabelle's sister* • Fred Personne *1st client* • Roland Amstutz *2nd client* • Nicole Jacquet *Woman* ■ *Dir* Jean-Luc Godard • *Scr* Jean-Luc Godard, Jean-Claude Carrière, Anne-Marie Miéville

Slow West ★★★★ 15
Western 2015 · UK/NZ/Aus · Colour · 79min

Slow West is a real treat. A western, most likely different from any western you'll have seen before, it is by turns funny, sad, tragic, comic and drily witty – it's a gem of the genre. Kodi Smit-McPhee (*The Road*, *Let Me In*) plays a young Scot who's crossing the US in pursuit of his lover and her father, who've fled Scotland after accidentally committing a capital crime. He's joined by gunfighter Michael Fassbender, who offers help for cash, but whose true motives seem much murkier. En route, they encounter such staples of the genre as outlaws and "injuns", all treated in a deliciously different, offbeat kind of way. *Slow West* is a must-see. DA Violence, swearing. *DVD* 🔵

Kodi Smit-McPhee *Jay Cavendish* • Michael Fassbender *Silas Selleck* • Ben Mendelsohn *Payne* • Caren Pistorius *Rose Ross* • Rory McCann *John Ross* • Andrew Robertt *Werner* ■ *Dir/Scr* John Maclean • *Cinematographer* Robbie Ryan

The Slugger's Wife ★ 15
Romantic comedy 1985 · US · Colour · 99min

Rebecca De Mornay looks jaded in the role of a rock singer who (inexplicably) falls for the crude charms of baseball star Michael O'Keefe. They marry and are soon beset by career conflicts, not to mention ridiculous baseball double entendres. This dismal comedy fails to provide either laughs or romance. A waste of a good cast and director. LH

Michael O'Keefe *Darryl Palmer* • Rebecca De Mornay *Debby Palmer* • Martin Ritt *Burly DeVito* • Randy Quaid *Moose Granger* • Cleavant Derricks *Manny Alvarado* • Lisa Langlois *Aline Cooper* • Loudon Wainwright III *Gary* ■ *Dir* Hal Ashby • *Scr* Neil Simon

Slumber Party '57 ★★
Comedy drama 1976 · US · Colour · 88min

Six high school girls at a slumber party recount how they lost their virginity via some variable flashbacks – the best revolving around making a movie. Sloppy direction and continuity matches the Golden Oldie soundtrack which is mainly comprised of 1960s hits. Debra Winger makes an inauspicious film debut, appearing topless and suggestively eating a banana. A mess, but not devoid of entertainment value. AJ

Noelle North *Angie* • Bridget Holloman *Bonnie May* • Debra Winger *Debbie* • Mary Ann Appleseth *Jo Ann* • Cheryl Smith *Sherry* • Janet Wood *Smitty* • *Scr* Frank Farmer, from a story by William A Levey

The Slumber Party Massacre ★ 18
Horror 1982 · US · Colour · 76min

Given the feminist credentials of author Rita Mae Brown and director Amy Jones, the most shocking thing about this addition to the stalk-and-slash cycle is that it's just as crass and exploitative as most other low-budget entries. Student Michele Michaels is holding a slumber party at her house while her parents are away. Homicidal gate-crasher Michael Villela spoils the fun, decimating her friends. Gory, stupid and sexist. AJ

Michele Michaels *Trish Devereaux* • Robin Stille *Valerie* • Michael Villela *Russ Thorn* • Andree Honore *Jackie* • Debra Deliso *Kim* ■ *Dir* Amy Jones [Amy Holden Jones] • *Scr* Rita Mae Brown

Slumdog Millionaire ★★★★ 15
Drama 2008 · UK · Colour · 115min

Shot almost entirely on the streets of Mumbai, British director Danny Boyle's

S

hyper-energetic rags-to-riches tale aims to dazzle and delight from the start, and for the most part it succeeds. Dev Patel plays the title "slumdog", a poverty-stricken orphan who's just one correct answer away from the *Who Wants to Be a Millionaire?* jackpot of 20 million rupees as the police are brought in. During his interrogation, episodes from his extraordinary life unfold, revealing that each quiz question relates to a different incident. Patel is an appealing lead and he is ably supported by Freida Pinto as his lifelong love interest and Madhur Mittal as his cynical, morally compromised brother Salim. But the movie's real star is the city itself, which is brought to exuberant life by the Oscar-winning Boyle and ace cinematographer Anthony Dod Mantle. AS English, Hindi, +subtitles. **DVD** **BL**

Dev Patel *Jamal Malik (older)* • Freida Pinto *Latika (older)* • Madhur Mittal *Salim Malik (older)* • Anil Kapoor *Prem* ■ *Dir* Danny Boyle • *Scr* Simon Beaufoy, from the novel *Q&A* by Vikas Swarup • *Cinematographer* Anthony Dod Mantle

Slums of Beverly Hills ★★★★ 15

Comedy drama   1998 · US · Colour · 87min

Writer/director Tamara Jenkins made her feature debut with this quirky comedy drama about the bizarreness of growing up. The Abramowitz family live on the slum fringes of Beverly Hills, and we see their problematic existence through the eyes of daughter Natasha Lyonne, who has to deal with her two brothers and a dad (Alan Arkin, superb as usual) trying hard to keep it all together. While all the family and their various acquaintances are both funny and well-realised, the film belongs to Lyonne, who gives a terrific turn as the girl finding pubescent life a very strange experience indeed. JB Swearing, sex scenes, drug abuse, nudity. **DVD**

Alan Arkin *Murray Abramowitz* • Natasha Lyonne *Vivian Abramowitz* • Kevin Corrigan *Eliot* • Jessica Walter *Doris* • Rita Moreno *Belle* • David Krumholtz *Ben Abramowitz* • Eli Marienthal *Rickey Abramowitz* • Carl Reiner *Mickey Abramowitz* • Marisa Tomei *Rita* • Mena Suvari *Rachel* ■ *Dir/Scr* Tamara Jenkins

A Small Act ★★★ 12A

Documentary   2010 · US/Aus · Colour · 88min

Writer/director Jennifer Arnold reveals the great significance of small acts of generosity in this touching, if conventional, documentary. Kenyan Chris Mburu escaped poverty to become a United Nations Human Rights advocate – his education was funded by Hilde Back, a teacher from Sweden who is now in her 80s. Now Mburu has established a fund for underprivileged Kenyan children in Back's name, and Arnold accompanies her to Africa to meet her star student. However, the storylines remain in stubborn isolation and Arnold clumsily attempts to drum up some dramatic tension as a trio of African children await their crucial exam results. The message here is certainly inspirational, but the film is cinematically conservative and fails to pack much political punch. DP English, Kikuyu, Swahili, Swedish +subtitles.

■ *Dir/Scr* Jennifer Arnold

Small Apartments ★★★ 15

Black comedy   2012 · US · Colour · 92min

Jonas Akerlund's quirky and cartoonish film stars Matt Lucas as a Y-front-wearing loner who wonders how to dispose of the body of his loathsome landlord Peter Stormare. But such is the focus on Lucas's desire to escape to Switzerland with cash provided by his mentally unstable brother (James Marsden) that the frantic storyline struggles to make room for such oddball neighbours as Billy Crystal, Johnny Knoxville, James Caan and Juno Temple. Despite the film's distinctive look and the best efforts of the willing cast, this amusing, morbid and mildly misanthropic melange always seems to be straining for effect. DP

Matt Lucas *Franklin Franklin* • James Caan *Mr Allspice* • Billy Crystal *Burt Walnut* • Juno Temple *Simone* • Johnny Knoxville *Tommy Balls* • James

Marsden *Bernard Franklin* • Peter Stormare *Mr Olivetti* ■ *Dir* Jonas Akerlund • *Scr* Chris Millis, from his novella

The Small Back Room ★★★ PG

Second World War drama
1949 · UK · BW · 102min

After the sumptuous theatrics of *Black Narcissus* and *The Red Shoes*, Michael Powell and Emeric Pressburger returned to the muted naturalism of their earlier collaborations for this adaptation of Nigel Balchin's novel about scientists feeling the strain in wartime. The pair were obviously uninspired by the lengthy passages of chat in which the backroom boffins bicker about their latest inventions, but their masterful use of camera angles and cutting gives the finale an unbearable tension. DP **DVD**

David Farrar *Sammy Rice* • Kathleen Byron *Susan* • Jack Hawkins *RB Waring* • Leslie Banks *Colonel Holland* • Cyril Cusack *Corporal Taylor* • Robert Morley *Minister* • Emrys Jones *Joe* • Renée Asherson *ATS Corporal* ■ *Dir* Michael Powell, Emeric Pressburger • *Scr* Michael Powell, Emeric Pressburger, from the novel by Nigel Balchin

Small Change ★★ PG

Drama   1976 · Fr · Colour · 102min

François Truffaut's anecdotal return to the charmed world of childhood suffers from protracted bouts of mawkishness and inconsequence. The linked episodes involving Geory Desmouceaux (a boy caring for his disabled father) and Philippe Goldman (a tearaway beaten by his parents) are the best developed, but even these are tainted by the moralising of their teacher, Jean-François Stévenin. DP In French. **DVD**

Geory Desmouceaux *Patrick* • Philippe Goldman *Julien* • Claudio Deluca *Mathieu Deluca* • Franck Deluca • Richard Golfier • Laurent Devlaeminck *Laurent Riffle* • Jean-François Stévenin *Jean-François Richet* ■ *Dir* François Truffaut • *Scr* François Truffaut, Suzanne Schiffman

Small Engine Repair ★★★ 15

Comedy drama   2006 · Ire · Colour · 117min

Heavily influenced by country music and American independent cinema, Irish director Niall Heery's debut feature piles on the clichés and stereotypes, but leaves an unexpected impression. As an aspiring country singer, Iain Glen has a suitably woe-filled life: his wife has kicked him out, forcing him to move in with garage-owning pal Steven Mackintosh, and he's being threatened by Stuart Graham, a hit-and-run killer recently released from prison. But Glen still dreams of stardom and when an opportunity to perform presents itself, he realises he has to shake off his past and grab his chance. The story offers nothing new, but the wry humour, capable performances and assured sense of place make this an unassuming treat. DP Swearing, some violence. **DVD**

Iain Glen *Doug* • Steven Mackintosh *Bill* • Stuart Graham *Burley* • Laurence Kinlan *Tony* • Tom Jordan Murphy *Christy* • Kathy Keira Clarke *Agnes* • Gary Lydon *Big Eddy* ■ *Dir/Scr* Niall Heery

Small Faces ★★★★ 15

Drama   1995 · UK · Colour · 104min

Gillies MacKinnon's excellent memoir of late-1960s Glasgow was co-written with his producer brother, Billy. Iain Robertson is absolutely superb as the razor-sharp teenager unsure which of his brothers is the best role model – emotionally stunted hardcase JS Duffy or art student Joseph McFadden. Whether running with street gangs, suffering the agonies of a family get-together or driving mother Clare Higgins to distraction, Robertson never fails to convince, which can't always be said for some of the period details. DP Violence, swearing, nudity. **DVD**

Iain Robertson *Lex Maclean* • Joseph McFadden *Alan Maclean* • JS Duffy *Bobby Maclean* • Laura Fraser *Joanne MacGowan* • Garry Sweeney *Charlie Sloan* • Clare Higgins *Lorna Maclean* •

Kevin McKidd *Malky Johnson* ■ *Dir* Gillies MacKinnon • *Scr* Gillies MacKinnon, Billy MacKinnon

Small Soldiers ★★★ PG

Fantasy action adventure
1998 · US · Colour · 105min

Action Man-type figures fitted with deadly microprocessors go on menacing manoeuvres in director Joe Dante's *Gremlins*-meets-*Toy Story* war fantasy. The slick professionalism and technical brilliance keep the awkward mixture of comedy and carnage from becoming too uncomfortable an experience. Crafty nods to classic war films such as *Patton*, the creepy Gwendy Doll sequence and the GI Joes being voiced by the likes of Tommy Lee Jones, Ernest Borgnine and Bruce Dern also help maintain the interest for adults as well as youngsters. AJ Violence, swearing. **DVD** **CS**

Kirsten Dunst *Christy Fimple* • Gregory Smith *Alan Abernathy* • Denis Leary *Gil Mars* • Tommy Lee Jones *Major Chip Hazard* • Frank Langella *Archer* • Ernest Borgnine *Kip Killagin* • Bruce Dern *Link Static* • George Kennedy *Brick Bazooka* • Clint Walker *Nick Nitro* • Sarah Michelle Gellar *Gwendy doll* • Christina Ricci *Gwendy doll* • Phil Hartman *Phil Fimple* • Ann Magnuson *Irene Abernathy* ■ *Dir* Joe Dante • *Scr* Gavin Scott, Adam Rifkin, Ted Elliott, Terry Rossio

Small Time Crooks ★★★ PG

Crime comedy   2000 · US · Colour · 90min

Woody Allen drops a couple of social rungs to lampoon his hermetically sealed Manhattan surroundings in this throwback to his earlier wisecracking comedies. There's much to enjoy in Tracey Ullman's splendid performance as the nouveau riche cookie tycoon who seeks acceptance by taking a culture crash-course with highbrow Hugh Grant. Allen's inverted snobbery is strewn with entertainingly sulky acid drops and Elaine May's ditzy turn as Ullman's cousin is priceless. It's a shame, however, that Allen the director adopts such a patronising approach to his proletarian characters while aiming to expose the pretensions of the chattering classes. DP **DVD**

Woody Allen *Ray Winkler* • Tracey Ullman *Frenchy Winkler* • Hugh Grant *David* • Elaine May *May* • Tony Darrow *Tommy* • George Grizzard *George Blint* • Jon Lovitz *Benny* • Michael Rapaport *Denny* • Elaine Stritch *Chi Chi Potter* ■ *Dir/Scr* Woody Allen

Small Town Girl ★★

Drama   1936 · US · BW · 105min

Robert Taylor had scored so well as a wastrel turned brain surgeon in *Magnificent Obsession* that he was obvious casting for the role in this romantic drama of a wealthy surgeon who marries Janet Gaynor's small-town girl while drunk. Jean Harlow, originally cast, would have given the proceedings more zest and it's a rising young actor called James Stewart who stands out in the thankless part of Gaynor's beau. Director William A Wellman, who fell out with Gaynor, brings no particular distinctiveness to the picture. AE

Janet Gaynor *Kay Brannan* • Robert Taylor (1) *Bob Dakin* • Binnie Barnes *Priscilla* • James Stewart *Elmer* • Lewis Stone *Dr Dakin* • Elizabeth Patterson *Ma Brannan* • Frank Craven *Pa Brannan* ■ *Dir* William A Wellman • *Scr* John Lee Mahin, Edith Fitzgerald, Frances Goodrich, Albert Hackett, from the novel by Ben Ames Williams

The Small Voice ★★★ PG

Thriller   1948 · UK · BW · 80min

Howard Keel made his screen debut in this tense adaptation. Although he eventually proves to have a streak of decency, Keel is imposingly menacing as a convict who exploits the charity of James Donald and Valerie Hobson to hold them and a couple of children hostage until he and confederates David Greene and Michael Balfour can make good their escape. His performance led to a contract with MGM and typecasting as a singing hunk that would prevent him from playing an equally challenging role for many years. DP **DVD**

Valerie Hobson *Eleanor Byrne* • James Donald *Murray Byrne* • Harold Keel [Howard Keel] *Boke* • David Greene *Jim* • Michael Balfour *Frankie* • Joan Young *Potter* • Angela Fouldes *Jenny* • Glynn Dearman *Ken* ■ *Dir* Fergus McDonell • *Scr* George Barraud, Derek Neame, Julian Orde, from the novel by Robert Westerby

The Small World of Sammy Lee ★★ 12

Comedy drama   1963 · UK · BW · 102min

This fast-moving drama, expanded from a BBC TV play, finds Anthony Newley as a smart-aleck strip-show compère, spending a frantic night trying to raise cash to pay off his gambling debts. Newley was involved with several offbeat and nearly forgotten projects, but this is worth seeing for a string of appearances by familiar British television faces. The black-and-white photography makes the suitably grim Soho locations even grimmer. JG **DVD**

Anthony Newley *Sammy Lee* • Julia Foster *Patsy* • Robert Stephens *Gerry* • Wilfrid Brambell *Harry* • Warren Mitchell *Lou* • Miriam Karlin *Milly* • Roy Kinnear *Lucky Dave* ■ *Dir* Ken Hughes • *Scr* Ken Hughes, from his TV play *Sammy*

The Smallest Show on Earth ★★★★ U

Comedy   1957 · UK · BW · 82min

This charming comedy will bring back happy memories for anyone who pines for the days when going to the pictures meant something more than being conveyor-belted in and out of a soulless multiplex. Fondly scripted by John Eldridge and William Rose and deftly directed by Basil Dearden, it stars Bill Travers and Virginia McKenna as a couple who inherit a crumbling cinema staffed by eccentrics. The cast alone makes the movie a must-see, and the sequence in which projectionist Peter Sellers, pianist Margaret Rutherford and doorman Bernard Miles relive the glories of the silent era is adorable. DP **DVD**

Virginia McKenna *Jean Spenser* • Bill Travers *Matt Spenser* • Peter Sellers *Percy Quill* • Margaret Rutherford *Mrs Fazackalee* • Leslie Phillips *Robin Carter* • Bernard Miles *Old Tom* • Sidney James *Mr Hogg* ■ *Dir* Basil Dearden • *Scr* William Rose, John Eldridge, from a story by William Rose

Smalltime ★★★ 18

Comedy drama   1996 · UK · Colour and BW · 58min

It was *TwentyFourSeven* that propelled Nottingham director Shane Meadows into the mainstream, but this earlier work, made on half a shoestring, is a welcome introduction to his raw, gritty and amusing universe. By turns amateurish and professional, funny and depressing, it follows the lives of a bunch of small-time crooks (all wearing the most ridiculous cheap wigs) whose botched attempts at crime make an art form out of incompetence. A sweet-and-sour suburban satire that's touching in a grotesque way. AJ Swearing. **DVD**

Mat Hand *Malc* • Dena Smiles *Kate* • Shane Meadows *Jumbo* • Gena Kawecka *Ruby* • Jimmy Hynd *Willy* • Leon Lammond *Bets* • Tim Cunningham *Lenny the Fence* • Dominic Dillon *Mad Terrance* ■ *Dir/Scr* Shane Meadows

Smart Ass ★ 18

Comedy drama   2014 · Fr · Colour · 85min

Misfit students at France's most exclusive business school apply market economics to sex lives on campus in this satirical offering released in France under the title *La Crème de la Crème*. Having set the story in motion however, writer/director Kim Chapiron fails to exploit it for either sharp humour or moral outrage, instead devoting much of the running time to the romantic foibles of the club's prime movers. TJ In French. Sex scenes, nudity. **DVD**

Thomas Blumenthal *Dan* • Alice Isaaz *Kelly* • Jean-Baptiste Lafarge *Louis* • Karim Ait M'Hand *Jaffar* ■ *Dir* Kim Chapiron • *Scr* Kim Chapiron, from a story by Noe Debre

Smart Blonde ★★★

Detective comedy drama
1936 · US · BW · 55min

This is the first in Warner Bros nine-film Torchy Blane franchise inspired by the crime stories of magazine writer Frederick Nebel, in which the intrepid reporter was actually a man. But Glenda Farrell sparks as the wiseacre news ace who seems to solve every case before lieutenant Barton MacLane (who's also her fiancée) and his doltish sidekick, Tom Kennedy. Lola Lane and Paul Kelly assumed the roles for Torchy Blane in Panama, while the series finale teamed Jane Wyman and Allen Jenkins. But the original, about the killing of a nightclub boss, was the best. DP

Glenda Farrell *Torchy Blane* · Barton MacLane *Steve McBride* · Winifred Shaw *Dolly Ireland* · Addison Richards *Fitz Mularkay* · David Carlyle [Robert Paige] *Louie Friel* · Craig Reynolds *Tom Carney* · Jane Wyman *Dixie* · Tom Kennedy *Gahagan* ■ *Dir* Frank McDonald · *Scr* Kenneth Gamet, Don Ryan, from a story by Frederick Nebel

Smart Money ★★★

Crime drama
1931 · US · BW · 83min

This is as tough as they come, and, incidentally, the only movie to co-star those two gangster heavyweights James Cagney and Edward G Robinson. Robinson plays a lucky small-time barber who hits it big, and Cagney is his mate. Both actors knew one another from the New York stage, and their naturalistic delivery owes much to their theatre background. Directed by Alfred E Green, this gambling-racket crime drama also features Boris Karloff. TS

Edward G Robinson *Nick Venezelos* · James Cagney *Jack* · Evalyn Knapp *Irene Graham* · Ralf Harolde *Sleepy Sam* · Noel Francis *Marie* · Margaret Livingston *District attorney's girl* · Maurice Black *Greek barber* · Boris Karloff *Sport Williams* ■ *Dir* Alfred E Green · *Scr* Kubec Glasmon, John Bright, Lucien Hubbard, Joseph Jackson, from the story *The Idol* by Lucien Hubbard, Joseph Jackson

Smart People ★★★ 15

Romantic comedy drama
2007 · US/Hun · Colour · 90min

Dennis Quaid piles on the pounds for this dysfunctional family tale, playing a widowed academic whose life has gone stale in every possible way. Though worshipped by his daughter (Juno's Ellen Page), he is increasingly estranged from his aspiring poet son (Ashton Holmes) and unfulfilled by work. The unhappy threesome stay locked in their routines until an accident leaves Quaid requiring the chauffeur services of his layabout adopted brother Thomas Haden Church (Sideways). Commercials whiz Noam Murro directs this funny look at people who should know better with a sure hand, but ultimately it's a movie that ends up engaging the head rather than the heart. KK Swearing, drug abuse. DVD

Dennis Quaid *Professor Lawrence Wetherhold* · Sarah Jessica Parker *Dr Janet Hartigan* · Thomas Haden Church *Chuck Wetherhold* · Ellen Page *Vanessa Wetherhold* · Ashton Holmes *James Wetherhold* · David Denman *William* ■ *Dir* Noam Murro · *Scr* Mark Jude Poirier

Smash and Grab ★★ U

Detective comedy drama
1937 · UK · BW · 73min

Jack Buchanan's name is prominent in the credits of this crime comedy as producer and star, but he tries too hard with a confection that exerts little appeal today. He and his frequent musical comedy co-star Elsie Randolph play an investigator and his wife. Randolph gains employment with the principal suspects behind a spate of jewel robberies, while Buchanan stays in his flat practising jujitsu with the butler. AE

Jack Buchanan *John Forrest* · Elsie Randolph *Alice Forrest* · Arthur Margetson *Malvern* · Antony Holles *Palmo* · Edmund Willard *Cappellano* · David Burns *Bellini* ■ *Dir* Tim Whelan · *Scr* Ralph Spence, from a story by Tim Whelan

Smash & Grab: the Story of the Pink Panthers ★★★★ 12A

Part-animated documentary
2012 · UK/US/Ser/Montenegro · Colour · 89min

This documentary takes a compelling look at the most successful jewel gang of modern times. With their roots in Serbia, the Pink Panthers have been linked to hundreds of high-end robberies across the globe, netting millions in the process. Director Havana Marking attempts to shed some light on the shady outfit, fashioning her film around the Dubai police's investigation into a 2007 mall heist and the testimonies of gang members. Without the benefit of a bling budget, proceedings sometimes look more like Crimewatch than Hollywood caper, but the rotoscope-style animated sequences lend it some finesse, there's a wealth of well-chosen archive footage, and the CCTV recording of the raids is as exhilarating as it is shocking. JH Swearing, sexual references. DVD

Tomislav Benzon *Mike* · Jasmin Topalusic *Lela* · Daniel Vivian *Mr Green* ■ *Dir* Havana Marking

Smash Palace ★★★★ 18

Drama
1981 · NZ · Colour · 108min

Among the films that put New Zealand cinema on the map, this is an engrossing study of one man's retreat into despair. Bruno Lawrence gives a painfully truthful performance as the one-time grand prix hero whose idyllic life as a mechanic in the middle of nowhere drives his French wife, Anna Jemison, to adultery. Equally impressive is ten-year-old Greer Robson, as the daughter who becomes a pawn in her parents' increasingly bitter wrangle. This deeply disturbing drama was directed by Roger Donaldson, who has yet to achieve anything of comparable power since his arrival in Hollywood. DP Violence, swearing, nudity.

Bruno Lawrence *Al Shaw* · Anna Jemison *Jacqui Shaw* · Greer Robson *Georgie Shaw* · Keith Aberdein *Ray Foley* · Desmond Kelly *Tiny* ■ *Dir* Roger Donaldson · *Scr* Roger Donaldson, Peter Hansard, Bruno Lawrence

Smash Up – the Story of a Woman ★★★

Drama
1947 · US · BW · 103min

Adapted from a story co-written by the estimable Dorothy Parker, this overblown melodrama seems to have been concocted by putting A Star Is Born and The Lost Weekend in a cocktail mixer and shaking well. Susan Hayward received an Oscar nomination for her performance as a singer who begins to view the world through the bottom of a glass at the same time as her shiftless husband's showbiz stock begins to rise. Lee Bowman's out of his depth as Hayward's husband, but it's still worth a watch. DP

Susan Hayward *Angie Evans Conway* · Lee Bowman *Ken Conway* · Marsha Hunt *Martha Gray* · Eddie Albert *Steve Anderson* · Carl Esmond *Dr Lorenz* · Carleton Young *Mr Elliott* · Charles D Brown *Mike Dawson* ■ *Dir* Stuart Heisler · *Scr* John Howard Lawson, Lionel Wiggam, from a story by Dorothy Parker, Frank Cavett

Smashed ★★★ 15

Comedy drama
2012 · US · Colour · 77min

A low-budget American indie movie about alcoholism would seem to promise a world of misery but, though slight, this well-played drama takes the opposite spin: that it's harder to commit to sobriety than kick dependency. Mary Elizabeth Winstead is cast perfectly against type as the dowdy though still pretty Kate, a kindergarten teacher with a drink problem. Finally forced to face up to her addiction, Kate starts to see her life through different eyes. While there really isn't much in the way of resolution, this thoughtful film does offer an alternative to the usual issue-led movie, thanks to a soulful performance from the underrated Winstead. DW DVD

Mary Elizabeth Winstead *Kate Hannah* · Aaron Paul *Charlie Hannah* · Nick Offerman *Dave Davies* · Megan Mullally *Principal Barnes* · Octavia Spencer *Jenny* · Mary Kay Place *Rochelle* ■ *Dir* James Ponsoldt · *Scr* James Ponsoldt, Susan Burke

The Smashing Bird I Used to Know ★★★ 18

Drama
1969 · UK · Colour · 91min

This prison drama provides an opportunity to see the youthful early careers of Dennis Waterman and Maureen Lipman. It's a rather bizarre tale concerning the murder of Madeline Hinde's mother's boyfriend and the attendant mayhem wreaked on several relationships and individual psyches. They used to crank them out in this mould by the cartload in the 1960s, and this is not the worst example of the genre by any means. Additional interest may come from spotting later sitcom stars. DP DVD

Madeline Hinde *Nicki Johnson* · Renée Asherson *Anne Johnson* · Dennis Waterman *Peter* · Patrick Mower *Harry Spenton* · Faith Brook *Dr Sands* · Maureen Lipman *Sarah* · Derek Fowlds *Geoffrey* · Sheila Steafel *Gilda* · Megs Jenkins *Matron* ■ *Dir* Robert Hartford-Davis · *Scr* John Peacock

Smashing the Rackets ★★

Crime drama
1938 · US · BW · 68min

This efficient, if undistinguished crime drama was the result of a conscious effort by RKO executives to produce the kind of topical, if sensationalist, fare known as "exploitation". Loosely based on the career of New York DA Thomas E Dewey, this fast-talking insight into underworld machinations and corruption in high places makes racket-busting look easy, as every illegal operation crumbles at the sight of Chester Morris and his team. DP

Chester Morris *Jim Conway* · Frances Mercer *Susan Lane* · Bruce Cabot *Steve Lawrence* · Rita Johnson *Letty Lane* · Donald Douglas [Don Douglas] *Spaulding* · Ben Welden *Whitey Clark* · Edward Pawley *Chin Martin* · Frank M Thomas *Judge Wend* ■ *Dir* Lew Landers · *Scr* Lionel Houser, from a story by Forrest Davis

Smashing Time ★★

Comedy
1967 · UK · Colour · 96min

The fact that some of the character names come from the poems of Lewis Carroll provides the clue that this Swinging Sixties comedy is trying too hard to be both clever and cool. It's scripted as satire by George Melly, with Lynn Redgrave and Rita Tushingham as the iconoclastic northern lasses trying to gate-crash the fame game. Director Desmond Davis draws some knowing cameos, but seems ill at ease with the slapstick excesses. DP

Rita Tushingham *Brenda* · Lynn Redgrave *Yvonne* · Michael York *Tom Wabe* · Anna Quayle *Charlotte Brilling* · Irene Handl *Mrs Gimble* · Ian Carmichael *Bobby Mome-Rothlan* · Jeremy Lloyd *Jeremy Tove* · Toni Palmer *Toni* · Arthur Mullard *Café boss* ■ *Dir* Desmond Davis · *Scr* George Melly

Smile ★★★★

Satire
1975 · US · Colour · 112min

Michael Ritchie's picture records the run-up to and the staging of the horrendous Young American Miss competition in Santa Rosa, California, in which 33 wide-eyed girls subject themselves to personality interviews, dance sessions, photo calls and every other cringe-making ritual known to man. Ritchie's camera is unblinking: it's like a documentary, but it isn't. Bruce Dern is the chief judge, a car salesman, and among the hopefuls are Melanie Griffith and Annette O'Toole. A minor masterpiece of wit and observation. AT Swearing.

Bruce Dern *"Big Bob" Freelander* · Barbara Feldon *Brenda DiCarlo* · Michael Kidd *Tommy French* · Geoffrey Lewis *Wilson Shears* · Nicholas Pryor *Andy DiCarlo* · Colleen Camp *Connie Thompson, "Miss Imperial County"* · Annette O'Toole *Doria Houston, "Miss Anaheim"* · Melanie Griffith *Karen Love, "Miss Simi Valley"* ■ *Dir* Michael Ritchie · *Scr* Jerry Belson

A Smile like Yours ★★ 12

Romantic comedy
1997 · US · Colour · 93min

Greg Kinnear and Lauren Holly are both miscast here, playing a couple whose happy marriage comes under fire when they realise they can't have children. Their troubles are compounded when Holly suspects Kinnear of beginning an affair. Sadly, their lack of chemistry is palpable. Cameos from Joan Cusack and Shirley MacLaine are entertaining, but the direction is unfocused. LH Swearing, sexual references.

Greg Kinnear *Danny Robertson* · Lauren Holly *Jennifer Robertson* · Joan Cusack *Nancy Tellen* · Jay Thomas *Steve Harris* · Jill Hennessy *Lindsay Hamilton* · Christopher McDonald *Richard Halstrom* · Shirley MacLaine *Jennifer's mother* ■ *Dir* Keith Samples · *Scr* Kevin Meyers, Keith Samples

Smiles of a Summer Night ★★★★★ PG

Romantic comedy
1955 · Swe · BW · 104min

Ingmar Bergman's sprightly comedy of sexual manners has a distinguished lineage, inspired as it is by Shakespeare's A Midsummer Night's Dream, the operas of Mozart, the plays of Marivaux and Mauritz Stiller's film Erotikon. Its progeny includes Stephen Sondheim's musical A Little Night Music and Woody Allen's A Midsummer Night's Sex Comedy. Bergman's comedies can be laboured and precious, but here he strikes exactly the right note of levity. Led by Eva Dahlbeck as the actress who assembles a weekend party of past, present and prospective lovers, the cast is excellent. DP Swedish +subtitles. DVD

Gunnar Björnstrand *Fredrik Egerman* · Eva Dahlbeck *Desirée Armfeldt* · Ulla Jacobsson *Anne Egerman* · Margit Carlquist [Margit Carlqvist] *Charlotte Malcolm* · Harriet Andersson *Petra the maid* · Birgitta Valberg *Actress* · Bibi Andersson *Actress* ■ *Dir/Scr* Ingmar Bergman

Smiley ★★ U

Adventure drama
1956 · UK · Colour · 96min

This British movie made entirely in Australia shows life in an outback town. Smiley (Colin Petersen) is a small boy obliged to become independent because his mum is a washer woman and his dad is a drunken stockman who spends months in the bush. So Smiley rings the church bells for the local vicar (Ralph Richardson no less), innocently gets involved with drug smugglers and yearns to own a bicycle. It's a rather sickly affair that trades on stereotypes. AT

Ralph Richardson *Rev Lambeth* · John McCallum *Rankin* · Chips Rafferty *Sgt Flaxman* · Colin Petersen *Smiley Greevins* · Jocelyn Hernfield *Miss Workman* ■ *Dir* Anthony Kimmins · *Scr* Moore Raymond, Anthony Kimmins, from the novel by Moore Raymond

Smiley Gets a Gun ★★ U

Comedy drama
1959 · UK · Colour · 89min

Smiley was a huge hit with British family audiences, many of whom were queuing up to emigrate Down Under. This sequel retains writer/director Anthony Kimmins but exchanges one grand thespian (Ralph Richardson) for another, namely Dame Sybil Thorndike. The story has the local copper, Chips Rafferty, promising to give Smiley (Keith Calvert) a gun if he can catch the man who stole Thorndike's horde of gold. AT

Sybil Thorndike *Granny McKinley* · Chips Rafferty *Sgt Flaxman* · Keith Calvert *Smiley Greevins* · Bruce Archer *Joey* · Margaret Christensen *Ma Greevins* · Reg Lye *Pa Greevins* ■ *Dir* Anthony Kimmins · *Scr* Anthony Kimmins, Rex Rienits, from the novel by Moore Raymond

Smilin' Through ★★★★

Melodrama
1932 · US · BW · 98min

The famous and much loved stage play Smilin' Through was filmed as a silent with Norma Talmadge in 1922. This first sound version, Oscar-nominated for best picture, showcases Norma Shearer - en route to mega-stardom - with Fredric March and Leslie Howard under the polished direction of Sidney Franklin. Set in England and

S

spanning the years from 1868 to 1918, the complicated plot involves Howard, reclusive and bitter after his adored bride (Shearer) was shot at the altar by a jealous suitor (March), his orphaned niece who is the spitting image of his dead beloved, and the anguish suffered by all when she falls in love with the killer's son. RK

Norma Shearer *Moonyean Clare/Kathleen* • Fredric March *Kenneth Wayne/Jeremy Wayne* • Leslie Howard *John Carteret* • OP Heggie *Dr Owen* • Ralph Forbes *Willie Ainley* • Beryl Mercer *Mrs Crouch* • Margaret Seddon *Ellen* ■ Dir Sidney Franklin • Scr Ernest Vajda, Claudine West, Donald Ogden Stewart, James Bernard Fagan, from the play by Jane Cowl, Jane Murfin, Langdon McCormick

Smilin' Through ★★
Musical drama   1941 · US · Colour · 100min

The second sound version of this romantic drama stars Jeanette MacDonald in the dual role of the dead wife and niece of bereaved husband Brian Aherne, and accordingly works in several songs. Director Frank Borzage hits new heights in treacly sentimentality here; MacDonald acts well, as does Aherne, but Gene Raymond (the star's real-life husband) is an unattractive disaster as a drunken jealous suitor and his son. RK

Jeanette MacDonald *Kathleen Clare/Moonyean Clare* • Brian Aherne *Sir John Carteret* • Gene Raymond *Kenneth Wayne/Jeremy Wayne* • Ian Hunter *Rev Owen Harding* • Frances Robinson *Ellen* • Patrick O'Moore *Willie* • Eric Lonsdale *Charles* ■ Dir Frank Borzage • Scr Donald Ogden Stewart, John Balderston, from the play by Jane Cowl, Jane Murfin, Langdon McCormick

The Smiling Lieutenant ★★★★★
Musical comedy   1931 · US · BW · 82min

Nowhere is director Ernst Lubitsch's famous "touch" more frequently in evidence than in this delicious trifle adapted from the stage operetta *A Waltz Dream*, its charming score given witty lyrics by Clifford Grey. Maurice Chevalier plays a sexy Viennese guards officer enjoying a love affair with Claudette Colbert, the fiddle-playing leader of a ladies' café orchestra, who attracts the attention of the prim and dowdy daughter (Miriam Hopkins) of a visiting monarch. Assigned, at her request, as official aide to the visitors, he is then ordered to marry her. The plot serves as a foundation on which to build a breathless series of heavenly encounters, alternating between the risqué, the romantic, the hilarious and the poignant. RK

Maurice Chevalier *Niki* • Claudette Colbert *Franzi* • Miriam Hopkins *Princess Anna* • George Barbier *King Adolf* • Charles Ruggles *Max* • Hugh O'Connell *Orderly* ■ Dir Ernst Lubitsch • Scr Ernest Vajda, Samson Raphaelson, Ernst Lubitsch, from the operetta *A Waltz Dream* by Leopold Jacobson, Felix Doermann, from the novel *Nux der Prinzgemahl* by Hans Müller

Smilla's Feeling for Snow ★★15
Mystery thriller   1996 · Ger/Den/Swe · Colour · 116min

Fans of the bestselling book will be disappointed by this plodding adaptation by Bille August. Julia Ormond doesn't have the depth or experience to carry the film as the scientist investigating the death of a young boy who plunges from the roof of her Copenhagen apartment building. While occasionally moody in places, this thriller never quite pushes you to the edge - or even the middle - of your seat, and Ormond is overshadowed at every turn by her impressive co-stars. JB Violence, swearing.

Julia Ormond *Smilla Jasperson* • Gabriel Byrne *Mechanic* • Richard Harris *Tork* • Vanessa Redgrave *Elsa Lubing* • Robert Loggia *Moritz Johnson* • Jim Broadbent *Lagermann* • Bob Peck *Ravn* ■ Dir Bille August • Scr Ann Biderman, from the novel *Miss Smilla's Feeling for Snow* by Peter Høeg

Smith! ★★U
Western comedy drama   1969 · US · Colour · 97min

This is a solidly crafted Disney western about a rancher who tries to prevent the

execution of a young American Indian in the custody of a racist sheriff. Glenn Ford is happily married to Nancy Olson and oozes decency and liberal values while Keenan Wynn pushes every button marked "hiss" or "villain". This also marked the screen debut of Chief Dan George, whose next film, *Little Big Man*, would earn him an Oscar nomination. AT

Glenn Ford *Smith* • Nancy Olson *Norah Smith* • Dean Jagger *Judge* • Keenan Wynn *Vince Heber* • Warren Oates *Walter Charlie* • Chief Dan George *Ol' Antoine* • Frank Ramirez *Gabriel Jimmyboy* • John Randolph *Mr Edwards* ■ Dir Michael O'Herlihy • Scr Louis Pelletier, from the novel *Breaking Smith's Quarter Horse* by Paul St Pierre

Smithereens ★★★15
Drama   1982 · US · Colour · 93min

This low-budget movie packs an adrenaline-charged punch. It features a raucously poignant portrayal by Susan Berman of a punkish, working-class girl trying to make it in the rock 'n' roll world of Manhattan's Lower East Side. The debut film of director Susan Seidelman, this has a terrific soundtrack, and what it lacks in production values it makes up for in verve and gaiety. TH

Susan Berman *Wren* • Brad Rinn *Paul* • Richard Hell *Eric* • Nada Despotovich *Cecile* • Roger Jett *Billy* ■ Dir Susan Seidelman • Scr Ron Nyswaner, Peter Askin, from a story by Ron Nyswaner, Susan Seidelman

Smoke ★★★★15
Drama   1995 · US · Colour and BW · 107min

Novelist Paul Auster's first original screenplay is clearly the product of a literary mind, as the dialogue hangs on the air like the aroma of a good cigar. But without director Wayne Wang's insouciant control and the nuanced performances, this episodic roundelay about the inevitability of chance and coincidence would have seemed stiff and unconvincing. Instead, it's a vibrant portrait of the small community that congregates around Harvey Keitel's Brooklyn cigar shop, whose customers meet fortune and tragedy with equanimity. DP DVD Blu

Harvey Keitel *Auggie Wren* • William Hurt *Paul Benjamin* • Harold Perrineau *Rashid* • Forest Whitaker *Cyrus* • Stockard Channing *Ruby* • Ashley Judd *Felicity* • Giancarlo Esposito *Tommy* • José Zuniga *Jerry* ■ Dir Wayne Wang • Scr Paul Auster, from his short story *Auggie Wren's Christmas Story*

Smoke Signal ★★U
Western   1955 · US · Colour · 87min

Dana Andrews leads the survivors of an Indian massacre to safety in a very routine western, distinguished only by its majestic Grand Canyon setting. Piper Laurie is the only woman in the cast, which includes Universal's handsome heart-throb Rex Reason and veteran Milburn Stone. TS

Dana Andrews *Brett Halliday* • Piper Laurie *Laura Evans* • Rex Reason *Lieutenant Wayne Ford* • William Talman *Captain Harper* • Gordon Jones *Corporal Rogers* • Milburn Stone *Sergeant Miles* • Douglas Spencer *Garode* ■ Dir Jerry Hopper • Scr George Slavin, George W George

Smoke Signals ★★★
Road movie   1998 · US · Colour · 89min

A double winner at the Sundance festival, this is the first US feature to be written, directed and performed solely by native Americans. Adapted by Sherman Alexie from stories in his own collection, it follows Adam Beach and Evan Adams on their trek to Phoenix to collect the ashes of Gary Farmer, the abusive father Beach despises and the hero who pulled Adams out of the fire that killed his parents. Chris Eyre's debut may be a cinematic landmark, but with its sharp, self-deprecating humour, it's also a warm, vibrant and human story. DP

Adam Beach *Victor Joseph* • Evan Adams *Thomas Builds-the-Fire* • Irene Bedard *Suzy Song* • Gary Farmer *Arnold Joseph* • Tantoo Cardinal *Arlene Joseph* • Cody Lightning *Young Victor Joseph* • Simon Baker (2) *Young Thomas Builds-*

the-Fire ■ Dir Chris Eyre • Scr Sherman Alexie, from his stories *The Lone Ranger and Tonto Fistfight in Heaven*

Smokescreen ★★★U
Thriller   1964 · UK · BW · 65min

This above-average programme filler is kept moving swiftly and painlessly by director Jim O'Connolly. Adultery, embezzlement and murder are all taken in his stride by Peter Vaughan as the insurance claims inspector who suspects that there is more to a blazing car wreck than meets the eye. While all around him give typically second-division performances, Vaughan plays with a dogged determination that is efficient, engaging and quite at odds with the more sinister characters he would essay later in his career. DP

Peter Vaughan *Ropey Roper* • John Carson *Trevor Baylis* • Yvonne Romain *Janet Dexter* • Gerald Flood *Graham Turner* • Glynn Edwards *Inspector Wright* ■ Dir/Scr Jim O'Connolly

Smokey and the Bandit ★★★★PG
Comedy   1977 · US · Colour · 91min

A smash hit in its day, this is a marvellously good-natured chase movie, as Burt Reynolds ("Bandit") carts a rather too obviously product-placed truckload of Coors beer across the state lines, outpacing sheriff Jackie Gleason ("Smokey" in the local lingo) by way of a variety of spectacular stunts. Unsurprising, since the movie is the directorial debut of former stuntman Hal Needham. Several sequels were spawned, but none captured the freshness and charm of this terrific original, which greatly benefits from the real-life, as well as on-screen, sexual chemistry between co-stars Burt Reynolds and the vivacious Sally Field. TS DVD Blu

Burt Reynolds *Bandit* • Sally Field *Carrie* • Jackie Gleason *Sheriff Buford T Justice* • Jerry Reed *Cledus Snow* • Mike Henry *Junior Justice* • Paul Williams *Little Enos Burdette* • Pat McCormick *Big Enos Burdette* ■ Dir Hal Needham • Scr James Lee Barrett, Charles Shyer, Alan Mandel, from a story by Hal Needham, Robert L Levy

Smokey and the Bandit II ★★★PG
Comedy   1980 · US · Colour · 96min

Not so much of a chase comedy as the first film, this battle of wits between trucker Burt Reynolds and dogged cop Jackie Gleason is more a series of sight gags that pile up like a motorway collision. The tone is set from the beginning when Reynolds emerges from behind a huge heap of beer cans. Reynolds has always been capable of much more than this genial, show-off role, but it's what he obviously likes best. TH Swearing. DVD

Burt Reynolds *Bandit* • Jackie Gleason *Sheriff Buford T Justice/Reginald Van Justice/Gaylord Van Justice* • Jerry Reed *Cledus* • Dom DeLuise *Doc* • Sally Field *Carrie* • Paul Williams *Little Enos* • David Huddleston *John Conn* ■ Dir Hal Needham • Scr Jerry Belson, Brock Yates, from a story by Michael Kane, from characters by Hal Needham, Robert L Levy

Smokey and the Bandit III ★18
Comedy   1983 · US · Colour · 81min

Jerry Reed (Burt Reynolds's sidekick from the first two movies) takes over as the number one bandit, once again setting off on a cross-country trek and being pursued by the moronic police force. Dick Lowry takes over the directorial reins, but he simply throws car crash after car crash at the screen in a desperate fashion. Dire. JF Swearing, nudity. DVD

Jackie Gleason *Buford T Justice* • Jerry Reed *Cletus/Bandit* • Paul Williams *Little Enos Burdette* • Pat McCormick *Big Enos* • Mike Henry *Junior* • Colleen Camp *Dusty Trails* • Faith Minton *Tina* • Burt Reynolds *The Real Bandit* ■ Dir Dick Lowry • Scr Stuart Birnbaum, David Dashev, from characters by Hal Needham, Robert L Levy

Smokin' Aces ★18
Black comedy action drama   2006 · US/UK/Fr · Colour · 104min

After his thoughtful and engaging cop thriller *Narc* (2001), writer/director Joe Carnahan wildly misses the mark with this Tarantino-style black comedy. When Las Vegas showman Buddy "Aces" Israel (*Entourage*'s Jeremy Piven) agrees to turn FBI informant, his former Mob cronies put out a hit on him. Enter a motley assortment of assassins ranging from Ben Affleck to singer Alicia Keys (who should stick to the day job), with Ray Liotta and Ryan Reynolds thrown into the mix as federal agents out to protect their asset. Instead of crafting characters to laugh with (or even at), Carnahan mistakenly indulges in a sniggering schoolboy obsession with casual mutilation and silly wigs. SP DVD Blu

Ben Affleck *Jack Dupree* • Jeremy Piven *Buddy "Aces" Israel* • Andy Garcia *Stanley Locke* • Alicia Keys *Georgia Sykes* • Jason Bateman *Rupert "Rip" Reed* • Ray Liotta *Donald Carruthers* • Ryan Reynolds *Richard Messner* • Peter Berg *"Pistol" Pete Deeks* ■ Dir/Scr Joe Carnahan • Cinematographer Mauro Fiore

Smoking/No Smoking ★★★★PG
Drama   1993 · Fr · Colour · 292min

The eight plays in Alan Ayckbourn's *Intimate Exchanges* cycle are presented in an unashamedly theatrical manner by Alain Resnais in this mammoth two-part adaptation. It takes a while to get used to hearing the clichéd expressions of the English middle classes in colloquial French, but the exceptional performances of Sabine Azéma and Pierre Arditi will soon have you hooked. It is worth trying to watch in one sitting as the interweaving between the two films is ingenious. DP French +subtitles. Swearing.

Sabine Azéma *Celia Teasdale/Rowena Coombes/Sylvie Bell/Irene Pridworthy/Josephine Hamilton* • Pierre Arditi *Toby Teasdale/Miles Coombes/Lionel Hepplewick/Joe Hepplewick* ■ Dir Alain Resnais • Scr Alan Ayckbourn, Agnès Jaoui, Jean-Pierre Bacri, from the plays *Intimate Exchanges* by Ayckbourn

Smoky ★★★U
Western   1946 · US · Colour · 84min

This heartbreaking tale of a horse will bring a lump to the hardest of throats. Based on the once-popular Will James story, the adventures of Smoky put *Black Beauty* to shame. This version is well photographed in glorious 1940s Technicolor and sympathetically directed by Louis King, lesser-known younger brother of veteran Henry King. Fred MacMurray and Anne Baxter are eminently likeable, but the real scene-stealer, making his movie debut here, is Burl Ives. TS

Fred MacMurray *Clint Barkley* • Anne Baxter *Julie Richards* • Burl Ives *Bill* • Bruce Cabot *Frank* • Esther Dale *Gram* • Roy Roberts *Jeff* ■ Dir Louis King • Scr Lillie Hayward, Dwight Cummins, Dorothy Yost, from the novel *Smoky, the Cowhorse* by Will James

Smooth Talk ★★★15
Drama   1985 · US · Colour · 87min

This American coming-of-age movie features Laura Dern as a gauche teenager unable to relate to her mother (Mary Kay Place), who unfavourably compares the 15-year-old to her peaches and cream sister. Rebelling, Dern hangs out with her girlfriends and gets up to mischief, finally biting off more than she can chew when she encounters the charismatic but sexually aggressive Treat Williams. It's a well-judged piece by director Joyce Chopra, with Dern excelling in the lead role. LH

Treat Williams *Arnold Friend* • Laura Dern *Connie* • Mary Kay Place *Katherine* • Levon Helm *Harry* • Sara Inglis [Sarah Inglis] *Jill* • Margaret Welsh *Laura* ■ Dir Joyce Chopra • Scr Tom Cole, from the short story *Where Are You Going, Where Have You Been* by Joyce Carol Oates

The Smurfs ★★ U
Part-animated comedy adventure
2011 · US/Bel · Colour · 98min

These little blue creatures have been charming – and sickening – children and adults since they were dreamt up by Belgian cartoonist Peyo in 1958. Now they're in a 3D film with Neil Patrick Harris and Jayma Mays as soon-to-be parents who find themselves protectors of Smurfs fleeing from the evil magician Gargamel (Hank Azaria) in modern-day New York. Adults will find it barely entertaining, but children will love the little blue folk, while extra points go to Harris for comedic grace in an otherwise banal role. KK *DVD* *BL* *3D*

Neil Patrick Harris *Patrick Winslow* · Jayma Mays *Grace Winslow* · Hank Azaria *Gargamel* · Jonathan Winters *Papa Smurf* · Katy Perry *Smurfette* · Alan Cumming *Gutsy Smurf* ■ *Dir* Raja Gosnell · *Scr* J David Stern, David N Weiss, Jay Scherick, David Ronn, from characters by Peyo

The Smurfs 2 ★★★ U
Part-animated comedy
2013 · US · Colour · 100min

Those little blue heroes are back. The first film, adapted from the Belgian comic and 1980s cartoon series, was good-natured fun and so, too, is this – if you're under seven and easily amused. This time, hapless returning human stars Neil Patrick Harris, Jayma Mays and Hank Azaria interact with the CG smurfs in Paris, where hiss-boo baddie Gargame (Azaria) has kidnapped Smurfette (voiced by singer Katy Perry). The rescue mission is daft, but it's a decent diversion for younger kids. *Smurfs: the Lost Village*, with Demi Lovato as Smurfette, is due in 2017. DA *DVD* *BL* *CS*

Neil Patrick Harris *Patrick Winslow* · Brendan Gleeson *Victor Doyle* · Jayma Mays *Grace Winslow* · Hank Azaria *Gargamel* · Katy Perry *Smurfette* · Jonathan Winters *Papa Smurf* · Christina Ricci *Vexy* · JB Smoove *Hackus* ■ *Dir* Raja Gosnell · *Scr* Karey Kirkpatrick, David Ronn, Jay Scherick, J David Stern, David N Weiss, from a story by Ronn, Scherick, Stern and Weiss, from characters by Peyo

The Snail's Strategy ★★★
Comedy
1993 · Col · Colour · 116min

Sergio Cabrera's sympathy for the common people is evident in this genial comedy, in which the squatters in a Bogota mansion vacillate between legal stalling and direct action to prevent an avaricious capitalist reclaiming his lapsed rights to ownership. Frank Ramirez's opportunist attorney and Fausto Cabrera's Spanish Civil War veteran stand out in an ensemble whose travails reflect the nation's plights and characteristics. The hilarious house-shifting scam is inspired. DP Spanish +subtitles.

Frank Ramirez · Humberto Dorado · Florina Lemaitre · Gustavo Angarita · Vicky Hernandez · Fausto Cabrera ■ *Dir* Sergio Cabrera · *Scr* Humberto Dorado, from a screenplay (unproduced) by Sergio Cabrera, Ramon Jimeno

Snake Eyes ★★★ 15
Mystery thriller
1998 · US · Colour · 94min

The US Secretary of Defense is assassinated in full view of a huge audience gathered in an Atlantic City casino for a boxing champion ship. Can supercharged detective Nicolas Cage use his own recollections and those of key witnesses to find out whodunnit and unravel an ever-widening conspiracy? Although a stunning visual tour de force by director Brian De Palma, this jigsaw murder mystery lacks suspense and disappoints as a thriller, with the expected slam-bang finale never materialising. AJ Violence, some swearing. *DVD*

Nicolas Cage *Rick Santoro* · Gary Sinise *Kevin Dunne* · John Heard *Gilbert Powell* · Carla Gugino *Julia Costello* · Stan Shaw *Lincoln Tyler* · Kevin Dunn *Lou Logan* ■ *Dir* Brian De Palma · *Scr* David Koepp, from a story by Brian De Palma, David Koepp · *Cinematographer* Stephen H Burum

Snake in the Eagle's Shadow ★★★★ 18
Martial arts action comedy
1978 · HK · Colour · 92min

Released just before Jackie Chan's breakout hit *Drunken Master*, this terrific action yarn was his first leading role. Ditching his previous attempts to become the new Bruce Lee, he unveiled his talent for slapstick comedy here. Chan plays Chien Fu, a cowardly, bumbling bumpkin who learns the fabled Snake Fist fighting style from an old beggar and becomes a hero despite himself. The silliness of the plot and the overbearing soundtrack are more than compensated for by the incredible fight sequences. JR Cantonese +subtitles.

Lung Cheng [Jackie Chan] *Chien Fu* · Yuen Hsiao-Tien [Simon Yuen] *Grandmaster Pai Cheng-Tien* · Huang Cheng Li [Hwang Jang Lee] *Lord Sheng Kuan* ■ *Dir* Yuen Woo-Ping · *Scr* Ng See Yuen, Tsai Chi-Kuang

A Snake of June ★★★★ 18
Drama
2002 · Jpn · BW · 76min

Although there's a metallic sheen to the monochrome imagery, there is little of the industrial dehumanisation that characterised Shinya Tsukamoto's *Tetsuo* pictures in this sinister, stylish and highly disconcerting rain-saturated study of sexual frustration and the torment of isolation. Decay remains a key theme, however, as both Tsukamoto's manipulative stalker and victim Asuka Kurosawa are suffering from malevolent illnesses. Yet notwithstanding the humiliation Kurosawa endures as Tsukamoto puts her through acts of public exhibitionism and the beating that her complacent husband Yuji Koutari sustains, the story ends on an unexpected note of optimism as the couple re-ignite their long-dormant passion. DP Japanese +subtitles. *DVD*

Asuka Kurosawa *Rinko Tatsumi* · Yuji Koutari *Shigehiko Tatsumi* · Shinya Tsukamoto *Michio Iguchi* ■ *Dir/Scr* Shinya Tsukamoto

The Snake Pit ★★★★ 12
Psychological drama
1948 · US · BW · 103min

In its day, this was a truly harrowing and extremely controversial adaptation of Mary Jane Ward's semi-autobiographical novel about life in a mental institution. In Britain, the film was perceived to be so disturbing that it suffered from over-zealous censor cuts. The film still retains its power to shock and, although the medical department may seem slightly antiquated, the performances of the women inmates are still incredibly moving, particularly Olivia de Havilland in the lead, and Celeste Holm, Beulah Bondi and a young Betsy Blair in support. Anatole Litvak's direction may seem on the strident side, but this still has impact. TS *DVD*

Olivia de Havilland *Virginia Stuart Cunningham* · Mark Stevens *Robert Cunningham* · Leo Genn *Dr Mark Kirk* · Celeste Holm *Grace* · Glenn Langan *Dr Terry* · Helen Craig *Miss Davis* · Leif Erickson *Gordon* · Beulah Bondi *Mrs Greer* ■ *Dir* Anatole Litvak · *Scr* Frank Partos, Millen Brand, from the novel by Mary Jane Ward

Snakes & Ladders ★★ 15
Comedy
1996 · Ire/Ger · Colour · 92min

Things go downhill rather rapidly in this would-be wacky comedy from Trish McAdam. Pom Boyd and Gina Moxley share a flat in Dublin, harbouring dreams that someone will see them performing on the city streets and whisk them off to cabaret celebrity. However, their friendship comes under threat when Boyd's indolent boyfriend, Sean Hughes, pops the question. This doggedly alternative romp might have passed muster as a sitcom subplot, but it works woefully as a feature. DP

Pom Boyd *Jean* · Gina Moxley *Kate* · Sean Hughes *Martin* · Paudge Behan *Dan* ■ *Dir/Scr* Trish McAdam

Snakes on a Plane ★★ 15
Action horror thriller
2006 · US · Colour · 101min

David R Ellis's much-anticipated slither-fest certainly generated a wave of internet hype, but this by-the-numbers thriller barely surpasses the standard of a straight-to-video movie. As the gimmicky title suggests, the poisonous reptiles are let loose on a Hawaii to LA flight. Their target is Nathan Phillips (*Wolf Creek*), the only witness in a major murder case, who is in the protective custody of FBI agent Samuel L Jackson. The script is a few one-liners short of an *Airplane!* sequel. And, yes, stewardess Julianna Margulies does have to fly the plane. AJ *DVD* *BL*

Samuel L Jackson *Neville Flynn* · Julianna Margulies *Claire Miller* · Nathan Phillips *Sean Jones* · Bobby Cannavale *Hank Harris* · Rachel Blanchard *Mercedes* · Flex Alexander *Three G's* · Kenan Thompson *Troy* · Terry Chen *Chen Leong* ■ *Dir* David R Ellis · *Scr* John Heffernan, Sebastian Gutierrez, from a story by Heffernan, David Dalessandro

Snapdragon ★ 18
Erotic thriller
1993 · US · Colour · 94min

This dire erotic thriller has Pamela Anderson playing an amnesiac who has dreams about killing the men she has sex with. Steven Bauer co-stars as the police psychologist who takes an awful long time to figure it all out. There is a twist in the tale, but don't expect too much in the way of a quality plot or decent acting. ST

Steven Bauer *David* · Chelsea Field *Sergeant Peckham* · Pamela Anderson *Felicity* · Matt McCoy *Bernie* · Kenneth Tigar *Captain* · Irene Tsu *Hua* ■ *Dir* Worth Keeter · *Scr* Gene Church

The Snapper ★★ 15
Comedy drama
1993 · UK · Colour · 90min

Adapted by Roddy Doyle from his own novel, this sassy comedy drama was something of a disappointment after his earlier slice of working-class Dublin life, *The Commitments*. Sometimes funny, sometimes touching, the film benefits from a few snorting one-liners and some solid ensemble playing, although the cast occasionally gets carried away during the very stagey shouting matches. The main problem, however, is that director Stephen Frears too often allows the comedy to slip into sitcom and the drama to come across as something from a social-conscience soap opera. *The Van*, the final part of the trilogy, was released in late 1996. DP

Tina Kellegher *Sharon Curley* · Colm Meaney *Dessie Curley* · Ruth McCabe *Kay Curley* · Eanna MacLiam *Craig Curley* · Peter Rowen *Sonny Curley* · Joanne Gerrard *Lisa Curley* · Colm O'Byrne *Darren Curley* · Brendan Gleeson *Lester* ■ *Dir* Stephen Frears · *Scr* Roddy Doyle, from his novel

Snatch ★★★ 18
Comedy crime drama
2000 · US/UK · Colour · 102min

You'd have thought that Guy Ritchie would've shied away from replicating *Lock, Stock and Two Smoking Barrels* after the current glut of British gangster movies. Sadly not. Although *Snatch* has its merits – among them originality and the talents of Brad Pitt, Benicio Del Toro, and Jasons Statham and Flemyng – the diamond heist and East End Mob plot are just more of the same. Gangs, cheeky chappies, bare-knuckle boxing and cameos from Vinnie Jones and Mike Reid merge into a "seen it all before" mix. Ritchie can direct, but perhaps it's time he got someone else to write the material. LH *DVD* *BL*

Brad Pitt *Mickey One Punch O'Neill* · Jason Statham *Turkish* · Benicio Del Toro *Franky Four Fingers* · Dennis Farina *Avi* · Vinnie Jones *Bullet Tooth Tony* · Rade Serbedzija *Boris the Blade* · Alan Ford *Brick Top* · Mike Reid *Doug the Head* · Ewen Bremner *Mullet* · Jason Flemyng *Darren* ■ *Dir/Scr* Guy Ritchie

Sneakers ★★★★ 15
Comedy thriller
1992 · US · Colour · 120min

This is a smart and snappy caper that is blessed with a sparkling script and an outstanding ensemble cast. Robert Redford, graciously sending himself up a little, plays the former student radical who now makes a living heading a team that is paid to break into hi-tech buildings to show up lapses in security systems. However, his past returns to haunt him when he is blackmailed into stealing the ultimate codebreaker. Ignore the holes in plot logic and savour the relaxed and unselfish comic interplay. JF Violence, swearing. *DVD*

Robert Redford *Martin Bishop* · Dan Aykroyd *"Mother"* · Ben Kingsley *Cosmo* · Mary McDonnell *Liz* · River Phoenix *Carl* · Sidney Poitier *Crease* · David Strathairn *Whistler* · Timothy Busfield *Dick Gordon* · James Earl Jones *Bernard Abbott* ■ *Dir* Phil Alden Robinson · *Scr* Phil Alden Robinson, Lawrence Lasker, Walter F Parkes

The Sniper ★★★★
Crime drama
1952 · US · BW · 87min

This is an excellent exploration of what drives one man to shoot at random with no apparent thought or feeling. The man in question has a deep grudge against women and the camera follows his gun as if we, the audience, are his eyes, the effect of this visual trick being both eerie and strangely compelling. Arthur Franz gives a powerful performance as the madman and this is neither a paean to violence, nor a total condemnation of society, but an intelligent movie that poses many complex questions. SH

Adolphe Menjou *Lieutenant Kafka* · Arthur Franz *Eddie Miller* · Gerald Mohr *Sergeant Ferris* · Marie Windsor *Jean Darr* · Frank Faylen *Inspector Anderson* · Richard Kiley *Dr James G Kent* ■ *Dir* Edward Dmytryk · *Scr* Harry Brown, from a story by Edward Anhalt, Edna Anhalt

Sniper ★★★ 15
Action thriller
1992 · US · Colour · 94min

Though it doesn't quite come off, this is an intelligent spin on the action thriller. Tom Berenger is a marksman on a covert mission to terminate a Panamanian rebel leader. However, he soon discovers he has more than enough on his plate dealing with his twitchy new partner, Billy Zane. The pair's claustrophobic relationship generates plenty of jungle-bound tension and the action set pieces are stylishly staged by director Luis Llosa. Two sequels to date. JF Swearing, violence. *DVD*

Tom Berenger *Tom Beckett* · Billy Zane *Richard Miller* · Aden Young *Doug Papich* · Ken Radley *El Cirujano* · JT Walsh *Chester Van Damme, Beckett's senior officer* · Reinaldo Arenas [Reynaldo Arenas] *Cacique* ■ *Dir* Luis Llosa · *Scr* Michael Frost Beckner, Crash Leyland

Snitch ★★★ 12
Crime thriller
2013 · US/Can/UAE · Colour · 107min

Dwayne "The Rock" Johnson stars in this solid crime thriller with a capable supporting cast. He plays a construction boss who poses as a truck-driving drugs trafficker to get his estranged son freed from prison. The action scenes, shootouts and car chases are efficiently handled by director and former stuntman Ric Roman Waugh, and Johnson genuinely impresses in the more emotional moments, too. If it's not quite the really good film that Johnson has in him, *Snitch* more than passes muster. DA Some violence, swearing. *DVD* *BL*

Dwayne Johnson *John Matthews* · Barry Pepper *Agent Billy Cooper* · Jon Bernthal *Daniel* · Michael K Williams [Michael Kenneth Williams] *Malik* · Melina Kanakaredes *Sylvie Collins* · Nadine Velazquez *Analisa* · Benjamin Bratt *Juan Carlos "El Topo" Pintera* · Susan Sarandon *Joanne Keeghan* ■ *Dir* Ric Roman Waugh · *Scr* Ric Roman Waugh, Justin Haythe

Snoopy and Charlie Brown: the Peanuts Movie ★★★★ U
Animated comedy adventure
2015 · US · Colour · 88min

Sixty-five years after US cartoonist Charles M Schulz first created Charlie Brown, Snoopy, Lucy and the rest of the *Peanuts* pack, and 35 years since the most recent feature release, they finally make a return to cinemas with this cute and charmingly computer-generated outing. There's a plot of sorts, which has Charlie Brown bidding to woo the town's new "red-haired girl". But it's really just a framework for some beautifully rendered *Peanuts* scenarios,

with determined but luckless Charlie as the "face of failure", Lucy as the queen of crabbiness, and Snoopy as the supreme fantasist. Adults will wallow in the nostalgia, and chances are kids will love it, too. **DA**
DVD **BL** **3D**

Noah Schnapp *Charlie Brown* • Hadley Belle Miller *Lucy* • Bill Melendez *Snoopy/Woodstock* • Mariel Sheets *Sally* • Alex Garfin [Alexander Garfin] *Linus* ■ *Dir* Steve Martino • *Scr* Cornelius Uliano, Bryan & Craig Schulz, from the comic strip by Charles M Schulz

Snoopy, Come Home ★★★ U

Animation	1972 · US · Colour · 81min

Second in the series of feature-length *Peanuts* adventures. Charles M Schulz's beagle takes centre stage, vowing that life *isn't* going to the dogs, and, with bird-brained buddy Woodstock in tow, heading off in search of something better. Cutely animated, and packed with all the gentle charm and humour of the *Peanuts* comic strip, this can still delight the kids. **DA** **DVD**

Chad Webber *Charlie Brown* • Robin Kohn *Lucy Van Pelt* • Stephen Shea *Linus Van Pelt* • David Carey *Schroeder* • Bill Melendez *Snoopy* ■ *Dir* Bill Melendez • *Scr* from the comic strip by Charles M Schulz

Snow ★★

Seasonal comedy
2004 · Can/US · Colour · 90min

Taking over the family business proves a headache for Santa's son (played by Tom Cavanagh from *The Flash* TV series), when his new reindeer, Buddy, is stolen just days before Christmas. In this flimsy but fun, festive diversion, slapstick and other kid-friendly goofiness follow, as the exaggeratedly flustered novice races to retrieve the critter from a zoo. Younger viewers will enjoy the bouncy last act, which culminates in an exciting chase once Buddy's magical abilities finally emerge. **SF**

Tom Cavanagh *Nick Snowden* • Ashley Williams *Sandy Brooks* • Patrick Fabian *Buck Seger* • Bobb'e J Thompson *Hector* • Jackie Burroughs *Lorna* ■ *Dir* Alex Zamm • *Scr* Rich Burns

Snow Cake ★★★★ 15

Tragicomedy
2005 · UK/Can/Neth · Colour · 107min

Sigourney Weaver turns in a bold performance as a high-functioning autistic woman in this potentially dour yet carefully balanced tragicomedy from Welsh director Marc Evans. Weaver's ordered life in a remote Canadian town is disrupted by the news that her daughter is dead. Alan Rickman plays the hangdog loner who was driving the car in which her child was killed. As Evans explores the relationship between Alex, Linda and her neighbour Maggie (Carrie-Anne Moss), he finds genuine laugh-out-loud moments amid the aching tragedy. Revelations about Rickman's past are perhaps too much icing on the cake, but this is still a thoroughly satisfying piece of cinema. **SP** Swearing. **DVD**

Alan Rickman *Alex Hughes* • Sigourney Weaver *Linda Freeman* • Carrie-Anne Moss *Maggie* • Emily Hampshire *Vivienne* • James Allodi *Clyde* ■ *Dir* Marc Evans • *Scr* Angela Pell

Snow Day ★★ PG

Comedy
2000 · US/Ger · Colour · 85min

A "snow day" is that special day in America when a freak blizzard causes an unexpected break from school. Mark Webber uses the opportunity to make a play for the glamorous Emmanuelle Chriqui, while his younger sister Zena Grey tries to keep the snow-plowman (Chris Elliott) occupied so that her school remains closed. Director Chris Koch piles on the teen movie clichés, but this is still good-natured. **TH** **DVD**

Chris Elliott *Snow-plowman* • Mark Webber *Hal Brandston* • Jean Smart *Laura Brandston* • Schuyler Fisk *Lane Leonard* • Iggy Pop *Mr Zellweger* • Pam Grier *Tina* • John Schneider *Chad Symmonz* • Chevy Chase *Tom Brandston* • Zena Grey *Natalie Brandston* • Emmanuelle Chriqui *Claire Bonner* ■ *Dir* Chris Koch • *Scr* Will McRobb, Chris Viscardi

Snow Dogs ★★ PG

Comedy adventure
2002 · US · Colour · 95min

A reconciliation between estranged father and son – a familiar Hollywood staple – provides the basis for this comedy adventure, sadly lacking in both thrills and jokes. Cuba Gooding Jr plays a successful Miami dentist who discovers he's adopted and has been left an Alaskan cabin and a pack of sled dogs by his real mother. Travelling to the small town of Tolketna, Gooding Jr encounters his white biological father, unwelcoming James Coburn. **TH**
DVD

Cuba Gooding Jr *Ted Brooks* • James Coburn *Thunder Jack* • Sisqo *Dr Rupert Brooks* • Nichelle Nichols *Amelia Brooks* • M Emmet Walsh *George* • Brian Doyle-Murray *Ernie* ■ *Dir* Brian Levant • *Scr* Jim Kouf, Tommy Swerdlow, Michael Goldberg, Mark Gibson, Philip Halprin, from the non-fiction book *Winterdance: the Fine Madness of Running the Iditarod* by Gary Paulsen

Snow Falling on Cedars ★★★★ 15

Courtroom drama
1999 · US · Colour · 121min

It's rare to experience an adaptation of a novel as true to the spirit of the original as director Scott Hicks's follow-up to the Oscar-winning *Shine*. David Guterson's book about prejudice within a small fishing community in the years following the Second World War is vivid, poetic and sensual, qualities this film shares in abundance. Ethan Hawke plays a local journalist fascinated by the trial of a Japanese-American war hero accused of murdering a fellow fisherman. The trial becomes the focus for fear and scapegoating in a mixed-race community torn apart by Pearl Harbor. Hicks sacrifices narrative thrust for atmosphere, resulting in a slow but very beautiful film. **LH** **DVD**

Ethan Hawke *Ishmael Chambers* • Youki Kudoh *Hatsue Miyamoto* • Reeve Carney *Young Ishmael Chambers* • Anne Suzuki *Young Hatsue Imada* • Rick Yune *Kazuo Miyamoto* • Max von Sydow *Nels Gudmundsson* • James Rebhorn *Alvin Hooks* • James Cromwell *Judge Fielding* • Sam Shepard *Arthur Chambers* ■ *Dir* Scott Hicks • *Scr* Ron Bass [Ronald Bass], Scott Hicks, from the novel by David Guterson

Snow Flower and the Secret Fan ★★★ 12

Historical drama
2011 · Chi/US · Colour · 99min

From Wayne Wang, director of *The Joy Luck Club*, comes a similarly sentimental sob story, this time one rooted in the Chinese notion of "laotong", the vow of eternal friendship between two women. The two parallel stories feature the same actress pairing of Bingbing Li and Gianna Jun, and concern two estranged modern-day Shanghai friends, Nina and Sophia, and their 19th-century ancestors. The cross-cutting between the foot-binding, arranged-marriage past and the fast-living, globe-trotting present is sometimes irksome, but is vital to emphasise the bonds of sisterhood that straddle history. It's a handsomely mounted if somewhat staid chick flick, and there's the added bonus of a sparkling cameo by *X-Men* star Hugh Jackman. **DA** English, Mandarin +subtitles. A sex scene. **DVD**

Gianna Jun *Snow Flower/Sophia* • Bingbing Li *Nina/Lily* • Hugh Jackman *Arthur* • Vivian Wu *Aunt* • Wu Jiang *Butcher* • Coco Chiang *Anna* ■ *Dir* Wayne Wang • *Scr* Ron Bass [Ronald Bass], Angela Workman, Michael K Ray, from the novel by Lisa See

Snow in Paradise ★★★ 18

Thriller based on a true story
2014 · UK · Colour · 103min

Unusually for a contemporary London-set gangster film, *Snow in Paradise* paints its native East End wide-boy hero as a dying breed, slowly squeezed out by gentrification and outnumbered as the city becomes more multicultural. Based on the real-life experiences of co-star and co-writer Martin Askew, it stars newcomer Frederick Schmidt as Dave, a small-time crook who accidentally leads his best friend into mortal danger when a drug deal goes wrong. The

film's subtle, underlying air of menace is nicely sustained throughout. **DW** **DVD**

Frederick Schmidt *Dave* • Aymen Hamdouchi *Tariq* • Martin Askew *Uncle Jimmy* • Claire-Louise Cordwell *Theresa* • Ashley Chin *Amjad* ■ *Dir* Andrew Hulme • *Scr* Martin Askew, Andrew Hulme

Snow Job ★★

Crime drama
1972 · US · Colour · 90min

In this vehicle for the former Olympic ski champion Jean-Claude Killy, the beauty of the Alpine scenery and Killy's sporting prowess are plain for all to see, but so is the fact that this crime caper is just no good. As the ski instructor who robs the local bank, Killy falls flat on his face every time he comes off the piste. The sole bright spot is provided by legendary director Vittorio De Sica, whose sly cameo shows why he was such a matinée idol in the 1930s and 40s. **DP**

Jean-Claude Killy *Christian Biton* • Danièle Gaubert *Monica Scotti* • Cliff Potts *Bob Skinner* • Vittorio De Sica *Enrico Dolphi* • Lelio Luttazzi *Bank manager* • Delia Boccardo *Lorraine Borman* ■ *Dir* George Englund • *Scr* Ken Kolb, Jeffrey Bloom, from the story *$125,000 Ski Bum Holdup* by Richard Gallagher

Snow White ★★ PG

Fairy tale
2001 · Can/US · Colour · 84min

Director Caroline Thompson here attempts to put the Grimm back into a story that has become surprisingly unfamiliar since Disney's fanciful cartoon became the standard version. Consequently, Snow White is imperilled by a wicked stepmother who has gained control of her grieving father through the machinations of a green-eyed genie. Miranda Richardson revels in the beauty-fixated queen's venomous villainy, but Kristin Kreuk's inanimate performance makes her a dull heroine. **DP** **DVD**

Miranda Richardson *Elspeth* • Kristin Kreuk *Snow White* • Tom Irwin *John* • Clancy Brown *Grandfather of Wishes* • José Zuniga *Hector* • Tyron Leitso *Prince Alfred* • Michael Gilden *Monday* • Mark J Trombino *Tuesday* • Vincent Schiavelli *Wednesday* • Penny Blake *Thursday* • Martin Klebba *Friday* • Warwick Davis *Saturday* • Michael J Anderson *Sunday* ■ *Dir* Caroline Thompson • *Scr* Caroline Thompson, Julie Hickson, from the fairy tale by Wilhelm Grimm, Jacob Grimm

Snow White: a Tale of Terror ★★★ 15

Gothic horror
1996 · UK/US · Colour · 96min

All Disney expectation is turned on its head as the sexual tensions and bloody obsessions are accentuated in this highly sinister fable with a richly textured Hammer horror look. The dwarfs are barbaric outcasts in this intriguing revision (scarred, simple-minded, branded) that's too sombre for kids, but too light in the fright department for adults. However, Sigourney Weaver gives the performance of her career as the wicked stepmother. **AJ** Swearing, violence. **DVD**

Sigourney Weaver *Claudia Hoffman* • Sam Neill *Frederick Hoffman* • Gil Bellows *Will* • Taryn Davis *Little Lilli* • Brian Glover *Lars* • David Conrad *Peter Gutenberg* • Monica Keena *Lilli Hoffman* • Anthony Brophy *Rolf* ■ *Dir* Michael Cohn • *Scr* Tom Szollosi, Deborah Serra, from the fairy tale by Jacob Grimm, Wilhelm Grimm

Snow White and the Huntsman ★★★ 12

Fantasy adventure
2012 · US · Colour · 121min

Twilight star Kristen Stewart seems ideally cast in this gloomy re-telling of the Snow White story, but Charlize Theron makes a deeper impact as the queen who wants her dead for fear of being usurped. Unfortunately, the love triangle between Snow White, the Huntsman who finds her in the woods (Chris Hemsworth) and the nobleman William (Sam Claflin) feels underdeveloped. Making his debut, British director Rupert Sanders shows a more confident hand with the visuals, creating a sumptuous fairy-tale world, and the dwarves (including Ray Winstone and Ian

McShane) add a welcome dash of humour. The overall look is seductively stormy, but looks are skin-deep – this is just a bit of fun dressed up as something more. A sequel, with the emphasis on the Huntsman, is due in 2016. **SP** Some violence. **DVD** **BL**

Kristen Stewart *Snow White* • Chris Hemsworth *The Huntsman* • Charlize Theron *Queen Ravenna* • Ian McShane *Beith* • Sam Claflin *William* • Toby Jones *Coll* • Nick Frost *Nion* • Ray Winstone *Gort* ■ *Dir* Rupert Sanders • *Scr* Hossein Amini, John Lee Hancock, Evan Daugherty

LANDMARK FILM ▬▬▬▬▬
Disney's first feature-length animation marks the birth of an entertainment empire

Snow White and the Seven Dwarfs ★★★★★ U

Classic animated fantasy
1937 · US · Colour · 83min

Disney's first animated feature pushed the art form in thrilling new directions, completely redrawing a much-loved fairy tale of bad stepmothers, forest glades and handsome princes that previously existed only on the printed page. (Indeed it opens with a storybook, a respectful nod that has been oft-repeated.) In places, it's cuter than the Brothers Grimm template – the adorable dwarfs with their pratfalls – but scenes with the Wicked Queen and the poisoned apple achieve a high new level of terror. Its ability to invoke German expressionism on the one hand while keeping the gallery entertained with Dopey's antics and *Whistle While You Work* on the other is why this classic has enduring appeal for all ages. **AC** **DVD** **BL**

Adriana Caselotti *Snow White* • Harry Stockwell *Prince Charming* • Lucille La Verne *The queen/The witch* • Moroni Olsen *Magic Mirror* • Billy Gilbert *Sneezy* • Pinto Colvig *Sleepy/Grumpy* • Otis Harlan *Happy* • Scotty Mattraw *Bashful* • Roy Atwell *Doc* ■ *Dir* David Hand • *Scr* Ted Sears, Richard Creedon, Otto Englander, Dick Rickard, Earl Hurd, Merrill De Maris, Dorothy Ann Blank, Webb Smith, from the fairy tale *Sneewittchen* in *Kinder und Haus-Marchen*, collected by Jacob Grimm, Wilhelm Grimm • *Music* Leigh Harline

Snow White in Happily Ever After ★★ U

Animation	1990 · US · Colour · 71min

While the animation is competent, what lets down this stubbornly unmagical fairy tale is the laboured plot, in which Snow White is aided by the seven dwarfs' cousins after her prince is snatched away by the wicked queen's vengeful brother Lord Maliss. The one bright spot, however, are the voiceovers, with Malcolm McDowell sneerily villainous as Maliss, Irene Cara tunefully vulnerable as Snow White and Tracey Ullman delightfully winsome as Moonbeam. **DP**

Irene Cara *Snow White* • Malcolm McDowell *Lord Maliss* • Dom DeLuise *Looking Glass* • Phyllis Diller *Mother Nature* • Zsa Zsa Gabor *Blossom* • Edward Asner *Scowl* • Sally Kellerman *Sunburn* • Carol Channing *Muddy* • Tracey Ullman *Moonbeam/Thunderella* • Michael Horton *Prince* ■ *Dir* John Howley • *Scr* Martha Moran, Robby London

Snowball Express ★★★ U

Comedy	1972 · US · Colour · 93min

Beating a retreat from the city is many a suburbanite's dream. This comedy shows that dream turning sour, when Manhattan family man Dean Jones inherits a ski-resort hotel in the Rockies and tries to make a go of it with wife Nancy Olson. Being a Disney confection that aims to please, the bad succumbs to the beautiful, with lots of ski sequences and a snowmobile race, and the tales of financial hardship tend to get buried under a pile of slush. **TH**

Dean Jones *Johnny Baxter* • Nancy Olson *Sue Baxter* • Harry Morgan *Jesse McCord* • Keenan Wynn *Martin Ridgeway* • Johnny Whitaker *Richard Baxter* • Michael McGreevey *Wally Perkins* ■ *Dir* Norman Tokar • *Scr* Don Tait, Jim Parker, from the novel *Chateau Bon Vivant* by Frankie O'Rear, John O'Rear

S

Snowbound ★★★ U
Adventure 1948 · UK · BW · 81min

This Alpine adventure too often betrays its pulp novel roots among resolutely studio-bound snow. Nevertheless, the cast is splendid, with Dennis Price and Robert Newton positively outdoing each other for the (over-) acting honours: the former plays a film extra-cum-scriptwriter sent by the latter, a film director, to write a script in the Dolomites, knowing full well there's Nazi gold in them there Alps. It becomes slightly less ludicrous when the snow traps everybody. TS

Robert Newton *Derek Engles* • Dennis Price *Neil Blair* • Herbert Lom *Keramikos* • Marcel Dalio *Stefan Valdini* • Stanley Holloway *Joe Wesson* • Guy Middleton *Gilbert Mayne* ■ *Dir* David MacDonald • *Scr* David Evans, Keith Campbell, from the novel *The Lonely Skier* by Hammond Innes

Snowden
Thriller based on a true story
2016 · Ger/US · Colour

This is a preview – no prints were available to review as we went to press: An analyst at America's National Security Agency, Edward Snowden became front page news in 2013 after leaking several thousand secret documents. He's a hero to some, a traitor to others, a split in opinion that makes him ideal as a subject for drama. Is co-writer/director Oliver Stone too partisan for the job, though? Or is his passion exactly what's needed? Joseph Gordon-Levitt must, surely, be a safe pair of hands as the young idealist. SvM

Joseph Gordon-Levitt *Edward Snowden* • Shailene Woodley *Lindsay Mills* • Nicolas Cage • Scott Eastwood *Trevor* • Timothy Olyphant • Zachary Quinto *Glenn Greenwald* • Melissa Leo *Laura Poitras* ■ *Dir* Oliver Stone • *Scr* Kieran Fitzgerald, Oliver Stone, from the non-fiction books *The Snowden Files* by Luke Harding and *Time of the Octopus* by Anatoly Kucherena • *Cinematographer* Anthony Dod Mantle

Snowman's Pass ★
Action adventure
2004 · Can/US · Colour · 96min

There's barely a shred of realism in this unconvincing action adventure. Instead Marc Singer's dodgy industrialist chews the scenery to unintentionally hilarious levels, as he and his sidekicks lure a bereaved climbing guide (Nicole Eggert) to a perilous mountain range under false pretences. The cat-and-mouse game that ensues is neither suspenseful nor particularly eventful, making the handsome landscape the main point of interest. SF

Nicole Eggert *Diana Pennington* • Marc Singer *Curt Seaver* • George Stults *Tyler* • Mike Dopud *Hugo* • Bruce Dawson *Ed* ■ *Dir* Rex Piano • *Scr* Peter Layton

Snowpiercer ★★★★
Science-fiction action drama
2013 · S Kor/US/Fr/Cz Rep · Colour · 126min

This uncompromising slice of dystopian sci-fi is that rarest of things: a thinking man's action film. It takes place in the year 2031, where the world has been plunged into a second ice age as a result of a failed global warming experiment. With the planet now uninhabitable, mankind's last survivors live on a self-sustaining train, but the poor inhabitants at the tail end decide to revolt. The film is blessed with the inventive craftsmanship of talented film-maker Bong Joon-Ho, who ensures that the set pieces are both thrilling and visually dynamic. SC In English, Korean, Japanese, French. Violence.

Chris Evans *Curtis* • Tilda Swinton *Mason* • Ed Harris *Wilford* • Jamie Bell *Edgar* • Octavia Spencer *Tanya* • John Hurt *Gilliam* ■ *Dir* Bong Joon-ho • *Scr* Kelly Masterson, Bong Joon-ho, from a story by Bong, from the graphic novel *Le Transperceneige* by Jacques Lob, Benjamin Legrand, Jean-Marc Rochette

The Snows of Kilimanjaro ★★★ PG
Romantic drama 1952 · US · Colour · 109min

This prettified 20th Century-Fox film version of Ernest Hemingway's novella is almost totally wrecked by the miscasting of Gregory Peck. He is much too nice to play the macho, hard-drinking, animal-hunting hero remembering his life as he lies injured in a camp beneath the mountain of the title. But Ava Gardner, Hildegarde Neff and Susan Hayward are spot-on, seductively rivalling the African and Riviera landscapes and making Peck's life a misery. AT [DVD]

Gregory Peck *Harry* • Susan Hayward *Helen* • Ava Gardner *Cynthia* • Hildegarde Neff *Countess Liz* • Leo G Carroll *Uncle Bill* • Torin Thatcher *Johnson* • Ava Norring *Beatrice* • Helene Stanley *Connie* ■ *Dir* Henry King • *Scr* Casey Robinson, from the short story by Ernest Hemingway

The Snows of Kilimanjaro ★★★ 15
Drama 2011 · Fr · Colour · 102min

Robert Guédiguian's film is a sentimental melodrama that wears its socialist heart on its sleeve. Inspired by Victor Hugo's poem *How Good Are the Poor*, the movie stars regular collaborators Ariane Ascaride and Jean-Pierre Darroussin, who excel as a Marseilles couple stoically celebrating their wedding anniversary in the face of his redundancy from the docks. The cloying contrivance and rhetorical earnestness of the set-up are undeniable. Yet this affectionate portrait of politicised people driven by conscience is also reminiscent of the 1930s masterpieces by Marcel Pagnol and Jean Renoir. DP French +subtitles. Swearing. [DVD]

Ariane Ascaride *Marie-Claire* • Jean-Pierre Darroussin *Michel* • Gérard Meylan *Raoul* • Maryline Canto [Marilyne Canto] *Denise* ■ *Dir* Robert Guédiguian • *Scr* Robert Guédiguian, Jean-Louis Milesi, from the poem *How Good Are the Poor* by Victor Hugo

Snowtown ★★★ 18
Crime drama based on a true story
2011 · Aus · Colour · 157min

Bleak social commentary combines with true-life horror in this impressive though relentlessly disturbing debut from Australian director Justin Kurzel, based on his homeland's notorious "Bodies in the Barrels" murders. Manipulative psychopath John Bunting (Daniel Henshall) grooms a 16-year-old boy (Lucas Pittaway) to participate in his shocking crimes. Henshall is startling, while the escalating sense of dread really crawls under the skin. But it's in the confusing time frame that this comes unstuck. SF [DVD] [Blu-ray]

Lucas Pittaway *Jamie Vlassakis* • Daniel Henshall *John Bunting* • Louise Harris *Elizabeth Harvey* • Anthony Groves *Troy* ■ *Dir* Justin Kurzel • *Scr* Shaun Grant, from a story by Grant, Justin Kurzel, from the non-fiction books *Killing for Pleasure* by Debi Marshall and *The Snowtown Murders* by Andrew McGarry

Snuff ★ 18
Horror 1976 · US/Arg · Colour · 76min

Rarely has a film been so mendaciously mythologised as this fifth-rate slasher. It began life in 1971 as a Manson murder cash-in called *Slaughter*, which was shot on a shoestring in Argentina by Michael and Roberta Findlay. It resurfaced under its new title five years later, featuring a gruesome four-minute insert, purporting to depict a real-life disembowelling (but which was actually shot in a Manhattan loft by one Simon Nuchtern using animal entrails). Opportunist distributor Allan Shackleton even launched a bogus morality campaign to garner extra publicity and the movie made a packet. Yet it remains amateurish, incoherent and unpleasant. DP Swearing, nudity, violence, drug abuse.

Ana Carro • Roberta Findlay • Alfredo Iglesias • Aldo Mayo ■ *Dir* Michael Findlay, Roberta Findlay, Simon Nuchtern • *Scr* Michael Findlay, Roberta Findlay

Snuff-Movie ★ 18
Horror 2005 · UK/Rom/US · Colour · 89min

Reclusive horror director Boris Arkadin (Jeroen Krabbé) invites four actors to his home in order to re-create the Manson-esque murder of his pregnant wife. Unknown to them, they are kept under constant surveillance from hidden video cameras, with the results broadcast on a pay-per-view website. But all is not what it seems in *Candyman* director Bernard Rose's limp mix of shocker satire and stale *Big Brother* social commentary. Cheaply shot in digital format, the film is a queasy brew of Ken Russell-style controversy and Dario Argento cliché. AJ [DVD]

Jeroen Krabbé *Boris Arkadin* • Lisa Enos *Wendy* • Hugo Myatt *Leon* • Joe Regan *Jack* • Teri Harrison *Pamela* • Sharif *Matt* • Alastair Mackenzie (2) *Andy* ■ *Dir/Scr* Bernard Rose

So Big ★★★ U
Period drama 1932 · US · BW · 81min

Barbara Stanwyck stars as the woman of indomitable character who becomes a schoolteacher in rural Illinois, marries a farmer and has a son, but is widowed and left to care for the land and her difficult child. This is the second of three feature versions of a Pulitzer Prize-winning novel, first filmed as a silent with Colleen Moore in 1924. This one benefits from solid direction by William A Wellman and the all-encompassing commitment of the great Stanwyck. Note the young Bette Davis in a small role. RK

Barbara Stanwyck *Selina Peake* • George Brent *Roelf Pool* • Dickie Moore *Dirk as a boy, "So Big"* • Bette Davis *Dallas O'Mara* • Mae Madison *Julie Hemple* • Hardie Albright *Dirk, adult* • *Scr* J Grubb Alexander, Robert Lord, from the novel by Edna Ferber

So Big ★★★ U
Period drama 1953 · US · BW · 101min

Jane Wyman, a huge star after her Oscar for *Johnny Belinda*, stars here as Edna Ferber's New Holland schoolmistress bringing up her son Steve Forrest against all odds in rural America. The Warner Bros gloss is not too intrusive, and there are nicely honed performances from big Sterling Hayden and lovely Nancy Olsen in support. TS

Jane Wyman *Selina Dejong* • Sterling Hayden *Pervus Dejong* • Nancy Olson *Dallas O'Mara* • Steve Forrest *Dirk Dejong* • Elisabeth Fraser *Julie Hempel* • Martha Hyer *Paula Hempel* ■ *Dir* Robert Wise • *Scr* John Twist, from the novel by Edna Ferber

So Close ★★★ 15
Science-fiction action
2002 · HK · Colour · 106min

Despite opening with a stunning office sequence in which Shu Qi redefines the term "computer virus") and closing with a spectacular rooftop swordfight, Corey Yuen's girlpower actioner loses its way in the interim amid a wealth of exposition and a tiresome narrative subplot. Clearly it helps to know why Shu and techno savvy sister Zhao Wei team up with cop Karen Mok to confound a malevolent tycoon. But it's much more fun watching them get on with the job. DP Cantonese, Mandarin +subtitles. [DVD]

Shu Qi *Lynn* • Zhao Wei *Sue* • Karen Mok *Hong Yat Hong* • Song Seoung Heon *Yan* • Michael Wei *Mark* • Yasuaki Kurata *Master* ■ *Dir* Corey Yuen • *Scr* Jeff Lau

So Close to Life ★★★ 12
Drama 1957 · Swe · BW · 78min

Ingrid Thulin, Eva Dahlbeck and Bibi Andersson shared the best actress prize at the 1958 Cannes film festival, but it's not just the performances that makes this significant. This is the film that signalled Ingmar Bergman's shift towards what are usually called "chamber dramas", intense conversation pieces that take place in symbolically confined spaces (in this case, a maternity ward). Bergman hedges his bets about the wisdom of bringing a child into such a troubled world but, for all its purple passages and cosy conclusions, the film leaves you with plenty to think about. DP Swedish +subtitles.

Eva Dahlbeck *Stina* • Ingrid Thulin *Cecilia* • Bibi Andersson *Hjordis* • Barbro Hiort Af Ornas *Brita* • Erland Josephson *Anders* • Max von Sydow *Harry* • Gunnar Sjöberg *Doctor* ■ *Dir* Ingmar Bergman • *Scr* Ingmar Bergman, from a story by Ulla Isaksson

So Dark the Night ★★★
Crime drama 1946 · US · BW · 70min

It's not often that character actors have the chance to play leading roles and Steven Geray, an east European actor usually cast as bartender, foreign agent or small-time criminal, does a splendid job in this outstanding B-feature. Playing a famous French detective on holiday, he finds himself investigating murders in a small village. Although the rest of the cast is little known, the well-written story has a memorably original twist and the setting is skilfully evoked. AE

Steven Geray *Henri Cassin* • Micheline Cheirel *Nanette Michaud* • Eugene Borden *Pierre Michaud* • Ann Codee *Mama Michaud* • Egon Brecher *Dr Boncourt* ■ *Dir* Joseph H Lewis • *Scr* Martin Berkeley, Dwight Babcock, from a story by Audrey Wisberg

So Dear to My Heart ★★★ U
Part-animated musical
1949 · US · Colour · 78min

The first actor to sign a long-term contract at Disney, Bobby Driscoll won a special Oscar for his work in 1949, although it clearly had more to do with *The Window*, than this slight blend of live-action and animation. Although the nominated song, *Lavender Blue*, was one of Uncle Walt's favourites, today's youngsters will get more enjoyment out of numbers like *Stick-with-it-ivity*, one of the many animated sequences in which farm boy Driscoll learns the lessons of life as he trains his black lamb, Danny, for a country fair. DP

Burl Ives *Uncle Hiram* • Beulah Bondi *Granny Kincaid* • Harry Carey [Harry Carey Jr] *Judge* • Bobby Driscoll *Jeremiah Kincaid* ■ *Dir* Harold Schuster, Hamilton Luske • *Scr* John Tucker Battle, Maurice Rapf, Ted Sears, from the novel *Midnight and Jeremiah* by Sterling North

So Ends Our Night ★★★
Wartime drama 1941 · US · BW · 121min

Released before the US entered the Second World War, this strong drama relates the experiences of three Germans who flee the rise of Hitler in 1937. Fredric March, an anti-Nazi German, risks danger to return to his dying wife (Frances Dee), while Jewish girl Margaret Sullavan and half-Jewish Glenn Ford make it to safety, falling in love en route. Adapted from Erich Maria Remarque's novel, the subject matter can hardly fail to be moving, and this is frequently tense and gripping. No thanks, though, to director John Cromwell, who tends to use a sledgehammer to kill a gnat. RK

Fredric March *Joseph Steiner* • Margaret Sullavan *Ruth Holland* • Frances Dee *Marie Steiner* • Glenn Ford *Ludwig Kern* • Anna Sten *Lilo* • Erich von Stroheim *Brenner* ■ *Dir* John Cromwell • *Scr* Talbot Jennings, from the novel *Flotsam* by Erich Maria Remarque

So Fine ★★★ 15
Comedy 1981 · US · Colour · 87min

Clever comic writer Andrew Bergman's directorial debut is an absolutely hilarious wacky comedy about the inventor of see-through jeans – yes, really! Although fresh-faced Ryan O'Neal isn't ideal as the intellectual heir of a New York City clothing manufacturer, his bookish quality is well-used, and his reluctance to make a career in the garment jungle is wittily observed, while the whole descends into a delirious farce. TS

Ryan O'Neal *Bobby Fine* • Jack Warden *Jack Fine* • Mariangela Melato *Lire* • Richard Kiel *Mr Eddie* • Fred Gwynne *Chairman Lincoln* • Mike Kellin *Sam Schlotzman* • David Rounds *Prof Dick McCarthy* • Joel Steadman *Prof Yarnell* ■ *Dir/Scr* Andrew Bergman

So Goes My Love ★★★ U
Period biographical comedy
1946 · US · BW · 91min

This light tale of eccentric family life in the 19th century features young Bobby Driscollm whose parents are inventor Don Ameche and the fussing Myrna Loy. It's not without period charm, but it needed a more forceful director than Frank Ryan. However, one should be thankful that Hollywood could at one time produce movies whose charm alone outweighed their content. **TS**

Myrna Loy *Jane* · Don Ameche *Hiram Stephen Maxim* · Rhys Williams *Magel* · Bobby Driscoll *Percy Maxim* · Richard Gaines *Mr Josephus* · Molly Lamont *Anty Gannet* ■ *Dir* Frank Ryan · *Scr* Bruce Manning, James Clifden, from the memoir *A Genius in the Family* by Hiram Percy Maxim

So I Married an Axe Murderer ★★★ 15
Comedy
1993 · US · Colour · 89min

Mike Myers's first stab at flying solo after his *Wayne's World* partner Dana Carvey is a mixed bag. He plays an aspiring poet who has a history of failed relationships. All that seems to change when he falls madly in love with Nancy Travis, until evidence starts mounting that she may be a black widow who has left a trail of dead husbands in her wake. There are some nicely black comic moments, but Myers tries too hard and mugs shamelessly to the camera. **JF**
Nudity, violence, swearing. *DVD*

Mike Myers *Charlie Mackenzie/Stuart Mackenzie* · Nancy Travis *Harriet Michaels* · Anthony LaPaglia *Tony Giardino* · Amanda Plummer *Rose Michaels* · Brenda Fricker *May Mackenzie* · Matt Doherty *Heed* · Charles Grodin *Comandeered car driver* · Phil Hartman *Park ranger "Vickie"* · Debi Mazar *Tony's girlfriend "Susan"* ■ *Dir* Thomas Schlamme · *Scr* Robbie Fox, Mike Myers, Neil Mullarkey, from a story by Robbie Fox

So Long at the Fair ★★ U
Mystery
1950 · UK · BW · 85min

Everything's set here for an attention-grabbing little mystery. In addition to David Tomlinson's unexplained disappearance, there's the unique backdrop of the 1889 Great Exhibition in Paris, a solid supporting cast and the exciting prospect of seeing Dirk Bogarde woo Jean Simmons. Yet, somehow, it fails to gel. Definitely a wasted opportunity. **DP**

Jean Simmons *Victoria Barton* · Dirk Bogarde *George Hathaway* · David Tomlinson *Johnny Barton* · Marcel Poncin *Narcisse* · Cathleen Nesbitt *Madam Herve* · Honor Blackman *Rhoda O'Donovan* · Betty Warren *Mrs O'Donovan* ■ *Dir* Terence Fisher, Anthony Darnborough · *Scr* Hugh Mills, Anthony Thorne, from a novel by Anthony Thorne

So Proudly We Hail ★★★
Second World War drama
1943 · US · BW · 125min

When major Hollywood stars such as John Wayne, Gary Cooper and James Stewart were winning the Second World War, major Hollywood actresses tended to lose out on heroism and were cast as *femme fatales* or dewy-eyed wives. But this lavish Paramount flag-waver puts Claudette Colbert, Paulette Goddard and Veronica Lake into army nurse uniform and packs them off to the Pacific where they get on in a no-nonsense, "pass the plasma please" way. Each of them has a personal problem to overcome and each of them battles with Miklos Rozsa's music. Overlong, but watchable for the stars on parade. **AT**

Claudette Colbert *Lt Janet Davidson* · Paulette Goddard *Lt Joan O'Doul* · Veronica Lake *Lt Olivia D'Arcy* · George Reeves *Lt John Summers* · Barbara Britton *Lt Rosemary Larson* · Walter Abel *Chaplain* · Sonny Tufts *Kansas* ■ *Dir* Mark Sandrich · *Scr* Allan Scott

So Red the Rose ★★★ U
Period war romance
1935 · US · BW · 82min

This is the period movie that convinced Hollywood producers that there was no money to be made in movies about the American Civil War, so they all rejected *Gone with the Wind*, letting it go to independent David O Selznick who turned it into screen history. This isn't at all bad, though, and Margaret Sullavan is particularly touching as she waits for Randolph Scott to return from the war between the states. King Vidor's direction is restrained and masterly, making this rewarding. **TS**

Margaret Sullavan *Vallette Bedford* · Walter Connolly *Malcolm Bedford* · Randolph Scott *Duncan Bedford* · Janet Beecher *Sally Bedford* · Elizabeth Patterson *Mary Cherry* · Robert Cummings *Archie Pendleton* · Harry Ellerbe *Edward Bedford* · Dickie Moore *Middleton Bedford* · Charles Starrett *George McGehee* ■ *Dir* King Vidor · *Scr* Laurence Stallings, Edwin Justus Mayer, Maxwell Anderson, from a novel by Stark Young

So This Is Love ★★ U
Biographical musical drama
1953 · US · Colour · 100min

Kathryn Grayson was undeniably talented, as her career-best work in *Show Boat* and *Kiss Me Kate* for MGM demonstrates. However, in this Warner Bros biopic she is seriously miscast, lacking the class to portray real-life tragic Metropolitan Opera star Grace Moore, whose screen career faded as her weight ballooned. The songs are worthy and the Technicolor is fine to watch, but leading man Merv Griffin (later a chat-show host) is dull, and in truth there's little of substance. **TS**

Kathryn Grayson *Grace Moore* · Merv Griffin *Buddy Nash* · Joan Weldon *Ruth Obre* · Walter Abel *Colonel Moore* · Rosemary DeCamp *Aunt Laura Stokley* · Jeff Donnell *Henrietta Van Dyke* · Ann Doran *Mrs Moore* ■ *Dir* Gordon Douglas · *Scr* John Monks Jr, from the autobiography *You're Only Human Once* by Grace Moore · *Music* Max Steiner

So This Is New York ★★★
Comedy
1948 · US · BW · 77min

This attractive vehicle for radio star Henry Morgan is an early effort from director Richard Fleischer. Based on Ring Lardner's autobiographical novel, his recollections, when transferred to film, are so good-natured they ultimately become tiresome. Still, there's no denying young Fleischer's talent behind the camera, and film buffs should note that this was also Hollywood legend Stanley Kramer's first producer credit. **TS**

Henry Morgan *Ernie Finch* · Virginia Grey *Ella Finch* · Dona Drake *Kate Goff* · Rudy Vallee *Herbert Daley* · Bill Goodwin *Jimmy Ralston* · Hugh Herbert *Mr Trumball* · Leo Gorcey *Sid Mercer* · Jerome Cowan *Francis Griffin* ■ *Dir* Richard O Fleischer [Richard Fleischer] · *Scr* Carl Foreman, Herbert Baker, from the novel *The Big Town* by Ring Lardner

So This Is Paris ★★★
Silent comedy
1926 · US · BW · 74min

German import Ernst Lubitsch's seventh American film is an elegant, sophisticated and satirical silent comedy, in which the unique Lubitsch touch, spoke as eloquently as any words could. It made a mint for Warner Bros and was voted one of the year's ten best by the *New York Times*. The plot revolves around the light-hearted complications that ensue when a husband-and-wife dance duo (Lilyan Tashman, André Beranger) decide to spice up their relationship by indulging in criss-cross flirtations with a dancer and his wife (Monte Blue, Patsy Ruth Miller). Very "French", very ooh-la-la, and a lot of fun. **RK**

Monte Blue *Dr Eisenstein* · Patsy Ruth Miller *Rosalind Eisenstein* · Lilyan Tashman *Adela, a dancer* · André Beranger *Alfred, her husband* · Myrna Loy *Maid* ■ *Dir* Ernst Lubitsch · *Scr* Hans Kräly, from the play *Le Réveillon* by Henri Meilhac, Ludovic Halévy

So This Is Paris ★★ U
Musical comedy
1954 · US · Colour · 96min

This retread of every tired old musical cliché about sailors on the town or Americans in Paris, stars Tony Curtis, Gene Nelson and Paul Gilbert as three mariners on the make in the French capital. The musical numbers are reasonably pleasing, if totally forgettable, but the script hits a level of such mind-numbing imbecility that the sentimental element – Gloria De Haven masquerading as French and dancing in a nightclub to help support a bunch of cute orphans – is actually a welcome relief. **RK**

Tony Curtis *Joe Maxwell* · Gloria De Haven [Gloria DeHaven] *Colette D'Avril/Jane Mitchell* · Gene Nelson *Al Howard* · Corinne Calvet *Suzanne Sorel* · Paul Gilbert *Davey Jones* · Mara Corday *Yvonne* ■ *Dir* Richard Quine · *Scr* Charles Hoffman, from a story by Ray Buffum

So Undercover ★★ 12
Action comedy
2012 · US · Colour · 89min

Miley Cyrus stars in this mildly diverting action comedy that's aimed squarely at her teenage female fan base. She plays a sassy private investigator who's assigned by the FBI to infiltrate a sorority house and protect the daughter of a witness in a big Mafia case. But first she has to endure a makeover that turns her from a streetwise private eye into a sophisticated college student (think *Miss Congeniality* and you have the general idea). Cyrus works hard and there are some decent support performances (including a nicely spiky one from Kelly Osbourne), but the result is all rather tame and derivative. **DA** Swearing, sexual references. *DVD* Blu

Miley Cyrus [Miley Ray Cyrus] *Molly Morris* · Jeremy Piven *Armon* · Mike O'Malley *Sam* · Joshua Bowman *Nicholas* · Kelly Osbourne *Becky* ■ *Dir* Tom Vaughan (1) · *Scr* Steven Pearl, Allan Loeb

So Well Remembered ★★★★
Second World War drama
1947 · UK · BW · 114min

Adapted from a novel by James Hilton (who narrates), this weighty and moving drama stars John Mills as a crusading newspaper editor in a depressed northern mill town. Directed with a vivid sense of place by Edward Dmytryk, the film chronicles the class and social problems and the struggling socialist politics of the era. Against this canvas, the crises for Mills, including his disastrous marriage to the mill-owner's ruthless daughter (Martha Scott) which brings personal tragedy, and his friendship with the equally dedicated town doctor (Trevor Howard) are played out. Powerful, gripping, and beautifully acted. **RK**

John Mills *George Boswell* · Martha Scott *Olivia* · Patricia Roc *Julie* · Trevor Howard *Whiteside* · Richard Carlson *Charles* · Reginald Tate *Mangin* · Juliet Mills *Baby Julie* · James Hilton *Narrator* ■ *Dir* Edward Dmytryk · *Scr* John Paxton, from a novel by James Hilton

Soapdish ★★★★ 15
Comedy
1991 · US · Colour · 92min

The inside dope on daytime soap features Sally Field, Carrie Fisher and Whoopi Goldberg among the stars and creators of a ghastly TV show called *The Sun Also Sets*. Actors are written out, has-beens stage comebacks, real life echoes fiction, emotional wreckage piles up, you know the rest. As for the always brilliant Kevin Kline, he's been off the show for years. But, executive producer Robert Downey Jr and Field's co-star and rival (Cathy Moriarty) want him back to induce Field to leave. Despite some longueurs, this farce has genuinely hysterical moments. **AT** Swearing. *DVD*

Sally Field *Celeste Talbert* · Kevin Kline *Jeffrey Anderson* · Robert Downey Jr *David Barnes* · Whoopi Goldberg *Rose Schwartz* · Carrie Fisher *Betsy Faye Sharon* · Cathy Moriarty *Montana Moorehead* · Teri Hatcher *Ariel Maloney* · Paul Johansson *Bolt Brennan* · Elisabeth Shue *Lori Craven* · Kathy Najimy *Tawny Miller* ■ *Dir* Michael Hoffman · *Scr* Robert Harling, Andrew Bergman, from a story by Robert Harling

Sobibor: 14 October 1943, 16:00 ★★★
Documentary
2001 · Fr · BW and Colour · 95min

With its title referring to the only successful concentration camp uprising to occur during the entire Second World War, director Claude Lanzmann's documentary may lack the scale of his masterpiece, *Shoah*, but it's still a compelling and provocative memoir of one survivor's extraordinary experiences. Recorded in 1979, the interview with Yehuda Lerner is hindered by the on-screen translation. Yet the insertion of new location footage and deeply moving bookend passages gives the story of Alexander Pechersky's audacious wartime revolt both a historical context and a contemporary resonance. **DP** French +subtitles.

■ *Dir/Scr* Claude Lanzmann

The Social Network ★★★★★ 12
Drama based on a true story
2010 · US · Colour · 120min

The foundation of online phenomenon Facebook comes in for scrutiny in this fact-based drama, which turns the site's formative years into a morality tale for our times. Computer-science student Mark Zuckerberg (Jesse Eisenberg) is an unloved outsider at Harvard in 2003, but circumvents the university's traditional elite by creating networking technology that eventually makes him one of the world's youngest billionaires. Along the way, there's camaraderie, betrayal, class tension and much litigation. The dazzling wordplay from screenwriter Aaron Sorkin (TV's *The West Wing*) and David Fincher's intensely focused direction work in concert to favour character conflict over computer geekery. This brilliantly assembled cautionary tale gets straight to the heart of the human needs and failings underpinning dizzying technological advancement, creating one of the truly defining films of its era. **TJ** Swearing, drug abuse. *DVD* Blu

Jesse Eisenberg *Mark Zuckerberg* · Andrew Garfield *Eduardo Saverin* · Justin Timberlake *Sean Parker* · Joseph Mazzello *Dustin Moskovitz* · Rooney Mara *Erica Albright* · Rashida Jones *Marylin Delpy* · Brenda Song *Christy* · Armie Hammer *Cameron Winklevoss/Tyler Winklevoss* · Max Minghella *Divya Narendra* · Patrick Mapel *Chris Hughes* ■ *Dir* David Fincher · *Scr* Aaron Sorkin, from the novel *The Accidental Billionaires: the Founding of Facebook: a Tale of Sex, Money, Genius and Betrayal* by Ben Mezrich

Society ★★★ 18
Horror
1989 · US · Colour · 94min

A truly unique shocker, this mixture of social comment and splatter horror will definitely not be to everyone's taste. Is Billy Warlock just paranoid about his well-respected Beverly Hills family? Or do they really get up to unspeakable taboo-breaking orgies when he's not around? The answer involves a great deal of special make-up effects, including torso distortion, melting flesh, deviant gender blurring and surreal spectacle. Disturbing and silly in roughly equal amounts, this over-the-top exposé of what the rich are really doing to the poor marked the directing debut of Brian Yuzna. **AJ** Swearing, nudity. *DVD* Blu

Billy Warlock *Bill Whitney* · Devin Devasquez *Clarisa* · Evan Richards *Milo* · Ben Meyerson *Ted Ferguson* · Charles Lucia *Jim* · Connie Danese *Nan* ■ *Dir* Brian Yuzna · *Scr* Woody Keith, Rick Fry · *Makeup Special Effects* Screaming Mad George

Sodbusters ★★ 12
Comedy western
1994 · Can · Colour · 94min

Is there anything more embarrassing than a spoof that isn't funny? Kris Kristofferson, as the battle-scarred gunslinger helping some Colorado farmers keep the railroad off their land, has only been armed with blanks, thanks to the leaden script co-written by director Eugene Levy. The inclusion of a couple of gay cowboys doesn't help this TV movie much, either. **AT** Violence, swearing. *DVD*

Kris Kristofferson *Destiny* · John Vernon *Slade Cantrell* · Fred Willard *Clarence Gentry* · Wendel Meldrum *Lilac Gentry* · Steve Landesberg *Gunther Schteuppin* · Max Gail *Tom Partridge* ■ *Dir* Eugene Levy · *Scr* Eugene Levy, John Hemphill

Sodom and Gomorrah
★★★ PG

Biblical epic　1962 · US/Fr/It · Colour · 111min

Lot (Stewart Granger) leads his people away from Sodom and Gomorrah, the twin cities of sin, just as God lays waste to them both. "Don't look back!" Lot tells his wife, but she does and is turned into a pillar of salt (one of the strangest special effects in movie history). Ridiculous in so many ways, Robert Aldrich's biblical epic has an energy and a knowing hypocrisy that makes it very watchable. Sergio Leone directed the Italian version and some of the action sequences. AT

Stewart Granger *Lot* • Anouk Aimée *Queen Bera* • Stanley Baker *Astaroth* • Pier Angeli *Ildith* • Rossana Podesta *Shuah* ■ *Dir* Robert Aldrich, Sergio Leone • *Scr* Hugo Butler, Giorgio Prosperi

Sofie
★★★ PG

Period drama　1992 · Den/Nor/Swe · Colour · 145min

Liv Ullmann's full-feature-length directorial debut is a Bergmanesque examination of the pressures placed on women in late 19th-century Denmark. A study in dignified strength amid the ruins of her romantic ideals, Karen-Lise Mynster gives a performance worthy of her director, as the mature Jewish woman who abandons a passionate Gentile painter to marry her repressed shopkeeping cousin and bear him a rebellious son. With Jorgen Persson's compositions suggesting the rigidity of the period, this is deliberate and theatrical, but heartfelt. DP Swedish +subtitles.

Karen-Lise Mynster *Sofie* • Erland Josephson *Semmy* • Ghita Nørby *Frederikke* • Jesper Christensen *Højby* • Torben Zeller *Jonas* ■ *Dir* Liv Ullmann · *Scr* Liv Ullmann, Peter Poulsen, from the novel *Mendel Philipsen and Son* by Henri Nathansen

Soft Beds, Hard Battles
★★ 12

Second World War comedy　1973 · UK · Colour · 90min

This film reunited Peter Sellers with the Boulting Brothers who had been responsible for one of his greatest screen triumphs, *I'm All Right Jack*. Alas this originally X-rated romp was not in the same class. Sellers plays multiple roles in a story of murder and duplicity set around a Parisian brothel in 1940. The production was reportedly dogged with problems and the cracks are all too evident on screen. DF **DVD**

Peter Sellers *General Latour/Major Robinson/Schroeder/Hitler/Prince Kyoto/President of France/Radio newsreader* • Lila Kedrova *Madame Grenier* • Curt Jurgens *General von Grotjahn* • Béatrice Romand *Marie-Claude* ■ *Dir* Roy Boulting · *Scr* Leo Marks, Roy Boulting

Soft Deceit
★★★ 18

Erotic thriller　1994 · US/Can · Colour · 91min

Made in Canada by writer/director Jorge Montesi, this erotic thriller is packed to the rafters with clichés and contrivances. Yet, you can't quite pull yourself away from watching undercover cop Kate Vernon struggle with her feelings for slippery crook Patrick Bergin. Every trick is thrown into the mix to keep the plot rattling along and Vernon gives a gutsy performance. TS Swearing, violence, sex.

Patrick Bergin *Adam Trent* • Kate Vernon *Anne Fowler* • John Wesley Shipp *Detective John Hobart* • Nigel Bennett *Ed McCullough* • Ted Dykstra *Don Froese* ■ *Dir/Scr* Jorge Montesi

Soft Fruit
★★ 18

Comedy drama　1999 · Aus/US · Colour · 97min

Jane Campion's former assistant, Christina Andreef, made her feature debut with this spikey, but unfocused comedy drama about a splintered family coming to terms with a mother's terminal cancer. Always a sympathetic matriarch, Jeanie Drynan provides a warm focus for the reunion of her larger-than-life siblings in the hellhole steel town of Port Kembla. The episodic structure deprives the action of dramatic

and emotional unity. DP Violence, swearing, drug abuse, nudity.

Jeanie Drynan *Patsy* • Linal Haft *Vic* • Russell Dykstra *Bo* • Geneviève Lemon *Josie* • Sacha Horler *Nadia* • Alicia Talbot *Vera* • Dion Bilios *Bud* ■ *Dir/Scr* Christina Andreef • *Executive Producer* Jane Campion

Soft Top, Hard Shoulder
★★ 15

Road movie　1992 · UK · Colour · 90min

From its contrived title downwards, virtually everything about this odd couple comedy (apart from the playing of Peter Capaldi and Elaine Collins) is ill-judged. Capaldi bases his script on a Frank Capra classic, with several situations here reminiscent of scenes from *It Happened One Night*. However, Capaldi not only misfires with the screwball antics, but is also wide of the mark with the Bill Forsyth-style whimsy he is obviously striving for. DP Swearing. **DVD**

Peter Capaldi *Gavin Bellini* • Elaine Collins *Yvonne* • Frances Barber *Miss Trimble* • Catherine Russell *Animal Rights activist* • Jeremy Northam *John* • Richard Wilson (3) *Uncle Salvatore* • Sophie Hall *Nancy* • Scott Hall *Mr Young* • Simon Callow *Eddie Cherdowski* • Phyllis Logan *Karla* ■ *Dir* Stefan Schwartz · *Scr* Peter Capaldi

Soigne Ta Droite
★★

Experimental fantasy　1986 · Fr/Swi · Colour · 82min

Jean-Luc Godard appears as the idiot and the prince in this impenetrable in-joke, complete with whispered mock-philosophical narration. There are several main stories, inseparable but unconnected, including one about an airline pilot apparently about to commit suicide in midair. The film has been described as a "metaphysical cartoon", but what it all means is anyone's guess. A cinematic doodle. AT In French.

Jean-Luc Godard *The idiot/The prince* • Jacques Villeret *The individua* • François Périer *The man* • Jane Birkin *The cricket* • Michel Galabru *The admiral* ■ *Dir/Scr* Jean-Luc Godard

Solace
★★★ 15

Mystery thriller　2015 · US · Colour · 97min

Anthony Hopkins stars as a clairvoyant enlisted by two FBI agents (Jeffrey Dean Morgan and Abbie Cornish) to stop a serial killer (Colin Farrell). Clearly influenced by *Seven*, this takes dark and creepy turns, offering a bleak exploration of what such a power can mean. Hopkins is often captivating, especially talking to a bereaved mother, but Morgan and Cornish are both decidedly lifeless. Despite getting bogged, this is a chilling supernatural thriller that takes its viewer on a sombre but satisfying journey. JL Violence, sex, swearing **DVD** **Blu-ray**

Anthony Hopkins *John Clancy* • Colin Farrell (2) *The Stranger/Charles Ambrose* • Jeffrey Dean Morgan *Agent Joe Merriweather* • Abbie Cornish *Agent Katherine Cowles* ■ *Dir* Afonso Poyart • *Scr* Sean Bailey, Ted Griffin

Solar Crisis
★★ 15

Science-fiction thriller　1990 · Jpn/US · Colour · 107min

This expensive co-production was filled with production problems, including director Richard C Sarafian opting for a pseudonym when the producers dictated additional shooting after the movie bombed in Japan. Despite the new footage, it's easy to see why the movie went straight to video in North America. Though the story of a 21st-century space station crew working to save the broiling Earth by firing a special bomb into the Sun has plenty of impressive special effects, the proceedings are bogged down by a lack of tension. KB **DVD**

Charlton Heston *Skeet Kelso* • Peter Boyle *Teague* • Tetsuya Bessho *Ken Minami* • Jack Palance *Travis* • Tim Matheson *Steve Kelso* • Annabel Schofield *Alex* • Corin "Corky" Nemec [Corin Nemec] *Mike Kelso* • Brenda Bakke *Claire* ■ *Dir* Alan Smithee [Richard C Sarafian] · *Scr* Joe Gannon, Crispan Bolt [Ted Sarafian], from a novel by Takeshi Kawata

Solaris
★★★★ PG

Science-fiction drama　1972 · USSR · Colour · 159min

For some, director Andrei Tarkovsky's philosophical cult movie is the Soviet equivalent of *2001*; for others, it's an obscure intellectual exercise. Based on Polish writer Stanislaw Lem's 1961 novel, the tale involves astronauts on an alien planet who are confronted by illusions from their subconscious memories (usually their morose girlfriends back on Earth). Tarkovsky's highly influential and cerebral science-fiction epic is ponderous, very talky and contains minimal special effects, but its remote strangeness exerts a compelling hypnotic power that's often extraordinarily potent. AJ Russian +subtitles. **DVD**

Donatas Banionis *Kris Kelvin* • Natalya Bondarchuk *Hari* • Juri Jarvet *Snow* • Anatoli Solonitsin [Anatoli Solonitsyn] *Sartorius* • Vladislav Dvorjetzki *Burton* ■ *Dir* Andrei Tarkovsky · *Scr* Andrei Tarkovsky, Friedrich Gorenstein, from the novel by Stanislaw Lem

Solaris
★★★ 12

Romantic science-fiction drama　2002 · US · Colour · 94min

To remake Andrei Tarkovsky's brilliant 1972 film might seem impertinent, but director Steven Soderbergh has crafted an original drama here. George Clooney, showcasing his acting talent, plays a psychologist who is called to a space station orbiting the planet Solaris. Clooney is joined by his wife Natascha McElhone, who had committed suicide on Earth some time before, but the nature of her presence is enigmatic. As a profound meditation on love, regret and desire, this dares to put dialogue before action. TH Swearing, a sex scene, nudity. **DVD**

George Clooney *Dr Chris Kelvin* • Natascha McElhone *Rheya* • Jeremy Davies *Snow* • Viola Davis *Gordon* • Ulrich Tukur *Gibarian* ■ *Dir* Steven Soderbergh · *Scr* Steven Soderbergh, from the novel by Stanislaw Lem

Solas
★★★★ 15

Drama　1998 · Sp · Colour · 96min

What would Hollywood's ageing actresses give for a role like this? Exuding battered dignity and stubborn devotion, Maria Galiana excels as the rural housewife who quietly transforms her unmarried daughter's life while her abusive, alcoholic husband recovers in a Seville hospital. Galiana's relationship with the prickly, pregnant and dubious Ana Fernández highlights both Spain's fierce conservatism and its shifting attitude to previously sacrosanct values. But it's her hesitant friendship with Carlos Alvarez Novoa's urbane octagenarian neighbour that gives the film its charm. Debuting film-maker Benito Zambrano's sedate pacing is perfect. DP Spanish +subtitles. **DVD**

Ana Fernández *María* • Maria Galiana *Rosa Jimenez Pena, María's mother* • Carlos Alvarez Novoa *Neighbour* • Paco de Osca *María's father* • Juan Fernandez *Juan* ■ *Dir/Scr* Benito Zambrano

Soldier
★ 18

Science-fiction action thriller　1998 · US · Colour · 94min

Shane goes to outer space in director Paul Anderson's depressingly unoriginal slice of science fiction. A near monosyllabic Kurt Russell plays the brainwashed army killing machine dumped on a garbage planet when a newer DNA manipulated model is developed. There he finds a forgotten outpost of stranded humans who adopt him as their warrior saviour. A by-the-numbers empty spectacle. AJ Violence, swearing. **DVD**

Kurt Russell *Todd* • Jason Scott Lee *Caine 607* • Connie Nielsen *Sandra* • Gary Busey *Captain Church* • Jason Isaacs *Colonel Mekum* • Sean Pertwee *Mace* ■ *Dir* Paul Anderson (1) • *Scr* David Webb Peoples

Soldier Blue
★★★ 18

Western drama　1970 · US · Colour · 114min

Very controversial on its release, this dramatisation of the Sand Creek Massacre

of 1864 does not stint on the appalling carnage meted out to the Cheyenne by the US Cavalry. Scenes of women and children being raped and mutilated were cut by the British censor and the film was widely condemned for its extreme violence. Candice Bergen is kidnapped by Cheyenne tribesmen and becomes culturally enriched rather than bigoted. Often vilified, this was considered by many contemporary viewers to be an allegory of the My Lai massacre in Vietnam. AT Violence, swearing. **DVD**

Candice Bergen *Cresta Marybelle Lee* • Peter Strauss *Private Honus Gant* • Donald Pleasence *Isaac Q Cumber* • Bob Carraway *Lieut John McNair* • Jorge Rivero *Spotted Wolf* • Dana Elcar *Captain Battles* • John Anderson *Colonel Iverson* ■ *Dir* Ralph Nelson · *Scr* John Gay, from the novel *Arrow in the Sun* by Theodore V Olsen

Soldier in the Rain ★★★★ U

Comedy drama　1963 · US · BW · 87min

This unfashionable film is one of the most neglected in Steve McQueen's filmography. The story of scamming and shirking at an army base is *Bilko* with bitterness and sentiment stirred in to give the comedy its unique flavour. McQueen engagingly blends naivety with nous, as he tries to persuade scheming sergeant Jackie Gleason to quit the service and cut a dash on civvy street. An odd couple, but they work well together and make the most of every nugget in an accomplished script. DP

Steve McQueen (1) *Supply Sgt Eustice Clay* • Jackie Gleason *Master Sgt Maxwell Slaughter* • Tuesday Weld *Bobby Jo Pepperdine* • Tony Bill *Private Jerry Meltzner* • Tom Poston *Lieutenant Magee* • Paul Hartman *Chief of Police* • Adam West *Captain Blekeley* ■ *Dir* Ralph Nelson · *Scr* Maurice Richlin, Blake Edwards, from the novel by William Goldman

Soldier of Fortune
★★★

Romantic adventure　1955 · US · Colour · 95min

This was Clark Gable's first movie as an independent freelancer, away from the shackles of his 25-year stint as "King" of MGM. Twentieth Century-Fox was trying out its new CinemaScope process in a variety of locations, and here Gable finds himself in Hong Kong as a smuggler, hired to locate Susan Hayward's husband Gene Barry, who's either dead or over in Red China. Skilled director Edward Dmytryk makes this melodramatic tosh seem exciting, and Gable and Hayward strike starry sparks. TS

Clark Gable *Hank Lee* • Susan Hayward *Jane Hoyt* • Michael Rennie *Inspector Merryweather* • Gene Barry *Louis Hoyt* ■ *Dir* Edward Dmytryk · *Scr* Ernest K Gann, from his novel

Soldier of Orange ★★★★ 15

Second World War drama　1977 · Neth · Colour · 147min

Paul Verhoeven's lavish, personal war epic re-creates the Nazi invasion of his native Holland and shows the effects it has on six university students, all but one of whom become involved in the Resistance. Known for his graphic depiction of sex and violence, Verhoeven's approach here is more traditional and boasts two splendid leading performances from Rutger Hauer and Jeroen Krabbé. Edward Fox appears as the head of British military intelligence and Susan Penhaligon is on hand to give both Hauer and Krabbé a squeeze when they escape to Britain. AT Dutch +subtitles. **DVD**

Rutger Hauer *Erik* • Jeroen Krabbé *Gus* • Peter Faber *Will* • Derek De Lint *Alex* • Edward Fox *Colonel Rafelli* • Susan Penhaligon *Susan* ■ *Dir* Paul Verhoeven · *Scr* Gerard Soeteman, Kees Holierhoek, Paul Verhoeven, from a autobiography by Erik Hazelhoff Roelfzema

A Soldier's Daughter Never Cries
★★★ 15

Drama　1998 · US · Colour · 121min

James Ivory may have freed himself from the Henry James/EM Forster orbit, but this remains a bookish story about a young girl and her relationship with her mum and novelist dad (loosely based on James Jones, author of *From Here to Eternity*). There are good performances behind that

S

terrible title, though Kris Kristofferson rather overdoes the Hemingway/James Jones routine. **AT** Swearing. **DVD**

Kris Kristofferson *Bill Willis* • Barbara Hershey *Marcella Willis* • Leelee Sobieski *Channe, aged 14* • Jesse Bradford *Billy, aged 14* • Dominique Blanc *Candida* • Jane Birkin *Mrs Fortescue* ■ *Dir* James Ivory • *Scr* James Ivory, Ruth Prawer Jhabvala, from the novel by Kaylie Jones • *Producer* Ismail Merchant

A Soldier's Love Story ★★
Romantic drama 2010 · US · Colour · 100min

A pen-pal correspondence between a lonely boy and a US soldier transforms both their lives in this simple celebration of love and family. Not only does the ten-year-old get the father figure he craves, but charming sergeant Johnny Messner also predictably finds romance with the youngster's newly divorced mum (Lori Loughlin) after deciding to visit the pair while on leave. Although the episodic narrative that unfolds hasn't much meat, it's packed with warmth and positive self-fulfilment messages, as the three emotionally scarred characters gradually reap the rewards of learning to trust again. Likeable central performances and some nice support, including Stefanie Powers playing a glam gran, add to the film's gentle appeal and help temper the heavy-handed faith references. **SF**

Lori Loughlin *Dana Marshall* • Johnny Messner *Sgt Vince Carerra* • Stefanie Powers *Louise Metcalf* • Charles Henry Wyson *Jared Marshall* ■ *Dir* Harvey Frost • *Scr* Pamela Wallace

Soldiers of Fortune ★★ 15
Action adventure
2012 · Rus/US · Colour · 89min

Stupidity is taken to the nth degree in this nonsense actioner. Strongly cast yet relentlessly unconvincing, this sees Christian Slater's ex-special forces officer play bodyguard to five excitement-hungry millionaires (including Sean Bean and James Cromwell) who've paid big money to participate in a real war zone mission. For the first hour, the absurdity of the plotting, characters and dialogue keep things guiltily entertaining, but insufficient thrills ruin the final section and the climax is a boring waste. **SF** Violence, swearing. **DVD**

Christian Slater *Craig McCenzie* • Sean Bean *Dimidov* • Ving Rhames *Grimaud Tourneur* • James Cromwell *Samuel Haussman* • Colm Meaney *Carter Mason* ■ *Dir* Maxim Korostyshevsky • *Scr* Robert Crombie, Alexandre Coscas, Joe Kelbley

A Soldier's Story ★★★★ 15
Mystery drama 1984 · US · Colour · 96min

Adapted by Charles Fuller from his own Pulitzer Prize-winning play, this is not just a gripping mystery, but also a far-reaching investigation into the widely differing aspirations and expectations that divide, as much as unite, America's black population. Howard Rollins gives a showy performance as the army captain sent to a camp in the Deep South to discover who murdered a black sergeant. Everyone has motive and opportunity and, under Norman Jewison's tight direction, the supporting cast, led by Denzel Washington and Adolph Caesar, gives nothing away. **DP** **DVD**

Howard E Rollins Jr *Capt Davenport* • Adolph Caesar *Master Sgt Vernon C Waters* • Art Evans *Pte Wilkie* • David Alan Grier *Cpl Cobb* • David Harris *Pte Smalls* • Dennis Lipscomb *Capt Taylor* • Larry Riley *CJ Memphis* • Robert Townsend *Cpl Ellis* • Denzel Washington *Pte Peterson* • Patti LaBelle *Big Mary* ■ *Dir* Norman Jewison • *Scr* Charles Fuller, from his play

A Soldier's Tale ★★★
Second World War drama
1988 · NZ · Colour · 99min

This touching, offbeat drama did not even get a video release in the UK. Gabriel Byrne is the British soldier in France in the latter years of the Second World War, who falls for a French girl (Marianne Basler) who may or may not be a collaborator. Although it's a little too downbeat, the two leads deliver moving performances and it's directed with

some sensitivity. **JF** Violence, swearing, nudity.

Gabriel Byrne *Saul* • Marianne Basler *Belle* • Paul Wyett *Charlie* • Judge Reinhold *Yank* ■ *Dir* Larry Parr • *Scr* Grant Hinden Miller, Larry Parr, from the novel by MK Joseph

Soldiers Three ★★★ U
Adventure 1951 · US · BW · 91min

Several Rudyard Kipling stories have been put through the MGM blender and reduced to pulp in this rumbustious North-West Frontier tale. The soldiers are a likeable bunch; Stewart Granger, Walter Pidgeon and David Niven among them. Whenever the plot stalls, which is often, a horde of Indians appears on the horizon. It's not as funny as *Carry On Up the Khyber*, but it is played for laughs. **AT**

Stewart Granger *Private Archibald Ackroyd* • Walter Pidgeon *Colonel Brunswick* • David Niven *Captain Pindenny* • Robert Newton *Private Jock Sykes* • Cyril Cusack *Private Dennis Malloy* • Greta Gynt *Crenshaw* • Frank Allenby *Colonel Groat* • Robert Coote *Major Mercer* • Dan O'Herlihy *Sergeant Murphy* • Michael Ansara *Manik Rao* ■ *Dir* Tay Garnett • *Scr* Marguerite Roberts, Tom Reed, Malcolm Stuart Boylan, from the short stories by Rudyard Kipling

The Solid Gold Cadillac ★★★ U
Comedy 1956 · US · BW and Colour · 95min

A clever idea and perfect casting make a delightful comedy. Judy Holliday is the small shareholder who embarrasses the crooked directors of a big company by innocently questioning their high salaries and is given a meaningless job to keep her quiet. In the tradition of Frank Capra, the little woman eventually triumphs over the pompous bosses. Paul Douglas figures as the former chairman who becomes her ally and romantic interest. Richard Quine ably directes in black-and-white with a flash of colour at the end. **AE**

Judy Holliday *Laura Partridge* • Paul Douglas *Edward L McKeever* • Fred Clark *Clifford Snell* • John Williams *John T Blessington* • Hiram Sherman *Harry Harkness* • Neva Patterson *Amelia Shotgraven* • Ralph Dumke *Warren Gillie* • Ray Collins *Alfred Metcalfe* • Arthur O'Connell *Jenkins* ■ *Dir* Richard Quine • *Scr* Abe Burrows, from the play by George S Kaufman, Howard Teichmann

Solitaire for 2 ★ 15
Romantic comedy 1994 · UK · Colour · 100min

This unwatchable romantic comedy left cinema audiences groaning in droves. Amanda Pays is a woman who reads minds, aware that all the men she dates are only interested in one thing. Academic philanderer Mark Frankel is determined to conquer Pays and their battle forms the bedrock of a bad film. Utterly ridiculous. **LH** Swearing, sex scenes.

Mark Frankel *Daniel Becker* • Amanda Pays *Katie* • Roshan Seth *Sandip Tamar* • Jason Isaacs *Harry* • Maryam D'Abo *Caroline* • Helen Lederer *Cop* • Malcolm Cooper *Cop* • Annette Crosbie *Mrs Dwyer* • Neil Mullarkey *Parris* ■ *Dir/Scr* Gary Sinyor

Solitary Man ★★★ 15
Comedy drama 2009 · US · Colour · 86min

This very decent Michael Douglas drama, which inexplicably went straight to DVD here last year, will appeal in particular to fans of his two *Wall Street* films. Douglas plays the former owner of a major car dealership who has fallen from grace because of dodgy business doings, and is now trying to rebuild both his personal and professional reputations. No one does desperate and dangerous like the urbane Douglas, and toss into the mix a crack support cast of Susan Sarandon, Danny DeVito and *Social Network* star Jesse Eisenberg, and you've a film well worthy of two hours of anyone's viewing time. **DA** In English, Spanish. Swearing. **DVD**

Michael Douglas (1) *Ben Kalmen* • Susan Sarandon *Nancy Kalmen* • Danny DeVito *Jimmy Marino* • Mary-Louise Parker *Jordon Karsch* • Jenna Fischer *Susan Porter* • Imogen Poots

Allyson Karsch • Jesse Eisenberg *Daniel Cheston* ■ *Dir* Brian Koppelman, David Levien • *Scr* Brian Koppelman

Solo ★★ 18
Science-fiction action thriller
1996 · US/Mex · Colour · 89min

A pumped-up Mario Van Peebles plays a cyber-soldier who refuses to kill innocent Latin American villagers and becomes their friend, in this derivative, but amiable, sci-fi action thriller. You'll recognise themes, scenes and characters from dozens of other movies – particularly *Terminator 2* – but Van Peebles isn't bad as a low-budget Arnie and the film has much less violence and more heart than you would expect. **JC** Violence, swearing. **DVD**

Mario Van Peebles *Solo* • Barry Corbin *General Clyde Haynes* • William Sadler *Colonel Madden* • Jaime Gomez *Lorenzo* • Adrien Brody *Bill Stewart* ■ *Dir* Norberto Barba • *Scr* David Corley, from the novel *Weapon* by Robert Mason

The Soloist ★★ 12
Biographical drama
2008 · UK/US · Colour · 111min

This saccharine fact-based tale stars Jamie Foxx as a musically gifted down-and-out with mental-health issues, with Robert Downey Jr as the jaded journalist who wants to elevate him from kerbside to concert stage after he hears him playing a beaten-up violin near his LA office. Essentially a buddy-movie version of *Shine*, this is adequately if unimaginatively directed by Joe Wright (*Atonement*), who is a little over-literal in his portrayal of the redemptive power of music. But the leads strike the right notes, in Foxx's case, maybe, rather too many of them - his *Rain Man* ramblings do get a little irritating. **DA** Drug abuse, brief swearing. **DVD**

Robert Downey Jr *Steve Lopez* • Jamie Foxx *Nathaniel Ayers* • Catherine Keener *Mary Weston* • Stephen Root *Curt* • Tom Hollander *Graham Claydon* • Lisagay Hamilton [Lisa Gay Hamilton] *Jennifer Ayres* ■ *Dir* Joe Wright • *Scr* Susannah Grant, from articles by Steve Lopez

Solomon and Gaenor ★★★ 15
Period romance 1998 · UK · Colour · 103min

Filmed in both Welsh and English, director/writer Paul Morrison's debut feature is a tragic tale of forbidden love. Set in 1911 in the Welsh valleys, the Romeo and Juliet-esque narrative finds chapel-goer Gaenor (Nia Roberts) falling for door-to-door salesman Solomon (Ioan Gruffudd). Yet Solomon has concealed his Jewish identity and, in a heated atmosphere of anti-Semitism, the couple take desperate measures to preserve their love. Both Gruffudd and Roberts are outstanding as the lovers; ultimately, however, this is a grim and sorry tale. **LH** English, Welsh, Yiddish +subtitles. Sex scenes, violence.

Ioan Gruffudd *Solomon* • Nia Roberts *Gaenor* • Sue Jones-Davies *Gwen* • William Thomas *Idris* • Mark Lewis Jones *Crad* • Maureen Lipman *Rezl* • David Horovitch *Isaac* • Bethan Ellis Owen *Bronwen* • Adam Jenkins *Thomas* ■ *Dir/Scr* Paul Morrison

Solomon and Sheba ★★ PG
Biblical epic 1959 · US · Colour · 135min

This generally stodgy epic has a black-wigged Yul Brynner courting scantily clad Gina Lollobrigida in days of Biblical yore. This has all the weaknesses of the genre, notably a script brimming with non sequiturs and inane Americanisms. Despite some eye-catching designs and photography by Freddie Young, the picture was probably doomed when the original star, Tyrone Power, died on set. That disaster, together with a critical drubbing and poor audiences, caused the director, King Vidor, to abandon the movie business. **AT** **DVD**

Yul Brynner *Solomon* • Gina Lollobrigida *Magda, Queen of Sheba* • George Sanders *Adonijah* • Marisa Pavan *Abishag* • David Farrar *Pharaoh* • John Crawford *Joab* • Laurence Naismith *Hezrai* • José Nieto *Ahab* • Alejandro Rey *Sittar* ■

Dir King Vidor, *Scr* Anthony Veiller, Paul Dudley, George Bruce, from a story by Crane Wilbur • *Art Directors* Richard Day, Alfred Sweeney

Solomon Kane ★★★ 15
Fantasy action horror
2009 · UK/Cz Rep/Fr · Colour · 99min

Writer/director Michael J Bassett's well-appointed, if rather old-fashioned, action fantasy epic brings Conan the Barbarian creator Robert E Howard's lesser-known Puritan hero Solomon Kane to centre stage. Provided here with an invented origins story, charismatic James Purefoy is terrific as the West Country-accented crusader trying to devote his life to good deeds after just escaping eternal damnation for past sins. It may be an obvious sword-and-sorcery affair, but decked out with terrific Czech locations, Klaus Badelt's rousing score, neat CGI visual effects, keen biblical imagery and a solid supporting cast, the imperfections can be forgiven. **AJ** **DVD** Blu-ray

James Purefoy *Solomon Kane* • Pete Postlethwaite *William Crowthorn* • Rachel Hurd-Wood *Meredith Crowthorn* • Alice Krige *Katherine Crowthorn* • Jason Flemyng *Malachi* • Mackenzie Crook *Father Michael* • Max von Sydow *Josiah Kane* ■ *Dir* Michael J Bassett • *Scr* Michael J Bassett, from the character created by Robert E Howard • *Music* Klaus Badelt

Sombrero ★★
Musical drama 1952 · US · Colour · 103min

A messy, meandering and overblown attempt to capture the flavour of Mexican life through three different love stories results in a colourfully filmed but bizarre mix of music and melodrama. The first tale, involving Ricardo Montalban and Pier Angeli in a Romeo and Juliet situation aims for comedy; romance between wealthy Vittorio Gassman and peasant Yvonne Carlo is a tear-jerker; and the marriage of bullfighter's dancing sister Cyd Charisse to a street trader ends in bloody violence. The last episode has an electrifying display of flamenco dancing by José Greco and a good bullfighting sequence. **RK**

Ricardo Montalban *Pepe Gonzales* • Pier Angeli *Eufemia Calderon* • Vittorio Gassman *Alejandro Castillo* • Yvonne De Carlo *Maria* • Cyd Charisse *Lola de Torrano* • Rick Jason *Ruben* • Nina Foch *Elena* • José Greco *Gintanillo de Torrano* ■ *Dir* Norman Foster • *Scr* Norman Foster, Josefina Niggli, from the novel *A Mexican Village* by Josefina Niggli

Some Came Running ★★★ PG
Drama 1958 · US · Colour · 130min

Adapted from the novel by *From Here to Eternity* writer James Jones, this is a highly stylised melodrama from ace director Vincente Minnelli. Frank Sinatra plays a writer who, returning home from the army, becomes involved with a happy-go-lucky gambler (Dean Martin) and two very different women (Shirley MacLaine and Martha Hyer). The fireworks of the finale are exemplary and the cast is extraordinarily watchable. **TS** **DVD**

Frank Sinatra *Dave Hirsh* • Dean Martin *Bama Dillert* • Shirley MacLaine *Ginny Moorhead* • Arthur Kennedy *Frank Hirsh* • Martha Hyer *Gwen French* • Nancy Gates *Edith Barclay* ■ *Dir* Vincente Minnelli • *Scr* John Patrick, Arthur Sheekman, from the novel by James Jones • *Music* Elmer Bernstein

Some Girls ★★ 15
Comedy 1988 · US · Colour · 89min

Also known as *Sisters*, this has Patrick Dempsey as the student who looks forward to spending Christmas with his girlfriend's family in Canada, only to fall prey to both of her sisters while trying to avoid the watchful eye of her eccentric parents. Directed by Michael Hoffman, this has some moments of hilarity, but not enough to sustain interest in what is supposed to be a funny film. **JB** Swearing, sex scenes, nudity.

Patrick Dempsey *Michael* • Jennifer Connelly *Gabby* • Sheila Kelley (1) *Irenka* • Andre Gregory *Father* • Ashley Greenfield *Simone* • Florinda Bolkan *Mother* ■ *Dir* Michael Hoffman • *Scr* Rupert Walters

S

Some Girls Do ★★ PG

Spy comedy thriller 1969 · UK · Colour · 87min

Having played Bulldog Drummond with some aplomb in *Deadlier than the Male* in 1966, Richard Johnson is left high and dry in this risible sequel about a gang targeting a prototype supersonic airliner. Desperately seeking to spoof James Bond and cash in on the swinging sauciness of the 1960s, director Ralph Thomas is content to operate with a plot that manages to be even flimsier than the costumes worn by the bevy of bad beauties. DP *DVD*

Richard Johnson *Hugh Drummond* • Daliah Lavi *Baroness Helga Hagen* • Beba Loncar *Pandora* • James Villiers *Carl Petersen* • Sydne Rome *Flicky* • Ronnie Stevens *Peregrine Carruthers* • Robert Morley *Miss Mary* • Maurice Denham *Mr Mortimer* ■ *Dir* Ralph Thomas • *Scr* David Osborn, Liz Charles-Williams, from the character created by HC "Sapper" McNeile

Some Kind of Wonderful ★★★★ 15

Romantic drama 1987 · US · Colour · 90min

Lea Thompson has one of her best roles as the spoilt girl for whom garage attendant Eric Stoltz falls, and Mary Stuart Masterson is delightful as the tomboy who secretly harbours deeper feelings for her male friend. Stoltz makes an effective leading man, giving a touching performance in a charming film. JB *DVD*

Eric Stoltz *Keith Nelson* • Mary Stuart Masterson *Watts* • Lea Thompson *Amanda Jones* • Craig Sheffer *Hardy Jenns* • John Ashton *Cliff Nelson* • Elias Koteas *Skinhead* • Molly Hagan *Shayne* • Chynna Phillips *Mia* ■ *Dir* Howard Deutch • *Scr* John Hughes

Some Like It Hot ★★ U

Musical comedy 1939 · US · BW · 64min

Based on Ben Hecht and Gene Fowler's Broadway flop *The Great Magoo*, this musical comedy was retitled *Rhythm Romance* for US television broadcast to avoid confusing it with Billy Wilder's 1959 cross-dressing classic. In only his sixth feature, Bob Hope ably holds the action together, as the fairground shyster exploiting girlfriend Shirley Ross's singing talent in the hope of making it big. This is moderate fare, despite being directed with brisk efficiency by journeyman George Archainbaud, but Gene Krupa's drum routine is worth catching. DP

Bob Hope *Nicky Nelson* • Shirley Ross *Lily Racquet* • Una Merkel *Flo Saunders* • Gene Krupa • Rufe Davis *Stoney* • Bernard Nedell *Stephen Hanratty* ■ *Dir* George Archainbaud • *Scr* Lewis R Foster, Wilkie Mahoney, from the play *The Great Magoo* by Gene Fowler, Ben Hecht

Some Like It Hot ★★★★★ U

Classic comedy 1959 · US · BW · 116min

Tony Curtis and Jack Lemmon are ideally matched in this crackling cross-dressing comedy, as the 1920s musicians who join an all-girl band to escape the Mob after witnessing the St Valentine's Day Massacre. Amazingly, Billy Wilder had originally wanted Bob Hope and Danny Kaye, and even considered casting Frank Sinatra instead of Lemmon. Curtis didn't always get along with Marilyn Monroe and compared their embraces to kissing Hitler (ironically, the name she gave the bullying Wilder). Yet sparks fly when she falls for Curtis's bogus oil tycoon – who not only boasts the voice of Cary Grant but also the body language of Grace Kelly! Clearly, the personality clashes both on- and off-screen were crucial to this becoming a true film classic, for, as Joe E Brown famously says in the last line, "Nobody's perfect!" DP *DVD* *Blu*

Marilyn Monroe *Sugar Kane* • Tony Curtis *Joe/Josephine* • Jack Lemmon *Jerry/Daphne* • George Raft *Spats Columbo* • Pat O'Brien *Mulligan* • Joe E Brown *Osgood E Fielding III* • Nehemiah Persoff *Little Bonaparte* • Joan Shawlee *Sweet Sue* • Billy Gray *Sig Poliakoff* ■ *Dir* Billy Wilder • *Scr* Billy Wilder, IAL Diamond, from the film *Fanfares of Love* by Robert Thoeren, M Logan • *Costume Designer* Orry-Kelly

Some Mother's Son ★★★★ 15

Political drama 1996 · Ire/US · Colour · 106min

This, while it touches the raw nerve of Northern Irish politics, shows Helen Mirren's formidable ability; she plays a widowed mother who discovers her son is involved with the IRA and fights for him when he is on the prison hunger strike during which ten activists died in the early 1980s. Director Terry George makes no secret of whose side he's on, but Helen Mirren extends propaganda into an unsentimental, but poignant, portrait of motherhood. TH Swearing, violence.

Helen Mirren *Kathleen Quigley* • Fionnula Flanagan *Annie Higgins* • Aidan Gillen *Gerard Quigley* • David O'Hara *Frank Higgins* • John Lynch *Bobby Sands* • Tom Hollander *Farnsworth* • Tim Woodward *Tim Harrington* • Ciaran Hinds *Danny Boyle* ■ *Dir* Terry George • *Scr* Jim Sheridan, Terry George

Some People ★★★ PG

Melodrama 1962 · UK · Colour · 89min

This coffee bar musical arrived two months before the Beatles, but its moral values are those of the early 1950s: motorbikes and pop music equal juvenile delinquency, and what young tearaways need is spiritual guidance. (The film's profits went to the Duke of Edinburgh's relatively new Award Scheme, which is heavily plugged.) Ray Brooks and David Hemmings are among the boys who are taken under the wing of church organist Kenneth More. Naively charming, with unusual Bristol locations and a bouncy title song. DM *DVD*

Kenneth More *Mr Smith* • Ray Brooks *Johnnie* • Annika Wills *Anne Smith* • David Andrews (1) *Bill* • Angela Douglas *Terry* • David Hemmings *Bert* • Timothy Nightingale *Tim* • Frankie Dymon Jr *Jimmy* ■ *Dir* Clive Donner • *Scr* John Eldridge

Some Voices ★★★ 15

Comedy drama 2000 · UK · Colour · 96min

Simon Cellan Jones makes his feature debut with this low-key study of psychiatric instability and its ramifications. The director occasionally allows Joe Penhall's adaptation of his own play to become stagey and soap-operatic, and there's a lack of impact in the conventional relationships the schizophrenic Daniel Craig has with his café-owning brother, David Morrissey, and sassy Scot Kelly Macdonald. Yet Cellan Jones gives an immediacy to the action by using flash-editing techniques to convey Craig's distorted world. Intense, well-acted and affecting. DP *DVD*

Daniel Craig *Ray* • David Morrissey *Pete* • Kelly Macdonald *Laura* • Julie Graham *Mandy* • Peter McDonald *Dave* ■ *Dir* Simon Cellan Jones • *Scr* Joe Penhall, from his play

Some Will, Some Won't ★ PG

Comedy 1969 · UK · Colour · 86min

If this insipid remake of *Laughter in Paradise* is supposed to be a comedy, it's not only an insult to the memory of the original, but it also breaches the Trades Descriptions Act. What makes this an even more depressing experience is the utter waste of fine cast, with Thora Hird, Michael Hordern, Ronnie Corbett and Leslie Phillips as the quartet forced to humiliate themselves to benefit from joker Wilfrid Brambell's will. DP *DVD*

Ronnie Corbett *Herbert Russell* • Thora Hird *Agnes Russell* • Michael Hordern *Deniston Russell* • Leslie Phillips *Simon Russell* • Barbara Murray *Lucille* • Wilfrid Brambell *Henry Russell* • Dennis Price *Benson* • James Robertson-Justice *Sir Charles Robson* ■ *Dir* Duncan Wood • *Scr* Lew Schwarz, from the film *Laughter in Paradise* by Jack Davies, Michael Pertwee

Somebody Killed Her Husband ★★ PG

Comedy mystery 1978 · US · Colour · 92min

Farrah Fawcett (in her first starring feature role) turns amateur detective with Jeff Bridges to find out who killed her husband in this lame comedy mystery. Director Lamont Johnson is clearly aiming for a sophisticated caper in the Hitchcock vein,

and the engaging climax during the Macy's Thanksgiving Parade almost gets there. The ex-Charlie's Angel isn't bad but she's a little too lightweight to carry the melodramatic load in such inconsequential fluff. AJ

Farrah Fawcett-Majors [Farrah Fawcett] *Jenny Moore* • Jeff Bridges *Jerry Green* • John Wood (2) *Ernest Van Santen* • Tammy Grimes *Audrey Van Santen* • John Glover *Hubert Little* • Patricia Elliott *Helene* • Mary McCarty *Flora* ■ *Dir* Lamont Johnson • *Scr* Reginald Rose

Somebody Loves Me ★★★ U

Musical biography 1952 · US · Colour · 90min

This typical highly fictionalised musical biopic was Betty Hutton's penultimate picture, and her last for Paramount. When studio executives refused to give in to her demand that her second husband, Charles O'Curran, who choreographed the film, be allowed to direct her subsequent pictures, she left, and her career was almost over. Hutton is as energetic as ever in this rags-to-riches story of vaudeville entertainer Blossom Seeley, and delivers several fine songs in her raucous and sentimental manner. RB

Betty Hutton *Blossom Seeley* • Ralph Meeker *Benny Fields* • Robert Keith (1) *Sam Doyle* • Adele Jergens *Nola Beach* • Billie Bird *Essie* • Henry Slate *Forrest* • Sid Tomack *Lake* • Ludwig Stossel *Mr Grauman* • Jack Benny ■ *Dir/Scr* Irving Brecher

Somebody to Love ★★ 18

Romantic drama 1994 · US · Colour · 98min

A meandering menagerie of characters merge here in this stream-of-consciousness urban drama. Steve Buscemi, Stanley Tucci, Quentin Tarantino and Anthony Quinn all have bizarre cameos in the story of the unrequited love felt by aspiring actress Rosie Perez for down-on-his-luck TV cowboy Harvey Keitel. Perez is the energy and fun in the film, and it needs her. However, though both an interesting and perceptive exercise by director Alexandre Rockwell, Perez just isn't dynamic enough. A strange and slightly nihilistic trip. LH

Rosie Perez *Mercedes* • Harvey Keitel *Harry* • Michael DeLorenzo *Ernesto* • Stanley Tucci *George* • Steve Buscemi *Mickey* • Anthony Quinn *Emilio* • Samuel Fuller *Old man on highway* • Quentin Tarantino *Bartender* ■ *Dir* Alexandre Rockwell • *Scr* Alexandre Rockwell, Sergei Bodrov

Somebody Up There Likes Me ★★★★ PG

Biographical sports drama 1956 · US · BW · 108min

The role of middleweight champ Rocky Graziano was intended for James Dean, who unfortunately had a date with destiny on the highway. Into the ring stepped Paul Newman, and he became a star overnight. Newman brings to the role a lot of Marlon Brando's Method mannerisms and the script drags in rather too many social issues for comfort. It's very much a product, albeit an important one, from the 1950s. Watch closely, and you'll catch Steve McQueen making his screen debut. AT

Paul Newman *Rocky Graziano* • Pier Angeli *Norma* • Everett Sloane *Irving Cohen* • Eileen Heckart *Ma Barbella* • Sal Mineo *Romolo* • Harold J Stone *Nick Barbella* • Steve McQueen (1) *Fidel* • Robert Loggia *Frankie Peppo* ■ *Dir* Robert Wise • *Scr* Ernest Lehman, from the autobiography by Rocky Graziano, Rowland Barber • *Cinematographer* Joseph Ruttenberg • *Art Directors* Cedric Gibbons, Malcolm Brown

Someone at the Door ★★ U

Crime comedy 1950 · UK · BW · 61min

A remake of Herbert Brenon's 1936 version of the hit West End play, this Hammer hokum of the hoariest kind. There isn't a semblance of suspense in the shenanigans that follow journalist Michael Medwin's bizarre decision to make headlines with the fake killing of his sister. Not even the arrival of jewel thieves at the haunted house they've inherited can revive one's fast-fading interest. DP

Michael Medwin *Ronnie Martin* • Garry Marsh *Kapel* • Yvonne Owen *Sally Martin* • Hugh Latimer *Bill Reid* • Danny Green *Price* • Campbell Singer *Inspector Spedding* • John Kelly (2) *PC O'Brien* ■ *Dir* Francis Searle • *Scr* AR Rawlinson, from the play by Dorothy Christie, Campbell Christie

Someone behind the Door ★★

Crime drama 1971 · Fr /UK · Colour · 95min

The strange pairing of Anthony Perkins and Charles Bronson (and Bronson's wife Jill Ireland) is the most interesting thing about this psychological suspense drama. Bronson plays a lost and befuddled amnesiac who doesn't know he's a dangerous fugitive. Doctor Perkins discovers who he is and decides to use him as a tool in his plans for revenge against his adulterous wife. The movie drifts along at a pretty slow pace. KB

Charles Bronson *Stranger* • Anthony Perkins *Laurence Jeffries* • Jill Ireland *Frances Jeffries* • Henri Garcin *Paul Damien* • Adriano Magestretti *Andrew* • Agathe Natanson *Lucy* ■ *Dir* Nicolas Gessner • *Scr* Marc Behm, Jacques Robert, Nicolas Gessner, Lorenzo Ventavoli, from the novel *Quelqu'un Derrière la Porte* by Jacques Robert

Someone Else ★★★ 15

Romantic comedy drama 2005 · UK · Colour · 76min

Former BBC TV director Col Spector co-wrote this unconventional romantic comedy with *Green Wing* star Stephen Mangan in mind. It's certainly a tailor-made role, with Mangan adeptly switching between cynicism, flirtatiousness and self-pity as London-based portrait photographer David, who breaks up with long-time girlfriend Lisa (Susan Lynch) after confessing to a crush on kooky stranger Nina (Lara Belmont). Mangan is never allowed to dominate proceedings – his byplay with Lynch, Belmont and loser buddy Christopher Coghill is always quirkily even-handed. This is a very British kind of comedy, but its wit and restraint give it a pleasing authenticity. DP *DVD*

Stephen Mangan *David* • Susan Lynch *Lisa* • Lara Belmont *Nina* • Christopher Coghill *Matt* • Shaun Dingwall *Michael* ■ *Dir* Col Spector • *Scr* Col Spector [Colin Spector], Rhada Chakraborty

Someone Else's America ★★★ 15

Comedy drama 1995 · Fr/UK/Ger · Colour · 95min

Winner of the audience prize at Cannes, this well-meaning drama gave Tom Conti another chance to play a heavily accented Mediterranean type. As the Spanish bar owner living in Brooklyn with his blind mother, Conti gives a heartfelt performance that's matched by Miki Manojlovic as the illegal immigrant from Montenegro who becomes his lodger. Released at a time when the Balkan crisis was front-page news, this gentle, if unfocused, fable takes on a more serious tone when Manojlovic's mother decides to leave Montenegro and head for the promised land of America to reunite her grandchildren with their father. AT English, Serbo-Croat +subtitles. Swearing.

Tom Conti *Alonso* • Miki Manojlovic *Bayo* • Maria Casarès *Alonso's mother* • Zorka Manojlovic *Bayo's mother* ■ *Dir* Goran Paskaljevic • *Scr* Gordon Mihic

Someone Is Bleeding ★★★ 15

Thriller 1974 · Fr · Colour · 105min

Mireille Darc plays against type in this engrossing psychological thriller. As the sociopathic drug addict who spells trouble for all the men she encounters, Darc displays an icy detachment that ensnares television writer Claude Brasseur. Although he usually injected a note of levity into his thrillers, Georges Lautner plays this adaptation of Richard Matheson's novel dead straight, casting a wintry pall over the Riviera coastline that not only reflects Darc's cold heart, but also the film's

S

downbeat ending. DP French dubbed. *DVD*

Alain Delon *Marc* • Claude Brasseur *Francois* • Mireille Darc *Peggy* • Nicoletta Machiavelli *Jacqueline* • Fiora Altoviti *Denis* ■ *Dir* Georges Lautner • *Scr* Georges Lautner, from the novel by Richard Matheson

Someone to Love ★★★ 15

Comedy drama   1987 · US · Colour · 104min

This discussion of love and loneliness was written and directed by leading independent Henry Jaglom. He also stars, playing a film-maker who seeks to solve his romantic problems by getting his friends to reveal their deepest emotions during a Valentine's party. While there are a few profound insights and the odd smart remark, it's not an easy picture to get involved in. The highlight is Orson Welles making his final film appearance. DP Swearing.

Orson Welles *Danny's friend* • Henry Jaglom *Danny Sapir* • Andrea Marcovicci *Helen Eugene* • Michael Emil *Mickey Sapir* • Sally Kellerman *Edith Helm* ■ *Dir/Scr* Henry Jaglom

Someone to Watch over Me
★★★★ 15

Thriller   1987 · US · Colour · 102min

This intelligent thriller remains one of Ridley Scott's most quietly satisfying works. Tom Berenger plays a tough police detective who gets to sample the high life when he is assigned to protect beautiful, wealthy Mimi Rogers, the key witness in a murder trial. It may lack the power of the some of Scott's other films, but this is still a beautifully shot, stylish affair. Howard Franklin's clever script touches upon issues of class and voyeurism, while still producing the goods in the suspense stakes. The performances are first rate. JF Swearing, violence, nudity. *DVD*

Tom Berenger *Mike Keegan* • Mimi Rogers *Claire Gregory* • Lorraine Bracco *Ellie Keegan* • Jerry Orbach *Lieutenant Garber* • John Rubinstein *Neil Steinhart* • Andreas Katsulas *Joey Venza* ■ *Dir* Ridley Scott • *Scr* Howard Franklin • *Cinematographer* Steven Poster

Someone's Watching Me!
★★★

Thriller   1978 · US · Colour · 100min

A rare excursion into TV movie thrillerdom for horror director John Carpenter. A peeping tom with a telescope bugs Lauren Hutton's apartment and terrorises her with scary phone calls. Only best friend Adrienne Barbeau believes her story and sets out to prove it. Taking all its cues from *Rear Window*, Carpenter's script and direction are full of tight, taut little touches that raise it above the TV norm and disguise its blatant Hitchcock homages. The atmosphere of unexpectancy and dread is well sustained even though Hutton leaves much to be desired as the central focus of the puzzle. AJ

Lauren Hutton *Leigh Michaels* • David Birney *Paul Winkless* • Adrienne Barbeau *Sophie* • Charles Cyphers *Gary Hunt* ■ *Dir/Scr* John Carpenter

Somers Town ★★★ 12

Black comedy drama   2008 · UK · BW · 67min

Director Shane Meadows follows up his Bafta-winning *This Is England* with this black comedy drama set in the multicultural area of London close to King's Cross that gives the film its name. Thomas Turgoose stars as Tommo, who arrives from Nottingham with dreams of making a better life, but is met instead by a welcoming committee who relieve him of his beer, bag and cash. He crosses paths with a young Polish lad Marek (Piotr Jagiello) and the pair become friends, earning money from a series of increasingly eccentric schemes dreamt up by a neighbour. It's an easy film to like, buoyed by a relaxed sense of humour and an amiable ensemble of characters. However, the brief running time does make this feel a little insubstantial after the bleak power of its predecessor. BP English, Polish, French +subtitles. Violence, sexual references, brief swearing. *DVD* *Blu*

Thomas Turgoose *Tommo* • Kate Dickie *Jane* • Piotr Jagiello *Marek* • Ireneusz Czop *Marius, Marek's dad* • Perry Benson *Graham* ■ *Dir* Shane Meadows • *Scr* Paul Fraser, from an idea by Mother Vision

Somersault ★★★★ 15

Drama   2004 · Aus · Colour · 101min

This moving coming-of-age drama deservedly cleaned up at the 2004 AFI awards (the Australian equivalent of the Oscars), bagging a record 13 gongs. Newcomer Abbie Cornish won the best actress award for her superb performance as a teenage girl who flees home after seducing her mother's partner. She ends up in a small town at the foot of a ski resort, where she begins a troubled relationship with a brooding local farmer (the equally good Sam Worthington, who won best actor). The story is familiar enough, but director Cate Shortland sympathetically catches the heartbreak and emotional confusion of her flawed characters, with an eye for quirky detail and fresh, haunting visuals. JF Swearing, violence, sex scenes. *DVD*

Abbie Cornish *Heidi* • Sam Worthington *Joe* • Lynette Curran *Irene* • Erik Thomson *Richard* • Hollie Andrew *Bianca* • Leah Purcell *Diane* • Olivia Pigeot *Nicole* • Blake Pittman *Karl* ■ *Dir/Scr* Cate Shortland

Something about Sex ★★★ 18

Comedy   1998 · US · Colour · 89min

Differing attitudes towards sexual fidelity are explored with humorous candour by writer/director Adam Rifkin. It may join a long list of contemporary movies in which affluent, attractive characters are handicapped by the hang-ups and neuroses of "ordinary people", but this is truthfully scripted and keenly acted by its young cast. Despite obvious insights, the unexpected sexiness of its bedroom scenes, coupled with some comical fantasy scenes, give the film some minor distinction. JC *DVD*

Jonathan Silverman *Joel* • Leah Lail *Sophie* • Ryan Alosio *Isaac* • Amy Yasbeck *Claudia* • Patrick Dempsey *Sam* • Christine Taylor *Sammie* • Jason Alexander *Art* ■ *Dir/Scr* Adam Rifkin

something big ★

Comedy western   1971 · US · Colour · 108min

This is the only other movie alongside *tom thumb* to insist on lower-case lettering in its original publicity – apt, because this would-be comedy western is very lower case indeed. Dean Martin enjoys his post-Matt Helm stardom by offering such a perilously lazy performance that you just want to shut your eyes and nod off. Tasteless and unfunny. TS

Dean Martin *Joe Baker* • Brian Keith *Colonel Morgan* • Honor Blackman *Mary Anna Morgan* • Carol White *Dover MacBride* • Ben Johnson (1) *Jesse Bookbinder* • Albert Salmi *Johnny Cobb* • Don Knight *Tommy MacBride* • Joyce Van Patten *Polly Standall* • Denver Pyle *Junior Frisbee* ■ *Dir* Andrew V McLaglen • *Scr* James Lee Barrett

Something Borrowed ★ 12

Romantic comedy drama   2011 · US · Colour · 108min

Director Luke Greenfield's first feature since 2004's *The Girl Next Door* isn't the world's worst romantic comedy. But it comes perilously close. Self-absorbed extrovert Kate Hudson and "nice girl" introvert Ginnifer Goodwin have been best friends since childhood. For years, Goodwin has secretly had the hots for mutual friend Colin Egglesfield (looking distractingly like a young Tom Cruise). But it's Hudson who's about to take him up the aisle. It's not surprising there was no critics' screening when a film is as overlong, overplayed and utterly without charm as this nonsense. DA Swearing, sexual references, brief gory moment. *DVD* *Blu*

Kate Hudson *Darcy* • Ginnifer Goodwin *Rachel* • Colin Egglesfield *Dex* • John Krasinski *Ethan* • Steve Howey *Marcus* • Ashley Williams *Claire* • Geoff Pierson *Dexter Thaler Sr* • Jill Eikenberry *Bridget Thaler* ■ *Dir* Luke Greenfield • *Scr* Jennie Snyder Urman, from the novel by Emily Giffin

Something Evil ★★★

Horror   1972 · US · Colour · 73min

The best Steven Spielberg film you've never heard of, this TV movie stars Sandy Dennis and Darren McGavin as a couple who move their family to a farmhouse in rural Pennsylvania. But Dennis's countryside idyll of baking, flower arranging and craft projects soon gives way to disturbing noises and things going bump in the night, as the house takes on a sinister aspect and the couple's young son begins to change. Dennis's excellent performance as a mother pushed to the edge gives the film real power and Spielberg shows off some inventive camerawork and sound design, which gives a hint of the career that was to follow. LB

Sandy Dennis *Marjorie Worden* • Darren McGavin *Paul Worden* • Ralph Bellamy *Harry Lincoln* • Jeff Corey *Gehrmann* • Johnny Whitaker *Stevie Worden* ■ *Dir* Steven Spielberg • *Scr* Robert Clouse

Something for Everyone ★★★

Black comedy   1970 · US · Colour · 112min

Celebrated theatre director Harold Prince made his feature debut with this pitch black adaptation. Walter Lassally's images of the Bavarian countryside are splendid, but otherwise Prince opts for a decidedly stagey approach, with the long-held shots designed to draw attention to the excellence of the cast. Michael York adds malevolence to his trademark charm, as the opportunist who attempts to exploit countess Angela Lansbury while serving as her footman. But it's Lansbury and her spiteful daughter, Jane Carr, who take the acting honours in a story notable for the dastardliness of just about every principal character. DP

Angela Lansbury *Countess Herthe von Ornstein* • Michael York *Konrad Ludwig* • Anthony Corlan [Anthony Higgins] *Helmuth von Ornstein* • Heidelinde Weis *Anneliese Pleschke* • Jane Carr *Lotte von Ornstein* • Eva-Maria Meineke *Mrs Pleschke* • John Gill *Mr Pleschke* ■ *Dir* Harold Prince • *Scr* Hugh Wheeler, from the novel *The Cook* by Harry Kressing

Something for Joey ★★★★

Drama based on a true story   1977 · US · Colour · 96min

A fine screenplay, superior acting and classy direction save this made-for-TV drama – based on the true-life relationship between a US college football star and his kid brother who is dying of leukaemia – from sentimentality. Geraldine Page and Steve Guttenberg both won praise for their performances and went on to greater fame and fortune. However, it is Jeff Lynas's sensitive portrayal of the afflicted brother that provides the key to making this such a surprisingly effective, moving and uplifting film. PF

Geraldine Page *Anne Cappelletti* • Gerald S O'Loughlin *John Cappelletti Sr* • Marc Singer *John Cappelletti* • Jeff Lynas [Jeffrey Lynas] *Joey Cappelletti* • Linda Kelsey *Joyce Cappelletti/Narrator* • Brian Farrell *Marty Cappelletti* • Kathleen Beller *Jean Cappelletti* • Steve Guttenberg *Mike Cappelletti* ■ *Dir* Lou Antonio • *Scr* Jerry McNeely

Something for the Boys ★★★ U

Musical   1944 · US · Colour · 86min

Cole Porter's 1943 stage production lost a lot on its transfer to the screen, including Ethel Merman and most of its score. What remains is a typically garish 20th Century-Fox musical, interesting today for the array of talent on display. The plot's about cousins Carmen Miranda, Vivian Blaine and Phil Silvers opening up their inherited southern plantation to army wives, and putting on a show to fund it. Silvers is terrific in a routine that owes much to his vaudeville background, while that new young crooner Perry Como puts over numbers with style and verve. TS

Carmen Miranda *Chiquita Hart* • Michael O'Shea (1) *Staff Sergeant Rocky Fulton* • Vivian Blaine *Blossom Hart* • Phil Silvers *Harry Hart* • Sheila

---

Ryan *Melanie Walker* • Perry Como *Sergeant Laddie Green* • Glenn Langan *Lieutenant Ashley Crothers* ■ *Dir* Lewis Seiler • *Scr* Robert Ellis, Helen Logan, Frank Gabrielson, from a musical comedy by Herbert Fields, Dorothy Fields, Cole Porter

Something from Nothing: the Art of Rap ★★★★ 15

Music documentary   2012 · UK/US · Colour · 111min

Rap pioneer Ice-T is our guide for this fascinating documentary about a controversial form of music that still struggles to receive its due. Guns and bling laid aside as co-director/interviewer Ice-T explores the craft, skill and mechanics of rapping. He's aided by anyone who is anyone in the rap firmament – Eminem, Dr Dre, Snoop Dogg, Ice Cube and Public Enemy's Chuck D, to name but a few. Ice-T himself is a refreshingly laid-back interviewer, and this terrific piece of work proves that rap is as deserving of respect as other art forms. JA Swearing, drug abuse. *DVD* *Blu*

Ice-T • Ice Cube • Eminem • Africa Bambaataa • Snoop Dogg • Dr Dre • KRS-One • Kanye West • Common • Chuck D ■ *Dir* Ice-T, Andy Baybutt

Something in the Air ★★★ 15

Drama   2012 · Fr · Colour · 121min

This 1970s-set rites-of-passage drama stars Clément Métayer as a Paris teenager torn between following activist students emulating the notorious protests of 1968 and pursuing his interests in art and film-making. Writer/director Olivier Assayas perfectly captures the mood through smart use of period music, hippy party scenes and the sloganeering clichés of right-on youth. However, a romantic subplot seems awkwardly tacked on, and some pedestrian performances curb any sympathy for these narcissistic would-be revolutionaries. TeS French, English, Italian +subtitles. *DVD* *Blu*

Clément Métayer *Gilles* • Lola Créton *Christine* • Felix Armand *Alain* • Carole Combes *Laure* • India Salvor Menuez *Leslie* ■ *Dir/Scr* Olivier Assayas • *Cinematographer* Eric Gautier

Something in the City ★★ U

Comedy   1950 · UK · BW · 74min

After 40 years as a circus clown and music-hall comic, Richard Hearne finally found fame on TV as the fumbling old fool, Mr Pastry. But the performer was less fond of the character to whom he owed his fortune than the public, and Hearne frequently sought to escape from the corny slapstick of his children's shows. Here, he plays a pavement artist who convinces his wife he is a high financier. The cheery street folk simply don't ring true and the pathos makes Chaplin look like a cynic. DP *DVD*

Richard Hearne *William Ningle* • Garry Marsh *Mr Holley* • Ellen Pollock *Mrs Holley* • Betty Sinclair *Mrs Ningle* • Tom Gill *Richard* • Dora Bryan *Waitress* ■ *Dir* Maclean Rogers • *Scr* HF Maltby

Something in the Wind ★★★ U

Musical romantic comedy   1947 · US · BW · 85min

Deanna Durbin would make only a couple more pictures after this engaging comedy of errors, but she's on fine form as a radio star who's kidnapped by John Dall, after he becomes convinced that she'd been gold-digging with his wealthy, late grandfather. Romantic twists and entanglements ensue, complicated by the involvement of Dall's livewire cousin, Donald O'Connor. Director Irving Pichel occasionally pads the action, but Durbin's rendition of a Verdi aria (with Metropolitan Opera star Jan Peerce) is splendid, as is O'Connor's athletic parody of pulp thriller clichés. DP *DVD*

Deanna Durbin *Mary Collins* • Donald O'Connor *Charlie Read* • John Dall *Donald Read* • Charles Winninger *Uncle Chester* • Helena Carter *Clarissa Prentice* • Margaret Wycherly *Grandma Read* • Jan Peerce *Tony* • Jean Adair *Aunt Mary*

Collins ■ *Dir* Irving Pichel • *Scr* Harry Kurnitz, William Bowers, from a story by Fritz Rotter, Charles O'Neal

Something Must Break
★★★ 18

Romantic drama   2014 · Swe · Colour · 81min

Stockholm is the setting for this troubled romance between a young self-destructive pre-op transsexual and a straight-looking punk struggling with his bisexuality. Sebastian (Saga Becker) has a dead-end warehousing job, loses his weekends in a haze of booze and self-abasing promiscuity, and is far from happy, until he's rescued from a gay-bashing thug by the leather-jacketed Andreas (Iggy Malmborg), sparking a highly charged liaison. Sexually forthright without getting too explicit, Ester Martin Bergsmark's film plots a convincing course for their relationship, but suffers from a decidedly tame ending. TJ In Swedish. Sex scenes. *DVD*

Saga Becker *Sebastian/Ellie* • Iggy Malmborg *Andreas* • Shima Navarani *Lea* • Mattias Ahlen *Mattias* ■ *Dir* Ester Martin Bergsmark • *Scr* Ester Martin Bergsmark, Eli Leven, from the novel *You Are the Roots That Sleep beneath My Feet and Hold the Earth in Place* by Leven

Something New   ★★★ PG

Romantic comedy   2006 · US · Colour · 100min

"New" is pushing it a bit, but Sanaa Hamri's thoughtful romantic comedy does at least attempt to say something different about modern relationships, particularly those of the interracial kind. Sanaa Lathan plays a go-getting black accountant who has set her sights on finding the "IBM" – Ideal Black Man. However, she is forced to examine her own prejudices when she falls for white landscape architect Simon Baker. While the film is a lot more subtle than the similarly themed *Guess Who*, Hamri struggles to keep the predictable romantic comedy clichés at bay. But the two leads spark off each other nicely and there are solid supporting turns from the likes of Alfre Woodard, Blair Underwood and Donald Faison. JF

Sanaa Lathan *Kenya McQueen* • Simon Baker (1) *Brian Kelly* • Mike Epps *Walter* • Donald Faison *Nelson McQueen* • Blair Underwood *Mark Harper* • Wendy Raquel Robinson *Cheryl* • Alfre Woodard *Joyce McQueen* ■ *Dir* Sanaa Hamri • *Scr* Kriss Turner

Something of Value   ★★★

Drama   1957 · US · BW · 113min

Directed by Richard Brooks, who adapted it from Robert Ruark's novel based on the Mau Mau uprisings in Kenya, the film graphically conveys the horror of slaughter, but is dull. The more personal plot at the centre of the upheaval between white farmers and black tribesman, focuses on Rock Hudson and Sidney Poitier, close friends plunged into conflicting loyalties by the bloody divide with Poitier, excellent in the role, succumbing to tribal allegiance. Vivid East African locations add to the reality of this tale. RK

Rock Hudson *Peter McKenzie* • Dana Wynter *Holly Keith* • Wendy Hiller *Elizabeth* • Sidney Poitier *Kimani* • Juano Hernandez *Njogu* • William Marshall (2) *Leader* • Robert Beatty *Jeff Newton* • Walter Fitzgerald *Henry McKenzie* ■ *Dir* Richard Brooks • *Scr* Richard Brooks, from a novel by Robert C Ruark

Something Short of Paradise   ★★★ 15

Romantic comedy   1979 · US · Colour · 86min

David Steinberg and Susan Sarandon star as a moviehouse manager and a journalist who fall in love, despite obstacles thrown in their paths by conniving acquaintances. Performances from the two leads are good, though Steinberg's character is perhaps more unlikeable than he needs to be. Film buffs will go ga-ga over the title sequence, which cleverly strings together old movie ads. DA

Susan Sarandon *Madeleine Ross* • David Steinberg *Harris Soane* • Jean-Pierre Aumont *Jean-Fidel Mileau* • Marilyn Sokol *Ruthie Miller* • Joe Grifasi *Barney Collins* ■ *Dir* David Helpern Jr [David Helpern] • *Scr* Fred Barron

Something to Believe In
★ PG

Romantic drama
1997 · UK/Ger · Colour · 108min

Schmaltz, saccharin and sentimentality overwhelm this melodrama, despite a strong cast of recognisable faces. William McNamara plays a concert pianist off to compete in Naples and en route he encounters terminally ill Las Vegas croupier Maria Pitillo, who's in Italy seeking a miracle cure. The cast flails about with this all too "sweet" material, but to no avail. LH Swearing.

William McNamara *Mike* • Maria Pitillo *Maggie* • Tom Conti *Monsignor Calogero* • Maria Schneider *Maria* • Ian Bannen *Dcn Pozzi* • Robert Wagner *Brad* • Jill St John *Dr Joann Anderson* • Roddy McDowall *Gambler* ■ *Dir* John Hough • *Scr* John Goldsmith, John Hough, from an idea by John Hough, David Purcell

Something to Hide   ★

Thriller   1971 · UK · Colour · 106min

For ten minutes, as Peter Finch and Shelley Winters hurl drunken abuse at each other, this melodrama looks as if it could be a scorcher. But then Winters departs the scene and Finch is left to wallow in what must be the worst movie hangover since Ray Milland had his lost weekend. Finch's encounter with pregnant waif Linda Hayden is utterly unbelievable, and the preposterous dialogue lacks insight, while the images are packed with thick-ear symbolism. DP

Peter Finch *Harry Field* • Shelley Winters *Gabrielle Field* • Colin Blakely *Blagdon* • John Stride *Sergeant Tom Winnington* • Linda Hayden *Lorelei* • Harold Goldblatt *Dibbick* • Rosemarie Dunham *Elsie* • Helen Fraser *Miss Bunyan* • Graham Crowden *Lay preacher* ■ *Dir* Alastair Reid • *Scr* Alastair Reid, from the novel by Nicholas Monsarrat

Something to Live For   ★★

Melodrama   1952 · US · BW · 89min

Seven years after winning his Oscar for playing an alcoholic in *The Lost Weekend*, Ray Milland was involved with booze again in this less ambitious vehicle, produced and directed by George Stevens. As a member of Alcoholics Anonymous, Milland helps actress Joan Fontaine battle the demon drink and falls for her in the process. Teresa Wright plays Milland's wife, and all three stars, though past the peak of their film careers, give excellent performances. Director Stevens must take the blame for the film's dull tone and turgid progress. TV

Joan Fontaine *Jenny Carey* • Ray Milland *Alan Miller* • Teresa Wright *Edna Miller* • Richard Derr *Tony Collins* • Douglas Dick *Baker* • Herbert Heyes *Mr Crawley* • Harry Bellaver *Billy* • Paul Valentine *Albert* ■ *Dir* George Stevens • *Scr* Dwight Taylor

Something to Sing About
★★ U

Musical comedy   1937 · US · BW · 87min

As this is one of James Cagney's all too few musicals, we should be grateful even for this mistitled low-budget affair in which he gets to sing and dance his way through a few numbers. (The film was released ten years later with the worse title: *The Battling Hoofer*.) Cagney plays a Hollywood star who discovers that the small print in his contract says that he must remain a bachelor while with the studio, so he can't marry his sweetheart Evelyn Daw. RB

James Cagney *Terry Rooney* • Evelyn Daw *Rita Wyatt* • William Frawley *Hank Meyers* • Mona Barrie *Stephanie Hajos* • Gene Lockhart *Bennett O Regan* ■ *Dir* Victor Schertzinger • *Scr* Austin Parker, from a story by Victor Schertzinger

---

Something to Talk About
★★ 15

Romantic drama   1995 · US · Colour · 100min

Reversing the tactics she employed in *Thelma & Louise*, screenwriter Callie Khouri has disgruntled wife Julia Roberts stand and fight rather than take to the road. But it's not much of a contest, as who could possibly have any sympathy for either play-away husband Dennis Quaid or her overbearing father Robert Duvall? It's directed with care, but no flair by Lasse Hallström, while Roberts is outclassed by both Kyra Sedgwick and Gena Rowlands. DP *DVD*

Julia Roberts *Grace* • Dennis Quaid *Eddie* • Robert Duvall *Wyly King* • Gena Rowlands *Georgia King* • Kyra Sedgwick *Emma Rae* • Brett Cullen *Jamie Johnson* ■ *Dir* Lasse Hallström • *Scr* Callie Khouri

Something Wicked This Way Comes   ★★★ PG

Gothic fantasy drama   1983 · US · Colour · 91min

Generally thought of as a disappointingly crude adaptation by Ray Bradbury of his own novel, this fantasy promises more than it delivers, but is still a good, spooky horror yarn for children with imagination. Jonathan Pryce is suitably evil as the owner of the Pandemonium Carnival, which appears to grant the wishes of the inhabitants of a small American town. Director Jack Clayton piles on the suspense and atmosphere, especially when Pryce goes in search of two young boys who have discovered too many of his secrets. DM

Jason Robards *Charles Halloway* • Jonathan Pryce *Mr Dark* • Diana Ladd *Mrs Nightshade* • Pam Grier *Dust Witch* • Royal Dano *Tom Fury* • Vidal Peterson *Will Halloway* • Shawn Carson *Jim Nightshade* • Arthur Hill *Narrator* ■ *Dir* Jack Clayton • *Scr* Ray Bradbury, from his novel

Something Wild   ★★★★ 18

Black comedy drama
1986 · US · Colour · 108min

Jonathan Demme's oddball "yuppie nightmare" finds meek Jeff Daniels dragged into boozing and bondage after an accidental meeting with flaky *femme fatale* Melanie Griffith, who persuades him to attend her high-school reunion. The film moves up a violent gear when her crazed ex-con husband Ray Liotta kidnaps them both for his own vengeful purposes. Constantly confounding expectations, Demme's jet-black anarchic comedy features a marvellous rock soundtrack and a great performance by Griffith. AJ Violence, swearing, nudity. *DVD*

Jeff Daniels *Charles Driggs* • Melanie Griffith *Audrey "Lulu" Hankel* • Ray Liotta *Max Sinclair* • Margaret Colin *Irene* • Tracey Walter *Country squire* • Dana Preu *"Peaches"* • Jack Gilpin *Larry Dillman* • Su Tissue *Peggy Dillman* ■ *Dir* Jonathan Demme • *Scr* E Max Frye

Something's Gotta Give
★★★ 12

Romantic comedy drama
2003 · US · Colour · 122min

Jack Nicholson and Diane Keaton star in this frothy portrayal of post-menopausal love from director Nancy Meyers. In a role that combines sassy sophistication and emotionally flummoxed charm, Keaton shines as a divorced playwright who thinks affairs of the heart are a folly of youth, until she reluctantly nurses her daughter's ageing lover (Nicholson). Drawn to the arrogant bachelor, she's surprised to find a mutual attraction, despite his assertion he only dates women under 30. While wolfish Nicholson plays to type, it's still thoroughly enjoyable watching the duo interact. SF Swearing. *DVD*

Jack Nicholson *Harry Sanborn* • Diane Keaton *Erica Barry* • Keanu Reeves *Dr Julian Mercer* • Frances McDormand *Zoe* • Amanda Peet *Marin* • Jon Favreau *Leo* • Paul Michael Glaser *David Klein* • Rachel Ticotin *Dr Martinez* ■ *Dir/Scr* Nancy Meyers

---

Sometimes a Great Notion
★★★ 12

Drama   1971 · US · Colour · 109min

Set in Oregon, Paul Newman's film of Ken Kesey's gargantuan novel tells of a family of lumberjacks who have no truck with the striking loggers' union. However, it's the family itself, led by Henry Fonda, that offers the meatiest bits of the drama, resulting in scenes that vaguely recall Newman's earlier fim, *Hud*. A strong cast and fine location work make this a gripping, if rather solemn effort. Newman took over from director Richard A Colla halfway through shooting. AT *DVD*

Paul Newman *Hank Stamper* • Henry Fonda *Henry Stamper* • Lee Remick *Viv Stamper* • Michael Sarrazin *Leeland Stamper* • Richard Jaeckel *Joe Ben Stamper* • Linda Lawson *Jan Stamper* ■ *Dir* Paul Newman • *Scr* John Gay, from the novel by Ken Kesey

Sometimes in April   ★★★ 15

Drama   2005 · US/Rwanda/Fr · Colour · 140min

Idris Elba (*Luther*) stars in this ambitious drama that provides sombre reflection on the Rwandan genocide of 1994. His naturally dignified air serves him well as a Hutu soldier married to a woman of Tutsi heritage who is therefore a target (along with their kids) in a campaign of ethnic cleansing. It's harrowing in places, leaving you breathless with the sheer scale of the killing, and yet too polite in others, with the apologetic tone distracting from a full examination of what went wrong. Debra Winger features in snapshots from Washington. SP Some violence, swearing. *DVD*

Idris Elba *Augustin* • Debra Winger *Prudence Bushnell* • Oris Erhuero *Honoré* • Carole Karemera *Jeanne* ■ *Dir/Scr* Raoul Peck

Sometimes They Come Back   ★★ 15

Horror   1991 · US · Colour · 96min

This is a so-so shocker from the Stephen King horror conveyor belt. Teacher Tim Matheson returns to his home town where he's haunted by the ghosts of the boys responsible for killing his brother 27 years before. Matheson stumbles with suitable dread through the fights with the juvenile delinquents from hell, but while director Tom McLoughlin aims to engross and gross-out in equal measure, the numerous plot inconsistencies scupper the good intentions. AJ *DVD*

Tim Matheson *Jim Norman* • Brooke Adams *Sally Norman* • Robert Rusler *Lawson* • Chris Demetral *Wayne* • Robert Hy Gorman *Scott Norman* • William Sanderson *Carl Mueller* ■ *Dir* Tom McLoughlin • *Scr* Lawrence Konner, Mark Rosenthal, from the short story by Stephen King

Sometimes They Come Back... Again   ★★ 18

Horror   1996 · US · Colour · 94min

Michael Gross returns to his home town after his mother dies, to take care of her estate, only to find the town absolutely awash with the occult. Alexis Arquette is the demonically powered teenager who has his eyes on Gross's daughter, played by Hilary Swank. Despite being a needless sequel to a movie that was barely based on a Stephen King short story, it's slickly produced. ST *DVD*

Michael Gross *Jon Porter* • Hilary Swank *Michelle Porter* • Jennifer Elise Cox *Jules Martin* • Alexis Arquette *Tony Reno* ■ *Dir* Adam Grossman • *Scr* Guy Reidel, Adam Grossman, from characters by Stephen King

Sometimes They Come Back... for More   ★★★ 15

Horror   1998 · US · Colour · 85min

The best of the three movies based on Stephen King's short story, mainly because director Daniel Zelik Berk's addition to the series has really nothing to do with its title source material. This is an effective variation on *The Thing from Another World* (1951). Sent to the Antarctic military ice station Erebus to investigate weird occurrences and unexplained deaths, Clayton Rohner uncovers a satanic power that kills and then revives the corpses. Berk uses the locations with considerable visual flair, but this does peter out as it wends its way to a hokey conclusion. AJ *DVD*

Faith Ford *Jennifer Wills* • Clayton Rohner *Capt Sam Cage* • Damian Chapa *Dr Karl Schilling* • Max Perlich *Lt Brian Shebanski* • Michael Stadvec *Capt Robert Reynolds* • Chase Masterson *Major Callie O'Grady* ■ *Dir* Daniel Zelik Berk • *Scr* Adam Grossman, Darryl Sollerh, from characters by Stephen King

Somewhere ★★★ 15

Comedy drama
2010 · US/UK/It/Jpn · Colour · 97min

From Sofia Coppola, the writer/director of *Lost in Translation*, comes another story of an older man and a younger woman, set against the backdrop of a luxury hotel. Stephen Dorff, cast against his usual villainous type, plays fading Hollywood actor Johnny Marco, who is left with his 11-year-old daughter (Elle Fanning) for a few more days than usual. Not much happens, and the measured, deliberate pace can be read as either stately or deathly. But as a slow-burn, poetic character piece it works just fine, with Dorff and especially Fanning making engaging leads. DW In English, Italian. Swearing, nudity. *DVD* [Blu]

Stephen Dorff *Johnny Marco* • Elle Fanning *Cleo Marco* • Chris Pontius *Sammy* • Michelle Monaghan *Rebecca* ■ *Dir/Scr* Sofia Coppola • *Cinematographer* Harris Savides

Somewhere I'll Find You ★★★

Second World War romantic drama
1942 · US · BW · 107min

The relationship of two brothers (Clark Gable, Robert Sterling), both war correspondents, is upset by their involvement with journalist Lana Turner, who is sent to report in Indochina. She becomes a nurse, they all go to Bataan, and one of them doesn't return. It's a standard romance, but was a huge box-office success in its day. The film is remembered because Gable's wife, Carole Lombard, was killed three days into shooting, becoming an early Hollywood war casualty. A grief-stricken Gable insisted on finishing the picture, but gives an understandably subdued performance. RK

Clark Gable *Jonathan "Johnny" Davis* • Lana Turner *Paula Lane* • Robert Sterling *Kirk Davis* • Reginald Owen *Willie Manning* • Lee Patrick *Eve Manning* • Charles Dingle *George L Stafford* • Van Johnson *Lt Wade Halls* • Keenan Wynn *Sgt Tom Purdy* ■ *Dir* Wesley Ruggles • *Scr* Marguerite Roberts, Walter Reisch, from a story by Charles Hoffman

Somewhere in Europe ★★★★

Drama
1947 · Hun · BW · 104min

This is a landmark film in that it was Hungary's first international success for decades and led to the Hungarian cinema becoming a nationalised industry. Bela Balazs – the film theorist and author who had returned from exile in the USSR – co-wrote the screenplay which dealt with the bitter realities of postwar Hungary in a direct manner. It involves a band of thieving, begging orphans who take refuge in a castle, where they find a better way of life. Despite its subject matter, this is lyrical and optimistic. RB In Hungarian.

Ladislas Horvath *Kuksi* • Arthur Somlay *Peter Simon* • Miklos Gabor *Ossup* • Zsuzsa Banky *The girl* ■ *Dir* Geza von Radvanyi • *Scr* Geza von Radvanyi, Bela Balazs, Judit Fejer, Felix Mariassy

Somewhere in the Night ★★★

Crime mystery
1946 · US · BW · 110min

US marine John Hodiak (the poor man's Clark Gable) is discharged from the service suffering from amnesia. The only lead to his past is an address in Los Angeles, where a series of clues involve him with nightclub singer Nancy Guild, club owner Richard Conte, a police detective, and a bruising encounter with a pair of thugs before he

discovers the truth about himself. The complicated plot, well handled by Joseph L Mankiewicz, unfolds as a tense and absorbing crime drama, which is well cast but for Guild, making an undistinguished debut to a career that never took off. RK

John Hodiak *George Taylor* • Nancy Guild *Christy Smith* • Lloyd Nolan *Lt Donald Kendall* • Richard Conte *Mel Phillips* • Josephine Hutchinson *Elizabeth Conroy* ■ *Dir* Joseph L Mankiewicz • *Scr* Howard Dimsdale, Joseph L Mankiewicz, Lee Strasberg, from a story by Marvin Borowsky

Somewhere in Time ★★★ PG

Romantic drama
1980 · US · Colour · 99min

Christopher Reeve stars as a disaffected playwright in this highly schmaltzy love story. Reeve is serviceable and moist-eyed enough, and Jane Seymour sleepwalks her way through a familiar role in a tale with a supernatural twist. This rather charming, old-fashioned love story is an entertaining tear-jerker for those in the mood. SH *DVD*

Christopher Reeve *Richard Collier* • Jane Seymour (2) *Elise McKenna* • Christopher Plummer *William Fawcett Robinson* • Teresa Wright *Laura Roberts* • Bill Erwin *Arthur* • Victoria Michaels *Maude* • William P O'Hagan *Rollo* ■ *Dir* Jeannot Szwarc • *Scr* Richard Matheson, from his novel

Somewhere on Leave ★★ U

Comedy
1942 · UK · BW · 96min

Of the music-hall turns who made films, Lancashire comedian Frank Randle was among the most successful. His appeal exemplifies the North-South divide and his success was largely confined to home ground. Here, Randle and three of his regular army pals are invited by a fellow private to have some off-duty fun at his stately home. Unsophisticated perhaps, but fun. BB

Frank Randle *Private Randle* • Harry Korris *Sgt Korris* • Robbie Vincent *Private Enoch* • Dan Young *Private Young* • Toni Lupino *Toni Beaumont* • Pat McGrath *Private Roy Desmond* ■ *Dir* John E Blakeley • *Scr* Roney Parsons, Anthony Toner, Frank Randle

Sommersby ★★★ 12

Period romantic drama
1993 · US · Colour · 108min

This is the American reworking of the Gérard Depardieu/Nathalie Baye modern classic *The Return of Martin Guerre*, and it isn't a patch on the original, either in terms of tension, intelligence or performance. Still, there is much to enjoy in the central mystery surrounding the true identity of returning American Civil War veteran Richard Gere, in particular the sensitive playing of Jodie Foster as his confused "widow". Unfortunately, neither Gere nor Bill Pullman, as Foster's embittered suitor, can hold a candle to her. DP Violence, swearing, sex scenes. *DVD*

Richard Gere *Jack Sommersby* • Jodie Foster *Laurel Sommersby* • Bill Pullman *Orin Meecham* • James Earl Jones *Judge Isaacs* • Lanny Flaherty *Buck* • William Windom *Reverend Powell* • Wendell Wellman *Travis* • Brett Kelley *Little Rob* • Clarice Taylor *Esther* • Frankie Faison *Joseph* • Ronald Lee Ermey [R Lee Ermey] *Dick Mead* ■ *Dir* Jon Amiel • *Scr* Nicholas Meyer, Sarah Kernochan, from a story by Nicholas Meyer, Anthony Schaffer, from the film *The Return of Martin Guerre* by Daniel Vigne, Jean-Claude Carrière

The Son ★★★★ 12

Drama
2002 · Bel/Fr · Colour · 100min

Belgian film-makers Jean-Pierre and Luc Dardenne apply their brand of social realism to the subject of masculine emotion in this unsettling account of a carpentry teacher's relationship with the teenager responsible for the death of his son. Yet there's also an element of suspense, as Olivier Gourmet's intentions towards student Morgan Marinne appear anything but honourable. Employing an aggressive hand-held camera to reinforce Gourmet's superb portrayal of the man's fraught state, the Dardenne brothers explore the nature of pain, forgiveness and redemption. DP French +subtitles. *DVD*

Olivier Gourmet *Olivier* • Morgan Marinne *Francis* • Isabella Soupart *Magali* • Remy Renaud *Philippo* • Nassim Hassaïni *Omar* • Kevin Leroy *Raoul* • Félicien Pitsaer *Steve* ■ *Dir/Scr* Jean-Pierre Dardenne, Luc Dardenne

Son Frère ★★★ 15

Drama
2003 · Fr · Colour · 88min

Director Patrice Chéreau here produces an intimate study of emotion in extremis with this adaptation about siblings repairing their strained relationship. Estranged brothers Bruno Todeschini and Eric Caravaca attempt to reconcile after the former is diagnosed with a potentially fatal illness. Caravaca seeks to console their parents and his brother's girlfriend, Nathalie Boutefeu, while dealing with his own rocky liaison with Sylvain Jacques. The intersecting time frames complicate matters unnecessarily. DP French +subtitles. Swearing, sex scenes, nudity. *DVD*

Bruno Todeschini *Thomas* • Eric Caravaca *Luc* • Nathalie Boutefeu *Claire* • Maurice Garrel *Old man* • Catherine Ferran *Head doctor* • Antoinette Moya *Mother* • Sylvain Jacques *Vincent* • Fred Ulysse *Father* ■ *Dir* Patrice Chéreau • *Scr* Patrice Chéreau, Anne-Louise Trividic, from the novel by Philippe Besson

Son of a Gun ★★★ 15

Action crime drama
2013 · Aus · Colour · 108min

Ewan McGregor makes a decent fist of playing against type in this debut movie from Australian director Julius Avery, but the film's determination to pack multiple genres into a single film will likely leave audiences wishing he'd concentrated on just the one. McGregor's hard-bitten professional bank robber is serving a 25-year prison sentence when he is befriended by a teenage petty criminal (Brenton Thwaites) struggling to survive his own six months inside. Sadly, the underwritten blackly comedic ending proves to be at least one genre shift too far. AS

Ewan McGregor *Brendan Lynch* • Brenton Thwaites *JR* • Alicia Vikander *Tasha* • Jacek Koman *Sam Lennox* • Matt Nable *Sterlo* ■ *Dir/Scr* Julius Avery

Son of a Gunfighter ★★★ U

Western
1964 · US/Sp · Colour · 91min

In an enjoyable "paella" western, Russ Tamblyn portrays the title character, a youngster out to kill the man who deserted his mother 20 years earlier. Many of the characters are Mexican, giving an opportunity for Spanish actors (including Fernando Rey as a cattle rancher) to speak English with appropriate accents. The complicated plot features warring American outlaws and Mexican *bandidos*, but the scenery is terrific, the score rousing and the action briskly handled. AE

Russ Tamblyn *Johnny* • Kieron Moore *Deputy Fenton* • James Philbrook *Ketchum* • Fernando Rey *Don Fortuna* • María Granada *Pilar* ■ *Dir* Paul Landres • *Scr* Clarke Reynolds

Son of Ali Baba ★★ U

Fantasy adventure
1952 · US · Colour · 74min

This is the sort of pantomime stuff Tony Curtis appeared in when good looks mattered more than good acting. As Kashma Baba, son of Ali, he must protect the Princess Kiki from an evil caliph, who also wants to get his greedy hands on Baba Sr's treasure. It's a satirical tale of kidnapping, sword crossing and falling in love, but without a genie or flying carpet, it's less than magical. TH

Tony Curtis *Kashma Baba* • Piper Laurie *Kiki* • Susan Cabot *Tala* • William Reynolds *Mustafa* • Hugh O'Brian *Hussein* • Victor Jory *Caliph* • Morris Ankrum *Ali Baba* ■ *Dir* Kurt Neumann • *Scr* Gerald Drayson Adams

Son of Babylon ★★★ 12

Drama
2009 · Iraq/UK/Fr/Neth/UAE/Egy · Colour · 87min

Set in the weeks following the fall of Saddam Hussein in 2003, this thoughtful neo-realist road movie follows a Kurdish

grandmother (Shezhad Hussein) and her 12-year-old grandson (Yasser Taleeb) as they embark on a 600-mile search for her son/ his father who's been missing since the end of the first Gulf War. Owing much to the humanist tradition of Iranian cinema, this visually striking and emotionally harrowing odyssey is played to the hilt by the non-professional cast. But despite his evident good intentions, director Mohamed Al-Daradji struggles to make the case that Arabs suffered as much as the ethnic minorities under Saddam. DP Arabic, Kurdish +subtitles. *DVD*

Shezhad Hussein *Um-Ibrahim* • Yasser Taleeb *Ahmed* • Bashir Al-Majid *Musa* ■ *Dir* Mohamed Al-Daradji • *Scr* Mohamed Al-Daradji, Jennifer Norridge, Mithal Ghazi

Son of Dracula ★★★ PG

Horror
1943 · US · BW · 77min

Lon Chaney Jr plays the famous Count under the pseudonym Alucard (Dracula spelt backwards, a device destined to be used in numerous inferior horrors), and recruits vampires in the Deep South because Universal wouldn't pay for Transylvanian sets. It didn't matter. This has atmosphere to spare, super make-up by *Frankenstein* genius Jack Pierce and fun man-to-bat transformations. A neglected highlight from the golden age of horror. AJ

Lon Chaney Jr *Count Alucard* • Robert Paige *Frank Stanley* • Louise Allbritton *Katherine Caldwell* • Evelyn Ankers *Claire Caldwell* • Frank Craven *Dr Harry Brewster* • J Edward Bromberg *Professor Lazlo* • Samuel S Hinds *Judge Simmons* ■ *Dir* Robert Siodmak • *Scr* Eric Taylor, from a story by Curtis Siodmak

Son of Flubber ★★ U

Comedy
1962 · US · BW · 98min

You will remember that "flubber" was the flying rubber invented by Fred MacMurray in the fun family comedy *The Absent-Minded Professor*. Disney reassembled many of the same cast two years later, but usually reliable director Robert Stevenson could not repeat the winning formula. Keenan Wynn enjoys himself as the villain, but the jokes are tired. DP *DVD*

Fred MacMurray *Prof Ned Brainard* • Nancy Olson *Betsy Brainard* • Keenan Wynn *Alonzo Hawk* • Tommy Kirk *Biff Hawk* • Elliott Reid *Shelby Ashton* • Joanna Moore *Desiree de la Roche* • Leon Ames *President Rufus Daggett* • Ed Wynn *AJ Allen* • Ken Murray *Mr Hurley* • Charlie Ruggles [Charles Ruggles] *Judge Murdock* • William Demarest *Mr Hummel* • Paul Lynde *Sportscaster* ■ *Dir* Robert Stevenson • *Scr* Bill Walsh, Don DaGradi, from the story *A Situation of Gravity* by Samuel W Taylor, from novels by Jay Williams, Raymond Abrashkin

Son of Frankenstein ★★★★ PG

Horror
1939 · US · BW · 95min

The third instalment of Universal's classic series features Boris Karloff's last fling as the Monster and is a superior shocker all round. Basil Rathbone (the Baron), Bela Lugosi (Ygor) and Lionel Atwill (the police chief with a noisy artificial arm) all turn in unforgettably eccentric performances along with the ever-imposing Karloff. Add Rowland V Lee's eerie direction and the result is a majestically macabre chiller. After this, the Monster became a cliché. AJ *DVD*

Basil Rathbone *Baron Wolf von Frankenstein* • Boris Karloff *The Monster* • Bela Lugosi *Ygor* • Lionel Atwill *Inspector Krogh* • Josephine Hutchinson *Elsa von Frankenstein* • Donnie Dunagan *Peter von Frankenstein* ■ *Dir* Rowland V Lee • *Scr* Willis Cooper, from characters by Mary Shelley

Son of Fury ★★★ U

Period adventure
1942 · US · BW · 94min

Tyrone Power, cheated out of his inheritance by George Sanders, falls in love with Frances Farmer and ends up on a Polynesian island with native girl Gene Tierney. Having cast its most alluring stars, 20th Century-Fox threw money (though not much-needed Technicolor) at the production and the result was big box office. The stars perform well, especially

Sanders as a snarling villain, and the supporting cast is worth a look, too. AT

Tyrone Power *Benjamin Blake* • Gene Tierney *Eve* • George Sanders *Sir Arthur Blake* • Frances Farmer *Isabel Blake* • Roddy McDowall *Benjamin as a boy* • John Carradine *Caleb Green* • Elsa Lanchester *Bristol Isabel* ■ *Dir* John Cromwell • *Scr* Philip Dunne

Son of Godzilla ★★ U
Monster horror   1967 · Jpn · Colour · 81min

Intense heat from Japanese weather experiments causes cute Godzilla offspring, Minya, to hatch. Then mother (and who knew Godzilla was female?) must protect her son from a giant hairy spider, and other insect life enlarged by the atmospheric conditions. The eighth in the Toho monster series is an inept juvenile adventure with comical episodes spliced into the miniature special effects mayhem. AJ Japanese dubbed.

Tadao Takashima *Dr Kuzumi* • Akira Kubo *Goro* ■ *Dir* Jun Fukuda • *Scr* Shinichi Sekizawa, Kazue Shiba

Son of Kong ★★★
Fantasy adventure   1933 · US · BW · 69min

Rushed out within a year of its predecessor *King Kong*'s release, the official sequel took a more light-hearted and whimsical approach and was dismissed by critics because of the accent on comedy. Today, it now plays as short, inoffensive and good fun. The ludicrous story has Carl Denham (Robert Armstrong) returning to Skull Island in a hunt for treasure in order to pay off Manhattan's rebuilding costs after Kong's destructive rampage, and finding the giant ape's cute albino offspring. AJ

Robert Armstrong *Carl Denham* • Helen Mack *Hilda Peterson* • Frank Reicher *Captain Englehorn* • John Marston *Helstrom* • Victor Wong (1) *Charlie* • Lee Kohlmar *Mickey* • Ed Brady *Red* • Clarence Wilson *Peterson* ■ *Dir* Ernest B Schoedsack • *Scr* Ruth Rose

Son of Lassie ★★★ U
Drama   1945 · US · Colour · 100min

This sequel to the tremendously popular *Lassie Come Home* consolidated the stardom of the most successful canine performer since Rin Tin Tin. It benefits from a fine supporting cast of caring humans, including Peter Lawford and June Lockhart, but is very much of its time, as Lassie's son Laddie accompanies Lawford into Nazi-occupied Norway. TS

Peter Lawford *Joe Carraclough* • Donald Crisp *Sam Carraclough* • June Lockhart *Priscilla* • Nigel Bruce *Duke of Rudling* • William Severn *Henrik* • Leon Ames *Anton* ■ *Dir* S Sylvan Simon • *Scr* Jeanne Bartlett, from characters by Eric Knight

Son of Monte Cristo ★★★ U
Swashbuckling adventure   1940 · US · BW · 95min

This long-gestating sequel to the marvellous 1934 *Count of Monte Cristo* features Louis Hayward (replacing Robert Donat, who refused to return) as the swashbuckling son of the famous Edmond Dantes, and Joan Bennett as an imprisoned queen. The plot assumes a deliberate political relevance as it deals with an evil Balkan dictator, suavely played by George Sanders, attempting to conquer her country. TS

Louis Hayward *Count of Monte Cristo* • Joan Bennett *Grand Duchess Zona* • George Sanders *Gurko Lanen* • Florence Bates *Mathilde* • Lionel Royce *Colonel Zimmerman* • Montagu Love *Baron von Neuhoff* ■ *Dir* Rowland V Lee • *Scr* George Bruce

Son of Paleface ★★★★ PG
Spoof western   1952 · US · Colour · 90min

In this very funny follow-up to *The Paleface* (1948) – one of the rare cases of a sequel being better than the original – Bob Hope plays his own son, a cowardly dude who gets entangled with Jane Russell, a bandit who sings in a saloon called "The Dirty Shame". Roy Rogers is delightfully self-mocking as himself, particularly when singing *A Four-Legged Friend* to Trigger. All the clichés of the western are played for

laughs by director Frank Tashlin, a former animator who sets up many of the sequences like a cartoon. RB

Bob Hope *Junior Potter* • Jane Russell *Mike* • Roy Rogers *Roy Barton* • Bill Williams *Kirk* • Harry Von Zell *Stoner* • Douglass Dumbrille *Sheriff McIntyre* • Lyle Moraine *Waverly* • Lloyd Corrigan *Doc Lovejoy* • Cecil B DeMille *Photographer* ■ *Dir* Frank Tashlin • *Scr* Frank Tashlin, Robert L Welch, Joseph Quillan

Son of Rambow ★★★★ 12
Comedy drama   2007 · UK/Fr/Ger/US · Colour · 91min

After bending time and space in *The Hitchhiker's Guide to the Galaxy*, writer/director Garth Jennings revisits his own childhood in this wonderful 1980s-set growing pains yarn. Bill Milner is adorable as Will Proudfoot, the timid boy who defies years of religious indoctrination by his devout Plymouth Brethren mother (Jessica Hynes) when he falls in with school bully and aspiring film-maker Lee (Will Poulter). Unfamiliar with TV, Will is transfixed by his new friend's pirated video of Sylvester Stallone in *First Blood*, and is soon enlisted as a stuntman in Lee's new action film. Together they re-create war-torn Vietnam in leafy English suburbia – only this time there's less gore and more belly laughs. It's a nostalgia trip with a slightly surreal twist, and it's occasionally indulgent, but the bond between the boys is strong enough to prevail in this poignant ode to friendship. SP Some swearing. *DVD* *Blu*

Bill Milner *Will Proudfoot* • Will Poulter *Lee Carter* • Neil Dudgeon *Joshue* • Jessica Hynes [Jessica Stevenson] *Mary Proudfoot* • Jules Sitruk *Didier Revol* • Eric Sykes *Frank* • Anna Wing *Grandma* • Adam Godley *Brethren leader* ■ *Dir/Scr* Garth Jennings

Son of Robin Hood ★★ U
Adventure   1958 · UK · Colour · 80min

The son of Sherwood's finest is in fact a girl, played by June Laverick, and she takes over the remnants of her father's outlaw band to fight against the Black Duke (David Farrar) who wants the British throne. All the most hilarious aspects of Hollywood-on-Trent are present in this jolly jape – the Middle Ages dialogue, the classy grovelling, as well as an undercurrent of cross-dressing – and Laverick makes a pleasing heroine. AT

Al Hedison [David Hedison] *Jamie* • June Laverick *Deering Hood* • David Farrar *Des Roches* • Marius Goring *Chester* • Philip Friend *Dorchester* • Delphi Lawrence *Sylvia* • George Coulouris *Alan A Dale* • George Woodbridge *Little John* ■ *Dir* George Sherman • *Scr* George W George, George Slavin

Son of Saul ★★★★★ 15
Wartime drama   2015 · Hun/Fr/Is/Bosnia/US · Colour · 102min

A stunningly original Hungarian drama that won 2015's Grand Prix at Cannes, this proves there is still room for another film about Nazi atrocities. A Jewish prison camp inmate forced to work for special privileges discovers the body of his illegitimate son in a pile of recently murdered corpses. To give the boy a proper burial, he searches the camp for a rabbi who will recite the Kaddish for him. The result is an intense, immersive experience that harrowingly but respectfully explores the personal and public horrors of the Holocaust. DW Hungarian, German, Yiddish +subtitles. *DVD* *Blu*

Géza Röhrig *Saul Ausländer* • Levente Molnár *Abraham Warszawski* • Urs Rechn *Oberkapo Biederman* ■ *Dir* Laszlo Nemes • *Scr* Laszlo Nemes, Clara Royer • *Cinematographer* Matyas Erdely

Son of Sinbad ★★ U
Fantasy adventure   1955 · US · Colour · 85min

Howard Hughes allegedly produced this frothy fantasy nonsense solely to placate the screen ambitions of all the starlets to whom he'd promised a career. There can be no other explanation for this "40 thieves" exotica. Even Vincent Price, as comical poet Omar Khayam, considered it the worst script ever written. Dale Robertson, playing

Sinbad with a Texas accent, seems perfectly in synch with the camp confection. AJ

Dale Robertson *Sinbad* • Sally Forrest *Ameer* • Vincent Price *Omar Khayham* • Lili St Cyr *Nerissa* • Mari Blanchard *Kristina* • Jay Novello *Jiddah* • Kim Novak • Dir Ted Tetzlaff • *Scr* Aubrey Wisberg, Jack Pollexfen

Son of the Bride ★★★ 15
Comedy drama   2001 · Arg/Sp · Colour · 125min

This comedy is both a bustling ensemble piece and a pensive insight into one man's midlife nightmare. Beset by domestic conflicts and the prospect of losing the family restaurant to a soulless chain, Ricardo Darin is the victim of his own errors of judgement. But, with his father determined to renew his marital vows with a wife suffering from Alzheimer's, Darin's presented with an unexpected opportunity to atone for his past and seize his destiny. Expertly marshalling his cast and capturing Buenos Aires's vibrancy, Juan José Campanella's satire is amusing and astute. DP Spanish +subtitles.

Ricardo Darin *Rafael Belvedere* • Héctor Alterio *Nino Belvedere* • Norma Aleandro *Norma Belvedere* • Eduardo Blanco *Juan Carlos* • Nàtalia Verbeke *Naty* ■ *Dir* Juan José Campanella • *Scr* Juan José Campanella, Fernando Castets

Son of the Mask ★ PG
Fantasy comedy   2004 · US/Ger · Colour · 90min

In this poor sequel to Jim Carrey's 1994 hit *The Mask*, the magical Nordic relic falls into the hands of an aspiring cartoonist (Jamie Kennedy), who fathers a son while wearing it. The baby is born with all the literally eye-popping powers of Carrey's original character, turning his dad's world upside down with nonstop mayhem. A barrel-scraping cash-in. SF *DVD*

Jamie Kennedy *Tim Avery* • Alan Cumming *Loki* • Bob Hoskins *Odin* • Traylor Howard *Tonya Avery* • Ben Stein *Dr Arthur Neuman* ■ *Dir* Lawrence Guterman • *Scr* Lance Khazei

Son of the Pink Panther ★ PG
Action comedy   1993 · US · Colour · 88min

One can understand Blake Edwards's frustration at seeing a successful series stopped in its tracks by the death of Peter Sellers. Yet surely the critical mauling meted out to those cut-and-paste jobs *Trail* and *Curse*, should have clued him in to the fact that the public were simply not interested in Clouseau clones. Here, he puts Italian comic Roberto Benigni through his paces. The kidnapping plot is inane, the slapstick inept and the cast ineffectual. DP

Roberto Benigni *Jacques Gambrelli* • Herbert Lom *Inspector Dreyfus* • Shabana Azmi *The Queen* • Debrah Farentino *Princess Yasmin* • Jennifer Edwards *Yussa* • Robert Davi *Hans* • Burt Kwouk *Cato* • Mark Schneider *Arnon* • Graham Stark *Dr Balls* • Liz Smith *Madame Balls* ■ *Dir* Blake Edwards • *Scr* Blake Edwards, Madeline Sunshine, Steve Sunshine, from a story by Blake Edwards, from characters by Maurice Richlin, Blake Edwards

The Son of the Sheik ★★★★ U
Silent adventure   1926 · US · BW · 68min

Abandon all resistance to the technique and conventions of blood-and-sand romance as filmed in the silent era. Remind yourself that there has been no greater male screen idol than Rudolph Valentino, and surrender to this, his last film before his premature death. The star plays two roles, Prince Ahmed, and his father, the all-powerful Sheik. Marvellously photographed by George Barnes, directed by George Fitzmaurice and drawing excellent work from Valentino, this tongue-in-cheek tale, combining passion, violence and swashbuckling action with humour, has lost none of its entertainment value. RK

Rudolph Valentino *Ahmed/The Sheik* • Vilma Banky *Yasmin* • George Fawcett *André* • Montague Love [Montagu Love] *Ghabah* • Karl Dane *Ramadan* ■ *Dir* George Fitzmaurice • *Scr*

Frances Marion, Fred De Gresac, George Marion Jr (titles), from the novel *The Sons of the Sheik* by Edith Maude Hull

Sonatine ★★★★★ 18
Crime drama   1993 · Jpn · Colour · 93min

This violent gang war thriller is a stunning piece of film-making. Director Takeshi "Beat" Kitano shows a complete understanding of the Hollywood gangster movie and its Japanese counterpart, the yakuza film. Moreover, he demonstrates a mastery of technique in the magnificent beach hideout segment in which he uses trick effects, imaginative camera angles and a range of comic styles to question the value of the yakuza's existence and build tension towards the superb silhouette shoot-out. He also gives a towering performance as a disillusioned hitman. DP Japanese +subtitles. Violence, nudity. *DVD*

"Beat" Takeshi [Takeshi Kitano] *Murakawa* • Aya Kokumai *Miyuki* • Tetsu Watanabe *Uechi* • Masanobu Katsumura *Ryoji* ■ *Dir/Scr* Takeshi Kitano • *Cinematographer* Katsumi Yanagijima

Song for a Raggy Boy ★★ 15
Drama based on a true story   2002 · Ire/UK/Sp/Den · Colour · 93min

Although less shocking than *The Magdalene Sisters*, Aisling Walsh's adaptation of Patrick Galvin's autobiographical tome exposes similar abuses that scarred religious education in bygone Ireland. As the socialist returning from the Spanish Civil War, Aidan Quinn has a touching influence over his charges at the Catholic reform school ruled by Iain Glen's sadistic cleric. But Walsh never strikes the right balance between cruelty and compassion, especially as Richard Blackford's score drenches the latter in gushing sentiment. DP Swearing, violence.

Aidan Quinn *William Franklin* • Iain Glen *Brother John* • Marc Warren (1) *Brother Mac* • Dudley Sutton *Brother Tom* • Alan Devlin *Father Damian* • Stuart Graham *Brother Whelan* • John Travers *Liam Mercier* • Chris Newman (1) *Patrick Delaney* ■ *Dir* Aisling Walsh • *Scr* Patrick Galvin, Aisling Walsh, Kevin Byron Murphy, from the autobiography by Patrick Galvin

A Song for Beko ★★★★
Wartime drama   1992 · Ger/Arm · Colour · 86min

A teacher not a fighter, Turkish Kurd Nizamettin Aric goes in search of his rebel brother with a diligence and dignity that characterises his relationship with orphan refugee Bezara Arsen. The first-ever Kurdish feature, Aric's directorial debut is remarkable not just for its courage, but also for the restraint with which it depicts everyday reality and passionately espouses its cause. The flashback-packed storyline contrasts the persistent prejudice of the Turks with Saddam Hussein's pitiless poison gas attack on a village returning to normality after the Iran-Iraq War. DP Kurdish +subtitles.

Nizamettin Aric *Beko* • Bezara Arsen *Zine* ■ *Dir/Scr* Nizamettin Aric

A Song for Europe ★★★ 15
Drama   1985 · UK/W Ger · Colour · 95min

David Suchet and star Maria Schneider head the mostly German cast of this international co-production. It tells the story of how a drug company executive was imprisoned for industrial espionage after taking evidence of his company's malpractice to Common Market officials. Focusing on the injustices suffered by the executive at the hands of the authorities, director John Goldschmidt offers a disturbing indictment of corporate power. DA

David Suchet *Stephen Dyer* • Maria Schneider *Madeline* • Anne-Marie Blanc *Maman* • Reinhard Glemnitz *Weigel* ■ *Dir* John Goldschmidt • *Scr* Peter Prince

Song for Marion ★★★ PG
Comedy drama   2012 · UK/Ger · Colour · 89min

Terence Stamp and Vanessa Redgrave prove that it can be fun to watch old pros at

S

work in this "feel-good" film about life, death and love. Redgrave plays terminally ill Marion, who derives comfort and distraction by singing in the local pensioners' choir. Stamp co-stars as her husband, Arthur, who is caring but curmudgeonly, a man of fewer outward emotions. He's disparaging about her involvement with the choir, which is run with disarming enthusiasm by Elizabeth (Gemma Arterton injecting much-needed youthful energy). But when tragedy strikes, it's the choir that calms Arthur's rage, allowing him to find both inner peace and a new lease of life. It's a surprisingly dyed-in-the-wool weepie from writer/director Paul Andrew Williams, who's better known for grittier fare like *London to Brighton*. **DA** Some swearing and sexual references.

DVD **SD**

Terence Stamp *Arthur* • Vanessa Redgrave *Marion* • Christopher Eccleston *James* • Gemma Arterton *Elizabeth* • Anne Reid *Brenda* • Ram John Holder *Charlie* ■ *Dir/Scr* Paul Andrew Williams

A Song Is Born ★★★ PG
Musical comedy 1948 · US · Colour · 119min

Howard Hawks here remakes his classic *Ball of Fire*, with Danny Kaye in the Gary Cooper role. Cooper played a gauche professor compiling a dictionary of slang; now the plot's updated to a study of jazz, and on hand are some of its greatest exponents, including Benny Goodman, Louis Armstrong, Charlie Barnet and Tommy Dorsey. In Hawks's canon this is a trifle, though it has interest as the director's first film in colour. **TS**

Danny Kaye *Professor Hobart Frisbee* • Virginia Mayo *Honey Swanson* • Benny Goodman *Professor Magenbruch* • Hugh Herbert *Professor Twingle* • Steve Cochran *Tony Crow* ■ *Dir* Howard Hawks • *Scr* Harry Tugend, from the story *From A to Z* by Thomas Monroe, Billy Wilder

Song o' My Heart ★★
Musical 1930 · US · BW · 85min

Designed as a vehicle for the film debut of the internationally popular Irish tenor, John McCormack, this blarney was directed by that skilful engineer of sentimentality, Frank Borzage. McCormack plays a singer whose great love (Alice Joyce) is forced to marry another. It allows McCormack to sing a clutch of songs, including *Rose of Tralee*. Ecstatically received in its day, it's all rather maudlin now, but McCormack fans are in for a treat. **RK**

John McCormack *Sean O'Carolan* • Maureen O'Sullivan *Eileen O'Brien* • John Garrick *Fergus O' Donnell* • JM Kerrigan *Peter Conlon* ■ *Dir* Frank Borzage • *Scr* Tom Barry

The Song of Bernadette
★★★★ U

Biographical drama 1943 · US · BW · 155min

This desperately sincere slice of now unfashionable Hollywood sermonising still contrives to move audiences, largely because of the amazing story of young Bernadette Soubirous, who, in 1858, saw a vision of the Virgin Mary in a grotto at Lourdes. Jennifer Jones won the best actress Oscar for her openly affecting Bernadette, the Virgin is portrayed by Linda Darnell and an unusually restrained Vincent Price is impeccable. Cynics won't be converted, but sceptics may find the movie posits a sincere argument. Another Oscar went to Arthur Miller's luminous photography. **TS** **DVD**

Jennifer Jones *Bernadette Soubirous* • William Eythe *Antoine* • Charles Bickford *Peyremale* • Vincent Price *Dutour* • Lee J Cobb *Dr Dozous* • Gladys Cooper *Sister Vauzous* • Anne Revere *Louise Soubirous* • Roman Bohnen *François Soubirous* • Linda Darnell *Blessed Virgin* ■ *Dir* Henry King • *Scr* George Seaton, from the novel by Franz Werfel

Song of Ceylon ★★★★★ U
Documentary 1934 · UK · BW · 39min

Although sponsored by the Ceylon Tea Propaganda Board, this extraordinarily beautiful film is far more concerned with the ancient customs and Buddhist heritage of what is now called Sri Lanka. Basil Wright divided his odyssey into four sections and used the 17th-century travelogue of Robert Knox to counterpoint his poetic and ethnographically invaluable images. Tea is only introduced in the third segment and is presented as a corrupting influence on an idyllic scene. Every bit as impressive as, but less celebrated than, *Night Mail* (which Wright co-directed with Harry Watt), this is one of the glories of the British documentary. **DP**

Lionel Wendt *Narrator* ■ *Dir* Basil Wright • *Scr* John Grierson, Basil Wright, from a travel book by Robert Knox • *Producer* John Grierson • *Cinematographer* Basil Wright

Song of Freedom ★★★★ U
Drama 1936 · UK · BW · 73min

Paul Robeson unearthed the legend of the singing king while shooting *Sanders of the River*. Even though he had just completed *Show Boat*, he considered this the first film to showcase his talent without demeaning his race. As the London stevedore who is discovered by an operatic impresario, only to cast off his fame to return to the island kingdom from which he was kidnapped years before, Robeson not only gets to sing several fine songs, but also explores such themes as interracial marriage, the evils of superstition and slavery, and the clash between tradition and progress. Dated, but still powerful. **DP** **DVD**

Paul Robeson *John Zinga* • Elisabeth Welch *Ruth Zinga* • Esme Percy *Gabriel Donezetti* • Robert Adams *Monty* • Ecce Homo Toto *Mandingo* ■ *Dir* J Elder Wills • *Scr* Fenn Sherie, Ingram D'Abbes, from a story by Claude Wallace, Dorothy Holloway

Song of Love ★★★ U
Musical biography 1947 · US · BW · 118min

Clara Wieck Schumann's story is not as awful as you might expect, thanks to Katharine Hepburn's portrayal. Hubby is an austere Paul Henreid and close mate Brahms is a beardless Robert Walker. Fictional tosh, certainly, but expertly produced with just the requisite amount of MGM gloss. Director Clarence Brown, who gave us *The Yearling* and stacks of Garbos, seems overawed by his subject, and his usual sureness of touch lapses into a slow pace. **TS**

Katharine Hepburn *Clara Wieck Schumann* • Paul Henreid *Robert Schumann* • Robert Walker *Johannes Brahms* • Henry Daniell *Franz Liszt* • Leo G Carroll *Prof Wieck* ■ *Dir* Clarence Brown • *Scr* Ivan Tors, Irmgard Von Cube, Allen Vincent, Robert Ardrey, from the play by Bernard Schubert, Mario Silva

Song of Norway ★ U
Musical biography 1970 · US · Colour · 138min

Let's be honest: this horrendously overlong biopic of composer Edvard Grieg has precious little going for it, except for the magnificent Scandinavian locations. Otherwise, one-time talented director Andrew L Stone has assembled a motley cast to surround the woefully ill-equipped Toralv Maurstad (who?) in this supremely uninteresting saga. **TS**

Toralv Maurstad *Edvard Grieg* • Florence Henderson *Nina Grieg* • Christina Schollin *Therese Berg* • Frank Porretta *Rikard Nordraak* • Harry Secombe *Bjornsterne Bjornson* • Robert Morley *Berg* • Edward G Robinson *Krogstad* • Elizabeth Larner *Mrs Bjornson* • Oscar Homolka *Engstrand* ■ *Dir* Andrew L Stone • *Scr* Andrew L Stone, from the musical by Milton Lazarus, Robert Wright and George Forrest, from a play by Homer Curran

Song of Scheherazade
★★★ PG

Musical biography 1947 · US · Colour · 101min

Supposedly a biopic of Rimsky-Korsakov, this is one of the campest of all Universal's gaudy costume pictures. Jean-Pierre Aumont plays the young Russian composer, who meets and falls for sultry dancer Yvonne De Carlo on his way back to Russia. They fall in love, she inspires him to write *Scherherazade* and dances at the premiere in St Petersburg. Eve Arden, only ten years De Carlo's senior, plays her wisecracking mother in this enjoyable nonsense. **RB**

DVD

Yvonne De Carlo *Cara de Talavera/Scheherazade* • Brian Donlevy *Captain Vladimir Gregovich* • Jean-Pierre Aumont *Nikolai Rimsky-Korsakov* • Eve Arden *Mme Conchita de Talavera* • Philip Reed *Prince Mischetsky* ■ *Dir/Scr* Walter Reisch • *Music Director* Miklos Rozsa

The Song of Songs ★★ U
Comedy drama 1933 · US · BW · 86min

After disappointing box-office returns for *Blonde Venus*, Paramount engineered a trial separation between Marlene Dietrich and director Josef von Sternberg. Rouben Mamoulian was entrusted with the task of making something of this tale about a German peasant girl who falls in love with a sculptor and becomes his model, but marries a baron, turns café singer, and has several lovers. The stylish and intelligent Mamoulian did what he could, but this tired old material obstinately refused to come to life. **RK** **DVD**

Marlene Dietrich *Lily Czepanek* • Brian Aherne *Richard Waldow* • Lionel Atwill *Baron von Merzbach* • Alison Skipworth *Mrs Rasmussen* ■ *Dir* Rouben Mamoulian • *Scr* Leo Birinski, Samuel Hoffenstein, the play by Edward Brewster Sheldon, from the novel *Das Hohe Lied* by Hermann Sudermann, and

Song of the Islands ★★★ U
Romantic musical 1942 · US · Colour · 75min

This entertaining 20th Century-Fox Technicolor romp stars pin-up Betty Grable as a Hawaiian "hula" girl in a sunny musical. Hunk Victor Mature claims her, despite interference from a pair of feudin' fathers. There's some robust comic playing from reliable Jack Oakie, who's involved in some super by-play with Hilo Hattie. Unsurprisingly, this movie was a massive wartime hit, and is still mightily pleasing today. **TS**

Betty Grable *Eileen O'Brien* • Victor Mature *Jefferson Harper* • Jack Oakie *Rusty Smith* • Thomas Mitchell *Dennis O'Brien* • George Barbier *Harper* • Billy Gilbert *Palola's father* • Hilo Hattie *Palola* ■ *Dir* Walter Lang • *Scr* Joseph Schrank, Robert Pirosh, Robert Ellis, Helen Logan

Song of the Open Road
★★ U

Musical comedy 1944 · US · BW · 93min

The only notable thing about this "let's-put-on-a-show" musical, was the screen debut of 15-year-old radio singing star Jane Powell. Virtually a showcase for her vocal talent, it soon led to an MGM contract and blonde star. Powell plays a juvenile movie star, who runs away from home to work on a youth farm where everyone seems to have a musical gift. **RB**

Edgar Bergen • Jane Powell • WC Fields • Bonita Granville *Bonnie* • Peggy O'Neill *Peggy* • Jackie Moran *Jack* • Bill Christy *Bill* ■ *Dir* S Sylvan Simon • *Scr* Albert Mannheimer, from a story by Irving Phillips, Edward Verdier

Song of the Road ★★★ U
Drama 1937 · UK · BW · 73min

John Baxter was one of the most original British film-makers. In addition to some rather clumsy (but surprisingly commercial) regional comedies, he also made a string of socially aware dramas in which the heroes were either everyday workers or outsiders unwilling to march in step with progress. A sobering, if sentimental view of Britain emerging from the Depression, this old-fashioned, but compelling picture follows Bransby Williams and his horse Polly as they tour the country looking for work. Keep an eye out for that barnstormer Tod Slaughter in a cameo as a travelling showman. **DP**

Bransby Williams *Old Bill* • Ernest Butcher *Foreman* • Muriel George *Mrs Trelawney* • Davy Burnaby *Mr Keppel* • Tod Slaughter *Showman* • John Turnbull *Bristow* • Edgar Driver *Titch* ■ *Dir* John Baxter • *Scr* John Baxter, from a story by Michael Kent

Song of the Sea ★★★★ PG
Animated fantasy 2014 · Ire/Den/Bel/Lux/Fr · Colour · 89min

This animated fairy tale casts an intoxicating spell. Steeped in Irish myth, it tells the enchanting story of a young boy (voiced by David Rawle), who lives on a tiny island off the coast of Ireland. During the first couple of scenes, we discover that Rawle resents his little sister(Lucy O'Connell), since her birth coincided with the sudden disappearance of their mother. After O'Connell falls ill, however, Rawle accompanies her on a fantastical journey involving an owl-witch and a trio of fairies. All of this plays out as a child-friendly adventure, but at the same time it also functions as a moving – and occasionally heartbreaking – exploration of grief and loss. **SC** In English, Irish, Scottish Gaelic.

DVD **BL**

David Rawle *Ben* • Brendan Gleeson *Conor/Mac Lir* • Fionnula Flanagan *Granny/Macha* • Lisa Hannigan *Bronach* • Lucy O'Connell *Saoirse* ■ *Dir* Tomm Moore • *Scr* William Collins

Song of the South ★★★ U
Part-animated fantasy 1946 · US · Colour · 90min

This wonderful Disney fantasy was a technical tour de force in its day, blending live action and animation with wit and brilliance, most notably in the now-classic *Zip-a-Dee Doo-Dah* sequence in which James Baskett's Oscar-winning Uncle Remus meets the woodland folk of his tales. Seen now, alas, such quaint simplicity looks patronising, and makes many contemporary viewers squirm. It's best to remember the film's period and attitudes, and thereby enjoy to the full the sheer innocence of the movie. The three animated adventures of Brer Rabbit, Brer Fox and Brer Bear will captivate adults as well as children. **TS**

Bobby Driscoll *Johnny* • James Baskett *Uncle Remus/Brer Fox* • Ruth Warrick *Sally* • Luana Patten *Ginny* • Lucile Watson *Grandmother* • Hattie McDaniel *Aunt Tempy* ■ *Dir* Wilfred Jackson, Harve Foster • *Scr* Dalton Raymond, Morton Grant, Maurice Rapf, from a story by Dalton Raymond, William Peet, Ralph Wright, George Stallings, from the story collection *Tales of Uncle Remus* by Joel Chandler Harris

Song of the Thin Man
★★★ U

Detective comedy 1947 · US · BW · 82min

The sixth and last of the popular *Thin Man* series that started in 1934, this is closer to *film noir* than the earlier films, with the sleuthing couple visiting several jazz clubs in their search for a killer. The sophisticated banter and the blend of screwball comedy and murder mystery survive, however, and the rapport between stars William Powell and Myrna Loy is still palpable (though actor Leon Ames claimed later that they never spoke to each other during the shooting). A satisfying finish to an enjoyable series. **TV** **DVD**

William Powell *Nick Charles* • Myrna Loy *Nora Charles* • Keenan Wynn *Clarence "Clinker" Krause* • Dean Stockwell *Nick Charles Jr* • Philip Reed *Tommy Edlon Drake* • Patricia Morison *Phyllis Talbin* • Leon Ames *Mitchell Talbin* ■ *Dir* Edward Buzzell • *Scr* Steve Fisher, Nat Perrin, from a story by Stanley Roberts, from characters by Dashiell Hammett

The Song Remains the Same
★★★ 15

Concert documentary 1976 · UK · Colour · 136min

The thunderous rock riffs of Led Zeppelin were a favourite among 1970s acid-droppers and it looks as if the makers of this odd documentary had more than their fair share. Footage of a 1973 New York concert (with the highlight being jukebox giant *Stairway to Heaven*) are interspersed with behind-the-scenes mishaps, trippy effects and ultra-weird fantasy sequences from the heads of Robert Plant, Jimmy Page *et al*, which makes *Tommy* look like social realism. The dated sound quality might bother those with a re-mastered Led Zep CD collection. JC **DVD** **Blu**

John Bonham · John Paul Jones · Jimmy Page · Robert Plant · Peter Grant ■ *Dir* Peter Clifton, Joe Massot

A Song to Remember
★★★ **U**

Biographical drama 1945 · US · Colour · 107min

Hollywood biographies of classical composers are usually fair game for jest, and this account of Chopin's life is no exception. It features some flowery dialogue, a wildly over-the-top performance by Paul Muni as the composer's tutor and Merle Oberon miscast as the trousered George Sand who tells her lover to "Discontinue that so-called *Polonaise* jumble you've been playing for days." But the melodies, gorgeous Technicolor photography, opulent production and the seductive piano playing of José Iturbi (who dubbed for Cornel Wilde in the title role) add up to a lush, irresistible experience. TV

Cornel Wilde *Chopin* · Paul Muni *Joseph Elsner* · Merle Oberon *George Sand* · Stephen Bekassy *Franz Liszt* · Nina Foch *Constantia* · George Coulouris *Louis Pleyel* · George Macready *Alfred de Musset* ■ *Dir* Charles Vidor · *Scr* Sidney Buchman, from a story by Ernst Marischka · *Cinematographers* Tony Gaudio, Allen M Davey

Song without End
★★★ **U**

Musical biography 1960 · US · Colour · 142min

Dirk Bogarde made his Hollywood debut playing Franz Liszt in this ultra-glamorous Columbia biopic, turning down the role of Gaston Lachaille in MGM's *Gigi* in the process. Bogarde swiftly returned to European film-making, and no wonder, for excellent though he is, this is preposterous tosh, redeemed only by Jorge Bolet's off-screen piano and the panache of cameraman James Wong Howe. Alas, the soul went out of the project when the original director, Charles Vidor, died and George Cukor took over. TS

Dirk Bogarde *Franz Liszt* · Capucine *Princess Carolyne* · Geneviève Page *Countess Marie* · Patricia Morison *George Sand* · Ivan Desny *Prince Nicholas* · Martita Hunt *Grand Duchess* ■ *Dir* Charles Vidor, George Cukor · *Scr* Oscar Millard

Songcatcher
★★

Period drama 1999 · US · Colour · 109min

Maggie Greenwald's tendency to melodrama allows stock characters to assume control of the intriguing early 20th-century scenario. Driven from academe by chauvinism, musicologist Janet McTeer's plan to record for posterity the ballads she hears in the remote mountain town where her sister teaches are jeopardised by the incursion of a ruthless mining company. Her relationship with frontiersman Aidan Quinn is more than a novelettish romance, but the story's real interest lies elsewhere. DP

Janet McTeer *Dr Lily Penlenic* · Aidan Quinn *Tom Bledsoe* · Pat Carroll *Viney Butler* · Jane Adams (2) *Elna Penlenic* · Greg Russell Cook *Fate Honeycutt* ■ *Dir/Scr* Maggie Greenwald

Songs from the Second Floor
★★★★ **15**

Drama 2000 · Swe/Den/Nor · Colour · 94min

Emerging from a 25-year exile, Roy Andersson has produced a virtuoso film that will infuriate as many people as it intrigues. Littered with eccentrics, it's a colliding series of vignettes that effectively convey the chaos and coldness of modern life. At its centre is Lars Nordh, whose midlife crisis coincides with millennial angst to create a character teetering on the brink of a cockeyed world. Completely improvised, and shot with a disquietingly static insistence, this astounding study of urban alienation eventually limps home. Yet it more than justifies Andersson's reputation as cinema's "unknown genius". DP Swedish +subtitles. **DVD**

Lars Nordh *Kalle* · Stefan Larsson *Stefan, Kalle's son* · Bengt CW Carlsson *Lennart* · Torbjörn Fahlström *Pelle Wigert, the manager* · Sten Andersson *Lasse* ■ *Dir/Scr* Roy Andersson

Songs in Ordinary Time
★★★

Period drama 2000 · US · Colour · 120min

In this shrewd TV adaptation of Mary McGarry Morris's bestseller, director Rod Holcomb nails the atmosphere of small-town America at the crossroads between the 1950s and 60s. There's something to hide behind the curtains of every home in Atkinson, Vermont, and this takes the melodramatic curse off divorcee Sissy Spacek's self-evidently dangerous liaison with the mysterious Beau Bridges. If there is a problem it's that there's too much going on to let the storylines gel. DP

Sissy Spacek *Marie Fermoyle* · Beau Bridges *Omar Duvall* · Tom Guiry *Norm Fermoyle* · Jordan Warkol *Ben Fermoyle* · Careena Melia *Alice Fermoyle* ■ *Dir* Rod Holcomb · *Scr* Malcolm MacRury, from the novel by Mary McGarry Morris

Songwriter
★★★ **15**

Musical comedy drama 1984 · US · Colour · 90min

This is sheer heaven for country music fans, with Willie Nelson and Kris Kristofferson as former singer-songwriter partners, who reunite to take on unscrupulous elements of the country music biz. The usual cocktail of drugs, booze and sleazy business professionals is enlivened by the requisite musical number. An amiable and entertaining work from Robert Altman protégé Alan Rudolph. DA

Willie Nelson *Doc Jenkins* · Kris Kristofferson *Blackie Buck* · Melinda Dillon *Honey Carder* · Rip Torn *Dino McLeish* · Lesley Ann Warren *Gilda* ■ *Dir* Alan Rudolph · *Scr* Bud Shrake

Sonny
★★ **18**

Drama 2002 · US · Colour · 106min

Nicolas Cage's New Orleans-set melodrama isn't a bad directorial debut, it's just a stale one, competently constructed but clichéd. James Franco is a handsome former gigolo who returns from the army in 1981 hoping to go straight, much to his trashy madam mother Brenda Blethyn's dismay. Though his performance is sympathetic, Blethyn wildly overacts, while Cage's cameo as a gay pimp is probably his career worst. SF Swearing, violence, sex scenes. **DVD**

James Franco *Sonny* · Brenda Blethyn *Jewel* · Mena Suvari *Carol* · Harry Dean Stanton *Henry* · Brenda Vaccaro *Meg* · Scott Caan *Jesse* · Seymour Cassel *Albert* · Nicolas Cage *Acid Yellow* ■ *Dir* Nicolas Cage · *Scr* John Carlen

Sons
★★★

Comedy drama 1989 · US · Colour · 85min

This is a modest but intriguing comedy drama about an attempt by three men to take their elderly father back to France to see the woman he fell in love with during the Second World War. While not saying anything particularly new, it benefits from the neat performances by the leads, and look out for appearances from American director Samuel Fuller, French actress Stéphane Audran and *Flashdance's* Jennifer Beals as a transvestite. JF Swearing.

William Forsythe *Mike* · DB Sweeney *Rich* · Robert Miranda *Fred* · Samuel Fuller *Father* · Stéphane Audran *Florence* · William Hickey *Roger* · Jennifer Beals *Transvestite* ■ *Dir* Alexandre Rockwell · *Scr* Alexandre Rockwell, Brandon Cole

Sons and Lovers
★★★ **PG**

Period drama 1960 · UK · BW · 98min

The great cameraman Jack Cardiff made a directorial outing with this forthright adaptation of DH Lawrence's semi-autobiographical novel, about a boy caught between the Nottinghamshire rock and the hard place of his possessive mother (Wendy Hiller) and miner father (Trevor Howard). The trouble is that Dean Stockwell, as the teenager, is unconvincing in such great acting company. Ironically, the film won an Oscar for Freddie Francis's cinematography, while Cardiff was nominated as director. TH **DVD**

Trevor Howard *Walter Morel* · Dean Stockwell *Paul Morel* · Wendy Hiller *Mrs Morel* · Mary Ure *Clara Dawes* · Heather Sears *Miriam Lievers* · William Lucas *William* · Conrad Phillips *Baxter Dawes* · Donald Pleasence *Pappleworth* · Ernest Thesiger *Henry Hadlock* ■ *Dir* Jack Cardiff · *Scr* Gavin Lambert, TEB Clarke, from the novel by DH Lawrence

The Sons of Katie Elder
★★★★ **U**

Western 1965 · US · Colour · 117min

This terrific western contains a wonderful score from Elmer Bernstein, and has brothers John Wayne and Dean Martin riding out to avenge the death of their father. It's stirring stuff, beautifully photographed, with a fine support cast headed by Martha Hyer, who dignifies the movie by making a heartfelt speech about matriarchal virtue, addressed to the late Katie Elder's empty chair. TS **DVD**

John Wayne *John Elder* · Dean Martin *Tom Elder* · Michael Anderson Jr *Bud Elder* · Earl Holliman *Matt Elder* · Martha Hyer *Mary Gordon* · George Kennedy *Curley* · Dennis Hopper *Dave Hastings* ■ *Dir* Henry Hathaway · *Scr* Allan Weiss, William H Wright, Harry Essex, from a story by Talbot Jennings · *Cinematographer* Lucien Ballard

Sons of the Desert
★★★★★ **U**

Comedy 1933 · US · BW · 64min

This is probably the finest, and fastest, Laurel and Hardy feature film, in which Stan and Ollie "fool" their intimidating wives (Mae Busch and Dorothy Christy) with a story of a recuperative ocean cruise so they can attend the Chicago convention of their fraternity lodge. The ridiculous men-only antics of the lodge are wonderfully exploited, especially by a bumptious Charley Chase. The international society devoted to Stan and Ollie bears the name of this comedy gem – an indication of how highly it is thought of. TH **DVD**

Stan Laurel *Stan* · Oliver Hardy *Ollie* · Charley Chase · Mae Busch *Mrs Lottie Chase Hardy* · Dorothy Christy *Mrs Betty Laurel* ■ *Dir* William A Seiter · *Scr* Frank Craven, Byron Morgan

Sons of the Musketeers
★★★ **U**

Swashbuckling adventure 1951 · US · Colour · 81min

This gloriously Technicolored hokum imagines that the offspring of the Musketeers are just as nifty with swords as their fathers. One of them is female (Athos's daughter, in fact), and played by Maureen O'Hara, who tosses her red tresses to the wind and buckles a swash as if to the manner born. Co-star Cornel Wilde, a former member of the US Olympic fencing team, is no match for our Maureen in what is splendid fun. TS

Maureen O'Hara *Claire* · Cornel Wilde *D'Artagan* · Robert Douglas *Lavalle* · Gladys Cooper *Queen Anne* · Dan O'Herlihy *Aramis* · Alan Hale Jr *Porthos* · June Clayworth *Claudine* · Blanche Yurka *Madame Michom* · Nancy Gates *Princess Henriette* ■ *Dir* Lewis Allen · *Scr* Walter Ferris, Joseph Hoffman, from a story by Aubrey Wisberg, Jack Pollexfen

Sons of the Sea
★★★ **U**

Wartime drama 1939 · UK · Colour · 108min

This routine spy drama is an early wartime flag-waver that provides a fascinating insight into the nation's mindset at the start of the Second World War. It follows navy commander Leslie Banks as he rallies to the cause when his son (Simon Lack) is accused of collaborating with the enemy from his naval training college. The actual drama is not really up to the propaganda value, but the movie looks great because it was filmed in the pioneering Dufaycolour process. DP

Leslie Banks *Captain Hyde* · Mackenzie Ward *Newton Hulls* · Kay Walsh *Alison Devar* · Simon Lack *Philip Hyde* · Cecil Parker *Commander Herbert* · Ellen Pollock *Margaret Hulls* · Peter Shaw (1) *Lt John Strepte* · Nigel Stock *Rudd* · Charles Eaton *Commander-in-chief* · Kynaston Reeves *Professor Devar* ■ *Dir* Maurice Elvey · *Scr* D William Woolf, Gerald Eliott, Maurice Elvey, from a story by D William Woolf, George Barraud

The Son's Room
★★★★★ **15**

Drama 2001 · It/Fr · Colour · 95min

Rarely has the raw subject of bereavement been so brilliantly portrayed than here in director Nanni Moretti's heart-wrenching account of how a provincial, middle-class family cope with the death of a child. The deserved winner of the 2001 Palme d'Or at Cannes, Moretti's pitch-perfect tragedy is almost unbearably moving and rings undeniably true. On a day he's supposed to spend with his son Giuseppe Sanfelice, psychoanalyst Moretti is called out on a patient emergency; Sanfelice goes scuba diving with friends instead and is accidentally killed. In the aftermath, Moretti introspectively obsesses over his actions on the fateful day, while his wife and daughter also begin to crack under the pressure of their inconsolable anguish. A near faultless masterpiece. AJ Italian +subtitles. **DVD**

Nanni Moretti *Giovanni* · Laura Morante *Paola* · Jasmine Trinca *Irene* · Giuseppe Sanfelice *Andrea* · Silvio Orlando *Oscar* · Claudia Della Seta *Raffaella* ■ *Dir* Nanni Moretti · *Scr* Linda Ferri, Nanni Moretti, Heidrun Schleef

Sophie Scholl: the Final Days
★★★★ **PG**

Second World War biographical drama 2005 · Ger/Fr · Colour · 115min

The activities of Sophie Scholl and the White Rose resistance movement have been dramatised twice before, but Marc Rothemund's starkly authentic drama has the advantage of being based on the Gestapo records of Scholl's interrogation, after she was caught distributing anti-Nazi leaflets around Munich in 1943. Julia Jentsch is sympathetically stoic in the title role, although her courage and conviction are powerfully matched by the disgust, disappointment and grudging respect exhibited by Gestapo interrogator Alexander Held during their intense confrontations. Fabian Hinrichs, as Jentsch's co-conspirator brother, and Johanna Gastdor, as her Communist cellmate, also impress. DP German +subtitles. **DVD** **Blu**

Julia Jentsch *Sophie Scholl* · Alexander Held *Robert Mohr* · Fabian Hinrichs *Hans Scholl* · Johanna Gastdorf *Else* ■ *Dir* Marc Rothemund · *Scr* Fred Breinersdorfer

Sophie's Choice
★★★★ **15**

Period drama 1982 · US · Colour · 144min

Meryl Streep confirmed her status as the Queen of Accents with her Oscar-winning performance in this moving adaptation of William Styron's bestselling novel. Yet, for all the significance of the revelations about Sophie's past, it is the interaction between the three central characters that gives the story its strength – in fact, it's quite bewildering that, in spite of the quality of Kevin Kline's temperamental zest and Peter MacNicol's adoring timidity, neither merited even a nomination. Alan J Pakula's direction is much less constricted than his overly reverential script, thanks to the beautiful and evocative photography by Nestor Almendros. DP **DVD** **Blu**

Meryl Streep *Sophie Zawistowska* · Kevin Kline *Nathan Landau* · Peter MacNicol *Stingo* · Rita Karin *Yetta Zimmerman* · Stephen D Newman *Larry Landau* · Greta Turken *Leslie Lapidus* · Josh Mostel *Morris Fink* · Marcel Rosenblatt *Astrid Weinstein* · Moishe Rosenfeld *Moishe Rosenblaum* ■ *Dir* Alan J Pakula · *Scr* Alan J Pakula, from the novel by William Styron

The Sorcerers
★★★ **15**

Science-fiction horror 1967 · UK · Colour · 81min

Prior to *Witchfinder General* and his death at the age of 24, Michael Reeves directed this intelligent shocker. Boris Karloff invents a mesmeric machine to control the mind of bored, swinging Londoner Ian Ogilvy, which can absorb and pass on the sensations he experiences. Karloff's wife gets hooked on the voyeuristic thrills, and wills the mod zombie to steal and kill. Cult brilliance on a small budget. AJ **DVD** **Blu**

Boris Karloff *Professor Monserrat* • Catherine Lacey *Estelle Monserrat* • Ian Ogilvy *Mike* • Elizabeth Ercy *Nicole* • Victor Henry *Alan* • Susan George *Audrey* ■ *Dir* Michael Reeves • *Scr* Michael Reeves, Tom Baker, from an idea by John Burke

The Sorcerer's Apprentice
★★★ **PG**

Action fantasy 2010 • US • Colour • 104min

Disney's attempt at *Harry Potter*-style magic is a barrage of spectacular special effects in search of an appealing story. Jay Baruchel exudes nerdy charm as a physics student told by immortal sorcerer Nicolas Cage that he's Merlin's descendant and must fight an army of the dead. Cue awkward spell-training sessions before the battle royale with evil Alfred Molina. *National Treasure* director Jon Turteltaub ensures the eye-candy action is never boring, yet it's never more than competent, either, failing to engage any sense of wonder. AJ *DVD* **BL**

Nicolas Cage *Balthazar Blake* • Jay Baruchel *Dave Stutler* • Alfred Molina *Maxim Horvath* • Teresa Palmer *Becky Barnes* • Monica Bellucci *Veronica* ■ *Dir* Jon Turteltaub • *Scr* Doug Miro, Carlo Bernard, Matt Lopez, from a story by Lopez, Lawrence Konner, Mark Rosenthal, from the poem *Der Zauberlehrling* by Johann Wolfgang von Goethe

Sorority Boys
★★ **15**

Comedy 2002 • US • Colour • 89min

Sexist frat boys learn valuable lessons about women in this watered-down college comedy that follows a macho trio masquerading as female students after being kicked out of their fraternity house. Though the film is often amusing with some laugh-out-loud sequences, it's too self-conscious to make a lasting impression. Corny innuendo and repetitive sight gags quickly go stale, while some of the subject matter is just bad taste. SF Swearing, nudity, drug abuse. *DVD* **CS**

Barry Watson *Dave/Daisy* • Michael Rosenbaum *Adam/Adina* • Harland Williams *Doofer/Roberta* • Melissa Sagemiller *Leah* • Tony Denman *Jimmy* • Brad Beyer *Spence* • Kathryn Stockwood *Patty* • Heather Matarazzo *Katie* ■ *Dir* Wallace Wolodarsky • *Scr* Joe Jarvis, Greg Coolidge

Sorority Row
★★ **15**

Horror thriller 2009 • US • Colour • 96min

Eight months after a sorority prank goes wrong, the remaining girls are celebrating graduation when a hooded killer starts picking them off, in a slapdash slasher update of 1983's *The House on Sorority Row* (renamed *House of Evil* in the UK) that fails to avoid the pitfalls plaguing other maniac-on-the-loose knock-offs. Carrie Fisher gives the dullness a lift as a gun-toting, no-nonsense den mother, but Rumer Willis (daughter of Bruce Willis and Demi Moore) barely convinces as one of the ill-fated girls of Theta Pi. AJ Violence, swearing, drug abuse, brief nudity. *DVD* **BL**

Briana Evigan *Cassidy* • Leah Pipes *Jessica* • Rumer Willis *Ellie* • Jamie Chung *Claire* • Margo Harshman *Chugs* • Audrina Partridge *Megan* • Caroline D'Amore *Maggie* • Carrie Fisher *Mrs Crenshaw* ■ *Dir* Stewart Hendler • *Scr* Josh Stolberg, Peter Goldfinger, from the 1983 film *House of Evil*

Sorority Wars
★★

Comedy drama 2009 • US • Colour • 89min

In this flimsy TV movie, student Lucy Hale causes family ructions by snubbing the sorority that her mother co-founded. Cue an increasingly silly examination of female and campus relationships, as her principled decision costs her best friend Phoebe Strole, alienates mum Courtney Thorne-Smith and her equally shallow alumni, and then kicks off a battle between the rival Delta and Kappa groups. The overall result is a clumsy mix of *Mean Girls*-style maliciousness and message-filled sentimentality. SF

Lucy Hale *Katie Parker* • Courtney Thorne-Smith *Lutie* • Amanda Schull *Gwen* • Phoebe Strole *Sara* • Kristen Hager *Heather* ■ *Dir* James Hayman • *Scr* Michelle Lovretta [MA Lovretta]

The Sorrow and the Pity
★★★★★

Political documentary 1969 • Fr/Swi/W Ger • BW • 248min

Divided into two parts – *The Collapse* and *The Choice* – Marcel Ophüls's monumental documentary is not just an investigation into what occurred in France during the Nazi Occupation, but how the nation has elected to remember it. Probing the selective memory of his occasionally evasive witnesses (who range from heroes and survivors to traitors and oppressors), he uncovers contradictions among the half-truths, as well as provoking outbursts of bitter fury and expressions of genuine remorse. Topics such as collaboration and co-operation, resistance and indifference are painfully explored. The archive material may be manipulative, but it retains the power to chill and cast doubt. DP French, German, English +subtitles. *DVD*

■ *Dir* Marcel Ophüls • *Scr* Marcel Ophüls, André Harris

Sorrowful Jones
★★★ **U**

Comedy 1949 • US • BW • 84min

Damon Runyon's warm-hearted story, *Little Miss Marker* – about a tightwad Broadway bookie forced to look after a gambler's child – had been a huge success as a film with Shirley Temple. Paramount then ingeniously adapted it into a Bob Hope vehicle, taking attention away from the moppet played competently by Mary Jane Saunders. Although well supplied with characteristic quips, a restrained Hope brings out the sentimentality inherent in the story. The film proved such a hit, that director and star teamed up for another Runyon adaptation, *The Lemon Drop Kid*. AE *DVD*

Bob Hope *Sorrowful Jones* • Lucille Ball *Gladys O'Neill* • William Demarest *Regret* • Bruce Cabot *Big Steve Holloway* • Thomas Gomez *Reardon* • Mary Jane Saunders *Martha Jane Smith* ■ *Dir* Sidney Lanfield • *Scr* Melville Shavelson, Edmund Hartmann [Edmund L Hartmann], Jack Rose, from the film *Little Miss Marker* by Gladys Lehman, William R Lipman, Sam Hellman, from the story by Damon Runyon

Sorry, Wrong Number
★★★★

Thriller 1948 • US • BW • 89min

This taut drama centres on a bedridden heiress who, left alone in her apartment, tries to call her husband and overhears her own murder being planned. Writer Lucille Fletcher opened out her original radio play screenplay just enough to allow beefy Burt Lancaster to share a crumb of the honours with Barbara Stanwyck, and heightened the claustrophobia of the victim's bedroom by contrasting it with a murky outside world. Anatole Litvak directed this classic *film noir*, which earned Stanwyck an Oscar-nomination for her performance. Remade in 1989 as a TV movie, improbably starring Loni Anderson in the Stanwyck role. RK

Barbara Stanwyck *Leona Stevenson* • Burt Lancaster *Henry Stevenson* • Ann Richards *Sally Lord Dodge* • Wendell Corey *Dr Alexander* • Ed Begley *James Cotterell* • Leif Erickson *Fred Lord* • William Conrad *Morano* ■ *Dir* Anatole Litvak • *Scr* Lucille Fletcher, from her radio play

Sorted
★★ **18**

Crime drama 2000 • UK • Colour • 98min

This is an energetic but utterly predictable crime drama from first-time director Alex Jovy, who was Oscar-nominated for his 1998 short film, *Holiday Romance*. Arriving from Scunthorpe to collect his dead brother's belongings, Matthew Rhys is sucked into the London club scene and its sleazy hinterland. Resisting the designer violence that has accompanied recent British gangster flicks, Jovy directs with pace and visual flourish, but his grasp of character is less assured. DP Swearing, drug abuse. *DVD*

Tim Vincent *Justin* • Mary Tamm *School mother* • Matthew Rhys *Carl* • Sienna Guillory *Sunny* • Fay Masterson *Tiffany* • Jason Donovan *Martin* • Tim Curry *Damian Kemp* • Alex Jovy *Club DJ* ■

Dir Alex Jovy • *Scr* Nick Villiers, from a story by Alexander Jovy, from a screenplay (unproduced) by Christian Spurrier, Malcolm Campbell

Le Souffle
★★★ **15**

Drama 2001 • Fr • Colour • 74min

Shot in a monochrome that's variously forbidding and fantastical, the events triggered by the drunken feast attended by 15-year-old Pierre-Louis Bonnetblanc ultimately lapse into melodrama in Damien Odoul's uncompromising rites-of-passage drama. The irregular fantasy sequences feel intrusive, even though their fairy-tale undertones are reinforced by the grandeur of girlfriend Laure Magadoux's house. DP French +subtitles. *DVD*

Pierre-Louis Bonnetblanc *David* • Dominique Chevallier *Jacques* • Maxime Dalbrut *Paul* • Jean-Claude Lecante *John* • Laure Magadoux *Aurore* • Stéphane Terpereau *Stef* ■ *Dir/Scr* Damien Odoul

Le Souffle au Coeur
★★★★ **18**

Drama 1971 • Fr/It/W Ger • Colour • 113min

On hearing the word incest, moral guardians almost fell over themselves in the rush to condemn this film. Even the critics got caught up in the fuss, and devoted more column space to a brief, tender scene at the end of the film than they did to the fond, very funny portrait of the French middle-classes in the mid-1950s. This classic rite-of-passage stuff from Louis Malle, with non-actor Benoît Ferreux giving a wonderfully natural performance as the Dijon teenager curious about everything from sex to art forgery. Lea Massari is equally outstanding as his flirtatious mother. DP French +subtitles. Sex scenes, nudity. *DVD*

Lea Massari *Clara Chevalier* • Benoît Ferreux *Laurent Chevalier* • Daniel Gélin *Father* • Marc Winocourt *Marc* • Fabien Ferreux *Thomas* • Michel Lonsdale *Father Henri* • Ave Ninchi *Augusta* ■ *Dir/Scr* Louis Malle

Soul Boys of the Western World
★★★ **12A**

Music documentary 2014 • UK • Colour • 110min

Only deep-seated musical snobbery would hinder enjoyment of this definitive, authorised, fastidious, and perhaps overlong telling of the Spandau Ballet story, which restores credibility to the "blue-eyed soul" quintet who were unjustly dismissed as opportunistic clotheshorses. George Hencken's stringently archive-built approach boasts the rollercoaster momentum of many classic rock and pop biopics, but it's illuminated with valuable home-movie footage, while commentary by the unseen band members lends first-person authenticity. AC *DVD* **BL**

Tony Hadley • Martin Kemp • Gary Kemp • John Keeble • Steve Norman ■ *Dir* George Hencken

Soul Food
★★★★ **15**

Drama 1997 • US • Colour • 110min

This well-acted and well-made drama focuses, as the title suggests, on the Sunday dinner get-togethers of a large African-American family. Matriarch Irma P Hall's home cooking just about keeps her three grown-up daughters and their partners from each other's throats, until a tragedy forces them to reconcile their differences. This is a terrific ensemble piece, boosted by the unfussy script and direction of George Tillman Jr. JB Swearing, sex scenes. *DVD*

Vanessa L Williams *Teri* • Vivica A Fox *Maxine* • Nia Long *Bird* • Michael Beach *Miles* • Mekhi Phifer *Lem* • Brandon Hammond *Ahmad* • Jeffrey D Sams *Kenny* ■ *Dir/Scr* George Tillman Jr

Soul in the Hole
★★★★ **15**

Sports documentary 1995 • US • Colour • 98min

Never has the human drama and the simple beauty of the game of basketball been combined with such pace, passion and personality as in Danielle Gardner's documentary. Following the fortunes of "Bed-Stuy" team Kenny's Kings, and

particularly its wayward star Ed "Booger" Smith, it may not break stylistic ground with its blend of talking heads and big game highlights. However, with its concentration on character and locale, this clipped, comic film takes a grip, but its real strength is that it never loses sight of life. DP *DVD*

■ *Dir* Danielle Gardner

Soul Man
★★ **12**

Comedy 1986 • US • Colour • 100min

This charade was supposed to be a daring and right-on attempt to explore the prejudices on both sides of the American racial divide, from the perspective of a middle-class white boy who is being penalised for not being black! Even though the social comment is totally subservient to the endless round of cheap-shot gags, the critics were inexplicably charitable to the film on its release, pointing to the sly satire and the courageous performance of C Thomas Howell as the kid who gulps down suntan pills in order to win a law school scholarship. Insidious and offensive. DP *DVD*

C Thomas Howell *Mark Watson* • Arye Gross *Gordon Bloomfield* • Rae Dawn Chong *Sarah Walker* • James Earl Jones *Professor Rutherford Banks* • Melora Hardin *Whitney Dunbar* • Leslie Nielsen *Mr Dunbar* • James B Sikking *Bill Watson* ■ *Dir* Steve Miner • *Scr* Carol Black

Soul Men
★★★ **15**

Road movie comedy 2008 • US • Colour • 95min

Samuel L Jackson and Bernie Mac (who, like a cameoing Isaac Hayes, died shortly after filming) prove a dream team in director Malcolm D Lee's formulaic musical comedy. Keeping the slight and predictable story afloat, the duo shares terrific chemistry as the feuding ex-soul performers who reluctantly reunite for a tribute show following the demise of their one-time lead singer. Both stars are having a ball and their energy is infectious, even if some of the slapstick is decidedly ordinary. SF Swearing, sexual references. *DVD* **BL**

Samuel L Jackson *Louis Hinds* • Bernie Mac *Floyd Henderson* • Sharon Leal *Cleo* • Sean Hayes *Danny Epstein* • Isaac Hayes ■ *Dir* Malcolm D Lee • *Scr* Robert Ramsey, Matthew Stone

The Soul of Flies
★★★ **15**

Road movie comedy 2011 • Sp • Colour • 79min

Made with a minuscule budget, Jonathan Cenzual Burley's debut feature is tantamount to *The Wizard of Oz* being reinvented by Samuel Beckett. Opening with a brief account of the eventful life of a Castilian lothario, the action centres on the journey of discovery made by his sons (Andrea Calabrese and Javier Sáez), who are blithely ignorant of each other's existence until they receive an invitation to their father's funeral. The imagery is sublime, and the themes of life being too short to waste and memory being the solace of old age are poignantly explored. DP Spanish +subtitles. Swearing, attempted hanging. *DVD*

Andrea Calabrese *Nero de la Sierra* • Javier Sáez *Miguel de la Sierra* • Norberto Gutiérrez *Federico/Thief* • Miriam Montero *Sofía* • Felix Cenzual *Evaristo de la Sierra* ■ *Dir/Scr* Jonathan Cenzual Burley

Soul of the Game
★★★★ **12**

Historical sports drama 1996 • US • Colour • 90min

A talented cast toplines this TV docudrama about the racial integration of American baseball, told from the point of view of three black baseball greats. Kevin Sullivan deftly directs Delroy Lindo, Mykelti Williamson and Blair Underwood in a tale that rises above the sports genre with its intense look at loyalty, racism and morality. Baseball fans will lap it up, but everyone will appreciate its authentic period locations and atmosphere. MC Swearing. *DVD*

S

Delroy Lindo *Satchel Paige* • Mykelti Williamson *Josh Gibson* • Blair Underwood *Jackie Robinson* • Edward Herrmann *Branch Rickey* • R Lee Ermey *Wilkie* ■ *Dir* Kevin Rodney Sullivan • *Scr* David Himmelstein, from a story by Gary Hoffman

Soul Plane ★ 18
Comedy 2004 · Colour · 88min

Kevin Hart uses a $100million settlement from an airline to start up his own carrier – one strictly designed for an African-American clientele. Unfortunately, instead of the urban take on comedy classic *Airplane!* that this was presumably intended to be, what we get is an offensive stream of sexual innuendo, drugs humour and "bling" jokes, delivered by a variety of trite homophobic, sexist and racist characters. KK Swearing, sex scenes, drug abuse. **DVD**

Kevin Hart *Nashawn* • Tom Arnold *Mr Hunkee* • Method Man *Muggsy* • Snoop Dogg *Captain Mack* • KD Aubert *Giselle* • Godfrey *Gaeman* • Brian Hooks *DJ* • DL Huchley *Johnny* ■ *Dir* Jessy Terrero • *Scr* Bo Zenga, Chuck Wilson

Soul Power ★★★ 12
Documentary 2008 · US · Colour · 92min

The long-overdue companion to Leon Gast's 1996 Oscar winner *When We Were Kings*, this documentary capably chronicles the concerts that were staged in Kinshasa in the weeks before Muhammad Ali's legendary 1974 'Rumble in the Jungle' with George Foreman. Confronted with masses of 16mm footage, director Jeffrey Levy-Hinte (who edited *When We Were Kings*) does well in conveying the chaos and excitement of the media scrums, though it's the quieter moments that prove more effective, including a jam session that takes place onboard a plane. Soul music fans will relish Bill Withers's *Hope She'll Be Happier*, Miriam Makeba's *The Click Song* and BB King's *Thrill Is Gone*. But the highlight is a storming James Brown set that includes *Soul Power* and *Say It Loud (I'm Black and I'm Proud)*. DP English, French, Spanish, Xhosa +subtitles. **DVD** **BD**

James Brown (2) *James Brown* • Bill Withers • BB King *BB King* • Miriam Makeba • Muhammad Ali ■ *Dir* Jeffrey Levy-Hinte

Soul Surfer ★★★ PG
Sports drama based on a true story
2011 · US · Colour · 105min

This decent drama tells the true story of Hawaiian teenager Bethany Hamilton (AnnaSophia Robb), a rising surf star who, in 2003, lost her left arm in a shark attack. You can praise or damn a film by describing it as "worthy" or "inspirational", and this certainly falls into both categories. Bethany's faith-fuelled fortitude is slapped on with a trowel as she overcomes adversity to get back on her board, but the surfing scenes are well handled, the CGI effects that transform Robb into an amputee are impressively realistic, and Helen Hunt and Dennis Quaid offer assured support as her parents. Sure, the film has its mawkish moments, but it's a remarkable, well-intentioned tale. DA

AnnaSophia Robb *Bethany Hamilton* • Helen Hunt *Cheri Hamilton* • Dennis Quaid *Tom Hamilton* • Lorraine Nicholson *Alana Blanchard* • Craig T Nelson *Dr David Rovinsky* • Kevin Sorbo *Holt Blanchard* ■ *Dir* Sean McNamara • *Scr* Sean McNamara, Michael Berk, Deborah and Douglas Schwartz, from the autobiography by Bethany Hamilton, Sheryl Berk, Rick Bundschuh

Soul Survivors ★★★ 12
Horror thriller 2001 · US · Colour · 81min

Melissa Sagemiller plays a college girl who survives the car crash that kills her boyfriend, following a wild night out at a club in a spooky old church. But back at school, she rapidly realises there's something wrong. Dead wrong. Her world's just not quite right anymore. And the key to its eeriness are the schoolmates who survived the crash with her. Featuring *Twilight Zone* qualities, some decent production values, and a teen-friendly cast, this teen film puts head-thrills before blood-spills. DA **DVD**

Melissa Sagemiller *Cassie* • Casey Affleck *Sean* • Wes Bentley *Matt* • Eliza Dushku *Annabel* • Angela Featherstone *Raven* • Luke Wilson *Father Jude* ■ *Dir/Scr* Steve Carpenter [Stephen Carpenter]

SoulBoy ★★★ 15
Coming-of-age comedy drama
2010 · UK/Ire · Colour · 80min

Martin Compston and Felicity Jones inject charm and sparkle into this tale of northern teenagers in the 1970s, whose humdrum lives are enlivened by a weekly trip to Wigan, then the soul capital of the world. Compston plays a happy-go-lucky van boy, Jones is the younger sister of one of Compston's old schoolfriends. She's secretly in love with him, but his attention is focused on a girl from the hair salon who's largely responsible for his sudden passion for northern soul. This is more than a little clichéd, with a disco-floor bully who's straight out of panto, but the music and period detail will help take your mind off such deficiencies. BP Swearing, drug abuse

Martin Compston *Joe McCain* • Felicity Jones *Mandy Hodgson* • Alfie Allen *Russ Mountjoy* • Nichola Burley *Jane* • Pat Shortt *Brendan* • Jo Hartley *Monica* ■ *Dir* Shimmy Marcus • *Scr* Jeff Williams

Souls at Sea ★★★
Drama 1937 · US · BW · 90min

This spectacular features Gary Cooper as the strong, silent opponent of slavery, on trial for shooting survivors of a sinking vessel who clung to the oars of his crowded lifeboat. Co-star George Raft revived his flagging career with a winning performance as Cooper's loyal, but slow-witted companion with a ring in his ear. The story is rather awkwardly presented, but Henry Hathaway's direction is swift and incisive, and the period setting is superbly evoked. AE

Gary Cooper *Michael "Nuggin" Taylor* • George Raft *Powdah* • Frances Dee *Margaret Tarryton* • Henry Wilcoxon *Lt Stanley Tarryton* • Harry Carey *Captain* • Olympe Bradna *Babsie* • Robert Cummings *George Martin* • Virginia Weidler *Tina* ■ *Dir* Henry Hathaway • *Scr* Grover Jones, Dale Van Every, Richard Talmadge, from a story by Ted Lesser

The Sound and the Fury ★★★
Drama 1959 · US · Colour · 115min

Joanne Woodward is the young misfit in this less intense companion piece to the earlier William Faulkner adaptation, *The Long Hot Summer*, by the same director, screenwriters and leading lady. But there's no escaping Jason, played by Yul Brynner (with hair), the cruel-to-be-kind outsider, who bullies a decayed southern family into some semblance of self respect. It's a delightfully layered battle of wills between Woodward and Brynner, with a fine supporting cast. AE

Yul Brynner *Jason* • Joanne Woodward *Quentin* • Margaret Leighton *Caddy* • Stuart Whitman *Charles Busch* • Ethel Waters *Dilsey* • Jack Warden *Ben* • Françoise Rosay *Mrs Compson* ■ *Dir* Martin Ritt • *Scr* Irving Ravetch, Harriet Frank Jr, from the novel by William Faulkner

The Sound Barrier ★★★★ U
Drama 1952 · UK · BW · 112min

Terence Rattigan's script was Oscar-nominated, but the main honours in this David Lean film are shared between the stunning aerial sequences and the fine performance by Ralph Richardson as an aeroplane designer driven to produce the first craft to outstrip the speed of sound. The film is an illustration of the dictum that history is made by unreasonable people or by those single-minded enough to pursue their visions, regardless of the cost. PF **DVD** **BD**

Ralph Richardson *John Ridgefield* • Ann Todd *Susan Garthwaite* • Nigel Patrick *Tony Garthwaite* • John Justin *Phillip Peel* • Dinah Sheridan *Jess Peel* • Joseph Tomelty *Will Sparks* • Denholm Elliott *Christopher Ridgefield* • Jack Allen *Windy Williams* • Ralph Michael *Fletcher* • Vincent Holman *ATA officer* • Douglas Muir *Controller* •

Leslie Phillips *Controller* ■ *Dir* David Lean • *Scr* Terence Rattigan • *Cinematographer* Jack Hildyard

Sound It Out ★★★ 12A
Documentary 2011 · UK · Colour · 77min

Jeanie Finlay's affectionate film focuses on what is billed as the last specialist record shop (we're talking vinyl here, not new-fangled CDs) in Teesside and the people who frequent it. They are a likeable and delightfully quirky bunch, from Tom the proprietor, the fount of all musical knowledge, to customers like Status Quo fan Shane, who has already made arrangements for his records to be melted down and made into his coffin. But while you share the enthusiasm of the shop's patrons, you're left with the melancholy feeling that this is the end of an era. TP Swearing. **DVD**

■ *Dir* Jeanie Finlay

The Sound of Fury ★★★ PG
Crime drama 1950 · US · BW · 88min

This extraordinarily stark and uncompromising low-budget drama features Lloyd Bridges as a hardened criminal of the Depression era who recruits an out-of-work family man, played by Frank Lovejoy, as his accomplice in a kidnapping. When their plan ends in tragedy, a journalist (Richard Carlson) whips up local feeling, leading to a terrifying climax. Only the unnecessary moral comments of an Italian doctor lessen the film's impact. The critical view of American mores contributed to the blacklisting of its director, Cyril Endfield, who moved to Britain. AE

Frank Lovejoy *Howard Tyler* • Lloyd Bridges *Jerry Slocum* • Kathleen Ryan *Judy Tyler* • Richard Carlson *Gil Stanton* • Katherine Locke *Hazel* • Adele Jergens *Velma* ■ *Dir* Cyril Endfield [Cy Endfield] • *Scr* Jo Pagano, from his novel *The Condemned*

The Sound of Music ★★★★★ U
Classic musical 1965 · US · Colour · 167min

At the time, the biggest money-maker in the history of cinema, this is an artful and professionally made crowd-pleaser that reaches out to every generation, thanks to expert and unsentimental handling from director Robert Wise (replacing William Wyler) and a magnificent performance from Julie Andrews. She is perfectly cast as Maria, the reluctant nun who discovers her true calling as governess to a houseful of youngsters. It still looks lovely, in particular the stunning opening panoramic sweep onto the mountain top and the *Do Re Mi* tour around Salzburg, and the Rodgers and Hammerstein score is as refreshing as ever. As fresh and as magical as Andrews's smile. TS **DVD** **BD**

Julie Andrews *Maria* • Christopher Plummer *Captain Von Trapp* • Eleanor Parker *Baroness* • Richard Haydn *Max Detweiler* • Peggy Wood *Mother Abbess* • Charmian Carr *Liesl* • Heather Menzies *Louisa* • Nicholas Hammond *Friedrich* • Duane Chase *Kurt* • Angela Cartwright *Brigitta* • Debbie Turner *Marta* • Kym Karath *Gretl* • Daniel Truhitte *Rolfe* ■ *Dir* Robert Wise • *Scr* Ernest Lehman, from the musical by Richard Rodgers, Oscar Hammerstein II, Howard Lindsay, Russel Crouse • *Cinematographer* Ted McCord • *Production Designer* Boris Leven • *Music Director* Irwin Kostal • *Editor* William Reynolds

Sound of My Voice ★★★ 15
Psychological drama 2011 · US · Colour · 81min

Admirers of movies that tease the audience will find plenty to savour in this psychological drama. Two documentary-makers (Christopher Denham and Nicole Vicius) infiltrate a cult with the intention of exposing its leader (Brit Marling), who claims to be from the future. At first, the investigation appears to uncover a clear-cut case of fraud, but how does Marling know what she knows, and what does she want? There are quite a few narrative gaps and unexplained occurrences, but it's these quirks that make the film so dreamlike, engaging and menacing. DW Swearing. **DVD** **BD**

Brit Marling *Maggie* • Christopher Denham *Peter Aitken* • Nicole Vicius *Lorna Michaelson* • Davinia McFadden *Carol Briggs* ■ *Dir* Zal Batmanglij • *Scr* Zal Batmanglij, Brit Marling

Sounder ★★★★ U
Drama 1972 · US · Colour · 105min

This is a sentimental, but still powerful movie about a family of black sharecroppers in 1930s Depression-hit Louisiana. Beautifully photographed, it boasts fine performances from Paul Winfield as the dad who is snatched from his family for stealing a ham and Cicely Tyson as the mother of three who struggles to carry on the farm without him. Kevin Hooks (who won a Golden Globe for best newcomer and went on to become a director) is the son who embarks on an odyssey to find Winfield. Accompanied by faithful dog Sounder, he meets schoolteacher Jane McLachlan, who irrevocably changes his life. A sequel (*Part 2, Sounder*) followed in 1976. FL

Cicely Tyson *Rebecca Morgan* • Paul Winfield *Nathan Lee Morgan* • Kevin Hooks *David Lee Morgan* • Carmen Mathews *Mrs Boatwright* • Taj Mahal *Ike* • James Best *Sheriff Young* ■ *Dir* Martin Ritt • *Scr* Lonne Elder III, from the novel by William H Armstrong • *Cinematographer* John A Alonzo

Sounds like Teen Spirit ★★★ 12A
Music documentary
2008 · UK/Cay · Colour · 93min

Anything Eurovision-related is an easy satirical target. And the kitsch factor, grand political illusions, tacky songs and exaggerated glitz are all present and correct in director Jamie J Johnson's thoroughly enjoyable documentary about the highs and lows of the Fifth Junior Eurovision Song Contest, held in 2007. It follows the fortunes of impoverished Mariam from Georgia, rich kid Marina from Bulgaria, bullied Yiorgos from Cyprus and raging hormonal school band Trust from Belgium, as they head to Rotterdam to sing their self-composed songs in the final. The impact that growing fame has on their personalities and the proud folks back home is well conveyed. Yet it's the way that Johnson subtly catches his subjects off-guard that gives this affectionate film poignancy and bite. AJ English, Flemish, Bulgarian, Georgian, Greek +subtitles.

■ *Dir* Jamie J Johnson

Sour Grapes ★ 15
Comedy 1998 · US · Colour · 88min

Two cousins hit it rich playing slot machines in Atlantic City – or rather, one of them does, using the quarters he borrowed from his relative. Craig Bierko's refusal to split the winnings with Steven Weber means the end of their friendship and the start of an endless round of recriminations. It's written and directed by Larry David, co-creator of sitcom *Seinfeld*, but the humour is missing from this misfire. ST Swearing.

Steven Weber *Evan* • Craig Bierko *Richie* • Karen Sillas *Joan* • Robyn Peterman *Roberta* • Jack Burns *Eulogist* • Viola Harris *Selma* ■ *Dir/Scr* Larry David

The Source ★★ 15
Comedy drama
2011 · Bel/It/Fr · Colour · 124min

In this overworked comedy drama set in a remote Maghreb village, Romanian-born writer/director Radu Mihaileanu uses an awkward mixture of satire and sentimentality to examine several weighty issues. Angry that so many neighbours have miscarried while hauling water along a dangerous mountain path, village outsider Leila Bekhti proposes a sex strike until the menfolk stop treating them like baby-making slaves. The film is never dull, and even features some heavy-handed song-and-dance numbers, but Mihaileanu and co-screenwriter Alain-Michel Blanc try to do too much and mistake clichéd exoticism for sociological insight. DP Arabic +subtitles. **DVD**

S

Leila Bekhti *Leila* • Hafsia Herzi *Loubna/Esmeralda* • Biyouna *Le Vieux Fusil* • Sabrina Ouazani *Rachida* • Saleh Bakri *Sami* ■ *Dir* Radu Mihaileanu • *Scr* Radu Mihaileanu, Alain-Michel Blanc

Source Code ★★★★ 12

Science-fiction thriller
2011 · US/Fr · Colour · 89min

In this speculative slice of suspense from *Moon* director Duncan Jones, we first meet Jake Gyllenhaal as a teacher on a Chicago commuter train. But unknown to him, he's on a mission to identify who's about to take the lives of all those on board. Blending elements of *Déjà Vu*, *Murder on the Orient Express* and even *Groundhog Day* (since the fateful events are replayed to clarify the killer's identity), the story's fascinating premise draws us in, while the whodunnit aspects keep us hooked. On reflection, the holes in the narrative are rather obvious, but while it's unfolding, the plight of a man battling against time isn't given a degree of emotional weight not always present in the realm of pulp sci-fi. Kudos also goes to Gyllenhaal, adeptly balancing vulnerability with muscle-bound action, amid solid supporting work from fellow passenger Michelle Monaghan and his sinister handlers Jeffrey Wright and Vera Farmiga. TJ Brief swearing. DVD BD
Jake Gyllenhaal *Captain Colter Stevens* • Michelle Monaghan *Christina* • Vera Farmiga *Colleen Goodwin* • Jeffrey Wright *Dr Walter Rutledge* • Russell Peters *Max Denoff* ■ *Dir* Duncan Jones • *Scr* Ben Ripley

Soursweet ★★★ 15

Drama 1988 · UK · Colour · 121min

Mike Newell directs this sweet and sour drama of immigrant life in London, about a Chinese couple who set up their own small restaurant. It could have been chop phooey, but, with the help of a fine screenplay by Ian McEwan, and thoughtful direction, it becomes a charming and moving character study of one of the many ethnic strands that make up multiracial Britain. DA DVD
Sylvia Chang *Lily* • Danny An-Ning Dun *Chen* • Jodi Long *Mui* • Soon-Teck Oh *Red Cudgel* • William Chow *White Paper Fan* • Jim Carter *Mr Constantinides* ■ *Dir* Mike Newell • *Scr* Ian McEwan, from the novel by Timothy Mo

Sous le Soleil de Satan ★★★★ 15

Religious drama 1987 · Fr · Colour · 97min

Since director Robert Bresson had already adapted two Georges Bernanos novels, *Diary of a Country Priest* and *Mouchette*, it was logical that Maurice Pialat should elect to emulate his stark authenticity in relating Bernanos's tale of the village cleric who comes to see Satan as the world's controlling force. Yet, this is clearly the work of an atheist, who considers that Father Gérard Depardieu's relentless self-flagellation is as much an act of pride as saintliness. The elliptical structure brings an intellectual rigour to the emotive exchanges, while the performances of Depardieu and Sandrine Bonnaire are riveting. DP French +subtitles.
Gérard Depardieu *Donissan* • Sandrine Bonnaire *Mouchette* • Maurice Pialat *Menou-Segrais* • Alain Artur *Cadignan* • Yann Dedet *Gallet* • Brigitte Legendre *Mouchette's mother* • Jean-Claude Bourlat *Malorthy* ■ *Dir* Maurice Pialat • *Scr* Sylvie Danton, Maurice Pialat, from the novel *Sous le Soleil de Satan* by Georges Bernanos

Sous les Toits de Paris ★★★★

Drama 1930 · Fr · BW · 91min

Deriving much neighbourhood charm from Lazare Meerson's sets and full of memorable songs and pleasing performances, René Clair's sound debut was a fluent delight at a time when everyone else's talkies were little more than animated radio. Indeed, he places so much emphasis on the narrative power of the image, that he mischievously stages conversations where the dialogue simply couldn't be heard. Keeping the camera on the move and the action light, he utterly enchants with the story of Parisian street singer, Albert Préjean, whose beloved, Pola Illery, is also pursued by his best friend, Edmond Gréville, and the lecherous Gaston Modot. DP French +subtitles.
Albert Préjean *Albert* • Pola Illery *Pola* • Gaston Modot *Fred* • Edmond T Gréville *Louis* • Bill Bocket *Bill* ■ *Dir/Scr* René Clair • *Cinematographer* Georges Périnal

South ★★★

Silent documentary 1919 · UK · Tinted · 81min

A milestone in Britain's documentary history, Frank Hurley's silent account of Sir Ernest Shackleton's doomed Antarctic expedition (1914-16) is heavily reliant on captions that don't always provide adequate information or explanation. Nor does Hurley come clean about the fate of the 70 sled dogs on whom he lavishes so much attention, until they are abandoned when the mission becomes a desperate bid for survival. However, the tinted footage is compelling, with the hauntingly beautiful night shots of the *Endurance* trapped among the ice floes standing out as symbols of our nation's love affair with flawed heroism. DP DVD
Ernest Shackleton ■ *Dir* Frank Hurley

South American George ★★★ U

Comedy 1941 · UK · BW · 88min

The first film that ukulele-playing comic George Formby made after he left Ealing Studios and signed with Columbia gives him a dual role as an opera singer and his double, a stagehand who agrees to take the singer's place then finds himself fleeing gangsters. Sometimes cited as the start of Formby's decline on the screen, this has more plot than usual for a Formby vehicle and although some of his fans missed the "old" George, they still turned out in their millions and maintained his position as Britain's top box-office draw. TV DVD
George Formby *George Butters/Gilli Vanetti* • Linden Travers *Carole Dean* • Enid Stamp-Taylor *Frances Martinique* • Jacques Brown *Enrico Richardo* • Felix Aylmer *Mr Appleby* • Ronald Shiner *Swifty* ■ *Dir* Marcel Varnel • *Scr* Leslie Arliss, Norman Lee, Austin Melford

South Central ★★★ 15

Drama 1992 · US · Colour · 94min

This stark look at life on the streets of South Central Los Angeles begins in standard *Boyz N the Hood* territory, but then the action takes a dramatic turn when jailed murderer Glenn Plummer discovers Islam. There's something of the Malcolm X story about this transformation, but the struggle for control of his ten-year-old between Plummer and gang leader Byron Keith Minns, and his girlfriend's descent into addiction and prostitution, make for powerful human drama. DP DVD
Glenn Plummer *Bobby Johnson* • Carl Lumbly *Ali* • Byron Keith Minns [Byron Minns] *Ray Ray* • Lexie D Bigham [Lexie Bigham] *Bear* • Vincent Craig Dupree *Loco* • LaRita Shelby *Carole* • Kevin Best *Genie Lamp* ■ *Dir* Steve Anderson (1) • *Scr* Steve Anderson (1), from the novel *Crips* by Donald Bakeer

South of Algiers ★★★ PG

Drama 1952 · UK · Colour · 86min

This is an exciting, richly Technicolored movie about a sun-scorched search in the Sahara for a fabled "golden mask" (the American title). Imaginatively shot by underrated documentarist Jack Lee, it features sturdy Van Heflin as the archaeologist with a mission and Eric Portman as his rapacious adversary. Stirring stuff, and beautifully filmed by veteran British cameraman Oswald Morris, with some strikingly authentic sequences. TS
Van Heflin *Nicholas Chapman* • Wanda Hendrix *Anne Burnet* • Eric Portman *Dr Burnet* • Charles Goldner *Petris* • Jacques François *Jacques Farnod* • Jacques Brunius *Kress* • Aubrey Mather *Professor Sir Arthur Young* ■ *Dir* Jack Lee (2) • *Scr* Robert Westerby

South of Heaven, West of Hell ★★

Western 2000 · US · Colour · 132min

Dwight Yoakam adds another hyphenated credit to his CV with this first outing as a writer-director-composer. But, despite its impressive ensemble, there's not much else to applaud in this sprawling western that is very much a tale of two halves. In the first, Yoakam's Arizona lawman turns on the outlaw family who raised him as an orphan, while in the second he returns, having thrown away his badge, to compete with bombastic brigadier Billy Bob Thornton for the affections of Bridget Fonda. DP
Dwight Yoakam *Valentine Casey* • Vince Vaughn *Taylor Henry* • Billy Bob Thornton *Brigadier Smalls* • Bridget Fonda *Adalyne* • Peter Fonda *Shoshone Bill* • Paul Reubens *Arvid Henry* • Bud Cort *Agent Otts* • Bo Hopkins *Doc Angus Dunfries* ■ *Dir* Dwight Yoakam • *Scr* Dwight Yoakam, Stan Bertheaud, from a story by Dwight Yoakam, Dennis Hackin, Otto Felix

South of Pago Pago ★★★ U

Adventure 1940 · US · BW · 97min

Pago Pago is the main town of American Samoa, where Victor McLaglen runs a pearl-diving operation while dodging hostile Polynesians and watching his divers fail to come up for air. Romance is supplied by the alluring Frances Farmer who catches the eye of native hunk Jon Hall. Exciting action and fine photography keep it above the merely routine. AT
Victor McLaglen *Bucko Larson* • Jon Hall *Kehane* • Frances Farmer *Ruby Taylor* • Olympe Bradna *Malia* • Gene Lockhart *Lindsay* • Douglass Dumbrille *Williams* • Francis Ford *Foster* ■ *Dir* Alfred E Green • *Scr* George Bruce • *Cinematographer* John J Mescall

South of St Louis ★★ U

Western 1949 · US · Colour · 86min

This relentlessly routine western about three ranchers wasn't particularly memorable in its day, but is worth a look for nostalgic value alone. The three leads – Joel McCrea, Alexis Smith and Zachary Scott – are watchable, their sheer professionalism a delight. Director Ray Enright proves as competent as ever, this time helped by the great cameraman Karl Freund's outdoor Technicolor photography. TS
Joel McCrea *Kip Davis* • Alexis Smith *Rouge de Lisle* • Zachary Scott *Charlie Burns* • Dorothy Malone *Deborah Miller* • Douglas Kennedy *Lee Price* • Alan Hale *Jake Evarts* • Victor Jory *Luke Cottrell* ■ *Dir* Ray Enright • *Scr* Zachary Gold, James R Webb

South of the Border ★★★ 15

Documentary 2009 · US · Colour · 77min

Oliver Stone downsizes from his usual high-profile fare with this polemical documentary about political change in South America. Obviously riled by what he sees as the misinformation being fed by TV news to US viewers, Stone determines to set the record straight, blending potted revisionist history and a series of cosy chats with Venezuelan president Hugo Chavez and other South American heads of state. Even if he's taking the politicians in question rather naively at face value, at least Stone is getting a provocative alternative viewpoint across – and in an engaging and entertaining way, too. TJ English, Spanish, Portuguese +subtitles.
Hugo Chávez • Raúl Castro • Rafael Correa ■ *Dir* Oliver Stone • *Scr* Tariq Ali, Oliver Stone

South Pacific ★★★ U

Musical 1958 · US · Colour · 151min

This screen version of the fabulous Rodgers and Hammerstein Broadway show has always been better liked by the public than the critics. It has several flaws, not least of which is the bizarre use of colour filters. Wonderful though Mitzi Gaynor is in the big numbers, her character's brashness grows tiresome and one longs for Doris Day's tenderness in the role, while Rossano Brazzi is wooden and the war sequences seem to belong to a different movie. But the score is wonderful, and no one could fail to be carried away by some of the finest songs ever written. TS DVD BD
Mitzi Gaynor *Nellie Forbush* • Rossano Brazzi *Emile de Becque* • John Kerr *Lieutenant Cable* • Ray Walston *Luther Billis* • Juanita Hall *Bloody Mary* • France Nuyen *Liat* • Russ Brown *Captain Brackett* • Joan Fontaine *Polynesian woman* ■ *Dir* Joshua Logan • *Scr* Paul Osborn, from the musical by Richard Rodgers, Oscar Hammerstein II, Joshua Logan, from the novel *Tales of the South Pacific* by James A Michener

South Pacific ★★★

Musical drama 2001 · US · Colour · 129min

In this small-screen remake of Rodgers and Hammerstein's hit musical, director Richard Pearce dispenses with the visual artiness of Joshua Logan's 1958 version and returns to James A Michener's source stories to re-emphasise the themes of racial prejudice and the human cost of war. But he doesn't neglect the musical interludes and the classic tunes are competently performed. DP
Glenn Close *Nellie Forbush* • Harry Connick Jr *Lieutenant Cable* • Rade Sherbedgia [Rade Serbedzija] *Emile de Beque* • Lori Tan Chinn *Bloody Mary* • Robert Pastorelli *Luther Billis* • Natalie Mendoza *Liat* ■ *Dir* Richard Pearce • *Scr* Lawrence D Cohen, from the musical by Richard Rodgers, Oscar Hammerstein II, Joshua Logan, from the novel *Tales of the South Pacific* by James A Michener

South Park: Bigger, Longer & Uncut ★★★★ 15

Animated comedy 1999 · US · Colour · 81min

Trey Parker and Matt Stone's tasteless animated TV series gets the big-screen treatment in this dark, demented and deliriously funny feature-length tale. Stan, Kyle, Cartman and Kenny go on an outing to see Terrance and Phillip's profanity-laced movie and their resultant change in vocabulary is the catalyst for an escalating bout of moral-guardian madness, culminating in the outbreak of World War Three (well, the USA versus Canada). This sharp, inventive TV spin-off doesn't pad its plot or waste widescreen opportunities. Bad taste at its best. JC Swearing. DVD CS
Trey Parker *Stan Marsh/Eric Cartman/Mr Garrison/Mr Hat/Officer Barbrady* • Matt Stone *Kyle Broflovski/Kenny McCormick/Pip/Jesus/Jimbo* • Mary Kay Bergman *Mrs Cartman/Sheila Broflovski/Sharon Manson/Mrs McCormick/Wendy Testaburger/Principal Victoria* • Isaac Hayes *Chef* • George Clooney *Doctor Gouache* • Brent Spiner *Conan O'Brien* • Minnie Driver • Brooke Shields • Eric Idle *Doctor Vosknocker* ■ *Dir* Trey Parker • *Scr* Trey Parker, Matt Stone, Pam Brady

South Riding ★★★

Romantic drama 1938 · UK · BW · 68min

Victor Saville makes an admirable job of bringing Winifred Holtby's bubbling cauldron of upper-class insanity, misguided philanthropy and council-chamber corruption to the screen. Deftly capturing the sights and sounds of this Yorkshire neverland, he only loses his grasp at the close as sentimentality is allowed to wash away the grit. Ralph Richardson reins in his customary screen excesses to give a sensitive reading of the misguided squire unable to come to terms with his wife's madness. DP
Ralph Richardson *Robert Carne* • Edna Best *Sarah Burton* • Ann Todd *Madge Carne* • Edmund Gwenn *Alfred Huggins* • John Clements *Joe Astell* • Marie Lohr *Mrs Beddows* • Milton Rosmer *Alderman Snaith* • Glynis Johns *Midge Carne* ■ *Dir* Victor Saville • *Scr* Ian Dalrymple, Donald Bull, from the novel by Winifred Holtby

South Sea Woman ★★

Comedy adventure 1953 · US · BW · 98min

Even stars as big as Burt Lancaster had to serve their Hollywood apprenticeship in tacky movies such as this, in which he's an eager-to-fight marine sparking with sultry Virginia Mayo on a tropical island. Director Arthur Lubin had made six movies about Francis the Talking Mule, so Burt's reported mulish behaviour off-set was forgivably in character. TH

U SUITABLE FOR ALL   Uc SUITABLE ESPECIALLY FOR YOUNG CHILDREN (DVD ONLY)   PG PARENTAL GUIDANCE   12A UNDER 12s TO BE ACCOMPANIED (CINEMA ONLY)

Burt Lancaster *Sergeant James O'Hearn* • Virginia Mayo *Ginger Martin* • Chuck Connors *Davey White* • Barry Kelley *Colonel Hickman* • Hayden Rorke *Lieutenant Fears* • Leon Askin *Marchand* ◼ *Dir* Arthur Lubin • *Scr* Edwin Blum, Earl Baldwin, Stanley Shapiro, from a play by William M Rankin

South West Nine ★★★ 18

Drama 2001 · UK/Ire · Colour · 94min

Low-budget films set in a distinctive London suburb have become a rather stale British subgenre of late, but this Brixton-based social tapestry has enough energy, personality and multicultural scope to make its own distinctive mark. Charting 24 hours in the lives of an eclectic bunch of local characters, writer/director Richard Parry combines such elements as a mysterious stolen briefcase, some accidentally ingested LSD and a climactic church rave. He also extracts bright, authentic performances from a largely unknown young cast. It's only real shortcoming is the ineffectual attempt to crank up tension with an unnecessary thriller plot. JC *DVD*

Wil Johnson *Fredcy* • Stuart Laing *Jake* • Mark Letheren *Mitch* • Amelia Curtis *Kat* • Orlessa Edwards *Helen* ◼ *Dir/Scr* Richard Parry

Southbound ★★★

Horror anthology 2015 · US · Colour · 89min

From contributors to the *V/H/S* franchise, five gritty tales of terror form a "circle of death" in this above average chiller compendium set around a remote stretch of desert highway. The best of the stylistically unified bunch sees a tired driver ploughing into a hapless victim and then, after taking her to an abandoned emergency room, being guided through surgery procedures by creepy 911 voices. It's a solid shocker throughout, with horror icon Larry Fessenden taking us through the menacing morality lessons. AJ *DVD* 🔵

Chad Villella *Mitch* • Matt Bettinelli-Olpin *Jack* • Fabienne Therese *Sadie* • Hannah Marks *Ava* • Nathalie Love *Kim* • Kate Beahan *Cait* ◼ *Dir* Roxanne Benjamin, David Bruckner, Patrick Horvath, Radio Silence [Matt Bettinelli-Olpin], Radio Silence [Tyler Gillett], Radio Silence [Justin Martinez], Radio Silence [Chad Villella] • *Scr* Roxanne Benjamin, Susan Burke, David Bruckner, Dallas Hallam [Dallas Richard Hallam], Patrick Horvath, Matt Bettinelli-Olpin

Southern Comfort ★★★★ 15

Action drama 1981 · US · Colour · 101min

Nine National Guardsmen – including Keith Carradine and Powers Boothe – are sent on exercises through the Louisiana swamplands and find themselves drawn into a guerrilla war with the local Cajuns. Set in 1973, Walter Hill's movie is evidently an allegorical treatment of the Vietnam conflict, with the Cajuns cast as the shadowy but lethal Vietcong. Few movies are as single-minded as this one: Hill establishes the bayou as a grey, formless labyrinth and creates a purely abstract action movie that's creepy, tense and never remotely comfortable. AT Violence, swearing, drug abuse. *DVD* 🔵

Keith Carradine *Spencer* • Powers Boothe *Hardin* • Fred Ward *Reece* • Franklyn Seales *Simms* • TK Carter *Cribbs* • Lewis Smith *Stuckey* • Les Lannom *Casper* • Peter Coyote *Poole* • Carlos Brown [Alan Autry] *Bowden* • Brion James *Trapper* ◼ *Dir* Walter Hill • *Scr* Michael Kane, Walter Hill, David Giler

Southern Softies ★★ U

Spoof documentary 2009 · UK · Colour · 78min

Sheffield-born writer/director Graham Fellows is the man behind John Shuttleworth, social commentator and maker of light-hearted spoof documentaries. In this ultra-low budget project, Shuttleworth visits each of the Channel Islands in pursuit of his producer, Ken Worthington (also the voice of Fellows), imparting his unique form of wisdom to camera while analysing the vexed question of whether it's soft down south. There are moments of wacky hilarity that raise the odd smile, but ultimately this comedy curio has decidedly limited appeal. SuR

John Shuttleworth [Graham Fellows] *John Shuttleworth* • Martin Parr • Graham Fellows *Ken Worthington* • Stuart Thom • Tim Humphries• Faye ◼ *Dir/Scr* Graham Fellows

The Southern Star ★★★ PG

Comedy adventure 1969 · Fr/UK · Colour · 101min

This splendidly photographed African adventure was filmed on authentic Senegalese locations, but alas bears the curse of international co-production. Underrated editor-turned-director Sidney Hayers tries to pull together the Jules Verne-inspired plot and a cast that verges on the preposterous, headed by George Segal (far too urban for this type of trek), Ursula Andress and Orson Welles, who was obviously in need of the money. This romp isn't sure whether it's comedy or adventure or both, but it looks good nevertheless. TS

George Segal *Dan* • Ursula Andress *Erica Kramer* • Orson Welles *Plankett* • Ian Hendry *Karl* • Harry Andrews *Kramer* ◼ *Dir* Sidney Hayers • *Scr* David Pursall, Jack Seddon, Jean Giono, from the novel *L'Etoile du Sud, le Pays des Diamants* by Jules Verne • *Cinematographer* Raoul Coutard

A Southern Yankee ★★★

Comedy 1948 · US · BW · 90min

Fans of Buster Keaton's *The General* may well recognise an occasional overlap here. That's because not only was Keaton happy for Red Skelton to borrow ideas from that silent classic, he was also in charge of many comic sequences, which unsurprisingly turn out to be those that make the film really sing. Otherwise proceedings oscillate from swirling exuberance to blandness, though Skelton's comic knack, as a foolish Civil War spy, is never in doubt. TS

Red Skelton *Aubrey Filmore* • Arlene Dahl *Sallyann Weatharby* • Brian Donlevy *Curt Devlynn* • George Coulouris *Major Jack Drumman* • Minor Watson *General Watkins* • Lloyd Gough *Captain Steve Lorford* • John Ireland *Captain Jed Calbern* ◼ *Dir* Edward Sedgwick • *Scr* Harry Tugend, from a story by Melvin Frank

The Southerner ★★★★★

Drama 1945 · US · BW · 92min

The only American film by the great French director Jean Renoir to receive critical praise and break even at the box office, the screenplay, on which Renoir was advised by William Faulkner, told of a year in the life of a cotton farmer who has to fight a malicious neighbour, the elements and malnutrition. In order to achieve pictorial splendour and realism, the film was shot almost entirely on location in the San Joaquin valley in California (standing in for Texas) and produced an effective slice of Americana. Zachary Scott, cast against type, gives one of his finest performances. RB

Zachary Scott *Sam Tucker* • Betty Field *Nona Tucker* • J Carrol Naish *Devers* • Beulah Bondi *Granny* • Jean Vanderwilt *Daisy* • Jay Gilpin *Jot* • Percy Kilbride *Harmie* • Blanche Yurka *Ma* • Charles Kemper *Tim* • Norman Lloyd *Finley* • Jack Norworth *Doctor* • Nestor Paiva *Bartender* • Estelle Taylor *Lizzie* ◼ *Dir* Jean Renoir • *Scr* Jean Renoir, Hugo Butler, from the novel *Hold Autumn in Your Hands* by George Sessions Perry

Southland Tales ★★ 15

Futuristic comedy thriller 2005 · US · Colour · 138min

After a poor reception at Cannes in 2006, director Richard Kelly's futuristic follow-up to *Donnie Darko* was recut into a shorter but no less self-indulgent version. The action begins with nuclear attacks on Texas in 2005 and moves forward to 2008, with a presidential election looming and America in the vice-like grip of a totalitarian government. Throw in a multitude of storylines involving "fluid karma" wonder fuel, neo-marxist plotting, and a porn star-turned-pundit (Sarah Michelle Gellar) dating an amnesiac movie hero (Dwayne "The Rock" Johnson) and you have the recipe for a fabulously contrived, unstructured mess. AJ *DVD* 🔵

Dwayne Johnson *Boxer Santaros/Jericho Cane* • Seann William Scott *Roland Taverner/Ronald Taverner* • Sarah Michelle Gellar *Krysta*

Kapowski/Krysta Now • Curtis Armstrong *Dr Soberin Exx* • Joe Campana *Brandt Huntington* • Nora Dunn *Cyndi Pinziki* • Miranda Richardson *Nana Mae Frost* • Kevin Smith (2) *Simon Thiery* • Mandy Moore *Madeline Frost Santaros* • David McDivitt *Marine sergeant* • Michele Durrett *Starla Von Luft* ◼ *Dir/Scr* Richard Kelly

Southpaw ★★★★ 15

Sports documentary 1998 · Ire/UK · Colour · 79min

This documentary charts the rise to fame of Francis Barrett, an Irish boxer and one of a community of Galway travellers. A national hero, he qualified for the Irish Olympic team, carrying his country's flag during the opening ceremony at Atlanta in 1996. Training in a ramshackle gym, under a boxing-addicted barber, he encounters bigotry, but settles into marriage easily – if not celebrity. Liam McGrath directs this hard-hitting account of a real-life fighter who is naturally appealing. TH Swearing.

◼ *Dir* Liam McGrath

Southpaw ★★★ 15

Sports drama 2015 · US · Colour · 118min

Jake Gyllenhaal's Billy Hope is the latest in a long line of blue-collar bruisers to fight his way out of the gutter, putting the orphanage behind him to find fame as a middleweight boxing champion in director Antoine Fuqua's visceral albeit somewhat familiar drama. A fracas with a trash-talking rival (Miguel Gomez) has tragic consequences and soon Hope is broke and alone, fighting to restore his reputation and win back his child. With any other star, this would be the stuff of soap opera, but Gyllenhaal gives a powerful performance that towers above the script. DW Violence, swearing. *DVD* 🔵

Jake Gyllenhaal *Billy Hope* • Forest Whitaker *Titus "Tick" Willis* • Rachel McAdams *Maureen Hope* • Naomie Harris *Angela Rivera* • 50 Cent [Curtis "50 Cent" Jackson] *Jordan Mains* ◼ *Dir* Antoine Fuqua • *Scr* Kurt Sutter

Southwest Passage ★★★ U

Western 1954 · US · Colour · 75min

An unusual aspect of western history lifts this drama out of the rut: it's the experimental use of pack camels with Arab drivers to create a shorter route across the American desert. Rod Cameron is surprisingly effective as the determined camel enthusiast and his story should have been enough in itself. But there's John Ireland and Joanne Dru doing their best with clichéd roles as the sympathetic bank robber on the run and his gal, who join the caravan. Originally seen by American audiences in 3D, the film was shown flat in Britain under the title *Camels West*. AE

Joanne Dru *Lilly* • Rod Cameron *Edward Fitzpatrick Beale* • John Ireland *Clint McDonald* • Guinn "Big Boy" Williams *Tall Tale* • Darryl Hickman *Jeb* • Morris Ankrum *Doc Stanton* ◼ *Dir* Ray Nazarro • *Scr* Harry Essex, Geoffrey Homes [Daniel Mainwaring], from a story by Harry Essex

Soylent Green ★★★ 15

Science-fiction thriller 1973 · US · Colour · 92min

Charlton Heston is in serious jaw-jutting mode as the lone honest cop in a polluted and over-populated 21st-century New York, investigating a murder at the company responsible for a new synthetic food product. Harry Harrison's sober novel has been rather ploddingly adapted as a curious update of the private eye genre with grim glimpses of a future consumer society run amok, though director Richard Fleischer still manages to retain the book's anti-utopian sentiments. Edward G Robinson, in his final performance, gives a very poignant turn. AJ Violence, swearing. *DVD*

Charlton Heston *Detective Robert Thorn* • Leigh Taylor-Young *Shirl* • Chuck Connors *Tab Fielding* • Joseph Cotten *William Simonson* • Brock Peters *Hatcher* • Edward G Robinson *Sol Roth* ◼ *Dir* Richard Fleischer • *Scr* Stanley R Greenberg, from the novel *Make Room! Make Room!* by Harry Harrison

Space Chimps ★★★ U

Animated comedy adventure 2008 · US · Colour · 77min

This modest piece of computer-generated fluff isn't a match for the more impressive likes of *WALL-E* and *Kung Fu Panda*. That said, *Space Chimps* is watchable enough, and will certainly keep smaller children entertained. After a space probe vanishes into a wormhole, it winds up in the hands of evil dictator Zartog (voiced by Jeff Daniels) on a distant planet. A crew of trained chimp astronauts are soon involved in all kinds of adventures as they try to thwart Zartog's nefarious plans. Bright, breezy and fun, *Space Chimps* is *The Right Stuff* simian-style. DA *DVD* 🔵 CS

Andy Samberg *Ham III* • Cheryl Hines *Luna* • Patrick Warburton *Titan* • Omid Abtahi *Dr Jagu* • Jeff Daniels *Zartog* • Patrick Breen *Dr Bob* • Stanley Tucci *The Senator* ◼ *Dir* Kirk De Micco • *Scr* Kirk De Micco, Robert Moreland

Space Chimps 2: Zartog Strikes Back ★★ U

Animated adventure 2009 · US · Colour · 72min

This lacklustre sequel to the 2008 original picks up where *Space Chimps* left off, following the astronaut apes as youngest recruit Comet (voiced by Zack Shada) accidentally blasts into space and returns to alien planet Malgor. Meanwhile, down on Earth frozen baddie Zartog thaws out and tries to cause chaos. Even the youngest viewers will probably agree that this adventure is for chumps. JR *DVD* 🔵 3D

Zack Shada *Comet* • Laura Bailey *Kilowatt* • Tom Kinney *Ham* • Cheryl Hines *Luna* • Patrick Warburton *Titan* • Stanley Tucci *The Senator* ◼ *Dir* John H Williams • *Scr* Rob Moreland [Robert Moreland]

Space Cowboys ★★★ PG

Space adventure 2000 · US/Aus · Colour · 125min

Houston, we have another problem. But, unlike the factual *Apollo 13*, director/producer/star Clint Eastwood's self-deprecating and winningly indulgent cosmic adventure is a complete macho-fuelled fantasy set in the ultra-realistic world of Nasa operations today. With an irresistible premise – four geriatric astronauts finally get the chance to go into orbit 40 years after being sidelined by a monkey – this slice of gung-ho wish-fulfilment is an entertaining feel-good pleasure, but lacks any real thrills or suspense because the outcome is obvious from the start. AJ Some swearing. *DVD* 🔵

Clint Eastwood *Frank D Corvin* • Tommy Lee Jones *Hawk Hawkins* • Donald Sutherland *Jerry O'Neill* • James Garner *Tank Sullivan* • James Cromwell *Bob Gerson* • Marcia Gay Harden *Sara Holland* • William Devane *Eugene Davis* • Loren Dean *Ethan Glance* • Courtney B Vance *Roger Hines* ◼ *Dir* Clint Eastwood • *Scr* Ken Kaufman, Howard Klausner

Space Jam ★★★ U

Part-animated fantasy comedy 1997 · US · Colour · 83min

American basketball star Michael Jordan makes a charismatic big screen acting debut alongside the entire Warner Bros cartoon catalogue. Aliens from an ailing intergalactic theme park want Bugs Bunny, Daffy Duck et al to be their new attraction. In a desperate attempt to keep their freedom, the animated superstars challenge their would-be captors to a basketball game and increase their odds of success by kidnapping Jordan. The humour cleverly mixes typical Looney Tunes gags with references to *Reservoir Dogs*, while Bill Murray provides some hilarious moments. SuR *DVD* CS

Michael Jordan • Wayne Knight *Stan Podolak* • Danny DeVito *Swackhammer* • Theresa Randle *Juanita Jordan* • Eric Gordon *Marcus Jordan* • Penny Bae Bridges *Jasmine Jordan* • Bill Murray ◼ *Dir* Joe Pytka • *Scr* Leo Benvenuti, Steve Rudnick, Timothy Harris, Herschel Weingrod

S

Space Master X 7 ★★

Science-fiction horror　1958 · US · BW · 70min

Fungus from a space probe mixes with human blood and turns deadly in this prime example of a 1950s copycat chiller. It's told in routine, and extremely padded out, semi-documentary style, the presence of Three Stooges funnyman Moe Howard (playing a cab driver), suggests director Edward Bernds thought it was a comedy, too. Unfortunately, the other actors take it all very seriously. AJ

Bill Williams *John Hand* • Lyn Thomas *Lora Greeling* • Robert Ellis *Radigan* • Paul Frees *Charles Palmer* • Joan Nixon Barry *Miss Meyers* • Thomas Browne Henry *Professor West* • Fred Sherman *Morse* • Rhoda Williams *Miss Archer* ■ *Dir* Edward Bernds • *Scr* George Worthing Yates, Daniel Mainwaring

Space Truckers ★★★ 12

Science-fiction adventure
1996 · US/Ire · Colour · 92min

A better than expected cast has an intergalactic brush with killer robots, pirates and motorised body parts in this off-the-wall sci-fi romp from *Re-Animator* director Stuart Gordon. Dennis Hopper, Stephen Dorff and Debi Mazar are among those on the receiving end, while Charles Dance's bio-mechanical adversary even out-camps his pantomime *Last Action Hero* villain. A colourful, unpretentious slice of entertaining nonsense. JC

Dennis Hopper *John Canyon* • Stephen Dorff *Mike Pucci* • Debi Mazar *Cindy* • George Wendt *Mr Keller* • Barbara Crampton *Carol* • Charles Dance *Nabel/Macanudo* • Shane Rimmer *EJ Saggs* ■ *Dir* Stuart Gordon • *Scr* Ted Mann, from a story by Stuart Gordon, Ted Mann

Spaceballs ★★ 12

Science-fiction spoof 1987 · US · Colour · 92min

Mel Brooks seems to think that just by appearing on screen, assembling assorted clowns (Rick Moranis and John Candy among them) and substituting noise for wit, hilarity will somehow ensue. In this limp spoof of *Star Wars* (where the obvious is never avoided), visual gags leap across the screen with manic abandon, but a handful of decent jokes and japes brighten the mundane proceedings. JM Swearing. *DVD*

Mel Brooks *President Skroob/Yogurt* • John Candy *Barf the Mawg* • Rick Moranis *Lord Dark Helmet* • Bill Pullman *Lone Starr* • Daphne Zuniga *Princess Vespa* • Dick Van Patten *King Roland* • George Wyner *Colonel Sandurz* • Michael Winslow *Radar technician* • Joan Rivers *Dot Matrix (voice only)* • Lorene Yarnell *Dot Matrix* • John Hurt • Dom DeLuise *Pizza the Hutt* ■ *Dir* Mel Brooks • *Scr* Mel Brooks, Thomas Meehan, Ronny Graham

SpaceCamp ★★ PG

Adventure　1986 · US · Colour · 103min

This space opera for youngsters brought Kate Capshaw down to earth with something of a bump from the heady heights of *Indiana Jones and the Temple of Doom*. Younger teenagers might well relish the idea of a group of aspiring astronauts who accidentally blast off into orbit, but they will be less forgiving about the cut-price special effects. DP *DVD*

Lea Thompson *Kathryn* • Tate Donovan *Kevin* • Kelly Preston *Tish* • Larry B Scott *Rudy* • Leaf Phoenix *[Joaquin Phoenix] Max* • Kate Capshaw *Andie Bergstrom* • Tom Skerritt *Zach Bergstrom* • Barry Primus *Brennan* ■ *Dir* Harry Winer • *Scr* WW Wicket, Casey T Mitchell, from a story by Patrick Bailey, Larry B Williams

Spacehunter: Adventures in the Forbidden Zone ★★ 15

Science-fiction adventure
1983 · US · Colour · 86min

In this messy jump on the science-fiction bandwagon, galactic adventurer Peter Strauss aims to rescue cosmic travellers held prisoner by an evil man-machine on the plague-ridden planet of Terra 11. Directed with a weary eye by Lamont Johnson, the feeble script gives Strauss's bratty sidekick Molly Ringwald nothing to do, but the sheer force of Michael Ironside's personality creates a hissable villain. AJ

Peter Strauss *Wolff* • Molly Ringwald *Niki* • Ernie Hudson *Washington* • Andrea Marcovicci *Chalmers* • Michael Ironside *Overdog McNabb* • Beeson Carroll *Grandma Patterson* ■ *Dir* Lamont Johnson • *Scr* David Preston, Edith Rey, Dan Goldberg, Len Blum, from a story by Stewart Harding, Jean LaFleur

The Spaceman and King Arthur ★★★ U

Adventure　1979 · US/UK · Colour · 89min

Also known, with delightful Disney whimsy, as *Unidentified Flying Oddball*, this reworking of Mark Twain's *A Connecticut Yankee in King Arthur's Court* has a frantic charm and provides a chance to see the desperately amiable Jim Dale as a baddie. The tale involves Nasa technician Dennis Dugan who, along with his lookalike robot, ends up in aristocratic Camelot with an engagingly silly King Arthur (Kenneth More) and John Le Mesurier as a hesitant Sir Gawain. TH

Dennis Dugan *Tom Trimble* • Jim Dale *Sir Mordred* • Ron Moody *Merlin* • Kenneth More *King Arthur* • John Le Mesurier *Sir Gawain* • Rodney Bewes *Clarence* • Sheila White *Alisande* • Robert Beatty *Senator Milburn* ■ *Dir* Russ Mayberry • *Scr* Don Tait, from the novel *A Connecticut Yankee in King Arthur's Court* by Mark Twain

Spaceways ★ U

Science-fiction fantasy 1953 · UK · BW · 73min

Why did anybody who read the radio play on which this is based think it was worth doing anything with it other than hurl it across the room? The plot has leads Howard Duff and Eva Bartok blasting off in pursuit of a satellite to prove Duff's innocence following an accusation of double murder. Terence Fisher's funereal pace kills this cheaply-made picture stone dead long before the dénouement. DP *DVD*

Howard Duff *Stephen Mitchell* • Eva Bartok *Lisa Frank* • Alan Wheatley *Smith* • Philip Leaver *Dr Keppler* • Michael Medwin *Toby Andrews* ■ *Dir* Terence Fisher • *Scr* Paul Tabori, Richard Landau, from the radio play by Charles Eric Maine

La Spagnola ★★ 15

Period comedy drama
2001 · Aus · Colour · 86min

Making his directorial debut, Australian actor Steve Jacobs merits praise for attempting such an ambitious enterprise as this florid melodrama, especially as it's played out almost entirely in Spanish and Italian. However, he errs in allowing Lola Marceli to give a spitfiring performance as the wronged wife whose desire to exact revenge on husband Simon Palomares's Aussie mistress (Helen Thomson) is a source of acute embarrassment to her gawky teenage daughter (Alice Ansara). Bravura stuff, but too brash to engross. DP English, Spanish, Italian +subtitles. *DVD*

Lola Marceli *Lola* • Alice Ansara *Lucia* • Lourdes Bardolomé *Manola* • Alex Dimitriades *Stefano* • Simon Palomares *Ricardo* • Silvio Ofria *Bruno* • Helen Thomson *Wendy* ■ *Dir* Steve Jacobs • *Scr* Anna Maria Monticelli [Anna Jemison]

Spanglish ★★★★ 12

Comedy drama　2004 · US · Colour · 125min

Spanish and English-speaking cultures collide to poignant effect in this engaging film that's anchored by strong performances. Mexican single mother Paz Vega becomes housekeeper to a rich but troubled Los Angeles couple (played by Adam Sandler and Téa Leoni). At first unable to communicate in English, she's thrown into an alien world, whose emotional mechanics she finds hard to understand. But it's Sandler's turn as the unhappy husband that's the real surprise, as he is both effortlessly natural and quietly charming. SF Swearing, sex scenes. *DVD*

Adam Sandler *John Clasky* • Téa Leoni *Deborah Clasky* • Paz Vega *Flor* • Cloris Leachman *Evelyn* • Shelbie Bruce *Cristina* • Sarah Steele *Bernice* • Ian Hyland *Georgie* ■ *Dir/Scr* James L Brooks

Spanish Fly ★★ 15

Comedy　1975 · UK/Sp/Can · Colour · 81min

Beloved comic actors Leslie Phillips and Terry-Thomas had definitely seen better days when they co-starred in this silly British sex farce. It sees Phillips encounter old school pal Thomas on sunny Menorca, as the cunning cad tries to flog off cheap plonk to the local tavernas. But then an aphrodisiac is added to the brew. This bawdy nonsense from the 1970s may not be as dire as the *On the Buses* movies, but it's not especially amusing and, despite the stars' consummate charm, looks awfully dated now. JA *DVD*

Leslie Phillips *Mike Scott* • Terry-Thomas *Sir Percy de Courcy* • Graham Armitage *Perkins* • Nadiuska *Julie* • Frank Thornton *Dr Johnson* ■ *Dir* Bob Kellett • *Scr* Robert Ryerson, from a story by Peter James, Kent Walwin, from the play *Die Spanische Fliege* by Franz Arnold [uncredited], José Luis Martínez Mollá [uncredited] • *Music* Ron Goodwin

The Spanish Gardener ★★★ U

Drama　1956 · UK · Colour · 91min

Dirk Bogarde posted notice that he was much more than Rank's "Mr Charm" in this brooding drama. Although it was supposed to be buried safely beneath the surface, the film's homosexual subtext is clearly detectable as diplomat Michael Hordern comes to resent his son's burgeoning relationship with gardener Bogarde. Thanks to Christopher Challis's sultry cinematography, director Philip Leacock is able to convey the rising emotional temperature of the action, while also coaxing a creditable performance from young Jon Whiteley. DP *DVD*

Dirk Bogarde *Jose* • Jon Whiteley *Nicholas Brande* • Michael Hordern *Harrington Brande* • Cyril Cusack *Garcia* • Maureen Swanson *Maria* • Lyndon Brook *Robert Burton* • Josephine Griffin *Carol Burton* • Bernard Lee *Leighton Bailey* ■ *Dir* Philip Leacock • *Scr* Lesley Storm, John Bryan, from the novel by AJ Cronin

The Spanish Main ★★ U

Swashbuckling adventure
1945 · US · Colour · 95min

This hopelessly inadequate swashbuckler is partially redeemed by its ravishing 1940s Technicolor, used to best effect when photographing red-headed Maureen O'Hara, who here proves more than a match for leading man Paul Henreid. Walter Slezak makes a splendidly corrupt villain, but director Frank Borzage hasn't a clue how to buckle a swash. TS

Maureen O'Hara *Francisca* • Paul Henreid *Laurent Van Horn, "The Barracuda"* • Walter Slezak *Don Alvarado* • Binnie Barnes *Anne Bonny* • John Emery *Maria Da Bilar* • Barton MacLane *Captain Benjamin Black* • JM Kerrigan *Pillory* ■ *Dir* Frank Borzage • *Scr* George Worthing Yates, Herman J Mankiewicz, from a story by Aeneas MacKenzie

The Spanish Prisoner ★★★★ PG

Mystery thriller　1997 · US · Colour · 105min

David Mamet returns to the themes of his first film (*House of Games*) in this adroit fable about the simple-mindedness of complex-minded executives. Campbell Scott is the corporation inventor, creator of "the Process", who's concerned about his employer's integrity. Cue a smoothly plausible Steve Martin and an elaborate and totally convincing con trick played on us as well as the hapless Scott. This is a tale told with all the entertaining sleight of hand of a three-card trick: now you see it, now you don't. TH *DVD*

Campbell Scott *Joe Ross* • Steve Martin *Jimmy Dell* • Rebecca Pidgeon *Susan Ricci* • Ben Gazzara *Joe Klein* • Ricky Jay *George Lang* • Felicity Huffman *Pat McCune* ■ *Dir/Scr* David Mamet

Spanking the Monkey ★★★★ 18

Drama　1994 · US · Colour · 95min

This low-budget cult hit caused a big stir owing to its story of incest between mother and son. It was not so much the subject matter but the movie's sanguine, almost blasé attitude towards its theme that offended many, yet this view profoundly misunderstood an original and daring film. A largely unknown cast brings great assurance and subtlety to an often funny, sometimes moving and always intriguing look at the essential complexities between parent and child. SH Swearing, sex scenes, drug abuse, nudity. *DVD*

Jeremy Davies *Raymond Aibelli* • Alberta Watson *Susan Aibelli* • Benjamin Hendrickson *Tom Aibelli* • Carla Gallo *Toni Peck* • Matthew Puckett *Nicky* • Zak Orth *Curtis* • Josh Weinstein *Joel* ■ *Dir/Scr* David O Russell

Spare a Copper ★★ U

Second World War comedy
1940 · UK · BW · 74min

Wartime audiences were grateful for any relief from the conflict and this did very tidy business at the box office, thanks largely to the jokes at the expense of the special constabulary. But the story, in which George Formby confounds a gang of Nazi saboteurs, is too far-fetched, and there were mutterings in high places that the depiction of the enemy as such easily defeated dolts could lull audiences into a false sense of security. DP

George Formby *George Carter* • Dorothy Hyson *Jane Grey* • Bernard Lee *Jake* • John Warwick *Shaw* • Warburton Gamble *Sir Robert Dyer* • John Turnbull *Inspector Richards* • George Merritt (1) *Edward Brewster* ■ *Dir* John Paddy Carstairs • *Scr* Roger Macdougall, Basil Dearden, Austin Melford

Spare Parts ★★★ 15

Drama　2003 · Slovenia · Colour · 86min

The gross iniquity of people-trafficking should never be diminished, but writer/director Damjan Kozole's bleak drama suggests that otherwise decent individuals can sometimes enter into this desperate trade, from motives other than naked greed. Former Slovenian speedway champion Peter Musevski's fall from grace, for example, followed the death of his wife from cancer. And his young apprentice Aljosa Kovacic demonstrates a compassion that stands in stark contrast to the exploitation of the pitiless thugs who force migrant Aleksandra Balmazovic into prostituting herself. Uncomfortable, but provocative. DP Slovenian +subtitles. Swearing.

Peter Musevski *Ludvik* • Aljosa Kovacic *Rudi* • Primoz Petkovsek *Rajc* • Valter Dragan *Drago* • Aleksandra Balmazovic *Angela* • Vladimir Vlaskalic *Geri* • Verica Nedeska *Ilinka* ■ *Dir/Scr* Damjan Kozole

Spare the Rod ★★★

Drama　1961 · UK · BW · 92min

Although he didn't make many films, Max Bygraves is a surprisingly sympathetic screen presence in this docudramatic story about a benevolent teacher in a tough inner-city school. Of course, he's not in the same league as those old pros Donald Pleasence and Geoffrey Keen, who give completely credible performances as the wishy-washy headmaster and the staffroom tyrant respectively. A young Richard O'Sullivan is his trademark perky self as a cheeky pupil. DP

Max Bygraves *John Saunders* • Donald Pleasence *Mr Jenkins* • Geoffrey Keen *Arthur Gregory* • Betty McDowall *Ann Collins* • Peter Reynolds *Alec Murray* • Jean Anderson *Mrs Pond* • Eleanor Summerfield *Mrs Harkness* • Richard O'Sullivan *Fred Harkness* ■ *Dir* Leslie Norman • *Scr* John Cresswell, from the novel by Michael Croft

Sparkle ★★★★ 15

Romantic comedy drama
2006 · UK · Colour · 99min

The directing/writing team of Neil Hunter and Tom Hunsinger (*Lawless Heart*) scores again with this emotionally rich tragicomedy. Shaun Evans (*Endeavour*) plays Liverpool chancer Sam, who moves to London with his aspiring chanteuse mum (Lesley Manville). There, he begins an affair with a PR boss (Stockard Channing) before falling for her estranged daughter (Amanda Ryan). Crackling with wry wit and bittersweet wisdom, it builds to a hugely affecting payoff **AJ**

Stockard Channing *Sheila* • Shaun Evans *Sam Sparks* • Anthony Head *Tony* • Bob Hoskins *Vince* • Lesley Manville *Jill* • Amanda Ryan *Kate* • John Shrapnel *Bernie* ■ *Dir* Neil Hunter, Tom Hunsinger • *Scr* Tom Hunsinger, Neil Hunter • *Cinematographer* Sean Van Hales

Sparkle ★★ 12
Musical drama 2012 · US · Colour · 111min

As swansongs go, this last film appearance by Whitney Houston was bound to be a disappointment. It was rushed into cinemas in mid-2012 after Houston's sudden death, and the haste shows. Houston is a wealthy mother to three talented daughters who perform songs composed by one of them, the eponymous Sparkle (2002 *American Idol* winner Jordin Sparks). The backstage drama that ensues includes a drug-induced domestic violence subplot, turning this into a pale imitation of *Dreamgirls*. What everyone's waiting for is the belter from Houston and when her big number comes, it's sadly underwhelming. The 1960s period detail is fabulous, however – just look at that hair and those dresses. **SuR** Some violence, swearing, racist language. **DVD**

Jordin Sparks *Sparkle* • Whitney Houston *Emma* • Derek Luke *Stix* • Mike Epps *Satin* • Carmen Ejogo *Sister* ■ *Dir* Salim Akil • *Scr* Mara Brock Akil, from the 1976 film by Joel Schumacher, Howard Rosenman

Sparks and Embers ★★ 15
Romantic comedy 2014 · UK · Colour · 84min

Kris Marshall (from TV's *Death in Paradise*) and French actress Annelise Hesme play exes who, six months after their break-up, meet up and reminisce about their relationship during an evening stroll along London's South Bank. The movie clearly strives for a *Before Sunrise/Before Sunset* sort of vibe. But Marshall and Hesme are no Ethan Hawke and Julie Delpy: there's not the chemistry. But it is a mildly diverting confection for a rainy day. **DA** Swearing, sexual references.

Kris Marshall *Tom Sanger* • Annelise Hesme *Eloise Martin* • Waleed Akhtar *Tariq Haq* • Valda Aviks *Rosa* • Sean Baker *Kenneth Fenton* ■ *Dir/Scr* Gavin Boyter

Sparrow ★ 12
Period drama 1993 · It/Ger · Colour · 102min

Franco Zeffirelli's most vilified film is set in the mid-1850s and tells the story of a young girl who enters a convent. A cholera outbreak results in her returning to her father's villa, where she falls in love with handsome young Johnathon Schaech. The plague over, she returns to the convent to battle with her religious calling and her love for Schaech. Zeffirelli lets rip with full-blown theatrics, but the story and the inexperienced leads are not enough to carry the film. **BB**

Angela Bettis *Maria* • Johnathon Schaech *Nino* • Sinead Cusack *Matilde* • John Castle *Giuseppe* • Vanessa Redgrave *Sister Agata* • Sara-Jane Alexander *Annetta* • Frank Finlay *Father Nunzio* ■ *Dir* Franco Zeffirelli • *Scr* Franco Zeffirelli, Allan Baker, from the novel *A Sparrow's Tale* by Giovanni Verga

Sparrow ★★★ 12
Crime drama 2008 · HK · Colour · 86min

Hong Kong maestro Johnnie To pays handsome tribute to 1960s Cantonese cinema with this crime drama that has all the lyricism, fluency and precision of a musical. Pickpocket Kei (Simon Yam) falls for the charms of gangster's moll Chung Chun-lei (Kelly Lin), who convinces him to disregard the advice of his criminal confederates, only to then systematically dupe each man in turn. Played out to a bluesy jazz score the action is lushly

photographed and slickly choreographed, but the visuals occasionally threaten to overwhelm a slender storyline. But the real pleasure lies in the set pieces, including an intricate ballet of a pickpocket contest beneath umbrellas on a rain-soaked pedestrian crossing. **DP** Cantonese, Mandarin +subtitles. Some violence. **DVD**

Simon Yam *Kei* • Kelly Lin *Chung Chun-lei* • Lam Ka Tung *Bo* • Lo Hoi-pang *Mr Fu* • Law Wing-cheong *Sak* • Kenneth Cheung *Mac* ■ *Dir* Johnnie To • *Scr* Milkway Creative Team, Chan Kin Chung, Fung Chih-chiang

Sparrows ★★★★
Silent melodrama 1926 · US · BW · 81min

A near classic of the silent era, this features 1920s superstar Mary Pickford in her last juvenile role. She plays Molly, the leader of a ragtag bunch of orphans treated as slaves by evil Mr Grimes on his farm in the Deep South swamplands. When a gang in league with Grimes kidnaps the daughter of a rich man and hides her on his farm, Molly leads her flock out through alligator-infested waters as the police close in. Although the film is poorly paced, Pickford is as touchingly poignant as ever in an American-style Grimm fairy tale. **AJ**

Mary Pickford *Mama Mollie* • Gustav von Seyffertitz *Grimes* • Roy Stewart (1) *Richard Wayne* • Mary Louise Miller *Doris Wayne* ■ *Dir* William Beaudine • *Scr* C Gardner Sullivan, George Marion Jr (titles), from a story by Winifred Dunn

Sparrows Can't Sing ★ PG
Comedy drama 1962 · UK · BW · 88min

You can't capture the sights and sounds of East End life simply by packing the cast with cockneys and touting a camera round the streets of Stepney. James Booth is eminently resistible as the sailor searching for wife Barbara Windsor and her bus-driving fancy man, George Sewell. Missing both social statement and fond characterisation, director Joan Littlewood has succeeded only in being patronising. **DP** **DVD** Blu-ray

James Booth *Charlie Gooding* • Barbara Windsor *Maggie Gooding* • Roy Kinnear *Fred Gooding* • Avis Bunnage *Bridgie Gooding* • Brian Murphy *Jack* • George Sewell *Bert* ■ *Dir* Joan Littlewood • *Scr* Stephen Lewis, Joan Littlewood, from the play by Stephen Lewis • *Music/lyrics* Lionel Bart

Spartacus ★★★★★ PG
Historical epic 1960 · US · Colour · 196min

The restored version of this Roman epic about the famous slave revolt has additional blood, more lingering death agonies of Kirk Douglas on the cross and a risible bath scene with Laurence Olivier and Tony Curtis, which was originally cut because of its alleged homosexual innuendo. Despite the film's length and overemphasis in the latter half on wordy speeches from Douglas, the action leading up to the revolt of the gladiators is brilliantly re-created, with Peter Ustinov, Charles Laughton and Olivier addictively greedy scene-stealers. The early sequences, set in the Libyan desert, were directed by Anthony Mann, who was fired by Douglas and replaced by Stanley Kubrick. **AT** Blu-ray

Kirk Douglas *Spartacus* • Laurence Olivier *Marcus Crassus* • Tony Curtis *Antoninus* • Jean Simmons *Varinia* • Charles Laughton *Gracchus* • Peter Ustinov *Batiatus* • John Gavin *Julius Caesar* • Nina Foch *Helena Glabrus* ■ *Dir* Stanley Kubrick • *Scr* Dalton Trumbo, from the novel by Howard Fast • *Cinematographer* Russell Metty • *Music* Alex North • *Costume Designers* Bill Thomas, Valles

Spartan ★★★ 15
Political thriller 2004 · US/Ger · Colour · 102min

David Mamet's sharp political thriller is a typically intelligent, yet irritatingly self-conscious film. The set-up is intriguingly simple: the daughter (Kristen Bell) of a high-ranking US official goes missing, and the Secret Service puts hardman Val Kilmer on the case. Though less stylised than usual, the rhythms and cadences in Mamet's dialogue always take some getting used to. Occasionally, these verbal flourishes come

across as po-faced, deflating the tension, but they also give the story a hypnotic quality. Visually, this is Mamet's best film, with a clean, economical style. **GM** Swearing, violence. **DVD**

Val Kilmer *Robert Scott* • Derek Luke *Curtis* • William H Macy *Stoddard* • Ed O'Neill *Burch* • Kristen Bell *Laura Newton* • Saïd Taghmaoui *Tariq Asani* • Linda Kimbrough *Donny* • Tia Texada *Jackie Black* ■ *Dir/Scr* David Mamet

Spawn ★★ 12
Supernatural horror adventure 1997 · US · Colour · 92min

This live-action comic book spin-off promised to duplicate the grim and extremely violent images that were the bestselling comic's hallmarks, but ended up being distributed in a toned-down "12" certificate version; a "15" certificate "Director's Cut" followed later. Michael Jai White plays Al Simmons, a special forces assassin betrayed by boss Martin Sheen and left to fry in a burning chemical factory. He is revived as Spawn, who becomes caught up in a plot to trigger the apocalypse. Dark in tone and crammed with computer-generated effects, it found a cult popularity and spawned a follow-up animated series. **JF** **DVD**

Michael Jai White *Al Simmons/Spawn* • Martin Sheen *Jason Wynn* • John Leguizamo *Clown* • Theresa Randle *Wanda* • Nicol Williamson *Cogliostro* • Melinda Clarke *Jessica Priest* • DB Sweeney *Terry Fitzgerald* ■ *Dir* Mark AZ Dippé • *Scr* Alan McElroy, from a story by Mark AZ Dippé, Alan McElroy, from the comic book by Todd McFarlane

Spawn of the North ★★★
Period adventure drama 1938 · US · BW · 105min

Henry Fonda stars as the skipper of an American fishing crew in Alaska, circa 1890, whose best buddy (George Raft) deserts him for some villainous Russian poachers, led by Akim Tamiroff. It's an entertaining action adventure, with some high drama, a little romance, satisfying heroics, and a convincing John Barrymore as a heavy-drinking newspaper reporter. A big hit in its day, superbly directed and with the authentic exteriors filmed on location in Alaska. **RK**

George Raft *Tyler Dawson* • Henry Fonda *Jim Kimmerlee* • Dorothy Lamour *Nicky Duval* • Akim Tamiroff *Red Skain* • John Barrymore *Windy Turlon* • Louise Platt *Dian Turlon* • Lynne Overman *Jackson* • Fuzzy Knight *Lefty Jones* ■ *Dir* Henry Hathaway • *Scr* Jules Furthman, Talbot Jennings, from the novel by Florence Barrett Willoughby

Speak Easily ★★★★ U
Comedy 1932 · US · BW · 81min

When Buster Keaton gave up independent production and signed with MGM in 1928 it was a move he later considered the worst of his career. But of the eight sound films he made for the studio, this was his favourite. It features Keaton as a sheltered university professor who decides to see life and becomes involved with a run-down theatrical troupe. Keaton's co-star Jimmy Durante has some fine moments, and though Keaton disliked working with the brash comic, the two became good friends. The film is a hit-and-miss affair but Keaton is superb as the innocent in a world of showbiz sharpies. **TV** **DVD**

Buster Keaton *Prof Post* • Jimmy Durante *James* • Ruth Selwyn *Pansy Peets* • Thelma Todd *Eleanor Espere* • Hedda Hopper *Mrs Peets* • William Pawley *Griffo* • Sidney Toler *Stage director* • Lawrence Grant *Dr Bolton* ■ *Dir* Edward Sedgwick • *Scr* Ralph Spence, Laurence E Johnson, from the novel by Clarence Budington Kelland

Speaking Parts ★★ 15
Drama 1989 · Can · Colour · 87min

Gabrielle Rose watches videos of her dead brother while pursuing a movie project about his life. She gets involved with aspiring actor Michael McManus who, coincidentally, resembles her sibling, and is himself a lust object for lovelorn Arsinée Khanjian. Writer/director Atom Egoyan

successfully connects the characters in his strange story, but in focusing on intellectual dissection the director sacrifices the emotional payoff essential in this story of a three-way relationship. **JM** Nudity. **DVD** Blu-ray

Michael McManus (2) *Lance* • Arsinée Khanjian *Lisa* • Gabrielle Rose *Clara* • Tony Nardi *Eddy* • David Hemblen *Producer* • Patricia Collins *Housekeeper* ■ *Dir/Scr* Atom Egoyan

Special Agent ★★
Crime drama 1935 · US · BW · 77min

"Miss Davis is too valuable a performer to be doing stories such as this one," said *Variety*, slamming this crime drama which Warners "encouraged" her to do. Bette Davis plays the secretary to a mobster, Ricardo Cortez, whose operation is being investigated by plucky newspaper man George Brent. Davis takes a shine to Brent and gives him secrets. **AT**

Bette Davis *Julie Carston* • George Brent *Bill Bradford* • Ricardo Cortez *Nick Cartson* • Joseph Sawyer [Joe Sawyer] *Rich* • Joseph Crehan *Chief of Police* • Henry O'Neill *District Attorney* • Irving Pichel *US District Attorney* ■ *Dir* William Keighley • *Scr* Laird Doyle, Abem Finkel, from an idea by Martin Mooney

A Special Day ★★
Period drama 1977 · It/Can · Colour · 105min

Marcello Mastroianni earned an Oscar nomination for performing so subtly against type in this contrived romance dressed up as a sweeping statement about the human condition and Italy's Fascist past. It's beautifully set up, with Mastroianni 's suicidal gay radio announcer and Sophia Loren's harassed mother of six meeting in a Roman tenement on the day in 1938 that Mussolini first played host to Hitler. But the symbolism is heavy-handed and the dialogue drips with portentous pronouncements. **DP**

Sophia Loren *Antonietta* • Marcello Mastroianni *Gabriele* • John Vernon *Emanuele* • Françoise Berd *Concierge* ■ *Dir* Ettore Scola • *Scr* Ettore Scola, Ruggero Maccari, Maurizio Costanzo, from a story by Ettore Scola

Special Delivery ★★ U
Political satirical comedy 1955 · US/W Ger · BW · 86min

Even when lumbered with a banal script and mediocre performances from everyone but Joseph Cotten, director John Brahm can't help but conjure atmosphere in this story of an American diplomat being assigned behind the Iron Curtain, where he has to cope with an abandoned baby. **TH**

Joseph Cotten *Jonathan Adams* • Eva Bartok *Sonia* • René Deltgen *Kovak* • Lexford Richards *Wayne* ■ *Dir* John Brahm • *Scr* Philip Reisman Jr, Dwight Taylor, from an idea by Geva Radvanyi

Special Delivery ★★★ 15
Crime comedy 1976 · US · Colour · 94min

Surprisingly, this Bo Svenson vehicle is a neat little caper movie, with Svenson doing a respectable job as a bank robber who stashes his loot in the mail while fleeing the police. But the real star of the movie is Cybill Shepherd, excellent as the woman who witnesses Svenson at the mailbox. The strength of the movie comes from the many interesting interactions the central characters have with other parties, all realistically done. **KB**

Bo Svenson *Jack Murdock* • Cybill Shepherd *Mary Jane* • Tom Atkins *Zabelski* • Sorrell Booke *Bank Manager* • Hubert Zane • Gerrit Graham *Swivot* • Michael C Gwynne *Carl Graff* • Jeff Goldblum *Snake* ■ *Dir* Paul Wendkos • *Scr* Don Gazzaniga, Gil Ralston

Special Forces ★★★ 15
Action drama 2011 · Fr · Colour · 104min

An elite team of soldiers is called in to rescue a crusading French journalist from the Taliban in this pacey, beautifully photographed action drama. However, the unusual thing here is that it's French Special Forces – led by Djimon Hounsou – unleashing lethally efficient mayhem rather

S

than their British or American counterparts. Yes, the enemy is portrayed in broad strokes but the cracking action is grippingly realistic and there's some genuine heart, too, with the men's camaraderie refreshingly believable. JA English, French +subtitles. *DVD*

Diane Kruger *Elsa Casanova* • Djimon Hounsou *Kovax* • Benoît Magimel *Tic Tac* • Denis Ménochet *Lucas* • Raphaël Personnaz *Elias* • Alain Figlarz *Victor* • Raz Degan (1) *Ahmed Zaief* • Tcheky Karyo *Guezennec* ■ *Dir/Scr* Stéphane Rybojad

Special People ★★★★ 12A
Comedy drama 2007 · UK · Colour · 81min

In this sharp British comedy drama, a pretentious film-maker teaches a class of teenage wheelchair-users how to "capture reality". Dominic Coleman (who co-wrote the screenplay with director Justin Edgar) is brilliant as Jasper who, despite being a know-it-all, can only find work in a community outreach programme. His students are utterly nonplussed by his artistic musings along with his cringeworthy short film about life on a council estate. Alas, they're obliged to help him craft "a visual poem" during a madcap outing to the countryside, where he forces them up and down hillsides as a metaphor for their daily struggles. Ultimately, the film is a triumph of understated, heartfelt humour for Edgar, who expanded the material from his own award-winning short. SP

Dominic Coleman *Jasper* • Robyn Frampton *Jess* • Sasha Hardway *Anais* • Jason Maza *Dave* • David Proud *Scott* • Lucinda Raikes *Ann* ■ *Dir* Justin Edgar • *Scr* Justin Edgar, Dominic Coleman, from the short film by Edgar

Special (PX) – Specioprin Hydrochloride ★★★ 15
Drama 2006 · US · Colour · 77min

The special thing about *Special (PX)* is the energetic and enthusiastic performance of its star, Michael Rapaport. He plays Les Franken, a parking attendant and comic-book fan who volunteers for the trials of an experimental antidepressant. But the drug's psychotic side-effect makes Les believe that he has super powers. The film then flits back and forth between Les's new world, in which his super powers exist, and the "real" world, in which they don't. The movie is distinctly low budget, but marshals its limited resources. Special effects are sparing, but effectively used. But it's Rapaport's intense and committed performance that is truly to be treasured. DA *DVD*

Michael Rapaport *Les Franken* • Paul Blackthorne *Jonas Exiler* • Josh Peck *Joey* • Robert Baker *Everett* • Jack Kehler *Dr Dobson* • Alexandra Holden *Maggie* ■ *Dir/Scr* Hal Haberman, Jeremy Passmore

The Specialist ★★★ 18
Thriller 1994 · US · Colour · 105min

James Woods has a knack for spotting mediocre movies with roles that give him the chance to shine when his co-stars are floundering. This is a case in point, as he strides off with Luis Llosa's bomb thriller without even getting his hair mussed. Sylvester Stallone stars as an explosives expert and former colleague of Woods, who reality. He is hired by the mysterious Sharon Stone to avenge the death of her parents. The leads generate some sparks, but the film belongs to the supporting cast. DP Swearing, violence, sex scenes, nudity. *DVD*

Sylvester Stallone *Ray Quick* • Sharon Stone *May Munro* • James Woods *Ned Trent* • Rod Steiger *Joel Leon* • Eric Roberts *Tomas Leon* • Mario Ernesto Sanchez *Charlie* • Sergio Dore Jr *Strongarm* ■ *Dir* Luis Llosa • *Scr* Alexandra Seros, from the novels by John Shirley

The Specials ★ 18
Action fantasy spoof 2000 · US · Colour · 78min

This abysmal copy of superhero spoof *Mystery Men* features a day in the life of a team of downbeat crime-fighters. The joke is that these heroes, including Rob Lowe's Weevil and Jamie Kennedy's Amok, are less than special, meaning there's absolutely no

reason to want to spend time with them. The performances are weak, the profane dialogue is grating, the suburban locations are dreary and there aren't even any visual effects until the final minutes. JC *DVD*

Rob Lowe *The Weevil* • Jamie Kennedy *Amok* • Thomas Haden Church *The Strobe* • Paget Brewster *Ms Indestructible* • Kelly Coffield *Power Chick* • Judy Greer *Deadly Girl* • James Gunn (2) *Minute Man* ■ *Dir* Craig Mazin • *Scr* James Gunn

Species ★★★ 18
Science-fiction horror 1995 · US · Colour · 103min

Natasha Henstridge plays the dangerous spawn of combined alien and human DNA in director Roger Donaldson's sexy sci-fi shocker. Ben Kingsley, Michael Madsen and Alfred Molina are among the inept government scientists speaking daft dialogue as they attempt to track down the genetic engineering experiment gone awry. Nifty designs by surrealist HR Giger (who gave the extraterrestrial in *Alien* its incredible look) and some engaging tongue-in-cheek thrills go part way to disguising the fact that this is a clichéd B-movie. AJ Violence, sex scenes, swearing, nudity. *DVD* *BL*

Ben Kingsley *Fitch* • Michael Madsen *Press* • Alfred Molina *Arden* • Forest Whitaker *Dan* • Marg Helgenberger *Laura* • Natasha Henstridge *Sil* ■ *Dir* Roger Donaldson • *Scr* Dennis Feldman

Species II ★★★ 18
Science-fiction horror 1998 · US · Colour · 89min

Exploding heads, torso-bursting and computer-generated aliens in heat: it's all here in Peter Medak's science-fiction howler that continues the half-human/half-alien DNA experiment as a sex rampage saga. Far gorier and camper than the original film, this lascivious popcorn treat is a spectacularly lunatic shocker that revels in soft-core sleaze and grisly death. A second, straight-to-video sequel followed in 2004. AJ Sex scenes, swearing, violence. *DVD*

Michael Madsen *Press Lennox* • Natasha Henstridge *Eve* • Marg Helgenberger *Doctor Laura Baker* • Mykelti Williamson *Dennis Gamble* • George Dzundza *Colonel Carter Burgess Jr* • James Cromwell *Senator Ross* • Myriam Cyr *Anne Sampas* • Justin Lazard *Patrick Ross* ■ *Dir* Peter Medak • *Scr* Chris Brancato, from characters by Dennis Feldman

Species: the Awakening ★ 15
Science-fiction horror thriller 2007 · US · Colour · 94min

Another gorgeous lab-grown spawn of alien/human crossbreeding (Helena Mattsson) learns her true murderous nature in the barely competent straight-to-DVD third sequel in the horny hybrid saga. So off she goes to Mexico with "uncle" Ben Cross for a human DNA transfusion (from a crazy prostitute, naturally!) in the hope it will stop her libidinous slaughter episodes. Those bothering to look past the plentiful nudity will notice the worst performance, and fake Australian accent, coming from Dominic Keating (*Enterprise*) as Cross's unethical former partner. AJ Violence, swearing, sex scenes, nudity. *DVD*

Ben Cross *Tom Hollander* • Helena Mattsson *Miranda* • Edy Arellano *Calderón* • Marco Bacuzzi *Rinaldo* • Jan Bouda *Student 2* • Dominic Keating *Forbes McGuire* ■ *Dir* Nick Lyon • *Scr* Ben Ripley

Specter of the Rose ★★★
Comedy drama 1946 · US · BW · 90min

An unusual and ambitious undertaking by Ben Hecht – one of the sharpest writers in Hollywood – this film purports to be based in part on the ballet *Spectre de la Rose*. One suspects, however, that Nijinsky couldn't have been far from Hecht's mind in this tale of a progressively deranged dancer (Ivan Kirov) driven to attempt murder and suicide by the eponymous ballet. Admittedly "arty", the film is also camp, inventive and eccentric. RK

Judith Anderson *Madame La Sylph* • Michael Chekhov *Max "Poli" Polikoff* • Ivan Kirov *Andre Sanine* • Lionel Stander *Lionel Gans* • Ben Hecht *Waiter* ■ *Dir* Ben Hecht • *Scr* Ben Hecht, from his short story

Spectre ★★
Horror thriller 2006 · Sp · Colour · 77min

Ignorance, superstition and jealousy bring predictably tragic results in this handsome but underwhelming ghost story. Produced for Spanish TV, it sees a bereaved man (Jordi Dauder) return to his home village after 44 years away to confront disturbing events from his adolescence. SF Spanish +subtitles.

Juan José Ballesta *Young Tomas* • Natalia Millán *Moira* • Jordi Dauder *Adult Tomas* • Victoria Mora *Carmen* ■ *Dir* Mateo Gil • *Scr* Mateo Gil, Igor Legarreta

Spectre ★★★ 12
Spy adventure 2015 · US/UK · Colour · 142min

The box office-busting *Skyfall* gave director Sam Mendes a licence to take the James Bond franchise in any direction he wanted. And with *Spectre* he draws upon the ultimate foe to pull together Daniel Craig's three previous missions into one ambitious story arc. The interesting conceit here is that Bond discovers he has a personal connection to the leader of shadowy organisation Spectre, played with smirking relish by Christoph Waltz. Once again, Mendes succeeds in delivering a prestige picture on a huge scale. But the film over-congratulates itself with a surfeit of in-jokes and knowing references – and this game of Bond Bingo soon becomes a distraction. JH Violence, swearing. *DVD* *BL*

Daniel Craig *James Bond* • Christoph Waltz *Franz Oberhauser* • Léa Seydoux *Madeleine Swann* • Ralph Fiennes *M* • Ben Whishaw *Q* • Naomie Harris *Moneypenny* ■ *Dir* Sam Mendes • *Scr* John Logan, Neal Purvis, Robert Wade, Jez Butterworth, from a story by Logan, Purvis and Wade, from Ian Fleming's characters • *Cinematographer* Hoyte Van Hoytema

Speechless ★★★ 12
Romantic comedy 1994 · US · Colour · 94min

Bewilderingly, this starry comedy bypassed cinemas and went straight to video in this country. It's a shame, because it's a smart and sassy affair from director Ron Underwood. Michael Keaton and Geena Davis spark off each other nicely, playing a pair of rival political speech writers who fall in and out of love with each other while on the campaign trail. There are excellent supporting turns from Bonnie Bedelia and Christopher Reeve, plus some gentle fun at the expense of the American political system. JF Swearing. *DVD*

Michael Keaton *Kevin Vallick* • Geena Davis *Julia Mann* • Christopher Reeve *Bob Freed* • Bonnie Bedelia *Annette* • Ernie Hudson *Ventura* • Charles Martin Smith *Kratz* ■ *Dir* Ron Underwood • *Scr* Robert King

Speed ★★
Sports drama 1936 · US · BW · 65min

This minor B-movie about motor racing is notable only for the presence of James Stewart. He plays a test-car driver who, when not romancing the boss's daughter (Wendy Barrie), finds time to develop a high-speed carburettor to use in the Indianapolis 500. The film's depiction of an ultra-modern auto-plant in 1936 makes interesting viewing, but there is too much back projection. TV

James Stewart *Terry Martin* • Wendy Barrie *Jane Mitchell* • Ted Healy *Gadget* • Una Merkel *Josephine Sanderson* • Weldon Heyburn *Frank Lawson* • Patricia Wilder *Fanny Lane* • Ralph Morgan *Mr Dean* • Robert Livingston *George Saunders* ■ *Dir* Edwin L Marin • *Scr* Michael Fessier, from a story by Milton Krims, Larry Bachman

Speed ★★★★★ 15
Action thriller 1994 · US · Colour · 111min

This pure adrenaline-pumping entertainment of the highest order has action man Keanu Reeves and Sandra Bullock trapped on a crowded LA bus that

crazed extortionist Dennis Hopper has primed to explode if its speed falls below 50mph. Slipping smoothly into top gear from the nail-biting scene-setting opening, director Jan De Bont's "*Die Hard* on the Buses" moves into the fast lane with a nonstop barrage of nerve-jangling thrills and death-defying stunts. Outrageous, over-the-top and as exciting as can be. AJ Swearing, violence. *DVD* *BL*

Keanu Reeves *Jack Traven* • Dennis Hopper *Howard Payne* • Sandra Bullock *Annie* • Joe Morton *Captain McMahon* • Jeff Daniels *Harry* • Alan Ruck *Stephens* • Glenn Plummer *Jaguar owner* • Richard Lineback *Norwood* ■ *Dir* Jan De Bont • *Scr* Graham Yost

Speed 2: Cruise Control ★★ PG
Action thriller 1997 · US · Colour · 119min

Director Jan De Bont's listlessly routine sequel to his own powerhouse original is a massive disappointment. Sandra Bullock reprises her role as Annie Porter who, with cop boyfriend Jason Patric, boards a luxury cruise liner for a holiday. Before you can say "Where's Keanu Reeves gone?", disgruntled computer genius Willem Dafoe puts his extortion plan into operation and turns their voyage into a titanic nightmare. AJ Swearing, some violence. *DVD* *BL*

Sandra Bullock *Annie* • Jason Patric *Alex* • Willem Dafoe *Geiger* • Temuera Morrison *Juliano* • Brian McCardie *Merced* • Christine Firkins *Drew* • Michael G Hagerty *Harvey* ■ *Dir* Jan De Bont • *Scr* Randall McCormick, Jeff Nathanson, from a story by Jan DeBont, Randall McCormick, from characters by Graham Yost

Speed Racer ★★★★ PG
Fantasy action adventure 2008 · US · Colour · 129min

The writer/directors of the *Matrix* trilogy, the Wachowski brothers, serve up a phenomenal reinvention of the cult 1960s *anime* TV series with this turbo-charged action adventure. It stars Emile Hirsch as racing driver Speed, who uncovers a race-fixing scam when he turns down an offer to drive for a large corporation. With the help of his parents (John Goodman and Susan Sarandon) and girlfriend Trixie (Christina Ricci), our hero sets out to prove that sportsmanship lives in an era of big business manipulation. Going beyond the mixing of live action and CGI, the Wachowskis create a vibrant Day-Glo world where nostalgic pasts and the highest-tech futures co-exist in a stunning range of cinematic styles. The high-calibre casting, particularly Roger Allam's delicious villain, ground the thrilling antics in a striking version of reality, one that tailspins the action genre into another dimension. AJ *DVD* *BL*

Emile Hirsch *Speed Racer* • Christina Ricci *Trixie* • John Goodman *Pops Racer* • Susan Sarandon *Mom Racer* • Matthew Fox *Racer X* • Roger Allam *Royalton* • Paulie Litt *Spritle* • Benno Fürmann *Inspector Detector* • Scott Porter *Rex Racer* ■ *Dir* The Wachowski Brothers [Lilly Wachowski], The Wachowski Brothers [Lana Wachowski] • *Scr* Andy and Larry Wachowski, from the TV series by Tatsuo Yoshida

Speedway ★ U
Musical drama 1968 · US · Colour · 90min

This bland, cheap and hopelessly unhip musical was made when both the recording and screen careers of Elvis Presley were at rock bottom. Recently wed to Priscilla Beaulieu, the rock 'n' roll king seems to be going through the motions as a stock car driver pursued by income tax investigator Nancy Sinatra. DM *DVD*

Elvis Presley *Steve Grayson* • Nancy Sinatra *Susan Jacks* • Bill Bixby *Kenny Donford* • Gale Gordon *RW Hepworth* • William Schallert *Abel Esterlake* • Victoria Meyerink *Ellie Esterlake* • Ross Hagen *Paul Dado* ■ *Dir* Norman Taurog • *Scr* Phillip Shuken

Speedy ★★★ U
Silent comedy 1928 · US · BW · 86min

Harold Lloyd's silent swan song is something of a disappointment considering

the glorious high-risk clowning that had gone before. Still nurturing go-getting ambitions, his baseball-crazy soda jerk takes on some ruthless traffic tycoons after they try to drive the last horse-drawn trolley bus off the road. Naturally, love is at the heart of Harold's heroism, although the romantic outing to Coney Island lacks both the period charm of the New York street scenes and the comic zest of the chase finale. DP
DVD *BL*

Harold Lloyd *Harold "Speedy" Swift* • Ann Christy *Jane Dillon* • Bert Woodruff *Pop Dillon* • Brooks Benedict *Steven Carter* • George Herman "Babe" Ruth [Babe Ruth] • ■ *Dir* Ted Wilde • *Scr* John Grey, Lex Neal, Howard Emmett Rogers, Jay Howe

The Spell ★ 15
Supernatural drama 2009 · UK · Colour · 87min

A young girl meets with scepticism when her ex-boyfriend has her put under a hex in this micro-budget British horror. Lead actress Rebecca Pitkin tries her best, but the minimal special-effects budget – which just about stretches to a shaking chest of drawers and intermittent vocal effects – generates not a frisson of terror, while the absurdly overcooked score, painfully poor performances and unspeakable dialogue provoke gales of unintentional laughter instead. A strong candidate for the worst British film of the noughties. TJ Swearing, nudity. *DVD*

Rebecca Pitkin *Jenny* • Pietro Herrera *Rick* • Amber Hodgkiss *Vicky* • Julia Curle *Clare* • Laura O'Donoughue *Kate* • Paul Hurstfield *Ian* ■ *Dir/Scr* Owen Carey Jones

Spellbinder ★ 18
Thriller 1988 · US · Colour · 94min

American TV actor Timothy Daly (brother of *Cagney & Lacey*'s Tyne) stars in this silly and completely unthrilling chiller about a lawyer who becomes obsessed with a woman (Kelly Preston) on the run from an evil coven. A disaster. JB

Timothy Daly *Jeff Mills* • Kelly Preston *Miranda Reed* • Rick Rossovich *Derek Clayton* • Audra Lindley *Mrs White* • Anthony Crivello *Aldys* • Diana Bellamy *Grace Woods* • Cary-Hiroyuki Tagawa *Lieutenant Lee* ■ *Dir* Janet Greek • *Scr* Tracey Torme

Spellbound ★★★ PG
Psychological thriller 1945 · US · BW · 109min

In his eagerness to make the first serious film about psychoanalysis, Alfred Hitchcock so diluted the fantastical elements in Francis Beeding's novel *The House of Dr Edwardes*, all that remained was a melodramatic plot and an awful lot of psychobabble. Not even dream sequences designed by Salvador Dali could enliven the turgid script, made all the less palatable by the robotic performance of Gregory Peck as the amnesiac trying to unravel his troubled past with the help of sympathetic shrink Ingrid Bergman. Hitch himself was disappointed with the picture, but there are enough masterly touches to keep your attention. DP *DVD*

Ingrid Bergman *Dr Constance Peterson* • Gregory Peck *John Ballantrae/Dr Anthony Edwardes* • Michael Chekhov *Dr Alex Brulov* • Leo G Carroll *Dr Murchison* • Rhonda Fleming *Mary Carmichael* • John Emery *Dr Fleurot* ■ *Dir* Alfred Hitchcock • *Scr* Ben Hecht, Angus MacPhail, from the novel *The House of Dr Edwardes* by Francis Beeding

Spellbound ★★★★ U
Documentary 2002 · US · Colour · 92min

This quirky documentary follows eight teenagers as they compete in the 1999 American National Spelling Bee. While the competition is exciting enough, it's the kids' differing backgrounds that give this film its real heart. From the daughter of Mexican immigrants whose father speaks no English to a gawky farmboy whose parents struggle to understand their talented offspring, this is really a story of the trials and occasional triumphs of what it's like to be young and "different" in America. First-time documentary director Jeff Blitz makes the odd forgivable lapse – trying to cover too many children and structuring the film in an

unimaginatively linear way – this is still a fascinating account of a slice of Americana. AS *DVD*

■ *Dir* Jeff Blitz [Jeffrey Blitz]

Spencer's Mountain ★★★
Drama 1963 · US · Colour · 119min

Although it was a commercial success, Henry Fonda loathed this cosy melodrama. With Fonda playing the church-hating head of a Wyoming hill family, it's not immediately apparent that Earl Hamner Jr's novel also provided the inspiration for that enduringly popular TV show, *The Waltons*. The connection becomes clearer as James MacArthur's character Clayboy struggles to choose between his education and his inheritance. As mom and grandpa, Maureen O'Hara and Donald Crisp provide expert support. DP

Henry Fonda *Clay Spencer* • Maureen O'Hara *Olivia* • James MacArthur *Clayboy Spencer* • Donald Crisp *Grandpa Spencer* • Wally Cox *Preacher Goodson* • Mimsy Farmer *Claris Coleman* • Virginia Gregg *Miss Parker* ■ *Dir* Delmer Daves • *Scr* Delmer Daves, from the novel by Earl Hamner Jr

Spendthrift ★★★
Comedy 1936 · US · BW · 77min

Millionaire playboy Henry Fonda is temporarily out of cash but can't bring himself to break the news to mercenary spouse Mary Brian. Eventually he gets to see how the other half lives when he takes a job as a sports announcer and falls for Pat Paterson. Action director Raoul Walsh has a light enough touch, and the streak of social conscience – very necessary at the time – is eased in almost painlessly. What's so delightfully manipulative about the movie is the way it shows us how the rich live, spiking those lush vistas with Depression era home truths. TH

Henry Fonda *Townsend Middleton* • Pat Paterson *Valerie "Boots" O'Connell* • Mary Brian *Sally Barnaby* • George Barbier *Uncle Morton Middleton* • Edward Brophy *Bill* • Richard Carle *Popsy* • JM Kerrigan *Pop O'Connell* • Spencer Charters *Col Barnaby* ■ *Dir* Raoul Walsh • *Scr* Raoul Walsh, Bert Hanlon, from the novella by Eric Hatch

Spetters ★★★★ 18
Drama 1980 · Neth · Colour · 117min

Fans of Paul Verhoeven's Hollywood output will be amazed by this garish Dutch take on the teen pic. Punctuated with graphic scenes of straight and gay sex, played to the melodramatic hilt and deliriously overstylised, it owes its greatest debt to Rainer Werner Fassbinder as a trio of dirt-bike dreamers strive to emulate their motocross hero, Rutger Hauer. Meanwhile, hot-dog seller Renée Soutendijk seeks to seduce one of them into delivering her from dead-end hell. You name it, Verhoeven nails it, whether it's religious fanaticism, homophobia, media manipulation or adolescent lust. DP Dutch +subtitles. *DVD*

Hans Van Tongeren *Reen* • Renée Soutendijk *Fientje* • Toon Agterberg *Eve* • Maarten Spanjer *Hans* • Marianne Boyer *Maya* • Rutger Hauer *Gerrit Witkamp* • Jeroen Krabbé *Frans Henkhof* ■ *Dir* Paul Verhoeven • *Scr* Gerard Soeteman

Sphere ★★★ 12
Science-fiction thriller 1998 · US · Colour · 128min

A submerged spacecraft from the future containing a golden sphere that has the ability to manifest the darkest fears of anyone who enters its enigmatic interior is at the centre of director Barry Levinson's cerebral adaptation of Michael Crichton's bestselling novel. Alternating between being genuinely creepy and overly tame, this underwater *Solaris* relies on moody dread rather than cheap thrills to weave its spell. A wittily scripted chamber piece. AJ Swearing, violence. *DVD*

Dustin Hoffman *Dr Norman Goodman* • Sharon Stone *Dr Beth Halperin* • Samuel L Jackson *Harry Adams* • Peter Coyote *Harold C Barnes* • Liev Schreiber *Dr Ted Fielding* • Queen Latifah *Fletcher* ■ *Dir* Barry Levinson • *Scr* Stephen Hauser, Paul Attanasio, from the novel by Michael Crichton

The Sphinx ★
Mystery 1933 · US · BW · 62min

The old evil twin device is given another airing in an unremarkable programmer. Lionel Atwill appears to have the perfect alibi for murder – he is deaf-mute, and a witness heard the killer speak. A sorry mix of low-grade suspense and comic relief means *The Sphinx* stinks! AJ

Lionel Atwill *Jerome Breen* • Sheila Terry *Jerry Crane, society editor* • Theodore Newton *Jack Burton, reporter* • Paul Hurst *Terrence Hogan* ■ *Dir* Phil Rosen • *Scr* Albert DeMond, from his story

Sphinx ★★ 15
Adventure 1980 · US · Colour · 112min

Rarely since *The Perils of Pauline* has so much been endured by a heroine as by Lesley-Anne Down here, starring as an Egyptologist who comes up against a gang smuggling artefacts from the Valley of the Kings. After witnessing John Gielgud's demise, she's shot at, nearly raped, attacked by bats, thrown into a dungeon of rotting corpses and has a tomb cave in on her. She screams a lot, though co-star Frank Langella seems not to hear. TH Swearing, violence.

Lesley-Anne Down *Erica Baron* • Frank Langella *Ahmed Khazzan* • Maurice Ronet *Yvon* • John Gielgud *Abdu Hamdi* • Vic Tablian *Khalifa* • John Rhys-Davies *Stephanos Markoulis* • Nadim Sawalha *Gamal* • Saeed Jaffrey *Selim* ■ *Dir* Franklin J Schaffner • *Scr* John Byrum, from the novel by Robin Cook

Spice World: the Movie ★★ PG
Musical comedy 1997 · UK · Colour · 88min

The first and, as it transpired, only feature film to exploit the enormous success of pop quintet the Spice Girls, this is an attempt to capture the comedic style of the Beatles films, and is not nearly as bad as it might have been. The girls themselves are engaging screen presences, if not much cop at acting, and seasoned TV sitcom director Bob Spiers corrals the parade of cameos with aplomb. AC Swearing. *DVD*

Victoria Adams *Posh Spice* • Melanie Brown *Scary Spice* • Emma Bunton *Baby Spice* • Melanie Chisholm *Sporty Spice* • Geraldine Halliwell *Ginger Spice* • Richard E Grant *Clifford* • Alan Cumming *Piers Cuthbertson-Smyth* • George Wendt *Martin Barnfield* ■ *Dir* Bob Spiers • *Scr* Kim Fuller, from an idea by the Spice Girls, Kim Fuller

Spider ★★★★ 15
Psychological drama 2002 · Can/UK/Jpn/Fr · Colour · 94min

An intense and complex exploration of mental illness, sociopathic existentialism and Freudian symbolism, director David Cronenberg's film combines pain, sadness and the shock of the new with innovative dexterity. It uses a visually emblematic inner monologue device to depict the destitute Spider (Ralph Fiennes in his finest performance) watching his younger self go through the harrowing motions of misunderstanding and misrepresenting his mother's "murder". Set in an East End London cunningly styled as an empty vacuum, Cronenberg's unravelling of Spider's delusional mind is both intellectually demanding and courageous. AJ Violence, swearing, sex scenes, nudity. *DVD*

Ralph Fiennes *Spider* • Miranda Richardson *Yvonne/Mrs Cleg* • Gabriel Byrne *Bill Cleg* • Lynn Redgrave *Mrs Wilkinson* • John Neville *Terrence* • Bradley Hall *Young Spider* • Gary Reineke *Freddy* • Philip Craig *John* • Cliff Saunders *Bob* ■ *Dir* David Cronenberg • *Scr* Patrick McGrath, from his novel

The Spider and the Fly ★★★★ U
Crime drama 1949 · UK · BW · 90min

Predating *Father Brown* by five years, this was Robert Hamer's first attempt at depicting the grudging respect that exists between a master thief and a brilliant detective. Evoking the Paris of Louis

Feuillade's *Fantômas* serials, Hamer superbly captures the conspiratorial pre-First World War atmosphere, while artfully keeping the tone as light as it is suspenseful, as Eric Portman initially attempts to capture Guy Cole and then enlists him to procure some top-secret German plans. A cat-and-mouse thriller of the highest order. DP

Eric Portman *Maubert* • Guy Rolfe *Philippe* • Nadia Gray *Madeleine* • George Cole *Marc* • Edward Chapman *Minister of War* • Maurice Denham *Col de la Roche* ■ *Dir* Robert Hamer • *Scr* Robert Westerby

Spider Baby ★★★ 15
Cult horror 1964 · US · BW · 80min

Director Jack Hill's fascinating curio features Lon Chaney Jr in one of his best Z-movie later roles, as chauffeur to the bizarre Merrye family, who have become cannibals because of inbreeding. That news comes as a shock to visiting relatives who must face death games devised by the tainted clan's demented children. Keeping his weird script perfectly balanced between macabre fable and black satire, the tongue-in-cheek aspects never lessen the chills. AJ *DVD* *BL*

Lon Chaney Jr *Bruno* • Carol Ohmart *Emily* • Quinn Redeker *Peter* • Mantan Moreland *Messenger* • Beverly Washburn *Elizabeth* • Mary Mitchel *Ann* • Sid Haig *Ralph* • Jill Banner *Virginia* ■ *Dir/Scr* Jack Hill

Spider-Man ★★★★ 12
Fantasy action adventure 2002 · US · Colour · 116min

Thanks in part to legal battles, Marvel Comics much-loved superhero took his time to reach the big screen. A self-confessed fan, director Sam Raimi sticks closely to the character's comic book roots with the creation of a colourful, visually striking frolic that's bubbling with energy and gleefully tongue-in-cheek, yet edged with pathos. Lead actor Tobey Maguire is unusual but inspired casting, exuding boy-next-door charm as the clandestine teen avenger. Indeed, it's his intense likeability that helps paper over the film's minor flaws. As for the all important villain, Willem Dafoe looks the part as the Green Goblin, but lacks charisma. SF *DVD*

Tobey Maguire *Peter Parker/Spider-Man* • Willem Dafoe *Green Goblin/Norman Osborn* • Kirsten Dunst *Mary Jane Watson* • James Franco *Harry Osborn* • Cliff Robertson *Ben Parker* • Rosemary Harris *May Parker* • JK Simmons *J Jonah Jameson* ■ *Dir* Sam Raimi • *Scr* David Koepp, from the comic books *Amazing Fantasy/The Amazing Spider-Man* by Stan Lee, Steve Ditko

Spider-Man 2 ★★★★ PG
Fantasy action adventure 2004 · US · Colour · 122min

Director Sam Raimi harnesses advances in technology to deliver a fantasy adventure sequel that's slicker and more stylish than its predecessor. Two years after events in the original, Tobey Maguire's web-slinger is struggling to cope with the responsibilities his powers bring, a task complicated by the appearance of multi-tentacled villain Doctor Octopus (Alfred Molina). Doc Ock's clashes with Spider-Man are the film's highlights, while the focus on Spidey's feelings for Mary Jane (Kirsten Dunst) adds emotional depth. Quibbles aside, the feature's still the most solid of the recent comic book adaptations, with wit, charm and imagination. SF Violence. *DVD* *BL*

Tobey Maguire *Peter Parker/Spider-Man* • Kirsten Dunst *Mary Jane Watson* • Alfred Molina *Doc Ock/Dr Otto Octavius* • James Franco *Harry Osborn* • Rosemary Harris *May Parker* • Donna Murphy *Rosalie Octavius* • JK Simmons *J Jonah Jameson* • Elizabeth Banks (2) *Betty Brant* ■ *Dir* Sam Raimi • *Scr* Alvin Sargent, from a story by Alfred Gough, Miles Millar, Michael Chabon, from the comic book *The Amazing Spider-Man* by Stan Lee, Steve Ditko

Spider-Man 3 ★★★ 12
Fantasy action adventure 2007 · US · Colour · 133min

Spider-Man turns bad and has a blast doing it, in Sam Raimi's second sequel to his 2002 hit. Swinging in at a hefty 140 minutes, it sees Peter Parker (Tobey Maguire) now at ease with his alter ego and the public adoration it attracts, leaving girlfriend Mary Jane (a sympathetic Kirsten Dunst) constantly neglected. Events are complicated when contact with a parasitical alien substance brings out Spidey's dark side and exacerbates a personal vendetta against one of the tale's three villains, Sandman (a molecularly displaced Thomas Haden Church). Visually, this comic-book spectacle can't be faulted, with eye-popping effects intensifying a clutch of exciting set pieces. However, the self-indulgent running time and cluttered plotline frequently render the scenes in-between unfocused and plodding. SF *DVD* *BL*

Tobey Maguire *Peter Parker/Spider-Man* • Kirsten Dunst *Mary Jane Watson* • James Franco *Harry Osborn/New Goblin* • Thomas Haden Church *Flint Marko/Sandman* • Topher Grace *Eddie Brock/Venom* • Bryce Dallas Howard *Gwen Stacy* • James Cromwell *Captain George Stacy* • Rosemary Harris *Aunt May* • Theresa Russell *Mrs Marko* • Cliff Robertson *Uncle Ben Parker* ■ *Dir* Sam Raimi • *Scr* Alvin Sargent, Ivan Raimi, Sam Raimi, from a story by Sam Raimi, Ivan Raimi, from characters by Stan Lee, Steve Ditko • *Cinematographer* Bill Pope

Spider-Man: Homecoming
Fantasy action adventure 2017 · US · Colour

This is a preview – no prints were available to review prior to publication: What? Another Spider-Man? Yes, the third in 15 years, with Tom Holland now donning the clingy costume recently modelled by Tobey Maguire and Andrew Garfield. This will be Holland's second time out as the webbed wonder, after his debut in *Captain America: Civil War*. In his favour is not just the fact that he can act – Holland was self-assured in tsunami disaster movie *The Impossible* – but also he actually is a teenager. SvM *3D*

Tom Holland (2) *Peter Parker/Spider-Man* • Marisa Tomei *Aunt May* • Zendaya *Michelle* • Robert Downey Jr *Tony Stark/Iron Man* • Michael Keaton *Vulture* ■ *Dir* Jon Watts • *Scr* John Francis Daley, Jonathan M Goldstein, from characters by Stan Lee, Steve Ditko

Spiderhole ★★ 18
Horror 2009 · Ire · Colour · 81min

The old dark house movie gets a torture porn makeover in Daniel Simpson's sick psycho-chiller. Desperate to find cheaper digs, four art students decide to squat in an abandoned London property. However, as they celebrate moving in, they quickly realise that they've been trapped in by a sinister, white-clad figure. Simpson keeps the camera prowling around the dankly claustrophobic sets, but he struggles to create much tension and invites even less sympathy for the imperilled quartet. DP *DVD*
Violence. ■

Emma Griffiths Malin *Molly* • Reuben-Henry Biggs *Luke* • Amy Noble *Zoe* • George Maguire *Toby* • John E Regan *Captor* ■ *Dir/Scr* Daniel Simpson

The Spiders ★★★★
Silent adventure 1919 · Ger · BW · 72min

Fritz Lang's first commercial success is an adventure melodrama on a theme popular at the time (and soon to become a reality): arch criminals hoping to take over the world. Inspired by the German pulp writer Karl May and the serials of Louis Feuillade, it was made in two parts, but broken up into episodes like a serial. It tells of a hero pitted against an Asian criminal and a gang called the Spiders, who are after a very special diamond. The earliest of Lang's surviving works, it already has many Langian elements: the use of mirrors, hypnosis and underground chambers. RB

Carl de Vogt *Kay Hoog* • Lil Dagover *Naela, Priestess of the Sun* • Ressel Orla *Lio Sha* • Georg John *Dr Telphas* • Rudolph Lettinger [Rudolf Lettinger] *John Terry, the Diamond King* • Edgar Pauly *Four Finger John* ■ *Dir/Scr* Fritz Lang

The Spider's Stratagem ★★★★★ PG
Drama 1970 · It · Colour · 94min

One of the all-time great movies of Italian cinema, this shows director Bernardo Bertolucci at the zenith of his consummate talent in the days when he excelled at illuminating the effect of cultural differences on the human spirit. His hero, brilliantly played by Giulio Brogi, returns home to find his sense of family shattered by unseen events from the past. As he struggles to attain greater knowledge of his heroic father's assassination, we are taken on a fascinating psychological journey with enormous verve and wit, while Italy's Po valley looks marvellous thanks to the luminous camerawork of Vittorio Storaro. A masterpiece. SH Italian +subtitles.

Giulio Brogi *Athos Magnani/His father* • Alida Valli *Draifa* • Tino Scotti *Costa* • Pippo Campanini *Gaibazzi* • Franco Giovanelli *Rasori* ■ *Dir* Bernardo Bertolucci • *Scr* Bernardo Bertolucci, Eduardo de Gregorio, Marilu Parolini, from the story *Theme of the Traitor and the Hero* by Jorge Luis Borges

The Spiderwick Chronicles ★★★★ PG
Fantasy adventure 2008 · US · Colour · 91min

Goblins, trolls and griffins populate this adaptation of the book series that plays like a horror movie for kids. Freddie Highmore stars as twins who move into a creepy old mansion with their sister (Sarah Bolger) and mother (Mary-Louise Parker) and discover a hidden world. The terrific CGI creatures are so un-cute that even the good characters – honey-eating sprite Thimbletack (voiced by Martin Short) and a bird-munching hobgoblin (voiced by Seth Rogen) – may frighten some younger viewers. But older children will love it. JR *DVD* *BL*

Freddie Highmore *Jared Grace/Simon Grace* • Sarah Bolger *Mallory Grace* • Mary-Louise Parker *Helen Grace* • Seth Rogen *Hogsqueal* • David Strathairn *Arthur Spiderwick* • Andrew McCarthy *Richard Grace* • Nick Nolte *Mulgarath* • Martin Short *Thimbletack* • Joan Plowright *Aunt Lucinda* ■ *Scr* Mark Waters (1) • *Scr* David Berenbaum, Karey Kirkpatrick, John Sayles, from the novels by Holly Black, Tony DiTerlizzi

Spies ★★★★ PG
Silent spy thriller 1928 · Ger · BW · 143min

Perhaps the most underrated of Fritz Lang's silent spectacles, this tale of master criminality has all the visceral thrill and visual atmospherics of one of Louis Feuillade's *Fantômas* serials. Many of the *Metropolis* alumni were reunited for the picture, with Karl Vollbrecht and Otto Hunte creating expressionist sets which added menace to the dastardly deeds laid at the door of the Mabuse-like Rudolf Klein-Rogge by Lang and Thea von Harbou's breathless script. However, once again, this is very much Lang's own vision, as he abandons political allegory to place the emphasis firmly on escapism and his genius for the awe-inspiring set piece. DP *DVD* *BL*

Rudolf Klein-Rogge *Haghi* • Gerda Maurus *Sonia Barranikova* • Willy Fritsch *Number 326* ■ *Dir* Fritz Lang • *Scr* Fritz Lang, Thea von Harbou, from their story

Spies like Us ★★ PG
Comedy 1985 · US · Colour · 97min

This highly resistible spoof is one of John Landis's failures. Paired for the first time in a film, former *Saturday Night Live* alumni Dan Aykroyd and Chevy Chase simply fail to gel, and there's little fun to be had once the boisterous training school gags are exhausted. Cold comfort can be obtained from a brief appearance by Bob Hope, and movie aficionados can while away the time playing spot the famous film-makers in a variety of cameo roles. DP *DVD*

Chevy Chase *Emmett Fitz-Hume* • Dan Aykroyd *Austin Millbarge* • Steve Forrest *General Sline* • Donna Dixon *Karen Boyer* • Bruce Davison *Mr Ruby* • Bernie Casey *Colonel Rhombus* • William Prince *Mr Keyes* • Tom Hatten *General Miegs* • Bob Hope ■ *Dir* John Landis • *Scr* Dan Aykroyd, Lowell Ganz, Babaloo Mandel, from a story by Dan Aykroyd, Dave Thomas

Spike Island ★★★ 15
Music drama 2012 · UK · Colour · 104min

Director Mat Whitecross's heartfelt drama is set around a seminal 1990 gig by iconic Manchester band the Stone Roses at Spike Island in Widnes. The fond fictional story of an unsigned local four-piece caught up in the heady anticipation has a lively young cast of small-screen repute including Elliott Tittensor (*Shameless*), Nico Mirallegro (*The Village*) and Emilia Clarke (*Game of Thrones*). Some of the drama is a little forced, but Whitecross is on surer footing with the era's colloquial bravado, comedic street slang and inter-band rivalry, and the music buoys the vibrant time-capsule mood. AC Swearing, sexual references, drug abuse.

Elliott Tittensor *Tits* • Emilia Clarke *Sally* • Nico Mirallegro *Dodge* • Jordan Murphy *Zippy* • Adam Long *Little Gaz* • Oliver Heald *Penfold* • Lesley Manville *Margaret* ■ *Dir* Mat Whitecross • *Scr* Chris Coghill

The Spikes Gang ★★ 12
Western 1974 · US · Colour · 92min

It's a shame that this was filmed in Spain, for it's the European look and corny Almeria locations that undermine any grit that director Richard Fleischer and star Lee Marvin can bring to this intriguing screenplay. This is a story of awestruck lads out West, who idolise Marvin's Harry Spikes (the film's original title), while he teaches them to rob banks. The then-fashionable dashes of violence don't help. TS *DVD*

Lee Marvin *Harry Spikes* • Gary Grimes *Will Young* • Ron Howard *Les Richter* • Charlie Martin Smith [Charles Martin Smith] *Tod Mayhew* • Arthur Hunnicutt *Kid White* • Noah Beery Jr *Jack Bassett* • Marc Smith *Abel Young* ■ *Dir* Richard Fleischer • *Scr* Irving Ravetch, Harriet Frank Jr

Spinout ★★ U
Musical comedy 1966 · US · Colour · 89min

This may not be Elvis Presley's most distinguished movie outing, but it's certainly one of the busiest. In all, three women have designs on the struggling singer, whose real ambition is to race fast cars. But who will be swooning in the final clinch: author Diane McBain; Shelley Fabares, whose millionaire father wants Presley to drive one of his racing cars; or Deborah Walley, who plays drums in the King's combo? Norman Taurog's direction is enthusiastic, but this is strictly for Elvis fans. DP *DVD*

Elvis Presley *Mike McCoy* • Shelley Fabares *Cynthia Foxhugh* • Diane McBain *Diana St Clair* • Deborah Walley *Les* • Dodie Marshall *Susan* • Jack Mullaney *Curly* ■ *Dir* Norman Taurog • *Scr* Theodore J Flicker, George Kirgo

The Spiral Road ★
Melodrama 1962 · US · Colour · 135min

American director Robert Mulligan followed this dire religious medical drama with *To Kill a Mockingbird*, thus making both his best and possibly worst films within the same 12 months. This jungle-set drama is disadvantaged from the start in its implausible casting of the amiable Rock Hudson as an aggressively ambitious doctor who, in the mid-1930s, travels to Java to learn and then profit from the ideas of guru physician Burl Ives. BB

Rock Hudson *Dr Anton Drager* • Burl Ives *Dr Brits Jansen* • Gena Rowlands *Els* • Geoffrey Keen *Willem Wattereus* • Neva Patterson *Louise Kramer* • Will Kuluva *Dr Sordjano* • Philip Abbott *Frolick* ■ *Dir* Robert Mulligan • *Scr* John Lee Mahin, Neil Paterson, from the novel by Jan de Hartog

The Spiral Staircase ★★★★ PG
Thriller 1946 · US · BW · 80min

Thought-provoking and disturbing, this masterly thriller is directed with touches of sheer genius by Robert Siodmak, who beckons us into a voyeuristic nightmare with taut, creeping camerawork that makes the hair on your neck stand up. However, while this is undoubtedly a classic of 1940s Hollywood gothic, the movie treads a fine line between acceptable menace and

uncomfortable sadism with its story of a serial killer murdering disabled and disfigured women. That said, this remains a masterwork, with a fine performance from Dorothy McGuire. An embarrassing TV movie remake appeared in 2000. SH *DVD*

Dorothy McGuire *Helen Capel* • George Brent *Professor Warren* • Ethel Barrymore *Mrs Warren* • Kent Smith *Dr Parry* • Rhonda Fleming *Blanche* • Gordon Oliver *Steve Warren* • Elsa Lanchester *Mrs Oates* • Sara Allgood *Nurse Barker* ■ *Dir* Robert Siodmak • *Scr* Mel Dinelli, from the novel *Some Must Watch* by Ethel Lina White • *Cinematographer* Nicholas Musuraca

The Spirit ★★ 12
Action crime drama 2008 · US · Colour · 97min

Writer/director Frank Miller builds on bringing his own *Sin City* graphic novel to the screen with this stylised superhero *noir*, based on Will Eisner's classic 1940s comic-book series. Gabriel Macht stars as the titular indestructible, masked crime fighter, who engages in a cat-and-mouse battle with megalomaniac villain the Octopus (Samuel L Jackson on autopilot) for an immortality serum. Retaining the look of Miller's earlier film, flesh-and-blood actors are shot against a green screen with everything else added in digitally. The black-and-white palette (with bursts of colour, mostly red) provides plenty of visually arresting images, but the overall tone of the story falls somewhere between camp excess and poker-faced pulp. AC *DVD* *BL*

Gabriel Macht *Denny Colt/The Spirit* • Samuel L Jackson *The Octopus* • Scarlett Johansson *Silken Floss* • Eva Mendes *Sand Saref* • Paz Vega *Plaster of Paris* • Jaime King *Lorelei* • Sarah Paulson *Ellen Dolan* • Stana Katic *Morgenstern* ■ *Dir* Frank Miller • *Scr* Frank Miller, from a comic book by Will Eisner

The Spirit of '45 ★★★
Documentary 2013 · UK · BW and Colour · 98min

This rare excursion into the documentary genre for veteran director Ken Loach is a rousing account of a period of unprecedented change in Britain. Following a landslide victory at the 1945 general election, Labour leader Clement Attlee nationalised the railway network, initiated a programme of house building and established the National Health Service. But just about everything he achieved was subsequently undone, and the blame is laid firmly at the door of Margaret Thatcher. Such a simplistic verdict ignores the tempestuous socio-political history of the subsequent years and the impact of factors beyond the control of successive Labour and Conservative administrations, while the noble and passionate utterances of politicians, union officials, academics and working people exhorting a socialist revival are ultimately undermined by Loach's narrow focus and revisionism. DP *DVD*

■ *Dir* Ken Loach • *Music* George Fenton

The Spirit of St Louis ★★★★ U
Historical drama 1957 · US · Colour · 129min

It is a staggering conceit to film such a seemingly uncinematic tale as Charles A Lindbergh's solo flight across the Atlantic, confined as it is to one man in a small cockpit. But director Billy Wilder makes it an emotional tour de force, utilising flashbacks and narration with wit and skill, aided by Franz Waxman's superb score and Robert Burks and J Peverell Marley's magnificent photography. James Stewart is a shade too old for Lindbergh, but no other actor could better his unique all-American combination of intensity, tenderness and wry concern. This underrated film is a great achievement. TS

James Stewart *Charles A Lindbergh* • Murray Hamilton *Bud Gurney* • Patricia Smith *Mirror girl* • Bartlett Robinson *BF Mahoney* • Robert Cornthwaite *Knight* • Sheila Bond *Model/dancer* • Marc Connelly *Father Hussman* ■ *Dir* Billy Wilder • *Scr* Billy Wilder, Wendell Mayes, Charles Lederer, from the autobiography by Charles A Lindbergh

U SUITABLE FOR ALL Uc SUITABLE ESPECIALLY FOR YOUNG CHILDREN (DVD ONLY) PG PARENTAL GUIDANCE 12A UNDER 12s TO BE ACCOMPANIED (CINEMA ONLY)

The Spirit of the Beehive
★★★★★ PG

Period drama | 1973 · Sp · Colour · 93min

Set in 1940, Victor Erice's remarkable debut is a controlled assault on the indolence into which Spain slipped under Franco, and a biting allegory on the evil of which the seemingly benevolent state could be capable. A vision of trust and gentleness, Ana Torrent is enchanting as the small girl who watches *Frankenstein* and becomes fascinated by the monster, mistakenly believing that its spirit is embodied in the fugitive soldier she has befriended. Told with a disarming realism and simplicity, this charming film is one of the gems of Spanish cinema. DP Spanish +subtitles. *DVD*

Ana Torrent *Ana* • Isabel Telleria *Isabel* • Fernando Fernán Gómez *Father* • Teresa Gimpera *Mother* • José Villasante *Frankenstein's monster* ■ *Dir* Victor Erice • *Scr* Francisco J Querejeta

Spirit of the Eagle ★★★ U
Adventure | 1991 · US · Colour · 88min

Those who have not had enough of Dan Haggerty in his "Grizzly" Adams incarnation will probably enjoy this good-natured, Great Outdoors adventure. Haggerty is Big Eli, a cartographer who makes the mistake of leaving son Little Eli home alone, only to find that he's been kidnapped. It's a great advertisement for the attractions of Oregon, even though the story itself could do with more hills and valleys, light and shade. Still, this peek into family harmony is affecting, and the sumptuous locations provide the eye with a rich, ready meal. JG

Dan Haggerty *Big Eli McDonaugh* • Bill Smith [William Smith] *Ore-Eye* • Trever Yarrish *Little Eli* • Jeri Arredondo *Watawna* • Taylor Lacher *Weasel* • Ken Carpenter *Jake* • Don Shanks *Running Wolf* ■ *Dir/Scr* Boon Collins

Spirit of the People ★★★ PG
Historical drama | 1940 · US · BW · 109min

Henry Fonda had just played the young Abraham Lincoln in John Ford's movie. Now it was the turn of Raymond Massey, who repeats his stage performance from the popular Robert E Sherwood play. The 30-year span of the story rather lumbers along but Massey conveys the private complexity of the man as well as his public eloquence, though the film was an expensive flop at the box office. Massey played Lincoln again – ever so briefly – in *How the West Was Won*. AT *DVD*

Raymond Massey *Abraham Lincoln* • Gene Lockhart *Stephen Douglas* • Ruth Gordon *Mary Todd Lincoln* • Mary Howard *Ann Rutledge* • Dorothy Tree *Elizabeth Edwards* • Harvey Stephens *Ninian Edwards* • Minor Watson *Joshua Speed* • Alan Baxter *Billy Herndon* ■ *Dir* John Cromwell • *Scr* Grover Jones, Robert E Sherwood, from the play *Abe Lincoln in Illinois* by Sherwood

Spirit: Stallion of the Cimarron ★★ U
Animated western | 2002 · US · Colour · 80min

Despite being beautifully animated (a flawless combination of old school hand-drawn animation and dazzling computer graphics), this wild mustang horse opera doesn't match the heart of classic Disney or the slick fun of modern digital efforts. Saddled with an overly moralistic and politically correct story, this is strictly kids stuff with Matt Damon providing the first person narration, and Bryan Adams crooning bland songs that pointlessly underline the action. AJ *DVD*

Matt Damon *Spirit* • James Cromwell *Colonel* • Daniel Studi *Little Creek* • Chopper Bernet *Sgt Adams* • Jeff LeBeau *Murphy/Railroad foreman* ■ *Dir* Kelly Asbury, Lorna Cook • *Scr* John Fusco

Spirit Trap ★ 15
Horror | 2004 · UK · Colour · 87min

Billie Piper moves into a creepy North London mansion with four other students and it's not long before they discover a supernatural link between their new home and the tragic fate of a widow and her black lover 100 years earlier. Former pop star Piper shot this movie in Romania before *Doctor Who* propelled her back into the limelight, but she's just going through the motions. AJ Violence, swearing, drug abuse, sex scenes. *DVD*

Billie Piper *Jenny* • Luke Mably *Tom* • Emma Catherwood *Adele* • Sam Troughton *Nick* • Alsou *Tina* ■ *Dir* David Smith • *Scr* Phil O'Shea

Spirited Away ★★★★ PG
Animated fantasy adventure
2001 · Jpn · Colour · 124min

Having broken box-office records and added an Oscar to its share of Berlin's Golden Bear, Hayao Miyazaki's follow-up to *Princess Mononoke* has become an instant Japanimation classic. The tale of a sulky girl who learns the importance of being true to one's self contains echoes of *Alice in Wonderland* that are reinforced by the gallery of rogues and grotesques that Chihiro encounters after she's trapped inside a fantasy world ruled by twin witches. Miyazaki's insistence on hand-drawn graphics gives the CGI visuals an ethereal charm that ensures the action is always a pleasure to behold, even during its rare moments of inaction. DP Japanese dubbed. *DVD* *BL*

Daveigh Chase *Chihiro* • Suzanne Pleshette *Yubaba/Zeniba* • Jason Marsden *Haku* • Susan Egan *Lin* • David Ogden Stiers *Kamaji* • Lauren Holly *Chihiro's mother* • Michael Chiklis *Chihiro's father* • John Ratzenberger *Assistant manager* • Tara Strong [Tara Charendoff] *Baby Boh* ■ *Dir* Hayao Miyazaki • *Scr* Hayao Miyazaki; Cindy Davis Hewitt, Donald H Hewitt (English version)

Spiritual Love ★★★ 15
Fantasy | 1987 · HK · Colour · 88min

Inspired by the writings of the 17th-century chronicler of the supernatural, Master Liaozhai, the female ghost story developed into a popular subgenre of Hong Kong fantasy horror in the 1980s. Made just before the emphasis shifted away from atmosphere and on to special effects, David Lai and Taylor Wong's film also slips in plenty of comedy, notably the bizarre manner in which Chow Yun-Fat's jealous lover, Pauline Wong, is transformed into his "girlfriend". DP Cantonese +subtitles.

Chow Yun-Fat *Pok* • Cherie Chung *Butterfly* • Pauline Wong ■ *Dir* David Lai, Taylor Wong • *Scr* Stephen Shiu

Spite Marriage ★★★
Silent comedy | 1929 · US · BW · 76min

Despite a couple of uproarious scenes, it was clear – in only his second feature for the studio – that MGM was slowly eroding Buster Keaton's creative autonomy and corrupting his comic instincts. Never had Keaton's stone-faced bewilderment been so apposite, as he hurtles through plot contrivances that culminate in him confronting a rum-runner on his yacht. Much more sure-footed are the scenes between his daydreaming dry cleaner and Dorothy Sebastian, the actress who exploits him to get back at her feckless beau. DP

Buster Keaton *Elmer Edgemont* • Dorothy Sebastian *Trilby Drew* • Edward Earle *Lionel Denmore* • Leila Hyams *Ethyle Norcrosse* • William Bechtel *Frederick Nussbaum* • John Byron *Giovanni Scarzi* ■ *Dir* Edward Sedgwick • *Scr* Richard Schayer, Ernest S Pagano, Robert Hopkins, from a story by Lew Lipton

Spitfire ★
Drama | 1934 · US · BW · 85min

This ludicrous melodrama was an early nail in the coffin of Katharine Hepburn's reputation, that would see her labelled as "box-office poison" by the end of the decade. Improbably cast as a badly educated, uncouth mountain girl, she alienates the backwoods community with her faith-healing ideas, and is caught in a dreary and unbelievable love triangle with Robert Young and Ralph Bellamy. The script is dreadful, and the patrician Hepburn is badly miscast. RK

Katharine Hepburn *Trigger Hicks* • Robert Young (1) *John Stafford* • Ralph Bellamy *George Fleetwood* • Martha Sleeper *Eleanor Stafford* ■ *Dir* John Cromwell • *Scr* Jane Murfin, Lula Vollmer, from the play *Trigger* by Lula Vollmer

The Spitfire Grill ★★★ 12
Drama | 1996 · US · Colour · 111min

A mesmerising performance from Alison Elliott (*The Wings of the Dove*) is the highlight of this moving if slightly unbelievable drama. Elliott plays Percy, the young ex-con paroled to a small (and small-minded) Maine town, where she goes to work at the local diner run by worldly-wise Ellen Burstyn. Well played by a cast that includes Marcia Gay Harden and the always watchable Will Patton, and featuring some luscious, rugged scenery, this is tear-jerking, female bonding stuff. JB

Alison Elliott (2) *Percy Talbott* • Ellen Burstyn *Hannah Ferguson* • Marcia Gay Harden *Shelby Goddard* • Will Patton *Nahum Goddard* ■ *Dir/Scr* Lee David Zlotoff

Splash ★★★★ PG
Romantic fantasy comedy
1984 · US · Colour · 105min

This charming romantic comedy touched a chord with audiences around the world and propelled its stars, Tom Hanks and Daryl Hannah, along with director Ron Howard, to Hollywood's front rank. Hannah is the innocent mermaid who docks on dry land to locate Hanks, whom she saved from drowning years ago. The two leads make a charismatic pair, although John Candy gets most of the best gags. Howard piles on the good-natured fun and keeps soppiness largely at bay. The film was followed four years later by a dismal TV-movie sequel, and is now being remade with Channing Tatum as the mermaid. JF *DVD*

Tom Hanks *Allen Bauer* • Daryl Hannah *Madison* • Eugene Levy *Walter Kornbluth* • John Candy *Freddie Bauer* • Dody Goodman *Mrs Stimler* • Shecky Greene *Mr Buyrite* • Richard B Shull *Dr Ross* ■ *Dir* Ron Howard • *Scr* Lowell Ganz, Babaloo Mandel, Bruce Jay Friedman, from a screen story by Bruce Jay Friedman from a story by Brian Grazer

Splendor ★★★ U
Melodrama | 1935 · US · BW · 73min

Producer Samuel Goldwyn commissioned playwright Rachel Crothers to write this as a vehicle for Miriam Hopkins. Joel McCrea marries poor girl Hopkins, instead of the rich heiress his mother has set her sights on. Hopkins is a take-her-or-leave-her actress, and she can't quite bring off the early stages of the movie, clearly being anything but a naive newlywed. Yet her later scenes with Helen Westley as McCrea's thwarted mother have a ferocity all their own. TS

Miriam Hopkins *Phyllis Manning Lorrimore* • Joel McCrea *Brighton Lorrimore* • Paul Cavanagh *Martin Deering* • Billie Burke *Clarissa* • David Niven *Clancey Lorrimore* ■ *Dir* Elliott Nugent • *Scr* Rachel Crothers, from her story

Splendor ★★★ 15
Romantic comedy | 1999 · US · Colour · 88min

Gregg Araki takes a tilt at the mainstream with this archly postmodern reworking of Noel Coward's *Design for Living*. Reining in his penchant for societal diatribes, he establishes the romantic triangle with sweeping satirical strokes. But once bespectacled rock critic Johnathon Schaech and primal punk drummer Matt Keeslar move in with aspiring actress Kathleen Robertson any finesse seeps away and the action becomes increasingly sitcomic, especially once a rival suitor appears on the scene. There are numerous neat touches and the leads spark brightly. DP Swearing, drug abuse, sexual situations.

Kathleen Robertson *Veronica* • Johnathon Schaech *Abel* • Matt Keeslar *Zed* • Kelly Macdonald *Mike* • Eric Mabius *Ernest* ■ *Dir/Scr* Gregg Araki

Splendor in the Grass ★★★★ 15
Period drama | 1961 · US · Colour · 118min

Warren Beatty couldn't have had a better start to his movie career than this, with co-star Natalie Wood and director Elia Kazan. Beatty and Wood play star-crossed lovers in playwright William Inge's tragi-romantic screenplay, set in 1920s Kansas. The young couple who spend the film attempting to cross the sexual morality divide are dominated by interfering parents (Audrey Christie, Pat Hingle), so that what should be splendid is seen to be squalid. The psychology may be simplistic, but the portrayals are powerful. TH Sexual references. *DVD*

Natalie Wood *Wilma Dean Loomis* • Warren Beatty *Bud Stamper* • Pat Hingle *Ace Stamper* • Audrey Christie *Mrs Loomis* • Barbara Loden *Ginny Stamper* • Zohra Lampert *Angelina* • Fred Stewart *Del Loomis* • Sandy Dennis *Kay* ■ *Dir* Elia Kazan • *Scr* William Inge

Splice ★★★ 15
Science-fiction horror thriller
2009 · Can/Fr · Colour · 102min

Cube director Vincenzo Natali merges David Cronenberg-style body horror with twisted fairy-tale fantasy to craft a *Frankenstein* fable for the modern era. Rebellious scientists Sarah Polley and Adrien Brody experiment with DNA splicing to create new life and the resultant deformed female infant develops into a beautiful chimera. As his potent allegory about child-rearing turns deadly, Natali deflates the most risible moments with well-judged levity, while, as the fully fledged creature, CGI-augmented actress Delphine Chaneac gives this oddly affecting monster movie its heart of dark fascination. AJ Violence, sex scenes. *DVD* *BL*

Adrien Brody *Clive* • Sarah Polley *Elsa* • Délphine Chaneac *Dren* • David Hewlett *Barlow* • Abigail Chu *Young Dren* • Stephanie Baird *Elsa/PD* ■ *Dir* Vincenzo Natali • *Scr* Vincenzo Natali, Antoinette Terry Bryant, Doug Taylor, from a story by Natali, Terry Bryant

Splintered ★★ 18
Horror thriller | 2008 · UK · Colour · 81min

A troubled young woman's fascination with the unexplained leads her into a deadly nightmare in this messy and underwhelming low-budget British horror. Throwing everything from clerical child abuse to werewolf mythology, first-time director Simeon Halligan gradually drowns under the weight of genre clichés, as his foolhardy characters find themselves being picked off while hunting for a wild beast in the remote Welsh countryside. Stylish visuals manufacture a rudimentary feeling of unease but poor pacing and predictability – not to mention amateurish performances – rob even the kills of genuine impact. SF Violence. *DVD*

Holly Weston *Sophie* • Stephen Martin Walters [Stephen Walters] *Gavin* • Sacha Dhawan *Sam* • Sadie Pickering *Jane* • Jonathan Readwin *Dean* ■ *Dir* Simeon Halligan • *Scr* Mat Archer, Simeon Halligan, Stephen Trimingham

The Split ★★★
Crime thriller | 1968 · US · Colour · 89min

This gutsy crime thriller boasts a splendid supporting cast of tough guys and a script based on a novel by Richard Stark, who also wrote *Point Blank*. The movie spins around Jim Brown, who plans to rob a football stadium and recruits his team in the manner of *The Dirty Dozen*. It's a formula picture, though director Gordon Flemyng makes the most of his Los Angeles locations. AT

Jim Brown *McClain* • Diahann Carroll *Ellie* • Julie Harris (2) *Gladys* • Ernest Borgnine *Bert Clinger* • Gene Hackman *Lt Walter Brill* • Jack Klugman *Harry Kifka* • Warren Oates *Marty Gough* • Donald Sutherland *Dave Negli* ■ *Dir* Gordon Flemyng • *Scr* Robert Sabaroff, from the novel *The Seventh* by Richard Stark [Donald E Westlake]

Split

Thriller   2017 · US · Colour

This is a preview – no prints were available to review as we went to press: If we'd only stop expecting writer/director M Night Shyamalan to make another *Sixth Sense*, we'd probably all enjoy his films more. That said, *Split* does have an intriguing premise. James McAvoy plays the abductor of three young women who, it turns out, has 23 separate personalities, one of which –The Beast –the abductees really don't want to meet. The smaller budget might encourage Shyamalan to up his game. **SvM**

James McAvoy *Kevin* • Kim Director • Anya Taylor-Joy *Casey* • Haley Lu Richardson • Brad William Henke [Brad Henke] *Uncle John* ■ *Dir/Scr* M Night Shyamalan

Split Image   ★★★ 15

Drama   1982 · US · Colour · 106min

The 1980s were a quiet time for Peter Fonda, but here he delivers a powerful performance that shows a different side to the counterculture hero. He plays a cult leader who ensnares Michael O'Keefe, only to discover that the latter's father (the ever-reliable Brian Dennehy) is not giving up without a fight. The film additionally provides juicy roles for James Woods and Karen Allen, while director Ted Kotcheff lends a dark edge to the proceedings. **JF** Swearing, nudity.

Michael O'Keefe *Danny Stetson* • Karen Allen *Rebecca* • Peter Fonda *Neal Kirklander* • James Woods *Charles Pratt* • Elizabeth Ashley *Diana Stetson* • Brian Dennehy *Kevin Stetson* • Ronnie Scribner *Sean Stetson* ■ *Dir* Ted Kotcheff • *Scr* Scott Spencer, Robert Kaufman, Robert Mark Kamen, from a story by Scott Spencer

Split Second   ★★★

Thriller   1953 · US · BW · 80min

Dick Powell makes his directorial debut with this cracking thriller and manages to crank up a fair amount of suspense. Slimy escaped convict Stephen McNally ends up in a Nevada ghost town with a clutch of hostages to keep the law at bay. The catch is that the town is actually part of a nuclear test site. This is clever stuff, particularly well cast. **TS**

Stephen McNally *Sam Hurley* • Alexis Smith *Kay Garven* • Jan Sterling *Dottie* • Keith Andes *Larry Fleming* • Arthur Hunnicutt *Asa* • Paul Kelly (1) *Bart Moore* • Robert Paige *Arthur Ashton* • Richard Egan *Dr Garven* ■ *Dir* Dick Powell • *Scr* William Bowers, Irving Wallace, from a story by Chester Erskine, Irving Wallace

Split Second   ★★ 18

Science-fiction horror thriller
1991 · UK · Colour · 86min

Rutger Hauer mugs shamelessly in this nonsensical science-fiction effort. He's an on-edge cop in the flooded London of 2008, in search of a monstrous heart-ripping serial killer with Satanic origins with whom he shares a psychic link. Sidekick Neil Duncan and love interest Kim Cattrall take their places for the daft battle dénouement in Cannon Street tube station. **AJ** *DVD*

Rutger Hauer *Harley Stone* • Kim Cattrall *Michelle* • Neil Duncan *Dick Durkin* • Michael J Pollard *The Rat Catcher* • Pete Postlethwaite *Paulsen* • Ian Dury *Jay Jay* • Roberta Eaton *Robin* • Alun Armstrong *Thrasher* ■ *Dir* Tony Maylam • *Scr* Gary Scott Thompson

Split Wide Open   ★★★ 15

Drama   1999 · Ind · Colour · 100min

Acclaimed for 1994's *English, August*, Dev Benegal launched another scathing attack on contemporary India with this messy, but provocative picture. Laila Rouass stars as a London expatriate whose celebrity rests on her muck-raking TV talk show. She alights on Bombay water-seller Rahul Bose to expose the gulf between the city's classes. But then a more sinister story breaks, as Bose's adopted sister, Farida Hyder Mullah, claims she's being stalked by wealthy paedophile Shivaji Satham. Benegal slyly mocks the flashy trashiness of daytime TV,

but lets the narrative slip out of his control. **DP** Hindi, English +subtitles.

Rahul Bose *KP* • Laila Rouass *Nandita Mehta* • Ayesha Dharker [Ayesha Dharkar] *Leela* • Farida Hyder Mullah *Didi* ■ *Dir* Dev Benegal

Splitting Heirs   ★★ 15

Comedy   1993 · UK · Colour · 83min

Eric Idle is mistakenly allowed to roam free here as both star and scriptwriter by director Robert M Young, who should have boxed him in tight. As a result, the story about an heir (Idle) who is switched at birth (with Rick Moranis) lacks focus, and the talented cast is left to fend for itself. Odd moments do resurrect the barmy surrealism so familiar from Monty Python, but on the whole this is a rather disorganised comedy. **JM** Some violence, swearing, sex scenes, nudity.

Eric Idle *Tommy* • Rick Moranis *Henry* • Barbara Hershey *Duchess Lucinda* • Catherine Zeta-Jones *Kitty* • John Cleese *Shadgrind* • Sadie Frost *Angela* • Stratford Johns *Butler* • Brenda Bruce *Mrs Bullock* • Eric Sykes *Jobson the doorman* ■ *Dir* Robert Young (2) • *Scr* Eric Idle

The Spoilers   ★★★ PG

Western   1942 · US · BW · 83min

Saloon keeper Marlene Dietrich reprises the role she played with much greater success in 1939's *Destry Rides Again*. What distinguishes movie versions of this Alaska-set western is the exciting fist-fight between the leading men that marks the story's climax. The macho cuffing here is between stars John Wayne and Randolph Scott, but watch out for a cameo appearance from silent heart-throb Richard Barthelmess, in his penultimate screen role. **TS** *DVD*

Marlene Dietrich *Cherry Malotte* • John Wayne *Roy Glennister* • Randolph Scott *McNamara* • Margaret Lindsay *Helen Chester* • Harry Carey *Dextry* • Richard Barthelmess *Bronco Kid* ■ *Dir* Ray Enright • *Scr* Lawrence Hazard, Tom Reed, from the novel by Rex Beach

The Spoilers   ★★ U

Western   1955 · US · Colour · 83min

This is another version of Rex Beach's novel about claim jumping during the Alaskan gold rush and the first to be filmed in colour with a new generation of stars. The preceding films have become noted for the climactic fist-fights between hero and villain and this makes a determined effort to compete as Jeff Chandler and Rory Calhoun (and their stunt doubles) slug it out from the floor above the saloon, but the story is tired and the picture is never more than mildly engrossing. **AE**

Anne Baxter *Cherry Malotte* • Jeff Chandler *Roy Glennister* • Rory Calhoun *Alex McNamara* • Ray Danton *"Bronco" Blackie* • Barbara Britton *Helen Chester* • John McIntire *Dextry* • Carl Benton Reid *Judge Stillman* • Wallace Ford *Flapjack Simms* ■ *Dir* Jesse Hibbs • *Scr* Oscar Brodney, Charles Hoffman, from the novel by Rex Beach

The SpongeBob SquarePants Movie   ★★★★ U

Animated comedy adventure
2004 · US · Colour · 83min

There's never a dull moment in this multi-level extravaganza featuring Nickelodeon's cartoon cult hero. Even those unfamiliar with the undersea fast-food employee will find the trippy action, hip absurdity and self-aware silliness of Stephen Hillenburg's joyful creation a lot more fun than expected. SpongeBob (voiced by Tom Kenny) and his dumb starfish buddy Patrick (Bill Fagerbakke) set out on a quest to reclaim the crown stolen from King Neptune (Jeffrey Tambor). They're helped by Neptune's daughter (Scarlett Johansson) and hindered by a hitman (Alec Baldwin). **AJ** *DVD*

Tom Kenny *SpongeBob* • Bill Fagerbakke *Patrick Star* • Clancy Brown *Mr Eugene H Krabs* • Rodger Bumpass *Squidward Tentacles* • Doug Lawrence *Plankton* • Alec Baldwin *Dennis* • David Hasselhoff • Scarlett Johansson *Mindy* • Jeffrey Tambor *King Neptune* ■ *Dir* Stephen Hillenburg • *Scr* Stephen Hillenburg, Derek Drymon, Tim Hill,

Kent Osborne, Aaron Springer, Paul Tibbitt, from a story by Stephen Hillenburg, from characters in the animated TV series by Stephen Hillenburg

The SpongeBob Movie: Sponge out of Water   ★★★★ U

Part-animated comedy adventure
2015 · US · Colour · 93min

Nothing has changed a decade on from the first movie, as dastardly pirate Burger Beard (an ever game Antonio Banderas) steals an ancient book Indiana Jones-style, then tells the story within to a flock of seagulls. The tale has SpongeBob and Plankton pooling resources to find the Krabby Patty recipe that's gone missing from Bikini Bottom. Under the expert guidance of Paul Tibbitt, sophisticated adult gags jostle with inspired silliness to provide a smart and infectiously anarchic mix. **AJ** *DVD* [blu] 🎬

Tom Kenny *SpongeBob* • Antonio Banderas *Burger Beard* • Clancy Brown *Mr Krabs* • Rodger Bumpass *Squidward* • Mr Lawrence [Doug Lawrence] *Plankton* • Bill Fagerbakke *Patrick Star* ■ *Dir* Paul Tibbitt • *Scr* Glenn Berger, Jonathan Aibel, Paul Tibbitt, from a story by Tibbitt, Stephen Hillenburg, from the TV series by Hillenburg

Spooks Run Wild   ★★ U

Comedy   1941 · US · BW · 63min

This entry in the East Side Kids series must have seemed something of a comedown for Bela Lugosi. However, an even more surprising credit for this harum-scarum old-dark-house adventure is that of co-scriptwriter Carl Foreman, who later received five Oscar nominations for pictures such as *High Noon*. Lugosi is mildly sinister, the Kids wisecrack like popcorn machines and there's a nice turn from Dave O'Brien. **DP** *DVD*

Bela Lugosi *Nardo, the monster* • Leo Gorcey *Muggsy* • Huntz Hall *Glimpy* • Bobby Jordan *Danny* • David Gorcey *Pee Wee* • "Sunshine Sammy" Morrison *Scruno* • Donald Haines *Skinny* ■ *Dir* Phil Rosen • *Scr* Carl Foreman, Charles Marion, Jack Henley

Spooks: the Greater Good   ★★ 15

Spy action thriller   2015 · UK · Colour · 99min

The BBC drama *Spooks* ended in 2011 and this first big-screen spin-off is essentially an extended bonus episode. Anchored to Peter Firth's MI5 boss Harry Pearce, the film's commercial asset is hairy Kit Harington, hot from *Game of Thrones*. His retired, sulky protégé is brought back into the fold to foil an imminent attack on the capital. A couple of effective set pieces aside, this strains to fill its extra 40 minutes and Harington proves an underpowered lead compared to his TV forebears. **AC** Violence, swearing, sexual references. *DVD* [blu]

Peter Firth *Harry Pearce* • Kit Harington *Will Holloway* • Jennifer Ehle *Geraldine Maltby* • Elyes Gabel *Adem Qasim* • Lara Pulver *Erin Watts* • Tim McInnerny *Oliver Mace* • Hugh Simon *Malcolm Wynn-Jones* • Tuppence Middleton *June Keaton* ■ *Dir* Bharat Nalluri • *Scr* Jonathan Brackley, Sam Vincent (2), from the TV series *Spooks* created by David Wolstencroft

Spooky House   ★★★

Adventure   1999 · US · Colour · 107min

How many children's films can boast a couple of Oscar winners in the leading roles? Well, Ben Kingsley and Mercedes Ruehl headline this entertaining tale of magic and malevolence that should amuse anyone hooked on the exploits of Harry Potter. Kingsley plays a reclusive magician who has shunned the limelight since his wife mysteriously disappeared during his act. A young quintet choose Halloween to seek his help in dealing with the ne'er-do-wells over-running their little town. **DP**

Ben Kingsley *The Great Zamboni* • Mercedes Ruehl *Boss* • Matt Weinberg *Max* • Jason Fuchs *Yuri* • Ronald Joshua Scott *Beans* • Simon Baker (2) *Prescott* • Myles Ferguson *Mike the Mouth* ■ *Dir* William Sachs • *Scr* William Sachs, Margaret Sachs

Sporting Blood   ★★★ U

Comedy drama   1931 · US · BW · 82min

Top-billed Clark Gable is the only big name in this "biography" of a horse named Tommy Boy, which follows him from a Kentucky stud farm, through the abuse he suffers at the hands of several racehorse owners, to his eventual rescue and triumph as the Derby winner. This unusual movie is part exposé of the ugly elements in the sport of kings, and part tribute to and plea on behalf of animals. **RK**

Clark Gable *Rid Riddell* • Ernest Torrence *Jim Rellence* • Madge Evans *Ruby* • Lew Cody *Tip Scanlon* • Marie Prevost *Angela* • Hallam Cooley *Ludeking* • J Farrell MacDonald *MacGuire* ■ *Dir* Charles Brabin • *Scr* Wanda Tuchock, from the novel *Horseflesh* by Frederick Hazlitt Brennan

The Sports Pages   ★★ 12

Sports comedy   2001 · US · Colour · 85min

This patchy two-part TV comedy examines downside of being an American sports fanatic. The first part sees Bob Newhart as a golfer trying to explain how his personal best was more important than the life of playing partner Kelsey Grammer. The second, unrelated tale is based on the real-life incident when an important American football match was taken off the air, 65 seconds before the final whistle and with the score at 32-29, for a scheduled showing of *Heidi*. It's tame, but quite well performed. **SuR**

Kelsey Grammer *Howard Greene* • Bob Newhart *Doc Waddems* • Brian Markinson *Robert Russo* • Graham Jarvis *Judge* • Ellie Harvie *Melinda* • Gary Basaraba *Frank* • John Kapelos *Marvin* ■ *Dir* Richard Benjamin • *Scr* Donald Todd (teleplay, segment "How Doc Waddems Finally Broke 100" with Don Marquis), George Zaloom (teleplay, segment "The Heidi Bowl", from the story "Why Doc Waddems Never Broke 100" by Marquis)

Spotlight   ★★★★★ 15

Drama based on a true story
2015 · US · Colour · 128min

In 2001, *The Boston Globe* ran a story about a priest accused of child abuse. After digging deeper, the members of the paper's Spotlight team (Michael Keaton, Mark Ruffalo, Rachel McAdams, Brian d'Arcy James) exposed a shocking, widespread cover-up that led to countless other priests who had molested young boys. Much like *All the President's Men*, this is utterly engrossing from start to finish, and was rewarded with Oscars for best picture and best original screenplay. **SC** Swearing. *DVD* [blu]

Mark Ruffalo *Michael Rezendes, "Mike"* • Michael Keaton *Walter "Robby" Robinson* • Rachel McAdams *Sacha Pfeiffer* • Liev Schreiber *Martin "Marty" Baron* • John Slattery *Ben Bradlee Jr* • Stanley Tucci *Mitchell Garabedian* • Len Cariou *Cardinal Law* ■ *Dir* Tom McCarthy [Thomas McCarthy] • *Scr* Tom McCarthy, Josh Singer • *Music* Howard Shore • *Editor* Tom McArdle

Spotswood   ★★★ PG

Comedy drama   1991 · Aus · Colour · 92min

Director Mark Joffe's appealing feature is similar to an Aussie Ealing comedy. At his most hesitant and human, Anthony Hopkins stars as a time-and-motion man whose dealings with the workers in a suburban moccasin factory cause him to re-evaluate a life dictated by emotional sterility and ruthless efficiency. The satire is gentle, the comedy often delightfully offbeat and the character traits neatly observed. **DP**

Anthony Hopkins *Wallace* • Ben Mendelsohn *Carey* • Toni Collette *Wendy* • Alwyn Kurts *Mr Ball* • Dan Wyllie *Frank Fletcher* • Bruno Lawrence *Robert* • Rebecca Rigg *Cheryl* • Russell Crowe *Kim Barrett* ■ *Dir* Mark Joffe • *Scr* Max Dann, Andrew Knight

Spread   ★★★ 18

Comedy   2008 · US · Colour · 93min

This portrait of a Hollywood stud who lives off the wealthy women in his life offers co-producer and star Ashton Kutcher a chance to match his own decorative looks with a role of some substance. Kutcher's flint-hearted, smart-talking professional is certainly a memorable creation, a variation on the male escort portrayed by Richard Gere in *American Gigolo*. However, when a young waitress enters the fray, the drama soon reveals a disappointingly mushy centre beneath the film's glittering façade. It's fun when it's at its bitchiest, and Kutcher's astute performance will surprise a few people. TL Swearing, sex scenes. **DVD BL**

Ashton Kutcher *Nikki* • Anne Heche *Samantha* • Margarita Levieva *Heather* • Sebastian Stan *Harry* • Rachel Blanchard *Emily* • Eric Balfour *Sean* • Ashley Johnson *Eva* ■ *Dir* David Mackenzie • *Scr* Jason Hall [Jason Dean Hall], from a story by Paul Kolsby, Hall

Spring ★★★ 15
Romantic horror   2014 · US/It · Colour · 104min

Every so often, a film comes along that takes so weird a turn that it completely discombobulates the viewer. Lou Taylor Pucci stars as a young American whose wanderlust lands him in a small Italian coastal town where he falls for fathomless local Nadia Hilker. But there's a twist that will please fans of HP Lovecraft. Part romance, part creep-out, it will definitely spring a surprise. DA **DVD**

Lou Taylor Pucci *Evan* • Nadia Hilker *Louise* • Francesco Carnelutti *Angelo* • Nick Nevern *Thomas* ■ *Dir* Justin Benson, Aaron Moorehead • *Scr* Justin Benson

Spring and Port Wine ★★★
Comedy drama   1969 · UK · Colour · 100min

Any film adaptation of a play in which the critical action takes place around a dining table is likely to be slightly stagebound. That Bill Naughton's screen version of his own generation-gap comedy works as a movie is partly down to its commonplace, yet utterly compelling content and director Peter Hammond's deft opening out of events. However, the key element is the playing of James Mason, Susan George and a host of sitcom celebrities, with Mason both infuriating and endearing as the Lancastrian feuding with daughter George. DP

James Mason *Rafe Crompton* • Susan George *Hilda Crompton* • Diana Coupland *Daisy Crompton* • Rodney Bewes *Harold Crompton* • Hannah Gordon *Florence Crompton* • Len Jones *Wilfred Crompton* • Keith Buckley *Arthur Gasket* ■ *Dir* Peter Hammond • *Scr* Bill Naughton, from his play

Spring Breakers ★★★★ 18
Crime drama   2012 · US · Colour · 90min

At 40 years old, film-maker and former *enfant terrible* Harmony Korine (writer of *Kids*) is still obsessed with youthful transgression. Here, American college kids look forward to spring break – notorious for sex, drugs and wild parties – but students Selena Gomez, Vanessa Hudgens, Ashley Benson and Rachel Korine, with help from sleazy rapper James Franco, go off the rails in their hedonistic quest. Franco gives an incredible performance, while Gomez and Hudgens impress with a brave (and successful) move to shed their squeaky clean image. But beneath the bikinis and beer bongs, Korine's film is a merciless examination of race and class privilege in America. This will appeal to the young crowd it depicts, but also as a twisted morality tale for those who are older and, hopefully, wiser. LB Violence, swearing, drug abuse, sex scenes, nudity. **DVD BL**

James Franco *Alien* • Selena Gomez *Faith* • Vanessa Hudgens [Vanessa Anne Hudgens] *Candy* • Ashley Benson *Brit* • Rachel Korine *Cotty* • Gucci Mane *Archie* ■ *Dir/Scr* Harmony Korine

Spring in a Small Town ★★★★ U
Drama   1948 · Chi · BW · 97min

This is usually considered the finest Chinese film ever made, and is remarkable for its use of voiceover and the subtlety of the lighting and camera movement. At its heart is a romantic triangle sparked when doctor Li Wei comes to visit his friend, the invalid Yu Shi. It transpires that Li is also the old flame of Yu's wife, Wei Wei. Fei Mu's

austere chamber drama was produced before the Communist revolution and promptly banned by the Party for failing to condemn bourgeois indolence and lacking instructive political content. However, accusations that it has a "narcotic effect" fall wide of the mark, as the emotional intensity and crushing air of melancholy make this study of dashed hope both compelling and poignant. DP Mandarin +subtitles. **DVD**

Wei Wei *Zhou Yuwen* • Yu Shi *Dai Liyan* • Li Wei *Zhang Zhichen* • Chaoming Cui *Lao Huang* • Zhang Hongmei *Dai Xiu* ■ *Dir* Fei Mu • *Scr* Li Tianji

Spring in Park Lane ★★★ U
Romantic comedy   1948 · UK · BW · 87min

Another of those fatuous fantasies about lords pretending to be servants, as wealthy Anna Neagle falls for footman Michael Wilding. Even though Herbert Wilcox's direction tends to be heavy-handed, there are many deft touches, mainly supplied by Nicholas Phipps's light-as-air screenplay. The two leads carry off the plot with some aplomb, and Wilding plays his role of charming wimp surprisingly well. A big hit in postwar Britain. TS

Anna Neagle *Judy Howard* • Michael Wilding *Richard* • Tom Walls *Uncle Joshua Howard* • Peter Graves (1) *Basil Maitland* • Marjorie Fielding *Mildred Howard* • Nicholas Phipps *Marquis of Borechester* ■ *Dir* Herbert Wilcox • *Scr* Nicholas Phipps, from the play *Come Out of the Kitchen* by Alice Duer Miller

Spring Reunion ★★ U
Romantic drama   1957 · US · BW · 79min

The once raucous, ebullient Hollywood hoyden Betty Hutton made her final screen appearance in this movie, before suffering psychiatric problems and sliding into bankruptcy. In an uncharacteristically subdued role, she is a spinster whose life is changed for the better when she meets up with Dana Andrews, the once golden student who has failed to fulfil his promise, at a high-school reunion. Palatable but run-of-the-mill. RK

Dana Andrews *Fred Davis* • Betty Hutton *Maggie Brewster* • Jean Hagen *Barna Forrest* • Sara Berner *Paula Kratz* • Robert F Simon *Harry Brewster* • Laura La Plante *May Brewster* • James Gleason *Mr Collyer* ■ *Dir* Robert Pirosh • *Scr* Elick Moll, Robert Pirosh, from a story by Robert Alan Aurthur

Spring, Summer, Autumn, Winter ... and Spring ★★★★★ 15
Drama   2003 · S Kor/Ger · Colour · 98min

South Korean director Kim Ki-Duk's exquisite meditation on the trials and burdens of life is not one for fans of intrigue, car chases or explosions. A tiny Buddhist hermitage floats on the glassy waters of a beautiful lake. Inside, a monk and a young boy live and contemplate. The boy grows up and leaves; the monk grows old; the boy returns to the temple as a man, and the cycle of life repeats itself. There you have pretty much the whole plot. But this is not a film greatly concerned with story or even dialogue (which is also minimal), but about image, emotional tone, ritual and symbolism, all of which are employed masterfully, leaving Kim's film moving, mysterious - and utterly unmissable. AS Korean +subtitles. Sex scenes. **DVD**

Oh Young-Su *Old monk* • Kim Ki-Duk *Adult monk* • Kim Young-Min *Young monk* • Kim Jong-Ho *Child monk* • Seo Jae-Kyung *Boy monk* • Ha Yeo-Jin *The girl* ■ *Dir/Scr* Kim Ki-Duk

Spring Thaw ★★
Drama   2007 · US · Colour · 90min

This well-meaning story about a macho farmer succumbing to Alzheimer's disease was written by Patti Davis, whose own father, Ronald Reagan, died of the disease in 2004. The insights into the diagnosis and development of the condition are perceptive enough and Ken Howard conveys the growing confusion and helplessness with admirable restraint. But

the narrative is strewn with melodramatic incidents, as city lawyer Melissa Gilbert leaves her job defending troubled delinquents to help her loyal brother Cyril O'Reilly nurse the father she's never forgiven for a childhood trauma. DP

Melissa Gilbert *Katelyn Weston* • Ken Howard *Thane Weston* • Cyril O'Reilly *Ryan Weston* • Andre Ware [Frank Andre Ware] *Jury Foreman* • Kevin Cooney *Doc Osborne* • Anthony De Marco *Zack Weston* ■ *Dir* David S Cass Sr • *Scr* Patti Davis

Springfield Rifle ★★ U
Western   1952 · US · Colour · 88min

In the same year that Gary Cooper won an Oscar for *High Noon* he also starred in this perfunctory Warner Bros western. Directed with some style by Andre De Toth, this feature still resembles a Randolph Scott programme filler, wherein Cooper instead of Scott rides with a batch of second-string actors to infiltrate a gang. Cooper is a little too old for this kind of lark, but there's a certain pleasure to be gained from watching a great star at work. TS

Gary Cooper *Major "Lex" Kearney* • Phyllis Thaxter *Erin Kearney* • David Brian *Austin McCool* • Paul Kelly (1) *Lt Col Hudson* • Philip Carey *Captain Tennick* • Lon Chaney Jr *Elm* • James Millican *Matthew Quint* • Martin Milner *Olie Larsen* ■ *Dir* Andre De Toth • *Scr* Charles Marquis Warren, Frank Davis, from a story by Sloan Nibley

Springsteen & I ★★★★ PG
Documentary   2013 · UK · Colour · 123min

A music documentary with a difference, director Baillie Walsh's film focuses not on Bruce Springsteen himself but on the devoted fans he's inspired during his lengthy career. It features archive footage of The Boss on stage, in particular from shows where he's interacted with specific members of the audience. Time and again, the documentary gives examples of how ordinary people connect to the man and his songs, providing a soundtrack to their personal triumphs and disappointments. This is a must-see for converts that also goes a long way towards explaining to the uninitiated why Springsteen attracts such avid worshippers. TeS

Bruce Springsteen • *Dir* Baillie Walsh

Springtime in a Small Town ★★★★ PG
Period drama   2002 · Chi/HK/Fr · Colour · 111min

Fei Mu's 1948 feature was among the last produced in China before the Communist takeover. So much can be read into the fact that this remake marks Tian Zhuangzhuang's return to film-making after a decade of state-proscribed silence. He certainly uses this sedate, yet intense study of a household coming to terms with the aftermath of war to comment on the equally momentous socio-economic transition currently taking place. But the impact of returning doctor Xin Baiqing upon ailing grandee Wu Jun and his wife Hu Jingfan and sister Lu Sisi works just as well as an exquisitely judged Chekhovian chamber drama. DP Mandarin +subtitles. **DVD**

Hu Jingfan *Yuwen, the wife* • Wu Jun *Dai Liyan, the husband* • Xin Baiqing *Zhang Zhichen, the visitor* • Ye Xiaokeng *Lao Huang, the retainer* • Lu Sisi *Dai Xiu, the sister* ■ *Dir* Tian Zhuangzhuang • *Scr* Ah Cheng, from a story by Li Tianji, from the 1948 film *Xiao Cheng zhi Chun* by Fei Mu

Springtime in the Rockies ★★★ U
Musical comedy   1942 · US · Colour · 87min

Betty Grable and John Payne play a sparring Broadway duo, and the music includes the wonderful Helen Forrest performing Harry Warren and Mack Gordon's *I Had the Craziest Dream*. The supporting cast includes such eccentrics as Carmen Miranda (attempting *Chattanooga Choo Choo*). Grable shows off her slim talents to best effect, and consolidates her stardom on her way to becoming the Forces' "pin-up". TS

Betty Grable *Vicky Lane* • John Payne *Dan Christy* • Carmen Miranda *Rosita Murphy* • Cesar Romero *Victor Prince* • Charlotte Greenwood *Phoebe Gray* • Edward Everett Horton *McTavish* • Jackie Gleason *The commissioner* • Harry James ■ *Dir* Irving Cummings • *Scr* Walter Bullock, Ken Englund, Jacques Thery, from the short story *Second Honeymoon* by Philip Wylie

Spud ★★★ 15
Comedy drama   2010 · S Afr · Colour · 102min

A sweet and raunchy coming-of-age comedy set in a South African boarding school. Sivan Troye plays the new boy whose slow progress towards puberty makes communal showers a trial and tangles with girls even more fraught. Luckily, Spud is taken under the wing of Mr Edly (John Cleese). Once a sub-plot about a school production of a musical *Oliver Twist* gets underway, Sivan really comes into his own, and the all-singing, all dancing numbers remind us that 2010 was the year of *Glee* on TV. Two sequels followed. SvM

Troye Sivan *John "Spud" Milton* • John Cleese *The Guv* • Mr Edly • Jamie Royal *Henry "Gecko" Barber* • Sven Ruygrok *Rambo* • Tanit Phoenix *Eve* ■ *Dir* Donovan Marsh • *Scr* Donovan Marsh, from John Van De Ruit's novel

Spun ★★★ 18
Part-animated satirical drama   2002 · US · Colour · 97min

Swedish music video director Jonas Akerlund's first foray into feature films is a grimy tale of "spun-out" crystal meth users. The action unfolds over three days, during which their dependency pushes them into increasingly bizarre situations. Frenetically shot, with enough jump-cuts and imaginative visuals to give viewers whiplash, the movie has cult cool written all over it. However, its lack of morality, cheap shock tactics and sewer-mouth script mean it really is an acquired taste. SF Violence, swearing, sex scenes, drug abuse, nudity. **DVD**

Jason Schwartzman *Ross* • John Leguizamo *Spider Mike* • Brittany Murphy *Nikki* • Patrick Fugit *Frisbee* • Mena Suvari *Cookie* • Mickey Rourke *The Cook* • Peter Stormare *Cop number one* • Alexis Arquette *Cop number two* • Deborah Harry *Neighbour* • Eric Roberts *The Man* • Chloe Hunter *April* ■ *Dir* Jonas Akerlund • *Scr* Will De Los Santos, Creighton Vero

Spy ★★★★ 15
Comedy   2015 · US · Colour · 115min

Melissa McCarthy becomes a bona-fide movie star in *Spy*, reteaming with Paul Feig who directed her in *Bridesmaids* and *The Heat*. She plays a CIA desk agent sent into the field to gather intelligence on Rose Byrne's criminal mastermind. Feig scores plenty of laughs by making McCarthy look laughably incongruous when she should be inconspicuous, and her banter with old *Bridesmaids* comrade Byrne, as she strikes up an unlikely friendship, is deliciously bitchy fun. Miranda Hart isa tad jarring as McCarthy's sidekick, but Jason Statham is Feig's secret weapon as a super-agent who thinks he's better qualified than McCarthy. But this is McCarthy's show. She carries the film with huge charm. SP Violence, swearing, sexual references. **DVD BL**

Melissa McCarthy *Susan Cooper* • Jason Statham *Rick Ford* • Rose Byrne *Rayna Boyanov* • Miranda Hart *Nancy* • Allison Janney *Elaine Crocker* • Jude Law *Bradley Fine* ■ *Dir/Scr* Paul Feig

Spy Game ★★★ 15
Spy thriller   2001 · US/Ger/Jpn/Fr · Colour · 121min

Looking for all the world like father and son, cinema's two golden "boys", Robert Redford and Brad Pitt, team up for this daftly implausible but diverting spy yarn from director Tony Scott. Redford's the old pro set to retire from the CIA. Pitt's the boy-wonder protégé banged up in a Chinese hellhole when failing to free old flame Catherine McCormack from custody. The 24 hours prior to Pitt's execution see Redford reminiscing about his partnership before running rings round his oblivious CIA

S

superiors to save his friend's life. DA Violence, swearing. *DVD*

Robert Redford *Nathan Muir* • Brad Pitt *Tom Bishop* • Catherine McCormack *Elizabeth Hadley* • Stephen Dillane *Charles Harker* • Larry Bryggman *Troy Folger* • Marianne Jean-Baptiste *Gladys Jennip* • David Hemmings *Harry Duncan* • Charlotte Rampling *Anne Cathcart* ■ *Dir* Tony Scott • *Scr* Michael Frost Beckner, David Arata, from a story by Michael Frost Beckner

Spy Hard ★★ PG
Spy spoof   1996 · US · Colour · 77min

The blockbuster action thriller genre is ripe for sending up, but this lazy effort has to go down as a miss despite the presence of spoofmeister Leslie Nielsen. The basic story is firmly rooted in James Bond – Nielsen is superagent Dick Steele battling supervillain Andy Griffith – but the cast is defeated by the determinedly juvenile script. JF *DVD*

Leslie Nielsen *Dick Steele* • Nicollette Sheridan *Veronique Ukrinsky* • Charles Durning *The Director* • Marcia Gay Harden *Miss Cheevus* • Barry Bostwick *Norman Coleman* • John Ales *Kabul* • Andy Griffith *General Rancor* ■ *Dir* Rick Friedberg • *Scr* Rick Friedberg, Dick Chudnow, Aaron Seltzer, from a story by Jason Friedberg, Aaron Seltzer

The Spy in Black ★★★ U
First World War spy drama
1939 · UK · BW · 79min

The first collaboration of celebrated film-makers Michael Powell and Emeric Pressburger, this is a bold and atmospheric spy drama set during the First World War. Conrad Veidt turns in a convincing performance as a German submarine commander on a mission to sink the British fleet. Dispatched to the Orkney Islands, Veidt makes contact with a German agent who turns out to be local schoolteacher Valerie Hobson, and is soon wondering whether she's on his side. Strong writing combines with striking cinematography and talented direction to make this a satisfying entertainment. PF *DVD*

Conrad Veidt *Captain Hardt* • Valerie Hobson *Joan, the schoolmistress* • Sebastian Shaw *Commander Davis Blacklock* • Marius Goring *Lieutenant Schuster* • June Duprez *Anne Burnett* • Athole Stewart *Reverend Hector Matthews* • Agnes Lauchlan *Mrs Matthews* • Helen Haye *Mrs Sedley* ■ *Dir* Michael Powell • *Scr* Emeric Pressburger, Roland Pertwee, from the novel by J Storer Clouston • *Cinematographer* Bernard Browne

The Spy in the Green Hat ★★★
Spy adventure   1966 · US · Colour · 92min

The Man from UNCLE TV show spawned a hit-and-miss series of spin-off movies of which this is arguably the most accomplished. It features the series' best villains in the guise of Jack Palance's pill-popping megalomaniac and his kinky female secretary/assassin, played with delicious malice by Janet Leigh. The plot is even more tongue in cheek than usual with the ever unflappable Napoleon Solo and Illya Kuryakin teaming up with a pack of stereotypical Italian-American gangsters to thwart THRUSH's latest plan for world domination. RS

Robert Vaughn (1) *Napoleon Solo* • David McCallum (1) *Illya Kuryakin* • Jack Palance *Louis Strago* • Janet Leigh *Miss Diketon* • Letitia Roman [Leticia Roman] *Pia Monteri* • Leo G Carroll *Alexander Waverly* • Eduardo Ciannelli *Arturo "Fingers" Stiletto* • Allen Jenkins *Enzo "Pretty" Stiletto* • Jack La Rue [Jack LaRue] *Federico "Feet" Stiletto* • Joan Blondell *Mrs "Fingers" Stiletto* • Elisha Cook [Elisha Cook Jr] *Arnold* ■ *Dir* Joseph Sargent • *Scr* Peter Allan Fields

SPYkids ★★★★ U
Fantasy action adventure
2001 · US · Colour · 84min

Antonio Banderas and Carla Gugino play married spies who get captured by a megalomaniac children's TV presenter (Alan Cumming) who's seeking world domination. To the rescue come the couple's pleasingly non-precocious kids (Alexa Vega and Daryl Sabara), aided and

abetted by a cool array of gizmos that range from rocket-packs to electromagnetic chewing gum. Smartly and sassily directed by Robert Rodriguez (who quite rightly pitches the film at youngsters, not down to them) and sporting some nifty special effects, this is rollicking family cinema as it should be. DA *DVD* *Blu*

Antonio Banderas *Gregorio Cortez* • Carla Gugino *Ingrid Cortez* • Alexa Vega *Carmen Cortez* • Daryl Sabara *Juni Cortez* • Alan Cumming *Fegan Floop* • Tony Shalhoub *Alexander Minion* • Teri Hatcher *Ms Gradenko* • Cheech Marin [Richard "Cheech" Marin] *Felix Gumm* • Danny Trejo *Machete* • Robert Patrick *Mr Lisp* • George Clooney *Devlin* ■ *Dir/Scr* Robert Rodriguez

SPYkids 2: the Island of Lost Dreams ★★★★ U
Fantasy action adventure
2002 · US · Colour · 95min

Children's action adventures don't come any more sophisticated than director Robert Rodriguez's slick and colourful sequel to his 2001 hit. This time around, Carmen and Juni (Alexa Vega and Daryl Sabara) are on a mission to investigate the mysterious volcanic island inhabited by a mad scientist (Steve Buscemi) and his hybrid animal creations. In a playful homage to effects specialist Ray Harryhausen's style of stop-motion animation, these mutant monsters add extra excitement to the thrill-packed feature. This pint-sized espionage caper is as stylish and inventive as a Bond film. SF *DVD* *Blu* *CS*

Antonio Banderas *Gregorio Cortez* • Carla Gugino *Ingrid Cortez* • Alexa Vega *Carmen Cortez* • Daryl Sabara *Juni Cortez* • Steve Buscemi *Romero* • Mike Judge *Donnagon* • Danny Trejo *Uncle Machete* • Cheech Marin [Richard "Cheech" Marin] *Felix Gumm* • Ricardo Montalban *Grandpa* • Holland Taylor *Grandma* ■ *Dir* Robert Rodriguez • *Scr* Robert Rodriguez, from his characters

SPYkids 3-D: Game Over ★★ U
Fantasy action adventure
2003 · US · Colour · 80min

Robert Rodriguez's franchise ditches plot sophistication in favour of pure visual spectacle for this second sequel, filmed predominantly in 3D. In this minutely detailed cyberspace fantasy, young agents Daryl Sabara and Alexa Vega journey into the virtual-reality world of a 3D video game to save mankind from its megalomaniac creator, Sylvester Stallone. The humorous cameos and witty banter do little to camouflage the limp storyline and weak characters. A fourth instalment is due in 2011. SF *DVD* *Blu* *SP* *CS*

Antonio Banderas *Gregorio Cortez* • Carla Gugino *Ingrid Cortez* • Alexa Vega *Carmen Cortez* • Daryl Sabara *Juni Cortez* • Ricardo Montalban *Grandpa* • Holland Taylor *Grandma* • Sylvester Stallone *Toymaker* • Mike Judge *Donnagon Giggles* • Cheech Marin [Richard "Cheech" Marin] *Felix Gumm* ■ *Dir/Scr* Robert Rodriguez

SPYkids 4: All the Time in the World ★★ PG
Fantasy action adventure
2011 · US · Colour · 88min

Director Robert Rodriguez's playful sense of fun deserts him in his frenetic and charmless fourth dip into the mini-spy pool. Retired secret agent Jessica Alba is called back into action, along with her two stepchildren and grown up spy kids Alexa Vega and Daryl Sabara, to take on a former nemesis, the maniacal Time Keeper (Jeremy Piven). Youngsters may find the nappy bombs, potty jokes and robot guard dog (flatly voiced by Ricky Gervais) amusing in this cardboard fantasy. Anyone else need not apply. AJ Some violence. *DVD* *Blu* *SP*

Jessica Alba *Marissa Cortez Wilson* • Jeremy Piven *TimeKeeper* • Joel McHale *Wilbur Wilson* • Alexa Vega *Carmen Cortez* • Daryl Sabara *Juni Cortez* • Rowan Blanchard *Rebecca Wilson* • Mason Cook *Cecil Wilson* • Ricky Gervais *Argonaut* ■ *Dir/Scr* Robert Rodriguez

The Spy Next Door ★★★ PG
Action comedy   2009 · US · Colour · 90min

In this family-friendly comedy, Jackie Chan stars as the retired secret agent whose attempt to sustain a relationship with next-door neighbour Amber Valletta is not only hampered by the antipathy of her three children, but also his previous profession coming back to haunt him. Here, his likeable presence is a major plus, and his target audience will respond to his baddie-bopping agility and not worry about the corny, predictable plot. The movie also gives smartly written roles to its junior cast (Will Shadley, Madeline Carroll) while the story is a tongue-in-cheek entertainment that sees Chan's superspy tangle with Russian villains while trying to babysit Valletta's terrible threesome. TJ *DVD* *Blu*

Jackie Chan *Bob Ho* • Amber Valletta *Gillian* • Madeline Carroll *Farren* • Will Shadley *Ian* • Magnus Scheving *Poldark* • Billy Ray Cyrus *Colton James* ■ *Dir* Brian Levant • *Scr* James Greer, Jonathan Bernstein, Gregory Poirier, from a story by Greer, Bernstein

The Spy Who Came In from the Cold ★★★★ PG
Spy drama   1965 · UK · BW · 112min

This gritty adaptation of John Le Carré's gruelling novel finally offered Richard Burton a role worthy of his wonderfully world-weary style. Bitterness seeps from every pore as he goes behind the Iron Curtain for a final showdown with his East German counterpart. With agents trapped behind state secrecy and false identities, this isn't the glitzy neverland of James Bond, but a dangerous reality in which suppressed emotion matters more than derring-do. Martin Ritt's icy direction and Oswald Morris's bleak black-and-white photography make this is one of the best Cold War films. DP

Richard Burton *Alec Leamas* • Claire Bloom *Nan Perry* • Oskar Werner *Fiedler* • Peter Van Eyck *Hans-Dieter Mundt* • Sam Wanamaker *Peters* • Rupert Davies *George Smiley* • Cyril Cusack *Control* ■ *Dir* Martin Ritt • *Scr* Paul Dehn, Guy Trosper, from the novel by John le Carré

The Spy Who Loved Me ★★★★ PG
Spy adventure   1977 · UK · Colour · 120min

"Nobody Does It Better" than Roger Moore in one of the best post-Connery James Bond adventures. Well-acted (with less reliance on slapstick humour than normal), smartly cast (metal-toothed Jaws, played by Richard Kiel, makes his first appearance) and lavishly directed (by Lewis Gilbert), this exceptional spy escapade is far-fetched mayhem of the highest order, with a welcome accent on character realism rather than just spectacular sets. Barbara Bach is the alluring Russian agent Anya Amasova. AJ Some violence. *DVD* *Blu*

Roger Moore *James Bond* • Barbara Bach *Major Anya Amasova* • Curt Jurgens *Karl Stromberg* • Richard Kiel *Jaws* • Caroline Munro *Naomi* • Walter Gotell *General Gogol* • Geoffrey Keen *Minister of Defence* • Bernard Lee *"M"* • Shane Rimmer *Captain Carter* • Bryan Marshall *Commander Talbot* • Desmond Llewelyn *"Q"* • Lois Maxwell *Miss Moneypenny* ■ *Dir* Lewis Gilbert • *Scr* Christopher Wood, Richard Maibaum, from the novel by Ian Fleming

The Spy with a Cold Nose ★★★ U
Comedy   1966 · UK · Colour · 98min

Ace sitcom writers Ray Galton and Alan Simpson here offer their contribution to the spy boom that was dominating popular cinema in the 1960s. Their sub-Bondian farce stars Laurence Harvey and fine comedy actor Lionel Jeffries in a story of Cold War espionage which features a bulldog with a listening bug grafted to its insides for spying on the Russians. The script was held up as a model of its type but the genius of the words lost a little something in translation, but much mirth remains. DF

Laurence Harvey *Dr Francis Trevellyan* • Lionel Jeffries *Stanley Farquhar* • Daliah Lavi *Princess Natasha Romanova* • Eric Sykes *Wrigley* • Eric Portman *British ambassador* • Colin Blakely *Russian prime minister* • Denholm Elliott *Pond-Jones* ■ *Dir* Daniel Petrie • *Scr* Ray Galton, Alan Simpson

The Spy with My Face ★★★ PG
Spy adventure   1966 · US · Colour · 82min

The Man from UNCLE was such a cult hit in this country that the seven movie spin-offs were made almost exclusively with the British box office in mind. In this second film in the series, Robert Vaughn's Napoleon Solo is sent to deal with a devilish doppelganger. As always David McCallum provides the dependable support as Illya Kuryakin, while Senta Berger is the naughty Napoleon's partner in crime. DP *DVD*

Robert Vaughn (1) *Napoleon Solo* • David McCallum (1) *Illya Kuryakin* • Senta Berger *Serena* • Leo G Carroll *Alexander Waverly* • Michael Evens *Darius Two* • Sharon Farrell *Sandy Wister* • Fabrizio Mioni *Arsena Coria* ■ *Dir* John Newland • *Scr* Clyde Ware, Joseph Caivelli, from a story by Clyde Ware

Spymaker: the Secret Life of Ian Fleming ★★ 15
Biographical drama 1990 · US · Colour · 95min

Fans of 007 will appreciate the Bond movie references (and the casting of Jason Connery, son of first Bond Sean, as Ian Fleming), but anyone who isn't a zealous Fleming fan may be left out in the cold by this semi-fictionalised made-for-TV account of the author's life. Mildly entertaining, but wouldn't you rather be watching a real Bond movie? JB Sex scenes.

Jason Connery *Ian Fleming* • Kristin Scott Thomas *Leda St Gabriel* • Joss Ackland *General Helstein* • David Warner *Admiral Godfrey* • Patricia Hodge *Lady Evelyn* • Colin Welland *George Fowler* • Richard Johnson *General Halmsden* ■ *Dir* Ferdinand Fairfax • *Scr* Robert J Avrech

Squanto: the Last Great Warrior ★★★ PG
Historical adventure 1994 · US · Colour · 97min

Swiss director Xavier Koller, who won a best foreign film Oscar for *Journey of Hope*, came to Disney to make this costume drama. This is far too fanciful in its description of a native American's adventures in 17th-century England. Adam Beach is suitably noble as the warrior who learns the value of life while taking sanctuary in a monastery. Younger viewers, however, will probably prefer his skirmishes with the wicked Michael Gambon to these spiritual asides. DP

Adam Beach *Squanto* • Sheldon Peters Wolfchild *Mooshawset* • Irene Bedard *Nakooma* • Eric Schweig *Epenow* • Leroy Peltier *Pequod* • Michael Gambon *Sir George* • Nathaniel Parker *Thomas Dermer* • Mandy Patinkin *Brother Daniel* • Donal Donnelly *Brother Paul* ■ *Dir* Xavier Koller • *Scr* Darlene Craviotto, Bob Dolman

The Square ★★★
Crime thriller   2008 · Aus · Colour · 105min

The *noir* trappings, the small-town setting and the fact that producers Nash and Joel Edgerton are siblings have invited comparisons with the Coen brothers. However, their striking debut feature – Nash directs, Joel co-writes and co-stars – is actually closer in feel to thrillers like *Shallow Grave* and *A Simple Plan*. A middle-aged construction manager (David Roberts) reluctantly agrees to help his mistress (Claire van der Boom) steal a stash of cash from her criminal husband (Anthony Hayes), but things don't go according to plan. The plotting relies too much on coincidence, but believable performances help the film along. JF

David Roberts (2) *Ray* • Claire van der Boom *Carla* • Joel Edgerton *Billy* • Anthony Hayes *"Smithy"* • Peter Phelps *Jake* ■ *Dir* Nash Edgerton • *Scr* Joel Edgerton, Matthew Dabner, from a story by Edgerton

The Square ★★★ 15
Documentary 2013 · Egy/US · Colour · 103min

Such is the immediacy afforded by social media that events like the Arab Spring happen in real time in our living rooms. The abundance of first-hand footage is a boon to documentarists, but events often move too quickly for cinema, and film-maker Jehane Noujaim's regular visits to Cairo's Tahrir Square continued to reshape her movie about the Egyptian Revolution even after she had finished editing. Consequently, this sometimes feels like a work in progress, as she follows various activists between the ousting of long-time president Hosni Mubarak February 2011 and the removal of his elected successor, Mohamed Morsi, in July 2013. DP Arabic +subtitles. Violence, swearing. 𝐃𝐕𝐃
• Dir Jehane Noujaim

Square Dance ★★★ 15
Drama 1987 · US · Colour · 107min

This was Winona Ryder's second film and her scripture-spouting role ultimately proves too much for her. But she is definitely one of the plus points in a film that deals solely with eccentrics. Jason Robards is lazily effective as Ryder's crotchety grandpa and Jane Alexander lets off plenty of steam as her city-corrupted mother. Rob Lowe is unbelievable as the mentally disabled Rory (and seems to belong to another film altogether). DP Swearing.

Jason Robards Jr [Jason Robards] Dillard • Jane Alexander Juanelle • Winona Ryder Gemma Dillard • Rob Lowe Rory • Deborah Richter Gwen • Guich Koock Frank • Elbert Lewis Beecham • Charlotte Stanton Aggie ■ Dir Daniel Petrie • Scr Alan Hines, from his novel

The Square Jungle ★★★
Sports drama 1955 · US · BW · 86min

Tony Curtis stars as a grocery-store clerk who joins the beasts of the "square jungle", otherwise known as the boxing ring, to earn the money to bail out his drunken father (Jim Backus). With Ernest Borgnine as Curtis's trainer, Paul Kelly as the cop who sponsors him, some peripheral romantic interest, and an appearance by heavyweight champ Joe Louis as himself, this is unremarkable but entertaining drama. RK

Tony Curtis Eddie Quaid/Packy Glennon • Patricia Crowley [Pat Crowley] Julie Walsh • Ernest Borgnine Bernie Browne • Paul Kelly (1) Jim McBride • Jim Backus Pat Quaid • Leigh Snowden Lorraine Evans • David Janssen Jack Lindsay • Joe Louis ■ Dir Jerry Hopper • Scr George Zuckerman, from his story

Square of Violence ★★★
Second World War drama
1961 · US/Yug · BW · 95min

Leonardo Bercovici's crisis of conscience drama avoids the longueurs that blighted so many stellar co-productions about the Second World War. In a rare sympathetic part, Broderick Crawford excels as the Yugoslavian partisan whose unintentionally reckless action prompts Nazi major Branko Plesa to threaten to execute hundreds of hostages unless the perpetrator of a bombing raid surrenders. Exploring the cruel realities of combat, the film eschews cheap heroics. DP

Broderick Crawford Dr Stefan Bernardi • Valentina Cortese Erica Bernardi • Branko Plesa Major Kohler • Bibi Andersson Maria • Anita Björk Sophia • Bert Sotlar Partisan leader ■ Dir Leonardo Bercovici • Scr Eric Bercovici, Leonardo Bercovici, from a story by Eric Bercovici

The Square Peg ★★ U
Second World War comedy
1958 · UK · BW · 85min

Norman Wisdom's comedy appeals because many in the audience can identify with the situations his "little man" character struggles valiantly to overcome. But here, Norman becomes a war hero by impersonating a top Nazi general, and it misfires because the commonplace is forsaken for the fantastic. It's hard to sympathise, let alone laugh, with him. DP 𝐃𝐕𝐃

Norman Wisdom Norman Pitkin/General Schreiber • Honor Blackman Lesley Cartland • Edward Chapman Mr Grimsdale • Campbell Singer Sergeant Loder • Hattie Jacques Gretchen von Schmetterling • Brian Worth Henri Le Blanc • Terence Alexander Captain Wharton • John Warwick Colonel Layton ■ Dir John Paddy Carstairs • Scr Jack Davies, Henry E Blyth, Norman Wisdom, Eddie Leslie

The Square Ring ★★ PG
Portmanteau drama 1953 · UK · BW · 79min

The portmanteau movie meets the boxing film in this clash of the genres. Covering one night at a seedy boxing ring allows this movie to veer off into separate mini-dramas, each dealing with one boxer – ranging from a wide-eyed beginner to a punch-drunk veteran. It's uneven, wavering between comedy and tragedy, but given the dangerous nature of the game there's uncertainty about the future of the pugilists. AT

Jack Warner Danny Felton • Robert Beatty Kid Curtis • Bill Owen Happy Burns • Maxwell Reed Rick Martell • George Rose Whitey Johnson • Bill Travers Rowdie Rawlings • Alfie Bass Frank Forbes • Ronald Lewis Eddie Lloyd • Sidney James Adams • Joan Collins Frankie • Kay Kendall Eve Lewis • Joan Sims Bunty ■ Dir Michael Relph, Basil Dearden • Scr Robert Westerby, Peter Myers, Alec Grahame, from the play by Ralph W Peterson

The Squeaker ★★★ U
Crime drama 1937 · UK · BW · 73min

Edmund Lowe reprises his stage role as the methodical Scotland Yard inspector who doggedly pursues arch criminal Sebastian Shaw. Confined within starchy studio sets, William K Howard directs steadily, but the removal of that touch of mystery leaves him with precious little to play with, to the extent that he has to bolster the action with protracted love scenes between Lowe and Ann Todd. Robert Newton and Alastair Sim put in pleasing support appearances. DP

Edmund Lowe Inspector Barrabal • Sebastian Shaw Frank Sutton • Ann Todd Carol Stedman • Tamara Desni Tamara • Robert Newton Larry Graeme • Allan Jeayes Inspector Elford • Alastair Sim Joshua Collie ■ Dir William K Howard • Scr Bryan Wallace, Edward O Berkman, from the novel by Edgar Wallace

The Squeeze ★★★ 18
Crime drama 1977 · UK · Colour · 102min

Comedian Freddie Starr shows that there's more to him than pratfalls and double entendres. He acquits himself surprisingly well as a small-time London crook, but the focus here falls firmly on Stacy Keach as the booze-sodden former cop who is forced to clean up his act when his ex-wife is kidnapped. This is a violent and abrasive thriller – creaky perhaps, but still disturbingly plausible. DP

Stacy Keach Naboth • Freddie Starr Teddy • Edward Fox Foreman • Stephen Boyd Vic • David Hemmings Keith • Carol White Jill • Alan Ford Taff • Roy Marsden Barry ■ Dir Michael Apted • Scr Leon Griffiths, from the novel Whose Little Girl Are You? by David Craig

The Squeeze ★ 15
Comedy thriller 1987 · US · Colour · 97min

Beetle Juice was arguably the only Michael Keaton film ever to make full use of its star's prodigious comic talents. This dreary comedy thriller, about a conman who gets caught up in murder and mayhem, is a case in point. Keaton provides a few laughs, but the remainder of this time-filler is a mirth-free zone. DA

Michael Keaton Harry Berg • Rae Dawn Chong Rachel Dobs • John Davidson Honest Tom T Murray • Ric Abernathy Bouncer • Danny Aiello III Ralph Vigo • Bobby Bass Poker player • Leslie Bevis Gem Vigo • Joohery Brown Poker player ■ Dir Roger Young • Scr Daniel Taplitz

Squibs ★★ U
Musical 1935 · UK · BW · 77min

Betty Balfour had been hailed as the English Mary Pickford during the silent era, but by the mid-1930s she was reduced to taking chirpy supports. Here she reprised the role of Squibs, the tousle-haired cockney flower girl she had played several times at the height of her fame. The story of the waif who becomes wealthy overnight was an old warhorse in the 1920s, and this has little new to offer. DP

Betty Balfour Squibs Hopkins • Gordon Harker Sam Hopkins • Stanley Holloway PC Charley Lee • Margaret Yarde Mrs Lee • Morris Harvey Inspector Lee • Michael Shepley Colin Barrett ■ Dir Henry Edwards • Scr Michael Hogan, H Fowler Mear, from the play by Clifford Seyler, George Pearson

The Squid and the Whale ★★★★ 15
Comedy drama 2005 · US · Colour · 77min

Noah Baumbach's Oscar-nominated drama is a serio-comic account of an intellectual New York couple's divorce as seen from the perspective of their two sons. It's beautifully played by the principals, with Jesse Eisenberg particularly good as the clever but callow teenager beginning the painful process of realising that his father (Jeff Daniels) is not as perfect as he once thought. But at the heart of the film is Daniels's astonishing performance as the paterfamilias whose intellectual arrogance and casual meanness are tempered by a wounded bewilderment, both at his own professional decline and at his abandonment by his wife (the excellent Laura Linney). AS Swearing. 𝐃𝐕𝐃

Jeff Daniels Bernard Berkman • Laura Linney Joan Berkman • Jesse Eisenberg Walt Berkman • Owen Kline Frank Berkman • William Baldwin Ivan • Halley Feiffer Sophie • Anna Paquin Lili • David Benger Carl ■ Dir/Scr Noah Baumbach

Squirm ★★★ 18
Black comedy horror 1976 · US · Colour · 92min

The worm turns in this cheap but cheerfully repellent horror film. A pylon, struck by lightning, electrifies the earth in typical small town, USA, and the worms go on the offensive. Writer/director Jeff Lieberman, making the most of a limited budget, builds the tension expertly, and limits the shock effects, giving full value to the scenes (created by master of the art Rick Baker) in which worms crawl through human flesh. DM

Don Scardino Mick • Patricia Pearcy Geri • RA Dow Roger • Jean Sullivan Naomi • Peter MacLean Sheriff • Fran Higgins Alma • William Newman Quigley ■ Dir/Scr Jeff Lieberman • Special Effects Rick Baker

Stacy's Knights ★★ PG
Drama 1983 · US · Colour · 90min

Kevin Costner's star did not begin to shine until he played Eliot Ness in The Untouchables, but his creative potential and charisma are evident even in this latter-day B-movie. The film has occasional tense moments in between rather too many fast sequences, though it benefits from Costner's lively performance and screenwriter Michael Blake's realistic portrayal of gambling addiction. JM Swearing, violence.

Andra Millian Stacy • Kevin Costner Will • Eve Lilith Jean • Mike Reynolds Shecky • Ed Semenza Kid • Don Hackstaff Lawyer ■ Dir Jim Wilson (2) • Scr Michael Blake

The Stag ★★ 15
Comedy 2013 · Ire · Colour · 90min

John Butler's broad, box-ticking comedy delivers all you might expect from a tale of high jinks on a bachelor weekend. Sensitive best man Andrew Scott (Moriarty in TV's Sherlock) organises a supposedly low-key camping trip in the Irish countryside, but things get out of hand as the bride's macho brother (co-writer Peter McDonald) leads the party into ever more outlandish scrapes. Scott does well as the pivotal voice of sanity trying to rein in the boorishness, but is fighting an uphill battle against the shock for shock's sake misogyny and stereotypical supporting characters. TeS Swearing, sexual references, drug abuse, brief nudity. 𝐃𝐕𝐃 🅑

Andrew Scott Davin • Hugh O'Conor Fionan • Peter McDonald The Machine • Brian Gleeson Simon • Andrew Bennett Large Kevin • Michael Legge Little Kevin ■ Dir John Butler (2) • Scr John Butler, Peter McDonald

Stage Beauty ★★★ 15
Period romantic comedy drama
2004 · US/UK/Ger · Colour · 105min

Set in the world of 17th-century London theatre, when female roles were played by men, this has as its protagonist Ned Kynaston (Billy Crudup), once London theatre's most celebrated "leading lady". The toast of society, Kynaston is oblivious to the romantic feelings of his dresser Maria (Claire Danes), who secretly reprises his performance as Desdemona in a small, illegal production of Othello. This promises much as an offbeat period romantic drama, but never quite overcomes the central problem of a "leading lady" who doesn't convince as a woman. BP Swearing, sex scenes, nudity. 𝐃𝐕𝐃

Billy Crudup Ned Kynaston • Claire Danes Maria • Rupert Everett King Charles II • Tom Wilkinson Thomas Betterton • Ben Chaplin George Villiars, Duke of Buckingham • Hugh Bonneville Samuel Pepys • Richard Griffiths Sir Charles Sedley • Edward Fox Sir Edward Hyde • Zoe Tapper Nell Gwyn ■ Dir Richard Eyre • Scr Jeffrey Hatcher, from his play Compleat Female Stage Beauty

Stage Door ★★★★ U
Comedy drama 1937 · US · BW · 90min

This is a marvellous adaptation of the witty Edna Ferber/George S Kaufman play set in a boarding house for theatrical hopefuls. Scintillating casting gives bravura roles to a batch of Hollywood greats, most notably the fabulous Katharine Hepburn and the sassy Ginger Rogers. Points, too, for acerbic Eve Arden, dippy Constance Collier and a teenaged Ann Miller. Only Andrea Leeds in the tragic role isn't up to the demands of the plot or her co-stars. A true joy, especially for stage-struck hopefuls. TS

Katharine Hepburn Terry Randall Sims • Ginger Rogers Jean Maitland • Adolphe Menjou Anthony "Tony" Powell • Gail Patrick Linda Shaw • Constance Collier Miss Catherine Luther • Andrea Leeds Kaye Hamilton • Samuel S Hinds Henry Sims • Lucille Ball Judith Canfield • Franklin Pangborn Harcourt • Jack Carson Mr Millbanks • Eve Arden Eve • Ann Miller Annie ■ Dir Gregory La Cava • Scr Morrie Ryskind, Anthony Veiller, William Slavens McNutt, from the play by Edna Ferber, George S Kaufman

Stage Door Canteen ★★★ U
Musical 1943 · US · BW · 131min

New York's Stage Door Canteen was the venue where servicemen on leave during the Second World War would meet, and be entertained by the stars of stage and screen. Producer Sol Lesser's film (directed by Frank Borzage) is a revue-style show, set in the Canteen and populated by countless entertainers giving their services free. A redundant wisp of romantic plot occasionally interrupts the parade of celebrities. RK

Cheryl Walker Eileen • William Terry Ed "Dakota" Smith • Marjorie Riordan Jean Rule • Lon McCallister "California" • Judith Anderson • Tallulah Bankhead • Ralph Bellamy • William Demarest • Gracie Fields • Billy Gilbert • Helen Hayes • Katharine Hepburn • Jean Hersholt • Sam Jaffe • Otto Kruger • Gertrude Lawrence • Gypsy Rose Lee • Peggy Lee • Harpo Marx • Yehudi Menuhin • Ethel Merman • Paul Muni • Merle Oberon • George Raft • Ethel Waters • Johnny Weissmuller ■ Dir Frank Borzage • Scr Delmer Daves

Stage Fright ★★★★ PG
Comedy thriller 1949 · UK · BW · 105min

Alfred Hitchcock's overlooked and underrated film stars Jane Wyman as a stage-struck drama student implausibly forced to require a real-life role in order to solve a murder. Marlene Dietrich is decidedly eye-catching as the jaded international singing star, with Richard Todd on the run as Wyman's former boyfriend. The film offers frequent teasing

S

diversions from great supporting players, and it's a comic charade, really – a whodunnit about role-playing and duplicity; even the flashback lies. AT *DVD*

Jane Wyman *Eve Gill/Doris Tinsdale* • Marlene Dietrich *Charlotte Inwood* • Michael Wilding *Inspector Wilfrid O "Ordinary" Smith* • Richard Todd *Jonathan Cooper* • Alastair Sim *Commodore Gill* • Sybil Thorndike *Mrs Gill* • Kay Walsh *Nellie Goode* • Miles Malleson *Mr Fortesque* • Hector MacGregor *Freddie Williams* • André Morell *Inspector Byard* • Joyce Grenfell *"Lovely Ducks"* • Patricia Hitchcock *Chubby Bannister* • Irene Handl *Mrs Mason, Mrs Gill's maid* ■ *Dir* Alfred Hitchcock • *Scr* Whitfield Cook, Alma Reville, James Bridie, from the stories *Man Running* and *Outrun the Constable* by Selwyn Jepson

Stage Fright – Aquarius ★★★ 18

Horror thriller 1987 · It · Colour · 90min

Michele Soavi, a former assistant to horror icon Dario Argento, makes his big screen directorial debut with an impressive horror movie which is not only packed with gross-out gore, but also hasn't forgotten how to frighten its audience. Soavi tackles the conventional storyline of an asylum escapee locked in a theatre where a dance company is rehearsing a ballet based on the Jack the Ripper legend in much the same style as Argento would. RS In Italian. *DVD* Blu

David Brandon • Barbara Cupisti • Robert Gligorov • Martin Philips • Mary Sellers ■ *Dir* Michele Soavi • *Scr* Michele Soavi, George Eastman [Luigi Montefiori]

Stage Struck ★★★

Silent comedy
1925 · US · BW and Colour · 76min

Gloria Swanson threw off her famous *haute couture* clothes to star as a grease-stained waitress trying to become an actress via mail order lessons in order to hang on to her stage-struck boyfriend (Lawrence Gray). As directed by Allan Dwan, it's knockabout comedy, and even has Gloria at one moment wearing trousers – and dropping them. It was her last major hit for Paramount. RK

Gloria Swanson *Jennie Hagen* • Lawrence Gray *Orme Wilson* • Gertrude Astor *Lillian Lyons* • Marguerite Evans *Hilda Wagner* • Ford Sterling *Waldo Buck* ■ *Dir* Allan Dwan • *Scr* Forrest Halsey, Sylvia La Varre, from a story by Frank R Adams

Stage Struck ★ U

Musical comedy 1936 · US · BW · 93min

Empty-headed Joan Blondell, with Broadway aspirations but no talent, backs a show but has problems with dance director Dick Powell (her real-life husband at the time). This miserable apology for a backstage musical was directed by Busby Berkeley but suffers from an almost total absence of music or dance numbers. The script is atrocious, and the comedy relief pathetic. RK

Dick Powell *George Randall* • Joan Blondell *Peggy Revere* • Warren William *Fred Harris* • Frank McHugh *Sid* • Jeanne Madden *Ruth Williams* • Carol Hughes (1) *Grace* • Craig Reynolds *Gilmore Frost* • Hobart Cavanaugh *Wayne* • Spring Byington *Mrs Randall* ■ *Dir* Busby Berkeley • *Scr* Tom Buckingham, Pat C Flick, Warren Duff, from a story by Robert Lord • *Cinematographer* Byron Haskin

Stage Struck ★★★ U

Drama 1958 · US · Colour · 94min

This interesting, sophisticated and compulsively watchable remake of *Morning Glory* is cleverly updated to the 1950s Broadway circuit and directed by Sidney Lumet. Susan Strasberg takes the lead, but isn't quite up to the demands of the role. Her distinguished co-stars include the brilliant Joan Greenwood, who has all the best dialogue as the temperamental actress Strasberg replaces. However, Henry Fonda and Christopher Plummer look as though they belong on Broadway, and the authentic use of Manhattan locations helps immensely. TS

Henry Fonda *Lewis Easton* • Susan Strasberg *Eva Lovelace* • Joan Greenwood *Rita Vernon* • Herbert Marshall *Robert Hedges* • Christopher Plummer *Joe Sheridan* • Daniel Ocko *Constantine* • Pat Harrington *Benny* • Frank Campanella *Victor* ■ *Dir* Sidney Lumet • *Scr* Ruth Goetz, Augustus Goetz, from the play *Morning Glory* by Zoe Akins

LANDMARK FILM
John Ford's tour de force turns John Wayne and Monument Valley into genre icons

Stagecoach ★★★★★ U

Classic western 1939 · US · BW · 91min

Orson Welles prepared for *Citizen Kane* by watching John Ford's masterpiece some 40 times. And why not, because this is textbook film-making by the only cinematic poet Hollywood ever produced. The plot is simplicity itself, but with just a few deft touches screenwriter Dudley Nichols creates a coachload of credible characters whose vices and virtues are not as apparent as they initially seem. Ford's first venture into Monument Valley was also his first picture starring John Wayne, the man with whom he would transform the very nature of the western. From Yakima Canutt's breathtaking stunts (although Wayne did most of his own) to the brilliant support playing, everything about this picture is perfection. DP *DVD*

John Wayne *Ringo Kid* • Claire Trevor *Dallas* • Thomas Mitchell *Dr Josiah Boone* • Andy Devine *Buck Rickabaugh, stagecoach driver* • John Carradine *Hatfield* • George Bancroft *Sheriff Curly Wilcox* • Louise Platt *Lucy Mallory* • Tim Holt *Lt Blanchard* • Chris-Pin Martin *Chris* • Donald Meek *Mr Samuel Peacock* ■ *Dir* John Ford • *Scr* Dudley Nichols, from the short story *Stage to Lordsburg* by Ernest Haycox • *Cinematographer* Bert Glennon

Stagecoach ★★

Western 1966 · US · Colour · 113min

This remake of John Ford's revered classic is no masterpiece, but it's not a total disaster, either. The producers shrewdly decided against filming in Monument Valley, electing for the plains and mountains of Colorado instead. Alex Cord is certainly no John Wayne, but Van Heflin and Ann-Margret contribute solid performances. It's also notable as being Bing Crosby's final big-screen appearance. AT

Ann-Margret *Dallas* • Bing Crosby *Doc Boone* • Red Buttons *Mr Peacock* • Alex Cord *Ringo* • Van Heflin *Curly* • Michael Connors [Mike Connors] *Hatfield* • Bob Cummings [Robert Cummings] *Mr Gatewood* • Slim Pickens *Buck* • Stefanie Powers *Lucy Mallory* • Keenan Wynn *Luke Plummer* ■ *Dir* Gordon Douglas • *Scr* Joseph Landon, from the 1939 film by Dudley Nichols

Stagecoach ★★ U

Western 1986 · US · Colour · 94min

John Ford's classic 1939 western starring John Wayne was remade in 1966 with Bing Crosby among the passengers desperate to survive attack from hostile Apaches. However, this 1986 take on Ernest Haycox's original yarn is less a remake than a gimmicky vehicle allowing country and western legends Kris Kristofferson, Johnny Cash and Willie Nelson to strap on a six-gun and save the day. It's serviceable enough, but there's no danger of Ted Post's western swan song threatening Ford's sublime masterpiece. JA

Willie Nelson *Doc Holliday* • Kris Kristofferson *Ringo/Ringo Kid/Bill Williams* • Johnny Cash *Marshal Curly Wilcox* • Waylon Jennings *Hatfield* • Elizabeth Ashley *Dallas* ■ *Dir* Ted Post • *Scr* James Lee Barrett, from the 1939 film

Stagecoach to Dancer's Rock ★★★

Western 1962 · US · BW · 72min

This unprepossessing but interesting minor Universal western deals with a tricky moral issue – the unceremonious dumping of six passengers from a stagecoach when it transpires that one of them has smallpox. Veteran western director Earl Bellamy makes the most of the film's short duration, and he's helped by the excellent performances of the underrated Warren Stevens, Jody Lawrence and the ineffable

Martin Landau. A bigger budget might have helped, though. TS

Warren Stevens *Jess Dollard* • Martin Landau *Dade Coleman* • Jody Lawrence [Jody Lawrance] *Dr Ann Thompson* • Judy Dan *Loi Yan Wu* • Del Moore *Hiram Best* • Don Wilbanks *Major John Southern* • Bob Anderson *Carl Whip Mott* ■ *Dir* Earl Bellamy • *Scr* Kenneth Darling

Staggered ★★★ 15

Comedy 1993 · UK · Colour · 95min

Martin Clunes's debut as actor/director is packed with neat cameos, tasty situations and well-timed gags. Yet it suffers from the cinematic equivalent of long stretches of motorway without a service station. Deposited on a Scottish island after his riotous stag night by a best man with designs on his bride, Clunes has to thumb his way across the country to make it to the church on time. Clunes is amiable, but the comedy is, occasionally, rather ridiculous. DP Swearing, nudity. *DVD*

Martin Clunes *Neil Price* • Michael Praed *Gary* • John Forgeham *Inspector Lubbock* • Anna Chancellor *Carmen Sfennipeg* • Sylvia Syms *Mother* • Sarah Winman *Hilary* • Griff Rhys Jones *Graham* • Michele Winstanley *Tina* • Kate Byers *Jackie* ■ *Dir* Martin Clunes • *Scr* Paul Alexander, Simon Braithwaite

Staircase ★

Comedy drama 1969 · UK · Colour · 97min

The sight of Richard Burton and Rex Harrison – two of the most notorious serial husbands and womanisers in showbusiness – parading about as ageing homosexual hairdressers made for one of the silliest sights in 1960s cinema. Both are desperately miscast and act accordingly, trying hard not to be camp and failing completely. AT

Richard Burton *Harry Leeds* • Rex Harrison *Charlie Dyer* • Cathleen Nesbitt *Harry's mother* • Beatrix Lehmann *Charlie's mother* • Stephen Lewis *Jack* ■ *Dir* Stanley Donen • *Scr* Charles Dyer, from his play

The Staircase Murders ★★

Crime thriller 2007 · US · Colour · 102min

Treat Williams delivers a considered and enigmatic performance in this dry yet twisting true-crime drama. He plays a bestselling American novelist and aspiring politician who is suspected of murdering his socialite wife. Ably supported by Kevin Pollak as his unprincipled defence lawyer, Williams elevates an otherwise episodic and pedestrian TV feature. But with variable acting from the rest of the cast, there's little authentic emotion to elicit any empathy, even for the grieving family members. SF Violence.

Treat Williams *Michael Peterson* • Kevin Pollak *David Rudolf* • Samaire Armstrong *Caitlin Atwater* • Laura Bailey *Margaret* • Kyle Clements [Kyle Russell Clements] *Clayton* ■ *Dir* Tom McLoughlin • *Scr* Donald Martin, from the novel *A Perfect Husband* by Aphrodite Jones

Stake Land ★★★ 15

Horror 2010 · US · Colour · 94min

As much a character-driven coming-of-age tale as a gritty horror fable, writer/director Jim Mickle's shocker is *The Road* with vampires. Mickle's co-writer Nick Damici stars as a vampire hunter roaming post-apocalyptic America after an epidemic has turned most of the population into blood-crazed feral creatures. He takes traumatised Connor Paolo under his wing and, along with pregnant teen Danielle Harris and abused nun Kelly McGillis, they journey through barricaded towns on the way to a New Eden. Despite a derivative story straight out of a John Ford western, this dark futuristic vision has pugnacious substance thanks to Mickle's direction, which is suffused with an intense John Carpenter vibe. AJ Violence, swearing, brief nudity. *DVD* Blu

Nick Damici *Mister* • Connor Paolo *Martin* • Kelly McGillis *Sister* • Danielle Harris *Belle* • Bonnie Dennison *Peggy* • Michael Cerveris *Jebedia Loven* ■ *Dir* Jim Mickle • *Scr* Nick Damici, Jim Mickle

Stakeout ★★★ 15

Comedy thriller 1987 · US · Colour · 112min

The always watchable Richard Dreyfuss elevates this thriller above the norm. For all its attempts to up the comedy content of the *Lethal Weapon* pictures without cutting down on their violence, it manages to be both too abrasive for family viewing and too soft for the six-pack brigade. Emilio Estevez struggles with the verbal ping-pong, but Dreyfuss's scenes with Madeleine Stowe more than atone. Both Dreyfuss and Estevez reprised their roles in the sequel *Another Stakeout*. DP Swearing, violence, sex scenes, nudity. *DVD*

Richard Dreyfuss *Chris Leece* • Emilio Estevez *Bill Reimers* • Madeleine Stowe *Maria McGuire* • Aidan Quinn *Richard "Stick" Montgomery* • Dan Lauria *Phil Coldshank* • Forest Whitaker *Jack Pismo* • Ian Tracey *Caylor Reese* • Earl Billings *Captain Giles* ■ *Dir* John Badham • *Scr* Jim Kouf

Stakeout on Dope Street ★★

Crime drama 1958 · US · BW · 75min

Irvin Kershner – who would go on to direct *Star Wars Episode V: the Empire Strikes Back* – made his feature debut with this would-be gritty crime drama. Mark Jeffrey's monochrome images of urban decay provide a credible backdrop, but any authenticity the story might have had is sapped by the ponderous performances of Yale Wexler, Jonathan Haze and Morris Miller, as the trio of street kids who come into possession of a stash of heroin, only to be pursued by a drug dealer. Underwhelming. DP

Yale Wexler *Jim* • Jonathan Haze *Ves* • Morris Miller *Nick* • Abby Dalton *Kathy* • Allen Kramer *Danny* • Herman Rudin *Mitch* • Phillip A Mansour *Lenny* • Frank Harding *Captain Allen* ■ *Dir* Irvin Kershner • *Scr* Andrew J Fenady, Irvin Kershner, Irwin Schwartz

Stalag 17 ★★★★ PG

Second World War drama
1953 · US · BW · 115min

William Holden won the best actor Oscar for his unsympathetic portrayal here of an imprisoned opportunist in a German PoW camp – an emotive subject just eight years after the end of the Second World War. Director Billy Wilder superbly balances elements of drama, satire and comedy, and captures the claustrophobia of camp life, aided by fine performances from inmates Robert Strauss and Harvey Lembeck, both of whom were veterans of the tale's original Broadway run. Director Otto Preminger is mesmerising as a Nazi. TS *DVD* Blu

William Holden (2) *Sefton* • Don Taylor *Dunbar* • Otto Preminger *Oberst Von Scherbach* • Robert Strauss *"Animal"* • Harvey Lembeck *Harry* • Neville Brand *Duke* • Richard Erdman *Hoffy* • Peter Graves (2) *Price* • Gil Stratton Jr [Gil Stratton] *Cookie* • Jay Lawrence *Bagradian* • Sig Rumann [Sig Ruman] *Schultz* ■ *Dir* Billy Wilder • *Scr* Billy Wilder, Edwin Blum, from the play by Donald Bevan, Edmund Trzcinski

Stalingrad ★★ 15

War action drama 2013 · Rus · Colour · 125min

The first Russian film to be produced in 3D IMAX aims for the epic by focusing on one of the bloodiest battles of the Second World War. Director Fyodor Bondarchuk centres on an imagined pocket of the conflict, where a ragtag band of Russians defends a strategically important building against overwhelming German forces. Subtlety isn't one of the film's strengths, but Thomas Kretschmann's committed performance and the sheer scope of the production at least ensure that it remains watchable to the end. JH Russian, German, Japanese +subtitles. *DVD* Blu 3D

Pyotr Fyodorov *Gromov* • Thomas Kretschmann *Hauptmann Peter Kahn* • Maria Smolnikova *Katya* • Yana Studilina *Masha* ■ *Dir* Fyodor Bondarchuk • *Scr* Sergey Snezhkin, Ilya Tilkin, from the novel *Life and Fate* by Vassili Grossman

Stalker ★★★★ PG
Science-fiction drama
1979 · USSR · Colour and BW · 154min

Andrei Tarkovsky could always be relied upon for visual lyricism, but the terrain traversed during this gruelling trek is anything but picturesque. Chillingly shot in muted colour by Aleksandr Knyazhinsky, the Zone is an area of the post-meteoric wilderness that can only be crossed by "stalkers" such as Aleksandr Kaidanovsky. He is hired to guide writer Anatoli Solonitsyn and professor Nikolai Grinko to the "Room", a place in which truth and innermost desire can be attained. The metaphysical discussion feels somewhat mundane after what has gone before, but this still leaves you questioning your own beliefs and values. DP Russian +subtitles. DVD

Alexander Kaidanovsky *Stalker* • Anatoly Solonitsin [Anatoli Solonitsyn] *Writer* • Nikolai Grinko *Professor* • Alisa Freindlikh *Stalker's wife* • Natasha Abramova *Stalker's daughter* ■ *Dir* Andrei Tarkovsky • *Scr* Arkady Strugatsky, Boris Strugatsky, from the book *Picnic by the Roadside* by Arkady Strugatsky

The Stalking Moon ★★ PG
Western 1968 · US · Colour · 103min

Charles Lang's Panavision landscape photography is the redeeming feature in this western, but the pacing leaves much to be desired. Gregory Peck is dull as the scout who agrees to lead Eva Marie Saint and her half-Apache son to safety. The boy's father has other ideas. The screenplay fails to convey the threat. TS

Gregory Peck *Sam Varner* • Eva Marie Saint *Sarah Carver* • Robert Forster *Nick Tana* • Noland Clay *Boy* • Russel Thorson *Ned* • Frank Silvera *Major* • Lonny Chapman *Purdue* • Lou Frizzell *Stationmaster* ■ *Dir* Robert Mulligan • *Scr* Alvin Sargent, Wendell Mayes, from the novel by Theodore V Olser

Stamboul Quest ★★★
First World War spy romance
1934 · US · BW · 85min

This espionage drama is conducted in shadows courtesy of some moody lighting by the ace cameraman James Wong Howe. Myrna Loy plays a German spy who claims to have ended Mata Hari's career, but in Istanbul she breaks her own rule by falling in love - with US medical student George Brent - right in the middle of the First World War. There's a preposterous ending, but fans of 1930s Hollywood will find much to enjoy. AT

Myrna Loy *Annemarie/Fraülein Doktor/Helena Bohlen* • George Brent *Douglas Beall* • Lionel Atwill *Von Strum* • C Henry Gordon *Ali Bey* • Douglass Dumbrille *General* • Mischa Auer *Ameel* ■ *Dir* Sam Wood • *Scr* Herman Mankiewicz, from a story by Leo Birinski

Stand and Deliver ★★★★ PG
Drama based on a true story
1988 · US · Colour · 98min

Edward James Olmos stars in this uplifting LA *barrio* tale, which he also helped power into existence. Based on the true story of teacher Jaime Escalante (Olmos), who transformed a classroom full of disaffected young gang members into such a top-scoring exam team that the examination board refused to believe it and made them sit everything again. Olmos gives an infectious, driven performance that carries everyone else along. SH Swearing.

Edward James Olmos *Jaime Escalante* • Lou Diamond Phillips *Angel* • Rosana De Soto *Fabiola Escalante* • Andy Garcia *Dr Ramirez* • Virginia Paris *Chairwoman* • Raquel Ortega • Carmen Argenziano *Principal Molina* • Mark Eliot *Tito* ■ *Dir* Ramon Menendez • *Scr* Ramon Menendez, Tom Musca

Stand by for Action ★★
Second World War drama
1942 · US · BW · 100min

Despite being co-written by Herman J Mankiewicz (of *Citizen Kane* fame) and boasting the heavyweight talents of Charles Laughton, the story of snooty Harvard graduate Robert Taylor coming to terms with the gritty reality of life on an ancient destroyer is as much junk as the ship itself. Sentimentality waterlogs the studio-harboured craft. TH

Robert Taylor (1) *Lt Gregg Mastermann* • Charles Laughton *Rear Adm Stephan "Iron Pants" Thomas* • Brian Donlevy *Lt Comdr Martin J Roberts* • Walter Brennan *Chief Yeoman Henry Johnson* • Marilyn Maxwell *Audrey Carr* ■ *Dir* Robert Z Leonard • *Scr* George Bruce, John L Balderston, Herman J Mankiewicz, from a story by Capt Harvey Haislip, RC Sherriff, from the story *A Cargo of Innocence* by Laurence Kirk

Stand by Me ★★★★★ 15
Coming-of-age drama
1986 · US · Colour · 84min

Rob Reiner's likeable but hard-centred 1950s drama is widely agreed to be one of the most successful adaptations of a Stephen King story. Blending the themes of childhood friendship, parental pressure and the loss of innocence into a roving adventure, it sees four friends (including River Phoenix) go on a rural camping odyssey to find the body of a missing boy. Each is something of a social misfit, subtly played by the cast, and their problems at home are deftly revealed against rollicking action sequences and an eventual showdown with bullies. AC Violence, swearing. DVD

Wil Wheaton *Gordie Lachance* • River Phoenix *Chris Chambers* • Corey Feldman *Teddy Duchamp* • Jerry O'Connell *Vern Tessio* • Richard Dreyfuss *The writer* • Kiefer Sutherland *Ace Merrill* • Casey Siemaszko *Billy Tessio* • John Cusack *Denny Lachance* ■ *Dir* Rob Reiner • *Scr* Raynold Gideon, Bruce A Evans, from the novella *The Body* by Stephen King

Stand-In ★★★ U
Satirical comedy 1937 · US · BW · 86min

This is a funny and perceptive tale about the dangers of non-film people involving themselves in making movies. Leslie Howard stars as an accountant sent west to audit the books of the fictional Colossal Studios, with the titular stand-in played by Joan Blondell, whose career is being guided by producer Humphrey Bogart. It's an independent satire produced by Walter Wanger, whose views on labour relations in Los Angeles as depicted here are still relevant today. The second half doesn't really live up to the wacky initial premise. TS

Leslie Howard *Atterbury Dodd* • Joan Blondell *Lester Plum* • Humphrey Bogart *Douglas Quintain* • Alan Mowbray *Koslofski* • Marla Shelton *Thelma Cheri* • C Henry Gordon *Ivor Nassau* • Jack Carson *Tom Potts* ■ *Dir* Tay Garnett • *Scr* Gene Towne, Graham Baker, from a story by Clarence Budington Kelland in *The Saturday Evening Post*

Stand Up and Cheer! ★★ U
Musical 1934 · US · BW · 81min

Broadway theatrical producer Warner Baxter is summoned to Washington by the president of the USA and appointed "Secretary of Entertainment" with a brief to cheer up a Depression-weary nation. This is the excuse for a revue featuring various musical entertainers and comedians, including a performing penguin, but the film is remembered for the attention it brought a four-year-old moppet named Shirley Temple. Relentlessly cheerful and cheerily propagandistic. RK

Warner Baxter *Lawrence Cromwell* • Madge Evans *Mary Adams* • Nigel Bruce *Eustace Dinwiddie* • Stepin Fetchit *Stepin Fetchit/George Bernard Shaw* • Frank Melton *Fosdick* • Lila Lee *Zelda* • Ralph Morgan *Secretary to the President* • Frank Mitchell *Senator Danforth* • Shirley Temple *Shirley Dugan* ■ *Dir* Hamilton MacFadden • *Scr* Lew Brown, Ralph Spence, Rian James, Edward T Lowe Jr, Malcolm Stuart Boylan, Hamilton MacFadden, from an idea by Will Rogers, Philip Klein

Stand Up Guys ★★★★ 15
Crime comedy drama 2012 · US · Colour · 91min

In this smart and hugely likeable little comedy drama, Al Pacino and Christopher Walken play best buddies and former partners in crime. Fresh from a 28-year prison stretch, Pacino spends his first night of freedom schmoozing with Walken, trawling old haunts. But there's a hidden agenda: one of them has been pressured into killing the other to settle an old gangland grudge. Pacino and Walken have rarely been better. Nor has Alan Arkin in a pivotal role as the duo's ageing former getaway driver. Sheer class. DA Violence, swearing. DVD BL

Al Pacino *Val* • Christopher Walken *Doc* • Alan Arkin *Hirsch* • Julianna Margulies *Nina Hirsch* • Lucy Punch *Wendy* ■ *Dir* Fisher Stevens • *Scr* Noah Haidle

Stand Up Virgin Soldiers ★★ 15
Comedy 1977 · UK · Colour · 87min

Writer Leslie Thomas revisits his Malayan war memoirs but this time the result is more akin to "Confessions of a National Serviceman". Nigel Davenport returns from the original *The Virgin Soldiers*, but Robin Askwith is a crude substitute for Hywel Bennett and the lavatorial humour sits uneasily alongside the stabs at drama. Look for Pamela Stephenson in an early film role. JF

Robin Askwith *Private Brigg* • George Layton *Private Jacobs* • Pamela Stephenson *Bernice* • Lynda Bellingham *Valerie* • Edward Woodward *Sergeant Wellbeloved* • Nigel Davenport *Sergent Driscoll* • John Le Mesurier *Colonel Bromley-Pickering* • Warren Mitchell *Morris Morris* • Irene Handl *Mrs Phillimore* • Miriam Margolyes *Elephant Ethel* ■ *Dir* Norman Cohen • *Scr* Leslie Thomas, from his novel

Standard Operating Procedure ★★ 15
Documentary 2008 · US · Colour · 111min

With his 1988 documentary *The Thin Blue Line*, director Errol Morris made film history by successfully clearing a man of murder. This picture is a similar attempt to exonerate the apparently guilty. However, his exposé of events surrounding the 2004 Abu Ghraib scandal - when pictures of abused prisoners at the notorious Iraqi jail found their way into the media - goes too far in protecting the not-so-innocent. In a long two hours, Morris does make a good case on behalf of those named and shamed, and there is an argument that the accused have been hung out to dry by the military machine. However, the absence of Iraqi voices is uncomfortable (although Morris did try to trace former detainees) and the lack of remorse by some of perpetrators leaves a very bad taste indeed. DW DVD BL

■ *Dir* Errol Morris • *Cinematographers* Robert Chappell, Robert Richardson • *Music* Danny Elfman

Stander ★★★ 15
Drama based on a true story
2003 · Can/Ger/S Afr/UK/US · Colour · 107min

Thomas Jane stars as Andre Stander, a Johannesburg police captain who, in 1976, suffers a crisis of conscience after killing an unarmed black man during a political protest. Rejecting the brutal system he's part of, Stander turns from cop to crook, committing a string of bold bank robberies and becoming an unlikely anti-establishment hero in the process. The film's sense of time and place is excellent, as is the acting, but it's flawed by sluggish pacing. DA English, Afrikaans +subtitles. Swearing, sex scenes, violence. DVD

Thomas Jane *Andre Stander* • Dexter Fletcher *Lee McCall* • David Patrick O'Hara [David O'Hara] *Allan Heyl* • Deborah Kara Unger *Bekkie Stander* • Ashley Taylor *Cor Van Deventer* • Marius Weyers *General Stander* • At Botha *General Viljoen* ■ *Dir* Bronwen Hughes • *Scr* Bronwen Hughes, Bima Stagg, from a story by Bima Stagg

Standing in the Shadows of Motown ★★★ PG
Documentary 2002 · US · Colour · 103min

Packed with anecdotes and insights, this documentary pays overdue tribute to the unheralded session musicians who created the unique Tamla Motown sound. What's remarkable about the Funk Brothers is their equanimity towards missing out on the fame and fortune the label's biggest stars enjoyed. What doesn't quite ring true is the contention that the musicianship is so impeccable that anyone could sing these legendary 1960s hits, as the disappointing reunion concert testifies. DP DVD

André Braugher *Narrator* • Jack "Black Jack" Ashford • Bob Babbitt • Johnny Griffith • Uriel Jones • Joe Messina • Eddie "Chank" Willis ■ *Dir* Paul Justman • *Scr* Walter Dallas, Ntozake Shange, from the book by Allan "Dr Licks" Slutsky

Standing Room Only ★★ U
Romantic comedy 1944 · US · BW · 82min

Fred MacMurray is an executive arriving in town in the hope of landing a government contract for his factory. Paulette Goddard is his inept secretary who bungles their accommodation, forcing them to take up work as husband-and-wife servants for somewhere to sleep. The comic highlight is probably MacMurray's efforts - while serving fruit salad - to retrieve a cherry that's dropped into a guest's lap without her noticing. Poorly written and contrived. AE

Paulette Goddard *Jane Rogers* • Fred MacMurray *Lee Stevens* • Edward Arnold *TJ Todd* • Roland Young *Ira Cromwell* • Hillary Brooke *Alice Todd* • Porter Hall *Hugo Farenhall* • Clarence Kolb *Glen Ritchie* ■ *Dir* Sidney Lanfield • *Scr* Darrell Ware, Karl Tunberg, from a story by Al Martin

The Stanford Prison Experiment ★★★★ 15
Prison drama based on a true story
2015 · US · Colour · 117min

This raw, often unbearably tense true-life drama is the second US feature to dramatise Stanford University's controversial 1971 study into prison life, where student volunteers assumed the roles of prisoners and guards to devastating effect. Screenwriter Tim Talbott applies an academic composure that's absent from the previous depiction. Aside from slo-mo for the first inevitable eruption of violence, director Kyle Patrick Alvarez directs without artifice, and Ezra Miller (*We Need to Talk about Kevin*) stands out as a victimised inmate. AC Violence, swearing.

Billy Crudup *Dr Philip Zimbardo* • Michael Angarano *Christopher Archer* • Moises Arias *Anthony Carroll* • Nicholas Braun *Karl Vandy* • Thomas Mann (2) *Prisoner 416* • Ezra Miller *Daniel Culp/8612* ■ *Dir* Kyle Patrick Alvarez • *Scr* Tim Talbott, from the book *The Lucifer Effect* by Philip Zimbardo

Stanley & Iris ★★★ 15
Drama 1989 · US · Colour · 100min

Although virtually unrecognisable from Pat Barker's source novel *Union Street*, this blue-collar drama is carried by striking performances from Robert De Niro and Jane Fonda. De Niro is the uneducated factory worker who is slowly drawn out of his shell by recently widowed Fonda. Martin Ritt's direction is curiously anonymous and if it weren't for the cast, this would be little more than just another "issue of the week" TV movie. JF Swearing. DVD

Jane Fonda *Iris King* • Robert De Niro *Stanley Cox* • Swoosie Kurtz *Sharon* • Martha Plimpton *Kelly King* • Harley Cross *Richard* • Jamey Sheridan *Joe* • Feodor Chaliapin [Feodor Chaliapin Jr] *Leonides Cox* • Zohra Lampert *Elaine* ■ *Dir* Martin Ritt • *Scr* Harriet Frank Jr, Irving Ravetch, from the novel *Union Street* by Pat Barker

Stanley and Livingstone ★★★★ U
Historical adventure 1939 · US · BW · 100min

This is one of the best 20th Century-Fox historical biopics, despite necessary tamperings with history to enable the inclusion of one of the most famous greetings in history. Avoiding any sense of parody whatsoever are the two fine main performances: the redoubtable Spencer Tracy as an obsessed, fever-ridden Henry Morton Stanley, and Cedric Hardwicke, genuinely convincing as Dr Livingstone.

S

Director Henry King is in his element, but he would have been surprised to see much footage from this film in *Monster from Green Hell* nearly 20 years later. **TS**

Spencer Tracy *Henry M Stanley* • Nancy Kelly *Eve Kingsley* • Richard Greene *Gareth Tyce* • Walter Brennan *Jeff Slocum* • Charles Coburn *Lord Tyce* • Cedric Hardwicke *Dr David Livingstone* • Henry Hull *James Gordon Bennett Jr* • Henry Travers *John Kingsley* ▪ *Dir* Henry King • *Scr* Philip Dunne, Julien Josephson, from research and story outline by Hal Long, Sam Hellman

Stanley's Magic Garden ★★ U

Animated musical fantasy
1994 · US · Colour · 72min

This instantly forgettable animated fantasy from Don Bluth (also known as *A Troll in Central Park*) geared towards a young audience is a sickly sweet tale about a benevolent troll with an overactive green finger who's banished to New York's Central Park. The voice cast is good, though. **JC** *DVD*

Dom DeLuise *Stanley* • Cloris Leachman *Queen Gnorga* • Phillip Glasser *Gus* • Tawney Sunshine Glover *Rosie* • Hayley Mills *Hilary* • Jonathan Pryce *Alan* ▪ *Dir* Gary Goldman, Don Bluth • *Scr* Stu Krieger

The Star ★★★

Drama
1953 · US · BW · 90min

The star is Bette Davis, three years after *All about Eve*, in a role with which she clearly identifies, as an over-the-hill movie star. This is a relatively low-budget independent feature, which gains great strength from the casting of Davis and Sterling Hayden, a pillar of integrity as her admirer. There's nice work, too, from a precocious Natalie Wood. Despite a few over-the-top scenes this minor movie echoes with a ring of truth. **TS**

Bette Davis *Margaret Elliot* • Sterling Hayden *Jim Johannson* • Natalie Wood *Gretchen* • Warner Anderson *Harry Stone* • Minor Watson *Joe Morrison* • June Travis *Phyllis Stone* • Katherine Warren *Mrs Morrison* ▪ *Dir* Stuart Heisler • *Scr* Katherine Albert, Dale Eunson

Star! ★★ PG

Biographical musical
1968 · US · Colour · 165min

Julie Andrews spends nearly three mind-boggling hours trying to convince us that she is the stage star Gertrude Lawrence. Daniel Massey does a rather better job portraying Noël Coward (his godfather in real life). Some believe Andrews is a deeply underrated actress while others think she can only portray herself. If you tend towards the latter view, then this is tedious fare, saved only by some spectacular production numbers. **SH** *DVD*

Julie Andrews *Gertrude Lawrence* • Richard Crenna *Richard Aldrich* • Michael Craig *Sir Anthony Spencer* • Daniel Massey *Noël Coward* • Robert Reed *Charles Fraser* • Bruce Forsyth *Arthur Lawrence* • Beryl Reid *Rose* • Jenny Agutter *Pamela* ▪ *Dir* Robert Wise • *Scr* William Fairchild

The Star Chamber ★★★ 15

Thriller
1983 · US · Colour · 104min

This gripping thriller revolves around the moral dilemma of a young judge having to free dangerous criminals because of legal technicalities. As a result, he discovers the existence of the "Star Chamber", a legal vigilante committee that takes the law into its own hands. The drawn-out storyline ultimately fails to convince, and Michael Douglas in the leading role is too inexperienced (at that time) as an actor to bring it off. Director Peter Hyams does well enough, despite having to film on confined sets. **TS** Swearing, violence. *DVD*

Michael Douglas (1) *Steven R Hardin* • Hal Holbrook *Benjamin Caulfield* • Yaphet Kotto *Detective Harry Lowes* • Sharon Gless *Emily Hardin* • James B Sikking *Dr Harold Lewin* • Joe Regalbuto *Arthur Cooms* ▪ *Dir* Peter Hyams • *Scr* Roderick Taylor, Peter Hyams, from a story by Roderick Taylor

Star Dust ★★★ U

Drama
1940 · US · BW · 85min

Walter Lang directs Linda Darnell in this tale of the struggles and disappointments suffered by an attractive young woman spotted by a Hollywood talent scout, only to be turned down by the studio boss. About to go home, she meets and falls in love with former singing football star John Payne, who pushes her into persevering. A familiar tale to be sure, but well told here with an unromantic air of authenticity that convinces. **RK**

Linda Darnell *Carolyn Sayres* • John Payne *Bud Borden* • Roland Young *Thomas Brooke* • Charlotte Greenwood *Lola Langdon* • William Gargan *Dane Wharton* • Mary Beth Hughes *June Lawrence* • Mary Healy *Mary Andrews* • Donald Meek *Sam Wellman* ▪ *Dir* Walter Lang • *Scr* Robert Ellis, Helen Logan, from a story by Jesse Malo, Kenneth Earl, Ivan Kahn

Star 80 ★★★★ 18

Biographical drama
1983 · US · Colour · 98min

The true story of Canadian *Playboy* playmate-turned-Hollywood actress Dorothy Stratten who was on the verge of stardom when she was murdered by her small-time hustler husband Paul Snider. Director Bob Fosse's last movie is a disturbing look at the high cost of fame. Stratten is brilliantly portrayed by Mariel Hemingway (complete with breast enlargements), but it's Eric Roberts as her psychotically jealous spouse who registers the strongest impact. A downbeat and dark fairy tale of Tinseltown's tarnished ethics. **AJ**

Mariel Hemingway *Dorothy Stratten* • Eric Roberts *Paul Snider* • Cliff Robertson *Hugh Hefner* • Carroll Baker *Dorothy's mother* • Roger Rees *Aram Nicholas* • David Clennon *Geb* • Josh Mostel *Private detective* ▪ *Dir* Bob Fosse • *Scr* Bob Fosse, from the story *Death of a Playmate* by Teresa Carpenter

Star in the Dust ★★★★ PG

Western
1956 · US · Colour · 76min

A very fine but generally underrated western, this taut film contains its action between twilight and dawn as sheriff John Agar gets ready to hang killer Richard Boone, while Boone's hired guns (at the behest of banker villain Leif Erickson) menace the town. Sultry 1950s icon Mamie Van Doren is Agar's gal and – to add to the plot – Erickson's relation. Watch closely for a very young Clint Eastwood. **TS** *DVD*

John Agar *Sheriff Bill Jorden* • Mamie Van Doren *Ellen Ballard* • Richard Boone *Sam Hall* • Coleen Gray *Nellie Mason* • Leif Erickson *George Ballard* • James Gleason *Orval Jones* • Randy Stuart *Nan Hogan* • Clint Eastwood *Ranch hand* ▪ *Dir* Charles F Haas [Charles Haas] • *Scr* Oscar Brodney, from the novel *Law Man* by Lee Leighton

A Star Is Born ★★★★ U

Drama
1937 · US · Colour · 110min

This is one of the most famous movie titles of all time, here in its second incarnation (the first was called *What Price Hollywood?*), with Janet Gaynor as the young star on the way up and Fredric March as the ageing star on the way out in Tinseltown. Gaynor and March are superb and Hollywood itself is well depicted in early three-strip Technicolor. The now classic screenplay by Dorothy Parker and Alan Campbell, among others, is still caustic and vibrant, and, of course, contains one of the greatest last lines in all cinema. **TS** *DVD*

Janet Gaynor *Esther Blodgett/Vicki Lester* • Fredric March *Norman Maine* • Adolphe Menjou *Oliver Niles* • May Robson *Lettie, Grandmother Blodgett* • Andy Devine *Danny McGuire* • Lionel Stander *Matt Libby* • Owen Moore *Casey Burke* • Peggy Wood *Miss Phillips, Central Casting Corp clerk* • Elizabeth Jenns *Anita Regis* ▪ *Dir* William A Wellman • *Scr* Dorothy Parker, Alan Campbell, Robert Carson, William A Wellman, Ring Lardner Jr, Bud Schulberg, John Le Mahin, from a story by Robert Carson, William A Wellman

A Star Is Born ★★★★★ U

Musical drama
1954 · US · Colour · 168min

One of the most outstanding melodramas in Hollywood's history, this remake contains the greatest ever performance by the lustrous Judy Garland, paired with the brilliant James Mason at the very zenith of their talents. Their portrayals, plus superb direction from George Cukor, ensure that this film enriches more lives each time it is screened. But on first release, the movie was overlong, and was trimmed. In the 1980s some of this missing material was discovered, with other scenes re-created using stills. This "restoration", though of historical value, may alienate a first-time viewer. In any case, this stunner superbly portrays Hollywood at its self-centred best, and when Judy Garland lost that year's Oscar to Grace Kelly, Groucho Marx quipped, "It's the biggest robbery since Brink's!". **TS** *DVD*

Judy Garland *Esther Blodgett/Vicki Lester* • James Mason *Norman Maine* • Jack Carson *Matt Libby* • Charles Bickford *Oliver Niles* • Tommy Noonan *Danny McGuire* • Lucy Marlow *Lola Lavery* • Amanda Blake *Susan Ettinger* • Irving Bacon *Graves* • Hazel Shermet *Miss Wheeler* • James Brown (1) *Glenn Williams* ▪ *Dir* George Cukor • *Scr* Moss Hart, from the 1937 film • *Cinematographer* Sam Leavitt

A Star Is Born ★★ 15

Musical drama
1976 · US · Colour · 133min

This remake, starring Barbra Streisand and Kris Kristofferson as the star-crossed lovers on self-destruct, doesn't quite work. They tried to bring the action screechingly up to date with a contemporary rock soundtrack, but there's little finesse as everyone rushes around in 1970s gear that already looked pretty dated on release. The movie's basic problem is that we simply cannot believe that Streisand and Kristofferson are in the throes of a passionate love affair. **SH** Swearing, brief nudity.

Barbra Streisand *Esther Hoffman* • Kris Kristofferson *John Norman Howard* • Gary Busey *Bobby Ritchie* • Oliver Clark *Gary Danziger* • Marta Heflin *Quentin* • MG Kelly *Bebe Jesus* • Sally Kirkland *Photographer* • Paul Mazursky *Brian* ▪ *Dir* Frank Pierson • *Scr* John Gregory Dunne, Joan Didion, Frank Pierson, from the 1937 film

Star Kid ★★★ PG

Science-fiction adventure
1997 · US · Colour · 96min

Joseph Mazzello gives an engaging performance as an ignored and bullied child who isn't having much luck with girls, either. In a scrapyard he comes across a combat-enhancement suit (with its own intelligence) belonging to an alien race. The garment takes everything Mazzello says literally, providing much amusement and the movie serves up enough action to satisfy the kids. **KB**

Joseph Mazzello *Spencer Griffith* • Richard Gilliland *Roland Griffith* • Corinne Bohrer *Janet Holloway* • Alex Daniels *Cyborsuit* • Joey Simmrin *Turbo Bruntley* • Ashlee Levitch *Stacey Griffith* • Jack McGee *Hank Bruntley* ▪ *Dir/Scr* Manny Coto

The Star Maker ★★ U

Musical drama
1939 · US · BW · 93min

This minor musical drama stars Bing Crosby as a showman and songwriter, inspired by the career of Gus Edwards (who discovered Eddie Cantor among others). Failed singer Edwards, forced to work as a store salesman, hits on the idea of setting up a vaudeville act with youngsters. Success is cut short when he falls foul of child labour laws, but he then turns to the new medium of radio. Crosby dispenses easy charm and croons a handful of numbers. **RK**

Bing Crosby *Larry Earl* • Linda Ware *Jane Gray* • Louise Campbell *Mary* • Ned Sparks *"Speed" King* • Walter Damrosch • Laura Hope Crews *Carlotta Salvina* • Thurston Hall *Mr Proctor* ▪ *Dir* Roy Del Ruth • *Scr* Frank Butler, Don Hartman, Arthur Caesar, from a story by Arthur Caesar, William A Pierce

Star of India ★ U

Period swashbuckling adventure
1954 · UK · Colour · 92min

This virtually unwatchable swashbuckler stars Cornel Wilde as the French nobleman who, stripped of his estates, starts a search for a priceless jewel. Jean Wallace isn't stripped of anything but tags along anyway. Herbert Lom hisses like a panto villain and seems to have an unhealthy relationship with his Siamese cats. **AT**

Cornel Wilde *Pierre St Laurent* • Jean Wallace *Katrina* • Herbert Lom *Narbonne* • Yvonne Sanson *Madame De Montespan* • John Slater *Emile* • Walter Rilla *Van Horst* • Basil Sydney *King Louis XIV* ▪ *Dir* Arthur Lubin • *Scr* Herbert Dalmas, Denis Freeman

Star of Midnight ★★★

Mystery comedy
1935 · US · BW · 89min

Capitalising on William Powell's success in *The Thin Man*, RKO plagiarised the attributes of both the Nick Charles character and the actor himself, casting him as a witty and debonair lawyer. Nicely directed by Stephen Roberts, this comedy suspenser sees Powell trying to prove himself innocent of the murder of a gossip columnist by turning sleuth, with the assistance of his girlfriend Ginger Rogers. A characteristic 1930s mixture of cops, criminals, and cocktails, it's sophisticated and entertaining. **RK**

William Powell *Clay Dalzell* • Ginger Rogers *Donna Mantin* • Leslie Fenton *Tim Winthrop* • Paul Kelly (1) *Jimmy Kinland* • Gene Lockhart *Horace Swayne* • Ralph Morgan *Roger Classon* • J Farrell MacDonald *Inspector Doremus* • Russell Hopton *Tommy Tennant* ▪ *Dir* Stephen Roberts • *Scr* Howard J Green, Anthony Veiller, Edward Kaufman, from the novel *Star of Midnight* by Arthur Somers Roche

The Star Packer ★★ U

Western
1934 · US · BW · 53min

This John Wayne programme filler for Monogram has a ludicrous plot about a mysterious "Shadow" who traverses the town via an underground tunnel is made palatable by sprightly casting: George Hayes, and the friendly Indian, played by ace stuntman Yakima Canutt, usually cast as the heavy in these B-movies. **TS** *DVD*

John Wayne *John Travers* • Verna Hillie *Anita Matlock* • George "Gabby" Hayes *Matt Matlock* • Yakima Canutt *Yak* • Earl Dwire *Mason* • Ed Parker [Eddie Parker] *Parker* • George Cleveland *Old Jake* • William Franey *Pete* ▪ *Dir/Scr* Robert N Bradbury

Star Spangled Rhythm ★★★ U

Musical comedy
1942 · US · BW · 100min

One of the better wartime revue-format shows, for which Paramount corralled just about everybody on the payroll. The screwy premise for the musical and comedy extravaganza is the impending visit of a sailor on leave (Eddie Bracken), who believes that his Paramount gateman father (Victor Moore) is really the studio's executive vice-president. Encouraged by switchboard operator Betty Hutton, Moore pretends he is the studio head, whereupon the mighty organisation co-operates in the deception and stages a show for Bracken and his pals. **RK**

Bing Crosby • Bob Hope *Master of Ceremonies* • Fred MacMurray *Man playing cards* • Ray Milland *Man playing cards* • Franchot Tone *Man playing cards* • Victor Moore *"Pop" Webster/"Bronco Billy"* • Dorothy Lamour • Paulette Goddard • Veronica Lake • Vera Zorina • Mary Martin • Dick Powell • Betty Hutton *Polly Judson* • Eddie Bracken *Johnny Webster* • Alan Ladd *Scarface* • William Bendix *Husband* • Macdonald Carey *Louie the Lug* • Walter Abel *BG De Soto* • Susan Hayward *Genevieve* • Cecil B DeMille • Preston Sturges • Anne Revere *Sarah* ▪ *Dir* George Marshall • *Scr* Harry Tugend, Arthur Phillips, George Kaufman, Arthur Ross, Fred Saidy, Norman Panama, Melvin Frank • *Music/lyrics* Harold Arlen, Johnny Mercer

Star Trek: the Motion Picture ★★★U

Science-fiction adventure
1979 · US · Colour · 124min

Dubbed "The Slow Motion Picture" when it was first released, the long-delayed big-screen debut of the cult TV series is rather talky, but does hit epic heights that fans can't fail to be moved by. Director Robert Wise purposely went for grandeur rather than mock heroics in an effort to give the beloved characters an enduring film career beyond TV repeats. And it worked, as time has shown, despite the familiar plot of the crew of the USS *Enterprise* confronting a mysterious alien menace. AJ *DVD* Blu

William Shatner *Admiral James T Kirk* • Leonard Nimoy *Mr Spock* • DeForest Kelley *Dr Leonard "Bones" McCoy* • Stephen Collins *Commander Willard Decker* • Persis Khambatta *Ilia* • James Doohan *Scotty* • George Takei *Sulu* • Nichelle Nichols *Uhura* • Walter Koenig *Chekov* • Majel Barrett *Dr Christine Chapel* ■ *Dir* Robert Wise • *Scr* Harold Livingston, Gene Roddenberry, from a story by Alan Dean Foster, from the TV series created by Gene Roddenberry

Star Trek II: the Wrath of Khan ★★★★12

Science-fiction adventure
1982 · US · Colour · 108min

The big screen sequel to the 1967 TV episode *Space Seed* is truer in spirit to the beloved space opera than the first feature. Here, genetic superman Ricardo Montalban wreaks vengeance against the *Enterprise* crew for sending him to a planetary wasteland. Director Nicholas Meyer stresses the narrative values that made the original series so compelling and vibrantly weaves the thematic motifs of life, loss and adventure together as he expertly continues the saga. Leonard Nimoy has rarely been so moving. AJ Violence. *DVD* Blu

William Shatner *Admiral James T Kirk* • Leonard Nimoy *Spock* • DeForest Kelley *Dr Leonard "Bones" McCoy* • James Doohan *Scotty* • Walter Koenig *Chekov* • George Takei *Sulu* • Nichelle Nichols *Commander Uhura* • Bibi Besch *Dr Carol Marcus* • Merritt Butrick *David* • Paul Winfield *Captain Terrell* • Kirstie Alley *Saavik* • Ricardo Montalban *Khan* ■ *Dir* Nicholas Meyer • *Scr* Jack B Sowards, from a story by Harve Bennett, Jack B Sowards, from the TV series created by Gene Roddenberry

Star Trek III: the Search for Spock ★★★PG

Science-fiction adventure
1984 · US · Colour · 100min

There are no real surprises in this ponderous journey to the final frontier, in which Admiral Kirk hijacks the starship *Enterprise* to help in the rejuvenation of the deceased Spock on the planet Genesis. It's a good character-driven story, marred by Leonard Nimoy's workmanlike direction, a pseudo-mystical ending and an all-pervasive funereal tone. Amazing special effects supply the wonder and emotional charge missing from what is nothing more than a bloated TV episode. AJ *DVD* Blu

William Shatner *Admiral James T Kirk* • DeForest Kelley *Dr Leonard "Bones" McCoy* • James Doohan *Scotty* • George Takei *Sulu* • Walter Koenig *Chekov* • Nichelle Nichols *Uhura* • Christopher Lloyd *Kruge* • Robin Curtis *Lieutenant Saavik* • Merritt Butrick *David Marcus* • James B Sikking *Captain Styles* • Mark Lenard *Ambassador Sarek* ■ *Dir* Leonard Nimoy • *Scr* Harve Bennett, from the TV series created by Gene Roddenberry

Star Trek IV: the Voyage Home ★★★★PG

Science-fiction adventure
1986 · US · Colour · 113min

After three impressive but rather po-faced adventures, the *Enterprise* regulars got the chance to let their hair down a little for this hugely enjoyable trek. The crew has to travel back to 1980s San Francisco to free a couple of whales that can save the Earth from a destructive space probe. While there is little in the way of sci-fi spectacle, the crew has a great time poking fun at the idiosyncrasies of life in modern-day California. JF Swearing. *DVD* Blu

William Shatner *Captain James T Kirk* • Leonard Nimoy *Spock* • Catherine Hicks *Dr Gillian Taylor* • DeForest Kelley *Dr Leonard "Bones" McCoy* • James Doohan *Scotty* • George Takei *Sulu* • Walter Koenig *Chekov* • Nichelle Nichols *Commander Uhura* • Jane Wyatt *Amanda, Spock's mother* • Mark Lenard *Sarek* • Robin Curtis *Lieutenant Saavik* ■ *Dir* Leonard Nimoy • *Scr* Harve Bennett, Steve Meerson, Peter Krikes, Nicholas Meyer, from a story by Leonard Nimoy, Bennett, from the TV series created by Gene Roddenberry

Star Trek V: the Final Frontier ★★★PG

Science-fiction adventure
1989 · US · Colour · 102min

With William Shatner in the director's chair, this lacks the wit and panache of its predecessor, but still makes for an enjoyable romp. A messianic figure (Laurence Luckinbill) is holding a distant planet hostage but, in reality, wants to lay his hands on the *Enterprise* and its creaky crew. Aiming for a more mystical plane than usual, the plot is embarrassingly trite at times. In the end it just about gets by, thanks to the interplay between Shatner, Leonard Nimoy and DeForest Kelley, and an action-packed finale. JF Swearing. *DVD* Blu

William Shatner *Captain James T Kirk* • Leonard Nimoy *Mr Spock* • DeForest Kelley *Dr Leonard "Bones" McCoy* • James Doohan *Scotty* • Walter Koenig *Chekov* • Nichelle Nichols *Lieutenant Uhura* • George Takei *Sulu* • Laurence Luckinbill *Sybok* • David Warner *St John Talbot* • Melanie Shatner *Yeoman* ■ *Dir* William Shatner • *Scr* David Loughery, from a story by William Shatner, Harve Bennett, David Loughery, from the TV series created by Gene Roddenberry

Star Trek VI: the Undiscovered Country ★★★★PG

Science-fiction adventure
1991 · US · Colour · 105min

The *Star Trek* movie series goes supernova with an outstanding episode directed by Nicholas Meyer, who also directed *The Wrath of Khan*. Mirroring world news events of the time (the Soviet Union's dissolution), Meyer crafts a near perfect blend of humanistic messages, affectionate lampooning, epic visuals and fairy-tale imagination as the classic *Enterprise* crew encounters treachery during prospective peace negotiations with the Klingons. Clever Shakespearean touches heighten the dramatic agony and ecstasy. AJ *DVD* Blu

William Shatner *Captain James T Kirk* • Leonard Nimoy *Spock* • DeForest Kelley *Dr Leonard "Bones" McCoy* • James Doohan *Montgomery "Scotty" Scott* • Walter Koenig *Pavel Chekov* • Nichelle Nichols *Lieutenant Uhura* • George Takei *Captain Hikaru Sulu* • Kim Cattrall *Lieutenant Valeris* • Mark Lenard *Sarek* • Christopher Plummer *General Chang* • Iman *Martia* • David Warner *Chancellor Gorkon* • Christian Slater *"Excelsior" crewman* ■ *Dir* Nicholas Meyer • *Scr* Nicholas Meyer, Denny Martin Flinn, from a story by Leonard Nimoy, Lawrence Konner, Mark Rosenthal, from the TV series created by Gene Roddenberry

Star Trek: Generations ★★★★PG

Science-fiction adventure
1994 · US · Colour · 113min

Some of the old *Star Trek* cast, led by William Shatner, unite with the *Next Generation* crew, commanded by Patrick Stewart, to stop mad scientist Malcolm McDowell tapping into an energy source that can bring one's most desired fantasies to life. If you can stay with the multilayered and self-referential plot, this fun saga builds up to warp speed for an exciting climax. A special-effects laden adventure, it trades on fan sentiment and nostalgia as the two much loved generations of space heroes merge into one space/time continuum. AJ Violence. *DVD* Blu

Patrick Stewart *Captain Jean-Luc Picard* • Jonathan Frakes *Commander William T Riker* • Brent Spiner *Lt Commander Data* • LeVar Burton *Lt Commander Geordi La Forge* • Michael Dorn *Lt Worf* • Gates McFadden *Dr Beverly Crusher* • Marina Sirtis *Counselor Deanna Troi* • Malcolm McDowell *Soran* • James Doohan *Scotty* • Walter Koenig *Chekov* • William Shatner *Captain James T Kirk* • Whoopi Goldberg *Guinan* ■ *Dir* David Carson • *Scr* Ronald D Moore, Brannon Braga, from a story by Brannon Braga, Ronald D Moore, Rick Berman, from characters by Gene Roddenberry

Star Trek: First Contact ★★★★★12

Science-fiction adventure
1996 · US · Colour · 106min

The Borg travel back in time to sabotage that pivotal moment in Earth's destiny when we first made contact with an alien race in this first-rate adventure. What else can Captain Picard do except follow and sort things out? Epic in scope, grandiose in emotional sweep and featuring awesome special effects, this is captivating science fiction packed with ideas, thrills, in-jokes and tense action. It's all expertly marshalled by director Jonathan Frakes (who also plays Commander Riker) with a keen visual eye and an inherent understanding of the history of the series. AJ Violence. *DVD* Blu

Patrick Stewart *Captain Jean-Luc Picard* • Jonathan Frakes *Commander William T Riker* • Brent Spiner *Lt Commander Data* • LeVar Burton *Lt Commander Geordi La Forge* • Michael Dorn *Lt Commander Worf* • Gates McFadden *Dr Beverly Crusher* • Marina Sirtis *Counselor Deanna Troi* • Alice Krige *Borg Queen* • James Cromwell *Zefram Cochrane* • Alfre Woodard *Lily Sloane* • Dwight Schultz *Lt Barclay* • Robert Picardo *Holographic doctor* ■ *Dir* Jonathan Frakes • *Scr* Brannon Braga, Ronald D Moore, from a story by Rick Berman, Brannon Braga, Ronald D Moore, from the TV series created by Gene Roddenberry

Star Trek: Insurrection ★★★PG

Science-fiction adventure
1998 · US · Colour · 98min

Ethnic cleansing gets the *Trek* treatment in the ninth feature, which is aimed squarely at fans. Travelling where *Star Trek* has boldly gone before, with the light-hearted tale of a planet of perpetual youth and the two races who are struggling for the right to use it, there's nothing new in this proficient cocktail of predictable space heroics and *Lost Horizon* homages. Visually impressive (marking the first use of computer digitals for the spaceship sequences), the film also features F Murray Abraham as an unusual villain. AJ Swearing, violence. *DVD* Blu

Patrick Stewart *Captain Jean-Luc Picard* • Jonathan Frakes *Commander William T Riker* • Brent Spiner *Lt Commander Data* • LeVar Burton *Lt Commander Geordi La Forge* • Michael Dorn *Lt Commander Worf* • Gates McFadden *Dr Beverly Crusher* • Marina Sirtis *Counselor Deanna Troi* • F Murray Abraham *Ru'afo* • Donna Murphy *Anij* • Anthony Zerbe *Dougherty* ■ *Dir* Jonathan Frakes • *Scr* Michael Piller, from a story by Rick Berman, Michael Piller, from the TV series created by Gene Roddenberry

Star Trek: Nemesis ★★★12

Science-fiction adventure
2002 · US · Colour · 111min

The tenth entry in the long-running *Star Trek* franchise sees the crew of the USS *Enterprise* about to split up after the nuptials of Commander Riker (Jonathan Frakes) and Counselor Troi (Marina Sirtis), and Riker's acceptance of his own starship command. However, their plans change when the Romulans offer a suspect peace treaty and Captain Picard (Patrick Stewart) encounters his evil clone twin, Shinzon (Tom Hardy). Like many of the previous big-screen adventures, this action-packed outing resembles a good episode of the TV series stretched to feature-film length. AS *DVD* Blu

Patrick Stewart *Jean-Luc Picard* • Jonathan Frakes *Cmdr William T Riker* • Brent Spiner *Lt Cmdr Data/B-4* • LeVar Burton *Lt Cmdr Geordi La Forge* • Michael Dorn *Lt Cmdr Worf* • Marina Sirtis *Counselor Deanna Troi* • Gates McFadden *Dr Beverly Crusher* • Tom Hardy *Shinzon* • Ron Perlman *Viceroy* • Kate Mulgrew *Admiral Janeway* • Wil Wheaton *Wesley Crusher* • Majel Barrett Roddenberry [Majel Barrett] *Computer* • Whoopi Goldberg *Guinan* ■ *Dir* Stuart Baird • *Scr* John Logan, from a story by John Logan, Rick Berman, Brent Spiner, from the TV series created by Gene Roddenberry

Star Trek ★★★★12

Science-fiction adventure
2009 · US/Ger · Colour · 121min

JJ Abrams's successful reboot – the 11th *Star Trek* motion picture – is a prequel to the original TV series. A big budget and top-flight digital effects designed to snare a new audience combine with enough in-jokes to satisfy the old guard. A young, impulsive James T Kirk (Chris Pine) reluctantly attends Starfleet Academy and stows aboard the USS *Enterprise*. Here his frosty relationship with Vulcan first officer Spock (Zachary Quinto) thaws in the grip of an epic battle with Eric Bana's impressive Romulan foe, Nero. Light relief is provided by Simon Pegg's offbeat engineer Scotty and an already grumpy Dr "Bones" McCoy (Karl Urban). AC *DVD* Blu

Chris Pine *James T Kirk* • Zachary Quinto *Spock* • Leonard Nimoy *Spock Prime* • Eric Bana *Nero* • Karl Urban *Dr Leonard "Bones" McCoy* • Simon Pegg *Montgomery "Scotty" Scott* • John Cho *Hikaru Sulu* • Zoë Saldana *Uhura* • Anton Yelchin *Pavel Chekov* • Winona Ryder *Amanda Grayson* • Bruce Greenwood *Captain Christopher Pike* • Ben Cross *Sarek* ■ *Dir* JJ Abrams • *Scr* Roberto Orci, Alex Kurtzman, from the TV series created by Gene Roddenberry

Star Trek into Darkness ★★★★12

Science-fiction adventure
2013 · US · Colour · 132min

In returning director JJ Abrams's thrill-a-minute blockbuster, Benedict Cumberbatch is sensational as the rogue Starfleet officer who turns intergalactic terrorist, prompting the *Enterprise* crew to track him to the planet Kronos where the Klingons are on war alert. The story is built primarily around the burgeoning friendship between Kirk (Chris Pine, more relaxed in his iconic role) and Spock (Zachary Quinto, finding the perfect Vulcan balance of logic and emotion), which means that other key characters are either sidelined or, in the case of Alice Eve's new recruit, weakly drawn. But Abrams pulls out all the action stops, beginning in full-throttle adventure mode and sustaining the warp-speed spectacle all the way through to an epic finale in San Francisco. A further sequel is due in 2016. AJ Some violence, swearing. *DVD* Blu 3D

Chris Pine *Captain James T Kirk* • Zachary Quinto *Spock* • Benedict Cumberbatch *John Harrison* • Karl Urban *Dr Leonard McCoy* • Zoë Saldana *Nyota Uhura* • Simon Pegg *Montgomery "Scotty" Scott* • Anton Yelchin *Pavel Chekov* • John Cho *Sulu* • Bruce Greenwood *Christopher Pike* • Noel Clarke *Thomas Harewood* • Leonard Nimoy *Spock Prime* ■ *Dir* JJ Abrams • *Scr* Alex Kurtzman, Damon Lindelof, Roberto Orci, from the TV series *Star Trek* by Gene Roddenberry

S

Star Trek Beyond ★★★★12A

Science-fiction adventure
2016 · US · Colour · 122min

The best since *Wrath of Khan*? Could be, as the 13th movie marries such quintessential Roddenberry material (co-written by fanboy Simon Pegg) as intense action, character-driven humour and philosophical musings with the most spectacular special effects in the entire canon. Lured by a bogus distress call, the Enterprise crew must regroup to thwart the war mongering desires of lizard-like ruler Krall (an underused Idris Elba). Paying moving tribute to Leonard Nimoy, director Justin Lin upscales the visually majestic spills into the hyperspeed stratosphere. Phenomenally entertaining. AJ 3D

Chris Pine *Kirk* • Zachary Quinto *Spock* • Karl Urban *Bones* • Zoe Saldana [Zoë Saldana] *Uhura* • Simon Pegg *Scotty* • Anton Yelchin *Chekov* • John Cho *Sulu* • Idris Elba *Krall* ■ *Dir* Justin Lin, Robert Orci • *Scr* Doug Jung, Simon Pegg, from characters by Gene Roddenberry

Star Wars Episode I: the Phantom Menace ★★★ U

Science-fiction epic adventure
1999 · US · Colour · 132min

No matter how hard George Lucas has tried to recapture the magic of the original films, that vital sense of wonder is missing from this first prequel. Instead, Lucas provides a welter of incident, cosmic dilemmas, cryptic forebodings and idiotic dialogue. It's absolutely phenomenal on the visual front, but completely mindless in the story department. Forget the overworked plot about Natalie Portman trying to stop the Trade Federation invading her planet with help from Jedi knights Liam Neeson and Ewan McGregor; marvel instead at the technical wizardry and fizzing action. AJ DVD Blu-ray SP CS

Liam Neeson *Qui-Gon Jinn* • Ewan McGregor *Obi-Wan Kenobi* • Natalie Portman *Queen Amidala/ Padmé* • Jake Lloyd *Anakin Skywalker* • Ian McDiarmid *Senator Palpatine* • Pernilla August *Shmi Skywalker* • Oliver Ford Davies *Sio Bibble* • Frank Oz *Yoda* • Anthony Daniels *C-3PO* • Kenny Baker (2) *R2-D2* • Terence Stamp *Chancellor Valorum* • Brian Blessed *Boss Nass* • Ray Park *Darth Maul* • Celia Imrie *Fighter Pilot Bravo 5* • Samuel L Jackson *Jedi Knight Mace Windu* • Sofia Coppola *Saché* • Greg Proops *Fode* • Scott Capurro *Beed* • Lindsay Duncan *TC-14* ■ *Dir/Scr* George Lucas • *Music* John Williams

Star Wars Episode II: Attack of the Clones

★★★ PG

Science-fiction epic adventure
2002 · US · Colour · 136min

This beats the underwhelming first prequel: more action, less politics and better gags. Ewan McGregor relaxes into the role of Obi-Wan Kenobi, playing master rather than pupil now, and combines withering humour with credible superheroics. By cutting between three major plot strands – Anakin Skywalker (Hayden Christensen) and Padmé Amidala (Natalie Portman) fall in love; Obi-Wan confronts bounty hunter Jango Fett (Temuera Morrison); the Jedi prepare for war – Lucas never loses our attention, and the computer-generated imagery is impeccable, not least when Yoda duels with Jedi gone bad Christopher Lee. AC DVD Blu-ray

Ewan McGregor *Obi-Wan Kenobi* • Natalie Portman *Padmé Amidala* • Hayden Christensen *Anakin Skywalker* • Christopher Lee *Count Dooku* • Samuel L Jackson *Mace Windu* • Frank Oz *Yoda* • Ian McDiarmid *Supreme Chancellor Palpatine* • Pernilla August *Shmi Skywalker* • Temuera Morrison *Jango Fett* • Jimmy Smits *Senator Bail Organa* • Ahmed Best *Jar Jar Binks* • Anthony Daniels *C-3PO* • Kenny Baker (2) *R2-D2* ■ *Dir* George Lucas • *Scr* George Lucas, Jonathan Hales, from a story by George Lucas

Star Wars Episode III: Revenge of the Sith ★★★ 12

Science-fiction epic adventure
2005 · US · Colour · 134min

The *Star Wars* saga finally concludes 28 years after the original instalment first hit cinemas. With the story's outcome predetermined, this crucial and much-anticipated segment details how and why dedicated Jedi knight Anakin Skywalker (Hayden Christensen) turned away from good to become the evil Darth Vader. Given that this involves love, loyalty, jealousy and betrayal, you'd expect an emotionally intense film. However, writer/director George Lucas's ridiculous dialogue and unconvincing plot developments play like second-rate soap opera, almost robbing this epic of pathos and tension. Fortunately, the superb visuals save the day, making for a breathtaking spectacle. SF DVD Blu-ray

Ewan McGregor *Obi-Wan Kenobi* • Hayden Christensen *Anakin Skywalker/Lord Darth Vader* • Natalie Portman *Senator Amidala/Padmé Naberrie-Skywalker* • Ian McDiarmid *Supreme Chancellor Palpatine* • Samuel L Jackson *Mace Windu* • Christopher Lee *Count Dooku/Darth Tyrannus* • Anthony Daniels *C-3PO* • Kenny Baker (2) *R2-D2* • Peter Mayhew *Chewbacca* • Frank Oz *Yoda* • James Earl Jones *Darth Vader* • Ahmed Best *Jar Jar Binks* ■ *Dir/Scr* George Lucas

Star Wars Episode IV: a New Hope ★★★★★ U

Classic science-fiction adventure
1977 · US · Colour · 115min

Endlessly imitated but never rivalled, this first instalment of George Lucas's space opera dresses up the timeless tale of good versus evil with ground-breaking special effects and a dazzling array of intergalactic characters. Mark Hamill plays Luke Skywalker, whose dull life on a remote planet is thrown into chaos when he intercepts a distress call from beleaguered Princess Leia (Carrie Fisher). With robots R2-D2 and C-3PO in tow, Luke teams up with an ageing Jedi warrior (Alec Guinness) and a cynical space rogue (a star-making turn from Harrison Ford) to rescue Leia from the clutches of the evil Darth Vader. Breathless action collides with sci-fi theatrics and more than a hint of mysticism to create a new style of cinema that remains unmatched for entertainment value. AJ DVD

Mark Hamill *Luke Skywalker* • Harrison Ford *Han Solo* • Carrie Fisher *Princess Leia Organa* • Peter Cushing *Grand Moff Tarkin* • Alec Guinness *Ben (Obi-Wan) Kenobi* • Anthony Daniels *C-3PO* • Kenny Baker (2) *R2-D2* • Peter Mayhew *Chewbacca* • Dave Prowse *Darth Vader* • James Earl Jones *Darth Vader* ■ *Dir/Scr* George Lucas • *Cinematographer* Gilbert Taylor • *Music* John Williams • *Art Director* John Barry (2)

Star Wars Episode V: the Empire Strikes Back ★★★★★ U

Classic science-fiction adventure
1980 · US · Colour · 124min

Director Irvin Kershner's imaginative supervision of George Lucas's brainchild gives this second part of the first *Star Wars* trilogy a truly epic dimension, adding a mature, philosophical aspect to the nonstop barrage of brilliant special effects. Events take place all over the universe – Darth Vader sends Imperial troops to crush the rebels on the ice planet Hoth, while Luke Skywalker searches out Jedi master Yoda for further instruction in the mysterious ways of "the Force" – and the much loved characters are developed in intriguing ways. Kershner darkens the imagery of Lucas's vibrant, futuristic fairy tale, giving this sequel a cynical, harder edge. AJ DVD Blu-ray

Mark Hamill *Luke Skywalker* • Harrison Ford *Han Solo* • Carrie Fisher *Princess Leia* • Billy Dee Williams *Lando Calrissian* • Anthony Daniels *C-3PO* • David Prowse [Dave Prowse] *Darth Vader* • James Earl Jones *Voice of Darth Vader* • Peter Mayhew *Chewbacca* • Kenny Baker (2) *R2-D2* • Frank Oz *Yoda* • Alec Guinness *Obi-Wan "Ben" Kenobi* ■ *Dir* Irvin Kershner • *Scr* Leigh Brackett, Lawrence Kasdan, from a story by George Lucas • *Music* John Williams • *Art Director* Norman Reynold

Star Wars Episode VI: Return of the Jedi ★★★★ U

Science-fiction epic adventure
1983 · US · Colour · 134min

Sequels are usually a case of diminishing returns, but this conclusion to the original *Star Wars* trilogy is still essential viewing. Director Richard Marquand jumps straight in where *The Empire Strikes Back* finished off with a stunning sequence involving the monstrous Jabba the Hutt and the pace rarely falters from then on, even if the plot is a dash stop-start at times. Mark Hamill still looks more like an enthusiastic schoolboy than an intergalactic hero, yet his climactic scenes with Darth Vader work a treat, and, while adults will probably cringe at the cutesy Ewoks, their presence makes this a particular favourite with younger viewers. JF DVD Blu-ray

Mark Hamill *Luke Skywalker* • Harrison Ford *Han Solo* • Carrie Fisher *Princess Leia* • Billy Dee Williams *Lando Calrissian* • Anthony Daniels *C-3PO* • Peter Mayhew *Chewbacca* • Sebastian Shaw *Anakin Skywalker* • Ian McDiarmid *Emperor Palpatine* • Frank Oz *Yoda* • David Prowse [Dave

Prowse] *Darth Vader* • James Earl Jones *Voice of Darth Vader* • Alec Guinness *Obi-Wan "Ben" Kenobi* • Kenny Baker (2) *R2-D2* ■ *Dir* Richard Marquand • *Scr* Lawrence Kasdan, George Lucas, from a story by George Lucas

Star Wars Episode VII: the Force Awakens ★★★★★ 12

Fantasy action adventure
2015 · US · Colour · 132min

The space opera franchise returns with a massive cosmic bang as co-writer/director JJ Abrams takes George Lucas's brainchild and guides it firmly towards a healthy series future. Winning newcomers Daisy Ridley and John Boyega are the scrap metal scavenger and renegade stormtrooper who escort a droid carrying an intergalactic map to where last remaining Jedi knight Luke Skywalker (Mark Hamill) is in hiding. Keeping the spirit of the original *Star Wars* intact, while tweaking its basic story, Abrams and returning classic cast members create a visually compelling and remarkably deft fantasy spectacle. AJ Some violence Blu-ray SP

Harrison Ford *Han Solo* • Mark Hamill *Luke Skywalker* • Carrie Fisher *Leia* • Daisy Ridley *Rey* • John Boyega *Finn* • Oscar Isaac *Poe Dameron* • Lupita Nyong'o *Maz Kanata* • Peter Mayhew *Chewbacca* • Anthony Daniels *C-3PO* • Kenny Baker (2) *R2-D2* • Andy Serkis *Supreme Leader Snoke* • Domhnall Gleeson *General Hux* • Simon Pegg *Unkar Plutt* • Warwick Davis *Wollivan* • Daniel Craig *Stormtrooper JB-007* ■ *Dir* JJ Abrams • *Scr* JJ Abrams, Lawrence Kasdan, Michael Arndt, from characters by George Lucas • *Cinematographer* Dan Mindel [Daniel Mindel] • *Music* John Williams • *Production Designers* Rick Carter, Darren Gilford • *Editors* Maryann Brandon, Mary Jo Markey

Star Wars Episode VIII

Fantasy action adventure 2017 · US · Colour

This is a preview – no prints were available to review as we went to press: Rian Johnson should feel the force of extreme pressure weighing on his shoulders as he's handed the directing reins to the eighth instalment of the blockbusting space franchise amid reports of re-shoots on spin-off *Rogue One*. Plot details have been jealously guarded but you can be fairly sure of seeing Rey (Daisy Ridley) in Jedi training under the tutelage of Luke Skywalker (Mark Hamill) while Kylo Ren (Adam Driver doing a junior Darth Vader) assembles the First Order for an all-lasers-blazing space battle. SP SP

Mark Hamill *Luke Skywalker* • Daisy Ridley *Rey* • John Boyega *Finn* • Oscar Isaac *Poe Dameron* ■ *Dir/Scr* Rian Johnson

Star Wars: The Clone Wars ★★ PG

Animated science-fiction adventure
2008 · US · Colour · 94min

If you've been following the labyrinthine myth that George Lucas began in 1977, then this animated offshoot from the *Star Wars* franchise fills in yet more convoluted gaps between Episodes II and III. The plot sees Anakin Skywalker (voiced by Matt Lanter) and his apprentice Ahsoka Tano (Ashley Eckstein) set out to rescue the son of Jabba the Hutt from renegades, a double-crossing scheme hatched by evil Count Dooku (Christopher Lee). The battle scenes are impressively flashy but the angular *manga* style and humourless character interplay reduce the movie to the standard of a banal children's cartoon. Not surprising, really, as this was originally intended to act as the opening episodes of a TV series. AJ DVD Blu-ray

Matt Lanter *Anakin Skywalker* • James Arnold Taylor *Obi-Wan Kenobi* • Christopher Lee *Count Dooku* • Samuel L Jackson *Mace Windu* • Tom Kane *Yoda* • Catherine Taber *Padmé Amidala* • Ian Abercrombie *Palpatine* • Anthony Daniels *C-3PO* • Ashley Eckstein *Ahsoka Tano* ■ *Dir* Dave Filoni • *Scr* Henry Gilroy, Steven Melching, Scott Murphy, from characters by George Lucas

Starbuck ★★★ 15

Comedy 2011 · Can · Colour · 109min

This comedy about a man who made a prodigious amount of sperm bank

donations in his youth was a huge hit across Canada. Now in his forties, but still not behaving like a grown-up, chubby schlub Patrick Huard is confronted with the fact that he has sired 533 children, and 142 of them want to know his identity. He anonymously inserts himself into some of their lives, while facing the prospect of knowingly becoming a father for the first time with his long-suffering girlfriend. That's on top of being in debt to some ruthless mobsters. Taking its title from a famously potent Holstein bull, this is an amiable enough rites-of-passage tale. But, while Huard makes an engaging antihero, there's a fair amount of manipulative mawkishness here, too. DP French +subtitles.

Patrick Huard *David Wozniak/Starbuck* • Julie Le Breton *Valérie* • Antoine Bertrand *David's lawyer* • Dominic Philie *Older brother* ■ *Dir* Ken Scott (2) • *Scr* Ken Scott (2), Martin Petit

Stardom ★★★

Satire 2000 · Can/Fr · Colour and BW · 100min

Atoning in perception for what it lacks in subtlety, Denys Arcand's sniping satire on the transient cult of celebrity is as brash as the worlds it depicts. Fittingly for a mockumentary about a life lived in the public gaze, the action is made up of clips from news reports, chat shows and actuality profiles, as Jessica Paré goes from small-town nobody to supermodel and cultural icon in the twinkling of a TV set. The writing is scattershot and the performances inconsistent, although Frank Langella and Dan Aykroyd are excellent. DP

Jessica Paré *Tina Menzhal* • Dan Aykroyd *Barry Levine* • Thomas Gibson *Renny Ohayon* • Charles Berling *Philippe Gascon* • Robert Lepage *Bruce Taylor* • Camilla Rutherford *Toni* • Frank Langella *Blaine de Castillon* ■ *Dir* Denys Arcand • *Scr* Denys Arcand, J Jacob Potashnik

Stardust ★★★ 15

Musical drama 1974 · UK · Colour · 106min

Singer David Essex reprises his role as Jim MacLaine, the working class boy who wanted to become a pop star in this dated but enjoyable sequel to *That'll Be the Day*. In this follow-up he becomes the biggest rock star in the world – so you just know it's going to all go horribly wrong. Most interesting here – apart from Essex's lame attempts at acting – is the supporting cast of 1960s warblers, including Adam Faith and Marty Wilde. JB

David Essex *Jim MacLaine* • Adam Faith *Mike* • Larry Hagman *Porter Lee Austin* • Ines Des Longchamps *Danielle* • Rosalind Ayres *Jeanette* • Marty Wilde *Colin Day* • Edd Byrnes *Television interviewer* • Keith Moon *JD Clover* • Dave Edmunds *Alex* • Paul Nicholas *Johnny* ■ *Dir* Michael Apted • *Scr* Ray Connolly

Stardust ★★★★ PG

Fantasy adventure
2007 · US/UK · Colour · 122min

This adaptation of the fantasy graphic novel by Neil Gaiman and Charles Vess invites comparison with *The Princess Bride* and Terry Gilliam's *The Adventures of Baron Munchausen* for its imagination, scale, humour and cross-generational appeal. Charlie Cox plays Tristan, a young shop assistant in rural Victorian England, who enters a magical parallel world in pursuit of a fallen star in order to prove his worth to indifferent sweetheart Victoria (Sienna Miller). The star has taken on the earthly shape of Yvaine (Claire Danes) and the two find themselves pursued by Lamia the witch (Michelle Pfeiffer) and a motley crew of murderous princes, several of whom are dead. The pace is brisk throughout and the story (co-written by Mrs Jonathan Ross, Jane Goldman) delightfully picaresque, while director Matthew Vaughn makes the most of some awesome Scottish and Icelandic backdrops. BP DVD Blu-ray

Claire Danes *Yvaine* • Charlie Cox *Tristan Thorne* • Michelle Pfeiffer *Lamia* • Robert De Niro *Captain Shakespeare* • Mark Strong *Septimus* • Ricky Gervais *Ferdy the fence* • Sienna Miller *Victoria* • Jason Flemyng *Primus* • Rupert Everett *Secondus* • Peter O'Toole *The King* ■ *Dir* Matthew Vaughn • *Scr* Matthew Vaughn,

Jane Goldman, from the graphic novel by Neil Gaiman, Charles Jess · *Cinematographer* Ben Davis

Stardust Memories
★★★★ **15**

Comedy 1980 · US · BW · 84min

Woody Allen vents his spleen against critics and audiences in this heavily autobiographical, but surprisingly funny comedy. He plays Sandy Bates, a director remarkably like Allen, who wants to break out of the comedy mould and make "serious" movies. Attending a weekend film festival of his work, he runs the gauntlet of fans and critics and muses on his complicated love life with Charlotte Rampling and Jessica Harper. This two-fingered salute to audiences deserves marks for audacity and is beautifully shot in black and white. TH Swearing. *DVD*

Woody Allen *Sandy Bates* · Charlotte Rampling *Dorrie* · Jessica Harper *Daisy* · Marie-Christine Barrault *Isobel* · Tony Roberts *Tony* · Helen Hanft *Vivian Orkin* · John Rothman *Jack Abel* · *Dir/Scr* Woody Allen

Starflight One
★★ **U**

Futuristic adventure
1983 · US · Colour · 109min

Director Jerry Jameson specialised in this type of jeopardy movie in the 1970s and 80s. Here, Lee Majors deals with a new-fangled jetliner in crisis, having been inadvertently chucked into outer space on its maiden flight. Naturally there's a sturdy cast of watchables on board, while the special effects are courtesy of *Star Wars* wizard John Dykstra, former head of Industrial Light & Magic. TS

Lee Majors *Capt Cody Briggs* · Hal Linden *Josh Gilliam* · Ray Milland *QT Thornwell* · Gail Strickland *Nancy Gilliam* · Lauren Hutton *Erika Hansen* · George DiCenzo *Bowdish* · Robert Englund ■ *Dir* Jerry Jameson · *Scr* Robert Malcolm Young, from a story by Gene Warren, Peter R Brooke

Stargate
★★★★ **PG**

Science-fiction adventure
1994 · US/Fr · Colour · 115min

Aliens colonised ancient Egypt through a space-time portal according to this derivative yet hugely enjoyable cosmic adventure. James Spader is terrific as the code-cracking archaeologist who accompanies soldier Kurt Russell across the universe to fight galactic tyrant Jaye Davidson. Simple in execution, yet classic in the nostalgic way it evokes the feel of vintage 1940s serials, director Roland Emmerich combines plot strands from literature and other films of the genre, with some imaginative special effects and impressive visuals. AJ Brief violence, swearing. *DVD*

Kurt Russell *Col Jonathan "Jack" O'Neil* · James Spader *Dr Daniel Jackson* · Jaye Davidson *Ra* · Viveca Lindfors *Catherine* · Alexis Cruz *Skaara* · Mili Avital *Sha'uri* · Leon Rippy *General WO West* · John Diehl *Lieutenant Kawalsky* ■ *Dir* Roland Emmerich · *Scr* Roland Emmerich, Dean Devlin · *Cinematographer* Karl Walter Lindenlaub · *Production Designer* Holger Gross

Stark Raving Mad
★★ **15**

Heist comedy drama 2002 · US · Colour · 99min

This highly derivative heist comedy patches together a ragtag assortment of multi-genre clichés, pop culture references and flashy camera techniques. It follows debt-ridden 20-something Seann William Scott and his slacker pals as they struggle to pull off a bank robbery using a nightclub rave as cover. Throw into the mix a vengeful Mob boss (a blond-haired Lou Diamond Phillips), undercover federal agents, Chinese gangsters and even a couple of transvestites, and you've got a moderately engaging, if predictable feature. SF *DVD*

Seann William Scott *Ben McGewan* · Timm Sharp *Rikki Simms* · Patrick Breen *Jeffrey Jay* · Lou Diamond Phillips *Mr Gregory* · John Crye [John B Crye] *Jake Nealson* · Suzy Nakamura *Betty Shin* · Dave Foley *Roy* ■ *Dir/Scr* Drew Daywalt, Dave Schneider [David Schneider (2)]

The Starmaker
★★★ **18**

Comedy drama 1994 · It · Colour · 102min

Giuseppe Tornatore (*Cinema Paradiso*) returns to similarly nostalgic territory with this drama set in the 1950s. Roving conman Sergio Castellitto poses as a movie talent scout who persuades Sicilian villagers to pay for their own screen tests and promises them a bright future. This is a smashing idea, intrinsically funny and flexible enough to combine the dreams and crushed hopes of any number of budding actors. But the film is oddly repetitive, and the touristy photography is a bit much. AT Italian +subtitles.

Sergio Castellitto *Joe Morelli* · Tiziana Lodato *Beata* · Franco Scaldati *Brigadiere Mastropaolo* · Leopoldo Trieste *Mute* ■ *Dir* Giuseppe Tornatore · *Scr* Giuseppe Tornatore, Fabio Rinaudo, from a story by Giuseppe Tornatore

Starman
★★★★ **PG**

Science-fiction romance
1984 · US · Colour · 110min

A curious alien responds to the *Voyager* spacecraft's invitation to visit Earth, lands in Wisconsin and takes the form of Karen Allen's late husband in a romantic road movie with a cosmic twist. John Carpenter's religious sci-fi parable has as much heart and emotion as it does special effects, and gives Oscar-nominated Jeff Bridges a real chance to stretch his acting talent as the extraterrestrial eager to learn about the pleasures and pain of human existence. Funny, suspenseful and moving, this engaging space odyssey is one of Carpenter's best efforts. AJ Swearing, violence. *DVD*

Jeff Bridges *Starman* · Karen Allen *Jenny Hayden* · Charles Martin Smith *Mark Shermin* · Richard Jaeckel *George Fox* · Robert Phalen *Major Bell* · Tony Edwards *Sergeant Lemon* ■ *Dir* John Carpenter · *Scr* Bruce A Evans, Raynold Gideon

Starred Up
★★★★ **18**

Prison drama 2013 · UK · Colour · 101min

A new British star is born in this brutal but rewarding drama, with Jack O'Connell as a violent young offender transferred to an adult prison. Scorning the best efforts of well-meaning volunteer counsellor Oliver (Rupert Friend), Eric stubbornly resists any attempt to rehabilitate him. However, a glimmer of hope appears in the unlikely form of older inmate Neville (Ben Mendelsohn), who happens to be Eric's father – but will his form of tough love be Eric's salvation? It's a question this moving but unsentimental film pursues to its stunning climax, and though the depiction of prison justice sometimes recalls an overcooked version of Hogarth's *A Rake's Progress*, O'Connell commands the screen as the troubled yet somehow sympathetic antihero. DW Violence, swearing, sexual references, nudity. *DVD*

Jack O'Connell (2) *Eric Love* · Ben Mendelsohn *Neville Love* · Rupert Friend *Oliver Baumer* · Sam Spruell *Deputy Governor Hayes* · Anthony Welsh *Hassan* ■ *Dir* David Mackenzie · *Scr* Jonathan Asser

Stars
★★★★

Drama 1959 · E Ger/Bul · BW · 93min

The first East German film to find favour abroad was written by a Bulgarian Jew and directed by a Red Army veteran. The combination of their experiences and a refusal to indulge in easy sentimentality enables director Konrad Wolf and screenwriter Anzel Wagenstein to impart realism, abhorrence and faint optimism to the story of the German soldier who falls in love while transporting Greek Jews from a Bulgarian detention centre. The dramatic onus rests on Jürgen Frohriep, as he realises the enormity of the Nazis' crimes and deserts to join the Partisans. DP German +subtitles.

Sascha Krusharska *Ruth* · Jürgen Frohriep *Walter* · Erik S Klein *Kurt* · Stefan Peichev *Uncle Petko* · Georgi Naumov *Blazhe* · Ivan Kondov *Ruth's father* ■ *Dir* Konrad Wolf, Rangel Vulchanov · *Scr* Angel Wagenstein

Stars and Bars
★ **15**

Comedy 1988 · US · Colour · 90min

It would be nice to recommend this picture and on paper it promises much: Daniel Day-Lewis and Harry Dean Stanton in the main roles, based on a novel by William Boyd and directed by Pat O'Connor, who made *Cal*. Sadly, something went horribly wrong with this comedy about an Englishman's misadventures in the American Deep South. What was quite funny in the novel becomes, in Boyd's script, trite and embarrassing. AT

Daniel Day-Lewis *Henderson Dores* · Harry Dean Stanton *Loomis Gage* · Laurie Metcalf *Melissa* · Martha Plimpton *Bryant* · Kent Broadhurst *Sereno* · Maury Chaykin *Freeborn Gage* · Matthew Cowles *Beckman Gage* · Joan Cusack *Irene Stein* ■ *Dir* Pat O'Connor · *Scr* William Boyd, from his novel

Stars and Stripes Forever
★★★ **U**

Musical biography 1952 · US · Colour · 89min

March king John Philip Sousa is waspishly incarnated by Clifton Webb, who portrays a composer desperate to write ballads, not marches. It may or may not be true, but who cares when his fabulous compositions are dispersed through the movie in superb Alfred Newman arrangements? Ruth Hussey makes a tolerant Mrs Sousa, and upcoming Fox stars Robert Wagner and Debra Paget enjoy themselves as the youngsters. TS

Clifton Webb *John Philip Sousa* · Debra Paget *Lily* · Robert Wagner *Willie* · Ruth Hussey *Jennie* · Finlay Currie *Colonel Randolph* · Benay Venuta *Madame Bernsdorff-Mueller* ■ *Dir* Henry Koster · *Scr* Lamar Trotti, Ernest Vajda, from the autobiography *Marching Along* by John Philip Sousa

The Stars Fell on Henrietta
★★★ **PG**

Drama 1995 · US · Colour · 105min

Barely released, this Depression-era drama stars Robert Duvall as a down-on-his-luck Texas oilman dreaming of one last big strike. Director James Keach (brother of Stacy) creates a fine atmosphere from the desolate landscape and gets some good performances – Duvall is excellent, as usual, and so are Aidan Quinn and Frances Fisher as the lowly farmers whose land may hold the key to Duvall's fortune. Fisher was the one-time partner of the film's producer, Clint Eastwood, and their daughter, Francesca, plays one of Fisher's daughters in the story. AT

Robert Duvall *Mr Cox* · Aidan Quinn *Don Day* · Frances Fisher *Cora Day* · Brian Dennehy *Big Dave* · Lexi Randall *Beatrice Day* · Kaytlyn Knowles *Pauline Day* · Francesca Ruth Eastwood *Mary Day* · Billy Bob Thornton *Roy* ■ *Dir* James Keach · *Scr* Philip Railsback

Stars in My Crown
★★★

Period religious drama 1950 · US · BW · 89min

Joel McCrea gives another sterling performance as the new parson appointed to a small Southern town. He proves to be of stern stuff as he encounters epidemics and the menace of the Ku Klux Klan, while shattering the superstitious illusions of the populace. Director Jacques Tourneur was better known for eerie horrors and brooding *films noirs*, but he neatly blends genre convention with period nostalgia to explore themes rarely tackled in the average B-western. DP

Ellen Drew *Harriet Gray* · Dean Stockwell *John Kenyon* · Alan Hale *Jed Isbell* · Lewis Stone *Dr DK Harris Sr* · James Mitchell *Dr DK Harris Jr* · Amanda Blake *Faith Radmore Samuels* · Ed Begley *Lon Backett* · Jim Arness [James Arness] *Rufe Isbell* ■ *Dir* Jacques Tourneur · *Scr* Margaret Fitts, from the novel by Joe David Brown

The Stars Look Down
★★★★ **PG**

Drama 1939 · UK · BW · 94min

Carol Reed's well-crafted drama, based on AJ Cronin's novel about life in an English mining town, is a precursor to the gritty northern school of socially conscious British film-making. Michael Redgrave tops the bill as the upwardly mobile son of a miner, while Margaret Lockwood is the woman he marries. The film is strong on detail in its portrayal of mining life and, although it creaks with age in parts, it remains powerful and moving. Novelist and sometime film critic Graham Greene rated this one of the best British movies he'd ever seen. PF *DVD*

Michael Redgrave *David Fenwick* · Margaret Lockwood *Jenny Sunley* · Emlyn Williams *Joe Gowan* · Nancy Price *Martha Fenwick* · Allan Jeayes *Richard Barras* · Edward Rigby *Robert Fenwick* ■ *Dir* Carol Reed · *Scr* JB Williams, from the novel by AJ Cronin

Starship Troopers
★★★★ **18**

Satirical science-fiction adventure
1997 · US · Colour · 129min

Director Paul Verhoeven's ultra-violent adaptation of science-fiction writer Robert A Heinlein's classic 1959 novel – a saga about Earth versus alien bugs - is popcorn exploitation at its lip-smacking, blood-spattered best. Whether portraying the chilling spectacle of millions of ugly giant insects swarming over the planet or the astonishing intergalactic battles, the digitally-created special effects are simply outstanding. It's when Verhoeven cuts to the teenage romance that his sensational cartoon carnage comes unstuck. This enjoyably absurd apocalyptic satire was followed by an inconsequential straight-to-video sequel in 2004. AJ Violence, some swearing. *DVD* *BL*

Casper Van Dien *Johnny Rico* · Dina Meyer *Dizzy Flores* · Denise Richards *Carmen Ibanez* · Jake Busey *Ace Levy* · Neil Patrick Harris *Carl Jenkins* · Clancy Brown *Sergeant Zim* · Michael Ironside *Jean Rasczak* ■ *Dir* Paul Verhoeven · *Scr* Edward Neumeier, from the novel by Robert A Heinlein

Starship Troopers 2: Hero of the Federation
★★ **18**

Science-fiction action horror
2004 · US · Colour · 87min

Having helped devise the effects for the Paul Verhoeven original, Phil Tippett was entrusted with the direction of this disappointing sequel. Dispensing with Verhoeven's dark humour, it follows the stand-off between a stranded squad of Troopers and the planet-seizing arachnids in an abandoned military base. Budget limitations clearly have an impact on the storyline, as both tension and creature sequences are at a premium. Casper Van Dien returned in 2008 for a second sequel, which went straight to DVD. DP Violence, swearing, a sex scene, brief nudity. *DVD*

Richard Burgi *Captain Dax* · Colleen Porch *Private Lei Sahara* · Lawrence Monoson *Lt Pavlov Dill* · Ed Lauter *Gen JG Shepherd* · Brenda Strong *Sgt Dede Rake* · Billy Brown [Bill Brown] *Private Ottis Brick* ■ *Dir* Phil Tippett · *Scr* Ed Neumeier

Starship Troopers 3: Marauder
★ **15**

Science-fiction action adventure
2008 · US/S Afr/Ger · Colour · 100min

Directly following on from the original movie (the first sequel was a stand-alone adventure), Casper Van Dien's Colonel Johnny Rico returns to squash more giant bugs with the help of high-powered mechanical suits. Anything good from Robert A Heinlein's classic sci-fi novel has long since been wrung out of the franchise; what's left is this jumble of explosions, flesh-ripping and reduced-to-clear special effects. AJ Violence, swearing. *DVD* *BL*

Casper Van Dien *Colonel Johnny Rico* · Jolene Blalock *Captain Lola Beck* · Amanda Donohoe *Admiral Enolo Phid* · Marnette Patterson *Holly Little* ■ *Dir/Scr* Edward Neumeier

Starsky & Hutch
★★★ **15**

Action crime comedy
2004 · US · Colour · 96min

By cleverly respecting his source material and skewering some much loved clichés, co-writer/director Todd Phillips nails the big screen version of TV cop show. The casting

S

of Ben Stiller as by-the-book Starsky and Owen Wilson as laid-back chancer Hutch couldn't be better. Grudgingly paired up, the mismatched detectives learn to rely on each other while bringing a drugs lord (Vince Vaughn) to justice. Phillips's eye for the show's kitsch iconography ensures a good time for all. AJ Drug abuse, violence.

DVD BL

Ben Stiller *Detective David Starsky* • Owen Wilson *Detective Ken "Hutch" Hutchinson* • Vince Vaughn *Reese Feldman* • Juliette Lewis *Kitty* • Snoop Dogg *Huggy Bear* • Fred Williamson *Captain Doby* • Carmen Electra *Staci* • Amy Smart *Holly* • Jason Bateman *Kevin* • Chris Penn *Manetti* ■ *Dir* Todd Phillips • *Scr* Todd Phillips, John O'Brien, Scot Armstrong, from a story by Stevie Long, John O'Brien, from characters by William Blinn

Starsuckers ★★★ 12

Documentary   2009 · UK · Colour · 103min

In this hit-and-miss documentary about the all-pervasive cult of celebrity, director Chris Atkins (*Taking Liberties*) effectively highlights how Britain is "Sleaze Central" for fake and fabricated celebrity stories in the media. The film also demonstrates how a public that can taste fame vicariously through reality TV shows, gossip magazines and tabloid kiss-and-tells is more than willing to do anything for its own 15 minutes of fame. The movie tilts at a few too many targets, and does not always hit them (a Live Aid/Live 8 coda is rather ill-thought through), but it does make for punchy, potent viewing. DA *DVD*

■ *Dir/Scr* Chris Atkins

Start the Revolution without Me ★★★★ PG

Period farce   1970 · US · Colour · 86min

In 18th-century France, two sets of identical twins get scrambled at birth thanks to an incompetent doctor, resulting in double helpings of Donald Sutherland and Gene Wilder. One pair of brothers grow up rich and privileged, while their less fortunate counterparts are peasants. Confused? You will be when the mismatched twins find themselves on opposing sides during some Revolutionary skirmishes. There's a *Monty Python* quality to some of the humour and verbal fireworks. TH

Gene Wilder *Claude Coupé/Philippe Di Sisi* • Donald Sutherland *Charles Coupé/Pierre Di Sisi* • Hugh Griffith *King Louis XVI* • Jack MacGowran *Jacques Cabriolet* • Billie Whitelaw *Queen Marie Antoinette* • Victor Spinetti *Duke d'Escargot* • Orson Welles *Narrator* ■ *Dir* Bud Yorkin • *Scr* Fred Freeman, Lawrence J Cohen, from the story *Two Times Two* by Fred Freeman

Starter for 10 ★★★★ 12

Period romantic comedy drama
2006 · US/UK · Colour · 92min

TV's *University Challenge* provides a hilarious framing device for debut director Tom Vaughan's spirited coming-of-age tale. Adapted by David Nicholls from his own bestselling novel, it stars a charismatic James McAvoy as a student navigating through his chaotic first year at Bristol University in the mid-1980s. Bittersweet lessons about life and love follow, precipitated by two headstrong girls and a dream opportunity to compete in his favourite academic telly quiz (whose catchphrase gives the film its title). With its smart, pop culture-infused dialogue and evocative period soundtrack, this has all the buoyancy of a John Hughes teen caper. But it's the sharp, distinctly British humour and nostalgic warmth that have most appeal. SF Swearing, some drug abuse. *DVD* BL

James McAvoy *Brian Jackson* • Alice Eve *Alice Harbinson* • Rebecca Hall *Rebecca Epstein* • Catherine Tate *Julie Jackson* • Dominic Cooper *Spencer* • Benedict Cumberbatch *Patrick* • James Corden *Tone* • Mark Gatiss *Bamber Gascoigne* • Charles Dance *Michael Harbinson* • Lindsay Duncan *Rose Harbinson* ■ *Dir* Tom Vaughan (1) • *Scr* David Nicholls, from his novel • *Cinematographer* Ashley Rowe

Starting Over ★★★ 15

Romantic comedy   1979 · US · Colour · 101min

Get the tissues out for this romantic comedy in which Burt Reynolds – in one of his most sensitive performances – stars as a man coping with his wife (Candice Bergen) leaving him to pursue a singing career. There are some funny and moving moments to be had as he consults his pals and even joins a divorced men's group. There's also much hilarity from Bergen's eye-wincingly awful singing. Nice support from Jill Clayburgh, too, as the commitment-shy teacher with whom Reynolds attempts a relationship. JB *DVD*

Burt Reynolds *Phil Potter* • Jill Clayburgh *Marilyn Holmberg* • Candice Bergen *Jessica Potter* • Charles Durning *Michael "Mickey" Potter* • Frances Sternhagen *Marva Potter* • Austin Pendleton *Paul* • Mary Kay Place *Marie* • MacIntyre Dixon *Dan Ryan* • Jay O Sanders *Larry* ■ *Dir* Alan J Pakula • *Scr* James L Brooks, from the novel by Dan Wakefield

Startup.com ★★★ 15

Documentary   2001 · US · Colour · 102min

As fly-on-the-wall documentaries go, this account of the rise and fall of an internet business set up by two college buddies is packed with commercial conflicts and human interest. The contrast between Kaleil Isaza Tuzman's ruthless belief in his business acumen and Tom Herman's more reckless approach to the project is fascinating as the ambitious pair build a website to ease everyday local government transactions such as paying taxes or renewing driving licences. But by adhering to a *cinéma vérité* style, directors Chris Hegedus and Jehane Noujaim allow their subjects to set the agenda, which leaves the audience with more questions than answers. There's a suspicion that a more revealing story somehow got away. DP *DVD*

■ *Dir* Chris Hegedus, Jehane Noujaim • *Producer* DA Pennebaker

State and Main ★★★★ 15

Comedy   2000 · US · Colour · 101min

Writer/director David Mamet shows his lighter side with this superb comedy about the havoc that results when a Hollywood film crew descends on a small New England town. There's the movie's star (played perfectly by Alec Baldwin) who has a preference for underage girls; the writer (Philip Seymour Hoffman) who is watching his beautiful words being twisted to suit the budget and the producer; and the actress (Sarah Jessica Parker) known for taking her top off, who is refusing to do any more nude scenes. Meanwhile, the harassed director (William H Macy) is trying to hold it all together. JB *DVD*

Alec Baldwin *Bob Barrenger* • Charles Durning *Mayor George Bailey* • Clark Gregg *Doug MacKenzie* • Philip Seymour Hoffman *Joseph Turner White* • Patti LuPone *Sherry Bailey* • William H Macy *Walt Price* • Sarah Jessica Parker *Claire Wellesley* • Rebecca Pidgeon *Ann Black* • Julia Stiles *Carla Taylor* ■ *Dir/Scr* David Mamet

State Fair ★★★ U

Comedy   1933 · US · BW · 99min

A day out at the Iowa state fair with the Frake family is the fulcrum for this folksy, good-humoured, idealised and beautifully performed piece of period Americana. Abel Frake (the much loved Will Rogers) is hoping his prize pig will win the Blue Ribbon; his wife, Louise Dresser, has entered her pickles and mincemeat. The young ones, meanwhile, are alive to romance, with daughter Janet Gaynor finding true love with newspaper reporter Lew Ayres and son Norman Foster faring less well in a fling with Sally Eilers. Delightful and innocent. RK

Will Rogers (1) *Abel Frake* • Janet Gaynor *Margy Frake* • Lew Ayres *Pat Gilbert* • Sally Eilers *Emily Joyce* • Norman Foster *Wayne Frake* • Louise Dresser *Melissa Frake* ■ *Dir* Henry King • *Scr* Paul Green, Sonya Levien, from the novel by Phil Stong

State Fair ★★★★ U

Musical   1945 · US · BW · 96min

The second and probably best of the three Hollywood movies inspired by Phil Stong's popular novel of country folk and their simple ways, set in the American Midwest. It takes the same story of pickles, pigs and boy-meets-girl at the country fair, as told in the 1933 movie, but sets it to music with some top-notch numbers by Rodgers and Hammerstein, including *That's for Me* and *It Might As Well Be Spring*, which bagged the Oscar for best song. Entertaining fare. PF

DVD

Jeanne Crain *Margy Frake* • Dana Andrews *Pat Gilbert* • Dick Haymes *Wayne Frake* • Vivian Blaine *Emily Joyce* • Charles Winninger *Abel Frake* • Fay Bainter *Melissa Frake* • Donald Meek *Hippenstahl* • Frank McHugh *McGee* • Percy Kilbride *Miller* ■ *Dir* Walter Lang • *Scr* Oscar Hammerstein II, Sonya Levien, Paul Green, from the novel by Phil Stong

State Fair ★★ U

Musical   1962 · US · Colour · 113min

A disappointment, this remake of the much loved musical is shackled by the leaden direction of José Ferrer. Even the legendary Alice Faye, returning to the screen after an absence of 17 years, seems dispirited. The Rodgers and Hammerstein songs are still wonderful, though the five new ones added by Rodgers alone are merely serviceable. Ann-Margret performs a torrid dance number which would have scandalised 1945 audiences. TV *DVD*

Pat Boone *Wayne Frake* • Bobby Darin *Jerry Dundee* • Pamela Tiffin *Margie Frake* • Ann-Margret *Emily Porter* • Alice Faye *Melissa Frake* • Tom Ewell *Abel Frake* • Wally Cox *Hipplewaite* • David Brandon *Harry* ■ *Dir* José Ferrer • *Scr* Richard L Breen, from the 1945 film, from the novel by Phil Stong

State of Grace ★★★★ 18

Crime thriller   1990 · US · Colour · 128min

Set in New York's Irish quarter, this glowering thriller makes so many blatant bids to be bracketed with the Mob movies of Martin Scorsese that it could justifiably be nicknamed *O'GoodFellas*. While not up to the Scorsese standard, this is still a cracking crime movie, with gutsy performances from Sean Penn, the underrated Ed Harris and that master of manic malevolence, Gary Oldman. Robin Wright gets slightly lost in the mêlée and director Phil Joanou might have kept the running time down, but it's violent, vibrant and very impressive. DP Swearing, violence, nudity. *DVD* BL

Sean Penn *Terry Noonan* • Gary Oldman *Jackie Flannery* • Ed Harris *Frankie Flannery* • Robin Wright *Kathleen Flannery* • John Turturro *Nick* • John C Reilly *Stevie* • Burgess Meredith *Finn* ■ *Dir* Phil Joanou • *Scr* Dennis McIntyre

State of Play ★★★★ 12

Crime thriller
2009 · US/Ger/UK/Fr/Jpn · Colour · 121min

Despite the flab, Russell Crowe proves he's definitely no slouch in this excellent conspiracy tale, based on the BBC TV mini-series. He brings a raw intensity to the role of a slovenly Washington journalist who smells a rat when a political aide employed by rising Congressman Ben Affleck turns up dead. The intricately weaved plot sees Crowe chasing down a high-ranking politician (an unusually sinister Jeff Daniels) and rankling his editor (a typically hard-nosed Helen Mirren). It's more overblown than *All the President's Men*, but as in that 1976 classic the real intrigue unfolds behind closed doors. SP *DVD* BL

Russell Crowe *Cal McAffrey* • Ben Affleck *Stephen Collins* • Rachel McAdams *Della Frye* • Helen Mirren *Cameron Lynne* • Robin Wright Penn [Robin Wright] *Anne Collins* • Jason Bateman *Dominic Foy* • Jeff Daniels *George Fergus* ■ *Dir* Kevin Macdonald • *Scr* Matthew Michael Carnahan, Tony Gilroy, Billy Ray, from the TV series by Paul Abbott

State of Siege ★★★ 15

Political thriller
1972 · Fr/US/It/W Ger · Colour · 115min

Although set in an unnamed state, this is clearly a film about the abduction by Uruguay's Tupamaro guerrillas of Daniel Mitrione. Mitrione was a member of the US Agency for International Development, whose traffic control brief provided a front for his expertise in the interrogation and torture of political prisoners. There was criticism of the casting of Yves Montand as the villain, while others complained that the director's sympathies lay with the kidnappers. Either way, despite reusing the reportage techniques he employed on *Z*, Costa-Gavras is less successful here. DP In French.

Yves Montand *Santore* • Renato Salvatori *Lopez* • OE Hasse *Ducas* • Jacques Weber *Hugo* • Jean-Luc Bideau *Este* • Evangeline Peterson *Mrs Santore* ■ *Dir* Constantin Costa-Gavras [Costa-Gavras] • *Scr* Constantin Costa-Gavras [Costa-Gavras], Franco Solinas

State of the Union ★★★★ PG

Political drama   1948 · US · BW · 117min

Originally released in the year of a presidential campaign, this concerns millionaire industrialist Spencer Tracy running for the highest office and unwittingly putting himself and his integrity at the mercy of other people's unprincipled ambition. When the candidate's estranged wife Katharine Hepburn is persuaded to return for a public reunion, there are unexpected consequences. Enthralling and astringently witty, the film boasts top-class supporting performances, while the star duo fires on all cylinders. RK *DVD*

Spencer Tracy *Grant Matthews* • Katharine Hepburn *Mary Matthews* • Van Johnson *Spike McManus* • Angela Lansbury *Kay Thorndyke* • Adolphe Menjou *Jim Conover* • Lewis Stone *Sam Thorndyke* ■ *Dir* Frank Capra • *Scr* Anthony Veiller, Myles Connolly, from a play by Howard Lindsay, Russel Crouse

The State of Things ★★★★

Drama   1982 · US/Por/W Ger · BW · 121min

Shot contemporaneously with the interminable production of *Hammett*, Wim Wenders's treatise on the uneasy relationship between the European art film and Hollywood was dubbed by its director as the last of the B-movies. The shifts between narrative and dissertation are superbly achieved, as the cast and crew of a poverty-stricken sci-fi remake are stranded in Portugal and left to cogitate on the ironies of life and illusion as their producer heads for the States in search of funds. Despite dividing the critics, this cameo-packed film won the Golden Lion award at the Venice film festival. DP

Patrick Bauchau *Friedrich "Fritz" Munro, the director* • Isabelle Weingarten *Anna* • Allen Garfield *Gordon* • Samuel Fuller *Joe Corby, the cameraman* • Viva Auder *Kate, the scriptgirl* • Jeffrey Kime *Mark* • Paul Getty III *Dennis, the writer* • Roger Corman *Lawyer* ■ *Dir* Wim Wenders • *Scr* Wim Wenders, Robert Kramer

State Secret ★★★ U

Thriller   1950 · UK · BW · 100min

This serviceable thriller from Frank Launder and Sidney Gilliat borrows its blend of comedy and suspense from their own spy caper *Night Train to Munich*. Douglas Fairbanks Jr stars as a surgeon lured to the Balkan state of Vosnia after its dictator is wounded in an assassination attempt. When his patient dies, Fairbanks has to take to the hills with plucky Glynis Johns at his side. Gilliat directs with panache and the location photography is stunning. DP

Douglas Fairbanks Jr *Dr John Marlowe* • Glynis Johns *Lisa* • Jack Hawkins *Colonel Galcon* • Herbert Lom *Karl Theodor* • Walter Rilla *General Niva* • Karel Stepanek *Dr Revo* • Carl Jaffe *Janovik Prada* ■ *Dir* Sidney Gilliat • *Scr* Sidney Gilliat, from the novel *Appointment with Fear* by Roy Huggins • *Producer* Frank Launder

The Statement ★★ 12

Drama 2003 · Can/Fr/UK/US · Colour · 114min

War-crime investigators Tilda Swinton and Jeremy Northam pursue ageing French collaborator Michael Caine for his involvement in the execution of seven Jews, but their prey stays one step ahead of them with the help of his high-level friends. Caine gives his usual solid performance, but Swinton and Northam struggle with their flimsy characters and Norman Jewison's film can't decide whether it's a chase thriller, a conspiracy yarn or a message movie. DA Violence.
DVD

Michael Caine *Pierre Brossard* • Tilda Swinton *Judge Annemarie Livi* • Jeremy Northam *Colonel Roux* • Alan Bates *Armand Bertier* • John Boswall *Father Léo* • Matt Craven *David Manenbaum* • Frank Finlay *Commissaire Vionnet* • Ciaran Hinds *Pochon* • Charlotte Rampling *Nicole* ■ *Dir* Norman Jewison • *Scr* Ronald Harwood, from the novel by Brian Moore

Staten Island ★★★ 15

Black comedy crime thriller
2009 · Fr/US · Colour · 95min

This offbeat but intriguing crime tale intersects the stories of three characters: Parmie Tarzo (Vincent D'Onofrio), a gangster betrayed by his confederates; intellectually challenged cleaner Sully (Ethan Hawke), who wants a better life for his unborn child; and a deaf-mute deli worker (Seymour Cassel), who disposes of bodies for the Mob. Although some of the twists and turns fail to convince, the action sequences are both original and technically impressive and while Hawke is miscast, outstanding character actor Cassel works wonders in a dialogue-free role. LF Violence, swearing.

Ethan Hawke *Sully Halverson* • Vincent D'Onofrio *Parmie Tarzo* • Seymour Cassel *Jasper Sabiano* • Julianne Nicholson *Mary Halverson* • Jeremy Schwartz *Eddie DeGiulio* • David Vadim *Tall man* ■ *Dir/Scr* James DeMonaco

Static ★★★ 15

Satirical drama 1985 · US · Colour · 90min

In this decidedly odd drama, Keith Gordon plays a guy who invents a TV that can supposedly tune in to heaven. It can't, of course, and simply shows static. But try telling that to spiritually isolated people who desperately need to believe in something bigger and better. By turns moving and amusing, but also drawn-out and dreary, This displays an obvious, if surreal, intelligence. DA

Keith Gordon *Ernie Blick* • Amanda Plummer *Julia Purcell* • Bob Gunton *Frank* • Lily Knight *Patty* • Barton Heyman *Sheriff William Orling* • Reathel Bean *Fred Savins* • Jane Hoffman *Emily Southwick* ■ *Dir* Mark Romanek • *Scr* Keith Gordon, Mark Romanek

The Station Agent ★★★★ 15

Comedy drama 2003 · US · Colour · 86min

Finbar McBride (Peter Dinklage) seems to have no emotions, he is a dwarf, and his hobbies are model railways and trainspotting. Finbar works in a model shop and when the owner dies, he inherits a disused rural railway station in New Jersey. He shuns attention, but finds himself befriended by Joe (Bobby Cannavale), a gregarious young Cuban who runs his father's fast-food van, and Olivia (Patricia Clarkson), a local artist grieving for a dead son and a dead marriage. A ragbag collection of misfits and losers, they end up sitting, talking and trainspotting together. The script strikes a fine balance between comedy and the pain of living, with the characters beautifully observed. BP Swearing. **DVD**

Peter Dinklage *Finbar "Fin" McBride* • Patricia Clarkson *Olivia Harris* • Bobby Cannavale *Joe Oramas* • Paul Benjamin *Henry Styles* • Raven Goodwin *Cleo* • Michelle Williams *Emily* • Josh Pais *Carl* ■ *Dir/Scr* Tom McCarthy [Thomas McCarthy]

Station Six-Sahara ★★★★

Drama 1962 · UK/W Ger · BW · 101min

Eroticism isn't something that the British cinema tackles very often, but this 1962 offering does. It's set on an oil pipeline in the middle of the Sahara where the blokes are muscular, sweaty and bad-tempered. Their frustration is palpable. Then out of the blue comes a provocative, unbuttoned Carroll Baker. Directed by former editor Seth Holt and co-written by Bryan Forbes, it makes the most of an intrinsically ridiculous situation, relishing the clichés, laying on the impudent symbolism and wringing out as much sexual tension as possible. AT

Carroll Baker *Catherine* • Peter Van Eyck *Kramer* • Ian Bannen *Fletcher* • Denholm Elliott *Macey* • Hansjörg Felmy *Martin* • Mario Adorf *Santos* • Biff McGuire *Jimmy* • Harry Baird *Sailor* ■ *Dir* Seth Holt • *Scr* Bryan Forbes, Brian Clemens, from the play *Men without a Past* by Jacques Maret

Station to Station ★★★ 15

Documentary 2015 · US · Colour · 70min

A concept film about a cross-country conceptual art project is hardly multiplex fodder. But the surprises come thick and fast in Doug Aitken's quirky account of the 24-day, 4000-mile journey aboard a train designed as an evocative kinetic light sculpture. The locomotive makes ten stops along the way to visit a series of arty happenings and pick up new passengers to be coaxed into doing a bit for the camera. The talent comes from across the artistic spectrum, but the emphasis is firmly on musicians like Patti Smith, Jackson Browne, Thurston Moore and Mavis Staples, but, whatever the subject, the vignettes provide plenty to admire, amuse, contemplate and provoke. DP Some swearing, brief nudity.

Giorgio Moroder • Patti Smith ■ *Dir* Doug Aitken

Station West ★★★ PG

Western 1948 · US · BW · 79min

Former crooner Dick Powell had just carved out a new career for himself as a tough guy in such taut thrillers as *Farewell My Lovely* (1945) and *Johnny O'Clock* (1947) and so brought a new, darker image to this cleverly scripted RKO western about an army investigator trying to sort out a series of gold heists. Jane Greer makes a feisty sparring partner, but what really gives this movie some distinction is the use of clever one-liners. TS **DVD**

Dick Powell *Lt John Martin Haven* • Jane Greer *Charlie* • Agnes Moorehead *Mrs Mary Caslon* • Burl Ives *Hotel clerk* • Tom Powers *Captain George Iles* • Gordon Oliver *Prince* • Steve Brodie *Lt Stellman* • [Guinn "Big Boy" Williams] *Mick Marion* • Raymond Burr *Mark Bristow* • Regis Toomey *James Goddard* ■ *Dir* Sidney Lanfield • *Scr* Frank Fenton, Winston Miller, from a novel by Luke Short as serialised in *The Saturday Evening Post*

Stations of the Cross ★★★ 15

Drama 2014 · Ger/Fr · Colour · 110min

The movies have provided some barbed satires of Christianity (*Monty Python's The Life of Brian*, *Dogma*), but director Dietrich Brüggemann takes aim at too many easy targets here. 14-year-old Maria, a devout member of a strict Catholic sect, tries to befriend a classmate without going against the stern teachings of her priest and her devout mother, and also decides to undertake a sacrificial fast. The use of a static camera imposes a stylistic rigour to match the religious intransigence. But the action veers between acerbic mockery and gauche melodrama, while the arguments are often leaden. DP German, French +subtitles. **DVD** **Blu**

Lea van Acken *Maria* • Franziska Weisz *Mother* • Florian Stetter *Father Weber* • Lucie Aron *Bernadette* • Moritz Knapp *Christian* ■ *Dir* Dietrich Brüggemann • *Scr* Anna Brüggemann, Dietrich Brüggemann

Status Quo: Hello Quo ★★★★ 15

Music documentary
2012 · UK · Colour and BW · 152min

In their 50 years together, the members of Status Quo have had more than their fair share of hit singles and must-tell anecdotes. In telling the full story, director Alan G Parker's definitive account clocks in at over two hours 30 minutes, but it is one of the best rockumentaries of recent times. Core members Francis Rossi, Rick Parfitt, Alan Lancaster and John Coghlan recall their journey from childhood friends to their 1970s heyday and subsequent rock legend status with clarity and affection, and fans, ranging from Cliff Richard and Jeff Lynne to Paul Weller and Brian May, dispel the idea of "The Quo" being three-chord thrashers by discussing the dynamism, distinctiveness and deftness of their sound. It's compelling stuff, and the climactic reunion performance of *In My Chair* will have toes tapping and stiff upper lips quivering. DP Swearing, sexual references.
DVD **Blu**

Francis Rossi • Rick Parfitt • Alan Lancaster • John Coghlan • Andrew Bown ■ *Dir* Alan G Parker • *Scr* Alan G Parker, Alexa Morris

Stavisky ★★★★ PG

Period drama based on a true story
1974 · Fr/It · Colour · 112min

With Jean-Paul Belmondo in the lead, a famous scandal as its subject, atmospheric art deco sets and a memorable Stephen Sondheim score, this is Alain Resnais's most commercial picture. Yet, with its temporal shifts and deft blend of fact, memory and fallacy, it also serves as a perfect vehicle for Resnais's trademark preoccupations, as he explores the legend grown up around a financial swindle that had the most sinister political implications. It's a technically accomplished film, too, with Resnais using filters to approximate 1930s Technicolor and only using angles extant in the period. DP French +subtitles. **DVD**

Jean-Paul Belmondo *Stavisky* • Charles Boyer *Baron Raoul* • François Périer *Albert Borelli* • Anny Duperey *Arlette Stavisky* • Michel Lonsdale *Dr Mezy* • Claude Rich *Bonny* ■ *Dir* Alain Resnais • *Scr* Jorge Semprun • *Cinematographer* Sacha Vierny

Stay ★★ 18

Psychological thriller
2005 · US · Colour · 94min

Distraught student Ryan Gosling announces to psychiatrist Ewan McGregor that he plans to commit suicide. In a desperate attempt to stop Gosling, McGregor goes on a nightmarish journey through a surreal version of Manhattan, until the "truth" of what we're really seeing is revealed. Tricksy, arty and pretentious - often all at once - it's hard to become sufficiently intrigued by the characters or situations to care about what's going on. AJ Swearing. **DVD**

Ewan McGregor *Sam Foster* • Naomi Watts *Lila* • Ryan Gosling *Henry Letham* • Janeane Garofalo *Dr Beth Levy* • BD Wong *Dr Ren* • Bob Hoskins *Dr Leon Patterson* • Kate Burton *Mrs Letham* ■ *Dir* Marc Forster • *Scr* David Benioff

Stay Alive ★ 15

Horror thriller 2006 · US · Colour · 82min

Die on screen playing the prototype video game "Stay Alive", and you are killed in the same way for real. This airs every chiller chestnut on the overfamiliar route of New Orleans teens locating the plantation source of the ancient evil possessing their consoles. Pre-gore cutaways to secure a wider audience sink any shock value, and even the game's computer graphics refuse to summon up the requisite gothic frisson. A complete waste of time and energy. AJ **DVD**

Jon Foster (1) *Hutch* • Samaire Armstrong *Abigail* • Frankie Muniz *Swink* • Jimmi Simpson *Phineus* • Wendell Pierce *Detective Thibodeaux* • Sophia Bush *October* • Adam Goldberg *Miller Banks* ■ *Dir* William Brent Bell • *Scr* William Brent Bell, Matthew Peterman

Stay Away, Joe ★★ U

Comedy drama 1968 · US · Colour · 96min

Shamefully depicting native Americans as dissolute wastrels obsessed with girls and grog, this Elvis Presley romp was uncharacteristically bawdy. Every bit as unenlightened is the chauvinistic story, Elvis takes a break from flirting with Joan Blondell's teenage daughter to help his shiftless father (Burgess Meredith) pull a cattle scam on the government. Rarely called upon to sing, Presley shambles along as he's upstaged by his co-stars. DP

Elvis Presley *Joe Lightcloud* • Burgess Meredith *Charlie Lightcloud* • Joan Blondell *Glenda Callahan* • Katy Jurado *Annie Lightcloud* • Thomas Gomez *Grandpa* • Jones Henry *Hy Slager* • LQ Jones *Bronc Hoverty* ■ *Dir* Peter Tewksbury • *Scr* Michael A Hoey, from the novel by Dan Cushman

Stay Hungry ★★★★ 15

Drama 1976 · US · Colour · 98min

Before Arnold Schwarzenegger found muscleman fame and Robert Englund became Elm Street's Freddy, they turned up as characters in Bob Rafelson's culture-clash tale about what happens when Alabama heir Jeff Bridges infiltrates a downtown gym for real-estate reasons and falls for Sally Field. Totally laid-back, this all seems pointlessly unstructured, until you realise that's the way it's supposed to be: an endearing look at barbell bums who may never win through, but have lots of fun trying. TH Violence, swearing, nudity. **DVD**

Jeff Bridges *Craig Blake* • Sally Field *Mary Tate Farnsworth* • Arnold Schwarzenegger *Joe Santo* • RG Armstrong *Thor Erickson* • Robert Englund *Franklin* • Helena Kallianiotes *Anita* • Roger E Mosley *Newton* • Scatman Crothers *Butler* ■ *Dir* Bob Rafelson • *Scr* Bob Rafelson, Charles Gaines, from the novel by Charles Gaines

Stay Tuned ★★ PG

Comedy fantasy 1992 · US · Colour · 84min

The central conceit is quite clever: TV-obsessed John Ritter sells his soul to the Devil (Jeffrey Jones) and finds himself literally trapped in the box with wife Pam Dawber. However, the execution is all wrong, and the result is a string of rather lame send-ups of popular television shows. Jones is as reliable as ever, but the two leads are bland and Peter Hyams never really gets a handle on the project. Watch for the splendid animation sequence directed by Chuck Jones. JF

John Ritter *Roy Knable* • Pam Dawber *Helen Knable* • Jeffrey Jones *Spike* • Eugene Levy *Crowley* • David Tom *Darryl Knable* • Heather McComb *Diane Knable* • Michael Hogan (3) *Duane* ■ *Dir* Peter Hyams • *Scr* Tom S Parker, Jim Jennewein, from a story by Tom S Parker, Jim Jennewein, Richard Siegel

Staying Alive ★★ PG

Dance drama 1983 · US · Colour · 92min

This sequel to *Saturday Night Fever*, the film that launched his career, isn't the lowest point in John Travolta's career, but one he would still probably love to forget. Warning bells should have started ringing over the involvement of Sylvester Stallone, who co-wrote and directed this clunker. The slim plot focuses on Travolta, now a professional dancer, being torn between two women as he prepares for a big show. Stallone's brother Frank, who was responsible for much of the music, is certainly no Bee Gee. JF Swearing. **DVD**

John Travolta *Tony Manero* • Cynthia Rhodes *Jackie* • Finola Hughes *Laura* • Steve Inwood *Jesse* • Julie Bovasso *Mrs Manero* • Charles Ward *Butler* ■ *Dir* Sylvester Stallone • *Scr* Sylvester Stallone, Norman Wexler, from characters by Nik Cohn

Staying Together ★★★ 15

Comedy drama 1989 · US · Colour · 87min

This is a sentimental, if well-intentioned little movie about a small-town family facing radical upheavals. The McDermotts own a fried chicken business and the three boys believe that is where their future lies. But when dad sells the restaurant and dies, the boys have to rethink. This character-driven movie doesn't sound like much, but this is engrossing, thanks to sensitive direction from actress Lee Grant. DA

Sean Astin *Duncan McDermott* • Stockard Channing *Nancy Trainer* • Melinda Dillon *Eileen McDermott* • Jim Haynie *Jake McDermott* • Levon Helm *Denny Stockton* • Dinah Manoff *Lois Cook* • Dermot Mulroney *Kit McDermott* • Tim Quill *Brian McDermott* ■ *Dir* Lee Grant • *Scr* Monte Merrick

The Steal ★★ PG
Crime comedy   1994 · UK · Colour · 90min

This has a strong cast, but the uninspired direction and script leave the talented players floundering. Alfred Molina and Helen Slater are the amateur crooks out to rob a City firm who get mixed up in an increasingly hysterical series of misadventures. The leads give of their best and there are enthusiastic turns from the good supporting cast, yet it must go down as another missed opportunity. JF Some swearing.

Alfred Molina *Cliff* • Helen Slater *Kim* • Peter Bowles *Lord Childwell* • Dinsdale Landen *Sir Wilmot* • Heathcote Williams *Jeremiah* • Stephen Fry *Wimborne* • Bryan Pringle *Cecil, bank doorman* • Jack Dee *Wilmot's servant* ■ *Dir/Scr* John Hay

Steal ★★ 15
Action crime drama
2002 · Fr/Can/UK · Colour · 80min

Featuring the first roller-skating crooks since Jean-Hugues Anglade trundled his way through *Subway*, the plot strives to provide a few novel twists on the last blag scenario. But Stephen Dorff's plan is doomed to misfire after someone tips off the cops and the gang steals a consignment of Mafia money. The stunt performers merit mention for the high-speed chases, but everything else is overly familiar, right down to Steven Berkoff's scenery-gnawing histrionics. DP Violence, swearing, a sex scene, nudity. DVD

Stephen Dorff *Slim* • Natasha Henstridge *Karen Svenson* • Bruce Payne *Lt Jake MacGruder* • Steven Berkoff *Surtayne* ■ *Dir* Gérard Pirès • *Scr* Mark Ezra, Gérard Pirès

Steal Big, Steal Little ★★ 12
Action comedy   1995 · US · Colour · 108min

This misguided comedy tale of greed and corruption stars Andy Garcia as the identical twin brothers battling over the estate left by their adoptive mother. As you would expect, one's a really nice guy and the other is a scheming rat. What sounds like a simple tale is in reality a confusing mess of too many plot strands and supporting characters. JC

Andy Garcia *Ruben Partida Martinez/Robert Martin* • Alan Arkin *Lou Perilli* • Rachel Ticotin *Laura Martinez* • Joe Pantoliano *Eddie Agopian* • Holland Taylor *Mona Rowland-Downey* • Ally Walker *Bonnie Martin* • David Ogden Stiers *Judge Winton Myers* ■ *Dir* Andrew Davis • *Scr* Andrew Davis, Lee Blessing, Jeanne Blake, Terry Kahn, from a story by Teresa Tucker-Davies, Frank Ray Perilli, Andrew Davis

Stealing Beauty ★★ 15
Romantic drama
1995 · It/UK/Fr · Colour · 113min

Accomplished director Bernardo Bertolucci stumbles into bathos with this pretentious drama. Liv Tyler stars as the American teenager who, after her mother's suicide, takes a summer holiday with an expatriate family in Tuscany. Anxious to lose her virginity and discover the identity of her biological father, she encounters a range of eccentric house guests, including Jeremy Irons as a terminally ill playwright and Jean Marais as an art dealer. TH Swearing, sex scenes. DVD

Sinead Cusack *Diana Grayson* • Jeremy Irons *Alex Parrish* • Liv Tyler *Lucy Harmon* • Jean Marais *Monsieur Guillaume* • Donal McCann *Ian Grayson* • DW Moffett *Richard Reed* • Stefania Sandrelli *Noemi* • Rachel Weisz *Miranda Fox* • Joseph Fiennes *Christopher Fox* ■ *Dir* Bernardo Bertolucci • *Scr* Susan Minot, from a story by Bernardo Bertolucci

Stealing Harvard ★ 12
Crime comedy   2002 · US · Colour · 81min

Tom Green applies the kiss of death to yet another film. Here the hugely unfunny comic may only play support to Jason Lee's lead, but he's enough to sink a mediocre movie. Lee plays a none-too-bright nice guy who's reminded of his vow to pay his trailer-trash niece's tuition fees if she gets into a good university – and she's just got a place at Harvard. Unfunny, overplayed and underplotted. DA DVD CS

Jason Lee *John Plummer* • Tom Green (1) *Walter "Duff" Duffy* • Leslie Mann *Elaine Warner* • Megan Mullally *Patty Plummer* • Dennis Farina *Mr Warner* • Tammy Blanchard *Noreen* • Richard Jenkins *Mr Cook* • Chris Penn *David Loach* • John C McGinley *Detective Charles* • Seymour Cassel *Uncle Jack* ■ *Dir* Bruce McCulloch • *Scr* Peter Tolan, from a story by Peter Tolan, Martin Hynes

Stealing Heaven ★★ 15
Historical romance
1988 · UK/Yug · Colour · 110min

The true story of medieval star-crossed lovers Abelard and Heloise gets an unsubtle and highly erotic treatment in director Clive Donner's soap-opera confection. Philosophy scholar Abelard, who is supposed to remain celibate, falls for the aristocratic Heloise and they flout both religion and society as they wend their romantic way towards tragedy. Despite the efforts of a good cast, the film remains ordinary. AJ

Derek De Lint *Abelard* • Kim Thomson *Heloise* • Denholm Elliott *Canon Fulbert* • Bernard Hepton *Bishop Martin* • Kenneth Cranham *Vice Chancellor Suger* • Patsy Byrne *Agnes* ■ *Dir* Clive Donner • *Scr* Chris Bryant, from the novel by Marion Meade

Stealing Home ★★★ 15
Drama   1988 · US · Colour · 93min

This should be seen if only for future Oscar winner Jodie Foster's fine performance as the wild Katie, whose death evokes troubled memories and regrets among her young contemporaries. Told in flashback, this is the cinematic autobiography of its two writer/directors, Steven Kampmann and Will Aldis. Earnest and personal. TS Swearing, sex scenes.

Mark Harmon *Billy Wyatt as an adult* • Jodie Foster *Katie Chandler* • Blair Brown *Ginny Wyatt* • Jonathan Silverman *Alan Appleby as a teenager* • Harold Ramis *Alan Appleby as an adult* • John Shea *Sam Wyatt* • William McNamara *Billy Wyatt as a teenager* ■ *Dir/Scr* Steven Kampmann, Will Aldis [Will Porter]

Stealing Paradise ★★
Thriller   2011 · Can · Colour · 100min

Poor casting and a dull script make for an ineffectual thriller, as aggrieved aeronautical engineer Rachael Leigh Cook is accused of murdering the sneaky colleague who stole her latest breakthrough design. Fortunately for the real culprit, her desperate-to-impress character behaves so foolishly that she almost frames herself, leading to dry legal scenes that threaten to obliterate the movie's limited energy levels. When events pick up pace away from the courtroom, they're as unconvincing as Cook's performance, with supposed twists intended to boost the plot proving both weak and predictable. SF

Rachael Leigh Cook *Amanda Collier* • Graham Abbey *Steven Collier* • Paula Jean Hixson *Det Maureen Usher* • Neil Napier *Det Mike Sanders* • Jonathan Higgins *Kevin Maknassy* ■ *Dir* Tristan Dubois • *Scr* Tom Gates

Stealth ★★ 12
Action adventure thriller
2005 · US · Colour · 115min

This exceptionally silly B-movie actioner stars Jessica Biel, Jamie Foxx and Josh Lucas as top secret US Navy pilots who find themselves attempting to regain control of a "drone" plane piloted by a rogue computer that has decided to bomb Tajikistan. Although Rob Cohen directs the aerial action with his usual hectic brio, the screenplay is lumpen, the dialogue inept

and the characters uninteresting. AS Swearing, violence. DVD 🔵 CS

Josh Lucas *Lt Ben Gannon* • Jessica Biel *Lt Kara Wade* • Jamie Foxx *Lt Henry Purcell* • Sam Shepard *Capt George Cummings* • Joe Morton *Capt Dick Marshfield* • Richard Roxburgh *Keith Orbit* • Ian Bliss *Lt Aaron Shaftsbury* • Ebon Moss-Bachrach *Josh Hudson* ■ *Dir* Rob Cohen • *Scr* WD Richter

Stealth Fighter ★★ 15
Action thriller   1999 · US · Colour · 83min

Ice-T plays a top pilot who steals a top of the range stealth fighter plane and then teams up with a drug baron to extort the US Government. Costas Mandylor is the naval officer assigned to bring the rogue pilot in, and there are fleeting appearances from an eclectic collection of vaguely familiar faces. However, no one makes an impression, while the action sequences are laughable. JF DVD

Ice-T *Owen Turner* • Costas Mandylor *Ryan Mitchell* • Ernie Hudson *President Westwood* • Andrew Divoff *Robert Menendez* • Erika Eleniak *Erin Mitchell* • William Sadler *Peterson* ■ *Dir* Jay Andrews [Jim Wynorski] • *Scr* Lenny Juliano

Steamboat Bill, Jr
★★★★★ U
Silent comedy   1928 · US · BW · 69min

One of Buster Keaton's greatest comedies, this stars the "Great Stone Face" as the saphead son of a steamboat operator, who arrives home from college a rather prissy figure, clearly disappointing his tough-guy dad. Keaton's efforts to please his despairing father, as well as his attempts to woo the daughter of his father's business rival, give rise to a series of wonderful gags and these alone would give this comedy classic status. But Keaton also produces the most spectacular and dangerous stunt sequence of his entire career – a cyclone that sweeps up everything in its path. This culminates in the entire front of a house falling on our hero in a scene of astonishing precision and daring. AT DVD

Buster Keaton *William "Willie" Canfield Jr* • Ernest Torrence *William "Steamboat Bill" Canfield Sr* • Tom Lewis *His first mate* • Tom McGuire *John James King, his rival* • Marion Byron *Kitty, his daughter* ■ *Dir* Charles Reisner • *Scr* Carl Harbaugh • *Cinematographers* J Devereaux Jennings, Bert Haines

Steamboat round the Bend
★★★ U
Drama   1935 · US · BW · 77min

This warm-hearted Will Rogers vehicle was released after his tragic death in a plane crash. With the distance of time, this may require tolerance from the viewer, but it's still fascinating to watch a riverboat battle between America's two folk philosophers of the time, Rogers himself and the garrulous Irvin S Cobb. Director John Ford was always prone to sentimentality, and this is no exception, but he achieves a sweet, elegiac feel for a more gentle, romantic past. TS DVD

Will Rogers (1) *Dr John Pearly* • Anne Shirley *Fleety Belle* • Eugene Pallette *Sheriff Rufe Jeffers* • John McGuire *Duke* • Berton Churchill *New Moses* • Stepin Fetchit *Jonah* ■ *Dir* John Ford • *Scr* Dudley Nichols, Lamar Trotti, from the novel by Ben Lucian Burman

Steamboat Willie ★★★★★
Animation   1928 · US · BW · 7min

Walt Disney's third Mickey Mouse cartoon has Mickey as the captain of a steamboat sailing up the Mississippi, and demonstrates Disney's use of music and sound to give additional weight to a production's narrative and structure. (This was the first animated film with sound.) In one memorable moment, a cow's teeth are played like a xylophone, while its udder is used as a bagpipe. The term "Mickey Mouse Music" – with the soundtrack covering all visual events – undoubtedly came from this cartoon, which was the first notable example of the audio-visual orchestration used so effectively in later Disney successes. TH

Walt Disney *Mickey Mouse* ■ *Dir* Walt Disney • *Scr* Walt Disney, Ub Iwerks • *Music* Carl Stalling [Carl W Stalling] • *Animator* Ub Iwerks

Steamboy ★★ PG
Animated fantasy adventure
2004 · Jpn · Colour · 99min

More than ten years in the making, Katsuhiro Otomo's first feature-length *anime* as director since 1988's dazzling *Akira* concerns the Steams, a family of Manchester inventors. Schoolboy Ray (poorly voiced by Anna Paquin) is forced to come between his feuding scientist father (Alfred Molina) and grandfather (Patrick Stewart) as their latest device is about to be unleashed on Victorian London. Yet, aside from the lengthy running time and a remarkable attention to detail, there's little to show for its $22 million budget. SF Japanese dubbed. DVD

Anna Paquin *Ray Steam* • Alfred Molina *Eddie Steam* • Patrick Stewart *Lloyd Steam* • Kari Wahlgren *Scarlett* • Robert Atkin Downes *David* • David Lee (1) *Jason* ■ *Dir* Katsuhiro Otomo • *Scr* Katsuhiro Otomo, Sadayuki Murai

Steaming ★★★★ 18
Drama   1985 · UK · Colour · 91min

If you liked Nell Dunn's breast-beating play about an all-women group at the local Turkish baths, you'll love Joseph Losey's movie, which sticks rigidly to text and scene. It is a tightly drawn, multi-charactered, often insightful look at the female condition, with a last, wonderful performance from Diana Dors as the surrogate mum in charge of the towels. Both achingly sad and funny. SH Nudity.

Vanessa Redgrave *Nancy* • Sarah Miles *Sarah* • Diana Dors *Violet* • Patti Love *Josie* • Brenda Bruce *Mrs Meadows* • Felicity Dean *Dawn Meadows* • Sally Sagoe *Celia* • Anna Tzelniker *Mrs Goldstein* ■ *Dir* Joseph Losey • *Scr* Patricia Losey, from the play by Nell Dunn

Steel ★★ PG
Action fantasy   1997 · US · Colour · 92min

Former basketball star Shaquille O'Neal suits up in a metal overcoat and butts heads with street gangs in this action fantasy that's loosely based on the DC Comics superhero of the same name. As an actor, Shaq makes a great basketball player, and one suspects that he finds remembering dialogue as hard as making free throw shots consistently. ST Violence, swearing.

Shaquille O'Neal *Steel/John Henry Irons* • Annabeth Gish *Susan Sparks* • Judd Nelson *Nathaniel Burke* • Richard Roundtree *Uncle Joe* • Irma P Hall *Grandma Odessa* • Ray J *Martin* • Charles Napier *Colonel David* ■ *Dir* Kenneth Johnson • *Scr* Kenneth Johnson, from the character created by Jon Bogdanove, Louise Simonson

The Steel Bayonet ★★
Second World War drama
1957 · UK · BW · 82min

Michael Carreras directs rather in the style of an American platoon picture – the title is reminiscent of a Sam Fuller movie – as it deals with Leo Genn and his battle-worn men who are ordered to hold a farmhouse during the Allied assault on Tunis. As in American movies, the men embody a variety of attitudes towards the morality of war, but, this being a British movie, it all comes down to class attitudes. AT

Leo Genn *Major Gerrard* • Kieron Moore *Captain Mead* • Michael Medwin *Lieutenant Vernon* • Robert Brown *Sgt Maj Gill* • Michael Ripper *Private Middleditch* • John Paul *Lt Col Derry* • Michael Caine ■ *Dir* Michael Carreras • *Scr* Howard Clewes

The Steel Helmet ★★★
War drama   1951 · US · BW · 84min

The first in a long line of Samuel Fuller war movies has Gene Evans as a seasoned sergeant in the thick of the Korean War. He survives a massacre, is saved by an orphan and injects a deep-rooted cynicism into the platoon he adopts as his own. Shot in a mere ten days and sometimes looking like it took only five, the movie has the energy so typical of its director. AT

Gene Evans *Sgt Zack* • Robert Hutton *Pte "Conchie" Bronte* Richard Loo *Sgt "Buddhahead" Tanaka* • Steve Brodie *Lt Driscoll* • James Edwards *Cpl "Medic" Thompson* • Sid Melton *Joe, 2nd G* • Richard Monahan *Pte Baldy* • William Chun *"Short Round"* • Lynn Stalmaster *2nd Lieutenant* ■ *Dir/Scr* Samuel Fuller

Steel Magnolias ★★★★ PG
Comedy drama 1989 · US · Colour · 113min

At a time when muscle-bound action heroes held sway at the box office, this provided juicy roles for some of Hollywood's leading ladies. Sally Field, Daryl Hannah, Olympia Dukakis and Julia Roberts interact so beautifully as they discuss men, the menopause, manicures and marriage in Dolly Parton's kitsch small-town beauty salon that it was something of a surprise that only Roberts scooped an Oscar nomination. A little too dependent on sassy one-liners and awash with sentiment by the end, this is still wonderful entertainment. DP Swearing. *DVD*

Sally Field *M'Lynn Eatenton* • Dolly Parton *Truvy Jones* • Shirley MacLaine *Ouiser Boudreaux* • Daryl Hannah *Annelle Dupuy Desoto* • Julia Roberts *Shelby Eatenton Latcherie* • Olympia Dukakis *Clairee Belcher* • Tom Skerritt *Drum Eatenton* • Dylan McDermott *Jackson Latcherie* • Sam Shepard *Spud Jones* ■ *Dir* Herbert Ross • *Scr* Robert Harling, from his play

The Steel Trap ★★★ U
Crime comedy 1952 · US · BW · 84min

Assistant bank manager Joseph Cotten steals money from his employer and attempts to flee to Brazil where there is no extradition treaty, but finds his plans thwarted when he misses his flight. Cotten and Teresa Wright, the uncle and niece from Hitchcock's *Shadow of a Doubt*, are reunited here as husband and wife, and both are excellent. The well-made film is directed from his own screenplay by Andrew L Stone. TS

Joseph Cotten *Jim Osborne* • Teresa Wright *Laurie Osborne* • Eddie Marr *Ken* • Aline Towne *Gail* • Bill Hudson *Paglin* ■ *Dir/Scr* Andrew Stone [Andrew L Stone]

Steelyard Blues ★★★ 15
Comedy 1973 · US · Colour · 89min

Whatever happened to director Alan Myerson, who announced himself as an offbeat original with this comic irreverence? Strung out attractively between dotty humour and period paranoia, this concerns a bunch of square pegs who plan to revive an abandoned seaplane and escape to a better life. The humour emerges naturally from the situation. JM Swearing.

Donald Sutherland *Jesse Veldini* • Jane Fonda *Iris Caine* • Peter Boyle *Eagle Throneberry* • Howard Hesseman *Frank Veldini* • Garry Goodrow *Duval Jacks* • John Savage *The Kid* • Richard Schaal *Zoo official* ■ *Dir* Alan Myerson • *Scr* David S Ward

Steep ★★★ PG
Sports documentary 2007 · US · Colour · 86min

Extreme sports documentaries have covered everything from surfing (*Riding Giants*) to skateboarding (*Dogtown and Z-Boys*). *Steep* does much the same for big-mountain skiing with a real-life cast of daredevil skiers who think nothing of trekking up to the top of some of the world's tallest peaks and hurtling back down 50 degree slopes at breakneck speeds. There's much jaw-dropping aerial photography here as director Mark Obenhaus reveals the early origins of the sport and catches up with some of its more colourful protagonists. It's just a pity that the film's treatment of the subject matter is so trite. JR

Peter Krause *Narrator* ■ *Dir/Scr* Mark Obenhaus • *Cinematographer* Erich Roland

Stella ★★★
Comedy mystery 1950 · US · BW · 75min

This frantic black comedy feels like an inversion of *The Trouble with Harry*, as all the fun stems from an accidental death and

the burial of a body. Victor Mature gives a sportingly self-ridiculing performance as the insurance investigator attempting to make sense of the rambling of Ann Sheridan's eccentric kin as they seek to pass off any old corpse to get their hands on the payout, while barking nephew David Wayne tries to recall where he interred his uncle. DP

Ann Sheridan *Stella* • Victor Mature *Jeff De Marco* • David Wayne *Carl Granger* • Randy Stuart *Claire Granger* • Marion Marshall *Mary* • Frank Fontaine *Don* • Leif Erickson *Fred Anderson* • Evelyn Varden *Flora Bevins* ■ *Dir* Claude Binyon • *Scr* Claude Binyon, from the novel *Family Skeleton* by Doris Miles Disney

Stella ★★★ PG
Drama 1955 · Gr · BW · 90min

Michael Cacoyannis's second feature made an instant star of its debuting lead, Melina Mercouri. Mercouri's hall singer is the Greek equivalent of Carmen, as she inflames passions with her smouldering availability and tempestuous spirit. Yet she herself only has eyes for footballer George Foundas – until, that is, she begins to perceive marriage as a trap and not a declaration of love. Despite bringing a raw realism to his depiction of backstreet Athens, Cacoyannis allows Mercouri too much latitude and her exuberance unbalances the narrative. DP In Greek. *DVD*

Melina Mercouri *Stella* • George Foundas *Milto* • Alekos Alexandrakis *Aleko* • Sophia Vembo *Maria* • Voula Zoumboulaki *Anneta* ■ *Dir* Michael Cacoyannis • *Scr* Michael Cacoyannis, from the play *Stella with the Red Gloves* by Iakovos Kabanellis

Stella ★★ 15
Melodrama 1990 · US · Colour · 104min

Battling Bette Midler takes on the old Barbara Stanwyck role of working-class mother Stella Dallas and loses. Not only does her character (here renamed Stella Claire) seem horribly politically incorrect in her efforts to get illegitimate daughter Trini Alvarado married to an upper-crust beau, but Midler is also far too feisty for this out-of-date melodrama. Even the starry cast is defeated by this over-sentimental stodge. TH Swearing, drug abuse, nudity.

Bette Midler *Stella Claire* • John Goodman *Ed Munn* • Trini Alvarado *Jenny Claire* • Stephen Collins *Stephen Dallas* • Marsha Mason *Janice Morrison* • Eileen Brennan *Mrs Wilkerson* • Linda Hart *Debbie Whitman* • Ben Stiller *Jim Uptegrove* ■ *Dir* John Erman • *Scr* Robert Getchell, from the novel *Stella Dallas* by Olive Higgins Prouty

Stella Dallas ★★★★
Silent drama 1925 · US · BW · 108min

Small-town Belle Bennett marries out of her class. When her husband Ronald Colman leaves their hopeless marriage and returns to New York, she lavishes love on their daughter Lois Moran, but later sacrifices the girl to a better life with her father and marriage to Douglas Fairbanks Jr. Down-at-heel Bennett, watching the wedding through a window with tears streaming down her face, gave the cinema of weepie melodrama one of its most famous and enduring images. RK

Ronald Colman *Stephen Dallas* • Belle Bennett *Stella Dallas* • Alice Joyce *Helen Morrison* • Jean Hersholt *Ed Munn* • Beatrix Pryor *Mrs Grovesnor* • Lois Moran *Laurel Dallas* • Douglas Fairbanks Jr *Richard Grovesnor* • Vera Lewis *Miss Tibbets* ■ *Dir* Henry King • *Scr* Frances Marion, from the novel by Olive Higgins Prouty

Stella Dallas ★★★★ U
Melodrama 1937 · US · BW · 101min

The magnificent Barbara Stanwyck never won a performance Oscar, the Academy making its usual reparation by presenting her with an honorary award in 1981. *Stella Dallas* is the movie for which she deserved the best actress Oscar, but that year the honour went to Luise Rainer in Sidney Franklin's *The Good Earth*. Stella is the ultimate soap-opera queen, a woman who, quite literally, sacrifices everything for her daughter's happiness, and this movie is the definitive version of the tale. Stanwyck is

brilliant, her own upbringing as a Brooklyn orphan giving added resonance to the story. TS

Barbara Stanwyck *Stella Martin Dallas* • John Boles *Stephen Dallas* • Anne Shirley *Laurel Dallas* • Barbara O'Neil *Helen Morrison* • Alan Hale *Ed Munn* • Marjorie Main *Mrs Martin* • Edmund Elton *Mr Martin* • Tim Holt *Richard* ■ *Dir* King Vidor • *Scr* Sarah Y Mason, Victor Heerman, from the play by Harry Wagstaff Gribble, Gertrude Purcell, from the novel by Olive Higgins Prouty

Stella Does Tricks ★★★ 18
Drama 1997 · UK · Colour · 94min

This bittersweet little story about teenage prostitution from director Coky Giedroyc is well-intentioned but ends up being rather voyeuristic. Kelly Macdonald is excellent as the feisty young girl, working for creepy pimp James Bolam, who wants to stop working the streets and go away with drug addict Hans Matheson. The film is not exactly heartening but remains compelling, thanks to Macdonald's winning performance. JB Drug abuse, swearing, violence.

Kelly Macdonald *Stella McGuire* • James Bolam *Mr Peters* • Hans Matheson *Eddie* • Ewan Stewart *McGuire* • Andy Serkis *Fitz* ■ *Dir* Coky Giedroyc • *Scr* AL Kennedy

Stella Maris ★★★★
Silent drama 1918 · US · BW · 84min

"Two Marys for the price of one!" gloated the poster for this weepie starring "America's Sweetheart", Mary Pickford, in a dual role. As Stella Maris she is a pretty and pampered invalid, and as Unity Blake she is a less attractive orphan girl. Both are in love with Conway Tearle. In order to ensure some sort of happy ending, it's the homely Unity who sacrifices herself for the happiness of the ringleted Stella. Director Marshall A Neilan pumped the tears without mercy, helped by a realistically successful double portrayal by Pickford. TH

Mary Pickford *Stella Maris/Unity Blake* • Conway Tearle *John Risca* • Marcia Manon *Louise Risca* • Ida Waterman *Lady Blount* • Herbert Standing *Sir Oliver Blount* ■ *Dir* Marshall A Neilan [Marshall Neilan] • *Scr* Frances Marion, from the novel by William J Locke

Stella Street ★★★ 15
Comedy 2004 · UK/US · Colour · 79min

Michael Caine is back in his suburban hideaway and he's brought a lot of Hollywood pals seeking anonymity in this sly satire on the ordinary folk whose personalities are hijacked by the media. Fans of the cult BBC series will be delighted to see Phil Cornwell and John Sessions being given the opportunity to flesh out their wicked caricatures, but there are longueurs and a number of misfiring gags. Yet, the concept remains inspired and the star re-imaginings are affectionate. DP Swearing. *DVD*

Phil Cornwell *Nicholson/Caine/Jagger/Bowie/Jimmy/Len/Vince/Nick* • John Sessions *Pacino/Mrs Hugget/Pesci/Richards/Hoffman/Dean* • Ronni Ancona *Tara/Madonna/Jerry Hall/Posh Spice/Stephanie* • Harry Enfield *Narrator* ■ *Dir* Peter Richardson • *Scr* Phil Cornwell, Peter Richardson, John Sessions

The Stendhal Syndrome ★★★ 18
Horror thriller 1996 · It · Colour · 110min

Director Dario Argento's daughter, Asia, plays the lead in this deeply disturbing thriller. However, she rarely convinces as the detective whose pursuit of serial rapist Thomas Kretschmann is hindered by the fact she secretly suffers from a condition that causes her to hallucinate in the presence of paintings. Even ignoring all the psychological ramifications, this is not one of the Italian horror maestro's finer hours. There are some bravura camera movements, Rome and Florence look stunning, and Ennio Morricone's score is superb, but the pacing is indifferent. DP Italian +subtitles. *DVD*

Asia Argento *Anna Manni* • Thomas Kretschmann *Alfredo Grossi* • Marco Leonardi *Marco Longhi* • Luigi Diberti *Inspector Manetti* ■

Dir Dario Argento • *Scr* Dario Argento, from the novel *La Sindrome di Stendhal* by Graziella Magherini

Step Brothers ★★★ 15
Comedy 2008 · US · Colour · 101min

Even at their most obnoxious, Will Ferrell and John C Reilly are strangely adorable together. Their brotherly bond was key to the success of *Talladega Nights* and in this equally zany comedy (also from director Adam McKay), they take the relationship to its natural conclusion. All the gags rest on these burly, 40-year-old men acting like children when their parents (Mary Steenburgen and Richard Jenkins) get hitched. They draw battle lines in the room they're forced to share, staring each other down at bedtime and trading peculiar insults. It's these exchanges, so specific in their weirdness, that get the biggest laughs. Things do get a little too weird, and the joke is overstretched, but that is, after all, the point. SP Swearing, sexual references. *DVD* *BL*

Will Ferrell *Brennan Huff* • John C Reilly *Dale Doback* • Mary Steenburgen *Nancy Huff* • Richard Jenkins *Robert Doback* • Adam Scott *Derek Huff* • Kathryn Hahn *Alice Huff* ■ *Dir* Adam McKay • *Scr* Will Ferrell, Adam McKay

Step Lively ★★★ U
Musical comedy 1944 · US · BW · 84min

Frank Sinatra's last film before his move to MGM is a musical remake of the comedy *Room Service* – also the basis for a Marx Brothers movie. Under the tutelage of Gene Kelly, Sinatra would finally prove that he was more than just the king of the bobbysoxers, but here he occasionally looks a little lost when he's not given some crooning to do. George Murphy is wildly over the top as a theatrical producer. DP

Frank Sinatra *Glen* • George Murphy *Miller* • Adolphe Menjou *Wagner* • Gloria DeHaven *Christine* • Walter Slezak *Gribble* • Eugene Pallette *Jenkins* • Wally Brown *Binion* • Alan Carney *Harry* ■ *Dir* Tim Whelan • *Scr* Warren Duff, Peter Milne, from the play *Room Service* by John Murray, Allen Boretz • *Music/lyrics* Sammy Cahn, Jule Styne

Step Lively, Jeeves ★★
Comedy 1937 · US · BW · 69min

This sequel to *Thank You, Jeeves* commits the ultimate heresy of featuring the world's most resourceful gentleman's gentleman without the young master himself, one Bertie Wooster. Owing nothing to the genius of creator PG Wodehouse, this is an amiable affair, but too much of the action centres on a couple of American conmen (Alan Dinehart and George Givot) who trick Jeeves (the superb Arthur Treacher) into believing he has come into a fortune. DP

Arthur Treacher *Jeeves* • Patricia Ellis *Patricia Westley* • Robert Kent *Gerry Townsend* • Alan Dinehart *Hon Cedric B Cromwell* • George Givot *Prince Boris Caminov* • Helen Flint *Babe Ross* • John Harrington *Barney Ross* ■ *Dir* Eugene Forde • *Scr* Frank Fenton, from a story by Lynn Root, Frances Hyland, from characters by PG Wodehouse

Step Up ★★ PG
Romantic dance drama 2006 · US · Colour · 99min

Love blooms between unlikely dance partners in this teen romance from choreographer-turned-director Anne Fletcher, but the moves are achingly predictable. Co-writer Duane Adler lazily reworks his 2000 film *Save the Last Dance* here, with Jenna Dewan (*Take the Lead*) playing a privileged ballet dancer opposite Channing Tatum (*She's the Man*) as a hip-hopping petty criminal. You're guaranteed always to be ten steps ahead of the plot, even in the closing scenes when the story takes a clumsy swerve into *Boyz N the Hood* territory. Despite the gunplay, Fletcher is unable to bring any tension to the mix. SP *DVD* *BL*

Channing Tatum *Tyler Gage* • Jenna Dewan *Nora Clark* • Mario Miles *Darby* • Drew Sidora *Lucy Avila* • Heavy D *Omar* • Damaine Radcliff *Mac Carter* • Rachel Griffiths *Director Gordon* ■

S

Dir Anne Fletcher • *Scr* Duane Adler, Melissa Rosenberg, from a story by Adler • *Choreographer* Anne Fletcher

Step Up 2 the Streets
★★★ PG

Romantic dance drama
2008 · US · Colour · 93min

It may be set in the modern urban sprawl of Baltimore and feature cutting-edge hip hop, but the chief inspiration for this freestyle dance movie is 1980s classic *Fame*. Winning a coveted place at the Maryland School of the Arts, teenager Andie (Briana Evigan) is torn between her dance crew, the 410, and the sedate demands of the academy. Then a blossoming romance with fellow student Chase (Robert Hoffman) sets Andie on a collision course with her street buddies. While its vision of the ghetto is sanitised to the point of ridiculousness, this scrappily produced teen flick showcases some astounding choreography, including a memorable sequence in a club fitted with floor trampolines. JR DVD 🅱

Briana Evigan *Andie* • Robert Hoffman *Chase Collins* • Will Kemp *Blake Collins* • Sonja Sohn *Sarah* • Adam G Sevani *Moose* • Cassie Ventura *Sophie* • Danielle Polanco *Missy* • Telisha Shaw *Felicia* ■ *Dir* Jon M Chu • *Scr* Toni Ann Johnson, Karen Barna, from characters by Duane Adler

Step Up 3
★★★ 12

Romantic dance drama
2010 · US · Colour · 107min

Even if you've heard the one about the high-stakes dance contest some street performers must win to hold on to their communal home, you've never seen it done quite like this. Jon Chu is back from directing the second in the franchise, but does little with the banal bumper-sticker dialogue ("We're part of something bigger") or predictable plot including star-crossed romance, in-house sabotage and last-minute victory. Yet none of that matters when the appealing cast of characters spin, break and move to the music, and the excitement and energy is palpable. A fourth instalment was released in summer 2012. AJ DVD 🅱

Harry Shum Jr *Cable* • Adam G Sevani *Moose* • Sharni Vinson *Natalie* • Kylie Goldstein *Ice cream truck kid* • Rick Malambri *Luke* ■ *Dir* , , [Jon M Chu] • *Scr* Amy Andelson, Emily Meyer, from characters by Duane Adler

Step Up: All In
★★ 12

Romantic dance drama
2014 · US · Colour · 107min

Stars from the previous four *Step Up* movies reunite here to compete in a reality TV contest. No Channing Tatum though, and if any instalment in this franchise needed the charisma of the star of the first two films, it was this one. There are still plenty of inventive routines, choreographed impressively and with gusto by music video director Trish Sie. It's the recycled plot, tired romantic complications, hackneyed rivalries and soap operatics between the dance-offs that are the trouble. AJ Brief swearing, sexual references. DVD 🅱

Ryan Guzman *Sean* • Briana Evigan *Andie* • Adam G Sevani *Moose* • Misha Gabriel *Eddy* • Alyson Stoner *Camille* • Izabella Miko *Alexxa* ■ *Dir* Trish Sie • *Scr* John Swetnam, from characters by Duane Adler

The Stepfather
★★★★ 18

Horror thriller
1986 · US · Colour · 85min

This sardonic and unerringly frightening B-movie classic strips down the American Dream to its maggot-ridden gory glory. Shelley Hack and daughter Jill Schoelen gradually come to realise that the charming, affable man of the house is actually a multiple murderer obsessed with middle-class values and establishing the perfect home. Their failure to live up to his pure vision of domestic bliss earmarks them as additions to his ever-growing list of victims. Joseph Ruben's faultless direction sets the mayhem against an unsettling backdrop of mundane normality. A remake is due out in late 2009. AJ DVD

Terry O'Quinn *Jerry Blake/Henry Morrison/Bill Hodgkins* • Jill Schoelen *Stephanie Maine* • Shelley Hack *Susan Blake* • Stephen Shellen *Jim Ogilvie* • Robyn Stevan *Karen* ■ *Dir* Joseph Ruben • *Scr* Donald E Westlake, from a story by Carolyn Lefcourt, Brian Garfield, Westlake

The Stepfather
★★ 15

Horror thriller
2009 · US · Colour · 97min

Director Nelson McCormick and writer JS Cardone (the men behind the *Prom Night* remake) here craft a slightly less disposable, if still redundant, retread of another noteworthy chiller. Like the 1986 original, the film revolves around a creepily charismatic central performance, this time from *Nip/Tuck's* Dylan Walsh, whose mercurial personality changes and icy delivery keep the basic scares fairly watchable. But without the dark Reagan-era satire or frighteningly inverted family values that made the original so memorable, McCormick's lacklustre reboot is just another psycho thriller. AJ In English, German. Violence. DVD

Dylan Walsh *David Harris* • Sela Ward *Susan Harding* • Penn Badgley *Michael Harding* • Amber Heard *Kelly Porter* • Jon Tenney *Jay* • Sherry Stringfield *Leah* • Paige Turco *Jackie Kerns* • Nancy Linehan Charles *Mrs Cutter* ■ *Dir* Nelson McCormick • *Scr* JS Cardone, from the 1986 film

Stepfather II
★★ 18

Horror
1989 · US · Colour · 84min

The psychotic super-dad (Terry O'Quinn) escapes from a Washington State mental institution, sets himself up as a marriage counsellor and has another go at perfect family life with real-estate agent Meg Foster in this lacklustre sequel. O'Quinn is as good as ever, yet even he can't make the jokey dialogue seem believable. A made-for-TV second sequel was produced in 1992. AJ DVD

Terry O'Quinn *The Stepfather* • Meg Foster *Carol Grayland* • Caroline Williams *Matty Crimmins* • Jonathan Brandis *Todd Grayland* • Henry Brown *Dr Joseph Danvers* • Mitchell Laurance *Phil Grayland* ■ *Dir* Jeff Burr • *Scr* John Auerbach, from characters by Carolyn Lefcourt, Brian Garfield, Donald E Westlake

The Stepford Wives
★★★★★ 15

Science-fiction thriller
1975 · US · Colour · 114min

Ira Levin's bestseller about suburban housewives becoming obedient robots is here turned into an intriguing thriller that highlights society's increasing obsession with perfection. Bryan Forbes's thoughtful direction and intelligent script unfold at a measured pace, so the suspenseful mystery can exert a chilling grip before it ultimately appals. Katharine Ross and Paula Prentiss shine as the nonconformist women fighting their animatronic fate. Followed by three inferior made-for-TV affairs. AJ Swearing, violence. DVD

Katharine Ross *Joanna* • Paula Prentiss *Bobby* • Peter Masterson *Walter* • Nanette Newman *Carol* • Patrick O'Neal *Dale Coba* • Tina Louise *Charmaine* • Carol Rosson *Dr Fancher* ■ *Dir* Bryan Forbes • *Scr* William Goldman, from the novel by Ira Levin

The Stepford Wives
★★ 12

Science-fiction comedy thriller
2004 · US · Colour · 89min

Ira Levin's bestselling tale of extreme female makeovers is given a satirical update in this clumsy comedy from director Frank Oz. Matthew Broderick moves his high-powered TV-executive wife (Nicole Kidman) to the pastel-perfect Connecticut community of Stepford for a flawless "fembot" overhaul under the management of mayor Christopher Walken. The black comedy isn't consistent, there's little in the way of tension or character development. AJ DVD

Nicole Kidman *Joanna Eberhart* • Matthew Broderick *Walter Kresby* • Bette Midler *Roberta "Bobbie" Markowitz* • Christopher Walken *Mike Wellington* • Roger Bart *Roger Bannister* • Faith Hill *Sarah Sunderson* • Glenn Close *Claire Wellington* • David Marshall Grant *Jerry Harmon* •

Jon Lovitz *David Markowitz* • Lorri Bagley *Charmaine Van Sant* ■ *Dir* Frank Oz • *Scr* Paul Rudnick, from the novel by Ira Levin

Stephen King's The Night Flier
★★★ 18

Horror thriller
1997 · US · Colour · 92min

Based on one of Stephen King's most peculiar short stories, this involves a vampire who pilots a Cessna plane and leaves a trail of bodies in his wake. Tabloid reporter Miguel Ferrer and young rival Julie Entwisle pursue the mysterious killer. Director Mark Pavia does wonders on a small budget, making the atmosphere genuinely tense and mysterious, and gruesome when it needs to be. KB DVD

Miguel Ferrer *Richard Dees* • Julie Entwisle *Katherine Blair* • Dan Monahan *Merton Morrison* • Michael H Moss *Dwight Renfield* • John Bennes *Ezra Hannon* • Beverly Skinner *Selida McCamon* ■ *Dir* Mark Pavia • *Scr* Mark Pavia, Jack O'Donnell, from the short story by Stephen King

Stephen King's Thinner
★ 18

Horror
1996 · US · Colour · 88min

The "thinner" end of the wedge as far as adaptations of Stephen King's books go. Robert John Burke is the grossly overweight lawyer cursed by the King of the Gypsies to fade away to nothing after killing a Romany in a hit-and-run car accident. Nothing convinces in this latex-heavy bust where the nightmare twists cause more yawns than terror. AJ Swearing, violence.

Robert John Burke [Robert Burke] *Billy Halleck* • Joe Mantegna *Richie Ginelli* • Lucinda Jenney *Heidi Halleck* • Joie Lenz *Linda Halleck* • Time Winters *Prosecutor* • Howard Erskine *Judge Phillips* ■ *Dir* Tom Holland (1) • *Scr* Michael McDowell, Tom Holland, from the novel by Richard Bachman [Stephen King]

Stepkids
★★ PG

Comedy
1992 · US · Colour · 100min

The problems of trying to survive in an overextended family form the basis of director Joan Micklin Silver's overlong and mawkish comedy. Disgruntled 13-year-old Hillary Wolf decides to run away to stepbrother Dan Futterman's lakeside cabin, following a row at home. Unfortunately, far from escaping her dysfunctional family, Wolf's disappearance makes them converge on the cabin. Despite the presence of Griffin Dunne, this is an overly cute and schematic tale. AJ

Hillary Wolf *Laura Chartoff* • David Strathairn *Keith Powers* • Margaret Whitton *Melinda Powers* • Griffin Dunne *David Chartoff* • Patricia Kalember *Barbara Chartoff* • Adrienne Shelly *Stephanie Miller* • Dan Futterman *Josh Powers* ■ *Dir* Joan Micklin Silver • *Scr* Frank Mugavero, from a story by Mark and Melissa Goddard, Mugavero

Stepmom
★★★★ 12

Drama
1998 · US/Ger · Colour · 119min

This is a touching and sophisticated film about post-divorce family life. As the girlfriend of divorcee Ed Harris, fashion photographer Julia Roberts starts off on the wrong foot when she meets his family. Attempting to win over his two children she finds herself competing with their "perfect" mother Susan Sarandon. However, when Sarandon falls seriously ill, the women must reappraise their priorities. Strong performances from actors who are not afraid to be unsympathetic and unpredictable narrative twists make this far from your average sentimental family drama. LH DVD

Julia Roberts *Isabel Kelly* • Susan Sarandon *Jackie Harrison* • Ed Harris *Luke Harrison* • Jena Malone *Anna Harrison* • Liam Aiken *Ben Harrison* • Lynn Whitfield *Dr Sweikert* ■ *Dir* Chris Columbus • *Scr* Gigi Levangie, Jessie Nelson, Steven Rogers, Karen Leigh Hopkins, Ron Bass, from a story by Gigi Levangie

Steppenwolf
★★★

Part-animated drama
1974 · US · Colour · 107min

Since 1927, Herman Hesse's novel has sold millions of copies and is regarded as an intensely personal work in its portrait of the intellectual and emotional crises facing a man nudging 50. Inevitably, the response to director Fred Haines's treatment of a seemingly unfilmable book has concentrated on the success in translating it to the screen, but for most people it will emerge as a very striking film visually, dominated by Max von Sydow's fine performance. BB

Max von Sydow *Harry* • Dominique Sanda *Hermine* • Pierre Clémenti *Pablo* • Carla Romanelli *Maria* • Roy Bosier *Aztec* • Alfred Baillou *Goethe* ■ *Dir* Fred Haines • *Scr* Fred Haines, from the novel by Hermann Hesse • *Cinematographer* Tomaslav Pinter

Stepping Out
★★ PG

Musical drama
1991 · Can/US · Colour · 104min

Lewis Gilbert's rather humdrum hymn to tap and shuffle stars Liza Minnelli as a Broadway hoofer attempting to transform a bunch of near-hopeless amateurs into a crack dancing troupe. All stereotypes are firmly in place, including Julie Walters as a germ-obsessed housewife and Shelley Winters as the cantankerous pianist. Obvious, but with pockets of fun. SH Some swearing.

Liza Minnelli *Mavis Turner* • Shelley Winters *Mrs Fraser* • Julie Walters *Vera* • Ellen Greene *Maxine* • Sheila McCarthy *Andy* • Bill Irwin *Geoffrey* • Carol Woods *Rose* • Robyn Stevan *Sylvia* • Jane Krakowski *Lynne* ■ *Dir* Lewis Gilbert • *Scr* Richard Harris, from his play

Steptoe and Son
★★★ PG

Comedy
1972 · UK · Colour · 93min

This is one of the better sitcom spin-offs, with Ray Galton and Alan Simpson contributing a script that not only has a half-decent story, but also gags that would not have disgraced the original TV series. Wilfred Brambell and Harry H Corbett reprise their roles to good effect, along with Carolyn Seymour, Corbett's new stripper-bride, whose mercenary intentions threaten the future of the rag-and-bone yard. DP DVD

Wilfred Brambell *Albert Steptoe* • Harry H Corbett *Harold Steptoe* • Carolyn Seymour *Zita* • Arthur Howard (2) *Vicar* • Victor Maddern *Chauffeur* • Fred Griffiths *Barman* ■ *Dir* Cliff Owen • *Scr* Ray Galton, Alan Simpson, from their TV series

Steptoe and Son Ride Again
★★ PG

Comedy
1973 · UK · Colour · 94min

This second movie featuring the nation's favourite junkmen is very much a rags-and-bones affair, with the material stretched to fraying point to justify the running time. Apart from the unnecessary crudeness of its humour, the main problem here is the dilution of the intense, disappointed fondness that made the pair's TV relationship so engaging. Weakly scripted. DP DVD

Wilfrid Brambell *Albert Steptoe* • Harry H Corbett *Harold Steptoe* • Diana Dors *Woman in flat* • Milo O'Shea *Doctor Popplewell* • Neil McCarthy *Lennie* • Bill Maynard *George* • George Tovey *Percy* • Sam Kydd *Claude* ■ *Dir* Peter Sykes • *Scr* Ray Galton, Alan Simpson, from their TV series

The Sterile Cuckoo
★★★

Romantic comedy drama
1969 · US · Colour · 107min

Liza Minnelli gives an Oscar-nominated performance, playing the sort of character who puts the "kook" into cuckoo. She's an insecure near-nutter who ropes a hapless college student into her neurotically self-centred world. Predictably, her grades go all to pot in the process. Wendell Burton beautifully plays the boy; curiously, he's been little heard of since. No such obscurity for Alan J Pakula, here making his directorial debut. The movie was originally released as *Pookie* in the UK. DA

U SUITABLE FOR ALL Uc SUITABLE ESPECIALLY FOR YOUNG CHILDREN (DVD ONLY) PG PARENTAL GUIDANCE 12A UNDER 12s TO BE ACCOMPANIED (CINEMA ONLY)

Liza Minnelli *Pookie Adams* • Wendell Burton *Jerry Payne* • Tim McIntire *Charlie Schumacher* • Elizabeth Harrower *Landlady* • Austin Green *Pookie's father* • Sandra Faison [Sandy Faison] *Nancy Putnam* • Chris Bugbee *Roe* • Jawn McKinley *Helen Upshaw* ■ *Dir* Alan J Pakula • *Scr* Alvin Sargent, from the novel *The Sterile Cuckoo* by John Treadwell Nichols [John Nichols]

Steve Jobs ★★★★ 15

Biographical drama 2015 · US · Colour · 117min

Not your typical biopic... Instead of portraying every notable moment in Jobs's life, it focuses on three events: the launch of the Mac in 1984, the launch of the NeXT Cube in 1988, and the unveiling of the iMac in 1998. Each act takes place backstage, unfolding in real time as Jobs (Michael Fassbender) prepares to present these products to an audience. The compelling Fassbender doesn't look like Steve Jobs, of course, and the story feels somewhat contrived, but these are minor complaints in a thoroughly enjoyable and witty film. SC Swearing

Michael Fassbender *Steve Jobs* • Kate Winslet *Joanna Hoffman* • Seth Rogen *Steve Wozniak* • Jeff Daniels *John Sculley* • Michael Stuhlbarg *Andy Hertzfeld* ■ *Dir* Danny Boyle • *Scr* Aaron Sorkin, from Walter Isaacson's biography • *Music* Daniel Pemberton

Steve McQueen: the Man & Le Mans ★★★ 15

Documentary
2015 · US/UK · Colour and BW · 102min

Using audio recordings and behind-the-scenes footage, this reveals how the 1971 drama about the Le Mans 24-hour motor race, starring Steve McQueen, flopped so badly. McQueen's obsession with authenticity resulted in reels of actual race footage but no script, which eventually caused original director John Sturges to quit in disgust. Petrolheads will revel in the race sequences but like *Le Mans* itself, this watchable documentary could have done with some judicious editing. JA Swearing.

Steve McQueen (1) *Steve McQueen* • Chad McQueen • Neile Adams • Derek Bell • Siegfried Rauch ■ *Dir* Gabriel Clarke, John McKenna

Stevie ★★★ 15

Biographical drama 1978 · UK · Colour · 101min

Glenda Jackson's typically terrific in this play-derived drama about a poetess living with her doting but dotty maiden aunt Mona Washbourne, giving Glenda Jackson a run for her money in the scene-stealing stakes. Trevor Howard narrates and co-stars. As a film, *Stevie* never quite escapes its obvious stage origins, but it's an intriguing character study, and worth watching for the quality of the performances alone. DA

Glenda Jackson *Stevie Smith* • Mona Washbourne *Aunt* • Alec McCowen *Freddy* • Trevor Howard *The Man* • Emma Louise Fox *Stevie as a child* ■ *Dir* Robert Enders • *Scr* Hugh Whitmore, from his play and the works of Stevie Smith

Stick ★ 18

Crime thriller 1985 · US · Colour · 104min

Elmore Leonard adapted his own novel about a flamboyant ex-con who goes down the vengeance trail after his best buddy is rubbed out. Set in the now familiar Leonard world of loan sharks, drug dealers and Palm Beach slimeballs with terrible taste in shirts and wallpaper, it squanders everything for the sake of making star/director Burt Reynolds a handsome, lovable rogue. Reynolds took all the guts out of the book and reshot the ending, but the result was still a critical passing and box-office disaster. AT

Burt Reynolds *Stick* • Candice Bergen *Kyle* • George Segal *Barry* • Charles Durning *Chucky* • José Perez (2) *Rainy* • Richard Lawson *Cornell* • Castulo Guerra *Nestor* ■ *Dir* Burt Reynolds • *Scr* Elmore Leonard, Joseph C Stinson, from the novel by Elmore Leonard

Stick It ★★★ PG

Sports comedy 2006 · US · Colour · 98min

After tackling the competitive world of high-school cheerleading in *Bring It On*, screenwriter Jessica Bendinger turns her attention to the cut-throat arena of teen gymnastics for this, her directorial debut. Jeff Bridges plays the hard-nosed head coach of a top gymnastics academy; Missy Peregrym the emotionally damaged but gifted teenager who's sent there after ending up in front of a judge on a charge of criminal damage. There's no prize for guessing that the collision of their personalities proves to be a learning experience for both. If there's one thing *Stick It* isn't, it's original. DA Some swearing. **DVD**

Jeff Bridges *Burt Vickerman* • Missy Peregrym *Haley Graham* • Vanessa Lengies *Joanne Charis* • Nikki Soohoo *Wei Wei Yong* • Maddy Curley *Mina Hoyt* • Kellan Lutz *Frank* • Julie Warner *Mrs Charis* ■ *Dir/Scr* Jessica Bendinger

Stickmen ★★★ 18

Comedy drama 2000 · NZ · Colour · 93min

Very much in the hip comic vein of *Lock, Stock and Two Smoking Barrels*, this Kiwi caper is a slick, likeable affair, in which three pool players get dragged into an underworld competition. As well as having to contend with a wacky collection of pool competitors, they also have to stay one step ahead of a Greek mobster, the excellent Enrico Mammarella. Hamish Rothwell's direction is suitably laddish and he and writer Nick Ward bring a winning collection of trick shots to the table. JF Violence, swearing, sex scenes. **DVD**

Robbie Magasiva *Jack* • Paolo Rotondo *Thomas* • Scott Wills *Wayne* • Simone Kessell *Karen* • Anne Nordhaus *Sarah* • Luanne Gordon *Lulu* • Enrico Mammarella *Daddy* ■ *Dir* Hamish Rothwell • *Scr* Nick Ward

The Stickup ★★★ 15

Crime thriller 2001 · US/Can · Colour · 92min

James Spader stars as a cop who quits the city after the death of his partner and heads into the backwoods. There his ambition to start afresh takes an unexpected twist when he falls for nurse Leslie Stefanson and finds himself lured on to the wrong side of the law. With a series of flashbacks deepening the mystery, this is a brisk, slickly plotted crime thriller that proves once again that no one does offbeat quite like Spader. DP Violence, swearing. **DVD**

James Spader *John Parker* • Leslie Stefanson *Natalie Wright* • David Keith *Ray DeCarlo* • John Livingston *FBI Agent Rick Kendall* • Robert Miano *Lt Vincent Marino* • A fred E Humphreys *Alf Humphreys* *Mike O'Grady* ■ *Dir/Scr* Rowdy Herrington

Sticky Fingers ★★★ 15

Comedy 1988 · US · Colour · 84min

There is a wonderful air of naive debauchery and jangling nerves about this story of two flat-sharing musicians who are left holding \$91,000 in a holdall. Piles of designer clothes and plentiful wild parties later, the hoods are on their trail. The film boasts lovely performances from Helen Slater and Melanie Mayron and a gloriously zany overview of immaturity and neurosis from debuting director Catlin Adams. SH Swearing.

Helen Slater *Hattie* • Melanie Mayron *Lolly* • Eileen Brennan *Stella* • Loretta Devine *Diane* • Christopher Guest *Sam* • Carol Kane *Kitty* • Stephen McHattie *Eddie* ■ *Dir* Catlin Adams • *Scr* Catlin Adams, Melanie Mayron

Stiff Upper Lips ★★★★ 15

Period drama parody 1997 · UK · Colour · 91min

This is a parody (long overdue, some might feel) of the "white flannel" school of British film-making that produced the likes of *Brideshead Revisited* and *Chariots of Fire*, which are all amusingly ridiculed here by co-writer/director Gary Sinyor. Prunella Scales is delightful as the aristocratic Aunt Agnes, who takes her soppy family on a Grand Tour, on which many awful mishaps occur. A genuinely witty script, and locations in

Italy and India, make one forget that it could have been done as a TV sketch. DM

Peter Ustinov *Horace* • Prunella Scales *Aunt Agnes Ivory* • Georgina Cates *Emily Ivory* • Samuel West *Edward Ivory* • Sean Pertwee *George* • Brian Glover *Eric* • Frank Finlay *Hudson Junior* ■ *Dir* Gary Sinyor • *Scr* Paul Simpkin, Gary Sinyor

Stigmata ★★ 18

Supernatural thriller 1999 · US · Colour · 97min

In this dumb religious horror, Patricia Arquette is the atheist hairdresser who suddenly starts suffering from vicious stigmata – wounds identical to the ones Christ received on the cross. When Vatican priest Gabriel Byrne is sent to investigate, he realises there are more to her gory wounds than meets the eye. A booming soundtrack (from Billy Corgan of the Smashing Pumpkins), flashy images and pop video-style direction add to the film's frenetic feel, while diverting us from some of the less plausible plot twists. JB **DVD**

Patricia Arquette *Frankie Paige* • Gabriel Byrne *Father Andrew Kiernan* • Jonathan Pryce *Cardinal Daniel Houseman* • Nia Long *Donna Chadway* • Thomas Kopache *Father Durning* • Rade Serbedzija *Marion Petrocelli* • Enrico Colantoni *Father Dario* • Dick Latessa *Father Gianni Delmonico* ■ *Dir* Rupert Wainwright • *Scr* Tom Lazarus, Rick Ramage, from a story by Tom Lazarus

Still ★★★ 15

Thriller 2014 · UK · Colour · 98min

Moody, bleak and uneven, this award-winning low-budget thriller rests on the able shoulders of Aiden Gillen (*Game of Thrones*) who stars as Carver, a North London photographer failing to cope with his son's apparently accidental death and the breakdown of his relationship with ex-wife Rachel (Amanda Mealing), the boy's mother. Strong performances and vivid production design buoy up this evocative, troubling film that shows flashes of brilliance from writer/director Simon Blake, making his feature debut. RSC star Jonathan Slinger, Elodie Yung as Carver's girlfriend and rapper Sonny Green also make an impression. KK

Aidan Gillen *Tom Carver* • Jonathan Slinger *Ed* • Elodie Yung *Christina* • Amanda Mealing *Rachel* • Sonny Green *Carl* • Kate Ashfield *Margaret* ■ *Dir/Scr* Simon Blake

Still Alice ★★★ 12

Drama 2014 · US · Colour · 100min

In Hollywood, Alzheimer's tends to afflict the comfortably off or brilliantly academic, but in this otherwise rather coy adaptation of neuroscientist Lisa Genova's novel, Julianne Moore's linguistics professor is diagnosed with the rare, early-onset strain. While Moore's Oscar- and Bafta-winning performance is subtle and intelligent, Alec Baldwin has less to conjure with as her physician husband and their adult children (Kate Bosworth, Hunter Parrish, Kristen Stewart) are mere cut-outs. AC Brief swearing, sexual references. **DVD** **Blu**

Julianne Moore *Dr Alice Howland* • Alec Baldwin *John Howland* • Kristen Stewart *Lydia Howland* • Kate Bosworth *Anna* • Hunter Parrish *Tom Howland* • Daniel Gerroll *Eric Wellman* ■ *Dir* Richard Glatzer, Wash Westmoreland • *Scr* Richard Glatzer, Wash Westmoreland, from Lisa Genova's novel

Still Bill: the Bill Withers Story ★★★

Music documentary 2009 · US · Colour · 78min

The Bill Withers story is like something from *The X Factor*: a 32-year-old factory worker becomes an overnight singing success after deciding to make a record despite never having written a song, played any instruments or sung anywhere except in the shower. But this warm documentary uses Withers's story to paint a picture of a down-to-earth man ill at ease with the music industry and the idea of fame. Which goes some way to explain why this most soulful of soul singers is also one of the most underrated. DC

Bill Withers ■ *Dir* Damani Baker, Alex Vlack

Still Crazy ★★★★ 15

Comedy 1998 · US/UK · Colour · 91min

Fans of the superb mockumentary *This Is Spinal Tap* will chortle at this 1990s British take on the theme. Ageing rockers Jimmy Nail, Timothy Spall, Stephen Rea and Bill Nighy (along with roadie Billy Connolly) reform the successful 1970s group Strange Fruit to go on the road one more time. There are all the clashing egos, old grudges and bad rock numbers you'd expect, plus a deft script from comedy writers Dick Clement and Ian La Frenais, but the true plaudits should go to the performances from Nighy (as the narcissistic lead singer) and Bruce Robinson (writer/director of *Withnail & I*) in a strangely moving cameo role. JB Swearing. **DVD** **CS**

Stephen Rea *Tony Costello* • Billy Connolly *Hughie* • Jimmy Nail *Les Wickes* • Timothy Spall *Beano Baggot* • Bill Nighy *Ray Simms* • Juliet Aubrey *Karen Knowles* • Helena Bergström *Astrid Simms* • Bruce Robinson *Brian Lovell* • Phil Daniels *Neil Gaydon* • Frances Barber *Woman in black* • Phil Davis [Philip Davis] *Limo driver* • Zoë Ball *Zoë* ■ *Dir* Brian Gibson • *Scr* Dick Clement, Ian La Frenais

Still Life ★★★★

Social drama 1974 · Iran · Colour · 93min

This measured study of social alienation from influential Iranian director Sohrab Shahid Saless earned him both the Silver Bear at the Berlin film festival and the enmity of the Shah that forced him into German exile. The superficially simple drama focuses on a veteran railwayman who is discarded in the interests of progress after uncomplainingly doing his monotonous job in near isolation for 30 years. By presenting the daily routines of Zadour Bonyadi and his carpet-weaving wife in such unfussy detail, Saless speaks volumes about the irrelevance of the individual to Iranian industrialisation. DP Farsi +subtitles.

Zadour Bonyadi *Mohamad Sardari* ■ *Dir/Scr* Sohrab Shahid Saless

Still Life ★★★ 12

Comedy drama 2013 · UK/It · Colour · 88min

In this melancholy drama, lonely council worker Eddie Marsan organises the burial service whenever someone in his borough dies alone. After being made redundant, he persuades his boss to let him finish a final case, which centres on a hot-tempered alcoholic who recently passed away. The story that follows is sombre and understated to a fault, but also quietly affecting, while Marsan is typically impressive in the lead role. SC **DVD**

Eddie Marsan *John May* • Joanne Froggatt *Kelly* • Karen Drury *Mary* • Andrew Buchan *Mr Pratchett* • Ciaran McIntyre *Jumbo* • Neil D'Souza *Shakthi* ■ *Dir/Scr* Uberto Pasolini

Still of the Night ★★★★ 15

Thriller 1982 · US · Colour · 87min

Occasionally as tense as *Jagged Edge*, with dramatic moments reminiscent of medium-grade Hitchcock, this never quite attains the status of classic suspense. On-the-move Meryl Streep stays around long enough to enthral psychiatrist Roy Scheider, one of whose patients winds up dead, in director Robert Benton's moral tale that proclaims doctors should not mix business and pleasure. For all its plot flaws, this is a sleekly crafted movie with performances to match. TH Some violence.

Roy Scheider *Sam Rice* • Meryl Streep *Brooke Reynolds* • Jessica Tandy *Grace Rice* • Joe Grifasi *Joe Vitucci* • Sara Botsford *Gail Phillips* • Josef Sommer *George Bynum* • Irving Metzman *Murray* ■ *Dir* Robert Benton • *Scr* Robert Benton, from a story by David Newman, Robert Benton

Still the Enemy Within ★★★ 15

Documentary 2014 · UK · Colour · 112min

This impassioned documentary chronicles the infamous miners' strike that took place between 1984 and 1985. Buoyed by two successful strikes in the early 70s, the

National Union of Mineworkers took action when it was announced that various pits were to be closed across the UK. Approximately 160,000 coal miners went on strike, resulting in an ongoing conflict with Margaret Thatcher's Conservative government. Owen Gower's film is told from the perspective of the miners, and alternates between grainy archive footage and frank interviews with the colliery workers who stood on the picket lines. It is unashamedly one-sided, but the testimonies from those involved are often insightful and revealing. SC *DVD*

■ *Dir* Owen Gower • *Cinematographer* Malcolm Hadley

Still Walking ★★★★ U
Drama   2008 · Jpn · Colour · 114min

In this consummate variation on director Yasujiro Ozu's 1953 masterpiece *Tokyo Story*, Hirokazu Koreeda allows an air of humanist compassion to pervade a provincial family's reunion to mark the anniversary of a deceased son, while also offering a cutting dissection of Japanese manners. Yoshio Harada's family patriarch may bemoan what his daughter (You) and art-restorer son (Hiroshi Abe) have amounted to, but his grumpy disapproval is positively benign beside the wounding bitterness his wife (Kiki Kirin) is capable of. Yutaka Yamazaki's photography and Gontiti's guitar score are as impeccable as the performances, but it's Koreeda's delicacy, wit and insight that make this so intricate, poignant and truthful. DP Japanese +subtitles.

Hiroshi Abe *Ryota Yokoyama* • Yui Natsukawa *Yukari Yokoyama* • You *Chinami Kataoka* • Kazuya Takahashi *Nobuo Kataoka* • Shohei Tanaka *Atsushi Yokoyama* • Kirin Kiki *Toshiko Yokoyama* • ■ *Dir/Scr* Hirokazu Koreeda

The Sting ★★★★★ PG
Period crime caper   1973 · US · Colour · 123min

These things rarely come off, but the reteaming of *Butch Cassidy and the Sundance Kid* stars Paul Newman and Robert Redford and their director George Roy Hill proved to be a glorious triumph, and this raced away with seven Oscars. Newman and Redford play conmen who, after the death of an old chum, set about fleecing mobster Robert Shaw out of a fortune. The sting itself is as audacious as it is elaborate, but the real pleasure comes from the easy, charismatic playing of the two leads, the lovingly created 1930s settings and Marvin Hamlisch's inspired reworking of Scott Joplin's music. JF Swearing. *DVD* Blu

Paul Newman *Henry Gondorff* • Robert Redford *Johnny Hooker* • Robert Shaw *Doyle Lonnegan* • Charles Durning *Lt William Snyder* • Ray Walston *JJ Singleton* • Eileen Brennan *Billie* • Harold Gould *Kid Twist* • John Heffernan *Eddie Niles* • *Dir* George Roy Hill • *Scr* David S Ward • *Costume Designer* Edith Head • *Cinematographer* Robert Surtees • *Art Director* Henry Bumstead • *Music* Scott Joplin

The Sting II ★★ PG
Period crime caper   1983 · US · Colour · 97min

Proof that lightning seldom strikes twice, this was the belated and unnecessary sequel to George Roy Hill's multi-Oscar-winning hit. Robert Redford and Paul Newman's scam on gangster Robert Shaw is reprised as a boxing set-up, with Jackie Gleason and Mac Davis as their inadequate replacements. TH

Jackie Gleason *Gondorff* • Mac Davis *Hooker* • Teri Garr *Veronica* • Karl Malden *Macalinski* • Oliver Reed *Lonnegan* ■ *Dir* Jeremy Paul Kagan • *Scr* David S Ward

Stir Crazy ★★★ 15
Comedy   1980 · US · Colour · 106min

As Sidney Poitier's direction and a firm script all but vanish beneath the clowning, Richard Pryor and Gene Wilder are, according to your taste, either highly creative, witty and inspired, or contrived, noisy and tedious. Relying more on mugging than acting, they play a couple of goons who leave New York for California

and are wrongly imprisoned for a bank robbery en route. Prison clichés are cleverly lampooned, and Pryor's chicken scene is one that will last. JM Violence, swearing. *DVD*

Gene Wilder *Skip Donahue* • Richard Pryor *Harry Monroe* • Georg Stanford Brown *Rory Schultebrand* • JoBeth Williams *Meredith* • Miguel Angel Suarez *Jesus Ramirez* • Craig T Nelson *Deputy Ward Wilson* • Barry Corbin *Warden Walter Beatty* • Charles Weldon *Blade* ■ *Dir* Sidney Poitier • *Scr* Bruce Jay Friedman

Stir of Echoes ★★★ 15
Supernatural thriller   1999 · US · Colour · 95min

David Koepp's creepy supernatural tale was completely overshadowed by *The Sixth Sense*. However, while it isn't as smart or satisfying, it delivers a handful of extremely frightening moments and a credible performance from Kevin Bacon as a man haunted by startling visions. Using jolting cuts and stylised camerawork to evoke fear, Koepp immerses the audience in a mystery involving psychic powers, a dead girl and Bacon's son, who seems to share his "gift". JC Swearing.

Kevin Bacon *Tom Witzky* • Kathryn Erbe *Maggie Witzky* • Illeana Douglas *Lisa* • Liza Weil *Debbie Kozac, the babysitter* • Kevin Dunn *Frank McCarthy* • Conor O'Farrell *Harry Damon* • Jenny Morrison [Jennifer Morrison] *Samantha* ■ *Dir* David Koepp • *Scr* David Koepp, from the novel by Richard Matheson

A Stitch in Time ★★ U
Comedy   1963 · UK · BW · 90min

Norman Wisdom relives a little of his youth in this sentimental comedy, as his first job at 13 was as a delivery boy. This was his final film in black and white and also his last big starring success at the box office, for he belonged to a more innocent age. The script sticks closely to the Wisdom formula and he knots his cap in shyness in his attempts to declare his love for a pretty nurse. DP *DVD*

Norman Wisdom *Norman Pitkin* • Edward Chapman *Grimsdale* • Jeannette Sterke *Janet Haskell* • Jerry Desmonde *Sir Hector Hardcastle* • Jill Melford *Lady Brinkley* • Glyn Houston *Welsh* • Hazel Hughes *Matron* ■ *Dir* Robert Asher • *Scr* Jack Davies, Norman Wisdom, Henry Blyth, Eddie Leslie

Stitches ★★ 18
Horror comedy   2012 · Ire/US · Colour · 82min

Cheap, cheesy and very 1980s, this killer-clown comedy is salvaged by some gorily gigglesome moments, several of which involve balloon pumps and human body bits. Stand-up comedian Ross Noble makes his feature debut as Stitches, a third-rate party clown who returns from the dead to take revenge on the kids who accidentally killed him years before at a birthday party. Noble acquits himself well, and his turn as the red-nosed, big-booted fiend is the best thing about this time-warped splatter-fest. DA Violence *DVD* Blu

Ross Noble *Richard "Stitches" Grindle* • Tommy Knight *Tommy* • Shane Murray Corcoran *Vinny* • Gemma-Leah Devereux *Kate* • Thommas Kane Byrne *Bulger* • Eoghan McQuinn *Richie* ■ *Dir* Conor McMahon • *Scr* Conor McMahon, David O'Brien

Stock Car ★ U
Sports drama   1955 · UK · BW · 66min

This road smash of a picture packs in every kind of quota quickie cliché, as plucky garage owner Rona Anderson turns to dashing driving ace Paul Carpenter to help her repulse the threat of a charlatan creditor. The mediocrity is unrelenting, with the race sequences every bit as hackneyed as the risible melodrama. DP

Paul Carpenter *Larry Duke* • Rona Anderson *Katie Glebe* • Harry Fowler *Monty Albright* • Paul Whitsun-Jones *Turk McNeil* • Susan Shaw *Gina* • Robert Rietty *Roberto* • Alma Taylor *Nurse Sprott* ■ *Dir* Wolf Rilla • *Scr* AR Rawlinson, Victor Lyndon

Stockade ★★★ 15
Drama   1991 · US · Colour · 93min

Sheen family projects tend to be more serious fare than usual (think of 1996's *The War at Home*) and this is no exception. In this gripping but talky drama, dad Martin is in the director's chair and also has a co-starring role, alongside son Charlie. There's even a part for a less well-known member of the family, Ramon Estevez. Sheen Jr plays a reluctant soldier sentenced to a term in a military stockade, where he gets locked into a dangerous battle of wills with a cruel NCO, played by Sheen Sr. This is solid if slightly familiar entertainment. JF Swearing, violence.

Charlie Sheen *Franklin Bean Jr* • Martin Sheen *Sergeant Otis V McKinney* • Larry Fishburne [Laurence Fishburne] *Stokes* • Blu Mankuma *Spoonman (Bryce)* • Michael Beach *Webb* • Harry Stewart *Sweetbread (Crane)* • John Toles-Bey *Lawrence* • James Marshall *Lamar* • Ramon Estevez [Ramon Sheen] *Gessner* • F Murray Abraham *Garcia* ■ *Dir* Martin Sheen • *Scr* Dennis Schryack, Martin Sheen, from the novel *Count a Lonely Cadence* by Gordon Weaver

Stoked: the Rise and Fall of Gator ★★★ 15
Documentary   2002 · US · Colour · 80min

Helen Stickler's study of skateboarding superstar Mark "Gator" Rogowski reveals the depressing extent to which youthful exuberance has been exploited by corporate America. One of the vertical-ramp legends of the 1980s, the Californian teenager had an unrivalled marketability that sustained his celebrity lifestyle. But his failure to make the transition to street skating saw his star plummet until he was given 31 years for raping and murdering his former fiancée's best friend. Stickler never excuses Gator's crime, but her precise evocation of a once-golden age makes his actions more comprehensible. DP Swearing, sexual references. *DVD*

■ *Dir* Helen Stickler

The Stoker ★★★★ 15
Crime drama   2010 · Rus · Colour · 87min

From his 1997 breakthrough film, *Brother*, onwards, Alexei Balabanov's work remains unblinkingly matter-of-fact regarding the value of human life. Set in St Petersburg in the 1990s, this chillingly deadpan saga centres on two veterans of the Afghan-Soviet War, an ethnic Yakut, Major Skryabin (Mikhail Skryabin) who stokes coal for a living and Sergeant, a mob hitman (Aleksander Mosin) who uses the furnace to dispose of his victims. The action would be disconcerting anyway, but being accompanied by a relentlessly jaunty score makes it all the more shocking. The overall look of the film and the impeccable performances serve Balabanov's unique vision, making it a riveting watch. DP Russian +subtitles. Violence, sex scenes, nudity, some swearing.

Mikhail Skryabin *Major Skryabin* • Aida Tumutova *Sasha* • Aleksander Mosin *Sergeant* • Yuriy Matveev *Bizon* • Anna Korotaeva *Masha* • Vyacheslav Paulyuts *Fedor Alexeevich* ■ *Dir/Scr* Alexei Balabanov

Stoker ★★★★ 18
Thriller   2013 · US/UK · Colour · 94min

South Korean director Park Chan-wook (*Oldboy*, *Thirst*) makes his Hollywood debut with this unsettling gothic thriller. On her 18th birthday, India Stoker (Mia Wasikowska) finds out that her father has been killed in an accident. She has never met her brother, but uncle Charlie (Matthew Goode) appears at the funeral and quickly makes himself at home. There are nods to Hitchcock's *Shadow of a Doubt* and Douglas Sirk's lush melodramas, but Park's usual themes of sex, death and revenge are still very much in evidence and – happily – they have been only slightly toned down. The potboiler script from *Prison Break* actor Wentworth Miller is elevated by the director's incredibly immersive visual style, Clint Mansell's superb score and expert performances from Goode, Nicole Kidman

and Wasikowska, who skilfully keeps you guessing as to whether India is an angel or a monster. LB Violence, swearing, sex scenes. *DVD* Blu

Mia Wasikowska *India Stoker* • Nicole Kidman *Evelyn "Evie" Stoker* • Matthew Goode *Charles Stoker* • Dermot Mulroney *Richard Stoker* • Jacki Weaver *Gwendolyn Stoker* • Phyllis Somerville *Mrs McGarrick* ■ *Dir* Park Chan-wook • *Scr* Wentworth Miller • *Music* Clint Mansell, Philip Glass

Stolen ★★ 12
Action thriller   2012 · US · Colour · 91min

This workmanlike thriller stars Nicolas Cage as a thief trying to go straight, but forced to confront his past when his daughter is kidnapped by an old gang member. As Cage sets about making up the missing millions from an earlier heist to secure his daughter's freedom, hard-nosed FBI man Danny Huston shadows his every move and is ready to pounce. It's a familiar premise, and was handled with some flair in the Liam Neeson action yarn *Taken*, but here there are just too many standard movie conventions and too few surprises. TeS *DVD* Blu

Nicolas Cage *Will Montgomery* • Danny Huston *Tim Harlend* • Malin Akerman *Riley Jeffers* • MC Gainey *Hoyt* • Sami Gayle *Alison* • Josh Lucas *Vincent* ■ *Dir* Simon West • *Scr* David Guggenheim

The Stolen Children ★★★★ 15
Drama   1992 · It/Fr/Swe · Colour · 110min

This heart-warming if occasionally sentimental story was inspired by a newspaper headline. In addition to highlighting a range of social issues, director Gianni Amelio also coaxes a quite remarkable performance from Valentina Scalici, as an 11-year-old Sicilian girl who is sent to an orphanage after her desperate mother sells her into prostitution in Milan. Enrico Lo Verso is equally impressive as the inexperienced cop escorting the girl and her younger brother. DP Italian +subtitles.

Enrico Lo Verso *Antonio* • Valentina Scalici *Rosetta* • Giuseppe Ieracitano *Luciano* • Renato Carpentieri *Marshal* • Vitalba Andrea *Antonio's sister* • Fabio Alessandrini *Grignani* ■ *Dir* Gianni Amelio • *Scr* Sandro Petraglia, Stefano Rulli, Gianni Amelio

Stolen Face ★★ PG
Drama   1952 · UK · BW · 69min

Take this early Hammer melodrama with a ton of salt and you may enjoy its wild fantasy about sexual obsession and the incredible achievements of plastic surgery. Two 1940s stars, past their prime, were dragged to Britain to boost international sales. Surgeon Paul Henreid falls in love with pianist Lizabeth Scott. Thwarted in his desire, he gives Scott's face to a woman convict (not a good move). DM *DVD*

Paul Henreid *Dr Philip Ritter* • Lizabeth Scott *Alice Brent/Lilly* • André Morell *David* • Mary Mackenzie *Lilly* • John Wood [1] *Dr Jack Wilson* • Susan Stephen *Betty* • Arnold Ridley *Dr Russell* ■ *Dir* Terence Fisher • *Scr* Martin Berkeley, Richard Landau

Stolen Hearts ★★ 15
Romantic comedy   1996 · US · Colour · 91min

Sandra Bullock has little to do in this romantic comedy caper but look gorgeous, leaving her co-star, American stand-up comedian Denis Leary, with the lion's share of the movie. Unfortunately, Leary's trademark put-downs are not enough to carry the film. He's a petty thief who steals a Matisse painting and goes on the run with his girlfriend (Bullock), holing up in a rich New England neighbourhood where the poverty-stricken twosome stand out like sore thumbs. The film shows some glimmers of sarcastic potential, but co-writer Leary's ego gets in the way. TH Swearing. *DVD*

Denis Leary *Frank* • Sandra Bullock *Roz* • Stephen Dillane *Evan Marsh* • Yaphet Kotto *O'Malley* • Mike Starr *Fitzie* • Jonathan Tucker *Todd* • Wayne Robson *Beano* • Michael

Badalucco *Quinn* ■ *Dir* Bill Bennett • *Scr* Denis Leary, Mike Armstrong, from a story by Denis Leary, Mike Armstrong, Ann Lembeck

Stolen Innocence ★★
Crime drama   2007 · Can/US · Colour · 120min

This manipulative yet efficient "parent's worst nightmare" scenario centres on single career woman Jenna, who is preparing for the birth of her first child. Advised to rest, she takes to her bed and is visited by a nurse who gives her some pills that are supposedly harmless vitamins, but Jenna quickly loses consciousness. When she wakes in hospital, she's told that the baby was stillborn and that she is suspected of infanticide. Reunited with her baby's father, Jenna determines to find the truth. SF

Gina Philips *Jenna Davis* • Leanne Adachi *Debbie* • Suzanne Bastien *Secretary* ■ *Dir* Neill Fearnley • *Scr* Don Nelson

Stolen Kisses ★★★★★ 15
Romantic comedy   1968 · Fr · Colour · 87min

After *The 400 Blows* and the *Antoine et Colette* episode of *Love at Twenty*, Truffaut catches up with Antoine Doinel as he leaves the army and becomes a private eye. Hired by shoeshop owner Michel Lonsdale to find out why the employees hate him, Doinel falls madly in love with Lonsdale's wife (Delphine Seyrig), while trying to remain faithful to his girlfriend (Claude Jade). Once again, Doinel is played to perfection by Jean-Pierre Léaud. Add some engaging subplots and a bit of Hitchcockian mischief with a man in a raincoat, and you have one of Truffaut's greatest movies, a slight but utterly magical romantic comedy set in the Paris of our dreams. AT French +subtitles.
DVD 🔵

Jean-Pierre Léaud *Antoine Doinel* • Delphine Seyrig *Fabienne Tabard* • Claude Jade *Christine Darbon* • Michel Lonsdale *Monsieur Tabard* • Harry-Max *Monsieur Henri* • André Falcon *Monsieur Blady* ■ *Dir* François Truffaut • *Scr* François Truffaut, Claude de Givray, Bernard Revon

Stolen Life ★★
Romantic drama   1939 · UK · BW · 90min

Legendary German actress Elisabeth Bergner stars in this British-made romantic melodrama, directed, as were most of her films, by her husband Paul Czinner. Bergner takes the dual role of identical twin sisters in love with the same man (in this case, Michael Redgrave). He is duped into marrying the wrong sister, who later conveniently drowns in his absence, allowing the other to deceive him by taking her place. And that's not all! Well-acted, and quite pleasing for fans of the genre, but more restrained and dull than the full-blooded Bette Davis version made seven years later. RK

Elisabeth Bergner *Sylvina Lawrence/Martina Lawrence* • Michael Redgrave *Alan McKenzie* • Wilfrid Lawson *Thomas Lawrence* • Mabel Terry Lewis *Aunt Helen* • Richard Ainley *Morgan* ■ *Dir* Paul Czinner • *Scr* Margaret Kennedy, from the novel by KJ Benes [Karel J Benes]

A Stolen Life ★★★
Melodrama   1946 · US · BW · 107min

The great Bette Davis often struggled to find vehicles worthy of her talent, but even in this relatively creaky melodrama, which is the only film she ever produced, she conveys the marvellous sense of the dramatics that made her a Hollywood great. Her star quality is particularly evident as she plays twins (one good, one bad), but unfortunately the men in the cast aren't up to her standard. Glenn Ford is callow and uninteresting, and both Dane Clark and Bruce Bennett offer period good looks, and do what little the script allows them to do well. TS

Bette Davis *Kate Bosworth/Pat Bosworth* • Glenn Ford *Bill Emerson* • Dane Clark *Karnock* • Walter Brennan *Eben Folgor* • Charles Ruggles *Freddie Lindley* • Bruce Bennett *Jack Talbot* • Peggy Knudsen *Diedra* ■ *Dir* Curtis Bernhardt • *Scr* Catherine Turney, Margaret Buell Wilder, from the novel by Karel J Benes

Stolen Summer ★★ PG
Comedy drama   2002 · US · Colour · 88min

Having won the Project Greenlight screenwriting contest and endured a documentary about his initiation into movie-making, Pete Jones delivered this sugar-coated paean to childhood and lost innocence. The concept of a 1970s Catholic kid trying to convert a Chicago rabbi's son to please God is not without its controversies. But Jones takes such a superficial approach that he neither offends nor enlightens. Bonnie Hunt rings true as the child's mother, but Aidan Quinn and Kevin Pollak are predictable as the respective fathers of do-gooding Adi Stein and the leukaemia-stricken Mike Weinberg. DP

Aidan Quinn *Joe O'Malley* • Bonnie Hunt *Margaret O'Malley* • Kevin Pollak *Rabbi Jacobsen* • Brian Dennehy *Father Kelly* • Eddie Kaye Thomas *Patrick O'Malley* • Adi Stein *Pete O'Malley* • Mike Weinberg *Danny Jacobsen* ■ *Dir/Scr* Pete Jones

Stomp the Yard ★★ 12
Dance drama   2006 · US · Colour · 109min

Director Sylvain White's film showcases stepping, an extreme mix of dance, gymnastics and poetry practised among students at traditionally African-American colleges. DJ (Columbus Short) arrives at university from the proverbial wrong side of the tracks, weighed down by guilt over the senseless murder of his brother (and a total lack of imagination on the part of the screenwriters). A step contest offers him a new sense of purpose, as does sexy fellow student Meagan Good – who just happens to be dating his arch rival in the stepping stakes. Short certainly boasts some impressive moves, but away from the dance floor the action is lethargic and full of clumsy contrivances. SP *DVD* 🔵

Columbus Short *DJ Williams* • Meagan Good *April* • Ne-Yo *Rich Brown* • Darrin Henson [Darrin DeWitt Henson] *Grant* • Brian White *Sylvester* • Laz Alonso *Zeke* • Valarie Pettiford *Aunt Jackie* ■ *Dir* Sylvain White • *Scr* Robert Adetuyi, from a screenplay (unproduced) by Gregory Anderson

Stone ★★ 15
Thriller   2010 · US · Colour · 100min

As with their underwhelming match-up in *The Score* (2001), this clash of Method titans Robert De Niro and Edward Norton has to go down as another missed opportunity. This time around Norton plays a convicted arsonist who must convince a soon-to-retire prison official (De Niro) that he is ready to be released. Milla Jovovich plays Norton's loyal wife, who will go to any lengths to secure her husband's freedom. Although the leads deliver compelling enough performances, they are undermined by a muddled script. JF Violence, swearing, sex scenes. *DVD* 🔵

Robert De Niro *Jack Mabry* • Edward Norton *Gerald "Stone" Creeson* • Milla Jovovich *Lucetta* • Frances Conroy *Madylyn* • Enver Gjokaj *Young Jack* • Pepper Binkley *Young Madylyn* ■ *Dir* John Curran • *Scr* Angus MacLachlan

The Stone Boy ★★★★
Drama   1984 · US · Colour · 93min

Robert Duvall, Frederic Forrest and Glenn Close head the terrific cast of this powerful rural drama. Young Jason Presson accidentally shoots and kills his older brother, then has to cope alone with the trauma of it after his farming family retreat into their own private grief. This is one of those rare films that seems quietly and accurately to convey the emotions of true tragedy. While downbeat, it remains a fine ensemble piece. DA

Robert Duvall *Joe Hillerman* • Jason Presson *Arnold Hillerman* • Frederic Forrest *Andy Jansen* • Glenn Close *Ruth Hillerman* • Wilford Brimley *George Jansen* • Gail Youngs *Lu Jansen* • Cindy Fisher *Amalie* • Dean Cain *Eugene Hillerman* ■ *Dir* Christopher Cain • *Scr* Gina Berriault, from her novel

Stone Cold ★★ 18
Action thriller   1991 · US · Colour · 88min

Former football player Brian Bosworth started his new thespian career in this bubble-brained action movie that required some cuts before obtaining an R rating in the US. There is still more than enough violence to satisfy action fans, though its frequent heavy-handedness and perversely cruel tone may cause some misgivings. Bosworth is a cop, working undercover with the FBI to infiltrate Lance Henriksen's biker/white militant gang. KB 🔵

Brian Bosworth *Joe Huff/John Stone* • Lance Henriksen *Chains Cooper* • William Forsythe *Ice* • Arabella Holzbog *Nancy* • Sam McMurray *Lance* • Richard Gant *Cunningham* ■ *Dir* Craig R Baxley • *Scr* Walter Doniger

Stone Cold ★★ 12
Crime drama   2005 · US · Colour · 83min

Tom Selleck is on strong form but his talent is wasted in this limp TV-movie crime drama. He gives a sympathetic performance as a former LA homicide detective turned New England police chief, whose sleepy small-town life is shattered by a string of murders and the rape of a high-school student. Yet despite its sensational set-up, this first in a series of films based on Robert B Parker's Jesse Stone books suffers from poor pacing, sketchy characters and zero tension. SF Some violence, sexual references. *DVD*

Tom Selleck *Chief Jesse Stone* • Mimi Rogers *Rita Fiore* • Jane Adams (2) *Brianna Lincoln* • Reg Rogers *Andrew Lincoln* • Viola Davis *Molly* • Alexis Dziena *Candace Pennington* • Stephen McHattie *Captain Healy* ■ *Dir* Robert Harmon • *Scr* John Fasano, Michael Brandman, from the novel by Robert B Parker

The Stone Killer ★★ 18
Action thriller   1973 · US · Colour · 91min

A Michael Winner film starring Charles Bronson immediately conjures up an image of violence, and both men live up to expectations in this nasty movie. Bronson plays a former New York cop now working in LA, who is almost indistinguishable from the killers he's trying to track down. Stomach-churning and predictable. SG Drug abuse, swearing, nudity.

Charles Bronson *Detective Lou Torrey* • Martin Balsam *Al Vescari* • David Sheiner *Detective Guido Lorenz* • Norman Fell *Detective Les Daniels* • Ralph Waite *Detective Mathews* • Eddie Firestone *George Armitage, the junkie* • Walter Burke *JD* ■ *Dir* Michael Winner • *Scr* Gerald Wilson, from the novel *A Complete State of Death* by John Gardner

Stone of Destiny ★★★ PG
Comedy adventure based on a true story   2008 · UK /Can · Colour · 96min

American writer/director Charles Martin Smith draws on an incident that is part of Scottish Nationalist legend, but creates a film that is more like an Ealing comedy than a stirring drama in the vein of *Braveheart*. On Christmas Day in 1950, four students broke into Westminster Abbey to return Scotland's coronation stone to its homeland. And while Mel Gibson overcame huge odds to turn the story of William Wallace into an international hit, Smith faced an even greater challenge in dramatising a story that lacks any genuine suspense. The result is a gentle and likeable comedy drama that is not only set in 1950, but could easily have been made back then, too. BP

Charlie Cox *Ian Hamilton* • Kate Mara *Kay Matheson* • Billy Boyd (1) *Bill Craig* • Ciaron Kelly *Alan Stuart* • Robert Carlyle *John MacCormick* • Peter Mullan *Ian's dad* ■ *Dir* Charles Martin Smith • *Scr* Charles Martin Smith, from the non-fiction book *The Taking of the Stone of Destiny* by Ian Hamilton

Stoned ★★★ 15
Biographical drama   2005 · UK · Colour · 98min

The death of Rolling Stone Brian Jones has fuelled no end of speculation since his body was found in his swimming pool in 1969. Stephen Woolley, making the transition to director after years as one of Britain's top producers, focuses on the relationship between Jones (played by Leo Gregory) and his oddball builder-cum-house guest Frank Thorogood (Paddy Considine). He does well to recapture the spirit of an era when the class system was breaking down, but Gregory's Jones is a curiously uncharismatic figure, and the film suffers from the absence of Stones' recordings. BP Swearing, sex scenes, drug abuse. *DVD*

Leo Gregory *Brian Jones* • Paddy Considine *Frank Thorogood* • David Morrissey *Tom Keylock* • Tuva Novotny *Anna Wohlin* • Amelia Warner *Janet* • Ben Whishaw *Keith Richards* • Monet Mazur *Anita Pallenberg* • Luke de Woolfson *Mick Jagger* ■ *Dir* Stephen Woolley • *Scr* Neal Purvis, Robert Wade, from the non-fiction books *Paint It Black* by Geoffrey Giuliano, *Who Killed Christopher Robin? The Murder of a Rolling Stone* by Terry Rawlings and *The Murder of Brian Jones* by Anna Wohlin

Stonehearst Asylum ★★ 15
Psychological thriller   2014 · US · Colour · 108min

Set in 1899, this gothic, twist-laden thriller sees medical school graduate Jim Sturgess arrive at an isolated lunatic asylum where he begins work for unorthodox superintendent (Ben Kingsley). Before long, however, Sturgess discovers that the patients have managed to seize control of the institution. Kingsley elevates every scene he appears in but, despite the presence of Kate Beckinsale as the inmate who doesn't deserve to be there, the tone is uneven and the various plot twists aren't as effective as they need to be. SC Violence. *DVD* 🔵

Kate Beckinsale *Eliza Graves* • Jim Sturgess *Edward Newgate* • Ben Kingsley *Dr Lamb* • Michael Caine *Dr Salt* • Brendan Gleeson *Alienist* • David Thewlis *Mickey Finn* • Jason Flemyng *Swanwick* ■ *Dir* Brad Anderson • *Scr* Joe Gangemi, from the short story *The System of Doctor Tarr and Professor Fether* by Edgar Allan Poe

Stones for Ibarra ★★★★ PG
Drama   1988 · US · Colour · 96min

This is a thoughtful and often moving TV drama about a San Francisco couple who move to a small Mexican village to reopen a copper mine, only to have their dreams turn sour when the husband learns he is suffering from cancer. Glenn Close and Keith Carradine give restrained and touching performances; they are well supported by Alfonso Arau, now better known as a director. Simple but poignant. JB

Glenn Close *Sara Everton* • Keith Carradine *Richard Everton* • Alfonso Arau *Chuy Santos* • Ray Oriel *Domingo Garcia* • Trinidad Silva *Basilio Garcia* ■ *Dir* Jack Gold • *Scr* Ernest Kinoy, from the novel by Harriett Doerr

Stones for the Rampart: Battle for Warsaw ★★★ 15
Wartime drama   2014 · Pol · Colour · 111min

Aleksander Kaminski's landmark 1943 novel celebrates the Polish Scouting Association who fought alongside the Home Army against the occupying Nazis under the code-name "Grey Ranks". This adaptation has good intentions and exceptional widescreen photography, but the result is a sometimes overly flashy treatise on patriotic heroism that reduces acts of selfless courage to stylised set pieces, seeming to owe more to video gaming than the proud tradition of Polish war cinema. DP In Polish.

Tomasz Zietek *Jan Bytnar "Rudy"* • Marcel Sabat *Tadeusz Zawadzki, "Zoska"* • Kamil Szeptycki *Aleksander Dawidowski, "Alek"* • Magdalena Kolesnik *Monia* • Sandra Staniszewska *Hala Glinska* ■ *Dir* Robert Glinski • *Scr* Dominik Wieczorkowski-Rettinger, Wojtek Palys, from Alexander Kaminski's novel

Stonewall ★★ 15
Drama   1995 · UK · Colour · 94min

The decision to introduce a fictional love story into this re-creation of the infamous 1969 riot at the Stonewall Inn in Greenwich Village was a serious misjudgement. It deflects from the more serious purpose of examining the penalties and prejudices suffered by the gay population in those pre-liberation days. The cast looks good but, sadly, lacks the necessary acting ability. **DP** Swearing.

Guillermo Díaz *La Miranda* • Frederick Weller *Matty Dean* • Brendan Corbalis *Ethan* • Duane Boutté *Bostonia* • Bruce MacVittie *Vinnie* • Peter Ratray *Burt* • Dwight Ewell *Helen Wheels* ■ *Dir* Nigel Finch • *Scr* Rikki Beadle Blair, from the book by Martin Duberman

Stonewall ★
Drama based on a true story
2015 · US · Colour · 129min

Loosely based on true events, this has Jeremy Irvine as a college student who becomes involved in the New York gay scene in 1969, fighting police oppression that would eventually lead to the Stonewall riots. It's hard to think of a film that misjudges the tone of an important historical event quite as dramatically as this brightly coloured melodrama. As it follows a group of broad stereotypes drenched in bad dialogue, there's a disturbing lack of diversity in a story meant to cover that very issue. A pantomime of a vital moment. **JL**

Jonathan Rhys Meyers *Trevor* • Joey King *Phoebe* • Ron Perlman *Ed Murphy* • Jeremy Irvine *Danny Winters* • Caleb Landry Jones *Orphan Annie* ■ *Dir* Roland Emmerich • *Scr* Jon Robin Baitz

The Stooge ★★★ U
Musical comedy 1951 · US · BW · 100min

This clever and prescient Dean Martin and Jerry Lewis vehicle sees Martin showing a marked antipathy to his partner – the titular stooge. There is a brilliant character study from Eddie Mayehoff, while Polly Bergen proves an attractive foil. With hindsight, it looks as though reality was intruding on the popular comedy team, as the Dino character learns how important his stooge is to his career. It wasn't until until after *Pardners* (when the pair split) that the paying public became aware of the truth. **TS**

Dean Martin *Bill Miller* • Jerry Lewis *Ted Rogers* • Polly Bergen *Mary Turner* • Marion Marshall *Frecklehead Tait* • Eddie Mayehoff *Leo Lyman* • Richard Erdman *Ben Bailey* ■ *Dir* Norman Taurog • *Scr* Fred F Finklehoffe, Martin Rackin, Elwood Ullman, from a story by Fred F Finklehoffe, Sid Silvers

Stop-Loss ★★★ 15
Military drama 2007 · US · Colour · 107min

Despite opening with a terrifying insurgent attack on an infantry checkpoint in Iraq, this low-key drama actually spends most of its time on American soil. The title refers to a controversial US government policy that can be used to send soldiers who have finished their tours of duty back to the front line. Returning home to Texas to find himself "stop-lossed", decorated war hero Staff Sergeant Brandon King (Ryan Phillippe) deserts and goes on the run with the help of a comrade's girlfriend (Abbie Cornish). Writer/director Kimberly Peirce (*Boys Don't Cry*) turns in a quietly intelligent film about one man's soul-searching that disappoints only in its lack of political bite. Still, Phillippe is superb as the traumatised veteran caught between duty and dishonour. **JR** *DVD*

Ryan Phillippe *Brandon King* • Joseph Gordon-Levitt *Tommy Burgess* • Rob Brown *Isaac "Eyeball" Butler* • Channing Tatum *Steve Shriver* • Victor Rasuk *Rico Rodriguez* • Terry Quay *Al "Preacher" Colson* • Timothy Olyphant *Lt Col Boot Miller* • Abbie Cornish *Michelle* ■ *Dir* Kimberly Peirce • *Scr* Kimberly Peirce, Mark Richard

Stop Making Sense ★★★★ PG
Concert documentary 1984 · US · Colour · 87min

Building from an image of a single pair of white sneakers into a sublime, almost surreal display of cerebral rock, this is simply one of the finest concert films ever made. Yet this enviable achievement isn't down to the understated direction of Jonathan Demme or the subtle photography of *Blade Runner* cameraman Jordan Cronenweth. What makes this such a memorable experience is the ingenuity of Talking Heads frontman David Byrne. In addition to writing and giving a mesmerising performance of the 16 songs on the soundtrack, he also designed the show, which includes some wonderfully atmospheric shadow mime sequences, played out on a triptych screen behind the minimalist stage. **DP** *DVD*

David Byrne • Chris Franz *Chris Frantz* • Jerry Harrison • Tina Weymouth ■ *Dir* Jonathan Demme • *Scr* David Byrne

Stop! or My Mom Will Shoot ★ PG
Action comedy 1992 · US · Colour · 87min

This was the comedy that finally seemed to convince Sylvester Stallone that he wasn't really very funny; after this he was back to the action-adventure genre with *Cliffhanger*. Stallone is the tough detective whose life is ruined when his fussy, dotty mother Estelle Getty turns up to stay with him. Inane and joke-free. **JF** Swearing, violence. *DVD*

Sylvester Stallone *Joe Bomowski* • Estelle Getty *Tutti* • JoBeth Williams *Gwen Harper* • Roger Rees *Parnell* • Martin Ferrero *Paulie* • Gailard Sartain *Munroe* • John Wesley Tony • Al Fann *Lou* ■ *Dir* Roger Spottiswoode • *Scr* Blake Snyder, William Osborne, William Davies

Stop the World, I Want to Get Off ★★
Musical 1966 · UK · Colour and BW · 99min

"What kind of fool am I?" bawls Tony Tanner, and what kind of musical is this, you might ask. It's a listless version of the Broadway and West End hit by Anthony Newley and Leslie Bricusse, which turns allegorical as it recounts the ups and downs of its Everyman hero Littlechap (Tanner), and is only kick-started into some sort of life by the delectable Millicent Martin. Too self-pitying for long-term tolerance, it was remade in 1978 as *Sammy Stops the World*, with Sammy Davis Jr. **TH** Swearing.

Tony Tanner *Littlechap* • Millicent Martin *Evie/Anya/Ara/Ginnie* • Leila Croft *Susan* • Valerie Croft *Jane* • Neil Hawley *Little Littlechap* • Graham Lyons *Father-in-law* ■ *Dir* Philip Saville • *Scr* Anthony Newley, Leslie Bricusse, David Donable, Al Ham, Marilyn Bergman, Alan Bergman, from the play by Anthony Newley, Leslie Bricusse

Stop, You're Killing Me ★★★
Musical comedy 1952 · US · Colour · 86min

This is an update of a marvellous Damon Runyon/Howard Lindsay play called *A Slight Case of Murder*, which in 1938 became one of Edward G Robinson's most popular film vehicles. Broderick Crawford, though personable, is no substitute for Edward G, and the film certainly doesn't need its musical moments. Nevertheless, this is still amusing and there's a nice piece of casting in the wonderful Margaret Dumont as the unlucky discoverer of the body. **TS**

Broderick Crawford *Remy Marko* • Claire Trevor *Nora Marko* • Virginia Gibson *Mary Marko* • Bill Hayes *Chance Whitelaw* • Margaret Dumont *Mrs Whitelaw* • Howard St John *Mahoney* • Charles Cantor *Mike* ■ *Dir* Roy Del Ruth • *Scr* James O'Hanlon, from the play *A Slight Case of Murder* by Damon Runyon, Howard Lindsay

Storage 24 ★★★★ 15
Science-fiction horror 2012 · UK · Colour · 83min

Director Johannes Roberts's follow-up to his compelling 2010 horror *F* is a perfectly crafted B-movie monster flick that scores high on fun, scares and gore. As a military plane crashes in central London, spilling its highly classified alien cargo, ex-lovers Noel Clarke (neatly cast against type) and Antonia Campbell-Hughes are acrimoniously dividing up their possessions in a nearby storage facility. Will they, their friends and the staff survive being trapped in the dark maze of corridors with the escaped predator? Roberts makes the most of a simple premise and single location setting, the cast are uniformly good, and the impressive creature delivers nastily effective splatter chaos. **AJ** Violence, swearing. *DVD* *BD*

Noel Clarke *Charlie* • Colin O'Donoghue *Mark* • Antonia Campbell-Hughes *Shelley* • Laura Haddock *Nikki* • Jamie Thomas King *Chris* • Ned Dennehy *David* ■ *Dir* Johannes Roberts • *Scr* Davie Fairbanks, Marc Small, Johannes Roberts, from an original idea and screenplay by Noel Clarke

Storefront Hitchcock ★★★ 12
Concert movie 1998 · US · Colour · 77min

A mix of alfresco music and off-the-wall musings from eccentric British songster Robyn Hitchcock. The film is directed by Jonathan Demme, of *The Silence of the Lambs* fame. He's a big Robyn Hitchcock fan, and patently regarded this small-scale spot of whimsy as a welcome change from the high-pressure world of big-bucks Hollywood film-making. Incidentally, new-ager Hitchcock is also one of the UK's leading authorities on ancient stone circles, ley lines and the like. **DA**

■ *Dir* Jonathan Demme

Storia di Piera ★★★
Drama 1983 · It/Fr/W Ger · Colour · 110min

Hanna Schygulla won the best actress prize at Cannes for her performance in Marco Ferreri's characteristically frank adaptation of actress Piera Degli Esposti's autobiography. Isabelle Huppert takes the title role, but it's Schygulla who dominates as the embittered mother who uses promiscuity as a weapon against her neglectful husband, Marcello Mastroianni. This discomforting blend of dark comedy and sordid melodrama is more concerned with the shock treatment meted out to Schygulla after she's committed to nymphomania and the family's eccentric sexual practices. **DP** In Italian.

Hanna Schygulla *Eugenia* • Isabelle Huppert *Piera as an adult* • Bettina Gruhn *Piera as a child* • Marcello Mastroianni *Lorenzo* ■ *Dir* Marco Ferreri • *Scr* Piera Degli Esposti, Dacia Maraini, Marco Ferreri, from the autobiography by Degli Esposti, Maraini

Stories We Tell ★★★★★ 12A
Documentary 2012 · Can · Colour and BW · 108min

Having set a successful acting career aside to move behind the camera, Canada's Sarah Polley turns to her own family history for this engrossing documentary portrait of seriously unusual domestic circumstances. It had long been an in-family joke that Sarah didn't look much like her siblings, but what did that say about her parents' marriage? The film finds Polley trying to make sense of a situation further complicated by her mother's untimely death. Intimate, thought-provoking and affecting, this is exceptional on every level. **TJ** Swearing, sexual references. *DVD* *BD*

Sarah Polley ■ *Dir/Scr* Sarah Polley

The Stork Club ★★★ U
Musical comedy 1945 · US · BW · 98min

This lightweight frivolity is at once a major plug for the legendary Manhattan nightspot, and a showcase for the energetic talents of Betty Hutton, who sings half-a-dozen made-to-order numbers. The plot has Stork Club hat-check girl Hutton saving a shabby tramp (Barry Fitzgerald) from drowning and being rewarded for her good deed when he turns out to be a millionaire. He sets her up in luxury, which causes a problem with her musician boyfriend (Don DeFore). **RK**

Betty Hutton *Judy Peabody* • Barry Fitzgerald *JB Bates* • Don DeFore *Danny Wilton* • Robert Benchley *Tom Curtis* • Bill Goodwin *Sherman Billingsley* • Iris Adrian *Gwen* ■ *Dir* Hal Walker • *Scr* BG De Sylva, John McGowan

Storks
Animated comedy 2016 · US · Colour

This is a preview – no prints were available to review as we went to press: If you remember *Presto*, the superb short that preceded *WALL-E* – about a magician getting into a fight with his stage rabbit – then you're already familiar with the work of Doug Sweetland. He's teamed up with co-director Nicholas Stoller for this animation about storks being presented with a delivery order for a baby – something they've forgotten how to do. Warner Bros is clearly hoping that they can give Pixar a run for their money. **SvM** 3D

Andy Samberg *Junior* • Kelsey Grammer *Hunter* • Katie Crown *Tulip* • Anton Starkman *Nate Gardner* • Jennifer Aniston *Sarah Gardner* • Danny Trejo *Jasper* ■ *Dir* Nicholas Stoller, Doug Sweetland • *Scr* Nicholas Stoller

Storm ★★ 12
Action thriller 1999 · US · Colour · 86min

Weather movies rarely fulfil their makers' expectations. Neither *Twister* nor *A Perfect Storm* lived up to the hype about their special effects, so what chance can a low-budget TV thriller such as this have of success? Martin Sheen gives his all as the leader of a government research programme that develops a weather controlling device, but Luke Perry is woefully miscast as the computer whizz who takes to the skies when the device threatens to destroy Los Angeles. **DP** *DVD*

Luke Perry *Dr Ron Young* • Martin Sheen *General Roberts* • Robert Knott *Tom Holt* • David Moses *Dr Platt* • Marc McClure *Brian Newmeyer* • Renée Estevez *Andrea* ■ *Dir* Harris Done, Vincent Spano • *Scr* Harris Done, Diane Fine

Storm ★★★★ 15
Political drama 2009 · Ger/Den/Neth/Swe · Colour · 102min

A former Bosnian Serb general goes on trial for war crimes in The Hague, leaving a prosecutor for the International Criminal Tribunal battling to balance justice with the complex court proceedings. There's a danger Hans-Christian Schmid's Euro-thriller could fall into the worthy-but-dull category, since it doesn't add pumped-up Hollywood action to get us interested in the issues surrounding such high-profile human rights cases. However, Kerry Fox's terrific performance as the decent, hard-working lawyer dedicated to bringing out the truth really draws the viewer into caring about achieving the only justice that many victims of the Balkan conflict are ever likely to see. Neither sexed-up nor dumbed-down, *Storm* is both absorbing and satisfying. **TJ** English, German, Bosnian, Serbian +subtitles.

Kerry Fox *Hannah Maynard* • Anamaria Marinca *Mira Arendt* • Stephen Dillane *Keith Haywood* • Rolf Lassgard *Jonas Dahlberg* • Alexander Fehling *Patrick Father* • Tarik Filipovic *Mladen Banovic* ■ *Dir* Hans-Christian Schmid • *Scr* Hans-Christian Schmid, Bernd Lange • *Cinematographer* Bogumi Godfrejow

Storm Catcher ★ 18
Action thriller 1999 · US · Colour · 91min

Faced with a minuscule budget, a few feet of stock aerial footage and a script with dialogue that amounts to an aural assault, director Anthony Hickox has done well to produce a film that's only as bad as this one. Dolph Lundgren is OK as the ace pilot who has to recover a top-secret plane that only he and colleague John Pennell can fly, but the supporting performances range from the rank to the ranting. **DP** *DVD*

Dolph Lundgren *Major Jack Holloway* • Mystro Clark *Sparks* • John Pennell *[Jon Pennell] Captain Lucas* • Robert Miano *General Jacob* • Yvonne Zima *Nicole* • Kylie Bax *Jessica Holloway* ■ *Dir* Tony Hickox [Anthony Hickox] • *Scr* Bill Gucwa, Ed Masterson

Storm Center ★★★
Drama 1956 · US · BW · 85min

This is a tremendously courageous subject for its period that is still relevant today, as librarian Bette Davis is fired for refusing to remove a book on communism from the shelves. Unfortunately, the movie is directed by one of the screenwriters (Daniel Taradash) and it apses too often into cliché and sentiment. Although the theme deserved more than this melodramatic treatment, it's also likely that a better movie would still have met with an uninterested public. TS

Bette Davis *Alicia Hull* • Brian Keith *Paul Duncan* • Kim Hunter *Martha Lockridge* • Paul Kelly (1) *Judge Robert Ellerbe* • Kevin Coughlin *Freddie Slater* • Joe Mantell *George Slater* • Sallie Brophy *Laura Slater* • Howard Wierum *Mayor Levering* ■ *Dir* Daniel Taradash • *Scr* Daniel Taradash, Elick Moll

Storm Chasers: Revenge of the Twister ★★
Action adventure 1998 · US · Colour · 96min

Kelly McGillis is a pale shadow of her *Witness* self in this perfunctory action adventure, playing the widow of a meteorologist whose plane was struck by lightning during a tornado. The sequence in which her passion for Colorado storm chaser Wolf Larsen is inflamed by a bolt from an angry sky sums up the cheesiness of the plot and the elementary nature of the special effects. But at least director Mark Sobel attempts to discuss the damage that industry is doing to the environment. DP Flashing images.

Kelly McGillis *Jamie Marshall* • Wolf Larson *Will Stanton* • Liz Torres *Wallace Houston* • Adrian Zmed *Smitty* • David Millbern *Tony Grant* • James MacArthur *Frank Del Rio* • Martin Evans *Jim Marshall* ■ *Dir* Mark Sobel • *Scr* Jeff Wynne

Storm in a Teacup ★★★
Comedy 1937 · UK · BW · 88min

When the authoritarian provost of a small Scottish town (Cecil Parker) orders an old lady's dog to be confiscated because she hasn't paid her fines, reporter Rex Harrison picks up the story and creates a national scandal. The furious provost institutes legal proceedings against the journalist, but his daughter Vivien Leigh, who is in love with the young man, intervenes. Well directed by Victor Saville, the film is an oh-so-English, pre-Second World War relic, that's sweet and funny. RK

Vivien Leigh *Victoria Gow* • Rex Harrison *Frank Burden* • Sara Allgood *Mrs Hegarty* • Cecil Parker *Provost Willie Gow* • Ursula Jeans *Lisbet Skirving* • Gus McNaughton *Horace Skirving* ■ *Dir* Victor Saville, Ian Dalrymple • *Scr* Ian Dalrymple, Donald Bull, from James Bridie's adaptation of the play *Sturm in Wassergläs* by Bruno Frank

A Storm in Summer ★★★
Drama 2000 · US · Colour · 94min

Originally aired in 1970, with Peter Ustinov in the lead, Rod Serling's TV drama has been respectfully revived by veteran director Robert Wise. Peter Falk assumes the role of the Fairview deli owner whose jaundiced outlook is slowly transformed by the arrival of Aaron Meeks, a young New Yorker afforded the opportunity of an upstate vacation by a charity. The focus falls firmly on the unlikely cross-generational rapport that develops between the embittered outsiders, who have both lost loved ones in war. DP

Peter Falk *Abel Shaddick* • Aaron Meeks *Herman Washington* • Nastassja Kinski *Gloria Ross* • Andrew McCarthy *Stanley Banner* • Ruby Dee *Grandmother* ■ *Dir* Robert Wise • *Scr* Rod Serling

Storm over Asia ★★★★★ PG
Classic silent drama 1928 · USSR · BW · 125min

The summit of Soviet cinema was reached in the 1920s with the films of Dovzhenko, Eisenstein and Pudovkin, whose last great silent film this was. It concerns nomadic fur-trapper, Blair, who is set up as a puppet monarch by the occupying British interventionist forces in Mongolia in 1918. But, realising his national identity, and believing himself to be a descendant of Genghis Kahn, he rouses the Asian hordes against their oppressors. A film of great visual beauty, dynamic montage, humour and compassion, it also has an ethnographic quality in the detailed depiction of the life of the Mongolian herdsmen. A new version with a sound track was released some 20 years later under Pudovkin's supervision. RB DVD

Valeri Inkishinov [Valery Inkijinoff] *Blair, a mongol huntsman* • I Inkishinov *Blair's father* • A Chistyakov *Commander of a partisan detachment* • A Dedintsev *Commander of the occupation forces* ■ *Dir* Vsevoloc I Pudovkin • *Scr* Osip Brik, from a story by I Novokshenov

Storm over the Nile ★★ U
Adventure 1955 · UK · Colour · 102min

Zoltan Korda made little effort to disguise the fact that this is a remake of his 1939 classic *The Four Feathers*. Some of the original location footage is also included, distorted to fit the new picture's CinemaScope format. Co-director Terence Young helps bring a touch of pizzazz to the action sequences, yet the story, of an officer who's branded a coward but who proves to have more pluck than his pals, has dated badly. DP

Laurence Harvey *John Durrance* • Anthony Steel *Harry Faversham* • James Robertson-Justice *General Burroughs* • Geoffrey Keen *Dr Sutton* • Ronald Lewis *Peter Burroughs* • Ian Carmichael *Tom Willoughby* • Michael Hordern *General Faversham* • Jack Lambert *Colonel* • Mary Ure *Mary Burroughs* • Christopher Lee *Karaga Pasha* ■ *Dir* Zoltan Korda, Terence Young • *Scr* RC Sherriff, Lajos Biró, Arthur Wimperis, from the novel *The Four Feathers* by AEW Mason

Storm Warning ★★
Drama 1950 · US · BW · 89min

Fashion model Ginger Rogers decides to visit her sister Doris Day in a small southern town. Arriving at night, she witnesses a Klan murder, and soon realises that one of the perpetrators is her brother-in-law, Steve Cochran. District attorney Ronald Reagan asks her to testify as a witness to the killing, leading to an agonising clash of loyalties. This punchy and intriguing little social conscience effort is ruined by its descent into crudely obvious melodrama. RK

Ginger Rogers *Marsha Mitchell* • Ronald Reagan *Burt Rainey* • Doris Day *Lucy Rice* • Steve Cochran *Hank Rice* • Hugh Sanders *Charlie Barr* • Lloyd Gough *Cliff Rummel* • Raymond Greenleaf *Faulkner* ■ *Dir* Stuart Heisler • *Scr* Daniel Fuchs, Richard Brooks, from their story *Storm Center*

Stormbreaker ★★★ PG
Action adventure 2006 · Ger/US/UK · Colour · 89min

A teenager turns super-spy to avenge the murder of his uncle (Ewan McGregor) in this British action thriller with Hollywood-style bombast. Leading the charge, Alex Pettyfer is California pretty, while Mickey Rourke is a campy arch villain. The film has its flaws, but director Geoffrey Sax ensures it's never dull. There are lots of audacious stunts featuring quirky gadgets, and extra laughs courtesy of Bill Nighy as a deadpan spook. Enjoyable family viewing. SP DVD

Alex Pettyfer *Alex Rider* • Ewan McGregor *Ian Rider* • Mickey Rourke *Darrius Sayle* • Bill Nighy *Alan Blunt* • Sophie Okonedo *Mrs Jones* • Alicia Silverstone *Jack Starbright* • Missi Pyle *Nadia Vole* • Sarah Bolger *Sabina Pleasure* • Damian Lewis *Yassen Gregorovich* ■ *Dir* Geoffrey Sax • *Scr* Anthony Horowitz from his novel

Stormy ★★ U
Western 1935 · US · BW · 66min

Noah Beery Jr may take the lead in this western melodrama about a thoroughbred colt that's lost after a train wreck, but his thunder is stolen by the Rex the Wonder Horse in the title role. Among the other supporting humans, J Farrell MacDonald, as the wonderfully named Trinidad Dorn, emerges with dignity. TS

Noah Beery Jr *Stormy* • Jean Rogers *Kerry Dorn* • J Farrell MacDonald *Trinidad Dorn* • Walter Miller *Craig* • James P Burtis *Greasy* • Charles Hunter *The Arizona Wrangler* ■ *Dir* Louis Friedlander [Lew Landers] • *Scr* George H Plympton, Ben G Kohn, from a story by Cherry Wilson

Stormy Monday ★★★ 15
Romantic thriller 1987 · UK · Colour · 88min

Mike Figgis marked himself out as a director to watch out for with this assured debut, which successfully transplants *film noir* to the unlikely surroundings of Newcastle upon Tyne. Sean Bean is the young innocent who falls for visiting American Melanie Griffith and gets caught between the machinations of sinister American developer Tommy Lee Jones and local jazz club owner Sting. It doesn't always convince, but Figgis summons up a melancholy air of menace, and the performances are memorable. JF Violence, swearing, sex scenes, nudity. DVD

Melanie Griffith *Kate* • Tommy Lee Jones *Cosmo* • Sting *Finney* • Sean Bean *Brendan* • James Cosmo *Tony* • Mark Long *Patrick* • Brian Lewis *Jim* ■ *Dir/Scr* Mike Figgis

Stormy Waters ★★★★
Romantic drama 1941 · Fr · BW · 90min

Tugboat captain Jean Gabin rescues Michèle Morgan from the sea and falls in love with her. The picture was begun in 1939, but the Nazi Occupation held up production. It was eventually completed in the studio, although director Jean Grémillon had earlier filmed a number of realistic sea scenes on location at Brest. A perceptive but gloomy study of passion and fidelity, the film benefits from the masterly performances of its trio of top stars. RB French +subtitles.

Jean Gabin *André Laurent* • Michèle Morgan *Catherine* • Madeleine Renaud *Yvonne Laurent* • Charles Blavette *Gabriel Tanguy* ■ *Dir* Jean Grémillon • *Scr* Roger Vercel, Charles Spaak, Jacques Prévert, André Cayatte, from the novel *Remorques* by Roger Vercel

Stormy Weather ★★★ U
Musical 1943 · US · BW · 74min

Little more than an excuse to feature some of the finest black American performers, this expertly made extravaganza may well seem tasteless today. Try to ignore the parade of grinning racial stereotypes, and concentrate on the star turns: the great Bill Robinson, Cab Calloway, Fats Waller and the lovely Lena Horne performing the title number and a wondrous *I Can't Give You Anything but Love, Baby*. The virtually nonexistent plot is trite, with Bill Robinson playing a musician looking back on his life. TS DVD

Lena Horne *Selina Rogers* • Bill Robinson *Corky* • Cab Calloway *Himself* • Katherine Dunham *Fats Waller* • Ada Brown • Dooley Wilson *Gabe* ■ *Dir* Andrew Stone [Andrew L Stone] • *Scr* Frederick Jackson, Ted Koehler, HS Kraft, from a story by Jerry Horwin, Seymour B Robinson

LANDMARK FILM
Jump cuts, audiovisual juxtapositions, in-jokes – this film anticipates the tricks of the French New Wave by 25 years

The Story of a Cheat ★★★★★
Comedy drama 1936 · Fr · BW · 83min

Though very much a man of the stage who only occasionally made films, Sacha Guitry was still capable of being highly cinematic. Here, for example, the entire story is enacted visually, with only Guitry's voiceover and Adolphe Borchard's score for accompaniment - although Marguerite Moreno does speak in a café scene. An under-acknowledged influence on the New Wave, this is a bravura auteurist exhibition. Guitry stars in this self-scripted picaresque about a cardsharp convinced that fortune can be seduced by deception; as director, he manipulates time and space with a masterly ease that perfectly complements the action's witty amorality. DP In French.

Sacha Guitry *The cheat* • Jacqueline Delubac *Young woman* • Rosine Deréan *The jewel thief* • Marguerite Moreno *The countess* ■ *Dir* Sacha Guitry • *Scr* Sacha Guitry, from the novel *Mémoires d'un Tricheur* by Sacha Guitry

Story of a Love Story ★★
Romantic fantasy drama 1973 · Fr · Colour · 110min

Give director John Frankenheimer a hard-hitting melodrama or a bruising action film and he'll produce a polished picture. However, when confronted with a romantic drama he's likely to be confounded by his own pretensions. That is exactly what has happened here: the film is so preoccupied with the fact or fiction game that the adulterous affair between author Alan Bates and Dominique Sanda is almost secondary. DP Nudity.

Alan Bates *Harry* • Dominique Sanda *Nathalie* • Evans Evans *Elizabeth* • Lea Massari *Woman* • Michael Auclair [Michel Auclair] *Georges* • Laurence De Monaghan *Cleo* ■ *Dir* John Frankenheimer • *Scr* Nicholas Mosley

The Story of Adèle H ★★★ 12
Biographical drama 1975 · Fr · Colour · 96min

In what was only her fourth feature, the 19-year-old Isabelle Adjani comes remarkably close to conveying the desolation of a passionate older woman broken by her own determination. She plays Victor Hugo's daughter Adèle, who followed a young English soldier (Bruce Robinson) from Nova Scotia to Barbados, despite the fact that her love was unreciprocated. Director François Truffaut relies heavily on Adjani's crestfallen beauty and the oppressive majesty of Nestor Almendros's photography to suggest the heroine's agonising hope and incipient madness. DP French +subtitles. DVD

Isabelle Adjani *Adèle Hugo* • Bruce Robinson *Lt Albert Pinson* • Sylvia Marriott *Mrs Saunders* • Joseph Blatchley *Mr Whistler* • Reuben Dorey *Mr Saunders* • M White *Colonel White* • Cal Hathwell *Lt Pinson's Batman* • Ivry Gitlis *Hypnotist* ■ *Dir* François Truffaut • *Scr* François Truffaut, Jean Gruault, Suzanne Schiffman, from *Le Journal d'Adèle Hugo* by Adèle Hugo, Frances V Guille

The Story of Alexander Graham Bell ★★ U
Biographical drama 1939 · US · BW · 98min

This biopic of the man who invented the telephone is straightforward, sentimental and slow. Don Ameche, then known as a light comedian and debonair leading man, tried to gain gravitas in the role as he teaches the deaf to communicate, while pioneering his research into transmitting speech over the telegraph wires. His loyal assistant is Henry Fonda, who is far more convincing as a visionary than the miscast Ameche. AT

Don Ameche *Alexander Graham Bell* • Loretta Young *Mrs Bell* • Henry Fonda *Tom Watson* • Charles Coburn *Gardner Hubbard* • Spring Byington *Mrs Hubbard* • Gene Lockhart *Thomas Sanders* ■ *Dir* Irving Cummings • *Scr* Lamar Trotti, from a story by Ray Harris

The Story of an African Farm ★★
Period drama 2004 · S Afr · Colour · 94min

If it weren't for the eccentric presence of Richard E Grant, this old-fashioned family drama set in the 1870s would be a lacklustre affair. He adds much-needed colour as con artist Bonaparte Blenkins - a Dickensian-style villain who appears at the remote South African farm of religious bigot Tant Sannie (a pantomimic Karin van der Laag) and proceeds to make life doubly unbearable for the three children residing there. Though the tale depicts the darker, more disturbing aspects of Victorian author Olive Schreiner's source novel, they're undermined by the predominantly comic tone. As a result, the narrative is bitty and emotionally uneven, while the conclusion feels far too convenient. SF

Richard E Grant *Bonaparte Blenkins* • Karin van der Laag *Tant Sannie* • Armin Mueller-Stahl *Otto* • Luke Gallant *Waldo* • Kasha Kropinski *Lyndall* • Anneke Weidemann *Em* ■ *Dir* David Lister • *Scr* Thandi Brewer, Bonnie Rodini, from the novel by Olive Schreiner

S

A Story of Children and Film ★★★★ PG

Documentary
2013 · UK · Colour and BW · 105min

Global cinema's capacity to capture all the emotions of childhood is put front and centre in this typically knowledgeable and idiosyncratic survey from critic-turned-filmmaker Mark Cousins. Familiar clips from Hollywood classics like Chaplin's *The Kid* and Spielberg's *ET* are joined by remarkable moments from countries as diverse as Japan, Iran, Denmark and... Albania. Cousins's sing-song delivery and gadfly attention span has its detractors, yet his delight and sincerity is obvious, even if the film's linking segments (taking in the asylum that hosted van Gogh, and Cousin's junior relatives at play) pan out a little self-consciously. Overall, though, this is captivating, educational stuff: ideal viewing for families looking to broaden their cinematic horizons. TJ English, Japanese, Russian, Swedish, Polish, Czech, Farsi +subtitles. Some swearing, brief nudity.

■ *Dir/Scr* Mark Cousins

The Story of Dr Wassell ★★

Second World War drama
1944 · US · Colour · 136min

Having won an Oscar as the First World War hero in *Sergeant York*, Gary Cooper played another real-life hero, Dr Corydon Wassell, who managed to evacuate nine wounded men from Java and get them safely to Australia, dodging Japanese bombs all the way. Wassell himself was awarded the Navy Cross and was commended in a Presidential radio broadcast. He was reluctant to give his co-operation to Cecil B DeMille's movie, which is overlong, sentimental, self-important and cliché-ridden. AT

Gary Cooper *Dr Corydon M Wassell* · Laraine Day *Madeline* · Signe Hasso *Bettina* · Dennis O'Keefe *"Hoppy" Hopkins* · Carol Thurston *Tremartini* · Carl Esmond *Lt Dirk Van Daal* ■ *Dir* Cecil B DeMille · *Scr* Alan LeMay, Charles Bennett, James Hilton, from the stories by Dr Corydon M Wassell, James Hilton

The Story of Esther Costello ★★★

Drama 1957 · UK · BW · 104min

This is melodrama in the grand Hollywood tradition as socialite Joan Crawford adopts an Irish girl (Heather Sears) who has lost her sight, speech and hearing as a result of an accident. Unfortunately, Crawford's estranged husband (Rossano Brazzi) turns her charitable deed into a shameless exploitation racket. Crawford adds high emotional gloss to a tailor-made role that successfully tugs the heartstrings and holds the interest. AJ

Joan Crawford *Margaret Landi* · Rossano Brazzi *Carlo Landi* · Heather Sears *Esther Costello* · Lee Patterson *Harry Grant* · Ron Randell *Frank Wenzel* · Fay Compton *Mother Superior* · John Loder *Paul Marchant* · Denis O'Dea *Father Devlin* · Sidney James *Ryan* ■ *Dir* David Miller (1) · *Scr* Charles Kaufman, from the novel by Nicholas Monsarrat

The Story of GI Joe ★★★★ PG

Biographical Second World War drama
1945 · US · BW · 107min

This salute to the ordinary foot soldier is based on the memoirs of war correspondent Ernie Pyle, who is played by Burgess Meredith. Dealing with the guys who yomped it all the way from North Africa to Rome via Sicily, it was hailed at the time as one of the most authentic war movies ever made. It's crudely manipulative yet often very moving, mainly thanks to Robert Mitchum's star-building, Oscar-nominated performance as the GI who rises to become the platoon's commander. AT *DVD*

Burgess Meredith *Ernie Pyle* · Robert Mitchum *Lt Bill Walker* · Freddie Steele *Sgt Steve Warnicki* · Wally Cassell *Pte Dondaro* · Jimmy Lloyd *Pte Spencer* · Jack Reilly *Pte Robert "Wingless" Murphy* · Bill Murphy *Pte Mew* · William Self *"Gawky" Henderson* ■ *Dir* William A Wellman ·

Scr Leopold Atlas, Guy Endore, Philip Stevenson, from the books *Here Is Your War* and *Brave Men* by Ernie Pyle

The Story of Gilbert and Sullivan ★★★ U

Biographical musical drama
1953 · UK · Colour · 111min

Splendidly Technicolored, though slow-moving, this is a British account of the Tim Rice and Andrew Lloyd Webber team of their day, incarnated by Robert Morley (a rare top-billed appearance as the volatile Gilbert) and Maurice Evans (a rather bloodless Sullivan). Chunks of the comic operettas are ladled out among the petty squabblings that constitute the plot. The movie is stolen by the urbane Peter Finch as the equally urbane Richard D'Oyly Carte. TS

Robert Morley *WS Gilbert* · Maurice Evans *Arthur Sullivan* · Eileen Herlie *Helen Lenoir* · Martyn Green *George Grossmith* · Peter Finch *Richard d'Oyly Carte* · Dinah Sheridan *Grace Marston* · Isabel Dean *Mrs Gilbert* · Wilfrid Hyde White *Mr Marston* ■ *Dir* Sidney Gilliat · *Scr* Sidney Gilliat, Leslie Bailey, Vincent Korda, from the book *The Gilbert and Sullivan Book* by Leslie Bailey

The Story of Louis Pasteur ★★★

Biographical drama 1936 · US · BW · 87min

Paul Muni won an Oscar and established a formula for Warner Bros biopics with his performance in the lead role of Louis Pasteur. The trick that Sheridan Gibney and Pierre Collings's Oscar-winning script pulls is to make scientific research into sterilisation and rabies interesting, and director William Dieterle pulls another trick by keeping a firm check on the running time. There's some minor love interest, of course, but it's Muni's picture – though today his acting style and the general hagiographic approach seem very old-fashioned. AT

Paul Muni *Louis Pasteur* · Josephine Hutchinson *Mme Pasteur* · Anita Louise *Annette Pasteur* · Donald Woods *Jean Martel* · Fritz Leiber *Dr Charbonnet* · Henry O'Neill *Roux* ■ *Dir* William Dieterle · *Scr* Sheridan Gibney, Pierre Collings, from a story by Sheridan Gibney, Pierre Collings

The Story of Mankind ★ U

Historical fantasy drama
1957 · US · Colour · 99min

Future disaster-movie king Irwin Allen made this portentous rubbish in which the question of whether or not the human race should be allowed to survive is debated in front of a heavenly tribunal. Ronald Colman (in his last film) is the Spirit of Man, advancing the argument in favour of human kind; Vincent Price gleams with wicked delight as the Devil. This is generally, and rightly, acknowledged as one of the worst films ever made. RK

Ronald Colman *Spirit of Man* · Hedy Lamarr *Joan of Arc* · Groucho Marx *Peter Minuit* · Harpo Marx *Isaac Newton* · Chico Marx *Monk* · Virginia Mayo *Cleopatra* · Agnes Moorehead *Queen Elizabeth* · Vincent Price *Devil* ■ *Dir* Irwin Allen · *Scr* Irwin Allen, Charles Bennett, from the book by Hendrik Willem Van Loon

The Story of O ★★★ 18

Erotic drama 1975 · Fr/W Ger · Colour · 92min

This tale of a woman who becomes a willing slave to the men she loves was banned in the UK for 25 years. Dramatising the controversial sadomasochistic novel by Pauline Réage, director Just Jaeckin takes a dreamy, soft-focus, shampoo commercial approach to the sexual content, though it remains eye-opening. The addition of then-fashionable feminism barely excuses the exploitative tableaux. However, Jaeckin's often unintentionally funny erotic epic still stands as a 1970s landmark. AJ French +subtitles. *DVD*

Corinne Cléry *O, a photographer* · Udo Kier *René* · Anthony Steel *Sir Stephen H* · Jean Gaven *Pierre, O's valet* · Christiane Minazzoli *Anne-Marie* · Martine Kelly *Thérèse* · Jean-Pierre Andréani *Eric, Master III* ■ *Dir* Just Jaeckin · *Scr* Sébastien Japrisot, from the novel *Histoire d'O* by Pauline Réage [Anne Desclos]

The Story of Qiu Ju ★★★★★ 15

Drama 1992 · HK/Chi · Colour · 96min

Scooping both the Golden Lion and the best actress award at Venice, this is an impeccable piece of film-making by Zhang Yimou. Gong Li gives an exceptional performance as the tenacious woman who is prepared to go to any lengths to secure justice after her husband is assaulted by the village elder. Exposing the flaws in the Communist legal system and the chasm between urban and rural living standards, this is Zhang's first study of contemporary China. As ever, the engrossing drama, which is underpinned with bitter humour, is tightly handled and the use of colour and landscape is exhilarating. DP Mandarin +subtitles.

Gong Li *Wan Qiu Ju* · Liu Peiqi *Wan Qing Lai* · Yang Liuchun *Meizi* · Lei Laosheng *Wang Shantang, village chief* · Ge Zhijun *Officer Li* ■ *Dir* Zhang Yimou · *Scr* Liu Heng, from the story *Wanjia Susong* by Chen Yuanbin

The Story of Robin Hood and His Merrie Men ★★★ U

Adventure 1952 · UK · Colour · 83min

This may not hold a candle to the Errol Flynn version, but at around 80 minutes and boasting authentic English locations and fine Technicolor photography, it's excellent family entertainment. Richard Todd enjoys himself as the famous outlaw, but is up against strong competition, with Peter Finch as the wicked Sheriff and the delightful Hubert Gregg cast against type as the evil King John. There's light-hearted humour, a tuneful Allan-a-Dale and some lively swordfights. Briskly directed by the highly professional Ken Annakin. BB

Richard Todd *Robin Hood* · Joan Rice *Maid Marian* · Peter Finch *Sheriff of Nottingham* · James Hayter *Friar Tuck* · James Robertson-Justice *Little John* · Martita Hunt *Queen Eleanor* · Hubert Gregg *Prince John* · Bill Owen *Stutely* · Reginald Tate *Hugh Fitzooth* ■ *Dir* Ken Annakin · *Scr* Lawrence E Watkin

The Story of Ruth ★★ U

Biblical drama 1960 · US · Colour · 126min

Twentieth Century-Fox was the studio behind this Hollywood makeover of the Old Testament. It's a lengthy and colourful but ultimately static version of the Sunday School favourite. Elana Eden plays Ruth, who renounces false gods in order to worship the true faith of her husband. Familiar faces Stuart Whitman and Tom Tryon are the men in her life. The clichés are strung together by Norman Corwin. TH *DVD*

Stuart Whitman *Boaz* · Tom Tryon *Mahlon* · Viveca Lindfors *Eleilat* · Peggy Wood *Naomi* · Jeff Morrow *Tob* · Elana Eden *Ruth* · Thayer David *Hedak* ■ *Dir* Henry Koster · *Scr* Norman Corwin

Story of the Late Chrysanthemums ★★★★★★

Period melodrama 1939 · Jpn · BW · 142min

Widely regarded as director Kenji Mizoguchi's finest accomplishment, this is notable for its humanist insight into the role of women in Japanese society. Composed in depth and shot primarily in stately long takes, the story follows the selfless trials of servant Kakuko Mori, as she tries to help the son of a wealthy family achieve his ambition of becoming a kabuki artist. While painting a harsh portrait of life in the 1880s, Mizoguchi warms the heart with his attention to detail and the understated way in which female impersonator Shotaro Hanayagi comes to appreciate his wife's sacrifice. Quite beautiful. DP Japanese +subtitles.

Shotaro Hanayagi *Kikunosuke Onoue* · Kakuko Mori *Otoku* · Gonjuro Kawarazaki *Kikugoro Onoue V* · Kokichi Takada *Fukusuke Nakamura* · Ryotaro Kawanami *Eiju Dayu* · Nobuko Fushimi *Onaka, a geisha* · Benkei Shiganoya *Genshun Anma* · Yoko Umemura *Osato, Kikugoro's wife* ■ *Dir* Kenji Mizoguchi · *Scr* Yoshikata Yoda, Matsutaro Kawaguchi, from a story by Shofu Muramatsu

The Story of the Weeping Camel ★★★★ U

Documentary
2003 · Ger/Mongolia · Colour · 86min

When Byambasuren Davaa and Luigi Falorni arrived in the Gobi Desert, they had only ten hours of Super-16 film stock. So the fact that this study of a family of Mongolian camel herders is both compelling and charming owes as much to luck as judgement. When a mother camel begins to neglect her newborn white calf, the action becomes increasingly affecting, especially when a local musician is summoned to perform a mystical ritual to bond the intransigent mother and her adorable offspring. But the human side of the story is equally poignant, with the final arrival of satellite television symbolising a threat to this ancient and arduous way of life. DP Mongolian +subtitles. *DVD*

■ *Dir* Byambasuren Davaa, Luigi Falorni

The Story of Three Loves ★★★★ U

Portmanteau romantic drama
1953 · US · Colour · 121min

This beautifully shot portmanteau romance, filmed by MGM with all stops out features a marvellously starry cast, impossibly romantic situations and a particularly fine score from Miklos Rozsa. The mood is bittersweet throughout, and the attitudes and settings resolutely Hollywood European, with wonderful resonances for film fans. Here's James Mason as a ballet impresario, touched by *Red Shoes* ballerina Moira Shearer. Here's Kirk Douglas playing a trapeze artist, partnered by tragic Pier Angeli. Best of all, in the weakest segment, is young Ricky Nelson, transformed by magic into Farley Granger. TS

Moira Shearer *Paula Woodward* · James Mason *Charles Coudray* · Agnes Moorehead *Aunt Lydia* · Miklos Rozsa *Conductor* · Ethel Barrymore *Mrs Pennicott* · Leslie Caron *Mademoiselle* · Farley Granger *Thomas Campbell Jr* · Ricky Nelson *Tommy, aged 12* · Pier Angeli *Nina* · Kirk Douglas *Pierre Narval* ■ *Dir* Gottfried Reinhardt, Vincente Minnelli · *Scr* John Collier, Jan Lustig, George Froeschel, John Collier, Jan Lustig, George Froeschel, from the stories by Arnold Phillips, Ladislas Vajda, Jacques Maret

The Story of Us ★★ 15

Romantic comedy 1999 · US · Colour · 91min

Director Rob Reiner tries to make another *When Harry Met Sally*-style romantic comedy, but clearly forgot to hire someone capable of turning in a funny or moving script. Bruce Willis and Michelle Pfeiffer do their best as an unhappily married couple who opt for a temporary separation when their kids go off to summer camp. However, what could have been a sweet and amusing tale of mid-marriage crisis is a rather one-sided affair. JB Swearing. *DVD*

Michelle Pfeiffer *Katie Jordan* · Bruce Willis *Ben Jordan* · Rita Wilson *Rachel* · Julie Hagerty *Liza* · Paul Reiser *Dave* · Tim Matheson *Marty* · Colleen Rennison *Erin aged 10* · Jake Sandvig *Josh aged 12* · Red Buttons *Arnie* ■ *Dir* Rob Reiner · *Scr* Alan Zweibel, Jessie Nelson

The Story of Vernon and Irene Castle ★★★★ U

Musical biography 1939 · US · BW · 89min

This was the last RKO teaming of its incomparable dance duo of Fred Astaire and Ginger Rogers. They are cleverly cast as their great predecessors the Castles, the foremost dance partners of the early 20th century, in a tale that took on new resonances at the outbreak of the Second World War. The period songs are spot-on, though the ever-sophisticated Astaire and Rogers look nothing like the bunny-hugging Castles (Irene was critical of Ginger's impersonation). The scripting leaves something to be desired, but despite its flaws, Ginger looks swell and Fred dances divinely. TS *DVD*

Fred Astaire *Vernon Castle* · Ginger Rogers *Irene Castle* · Edna May Oliver *Maggie Sutton* · Walter Brennan *Walter* · Lew Fields · Etienne Girardot *Papa Aubel* · Janet Beecher *Mrs Foote* · Rolfe

Sedan *Emile Aubel* ■ *Dir* HC Potter • *Scr* Richard Sherman, Oscar Hammerstein, Dorothy Yost, from the books *My Husband* and *My Memories of Vernon Castle* by Irene Castle

The Story on Page One ★★
Courtroom drama 1959 · US · BW · 123min

Given that this was written and directed by hard-hitting playwright Clifford Odets, it should have been a cracker, but it's a damp squib, thanks to inept plotting and sloppy assembly. It does have its moments, and Rita Hayworth, though past her sex symbol days, is on excellent acting form. The story concerns the trial of adulterous Hayworth and her lover Gig Young, accused of murdering her husband and defended by an over-the-top Anthony Franciosa. RK

Rita Hayworth *Jo Morris* • Anthony Franciosa *Victor Santini* • Gig Young *Larry Ellis* • Mildred Dunnock *Mrs Ellis* • Hugh Griffith *Judge Nielsen* ■ *Dir/Scr* Clifford Odets

Storytelling ★★18
Black comedy 2001 · US · Colour · 83min

Todd Solondz's focus here seems less on a coherent story than on satirising the art of storytelling itself. He employs a two-part structure, "Fiction" and "Non-fiction", to mock both the art of the written word (involving student Selma Blair's creative writing course) and documentary-making (Paul Giamatti examines disaffected teenage life), as well as the dark side of suburban folk. The thinly developed characters fail to rouse much interest or empathy, and some witty notions about fiction versus reality are lost in the director's apparent desire to be disturbing, offensive and cruel. JC Violence, swearing, a sex scene, nudity. *DVD*

John Goodman *Marty Livingston* • Julie Hagerty *Fern Livingston* • Mark Webber *Scooby Livingston* • Paul Giamatti *Toby Oxman* • Selma Blair *Vi* • Jonathan Osser *Mikey Livingston* ■ *Dir/Scr* Todd Solondz

Storyville ★★★15
Mystery drama 1992 · US · Colour · 113min

Mark Frost, David Lynch's unsung partner on the cult TV series *Twin Peaks*, made his directorial debut with this nasty story of dark deeds in the Deep South. As if adultery, corruption, blackmail and murder weren't enough, Frost throws in a little video voyeurism and an upcoming election to keep the plot simmering. James Spader disappoints as the politically ambitious lawyer at the centre of events, but there are some choice performances from Jason Robards, Joanne Whalley-Kilmer and Piper Laurie. Engagingly offbeat, but the action loses its way. DP Violence, sex scenes, swearing.

James Spader *Cray Fowler* • Joanne Whalley-Kilmer [Joanne Whalley] *Natalie Tate* • Jason Robards *Clifford Fowler* • Charlotte Lewis *Lee* • Michael Warren *Nathan LeFleur* • Michael Parks *Michael Trevallian* • Chuck McCann *Pudge Herman* • Charles Haid *Abe Choate* • Woody Strode *Charlie Sumpter* ■ *Dir* Mark Frost • *Scr* Mark Frost, Lee Reynolds, from the book *Juryman* by Frank Galbally, Robert Macklin

Stowaway ★★★★U
Musical comedy 1936 · US · BW · 83min

Talented child star Shirley Temple plays the daughter of a slain Chinese missionary, who stows away on a playboy's yacht. This prime vehicle is one of Temple's best, with an excellent cast, just enough plot and some splendid musical moments. She sings, dances and, in one memorable sequence, impersonates Al Jolson, Eddie Cantor and Ginger Rogers. The moppet even converses in Chinese in this entertaining movie, which was one of the biggest box-office hits of its year. TV *DVD*

Shirley Temple *Ching-Ching, daughter of missionaries* • Robert Young (1) *Tommy Randall* • Alice Faye *Susan Parker* • Eugene Pallette *The Colonel* • Helen Westley *Mrs Hope* • Arthur Treacher *Atkins* • J Edward Bromberg *Judge Booth* ■ *Dir* William A Seiter • *Scr* William Conselman, Arthur Sheekman, Nat Perrin, from the story by Samuel G Engel

---

La Strada ★★★★PG
Drama 1954 · It · BW · 103min

This Federico Fellini classic about a brutal circus strong man and a childlike woman was dismissed in Italy on release, but hailed abroad as a masterpiece, sealing Fellini's reputation as a "great artist". Fellini's wife Giulietta Masina gives a touching perfomance, but viewed today the movie might seem crudely sentimental, its love story between a human animal and a simple waif hardly able to contain all the messages and symbols about humanity that the Italian maestro tosses at it. Combining the neorealism of Fellini's early career and the outright fantasies of his later work, this is well worth seeing, if only for its historical impact and striking influence. AT Italian +subtitles. *DVD*

Anthony Quinn *Zampano* • Giulietta Masina *Gelsomina* • Richard Basehart *Il Matto/"The Fool"* • Aldo Silvani *Il Signor Giraffa* ■ *Dir* Federico Fellini • *Scr* Federico Fellini, Tullio Pinelli, Ennio Flaiano

Straight from the Heart ★★
Romantic drama 2003 · US · Colour · 100min

Teri Polo and Andrew McCarthy learn the well-worn lesson that opposites attract in this pleasant romantic drama. Polo plays a budding New York photographer who visits Wyoming for a blind-date weekend with a widowed rancher (McCarthy). Predictably, their chalk-and-cheese personalities slowly find common ground – but not before a dose of mutual dislike and poignant soul-searching, brought about by McCarthy's preoccupation with his wife's death. Polo and McCarthy never really stretch themselves, but their performances are charming. SF

Teri Polo *Jordan Donavan* • Andrew McCarthy *Tyler Ross* • Greg Evigan *Edward Morgan* • Patricia Kalember *Laurie Woods* • Christine Tucci *Carla DiMaggio* ■ *Dir* Dave Cass [David S Cass Sr] • *Scr* Pamela Wallace, from her novel

Straight out of Brooklyn ★★★15
Drama 1991 · US · Colour · 82min

With its firm grasp of the realities of Brooklyn street life and its uncompromising use of realistic language and violence, this bruising account of what it's like to be black in urban America is all the more remarkable considering its debuting writer/director, Matty Rich, was only 19 when he completed it. There are jagged edges, but, like the rawness of the performances, they only add to the power of the picture. DP Sex scenes, drug abuse.

George T Odom *Ray Brown* • Ann D Sanders *Frankie Brown* • Lawrence Gilliard Jr [Larry Gilliard Jr] *Dennis Brown* • Barbara Sanon *Carolyn Brown* • Reana E Drummond *Shirley* • Matty Rich *Larry Love* • Mark Malone *Kevin* • Ali Shahid Abdul Wahha *Luther* ■ *Dir/Scr* Matty Rich

Straight Outta Compton ★★★★18
Biographical music drama 2015 · US · Colour · 166min

Gangsta rap pioneers NWA released their first album in 1988, and it shares its title with this juggernaut of a biopic. With songs like F*** tha Police, the group brought the everyday struggles of black youth in LA to international audiences, attracting controversy and acclaim in equal measure. Director F Gary Gray's stroke of genius is to shoot the rags to riches tale in the style of an action movie, and it's an undeniably thrilling move. The young actors playing the rappers are uniform y charismatic, particularly Jason Mitchell as reformed real-life gangster Eazy-E. The visceral impact of NWA's music is lovingly (and loudly) recreated. LB Violence, swearing, a sex scene, nudity, drug abuse. *DVD*

O'Shea Jackson Jr *Ice Cube* • Corey Hawkins *Dr Dre* • Jason Mitchell *Eazy-E* • Paul Giamatti *Jerry Heller* • Neil Brown Jr *DJ Yella* • R Marcus Taylor

---

Suge Knight ■ *Dir* F Gary Gray • *Scr* Andrea Berloff, Jonathan Herman, from a story by Berloff, S Leigh Savidge, Alan Wenkus

Straight Shooting ★★★
Silent western 1917 · US · BW · 75min

Long believed to be lost until it was rediscovered in a Czech film archive in the 1960s, this very early western is part of a series that starred Harry Carey as Cheyenne Harry under the direction of John Ford. During production it crept up to five reels, becoming Ford's first feature. It develops a cattlemen versus homesteaders conflict, with Cheyenne Harry changing sides. Ford's visual style is already often striking. AE

Harry Carey *Cheyenne Harry* • Duke Lee *Thunder Flint* • George Berrell *Sweetwater Sims* • Molly Malone *Joan Sims* • Ted Brooks *Tom Sims* • Hoot Gibson *Danny Morgan* ■ *Dir* Jack Ford [John Ford] • *Scr* George Hively

The Straight Story ★★★★★U
Biographical road movie 1999 · US/Fr/UK · Colour · 106min

David Lynch is in a mellow mood with this whimsical road movie that slyly dissects middle-American mores with disarming precision. Exhibiting dignified self-assurance, Richard Farnsworth gives an Oscar-nominated performance as the Iowa farmer travelling by lawnmower to visit his dying brother in Wisconsin. There's selfless support from Sissy Spacek, as his traumatised daughter, and from the various eccentrics he meets en route. It's hard to imagine a gentler film, yet Lynch exploits the stately pace to gaze fondly upon life's rich pageant. DP *DVD*

Richard Farnsworth *Alvin Straight* • Sissy Spacek *Rose Straight* • Harry Dean Stanton *Lyle Straight* • Everett McGill *Tom the John Deere dealer* • John Farley *Thorvald Olsen* • Kevin Farley *Harald Olsen* • Jane Galloway Heitz *Dorothy* • Joseph A Carpenter *Bud* ■ *Dir* David Lynch • *Scr* John Roach, Mary Sweeney • *Cinematographer* Freddie Francis • *Music* Angelo Badalamenti

Straight Talk ★★★★PG
Romantic comedy 1992 · US · Colour · 86min

Both Dolly Parton and James Woods are perfectly cast as the bogus radio agony aunt and the sleazy reporter investigating her in this fun romantic comedy, which was filmed on location in Chicago. Woods's reporter wants to expose Parton as a sham, but soon finds he wants to get her into bed along the way. What makes this work so well is the sparring double act of the two leads. JB Some swearing. *DVD*

Dolly Parton *Shirlee Kenyon* • James Woods *Jack Russell* • Griffin Dunne *Alan Riegert* • Michael Madsen *Steve Labell* • Deirdre O'Connell *Lily* • John Sayles *Guy Girardi* • Teri Hatcher *Janice* • Spalding Gray *Dr Erdman* • Jerry Orbach *Milo Jacoby* ■ *Dir* Barnet Kellman • *Scr* Craig Bolotin, Patricia Resnick

Straight Time ★★★18
Crime drama 1978 · US · Colour · 109min

This terrific if sordid little opus was originally begun with the film's star Dustin Hoffman directing himself, but he handed the reins over to Broadway veteran Ulu Grosbard when the strain of juggling both tasks got too much for him. Hoffman is brilliant as a petty hood, and there are marvellous supporting performances. TS Violence, swearing, nudity.

Dustin Hoffman *Max Dembo* • Theresa Russell *Jenny Mercer* • Harry Dean Stanton *Jerry Schue* • Gary Busey *Willy Darin* • M Emmet Walsh *Earl Frank* • Sandy Baron *Manny* • Kathy Bates *Selma Darin* ■ *Dir* Ulu Grosbard • *Scr* Alvin Sargent, Edward Bunker, Jeffrey Boam, from the novel *No Beast So Fierce* by Edward Bunker

Straight to Hell ★15
Spoof spaghetti western 1987 · UK · Colour · 82min

This awful spoof spaghetti western is directed by Alex Cox, who took all his pop star friends to Spain to shoot what is essentially an expensive home movie. Sy Richardson, Joe Strummer and Dick Rude

---

play desperados on the run after a bank robbery. The Pogues are the gang who want them out of the one-horse town they control. Stilted and boring. AJ *DVD*

Sy Richardson *Norwood* • Joe Strummer *Simms* • Dick Rude *Willy* • Courtney Love *Velma* • Zander Schloss *Karl* • Del Zamora *Poncho* • Luis Contreras *Sal* • Dennis Hopper *IG Farben* • Elvis Costello *Hives, the butler* • Grace Jones *Sonya* ■ *Dir* Alex Cox • *Scr* Alex Cox, Dick Rude

Straightheads ★★18
Thriller 2007 · UK · Colour · 76min

Scenes of stomach-churning violence are the focus of this British revenge thriller by writer/director Dan Reed. Gillian Anderson and Danny Dyer play a couple of hard-bitten urbanites who enjoy a brief sexual encounter at a country house just before being attacked by a ferocious gang of thugs. Their relationship undergoes a deep and dramatic shift as Anderson formulates a plan for revenge. Her portrayal of an outwardly self-assured woman who begins to emotionally unravel is by far the most convincing aspect of the story. SP *DVD* *Blu-ray*

Gillian Anderson *Alice* • Danny Dyer *Adam* • Anthony Calf *Heffer* • Ralph Brown *Jamie* • Steven Robertson *Bill* • Francesca Fowler *Sophie* ■ *Dir/Scr* Dan Reed

Strait-Jacket ★★★
Horror 1963 · US · BW · 92min

"When the axe swings, the excitement begins!" screamed the original poster for William Castle's showy horror tale. But you'll be screaming louder with laughter watching trampy Joan Crawford playing a rehabilitated convicted murderess who may, or may not, be returning to her old head-severing habits. Scripted by *Psycho*'s Robert Bloch, it was the writer's favourite because it was filmed intact. Castle provided restrictive seat belts in cinemas, plus free cardboard axes to wave during the mayhem. AJ

Joan Crawford *Lucy Harbin* • Diane Baker *Carol* • Leif Erickson *Bill Cutler* • Howard St John *Raymond Fields* • John Anthony Hayes *Michael Fields* • Rochelle Hudson *Emily Cutler* • George Kennedy *Leo Krause* ■ *Dir* William Castle • *Scr* Robert Bloch

The Strange Affair ★★★
Crime drama 1968 · UK · Colour · 104min

Failed student Michael York becomes a policeman and gets entangled with bent cops, drug dealing and lustful Susan George. This film's swinging London trappings – Indian mystics, flower people, garish decor, circular beds, touristy locations – tend to work against the underworld elements. On the plus side are some diverting supporting performances and flashes of quirky humour. AT

Michael York *Peter Strange* • Jeremy Kemp *Detective Sgt Pierce* • Susan George *Frederika "Fred" March* • Jack Watson *Daddy Quince* • George A Cooper (2) *Superintendent Kingley* • Barry Fantoni *Charley Small, informer* ■ *Dir* David Greene • *Scr* Stanley Mann, from the novel by Bernard Toms

A Strange Affair ★★★
Psychological drama 1981 · Fr · Colour · 100min

There's a Capra-esque feel to this drama, which begins with an air of despondent realism only to suddenly soar into flights of inexplicable fantasy. The reason for this sudden change in the fortunes of Gérard Lanvin is Michel Piccoli, who not only takes over the shop where he works, but also insinuates himself into other areas of his life. But Pierre Granier-Deferre's lightness of touch gives this a disarming stealth that prevents the action from becoming tacky or twee. DP French dubbed.

Michel Piccoli *Bertrand Malair* • Nathalie Baye *Nina Coline* • Gérard Lanvin *Louis Coline* • Jean-Pierre Kalfon *François Lingre* • Jean-François Balmer *Paul Belais* • Madeleine Cheminat *Yette* ■ *Dir* Pierre Granier-Deferre • *Scr* Christopher Frank, Pierre Granier-Deferre

S

The Strange Affair of Uncle Harry ★★ 15

Mystery drama   1945 · US · BW · 77min

Released as plain *Uncle Harry* in the USA, this Broadway-based thriller stars George Sanders as a textile designer who lives with his two spinster sisters. When he falls in love with Ella Raines, one of the sisters is consumed with jealousy. While Sanders gives an excellent, multilayered performance, the dreadful studio-imposed ending precipitated the resignation of the producer, Joan Harrison, a regular associate of Hitchcock. **AT**

George Sanders *Harry Melville Quincy* • Geraldine Fitzgerald *Lettie Quincy* • Ella Raines *Deborah Brown* • Sara Allgood *Nona* • Moyna MacGill *Hester Quincy* • Samuel S Hinds *Dr Adams* ■ *Dir* Robert Siodmak · *Scr* Stephen Longstreet, Keith Winter, from the play *Uncle Harry* by Thomas Job

Strange Bedfellows ★★★

Romantic comedy   1965 · US · Colour · 98min

Executive Rock Hudson and his Italian wife Gina Lollobrigida have been separated for five years. When they come across each other in London, it is obvious there is still a spark between them, but after one passionate night they start bickering all over again. Their plans to part are complicated by Gig Young, a PR man determined to keep them together for the sake of Hudson's firm. Old hand Melvin Frank here turns in another smooth but unexceptional romantic comedy, enlivened by the talents of Terry-Thomas and Arthur Haynes. **DF**

Rock Hudson *Carter Harrison* • Gina Lollobrigida *Toni* • Gig Young *Richard Bramwell* • Edward Judd *Harry Jones* • Terry-Thomas *assistant mortician* • Arthur Haynes *Carter's taxi driver* • Howard St John *JL Stevens* • David King *Toni's taxi driver* ■ *Dir* Melvin Frank · *Scr* Melvin Frank, Michael Pertwee, from a story by Norman Panama, Melvin Frank

Strange Boarders ★★★

Comedy thriller   1938 · UK · BW · 74min

The spy thriller meets the bedroom farce in this sprightly suspense comedy. Tom Walls plays an investigator called away from his honeymoon with Renée Saint-Cyr to discover which of the guests at Irene Handl's boarding house has stolen some top-secret blueprints. Walls was never the most understated of screen performers, but he keeps this enjoyable mystery breezy. **DP**

Tom Walls *Tommy Blythe* • Renée Saint-Cyr *Louise Blythe* • Googie Withers *Elsie* • Ronald Adam *Barstow* • CV France *Colonel Anstruther* • Nina Boucicault *Mrs Anstruther* • Irene Handl *Mrs Dewar* ■ *Dir* Herbert Mason · *Scr* AR Rawlinson, Sidney Gilliat, from the novel *The Strange Boarders of Paradise Crescent* by E Phillips Oppenheim

Strange Cargo ★★★

Drama   1940 · US · BW · 113min

Clark Gable and Joan Crawford's eighth and last picture together is a jungle adventure that turns into a religious parable about redemption. Gable, Paul Lukas and Peter Lorre hack their way through the jungle together with Ian Hunter, Christ's disciple in French Guiana, in a bid to escape from Devil's Island. Crawford, meanwhile, turns in another Sadie Thompson routine. Banned in Boston, when the Catholic Legion of Decency condemned it as blasphemous. Recommended for connoisseurs of studio foliage. **AT**

Clark Gable *Andre Verne* • Joan Crawford *Julie* • Ian Hunter *Cambreau* • Peter Lorre *Cochon* • Paul Lukas *Hessler* • Albert Dekker *Moll* • J Edward Bromberg *Flaubert* • Eduardo Ciannelli *Telez* ■ *Dir* Frank Borzage · *Scr* Lawrence Hazard, Lesser Samuels, Anita Loos (adaptation), from the book *Not Too Narrow... Not Too Deep* by Richard Sale

The Strange Colour of Your Body's Tears ★★★ 18

Horror thriller   2013 · Bel/Fr/Lux · Colour · 97min

The influence of Italian horror maestro Dario Argento looms large over the second feature from Belgium-based directors Hélène Cattet and Bruno Forzani. A businessman (Klaus Tange) returns to his Brussels apartment, only to find his wife has vanished with no clue as to her whereabouts. Cattet and Forzani unleash a cornucopia of eye-popping images backed up by slick editing and cracking sound. Those who prefer substance over style may baulk at the sensory overkill here, but it will be intriguing to see what this talented duo do next. **JA** In French, Dutch. Violence, sex scenes, nudity. *DVD*

Klaus Tange *Dan Kristensen/Detective Vincentelli* • Ursula Bedena *Edwige* • Birgit Yew *Dora* ■ *Dir/Scr* Hélène Cattet, Bruno Forzani

Strange Confession ★★

Mystery   1945 · US · BW · 62min

In this mediocre *Inner Sanctum* entry, novice director John Hoffman fails to seize the attention, despite the urgency with which series regular Lon Chaney Jr starts to relate the events that lead to a murder rap. The opening segment, in which Chaney's chemist endures the bullying of boss J Carrol Naish (who also has designs on his wife, Brenda Joyce), offers the occasional morsel of juicy melodrama. But time hangs heavy during the South American exile sequences. **DP**

Lon Chaney [Lon Chaney Jr] *Jeff Carter* • Brenda Joyce *Mary Carter* • J Carrol Naish *Roger Graham* • Milburn Stone *Stevens* • Lloyd Bridges *Dave Curtis* ■ *Dir* John Hoffman (1) · *Scr* M Coates Webster, from the play *The Man Who Reclaimed His Head* by Jean Bart

Strange Days ★★★★ 18

Science-fiction action thriller
1995 · US · Colour · 139min

Ralph Fiennes plays a dealer in virtual reality clips that replicate sensory perceptions in director Kathryn Bigelow's dazzling sci-fi thriller. As New Year's Eve 1999 approaches, he tries to track down a killer recording his crimes for the ultimate "snuff" experience. This controversial, highly imaginative and inventively staged movie is a fascinating look at the moral implications of advanced technology. Using subjective camerawork to place the viewer in the voyeuristic frame, Bigelow reinvents *film noir* for contemporary audiences. **AJ** Violence, swearing, drug abuse, nudity. *DVD*

Ralph Fiennes *Lenny Nero* • Angela Bassett *Lornette "Mace" Mason* • Juliette Lewis *Faith Justin* • Tom Sizemore *Max Peltier* • Michael Wincott *Philo Gant* • Vincent D'Onofrio *Burton Steckler* • Glenn Plummer *Jeriko One* ■ *Dir* Kathryn Bigelow · *Scr* James Cameron, Jay Cocks, from a story by James Cameron

The Strange Door ★★ U

Horror   1951 · US · BW · 80min

A contrived melodrama is heightened in stature by the presence of Boris Karloff and Charles Laughton. The latter is a sadistic French nobleman who imprisons his brother in the basement for marrying a woman they both loved. It's when Laughton tries to marry his brother's daughter to an infamous brigand in revenge that manservant Karloff rebels. More histrionic than horror historic. **AJ**

Charles Laughton *Sire Alan de Maletroit* • Boris Karloff *Voltan* • Sally Forrest *Blanche de Maletroit* • Richard Stapely *Denis de Beaulieu* • Michael Pate *Talon* • Paul Cavanagh *Edmond de Maletroit* ■ *Dir* Joseph Pevney · *Scr* Jerry Sackheim, from the story *The Sire de Maletroit's Door* by Robert Louis Stevenson

Strange Gardens ★★★ 15

Second World War comedy drama
2003 · Fr · Colour · 97min

Jean Becker's adaptation is perfectly pitched between whimsical nostalgia and genuinely moving human drama. Teacher Jacques Villeret and aristocratic milliner André Dussollier come to appreciate the unexpected moment of human warmth shown them by a Nazi soldier detailed to guard a quartet of Resistance actors during a mischievous act of sabotage escalates into a major incident. This thoughtful film's emphasis is firmly on character and how a seemingly minor moment can change someone's life forever. Impeccably judged and played with restraint. **DP** French +subtitles. Violence.

Jacques Villeret *Jacques Pouzay* • André Dussollier *André Designy* • Thierry Lhermitte *Thierry Plaisance* • Benoît Magimel *Emile Bailleul* • Suzanne Flon *Marie Gerbier* • Isabelle Candelier *Louise* ■ *Dir* Jean Becker · *Scr* Jean Becker, Jean Cosmos, Guillaume Laurant, from the novella *In Our Strange Gardens* by Michel Quint

Strange Holiday ★

Second World War drama
1942 · US · BW · 61min

One of the more bizarre artefacts to have survived from the Second World War, this propaganda piece was financed by General Motors and stars Claude Rains, who returns from a holiday in the backwoods to find America transformed into a Nazi dictatorship. It was made in 1942 and shelved until 1945 when Rains himself arranged its limited release. **AT**

Claude Rains *John Stevenson* • Bobbie Stebbins *John Jr* • Barbara Bates *Peggy Lee* • Paul Hilton *Woodrow Jr* • Gloria Holden *Mrs Jean Stevenson* • Milton Kibbee *Sam Morgan* ■ *Dir/Scr* Arch Oboler

Strange Interlude ★★★★

Melodrama   1932 · US · BW · 109min

Norma Shearer, distraught at the death of her beloved in war, makes a self-sacrificing marriage to Alexander Kirkland and is then forced by circumstance to have her child by Clark Gable and falls in love with him. MGM's attempt to film Eugene O'Neill's complex Pulitzer Prize-winning play was either foolhardy or a brave bid for intellectual respectability. Critics were divided over the merits of the play and few people liked (or saw) the lavish film, which is an experimental delve into the torment of an idealistic, highly strung and strong woman, and the weak men around her. **RK**

Norma Shearer *Nina Leeds* • Clark Gable *Ned Darrell* • Alexander Kirkland *Sam Evans* • Ralph Morgan *Charlie Marsden* • Robert Young (1) *Gordon, as a young man* • May Robson *Mrs Evans* • Maureen O'Sullivan *Madeleine* • Henry B Walthall *Prof Leeds* ■ *Dir* Robert Z Leonard · *Scr* Bess Meredyth, C Gardner Sullivan, from the play by Eugene O'Neill

Strange Invaders ★★★★ 12

Science fiction   1983 · US · Colour · 89min

An affectionate parody of 1950s alien invasion B-movies, this film's simple premise evokes memories of *It Came from Outer Space*, with co-writer/director Michael Laughlin bringing the genre bang up to date courtesy of the marvellous special effects, warmly comic overtones and a sharply observed script. This recaptures the heady atmosphere and demented imagery of its major inspirations. **AJ** Swearing.

Paul Le Mat *Charles Bigelow* • Nancy Allen *Betty Walker* • Diana Scarwid *Margaret* • Michael Lerner *Willie Collins* • Louise Fletcher *Mrs Benjamin* • Wallace Shawn *Earl* • Fiona Lewis *Waitress/Avon Lady* • Kenneth Tobey *Arthur Newman* ■ *Dir* Michael Laughlin · *Scr* William Condon, Michael Laughlin

Strange Justice ★★★ 15

Political documentary drama
1999 · US · Colour · 107min

In 1991, the American legal system was rocked when President Bush's African-American candidate for the Supreme Court, Clarence Thomas, was accused of sexual harassment by Anita Hill during his confirmation hearing. It was a critical and compelling case. In Ernest R Dickerson's made-for-TV reconstruction it's less the morality of the establishment that comes under scrutiny than the advisability of allowing women access to the corridors of power. Delroy Lindo and Regina Taylor impress as the main protagonists, but they're overshadowed by the hissably persuasive performance of Mandy Patinkin as White House spin doctor Kenneth Duberstein. **DP**

Delroy Lindo *Clarence Thomas* • Mandy Patinkin *Kenneth Duberstein* • Regina Taylor *Anita Hill* • Stephen Young *Senator Danforth* • Paul Windfield *Thurgood Marshall* • Louis Gossett Jr *Vernon Jordan* ■ *Dir* Ernest R Dickerson · *Scr* Jacob Epstein, from the non-fiction book *Strange Justice: the Selling of Clarence Thomas* by Jane Mayer, Jill Abramson

Strange Lady in Town ★★★ U

Western   1955 · US · Colour · 111min

Doctor Greer Garson is peddling pills to the good citizens of Santa Fe in the late 19th century. Glossily shot by Harold Rosson, this is more melodrama than western, with Garson having trouble with her outcast brother Cameron Mitchell as well as confronting the usual ignorance and prejudice among her patients. As with many of director Mervyn LeRoy's later films, this is polished stuff, but paste rather than a real gem. **DP**

Greer Garson *Dr Julia Winslow Garth* • Dana Andrews *Rork O'Brien* • Cameron Mitchell *David Garth* • Lois Smith *Spurs O'Brien* • Walter Hampden *Father Gabriel* ■ *Dir* Mervyn LeRoy · *Scr* Frank Butler

The Strange Love of Martha Ivers ★★★★★ PG

Film noir   1946 · US · BW · 115min

A critical and commercial hit for Barbara Stanwyck, Van Heflin and, making his debut, Kirk Douglas, this high-voltage portrait of evil and greed remains blissfully absorbing and entertaining. Stanwyck plays manipulative millionairess Martha, married to Douglas, a weak-willed district attorney with a drink problem, whom she despises. Enter Van Heflin, Stanwyck's nemesis from the past, and the fun begins. Robert Rossen has a hand in the screenplay, and Lewis Milestone directs for maximum effect. The *New York Times* accurately defined Martha and her hubby as "two of the meanest and most seriously interesting characters that addicts of homicidal melodrama are likely to meet on the screen". **RK** *DVD*

Barbara Stanwyck *Martha Ivers* • Van Heflin *Sam Masterson* • Kirk Douglas *Walter O'Neil* • Lizabeth Scott *Toni Marachek* • Judith Anderson *Mrs Ivers* • Roman Bohnen *Mr O'Neil* • Ann Doran *Secretary* ■ *Dir* Lewis Milestone · *Scr* Robert Rossen, from the story *Love Lies Bleeding* by Jack Patrick

The Strange Love of Molly Louvain ★★

Melodrama   1932 · US · BW · 70min

Ann Dvorak, abandoned in childhood to the wrong side of the tracks but determined to be respectable, is courted by a wealthy young man. He deserts her, leaving her pregnant. She boards out her daughter, but her liaison with a scumbag (Leslie Fenton) implicates her in a murder. In hiding with Richard Cromwell, long in love with her, she falls for fast-talking newspaperman Lee Tracy who is unaware she's the fugitive. Unbelievable, but not uninvolving. **RK**

Ann Dvorak *Molly Louvain* • Lee Tracy *Scottie Cornell* • Richard Cromwell *Jimmy Cook* • Guy Kibbee *Pop* • Leslie Fenton *Nicky Grant* • Frank McHugh *Skeets* ■ *Dir* Michael Curtiz · *Scr* Erwin Gelsey, Brown Holmes, from the play *Tinsel Girl* by Maurine Dallas Watkins

Strange Magic ★★ U

Animated musical fantasy
2015 · US · Colour · 99min

George Lucas came up with the original story for this animated musical saga of fairies, elves and a magic elixir, but the result is not Lucasfilm's finest hour. With the cast (led by Evan Rachel Wood) breaking into song – from Elvis oldies to Lady Gaga, and even the ELO title tune – at a moment's notice, the effect is bright and busy, but too frenetic for its own good. Ultimately, the impressively ornate visuals don't make up for a lack of genuine emotional impact. **TJ**

Evan Rachel Wood *Marianne* • Alan Cumming *Bog King* • Elijah Kelley *Sunny* • Sam Palladio *Roland* • Meredith Anne Bull *Dawn* ■ *Dir* Gary Rydstrom • *Scr* Gary Rydstrom, Irene Mecchi, David Berenbaum, from a story by George Lucas

Strange Planet ★★★ 15
Romantic comedy   1999 · Aus · Colour · 91min

This episodic romantic comedy from Australia is about a year in the love lives of six men and women. Perceptive and engaging, Emma-Kate Croghan's film features a trio of delightful performances from career girl Claudia Karvan, sweet but insecure Naomi Watts and quirky Alice Garner. The male characters are incredibly dull and self-absorbed in comparison. The film loses its perky momentum after a cracking first half. JC Sex scenes, swearing, drug abuse.

Claudia Karvan *Judy* • Naomi Watts *Alice* • Alice Garner *Sally* • Tom Long *Ewan* • Aaron Jeffery *Joel* • Felix Williamson *Neil* • Hugo Weaving *Steven* • Rebecca Frith *Amanda* ■ *Dir* Emma-Kate Croghan • *Scr* Stavros Kazantzidis, Emma-Kate Croghan

The Strange Vengeance of Rosalie ★
Drama   1972 · US · Colour · 107min

This pointless, ill-conceived and painfully contrived thriller revives the old chestnut of the kidnapped falling in love with the kidnapper. In this instance it's travelling salesman Ken Howard who is abducted by young native American girl Bonnie Bedelia. The dumb plot about a stash of gold descends into mass confusion. AJ

Bonnie Bedelia *Rosalie* • Ken Howard *Virgil* • Anthony Zerbe *Fry* ■ *Dir* Jack Starrett • *Scr* Anthony Greville-Bell, John Kohn

Strange Wilderness ★★ 15
Comedy   2007 · US · Colour · 81min

From Cheech and Chong going up in smoke to Harold and Kumar getting the munchies, stoner comedies are nothing new. This inane addition to the genre stars Steve Zahn as the host of a cable-TV nature show that's about to be axed unless the potheads behind it can pull off something sensational... like finding Bigfoot. Cue a skittish collection of drug gags and bad Spanish as Zahn and his crew head off to Central America in search of the hairy beast. Among the players demeaning themselves are Jonah Hill from *Superbad* and veteran actors Joe Don Baker and Ernest Borgnine - both of whom are old enough to know better. There are a couple of amusing moments, but on the whole this is dopey in every sense. JR DVD

Steve Zahn *Peter Caulke* • Allen Covert *Fred Wolf* • Jeff Garlin *Ed Lawson* • Justin Long *Junior* • Jonah Hill *Cooker* • Robert Patrick *Gus Hayden* • Harry Hamlin *Sky Pierson* • Joe Don Baker *Bill Calhoun* • Ernest Borgnine *Milas* • Kevin Heffernan *Bill Whitaker* ■ *Dir* Fred Wolf • *Scr* Peter Gaulke, Fred Wolf

The Strange Woman ★★★
Period melodrama   1946 · US · BW · 101min

This is a rare examples of ace cult director Edgar G Ulmer (*Detour, Bluebeard*) working with major stars and he coaxes what is possibly a career best performance from Hedy Lamarr. Lamarr stars as a social-climbing beauty who ensnares boring Gene Lockhart, suave George Sanders and gauche Louis Hayward during her rise from a deprived childhood. It's enjoyable tosh, glamorous to look at and played to perfection. TS

Hedy Lamarr *Jenny Hager* • George Sanders *John Evered* • Louis Hayward *Ephraim Poster* • Gene Lockhart *Isaiah Poster* • Hillary Brooke *Meg Saladine* • Rhys Williams *Deacon Adams* • June Storey *Lena Tempest* ■ *Dir* Edgar G Ulmer • *Scr* Herb Meadow, from the novel by Ben Ames Williams

The Strange World of Planet X ★★
Science-fiction thriller   1957 · UK · BW · 75min

Perhaps because the hysterical levels of 1950s Cold War paranoia that swept America did not reach the same heights here, Britain never really went for big insect movies. However, the odd ones did slip out and here Forrest Tucker is the obligatory square-jawed imported American out to stop irradiated bugs taking over the world. Cheap and cheerful fun. JF

Forrest Tucker *Gil Graham* • Gaby André *Michele Dupont* • Martin Benson *Smith* • Hugh Latimer *Jimmy Murray* • Wyndham Goldie *Brigadier Cartwright* • Alec Mango *Dr Laird* ■ *Dir* Gilbert Gunn • *Scr* Paul Ryder, Joe Ambor, from a story by René Ray

The Stranger ★★★ PG
Thriller   1946 · US · BW · 94min

Orson Welles was said to have had little time for this thriller about the search for a Nazi war criminal in small-town America, but it helped put him back on the Hollywood map after a series of box-office failures. There are some of his characteristic directorial touches on view, as well as some of the actorly excesses that typified the performances he gave when he was jobbing to fund his more personal projects. Russell Metty's stylish, shadowy black-and-white photography is so superb, it beggars belief the film was also released in a colourised version. DP DVD Blu

Edward G Robinson *Wilson* • Loretta Young *Mary Longstreet* • Orson Welles *Professor Charles Rankin/Franz Kindler* • Philip Merivale *Judge Longstreet* • Richard Long *Noah Longstreet* • Byron Keith *Dr Jeff Lawrence* ■ *Dir* Orson Welles • *Scr* Anthony Veiller, John Huston (uncredited), Orson Welles, from a story by Victor Trivas, Decla Dunning

The Stranger ★★
Drama   1967 · Alg/Fr/It · Colour · 104min

Despite the insistence of the author's widow, Luchino Visconti was totally the wrong director to adapt Albert Camus's stark, existential tale of the outsider whose irrational act of murder lands him on death row. His visuals are too ornate, his grasp of 1930s Franco-Algerian politics too tenuous and his sympathy for the alienated killer too superficial. Yet, he still succeeds in drawing an undervalued performance from Marcello Mastroianni. Fascinating, but a failure nonetheless. DP In Italian.

Marcello Mastroianni *Arthur Meursault* • Anna Karina *Marie Cardona* • Georges Wilson *Examining magistrate* • Bertrand Blier *Defense counsel* • Pierre Bertin *Judge* • Georges Geret *Raymond* • Bruno Cremer *Priest* ■ *Dir* Luchino Visconti • *Scr* Suso Cecchi D'Amico, Georges Conchon, Emmanuel Robles, Luchino Visconti, from the novel *L'Étranger* by Albert Camus • *Cinematographer* Giuseppe Rotunno

The Stranger ★★ U
Drama   1991 · Ind · Colour · 115min

With a nod towards the story of Martin Guerre, this was Satyajit Ray's final film, but still very much a minor work. Utpal Dutt is suitably ambiguous as the returning prodigal who may or may not be the uncle Mamata Shankar has not seen since 1955. While Ray handles the awkward civilities of the homecoming in his typically unassuming manner, he fails to build the tension as Shankar's husband (Dipankar De) decides to put the stranger to the test. Subtly satirical, allegorically autobiographical, yet disappointingly formal. DP Bengali +subtitles.

Dipankar Dey *Sudhindra Bose* • Mamata Shankar *Anila Bose* • Bikram Bhattacharya *Satyaki/Bablu* • Utpal Dutt *Manmohan Mitra* • Dhritiman Chatterjee *Prithwish Sen Gupta* ■ *Dir/Scr* Satyajit Ray

A Stranger among Us ★★ 15
Crime drama   1992 · US · Colour · 104min

Released in British cinemas as *Close to Eden*, this is a flop under any name, with Melanie Griffith woefully miscast as a cop investigating a murder in New York's tightknit Hassidic community. Throw in a romantic interest in the form of Eric Thal and you have an uneven thriller from director Sidney Lumet, who has certainly had his share of career ups and downs. JB Some violence, swearing.

Melanie Griffith *Emily Eden* • Eric Thal *Ariel* • John Pankow *Levine* • Tracy Pollan *Mara* • Lee Richardson *Rebbe* • Mia Sara *Leah* • Jamey Sheridan *Nick Kemp* ■ *Dir* Sidney Lumet • *Scr* Robert J Avrech

Stranger by the Lake ★★★★ 18
Drama   2013 · Fr · Colour · 99min

A fascinating drama that's part-thriller, part-study in homoerotic psychology, and sticks rigorously to just one location - a French lakeside bathing area and its surrounding cruising grounds in high summer. One night, Franck (Pierre Deladonchamps) sees Michel (Christophe Paou), the hunkiest guy at the lake, drown his lover, which only increases his attraction to the ruthless Adonis. The film's sticky brew of sex, death and neediness offers a bold, troubling exploration of the murkier regions of desire. LF French +subtitles. Sex scenes. DVD Blu

Pierre Deladonchamps *Franck* • Christophe Paou *Michel* • Patrick D'Assumçao *Henri* • Jérôme Chappatte *Inspecteur Damroder* ■ *Dir/Scr* Alain Guiraudie

The Stranger Came Home ★
Crime mystery   1954 · UK · BW · 78min

Paulette Goddard gave up her screen career (apart from one Italian job ten years later) after being reduced to this dreary non-thriller from Hammer Films. Supposedly irresistible as the wife of a vanished businessman, she is favoured by Hollywood-style soft-focus close-ups. Husband William Sylvester reappears with amnesia, seeking to find out which of three former associates had tried to kill him. AE

Paulette Goddard *Angie* • William Sylvester *Philip Vickers* • Patrick Holt *Job Crandall* • Paul Carpenter *Bill Saul* • Alvys Maben *Joan Merrill* • Russell Napier *Inspector Treherne* • David King-Wood *Sessions* ■ *Dir* Terence Fisher • *Scr* Michael Carreras, from the novel *Stranger at Home* by George Sanders

Stranger from Venus ★ U
Science fiction   1954 · UK · BW · 74min

This is directed by Burt Balaban, who adds a mere hint of American zip to the stiff upper lip atmosphere and limited public house setting. After crashing her car, Patricia Neal meets mysterious Helmut Dantine who has travelled from Venus to persuade mankind to abandon their nuclear power experiments. This is lacklustre and too restrained. AJ

Patricia Neal *Susan North* • Helmut Dantine *The Stranger* • Derek Bond *Arthur Walker* • Cyril Luckham *Dr Meinard* • Willoughby Gray *Tom* • Marigold Russell *Gretchen* • Arthur Young (1) *Scientist* • Kenneth Edwards *Charles Dixon* ■ *Dir* Burt Balaban • *Scr* Hans Jacoby, from a story by Desmond Leslie

A Stranger in My Arms ★★
Melodrama   1959 · US · BW · 88min

June Allyson plays a war widow whose husband has been killed in Korea in this not-so-classic melodrama from Ross Hunter, producer of many of Douglas Sirk's best films. She has to deal with her difficult mother-in-law (Mary Astor), a woman ruthlessly intent on seeing that her adored son is posthumously honoured, and with the air force officer (Jeff Chandler) asked to testify to the dead man's heroism. The earnest stars lack the charisma to lift the material, leaving the polished veteran Astor to provide what little spark there is. RK

June Allyson *Christina Beasley* • Jeff Chandler *Pike Yarnell* • Sandra Dee *Pat Beasley* • Charles Coburn *Vance Beasley* • Mary Astor *Mrs Beasley* • Peter Graves (2) *Donald Beasley* • Conrad Nagel *Harley Beasley* • Hayden Rorke *Marcus Beasley* • Reita Green *Bessie Logan* ■ *Dir* Helmut Käutner • *Scr* Peter Berneis, from the novel *And Ride a Tiger* by Robert Wilder

Stranger in the Family ★★ PG
Drama   1991 · US · Colour · 95min

It's amnesia again, this time involving the teenage victim of a car crash having to learn how to do everything all over again.

Glum stuff, not mitigated by the earnest and tortuous family saga woven around the sorrowful central theme. Talented Teri Garr is wasted in this TV movie, but nonetheless is excellent, as are all the cast. But did it all have to be so strained? The family members experience the whole gamut of emotions and crises: guilt, anger, interdependency. It's all very American, and maybe a little too intense for UK palates. TS

Neil Patrick Harris *Steve Thompson* • Teri Garr *Randi Thompson* • Randle Mell *Alan Thompson* • Sierra Samuel *Shari Thompson* • Kathryn Dowling *Dr Webb* • Cully Fredricksen *Principal Kadinski* • Mag Ruffman *Mrs Kessler* ■ *Dir* Donald Wrye • *Scr* Hal Sitowitz

Stranger in the House ★★
Mystery melodrama   1967 · UK · Colour · 111min

Also known as *Cop-Out*, the highlight here is a solid performance from James Mason as a depressed, drunken ex-barrister who comes out of retirement for a seemingly hopeless murder case involving his daughter's boyfriend. Georges Simenon's novel makes an uneasy transfer to sleepy Hampshire, but reliable British performers are worth picking out in small parts. JG

James Mason *John Sawyer* • Geraldine Chaplin *Angela Sawyer* • Bobby Darin *Barney Teale* • Paul Bertoya *Jo Christophorides* • Ian Ogilvy *Desmond Flower* • Bryan Stanyon *Peter Hawkins* • Pippa Steel *Sue Phillips* • Clive Morton *Col Flower* • Moira Lister *Mrs Flower* • Yootha Joyce *Girl at shooting range* • Rita Webb *Mrs Plaskett* ■ *Dir* Pierre Rouve • *Scr* Pierre Rouve, from the novel *Les Inconnus dans la Maison* by Georges Simenon

Stranger Inside ★★★ 18
Drama   2001 · US · Colour · 86min

Pitching itself well above the usual lesbian prison drama by taking time to explore key issues of Afro-American race and the social damage done by incarceration, Cheryl Dunye's unflinching made-for-cable movie is a worthy if intermittently affecting polemic. Tough young offender Yolanda Ross gets herself transferred to the same prison where her mother is serving a life sentence. As they uneasily bond behind bars, and hardened mother shows long-lost daughter the inside ropes, both must face each others' hurt and dark past secrets. Gritty, realistic and compelling. AJ DVD

Yolanda Ross *Treasure* • Davenia McFadden *Brownie* • Rain Phoenix *Kit* • LaTonya "T" Hagan *Shadow* • Mary Mara *Tanya* • Marc Vann *Nelson* • Conchata Ferrell *Mama Cass* ■ *Dir* Cheryl Dunye • *Scr* Cheryl Dunye, Catherine Crouch

Stranger on Horseback ★★★ PG
Western   1955 · US · Colour · 65min

Joel McCrea brings his calm authority to this strong but brief western, playing the circuit judge who dares to arrest Kevin McCarthy, the spoiled killer son of the local land baron (John McIntire) and then has to coax witnesses to testify. The film was shot in Mexico using an unsatisfactory colour process. However, director Jacques Tourneur draws effective performances from his cast. AE Some violence DVD

Joel McCrea *Rick Thorne* • Miroslava *Amy Lee Bannerman* • Kevin McCarthy *Tom Bannerman* • John McIntire *Josiah Bannerman* • Nancy Gates *Caroline Webb* • John Carradine *Colonel Streeter* • Emile Meyer *Sheriff Nat Bell* ■ *Dir* Jacques Tourneur • *Scr* Herb Meadow, Don Martin, from a story by Louis L'Amour

Stranger on the Run ★★★
Western   1967 · US · Colour · 97min

This intelligent western drama stars Henry Fonda as an ex-con who finds himself arrested for murder by perverse lawman Michael Parks, who has the habit of releasing drifters into the desert to be chased by his brutal railway posse. This TV movie has a strong cast, workmanlike direction by Don Siegel and an intelligent script that lifts it above the average. JG Violence.

Henry Fonda *Ben Chamberlain* • Anne Baxter *Valverda Johnson* • Michael Parks *Vince McKay* • Dan Duryea *OE Hotchkiss* • Sal Mineo *George*

S

Blaylock • Lloyd Bochner *Mr Gorman* • Michael Burns *Matt Johnson* • Tom Reese *Leo Weed* • *Dir* Don Siegel • *Scr* Dean E Riesner, from a story by Reginald Rose

Stranger on the Third Floor ★★★

Thriller   1940 · US · BW · 62min

Although John Huston's *The Maltese Falcon* is usually regarded as the first authentic *film noir*, this gripping thriller from RKO came out a year earlier. All the requisite *noir* elements are present: the fatalistic, paranoid mood, the corkscrew murder plot and bug-eyed Peter Lorre as the "stranger". The violent story, including knifings and capital punishment, is remarkably compressed by Boris Ingster's direction. But the star is the expressionistic camerawork of maestro Nicholas Musuraca. AT

Peter Lorre *The Stranger* • John McGuire *Michael Ward* • Margaret Tallichet *Jane* • Elisha Cook Jr *Joe Briggs* • Charles Waldron *District attorney* • Charles Halton *Meng* • Ethel Griffies *Mrs Kane* • Cliff Clark *Martin* ■ *Dir* Boris Ingster • *Scr* Frank Partos, from his story

Stranger than Fiction ★★ 18

Black comedy thriller 1999 · US · Colour · 95min

A dark comedy thriller that is just a little clever for its own good, this begins intriguingly, but eventually spirals out of control. The plot revolves around a group of young friends who agree to cover up an accidental killing one of their number has committed. However, as they dig themselves deeper and deeper into trouble, it transpires that some of them may have been a little economical with the truth. JF *DVD*

MacKenzie Astin *Jared* • Todd Field *Austin* • Dina Meyer *Emma* • Natasha Gregson Wagner *Violet* ■ *Dir* Eric Bross • *Scr* Tim Garrick, Scott Russell

Stranger than Fiction ★★★★ 12

Fantasy comedy drama
2006 · US · Colour · 108min

Following in the footsteps of *Being John Malkovich* and *I ♥ Huckabees*, the loopy premise here is that mild-mannered Will Ferrell begins to hear voices – well, actually one voice, which seems to be narrating his life. A visit to a literature professor (Dustin Hoffman) reveals that the author of his story is Kay Eiffel (Emma Thompson) and she is indeed in control of his destiny. The trouble is that all her novels end in death. In less talented hands, this kind of forced intellectual whimsy can be irritating, but with the understated direction of *Finding Neverland*'s Marc Forster, the decidedly odd is perfectly believable. And Ferrell, like Bill Murray and Robin Williams, proves that comic actors can give affecting dramatic performances. AS Some swearing. *DVD* ♪

Will Ferrell *Harold Crick* • Maggie Gyllenhaal *Ana Pascal* • Dustin Hoffman *Professor Jules Hilbert* • Queen Latifah *Penny Escher* • Emma Thompson *Karen "Kay" Eiffel* • Tom Hulce *Dr Cayly* • Linda Hunt *Dr Mittag-Leffler* ■ *Dir* Marc Forster • *Scr* Zach Helm

Stranger than Paradise ★★★★ 15

Road movie drama 1984 · US · BW · 85min

Developed from a 30-minute short and made for a mere $120,000, this chilled-out road movie could be seen as the first slacker picture. Shot in long takes, each ending with a dawdling fade to black, the action (if that's the word) centres on Hungarian immigrant John Lurie, his cousin Eszter Balint and his mate Richard Edson, and their driftings between New York, Cleveland and Florida. The winner of the Caméra d'Or at Cannes, this is an irresistible film, which warned us all that the only thing to expect from Jim Jarmusch is the unexpected. DP Swearing. *DVD* ♪

John Lurie *Willie* • Eszter Balint *Eva* • Richard Edson *Eddie* • Cecilia Stark *Aunt Lottie* • Danny Rosen *Billy* • Sara Driver *Girl with hat* ■ *Dir/Scr* Jim Jarmusch • *Cinematographer* Tom DiCillo

Stranger with My Face ★★

Mystery thriller 2009 · Can · Colour · 96min

Adopted teen Alexz Johnson uncovers dark and dangerous secrets following her dad's unexpected death in this far-fetched supernatural chiller. A loose adaptation of Lois Duncan's popular novel, the TV movie falls over itself to be spooky, becoming dafter in the process. Doppelgangers, astral projection and trapped souls are just part of the chuck-everything-in mumbo-jumbo; keeping the narrative intriguing, admittedly, but being too unconvincingly handled to have much impact. Thankfully, Johnson's emotionally subtle double performance holds the feature together, even in the weak final act. SF

Catherine Hicks *Shelley Stratton* • Alexz Johnson *Laurie Stratton/Lia Abbot* • Beau Mirchoff *Gordon* • Leah Gibson *Lia's nurse* • Luisa D'Oliveira *Nat* • Emily Hirst *Alexis Stratton* ■ *Dir* Jeff Renfroe • *Scr* Jamie Pachino, Eric Tuchman, from the novel by Lois Duncan

Strangerland ★★★ 15

Thriller 2015 · Aus/Ire · Colour · 106min

While director Kim Farrant superbly captures the haunting beauty of the Aussie interior in her debut feature, she stumbles when it comes to the emotional landscape. The strained marriage of Nicole Kidman and Joseph Fiennes disintegrates further when their two children disappear into the wilderness. But the intriguing mystery becomes submerged in melodrama, as Kidman's grip on reality begins to crumble. A missed opportunity, though the performances are first-rate. JF *DVD* *BD*

Nicole Kidman *Catherine Parker* • Joseph Fiennes *Matthew Parker* • Hugo Weaving *Detective Rae* • Maddison Brown *Lily Parker* • Nicholas Hamilton *Tom Parker* ■ *Dir* Kim Farrant • *Scr* Fiona Seres, Michael Kinirons, from a story by Seres

The Strangers ★★★ 15

Horror thriller 2007 · US · Colour · 81min

Writer/director Bryan Bertino makes an impressive debut with this lean, chilling home-invasion thriller. Liv Tyler and Scott Speedman play the couple returning from a friend's wedding to his family's secluded holiday home. Tired and drunk, their relationship has a crisis and it's about to get a lot worse as a knock on their door heralds a night of terror from three masked assailants. With a clear grasp of the mechanics of suspense, and a crisp, spare style, Bertino employs long periods of unbearably potent silence to ramp up the ominous atmosphere and let his unsettling images do the stalking. Tense, scary and nail-bitingly effective. AJ *DVD* *BD*

Liv Tyler *Kristen McKay* • Scott Speedman *James Hoyt* • Gemma Ward *Dollface* • Kip Weeks *The Man in the Mask* • Laura Margolis *Pin-Up Girl* • Glenn Howerton *Mike* ■ *Dir/Scr* Bryan Bertino

The Stranger's Hand ★★★ U

Spy thriller 1953 · It/UK · BW · 85min

This intriguing Cold War thriller is most memorable for director Mario Soldati's inspired use of the magic and mystery of Venice. Richard O'Sullivan impresses as the young boy who goes in search of his kidnapped father, receiving sympathetic support from unlikely hero Richard Basehart and hotel receptionist Alida Valli. Trevor Howard appears all too briefly as the missing major, but author Graham Greene contributes a cameo, as the hand untying the mooring rope of one of the gondolas. DP

Trevor Howard *Major Court* • Alida Valli *Roberta* • Richard Basehart *Joe Hamstringer* • Eduardo Ciannelli *Dr Vivaldi* • Richard O'Sullivan *Roger Court* ■ *Dir* Mario Soldati • *Scr* Guy Elmes, Giorgio Bassani, from the story by Graham Greene

A Stranger's Heart ★★

Romantic drama 2007 · US · Colour · 85min

This syrupy and contrived romantic drama sees writer Samantha Mathis gradually fall in love with practical joker Peter Dobson as

they both undergo heart transplant operations. Though the hospital scenes are realistically moving, with Mathis capturing the fear and confusion of her situation, the button-pushing events that follow seriously stretch credibility. The notion that two people should be linked literally by their hearts is charming but overly convenient, while the duo's obsession with their donors' orphaned daughter feels more bizarre than poignant. SF

Samantha Mathis *Callie* • Peter Dobson *Jasper* • Mary Matilyn Mouser *Sarah "Cricket" Cummings* • Gina Hecht *Darlene* • Kevin Kilner *Doc Jackson* • Raynor Scheine *Frank* ■ *Dir* Andy Wolk • *Scr* Kelli Pryor

Strangers Kiss ★★★★ 15

Romantic drama
1983 · US · Colour and BW · 93min

This cleverly conceived and well-executed drama has as its obvious inspiration Stanley Kubrick's *Killer's Kiss*, but without that film's steely black-and-white photography. Mikhail Suslov's colour shots are more akin to the lush melodramas that Douglas Sirk used to make for producer Ross Hunter. Peter Coyote is outstanding as the obsessive director prepared to endanger the life of his star Victoria Tennant to complete his picture. Intricate, astute and very classy. DP

Peter Coyote *Stanley* • Victoria Tennant *Carol Redding* • Blaine Novak *Stevie Blake* • Dan Shor *Farris* • Richard Romanus *Frank Silva* • Linda Kerridge *Shirley* • Carlos Palomino *Estoban* ■ *Dir* Matthew Chapman • *Scr* Blaine Novak, Matthew Chapman, from a story by Blaine Novak

Strangers May Kiss ★★★

Romantic drama 1931 · US · BW · 83min

In love with foreign correspondent Neil Hamilton, Norma Shearer is heartbroken when he goes off on an assignment. She dallies with a series of lovers in Europe and finally decides to go home and marry her faithful suitor Robert Montgomery, whereupon Hamilton reappears. Shearer holds the screen in the kind of role she played almost peerlessly countless times. Typical of its time, this is very good if not quite the very best. RK

Norma Shearer *Lisbeth Corbin* • Robert Montgomery *Steve* • Neil Hamilton *Alan* • Marjorie Rambeau *Geneva* • Irene Rich *Celia* • Hale Hamilton *Andrew* ■ *Dir* George Fitzmaurice • *Scr* John Meehan, from the novel by Ursula Parrott • *Cinematographer* William Daniels (1)

Strangers on a Train ★★★★★ PG

Classic thriller 1951 · US · BW · 96min

This splendid thriller is testimony to Alfred Hitchcock's mastery of technique and his ability to transform even the most unpromising start into a gripping movie. After nearly a dozen writers had turned down the chance to adapt Patricia Highsmith's novel, Raymond Chandler stepped into the breach, only to disagree with Hitch on several key scenes and suffer the humiliation of having his dialogue polished by Czenzi Ormonde, a staff writer. Hitchcock was also underwhelmed by Farley Granger in a role he felt cried out for William Holden. Nevertheless, he turns the murderous proposal of eccentric playboy Robert Walker to tennis champ Granger into a veritable nail-biter, with the two fairground scenes outstanding. DP *DVD*

Farley Granger *Guy Haines* • Ruth Roman *Anne Morton* • Robert Walker *Bruno Antony* • Leo G Carroll *Senator Morton* • Patricia Hitchcock *Barbara Morton* • Laura Elliot *Miriam* • Marion Lorne *Mrs Antony* • Jonathan Hale *Mr Antony* ■ *Dir* Alfred Hitchcock • *Scr* Raymond Chandler, Czenzi Ormonde, Whitfield Cook, from the novel by Patricia Highsmith

The Stranger's Return ★★ U

Drama 1933 · US · BW · 87min

Having left her husband, Miriam Hopkins goes to live with her grandfather Lionel Barrymore on his farm in the Midwest, where she becomes passionately involved with married man and father Franchot Tone. Meanwhile, Barrymore, who is facing

approaching death, has to fend off the grasping relatives who are trying to get their clutches on his land. King Vidor directs this dour drama which, despite its excellent cast, remains unappealing. RK

Lionel Barrymore *Grandpa Storr* • Miriam Hopkins *Louise Storr* • Franchot Tone *Guy Crane* • Stuart Erwin *Simon, farmhand* • Irene Hervey *Nettie Crane* • Beulah Bondi *Beatrice* ■ *Dir* King Vidor • *Scr* Brown Holmes, Phil Stong, from the novel by Phil Stong

Strangers When We Meet ★★★ 15

Romantic drama 1960 · US · Colour · 112min

A sophisticated study of compulsive marital infidelity starring Kirk Douglas and Kim Novak, beautifully acted and glamorously photographed, this is marred only by a syrupy music score that undermines the bittersweet pathos of the events portrayed. Director Richard Quine's use of landscape and roadside assignations works well, and the supporting cast is exemplary. Despite censorship limitations at the time, Evan Hunter's adaptation of his own novel has the ring of truth to it. TS

Kirk Douglas *Larry Coe* • Kim Novak *Maggie Gault* • Ernie Kovacs *Roger Altar* • Barbara Rush *Eve Coe* • Walter Matthau *Felix Anders* • Virginia Bruce *Mrs Wagner* • Kent Smith *Stanley Baxter* ■ *Dir* Richard Quine • *Scr* Evan Hunter, from his novel

Strapless ★★ 15

Romantic drama 1988 · UK · Colour · 95min

This is a rather jarring and unconvincing look at romance from David Hare. Blair Brown is the 40-something doctor who re-evaluates her life when she is wooed by charming but unreliable Bruno Ganz. More believable is the relationship between Brown and her younger, freer – and pregnant – sister played by Bridget Fonda. This drama suffers from stilted dialogue and direction and an overall condescending attitude towards female independence. JB

Blair Brown *Lillian Hempel* • Bridget Fonda *Amy Hempel* • Bruno Ganz *Raymond Forbes* • Alan Howard *Mr Cooper* • Michael Gough *Douglas Brodie* • Hugh Laurie *Colin* • Suzanne Burden *Romaine Salmon* • Rohan McCullough *Annie Rice* ■ *Dir/Scr* David Hare

Strategic Air Command ★★★ U

Drama 1955 · US · Colour · 113min

In this unconvincing combination of domestic melodrama and high-flying flag-waving, James Stewart plays a baseball player-turned-bomber pilot, with June Allyson as his wife. Paramount's biggest money-spinner of 1955, the film is most effective during the thrilling aerial sequences. Director Anthony Mann seems more at home with the male-bonding between Stewart and his fellow trainee pilots, but Allyson still makes an impact in a role less saccharine than usual. DP

James Stewart *Lt Col Robert "Dutch" Holland* • June Allyson *Sally Holland* • Frank Lovejoy *General Ennis C Hawkes* • Barry Sullivan *Lt Col Rocky Samford* • Alex Nicol *Ike Knowland* • Bruce Bennett *General Espy* • Jay C Flippen *Doyle* ■ *Dir* Anthony Mann • *Scr* Valentine Davies, Beirne Lay Jr, from a story by Beirne Lay Jr • *Cinematographers* William Daniels (1), Tom Tutwiler

The Stratford Adventure ★★★ U

Documentary 1954 · Can · Colour · 44min

This Oscar-nominated documentary chronicles the sterling efforts of Stratford, Ontario, to stage an annual festival of Shakespeare. The local bigwigs get together, raise enough for a shoestring budget and persuade Tyrone Guthrie to produce the plays. Guthrie in turn persuades Alec Guinness to star in *All's Well That Ends Well* and *Richard III*, with a cast that also includes Irene Worth (who later starred with Guinness in *The Scapegoat*). Theatre fans won't want to miss this chance to see snatches of Guinness in these classic plays; they should also read his marvellous account of the festival in his 1985 memoir *Blessings in Disguise*. AT

■ *Dir* Morten Parker • *Scr* Gudrun Parker

The Stratton Story ★★★ U

Biographical sports drama
1949 · US · BW · 106min

Douglas Morrow won a best original story Oscar for this biopic of Monty Stratton, the impoverished southern cotton picker who became a baseball star with the Chicago White Sox until a freak hunting accident threatened his career. James Stewart is typically affable in the lead, but he also does a good job of conveying Stratton's post-injury bitterness. In the first of a trio of collaborations with Stewart, June Allyson is just a tad too perfect. DP

James Stewart *Monty Stratton* • June Allyson *Ethel Stratton* • Frank Morgan *Barney Wile* • Agnes Moorehead *Ma Stratton* • Bill Williams *Eddie Dibson* • Bruce Cowling *Ted Lyons* • Cliff Clark *Josh Higgins* ■ *Dir* Sam Wood • *Scr* Douglas Morrow, Guy Trosper, from a story by Douglas Morrow

Straw Dogs ★★★★ 18

Thriller
1971 · UK · Colour · 116min

Mild-mannered maths teacher Dustin Hoffman finds his manhood tested when, after he moves to a Cornish village, the local toughs viciously rape his wife Susan George and threaten his home. One of the key movies in the controversial 1970s debate about unacceptable screen violence, director Sam Peckinpah's cynical parable virtually states that all pacifists are cowardly thugs under their liberal exteriors. Reprehensible and disturbing in equal measure, this pitch black revenge drama remains potent and shocking, particularly the much-discussed rape scene. AJ Graphic violence, swearing, nudity. *DVD* Bl

Dustin Hoffman *David Sumner* • Susan George *Amy Sumner* • Peter Vaughan *Tom Hedden* • TP McKenna *Major Scott* • Del Henney *Venner* • Ken Hutchison *Scutt* • Colin Welland *Reverend Hood* • Jim Norton *Cawsey* ■ *Dir* Sam Peckinpah • *Scr* David Zelag Goodman, Sam Peckinpah, from the novel *The Siege of Trencher's Farm* by Gordon M Williams

Straw Dogs ★★ 18

Thriller
2011 · US · Colour · 105min

If you've never seen Sam Peckinpah's 1971 controversial original, or if you've seen it but don't rate it, then this slick remake is adequate enough. Here, the action is relocated from rural England to redneck America as newlyweds David (James Marsden) and Amy (Kate Bosworth) move to her Mississippi home town, where Amy is soon back on the radar of an ex-boyfriend (*True Blood's* Alexander Skarsgard) and his bozo buddies. The acting is OK and, if the scenes of rape and violence are no longer as shocking as they were 40 years ago, that may be more a reflection of how audiences have become inured to such things than of any shortcomings in the way it's directed by Rod Lurie (*The Contender*). DA *DVD* Bl

James Marsden *David Sumner* • Kate Bosworth *Amy Sumner* • Alexander Skarsgård *Charlie* • James Woods *Tom Heddon* • Dominic Purcell *Jeremy Niles* • Laz Alonso *John Burke* • Willa Holland *Janice Hedaon* ■ *Dir* Rod Lurie • *Scr* Rod Lurie, from the 1971 film

Strawberry and Chocolate ★★★ 18

Drama
1993 · Cub · Colour · 105min

Considering that America has tried to prevent the worldwide distribution of Cuban films, it is remarkable that the island's first gay movie should have been nominated for the best foreign film Oscar. It was co-directed by Juan Carlos Tabio and Tomás Gutiérrez Alea, the latter perhaps the most gifted of all Cuban film-makers. However, what should have been a witty and subversive aside on Cuban socio-sexual politics is, in fact, a showy, rather obvious film. DP Spanish +subtitles. Sex scenes, nudity.

Jorge Perugorría *Diego* • Vladimir Cruz *David* • Mirta Ibarra *Nancy* • Francisco Gattorno *Miguel* ■ *Dir* Tomás Gutiérrez Alea, Juan Carlos Tabío • *Scr* Senel Paz, from his story *El Lobo, El Bosque y el Hombre Nuevo*

The Strawberry Blonde ★★★★ U

Romantic comedy
1941 · US · BW · 94min

Dentists don't often get to play romantic leads in the movies, but James Cagney does his bit by playing a struggling tooth-doctor. It's an agreeable comedy, set in late 19th-century New York, with the action flashing back to tell of Cagney's enduring passion for Rita Hayworth (in the title role). But his ultimate discovery is that, in nice, sweet Olivia de Havilland, he has married the right woman all along. PF

James Cagney *Biff Grimes* • Olivia de Havilland *Amy Lind* • Rita Hayworth *Virginia Brush* • Alan Hale *Old Man Grimes* • Jack Carson *Hugo Barnstead* • George Tobias *Nicholas Pappalas* • Una O'Connor *Mrs Mulcahey* ■ *Dir* Raoul Walsh • *Scr* Julius J Epstein, Philip G Epstein, from the play *One Sunday Afternoon* by James Hogan

Strawberry Fields ★★★ 15

Drama
2011 · UK · Colour · 83min

Strawberry-picking season on a Kent farm is the unusual setting for a rites-of-passage psychological drama from a BBC-supported scheme designed to foster new film-making talent. Two sisters arrive at the farm, only for it to become clear that flamoyant yet needy sister Gillian is determined to crush her sibling's independence. Convincing performances from the female leads create the sense of an intimate yet hopelessly conflicted family bond with a history that's led up to this flashpoint. TJ Violence, swearing, sex scenes, drug abuse. *DVD*

Anna Madeley *Gillian* • Christine Bottomley *Emily* • Emun Elliott *Kev* • Florence Bell *Sammy* ■ *Dir* Frances Lea • *Scr* Frances Lea, Judith Johnson

The Strawberry Statement ★★★

Political drama
1970 · US · Colour · 108min

Easy Rider showed studio executives that there was a huge, untapped youth audience out there, running riot on the nation's campuses to protest against the Vietnam War. So Hollywood quickly came over all radical with movies such as this, in which student Bruce Davison is turned into a militant and free love advocate by fellow student Kim Darby. It all ends with a frenzied riot and a stand-off with the National Guard while John Lennon sings *Give Peace a Chance*. AT

Bruce Davison *Simon* • Kim Darby *Linda* • Bud Cort *Elliot, the coxswain* • Murray MacLeod *George* ■ *Dir* Stuart Hagmann • *Scr* Israel Horovitz, from the novel *The Strawberry Statement: Notes of a College Revolutionary* by James Simon Kunen

Stray Dog ★★★ PG

Crime drama
1949 · Jpn · BW · 117min

As is often the case with Akira Kurosawa, this is a film in which a quest results in self-discovery. Here, rookie detective Toshiro Mifune has his pistol stolen on a crowded bus and begins painstakingly tracking down the culprit as the gun is used in a series of crimes. Kurosawa gives the action an authentic feel by shooting in the more run-down areas of Tokyo, emphasising the sticky summer heat and Mifune's self-loathing. A minor but compelling work. DP Japanese +subtitles. *DVD*

Toshiro Mifune *Murakami* • Takashi Shimura *Sato* • Ko Kimura [Isao Kimura] *Yuro* • Keiko Awaji *Harumi* • Reisaburo Yamamoto *Hondo* ■ *Dir* Akira Kurosawa • *Scr* Ryuzo Kikushima, Akira Kurosawa, from a novel by Akira Kurosawa

Stray Dogs ★★★ 12

Drama
2004 · Iran/Fr · Colour · 88min

Iranian director Marziyeh Meshkini makes discomforting use of the desolate conditions in post-Taliban Afghanistan in this effective, but rather contrived reworking of Vittorio De Sica's neorealist classic, *Bicycle Thieves* (1948). Non-professionals Zahed and Gol-Ghotai deliver miraculous performances as the young siblings left to fend for themselves after their mother is imprisoned on adultery charges. But while the waifs' attachment to a frisky terrier rescued from the bombed-out ruins is quaint and their resourceful approach to survival is endearing, Meshkini isn't always able to keep sentimentality at bay. DP Farsi +subtitles. *DVD*

Gol-Ghotai *Girl* • Zahed *Boy* • Agheleh Rezaie *Mother* • Sohrab Akbari *Atef, guard* • Jamil Ghanizadeh *Angry guard* ■ *Dir/Scr* Marziyeh Meshkini

Strayed ★★★ 15

Second World War romantic drama
2003 · Fr/UK · Colour · 95min

Director André Téchiné's recurrent fascination with the emotional vagaries of youth informs this typically efficient adaptation. But, although this is a consistently intriguing insight into the unspoken suspicions and unholy alliances that dominated French life during the Second World War, Parisian widow Emmanuelle Béart's dependence on opportunistic country boy Gaspard Ulliel doesn't always ring true. Despite making evocative use of his locations and generating a disconcerting mood of ambiguity, Téchiné succumbs to rose-tinted lapses that undermine the story's credibility. DP French +subtitles. Sex scenes.

Emmanuelle Béart *Odile* • Gaspard Ulliel *Yvan* • Grégoire Leprince-Ringuet *Philippe* • Clémence Meyer *Cathy* • Jean Fornerod *Georges* ■ *Dir* André Téchiné • *Scr* Gilles Taurand, André Téchiné, from the novel *Le Garçon aux Yeux Gris* by Gilles Perrault

Streamers ★★★ 15

Drama
1983 · US · Colour · 113min

Up close and personal animosity comes to the boil in the one-set locality of an army barracks dormitory. Director Robert Altman developed the film from its original stage context, in much the same way as he did with his earlier offering, *Come Back to the Five and Dime, Jimmy Dean, Jimmy Dean*. The screenplay is an adaptation by David Rabe of his own Broadway venture and its claustrophobic tensions are expanded thanks to fine acting, especially from Matthew Modine and Michael Wright. TH *DVD*

Matthew Modine *William "Billy" Wilson* • Michael Wright *Carlyle* • Mitchell Lichtenstein *Richard "Richie" Douglas* • David Alan Grier *Roger Hicks* • Guy Boyd *Sergeant Rooney* • George Dzundza *Sergeant Cokes* ■ *Dir* Robert Altman • *Scr* David Rabe, from his play

Street Angel ★★ PG

Silent drama
1928 · US · BW · 97min

At the first Academy Awards, Janet Gaynor was voted best actress winner for three films: director Frank Borzage's *7th Heaven* and *Street Angel* and, best of all, FW Murnau's *Sunrise*. The least of these is *Street Angel*, a turgidly sentimental melodrama. It's the tale of a Neapolitan slum girl who resorts to illegal means to procure medicine for her sick mother. She temporarily avoids arrest by joining a circus, where artist Charles Farrell paints her as the Madonna. The film is now little more than a barely tolerable collector's item. Principally silent, it includes some sound sequences. RK *DVD*

Janet Gaynor *Angela* • Charles Farrell (1) *Gino* • Alberto Rabagliati *Policeman* • Gino Conti *Policeman* • Guido Trento *Neri, police sergeant* ■ *Dir* Frank Borzage • *Scr* Marion Orth, Katherine Hilliker (titles), HH Caldwell (titles), Philip Klein, Henry Roberts Symonds, from the novel *Cristilina* by Monckton Hoffe

Street Angel ★★★★

Romance
1937 · Chi · BW · 100min

Yuan Muzhi reaffirmed his left-wing credentials with this socially critical, yet warmly human drama, which proved to be his final feature. Both a tribute to the spirit of the poor and an indictment of Shanghai's post-colonial indifference, it is, essentially, a moving love story in which naive musician Zhao Dan attempts to rescue Manchurian exile Zhou Xuan from prostitution. However, with its frank discussion of contentious issues, its roots in traditional Chinese art and its stylistic debt to Hollywood and Soviet cinema, it merits its reputation as a proto-neorealist study. DP Mandarin +subtitles.

Zhao Dan *Chen Shaoping* • Wei Heling *Wang, newspaper seller* • Zhou Xuan *Xiao Hong, little singer* • Zhao Huishen *Xiao Yun* ■ *Dir/Scr* Yuan Muzhi

The Street Fighter ★★★ 18

Martial arts action
1974 · Jpn · Colour and BW · 86min

After more than a decade jobbing in Japanese B-movies, Sonny Chiba found international fame in this shameless Bruce Lee rip-off. Echoes of Akira Kurosawa's samurai masterpiece, *Yojimbo*, also abound as Chiba lets rip aboard an oil tanker after discovering that the yakuza who hired him to kidnap an heiress has reneged on the deal. The brutality of the fight sequences would recur in the sequels *Return of the Street Fighter* and *The Street Fighter's Last Revenge*. DP In Japanese. *DVD*

Shinichi Chiba [Sonny Chiba] *Terry Tsuguri* • Waichi Yamada [Gerald Yamada] *Ratnose* • Yutaka Nakajima *Sarai* • Tony Cetera *Jadot* • Masashi Ishibashi *Junjou* ■ *Dir* Shigehiro Ozawa • *Scr* Koji Takada, Motohiro Torii

Street Fighter ★ 12

Action adventure
1994 · US · Colour · 97min

Jean-Claude Van Damme and Kylie Minogue team up for a movie adaptation of the popular computer game. If that unlikely pairing isn't enough to put you off, the simple-minded plot will. It concerns an assignment to overthrow dictator Raul Julia. Laughably bad. AJ Violence, swearing. *DVD* Bl *CS*

Jean-Claude Van Damme *Colonel William F Guile* • Raul Julia *Bison* • Wen Ming-Na [Ming-Na] *Chun-Li* • Damian Chapa *Ken* • Kylie Minogue *Cammy* • Simon Callow *AN official* • Roshan Seth *Dhalsim* • Wes Studi *Sagat* ■ *Dir/Scr* Steven E de Souza

Street Kings ★★ 15

Crime drama
2008 · US · Colour · 104min

James Ellroy, the author of *LA Confidential*, returns to familiar territory co-writing this brooding cop drama. In fact, it's a tad too familiar. Hugh Laurie plays the Internal Affairs honcho who suspects that Keanu Reeves's widowed policeman has killed a fellow policeman to cover previous violations. Director David Ayer (who wrote the Oscar-winning *Training Day*) generates a fair amount of intrigue as he examines the rogue cop's motives. It's just a shame that Reeves can't put across the same complexity, and that the script succumbs to cliché. SP *DVD* Bl

Keanu Reeves *Detective Tom Ludlow* • Forest Whitaker *Captain Jack Wander* • Hugh Laurie *Captain James Biggs* • Chris Evans *Detective Paul Diskant* • Cedric "The Entertainer" *Kyles [Cedric the Entertainer] Scribble* • Jay Mohr *Sergeant Mike Clady* • Terry Crews *Detective Terrence Washington* • Naomie Harris *Linda Washington* • Common *Coates* ■ *Dir* David Ayer • *Scr* James Ellroy, Kurt Wimmer, Jamie Moss, from a story by Ellroy

Street of Crocodiles ★★★ PG

Animation
1986 · UK · Colour and BW · 20min

A puppet warily explores the darkened rooms of a deserted lecture hall and finds other dolls acting in strange ways in a typical stop-motion animation production from the idiosyncratic Brothers Quay. This is gloomy, creepy and quite unsettling – Stephen and Timothy Quay tap into our worst childhood nightmares and the claustrophobic end result couldn't be further from the colourful fantasy of Ray Harryhausen. A relentlessly downbeat and unique nightmare, which continuously offers up one startling image after another. AJ

S

Street of No Return ★★ 18
Action crime thriller
1989 · Fr/Por · Colour · 88min

Forty years after making his debut, Samuel Fuller wound up his directorial career with this disappointing adaptation. Here Keith Carradine plays a singer who falls foul of the underworld after he decides to take a sabbatical from stardom in the company of gangster's moll, Valentina Vargas. But once Carradine begins skulking round the backstreets seeking revenge on those who slit his throat, the action descends into thick-ear violence. DP

Keith Carradine *Michael* · Valentina Vargas *Celia* · Bill Duke *Ltt Borel* · Andréa Ferréol *Rhoda* · Bernard Fresson *Morin* ■ *Dir* Samuel Fuller · *Scr* Samuel Fuller, Jacques Bral, from the novel by David Goodis

Street of Shadows ★★ PG
Thriller
1953 · UK · BW · 80min

They used to churn out these pseudo *noir* thrillers by the van load in the early 1950s with varying degrees of success. This one moves along at a brisk trot, but basically there is little else to commend it, apart from a workmanlike performance by Cesar Romero as a casino owner madly in love with Kay Kendall. The consistently underrated Kendall often had a strange luminescent quality on screen and this film shows it to moody advantage. SH

Cesar Romero *Luigi* · Kay Kendall *Barbara Gale* · Edward Underdown *Inspector Johnstone* · Victor Maddern *Limpy* · Simone Silva *Angele Abbe* · Liam Gaffney *Fred Roberts* · Robert Cawdron *Sergeant Hadley* · John Penrose *Captain Gerald Gale* · Bill Travers *Nigel Langley* ■ *Dir* Richard Vernon · *Scr* Richard Vernon, from the novel *The Creaking Chair* by Lawrence Meynall

Street of Shame ★★★★ 12
Drama
1955 · Jpn · BW · 85min

Set in Dreamland, in Tokyo's Yoshiwara red-light district, this study of oppressed womanhood was the final feature of Kenji Mizoguchi. Though denied the chance to shoot on location in docudramatic style, he exposes the exploitation and hypocrisy of bordello life with such power that the film was credited at the time with swaying the Diet during its debates on prostitution. The most impressive performance comes from Machiko Kyo as the flint-hearted hooker, who mercilessly denounces the father whose excesses have condemned her to unrelenting misery. Not the great director's most accomplished picture, but still a fitting swan song. DP Japanese +subtitles. DVD

Machiko Kyo *Mickey* · Ayako Wakao *Yasumi* · Aiko Mimasu *Yumeko* · Michiyo Kogure *Hanae* · Kumeko Urabe *Otane* · Yasuko Kawakami *Shizuko* · Hiroko Machida *Yorie* · Eitaro Shindo *Kurazo Taya, proprietor of Dreamland* ■ *Dir* Kenji Mizoguchi · *Scr* Masashige Narusawa, from the story *Susaki no Onna* by Yoshiko Shibaki

Street Scene ★★★★
Drama
1931 · US · BW · 80min

Adapted by Elmer Rice from his play and directed by King Vidor, the film covers the events of a night and morning in the lives of tenement dwellers during a stifling Manhattan summer. It centres on young Sylvia Sidney and her unhappy mother's illicit affair, which leads to tragedy. Dated, and sometimes stagey, this is still riveting as an early attempt to capture a slice of tenement life and as an evocation of New York's melting pot of immigrants. It was a step on the way to stardom for Sidney, young, beautiful and demonstrating the poignant quality that became her trademark. RK

Sylvia Sidney *Rose Maurrant* · William Collier [William Collier Jr] *Sam Kaplan* · Estelle Taylor *Anna Maurrant* · Beulah Bondi *Emma Jones* · Max Montor *Abe Kaplan* · David Landau *Frank Maurrant* · Matt McHugh *Vincent Jones* ■ *Dir* King Vidor · *Scr* Elmer Rice, from his play

Street Smart ★★ 18
Thriller based on a true story
1987 · US · Colour · 92min

Journalistic ethics come under rather fuzzy scrutiny in a tepid thriller based on a true story. Christopher Reeve plays a struggling magazine writer who finds his career taking off after the publication of his fictional exposé of Manhattan prostitution. Despite his success, Reeve soon discovers that his story has some very deadly consequences in a slow-moving melodrama sparked into sporadic life by Morgan Freeman's Oscar-nominated portrayal of a lowlife pimp. AJ

Christopher Reeve *Jonathan Fisher* · Morgan Freeman *Fast Black* · Kathy Baker *Punchy* · Mimi Rogers *Alison Parker* · Jay Patterson *Leonard Pike* · Andre Gregory *Ted Avery* ■ *Dir* Jerry Schatzberg · *Scr* David Freeman

A Street to Die ★★ PG
Drama
1985 · Aus · Colour · 92min

This is a brave drama about the effect on humans of the defoliant Agent Orange used during the Vietnam War. When an Australian ex-soldier with leukaemia discovers many of his fellow veterans are also afflicted with the condition, he initiates a lawsuit against the authorities. Well made and well acted (particularly by Chris Haywood), it's a sympathetic demonstration of the hidden casualties of war. JG

Chris Haywood *Col Turner* · Jennifer Cluff *Lorraine Turner* · Peter Hehir *Peter Townley* · Arianthe Galani *Dr Walsea* · Peter Kowitz *Craig* ■ *Dir/Scr* Bill Bennett

The Street with No Name ★★★★ PG
Crime thriller
1948 · US · BW · 87min

When, in his screen debut in *Kiss of Death*, Richard Widmark giggled as he pushed an old lady in a wheelchair down the stairs, 20th Century-Fox knew it had a star on its books. This follow-up casts him as a psychotic hypochondriac, always snorting on an inhaler and beating his wife. Not many screen villains looked nastier than Widmark in those days, his thin-lipped mouth and bony face epitomising the look of a man with antisocial tendencies. FBI agent Mark Stevens is the nominal hero, but he's no match for Widmark. AT DVD

Mark Stevens *Cordell* · Richard Widmark *Alec Stiles* · Lloyd Nolan *Inspector Briggs* · Barbara Lawrence *Judy Stiles* · Ed Begley *Chief Harmatz* · Donald Buka *Shivvy* · Joseph Pevney *Matty* · John McIntire *Cy Gordon* ■ *Dir* William Keighley · *Scr* Harry Kleiner

A Streetcar Named Desire ★★★★★ 12
Classic drama
1951 · US · BW · 124min

Marlon Brando is at the height of his powers here, reprising his acclaimed Broadway role as the brutal Stanley Kowalski in director Elia Kazan's classic adaptation of Tennessee Williams's play. Brando's bravura performance is matched by that of Vivien Leigh (as the neurotic southern belle Blanche DuBois) and their scenes together sizzle with sexual tension. The play's homosexual references were cut to comply with censorship rules of the day, though Blanche's implied violation and references to her sordid past remain. The film won four Oscars – awards for Leigh, Kim Hunter, Karl Malden and art director Richard Day – but Brando missed out to Humphrey Bogart for *The African Queen*. TH DVD

Vivien Leigh *Blanche DuBois* · Marlon Brando *Stanley Kowalski* · Kim Hunter *Stella Kowalski* · Karl Malden *Mitch* · Rudy Bond *Steve Hubbell* · Nick Dennis *Pablo Gonzales* · Peg Hillias *Eunice Hubbell* ■ *Dir* Elia Kazan · *Scr* Tennessee Williams, from his play, adapted by Oscar Saul · *Cinematographer* Harry Stradling · *Set Designer* George James Hopkins

StreetDance ★★★★ PG
Dance drama
2010 · UK · Colour · 94min

Stereotypes and stock situations are sprinkled across familiar territory in a nonetheless winning British take on *Save the Last Dance*. The plot sees street-dancer

Nichola Burley and ballet student Richard Winsor grudgingly bring out the best in each other as a contest looms, but the vitality in the direction makes the clichés feel fresh and even uplifting, turning this into a real crowd-pleaser. The dancing is ace, too, with show-stopping turns from *Britain's Got Talent* alumni George Sampson, Flawless and Diversity, and a smoking classical/hip-hop soundtrack. And Charlotte Rampling as a ballet teacher adds a touch of class. *StreetDance 2* came out in 2012. AJ Brief swearing. DVD Blu 3D

Nichola Burley *Carly* · Richard Winsor *Tomas* · Charlotte Rampling *Helena* · Ukweli Roach *Jay* · Frank Harper *Fred* · George Sampson *Eddie* · Eleanor Bron *Madame Fleurie* · Ashley Banjo *Aaron* · Diversity *Aaron's Crew* · Flawless *The Surge* ■ *Dir* Max [Max Giwa], Dania [Dania Pasquini] · *Scr* Jane English

StreetDance 2 ★★★★ PG
Dance drama
2012 · UK · Colour · 81min

The follow-up to the hit 2010 dance extravaganza has exactly the same recipe as before, only played out on a slicker canvas. Returning directors Max and Dania keep the easy charm intact, the characterisation on the right side of minimal and the tone consistently appealing. Falk Hentschel stars here as Ash, a freestyle dancer who combs Europe to find the best performers to win the Final Clash in Paris. But will his fusion of Latin and street thrill the hip-hop brigade, and can he learn to "share the moment" with hot salsa partner Sofia Boutella? Forget the plot as it's once again the dancing that counts here, and this is a sure-fire crowd-pleaser. AJ Some swearing, sexual references. DVD Blu

Falk Hentschel *Ash* · Sofia Boutella *Eva* · Tom Conti *Manu* · George Sampson *Eddie* · Akai Osei-Mansfield *Junior* · Flawless *The Surge Crew* ■ *Dir* Max [Max Giwa], Dania [Dania Pasquini] · *Scr* Jane English, from her characters

Streets ★★★ 18
Thriller
1990 · US · Colour · 80min

In a gritty, often gripping drama about teen runaways in LA, Christina Applegate plays a 14-year-old junkie prostitute. David Mendenhall is a clean-cut suburban boy who arrives in LA with the vague idea of becoming a rock star and saves Applegate from a violent punter. The movie follows the couple as the psychotic punter tries to track them down. Neither tub-thumping nor slick, the movie says what it has to say without sentimentality or toning down the violence, with a great performance from Applegate. DA

Christina Applegate *Dawn* · David Mendenhall *Sy* · Eb Lottimer *Lumley* · Patrick Richwood *Bob* · Kady Tran *Dawn's blonde roommate* · Mel Castelo *Elf* ■ *Dir* Katt Shea Ruben [Katt Shea] · *Scr* Katt Shea Ruben, Andy Ruben

Streets of Fire ★★★ 15
Romantic action fantasy
1984 · US · Colour · 89min

Director Walter Hill obviously had fun with this violent rock-fuelled fantasy shot in a sort of youth culture neverland. Viewers will have fun spotting the faces of future stars, although for Michael Paré, who plays the brooding loner hero, this was probably his career high spot. Paré arrives back in town just in time to gather up a posse of old friends and rescue his rock-star ex-girlfriend from the clutches of a merciless biker gang. Scored by the peerless Ry Cooder, the music also comes courtesy of retro-rockers the Blasters. JF DVD Blu

Michael Paré *Tom Cody* · Diane Lane *Ellen Aim* · Rick Moranis *Billy Fish* · Willem Dafoe *Raven* · Amy Madigan *McCoy* · Deborah Van Valkenburgh *Reva* · Bill Paxton *Clyde* · Lee Ving *Greer* · Robert Townsend *Lester* ■ *Dir* Walter Hill · *Scr* Walter Hill, Larry Gross

Streets of Gold ★★ 15
Sports drama
1986 · US · Colour · 89min

Distinguished Austrian actor Klaus Maria Brandauer swaps meaningful European cinema for big American clichés in this boxing drama. He brings detail and a hint of

depth to his role of Soviet champ turned dishwasher turned trainer, in a thrusting but dull outing. DP Swearing.

Klaus Maria Brandauer *Alek Neuman* · Wesley Snipes *Roland Jenkins* · Adrian Pasdar *Timmy Boyle* · Angela Molina *Elena Gitman* · Elya Baskin *Klebanov* ■ *Dir* Joe Roth · *Scr* Heywood Gould, Richard Price, Tim Cole, from a story by Dezso Magyar

Streets of Laredo ★★★ U
Western
1949 · US · Colour · 92min

This is an inferior remake of King Vidor's splendid 1936 western *The Texas Rangers*, in which three outlaw pals go their separate ways, with two becoming lawmen and ending up chasing the third. Nevertheless, there is a fine star-making performance from a deceptively casual William Holden, whose burgeoning screen presence demands attention, especially when dull co-star Macdonald Carey is on screen. The stunning Technicolor photography is really what gives this western its distinction. TS

William Holden (2) *Jim Dawkins* · Macdonald Carey *Lorn Reming* · Mona Freeman *Rannie Carter* · William Bendix *Wahoo Jones* · Stanley Ridges *Major Bailey* · Alfonso Bedoya *Charley Calico* ■ *Dir* Leslie Fenton · *Scr* Charles Marquis Warren, from a story by Louis Stevens, Elizabeth Hill · *Cinematographer* Ray Rennahan

Streetwise ★★★ 18
Documentary
1985 · US · Colour · 96min

This Academy Award-nominated documentary examines the nightmare flip side of the American Dream. Martin Bell's "shock doc" focuses on the teenagers who live rough on the streets of Seattle, where they earn what passes for a living as prostitutes, pimps, muggers and petty drug dealers. The film makes no judgements and offers no answers. This litany of lost souls is tough viewing. DA

■ *Dir* Martin Bell · *Scr* from the article *Streets of the Lost* in *Life* magazine by Mary Ellen Mark, Cheryl McCall · *Editor* Nancy Baker · *Music* Tom Waits

Strictly Ballroom ★★★★★ PG
Romantic comedy drama
1992 · Aus · Colour · 90min

Feel-good movies don't come any better than this Australian smash hit, which is an exuberant joy from sequined start to feathered finish. *Come Dancing* meets *Footloose* when rebel ballroom star Paul Mercurio hesitantly teams up with ugly duckling novice Tara Morice for an important contest. He wants to perform his own Latin routine, however, rather than the boring steps set by the conservative dancing federation. Will love be in the air? What do you think! As kitsch and as corny as anything, this hilariously heart-warming romantic comedy drama is the ideal pick-me-up. AJ Swearing. DVD Blu

Paul Mercurio *Scott Hastings* · Tara Morice *Fran* · Bill Hunter *Barry Fife* · Pat Thomson *Shirley Hastings* · Gia Carides *Liz Holt* · Peter Whitford *Les Kendall* · Barry Otto *Doug Hastings* · John Hannan *Ken Railings* · Sonia Kruger *Tina Sparkle* ■ *Dir* Baz Luhrmann · *Scr* Baz Luhrmann, Craig Pearce, from a story by Luhrmann, Andrew Bovell, from an original idea by Luhrmann and the NIDA stage production

Strictly Sinatra ★★ 15
Romantic crime drama
2000 · UK · Colour · 92min

Despite the efforts of actor/director Peter Capaldi in his feature debut and a strong cast, this takes us on yet another trip to turgid *Lock, Stock* territory. Ian Hart as the pseudo-Sinatra is sad, clad in shiny suits and sporting a dreadful perm. There's something inherently depressing about him as the film's focus; he sells out his pianist mentor Alun Armstrong and girlfriend Kelly Macdonald all too easily, and for a world that is so obviously full of hollow promises. Ironically the only great thing here is the Sinatra soundtrack. LH Swearing, violence. DVD

Street of No Return

■ *Dir* Stephen Quay, Timothy Quay · *Scr* Brothers Quay [Stephen Quay, Timothy Quay], from the short story collection *Ulica Krokodyli* by Bruno Schulz

Ian Hart *Toni Cocozza* • Kelly Macdonald *Irene* • Brian Cox (1) *Chisholm* • Alun Armstrong *Bill* • Tommy Flanagan *Michelangelo* • Iain Cuthbertson *Connolly* • Richard E Grant • Jimmy Tarbuck ■ *Dir/Scr* Peter Capaldi

Strike ★★★★ 12
Silent political drama 1924 · USSR · BW · 86min

Sergei Eisenstein's debut feature was an electrifying testament to the dramatic and intellectual power of cinema. It chronicles the suppression of a 1912 factory uprising after one of the workers committed suicide. The bold decision to focus on collective heroism invests the film with a scale and energy that is intensified by the brilliance of Eisenstein's rhythmic editing of Edouard Tissé's starkly realistic visuals. Juxtaposing images to give them satirical, metaphorical or emotional weight (the massacre being intercut with slaughterhouse scenes), Eisenstein transformed "kino-eye" footage into the "kino-fist" he hoped would inspire revolutionary endeavour. DP *DVD*

Grigori Alexandrov *Factory foreman* • Aleksandr Antonov [Aleksander Antonov] *Member of strike committee* • Yduit Glizer *Queen of Thieves* • Mikhail Gomorov *Worker* • I Ivanov *Chief of police* ■ *Dir* Sergei Eisenstein • *Scr* Sergei Eisenstein, Grigor Alexandrov, V Pletniev, I Kravtchunovsky

Strike! ★★★ 12
Comedy drama 1998 · US/Can · Colour · 93min

The girls of St Trinian's meet the *Dead Poets Society* in this sharp, witty tale of pupil power set in an exclusive American school in the early 1960s. Kirsten Dunst and Gaby Hoffmann are two of the students waging a campaign to prevent male pupils from being admitted to their beloved school. Rachael Leigh Cook and Lynn Redgrave are among the strong supporting cast. JF

Kirsten Dunst *Verena Von Stefan* • Gaby Hoffmann *Odette Sinclair* • Lynn Redgrave *Miss McVane* • Rachae Leigh Cook *Abby* • Tom Guiry *"Frosty" Frost* • Vincent Kartheiser *Snake* ■ *Dir/Scr* Sarah Kernochan

Strike Me Pink ★★★ U
Musical comedy 1936 · US · Colour · 95min

The last, but by no means least, of the six films Eddie Cantor made for Samuel Goldwyn is a wacky comedy with songs that allegedly utilised many more writers than those credited. Cantor is a mild tailor who, inspired by a book called *Man or Mouse: What Are You?*, agrees to run an amusement park that gangsters have targeted for their slot-machine business. The farcical consequences become surreal at times – tough guy Edward Brophy breaks into a ballet routine in one priceless sequence. TV

Eddie Cantor *Eddie Pink* • Ethel Merman *Joyce Lenox* • Sally Eilers *Claribel Hayes* • Parkyakarkus [Harry Einstein] *Harry Parke* • William Frawley *Copple* • Helen Lowell *Ma Carson* • Gordon Jones *Butch Carson* • Brian Donlevy *Vance* • Edward Brophy *Killer* ■ *Dir* Norman Taurog • *Scr* Frank Butler, Walter DeLeon, Francis Martin, Philip Rapp, from the novel *Dreamland* by Clarence Buddington Kelland • *Choreographer* Robert Alton

Strike Up the Band ★★★★ U
Musical 1940 · US · BW · 119min

This is one of the great MGM Judy Garland/ Mickey Rooney collaborations, a super Busby Berkeley-directed heartwarmer with a major bonus in a fine score. Very much of its period, from a time when band contests on radio were the peak of public entertainment and Paul Whiteman (here playing himself) was the "King of Jazz", this vehicle creates several marvellous moments for the two leads. The movie never palls during its long running time, and, despite the rubber-boned June Preisser, it's never unwatchable, avoiding the sentimentality that so often ruins these "let's put on a show" plots. TS

Mickey Rooney *Jimmy Connors* • Judy Garland *Mary Holden* • June Preisser *Barbara Frances Morgan* • William Tracy *Phillip Turner* • Ann Shoemaker *Mrs Connors* • Larry Nunn *Willie*

Brewster • George Lessey *Mr Morgan* • Phil Silvers *Pitch man* ■ *Dir* Busby Berkeley • *Scr* John Monks [John Monks Jr], Fred F Finklehoffe, Herbert Fields (uncredited), Kay Van Riper (uncredited)

Striking Distance ★★★ 18
Crime thriller 1993 · US · Colour · 97min

Bruce Willis plays his usual hard-nosed loner, who here finds himself relegated to the unfashionable water cops (and partnered with Sarah Jessica Parker) when he breaks ranks and testifies against a policeman. However, a serial killer with an unhealthy interest in Willis's life offers the chance of redemption. The aptly named Rowdy Herrington ensures the action roars along and that the set pieces are big and brash. JF A sex scene, swearing, violence. *DVD* *BL*

Bruce Willis *Tom Hardy* • Sarah Jessica Parker *Jo Christman* • Dennis Farina *Nick Detillo* • Tom Sizemore *Danny Det.llo* • Brion James *Detective Eddie Eiler* • Robert Pastorelli *Jimmy Detillo* • Timothy Busfield *Tony Sacco* • John Mahoney *Vince Hardy* ■ *Dir* Rowdy Herrington • *Scr* Rowdy Herrington, Martin Kaplan

The Stringer ★★★
Romantic drama 1997 · Rus/UK · Colour · 88min

Pawel Pawlikowski made his feature debut with this piercing insight into democratic Russia. The scene-setting sequences depicting the decay and potential for corruption and crime after decades of Communist misrule are both revealing and sobering. But the focus blurs once it falls on tele-news cameraman Sergei Bodrov Jr's relationships with British producer Anna Friel and Vladimir Ilyin's charismatic nationalist. The romantic subplot is pretty routine, while the thriller element that builds around a faked assassination attempt falters short of suspense. DP Russian, English +subtitles.

Anna Friel *Helen* • Sergei Bodrov Jr *Vadik Chernyshov* • Vladimir Ilyin *Yarvovsky* • Rob Knepper [Robert Knepper] *John* • Anna Kamenkova *Mother* ■ *Dir* Paul Pavlikovsky [Pawel Pawlikowski] • *Scr* Paul Pavlikovsky, Gennadi Ostrovsky

Strings ★★★★ PG
Puppet fantasy drama 2004 · Den/UK/Swe/Nor · Colour · 87min

This puppet fantasy drama from Danish director Anders Ronnow Klarlund dazzles with its technical virtuosity, inventiveness and scope. The story follows Hal (voiced by James McAvoy), the prince of Hebalon who infiltrates the kingdom of his people's bitter enemies, the Zeriths, in an attempt to avenge the apparent murder of his father. There he falls for the mysterious Zita (Catherine McCormack), while at home his wicked Uncle Nezo (Derek Jacobi) tries to take control. The film's strength comes from the wholly credible universe it establishes for its characters. This is an impressive piece of work that dares to be political while remaining consistently imaginative. AJ *DVD*

James McAvoy *Hal* • Catherine McCormack *Zita* • Julian Glover *Kahro* • Derek Jacobi *Nezo* • Ian Hart *Ghrak* • Claire Skinner *Jhinna* • David Harewood *Erito* • Samantha Bond (2) *Eike* ■ *Dir* Anders Ronnow Klarlund • *Scr* Naja Maria Aidt, Anders Ronnow Klarlund

The Strip ★★★
Crime drama 1951 · US · BW · 85min

Although *A Kiss to Build a Dream On* landed an Oscar nomination, turns by jazz greats such as Louis Armstrong and Vic Damone prove the highlight of this noirish story with music. Mickey Rooney, playing the drummer at a nightclub owned by William Demarest, demonstrates a talent for downbeat drama when his passion for dancer and would-be actress Sally Forrest lands him in deep with ruthless bookie James Craig. Offering intriguing insights into the seedier side of showbiz, this unsung film merits more than its minor cult status. DP

Mickey Rooney *Stanley Maxton* • Sally Forrest *Jane Tafford* • William Demarest *Fluff* • James Craig *Delwyn "Sonny" Johnson* • Kay Brown *Edna* • Tommy Rettig *Artie* • Tom Powers *Detective Bonnabel* ■ *Dir* Leslie Kardos • *Scr* Allen Rivkin

Strip Search ★★★
Political drama 2004 · US · Colour · 86min

At what point does healthy political dissent constitute disloyalty and a potential threat to national security? That's one of many difficult questions raised by Sidney Lumet's thought-provoking TV drama in which two graduate students (an American woman in China and an Arab man in New York) are arrested and questioned about suspected terrorist activities. The use of archive footage to make political points is sometimes heavy-handed, but Maggie Gyllenhaal and Bruno Lastra strike exactly the right balance as the detainees, while Glenn Close is mesmerising as an FBI interrogator. SS

Glenn Close *Karen Moore* • Maggie Gyllenhaal *Linda Sykes* • Bruno Lastra *Sharaf Bin Said* • Ken Leung *Liu Tsung-Yuan* • Tom Guiry *Gerry Sykes* ■ *Dir* Sidney Lumet • *Scr* Tom Fontana

Stripes ★★★ 15
Comedy 1981 · US · Colour · 101min

This was the breakthrough film for Bill Murray, whose sleazy charisma helps disguise the formulaic "you're in the army now" plotting. Layabout Murray and chum Harold Ramis (also co-writer) are conned into joining up, and Murray's sparring with the obligatory hard-nosed NCO (Warren Oates, in one of his last film roles) is a constant delight. A surprise hit, this comedy also provided early high profile roles for Judge Reinhold, John Candy and Sean Young. JF Violence, swearing, nudity. *DVD*

Bill Murray *John* • Harold Ramis *Russell* • Warren Oates *Sergeant Hulka* • PJ Soles *Stella* • Sean Young *Louise* • John Candy *Ox* • John Larroquette *Captain Stillman* • Judge Reinhold *Elmo* ■ *Dir* Ivan Reitman • *Scr* Len Blum, Dan Goldberg, Harold Ramis

The Stripper ★★★
Melodrama 1963 · US · BW · 94min

Politely retitled *Woman of Summer* in Britain, this is an atmospheric drama about a woman from small-town Kansas who, having failed as a movie actress, returns home as part of a sleazy dance troupe. There she gets involved with Claire Trevor's teenage son (Richard Beymer). Joanne Woodward is beautifully cast as the woman whose life resembles a never-ending car crash, though she's more self-reliant than wallowing in self-pity. The story is based on a play by William Inge and is fairly restrained compared to his other melodramas. AT

Joanne Woodward *Lila Green* • Richard Beymer *Kenny Baird* • Claire Trevor *Helen Baird* • Carol Lynley *Miriam Caswell* • Robert Webber *Ricky Powers* • Louis Nye *Ronnie Cavendish* • Gypsy Rose Lee *Madame Olga* ■ *Dir* Franklin J Schaffner • *Scr* Meade Roberts, from the play *A Loss of Roses* by William Inge

Stripper ★★★ 18
Documentary 1985 · US · Colour · 86min

This documentary is a brave attempt to come up with a non-exploitative insight into the world of stripping. Against the backdrop of the first annual convention for the trade, Janette Boyd, Sara Costa and Kimberly Holcomb are among the dancers who speak frankly about the job, while director Jerome Gary keeps the actual scenes of stripping down to a minimum. The soundtrack is from ace composer Jack Nitzsche, who is responsible for the music for films such as *The Exorcist* and *One Flew over the Cuckoo's Nest*. JF Swearing, nudity.

■ *Dir* Jerome Gary

Strippers vs Werewolves ★★ 15
Comedy horror 2012 · UK · Colour · 89min

High in concept but sadly low in quality, this determinedly B-grade movie has werewolf

---

Martin Kemp getting killed by an exotic dancer, only for his hairy mates to seek retribution against her strip club. Surprisingly, the girls are decently portrayed; it's the monsters that let the movie down. Their make-up is little more than kids' party standard – you half expect to see a credit for a face painter. As comedy horror, it offers a few cheesily chucklesome moments, but you wonder how such tosh attracted the participation of not only Kemp, but also Robert Englund (*A Nightmare on Elm Street*). DA *DVD* *BL*

Billy Murray *Ferris* • Sarah Douglas *Jeanette* • Robert Englund *Tapper* • Steven Berkoff *Flett* • Lysette Anthony *Jilly* ■ *Dir* Jonathan Glendening • *Scr* Phillip Barron, Pat Higgins

Striptease ★★ 15
Crime comedy drama 1996 · US · Colour · 112min

When devoted mother Demi Moore loses custody of her daughter to her lowlife erstwhile husband Robert Patrick because she's unemployed, she finds work as a stripper in a Florida topless bar to earn money and get the child back. She becomes the object of oily, corrupt politician Burt Reynolds's lust, and finds herself involved in murder and blackmail. Andrew Bergman's direction makes this watchable, but his screenplay pulls its punches on the sleaze, and tear-jerking sentimentality and inadequate humour don't combine well with the drama. RK Violence, swearing, nudity. *DVD*

Demi Moore *Erin Grant* • Armand Assante *Al Garcia* • Ving Rhames *Shad* • Robert Patrick *Darrell Grant* • Burt Reynolds *Congressman Dilbeck* • Paul Guilfoyle (2) *Malcolm Moldovsky* • Jerry Grayson *Orly* • Rumer Willis *Angela Grant* ■ *Dir* Andrew Bergman • *Scr* Andrew Bergman, from the novel by Carl Hiaasen

Stroker Ace ★ PG
Comedy 1983 · US · Colour · 90min

Burt Reynolds stars in a lame comedy about the larger-than-life exploits of racing car driver who is forced into loony promotional work (such as dressing up as a giant chicken) by his sponsor (Ned Beatty), who is the owner of a chain of fried chicken shops. The clash between the two loud personalities forms the core of the film. This one's the pits. DF

Burt Reynolds *Stroker Ace* • Ned Beatty *Clyde Torkle* • Jim Nabors *Lugs* • Parker Stevenson *Aubrey James* • Loni Anderson *Pembrook Feeney* • Bubba Smith *Arnold* • John Byner *Doc Seegle* ■ *Dir* Hal Needham • *Scr* Hal Needham, Hugh Wilson, from the novel *Stand On It* by William Neely, Robert K Ottum

Stromboli ★★ PG
Drama 1950 · It/US · BW · 101min

When Ingrid Bergman abandoned her husband (and Hollywood) for Italian director Roberto Rossellini, she found herself at the centre of the first major showbiz scandal of the postwar era. Denounced by religious groups, blacklisted by the studios and called "Hollywood's apostle of degradation" by a US senator, Bergman made this film with Rossellini (whom she soon married). Launched with a fanfare, it flopped noisily. Bergman is ill at ease as the refugee who marries an Italian fisherman, while the island of Stromboli's volcano simmers symbolically in the background. Part melodrama, part neorealist exercise, it never gels. AT

Ingrid Bergman *Karin Bjiorsen* • Mario Vitale *Antonio* • Renzo Cesana *Priest* • Mario Sponza *Lighthouse keeper* ■ *Dir* Roberto Rossellini • *Scr* Roberto Rossellini, Art Cohn, Renzo Cesana, Sergio Amidei, CP Callegari

Strong Language ★ 18
Comedy drama 1998 · UK · Colour · 76min

First-timer Simon Rumley is to be congratulated for his persistence in making this talking-heads scrapbook for a hard-earned £30,000. However, his portrait of 1990s London 20-somethings is as disappointingly contrived as its visual style is simple. In the mouths of a largely inexperienced cast, Rumley's ruminations sound self-conscious and too obviously

S

12 15 18 PASSED FOR PEOPLE OF THESE AGES AND OVER *DVD* RELEASED ON DVD *BL* RELEASED ON BLU-RAY *3D* RELEASED IN 3D *CS* END CREDIT SEQUENCE **1217**

scripted. DP Swearing, sexual references. *DVD*

David Groves *Narrator* • Al Nedjari *Pete, unemployed* • Paul Tonkinson *Danny, lift attendant* • Julie Rice *Tatty, astrologer & tarot card reader* • Charlie De'Ath *Stuart, video director* • Kelly Marcel *Philippa, magazine production assistant* ■ *Dir/Scr* Simon Rumley

The Strong Man ★★★★ U
Silent comedy　　1926 · US · BW · 73min

Of the four great silent comedians, Harry Langdon is virtually forgotten – though, in popularity terms, he once stood beside Chaplin, Keaton and Harold Lloyd. The puny, sad-faced clown plays a Belgian immigrant who tours America with circus strong man Arthur Thalasso, while searching for his pen pal, who turns out to be a blind girl. It's not as sentimental as it sounds, and the sequences with Langdon being ravished by Gertrude Astor and labouring under the effects of a heavy cold are superb. As much a social drama about the immigrant experience as a comedy, this was probably Langdon's best movie and gave Frank Capra his first official directorial credit. AT *DVD*

Harry Langdon *Paul Bergot* • Priscilla Bonner *Mary Brown* • Gertrude Astor *"Gold Tooth"* • William V Mong *Parson Brown* • Robert McKim *Roy McDevitt* • Arthur Thalasso *Zandow the Great* ■ *Dir* Frank Capra • *Scr* Arthur Ripley, Frank Capra, Hal Conklin, Robert Eddy, Reed Heustis (titles), from the story by Arthur Ripley

The Strongest Man in the World ★★★ U
Comedy　　1975 · US · Colour · 88min

This was Kurt Russell's third outing as Disney's super-teen Dexter Riley (after *The Computer Wore Tennis Shoes* and *Now You See Him, Now You Don't*). This time his misadventures begin when he accidentally acquires phenomenal strength. Russell is amiable enough, but the real fun comes from the film's seasoned stars (Phil Silvers, Eve Arden, Cesar Romero), who wring smiles out of some pretty tired gags. DP

Kurt Russell *Dexter Riley* • Joe Flynn *Dean Higgins* • Eve Arden *Aunt Harriet Crumply* • Cesar Romero *AJ Arno* • Phil Silvers *Kirwood Krinkle* • Dick Van Patten *Harry* • Harold Gould *Dietz* ■ *Dir* Vincent McEveety • *Scr* Herman Groves, Joseph L McEveety

Strongroom ★
Crime drama　　1961 · UK · BW · 80min

This low-budget thriller has all the mystery and tension of a shelved *Thunderbirds* episode. Two petty crooks discover their consciences after their accomplice dies in a hit-and-run accident, and they decide to break back into the bank they have just robbed, to prevent the manager and his secretary from suffocating in the safe. If the anxious expressions and banal utterances of the villains aren't bad enough, there are glutinous exchanges between the stuffy boss and his assistant. DP

Derren Nesbitt *Griff* • Colin Gordon *Mr Spencer* • Ann Lynn *Rose Taylor* • John Chappell *John Musgrove* • Keith Faulkner *Len* • Dir Vernon Sewell • *Scr* Max Marquis, Richard Harris, from an idea by Harris

Stroszek ★★★ 15
Satirical drama　　1977 · W Ger · Colour · 103min

Tired of the degradation of Berlin, street singer Bruno S, prostitute Eva Mattes and the diminutive Clemens Scheitz head for freedom in Wisconsin. However, this being a Werner Herzog film, it proves to be anything but a land of opportunity and the troubled trio are forced apart after a bungled robbery. This is a sobering portrait of America as a desolate, unwelcoming wilderness and while some of the culture clash jokes are rather obvious, there's still a visionary surrealism to the story that renders it a road movie like no other. DP German, English +subtitles. *DVD*

Bruno S *Bruno Stroszek* • Eva Mattes *Eva* • Clemens Scheitz *Scheitz* • Clayton Szalpinski *Scheitz's nephew* • Ely Rodriguez *Ely* ■ *Dir/Scr* Werner Herzog

Struck by Lightning ★★★ 15
Comedy drama　　1990 · Aus · Colour · 91min

This Australian drama takes a refreshing and honest look at the subject of Down's syndrome. Director Jerzy Domaradzki refuses to wallow in sentimentality and draws lively performances from his Down's syndrome cast. There's also solid work from Garry McDonald and Brian Vriends, as the senior teachers at a special school who come into conflict. Compassionate but never corny, this is rewarding. DP Swearing.

Gary McDonald *Ollie Rennie* • Brian Vriends *Pat Cannizzaro* • Catherine McClements *Jill McHugh* • Jocelyn Betheras *Jody* • Dick Tomkins *Donald* • Roger Haddad *Peter* ■ *Dir* Jerzy Domaradzki • *Scr* Trevor Farrant

The Struggle ★★
Drama　　1931 · US · BW · 77min

Blaming his recent failures on a lack of independence, DW Griffith, the once-great director, decided to produce his final film quickly and cheaply himself. The title, which accurately reflects the last decade of Griffith's working life, refers to a millworker's struggle to give up the demon drink. Anita Loos and her husband John Emerson meant their screenplay, reminiscent of Emile Zola's *The Drunkard*, to be humorous, but Griffith turned it into a rather maudlin and naive morality tale. RB

Hal Skelly *Jimmie Wilson* • Zita Johann *Florrie Wilson* • Charlotte Wynters *Nina* • Evelyn Baldwin *Nan Wilson* • Jackson Halliday *Johnnie Marshall* ■ *Dir* DW Griffith • *Scr* Anita Loos, John Emerson

Stuart Little ★★★ U
Part-animated fantasy adventure
1999 · US · Colour · 81min

Based on the much-loved novel by EB White, this charming part-animated fantasy adventure ought to be better. For while the animation is pixel-perfect, the narrative is short on inspiration and awash with sentiment. Both Stuart the orphan mouse and Snowbell, his feline nemesis, are expertly realised and superbly voiced by Michael J Fox and Nathan Lane, respectively. But the humans are awkward interlopers, with Geena Davis and Hugh Laurie overeager and Jonathan Lipnicki lacking his *Jerry Maguire* cuteness. Visually it's vibrant, inventive and inviting, but overall it's less adorable than *Babe*. DP *DVD* 🔵

Michael J Fox *Stuart Little* • Geena Davis *Mrs Little* • Hugh Laurie *Mr Little* • Jonathan Lipnicki *George Little* • Nathan Lane *Snowbell* • Jennifer Tilly *Camille Stout* • Chazz Palminteri *Smokey* • Jeffrey Jones *Uncle Crenshaw* • Steve Zahn *Monty* ■ *Dir* Rob Minkoff • *Scr* M Night Shyamalan, Greg Brooker, from the novel by EB White

Stuart Little 2 ★★★ U
Part-animated fantasy adventure
2002 · US · Colour · 74min

Despite lacking the wit that distinguished Stuart's first film outing, this amusing sequel will still appeal to those who were delighted by the original. Stuart (expertly voiced by Michael J Fox) falls for a flighty little bird, Margalo (Melanie Griffith), but doesn't realise that she's under the control of a villainous falcon (James Woods). Directed by Rob Minkoff, this blend of live action and animation is technically superb, but its real charm lies in the balance it maintains between enchantment and the everyday. TH *DVD* 🔵

Michael J Fox *Stuart Little* • Geena Davis *Eleanor Little* • Hugh Laurie *Fredrick Little* • Nathan Lane *Snowbell* • Melanie Griffith *Margalo* • Jonathan Lipnicki *George Little* • James Woods *Falcon* • Steve Zahn *Monty* ■ *Dir* Rob Minkoff • *Scr* Bruce Joel Rubin, from a story by Bruce Joel Rubin, Douglas Wick, from characters by EB White

Stuart Little 3: Call of the Wild ★★ U
Animated fantasy adventure
2005 · US · Colour · 72min

The quality plunges drastically in this uninspired direct-to-video sequel. Gone is the charming mix of live action and CGI

used in the original two films, replaced by full animation whose flatness and simplicity is symbolic of the entire tale. Surprisingly, the core voice talent remains the same with Michael J Fox, Geena Davis and Hugh Laurie wasting their efforts on a weak plot that sees boy mouse Stuart demonstrate his bravery when Snowbell the family cat is kidnapped during the Little clan's lakeside vacation. Undemanding humour, a sprinkling of mild peril and the obligatory life lessons offer enough substance to keep the very young happy, but only the short running time will impress anyone older. SF *DVD*

Michael J Fox *Stuart Little* • Hugh Laurie *Mr Frederick Little* • Geena Davis *Mrs Eleanor Little* • Virginia Madsen *The Beast* • Wayne Brady *Reeko* • Jonathan Lipnicki *George Little* • Nathan Lane *Snowbell* • Peter MacNicol *Troopmaster* ■ *Dir* Audu Paden • *Scr* Bill Motz, Bob Roth, from characters by EB White

Stuart Saves His Family ★★★ 12
Comedy　　1995 · US · Colour · 93min

This feature-length adaptation of Al Franken's Stuart Smalley sketches from TV's *Saturday Night Live* didn't deserve the critical and commercial panning it received on its release. The problem lies with the movie's attempt to combine serious drama with the mocking of neurotic TV host Stuart Smalley. Stuart's interactions with his equally neurotic friends on and off his self-help TV show are realistic, yet amusing all the same. The second half of the movie brings a change of pace, with Stuart rejoining his estranged and extremely dysfunctional family, prompting a number of heartbreaking confessions and outbursts. KB

Al Franken *Stuart Smalley* • Laura San Giacomo *Julia* • Vincent D'Onofrio *Donnie* • Shirley Knight *Stuart's mom* • Harris Yulin *Stuart's dad* • Lesley Boone *Jodie* • John Link Graney *Kyle* ■ *Dir* Harold Ramis • *Scr* Al Franken, from his book

Stuck ★★★ 15
Horror thriller
2007 · Can/US/UK/Ger · Colour · 85min

Jobless and homeless Stephen Rea finds himself in the wrong place at the wrong time in this slow-burning horror thriller inspired by a true story. Just when he thinks his day couldn't get any worse, Rea is hit by a car driven by inebriated nursing assistant Mena Suvari, and ends up wedged in her windscreen. In fear of losing her job, the desperate woman leaves the ensnared pedestrian in her garage in the hope that he will die. As with his previous horror outings, director Stuart Gordon is adept at blending tongue-in-cheek moments with scenes of eye-watering violence, and he is also rewarded here with full-blooded performances from his two leads. JA English, Spanish +subtitles.

Mena Suvari *Brandi Boski* • Stephen Rea *Tom Bardo* • Russell Hornsby *Rashid* • Rukiya Bernard *Tanya* ■ *Dir* Stuart Gordon • *Scr* John Strysik, from a story by Stuart Gordon

Stuck in Love ★★★ 15
Comedy drama　　2012 · US · Colour · 92min

The romantic trials of a father and his two teenage children are at the heart of this low-key comedy drama. The almost-too-beautiful cast is led by Greg Kinnear as a famous novelist who refuses to give up hope of reconciliation with his ex-wife (Jennifer Connelly), despite that fact that she has remarried. As this gentle tale unfolds, Kinnear's kids (Lily Collins and Nat Wolff) gain new and – naturally – complicated love interests, while Kinnear stubbornly refuses to move on. Writer/director Josh Boone's quiet romantic fantasy is, in its own way, as unrealistic as any blockbuster, but a perfectly pleasant watch. KK Swearing, drug abuse, a sex scene. *DVD* 🔵

Greg Kinnear *Bill Borgens* • Jennifer Connelly *Erica* • Lily Collins *Samantha Borgens* • Nat Wolff *Rusty Borgens* • Logan Lerman *Louis* • Kristen Bell *Tricia* ■ *Dir/Scr* Josh Boone

Stuck on You ★★★ 12
Comedy　　2003 · US · Colour · 113min

The Farrelly brothers here shine their bad-taste spotlight on conjoined twins and deliver a slapstick tale that's full of fun. Matt Damon and Greg Kinnear play the brothers, a well-liked duo who quit their sleepy home town in favour of exploitative LA when amateur dramatics performer Kinnear decides he wants to become a serious actor. Despite the questionable subject matter, the film is not nearly as outrageous as it sounds. Where the movie excels is in the obvious sight gags afforded by the twins' condition, Damon and Kinnear's strong chemistry and a great send-up performance by Cher. SF *DVD*

Matt Damon *Bo* • Greg Kinnear *Walt* • Eva Mendes *April* • Wen Yann Shih *May* • Pat Crawford Brown *Mimmy* • Ray "Rocket" Valliere *Rocket* • Tommy Songin *Tommy* • Cher ■ *Dir* Bobby Farrelly, Peter Farrelly • *Scr* Bobby Farrelly, Peter Farrelly, from a story by Bobby Farrelly, Peter Farrelly, Charles B Wessler, Bennett Yellin

The Stud ★★ 18
Sex drama　　1978 · US · Colour · 91min

The Jackie Collins novel about jet-set sex in swinging London was updated for this celebrated (for all the wrong reasons) example of disco and sexploitation, but it still looked coy and old-fashioned in 1978. Jackie's sister Joan revived her career as the rich bitch whose toy boy (Oliver Tobias) makes fruitless attempts to escape her clutches. The shallow plot and paper-thin characterisations matter little today, compared to the kitsch appeal of the Collins sisters and the dodgy disco milieu. Followed by *The Bitch* (1979). DM *DVD*

Joan Collins *Fontaine Khaled* • Oliver Tobias *Tony Blake* • Emma Jacobs *Alex Khaled* • Sue Lloyd *Vanessa* • Walter Gotell *Ben Khaled* ■ *Dir* Quentin Masters • *Scr* Jackie Collins, Humphries Dave, Christopher Stagg, from the novel by Jackie Collins

Student Bodies ★ 15
Horror spoof　　1981 · US · Colour · 81min

This has a masked killer cutting a swathe through his sassy classmates using an inventive array of sharp school supplies. The rare amusing moments include one victim being paper-clipped to death and the "producer" putting in an on-screen appearance to apologise for the lack of gore and then swearing to make up for it in ratings terms. AJ

Kristen Riter *Toby* • Matthew Goldsby *Hardy* • Richard Brando *The Breather* • Joe Flood *Mr Dumpkin* • Joe Talarowski *Principal Peters* • Mimi Weddell *Miss Mumsley* • Carl Jacobs *Dr Sigmund* • Peggy Cooper *Ms Van Dyke* ■ *Dir/Scr* Mickey Rose

The Student Prince ★★★ U
Musical　　1954 · US · Colour · 107min

This was to have starred romantic tenor Mario Lanza as the prince who falls for a barmaid, only Lanza grew too obese to wear the period costumes, economically handed over from MGM's *The Prisoner of Zenda* remake. While his voice remains on the rousing soundtrack, he was replaced in the film by stiff British actor Edmund Purdom. The film sounds magnificent and looks sumptuous, and the plot about the duties of royalty has resonances today. TS *DVD*

Ann Blyth *Kathie* • Edmund Purdom *Prince Karl* • John Ericson *Count Von Asterburg* • Louis Calhern *King of Karlsburg* • Edmund Gwenn *Professor Juttner* • John Williams *Lutz* • SZ Sakall *Joseph Ruder* • Betta St John *Princess Johanna* • Mario Lanza *Prince Karl's singing voice* ■ *Dir* Richard Thorpe • *Scr* William Ludwig, Sonya Levien, from the operetta *The Student Prince* by Dorothy Donnelly, Sigmund Romberg, from the play *Alt Heidelberg (Old Heidelberg)* by Wilhelm Meyer-Förster • *Music* Sigmund Romberg

The Student Prince in Old Heidelberg ★★★
Silent romantic comedy 1927 · US · BW · 102min

This is a silent screen version of a play and a popular operetta about a Ruritanian prince, studying at Heidelberg university, who falls for the local innkeeper's pretty niece. Norma Shearer and "Latin lover" Ramon Novarro star in this early example of MGM in lavish mode. The absence of sound is well compensated for by the great Ernst Lubitsch's direction, as he stylishly extracts every ounce of charm and wistful romance from the piece and its stars. RK

Ramon Novarro *Prince Karl Heinrich* · Norma Shearer *Kathi* · Jean Hersholt *Dr Juttner* · Gustav von Seyffertitz *King Karl VII* · Philippe De Lacy *Heir apparent* ■ *Dir* Ernst Lubitsch · *Scr* Hans Kräly, Marian Ainslee (titles), Ruth Cummings (titles), from the operetta *The Student Prince* by Dorothy Donnelly, Sigmund Romberg and the play *Alt Heidelberg* (Old Heidelberg) by Wilhelm Meyer-Förster

Student Seduction ★★
Thriller 2003 · US/Can · Colour · 95min

Misconceptions and lies bring life-wrecking consequences for an attractive chemistry teacher in this predictable thriller. Elizabeth Berkley stars as the high-school newcomer whose offer to coach failing student Corey Sevier is disturbingly misinterpreted by the obsessive teen. Yet while Berkley fits the bill visually which makes the fragmented narrative watchable, her bland performance lacks integrity and this just dilutes its emotional impact. The overall result plays like a cheaply shot soap opera rather than a credible exploration of the potential dangers of tutor/pupil relationships. SF

Elizabeth Berkley *Christie Dawson* · Corey Sevier *Josh Gaines* · Rick Roberts *Drew Dawson* · Karen Robinson *Lorraine Boyle* · Sarah Allen *Jenna* · Lois Dellar *Jane Stanley* · Al Dubois *Harold Lang* ■ *Dir* Peter Svatek · *Scr* Edithe Swensen

A Study in Terror ★★★ 15
Mystery 1965 · UK · Colour · 90min

No fictional character has been portrayed more often on screen than Sherlock Holmes, but of the scores of actors to tackle the role, few deserved a second outing beneath the famous deerstalker more than John Neville. In this neatly plotted, at times gruesome, picture, he gives a stylish performance as Baker Street's most famous tenant – a portrayal that is all the more impressive for the lack of acting support he receives from Donald Houston as Watson. Director James Hill recreates the Whitechapel of the Jack the Ripper era with relish, and the solution is a corker. DP *DVD* *BL*

John Neville *Sherlock Holmes* · Donald Houston *Dr John Watson* · John Fraser *Lord Edward Carfax* · Anthony Quayle *Dr Murray* · Robert Morley *Mycroft Holmes* · Barbara Windsor *Annie Chapman* · Adrienne Corri *Angela* · Frank Finlay *Lestrade* · Judi Dench *Sally* ■ *Dir* James Hill · *Scr* Derek Ford, Donald Ford, from a novel by Ellery Queen [Frederic Dannay, Manfred B Lee], from the characters by Sir Arthur Conan Doyle

The Stuff ★★★ 15
Comedy horror 1985 · US · Colour · 82min

Director Larry Cohen has one of the quirkiest minds in the fantasy genre and this gory junk-food horror satire is one of his best ever ideas. For here's a monster movie where the monster doesn't eat, you eat it! "The Stuff" is a delicious new fast-food dessert that becomes a marketing sensation. But the bubbly goo turns out to be a living substance, a killer product that turns the nation into crazed, foaming addicts. A blackly comic attack on American consumerism, the military and the advertising world, this is a fun shocker chock full of spoof ingredients. AJ Swearing. *DVD* *BL*

Michael Moriarty *David "Mo" Rutherford* · Andrea Marcovicci *Nicole* · Garrett Morris *"Chocolate Chip" Charlie* · Paul Sorvino *Colonel Spears* · Scott Bloom *Jason* · Danny Aiello *Vickers* · Patrick O'Neal (1) *Fletcher* · James Dixon *Postman* ■ *Dir/Scr* Larry Cohen

The Stunt Man ★★★ 15
Drama 1980 · US · Colour · 125min

Peter O'Toole soars off the overacting scale as a film director trying to make a war movie and hiring the fugitive Vietnam veteran who killed his chief stuntman. O'Toole later claimed that he based his character on the intimidating, ruthless perfectionist David Lean – and he got an Oscar nomination for it. If you can see through the smokescreen of O'Toole's performance, you'll find a slightly ramshackle satire about movies, illusion and politics. AT *DVD*

Peter O'Toole *Eli Cross* · Barbara Hershey *Nina Franklin* · Steve Railsback *Cameron* · Sharon Farrell *Denise* · John Garwood *Gabe* · Allen Goorwitz [Allen Garfield] *Sam* · Alex Rocco *Jake* ■ *Dir* Richard Rush · *Scr* Lawrence B Marcus, Richard Rush (adaptation), from the novel by Paul Brodeur

The Stupids ★★ PG
Comedy 1995 · US · Colour · 89min

This misfiring comedy from director John Landis features Tom Arnold as the head of a family unable to cope with life in the 1990s. Thanks to the energetic efforts of the cast, this is not a total disaster, and there are even occasional moments of pleasing surrealism. But, for the most part, this is a loosely linked collection of crass slapstick gags. Bizarrely, several film-makers have cameo roles. DP

Tom Arnold *Stanley Stupid* · Jessica Lundy *Joan Stupid* · Bug Hall *Buster Stupid* · Alex McKenna *Petunia Stupid* · Scott Kraft *Policeman* · Christopher Lee *Evil Sender* · David Cronenberg *Postal supervisor* · Norman Jewison *TV director* · Costa-Gavras *Gas station guy* ■ *Dir* John Landis · *Scr* Brent Forrester, from the characters by James Marshall, Harry Allard

Styx ★★ 18
Action thriller 2000 · S Afr/US · Colour · 89min

The ingenious robbery enacted in the opening sequence holds out the hope that this could be a better than average crime thriller. Sadly, it's pretty much downhill after that as three of the original robbers – the reluctant Peter Weller, his debt-ridden brother Angus MacFadyen and Bryan Brown, who everyone thought was dead – are reunited for one final job. Even in second gear, Brown and Weller are effortlessly watchable, but the rest of the cast isn't in the same class, and the action sequences are embarrassingly inept. JF *DVD*

Peter Weller *Nelson* · Bryan Brown *Art* · Angus MacFadyen *Mike* · Gerard Rudolph *Sloan* · Spencer Sykes *Ricky* ■ *Dir* Alex Wright · *Scr* George Ferris

Sub Zero ★
Action adventure 2005 · Can · Colour · 86min

Expert mountaineer Costas Mandylor and his crack team risk their lives to retrieve a world-threatening device from the top of K2 in this goofy adventure. Yet though the clock's ticking, there's more agitated talk than rock face action for the film's first hour, as the reluctant heroes trade bitchy insults and naff one-liners with their amusingly gung-ho military clients. A flurry of activity immediately prior to their ascent brings sabotage and murder into the increasingly preposterous mix, but instead of adding drama, it just feels like further plot-padding. Sadly, after all the waiting, the climactic climbing scenes are neither dynamic nor convincing, while an emotional ending is obliterated by poor acting and weak special effects. SF

Costas Mandylor *Jonny Deckert* · Nia Peeples *Kelli Paris* · Linden Ashby *Soloman Davis* · Colin Lawrence *Pete Tanner* · Jackie Samuda *Sasha Mirov* ■ *Dir* Jay Andrews [Jim Wynorski] · *Scr* Jay Andrews [Jim Wynorski], William Langlois, Jonas Quastel

The Subject Was Roses ★★★★
Drama 1968 · US · Colour · 108min

Based on Frank D Gilroy's Pulitzer Prize-winning Broadway play about a young Second World War veteran's troubled relationship with his parents, this is famous as the movie comeback of Patricia Neal after a near-fatal stroke, and her Oscar-nominated performance is all the more affecting with this knowledge. Martin Sheen plays the returning serviceman in only his second film role. The action is a trifle enclosed and theatrical, but this actually enhances the emotional punch of the drama. It's a film that requires work, but if you can stay the course, it's hugely rewarding. SH

Patricia Neal *Nettie Cleary* · Jack Albertson *John Cleary* · Martin Sheen *Timmy Cleary* · Don Saxon *Nightclub master of ceremonies* · Elaine Williams *Woman* · Grant Gordon *Man in a restaurant* ■ *Dir* Ulu Grosbard · *Scr* Frank D Gilroy, from his play

The Subjects ★★
Fantasy thriller 2015 · Aus · Colour · 80min

Eight strangers are locked in a room as part of a clinical drug study. They soon find that the drug gives them superpowers, but all of these new "gifts" come with a sting in the tail. This Australian fantasy certainly has an intriguing set-up, which takes the superhero idea to a dark and grisly new place. It's also quite funny in places, with a musical credits sequence providing one of the highlights of the film (make of that what you will). It's a shame, then, that more was not done to flesh out the characters. JL

Frank Magree *Giggles* · Charlotte Nicdao *Lilly* · Paul Henri *Corey* · Paul O'Brien (2) *John* · Katharine Innes *Nikki* ■ *Dir/Scr* Robert Mond

Submarine ★★★ 15
Comedy drama 2010 · UK · Colour · 92min

This sweet-natured feature debut from Richard Ayoade (Channel 4's *The IT Crowd* centres around the utterly self-obsessed yet likeable character of 15-year-old Oliver Tate (Craig Roberts). The film charts Oliver's first love affair and the troubled marriage of his middle-class parents (excellently played by Sally Hawkins and Noah Taylor), whose relationship is heading down the tubes owing to the arrival of old flame Graham (Paddy Considine), a mullet-sporting new ager. Ayoade impresses with his sure, sympathetic handling of character, generating a real warmth for Oliver and his travails where a lesser director might have contented themselves with cheap laughs at the love-struck teen's expense. AS *DVD* *BL*

Noah Taylor *Lloyd Tate* · Paddy Considine *Graham Purvis* · Craig Roberts *Oliver Tate* · Yasmin Paige *Jordana Bevan* · Sally Hawkins *Jill Tate* · Gemma Chan *Kim-Lin* ■ *Dir* Richard Ayoade · *Scr* Richard Ayoade, from the novel by Joe Dunthorne · *Music* Alex Turner (2)

Submarine Command ★★★ U
War drama 1951 · US · BW · 82min

So many Hollywood naval pictures have focused on skippers whose courage is called into question by a bullish member of the crew. But, while this adventure isn't of the calibre of *Run Silent, Run Deep* (1958) or *Crimson Tide* (1995), it's still a tautly told tale of redemption. William Holden is persuasive as the tormented commander whose evasive action costs lives. But William Bendix is even more impressive as the resentful torpedo chief. DP

William Holden (2) *Lt Commander Ken White* · Don Taylor *Lt Commander Pete Morris* · Nancy Olson *Carol* · William Bendix *Boyer* · Moroni Olsen *Commander Joshua Rice* · Peggy Webber *Alice Rice* ■ *Dir* John Farrow · *Scr* Jonathan Latimer

Submarine Patrol ★★★
First World War action adventure 1938 · US · BW · 95min

This is directed by the great John Ford, but it sure doesn't look like a John Ford movie. The director had been underwater before, for the submarine drama *Men without Women*, and this film about sub searchers contains several themes from the earlier tale. There is a love interest this time, with captain's daughter Nancy Kelly falling for

playboy sailor Richard Greene. Before they set sail, there's a fair amount of those good-natured high jinks that tend to irritate Ford's detractors, but, once they cast off, suspense abounds and the well-handled climax is full of action. TS

Richard Greene *Perry Townsend III* · Nancy Kelly *Susan Leeds* · Preston Foster *Lieutenant John C Drake* · George Bancroft *Captain Leeds* · Slim Summerville *Ellsworth "Spotts" Ficketts* · Joan Valerie *Anne* · John Carradine *McAllison* · Ward Bond *Olaf Swanson* ■ *Dir* John Ford · *Scr* Rian James, Darrell Ware, Jack Yellen, from the novel *The Splinter Fleet* by John Milholland

Submarine X-1 ★★★ U
Second World War drama 1967 · UK · Colour · 89min

One of the few cinema features made by prolific TV-movie director William Graham, this Second World War action film would never win any prizes for originality. But the story of a mini-sub raid on a German battleship is decently acted by James Caan and a supporting cast of British and American second-stringers. Graham brings an unexpected tension to the underwater finale, in spite of having to accommodate virtually every submarine cliché in the book. DP

James Caan *Lt Commander Bolton* · Rupert Davies *Vice-Admiral Redmayne* · Norman Bowler *Sub-Lt Pennington* · David Sumner *Lt Davies* · William Dysart *Lt Gogan* ■ *Dir* William Graham [William A Graham] · *Scr* Donald S Sanford, Guy Elmes, from a story by John C Champion, Edmund H North

Subspecies ★ 18
Horror 1991 · Rom/US · Colour · 80min

Good vampire Michael Watson seeks to inherit a Transylvanian bloodstone's powers, but his evil brother Anders Hove wins the battle to put the bite on his former co-ed classmates from America who are visiting Romania. *Nosferatu* is shamelessly ripped-off by director Ted Nicolau in these relentlessly drab proceedings. Three equally feeble sequels followed. AJ *DVD*

Michael Watson *Stefan* · Michele McBride *Lillian* · Anders Hove *Radu* · Laura Tate *Michele* · Angus Scrimm *King Vlad* ■ *Dir* Ted Nicolaou · *Scr* Jackson Barr, David Pabian · *Special Effects* David Allen

The Substance of Fire ★★ 15
Drama 1996 · US · Colour · 97min

Tony Goldwyn plays the gay son who coaxes his siblings – cancer patient Timothy Hutton and adulterous TV celebrity Sarah Jessica Parker – into thwarting their father's ambition to publish a worthy but commercially ruinous history of Nazi atrocities. Director Daniel G Sullivan is enslaved by the rigid characters and overfamiliar themes, but Ron Rifkin, reprising his award-winning stage role, turns in a tour de force performance as the latter-day Lear, whose guilt at surviving the war has dictated his life. DP Swearing.

Timothy Hutton *Martin Geldhart* · Sarah Jessica Parker *Sarah Geldhart* · Ron Rifkin *Isaac Geldhart* · Tony Goldwyn *Aaron Geldhart* · Lee Grant *Cora Cahn* · Eric Bogosian *Gene Byck* · Roger Rees *Max* · Gil Bellows *Val Chenard* ■ *Dir* Daniel G Sullivan · *Scr* Jon Robin Baitz, from his play

The Substitute ★★ 18
Action drama 1996 · US · Colour · 109min

When his teacher girlfriend, Diane Venora, is savagely beaten up by one of her disgruntled students, ex-soldier of fortune Tom Berenger takes over her job at Columbus High School and uses mercenary tactics to exact revenge on the drug gang behind the attack. Director Robert Mandel's contemporary *Blackboard Jungle* meets *Rambo* nudges towards mindless camp far too often to be taken as anything but trashy exploitation. A straight-to-video sequel (without Berenger) followed in 1997. AJ Violence, swearing, brief nudity.

Tom Berenger *Shale* · Ernie Hudson *Principal Claude Rolle* · Diane Venora *Jane Hetzko* · Glenn Plummer *Darryl Sherman* · Marc Anthony *Juan* · Raymond Cruz *Joey Six* · William Forsythe *Hollan* · Luis Guzman *Rem* ■ *Dir* Robert Mandel · *Scr* Alan Ormsby, Roy Frumkes, Rocco Simonelli

S

The Subterraneans ★★

Drama   1960 · US · Colour · 88min

A former graduate and sportsman abandons himself to looking for the meaning of life in San Francisco and takes up with acolytes of the Beat generation. He has an affair with a free-spirited member of the group and, when she becomes pregnant, they decide to rejoin conventional society. Starring George Peppard and Leslie Caron, this unsatisfying bowdlerisation of Jack Kerouac's novel entirely misses the point of Beat philosophy. It does at least offer an evocative atmosphere, along with a generous helping of jazz. RK

Leslie Caron *Mardou Fox* • George Peppard *Leo Percepied* • Janice Rule *Roxanne* • Roddy McDowall *Yuri Gligoric* • Anne Seymour *Charlotte Percepied* • Jim Hutton *Adam Moorad* • Ruth Storey *Analyst* ■ *Dir* Ranald MacDougall • *Scr* Robert Thom, from the novel by Jack Kerouac • *Cinematographer* Joseph Ruttenberg • *Music* André Previn

Suburban Commando

★★★ PG

Comedy adventure   1991 · US · Colour · 86min

The appeal of Hulk Hogan may seem bewildering unless you enjoy seeing chaps pretending to throw each other around a wrestling ring, but at least he is well aware of his limitations when it comes to films. This is one of Hogan's more enjoyable efforts, in which he is the alien warrior who lands on Earth and struggles to blend in with Christopher Lloyd's puzzled family. Hogan makes Arnold Schwarzenegger look like an actor of great subtlety, but there are some nice one-liners and director Burt Kennedy ropes in a classy supporting cast. JF Swearing, violence.

Hulk Hogan *Shep Ramsey* • Christopher Lloyd *Charlie Wilcox* • Shelley Duvall *Jenny Wilcox* • Larry Miller *Adrian Beltz* • William Ball *General Suitor* • JoAnn Dearing *Margie Tanen* • Jack Elam *Colonel Dustin "Dusty" McHowell* ■ *Dir* Burt Kennedy • *Scr* Frank Cappello

Suburban Madness ★★

Crime drama based on a true story
2004 · US · Colour · 89min

On 24 July 2002, Houston dentist Clara Harris killed her adulterous husband by running over him three times in her car. Harris is ably played by the ever-reliable Elizabeth Peña, but this patchy TV movie concentrates on exploring the psyche of Bobbi Bacha (Sela Ward), the private eye hired by Harris to keep tabs on her cheating spouse. As a result, this lacks focus and drifts into melodrama. DP

Elizabeth Peña *Clara Harris* • Sela Ward *Bobbi Bacha* • Brett Cullen *David Harris* • Rheagan Wallace *Amy Harris* • Heather Allin *Mary Louise* • Kirsten Bishop *Pam Wright* ■ *Dir* Robert Dornhelm • *Scr* Kimberlee Reed, from an article by Skip Hollandsworth

Suburban Mayhem

★★★★ 15

Crime drama   2006 · Aus · Colour · 85min

Here's a movie that Jerry Springer couldn't have scripted better. This hilariously dark Australian tale – rather scarily based on a true-life case – finds a teenage vixen, Emily Barclay, plotting the murder of her father after he refuses to pay for her beloved brother's appeal (he's been jailed for beheading a shop worker). Director Paul Goldman elicits great performances from Michael Dorman (TV's *The Secret Life of Us*) and Anthony Hayes (*Look Both Ways*) as the gormlessly besotted men in Barclay's life. But the film belongs to the young Kiwi actress, who deservedly picked up the Australian equivalent of the best actress Oscar for her fearless performance. JF Violence, swearing, sex scenes, drug abuse.

DVD

Emily Barclay *Katrina Skinner* • Michael Dorman *Rusty* • Robert Morgan *John Skinner* • Anthony Hayes *Kenny* • Laurence Breuls *Danny* • Steve Bastoni *Detective Robert Andretti* ■ *Dir* Paul Goldman • *Scr* Alice Bell

The Suburbans ★★ 15

Satirical comedy drama
1999 · US · Colour · 83min

After a very promising start, director Donal Lardner Ward's pop music satire soon crashes and burns. That's a shame because the game cast injects a great deal of life into the obvious script. The Suburbans is the name of a rock group who acrimoniously disbanded after one mega-hit single. Now in boring jobs, they are given a second chance at stardom by hotshot record producer Jennifer Love Hewitt. Ward's flat direction and lack of dramatic smarts result in a morass of showbiz clichés. AJ

Jennifer Love Hewitt *Kate* • Craig Bierko *Mitch* • Amy Brenneman *Grace* • Will Ferrell *Gil* • Donal Lardner Ward *Danny* • Tony Guma *Rory* • Ben Stiller *Jay Rose* ■ *Dir* Donal Lardner Ward • *Scr* Donal Lardner Ward, Tony Guma

subUrbia ★★★ 15

Comedy drama   1996 · US · Colour · 95min

Richard Linklater, king of the slacker movie, here brings a perfect slacker-type story to the screen. It's based on the stage play by Eric Bogosian and the story is inspired by his early life. Set in a parking lot during one long night, it's an ensemble piece about a group of aimless 20-somethings and their meeting with old friend Pony (Jayce Bartok) who's gone on to become a successful rock star. Dark and absorbing. DF Swearing, sexual references, violence.

Giovanni Ribisi *Jeff* • Steve Zahn *Buff* • Amie Carey *Sooze* • Ajay Naidu *Nazeer* • Jayce Bartok *Pony* • Nicky Katt *Tim* • Parker Posey *Erica* ■ *Dir* Richard Linklater • *Scr* Eric Bogosian, from his play

Suburra ★★★★ 18

Crime drama   2015 · It/Fr · Colour · 129min

Based on a novel taking its title from the ancient Roman quarter where senators consorted with lowlifes, this is a wrenchingly gritty and intricate thriller. Its twisting tale is set during a fictionalised week in 2011 when Pope Benedict abdicates, Silvio Berlusconi loses office and a deluge is lashing the Eternal City. The plot turns on a lucrative property development, but it's the human interactions that are of greater interest. Sollima's sense of pace and place is impeccable, while the performances seethe with decadence, danger and despair. DP In Italian, Romany. Strong sex, violence, drug abuse

Pierfrancesco Favino *Filippo Malgradi* • Elio Germano *Sebastiano* • Claudio Amendola *Samurai* • Alessandro Borghi *Number 8* • Greta Scarano *Viola* ■ *Dir* Stefano Sollima • *Scr* Carlo Bonini, Giancarlo De Cataldo, Sandro Petraglia, Stefano Rulli, from a story by Bonini, De Cataldo, Petraglia, Rulli, from the novel by Bonini, De Cataldo

Subway ★★★★ 15

Thriller   1985 · Fr · Colour · 97min

Christopher Lambert goes underground in director Luc Besson's chic cult classic. He's a safe-cracker who falls in love with Isabelle Adjani while turning over her husband's strongbox and finds refuge from the authorities among the oddballs inhabiting the shady world of the Paris metro. Besson's darkly humorous script and spiky style, combined with the starkly depressing environment and weird subculture, give this New Wave suspense thriller a delightful edginess. AJ French +subtitles. DVD

Isabelle Adjani *Helena* • Christopher Lambert *Fred* • Richard Bohringer *Florist* • Michel Galabru *Commisioner Gesberg* • Jean-Hugues Anglade *The Roller Skater* • Jean-Pierre Bacri *Batman* • Jean Reno *Drummer* ■ *Dir* Luc Besson • *Scr* Luc Besson, Pierre Jolivet, Alain Le Henry, Marc Perrier, Sophie Schmit • *Art Director* Alexandre Trauner

Subway in the Sky ★★★

Crime drama   1958 · UK · BW · 86min

Though not highly regarded on its release, thanks to its cast, subject matter and director, this crime drama bears re-evaluation today. It's set in postwar

Germany and features two particularly watchable stars, both of whom have done better work. Ageing bobby-sox idol Van Johnson is a better actor than is generally acknowledged. Here he's hiding from the authorities in the flat of cabaret singer Hildegarde Neff. Director Muriel Box was one of the few English women directors to have had a successful screen career, but she struggles to conceal the stage origins of the material. TS

Van Johnson *Major Baxter Grant* • Hildegarde Neff *Lilli Hoffman* • Albert Lieven *Carl von Schecht* • Cec Linder *Captain Carson* • Katherine Kath *Anna Grant* • Vivian Matalon *Stefan* • Carl Jaffe *Adler* ■ *Dir* Muriel Box • *Scr* Jack Andrews, from a play by Ian Main

Subway Stories: Tales from the Underground ★★★ 15

Portmanteau drama   1997 · US · Colour · 80min

The result of a competition in which habitual users of the New York subway system were encouraged to submit their true-life experiences, this diverse portmanteau drama sees the ten most original entries interpreted by a host of stars and directors. Although the stories vary in quality, there are notable contributions from Denis Leary as a Vietnam veteran and Gregory Hines as a benevolent bystander. The overall result is a worthwhile, dramatically affecting TV movie. JF Swearing.

Bill Irwin • Denis Leary *Guy in wheelchair* • Christine Lahti *Red shoes woman* • Steve Zahn *Tucker* • Jerry Stiller *Old man* • Bonnie Hunt *Fern McDermott* • Lili Taylor *Belinda* • Michael Rapaport *Jake* • Mercedes Ruehl *Leyla* • Sarita Choudhury *Humera* • Nicole Ari Parker *Sharon* • Kenny Garrett *Sax player* • Rosie Perez *Mystery girl* • Gretchen Mol *Wife* • Gregory Hines *Jack* • Anne Heche *Pregnant girl* ■ *Dir* Bob Balaban, Patricia Benoit, Julie Dash, Jonathan Demme, Ted Demme, Abel Ferrara, Alison Maclean, Craig McKay, Lucas Platt, Seth Zvi Rosenfeld • *Scr* Adam Brooks, Julie Dash, Lynn Grossman, John Guare, Marla Hanson, Angela Todd, Seth Zvi Rosenfeld, Albert Innaurato, Danny Hoch, Joe Viola

Success Is the Best Revenge ★★★ 15

Drama   1984 · UK/Fr · Colour · 85min

Following *Moonlighting*, director Jerzy Skolimowski continued his theme of Polish exiles in London. Very much a family affair, in terms of the plot and the filming, it was shot at Skolimowski's Kensington home and co-written by his son, Michael Lyndon, who also appears in a main role. A Polish theatre director (Michael York) becomes totally absorbed with the play he is staging, to the point where his family feel alienated by his behaviour. The film suffers from being slightly unfocused, but cinematically there is much to admire. TH

Michael York *Alex Rodak* • Joanna Szczerbic *Wife* • Michael Lyndon *Adam* • Michel Piccoli *French official* • Anouk Aimée *Monique de Fontaine* • John Hurt *Dino Montecurva* ■ *Dir* Jerzy Skolimowski • *Scr* Michael Lyndon, Jerzy Skolimowski • *Cinematographer* Mike Fash

A Successful Calamity ★★★

Comedy   1932 · US · BW · 72min

In his later years, British theatre actor George Arliss unexpectedly became a major Hollywood film star, usually playing an upper-class or royal role. Here he is a millionaire who returns home after a prolonged business trip in Europe to find his self-centered family are taking their money for granted. To teach them a lesson he feigns bankruptcy, sparking several amusing scenes. This deft morality tale, while somewhat dated, still has much to recommend it. DF

George Arliss *Henry Wilton* • Mary Astor *Emmie Wilton* • Evalyn Knapp *Peggy Wilton* • Grant Mitchell *Connors* • David Torrence *Partington* • William Janney *Eddie Wilton* ■ *Dir* John G Adolfi • *Scr* Austin Parker, Maude Howell, Julien Josephson, from the play by Clare Kummer

Such a Long Journey

★★★ 15

Drama   1998 · Can/UK · Colour · 108min

This allegorical study of India's socio-political problems in the early 1970s is held together by a performance of muddled idealism and dignified pride from Roshan Seth, as a Parsi bank clerk whose world begins to crumble after he agrees to do a favour for a friend in the Secret Service. This slowly simmering story is handled with care by director Sturla Gunnarsson, who exploits the contrasting colours and moods of Bombay to heighten the authenticity. DP Swearing, sexual situations.

Roshan Seth *Gustad Noble* • Om Puri *Ghulam* • Soni Razdan *Dilnavaz Noble* • Naseeruddin Shah *Jimmy Bilimoria* • Sam Dastor *Dinshawji* • Vrajesh Hirjee *Sohrab Noble* ■ *Dir* Sturla Gunnarsson • *Scr* Sooni Taraporevala, from the novel by Rohinton Mistry

Such Good Friends ★★★★

Black comedy   1971 · US · Colour · 101min

This witty Otto Preminger film gives Dyan Cannon her best screen role to date. She's the wife of hospitalised New Yorker Laurence Luckinbill who discovers an awful lot about her hubby while he's in care. Sexy and clever by turns, the screenplay is by a pseudonymous Elaine May. The film contains one of the great telephone scenes, as Dyan prepares to "service" James Coco solicitously while he's engaged in conversation. Very funny and about as black as black comedies get – its ultra-sophisticated subtext bears repeated reviewings. TS

Dyan Cannon *Julie Messenger* • James Coco *Dr Timmy Spector* • Jennifer O'Neill *Miranda Graham* • Ken Howard *Cal Whiting* • Nina Foch *Mrs Wallman* • Laurence Luckinbill *Richard Messenger* • Louise Lasser *Marcy Berns* • Burgess Meredith *Bernard Kalman* • Doris Roberts *Mrs Gold* ■ *Dir* Otto Preminger • *Scr* Esther Dale [Elaine May], David Shaber, from the novel by Lois Gould

Sucker Punch ★★ 12

Fantasy thriller   2011 · US · Colour · 109min

Zack Snyder's elaborate but often bewildering fantasy centres on Babydoll (Emily Browning), a young woman committed to a creepy asylum by her abusive stepfather, who blocks out the horrors by imagining the institution as a sleazy bordello. Deeper in her troubled mind she acts out battles against dragons, robot Nazis and sword-wielding giant samurai, in search of the prizes that will secure her escape. The over-the-top action sequences occasionally thrill, although the sight of scantily clad women in balletically choreographed fisticuffs has the air of a bombastic heavy metal rock video. TeS Violence, swearing, sexual references.

DVD Blu

Emily Browning *Babydoll* • Abbie Cornish *Sweet Pea* • Jena Malone *Rocket* • Vanessa Hudgens [Vanessa Anne Hudgens] *Blondie* • Carla Gugino *Madam Gorski* • Oscar Isaac *Blue Jones* ■ *Dir* Zack Snyder • *Scr* Zack Snyder, Steve Shibuya, from a story by Snyder

Sudan ★★

Period romantic adventure
1945 · US · Colour · 76min

This was the sixth and final teaming of the King and Queen of Technicolor. Yet, Jon Hall and Maria Montez weren't the romantic leads in this ancient Egyptian fantasy. However, they share several scenes, as Hall and sidekick Andy Devine rescue Montez from the desert when she goes in search of those responsible for her father's assassination. Only the hissing villainy of George Zucco prevents the onset of tedium. DP

Maria Montez *Naila* • Jon Hall *Merab* • Turhan Bey *Herua* • Andy Devine *Nebka* • George Zucco *Horadef* ■ *Dir* John Rawlins • *Scr* Edmund L Hartmann

Sudden Death ★★★★ 18
Action thriller 1995 · US · Colour · 105min

This is one of Jean-Claude Van Damme's best thrillers. As a fire officer at an ice-hockey stadium he is given the task of thwarting the deliciously menacing Powers Boothe, who plans to blow up the spectators – among them Van Damme's kids and the US vice president. Who can resist a movie in which the Muscles from Brussels has to fight an assassin dressed as a penguin? Although plausibility isn't its strongest suit, it moves at a rollicking pace and never takes itself too seriously. SR ᴅᴠᴅ Bʟᴜ

Jean-Claude Van Damme *Darren McCord* • Powers Boothe *Joshua Foss* • Raymond J Barry *Vice-president* • Whitni Wright *Emily McCord* • Ross Malinger *Tyler McCord* • Dorian Harewood *Hallmark* • Jophery Brown *Wootton* ■ *Dir* Peter Hyams • *Scr* Gene Quintano, from a story by Karen Baldwin

Sudden Fear ★★★
Thriller 1952 · US · BW · 110min

Joan Crawford has a splendid opportunity to suffer agonies in this contrived but lively thriller in which she accidentally discovers her husband is plotting to kill her. The woman's whirlwind passion for someone as sinister as Jack Palance does strain credulity, although her career as a playwright serves to explain why she devises her own scheme to trap Palance and his grasping girlfriend, Gloria Grahame. Dramatically photographed by Charles Lang Jr and forcefully acted, the film is always a visual treat. AE

Joan Crawford *Myra Hudson* • Jack Palance *Lester Blaine* • Gloria Grahame *Irene Neves* • Bruce Bennett *Steve Kearney* • Touch Connors [Mike Connors] *Junior Kearney* ■ *Dir* David Miller (1) • *Scr* Lenore Coffee, Robert Smith, from the novel by Edna Sherry

Sudden Impact ★★★ 18
Crime thriller 1983 · US · Colour · 112min

This fourth outing for Clint Eastwood's "Dirty" Harry Callahan has the big man with the big magnum hunting a woman who's systematically tracking down and terminating the sickos who raped her and her sister. Sondra Locke, Eastwood's partner at the time, plays the ladykiller. More down and dirty than previous *Harrys*, it won't disappoint series fans, even if the formula is starting to wear a little thin. Incidentally, this is the film in which Eastwood delivers his much quoted "Go ahead, make my day" quip. In 1988, *The Dead Pool* concluded Harry's run. DA Violence, swearing, sex scenes, drug abuse, brief nudity. ᴅᴠᴅ Bʟᴜ

Clint Eastwood *Inspector Harry Callahan* • Sondra Locke *Jennifer Spencer* • Pat Hingle *Chief Jannings* • Bradford Dillman *Captain Briggs* • Paul Drake *Mick* • Audrie J Neenan *Ray Parkins* ■ *Dir* Clint Eastwood • *Scr* Joseph C Stinson, from a story by Earl E Smith, Charles B Pierce, from characters by Harry Julian Fink, RM Fink

Suddenly ★★★ PG
Thriller 1954 · US · BW · 75min

Withdrawn from distribution for years because star Frank Sinatra found out Lee Harvey Oswald had watched it only days before assassinating President Kennedy, this is a must-see rarity, if for that reason alone. Ol' Blue Eyes is the killer who holds a family hostage in the hick town of Suddenly, California, as part of a plot to kill the President, who's passing through on a holiday. Sinatra plays this tension-laden thriller to the hilt, and he's given top-notch support by Sterling Hayden as the sheriff and James Gleason as the retired Secret Service agent whose house is taken over by the would-be assassin. AJ ᴅᴠᴅ

Frank Sinatra *John Baron* • Sterling Hayden *Sheriff Tod Shaw* • James Gleason *Pop Benson* • Nancy Gates *Ellen Benson* • Kim Charney *Pidge Benson* • Paul Frees *Benny Conklin* • Christopher Dark *Bart Wheeler* ■ *Dir* Lewis Allen • *Scr* Richard Sale

Suddenly ★★★ 15
Comedy drama 2002 · Arg/Neth · BW · 88min

Diego Lerman's stylish study of sexual awakening begins in sinister fashion, as country girl Tatiana Saphir is kidnapped outside the Buenos Aires lingerie shop where she works by lesbian ladettes Carla Crespo and Verónica Hassan. But the tone soon shifts as the trio head south to stay with Hassan's ageing aunt, Beatriz Thibaudín, whose tenants find the newcomers intriguing. Evocatively shot in black and white by Luciano Zito and Diego del Piano, this provides a seductive insight into life in a little-seen part of Argentina. DP Spanish +subtitles. ᴅᴠᴅ

Tatiana Saphir *Marcia* • Carla Crespo *Mao* • Verónica Hassan *Lenin* • Beatriz Thibaudín *Blanca* • María Merlino *Delia* • Marcos Ferrante *Felipe* ■ *Dir* Diego Lerman • *Scr* Diego Lerman, María Meira, from the short film *La Prueba* by Diego Lerman, from the novel *La Prueba* by César Aira

Suddenly It's Spring ★★★
Romantic comedy 1947 · US · BW · 88min

Paulette Goddard returns from the war as an officer to find that her lawyer husband, Fred MacMurray, has found someone else and wants a divorce, which she refuses. A woman's place is usually at the centre of director Mitchell Leisen's movies, and role-reversal is a constant theme. The gender switch is about the only novelty in this pleasantly familiar, lightweight comedy. RB

Paulette Goddard *WAC Captain Mary Morely/ "Captain Lonelyhearts"* • Fred MacMurray *Peter Morely* • MacDonald Carey *[Macdonald Carey] Jack Lindsay* • Arleen Whelan *Gloria Fay* • Lilian Fontaine *Mary's mother* • Frank Faylen *Harold Michaels* ■ *Dir* Mitchell Leisen • *Scr* Claude Binyon, PJ Wolfson, from the story *Sentimental Journey* by PJ Wolfson

Suddenly, Last Summer ★★★★ 15
Drama 1959 · UK · BW · 109min

This wonderfully overheated drama by Tennessee Williams, who wrote the screenplay with Gore Vidal, is animated by two ultra-powerful performances by Elizabeth Taylor and Katharine Hepburn. Taylor is the niece about to be committed to a mental institution by southern matriarch Hepburn after witnessing the violent death of a homosexual cousin. Montgomery Clift is the neurosurgeon called in to assess the girl's sanity rating before a possible lobotomy. Director Joseph L Mankiewicz makes it a class act all round. TH ᴅᴠᴅ

Elizabeth Taylor *Catherine Holly* • Montgomery Clift *Dr John Cukrowicz* • Katharine Hepburn *Mrs Violet Venable* • Albert Dekker *Dr Hockstader* • Mercedes McCambridge *Mrs Holly* • Gary Raymond *George Holly* • Mavis Villiers *Mrs Foxhill* • Patricia Marmont *Nurse Benson* • Joan Young *Sister Felicity* ■ *Dir* Joseph L Mankiewicz • *Scr* Gore Vidal, Tennessee Williams, from the play by Tennessee Williams

Suez ★★★
Biographical drama 1938 · US · Sepia · 104min

Twentieth Century-Fox was marvellously adept high-budget biopics. But one of the most unlikely candidates for Fox screen canonisation must surely have been 19th-century French engineer Ferdinand de Lesseps, who was the force behind the construction of the Suez Canal. Fox turned his story into a slice of romantic hokum for their contractee, popular matinée idol Tyrone Power, and the whole saga became a rattlingly entertaining melodrama under the expert direction of Allan Dwan and Otto Brower. TS

Tyrone Power *Ferdinand de Lesseps* • Loretta Young *Empress Eugenie* • Annabella *Toni* • J Edward Bromberg *Said* • Joseph Schildkraut *La Tour* • Henry Stephenson *Count de Lesseps* • Sidney Blackmer *du Brey* • Maurice Moscovich *Mohammed Ali* • Sig Rumann [Sig Ruman] *Sergeant Fellerin* ■ *Dir* Allan Dwan, Otto Brower • *Scr* Philip Dunne, Julien Josephson, from a story by Sam Duncan

Suffering Bastards ★★★
Comedy 1989 · US · Colour · 95min

This is a provocative title for a well-crafted but chat-heavy comedy in which a guy regales a girl he meets in a bar with tall tales about his hard-luck past. Are they fact or fiction? And does it matter if they're just a weapon in his chat-up arsenal? Eric Bogosian and Gina Gershon star, with John C McGinley at the top of a talented support cast. McGinley also wrote the piece, which looks as if it would have been better suited to the stage than the cinema screen. DA

Eric Bogosian *Mr Leech* • Gina Gershon *Sharnetta* • John C McGinley *Buddy Johnson* • David Warshofsky *Al Johnson* • Michael Wincott *Chazz* ■ *Dir* Bernard McWilliams • *Scr* John C McGinley

Suffragette ★★★★ 12
Historical drama 2015 · UK/France · Colour · 101min

Director Sarah Gavron and writer Abi Morgan beat their feminist drum proudly as they bring to screen the fight for the female vote. The film centres on a group of largely fictional women, although Meryl Streep appears as Emmeline Pankhurst. During the escalating civil disobedience, we follow a wrung-out laundress (Carey Mulligan), her feisty colleague (Anne-Marie Duff) and local ringleader (Helena Bonham Carter). There are real women's stories here that intersect too briefly but *Suffragette* is an inspiring introduction to a chapter of history that's been disgracefully ignored and in the hands of these film-makers becomes, finally, unforgettable. EAS Some violence. ᴅᴠᴅ Bʟᴜ

Carey Mulligan *Maud Watts* • Helena Bonham Carter *Edith Ellyn* • Meryl Streep *Emmeline Pankhurst* • Brendan Gleeson *Inspector Arthur Steed* • Anne-Marie Duff *Violet Miller* • Ben Whishaw *Sonny Watts* • Romola Garai *Alice Haughton* • Samuel West *Benedict Haughton* ■ *Dir* Sarah Gavron • *Scr* Abi Morgan • *Cinematographer* Eduard Grau

Sugar ★★★ 15
Sports drama 2008 · US · Colour · 109min

American sports movies are something of a niche market over here, and a familiarity with baseball is probably crucial to getting the most out of this quiet, absorbing drama. Made by the team behind the superb, Oscar-nominated teaching drama *Half Nelson*, it is a similarly low-key, beautifully observed, but frustratingly slight fish-out-of-water tale. Algenis Perez Soto plays the 19-year-old Dominican sportsman Miguel "Sugar" Santos, who is talent-scouted in his native country and fast-tracked to the US minor leagues. Much of the baseball detail will leave non-fans cold, but there's a very human element that makes the movie worth sticking with. DW Spanish, English +subtitles. ᴅᴠᴅ

Algenis Perez Soto *Miguel "Sugar" Santos* • Rayniel Rufino *Jorge Ramirez* • Andre Holland *Brad Johnson* • Michael Gaston *Stu Sutton* • Jose Rijo *Alvarez* • Ann Whitney *Helen Higgins* ■ *Dir/Scr* Anna Boden, Ryan Fleck

Sugar & Spice ★★★ 15
Black comedy 2001 · US · Colour · 77min

The cast list – Mena Suvari, James Marsden, Rachel Blanchard – is an impressive roster of 20-something American actors, and they all look as if they had fun making this broad, if not always successful comedy about a group of cheerleaders who turn to bank robbery when one of their number (Marley Shelton) gets pregnant and is disowned by her parents. Mildly amusing teen fare, with a grown-up cast that includes Sean Young and king of the annoying cameos, Jerry Springer. JB ᴅᴠᴅ

Marla Sokoloff *Lisa* • Marley Shelton *Diane* • Melissa George *Cleo* • Mena Suvari *Kansas* • Rachel Blanchard *Hannah* • Alexandra Holden *Fern* • Sara Marsh *Lucy* • James Marsden *Jack Barlett* • Sean Young *Mrs Hill* ■ *Dir* Francine McDougall • *Scr* Mandy Nelson

Sugar Hill ★★★ 15
Blaxploitation horror 1974 · US · Colour · 87min

When her boyfriend is brutally murdered for standing up to a Mafia syndicate, fashion photographer Marki Bey visits a voodoo queen who summons up evil baron Don Pedro Colley and his zombie hordes to take revenge. Mainly because first-time director Paul Maslansky learnt from producing such gruesome gems as *Death Line*, this blaxploitation horror is one of the best. The gore is leavened with a keen sense of genre ridiculousness that a knowing audience can share and a "right on" attitude is on show with the cobwebbed zombies all being former slaves. AJ ᴅᴠᴅ

Marki Bey *Diana "Sugar" Hill* • Robert Quarry *Morgan* • Don Pedro Colley *Baron Samedi* • Richard Lawson *Valentine* • Betty Anne Rees *Celeste* • Zara Culley *Mama Maitresse* ■ *Dir* Paul Maslansky • *Scr* Tim Kelley

Sugar Hill ★★★ 18
Crime thriller 1993 · US · Colour · 118min

Director Leon Ichaso explores the difficulties involved in quitting the ghetto and starting over. As the dealer determined to leave behind the trade that has destroyed his family, Wesley Snipes is convincingly torn between a romance with well-heeled Theresa Randle and his loyalty to his brother (Michael Wright), who's in thrall to gangster Abe Vigoda. However, the wordiness of Barry Michael Cooper's script detracts from the film's authenticity. AT Violence, swearing, drug abuse, nudity.

Wesley Snipes *Roemello Skuggs* • Michael Wright *Raynathan Skuggs* • Theresa Randle *Melissa* • Clarence Williams III *Ar Skuggs* • Abe Vigoda *Gus Molino* • Larry Joshua *Harry Molino* • Ernie Hudson *Lolly* ■ *Dir* Leon Ichaso • *Scr* Barry Michael Cooper

Sugar Town ★★ 18
Spoof music comedy 1999 · US/UK · Colour · 89min

Allison Anders turns her attention to the downside of the music business in this eager, but overfamiliar satire. Despite the presence of Duran Duran's John Taylor and Spandau Ballet's Martin Kemp, the music is neither intriguing nor good pastiche, while caricatures such as Ally Sheedy's neurotic New Age designer, Rosanna Arquette's ageing ingénue and Beverly D'Angelo's sugar mommy feel underwritten and overplayed. DP Swearing, drug abuse.

Rosanna Arquette *Eva* • Ally Sheedy *Liz* • Jade Gordon *Gwen* • Lumi Cavazos *Rosio* • John Taylor (3) *Clive* • Michael Des Barres *Nick* • Beverly D'Angelo *Jane* • Martin Kemp *Jonesy* • John Doe *Carl* ■ *Dir* Allison Anders • *Scr* Kurt Voss, Allison Anders

Sugarbaby ★★★★ 15
Romantic comedy 1985 · W Ger · Colour · 85min

Percy Adlon's unconventional romantic comedy was rightly hailed as a triumph for its star, Marianne Sägebrecht. She excels as the generously proportioned Munich mortuary assistant whose obsession with a married underground train driver (Eisi Gulp) inspires a scheme to seduce him. However, this is also a skilfully directed film, with the candied neon colour schemes suggesting a fairy-tale atmosphere that is reinforced by the wicked witch-like appearance of Gulp's wife, Manuela Denz. Remade as a TV movie in 1989, starring Ricki Lake. DP German +subtitles.

Marianne Sägebrecht *Marianne* • Eisi Gulp *Eugen Huber* • Toni Berger *Funeral parlor boss* • Manuela Denz *Huber's wife* • Will Spindler *1st train driver* ■ *Dir* Percy Adlon • *Scr* Percy Adlon, Gwendolyn von Ambesser, from a story by Percy Adlon • *Cinematographer* Johanna Heer

Sugarfoot ★★ U
Western 1951 · US · Colour · 79min

An undistinguished Warner Bros western, this pairs rugged Randolph Scott with suave Raymond Massey as his nemesis. It is better remembered today as one of the first western TV series based on a feature film. This is very average, and really only for fans of Scott, though the super 1950s Technicolor gives it a certain class. TS

Randolph Scott *Sugarfoot* • Adele Jergens *Reva Cairn* • Raymond Massey *Jacob Stint* • SZ Sakall *Don Miguel* • Robert Warwick *JC Crane* • Arthur Hunnicutt *Fly-up-the-Creek Jones* • Hugh

S

Sanders *Asa Goodhue* ■ *Dir* Edwin L Marin • *Scr* Russell Hughes, from a novel by Clarence Budington

Sugarhouse ★★ 15

Crime thriller   2007 · UK · Colour · 90min

This British "gangster" drama may cover familiar territory, but it does boast good performances and some moments of genuine screen power. In a grotty London café middle-class Tom (Steven Mackintosh) negotiates with crack addict D (Ashley Walters) to buy a gun. The weapon turns out to have been stolen from local dealer Hoodwink (Andy Serkis) and he wants his property back because it links him to a murder. There's some overacting – and a lot of shouting – in this overwrought three-hander, but the chief attraction is the bald and bullish Serkis. Subtle he isn't. DA **DVD**

Steven Mackintosh *Horatio ("Tom")* • Ashley Walters *D* • Andy Serkis *Hoodwink* • Adam Deacon *Ray* ■ *Dir* Gary Love • *Scr* Dominic Leyton, from his play *Collision*

The Sugarland Express ★★★ PG

Action adventure based on a true story
1974 · US · Colour · 104min

This is a marvellously constructed chase movie from a young Steven Spielberg, about a young couple heading for Sugarland, Texas, pursued by the police as they race across the state. As written, the couple are not particularly likeable, but as played by Goldie Hawn and William Atherton they're funny and sympathetic, even when they capture patrolman Michael Sacks and hold him hostage. The set pieces are beautifully handled and Ben Johnson is watchable as the head cop on their tail. TS Violence, swearing. **DVD** Blu-ray

Goldie Hawn *Lou Jean Poplin* • Ben Johnson (1) *Captain Tanner* • Michael Sacks *Officer Maxwell Slide* • William Atherton *Clovis Poplin* • Gregory Walcott *Officer Mashburn* • Steve Kanaly *Jessup* • Louise Latham *Mrs Looby* ■ *Dir* Steven Spielberg • *Scr* Hal Barwood, Matthew Robbins, from a story by Steven Spielberg, Hal Barwood, Matthew Robbins

Suicide Battalion ★★ U

Second World War adventure
1958 · US · BW · 78min

This static action adventure is directed by Edward L Cahn, who churned out roughly ten similarly uninspired films a year during this period. This was drive-in fodder, made to support a horror or beach party flick and featuring actors who would appeal to the teenage market. Here, Michael Connors and John Ashley break into a captured American base to destroy some top secret papers. TS

Michael Connors [Mike Connors] *Major Matt McCormack* • John Ashley *Tommy Novello* • Jewell Lian *Elizabeth Ann Mason* • Russ Bender *Harry Donovan* • Bing Russell *Lt Chet Hall* • Scott Peters *Wally Skilzowski* ■ *Dir* Edward L Cahn • *Scr* Lou Rusoff

Suicide Kings ★★★ 15

Black comedy thriller
1997 · US · Colour · 102min

Despite its tortuous plot, this black comedy provides a rewarding mix of amoral laughs and suspense. Christopher Walken stars as a Mob boss kidnapped by a group of youngsters who need to raise their own ransom to rescue one of their girlfriends. Henry Thomas, Jay Mohr and Sean Patrick Flanery more than hold their own with the experienced Walken, and there's also a nice turn from Denis Leary. A little too clever for its own good, this still holds the attention. JF Violence, swearing, drug abuse, nudity.

Christopher Walken *Charles Barrett* • Denis Leary *Lono Vecchio* • Sean Patrick Flanery *Max Minot* • Johnny Galecki *Ira Reder* • Jay Mohr *Brett Campbell* • Jeremy Sisto *TK* ■ *Dir* Peter O'Fallon • *Scr* Josh McKinney, Wayne Rice, Gina Goldman, from the story *The Hostage* by Don Stanford

Suicide Squad ★★ 15

Action adventure   2016 · US · Colour · 122min

Never mind the good, only the bad and the ugly can be members of the superteam at the heart of this underpowered comic-book adaptation. Following the catastrophic events of *Batman v Superman: Dawn of Justice*, the US government sanctions hard-as-nails Amanda Waller (a menacing Viola Davis) to press-gang incarcerated villains into doing its dirty work – hitman supreme Deadshot (Will Smith), cannibal Killer Croc (Adewale Akinnuoye-Agbaje) and the Joker's madcap moll, Harley Quinn (Margot Robbie). It's all in stark contrast to the breeze and banter of Marvel's *Avengers* series, though the cast is undoubtedly game. However, character chemistry is limited and there's a distinct lack of suspense. JA Violence, swearing. 3D CS

Will Smith *Floyd Lawton/Deadshot* • Jared Leto *The Joker* • Margot Robbie *Dr Harleen Quinzel/ Harley Quinn* • Joel Kinnaman *Rick Flag* • Jai Courtney *Boomerang* • Scott Eastwood *Lieutenant GQ Edwards* • Cara Delevingne *June Moone/Enchantress* ■ *Dir* David Ayer • *Scr* David Ayer, from the comic book by Robert Kanigher (original writer), Ross Andru (original artist), John Ostrander (relaunch writer) (uncredited)

Suite Française ★★★★ 15

Wartime romantic drama
2014 · UK/Fr/Can · Colour · 107min

In the early 1940s the Nazis have swept through France and Michelle Williams finds herself drawn to the German officer billeted in her grand house – even while her husband languishes in a prison camp. Once again, romance proves no respecter of nationality or creed in this adaptation of the novel by Irene Nemirovsky who, in a tragic irony, wrote it just before being deported to Auschwitz where she died in 1942. Williams is utterly convincing, while Matthias Schoenaerts proves gallant and sensitive in what could have been a clichéd role. TJ In English, German. Violence, swearing.

Michelle Williams *Lucile Angellier* • Kristin Scott Thomas *Madame Angellier* • Matthias Schoenaerts *Bruno von Falk* • Sam Riley *Benoit Labarie* • Ruth Wilson *Madeleine Labarie* • Margot Robbie *Celine Joseph* ■ *Dir* Saul Dibb • *Scr* Saul Dibb, Matt Charman, from Irene Nemirovsky's novel

Suite 16 ★★★ 18

Erotic drama
1994 · UK/Bel/Neth · Colour · 106min

A wealthy paraplegic offers sanctuary to a fleeing felon in return for his aiding him with his erotic fantasies. Pete Postlethwaite is the dirty old man, Antonie Kamerling his hunky helper, in an intriguing if somewhat pretentious piece that was badly mismarketed as soft-core porn by most of its distributors. Considering the presence of Postlethwaite and the co-scripting of *The Fast Show*'s Charlie Higson, it deserves a little more attention. DA English, French +subtitles. Swearing, sex scenes, violence. **DVD**

Pete Postlethwaite *Glover* • Antonie Kamerling *Chris* • Géraldine Pailhas *Helen* • Tom Jansen *Paul* • Bart Slegers *Rudy* ■ *Dir* Dominique Deruddere • *Scr* Charles Higson, Lise Mayer

Sukiyaki Western Django ★★ 15

Western   2007 · Jpn · Colour · 94min

Cult appeal is stamped all over Japanese film-maker Takashi Miike's eccentric homage to the spaghetti western. The familiar scenario sees a gun-slinging stranger (Hideaki Ito) arrive in a town controlled by two violent, rival gangs. Miike's more interesting creative touches prevent it from descending into a straight genre piece but the dialogue (made up of western clichés) is delivered in such heavily accented English that subtitling is a necessity. Kaori Momoi stands out as a granny with a violent secret, while sole credited "gaijin" (non-Japanese) performer Quentin Tarantino offers a predictably toe-curling cameo. JH English +subtitles. Violence, swearing. **DVD**

Hideaki Ito *Gunslinger* • Koichi Sato *Kiyomori* • Yusuke Iseya *Yoshitsune* • Quentin Tarantino *Piringo* ■ *Dir* Takashi Miike • *Scr* Takashi Miike, Masa Nakamura

Sullivan's Travels ★★★★★ PG

Satirical comedy drama 1941 · US · BW · 86min

A sparkling satire from writer/director Preston Sturges, this centres on the age-old Hollywood dilemma of art versus entertainment. Giving perhaps his best performance, Joel McCrea plays a hugely successful slapstick comedy director who yearns to make a serious movie. So he hits the road, disguised as a tramp, in a concerted attempt to find out what it means to suffer. With Veronica Lake in a star-making turn as McCrea's travelling companion, the plot veers from inspired insight to corny contrivance at such a rattling pace the sheer vigour of the action carries you along. This classic comedy should leave you in no doubt where Sturges thought a movie's first duty lay, yet it's also one of the few films that manages to strike a winning balance between entertainment and conscience. DP **DVD** Blu-ray

Joel McCrea *John L Sullivan* • Veronica Lake *The girl* • William Demarest *Mr Jones* • Robert Warwick *Mr Lebrand* • Franklin Pangborn *Mr Casalais* • Porter Hall *Mr Hadrian* • Robert Greig *Sullivan's butler* • Eric Blore *Sullivan's valet* • Arthur Hoyt *Preacher* • Preston Sturges *Man in film studio* ■ *Dir/Scr* Preston Sturges

Sully

Drama based on a true story 2016 · US · Colour

This is a preview – no prints were available to review prior to publication: Chesley "Sully" Sullenberger was the pilot who, in January 2009, after multiple bird strikes caused both his engines to fail, managed to land his plane containing 155 passengers on the Hudson River. The remarkable unpowered landing turned Sully into an instant YouTube hero. Now, director Clint Eastwood comes up with the more considered response. And who better to play Sully than Tom Hanks, who has built a career out of everyman heroes? Expect grace under pressure and maturity winning the day. SvM

Tom Hanks *Chesley "Sully" Sullenberger* • Anna Gunn *Dr Elizabeth Davis* • Laura Linney *Lorraine Sullenberger* • Autumn Reeser *Tess Sosa* • Aaron Eckhart *Jeff Skiles* ■ *Dir* Clint Eastwood • *Scr* Todd Komarnicki, from the non-fiction book *Highest Duty* by Chesley Sullenberger, Jeffrey Zaslow

The Sum of All Fears ★★★ 12

Political action thriller
2002 · US/Ger · Colour · 118min

This absorbing adaptation of a typically intricate Tom Clancy novel takes a couple of big gambles. The first is replacing Harrison Ford as CIA analyst Jack Ryan with Ben Affleck, who's 30 years younger, and the story has been re-written to accommodate a less savvy, lower-ranking hero. The other is a shocking act of international terrorism that takes place around the halfway mark and transforms the film from a thinking person's thriller into a contemporary version of Sidney Lumet's doom-laden *Fail-Safe*. The appealing Affleck and director Phil Alden Robinson pull it off, thanks to a superior supporting cast, intelligent twists and taut pacing. JC **DVD**

Ben Affleck *Jack Ryan* • Morgan Freeman *DCI William Cabot* • James Cromwell *President Fowler* • Liev Schreiber *John Clark* • Bridget Moynahan *Dr Cathy Muller* • Alan Bates *Richard Dressler* • Ciaran Hinds *President Nemerov* • Philip Baker Hall *Defense Secretary Becker* • Ron Rifkin *Secretary of State Owens* • Bruce McGill *National Security Advisor Revell* • Colm Feore *Olson* ■ *Dir* Phil Alden Robinson • *Scr* Paul Attanasio, Daniel Pyne, from the novel by Tom Clancy

The Sum of Us ★★★ 15

Comedy   1995 · Aus · Colour · 95min

Although set against the familiar landmarks of Sydney, this well-meaning plea for sexual tolerance never quite escapes its theatrical origins. Too many stagey lines and matey

nods to camera intrude upon widower Jack Thompson's eager efforts to make plumber son Russell Crowe feel at home with his homosexuality. Yet, such is the geniality of Thompson's one-man assault on Aussie macho culture that it's easy to forgive the contrivances. DP Swearing.

Jack Thompson *Harry Mitchell* • Russell Crowe *Jeff Mitchell* • John Polson *Greg* • Deborah Kennedy *Joyce Johnson* • Joss Morony *Young Jeff* • Mitch Mathews *Gran* • Julie Herbert *Mary* ■ *Dir* Kevin Dowling, Geoff Burton • *Scr* David Stevens, from his play

Summer ★★★★ 15

Drama   2008 · UK/Ger · Colour · 79min

After working up a sweat in adventure flicks like *28 Weeks Later*, Robert Carlyle slows the pace in this excellent, contemplative drama. He says little as Shaun, a man haunted by the events of one summer in his misspent youth, but his frustration is palpable. It's an absorbing performance and director Kenneth Glenaan takes us even deeper into Shaun's inner world with dreamy and evocative snapshots from the past. These clash with the bitter reality of Shaun's adult life, which is sacrificed in caring for his best pal Daz (Steve Evets), who is confined to a wheelchair for reasons that become poignantly clear. Some patience is required as fractured memories are pieced together, but it's definitely time well spent. SP **DVD**

Robert Carlyle *Shaun* • Steve Evets *Daz* • Rachael Blake *Katy* • Joanna Tulej *Young Katy* ■ *Dir* Kenny Glenaan [Kenneth Glenaan] • *Scr* Hugh Ellis

Summer and Smoke ★★

Drama   1961 · US · Colour · 118min

Tennessee Williams's play, spanning several years in the life of the timid, sexually repressed and neurotic daughter of a minister in a small Southern town, won Geraldine Page plaudits and fame in the 1952 Broadway production. She repeated it on screen, with Laurence Harvey co-staring as the wild young doctor for whom Page harbours a passion, and Rita Moreno as the dance-hall girl who's much more his cup of tea. However, the material simply fails to ignite and is worth enduring only for Page's performance. RK

Geraldine Page *Alma Winemiller* • Laurence Harvey *John Buchanan* • Una Merkel *Mrs Winemiller* • Rita Moreno *Rosa Zacharias* • John McIntire *Dr Buchanan* ■ *Dir* Peter Glenville • *Scr* James Poe, Meade Roberts, from the play by Tennessee Williams • *Music* Elmer Bernstein

A Summer at Grandpa's ★★★★ PG

Drama   1984 · Tai · Colour · 97min

Such is the mastery of Hou Hsiao-Hsien that he takes a situation ripe for sentimentalising and fills it with small moments of truth and insight into how kids relate to grown-ups. As Wang Qiguang and his younger sister witness the rivalry between their grandpa and uncle, it's the innocent immediacy of children's preoccupations that is most keenly observed. This rite-of-passage film offers no easy lessons and cosy resolutions, and is all the more charming and effective for it. DP Mandarin +subtitles.

Wang Qiguang *Tung-Tung* • Gu Jun *Grandpa* • Mei Fang *Grandma* • Lin Xiuling *Pi-Yun* • Edward Yang ■ *Dir* Hou Hsiao-Hsien • *Scr* Zhu Tianwen, Hou Hsiao-Hsien

Summer Catch ★★ 12

Sports comedy drama
2001 · US · Colour · 99min

Not even a cast of fresh-faced acting hotshots can give flavour to this bland and undistinguished teen sporting romance. The film applies all the usual strength-through-adversity clichés, and wraps them up in a poor-boy-meets-rich-girl subplot. Freddie Prinze Jr is the quick-tempered lawn boy given a shot at major league baseball success, only to jeopardise his chances by falling for Jessica Biel, daughter of one of his rich clients. SF **DVD**

Freddie Prinze Jr *Ryan Dunne* • Jessica Biel *Tenley Parrish* • Matthew Lillard *Billy Brubaker* • Brian Dennehy *John Schiffner* • Fred Ward *Sean Dunne* • Jason Gedrick *Mike Dunne* • Brittany Murphy *Dede Mulligan* • Bruce Davison *Rand Parrish* ■ *Dir* Mike Tollin • *Scr* Kevin Falls, John Gatins, from a story by Kevin Falls

Summer Holiday ★★★

Musical comedy
1948 · US · Colour and BW · 92min

This musical version of Eugene O'Neill's play *Ah, Wilderness* (already filmed in 1935) is a spirited, if low-key, MGM production with little of lasting value, unless you warm to the brash Mickey Rooney in the lead. He plays the lovestruck scion of a small-town American family. Co-star Gloria DeHaven is certainly mouthwatering, and the film does look superb. **TS**

Mickey Rooney *Richard Miller* • Gloria DeHaven *Muriel McComber* • Walter Huston *Nat Miller* • Frank Morgan *Uncle Sid* • Jackie "Butch" Jenkins *Tommy Miller* • Marilyn Maxwell *Belle* • Agnes Moorehead *Cousin Lily* ■ *Dir* Rouben Mamoulian • *Scr* Frances Goodrich, Albert Hackett, Irving Brecher, Jean Holloway, from the play *Ah, Wilderness* by Eugene O'Neill

Summer Holiday ★★★ U

Musical comedy 1962 · UK · Colour · 103min

Cliff Richard was still making hit records decades after this high-spirited romp. It's unlikely that his knighthood was awarded solely on the strength of this wholesome road movie (the less than august debut of director Peter Yates), in which four youths cross Europe in a London Transport double-decker bus. But there are plenty of fondly remembered songs, some splendid scenery and a willing supporting cast. **DP** *DVD*

Cliff Richard *Don* • Lauri Peters *Barbara* • Melvyn Hayes *Cyril* • Una Stubbs *Sandy* • Teddy Green *Steve* • Pamela Hart (1) *Angie* • Jeremy Bulloch *Edwin* • Hank Marvin • Bruce Welch • Jet Harris • Tony Meehan ■ *Dir* Peter Yates • *Scr* Peter Myers, Ronald Cass

Summer Hours ★★★★ 12

Drama 2008 · Fr · Colour · 98min

This drama from Olivier Assayas tells the story of adult siblings who squabble over what to do with their late mother's estate and, in particular an art collection of which she was the custodian. While Frédéric (Charles Berling) seems the most cultured of the children and is genuinely concerned about the artifacts, he is patently at odds with career-minded Adrienne (Juliette Binoche) and younger brother Jérémie (Jérémie Renier) who are eager to sell up as quickly as possible. Assayas's film is a compelling treatise on heritage, ancestral ties and the true value of art, and also typifies his habit of littering his pictures with homages to favourite film-makers such as Jean Renoir, Eric Rohmer and Louis Malle. **DP** French +subtitles. *DVD*

Juliette Binoche *Adrienne* • Charles Berling *Frédéric* • Jérémie Renier [Jérémie Rénier] *Jérémie* • Edith Scob *Hélène* • Dominique Reymond *Lisa* • Valérie Bonneton *Angela* • Isabelle Sadoyan *Éloïse* • Kyle Eastwood *James* ■ *Dir/Scr* Olivier Assayas

Summer House ★★

Mystery thriller 2008 · US/Can · Colour · 90min

Lipstick Jungle's Lindsay Price adds good looks but very little else to this banal haunted house tale, as an introverted artist who's desperate to break a curse that's afflicted the male heirs in her husband's family for centuries. Despite the cast's best efforts, it's only the bursts of foreboding music that provide any sense of eerie atmosphere – a lazy device ill-served by the preposterous dialogue and lame finale. **SF**

Lindsay Price *Nikki Wickersham* • David Hadyn-Jones [David Jones (5)] *George Wickersham IV* • Sadie LeBlanc *Margie Mancuso* • Niall Matter *Peter Hughes* • Emma Stevens *Virginia Roberts* • Susan Bain *Celia Calvert* ■ *Dir* Jean-Claude Lord • *Scr* John Benjamin Martin, Donald David Martin

Summer in February ★★★ 15

Period romantic drama
2012 · UK · Colour · 96min

Teacher Jonathan Smith's novel about a real-life group of bohemian artists living on the Cornish coast just before the First World War came to the big screen with one of his former pupils, *Downton Abbey* star Dan Stevens, as producer and co-star. Stevens gives a touching performance as Gilbert Evans, the land agent in charge of the Lamorna Estate, while Dominic Cooper oozes charisma as roguish artist AJ Munnings, and Emily Browning plays Florence Carter-Wood, who steals the hearts of both men. They are all upstaged, however, by the Cornish landscape. **AIS** Swearing, nudity. *DVD* *BL*

Dominic Cooper *AJ Munnings* • Emily Browning *Florence Carter-Wood* • Dan Stevens *Gilbert Evans* • Hattie Morahan *Laura Knight* • Shaun Dingwall *Harold Knight* • Mia Austen *Dolly* ■ *Dir* Christopher Menaul • *Scr* Jonathan Smith, from his novel

Summer Interlude ★★★★ PG

Drama 1950 · Swe · BW · 91min

This is the picture that established Ingmar Bergman's international reputation. It contains the first intimations of the dramatic intensity and structural complexity that would characterise his more mature work. As the world-weary ballerina recalling her teenage affair with timid student Birger Malmsten, May-Britt Nilsson gives a performance of such sensitivity that one is at a loss to explain why Bergman dropped her from his stock company after *Secrets of Women* a couple of years later. Gunnar Fischer and Bengt Jarnmark's shimmering images of the sunny Swedish countryside further enhance this subtle, moving film. **DP** Swedish +subtitles. *DVD*

Maj-Britt Nilsson *Marie* • Birger Malmsten *Henrik* • Alf Kjellin *David Nyström* • Georg Funkquist *Uncle Erland* • Mimi Pollak *Aunt Elizabeth* ■ *Dir* Ingmar Bergman • *Scr* Ingmar Bergman, Herbert Grevenius, from a story by Ingmar Bergman

Summer Lovers ★★ 18

Erotic comedy 1982 · US · Colour · 98min

After 1980's *The Blue Lagoon*, director Randal Kleiser chose another, equally exotic, location for this slightly more grown-up tale of young romance. The setting this time is a sun-drenched Greek island, where poor old Peter Gallagher finds himself torn between Daryl Hannah and Valérie Quennessen. It looks great, but there's more depth in a teen magazine picture story than in this empty-headed nonsense. **JF** Sex scenes, nudity.

Peter Gallagher *Michael Papas* • Daryl Hannah *Cathy Feathererst* • Valérie Quennessen *Lina* • Barbara Rush *Jean Feathererst* • Carole Cook *Barbara Foster* • Hans Van Tongeren *Jan Tolin* ■ *Dir/Scr* Randal Kleiser

Summer Magic ★★★ U

Period comedy 1963 · US · Colour · 109min

Co-produced by Walt Disney and starring Hayley Mills, this lovingly re-creates the atmosphere of 1900s Maine. Mills is not at her effervescent best, but she's still suitably fresh-faced, as she finds time for a little innocent romance while helping widowed mother Dorothy McGuire raise her brothers. One of the highlights is Burl Ives's rendition of *The Ugly Bug Ball*, which became a popular song of the time. **DP**

Hayley Mills *Nancy Carey* • Burl Ives *Osh Popham* • Dorothy McGuire *Margaret Carey* • Deborah Walley *Julia Carey* • Una Merkel *Maria Popham* • Eddie Hodges *Gilly Carey* • Michael J Pollard *Digby Popham* ■ *Dir* James Neilson • *Scr* Sally Benson, from the novel *Mother Carey's Chickens* by Kate Douglas Wiggin

The Summer of Ben Tyler ★★★★

Period drama 1996 · US · Colour · 134min

James Woods delivers a stirring performance as an ethical attorney who rocks a small southern town when he chooses to take in the mentally disadvantaged teenage son of his recently deceased black housekeeper. Set during the Second World War, this highly emotional production eloquently illuminates the nature of racial prejudice and intolerance. It's a poignant TV drama with superb performances by Woods and a stunning supporting cast. **MC**

James Woods *Temple Rayburn* • Elizabeth McGovern *Celia Rayburn* • Charles Mattocks *Ben Tyler* • Len Cariou *Spencer Maitland* • Julia McIlvaine *Nell Rayburn* ■ *Dir* Arthur Allan Seidelman • *Scr* Robert Inman

Summer of '42 ★★ 15

Wartime drama 1971 · US · Colour · 99min

Robert Mulligan's surprisingly popular rite-of-passage picture is so shrouded in nostalgia that it arouses your suspicions. Home-front life in the year after America entered the Second World War simply couldn't have been this good. But there is something undeniably touching about 15-year-old Gary Grimes's relationship with war bride Jennifer O'Neill, which almost atones for the adolescent humour and the cosiness of the period detail. A sequel, *Class of '44*, was even less convincing. **DP** Swearing, violence, sex scenes.

Jennifer O'Neill *Dorothy* • Gary Grimes *Hermie* • Jerry Houser *Oscy* • Oliver Conant *Benjie* • Katherine Allentuck *Aggie* • Christopher Norris *Miriam* • Robert Mulligan *Narrator, older Hermie* ■ *Dir* Robert Mulligan • *Scr* Herman Raucher • *Music* Michel Legrand

Summer of My German Soldier ★★★★★★

Second World War romantic drama
1978 · US · Colour · 98min

A contender for the accolade as the best-ever TV movie, this moving work occasionally has sentimental moments but is never false in its emotions. The setting is Georgia, USA, where a group of German PoWs is interned to the dismay of the locals, apart from Jewish teenager Kristy McNichol. She befriends young soldier Bruce Davison, only to have her life turned upside down by bigotry and misunderstanding. Esther Rolle won an Emmy for her performance, but all the acting is memorable in a film of resonance, power and conviction. **BB**

Kristy McNichol *Patty Bergen* • Bruce Davison *Anton Reiker* • Esther Rolle *Ruth* • Michael Constantine *Harry Bergen* • Barbara Barrie *Mrs Bergen* • James Noble *Pierce* ■ *Dir* Michael Tuchner • *Scr* Jane-Howard Hammerstein, from the novel by Bette Greene

Summer of Sam ★★★ 18

Drama 1999 · US · Colour · 136min

Full marks to Spike Lee for tackling a movie where all the main characters are white, in this case Italian-American. The year is 1977, and New York is being terrorised by David Berkowitz, the serial killer dubbed "Son of Sam". However, the focus here is on the troubled marriage of John Leguizamo and Mira Sorvino, and the rather seedy life of fledgeling punk rocker and part-time male hooker Adrien Brody. The scenes involving Berkowitz are disturbingly creepy, while Lee successfully evokes the seedy side of the late 1970s. **JF** Swearing, violence, drug abuse, nudity. *DVD*

John Leguizamo *Vinny* • Adrien Brody *Ritchie* • Mira Sorvino *Dionna* • Jennifer Esposito *Ruby* • Ben Gazzara *Luigi* • Michael Rispoli *Joey T* • Saverio Guerra *Woodstock* • Brian Tarantino *Bobby Del Fiore* • Al Palagonia *Anthony* • Spike Lee *John Jeffries* • John Turturro *Harvey the black dog* ■ *Dir* Spike Lee • *Scr* Victor Colicchio, Michael Imperioli, Spike Lee

A Summer Place ★★★

Melodrama 1959 · US · Colour · 129min

A lush assemblage of sexual matters dominates Delmer Daves's adaptation of Sloan Wilson's steamy bestseller about the middle-classes at play on the beaches of New England. This glossy affair was quite outspoken for its time and cleaned up at the box office. The youthful focus is on pretty-boy Troy Donahue's romance with Sandra Dee, while the adult coupling mainly involves married Dorothy McGuire and her lover Richard Egan. The soapy score and the hit title song, composed by Max Steiner, contribute greatly to this enjoyable trash. **RK**

Richard Egan *Ken Jorgenson* • Dorothy McGuire *Sylvia Hunter* • Sandra Dee *Molly Jorgenson* • Arthur Kennedy *Bart Hunter* • Troy Donahue *Johnny Hunter* • Constance Ford *Helen Jorgenson* ■ *Dir* Delmer Daves • *Scr* Delmer Daves, from the novel by Sloan Wilson

Summer Rental ★★ PG

Comedy 1985 · US · Colour · 83min

Harassed and overworked air-traffic controller John Candy badly needs a vacation and takes his family away to holiday on a beach. But almost from the moment they arrive, things start to go wrong and the supposedly restful trip turns into a nightmare every bit as stressful as work. This thin comedy fails to exploit its promising premise. **JG**

John Candy *Jack Chester* • Richard Crenna *Al Pellet* • Karen Austin *Sandy* • Rip Torn *Scully* • Kerri Green *Jennifer* • Joey Lawrence *Bobby* • John Larroquette *Don Moore* ■ *Dir* Carl Reiner • *Scr* Jeremy Stevens, Mark Reisman

Summer Scars ★★★ 15

Horror thriller 2007 · US · Colour · 67min

British director Julian Richards highlights the perils of talking to strangers in this disturbing coming-of-age thriller. Richards twists a personal childhood incident into a bare-bones terror tale in which teens playing truant are caught up in the sadistic mind games of a deranged drifter (Kevin Howarth, who also starred in the director's 2003 horror *The Last Horror Movie*). The briskly paced action is intense and character driven, and, though the young delinquents start out as unlikeable stereotypes, it's the unmasking of the vulnerability beneath that gives depth to an otherwise simple narrative. Howarth's impressively subtle performance provides the film's purest note. **SF**

Kevin Howarth *Peter* • Ciaran Joyce *Bingo* • Amy Harvey *Leanne* • Jonathan Jones *Paul* • Darren Evans *Jonesy* • Chris Conway *Ben* • Ryan Conway *Mugsey* ■ *Dir* Julian Richards • *Scr* Al Wilson, from an idea by Julian Richards

Summer School ★★★ 15

Comedy 1987 · US · Colour · 92min

This genial teen comedy has Mark Harmon as the teacher who reluctantly agrees to cancel his vacation and teach English to a class of misfits over the summer holidays. It's a bit of a disappointment when you realise it was directed by Carl Reiner, but Harmon and co-star Kirstie Alley are funny and they are ably abetted by the teenage supporting cast. **JB** Swearing, violence.

Mark Harmon *Freddy Shoop* • Kirstie Alley *Robin Bishop* • Robin Thomas *Phil Gills* • Dean Cameron *Francis "Chainsaw" Gremp* • Gary Riley *Dave Frazier* • Shawnee Smith *Rhonda Altobello* • Courtney Thorne-Smith *Pam House* ■ *Dir* Carl Reiner • *Scr* Jeff Franklin, from a story by Stuart Birnbaum, David Dashev, Jeff Franklin

Summer Stock ★★★★ U

Musical 1950 · US · Colour · 108min

Also known in the UK as *If You Feel like Singing*, this was Judy Garland's last MGM feature and, despite rather obvious scene-by-scene weight fluctuations stemming from her attempts to withdraw from drug dependency, she managed to deliver another wonderful musical. Pure joy from beginning to end, this quintessential "let's put on a show in a barn" movie contains moments that are among the career highlights of the film's two stars. Gene Kelly's newspaper dance is a treat and Garland's *Get Happy* finale became an instant classic. There's a fabulous rapport between the two leads and the whole is wrapped up in that sumptuous MGM Technicolor. **TS**

Judy Garland *Jane Falbury* • Gene Kelly *Joe D Ross* • Eddie Bracken *Orville Wingait* • Gloria DeHaven *Abigail Falbury* • Marjorie Main *Esme* •

S

Phil Silvers *Herb Blake* • Ray Collins *Jasper G Wingait* • Nita Bieber *Sarah Higgins* ■ *Dir* Charles Walters • *Scr* George Wells, Sy Gomberg, from a story by Sy Gomberg

Summer Storm ★★★

Period romantic drama 1944 · US · BW · 106min

Based on Anton Chekhov's story *The Shooting Party*, this offering from director Douglas Sirk stars Linda Darnell as the wife of the manager of a country estate, whose affair with local judge George Sanders leads to murder and disintegration. Events take place both before and after the Russian Revolution in this interesting – if only partially successful – attempt to venture away from the Hollywood mainstream. RK

George Sanders *Fedor Petroff* • Linda Darnell *Olga* • Anna Lee *Nadina* • Edward Everett Horton *Count Volsky* • Hugo Haas *Urbenin* • Lori Lahner *Clara* • John Philliber *Polycarp* • Sig Ruman *Kuzma* ■ *Dir* Douglas Sirk • *Scr* Rowland Leigh, Douglas Sirk, Robert Thoeren, from the story *The Shooting Party* by Anton Chekhov

Summer Storm ★★★ 15

Coming-of-age comedy drama
2004 · Hun/Ger · Colour · 93min

This tender and kind-hearted drama about mixed-up teens at a summer rowing camp discovering their sexuality is a coming-of-age and a coming-out story in one tidy package. Handsome blond Tobi (Robert Stadlober, in a naturalistic performance), the captain of a Bavarian rowing team, feels something more than sporting camaraderie for his team-mate and best friend, Achim (Kostja Ullmann). A charming comedy drama, if occasionally melodramatic and a little right on. LF German +subtitles. *DVD*

Robert Stadlober *Tobi* • Kostja Ullmann *Achim* • Alicja Bachleda-Curus *Anke* • Miriam Morgenstern *Sandra* • Jürgen Tonkel *Hansi* • Hanno Koffler *Malte* • Tristano Casanova *Georg* ■ *Dir* Marco Kreuzpaintner • *Scr* Tom Bahmann, Marco Kreuzpaintner

A Summer Story ★★★★ 15

Period romantic drama
1987 · UK · Colour · 92min

This beautifully filmed early 20th-century romance is based on John Galsworthy's tale *The Apple Tree*. James Wilby is the lawyer who falls for Devon country girl Imogen Stubbs while recuperating from an accident. When he has to leave, he promises to take her with him, but things don't go as planned. Wilby and Stubbs are ideally cast, and director Piers Haggard keeps the sentiment in check, so it never wanders into Mills and Boon territory. JB

Imogen Stubbs *Megan David* • James Wilby *Frank Ashton* • Kenneth Colley *Jim* • Sophie Ward *Stella Halliday* • Susannah York *Mrs Narracombe* • Jerome Flynn *Joe Narracombe* • Lee Billett *Nick Narracombe* • Oliver Perry *Rick Narracombe* ■ *Dir* Piers Haggard • *Scr* Penelope Mortimer, from the short story *The Apple Tree* by John Galsworthy • *Cinematographer* Kenneth MacMillan

Summer Things ★★★★ 15

Comedy 2002 · Fr/UK/It · Colour · 99min

Shifting effortlessly between seaside farce and social satire, this touches on serious topics while remaining acerbically amusing. Director Michel Blanc revels in a cameo as Carole Bouquet's insanely jealous spouse, but it's Charlotte Rampling's delicious display of careless snobbery that dominates, as she interferes in impoverished friend Karin Viard's domestic travails and is blissfully unaware that her own privileged lifestyle is under threat from her reckless daughter and bisexual husband. The resolution is overly neat, but the ensemble's polished expertise ensures events remain irresistibly entertaining. DP French +subtitles. Swearing, sex scenes. *DVD*

Charlotte Rampling *Elizabeth Lannier* • Jacques Dutronc *Bertrand Lannier* • Carole Bouquet *Lulu* • Michel Blanc *Jean-Pierre* • Karin Viard *Véronique* • Denis Podalydès *Jérôme* ■ *Dir* Michel Blanc • *Scr* Michel Blanc, from the novel by Joseph Connolly

Summer Vacation: 1999 ★★★★ 15

Drama 1988 · Jpn · Colour · 89min

Following the Japanese stage tradition of *Takurazuka* in which girls play the story's teenaged boys, this is a dream-like study of the adolescent agonies that arise from the pangs of first love. After one of their number seems to commit suicide on account of unrequited passion, three sexually awakening boarding school students are thrown into confusion by the arrival of another youth who bears an eerie resemblance to their friend. Both a gay ghost story and a hymn to lost innocence, Shusuke Kaneko's unique film combines disarmingly androgynous performances with lush visuals to hauntingly romantic effect. DP Japanese +subtitles.

Eri Miyajima *Yu/Kaoru/Last new boy* • Tomoko Otakara *Kazuhiko* • Miyuki Nakano *Naoto* • Rie Mizuhara *Norio* ■ *Dir* Shusuke Kaneko • *Scr* Rio Kishida

Summer Wars ★★★ 12

Animated comedy drama
2009 · Jpn · Colour · 109min

Traditional Japanese family values collide with state-of-the-art technology in this fun if overly ambitious animated tale. Life is looking up for geeky maths whizz Kenji: he works for Oz, the world's premier online social network, and the girl of his dreams, Natsuki, has asked him to come to her grandmother's birthday party. But when the pair get to Natsuki's ancestral family home, Kenji has to deal with her highly eccentric – and not especially welcoming – relatives. The incredibly detailed animation is delightful, if sometimes confusing, but it's actually the relationships that convince the most. And while the central message of the importance of friendship, family and forgiveness is far from original, it's still valid. LB *DVD*

Michael Sinterniklaas *Kenji Koiso* • Brina Palencia *Natsuki Shinohara* • Pam Dougherty *Sakae Jinnouchi* • Todd Haberkorn *Sakuma* ■ *Dir* Mamoru Hosoda • *Scr* Satoko Okudera, from a story by Mamoru Hosoda

Summer Wishes, Winter Dreams ★★

Drama 1973 · US · Colour · 88min

When Joanne Woodward rails about her disappointing life and desperately dull husband to Martin Balsam, and then concludes "I had no business inflicting all of this on you", audiences are likely to concur. This serious, well-intentioned drama is believably written, capably directed and beautifully acted (with Sylvia Sidney, making a comeback after 17 years, as Woodward's aged mother), but it fails to make these characters anything but tedious. AE

Joanne Woodward *Rita Walden* • Martin Balsam *Harry Walden* • Sylvia Sidney *Mrs Pritchett, Rita's mother* • Dori Brenner *Anna* • Win Forman *Fred Goody* • Tresa Hughes *Betty Goody* ■ *Dir* Gilbert Cates • *Scr* Stewart Stern

Summer with Monika ★★★★★ PG

Romantic drama 1952 · Swe · BW · 91min

The last of Ingmar Bergman's studies of young love and the alienating effects of city life, this is a masterpiece of contrasting images and emotions. The brilliant, sunlit scenes set on the isolated islands perfectly capture the joy and innocence of summer love, as sassy teenager Harriet Andersson and adoring Lars Ekborg splash in the dappled water and kiss beneath the stars. But Gunnar Fischer's stifling shots of Stockholm are perhaps even more impressive, as he sets the visual tone for the drift into disillusionment. DP Swedish +subtitles. *DVD*

Harriet Andersson *Monika* • Lars Ekborg *Harry* • John Harryson *Lelle* • Georg Skarstedt *Harry's father* • Dagmar Ebbesen *Harry's aunt* ■ *Dir* Ingmar Bergman • *Scr* Per-Anders Fogelstrom, Ingmar Bergman

A Summer's Tale ★★★★ U

Romantic comedy 1996 · Fr · Colour · 109min

This is a sunny treatise on the agonies of holiday romance from director Eric Rohmer. Graduate student Melvil Poupaud is torn between his love of music and his infatuations with girlfriend Aurélia Nolin, waitress Amanda Langlet and her friend Gwenaëlle Simon. His prevarications are as natural as they are frustrating, as comic as they are suspenseful. Displaying again Rohmer's gift for capturing the vernacular and behaviour of youth, this is a delight. DP French +subtitles. *DVD*

Melvil Poupaud *Gaspard* • Amanda Langlet *Margot* • Aurélia Nolin *Léna* • Gwenaëlle Simon *Solène* ■ *Dir/Scr* Eric Rohmer

Summertime ★★★★ PG

Romantic drama 1955 · US/UK · Colour · 95min

This was the movie that whetted director David Lean's appetite for location filming with international stars. It's a touching take on Arthur Laurent's play about a lonely spinster enjoying a summer fling in Venice. In a piece of unlikely casting, Katharine Hepburn plays the sheltered secretary, with Rossano Brazzi as the married object of her affection. Hepburn turns out to be an inspired choice, her reserve melting under the liberating effect of the city and the charming Brazzi. Venice looks fabulous, thanks to cameraman Jack Hildyard, and the whole thing is perfect matinée fare. Originally released in the UK as *Summer Madness*. TS *DVD*

Katharine Hepburn *Jane Hudson* • Rossano Brazzi *Renato Di Rossi* • Isa Miranda *Signora Fiorina* • Darren McGavin *Eddie Jaeger* • Mari Aldon *Phyl Jaeger* • Jane Rose *Mrs McIlhenny* • MacDonald Parke *Mr McIlhenny* • Gaitano Audiero *Mauro* ■ *Dir* David Lean • *Scr* David Lean, HE Bates, from the play *The Time of the Cuckoo* by Arthur Laurents

Summertime ★★★ 15

Romantic drama 2015 · Fr · Colour · 105min

Director Catherine Corsini and producer and life-partner Elisabeth Perez draw on their own experiences for this touching, if occasionally affected love story set in Paris and Limousin in the early 1970s. Izïa Higelin plays the twentysomething farm girl who connects with Cécile de France's older Spanish teacher through feminist politics before they tumble into bed. But Higelin must return to Limousin to help her mother, and her family's fate depends on the support of its highly conservative neighbours. DP In French. Swearing, sex scenes, drug abuse.

Cécile de France *Carole* • Izïa Higelin *Delphine* • Noémie Lvovsky *Monique* • Kévin Azaïs *Antoine* • Laetitia Dosch *Adeline* ■ *Dir* Catherine Corsini • *Scr* Catherine Corsini, Laurette Polmanss

Summertree ★★

Drama 1971 · US · Colour · 88min

Michael Douglas plays a young man who drops out of college to pursue his interest in music, and finds himself mentoring a troubled, black Kirk Callaway as part of the Big Brother youth programme. He also moves in with nurse Brenda Vaccaro, whose husband is fighting in Vietnam. The war and the counterculture are somewhat shoehorned in and, frustratingly, British director Anthony Newley resorts to melodrama as he tries to capture the mood of a nation divided along racial, social and gender lines. DP

Michael Douglas *Jerry* • Jack Warden *Herb* • Brenda Vaccaro *Vanetta* • Barbara Bel Geddes *Ruth* ■ *Dir* Anthony Newley • *Scr* Edward Hume, Stephen Yafa, from Ron Cowen's play

Sumuru ★★★

Cult science-fiction fantasy
1967 · UK · Colour · 87min

Producer and writer Harry Alan Towers, who made several films based on the exploits of Sax Rohmer's Fu Manchu, also made two featuring Rohmer's lesser-known female "evil genius" Sumuru (Shirley Eaton). In this, the first, George Nader and Frankie Avalon, both looking ill at ease, discover that Eaton and her beautiful female warriors want nothing less than world domination. The stuff of a 1930s serial, spoofed 1960s-style and combining feeble humour with an international cast of shapely starlets, this may be too rich a mix for some. The 1969 sequel, released under several titles including *Rio 70* and *Future Women*, is hard to find. DM

Shirley Eaton *Sumuru* • Frankie Avalon *Tommy Carter* • George Nader *Nick West* • Wilfrid Hyde White *Colonel Baisbrook* • Klaus Kinski *President Boong* ■ *Dir* Lindsay Shonteff • *Scr* Kevin Kavanagh, from a story by Peter Welbeck [Harry Alan Towers], from the books by Sax Rohmer

The Sun ★★★★ PG

Historical drama
2005 · Rus/It/Fr/Swi · Colour · 114min

Following his studies of Hitler (*Moloch*) and Lenin (*Taurus*), director Aleksandr Sokurov examines the strains endured by the Emperor Hirohito as Japan succumbed to the Americans in 1945. More humanist than its predecessors in this remarkable series, the film is a warm and amusing insight into a man who appears more comfortable devoting his time to marine biology than fanatical militarism. Shifting between disarming vulnerability and pragmatic decency, Issey Ogata is superb as the fastidious, lonely man, who is as uncomfortable with his divine status as he is stubbornly proud in the company of a victorious General MacArthur. This is a compelling exploration of the accidents of history and the pressures of power. DP Japanese, English +subtitles. *DVD*

Issey Ogata *Emperor* • Robert Dawson *General MacArthur* • Kaori Momoi *Empress* • Shiro Sano *Chamberlain* • Shinmei Tsuji *Old servant* • Taijiro Tamura *Director of the institute* • Georgy Pitskhelauri *General MacArthur's adjutant* • Hiroya Morita *Prime Minister Suzuki Kantaro* ■ *Dir* Aleksandr Sokurov • *Scr* Yury Arabov

The Sun Also Rises ★★★★ PG

Drama 1957 · US · Colour · 124min

An expansive version of Ernest Hemingway's great "lost generation" novel, this has a slightly too old Tyrone Power in the leading role of the impotent wartime flier adrift in Paris. Ava Gardner is a dissolute sensualist roaming Europe, and Errol Flynn is simply magnificent as an alcoholic. Also particularly fine are Mel Ferrer and Eddie Albert as Power's cronies, and take note of the actor playing Gardner's bullfighter lover – Robert Evans, future producer of *Chinatown*. TS *DVD*

Tyrone Power *Jake Barnes* • Ava Gardner *Lady Brett Ashley* • Mel Ferrer *Robert Cohn* • Errol Flynn *Mike Campbell* • Eddie Albert *Bill Gorton* • Gregory Ratoff *Count Mippipopolous* • Juliette Greco *Georgette* • Robert Evans *Pedro Romero* ■ *Dir* Henry King • *Scr* Peter Viertel, from the novel by Ernest Hemingway

The Sun Shines Bright ★★★ PG

Period drama 1953 · US · BW · 100min

Charles Winninger inherits the role of Judge Priest from Will Rogers, who played him in Ford's 1934 movie *Judge Priest*. This time the benevolent judge is standing for re-election in Fairfield, Kentucky, in 1905, but he has some serious competition. There are comic and romantic strands to the story as well as serious subplots involving rape and racism – a mix that modern audiences may find naive or offensive, or both. Whatever the views of the critics or the public, Ford cited this as one of his personal favourites, and his feeling for the story and the period is easy to see. AT

Charles Winninger *Judge Priest* • Arleen Whelan *Lucy Lee Lake* • John Russell *Corwin* • Stepin Fetchit *Jeff Poindexter* • Russell Simpson *Dr Lewt Lake* • Ludwig Stossel *Herman Felsburg* • Francis Ford *Feeney* ■ *Dir* John Ford • *Scr* Laurence Stallings, from stories by Irvin S Cobb

Sun Valley Serenade
★★★ U

Musical   1941 · US · BW · 82min

Norwegian ice-skating champion Sonja Henie returned to the screen after a two-year absence for this smash hit. The movie's success was doubtless helped by the presence of Glenn Miller in one of only two films he made, and the Mack Gordon/Harry Warren score. The characteristic candy-floss plot – Miller's star pianist (John Payne) is assigned to take care of refugee Henie – is only an excuse on which to hang the numbers. RK

Sonja Henie *Karen Benson* · John Payne *Ted Scott* · Glenn Miller *Phil Carey* · Milton Berle *Nifty Allen* · Lynn Bari *Vivian Dawn* · Joan Davis *Miss Carstairs* · Dorothy Dandridge *Vocalist* ■ *Dir* H Bruce Humberstone · *Scr* Robert Ellis, Helen Logan, from a story by Art Arthur, Robert Harari · *Choreographer* Hermes Pan · *Cinematographer* Edward Cronjager · *Music Director* Emil Newman

Sunburn
★★

Detective comedy   1979 · US · Colour · 110min

Those more inclined to swallow the idea of detective Charles Grodin and Farrah Fawcett (as the model he hires to pose as his wife) falling in love while investigating an insurance case in Mexico may enjoy this otherwise forgettable mystery romp. Fawcett is actually one of the better aspects of the movie, but she and the rest of the cast are unfortunately saddled with a story that has little mystery. KB

Farrah Fawcett-Majors [Farrah Fawcett] *Ellie Morgan* · Charles Grodin *Jake Dekker* · Art Carney *Al Marcus* · Joan Collins *Nera* · William Daniels (2) *Crawford* · John Hillerman *Webb* · Eleanor Parker *Mrs Thoren* · Keenan Wynn *Mark Elmes* ■ *Dir* Richard C Sarafian · *Scr* John Daly, Stephen Oliver, James Booth, from the novel *The Bind* by Stanley Ellin

Sunchaser
★★ 15

Road movie   1996 · US · Colour · 117min

Michael Cimino's over-egged pudding ambitiously seeks to mix elements of road and male-bonding movies, and to toss in some native American mysticism for good measure. Jon Seda is impressive as a teen hoodlum dying of cancer. After breaking out of prison, he takes a miscast Woody Harrelson hostage and forces him to drive to a mystical lake that, according to legend, has healing properties. Though well intentioned, it's somewhat pretentious. DA
Swearing, violence.

Woody Harrelson *Dr Michael Reynolds* · Jon Seda *Brandon "Blue" Monroe* · Anne Bancroft *Dr Renata Baumbauer* · Alexandra Tydings *Victoria Reynolds* · Matt Mulhern *Dr Chip Byrnes* · Talisa Soto *Navajo woman* ■ *Dir* Michael Cimino · *Scr* Charles Leavitt

Sunday
★★★

Drama   1997 · US · Colour · 93min

Winner of the Grand Jury Prize at the Sundance film festival, this is a fascinating look at being lonely, and the lengths we'll go to to kid ourselves we're not. Spanning a single day, this duality character study stars David Suchet as a downsized executive, now homeless, who pretends to be a famous art-film director to woo washed-up actress Lisa Harrow. The pretence becomes an intrinsic part of their day's mating rituals. The film's a little arty and won't appeal to everyone, but there's much here to admire, not least the performances of the two leads. DA

David Suchet *Oliver/Matthew* · Lisa Harrow *Madeleine Vesey* · Jared Harris *Ray* · Larry Pine *Ben Vesey* · Joe Grifasi *Scottie Elster* · Arnold Barkus *Andy* · Batman Soltani *Abram* ■ *Dir* Jonathan Nossiter · *Scr* James Lasdun, Jonathan Nossiter

Sunday, Bloody Sunday
★★★★ 15

Drama   1971 · UK · Colour · 105min

Divorced Glenda Jackson shares bisexual Murray Head with gay Peter Finch in John Schlesinger's ground-breaking exploration of heterosexual and homosexual relationships. This 1970s moral tale caused shock waves thanks to Finch and Head sharing one of the first all-male on-screen kisses. Finch steals the acting honours with a sympathetic performance among the tangled web of verbalised angst about the real meaning of communication, sexual and otherwise, as symbolised by telephone wires linking the busy eternal triangle's lives. AJ *DVD*

Glenda Jackson *Alex Greville* · Peter Finch *Dr Daniel Hirsh* · Murray Head *Bob Elkin* · Peggy Ashcroft *Mrs Greville* · Maurice Denham *Mr Greville* · Vivian Pickles *Alva Hodson* · Frank Windsor *Bill Hodson* · Thomas Baptiste *Professor Johns* · Tony Britton *Mr Harding* ■ *Dir* John Schlesinger · *Scr* Penelope Gilliatt

Sunday Dinner for a Soldier
★★★ U

Romantic drama   1944 · US · BW · 86min

Some find this whimsy charming, others glutinous, but in its day it chimed perfectly with popular taste, as lovely Anne Baxter yearned for just what it says – a GI to bring home for lunch on Sunday. Handsome John Hodiak turns up just in time. Expertly made schmaltz, this is one of those movies about impoverished people who don't actually suffer from being poor, but just get all philosophical with a foxy twinkle in their eye. TS

Anne Baxter *Tessa Osborne* · John Hodiak *Eric Moore* · Charles Winninger *Grandfather Osborne* · Anne Revere *Agatha* · Connie Marshall *Mary Osborne* · Chill Wills *Mr York* ■ *Dir* Lloyd Bacon · *Scr* Wanda Tuchock, Melvin Levy, from the story by Martha Cheavens

Sunday in August
★★★ U

Comedy drama   1949 · It · BW · 83min

In his feature debut, Luciano Emmer captures the carefree spirit of this witty neorealist satire on middle-class morality, which numbers among its co-scenarists Cesare Zavattini and Sergio Amidei, who had collaborated on Vittorio De Sica's *Shoeshine* (1946). Prominent among the ensemble cast decamping for the day to the Roman resort of Ostia are two of Federico Fellini's protégés, Franco Interlenghi and Marcello Mastroianni. DP Italian +subtitles.

Anna Baldini *Marcella* · Vera Carmi *Adriana* · Emilio Cigoli *Mantovani* · Andrea Compagnoni *Cesare Meloni* · Franco Interlenghi *Enrico* · Marcello Mastroianni *Ercole* ■ *Dir* Luciano Emmer · *Scr* Franco Brusati, Luciano Emmer, Giulio Macchi, Cesare Zavattini, from a story by Sergio Amidei

Sunday in New York
★★★

Comedy   1963 · US · Colour · 104min

This is one of those early 1960s capers in which provincial innocents, in this case Jane Fonda, head for the big city and fall madly in love with life in the fast lane. It's a delightfully skittish romp in the Big Apple, showing off Fonda's youthful charisma to best advantage. Peter Nero's memorable score is the perfect complement to a film that harks back to those days when sex came tiptoeing out of the celluloid closet and everyone thought they were being daring. SH

Cliff Robertson *Adam Tyler* · Jane Fonda *Eileen Tyler* · Rod Taylor *Mike Mitchell* · Robert Culp *Russ Wilson* · Jo Morrow *Mona Harris* · Jim Backus *Flight dispatcher* · Peter Nero ■ *Dir* Peter Tewksbury · *Scr* Norman Krasna, from his play

Sunday in the Country
★★ 18

Crime thriller   1975 · Can · Colour · 87min

Ernest Borgnine plays a farmer in the backwoods of America who takes the law into his own hands when three dangerous fugitives attempt to take him and his granddaughter hostage. John Trent's decidedly cruel and violent crime drama is distinguished by Borgnine's performance as the calm countryman who coolly exacts a terrible revenge against Michael J Pollard and his cronies. The whole premise is decidedly questionable. AJ

Ernest Borgnine *Adam Smith* · Michael J Pollard *Leroy* · Hollis McLaren *Lucy* · Louis Zorich *Dinelli* · Cec Linder *Ackerman* · Vladimir Valenta *Luke* · Al Waxman *Sergeant* ■ *Dir* John Trent · *Scr* Robert Maxwell, John Trent, from a story by David Main

Sunday in the Country
★★★★ U

Period drama   1984 · Fr · Colour · 90min

This lyrical conversation piece deservedly won Bertrand Tavernier the best director award at Cannes. Beautifully evoking a balmy Sunday afternoon in the late summer of 1912, the film eavesdrops on the subtly charged encounters between ageing painter Louis Ducreux, his beloved but unreliable daughter Sabine Azéma and his married son Michel Aumont. All the performances are impeccable and Tavernier alights on such topics as Impressionism, family allegiances and the purpose of life with a light but restless touch. Bruno de Keyzer's gorgeous photography makes this serene drama quite irresistible. DP French +subtitles.

Louis Ducreux *Monsieur Ladmiral* · Sabine Azéma *Irène* · Michel Aumont *"Gonzague" Edouard* · Geneviève Mnich *Marie-Thérèse* · Monique Chaumette *Mercédès* · Claude Winter *Madame Ladmiral* ■ *Dir* Bertrand Tavernier · *Scr* Bertrand Tavernier, Colo Tavernier, from the novella *Monsieur Ladmiral Va Bientôt Mourir* by Pierre Bost

Sunday Too Far Away
★★★★

Drama   1974 · Aus · Colour · 94min

Life as a sheep-shearer can be rather monotonous, but had man Jack Thompson has enough star power to keep us watching this tale of rivalry and hardship. He's chief shearer and troubleshooter, calling the men out on strike when the bosses try to introduce non-union labour. There's real integrity in Ken Hannam's direction, as he takes us right into the heart of a world very like that of the Wild West where rivalries are fuelled by booze and life is a real struggle. Men at work have rarely been so convincingly portrayed. TH

Jack Thompson *Foley* · Phyllis Ophel *Ivy* · Peter Cummins *"Black" Arthur* · Reg Lye *Old Garth* · John Charman *Barman* · Gregory Apps *Michael Simpson* · Max Cullen *Tim King* ■ *Dir* Ken Hannam · *Scr* John Dingwall

Sundays and Cybèle
★★★

Drama   1962 · Fr · BW · 110min

Debutant director Serge Bourguignon won the Oscar for best foreign language film with this self-promoting, arty affair. Hardy Kruger is the amnesiac German pilot who forges a friendship with pre-teen orphan Patricia Gozzi. There is an undeniable tenderness in their relationship, even though there's an inevitability about the consequences of their innocent Christmas sojourn in the woods. Cinematographer Henri Decaë's compositions, though elegant, strain too hard for lyrical effect. DP In French.

Hardy Kruger *Pierre* · Nicole Courcel *Madeleine* · Patricia Gozzi *Françoise/Cybèle* · Daniel Ivernel *Carlos* · Michel de Re *Bernard* · André Oumansky *Nurse* ■ *Dir* Serge Bourguignon · *Scr* Antoine Tudal, Serge Bourguignon, Bernard Eschassériaux, from the novel *Les Dimanches de Ville D'Avray* by Eschassériaux

Sunday's Children
★★★★

Drama   1992 · Swe · Colour · 118min

It's apt that this study of fathers and sons (the second part of the autobiographical trilogy scripted by Ingmar Bergman that began with *Best Intentions*) should be directed by Bergman's own son, Daniel. Recalling the summer of 1926, when the young Ingmar tried to become closer to his strict father (a chaplain to the Swedish royal family), this is such an assured film that it could easily have been directed by the master himself. The sunlit country picnics and cycle rides are joyous evocations of past times, but they also make the darker moments of doubt and the confrontations between Thommy Berggren and Henrik Linnros all the more powerful. *Private Confessions* (1996) completes the trilogy. DP Swedish +subtitles.

Henrik Linnros *Pu* · Thommy Berggren *Pu's father* · Börje Ahlstedt *Uncle Carl* ■ *Dir* Daniel Bergman · *Scr* Ingmar Bergman, from his autobiography *The Magic Lantern*

Sundown
★★★

Second World War adventure
1941 · US · BW · 90min

Gene Tierney's sultry looks are used to good effect in this wartime yarn set in Africa, where a band of Nazis are supplying weapons to tribesmen in the hope that they will rise up against the British. Commissioner Bruce Cabot befriends the locals, while English major George Sanders wrestles with his distrust of Arabs. Tierney is the linchpin, working undercover for the Allies but arousing Sanders's suspicions as she romances Cabot. The film is well photographed and rattles along efficiently. SuR

Gene Tierney *Zia* · Bruce Cabot *Captain Bill Crawford* · George Sanders *Major Coombes* · Cedric Hardwicke *Bishop Coombes* · Harry Carey Dewey · Joseph Calleia *Pallini* · Reginald Gardiner *Lt Turner* · Dorothy Dandridge *Kipsang's bride* ■ *Dir* Henry Hathaway · *Scr* Barre Lyndon, Charles G Booth, from a story by Lyndon · *Cinematographer* Charles Lang

The Sundowners
★★★ U

Western   1950 · US · Colour · 83min

This agreeable western, filmed entirely on location in Texas, rests on the roguish charm of Robert Preston and the superb Technicolor photography by Winton Hoch. The film introduces John Barrymore Jr, who is unexceptional as the teenage kid idolising Preston as his bad outlaw brother. Leading western novelist Alan LeMay (*The Searchers*) produced and scripted this adaptation of one of his early pieces, as well as appearing uncredited as Preston's companion. AE *DVD*

Robert Preston *Kid Wichita* · Robert Sterling *Tom Cloud* · Chill Wills *Sam Beard* · John Litel *John Gaul* · Cathy Downs *Kathleen Boyce* · Jack Elam *Earl Boyce* · Don Haggerty *Elmer Gaul* · John Barrymore Jr [John Drew Barrymore] *Jeff Cloud* ■ *Dir* George Templeton · *Scr* Alan LeMay, from his story *Thunder in the Dust*

The Sundowners
★★★★ U

Adventure   1960 · US · Colour · 124min

This marvellously authentic family epic from Warner Bros is set in Australia and contains superb performances (and moderately believable Australian accents) from Robert Mitchum and Deborah Kerr. Backing up the two leads in this sheep-shearing saga is a strong cast and excellent technical credits, notably the striking Technicolor photography from Jack Hildyard and an atmospheric Dimitri Tiomkin score. The film earned five Oscar nominations, a tribute to its director Fred Zinnemann, whose exquisite handling of the personal drama proves once again what a fine film-maker he was. TS

Deborah Kerr *Ida Carmody* · Robert Mitchum *Paddy Carmody* · Peter Ustinov *Venneker* · Michael Anderson Jr *Sean* · Glynis Johns *Mrs Firth* · Dina Merrill *Jean Halstead* · Ewen Solon *Bob Halstead* · Chips Rafferty *Quinlan* ■ *Dir* Fred Zinnemann · *Scr* Isobel Lennart, from the novel by Jon Cleary

Sunflower
★★ 15

Drama   1969 · It/Fr · Colour · 102min

Co-screenwriter Cesare Zavattini and director Vittorio De Sica were two of the key figures in the neorealist movement that dominated Italian cinema in the postwar era. But there is little evidence of their celebrated humanism in this preposterous nonsense in which Sophia Loren goes to the USSR in search of missing husband Marcello Mastroianni only to find him married to Lyudmila Savelyeva and blissfully ignorant of her existence. DP Italian +subtitles.

Sophia Loren *Giovanna* · Marcello Mastroianni *Antonio* · Lyudmila Savelyeva *Mascia* ■ *Dir* Vittorio De Sica · *Scr* Tonino Guerra, Cesare Zavattini, Georgi Mdivani

S

Sunny ★★
Musical comedy 1930 · US · BW · 78min

A very early, creaky and mind-bendingly idiotic romantic comedy musical, this relies on low vaudeville gags for much of its dated humour. However, those who can survive the first 15 minutes will find that this tale of a circus bareback rider, who stows away on a New York-bound ship in order to follow her heart, does have a certain charm. More importantly, it's a rare opportunity to see the multi-talented all-singing, all-dancing Broadway legend Marilyn Miller in action. This was remade in 1941 with Anna Neagle. RK

Marilyn Miller *Sunny* • Lawrence Gray *Tom Warren* • Joe Donahue *Jim Deming* • Mackenzie Ward *Wendell-Wendell* ■ *Dir* William Seiter [William A Seiter] • *Scr* Humphrey Pearson, Henry McCarty, from the musical by Otto Harbach, Oscar Hammerstein II, Jerome Kern

Sunny ★★ U
Romance 1941 · US · BW · 97min

Producer/director Herbert Wilcox remade this hit Broadway musical for his wife, the oh-so-charming, restrained English actress Anna Neagle. Wilcox reworked the original book, cutting out most of the (admittedly silly) plot, and leaving a thin tale about a bareback-riding circus performer (Neagle) who marries New Orleans aristocrat John Carroll, despite his stiff-necked family's disapproval. RK

Anna Neagle *Sunny O'Sullivan* • Ray Bolger *Bunny Billings* • John Carroll *Larry Warren* • Edward Everett Horton *Henry Bates* • Grace Hartman *Juliet Runnymede* • Paul Hartman *Egghead* • Frieda Inescort *Elizabeth Warren* ■ *Dir* Herbert Wilcox • *Scr* Sid Herzig, from a play by Otto Harbach, Oscar Hammerstein II • *Music* Jerome Kern

Sunny Side Up ★★★
Musical comedy drama 1929 · US · BW and Colour · 80min

A charming but creaky film from the early days of the talkies, this is a lightweight offering from 20th Century-Fox. It stars popular screen sweethearts Janet Gaynor and the lovable Charlie Farrell, and is almost a singing version of their standard tenement-girl-falls-for-Farrell plot. But who cares when the songs are such fabulous classics as *I'm a Dreamer (Aren't We All?)* and *If I Had a Talking Picture of You*. TS

Janet Gaynor *Molly Carr* • Charles Farrell (1) *Jack Cromwell* • El Brendel *Eric Swenson* • Marjorie White *Bee Nichols* • Frank Richardson *Eddie Rafferty* • Sharon Lynn [Sharon Lynne] *Jane Worth* • Mary Forbes *Mrs Cromwell* • Joe Brown [Joe E Brown] *Joe Vitto* ■ *Dir* David Butler • *Scr* David Butler, Buddy De Sylva [BG De Sylva], Ray Henderson, Lew Brown, from a story by De Sylva, Henderson, Brown

Sunnyside ★★★
Silent satirical drama 1919 · US · BW · 41min

In this pastoral fairy tale, Charlie Chaplin is a farm hand in love with Edna Purviance (again!). Chaplin said the production of *Sunnyside* was "like pulling teeth", and he must have appreciated the great ballet dancer Vaslav Nijinsky telling him that the dance with four nymphs was "pure delight". TH

Charlie Chaplin [Charles Chaplin] *Handyman* • Edna Purviance *Woman* • Tom Wilson *Boss* • Henry Bergman *Father* ■ *Dir* Charles Chaplin • *Scr* Charles Chaplin, from his story

Sunrise ★★★★★ U
Silent romantic drama 1927 · US · BW · 90min

Janet Gaynor won the first ever best actress Oscar for her work in this exquisite silent feature, subtitled *A Song of Two Humans*. Emigré director FW Murnau has reduced a tale of threatened marriage to its bare essentials, as George O'Brien's farmer falls for visiting city girl Margaret Livingston. It is hard to convey briefly the wonder of imagery on display here, as Murnau both wittily and stylistically uses every aspect of visual storytelling, even making imaginative use of the back projection itself. Perspective design and stunning photography (by Charles Rosher

and Karl Struss) help immeasurably. The tale is timeless, the setting nameless and the mood resolutely central European, though it was filmed in America. O'Brien brings a distinctively American presence to the romantically tortured hero, and Gaynor is perfection as his wife. TS **DVD BL**

George O'Brien *The Man* • Janet Gaynor *The Wife* • Bodil Rosing *Maid* • Margaret Livingston *Woman from the city* • J Farrell MacDonald *Photographer* ■ *Dir* FW Murnau • *Scr* Carl Mayer, from the novel *Die Reise nach Tilsit* by Hermann Sudermann • *Production Designer* Rochus Gliese

Sunrise at Campobello ★★★ U
Biographical drama 1960 · US · Colour · 143min

This is a moving account of Franklin D Roosevelt's life during his battle with polio. Although the film at times betrays its theatrical origins, it remains enthralling, and it also leaves posterity a record of Ralph Bellamy's extraordinary stage performance, re-created here. Curiously, the Oscar nomination went to Greer Garson as Roosevelt's wife, Eleanor. The supporting cast is first class. RK

Ralph Bellamy *Franklin Delano Roosevelt* • Greer Garson *Eleanor Roosevelt* • Hume Cronyn *Louis Howe* • Jean Hagen *Missy Le Hand* • Ann Shoemaker *Sara Roosevelt* • Alan Bunce *Al Smith* • Tim Considine *James Roosevelt* ■ *Dir* Vincent J Donehue • *Scr* Dore Schary, from his play

Sunset ★★ 15
Period comedy thriller 1988 · US · Colour · 102min

As with many of Blake Edwards's films, the concept is great, but the execution disastrous. Set in silent-era Hollywood, this would-be comedy thriller finds the film industry's first western star Tom Mix (Bruce Willis) joining forces with the ageing Wyatt Earp (James Garner) to solve a murder involving corrupt studio chiefs. Edwards's clumsily fails to blend the comic and action elements, while Willis irritates in the lead role. Garner rises above the material. JF Violence, swearing, nudity. **DVD**

Bruce Willis *Tom Mix* • James Garner *Wyatt Earp* • Malcolm McDowell *Alfie Alperin* • Mariel Hemingway *Cheryl King* • Kathleen Quinlan *Nancy Shoemaker* • Jennifer Edwards *Victoria Alperin* • Patricia Hodge *Christina Alperin* • Richard Bradford *Captain Blackworth* • M Emmet Walsh *Chief Dibner* • Joe Dallesandro *Dutch Kieffer* ■ *Dir* Blake Edwards • *Scr* Blake Edwards, from a story by Rod Amateau

Sunset Blvd ★★★★★ PG
Satirical drama 1950 · US · BW · 105min

Even the title of this dark, deeply satisfying work of cinematic genius can be read as a metaphor for the Hollywood machine. Master director Billy Wilder's witty, brilliantly constructed Tinseltown satire is both canny and knowing about the film industry and those souls unfortunate, and yet willing, enough to be caught in its wheels. The stark story of former movie queen Norma Desmond, haunted by memories of her past greatness ("I am big. It's the pictures that got small"), is greatly aided by superb casting, notably of silent-movie siren Gloria Swanson, who brings a desperate, vampiric glamour to her role. William Holden, a last minute replacement for Montgomery Clift, is also excellent as the doomed writer, who narrates the film in flashback from the scene of his death. Savage, dark and wholly original. TS **DVD BL**

William Holden (2) *Joe C Gillis* • Gloria Swanson *Norma Desmond* • Erich von Stroheim *Max Von Mayerling* • Nancy Olson *Betty Schaefer* • Fred Clark *Sheldrake* • Lloyd Gough *Morino* • Jack Webb *Artie Green* ■ *Dir* Billy Wilder • *Scr* Billy Wilder, Charles Brackett, DM Marshman Jr, from the story *A Can of Beans* by Charles Brackett, Billy Wilder • *Costume Designer* Edith Head • *Cinematographer* John F Seitz • *Music* Franz Waxman

Sunset Grill ★★ 18
Thriller 1992 · US · Colour · 99min

A weary LA private detective gets more than he bargained for when he attempts to

avenge the murder of his wife. For he uncovers a sinister conspiracy revolving around Mexicans being killed and sold for their body parts. Directed by former horror veteran Kevin Connor, this decidedly odd thriller is a mix of the bizarre and the mundane. AJ Swearing, violence, sex scenes, nudity.

Peter Weller *Ryder Hart* • Lori Singer *Loren Duquesne* • Stacy Keach *Harrison Shelgrove* • Michael Anderson Jr *Carruthers* • Alexandra Paul *Anita* • John Rhys-Davies *Stockton* • Pete Koch [Peter Koch] *Christian* ■ *Dir* Kevin Connor • *Scr* Marcus Wright, Faruque Ahmed

Sunset Heights ★★ 15
Science-fiction thriller 1996 · UK/Ire · Colour · 91min

Set in the near future, this flawed but intriguing thriller presents a nightmare vision of life in Northern Ireland. Two gangs police their communities using fear and violence. Caught between them is Toby Stephens, whose child is believed to be latest victim of a serial killer known as The Preacher. The plotting is confused but there are strong performances from the cast, and director Colm Villa displays some stylish visual touches. JF Violence. **DVD**

Toby Stephens *Luke* • Jim Norton *Sam Magee* • Patrick O'Kane *Friday Knight* • Joe Rea *Victor* • James Cosmo *MacDonald* ■ *Dir/Scr* Colm Villa

The Sunset Limited ★★★★
Drama 2010 · US · Colour · 91min

Tommy Lee Jones's latest directorial effort is based on Cormac McCarthy's "novel in dramatic form", a two-hander in which he and Samuel L Jackson are given free rein to make the most of the powerful (and plentiful) dialogue. Their two characters are holed up in a run-down apartment throughout and become engaged in a theological debate after Jackson foils Jones's suicide attempt. Despite Jones's best efforts behind the lens, it's clear that this is a work whose natural home is on the stage. JoC

Samuel L Jackson *"Black"* • Tommy Lee Jones *"White"* ■ *Dir* Tommy Lee Jones • *Scr* Cormac McCarthy, from his play

Sunset Park ★★ 15
Sports comedy drama 1996 · US · Colour · 94min

A rare lead outing for Rhea Perlman, this is an uneasy amalgam of comedy and ghetto drama. The former *Cheers* star plays a basketball novice who reluctantly becomes the unlikely trainer to a struggling team from a deprived, inner city high school. Of course, it's not long before she is won over. It's a familiar enough tale, enthusiastically played, but the laughs are dampened by waves of sentimentality. JF

Rhea Perlman *Phyllis Saroka* • Fredro Starr *Shorty* • Carol Kane *Mona* • Terrence Dashon Howard [Terrence Howard] *Spaceman* • Camille Saviola *Barbara* • De'Aundre Bonds *Busy-Bee* • James Harris *Butter* ■ *Dir* Steve Gomer • *Scr* Seth Zvi Rosenfeld, Kathleen McGhee-Anderson

Sunset Song ★★★ 15
Coming-of-age period drama 2015 · UK/Lux · Colour · 130min

This understated drama is a story of hope and tragedy. It begins on a remote farm in rural Scotland, where we find a young woman (model-turned-actress Agyness Deyn) whose life is plagued by the suffering inflicted by her father (Peter Mullan), a monstrous man who runs the family estate. Her eventual happiness is short-lived owing to the outbreak of war. It's superbly acted, and beautifully crafted by Terence Davies, but certain plot developments are unconvincing and Deyn makes for a rather passive heroine. SC Sexual violence **DVD BL**

Peter Mullan *John Guthrie* • Agyness Deyn *Chris Guthrie* • Kevin Guthrie *Ewan Tavendale* • Ian Pirie *Chae Strachan* • Hugh Ross *Inspector* ■ *Dir* Terence Davies • *Scr* Terence Davies, from Lewis Grassic Gibbon's novel

Sunset Strip ★ 15
Comedy drama 2000 · US · Colour · 86min

This film about friends in 1970s LA desperately wants to be *American Graffiti* meets *Reality Bites*, but doesn't capture the nostalgia of one nor the humour, writing or skilled performances of either. Anna Friel is unconvincing as the fashion designer sleeping her way around LA's trendy people when her friend (played by Simon Baker) is the one everyone but her realises is the man for her. JB

Simon Baker (1) *Michael Scott* • Anna Friel *Tammy Franklin* • Nick Stahl *"Zach" Zachary* • Rory Cochrane *Felix* • Adam Goldberg *Marty Shapiro* • Jared Leto *Glen Walker* ■ *Dir* Adam Collis • *Scr* Russell DeGrazier, Randall Jahnson, from a story by Randall Jahnson

Sunshine ★★★★ 15
Epic romantic drama 1999 · Hun/Ger/Can/Austria · Colour · 172min

This sprawling epic is a glorious summation of the themes that have preoccupied István Szabó over the last 20 years. Ralph Fiennes essays a trio of flawed ancestors whose personal tragedies are enacted against the great events of the 20th century. Passing through Hungary's imperial, fascist and communist phases, the action chronicles the history of a Jewish family whose bid to belong is undermined by successive generations' susceptibility to passion, vanity and lust for power. DP **DVD**

Ralph Fiennes *Ignatz Sonnenschein/Adam Sors/Ivan Sors* • Rosemary Harris *Valerie Sors* • Rachel Weisz *Greta Sors* • Jennifer Ehle *Valerie Sonnenschein* • ig *Major Carole Kovacs* • Molly Parker *Hannah Wippler* • James Frain *Gustave Sonnenschein* • David De Keyser *Emmanuel Sonnenschein* • William Hurt *Andor Knorr* ■ *Dir* István Szabó • *Scr* Istvan Szabo, Israel Horovitz, from a story by Istvan Szabo

Sunshine ★★★ 15
Science-fiction thriller 2007 · US/UK · Colour · 103min

Slumdog Millionaire director Danny Boyle's first foray into pure science fiction starts out as a philosophical epic along the lines of *2001: a Space Odyssey* and *Solaris* before lurching inexplicably into action horror territory previously charted by *Alien* and *Event Horizon*. Set in 2057, the film boasts crisp performances from Cillian Murphy, Chris Evans and Rose Byrne as the astronauts who are sent on a hazardous mission to rekindle the dying Sun by firing a giant bomb into its core. Throwing in nods to genre classics *Silent Running* and *Dark Star*, Boyle succeeds admirably in cranking up the tension but, despite a strong first half, the film loses its way as the spaceship nears its fiery destination. AS **DVD BL**

Chris Evans *Mace* • Cillian Murphy *Capa* • Rose Byrne *Cassie* • Michelle Yeoh *Corazon* • Mark Strong *Pinbacker* • Cliff Curtis *Searle* • Troy Garity *Harvey* ■ *Dir* Danny Boyle • *Scr* Alex Garland

The Sunshine Boys ★★★★ PG
Comedy 1975 · US · Colour · 106min

George Burns, who died just a cigar length past his 100th birthday, made his big-screen comeback in this Neil Simon-scripted comedy about two ageing, rival vaudevillians. Burns stepped in when Jack Benny died and found himself co-starring with the best scene-stealer in the business, Walter Matthau. As with many of Simon's confections, it's a New York Jewish odd couple sort of story, overtly sentimental but played to perfection. Richard Benjamin also makes an impact as Matthau's nephew and agent, who tries to reconcile the two old boys. AT Swearing.

Walter Matthau *Willy Clark* • George Burns *Al Lewis* • Richard Benjamin *Ben Clark* • Lee Meredith *Nurse in sketch* • Carol Arthur *Doris* • F Murray Abraham *Mechanic* • Howard Hesseman *Commercial director* ■ *Dir* Herbert Ross • *Scr* Neil Simon, from his play

The Sunshine Boys ★★★ U
Comedy 1997 · US · Colour · 84min

The words Woody Allen and TV movie were once mutually exclusive, but here he's back as a jobbing actor in this update of Neil Simon's classic comedy. Allen takes on the role that won George Burns an Oscar, while Peter Falk steps into Walter Matthau's shoes as the struggling entertainer who calls on his now-detested partner to revive his fortunes. Simon's acerbic wit is as amusing as ever, but the original is unsurpassable. DP DVD

Woody Allen *Al Lewis* • Peter Falk *Willie Clark* • Sarah Jessica Parker *Nancy* • Michael McKean *Peter* • Liev Schreiber *Ricky Gregg* • Edie Falco ■ *Dir* John Erman • *Scr* Neil Simon, from his play

Sunshine Cleaning ★★★ 15
Comedy drama 2008 · US · Colour · 87min

In this dark comedy, Amy Adams and Emily Blunt play disparate sisters – Adams a single mum still in love with her married high-school sweetheart who fathered her eccentric son, Blunt a grumpy slacker. When Adams's eccentric son is kicked out of state education, the sisters set up a crime scene clean-up service, without a clue as to what it involves, so he can go to private school. The interplay between the leads makes for lively entertainment that's both funny and unpredictable as their characters haplessly work their way through adversity. KK DVD

Amy Adams *Rose Lorkowski* • Emily Blunt *Norah Lorkowski* • Alan Arkin *Joe Lorkowski* • Jason Spevack *Oscar Lorkowski* • Steve Zahn *Mac* • Mary Lynn Rajskub *Lynn* • Clifton Collins Jr *Winston* • Eric Christian Olsen *Randy* • Kevin Chapman *Carl* • Josh Berry *TV detective* ■ *Dir* Christine Jeffs • *Scr* Megan Holley

Sunshine on Leith ★★★★ PG
Musical 2013 · UK · Colour · 95min

The boisterous back catalogue of militantly Scottish folk-pop duo the Proclaimers forms the backbone to actor-turned-director Dexter Fletcher's often irresistible Edinburgh-set musical. Based on Stephen Greenhorn's hit stage play, it tells the story of two soldiers –George MacKay and Kevin Guthrie), who return to Leith after a traumatic tour of duty in Afghanistan. Elegantly balancing poignant drama and broad comedy, the movie adopts the *Mamma Mia!* formula in that the songs are interpreted by the actors using their own voices, creating an effect that's immediate, intimate and heartfelt. The music may not suit all tastes but the charismatic characters will, in a study of family life that's raw, romantic and real. DW Some violence, swearing, sexual references. DVD

Peter Mullan *Rab* • Jane Horrocks *Jean* • George MacKay *Davy* • Freya Mavor *Liz* • Kevin Guthrie *Ally* ■ *Dir* Dexter Fletcher • *Scr* Stephen Greenhorn, from his musical

Sunshine State ★★★★ 15
Drama 2002 · US · Colour · 134min

This multilayered ensemble piece from writer/director/editor John Sayles takes as its notional theme the development of swampland for profit. In Florida's Delrona Beach, Edie Falco's motel owner sees the chance of escape from small-town drudgery with Timothy Hutton's visiting architect, who is paradoxically there, effectively, to run her out of town. Meanwhile, Angela Bassett returns to face her past, corruption rages from within the town council and a historical pageant is threatened by apathy. Too talky for a wide audience, it's intelligent, cool, questioning and humane – a small film that leaves a big impression. AC Swearing. DVD

Edie Falco *Marly Temple* • Jane Alexander *Delia Temple* • Ralph Waite *Furman Temple* • Angela Bassett *Desiree Perry* • James McDaniel *Reggie Perry* • Mary Steenburgen *Francine Pickney* • Timothy Hutton *Jack Meadows* ■ *Dir/Scr* John Sayles

Sunstruck ★ PG
Comedy drama 1972 · Aus/UK · Colour · 88min

This star vehicle for singer and comedian Harry Secombe was made Down Under back in the days when the Welsh warbler used to summer there. Daft and dated, even at the time, the slight tale has Secombe playing a dimwit Welsh schoolteacher who emigrates to the Aussie outback. The simple-minded humour derives from his patent unsuitability for the new way of life. Thankfully, the sort of film they don't make any more. DA DVD

Harry Secombe *Stanley Evans* • Maggie Fitzgibbon *Shirley Marshall* • John Meillon *Mick Cassidy* • Dawn Lake *Sal Cassidy* • Peter Whittle *Pete Marshall* • Dennis Jordan *Steve Cassidy* • Donald Houston ■ *Dir* James Gilbert (2) • *Scr* James Grafton, Stan Mars

The Super ★★★ 15
Comedy 1991 · US · Colour · 85min

Joe Pesci's Oscar for *GoodFellas* earned him the opportunity to become an unlikely leading man, but he enjoys mixed success here in his first such role. On paper it sounds great: Pesci plays a sleazy New York landlord who is taken to court and sentenced to living in one of his own rat-filled apartments. The star is fine, and there's good support from Rubén Blades and Vincent Gardenia, but director Rod Daniel indulges in too much soppy moralising, and the film veers uncomfortably between comedy and drama. JF Swearing.

Joe Pesci *Louie Kritski* • Vincent Gardenia *Big Lou Kritski* • Madolyn Smith Osborne [Madolyn Smith] *Naomi Bensinger* • Rubén Blades *Marlon* • Stacey Travis *Heather* ■ *Dir* Rod Daniel • *Scr* Sam Simon

Super ★★★ 18
Action comedy drama 2010 · UK/US · Colour · 91min

Released at the same time as *Kick-Ass*, *Super* takes a different – and more extreme – slant on the same theme. Rainn Wilson plays the short-order cook who responds to his wife's departure and a religious experience by sewing a red superhero costume and roaming the streets attacking drug dealers and queue-jumping cinema-goers with a monkey wrench. Written and directed by former Troma Studios intern James Gunn, this seriously deranged fantasy is abhorrent, hilarious and destined for cult status. JR Violence, swearing, drug abuse, sex scenes. DVD

Rainn Wilson *Frank D'Arbo/The Crimson Bolt* • Ellen Page *Libby/Boltie* • Liv Tyler *Sarah* • Kevin Bacon *Jacques* • Michael Rooker *Abe* • Nathan Fillion *The Holy Avenger* ■ *Dir/Scr* James Gunn (2)

The Super Cops ★★★ 15
Detective comedy drama 1973 · US · Colour · 90min

This is a fine telling of the true story of two cops, nicknamed "Batman and Robin", who used unconventional crime-busting techniques to stop drug dealing in the Bedford-Stuyvesant area of New York's Brooklyn. The film is fast, furious, and often very funny, and it benefits from using the actual locations where real-life events occurred. Ron Leibman and David Selby play the super cops, with the bona fide detectives popping up in bit parts. DA

Ron Leibman *David Greenberg* • David Selby *Robert Hantz* • Sheila Frazier *Sara* • Pat Hingle *Lieutenant Novick* • Dan Frazer *Krasna* • Joseph Sirola *Lieutenant O'Shaughnessy* • Arny Freeman *Judge Kellner* ■ *Dir* Gordon Parks • *Scr* Lorenzo Semple Jr, from the non-fiction book by LH Whittemore

Super 8 ★★★★ 12
Science-fiction adventure 2011 · US · Colour · 107min

Named after the old film format used by home-movie hobbyists, this 1970s-set adventure follows a bunch of schoolkids who accidentally capture footage of a spectacular train crash while filming their own low-budget zombie flick. In an age of relentlessly spectacular, often emotionally vacant blockbusters, it's a real pleasure to see a big movie thrumming with genuine feeling for characters touchingly poised on the cusp of adulthood. Writer/director JJ Abrams has clearly soaked up the early work of fellow producer Steven Spielberg, and here he reproduces not only the visual style of *Close Encounters* and *ET* but also their affecting humanity. TJ Some swearing, drug abuse. DVD BD

Kyle Chandler *Jackson Lamb* • Elle Fanning *Alice Dainard* • Noah Emmerich *Nelec* • Ron Eldard *Louis Dainard* • AJ Michalka [Amanda Michalka] *Jen Kaznyk* ■ *Dir/Scr* JJ Abrams

Super 8 Stories ★★★★
Music documentary 2001 · Ger/It · BW and Colour · 90min

Fronted by doctor Nele Karajlic and boasting film-maker Emir Kusturica on guitar, the No Smoking Orchestra has been entertaining and outraging Yugoslavia and its derivatives since 1980. Fusing rock, punk, jazz and traditional Romany folk, the band's musical style is as refreshing as its lyrics are irreverent. Yet, as this self-consciously grungy tour documentary reveals, the NSO – which comes across as Bosnia's raucous answer to the Leningrad Cowboys – is as committed to political comment as it is to crowd pleasing. Moreover, each of its ten members is a fully paid-up eccentric, whose opinions and backstage antics make for provocative and amusing viewing. DP German, Serbo-Croat +subtitles.

■ *Dir* Emir Kusturica

Super Mario Bros ★★ PG
Fantasy adventure 1993 · US · Colour · 104min

How do you turn a popular interactive video game into an equally engaging and exciting movie? Not like this, you don't! This awkward fantasy contains few trace elements from the "Super Mario Land" games themselves, thereby instantly betraying the very audience it was made for. Bob Hoskins and John Leguizamo try their best as the two plumbers adrift in a parallel dinosaur dimension, but it isn't super, amusing or thrilling by any stretch of the imagination. AJ Swearing, violence. DVD BD CS

Bob Hoskins *Mario Mario* • Dennis Hopper *King Koopa* • John Leguizamo *Luigi Mario* • Samantha Mathis *Daisy* • Fisher Stevens *Iggy* • Richard Edson *Spike* • Fiona Shaw *Lena* ■ *Dir* Rocky Morton, Annabel Jankel • *Scr* Parker Bennett, Terry Runté, Ed Solomon, from the characters by Shigeru Miyamoto, Takashi Tezuka

Super Size Me ★★★★ 12
Documentary 2004 · US · Colour · 99min

Describing himself as the "producer/director/guinea pig" of this, his first feature documentary, healthy 30-something Morgan Spurlock wondered what would happen if he ate nothing but McDonald's food for a month. With this headline-grabbing experiment at its core, *Super Size Me* looks more broadly at the hold fast food has over Americans in an age of ever-increasing obesity. An initially chipper host without a political axe to grind, Spurlock soon finds his strict new diet hard to stomach. After a few weeks, Spurlock's doctor tells him his "liver is like pâté" and the gross-out comedy takes a darker turn. Like Michael Moore, Spurlock presents his statistical material light-heartedly to make a serious point, but the success of his film depends on the likeability of his ubiquitous presence. AC DVD

■ *Dir/Scr* Morgan Spurlock

Super Troopers ★ 15
Comedy 2001 · US · Colour · 95min

This juvenile cop comedy resembles a cruder version of the *Police Academy* films. Written and performed by the five-man comedy group Broken Lizard, this puerile affair concerns a bunch of idiotic Vermont State Troopers who enjoy nothing more than tormenting drivers with bizarre, unfunny pranks. There is a vague plot about the rivalry between the Troopers and the local police, but it's really just a series of sketches in which the lawmen behave like members of a particularly dim fraternity. JC DVD

Brian Cox (1) *Capt John O'Hagan* • Daniel Von Bargen *Police Chief Grady* • Marisa Coughlan *Officer Ursula Hanson* • Lynda Carter *Governor Jessman* • Erik Stolhanske *Robert "Rabbit" Roto* • Steve Lemme *MacIntyre "Mac" Womack* • Paul Soter *Jeff Foster* • Jay Chandrasekhar *Arcot "Thorny" Ramathorn* ■ *Dir* Jay Chandrasekhar • *Scr* Jay Chandrasekhar, Kevin Heffernan, Steve Lemme, Paul Soter, Erik Stolhanske [Broken Lizard]

Superbad ★★★★ 15
Comedy 2007 · US · Colour · 108min

This post-*American Pie* teen movie serves up all the essential elements of the genre, but does it with a scabrous and intelligent wit. Seth (Jonah Hill) and Eric (Michael Cera, from TV's *Arrested Development*) are high schoolers who plan to provide booze for a party and thus ensure the gratitude (and sexual favours) of its female attendees. Sadly, an idiot friend going by the fake-ID pseudonym of "McLovin" and two utterly corrupt and drunken cops are among the characters that foil their plans. *Superbad* stands out from the standard teen-movie crowd with its slacker dialogue, universally funny performances and an unexpected sweetness in the friendship between the sex-crazed Seth and the slightly more diffident Eric. For those with a high tolerance for exuberant crudity, belly laughs are guaranteed. AS DVD BD

Jonah Hill *Seth* • Michael Cera *Evan* • Christopher Mintz-Plasse *Fogell* • Bill Hader *Officer Slater* • Seth Rogen *Officer Michaels* • Martha MacIsaac *Becca* ■ *Dir* Greg Mottola • *Scr* Seth Rogen, Evan Goldberg

SuperBob ★★★ 15
Romantic action comedy 2015 · UK · Colour · 82min

The dull side of being a superhero is explored in this independent comedy about Bob, a government-sanctioned caped saviour who uses his day off to go out on a date. Opting for a low-fi approach, the film wins you over with a funny script rather than elaborate action scenes. Writer/star Brett Goldstein is likeable in the lead, a timid everyman overwhelmed by what has happened to him. Working within its low budget limitations without ever feeling cheap, this light but effective comedy offers something new to its genre. JL Swearing.

Brett Goldstein *Robert Kenner "SuperBob"* • Natalia Tena *Dorris* • Laura Haddock *June* • Ruth Sheen *Pat* • David Harewood *Simon* ■ *Dir* Jon Drever • *Scr* William Bridges, Brett Goldstein, from a story by Bridges, Goldstein, Jon Drever, from his short film

Superfly ★★★ 18
Cult blaxploitation 1972 · US · Colour · 88min

This notorious film exploited the conventions of the blaxploitation genre to the hilt. The antihero, played by flamboyent, supercool Ron O'Neal, is a cocaine pusher who plans one last deal before retirement. Director Gordon Parks Jr has a feel for gritty locations and the language of the residents. The movie was a huge success in the US and abroad, although it may appear somewhat dated now – the black men are little more than robots, the white men are crooked and the women (black and white) are mere sex objects. However, what really keeps this cult drama alive is the fantastic Curtis Mayfield score, especially the groovy title track. Two sequels followed. DM Sex scenes, swearing, violence.

Ron O'Neal *Youngblood Priest* • Carl Lee *Eddie* • Sheila Frazier *Georgia* • Julius Harris *Scatter* • Charles McGregor *Fat Freddie* • Nate Adams *Dealer* • Polly Niles *Cynthia* ■ *Dir* Gordon Parks Jr • *Scr* Phillip Fenty

Supergirl ★★ PG
Fantasy adventure 1984 · UK · Colour · 111min

This is a disastrous attempt to extend the *Superman* series by bringing the Man of Steel's comic book cousin (played here by Helen Slater) to Earth, to retrieve a vital power source that has fallen into the hands of the evil Faye Dunaway. The story is pretty daft, the special effects merely ordinary and Slater is a weak superheroine. JF **DVD**

Helen Slater *Kara, Supergirl/Linda Lee* • Faye Dunaway *Selena* • Peter O'Toole *Zaltar* • Mia Farrow *Alura* • Brenda Vaccaro *Bianca* • Peter Cook *Nigel* • Simon Ward *Zor-El* ■ *Dir* Jeannot Szwarc • *Scr* David Odell

The Supergrass ★★ 15

Comedy   1985 · UK · Colour · 93min

In a so-so comedy, a spin-off from *The Comic Strip* TV series, Ade Edmondson poses as a drug dealer to impress a girlfriend. However he finds that the pretence also fools the police, who pressure him into grassing on his nonexistent drugs ring. There's strong support from Dawn French, Jennifer Saunders and Peter Richardson, who also co-wrote and directed, but this is small-screen stuff that doesn't stand up to big-screen scrutiny. DA

Adrian Edmondson *Dennis* • Jennifer Saunders *Lesley* • Peter Richardson *Harvey Duncan* • Dawn French *Andrea* • Keith Allen *Wong* • Nigel Planer *Gunter* • Robbie Coltrane *Troy* ■ *Dir* Peter Richardson • *Scr* Pete Richens, Peter Richardson

Superhero Movie ★★★ 12

Fantasy action spoof
2008 · US · Colour · 82min

A bite turns geeky Rick Riker (Drake Bell) into the Dragonfly, in this far-from-subtle superhero satire. It's a cut-and-paste of *Batman Begins*, *X-Men* and *Fantastic Four* references, all shoehorned into the *Spider-Man* template, with the usual mix of sexual crudity, fart gags and patented schtick from *Naked Gun* warhorse Leslie Nielsen. There are more laughs than might be expected, though, considering several cast and crew members are veterans of the *Scary Movie* franchise, and writer/director Craig Mazin's easy-going style ensures a smooth ride through the rapid-fire gag delivery. His cheesy comic-book dialogue is amusingly spot-on, too, and some moments – like the pheromone-crazed lab animals attacking Riker – prove impossible to resist. AJ **DVD**

Drake Bell *Rick Riker/The Dragonfly* • Sara Paxton *Jill Johnson* • Leslie Nielsen *Uncle Albert* • Marion Ross *Aunt Lucille* • Christopher McDonald *Lou Landers/The Hourglass* • Brent Spiner *Dr Strom* • Kevin Hart *Trey* • Tracy Morgan *Dr Xavier* • Pamela Anderson *The Invisible Girl* ■ *Dir/Scr* Craig Mazin

LANDMARK FILM
Epic in its vision, this sets the standard for comic-book adaptations to come

Superman ★★★★★ PG

Fantasy adventure   1978 · US · Colour · 137min

This big-budget, epic-scale version of the Man of Steel legend is irresistible, fabulous entertainment. The elegiac opening – from the destruction of Krypton to Clark Kent's arrival at the *Daily Planet* in Metropolis – turns more traditional comic book when Clark falls for Lois Lane, before a bright and breezy confrontation with comedic criminal Lex Luthor. The deliberate clash of styles generates much excitement and, yes, you'll believe a man can fly. Christopher Reeve is perfectly cast, and as a spectacle it's a masterful confection. AJ **DVD** ⟶

Christopher Reeve *Clark Kent/Superman* • Gene Hackman *Lex Luthor* • Margot Kidder *Lois Lane* • Marlon Brando *Jor-El* • Ned Beatty *Otis* • Jackie Cooper *Perry White* • Glenn Ford *Pa Kent* • Trevor Howard *First Elder* • Valerie Perrine *Eve Teschmacher* • Terence Stamp *General Zod* • Susannah York *Lara* • Larry Hagman *Major* ■ *Dir* Richard Donner • *Scr* Mario Puzo, David Newman, Leslie Newman, Robert Benton, from the story by Mario Puzo, from the comic strip by Jerry Siegel, Joe Shuster • *Cinematographer* Geoffrey Unsworth • *Music* John Williams • *Production Designer* John Barry (2)

Superman II ★★★★ PG

Fantasy adventure
1980 · UK/US · Colour · 122min

Director Richard Lester delivers a knowing, knockabout cartoon when Superman (Christopher Reeve) finding out that he is no longer the toughest guy around when three baddies are exiled from his home planet and arrive on Earth. The effects are equal to the first film and there's a strong supporting cast, including an irascible Gene Hackman and the excellent Terence Stamp. JF **DVD** **BL**

Christopher Reeve *Clark Kent/Superman* • Gene Hackman *Lex Luthor* • Margot Kidder *Lois Lane* • Terence Stamp *General Zod* • Ned Beatty *Otis* • Sarah Douglas *Ursa* • Jack O'Halloran *Non* • Valerie Perrine *Eve Teschmacher* • Susannah York *Lara* • Jackie Cooper *Perry White* • EG Marshall *President* ■ *Dir* Richard Lester • *Scr* Mario Puzo, David Newman, Leslie Newman, from the story by Mario Puzo, from the characters by Jerry Siegel, Joe Shuster

Superman III ★★★ PG

Fantasy adventure   1983 · US · Colour · 119min

Director Richard Lester injected a much needed irreverence into *Superman II*, but can't quite sustain the humour for this third instalment of "the man from Krypton" saga. Superman battles against a tycoon with plans for world domination, while Richard Pryor features as a bumbling computer genius. There are a few nice touches – particularly when Superman turns nasty – and for fans of superhero action this is still enjoyable enough entertainment. JF **DVD** ⟶

Christopher Reeve *Superman/Clark Kent* • Richard Pryor *Gus Gorman* • Robert Vaughn (1) *Ross Webster* • Annette O'Toole *Lana Lang* • Annie Ross *Vera Webster* • Pamela Stephenson *Lorelei Ambrosia* • Margot Kidder *Lois Lane* • Jackie Cooper *Perry White* ■ *Dir* Richard Lester • *Scr* David Newman, Leslie Newman, from the characters by Jerry Siegel, Joe Shuster

Superman IV: the Quest for Peace ★★ PG

Fantasy adventure   1987 · US · Colour · 86min

Despite the return of Gene Hackman as the evil Lex Luthor, this creaky, tired third sequel sounded the final death knell for the *Superman* saga. In this one, Christopher Reeve's man in tights has finally brought about peace in our time, but soon finds himself up against Luthor (now a budding arms baron), his irritating nephew (Jon Cryer) and a powerful new foe called Nuclear Man. However, the enthusiastic hamming can't hide the clunking direction and poor special effects. JF **DVD** **BL** ⟶

Christopher Reeve *Superman/Clark Kent* • Gene Hackman *Lex Luthor* • Margot Kidder *Lois Lane* • Jackie Cooper *Perry White* • Marc McClure *Jimmy Olsen* • Jon Cryer *Lenny* • Sam Wanamaker *David Warfield* • Mark Pillow *Nuclear Man* • Mariel Hemingway *Lacy Warfield* ■ *Dir* Sidney J Furie • *Scr* Lawrence Konner, Mark Rosenthal, from a story by Christopher Reeve, Lawrence Konner, Mark Rosenthal, from characters by Jerry Siegel, Joe Shuster

Superman Returns ★★★★ 12

Fantasy adventure
2006 · US/Aus · Colour · 147min

Newcomer Brandon Routh dons the cape as Superman and he carries the preposterous plot with sheer charm, growing in confidence even as the plausibility of Clark Kent's dual existence is stretched to breaking point. Routh's eerie resemblance to Christopher Reeve is a bonus that also reflects director Bryan Singer's back-to-basics approach: the film is tinged with nostalgia for the original franchise, from the cheeky humour to John Williams's trumpeting score. But Singer also takes advantage of new technology to create even more breathtaking special effects. Kevin Spacey is adeptly sinister as Lex Luthor, although Parker Posey steals his thunder as a sassy gangster's moll. SP **DVD** ⟶

Brandon Routh *Superman/Clark Kent* • Kevin Spacey *Lex Luthor* • Kate Bosworth *Lois Lane* • Parker Posey *Kitty Kowalski* • James Marsden *Richard White* • Sam Huntington *Jimmy Olsen* • Eva Marie Saint *Martha Kent* • Frank Langella *Perry White* • Marlon Brando *Jor-El* • Richard Branson *Shuttle engineer* ■ *Dir* Bryan Singer • *Scr* Michael Dougherty, Dan Harris, from a story by Bryan Singer, Dougherty, Harris, from characters by Jerry Siegel, Joe Shuster

SuperMensch: the Legend of Shep Gordon ★★★ 15

Documentary   2013 · US · Colour · 85min

This is one of those documentaries that takes a figure most viewers have probably never heard of and builds a persuasive case as to why they are really important. In this instance the subject is Shep Gordon, who is best known for being Alice Cooper's manager for over 40 years. Co-director Mike Myers explains how Gordon also managed many other artists, including folk singer Anne Murray and soul star Teddy Pendergrass. He also crusaded for fairer pay for black artists, took drugs with Janis Joplin and Jimi Hendrix, slept with oodles of women and came up with the idea of celebrity chefs. Maybe Gordon wasn't always that nice a guy in real life, but he charms Myers, the camera and the viewer throughout this lively account. LF

Shep Gordon • Alice Cooper • Michael Douglas • Emeril Lagasse ■ *Dir* Mike Myers

Supernatural ★★

Mystery melodrama   1933 · US · BW · 65min

Heiress Carole Lombard becomes involved with fake medium Alan Dinehart, who says he can put her in touch with her dead brother. Of course, he's only after her money. The extraordinarily convoluted plot then sees Lombard possessed by the spirit of a dead murderess as she threatens to exact revenge on the fraudulent Dinehart. This is a disappointing vehicle for the talents of the lovely Lombard, though it remains a collectable curiosity for her fans. RK

Carole Lombard *Roma Courtney* • Randolph Scott *Grant Wilson* • Vivienne Osborne *Ruth Rogen* • Alan Dinehart *Paul Bavian* • HB Warner *Dr Houston* • Beryl Mercer *Madame Gourjan* • William Farnum *Robert Hammond* ■ *Dir* Victor Halperin • *Scr* Harvey Thew, Brian Marlow, from the story by Garnett Weston

Supernova ★ 15

Science-fiction adventure
2000 · US · Colour · 90min

Credited to a bogus name – Thomas Lee, the new century's Alan Smithee replacement – this relentlessly mediocre *Alien* rip-off at least looks good, as it shambles through the familiar conventions of the genre. A medical crew in deep space answer a distress call and take on board the only survivor of a mysterious mining accident. James Spader and Angela Bassett try in vain to soften the ridiculous impact of the clumsy theatrics, while the rest of the cast do little but disrobe. AJ **DVD**

James Spader *Nick Vanzant* • Angela Bassett *Kaela Evers* • Robert Forster *AJ Marley* • Lou Diamond Phillips *Yerzy Penalosa* • Peter Facinelli *Karl Larson* • Robin Tunney *Danika Lund* • Wilson Cruz *Benj Sotomejor* • Eddy Rice Jr *Flyboy* ■ *Dir* Thomas Lee [Walter Hill] • *Scr* David Campbell Wilson, from a story by William Malone

Superstar ★★ 15

Comedy   1999 · US · Colour · 78min

Calling this particular *Saturday Night Live* spin-off a cut above their usual product isn't exactly a compliment. It does have its moments, but it sometimes has to go wildly out of its way to get to them. Molly Shannon's character is a nerdy Catholic high-school girl who is determined not to let her dizzy nature or her snotty classmates stop her from becoming a star. The supporting characters are underused, and much of the action is generally lame. KB **DVD**

Molly Shannon *Mary Katherine Gallagher* • Will Ferrell *Sky Corrigan/Jesus* • Elaine Hendrix *Evian* • Harland Williams *Slater* • Mark McKinney *Father Ritley* • Glynis Johns *Grandma* • Jason Blicker *Howard* • Gerry Bamman *Father John* ■ *Dir* Bruce McCulloch • *Scr* Steven Wayne Koren, from the character created by Molly Shannon

Superstar: the Karen Carpenter Story ★★★★

Experimental biographical fantasy
1987 · US · Colour · 43min

Making unauthorised use of The Carpenters' music, director Todd Haynes presents a surreal re-enactment of the ill-fated life and career of singer Karen Carpenter and her brother Richard, using Barbie dolls instead of actors. Despite the superficially camp treatment, there's a serious message behind Haynes's portrayal of the doomed Karen, as she battles with overnight success, family pressures and the anorexia nervosa that would cause her death. Contemporary newsreel and TV-show footage provides the background to this bizarre yet moving examination of the dark side of 1970s pop culture. AJ

Gwen Kraus *Voice* • Bruce Tuthill *Voice* ■ *Dir* Todd Haynes • *Scr* Todd Haynes, Cynthia Schneider

Superstar: the Life and Times of Andy Warhol ★★★★

Documentary   1991 · US · Colour · 87min

This absorbing documentary was made three years after the death of pop artist and film-maker Warhol. Extremely well researched and well put together by Chuck Workman, it includes interviews with Warhol's relatives and famous friends, fascinating footage from the Warhol Factory, and clips from early films that many may not have been seen. Paul Morrissey, who directed Warhol's biggest hits, is noticeably absent, and there is a tendency to eulogise rather than analyse, but anyone interested in the zeitgeist of the 1960s will not be disappointed. DM **DVD**

■ *Dir/Scr* Chuck Workman • *Cinematographer* Burleigh Wartes

Supervixens ★★★★ 18

Satirical sex thriller   1975 · US · Colour · 104min

Cult sexploiter Russ Meyer cranked up to overdrive his giddy formula of fast pacing, breathless editing and weird camera angles with this exaggerated cartoon romp, complete with a "That's all, folks!" ending. The convoluted plot, detailing the sexual misadventures of a man on the run for a murder he didn't commit, includes escaped Nazis and psycho cops alongside the usual bevy of well-proportioned fantasy females. A delightfully manic rollercoaster ride through the sexual mores of mid-1970s America, laced with outrageous comedy and extreme violence. AJ Violence, swearing, sex scenes, nudity. **DVD**

Shari Eubank *Superangel/Supervixen* • Charles Pitts *Clint Ramsey* • Charles Napier *Harry Sledge* • Uschi Digard *Supersoul* • Henry Rowland *Martin Bormann* • Christy Hartburg *Superlorna* • Sharon Kelly *Supercherry* ■ *Dir/Scr* Russ Meyer

Support Your Local Gunfighter ★★★★ U

Comedy western   1971 · US · Colour · 88min

Amiable James Garner polished up his TV *Maverick* persona in a wonderfully witty pair of cowboy satires directed by Burt Kennedy, who had secured his spurs by writing a cycle of Randolph Scott westerns. This isn't exactly a sequel to *Support Your Local Sheriff!*, except perhaps in tone, but it's equally funny, as conman Garner passes himself off as a deadly gunman. Bumbling Jack Elam walks away with the movie as Garner's buddy and delivers one of the funniest last lines in American screen comedy. A side-splitting treat. TS **DVD**

James Garner *Latigo Smith* • Suzanne Pleshette *Patience Barton* • Jack Elam *Jug May* • Joan Blondell *Jenny* • Harry Morgan *Taylor Barton* • Marie Windsor *Goldie* • Henry Jones *Ez* • Chuck Connors *Swifty Morgan* • Grady Sutton *Storekeeper* ■ *Dir* Burt Kennedy • *Scr* James Edward Grant

Support Your Local Sheriff! ★★★★ PG

Comedy western   1969 · US · Colour · 89min

This is one of a pair of priceless comedy gems (*Support Your Local Gunfighter* followed in 1971) from director Burt Kennedy, which spoof the western genre with great affection and provide marvellous roles for James Garner. Here he utilises his easy-going, wry charm as a put-upon

U SUITABLE FOR ALL   Uc SUITABLE ESPECIALLY FOR YOUNG CHILDREN (DVD ONLY)   PG PARENTAL GUIDANCE   12A UNDER 12s TO BE ACCOMPANIED (CINEMA ONLY)

lawman. Western fans will enjoy the clever casting. Walter Brennan virtually reprises the role of Ike Clanton in *My Darling Clementine*, only this time for laughs, and there's Joan Hackett from *Will Penny*. Jack Elam and Bruce Dern are hysterically funny. **TS** *DVD*

James Garner *Jason McCullough* • Joan Hackett *Prudy Perkins* • Walter Brennan *Pa Danby* • Harry Morgan *Mayor Oly Perkins* • Jack Elam *Jake* • Bruce Dern *Joe Danby* • Henry Jones *Preacher Henry Jackson* ■ *Dir* Burt Kennedy • *Scr* William Bowers

Suppose They Gave a War and Nobody Came? ★★★ 15
Satirical comedy drama
1970 · US · Colour · 112min

A commander of a US army base in the American South hopes to foster good will with the nearby town by organising a dance. All seems well at first, but when army sergeant Tony Curtis is caught canoodling with local beauty Suzanne Pleshette, the resulting fracas leads to war breaking out between the town and the military. Sometimes farcical, sometimes satirical, it's a crazy sprawling mess of a comedy that manages to entertain, despite its many flaws. **DF**

Brian Keith *Nace* • Tony Curtis *Shannon Gambroni* • Ernest Borgnine *Sheriff Harve* • Ivan Dixon *Sgt Jones* • Suzanne Pleshette *Ramona* • Tom Ewell *Billy Joe Davis* • Bradford Dillman *Capt Myerson* • Don Ameche *Col Flanders* ■ *Dir* Hy Averback • *Scr* Don McGuire, Hal Captain, from a story by Hal Captain

Supreme Sanction ★★ 18
Action thriller
1999 · US · Colour · 89min

Michael Madsen sleepwalks through yet another ho-hum action thriller that offers little but some efficiently staged action pieces. He's the bad guy here, a hitman for a secret government-sponsored agency on the trail of old colleague Kristy Swanson, who has baulked at her latest assignment – the killing of journalist David Dukes. Even on autopilot, Madsen is alway watchable, while Swanson makes for a feisty heroine, but this is instantly forgettable. **JF** *DVD*

Michael Madsen *Dalton* • Kristy Swanson *Jenna* • Holliston Coleman *Bailey* • David Dukes *Jordan McNamara* • Ron Perlman *The Director* • Tom "Tiny" Lister Jr *Lester* ■ *Dir/Scr* John Terlesky

El Sur ★★★★ U
Drama
1983 · Sp/Fr · Colour · 94min

Victor Erice's first film in the decade since completing his masterpiece, *Spirit of the Beehive*, returns to the idea of cinema reflecting the hopes and misconceptions of an intense young girl. The poster advertising Alfred Hitchcock's *Shadow of a Doubt* suggests the notion of betrayal that is then confirmed by the film-within-the-film, *Flor en la Sombre*. But even more effective is the leisurely, lyrical manner in which Erice allows 1950s adolescent Iciar Bollain to realise the fragility of the dreams her younger self (Sonsoles Aranguren) has woven around her doting – and now mysteriously disappeared – father, Omero Antonutti. **DP** Spanish +subtitles.

Omero Antonutti *Agustín* • Sonsoles Aranguren *Estrella, aged 8* • Iciar Bollain *Estrelle, teenager* • Lola Cardona *Julia* • Rafaela Aparicio *Milagros* • Aurore Clément *Irene Ríos* ■ *Dir* Victor Erice • *Scr* Victor Erice, from the novel by Adelaida García Morales

Sur ★★★★ 15
Drama
1987 · Arg/Fr · Colour · 118min

Following his treatise on physical exile, *Tangos, Exilo de Gardel* (1985), Argentinian director Fernando E Solanas (himself heading home after a prolonged absence) explores the pain of the prisoner in this vibrant, lyrical, political and poignant study of national transition and individual turmoil. Consciously employing a theatrical style, he uses tango, poetry and song to counterpoint the jumble of emotions, memories, hopes and fears that beset newly released Miguel Angel Sola as he returns to his Buenos Aires neighbourhood. However, his wife, Susu Pecoraro, also has

to readjust, having turned to close friend Philippe Léotard for solace in her isolation. **DP** In Spanish.

Susu Pecoraro *Rosi Echegoyen* • Miguel Angel Sola *Floreal Echegoyen* • Philippe Léotard *Roberto* • Lito Cruz *El Negro* • Ulises Dumont *Emilio* ■ *Dir/Scr* Fernando E Solanas

Sur ★★★ U
Musical drama
2002 · Ind · Colour · 137min

After years of singing for others, playback vocalist Lucky Ali makes his screen debut in this Bollywood take on the Svengali story (with a smattering of *A Star Is Born* thrown in for good measure). Not content with being a musical superstar, he becomes obsessed with fincing a student whom he can train to be his equal. But no sooner has the demure Gauri Karnik found fame than he becomes destructively jealous. Revelling in its melodramatic clichés, Tanuja Chandra's tear-jerker is undemanding entertainment. **DP** Hindi +subtitles. *DVD*

Lucky Ali *Vikramaditya Singh* • Gauri Karnik *Tina Marie* ■ *Dir/Scr* Tanuja Chandra

The Sure Thing ★★★★ 15
Comedy
1985 · US · Colour · 90min

This delightful comedy from director Rob Reiner should have made John Cusack a star. He's superb as a beer-guzzling, sex-obsessed freshman who travels from his eastern college to California during the holidays to meet up with a beautiful girl who's a "sure thing". However, during a series of misadventures he ends up on the road with clean-living Daphne Zuniga, and that's where the fun really begins. Both the leads are enjoyable to watch, and look out for a young Tim Robbins as the driver with whom no one should ever hitch a ride. **JB** Some swearing. *DVD*

John Cusack *Walter "Gib" Gibson* • Daphne Zuniga *Alison Bradbury* • Anthony Edwards *Lance* • Boyd Gaines *Jason* • Lisa Jane Persky *Mary Ann* • Viveca Lindfors *Professor Taub* • Nicollette Sheridan *The Sure Thing* • Tim Robbins *Gary* ■ *Dir* Rob Reiner • *Scr* Steven L Bloom, Jonathan Roberts

Surf Crazy ★★★
Documentary
1959 · US · Colour · 72min

Hawaii had only just achieved statehood when Bruce Brown made his second surfing documentary there. So there's a sense of moment about the sequences filmed at the Waimea and Sunset beaches on Oahu. But this was a cross-continental odyssey, which sees Brown and his buddies push their Ford through 7,000 miles in search of breakers. The California sequences at Rincon and Cottons are spectacular. But the film's real interest lies in the Mexican segment, as it was still virgin surf territory. **DP** *DVD*

■ *Dir* Bruce Brown

Surf Nazis Must Die ★ 18
Futuristic satire
1987 · US · Colour · 85min

This is one of cinema's most notoriously titled movies and a typical release from Troma – the studio that gave us *Rabid Grannies* and *The Toxic Avenger* – featuring bad acting, a nonexistent budget and a ludicrous plotline. It's set in a future California, where an earthquake has left millions homeless and the beaches have turned into battlegrounds, as surf gangs vie for control. **RS** *DVD*

Barry Brenner *Adolf* • Gail Neely *Mama Washington* • Michael Sonye *Mengele* • Dawn Wildsmith *Eva* • Jon Ayre *Narrator* ■ *Dir* Peter George • *Scr* Jon Ayre

Surf Ninjas ★ PG
Comedy adventure
1993 · US · Colour · 83min

Isn't it amazing that, in the midst of the 1990s ninja craze, not one of them had a decent martial arts sequence or a single line of decent dialogue? This one has the audacity to include both Rob Schneider and Leslie Nielsen for its odious comic relief. Polynesian brothers Ernie Reyes Jr and Nicholas Cowan discover that they are the royal heirs to an island nation, which was overthrown by evil warlord Nielsen. **ST**

Ernie Reyes Sr *Zatch* • Ernie Reyes Jr *Johnny* • Nicholas Cowan *Adam* • John Karlen *Mac* • Rob Schneider *Iggy* • Leslie Nielsen *Colonel Chi* ■ *Dir* Neal Israel • *Scr* Dan Gordon

Surf's Up ★★★ PG
Animated action comedy
2007 · US · Colour · 81min

There's nothing childish about the animated penguins in directors Ash Brannon (*Toy Story 2*) and Chris Buck's (*Tarzan*) action cartoon. The script is smart, the vocal acting smarter, and its presentation as a fake documentary cleverest of all. The fun begins with a surfing penguin history lesson using scratchy "archival" footage, then switches to a TV crew covering cocky rockhopper Cody's (Shia LaBeouf) journey to a surf competition in Hawaii. It's the Spinal Tap-style jibes at televised sports/ reality shows, the warmth of the supporting characters (Zooey Deschanel, Jon Heder) and memorable one-liners that make this almost as delightful as *Happy Feet*. **AJ** Brief swearing. *DVD* CS

Shia LaBeouf *Cody Maverick* • Jeff Bridges *Zeke "Big Z" Topanga/"Geek"* • Zooey Deschanel *Lani Aliikai* • Jon Heder *Chicken Joe* • James Woods *Reggie Belafonte* • Diedrich Bader *Tank "The Shredder" Evans* • Jane Krakowski • Michael McKean ■ *Dir* Ash Brannon, Chris Buck • *Scr* Ash Brannon, Chris Buck, Christopher Jenkins, Don Rhymer, from a story by Jenkins, Christian Darren

Surprise Package ★★★ U
Comedy
1960 · UK · BW · 99min

By now a major international star, Yul Brynner was given his first comic role as a mobster deported to a Greek island, where deposed king Noël Coward is already ensconced. Mitzi Gaynor is the surprise package, flown in for Brynner's delectation. The trio's nefarious adventures are fun, but not as funny as they should have been considering that the script is by Harry Kurnitz, writer of very polished comedies, and based on a novel by the great satirist Art Buchwald. **DM**

Yul Brynner *Nico March* • Bill Nagy *Johnny Stettina* • Mitzi Gaynor *Gabby Rogers* • Lionel Murton *US Marshall* • Barry Foster *US Marshall* • Eric Pohlmann *Stefan Miralis* • Noël Coward *King Pavel II* • George Coulouris *Dr Hugo Panzer* • Warren Mitchell *Klimatis* ■ *Dir* Stanley Donen • *Scr* Harry Kurnitz, from the novel *A Gift from the Boys* by Art Buchwald

Surrender ★★★ PG
Romantic comedy
1987 · US · Colour · 91min

This light courtship comedy is about a confused woman caught in two minds about the men in her life. Sally Field is Little Miss Muddle; Michael Caine and Steve Guttenberg are the twin objects of her affections. Though the film is trite and contrived at times, strong performances, in particular from the two male leads, just about carry it through. **DA**

Sally Field *Daisy Morgan* • Michael Caine *Sean Stein* • Steve Guttenberg *Marty Caesar* • Peter Boyle *Jay Bass* • Julie Kavner *Ronnie* • Jackie Cooper *Ace Morgan* • Louise Lasser *Joyce* • Iman *Hedy* ■ *Dir/Scr* Jerry Belson

Surrender Dorothy ★★
Drama
2006 · US · Colour · 86min

In this undemanding melodrama, Diane Keaton is in hyperactive mode as an overbearing divorcee who's forced to face a few home truths after the death of her daughter. Lots of shouting and overdramatic soul-searching follow, as Keaton discovers the relationship with her child was not as close as she thought. Though the lessons learnt are both harsh and monumental, the movie lacks the poignancy you'd expect. **SF** Violence, swearing, sexual references, drug abuse.

Diane Keaton *Natalie* • Alexa Davalos *Sara* • Tom Everett Scott *Adam* • Chris Pine *Shawn* • Lauren German *Maddy* • Josh Hopkins *Peter* • Peter Riegert *Mel* ■ *Dir* Charles McDougall • *Scr* Matthew McDuffie, from the novel by Meg Wolitzer

Surrogates ★★★ 12
Science-fiction action thriller
2009 · US · Colour · 84min

This intriguing sci-fi thriller poses some big questions about what it means to be human. In a future where much of the population has robotic alter egos to take care of their day-to-day work, dogged FBI agent Bruce Willis discovers that all is not well in this brave new world of "surrogates" – whose chiselled forms represent the users' idealised versions of themselves (Willis's model even has a thick head of hair!). A murder case where the destruction of a surrogate also effects a splattery demise for its human master sets in motion what becomes an increasingly plodding conspiracy plot, yet it's the underlying story of Willis's failing relationship with wife Rosamund Pike (who's excellent) that adds a resonant emotional layer not often found in action flicks. **TJ** Violence, swearing, sexual references, drug abuse. *DVD* *Blu*

Bruce Willis *Agent Greer* • Radha Mitchell *Agent Peters* • Rosamund Pike *Maggie Greer* • Boris Kodjoe *Stone* • James Francis Ginty *Canter* • Ving Rhames *The Prophet* • James Cromwell *Older Canter* ■ *Dir* Jonathan Mostow • *Scr* Michael Ferris, John Brancato, from the graphic novel *The Surrogates* by Robert Venditti, Brett Weldele

Surveillance ★★ 18
Crime thriller
2007 · US/Ger/Can/Aus · Colour · 97min

Jennifer Lynch's belated follow-up to *Boxing Helena* (1993) is a dark, violent psycho-thriller. In a nod to her father David Lynch's cult TV series *Twin Peaks*, the protagonists here are FBI agents (played by Bill Pullman and Julia Ormond) who arrive in a small town to investigate a string of recent murders on a local highway. One or two fine shock moments that are certainly not for the squeamish prevent the film from becoming boring. Unfortunately, such flashes of originality aren't enough to compensate for Lynch's failure to emulate her father's mastery of mood and tension as she smothers a very simple story with irritating flourishes. **DW** *DVD* *Blu*

Julia Ormond *Elizabeth Anderson* • Bill Pullman *Sam Hallaway* • Pell James *Bobbi Prescott* • Ryan Simpkins *Stephanie* • Cheri Oteri *Mom* • Michael Ironside *Captain Billings* ■ *Dir* Jennifer Lynch [Jennifer Chambers Lynch] • *Scr* Jennifer Lynch, Kent Harper

The Survivalist ★★★★ 18
Futuristic thriller
2015 · UK/Ger · Colour · 99min

A stark corrective to the garish dystopia of films like *Mad Max: Fury Road*, this brutal Northern Ireland-set drama takes a more realistic look at a world driven to near-collapse by the steady depletion of its resources. Scavenging to get by in a remote woodland shack, the nameless hunter of the title lives in isolation, his senses perpetually primed for intruders. The sweat and filth of life in the wilderness are evoked without mercy, but like in *Fury Road*, there's an accent on the feminine here that offers hope. **DW** Sex, violence *DVD* *Blu*

Martin McCann *Survivalist* • Mia Goth *Milja* • Olwen Fouéré *Kathryn* • Douglas Russell *Snatcher* ■ *Dir/Scr* Stephen Fingleton

Surviving ★★★★ 15
Drama
1985 · US · Colour · 137min

This is an often fascinating and powerful TV movie about the devastating consequences of thwarted teenage romance. Zach Galligan and Molly Ringwald are the young lovers, driven to desperate measures when their parents oppose their relationship. A strong cast includes Ellen Burstyn and Marsha Mason as the mothers confronting this teenage angst and struggling to deal with their own feelings of guilt. **JB**

Ellen Burstyn *Tina Morgan* • Len Cariou *David Morgan* • Zach Galligan *Rick Morgan* • Marsha Mason *Lois Carlson* • Molly Ringwald *Lonnie Carlson* • Paul Sorvino *Harvey Carlson* • River Phoenix *Philip Morgan* • Heather O'Rourke *Sarah Morgan* ■ *Dir* Waris Hussein • *Scr* Joyce Eliason

S

Surviving Christmas ★ 12
Seasonal comedy   2004 · US · Colour · 86min

Ben Affleck plays a rich advertising executive who returns to his former home where he pays the blue-collar Valco family that now lives there to let him spend the holiday period with them as their son. Cue a mess of clichés, pratfalls and limp jokes. Even co-stars James Gandolfini and Catherine O'Hara as the Valco parents, who at least realise less is more, cannot rescue the movie. SF Swearing. *DVD*

Ben Affleck *Drew Latham* · James Gandolfini *Tom Valco* · Christina Applegate *Alicia Valco* · Catherine O'Hara *Christine Valco* · Josh Zuckerman *Brian Valco* · Bill Macy *Doo-Dah* · Jennifer Morrison *Missy Vangilder* · Udo Kier *Heinrich* ■ *Dir* Mike Mitchell · *Scr* Deborah Kaplan, Harry Elfont, Jeffrey Ventimilia, Joshua Sternin, from a story by Kaplan, Elfont

Surviving Life ★★★★ 15
Part-animated comedy fantasy
2010 · Cz Rep/Jpn · Colour · 104min

This psychological satire from Czech master surrealist Jan Svankmajer, inspired by one of his own dreams, chronicles the failing efforts of a middle-aged Mr Average, Evzen (Vaclav Helsus), to distinguish between his waking and sleeping worlds. In the former, he's been married to Milada (Zuzana Kronerova) for 25 years, but in the latter he is besotted with Evzenie (Klara Issova) whose name changes with each encounter, though she bears a striking resemblance to his mother. All manner of bizarre events befall Evzen as his conscious and subconscious states become entwined. But it's pointless trying to figure this all out, as the enjoyment comes from admiring Svankmajer's intellectual audacity and technical brilliance as he laces the live action with animated photographic cut-outs that are simultaneously subversive, hilarious and grotesquely disconcerting. DP *DVD*

Vaclav Helsus *Evzen/Milan* · Klara Issova *Evzenie* · Zuzana Kronerova *Milada* · Daniela Bakerova *Dr Holubova* · Emilia Dosekova *Super-ego* · Marcel Nemec *Colleague* ■ *Dir/Scr* Jan Svankmajer

Surviving Love ★★
Romantic comedy drama
2004 · US · Colour · 87min

Pulitzer Prize-winning playwright Beth Henley scripted this study of marital discord, and the performances of stars Ted Danson and Mary Steenburgen give the slightly wordy melodrama its core credibility. Following a fiasco at their daughter's wedding, the bickering couple plan to discuss their proposed divorce during a road trip. The exchanges occasionally have a theatrical feel, but there's guilty pleasure to be had in watching real-life couple Danson and Steenburgen patch things up. DP

Ted Danson *George Gazelle* · Mary Steenburgen *Clem Gazelle* · Erin Karpluk [Erin Karpluk] *Tess Gazelle* · Adam Nicholas Frost [Adam Frost] *Joe Gazelle* · Bonnie Bartlett *Kate Gazelle* · Danny Dorosh *Tad Neill* · Emma Duncan *Thelma Bridgewater* ■ *Dir* Steven Schachter · *Scr* Beth Henley, from the short story *Rediscovered Love* by Nancy Whitmore and the book *Meant to Be* by Barry & Joyce Vissell

Surviving Picasso ★★★★ 15
Biographical drama   1996 · US · Colour · 120min

James Ivory directs Anthony Hopkins in a vision of Picasso's life that argues his passion for women equalled his passion for painting. His objects of desire are all stunning – Natascha McElhone, Julianne Moore, Susannah Harker – but which of them will prove a match for him? Hopkins is excellent as the self-centred artist and McElhone makes a very impressive impact in her first major role. As ever Ivory directs with flair and aesthetic insight. LH Swearing, violence, nudity.

Anthony Hopkins *Pablo Picasso* · Natascha McElhone *Françoise Gilot* · Julianne Moore *Dora Maar* · Joss Ackland *Henri Matisse* · Jane Lapotaire *Olga Koklova* · Joseph Maher *Kahnweiler* · Bob Peck *Françoise's father* · Diane Venora *Jacqueline Rocque* · Joan Plowright

Françoise's grandmother · Susannah Harker *Marie-Thérèse* · *Dir* James Ivory · *Scr* Ruth Prawer Jhabvala, from the non-fiction book *Picasso: Creator and Destroyer* by Arianna Stassinopoulos Huffington

Surviving the Game ★★ 15
Action thriller   1994 · US · Colour · 92min

Another variant on the shopworm manhunt premise, best exhibited back in the 1930s with *The Most Dangerous Game*. This time, rapper-cum-thespian Ice-T is a homeless derelict conned out of the city and into the wilderness to act as prey for a bunch of thrill-seeking high rollers including Gary Busey's ex-CIA agent, F Murray Abraham's Wall Street executive and Rutger Hauer. Former Spike Lee cinematographer Ernest R Dickerson brings technical bravado to the proceedings, but the whole premise of wealthy whites hunting homeless blacks is tasteless. RS *DVD*

Ice-T *Jack Mason* · Rutger Hauer *Burns* · Charles S Dutton *Cole* · Gary Busey *Hawkins* · F Murray Abraham *Wolf Sr* · John C McGinley *Griffin* · William McNamara *Wolf Jr* · Jeff Corey *Hank* ■ *Dir* Ernest R Dickerson · *Scr* Eric Bernt

The Survivor ★ 15
Supernatural thriller   1981 · Aus · Colour · 95min

Robert Powell puts on that martyred look he keeps handy in lieu of acting, here as a pilot who's the sole survivor of a crashed jet and is prey to visions of dead passengers. Jenny Agutter simpers while Powell whimpers in this Australian oddity directed by David Hemmings, a would-be thriller that's sadly lacking in suspense. TH Violence, swearing. *DVD*

Robert Powell *Keller* · Jenny Agutter *Hobbs* · Joseph Cotten *Priest* · Angela Punch McGregor *Beth Rogan* · Ralph Cotterill *Slater* · Peter Sumner *Tewson* ■ *Dir* David Hemmings · *Scr* David Ambrose, from the novel by James Herbert

Survivor ★★ 12
Action thriller   2015 · US · Colour · 92min

Milla Jovovich stars in this standard action thriller, playing a US government officer in London who must prove her innocence and evade a terrorist assassin (Pierce Brosnan) after being framed for a bombing in the British capital. Slick action unfolds in various London and New York locations, but production values are just window dressing for what is a quite straightforward "woman on the run" story directed by *V for Vendetta* and *The Raven*'s James McTeigue. JL Violence, swearing.

Milla Jovovich *Kate Abbott* · Pierce Brosnan *Nash, "The Watchmaker"* · Dylan McDermott *Sam Parker* · Angela Bassett *Ambassador Maureene Crane* · Robert Forster *Bill Talbot* · James D'Arcy *Inspector Paul Anderson* ■ *Dir* James McTeigue · *Scr* Philip Shelby

The Survivors ★★ 15
Comedy   1983 · US · Colour · 98min

What starts as a promising social satire soon descends into coarse slapstick and manic babble as Robin Williams and Walter Matthau come to terms with life after foiling a crime, but being identified from mild-mannered executive into gun-toting survivalist, while his fellow hero Matthau stays cynically calm. Director Michael Ritchie lets the picture and his stars run out of control. DP Swearing, violence. *DVD*

Walter Matthau *Sonny Paluso* · Robin Williams *Donald Quinelle* · Jerry Reed *Jack Locke* · James Wainwright *Wes Huntley* · Kristen Vigard *Candice Paluso* · Annie McEnroe *Doreen* · Anne Pitoniak *Betty* ■ *Dir* Michael Ritchie · *Scr* Michael Leeson

Sus ★★ 15
Drama   2009 · UK · Colour · 90min

It's election night, 1979, and at a London police station, a black suspect under interrogation fears he's being "fitted up" for his wife's murder in this disappointing drama from *Long Good Friday* writer Barrie Keefe. As a three-hander unfolding in a single room, you'd expect a confrontation of escalating intensity and no little claustrophobia, yet director Robert Heath's

widescreen compositions are contrived and artificial. And the script's carefully weighted revelations are reduced by the over-theatrical performances of Clint Dyer, Ralph Brown and Rafe Spall. TJ Violence, swearing. *DVD*

Ralph Brown *DS Karn* · Rafe Spall *DC Wilby* · Clint Dyer *Leon Delroy* · Anjela Lauren Smith *Georgie* ■ *Dir* Robert Heath · *Scr* Barrie Keeffe

Susan and God ★★★
Comedy drama   1940 · US · Colour · 115min

Shallow and narcissistic society wife and mother Joan Crawford, whose disregard is alienating her husband Fredric March, returns from a European trip with a new fad – religion. Her verbal zealotry and pious interference in other people's lives causes havoc and drives her husband to drink. An unusual drama, it's directed by George Cukor, who draws a persuasive performance from Crawford. RK

Joan Crawford *Susan Trexel* · Fredric March *Barry Trexel* · Ruth Hussey *Charlotte* · John Carroll *Clyde Rochester* · Rita Hayworth *Leonora Stubbs* · Nigel Bruce *Hutchins Stubbs* · Bruce Cabot *Michael O'Hara* ■ *Dir* George Cukor · *Scr* Anita Loos, from a play by Rachel Crothers

Susan Lenox: Her Fall and Rise ★★★
Romantic melodrama   1931 · US · BW · 76min

This steamy movie seems tame today, save for the undeniable sexual magnetism between Greta Garbo and Clark Gable in their only screen pairing. But the British film censor was having none of it, lopped out several key seconds and changed the title to *The Rise of Helga*. Garbo is magic, however, playing a farmer's illegitimate daughter who flees rather than go through with an arranged marriage. She meets and falls in love with Gable, but her oppressive father is hot on the trail. TS

Greta Garbo *Susan Lenox* · Clark Gable *Rodney* · Jean Hersholt *Ohlin* · John Miljan *Burlingham* · Alan Hale *Mondstrum* · Hale Hamilton *Mike Kelly* · Hilda Vaughn *Astrid* · Russell Simpson *Doctor* ■ *Dir* Robert Z Leonard · *Scr* Wanda Tuchock, Zelda Sears, Leon Gordon, Edith Fitzgerald, from the novel by David Graham Phillips

Susan Slade ★
Melodrama   1961 · US · Colour · 116min

The daughter of a respectable engineer falls pregnant by a mountaineer who is promptly killed in an accident. After hiding in South America, she returns to California with her illegitimate baby and has to deal with the consequences of her father's unexpected death. Turgid, unconvincing and boring. RK

Troy Donahue *Hoyt Brecker* · Connie Stevens *Susan Slade* · Dorothy McGuire *Leah Slade* · Lloyd Nolan *Roger Slade* · Brian Aherne *Stanton Corbett* · Grant Williams *Conn White* ■ *Dir* Delmer Daves · *Scr* Delmer Daves, from the novel *The Sin of Susan Slade* by Doris Hume · *Music* Max Steiner

Susan Slept Here ★★★
Comedy   1954 · US · Colour · 97min

This super-sophisticated farce is as funny and risqué now as it was back in 1954, and Debbie Reynolds is simply terrific in one of her rare naughty-but-nice roles as a sexy teenage delinquent foisted on screenwriter Dick Powell. The Hollywood scene is well observed by director Frank Tashlin, and the humour is peppered with in-jokes. (The narrator is an Oscar statuette!) The Technicolor is particularly rich, and the Oscar-nominated theme song *Hold My Hand* went to number one in the charts. A film for 1950s freaks. TS

Dick Powell *Mark Christopher* · Debbie Reynolds *Susan* · Anne Francis *Isabella* · Glenda Farrell *Maude* · Alvy Moore *Virgil* · Horace McMahon *Maizel* ■ *Dir* Frank Tashlin · *Scr* Alex Gottlieb, from the play *Susan* by Alex Gottlieb, Steve Fisher

Susannah of the Mounties ★★★ U
Adventure   1939 · US · BW · 75min

Having survived a tribal massacre, little Shirley Temple is taken in by Mountie

Randolph Scott and duly helps him get both his man (the truly villainous Victor Jory) and his woman (Margaret Lockwood, making her Hollywood debut). There's some toned-down action and a teeth-grinding sequence in which Scott is taught to tap dance, but it's mostly harmless. Avoid the colourised version. DP *DVD*

Shirley Temple *Susannah* · Randolph Scott *Inspector Angus "Monty" Montague* · Margaret Lockwood *Vicky Standing* · Martin Good Rider *Little Chief* · J Farrell MacDonald *Pat O'Hannegan* · Maurice Moscovich *Chief Big Eagle* · Victor Jory *Wolf Pelt* ■ *Dir* William A Seiter · *Scr* Robert Ellis, Helen Logan, from a story by Fidel La Barba, Walter Ferris, from the novel *Susannah, a Little Girl of the Mounties* by Muriel Denison

Susan's Plan ★★★ 18
Comedy   1998 · US · Colour · 84min

This is a contrived, complex and intermittently hilarious comedy from John Landis, returning somewhat to form. Nastassja Kinski plays Susan, who's desperate to bump off her reprehensible ex-hubby for cash and hires a string of bumbling hitmen to do it. Routine stuff, elevated above the ordinary by a cracking cast. DA Swearing, violence, nudity. *DVD*

Nastassja Kinski *Susan* · Billy Zane *Sam* · Michael Biehn *Bill* · Dan Aykroyd *Bob* · Lara Flynn Boyle *Betty* · Rob Schneider *Steve* · Adrian Paul *Paul* ■ *Dir/Scr* John Landis

The Suspect ★★★
Period thriller   1944 · US · BW · 85min

Directed by German émigré Robert Siodmak, this Edwardian drama stars Charles Laughton in the kind of role in which he excelled. He plays a decent, ordinary shopkeeper whose life is made a misery by his deeply unpleasant wife Rosalind Ivan. Smitten with pretty stenographer Ella Raines, he beats his wife to death with a cane, but gets away with claiming she died in an accidental fall. He marries Raines and all is well until his blackmailing neighbour Henry Daniell begins to suspect the truth. Modest, suspenseful and absorbing. RK

Charles Laughton *Philip Marshall* · Ella Raines *Mary Gray* · Dean Harens *John Marshall* · Stanley C Ridges [Stanley Ridges] *Inspector Huxley* · Henry Daniell *Mr Gilbert Simmons* · Rosalind Ivan *Cora Marshall* · Molly Lamont *Mrs Edith Simmons* · Raymond Severn *Merridew* ■ *Dir* Robert Siodmak · *Scr* Bertram Millhauser, Arthur T Hormen, from the novel *This Way Out* by James Ronald

Suspect ★★ PG
Spy drama   1960 · UK · BW · 77min

This story of spies at a chemical research lab betrays its secret through casting. Nominal stars Tony Britton and Virginia Maskell are awful, and you soon wish splendid supports Peter Cushing, Donald Pleasence, Raymond Huntley and Ian Bannen had more to do. The Boulting brothers fail to create the claustrophobia that might have intensified the climate of suspicion, and the casting of Spike Milligan in an espionage drama is the only real talking point. DP *DVD*

Tony Britton *Bob Marriott* · Virginia Maskell *Lucy Byrne* · Peter Cushing *Professor Sewall* · Ian Bannen *Alan Andrews* · Raymond Huntley *Sir George Gatling* · Thorley Walters *Mr Prince* · Donald Pleasence *Brown* · Spike Milligan *Arthur* ■ *Dir* Roy Boulting, John Boulting · *Scr* Nigel Balchin, Jeffrey Dell, Roy Boulting, from the novel *A Sort of Traitors* by Nigel Balchin

Suspect ★★★ 15
Courtroom thriller   1987 · US · Colour · 116min

This is an early Hollywood role for Liam Neeson, playing a deaf-mute Vietnam veteran accused of murder. Cher is his lawyer and Dennis Quaid provides a glimmer of hope in a seemingly hopeless case. Director Peter Yates winds up the courtroom tension to some effect, but any sympathy for Neeson's plight soon gets lost as suspicion shifts to a higher legal authority and the plot becomes too far-fetched. TH Violence, swearing. *DVD*

Cher *Kathleen Riley* • Dennis Quaid *Eddie Sanger* • Liam Neeson *Carl Wayne Anderson* • John Mahoney *Judge Matthew Helms* • Joe Mantegna *Charlie Stella* • Philip Bosco *Paul Gray* • E Katherine Kerr *Grace Comisky* • Fred Melamed *Morty Rosenthal* ■ Dir Peter Yates • Scr Eric Roth

Suspect Zero ★★ 15
Crime thriller   2004 · US · Colour · 95min

In this depressingly formulaic stab at the serial-killer genre, Aaron Eckhart plays an FBI agent who finds a formidable new adversary in the shape of Ben Kingsley, a former agent with a unique insight into the minds of murderers who seems to be specialising in dispatching other serial killers. Despite the good cast and the glimmer of an intriguing idea in the plot, director E Elias Merhige generates little in the way of menace or tension. JF *DVD*

Aaron Eckhart *Thomas Mackelway* • Ben Kingsley *Benjamin O'Ryan* • Carrie-Anne Moss *Fran Kulok* • Harry J Lennix [Harry Lennix] *Rick Charleton* • Kevin Chamberlin *Harold Speck* • Julian Reyes *Highway patrolman* • Keith Campbell *Raymond Starkey* ■ Dir E Elias Merhige • Scr Zak Penn, Billy Ray, from a story by Zak Penn

Suspension of Disbelief ★★ 15
Crime thriller   2012 · UK · Colour · 111min

Director Mike Figgis's self-conscious stylings undo this otherwise entertaining *film noir* that blurs the line between fact and fiction. Sebastian Koch plays a haunted London-based screenwriter who is seduced by a French woman (Lotte Verbeek) whose subsequent death brings Koch into contact with a police inspector who fancies writing whodunnits (Kenneth Cranham) and the victim's twin sister (also Verbeek). It's certainly an intriguing set-up, but Figgis's presentation quickly becomes intrusive and tiresome. DP Swearing, sexual references, drug abuse, some violence, brief nudity.

Sebastian Koch *Martin Ehrlichmann* • Lotte Verbeek *Therese/Angelique* • Emilia Fox *Claire Jones* • Rebecca Night *Sarah Jones* • Eoin Macken *Gregory O'Hanlon* • Lachlan Nieboer *Dominic* ■ Dir/Scr Mike Figgis

Suspicion ★★★★ PG
Psychological thriller   1941 · US · BW · 99min

In this marvellous Hitchcock thriller, timid Joan Fontaine is in mortal fear of being bumped off by her husband, amoral Cary Grant. Fontaine won the best actress Oscar for her pouting female-in-trouble portrayal, though some believe it was to compensate her for not winning the award for *Rebecca* the previous year. It all begins well enough, with Grant's bounder a most unlikeable cad, but the film is hopelessly crippled by the censorship of the time, and is ultimately both predictable and implausible. But there's much to enjoy, not least a totally phoney Hollywood England and sterling support from British expatriates Nigel Bruce and Cedric Hardwicke. TS *DVD*

Cary Grant *Johnnie Aysgarth* • Joan Fontaine *Lina McLaidlaw* • Cedric Hardwicke *General McLaidlaw* • Nigel Bruce *Gordon Cochran "Beaky" Thwaite* • Dame May Whitty *Mrs McLaidlaw* • Isabel Jeans *Mrs Newsham* ■ Dir Alfred Hitchcock • Scr Samson Raphaelson, Joan Harrison, Alma Reville, from the novel *Before the Fact* by Frances Iles [Anthony Berkeley Cox]

Suspicious River ★★ 18
Psychological drama   2000 · Can · Colour · 89min

In this dark study of small-town sexuality, Molly Parker, as a married motel receptionist who prostitutes herself to guests, ably suggests the dazed fragility that delivers her into the clutches of brutal redneck Callum Keith Rennie. Lynne Stopkewich's direction chillingly reduces sex to its bestial basics, while her refusal to clarify whether young Mary Kate Welsh's brush with abuse is a parallel story or a flashback to Parker's own childhood adds tension. But her concern with shocking rather than intriguing the audience

ultimately results in disappointment. DP *DVD*

Molly Parker *Leila Murray* • Callum Keith Rennie *Gary Jensen* • Mary Kate Welsh *Young girl* • Joel Bissonnette *Rick Schmidt* • Deanna Milligan *Millie* ■ Dir Lynne Stopkewich • Scr Lynne Stopkewich, from the novel by Laura Kasischke

Suspiria ★★★★ 18
Supernatural horror   1976 · It · Colour · 94min

In this landmark horror fantasy from cult director Dario Argento – dubbed the Italian Hitchcock for his mastery of suspense – Jessica Harper plays a dancer at a German ballet school where witches prowl the corridors. The famous opening 20 minutes of this *Snow White* fairy tale (by way of Thomas De Quincey's hallucinatory *Confessions of an Opium Eater*) are an unforgettable experience, and the whole is a stunning combination of menacing *Grand Guignol* atmosphere, dazzling colours, gory violence, lush decor and pounding soundtrack. AJ Violence. *DVD*

Jessica Harper *Susy Bannion* • Joan Bennett *Madame Blanc* • Alida Valli *Miss Tanner* • Udo Kier *Frank* • Flavio Bucci *Daniel* • Stefania Casini *Sara* • Miguel Bose *Mark* • Rudolf Schündler *Professor Milius* ■ Dir Dario Argento • Scr Dario Argento, Dario Nicclodi

Suture ★★★ 15
Thriller   1993 · US · BW · 91min

Great things were predicted for Scott McGehee and David Siegel after they debuted with this ultra-stylised *film noir*, a postmodern monochrome melodrama that delights in disorientating the viewer. At the centre of the confusion are half-brothers Dennis Haysbert and Michael Harris, whose racial and physical dissimilarity is turned into a mischievous lookalike gag on which depends the plot's dastardly game of interchangeable identities. It stumbles towards the end, but intrigues throughout. DP *DVD*

Dennis Haysbert *Clay Arlington* • Mel Harris *Dr Renée Descartes* • Sab Shimono *Dr Max Shinoda* • Dina Merrill *Alice Jameson* ■ Dir/Scr Scott McGehee, David Siegel

Suzhou River ★★★★ 12
Romantic drama   2000 · Chi/Ger/Neth/Jpn/Fr · Colour · 78min

With an unseen videographer giving the action an intriguingly subjective viewpoint, Lou Ye's teasing treatise on perspective and identity irresistibly recalls Alfred Hitchcock's *Rear Window* and *Vertigo*. Hired by a vodka racketeer to chaperone his daughter Zhou Xun, motorcycle courier Jia Hongsheng connives at her kidnapping, only to be jailed for murder when she seems to commit suicide. On his release, Jia becomes besotted with an aquarium mermaid (Zhou again), with tragic consequences. With its world-weary narration, oppressive cityscapes and dangerous passions, this blend of *film noir* and psychological drama is as edgy as it's engrossing. DP Mandarin +subtitles. Violence, swearing. *DVD*

Zhou Xun *Meimei/Moudan* • Jia Hongshen *Mardar* • Yao Anlian *Boss* • Nai An *Mada* ■ Dir/Scr Lou Ye

Suzie Gold ★★ 15
Romantic comedy drama   2003 · UK · Colour · 89min

This broad British comedy stars American actress Summer Phoenix as a north London Jewish "princess" defying her traditional family for the love of a non-Jewish boy. First-time director Ric Cantor leaves no stereotype unturned in the telling of this cross-cultural romance and as much as one might wish the film occasionally to confound one's expectations, it never does. DA Swearing, sex scenes, drug abuse. *DVD*

Summer Phoenix *Suzie Gold* • Leo Gregory *Darren* • Stanley Townsend *Irving Gold* • Rebecca Front *Barbara Gold* • Frances Barber *Joy Spencer* • Iddo Goldberg *Anthony Silver* • Miriam Karlin *Nana* ■ Dir Ric Cantor • Scr Ric Cantor, Carry Franklin, Lisa Ratner, from a story by Rebecca Green

Suzy ★★★
Romantic melodrama   1936 · US · BW · 99min

In London, penniless American chorus girl Jean Harlow marries Irish would-be inventor Franchot Tone but flees to a cabaret job in Paris after she believes him shot dead by a female spy. When the First World War breaks out, she marries French flying ace Cary Grant. Drama escalates when Tone, not dead after all, turns up in uniform. George Fitzmaurice directs this rather curious but effective piece that begins as romantic comedy and switches to espionage thriller. Harlow is ingenuous and charming, Tone is an attractive hero and Grant does well as a cad. RK

Jean Harlow *Suzy Trent* • Cary Grant *André Charville* • Franchot Tone *Terry Moore* • Benita Hume *Mme Diane Eyrelle* • Lewis Stone *Baron Charville* ■ Dir George Fitzmaurice • Scr Dorothy Parker, Alan Campbell, Horace Jackson, Lenore Coffee, from the novel by Herbert Gorman

Svengali ★★
Drama   1931 · US · BW · 76min

George du Maurier's famous Victorian novel, *Trilby*, tells of a beautiful young girl whose singing teacher uses hypnotism to turn her into a great opera singer. This version shifts the novel's emphasis on to Svengali himself, played in his most uninhibited, histrionic style by John Barrymore, while Marian Marsh is the artist's model who falls under his spell. Apart from the Oscar-nominated cinematography and the pleasure of watching Barrymore in action, there's not much of interest in this melodrama. RK

John Barrymore *Svengali* • Marian Marsh *Trilby* • Bramwell Fletcher *Billee* • Donald Crisp *The Laird* • Lumsden Hare *Taffy* ■ Dir Archie Mayo • Scr J Grubb Alexander, from the novel *Trilby* by George du Maurier • Cinematographer Barry McGill

Svengali ★★ 15
Comedy   2013 · UK · Colour · 92min

Stuffed with clichés, caricatures and guest stars, this genial adaptation of Jonny Owen's cult internet series has an infectious energy (and a more than decent soundtrack) that carries it over the contrivances. Owen plays the Welsh postman and music fanatic whose campaign to interest London record mavens in his undiscovered combo, the Premature Congratulations, includes sending the band's demo out on cassette tape. The haphazard plot consistently feels webisodic, and few of the cameos by the likes of Martin Freeman, Maxine Peake and Katy Brand work, but this still wears its sentimentality with pride. DP Swearing, sexual references.

Jonny Owen *Dixie* • Vicky McClure *Michelle, "Shell"* • Roger Evans *Horsey* • Martin Freeman *Don* • Maxine Peake *Angie* ■ Dir John Hardwick • Scr Jonny Owen, from an original concept by Owen, Dean Cavanagh

Swades ★★★ U
Social drama   2004 · Ind · Colour · 172min

Ashutosh Gowariker (*Lagaan*) here directs another patriotic and thoughtful epic. Shah Rukh Khan stars as an ambitious Nasa scientist who returns to his native India in search of his childhood nanny (Kishori Ballal). This nostalgic journey soon finds him in the heartland of rural India, where Khan encounters poverty, injustice and a young village girl (Gayatri Joshi) with whom he falls in love. Khan rises to the challenge of portraying a frustrated patriot, perturbed by the lack of progress. OA Hindi +subtitles. *DVD*

Shah Rukh Khan *Mohan Bhargava* • Gayatri Joshi *Gita* • Kishori Ballal *Kaveriamma* • Master Smit Sheth *Chikku* • Farrukh Jaffar *Fatimabi* • Dayashankar Pandey *Mela Ram* ■ Dir Ashutosh Gowariker • Scr Ashutosh Gowariker, from his story

Swallows and Amazons ★★★ U
Adventure   1974 · UK · Colour · 89min

Lovingly photographed by Denis Lewiston, this is an engaging if hardly enthralling adaptation of the Arthur Ransome novel. Director Claude Whatham clearly revels in the innocence of a 1920s summer, when the four swallows and two amazons embark upon their adventures, and he makes the most of the beautiful Lake District scenery. But the story stubbornly refuses to come to life and, sadly, few modern youngsters will relate to such old-fashioned game-playing. DP *DVD*

Virginia McKenna *Mrs Walker* • Ronald Fraser *Uncle Jim* • Brenda Bruce *Mrs Dixon* • Jack Woolgar *Old Billy* • John Franklyn-Robbins *Young Billy* • Simon West *John* • Zanna Hamilton *Susan* • Sophie Neville *Titty* ■ Dir Claude Whatham • Scr David Wood, from the novel by Arthur Ransome

Swallows and Amazons ★★★★ PG
Adventure   2016 · UK · Colour · 96min

Arthur Ransome's classic children's story of boating fun in the Lake District gets a fresh screen adaptation that preserves the spirit and period charm of the original but bumps up the action for modern audiences. Two boys and two girls on holiday in the Lake District are soon tussling in their sailboat the Swallow with rival crew the Amazons. The major difference here is an added subplot, involving travel writer Rafe Spall and the foreign spies out to get him, bringing shades of *The 39 Steps* to the proceedings. With more at stake, the drama's intensified, while still retaining the nostalgic appeal of bygone days. An intelligent, involving, beautifully performed and mounted adaptation of material that could easily have seemed old-fashioned. TJ

Kelly Macdonald *Mrs Walker* • Rafe Spall *Captain Flint* • Dane Hughes *John Walker* • Jessica Hynes [Jessica Stevenson] *Mrs Jackson* • Harry Enfield *Mr Jackson* • Teddie-Rose Malleson-Allen *Tatty Walker* • Bobby McCulloch *Roger Walker* • Seren Hawkes *Nancy Blackett* • Hannah Jayne Thorp *Peggy Blackett* ■ Dir Philippa Lowthorpe • Scr Andrea Gibb, from Arthur Ransome's novel

Swamp Thing ★★ 15
Horror   1982 · US · Colour · 84min

Wes Craven's terminally campy adaptation of the eco-friendly DC comic book character is a trivial pursuit into juvenile territory for the horror director. Ray Wise is transformed into the half-man/half-slime creature after an accident with a plant growth stimulant and battles evil genius Louis Jourdan, who sees the formula as a way to gain world domination. Adrienne Barbeau goes way beyond the call of duty as the vague heroine valiantly getting knocked around. Despite the tacky special effects, cheap budget and banal dialogue, this was successful enough for a sequel, *The Return of Swamp Thing* (1989). AJ *DVD*

Louis Jourdan *Arcane* • Adrienne Barbeau *Alice Cable* • Ray Wise *Dr Alec Holland* • David Hess *Ferret* • Nicholas Worth *Bruno* • Don Knight *Ritter* • Al Ruban *Charlie* • Dick Durock *Swamp Thing* ■ Dir/Scr Wes Craven

Swamp Water ★★ PG
Thriller   1941 · US · BW · 86min

Like other European émigrés, the gifted French director Jean Renoir went to Hollywood to escape the Nazi occupation. But this, the first of his American films, was a disappointment. He was plunged in at the deep end in the isolated setting of the Georgia swampland, where escaped convict Walter Brennan hides and befriends trapper Dana Andrews. It's a story that needs more explanation and a deeper understanding. TH *DVD*

Walter Brennan *Tom Keefer* • Walter Huston *Thursday Ragan* • Anne Baxter *Julie* • Dana Andrews *Ben Ragan* • Virginia Gilmore *Mabel Mckenzie* • John Carradine *Jesse Wick* • Mary Howard *Hannah* • Eugene Pallette *Jeb McKane* ■ Dir Jean Renoir • Scr Dudley Nichols, from a story by Vereen Bell

The Swan ★★★ U
Romantic drama 1956 · US · Colour · 107min

Best known today as Grace Kelly's final Hollywood production (it was released before *High Society*, though made after it), this features the star playing a very MGM version of a princess in a lavish adaptation of a hoary old play by Ferenc Molnar. The beautiful Kelly is in love with handsome tutor Louis Jourdan, but she's officially betrothed to prince Alec Guinness. Director Charles Vidor understands this glossy tosh and films it beautifully, but Guinness (in his first American film) is miscast. **TS**

Grace Kelly *Princess Alexandra* · Alec Guinness *Prince Albert* · Louis Jourdan *Dr Nicholas Agi* · Agnes Moorehead *Queen Maria Dominika* · Jessie Royce Landis *Princess Beatrix* · Brian Aherne *Father Hyacinth* · Leo G Carroll *Caesar* · Estelle Winwood *Symphorosa* ■ *Dir* Charles Vidor · *Scr* John Dighton, from the play by Ferenc Molnar

The Swan Princess ★★★ U
Animated musical fairy tale 1994 · US · Colour · 85min

A brave bid to produce a Disneyesque feature on a fraction of the budget, this politically correct fairy tale is entertaining enough, but it lacks the sparkle of the films it's trying to emulate. Director Richard Rich and character designer Steve Gordon, both Disney old boys, know the formula, but some rather uninspired artwork and the feeble songs undercut the neat reworking of *Swan Lake*. Jack Palance makes a booming Rothbart, while John Cleese is great fun as a French frog. Odette is feisty, but Prince Derek is a bit of a drip. Two modest sequels followed. **DP** *DVD*

Jack Palance *Rothbart* · John Cleese *Jean-Bob* · Howard McGillin *Prince Derek* · Michelle Nicastro *Princess Odette* · Steven Wright *Speed* ■ *Dir* Richard Rich · *Scr* Brian Nissen, from a story by Richard Rich, Brian Nissen · *Animator* Steven E Gordon

Swanee River ★★ U
Musical biography 1939 · US · Colour · 86min

Don Ameche plays composer Stephen Foster (*Beautiful Dreamer*) in 20th Century-Fox's unintentionally camp biopic, in which every cliché uttered becomes a cue for a song. Naturally enough, he wants to pen symphonies, but finds he can't stop drowning his sorrows. Andrea Leeds is his luckless spouse, but the surprise casting of the movie is the great Al Jolson himself as EP Christy, the forerunner of the black-faced minstrels. Unfortunately, Fox's garish Technicolor makes him look as though he's fallen into a tub of boot polish. Not high on taste. **TS**

Don Ameche *Stephen Foster* · Al Jolson *EP Christy* · Andrea Leeds *Jane* · Felix Bressart *Henry Kleber* · Chick Chandler *Bones* · Russell Hicks *Andrew McDowell* · George Reed *Old Joe* ■ *Dir* Sidney Lanfield · *Scr* John Taintor Foote, Philip Dunne

Swann ★★★★ 15
Drama 1996 · Can/UK · Colour · 91min

Bestselling author Miranda Richardson arrives at a small Canadian town to prepare a biography of local poet, Mary Swann, murdered by her husband. Brenda Fricker was Mary's closest friend and the film examines Richardson's growing relationship with her as she unravels the secrets of Swann's tragic death. Adapted from a novel by Carol Shields and directed by Anna Benson Gyles, it's a small film of great impact - an elegant, passionate meditation on feminism. **TH** *DVD*

Miranda Richardson *Sarah Maloney* · Brenda Fricker *Rose Hindmarch* · Michael Ontkean *Stephen* · David Cubitt *Brownie* · John Neville *Cruzzi* · Sean McCann *Homer* · Sean Hewitt *Morton Jimroy* ■ *Dir* Anna Benson Gyles · *Scr* David Young, from the novel by Carol Shields

Swann in Love ★★ 18
Drama 1984 · Fr/W Ger · Colour · 105min

Jeremy Irons makes a pig's ear out of Proust's novel *Un Amour de Swann*. As the French aristocrat, Irons scampers after working-class totty Ornella Muti through the scummy streets of Paris. His lust is fulfilled, but he remains lovelorn, troubled by the fact that he genuinely cares for her. Alain Delon is more charismatic as the gay, butch Baron and Muti is suitably smutty and sexy, but this is an awkward affair that lacks any true passion. **LH** French +subtitles.

Jeremy Irons *Charles Swann* · Ornella Muti *Odette de Crecy* · Alain Delon *Baron de Charlus* · Fanny Ardant *Duchesse de Guermantes* · Marie-Christine Barrault *Mrs Vedurin* · Anne Bennent *Chloe* · Nathalie Juvet *Madame Cottard* ■ *Dir* Volker Schlöndorff · *Scr* Peter Brook, Jean-Claude Carrière, Marie-Hélène Estienne, Volker Schlöndorff, from the novel *Un Amour de Swann* by Marcel Proust

The Swarm ★ 12
Disaster movie 1978 · US · Colour · 148min

African killer bees are moving west and threatening to engulf Houston, Texas. Quick, call on entomologist Michael Caine and a hive of Hollywood has-beens to out-ham each other while reciting terrible dialogue and getting stung by coloured Styrofoam pellets! A bumbled B-movie. **AJ** *DVD*

Michael Caine *Brad Crane* · Katharine Ross *Helena* · Richard Widmark *General Slater* · Richard Chamberlain *Dr Hubbard* · Olivia de Havilland *Maureen Schuster* · Ben Johnson (1) *Felix* · Lee Grant *Anne MacGregor* · José Ferrer *Dr Andrews* · Patty Duke Astin [Patty Duke] *Rita Bard* · Fred MacMurray *Clarence* ■ *Dir* Irwin Allen · *Scr* Stirling Silliphant, from the novel by Arthur Herzog

Swashbuckler ★★★ PG
Swashbuckling adventure 1976 · US · Colour · 96min

Unfairly dismissed at the time, this was a genuine attempt by Universal to re-create the kind of adventure film it used to deliver by the dozen: the good-natured pirate romp. Originally retitled *The Scarlet Buccaneer* for the UK, it evoked fond memories of its star's foray into similar territory on TV: a generation will recall a pre-*Jaws* Robert Shaw as swashbuckling Dan Tempest in the 1950s series *The Buccaneers*. Shaw does well here, romancing lovely Geneviève Bujold and swapping riddles with James Earl Jones. **TS**

Robert Shaw *Ned Lynch* · James Earl Jones *Nick Debrett* · Peter Boyle *Lord Durant* · Geneviève Bujold *Jane Barnet* · Beau Bridges *Major Folly* · Geoffrey Holder *Cudjo* · Avery Schreiber *Polonski* · Anjelica Huston *Woman of Dark Visage* ■ *Dir* James Goldstone · *Scr* Jeffrey Bloom, from a story by Paul Wheeler

SWAT ★★ 12
Police action thriller 2003 · US · Colour · 112min

A billionaire international terrorist offers $100 million to the criminal who springs him from US custody. Then a SWAT (Special Weapons and Tactics) team has to escort him across LA while every hoodlum not locked up tries for the bounty. But before this highlight, this half-baked misfire follows Colin Farrell's interminable retraining as a SWAT officer. Farrell is bland, Samuel L Jackson appears to be aware he's slumming it and the result is leaden. **AS** *DVD* Blu

Samuel L Jackson *Sgt Dan "Hondo" Harrelson* · Colin Farrell (2) *Jim Street* · Michelle Rodriguez *Chris Sanchez* · James Todd Smith [LL Cool J] *Deacon "Deke" Kaye* · Josh Charles *TJ McCabe* · Jeremy Renner *Brian Gamble* · Brian Van Holt *Michael Boxer* · Olivier Martinez *Alex Montel* ■ *Dir* Clark Johnson · *Scr* David Ayer, David McKenna, from a story by Ron Mita, Jim McClain, from characters by Robert Hamner

Swearing Allegiance ★★ 15
Crime drama based on a true story 1997 · US · Colour · 89min

The real-life case on which this TV movie is based made headline news all over the US, although British viewers may wonder what all the fuss is about. The story involves childhood sweethearts Diane Zamora and David Graham (played by Holly Marie Combs and David Lipper), who make a murderous pact after Graham confesses to sleeping with another girl. The performances can't be faulted, but director Richard A Colla's execution is nothing special. **JF** *DVD*

Holly Marie Combs *Diane Zamora* · David Lipper *David Graham* · Cassidy Rae *Adrienne Jones* · Dee Wallace Stone *Linda Jones* ■ *Dir* Richard A Colla · *Scr* Steve Johnson

Swedenhielms ★★★
Drama 1935 · Swe · BW · 92min

Directed by the great Gustav Molander, this was Ingrid Bergman's third film and, while she gives a wholehearted performance as an heiress hoping to marry into the family of a talented but poor scientist, the critics of the day considered her no more than "feelingful". The real star of the show, however, is Gösta Ekman as the scientist, while Karin Swanstrom also impresses as the sister-in-law who averts a scandal. **DP** Swedish +subtitles.

Gösta Ekman (1) *Rolf Swedenhielm* · Karin Swanstrom *Marta Boman* · Bjorn Berglund *Rolf Swedenhielm Jr* · Håkan Westergren *Bo Swedenhielm* · Tutta Rolf *Julia Swedenhielm* · Ingrid Bergman *Astrid* ■ *Dir* Gustaf Molander · *Scr* Stina Bergman, Gustaf Molander, from the play by Hjalmar Bergman

Sweeney! ★★★ 18
Police drama 1976 · UK · Colour · 92min

Not in the same manor as the legendary TV series, this spin-off is a reasonable reminder of what made John Thaw and Dennis Waterman the icons of 1970s law enforcement. Screenwriter Ranald Graham's unfamiliarity with the characters occasionally brings the action to a screeching halt. However, he cranks out a typically abrasive plot, which sees the boys investigating a suicide only to find themselves knee-deep in vice, blackmail and corruption. **DP** Violence, swearing, nudity. *DVD*

John Thaw *Detective Inspector Regan* · Dennis Waterman *Detective Sergeant Carter* · Barry Foster *McQueen* · Ian Bannen *Baker* · Colin Welland *Chadwick* · Diane Keen *Bianca* · Brian Glover *Mac* · Lynda Bellingham *Janice* ■ *Dir* David Wickes · *Scr* Ranald Graham, from the TV series by Ian Kennedy Martin

The Sweeney ★★ 15
Crime drama 2012 · UK · Colour · 107min

This re-boot shares little with the iconic 1970s TV series beyond the names of the three principle characters. Flying Squad maverick Jack Regan (Ray Winstone) employs dubious methods to bring down a ruthless gang, ruffling the feathers of his superiors (Damian Lewis, Steven Mackintosh), while his right-hand man George Carter (Ben Drew, aka rapper Plan B) faces a dilemma as to which arm of the law to follow. The requisite shoot-outs and car chases are well staged, but there's no papering over the confused plot. **TeS** Violence, swearing. *DVD* Blu

Ray Winstone *Jack Regan* · Ben Drew *George Carter* · Hayley Atwell *Nancy Lewis* · Steven Mackintosh *Ivan Lewis* · Damian Lewis *Frank Haskins* ■ *Dir* Nick Love · *Scr* Nick Love, Alex Garland, from characters by Ian Kennedy Martin

Sweeney 2 ★★ 18
Police drama 1978 · UK · Colour · 103min

In this second, dated-looking spin-off from the popular 1970s TV series, flying-squadders John Thaw and Dennis Waterman tackle upper-bracket bank robbers who fly in for each job to maintain their Mediterranean lifestyle. The leads struggle with material that would have barely filled a 50-minute television slot, let alone a full-length cinema feature. **DA** *DVD*

John Thaw *Detective Inspector Jack Regan* · Dennis Waterman *Detective Sergeant George Carter* · Denholm Elliott *Jupp* · David Casey *Goodyear* · Ken Hutchison *Hill* · Nigel Hawthorne *Dilke* · John Flanagan *Willard* · Derrick O'Connor *Llewellyn* ■ *Dir* Tom Clegg · *Scr* Troy Kennedy Martin, from the TV series by Ian Kennedy Martin

The Sweeney: Paris ★★★ 15
Crime action drama 2015 · UK/Fr · Colour · 89min

Although a faithful adaptation of *The Sweeney*, itself loosely based on the 1970s cop show, *The Sweeney: Paris* has a distinctly French accent. When a ruthless crime ring take aim at high-profile targets in the city, the case is duly assigned to rabid old dog Serge (Jean Reno) and his youthful sidekick Cartier (Alban Lenoir). The pleasure is in the details as Reno, looking weary, anchors the predictable and strangely flat-feeling crime drama. A solid if lacklustre police caper with some sparkling moments. **KK** French, English +subtitles. Violence, swearing. *DVD*

Jean Reno *Serge Buren* · Alban Lenoir *Cartier* · Caterina Murino *Margaux* · Oumar Diaw *Manu* ■ *Dir* Benjamin Rocher · *Scr* Tristan Schulmann, from an original story by John Hodge, Nick Love

Sweeney Todd, the Demon Barber of Fleet Street ★★★ PG
Horror 1936 · UK · BW · 65min

Tod Slaughter was billed as "the Horror Man of Europe" for his forays into early chiller territory with titles such as *Murder in the Red Barn* and *Crimes at the Dark House*. As the legendary throat-slitting barber, the aptly named Slaughter turns in what every genre historian agrees is a quintessential performance. He's at his highly theatrical, villainous best in this dainty slice of British horror and, if you can ignore the creaks, this film is melodramatic fun. **AJ**

Tod Slaughter *Sweeney Todd* · Eve Lister *Johanna* · Bruce Seton *Mack* · Davina Craig *Nan* · DJ Williams *Stephen Oakley* · Jerry Verno *Pearley* ■ *Dir* George King · *Scr* Frederick Hayward, HF Maltby, from the play by George Dibdin-Pitt

Sweeney Todd: the Demon Barber of Fleet Street ★★★★ 18
Horror musical 2007 · US · Colour · 111min

After making dark Gothic fantasies like *Sleepy Hollow* and *Corpse Bride*, Tim Burton puts his unique stamp on Stephen Sondheim's award-winning musical. Johnny Depp stars as the barber of the title who takes (very, very) bloody revenge on the men who wronged his family, before serving up their remains in meat pies made by his partner in crime Mrs Lovett (Helena Bonham Carter). Burton's production design is astoundingly detailed - the near-monochrome palette of blacks and greys a perfect contrast to the arterial spray from Todd's cut-throat razor. Neither Depp nor Bonham Carter is a trained vocalist, but both tackle Sondheim's musical numbers with gusto, not to mention entertaining cockney accents. Easily one of Burton's most deftly realised films. **JR** *DVD* Blu

Johnny Depp *Sweeney Todd* · Helena Bonham Carter *Mrs Nellie Lovett* · Alan Rickman *Judge Turpin* · Timothy Spall *Beadle Bamford* · Sacha Baron Cohen *Signor Adolfo Pirelli* · Edward Sanders *Toby* · Laura Michelle Kelly *Lucy* · Jayne Wisener *Johanna* · Jamie Campbell Bower *Anthony Hope* · Christopher Lee *Gentleman ghost* ■ *Dir* Tim Burton · *Scr* John Logan, from the musical by Stephen Sondheim, Hugh Wheeler, from a play by Christopher Bond

Sweepers ★★ 15
Action thriller 1999 · US · Colour · 92min

In a standard action movie that has a veneer of political correctness, Dolph Lundgren plays a landmine clearance expert who disappears into the Angolan wilderness after his young son is killed. Lundgren is found by bomb squad boffin Clare Stansfield and recruited to track down the lethal new A6 super-mine that's in the hands of terrorists. Video favourite Bruce Payne offers solid support. **JF** *DVD*

Dolph Lundgren *Christian Erickson* · Bruce Payne *Cecil Hopper* · Claire Stansfield *Michelle Flynn* · Ian Roberts (1) *Yager* · Fats Bookholane *Old Mo* ·

S

Sifiso Maphanga *Arthur* ■ *Dir* Darby Black [Keoni Waxman] • *Scr* Darby Black [Keoni Waxman], Kevin Bernhardt

Sweet Adeline ★★
Period musical   1935 · US · BW · 87min

A sweet-as-honey Irene Dunne takes the title role in this period (late 19th-century) musical, set in Hoboken, New Jersey where Adeline is adored by all the men who frequent her father's lovely beer garden. Spoilt for choice, she finally settles for songwriter Donald Woods. Directed by Mervyn LeRoy with dances staged by Bobby Connolly, this otherwise unremarkable, overly winsome and dull movie is partly redeemed by the Jerome Kern-Oscar Hammerstein II songs. RK

Irene Dunne *Adeline Schmidt* • Donald Woods *Sid Barnett* • Hugh Herbert *Rupert Rockingham* • Ned Sparks *Dan Herzig* • Joseph Cawthorn *Oscar Schmidt* ■ *Dir* Mervyn LeRoy • *Scr* Irwin S Gelsey, from a musical by Jerome Kern, Oscar Hammerstein II

Sweet and Lowdown ★★ⓤ
Musical romantic drama 1944 · US · BW · 75min

Aspiring trombone player (James Cardwell) is given his chance by Benny Goodman and goes on the road with the orchestra. But his youthful arrogance and swollen head almost put him back where he started. A minor entry from Fox, this moral tale-cum-romance with a fairy-tale outcome, directed by journeyman Archie Mayo, is anodyne entertainment but with enough music to please fans of Goodman, who plays himself. RK

Linda Darnell *Trudy Wilson* • James Cardwell *Johnny Birch* • Lynn Bari *Pat Sterling* • Jack Oakie *Popsy* • Allyn Joslyn *Lester Barnes* • John Campbell *Dixie Zang* • Roy Benson *Skeets McCormick* • Dickie Moore *General Carmichael* • Benny Goodman ■ *Dir* Archie Mayo • *Scr* Richard English, from a story by Richard English, Edward Haldeman

Sweet and Lowdown
★★★★ⓅⒼ
Period comedy drama 1999 · US · Colour · 91min

After the disappointing *Celebrity*, Woody Allen returned to form with this sparkling comedy drama about a fictional 1930s jazz man whose life only makes sense when he's playing guitar. Sean Penn plays a kleptomaniac musical genius whose idea of a good time is to watch trains, shoot rats and seduce women. Happiness comes in a sweetly fulfilling relationship with mute innocent Samantha Morton, though the feckless Penn is soon up to his old tricks with society gal Uma Thurman. The costumes and production design are splendidly opulent, but it's Morton who steals the show. NS 𝗗𝗩𝗗

Sean Penn *Emmet Ray* • Samantha Morton *Hattie* • Uma Thurman *Blanche* • Brian Markinson *Bill Shields* • Anthony LaPaglia *Al Torrio* • Gretchen Mol *Ellie* • Vincent Guastaferro *Sid Bishop* • John Waters (2) *Mr Haynes* • Woody Allen ■ *Dir/Scr* Woody Allen • *Cinematographer* Zhao Fei • *Production Designer* Santo Loquasto

Sweet Bird of Youth ★★★⓯
Melodrama   1962 · US · Colour · 115min

The ingredients of Tennessee Williams's original stage play (racism, substance abuse, male prostitution, castration) are present, if muted, in this bleak entertainment. The play, directed by Elia Kazan, starred Paul Newman and Geraldine Page. The movie, directed by Richard Brooks, retained the original leads and toned down the text. Despite obvious flaws, it's a polished production, with fine supporting performances from Rip Torn and Ed Begley, who won the best supporting actor Oscar. Elizabeth Taylor starred in a 1989 TV movie remake. AT 𝗗𝗩𝗗

Paul Newman *Chance Wayne* • Geraldine Page *Alexandra Del Lago* • Ed Begley *"Boss" Finley* • Shirley Knight *Heavenly Finley* • Rip Torn *Thomas J Finley Jr* • Mildred Dunnock *Aunt Nonnie* • Madeleine Sherwood *Miss Lucy* • Philip Abbott *Dr George Scudder* ■ *Dir* Richard Brooks • *Scr* Richard Brooks, from the play by Tennessee Williams

Sweet Bird of Youth ★★★
Drama   1989 · US · Colour

This TV-movie version of Tennessee Williams's celebrated play is perhaps more significant for academic reasons than cinematic ones. Based on screenwriter Gavin Lambert's exhaustive research, it's less a remake than a reinvention that draws on a range of Williams's writings to reinterpret several key scenes. Elizabeth Taylor, something of a Williams specialist after *Cat on a Hot Tin Roof* and *Suddenly, Last Summer*, does well enough in the role made famous by Geraldine Page, while Rip Torn (who has been involved with the play on stage, cinema and TV) shows he knows the material inside out. Studious rather than steamy, and somewhat staid. DP Nudity.

Elizabeth Taylor *Alexandra Del Lago* • Mark Harmon *Chance Wayne* • Rip Torn *Tom "Boss" Finley* • Valerie Perrine *Miss Lucy* • Kevin Geer *Tom Jr* • Seymour Cassel *Hatcher* • Cheryl Paris *Heavenly Finley* ■ *Dir* Nicolas Roeg • *Scr* Gavin Lambert, from the play by Tennessee Williams

Sweet Charity ★★★ⓅⒼ
Musical comedy   1968 · US · Colour · 142min

Dancer, theatre director and choreographic genius Bob Fosse made his film directing debut when he brought his Broadway hit to the screen. Based on Fellini's *Nights of Cabiria*, the musical was transposed to New York and chronicles the sad life of a dance-hall hostess whose sleazy experiences fail to dampen her belief in fairy-tale romance. Though it's jam-packed with stunning numbers, the film is brash and gaudy lacks the sophisticated edge of the movie original, with Shirley MacLaine's turbine-powered Charity substituting energy for subtlety. However Sammy Davis Jr, Chita Rivera and Paula Kelly are as electrifying as Fosse's choreography. RK 𝗗𝗩𝗗

Shirley MacLaine *Charity Hope Valentine* • Sammy Davis Jr *Big Daddy* • Ricardo Montalban *Vittorio Vitale* • John McMartin *Oscar* • Chita Rivera *Nickie* • Paula Kelly *Helene* • Stubby Kaye *Herman* ■ *Dir* Bob Fosse • *Scr* Peter Stone, from the musical by Neil Simon, Cy Coleman, Dorothy Fields, from the 1957 film *Nights of Cabiria*

Sweet Dreams ★★★⓯
Biographical drama 1985 · US · Colour · 110min

Having already produced the Loretta Lynn biopic *Coal Miner's Daughter*, Bernard Schwartz here turned his attention to her friendly rival for the Queen of Country title, Patsy Cline. The result is a film packed with fine acting and superb singing (provided, via record, by Cline herself). Unfortunately, the life story is pretty unremarkable, consequently, the sparks between Jessica Lange and Ed Harris ignite nothing but their scenes together, giving the action a staccato rhythm. DP 𝗗𝗩𝗗

Jessica Lange *Patsy Cline* • Ed Harris *Charlie Dick* • Ann Wedgeworth *Hilda Hensley* • David Clennon *Randy Hughes* • James Staley *Gerald Cline* • Gary Basaraba *Woodhouse* • John Goodman *Otis* • PJ Soles *Wanda* ■ *Dir* Karel Reisz • *Scr* Robert Getchell

Sweet Emma Dear Böbe
★★★★⓲
Drama   1992 · Hun · Colour · 77min

István Szabó demonstrates a sure grasp of contemporary reality in this despondent study of the newly liberated Hungary. Forced to abandon their careers as Russian teachers on the fall of Communism, Johanna Ter Steege and Eniko Borcsok personify the options open to a society emerging from decades of oppression. Reining in his fondness for stylistic flourish – yet barely suppressing his anger – Szabó struggles to find the light at the end of this dark passage of transition, as Ter Steege pursues a hopeless affair with her tyrannical headmaster and Borcsok flirts with rich tourists. DP In Hungarian.

Johanna Ter Steege *Emma* • Eniko Borcsok *Böbe* • Peter Andorai *Stefanics* • Eva Kerekes *Sleepy* ■ *Dir* István Szabó • *Scr* István Szabó, from an idea by Andrea Veszits

Sweet Hearts Dance
★★★⓯
Comedy drama 1988 · US · Colour · 96min

Don Johnson and Susan Sarandon are high school sweethearts who've been married for 15 years and have three children. Then Johnson realises he doesn't love his wife any more, just as his best buddy, Jeff Daniels, gets himself a new girlfriend. Scripted by Ernest Thompson, writer of *On Golden Pond*, this is a slightly ponderous study of marital angst, often warm and witty but lacking real bite. There are good performances, though. AT Swearing, nudity.

Don Johnson *Wiley Boon* • Susan Sarandon *Sandra Boon* • Jeff Daniels *Sam Manners* • Elizabeth Perkins *Adie Nims* • Kate Reid *Pearne Manners* • Justin Henry *Kyle Boon* • Holly Marie Combs *Debs Boon* • Heather Coleman *BJ Boon* ■ *Dir* Robert Greenwald • *Scr* Ernest Thompson

The Sweet Hereafter
★★★★⓯
Psychological drama
1997 · Can · Colour · 107min

Atom Egoyan won the Grand Jury prize at Cannes and was also Oscar nominated for his direction and adaptation of Russell Banks's novel about the impact of a schoolbus crash (which kills 14 children) on a small Canadian community. Although the Pied Piper analogy is overemphasised, this is still an intricate and involving drama, in which the town's guilty secrets are slowly revealed as ambulance-chasing lawyer Ian Holm tries to persuade the bereaved to sue for damages. With Sarah Polley outstanding as a survivor paralysed by the accident, this is intense, atmospheric and deeply moving. DP Swearing, nudity. 𝗗𝗩𝗗

Ian Holm *Mitchell Stephens* • Sarah Polley *Nicole Burnell* • Bruce Greenwood *Billy Ansell* • Tom McCamus *Sam Burnell* • Gabrielle Rose *Dolores Driscoll* • Arsinée Khanjian *Wanda Otto* • Alberta Watson *Risa Walker* • Maury Chaykin *Wendell Walker* ■ *Dir* Atom Egoyan • *Scr* Atom Egoyan, from the novel by Russell Banks

Sweet Home Alabama ★★⓬
Romantic comedy 2002 · US · Colour · 104min

Reese Witherspoon stars here as a New York-residing, Alabama-raised fashion designer who needs a divorce from her childhood sweetheart in order to marry socialite Patrick Dempsey. She heads home, bristling with snobbish attitude, only to step into a corny Dixieland fantasy that opens her eyes sufficiently to blind her to the problems that caused her to abandon husband Josh Lucas in the first place. Negligible, but charming. DP 𝗗𝗩𝗗

Reese Witherspoon *Melanie Carmichael* • Josh Lucas *Jake Perry* • Patrick Dempsey *Andrew Hennings* • Candice Bergen *Kate* • Mary Kay Place *Pearl Smooter* • Fred Ward *Earl Smooter* • Jean Smart *Stella Kay* • Ethan Embry *Bobby Ray* ■ *Dir* Andy Tennant • *Scr* C Jay Cox, from a story by Douglas J Eboch

Sweet Hunters ★★★★
Drama   1969 · Pan · Colour · 100min

This resolutely arty effort is about an American who lives with his wife and son on a private island. The arrival of the professor's sister-in-law starts to upset the already delicate balance of relationships. Then an escaped convict lands on the island. Some viewers may tire of this soul-searching drama after 20 minutes, but others will find it riveting, mainly due to Sterling Hayden's performance in which all of the actor's physical power and emotional weakness, as well as his troubled history, are laid open like a festering wound. AT

Sterling Hayden *Allan* • Maureen McNally *Clea* • Susan Strasberg *Lis* • Andrew Hayden *Bob* • Stuart Whitman *Prisoner* ■ *Dir* Ruy Guerra • *Scr* Ruy Guerra, Philippe Dumarçay, Gérard Zingg

Sweet Land ★★★ⓅⒼ
Drama   2005 · US · Colour · 106min

Moving in flashback from a contemporary agricultural recession to 1920s Minnesota, this handsome, restrained and consistently intelligent drama unflinchingly explores the concept of the United States as a melting pot. Elizabeth Reaser stars as the cultured German mail-order bride who's subjected to a backlash of postwar xenophobia when she arrives to marry Norwegian sodbuster Tim Guinee. Ned Beatty's grasping banker, John Heard's judgemental minister, and Alan Cumming and Alex Kingston's quirkily accommodating neighbours head an admirable ensemble cast, while David Tumblety's camera captures both the inhospitable prairies and the cosiness of the settlers' homes. A compelling story of communication and acceptance. DP In English, German, Norwegian. 𝗗𝗩𝗗

Elizabeth Reaser *Young Inge* • Tim Guinee *Young Olaf* • Alan Cumming *Young Frandsen* • Lois Smith *Old Inge* • Ned Beatty *Harmo* • John Heard *Minister Sorrensen* • Alex Kingston *Brownie* ■ *Dir* Ali Selim • *Scr* Ali Selim, from the short story *A Gravestone Made of Wheat* by Will Weaver • *Cinematographer* David Tumblety

Sweet Liberty ★★★⓯
Comedy   1986 · US · Colour · 101min

Compared with *The Player*, this is little more than a mild nip at the movie world. However, there are still plenty of laughs to be had as small-town college professor Alan Alda (writer/director/star) gets sucked into the ego-ridden lives of a movie crew when they make a film based on his American War of Independence novel. Michael Caine steals the show as the womanising lead, but there is handsome support from Michelle Pfeiffer, Bob Hoskins and Saul Rubinek. Overall, though, the requisite bite is missing. JF Some swearing, brief nudity.

Alan Alda *Michael Burgess* • Michael Caine *Elliott James* • Michelle Pfeiffer *Faith Healy* • Bob Hoskins *Stanley Gould* • Lise Hilboldt *Gretchen Carlsen* • Lillian Gish *Cecelia Burgess* • Saul Rubinek *Bo Hodges* • Lois Chiles *Leslie* ■ *Dir/Scr* Alan Alda

Sweet Nothing ★★⓲
Drama   1995 · US · Colour · 85min

Mira Sorvino stars in this grim drama is about a white-collar worker who gets dragged into drug addiction. Three years after Michael Imperioli persuades his reluctant wife to agree to a three-month limited term of dealing crack in order to provide money for his family, they're both hooked: he to the drug, his wife to the money. His descent to rock bottom is portrayed without mercy to either the characters or the audience. FL Swearing, violence.

Michael Imperioli *Angel* • Mira Sorvino *Monika* • Paul Calderon *Raymond* • Patrick Breen *Greg* • Richard Bright *Jack the Cop* • Billie Neal *Rio* ■ *Dir* Gary Winick • *Scr* Lee Drysdale

Sweet November ★★
Comedy drama 1968 · US · Colour · 112min

Suffering from a chronic case of the cutes, Sandy Dennis and Anthony Newley star in an oddly effective, but undoubtedly eccentric tragicomedy. She's doing her best, as an amateur sex therapist, to take a lover a month to rid them of their inhibitions. Trouble is that November's lodger, tycoon Newley, wants to claim her permissive life all to himself. The idea works surprisingly well at first, but both stars seem to be in competition, trying to make irritating ad libs out of Herman Raucher's script. TH

Sandy Dennis *Sara Deever* • Anthony Newley *Charlie Blake* • Theodore Bikel *Alonzo* • Burr DeBenning *Clem Batchman* • Sandy Baron *Richard* • Marj Dusay *Carol* • Martin West *Gordon* ■ *Dir* Robert Ellis Miller • *Scr* Herman Raucher

Sweet November ★★⓬
Romantic drama 2001 · US · Colour · 115min

Keanu Reeves takes the lead role of a narcissistic ad executive who gets too big for his Gucci slip-ons and ends up jobless. Vexed and confused, he encounters free-spirited Charlize Theron who out of the blue offers to be his November – she will commit herself to him for one month and in that time turn him into a nicer person. Love is in the air, but when Reeves wants to continue into December, he uncovers Theron's deep dark secret. The two leads are endearing, but this is too sickly sweet. LH **DVD**

Keanu Reeves *Nelson Moss* • Charlize Theron *Sara Deever* • Jason Isaacs *Chaz* • Frank Langella *Edgar Price* ■ *Dir* Pat O'Connor • *Scr* Kurt Voelker, from a story by Paul Yurick, Kurt Voelker, from the 1968 film

Sweet Revenge ★★ PG

Romantic comedy 1990 · US/Fr · Colour · 84min

This mildly amusing TV movie has a clever plot that never quite leaves the starting blocks despite the efforts of its stars Rosanna Arquette and Carrie Fisher. Basically the plot revolves around a divorce settlement that goes haywire when attorney Carrie Fisher finds that she must pay alimony to her ex-husband John Sessions, a struggling writer, until he remarries. In desperation, she recruits actress Rosanna Arquette to lure him into matrimony. This tepid tale does try hard with a cute plot twist, but ultimately it fails to be nothing more than standard TV movie fluff. MC

Rosanna Arquette *Kate Williams* • Carrie Fisher *Linda Michaels* • John Sessions *John Michaels* • John Hargreaves *Jim Harris* • François-Eric Gendron *Frank Marsh* • Myriam Moszko *Ruth* ■ *Dir* Charlotte Brandstrom • *Scr* Janet Brownell

The Sweet Ride ★★

Drama 1967 · US · Colour · 109min

Jacqueline Bisset fans covet this picture about the beach culture of southern California. It was Bisset's first major role in a Hollywood picture. Yes, one does miss Frankie Avalon, Fabian and Annette Funicello, but this is much more grown-up stuff that even alludes to the Vietnam war. Bisset plays a TV soap star who drops her producer for an affair with Michael Sarrazin, a tennis hustler. AT

Tony Franciosa [Anthony Franciosa] *Collie Ransom* • Michael Sarrazin *Denny McGuire* • Jacqueline Bisset *Vicki Cartwright, actress* • Bob Denver *Choo-Choo Burns, jazz pianist* • Michael Wilding *Mr Cartwright* • Michele Carey *Thumper* • Norma Crane *Mrs Cartwright* ■ *Dir* Harvey Hart • *Scr* Tom Mankiewicz, from the novel by William Murray

Sweet Rosie O'Grady ★★★ U

Musical comedy 1943 · US · Colour · 75min

An extremely entertaining 20th Century-Fox Technicolor musical and a vehicle for Betty Grable – for many, that's recommendation enough. It's all about a burlesque queen and an inquisitive reporter (Robert Young). Set in late-19th century London, Adolphe Menjou is particularly watchable as the editor of the *Police Gazette*. TS

Betty Grable *Madeleine Marlowe* • Robert Young (1) *Sam MacKeever* • Adolphe Menjou *Morgan* • Reginald Gardiner *Duke Charles* • Virginia Grey *Edna Van Dyke* • Phil Regan *Composer* • Sig Rumann [Sig Ruman] *Joe Flugelman* • Alan Dinehart *Arthur Skinner* ■ *Dir* Irving Cummings • *Scr* Ken Englund, from a story by William R Lipman, Frederick Stephani, Edward Van Every

Sweet Sixteen ★★★★ 18

Drama 2002 · UK/Ger/Sp/Fr/It · Colour · 101min

This grim, but slice of life is the fourth collaboration between Ken Loach and writer Paul Laverty. Liam, whose approaching birthday gives the film its title, is played with astonishing clarity and depth by non-professional actor Martin Compston. He is chasing the dream of a caravan for his currently imprisoned, ex-junkie mum and, paradoxically, it is through drug-dealing that he hopes to pay for it. In the process he crosses local gangsters and jeopardises relationships with his older sister and joyriding best pal, William Ruane. Hopes may be systematically dashed in this unforgiving world, but Loach and Laverty invest maximum humanity in the central character. AC +subtitles. Violence, swearing, drug abuse. **DVD**

Martin Compston *Liam* • William Ruane *Pinball* • Annmarie Fulton *Chantelle* • Michelle Abercromby *Suzanne* • Michelle Coulter *Jean* • Gary McCormack *Stan* • Tommy McKee *Rab* ■ *Dir* Ken Loach • *Scr* Paul Laverty

Sweet Smell of Success ★★★★★ PG

Satirical drama 1957 · US · BW · 95min

Not a box-office success in its day, this mordant satire has rightly picked up admirers over the years, and is at long last recognised for the classic that it is. It contains key career highs for Burt Lancaster, as a vicious Broadway columnist, and Tony Curtis as the hustling press agent totally under his all-powerful thumb. Lancaster's relationship with his sister Susan Harrison is particularly perverse, and provides the plot thrust for the Faustian pact, which is still relevant in an era of dubious media ethics. Diamond-hard photography from the great James Wong Howe and a sizzling Clifford Odets screenplay contribute immeasurably to this film's brutal quality, and it remains a tribute to its canny British director Alexander Mackendrick. TS **DVD** **Blu**

Burt Lancaster *JJ Hunsecker* • Tony Curtis *Sidney Falco* • Susan Harrison *Susan Hunsecker* • Marty Milner [Martin Milner] *Steve Dallas* • Sam Levene *Frank D'Angelo* • Barbara Nichols *Rita* • Jeff Donnell *Sally* • Joseph Leon *Robard* ■ *Dir* Alexander Mackendrick • *Scr* Clifford Odets, Ernest Lehman, from the short story *Tell Me about It* by Lehman • *Music* Elmer Bernstein

LANDMARK FILM

Melvin Van Peebles makes the first blaxploitation movie to counter racial stereotyping in Hollywood

Sweet Sweetback's Baad Asssss Song ★★★★ 18

Blaxploitation 1971 · US · Colour · 97min

An important feature in the history of black film-making in the US, this is an angry riposte to the stereotypical characters that exist in both mainstream and blaxploitation pictures. Written, directed, edited and scored by its star, Melvin Van Peebles, it can be loosely labelled a road movie, yet the relentless stream of sex, violence and prejudice, described with a mixture of realism, artifice and grim humour, isn't supposed to entertain, but rather incite. Still astonishing 30 years after its controversial release. DP Violence, swearing, nudity, sex scenes. **DVD**

Melvin Van Peebles *Sweetback* • Simon Chuckster *Beetle* • Hubert Scales *Mu-Mu* • John Dullaghan (1) *Commissioner* • Rhetta Hughes *Old girlfriend* ■ *Dir/Scr* Melvin Van Peebles

Sweet William ★★ 15

Drama 1980 · UK · Colour · 87min

Beryl Bainbridge adapted her own novel for this rather languid drama directed by Claude Whatham. Sam Waterston plays a Scot with a bevy of ex-wives and girlfriends; Jenny Agutter falls for him and lives to regret it. Despite the presence of a decent cast, this portrait of a rather unpleasant cad lacks a real cutting edge. AT Some swearing, nudity. **DVD**

Sam Waterston *William McClusky* • Jenny Agutter *Ann Walton* • Anna Massey *Edna* • Geraldine James *Pamela* • Daphne Oxenford *Mrs Walton* • Rachel Bell *Mrs Kershaw* • David Wood *Vicar* • Tim Pigott-Smith *Gerald* ■ *Dir* Claude Whatham • *Scr* Beryl Bainbridge, from her novel

The Sweetest Thing ★★★ 15

Romantic comedy 2002 · US · Colour · 86min

Director Roger Kumble gives crass humour a feminine edge in this bright and frothy take on the "chick flick". Essentially a straight romantic comedy clothed in Farrelly brothers-style laughs, it emphasises that women can be just as irreverent as their male counterparts. The end result is something akin to a celluloid hen night, as serial heartbreaker Cameron Diaz and her two brash best friends (the hilarious Selma Blair and Christina Applegate) encounter the highs and lows of commitment-free love. SF Swearing, nudity. **DVD**

Cameron Diaz *Christina Walters* • Christina Applegate *Courtney Rockliffe* • Thomas Jane *Peter Donahue* • Selma Blair *Jane Burns* • Jason Bateman *Roger Donahue* • Parker Posey *Judy Webb* • Lillian Adams *Aunt Frida* • Georgia B Engel [Georgia Engel] *Vera* ■ *Dir* Roger Kumble • *Scr* Nancy M Pimental

Sweetheart of the Campus

Musical 1941 · US · BW · 64min

This small-scale clanger of a campus musical marked both the return to the screen after a three-year absence of Ruby Keeler and (with the exception of a forgotten cameo) her permanent exit remarriage and retirement. The one-note, boring plot has something to do with bandleader Ozzie Nelson and his troupe involved in attempts to encourage intake at a college where student enrolment has dropped. RK

Ruby Keeler *Betty Blake* • Ozzie Nelson *Ozzie Norton* • Harriet Hilliard [Harriet Nelson] *Harriet Hale* • Gordon Oliver *Terry Jones* • Don Beddoe *Sheriff Denby* • Charles Judels *Victor Demond* • Kathleen Howard *Mrs Minnie Sparr* • Alan Hale Jr *Football player* ■ *Dir* Edward Dmytryk • *Scr* Robert D Andrews, Edmund [Edmund L] Hartmann, from a story by Andrews

Sweethearts ★★★

Musical comedy 1938 · US · Colour · 120min

As the first-ever MGM feature filmed wholly in three-strip Technicolor (*The Wizard of Oz* was part colour, part sepia), this musical comedy has historical significance, though that same process tends to overshadow the popular star team of Jeanette MacDonald and Nelson Eddy. They warble through the Victor Herbert score and struggle through a brand new Dorothy Parker–Alan Campbell screenplay, but much of their thunder is stolen by dance-whiz Ray Bolger. The Broadway to Hollywood plot was well worn even then. TS

Jeanette MacDonald *Gwen Marlowe* • Nelson Eddy *Ernest Lane* • Frank Morgan *Felix Lehman* • Ray Bolger *Hans the dancer* • Florence Rice *Kay Jordan* • Mischa Auer *Leo Kronk* • Fay Holden *Hannah the dresser* ■ *Dir* WS Van Dyke II [WS Van Dyke] • *Scr* Dorothy Parker, Alan Campbell, from the operetta by Harry B Smith, Fred DeGresac, Robert B Smith, Victor Herbert

Sweetie ★★★★ 15

Comedy drama 1989 · Aus · Colour · 95min

Director Jane Campion's first film for the cinema, this quickly established her as one of the most interesting directors working today. Part comedy, part drama, it follows the lives of two eccentric sisters and their equally unstable lovers when they come together under one roof. Like David Lynch's *Blue Velvet*, the film shows us the surreal side of surburbia, where even the most ordinary person is not what he or she seems. Funny, affecting and wonderful. JB Swearing, nudity.

Geneviève Lemon *Dawn, "Sweetie"* • Karen Colston *Kay* • Tom Lycos *Louis* • Jon Darling *Gordon* • Dorothy Barry *Flo* • Michael Lake *Bob* • André Pataczek *Clayton* ■ *Dir* Jane Campion • *Scr* Gerard Lee, Jane Campion, from an idea by Campion

Swept Away ★ 15

Romantic comedy drama 2002 · UK/It · Colour · 85min

Guy Ritchie's insipid vehicle for his then-wife, Madonna, went straight to video in the UK and it's obvious to see why. This romantic comedy is a lifeless and occasionally misogynistic bore. Madonna's role here as a spoilt socialite stranded on an island with one of her hired boat's crew only cements her less than distinguished reputation as an actress. Ritchie's direction and script are unimaginative, and only Adriano Giannini as the boat slave-turned-desert-island master has any spark. SF **DVD**

Madonna *Amber* • Adriano Giannini *Giuseppe* • Jeanne Tripplehorn *Marina* • Bruce Greenwood *Anthony* • Elizabeth Banks (2) *Debi* • David Thornton *Michael* • Michael Beattie *Todd* • Yorgo Voyagis *Captain* ■ *Dir* Guy Ritchie • *Scr* Guy Ritchie, from the film *Swept Away… by an Unusual Destiny in the Blue Sea of August* by Lina Wertmuller

Swimfan ★★★ 12

Psychological thriller 2002 · US/UK · Colour · 81min

A tautly paced and sharply executed thriller, this reworks the familiar cycle of female obsession and revenge. It's a cautionary tale, apparently unaware of its own clichés, as new-girl-in-town Erika Christensen unleashes her fury on handsome high-school swimming champ Jesse Bradford when she realises her affection for him is unrequited. Despite the obvious plot, what viewers won't anticipate is just how nasty Christensen gets – Glenn Close's Alex was a mere pussycat compared to this nightmare incarnate. Intelligent and non-patronising. SF **DVD**

Jesse Bradford *Ben Cronin* • Erika Christensen *Madison Bell* • Shiri Appleby *Amy* • Dan Hedaya *Coach Simkins* • Kate Burton *Carla Cronin* • Clayne Crawford *Josh* • Jason Ritter *Randy* • Kia Joy Goodwin *Rene* ■ *Dir* John Polson • *Scr* Charles Bohl, Phillip Schneider

The Swimmer ★★★★ PG

Drama 1968 · US · Colour · 90min

Based on a short story by cult writer John Cheever, this stars Burt Lancaster as a washed-up suburban man who decides to swim home, using all the pools in his neighbourhood en route. This is not only healthy – and Lancaster looks terrific in his trunks – it's a metaphor for alienation from affluence, sexual desire, Vietnam – you name it, it's all at the bottom of the deep end. Not to everyone's taste, this weird picture now seems an oddly powerful companion piece to *The Graduate*. AT **DVD**

Burt Lancaster *Ned Merrill* • Janet Landgard *Julie Hooper* • Janice Rule *Shirley Abbott* • Tony Bickley *Donald Westerhazy* • Marge Champion *Peggy Forsburgh* • Nancy Cushman *Mrs Halloran* • Bill Fiore *Howie Hunsacker* ■ *Dir* Frank Perry • *Scr* Eleanor Perry, from the short story by John Cheever

The Swimming Pool ★★ 12

Drama 1968 · Fr/It · Colour · 118min

A pool in St Tropez provides the setting for this sexual roundelay. The men are Alain Delon and Maurice Ronet – two of France's biggest stars – and the women are Romy Schneider and Jane Birkin, in her first major role. It's a case of he fancies her, she fancies him and round and round they go, until someone ends up in the deep end. It's a bit too long and the plot doesn't really go anywhere, but the glam trappings have a certain retro appeal. AT French, English +subtitles. **DVD** **Blu**

Alain Delon *Jean-Paul* • Romy Schneider *Marianne* • Maurice Ronet *Harry* • Jane Birkin *Penelope* • Paul Crauchet *Inspector Levêque* ■ *Dir* Jacques Deray • *Scr* Jean-Emmanuel Conil, Jean-Claude Carrière, Jacques Deray

Swimming Pool ★★★★ 15

Psychological mystery drama 2002 · Fr/UK · Colour · 98min

François Ozon continues to pry into the psyche of the vulnerable in this teasingly ambiguous study of creative angst and sexual tension. Yorick Le Saux's cinematography is key to establishing the contrast between the drab frustration of London and the scorching temptation of the southern French hideaway of Luberon. This in turn serves to reinforce the differences between Charlotte Rampling's emotionally repressed crime writer and publisher Charles Dance's carefree daughter, Ludivine Sagnier. This knowing film compels right up to its mischievous conclusion. DP English, French +subtitles. **DVD**

Charlotte Rampling *Sarah Morton* • Ludivine Sagnier *Julie* • Charles Dance *John Bosload* • Marc Fayolle *Marcel* • Jean-Marie Lamour *Franck* • Mireille Mossé *Marcel's daughter* ■ *Dir* François Ozon • *Scr* François Ozon, Emmanuèle Bernheim

Swimming to Cambodia

★★★ 18

Satirical monologue · 1987 · US · Colour · 77min

Spalding Gray described his experiences filming *The Killing Fields* in a one-man stage show, here condensed into a shorter film by director Jonathan Demme. Covering the same ground – the appalling conflict and atrocities which happened in Cambodia – Gray basically delivers a monologue to camera, explaining his experiences in the film from casting to finding out about the Khmer Rouge. Criticised for being a self-aggrandising attempt to capitalise on his small role in the film, Gray insisted that he was trying to show how his experiences as an actor helped him understand the nature of war. He succeeds in his objective, making the horror of war clearer to the audience, too. LH

Spalding Gray · Sam Waterston *Sydney Schanberg* · Ira Wheeler *Ambassador Wade* ■ *Dir* Jonathan Demme · *Scr* Spalding Gray, from his play

Swimming Upstream   ★★ 12

Biographical sports drama
2003 · Aus · Colour · 93min

This classy, if somewhat bloodless true story is based on the life of Australian swimming champion Anthony Fingleton. Set mainly in the 1950s and 60s, it focuses on the troubled relationship between Tony (Jesse Spencer) and his father and coach (Geoffrey Rush). The alcoholic Fingleton Senior prefers to lavish his attention on Tony's brother John (Tim Draxl), a successful swimmer in his own right, which leads to increasing tension within the family. As good as Rush is, Judy Davis steals the show as his long-suffering wife, but even they struggle to make this any more than a standard sporting biopic. JF
DVD

Geoffrey Rush *Harold Fingleton* · Judy Davis *Dora Fingleton* · Jesse Spencer *Tony Fingleton* · Tim Draxl *John Fingleton* · David Hoflin *Harold Fingleton Jr* · Craig Horner *Ronald Fingleton* · Brittany Byrnes *Diane Fingleton* · Deborah Kennedy *Billie* ■ *Dir* Russell Mulcahy · *Scr* Anthony Fingleton, from the memoirs by Anthony Fingleton, Diane Fingleton

Swimming with Sharks

★★★ 15

Comedy · 1994 · US · Colour · 89min

This savage Tinseltown satire from director George Huang is often hilarious in between its bouts of numbingly bleak cynicism. Unfolding its story in a series of flashbacks, it features Frank Whaley as the hapless assistant of heartless Hollywood mogul Kevin Spacey, who enjoys exercising his power right down to the brand of sweetener he wants in his coffee. Spacey's dazzling portrayal of the acid-tongued executive is the most memorable facet of this tar-black comedy, which is heavy on industry in-jokes and vicious put-downs. AJ Swearing, violence. *DVD*

Kevin Spacey *Buddy Ackerman* · Frank Whaley *Guy* · Michelle Forbes *Dawn Lockard* · Benicio Del Toro *Rex* · TE Russell *Foster Kane* · Roy Dotrice *Cyrus Miles* · Matthew Flynt *Manny* ■ *Dir/Scr* George Huang

The Swindle   ★★★ 12

Crime drama · 1955 · Fr/It · BW · 91min

The fabled prospect of Federico Fellini directing Humphrey Bogart haunts this biting tragicomedy, although Broderick Crawford still makes a decent fist of playing alongside Richard Basehart and Franco Fabrizi as the provincial conmen out to fleece the desolate, the devout and the disabled. Having posed as priests and petty bureaucrats, the gang disperses, only for Crawford to hook up with new confrères and be undone by a fatal pang of conscience. Determined to bury his neorealist past, Fellini achieves a cynical authenticity here that even undermines the faint optimism of his ambiguous finale. DP Italian +subtitles. *DVD* 🔵

Broderick Crawford *Augusto* · Richard Basehart *Picasso* · Franco Fabrizi *Roberto* · Giulietta Masina *Iris* · Lorella De Luca *Patrizia* ■ *Dir* Federico Fellini · *Scr* Federico Fellini, Ennio Flaiano, Tullio Pinelli, from a story by Fellini, Flaiano

Swing   ★★ 15

Musical comedy drama
1998 · UK · Colour · 93min

In a piece of uninspired casting, singer Lisa Stansfield plays a singer in this run-of-the-mill Liverpudlian romantic comedy. She's the ex-girlfriend of ex-con Hugo Speer, who joins his swing band against the wishes of her policeman husband Danny McCall. It's predictable but likeable fare, with a nice performance (and even better vocals) from Stansfield. JB Swearing.

Hugo Speer *Martin Luxford* · Lisa Stansfield *Joan Woodcock* · Tom Bell *Sid Luxford* · Rita Tushingham *Mags Luxford* · Alexei Sayle *Mighty Mac* · Paul Usher *Liam Luxford* · Danny McCall *Andy* · Clarence Clemons *Jack* ■ *Dir* Nick Mead · *Scr* Nick Mead, from a story by Su Lim, Mead

Swing High, Swing Low

★★★

Drama · 1937 · US · BW · 92min

Here, comedy is effectively mixed in to the drama about a newly married showbiz couple who come unstuck when he, a trumpeter, gets a job in a New York nightclub and is seduced by the singer (Dorothy Lamour). Mitchell Leisen is in full command of this backstage drama. RK

Carole Lombard *Maggie King* · Fred MacMurray *Skid Johnson* · Charles Butterworth *Harry* · Jean Dixon *Ella* · Dorothy Lamour *Anita Alvarez* · Harvey Stephens *Harvey Howel* · Anthony Quinn *The Don* ■ *Dir* Mitchell Leisen · *Scr* Virginia Van Upp, Oscar Hammerstein II, from the play *Burlesque* by George Manker Watters, Arthur Hopkins

Swing Kids   ★★ 15

Drama · 1993 · US · Colour · 109min

Set in Germany during the Nazi uprising, this film poses an interesting dilemma. A group of youngsters, led by Robert Sean Leonard and Christian Bale, are torn between the rise of Hitler Youth and the popularity of American Swing music and dance. The premise, however, is muted by a lack of directorial punch from Thomas Carter and though the actors are appealing, lack of period detail and overly long sequences of swing dull down a good idea. LH *DVD*

Robert Sean Leonard *Peter* · Christian Bale *Thomas* · Frank Whaley *Arvid* · Barbara Hershey *Frau Muller* · Kenneth Branagh *SS official* · Tushka Bergen *Evey* · David Tom *Willi* · Julia Stemberger *Frau Linge* ■ *Dir* Thomas Carter · *Scr* Jonathan Marc Feldman

Swing Shift   ★★★★ PG

Romantic drama · 1984 · US · Colour · 95min

Directed by Jonathan Demme, this is a small but often delightful romantic drama that went by largely unnoticed on its limited cinema release in Britain. Goldie Hawn is the unassuming housewife who goes to work in a factory during the Second World War while her husband Ed Harris is away fighting, and it is there that she meets free spirit Christine Lahti and cool trumpeter Kurt Russell. It was allegedly during filming that Hawn and Russell fell in love in real life, and they are certainly convincing as the two poles-apart lovers drawn together. JB Swearing.

Goldie Hawn *Kay Walsh* · Kurt Russell *Lucky Lockhart* · Christine Lahti *Hazel Zanussi* · Fred Ward *Biscuits Toohey* · Ed Harris *Jack Walsh* · Holly Hunter *Jeannie Sherman* · Belinda Carlisle *Jamboree singer* ■ *Dir* Jonathan Demme · *Scr* Rob Morton

Swing Time   ★★★★★ U

Classic musical comedy · 1936 · US · BW · 99min

Top Hat might have been more popular, but this is actually the finest of the Fred Astaire/Ginger Rogers movies. Working with a major director in George Stevens, Fred and Ginger achieve such heights that to single out a particular instance might seem invidious. But the climactic *Never Gonna Dance* seems to provide the perfect example of the effortless style Astaire conveyed, and the dialogue between the pair that precedes the dance is among their most poignant. The plot? When Astaire is late for his own wedding, the bride's father forbids the marriage until the groom has made his fortune. TS *DVD*

Fred Astaire *John "Lucky" Garnett* · Ginger Rogers *Penelope "Penny" Carrol* · Victor Moore *Dr Cardetti, "Pop"* · Helen Broderick *Mabel Anderson* · Eric Blore *Mr Gordon* · Betty Furness *Margaret Watson* · George Metaxa *Ricardo Romero* ■ *Dir* George Stevens · *Scr* Howard Lindsay, Allan Scott, from a story by Erwin Gelsey · *Music* Jerome Kern · *Choreographer* Hermes Pan

Swing Vote   ★★ PG

Courtroom drama · 1999 · US · Colour · 89min

Despite a splendid cast and a contentious topic, this courtroom TV movie loses its nerve and settles for melodrama instead of exploring its compelling moral dilemma. It's set in a near future, in which the celebrated Roe v Wade judgement has been overturned and abortion is again illegal in several American states. Alabama is one such place and Lisa Gay Hamilton is on trial for murder after terminating her pregnancy. Supreme Court judge Andy Garcia finds himself with the casting vote. And that's where the film stumbles, as it plumps for suspense instead of debate. DP

Andy Garcia *Joseph Michael Kirkland* · Harry Belafonte *Justice Will Dunn* · Robert Prosky *Chief Justice* · Ray Walston *Justice Clore Cawley* · James Whitmore *Daniel Morrissey* · Kate Nelligan *Justice Sara Marie Brandwynne* · Milo O'Shea *Justice Harlan Greene* · Bob Balaban *Eli "The Cork" MacCorckle* · Lisa Gay Hamilton *Virginia Mapes* ■ *Dir* David Anspaugh · *Scr* Ron Bass [Ronald Bass], Jane Rusconi

Swing Vote   ★★★ 12

Political comedy · 2008 · US · Colour · 114min

One man's vote decides the fate of the world's greatest superpower in this improbable yet endearing yarn. Kevin Costner is the beer-swilling slacker forced to assume his civic responsibility in the full glare of the media spotlight. But the real crowd-pleaser is 12-year-old Madeline Carroll as his daughter, the most intriguing character in a line-up of caricatures. It helps that co-writer/director Joshua Michael Stern has assembled a cast of comedy naturals, including Kelsey Grammer (aka Frasier) and Dennis Hopper as the rival presidential candidates whose measures to secure Costner's vote become increasingly ridiculous. The film's energy flags midway, but this is still a rare treat: a family film with brains as well as heart. SP Brief swearing.
DVD 🔵

Kevin Costner *Ernest "Bud" Johnson* · Kelsey Grammer *President Andrew Boone* · Dennis Hopper *Donald Greenleaf* · Nathan Lane *Art Crumb* · Stanley Tucci *Martin Fox* · Madeline Carroll *Molly Johnson* · Paula Patton *Kate Madison* · George Lopez *John Sweeney* · Judge Reinhold *Walter* · Mare Winningham *Larissa Johnson* ■ *Dir* Joshua Michael Stern · *Scr* Joshua Michael Stern, Jason Richman

Swing Your Lady   ★

Comedy · 1937 · US · BW · 72min

With five song-and-dance numbers appended to it, this really pitiful effort from Warner Bros qualifies as a musical of sorts. The plot concerns a wrestling promoter who, heading for financial ruin, decides to mount a match in which an Amazon of a lady blacksmith (Louise Fazenda) takes on a dim-witted hulk (Nat Pendleton). The big surprise is the appearance of an understandably uncomfortable-looking Humphrey Bogart as the promoter, while the supporting cast includes Ronald Reagan in a small part. RK

Humphrey Bogart *Ed* · Frank McHugh *Popeye* · Louise Fazenda *Sadie* · Nat Pendleton *Joe Skopapolous* · Penny Singleton *Cookie* · Allen Jenkins *Shiner* · Ronald Reagan *Jack Miller* ■ *Dir* Ray Enright · *Scr* Joseph Schrank, Maurice Leo, from the play by Kenyon Nicholson, Charles Robinson

Swingers   ★★★★ 15

Comedy drama · 1996 · US · Colour · 92min

This honest exploration of male friendship is based on lead actor Jon Favreau's autobiographical script about his first years in Hollywood. He and three other out-of-work buddies bar-hop around LA, bitch nonstop, try to pick up women and wait endlessly by the phone for that all-important call. A highly original and entertaining delight using hilarious situations to illuminate male neuroses in an uncompromising way. This independent labour of love carries the solid ring of truth and features superb performances by Vince Vaughn and Favreau. AJ Swearing. *DVD* 🔵

Jon Favreau *Mike* · Vince Vaughn *Trent* · Ron Livingston *Rob* · Patrick Van Horn *Sue* · Alex Desert *Charles* · Heather Graham *Lorraine* · Deena Martin *Christy* ■ *Dir* Doug Liman · *Scr* Jon Favreau · *Cinematographer* Doug Liman

Swinging with the Finkels

★ 15

Romantic comedy
2010 · US/UK · Colour · 84min

This largely laugh-free sex comedy doesn't plumb quite the depths that the notorious *Sex Lives of the Potato Men* did, but it comes perilously close. Martin Freeman and Mandy Moore play a married couple whose sex life has lost its zing. They decide to spice it up by partner-swapping – cue some tepid swinging with the likes of Angus Deayton – but the film quickly abandons sex in favour of schmaltz. Freeman, in particular, could and should do better. DA Sex scenes, sexual references. *DVD*

Mandy Moore *Ellie Finkel* · Martin Freeman *Alvin Finkel* · Melissa George *Janet* · Jerry Stiller *Mr Winters* · Jonathan Silverman *Peter* · Daisy Beaumont *Clementine* · Angus Deayton *Richard* ■ *Dir/Scr* Jonathan Newman

Swiss Army Man   ★★★

Adventure · 2016 · US · Colour · 95min

A curious fable of an imaginary friendship between a suicidal loser (Paul Dano) and the decomposing corpse he finds on a beach (Daniel Radcliffe), this could be seen as a combination of *Castaway* and *Weekend at Bernie's*. It's an uncompromising journey into unexpected laughter, off-putting shock and emotional suspense that has sparked division and heated debate. It's consistently inventive in ways you won't forget, but it's the inconsistency in tone that ultimately dooms this sporadically fun but over-reaching surreal bromance. AJ

Paul Dano *Hank* · Daniel Radcliffe *Manny* · Mary Elizabeth Winstead *Sarah* · Timothy Eulich *Preston* · Antonia Ribero *Chrissy* ■ *Dir* Dan Kwan, Daniel Scheinert · *Scr* Daniel Scheinert, Dan Kwan

The Swiss Conspiracy   ★ 15

Thriller · 1975 · US/W Ger · Colour · 85min

This dismal thriller features David Janssen, who is hired to protect high-class Swiss banking customers (at the same time proving you can still be a star with a face that completely lacks expression). At least John Ireland and Ray Milland display a few emotions, but they come across as too inhuman to elicit any sympathy. TH

David Janssen *David Christopher* · Senta Berger *Denise Abbott* · John Ireland *Dwight McGowan* · John Saxon *Robert Hayes* · Ray Milland *Johann Hurtil* · Elke Sommer *Rita Jensen* · Anton Diffring *Franz Benninger* ■ *Dir* Jack Arnold · *Scr* Norman Klenman, Philip Saltzman, Michael Stanley, from the novel by Stanley

Swiss Family Robinson

★★★ U

Period adventure · 1940 · US · BW · 93min

This is a modest film version of Johann David Wyss's once popular novel about a family, shipwrecked during the Napoleonic wars, who set about building a house and a new life on a desert island. Four-square and agreeably old-fashioned "family" entertainment with a mild message about values, the film boasts the rich voice of

S

Orson Welles as its narrator and a good cast headed by Thomas Mitchell as William Robinson and child star Freddie Bartholomew on loan from MGM. Inexplicably, the production was a box-office disaster for RKO. **RK**

Orson Welles *Narrator* • Thomas Mitchell *William Robinson* • Edna Best *Elizabeth Robinson* • Freddie Bartholomew *Jack Robinson* • Terry Kilburn *Ernest Robinson* • Tim Holt *Fritz Robinson* • Baby Bobby Quillan *Francis Robinson* ■ *Dir* Edward Ludwig • *Scr* Walter Ferris, Gene Towne, Graham Baker, from the novel by Johann David Wyss

Swiss Family Robinson
★★★★ U

Period adventure 1960 · US · Colour · 121min

John Mills and Dorothy McGuire leading their family in a chorus of *Oh, Christmas Tree* (in an impossibly luxurious desert-island tree house) is, for many, an abiding memory of childhood cinema-going. Viewed today, this lavish (if overlong) Disney version of Johann David Wyss's novel has lost little of its appeal. British director Ken Annakin shot the film on the Caribbean island of Tobago and keeps the action brisk. Compared to state-of-the-art sequences in modern action adventures, though, the shipwreck, the raft rescue and the pirate raid are perhaps not as thrilling as they once seemed. **DP**

John Mills *Father Robinson* • Dorothy McGuire *Mother Robinson* • James MacArthur *Fritz Robinson* • Janet Munro *Roberta* • Sessue Hayakawa *Pirate chief* • Tommy Kirk *Ernst* • Kevin Corcoran *Francis* • Cecil Parker *Captain Moreland* ■ *Dir* Ken Annakin • *Scr* Lowell S Hawley, from the novel by Johann David Wyss

Swiss Miss
★★★ U

Comedy 1938 · US · BW · 64min

Even the staunchest Laurel and Hardy fan won't overpraise this middling outing, in which their failed mousetrap salesmen become involved with a composer and his opera-singing wife. However, the film still contains a couple of classic sequences, most notably Stan's attempt to trick a St Bernard dog into letting him at its brandy keg and Ollie singing *Let Me Call You Sweetheart* to Stan's sousaphone accompaniment. **DA**

Stan Laurel *Stan* • Oliver Hardy *Ollie* • Della Lind *Anna Hoeful Albert* • Walter Woolf King *Victor Albert* • Eric Blore *Edward* ■ *Dir* John G Blystone • *Scr* James Parrott, Felix Adler, from a story by Jean Negulesco, Charles Rogers, Stan Laurel

Switch
★★ 15

Comedy 1991 · US · Colour · 98min

This is a rather disappointing and lewd gender-swap tale from Blake Edwards. Perry King is the ladykiller, killed by ladies and reincarnated as Ellen Barkin. It's a story that has a lot going for it, but it cops out as soon as lesbianism rears its alternative head. Barkin has proved herself worthy of much better material than this, but here she made a grave mistake in putting her faith in Edwards's slapstick brand of humour. **TH** Swearing, brief nudity.

Ellen Barkin *Amanda Brooks* • Jimmy Smits *Walter Stone* • JoBeth Williams *Margo Brofman* • Lorraine Bracco *Sheila Faxton* • Tony Roberts *Arnold Freidkin* • Perry King *Steve Brooks* • Bruce Martyn Payne [Bruce Payne] *Devil* • Lysette Anthony *Liz* ■ *Dir/Scr* Blake Edwards

The Switch
★★★★ PG

Drama based on a true story 1993 · US · Colour · 91min

Presumably because of Tinseltown prejudice against the TV movie, there are perfectly decent actors who have practically no life beyond the small screen. Gary Cole and Craig T Nelson are a case in point. They have no trouble at all bringing an emotional and psychological authenticity to their respective roles as a seriously injured biker who wants to die and a DJ who is his political, and personal, opposite. Issues of life and death, responsibility and freedom are woven in with style. **JM** DVD

Gary Cole *Larry McAfee* • Craig T Nelson *Russ Fine* • Beverly D'Angelo *Dee Fine* • Kathleen Nolan *Amelia McAfee* • Chris Mulkey *Bill* • L Scott Caldwell *Mrs Linson* • Max Gail *Judge Johnson* ■ *Dir* Bobby Roth • *Scr* TS Cook, from a story by Cook, Ron Schultz

The Switch
★★★ 12

Romantic comedy 2010 · US · Colour · 97min

Jennifer Aniston tops the bill of this romantic comedy as an unmarried 40-year-old whose biological clock is screaming "baby" but not "commitment". So she turns to goofy but willing sperm donor Patrick Wilson. Come basting night, Aniston's best friend (the borderline-neurotic Jason Bateman who is none too keen on her plan) drunkenly swaps his own sperm for Wilson's. This is far more the under-rated Bateman's film than the adequate Aniston's, and he is well supported by a cracklingly quirky support cast. You know five minutes in exactly where *The Switch* is heading, but getting there is a surprisingly entertaining journey. **DA** Some swearing, sexual references, drug abuse. DVD BL

Jennifer Aniston *Kassie Larson* • Jason Bateman *Wally Mars* • Patrick Wilson *Roland* • Juliette Lewis *Debbie* • Jeff Goldblum *Leonard* • Thomas Robinson *Sebastian* • Todd Louiso *Artie* ■ *Dir* Josh Gordon, Will Speck • *Scr* Allan Loeb, from the short story *Baster* by Jeffrey Eugenides

Switchback
★★★ 15

Action thriller 1997 · US · Colour · 113min

This refreshingly different variation on the overused serial killer plot cuts between Dennis Quaid's miserable FBI man on the trail of the killer he believes has kidnapped his son, and travelling companions Danny Glover and Jared Leto, both of whom are just suspicious enough to be the culprit. Writer/director Jeb Stuart is confident enough to make the "suspects" more interesting than the hero, although his shaky plotting throws up its share of unlikely contrivances. **JC** Violence, nudity, swearing.

Dennis Quaid *Agent Frank LaCrosse* • Danny Glover *Bob Goodall* • Jared Leto *Lane Dixon* • Ted Levine *Nate Booker* • R Lee Ermey *Sheriff Buck Olmstead* ■ *Dir/Scr* Jeb Stuart

Switchblade Romance
★★★★ 18

Horror thriller 2003 · Fr/Rom · Colour · 88min

When French director and co-writer Alexandre Aja called this chiller *Haute Tension* (*High Tension*), he certainly picked the right title. Renamed less aptly for English audiences, it's still a nail-biter. Desperate student Cécile de France tries to rescue her best friend (Maïwenn) after she's kidnapped from a remote farmhouse by a psychopath who's slaughtered her entire family. Though relentlessly gruesome, the feature is more about atmosphere than gore. Every single frame is meticulously composed for maximum effect, while the ultra-glossy production values take it far beyond the realms of the traditional slasher flick. **SF** French +subtitles. DVD BL

Cécile de France *Marie* • Maïwenn *Alex* • Philippe Nahon *Killer* • Franck Khalfoun *Jimmy* • Andrei Finti *Alex's father* • Oana Pellea *Alex's mother* • Marco Claudiu Pascu *Tom* • Jean-Claude de Goros *Police captain* ■ *Dir* Alexandre Aja • *Scr* Alexandre Aja, Grégory Levasseur

Switchblade Sisters
★★ 18

Crime action adventure 1975 · US · Colour · 86min

Quentin Tarantino tried re-releasing this exploitation cheapie in 1999, though it still didn't really find an audience. Indeed, the movie has dated in a way that makes it more tacky than actually hilarious, and though a director known for campy exploitation movies was at the helm, the very low budget results in the characters providing more "attitude" and arguments than violence or sexual material. Still, this saga of the trials and battles of an all-girl gang does have its moments. **KB** Violence, drug abuse.

Robbie Lee *Lace* • Joanne Nail *Maggie* • Monica Gayle *Patch* • Asher Brauner *Dominic* • Chase Newhart *Crabs* • Marlene Clark *Muff* • Kitty Bruce *Donut* • Janice Karman *Bunny* ■ *Dir* Jack Hill • *Scr* FX Maier, from a story by FX Maier, Jack Hill, John Prizer

Switching Channels ★★★ PG

Romantic comedy 1987 · US · Colour · 100min

After three screen versions of *The Front Page* set in a newspaper office (including the best of them all, *His Girl Friday*), it was only a matter of time before someone brought the story into the TV age. Canadian director Ted Kotcheff never quite comes to grips with the pace of either the story or the humour, and his uncertain handling hampers his capable cast. Burt Reynolds keeps threatening to match two of his predecessors in the role, but Kathleen Turner and Christopher Reeve leave you longing for Rosalind Russell and Ralph Bellamy. **DP** Swearing. DVD

Kathleen Turner *Christy Colleran* • Burt Reynolds *John L Sullivan IV* • Christopher Reeve *Blaine Bingham* • Ned Beatty *Roy Ridnitz* • Henry Gibson *Ike Roscoe* • George Newbern *Siegenthaler* • Al Waxman *Berger* ■ *Dir* Ted Kotcheff • *Scr* Jonathan Reynolds, from the play *The Front Page* by Ben Hecht, Charles MacArthur

Swoon
★★★ 18

Crime drama 1992 · US · BW · 93min

Overly arty and surrealistic it might be, but writer/director Tom Kalin's take on the famous Leopold and Loeb murder case is still provocative, gripping and chilling, raising clever contemporary issues within its period confines. Using monochrome melodrama, archive footage and experimental narrative, Kalin starkly examines with haunting effectiveness the homophobia behind the conviction of the two wealthy gay Chicago college kids who killed a schoolboy for kicks in 1924. **AJ** Swearing.

Daniel Schlachet *Richard Loeb* • Craig Chester *Nathan Leopold Jr* • Ron Vawter *State's Attorney Crowe* • Michael Kirby *Detective Savage* • Michael Stumm *Doctor Bowman* • Valda Z Drabla *Germaine Reinhardt* • Natalie Stanford *Susan Lurie* • Paul Connor *Bobby Franks* ■ *Dir/Scr* Tom Kalin

The Sword and the Cross
★★

Biblical drama 1958 · It · Colour · 93min

The success of such films as MGM's *Quo Vadis* and *Ben-Hur* must have left a lot of props and costumes in the scene docks at Cinecittà studios in Rome. A whole subgenre arose utilising existing materials with quasi-religious plots, invariably importing a Hollywood name to add international lustre. This one finds Yvonne De Carlo as Mary Magdalene in a fictional romance set during the last days of Christ. Not unwatchable, but don't expect taste. **TS** Italian dubbed.

Yvonne De Carlo *Mary Magdalene* • Jorge Mistral *Caius Marcellus* • Rossana Podesta *Marthe* • Philippe Hersent *Pontius Pilate* • Mario Girotti [Terence Hill] *Lazarus* ■ *Dir* Carlo Ludovico Bragaglia

The Sword and the Rose
★★ U

Historical drama 1952 · US · Colour · 87min

In days of old when knights were bold and painted scenery was a cutting-edge special effect, this Disney costume drama would have had children in raptures. This corny romp has Michael Gough's pantomimically wicked lord standing between Glynis Johns's winsome Mary Tudor and true happiness. Gleefully dispensing with historical fact, it's all simply an excuse for Richard Todd to prance about in brightly coloured tights (again), while James Robertson-Justice demonstrates what a Scottish Henry VIII might have sounded like. **DP**

Richard Todd *Charles Brandon* • Glynis Johns *Princess Mary Tudor* • James Robertson-Justice *King Henry VIII* • Michael Gough *Duke of Buckingham* • Jane Barrett *Lady Margaret* • Peter Copley *Sir Edwin Caskoden* • Rosalie

Crutchley *Queen Catherine of Aragon* ■ *Dir* Ken Annakin • *Scr* Lawrence E Watkin, from the novel *When Knighthood Was in Flower* by Charles Major

The Sword in the Stone
★★★ U

Animated adventure 1963 · US · Colour · 76min

Disney's feature-length cartoon account of young King Arthur's magical misadventures may feature unmemorable songs by the Sherman brothers, but the film makes good use of its limited animation techniques (Disney was on a cost-cutting drive at the time) in relating the legend of Arthur, here nicknamed Wart, and the valuable life lessons taught to him by wizard Merlin. Memorable sequences include Wart's transformation into a fish to witness the wonders of the underwater world before pulling Excalibur from the stone and claiming his rightful inheritance. **AJ** DVD BL

Rickie Sorensen *Wart* • Sebastian Cabot *Sir Ector* • Karl Swenson *Merlin, the magician* • Junius Matthews *Archimedes* • Norman Alden *Kay* • Martha Wentworth *Mad Madame Mim/Granny Squirrel* • Alan Napier *Sir Pelinore* ■ *Dir* Wolfgang Reitherman • *Scr* Bill Peet, from the novel *The Once and Future King* by TH White

The Sword of Monte Cristo
★★ U

Swashbuckling adventure 1951 · US · Colour · 79min

Some vigorous swordplay, handsome settings and lavish costumes fail to make up for the convoluted plot and general shortcomings of this second-rate action adventure tale, very loosely inspired by Alexandre Dumas's classic novel. George Montgomery is merely adequate as the loyal French officer who helps save Napoleon III from the treachery of his tyrannical chief minister, and this sort of Gallic swashbuckler has been done far better many times before and since. **PF**

George Montgomery *Captain Renault* • Paula Corday [Rita Corday] *Lady Christiane* • Berry Kroeger *Minister Charles La Roche* • William Conrad *Major Nicolet* • Rhys Williams *Major of Varonne* • Steve Brodie *Sergeant* • Robert Warwick *Marquis de Montableau* • David Bond (1) *Louis Napoleon III* ■ *Dir* Maurice Geraghty • *Scr* Maurice Geraghty, from the novel *The Count of Monte Cristo* by Alexandre Dumas

Sword of Sherwood Forest
★★ U

Adventure 1960 · UK · Colour · 76min

To many, Richard Greene was the definitive Robin Hood, ushering in ITV in a cleverly cast (though cheaply made) television series with a remarkably catchy theme tune. This is the feature, co-produced by Greene for Hammer Films. Alan Wheatley makes way for Peter Cushing as the villainous Sheriff of Nottingham, and the film is directed by Cushing's Hammer colleague, Terence Fisher. Technicolor adds some scale, but this is really a cheap and cheerful affair. **TS** DVD

Richard Greene *Robin Hood* • Peter Cushing *Sheriff of Nottingham* • Niall MacGinnis *Friar Tuck* • Sarah Branch *Maid Marian Fitzwalter* • Richard Pasco *Earl of Newark* • Nigel Green *Little John* • Jack Gwillim *Archbishop of Canterbury, Hubert Walter* • Oliver Reed *Melton* ■ *Dir* Terence Fisher • *Scr* Alan Hackney

Sword of the Valiant
★ PG

Fantasy adventure 1984 · UK · Colour · 97min

This is tantamount to a star-studded remake of Stephen Weeks's low-budget 1973 film *Gawain and the Green Knight*. He has made little improvement on his own original, however. Miles O'Keeffe is quite dreadful in the role of the squire Gawain, challenged by Sean Connery's Green Knight to answer a riddle within a year or risk having his head chopped off. Barely on screen, Trevor Howard and Peter Cushing are shamefully wasted, as are the locations. **DP**

Miles O'Keeffe *Gawain* • Cyrielle Claire *Linet* • Leigh Lawson *Humphrey* • Sean Connery *Green Knight* • Trevor Howard *King Arthur* • Peter

Cushing *Seneschal* • Ronald Lacey *Oswald* • Lila Kedrova *Lady of Lyonesse* ■ *Dir* Stephen Weeks • *Scr* Stephen Weeks, Philip M Breen, Howard C Pen

Sword of Vengeance ★★★ 18
Period martial arts adventure
1972 · Jpn · Colour · 83min

This is the first of the original six *Lone Wolf and Cub* adventures produced by Toho studios. Incredibly, the series flopped commercially and remained forgotten until the character of samurai Ogami Itto was revived for television in the early 1980s. However, they rank among the most visceral movies in the warrior genre, with Tomisaburo Wakayama as the embittered widower, who wheels his infant son around the 17th-century countryside, righting wrongs and seeking vengeance on the Yagyu clan. Followed by *Baby Cart at the River Styx*. DP Japanese +subtitles. DVD

Tomisaburo Wakayama *Ogami Itto* • Akihiro Tomikawa *Daigoro* ■ *Dir* Kenji Misumi • *Scr* Kazuo Koike, from a story by Kazuo Koike, Goseki Kojima

Sword of Vengeance ★★ 15
Action adventure 2015 · US · Colour · 83min

A grisly action film starring Stanley Weber as a prince out for bloody revenge in England in the years after the Battle of Hastings. It's about as straightforward a film as you are ever likely to see – Weber's Shadow Walker's out for vengeance (with a sword), and that's about as much plot development as the film chooses to include. As for the rest, it's a succession of gruesome fights, with enough eye-gouging and throat-slitting to make it seem more like one long, senseless action scene than a coherent story. Weber has leading-man looks, but his sullen medieval Superman says little and does little, other than dispatch numbers of snarling villains in elaborate ways. There is a brutal simplicity to the action that will appeal to some, but in terms of non-violent content *Sword of Vengeance* seems stretched even for a relatively short film. JL DVD

Stanley Weber *Shadow Walker* • Annabelle Wallis *Anna* • Karel Roden *Durant* • Ed Skrein *Treden* • Dave Legeno *Osger* • Edward Akrout *Romain* ■ *Dir* Jim Weedon • *Scr* Julian Unthank, from a story by Matthew Read

Sword of Xanten ★★ 12
Fantasy adventure
2004 · Ger/S Afr/UK/It · Colour · 176min

German director Uli Edel delves into Nordic and Germanic mythology for this ambitious fantasy adventure that was originally made for television. Prince Siegfried (Benno Fürmann) is raised as a blacksmith's son and only discovers his true heritage after slaying a dragon. The beast is hoarding stolen gold that belongs to the ghostly Nibelungs, and when Siegfried claims it, he unleashes a terrible curse. An enthralling though badly acted story, the film is adequately executed, but can't escape its low-budget roots. SF Violence. DVD

Benno Fürmann *Siegfried* • Kristanna Loken *Brunhild* • Alicia Witt *Kriemhild* • Julian Sands *Hagen* • Samuel West *King Gunther* • Max von Sydow *Eyvind* • Robert Pattinson *Giselher* • Mavie Hörbiger *Lena* ■ *Dir* Uli Edel • *Scr* Diane Duane, Peter Morwood, Uli Edel

Swordfish ★★ 15
Action thriller 2001 · US · Colour · 95min

This is a glossy, expensive computer-heist thriller that amounts to very little behind all the fireworks. If you've seen the trailer, you've seen the film, as it gives away the ending and shows part of a technically brilliant 360-degree explosion that director Dominic Sena obviously saw as his calling card. He's so proud of it, in fact, he gives it to us twice, such is the superficial nature of this film. The only saving grace is Hugh Jackman's performance as the cool super-hacker hired by John Travolta to help steal $9.5 billion. AC Nudity, violence, swearing. DVD

John Travolta *Gabriel Shear* • Hugh Jackman *Stanley Jobson* • Halle Berry *Ginger* • Don Cheadle *Agent Roberts* • Vinnie Jones *Marco* • Sam Shepard *Senator Reisman* ■ *Dir* Dominic Sena • *Scr* Skip Woods

The Swordsman of Siena ★★ U
Swashbuckling adventure
1962 · Fr/It · Colour · 96min

British actor Stewart Granger flails around with sabre and rapier in this Italian swashbuckler, set in the 16th century. Our hero plays a soldier of fortune who gets caught up in a struggle between a brutal nobleman and a rebel underground movement. He also gets to stretch his romantic muscles in dallying with Sylva Koscina and Tony Curtis's ex-wife, Christine Kaufmann. There's plenty of colourful costumes and swordfights, but the plot is as predictable as a calendar. TH Italian dubbed.

Stewart Granger *Thomas Stanwood* • Sylva Koscina *Orietta Arconti* • Christine Kaufmann *Serenella Arconti* • Riccardo Garrone *Don Carlos* • Tullio Carminati *Father Giacomo* ■ *Dir* Etienne Périer, Baccio Bandini • *Scr* Michael Kanin, Fay Kanin, Alec Coppel, Sandro Continenza, Dominique Fabre, from a story by Anthony Marshall

Sydney White ★★ 12
Comedy 2007 · US · Colour · 103min

The nerds get their revenge in this occasionally funny campus comedy that's a modern take on *Snow White*. Amanda Bynes stars as geeky new girl Sydney White, who's cast out of an uppity sorority house when wicked nemesis Rachel (Sara Paxton) wants to be the undisputed fairest of them all. So Sydney enrols the assistance of the seven dorks – a bunch of dopey, bashful and sleepy dropouts – to help her win her Prince Charming (Matt Long). Joe Nussbaum's film offers a couple of genuinely witty gags, but more often retreats into platitudes about popularity and acceptance, mouthed by questionable comic stereotypes. JR DVD

Amanda Bynes *Sydney White* • Sara Paxton *Rachel* • Matt Long *Tyler Prince* • Jack Carpenter *Lenny* • Jeremy Howard *Terrance* • John Schneider *Paul White* ■ *Dir* Joe Nussbaum • *Scr* Chad Gomez Creasey

Sylvester ★★★ PG
Drama 1985 · US · Colour · 99min

Melissa Gilbert stars as the tomboy who rides her horse Sylvester to victory in the Olympics three-day event at Lexington, Kentucky. The plot superficially resembles *National Velvet*, but Hunter brings a darker touch to the proceedings by making Gilbert's character rather unlikeable. Veteran Richard Farnsworth gives a fine performance as Gilbert's tipsy but tough mentor. DA

Richard Farnsworth *Foster* • Melissa Gilbert *Charlie* • Michael Schoeffling *Matt* • Constance Towers *Muffy* • Pete Kowanko *Harris* ■ *Dir* Tim Hunter • *Scr* Carol Sobieski

Sylvia ★★★★
Drama 1964 · US · BW · 114min

Hollywood's sex siren in residence – the one and only Carroll Baker – is about to marry a millionaire, so he hires a private detective to shed some light on her past. She's a champion rose grower and a published poet, so there shouldn't be too many surprises. But then comes the bad news: after being abused as a child, she became a prostitute and fell in with some very bad company indeed. As prurient and lurid as a mainstream Hollywood movie could be in 1965, this is superbly filmed and with a whole line of feeble, emasculated or disturbed men to trample over Baker's eventful life. AT

Carroll Baker *Sylvia West* • George Maharis *Alan Macklin* • Joanne Dru *Jane Philips* • Peter Lawford *Frederick Summers* • Viveca Lindfors *Irma Olanski* • Edmond O'Brien *Oscar Stewart* • Aldo Ray *Jonas Karoki* • Ann Sothern *Mrs Argona* ■ *Dir* Gordon Douglas • *Scr* Sydney Boehm, from the novel by EV Cunningham

Sylvia ★★★ PG
Drama 1984 · NZ · Colour · 94min

This moving biopic from the fledgeling days of New Zealand cinema recounts the early life of acclaimed novelist Sylvia Ashton-Warner, who, before finding fame as a writer, pioneered a radical new teaching programme to help Maori children. Eleanor David shines in the lead role, and there is sterling support from Tom Wilkinson and Nigel Terry. Director Michael Firth admirably evokes the conservatism and prejudices of post-Second World War New Zealand. JF

Eleanor David *Sylvia Henderson* • Nigel Terry *Aden* • Tom Wilkinson *Keith Henderson* • Mary Regan *Opal* • Martyn Sanderson *Inspector Gulland* • Terence Cooper *Inspector Bletcher* • David Letch *Inspector Scragg* ■ *Dir* Michael Firth • *Scr* Michael Quill, F Fairfax, Michael Firth, from the books *Teacher* and *I Pass This Way* by Sylvia Ashton-Warner

Sylvia ★★★ 15
Biographical drama
2003 · UK/US · Colour · 109min

Who was Sylvia Plath? According to this patchy, dislocated biopic, the American poet was a suicidal, husband-obsessed woman whose creative flame was prematurely extinguished when she took her own life in 1963. Relegating the people and events of the period to the background, the film centres on the love affair between Plath and her husband, future poet laureate Ted Hughes. What draws us in is the central performance of Gwyneth Paltrow – as steely as it is vulnerable – while Daniel Craig's turn as Hughes is also superbly conveyed. TH DVD

Gwyneth Paltrow *Sylvia Plath* • Daniel Craig *Ted Hughes* • Jared Harris *Al Alvarez* • Amira Casar *Assia Wevill* • Andrew Havill *David Wevill* • Sam Troughton *Tom Hadley-Clarke* • Lucy Davenport *Doreen* • Antony Strachan *Michael Boddy* • Blythe Danner *Aurelia Plath* • Michael Gambon *Professor Thomas* ■ *Dir* Christine Jeffs • *Scr* John Brownlow

Sylvia Scarlett ★★ U
Comedy drama 1936 · US · BW · 86min

Petty fraudster Edmund Gwenn and his daughter Katharine Hepburn (disguised as a boy to fool pursuing cops) join forces in England with cockney jewel thief Cary Grant. Their picaresque escapades and emotional entanglements defeat the script and George Cukor's direction. A bemused public gave the thumbs down to this sprawling and tedious adaptation that hasn't improved with age. RK

Katharine Hepburn *Sylvia Scarlett* • Cary Grant *Jimmy Monkley* • Brian Aherne *Michael Fane* • Edmund Gwenn *Henry Scarlett* • Natalie Paley *Lily Levetsky* • Dennie Moore *Maudie Tilt* ■ *Dir* George Cukor • *Scr* Gladys Unger, John Collier, Mortimer Offner, from the novel *The Early Life and Adventures of Sylvia Scarlett* by Compton Mackenzie

Sympathy for Lady Vengeance ★★★ 18
Action thriller 2005 · S Kor · Colour · 115min

The final part of director Park Chan-wook's trilogy (after *Sympathy for Mr Vengeance* and *Oldboy*) proves to be slightly disappointing when compared to its predecessors. Lee Young-ae, released from prison after serving more than 13 years for the kidnap and murder of a young boy, has been planning the downfall of ex-teacher Choi Min-sik, who implicated her in the crime and allowed her own daughter to be given up for adoption. Park's stylish direction may be too self-conscious for some tastes, but he laces the action with plenty of macabre humour. DP Korean, English +subtitles. Violence. DVD

Lee Young-ae *Lee Geum-ja* • Choi Min-sik *Mr Baek, teacher* • Kim Si-hu *Keun Shik* • Nam Il-woo *Detective Choi* • Kim Byeong-ok *Preacher* • Oh Dal-su *Jang* • Lee Seung-shin *Park Yi-jeong* • Kim Bu-sun *Woo So-young* ■ *Dir* Park Chan-wook • *Scr* Park Chan-wook, Chung Seo-kyung

Sympathy for Mr Vengeance ★★★★ 18
Action thriller 2002 · S Kor · Colour · 120min

Director Park Chan-wook examines the tensions inherent within South Korean society in this combustible tale of exploitation, despair and revenge. The opening section combines social critique, black comedy and domestic melodrama, as unemployed smelter Shin Ha-gyun decides to kidnap his ex-boss's daughter after he's cheated out of the savings intended for his sister's kidney transplant. The tone darkens after the plan backfires and the girl's father, Song Kang-ho, comes after them. Some may bridle at the violence, but Park's control over his bleak vision is impressive. DP Korean +subtitles. DVD

Song Kang-ho *Park Dong-jin* • Shin Ha-gyun *Ryu* • Bae Doo-na *Cha Yeong-mi* • Lim Ji-eun *Ryu's sister* • Han Bo-bae *Yu-sun* ■ *Dir* Park Chan-wook • *Scr* Lee Jae-sun, Lee Mu-yeong, Lee Yong-jong, Park Chan-wook

Sympathy for the Devil ★★ 15
Experimental documentary drama
1968 · UK · Colour · 96min

Intended for large audiences because of the presence of the Rolling Stones, this turned out to be one of Jean-Luc Godard's most cryptic, fragmentary and irritating works. The Stones rehearsing their song *Sympathy for the Devil* in a recording studio is intercut with shots of a black man reading anticolonial texts, as well as a girl (Anne Wiazemsky, for whom Godard had left his wife Anna Karina) contemplating suicide when her boyfriend joins the Black Panther movement. RB DVD

Anne Wiazemsky *Eve Democracy* • Iain Quarrier *Bookman* • Frankie Dymon Jr *Black Power militant* • Sean Lynch *Narrator* ■ *Dir/Scr* Jean-Luc Godard

La Symphonie Pastorale ★★★★★
Drama 1946 · Fr · BW · 107min

Blind orphan girl Michèle Morgan is brought up by pastor Pierre Blanchar and his wife in a small mountain village, where the pastor teaches his charge to understand the world as a place of beauty and serenity. However, he and his son Jean Desailly both fall in love with her, and the latter, hopeful of marriage, arranges an operation to restore her sight. Adapted from André Gide's painfully sad novella and filmed against a background of exquisite visuals, the film won the Grand Prix at Cannes in 1946, while Morgan's expressive performance saw her voted best actress. A French gem, redolent with beauty and despair. RK French +subtitles.

Michèle Morgan *Gertrude* • Pierre Blanchar *Pastor Jean Martin* • Line Noro *Amélie Martin* • Jacques Louvigny *Casteran* • Jean Desailly *Jacques Martin* • Andrée Clément *Piette Casteran* ■ *Dir* Jean Delannoy • *Scr* Pierre Bost, Jean Aurenche, Jean Delannoy, from the novel by André Gide

Symphony of Six Million ★★★
Drama 1932 · US · BW · 85min

Directed by the efficient Gregory La Cava, this concerns Ricardo Cortez, a doctor of humble origins, who sells out his high ideals for money and status, only to fail in performing an operation on his father Gregory Ratoff. He redeems himself, however, by saving Irene Dunne, the woman he loves. Max Steiner's emotive score heightens the drama without disguising Cortez's wooden acting, but the film, complete with then rare scenes of surgical procedure, is a good wallow. RK

Ricardo Cortez *Dr Felix Klauber* • Irene Dunne *Jessica* • Anna Appel *Hannah Klauber* • Gregory Ratoff *Meyer "Lansman" Klauber* ■ *Dir* Gregory La Cava • *Scr* Bernard Schubert, J Walter Ruben, James Seymour, from a story by Fannie Hurst

S

Syncopation ★★ U
Period drama 1942 · US · BW · 88min

Eleven musical numbers and the participation of Benny Goodman, Harry James, Gene Krupa, Charlie Barnet and Joe Venuti are the only possible reasons to sit through this dreary tale of a young trumpeter from Chicago (Jackie Cooper) and a New Orleans girl (Bonita Granville) who share an obsession with jazz and Walt Whitman. Top-billed Adolphe Menjou barely figures as Granville's father. RK

Adolphe Menjou *George Latimer* · Jackie Cooper *Johnnie* · Bonita Granville *Kit Latimer* · George Bancroft *Mr Porter* · Ted North *Paul Porter* · Todd Duncan *Rex Tearbone* · Connee Boswell *Café singer* ■ *Dir* William Dieterle · *Scr* Philip Yordan, Frank Cavett, from the story *The Band Played On* by Valentine Davies

Synecdoche, New York ★★★ 15
Drama 2008 · US · Colour · 118min

Writer Charlie Kaufman (*Adaptation.*, *Eternal Sunshine of the Spotless Mind*) makes an ambitious directorial debut with this high-concept comedy drama. It starts as a breezy tale of midlife, middle-class dysfunction, until neurotic New York theatre director Philip Seymour Hoffman begins an ambitious theatrical project to re-create his life inside a vast warehouse. Hoffman holds this sometimes baffling piece together with a multilayered performance, and there's excellent support from Samantha Morton, Emily Watson, Michelle Williams and Dianne Wiest. Despite its flaws, this is light years ahead of the average Hollywood comedy. SS Swearing, nudity. DVD BL

Philip Seymour Hoffman *Caden Cotard* · Samantha Morton *Hazel* · Michelle Williams *Claire Keen* · Catherine Keener *Adele Lack* · Emily Watson *Tammy* · Dianne Wiest *Ellen Bascomb/Millicent Weems* · Jennifer Jason Leigh *Maria* · Hope Davis *Madeleine Gravis* ■ *Dir/Scr* Charlie Kaufman · *Cinematographer* Fred Elmes [Frederick Elmes]

Syngenor ★★ 18
Science fiction 1989 · US · Colour · 98min

A sequel of sorts to the equally unimpressive *Scared to Death*, this is a lurid, cheapo slice of mutant mayhem. The syngenors of the titles are genetically engineered creatures, programmed to kill anyone who crosses their path and who go on to create havoc when they escape from a mad boffin's lab. Horror fans will appreciate another deranged turn from *Re-Animator's* David Gale and fans of the *Alien Nation* TV series will recognise Jeff Doucette. JF

Starr Andreeff *Susan* · Mitchell Laurance *Nick* · David Gale *Carter Brown* ■ *Dir* George Elanjian Jr · *Scr* Brent V Friedman, from a story by Michael Carmody

A Syrian Love Story ★★★★ 12A
Documentary 2015 · UK · Colour · 75min

Sean McAllister spent time behind bars to chronicle this struggle of a couple torn between raising their four sons and exposing the iniquities of the Syrian dictatorship. Palestinian Amer Daoud met Syrian Raghda Hassan through a hole in the wall while both were political prisoners in Syria in the 1990s. After Hassan was imprisoned for publishing a book about their romance, Daoud sought the help of McAllister and the US State Department in highlighting her plight. Providing an intimate insight into the realities behind the headlines, this provocative and compassionate study is both timely and essential viewing. DP Swearing, disturbing images.

■ *Dir* Sean McAllister

Syriana ★★★★ 15
Political thriller 2005 · US · Colour · 122min

Using the same multi-stranded technique as he did for his Oscar-winning screenplay of the drugs drama *Traffic*, writer/director

Stephen Gaghan here weaves the threads of apparently barely linked narratives into a giant tapestry, revealing the global oil industry in all its venal and corrupt glory. The story is labyrinthine, but individual plot elements include George Clooney as a worn-out CIA agent, Matt Damon as a grief-stricken energy analyst and Christopher Plummer as the head of a powerful law firm. The seemingly disparate tales move at a relentless pace and, as a result, the whole picture is sometimes difficult to grasp, but this is compelling, richly detailed and terrifying. AS English, Arabic, Farsi +subtitles. Violence, swearing. DVD BL

George Clooney *Bob Barnes* · Matt Damon *Bryan Woodman* · Jeffrey Wright *Bennett Holiday* · Chris Cooper *Jimmy Pope* · William Hurt *Stan Goff* · Mazhar Munir *Wasim Ahmed Khan* · Tim Blake Nelson *Danny Dalton* · Amanda Peet *Julie Woodman* · Christopher Plummer *Dean Whiting* · Alexander Siddig *Prince Nasir Al-Subaai* ■ *Dir* Stephen Gaghan · *Scr* Stephen Gaghan, suggested by the non-fiction book *See No Evil* by Robert Baer

The System ★★★
Romantic drama 1964 · UK · BW · 92min

Once upon a time, teenage boys used to go to the unromantic English seaside to pick up their girls, before cheap air travel to the Costa Brava was introduced. This quaint period romp provides a mirror of those not-so-innocent times, elegantly photographed in black-and-white by cinematographer Nicolas Roeg and oozing early 1960s charm from Peter Draper's clever screenplay. The young, talented cast is headed by Oliver Reed, Jane Merrow, Barbara Ferris and Julia Foster, and watch closely for Michael Winner in shot on the platform as the train arrives at Torquay. TS

Oliver Reed *Tinker* · Jane Merrow *Nicola* · Barbara Ferris *Suzy* · Julia Foster *Lorna* · Harry Andrews *Larsey* · Ann Lynn *Ella* · David Hemmings *David* · John Alderton *Nidge* ■ *Dir* Michael Winner · *Scr* Peter Draper

THX 1138 ★★★★ 15
Science-fiction drama 1971 · US · Colour · 82min

The debut feature from *Star Wars* maestro George Lucas is a bleak, claustrophobic affair. The always excellent Robert Duvall takes the title role as a man quietly rebelling against a repressive world where everyone has to have Yul Brynner haircuts, and the police are as frighteningly bland as a McDonald's assistant. The obtuse script doesn't help, but it looks wonderful and Lucas conjures up a genuinely chilling air. JF DVD BL

Robert Duvall *THX 1138* · Donald Pleasence *SEN 5241* · Don Pedro Colley *SRT* · Maggie McOmie *LUH 3417* · Ian Wolfe *PTO* · Sid Haig *NCH* ■ *Dir* George Lucas · *Scr* George Lucas, Walter Murch, from a story by Lucas

TMNT ★★★ PG
Animated action adventure 2007 · US/HK · Colour · 83min

While previous Teenage Mutant Ninja Turtle movies saw live action, this new adventure employs CGI animation – presumably in an attempt to appeal to both ageing fans of the original 1980s comics and a new generation of kids. Writer/director Kevin Munroe tones down the turtles' usual pizza-munching comedy in favour of something slightly darker and less camp. A routine plot about an army of monsters terrorising Manhattan allows Leonardo, Michelangelo, Donatello and Raphael to do their ninja stuff, while showcasing state-of-the-art visuals and supporting vocal work from the likes of Sarah Michelle Gellar and Patrick Stewart. It's not quite as grown-up as it wants to be, but it's still a polished revival of the franchise. JR In English. DVD BL

Chris Evans *Casey Jones* · Sarah Michelle Gellar *April O'Neil* · Mako *Splinter* · Patrick Stewart *Max Winters* · Mitchell Whitfield *Donatello* · Mikey Kelley *Michelangelo* · James Arnold Taylor *Leonardo* · Nolan North *Raphael/Nightwatcher* · Laurence Fishburne *Narrator* · Ziyi Zhang [Zhang Ziyi] *Karai* · Kevin Smith (2) *Diner cook* ■ *Dir* Kevin Munroe · *Scr* Kevin Munroe, from characters by Kevin Eastman, Peter Laird

T-Men ★★★★
Film noir 1947 · US/UK · BW · 92min

The "T" refers to Treasury Agents, as opposed to G-Men (FBI), and the picture is a real humdinger, one of director Anthony Mann's early works. It's a testament to the brilliance of cameraman John Alton, whose lighting can make a concrete wall as expressive as a Turner landscape. The story is hardly original – agents are assigned to smash a counterfeiting racket – but Mann's inventive telling belies the bargain-basement budget. Audiences at the time marvelled at Dennis O'Keefe's performance as one of the agents. AT

Dennis O'Keefe *Dennis O'Brien* · Alfred Ryder *Tony Genaro* · Mary Meade *Evangeline* · Wallace Ford *Schemer* · June Lockhart *Mary Genaro* · Charles McGraw *Moxie* · Jane Randolph *Diana* · Art Smith *Gregg* ■ *Dir* Anthony Mann · *Scr* John C Higgins, from a story by Virginia Kellogg

TR Baskin ★★
Comedy drama 1971 · US · Colour · 89min

This handsome but muddled comedy drama was released in the UK as *A Date with a Lonely Girl*. As the country girl trying to make it as a typist in Chicago, Candice Bergen is simply too glamorous and assured to convince us she's a timid waif. However, director Herbert Ross's clumsy handling of the interminable flashbacks give

her some sort of alibi. James Caan is a standout as a sympathetic admirer. DP

Candice Bergen *TR Baskin* · Peter Boyle *Jack Mitchell* · James Caan *Larry Moore* · Marcia Rodd *Dayle* · Erin O'Reilly *Kathy* · Howard Platt *Arthur* · William Wise *Gary* ■ *Dir* Herbert Ross · *Scr* Peter Hyams

Taal ★★★ U
Romantic musical melodrama 1999 · Ind · Colour · 178min

This masala melodrama has the distinction of being the first Bollywood production to make it into the top 20 of the US box office. Director Subhash Ghai borrows liberally from recent blockbusters to fashion this star-crossed romance, which features Akshaye Khanna as a millionaire's son who teams up with his loyal friend Anil Kapoor to defy class prejudice and the ruthless materialism of modern society in order to win the heart of folk singer Aishwarya Rai. DP Hindi +subtitles. DVD

Anil Kapoor *Vikrant Kapoor/Kapu* · Aishwarya Rai *Manasi* · Akshaye Khanna *Manav Mehta* · Alok Nath *Tara Babu* · Amrish Puri *Jagmohan* ■ *Dir/Scr* Subhash Ghai

Table for Five ★★★ PG
Drama 1983 · US · Colour · 116min

Hankies at the ready for this sentimental heartstring-tugger: Jon Voight stars as the divorced dad who takes his kids on a Mediterranean holiday, only to learn while they are away that his ex-wife has died and her husband may want custody of the children. While gushy towards the finale, this is best enjoyed for the earlier scenes of Voight trying to get to know his children again. JB

Jon Voight *JP Tannen* · Richard Crenna *Mitchell* · Marie-Christine Barrault *Marie* · Millie Perkins *Kathleen* · Roxana Zal *Tilde* · Robby Kiger *Truman-Paul* ■ *Dir* Robert Lieberman · *Scr* David Seltzer

Tabloid ★★★
Documentary 2010 · US · Colour and BW · 87min

Acclaimed documentary maker Errol Morris returns to his favourite "stranger than fiction" territory with this playful yet poignant portrait of romantic obsessive Joyce McKinney. An American former beauty queen, McKinney became a 1970s UK tabloid sensation after allegedly kidnapping, imprisoning and indecently assaulting her estranged Mormon boyfriend. This is a juicy though superficial movie, as interviews with the bubbly, now 60-something McKinney and other key figures quirkily combine with animation, stock footage and archival clips to detail the story behind the salacious headlines. The end result is concerned with the subjective nature of truth, rather than actual facts, but its overall effectiveness is weakened as Morris neither challenges statements, nor looks at their wider significance. SF DVD

■ *Dir* Errol Morris

Tabu ★★★ PG
Silent drama 1931 · US · BW · 82min

After creative differences caused him to leave WS Van Dyke to complete *White Shadows in the South Seas* (1928), the father of the documentary film, Robert Flaherty, found the same thing happening to him with his collaborator on another Polynesian project, the great German expressionist, FW Murnau. Overruled in his bid to promote the ethnographical aspect above the film's melodramatic storyline, he left Murnau and Oscar-winning cameraman Floyd Crosby to tell the tale of forbidden love and tyrannical superstition, which they did with lyrical integrity. DP DVD BL

Reri [Anna Chevalier] *The girl* · Matahi *The boy* · Robert J Flaherty [Robert Flaherty] *Narrator* ■ *Dir* FW Murnau · *Scr* from the story *Turia* by FW Murnau, Robert J Flaherty [Robert Flaherty]

Tabu ★★★★ 15
Drama 2012 · Por/Ger/Bra/Fr · BW · 113min

This beguiling Portuguese film is an oddly simpatico companion piece to 2012 Oscar

winner *The Artist* and pays homage to the less populist, more atmospheric films of the same silent era. Moving between the present day and the past, it sees Pilar (Teresa Madruça) doing some detective work about her flaky, elderly, gambling-addicted neighbour Aurora (Laura Soveral). What initially appears to be a social drama about the aged and infirm transforms into a very beautiful meditation on memory that never strays into sentiment. DW
Portuguese +subtitles. *DVD* *Blu-ray*

Teresa Madruga *Pilar* • Laura Soveral *Old Aurora* • Ana Moreira *Young Aurora* • Henrique Espirito Santo *Old Ventura* ■ *Dir* Miguel Gomes • *Scr* Miguel Gomes, Mariana Ricardo

Tactical Assault ★★ 15
Action thriller   1998 · US · Colour · 86min

Rutger Hauer stars in this implausible revenge adventure. We learn through flashbacks that Rutger's USAF ace went a little battle crazy during the Gulf War and was only prevented from shooting down an Iraqi passenger jet by the quick thinking of fellow fighter pilot Robert Patrick. Hauer believes Patrick is out to sabotage his career and seeks revenge in the skies over Bosnia. The conflicts may be contemporary, but the flyboy action is dated. DP

Rutger Hauer *Captain John "Doc" Holiday* • Robert Patrick *Colonel Lee Banning* • Isabel Glasser *Jennifer Banning* • Ken Howard *General Horace White* • Dey Young *Doctor Baxter* ■ *Dir* Mark Griffiths • *Scr* David Golden

Tadpole ★★★ 15
Comedy   2002 · US · Colour · 75min

This wry comedy is a variant on the theme of inter-generational lust; a low-budget, digital-video rendering of the obsession felt by 15-year-old Aaron Stanford for his 40-something stepmother (Sigourney Weaver) and the fallout from his unexpected liaison with her best friend (Bebe Neuwirth). The film's brevity means that the one-liners come thick and fast, but that very economy gives the movie an offhand attitude, despite the uniformly strong performances. Character and situation seem skimped on and the Voltaire-quoting Stanford is far too self-confident for the audience to feel any sympathy for him. TH *DVD*

Sigourney Weaver *Eve Grubman* • Aaron Stanford *Oscar Grubman* • John Ritter *Stanley Grubman* • Bebe Neuwirth *Diane* • Robert Iler *Charlie* • Adam LeFevre *Phil* • Peter Appel *Jimmy* • Ron Rifkin *Professor Tisch* ■ *Dir* Gary Winick • *Scr* Heather McGowan, Niels Mueller

Taffin ★★ 18
Action thriller   1988 · US/UK · Colour · 92min

In this dull thriller, Pierce Brosnan stars as a tough-guy debt collector confronting unscrupulous developers who want to build a chemical plant in a quiet Irish town. Brosnan's watchable, but displays little of the charisma that he'd bring years later to Bond. A rock-solid support cast includes Patrick Bergin, Alison Doody and Ray McAnally. DA

Pierce Brosnan *Mark Taffin* • Ray McAnally *O'Rourke* • Alison Doody *Charlotte* • Jeremy Child *Martin* • Dearbhla Molloy *Mrs Martin* • Jim Bartley *Conway* • Patrick Bergin *Mo Taffin* ■ *Dir* Francis Megahy • *Scr* David Ambrose, from a novel by Lyndon Mallett

Taggart ★★
Western   1964 · US · Colour · 84min

Here, Dan Duryea holds sway as the hired gunslinger out to kill Tony Young for his part in a land feud, but Dick Foran as a miner and Elsa Cardenas as his opportunistic wife also show well. Undaunted by the amount of incident he has to pack into a modest running time, director RG Springsteen takes the action at a steady clip, and still finds time to flesh out his lowlife characters. DP

Tony Young *Kent Taggart* • Dan Duryea *Jason* • Dick Foran *Stark* • Elsa Cardenas *Consuela Stark* • Jean Hale *Miriam Stark* • David Carradine *Cal Dodge* ■ *Dir* RG Springsteen • *Scr* Robert Creighton Williams [Bob Williams], from the novel by Louis L'Amour

Tai-Pan ★★ 18
Period adventure drama
1986 · US · Colour · 121min

Bryan Brown plays a 19th-century European trader who establishes his headquarters in Hong Kong, despite opposition from and frequent attacks by rivals, in this inept and lengthy adaptation of James Clavell's bestseller. Brown is the hero we're supposed to like but don't, while Joan Chen adds a touch of Oriental elegance to the sprawling plot over which director Daryl Duke seems to have no control. TH
Violence, nudity. *DVD*

Bryan Brown *Dirk Struan/Tai-Pan* • John Stanton *Tyler Brock* • Joan Chen *May-May* • Tim Guinee *Culum* • Bill Leadbitter *Gorth* • Russell Wong *Gordon* • Kyra Sedgwick *Tess* ■ *Dir* Daryl Duke • *Scr* John Briley, Stanley Mann, from the novel by James Clavell

The Tailor of Panama ★★★ 15
Spy drama   2000 · US/Ire · Colour · 105min

Although this movie is about a spy and stars Pierce Brosnan, don't expect Bond-style heroics from our man abroad. In fact, Brosnan's character is a rotter of a Secret Service agent, sent to Panama after one too many misadventures. Once there, he causes more problems by enlisting the information services of expatriate tailor Geoffrey Rush. Based on the John le Carré bestseller, this is one of those movies that you'll either love or detest with a vengeance, as Pierce looks handsome but devious, Rush bumbles and Jamie Lee Curtis is given little to do. JB Swearing, sex scenes. *DVD*

Pierce Brosnan *Andrew Osnard* • Geoffrey Rush *Harry Pendel* • Jamie Lee Curtis *Louisa Pendel* • Brendan Gleeson *Mickie Abraxas* • Catherine McCormack *Francesca* • Leonor Varela *Marta* • Martin Ferrero *Teddy* • Harold Pinter *Uncle Benny* ■ *Dir* John Boorman • *Scr* Andrew Davies, John le Carré, John Boorman, from the novel by le Carré

Taipei Story ★★★★
Romantic drama   1984 · Tai · Colour · 110min

Edward Yang confirmed his place in the vanguard of New Taiwanese Cinema with this episodic insight into the consumerist erosion of traditional values and the role of women in an increasingly emasculated patriarchal society. Cai Qin gradually comes to realise that she's being exploited by her reckless father and self-centred sister and has nothing in common with her fiancé Hou Hsiao-Hsien, as he subsists on nostalgia for his days as a baseball star and his relationship with a newly returned old flame. Played against harsh neon cityscapes, this is an uncompromising study of urban alienation and wasted lives. DP
Mandarin +subtitles.

Cai Qin *Chin* • Hou Xiaoxian [Hou Hsiao-Hsien] *Lon* • Ke Suyuan *Gwan* • Wu Hinnan *Chin's father* • Lin Xiuling *Ling* • Wu Nianzhen *Kim* ■ *Dir* Edward Yang • *Scr* Edward Yang, Hou Xiaoxian, Zhu Tianwen

Take a Chance ★★ PG
Comedy   1937 · UK · BW · 71min

Following a prolific silent career, Sinclair Hill entered his penultimate year as a film director with this adaptation of a long-forgotten Walter C Hackett play. Although the shots of the Sussex Downs open out the action (about horse-racing intrigue) a little, this remains a stubbornly stagey affair, with oodles of expository dialogue and a shortage of good jokes, but performances that are better than the material deserves. DP *DVD*

Claude Hulbert *Alastair Pallivant* • Binnie Hale *Wilhelmina Ryde* • Henry Kendall *Archie Burton* • Enid Stamp-Taylor *Cicely Burton* • Gwen Farrar *Lady Meriton* ■ *Dir* Sinclair Hill • *Scr* GH Moresby-White, DB Wyndham-Lewis, from a play by Walter C Hackett [Walter Hackett]

Take a Giant Step ★★★
Drama   1959 · US · BW · 99min

A black boy (Johnny Nash), sent to a white New England school in order to give him a better chance in life, has his adolescence complicated by the racial discrimination and hostility he encounters. He finds comfort with black maid Ruby Dee and wise counsel from his grandmother Estelle Hemsley. This modest film represents an earnest attempt to confront the race issue before it was fashionable to do so. It's very well played by Nash, but lacks both incisiveness of approach and depth of feeling. RK

Johnny Nash *Spencer Scott* • Ruby Dee *Christine the maid* • Estelle Hemsley *Grandma* • Frederick O'Neal *Lem Scott* • Ellen Holly *Carol* • Pauline Meyers *Violet* ■ *Dir* Philip Leacock • *Scr* Louis S Peterson, Julius J Epstein, from a play by Peterson

Take a Girl like You ★★ 15
Comedy drama   1970 · UK · Colour · 99min

Kingsley Amis's novel about a northern girl who teaches in a London grammar school was published in 1960 and fed off the 1950s atmosphere of frugality and furtive sex. Filmed at the tail end of the 1960s, it seemed dated on release, with Hayley Mills valiantly trying to remain virginal despite the best efforts of Labour councillor and landlord John Bird and art teacher Oliver Reed, who of course is a bit of a bohemian. It's directed with an uncertain feeling by Jonathan Miller. AT

Noel Harrison *Julian Ormerod* • Oliver Reed *Patrick Standish* • Hayley Mills *Jenny Bunn* • Sheila Hancock *Martha Thompson* • John Bird *Dick Thompson* • Aimi MacDonald *Wendy* • Ronald Lacey *Graham* • Geraldine Sherman *Anna* ■ *Dir* Jonathan Miller (1) • *Scr* George Melly, from the novel by Kingsley Amis

Take a Hard Ride ★★
Western   1975 · US/It · Colour · 102min

The spaghetti western meets blaxploitation industry in this violent example of genre crossbreeding. Cowboy Jim Brown, on a mission to deliver $86,000 to his dying boss's wife, teams up with gambler Fred Williamson. Unfortunately word gets around about the money and they become the target of bounty hunter Lee Van Cleef's ruthless posse. Williamson gives a nicely laconic performance in this Canary Islands shot shoot-em-up, where deft humour rides uncomfortable side-saddle with hosts of bloody corpses. AJ

Jim Brown *Pike* • Lee Van Cleef *Kiefer* • Fred Williamson *Tyree* • Catherine Spaak *Catherine* • Jim Kelly *Kashtok* • Barry Sullivan *Sheriff Kane* • Dana Andrews *Morgan* • Harry Carey Jr *Dumper* ■ *Dir* Anthony M Dawson [Antonio Margheriti] • *Scr* Eric Bercovici, Jerry Ludwig

Take a Letter, Darling ★★★
Comedy   1942 · US · BW · 93min

Rosalind Russell replaced Claudette Colbert in this agreeable romantic comedy in which Russell portrays the sort of career woman with whom she became identified and brilliantly gets laughs from occasionally thin material. As a high-flying advertising executive, she hires Fred MacMurray as a private secretary and escort to keep wolves at bay, but what ensues is not as predictable as it may sound. Good fun, expertly played, with all the trappings – gorgeous costumes, lush settings – of Hollywood escapism. TV

Rosalind Russell *AM MacGregor* • Fred MacMurray *Tom Verney* • Macdonald Carey *Jonathan Caldwell* • Constance Moore *Ethel Caldwell* • Robert Benchley *GB Atwater* • Charles Arnt *Fud Newton* • Cecil Kellaway *Uncle George* • Kathleen Howard *Aunt Minnie* ■ *Dir* Mitchell Leisen • *Scr* Claude Binyon, from a story by George Beck

Take Care of My Cat ★★★ PG
Drama   2002 · S Kor · Colour · 111min

Exploiting Inchon's industrial landscape and the false glamour of Seoul, this thoughtful drama delves deeply into the psyche of the single girl. Jeong Jae-eun's directorial debut succeeds in both exploring the ties that bind five former schoolfriends and assessing the status of women in South Korean society. There's an occasional tendency to meander, as introverted artist Ok Ji-young becomes increasingly dependent on the unconventional Bae Doo-na, but Jeong is more interested in personality than story and, consequently, the ambitions and insecurities of this disparate group begin to exert a fascination that is both touching and intriguing. DP
Korean +subtitles.

Bae Doo-na *Tae-hee* • Lee Yo-won *Hae-joo* • Ok Ji-young *Ji-young* • Lee Eun-shil *Bi-ryu* • Lee Eun-joo *Ohn-jo* ■ *Dir/Scr* Jeong Jae-eun

Take Care of Your Scarf, Tatjana ★★★★
Comedy   1994 · Fin · BW · 65min

Set in the early 1960s, this road movie is a brilliant study of sexual and cultural unease expressed almost exclusively in pregnant pauses and meaningful gestures, as a pair of morose music-loving Finns give a couple of Russian women a lift, against a soundtrack of suitably miserable rhythm-and-blues music. Aki Kaurismäki regulars Kati Outinen and Matti Pellonpaa give what amount to masterclasses in comic understatement. Sharp and hilarious. DP
Finnish +subtitles.

Kati Outinen *Tatjana* • Matti Pellonpaa *Reino* • Kirsi Tykkylainen *Klavdia* • Mato Valtonen *Valto* • Elina Salo *Hotel manageress* • Irma Junnilained *Valto's mother* • Veikko Lavi *Vepe* • Pertti Husu *Pepe* ■ *Dir* Aki Kaurismäki • *Scr* Aki Kaurismäki, Sakke Jarvenpaa

Take Her, She's Mine ★★★
Comedy   1963 · US · Colour · 97min

James Stewart is the doting but conservative father who goes into panic mode when his teenage daughter Sandra Dee exhibits the traits of her generation by supporting ban the bomb and espousing the hippy ethos. The situation is aggravated when the girl goes to Paris to study art and gets involved with painter Philippe Forquet. This pleasing, if now dated, family comedy, takes a light-hearted approach to the political and cultural upheavals of the 1960s. RK

James Stewart *Frank Michaelson* • Sandra Dee *Mollie Michaelson* • Audrey Meadows *Anne Michaelson* • Robert Morley *Pope-Jones* • Philippe Forquet *Henri Bonnet* • John McGiver *Hector G Ivor* ■ *Dir* Henry Koster • *Scr* Nunnally Johnson, from a play by Phoebe Ephron, Henry Ephron

Take Me High ★ U
Musical comedy   1973 · UK · Colour · 86min

Cliff Richard plays a bank manager who recaptures his youth by helping a failing restaurant become the most talked-about eatery in the West Midlands. The songs are confined to the soundtrack, while the "comedy" plods along with all the zip of Spaghetti Junction at rush hour. Indigestible. DP *DVD*

Cliff Richard *Tim Matthews* • Debbie Watling *Sarah* • Hugh Griffith *Sir Harry Cunningham* • George Cole *Bert Jackson* • Anthony Andrews *Hugo Flaxman* • Richard Wattis *Sir Charles Furness* • Madeline Smith *Vicki* ■ *Dir* David Askey • *Scr* Christopher Penfold

Take Me Home: the John Denver Story ★★ PG
Biographical drama   2000 · US · Colour · 86min

Recalling the fanciful musical biopics of the studio era, this TV movie seeks out the domestic misery behind the public persona of one of the few folk singers to make an impact on the pop scene. The son of a hectoring USAF pilot, Henry John Deutchendorf only came into his own after he quit the Chad Mitchell Trio. In the 1970s, as John Denver, he scored a string of hits. Sincere this may be, but also unpersuasive. DP *DVD*

Chad Lowe *John Denver* • Kristin Davis *Annie Denver* • Gerald McRaney *Dutch* • Brian Markinson *Hal Thau* ■ *Dir* Jerry London • *Scr* Stephen Harrigan, from the autobiography by John Denver, Arthur Tobier

Take Me Home Tonight ★★15

Comedy drama 2011 · US/Ger · Colour · 97min

The John Hughes-style action in this creaky 1980s nostalgia trip kicks off for nerdy MIT graduate Topher Grace when high-school crush Teresa Palmer walks into the video store where he's working. Grace's errant best friend (Dan Fogler) and sister (Anna Faris) bring mayhem to a teetering storyline: getting fired, cocaine, car theft, idiocy and an unopened letter from Cambridge university. More 80s than the 80s, this throwback tries a little too hard to be madcap and carefree, ending up instead as a juddering wad of big hair, great songs and bad fashion. Michael Biehn shines in his tiny role as Matt's cop father but Faris is wasted as the sister who can't put on lip gloss. There's a good, snappy screwball comedy buried somewhere in the movie, but director Michael Dowse can't unearth it. KK Swearing, sex scenes, drug abuse. DVD Blu

Topher Grace *Matt Franklin* · Anna Faris *Wendy Franklin* · Dan Fogler *Barry Nathan* · Teresa Palmer *Tori Frederking* · Chris Pratt *Kyle Masterson* · Michael Biehn *Bill Franklin* · Lucy Punch *Shelly* ■ *Dir* Michael Dowse · *Scr* Jackie Filgo, Jeff Filgo, from a story by Topher Grace, Gordon Kaywin

Take Me Out to the Ball Game ★★★★U

Musical 1949 · US · Colour · 89min

This wonderful MGM musical has super songs, ravishing Technicolor and extraordinary talent both behind and in front of the camera. Star Gene Kelly and director Stanley Donen provide the original story, and take over both choreography and some directing chores from ailing veteran Busby Berkeley. The movie's enchanting, not just for Kelly's great all-stops-out Irish solo and the fabulous trio of Kelly, Frank Sinatra and the underrated Jules Munshin, but also for a delightfully no-nonsense Esther Williams as the girl who inherits a baseball team. TS

Frank Sinatra *Dennis Ryan* · Esther Williams *KC Higgins* · Gene Kelly *Eddie O'Brien* · Betty Garrett *Shirley Delwyn* · Edward Arnold *Joe Lorgan* · Jules Munshin *Nat Goldberg* · Richard Lane *Michael Gilhuly* · Tom Dugan (1) *Slappy Burke* ■ *Dir* Busby Berkeley · *Scr* Harry Tugend, George Wells, Harry Crane (uncredited), from a story by Gene Kelly, Stanley Donen

Take Me to Town ★★U

Musical comedy adventure 1953 · US · Colour · 80min

Ann Sheridan is a saloon singer with a past who takes refuge from the law in a remote lumber-jacking community where woodsman Sterling Hayden is also the local preacher. His three young sons decide that Sheridan would make them a perfect mom, but the locals are hostile. Needless to say, she wins them all over. Folksy, saccharine-coated gloop, directed by Douglas Sirk and hard to swallow. RK

Ann Sheridan *Vermilion O'Toole* · Sterling Hayden *Will Hall* · Philip Reed *Newton Cole* · Phyllis Stanley *Mrs Stoffer* · Larry Gates *Ed Daggett* · Lee Patrick *Rose* · Forrest Lewis *Ed Higgins* ■ *Dir* Douglas Sirk · *Scr* Richard Morris, from his story *Flame of the Timberline*

Take My Eyes ★★★★15

Relationship drama 2003 · Sp · Colour · 102min

This award-winning film from Iciar Bollain is a painful and unforgettable experience. Having walked out after suffering years of physical and mental humiliation, Laia Marull contemplates returning to her husband Luis Tosar when he claims to have finally controlled his violent temper. Marull's anguish is heart-rending; her portrayal of a broken spirit on the verge of repair too touching for words. Equally, Tosar's gruffly tender brute makes one understand why his wife wants their marriage to work. Bollain directs with astonishing deftness and an even-handed tone, building to a dénouement of incredible power. AJ

Spanish +subtitles. Violence, swearing. DVD

Laia Marull *Pilar* · Luis Tosar *Antonio* · Candela Peña *Ana* · Rosa Maria Sarda *Aurora* · Kiti Manver *Rosa* · Sergi Calleja *Therapist* · Elisabet Gelabert *Lola* · Nicolás Fernández Luna *Juan* ■ *Dir* Iciar Bollain · *Scr* Iciar Bollain, Alicia Luna

Take My Life ★★★★PG

Murder mystery 1947 · UK · BW · 75min

This marks the impressive directorial debut from British cinematographer Ronald Neame. Hugh Williams is accused of murder and his opera singer wife Greta Gynt is determined to find out who really did it. This was the kind of intelligent thriller that Hollywood directors could churn out in their sleep and it is to Neame's credit that he makes it clever, convincing and, above all stylish. TS

Hugh Williams *Nicholas Talbot* · Greta Gynt *Philippa Bentley* · Marius Goring *Sidney Flemming* · Francis L Sullivan *Prosecuting counsel* · Henry Edwards *Inspector Archer* · Rosalie Crutchley *Elizabeth Rusman* · Maurice Denham *Defending counsel* ■ *Dir* Ronald Neame · *Scr* Winston Graham, Valerie Taylor, Margaret Kennedy, from a story by Winston Graham, Valerie Taylor

Take Shelter ★★★15

Psychological thriller 2011 · US · Colour · 116min

It's difficult to pigeonhole *Take Shelter*. Ohio blue-collar worker Curtis LaForche (an intense Michael Shannon) gets caught in a storm that no one else sees; he is bitten by his dog in what appears to be a dream, though his arm aches all day; he is attacked in his car by people who may be zombies. Curtis believes his hallucinations are a prophecy and upsets his wife (Jessica Chastain) by taking out a loan to turn their storm shelter into an underground fortress. The film then segues from psychological horror into a study of mental illness and alienation, but all the time the question lingers – what if Curtis is right? It is to writer/director Jeff Nichols's credit that he is prepared not just to mix genres but to do so with such difficult subject matter. There are a few longueurs in the middle, but this proves that not all films need to move with the pace of a rollercoaster. BP DVD Blu

Michael Shannon *Curtis LaForche* · Jessica Chastain *Samantha* · Shea Whigham *Dewart* · Katy Mixon *Nat* · Kathy Baker *Sarah* · Ray McKinnon *Kyle* ■ *Dir/Scr* Jeff Nichols

Take the High Ground ★★

War drama 1953 · US · Colour · 101min

Screenwriter Millard Kaufman was nominated for an Oscar for this insight into the realities of basic training for the Korean War. Carleton Carpenter seems suitably intimidated as the private singled out for especial ire by sergeant Richard Widmark, but the unit is comprised of stereotypical grunts. Much more convincing is the barely suppressed sadism with which Widmark barks out his orders. DP

Richard Widmark *Sergeant Thorne Ryan* · Karl Malden *Sergeant Laverne Holt* · Elaine Stewart *Julie Mollison* · Russ Tamblyn *Paul Jamison* · Carleton Carpenter *Merton Tolliver* · Steve Forrest *Lobo Naglaski* ■ *Dir* Richard Brooks · *Scr* Millard Kaufman

Take the Lead ★★★12

Drama based on a true story 2006 · US · Colour · 112min

Antonio Banderas struts his stuff as real-life ex-ballroom champion Pierre Dulaine – the man behind the school dance programme documented in *Mad Hot Ballroom* – who provides inspiration to New York high-school detention students via waltz and salsa lessons. A vibrant package of high-energy dance routines and soft social relevance, this diverting drama from music video director Liz Friedlander makes the right moves even when it's glossing over grim issues. AJ Swearing. DVD

Antonio Banderas *Pierre Dulaine* · Rob Brown *Rock* · Yaya DaCosta *LaRhette* · Dante Basco *Ramos* · John Ortiz (1) *Mr Temple* · Laura Benanti *Tina* · Marcus T Paulk *Eddie* · Jenna Dewan *Sasha* · Alfre Woodard *Augustine James* ■ *Dir* Liz Friedlander · *Scr* Dianne Houston

Take the Money and Run ★★★PG

Comedy 1969 · US · Colour · 81min

After years of writing for TV and doing his own stand-up routine, Woody Allen finally made his debut as co-writer, director and star with this ambitious cod documentary. Nicely joshing the "Voice of Doom" style of narration and such Hollywood movies as *The Defiant Ones*, the film gets off to a flying start, with public enemy Virgil Starkwell's childhood remaining among the funniest things Allen has ever done. The inspiration slowly ebbs away though, and the last ten minutes are something of a chore. DP DVD

Woody Allen *Virgil Starkwell* · Janet Margolin *Louise* · Marcel Hillaire *Fritz* · Jacquelyn Hyde *Miss Blaire* · Lonny Chapman *Jake* · Jan Merlin *Al* · James Anderson (2) *Chain gang warden* ■ *Dir* Woody Allen · *Scr* Woody Allen, Mickey Rose

Take This Waltz ★★★15

Romantic drama 2011 · Can · Colour · 111min

Michelle Williams stars as a slightly bored married woman who enjoys a brief flirtation on a flight to Toronto, only to face temptation when the handsome stranger (Luke Kirby) turns out to be her new neighbour. Williams is excellent but the casting of comedic actors in straight roles proves a little hit and miss: Seth Rogen has a certain hangdog charm as Williams's underachieving husband, but Sarah Silverman is less than impressive as his recovering alcoholic sister. Luckily, writer/director Sarah Polley is very good at depicting the small highs and lows of modern relationships. DW Swearing, sex scenes. DVD Blu

Michelle Williams *Margot* · Seth Rogen *Lou* · Luke Kirby *Daniel* · Sarah Silverman *Geraldine* · Jennifer Podemski *Karen* · Diane D'Aquila *Harriet* ■ *Dir/Scr* Sarah Polley

Taken ★★★★18

Action drama 2007 · Fr · Colour · 93min

Liam Neeson turns middle-aged action hero in this gritty thriller from French director Pierre Morel. Neeson plays an ex-serviceman who runs, kicks, shoots and punches a bloody swathe through Paris to find the men who've kidnapped his daughter (Maggie Grace). It soon becomes apparent that she's the victim of a major sex-trafficking operation, but any attempt to engage with this serious issue is drowned out by the crash, bang, wallop of bad guys (invariably swarthy immigrants) being dispensed with. Morel does counter the ludicrous Rambo-style moments with a bristling, raw energy to his camerawork. The physical punishment Neeson inflicts is almost palpable, but to his credit it's never at the expense of conveying his own sense of pain. SP English, French, Albanian, Arabic +subtitles. Violence, swearing, sex scenes, drug references. DVD Blu

Liam Neeson *Bryan Mills* · Maggie Grace *Kim* · Famke Janssen *Lenore* · Holly Valance *Diva* · Xander Berkeley *Stuart* ■ *Dir* Pierre Morel · *Scr* Luc Besson, Robert Mark Kamen · *Cinematographer* Michel Abramowicz

Taken 2 ★★★15

Action drama 2012 · Fr · Colour · 88min

The first *Taken* movie established Liam Neeson as a bona fide action star in his mid-50s, and made a sequel inevitable. Plotwise, this is pretty much the same as the first film, the twist here being that it's Neeson's retired CIA agent who gets kidnapped along with his ex-wife (Famke Janssen), leaving it to daughter Maggie Grace to help free them. It's certainly a dafter proposition than the original, with some unintentionally funny moments along the way. Equally, though, Olivier Megaton's film is often aware of its own stupidity, and doesn't take itself too seriously. A third instalment is due in early 2015. DA In English, Albanian, Turkish. Violence, some swearing. DVD Blu

Liam Neeson *Bryan Mills* · Maggie Grace *Kim* · Famke Janssen *Lenore* · Rade Serbedzija *Murad Krasniqi* · Leland Orser *Sam* · DB Sweeney *Bernie* ■ *Dir* Olivier Megaton · *Scr* Luc Besson, Robert Mark Kamen, from their characters

Taken 3 ★★12

Action drama 2014 · Fr/US · Colour · 104min

Liam Neeson draws upon his "particular set of skills" for a third time, tearing through the streets of LA to find the people who have framed him for murder. Neeson's "skills" become increasingly improbable, while the obvious plot twists and Sam Spruell's cartoonish Russian villain seem too outlandish even by the franchise's none-too-subtle standards. Not original enough to be truly excite, *Taken 3* may satisfy action fans but it's unlikely anybody will be begging for part four. JL English, Russian +subtitles. Violence, swearing. DVD Blu

Liam Neeson *Bryan Mills* · Forest Whitaker *Franck Dotzler* · Famke Janssen *Lenore St John* · Maggie Grace *Kim* · Dougray Scott *Stuart St John* · Sam Spruell *Oleg Malankov* · Leland Orser *Sam* · Jonny Weston *Jimy* ■ *Dir* Olivier Megaton · *Scr* Luc Besson, Robert Mark Kamen, from their characters

Taken Away ★★12

Drama based on a true story 1996 · US · Colour · 85min

Since making their names in *LA Law*, real-life married couple Michael Tucker and Jill Eikenberry have regularly teamed up in TV movies. Here, Eikenberry plays a kidnap victim with a heart condition who has been left bound and gagged in her car; Tucker is her frantic husband who's desperately trying to locate her. The two leads turn in believable performances and, although it hardly taxes the brain, this is an intriguing enough time-passer. JF Some swearing. DVD

Michael Tucker *Mark Hale* · Jill Eikenberry *Jan Hale* · James Marsden *Michael Galler* · Shane Meier *David Rattray* · Robert Wisden *Chief Ben Alpert* ■ *Dir* Jerry Jameson · *Scr* Ronald Parker

Taken in Broad Daylight ★★

Crime thriller based on a true story 2009 · Can · Colour · 89min

The 2001 kidnap of American teen Anne Sluti is re-enacted in this lacklustre crime thriller. As abductor and victim, James Van Der Beek and Sara Canning deliver unconvincing movie clichés – and, with such lazy characterisation, the events of the six-day ordeal have little tension or emotional impact. The plodding police procedural element of the film compounds this flat atmosphere, leaving it to the foreboding soundtrack to generate interest and unease. SF Some violence.

Sara Canning *Anne Sluti* · James Van Der Beek *Tony Zappa* · LeVar Burton *Mike Timbrook* · Diana Reis *Elaine Sluti* ■ *Dir* Gary B Yates [Gary Yates (1)] · *Scr* Charlene Blaine [Charlene Blaine-Schulenberg], Kim Delgado, from their story

Takers ★★★12

Action crime drama 2010 · US · Colour · 102min

This smart take on the classic cop v robbers formula stars Idris Elba and Paul Walker as the leaders of a veritable Rat Pack of robbers, while Matt Dillon plays the detective obsessed with finding them. When the gang are tempted into pulling one more job by a former associate, the scene is set for a showdown. There's an easy chemistry about Elba and co, which is only undermined by Tip "TI" Harris's terrible gangsta performance as the interloper in the outfit. Still, *Takers* compensates with its edge-of-the-seat thrills and rollicking action. KK Violence, some swearing. DVD Blu

Matt Dillon *Jack Welles* · Paul Walker *John Rahway* · Idris Elba *Gordon Jennings* · Hayden Christensen *AJ* · Jay Hernandez *Eddie Hatcher* · Tip "TI" Harris [Tip Harris] *Ghost* · Zoë Saldana *Lilli* · Marianne Jean-Baptiste *Naomi* ■ *Dir* John Luessenhop · *Scr* Peter Allen, Gabriel Casseus, John Luessenhop, Avery Duff

Taking a Chance on Love
★★

Romantic drama   2009 · Can · Colour · 103min

The lasting perils of letting caution impede true love are hammered home in actor-turned-director Douglas Barr's sequel to his 2007 TV melodrama The Note. Genie Francis returns as newspaper agony aunt Peyton McGruder, this time gaining a new perspective on life when a reader contacts her disagreeing with her latest column. Events go into saccharine overdrive as flashbacks to the woman's past explain her impassioned reasoning, while adding depth and interest to an otherwise slight feature. SF

Genie Francis Peyton MacGruder • Kate Trotter Eve Miller (older) • Katie Boland Christine • Joanna Douglas Eve Miller ■ Dir/Scr Douglas Barr (2)

Taking Care of Business
★★ 15

Comedy   1990 · US · Colour · 107min

This is a rather slight Trading Places rip-off with James Belushi as the prisoner on the run who finds wealthy Charles Grodin's Filofax and proceeds to steal his identity. The talented Belushi doesn't have enough good material here, while the usually excellent Grodin forfeits some of his substantial charm to the demands of the over-frenetic comedy. This is too uneven to be riproaring entertainment, but it's still harmless fun. Also known as Filofax in the UK. JB Swearing. DVD

James Belushi Jimmy Dworski • Charles Grodin Spencer Barnes • Anne De Salvo Debbie • Loryn Locklin Jewel • Stephen Elliott (1) Walter Bentley • Hector Elizondo Warden • Veronica Hamel Elizabeth Barnes ■ Dir Arthur Hiller • Scr Jill Mazursky, Jeffrey Abrams

Taking Liberties
★★★ 12

Documentary   2007 · UK · Colour · 101min

Much has been made of Tony Blair's legacy and, to many eyes, this uncompromising documentary will stand as a pretty damning summation. During Blair's decade in office, his government passed more laws than any of its predecessors and categorised over 3,000 actions as criminal offences. Touching on everything from protests in Parliament Square and the NatWest Three to Guantanamo Bay and the CIA's supposed access to Prestwick fuel supplies, this is combative stuff – even when David Morrissey and Ashley Jensen's narration occasionally adopts a misjudged comic tone). DP DVD

Ashley Jensen Narrator • Tony Benn • Ken Clarke • Andrew Gilligan • Boris Johnson • Clare Short ■ Dir Chris Atkins • Animator Simon Robson • Editor Nick Fenton

Taking Lives
★★ 15

Psychological thriller   2004 · US/Aus · Colour · 98min

Director DJ Caruso stumbles his way through the conventions of the psychological thriller in this dreary, by-the-numbers serial-killer film. Angelina Jolie plays a top FBI profiler, called in to help Canadian homicide detectives Jean-Hugues Anglade and Olivier Martinez catch a chameleon-like murderer who assumes his victims' identities. Ethan Hawke looks uncomfortable throughout, while the appearance of Kiefer Sutherland is lazy typecasting. SF Swearing, violence, sex scenes. DVD

Angelina Jolie Special Agent Illeana Scott • Ethan Hawke James Costa • Kiefer Sutherland Hart • Olivier Martinez Paquette • Tcheky Karyo Leclair • Jean-Hugues Anglade Duval • Gena Rowlands Mrs Asher • Paul Dano Young Asher ■ Dir DJ Caruso • Scr Jon Bokenkamp, from a story by Jon Bokenkamp, from the novel by Michael Pye

The Taking of Pelham One Two Three
★★★★ 15

Thriller   1974 · US · Colour · 102min

Gerald Greenberg and Robert Q Lovett are the "stars" of this tough and compelling thriller about the hijacking of a New York subway train. As the film's editors, their superb sense of rhythm and pace brings real tension to the radio exchanges between villain Robert Shaw and transport cop Walter Matthau, who tries to prevent Shaw and his gang from killing hostages while waiting for the payment of a $1 million ransom. The motley collection of clichéd passengers doesn't deserve to be rescued, but director Joseph Sargent keeps the focus firmly on his leads. Shaw is admirably fanatical, and the world-weary, wisecracking Matthau is magnificent. DP Violence, swearing. DVD BL

Walter Matthau Lieutenant Garber • Robert Shaw Blue • Martin Balsam Green • Hector Elizondo Grey • Earl Hindman Brown • James Broderick Denny Doyle • Dick O'Neill Correll • Lee Wallace Mayor • Jerry Stiller Lieutenant Rico Patrone ■ Dir Joseph Sargent • Scr Peter Stone, from the novel by John Godey

The Taking of Pelham 123
★★ 15

Crime thriller   2009 · US/UK · Colour · 101min

The pointless transformation of the title of this remake of the 1974 New York subway hijacking classic (123, instead of One Two Three) is the first clue that it has little original to add. A slightly ragged Denzel Washington fails to capture the weary sang-froid of the late Walter Matthau in the role of the subway train controller tensely negotiating with a crazed hijacker, here played by John Travolta in full scenery-chewing mode. Director Tony Scott adds his trademark visual pyrotechnics but little else. Worse, Brian Helgeland's screenplay strips the mordant wit of the original – in which the hostages were, if anything, even more unlikeable than the hostage-takers. A hijacking movie that's been hijacked, then. AS Violence, swearing. DVD BL

Denzel Washington Walter Garber • John Travolta "Ryder" • Luis Guzman Phil Ramos • Victor Gojcaj Bashkin • Gbenga Akinnagbe Wallace • John Turturro Lieutenant Camonetti • James Gandolfini Major • Ramon Rodriguez Delgado ■ Dir Tony Scott • Scr Brian Helgeland, from the novel by John Godey

Taking Off
★★★★ 18

Comedy drama   1971 · US · Colour · 88min

Director Milos Forman's (Amadeus, One Flew over the Cuckoo's Nest) first American movie is a comedy of manners. Like the Czech quasi-comedies that brought him international acclaim, it's charming, sexy, bittersweet, and, in truth, a trifle plotless, but, like them it contains gems of observation and a wondrous understanding of human nature. This deals with a dropout teenager's effect on her parents, with Buck Henry (who co-wrote The Graduate) playing the runaway's father, getting out of his depth in the permissive world. TS BL

Lynn Carlin Lynn Tyne • Buck Henry Larry Tyne • Linnea Heacock Jeannie Tyne • Georgia Engel Margot • Tony Harvey Tony • Audra Lindley Ann Lockston • Paul Benedict Ben Lockston • Ike Turner • Tina Turner • Carly Simon Audition singer ■ Dir Milos Forman • Scr Milos Forman, John Guare, Jean-Claude Carrière, John Klein

Taking Sides
★★★ 15

Second World War biographical drama   2001 · Ger/Fr/UK/Austria · Colour · 105min

Hungarian director István Szabó returns to Central Europe in the mid-20th century for this intelligent adaptation of Ronald Harwood's stage play. However, a resounding denunciation of America's current posturing as the world's policeman is also apparent in the way a defiantly uncultured war-crimes investigator (Harvey Keitel) attempts to impose his perceived moral superiority on an orchestra conductor accused of glorifying the Nazis. Keitel's blustering performance exaggerates the significance of this theme, whereas Stellan Skarsgård's nuanced depiction of Wilhelm Furtwängler explores the link between art and power. DP Swearing. DVD

Harvey Keitel Maj Steve Arnold • Stellan Skarsgård Dr Wilhelm Furtwängler • Moritz Bleibtreu Lt David Wills • Birgit Minichmayr Emmi Straube • Oleg Tabakov Col Dymshitz • Ulrich Tukur Helmuth Rode • Hanns Zischler Rudolf Werner • Armin Rohde Schlee • R Lee Ermey Gen Wallace ■ Dir István Szabó • Scr Ronald Harwood, from his play

Taking Woodstock
★★★ 15

Comedy based on a true story   2009 · US · Colour · 115min

The latest slice of American history from director Ang Lee (The Ice Storm, Brokeback Mountain) is his gentlest and frothiest movie yet. It's based on the memoir of Elliot Tiber, a young gay Jewish man who in 1969 became a key player in the staging of the Woodstock rock festival in Bethel, New York, where his immigrant family's dilapidated motel became centre of operations. The festival itself takes a back seat, with the music mostly heard from a distance, as the film focuses on the cultural collisions taking place on the sidelines. Deadpan comedian Demitri Martin plays Elliot as an innocent abroad – he's wide-eyed and stoic as the hippies descend in their thousands upon the neighbouring dairy farm of laid-back Max Yasgur (Eugene Levy). AC Swearing, nudity, drug abuse. DVD BL

Demetri Martin Elliot Teichberg • Dan Fogler Devon • Henry Goodman Jake Teichberg • Jonathan Groff Michael Lang • Eugene Levy Max Yasgur • Jeffrey Dean Morgan Dan • Imelda Staunton Sonia Teichberg • Emile Hirsch Billy • Liev Schreiber Vilma ■ Dir Ang Lee • Scr James Schamus, from the non-fiction book Taking Woodstock: A True Story of a Riot, a Concert and a Life by Elliot Tiber, Tom Monte

Tale of a Vampire
★★ 18

Horror   1992 · UK/Jpn · Colour · 92min

Melancholic bloodsucker Julian Sands prowls suburban London searching for the double of his lost lover, in this arty postmodern Hammer homage. When Sands eventually finds her in the guise of librarian Suzanna Hamilton (giving a dreadful performance) he must battle occult historian Kenneth Cranham for her spirit. Depressingly ordinary, despite a few oriental flourishes, this Mills and Boon vampire romance is far too low-key. AJ DVD

Julian Sands Alex • Suzanna Hamilton Anne/Virginia • Kenneth Cranham Edgar • Marian Diamond Denise • Michael Kenton Magazine man • Catherine Blake Virginia, aged 5 ■ Dir Shimako Sato • Scr Shimako Sato, Jane Corbett, from a story by Sato, from the poem Annabel Lee by Edgar Allan Poe

The Tale of Despereaux
★★ U

Animated comedy adventure   2008 · US/UK · Colour · 89min

A little mouse with big ears saves a mythical kingdom in this animated tale, but the story feels more like a background event than a plot. Matthew Broderick voices Despereaux, the tiny tyke who refuses to cower in corners as taught in mouse school and, instead, sets forth to save Princess Pea (voiced by Harry Potter's Emma Watson), make it rain and restore the flow of soup to the castle kitchen. It's a messy hotchpotch of fairy-tale incidents, and Broderick's deep tones make Despereaux feel a little too grown-up. SP DVD BL

Matthew Broderick Despereaux • Emma Watson Princess Pea • Sigourney Weaver The narrator • Dustin Hoffman Roscuro • Kevin Kline Andre • Tracey Ullman Miggery Sow ■ Dir Sam Fell, Robert Stevenhagen • Scr Will McRobb, Gary Ross, Chris Viscardi, from the novel by Kate DiCamillo

A Tale of Springtime
★★★★ U

Romantic drama   1989 · Fr · Colour · 102min

Eric Rohmer's film shows keen intelligence, insight into the emotions of youth and an unrivalled genius for chamber drama. As ever in Rohmer's features, we feel we are eavesdropping on real people, with their behaviour, conversation and sheer unpredictability the very stuff of human nature. Deftly handled and effortlessly played, particularly by Anne Teyssèdre and Hugues Quester, this tale of matchmaking and friendship is beguiling. DP French +subtitles. DVD

Anne Teyssèdre Jeanne • Hugues Quester Igor • Florence Darel Natasha • Eloise Bennett Eve • Sophie Robin Gaelle ■ Dir/Scr Eric Rohmer

Tale of Tales
★★★★ 15

Period romantic fantasy   2015 · It/Fr/UK · Colour · 133min

Matteo Garrone (Gomorrah) gives us the scrumptiously deranged, gorgeously ornate Tale of Tales, a welcome return to the grimmer reaches of the fairy tale as it bucks the trend toward redemptive origin stories. Inspired by the work of Italian author Giambattista Basile, this European co-production comprises a trio of briefly intersecting stories taking place in three adjacent kingdoms. The pace of this baroque beauty can be indulgently languorous, and the runtime is a shade stretched out. But it's worth your immersion: the cast (Salma Hayek, Toby Jones, Vincent Cassel) is divine, the cinematography, costuming and production design are to die for, and smatterings of absurdity and black humour never compromise what is primarily a satisfyingly sincere treatment of the material. EAS Violence, sex scenes, nudity.

Salma Hayek Queen of Longtrellis • John C Reilly King of Longtrellis • Toby Jones King of Highhills • Bebe Cave Violet • Vincent Cassel King of Strongcliff • Shirley Henderson Imma ■ Dir Matteo Garrone • Scr Edoardo Albinati, Ugo Chiti, Matteo Garrone, Massimo Gaudioso, from the fairy tales Lo cunto de li cunti overo lo trattenemiento de peccerille by Giambattista Basile • Music Alexandre Desplat

The Tale of the Fox
★★★★

Satirical fantasy   1931 · Fr · BW · 65min

Ladislaw Starewicz's only feature contains 100 different puppet characters and took a decade to prepare and 18 months to film. The story of the mischievous fox who is called to the court of the Lion King to explain his pranks works well as a children's film, thanks to the superbly judged blend of animal and human traits and the painstaking attention to natural detail. But it's also a subtle political satire that simmers with a deliciously naughty sexual tension. DP In French.

■ Dir Ladislaw Starewicz, Irène Starewicz • Scr Wladyslaw Starewicz, Irène Starewicz, Roger Richebé, Jean Nohain, Antoinette Nordmann, from the story Die Reineke Fuchs by Johann Wolfgang von Goethe • Animators Ladislaw Starewicz, Irene Starewicz

The Tale of the Princess Kaguya
★★★ U

Animated fantasy drama   2013 · Jpn · Colour · 131min

Inspired by a folk tale about a magical princess found in a bamboo shoot, this Japanese film controversially made the shortlist for best animated feature at the Oscars when The Lego Movie didn't. The delicate, handcrafted work certainly showcases the exemplary draughtsmanship of its director Isao Takahata (Grave of the Fireflies). Nevertheless, although some sequences are exquisitely rendered, it is also overlong and the narrative may alienate viewers expecting neat dramatic arcs and comforting conclusions. LF Japanese dubbed. DVD BL

Chloë Grace Moretz Princess Kaguya • Darren Criss Sutemaru • James Caan Okina, the bamboo cutter • Mary Steenburgen Ona, the bamboo cutter's wife/Narrator • Lucy Liu Lady Sagami • George Segal Inbe no Akita ■ Dir Isao Takahata • Scr Isao Takahata, Riko Sakaguchi, Mike Jones (2), from a story by Isao Takahata

A Tale of Two Cities
★★★★★ U

Period drama   1935 · US · BW · 120min

Ronald Colman is convincingly noble as lawyer Sydney Carton, a victim of unrequited love, who finds purpose in an act of self-sacrifice during the ruthless period of the French Revolution. The other actors – Elizabeth Allan, Basil Rathbone and Edna May Oliver – are at the mercy of some massive crowd scenes, for which thousands of extras were recruited. The featured players survive very well through a magnificent storming of a rather flimsy Bastille, while the cut-off point of the final scene with Madame la Guillotine and Sydney Carton will bring tears to your eyes. It is a far, far better movie of the classic than they were to make thereafter with Dirk Bogarde. TH

Ronald Colman *Sydney Carton* • Elizabeth Allan *Lucie Manette* • Edna May Oliver *Miss Pross* • Blanche Yurka *Mme Defarge* • Reginald Owen *Stryver* • Basil Rathbone *Marquis St Evremonde* • Henry B Walthall *Dr Manette* • Donald Woods *Charles Darnay* ■ *Dir* Jack Conway • *Scr* WP Lipscomb, SN Behrman, from the novel by Charles Dickens

A Tale of Two Cities ★★★ U
Period drama 1957 · UK · BW · 112min

Dirk Bogarde gives a good account of himself in this Rank remake of Dickens's French Revolution novel. TEB Clarke, who scripted many of the best Ealing comedies, was perhaps an odd choice for such a prestigious project and, in striving for dramatic weight, he is occasionally guilty of being both pompous and ponderous. But director Ralph Thomas brings the best out of his cast, with Dorothy Tutin making a fetching Lucie Manette and Christopher Lee a truly hissable Marquis St Evremonde. DP 𝔇𝔳𝔡

Dirk Bogarde *Sydney Carton* • Dorothy Tutin *Lucie Manette* • Cecil Parker *Jarvis Lorry* • Stephen Murray *Dr Manette* • Athene Seyler *Miss Pross* • Christopher Lee *Marquis St Evremonde* • Donald Pleasence *John Barsad* • Rosalie Crutchley *Madame Defarge* ■ *Dir* Ralph Thomas • *Scr* TEB Clarke, from the novel by Charles Dickens

A Tale of Two Sisters ★★★ 15
Horror 2003 · S Kor · Colour · 109min

South Korean film-maker Kim Ji-woon's atmospheric gothic horror may not be the most original tale, but with its sumptuous, colour-saturated visuals, it's certainly among the most beautiful. The feature is an eerie account of two sisters (Moon Geun-young and Im Soo-jung), who return home after a long psychiatric illness, only to grow increasingly fearful of their strange new stepmother. Yet for all its derivative elements, the meticulous direction and cinematography lend the picture a sense of freshness. SF Korean +subtitles. 𝔇𝔳𝔡

Kim Kab-su *Mu-hyun* • Yeom Jeong-ah *Eun-joo* • Im Soo-jung *Su-mi* • Moon Geun-young *Su-yeon* ■ *Dir* Kim Ji-woon • *Scr* Kim Ji-woon, Lee Byung-woo

A Tale of Two Thieves ★★★★ 15
Documentary drama 2014 · UK · Colour · 69min

Five decades after the most famous heist in British criminal history, 84-year-old Gordon Goody breaks his silence to provide an inside account of the 1963 Great Train Robbery, which saw £2.6 million robbed from the Glasgow to London mail train. Goody is keen to put things straight before he dies and so he reveals who struck train driver Jack Mills and, in the film's most memorable moment, also identifies the postal worker (and inside man) nicknamed "The Ulsterman". Director Chris Long avoids sensationalism and romanticism, but the lingering fascination here lies in Goody's analysis of celebrity cohorts Buster Edwards and Ronnie Biggs. DP Swearing. 𝔇𝔳𝔡

■ *Dir* Chris Long • *Scr* Erin Donovan

Talent for the Game ★★★ PG
Sports drama 1991 · US · Colour · 87min

A modest but watchable entry in the baseball genre, this stars Edward James Olmos as a baseball scout who discovers a brilliant young pitcher in an Idaho backwater, but watches in dismay as he is ruthlessly exploited by his club. Olmos delivers a typically gutsy performance and, although the story is slight, director Robert

M Young handles the proceedings commendably. JF Some swearing. 𝔇𝔳𝔡

Edward James Olmos *Virgil Sweet* • Lorraine Bracco *Bobbie Henderson* • Jamey Sheridan *Tim Weaver* • Terry Kinney *Gil Lawrence* • Jeff Corbett *Sammy Bodeen* • Tom Bower *Reverend Bodeen* • Janet Carroll *Rachel Bodeen* ■ *Dir* Robert M Young • *Scr* David Himmelstein, Tom Donnelly [Thomas Michael Donnelly], Larry Ferguson

The Talented Mr Ripley ★★★★ 15
Crime thriller 1999 · US · Colour · 142min

Director Anthony Minghella follows his award-winning *The English Patient* with this absorbing thriller, based on the novel by Patricia Highsmith. Matt Damon plays the eponymous Ripley, a young opportunist who seeks out Jude Law (Oscar-nominated), an American playboy living it up in Europe. Ripley becomes friends with Law, but gradually comes to covet the carefree lifestyle he shares with his glamorous girlfriend (Gwyneth Paltrow). Minghella's classy direction and the superior cast make this never less than compelling. LH Swearing. 𝔇𝔳𝔡 ʙʟᵘ

Matt Damon *Tom Ripley* • Gwyneth Paltrow *Marge Sherwood* • Jude Law *Dickie Greenleaf* • Cate Blanchett *Meredith Logue* • Philip Seymour Hoffman *Freddie Miles* • Jack Davenport *Peter Smith-Kingsley* • James Rebhorn *Herbert Greenleaf* • Philip Baker Hall *Alvin MacCarron* ■ *Dir* Anthony Minghella • *Scr* Anthony Minghella, from the novel by Patricia Highsmith

Tales from Earthsea ★★★ PG
Animated fantasy adventure 2006 · Jpn · Colour · 111min

Japanese animation house Studio Ghibli has developed a reputation for producing top-class fantasy animation with films like *Spirited Away/* and *Howl's Moving Castle*. Adapted from Ursula K Le Guin's celebrated *Earthsea* series, this lacks the technical sheen and warm sentimentality of some of Ghibli's other films. Taking over the reins from his father Hayao, debut director Goro Miyazaki delivers an over-complicated, slightly dour tale of dragons, wizards and teenage rebellion, as prince Arren (voiced by Matt Levin) battles evil villain Cob to save the land of Earthsea from environmental disaster. Willem Dafoe gives a sterling turn as the androgynous, blue-haired Cob – the film's most memorable creation. But gaping plot-holes, lengthy exposition and muted, joyless visuals won't endear this to younger audiences. JR Japanese dubbed. 𝔇𝔳𝔡

Timothy Dalton *Sparrowhawk* • Willem Dafoe *Cob* • Matt Levin [Matthew Levin] *Arren* • Cheech Marin [Richard "Cheech" Marin] *Hare* • Mariska Hargitay *Tenar* • Blaire Restaneo *Therru* ■ *Dir* Goro Miyazaki • *Scr* Goro Miyazaki, Keiko Niwa, with Jim Hubbert, Bob Buchholz and others (English version) from the *Earthsea* series of books by Ursula K Le Guin, and the comic book *Shuna's Journey* by Hayao Miyazaki

Tales from the Crypt ★★★★ 18
Portmanteau horror 1972 · UK · Colour · 91min

This excellent anthology of scares-with-a-smile stories drawn from EC horror comics has Ralph Richardson as the crypt keeper revealing a quintet of fearsome futures to a veteran British cast of terror troupers. Peter Cushing returns from the grave, Patrick Magee is a victimised blind man, Joan Collins battles a deranged Santa Claus, Richard Greene does a variation on *The Monkey's Paw* and Ian Hendry can't get used to being dead. Ace direction by genre favourite Freddie Francis adeptly leavens the horror with serio-comic interludes. AJ

Ralph Richardson *Crypt keeper* • Geoffrey Bayldon *Guide* • Joan Collins *Joanne Clayton* • Ian Hendry *Carl Maitland* • Nigel Patrick *William Rogers* • Patrick Magee *George Carter* • Peter Cushing *Grimsdyke* • Richard Greene *Ralph Jason* • Roy Dotrice *Charles Gregory* ■ *Dir* Freddie Francis • *Scr* Milton Subotsky, from stories from the comic books *Tales from the Crypt* and *The Vault of Horror* by Al Feldstein, Johnny Craig, William Gaines

Tales from the Crypt: Demon Knight ★★ 18
Horror fantasy 1995 · US · Colour · 92min

Not an anthology in the fondly remembered tradition of the original *Tales from the Crypt*, just one duff story ripped off from *Night of the Living Dead*. Billy Zane is the evil force who hounds an assortment of misfits trapped in a Texas motel in his search for an ancient talisman containing the blood of Jesus Christ. Crude sight gags and slimy schlock are accented over mordant humour. AJ Swearing, violence.

Billy Zane *The Collector* • William Sadler *Brayker* • Jada Pinkett [Jada Pinkett Smith] *Jeryline* • Brenda Bakke *Cordelia* • CCH Pounder *Irene* • Dick Miller *Uncle Willy* ■ *Dir* Ernest R Dickerson • *Scr* Ethan Reiff, Cyrus Voris, Mark Bishop

Tales from the Darkside: the Movie ★★★ 18
Portmanteau horror 1991 · US · Colour · 89min

A 3,000-year-old mummy, a malignant moggy and a gruesome gargoyle take their monstrous turns in a taut, tight and fun trio of terror tales drawn from the work of authors Sir Arthur Conan Doyle and Stephen King. High on creepy atmosphere, low on boring exposition, this well-crafted movie version of its duff namesake TV series is an agreeably ambitious and solidly shocking outing. AJ Violence, swearing. 𝔇𝔳𝔡

Deborah Harry *Betty* • David Forrester *Priest* • Matthew Lawrence *Timmy* • Christian Slater *Andy* • Steve Buscemi *Edward Bellingham* • Julianne Moore *Susan* • Michael Deak *Mummy* • David Johansen *Halston* • William Hickey *Drogan* • James Remar *Preston* • Rae Dawn Chong *Carola* ■ *Dir* John Harrison • *Scr* Michael McDowell, George Romero, from the story *Lot 249* by Sir Arthur Conan Doyle, from the story *Cat from Hell* by Stephen King

Tales from the Golden Age ★★★ 12
Portmanteau comedy 2009 · Rom · Colour · 146min

The darkest days under dictator Nicolae Ceausescu are recalled with ironic nostalgia in this ribald collection of urban myths. The brainchild of Cristian Mungiu (*4 Months, 3 Weeks and 2 Days*), the five vignettes are directed by – and credited collectively to – himself and four first-time feature-makers. The standout is the opener, "The Legend of the Official Visit", in which residents of a rural community strain to accommodate the requests of the apparatchiks organising a fleeting inspection by some Communist dignitaries. As with all portmanteau films, the whole is somewhat patchy. But the incidents are linked by a keen appreciation of the fear, suspicion, confinement, corruption and venality that blighted daily life for most Romanians in the 1970s and 80s. DP Romanian +subtitles. Swearing. 𝔇𝔳𝔡

Alexandru Potocean *Secretary* • Teo Corban [Teodor Corban] *Mayor* • Avram Birau *Photographer* • Vlad Ivanov *Grigore* • Ion Sapdaru *Policeman Alexa* • Radu Iacoban *Bughi* ■ *Dir* Hanno Hofer, Razvan Marculescu, Cristian Mungiu, Constantin Popescu, Ioana Uricaru • *Scr* Cristian Mungiu

The Tales of Beatrix Potter ★★★ U
Dance fantasy 1971 · UK · Colour · 86min

This big 1971 hit slips into ballet slippers to tell the lovely stories of Beatrix Potter, set in their original Lakeland landscape. Ballet maestro Frederick Ashton choreographs and makes an outstanding appearance as a fussy Mrs Tiggy-Winkle The *corps de ballet* comes with realistic-looking mouse heads, Mrs Puddleduck is a treat and there's a midnight *pas de deux* between two piglets. But the noteworthy costumes tend toward the bulky with a rather smothering effect, and though intended for children, its Peter Rabbit charm is too manipulative and humdrum to urge many balletomane stirrings. FL 𝔇𝔳𝔡

Frederick Ashton *Mrs Tiggy-Winkle* • Alexander Grant *Pigling Bland/Peter Rabbit* • Julie Wood *Mrs Tittlemouse* • Keith Martin *Johnny Town Mouse* • Ann Howard *Jemima Puddle-Duck* • Robert Mead *Fox* • Wayne Sleep *Tom Thumb/Squirrel Nutkin* ■ *Dir* Reginald Mills • *Scr* Richard Goodwin, Christine Edzard, from the stories by Beatrix Potter • *Costume Designer* Christine Edzard

The Tales of Hoffmann ★★★★ U
Opera 1951 · UK · Colour · 127min

Three years after the success of *The Red Shoes*, Michael Powell and Emeric Pressburger returned to the world of ballet at the behest of Sir Thomas Beecham for this irresistible confection. With Moira Shearer and Frederick Ashton dancing superbly and Hein Heckroth's art design and costumes worthy of their Oscar nominations, this sumptuous adaptation of Offenbach's opera is a visual delight. With the Sadler's Wells Chorus backing singers of the calibre of Robert Rounseville and Ann Ayars, it sounds pretty good, too. Only the slightly muddled structure detracts from what is otherwise an audacious cinematic experiment. DP 𝔇𝔳𝔡 ʙʟᵘ

Robert Rounseville *Hoffmann* • Moira Shearer *Stella/Olympia* • Robert Helpmann *Lindorff/Coppelius/Dapertutto* • Pamela Brown *Nicklaus* • Frederick Ashton *Kleinzack/Cochenille* • Léonide Massine *Spalanzani* • Ludmilla Tcherina *Giulietta* • Ann Ayars *Antonia* • John Ford *Nathaniel* ■ *Dir/Scr* Michael Powell, Emeric Pressburger

Tales of Manhattan ★★★ PG
Portmanteau comedy 1942 · US · BW · 118min

That title is really an awkward pun: the "tales" are those of a tail coat, and this charming all-star portmanteau comedy is a collection of playlets about the coat's adventures. Very much of its time and less than charming today, the episode involving the great Paul Robeson looks quite racist in its Uncle Remus sort of way, and one wonders why it wasn't deleted, instead of the notoriously missing WC Fields sequence. Edward G Robinson has a splendid moment, as does Charles Laughton at Carnegie Hall, and Rita Hayworth looks simply ravishing in the first story, but this movie is a curate's egg. TS 𝔇𝔳𝔡

Charles Boyer *Paul Orman* • Rita Hayworth *Ethel Halloway* • Ginger Rogers *Diane* • Henry Fonda *George* • Cesar Romero *Harry Wilson* • Charles Laughton *Charles Smith* • Elsa Lanchester *Elsa Smith* • Edward G Robinson *Larry Browne* • George Sanders *Williams* • Paul Robeson *Luke* • Ethel Waters *Esther* ■ *Dir* Julien Duvivier • *Scr* Ben Hecht, Ferenc Molnar, Donald Ogden Stewart, Samuel Hoffenstein, Alan Campbell, Ladislas Fodor, Laszlo Vadnai, Laslo Gorog, Lamar Trotti, Henry Blankford, Ed Beloin, Bill Morrow

Tales of Ordinary Madness ★★ 18
Drama 1981 · It/Fr · Colour · 101min

Italian director Marco Ferreri adapted this film from the autobiographical writings of the alcoholic Beat poet Charles Bukowski. Set mainly in Los Angeles, it stars Ben Gazzara as the disillusioned, womanising poet and he certainly gives a remarkable performance. But what might be wonderful pronouncements on paper certainly don't come across on screen and the effect is pretentious, tedious and very dated. BB Violence, nudity, sex scenes, drug abuse, swearing. 𝔇𝔳𝔡

Ben Gazzara *Charles Serking* • Ornella Muti *Cass* • Susan Tyrrell *Vera* • Tanya Lopert *Vicky* • Roy Brocksmith *Barman* ■ *Dir* Marco Ferreri • *Scr* Sergio Amidei, Marco Ferreri, Anthony Foutz, from the short story collection *Erections, Ejaculations, Exhibitions and General Tales of Ordinary Madness* by Charles Bukowski

Tales of Terror ★★★ 15
Portmanteau horror 1962 · US · Colour · 84min

This is one of cult director Roger Corman's classier productions, helped by ace genre writer Richard Matheson's skilled if loose adaptations of three Edgar Allan Poe stories. Ranging between macabre *Grand Guignol* and broad comedy, this cheerfully chilling collection is further boosted by the memorable teaming of Vincent Price and Peter Lorre, the latter in excellent scene-stealing form. AJ *DVD*

Vincent Price *Locke/Fortunato/Valdemar* • Maggie Pierce *Lenora* • Leona Gage *Morella* • Peter Lorre *Montresor* • Joyce Jameson *Annabel* • Basil Rathbone *Carmichael*, Debra Paget *Helene* ■ Dir Roger Corman • Scr Richard Matheson, from the stories *Morella, The Black Cat, The Facts in the Case of M Valdemar* and *The Cask of Amontillado* by Edgar Allan Poe

Tales of the Grim Sleeper ★★★★ 15

Documentary 2014 · US/UK · Colour · 109min

After his films about Aileen Wuornos, Nick Broomfield delves into another serial-killer case – the Grim Sleeper murders that plagued South Central LA for 25 years. It begins with the 2010 arrest of Lonnie Franklin, accused of 10 homicides but suspected of scores more. Franklin was awaiting trial during filming, so Broomfield decamps to the suburban area where he lived to find out how this family man had evaded capture for so long. Broomfield is initially ridiculed by Franklin's pals, only for them to co-operate as it transpires that their friend could be guilty. JA

■ Dir Nick Broomfield

Tales of the Night ★★★ PG

Animated fantasy 2011 · Fr · Colour · 80min

Portmanteau pictures will always be inconsistent and this sextet of stories from French animator Michel Ocelot is not only hampered by some underwhelming sections, but also by the clumsy linking device that sees a boy, a girl and an elderly man stage the enchanting fables in the latter's run-down theatre. Easily the most visually striking vignette is *The Doe Girl and the Architect's Son*, which relates how a medieval suitor outwits a sorcerer to win the heart of his beloved. Some of the tales are more reminiscent of *Aesop's Fables* in their moralising, yet such is Ocelot's mastery of shadow craft, that the movie is always engaging. DP French +subtitles. *DVD* 3D

Julien Béramis *Boy* • Marine Griset *Girl* • Yves Barsacq *Théo* ■ Dir/Scr Michel Ocelot

Tales of the Taira Clan ★★★ U

Historical drama 1955 · Jpn · Colour · 102min

Set in a turbulent 12th-century Japan, when Buddhist monks, backed by the indolent nobility, took up arms against the rebellious samurai, the action is efficiently staged in the manner of John Ford. However, the rise of Raizo Ichikawa and his Taira kinsmen at the expense of the tyrannical Minamoto clan lacks the character complexity in which Kenji Mizoguchi revelled. His heart was clearly not in what was to be his penultimate picture. DP Japanese +subtitles.

Raizo Ichikawa *Taira no Kiyomori* • Yoshiko Kuga *Tokiko* • Narutoshi Hayashi *Tokitada* • Michiyo Kogure *Yasuko* ■ Dir Kenji Mizoguchi • Scr Yoshikata Yoda, Masashige Narusawa, Hisakazu Miyagawa, from the novel by Eiji Yoshikawa

Talihina Sky: the Story of Kings of Leon ★★★ 15

Music documentary 2011 · US · Colour · 86min

Stephen C Mitchell, a long-time friend of Kings of Leon (brothers Nathan, Caleb and Jared Followill, and their cousin Matthew), traces their journey from impoverished childhood to stardom, employing old home videos, talking heads and fly-on-the-wall observation at a family reunion in small-town Oklahoma. The documentary is brutally honest in its depiction of the Followill clan, but rather disjointed in the way it bobs back and forth in time. You don't need to be a fan to appreciate this as an insight into rural America. BP *DVD* 📀

Caleb Followill • Jared Followill • Nathan Followill • Matthew Followill ■ Dir Stephen C Mitchell

Talk of Angels ★★ 12

Period romantic drama
1998 · US · Colour · 93min

Though it's pretty to look at and finely acted, there is something missing from this rather insubstantial 1930s-set romantic tale. Polly Walker plays a young Irish woman who goes to Spain, which is on the brink of civil war. She is employed to look after the young daughters of a wealthy liberal doctor (Franco Nero), but her life becomes complicated when she catches the eye of his idealistic (and married) young son, Vincent Perez. JF Violence.

Polly Walker *Mary Lavelle* • Vincent Perez *Francisco Areavaga* • Franco Nero *Dr Vicente Areavaga* • Marisa Paredes *Dona Consuelo* • Leire Berrocal *Milagros* • Penélope Cruz *Pilar* • Frances McDormand *Conlon* • Ruth McCabe *O'Toole* ■ Dir Nick Hamm • Scr Ann Guedes, Frank McGuinness, from the novel *Mary Lavelle* by Kate O'Brien

The Talk of the Town ★★★★ U

Comedy drama 1942 · US · BW · 113min

The eternal triangle – two men besotted by the same woman who is attracted to both – is the central ingredient of this classy, intelligent and witty romantic comedy. However, skilfully interwoven into the mix is an examination of hypocrisy, the inequities of the law and a measure of suspense. Cary Grant, a politically reformist factory worker, is wrongfully accused of murder and hides out in Jean Arthur's house, where he becomes friends with Ronald Colman, a distinguished legal academic and Supreme Court judge lodging there. Ideas are exchanged and both fall for their hostess. Story, script and picture were Oscar-nominated, and the stars deserved to be. RK *DVD*

Cary Grant *Leopold Dilg* • Jean Arthur *Nora Shelley* • Ronald Colman *Michael Lightcap* • Edgar Buchanan *Sam Yates* • Glenda Farrell *Regina Bush* • Charles Dingle *Andrew Holmes* ■ Dir George Stevens • Scr Irwin Shaw, Sidney Buchman, Dale Van Every, from a story by Sidney Harmon

Talk Radio ★★★★ 15

Drama 1988 · US · Colour · 104min

This gripping picture dates from the time when director Oliver Stone made good films rather than sensational headlines, featuring a tour de force performance from Eric Bogosian as the DJ who lets fly with a series of blistering diatribes against the callers to his late night radio show. The subplots rather get in the way of the monologues, which are delivered with such power and passion that one can only wonder why Bogosian's career has gone nowhere since. DP Swearing, violence. *DVD*

Eric Bogosian *Barry Champlain* • Alec Baldwin *Dan* • Ellen Greene *Ellen* • Leslie Hope *Laura* • John C McGinley *Stu* • John Pankow *Dietz* • Michael Wincott *Kent* • Linda Atkinson *Sheila Fleming* ■ Dir Oliver Stone • Scr Eric Bogosian, Oliver Stone, from the play by Eric Bogosian, Ted Savinar, from the non-fiction book *Talked to Death: the Life and Murder of Alan Berg* by Stephen Singular

Talk to Her ★★★★ 15

Romantic drama 2001 · Sp · Colour · 108min

Pedro Almodóvar's genius as a creator of memorable images takes centre stage in this intriguing and sometimes controversial insight into survival, male bonding and the nature of love. The emotional core forms around the friendship forged between nurse Javier Cámara and travel writer Darío Grandinetti, as they wait, respectively, for ballerina Leonor Watling and bullfighter Rosario Flores to emerge from their comas. Amid the shifting time frames and perspectives, it's the stylised set pieces rather than the unfolding story that really fire the imagination. DP Spanish +subtitles. Violence, a sex scene, swearing, nudity. *DVD*

Javier Cámara *Benigno* • Darío Grandinetti *Marco* • Leonor Watling *Alicia* • Rosario Flores *Lydia* • Geraldine Chaplin *Katerina Bilova* • Mariola Fuentes *Nurse Rosa* • Pina Bausch ■ Dir/Scr Pedro Almodóvar

Talk to Me ★★★★ 15

Biographical drama 2007 · US · Colour · 113min

The chemistry between lead actors Don Cheadle and Chiwetel Ejiofor lights up this vibrant biopic about ex-con Ralph Waldo "Petey" Greene, who became an iconic radio DJ in 1960s Washington DC. Director Kasi Lemmons's story of Greene (Cheadle) evolves into an emotionally rewarding journey, from his hustling a morning slot at a conservative radio station and becoming a shock jock sensation, to defusing street riots in the aftermath of the Martin Luther King assassination. It's when programme director Dewey Hughes (Ejiofor) tries to broaden his appeal into national celebrity that it all comes unstuck. What makes this superb portrait of a self-destructive free spirit work is the director's sociopolitical sensitivities, their placement against the turbulent civil rights backdrop of the era and a clear understanding of the rise in "Black is Beautiful" culture that followed. AJ *DVD* 📀

Don Cheadle *Ralph Waldo "Petey" Greene* • Chiwetel Ejiofor *Dewey Hughes* • Cedric the Entertainer *"Nighthawk" Bob Terry* • Taraji P Henson *Vernell Watson* • Mike Epps *Milo Hughes* • Martin Sheen *EG Sonderling* • Vondie Curtis-Hall *Sunny Jim Kelsey* ■ Dir Kasi Lemmons • Scr Michael Genet, Rick Famuyiwa, from a story by Genet

Talkin' Dirty after Dark ★★★ 18

Comedy 1991 · US · Colour · 86min

This is set around John Witherspoon's LA comedy club where stand-up acts rub shoulders with the equally crazy staff of the late night cabaret venue. Amid the joke-telling there is a complex web of romantic entanglements and sexual liaisons. A good showcase for a bunch of young comedians, the film particularly highlights the amiable, fast-talking Martin Lawrence who wins over the crowd with blue routines about sex. This profane, undisciplined romp is often very funny. DF

Martin Lawrence *Terry* • John Witherspoon *Dukie* • Jedda Jones *Rubie Lin* • "Tiny" Lister Jr [Tom "Tiny" Lister Jr] *Bigg* • Phyllis Yvonne Stickney *Aretha* • Renee Jones *Kimmie* • Darryl Sivad *Percy* • Yolanda King *Mother* ■ Dir/Scr Topper Carew

The Tall Blond Man with One Black Shoe ★★★ PG

Spy comedy 1972 · Fr · Colour · 85min

Physical French comedy, for those who like physical French comedies, and highly rated by those who do. This farce stars Pierre Richard as a bumbling innocent whose life becomes hectic when he is mistaken for a spy by rival groups of secret agents. Easy to watch, and surprisingly action-packed, with Richard showing himself to be a talented slapstick comic. The film spawned one French sequel, *The Return of...*, two years later, and was oddly retitled *The Man With One Red Shoe* for the US remake. DA In French.

Pierre Richard *François* • Bernard Blier *Milan* • Jean Rochefort *Toulouse* • Mireille Darc *Christine* • Jean Carmet *Maurice* • Colette Castel *Paulette* • Jean Obe *Botrel* ■ Dir Yves Robert • Scr Yves Robert, Francis Veber

Tall, Dark and Handsome ★★★

Crime comedy 1941 · US · BW · 78min

Cesar Romero's genial gangster and nightclub owner pretends to be a banker and father to impress childminder and would-be singer Virginia Gilmore. The subterfuge seems quite unnecessary for a man of Romero's dashing good looks (the remake, *Love That Brute*, got it right by casting burly Paul Douglas) but, then, this is a hoodlum who's too softhearted to kill anyone. This lacks the requisite wit and lightness of touch except when Charlotte

Greenwood's high-kicking housekeeper and Barnett Parker's gun-toting butler are around. AE

Cesar Romero *Shep Morrison* • Virginia Gilmore *Judy Miller* • Charlotte Greenwood *Winnie* • Milton Berle *Frosty Welch* • Sheldon Leonard *Pretty Willie* • Stanley Clements *Detective Harry Jr* • Barnett Parker *Quentin* ■ Dir H Bruce Humberstone • Scr Karl Tunberg, Darrell Ware

The Tall Guy ★★★ 15

Romantic comedy 1989 · UK · Colour · 88min

Now that she's regarded as one of Hollywood's leading thespians, it's unlikely that you'll ever see Emma Thompson like this again. So make the most of this often hilarious comedy directed by Mel Smith and written by Richard Curtis, particularly the brilliant knockabout love scene with the gangling Jeff Goldblum. They work well together throughout the film, with her deadpan approach and his neuroses perfectly matched. Rowan Atkinson's knowing send-up of his own image is both funny and generous. DP Swearing, nudity. *DVD*

Jeff Goldblum *Dexter King* • Emma Thompson *Kate Lemon* • Rowan Atkinson *Ron Anderson* • Geraldine James *Carmen* • Emil Wolk *Cyprus Charlie* • Kim Thomson *Cheryl* • Harold Innocent *Timothy* • Anna Massey *Mary* ■ Dir Mel Smith • Scr Richard Curtis

Tall in the Saddle ★★★ U

Western 1944 · US · BW · 87min

If ever there was a title made for Big John Wayne, this is it. However, the Duke barely gets a look-in, as in reality it's more of a vehicle for his tempestuous co-star Ella Raines, who goes gunning for the Duke in order to woo him. The complex plot has Wayne framed for murder as he discovers Ward Bond's crooked plans to steal Audrey Long's ranch. Edwin L Marin's direction is fast-moving, and there are two terrific fist fights. TS

John Wayne *Rocklin* • Ella Raines *Arly Harolday* • Ward Bond *Robert Garvey* • George "Gabby" Hayes *Dave* • Audrey Long *Clara Cardell* • Elisabeth Risdon *Miss Elizabeth Martin* • Don Douglas *Harolday* • Paul Fix *Bob Clews* ■ Dir Edwin L Marin • Scr Michael Hogan, Paul Fix, from the novel by Gordon Ray Young

Tall Man Riding ★★ U

Western 1955 · US · Colour · 81min

Randolph Scott returns to town to avenge a bullwhipping he received for daring to court a cattle baron's daughter some years earlier, and finds that she has married another. Her father, meanwhile, is now almost blind and about to lose his spread. With outlaws and landgrabbers stirring up trouble, Scott has his hands full. Dorothy Malone plays the girl he left behind, with Peggie Castle as the usual contrast, a saloon singer hooked up with the bad guys. AE

Randolph Scott *Larry Madden* • Dorothy Malone *Corinna Ordway* • Peggie Castle *Reva* • Bill Ching [William Ching] *Rex Willard* • John Baragrey *Cibo Pearlo* • Robert Barrat *Tucker "Tuck" Ordway* ■ Dir Lesley Selander • Scr Joseph Hoffman, from a novel by Norman A Fox

The Tall Men ★★★★ PG

Western 1955 · US · Colour · 117min

Clark Gable rarely ventured out West, but on the evidence of this impressive picture he should have done so more often. Few directors understood the nature of action better than Raoul Walsh, who draws bristling performances from both Gable and Robert Ryan in a tough trail-driving tale. Jane Russell is also on top form, giving as good as she gets as the boys bid for her affections. Walsh stages the action sequences with typical bravado and handles the more intimate moments with great finesse. Superbly photographed by Leo Tover, this is one of the genre's most unjustly overlooked films. DP *DVD*

Clark Gable *Ben Allison* • Jane Russell *Nella Turner* • Robert Ryan *Nathan Stark* • Cameron Mitchell *Clint Allison* • Juan Garcia *Luis* • Harry Shannon *Sam* • Emile Meyer *Chickasaw* ■ Dir Raoul Walsh • Scr Sydney Boehm, Frank Nugent, from a novel by Clay Fisher [Heck Allen]

T

The Tall Stranger ★★ PG
Western · 1957 · US · Colour · 79min

This very routine western is mainly of interest for reuniting the stars of Raoul Walsh's *Colorado Territory*, Joel McCrea and Virginia Mayo. Despite the spurious grandeur achieved by filming in CinemaScope, the two leads look too old and Thomas Carr's direction lacks focus. **TS**

Joel McCrea *Ned Bannon* · Virginia Mayo *Ellen* · Barry Kelley *Hardy Bishop* · Michael Ansara *Zarata* · Whit Bissell *Judson* · James Dobson *Dud* · George Neise [George N Neise] *Harper* ■ *Dir* Thomas Carr · *Scr* Christopher Knopf, from a story by Louis L'Amour

The Tall T ★★★★ PG
Western · 1957 · US · Colour · 74min

Randolph Scott plays the very ordinary cowpoke who stumbles into the hands of kidnappers, carefully biding his time to turn the tables and free their captive, a rich man's wife played by Maureen O'Sullivan. The outlaws are finely etched in Burt Kennedy's screenplay as both ruthless and human, especially Richard Boone as their leader, a lonely, intelligent figure who cannot escape his nature. It is superbly filmed by director Budd Boetticher, and the vivid, desolate landscape enhances the drama. **AE** *DVD*

Randolph Scott *Pat Brennan* · Richard Boone *Usher* · Maureen O'Sullivan *Doretta Mims* · Arthur Hunnicutt *Ed Rintoon* · Skip Homeier *Billy Jack* · Henry Silva *Chink* ■ *Dir* Budd Boetticher · *Scr* Burt Kennedy, from the story *The Captives* by Elmore Leonard · *Cinematographer* Charles Lawton Jr

Tall Tale ★★★ PG
Western adventure · 1994 · US · Colour · 99min

Jeremiah Chechik, who directed the disappointing movie version of *The Avengers*, also made this amiable western for Disney. Patrick Swayze has a lot of fun portraying the folk hero Pecos Bill who, with two companions, helps a family battle a greedy land agent (Scott Glenn in enjoyably pantomimic form). Chechik certainly seems at home on the range and children will lap up this updated version of good old-fashioned western action. **JF** *DVD*

Patrick Swayze *Pecos Bill* · Oliver Platt *Paul Bunyan* · Roger Aaron Brown *John Henry* · Nick Stahl *Daniel Hackett* · Scott Glenn *JP Stiles* · Stephen Lang *Jonas Hackett* · Jared Harris *Head Thug Pug* · Catherine O'Hara *Calamity Jane* ■ *Dir* Jeremiah Chechik · *Scr* Steven L Bloom, Robert Rodat

The Tall Target ★★★★ U
Period thriller · 1951 · US · BW · 77min

This ingeniously plotted, moody period thriller is a hidden nugget of gold among a great deal of early 1950s tosh. An exemplary Dick Powell plays Abraham Lincoln's bodyguard, a lone cop searching for an assassin as the newly elected president travels to Baltimore aboard a train in 1861. Director Anthony Mann's beautifully paced, atmospherically shot movie hums with intelligent intrigue and some neatly paced performances, particularly from Powell, who shines as the maverick with a mission. **SH**

Dick Powell *John Kennedy* · Paula Raymond *Ginny Beaufort* · Adolphe Menjou *Colonel Caleb Jeffers* · Marshall Thompson *Lance Beaufort* · Ruby Dee *Rachel* · Will Geer *Homer Crowley* · Richard Rober *Lieutenant Coulter* ■ *Dir* Anthony Mann · *Scr* Art Cohn, George Worthing Yates, from a story by Yates, Geoffrey Homes [Daniel Mainwaring]

Talladega Nights: the Ballad of Ricky Bobby ★★ 15
Sports comedy · 2006 · US · Colour · 103min

Will Ferrell, here looking for a big hit following the underwhelming box-office performances of *Bewitched* and *The Producers*, stars as the eponymous Nascar champion who is forced to take on his nemesis, gay French driver Jean Girard (Sacha Baron Cohen). Director Adam McKay (*Anchorman: the Legend of Ron Burgundy*) and Ferrell apparently improvised a great deal of the screenplay and the result is sloppy and self-indulgent. There's the odd funny moment, but the film is undermined by a homophobic undertone, which wouldn't be so irritating if the jokes were at least mildly amusing. **AS** *DVD Blu CS*

Will Ferrell *Ricky Bobby* · John C Reilly *Cal Naughton Jr* · Sacha Baron Cohen *Jean Girard* · Gary Cole *Reese Bobby* · Michael Clarke Duncan *Lucius Washington* · Leslie Bibb *Carley Bobby* · Jane Lynch *Lucy Bobby* · Molly Shannon *Mrs Dennit* ■ *Dir* Adam McKay, *Scr* Adam McKay, Will Ferrell

Talos the Mummy ★★★ 15
Horror adventure thriller · 1997 · US/Lux · Colour · 114min

A "me-too" Mummy quickie that cashed in on video while the Brendan Fraser blockbuster was cleaning up at the box office. The film is inventively cast, with martial arts star Jason Scott Lee popping up as a gun-toting detective and Louise Lombard providing the glamour. The strong pre-title sequence features horror great Christopher Lee. The story follows traditional bandaged lines as the remains of Talos, a very bad ancient Egyptian indeed, are disturbed by archaeologists, resulting in mayhem in modern-day London. **JF**

Jason Scott Lee *Riley* · Louise Lombard *Samantha Turkel* · Sean Pertwee *Bradley Cortese* · Lysette Anthony *Dr Claire Mulrooney* · Michael Lerner *Professor Marcus* · Jack Davenport *Detective Bartone* · Honor Blackman *Captain Shea* · Christopher Lee *Sir Richard Turkel* · Shelley Duvall *Edith Butros* ■ *Dir* Russell Mulcahy · *Scr* John Esposito, Russell Mulcahy, from a story by Keith Williams, Russell Mulcahy

Tamahine ★★ 12
Comedy · 1963 · UK · Colour · 92min

Back in the 18th century, Captain Cook brought to England a Tahitian named Omai who caused considerable cultural uproar and became a sexual magnet for ladies of wealth and discrimination. Transposed to an English boys' public school in 1963 with Nancy Kwan playing a Tahitian, the cultural collision doesn't have quite the same impact. Even so, the demure Miss Kwan drives everyone into a lather, including art master Derek Nimmo, posh pupil James Fox and supercilious headmaster Dennis Price. **AT** *DVD*

Nancy Kwan *Tamahine* · John Fraser *Richard* · Dennis Price *Poole* · Coral Browne *Madam Becque* · Dick Bentley *Storekeeper* · Derek Nimmo *Clove* · Justine Lord *Diana* · Michael Gough *Cartwright* · Allan Cuthbertson *Housemaster* · James Fox *Oliver* ■ *Dir* Philip Leacock · *Scr* Denis Cannan, from the novel by Thelma Nicklaus

Tamara Drewe ★★★ 15
Comedy drama · 2010 · UK · Colour · 106min

A sleepy Dorset village becomes a hotbed of scandal after an "It girl" newspaper columnist returns home to set local menfolk's hearts fluttering in this comedy drama adapted from Posy Simmonds's *Guardian* newspaper cartoon strip. As played by Gemma Arterton, the eponymous Tamara certainly doesn't lack charm, yet somehow the other characters in this ensemble piece prove more emotionally engaging. Director Stephen Frears juggles the various plotlines with assurance and the spot-on performances leave us with lots to enjoy. It's just a shame that the title character is perhaps the least interesting. **TJ** *DVD Blu*

Gemma Arterton *Tamara Drewe* · Roger Allam *Nicholas Hardiment* · Bill Camp *Glen McCreavy* · Dominic Cooper *Ben Sergeant* · Luke Evans *Andy Cobb* · Tamsin Greig *Beth Hardiment* · Jessica Barden *Jody Long* ■ *Dir* Stephen Frears · *Scr* Moira Buffini, from the graphic novel by Posy Simmonds

The Tamarind Seed ★★ 15
Romantic thriller · 1974 · UK · Colour · 119min

"I am a man and I want you," Omar Sharif says to Julie Andrews. "I know we are dialectically opposed to each other, but we must keep materialist thinking out of it." Julie thinks for a minute, maybe of England, and then says, "Are you trying to enrol me in the KGB or are you really defecting?" Omar is the most gorgeous spy in the Soviet bloc and Julie is the prettiest Foreign Office employee, so why shouldn't the Iron Curtain melt? There are hints that Blake Edwards saw this as a satire on spy melodramas, but mostly it's tosh. **AT** *DVD Blu*

Julie Andrews *Judith Farrow* · Omar Sharif *Feodor Sverdlov* · Anthony Quayle *Jack Loder* · Sylvia Syms *Margaret Stephenson* · Daniel O'Herlihy [Dan O'Herlihy] *Fergus Stephenson* · Oscar Homolka *Gen Golitsyn* ■ *Dir* Blake Edwards · *Scr* Blake Edwards, from the novel by Evelyn Anthony

The TAMI Show ★★★★★
Music concert documentary · 1964 · US · BW · 113min

This captures practically every significant chart act of the day at the height of their explosive performance powers. Filmed at the Santa Monica Civic Auditorium on 24 October 1964, the Teenage Awards Music International show begins with hosts Jan and Dean introducing Chuck Berry with Gerry and the Pacemakers and ends with the Rolling Stones whipping the crowd into an hysterical frenzy. In between, the Supremes and Lesley Gore boast huge hairdos, Billy J Kramer sings Lennon and McCartney, the Beach Boys surf through their California sound and James Brown struts his funky stuff. Fabulous talent in an amazingly witty and vivacious time capsule. **AJ** *DVD*

■ *Dir* Steve Binder

Taming Andrew ★★ PG
Drama based on a true story · 2000 · US · Colour · 87min

This TV movie explores similar territory to François Truffaut's *The Wild Child*. Returning to his mother (Park Overall) after five years living with the father who abducted him, Seth Adkins has none of the social or educational skills expected of a ten-year-old. The leads give it their all, but they're never entirely convincing, and the story lacks emotional insight. **DP** *DVD*

Park Overall *Gail* · Seth Adkins *Andrew* · Jason Beghe *Eddie* · Shane Daly *Police officer* ■ *Dir* Artie Mandelberg · *Scr* Susan Rice

The Taming of the Shrew ★★ U
Comedy · 1929 · US · BW · 65min

Shakespeare's comedy has been much filmed, perhaps most popularly as the musical *Kiss Me Kate*. This version co-stars the King and Queen of Hollywood, Douglas Fairbanks and Mary Pickford, paired for the first and last time. Unfortunately, working together revealed severe differences in temperament and approach – the battle between Shakespeare's lovers carried on and off the screen and ended their marriage. The Bard's verse takes second place to the stars' energetic mugging. **RK** *DVD*

Mary Pickford *Katherine* · Douglas Fairbanks *Petruchio* · Edwin Maxwell *Baptista* · Joseph Cawthorn *Gremio* · Clyde Cook *Grumio* ■ *Dir* Sam Taylor · *Scr* Sam Taylor, from the play by William Shakespeare

The Taming of the Shrew ★★★★ U
Comedy · 1967 · US/It · Colour · 116min

Richard Burton and Elizabeth Taylor, at the height of one of their own violent love affairs, breathe their personal life into Shakespeare's not so politically correct tale of Petruchio subduing his shrewish wife. It's a lush version in which director Franco Zeffirelli opts for colourful action rather than well-wrought articulation. It's certainly a feast for the eye - ravishing photography, impressive sets and costumes - and benefits from the ebullient performances of one of film's greatest couples. **TH** *DVD*

Richard Burton *Petruchio* · Elizabeth Taylor *Katharina* · Michael Hordern *Baptista* · Cyril Cusack *Grumio* · Michael York *Lucentio* · Alfred Lynch *Tranio* · Natasha Pyne *Bianca* · Alan Webb *Gremio* · Victor Spinetti *Hortensio* ■ *Dir* Franco Zeffirelli · *Scr* Paul Dehn, Suso Cecchi D'Amico, Franco Zeffirelli, from the play by William Shakespeare · *Cinematographers* Oswald Morris, Luciano Trasatti · *Costume Designers* Irene Sharaff, Danilo Donati

Tamla Rose ★ 12A
Musical · 2013 · UK · Colour · 108min

A Merseyside girl band hits the big time delivering old-fashioned soul numbers in this micro-budget home-grown offering. It's a familiar showbiz trajectory, but writer/director Joe Scott struggles to bring any freshness to it: his script is poorly organised, his cast merely adequate, and his production resources too meagre to convince us that the girls (played by Adi Alfa, Alexandra Johnston and Tisha Merry) are indeed wowing huge audiences. It's a shame, as Robbie Pollard and Laura Walton's tuneful Motown pastiches clearly deserve a better context. **TJ** Some swearing.

Adi Alfa *Tamla Rose Miller* · Alexandra Johnston *Lily* · Tisha Merry *Candi Shimm* · Jake Abraham *Jim* · Philip Olivier *Kyle* · Errol Smith *Shane Hunter* ■ *Dir/Scr* Joe Scott (2) · *Music* Robbie Pollard, Laura Walton

Tammy ★★ 15
Road movie comedy · 2014 · US · Colour · 92min

With hit comedies *Bridesmaids* and *The Heat* under her belt, Melissa McCarthy reveals bigger ambitions by co-writing and producing as well as starring in this road movie. Directed by McCarthy's husband, Ben Falcone, from a script the couple wrote together, this freewheeling trip is sadly lacking in drive, rhythm or laughs. McCarthy's Tammy is likeably brash, but the gags don't have the killer blow you might expect. **SP** Swearing, sexual references. *DVD Blu*

Melissa McCarthy *Tammy* · Susan Sarandon *Pearl* · Allison Janney *Deb* · Gary Cole *Earl* · Dan Aykroyd *Don* · Kathy Bates *Lenore* ■ *Dir* Ben Falcone · *Scr* Ben Falcone, Melissa McCarthy

Tammy and the Bachelor ★★★ U
Comedy · 1957 · US · Colour · 89min

Something of a surprise smash hit in its day, this modest but utterly charming piece of whimsy started a series featuring the guileless heroine, who came from the backwoods to charm Louisiana society. Debbie Reynolds is endearingly energetic as the heroine with a talent for sorting out problems and wistfully sings the song *Tammy*, that topped the Hit Parade in both the USA and UK. **TV**

Debbie Reynolds *Tammy Tyree* · Leslie Nielsen *Peter Brent* · Walter Brennan *Grandpa* · Mala Powers *Barbara* · Sidney Blackmer *Professor Brent* · Mildred Natwick *Aunt Renie* · Fay Wray *Mrs Brent* ■ *Dir* Joseph Pevney · *Scr* Oscar Brodney, from the novel *Tammy out of Time* by Cid Ricketts Sumner

Tammy and the Doctor ★★ U
Comedy · 1963 · US · Colour · 88min

Quintessential 1950s cutie Sandra Dee takes on the Debbie Reynolds mantle for the second time as the country girl among city folk, falling hook, line and sinker for handsome white-coated doctor Peter Fonda, here making his screen debut. This is truly a slight piece, but not without charm thanks to Universal's shrewd casting of a horde of veterans. **TS**

Sandra Dee *Tammy Tyree* · Peter Fonda *Dr Mark Cheswick* · Macdonald Carey *Dr Wayne Bentley* · Beulah Bondi *Mrs Call* · Margaret Lindsay *Rachel Coleman, Head Nurse* · Reginald Owen *Jason Tripp* · Adam West *Dr Eric Hassler* ■ *Dir* Harry Keller · *Scr* Oscar Brodney, from the character created by Cid Ricketts Sumner

Tammy Tell Me True ★★ U
Comedy · 1961 · US · Colour · 96min

Sandra Dee took over from Debbie Reynolds for the second of the three original movies featuring the character created by Cid Ricketts Sumner. She does a nice line in country cute as she sails down river to the college town where her errant boyfriend is studying. But she's quickly upstaged by Julia Meade, as the sniping niece who accuses Dee of doing away with her aunt, Virginia Grey. However, the acting honours undoubtedly go to the veteran trio of Beulah Bondi, Cecil Kellaway and Edgar Buchanan. DP

Sandra Dee *Tammy Tyree* • John Gavin *Tom Freeman* • Charles Drake *Buford Woodly* • Virginia Grey *Miss Jenks* • Julia Meade *Suzanne Rook* • Beulah Bondi *Mrs Call* • Cecil Kellaway *Captain Joe* • Edgar Buchanan *Judge Carver* ■ *Dir* Harry Keller • *Scr* Oscar Brodney, from the character created by Cid Ricketts Sumner

Tampopo ★★★★ 18
Satire　　　　1986 · Jpn · Colour · 109min

Juzo Itami's busy satire not only gives hungry viewers more than their fill of delicious food, but also satisfies the film gourmet. In addition to homages to *Shane*, *Seven Samurai* and *Death in Venice*, this story of a trucker (Tsutomu Yamazaki), who turns a roadside noodle bar owned by Nobuko Miyamoto (Itami's wife and regular star) into Tokyo's finest restaurant, is packed with parodies of westerns, samurai pictures and Japanese gangster and porn films. DP Japanese +subtitles.

Tsutomu Yamazaki *Goro* • Nobuko Miyamoto *Tampopo* • Koji Yakusho *Gangster* • Ken Watanabe *Gun* ■ *Dir/Scr* Juzo Itami

Tanganyika ★★ U
Adventure drama　1954 · US · Colour · 81min

In East Africa around 1900, murderer Jeff Morrow is exerting an evil influence over the warlike Nakumbi natives, thus endangering the lives of white settlers in the colony. A safari, led by Van Heflin and including Morrow's decent brother Howard Duff, sets off on a manhunt to catch the renegade. A bizarre combination of jungle adventure and thriller, this is absolute piffle, but it's awful enough to be quite entertaining. RK

Van Heflin *John Gale* • Ruth Roman *Peggy Merion* • Howard Duff *Dan Harder* • Jeff Morrow *Abel McCracken* • Joe Comadore *Andolo* • Gregory Marshall *Andy Merion* • Noreen Corcoran *Sally Merion* ■ *Dir* Andre De Toth • *Scr* William Sackheim, Richard Alan Simmons, from a story by William R Cox

Tangerine ★★★★ 15
Comedy drama　　2015 · US · Colour · 84min

Director Sean Baker (*Starlet*) triumphs once again with this raw and hilariously vulgar look at life on the Hollywood mean streets for two black transgender hookers on Christmas Eve. One is looking for her cheating boyfriend after a stint in jail. Her best friend, while sympathetic to her misguided pain, is more interested in touting a cabaret appearance at a local bar. Shot entirely on three iPhones, often resembling a crazed reality show, this big-hearted odyssey is unexpectedly charming and ultimately rather moving. AJ Swearing, sex scenes, drug abuse. DVD

Kiki Kitana Rodriguez [Kitana Kiki Rodriguez] *Sin-Dee* • Mya Taylor *Alexandra* • Karren Karagulian *Razmik* • Mickey O'Hagan *Dinah* ■ *Dir* Sean Baker, Chris Bergoch

Tangerines ★★★★ 15
War drama　　2013 · Est/Georgia · Colour · 83min

In Georgia in 1992, a harvest of tangerines becomes a metaphor for the struggles of war. An idyllic mountain village is readying for a bumper fruit crop, but the quiet is short-lived as two badly injured soldiers, one Georgian (Mikhail Meskhi) and one Chechen (Giorgi Nakhashidze), wage war on each other from one rustic home. Beautifully acted and directed, this alluring drama was nominated for the best foreign film Oscar. It's a filmic short story, concise, direct and simple that credibly reveals the tragedy of war. KK Russian, Estonian +subtitles. Violence, swearing.

Mikhail Meskhi *Nika* • Giorgi Nakhashidze *Ahmed* • Lembit Ulfsak *Ivo* • Elmo Nuganen *Margus* ■ *Dir/Scr* Zaza Urushadze

Tangled ★★★★ PG
Animated comedy adventure
2010 · US · Colour · 96min

Tangled is Disney's 50th animated movie and this deft version of a Brothers Grimm fairy tale, drawn with clever CGI panache, is a resounding success. Rapunzel (voiced by Mandy Moore) was kidnapped from her royal parents as a baby and trapped in a tower by Mother Gothel so that she could use the princess's long magical hair to stay forever young. Flynn Rider (Zachary Levi) is a cocksure thief who provides the sassy princess with a possible escape route. Their ensuing adventures are great fun with Rapunzel's multitasking flowing tresses used to great effect in lively action sequences. *Bolt* directors Nathan Greno and Byron Howard's film combines polished storytelling, witty scripting and relatable emotions to create a smart, snappy and sparkling tale that will appeal to both kids and adults. AJ Some violence. DVD BLU 3D

Mandy Moore *Rapunzel* • Zachary Levi *Flynn Rider* • Donna Murphy *Mother Gothel* • Ron Perlman *Stabbington Brother* • Jeffrey Tambor *Big Nose* • MC Gainey *Captain of the guard* ■ *Dir* Nathan Greno, Byron Howard • *Scr* Dan Fogelman, from a fairy tale by Jacob Grimm, Wilhelm Grimm

Tango & Cash ★★★ 18
Action thriller　1989 · US · Colour · 99min

Sylvester Stallone and Kurt Russell star in this hugely silly, hugely enjoyable action thriller. The main twist in this buddy caper is that Stallone is actually quite sophisticated, while Russell is the no-brain, all-brawn thug. The plot follows the bickering duo who become reluctant partners when they are framed by evil drugs baron Jack Palance. Russian director Andrei Konchalovsky produces lots of big explosions and brainless fun. JF Swearing, violence, drug abuse, sex scenes, nudity. DVD BLU

Sylvester Stallone *Ray Tango* • Kurt Russell *Gabe Cash* • Jack Palance *Yves Perret* • Teri Hatcher *Kiki* • Michael J Pollard *Owen* • Brion James *Requin* • Geoffrey Lewis *Police captain* • James Hong *Quan* • Robert Z'Dar *Face* ■ *Dir* Andrei Konchalovsky • *Scr* Randy Feldman

Tango Bar ★★★ PG
Dance documentary drama
1988 · P Ric/Arg · Colour · 89min

The tango is so inextricably woven into the fabric of Argentinian history that any socio-cultural overview is bound to have political implications. Thus, the live numbers performed by the Tango Argentino troupe and the film clips revealing how the dance has been depicted down the years are pregnant with a significance that is reinforced by the tense relationship between piano player Raul Julia, long-exiled bandoneonist Ruben Juarez and their mutual mistress, singer Valeria Lynch. Tango aficionados will revel in the performances, although film fans will be more intrigued by the juxtaposed classic clips. DP Spanish +subtitles.

Raul Julia *Ricardo* • Valeria Lynch *Elena* • Ruben Juarez *Antonio* ■ *Dir* Marcos Zurinaga • *Scr* Marcos Zurinaga, Juan Carlos Codazzi, Jose Pablo Feinman

The Tango Lesson ★★ PG
Dance drama
1997 · UK/Fr/Arg/Jpn/Ger · BW and Colour · 97min

Writer/director Sally Potter plays herself, taking a break from writing her latest screenplay to attend a tango exhibition. So struck is she by the super-sexy rhythms, that she reshapes her film around the dance and the man who teaches it. This is the film about that film. The idea of dispensing with the distinction between life and art is interesting, if not exactly original. DA English, French, Spanish +subtitles.

Sally Potter *Sally* • Pablo Veron *Pablo* • Gustavo Naveira *Gustavo* • Fab an Salas *Fabian* • David Toole *Fashion designer* • Carolina Iotti *Pablo's partner* • Carlos Copello *Carlos* ■ *Dir/Scr* Sally Potter

Tangos, Exilo de Gardel ★★★
Drama　　　1985 · Arg/Fr · Colour · 119min

One of the founders of Third Cinema, Argentinian director Fernando E Solanas explores the agony of exile in this politically charged variation on the "putting on a show" theme. Taking as his subject the life of tango star Carlos Gardel, who was killed in 1935, playwright Miguel Angel Sola smuggles the manuscript out of Buenos Aires to compatriots, who sacrifice both personal and national identities in Paris. Very much a patchwork of emotions, events and ideas, the film leavens its melancholy with sublime moments of symbolic music. DP Spanish +subtitles.

Marie Laforêt • Philippe Léotard • Miguel Angel Sola • Marina Vlady ■ *Dir/Scr* Fernando E Solanas

Tank Girl ★★ 15
Science-fiction comedy
1995 · US · Colour · 99min

This gets nowhere near the sassy black spark of the original comic strip, yet those unfamiliar with its source will find it goofy, undemanding fare. Lori Petty is the Tank Girl of the title, demonstrating an early manifestation of "girl power" as she takes on evil Malcolm McDowell in a water-starved post-apocalyptic world. Director Rachel Talalay never quite gets a handle on the mix of comedy and action, but Petty is credible in the lead and McDowell is suitably over the top as the villain. JF Violence, swearing. DVD

Lori Petty *Rebecca Buck/Tank Girl* • Ice T [Ice-T] *T-Saint* • Malcolm McDowell *Kesslee* • Naomi Watts *Jet Girl* • Don Harvey *Sergeant Small* • Jeff Kober *Booga* ■ *Dir* Rachel Talalay • *Scr* Tedi Sarafian, from the comic strip by Alan Martin, Jamie Hewlett

Tantric Tourists ★★
Documentary　2008 · UK · Colour · 80min

In director Alexander Snelling's first feature documentary, a group of American tourists on a whirlwind tour of holy sites search in vain for "the real India". Led by ebullient tantric teacher Laurie Handlers, who hopes to initiate a deep, inner transformation among her disciples, the group soon finds its dreams of nirvana clashing with the frantic reality of day-to-day life. Whilst Snelling's attempts to capture the clamour of street life and the tourists' moments of serenity may reflect the duality of Indian life, neither truly engages the viewer, leading to a rather unenlightening experience. DC

■ *Dir* Alexander Snelling

The Tao of Steve ★★★ 15
Romantic comedy　2000 · US · Colour · 83min

Donal Logue impresses as a part-time kindergarten teacher whose success with the opposite sex can be attributed to his philosophy of cool. His Tao is based on a mythical Steve, who embodies the qualities of those cultural icons Steve McQueen, Steve McGarrett (*Hawaii Five-O*) and "Six Million Dollar Man" Steve Austin. Logue has to rethink his slacker lifestyle when he decides to pursue the equally excellent Greer Goodman, a set designer tired of dating silly boys. Jennipher Goodman's directorial debut labours the point, but it's still a film of intelligence and charm. DP DVD

Donal Logue *Dex* • Greer Goodman *Syd* • Kimo Wills *Dave* • Ayelet Kaznelson *Beth* • David Aaron Baker *Rick* • Nina Jaroslaw *Maggie* ■ *Dir* Jennipher Goodman • *Scr* Jennipher Goodman, Greer Goodman, Duncan North, from a story by North

Tap ★★ 15
Drama　　　　1989 · US · Colour · 106min

If the title had not already worked against this dull movie, then the improbable story certainly would have. Burglar Gregory Hines plays the nimble-footed son of a legendary dancer, who's released from prison faced with two options. He can either join mentor Sammy Davis Jr at his tap dancing club or regroup with his old partners in crime for one last job. Tap dance fanatics may enjoy film but few will be engaged by its clichéd characters. BB DVD

Gregory Hines *Max Washington* • Suzanne Douglas *Amy* • Sammy Davis Jr *Little Mo* • Savion Glover *Louis* • Joe Morton *Nicky* • Dick Anthony Williams *Francis* • Sandman Sims *Sandman* • Bunny Briggs *Bunny* ■ *Dir/Scr* Nick Castle

Tape ★★ 15
Drama　　　　2001 · US · Colour · 83min

Director Richard Linklater demonstrates why the physical restrictions of theatre commonly make stage-play adaptations big-screen mistakes. In filming the action of this unconventional reunion tale within a motel room in real time, without music, camera trickery or effects, Linklater tips his hat to the Dogme school of movie-making. But what begins as an interesting exercise in character-based drama - as three former friends reveal long-held resentments - soon turns into a self-indulgent bore. SF Swearing, drug abuse. DVD

Ethan Hawke *"Vin" Vince* • Robert Sean Leonard *"Jon" Johnny* • Uma Thurman *Amy Randall* ■ *Dir* Richard Linklater • *Scr* Stephen Belber, from his play

Tapeheads ★★ 15
Comedy　　　1988 · US · Colour · 87min

John Cusack and Tim Robbins star in this lightweight offering from director Bill Fishman. The two play ex-security guards trying to make it as music-video producers and setting their sights on becoming MTV's finest. Given that the film credits every bigwig in the music industry, one might expect more than this series of skits with Cusack and Robbins going from disaster to success. LH DVD

John Cusack *Ivan Alexeev* • Tim Robbins *Josh Tager* • Mary Crosby *Samantha Gregory* • Clu Gulager *Norman Mart* • Katy Boyer *Belinda Mart* • Jessica Walter *Kay Mart* • Sam Moore *Billy Diamond* • Junior Walker *Lester Diamond* • Doug McClure *Sid Tager* • Connie Stevens *June Tager* ■ *Dir* Bill Fishman • *Scr* Bill Fishman, Peter McCarthy, from a story by Ryan Rowe, Jim Herzfeld, Bill Fishman, Peter McCarthy

Taps ★★★ PG
Drama　　　　1981 · US · Colour · 121min

This marked Tom Cruise's first impact in the movies, Sean Penn's debut and Timothy Hutton's follow-up to his Oscar-winning role in *Ordinary People*. They play cadets who take over their military academy when it's threatened with redevelopment in Harold Becker's fascinating film. It sometimes gets hysterical and loses its narrative way, but the bright young stars and George C Scott as the commander see it through. JA DVD

George C Scott *General Harlan Bache* • Timothy Hutton *Brian Moreland* • Ronny Cox *Colonel Kerby* • Sean Penn *Alex Dwyer* • Tom Cruise *David Shawn* • Brendan Ward *Charlie Auden* ■ *Dir* Harold Becker • *Scr* Darryl Ponicsan, Robert Mark Kamen, from the story *Father Sky* by Devery Freeman, James Lineberger

T

Tara Road ★★★ PG
Drama　　　　2005 · Ire · Colour · 96min

Andie MacDowell and Olivia Williams add class to a predictable yet engaging drama, playing two women from opposite sides of the Atlantic who swap homes in a bid to escape their problems. While their characters are exaggerated stereotypes - just like everyone else in the film - they enrich the roles with a warmth and poignancy that make the soap opera-style events seem more real. The project's barely a stretch for director Gillies MacKinnon (*Hideous Kinky*) but he mirrors his leading ladies' proficiency, applying a light touch and striking a balance between humour and serious emotion. SF DVD

Olivia Williams *Ria* • Andie MacDowell *Marilyn* • Johnny Brennan *Brian* • Iain Glen *Danny* • Stephen Rea *Colm* • Virginia Cole *Mrs Doyle* • Jean-Marc Barr *Andy* • Brenda Fricker *Mona* ■ *Dir* Gillies MacKinnon • *Scr* Cynthia Cidre, Shane Connaughton, from the novel by Maeve Binchy

Tarana ★★★ PG
Drama 1951 · Ind · BW · 137min

Although it's best known for its spectacular masala musicals, Bollywood also has a social conscience. Director Ram Daryani was renowned for the intelligence with which he tackled controversial issues, without ever losing sight of the central story. Here, he passes some pointed observations on arranged marriages, the class divide and the struggle between progress and tradition, but most eyes will be on regular co-stars Madhubala and Dilip Kumar as the star-crossed lovers whose path to happiness is strewn with prejudice. DP Hindi +subtitles.
Madhubala *Tarana* · Dilip Kumar · Kumar Shyama · Jeevan ■ *Dir* Ram Daryani

Tarantula ★★★ PG
Science-fiction horror 1955 · US · BW · 76min

Director Jack Arnold's big bug shocker features excellent special effects and the potent use of haunting desert locations. Scientist Leo G Carroll is working in an isolated laboratory trying to solve world famine and injects a spider with special nutrients that cause it to grow to enormous size. The giant arachnid escapes, decimates cattle and then eats people. The stillness of the desert allows Arnold to mount the tension impeccably. Look for Clint Eastwood as a jet pilot. AJ DVD
John Agar *Dr Matt Hastings* · Mara Corday *Stephanie Clayton* · Leo G Carroll *Prof Gerald Deemer* · Nestor Paiva *Sheriff Jack Andrews* · Ross Elliott *Joe Burch* · Edwin Rand *Lt John Nolan* · Clint Eastwood *First pilot* ■ *Dir* Jack Arnold · *Scr* Robert M Fresco, Martin Berkeley, from a story by Jack Arnold, Robert M Fresco · *Special Effects* Clifford Stine, David S Horsley

Taras Bulba ★★ U
Period epic 1962 · US · Colour · 123min

This is real junk, but of a splendid, watchable awfulness that is absolutely compulsive. This would-be swashbuckling saga set in the Ukraine in the 16th century achieves some uniqueness for being filmed in Argentina. The locations are indeed impressive, as is the score by the distinguished Franz Waxman, but the casting is ludicrous and director J Lee Thompson fails to find the necessary scale. Of the leads Tony Curtis and Yul Brynner as Cossack son and father, the less said the better. TS
Tony Curtis *Andrei Bulba* · Yul Brynner *Taras Bulba* · Christine Kaufmann *Natalia Dubrov* · Sam Wanamaker *Filipenko* · Brad Dexter *Shilo* · Guy Rolfe *Prince Grigory* · Perry Lopez *Ostap Bulba* · George Macready *Governor* ■ *Dir* J Lee Thompson · *Scr* Waldo Salt, Karl Tunberg, from the novel by Nikolai Gogol

Target ★★ 15
Spy thriller 1985 · US · Colour · 112min

Arthur Penn has had an indifferent directorial career since the glories of the 1960s and 1970s. Here he directs Gene Hackman, starring as a seemingly ordinary American businessman who gets drawn into Cold War intrigue when his wife Gayle Hunnicutt is kidnapped in Paris. At the same time Hackman has to rebuild a relationship with his surly adolescent son Matt Dillon. Sadly, Penn never successfully marries the two conflicting elements. JF Violence, swearing, nudity. DVD
Gene Hackman *Walter Lloyd* · Matt Dillon *Chris Lloyd* · Gayle Hunnicutt *Donna Lloyd* · Victoria Fyodorova *Lise* · Ilona Grubel *Carla* · Herbert Berghof *Schroeder* · Josef Sommer *Barney Taber* · Guy Boyd *Clay* ■ *Dir* Arthur Penn · *Scr* Howard Berk, Don Petersen, from a story by Leonard Stern

Target Eagle ★★ PG
Action adventure 1982 · Sp/Mex · Colour · 94min

Clever casting injects some life into a predictable action thriller centred around mercenaries hired to smash a smuggling ring. George Peppard, better known for his good guy TV roles in *Banacek* and *The A-Team*, relishes the chance to be the chief

baddie, and Max von Sydow is also unusually cast as a police chief. NF
George Rivero [Jorge Rivero] *David* · Maud Adams *Carmen* · George Peppard *Ronald McFadden* · Max von Sydow *Spanish police chief* · Chuck Connors *Sam Fisher* · Susana Dosamantes *Laura* ■ *Dir/Scr* J Anthony Loma

Target Unknown ★★ U
Second World War drama 1951 · US · BW · 89min

The interrogation of an American aircrew by a Nazi intelligence unit is the intriguing premise of this wartime drama set in occupied France. There is some splendid aerial combat footage, but director George Sherman allows the plot to develop in a wholly predictable manner, as Mark Stevens and his crew play mind games with Robert Douglas's smug German colonel, who wants to uncover the target of the next USAF raid. The subplot involving quisling Malu Gatica and resistance fighter Suzanne Dalbert is no more inspired. DP
Mark Stevens *Captain Jerome Stevens* · Alex Nicol *Al Mitchell* · Robert Douglas *Colonel von Broeck* · Don Taylor *Lieutenant Webster* · Gig Young *Captain Reiner* · Suzanne Dalbert *Theresa* · Malu Gatica *French entertainer* ■ *Dir* George Sherman · *Scr* Harold Medford, from his story

Targets ★★★★ 15
Crime thriller 1968 · US · Colour · 86min

The stunning feature debut of film critic-turned-writer/director Peter Bogdanovich is graced by a marvellous valedictory performance from Boris Karloff. Karloff plays Byron Orlok, an ageing horror star who finds himself in the gun sights of that scourge of contemporary America, a random sniper, chillingly portrayed by Tim O'Kelly. Based on the real-life killing spree of Charles Whitman in 1966, this is genuinely disturbing and immaculately crafted, with themes that are still relevant today. The cinematography, by debuting émigré Laszlo Kovacs, is superb. TS DVD
Boris Karloff *Byron Orlok* · Tim O'Kelly *Bobby Thompson* · Nancy Hsueh *Jenny* · James Brown (1) *Robert Thompson* · Sandy Baron *Kip Larkin* · Arthur Peterson *Ed Loughlin* · Mary Jackson *Charlotte Thompson* · Tanya Morgan *Ilene Thompson* · Monty Landis [Monte Landis] *Marshall Smith* · Peter Bogdanovich *Sammy Michaels* ■ *Dir* Peter Bogdanovich · *Scr* Peter Bogdanovich, from a story by Polly Platt, Peter Bogdanovich

Tarka the Otter ★★★ PG
Adventure 1978 · UK · Colour · 87min

Author Henry Williamson refused to allow Disney to film his much loved wildlife novel. Instead, he entrusted the story of Tarka to director David Cobham, who co-wrote the script with Gerald Durrell. Cobham remains faithful to the original and, in collaboration with cameraman John McCallum, paints a glorious picture of the Devon countryside. Although the action is occasionally deflected by a nature ramble approach, Tarka's adventures are skilfully staged and vividly brought to life by Peter Ustinov's narration. DP DVD
Peter Bennett *Master of the otter hounds* · Edward Underdown *Hibbert* · Brenda Cavendish *Lucy* · John Leeson *Hunt secretary* · Reg Lye *Farmer* · Peter Ustinov *Narrator* ■ *Dir* David Cobham · *Scr* Gerald Durrell, David Cobham, from the novel by Henry Williamson

The Tarnished Angels ★★★★ U
Adventure drama 1957 · US · BW · 87min

Journalist Rock Hudson joins ace barnstorming pilot Robert Stack and his sexy wife Dorothy Malone. Hudson's character is embarrassingly underwritten, but he manages to make his newshound eminently watchable, and the film never looks less than splendid in black-and-white CinemaScope. Shallow but well made, this melodrama fails to disguise the innate misanthropy of its literary source, though many have found much to admire in its sleazy bitterness. TS DVD Blu

Rock Hudson *Burke Devlin* · Robert Stack *Roger Shumann* · Dorothy Malone *Laverne Shumann* · Jack Carson *Jiggs* · Robert Middleton *Matt Ord* · Alan Reed *Colonel Fineman* · Alexander Lockwood *Sam Hagood* · Chris Olsen [Christopher Olsen] *Jack Shumann* · Robert J Wilke *Hank* · Troy Donahue *Frank Burnham* ■ *Dir* Douglas Sirk · *Scr* George Zuckerman, from the novel *Pylon* by William Faulkner

Tarnished Lady ★★
Drama 1931 · US · BW · 80min

This film marked the talkie debut of the already legendary, husky-voiced stage star Tallulah Bankhead, who returned to Hollywood after several years as the toast of London's West End stage. Sadly, Tallulah's exotic, erotic charms failed to make much impact on the camera. Despite glossy production, a Donald Ogden Stewart screenplay and direction by George Cukor, this tale of a Park Avenue girl who grows bored with marriage and leaves her husband (Clive Brook) to seek a more interesting life is no more than an efficient plod. RK
Tallulah Bankhead *Nancy Courtney* · Clive Brook *Norman Cravath* · Phoebe Foster *Germaine Prentiss* · Alexander Kirkland *DeWitt Taylor* · Osgood Perkins *Ben Sterner* · Eric Blore *Jewelry counter clerk* ■ *Dir* George Cukor · *Scr* Donald Ogden Stewart, from his story *New York Lady*

Tartuffe ★★★★ U
Silent drama 1926 · Ger · BW · 63min

Although his Nazi sympathies permanently tarnished his reputation, Emil Jannings remains one of the finest actors of the silent era and he delivers a performance of relishable roguery in this hilarious adaptation of Molière's scathing satire on religious hypocrisy. He's well supported by Lil Dagover as the wife willing to risk her honour in her determination to prevent gullible husband Werner Krauss from handing over his worldly goods. This sadly incomplete gem is also notable for Karl Freund's sombrely atmospheric cinematography. DP DVD Blu
Emil Jannings *Tartuffe* · Lil Dagover *Elmire* · Werner Krauss *Orgon* · André Mattoni *Grandson* · Rosa Valetti *Housekeeper* · Lucy Höflich *Dorine* · Hermann Picha *Old councillor* ■ *Dir* FW Murnau · *Scr* Carl Mayer, from the play by Molière

Tarzan ★★ U
Animated adventure 1999 · US · Colour · 84min

Despite some visually arresting action scenes, the first ever cartoon based on the classic jungle hero falls short of Disney's recent output. With weak comic relief provided by assorted "Animalz N the Hood", this is a frenetic mix of *George of the Jungle* and *Gorillas in the Mist*, with constant bouts of animated mayhem to keep the kids amused. Laced with feeble background songs from Phil Collins (inexplicably awarded an Oscar), this is no jungle VIP. AJ DVD Blu
Tony Goldwyn *Tarzan* · Minnie Driver *Jane* · Glenn Close *Kala* · Brian Blessed *Clayton* · Nigel Hawthorne *Professor Porter* · Lance Henriksen *Kerchak* ■ *Dir* Chris Buck, Kevin Lima · *Scr* Tab Murphy, Bob Tzudiker, Noni White, David Reynolds, Jeffrey Stepakoff, from the novel *Tarzan of the Apes* by Edgar Rice Burroughs · *Music/Lyrics* Phil Collins

Tarzan ★★★ PG
Animated adventure 2013 · Ger · Colour · 94min

Over 100 years since the first appearance of Edgar Rice Burroughs's apeman creation comes this motion-capture cartoon, which grafts some surprising visual nods to *Avatar* and *Jurassic Park* on to the basic plot. Young JJ Greystoke survives a helicopter crash that kills his family, and is raised by gorillas to become the legendary vine-swinger (voiced by Kellan Lutz). Years later, the evil head of the family firm resumes the search, threatening Tarzan's animal family. While not of Disney/Pixar animation quality, this lively fantasy packs in enough incident and vivid action to pass muster. AJ DVD Blu

Kellan Lutz *Tarzan* · Spencer Locke *Jane Porter* · Les Bubb *Jim Porter* · Mark Deklin *John Greystoke* · Jaime Ray Newman *Alice Greystoke* ■ *Dir* Reinhard Klooss · *Scr* Reinhard Klooss, from characters by Edgar Rice Burroughs

Tarzan II ★★ U
Animated adventure 2005 · US · Colour · 68min

This straight-to-DVD sequel to Disney's 1999 theatrically released adventure details the young Tarzan's exploits in the jungle. Small children will be entertained by the bright animation, the bouncy soundtrack and Phil Collins's engaging tunes (though adults may wonder again how he managed to win the best song Oscar for *You'll Be in My Heart* in the first film). This is really for the target audience only, and if your youngsters aren't very demanding they won't be disappointed. SuR
Harrison Chad *Tarzan* · George Carlin *Zugor* · Brad Garrett *Uto* · Glenn Close *Kala* · Ron Perlman *Kago* · Lance Henriksen *Kerchak* · Estelle Harris *Mama Gunda* ■ *Dir* Brian Smith (3) · *Scr* From characters by Edgar Rice Burroughs · *Music/Lyrics* Phil Collins

Tarzan and His Mate ★★★★ U
Adventure 1934 · US · BW · 86min

Generally regarded as the best of the Johnny Weissmuller MGM *Tarzans*, this is notable for being extremely raunchy, even by present-day standards, since it predates Hollywood's notorious censorship code. Cavorting semi-naked under the studio undergrowth is the lovely Maureen O'Sullivan as Jane. After this, the loincloths grew less revealing, but Weissmuller continued to cut a fine figure as the Lord of the Jungle. TS
Johnny Weissmuller *Tarzan* · Maureen O'Sullivan *Jane Parker* · Neil Hamilton *Harry Holt* · Paul Cavanagh *Martin Arlington* · Forrester Harvey *Beamish* · William Stack *Tom Pierce* · Desmond Roberts *Van Ness* ■ *Dir* Cedric Gibbons · *Scr* Howard Emmett Rogers, Leon Gordon, from a story by James Kevin McGuinness, from characters by Edgar Rice Burroughs

Tarzan and the Amazons ★★ U
Adventure 1945 · US · BW · 75min

It's not very good, and the Sol Lesser production values are decidedly cheesy, but any movie proffering tiny Maria Ouspenskaya as the queen of the Amazons has camp appeal - if little else. This reintroduced Jane, in the lacklustre person of Brenda Joyce, with Johnny Sheffield on hand as Boy, so it's down to a tired Johnny Weissmuller to make this tosh bearable. Fun of sorts, though, and certainly ecologically sound. TS
Johnny Weissmuller *Tarzan* · Johnny Sheffield *Boy* · Brenda Joyce *Jane* · Henry Stephenson *Henderson* · Maria Ouspenskaya *Amazon queen* · Barton MacLane *Ballister* ■ *Dir* Kurt Neumann · *Scr* Hans Jacoby, Marjorie L Pfaelzer, from characters by Edgar Rice Burroughs

Tarzan and the Great River ★★ U
Adventure 1967 · US/Swi · Colour · 88min

The Lord of the Jungle swings into action when an old zoo curator friend is murdered by a vicious cult of Leopard Men. Journeying up river towards the leader's hideout, accompanied by his trusty chimp and lion, Tarzan helps the local doctor to halt an epidemic. Not one of the best adventures, but Mike Henry makes a decent job of the hero, and the Brazilian locations are watchable. JG
Mike Henry *Tarzan* · Jan Murray *Captain Sam Bishop* · Manuel Padilla Jr *Pepe* · Diana Millay *Dr Ann Phillips* ■ *Dir* Robert Day · *Scr* Bob Barbash, from a story by Bob Barbash, Lewis Reed, from characters by Edgar Rice Burroughs

Tarzan and the Green Goddess ★★
Adventure 1938 · US · BW · 72min

This feature is one of two culled from episodes of *The New Adventures of Tarzan*. It combines some previously unseen material with footage edited from the last ten reels of the 1935 serial. Its star was Herman Brix, but he changed his name to Bruce Bennett and enjoyed a long career, albeit not as the ape man. The story is as evergreen as the jungle, with Tarzan out to protect civilisation from evil men who want a secret explosive formula hidden in a Mayan idol. BB

Herman Brix [Bruce Bennett] *Tarzan* • Ula Holt *Ula Vale* • Frank Baker (1) *Major Martling* • Don Castello *Raglan* ■ *Dir* Edward Kull • *Scr* Charles F Royal, from characters by Edgar Rice Burroughs

Tarzan and the Huntress ★★ U

Adventure 1947 · US · BW · 72min

The greatest Tarzan of them all, Johnny Weissmuller, was looking old and tired by this 11th film in his series. After *Tarzan and the Mermaids* the role of King of the Jungle passed to Lex Barker. Here, Brenda Joyce as Jane and Johnny Sheffield as Boy have more of a part to play than usual, as evil zoologist Patricia Morison plots to spirit animals into her private menagerie. All ecologically interesting, and certainly never boring. TS

Johnny Weissmuller *Tarzan* • Johnny Sheffield *Boy* • Brenda Joyce *Jane* • Patricia Morison *Tanya* • Barton MacLane *Weir* • John Warburton *Marley* • Wallace Scott *Smithers* • Charles Trowbridge *King Farrod* ■ *Dir* Kurt Neumann • *Scr* Jerry Gruskin, Rowland Leigh, from characters by Edgar Rice Burroughs

Tarzan and the Jungle Boy ★★ U

Adventure 1968 · US/Swi · Colour · 90min

Mike Henry was an engaging Tarzan, but he couldn't take the pace. Indeed, declining health while filming (including a chimp bite) prompted him to sue the producer. Tarzan is asked by a journalist to enter hostile territory to rescue a boy who has been lost for seven years. The area is dominated by an angry tribe whose dying chief is choosing which of his two sons - one bad, one good - should succeed him. Location photography means that the movie looks good. JG

Mike Henry *Tarzan* • Rafer Johnson *Nagambi* • Alizia Gur *Myrna Claudel* • Ed Johnson *Buhara* • Ronald Gans [Ron Gans] *Ken* • Steven Bond [Steve Bond] *Erik* ■ *Dir* Robert Gordon • *Scr* Stephen Lord, from characters by Edgar Rice Burroughs

Tarzan and the Leopard Woman ★★ U

Adventure 1946 · US · BW · 72min

Murder cults aren't a subject to be treated light-heartedly these days, but back in the mid-1940s they could still be wheeled out as a plot device. Here Tarzan, hindered and aided by Jane and Boy (Brenda Joyce and Johnny Sheffield) does what he can to destroy the titular villain, splendidly incarnated by Acquanetta. It's all jolly silly, but Johnny Weissmuller was getting a bit old for the role. TS

Johnny Weissmuller *Tarzan* • Johnny Sheffield *Boy* • Brenda Joyce *Jane* • Acquanetta *Lea* • Edgar Barrier *Lazar* • Tommy Cook *Kimba* ■ *Dir* Kurt Neumann • *Scr* Carroll Young, from characters by Edgar Rice Burroughs

Tarzan and the Lost City ★★ PG

Action adventure 1998 · Aus/US · Colour · 80min

Casper Van Dien dons the famous loincloth in this unambitious but enjoyable family adventure. Tarzan, now Lord Greystoke, has been fully integrated into British high society and is set to wed the beautiful Jane (Jane March). However, after experiencing a disturbing vision of the destruction of his childhood home, he's soon back swinging through the jungle. JF DVD

Casper Van Dien *Tarzan* • Jane March *Jane* • Steven Waddington *Nigel Ravens* • Winston Ntshona *Mugambi* • Rapulana Seiphemo *Kaya* • Ian Roberts (1) *Captain Dooley* ■ *Dir* Carl Schenkel • *Scr* Bayard Johnson, J Anderson Black, from characters by Edgar Rice Burroughs

Tarzan and the Lost Safari ★★★ U

Adventure 1956 · UK · Colour · 81min

One of the best 1950s episodes in the jungle saga brought a welcome mid-period lift to the series by being the first to venture into CinemaScope and Technicolor. Gordon Scott rescues the members of a safari team from the evil clutches of white hunter Robert Beatty. Thankfully, old stock footage was discarded and the movie was filmed on location in Africa, with studio scenes shot in England. RK

Gordon Scott *Tarzan* • Robert Beatty "*Tusker" Hawkins* • Yolande Donlan *Gamage Dean* • Betta St John *Diana* • Wilfrid Hyde White "*Doodles" Fletcher* • George Coulouris *Carl Kraski* ■ *Dir* H Bruce Humberstone • *Scr* Montgomery Pittman, Lillie Hayward, from characters by Edgar Rice Burroughs

Tarzan and the Mermaids ★★ U

Adventure 1948 · US · BW · 67min

Filmed in Mexico (mainly Acapulco) with an ambitious music score by Dimitri Tiomkin, this is less of a jungle adventure than most Tarzan films, as water and swimming sequences dominate. The spectacular scenery is the film's main asset as the story is a slow-moving affair in which Tarzan helps Linda Christian from being forced into marriage to a phoney island god. During the shooting of the cliff diving sequence, Johnny Weissmuller's double was killed. This was Weissmuller's 12th and last screen portrayal of Tarzan. TV

Johnny Weissmuller *Tarzan* • Brenda Joyce *Jane* • Linda Christian *Mara* • George Zucco *Palanth* • Andrea Palma *Luana* • Fernando Wagner *Varga* • Edward Ashley *Commissioner* ■ *Dir* Robert Florey • *Scr* Carroll Young, from characters by Edgar Rice Burroughs

Tarzan and the She-Devil ★★ U

Adventure 1953 · US · BW · 75min

Despite a great villain in Raymond Burr, this is a standard tale of ivory-seeking elephant hunters being stymied by the king of the jungle. Tarzan spends a good deal of the film in tied-up captivity, and director Kurt Neumann allows the pace to slacken too often before the climactic elephant stampede. This was the fifth and final Tarzan film for Lex Barker. TV

Lex Barker *Tarzan* • Joyce MacKenzie *Jane* • Raymond Burr *Vargo* • Monique Van Vooren *Lyra* • Tom Conway *Fidel* • Henry Brandon *M'Tara* • Michael Granger *Lavar* ■ *Dir* Kurt Neumann • *Scr* Karl Kamb, Carroll Young, from characters by Edgar Rice Burroughs

Tarzan and the Slave Girl ★★ U

Adventure 1950 · US · BW · 74min

The plotting of this adventure is exceptionally fanciful, as Jane is kidnapped by a tribe of lion worshippers who are being decimated by a strange malady and want to repopulate their civilisation. Tarzan finds himself fighting a native tribe called the Waddies, and fighting off the advances of a seductive nurse (Denise Darcel). Vanessa Brown is the first of several actresses to play Jane after the departure of Brenda Joyce. TV

Lex Barker *Tarzan* • Vanessa Brown *Jane* • Robert Alda *Neil* • Hurd Hatfield *Prince* • Arthur Shields *Dr Campbell* • Tony Caruso [Anthony Caruso] *Sengo* • Denise Darcel *Lola* ■ *Dir* Lee Sholem • *Scr* Hans Jacoby, Arnold Belgard, from characters by Edgar Rice Burroughs

Tarzan and the Trappers ★ U

Adventure 1958 · US · BW · 69min

The theme of white hunters searching for a lost city - said to be full of untold treasure - is so overworked that it needs the sort of production and cast that is totally missing in this compilation of three television episodes made for a series that failed to happen. Gordon Scott and Eve Brent are an acceptable Tarzan and Jane, but other

elements on display are under par. A successful Tarzan television series was made in 1966, starring Ron Ely. TV DVD

Gordon Scott *Tarzan* • Eve Brent *Jane* • Rickie Sorensen *Boy* ■ *Dir* Charles Haas, Sandy Howard • *Scr* Frederick Schlick, Robert Leach, from characters by Edgar Rice Burroughs

Tarzan and the Valley of Gold ★★★ U

Adventure 1966 · US/Swi · Colour · 89min

Mike Henry was poached from US pro football for this better than average jungle romp. A gold-obsessed archvillain, played with gusto by goateed David Opatoshu, kidnaps a boy, believing he holds the secret to a lost civilisation of gold. Enter a more gentlemanly Tarzan (by aircraft), who is persuaded to strip off his groovy suit, don a loincloth and re-enter the jungle to sort it all out. Those expecting a standard ape man adventure will be surprised by the sharp script and playful tone. JG

Mike Henry *Tarzan* • Nancy Kovack *Sophia Renault* • David Opatoshu *Vinaro* • Manuel Padilla Jr *Ramel* • Don Megowan *Mr Train* • Enrique Lucero *Perez* • Eduardo Noriega (1) *Talmadge* • John Kelly (3) *Voss* ■ *Dir* Robert Day • *Scr* Clair Huffaker, from characters by Edgar Rice Burroughs

Tarzan Escapes ★★★ U

Adventure 1936 · US · BW · 85min

The third entry in MGM's legendary jungle series was easily the most problematic, with a number of scenes being reshot from scratch. Much to the disgust of director Richard Thorpe, studio boss Louis B Mayer insisted that the more violent action be toned down. Yet this is still a full-blooded adventure, as Johnny Weissmuller resists John Buckler's attempts to exhibit him as a freak of nature back in Britain. DP

Johnny Weissmuller *Tarzan* • Maureen O'Sullivan *Jane Parker* • John Buckler *Captain Frye* • Benita Hume *Rita Parker* • William Henry *Eric Parker* • Herbert Mundin *Herbert Henry Rawlins* • EE Clive *Masters* ■ *Dir* Richard Thorpe • *Scr* Cyril Hume, Jack Cummings (uncredited), from characters by Edgar Rice Burroughs

Tarzan Finds a Son! ★★★ U

Adventure 1939 · US · BW · 78min

This is one of the splendid MGM Tarzans, starring the popular Johnny Weissmuller as the ape man and lovely Maureen O'Sullivan as Jane. Forbidden to produce children outside wedlock by the new film censorship code, the couple find a boy whose parents were killed in a plane crash, and begin a jungle version of a custody battle. It's a cleverly scripted and generally satisfying tale. TS

Johnny Weissmuller *Tarzan* • Maureen O'Sullivan *Jane* • John Sheffield [Johnny Sheffield] *Boy* • Ian Hunter *Austin Lancing* • Henry Stephenson *Sir Thomas Lancing* • Frieda Inescort *Mrs Lancing* • Henry Wilcoxon *Mr Sande* • Laraine Day *Mrs Richard Lancing* ■ *Dir* Richard Thorpe • *Scr* Cyril Hume, from characters by Edgar Rice Burroughs

Tarzan Goes to India ★★★ U

Adventure 1962 · UK · Colour · 86min

After playing a villain to Gordon Scott's King of the Jungle in *Tarzan the Magnificent*, former stuntman and western heavy Jock Mahoney took over the title role. This episode lifts the material out of its familiar rut by sending the hero to India for an elephant-rescuing operation, during which he encounters a company of Indians as well as Gajendra, King of the Elephants. RK

Jock Mahoney *Tarzan* • Mark Dana *O'Hara* • Jai *Jai the Elephant Boy* • Simi *Princess Kamara* • Leo Gordon *Bryce* ■ *Dir* John Guillermin • *Scr* Robert Hardy Andrews, John Guillermin, from characters by Edgar Rice Burroughs

Tarzan of the Apes ★★★

Silent adventure 1918 · US · BW · 55min

The first of the adventures of the jungle swinger, this has a rather wan Elmo Lincoln as the aristocrats' child reared by the apes. Years later, explorer Jane (Enid Markey)

comes looking for the Greystoke heir, prompting some heroics from the smitten Tarzan. The series didn't really get going until Johnny Weissmuller donned the loincloth but, as a curiosity, this is well worth seeing. Existing versions of the film run at less than half the length of the original 130 minute running time. TH

Elmo Lincoln *Tarzan* • Enid Markey *Jane Porter* • Gordon Griffith *Tarzan as a child* • True Boardman (1) *Lord Greystoke* • Kathleen Kirkham *Lady Greystoke* ■ *Dir* Scott Sidney • *Scr* William E Wing, from the novel by Edgar Rice Burroughs

Tarzan, the Ape Man ★★★★ PG

Adventure 1932 · US · BW · 96min

This is the first, and classiest, movie in the series starring Olympic swimming champion Johnny Weissmuller as the jungle swinger. Directed by WS Van Dyke with skill, the tale introduces the ape-reared boy to future partner Jane (Maureen O'Sullivan). Fighting a variety of big cats, armed with only a knife, may look unrealistic - as does some of the in-cut library material - but the fun at the expense of city dwellers on safari and the atmosphere of studio fantasy make it a living museum piece. TH DVD

Johnny Weissmuller *Tarzan* • Maureen O'Sullivan *Jane Parker* • Neil Hamilton *Harry Holt* • C Aubrey Smith *James Parker* • Doris Lloyd *Mrs Cutten* • Forrester Harvey *Beamish* • Ivory Williams *Riano* ■ *Dir* WS Van Dyke • *Scr* Cyril Hume, Ivor Novello, from characters by Edgar Rice Burroughs

Tarzan, the Ape Man ★ U

Adventure 1959 · US · Colour · 81min

Twenty-seven years after MGM unveiled the now-legendary Johnny Weismuller in the film of the same title, the studio had the temerity to remake it with one of the most lacklustre of all Tarzans, Denny Miller, in his only outing in the role. Since the company owned the original they tinted some footage from that and, apparently, even earlier silent Tarzan films. Nothing helped. BB

Denny Miller *Tarzan* • Joanna Barnes *Jane Parker* • Cesare Danova *Holt* • Robert Douglas *Col Parker* • Thomas Yangha *Riano* ■ *Dir* Joseph M Newman • *Scr* Robert Hill, from characters by Edgar Rice Burroughs

Tarzan, the Ape Man ★ 15

Adventure 1981 · US · Colour · 110min

This legendary turkey has Bo Derek traipsing through the greenery looking for excuses to disrobe more often than Edgar Rice Burroughs's jungle king himself. Directed by Bo's husband, John Derek, this actionless soft-core spectacular is a demented vanity production on such an epic scale that all you can do is stare in disbelief. Wooden Miles O'Keeffe must be the worst screen Tarzan ever. AJ Swearing, nudity. DVD

Bo Derek *Jane Parker* • Richard Harris *James Parker* • John Phillip Law *Harry Holt* • Miles O'Keeffe *Tarzan* • Akushula Selayah *Nambia, "Africa"* • Steven Strong *Ivory King* • Maxime Philoe *Riano* • Leonard Bailey *Feathers* • Wilfrid Hyde White *Club member* ■ *Dir* John Derek • *Scr* Tom Rowe, Gary Goddard, from characters by Edgar Rice Burroughs

Tarzan the Fearless ★★ U

Adventure 1933 · US · BW · 85min

Made by independent producer Sol Lesser just after MGM had released its first Tarzan blockbuster with Johnny Weissmuller, this starred the equally muscular Buster Crabbe, and followed MGM's portrayal of Tarzan as a grunting ape man rather than the educated hero of the original stories. Made simultaneously as a serial, this feature version is episodic and crudely edited. Crabbe's athleticism is fine, but his acting consists mainly of showing his teeth. TV DVD

Buster Crabbe [Larry "Buster" Crabbe] *Tarzan* • Jacqueline Wells [Julie Bishop] *Mary Brooks* • E Alyn Warren *Dr Brooks* • Edward Woods *Bob Hall* • Philo McCollough *Jeff Herbert* • Mischa Auer *High Priest* ■ *Dir* Robert F Hill • *Scr* Basil Dickey,

T

George H Plympton, Ford Beebe, Walter Anthony, from characters by Edgar Rice Burroughs

Tarzan the Magnificent
★★★ U

Adventure 1960 · UK · Colour · 86min

This was the last of Gordon Scott's six outings as Edgar Rice Burroughs's jungle hero. His adversary here, Jock Mahoney, would succeed him two years later in *Tarzan Goes to India*. The real star of the show, however, is veteran John Carradine, who throws restraint to the wind as the head of Mahoney's clan intent on ambushing the ape man before he can turn him over for trial. DP

Gordon Scott *Tarzan* • Jock Mahoney *Coy Banton* • Betta St John *Fay Ames* • John Carradine *Abel Banton* • Lionel Jeffries *Ames* • Alexandra Stewart *Laurie* ■ *Dir* Robert Day • *Scr* Berne Giler, Robert Day, from characters by Edgar Rice Burroughs

Tarzan Triumphs
★★★

Second World War adventure
1943 · US · BW · 76min

The first of the RKO Tarzan movies, produced by Sol Lesser, pits our hero, still in the brawny form of Johnny Weissmuller, against a topical German foe. The plot this time has Nazi paratroopers landing in a lost city and, sadly, leaves no room for Jane. Instead there's a fabulous performance from Cheetah, who here gets a super coda as he does something quite ingenious with the Nazis' short-wave radio – so it's worth sitting tight until the very end. TS

Johnny Weissmuller *Tarzan* • Johnny Sheffield *Boy* • Frances Gifford *Zandra* • Stanley Ridges *Col Von Reichart* • Rex Williams *Schmidt* • Sig Ruman *Sergeant* • Pedro De Cordoba *Patriarch* ■ *Dir* William Thiele • *Scr* Carroll Young, Roy Chanslor, from a story by Carroll Young, from characters by Edgar Rice Burroughs

Tarzan's Desert Mystery
★★★ U

Adventure 1943 · US · BW · 69min

Johnny Weissmuller's second jungle adventure for RKO is energetic hokum, a piece of lively wartime propaganda directed with zip by William Thiele. With Jane absent, the heroine is a chirpy showgirl (Nancy Kelly) with a secret message for a sheik, warning of foreign spies in his midst. The fast-moving action incorporates prehistoric monsters, man-eating plants and a totally unconvincing yet still gruesome giant spider which nearly devours Boy before turning its attention to the nasty Nazis. One of the most entertaining of the series. TV

Johnny Weissmuller *Tarzan* • Johnny Sheffield *Boy* • Nancy Kelly *Connie Bryce* • Otto Kruger *Paul Hendrix* • Joe Sawyer *Karl Straeder* • Lloyd Corrigan *Sheik Abdul El Khim* ■ *Dir* William Thiele • *Scr* Edward T Lowe, from a story by Carroll Young, from characters by Edgar Rice Burroughs

Tarzan's Fight for Life
★★ U

Adventure 1958 · US · Colour · 86min

In the third of six films in which he starred as Tarzan, former lifeguard Gordon Scott gets a new Jane, Eve Beck, and wrestles a live python in the film's best sequence. Otherwise it is business as usual when Tarzan's friendship with a doctor running a hospital in the jungle brings him into conflict with a tribal witch doctor and his superstitious followers. TV

Gordon Scott *Tarzan* • Eve Brent *Jane* • Rickie Sorensen *Tartu* • James Edwards *Futa* • Carl Benton Reid *Dr Sturdy* ■ *Dir* H Bruce Humberstone • *Scr* Thomas Hal Phillips, from characters by Edgar Rice Burroughs

Tarzan's Greatest Adventure
★★★ U

Adventure 1959 · UK · Colour · 84min

One of the best Tarzan movies, this was filmed on authentic African locations, with a fine plot and reliable direction from John Guillermin. Gordon Scott is Tarzan, with a greatly increased vocabulary compared with his predecessors, and the British co-stars are impressive. This is a splendid romp, beautifully photographed and edited, and it may even convert non-Tarzan fans. Watch out for Sean Connery as the diamond hunter. TS

Gordon Scott *Tarzan* • Anthony Quayle *Slade* • Sara Shane *Angie* • Niall MacGinnis *Kruger* • Sean Connery *O'Bannion* • Al Mulock *Dino* • Scilla Gabel *Toni* ■ *Dir* John Guillermin, Berne Giler, from a story by Les Crutchfield, from characters by Edgar Rice Burroughs

Tarzan's Magic Fountain
★★★ U

Adventure 1949 · US · BW · 72min

The first film Lex Barker made as Tarzan is also his best. The narrative, dealing with an elixir of youth, is intriguing and gripping with a neat mixture of humour and suspense. Evelyn Ankers, one of the screen's great B-movie heroines, is an aviatrix who crashed in the jungle 20 years earlier and still looks youthful, and Albert Dekker is a convincingly duplicitous villain who sights a fortune in marketing the secret of eternal youth. Brenda Joyce, considered second only to Maureen O'Sullivan as an effective "Jane", retired from the screen after this movie. TV

Lex Barker *Tarzan* • Brenda Joyce *Jane* • Albert Dekker *Trask* • Evelyn Ankers *Gloria James* • Charles Drake *Dodd* • Alan Napier *Douglas Jessup* ■ *Dir* Lee Sholem • *Scr* Curt Siodmak, Harry Chandlee, from characters by Edgar Rice Burroughs

Tarzan's New York Adventure
★★★ U

Adventure 1942 · US · BW · 70min

One of the best-loved and best-remembered of all the MGM Johnny Weissmuller *Tarzans*, this might not seem quite so original today, and perhaps it owed more than a little to *King Kong* even then. Still, Tarzan's confrontation with interior plumbing is still mightily amusing, funny enough to make you forget the nastiness of the abduction plot, as Boy is snatched from his ersatz jungle "parents" by unscrupulous circus folk. Sadly, this was the last time the lovely Maureen O'Sullivan played Jane. TS

Johnny Weissmuller *Tarzan* • Maureen O'Sullivan *Jane* • Johnny Sheffield *Boy* • Chill Wills *Manchester Mountford* • Paul Kelly (1) *Jimmie Shields* • Charles Bickford *Buck Rand* • Virginia Grey *Connie Beach* • Cy Kendall *Colonel Ralph Sargent* ■ *Dir* Richard Thorpe • *Scr* William R Lipman, Myles Connolly, from a story by Myles Connolly, from characters by Edgar Rice Burroughs

Tarzan's Peril
★★★ U

Adventure 1951 · US · BW · 78min

Filmed largely in Africa, this is one of the better Tarzan films, with fascinating shots of wildlife and plenty of action in its tale of gunrunners attempting to start a war between tribes. Though Virginia Huston is ineffectual as Jane, there is a striking performance by Dorothy Dandridge, in a small role as a jungle queen who wants peace, and George Macready, one of the screen's most hissable villains, proves a worthy adversary for hero Tarzan. The film was also supposed to be the first of the series in colour, but after much of the colour footage was destroyed in an accident, it was decided to switch to black and white. TV

Lex Barker *Tarzan* • Virginia Huston *Jane* • George Macready *Radijek* • Douglas Fowley *Trask* • Glenn Anders *Andrews* • Dorothy Dandridge *Melmendi* ■ *Dir* Byron Haskin • *Scr* Samuel Newman, Francis Swann, John Cousins, from characters by Edgar Rice Burroughs

Tarzan's Savage Fury
★★ U

Adventure 1952 · US · BW · 80min

This was the first movie to be directed by Cyril "Cy" Endfield in Britain, after he became one of the blacklisted Hollywood exiles. It was the beginning of a long career in Britain where his most famous film proved to be *Zulu*. Lex Barker becomes caught up in a typical adventure when his cousin, visiting him in Africa to obtain his help for Britain's military security, is killed. Plenty of action keeps the story bubbling along. BB

Lex Barker *Tarzan* • Dorothy Hart *Jane* • Patric Knowles *Edwards* • Charles Korvin *Rokov* • Tommy Carlton *Joey* ■ *Dir* Cyril Endfield [Cy Endfield] • *Scr* Cyril Hume, Hans Jacoby, Shirley White, from characters by Edgar Rice Burroughs

Tarzan's Secret Treasure
★★ U

Adventure 1941 · US · BW · 81min

High production values can't compensate for a ridiculous plot, but there is a certain perverse delight in watching Johnny Weissmuller's ape man and Maureen O'Sullivan's Jane cohabit in a tree house the like of which only the MGM art department could provide. There's a slew of dignified character players all looking worried, as well they might; after all, they're trying to fool Tarzan into helping them find gold. He may be big, but he certainly ain't stupid. TS

Johnny Weissmuller *Tarzan* • Maureen O'Sullivan *Jane* • Johnny Sheffield *Boy* • Reginald Owen *Professor Elliot* • Barry Fitzgerald *O'Doul* • Tom Conway *Medford* • Philip Dorn *Vandermeer* ■ *Dir* Richard Thorpe • *Scr* Myles Connolly, Paul Gabeglin, from characters by Edgar Rice Burroughs

Tarzan's Three Challenges
★★ U

Adventure 1963 · US · Colour · 92min

The producers dropped some Tarzan staples, such as Jane and Cheetah, in this episode of the jungle-fresh franchise, added Far Eastern locations and spent some money – all to good effect. A wise Oriental ruler is near death, and Tarzan has to prove himself a worthy minder to take the shrewd boy successor safely to the throne. On location, Jock Mahoney, in his second outing as the ape man, lost lots of weight during several bouts of illness; his constantly changing body is one of this picture's incidental pleasures. JG

Jock Mahoney *Tarzan* • Woody Strode *Khan/Tarim* • Tsu Kobayashi *Cho San* • Earl Cameron *Mang* ■ *Dir* Robert Day • *Scr* Berne Giler, Robert Day, from characters by Edgar Rice Burroughs

Task Force
★★ U

Action drama
1949 · US · BW and Colour · 116min

This long-winded account of the struggle to persuade the American navy to develop aircraft carriers opens with Gary Cooper as the retiring admiral looking back on his days as an early advocate of their use, arguing with politicians, newspaper proprietors and stubborn navy bigwigs. Only as the film bursts into colour towards the end, to work in documentary footage from the Second World War and demonstrate the carriers' worth in the Battle of Okinawa, does Delmer Daves's picture achieve liftoff. AE

Gary Cooper *Jonathan L Scott* • Jane Wyatt *Mary Morgan Scott* • Wayne Morris *McKinney* • Walter Brennan *Pete Richard* • Julie London *Barbara McKinney* • Bruce Bennett *McCluskey* • Jack Holt *Reeves* ■ *Dir/Scr* Delmer Daves

A Taste of Cherry
★★★★ PG

Drama 1997 · Iran · Colour · 94min

Sharing the Palme d'Or at Cannes with Shohei Imamura's *The Eel*, Abbas Kiarostami's unconventional road movie is as much about the filmic process as morality, mortality or modern Iran. World-weary, middle-aged Homayoon Irshadi cruises the suburbs of Tehran in search of someone willing to transgress Islamic law by burying him after his suicide. Each person he propositions has symbolic significance, including a Kurdistani soldier and an Afghan seminary student, before he finally finds a taxidermist, who accepts the reward to pay his son's medical bills. Endlessly fascinating, with the subtle shifts in landscape and palette quite masterly. DP Farsi +subtitles. *DVD*

Homayoon Irshadi *Mr Badiei* • Abdol Hossain Bagheri *Mr Bagheri, taxidermist in Natural History Museum* • Afshin Khorshid Bakhtari *Worker* • Safar Ali Moradi *Soldier from Kurdistan* • Mir Hossain Nouri *Clergyman* ■ *Dir/Scr* Abbas Kiarostami

Taste of Fear
★★★★ 12

Psychological thriller 1961 · UK · BW · 78min

Hammer's first *Psycho*-inspired thriller, also known as *Scream of Fear*, is the best House of Horror ever made. Squeezing maximum shocks from a clichéd story – a plot to drive someone insane – Seth Holt dazzles with his direction and gives Susan Strasberg her greatest role as the disabled young woman haunted by her father's corpse at his French villa. Just when you think you know what's going on, the marvellous script takes another labyrinthine twist into the unknown. Shot in moody black and white, the creepy swimming pool scene is justifiably famous. AJ *DVD*

Susan Strasberg *Penny Appleby* • Ronald Lewis *Bob, the chauffeur* • Ann Todd *Jane Appleby* • Christopher Lee *Dr Gerrard* • John Serret *Inspector Legrand* • Leonard Sachs *Spratt* ■ *Dir* Seth Holt • *Scr* Jimmy Sangster

A Taste of Honey
★★★★★ 15

Social drama 1961 · UK · BW · 96min

A ground-breaking movie of its time, this features the mousy Rita Tushingham in her screen debut as the unwanted teenage daughter of Dora Bryan, a hilariously vulgar Salford lass who is being courted by a flash and pimpish Robert Stephens. Our Rita is saved from her living hell by two social exiles – a black sailor, who makes her pregnant, and a homosexual who makes her happy – until the poverty trap snaps shut around her. Set in dank bedsits amid the grimy smokestacks, polluted canals and the tacky prom at Blackpool, this movie – a romance of sorts, and a comedy – survives as a priceless barometer of England in 1961. AT *DVD*

Rita Tushingham *Jo* • Dora Bryan *Helen* • Murray Melvin *Geoffrey* • Robert Stephens *Peter* • Paul Danquah *Jimmy* • David Boliver *Bert* • Moira Kaye *Doris* ■ *Dir* Tony Richardson • *Scr* Shelagh Delaney, Tony Richardson, from the play by Shelagh Delaney

The Taste of Money
★★ 15

Drama 2012 · S Kor · Colour · 114min

A super-rich Korean dynasty proves a law unto itself in this drama of entwining sharp business practices and tangled family relations. Kim Kang-woo plays the earnest right-hand man who struggles to maintain his own integrity while his employers bribe their way past the justice system. Director Im Sang-soo (*The Housemaid*, *The President's Last Bang*) utilises elegant production design and gorgeous camerawork, but the theme of corrupting wealth is just a bit too obvious. TJ Korean, English, Tagalog +subtitles. Swearing, a sex scene, nudity, some violence.

Kim Kang-woo *Young-jak Joo* • Baek Yun-shik *Chairman Yoon, the father* • Yoon Yeo-jung *Keumok "Baek", the mother* • Kim Hyo-jin *Nami, the daughter* ■ *Dir/Scr* Im Sang-soo

Taste the Blood of Dracula
★★★ 15

Horror 1969 · UK · Colour · 91min

Three Victorian gentlemen get more than they bargained for when they indulge in Satanism for fun with the assistance of Ralph Bates. They inadvertently resurrect Count Dracula (Christopher Lee), who sends their sons and daughters on a killing spree. Although Lee is given little to do apart from look suavely menacing, he does metamorphose into a caped hero battling the hypocrisy of Victorian family values in this flamboyantly grim fairy tale. AJ Violence. *DVD*

Christopher Lee *Dracula* • Geoffrey Keen *William Hargood* • Gwen Watford *Martha Hargood* • Linda Hayden *Alice Hargood* • Peter Sallis *Samuel Paxton* • Anthony Corlan [Anthony Higgins] *Paul Paxton* • Roy Kinnear *Weller* ■ *Dir* Peter Sasdy • *Scr* John Elder [Anthony Hinds], from the character created by Bram Stoker

U SUITABLE FOR ALL Uc SUITABLE ESPECIALLY FOR YOUNG CHILDREN (DVD ONLY) PG PARENTAL GUIDANCE 12A UNDER 12s TO BE ACCOMPANIED (CINEMA ONLY)

Tatie Danielle ★★ 15
Black comedy 1990 · Fr · Colour · 107min

Having mauled the middle-classes in *Life Is a Long Quiet River*, Etienne Chatiliez gives them an even more torrid time here at the hands of the auntie from hell, Tsilla Chelton. Relishing every little torture she inflicts upon Catherine Jacob and her dull, but decent family, Chelton gives a wonderfully malicious performance, but what began as a wicked satire ends up getting lost in the darkness of its own comedy, and we become increasingly drawn to the put-upon relatives. DP French +subtitles. Swearing, nudity. *DVD*

Tsilla Chelton *Aunt'e Danielle* · Catherine Jacob *Catherine Billard* · Isabelle Nanty *Sandrine* · Neige Dolsky *Odile* · Eric Pratt *Jean-Pierre Billard* · Laurence Février *Jeanne Billard* · Virginie Pradal *Madame La'osse* · Mathieu Foulon *Jean-Marie Billard* ■ *Dir* Etienne Chatiliez · *Scr* Florence Quentin, Etienne Chatiliez

The Tattered Dress ★★
Crime drama 1957 · US · BW · 92min

Jack Arnold directs this overheated, *film noir*-styled pompous melodrama. Monotone as ever, Jeff Chandler plays the defence lawyer who gets wealthy client Philip Reed acquitted of gunning down the man who attacked his wife (Gail Russell). Unfortunately for Chandler, the murdered man was the best friend of sheriff Jack Carson, who is determined to get revenge. The lurid paperback pulp-fiction thrust sits uneasily with a half-hearted indictment of the American judicial system. AJ

Jeff Chandler *James Gordon Blane* · Jeanne Crain *Dianne Blane* · Jack Carson *Sheriff Nick Hoak* · Gail Russell *Carol Morrow* · Elaine Stewart *Charleen Reston* · George Tobias *Billy Giles* · Edward Andrews *Lester Rawlings* · Philip Reed *Michael Reston* ■ *Dir* Jack Arnold · *Scr* George Zuckerman

Tattoo ★ 18
Drama 1980 · US · Colour · 98min

Bruce Dern kidnaps model Maud Adams in a sleazy psycho-drama. Written by Joyce Buñuel, daughter of Luis, it's supposed to be an insightful study of psychopathic behaviour; tattoo artist Dern's enforced needlework on Bond girl Adams is presented as a rape substitute. But, while it may have been Buñuel's intention to shower her controversial material in allegorical significance, former commercials director Bob Brooks isn't up to the job. AJ Swearing, nudity.

Bruce Dern *Karl Kinsky* · Maud Adams *Maddy* · Leonard Frey *Halsey* · Rikke Borge *Sandra* · John Getz *Buddy* · Peter Iacangelo *Dubin* · Alan Leach *Customer* · Cynthia Nixon *Cindy* ■ *Dir* Bob Brooks · *Scr* Joyce Buñuel, from a story by Bob Brooks

Tattoo ★★★ 18
Crime thriller 2002 · Fr/Ger · Colour · 108min

Christian Redl and August Diehl spark as the maverick veteran and his rookie partner who are assigned to the case of a demented collector of tattoos, who is prepared to kill in order to possess a series of prized ornate Japanese designs. Director Robert Schwentke's thriller favours atmosphere over character and incident, and the result is visually striking. DP German +subtitles. Violence.

August Diehl *Marc Schrader* · Christian Redl *Detective Minks* · Nadeshda Brennicke *Maya Kroner* · Ilknur Bahadir *Meltem* · Jasmin Schwiers *Marie Minks* · Johan Leysen *Frank Schoubya* · Monica Bleibtreu *Snr Detective Roth* ■ *Dir/Scr* Robert Schwentke

The Tattooed Stranger ★★★
Crime drama 1950 · US · BW · 64min

Producer Edward J Montagne demonstrates a fair for gritty realism as director of this police procedural, which not only makes evocative use of New York's backstreet locations, but also benefits from the deadpan performances of the largely unknown cast. Walter Kinsella and John Miles are particularly well matched as the dour veteran and forensics graduate whose differing approaches to the discovery of a serial bride's corpse add to an already intriguing case. A cult favourite among cineastes, this is taut, tough stuff. DP

John Miles *Detective Tobin* · Patricia White *[Patricia] Mary Mahan* · Walter Kinsella *Lieutenant Corrigan* · Frank Tweddell *Captain Lundquist* · Rod McLennan *Captain Gavin* · Henry Lasko *Joe Canko* ■ *Dir* Edward J Montagne · *Scr* Phil Reisman Jr [Phil Reisman Jr]

Tawny Pipit ★★★ U
Comedy 1944 · UK · BW · 77min

It was almost unthinkable in wartime that a British picture should criticise officialdom and poke fun at the eccentricities of national life. In Bernard Miles's independently produced feature, the only problem is that the satire is too gentle and the humour too whimsical. However, the story about rare birds that nest in a field outside a Cotswolds village is not without its charm, the excellent cast is a pleasure to watch and the photography is quite exquisite. DP

Bernard Miles *Colonel Barton-Barrington* · Rosamund John *Hazel Broome* · Niall MacGinnis *Jimmy Bancroft* · Jean Gillie *Nancy Forester* · Lucie Mannheim *Russian sniper* · Christopher Steele *Reverend Kingsley* ■ *Dir* Bernard Miles, Charles Saunders · *Scr* Bernard Miles, Charles Saunders, from a story by Miles · *Cinematographers* Eric Cross, Ray Sturgess

Taxi! ★★★
Crime drama 1932 · US · BW · 70min

This is a fast-paced, tough-as-nails Warner Bros melodrama with crackling dialogue, starring the great James Cagney as the New York cabbie involved in some inter-taxi-company rivalry. The opening sequence is a real surprise, with Cagney speaking fluent Yiddish, learned during his East Side childhood. There's some early fancy footwork from George Raft, who, like Cagney, was better known as a screen gangster than for what was his real forte – hoofing. TS

James Cagney *Matt Nolan* · Loretta Young *Sue Riley* · George E Stone *Skeets* · Guy Kibbee *Pop Riley* · David Landau *Buck Gerard* · Ray Cooke *Danny Nolan* · Leila Bennett *Ruby* · Dorothy Burgess *Marie Costa* · Matt McHugh *Joe Silva* · George Raft *William "Willie" Kenny* ■ *Dir* Roy Del Ruth · *Scr* Kubec Glasmon, John Bright, from the play *The Blind Spot* by Kenyon Nicholson

Taxi ★★
Comedy drama 1953 · US · BW · 77min

Directing his first movie in three years, Gregory Ratoff is deserted by the sure touch that persuaded 20th Century-Fox to entrust him with so many minor A features during the Second World War. Too many cooks were involved in concocting a script with little flavour of the New York streets. Dan Dailey plays a world-weary cabbie, who has to shrug off the loan sharks on his tail to help Irish immigrant Constance Smith locate her husband. DP

Dan Dailey *Ed Nielson* · Constance Smith *Mary* · Neva Patterson *Miss Millard* · Blanche Yurka *Mrs Nielson* · Geraldine Page *Florence Albert* · Rex O'Malley *Butler* · John Cassavetes *Cab driver* ■ *Dir* Gregory Ratoff · *Scr* DM Marshman Jr, Daniel Fuchs, Alex Joffe, Jean Paul Le Chanois, from the story *Sans Laisser d'Adresse* by Hans Jacoby, Fred Brady

Taxi ★★ 15
Action comedy thriller 1998 · Fr · Colour · 86min

The fancy automobile stunts are everything in this puerile, paper-thin comedy thriller scripted by Luc Besson. Speed-freak taxi driver Samy Naceri and timid cop Frédéric Diefenthal team up to catch a slick bunch of bank robbers, leading to much squealing of tyres through the streets of Marseille. Director Gérard Pirès adds feeble *Carry On*-style stabs at slapstick humour as the couple screw up the case and the bumbling Diefenthal attempts to woo statuesque police officer Emma Sjöberg. JC French +subtitles. Violence, sex scenes, nudity. *DVD*

Samy Naceri *Daniel* · Frédéric Diefenthal *Emilien* · Marion Cotillard *Lilly* · Emma Sjöberg *Petra* · Manuela Gouary *Camille* ■ *Dir* Gérard Pirès · *Scr* Luc Besson

Taxi ★★ 12
Action comedy 2004 · US/Fr · Colour · 93min

This reworking of the 1998 French smash takes knockabout stupidity to new levels. Thrown together by fate, useless New York cop Jimmy Fallon and speed-demon taxi driver Queen Latifah try to nab a gang of female Brazilian bank robbers, headed by supermodel Gisele Bundchen. All screeching brakes and no real excitement, this buddy movie is just a series of car chases linked together by tragically unfunny comedy. Latifah's wannabe racing champion has an easy charm, but Fallon's dumb schtick is annoying and tired. SF In English, Portuguese. Swearing, sexual references. *DVD* *Blu-ray*

Queen Latifah *Belle Williams* · Jimmy Fallon *Andy Washburn* · Gisele Bundchen *Vanessa* · Jennifer Esposito *Lt Marta Robbins* · Ann-Margret *Washburn's mom* · Henry Simmons *Jesse* · Christian Kane *Agent Mullins* ■ *Dir* Tim Story · *Scr* Robert Ben Garant, Thomas Lennon, Jim Kouf, from the film by Luc Besson

Taxi 2 ★★★ 12
Action drama 2000 · Fr · Colour · 84min

This harum scarum sequel reteams daredevil Marseille taxi driver Samy Naceri and laconic cop Frédéric Diefenthal. However, it benefits considerably from the snappier direction of Gérard Krawczyk, who not only keeps the plot ticking over, but also invests a Hollywood gusto into the action sequences. There's even some efficiently staged chop socky by way of variation, as a gang of ruthless ninjas kidnap a Japanese politician and Diefenthal's statuesque partner, Emma Sjöberg. DP French, Japanese +subtitles. *DVD*

Samy Naceri *Daniel* · Frédéric Diefenthal *Emilien* · Marion Cotillard *Lilly* · Emma Sjöberg *Petra* · Bernard Farcy *Chief Inspector Gibert* ■ *Dir* Gérard Krawczyk · *Scr* Luc Besson

Taxi Blues ★★★
Drama 1990 · Fr/USSR · Colour · 110min

Despite the visual excesses of a debutant, Pavel Lounguine won the best director prize at Cannes for this pioneering allegory on Russia at the crossroads. Alcoholic Jewish saxophonist Pyotr Nikolajevitch Mamonov epitomises the liberated intellectualism of the new era, while conservative Muscovite cabbie Piotr Zaitchenko represents the hard-pressed proletariat. The film can hardly be said to be subtle in its symbolism, especially once their unlikely camaraderie is soured by sudden wealth and romantic rivalry. DP Russian +subtitles.

Pyotr Nikolajevitch Mamonov *Liocha* · Piotr Zaitchenko *Schlikov* · Vladimir Kachpour *Old Netchiporenko* · Natalia Koliakanova *Christina* · Hal Singer ■ *Dir/Scr* Pavel Lounguine

Taxi Driver ★★★★★ 18
Psychological drama 1976 · US · Colour · 109min

Robert De Niro is mesmerising as the Vietnam veteran trapped in one of director Martin Scorsese's most frightening circles of hell, as he seeks a twisted redemption by saving the soul of New York child prostitute Jodie Foster. This time the bustling helter-skelter of Scorsese's *Mean Streets* gives way to a measured, chilly calm, and cinematographer Michael Chapman ensures the Big Apple glistens with barely concealed menace. It's De Niro's show, but the supporting players (Foster, Harvey Keitel, Cybill Shepherd) are almost as good, and there's a genuinely scary cameo from the director himself. This deeply disturbing modern masterpiece established Scorsese as a major figure in world cinema, and it has not lost any of its power to shock. JF Violence, swearing. *DVD* *Blu-ray*

Robert De Niro *Travis Bickle* · Cybill Shepherd *Betsy* · Jodie Foster *Iris* · Peter Boyle *Wizard* · Leonard Harris *Charles Palantine* · Harvey Keitel *Sport* · Albert Brooks *Tom* · Martin Scorsese *Passenger* ■ *Dir* Martin Scorsese · *Scr* Paul Schrader

Taxi to the Dark Side ★★★★ 15
Documentary 2007 · US · Colour and BW · 108min

Writer/director Alex Gibney confronts the horrifying reality of the "war on terror" with this Oscar-winning documentary. In December 2002, an innocent Afghan cab driver named Dilawar was detained at Bagram Air Force Base and subjected to brutal interrogation by US military personnel: he died five days later from his injuries. The murder was eventually exposed in an article in the *New York Times* and a handful of rank-and-file soldiers were prosecuted. But the film makes it clear that they were scapegoats for a crime that conformed to procedures sanctioned by both the White House and the Pentagon. Gibney combines stills, reconstructions and interviews with detainees, politicians and soldiers to devastating effect, constructing a damning case against both the military brass and a bellicose US Administration that tacitly encourages the employment of illegal torture techniques. DP *DVD*

■ *Dir/Scr* Alex Gibney

Taxi zum Klo ★★★★ 18
Erotic comedy 1980 · W Ger · Colour · 90min

A distinctive progenitor of "queer cinema", Frank Ripploh's first, highly accomplished movie is a light-hearted, sometimes farcical, but always uncompromising honest depiction of his own life, in which he and his former lover Bernd Broaderup play themselves. Ripploh, a schoolteacher in Berlin, is torn between his reliable domesticity and the excitement of extracurricular sex. In 1981 it was startling but refreshing to see such material played as sexually uninhibited romantic comedy, with no political message. Now, post-Aids, the film is a museum piece, but none the less enjoyable. After making an unsuccessful sequel, Ripploh faded from view. DM German +subtitles. Violence, swearing, sex scenes. *DVD*

Frank Ripploh *Frank* · Bernd Broaderup *Bernd* · Orpha Termin *Female neighbour* · Dieter Godde *Masseur* ■ *Dir/Scr* Frank Ripploh

Taxidermia ★★★ 18
Black comedy horror 2006 · Hun/Austria/Fr · Colour · 90min

The grotesqueries of the flesh are celebrated in all their stomach-churning glory in this outrageous black comedy horror. An explicit tale of three generations of men, each with their own bodily obsession, it's a sensory assault that's definitely not for the squeamish. Hungarian director/co-writer Gyorgy Palfi seems to revel in pressing viewers' shock buttons, as he introduces us briefly to a sexually frustrated military orderly during the Second World War, before focusing on his son, an obese speed-eating champion, and finally to his son, a skinny taxidermist. The baroque visuals and surreal scenarios play like a warped version of *Monty Python*, skilfully diverting attention from the uneven plot. SF Hungarian +subtitles. *DVD*

Csaba Czene *Vendel Morosgovanyi* · Gergo Trocsanyi *Kalman Balatony* · Marc Bischoff *Lajoska Balatony* · Adel Stanczel *Gizella "Gizi" Aczel* · Istvan Gyuricza *Lieutenant* · Piroska Molnar *Lieutenant's wife* · Gabor Mate *Older Kalman* ■ *Dir* Gyorgy Palfi · *Scr* Zsofia Ruttkay, Gyorgy Palfi, from stories by Lajos Parti Nagy · *Cinematographer* Gergely Poharnok

A Taxing Woman ★★★★ 18
Comedy drama 1987 · Jpn · Colour · 127min

The sharpest critic of Japanese mores in the 1980s, Juzo Itami focuses on the national obsession with all things material in this supremely controlled satire. His wife, Nobuko Miyamoto, is hilariously tenacious as the demure tax inspector whose slavish attention to detail is rewarded when she's given a pop at seedy motel mobster Tsutomu Yamazaki. With an unlikely romance, this blend of yakuza comedy and procedural thriller is both socially revealing and slyly entertaining. DP Japanese +subtitles.

Nobuko Miyamoto *Ryoko Itakura* • Tsutomu Yamazaki *Hideki Gondo* • Masahiko Tsugawa *Assistant Chief Inspector Hanamura* • Eitaro Ozawa *Tax accountant* ■ *Dir/Scr* Juzo Itami

Taxman ★★ 15

Crime action thriller 1998 · US · Colour · 96min

Whether many people will be rooting for a heroic tax inspector remains to be seen, but this no-frills thriller at least provides a rare leading role for Joe Pantoliano, who makes the most of the opportunity. As a tough-talking investigator he sets out on a personal crusade to expose the murky dealings of the Russian Mob with the help of a young cop (the late Wade Dominguez). The two leads spark off each other nicely and there are strong straight turns from Michael Chiklis and Robert Townsend, both better known for their comic work. JF DVD

Joe Pantoliano *Al Benjamin* • Wade Dominguez *Joseph Romero* • Elizabeth Berkley *Nadia Rubakov* • Michael Chiklis *Andre Rubakov* • Robert Townsend *Peyton Cody* ■ *Dir* Avi Nesher • *Scr* Avi Nesher, Robert Berger

Taza, Son of Cochise ★★ U

Western 1954 · US · Colour · 79min

This very average western starts with an uncredited Jeff Chandler making a third, brief appearance as the wise warrior chief Cochise, passing on the pipe of peaceful co-existence to his son, played rather stiffly by Rock Hudson. Unfortunately, a dissenting Geronimo and others stir up some predictable trouble. Shot entirely on location in Utah, it's vigorously staged by director Douglas Sirk. Although it's photographed in 3D, interest had peaked by this time and the film was mainly shown "flat". AE SP

Rock Hudson *Taza* • Barbara Rush *Oona* • Gregg Palmer *Captain Burnett* • Bart Roberts [Rex Reason] *Naiche* • Morris Ankrum *Gray Eagle* • Gene Iglesias [Eugene Iglesias] *Chato* ■ *Dir* Douglas Sirk • *Scr* George Zuckerman, Gerald Grayson Adams, from a story by Gerald Grayson Adams

Tea & Sangría ★★

Romantic comedy
2014 · UK/Sp · Colour · 110min

An Englishman gives up everything to live with his Spanish girlfriend in Madrid, and a romantic comedy of cross-cultural misunderstanding ensues after things don't work out and he becomes stranded in the city. Writer/producer/director Peter Domankiewicz shot this semi-autobiographical tale on a tiny budget, and also takes the central role, where his lack of leading-man charisma rather scuppers the film's chances. It's all a bit third-division Woody Allen, but at least the Spanish-speaking cast prove an endearing lot. TJ In English, Spanish.

Peter Domankiewicz *David* • Angela Boix *Marisa* • Daniel Albaladejo *Jose Maria* • Carlos Pontini *Ricardo* • Agnes Kiraly *Tamara* • Jorge Berges *Ignacio* ■ *Dir/Scr* Peter Domankiewicz

Tea and Sympathy ★★★★

Drama 1956 · US · Colour · 121min

"So the boy think's he's homosexual and the teacher's wife seduces him to prove he isn't, so what's the problem?", said a perplexed French producer to director Vincente Minnelli. But in its day this was notorious, the play banned in the UK and the film X certificated. Re-creating their Broadway roles are Deborah Kerr, John Kerr (no relation) and Leif Erickson, who are all superbly cast, though the honesty of their performances is slightly threatened by the gloss in which MGM has almost drowned the tale. Forty years ago its dialogue was ground-breaking. TS

Deborah Kerr *Laura Reynolds* • John Kerr *Tom Robinson Lee* • Leif Erickson *Bill Reynolds* • Edward Andrews *Herb Lee* • Darryl Hickman *Al* • Norma Crane *Ellie Martin* • Dean Jones *Ollie* • Jacqueline de Wit *Lilly Sears* ■ *Dir* Vincente Minnelli • *Scr* Robert Anderson, from his play

Tea for Two ★★ U

Musical comedy 1950 · US · Colour · 93min

Though popular enough in its day, this Technicolored Doris Day vehicle is not one of her better musicals, suffering greatly from lacklustre direction and an astoundingly stupid plotline. It's a loose remake of *No, No, Nanette*, in which the heroine has to reply "no" to every question asked of her in an otherwise uneventful weekend in order to fulfil a bet. A daft tale that's not even cute enough to be camp. TS

Doris Day *Nanette* • Gordon MacRae *Jimmy* • Gene Nelson *Tommy* • Eve Arden *Pauline* • Billy De Wolfe *Larry* • SZ Sakall *Max* • Patrice Wymore *Beatrice* ■ *Dir* David Butler • *Scr* Harry Clork, from the musical play *No, No, Nanette* by Frank Mandel, Otto Harbach, Vincent Youmans, Emil Nyitray

Tea with Mussolini ★★★ PG

Period comedy drama 1998 · It · Colour · 112min

Franco Zeffirelli here turns his camera on to his own life as a young boy growing up in Mussolini's Italy of the 1930s. Following his mother's death, young Baird Wallace is rescued from the prospect of life in an orphanage by an eccentric group of expatriate women dubbed "Scorpioni". Through his eyes we see the corseted and costumed women: Judi Dench, Joan Plowright, Maggie Smith, Lily Tomlin and Cher, giving boisterously strong performances. An interesting series of anecdotes rather than a rich character piece. JB English, Italian +subtitles. Swearing. DVD

Cher *Elsa* • Judi Dench *Arabella* • Joan Plowright *Mary* • Maggie Smith *Lady Hester* • Lily Tomlin *Georgie* • Baird Wallace *Luca* ■ *Dir* Franco Zeffirelli • *Scr* John Mortimer, Franco Zeffirelli, from an autobiography by Franco Zeffirelli

Teachers ★★ 15

Comedy 1984 · US · Colour · 102min

Nick Nolte is a cynical teacher at the overcrowded and undisciplined John F Kennedy High School. When a graduating student is found to be illiterate, his family sue the school causing vice-principal Judd Hirsch to rally the staff in defence of their teaching methods. The prosecuting lawyer, JoBeth Williams, turns out to have been a student at the school. A by-the-numbers story of a good teacher inspiring the kids others ignore. Predictable. DF

Nick Nolte *Alex* • JoBeth Williams *Lisa* • Judd Hirsch *Roger* • Ralph Macchio *Eddie* • Lee Grant *Dr Burke* • Richard Mulligan *Herbert* • Allen Garfield *Rosenberg* • Royal Dano *Ditto* • Laura Dern *Diane* • Crispin Glover *Danny* • Morgan Freeman *Lewis* ■ *Dir* Arthur Hiller • *Scr* WR McKinney

Teacher's Pet ★★★★ U

Comedy 1958 · US · BW · 115min

In this delightful comedy, Clark Gable stars as a crusty, hard-bitten newspaper editor who, instead of lecturing to Doris Day's journalism class, decides to enrol as a pupil. And, of course, his initial disdain of reporters who learn from books is swayed by his attraction to the teacher. Fay and Michael Kanin's screenplay becomes thin by the end, but Gable and Day fill it out with boisterous enthusiasm, while the great Gig Young, Doris's other beau, was Oscar-nominated. TH DVD

Clark Gable *James Gannon* • Doris Day *Erica Stone* • Gig Young *Dr Hugo Pine* • Mamie Van Doren *Peggy DeFore* • Nick Adams *Barney Kovac* • Peter Baldwin *Harold Miller* • Charles Lane (2) *Roy* • Harry Antrim *Lloyd Crowley* ■ *Dir* George Seaton • *Scr* Fay Kanin, Michael Kanin

Teacher's Pet ★★★ U

Animated comedy musical
2004 · US · Colour · 70min

There's fun for pre-teens and adults alike in this zany animated comedy in which an ultra-smart talking dog will do anything to become a real boy. Spinning off from a Disney TV cartoon series, the outlandish, modern fairy tale combines a breakneck barrage of pop-culture references, catchy tunes and madcap sight gags. An exuberant Nathan Lane voices the sarcastic, titular canine Spot, while a vivid retro style adds to the energy. SF DVD

Nathan Lane *Spot/Scott* • Kelsey Grammer *Dr Krank* • Shaun Fleming *Leonard* • Debra Jo Rupp *Mrs Helperman* • David Ogden Stiers *Jolly* • Jerry Stiller *Pretty Boy* • Paul Reubens *Dennis* ■ *Dir* Timothy Björklund • *Scr* Bill Steinkellner, Cheri Steinkellner, from the TV series by Gary Baseman, Bill Steinkellner, Cheri Steinkellner

Teaching Mrs Tingle ★★ 15

Black comedy thriller 1999 · US · Colour · 90min

Even a central performance by Helen Mirren and script packed with bitchy one-liners cannot rescue Kevin Williamson's directorial debut. In this bungled black comedy, Mirren is the mean-spirited teacher who stands in the way of student Katie Holmes and a scholarship. The tables are turned when Holmes and two friends hold their teacher hostage after an incident with an exam paper. AC Violence, drug abuse. DVD Blu

Helen Mirren *Mrs Tingle* • Katie Holmes *Leigh Ann Watson* • Jeffrey Tambor *Coach Wenchell* • Barry Watson *Luke Churner* • Marisa Coughlan *Jo Lynn Jordan* • Liz Stauber *Trudie Tucker* • Michael McKean *Principal Potter* • Molly Ringwald *Miss Banks* ■ *Dir/Scr* Kevin Williamson

The Teahouse of the August Moon ★★★ U

Comedy 1956 · US · Colour · 122min

Marlon Brando stars as the Japanese interpreter who comes into conflict with Glenn Ford, as the latter attempts to bring American democracy and materialism to the Japanese island of Okinawa. As a satire on the culture clash it has some teeth, though not quite as lethal-looking as those worn by Brando as part of his hilarious make-up. Brando made the film partly to raise money to make a documentary about the UN's role in Asia, but he disliked the result. AT

Marlon Brando *Sakini* • Glenn Ford *Captain Fisby* • Machiko Kyo *Lotus Blossom* • Eddie Albert *Captain McLean* • Paul Ford *Colonel Purdy* • Jun Negami *Mr Seiko* • Henry Morgan [Harry Morgan] *Sgt Gregovich* ■ *Dir* Daniel Mann • *Scr* John Patrick, from the play by John Patrick and the novel by Vern J Sneider

Team America: World Police ★★★ 15

Satirical comedy
2004 · US/Ger · Colour · 93min

Trey Parker and Matt Stone here admirably live up to their reputation for scatological high jinks. The film, performed by Thunderbirds-style marionettes, follows the team of the title as they battle terrorism across the world as well as tackling an enemy closer to home, the ultra-liberal Film Actors Guild (if you examine the acronym, you'll get an idea of the level of the film's humour). The running joke is that Team America invariably cause more damage battling terror than do the terrorists themselves. Sporadically very funny and astonishingly offensive. AS Swearing, violence, sex scenes. DVD Blu

Trey Parker *Gary/Joe/Kim Jong Il/Hans Blix* • Matt Stone *Chris* • Kristen Miller *Lisa* • Masasa *Sarah* • Daran Norris *Spottswoode* • Phil Hendrie *I.N.T.E.L.L.I.G.E.N.C.E.* • Maurice LaMarche *Alec Baldwin* ■ *Dir* Trey Parker • *Scr* Trey Parker, Matt Stone, Pam Brady

Tears of the Black Tiger ★★★ 18

Action melodrama 2000 · Thai · Colour · 97min

The first Thai film ever to screen in competition at Cannes, Wisit Sasanatieng's directorial debut resembles a strikingly stylised hybrid of Bollywood masala movie and spaghetti western. But it's actually a pastiche of 1950s Thai films typified by the work of pioneer film-maker Ratana Pestonji. Using digital video techniques and computer manipulation to heighten the film's colour, Sasanatieng enhances the kitsch value of a routine story about childhood sweethearts, separated by class and now on opposite sides of the law. It's a pastel-shaded magpie of a movie, in which old-fashioned narrative devices rub shoulders with ham acting, eruptions of violence and obvious budget limitations. DP Thai +subtitles. DVD

Chartchai Ngamsan *Seua Dum, "Black Tiger"* • Stella Malucchi *Rumpoey* • Suppakorn Kitsuwan *Mahesuan* • Arawat Ruangvuth *Police Captain Kumjorn* ■ *Dir/Scr* Wisit Sasanatieng

Tears of the Sun ★★ 15

War action thriller 2003 · US · Colour · 115min

Bruce Willis is up to his neck in mud and bullets in this passable action thriller, playing the gruff, tough leader of an elite marine squad that's sent into civil war-torn Nigeria to extricate a mission worker (Monica Bellucci). But Willis's position is complicated by the fact that the mission medic wants to bring half the neighbourhood back with her. Cue two hours of bullets, blood and bombast. DA Violence, swearing. DVD Blu

Bruce Willis *Lt AK Waters* • Monica Bellucci *Dr Lena Kendricks* • Cole Hauser *James "Red" Atkins* • Eamonn Walker *Ellis "Zee" Pettigrew* • Nick Chinlund *Michael "Slo" Slowenski* • Fionnula Flanagan *Sister Grace* • Malick Bowens *Col Idris Sadick* • Tom Skerritt *Capt Bill Rhodes* ■ *Dir* Antoine Fuqua • *Scr* Alex Lasker, Patrick Cirillo

Teaserama ★★ 15

Cult burlesque revue 1955 · US · Colour · 64min

Tempest Storm was one of the last of the classic strippers of the burlesque era. In this poverty-row record of her revue, she's joined by other disrobing artists, dancing girls and comedians, including, in one legendary mistress/maid scenario, queen of the 1950s pin-ups, Betty Page. Shot (saying directed would give completely the wrong impression!) with a single, static camera, this "adults only" antique is so coy and innocent by today's standards it's hard to believe it was ever considered controversial or racy. AJ Semi-nudity.

Tempest Storm • Bettie Page • Honey Baer • Cherry Knight • Chris LaChris • Vicki Lynn • Joe E Ross • Dave Starr • Trudy Wayne • Twinnie Wallen ■ *Dir* Irving Klaw

The Teckman Mystery ★★ PG

Thriller 1954 · UK · BW · 86min

There's more than a hint of *The Third Man* in this passable thriller. John Justin looks suitably bemused as an author who discovers that the dead air ace whose biography he's been commissioned to write may not have perished after all. Director Wendy Toye makes a reasonable fist at keeping the pace up and the clues hidden, but she's no Carol Reed. DP Some violence DVD

Margaret Leighton *Helen Teckman* • John Justin *Philip Chance* • Roland Culver *Inspector Harris* • Michael Medwin *Martin Teckman* • George Coulouris *Garvin* • Duncan Lamont *Inspector Hilton* ■ *Dir* Wendy Toye • *Scr* Francis Durbridge, James Matthews, from the BBC TV serial *The Teckman Biography* by Durbridge

Ted ★★★★ 15

Comedy 2012 · US · Colour · 101min

Imagine Bernard Manning as a teddy bear – that's the essence of this off-the-wall and very vulgar comedy from *Family Guy* creator Seth McFarlane, who also provides the voice for Ted. The fact that Ted can walk and talk (and swear) adds a hilarious twist to a conventional battle of wills between 30-something slacker Mark Wahlberg and girlfriend Mila Kunis over his refusal to grow up. The outlandish premise lightens the offensiveness, somehow, though Giovanni Ribisi, as Ted's stalker, turns the humour a shade darker. SP Swearing, sexual references, drug abuse, brief nudity. Blu

Mark Wahlberg *John Bennett* • Mila Kunis *Lori Collins* • Seth MacFarlane *Ted* • Joel McHale *Rex* • Giovanni Ribisi *Donny* • Patrick Stewart *Narrator* • Sam J Jones • Norah Jones ■ *Dir* Seth MacFarlane • *Scr* Seth MacFarlane, Alec Sulkin, Wellesley Wild

U SUITABLE FOR ALL Uc SUITABLE ESPECIALLY FOR YOUNG CHILDREN (DVD ONLY) PG PARENTAL GUIDANCE 12A UNDER 12s TO BE ACCOMPANIED (CINEMA ONLY)

Ted 2 ★★★ 🄵
Comedy   2015 · US · Colour · 112min

The trash-talking teddy bear has plenty to say in this sequel, although director Seth MacFarlane – who is also the voice of Ted – has padded the story a little heavily. Ted is fighting for his civil rights after being told he can't adopt a child, aided by old pal John (Mark Wahlberg) and Amanda Seyfried as a pot-smoking lawyer. As before, it's the bond between John and Ted that ties the movie together – and the cheeky banter between them that ensures plenty of laughs. Even though it isn't as lean and mean as the first film, Ted 2 is still a bagful of naughty fun. SP Swearing, sexual references, drug abuse DVD Blu

Mark Wahlberg *John Bennett* • Seth MacFarlane *Ted* • Amanda Seyfried *Samantha* • Jessica Barth *Tami-Lyn* • Giovanni Ribisi *Donny* • Morgan Freeman *Patrick Meighan* • Liam Neeson *Customer* • Patrick Stewart *Narrator* ■ *Dir* Seth MacFarlane • *Scr* Seth MacFarlane, Alec Sulkin, Wellesley Wild

Teen Agent ★★★ 🄿🄶
Spy comedy   1991 · US · Colour · 84min

Richard Grieco stars in a fun spy spoof laced with sly Ian Fleming references and 007-inspired gimmicks. He's mistaken for an undercover CIA agent when he flies to Paris for French lessons. Armed by MI5 with suction sneakers, X-ray specs and a tank-cum-sports car, he's sent to investigate Roger Rees, a megalomaniac in high camp *Goldfinger* mode. Although predictable every step of the way, this will leave you enjoyably shaken and pleasantly stirred. AJ Swearing, violence.

Richard Grieco *Michael Corben* • Linda Hunt *Ilsa Grunt* • Roger Rees *Augustus Steranko* • Robin Bartlett *Mrs Grober* • Gabrielle Anwar *Mariska* • Geraldine James *Vendetta Galante* • Michael Siberry *Richardson* • Roger Daltrey *Blade* ■ *Dir* William Dear • *Scr* Darren Star, from a story by Fred Dekker

Teen Kanya ★★★ 🅄
Comedy drama   1961 · Ind · BW · 114min

Satyajit Ray filmed two of Tagore's stories on the centenary of the author's birth. Both are charming tales about the difficulties faced by young women in love. In *The Postmaster* an orphaned girl becomes attached to her employer, who repays her affection by helping with her education. A young man rejects an arranged marriage in *The Conclusion*, but finds that his own choice of bride resents being forced into matrimony. The film's success is due as much to the gifted playing and Ray's observant eye, as to Tagore's skills as a storyteller. DP Bengali +subtitles.

Anil Chatterjee *Nandalal* • Chandana Bannerjee *Ratan* • Aparna Das Gupta *Mrinmoyee* • Soumitra Chatterjee *Amulya* ■ *Dir* Satyajit Ray • *Scr* Satyajit Ray, from the stories *The Postmaster* and *The Conclusion* by Rabindranath Tagore

Teen Wolf ★★★ 🄿🄶
Comedy   1985 · US · Colour · 91min

In this likeable, if lightweight, comedy, a teenager who longs to be a little less ordinary discovers a family curse that kicks in when the Moon is full. Beneath the facial fur, this is just another film about growing pains, although it does feature cinema's only werewolf slam dunk sequence. As the unfortunate teenager, the engaging Michael J Fox is doing what he does best – turning a loser into a winner. Jason Bateman took over in the needless sequel *Teen Wolf Too*. JC DVD Blu

Michael J Fox *Scott Howard* • James Hampton *Harold Howard* • Susan Ursitti *Lisa "Boof" Marconi* • Jerry Levine *Stiles* • Matt Adler *Lewis* • Lorie Griffin *Pamela* • Jim MacKrell [James MacKrell] *Mr Thorne* • Mark Arnold *Mick McAllister* • Jay Tarses *Coach Finstock* ■ *Dir* Rod Daniel • *Scr* Joseph Loeb III, Matthew Weisman

Teen Wolf Too ★★ 🄿🄶
Comedy   1987 · US · Colour · 90min

Arrested Development star Jason Bateman replaces Michael J Fox in a lazy retread of the first film, playing the cousin of Fox's character. He soon discovers that his lycanthropic genes work wonders for his sporting prowess (boxing rather than basketball) and his standing in high school society. Juvenile slapstick is the order of the day, with Bateman showing little early sign of his now-proven comic timing. JF DVD

Jason Bateman *Todd Howard* • Kim Darby *Professor Tanya Brooks* • John Astin *Dean Dunn* • Paul Sand *Coach Finstock* • James Hampton *Uncle Harold* • Mark Holton *Chubby* ■ *Dir* Christopher Leitch • *Scr* R Timothy Kring, from characters by Joseph Loeb III, Matthew Weisman

Teenage ★★★ 🄸🄰
Documentary   2013 · US/Ger · BW and Colour · 77min

Archive footage and artful reconstruction shape this film on the creation of the teenager, marking a journey from the child labour of the Victorian era to the postwar cultural recognition of a transitional period between childhood and adult responsibility. Matt Wolf's film is fascinating for the way it shows young people sent off to work or off to fight before they had a chance to grow up, seeking an identity in organisations like the Scout movement, and shocking their parents with wild new dance crazes like the jitterbug. However, filtering writer Jon Savage's non-fiction doorstopper into a mere 78 minutes also makes this feel like a taster for a more in-depth TV series – but one well worth seeing, nonetheless. TJ Some swearing, drug abuse, nudity.

Jena Malone *American girl* • Ben Whishaw *British boy* • Julia Hummer *German girl* • Jessie Usher *American boy* ■ *Dir* Matt Wolf • *Scr* Matt Wolf, Jon Savage, from Savage's book *Teenage: the Creation of Youth 1875-1945*

Teenage Caveman ★★ 🅄
Fantasy adventure   1958 · US · BW · 65min

Cult director Roger Corman's prehistoric *Rebel without a Cause* is justly famous for its catchpenny title, cheap dinosaurs (borrowed from *One Million BC*), the "stuffed deer" scene and lead actor Robert Vaughn in his pre-*Man from UNCLE* days. He's the titular boy who breaks tribal rules and ventures into the "forbidden land", where he learns his violent society is really a post-apocalyptic one. Vaughn calls this "one of the best-worst films of all time". AJ

Robert Vaughn (1) *Boy* • Leslie Bradley *Symbol Maker* • Darrah Marshall *Maiden* • Frank De Kova *Villain* ■ *Dir* Roger Corman • *Scr* R Wright Campbell

Teenage Monster ★ 🄿🄶
Science-fiction horror   1958 · US · BW · 65min

This ho-hum science-fiction horror movie was titled *Meteor Monster* until the success of *I Was a Teenage Werewolf* caused every horror film to jump on the same bandwagon. In a plot that drags western clichés into its juvenile delinquent mix, teenager Gilbert Perkins is infected by rays from a weird meteor and slowly turns into a hairy monster. AJ DVD

Anne Gwynne *Ruth Cannon* • Gloria Castillo *Kathy North* • Stuart Wade *Sheriff Bob* • Gilbert Perkins *Charles Cannon* • Charles Courtney [Chuck Courtney] *Marv Howell* ■ *Dir* Jacques Marquette • *Scr* Ray Buffum

Teenage Mutant Ninja Turtles ★★ 🄿🄶
Fantasy adventure   1990 · US · Colour · 89min

Those kickboxing Teletubbies of yesteryear made their feature debut in this uneven comic-strip fantasy directed by pop-video whizzkid Steve Barron. In case you'd forgotten, the awesome foursome are pizza-munching, kung fu fighting, sewer-dwelling super-reptiles who, in this mindless adventure, help perky TV reporter Judith Hoag solve a Manhattan crime spree masterminded by the Shredder, a Darth Vader-voiced rogue ninja master. Elias Koteas scores as a mock turtle vigilante, but little else in this garish affair hits the target. AJ DVD Blu

Judith Hoag *April O'Neil* • Elias Koteas *Casey Jones* • Josh Pais *Raphael* • Michelan Sisti *Michelangelo* • Leif Tilden *Donatello* • David Forman *Leonardo* • Michael Turney *Danny Pennington* • Jay Patterson *Charles Pennington* ■ *Dir* Steve Barron • *Scr* Todd W Langen, Bobby Herbeck, from a story by Bobby Herbeck, from characters by Kevin Eastman, Peter Laird

Teenage Mutant Ninja Turtles II: the Secret of the Ooze ★★ 🄿🄶
Fantasy adventure   1991 · US · Colour · 84min

This sequel is less abrasive than its predecessor and was considerably less successful at the box office. Seeking once more to stamp out the Foot clan, the turtles team up with reporter Paige Turco and gormless delivery boy Ernie Reyes Jr, but the human characters (even scientist David Warner) are pretty pointless. If you didn't know, Ooze is the nasty stuff that caused our heroes to live underground, shout "cowabunga" and gorge themselves on bizarre flavoured pizzas in the first place. DP DVD

Paige Turco *April O'Neil* • David Warner *Professor Jordan Perry* • Michelan Sisti *Michelangelo* • Leif Tilden *Donatello* • Kenn Troum *Raphael* • Mark Caso *Leonardo* • Kevin Clash *Splinter* • Ernie Reyes Jr *Keno* • François Chau *Shredder* • Toshishiro Obata *Tatsu* ■ *Dir* Michael Pressman • *Scr* Todd W Langen, from characters by Kevin Eastman, Peter Laird

Teenage Mutant Ninja Turtles III ★★ 🄿🄶
Fantasy adventure   1992 · US · Colour · 91min

This second sequel was, by this stage, a largely irrelevant one, as the equally irritating Power Rangers had succeeded the Pizza-loving reptiles in the children's popularity stakes. Writer/director Stuart Gillard tries to inject some life into the project by including some tongue-in-cheek scenes in 17th-century Japan, but it quickly degenerates into half-hearted cartoonish action. JF DVD

Elias Koteas *Casey Jones/Whit Whitley* • Paige Turco *April O'Neil* • Stuart Wilson (1) *Captain Dirk Walker* • Sab Shimono *Lord Norinaga* • Vivian Wu *Princess Mitsu* • Mark Caso *Leonardo* • Matt Hill *Raphael* • Jim Raposa *Donatello* • David Fraser *Michelangelo* • James Murray (2) *Splinter* ■ *Dir* Stuart Gillard • *Scr* Stuart Gillard, from characters by Kevin Eastman, Peter Laird

Teenage Mutant Ninja Turtles ★★★ 🄸🄸
Fantasy action adventure   2014 · US · Colour · 101min

Director Jonathan Liebesman's "Turtle Recall" origin story is an entertaining and smooth ride. Frustrated TV news reporter Megan Fox discovers the existence of the four half-shelled heroes, and realises her connection via her late researcher father's experiments. The movie strikes a fluid balance between pop-culture banter, cartoon fisticuffs and family friendliness, and the grit of the source material peeps through in the hi-octane action sequences. AJ Some violence, swearing. DVD Blu 3D

Megan Fox *April O'Neil* • Will Arnett *Vernon Fenwick* • William Fichtner *Eric Sacks* • Danny Woodburn *Splinter* • Alan Ritchson *Raphael* • Noel Fisher *Michelangelo* • Pete Ploszek *Leonardo* ■ *Dir* Jonathan Liebesman • *Scr* Josh Applebaum, André Nemec, Evan Daugherty, from characters by Kevin Eastman, Peter Laird

Teenage Mutant Ninja Turtles – Out of the Shadows ★★★ 🄸🄰
Fantasy action adventure   2016 · US · Colour · 111min

Transformers supremo Michael Bay doesn't actually direct here, but his wham-bam style is very much in evidence. Our secretive half-shell heroes break cover to thwart plans by an unholy alliance of arch-baddie Shredder, minions Rhino and Warthog, and a disembodied brain from another dimension. Megan Fox's TV reporter returns and Stephen Amell (from TV's *Arrow*) debuts as a vigilante good guy in a visually spectacular and fun family film in which the action sequences, though intense, are bloodless and comic. DA Some violence, swearing. 3D

Megan Fox *April O'Neil* • Stephen Amell *Casey Jones* • Laura Linney *Rebecca Vincent* • Will Arnett *Vernon Fenwick* • Pete Ploszek *Leonardo* • Noel Fisher *Michelangelo* • Alan Ritchson *Raphael* • Jeremy Howard *Donatello* • Danny Woodburn *Splinter* • Tyler Perry *Baxter Stockman* ■ *Dir* Dave Green • *Scr* Josh Applebaum, André Nemec, from characters by Kevin Eastman, Peter Laird

Teenage Rebel ★★
Comedy drama   1956 · US · BW · 94min

This is a misleading title for a mediocre family picture about teenager Betty Lou Keim who, having lived with her father after her parents' divorce, is sent back to her mother Ginger Rogers when dad decides to remarry. Initially resentful of both maternal control and her stepfather Michael Rennie, she gradually warms to her surroundings. Entirely forgettable despite Oscar nominations for costume, art direction and set decoration. RK

Ginger Rogers *Nancy Fallon* • Michael Rennie *Jay Fallon* • Mildred Natwick *Grace Hewitt* • Betty Lou Keim *Dodie* • Warren Berlinger *Dick Hewitt* • Rusty Swope *Larry Fallon* ■ *Dir* Edmund Goulding • *Scr* Walter Reisch, Charles Brackett, from the play *A Roomful of Roses* by Edith Sommer

Teeth ★★★ 🄸🄸
Black comedy horror   2007 · US · Colour · 90min

In this comedy horror with bite, Jess Weixler plays a high-school student with a second set of teeth. Where? That is for her gynaecologist to know, and for her hapless lovers to find out if they get violent. Though the plot may sound like Z-grade horror, this is in fact a female-empowerment film of some subtlety and no small amount of charm. That is thanks largely to a bright and breezy performance by leading lady Weixler. The film's gorier moments may prove too much for some, but if you like your horror with a blackly comic edge, then you will be pleasantly surprised. DA DVD

Jess Weixler *Dawn* • John Hensley *Brad* • Josh Pais *Dr Godfrey* • Hale Appleman *Tobey* • Lenny Von Dohlen *Bill* • Vivienne Benesch *Kim* ■ *Dir/Scr* Mitchell Lichtenstein

Telefon ★★★ 🄿🄶
Spy thriller   1977 · US · Colour · 98min

This is far from director Don Siegel's best work, but it's a more than acceptable thriller with a nifty plot and a couple of cracking performances. Charles Bronson is solid enough as a KGB troubleshooter sent to the USA to prevent "sleeping" agents from carrying out their missions, and Lee Remick is typically assured as his contact. But the film belongs to Donald Pleasence as a Stalinist spymaster and Tyne Daly as a CIA computer boffin. DP Violence.

Charles Bronson *Grigori Borzov* • Lee Remick *Barbara* • Donald Pleasence *Nicolai Dalchimsky* • Tyne Daly *Dorothy Putterman* • Alan Badel *Colonel Malchenko* • Patrick Magee *General Strelsky* • Sheree North *Marie Wills* • Frank Marth *Harley Sandburg* ■ *Dir* Don Siegel • *Scr* Peter Hyams, Stirling Silliphant, from the novel by Walter Wager

The Telephone ★ 🄵
Comedy drama   1988 · US · Colour · 78min

Poor Whoopi Goldberg has been involved in a number of dubious big screen projects in her time but this plumbs new depths. With a script by the unlikely pairing of musician Harry Nilsson and Terry Southern (co-writer of *Easy Rider*), and direction by dependable character actor Rip Torn, an intriguing project was on the cards, but it wasn't to be. This is virtually a one-woman show with Whoopi as a "resting" actress constantly ranting into her pet owl. DF

Whoopi Goldberg *Vashti Blue* • Severn Darden *Max* • Elliott Gould *Rodney* • John Heard *Telephone man* • Amy Wright *Honey Boxe/Irate neighbor/Jennifer, answering machine voice* ■ *Dir* Rip Torn • *Scr* Terry Southern, Harry Nilsson

T

Tell It to the Judge ★★
Romantic comedy 1949 · US · BW · 85min

Co-stars Rosalind Russell and Robert Cummings have to employ all their considerable skill as *farceurs* to keep this lightweight comedy afloat. The plot concerns the attempts of lawyer Cummings to get back with his ex-wife Russell, but the cause of their split – dumb blonde Marie McDonald – is the key witness in a case Cummings is working on. It's thin stuff, and Russell allows herself to be put through some undignified slapstick. TV

Rosalind Russell *Marsha Meredith* • Robert Cummings *Peter Webb* • Gig Young *Alexander Darvac* • Marie McDonald *Ginger Simmons* • Harry Davenport *Judge Meredith* • Fay Baker *Valerie Hobson* • Katharine Warren [Katherine Warren] *Kitty Lawton* • Douglass Dumbrille *George Ellerby* ■ *Dir* Norman Foster • *Scr* Nat Perrin, Roland Kibbee, from a story by Devery Freeman

Tell Me a Riddle ★★★
Drama 1980 · US · Colour · 90min

Unaware that the illness from which she is suffering is terminal, elderly Lila Kedrova, who has been locked in mutually unsatisfying 40-year-marriage to Melvyn Douglas, visits her granddaughter Brooke Adams in San Francisco. There, she reflects on her unfulfilled life and, before her death, finds reconciliation with her husband. Marking the directorial debut of Oscar-winning actress Lee Grant (*Shampoo*), this is a truthful, perceptive and intelligent film, that is well-made and well-acted, but perhaps too sad and sombre to hold a broad appeal. RK

Melvyn Douglas *David* • Lila Kedrova *Eva* • Brooke Adams *Jeannie* • Lili Valenty *Mrs Mays* • Dolores Dorn *Vivi* • Bob Elross *Sammy* • Jon Harris *Mathew* • Zalman King *Paul* ■ *Dir* Lee Grant • *Scr* Joyce Eliason, Alev Lytle, from a novel by Tillie Olsen

Tell Me Lies ★★
Drama 1967 · UK · Colour and BW · 116min

Following the disturbing film version of Peter Weiss's *Marat/Sade*, theatre director Peter Brook and Glenda Jackson reteamed for another all-out assault on the senses with this satirical swipe at the Vietnam War. This time, however, the chaotic structure (it's a mixture of sketches, music and news footage) fails to hold the attention and now seems self-indulgent rather than radical. Worth a look, if only for the eclectic cast. JF

Mark Jones (1) *Mark* • Pauline Munro *Pauline* • Robert Lloyd *Bob* • Kingsley Amis • Peggy Ashcroft • Glenda Jackson • Paul Scofield • Patrick Wymark • James Cameron • Ian Hogg ■ *Dir* Peter Brook • *Scr* Denis Cannan, Michael Kustow, Michael Scott, from the play *US* by Denis Cannan

Tell Me Something ★★★ 18
Horror thriller 1999 · S Kor · Colour · 117min

When body parts begin turning up in grotesque combinations in bin bags across Seoul, hangdog detective Han Suk-kyu and his loyal sidekick Chang Hang-seon begin to wonder whether the culprit is museum curator Shim Eun-ha or one of the many sadistic characters who have contributed to her traumatic past. Making splendid use of his rain-soaked locations and littering the action with moments of forensic nastiness, director Chang Youn-hyun mercilessly builds the suspense, only to allow much of it to dissipate during a dissatisfying final showdown. DP Korean +subtitles. *DVD*

Han Suk-kyu *Detective Cho* • Shim Eun-ha *Chae Su-Yeon* • Chang Hang-seon *Detective Oh* • Yum Jung-ah *Sung-min Oh* ■ *Dir* Chang Youn-hyun • *Scr* Chang Youn-hyun, In Eun-ah, Kim Eun-jeong, Kong Su-chang, Shim Hye-weon, from a story by Koo Bon-han

Tell Me That You Love Me, Junie Moon ★★
Comedy drama 1970 · US · Colour · 112min

One of Hollywood's most incisive, intelligent and provocative directors, Otto Preminger had seemingly lost his grip by the end of the 1960s, his judgement and objectivity replaced by trendy issues and glutinous sentimentality. A wildly over-emotional Liza Minnelli is Junie Moon while non-names Robert Moore and Ken Howard are her co-stars in this account of a facially disfigured young woman, a wheelchair-using homosexual and an epileptic drop-out. It should be inspiring, but it isn't. RK

Liza Minnelli *Junie Moon* • Ken Howard *Arthur* • Robert Moore *Warren* • James Coco *Mario* • Kay Thompson *Miss Gregory* • Ben Piazza *Jesse* ■ *Dir* Otto Preminger • *Scr* Marjorie Kellogg, from her novel

Tell No One ★★★★ 15
Thriller 2006 · Fr · Colour · 125min

An air of calculation pervades actor/director Guillaume Canet's adaptation of American thriller writer Harlan Coben's bestselling novel. Set in Paris, it's a well-told tale of sinister connivance that stars an impressive François Cluzet as the Hitchcockian everyman whose life is shattered by the murder of his wife (Marie-Josée Croze). Eight years later he becomes the chief suspect when fresh clues relating to her death emerge – just as he receives an email suggesting that she's actually alive and in trouble. Adroitly alternating between mysterious revelation and moments of abrasive action, Canet is assisted by committed performances from an excellent cast. But he fails to paper over all the cracks in the narrative logic, as he draws us into a sordid conspiracy that's saddled with the nastiest of MacGuffins. DP French +subtitles. *DVD* ◈

François Cluzet *Alexandre "Alex" Beck* • Marie-Josée Croze *Margot Beck* • André Dussollier *Jacques Laurentin* • Kristin Scott Thomas *Hélène Perkins* • François Berléand *Eric Levkowitch* • Nathalie Baye *Elysabeth Feldman* • Jean Rochefort *Gilbert Neuville* • Philippe Lefebvre (2) *Philippe Meynard* • Guillaume Canet *Philippe Neuville* ■ *Dir* Guillaume Canet • *Scr* Guillaume Canet, Philippe Lefebvre (2), from the novel by Harlan Coben

Tell No Tales ★★★
Crime drama 1939 · US · BW · 68min

An excellent second-feature drama, utilising those familiar Hollywood companions, crime and newspapers, this stars Melvyn Douglas as the editor of a daily newspaper that is about to close. When Douglas gets a scoop on a kidnapping case, his troubles appear to be over, but then he finds his involvement plunging him into danger. Well characterised and tightly constructed for maximum tension, this is enhanced by the commanding presence of the star in a less suave man-about-town role than usual. RK

Melvyn Douglas *Michael Cassidy* • Louise Platt *Ellen Frazier* • Gene Lockhart *Arno* • Douglass Dumbrille [Douglass Dumbrille] *Matt Cooper* • Florence George *Lorna Travers* ■ *Dir* Leslie Fenton • *Scr* Lionel Houser, from a story by Pauline London, Alfred Taylor

Tell Them Willie Boy Is Here ★★★ 15
Western 1969 · US · Colour · 93min

This sombre, allegorical western may seem too arty and introspective for today's tastes since the main thread of the story – a traditional pursuit across fine landscapes – is frequently broken for homilies on life and liberty. Even so, Robert Redford is excellent as the deputy sheriff chasing the Indian who's killed his prospective father-in-law. Robert Blake, as the fugitive, and Katharine Ross as his girlfriend, are less impressive. AT

Robert Redford *Christopher Cooper* • Katharine Ross *Lola Boniface* • Robert Blake *Willie Boy* • Susan Clark *Dr Elizabeth Arnold* • Barry Sullivan *Ray Calvert* • Charles McGraw *Frank Wilson* • John Vernon *Hacker* ■ *Dir* Abraham Polonsky • *Scr* Abraham Polonsky, from the book *Willie Boy* by Harry Lawton

Telling Lies in America ★★★★ 15
Drama 1997 · US · Colour · 97min

This sweet and subtle coming-of-age story was written by Joe Eszterhas, who is more noted for steamy material like *Basic Instinct* and *Showgirls*. Partly autobiographical, the film tells of an immigrant Hungarian kid (Brad Renfro) who falls under the spell of Kevin Bacon's charismatic but ethic-free radio DJ. When Bacon is accused of taking record company backhanders, Renfro has to decide whether to jeopardise his father's citizenship assessment by lying for a friend. Terrific performances from Bacon and Renfro, and solid support from Maximilian Schell and Calista Flockhart. DA Swearing.

Kevin Bacon *Billy Magic* • Brad Renfro *Karchy Jonas* • Maximilian Schell *Dr Istvan Jonas* • Calista Flockhart *Diney Majeski* • Paul Dooley *Father Norton* • Luke Wilson *Henry* ■ *Dir* Guy Ferland • *Scr* Joe Eszterhas

Telling You ★ 15
Romantic comedy drama 1998 · US · Colour · 90min

This debut indie written and directed by Robert DeFranco (who also features) has Jennifer Love Hewitt and Matthew Lillard to recommend it but very little else. Set in a pizzeria, this follows no-hopers Dash Mihok and Peter Facinelli as they return home from college and face a future of applying toppings to bases. When money goes missing, they scramble to replace it. LH *DVD*

Peter Facinelli *Phil Fazzulo* • Dash Mihok *Dennis Nolan* • Jennifer Love Hewitt *Deb Friedman* • Jennifer Jostyn *Beth Taylor* • Frank Medrano *Sal Lombardo* • Richard Libertini *Mr P* • Robert DeFranco *Steve Fagan* • Matthew Lillard *Adam Ginesberg* ■ *Dir* Robert DeFranco • *Scr* Robert DeFranco, Marc Palmieri, from a story by Marc Palmieri, from a story by Denis Flood

Telstar: the Joe Meek Story ★★★ 15
Biographical drama 2008 · UK · Colour · 111min

The life and death of influential 1960s record producer Joe Meek (Britain's unsung answer to Phil Spector) is brought efficiently to the screen in the directorial debut of actor Nick Moran (*Lock, Stock and Two Smoking Barrels*). Adapted from the acclaimed play, the film often betrays its stagey origins, although Con O'Neill (re-creating his award-winning stage performance) expertly captures Meek's fey arrogance in a biopic that's a must for pop music fans. There's also a wealth of supporting talent, including Kevin Spacey, James Corden and a number of rock star cameos. AJ Violence, swearing, sex scenes, drug abuse.

Con O'Neill *Joe Meek* • Kevin Spacey *Major Wilfred Banks* • Pam Ferris *Mrs Violet Shenton* • James Corden *Clem Cattini* • JJ Feild *Heinz Burt* • Tom Burke *Geoff Goddard* • Ralf Little *Chas Hodges* • Jon Lee *Billy Fury* ■ *Dir* Nick Moran • *Scr* Nick Moran, James Hicks, from a play by Moran, Hicks

The Temp ★★ 15
Thriller 1993 · US · Colour · 92min

After the nanny from hell (*The Hand That Rocks the Cradle*) and the lodger from hell (*Pacific Heights*), meet Satan's secretary. Lara Flynn Boyle is the shorthand expert wanting to make her way to the top no matter who stands in her way in this at times rather ludicrous thriller. Unfortunately, this film is neither as scary nor as funny as its predecessors, and serves only to embarrass a usually competent cast that includes Timothy Hutton and Faye Dunaway. JB Swearing, sex scenes, violence. *DVD*

Timothy Hutton *Peter Derns* • Lara Flynn Boyle *Kris Bolin* • Dwight Schultz *Roger Jasser* • Oliver Platt *Jack Hartsell* • Steven Weber *Brad Montroe* • Colleen Flynn *Sara Meinhold* • Faye Dunaway *Charlene Towne* • Scott Coffey *Lance* ■ *Dir* Tom Holland (1) • *Scr* Kevin Falls, from a story by Kevin Falls, Tom Engelman

Tempest ★★
Period drama 1959 · It/Yug/Fr · Colour · 120min

Producer Dino de Laurentiis's attempt to do cinematically for Pushkin what his *War and Peace* did for Tolstoy. While the spectacle (Technicolor and Technirama photography by the great Aldo Tonti) certainly passes muster, the direction by former Italian neorealist Alberto Lattuada isn't up to the task. Some thought has gone into the retelling of the overthrow of Russia's Catherine the Great, and Viveca Lindfors makes a striking Empress, but the whole is undermined by a trashy, sexy subplot involving gauche Geoffrey Horne and an over-ripe Silvana Mangano. TS Italian, Serbo-Croat, French dubbed.

Silvana Mangano *Masha* • Van Heflin *Pugacev* • Viveca Lindfors *Catherine II* • Geoffrey Horne *Peter Griniev* • Robert Keith (1) *Captain Mironov* • Agnes Moorehead *Vassilissa* • Oscar Homolka *Savelic* • Helmut Dantine *Svabrin* • Finlay Currie *Count Griniev* ■ *Dir* Alberto Lattuada • *Scr* Alberto Lattuada, Ivo Perilli, from stories by Alexander Pushkin

The Tempest ★★★★ 15
Fantasy drama 1979 · UK · Colour · 87min

Derek Jarman's experience as an art director is the key factor in this adaptation of Shakespeare's play, as his use of the Stoneleigh Abbey location is as inspired as his reworking of the material is audacious. Purists will bridle at the bowdlerisation of the action, but the shifting of emphasis to explore contemporary themes, the sensuality of Toyah Willcox's Miranda, the eccentricity of Heathcote Williams's Prospero and the carnality of Jack Birkett's Caliban make for provocative viewing. DP *DVD*

Heathcote Williams *Prospero* • Karl Johnson (2) *Ariel* • Toyah Willcox *Miranda* • Peter Bull *Alonso* • Richard Warwick *Antonio* • Elisabeth Welch *Goddess* • Jack Birkett *Caliban* • Ken Campbell *Gonzalo* • Christopher Biggins *Stephano* • David Meyer *Ferdinand* • Neil Cunningham *Sebastian* ■ *Dir* Derek Jarman • *Scr* Derek Jarman, from the play by William Shakespeare

Tempest ★★ 15
Fantasy drama 1982 · US · Colour · 136min

Director Paul Mazursky's transposition of Shakespeare's play into a modern setting is a lengthy, self-indulgent folly. As the architect who seeks solace on a Greek island, John Cassavetes introduces an unexpected conviction to an otherwise uninspired story, which, for all the beauty of Donald McAlpine's seascapes, is nothing more than another study in Manhattan angst. The Shakespearean links are clumsily forged, and the whole conceit is made faintly ridiculous by the zealous significance of the performances. DP Swearing, nudity.

John Cassavetes *Phillip Dimitrious* • Gena Rowlands *Antonia Dimitrious* • Susan Sarandon *Aretha* • Vittorio Gassman *Alonzo* • Raul Julia *Kalibanos* • Molly Ringwald *Miranda* • Sam Robards *Freddy* ■ *Dir* Paul Mazursky • *Scr* Paul Mazursky, Leon Capetanos, from the play by William Shakespeare

The Tempest ★★★ PG
Fantasy drama 2010 · US/UK/Ind · Colour · 105min

Shakespeare's play comes to the screen with the leading role of Prospero, the Milanese nobleman practising his dark arts on a Mediterranean island, changed to Prospera so that Helen Mirren can play the part. She's predictably splendid – bringing the verse to life, attuned to the rage and compassion in the material – though the gender switch gives the impression that director Julie Taymor's adaptation is a more radical beast than it actually is. For all Taymor's superficial computer-generated frippery, it works best when she lets her actors simply get on with it, thereby matching Mirren's accomplishment. All that's missing is the interpretative authority that would have made it something special. TJ Sexual references.

Helen Mirren *Prospera* • Russell Brand *Trinculo* • Alfred Molina *Stephano* • Chris Cooper *Antonio* • Djimon Hounsou *Caliban* • Felicity Jones *Miranda* • David Strathairn *King Alonso* • Ben Whishaw *Ariel* ■ *Dir* Julie Taymor • *Scr* Julie Taymor, from the play by William Shakespeare

Tempest ★★★ 12A
Drama documentary 2012 · UK · Colour and BW · 76min

When a movie about urban youth is located in south London, it is too often a bleak tale

---

U SUITABLE FOR ALL **Uc** SUITABLE ESPECIALLY FOR YOUNG CHILDREN (DVD ONLY) **PG** PARENTAL GUIDANCE **12A** UNDER 12s TO BE ACCOMPANIED (CINEMA ONLY)

about teen alienation, drugs and violence. It's refreshing, then, that this inspiring film focuses on a multiracial group of 17 young people as they workshop Shakespeare's *Tempest* in and around their home patch. Switching between performance and rehearsal, the documentary – which is mercifully free of explanatory narration – allows the teenagers to provide the commentary on their lives, their interest in drama and their hopes for the future. A much-needed reminder that investment in the young remains as important now as it's ever been. JA

Zephryn Taitte *Prospero* • Paris Campbell *Miranda* ■ *Dir* Rob Curry, Anthony Fletcher • *Scr* Based on *The Tempest* by William Shakespeare

Temple Grandin ★★★★
Biographical drama 2010 · US · Colour · 103min

This could so easily have been one of those disease-of-the-week, triumph over adversity TV movies. The story of a remarkable autistic woman, Temple Grandin (Claire Danes), and her fight for acceptance and a comfortable place in the world, this features little dramatic content outside of her fragile emotional state. But it is the visually stunning realisation of Temple's inner world – how she sees the world in pictures – that makes this such an absorbing character study. DC

Claire Danes *Temple Grandin* • Julia Ormond *Eustacia* • David Strathairn *Dr Carlock* • Catherine O'Hara *Aunt Ann* ■ *Dir* Mick Jackson • *Scr* Christopher Monger, William Merritt Johnson, from the autobiography *Emergence* by Temple Grandin, Margaret Scarciano, and the autobiography *Thinking in Pictures* by Grandin

Tempted ★★★
Thriller 2001 · Fr/US/Aus · Colour · 95min

Director Bill Bennett made his name with the unnerving, dislocated road movie *Kiss or Kill* and he brings some of the same edgy improvisational techniques to this, his first American movie. Burt Reynolds is the rich businessman who is the instigator of a dangerous *ménage à trois* when he hires a young carpenter (Peter Facinelli) to test the fidelity of his trophy wife Saffron Burrows. The three leads are excellent and Bennett avoids the usual tourist clichés in evoking the atmosphere of New Orleans. JF

Burt Reynolds *Charlie Le Blanc* • Saffron Burrows *Lilly Le Blanc* • Peter Facinelli *Jimmy Mulate* • Mike Starr *Dot Collins* • George DiCenzo *Byron Blades* ■ *Dir/Scr* Bill Bennett

The Temptress ★★★
Silent drama 1926 · US · BW · 117min

A Parisian aristocrat "sells" his wife Greta Garbo to a banker to secure himself a life of material luxury. She falls madly in love with Antonio Moreno, an Argentinian engineer who leaves her when he learns she is married. Following him to Argentina, Garbo inflames the passions of several men en route to a climactic fall-out. Begun under the direction of Garbo's Swedish mentor Mauritz Stiller, who was replaced by Fred Niblo, this raging inferno of lust, love and degeneracy was her second American film and it attracted ecstatic reviews. RK

Greta Garbo *Elena* • Antonio Moreno *Robledo* • Roy D'Arcy *Manos Duros* • Marc MacDermott *M Fontenoy* • Lionel Barrymore *Canterac* • Virginia Brown Faire *Celinda* ■ *Dir* Fred Niblo • *Scr* Dorothy Farnum, Mauritz Stiller, Marian Ainslee, from the novel *La Tierra de Todos* by Vicente Blasco Ibañez, Leo Ongley (translation)

Temptress ★★ 18
Erotic thriller 1995 · US · Colour · 89min

This lavishly produced erotic chiller is a class above the usual soft-core fare. Kim Delaney is transformed into the bad girl of the title after being possessed by the goddess Kali on a trip to India. There are sound supporting turns, and director Lawrence Lanoff brings at least a hint of style to the usual genre clichés. JF Sex scenes, nudity.

Kim Delaney *Karin Swann* • Chris Sarandon *Matthew Christianson* • Corbin Bernsen *Nick* • Dee Wallace Stone *Allison Mackie* • Ben Cross *Dr*

Samudaya • Jessica Walter *Dr Phyllis Evergreen* ■ *Dir* Lawrence Lanoff • *Scr* Melissa Mitchell

Temptress Moon ★★★ 15
Romantic period drama 1996 · HK/Chi · Colour · 115min

Following its indifferent reception at Cannes, Chen Kaige's visually stunning period piece suffered substantial cuts and the imposition of gutsier subtitles. But this remains an overwrought melodrama, complete with operatic emotions, two-dimensional performances (even from Gong Li and Leslie Cheung) and fumbling attempts to depict passion. The tale of a country boy caught up in both the aftermath of the 1911 Revolution and the opium-induced decline of his Shanghai family is a disappointment. DP Mandarin +subtitles. Swearing, sex scenes.

Leslie Cheung *Yu Zhongliang* • Gong Li *Pang Ruyi* • Kevin Lin *Pang Duanwu* • He Caifei *Yu Xiuyi, Zhongliang's sister* • Zhang Shi *Li Niangjui* • Lin Lianqun *Pang An* • Ge Xiangting *Elder Qi* ■ *Dir* Chen Kaige • *Scr* Shu Kei, from a story by Chen Kaige, Wang Anyi

10 ★★★★ 18
Comedy 1979 · US · Colour · 122min

If George Segal hadn't walked off the set of this Blake Edwards film, would Dudley Moore have become a movie star? He plays the middle-aged man who pursues the newly married woman of his dreams in this acerbic look at Los Angeles in a fishbowl. It may be desperately sexist, but it's still relentlessly funny, mixing satire and observation together with some really rude gags. Ravel's *Bolero* will never be the same after you see what our Dud and Bo Derek get up to during its strains. It's as dated as Derek's hair plugs, but still very perceptive, occasionally vulgar and a lot of fun. TS Swearing, sex scenes, nudity. *DVD*

Dudley Moore *George* • Julie Andrews *Sam* • Bo Derek *Jenny* • Robert Webber *Hugh* • Dee Wallace [Dee Wallace Stone] *Mary Lewis* • Sam Jones *David* • Brian Dennehy *Bartender* ■ *Dir/Scr* Blake Edwards

Ten ★★★★ 12
Drama 2002 · Fr/Iran · Colour · 89min

Taking a technical gamble by filming only the interior of a car from a camera fixed to the windscreen, Abbas Kiarostami provides a compelling insight into the current status of Iranian women in the light of recent liberalisation. As the divorcee ferrying her petulant eight-year-old son Amin Maher around town, Mania Akbari succeeds in moving between chic assurance and disconsolate fortitude as she encounters a variety of women, including a prostitute, a widow and a discarded bride, whose problems far outweigh her own. The issues raised are already momentous, but the simple immediacy of Kiarostami's approach makes them all the more poignant. DP Farsi +subtitles. *DVD*

Mania Akbari *Driver* • Amin Maher *Amin* ■ *Dir/Scr* Abbas Kiarostami

Ten Canoes ★★★★ 15
Comedy adventure 2006 · Aus · Colour and BW · 87min

Although this Australian feature is filmed almost entirely in the language of the country's indigenous people, it is an enjoyable and accessible piece of work. Shot in stunning black-and-white and colour, the film centres on a group of men – the majority of whom had never acted before – who set out on an expedition into the northern Australian wetlands to harvest bark for canoes and collect goose eggs. Instead of a politically correct, reverential story of a proud people, director Rolf de Heer (*The Tracker*) serves up a respectful but splendidly raucous and earthy mix of ancient myth and knockabout comedy. Much of that is down to the knowing English-language narration of *Walkabout* star David Gulpilil (father of Jamie who acts here). JF Aboriginal, English +subtitles. *DVD*

*Crusoe Kurddal *Ridjimiraril* • Jamie Dayindi Gulpilil *Dayindi/Yeeralparil* • Richard Birrinbirrin *Birrinbirrin* • Peter Minygululu *Minygululu* • Frances Djulibing *Nowalingu* • Philip Gudthaykudthay *The sorcerer* ■ *Dir* Rolf de Heer [Rolf De Heer], Peter Djigirr • *Scr* Rolf de Heer [Rolf De Heer]

10 Cloverfield Lane ★★★★ 12A
Science-fiction thriller 2016 · US · Colour · 103min

Effective psychological horror bursts into full-blown sci-fi in Dan Trachtenberg's debut feature. A young woman (Mary Elizabeth Winstead) awakens after a car crash to find herself held captive in a doomsday shelter by a menacing survivalist (John Goodman) and his bunker buddy (John Gallagher Jr). The acting trio mesh well – Goodman is outstanding as the "is-he-or-isn't-he?" crazed fanatic – and make the nasty twists and gory turns riveting to watch, while the involving scenario keeps you guessing. AJ Violence, swearing. *DVD* *BLU*

Mary Elizabeth Winstead *Michelle* • John Goodman *Howard* • John Gallagher Jr *Emmett* • Bradley Cooper *Ben* ■ *Dir* Dan Trachtenberg • *Scr* Josh Campbell, Matt Stuecken [Matthew Stuecken], Damien Chazelle, from a story by Campbell, Stuecken

The Ten Commandments ★★★★
Silent biblical epic 1923 · US · BW and Colour · 146min

Cecil B DeMille's first silent version marked his emergence as an epic showman. Despite its odd combination of two unconnected tales, ancient and modern, the film is a "must see" combination of interesting curiosity, historical document, lavish spectacle and entertaining melodrama. The first section covers Old Testament episodes. The modern story is a parable of two brothers, bad Rod La Rocque and good Richard Dix. It's ludicrous, but done with full-blooded conviction and panache. RK

Theodore Roberts *Moses* • Charles De Roche *Rameses* • Estelle Taylor *Miriam* • Julia Faye *Pharaoh's wife* • Terrence Moore *Pharaoh's son* • James Neill *Aaron* • Lawson Butt *Dathan* • Edythe Chapman *Mrs Martha McTavish* • Richard Dix *John McTavish* • Rod La Rocque *Dan McTavish* • Leatrice Joy *Mary Leigh* ■ *Dir* Cecil B DeMille • *Scr* Jeanie Macpherson

The Ten Commandments ★★★★ U
Biblical epic 1956 · US · Colour · 222min

This masterpiece of heroic vulgarity represents the Hollywood epic at the peak of its all-American powers. Cecil B DeMille's remake of his 1923 silent movie, about the life of Moses and his leadership of the Israelites in their exodus from Egypt, adds over an hour to his first telling of the story, but, with untypical restraint, sticks to the original ten commandments. It's a movie to savour, less for the sparkle of its dialogue or the complexity of its characterisations, than for the sheer magnificence of its set pieces and its casual deployment of 25,000 extras at the drop of a tablet. PF *BLU*

Charlton Heston *Moses* • Yul Brynner *Rameses* • Anne Baxter *Nefretiri* • Edward G Robinson *Dathan* • Yvonne De Carlo *Sephora* • Debra Paget *Lilia* • John Derek *Joshua* • Nina Foch *Bithiah* • John Carradine *Aaron* • Vincent Price *Baka* • Cedric Hardwicke *Sethi* ■ *Dir* Cecil B DeMille • *Scr* Aeneas MacKenzie, Jesse L Lasky Jr [Jesse Lasky Jr], Jack Gariss, Fredric M Frank, from the novel *The Prince of Egypt* by Dorothy Clarke Wilson, from the novel *Pillar of Fire* by Rev JH Ingraham, from the novel *On Eagle's Wings* by Rev GE Southon

Ten Days' Wonder ★★★ 15
Mystery drama 1971 · Fr · Colour · 104min

Orson Welles plays Theo Van Horn, representing God no less, in Claude Chabrol's portentous and enigmatic theological thriller, in which the ten days of the action represent each of the Ten Commandments. In a magnificent private estate in Alsace, old patriarch Welles dictates to his child bride Marlène Jobert

and adopted son (Anthony Perkins). The film was shot in a virtuoso, high-gothic style, while Perkins gives a typically nervous, agitated performance which the restless camera mirrors. RB French dubbed.

Orson Welles *Theo Van Horn* • Marlène Jobert *Helene Van Horn* • Michel Piccoli *Paul Regis* • Anthony Perkins *Charles Van Horn* • Guido Alberti *Ludovic* ■ *Dir* Claude Chabrol • *Scr* Paul Gardner, Paul Gégauff, Eugene Archer, from a novel by Ellery Queen [Frederic Dannay, Manfred B Lee]

Ten Gentlemen from West Point ★★ U
Drama 1942 · US · BW · 103min

Not quite the *Top Gun* of its day, though very gung ho, this propagandist frolic charts the founding in 1802 of West Point military academy. Directed by action maestro Henry Hathaway, it stars George Montgomery as one of the cadets and Maureen O'Hara, who appears for no other reason than to provide some romance and respite from all the scenes of men training. Episodic and contrived. AT

George Montgomery *Dawson* • Maureen O'Hara *Carolyn Bainbridge* • John Sutton *Howard Shelton* • Laird Cregar *Major Sam Carter* • John Shepperd [Shepperd Strudwick] *Henry Clay* • Victor Francen *Florimond Massey* • Harry Davenport *Bane* • Ward Bond *Scully* • Douglass Dumbrille *General William Henry Harrison* ■ *Dir* Henry Hathaway • *Scr* Richard Maibaum, George Seaton, from a story by Malvin Ward

Ten Little Indians ★★ 12
Thriller 1965 · UK · BW · 87min

This is the second film version of Agatha Christie's ever-popular whodunnit (after 1945's *And Then There Were None*), complete with a hugely irritating "guess-the-killer" break. It's hard to think of Dame Agatha as the originator of the serial killer thriller, but that's essentially what this ingenious mystery is. The cast of fading British stars doesn't seem particularly enthralled, while director George Pollock might have injected the film with a little more enthusiasm. DP *DVD*

Hugh O'Brian *Hugh Lombard* • Shirley Eaton *Ann Clyde* • Fabian *Mike Raven* • Leo Genn *General Mandrake* • Stanley Holloway *William Blore* • Wilfrid Hyde White *Judge Cannon* • Daliah Lavi *Ilona Bergen* • Dennis Price *Dr Armstrong* ■ *Dir* George Pollock • *Scr* Peter Yeldham, Dudley Nichols, Peter Welbeck [Harry Alan Towers], from the novel and play *Ten Little Niggers* by Agatha Christie

Ten Minutes Older: the Cello ★★ 15
Portmanteau drama 2002 · Ger/UK/US · BW and Colour · 100min

One Moment, Jiri Menzel's affectionate montage tribute to Czech actor Rudolf Hrusinsky, is the pick of this largely self-indulgent collection of musings on memory, fate and time. Bernardo Bertolucci's *Histoire d'Eaux* and István Szabó's *Ten Minutes After* are shrewd "cinecdotes", told with economy and wit. But the intriguing ideas in Claire Denis's *Vers Nancy* and Volker Schlöndorff's *The Enlightenment* are diluted respectively by inert visuals and trite melodramatics. Jean-Luc Godard revisits the iconic imagery of his past in *Dans le Noir du Temps*, while Mike Figgis recalls *Timecode* by quartering the screen for the negligible *About Time 2*. However, the nadir of this inconsistent collection is Michael Radford's interminable sci-fi parable, *Addicted to the Stars*. DP *DVD*

Valéria Bruni-Tedeschi *Marcellina* • Amit Arroz *Narada* • Mark Long *Man* • Alexandra Staden *Young woman* • Dominic West *Young man* • Ildiko Bansagi • Gabor Mate • Jean-Luc Nancy *The philosopher* • Ana Samardzija *The student* • Bibiana Beglau *Girl* • Irm Herrmann [Irm Hermann] *Mother* • Mario Irrek *Brother* • Daniel Craig *Cecil Thomas* • Charles Simon *Martin* ■ *Dir* Bernardo Bertolucci, Mike Figgis, Jiri Menzel, István Szabó, Claire Denis, Volker Schlöndorff, Michael Radford, Jean-Luc Godard • *Scr* Bernardo Bertolucci, Mike Figgis, Jiri Menzel, István Szabó, Claire Denis, Max E Frye from the religious text *Confessions* by Augustinus, Michael Radford, Anne-Marie Miéville

Ten Minutes Older: the Trumpet ★★★ 15

Portmanteau drama
2002 · Ger/UK/US · BW and Colour · 87min

Seven directors took up the challenge of interpreting Marcus Aurelius's maxim that time is as relentless as a river. Aki Kaurismäki's wry romance *Dogs Have No Hell* and Chen Kaige's whimsical *1000 Flowers Hidden Deep* make effective bookmarks, but Jim Jarmusch's on-set snapshot *Int.Trailer.Night* and Wim Wenders's gimmicky road movie *Twelve Miles to Trona* are disappointing. So, too, is Werner Herzog's well-meaning but rather trivial eco-documentary *Ten Thousand Years Older*. Much better is *We Wuz Robbed*, Spike Lee's pointed take on the 2000 US Presidential election. But easily outshining the rest is Victor Erice's superbly constructed, monochrome mini-masterpiece, *Lifeline*. DP English, German, Mandarin, Spanish, Portuguese, Finnish +subtitles. *DVD*

Kati Outinen *Woman* • Markku Peltola *Man* • Ana Sofia Liano *Young mother* • Celia Poo *Midwife* • Chloë Sevigny *Actress* • Charles Esten *Bill* • Amber Tamblyn *Kate* • Feng Yuanzheng *Mr Feng* ■ *Dir* Aki Kaurismäki, Victor Erice, Werner Herzog, Jim Jarmusch, Wim Wenders, Spike Lee, Chen Kaige • *Scr* Aki Kaurismäki, Victor Erice, Werner Herzog, Jim Jarmusch, Wim Wenders, Zhang Tan

Ten North Frederick ★★★★

Drama   1958 · US · BW · 101min

One of those fabulous extended soapy dramas based on the kind of bestselling doorstop novel that 20th Century-Fox seemed to specialise in during the early CinemaScope period. Gary Cooper stars as a successful lawyer, shoved into the political big time by grasping wife Geraldine Fitzgerald, who finds brief solace in the arms of ex-model Suzy Parker. Sit back and enjoy a good wallow. TS

Gary Cooper *Joe Chapin* • Diane Varsi *Ann Chapin* • Suzy Parker *Kate Drummond* • Geraldine Fitzgerald *Edith Chapin* • Tom Tully *Slattery* • Ray Stricklyn *Joby* • Philip Ober *Lloyd Williams* • John Emery *Paul Donaldson* • Stuart Whitman *Charley Bongiorno* ■ *Dir* Philip Dunne • *Scr* Philip Dunne, from the novel by John O'Hara

10 Rillington Place ★★★★★ 15

Biographical crime drama
1970 · UK · Colour · 106min

Three years after Timothy Evans went to the gallows for the murder of his daughter Geraldine, John Reginald Christie, the family's landlord and a wartime special constable, was convicted at the Old Bailey of murdering his wife and was also shown to be responsible for the deaths of five other women, and, by his own admission, for the death of Mrs Evans. Although Christie denied killing the infant, Evans was found not to have killed his child in a subsequent inquiry. Richard Fleischer's film is not as visually audacious as his *Boston Strangler*, but it does contain an acting tour de force from Richard Attenborough as the seedy killer. Superbly re-creating the atmosphere of late-1940s London, this is a chilling study of an evil mind. DP Swearing. *DVD*

Richard Attenborough *John Reginald Christie* • Judy Geeson *Beryl Evans* • John Hurt *Timothy John Evans* • Pat Heywood *Mrs Ethel Christie* • Isobel Black *Alice* • Miss Riley *Baby Geraldine* • Phyllis McMahon *Muriel Eady* ■ *Dir* Richard Fleischer • *Scr* Clive Exton, from the book by Ludovic Kennedy

Ten Seconds to Hell ★★

Drama   1959 · US · BW · 93min

A typically catchpenny title for a typically brash Robert Aldrich movie about German bomb-disposal experts in postwar Berlin coming to explosive blows over Martine Carol, a French sex symbol in the 1950s. Jack Palance and Jeff Chandler rant eloquently enough, but it's too stridently contrived for any credibility. A dampish squib. TH

Jeff Chandler *Karl Wirtz* • Jack Palance *Eric Koertner* • Martine Carol *Margot Hofer* • Robert Cornthwaite *Loeffler* • Dave Willock *Tillig* • Wesley Addy *Sulke* • Jimmy Goodwin *Globke* • Virginia Baker *Frau Bauer* • Robert Wattis *Major Haven* ■ *Dir* Robert Aldrich • *Scr* Robert Aldrich, Teddi Sherman, from the novel *The Phoenix* by Lawrence P Bachmann

Ten Tall Men ★★★ U

Comedy adventure   1951 · US · Colour · 96min

Dr Kildare's veteran writer/director Willis Goldbeck fashioned a more-than-passable film from this robust tale of the Foreign Legion, but *Beau Geste* it isn't. Nevertheless, with Burt Lancaster at the peak of his teeth-and-glory years in the lead, and tough hombres Gilbert Roland and Kieron Moore in support, this comedy adventure is well worth catching, especially since it's in sharp 1950s Technicolor. TS

Burt Lancaster *Sergeant Mike Kincaid* • Jody Lawrance *Mahla* • Gilbert Roland *Corporal Luis Delgado* • Kieron Moore *Corporal Pierre Molier* • George Tobias *Londos* • John Dehner *Jardine* • Nick Dennis *Mouse* • Mike Mazurki *Roshko* ■ *Dir* Willis Goldbeck • *Scr* Roland Kibbee, Frank Davis, from a story by James Warner Bellah, Willis Goldbeck

10 Things I Hate about You ★★★★ 12

Romantic comedy   1999 · US · Colour · 93min

Shakespeare's *The Taming of the Shrew* gets updated *Clueless*-style to high-school America for this engaging romantic comedy from debut director Gil Junger. Julia Stiles is the sulky teen who doesn't like anybody. This causes a problem for her hormonally charged younger sister Larisa Oleynik, who has been told by their dad that she can't date until Stiles does. Newcomer Heath Ledger plays the unfortunate lad picked to introduce Stiles to the dating scene, while the rest of the cast is peppered with equally good-looking youngsters. Smartly paced, fun and funny. JB Sexual references. *DVD*

Heath Ledger *Patrick Verona* • Julia Stiles *Katarina Stratford* • Joseph Gordon-Levitt *Cameron James* • Larisa Oleynik *Bianca Stratford* • David Krumholtz *Michael Eckman* • Andrew Keegan *Joey Donner* • Susan May Pratt *Mandella* ■ *Dir* Gil Junger • *Scr* Karen McCullah Lutz, Kirsten Smith

10:30 PM Summer ★

Drama   1966 · US/Sp · Colour · 84min

French novelist Marguerite Duras and director Jules Dassin adapted the former's novel as a vehicle for Dassin's wife, Melina Mercouri. She brings her strident Greek passion to the role of a wife, holidaying in Spain with her husband Peter Finch and best friend Romy Schneider. While troubled with erotic and alarming dreams about hubby and friend getting together, she wanders the streets and meets Julian Mateos who has killed his wife and her lover. Intensely irritating drivel. RK

Melina Mercouri *Maria* • Romy Schneider *Claire* • Peter Finch *Paul* • Julian Mateos *Rodrigo Palestra* • Isabel Maria Perez *Judith* • Beatriz Savon *Rodrigo's wife* ■ *Dir* Jules Dassin • *Scr* Jules Dassin, Marguerite Duras, from a novel by Marguerite Duras

10,000 BC ★★ 12

Prehistoric adventure
2008 · US/NZ · Colour · 104min

Nothing much has changed when it comes to prehistoric adventures since *One Million Years BC* featured Raquel Welch running around in a fur-skinned bikini in 1966. The same lovelorn cavemen fight the same primitive predators with the same historical inaccuracy. This messy melange of *Apocalypto* and TV series *Primeval* from *Day after Tomorrow* director Roland Emmerich sees brave young hunter Steven Strait embark on a quest to rescue blue-eyed Camilla Belle when she's taken to a faraway land by mysterious invaders. With plenty of mindless spectacle, chintzy computerised creature effects and sweeping *Stargate*-style Egyptian vistas, this epic nonsense isn't silly enough to even be entertaining. AJ *DVD*

Steven Strait *D'Leh* • Camilla Belle *Evolet* • Cliff Curtis *Tic'Tic* • Joel Virgel *Nakudu* • Nathanael Baring *Baku* • Omar Sharif *Narrator* ■ *Dir* Roland Emmerich • *Scr* Roland Emmerich, Harald Kloser

Ten Thousand Bedrooms ★★ U

Musical comedy   1957 · US · Colour · 114min

Millionaire hotel owner Dean Martin visits Rome to check out his latest acquisition and becomes romantically entangled with four Italian sisters, particularly the eldest, Eva Bartok. Anna Maria Alberghetti, Lisa Montell, and Lisa Gaye are the other girls in a large cast, which also includes Walter Slezak as the girls' Italian papa. A witless and interminable romantic comedy, this was Martin's first film without Jerry Lewis. RK

Dean Martin *Ray Hunter* • Anna Maria Alberghetti *Maria* • Eva Bartok *Maria Martelli* • Dewey Martin *Mike Clark* • Walter Slezak *Papa Vittorio Martelli* • Paul Henreid *Anton* • Lisa Montell *Diana Martelli* • Lisa Gaye *Anna Martelli* ■ *Dir* Richard Thorpe • *Scr* Laslo Vadnay, Art Cohn, William Ludwig, Leonard Spigelgass

10 to Midnight ★★ 18

Thriller   1983 · UK · Colour · 95min

Selecting the worst Charles Bronson film of the 1980s provides an embarrassment of riches. Not only are all of them pretty awful, but the plots are often strikingly similar. This nasty thriller, for example, could just have easily been an entry in the *Death Wish* series. This time Bronson plays a cop tracking down a serial killer of women. When orthodox methods fail, he's reduced to planting evidence and then stalking the murderer himself. JF

Charles Bronson *Leo Kessler* • Lisa Eilbacher *Laurie Kessler* • Andrew Stevens *Paul McAnn* • Gene Davis *Warren Stacey* • Geoffrey Lewis *Dave Dante* • Wilford Brimley *Captain Malone* • Robert F Lyons *Nathan Zager* • Bert Williams *Mr Johnson* ■ *Dir* J Lee Thompson • *Scr* William Roberts

Ten Wanted Men ★★ U

Western   1955 · US · Colour · 80min

Produced for the Ranown company that Randolph Scott formed with producer Harry Joe Brown, this routine western only emphasises the debt that Scott owed to Budd Boetticher and Andre De Toth, who directed his better genre outings. Journeyman H Bruce Humberstone simply points the camera and lets the cast get on with telling the story of an Arizona rancher who falls foul of neighbour Richard Boone after he offers his frightened ward (Donna Martell) sanctuary. Lee Van Cleef snarls effectively among the gunslingers that Boone hires to menace Scott, but the action remains stubbornly pedestrian. DP

Randolph Scott *John Stewart* • Jocelyn Brando *Corinne Michaels* • Richard Boone *Wick Campbell* • Alfonso Bedoya *Hermando* • Donna Martell *Maria Segura* • Skip Homeier *Howie Stewart* • Lee Van Cleef *Al Drucker* ■ *Dir* H Bruce Humberstone • *Scr* Kenneth Gamet, from a story by Irving Ravetch, Harriet Frank Jr

Ten Who Dared ★★ PG

Historical adventure   1960 · US · Colour · 92min

Set in the 19th century, this Disney production is based on the real-life diary chronicling the adventures of Major John Wesley Powell, an explorer/geologist/botanist who lost his arm in the Civil War but undaunted traversed nearly a thousand miles of the American west. The film features John Beal as Powell and Brian Keith as William Dunn negotiating uncharted territories. Opting for an episodic approach, veteran director William Beaudine fails to translate a scientific expedition into entertainment. TH

Brian Keith *William Dunn* • John Beal *Major John Wesley Powell* • James Drury *Walter Powell* • RG Armstrong *Oramel Howland* • Ben Johnson (1) *George Bradley* • LQ Jones *Billy Hawkins* ■ *Dir* William Beaudine • *Scr* Lawrence Edward Watkin, from the journal of Major John Wesley Powell

10 Years ★★ 12

Comedy drama   2011 · US · Colour · 96min

Channing Tatum produces and headlines this low-key comedy drama about a group of old high-school buddies who get together for their ten-year reunion. It's hardly a novel idea, and the stock characters are all present and correct: drunken former bully Chris Pratt, geek-made-good Justin Long, prom king Tatum and his lost love Rosario Dawson. But *American Pie* this ain't. While the lack of soap opera-style revelations, fist-fights and drunken shenanigans is probably closer to reality, it's difficult to get involved when their lives are so dull. LB *DVD* Blu

Channing Tatum *Jake* • Rosario Dawson *Mary* • Justin Long *Marty* • Max Minghella *AJ* • Chris Pratt *Cully* ■ *Dir/Scr* Jamie Linden

Tenacious D in The Pick of Destiny ★★★ 15

Musical comedy   2006 · US · Colour · 90min

Jack Black's twin careers as actor and rock musician merge in this fantastical tale of his band's humble beginnings and the search for the demonic guitar pick that will turn them into rock gods. He's joined in his quest by fellow Tenacious D band member Kyle Gass, and ropes in cameos from real-life rock gods Meat Loaf (as his dad), Ronnie James Dio (as his heavy metal muse) and Dave Grohl of the Foo Fighters (as Satan!). It's an over-the-top and endearingly self-indulgent slice of *Spinal Tap*-style self-mythologising that sadly, after a wildly funny start, rather runs out of comic steam. DA *DVD* CS

Jack Black *JB* • Kyle Gass *KG* • JR Reed *Lee* • Fred Armisen *Security guard 2* • Ned Bellamy *Security guard 1* • Ronnie James Dio • Meat Loaf *Bud Black* • Tim Robbins *The Stranger* • Ben Stiller *Guitar store dude* ■ *Dir* Liam Lynch • *Scr* Jack Black, Kyle Gass, Liam Lynch

The Tenant ★★★ 18

Psychological thriller   1976 · Fr · Colour · 119min

Roman Polanski directs a male take on the themes of paranoia and delusion that he explored from a female perspective in *Repulsion* ten years earlier. Polanski also stars, playing an expatriate Pole in Paris who comes to believe that the tenants of his apartment block are devilishly conspiring to drive him to suicide. Melvyn Douglas and Shelley Winters co-star in a puzzling and absorbing thriller. DA *DVD*

Roman Polanski *Trelkovsky* • Isabelle Adjani *Stella* • Melvyn Douglas *Mr Zy* • Jo Van Fleet *Madame Dioz* • Bernard Fresson *Scope* • Lila Kedrova *Madame Gaderian* • Shelley Winters *Concierge* ■ *Dir* Roman Polanski • *Scr* Roman Polanski, Gérard Brach, from the novel *Le Locataire Chimérique* by Roland Topor

Tender Comrade ★★★ U

Second World War drama
1943 · US · BW · 102min

On the surface, this is a harmless tale about women living together while their menfolk are off at war, but this slight drama had serious repercussions. Ginger Rogers's mother objected to her daughter uttering the sentiment "Share and share alike" in the film, and four years later writer Dalton Trumbo and director Edward Dmytryk were hauled before the House Un-American Activities Committee and imprisoned as "unfriendly" witnesses and alleged communists all because the women lived and worked communally in the movie! TS

Ginger Rogers *Jo Jones* • Robert Ryan *Chris Jones* • Ruth Hussey *Barbara* • Patricia Collinge *Helen Stacey* • Mady Christians *Manya* • Kim Hunter *Doris* • Jane Darwell *Mrs Henderson* • Mary Forbes *Jo's mother* • Richard Martin (1) *Mike* ■ *Dir* Edward Dmytryk • *Scr* Dalton Trumbo, from his story

Tender Is the Night ★★

Drama   1961 · US · Colour · 146min

This adaptation of Scott Fitzgerald's semi-autobiographical novel fails to achieve a coherent film from the complex, opaque material. Jason Robards and Jennifer Jones are Dick and Nicole Diver, the "beautiful people" of the 1920s, squandering their lives on a hedonistic existence among the Jazz Age jet set on the French Riviera. Robards and a too-old Jones make a good stab at their roles and the enormous cast includes Joan Fontaine, Tom Ewell and Jill St John in the major supporting parts. There is some vicarious entertainment to be had from watching the unstable, amoral, idle rich playing and disintegrating, but to date the book remains unfilmable. RK

Jason Robards Jr [Jason Robards] *Dick Diver* • Jennifer Jones *Nicole Diver* • Joan Fontaine *Baby Warren* • Jill St John *Rosemary Hoyt* • Tom Ewell *Abe North* • Cesare Danova *Tommy Barban* • Paul Lukas *Dr Dohmler* • Carole Mathews *Mrs Hoyt* ■ *Dir* Henry King • *Scr* Ivan Moffat, from the novel by F Scott Fitzgerald

Tender Mercies ★★★★ PG

Drama 1982 · US · Colour · 87min

A spare, lean performance from spare, lean Robert Duvall won him an Oscar. Duvall wakes up, after a drunken binge, in a Texan motel owned by religious widow Tess Harper and her young son Allan Hubbard. Having failed once in both his life and career as a country singer, he hesitatingly tries again with Harper. Australian director Bruce Beresford shows a sympathetic connection to the hot dusty Texan locations for his first Hollywood film and screenwriter Horton Foote (who also won an Oscar) provides a realistic pace. A poignant portrayal of redemption. FL *DVD*

Robert Duvall *Mac Sledge* • Tess Harper *Rosa Lee* • Allan Hubbard *Sonny* • Betty Buckley *Dixie* • Ellen Barkin *Sue Anne* • Wilford Brimley *Harry* • Michael Crabtree *Lewis Menefee* • Lenny Von Dohlen *Robert Dennis* ■ *Dir* Bruce Beresford • *Scr* Horton Foote

The Tender Trap ★★★★ U

Romantic comedy 1955 · US · Colour · 106min

A single swinger – the perfectly cast Frank Sinatra – falls into marriage (that's the "trap" of the title), but it's the wit and style of the ensemble playing that gives the film such charm. Debbie Reynolds co-stars, and Celeste Holm and David Wayne are the other principals, with Wayne's morning-after scene a particular joy to watch. TS *DVD*

Frank Sinatra *Charlie Y Reader* • Debbie Reynolds *Julie Gillis* • David Wayne *Joe McCall* • Celeste Holm *Sylvia Crewes* • Jarma Lewis *Jessica Collins* • Lola Albright *Poppy Matson* • Carolyn Jones *Helen* • Howard St John *Sam Sayers* ■ *Dir* Charles Walters • *Scr* Julius J Epstein, from the play by Max Shulman, Robert Paul Smith

Tenderness ★★ 15

Crime drama 2007 · US · Colour · 100min

Russell Crowe stars here as a semi-retired cop whose "hobby" is a young man (Jon Foster) who committed parenticide and is newly released from prison. Although Crowe and Foster acquit themselves well, the film's strongest performance is from remarkable newcomer Sophie Traub as an obsessed teenager, who is by turns alluring, irritating and pathetic. Director John Polson (*Swimfan*) has created an uneven, foreboding thriller, which takes unbelievable turns that highlight the contradictions plaguing the main characters, yet is at its best showing the inner conflicts of people in pain. KK Swearing.

Russell Crowe *Detective Cristofuoro* • Jon Foster (1) *Eric Poole* • Laura Dern *Aunt Teresa* • Sophie Traub *Lori* • Arija Bareikis *Marsha* • Alexis Dziena *Maria* • Michael Kelly (2) *Gary* ■ *Dir* John Polson • *Scr* Emil Stern, from the novel by Robert Cormier

Tenebrae ★★★ 18

Horror thriller 1982 · It · Colour · 96min

This is one of the best thrillers from Dario Argento, the Italian Hitchcock, full of stylish camerawork, kinky flashbacks, impressive gore and an ace electronic soundtrack. Novelist Anthony Franciosa visits Rome to promote his latest bestseller, only to find a murderer is copying the killings in his book. It's enormous fun sifting out the red herrings in this ultra-violent Agatha Christie-style whodunnit, and the twist

ending really is twisted. AJ Italian dubbed. Violence, sex scenes, some swearing. *DVD* 🔵

John Saxon *Bullmer* • Anthony Franciosa *Peter Neal* • Christian Borromeo *Gianni* • Mirella D'Angelo *Tilde* • Veronica Lario *Jane* • Ania Pieroni *Elsa* ■ *Dir/Scr* Dario Argento

Tennessee Champ ★★ U

Sports drama 1954 · US · Colour · 72min

Dewey Martin, a religious young Southern boxer, gets his break when he is taken up by fight manager Keenan Wynn, but is horrified to learn that Wynn is fixing a match. Preaching his own message about morality and God, he eventually gets a clean fight with Charles Buchinsky. This sentimental minor entry from MGM doesn't exactly compel one's attention. Buchinsky, of course, would do rather more as Charles Bronson. RK

Shelley Winters *Sarah Wurble* • Keenan Wynn *Willy Wurble* • Dewey Martin *Daniel Norson* • Earl Holliman *Happy Jackfield* • Dave O'Brien *Luke MacWade* • Charles Buchinsky [Charles Bronson] *Sixty Jubel* ■ *Dir* Fred M Wilcox • *Scr* Art Cohn, from the story *The Lord in His Corner* and other stories by Eustace Cockrell

Tennessee Johnson ★★★ U

Biographical drama 1942 · US · BW · 103min

Directed by experienced old hand at the genre William Dieterle, this above-average biopic of Andrew Johnson, who became president following Lincoln's assassination, stars Van Heflin in the title role. Johnson's rise from illiterate backwoods boy to holder of the highest office in the land, until politically conservative enemies led by Senator Stevens (Lionel Barrymore) determine to get rid of him by impeachment, is carefully detailed, with an appreciation of the moral issues as well as the intrigues. RK

Van Heflin *Andrew Johnson* • Lionel Barrymore *Thaddeus Stevens* • Ruth Hussey *Eliza McCardle* • Marjorie Main *Mrs Fisher* • Regis Toomey *Blackstone McDaniel* • J Edward Bromberg *Coke* • Grant Withers *Moreecai Milligan* ■ *Dir* William Dieterle • *Scr* John L Balderston, Wells Root, from a story by Milton Gunzberg, Alvin Meyers

Tension ★★★

Crime drama 1949 · US · BW · 90min

A title to take seriously, as in this case the film does pile on the suspense. Cyd Charisse is out of her ballet shoes for a low-budgeter, in which she plays the girl who falls for troubled Richard Basehart while he is trying to establish a new identity after plotting the murder of his wife's lover. Director John Berry was one of the best of the period's B-picture craftsmen until he was "named" as a communist and blacklisted. TH

Richard Basehart *Warren Quimby* • Audrey Totter *Claire Quimby* • Cyd Charisse *Mary Chanler* • Barry Sullivan *Lieutenant Collier Bonnabel* • Lloyd Gough *Barney Deager* • Tom D'Andrea *Freddie* • William Conrad *Lieutenant Edgar Gonsales* ■ *Dir* John Berry • *Scr* Allen Rivkin, from a story by John Klorer

Tension at Table Rock ★★★ U

Western 1956 · US · Colour · 93min

Charles Marquis Warren was the creative force behind such great TV western shows as *Gunsmoke*, *Rawhide* and *The Virginian* and here directs a tale of smoking guns and smouldering passions. In an era when action men were second-class citizens in Hollywood, Richard Egan never quite made the big time, but here he gives a sterling and convincing performance alongside Dorothy Malone and Cameron Mitchell. DP

Richard Egan *Wes Tancred* • Dorothy Malone *Lorna Miller* • Billy Chapin *Jody Burrows* • Cameron Mitchell *Sheriff Miller* • Joe De Santis *Ed Barrows* • Royal Dano *Jameson* • Edward Andrews *Kirk* • DeForest Kelley *Breck* • Angie Dickinson *Cathy Murdock* ■ *Dir* Charles Marquis Warren • *Scr* Winston Miller, from the novel *Bitter Sage* by Frank Gruber

Tentacles ★★

Horror 1977 · It · Colour · 101min

A giant octopus goes on a murderous rampage during a resort's annual yacht race. John Huston is the reporter trying to get to the bottom of why the scary squid is acting so nasty. Shelley Winters is Huston's sister whose son nearly goes missing during one attack. This lively enough rip-off features direct lifts from the Spielberg shock handbook, all wrapped up in a gorgeous Euro-pop score by Stelvio Cipriani. AJ Some dialogue dubbed.

John Huston *Ned Turner* • Shelley Winters *Tillie Turner* • Bo Hopkins *Will Gleason* • Henry Fonda *Mr Whitehead* • Delia Boccardo *Vicky Gleason* • Cesare Danova *John Corey* • Claude Akins *Captain Robards* ■ *Dir* Ovidio G Assonitis • *Scr* Jerome Max, Tito Carpi, Steven W Carabatsos, Sonia Molteni

The Tenth Circle ★★

Mystery thriller 2008 · Can/US · Colour · 103min

Dark secrets threaten a family's fragile unity in this contrived TV adaptation of Jodi Picoult's bestselling novel. Ron Eldard and a largely sidelined Kelly Preston play the parents thrown into a living hell after their teenage offspring (Brittany Robertson) makes a rape accusation against her ex-boyfriend. Despite its emotive subject matter, the film struggles to engage viewers and mistakes manipulative melodrama for narrative meat. SF

Kelly Preston *Laura Stone* • Ron Eldard *Daniel Stone* • Jamie Johnston *Jason Underhill* • Michael Riley *Mike* • Britt Robertson [Brittany Robertson] *Trixie Stone* ■ *Dir* Peter Markle • *Scr* Maria Nation, from the novel by Jodi Picoult

The Tenth Man ★★★ PG

Drama 1988 · US/UK · Colour · 94min

During the war, Graham Greene had a contract with MGM where he wrote what he later remembered as a two-page treatment for a movie that was never made. When the treatment was discovered some 40 years later, it turned out to be a 60,000-word novel set in France after the Liberation, which tells the story of a once wealthy lawyer who gave away his fortune in exchange for his life. The book was published in 1985, and this TV-movie version is impeccably directed by Jack Gold, with Anthony Hopkins among the starry cast. AT *DVD*

Anthony Hopkins *Jean Louis Chavel* • Derek Jacobi *Imposter* • Kristin Scott Thomas *Thérèse* • Cyril Cusack *Parish priest* • Brenda Bruce *Madame Mangeot* • Timothy Watson *Michel Mangeot* • Paul Rogers *Breton* ■ *Dir* Jack Gold • *Scr* Lee Langley, from the novel by Graham Greene

The Tenth Victim ★★★ 12

Science-fiction thriller 1965 · It · Colour · 88min

Famous now as one of the inspirations for *Austin Powers* (Ursula Andress wore the first bullet-firing bra as sported by the "fembots"), this erratically engrossing science-fiction thriller has a fabulous 1960s pop art look. In the 21st century, war has been replaced with a legalised game in which the participants are licensed-to-kill assassins, and anyone reaching the score of ten victims hits the financial jackpot. Andress is assigned to kill a cropped blond Marcello Mastroianni, but he falls in love with his huntress in this convincing futuristic satire. AJ Italian dubbed. Some violence *DVD*

Ursula Andress *Caroline Meredith* • Marcello Mastroianni *Marcello Polletti* • Elsa Martinelli *Olga* • Salvo Randone *Professor* • Massimo Serato *Lawyer* • Evi Rigano *Victim* ■ *Dir* Elio Petri • *Scr* Elio Petri, Tonino Guerra, Giorgio Salvioni, Ennio Flaiano, from the novel *The Seventh Victim* by Robert Sheckley

Tenue de Soirée ★★★ 18

Comedy 1986 · Fr · Colour · 84min

Although this scurrilous comedy reunited Bertrand Blier with the co-stars of *Les Valseuses*, Miou-Miou and Gérard Depardieu, it was the newcomer Michel Blanc who stole the picture and won himself

the best actor prize at Cannes. Smugly iconoclastic, gleefully picaresque, hopelessly misogynistic and outrageously funny are all descriptions that could aptly be applied to the ménage that develops between Depardieu's larger-than-life bisexual crook, Blanc's timid husband and Miou-Miou's opportunistic wife. DP French +subtitles.

Gérard Depardieu *Bob* • Michel Blanc *Antoine* • Miou-Miou *Monique* • Bruno Cremer *Art collector* • Jean-Pierre Marielle *Depressed man* • Caroline Sihol *Depressed woman* ■ *Dir/Scr* Bertrand Blier

Tequila Sunrise ★★★ 15

Thriller 1988 · US · Colour · 110min

Kurt Russell and Mel Gibson star as the former schoolfriends who have gone their separate ways, Russell into the police force and Gibson into drug dealing. When Gibson plans a final trade-off, Russell tries to persuade his old chum against the deal. Michelle Pfeiffer becomes romantically involved with both men. Writer/director Robert Towne occasionally allows his wordiness to get between the viewer and the characters, but the fine cast and Conrad Hall's Oscar-nominated cinematography provide some compensation. TH Swearing, drug abuse, nudity. *DVD*

Mel Gibson *Dale McKussic* • Michelle Pfeiffer *Jo Ann Vallenari* • Kurt Russell *Lieutenant Nick Frescia* • Raul Julia *Carlos/Commandante Escalante* • JT Walsh *Maguire* • Arliss Howard *Gregg Lindroff* • Ann Magnuson *Shaleen* ■ *Dir/Scr* Robert Towne

The Terence Davies Trilogy ★★★ 15

Drama 1984 · UK · BW · 91min

Made over a seven-year period, these three short films from the writer/director of *Distant Voices, Still Lives* record a man's singularly bleak life. In *Children* (1976), the young Robert Tucker is bullied at home and school. In *Madonna and Child* (1980), the middle-aged Robert appears to lead a nondescript life, but secretly haunts gay bars. In *Death and Transfiguration* (1983), the elderly Robert remembers. Made before, during and after Terence Davies's time at film school, these are clearly the work of a major visual artist; but his complex and austere material makes great demands on the viewer. The most touching episode is the first; thereafter the gloom is unrealistically relentless, and some may find the misery, tears and deaths almost ludicrous. DM

Phillip Mawdsley *Robert Tucker, boy* • Terry O'Sullivan *Robert Tucker, middle age* • Wilfrid Brambell *Robert Tucker, old age* ■ *Dir/Scr* Terence Davies

Teresa ★★★

Romantic drama 1951 · US · BW · 101min

Director Fred Zinnemann's tale of an imported GI bride was a courageously topical subject, and indicative of a now-forgotten trend at MGM to confront burning contemporary issues. Lovely Italian actress Pier Angeli brings great honesty and truth to the title role, and there are echoes of her own real-life plight in the plot, as she encounters small-town bigotry in the role of GI John Ericson's girl. As her psychiatrist, young Rod Steiger makes an impressive movie debut. Zinnemann's documentary-style treatment is winning. TS

Pier Angeli *Teresa* • John Ericson *Philip Quas* • Patricia Collinge *Philip's mother* • Richard Bishop *Philip's father* • Peggy Ann Garner *Susan* • Ralph Meeker *Sergeant Dobbs* • Rod Steiger *Frank* ■ *Dir* Fred Zinnemann • *Scr* Stewart Stern, from the story by Stewart Stern, Alfred Hayes

Terkel in Trouble ★★★ 15

Animated black comedy musical 2006 · Den/UK · Colour · 80min

In its native Denmark, the voices for this CGI animation were all provided by stand-up comedian Anders Matthesen. For the UK release, a host of British talent has been assembled to enliven a dark and dirty teen romp. Adrian Edmondson takes on the role of hapless hero Terkel who causes an obese, lovesick classmate to commit suicide, alienates his best mate by hooking

T

up with the school bullies and falls foul of a new teacher (Toby Stephens) on a field trip. Johnny Vegas steals the show as Terkel's alcoholic relative, Uncle Stewart, but credit also goes to designer/co-director Stefan Fjeldmark for giving his Jimmy Neutron-like characters a bit of *South Park* attitude. DP Danish dubbed.

Adrian Edmondson *Terkel* • Bill Bailey *Barry* • Ben Bishop *Jason/Osprey/Nigel/Saki* • Olivia Colman *Sheila* • Toby Stephens *Justin* • Johnny Vegas *Uncle Stewart* ■ *Dir* Kresten Vestbjerg Andersen [Kresten Andersen], Stefan Fjeldmark, Thorbjorn Christoffersen, Ray Gillon • *Scr* Mette Heeno, from a story by Anders Matthesen, from the radio series *Arne Fortoeller – Terkel i Knibe* by Matthesen

Term of Trial ★★★★

Drama   1962 · UK · BW · 138min

Made at the height of the "kitchen sink" boom in British cinema, this rather neglected drama boasts one of Laurence Olivier's most uncharacteristic and underrated performances. As the teacher at an inner-city school who is looked down upon by everyone from his blowsy wife Simone Signoret to class bully Terence Stamp, he conveys a sense of both seedy decency and wounded resignation that makes his prosecution for molestation and persecution by Signoret all the more painful to endure. In her screen debut, Sarah Miles is superb as the scorned teenager and Thora Hird bristles with indignation as her grasping mother. DP

Laurence Olivier *Graham Weir* • Simone Signoret *Anna Weir* • Sarah Miles *Shirley Taylor* • Hugh Griffith *O'Hara* • Terence Stamp *Mitchell* • Roland Culver *Trowman* • Thora Hird *Mrs Taylor* ■ *Dir* Peter Glenville • *Scr* Peter Glenville, from the novel by James Barlow

The Terminal ★★★ 12

Comedy drama   2004 · US · Colour · 123min

Tom Hanks is superb as the Eastern European who becomes trapped in visa hell after a military coup in his native Krakozhia means his country is no longer recognised by the US government. Stranded indefinitely at JFK airport, he learns English from TV, eats leftover fast food, finds work renovating the building, falls for ditzy flight attendant Catherine Zeta-Jones and is harassed by Stanley Tucci's power-hungry official. While the performances are appealing, director Steven Spielberg relies too heavily on the airport-terminal-as-microcosm-of-society angle and the saccharine sentimentality gets piled on as the credibility decreases. AJ Swearing. DVD

Tom Hanks *Viktor Navorski* • Catherine Zeta-Jones *Amelia Warren* • Stanley Tucci *Frank Dixon* • Chi McBride *Joe Mulroy* • Diego Luna *Enrique Cruz* • Barry Shabaka Henley [Barry "Shabaka" Henley] *Ray Thurman* • Kumar Pallana *Gupta Rajan* • Zoë Saldana *Dolores Torres* ■ *Dir* Steven Spielberg • *Scr* Jeff Nathanson, Sacha Gervasi, from a story by Andrew Niccol, Sacha Gervasi

Terminal Choice ★★★ 18

Medical thriller   1983 · Can · Colour · 94min

In this suspenseful little chiller, hospital staff lay wagers as to when patients will pop their clogs, and aren't above manipulating the odds in their favour. Rather bloodier than it needs to be, the film still manages to generate surprising tension, partly because of taut and economic direction, and partly because it's played dead straight by its high-calibre cast. DA

Joe Spano *Dr Frank Holt* • Diane Venora *Anna Lang* • David McCallum (1) *Dr Dodson* • Robert Joy *Dr Harvey Rimmer* • Don Francks *Chauncey Rand* • Nicholas Campbell *Henderson* • Ellen Barkin *Mary O'Connor* ■ *Dir* Sheldon Larry • *Scr* Neal Bell, from a story by Peter Lawrence

Terminal Island ★

Futuristic prison drama
1973 · US · Colour · 87min

This crummy exploitation pic – terminal in all departments – is about a future offshore prison colony where California's killers are sent because the death penalty has been abolished. The arrival of women prisoners results in their being treated as sex slaves.

The sole point of interest is an early screen appearance by Tom Selleck. DA

Phyllis Davis *Joy Lang* • Don Marshall *AJ Thomas* • Ena Hartman *Carmen Sims* • Marta Kristen *Lee Phillips* • Tom Selleck *Dr Milford* ■ *Dir* Stephanie Rothman • *Scr* Jim Barnett, Charles S Swartz, Stephanie Rothman

The Terminal Man ★★★★ 15

Science-fiction thriller
1974 · US · Colour · 99min

An intense performance from the usually laid-back George Segal nicely matches the desolation of this futuristic thriller, in which a scientist has a computer implant connected to his brain and becomes addicted to its killer vibes. Mike Hodges brilliantly creates a hi-tech parable in which meddling scientists get a moral comeuppance. Its implications are as thought-provoking as they are scary. TH Violence, swearing, brief nudity.

George Segal *Harry Benson* • Joan Hackett *Dr Janet Ross* • Richard A Dysart [Richard Dysart] *Dr John Ellis* • Jill Clayburgh *Angela Black* • Donald Moffat *Dr Arthur Mcpherson* • Matt Clark *Gerhard* • Michael C Gwynne *Dr Robert Morris* • Normann Burton [Norman Burton] *Detective Captain Anders* • William Hansen *Dr Ezra Manon* ■ *Dir* Mike Hodges • *Scr* Mike Hodges, from the novel by Michael Crichton

Terminal Velocity ★★ 15

Action thriller   1994 · US · Colour · 97min

Terminal stupidity, more like it. The second in a brief Hollywood flirtation with skydiving movies – *Drop Zone* came out in the same year – this is a big, dumb action thriller that exhilarates when airborne, but drags dangerously when on solid ground. Charlie Sheen is the parachuting instructor investigating the death of a pupil, who gets mixed up with Russian gangsters. JF Violence, swearing, nudity. DVD

Charlie Sheen *Ditch Brodie* • Nastassja Kinski *Chris Morrow* • James Gandolfini *Ben Pinkwater* • Christopher McDonald *Kerr* • Gary Bullock *Lex* • Hans R Howes [Hans Howes] *Sam* • Melvin Van Peebles *Noble* • Suli McCullough *Robocam* • Cathryn De Prume *Karen* • Richard Sarafian Jr *Dominic* ■ *Dir* Deran Sarafian • *Scr* David N Twohy [David Twohy]

The Terminator ★★★★★ 15

Science-fiction action thriller
1984 · US · Colour · 107min

Arnold Schwarzenegger said "I'll be back," and he was, seven years later. But the success of the subsequent sequels should not undermine the powerhouse strengths of James Cameron's original hi-tech nightmare, with violent cyborg Arnie time-warped from the future to alter the nuclear war-torn course of history. Generating maximum excitement from the first frame, the dynamic thrills are maintained right up to the nerve-jangling climax. Wittily written with a nice eye for sharp detail, it's hard sci-fi action all the way, and Linda Hamilton shines as the bewildered waitress who unwittingly becomes the saviour of the human race. AJ Swearing, violence, a sex scene, nudity. DVD BD

Arnold Schwarzenegger *The Terminator* • Michael Biehn *Kyle Reese* • Linda Hamilton *Sarah Connor* • Paul Winfield *Traxler* • Lance Henriksen *Vukovich* • Rick Rossovich *Matt* • Bess Motta *Ginger* • Earl Boen *Silberman* • Dick Miller *Pawn shop clerk* • Shawn Schepps *Nancy* ■ *Dir* James Cameron • *Scr* James Cameron, Gale Anne Hurd, William Wisher Jr

Terminator 2: Judgment Day ★★★★★ 15

Science-fiction action thriller
1991 · US · Colour · 145min

Director James Cameron piles on the hard-edged humour and rollercoaster action in a worthy sequel to his own 1984 horror fantasy classic. Adrenaline junkies get epic value for money, as cyborg Arnold Schwarzenegger comes back from the future to save our world from the T-1000 model, whose liquid metal shape-changing abilities set a new cinematic standard for stunning computer graphic special effects. Linda Hamilton turns in another marvellous performance as the fiercely committed

heroine who puts a necessary human face on Cameron's high-decibel mayhem and pyrotechnical bravura. AJ Swearing, violence. DVD BD

Arnold Schwarzenegger *The Terminator* • Linda Hamilton *Sarah Connor* • Edward Furlong *John Connor* • Robert Patrick *T-1000* • Earl Boen *Dr Silberman* • Joe Morton *Miles Dyson* • S Epatha Merkerson *Tarissa Dyson* • Castulo Guerra *Enrique Salceda* • Michael Biehn *Kyle Reese* ■ *Dir* James Cameron • *Scr* James Cameron, William Wisher

Terminator 3: Rise of the Machines ★★★ 12

Science-fiction action thriller
2003 · US/Ger · Colour · 104min

With a reported $170-million budget, this buys its way into public affection. Accordingly, the latest addition to the saga is bigger, louder and darker. Arnie's T-101 cyborg arrives in the present to protect future saviour of the human race John Connor (an unprepossessing Nick Stahl); the twist here is that the TX killing machine sent to kill Connor takes telepathic female form (a poised performance from former model Kristanna Loken). Other than that it's more of the same – the thrills are expensive, the chase highly charged and Arnie's one-liners suitably wry. AC DVD BD

Arnold Schwarzenegger *Terminator* • Nick Stahl *John Connor* • Claire Danes *Kate Brewster* • Kristanna Loken *TX* • David Andrews (2) *Robert Brewster* • Mark Famiglietti *Scott Petersen* • Earl Boen *Dr Silberman* ■ *Dir* Jonathan Mostow • *Scr* John Brancato, Michael Ferris, from a story by John Brancato, Michael Ferris, Tedi Sarafian

Terminator: Salvation ★★ 12

Science-fiction action thriller
2009 · US/Ger/UK · Colour · 110min

The fourth entry in the *Terminator* series continues the franchise stumble that began with *Terminator 3: Rise of the Machines*. Set in the aftermath of "Judgement Day", it's a glum, post-apocalyptic mess that can't decide which of its two lead characters is most interesting – Christian Bale's gruff resistance leader John Connor or a mysterious stranger from the past played by Sam Worthington. Worthington gives the film's stand-out performance, but Bale is completely wasted, left with little to do but shout orders into walkie-talkies. At least, the franchise's most familiar face keeps his "I'll be back" promise, thanks to some digital trickery, but even that moment seems more desperate than inventive. Let's hope *Terminator: Genisys* has more to offer in summer 2015. JR DVD BD

Christian Bale *John Connor* • Sam Worthington *Marcus Wright* • Anton Yelchin *Kyle Reese* • Moon Bloodgood *Blair Williams* • Bryce Dallas Howard *Kate Connor* • Helena Bonham Carter *Dr Serena Kogan* • Common *Barnes* • Jane Alexander *Virginia* ■ *Dir* McG [Joseph McGinty Nichol] • *Scr* John D Brancato, Michael Ferris

Terminator: Genisys ★★ 12

Science-fiction action thriller
2015 · US · Colour · 125min

Confusing time travel, lacklustre spectacle and a bland cast earmark this unexceptional reboot of James Cameron's classic cyborg v man franchisen. Emilia Clarke (*Game of Thrones*) stars as Sarah Connor, all clued-up about Skynet's plans for world domination, and is aided by a rock-solid Arnold Schwarzenegger, still unstoppable and uttering those famous one-liners.It should have been a simple story but complex jargon about nexus points, alternate childhood realities and bewildering parallel universes, makes for a head-scratching narrative. AJ Violence, some swearing. DVD BD 3D CS

Arnold Schwarzenegger *Guardian* • Jason Clarke (2) *John Connor* • Emilia Clarke *Sarah Connor* • Jai Courtney *Kyle Reese* • JK Simmons *O'Brien* • Matthew Smith [Matt Smith] *Alex* • Lee Byung-hun *Cop/T-1000* ■ *Dir* Alan Taylor • *Scr* Laeta Kalogridis, Patrick Lussier, from characters by James Cameron, Gale Anne Hurd

Terms of Endearment ★★★★ 15

Melodrama   1983 · US · Colour · 126min

Showered with Oscars (it won five and was nominated for a further seven), this is American mainstream movie-making at its best. Director James L Brooks largely succeeds in keeping sticky sentiment at bay in this story of the often strained mother-daughter relationship between Shirley MacLaine and Debra Winger. Jack Nicholson delivers one of his effortless scene-stealing supporting roles, and other familiar faces include Danny DeVito, Jeff Daniels and John Lithgow. MacLaine and Nicholson returned for the sequel, *Evening Star* (1996). JF Swearing. DVD BD

Shirley MacLaine *Aurora Greenway* • Debra Winger *Emma Horton* • Jack Nicholson *Garrett Breedlove* • Danny DeVito *Vernon Dahlart* • Jeff Daniels *Flap Horton* • John Lithgow *Sam Burns* • Lisa Hart Carroll *Patsy Clark* • Betty R King *Rosie Dunlop* • Huckleberry Fox *Teddy Horton* • Troy Bishop *Tommy Horton* ■ *Dir* James L Brooks • *Scr* James L Brooks, from the novel by Larry McMurtry

La Terra Trema ★★★★ U

Drama   1947 · It · BW · 153min

Intended as the first instalment of a trilogy on the exploitation of Sicilian labour (the other parts were to have focused on farmers and miners), this is much more of a neorealist document than Luchino Visconti's previous picture, *Ossessione*. Shooting without a script and using only non-professionals, he explores the trials of the fishermen of Aci Trezza as they are fleeced by worldly wholesalers and middlemen. Yet, despite the fact that the film was partially funded by the Communist Party, it still has an operatic realism, thanks to Visconti's editing of Graziati Aldo's meticulously composed vistas. DP Italian +subtitles. DVD

Luchino Visconti *Narrator* • Antonio Pietrangeli *Narrator* • Antonio Arcidiacono *Narrator* ■ *Dir* Luchino Visconti • *Scr* Luchino Visconti, from the novel *I Malavoglia* by Giovanni Verga

A Terrible Beauty ★★ U

Second World War drama
1960 · UK · BW · 90min

Stressing dramatic cliché, racial stereotyping and local colour over any kind of political analysis, this is a typical Hollywood yarn. Robert Mitchum is a reluctant recruit to the IRA, who finds leaving rather more difficult after the discovery that his new colleagues are collaborating with the Nazis to defeat the British. Made in Dublin, mainly on a studio set, with Mitchum well cast and ably supported by Richard Harris in an early role. AT

Robert Mitchum *Dermot O'Neill* • Anne Heywood *Neeve Donnelly* • Dan O'Herlihy *Don McGinnis* • Cyril Cusack *Jimmy Hannafin* • Richard Harris *Sean Reilly* • Marianne Benet *Bella O'Neill* • Niall MacGinnis *Ned O'Neill* ■ *Dir* Tay Garnett • *Scr* Robert Wright Campbell, from the novel by Arthur Roth

The Terror ★★ 12

Horror   1963 · US · Colour · 79min

More famous for being made in three days with leftover actors and sets from *The Raven* than anything else, Roger Corman's impromptu ghost story is incomprehensible. Lost Napoleonic soldier Jack Nicholson follows spectral Sandra Knight (Nicholson's wife at the time) to a cliff-top mansion owned by the demented Boris Karloff where mysterious things are going on - so mysterious in fact, neither the film-makers nor the audience can work out what's happening! Although Corman took the overall credit, scenes were also directed by Francis Ford Coppola, Monte Hellman, Jack Hill, Dennis Jacob and Nicholson (all uncredited). A legendary mess. AJ DVD

Boris Karloff *Baron von Leppe* • Jack Nicholson *Lt André Duvalier* • Sandra Knight *Hélène* • Richard Miller [Dick Miller] *Stefan* • Dorothy Neumann *Old woman* ■ *Dir* Roger Corman • *Scr* Leo V Gordon, Jack Hill

---

Terror ★★ 18
Horror 1979 · UK · Colour · 79min

In this efficient if rather nonsensical horror, a witch's curse is reactivated when surviving members of the family that persecuted her (including Carolyn Courage and John Nolan) base a horror film on the hex. *Inseminoid* director Norman J Warren piles on the gleefully gory chills, sleazy thrills and showbiz send-ups (courtesy of David McGillivray's endearingly wonky script), and the plot detours just about manage to belie the movie's micro-budget. AJ Swearing, violence, nudity. 📀

John Nolan *James Garrick* • Carolyn Courage *Ann Garrick* • James Aubrey *Phillip* • Sarah Keller *Suzy* • Trishia Walsh *Viv* • Glynis Barber *Carol Tucker* • Michael Craze *Gary* • Patti Love *Hannah* ■ *Dir* Norman J Warren • *Scr* David McGillivray, from a story by Les Young, Moira Young

Terror by Night ★★★ U
Mystery 1946 · US · BW · 60min

This Sherlock Holmes thriller moves fast enough to skim over the potholes in the plot. Basil Rathbone and Nigel Bruce are hired to safeguard a gem called the "Star of Rhodesia". Three murders later, the air-gun killer is revealed, and Dennis Hoey has overdone his comic act as Inspector Lestrade to an irritating degree. Years before, Alan Mowbray had appeared in the Clive Brook and Reginald Owen movies about Holmes, but he wrote that Rathbone's version of the sleuth was the best. TH 📀

Basil Rathbone *Sherlock Holmes* • Nigel Bruce *Dr John H Watson* • Alan Mowbray *Major Duncan Bleek* • Dennis Hoey *Inspector Lestrade* • Renee Godfrey *Vivian Vedder* • Skelton Knaggs *Sands* ■ *Dir* Roy William Neill • *Scr* Frank Gruber, from a story by Sir Arthur Conan Doyle

Terror Firmer ★★★
Comedy horror 1999 · US · Colour · 98min

Taking postmodernism to new depths, this is a hilarious exercise in self-reflection and bad taste from Lloyd Kaufman, co-founder of schlock-horror film company Troma. Based on his knowing memoir *All I Need to Know about Film-making I Learned from the Toxic Avenger*, the action centres on Kaufman's blind director, as he tries to make a slasher movie in spite of the fact that someone is butchering his cast and crew. The humour is gross, but should keep fans amused. D📀

Will Keenan *Casey* • Alyce LaTourelle *Jennifer* • Lloyd Kaufman *Larry Benjamin* • Trent Haaga *Jerry* ■ *Dir* Lloyd Kaufman • *Scr* Douglas Buck, Patrick Cassidy, Lloyd Kaufman

Terror in a Texas Town ★★★ PG
Western 1958 · US · BW · 77min

This B-western has attracted a cult following over the years. It's directed by Joseph H Lewis, and is an extraordinary work, featuring harpoon-wielding hero Sterling Hayden facing up to black-clad gunman Ned Young. Many hardened western admirers consider the contrivances of this movie and its elegiac camera style phoney and theatrical, but there's no denying this film's originality, given the obvious constraints of plot and budget. TS 📀

Sterling Hayden *George Hansen* • Sebastian Cabot *Ed McNeil* • Carol Kelly *Molly* • Eugene Martin *Pepe Mirada* • Ned Young *Nedrick Young* *Johnny Crale* • Victor Millan *José Mirada* ■ *Dir* Joseph H Lewis • *Scr* Ben L Perry

Terror in the Wax Museum ★★
Horror 1973 · US · Colour · 93min

Exhibits apparently come to life and commit murder in a very ordinary variation on the wax museum theme, with a mundane explanation for all the creepy goings-on. Poor scripting and direction doom the pedestrian plot further, although the cast – studded with an amazing array of intrepid old-timers – is enough of an attraction in itself to make this tired *House of Wax* retread worth watching. AJ

Ray Milland *Harry Flexner* • Broderick Crawford *Amos Burns* • Elsa Lanchester *Julia Hawthorn* • Maurice Evans *Inspector Daniels* • Shani Wallis *Laurie Mell* • John Carradine *Claude Dupree* ■ *Dir* Georg Fenady • *Scr* Jameson Brewer, from a story by Andrew Fenady

Terror Island ★★
Silent mystery adventure 1920 · US · BW · 55min

The third and most expensive major movie flop to star world-famous escapologist Harry Houdini borrows heavily from Jules Verne's underwater fantasy novels. As the inventor of a submarine device, he is asked to rescue Lila Lee's hostage father from cannibals on a South Sea island. However, it's really nothing more than an excuse to put Houdini in extreme situations so he can execute a series of amazing escapes. AJ

Houdini [Harry Houdini] *Harry Harper* • Jack Brammall *Starkey* • Lila Lee *Beverly West* • Wilton Taylor *Job Mourdant* • Eugene Pallette *Guy Mourdant* ■ *Dir* James Cruze • *Scr* Walter Woods, from a story by Arthur B Reeve, John W Grey

Terror of Mechagodzilla ★★★ 15
Monster horror 1975 · Jpn · Colour · 79min

The last of the original cycle of Godzilla movies picks up the action after the defeat of his robotic alter ego, whose remains have mysteriously vanished from the sea bed. Cue a daffy plot that sees a discredited scientist and his cyborg daughter teaming up with aliens to wipe out humanity through controlling both the fin-flapping Titanosaurus and a rebuilt and retooled Mechagodzilla. Our radioactive-breath lizard hero makes a fine entrance some way in, while the three-way smackdown finale is explosive. JH Japanese dubbed.

Tomoko Ai • Akihiko Hirata ■ *Dir* Inoshiro Honda • *Scr* Katsuhiko Sasaki

Terror on a Train ★★ U
Thriller 1953 · UK · BW · 72min

There are few more effective situations for building up tension than the race to defuse a ticking bomb. Glenn Ford plays a Canadian engineer searching for a bomb placed on a freight train. Meanwhile, the police hunt the saboteur. The direction is by former cameraman Ted Tetzlaff and he does an effective job visually, but the details of British everyday life sometimes ring false and the story is somewhat padded out. AE

Glenn Ford *Peter Lyncourt* • Anne Vernon *Janine Lyncourt* • Maurice Denham *Jim Warrilow* • Harcourt Williams *Vicar* • Victor Maddern *Saboteur* ■ *Dir* Ted Tetzlaff • *Scr* Kem Bennett, from his novel *Death at Attention*

Terror Train ★★★ 18
Horror 1980 · Can · Colour · 92min

Several years after participating in a cruel fraternity initiation that backfired and traumatised the victim, scream queen Jamie Lee Curtis and her college buddies rent a train for a party, with conductor Ben Johnson and young magician David Copperfield along for the ride. It doesn't take long for one of the many masked party-goers on board to start bumping people off. Director Roger Spottiswoode generates a noticeable amount of atmosphere, making the most of the superior production values and the talented cast. KB 📀

Ben Johnson (1) *Carne* • Jamie Lee Curtis *Alana* • Hart Bochner *Doc Manley* • David Copperfield *Magician* • Derek MacKinnon *Kenny Hampson* • Sandee Currie *Mitchy* ■ *Dir* Roger Spottiswoode • *Scr* TY Drake

The Terrorist ★★★★ 12
Political drama 1998 · Ind/US · Colour · 95min

Bollywood cinematographer Santosh Sivan proves himself a natural film-maker with this powerful study of the human aspect of political extremism. He makes audacious use of close-ups to register the bewildering range of emotions passing through the mind of teenage terrorist Ayesha Dharkar, as a combination of simple charity and an unexpected pregnancy cause her to doubt the value of her suicide bombing mission. But perhaps the film would have been more provocative without the 11th-hour optimism. DP Hindi +subtitles. Violence. 📀

Ayesha Dharkar *Milla* • Vishnu Vardhan *Thyagu* • Bhanu Prakash *Perumal* • K Krishna *Lover* • Sonu Sisupal *Leader* ■ *Dir* Santosh Sivan • *Scr* Santosh Sivan, Ravi Deshpande, Vijay Deveshwar, from a story by Santosh Sivan

TerrorVision ★ 15
Science-fiction comedy 1986 · US · Colour · 81min

This supposed satire on the media-obsessed, suburban middle classes is in fact a toe-curlingly embarrassing *Poltergeist* rip-off featuring a cartoonishly dysfunctional family. A new satellite dish accidentally beams an alien into the Putterman's living room. Writer/director Ted Nicolaou intentionally parodies those Z-grade monster movies of the 1950s, but has produced something of which Ed Wood would be proud. RS

Diane Franklin *Suzy Putterman* • Gerrit Graham *Stanley Putterman* • Mary Woronov *Raquel Putterman* • Chad Allen *Sherman Putterman* • Jonathan Gries *OD* • Jennifer Richards *Medusa* • Alejandro Rey *Spiro* • Bert Remsen *Grampa* ■ *Dir/Scr* Ted Nicolaou

Terry ★★★
Drama based on a true story 2005 · Can · Colour · 90min

The inspirational true story of Canadian national hero Terry Fox is told in simple style in this well-made TV drama. Anchored by Shawn Ashmore's strong lead performance, it poignantly re-enacts Fox's incredible 1980 "Marathon of Hope" in which the 21-year-old ran across Canada to raise money for cancer research – despite having lost a leg to the disease. Though Fox is portrayed in an almost saintly light (1983's *The Terry Fox Story* gives him a more balanced character), the film resists excessive sentimentality, leaving it to the events themselves to tug at the heartstrings. Drab soundtrack aside, it's deeply moving, with the end footage of the real Terry liable to bring on the tears. SF

Shawn Ashmore *Terry Fox* • Ryan McDonald *Doug Alward* • Noah Reid *Darrell Fox* • Matt Gordon *Bill Vigars* • Catherine Disher *Betty Fox* • David Huband *Rolly Fox* ■ *Dir* Don McBrearty • *Scr* Dennis Foon

Tesis ★★★ 18
Thriller 1996 · Sp · Colour · 118min

How is it possible to condemn our morbid fascination with violence without delivering the very imagery under scrutiny? It's a problem that Spanish director Alejandro Amenábar fails to solve in this otherwise compelling thriller. Yet, he can't be faulted for the way in which the story twists and turns, as post-graduate student Ana Torrent teams up with geek Fele Martínez to trace the origins of a snuff movie in a university's film vault. There may be only a handful of suspects, but even the most acute armchair detective will remain baffled. The suspense in the tunnel sequence is taken to almost sadistic levels. DP Spanish +subtitles. Swearing, violence, sex scenes. 📀

Ana Torrent *Angela* • Fele Martínez *Chema* • Eduardo Noriega (2) *Bosco* • Nieves Harranz *Sena* • Rosa Campillo *Yolanda* ■ *Dir/Scr* Alejandro Amenábar

Tess ★★★★ 12
Period drama 1979 · Fr/UK · Colour · 164min

Roman Polanski's now classic adaptation of Hardy's black and ironic tragedy is not as good as the novel, but still has much to recommend it, not least the evocative Oscar-winning photography. Nastassja Kinski rocketed to stardom after her starring role as the country girl, whose disastrous sexual encounters with her rakish cousin come back to haunt her when she finally finds love in the arms of Peter Firth. Devastating and powerful, Polanski's film achieves the requisite pathos and the director shoots a stunning dénouement against the backdrop of Stonehenge. The movie also won Oscars for costumes and art direction. LH 📀 🔵

Nastassia Kinski [Nastassja Kinski] *Tess* • Leigh Lawson *Alec d'Urberville* • Peter Firth *Angel Clare* • John Collin *John Durbeyfield* • David Markham *Rev Mr Clare* • Rosemary Martin *Mrs Durbeyfield* • Richard Pearson (1) *Vicar of Marlott* • Carolyn Pickles *Marian* ■ *Dir* Roman Polanski • *Scr* Roman Polanski, Gérard Brach, John Brownjohn, from the novel *Tess of the d'Urbervilles* by Thomas Hardy • *Cinematographers* Geoffrey Unsworth, Ghislain Cloquet • *Music* Philippe Sarde • *Production Designer* Pierre Guffroy • *Costume Designer* Anthony Powell

Tess of the Storm Country ★★
Silent melodrama 1922 · US · BW · 137min

This second adaptation of Grace Miller White's novel stars Mary Pickford – who'd starred in the 1914 original – as a fisherman's daughter who comes to the rescue of a woman about to be ostracised for her illegitimate baby. Pickford claims the baby as her own, admirably deflecting scorn away from the other woman. Naturally, it all comes right in the end. Pickford, a screen veteran at 21, acquired her top star status in the earlier version for Famous Players. RK

Mary Pickford *Tessibel Skinner* • Lloyd Hughes *Frederick Graves* • Gloria Hope *Teola Graves* • David Torrence *Elias Graves* • Forrest Robinson *Daddy Skinner* • Jean Hersholt *Ben Letts* ■ *Dir* John S Robertson • *Scr* Elmer Harris, from the novel by Grace Miller White

Tess of the Storm Country ★
Melodrama 1932 · US · BW · 75min

The appealing and talented Janet Gaynor is the heroine in this remake of a melodrama, popularised twice in the silent era by Mary Pickford. Gaynor was teamed with her frequent co-star, Charles Farrell, for maximum box-office potential, but this lachrymose tale of the gutsy, self-sacrificing daughter of an old seafarer was already past its sell-by date. RK

Janet Gaynor *Tess Howland* • Charles Farrell (1) *Frederick Garfield Jr* • Dudley Digges *Captain Howland* • June Clyde *Teola Garfield* • Claude Gillingwater *Frederick Garfield Sr* • George Meeker *Dan Taylor* ■ *Dir* Alfred Santell • *Scr* SN Behrmann, Sonya Levien, from the novel by Grace Miller White

Tess of the Storm Country ★★ U
Melodrama 1960 · US · Colour · 84min

Amazingly, the fourth screen version of the popular Grace Miller White family novel about a Scottish girl growing up among the Pennsylvania Dutch. Beautifully shot on location in CinemaScope by 20th Century-Fox as a vehicle for Diane Baker, who became a successful producer and in-demand character actress. Trouble is, time hasn't been kind to this sentimental tale, and, although it worked twice for Mary Pickford (in 1914 and again in 1922), the 1960s found this good-looking opus reduced to being released as a supporting feature. TS

Diane Baker *Tess Maclean* • Jack Ging *Peter Graves* • Lee Philips *Eric Thorson* • Archie Duncan *Hamish Maclean* • Nancy Valentine *Teola Graves* • Bert Remsen *Mike Foley* • Wallace Ford *Fred Thorson* ■ *Dir* Paul Guilfoyle (1) • *Scr* Charles Lang, Rupert Hughes, from the novel by Grace Miller White

Test Pilot ★★★★
Romantic drama 1938 · US · BW · 118min

Clark Gable stars in this top-notch MGM vehicle that teams him with ace director Victor Fleming. This is one of those flying movies based on the work of pioneering pilot-turned-writer Frank "Spig" Wead whose own courageous story was filmed in *The Wings of Eagles* and, like many such films, it rings true in the skies, but less so on the ground. Still, Gable's belle is sparky Myrna Loy and his mechanic pal is Spencer

T

Tracy, so whatever the weaknesses in the action, it's certainly watchable. Acting honours, though, are stolen by crusty Lionel Barrymore as an aeronautic tycoon. **TS**

Clark Gable *Jim Lane* • Myrna Loy *Ann Barton* • Spencer Tracy *Gunner Sloane* • Lionel Barrymore *Howard B Drake* • Samuel S Hinds *General Ross* • Arthur Aylesworth *Frank Barton* • Claudia Coleman *Mrs Barton* ■ *Dir* Victor Fleming • *Scr* Vincent Lawrence, Waldemar Young, Howard Hawks (uncredited), from a story by Frank Wead

Testament ★★★★★ PG
Disaster drama   1983 · US · Colour · 85min

This sobering and moving movie details with chilling accuracy how a typical family copes after an unspecified nuclear attack devastates America. There are no fancy special effects, just a shocking interruption during *Sesame Street*, followed by a blinding flash. In the aftermath, Jane Alexander (giving a stunning performance) must cope with situations she has always dreaded – mourning her missing husband, burying her children and coming to terms with the stark reality that she too will eventually die of radiation sickness. Director Lynne Littman accomplishes so much without hammering home the points or preaching. This is one of the best movies ever made about the futility of nuclear war. **AJ**

Jane Alexander *Carol Wetherly* • William Devane *Tom Wetherly* • Ross Harris [Rossie Harris] *Brad Wetherly* • Roxana Zal *Mary Liz Wetherly* • Lukas Haas *Scottie Wetherly* • Lilia Skala *Fania* • Leon Ames *Henry Abhart* • Rebecca De Mornay *Cathy Pitkin* • Kevin Costner *Phil Pitkin* ■ *Dir* Lynne Littman • *Scr* John Sacret Young, from the story *The Last Testament* by Carol Amen

Testament ★★ PG
Drama   1988 · UK · Colour · 79min

TV journalist Tania Rogers returns to her Ghanaian homeland in search of Werner Herzog on the set of *Cobra Verde*. Working under the auspices of the Black Audio Film Collective, writer/director John Akomfrah demonstrates admirable control in leaking fragments of information that enable us to piece together the horrifying experience that scarred Rogers during the fall of the Nkrumah regime. But, in order to achieve this "War Zone of Memories", Akomfrah is occasionally obscure and inconsequential. **DP**

Tania Rogers *Abena* • Evans Hunter *Rashid* • Emma Francis Wilson *Danso* • Frank Parkes *Mr Parkes* ■ *Dir/Scr* John Akomfrah

Le Testament d'Orphée ★★★★ PG
Experimental drama   1960 · Fr · BW · 76min

Testament to Jean Cocteau's influence on the New Wave, his final feature (a sequel to 1950's *Orphée*) was partly financed and produced by François Truffaut. But, while he exhorts the younger generation to bear his legacy, Cocteau is more interested here in looking back, with a potent mix of nostalgia and disillusionment, to the worlds and characters he created. No wonder this ragbag of references to his gloriously diverse artistic output is subtitled *Don't Ask Me Why*. Anyone coming to this poetic sojourn seeking revelation is going to be disappointed, as it's strictly for aficionados. **DP** French +subtitles. *DVD*

Jean Cocteau *Jean Cocteau, the Poet* • Jean-Pierre Léaud *The Schoolboy* • Edouard Dermithe *Cegeste* • Henri Cremieux *The Professor* • Françoise Christophe *The Nurse* • Maria Casarès *The Princess* • Jean Marais *Oedipus* • Pablo Picasso • Charles Aznavour • Roger Vadim • Brigitte Bardot • Yul Brynner ■ *Dir/Scr* Jean Cocteau

The Testament of Dr Cordelier ★★★★ PG
Horror drama   1959 · Fr · BW · 92min

Jean Renoir was one of the first great directors to make a film using television methods. The shooting of this updated free adaptation of Robert Louis Stevenson's *Dr Jekyll and Mr Hyde* took around ten days at the Radio-Télévision Française studios. The

use of multiple cameras gives the film the fluid, rough-edged spontaneous appeal of a live TV play. The switch between the cheap-looking studio interiors and the streets of Paris produces an appropriate sense of displacement and schism. Jean-Louis Barrault is extraordinary as the shaggy, bestial Monsieur Opale, the evil alter ego of the silver-haired, dignified Dr Cordelier. The film had to wait at least two years for a release. **RB** French +subtitles. *DVD*

Jean-Louis Barrault *Dr Cordelier/Opale* • Teddy Bilis *Maître Joly* • Michel Vitold *Dr Severin* • Jean Topart *Désiré* • Micheline Gary *Marguerite* • Jean Renoir *Narrator* ■ *Dir* Jean Renoir • *Scr* Jean Renoir, from the novel *Dr Jekyll and Mr Hyde* by Robert Louis Stevenson • *Cinematographer* Georges Leclerc

The Testament of Dr Mabuse ★★★★ 12
Classic horror   1932 · Ger · BW · 88min

Fritz Lang always liked to boast that the second part of his celebrated crime trilogy (after 1922's *Dr Mabuse, the Gambler*) was such a calculated insult to the Nazis that he feared for his life. Always one to embroider his own legend, Lang was nevertheless correct in claiming that the depiction of a master criminal who hypnotised people into doing his evil bidding was a bit near the knuckle for Goebbels, who had the film banned. Yet Lang's wife and co-scenarist, Thea von Harbou, was a committed Nazi who refused to follow her husband into French exile. This is a dark tale, told with atmospheric panache. Lang's final film was 1960's *The Thousand Eyes of Dr Mabuse*. **DP** German +subtitles. *DVD* Blu

Rudolf Klein-Rogge *Dr Mabuse* • Otto Wernicke *Insp Karl Lohmann* • Oskar Beregi [Oscar Beregi (1)] *Professor Baum* • Gustav Diessl *Thomas Kent* • Wera Liessem *Lilli* ■ *Dir* Fritz Lang • *Scr* Thea von Harbou, Fritz Lang, from characters by Norbert Jacques

Testament of Youth ★★★★ 12
Biographical drama   2014 · UK/Den · Colour · 124min

The futility of war is explored from a female perspective in this moving British period drama based on the beloved memoir by Vera Brittain. Alicia Vikander stars as Brittain in a beautiful-looking film that follows her trials and tribulations during the First World War. The feature debut of James Kent is overly familiar in places but it's nicely shot and there are affecting moments, while Vikander delivers an engaging, sympathetic turn that elevates what could have been merely worthy to the definitely worthwhile. **SC** *DVD* Blu

Alicia Vikander *Vera Brittain* • Kit Harington *Roland Leighton* • Taron Egerton *Edward Brittain* • Emily Watson *Mrs Brittain* • Hayley Atwell *Hope Milroy* • Dominic West *Mr Brittain* ■ *Dir* James Kent • *Scr* Juliette Towhidi, from Vera Brittain's autobiography • *Cinematographer* Rob Hardy

Testimony ★★ PG
Biographical drama   1987 · UK · BW and Colour · 150min

This heavy and long-winded biopic of the Russian composer Dmitri Shostakovich, was directed by one of the *enfants terribles* of 1980s UK cinema and television, Tony Palmer. Ben Kingsley brings his customary excellence to the leading role, but he can't quite compensate for a dull narrative, and for the film's ponderous overemphasis on Shostakovich's clashes with the Soviet authorities. A plus though, is the excellent photography, mainly black and white but with bursts of colour. **DA**

Ben Kingsley *Dmitri Shostakovich* • Sherry Baines *Nina Shostakovich* • Magdalen Asquith *Galya* • Mark Asquith *Maxim* • Terence Rigby *Stalin* • Ronald Pickup *Tukhachevksy* • John Shrapnel *Zhdanov* • Frank Carson *Carnival fat man* • Chris Barrie *Carnival thin man* ■ *Dir* Tony Palmer • *Scr* David Rudkin, Tony Palmer, from the memoirs *The Memoirs of Dmitri Shostakovich* by Dmitri Shostakovich • *Cinematographer* Nicholas D Knowland [Nic Knowland]

The Testimony of Taliesin Jones ★★★
Coming-of-age drama   2000 · US/UK · Colour · 93min

Jonathan Pryce heads an impressive cast in this unusual coming-of-age drama that blends nascent spirituality with domestic travails. In rural Wales, bookish 12-year-old Taliesin (John-Paul MacLeod) struggles to deal with the ridicule of his schoolmates and the fallout from his mum's affair with a hairdresser. But when he witnesses ageing piano teacher Billy Evans (Ian Bannen in his final role) performing a miraculous "healing" Taliesin's own faith in God is awakened. There are elements of Rhidian Brook's novel that translate awkwardly here to the screen – the protagonist's relief from the affliction of warts may stretch your credibility. But the sincerity of the performances makes this gentle tale a welcome contrast to more crude and worldly depictions of adolescent angst. **SS**

Jonathan Pryce *Tal's dad* • Ian Bannen *Billy Evans* • Geraldine James *Tal's mum* • Griff Rhys Jones *Caesar* • John-Paul MacLeod *Taliesin Jones* • Matthew Rhys *Jonathan* • Robert Pugh *Handycott* • Sophie Sherrington *Julie Dyer* • Mark Bishop *Luc Daniels* ■ *Dir* Martin Duffy • *Scr* Maureen Tilyou, from the novel by Rhidian Brook

Tetro ★★★ 15
Drama   2009 · US/Arg/Sp /It · BW and Colour · 121min

Having secured the 1970s with two *Godfathers* and *Apocalypse Now*, Francis Ford Coppola has seemed more of a director-for-hire in the last 25 years. Following 2007's unfathomable *Youth without Youth*, *Tetro* is another attempt to create something more personal. The intense Vincent Gallo plays the title character, a blocked writer living in Buenos Aires, who is visited by his much younger half-brother, Bennie (newcomer Alden Ehrenreich). The film is beautifully crafted and the complicated sibling relationship is well-handled, but Coppola's ham-fisted attempts to wrestle with ideas about art and artistry are just banal. **DW** In English, Spanish. Some swearing, sex scenes, nudity. *DVD* Blu

Vincent Gallo *Angelo Tetrocini "Tetro"* • Maribel Verdú *Miranda* • Alden Ehrenreich *Bennie Tetrocini* • Klaus Maria Brandauer *Carlo Tetrocini/Alfie* • Carmen Maura *Alone* • Rodrigo De La Serna *Jose* • Leticia Bredice *Josefina* • Mike Amigorena *Abelardo* ■ *Dir/Scr* Francis Ford Coppola • *Cinematographer* Mihai Malaimare Jr

Tetsuo: the Iron Man ★★ 18
Science-fiction horror   1989 · Jpn · BW · 64min

A Japanese businessman, apparently involved in a road accident, suddenly finds himself turning into a metallic mutant monster, providing an excuse for cult Japanese director Shinya Tsukamoto to bombard the viewer with surreal and nightmarish images. Employing grainy black-and-white photography, minimal dialogue and a pounding techno soundtrack this will either be seen as pretentious rubbish or a classy art movie. **RS** Japanese +subtitles. *DVD*

Tomoroh Taguchi *Salaryman* • Kei Fujiwara *Salaryman's girlfriend* • Nobu Kanaoka *Woman in glasses* • Shinya Tsukamoto *Young metals fetishist* ■ *Dir/Scr* Shinya Tsukamoto

Tetsuo II: Body Hammer ★★★ 18
Science-fiction horror   1991 · Jpn · Colour · 78min

Not so much a sequel to Shinya Tsukamoto's cult movie *Tetsuo*, as a radical reworking of that "body horror" study in mutant machine madness. Don't try and make sense of the story – bizarre experiments turn people into weapons – just savour the shiny images as Tsukamoto highlights "the beauty in destruction" in retina-scorching metallic hues. The central body-machine melding is well worth waiting for in this homo- and sado-erotic avant-garde abstraction. **AJ** Japanese +subtitles. *DVD*

Tomoroh Taguchi *Taniguchi Tomo* • Nobu Kanaoka *Kana* • Shinya Tsukamoto *Yatsu, "The Guy"* • Keinosuke Tomioka *Minori* ■ *Dir/Scr* Shinya Tsukamoto

Tex ★★★★ PG
Drama   1982 · US · Colour · 98min

There are early roles for Matt Dillon, Meg Tilly and Emilio Estevez in this terrific coming-of-age yarn, based on a book by SE Hinton, who also wrote *The Outsiders*. It focuses on the trials and tribulations of teenager Dillon and his elder brother, growing up footloose and parent-free in Oklahoma. Director Tim Hunter seemed to have the knack of drawing great performances from relatively inexperienced kids. Five years later, he'd do it again with *River's Edge*. **DA**

Matt Dillon *Tex McCormick* • Jim Metzler *Mason McCormick* • Meg Tilly *Jamie Collins* • Bill McKinney *Pop McCormick* • Frances Lee McCain *Mrs Johnson* • Ben Johnson (1) *Cole Collins* • Emilio Estevez *Johnny Collins* ■ *Dir* Tim Hunter • *Scr* Charlie Haas, Tim Hunter, from a novel by SE Hinton

The Texan ★★
Western   1930 · US · BW · 72min

One of Gary Cooper's first starring vehicles, this Paramount western presents him as a cocky bandit who is persuaded to impersonate the missing son of wealthy aristocrat Emma Dunn. Predictably, his innate good nature rebels at the deception, especially when he falls for one of the family, the lovely Fay Wray. Directed by John Cromwell from an O Henry's story, it has one of the celebrated storyteller's twists – a mild one – at the end. **AE**

Gary Cooper *Enrique "Quico", The Llano Kid* • Fay Wray *Consuelo* • Emma Dunn *Señora Ibarra* • Oscar Apfel *Thacker* • James A Marcus *John Brown* • Donald Reed *Nick Ibarra* ■ *Dir* John Cromwell • *Scr* Daniel N Rubin, Oliver HP Garrett, from the story *The Double-Dyed Deceiver* by O Henry

The Texans ★★★
Western   1938 · US · BW · 92min

There's nothing really special here, but this would-be epic from Paramount is still interesting to watch for its period setting and a fine cast. It tells the tale of the opening up of the West, including the formation of the Ku Klux Klan and the first cattle drive along the Chisholm Trail. Randolph Scott is the trail boss, but he's second-billed to Joan Bennett (in her only western), who gives the impression that she'd rather be somewhere else. **TS**

Joan Bennett *Ivy Preston* • Randolph Scott *Kirk Jordan* • May Robson *Granna* • Walter Brennan *Chuckawalla* • Robert Cummings *Captain Alan Sanford* • Raymond Hatton *Cal Tuttle* • Robert Barrat *Isaiah Middlebrack* ■ *Dir* James Hogan • *Scr* Bertrand Millhauser, Paul Sloane, William Wister Haines, from the story *North of '36* by Emerson H Hough

Texas ★★★ PG
Western   1941 · US · BW · 89min

This classy western from Columbia teams two matinee idols (and drinking buddies) William Holden and Glenn Ford, competing for the love of *Stagecoach*'s Claire Trevor. To be appreciated today it really needs colour, but it stems from the period when you didn't waste your budget if you had stars who would attract an audience regardless. George Marshall directs like a man who knows his territory, and turns out a satisfying and well-crafted movie. **TS**

William Holden (2) *Dan Thomas* • Glenn Ford *Tod Ramsey* • Claire Trevor *"Mike" King* • George Bancroft *Windy Miller* • Edgar Buchanan *Doc Thorpe* • Don Beddoe *Sheriff* ■ *Dir* George Marshall • *Scr* Horace McCoy, Lewis Meltzer, from his story Lewis Meltzer

Texas across the River ★★★ PG
Comedy western   1966 · US · Colour · 96min

Pairing likeable Dean Martin with French heart-throb Alain Delon, this was the first of a series of interesting, but failed attempts to turn Delon into a Hollywood star. There

T

are simplistic pleasures to be had here, though not if you're a die-hard western fan. Others will delight in the performance of Rat Pack member Joey Bishop as a deadpan Indian, and there's super cinematography by the great Russell Metty. Amiable. TS

Dean Martin *Sam Hollis* • Alain Delon *Don Andrea Baldasar* • Rosemary Forsyth *Phoebe Ann Taylor* • Joey Bishop *Kronk* • Tina Marquand *Lonetta* • Peter Graves (2) *Captain Stimpson* ■ *Dir* Michael Gordon • *Scr* Wells Root, Harold Greene, Ben Star

Texas Adios ★★★ 15
Spaghetti western 1966 · US · Colour · 88min

This lacks the stylisation and darkly comic touches that characterised the films of Italian western supremos Sergio Leone and Sergio Corbucci, with whom Franco Nero, the hero of this film, would team later in the same year for the cult classic *Django*. Nero plays a dutiful son who sets about avenging his father's death, but director Ferdinando Baldi's script lacks an innovative set piece that might have enlivened the all-too-familiar plotline. DP Italian dubbed. *DVD*

Franco Nero *Burt Sullivan* • Cole Kitosch *Jim* • José Suarez *Cisco Delgado* • Elisa Montés *Girl* ■ *Dir* Ferdinando Baldi • *Scr* Ferdinando Baldi, Franco Rossette

Texas Carnival ★★ U
Musical comedy 1951 · US · Colour · 76min

Supposedly a vehicle for Esther Williams, much of this musical appears to have landed on the cutting-room floor, since Williams – playing a carnival performer who is immersed in a barrel of water when customers hit the target in a ball-and-target game – barely swims at all. Ann Miller's part is downsized to one dance number (a highlight) and Howard Keel is similarly underemployed. At the centre of the unengaging plot is comedian Red Skelton, playing a carnival barker who is mistaken for a Texas oil baron. RK

Esther Williams *Debbie Telford* • Red Skelton *Cornie Quinell* • Howard Keel *Slim Shelby* • Ann Miller *Sunshine Jackson* • Paula Raymond *Marilla Sabinas* • Keenan Wynn *Dan Sabinas* ■ *Dir* Charles Walters • *Scr* Dorothy Kingsley, from a story by Dorothy Kingsley, George Wells

LANDMARK FILM
A savvy use of visual and editing techniques shows that suggestion and anticipation can be more effective than gore, and spawns the splatter sub-genre

The Texas Chain Saw Massacre ★★★★★ 18
Horror 1974 · US · Colour · 79min

Time has not dimmed the shock value of this seminal classic from director Tobe Hooper that's based on the same real-life case that inspired *Psycho*. This scream-filled chiller, which was finally granted a certificate from the British Board of Film Classification for its 25th anniversary re-release, tells the story of five Texas teenagers who come across a demented family of murderous cannibals. Hooper masterfully uses a documentary-style realism, coupled with the horror of anticipation and suggestion, to take the terror factor into stunning and disturbing areas. Low on gore (the three sequels aren't) and made on a micro-budget that adds to the harsh tone, this razor-sharp nightmare is a must-see for fans of the genre. AJ Violence, swearing. *DVD* *BL*

Marilyn Burns *Sally* • Allen Danziger *Jerry* • Paul A Partain *Franklin* • William Vail *Kirk* • Teri McMinn *Pam* • Edwin Neal *Hitch-hiker* • Jim Siedow *Old man* • Gunnar Hansen *Leatherface* ■ *Dir* Tobe Hooper • *Scr* Kim Henkel, Tobe Hooper, from their story

The Texas Chainsaw Massacre Part 2 ★★★★ 18
Horror 1986 · US · Colour · 96min

Evangelical ex-Texas Ranger Dennis Hopper is determined to bring the demented cannibal family to justice after the disappearance of his nephew (the wheelchair victim in the original). He's helped by DJ Caroline Williams who taped one of their atrocities during a live phone-in.

With its power to shock, outrage and disturb still intact, Tobe Hooper's masterful sequel is a rich slice of unrelenting American Gothic. Jeff Burr took over as director for the second sequel, *Leatherface: the Texas Chainsaw Massacre III*. AJ Violence, swearing. *DVD* *BL*

Dennis Hopper *Lieutenant "Lefty" Enright* • Caroline Williams *Vanita "Stretch" Block* • Jim Siedow *Drayton "Cook" Sawyer* • Bill Moseley *Chop-Top* • Bill Johnson (3) *Leatherface* • Ken Evert *Grandpa* ■ *Dir* Tobe Hooper • *Scr* LM Kit Carson, from characters by Kim Henkel, Tobe Hooper

Texas Chainsaw Massacre: the Next Generation ★★★ 18
Horror 1994 · US · Colour · 83min

Written and directed by Kim Henkel – the co-scripter of Tobe Hooper's original – this third sequel still shocks and horrifies. An unofficial remake of the first film, which rings weird changes on the whole demented, ultra-sadistic atmosphere, this has four senior prom revellers taking a wrong turning down a dark Texas road and coming into contact with the cannibal clan. This makes explicit what the original only hinted at. AJ *DVD*

Renée Zellweger [Renée Zellweger] *Jenny* • Matthew McConaughey *Vilmer* • Robert Jacks *Leatherface* • Tonie Perenski *Darla* • Joe Stevens *W E* • Lisa Newmyer *Heather* • John Harrison *Sean* • Tyler Cone *Barry* ■ *Dir* Kim Henkel • *Scr* Kim Henkel, from characters by Kim Henkel, Tobe Hooper

The Texas Chainsaw Massacre ★★★ 18
Horror 2003 · US · Colour · 94min

The raw terror of the 1974 original isn't replicated here, but director Marcus Nispel provides some great shocks in his gorgeous-looking update of Tobe Hooper's horror classic. Here, once again, five young people fight for their lives against the deranged Hewitts and their disfigured son, Leatherface. With just a hint of cannibalism, a leering upgrade in sexual content and more gore than the relatively bloodless original, this refit still manages to retain a grungy, unsavoury atmosphere as Scott Kosar's effective screenplay filters the now *déjà-vu* plot through seen-it-all slasher imagery and *Blair Witch* docu-realism. AJ *DVD* *BL*

Jessica Biel *Erin* • Jonathan Tucker *Morgan* • Erica Leerhsen *Pepper* • Mike Vogel *Andy* • Eric Balfour *Kemper* • David Dorfman *Jedidiah* • R Lee Ermey *Sheriff Hoyt* • Andrew Bryniarski *Thomas Hewitt/Leatherface* ■ *Dir* Marcus Nispel • *Scr* Scott Kosar, from the film by Kim Henkel, Tobe Hooper

The Texas Chainsaw Massacre: the Beginning ★★ 18
Horror thriller 2006 · US · Colour · 92min

Not content with remaking Tobe Hooper's landmark horror movie *The Texas Chain Saw Massacre* in 2003, producer Michael Bay returns with this lacklustre prequel. Set in 1969, it promises to reveal the origins of chainsaw killer Leatherface (Andrew Bryniarski), a social misfit goaded into murder by his sadistic adoptive father (R Lee Ermey). Unfortunately, Sheldon Turner's inane script saddles this once-great horror movie icon with such an uninspired backstory that it would have been better left untold. JR *DVD* *BL*

Jordana Brewster *Chrissie* • Taylor Handley *Dean* • Diora Baird *Bailey* • Matthew Bomer [Matt Bomer] *Eric* • R Lee Ermey *Sheriff Hoyt* • Andrew Bryniarski *Thomas Hewitt/Leatherface* • Cyia Batten *Alex* ■ *Dir* Jonathan Liebesman • *Scr* Sheldon Turner, from a story by Turner, David J Schow, from characters by Kim Henkel, Tobe Hooper

Texas Chainsaw ★ 18
Horror 2013 · US · Colour · 91min

Leatherface is back, and in gloriously indifferent 3D for this semi-coherent, morally confused, clumsy and superfluous sequel. It offers more slicing and dicing by

filmdom's favourite chainsaw-toting cannibal, who emerges implausibly from the basement of the old family home to butcher its new occupants. Almost 40 years separate this and Tobe Hooper's original everyday story of flesh-eating folk, but there's no Hooper this time and director John Luessenhop fails to match the short, sharp shock of the 1974 classic. DA Violence. *DVD* *BL* *3D*

Alexandra Daddario *Heather Miller* • Dan Yeager *Leatherface* • Tremaine "Trey Songz" Neverson [Trey Songz] *Ryan* • Scott Eastwood *Carl* • Marilyn Burns *Verna Carson* • Bill Moseley *Drayton Sawyer* ■ *Dir* John Luessenhop • *Scr* Kirsten Elms, Adam Marcus, Debra Sullivan, from a story by Marcus, Sullivan, Stephen Susco, from characters by Kim Henkel, Tobe Hooper

Texas Killing Fields ★★★ 15
Crime thriller based on a true story 2011 · US · Colour · 100min

This involving, atmospheric but often scrappy thriller marks the Hollywood feature debut of Ami Canaan Mann, the daughter of *Heat* director Michael Mann. Sam Worthington stars as a Texas cop who reluctantly joins forces with a New York detective (Jeffrey Dean Morgan) to solve a baffling series of murders that seem to criss-cross local state boundaries. While the film never delivers on its initial splurge of whodunnit intrigue, it does sustain a pleasurable intensity – largely due to an excellent supporting cast that includes Jessica Chastain, Chloë Grace Moretz and Stephen Graham. However, the standout here is Morgan, who gets a rare showcase to demonstrate his leading-man credentials. DW Violence, swearing. *DVD* *BL*

Sam Worthington *Detective Mike Souder* • Jeffrey Dean Morgan *Detective Brian Heigh* • Chloë Grace Moretz *Little Anne Sliger* • Jessica Chastain *Detective Pam Stall* • Stephen Graham *Rhino* • Annabeth Gish *Gwen Heigh* • Sheryl Lee *Lucie Sliger* ■ *Dir* Ami Canaan Mann • *Scr* Donald F Ferrarone [Don Ferrarone]

Texas Lady ★★ U
Western 1955 · US · Colour · 81min

This routine western is made mesmerisingly watchable by the sheer force of its star, Claudette Colbert, playing a crusading journalist in town to take over her father's newspaper against all odds. She looks splendid, and is well supported by goodies Barry Sullivan and John Litel, and baddies Ray Collins and Walter Sande. The Technicolor's nice, but then the cinematographer was *Duel in the Sun's* Ray Rennahan, one of Hollywood's finest. TS *DVD*

Claudette Colbert *Prudence Webb* • Barry Sullivan *Chris Mooney* • Gregory Walcott *Jess Foley* • Ray Collins *Ralston* • Walter Sande *Sturdy* • James Bell *Cass Gower* ■ *Dir* Tim Whelan • *Scr* Horace McCoy

The Texas Rangers ★★★★ U
Western 1936 · US · BW · 94min

Released to coincide with the Lone Star state's centennial celebrations, this roistering, good-natured adventure had the commercial effect of bringing the western back into public favour, rescuing it from poverty row B-movie obscurity. Allegedly based on official Texas Rangers records, this is a loosely woven tale about three buddies – Fred MacMurray, Jack Oakie and baddie Lloyd Nolan – who fall out. Director King Vidor has a firm grasp on the action sequences in what is a very satisfying western. TS *DVD*

Fred MacMurray *Jim Hawkins* • Jack Oakie *Wahoo Jones* • Jean Parker *Amanda Bailey* • Lloyd Nolan *Sam McGee* • Edward Ellis *Major Bailey* • Bennie Bartlett *David* • Frank Shannon *Captain Stafford* ■ *Dir* King Vidor • *Scr* Louis Stevens, from a story by King Vidor, Elizabeth Hill Vidor, from the book by Walter Prescott Webb

Texas Rangers ★ 12
Western adventure based on a true story 2001 · US · Colour · 86min

This crass postmodern western about the famous border force pitches itself as a *Young Guns*-style adventure for a new generation of teen pin-ups, as dying sheriff Dylan McDermott turns James Van Der Beek, Ashton Kutcher and Usher Raymond into a fighting force capable of taming Alfred Molina's bandits. It's a lamentable tale, and Steve Miner's direction is consistently uninspired. DP *DVD*

James Van Der Beek *Lincoln Rogers Dunnison* • Dylan McDermott *Leander McNelly* • Usher Raymond *Randolph Douglas Scipio* • Ashton Kutcher *George Durham* • Rachael Leigh Cook *Caroline Dukes* • Robert Patrick *John B Armstrong* • Randy Travis *Frank Bones* • Alfred Molina *John King Fisher* • Leonor Varela *Perdita* ■ *Dir* Steve Miner • *Scr* Scott Busby, Martin Copeland, from the memoir *Taming the Nueces Strip: the Story of McNelly's Rangers* by George Durham

Texas Terror ★★ U
Western 1935 · US · BW · 51min

In the mid-1930s, John Wayne was busy releasing a string of movies, many of them B-westerns that were made for producer Paul Malvern at Monogram Pictures, a poverty row outfit known for such westerns and the *Bowery Boys* series. Wayne was their workhorse and *Texas Terror* sticks to the formula, with Lucile Brown, plus his regular collaborator in these movies, famed stuntman Yakima Canutt. AT *DVD*

John Wayne *John Higgins* • Lucile Brown *Beth Matthews* • LeRoy Mason *Joe Dickson* • George Hayes [George "Gabby" Hayes] *Sheriff Williams* • Buffalo Bill Jr *Blackie* ■ *Dir/Scr* Robert N Bradbury

Texasville ★ 15
Comedy drama 1990 · US · Colour · 120min

The Last Picture Show was one of the iconic movies of early 1970s America, and its director Peter Bogdanovich was inevitably going to be drawn to novelist Larry McMurtry's 1987 sequel. The book was disappointing, but no one could have envisaged that the film version was going to be so mind-numbingly bad. The out-of-form Bogdanovich simply tries too hard, spending the first part of the picture debunking the original and longing despairingly for past glories in the cloying closing stages. DP *DVD*

Jeff Bridges *Duane Jackson* • Cybill Shepherd *Jacy Farrow d'Olonne* • Annie Potts *Karla Jackson* • Cloris Leachman *Ruth Popper* • Timothy Bottoms *Sonny Crawford* • Eileen Brennan *Genevieve* • Randy Quaid *Lester Marlow* • William McNamara *Dickie Jackson* ■ *Dir* Peter Bogdanovich • *Scr* Peter Bogdanovich, from the novel by Larry McMurtry

Thank God He Met Lizzie ★★★ 15
Romantic comedy 1997 · Aus · Colour · 86min

This quirky Australian comedy, starring a pre-*Elizabeth* Cate Blanchett, is no skeleton in the closet. Instead, it's a charming, amusingly eccentric affair, which tracks the romantic dilemmas of loner Richard Roxburgh (who co-starred with Blanchett in *Oscar and Lucinda*), who has reservations on the day of his wedding to Blanchett. JF

Richard Roxburgh *Guy Jamieson* • Cate Blanchett *Lizzie O'Hara* • Frances O'Connor *Jenny Follett* • Linden Wilkinson *Poppy O'Hara* • John Gaden *Dr O'Hara* • Genevieve Mooy *Mrs Jamieson* • Michael Ross *Mr Jamieson* ■ *Dir* Cherie Nowlan • *Scr* Alexandra Long

Thank God It's Friday ★★★ 15
Musical 1978 · US · Colour · 85min

Here's what disco was really like circa 1978. The flipside of *Saturday Night Fever*, director Robert Klane's exploitative movie doesn't carry any message as it focuses on different people assembling at the Zoo disco in Hollywood for that pop movie staple – a dance contest. Using a nonstop soundtrack of disco hits, it expertly communicates the exciting, buzzy and hip atmosphere of 1970s clubland. More fun than it pretends to be, Jeff Goldblum and Debra Winger make early movie appearances as disco queen Donna Summer belts out the Oscar-winning song *Last Dance*. AJ Swearing.

Donna Summer *Nicole Sims* • Valerie Landsburg *Frannie* • Terri Nunn *Jeannie* • Chick Vennera *Marv Gomez* • Ray Vitte *Bobby Speed* • Mark Lonow *Dave* • Andrea Howard *Sue* • Jeff Goldblum *Tony* • Robin Menken *Maddy* • Debra Winger *Jennifer* ■ *Dir* Robert Klane • *Scr* Barry Armyan Bernstein

Thank You and Good Night!
★★★

Documentary   1991 · US · Colour · 82min

This moving documentary charts the physical decline and ultimate death of film-maker Jan Oxenberg's Jewish grandmother, Mae Joffe. This isn't just a conventional documentary though, as Oxenberg experiments freely with various styles and techniques, from using cutout characters to home movie and outright fantasy sequences. Apart from the loss of a grandparent, there's a wider message here about family relationships and dealing with illness and bereavement. But the various elements combine beautifully in an offbeat movie, that's also tender-hearted and touching. DA

■ *Dir/Scr* Jan Oxenberg

Thank You for Smoking
★★★★15

Satirical black comedy
2005 · US · Colour · 88min

Jason Reitman's feature debut is a satire on the big businesses of smoking and spin doctoring that gleefully blasts away at unscrupulous lobbyists, hand-wringing liberals and most points in-between. Aaron Eckhart plays the antihero, a frighteningly convincing lobbyist for Big Tobacco, who dubs himself a "Merchant of Death". Also in his "MoDs" club are Maria Bello (alcohol) and David Koechner (firearms). This hits most of its targets with such artful elegance that it almost diffuses the impact, but there is great pleasure to be taken in its daring wit and excellent performances. AR Swearing. *DVD*

Aaron Eckhart *Nick Naylor* • Maria Bello *Polly Bailey* • Cameron Bright *Joey Naylor* • Adam Brody *Jack* • Sam Elliott *Lorne Lutch* • Katie Holmes *Heather Holloway* • David Koechner *Bobby Jay Bliss* • Rob Lowe *Jeff Megall* • William H Macy *Senator Ortolan Finistirre* ■ *Dir* Jason Reitman • *Scr* Jason Reitman, from the novel by Christopher Buckley

Thank You, Jeeves
★★

Comedy   1936 · UK · BW · 57min

Jeeves and Wooster have been firm favourites with readers and TV audiences for many years, but their antics have yet to be brought to the big screen with any degree of success. There is only the faintest echo of the Wodehouse wit and brio in this silly story about industrial espionage and gunrunning. The excellent Arthur Treacher is the fish-eating valet for whom no crisis is insurmountable, but David Niven (in his first Hollywood starring role) is far too suave and knowing to convince as Bertie Wooster. Jeeves only appeared in the 1937 follow-up, *Step Lively, Jeeves*. DP

David Niven *Bertie Wooster* • Arthur Treacher *Jeeves* • Virginia Field *Marjorie Lowman* • Lester Matthews *Elliott Manville* • Colin Tapley *Tom Brock* ■ *Dir* Arthur Greville Collins • *Scr* Joseph Hoffman, Stephen Gross, from the story by PG Wodehouse

Thank You, Mr Moto
★★★

Crime mystery   1937 · US · BW · 66min

The second series entry (after *Think Fast, Mr Moto*) featuring Peter Lorre as John P Marquand's Japanese sleuth, is perhaps the least tangled and most enjoyable, although the atmosphere is surprisingly sinister for a B-movie. The picture opens with Moto, disguised as a Gobi nomad, trying to infiltrate a gang preying on the desert's ancient treasure troves. The clues bring him

into contact with a Chinese prince, his overprotective mother and some ruthless gangsters. Lorre bustles around to good effect, and John Carradine is excellent as a shady antiques dealer. DP

Peter Lorre *Mr Moto* • Thomas Beck *Tom Nelson* • Pauline Frederick *Madame Chung* • Jayne Regan *Eleanor Joyce* • Sidney Blackmer *Eric Koerger* • Sig Rumann [Sig Ruman] *Colonel Tchernov* • John Carradine *Pereira* ■ *Dir* Norman Foster • *Scr* Norman Foster, Willis Cooper, from a story by John P Marquand

Thank Your Lucky Stars
★★★★U

Musical   1943 · US · BW · 122min

One of the most enjoyable of Hollywood's patriotic, star-studded wartime concoctions, this Warner Bros extravaganza is a joy, as Eddie Cantor takes us on a magic carpet ride through show-biz land. Here are unlikely and delightful songbirds Errol Flynn and Bette Davis singing, respectively, *That's What You Jolly Well Get* and *They're Either Too Young or Too Old*; and there's also a particularly fine production number involving Hattie McDaniel. Watch also for tough guys John Garfield and Humphrey Bogart sending themselves up. TS

Eddie Cantor *Joe Sampson/Himself* • Joan Leslie *Pat Dixon* • Dennis Morgan *Tommy Randolph* • Dinah Shore • SZ Sakall *Dr Schlenna* • Edward Everett Horton *Farnsworth* • Humphrey Bogart • John Garfield ■ *Dir* David Butler • *Scr* Norman Panama, Melvin Frank, James V Kern, from a story by Everett Freeman, Arthur Schwartz

Thanks a Million
★★

Musical comedy   1935 · US · BW · 85min

This minor but nevertheless enjoyable musical comedy from 20th Century-Fox is effectively a star vehicle for crooner Dick Powell, with some interesting but now dated sideswipes at political chicanery. Radio comedian Fred Allen has some moments as the troubled wisecracking manager pushing Powell for governor, and there's splendid period music from Paul Whiteman and his band and the Yacht Club Boys. TS

Dick Powell *Eric Land* • Ann Dvorak *Sally Mason* • Fred Allen (2) *Ned Lyman* • Patsy Kelly *Phoebe Mason* • Raymond Walburn *Judge Culliman* • David Rubinoff *Orchestra Leader* • Benny Baker *Tammany* ■ *Dir* Roy Del Ruth • *Scr* Nunnally Johnson, from a story by Melville Crossman [Darryl F Zanuck]

Thanks for Everything
★★★

Comedy   1938 · US · BW · 70min

Jack Haley is an unexceptional chap who wins a radio competition to find "Mr Average American". Unscrupulous advertising men Adolphe Menjou and Jack Oakie seize the opportunity to exploit Smith using his very averageness to sell any number of items. This fast paced satire on the advertising world benefits from the strong playing. DF

Adolphe Menjou *JB Harcourt* • Jack Oakie *Brady* • Jack Haley *Henry Smith* • Arleen Whelan *Madge Raines* • Binnie Barnes *Kay Swift* ■ *Dir* William A Seiter • *Scr* Harry Tugend, Curtis Kenyon, Art Arthur, from a story by Gilbert Wright

Thanks for Sharing
★★15

Sex comedy drama   2012 · US · Colour · 107min

There's plenty of sharing, but not enough caring in this edgy comedy drama from Stuart Blumberg, the co-writer of 2010 indie hit *The Kids Are All Right*. Mark Ruffalo plays Adam, a member of a support group for sex addicts who meets the girl of his dreams (Gwyneth Paltrow). Also part of the group is Josh Gad who gets a few cheap and easy laughs as an overweight sex fiend. However, the light-hearted approach means it's difficult to take the issues seriously. It works in fits and starts, and some scenes are boldly funny, but there's still an emotional void that Blumberg cannot fill. SP Swearing, sex scenes, nudity. *DVD*

Mark Ruffalo *Adam* • Tim Robbins *Mike* • Gwyneth Paltrow *Phoebe* • Josh Gad *Neil* • Joely Richardson *Katie* • Patrick Fugit *Danny* • Alecia Moore [Pink] *Dede* ■ *Dir* Stuart Blumberg • *Scr* Stuart Blumberg, Matt Winston

That Awkward Moment
★★★15

Romantic comedy   2013 · US · Colour · 90min

Zac Efron headlines a lightweight but quite likeable comedy "bromance" about Jason (Efron), Mikey (Michael B Jordan) and Daniel (Miles Teller), three New York friends at critical junctures in their love lives. When Mikey's wife is caught playing away with her lawyer, Jason and Daniel vow to stay single in sympathy. But love doesn't work like that. The threesome's plans for non-committal sex with a whole roster of girls is soon thwarted. It's corny, contrived and rather uneven in tone but there's genuine charisma between the three leads, and is amiable undemanding entertainment. DA Swearing, sex scenes. *DVD* *BL*

Zac Efron *Jason* • Imogen Poots *Ellie* • Miles Teller *Daniel* • Michael B Jordan *Mikey* • Mackenzie Davis *Chelsea* • Jessica Lucas *Vera* ■ *Dir/Scr* Tom Gormican

That Certain Age
★★★

Musical comedy   1938 · US · BW · 96min

In her fourth feature, 17-year-old Deanna Durbin was allowed a boyfriend (Jackie Cooper, who was the same age), but no kiss yet. This amiable comedy has Durbin neglecting Cooper while developing a crush on her parents' houseguest, man-of-the-world journalist Melvyn Douglas. She also finds time to warble six songs. Former silent film star Irene Rich plays Deanna's mother. RB *DVD*

Deanna Durbin *Alice Fullerton* • Melvyn Douglas *Vincent Bullitt* • Jackie Cooper *Ken* • Irene Rich *Mrs Fullerton* • Nancy Carroll *Grace Bristow* • John Halliday *Mr Fullerton* • Jackie Searl [Jackie Searle] *Tony* • Charles Coleman *Stephens* • Peggy Stewart *Mary Lee* ■ *Dir* Edward Ludwig • *Scr* Bruce Manning, Billy Wilder, Charles Brackett, from a story by F Hugh Herbert

That Certain Feeling
★★

Romantic comedy   1956 · US · Colour · 102min

A romantic comedy that is neither romantic nor funny, this does at least offer the bizarre combination of George Sanders and Bob Hope competing for the favours of Sanders's fiancée, Eva Marie Saint, who happens to be Hope's ex-wife. The complications ensue when top cartoonist Sanders loses his touch and hires bumbling artist Hope to "ghost" his strip. Also involved in this inferior offering is the splendid Pearl Bailey as Sanders's maid and Hope's ally. RK

Bob Hope *Francis X Dignan* • Eva Marie Saint *Dunreath Henry* • George Sanders *Larry Larkin* • Pearl Bailey *Gussie* • David Lewis (1) *Joe Wickes* • Al Capp • Jerry Mathers *Norman Taylor* ■ *Dir* Norman Panama, Melvin Frank • *Scr* Norman Panama, Melvin Frank, IAL Diamond, William Altman

That Certain Woman
★★★U

Melodrama   1937 · US · BW · 94min

An example of a movie remade by its original director, this is a new version of the 1929 Gloria Swanson early talkie *The Trespasser*, with a simmering Bette Davis as the gangster's widow trying to go straight. Director Edmund Goulding has less luck with Bette than he did with Gloria in this overblown melodrama, though a young and gauche Henry Fonda does impress as a playboy, vying with lawyer Ian Hunter for Davis's affections. TS

Bette Davis *Mary Donnell* • Henry Fonda *Jack Merrick* • Ian Hunter *Lloyd Rogers* • Anita Louise *Flip* • Donald Crisp *Mr Merrick Sr* • Hugh O'Connell *Virgil Whitaker* • Katherine Alexander *Mrs Rogers* ■ *Dir* Edmund Goulding • *Scr* Edmund Goulding, from his film *The Trespasser*

That Championship Season
★★★15

Drama   1982 · US · Colour · 104min

Jason Miller is probably best known for his role as Father Karras in *The Exorcist* and for being the father of Jason Patric. But Miller was really a playwright who dabbled in acting, and this movie marked his sole effort as a director, adapting his own

Pulitzer Prize-winning play which also won a Tony Award and the New York Drama Critics' Award in 1972. It's the story of four former basketball players and their coach, who have a reunion and engage in the sort of bonding dialogue and down home wisdom, beloved of American playwrights. Some may find it smug and a bit too wordy. AT

Bruce Dern *George Sitkowski* • Stacy Keach *James Daley* • Robert Mitchum *Coach Delaney* • Martin Sheen *Tom Daley* • Paul Sorvino *Phil Romano* • Arthur Franz *Macken* • Michael Bernosky *Jacks* • Joseph Kelly *Malley* ■ *Dir* Jason Miller • *Scr* Jason Miller, from his play

That Cold Day in the Park
★★★

Psychological drama
1969 · US/Can · Colour · 113min

This early Robert Altman film features the brilliant Sandy Dennis as an emotionally disturbed spinster who becomes infatuated with a young man she meets in the park, and takes him home to live with her. But her possessive jealousy soon renders him more prisoner than partner. The main theme of this rather disturbing film is repressed sexuality, but there are also odd hints of things darker and more taboo. Altman directs with aplomb. DA *DVD* *BL*

Sandy Dennis *Frances Austen* • Michael Burns *Boy* • Susanne Benton *Nina* • Luana Anders *Sylvie* • John Garfield Jr *Nick* ■ *Dir* Robert Altman • *Scr* Gillian Freeman, from a novel by Richard Miles

That Dangerous Age
★★

Romantic drama   1949 · UK · BW · 100min

Eminent barrister Roger Livesey, in Capri with his wife Myrna Loy and daughter Peggy Cummins to recover from a nervous breakdown, is visited by young barrister Richard Greene with whom Loy has an illicit affair. Produced and directed by the Russian-born Gregory Ratoff - imported from Hollywood along with Loy - for Alexander Korda's London Films, this part fraught, part sentimental melodrama is too old-fashioned to convince, despite decent production values and the best efforts of its polished leads. RK

Myrna Loy *Lady Cathy Brooke* • Roger Livesey *Sir Brian Brooke, KC* • Peggy Cummins *Monica Brooke* • Richard Greene *Michael Barclaigh* • Elizabeth Allan *Lady Sybil* • Gerard Heinz *Dr Thorvald* ■ *Dir* Gregory Ratoff • *Scr* Gene Markey, from the play *Autumn* by Margaret Kennedy, Ilya Surgutchoff

That Darn Cat!
★★U

Comedy   1965 · US · Colour · 111min

All the pieces slot together with ease in this lively, if overlong, Disney caper. Yet, while it makes efficient entertainment, the film is not as much fun as it should be, bearing in mind its exceptional cast. The cat steals the show by a whisker from nosey neighbours William Demarest and Elsa Lanchester. Hayley Mills is perky enough as the cat's owner, but all roles are dull compared to those of Dean Jones as the FBI agent with a cat allergy and Roddy McDowall as a drip whose ducks are the frisky feline's favourite playmates. DP *DVD*

Hayley Mills *Patti Randall* • Dean Jones *Zeke Kelso* • Roddy McDowall *Gregory Benson* • Dorothy Provine *Ingrid Randall* • Neville Brand *Dan* • Elsa Lanchester *Mrs MacDougall* • William Demarest *Mr MacDougall* ■ *Dir* Robert Stevenson • *Scr* Gordon Gordon, Mildred Gordon, Bill Walsh, from the novel *Undercover Cat* by Gordon Gordon, Mildred Gordon

That Darn Cat
★★U

Comedy   1997 · US · Colour · 85min

This watchable enough remake of the lively 1965 comedy stars Christina Ricci in the role originally played by Hayley Mills. The story is much the same as Ricci and rookie FBI agent Doug E Doug team up with a talented moggy to pursue a gang of kidnappers. But there's nothing new or any improvement from the unexceptional original, which makes one wonder why Disney bothered making an almost exact copy. DA *DVD*

Christina Ricci *Patti* • Doug E Doug *Zeke Kelso* • Dean Jones *Mr Flint* • George Dzundza *Boetticher* • Peter Boyle *Pa* • Michael McKean • Peter Randall • Bess Armstrong *Judy Randall* • Dyan Cannon *Mrs Flint* • John Ratzenberger *Dusty* • Estelle Parsons *Old Lady McCracken* ■ *Dir* Bob Spiers • *Scr* LA Karaszewski [Larry Karaszewski], SM Alexander [Scott Alexander], from a 1965 film, from the novel *Undercover Cat* by Mildred Gordon, Gordon Gordon

That Eye, the Sky ★★★
Fantasy drama 1994 · Aus · Colour · 105min

A far cry from the black comedy of *Death in Brunswick*, John Ruane's second feature is a mystical melodrama. Peter Coyote gives a memorable performance as the mysterious wandering evangelist who comes to the aid of a crisis-stricken farming family, though never quite assuaging the doubts of teenager Amanda Douge. With Lisa Harrow also impressive as the tether's-end wife taken by the stranger's charm and Jamie Croft suitably wide-eyed as her impressionable son, this is a film that will either enchant or infuriate. DP

Peter Coyote *Henry Warburton* • Lisa Harrow *Alice Flack* • Amanda Douge *Tegwyn Flack* • Jamie Croft *Ort* • Paul Sonkkila *Mr Cherry* • Louise Silversen *Mrs Cherry* ■ *Dir* John Ruane • *Scr* Jim Barton, John Ruane, from the novel by Tim Winton

That Funny Feeling ★★
Romantic comedy 1965 · US · Colour · 93min

This is one of those familiar romantic comedies in which the leads continually cross each other's path before they get together. This time, pleasant performances from Bobby Darin and his then wife Sandra Dee distract attention from the coincidences. Dee is an aspiring actress who entertains rich publisher Darin in an apartment that she doesn't own, but works in as a maid. Unbeknown to her, it's his apartment. Daft, but you've seen worse. JG

Sandra Dee *Joan Howell* • Bobby Darin *Tom Milford* • Donald O'Connor *Harvey Granson* • Nita Talbot *Audrey* • Larry Storch *Luther* • James Westerfield *Officer Brokaw* • Leo G Carroll *O'Shea* ■ *Dir* Richard Thorpe • *Scr* David R Schwartz, from a story by Norman Barasch, Carroll Moore

That Good Night
Drama 2017 · UK · Colour

This is a preview – no prints were available to review as we went to press: An adaptation of NJ Crisp's play – which the *British Theatre Guide* described as "brave and profound" – with John Hurt as the cantankerous author refusing to "go gentle into that good night", in the words of Dylan Thomas, but knowing he must and trying to iron things out with his estranged son before he goes. Seeing Hurt once more in a decent lead role is bound to whet the appetite, but for many the presence of Sofia Helin – Saga Noren in the Nordic TV series *The Bridge* – is enough to make this a must-see. SvM

John Hurt *Ralph* • Sofia Helin *Anna* • Erin Richards *Cassie* • Max Brown *Michael, Ralph's son* ■ *Dir* Eric Styles • *Scr* Charles Savage, from NJ Crisp's play

That Hamilton Woman ★★★ PG
Historical drama 1941 · UK · BW · 119min

"You cannot make peace with dictators," says Laurence Olivier as Lord Nelson, "You have to destroy them, wipe them out!" Audiences being bombed in London in 1941 caught the drift immediately and it was rumoured that Churchill not only urged Alexander Korda to make the film, but that he also wrote Nelson's maiden speech in the House of Lords. As propaganda, the picture is as single-minded as Olivier's later *Henry V*. But this is mainly a turgid love story, with Vivien Leigh as Lady Hamilton, whose adulterous affair with the naval hero was just as newsworthy as Napoleon's campaigns. AT

Vivien Leigh *Emma Hart Hamilton* • Laurence Olivier *Lord Horatio Nelson* • Alan Mowbray *Sir William Hamilton* • Sara Allgood *Mrs Cadogan-Lyon* • Gladys Cooper *Lady Nelson* • Henry

Wilcoxon *Captain Hardy* ■ *Dir* Alexander Korda • *Scr* Walter Reisch, RC Sherriff • *Production Designer* Vincent Korda • *Set Designer* Julia Heron

That Kind of Woman ★★
Romantic drama 1959 · US · Colour · 94min

Sophia Loren, the mistress of millionaire George Sanders, meets a group of GIs during a train trip and ends up spending the night with Tab Hunter. To her, it's a one-night stand, but for him it's love eternal: he proposes marriage, thus presenting her with the conflict of choice between a fresh new life and her old one. Directed by Sidney Lumet, the movie can hardly fail to be competently made, but is actually an embarrassingly miscast and unconvincing bucketful of soap. RK

Sophia Loren *Kay* • Tab Hunter *Red* • George Sanders *The Man* • Barbara Nichols *Jane* • Jack Warden *Kelly* ■ *Dir* Sidney Lumet • *Scr* Walter Bernstein

That Lady ★★
Historical drama 1955 · UK · Colour · 100min

Once mooted as a comeback vehicle for the great Garbo, it fell to an ill-cast Olivia de Havilland to portray the lusty one-eyed Princess of Eboli in this would-be spectacular 16th-century Spanish epic. Gilbert Roland is splendid, though, as de Havilland's lover, and King Philip II is played with intelligence by Paul Scofield, making his movie debut. The novelty of the CinemaScope process reduces director Terence Young to providing little more than a series of tableaux. TS

Olivia de Havilland *Ana De Mendoza, Princess of Eboli* • Gilbert Roland *Antonio Perez* • Paul Scofield *Philip II* • Françoise Rosay *Bernadina* • Dennis Price *Mateo Vasquez* • Robert Harris *Cardinal* • Christopher Lee *Captain* ■ *Dir* Terence Young • *Scr* Anthony Veiller, Sy Bartlett, from a novel by Kate O'Brien

That Lady in Ermine ★★★ U
Musical 1948 · US · Colour · 89min

This richly Technicolored Betty Grable fantasy musical with a genuinely mythic sense to it is remembered more today for the fact that it was, sadly, the last movie of the great Ernst Lubitsch. The director famed for the stylish wit of his "Lubitsch Touch" died after only eight days shooting and was replaced by another notable European exile, Otto Preminger. The original wafer-thin material revolves around a 19th-century European army officer billeting his men in a castle with a past. The result is entertaining, if not particularly memorable. TS

Betty Grable *Francesca/Angelina* • Douglas Fairbanks Jr *Colonel Teglash/The Duke* • Cesar Romero *Mario* • Walter Abel *Major Horvath/benvenuto* • Reginald Gardiner *Alberto* • Harry Davenport *Luigi* ■ *Dir* Ernst Lubitsch, Otto Preminger • *Scr* Samson Raphaelson, from an operetta by Rudolph Schanzer, Ernest Welisch

That Lucky Touch ★★★ PG
Romantic comedy 1975 · UK · Colour · 89min

The setting is Brussels and a Nato war games event, with Roger Moore as an arms dealer and Susannah York a leftie *Washington Post* journalist. It breezes along nicely, has some barbed comments about American imperialism and a federal Europe, and Moore and York are attractive and relaxed. In his final screen role, Lee J Cobb adds some class playing a general married to Shelley Winters, who sets everyone's teeth on edge. AT

Roger Moore *Michael Scott* • Susannah York *Julia Richardson* • Shelley Winters *Diana Steedeman* • Lee J Cobb *General Steedeman* • Jean-Pierre Cassel *Leo* • Raf Vallone *General Peruzzi* • Sydne Rome *Sophie* • Donald Sinden *General Armstrong* ■ *Dir* Christopher Miles • *Scr* John Briley, from an idea by Moss Hart

That Man from Rio ★★★★ U
Crime comedy adventure 1964 · Fr/It · Colour · 112min

How many other James Bond spoofs received an Oscar nomination for their screenplay? Moreover, how many could call

upon Jean-Paul Belmondo in this kind of form – as a French air force pilot who spends his eight-day leave traversing the Atlantic and the Brazilian mainland, in a frantic bid to rescue feisty girlfriend Françoise Dorléac from the Amazon natives intent on finding a horde of lost jungle treasure. With Philippe de Broca roaring through the set pieces (which just get gleefully more preposterous) and exploiting every one of his exotic locations, this is hectic, hilarious and more than a match for Indiana Jones. DP French +subtitles.

Jean-Paul Belmondo *Adrien Dufourquet* • Françoise Dorléac *Agnes* • Jean Servais *Professor Catalan* • Simone Renant *Lola* • Milton Ribeiro *Tupac* • Ubiracy De Oliveira *Sir Winston* • Adolfo Celi *Senor De Castro* ■ *Dir* Philippe de Broca • *Scr* Philippe de Broca, Jean-Paul Rappeneau, Ariane Mnouchkine, Daniel Boulanger

That Man George ★★
Crime adventure 1965 · Fr/It/Sp · Colour · 91min

This is the type of colourful thriller that kept international audiences entertained throughout the 1960s, but generally didn't play too well in English-speaking territories owing to wholesale dubbing of the bulk of the cast. American lead George Hamilton lets his tan do the acting as he romances Claudine Auger and combats assorted other villains as he takes a shipment of gold bullion across Morocco. Mindless, although there's a nice twist at the end. TS French dubbed.

George Hamilton *George* • Claudine Auger *Lila* • Alberto de Mendoza *Travis* • Daniel Ivernel *Vibert* • Tiberio Murgia *Jose* ■ *Dir* Jacques Deray • *Scr* Henri Lanoë, Jose Giovanni, Suzanne Arduini, Jacques Deray, from the novel *The Heisters* by Robert Page Jones

That Midnight Kiss ★★★ U
Romantic musical 1949 · US · Colour · 97min

This MGM musical is noteworthy as the feature debut of Mario Lanza, the star who brought opera to the movies and became the first tenor since Caruso to achieve massive popularity. It is virtually his biography, as Philadelphia opera patroness Ethel Barrymore has problems with the male lead of daughter Kathryn Grayson's stage debut, then Grayson discovers that local truck driver Lanza can more than hold his own with an aria. TS

Kathryn Grayson *Prudence Budell* • José Iturbi • Ethel Barrymore *Abigail Budell* • Mario Lanza *Johnny Donnetti* • Keenan Wynn *Artie Glenson* • J Carrol Naish *Papa Donnetti* • Jules Munshin *Michael Pemberton* • Thomas Gomez *Guido Betelli* ■ *Dir* Norman Taurog • *Scr* Bruce Manning, Tamara Hovey

That Night ★★★ 12
Drama 1992 · US/Jpn/Ger/Fr · Colour · 85min

This is an affectionate portrait of adolescent nostalgia from first-time director Craig Bolotin. The setting is the Long Island suburbia of the early 1960s, where impressionable youngster Eliza Dushku becomes the fascinated witness to a generation-gap battle between her neighbours – daughter Juliette Lewis and mum Helen Shaver. The story is very slight, but the young Dushku is a revelation, and Lewis and C Thomas Howell, Lewis's unsuitable beau, also deliver convincing performances. JF Swearing, sexual references.

C Thomas Howell *Rick* • Juliette Lewis *Sheryl* • Helen Shaver *Ann* • Eliza Dushku *Alice Bloom* • John Dossett *Larry Bloom* • J Smith-Cameron *Carol Bloom* • Katherine Heigl *Kathryn* ■ *Dir* Craig Bolotin • *Scr* Craig Bolotin, Alice McDermott

That Night in Rio ★★★
Musical comedy 1941 · US · Colour · 90min

"I-yi-yi-yi-yi I like you vairy much" sings Carmen Miranda in, arguably, her greatest screen musical. This remake of *Folies Bergère*, later itself remade as *On the Riviera* (20th Century-Fox was renowned for recycling it's plots) is really a vehicle for Don Ameche, in a dual role, and Alice Faye. But, from the opening, it's Miranda who

runs away with the film. By the way, if you're lusting for Rio, this movie never leaves the back lot. TS

Alice Faye *Baroness Cecilia Duarte* • Don Ameche *Larry Martin/Baron Duarte* • Carmen Miranda *Carmen* • SZ Sakall *Arthur Penna* • J Carrol Naish *Machado* • Curt Bois *Felicio Salles* • Leonid Kinskey *Pierre Dufont* • Frank Puglia *Pedro, the valet* • Maria Montez *Inez* ■ *Dir* Irving Cummings • *Scr* George Seaton, Bess Meredyth, Hal Long, Samuel Hoffenstein, Jessie Ernst, from a play by Rudolph Lothar, Hans Adler

That Obscure Object of Desire ★★★★★ 15
Drama 1977 · Fr/Sp · Colour · 99min

Luis Buñuel's final film is a fitting end to a dazzling career. A witty, ironic and barbed morality tale, it follows the increasingly desperate attempts of wealthy businessman Fernando Rey to seduce his maid, unaware that his world is collapsing around his ears. Buñuel only hit upon the intriguing idea of casting two actresses in the role of Conchita after Maria Schneider walked off the set, but it proved to be a creative masterstroke, as the switches between Carole Bouquet and Angela Molina teasingly suggest the indecision in Rey's mind as he searches for the woman of his dreams. DP French +subtitles. DVD Blu-ray

Fernando Rey *Mathieu* • Carole Bouquet *Conchita* • Angela Molina *Conchita* • Julien Bertheau *Edouard/d'Oleargues* • André Weber *Martin* • Piéral [Pierre Piéral] *Psychology professor* • Bernard Musson *Police inspector* ■ *Dir* Luis Buñuel • *Scr* Luis Buñuel, Jean-Claude Carrière, from the novel *La Femme et le Pantin* by Pierre Loüys

That Old Feeling ★★ 12
Romantic comedy 1997 · US · Colour · 100min

Bette Midler and Dennis Farina play feuding divorcees, meeting up at their daughter's wedding to a politician who trades on his squeaky clean image. It's not too long before they realise they still fancy each other. Although there's a nice quick-fire repartee between Midler and Farina, they aren't exactly in the Hepburn and Tracy class when it comes to bickering. More schmaltz than the average person can stomach. LH Swearing.

Bette Midler *Lilly Leonard* • Dennis Farina *Dan De Mora* • Paula Marshall *Molly De Mora* • Gail O'Grady *Rowena* • David Rasche *Alan* • Jamie Denton *Keith Marks* • Danny Nucci *Joey Donna* ■ *Dir* Carl Reiner • *Scr* Leslie Dixon

That Riviera Touch ★★ PG
Comedy 1966 · UK · Colour · 93min

Morecambe and Wise head for the south of France in what starts out looking like a customised remake of the old Laurel and Hardy comedy *Saps at Sea*. But Eric and Ernie's regular writers, Sid Green and Dick Hills, quickly run into the problem that blighted all three of their movies; the pair's relaxed, intimate style might have been perfect for the sketch format of their TV show, but it was totally wrong for sustaining narratives. Few laughs. DP DVD

Eric Morecambe *Eric* • Ernie Wise *Ernie* • Suzanne Lloyd *Claudette* • Paul Stassino *Le Pirate* • Armand Mestral *Inspector Duval* ■ *Dir* Cliff Owen • *Scr* Sidney C Green [SC Green], Richard M Hills [RM Hills], Peter Blackmore

That Sinking Feeling ★★★ 12
Crime caper 1979 · UK · Colour · 86min

Bill Forsyth made his directorial debut with this thin, but still enjoyable, comedy. This established the Forsyth style: underplayed humour and seemingly irrelevant gags, with a subtle payoff and the quirky use of the local idiom. The theft of a consignment of sinks is planned with the intricacy of a *Rififi*-like heist but, as in so many caper movies, it just didn't go smoothly. DP DVD Blu-ray

Robert Buchanan *Ronnie* • John Hughes *Vic* • Billy Greenlees *Wal* • Douglas Sannachan *Simmy* • Alan Love *Alec* • Danny Benson *Policeman* • Eddie Burt *Van Driver* • Tom Mannion *Doctor* • Eric Joseph *The Wee Man* • Gordon John Sinclair [John Gordon-Sinclair] *Andy* ■ *Dir/Scr* Bill Forsyth

T

That Sugar Film ★★ 12
Documentary   2014 · Aus · Colour · 97min

Here, Australian actor Damon Gameau seeks to consume 40 teaspoons of sugar a day in order to prove that seemingly healthy, low-fat foods are as bad for people as the fast food that Morgan Spurlock tucked into in *Super Size Me*. Gameau clearly means well, but his experiment is scientifically sloppy, while his smarminess does little to support his position. It's a case that's well-worth making, but the pill should be more potent, with less sugar-coating. DP *DVD*

■ *Dir/Scr* Damon Gameau

That Thing You Do!
★★★★ PG
Musical comedy   1996 · US · Colour · 103min

Tom Hanks's directorial debut is an immensely likeable pop fable about the meteoric rise and fall of the mythical Wonders, an all-American small-town rock 'n' roll band. Set in a period-perfect 1964, and featuring a marvellously evocative soundtrack of cod-Golden Oldies, it deliberately emphasises the *Forrest Gump*-style feel-good nostalgia, rather than making any hard-hitting statement about the price of fame. Hanks also plays the group's opportunistic manager, but it's sweet-natured Tom Everett Scott who registers strongest as the drumming driving force behind the band, with Liv Tyler affecting as their mascot. AJ *DVD*

Tom Everett Scott *Guy Patterson* • Liv Tyler *Faye* • Johnathon Schaech *Jimmy* • Steve Zahn *Lenny* • Ethan Embry *The Bass Player* • Tom Hanks *Mr White* • Charlize Theron *Tina* • Chris Isaak *Uncle Bob* • Kevin Pollak *Boss Vic Koss* ■ *Dir/Scr* Tom Hanks

That Touch of Mink ★★★ U
Romantic comedy   1962 · US · Colour · 94min

This very popular Doris Day vehicle only works if you accept that she won't sleep with co-star Cary Grant, which might have made sense back in 1962 but hardly makes any sense at all now – after all, these are two of the best-looking and most sophisticated people in the world. But that's the plot: will she or won't she, and we know she won't. This is quintessential Day fluff, complete with quite unnecessary heavily gauzed close-ups, and Grant can barely disguise the fact that he's getting a little too long in the tooth for such foolishness. TS *DVD*

Cary Grant *Philip Shayne* • Doris Day *Cathy Timberlake* • Gig Young *Roger* • Audrey Meadows *Connie* • Alan Hewitt *Dr Gruber* • John Astin *Beasley* • John McKee *Collins, chauffeur* ■ *Dir* Delbert Mann • *Scr* Stanley Shapiro, Nate Monaster

That Uncertain Feeling ★★★
Romantic comedy   1941 · US · BW · 81min

Ernst Lubitsch directed this remake of *Kiss Me Again* (1925), one of his best silent pictures, with that uncertain touch. Something was lost when sound was added, although the screenplay crackles wittily for the first quarter of the picture afterwards it becomes ever sillier and more desperate. Merle Oberon gets recurring hiccups after six years of marriage to insurance salesman Melvyn Douglas, and her psychiatrist diagnoses marriage trouble. She then has a brief flirtation with Burgess Meredith, who has the best zany moments in the film. RB

Merle Oberon *Jill Baker* • Melvyn Douglas *Larry Baker* • Burgess Meredith *Alexander Sebastian* • Alan Mowbray *Dr Vengard* • Olive Blakeney *Margie* • Harry Davenport *Jones* • Eve Arden *Sally Aikens* ■ *Dir* Ernst Lubitsch • *Scr* Donald Ogden Stewart, Walter Reisch, from the play *Divorçons* by Victorien Sardou, Emile de Najac

That Was Then... This Is Now ★★★ 15
Drama   1985 · US · Colour · 97min

Emilio Estevez's directorial career has been largely undistinguished, but when he scripted this respectful adaptation of the SE

Hinton novel, it seemed he might well have a career behind as well as in front of the camera. He and Craig Sheffer take the roles of two troubled adolescents whose friendship is threatened when romance rears its head. Although it is a little downbeat, this remains a moving drama about the traumas of growing up. JF Swearing, violence.

Emilio Estevez *Mark Jennings* • Craig Sheffer *Bryon Douglas* • Kim Delaney *Cathy Carlson* • Jill Schoelen *Angela Shepard* • Barbara Babcock *Mrs Douglas* • Frank Howard *"M & M" Carlson* • Frank McCarthy *Mr Carlson* • Larry B Scott *Terry Jones* • Morgan Freeman *Charlie Woods* ■ *Dir* Christopher Cain • *Scr* Emilio Estevez, from the novel

That Woman Opposite ★★ PG
Murder mystery   1957 · UK · BW · 80min

Don't expect too much of this modest film, and you'll be agreeably entertained by an efficiently directed work graced by many recognisable faces. The setting is a small French town where an English antique dealer is found murdered. An inconsequential plot of intrigue and romance follows, as private detective Dan O'Herlihy attempts to solve the mystery. BB *DVD*

Phyllis Kirk *Eve* • Dan O'Herlihy *Dermot Kinross* • Wilfrid Hyde White *Sir Maurice Lawes* • Petula Clark *Janice* • Jack Watling *Toby* • William Franklyn *Ned* ■ *Dir* Compton Bennett • *Scr* Compton Bennett, from the novel *The Emperor's Snuffbox* by John Dickson Carr

That Wonderful Urge ★★★
Comedy   1948 · US · BW · 81min

Tyrone Power is a cocky and insistent reporter who ridicules heiress Gene Tierney. To get her own back, she declares to the world that he has married her for money. The plot was familiar to those who remembered the earlier version called *Love Is News* (1937). Suitably witty and slick, this is less good, but shows off Tierney's talent for light comedy. RB

Tyrone Power *Thomas Jefferson Tyler* • Gene Tierney *Sara Farley* • Reginald Gardiner *Count Andre de Guyon* • Arleen Whelan *Jessica Woods* • Lucile Watson *Aunt Cornelia* • Gene Lockhart *Judge* • Lloyd Gough *Duffy* • Porter Hall *Attorney Ketchell* ■ *Dir* Robert B Sinclair • *Scr* Jay Dratler, from the story *Love Is News* by William R Lipman, Frederick Stephani

That'll Be the Day ★★★★ 15
Musical drama   1973 · UK · Colour · 87min

With the glint in his eye that made him a 1970s pop favourite, David Essex is perfect for the role of Jim MacLaine, the teenager with itchy feet who dreams of rock 'n' roll stardom and a life away from austere 50s Britain. Director Claude Whatham offers a more knowing view of teenage life than most films of the time and there's a nice turn from Ringo Starr as the pal who schools MacLaine in the ways of the world. TP Swearing. *DVD*

David Essex *Jim MacLaine* • Ringo Starr *Mike* • Rosemary Leach *Mrs MacLaine* • James Booth *Mr MacLaine* • Billy Fury *Stormy Tempest* • Keith Moon *JD Clover* • Rosalind Ayres *Jeanette* • Robert Lindsay *Terry Sutcliffe* ■ *Dir* Claude Whatham • *Scr* Ray Connolly

That's Carry On ★★★ PG
Comedy compilation   1977 · UK · Colour and BW · 91min

You can almost guarantee that your favourite *Carry On* clip will be missing from this compilation, which sticks to all the obvious moments that had already been aired on the TV "best of" series. Kenneth Williams and Barbara Windsor shot a few linking scenes that contain some of the biggest laughs, but there's more than a ring of truth in Williams's contention that the later films scripted by Talbot Rothwell were overly dependent on smut and lacked the sharpness of his earlier efforts. With a little more imagination and discrimination, this

---

could have been a cracking collection, but it's still well worth watching. DP *DVD*

Kenneth Williams • Barbara Windsor ■ *Dir* Gerald Thomas • *Scr* Tony Church

That's Dancing! ★★★★ U
Dance compilation   1985 · US · Colour and BW · 100min

Top-of-the-range tappers are featured in this all-dancing spectacular from Jack Haley Jr, who also made the *That's Entertainment!* films. And exhilarating fun it is, too, featuring not just tap-dancing, but many other forms of dance, from early Busby Berkeley extravaganzas to Michael Jackson, via ballet and acrobatics. Like those earlier compilation films, the movie is the best bits of numerous musicals, but within the limitations of the format, it's highly enjoyable. SG

■ *Dir/Scr* Jack Haley Jr

That's Entertainment! ★★★★★ U
Compilation   1974 · US · BW and Colour · 122min

Here, lovingly assembled, is MGM's compilation of its greatest triumphs in a field that it had made its own: the musical. Wittily discussed and cleverly edited are some of the Crown Jewels of Hollywood, linked by a superb cast of compères, including Frank Sinatra, Elizabeth Taylor and Liza Minnelli, whose tribute to her mother Judy Garland is both exquisite and moving. This is entertainment on a grand scale, the snippets making you ache to see the originals. Two sequels followed, but this was the great forerunner, and a big box-office hit. TS *DVD* *Blu*

■ *Dir* Jack Haley Jr

That's Entertainment, Part II ★★★★ U
Compilation   1976 · US · Colour and BW · 123min

The first film was a hard act to follow, but director Gene Kelly's sequel is satisfying and includes a memorable sequence of new material featuring the ageing Kelly dancing again with the great Fred Astaire. There's also a witty Saul Bass title sequence: watch how the graphics mirror the artists' names. Although this MGM compilation is not as powerful as its predecessor, it still recaptures the lovely golden glow that watching an MGM musical can bring. TS *DVD*

Gene Kelly • Fred Astaire ■ *Dir* Gene Kelly

That's Entertainment! III ★★★★ U
Compilation   1994 · US · Colour and BW · 108min

There may be the suspicion that MGM was scraping the barrel for this third compilation from its vaults, but it's a gold plated barrel! It also provides an answer for all those who thought the 1946 musical comedy *The Harvey Girls* lacked a third act number – it's here, as Judy Garland belts out *March of the Doggies*, in a restored and remixed version. Another highlight is Garland performing Irving Berlin's *Mr Monotony*, which was cut from 1948's *Easter Parade*. Beautifully assembled and immaculately edited. TS

■ *Dir* Bud Friedgen, Michael J Sheridan

That's Life ★★★ 15
Comedy drama   1986 · US · Colour · 101min

Failing to realise that smug, affluent Californians are of interest mainly to themselves, Blake Edwards invites us to share in their every tiny worry. Stepping into the shoes of another midlife neurotic, Jack Lemmon succeeds in making him both sympathetic and irksome. Meanwhile his introspection has blinded him to the more pressing needs of his wife (Julie Andrews). Shot in the Malibu home of director Edwards and his real-life wife Andrews, the cast includes members of their family as well as appearances from Lemmon's wife Felicia Farr and son Chris. JM

Jack Lemmon *Harvey Fairchild* • Julie Andrews *Gillian Fairchild* • Sally Kellerman *Holly Parrish* • Robert Loggia *Father Baragone* • Jennifer Edwards *Megan Fairchild Bartlet* • Chris Lemmon *Josh Fairchild* • Felicia Farr *Madame Carrie* ■ *Dir* Blake Edwards • *Scr* Milton Wexler, Blake Edwards

That's My Boy ★★ U
Comedy   1951 · US · BW · 98min

This is a college football caper redesigned as a vehicle for Dean Martin and Jerry Lewis. Lewis is the son of a wealthy college alumnus father, who wants his unathletic student son to play for his own old football team, and hires fellow-student and pigskin star Martin to train him. The movie, sparse on laughs, is even less amusing to those with no understanding of the intricacies of American football. RK

Dean Martin *Bill Baker* • Jerry Lewis *"Junior" Jackson* • Ruth Hussey *Ann Jackson* • Eddie Mayehoff *"Jarring Jack" Jackson* • Marion Marshall *Terry Howard* • Polly Bergen *Betty Hunter* • Hugh Sanders *Coach Wheeler* • John McIntire *Benjamin Green* ■ *Dir* Hal Walker • *Scr* Cy Howard, from his story

That's My Boy ★★ 15
Comedy   2012 · US · Colour · 109min

This Adam Sandler comedy is largely a laugh-free zone, a lazy amalgam of shoddy slapstick, stereotypes and sentimentality, with added gross-out moments. Sandler plays a struggling former tabloid celebrity who signs a deal with a TV show to set up a family reunion. However, his estranged financier son (Andy Samberg) wants nothing to do with him. Samberg gives it his all in a thankless role and there are some amusing supporting turns from an eclectic cast, but, overall, the kindest thing you can say about this movie is that it's not as bad as Sandler's previous, *Jack and Jill*. JF Violence, swearing, sexual references, drug abuse. *DVD* *Blu*

Adam Sandler *Donny Berger* • Andy Samberg *Han Solo, "Todd"* • James Caan *Father McNally* • Leighton Meester *Jamie* • Vanilla Ice • Susan Sarandon *Mary McGarricle (present day)* • Eva Amurri Martino *[Eva Amurri] Mary McGarricle (in past)* ■ *Dir* Sean Anders • *Scr* David Caspe

That's My Man ★★
Comedy   1947 · US · BW · 101min

A compulsive gambler neglects his wife and baby in favour of the racetrack and card table, leading, inevitably, to a decline in his fortunes and marital break-up. Tear-master Frank Borzage, with no ace up his sleeve, employs every possible sentimental cliché on the slow journey to the predictable resolution. Don Ameche is the star, bravely battling with the script and direction. RK

Don Ameche *Joe Grange* • Catherine McLeod *Ronnie* • Roscoe Karns *Toby Gleeton* • Joe Frisco *Willie Wagonstatter* ■ *Dir* Frank Borzage • *Scr* Steve Fisher, Bradley King, from their story

That's Right – You're Wrong ★★★ U
Musical comedy   1939 · US · Colour · 94min

The first – and best – of an increasingly inane series of comedy musicals starring popular radio bandleader Kay Kyser. Here, Kyser makes his screen debut with his musicians and his nonsensical "Kollege of Musical Knowledge" quiz. The plot involves a reluctant Kyser being lured to Hollywood, where producer Adolphe Menjou is under orders to star him in a hit. Chaos and confusion ensue when the scriptwriters are unable to come up with a plot. This is a mix of childish rubbish with a nice spoof on Hollywood studio methods. RK

Kay Kyser *Kay* • Adolphe Menjou *Delmore* • Lucille Ball *Sandra Sand* • May Robson *Grandma* • Dennis O'Keefe *Chuck Deems* • Edward Everett Horton *Village* ■ *Dir* David Butler • *Scr* William Conselman, James V Kern, from a story by David Butler, William Conselmann

That's Your Funeral ★
Comedy   1972 · UK · Colour · 81min

In all its long years, the Hammer House of Horror never churned out anything as gruesome as this abysmal comedy. The

---

original TV sitcom only ran for one six-part series, so why anyone thought it was worth making a feature version is beyond comprehension. Bill Fraser sledgehammers his way through gags that should have been allowed to rest in peace years ago, while even the usually reliable Raymond Huntley struggles to raise a smile. DP Swearing, drug abuse.

Bill Fraser *Basil Bulstrode* • Raymond Huntley *Emanuel Holroyd* • David Battley *Percy* • John Ronane *Mr Smallbody* • Sue Lloyd *Miss Peach* • Dennis Price *Mr Soul* • Roy Kinnear *Mr Purvis* ■ *Dir* John Robins • *Scr* Peter Lewis

Theatre of Blood ★★★★⅖
Comedy horror   1973 · UK · Colour · 102min

The magnum opus of Vincent Price's film career, this stylish, witty comedy horror boasts an irresistible premise, an inspired ensemble cast, fabulous music and first-rate production values. Price is classically trained actor Edward Lionheart, who murders theatre critics using famous death scenes from Shakespeare's plays as payback for being dismissive of his talents. Aided by his faithful daughter Edwina (Diana Rigg) and a group of tramps, Lionheart plans each killing with elaborate inventiveness and cunning disguise. Price does a superior job portraying an inferior actor and mines every nuance of tragedy and comedy with delicious gusto. AJ Violence. DVD Blu-ray

Vincent Price *Edward Lionheart* • Diana Rigg *Edwina Lionheart* • Ian Hendry *Peregrine Devlin* • Harry Andrews *Trevor Dickman* • Coral Browne *Chloe Moon* • Robert Coote *Oliver Larding* • Jack Hawkins *Solomon Psaltery* • Michael Hordern *George Maxwell* • Arthur Lowe *Horace Sprout* • Robert Morley *Meredith Merridrew* • Dennis Price *Hector Snipe* ■ *Dir* Douglas Hickox • *Scr* Anthony Greville-Bell

Theatre of Death ★★★⅖
Horror   1966 · UK · Colour · 89min

Is Christopher Lee, the obsessive director of a *Grand Guignol* theatre, responsible for a series of vampire-like killings terrorising Paris? It's fearful fun finding out in this odd horror whodunnit, played out against a neatly realised backdrop of fake gore, backstage seediness and macabre motives. Long revered by Lee cultists as a showcase for one of the actor's best performances, this baroque, moody murder mystery also features a rare screen role for 1930s musical comedy star Evelyn Laye, and is impressively photographed by Gilbert Taylor. AJ DVD

Christopher Lee *Philippe Darvas* • Lelia Goldoni *Dani Cirreaux* • Julian Glover *Charles Marquis* • Evelyn Laye *Madame Angele* • Jenny Till *Nicole Chapel* • *Dir* Samuel Gallu • *Scr* Ellis Kadison, Roger Marshall, from a story by Ellis Kadison

Theeb ★★★⅖
Coming-of-age adventure
2014 · UAE/Qatar/Jordan/UK · Colour · 100min

Sharing Jordanian locations with *Lawrence of Arabia*, Naji Abu Nowar's debut tale of Great War mettle and treachery feels like an adaptation of a classic adventure book for boys. At its heart is Bedouin youngster Jacir Eid, who follows big brother Hussein Salameh into the desert when the older boy offers to escort army officer Jack Fox to a well. Using imposing widescreen vistas to capture the beauty of the terrain, Nowar explores such potent themes as tradition, honour and duty via the alertly expressive Eid. DP In Arabic, English. Violence.

Jacir Eid *Theeb* • Hussein Salameh *Hussein* • Hassan Mutlag *The Stranger* • Jack Fox *Edward* • *Dir* Naji Abu Nowar • *Scr* Bassel Ghandour, Naji Abu Nowar

Their Eyes Were Watching God ★★
Period romantic drama
2005 · US · Colour · 113min

Halle Berry stars in this handsome but shallow drama about a black woman's search for romantic happiness in 1920s Florida. Zora Neale Hurston's original novel was a lyrical evocation of the period, but this adaptation is better treated as a straightforward romantic drama. It's executive-produced by Oprah Winfrey, which should give some indication of its flavour. This is Berry's second outing under Winfrey; the first, 1998's *The Wedding*, was made before she found fame in *Monster's Ball*, but the pair has yet to combine for a memorable movie. SuR

Halle Berry *Janie Crawford* • Michael Ealy *Tea Cake* • Ruben Santiago-Hudson *Major Joe Starks* • Ruby Dee *Nanny* • Terrence Dashon Howard [Terrence Howard] *Amos Hicks* ■ *Dir* Darnell Martin • *Scr* Suzan-Lori Parks, Misan Sagay, Bobby Smith Jr, from the novel by Zora Neale Hurston

Their First Mistake ★★★★Ⓤ
Comedy   1932 · US · BW · 20min

This brilliant Laurel and Hardy short features a nonstop array of gags around the subject of the boys and a baby. Ollie's wife is angry that he spends so little time with her and so much time with Stan. The boys come to the conclusion that if she had a baby, she wouldn't have time to harangue Ollie. So they adopt a child, only to find, when they return home, that the wife has left, leaving the lads holding the baby. DF DVD

Stan Laurel *Stan* • Oliver Hardy *Ollie* • Mae Busch *Mrs Arabella Hardy* • Billy Gilbert *Process server* • George Marshall *Neighbour* ■ *Dir/Scr* George Marshall

Thelma & Louise ★★★★★⅖
Road movie   1991 · US · Colour · 129min

In this hugely entertaining and controversial road movie, Geena Davis and Susan Sarandon star as the two friends whose weekend spree to escape the boredom of their small-town routines is curtailed when Louise (Sarandon) kills a man who's trying to rape Thelma (Davis). They flee, and thus begins their voyage of self-discovery. Ridley Scott's film sparked a row at the time over whether the sight of gals with guns was a symbol of liberated equality or depressing defeminisation. Whatever your viewpoint, films have a duty to provoke as well as entertain, and it's impossible to watch the plight of Thelma and Louise without feeling indignation. DP Swearing, violence, a sex scene. DVD Blu-ray

Susan Sarandon *Louise Sawyer* • Geena Davis *Thelma Dickinson* • Harvey Keitel *Hal Slocombe* • Michael Madsen *Jimmy* • Christopher McDonald *Darryl* • Stephen Tobolowsky *Max* • Brad Pitt *JD* • Timothy Carhart *Harlan* • Lucinda Jenney *Lena, Waitress* • Jason Beghe *State Trooper* • Sonny Carl Davis *Albert* • Ken Swofford *Major* ■ *Dir* Ridley Scott • *Scr* Callie Khouri

Thelonious Monk: Straight No Chaser ★★★Ⓟ
Music documentary
1988 · US · BW and Colour · 89min

Jazz buff Clint Eastwood acted as executive producer on this documentary about the great jazz pianist and composer of standards such as *Round Midnight*. Director Charlotte Zwerin uses concert footage of Monk on tour in the late 1960s, shot by Christian Blackwood with new interviews and biographical material about Monk, who died in 1982. TH

Samuel E Wright *Narration* • Thelonious Monk ■ *Dir* Charlotte Zwerin

Them! ★★★★★Ⓟ
Science fiction   1954 · US · BW · 88min

The best of the giant bug movies of the 1950s is a science-fiction classic. Spawned by atomic radiation, mutant ants arrive in Los Angeles from the New Mexico desert and infest the sewer system in a taut, atmospheric and totally convincing shocker laden with clever visual and verbal puns. Terrific special effects, noble humanitarian sentiments, involving performances and a first-class script make for monster thrills. AJ DVD

James Whitmore *Sgt Ben Peterson* • Edmund Gwenn *Dr Harold Medford* • Joan Weldon *Dr Patricia Medford* • James Arness *Robert Graham* • Onslow Stevens *Brig Gen O'Brien* • Leonard

Nimoy *Sergeant* ■ *Dir* Gordon Douglas • *Scr* Ted Sherdeman, Russell Hughes, from a story by George Worthing Yates

Them ★★★★⅖
Horror thriller   2006 · Fr/Rom · Colour · 73min

When it comes to crafting suspense in movies, what you can't see is often more effective than what you can. Which is why this ultra-taut Gallic tale works so well. A cat-and-mouse chiller based on real events, it centres on hidden assailants terrorising French schoolteacher Clémentine (Olivia Bonamy) and her husband (Michaël Cohen) during a weekend at their secluded country home in Romania. The tension is relentless and, at less than 80 minutes, there's no flab to detract from the scares. The only minor qualm is the ultimate reveal, which, although still disturbing, is slightly underwhelming compared to the breathless build-up. SF French +subtitles. DVD

Olivia Bonamy *Clémentine* • Michaël Cohen *Lucas* • Adriana Moca *Ileana* • Maria Roman *Sanda* ■ *Dir/Scr* Xavier Palud, David Moreau

Them Thar Hills! ★★★★Ⓤ
Comedy   1934 · US · BW · 18min

Stan Laurel believed that he and Ollie should have "stayed in the short film category" and watching gems like this one can understand his reluctance to milk a comic situation beyond a perfectly realised twenty minutes. Oliver has been told to take it easy, so the duo head for the hills and a caravan site. Disaster follows when bootleggers fill the nearby well with moonshine whisky. A camper's wife joins the boys and by the time her husband arrives the trio are plastered. The inevitable destructive tit-for-tat routine follows. A lesser sequel with the same couple followed the next year, called *Tit-for-Tat*. BB DVD

Stan Laurel *Stan* • Oliver Hardy *Ollie* • Billy Gilbert *Doctor* • Charlie Hall *Motorist who runs out of gas* • Mae Busch *Motorist's wife* ■ *Dir* Charles Rogers • *Scr* Stan Laurel, HM Walker

The Theme ★★★★
Drama   1979 · USSR · Colour · 99min

This was among the first films to benefit from the thawing of Soviet cinema in the Gorbachev era. Michael Ulyanov stars as a pulp novelist whose subservience to the Party line has led to his advancement in Moscow's literary circles. Seeking inspiration, he travels to the country where he becomes infatuated with Inna Churikova, a suppressed artist who shames him for his compromises. The winner of the Golden Bear at the 1987 Berlin film festival, Gleb Panfilov's searching study of artistic integrity and freedom of movement is not an easy watch, but it rewards the effort. DP Russian +subtitles.

Mikhail Ulyanov *Esenin* • Inna Churikova *Sasa Nikolaeva* ■ *Dir* Gleb Panfilov • *Scr* Gleb Panfilov, Aleksander Cervinski

Then She Found Me ★★★⅖
Comedy drama   2007 · US · Colour · 96min

Humour and heart combine to bittersweet effect in Helen Hunt's confident feature debut as writer/director. She also plays a teacher whose desire for a baby intensifies after her husband (Matthew Broderick) leaves. Events are complicated by her adoptive mother's death and the subsequent appearance of her biological parent – a brash talk-show host portrayed by a typically exuberant Bette Midler. Situations can feel contrived, particularly with Hunt's love interest (Colin Firth), but this has a warmth that shines through. SF In English, Hebrew. DVD Blu-ray

Helen Hunt *April Epner* • Colin Firth *Frank* • Bette Midler *Bernice Graves* • Matthew Broderick *Ben* • Lynn Cohen *Trudy* • Ben Shenkman *Freddy* ■ *Dir* Helen Hunt • *Scr* Alice Arlen, Victor Levin, Helen Hunt, from the novel by Elinor Lipman

Theodora Goes Wild ★★★★
Screwball comedy   1936 · US · BW · 94min

This wonderful madcap comedy from the genre's golden period stars the utterly enchanting Irene Dunne her first comic role.

She plays an author who hits the big city and falls for debonair Melvyn Douglas. They make a delightful couple, for a while, and that's the main theme of Sidney Buchman's clever, twist-laden screenplay. Stanislavsky-trained émigré director Richard Boleslawski has the good sense to sit back and let the cast get on with it. TS

Irene Dunne *Theodora Lynn* • Melvyn Douglas *Michael Grant* • Thomas Mitchell *Jed Waterbury* • Thurston Hall *Arthur Stevenson* • Rosalind Keith *Adelaide Perry* • Spring Byington *Rebecca Perry* • Elisabeth Risdon *Aunt Mary* • Margaret McWade *Aunt Elsie* ■ *Dir* Richard Boleslawski • *Scr* Sidney Buchman, from a story by Mary E McCarthy

Theodore Rex ★Ⓟ
Comedy fantasy   1995 · US · Colour · 87min

Only the threat of litigation kept Whoopi Goldberg on board this turkey and it is to her credit that she does her best to make it fly. But she clearly didn't regard being teamed with a doltish detective (who just happens to be a tyrannosaurus) as one of the highlights of her career. And the audience needs someone more menacing than mad scientist Armin Mueller-Stahl to distract from the woeful special effects. DP Violence, swearing.

Whoopi Goldberg *Katie Coltrane* • Armin Mueller-Stahl *Dr Edgar Kane* • Juliet Landau *Dr Shade* • Bud Cort *Spinner* • Stephen McHattie *Edge* • Richard Roundtree *Commissioner Lynch* • Peter Mackenzie *Alex Summers* • Peter Kwong *Toymaker* • George Newbern *Theodore Rex* • Carol Kane *Molly Rex* ■ *Dir/Scr* Jonathan Betuel

Theorem ★★★★⅖
Drama   1968 · It · Colour · 94min

Pier Paolo Pasolini found himself on an obscenity charge for this adaptation of his own novel, in which a handsome stranger seduces every member of a wealthy household before departing abruptly. Oblivious to whether Terence Stamp's intruder was messiah or demon, the Italian government banned the film, recognising that in its blend of Marxism and religion, Pasolini had created a scathing indictment of the sexually repressed bourgeoisie. Laura Betti won the best actress prize at Venice for her performance as the skittish maid, but it's Stamp's ethereal presence that dominates. DP Italian +subtitles. Sex scenes, nudity, some swearing. DVD Blu-ray

Terence Stamp *Visitor* • Silvana Mangano *Mother* • Massimo Girotti *Father* • Anne Wiazemsky *Daughter* • Laura Betti *Maid* • Andrés José Cruz *Son* ■ *Dir* Pier Paolo Pasolini • *Scr* Pier Paolo Pasolini, from his novel

The Theory of Everything ★★★★⅓
Biographical drama   2015 · UK · Colour · 118min

Despite its title, this version of Jane Hawking's memoir cleverly foregrounds her relationship with Stephen, spanning young love, family life, practicality in the face of illness and eventually divorce. Director James Marsh skilfully captures the moments of change: Hawking's first fall (Oscar winner Eddie Redmayne's transformation is remarkable); the friction when Jane (Felicity Jones, the drama's secret weapon) befriends Charlie Cox's widower; the decisive instant when new nurse Maxine Peake takes control. A grandly photogenic adaptation, it also provides a way in to Hawking's academic brilliance. AC DVD Blu-ray

Eddie Redmayne *Stephen Hawking* • Felicity Jones *Jane Hawking* • Charlie Cox *Jonathan Hellyer Jones* • Emily Watson *Beryl Wilde* • David Thewlis *Dennis Sciama* • Maxine Peake *Elaine Mason* ■ *Dir* James Marsh • *Scr* Anthony McCarten, from the non-fiction book *Travelling to Infinity: My Life with Stephen* by Jane Hawking

The Theory of Flight ★★★★⅖
Romantic drama   1998 · UK/US · Colour · 101min

Depicting human fallibility – both mental and physical – this very tender and honest romantic drama was originally made as a BBC film for television and later reconsidered for theatrical release. Kenneth Branagh plays a man re-inventing the

T

aeroplane as a futile expression of his lack of emotional freedom. After an attempted flight off a public building lands him on probation, he is assigned to take care of Helena Bonham Carter who, though terminally ill, is determined to lose her virginity before she dies. Together they pursue their dreams of literal and sexual flight; handled with sensitivity, this is very touching. **LH** Swearing.

Kenneth Branagh *Richard* • Helena Bonham Carter *Jane Hatchard* • Gemma Jones *Anne* • Holly Aird *Julie* • Ray Stevenson *Gigolo* • *Dir* Paul Greengrass • *Scr* Richard Hawkins

There Ain't No Justice
★★★ PG

Sports drama 1939 · UK · Colour · 76min

The great-grandson of poet Alfred, Lord Tennyson made his directorial debut with this sturdy, if overly cosy exposé of the seedy side of prize-fighting. Socialist Pen Tennyson may not have been entirely familiar with tight-knit, working-class London enclaves, but he ably conveys a vibrant sense of community spirit, and a subplot involving Phyllis Stanley and the roguish Michael Wilding is well staged. However, while the crowd's roar feels authentic, the fights are clumsily unpersuasive. **DP** DVD

Jimmy Hanley *Tommy Mutch* • Edward Rigby *Pa Mutch* • Mary Clare *Ma Mutch* • Edward Chapman *Sammy Sanders* • Michael Wilding *Len Charteris* ■ *Dir* Penrose Tennyson [Pen Tennyson] • *Scr* Penrose Tennyson [Pen Tennyson], Sergei Nolbandov, James Curtis, from Curtis's novel

There Goes My Baby ★★★

Period drama 1994 · US · Colour · 98min

If imitation is the sincerest form of flattery, *American Graffiti* must be feeling very flattered indeed. This is one of the many attempts to recapture its teen angst, and it's better than some. Set in 1965, the film focuses on a clichéd bunch of senior high school students as they prepare to enter the real world. The characters are stereotypes, but the quality of the film's ensemble cast just about brings them to life. **DA**

Dermot Mulroney *Pirate* • Rick Schroder *Stick* • Kelli Williams *Sunshine* • Noah Wyle *Finnegan* • Jill Schoelen *Babette* • Kristin Minter *Tracy* • Lucy Deakins *Mary Beth* • Kenny Ransom [Kenneth Ransom] *Calvin* ■ *Dir/Scr* Floyd Mutrux

There Goes My Heart ★★

Romantic comedy 1938 · US · BW · 81min

Fredric March stars as a newspaperman trying to interview heiress Virginia Bruce, in this comedy directed by Norman Z McLeod. Unfortunately she's escaped the control of her department store-owner grandfather and decamped to New York. Clearly lost for inspiration, the unbelievably convoluted plot sees Bruce adopting an alias, rooming with salesgirl Patsy Kelly and ending up as one herself in grandpa's department store, before March discovers her true identity. Well done, but predictable. **RK**

Fredric March *Bill Spencer* • Virginia Bruce *Joan Butterfield/Joan Baker* • Patsy Kelly *Peggy O'Brien* • Alan Mowbray *Pennypepper E Pennypepper* • Nancy Carroll *Dorothy Moore* ■ *Dir* Norman Z McLeod • *Scr* Eddie Moran, Jack Jevne, from a story by Ed Sullivan

There Goes the Bride ★ PG

Farce 1979 · UK · Colour · 86min

On the day of his daughter's wedding in Florida, an advertising executive takes a couple of accidental bumps on the head – each of which, in the time-honoured tradition of this sort of thing, causes embarrassing and supposedly hilarious hallucinations. An unamusing Ray Cooney farce with a curious melange of British and US actors. Contains poor jokes. **JG**

Tom Smothers *Timothy Westerby* • Twiggy *Polly Perkins* • Sylvia Syms *Ursula Westerby* • Michael Witney *Bill Shorter* • Martin Balsam *Elmer Babcock* • Phil Silvers *Psychiatrist* ■ *Dir* Terence Marcel [Terry Marcel] • *Scr* Ray Cooney, Terence Marcel, John Chapman, from a play by Ray Cooney

There Is Another Sun ★★★

Crime thriller 1951 · UK · BW · 97min

This seedy tale of greed and betrayal among funfair folk focuses on a stunt rider and a boxer, who put aside their rivalries to steal the boss's life savings. There's nothing new in the story and the performances of Maxwell Reed and Laurence Harvey have little to commend them. But director Lewis Gilbert's thoroughly nasty atmosphere conjured up in a place dedicated to enjoyment makes this unusually effective movie worth watching. **DP**

Maxwell Reed *Racer* • Susan Shaw *Lillian* • Laurence Harvey *Maguire* • Hermione Baddeley *Gypsy Sarah* • Meredith Edwards *Bratcher* • Robert Adair *Sarno* • Leslie Dwyer *Foley* ■ *Dir* Lewis Gilbert • *Scr* Guy Morgan, from a story by James Raisin

There Was a Crooked Man
★★★★ U

Comedy 1960 · UK · BW · 106min

Even some of those generally left cold by clown Norman Wisdom admit that this is one of his best films. This comedy allowed him to show more versatility, although he holds fast to his "poor but honest" persona, inspired by Chaplin. Released from jail, Wisdom teams up with crooks to outwit the venal mayor of a northern town. Alfred Marks as the gang boss and Andrew Cruickshank as the mayor are excellent foils. **DM**

Norman Wisdom *Davy Cooper* • Alfred Marks *Adolf Carter* • Andrew Cruickshank *McKillup* • Reginald Beckwith *Station master* • Susannah York *Ellen* • Jean Clarke *Freda* • Timothy Bateson *Flash Dan* ■ *Dir* Stuart Burge • *Scr* Reuben Ship, from the play *The Odd Legend of Schultz* by James Bridie

There Was a Crooked Man... ★★ 15

Western 1970 · US · Colour · 118min

Kirk Douglas and Henry Fonda – actors as different in style and persona as could be – are pitted against each other in this period crime movie with a western flavour. Douglas is a tough outlaw who escapes from jail and goes in search of his hidden booty; Fonda is the gentle sheriff-turned-prison warden who pursues Douglas in the hope of rehabilitating him. The movie promises much, but delivers little. **RK**

Kirk Douglas *Paris Pitman Jr* • Henry Fonda *Woodward Lopeman* • Hume Cronyn *Dudley Whinner* • Warren Oates *Floyd Moon* • Burgess Meredith *The Missouri Kid* • John Randolph *Cyrus McNutt* • Arthur O'Connell *Mr Lomax* ■ *Dir* Joseph L Mankiewicz • *Scr* David Newman, Robert Benton, from the story *Prison Story* by David Newman, Robert Benton

There Was a Father ★★★★

Drama 1942 · Jpn · BW · 94min

Filmed in accordance with wartime strictures and reminiscent of his earlier drama, *The Only Son*, this remains among Yasujiro Ozu's most unusual pictures, with its broad narrative span and diversity of setting standing in contrast to his more typically intense insularity. Its essential themes are patriarchy and patriotism. But the story of widowed Chishu Ryu's self-sacrificing devotion to his son also contains an element of Buddhist passivity, as each endures the pain of separation to make the best of their limited opportunities. Making symbolic use of train journeys and fishing trips, Ozu brings a human touch to the prescribed topic. **DP** Japanese +subtitles.

Chishu Ryu *Shuhei Horikawa* • Shuji Sano *Ryohei, Horikawa's son* • Mitsuko Mito *Fumiko* • Takeshi Sakamoto *Makota Hirata* • Shin Saburi *Yasutaro Kurokawa* ■ *Dir* Yasujiro Ozu • *Scr* Tadao Ikeda, Takao Yanai

There Will Be Blood
★★★★★ 15

Period drama 2007 · US · Colour · 158min

Writer/director Paul Thomas Anderson's magnificent oil-prospecting saga tells the story of one man, Daniel Plainview. An old-fashioned epic, forged self-consciously in the mould of *Citizen Kane* and *Giant*, it begins in 1898 with Plainview (an Oscar-winning Daniel Day-Lewis) perilously mining silver from the unyielding rock of Southern California. Four years later he strikes "black gold" and soon expands his operation to become one of the 20th century's new industrial tycoons. While not exactly a villain – he seems to care for his adopted son HW (Dillon Freasier) – he's certainly monstrous, his cold-hearted capitalism standing in opposition to the empire of his nemesis Paul Dano's local brimstone priest. Visually resplendent, thematically rich and by turns lyrical, hysterical and baffling, Anderson has made his finest film yet. **AC** Violence. DVD Blu-ray

Daniel Day-Lewis *Daniel Plainview* • Paul Dano *Eli Sunday/Paul Sunday* • Kevin J O'Connor *Henry* • Ciarán Hinds [Ciaran Hinds] *Fletcher* • Dillon Freasier *HW* • Sydney McCallister *Mary Sunday* ■ *Dir* Paul Thomas Anderson • *Scr* Paul Thomas Anderson, from the novel *Oil!* by Upton Sinclair • *Cinematographer* Robert Elswit • *Music* Jonny Greenwood

There's a Girl in My Soup
★★ 15

Comedy 1970 · UK · Colour · 91min

This is a very tame version of a sex comedy that ran and ran on both sides of the Atlantic. Roy Boulting directs without much enthusiasm for his tale of womanising TV celebrity Peter Sellers, who is knocked off his stride by a chance encounter with dippy waif Goldie Hawn. Content to cruise through his meagre repertoire of wisecracks, the miscast Sellers still teams well with Hawn, who also has some funny scenes with ditched boyfriend Nicky Henson. **DP** Swearing. DVD

Peter Sellers *Robert Danvers* • Goldie Hawn *Marion* • Tony Britton *Andrew Hunter* • Nicky Henson *Jimmy* • John Comer *John* • Diana Dors *John's wife* • Gabrielle Drake *Julia Halforde-Smythe* • Geraldine Sherman *Caroline* • Judy Campbell *Lady Heather* • Nicola Pagett *Clare* ■ *Dir* Roy Boulting • *Scr* Terence Frisby, Peter Kortner, from a play by Terence Frisby

There's Always a Woman
★★★

Detective crime comedy 1938 · US · BW · 82min

Private eye Melvyn Douglas is hired by Mary Astor for a routine investigation that soon escalates into a murder case. His wife, Joan Blondell, an enthusiastic and charmingly meddlesome amateur sleuth, involves herself in the mystery. Directed by Alexander Hall from a zany script, with Blondell the standout in an excellent cast, this was planned as the first part of a series, but Blondell withdrew, and the idea petered out after *There's That Woman Again*, a disappointing follow-up with Douglas and Virginia Bruce. **RK**

Joan Blondell *Sally Reardon* • Melvyn Douglas *William Reardon* • Mary Astor *Lola Fraser* • Frances Drake *Anne Calhoun* • Jerome Cowan *Nick Shane* • Rita Hayworth *Ketterling's secretary* ■ *Dir* Alexander Hall • *Scr* Gladys Lehman, Joel Sayre, Philip Rapp, Morrie Ryskind, from a short story by Wilson Collison

There's Always Tomorrow
★★ PG

Melodrama 1956 · US · BW · 80min

Fred MacMurray is the model husband who feels that he is taken for granted by his family. The reappearance of old flame Barbara Stanwyck revitalises him and he dreams of starting a new life with her. His wife Joan Bennett remains blissfully unaware of the situation, but it's not long before his children sense that something is going on. Douglas Sirk directs and Stanwyck is terrific, but the soap opera fails to ignite due to a dull screenplay. **RK** DVD

Barbara Stanwyck *Norma Miller* • Fred MacMurray *Clifford Groves* • Joan Bennett *Marion Groves* • Pat Crowley *Ann* • William Reynolds *Vinnie Groves* • Gigi Perreau *Ellen Groves* • Judy Nugent *Frankie Groves* ■ *Dir* Douglas Sirk • *Scr* Bernard C Schoenfeld, from a story by Ursula Parrott

There's No Business like Show Business ★★★★ U

Musical 1954 · US · Colour · 112min

The title was so long it filled the CinemaScope screen and that was exactly what 20th Century-Fox intended, to show off its new (and then virtually exclusive) letterbox screen process. Fox also crammed this musical with as many stars as possible, adding zest to its hokey old "Broadway family" plot. The story rarely matters in this kind of film, though this does take a dive when "Prince of Wails" Johnnie Ray shows a serious inclination towards the priesthood. Marilyn Monroe hangs out with Donald O'Connor, while Ethel Merman, Dan Dailey and Mitzi Gaynor are all in good voice. **TS** DVD

Ethel Merman *Molly Donahue* • Donald O'Connor *Tim Donahue* • Marilyn Monroe *Vicky* • Dan Dailey *Terrance Donahue* • Johnnie Ray *Steve Donahue* • Mitzi Gaynor *Katy Donahue* • Richard Eastham *Lew Harris* • Hugh O'Brian *Charles Gibbs* ■ *Dir* Walter Lang • *Scr* Phoebe Ephron, Henry Ephron, from a story by Lamar Trotti

There's One Born Every Minute ★★ U

Comedy 1942 · US · BW · 59min

Veteran comic actors Hugh Herbert, Guy Kibbee and Edgar Kennedy get what mileage they can from a plot which has Herbert as a small-town pudding manufacturer whose secret ingredient, Vitamin Z, puts "Zumph" into his product and gets him elected mayor. The Universal production's one claim to cinematic fame is that it was the screen debut of ten-year-old Elizabeth Taylor. The studio dropped Taylor shortly afterwards and its casting director spent the rest of his life living down his verdict on the young star: "The kid has nothing." **TV**

Hugh Herbert *Lemuel P Twine/Ghost of Elmer Twine/Ghost of Claudius Twine* • Peggy Moran *Helen Barbara Twine* • Tom Brown *Jimmie Hanagan* • Guy Kibbee *Lester Cadwalader Sr* • Catharine Doucet [Catherine Doucet] *Minerva Twine* • Elizabeth Taylor *Gloria Ann Twine* • Carl "Alfalfa" Switzer *Junior Twine* ■ *Dir* Harold Young • *Scr* Robert B Hunt, Brenda Weisberg, from the story *Man or Mouse* by Robert B Hunt

There's Only One Jimmy Grimble ★★★ 12

Sports drama 2000 · UK/Fr · Colour · 101min

In this feel-good fantasy football yarn, Lewis McKenzie plays Manchester teen Jimmy, a budding George Best, but only in the privacy of practice. Play him in a game and he's tackled by lack of confidence. Then an old crone gifts him a pair of "magic" football boots, and McKenzie is soon inspiring his school to the finals of the inter-school championships. With big guns Robert Carlyle (as his sports teacher) and Ray Winstone (as an ardent suitor in a subplot involving Jimmy's single mum), this has moments that are corny, clunky and crass, but it's still hard to dislike. **DA** DVD

Robert Carlyle *Eric Wirral* • Ray Winstone *Harry* • Gina McKee *Donna* • Lewis McKenzie *Jimmy Grimble* • Jane Lapotaire *Alice Brewer* ■ *Dir* John Hay • *Scr* Simon Mayle, John Hay, Rik Carmichael, from a story by Simon Mayle

There's Something about Mary ★★★★ 15

Romantic comedy 1998 · US · Colour · 114min

Those kings of bad taste Peter and Bobby Farrelly (*Dumb and Dumber*, *Kingpin*) surpassed themselves with this defiantly non-PC but wickedly funny Hollywood smash. Ben Stiller plays a writer who, 13 years later, is still obsessed by his prom date, Cameron Diaz, even though the occasion ended in disaster. The problem is that a queue of fellow misfits have also fallen under her spell, including British comic Lee Evans and the seedy private eye (Matt Dillon) Stiller hired to find her. With gags about the mentally and physically disabled, dead dogs and serial killers, not to mention the now infamous "hair gel" scene, this is unwholesome entertainment for

U SUITABLE FOR ALL Uc SUITABLE ESPECIALLY FOR YOUNG CHILDREN (DVD ONLY) PG PARENTAL GUIDANCE 12A UNDER 12s TO BE ACCOMPANIED (CINEMA ONLY)

older members of the family. JF Swearing, sexual references. 📀 💿

Cameron Diaz *Mary Jenson* • Matt Dillon *Pat Healy* • Ben Stiller *Ted Stroehmann* • Lin Shaye *Magda* • Lee Evans *Tucker* • Chris Elliott *Dom* • Jonathan Richman *Jonathan* • Jeffrey Tambor *Sully* • Markie Post *Mary's mom* ■ *Dir* Peter Farrelly, Bobby Farrelly • *Scr* Peter Farrelly, Bobby Farrelly, Ed Decter, John J Strauss, from a story by Ed Decter, John J Strauss

Thérèse ★★★★ PG
Drama   1986 · Fr · Colour · 91min

Taking a leaf out of Robert Bresson's stark book, director Alain Cavalier has created a film that has the purity and simplicity of its subject - the devout life of Thérèse Martin spent as a Carmelite nun in the convent at Lisieux. Thérèse, who was canonised in 1924, is serenely played by stage actress Catherine Mouchet from the age of 15 until her death of TB, aged 24, in 1897. Cavalier presents the story in a series of tableaux that recount, with little dialogue and action, the everyday existence of the nuns, without preaching or religiosity. RB In French.

Catherine Mouchet *Thérèse Martin* • Aurore Prieto *Celine* • Sylvie Habault *Pauline* • Ghislaine Mona *Marie* • Hélène Alexandridis *Lucie* ■ *Dir* Alain Cavalier • *Scr* Alain Cavalier, Camille de Casabianca

Thérèse Desqueyroux ★★★★
Drama   1962 · Fr · BW · 107min

Emmanuelle Riva won the best actress prize at Venice for her controlled portrayal of a bored provincial poisoner in this faithful adaptation of François Mauriac's novel. Director Georges Franju was attacked by contemporary critics for adhering so closely to the text, yet with its stately pace, flashback structure, steely detachment, enigmatic characterisation and minimalist performances, this is an unnerving Bressonian study in both the ennui that sets Riva against her husband, Philippe Noiret, and the charity that prompts his family to forgive her. DP French +subtitles.

Emmanuelle Riva *Thérèse Desqueyroux* • Philippe Noiret *Bernard Desqueyroux* • Edith Scob *Anne de la Trave* • Sami Frey *Jean Azevedo* • Renée Devillers *Mme de la Trave* • Richard Saint-Bris *Hector de la Trave* • Lucien Nat *Jérôme Larroque* ■ *Dir* Georges Franju • *Scr* Georges Franju, Claude Mauriac, François Mauriac, from his novel

Thérèse Desqueyroux ★★★ 12A
Drama   2012 · Fr · Colour · 110min

An independent-minded young woman marries into a conventional land-owning family with disastrous results in this adaptation of Nobel winner François Mauriac's 1927 novel. Audrey Tautou shines as the eponymous anti-heroine, whose actions scandalise local society and bitterly confuse her well-meaning husband Bernard (Gilles Lellouche). This final film from respected French director Claude Miller adopts a more straightforward timeline than the book, and makes a brave decision not to over-explain Therese's dark motivations. The undeniably atmospheric result boasts an abiding sense of ominous intrigue, which will draw in some viewers but might prove too enigmatic for some tastes. What's not in doubt, however, is the quality of Tautou's utterly mesmerising central performance. TJ French +subtitles.

Audrey Tautou *Thérèse Desqueyroux* • Gilles Lellouche *Bernard Desqueyroux* • Anaïs Demoustier *Anne de la Trave* • Catherine Arditi *Madame de la Trave* • Stanley Weber *Jean Azevedo* • Isabelle Sadoyan *Aunt Clara* ■ *Dir* Claude Miller • *Scr* Claude Miller, Natalie Carter, from the novel by François Mauriac

Thérèse Raquin ★★★★ PG
Crime drama   1953 · Fr · BW · 102min

Marcel Carné updates the action of Emile Zola's dark psychological novel and relocates it to the backstreets of Lyons. However, all the naturalistic intensity of the original has been retained, as frustrated housewife Simone Signoret and trucker Raf

Vallone suffer much more than pangs of conscience after they murder her husband. The deterioration of their relationship is charted with a lyrical realism that often approaches vintage Carné. Sylvie is superb as the mute mother-in-law, watching their torment with malicious satisfaction. DP French +subtitles. 📀

Simone Signoret *Thérèse Raquin* • Raf Vallone *Laurent* • Jacques Duby *Camille Raquin* • Roland Lesaffre *The sailor* • Sylvie *Mme Raquin* ■ *Dir* Marcel Carné • *Scr* Charles Spaak, Marcel Carné, from the novel by Emile Zola

These Final Hours ★★★★ 15
Thriller   2013 · Aus · Colour · 86min

At the start of this apocalyptic drama, we discover that Earth has just been hit by an asteroid, and life as we know it is about to end. The story takes place in the suburbs of Australia, where Nathan Phillips is planning to spend his final hours at a wild party. But he witnesses young Angourie Rice being abducted, which is something he can't ignore. After saving her, Phillips has to reshape his priorities as he shepherds Rice through the anarchy on the streets. The plot might suggest a large-scale epic, but what emerges is an intimate film about the end of the world, with strong performances and compelling direction. SC Violence, swearing, drug abuse, sex scenes, nudity.

Nathan Phillips *James* • Angourie Rice *Rose* • Jessica De Gouw *Zoe* • Kathryn Beck *Vicky* • Daniel Henshall *Freddy* • Sarah Snook *Mandy's mum* ■ *Dir/Scr* Zak Hilditch

These Foolish Things ★★★★ PG
Drama   1990 · Fr · Colour · 102min

This is a nicely underplayed domestic drama from top French director Bertrand Tavernier. Jane Birkin plays a screenwriter who returns home to re-establish her interrupted relationship with her dying dad Dirk Bogarde. The film follows them as they work out their differences, reminisce about times past, and restore mutual respect and understanding. Smashing stuff, very moving, with terrific performances from the two leads. DA French +subtitles.

Dirk Bogarde *Daddy* • Jane Birkin *Caroline* • Odette Laure *Miche* • Emmanuelle Bataille *Juliette* • Charlotte Kady *Barbara* ■ *Dir* Bertrand Tavernier • *Scr* Colo Tavernier

These Foolish Things ★★ 12
Period romantic drama   2006 · UK · Colour · 132min

Julia Taylor-Stanley's debut is set in 1930s London theatreland and follows the trials and tribulations of aspiring young actress Zoe Tapper as she attempts to follow in the career footsteps of her dead mother. In her search for stardom, Tapper becomes involved with a playwright (David Leon) and a director (Andrew Lincoln). With its clichéd storyline and corny acting, this often ends up being unintentionally funny. DA 📀

Zoe Tapper *Diana Shaw* • David Leon *Robin Gardner* • Andrew Lincoln *Christopher Lovell* • Mark Umbers *Douglas Middleton* • Terence Stamp *Baker* • Leo Bill *Garstin* • Anjelica Huston *Lottie Osgood* • Julia McKenzie *Miss Abernethy* • Lauren Bacall *Dame Lydia Simons* ■ *Dir* Julia Taylor-Stanley • *Scr* Julia Taylor-Stanley, from the novel *There's a Porpoise Close behind Us* by Noel Langley

These Old Broads ★★
Comedy   2001 · US · Colour · 100min

The producers must have thought they were on to a winner when they succeeded in assembling the superstellar cast for this TV-movie comedy. But the harder the veteran quartet tries, the more their schtick begins to grate. As the ageing starlets forced to reunite after the reissue of their 1960s movie becomes a hit, Shirley MacLaine, Debbie Reynolds and Joan Collins sportingly throw themselves into the bitching and hoofing. But Elizabeth Taylor merely settles for hamming it up as the bickering trio's conniving agent. DP

Shirley MacLaine *Kate Westbourne* • Joan Collins *Addie Holden* • Debbie Reynolds *Piper Grayson* • Elizabeth Taylor *Beryl Mason* • Jonathan

Silverman *Wesley Westbourne* • Peter Graves (2) *Bill* • Gene Barry *Mr Stern* ■ *Dir* Matthew Diamond • *Scr* Carrie Fisher, Elaine Pope

These Thousand Hills ★★
Western   1959 · US · Colour · 95min

This is a solid 20th Century-Fox western featuring a long list of contract players, having been made toward the end of the studio contract system. It's a long-winded saga about a cowboy's loyalties and responsibilities, but talented director Richard Fleischer seems at a loss as to how to present the story with any degree of dynamism. TS

Don Murray *Lat Evans* • Richard Egan *Jehu* • Lee Remick *Callie* • Patricia Owens *Joyce* • Stuart Whitman *Tom Ping* • Albert Dekker *Conrad* • Harold J Stone *Ram Butler* ■ *Dir* Richard Fleischer • *Scr* Alfred Hayes, from the novel by AB Guthrie Jr

These Three ★★★ U
Drama   1936 · US · BW · 88min

Time hasn't been kind to this fine adaptation of Lillian Hellman's play *The Children's Hour*. Deprived of its original sinister title, and with all references to lesbianism removed by the censors of the day, this still offers a stronger impact than the 1961 remake with Audrey Hepburn and Shirley MacLaine, which was also directed by William Wyler. What keeps this tale riveting is the superbly skilled portrayal by child actress Bonita Granville as the little horror who spreads the initial lie, and the well-matched teaming of Merle Oberon and Miriam Hopkins as the schoolteachers involved. TS

Miriam Hopkins *Martha Dobie* • Merle Oberon *Karen Wright* • Joel McCrea *Dr Joseph Cardin* • Catherine Doucet *Mrs Lily Mortar* • Alma Kruger *Mrs Tilford* • Bonita Granville *Mary Tilford* ■ *Dir* William Wyler • *Scr* Lillian Hellman, from her play *The Children's Hour*

These Wilder Years ★★
Drama   1956 · US · BW · 90min

It's a shame that two such powerful performers as Barbara Stanwyck and James Cagney met so late in their careers on such a mushy little picture. Directed with dull restraint, this old-fashioned weepie has unmarried millionaire Cagney trying to persuade Stanwyck, the head of a children's home, to reveal the whereabouts of the illegitimate son he handed over for adoption years before. AE

James Cagney *Steve Bradford* • Barbara Stanwyck *Ann Dempster* • Walter Pidgeon *James Rayburn* • Betty Lou Keim *Suzie* • Don Dubbins *Mark* • Edward Andrews *Mr Spottsford* • Basil Ruysdael *Judge* • Dean Jones *Hardware clerk* • Tom Laughlin *Football player* ■ *Dir* Roy Rowland • *Scr* Frank Fenton, from a story by Ralph Wheelwright

They ★★★ 15
Psychological horror thriller   2002 · US · Colour · 85min

Director Robert Harmon returns to form with this nervy horror that makes up for a lack of originality with its dream-like style and tense atmosphere. Revolving around the monster-in-the-closet nightmares of childhood, it follows ambitious student Laura Regan and her pals as they're terrorised by inhuman creatures that materialise when the lights go out. Harmon harnesses the power of imagination, creating fear by suggestion with creepy sound effects and shadowy visuals. The end result is basic and manipulative, but also ruthlessly effective. SF 📀

Laura Regan *Julia Lund* • Marc Blucas *Paul* • Ethan Embry *Sam* • Dagmara Dominczyk *Terry* • Jon Abrahams *Billy* • Wanda Cannon *Mrs Levin* • Desiree Zurowski *Mary Parks* ■ *Dir* Robert Harmon • *Scr* Brendan William Hood

They All Kissed the Bride ★★ U
Romantic comedy   1942 · US · BW · 87min

In an unexceptional and rather long-winded comedy, Joan Crawford spends much of the time arguing with, and ultimately romancing, reporter Melvyn Douglas.

Crawford copes well enough with her bossy-boots role, but her character isn't likeable, and as a result the film isn't very watchable, despite sterling support from the likes of Roland Young and Billie Burke. Director Alexander Hall does what he can, but this is no *Philadelphia Story*, to which it rather obviously aspires. TS

Joan Crawford *Margaret J "Maggie" Drew* • Melvyn Douglas *Michael Holmes* • Roland Young *Marsh* • Billie Burke *Mrs Drew* • Allen Jenkins *Johnny Johnson* • Andrew Tombes *Crane* ■ *Dir* Alexander Hall • *Scr* PJ Wolfson, Andrew P Solt, Henry Altimus, from a story by Gina Kaus, Andrew P Solt

They All Laughed ★★★★
Comedy   1981 · US · Colour · 115min

This is a stylish and splendidly wacky comedy about detectives who can't help getting involved with the women they are tailing. It's important as a late Audrey Hepburn entry, and she looks as lovely as ever, co-starring here with Ben Gazzara on wonderfully evocative New York locations. Director Peter Bogdanovich, seriously underrated these days, pulls it all together with great élan, aided by a quirky cast. There's a morbid interest in watching murdered centrefold Dorothy Stratten, directed by lover Bogdanovich. She died before the film came out. TS

Audrey Hepburn *Angela Niotes* • Ben Gazzara *John Russo* • John Ritter *Charles Rutledge* • Colleen Camp *Christy Miller* • Patti Hansen *Deborah "Sam" Wilson* • Dorothy Stratten *Dolores Martin* ■ *Dir/Scr* Peter Bogdanovich

They Call Me Mister Tibbs! ★★★ 15
Police thriller   1970 · US · Colour · 105min

With the emphasis on the Mister, it's Sidney Poitier, back again as the black detective after his love/hate relationship with sheriff Rod Steiger worked so well in *In the Heat of the Night*. This time he's investigating the killing of a prostitute who was close to his friend, reverend Martin Landau, and the usual clichés about a cop's fraught domestic life form a counterpoint to the main action. Poitier is impressive in his ruthless integrity, but the character contrast of the original is sorely missed. TH Violence, swearing. 📀

Sidney Poitier *Virgil Tibbs* • Martin Landau *Reverend Logan Sharpe* • Barbara McNair *Valerie Tibbs* • Anthony Zerbe *Rice Weedon* • Jeff Corey *Captain Marden* • David Sheiner *Herbert Kenner* • Juano Hernandez *Mealie* • Norma Crane *Marge Garfield* • Edward Asner *Woody Garfield* ■ *Dir* Gordon Douglas • *Scr* Alan R Trustman, James R Webb, from a story by Alan R Trustman, from the character created by John Ball

They Call Me Trinity ★★★ PG
Spaghetti western comedy   1970 · It · Colour · 105min

This successful spaghetti western made international superstars out of B-movie Italian actors Carlo Pedersoli (Bud Spencer) and Mario Girotti (Terence Hill). They play trouble-making brothers leading a group of Mormons against an outlaw band in journeyman director Enzo Barboni's easygoing cowboy comedy geared around slapstick saloon brawls, romantic farce and pratfall stunts. Lightweight, unpretentious and amiable fun. Followed by a number of sequels, including *Trinity Is Still My Name*. AJ Italian dubbed. 📀

Terence Hill *Trinity* • Bud Spencer *Bambino* • Farley Granger *Major Harriman* • Remo Capitani *Mezcal* • Elena Pedemonte *Judith* ■ *Dir/Scr* EB Clucher [Enzo Barboni]

They Came from beyond Space ★★ PG
Science-fiction thriller   1967 · UK · Colour · 82min

This is a pallid attempt by Hammer rivals Amicus to rehash some of the thematic lines from the *Quatermass* series. Astral invaders take over a Cornish factory to enslave Earthlings so they'll repair a spaceship that has crashed on the moon.

Fortunately, astrophysicist Robert Hutton has a metal plate in his head, which makes him immune from alien control, and he single-handedly combats the evil extraterrestrials, led by stalwart genre icon Michael Gough. AJ *DVD*

Robert Hutton *Dr Curtis Temple* • Jennifer Jayne Lee *Mason* • Michael Gough *Monj* • Zia Mohyeddin *Dr Farge* • Geoffrey Wallace *Alan Mullane* • Bernard Kay *Richard Arden* ■ *Dir* Freddie Francis • *Scr* Milton Subotsky, from the novel *The Gods Hate Kansas* by Joseph Millard

They Came to Cordura
★★★★ PG

Period drama   1959 · US · Colour · 118min

This grim but satisfying drama stars a gaunt Gary Cooper as an army major accused of cowardice during an expedition against Pancho Villa in 1916 Mexico. Cooper can only avoid disgrace if he recommends five men from his regiment who are worthy of receiving the Congressional Medal of Honor. There's a magnificent line-up of co-stars, including Rita Hayworth, but none of the characters they portray emerges with much credit as director Robert Rossen examines issues of bravery and cowardice. The location photography is stunning and the effect richly rewarding. TS *DVD*

Gary Cooper *Major Thomas Thorn* • Rita Hayworth *Adelaide Geary* • Van Heflin *Sergeant John Chawk* • Tab Hunter *Lieutenant William Fowler* • Richard Conte *Corporal Milo Trubee* • Michael Callan *Private Andrew Hetherington* ■ *Dir* Robert Rossen • *Scr* Ivan Moffat, Robert Rossen, from the novel by Glendon F Swarthout • *Cinematographer* Burnett Guffey

They Came to Rob Las Vegas
★★

Action thriller
1968 · It/Sp/Fr/W Ger · Colour · 99min

After his brother is killed during a Las Vegas heist, Gary Lockwood plans to do the job right. With a little help from Elke Sommer, he robs a heavily armoured truck, but agent Jack Palance is soon on his trail. Although let down slightly by some stiff dialogue, the film boasts a rock-solid cast and is a slick and ingenious computer-age thriller with a suggestion of humanity versus technology conflict. JG

Gary Lockwood *Tony* • Elke Sommer *Anne* • Lee J Cobb *Skorsky* • Jack Palance *Douglas* • Jean Servais *Gino* • Roger Hanin *Boss* • Georges Geret *Leroy* ■ *Dir* Antonio Isasi • *Scr* Antonio Isasi, J Eisinger, L Comeron, J Illa

They Came Together ★★ 15
Romantic comedy satire
2014 · US · Colour · 79min

Wet Hot American Summer director David Wain tries to do for the romcom what *The Naked Gun* did for the cop movie with this supposedly zany deconstruction of the fluffy genre. But the jokes miss much more frequently than they hit and the tone lurches from observational to lazily scatological too randomly for it to be ever more than fitfully amusing. Paul Rudd and Amy Poehler are game enough as the winsome couple clearly destined for each other, but the occasional sharply observed moment only throws the poorly judged gross-out elements into sharp relief. AS

Paul Rudd *Joel* • Amy Poehler *Molly* • Bill Hader *Kyle* • Ellie Kemper *Karen* • Cobie Smulders *Tiffany* • Jason Mantzoukas *Bob* • Michael Ian Black *Trevor* • Christopher Meloni *Roland* • Ed Helms *Eggbert* • Michael Shannon *Spike* ■ *Dir* David Wain • *Scr* Michael Showalter, David Wain

They Can't Hang Me ★★
Spy drama   1955 · UK · BW · 66min

The themes of atomic secrets and double agents may have lost some of their resonance, but director Val Guest puts a neat spin on events by having condemned killer André Morell strike a death row deal with cop Terence Morgan to deliver a treacherous scientist in return for leniency. The back-up cast is as solid as a rock, with Guest's wife Yolande Donlan putting in an effective appearance. DP

Terence Morgan *Inspector Brown* • Yolande Donlan *Jill* • André Morell *Robert Pitt* • Ursula Howells *Antonia Pitt* • Anthony Oliver *Newcome* • Reginald Beckwith *Harold* ■ *Dir* Val Guest • *Scr* Val Guest, Val Valentine, from a novel by Leonard Mosley

They Come Back ★★
Supernatural mystery   2007 · US/Can · Colour

Mia Kirshner wears a permanent expression of angst as a guilt-riddled psychologist in this nonetheless watchable, *Sixth Sense*-style TV movie. Yet it's her orphaned ten-year-old patient (Niamh Wilson) who makes the drama. Menaced by unseen supernatural forces, the youngster convincingly captures her character's haunted vulnerability. Gloomy hues and a jangling score add to the atmosphere and, although events have a feeling of *déjà vu*, the focus on relationships and emotions keeps them interesting. SF

Mia Kirshner *Dr Faith Hardy* • Jonathan Watton *Mason* • Niamh Wilson *Marley* • Rosemary Dunsmore *Mrs Carr* • Charlotte Arnold *Megan* ■ *Dir* John Bradshaw • *Scr* Gary Boulton-Brown

They Crawl ★★ 15
Horror   2001 · US · Colour · 89min

Convinced his wacko student brother's fireball death isn't an accident (the missing internal organs being something of a giveaway), Daniel Cosgrove teams with detective Tamara Davies to investigate. Cue army of genetically modified cockroaches developed for the US military. This is worth seeing only for Mickey Rourke's eccentric turn – and that's not a recommendation. DP *DVD*

Daniel Cosgrove *Ted Cage* • Tamara Davies *Gina O'Bannon* • Dennis Boutsikaris *Professor* • Grace Zabriskie *Ted's mother* • Mickey Rourke *Tiny* • Tim Thomerson *Exterminator* • Tone Loc *Clarence* ■ *Dir* John Allardice • *Scr* Joseph Curtis, David Mason

They Dare Not Love ★★ U
Second World War romantic drama
1941 · US · BW · 75min

This wartime propaganda movie was a disappointing swan song for director James Whale (he later directed a segment of the unreleased portmanteau film *Hello Out There*). A clichéd romantic drama, it stars George Brent as an Austrian playboy prince and Martha Scott as a Viennese girl, both fleeing the Nazis. They fall in love on board the ship taking them to America, but her father forbids marriage and they go their separate ways. Later they meet again. RK

George Brent *Prince Kurt von Rotenburg* • Martha Scott *Marta Keller* • Paul Lukas *Baron von Helsing* • Egon Brecher *Professor Keller* • Roman Bohnen *Baron Shafter* • Edgar Barrier *Captain Wilhelm Ehrhardt* • Lloyd Bridges *Blonde officer* ■ *Dir* James Whale, Charles Vidor • *Scr* Charles Bennett, Ernest Vajda, from a story by James Edward Grant

They Died with Their Boots On
★★★★ U

Biographical western   1941 · US · BW · 134min

Errol Flynn stars in this rip-roaring biopic as General George Armstrong Custer, who works his way up the ranks and dies heroically at the Battle of the Little Bighorn. History is cast to the wind as Flynn's hero becomes sympathetic to the Indian cause, while Mrs Custer (Olivia de Havilland) fusses about trying to get her husband to settle down. Cast as Custer's chief adversary Crazy Horse is Anthony Quinn, who said of his director, Raoul Walsh, "He was the least technical director I knew, but he relished the process with such a fire that I could almost taste it with him." AT

Errol Flynn *George Armstrong Custer* • Olivia de Havilland *Elizabeth Libby Bacon* • Arthur Kennedy *Ned Sharp* • Charley Grapewin *California Joe* • Gene Lockhart *Samuel Bacon, Esq* • Anthony Quinn *Crazy Horse* • Stanley Ridges *Major Romulus Taipe* • John Litel *General Phil Sheridan* • Walter Hampden *William Sharp* • Sydney Greenstreet *Lt Gen Winfield Scott* • Regis Toomey *Fitzhugh Lee* • Hattie McDaniel *Callie* ■ *Dir* Raoul Walsh • *Scr* Wally Klein, Aeneas MacKenzie

They Drive by Night
★★★★ PG

Drama   1940 · US · BW · 91min

A knockout cast stars in a "love and glory" saga of life among long-distance truck drivers on the Frisco Road. The movie neatly snaps into two thematically linked halves: the first a tale of perils on the road, the second a virtual reworking of Warner Bros' earlier *Bordertown*, with George Raft and Ida Lupino in the old Paul Muni/Bette Davis roles. Co-stars Humphrey Bogart and sizzling Ann Sheridan also draw the attention in a cracklingly directed film from Raoul Walsh. Lupino is superb, and the dialogue is as crisp as it comes. TS *DVD*

George Raft *Joe Fabrini* • Ann Sheridan *Cassie Hartley* • Ida Lupino *Lana Carlsen* • Humphrey Bogart *Paul Fabrini* • Gale Page *Pearl Fabrini* • Alan Hale *Ed J Carlsen* • Roscoe Karns *"Irish" McGurn* ■ *Dir* Raoul Walsh • *Scr* Jerry Wald, Richard Macaulay, from Al Bezzerides's novel *The Long Haul*

They Flew Alone ★★ U
Biographical drama   1941 · UK · BW · 94min

This is producer/director Herbert Wilcox's version of the life of pioneer female flier Amy Johnson. Anna Neagle plays Johnson with vim and vigour, while her playboy husband is portrayed by Robert Newton as little more than an alcoholic co-pilot. Johnson perished in a plane crash in the Thames Estuary in 1941, and Wilcox's device of having the character return from beyond the grave to deliver a patriotic wartime sermon now seems mawkish. TS *DVD*

Anna Neagle *Amy Johnson* • Robert Newton *Jim Mollison* • Edward Chapman *Mr Johnson* • Joan Kemp-Welch *Mrs Johnson* • Nora Swinburne *ATA commandant* ■ *Dir* Herbert Wilcox • *Scr* Miles Malleson, from the story by Lord Castlerosse

They Gave Him a Gun ★★★
Drama   1937 · US · BW · 93min

Young First World War recruit Franchot Tone is so sickened by the idea of killing a man, he wants to go AWOL. But, propped up by his friend Spencer Tracy, he sticks it out and turns into a gun-happy hero. Later he carries the weaponry and new attitude into civilian life to become a mobster. WS Van Dyke directs this interesting melodrama with a pacifist and anti-crime message, and a love story that involves both men committed to the same girl (Gladys George). Quite absorbing, despite a few credibility gaps. RK

Spencer Tracy *Fred Willis* • Gladys George *Rose Duffy* • Franchot Tone *Jimmy Davis* • Edgar Dearing *Sgt Meadowlark* • Mary Lou Treen *[Mary Treen] Saxe* • Cliff Edwards *Laro* ■ *Dir* WS Van Dyke II [WS Van Dyke] • *Scr* Cyril Hume, Richard Maibaum, Maurice Rapf, from the novel by William Joyce

They Got Me Covered
★★★ U

Second World War comedy
1943 · US · BW · 89min

Only Bing Crosby was missing from this wartime flag-waver that might otherwise have been called *The Road to Victory*. Bob Hope zings his way through a generous ration of wisecracks, as he and Dorothy Lamour root out Otto Preminger and his fellow Nazis. Screenwriter Harry Kurnitz, who was something of a dab hand at both comedies and thrillers, adeptly judges the mix of suspense and silliness, leaving director David Butler with little to do but keep up the tempo and show off the lavish sets. DP

Bob Hope *Robert "Kit" Kittredge* • Dorothy Lamour *Christina Hill* • Lenore Aubert *Mrs Vanescu, assumed name of Olga* • Otto Preminger *Otto Fauscheim* • Edward Ciannelli [Eduardo Ciannelli] *Baldanacco* • Marion Martin *Gloria, The "Glow Girl"* • Donald Meek *Little old man* • Phyllis Ruth *Sally Branch* ■ *Dir* David Butler • *Scr* Harry Kurnitz, Arthur Kober, Frank Fenton, Lynn Root, Don Hartman (uncredited), from a story by Leonard Q Ross, Leonard Spigelgass

They Had to See Paris ★★★
Comedy   1929 · US · BW · 96min

When simple Oklahoma family man Will Rogers unexpectedly strikes oil and comes into a great deal of money, his wife Irene Rich develops delusions of grandeur. She drags the family to Paris, buys a chateau, tries to marry off her daughter Marguerite Churchill to a title, and battles to transform her husband from hick to gentleman. Rogers, America's favourite homespun philosopher and wit, entered talkies in this comedy, with director Frank Borzage pressing the laughter buttons as well as he does the tear ducts. RK

Will Rogers (1) *Pike Peters* • Irene Rich *Mrs Peters* • Owen Davis Jr *Ross Peters* • Marguerite Churchill *Opal Peters* • Fifi D'Orsay *Claudine* ■ *Dir* Frank Borzage • *Scr* Sonya Levien, from a novel by Homer Croy

They Knew What They Wanted
★★

Drama   1940 · US · BW · 88min

Charles Laughton stars as an Italian-American winemaker who cons pen pal waitress Carole Lombard into marriage by sending her a picture not of himself, but of his beefcake employee, William Gargan. The plan backfires when Lombard falls in love with Gargan. It's like a French farce transplanted to the Napa Valley, but it isn't played for laughs. AT

Carole Lombard *Amy Peters* • Charles Laughton *Tony Patucci* • William Gargan *Joe* • Harry Carey *Doctor* • Frank Fay *Father McKee* • Joe Bernard [Joseph Bernard] *RFD* • Janet Fox *Mildred* • Lee Tung-Foo *Ah Gee* • Karl Malden *Red* ■ *Dir* Garson Kanin • *Scr* Robert Ardrey, from the play by Sidney Howard

They Live ★★★ 18
Science-fiction thriller
1988 · US · Colour · 93min

A return to his B-movie roots for John Carpenter, this is a knockabout salute to the alien invasion movies of the 1950s. Wrestler-turned-actor Roddy Piper is the working-class hero who, on finding a special pair of sunglasses, discovers that alien-like creatures appear to have taken over Los Angeles and are controlling the remaining human residents with subliminal advertising. There's a nicely relaxed feel to Carpenter's direction and he keeps the action roaring along, stopping only to take a few satirical swipes at yuppie life. JF
Violence, swearing. *DVD* *BL*

Roddy Piper *Nada* • Keith David *Frank* • Meg Foster *Holly Thompson* • George "Buck" Flower *Drifter* • Peter Jason *Gilbert* • Raymond St Jacques *Street preacher* • Jason Robards III *Family man* ■ *Dir* John Carpenter • *Scr* Frank Armitage [John Carpenter], from the short story *Eight O'Clock in the Morning* by Ray Nelson

They Live by Night ★★★★
Romantic film noir   1948 · US · BW · 95min

Nicholas Ray made his directorial debut with this Depression-era drama of young lovers on the run from the law, who find themselves staring into the abyss. Cathy O'Donnell and Farley Granger play the misfits who meet in the aftermath of a prison break-out. They fall in love and marry, but Granger is unable to shake off his criminal associations, leaving little prospect of a happy ending. This is a poignant story of idealism and romanticism betrayed by corruption, and a stunning debut from a future cult director. PF

Farley Granger *Bowie* • Cathy O'Donnell *Keechie* • Howard Da Silva *Chickamaw* • Jay C Flippen *T-Dub* • Helen Craig *Mattie* • Will Wright *Mobley* • Marie Bryant *Singer* • Ian Wolfe *Hawkins* ■ *Dir* Nicholas Ray • *Scr* Charles Schnee, Nicholas Ray, from the novel *Thieves Like Us* by Edward Anderson

They Made Me a Criminal
★★★ PG

Drama   1939 · US · BW · 87min

John Garfield stars as a hard-boiled boxing champion on the run from what he believes is a murder rap in this rollicking tale that goes at breakneck pace and contains strong, well-played performances from the likes of Gloria Dickson, May Robson, Claude Rains and Ann Sheridan. Essentially, it's an ensemble piece, with everyone getting a stab at the limelight. Not to everyone's taste, but admirable for its impudent tone. **SH**

John Garfield *Johnny Bradfield/"Jack Dorney"* • Gloria Dickson *Peggy* • Claude Rains *Detective Monty Phelan* • Ann Sheridan *Goldie* • May Robson *Gramma* • Billy Halop *Tommy* • Bobby Jordan *Angel* • Leo Gorcey *Spit* • Huntz Hall *Dippy* ■ *Dir* Busby Berkeley • *Scr* Sid Herzig, from the book by Bertram Millhauser, Beulah Marie Dix

They Made Me a Fugitive ★★★ PG

Crime thriller   1947 · UK · BW · 96min

Alberto Cavalcanti was a Brazilian-born, Swiss-educated architect and lawyer, who went on to direct a number of praised British films, while also turning out this grim, but largely absorbing example of British *film noir*. Trevor Howard leads a strong cast in the story of an ex-RAF pilot for whom things go from bad to worse. **PF DVD**

Trevor Howard *Clem Morgan* • Sally Gray *Sally* • Griffith Jones *Nancey* • René Ray *Cora* • Mary Merrall *Aggie* • Vida Hope *Mrs Fenshawe* ■ *Dir* Alberto Cavalcanti • *Scr* Noel Langley, from the novel *A Convict Has Escaped* by Jackson Budd

They Met in Bombay ★★★ U

Comedy adventure   1941 · US · BW · 91min

Rosalind Russell and Clark Gable are rival thieves, both after a priceless necklace belonging to an English duchess in a movie that combines comedy with topical wartime flag-waving. They work well together in the sophisticated first half of the film. The second half isn't so good, with Gable going all heroic and winning the Victoria Cross after impersonating a British army officer. **AT**

Clark Gable *Gerald Meldrick* • Rosalind Russell *Anya Von Duren* • Peter Lorre *Captain Chang* • Jessie Ralph *Duchess Of Beltravers* • Reginald Owen *General* • Matthew Boulton *Inspector Cressney* ■ *Dir* Clarence Brown • *Scr* Edwin Justus Mayer, Anita Loos, Leon Gordon, from a story by John Kafka

They Met in the Dark ★★ U

Mystery spy thriller   1943 · UK · BW · 91min

Framed by Naz agents, navy commander James Mason loses his job for accidentally revealing secret information. Determined to clear his name, he goes in search of the woman who set him up, only to find her dead. Joining forces with visiting Canadian Joyce Howard, they set out to unmask theatrical agent Tom Walls whose business is a front for Nazi spies. An old-fashioned, run-of-the-mill and unlikely espionage thriller, topical during the Second World War years, but rather unrewarding now. **RK**

James Mason *Comdr Richard Heritage* • Joyce Howard *Laura Verity* • Tom Walls *Christopher Child* • Phyllis Stanley *Lily Bernard* • Edward Rigby *Mansel* • Ronald Ward *Carter* • Ian Fleming ■ *Dir* Karel Lamac • *Scr* Anatole de Grunwald, Miles Malleson, Basil Bartlett, Victor McClure, James Seymour, from the novel *The Vanished Corpse* by Anthony Gilbert

They Might Be Giants ★★★ U

Mystery drama   1971 · US · Colour · 85min

This curio features George C Scott as a New Yorker who thinks he's Sherlock Holmes. Donning the deerstalker, puffing on the pipe and adopting a quizzical look, Scott encounters a psychiatrist, Dr Watson, who declares him to be suffering from classic paranoia. And since this Dr Watson is played by Joanne Woodward, the tale also gains a weird romantic angle. Some may find this silly and sentimental, others a captivating romantic fantasy. Studio cuts certainly don't help matters, but it remains a rarity of some distinction. **AT**

George C Scott *Justin Playfair* • Joanne Woodward *Dr Mildred Watson* • Jack Gilford *Peabody* • Lester Rawlins *Blevins Playfair* • Rue McClanahan *Daisy* ■ *Dir* Anthony Harvey • *Scr* James Goldman

They Only Kill Their Masters ★★★

Crime mystery   1972 · US · Colour · 97min

Police chief James Garner has a tough case on his hands: the death of a local divorcee and a suspect who's a dog, a doberman called Murphy. Despite the presence of the amiable Garner and the dog, however, this isn't a cutesy Disney movie, but a rather clever thriller about the sexual shenanigans that go on in a tightly knit coastal community. The cast is guaranteed to make older film fans happy. **AT**

James Garner *Police Chief Abel Marsh* • Katharine Ross *Kate* • Hal Holbrook *Watkins* • Harry Guardino *Capt Streeter, sheriff* • June Allyson *Mrs Watkins* • Christopher Connelly *John, cop* • Tom Ewell *Walter, cop* • Peter Lawford *Campbell* • Ann Rutherford *Gloria* ■ *Dir* James Goldstone • *Scr* Lane Slate

They Passed This Way ★★ U

Western   1948 · US · BW · 89min

This surprisingly low-key western from the short-lived independent Liberty production unit, releasing through Eagle-Lion, co-stars the bland (and married) star couple Joel McCrea and Frances Dee. Veteran Charles Bickford steals the acting honours as the lawman searching for McCrea, but Alfred E Green's direction seems in no hurry to advance the plot. This is almost a "western noir" in style. **TS**

Joel McCrea *Ross McEwen* • Frances Dee *Fay Hollister* • Charles Bickford *Pat Garrett* • Joseph Calleia *Monte Marquez* • Martin Garralaga *Florencio* ■ *Dir* Alfred E Green • *Scr* Graham Baker, Teddi Sherman, from the novel *Paso Por Aqui* by Eugene Manlove Rhodes, adapted by William Brent, Milarde Brent

They Rode West ★★★ U

Western   1954 · US · Colour · 84min

This exciting western reunites the popular lovers from *The Caine Mutiny*, handsome Robert Francis and lovely May Wynn. The story deals with medical ethics, as medical officer Francis uses his skill to help the Kiowa Indians, to the disgust of the soldiers at his fort. It's directed with skill by Phil Karson, and also stars Donna Reed. Francis, a contemporary of James Dean, was tragically killed at the age of 25 in a plane crash soon after this film was released. **TS**

Robert Francis *Doctor Allen Seward* • Donna Reed *Laurie MacKaye* • May Wynn *Manyi-ten* • Phil Carey [Philip Carey] *Captain Peter Blake* • Onslow Stevens *Colonel Ethan Waters* ■ *Dir* Phil Karlson • *Scr* DeVallon Scott, Frank Nugent, from a story by Leo Katcher

They Shall Have Music ★★★ U

Musical drama   1939 · US · BW · 97min

Producer Samuel Goldwyn fought a long, losing battle to make classical music popular on the big screen, but it certainly wasn't through lack of trying. Here, Archie Mayo directs a tale that finds room for top-billed virtuoso Jascha Heifetz to play no less than five violin pieces. In the story, tough youngster Gene Reynolds takes up the violin after hearing Heifetz perform, enrolling in music classes as a way out of the slums. **TS**

Jascha Heifetz • Joel McCrea *Peter McCarthy* • Walter Brennan *Professor Lawson* • Andrea Leeds *Ann Lawson* • Gene Reynolds *Frankie* • Terry Kilburn *Dominick* • Tommy Kelly *Willie* • Dolly Loehr [Diana Lynn] ■ *Dir* Archie Mayo • *Scr* Irmgard von Cube, John Howard Lawson, Robert Presnell and Anthony Veiller, from the novel by Charles L Clifford

They Shoot Horses, Don't They? ★★★ 15

Period drama   1969 · US · Colour · 119min

Portraying the dance-marathon craze that swept America during the Depression in the 1930s, director Sydney Pollack gives us plenty of cause for compassion in this hard-hitting adaptation of Horace McCoy's novel. Jane Fonda and Michael Sarrazin are among the partners wearily dragging themselves beyond the end of their tethers, spurred on by the monstrous master of ceremonies (an Oscar-winning Gig Young). It's too tunnel-visioned to work as the intended microcosm of America and the flash-forward narrative is peculiar, but the photography is suitably sickly hued and the performances are wittily authentic. **TH** Violence, swearing, sex scenes. **DVD**

Jane Fonda *Gloria Beatty* • Michael Sarrazin *Robert Syverton* • Susannah York *Alice* • Gig Young *Rocky* • Red Buttons *Sailor* • Bonnie Bedelia *Ruby* • Michael Conrad *Rollo* • Bruce Dern *James* • Al Lewis *Turkey* ■ *Dir* Sydney Pollack • *Scr* James Poe, Robert E Thompson, from the novel by Horace McCoy

They Were Expendable ★★★ U

Second World War drama   1945 · US · BW · 129min

During the Second World War, John Ford served in the navy, attaining the rank of rear admiral, and made several documentaries. When the war looked like being won, he enlisted with MGM to make this drama about buying time for the navy after the disaster of Pearl Harbor. It's an epic that follows the struggle of two officers (Robert Montgomery and John Wayne) to persuade the navy top brass that motor torpedo boats could play a useful role in the battle against the Japanese. Bursting with incident as the action crosses the Pacific, it contains many fine performances. **AT DVD**

Robert Montgomery *Lt John Brickley* • John Wayne *Lt RG "Rusty" Ryan* • Donna Reed *Lt Sandy Davyss* • Jack Holt *General Martin* • Ward Bond *"Boats" Mulcahey* • Marshall Thompson *Ensign Snake Gardner* • Paul Langton *Ensign Andy Andrews* ■ *Dir* John Ford • *Scr* Frank W Wead [Frank Wead], from the book by William L White

They Were Not Divided ★★ PG

Second World War drama   1950 · UK · BW · 97min

There's not much evidence in this stiff-upper-lipped Second World War drama to suggest that Terence Young would go on to direct three of the best Bond movies in the early 1960s. The action is almost totally reliant on the sort of gung-ho camaraderie that was characteristic of the recruiting propaganda that filled British screens in the first days of the conflict. Edward Underdown's Guards officer and Ralph Clanton's have-a-go Yank are nothing more than caricatures, but contemporary audiences queued round the block to see their exploits as they drove the Nazis back to Berlin. **DP DVD**

Edward Underdown *Philip* • Ralph Clanton *David* • Helen Cherry *Wilhelmina* • Stella Andrews *Jane* • Michael Brennan *Smoke O'Connor* • Michael Trubshawe *Major Bushy Noble* • John Wynn *45 Jones* ■ *Dir/Scr* Terence Young

They Were Sisters ★★★ U

Drama   1945 · UK · BW · 109min

This quintessential Gainsborough melodrama follows the marriages of three sisters, whose husbands, it turns out, range from the tolerant to the tyrannical. The sisters are played by three splendid actresses whose looks (and diction) epitomise a long-gone era: Phyllis Calvert, Dulcie Gray and Anne Crawford. Today, though, the main interest is a young James Mason, giving a performance every bit as vicious as his work in *The Seventh Veil* and *The Man in Grey*. **TS**

Phyllis Calvert *Lucy* • James Mason *Geoffrey* • Hugh Sinclair *Terry* • Anne Crawford *Vera* • Peter Murray Hill *William* • Dulcie Gray *Charlotte* • Barrie Livesey *Brian* ■ *Dir* Arthur Crabtree • *Scr* Roland Pertwee, Katherine Strueby, from the novel by Dorothy Whipple

They Who Dare ★★ U

Second World War drama   1953 · UK · Colour · 103min

Considering director Lewis Milestone was responsible for those combat classics *All Quiet on the Western Front* and *A Walk in the Sun*, this is a very disappointing account of an Allied commando raid on Rhodes. Ordered to knock out a couple of airfields, Dirk Bogarde and Denholm Elliott spend as much time squabbling as they do confronting the enemy. The dialogue (much of which was improvised) is sloppy, but the action sequences are convincing. **DP DVD**

Dirk Bogarde *Lieutenant Graham* • Denholm Elliott *Sergeant Corcoran* • Akim Tamiroff *Captain George One* • Gérard Oury *Captain George Two* • Eric Pohlmann *Captain Papadopoulos* • Alec Mango *Patroklis* • Kay Callard *Nightclub singer* ■ *Dir* Lewis Milestone • *Scr* Robert Westerby

They Won't Believe Me ★★★

Crime drama   1947 · US · BW · 95min

Robert Young sheds his good guy image to play a heel on trial for murder. He's cheated on his wealthy wife Rita Johnson, been involved with young writer Jane Greer and then with gold-digging secretary Susan Hayward. One has died in a car accident, one has committed suicide, but can Young persuade the jury that he didn't kill anybody? Told as a long flashback, this is slick and artificial but still engrossing. **AE**

Robert Young (1) *Larry Ballentine* • Susan Hayward *Verna Carlson* • Jane Greer *Janice Bell* • Rita Johnson *Gretta Ballentine* • Tom Powers *Trenton* • George Tyne *Lt Carr* ■ *Dir* Irving Pichel • *Scr* Jonathan Latimer, from a story by Gordon McDonell

They Won't Forget ★★★

Courtroom drama   1937 · US · BW · 95min

Starring Claude Rains as a Deep South DA, the story spins on the murder of a student (Lana Turner) and the suspicion that falls on a black janitor and a college lecturer. When the politically ambitious Rains clears the janitor and condemns the lecturer, a smart-aleck lawyer arrives to defend him, leading us into a courtroom drama in which the real defendant is bigotry. Featuring strong performances and a deal of moralising. **AT**

Claude Rains *Andrew J Griffin* • Gloria Dickson *Sybil Hale* • Edward Norris *Robert Perry Hale* • Otto Kruger *Michael Gleason* • Allyn Joslyn *William P Brock* • Lana Turner *Mary Clay* • Linda Perry *Imogene Mayfield* • Elisha Cook Jr *Joe Turner* ■ *Dir* Mervyn LeRoy • *Scr* Robert Rossen, Aben Kandel, from the novel *Death in the Deep South* by Ward Greene

They're a Weird Mob ★ U

Romantic comedy   1966 · Aus · Colour · 112min

This is a dire and rightly neglected Michael Powell/Emeric Pressburger collaboration. The lacklustre would-be comedy derives most of its laughs from Italian immigrant Walter Chiari battling with the Aussie dialect, while trying to locate his female cousin. All performances, with the honourable exception of Australian veteran Chips Rafferty, are deplorable. **TS**

Walter Chiari *Nino Culotta* • Clare Dunne *Kay Kelly* • Chips Rafferty *Harry Kelly* • Alida Chelli *Giuliana* • Ed Devereaux *Joe* ■ *Dir* Michael Powell • *Scr* Richard Imrie [Emeric Pressburger], from the novel by Nino Culotta

The Thick-Walled Room ★★★

Drama   1953 · Jpn · BW · 110min

Convinced that films should focus on emotion not theory, the Sochiku company decided to withhold for three years Masaki Kobayashi's drama, which used the case of a soldier who killed an innocent Indonesian civilian to raise the issue of war guilt. The characters are underdeveloped and few answers are provided, but novelist Kobo Abe's debut screenplay provocatively suggests that Japan's real warmongers had escaped punishment by drawing on the diaries of war criminals. **DP** In Japanese.

T

Ko Mishima • Torahiko Hamada • Keiko Kishi • Toshiko Kobayashi • Eitaro Ozawa ■ *Dir* Masaki Kobayashi • *Scr* Kobo Abe

Thicker than Water ★★★ U
Comedy 1935 · US · BW · 20min

In the last ever Laurel and Hardy short, Stan and Ollie squander their family savings on a grandfather clock. Though not as brilliant as some of their earlier shorts, this still has some rib-tickling moments. After 1935, the duo concentrated on feature-length movies, although they did make a cameo appearance in the Charley Chase short, *On the Wrong Trek*. DF **DVD**

Stan Laurel *Stan* • Oliver Hardy *Ollie* • Daphne Pollard *Mrs Daphne Hardy* • James Finlayson *Auction operator* • Harry Bowen *Auctioneer* • Charlie Hall *Bank teller* ■ *Dir* James W Horne • *Scr* from a story by Stan Laurel, HM Walker, Charles Rogers

Thicker than Water ★★
Drama 2005 · US · Colour · 87min

Melissa Gilbert is still best known for playing Laura Ingalls in the 1970s series *Little House on the Prairie*. So it will come as no great surprise to viewers of this over-sentimental drama that her high-powered lawyer would give up her stressful life to follow the trail of her recently deceased father's secret past in the country. Perhaps less blatant casting might have given David S Cass Sr's TV movie some much-needed edge. DP

Melissa Gilbert *Natalie Jones* • Brian Wimmer *Sam* • Lindy Newton *Lulu Nichols* • Grainger Hines *Tom Grove* • Robert Mailhouse *Larry Gorman* • Nan Martin *Abygail Jordan* • Nancy Atkinson *Receptionist* • Lindsay Wagner *Jess Jarrett* ■ *Dir* David S Cass Sr • *Scr* JP Martin

Thief ★★★★ 18
Crime drama 1981 · US · Colour · 119min

Director Michael Mann's auspicious feature debut pins its story of a professional jewel thief (James Caan) to a near-abstract idea about the criminal's urge to self-destruct, despite the meticulous way he plans his life. The terrific opening sequence involving a diamond robbery set to the music of Tangerine Dream establishes the mood and style for a crime drama that's almost too intellectual for its own genre. TH Swearing, violence, brief nudity. **DVD** Blu

James Caan *Frank* • Tuesday Weld *Jessie* • Willie Nelson *Okla* • James Belushi *Barry* • Robert Prosky *Leo* • Tom Signorelli *Attaglia* • Dennis Farina *Carl* ■ *Dir* Michael Mann • *Scr* Michael Mann, from the book *The Home Invaders* by Frank Hohimer

The Thief ★★★★ 15
Drama 1997 · Rus/Fr · Colour · 93min

Echoing his father Grigori's socialist realist masterpiece, *Ballad of a Soldier* (1960), Pavel Chukrai's Oscar-nominated drama, chronicles the crimes of a very different type of trooper. Seen through the eyes of her six year-old son, Misha Filipchuk, Ekaterina Rednikova's abrupt romance with Vladimir Mashkov is both intimidating and bewildering, as the threesome flits between provincial towns exploiting Mashkov's Red Army respectability. Contrasting the conditions of postwar austerity with the post-Communist present, this allegory on Yeltsin's Russia is stylishly composed and superbly acted. DP Russian +subtitles. Sex scenes, swearing, violence.

Vladimir Mashkov *Tolian* • Ekaterina Rednikova *Katia* • Misha Filipchuk *Sania, aged six* • Amaliia Mordvinova *Doctor's wife* • Dima Chigarev *Sania, aged 12* ■ *Dir/Scr* Pavel Chukhrai

The Thief Lord ★★ PG
Fantasy adventure 2005 · Ger/UK/Lux/Aus · Colour · 94min

After escaping their cruel aunt and uncle, orphans Aaron Johnson and Jasper Harris head to Venice and fall in with a group of fellow child runaways, led by Rollo Weeks, the teenage self-styled "Thief Lord". Supporting themselves by stealing for a crooked antiques dealer (a cartoonish Alexei Sayle), the gang end up commissioned to find a magical artefact.

Though the events that follow contain a sprinkling of mystery and enchantment, the storyline is underdeveloped. SF **DVD**

Jim Carter *Victor* • Caroline Goodall *Ida* • Rollo Weeks *Scipio* • Aaron Johnson *Prosper* • George MacKay *Riccio* • Jasper Harris *Bo* • Alice Connor *Hornet* • Lathaniel Dyer *Mosca* • Alexei Sayle *Barbarossa* • Vanessa Redgrave *Sister Antonia* ■ *Dir* Richard Claus • *Scr* Richard Claus, Daniel Musgrave, from the novel by Cornelia Funke

The Thief of Bagdad ★★★★ U
Silent fantasy adventure 1924 · US · BW · 210min

A grinning, bare-chested Douglas Fairbanks shimmies up a rope and enters a room in the palace, intending to steal a casket of baubles. Instead, his eyes fall on Princess Julanne Johnston, and he swears there and then to be worthy of her and take her for a ride on a magic carpet. Of such things movie myths are made, effortlessly embodied by Fairbanks in one of his most famous roles. Maybe it dawdles in some sections and some performances are distinctly wobbly, but even those, like the special effects, have a charm all their own. William Cameron Menzies provided the memorable sets, a clever combination of real structures and painted pieces of glass placed right next to the camera lens. AT **DVD** Blu

Douglas Fairbanks *The Thief of Bagdad* • Snitz Edwards *His evil associate* • Charles Belcher *The holy man* • Julanne Johnston *The princess* • Anna May Wong *The Mongol slave* • Winter Blossom *The slave of the lute* • Etta Lee *The slave of the sand board* • Brandon Hurst *The caliph* ■ *Dir* Raoul Walsh • *Scr* Lotta Woods, from a story by Elton Thomas [Douglas Fairbanks] • *Cinematographer* Arthur Edeson

The Thief of Bagdad ★★★★★ U
Fantasy adventure 1940 · UK · Colour · 101min

Producer and co-director Alexander Korda spared no expense to bring the magic of this wonderfully atmospheric *Arabian Nights* adventure to the screen, undeterred by the outbreak of war which necessitated decamping from England to Hollywood. Oscar-winning Technicolor photography and sumptuous art direction make this the definitive movie of this particular tale. With a giant genie, flying carpets, magical mechanical horses, a beautiful princess, Sabu himself, and a wickedly wicked grand vizier in the person of Conrad Veidt, what more could any one ask for? TS **DVD**

Conrad Veidt *Jaffar* • Sabu *Abu* • June Duprez *Princess* • John Justin *Ahmad* • Rex Ingram (2) *Djinni* • Miles Malleson *Sultan* • Morton Selten *King* • Mary Morris *Halima* • Hay Petrie *Astrologer* ■ *Dir* Ludwig Berger, Michael Powell, Tim Whelan, Zoltan Korda, William Cameron Menzies, Alexander Korda • *Scr* Lajos Bíró, Miles Malleson • *Cinematographers* Georges Périnal, Osmond Borradaile • *Art Director* Vincent Korda • *Music* Miklos Rozsa

The Thief of Baghdad ★ U
Fantasy adventure 1978 · UK/Fr · Colour · 96min

This version of the *Arabian Nights* fantasy was filmed in France and uses the Zoptic system that also featured in *Superman* for the flying scenes. Otherwise, the effects are not special at all, and the whole enterprise has a listless air. Enjoyment depends on one's tolerance of Peter Ustinov's ad-libbing sprees and Roddy McDowall's tendency to camp everything up. Former ballerina Marina Vlady behaves like a zombie. AT

Roddy McDowall *Hasan* • Peter Ustinov *Caliph* • Kabir Bedi *Prince Taj* • Terence Stamp *Wazir Jaudur* • Frank Finlay *Abu Bakar* • Marina Vlady *Perizadah* • Pavla Ustinov *Princess Yasmine* • Ian Holm *Gatekeeper* ■ *Dir* Clive Donner • *Scr* AJ Carothers

Thief of Damascus ★★★ U
Adventure 1952 · US · Colour · 78min

This light-hearted *Arabian Nights* adventure features Paul Henreid, Robert Clary and Lon Chaney Jr as Abu Andar, Aladdin and Sinbad. The band members pool their magical talents in order to rescue Princess

Elena Verdugo from the nasty likes of desert mogul John Sutton. Despite its hotch-potch pantomime, it's likeable. TH

Paul Henreid *Abu Andar* • John Sutton *Khalid* • Jeff Donnell *Sheherazade* • Lon Chaney Jr *Sinbad* • Elena Verdugo *Neela* • Robert Clary *Aladdin* • Edward Colmans *Sultan Raudah* • Nelson Leigh *Ben Jammal* • Philip Van Zandt *Ali Baba* ■ *Dir* Will Jason • *Scr* Robert E Kent

Thief of Hearts ★★★ 18
Thriller 1984 · US · Colour · 95min

This slick and sensual psychological drama stars Steven Bauer as a burglar who breaks into a married woman's home and steals a diary detailing her innermost sexual fantasies. He then uses them to woo the woman, who hasn't the faintest idea that he's acting on inside information. Sounds sleazy, and up to a point it is. But it's well-made with strong performances from Bauer and Barbara Williams, and fairly subtle sex scenes. Spicier ones were reportedly added for the film's video release. DA **DVD**

Steven Bauer *Scott Muller* • Barbara Williams (2) *Mickey Davis* • John Getz *Ray Davis* • David Caruso *Buddy Calamara* • Christine Ebersole *Janie Pointer* • George Wendt *Marty Morrison* ■ *Dir/Scr* Douglas Day Stewart

The Thief of Paris ★★★★
Period comedy drama 1967 · Fr/It · Colour · 120min

This is a melancholy, even pessimistic, work from the fine French director, Louis Malle, set in and around 1900. Jean-Paul Belmondo stars as a wealthy young Parisian whose uncle squanders his fortune, then marries off the cousin he loves to a rich neighbour. Belmondo steals the jewels of the neighbour's family and, obsessed by the notion of revenge against bourgeois society and its hypocrisies, embarks on a life of crime as a master thief. Enriched by warm colour photography and a marvellous sense of period. BB In French.

Jean-Paul Belmondo *Georges Randal* • Geneviève Bujold *Charlotte* • Marie Dubois *Geneviève* • Françoise Fabian *Ida* • Julien Guiomar *Lamargelle* • Paul Le Person *Roger La Honte* ■ *Dir* Louis Malle • *Scr* Louis Malle, Jean-Claude Carrière, Daniel Boulanger, from a story by Georges Darien • *Cinematographer* Henri Decaë

The Thief Who Came to Dinner ★★★ 15
Crime comedy drama 1973 · US · Colour · 100min

Written by Walter Hill, this has moments of originality, but is otherwise a tepid, episodic comedy thriller. Ryan O'Neal plays the computer analyst-turned-jewel thief, with Jacqueline Bisset as his girl. But it's support actors Warren Oates, playing a bemused insurance investigator, and Austin Pendleton, as an exasperated editor, who make the most of the predictable plot. TH

Ryan O'Neal *Webster Mcgee* • Jacqueline Bisset *Laura Keaton* • Warren Oates *Dave Reilly* • Jill Clayburgh *Jackie* • Charles Cioffi *Henderling* • Ned Beatty *Deams* • Austin Pendleton *Zukovsky* • George Morfogen *Rivera* • Gregory Sierra *Dynamite* • Michael Murphy (1) *Ted* ■ *Dir* Bud Yorkin • *Scr* Walter Hill, from the novel by Terence Lore Smith

Thieves' Highway ★★★★
Thriller 1949 · US · BW · 92min

This is a superb 20th Century-Fox melodrama from a great *film noir* period, about a tough soldier out to get the racketeer who ruined his dad when he was away fighting in the Second World War. Jules Dassin directs this committed socialist work, and his fine cast includes Lee J Cobb and the great Morris Carnovsky. This is American cinema at its most exciting: absorbing European influences and spitting them out in a tough, uniquely American way. TS

Richard Conte *Nick Garcos* • Valentina Cortesa [Valentina Cortese] *Rica* • Lee J Cobb *Mike Figlia* • Barbara Lawrence *Polly Faber* • Jack Oakie *Slob* • Millard Mitchell *Ed* • Joseph Pevney *Pete* • Morris Carnovsky *Yanko Garcos* ■ *Dir* Jules Dassin • *Scr* AI Bezzerides, from his novel *Thieves' Market*

Thieves' Holiday ★★★
Crime biography 1946 · US · BW · 99min

This diversion utilises the suave persona and polished style of George Sanders in the unusual guise of an 18th-century Parisian. Drawing its story from the memoirs of Eugene Vidocq, a thief who mended his ways to become Prefect of Police and first chief of the Sûreté, the movie concerns his relationship with cabaret entertainer Carole Landis for whom he steals a bejewelled garter, his imprisonment, and his reformation under the influence of Signe Hasso. A light mix of drama and romantic comedy directed by Douglas Sirk and easy to digest. RK

George Sanders *Eugene-François Vidocq* • Signe Hasso *Thérèse* • Carole Landis *Loretta* • Akim Tamiroff *Emile Vernet* • Gene Lockhart *Chief of Police Richet* • Jo Ann Marlowe *Mimi* ■ *Dir* Douglas Sirk • *Scr* Ellis St Joseph, from a memoir by François Eugene Vidocq

Thieves like Us ★★★★ 15
Period crime drama 1974 · US · Colour · 117min

Robert Altman's remake of Nicholas Ray's doom-laden *film noir* *They Live by Night*, has Shelley Duvall and Keith Carradine convincing and touching as the young lovers adrift in the poverty-stricken Deep South. Set in the 1930s and shot in Mississippi, the picture is classically made, lacking the "innovations" that were Altman's trademarks. Louise Fletcher, later an Oscar winner for *One Flew over the Cuckoo's Nest*, appears in her screen debut. AT Nudity. **DVD**

Keith Carradine *Bowie* • Shelley Duvall *Keechie* • John Schuck *Chicamaw* • Bert Remsen *T-dub* • Louise Fletcher *Mattie* • Ann Latham *Lula* • Tom Skerritt *Dee Mobley* ■ *Dir* Robert Altman • *Scr* Calder Willingham, Joan Tewkesbury, Robert Altman, from the novel by Edward Anderson

The Thin Blue Line ★★★★★ 15
Documentary 1988 · US · Colour · 97min

In 1976 a Dallas policeman, Robert Wood, routinely stopped a car and was shot dead. Later, a known delinquent, 16-year-old David Harris, was arrested after boasting about the murder. Under questioning, Harris protested his innocence and blamed a hitch-hiker he had picked up, Randall Adams. Adams was tried and sentenced to death, later commuted to life imprisonment. Twelve years after the crime, documentary film-maker Errol Morris reopened the case and produced this stunning film, an unsurpassed blend of interviews and reconstruction. Our journey into the case is also Morris's, as he slowly uncovers a symphony of doubt and a miscarriage of justice. The sense of unease, heightened by an enthralling collection of witnesses, accumulates so that a random murder in Dallas puts all of America under the microscope. The picture earned its ultimate prize – not an Oscar but a retrial and, in the end, Adams's release. AT Swearing. **DVD**

■ *Dir/Scr* Errol Morris • *Music* Philip Glass

Thin Ice ★★
Romantic musical comedy 1937 · US · BW · 78min

This lightweight trifle stretches Norwegian skating star Sonja Henie's acting ability more than a little, as she plays an ice-skating coach who falls in love with a prince (Tyrone Power). His sly, knowing performance suggests that the plot is not exactly coincidental in the heady days of the romance between Edward VIII and Mrs Simpson. To follow Henie's movements on the ice, 20th Century-Fox constructed a special camera rig. TS

Sonja Henie *Lili Heiser* • Tyrone Power *Prince Rudolph* • Arthur Treacher *Nottingham* • Raymond Walburn *Uncle Dornic* • Joan Davis *Orchestra Leader* ■ *Dir* Sidney Lanfield • *Scr* Boris Ingster, Milton Sperling, from the play *Der Komet* by Attila Obok

A Thin Line between Love and Hate ★ 18
Comedy thriller 1996 · US · Colour · 103min

Comedian Martin Lawrence has no one else to blame considering he's the executive producer, director, co-writer and star of this feeble *Fatal Attraction* clone. He plays a vulgar Casanova with limited ambitions, who gets his comeuppance after romancing glamorous real estate tycoon Lynn Whitfield and dumping her for his true love, Regina King. Unfunny and uncouth. AJ

William Lawrence *Darnell* • Lynn Whitfield *Brandi* • Regina King *Mia* • Bobby Brown *Tee* • Della Reese *Ma Wright* • Malinda Williams *Erica* • Daryl Mitchell *Earl* • Roger E Mosley *Smitty* ■ *Dir* Martin Lawrence • *Scr* Martin Lawrence, Bentley Kyle Evans, Kenny Buford, Kim Bass, from a story by Martin Lawrence

The Thin Man ★★★★ U
Classic detective comedy
1934 · US · BW · 87min

This is the first in a popular series, based on Dashiell Hammett's characters, with William Powell and Myrna Loy as Nick and Nora Charles, amateur sleuths and the epitome of 1930s style and sophistication. Hammett had written a thriller, but MGM turned it into a screwball comedy, with Powell and Loy making a sizzling couple. Their excessive drinking and other shocking habits (the characters are based on Hammett and Lillian Hellman) delighted audiences at the time and still do today, even if the pacing now seems rather slow. Five more films followed, beginning with 1936's *After the Thin Man*. AT DVD

William Powell *Nick Charles* • Myrna Loy *Nora Charles* • Maureen O'Sullivan *Dorothy Wynant* • Nat Pendleton *Lieutenant John Guild* • Minna Gombell *Mimi Wynant* • Porter Hall *MacCauley* • Henry Wadsworth *Tommy* ■ *Dir* WS Van Dyke • *Scr* Albert Hackett, Frances Goodrich, from the novel by Dashiell Hammett

The Thin Man Goes Home ★★★ PG
Detective comedy 1944 · US · BW · 96min

In the fifth in the Dashiell Hammett-inspired series, William Powell once again plays Nick Charles, a man aided by a sharp mind, several dry martinis and a glamorous wife Nora (Myrna Loy). In this film he's on a visit to his home town and as usual, the amateur sleuths and Asta the dog are up to their elegant necks in solving a murder mystery. The series concluded with *Song of the Thin Man*. BB DVD

William Powell *Nick Charles* • Myrna Loy *Nora Charles* • Lucile Watson *Mrs Charles* • Gloria De Haven [Gloria DeHaven] *Laura Ronson* • Anne Revere *Crazy Mary* • Helen Vinson *Helena Draque* • Harry Davenport *Dr Bertram Charles* • Leon Ames *Edgar Draque* ■ *Dir* Richard Thorpe • *Scr* Robert Riskin, Dwight Taylor, from a story by Robert Riskin, from a story by Harry Kurnitz, from characters by Dashiell Hammett

The Thin Red Line ★★★ 12
Second World War drama
1964 · US · BW · 95min

Admirers of Terrence Malick's excellent 1998 version of James Jones' epic Second World War novel may find this disappointing. But this well-acted picture takes a more conventional approach, focusing on the spiky relationship between veteran first sergeant Jack Warden and raw private Keir Dullea. In the bitter conflict in Guadalcanal in the Pacific, the two men's loathing for each other develops into mutual respect. The combat sequences are first class, without glorifying war. JG DVD

Keir Dullea *Private Doll* • Jack Warden *1st Sgt Welsh* • James Philbrook *Colonel Tall* • Ray Daley *Captain Stone* ■ *Dir* Andrew Marton • *Scr* Bernard Gordon, from the novel by James Jones

The Thin Red Line ★★★★★ 15
Second World War drama
1998 · US · Colour · 163min

After 20 years in the film-making wilderness, Terrence Malick released this belated third feature – a magnificent

account of the Second World War battle for Guadalcanal island in the South Pacific. It's a long, discursive and deeply philosophical evocation of war, beautifully shot by John Toll. The film boasts an all-star cast, with Sean Penn as a cynical sergeant and Nick Nolte as an uncompromising lieutenant colonel making deep impressions. The principal role, however, goes to the little known Jim Caviezel as the nonconformist and idealist who seems completely at one with the tropical surroundings, while British actor Ben Chaplin gives a convincing performance as the ordinary Joe who dreams of his wife back home. Malick's extraordinary direction is the real star turn, however. A modern masterpiece. AT Swearing, violence. DVD

Sean Penn *First Sgt Welsh* • Jim Caviezel *Private Witt* • John Cusack *Captain Gaff* • Ben Chaplin *Private Bell* • Nick Nolte *Lt Col Tall* • Woody Harrelson *Keck* • Elias Koteas *Captain "Bugger" Staros* • John Travolta *Qintard* • George Clooney *Bosche* ■ *Dir* Terrence Malick • *Scr* Terrence Malick, from the novel by James Jones

The Thing ★★★★ 18
Science-fiction horror
1982 · US · Colour · 108min

John Carpenter's remake of Howard Hawks and Christian Nyby's influential 1951 creature feature *The Thing from Another World*, is a special-effects extravaganza of the highest order. The updated screenplay by Bill Lancaster (son of Burt) has the occupants of a polar research station menaced by an alien with the ability to change its shape and impersonate its enemies. Carpenter stresses the slimy ET at the expense of characterisation and mood, yet it's precisely this one grisly facet that makes it so compelling. AJ Violence, swearing. DVD

Kurt Russell *MacReady* • A Wilford Brimley [Wilford Brimley] *Blair* • TK Carter *Nauls* • David Clennon *Palmer* • Keith David *Childs* • Richard Dysart *Dr Copper* • Charles Hallahan *Norris* • Peter Maloney *Bennings* • Richard Masur *Clark* • Donald Moffat *Garry* • Joel Polis *Fuchs* • Thomas Waites [Thomas G Waites] *Windows* ■ *Dir* John Carpenter • *Scr* Bill Lancaster, from the story *Who Goes There?* by John Wood Campbell Jr

The Thing ★★★★ 15
Science-fiction horror
2011 · US/Jpn · Colour · 98min

Director Matthijs van Heijningen's feature debut is pitched as a prequel to John Carpenter's 1982 classic –it ends where that film begins – but it's really more of a remake, down to the many grotesque, surreal shock moments. Mary Elizabeth Winstead plays a palaeontologist who is whisked to an Antarctic research base when an alien is found embedded in the ice. Once defrosted, the shape-shifting thing causes paranoia on a grand scale, and that's even before the gory mayhem begins. Van Heijningen creates an edgy atmosphere, and the restaged gross-out scenes are enhanced rather than overwhelmed by the slick CGI work, and the horrific sights that greeted Kurt Russell's crew at the base are cleverly explained. Tense, smart and suitably gruesome, this certainly delivers the goods. AJ DVD

Mary Elizabeth Winstead *Kate Lloyd* • Joel Edgerton *Carter* • Adewale Akinnuoye-Agbaje *Jameson* • Eric Christian Olsen *Adam Finch* • Kim Bubbs *Juliette* ■ *Dir* Matthijs van Heijningen • *Scr* Eric Heisserer, from the short story *Who Goes There?* by John W Campbell Jr

The Thing Called Love ★★ 15
Drama 1993 · US · Colour · 109min

Peter Bogdanovich directs River Phoenix in one of his final roles, in a run-of-the-mill drama about love and fame among a group of aspiring country singers. Phoenix is fine as the young singer trying to make a name for himself in Nashville, and he's backed up by a competent young cast as well as a handful of bona fide country singers. But despite the authenticity of the music and winning performances, it never really kicks into gear and ends up as a brief footnote to Phoenix's promising career. JB DVD

River Phoenix *James Wright* • Samantha Mathis *Miranda Presley* • Dermot Mulroney *Kyle Davidson* • Sandra Bullock *Linda Lue Linden* • KT Oslin *Lucy* • Anthony Clark *Billy* • Webb Wilder *Ned* ■ *Dir* Peter Bogdanovich • *Scr* Carol Heikkinen

The Thing from Another World ★★★★ PG
Science-fiction horror 1951 · US · BW · 83min

This pioneering science-fiction outing emphasises suspense and atmosphere, rather than the shock special effects of John Carpenter's 1982 remake *The Thing*, in a tense story of arctic scientists trying to cope with the first of Hollywood's Cold War aliens. Howard Hawks is only credited as producer, but the film is suspiciously full of his signature flourishes (camaraderie in the face of ambush, for instance) and director Christian Nyby never made anything half as good again. AJ

Kenneth Tobey *Captain Patrick Hendry* • Margaret Sheridan *Nikki* • Robert Cornthwaite *Dr Carrington* • Douglas Spencer *Scotty* • James Young (2) *Lt Eddie Dykes* • Dewey Martin *Crew Chief* • James Arness *The "Thing"* ■ *Dir* Christian Nyby • *Scr* Charles Lederer, from the story *Who Goes There?* by Don A Stuart [John Wood Campbell Jr]

The Thing with Two Heads ★★

Blaxploitation horror 1972 · US · Colour · 87min

This is probably the most lunatic blaxploitation horror film ever made, and also the genre's biggest missed opportunity to say something profound. Bigoted brain surgeon Ray Milland learns he's dying of cancer, so needs to transplant his head on to a healthy body. Unfortunately, racist Milland wakes to find his head next to that of condemned black killer Rosey Grier, who is intent on clearing his name. With each head trying to seek control of Grier's body, the jokes should have been funnier, the racist allegory more up-front and the pacing more breakneck to cover the absolute idiocy of the premise. AJ

Ray Milland *Dr Maxwell Kirshner* • Rosey Grier *Jack Moss* • Don Marshall *Dr Fred Williams* • Roger Perry *Dr Philip Desmond* • Chelsea Brown *Lila* • Kathy Baumann [Katherine Baumann] *Patricia* • John Dullaghan (1) *Thomas* • John Eliss Donald ■ *Dir* Lee Frost • *Scr* Lee Frost, James Gordon White, Wes Bishop

Things Change ★★★★ PG
Crime comedy 1988 · US · Colour · 96min

Hollywood veteran Don Ameche stars as an ageing shoeshine man who's persuaded to take the rap for a Mafia murder in return for the fulfilment of his lifelong dream in director David Mamet's charming follow-up to *House of Games*. Mamet regular Joe Mantegna co-stars as the well-meaning minder assigned to take care of Ameche, who decides to allow his charge one final fling. Ameche and Mantegna shared the best actor prize at Venice for their roles in this beautifully crafted film. DA

Don Ameche *Gino* • Joe Mantegna *Jerry* • Robert Prosky *Joseph Vincent* • JJ Johnston *Frankie* • Ricky Jay *Mr Silver* • Mike Nussbaum *Mr Green* ■ *Dir* David Mamet • *Scr* David Mamet, Shel Silverstein

The Things of Life ★★★ 15
Drama 1969 · Fr/It/Swi · Colour · 82min

An opening car crash, spectacularly filmed, sends this glossy marital drama into flashback mode, in which Michel Piccoli vacillates between estranged wife Lea Massari and mistress Romy Schneider. This is a movie of shifting moods and allegiances rather than substance, well acted by the three leads although Piccoli is too rough-edged to be a sympathetic hero. It was a huge hit in France and was remade in 1994 as *Intersection* with Sharon Stone and Richard Gere. AT French dubbed.

Michel Piccoli *Pierre Berard* • Romy Schneider *Hélène* • Lea Massari *Catherine Berard* • Gerard Lartigau *Bertrand Berard* • Jean Bouise *François* • Hervé Sand *Truck driver* ■ *Dir* Claude Sautet • *Scr* Paul Guimard, Jean-Loup Dabadie, Claude Sautet, from the novel *Les Choses de la Vie* by Guimard

Things to Come ★★★★ PG
Science-fiction epic 1936 · UK · BW · 92min

Although a classic slice of British sci-fi, Alexander Korda's elaborate production of HG Wells's prophetic novel is weakened by a prevailing air of over-theatricality and naivety. Spanning almost 100 years from 1940 to 2036, it begins during a world war and goes through plague and a technological revolution, ending with everyone living in an enormous Art Deco underground city run by Raymond Massey. Awesome sets and magnificent design make this hugely ambitious antique vision of the future Britain's answer to *Metropolis*. Amazingly, Wells actually visited the studio while it was being made. AJ DVD BLU

Raymond Massey *John Cabal/Oswald Cabal* • Edward Chapman *Pippa Passworthy/Raymond Passworthy* • Ralph Richardson *The Boss* • Margaretta Scott *Roxana/Rowena* • Cedric Hardwicke *Theotocopulos* • Maurice Braddell *Dr Harding* • Sophie Stewart *Mrs Cabal* • Derrick de Marney *Richard Gordon* • Ann Todd *Mary Gordon* • George Sanders *Pilot* ■ *Dir* William Cameron Menzies • *Scr* HG Wells, Lajos Bíró, from the book *The Shape of Things to Come* by HG Wells • *Cinematographer* Georges Périnal • *Production Designer* Vincent Korda

Things to Come ★★★★ 12A
Drama 2016 · Fr/Ger · Colour · 101min

There's an irony in the title of this drama, since philosophy lecturer Isabelle Huppert wonders if she actually has much of a future after an annus horibilis turns her life upside down. In the wake of marital dissolution and the passing of her mother, there's grief and loss, of course, but also a sense of liberation – something she's not exactly used to. The story unfolds gently, showcasing a central performance that is truly superb even by Huppert's elevated standards. A wise and affecting look at things that really matter. TJ In French. Some swearing, drug abuse.

Isabelle Huppert *Nathalie* • André Marcon *Heinz* • Roman Kolinka *Fabien* • Edith Scob *Yvette* ■ *Dir/Scr* Mia Hansen-Løve

Things to Do before You're 30 ★ 15
Comedy drama 2004 · UK · Colour · 96min

Dougray Scott and Jimi Mistry are an ensemble of man-children who'd rather play football than tackle adult responsibilities. Scott is the incorrigible womaniser who cheats on his pregnant girlfriend (Emilia Fox), and Mistry is a struggling musician at loggerheads with his entrepreneurial dad. Their dilemmas are limply written and drearily staged, and it's neither funny nor dramatic. SP Swearing, sex scenes. DVD

Dougray Scott *Cass* • Emilia Fox *Kate* • Jimi Mistry *Dylan* • Billie Piper *Vicky* • Shaun Parkes *Adam* • Donna Air *Fiona* • George Innes *Don* • Bruce Mackinnon *Colin* • Danny Nussbaum *Johnny* ■ *Dir* Simon Shore • *Scr* Patrick Wilde, from the film *All Stars* by Jean van de Velde, Mischa Alexander

Things to Do in Denver When You're Dead ★★★★ 18
Crime drama 1995 · US · Colour · 110min

The comparisons to Quentin Tarantino's work are inevitable, but Gary Fleder's witty take on the gangster movie marked him out as an individual talent to watch. Andy Garcia plays a retired mobster who is called in by his ailing former boss, Christopher Walken, to carry out one last job. When it goes badly wrong, Garcia and his pals find themselves on the hit list. The vivid splashes of violence are ably handled by Fleder, but he also delights in the rich dialogue of his oddball characters, warmly brought to life by an eclectic cast. JF Sex scenes, violence, swearing. DVD

Andy Garcia *Jimmy "the Saint" Tosnia* • Christopher Lloyd *Pieces* • William Forsythe *Franchise* • Bill Nunn *Easy Wind* • Treat Williams *Critical Bill Dooley* • Jack Warden *Joe Heff* • Steve Buscemi *Mr Shhh* • Fairuza Balk *Lucinda* • Gabrielle Anwar *Dagney* • Christopher Walken *The Man with the Plan* ■ *Dir* Gary Fleder • *Scr* Scott Rosenberg

T

Things We Lost in the Fire
★★ 15

Drama   2007 · US/UK/Can · Colour · 113min

Halle Berry stars in this overwrought domestic melodrama as a well-to-do mother whose doting husband (David Duchovny) loses his life in a random act of violence. To get closure she strikes up a friendship with his heroin-addicted best mate (a suspiciously dapper Benicio Del Toro) and invites him into the family home. Berry gives it her all and Del Toro is a suitably pitiable presence. But there's something so false here - why would such a devoted mother bring a thieving junkie into her children's home in the first place? - that it never comes anywhere near the heights of honesty and realism it was trying to achieve. DW Swearing, drug abuse. *DVD* ⊡

Halle Berry *Audrey Burke* • Benicio Del Toro *Jerry Sunborne* • David Duchovny *Brian Burke* • Alison Lohman *Kelly* • Omar Benson Miller *Neal* • John Carroll Lynch *Howard Glassman* • Robin Weigert *Brenda* • Alexis Llewellyn *Harper Burke* ■ *Dir* Susanne Bier • *Scr* Allan Loeb

Things You Can Tell Just by Looking at Her ★★★★ 12

Romantic comedy   2000 · US · Colour · 109min

Former cinematographer Rodrigo Garcia's feature debut is a set of five loosely overlapping stories. However, though blessed with a fine cast of performers, this film didn't get a cinematic release in the United States and only goes to show that distributors underestimate their audience and their ability to see A-list actresses in a new light. So what if Glenn Close is a lonely doctor, tending a senile mother? So what if Holly Hunter is an adulteress with an unwanted pregnancy? Yes, Calista Flockhart is a lesbian nursing her dying lover and Cameron Diaz is a blind bitch undermining her seeing sister's confidence. But that's what makes this original, interesting and honest. LH

Glenn Close *Dr Elaine Keener* • Holly Hunter *Rebecca* • Gregory Hines *Robert* • Miguel Sandoval *Sam* • Kathy Baker *Rose* • Calista Flockhart *Christine Taylor* • Valeria Golino *Lilly* • Cameron Diaz *Carol* • Amy Brenneman *Kathy* ■ *Dir/Scr* Rodrigo Garcia

Think Fast, Mr Moto ★★★

Crime mystery   1937 · US · BW · 66min

The first in the eight-strong series featuring Peter Lorre as Mr Moto, the master of blindingly obvious disguises. Here, the Japanese sleuth is on the track of diamond smugglers operating out of San Francisco. Starting with the discovery of a body in an antique shop during Chinese New Year and transporting us, via a murderous ocean cruise, to the gambling joints of Shanghai, the story rapidly becomes impenetrable, with virtually every character acting shiftily. But, thanks to director Norman Foster and a wholehearted cast, the film has an irresistible momentum. DP

Peter Lorre *Mr Moto* • Virginia Field *Gloria Danton* • Thomas Beck *Bob Hitchings* • Sig Rumann [Sig Ruman] *Nicholas Marloff* • Murray Kinnell *Mr Joseph Wilkie* • Lotus Long *Lela Liu* • John Rogers (1) *Carson* • George Cooper (1) *Muggs Blake* ■ *Dir* Norman Foster • *Scr* Norman Foster, Howard Ellis Smith, from the novel by John P Marquand

Think like a Man ★★★ 12

Relationship comedy   2012 · US · Colour · 116min

Basically a long infomercial for American comedian Steve Harvey's bestselling self-help book on romance, this is a simple-minded, earthy look at the snarls of modern relationships. It centres on a group of women who test out Harvey's man-handling advice while the men they are pursuing undermine them by using the same DIY manual. Although the film is energetically directed, the snippets of advice delivered by Harvey himself are awkwardly interwoven with the narrative. There are some amusing set pieces and asides, but mainly this is as stereotypical as it comes. KK *DVD*

Michael Ealy *Dominic* • Jerry Ferrara *Jeremy* • Meagan Good *Mya* • Regina Hall *Candace* • Kevin Hart *Cedric* • Steve Harvey ■ *Dir* Tim Story • *Scr* Keith Merryman, David A Newman, from the non-fiction book *Act like a Lady, Think like a Man* by Steve Harvey

Think like a Man Too ★★ 12

Relationship comedy   2014 · US · Colour · 101min

The sequel to the smash hit *Think like a Man* sees the original cast reunite in Vegas for a wedding. Both bachelor and bachelorette parties begin in style, but mishaps and relationship problems threaten to derail the nuptials. Mixing comedy tropes that have either run their course or didn't work in the first place, the film settles for simply bringing the cast back, ignoring the need for purpose and wasting the variety of talent on offer. JL Drug abuse, some swearing, sexual references. *DVD*

Kevin Hart *Cedric* • Michael Ealy *Dominic* • Terrence J [Terrence Jenkins] *Michael* • Romany Malco *Zeke* ■ *Dir* Tim Story • *Scr* Keith Merryman, David A Newman, from the non-fiction book *Act like a Lady, Think like a Man: What Men Really Think about Love, Relationships, Intimacy and Commitment* by Steve Harvey

The Third Alibi ★

Thriller   1961 · UK · BW · 68min

This is the kind of shoddy crime thriller that gives even low-budget features a bad name. The action never for a second escapes its stage origins as composer Laurence Payne and his pregnant mistress Jane Griffiths plot to murder Payne's wife Patricia Dainton. Blame playwrights Pip and Jane Baker for the elaborate murder games, but even they are betrayed by a cast incapable of holding its own in an amateur theatrical. DP

Laurence Payne *Norman Martell* • Patricia Dainton *Helen Martell* • Jane Griffiths *Peggy Hill* • Edward Underdown *Dr Murdoch* • John Arnatt *Supt Ross* • Humphrey Lestocq *Theatre producer* • Lucy Griffiths *Miss Potter* • Cleo Laine *Singer* ■ *Dir* Montgomery Tully • *Scr* Maurice J Wilson, from the play *Moment of Blindness* by Pip Baker, Jane Baker

The Third Day ★★★

Drama   1965 · US · Colour · 102min

Despite some lapses in the screenplay, this amnesia thriller works well as a psychodrama. There are convincing leading performances from George Peppard and Elizabeth Ashley, whose real-life marriage was heading for the rocks at the time, and an eclectic cast that includes Roddy McDowall, Mona Washbourne and Herbert Marshall. TS

George Peppard *Steve Mallory* • Elizabeth Ashley *Alexandria Mallory* • Roddy McDowall *Oliver Parsons* • Arthur O'Connell *Dr Wheeler* • Mona Washbourne *Catherine Parsons* • Herbert Marshall *Austin Parsons* ■ *Dir* Jack Smight • *Scr* Burton Wohl, Robert Presnell Jr, from the novel by Joseph Hayes

Third Finger, Left Hand ★★ U

Comedy   1940 · US · BW · 96min

A perky Myrna Loy vehicle with a bogglingly unbelievable plot, this is pleasant, but undemanding. Here, as Melvyn Douglas's reluctant fiancée, Loy shines with her usual panache. But the script is thin and what starts out as a moderately pleasing soufflé, falls flat well before the final reel. SH

Myrna Loy *Margot Sherwood Merrick* • Melvyn Douglas *Jeff Thompson* • Raymond Walburn *Mr Sherwood* • Lee Bowman *Philip Booth* • Bonita Granville *Vicky Sherwood* • Felix Bressart *August Winkel* ■ *Dir* Robert Z Leonard • *Scr* Lionel Houser

The Third Generation ★★★ 15

Black comedy   1979 · W Ger · Colour · 104min

Not one of Rainer Werner Fassbinder's best films, but still an interesting depiction of middle-class urban radicals, dealing with a group of Berlin terrorists whose conflicts are gradually eating away at their nucleus. The director, who constantly ran out of money during the film's making, called it "a comedy in six parts", and it is played as political farce. It provoked violent controversy in Germany, where it was attacked by the left and right - the latter for glorifying terrorists and the former for betraying the heirs of the Baader-Meinhof gang. RB German +subtitles. Violence, drug abuse.

Volker Spengler *August Brem* • Bulle Ogier *Hilde Krieger* • Hanna Schygulla *Susanne Gast* • Harry Baer *Rudolf Mann* • Vitus Zeplichal *Bernhard von Stein* • Udo Kier *Edgar Gast* • Margit Carstensen *Petra Vielhaber* • Günther Kaufmann *Franz Walsch* • Eddie Constantine *Peter Lurz* ■ *Dir/Scr* Rainer Werner Fassbinder

The Third Man ★★★★★ PG

Classic thriller   1949 · UK · BW · 101min

Developed by Graham Greene from an idea jotted down on the flap of an envelope, this virtually flawless feature is one of the best British films of all time. Set in postwar occupied Vienna, the plot is a corker, littered with memorable moments and played to perfection by an unforgettable cast, led with distinction by Orson Welles and Joseph Cotten. A master of place, angle and shade, director Carol Reed (helped by his Oscar-winning cinematographer Robert Krasker) fashions a city in which menace lurks round every corner, while Anton Karas's jaunty zither music echoes the wit and drama of this dark, yet daringly playful, picture. DP *DVD* ⊡

Joseph Cotten *Holly Martins* • Valli [Alida Valli] *Anna Schmidt* • Orson Welles *Harry Lime* • Trevor Howard *Major Calloway* • Bernard Lee *Sergeant Paine* • Paul Hoerbiger [Paul Hörbiger] *Harry's porter* • Ernst Deutsch *"Baron" Kurtz* • Siegfried Breuer *Popescu* • Erich Ponto *Dr Winkel* • Wilfrid Hyde-White [Wilfrid Hyde White] *Crabbin* • Hedwig Bleibtreu *Anna's "old woman"* ■ *Dir* Carol Reed • *Scr* Graham Greene, from his story

Third Person ★★ 15

Romantic drama
2013 · US/It/Ger/Bel · Colour · 131min

Three interlinked dramas (featuring Mila Kunis, Adrien Brody and Liam Neeson respectively) unfold in this seemingly personal project from writer/director Paul Haggis. Clearly, there's ambition here in the switchback editing and thematic connections (parental guilt runs throughout), while Haggis certainly gives his performers flamboyantly emotive roles. However, the whole teetering edifice seriously outstays its welcome and the final twist is anything but a surprise. TJ In English, Italian. Swearing, sex scenes. *DVD*

Liam Neeson *Michael* • Mila Kunis *Julia* • Adrien Brody *Scott* • Olivia Wilde *Anna* • James Franco *Rick* • Kim Basinger *Elaine* ■ *Dir/Scr* Paul Haggis

The Third Secret ★★★ PG

Psychological thriller   1964 · UK · BW · 98min

A psychiatrist is found shot dead. Did he kill himself or is something sinister going on? Directed by Charles Crichton, this is never as clever as it thinks it is, though the cast is outstanding, with the star of the show, as one of the dead shrink's patients trying to establish the truth, being Stephen Boyd, an Irish actor who, notwithstanding a riveting performance as Messala in *Ben-Hur*, never quite made it to the top. AT *DVD*

Stephen Boyd *Alex Stedman* • Jack Hawkins *Sir Frederick Belline* • Richard Attenborough *Alfred Price-Gorham* • Diane Cilento *Anne Tanner* • Pamela Franklin *Catherine Whitset* • Paul Rogers *Dr Milton Gillen* • Alan Webb *Alden Hoving* • Rachel Kempson *Mildred Hoving* • Peter Sallis *Lawrence Jacks* • Judi Dench *Miss Humphries* • Nigel Davenport *Lew Harding* ■ *Dir* Charles Crichton • *Scr* Robert L Joseph

Third Star ★★ 15

Comedy drama   2010 · UK · Colour · 92min

Lifelong friendships come under scrutiny in this well-meaning drama about a dying man who calls on his best friends to ferry him to a remote beach in Wales for a final holiday. Leaving aside the wisdom of transporting someone so frail away from the reach of any doctor, Hattie Dalton's debut feature never quite generates the intimacy needed to land the right emotional punches. The cancer-stricken James (Benedict Cumberbatch) comes across as waspish and even cruel at times, while his entourage (JJ Feild, Tom Burke and Adam Robertson) are a bumbling, self-centred bunch whose characters are rarely developed beyond their occupations. DW *DVD*

Benedict Cumberbatch *James* • Tom Burke *Davy* • JJ Feild *Miles* • Hugh Bonneville *Beachcomber* • Rupert Frazer *James's father* • Nia Roberts *Chloe* ■ *Dir* Hattie Dalton • *Scr* Vaughan Sivell

Third Time Lucky ★★

Drama   1949 · UK · BW · 90min

A gambler doesn't realise that he loves his lucky mascot until the chips are down. Dermot Walsh and Glynis Johns just don't set the screen alight and similarly, Gordon Parry (in fairness, directing only his second feature) fails to capture the seedy world of gambling dens and backstreet drinking joints. The ending is corny and moralising. DP

Glynis Johns *Joan* • Dermot Walsh *Lucky* • Charles Goldner *Flash* • Harcourt Williams *Doc* • Yvonne Owen *Peggy* • Helen Haye *Old Lady* ■ *Dir* Gordon Parry • *Scr* Gerald Butler, from his novel *They Cracked Her Glass Slipper*

The Third Voice ★★★★

Thriller   1960 · US · BW · 78min

Writer/director Hubert Cornfield's extraordinarily stylish thriller is adapted from Charles Williams's novel, *All the Way*. The story - in which a woman kills her wealthy lover and an accomplice impersonates him through some financial processes - never zigs the way you expect it to zag. Edmond O' Brien, Laraine Day and Julie London form a suspenser-à-trois that lends credibility to an artificial situation. TH

Edmond O'Brien *The Voice* • Laraine Day *Marian Forbes* • Julie London *Corey Scott* • Ralph Brooks *Harris Chapman* • Roque Ybarra *Fisherman* • Ruben Moreno *Fisherman* ■ *Dir* Hubert Cornfield • *Scr* Hubert Cornfield, from the novel *All the Way* by Charles Williams

Third World Cop ★★★ 15

Crime drama   1999 · Jam · Colour · 98min

Dirty Harry, Jamaican style: a rogue cop with a big gun and a disdain for police procedure is withdrawn from rural duties and transferred to Kingston, the island's front line of crime. There his maverick approach to policing brings him into conflict with a former best buddy who's now right-hand man to a vicious gunrunner. Filmed in the flashy fashion of a Hong Kong martial arts movie, this is neatly directed and solidly acted. DA +subtitles. *DVD*

Paul Campbell (2) *Capone* • Mark Danvers *Ratty* • Carl Bradshaw *Wonie* • Audrey Reid *Rita* ■ *Dir* Chris Browne • *Scr* Suzanne Fenn, Chris Browne, Chris Salewicz

Thirst ★★ 18

Horror   1979 · Aus · Colour · 90min

This intriguing modern-day vampire parable is set in a hospital in Australia's outback, where the hapless patients are "milked" for their blood by a secret society that believes its consumption bestows upon them great power. Sadly, Rod Hardy plays the whole thing totally deadpan, as if he's directing Chekhov. More ironic humour might have made the outrageous premise more effective. RS *DVD*

Chantal Contouri *Kate Davis* • David Hemmings *Dr Fraser* • Henry Silva *Dr Gauss* • Max Phipps *Hodge* • Shirley Cameron *Mrs Barker* • Rod Mullinar *Derek* • Robert Thompson *Sean* • Walter Pym *Dichter* ■ *Dir* Rod Hardy • *Scr* John Pinkney

Thirst ★★★

Disaster movie   1998 · US · Colour · 120min

During a withering heat wave, deadly parasites infect a town's water supply and water filtration engineer Adam Arkin struggles to find a way to kill the pernicious microbe before everyone dies of dehydration. Mirroring actual events in the American Midwest, this TV movie is kept believable by John Mandel's purposeful script and Bill L Norton's taut direction. MC

U SUITABLE FOR ALL • Uc SUITABLE ESPECIALLY FOR YOUNG CHILDREN (DVD ONLY) • PG PARENTAL GUIDANCE • 12A UNDER 12s TO BE ACCOMPANIED (CINEMA ONLY)

Adam Arkin *Bob Miller* • Joely Fisher *Susan Miller* • Giancarlo Esposito *Dr Carver* • Ken Jenkins *Lou Wolford* • Phyllis Lyons *Allison* • Michael Cudlitz *Andy* ■ *Dir* Bill L Norton • *Scr* John Mandel, Paul A Kaufman

Thirst ★★★ 18

Horror drama
2009 · S Kor/US · Colour · 128min

Oldboy director Park Chan-wook sinks his teeth into the vampire subgenre in this audacious tale of sin and redemption. Taking another twisted journey into the heart of human darkness, the South Korean innovator uses bloodsucking as the ultimate moral challenge for small-town priest Sang-hyun (Song Kang-ho) after an infected transfusion leaves him undead. The macabre farce that ensues borrows from Emile Zola's *Thérèse Raquin*, ramping up the novel with stylish visuals that even give the film's visceral splashes of eroticism and violence an intoxicating beauty. SF Korean, English +subtitles. Violence, swearing, sex scenes, nudity. DVD

Song Kang-ho *Sang-hyun* • Kim Ok-vin *Tae-ju* • Kim Hae-sook *Madame Ra* • Shin Ha-gyun *Kang-woo* • Park In-hwan *Old priest* • Song Young-chang *Seung-dae* ■ *Dir* Park Chan-wook • *Scr* Park Chan-wook, Chung Seo-kyung, from the novel *Thérèse Raquin* by Emile Zola

Thirteen ★★★ 18

Drama
2003 · US/UK · Colour · 95min

Based on the adolescent experiences of 13-year-old Nikki Reed (who co-scripted and plays the vivacious "It Girl" Evie), this emotionally intense drama stars Evan Rachel Wood as a model daughter who goes off the rails. Director Catherine Hardwicke's spiky character study has low-budget, hand-held panache. Yet its spark comes principally from the bewitching young leads and a powerhouse turn from Holly Hunter as Wood's single mother. To its detriment, the film at times seems to be deliberately courting controversy and repetition creeps into the confrontation-heavy second half. JC Violence, swearing, a sex scene, drug abuse. DVD

Holly Hunter *Melanie* • Evan Rachel Wood *Tracy* • Nikki Reed *Evie* • Jeremy Sisto *Brady* • Brady Corbet *Mason* • Deborah Kara Unger *Brooke* • Kip Pardue *Luke* • Sarah Clarke *Birdie* • DW Moffett *Travis* ■ *Dir* Catherine Hardwicke • *Scr* Catherine Hardwicke, Nikki Reed

13 ★★ 15

Thriller
2010 · US · Colour · 86min

Even though Georgian film-maker Gela Babluani helms this US remake of his cult hit *13 Tzameti*, something has been lost in translation. The premise is still pretty mind-blowing: desperate for money, electrician Sam Riley steals an envelope containing a mysterious invitation that could earn him loads of cash, only to find himself entered into an underground Russian Roulette game. Babluani once again ratchets up the tension during the chilling roulette sequences, but the dull subplots means the story flags badly. JF Violence, swearing, drug abuse. DVD

Jason Statham *Jasper* • Alexander Skarsgård *Jack* • Mickey Rourke *Jefferson* • Ray Winstone *Ronald Lynn* • Sam Riley *Vince* • Michael Shannon *Henry* ■ *Dir* Gela Babluani • *Scr* Gela Babluani, Gregory Pruss, from the 2005 film

13 Assassins ★★★★ 15

Period martial arts adventure
2010 · Jpn/UK · Colour · 120min

There's a whiff of the classic *Seven Samurai* about this excellent re-imagining of a little-seen 1960s Japanese action film. But, in the hands of cult director Takashi Miike, maker of the horror film *Audition*, this remake transcends its humble origins to become a minor masterpiece. Koji Yakusho stars as the respected samurai who is charged with assembling a team of assassins to kill a brutal lord (Goro Inagaki) whose ascendancy would spell disaster for a peaceful Japan. The controlled set-up gives way to a terrific climax that's sheer martial artistry in all its mud-splattered glory. DA

Japanese +subtitles. Violence, nudity. DVD Blu

Koji Yakusho *Shinzaemon Shimada* • Takayuki Yamada *Shinrokuro* • Yusuke Iseya *Koyata* • Goro Inagaki *Lord Naritsugu Matsudaira* • Masachika Ichimura *Hanbei Kitou* • Mikijiro Hira *Sir Doi* ■ *Dir* Takashi Miike • *Scr* Daisuke Tengan, from the 1963 film *Jûsan-nin no shikaku* by Shoichirou Ikemiya [Kaneo Ikegami]

Thirteen at Dinner ★★★ U

Murder mystery
1985 · US · Colour · 90min

Peter Ustinov gives another performance as Hercule Poirot, troubled by the murder of a peer. It's glossy, efficient entertainment, with a highly contrived dénouement, but Ustinov is fine and Faye Dunaway holds back nothing as the widow who's prime suspect. DP

Peter Ustinov *Hercule Poirot* • Faye Dunaway *Jane Wilkinson/Carlotta Adams* • David Suchet *Inspector Japp* • Jonathan Cecil *Arthur Hastings* • Bill Nighy *Ronald Marsh* • Diane Keen *Jenny Driver* • John Stride *Film director* • Benedict Taylor *Donald Ross* ■ *Dir* Lou Antonio • *Scr* Rod Browning, from the novel *Lord Edgware Dies* by Agatha Christie

Thirteen Conversations about One Thing ★★★ 15

Drama
2001 · US · Colour · 99min

The lives of disparate New Yorkers intertwine to poignant effect in this gentle, low-budget drama. Loosely themed around the topic of happiness, the unhurried film is composed of a series of dialogue-driven vignettes about four key characters linked together by fate. Matthew McConaughey and Alan Arkin elicit deep empathy in their respective roles as a cocksure attorney who falls foul of the law and a bitter office middleman. Less successful are the strands concerning cleaner Clea DuVall and physics professor John Turturro. Yet, though these weaker segments drag slightly, the mostly well-written script and subtle acting shine through. SF Swearing. DVD

Matthew McConaughey *Troy* • John Turturro *Walker* • Alan Arkin *Gene* • Clea DuVall *Beatrice* • Amy Irving *Patricia* • Barbara Sukowa *Helen* • Tia Texada *Dorrie* • Frankie Faison *Dick Lacey* • Shawn Elliott *Mickey Wheeler* • William Wise *Wade Bowman* ■ *Dir* Jill Sprecher • *Scr* Karen Sprecher, Jill Sprecher

Thirteen Days ★★★★ 12

Historical drama
2000 · US · Colour · 139min

The Cuban Missile Crisis – a key event in the Kennedy presidency – is brought to life in this fascinating drama starring Kevin Costner and directed by Roger Donaldson. In October 1962, President John F Kennedy (a mesmerising performance by Canadian actor Bruce Greenwood) was faced with the prospect of a nuclear showdown, following the discovery of Soviet missile bases in Cuba. Costner is superb as Kenny O'Donnell, a real-life adviser to the President. Part history lesson and part political drama, Donaldson's film is gripping and powerful, despite the essentially static nature of the story. JB Swearing. DVD

Kevin Costner *Kenny O'Donnell* • Bruce Greenwood *John F Kennedy* • Steven Culp *Robert F Kennedy* • Dylan Baker *Robert McNamara* • Michael Fairman *Adlai Stevenson* • Henry Strozier *Dean Rusk* • Frank Wood *McGeorge Bundy* • Len Cariou *Dean Acheson* ■ *Dir* Roger Donaldson • *Scr* David Self, from the book *The Kennedy Tapes – Inside the White House During the Cuban Missile Crisis* by Ernest R May, Philip D Zelikow

13 Ghosts ★★★ PG

Horror
1959 · US · Colour and BW · 78min

Forget the soulless 2001 remake and stick with gimmick king William Castle's campy and still spookily entertaining original. Donald Woods inherits a haunted mansion from an eccentric uncle under strict instructions from his last will to move his family in. Unaware that a vast fortune lies hidden in the house, the family is terrified they will soon join the poltergeist inmates, especially when somebody else is out to kill them and get the treasure. Originally filmed in Illusion-O, a 3D variant allowing the viewer to see the ghosts (or not depending

on their nervousness), Castle's juvenile shocker is one of his most endearing romps. AJ

Charles Herbert *Buck Zorba* • Jo Morrow *Medea Zorba* • Martin Milner *Ben Rush* • Rosemary DeCamp *Hilda Zorba* • Donald Woods *Cyrus Zorba* • Margaret Hamilton *Elaine Zacharides* ■ *Dir* William Castle • *Scr* Robb White

Thir13en Ghosts ★★ 15

Horror thriller
2001 · US · Colour · 87min

All fabulous production design and nothing else, this fails to capture the frightening fun of William Castle's 1959 original. Recently widowed Tony Shalhoub inherits the spectacular house of his late uncle F Murray Abraham, and learns that the 12 ghosts of the Black Zodiac are imprisoned there as part of uncle's plan to unlock the gateway to hell. Saddled with predictable twists and a plodding pace, this is just another dreaded remake. AJ Violence, swearing, nudity. DVD Blu

Tony Shalhoub *Arthur Kriticos* • Embeth Davidtz *Kalina* • Matthew Lillard *Dennis Rafkin* • Shannon Elizabeth *Kathy Kriticos* • Alec Roberts *Bobby Kriticos* • JR Bourne *Ben Moss* • F Murray Abraham *Cyrus Kriticos* ■ *Dir* Steve Beck • *Scr* Neal Marshall Stevens [Neal Stevens], Richard D'Ovidio, from a story by Robb White

13 Going on 30 ★★★ 12

Romantic comedy fantasy
2004 · US · Colour · 93min

Cute and frothy, this body-swap comedy is an ultra-girlie, wish-fulfilment fantasy that plays like a teen magazine come to life. In it, a nerdy 13-year-old girl's dreams become reality when she's miraculously transformed into gorgeous and successful 30-year-old Jennifer Garner. Though the events that follow are unrealistic fancy, Garner's delightful and authentic turn helps paper over many of the plot holes. Her adolescent take on the adult world is completely charming, infusing the film with a scatty innocence. SF Sexual references. DVD

Jennifer Garner *Jenna Rink* • Mark Ruffalo *Matt Flamhaff* • Judy Greer *Lucy Wyman* • Andy Serkis *Richard Kneeland* • Kathy Baker *Bev Rink* • Phil Reeves *Wayne Rink* • Samuel Ball *Alex Carlson* ■ *Dir* Gary Winick • *Scr* Josh Goldsmith, Cathy Yuspa

13 Hours: the Secret Soldiers of Benghazi ★★★ 15

Action thriller based on a true story
2016 · US · Colour · 144min

Michael Bay calls his blow-by-blow procedural detailing the 2012 terror attack on a US compound in Libya his "most real movie". But it has more in common with the jingoism of *Rambo* than the sobering analysis of something like *Black Hawk Down*. Bay treats the adaptation of Mitchell Zuckoff's politically divisive book in simplistic terms: it's basically *The Alamo*, only in Benghazi. As a tribute to heroic courage, this works best when being visually dynamic and brutally immersive in its sensational combat sequences – it's certainly hard to ignore. AJ Violence, swearing.

John Krasinski *Jack Da Silva* • James Badge Dale *Tyrone "Rone" Woods* • Pablo Schreiber *Kris "Tanto" Paronto* • David Denman *Dave "Boon" Benton* • Dominic Fumusa *John "Tig" Tiegen* • Toby Stephens *Glen "Bub" Doherty* ■ *Dir* Michael Bay • *Scr* Chuck Hogan, from the non-fiction book *13 Hours: the Inside Account of What Really Happened in Benghazi* by Mitchell Zuckoff

13 Minutes ★★★ 15

Wartime drama
2015 · Ger · Colour · 114min

Although director Oliver Hirschbiegel made the superb *Downfall*, this is a disappointingly superficial account of Georg Elser's attempt to blow up Hitler in Munich in November 1939. The production values are impeccable and Christian Friedel bears a resemblance to the 36-year-old carpenter, who was pitilessly tortured by the Gestapo. But a hallucinatory truth-serum sequence feels as much a miscalculation as not dwelling in depth on the practical

preparations for the attack. This compelling moment in history really deserves a more insightful reconstruction. DP German +subtitles.

Christian Friedel *Georg Elser* • Katharina Schüttler *Elsa* • Burghart Klaussner *Nebe* • Johann von Bülow *Heinrich Müller* • Felix Eitner *Eberle* ■ *Dir* Oliver Hirschbiegel • *Scr* Léni-e-Claire Breinersdorfer, Fred Breinersdorfer

13 Rue Madeleine ★★ U

Second World War spy drama
1946 · US · BW · 95min

This is one of several documentary-style dramas, produced by Louis de Rochemont and adopting the stentorian style of the *March of Time* newsreels he co-created. A narrator intones, the images look snatched from real-life... and a Hollywood star gives the game away. In this case it's James Cagney, slightly miscast as an American agent training spies for service in occupied Europe. Directed by that notorious on-set bully Henry Hathaway, the picture was shot in New England and Quebec, which was, as far as Hollywood was concerned, halfway to France. AT DVD

James Cagney *Robert Sharkey* • Annabella *Suzanne de Beaumont* • Richard Conte *Bill O'Connell/Wilhelm Kuncel* • Frank Latimore *Jeff Lassiter* • Walter Abel *Charles Stevenson Gibson* • Melville Cooper *Pappy Simpson* • Sam Jaffe *Mayor Galimard* ■ *Dir* Henry Hathaway • *Scr* John Monks Jr, Sy Bartlett

13 Sins ★★★ 15

Horror thriller
2013 · US · Colour · 88min

Last Exorcism director Daniel Stamm remains in scary movie territory with this taut little chiller. Mark Webber is the good-natured loser who's cajoled into completing 13 tasks for ever-increasing reward by an unseen games-master. With a cast including *True Blood* regular Rutina Wesley and genre veterans Ron Perlman and Pruitt Taylor Vince, it's always morbidly enjoyable with plenty of gruesome twists and turns. JA Violence, swearing. DVD

Mark Webber *Elliot Brindle* • Devon Graye *Michael* • Ron Perlman *Chilcoat* ■ *Dir* Daniel Stamm • *Scr* Daniel Stamm, David Birke, from the film *13: Game of Death* by Chookiat Sakveerakul

13 (Tzameti) ★★★★ 15

Psychological thriller
2005 · Fr/Georgia · BW · 89min

There's a near-Hitchcock feel to the opening segment of Gela Babluani's feature debut, as immigrant Georges Babluani decides to pose as his deceased employer to fulfil a mysterious rendezvous. But the suspense of the journey through the French countryside suddenly gives way to the macabre realisation that the 20-something has volunteered himself for a Russian-roulette tournament. Solidly played and superbly photographed by Tariel Meliava in a steely monochrome that reinforces the action's chilling authenticity, this is teasing, stylish and shocking. DP French +subtitles. DVD

Georges Babluani *Sébastien* • Aurélien Recoing *Player 6* • Philippe Passon *Jean François Godon* • Pascal Bongard *Master of ceremonies* • Augustin Legrand *José* ■ *Dir/Scr* Gela Babluani

13 West Street ★★

Drama
1962 · US · BW · 79min

Alan Ladd makes his penultimate screen appearance in this early example of a *Death Wish* movie, a cynical attempt to tap into the burgeoning youth market. With a touch more thought, it could have offered an intriguing insight into the reasons why well-heeled kids become involved in violence just like their counterparts across the tracks. While Ladd conducts his vendetta against Michael Callan's gang with typically repressed rage, his performance lacks the conviction of Rod Steiger's as the cop who fails to bring the gang to book. DP

Alan Ladd *Walt Sherill* • Rod Steiger *Det Sgt Koleski* • Michael Callan *Chuck Landry* • Dolores Dorn *Tracey Sherill* • Kenneth MacKenna *Paul Logan* • Margaret Hayes *Mrs Landry* ■ *Dir* Philip Leacock • *Scr* Bernard Schoenfeld, Robert Presnell Jr, from the novel *The Tiger among Us* by Leigh Brackett

The Thirteenth Floor

★★★ 🅸🅵

Science-fiction mystery thriller
1999 · US · Colour · 96min

Computer technician Craig Bierko finds himself the main suspect when his boss – the mastermind behind a computer simulation of 1937 Los Angeles populated with programmed inhabitants who are oblivious to their actual origin – is found murdered. Though Bierko's subsequent investigation uncovers plenty of twists and turns, this unravels predictably but still retains interest. The computer simulation of the 1930s world perfectly re-creates the era, the performances are acceptable and the script is intelligent and plausible. KB Violence, swearing. 📀 🅱🅻

Craig Bierko *Douglas Hall* • Armin Mueller-Stahl *Hannon Fuller* • Gretchen Mol *Jane Fuller* • Vincent D'Onofrio *Whitney/Ashton* • Dennis Haysbert *Detective Larry McBain* • Steven Schub *Zev Bernstein* • Jeremy Roberts *Tom* ■ *Dir* Josef Rusnak • *Scr* Josef Rusnak, Ravel Centeno-Rodriguez, from the novel *Simulacron 3* by Daniel Galouye

The Thirteenth Guest

★★

Murder mystery comedy 1932 · US · BW · 69min

In this low-budget ensemble mystery story from the tiny Monogram studio, 13 guests – who were all present 13 years earlier at a dinner that saw the sudden death of their host – reassemble, and find themselves under collective threat from a mysterious, hooded killer. Ginger Rogers is the leading lady of this old-fashioned but quite entertaining comedy thriller. RK

Ginger Rogers *Marie Morgan/Lela* • Lyle Talbot *Phil Winston* • J Farrell MacDonald *Capt Ryan* • James C Eagles *Harold "Bud" Morgan* • Eddie Phillips *Thor Jensen* • Erville Alderson *John Adams* • Robert Klein *John Barksdale* • Crauford Kent *Dr Sherwood* ■ *Dir* Albert Ray • *Scr* Frances Hyland, Arthur Hoerl, Armitage Trail, from the novel by Armitage Trail

The 13th Letter

★★★

Film noir mystery drama
1950 · US · BW · 85min

Using a mixed French and American cast (along with Englishman Michael Rennie), producer/director Otto Preminger turned to Henri-George Clouzot's masterly French thriller, *The Raven*, for this tale about a series of poison-pen letters that cause havoc in a provincial French-Canadian town. Charles Boyer as a doctor, Constance Smith as his wife, Rennie – the object of Smith's unwelcome attentions – and Linda Darnell, as a woman whose beauty is marred by a club foot, all convince in the central roles. A little melodramatic, this is still suspenseful entertainment. RK

Linda Darnell *Denise* • Charles Boyer *Dr Laurent* • Michael Rennie *Dr Pearson* • Constance Smith *Cora Laurent* • Françoise Rosay *Mrs Sims* • Judith Evelyn *Sister Marie* • Guy Sorel *Robert Helier* ■ *Dir* Otto Preminger • *Scr* Howard Koch, from the story *Le Corbeau* by Louis Chavance

The 13th Warrior

★★★ 🅸🅵

Period action adventure
1999 · US · Colour · 98min

Director John McTiernan's old-fashioned horror adventure stars Antonio Banderas (looking decidedly uncomfortable) as a tenth-century Arab emissary abducted by Norsemen to fight the barbaric cannibals who are terrorising their countrymen. How Banderas adapts to a totally alien culture and uncovers the secrets of the feared "spirits in the mist" makes for a visually arresting, if half-baked, saga. The film is never boring, but it's not really that exciting either. Jerry Goldsmith's marvellously stirring soundtrack is a major plus, however. AJ Violence. 📀

Antonio Banderas *Ahmed Ibn Fahdlan* • Diane Venora *Queen Weilew* • Omar Sharif *Melchisidek* • Dennis Storhoi *Herger/Joyous* • Vladimir Kulich *Buliwyf* • Anders T Andersen *Wiglift, King's son* • Richard Bremmer *Skeld/Superstitious* • Tony Curran *Weath, musician* ■ *Dir* John McTiernan • *Scr* William Wisher, Warren Lewis, from the novel *Eaters of the Dead* by Michael Crichton

-30-

★★★ 🆄

Drama 1959 · US · BW · 96min

Jack Webb brought the deadpan *Dragnet* style to a select number of cinema features as producer, director and star. This one provides a documentary-like treatment of the few hours before a Los Angeles newspaper reaches its deadline. (The American title refers to the traditional sign for the end of a reporter's copy – in Britain, the film was retitled *Deadline Midnight*.) A story is breaking: a three-year-old girl and her dog have disappeared. It turns out she is lost down a storm drain and a massive search is launched. Night editor Webb and a cast of little-known actors bring the characters to life. AE

Jack Webb *Sam Gatlin* • William Conrad *Jim Bathgate* • David Nelson (1) *Earl Collins* • Whitney Blake *Peggy Gatlin* • Louise Lorimer *Bernice Valentine* • James Bell *Ben Quinn* • Nancy Valentine *Jan Price* ■ *Dir* Jack Webb • *Scr* William Bowers

Thirty-Day Princess ★★★

Romantic comedy 1934 · US · BW · 73min

Sylvia Sidney stars in a dual role here. She's a foreign princess, in New York for a series of public appearances to raise money, and a down-on-her-luck actress and lookalike, hired to impersonate the royal visitor when the latter gets mumps. Cary Grant is an upper-crust newspaper publisher and the romantic interest, Edward Arnold the banker behind the deception. This small-scale romantic comedy overcomes its well-worn plot, thanks to the performances, the Paramount house-style and a charming script. RK

Sylvia Sidney *Nancy Lane/Princess "Zizzi" Catterina* • Cary Grant *Porter Madison III* • Edward Arnold *Richard Gresham* • Henry Stephenson *King Anatole XII* ■ *Dir* Marion Gering • *Scr* Sam Hellman, Edwin Justus Mayer, Preston Sturges, Frank Partos, from the story by Clarence Budington Kelland

30 Days of Night ★★★ 🅸🆈

Horror thriller 2007 · NZ/US · Colour · 108min

The Alaskan town of Barrow spends 30 days each year cut off from the outside world in polar winter darkness, which makes it ideal territory for feral bloodsuckers looking for an uninterrupted buffet of human flesh. After the initial invasion, survivors led by sheriff Josh Hartnett attempt to wait out the interminable month without attracting the attention of the screeching fiends. Director David Slade's solid – and gory – adaptation of the cult graphic novel is a variation on the classic siege-by-monsters scenario with snowy landscapes adding to the chill of the slow-building tale and Danny Huston's speaking-in-tongues pack leader grabbing the most attention. AJ 📀 🅱🅻

Josh Hartnett *Eben Oleson* • Melissa George *Stella Oleson* • Danny Huston *Marlow* • Ben Foster *The Stranger* • Mark Boone Junior *Beau Brower* • Mark Rendall *Jake Oleson* ■ *Dir* David Slade • *Scr* Steve Niles, Stuart Beattie, Brian Nelson, from the comic book by Niles, Ben Templesmith

35 Shots of Rum ★★★★ 🅸🅴

Drama 2008 · Fr/Ger · Colour · 96min

Writer/director Claire Denis draws on her own family history to depict the relationship between widowed Parisian train driver Lionel (Alex Descas) and his student daughter Joséphine (Mati Diop) in this drama that's also suffused with the spirit of Japanese maestro Yasujiro Ozu. The performances are taciturnly authentic, but it's Denis's use of cinematographer Agnès Godard's meticulously composed imagery that leaves the deepest impression. Whether watching trains snaking through the Paris suburbs or lingering on slow dancers in a cosy bar, Denis is more interested in the trust, understanding and love that exists between her characters than any domestic melodrama, and her discretion makes this movie unforgettable. DP French, German +subtitles. Some swearing. 📀

Alex Descas *Lionel* • Mati Diop *Joséphine* • Nicole Dogue *Gabrielle* • Grégoire Colin *Noé* • Ingrid Caven *The Aunt* • Jean-Pol Fargeau • *Cinematographer* Agnès Godard

30 Is a Dangerous Age, Cynthia

★★★ 🆄

Romantic comedy 1968 · US · Colour · 85min

This is one of those 1960s oddities, with everyone rushing around being breezily neurotic as nightclub musician Dudley Moore panics at the thought of imminently turning 30. Moore basically plays himself, even fronting his real-life jazz trio, and it works enjoyably enough, with Suzy Kendall suitably kooky and charming as the girl he chases. Not a movie that has aged with any dignity, but there are considerably worse examples of "swinging" celluloid than this. SH

Dudley Moore *Rupert Street* • Eddie Foy Jr *Oscar* • Suzy Kendall *Louise Hammond* • John Bird *Herbert Greenslade* • Duncan Macrae *Jock McCue* • Patricia Routledge *Mrs Woolley* • Peter Bayliss *Victor* • John Wells *Hon Gavin Hopton* ■ *Dir* Joseph McGrath • *Scr* Dudley Moore, Joseph McGrath, John Wells

30 Minutes or Less ★★★ 🅸🅵

Crime action comedy
2011 · US/Can /Ger · Colour · 79min

This knockabout action comedy features Jesse Eisenberg (*The Social Network*) as Nick, a slacker pizza delivery boy kidnapped by small-time hoodlums Dwayne (Danny McBride) and Travis Nick Swardson who then force him to rob a bank – with an explosive vest strapped to his torso. The bungling criminals scenario has been done better many times before, although director Ruben Fleischer makes his protagonists fairly likeable, if a little annoying at times, and the script adds some inventive and near-the-knuckle wit to the slapstick set pieces. TeS Swearing, nudity. 📀 🅱🅻

Jesse Eisenberg *Nick* • Danny McBride (2) *Dwayne* • Aziz Ansari *Chet* • Nick Swardson *Travis* • Michael Peña [Michael Pena] *Chango* • Fred Ward *The Major* ■ *Dir* Ruben Fleischer • *Scr* Michael Diliberti, from a story by Diliberti, Matthew Sullivan

The 39 Steps

★★★★★ 🆄

Classic spy thriller 1935 · UK · BW · 83min

Alfred Hitchcock brings John Buchan's novel to the screen with characteristic wit and verve, a style he forged in 1930s Britain with this, *The Man Who Knew Too Much* and *The Lady Vanishes*. *The 39 Steps* has all the ingredients of classic Hitch, not least the innocent-man-on-the-run plot, a staple all the way through to 1959's *North by Northwest*. In this case, it's visiting Canadian Richard Hannay (a winning Robert Donat), who gets dragged into an espionage conspiracy after an outing to a London music hall and ends up in Scotland handcuffed to an icy blonde (Madeleine Carroll). Playing "spot the recurring Hitchcock motif" is almost as thrilling as the chase itself and the chemistry between Donat and Carroll is a rare treat – particularly when they are forced to share a room (quite shocking in 1935). AC 📀 🅱🅻

Robert Donat *Richard Hannay* • Madeleine Carroll *Pamela* • Lucie Mannheim *Miss Smith* • Godfrey Tearle *Professor Jordan* • Peggy Ashcroft *Crofter's wife* • John Laurie *Crofter* • Helen Haye *Mrs Jordan* • Frank Cellier *Sheriff Watson* • Wylie Watson *Memory* ■ *Dir* Alfred Hitchcock • *Scr* Charles Bennett, Alma Reville, Ian Hay, from the novel by John Buchan

The Thirty-Nine Steps

★★ 🆄

Spy thriller 1959 · UK · Colour · 91min

Alfred Hitchcock cast a long and large shadow, leaving many a director in debt to a master film-maker. But this remake of his 1935 classic thriller is totally overwhelmed by the original. Kenneth More battles bravely to take on the role of Richard Hannay that Robert Donat made so very suavely his own, but succumbs to a bout of overplayed bravado. TH 📀

Kenneth More *Richard Hannay* • Taina Elg *Fisher* • Brenda de Banzie *Nellie Lumsden* • Barry Jones *Professor Logan* • Reginald Beckwith *Lumsden* • Faith Brook *Nannie* • Michael Goodliffe *Brown* • James Hayter *Mr Memory* ■ *Dir* Ralph Thomas, from the novel by John Buchan

The Thirty-Nine Steps

★★★ 🅿🅶

Period spy thriller 1978 · UK · Colour · 98min

The third film of John Buchan's novel goes back to the story's original era (the eve of the First World War), but lays on a little too much period colour along the way. Robert Powell has the bearing but not the charm as hero Richard Hannay, on the run in the Scottish Highlands from foreign agents. The sinister mystery at the beginning and the famous climax are good, exciting fun in the best daredevil tradition. DM 📀

Robert Powell *Richard Hannay* • David Warner *Appleton* • Eric Porter *Chief Supt Lomas* • Karen Dotrice *Alex Mackenzie* • John Mills *Scudder* • George Baker *Sir Walter Bullivant* • Ronald Pickup *Bayliss* • Donald Pickering *Marshall* • Timothy West *Porton* ■ *Dir* Don Sharp • *Scr* Michael Robson, from the novel by John Buchan

31 North 62 East

★ 🅸🅵

Political thriller 2009 · UK · Colour · 121min

The spin doctors from BBC sitcom *The Thick of It* could probably hatch a more credible story than this one from writer/director Tristan Loraine. It's woefully ill-judged from the start, when John Rhys-Davies blunders cartoonishly onto the scene as the British Prime Minister and negotiates an arms deal with a sinister sheik. In exchange for the contract, he divulges the co-ordinates of an elite SAS unit as casually as if he were ordering takeaway food. Revealing the conspiracy in the introduction means the only real mystery is how this film got made, and you'll want this pain to end long before the last ludicrous twist. SP Violence, swearing. 📀

John Rhys-Davies *John Hammond* • Marina Sirtis *Sarah Webber* • Heather Peace *Jill Mandelson/Kimberley Mandelson* • Craig Fairbrass *Major Paul Davidson* • George Calil *Jacob* • Nathalia Ramos *Rachel* • Kammy Darweish *Sheik Kaseem* • Ian Lavender *John Mandelson* ■ *Dir* Tristan Loraine • *Scr* Tristan & Leofwine Loraine

Thirty Seconds over Tokyo

★★★ 🆄

Second World War drama
1944 · US · BW · 132min

This overlong but impressively-staged war drama depicts America's first secret bombing raid over Tokyo, just four months after Pearl Harbor. Apart from the inevitable "woman's angle" – scenes with Van Johnson's wife back home – the first part of the film concentrates on military planning, led by Spencer Tracy as the real-life Lt Col James Doolittle. The script, by future blacklistee Dalton Trumbo, is full of heroic speeches, and the special effects won an Oscar. AT

Spencer Tracy *Lt Col James H Doolittle* • Van Johnson *Capt Ted W Lawson* • Robert Walker *David Thatcher* • Phyllis Thaxter *Ellen Jones Lawson* • Tim Murdock *Dean Davenport* • Scott McKay *Davey Jones* • Robert Mitchum *Bob Gray* ■ *Dir* Mervyn LeRoy • *Scr* Dalton Trumbo, from the novel by Capt Ted W Lawson, Robert Considine

36 Chowringhee Lane

★★★ 🅿🅶

Drama 1982 · Ind · Colour · 107min

Produced by Bollywood superstar Shashi Kapoor, Aparna Sen's directorial debut has the chintzy feel of an early Merchant Ivory picture. Yet it also contains several elements that go against the general atmosphere of post-colonial purdah and regret, notably a surreal dream sequence and some extravagant editing. Jennifer Kendal is magnificent as the 60-something teacher who seizes upon the presence of writer Dhritiman Chatterjee and his lover, Debashree Roy, in her Calcutta apartment as a release from a life tinged with sadness and disappointment. Melancholic, melodramatic and affecting. DP **DVD**

Jennifer Kendal *Miss Violet Stoneham* • Dhritiman Chatterjee *Samaresh Moitra* • Geoffrey Kendal *Eddie Stoneham* ■ *Dir/Scr* Aparna Sen

36 Hours ★★★★
Second World War spy thriller
1964 · US · BW · 114min

An American intelligence officer is kidnapped by Nazi agents who want him to reveal the D-Day invasion plans in this ingeniously scripted film that was a substantial hit in the UK. It's often remembered more for its plot than its title – there can't be many movie buffs around who haven't been asked: "What was the name of that film where James Garner is captured by the Germans and told that he's spent the last six years in an amnesiac state?" Well, it's this one, in all its black-and-white splendour, with a Rod Taylor as a Nazi major. TS

James Garner *Major Jefferson Pike* • Rod Taylor *Major Walter Gerber* • Eva Marie Saint *Anna Hedler* • Werner Peters *Otto Schack* • Alan Napier *Colonel Peter MacLean* • Celia Lovsky *Elsa* ■ *Dir* George Seaton • *Scr* George Seaton, from a story by Carl K Hittleman, Luis H Vance and the story *Beware of the Dog* by Roald Dahl in *Harper's*

36 Hours to Die ★★ 18
Crime thriller 1999 · US/Can · Colour · 90min

Recuperating from a heart attack, brewery owner Treat Williams learns that his brother has managed to embroil them in a deadly, Mob-run extortion scheme. His family and business are suddenly threatened, and he finds he has only 36 hours to fend off the gangsters. While the ending of this TV movie is never much in doubt, the script by Robert Rodat contains enough twists and idiosyncrasies to make it seem fresh. MC **DVD**

Treat Williams *Noah Stone* • Kim Cattrall *Kim Stone* • Saul Rubinek *Morano* • Carroll O'Connor *Uncle Jack O'Malley* • Alain Goulem *Frank Stone* • Barbara Eve Harris *Barbara Woods* • Stewart Bick *Sam* ■ *Dir* Yves Simoneau • *Scr* Robert Rodat

The 36th Chamber of Shaolin ★★★ 18
Martial arts action adventure
1978 · HK · Colour · 88min

Despite its relative lack of star power and modest budget, this Shaw Brothers kung fu movie was acclaimed in its day and is regarded as a landmark of the genre. Gordon Liu (credited here as Liu Chia-hui) plays a fugitive from Manchu forces who smuggles himself into the Shaolin temple to learn how to fight in order to avenge the deaths of his family and friends. Liu's dedication wins the respect of the monk elders as he works his way though various chambers that test mind, body and fighting skills. It's these inventive labours that lift what is an otherwise formulaic revenge picture into something a little more memorable. JH Cantonese dubbed.

Liu Chia-hui [Gordon Liu] *Liu Yu-te* • Lo Lieh *General Tien* • Yu Wang [Yue Wong] ■ *Dir* Lau Kar-leung • *Scr* I Kuang [Ni Kuang]

The 33 ★★★ 12A
Disaster drama based on a true story
2014 · US/Chil · Colour · 126min

A dramatisation of the 69-day operation to rescue 33 Chilean miners trapped in a collapsed mine, this uplifting true story should have been box-office gold. Antonio Banderas, Lou Diamond Phillips, Juliette Binoche and Gabriel Byrne are among the starry cast, though the people they play are roughly drawn and director Patricia Riggen doesn't quite achieve that air of uncertainty needed to convey the drama of this well-publicised disaster (as Ron Howard did in *Apollo 13*). So in the end *The 33* only grabs on a superficial level. SP In English, Spanish. Some swearing **DVD** **Blu-ray**

Antonio Banderas *Mario Sepulveda* • Rodrigo Santoro *Laurence Golborne* • Juliette Binoche *Maria Segovia* • James Brolin *Jeff Hart* • Gabriel Byrne *Andre Sougarret* ■ *Dir* Patricia Riggen •

Scr Mikko Alanne, Craig Borten, Michael Thomas, from a story by José Rivera, from the non-fiction book *Deep Down Dark* by Hector Tobar • *Music* James Horner

Thirty Two Short Films about Glenn Gould ★★★★★ U
Biographical drama 1993 · Can · Colour · 93min

It's too close to say which is the better pianist biopic: this exceptional Canadian film inspired by Bach's *Goldberg Variations* or *Shine*, Scott Hicks's outstanding feature on the life of Australian David Helfgott. The key to François Girard's picture is that he leaves Gould an enigma, allowing us to draw our own conclusions from the 32 vignettes that range from childhood to his sudden decision to quit the concert hall and concentrate on recording. Colm Feore's performance is remarkable, while Girard's use of sound is as masterly as his visual ingenuity and his sense that the minor episode is often as revealing as a major turning point. DP English, French +subtitles.

Colm Feore *Glenn Gould* • Derek Keurvorst *Gould's father* • Katya Ladan *Gould's mother* • Devon Anderson *Glenn aged 3* • Joshua Greenblatt *Glenn aged 8* • Sean Ryan *Glenn aged 12* • Kate Hennig *Chambermaid* ■ *Dir* François Girard • *Scr* François Girard, Don McKellar, Nick McKinney

This above All ★★★
Second World War drama
1942 · US · BW · 109min

This soapy wartime drama, produced by 20th Century-Fox with all the patriotic stops out, stars Tyrone Power as an unlikely working-class British soldier, who romances upper-class WAAF Joan Fontaine while struggling with pacifist urges. There's a marvellous supporting cast of British expats, and director Anatole Litvak does so well by RC Sherriff's script that even the most cynical might be reaching for the tissues. TS

Tyrone Power *Clive Briggs* • Joan Fontaine *Prudence Cathaway* • Thomas Mitchell *Monty* • Henry Stephenson *General Cathaway* • Nigel Bruce *Ramsbottom* • Gladys Cooper *Iris* • Philip Merivale *Dr Roger Cathaway* • Alexander Knox *Rector* ■ *Dir* Anatole Litvak • *Scr* RC Sherriff, from the novel by Eric Knight

This Ain't California ★★★ 15
Drama documentary
2012 · Ger · Colour and BW · 100min

The underground skateboard scene in 1980s East Germany provides the focus for this look at a society unwittingly nearing the end of its existence. Billed as a documentary about a bunch of 30-somethings reassembling to mourn the death of their charismatic leader, Marten Persiel's artfully assembled film actually plays fast and loose. It mixes actors with "real" people and animated sequences with news archive, into which is interspersed lots of questionably original footage of their youthful high jinks. That's not to say Persiel's points about a culture blind to the writing on the Berlin Wall aren't valid, nor that his film isn't fresh, energetic and full of nostalgia for lost youth. SvM German +subtitles. Nudity, drug abuse.

Kai Hillebrand *Denis "Panik" Paraceck* • David Nathan *Nico* ■ *Dir* Marten Persiel • *Scr* Martin Persiel, Ira Wedel

This Angry Age ★★★
Drama 1957 · It/US · Colour · 111min

Shot by French director René Clement on an island off Thailand with a cast that included Italians Silvana Mangano and Alida Valli and Americans Jo Van Fleet and Anthony Perkins playing French colonials in Indochina, the film sufferes from its hybrid parentage and over-melodramatic moments. But it caught the rich hues of the tropics in Technirama, and is an absorbing enough study of a colonial family. RB

Anthony Perkins *Joseph Dufresne* • Silvana Mangano *Suzanne Dufresne* • Richard Conte *Michael* • Jo Van Fleet *Madame Dufresne* • Nehemiah Persoff *Albert* • Alida Valli *Claude* ■

Dir René Clément • *Scr* Irwin Shaw, Rene Clement, from the novel *Un Barrage contre le Pacifique (Sea Wall)* by Marguerite Duras

This Boy's Life ★★★★ 15
Biographical drama 1993 · US · Colour · 110min

Anyone who doubts Leonardo DiCaprio's acting abilities should check out this moving coming-of-age drama. In this troubling tale set in Seattle in the 1950s, he plays the rebellious teenage son of struggling mum Ellen Barkin who finds himself locked in a battle of wills with bullying stepfather Robert De Niro. After the lightweight antics of his first American movie, *Doc Hollywood*, British director Michael Caton-Jones relishes the opportunity to try out meatier material and makes the most of Robert Getchell's largely unsentimental adaptation of Tobias Wolff's acclaimed autobiography. JF Violence, swearing, sex scenes. **DVD**

Robert De Niro *Dwight Hansen* • Ellen Barkin *Caroline Wolff* • Leonardo DiCaprio *Toby* • Jonah Blechman *Arthur Gayle* • Eliza Dushku *Pearl* • Chris Cooper *Roy* • Carla Gugino *Norma* • Tobey Maguire *Chuck Bolger* ■ *Dir* Michael Caton-Jones • *Scr* Robert Getchell, from the autobiography by Tobias Wolff

This Christmas ★★★ 12
Seasonal comedy drama
2007 · US · Colour · 113min

Christmas with the Whitfield family is eventful: matriarch Ma'Dere (Loretta Devine) is cooking, daughter Lisa (Regina King) is about to discover her husband's extramarital activities, deadbeat son Quentin (Idris Elba) is being chased by loan sharks, Claude (Columbus Short) is AWOL from the marines and Kelli (Sharon Leal) has just fallen for a fireman (*ER's* Mekhi Phifer). This saccharine holiday movie delivers plenty of cheer as it zips through its soap-opera plotting with a dash of wit and plenty of enthusiastic performances from its African-American cast. As the family elders, Loretta Devine and the stately Delroy Lindo add a touch of gravitas to the proceedings. With so many storylines and characters, the film inevitably overstays its welcome, but only a Scrooge could fail to be warmed by the seasonal goodwill. JR Violence, sexual references. **DVD**

Delroy Lindo *Joseph Black* • Idris Elba *Quentin Whitfield* • Loretta Devine *Ma'Dere* • Chris Brown *Michael "Baby" Whitfield* • Laz Alonso *Malcom Moore* • Columbus Short *Claude Whitfield* • Sharon Leal *Kelli Whitfield* • Lauren London *Mel Whitfield* • Mekhi Phifer *Gerald* • Regina King *Lisa Moore* ■ *Dir/Scr* Preston A Whitmore II

This Could Be the Night ★★★ U
Romantic comedy 1957 · US · BW · 104min

Virginal New England college graduate Jean Simmons takes a night job as secretary to a Manhattan club owner with underworld connections (Paul Douglas). She clashes with his aggressive partner Anthony Franciosa and affects the lives of everybody connected with the establishment. Simmons is excellent and Douglas is terrific as the gentlemanly rough diamond who takes her to his heart. A lively case of wishful thinking. RK

Jean Simmons *Anne Leeds* • Paul Douglas *Rocco* • Anthony Franciosa *Tony Armotti* • Julie Wilson *Ivy Corlane* • Neile Adams *Patsy St Clair* • Joan Blondell *Crystal St Clair* ■ *Dir* Robert Wise • *Scr* Isobel Lennart, from stories by Cordelia Baird Gross

This Day and Age ★
Crime drama 1933 · US · BW · 82min

Cecil B DeMille offers an extreme right-wing solution to the problem of the American gangster. When the law can't convict a known killer (Charles Bickford), a group of decent high school kids, led by Richard Cromwell, steps in to kidnap him and extract a confession by dangling him over a pitful of rats. The gangster is so broken by the experience that he signs a confession before the authorities. A hysterical and dangerous film. AE

Charles Bickford *Louis Garrett* • Richard Cromwell *Steve Smith* • Judith Allen *Gay Merrick* • Harry Green *Herman* • Bradley Page *Toledo* • Eddie Nugent [Edward Nugent] *Don Merrick* ■ *Dir* Cecil B DeMille • *Scr* Bartlett Cormack

This Earth Is Mine ★★★
Drama 1959 · US · Colour · 123min

A melodrama on an epic scale, this enjoyable tosh provides ideal, undemanding matinée fare. Rock Hudson and Jean Simmons barely flex their acting muscles but look superb. The real acting comes from Dorothy McGuire and Claude Rains, who virtually steal this Prohibition-era saga of uproar in the Napa Valley vineyards from their co-stars. Although his eye for landscape never falters, director Henry King has problems pulling together the sprawling script. TS

Rock Hudson *John Rambeau* • Jean Simmons *Elizabeth* • Dorothy McGuire *Martha* • Claude Rains *Philippe Rambeau* • Kent Smith *Francis Fairon* ■ *Dir* Henry King • *Scr* Casey Robinson, from the novel *The Cup and the Sword* by Alice Tisdale Hobart

This Film Is Not Yet Rated ★★★★ 18
Documentary 2006 · US · Colour · 100min

A fascinatingly acerbic documentary that lays charges of protectionism and moral hypocrisy at the door of the Motion Picture Association of America – the body that dictates through certification what Americans can and can't see on their cinema screens. Director Kirby Dick allows himself to be sidetracked by his bid to unmask the members of this secretive cabal, when the real issue is artists' freedom being curtailed for commercial as much as ethical reasons. However, with some splendidly arch graphics and contributions from the likes of John Waters, Atom Egoyan and Kimberly Peirce (*Boys Don't Cry*) that range from the funny to the furious, this is a heroic bid by the independent sector against the major studios and the big business that controls them. DP Sex scenes. **DVD**

Kirby Dick • Allison Anders • Darren Aronofsky • Atom Egoyan • Kimberly Peirce • Kevin Smith (2) • Kevin Smith • Matt Stone • John Waters (2) *John Waters* ■ *Dir* Kirby Dick • *Scr* Kirby Dick, Eddie Schmidt, Matt Patterson

This Filthy Earth ★★ 15
Drama 2001 · UK · Colour · 106min

As a celebration of the soil, Andrew Kötting's highly individual adaptation of Emile Zola's novel is a laudable attempt at capturing the essence of its literary source. But the combination of naturalism and stylisation that so effectively informs the visuals proves the undoing of this film as a drama. Set in a remote rural community, it's a stormy tale of two sisters working the family farm until their relationships with men threaten to destroy their livelihood. Much of the dialogue is so fruity that experienced actors and non-professionals alike are lured into overplaying the already fraught situations. DP

Rebecca Palmer *Francine* • Shane Attwooll *Buto* • Demelza Randall *Kath* • Xavier Tchili *Lek* • Dudley Sutton *Papa* ■ *Dir* Andrew Kötting • *Scr* Andrew Kötting, Sean Lock, from the novel *La Terre* by Emile Zola

This Gun for Hire ★★★ PG
Crime drama 1942 · US · BW · 77min

This is a tale involving ruthless fifth columnists, the cold-blooded hitman they hire and then try to dispose of, and the cabaret entertainer who gets caught up in the ensuing mess. The movie rocketed the unknown Alan Ladd to stardom on the strength of his performance as the loner killer. It also began his popular teaming with Veronica Lake, whose combination of blonde cool and touching vulnerability clicked into box-office chemistry with the laconic and charismatic actor. RK **DVD**

Veronica Lake *Ellen Graham* • Robert Preston *Michael Crane* • Laird Cregar *Willard Gates* • Alan Ladd *Philip Raven* • Tully Marshall *Alvin*

Brewster ▪ *Dir* Frank Tuttle • *Scr* Albert Maltz, WR Burnett, from the novel *A Gun for Sale* by Graham Greene

This Happy Breed ★★★★★ U
Drama   1944 · UK · Colour · 105min

The second of David Lean's four collaborations with Noël Coward provides a fascinating picture of the way we were. The action is largely confined to an unremarkable but lovingly re-created Clapham home, but such is the ebb and flow of events (both domestic and historical) that the two hours it takes to cover the 20 inter-war years seem to fly by. Celia Johnson is superb as the eminently sensible suburban housewife, while Kay Walsh gives a spirited performance as her mouthy daughter. But the best scenes belong to neighbours Robert Newton and Stanley Holloway, as a couple of very British chroniclers of their times. DP *DVD* ꞎ

Robert Newton *Frank Gibbons* • Celia Johnson *Ethel Gibbons* • John Mills *Billy Mitchell* • Kay Walsh *Queenie Gibbons* • Stanley Holloway *Bob Mitchell* • Amy Veness *Mrs Flint* • Alison Leggatt *Aunt Sylvia* • Laurence Olivier *Narrator* ▪ *Dir* David Lean • *Scr* David Lean, Ronald Neame, Anthony Havelock-Allan, Noël Coward (uncredited), from the play by Noël Coward

This Happy Feeling ★★ U
Romantic comedy   1958 · US · Colour · 92min

Hoping to repeat the success of the previous year's *Tammy and the Bachelor*, producer Ross Hunter put Debbie Reynolds in the path of another unsuspecting swain in this over-eager comedy, written and directed by Blake Edwards. But we're never quite caught up in the fun as Reynolds tilts her cap at retired film star Curt Jurgens. Nor are we convinced by the arch quirkiness of such supporting characters as Estelle Winwood's tipsy cook. DP

Debbie Reynolds *Janet Blake* • Curt Jurgens *Preston Mitchell* • John Saxon *Bill Tremaine* • Alexis Smith *Nita Holloway* • Mary Astor *Mrs Tremaine* ▪ *Dir* Blake Edwards • *Scr* Blake Edwards, from the play *For Love or Money* by F Hugh Herbert

This Is Elvis ★★ 12
Biographical documentary drama
1981 · US · Colour and BW · 97min

This is not in the same league as John Carpenter's faithful biopic starring Kurt Russell (*Elvis – the Movie*), but an engaging failure, nevertheless. Writers/directors Malcolm Leo and Andrew Solt blend in real footage with the staged scenes but, for all their efforts, do little more than scratch the surface of the myth behind the king of rock 'n' roll. JF Swearing. *DVD*

David Scott *Elvis, aged 18* • Paul Boensch III *Elvis, aged ten* • Johnny Harra *Elvis, aged 42* • Lawrence Koller *Vernon Presley* • Rhonda Lyn *Priscilla Presley* • Dana Mackay *Elvis, aged 35* ▪ *Dir/Scr* Malcolm Leo, Andrew Solt

This Is England ★★★★ 18
Drama   2006 · UK · Colour · 97min

The sixth feature from British film-maker Shane Meadows (*Dead Man's Shoes*, *TwentyFourSeven*) offers a semi-autobiographical portrait of skinheads in the 1980s. Set in a bleak (and unnamed) northern town just after the Falklands War, the film follows 12-year-old Shaun (newcomer Thomas Turgoose) as he's adopted by a group of kindly, multiracial skinheads. A touchingly funny first half gives way to something more disturbing as Shaun is drawn to a group of National Front supporters. Coaxing a superb performance from his young lead and brilliantly evoking the working-class despair of the Thatcher era, Meadows has created a film to be reckoned with. JR Violence, swearing. *DVD* ꞎ

Thomas Turgoose *Shaun Fields* • Stephen Graham *Combo* • Jo Hartley *Cynth* • Andrew Shim *Milky* • Vicky McClure *Lol* • Joe Gilgun *Woody* • Rosamund Hanson *Smell* ▪ *Dir/Scr* Shane Meadows • *Cinematographer* Danny Cohen

This Is 40 ★★★ 15
Comedy   2012 · US · Colour · 128min

Sold as a sort-of sequel to *Knocked Up*, Judd Apatow's midlife comedy returns to the bumpy family life of likeable LA married couple Pete (Paul Rudd) and Debbie (Leslie Mann). The couple has to deal with strains domestic, sexual and financial, not to mention a calamitous 40th birthday party. Turns from Apatow regulars Chris O'Dowd, Jason Segel and a freewheeling Melissa McCarthy add to the familiarity of the milieu. The surprise is just how sad and honest it all is beneath the scatology and quipping, with themes of regret, estrangement, emotional stalemate and the passage of time. Regular belly laughs help the medicine go down, although, like Apatow's last directorial effort, *Funny People*, it's about 20 minutes too long. And the so-called "unrated" version is even longer. AC Swearing, sexual references, drug abuse, sex scenes, some nudity. *DVD* ꞎ

Paul Rudd *Pete* • Leslie Mann *Debbie* • John Lithgow *Oliver* • Albert Brooks *Larry* • Megan Fox *Desi* • Maude Apatow *Sadie* • Iris Apatow *Charlotte* • Chris O'Dowd *Ronnie* • Jason Segel *Jason* • Melissa McCarthy *Catherine* ▪ *Dir* Judd Apatow • *Scr* Judd Apatow, from characters by Apatow

This Is My Affair ★★★
Crime drama   1937 · US · BW · 99min

This is a cracking crime story, set in the early 20th century. The "affair" turns out to be Robert Taylor's mission: he's been sent to the Midwest by President McKinley to root out bank robbers. Barbara Stanwyck is absolutely wonderful in an atypical role as a saloon singer, and it's easy to see how Taylor fell for her. They married for real two years later. TS

Robert Taylor (1) *Lieutenant Richard L Perry* • Barbara Stanwyck *Lil Duryea* • Victor McLaglen *Jock Ramsey* • Brian Donlevy *Batiste Duryea* • Sidney Blackmer *President Theodore Roosevelt* • John Carradine *Ed* • Alan Dinehart *Doc Keller* ▪ *Dir* William A Seiter • *Scr* Allen Rivkin, Lamar Trotti, from the novel *The McKinley Case* by Melville Crossman

This Is My Father ★★★ 15
Romantic drama   1999 · Can/Ire · Colour · 114min

Teacher James Caan learns a life lesson when a photo from his mother's past causes him to wonder about the identity of his father. This search for truth takes him to Ireland, where details of an unsuspected past romance emerge. Written and directed by Paul Quinn, and starring brother Aidan, James Caan, Stephen Rea, John Cusack and a who's who of Irish supporting actors. DA *DVD*

Aidan Quinn *Kieran O'Day* • Moya Farrelly *Fiona Flynn* • Stephen Rea *Father Quinn* • John Cusack *Eddie Sharp, the pilot* • James Caan *Kieran Johnson* • Jacob Tierney *Jack, Kieran Johnson's nephew* • Colm Meaney *Seamus* ▪ *Dir/Scr* Paul Quinn

This Is My Life ★★★ 15
Comedy drama   1992 · US · Colour · 89min

The formidable Nora Ephron made her directorial debut with this tale of single mum Julie Kavner trying to pursue a career in the world of stand-up comedy. Her daughters (Gaby Hoffmann and Samantha Mathis) soon find that their increasingly absentee mother is using their experiences as material for her act. The cast is certainly a treat, while Ephron's writing is at her sharpest. Quite why the whole fails to gel is a great mystery, but there is definitely too much slack around the middle. SH

Julie Kavner *Dottie Ingels* • Samantha Mathis *Erica Ingels* • Gaby Hoffmann *Opal Ingels* • Carrie Fisher *Claudia Curtis* • Dan Aykroyd *Arnold Moss* • Bob Nelson *Ed* • Marita Geraghty *Mia Jablon* ▪ *Dir* Nora Ephron • *Scr* Nora Ephron, Delia Ephron, from the novel *This Is Your Life* by Meg Wolitzer

This Is My Love ★★
Drama   1954 · US · Colour · 90min

Linda Darnell moves in to help her sister Faith Domergue and her brother-in-law Dan Duryea, who is confined to a wheelchair

after an accident. Into this sad household comes dishy Rick Jason, with whom Darnell is desperately in love, but it is Domergue who captures his fancy. This is a high-octane mix of sexual frustration and passion, jealousy, deception and murder to be relished – but definitely not taken seriously – by fans of overheated melodrama. RK

Linda Darnell *Vida* • Rick Jason *Glenn* • Dan Duryea *Murray* • Faith Domergue *Evelyn* • Hal Baylor *Eddie* • Connie Russell ▪ *Dir* Stuart Heisler • *Scr* Hugh Brooke, Hagar Wilde, from the story *Fear Has Black Wings* by Hugh Brooke

This Is My Street ★★ PG
Drama   1963 · UK · BW · 90min

The street of the title is a rather grim one in London's Battersea, before the place became gentrified, wherein a womanising lodger (Ian Hendry) seduces overburdened mother (June Ritchie). She becomes infatuated with him, but he dumps her for her sister. A well-written, nicely shot squalor fest. Fascinating fact: Mike Pratt and Annette Andre later starred together in the original TV series, *Randall and Hopkirk (Deceased)*. JG *DVD*

Ian Hendry *Harry King* • June Ritchie *Margery Graham* • John Hurt *Charlie* • Avice Landone *Lily* • Meredith Edwards *Steve* • Madge Ryan *Kitty* • Annette Andre *Jinny* • Mike Pratt *Sid* ▪ *Dir* Sidney Hayers • *Scr* Bill MacIlwraith, from the novel by Nan Maynard

> **LANDMARK FILM**
> This affectionate heavy metal parody
> trademarks the "rockumentary"

This Is Spinal Tap ★★★★★ 15
Spoof documentary   1984 · US · Colour · 79min

This brilliantly crafted and completely on-target satire of the rock 'n' roll industry is filmed in mock documentary style, with every rock-music cliché savagely lampooned for maximum hilarity, as director Rob Reiner follows a fictitious British heavy metal band on tour. The Stonehenge-inspired production number is a showstopping highlight, but there's also immense pleasure to be had in the details, particularly the unbelievably crass song lyrics. Christopher Guest and Michael McKean are perfect as the group's incredibly stupid lead guitarist and singer, and Reiner's unsurpassed spoof never hits a false note. A cult classic and a pop send-up landmark. AJ Swearing. *DVD* ꞎ

Christopher Guest *Nigel Tufnel (lead guitar)* • Michael McKean *David St Hubbins (lead guitar)* • Harry Shearer *Derek Smalls (bass)* • RJ Parnell *Mick Shrimpton (drums)* • David Kaff *Viv Savage (keyboards)* • Rob Reiner *Marti DiBergi* • Bruno Kirby *Tommy Pischedda* • Anjelica Huston *Designer* • Billy Crystal *Mime artist* • Patrick Macnee *Sir Denis Eaton-Hogg* ▪ *Dir* Rob Reiner • *Scr* Christopher Guest, Michael McKean, Harry Shearer, Rob Reiner

This Is the Army ★★★ U
Musical revue   1943 · US · Colour · 116min

Mainly of historical interest, this filmed record of Irving Berlin's patriotic 1940s stage revue is performed partly by amateur military personnel supported by a flock of Warner Brothers contract players, including hoofer and future Republican senator George Murphy, bizarrely playing the father of actor and future US president Ronald Reagan (Murphy was nine years Reagan's senior). Also in the cast is world heavyweight champion Joe Louis, and Berlin himself singing *Oh, How I Hate To Get Up In The Morning*. RB

Irving Berlin • George Murphy *Jerry Jones* • Joan Leslie *Eileen Dibble* • George Tobias *Maxie Twardofsky* • Alan Hale *Sgt McGee* • Charles Butterworth *Eddie Dibble* • Rosemary DeCamp *Ethel* • Kate Smith • Ronald Reagan *Johnny Jones* • Joe Louis ▪ *Dir* Michael Curtiz • *Scr* Casey Robinson, Capt Claude Binyon, Philip G Epstein, Julius G Epstein, from the play by Irving Berlin

This Is the End ★★★★ 15
Satirical comedy   2013 · US · Colour · 105min

Hollywood stars send themselves up to riotous effect in the directorial debut of Seth Rogen and his writing partner Evan

Goldberg. A party at James Franco's palatial LA home (attended by familiar faces from the big and small screens, all playing themselves) descends into chaos when the apocalypse strikes, and the pampered actors are forced to rely on their limited wits in order to survive. An over-the-top but whip-smart satire on the narcissism of Tinseltown, with the cast of celebs relishing the opportunity to indulge in self-mockery and the laugh-out-loud script sparing no egos. TeS Violence, swearing, sexual references, drug abuse. *DVD* ꞎ

James Franco • Jonah Hill • Seth Rogen • Jay Baruchel • Danny McBride (2) *Danny McBride* • Emma Watson ▪ *Dir* Evan Goldberg, Seth Rogen • *Scr* Evan Goldberg, Seth Rogen, from their story

This Is the Night ★★★
Romantic comedy   1932 · US · BW · 78min

Fifth-billed Cary Grant plays his first featured role at Paramount as an Olympic javelin champion and husband of Thelma Todd, who arrives at her Paris hotel with her lover Roland Young in tow, to find Grant unexpectedly there. The three of them, plus Young's pal Charlie Ruggles and Lily Damita, an actress hired to pose as Young's nonexistent wife, go to Venice where the male trio and Charlie are captivated by Damita. Directed with brio by Frank Tuttle, it's mildly risqué, sophisticated and entertaining. RK

Lili Damita *Germaine* • Charlie Ruggles [Charles Ruggles] *Bunny West* • Roland Young *Gerald Gray* • Thelma Todd *Claire* • Cary Grant *Stephen* ▪ *Dir* Frank Tuttle • *Scr* Benjamin Glazer, George Marion, from the play *Pouche* by René Peter, Henri Falk and the English-language adaptation, *Naughty Cinderella* by Avery Hopwood

This Is the Sea ★★ 15
Drama   1996 · Ire/UK/US · Colour · 103min

It's hard on well-intentioned films with good moments to condemn them with faint praise, but that's the case with this *Romeo and Juliet* story set in Ireland just after the 1994 ceasefire. The film's chief merit is in the young performers. Samantha Morton plays a protestant much sheltered by her mother. When she goes to Belfast she meets Ross McDade, a Catholic with ties to the IRA. Honest and non-partisan. BB Swearing.

Richard Harris *Old Man Jacobs* • Gabriel Byrne *Rohan* • John Lynch *Padhar McAliskey* • Dearbhla Molloy *Ma Stokes* • Ian McIlhinney *Da Stokes* • Samantha Morton *Hazel Stokes* • Ross McDade *Malachy McAliskey* • Rick Leaf *Pastor Lamthorn* ▪ *Dir/Scr* Mary McGuckian

This Is Where I Leave You ★★★ 15
Comedy   2014 · US · Colour · 98min

An incredible cast led by Jason Bateman and Tina Fey star in Shawn Levy's comedy drama about a dysfunctional family forced to "sit Shiva" for a week (the mourning period in Judaism) after their father passes away. The mouth-watering ensemble is endlessly watchable, even if the story doesn't take them anywhere particularly surprising. Bateman is the eye-rolling focus of the film, but Fey gets a lot of the best lines as the eldest sibling. If only the script had been a little more daring... JL Swearing, sex scenes.

Jason Bateman *Judd Altman* • Tina Fey *Wendy Altman* • Jane Fonda *Hillary Altman* • Adam Driver *Phillip Altman* • Rose Byrne *Penny Moore* ▪ *Dir* Shawn Levy • *Scr* Jonathan Tropper, from his novel • *Cinematographer* Terry Stacey

This Island Earth ★★★★ PG
Science-fiction adventure
1955 · US · Colour · 82min

This intelligent slice of 1950s sci-fi ranks among the best and most cleverly conceived of the genre. Really it's a film of two parts. A talky earthbound section finds brainy boffins being recruited by the otherworldly Jeff Morrow to save his distant homeland from destruction by interplanetary warfare. That's followed by a full-blooded space opera featuring astounding surrealistic landscapes on the planet Metaluna and fearsome insect-like mutations with huge bulbous craniums. RS

Jeff Morrow *Exeter* • Faith Domergue *Dr Ruth Adams* • Rex Reason *Dr Cal Meacham* • Lance Fuller *Brack* • Russell Johnson *Steve Carlson* • Richard Nichols *Joe Wilson* • Karl Lindt [Karl Ludwig Lindt] *Engelborg* • Douglas Spencer *Monitor* ■ *Dir* Joseph M Newman • *Scr* Franklin Coen, Edward G O'Callaghan, from the novel *The Alien Machine* by Raymond F Jones

This Land Is Mine ★★🅿🄶
Second World War drama
1943 · US · BW · 103min

Throughout the Second World War, Hollywood failed to capture the fear and suspicion that pervaded occupied Europe. This tale of a cowardly schoolteacher, played by Charles Laughton, who is inspired to heroism by his love for a Resistance fighter, Maureen O'Hara, is no exception. Jean Renoir's inability to re-create the atmosphere of Vichy France is partly excused by the fact that he had been living in exile from his homeland since 1940, after the Nazis placed him on a death list for his socialist sympathies. This bland picture is directed with virtually no enthusiasm for its clichéd villagers and hysterical Nazis. DP
DVD

Charles Laughton *Albert Lory* • Maureen O'Hara *Louise Martin* • George Sanders *George Lambert* • Walter Slezak *Major Erich von Keller* • Kent Smith *Paul Martin* ■ *Dir* Jean Renoir • *Scr* Dudley Nichols

This Love of Ours ★★
Melodrama
1945 · US · BW · 90min

Merle Oberon and Charles Korvin star in this banal melodrama about a jealous husband who unjustly deserts his wife. Years later, he discovers her in a Chicago nightclub, assisting Claude Rains in his act, and begs her forgiveness. Director William Dieterle, given a budget of $2 million, expertly attempts to extract every ounce of drama he can from his low-voltage cast and the pitiful script, recycled in 1955 as *Never Say Goodbye* with Rock Hudson and Cornell Borchers. RK

Merle Oberon *Karin Touzac/Florence Hale* • Charles Korvin *Michel Touzac* • Claude Rains *Dr Joseph Targel* • Carl Esmond *Uncle Robert* • Sue England *Susette Touzac* • Jess Barker *Chadwick* • Harry Davenport *Dr Jerry Wilkerson* ■ *Dir* William Dieterle • *Scr* Bruce Manning, John Klorer, Leonard Lee, from the play *Come Prima Meglio di Prima* by Luigi Pirandello

This Man Is Mine ★★
Drama
1934 · US · BW · 75min

RKO and director John Cromwell surrounded the lovely Irene Dunne with all the elegant accoutrements – sets, clothes and a Max Steiner score – that her fans would expect, but neglected to give her a convincing script or a sufficiently attractive leading man. The plot has Dunne battling to keep the affections of her philandering husband (Ralph Bellamy) when he falls into the seductive clutches of Constance Cummings. Wafer-thin and disappointingly dull, but it's all over swiftly. RK

Irene Dunne *Tony Dunlap* • Ralph Bellamy *Jim Dunlap* • Constance Cummings *Francesca "Fran" Harper* • Kay Johnson *Bee McCrea* • Charles Starrett *Jud McCrea* • Sidney Blackmer *Mort Holmes* ■ *Dir* John Cromwell • *Scr* Jane Murfin, from the play *Love Flies in the Window* by Anne Morrison Chapin

This Means War ★★🄓
Romantic action comedy
2012 · US · Colour · 93min

This slapdash movie sees best-buddy CIA operatives Chris Pine and Tom Hardy pitched against each other when they discover they're dating the same woman, perky Reese Witherspoon. They then brazenly stalk the object of their affections in the hope of winning the battle for her heart. Although director McG is clearly aiming for a frothy romance, the dubious methods employed by the love rivals make for uncomfortable viewing, and their characters are painted so stereotypically

that it's hard to care for either. TeS **DVD** **Blu**

Tom Hardy *Tuck* • Abigail Leigh Spencer [Abigail Spencer] *Katie* • Reese Witherspoon *Lauren* • Chris Pine *FDR Foster* • Til Schweiger *Heinrich* • Angela Bassett *Collins* • Chelsea Handler *Trish* • John Paul Ruttan *Joe* ■ *Dir* McG [Joseph McGinty Nichol] • *Scr* Timothy Dowling, Simon Kinberg, from a story by Dowling, Marcus Gautesen

This Modern Age ★★
Romantic drama
1931 · US · BW · 68min

Joan Crawford arrives in Paris to seek Pauline Frederick, the mother who left when she was a child. The reunion is a success until Crawford's association with drunkard Monroe Owsley breaks up her engagement to the whiter-than-white knight Neil Hamilton. His discovery that her mother is the kept mistress of a wealthy married man sends the girl hurtling into bitter debauchery. Unconvincing, even by the standards of the genre, but this dated melodrama is an absolute must for collectors of early Crawford, here uncharacteristically innocent, arch and winsome, and blonde! RK

Joan Crawford *Valentine Winters* • Pauline Frederick *Diane Winters* • Neil Hamilton *Bob Blake* • Monroe Owsley *Tony* • Hobart Bosworth *Mr Blake* • Emma Dunn *Mrs Blake* ■ *Dir* Nicholas Grindé [Nick Grinde] • *Scr* Sylvia Thalberg, Frank Butler, John Meehan, from the short story *Girls Together* by Mildred Cram

This Must Be the Place ★★🄵
Comedy drama
2011 · It/Fr/Ire · Colour · 113min

A retired pop star finds renewed purpose after his father's death returns him to the United States, in this first English-language offering from acclaimed Italian writer/director Paolo Sorrentino (*Il Divo*). An almost unrecognisable Sean Penn sports black eyeliner and a back-combed goth hairdo as the central character, delivering a witty and endearing performance that almost makes amends for the film's wayward storytelling. The movie's constituent elements are nearly always striking, yet somehow they never add up to anything that speaks clearly to the head or the heart. This has to go down as a misfire from a maverick talent. TJ Swearing, sexual references. **DVD** **Blu**

Sean Penn *Cheyenne* • Frances McDormand *Jane* • Judd Hirsch *Mordecai Midler* • Eve Hewson *Mary* • Kerry Condon *Rachel* • Harry Dean Stanton *Robert Plath* ■ *Dir* Paolo Sorrentino • *Scr* Paolo Sorrentino, Umberto Contarello, from a story by Sorrentino

This Other Eden ★★🅄
Comedy
1959 · UK · BW · 80min

This is an overwrought tale about the emotions that erupt when the statue of a long-dead IRA hero is blown up in the square of a sleepy Irish village. Leslie Phillips is fine as the son of the Black and Tan who shot the gunman, and who is blamed for the explosion. He is adequately supported by Audrey Dalton as his lover and Norman Rodway as the terrorist's seminarian son, but the film lacks power. DP

Audrey Dalton *Maire McRoarty* • Leslie Phillips *Crispin Brown* • Niall MacGinnis *Devereaux* • Geoffrey Golden *McRoarty* • Norman Rodway *Conor Heaphy* • Milo O'Shea *Pat Tweedy* ■ *Dir* Muriel Box • *Scr* Patrick Kirwan, Blanaid Irvine, from the play by Louis d'Alton

This Property Is Condemned ★★★🄵
Drama
1966 · US · Colour · 105min

This adaptation of Tennessee Williams's early one-act play is set in a boarding house during the Depression. Landlady Kate Reid exploits her daughter Natalie Wood's charms to attract custom, but Wood has her eye on nice Robert Redford, who has arrived in town to lay off the railroad men. The beautiful camerawork of James Wong Howe, the fresh performances and Sydney Pollack's assured direction keep this from

overheating in the usual Williams manner. AT **DVD**

Natalie Wood *Alva Starr* • Robert Redford *Owen Legate* • Charles Bronson *JJ Nichols* • Kate Reid *Hazel Starr* • Mary Badham *Willie Starr* • Alan Baxter *Knopke* • Robert Blake *Sidney* • John Harding *Johnson* • Dabney Coleman *Salesman* ■ *Dir* Sydney Pollack • *Scr* Francis Ford Coppola, Fred Coe, Edith Sommer, from the play by Tennessee Williams

This Rebel Breed ★
Crime drama
1960 · US · BW · 92min

Rita Moreno is the best thing about this crude and exploitative story of racial strife among teenage gangs of black, white and Latin Americans. A brief lecture at the end by a police officer hardly overcomes the relish with which the final riot is staged or the general air of sensationalism. AE

Rita Moreno *Lola* • Mark Damon *Frank* • Gerald Mohr *Lt Brooks* • Jay Novello *Papa* • Eugene Martin *Rudy* • Tom Gilson *Muscles* • Diane Cannon [Dyan Cannon] *Wiggles* ■ *Dir* Richard L Bare • *Scr* Morris Lee Green, from the story *All God's Children* by William Rowland, Irma Berk

This Side of Heaven ★★
Comedy drama
1934 · US · BW · 76min

This is a misleading title for what is essentially a heart-warming, albeit drama-filled, domestic tale. Lionel Barrymore and Fay Bainter star as a businessman and his wife who are parents to three grown-up children. When their eldest daughter's accountant fiancé uncovers an irregularity in the books of Barrymore's company, a series of crises and upheavals is unleashed, almost leading to tragedy. RK

Lionel Barrymore *Martin Turner* • Fay Bainter *Francene Turner* • Mae Clarke *Jane Turner* • Tom Brown *Seth Turner* • Una Merkel *Birdie* • Mary Carlisle *Peggy Turner* ■ *Dir* William K Howard • *Scr* Edgar Allan Woolf, Florence Ryerson, Zelda Sears, Eve Greene, from the novel *It Happened One Day* by Marjorie Bartholomew Paradis

This Sporting Life ★★★★★🄓
Drama
1963 · UK · BW · 128min

Director Lindsay Anderson's first feature film is his best, giving Richard Harris and Rachel Roberts the roles of their lives. Harris stars as the miner who becomes a ruthless professional rugby player; Roberts plays the repressed, widowed landlady with whom he can only communicate through violence. There are some remarkable scenes of confrontation – one particular quarrel between the two is painfully honest – and the northern town where it all takes place is evocatively realised. This numbers among the early ripples of the British New Wave. TH **DVD** **Blu**

Richard Harris *Frank Machin* • Rachel Roberts (1) *Mrs Hammond* • Alan Badel *Weaver* • William Hartnell *Johnson* • Colin Blakely *Maurice Braithwaite* • Vanda Godsell *Mrs Weaver* • Arthur Lowe *Slomer* • Anne Cunningham *Judith* • Jack Watson *Len Miller* ■ *Dir* Lindsay Anderson • *Scr* David Storey, from his novel

This Thing Called Love★★★
Romantic comedy
1940 · US · BW · 94min

This film not only acknowledges the existence of sex as a component of love and marriage, but actually builds its jokes on that fact of life. As a result, the Legion of Decency banned this otherwise innocuous offering. The story concerns Rosalind Russell's belief that marriages are best cemented on a celibate start, and she decides to keep her groom, Melvyn Douglas, waiting three months for her favours. This bright romantic farce is elegantly played. RK

Rosalind Russell *Ann Winters* • Melvyn Douglas *Tice Collins* • Binnie Barnes *Charlotte Campbell* • Allyn Joslyn *Harry Bertrand* • Gloria Dickson *Florence Bertrand* • Lee J Cobb *Julio Diestro* • Gloria Holden *Genevieve Hooper* ■ *Dir* Alexander Hall • *Scr* George Seaton, Ken Englund, PJ Wolfson, from the play by Edwin Burke

This Time for Keeps ★★🅄
Musical
1947 · US · Colour · 104min

Everything from Wagnerian tenor Lauritz Melchior belting a couple of popular opera

arias, through Jimmy Durante delivering his deathless *Inka Dinka Doo* to Xavier Cugat and his orchestra letting rip is thrown into the mix in an attempt to liven up a desperately unoriginal and feeble vehicle for Esther Williams. The famous aquatic star plays a famous aquatic star, caught in an on-again, off-again, on-again romance with Johnnie Johnson. RK

Esther Williams *Leonora "Nora" Cambaretti* • Jimmy Durante *Ferdi Farro* • Lauritz Melchior *Richard Herald* • Johnnie Johnson *Dick Johnson* ■ *Dir* Richard Thorpe • *Scr* Gladys Lehman, from a story by Erwin Gelsey, Lorraine Fielding

This Woman Is Dangerous ★★
Melodrama
1952 · US · BW · 97min

Not here she isn't, as ageing movie queen Joan Crawford nears the end of her glory days at Warner Bros. This was her last movie for the studio, and she's always watchable, but this vehicle strains credibility as the star assists at operations, cares for the daughter of widower doctor Dennis Morgan and tries to free herself from the clutches of gangster boyfriend David Brian. The kind of movie that gives Hollywood a bad name. TS

Joan Crawford *Beth Austin* • Dennis Morgan *Dr Ben Halleck* • David Brian *Matt Jackson* • Richard Webb *Franklin* • Mari Aldon *Ann Jackson* • Philip Carey *Will Jackson* • Ian MacDonald *Joe Grossland* ■ *Dir* Felix Feist • *Scr* Geoffrey Homes, George W Yates, from the story *Stab of Pain* by Bernard Girard

This World, Then the Fireworks ★★★🄙
Crime drama
1996 · US · Colour · 95min

This is a contrived but decent stab at contemporary *film noir*, with Billy Zane as an investigative reporter forced to hide out at the home of his sister Gina Gershon. Following a childhood trauma, Zane and his sibling enjoy a relationship that extends beyond the warm and loving. Soon they embark on a scam aimed at conning a pretty local policewoman out of her beach-front home. This may not produce true fireworks, but it's no damp squib either. DA Swearing, violence, sex scenes.

Billy Zane *Marty Lakewood* • Gina Gershon *Carol Lakewood-Wharton* • Sheryl Lee *Patrolwoman Lois Archer* • Rue McClanahan *Mom Lakewood* • Seymour Cassel *Detective Harris* • William Hootkins *Jake Krutz, private investigator* • Will Patton *Police Lt Morgan* ■ *Dir* Michael Oblowitz • *Scr* Larry Gross, from the story by Jim Thompson

This Year's Love ★★★🄙
Romantic comedy
1999 · UK · Colour · 104min

Writer/director David Kane tries hard to tap into the "Cool Britannia" zeitgeist with this breezy romantic comedy, set in and around funky Camden Lock and charting three years in the lives of six London dropouts. However, while Catherine McCormack, Douglas Henshall and Dougray Scott deliver spunky, dynamic performances, the episodic script gives them little to work with. Sadly, the schematic plotting soon becomes yawningly predictable. NS Drug abuse, swearing, sex scenes. **DVD**

Ian Hart *Liam* • Kathy Burke *Marey* • Jennifer Ehle *Sophie* • Douglas Henshall *Danny* • Catherine McCormack *Hannah* • Dougray Scott *Cameron* • Emily Woof *Alice* • Sophie Okonedo *Denise* ■ *Dir/Scr* David Kane

Thomas & Friends - Sodor's Legend of the Lost Treasure: the Movie ★★★★🅄
Animated adventure
2015 · UK · Colour · 67min

This finely judged children's adventure has just about enough feature-length pizzazz – and features Oscar-winner Eddie Redmayne in the cast – but doesn't deviate too much from the original books by the Reverend W Awdry. The treasure-hunting story starts with Thomas annoying the Fat Controller and ends up with Thomas falling down a mine shaft and meeting a dastardly seafarer (voiced by John Hurt). This never feels like an expanded TV episode – the animation is pretty much the same as you get in the TV show, but there are added dramatic set pieces and the narrative arc is well plotted. There's also a great song, *Never Overlook a Little Engine*. As if you would. **BD** *DVD*

Mark Moraghan *Narrator* • John Hasler *Thomas* • Keith Wickham *Edward/Henry/Gordon/Percy/James/Glynn/Sir Topham Hatt/Gordon's Driver/James's Guard/Knapford Station speaker* • Olivia Colman *Marion* • Eddie Redmayne *Ryan* • John Hurt *Sailor John* ■ *Dir* David Stoten • *Scr* Andrew Brenner, from characters by Rev W Awdry

Thomas & Friends: Tale of the Brave ★★★ U
Animated adventure 2014 · UK · Colour · 60min

Things have changed on the island of Sodor since the days of Ringo Starr (who narrated the original TV series), let alone original author the Reverend W Awdry, with this adventure a little darker than some young fans may be used to. Thomas sees a giant footprint while being rescued from a landslide at the Clay Pits and Percy convinces himself that a monster is on the loose. The plot is packed with incident and there are plenty of familiar faces along the way, while Olivia Colman is a welcome addition to the voice cast. **DP** *DVD* Ⓢ

Mark Moraghan *Narrator* • Ben Small *Thomas* • Keith Wickham *The Fat Controller/Percy/Salty/James* • Jonathan Broadbent *Bill/Ben* • Olivia Colman *Marion* ■ *Dir* Rob Silvestri • *Scr* Andrew Brenner, from the TV series by Britt Allcroft, from characters by Rev W Awdry

Thomas and the Magic Railroad ★ U
Adventure 2000 · UK/US · Colour · 85min

Writer/director Britt Allcroft may have translated the magic of the Rev W Awdry's books to the small screen, but this feature adaptation is crass, impenetrable and embarrassing. Clumsily Americanised, the story has Mara Wilson and her grandfather Peter Fonda help a marginalised Thomas and miniature conductor Alec Baldwin confound Diesel 10's dastardly plan to eradicate steam trains. A shameful betrayal of a national institution (and the songs are ghastly). **DP** *DVD*

Alec Baldwin *Mr Conductor* • Peter Fonda *Burnett Stone* • Mara Wilson *Lily* • Russell Means *Billy Two-Feathers* • Didi Conn *Stacy* ■ *Dir* Britt Allcroft • *Scr* Britt Allcroft, from the books by Rev W Awdry

The Thomas Crown Affair ★★★ PG
Romantic crime caper
1968 · US · Colour · 97min

Wound up by its Oscar-winning song, *The Windmills of Your Mind*, this is a movie of clockwork precision from director Norman Jewison and his cameraman Haskell Wexler, who give what is essentially a caper movie a reverent sheen. Steve McQueen is the businessman organising a bank heist out of boredom, while Faye Dunaway is the insurance investigator who falls for the bad guy. You can take or leave the story, but the style is something else. **TH** Some violence. *DVD* Ⓢ

Steve McQueen (1) *Thomas Crown* • Faye Dunaway *Vicky Anderson* • Paul Burke *Eddy Malone* • Jack Weston *Erwin Weaver* • Biff McGuire *Sandy* • Yaphet Kotto *Carl* • Todd Martin *Benjy* • Sam Melville *Dave* ■ *Dir* Norman Jewison • *Scr* Alan R Trustman • *Music* Michel Legrand

The Thomas Crown Affair ★★★ 15
Romantic crime caper
1999 · US/Ire · Colour · 108min

This loose remake of the 1968 caper has Pierce Brosnan as the millionaire who steals art in his spare time, and Rene Russo as the sultry insurance investigator with an unusually close interest in his extracurricular activities. It's considerably steamier than the original, and it's stylishly done by *Die Hard* director John McTiernan.

But though Brosnan and Russo are a sexy and believable match, this cat-and-mouse thriller lacks the 1960s cool of the original. **JB** Swearing, a sex scene, nudity. *DVD* Ⓑ

Pierce Brosnan *Thomas Crown* • Rene Russo *Catherine Banning* • Denis Leary *Detective Michael McCann* • Ben Gazzara *Andrew Wallace* • Frankie Faison *Detective Paretti* • Fritz Weaver *John Reynolds* • Charles Keating *Golchan* • Faye Dunaway *Psychiatrist* ■ *Dir* John McTiernan • *Scr* Leslie Dixon, Kurt Wimmer, from a story by Alan R Trustman

Thomas the Imposter ★★★★
First World War fantasy 1964 · Fr · BW · 94min

Partly inspired by his own experiences with an ambulance unit during the First World War, Jean Cocteau's 1923 novel explored both the horrors of war and the creation of a personal myth. Drawing comparisons between combat and theatre, Georges Franju plays heavily on the notion of illusion, both in his baroque visuals (notably in the fantasy dream sequences) and in presenting teenager Fabrice Rouleau's deceptions as a morally inspired sleight of hand when he poses as a famous general's nephew to help princess Emmanuelle Riva's ambulance service return to Paris. **DP** French +subtitles.

Emmanuelle Riva *Princess de Bormes* • Jean Servais *Pesquel-Duport* • Fabrice Rouleau *Guillaume Thomas* • Sophie Darès *Henriette* • Michel Vitold *Dr Vernes* • Rosy Varte *Mme Valiche* • Bernard Lavalette *Dr Gentil* ■ *Dir* Georges Franju • *Scr* Jean Cocteau, Georges Franju, Michel Worms, Raphael Cluzel, from the novel by Jean Cocteau

Thor ★★★ 12
Fantasy adventure 2011 · US · Colour · 110min

When Marvel Comics decided to add Thor, the Norse god of thunder, to their roster of characters in 1962, it certainly inspired a young Kenneth Branagh. For the director has packed the hammer-wielding hero's first big-screen appearance with nods to the original source material. The story sees the brash immortal (played to the hilt by Aussie actor Chris Hemsworth) stripped of his powers and banished to Earth by all-powerful father Odin (Anthony Hopkins) after a reckless attack on their frost giant enemies. True, the film has some scene-setting longueurs, but Hopkins brings gravitas to his role and the action is suitably earth-shattering. **JA** *DVD* Ⓑ Ⓢᴅ Ⓒˢ

Chris Hemsworth *Thor* • Natalie Portman *Jane Foster* • Anthony Hopkins *Odin* • Tom Hiddleston *Loki* • Stellan Skarsgård *Dr Erik Selvig* • Idris Elba *Heimdall* • Rene Russo *Frigga* • Samuel L Jackson *Nick Fury* • Stan Lee *Driver* ■ *Dir* Kenneth Branagh • *Scr* Ashley Miller, Mark Protosevich, Zak Stentz, from a story by Protosevich, J Michael Straczynski, from characters by Jack Kirby, Stan Lee, Larry Lieber

Thor: the Dark World ★★★★ 12
Action adventure 2013 · US · Colour · 107min

Chris Hemsworth makes a robust return as Marvel's hammer-hurling thunder god in this bigger, bolder second solo epic. No sooner has Thor returned his trickster sibling, Loki (a terrific Tom Hiddleston), to face justice in Asgard following the events of *Avengers Assemble* than dark elf Malekith (Christopher Eccleston) emerges to destroy the cosmos and Thor's mortal love Jane Foster (Natalie Portman) is the key to stopping him. The 2011 *Thor* flick was good entertainment and director Alan Taylor has built on that to produce a thrill-packed extravaganza, with large-scale battles, vivid locations and laugh-out moments of humour. The top-class cast has more to do, but it's the sparring between the bickering brothers that really crackles – Hiddleston is at his mellifluously malevolent best while Hemsworth shows genuine godlike poise as he puts the hammer down on his numerous foes. This branch of the franchise continues with *Thor: Ragnarok* in 2017. **JA** Some violence, swearing. *DVD* Ⓑ Ⓢᴅ Ⓒˢ

Chris Hemsworth *Thor* • Natalie Portman *Jane Foster* • Tom Hiddleston *Loki* • Idris Elba *Heimdall* • Anthony Hopkins *Odin* • Stellan Skarsgård *Erik Selvig* • Alan Taylor • *Scr* Christopher L Yost, Christopher Markus, Stephen McFeely, from a story by Don Payne, Robert Rodat, from characters by Jack Kirby, Stan Lee, Larry Lieber, Walt Simonson

Thor: Ragnarok
Action adventure 2017 · US · Colour

This is a preview – no prints were available to review as we went to press: In this next adventure for Chris Hemsworth's errant thunder god, Mark Ruffalo's Hulk is set to team up with Thor to stop the destruction of the Asgardian gods (or Ragnarok, as it's known in Norse legend). It should be a face-off to savour, with adversaries like Cate Blanchett's death god Hela, Karl Urban's Skurge the Executioner and slippery stepbrother Loki (Tom Hiddleston) out to thwart our muscular heroes. Let the wisecracks and walloping begin... **JA**

Chris Hemsworth *Thor* • Tom Hiddleston *Loki* • Mark Ruffalo *Bruce Banner/Hulk* • Cate Blanchett *Hela* • Anthony Hopkins *Odin* • Idris Elba *Heimdall* ■ *Dir* Taika Waititi • *Scr* Christopher L Yost, Craig Kyle, from characters by Jack Kirby, Stan Lee, Larry Lieber

The Thorn in the Heart ★★★ PG
Documentary
2009 · Fr · Colour and BW · 86min

This documentary from director Michel Gondry (*Eternal Sunshine of the Spotless Mind*, *Be Kind Rewind*) is a portrait of his elderly Aunt Suzette, a retired teacher who changed the lives of her many pupils, but whose private life had its fair share of heartbreak. If it wasn't for the work of a much-lauded cinematic maverick, perhaps we wouldn't be interested, but what emerges is an occasionally troubling picture of a woman whose iron will shaped a career of quiet heroism. Those prepared to make the effort will find this a low-key yet rewarding study of how time, personalities and social mores shape individual fortunes. **TJ** French +subtitles.

Suzette Gondry • Jean-Yves Gondry • Michel Gondry ■ *Dir/Scr* Michel Gondry

Thoroughbreds Don't Cry ★★
Sports comedy drama 1937 · US · BW · 80min

Young jockey Mickey Rooney is hired to ride a dead cert for visiting English aristocrat C Aubrey Smith, but he is forced by his no-good father to lose the race. Directed by Alfred E Green for MGM, this undistinguished little racetrack tale is remembered for the first joint appearance of Rooney and Judy Garland, the latter as his friend and niece of Sophie Tucker, who runs the boarding house where Rooney lodges. **RK**

Judy Garland *Cricket West* • Mickey Rooney *Tim Donahue* • Sophie Tucker *Mother Ralph* • C Aubrey Smith *Sir Peter Calverton* • Ronald Sinclair *Roger Calverton* • Forrester Harvey *Wilkins* ■ *Dir* Alfred E Green • *Scr* Lawrence Hazard, from a story by Eleanore Griffin, J Walter Ruben

Thoroughly Modern Millie ★★★ PG
Musical 1967 · US · Colour · 145min

This popular but overlong vehicle for Julie Andrews succeeds despite a confusing plot and a screenplay that never seems to know when to say "enough". But there's still much to enjoy, not least the bizarre appearances by Broadway divas Beatrice Lillie and Carol Channing, of whom a little goes an awfully long way. The real delight is co-star James Fox, dancing and romancing as if to the musical born, plus Mary Tyler Moore, whose natural good-naturedness proves a fine counterpoint to Andrews's studied brittleness. Sumptuous, but dated. **TS** *DVD*

Julie Andrews *Millie Dillmount* • Mary Tyler Moore *Dorothy Brown* • Beatrice Lillie *Mrs Meers* • James Fox *Jimmy Smith* • John Gavin *Trevor*

Graydon • Carol Channing *Muzzy Van Hossmere* ■ *Dir* George Roy Hill • *Scr* Richard Morris • *Music* Elmer Bernstein

Those Calloways ★★★ PG
Drama 1964 · US · Colour · 125min

Trapper Brian Keith spends his savings on some land by a lake in Maine to establish a sanctuary and protect the geese, and moves there with his wife Vera Miles and 19-year-old son Brandon de Wilde. The family's idealistic ambitions are beset with problems and danger, and Keith has to fend off the attentions of a fake conservationist who wants to develop the land for goose-hunters. This family film from Disney suffers from too many plot strands, but is well acted and entertaining. **RK** *DVD*

Brian Keith *Cam Calloway* • Vera Miles *Liddy Calloway* • Brandon de Wilde *Bucky Calloway* • Walter Brennan *Alf Simes* • Ed Wynn *Ed Parker* • Linda Evans *Bridie Mellot* • Philip Abbott *Dell Fraser* • John Larkin *Jim Mellot* • Tom Skerritt *Whit Turner* ■ *Dir* Norman Tokar • *Scr* Louis Pelletier, from the novel *Swiftwater* by Paul Annixter

Those Endearing Young Charms ★★★
Romance 1945 · US · BW · 82min

Many wartime romances have a certain endearing, if not enduring charm, and this is no exception. Shop assistant Laraine Day has to choose between army officer Robert Young, who is a bit of a heel, and nice but dull Bill Williams (in his film debut) from back home. There is no doubt who is the more attractive for her, despite the warnings of her sensible mother, played beautifully by Ann Harding. **RB**

Robert Young (1) *Hank* • Laraine Day *Helen* • Ann Harding *Mrs Brandt* • Marc Cramer *Capt Larry Stowe* • Anne Jeffreys *Suzanne* ■ *Dir* Lewis Allen • *Scr* Jerome Chodorov, from a play by Edward Chodorov

Those Glory, Glory Days ★★★ PG
Biographical drama 1983 · UK · Colour · 90min

Written by *The Observer's* football correspondent, Julie Welch, this amusing slice of pre-Swinging Sixties nostalgia was originally shown on Channel 4's *First Love* series. It enjoyed a brief theatrical run, following some glowing reviews by the nation's TV critics. Zoe Nathenson gives a wholehearted performance as the teenager obsessed with Tottenham Hotspur and their Northern Irish skipper, Danny Blanchflower (who crops up in a cameo). Some of the freshness might have worn off, but this is still unusual and enjoyable. **DP**

Zoe Nathenson *Julia, "Danny"* • Sara Sugarman *Toni* • Cathy Murphy *Tub* • Liz Campion *Jailbird* • Amelia Dipple *Petrina* • Elizabeth Spriggs *School mistress* • Julia McKenzie *Mrs Herrick* • Peter Tilbury *Mr Herrick* ■ *Dir* Philip Saville • *Scr* Julie Welch

Those Lips, Those Eyes ★★★★
Romantic comedy drama
1980 · US · Colour · 107min

Michael Pressman directs this cute little movie about the lessons young student Tom Hulce learns when he spends one summer in the 1950s working for a theatre company. There's love, of course, with the older leading lady Glynnis O'Connor, but the best lines and performance come from Frank Langella as the troupe's ageing leading man. **JB**

Frank Langella *Harry Crystal* • Glynnis O'Connor *Ramona* • Tom Hulce *Artie Shoemaker* • George Morfogen *Sherman Spratt* • Jerry Stiller *Mr Shoemaker* • Rose Arrick *Mrs Shoemaker* • Herbert Berghof *Dr Julius Fuldauer* ■ *Dir* Michael Pressman • *Scr* David Shaber

Those Magnificent Men in Their Flying Machines ★★★★ U
Period comedy 1965 · UK · Colour · 132min

A host of international comedians don period garb, climb aboard wondrously ramshackle aircraft and dominate the screen over top-billed stars Stuart Whitman and Sarah Miles in this very entertaining comedy. Co-writer and director Ken Annakin keeps the action rattling along at a rate of knots, never slowing the pace for the romance, and allocates equal screen time to the different nationalities competing in the race. Wonderfully wacky and gloriously photographed. *Monte Carlo or Bust* is the 1969 sequel. TS **DVD**

Sarah Miles *Patricia Rawnsley* • James Fox *Richard Mays* • Stuart Whitman *Orvil Newton* • Alberto Sordi *Count Emilio Ponticelli* • Robert Morley *Lord Rawnsley* • Gert Fröbe [Gert Fröbe] *Colonel Manfred Von Holstein* • Jean-Pierre Cassel *Pierre Dubois* • Eric Sykes *Courtney* • Terry-Thomas *Sir Percival Ware-Armitage* • Tony Hancock *Harry Popperwell* • Benny Hill *Fire Chief Perkins* • Flora Robson *Mother Superior* ■ *Dir* Ken Annakin • *Scr* Jack Davies, Ken Annakin • *Cinematographer* Christopher Challis

Those Were the Days
★★★ PG

Comedy   1934 · UK · BW · 77min

Will Hay plays a Victorian magistrate in this enjoyable adaptation of Arthur Wing Pinero's brisk stage farce. Making his feature debut, Hay doesn't look totally at ease, having not yet mastered playing down for the camera. But no one could do pompous bemusement quite like him and his scenes with stepson John Mills are good value. DP **DVD**

Will Hay *Brutus Poskett* • Iris Hoey *Agatha Poskett* • Angela Baddeley *Charlotte* • Claud Allister *Captain Horace Vale* • George Graves *Colonel Alexander Lukyn* • John Mills *Bobby* • Jane Carr (1) *Minnie Taylor* ■ *Dir* Thomas Bentley • *Scr* Frec Thompson, Frank Miller, Frank Launder, Jack Jordan, from the play *The Magistrate* by Arthur Wing Pinero

Those Who Love Me Can Take the Train
★★★★ 15

Drama   1998 · Fr · Colour · 116min

Patrice Chéreau explores the dysfunctional dynamic between the members of a crumbling family and its immediate entourage. Shooting initially with hand-held cameras on a Limoges-bound train, he bewilders with the sheer number of people heading for a once-great artist's funeral and the complexity of their relationships. But the skeletons and revelations soon fall into place as marriages, pregnancies, addictions, gay affairs, sex changes and all manner of ambitions and celusions are dragged into the open. What follows is soap opera of a sophistication even Douglas Sirk would have envied. DP French +subtitles. **DVD**

Pascal Greggory *François* • Jean-Louis Trintignant *Lucien* • Valéria Bruni-Tedeschi *Claire* • Charles Berling *Jean-Marie* • Bruno Todeschini *Louis* • Sylvain Jacques *Bruno* • Vincent Perez *Viviane* ■ *Dir* Patrice Chéreau • *Scr* Danièle Thompson, Patrice Chéreau, Pierre Trividic

Though None Go with Me
★★

Period drama   2006 · US · Colour · 100min

This tale of female duty would have seemed old-fashioned had it been made – let alone set – in the 1950s. With the framing device of Cheryl Ladd telling her restless granddaughter a few home truths, the action is staged as an extended flashback that follows a prim small-town girl who gives her heart to the new minister (played by Brad Rowe). She then loses him in the Korean War just as her father dies and leaves her destitute. It's a textbook case of "woman's picture" suffering, but Ladd's eventual romance with her childhood sweetheart makes it both corny and melodramatic. DP

Cheryl Ladd *Elizabeth Bishop* • Amy Grabow *Young Elizabeth* • David Norona *Young Will Bishop* • Brad Rowe *Young Ben Phillips* • Christopher Allpcrt *Dr James Leroy* • Emily Hardy *Young Frances* ■ *Dir* Armand Mastroianni • *Scr* Pamela Wallace, from the novel by Jerry B Jenkins

A Thousand Acres
★★★ 15

Drama   1997 · US · Colour · 101min

This modern reworking of *King Lear*, based on Jane Smiley's Pulitzer Prize-winning novel, is given weight and class by its three female leads – Michelle Pfeiffer, Jessica Lange and Jennifer Jason Leigh. They play the sisters who fall out over some family land that is to be divided up by their gruff father Jason Robards. Their conflict and their relationships with the men in their lives form the centre of the film. While downbeat, thanks to Jocelyn Moorhouse's pedestrian direction, this is still a rare showcase for three of Hollywood's best actresses. JB Some swearing, sexual references, violence. **DVD**

Michelle Pfeiffer *Rose Cook Lewis* • Jessica Lange *Ginny Cook Smith* • Jason Robards *Larry Cook* • Jennifer Jason Leigh *Caroline Cook* • Colin Firth *Jess Clark* • Keith Carradine *Ty Smith* • Kevin Anderson *Peter Lewis* • Pat Hingle *Harold Clark* ■ *Dir* Jocelyn Moorhouse • *Scr* Laura Jones, from the novel by Jane Smiley

A Thousand and One Nights
★★★ U

Fantasy comedy adventure   1945 · US · Colour · 89min

This high-spirited Columbia comedy pokes gentle fun at the *Arabian Nights* genre, with a singing Cornel Wilde quite dashing as Aladdin. Wilde is well supported by a genial Phil Silvers and canny genie Evelyn Keyes. Much of this is genuinely spectacular, while director Alfred E Green proves *The Jolson Story* was no fluke. Rex Ingram, the "real" genie from the immortal 1940 movie *The Thief of Bagdad*, makes a knowing guest appearance. Fun for all ages. TS

Cornel Wilde *Aladdin* • Evelyn Keyes *Genie* • Phil Silvers *Abdullah* • Adele Jergens *Princess Armina* • Dusty Anderson *Novira* • Dennis Hoey *Sultan Kamar Al-Kir/Prince Hadji* • Philip Van Zandt *Grand Wazir Abu-Hassan* • Rex Ingram (2) *Giant* • Shelley Winter [Shelley Winters] *Handmaiden* ■ *Dir* Alfred E Green • *Scr* Wilfred H Pettitt, Richard English, Jack Henley, from a story by Wilfred H Pettitt

A Thousand Clowns ★★★ U

Comedy drama   1965 · US · BW · 115min

Jason Robards, a free-spirited writer, quits his job on a kid's television series, mainly due to a personality clash with the show's star, Gene Saks. Robards is guardian to his precocious 12-year-old nephew Barry Gordon, but this arrangement is threatened by his unemployed status. This thoughtful and intriguing comedy was nominated for four Oscars, with Martin Balsam winning as best supporting actor for his role as Robard's brother. DF

Jason Robards Jr [Jason Robards] *Murray Burns* • Barbara Harris *Sandra* • Martin Balsam *Arnold Burns* • Barry Gordon *Nick* • Gene Saks *Leo* • William Daniels (2) *Albert* ■ *Dir* Fred Coe • *Scr* Herb Gardner, from his play

The Thousand Eyes of Dr Mabuse ★★★

Crime drama   1960 · W Ger/It/Fr · BW · 103min

Fritz Lang returned to the criminal underworld for his swan song feature. The narrative owes much to the serials of yesteryear; the imagery is shot through with expressionist leitmotifs and the gadgetry is high kitsch rather than hi-tech. But the emphasis was very much on the extent to which the Nazi ethos, symbolised by Wolfgang Preiss's sinister mastermind, still pervaded contemporary Berlin. Critics detested it, but there are enough flashes of mastery to engross. DP German +subtitles. **DVD**

Dawn Addams *Marion Menil* • Peter Van Eyck *Henry B Travers* • Wolfgang Preiss *Dr Jordan* • Gert Fröbe *Inspector Krass* • Werner Peters *Hieronymous P Mistelzweig* • Andrea Checchi *Inspector Berg* • Howard Vernon *"No 12"* ■ *Dir* Fritz Lang • *Scr* Heinz Oskar Wuttig, Fritz Lang, from an idea by Jan Fethke, from characters by Norbert Jacques • *Cinematographer* Karl Löb

A Thousand Kisses Deep
★★ 15

Psychological thriller   2011 · US/UK · Colour · 84min

This time-travelling melodrama feels like a Mills & Boon reworking of *The Terminator*.

The sight of her elderly neighbour plunging from the roof of her apartment block sets nurse Jodie Whittaker on a journey of discovery into her former life with jazz trumpeter Dougray Scott, courtesy of caretaker David Warner and his rickety Victorian lift. The sequences set in the past are admirably authentic, and the performances are spirited. But Dana Lustig's laboured direction only accentuates the implausibilities in the plot. DP Swearing, sex scenes, drug abuse. **DVD**

Jodie Whittaker *Mia* • Dougray Scott *Ludwig* • David Warner *Max* • Emilia Fox *Doris* • Allan Corduner *Buddy* ■ *Dir* Dana Lustig • *Scr* Alex Kustanovich, Vadim Moldovan

A Thousand Months ★★★ 12

Drama   2003 · Fr/Bel/Mor · Colour · 119min

Moroccan Faouzi Bensaïdi makes his directorial debut with this engaging, episodic study of a young boy's initiation into the realities of village life. Unaware that his father is in jail for his political views, Fouad Labied is more devoted to the mayor's rebellious daughter than the mother and grandfather who sacrifice everything for his welfare. Cinematographer Antoine Heberle captures a landscape populated with survivors and eccentrics. DP Arabic +subtitles. **DVD**

Fouad Labied *Mehdi* • Nezha Rahile *Amina* • Mohamed Majd *Grandfather* • Abdelati Lambarki *Caïd* • Mohamed Bastaoui *Caïd's brother* ■ *Dir* Faouzi Bensaïdi • *Scr* Faouzi Bensaïdi, Emmanuelle Sardou

The 1,000 Plane Raid ★★ U

Second World War adventure   1969 · US · Colour · 93min

Christopher George delivers a thick-eared performance in this thoroughly routine war movie. As the abrasive USAF colonel who is convinced that his unit of B-17 bombers can knock out a key German aeroplane factory, despite the huge risks, he picks a fight with just about everyone he encounters. Even his girlfriend Laraine Stephens has to suffer his macho ire. The flying footage is fine, but somewhat repetitive. DP

Christopher George *Col Greg Brandon* • Laraine Stephens *Lt Gabrielle Ames* • JD Cannon *General Cotten Palmer* • Gary Marshall *Wing Commander Trafton Howard* • Michael Evans (1) *British Group Commander Leslie Hardwicke* • Ben Murphy *Lt Archer* • James Gammon *Major Varga* • Gavin Macleod *Sgt Kruger* ■ *Dir* Boris Sagal • *Scr* Donald S Sanford, from a story by Robert Vincent Wright, from a novel by Ralph Barker

A Thousand Times Good Night
★★★★ 15

Drama   2013 · Nor/Ire/Swe · Colour · 112min

When she's almost killed during an assignment in Kabul, photographer Juliette Binoche must confront the anguish she's causing her family in this globe-trotting English-language drama from Norwegian film-maker (and former photojournalist) Erik Poppe. Even by her own high standards, Binoche is utterly compelling here, ravaged by guilt back home in Ireland when she sees the anguish she's visiting on her daughter and husband, yet still driven to experience the adrenaline rush of taking pictures in the world's hottest spots. Binoche's fierce commitment and ever-beguiling screen presence make the story vividly convincing. TJ In Norwegian, English. Violence. **DVD** **BL**

Juliette Binoche *Rebecca* • Nikolaj Coster-Waldau *Marcus* • Lauryn Canny *Stephanie* • Adrianna Cramer Curtis *Lisa* • Maria Doyle Kennedy *Theresa* ■ *Dir* Erik Poppe • *Scr* Harald Rosenløw Eeg

Thousands Cheer ★★★ U

Second World War musical   1943 · US · Colour · 125min

Pianist/conductor José Iturbi made his film debut in this blockbusting wartime musical romance, whose witless script is the excuse for a grand finale ostensibly staged for the boys at an army camp, compèred by Mickey Rooney and parading a host of MGM stars in songs, dances and sketches. The nominal stars are Kathryn Grayson and Gene Kelly.

She's a singer who, while visiting her colonel father, organises the show, falls for private Kelly, a circus aerialist, and tries to bring her long-separated parents (John Boles, Mary Astor) together again. RK

Kathryn Grayson *Kathryn Jones* • Gene Kelly *Eddie Marsh* • Mary Astor *Hyllary Jones* • José Iturbi • John Boles *Col Bill Jones* • Dick Simmons *Captain Fred Avery* ■ *Dir* George Sidney (2) • *Scr* Paul Jarrico, Richard Collins

Thrashin'
★ 15

Action drama romance   1986 · US · Colour · 88min

Josh Brolin stars in yet another *Romeo and Juliet* retread – this time on skateboards. Brolin falls for Pamela Gidley, little sister of rival skater gang leader Robert Rusler. The acting is terrible, the story is worse, and the film is only notable for the appearance of rock group the Red Hot Chili Peppers. ST

Josh Brolin *Corey Webster* • Robert Rusler *Tommy Hook* • Pamela Gidley *Chrissy* • Brooke McCarter *Tyler* • Brett Marx *Bozo* • Josh Richman *Radley* • David Wagner *Little Stevie* • Sherilyn Fenn *Velvet* ■ *Dir* David Winters • *Scr* Paul Brown, Alan Sacks

Three
★★★

Drama   1969 · UK · Colour · 104min

In a modish but offbeat adult drama, two American guys on a European tour find their friendship strained when they become attracted to sexy Charlotte Rampling, who joins them on their trip. The story could easily have strayed into soap opera, but a mature script keeps the cast's heads above water. JG

Charlotte Rampling *Marty* • Robie Porter *Bert* • Sam Waterston *Taylor* • Pascale Roberts *Claude* • Edina Ronay *Liz* ■ *Dir* James Salter • *Scr* James Salter, from the story *Then There Were Three* by Irwin Shaw

Three – III
★ 15

Thriller   2006 · UK/Lux · Colour · 91min

The tiresomely regular unveiling of Kelly Brook's breasts is the most obvious draw for this inept desert island-set farrago. But even they can't obscure the lackadaisical performances, bottom-rung production values and dim-witted screenplay. Brook is the only female washed up on a desert island with her jealous husband (Billy Zane) and a studly ship's mate (Juan Pablo Di Pace), who predictably develops the hots for her. AS Swearing, sex scenes, nudity, violence. **DVD**

Billy Zane *Jack* • Kelly Brook *Jennifer* • Juan Pablo Di Pace *Manuel* • Todd Collins *Bill* ■ *Dir/Scr* Stewart Raffill

Three Ages
★★★★ U

Silent comedy   1923 · US · BW · 61min

Buster Keaton's delightful parody of DW Griffith's epic *Intolerance* tells the same story intercut between different time periods, with Buster as the hero, Wallace Beery as the villain and Margaret Leahy as the girl. In the Stone Age, there's a mortal combat for love; in Roman times it is a battle to the death in the arena; while the Present Day sees a play-off on the football field. The first of three full-length features for Metro, it was a box-office investment they never regretted. TH **DVD**

Buster Keaton *The hero* • Margaret Leahy *The girl* • Joe Roberts *Her father* • Lillian Lawrence *Her mother* • Wallace Beery *Rival* • Oliver Hardy *Rival's Roman helper* • Horace "Cupid" Morgan [Horace Morgan] *Emperor* • Blanche Payson *Amazon cavewoman* • Lionel Belmore ■ *Dir* Buster Keaton, Eddie Cline [Edward Cline] • *Scr* Clyde Bruckman, Jean Havez, Joseph Mitchell

Three Amigos!
★★★ PG

Comedy western   1986 · US · Colour · 103min

This enjoyably indulgent comedy features Chevy Chase, Steve Martin and Martin Short. The leads play stars of silent westerns who end up in Mexico on what they think is a publicity tour, only to discover that they are expected to defend a village from an evil group of bandits. It's nowhere near as funny as it should have been, but the chemistry between the stars and the gentle digs at the western genre make for a diverting enough entertainment. JF Swearing. DVD BL

Chevy Chase *Dusty Bottoms* • Steve Martin *Lucky Day* • Martin Short *Ned Nederlander* • Patrice Martinez *Carmen* • Philip Gordon *Rodrigo* • Michael Wren *Cowboy* • Fred Asparagus *Bartender* ■ *Dir* John Landis • *Scr* Steve Martin, Lorne Michaels, Randy Newman

Three and Out ★★ 15

Black comedy drama
2008 · UK · Colour · 95min

Mackenzie Crook stars in this horribly misconceived black comedy, playing a London tube driver who accidentally kills two commuters within a matter of days. Staff gossip tells him that if he kills someone else before the month is up, he'll be pensioned off with stress and given ten years' pay for his troubles. So he goes looking for a person depressed enough to jump under his train voluntarily, and finds the suicidal Tommy (Colm Meaney). From here, the story springs to picaresque life, with Tommy reconnecting with his abandoned wife and daughter. Although these scenes have a bittersweet appeal, the grotesque subject matter lingers like a bad smell as the film propels its way to a bleak, harrowing climax. DW DVD

Mackenzie Crook *Paul Callow* • Colm Meaney *Tommy* • Imelda Staunton *Rosemary* • Gemma Arterton *Frankie* • Gary Lewis *Callaghan* • Rhashan Stone *Ash* • Antony Sher *Maurice* • Kerry Katona *Mary* ■ *Dir* Jonathan Gershfield • *Scr* Steve Lewis, Tony Owen

[Three] Après la Vie ★★★★ 15

Melodrama
2002 · Fr/Bel · Colour · 119min

Although Lucas Belvaux's Grenoble trilogy can be watched in any order, this harrowing drama - the concluding instalment after *[One] Cavale* and *[Two] Un Couple Epatant*– makes the most impact, as it audaciously focuses on a peripheral character from the previous episodes and transforms our perceptions of her. Instead of being the timid victim of a flirtatious husband, Dominique Blanc emerges as a desperate junkie whose calculating manipulation of cop Gilbert Melki stands in stark contrast to the selfless risks he takes to keep her addiction both secret and satisfied. Moreover, her duplicity enables Belvaux to complete his shrewd and assured exposé of middle-class hypocrisy and superficiality on a note of both pity and disdain. DP French +subtitles. Swearing, drug abuse, violence. DVD

Dominique Blanc *Agnès Manise* • Gilbert Melki *Pascal Manise* • Ornella Muti *Cécile Costes* • Catherine Frot *Jeanne Rivet* • Lucas Belvaux *Bruno Le Roux* • François Morel *Alain Costes* • Valérie Mairesse *Claire* • Patrick Descamps *Jaquillat* ■ *Dir/Scr* Lucas Belvaux

3 Bad Men ★★★★

Silent western
1926 · US · BW · 92min

The second of John Ford's epic silent westerns - after *The Iron Horse* (1924) – had its contemporary appeal dented by the director's insistence on giving the prominent outlaw roles to grizzled character actors - J Farrell MacDonald, Tom Santschi and Frank Campeau. He did have the popular but bland George O'Brien as the young settler and Olive Borden as his sweetheart, both of whom are protected by the wanted threesome from a crooked sheriff and his gang. Ford shot much of the film on remote locations and re-created the spectacular Cherokee Strip land rush near Los Angeles, where the memorable shot of a baby being snatched to safety was done with a real infant. AE

George O'Brien *Dan O'Malley* • Olive Borden *Lee Carlton* • Lou Tellegen *Layne Hunter* • J Farrell MacDonald *Mike Costigan* • Tom Santschi *Bull Stanley* • Frank Campeau *Spade Allen* • George Harris (1) *Joe Minsk* ■ *Dir* John Ford • *Scr* John Stone, Ralph Spence (titles), Malcolm Stuart Boylan (titles)

Three Blind Mice ★★★

Romantic comedy
1938 · US · BW · 75min

Fed up with running their Kansas chicken farm, three sisters take off to a fashionable Californian resort in search of rich husbands. There, the eldest and most determined (Loretta Young) masquerades as a wealthy socialite, while the other two pose as her maid and secretary. Situations go from mad to worse as events involving David Niven and Joel McCrea take several unexpected turns. Despite some limp moments, it's enjoyable romantic comedy nonsense, remade as *Moon over Miami* (1941) and *Three Little Girls in Blue* (1946). RK

Loretta Young *Pamela Charters* • Joel McCrea *Van Dam Smith* • David Niven *Steve Harrington* • Stuart Erwin *Mike Brophy* • Marjorie Weaver *Moira Charters* • Pauline Moore *Elizabeth Charters* • Binnie Barnes *Miriam Harrington* ■ *Dir* William A Seiter • *Scr* Brown Holmes, Lynn Starling, from the play by Stephen Powys

Three Brothers ★★★

Drama
1980 · It/Fr · Colour · 111min

Returning to their hilltop village for the funeral of their mother, Roman judge Philippe Noiret, teacher of underprivileged Neapolitan children Vittorio Mezzogiorno and Turin mechanic with marital problems Michele Placido end up discussing how they've drifted apart and try to renew ties with their ageing father Charles Vanel. This is a laboured, if unexpectedly lyrical allegory on the social, cultural and political antagonisms that divide modern Italy. DP Italian +subtitles.

Philippe Noiret *Raffaele Giuranna* • Michele Placido *Nicola Giuranna* • Vittorio Mezzogiorno *Rocco Giuranna/Young Donato* • Charles Vanel *Donato Giuranna* • Andréa Ferréol *Raffael's wife* ■ *Dir* Francesco Rosi • *Scr* Tonino Guerra, Francesco Rosi, from the story *The Third Son* by A Platonov

The Three Burials of Melquiades Estrada ★★★★ 15

Western drama
2005 · US/Fr · Colour · 116min

Tommy Lee Jones's feature directorial debut is the finest western since Clint Eastwood's 1992 film *Unforgiven*. Jones won best actor at Cannes for his role as the ranch foreman honouring illegal immigrant Julio César Cedillo's request to be buried in his native Mexico should he die in Texas. But his performance behind the camera is even more assured, as he neatly sustains the small-town subplots and uses Chris Menges's widescreen cinematography to mirror the Texan's near-fanatical dedication to delivering the mouldering corpse of his friend and forcing Cedillo's killer, border patrol officer Barry Pepper, to apologise to the man's family. DP English, Spanish +subtitles. Swearing, violence. DVD BL

Tommy Lee Jones *Pete Perkins* • Barry Pepper *Mike Norton* • Julio César Cedillo *Melquiades Estrada* • Dwight Yoakam *Sheriff Frank Belmont* • January Jones *Lou Ann Norton* • Melissa Leo *Rachel* ■ *Dir* Tommy Lee Jones • *Scr* Guillermo Arriaga

The Three Caballeros ★★★ U

Part-animated fantasy
1944 · US · Colour · 68min

This wonderful slice of richly-Technicolored magic from Walt Disney was a follow-up to the short *Saludos Amigos*, a product of the US "Good Neighbour" policy towards Latin America. Combining live-action and animation, it stars Joe Carioca, his friend Panchito and Donald Duck himself, enjoying a musical spree which gives vent to a marvellously creative burst of cartoon energy. There's more wizardry as Donald gets tied up with the soundtrack and falls in love with Carmen Miranda's sister Aurora. Bear with the coy opening scenes; this is a treat. TS DVD

■ *Dir* Norman Ferguson, Clyde Geronimi, Jack Kinney, Bill Roberts, Harold Young • *Scr* Homer Brightman, Ernest Terrazzas, Ted Sears, Bill Peet, Ralph Wright, Elmer Plymmer, Roy Williams, William Cottrell, Del Connell, James Bodrero

Three Came Home ★★★★ 12

War drama based on a true story
1950 · US · BW · 105min

This intensely moving and superbly acted adaptation of a true story features magnificent performances from Claudette Colbert and Sessue Hayakawa as a Second World War internee and a cultured Japanese officer respectively. Generally underrated, this is a particularly fine example of postwar cinema, dealing with moral issues raised by the war itself. Although the Borneo setting is clearly a Hollywood soundstage, director Jean Negulesco creates a totally believable environment, and Hayakawa's performance prompted David Lean to cast him in *The Bridge on the River Kwai*. TS DVD

Claudette Colbert *Agnes Newton Keith* • Patric Knowles *Harry Keith* • Florence Desmond *Betty Sommers* • Sessue Hayakawa *Colonel Suga* • Sylvia Andrew *Henrietta* • Mark Keuning *George* • Phyllis Morris *Sister Rose* ■ *Dir* Jean Negulesco • *Scr* Nunnally Johnson, from the autobiography by Agnes Newton Keith

Three Cases of Murder ★★★

Portmanteau murder mystery
1953 · UK · BW · 88min

This compendium of three tales of the not-entirely-unexpected variety is notable mainly for a typically larger-than-life performance from Orson Welles. He plays an aristocratic politician who undergoes a disturbing penance for a wrong-doing he perpetuated on a colleague. The other stories feature able performances from a reliable British cast. JF

Alan Badel *Mr X/Harry/Owen* • Hugh Pryse *Jarvis* • John Salew *Mr Rooke* • Emrys Jones *George Wheeler* • John Gregson *Edgar Curtain* • Elizabeth Sellars *Elizabeth* • Orson Welles *Lord Mountdrago* • Helen Cherry *Lady Mountdrago* ■ *Dir* Wendy Toye, David Eady, George More O'Ferrall • *Scr* Donald Wilson, Sidney Carroll, Ian Dalrymple, from stories by Roderick Wilkinson, Brett Halliday, W Somerset Maugham

Three Coins in the Fountain ★★★★ U

Romantic comedy
1954 · US · Colour · 97min

Twentieth Century-Fox's stand-by plot was the one involving three assorted girls in any location, and here they're in Rome, throwing money for wishes into the Trevi Fountain. Their wishes are granted by Clifton Webb, Louis Jourdan and Rossano Brazzi. Milton Krasner's cinematography won an Oscar, as did the (uncredited) Frank Sinatra title song. In its day, the movie's dialogue was considered quite risqué, and the clothes and performances were the epitome of sophisticated chic. Jean Negulesco remade his movie ten years later as *The Pleasure Seekers*. TS DVD

Clifton Webb *Shadwell* • Dorothy McGuire *Miss Francis* • Jean Peters *Anita* • Louis Jourdan *Prince Dino Di Cessi* • Maggie McNamara *Maria* • Rossano Brazzi *Georgio* • Howard St John *Burgoyne* • Kathryn Givney *Mrs Burgoyne* • Cathleen Nesbitt *Principessa* ■ *Dir* Jean Negulesco • *Scr* John Patrick, from the novel by John H Secondari • *Music* Victor Young

Three Colours Blue ★★★★★ 15

Drama
1993 · Fr/Swi/Pol · Colour · 93min

Polish director Krzysztof Kieslowski already had the sublime and unsurpassable *Dekalog* series to his credit when he embarked upon this trilogy, named after the colours of the French flag and derived from the Revolutionary principles of liberty, equality and fraternity. Juliette Binoche gives an intense yet sensitive performance as the survivor of a car crash that killed her family, who discovers that, no matter how great her pain, she doesn't have the freedom to give up life. The process by which she deals with her grief is minutely observed, yet Kieslowski's direction is never intrusive, and his use of Zbigniew Preisner's score is

inspired. DP French +subtitles. Swearing, a sex scene, nudity. DVD BL

Juliette Binoche *Julie* • Benoît Régent *Olivier* • Florence Pernel *Sandrine* • Charlotte Véry *Lucille* • Hélène Vincent *Journalist* • Philippe Volter *Estate agent* • Claude Duneton *Doctor* ■ *Dir* Krzysztof Kieslowski • *Scr* Krzysztof Piesiewicz, Krzysztof Kieslowski

Three Colours White ★★★★ 15

Comedy drama
1993 · Fr/Swi/Pol · Colour · 91min

The second film in Krzysztof Kieslowski's trilogy is the slightest of the series, yet there is still much to admire in a movie intended as a tribute to Charlie Chaplin. Although a comedy, *White* is an examination of the aftermath of the Communist regime in Poland under which everyone was supposed to be equal. The picture painted of democratic Warsaw, with its shady deals and run-down streets, is both unflattering and affectionate, providing an animated backdrop to the droll story of jilted hairdresser Zbigniew Zamachowski, who's determined never to feel inferior again. DP Polish, French +subtitles. Violence, nudity. DVD BL

Zbigniew Zamachowski *Karol Karol* • Julie Delpy *Dominique* • Janusz Gajos *Mikolaj* • Jerzy Stuhr *Jurek* • Grzegorz Warchol *Elegant man* • Jerzy Nowak *Old farmer* ■ *Dir* Krzysztof Kieslowski • *Scr* Krzysztof Piesiewicz, Krzysztof Kieslowski

Three Colours Red ★★★★★ 15

Drama
1994 · Fr/Swi/Pol · Colour · 99min

Earning Krzysztof Kieslowski Oscar nominations for both script (co-written by Krzysztof Piesiewicz) and direction, the concluding part of his tricolor trilogy has much in common with his earlier *The Double Life of Véronique*. Not only does it reunite him with Irène Jacob, but it also explores the theme that people are bound together by fraternal ties that they can never fully understand. Gloriously shot on location in Geneva by Oscar-nominated cinematographer Piotr Sobocinski, the film's use of colour and sound is unparalleled in 1990s cinema, while the intricate plot linking model Jacob with snooping judge Jean-Louis Trintignant is spellbinding. DP French +subtitles. Sex scenes, nudity. DVD BL

Irène Jacob *Valentine Dussaut* • Jean-Louis Trintignant *Judge Joseph Kern* • Frédérique Feder *Karin* • Jean-Pierre Lorit *Auguste Bruner* • Samuel Le Bihan *Photographer* • Marion Stalens *Veterinary surgeon* • Teco Celio *Barman* ■ *Dir* Krzysztof Kieslowski • *Scr* Krzysztof Kieslowski, Krzysztof Piesiewicz

Three Comrades ★★★

Drama
1938 · US · BW · 100min

Three Germans who fought in the First World War run a repair shop and all are in love with the same girl - Margaret Sullavan - who just happens to have terminal tuberculosis. This overblown melodrama was intended to make American audiences cry buckets yet, at the same time, comprehend Hitler's Reich, though the word "Nazi" was *verboten*. F Scott Fitzgerald received credit for the script, though it was extensively rewritten by Joseph L Mankiewicz after Sullavan protested that Fitzgerald's dialogue was unplayable. AT

Robert Taylor (1) *Erich Lohkamp* • Margaret Sullavan *Pat Hollmann* • Franchot Tone *Otto Koster* • Robert Young (1) *Gottfried Lenz* • Guy Kibbee *Alfons* • Lionel Atwill *Franz Breuer* • Henry Hull *Dr Heinrich Becker* • George Zucco *Dr Plauten* ■ *Dir* Frank Borzage • *Scr* F Scott Fitzgerald, Edward Paramore [Edward E Paramore Jr], from the novel by Erich Maria Remarque

Three Daring Daughters ★★★ U

Musical comedy
1948 · US · Colour · 113min

This schmaltzy, formula MGM musical is typical of the Joe Pasternak stable from which it came. Jeanette MacDonald stars as the divorced mother of three daughters (Jane Powell among them) who do not take kindly to mother's romance with a pianist (José Iturbi). Delightfully predictable, this is crammed with musical numbers both classical and popular and Iturbi's dazzling pyrotechnics. It's old-fashioned, but still fun. RK

Jeanette MacDonald *Louise Rayton Morgan* • José Iturbi • Jane Powell *Tess Morgan* • Edward Arnold *Robert Nelson* • Harry Davenport *Dr Cannon* • Mary Eleanor Donahue *Alix Morgan* • Ann E Todd *Ilka Morgan* ■ *Dir* Fred M Wilcox • *Scr* Albert Mannheimer, Frederick Kohner, Sonya Levien, John Meehan, from Kohner and Mannheimer's play *The Birds and the Flowers*

Three Days of the Condor
★★★★ 15
Thriller 1975 · US · Colour · 117min

Conspiracy theories abounded in Hollywood in the 1970s, as film-makers began to explore the nation's dark underside in the wake of Vietnam and Watergate. Directed by Sydney Pollack and starring Robert Redford, this terse thriller is a polished piece of work, as Redford holds photographer Faye Dunaway hostage while he tries to ascertain Max von Sydow's role in the murder of his undercover colleagues. The excellent cast makes up for Pollack's occasional lapses in pacing. DP Violence, swearing, a sex scene. DVD BD

Robert Redford *Turner* • Faye Dunaway *Kathy Hale* • Cliff Robertson *Higgins* • Max von Sydow *Joubert* • John Houseman *Mr Wabash* • Addison Powell *Atwood* • Walter McGinn *Sam Barber* • Tina Chen *Janice* ■ *Dir* Sydney Pollack • *Scr* Lorenzo Semple Jr, David Rayfiel, from the novel *Six Days of the Condor* by James Grady

3 Days to Kill
★★ 12
Action thriller 2014 · US/Fr · Colour · 117min

Kevin Costner emulates Liam Neeson in *Taken* in this lacklustre genre flick. Costner plays a veteran CIA agent diagnosed with a fatal disease who accepts one last assignment in order to get his hands on an new drug. However, his mission is complicated by the fact that he is also trying to reconnect with his surly teenage daughter (Hailee Steinfeld). The performances can't be faulted, and the action sequences have plenty of verve, but director McG interrupts them with tedious comedy sequences and some overly sentimental family moments. JF Violence, swearing, sexual references. DVD BD

Kevin Costner *Ethan Renner* • Amber Heard *Vivi Delay* • Hailee Steinfeld *Zooey Renner* • Connie Nielsen *Christine Renner* • Tomas Lemarquis *The Albino* • Richard Sammel *The Wolf* ■ *Dir* McG [Joseph McGinty Nichol] • *Scr* Luc Besson, Adi Hasak, from a story by Besson

The Three Faces of Eve
★★★ PG
Psychological drama 1957 · US · BW · 91min

An Oscar-winning performance from Joanne Woodward is the highlight of writer/director Nunnally Johnson's uneven film. Woodward is a young wife and mother who has three split personalities – insecure housewife, irresponsible floozy and educated woman. Her husband David Warner is sceptical, but psychiatrist Lee J Cobb soon sees all three personalities and takes on the task of trying to merge them into one again. Alistair Cooke adds some weight as the narrator, but despite the fact that it's based on a real case history, the movie falters when Woodward interacts with anyone except her doctor. JB

Joanne Woodward *Eve* • David Wayne *Ralph White* • Lee J Cobb *Dr Luther* • Edwin Jerome *Dr Day* • Alena Murray *Secretary* • Nancy Kulp *Mrs Black* • Douglas Spencer *Mr Black* • Terry Ann Ross *Bonnie* • Alistair Cooke *Narrator* ■ *Dir* Nunnally Johnson • *Scr* Nunnally Johnson, from a book by Corbett H Thigpen, Hervey M Cleckley

Three Faces West
★★ U
Drama 1940 · US · BW · 75min

This modern western attempted to cash in on John Ford's *The Grapes of Wrath* by featuring the plight of Dust Bowl farmers as well as being a story of refugees from Nazi Germany settling in America. John Wayne

arranges for Charles Coburn's eminent Viennese surgeon and his daughter, played by Norwegian actress Sigrid Gurie, to move away from the doomed farming area and settle in Oregon. Preaching self-help and optimism, the film shows no sign of a left-wing viewpoint, though the director, Bernard Vorhaus, and one of the writers, Samuel Ornitz, were later blacklisted. AE DVD

John Wayne *John* • Sigrid Gurie *Leni* • Charles Coburn *Dr Braun* • Spencer Charters *Nunk* • Helen MacKellar *Mrs Welles* • Roland Varno *Eric* • Sonny Bupp *Billy Welles* ■ *Dir* Bernard Vorhaus • *Scr* Frederick Hugh Herbert [F Hugh Herbert], Samuel Ornitz, Doris Anderson, Joseph Moncure March

3:15
★★ 18
Action drama 1986 · US · Colour · 80min

Larry Gross, who co-wrote *48 HRS* and has enjoyed a successful screenwriting career since, directs this action drama. However, the chief point of interest in this derivative teen-gang thriller is looking out for upcoming stars in early outings. The lead role goes to Adam Baldwin, as a reformed gang thug who is dragged back into that violent world when his girlfriend is attacked. JF

Adam Baldwin *Jeff Hannah* • Deborah Foreman *Sherry Havilland* • René Auberjonois *Principal Horner* • Ed Lauter *Moran* • Scott McGinnis *Chris* • Danny De La Paz *Cinco* • Mario Van Peebles *Whisperer* • Gina Gershon *Cobrette* ■ *Dir* Larry Gross • *Scr* Sam Bernard, Michael Jacobs

Three for the Road
★★ 15
Drama 1987 · US · Colour · 87min

Even after *Platoon*, Charlie Sheen was demonstrating his unerring ability to pick turkeys, and this would-be road movie was never released in cinemas in the UK. Sheen and the underrated Alan Ruck bite off more than they can chew when they are asked to escort the rebellious daughter of a politician to a reform school. JF

Charlie Sheen *Paul Tracy* • Kerri Green *Robin Kitteridge* • Alan Ruck *Tommy, "TS"* • Sally Kellerman *Blanche* • Blair Tefkin *Missy* • Raymond J Barry *Senator Kitteridge* • Alexa Hamilton *Virginia* • Bert Remsen *Stu* ■ *Dir* BWL Norton [Bill L Norton] • *Scr* Richard Martini, Tim Metcalfe, Miguel Tejada-Flores, from a story by Richard Martini

Three for the Show
★★★
Musical 1955 · US · Colour · 91min

This is the one about the girl who, believing her husband dead, has remarried only for him to reappear and confront her with a dilemma. It was a successful romantic comedy as *Too Many Husbands* in 1940, and would resurface in reverse – James Garner playing a husband with two wives – as *Move Over, Darling* in 1963. Here, showgirl Betty Grable is caught between returning Jack Lemmon and incumbent Gower Champion in a lively musical version of the tale. RK

Betty Grable *Julie* • Marge Champion *Gwen Howard* • Gower Champion *Vernon Lowndes* • Jack Lemmon *Marty Stewart* • Myron McCormick *Mike Hudson* • Paul Harvey *Colonel Wharton* • Robert Bice *Sergeant O'Hallihan* ■ *Dir* HC Potter • *Scr* Edward Hope, Leonard Stern [Leonard B Stern], from the play *Too Many Husbands* by W Somerset Maugham

Three Fugitives
★★★ 15
Crime comedy 1989 · US · Colour · 92min

French director Francis Veber made his Hollywood debut with this enjoyable remake of his own 1986 French odd-couple farce, *Les Fugitifs*. Nick Nolte does well enough as the armed robber out on parole, while Martin Short gets plenty of slapstick laughs as the incompetent bank robber who drags the unwilling Nolte into his bungled caper. The action gets off to a good start and, despite sentimental moments, keeps up a fair pace, with a healthy ration of amusement. PF Violence, swearing. DVD

Nick Nolte *Daniel Lucas* • Martin Short *Ned Perry* • Sarah Rowland Doroff *Meg Perry* • James Earl Jones *Detective Dugan* • Alan Ruck *Tener* • Kenneth McMillan *Horvath* ■ *Dir/Scr* Francis Veber

Three Godfathers
★★★ U
Western 1948 · US · Colour · 102min

The first half-hour of this western ranks among the very best of ace director John Ford's work. But then the plot starts, and the film turns out to be a western precursor of *Three Men and a Baby*, only here the trio is on the run from sheriff Ward Bond. Excellent though the three leads are, they only just manage to keep their embarrassment at bay, despite the sheer daftness of the whole exercise with its bizarre religious and allegorical connotations. TS DVD

John Wayne *Robert Hightower* • Pedro Armendáriz *Pete* • Harry Carey Jr *Kid* • Ward Bond *"Buck" Perley Sweet* • Mae Marsh *Mrs Perley Sweet* • Mildred Natwick *Mother* • Jane Darwell *Miss Florie* • Guy Kibbee *Judge* ■ *Dir* John Ford • *Scr* Laurence Stallings, Frank S Nugent, from the story by Peter B Kyne

Three Guns for Texas
★★ U
Western 1968 · US · Colour · 98min

Three episodes of the hit TV western *Laredo* are shoehorned into this theatrical release, but the result leaves a lot to be desired. Shelley Morrison's native American outlaw features, kidnapping Texas Ranger William Smith as a prospective groom. But plotlines involving pompous lawman Philip Carey and Neville Brand's paranoid pal Albert Salmi are bland. DP

Neville Brand *Reese Bennett* • Peter Brown *Chad Cooper* • William Smith *Joe Riley* • Martin Milner *MacMillan* • Philip Carey *Captain Parmalee* • Albert Salmi *Cleetus Grogan* ■ *Dir* David Lowell Rich, Paul Stanley, Earl Bellamy • *Scr* John DF Black

Three Hats for Lisa
★★ U
Musical 1965 · UK · Colour · 95min

Joe Brown stars in this trite tosh about a docker, a cabbie and a foreign film star. Not even the presence of the great Sidney James can elevate this story of Sophie Hardy's search for three typically English hats. The script, co-written by *Carry On* regular Talbot Rothwell, raises a few smiles, but the songs signified a new low in screen pop music. DP DVD

Joe Brown (2) *Johnny Howjego* • Sophie Hardy *Lisa Milan* • Sidney James *Sid Marks* • Una Stubbs *Flora* • Peter Bowles *Sammy* • Seymour Green *Signor Molfino* • Josephine Blake *Miss Penny* ■ *Dir* Sidney Hayers • *Scr* Leslie Bricusse, Talbot Rothwell, from a story by Leslie Bricusse

300
★★★★ 15
Historical action adventure 2006 · US · Colour · 111min

Director Zack Snyder brings Frank Miller's celebrated graphic novel to the big screen with this terrific re-creation of the Battle of Thermopylae in 480 BC. Staging live-action combat against virtual backgrounds, this is the second film to render Miller's visual panache in pure cinematic flash, bang and wallop, following the neo-*noir* atmospherics of *Sin City* (2005). The story is a simple one: Sparta's King Leonidas (Gerard Butler) rallies 300 of his finest warriors to fight to the death against a massive invading Persian army. Breathtaking choreography consistently erupts with gory violence as Snyder marshals his red-caped Spartans against the hordes. Both fun and exciting, this is a stunning technical accomplishment. A belated follow-up, *300: Rise of an Empire* starring Eva Green and Lena Headey, is due in 2014. AJ DVD BD

Gerard Butler *King Leonidas* • Lena Headey *Queen Gorgo* • David Wenham *Dilios* • Dominic West *Theron* • Vincent Regan *Captain* • Michael Fassbender *Stelios* ■ *Dir* Zack Snyder • *Scr* Zack Snyder, Kurt Johnstad, Michael B Gordon, from the graphic novel by Frank Miller, Lynn Varley • *Cinematographer* Larry Fong

300: Rise of an Empire
★★★★ 15
Historical action adventure 2013 · US · Colour · 98min

This worthy companion piece to Zack Snyder's *300* depicts events that run parallel to the Spartan massacre. General Themistocles (Sullivan Stapleton) rallies his

fellow Grecians together against the massive Persian navy led by ruthless commander Artemisia (Eva Green). Like *300*, the film is based on a Frank Miller graphic novel, and director Noam Murro skilfully sticks to what worked the first time in terms of raw, full-blooded violence and rugged, thunderous action. While Stapleton can't quite match the charisma of Gerard Butler's King Leonidas, a breathtaking Green does evil in the highest style possible, despite being saddled with the most risible dialogue. AJ Violence, a sex scene, nudity. DVD BD

Eva Green *Artemisia* • Sullivan Stapleton *Themistocles* • Rodrigo Santoro *Xerxes* • Lena Headey *Queen Gorgo* • David Wenham *Dilios* • Jack O'Connell (2) *Calisto* ■ *Dir* Noam Murro • *Scr* Kurt Johnstad, Zack Snyder, from the graphic novel *Xerxes* by Frank Miller

The 300 Spartans
★★★ PG
Historical adventure 1962 · US · Colour · 113min

At a time when the sword-and-sandal epic was flourishing in Italy, 20th Century-Fox went to Greece to shoot this antiquarian adventure about the stalwart defence of Thermopylae in 480 BC. The production looks a little threadbare, but the locations are intelligently used by director Rudolph Maté, who also manages to stage the battle sequences on a reasonably convincing scale. Less authentic, however, is the dialogue, which defeats an actor of the calibre of Ralph Richardson, and gives an animated statue like Richard Egan no chance at all. DP DVD

Richard Egan *King Leonidas of Sparta* • Ralph Richardson *Themistocles of Athens* • Diane Baker *Ellas* • Barry Coe *Phylon* • David Farrar *Xerxes* • Donald Houston *Hydarnes* ■ *Dir* Rudolph Maté • *Scr* George St George, from the original story material by Ugo Liberatore, Remigio Del Grosso, Giovanni D'Eramo, Gian Paolo Callegari

Three into Two Won't Go
★★★
Sex drama 1969 · UK · Colour · 93min

This seminal 1960s sex drama has Rod Steiger as a salesman who picks up sexy hitch-hiker Judy Geeson, has a fling with her, and then finds his marriage to Claire Bloom under threat when the girl brazenly moves in with them. Directed by Peter Hall, this has obvious class, but passing time and changing moral values have done it no favours. Considered quite shocking in its day, it's now hard to see what all the fuss was about. DA

Rod Steiger *Steve Howard* • Claire Bloom *Frances Howard* • Judy Geeson *Ella Patterson* • Peggy Ashcroft *Belle* • Paul Rogers *Jack Roberts* • Lynn Farleigh *Janet* • Elizabeth Spriggs *Marcia* ■ *Dir* Peter Hall • *Scr* Edna O'Brien, from a novel by Andrea Newman

3-iron
★★★★ 15
Romantic drama 2004 · S Kor/Jpn · Colour · 87min

Korean director Kim Ki-Duk's captivating Zen romance combines the calm gentility of his *Spring, Summer, Autumn, Winter ... and Spring* with the wincing violence of *The Isle* to ethereally fascinating effect. Jae Hee illegally occupies vacant homes for as long as the real tenants are away, until in one dwelling he finds battered wife Lee Seung-yeon who joins his hand-to-mouth existence. It's when they find a dead man in another house, get accused of murder, and Lee is returned to her abusive husband (Kwon Hyuk-ho) that the mystical elements come to the fore. AJ Korean +subtitles. Sex scenes, violence. DVD

Lee Seung-yeon *Sun-hwa* • Jae Hee *Tae-suk* • Kwon Hyuk-ho *Min-kyu* • Joo Jin-mo *Detective Cho* • Choi Jeong-ho *Jailor* • Lee Joo-suk *Son of old man* • Lee Mi-sook *Daughter-in-law of old man* • Moon Sung-hyuk *Sung-hyuk* ■ *Dir/Scr* Kim Ki-Duk

Three Kings
★★★★ 15
Wartime action adventure 1999 · US · Colour · 110min

This superb, though very violent – mix of comedy, drama and action is set at the end of the Gulf War. Hearing a rumour that

Saddam Hussein has stashed stolen gold in bunkers, US soldiers George Clooney, Ice Cube and Mark Wahlberg embark on a secret field trip. It seems simple enough: grab the bullion and be rich for the rest of their lives. However, when they encounter villagers being tortured by Saddam's men, the guys reluctantly agree to help them. This boasts terrific performances, while taking some well-aimed stabs at the late 20th-century phenomenon of war waged on television. JB Swearing, violence, sex scenes. **DVD** **BLU**

George Clooney *Major Archie Gates* • Mark Wahlberg *Sergeant Troy Barlow* • Ice Cube *Staff Sergeant Chief Elgin* • Spike Jonze *Private Conrad Vig* • Nora Dunn *Adriana Cruz* • Jamie Kennedy *Walter Wogaman* • Mykelti Williamson *Colonel Horn* • Cliff Curtis *Amir Abdulah* ■ *Dir* David O Russell • *Scr* David O Russell, from a story by John Ridley

Three Little Girls in Blue ★★★ U

Musical 1946 · US · Colour · 90min

This is a light and chirpy musical remake of 1938's *Three Blind Mice* (the plot was later rehashed for *How to Marry a Millionaire* in 1953). Take three girls, bored with life down on the chicken farm, and each wanting to find a rich husband. Cut to the big city, add a handful of musical numbers, some frisky hoofing and lavish period art direction. Stir gently and end up with an agreeable movie that is unmomentous but entertaining. PF

June Haver *Pam Charters* • George Montgomery *Van Damm Smith* • Vivian Blaine *Liz Charters* • Celeste Holm *Miriam Harrington* • Vera-Ellen *Myra Charters* • Frank Latimore *Steve Harrinton* • Charles Smith *Mike Bailey* • Charles Halton *Hoskins* ■ *Dir* H Bruce Humberstone • *Scr* Valentine Davis, Brown Holmes, Lynn Starling, Robert Ellis, Helen Logan, from the play by Stephen Powys

The Three Little Pigs ★★★★★ U

Animated musical comedy
1933 · US · Colour · 8min

This Oscar-winning short cartoon – one of the most popular in film history – was significant for a number of reasons. It introduced the concept of "squash and stretch", the technique by which a character retains believability by maintaining a constant volume as its body distorts. Additionally, it was the first true example of "personality animation" – although the three pigs look identical, they behave differently. And then there was Frank Churchill and Ann Ronell's theme song *Who's Afraid of the Big Bad Wolf?* To Depression-era audiences, this cheerful ditty of defiance was symbolically encouraging. CLP **DVD**

Mary Moder *Fiddler Pig* • Dorothy Compton *Fife Pig* • Pinto Colvig *Practical Pig* • Billy Bletcher *Zeke Wolf* ■ *Dir* Burt Gillett

T Three Little Words ★★★★ U

Musical biography 1950 · US · Colour · 102min

A top-notch cast and a clutch of hit songs make this film biography of songwriters Bert Kalmar and Harry Ruby perfect matinée material. Kalmar and Ruby bore as much resemblance to Fred Astaire and Red Skelton as the story bears to their lives. But with Astaire in three dances, two with Vera-Ellen, and Skelton, funny but more restrained than usual, it can't miss as light entertainment. In her third film, Debbie Reynolds has a cameo as Helen Kane, the "Boop-Boop-a-Doop" girl in *I Wanna Be Loved By You*, singing dubbed by Miss Kane. RB

Fred Astaire *Bert Kalmar, "Kendall the Great"* • Red Skelton *Harry Ruby* • Vera-Ellen *Jessie Brown Kalmar* • Arlene Dahl *Eileen Percy* • Keenan Wynn *Charlie Kope* • Gale Robbins *Terry Lordel* • Gloria DeHaven *Mrs Carter DeHaven* • Debbie Reynolds *Helen Kane* ■ *Dir* Richard Thorpe • *Scr* George Wells, from an autobiography by Bert Kalmar, Harry Ruby

Three Lives and Only One Death ★★★★

Fantasy comedy drama
1996 · Fr · Colour · 124min

The genius of Marcello Mastroianni illuminates this amusing diversion from Raúl Ruiz. He plays four different roles in a seemingly disconnected quartet of stories: a travelling salesman who surprises his ex-wife and her new husband; a Sorbonne professor who takes up with a similarly detached prostitute; a sinister butler trying to poison his employers; and a tycoon with a tendency to panic in a crisis. The aim of this delicious mêlée of running gags and visual puns is to question the validity of a single European culture. DP French +subtitles.

Marcello Mastroianni *Mateo Strano/Georges Vickers/Butler/Luc Allamand* • Anna Galiena *Tania* • Marisa Paredes *Maria* • Melvil Poupaud *Martin* • Chiara Mastroianni *Cecile* • Arielle Dombasle *Helene* • Féodor Atkine *André* • Jean-Yves Gautier *Mario* ■ *Dir* Raúl Ruiz • *Scr* Raúl Ruiz, Pascal Bonitzer

The Three Lives of Thomasina ★★★ U

Period fantasy 1963 · US/UK · Colour · 94min

Patrick McGoohan is superb in this British-made Disney fantasy about a veterinary surgeon whose decision to put down his daughter's ailing cat leads to magical encounters with a mysterious stranger. McGoohan is nicely supported by Susan Hampshire and Finlay Currie, but the adult leads are no match for the delightful Karen Dotrice as McGoohan's daughter and a very scene-stealing feline. TS

Patrick McGoohan *Andrew MacDhui* • Susan Hampshire *Lori MacGregor* • Karen Dotrice *Mary MacDhui* • Laurence Naismith *Reverend Angus Peddie* • Jean Anderson *Mrs MacKenzie* • Finlay Currie *Grandpa Stirling* ■ *Dir* Don Chaffey • *Scr* Robert Westerby, from the novel *Thomasina, the Cat Who Thought She Was God* by Paul Gallico

Three Loves ★★★

Silent romantic thriller 1929 · Ger · BW · 75min

In this strange, dream-like, threatening and romantic story, young Frenchman Uno Henning, who has married for money rather than love, then meets the intriguing Marlene Dietrich on his honeymoon. He falls in love with her, and she begs him to save her from sinister Fritz Kortner. Directed by Kurt (later Curtis) Bernhardt, this is the film that first gained American attention for Dietrich, with *Variety* drawing comparisons to Garbo and pronouncing the German star "a strong contender for international honours". RK

Marlene Dietrich *Stascha* • Fritz Kortner *Dr Karoff* • Frida Richard *Frau Leblanc* • Oskar Sima *Charles Leblanc* • Uno Henning *Henry Leblanc* ■ *Dir* Kurt Bernhardt [Curtis Bernhardt] • *Scr* Ladislaus Vajda, from the novel *Die Frau, nach der Man sich Sehnt* by Max Brod

Three Loves Has Nancy ★

Romantic comedy 1938 · US · BW · 69min

Janet Gaynor, a naive and irritating girl from a hick town down South, comes to New York to look for her missing fiancé, and seeks refuge with novelist Robert Montgomery whom she'd met earlier. Her presence, cooking and homespun simplicity cause general mayhem for Montgomery and his drunken friend and neighbour Franchot Tone. An absurd and unconvincing attempt at screwball comedy. RK

Janet Gaynor *Nancy Briggs* • Robert Montgomery *Malcolm Niles* • Franchot Tone *Robert Hansen* • Guy Kibbee *Pa Briggs* • Claire Dodd *Vivian Herford* • Reginald Owen *Valet* • Cora Witherspoon *Mrs Herford* ■ *Dir* Richard Thorpe • *Scr* Bella Spewack, Sam Spewack, George Oppenheimer, David Hertz, from a story by Lee Loeb, Mort Braus

The Three Marias ★★★ 15

Revenge drama
2002 · Bra/It/Neth · Colour · 106min

Director Aluizio Abranches reworks many of the conventions of Brazilian revenge dramas in this wry blend of naturalism and surrealism. The most significant departure is that the task of avenging the family honour falls to Marieta Severo's daughters – Julia Lemmertz, Maria Luisa Mendonca and Luiza Mariani – each of whom must locate a specialist assassin. Their encounters all have their own distinctive tone that adds to the atmosphere of tension and intrigue. DP Portuguese +subtitles. Violence. **DVD**

Marieta Severo *Filomena Capadocio* • Julia Lemmertz *Maria Francisca* • Maria Luisa Mendonca *Maria Rosa* • Luiza Mariani *Maria Pia* • Carlos Vereza *Firmino Santos Guerra* • Enrique Diaz *Ze das Cobras* • Tuca Andrada *Chief Tenorio* • Wagner Moura *Jesuino Cruz* ■ *Dir* Aluizio Abranches • *Scr* Heitor Dhalia, Wilson Freire

Three Men and a Baby ★★★★ PG

Comedy 1987 · US · Colour · 98min

The title says it all – bachelors Ted Danson, Steve Guttenberg and Tom Selleck are left holding the baby abandoned on their doorstep, and it's not long before they are knee-deep in bottles, nappies and gooey moments. The three leads look suitably harassed as they adapt to changing, feeding and burping duties, and director Leonard Nimoy (Mr Spock himself) keeps the comedy and entertainment coming thick and fast. Based on the French film *3 Men and a Cradle*, this is thoroughly enjoyable family fare. JB Swearing. **DVD**

Tom Selleck *Peter Mitchell* • Steve Guttenberg *Michael Kellam* • Ted Danson *Jack Holden* • Nancy Travis *Sylvia* • Margaret Colin *Rebecca* • Celeste Holm *Jack's mother* • Philip Bosco *Det Melkowitz* ■ *Dir* Leonard Nimoy • *Scr* James Orr, Jim Cruickshank, from the film *3 Men and a Cradle/Trois Hommes et un Couffin* by Coline Serreau

3 Men and a Cradle ★★★★ 12

Comedy 1985 · Fr · Colour · 101min

Former actress Coline Serreau hit the jackpot as a writer/director with this box-office smash about three die-hard bachelors who have to look after a baby girl. The plot centres around the allegation that one of the men is the baby's father. There's also a stash of drugs hidden in the cradle that attracts the attentions of the underworld and the cops. Smartly paced and engagingly acted, it's a sweet little satire about the demolition of the male ego in the era of feminism. Hollywood snapped up the remake rights and made the monster hit *Three Men and a Baby*. Belatedly followed by a disappointing sequel, *18 Years Later*. AT French dubbed. **DVD**

Roland Giraud *Pierre* • Michel Boujenah *Michel* • André Dussollier *Jacques* • Philippine Leroy-Beaulieu *Sylvia* • Gwendoline Mourlet *First Marie* • Jennifer Moret *Second Marie* • Dominique Lavanant *Madame Rapons* ■ *Dir/Scr* Coline Serreau

Three Men and a Little Lady ★★ PG

Comedy 1990 · US · Colour · 99min

In this decidedly lacklustre comedy sequel to *Three Men and a Baby*, Tom Selleck, Steve Guttenberg and Ted Danson travel to London to try to prevent their adopted daughter from being sent to – horrors! – boarding school. As an insult to Britain it would have been more effective if it had been better made, but it wasn't. In addition, casting British actors to perform as if they are the befuddled eccentrics of an imaginary England of the 1950s seems almost contemptuous. TH **DVD**

Tom Selleck *Peter Mitchell* • Steve Guttenberg *Michael Kellam* • Ted Danson *Jack Holden* • Nancy Travis *Sylvia Bennington* • Robin Weisman *Mary Bennington* • Christopher Cazenove *Edward* • Sheila Hancock *Vera* • Fiona Shaw *Miss Lomax* • John Boswall *Barrow* ■ *Dir* Emile Ardolino • *Scr* Charlie Peters, from a story by Sara Parriott, Josann McGibbon

Three Men in a Boat ★★★★ U

Comedy 1956 · UK · Colour · 87min

The nostalgic appeal of Jerome K Jerome's Victorian trio is undimmed – and perhaps even enhanced – by a rather childish approach to their messing about on the Thames with a scene-stealing dog. Despite a pretend feud between Jimmy Edwards and Laurence Harvey, kept up throughout filming for publicity purposes, the ensemble, including David Tomlinson, is amiability itself, while the parasol-toting girls are as radiant as the golden days of yesteryear. TH **DVD**

Laurence Harvey *George* • Jimmy Edwards *Harris* • David Tomlinson *J* • Shirley Eaton *Sophie Clutterbuck* • Jill Ireland *Bluebell Porterhouse* • Lisa Gastoni *Primrose Porterhouse* • Martita Hunt *Mrs Willis* • Campbell Cotts *Ambrose Porterhouse* • Joan Haythorne *Mrs Porterhouse* ■ *Dir* Ken Annakin • *Scr* Hubert Gregg, Vernon Harris, from the novel by Jerome K Jerome

Three Men in White ★★ U

Medical drama 1944 · US · BW · 84min

The 1942 departure of its title star, Lew Ayres, ended the popular series of *Dr Kildare* films. However, with Lionel Barrymore still on hand, MGM segued into the *Dr Gillespie* series, focusing on the crusty old wheelchair-using physician for six increasingly feeble movies, which finally put paid to Blair Hospital in 1947. This one has Gillespie seeking a new assistant and having to choose between Van Johnson and Keye Luke. RK

Lionel Barrymore *Dr Leonard Gillespie* • Van Johnson *Dr Randall Adams* • Keye Luke *Dr Lee Wong How* • Ava Gardner *Jean Brown* • Alma Kruger *Molly Byrd* ■ *Dir* Willis Goldbeck • *Scr* Martin Berkeley, Harry Ruskin, from the characters by Max Brand

Three Men to Destroy ★★★

Crime thriller 1980 · Fr · Colour · 90min

Stopping to help an accident victim, Alain Delon finds himself caught up in a bungled underworld hit and becomes the target of mobster Pierre Dux. However, when he turns himself into an efficient killing machine, the pursuit takes on a very different nature. This is a dark, almost Darwinian treatise on our potential for violence. Edgily directed, it's played with plenty of steel by Delon. DP French dubbed.

Alain Delon *Michel Gerfaut* • Dalila DiLazzaro *Bea* • Pierre Dux *Emmerich* • Michel Auclair *Leprince* ■ *Dir* Jacques Deray • *Scr* Jacques Deray, Christopher Franck, from the novel by Jean-Patrick Manchette

Three Miles North of Molkom... ★★★ 15

Documentary 2009 · UK · Colour · 103min

The annual No Mind festival held in the Swedish forest retreat of Angsbacka attracts a variety of people seeking enlightenment and inner peace. Among the crop allowing themselves to be filmed are glamorous pop singer Regina Lund, emotionally fragile Mervi and the gregarious Australian rugby coach, Nick. It's the latter, who provides a way in for the viewer – he initially derides what he fears before falling under the gathering's unique and delightfully eccentric spell. Despite pleading with viewers not to mock New Age philosophy and practices such as firewalking, tantric sex and trance healing until they've tried them, this amusing study of the lengths to which people will go to solve their problems also warns that for every shaman there's also a charlatan. DP Swearing, nudity. **DVD**

■ *Dir* Robert Cannan, Corinna Villari-McFarlane

Three Monkeys ★★★★ 15

Drama 2008 · Fr/It/Tur · Colour · 109min

Director Nuri Bilge Ceylan pulls few punches in this darkly melodramatic inquiry into the consequences of seeing, hearing and speaking no evil. Having killed a pedestrian while asleep at the wheel, a Turkish politician (Ercan Kesal) promises his chauffeur, Eyup (Yavuz Bingol), a handsome reward if he takes the blame. However, Eyup's incarceration takes such a toll on his wife (Hatice Aslan) and teenage son (Ahmet Rifat Sungar) that she is forced to throw herself on the politician's mercy. But the nature of their bargain soon becomes apparent as her much-changed husband emerges from jail. The film's strength lies in the way it expresses psychological, political and sexual corruption in terms of accessible human drama. DP Turkish +subtitles.

Yavuz Bingol *Eyup* • Hatice Aslan *Hacer* • Ahmet Rifat Sungar *Ismail* • Ercan Kesal *Servet* ■ *Dir* Nuri Bilge Ceylan • *Scr* Nuri Bilge Ceylan, Ebru Ceylan, Ercan Kesal

The Three Musketeers ★★★★★ U

Silent swashbuckling adventure
1921 · US · BW · 131min

This was the first major screen version of Alexandre Dumas's literary romp, though it had been filmed several times since 1911. Douglas Fairbanks had himself dipped a toe in the Dumasian sea in 1917 with *A Modern Musketeer*, in which he played D'Artagnan of Kansas. But in 1921 it was all stops out, with lavish sets, slavish attention to detail and knavish behaviour on the screen. Producer/star Fairbanks and director Fred Niblo were fresh from *The Mark of Zorro* and they made this swordfest just as exuberantly entertaining. It was a smash hit everywhere and remained the definitive version until Richard Lester's two-parter of 1973. AT

Douglas Fairbanks *D'Artagnan* • Leon Barry *Athos* • George Siegmann *Porthos* • Eugene Pallette *Aramis* • Boyd Irwin *De Rochefort* • Thomas Holding *George Villiers, Duke of Buckingham* • Sidney Franklin *Bonacieux* • Charles Stevens *Planchet, D'Artagnan's lackey* • Nigel de Brulier *Cardinal Richelieu* • Willis Robards *Capt de Treville* • Adolphe Menjou *Louis XIII, King of France* ■ *Dir* Fred Niblo • *Scr* Edward Knoblock, Lotta Woods, from the novel by Alexandre Dumas

The Three Musketeers ★ U

Swashbuckling adventure
1935 · US · BW · 96min

The first talkie version of the Dumas classic was slated at the time and remains a catastrophe, due mainly to the unappealing cast. The hangdog Walter Abel, who was imported from Broadway with much fanfare to play D'Artagnan, seems hopelessly lost, as do his uncharismatic co-stars. AT *DVD*

Walter Abel *D'Artagnan* • Paul Lukas *Athos* • Margot Grahame *Milady de Winter* • Heather Angel *Constance* • Ian Keith *De Rochefort* • Moroni Olsen *Porthos* • Onslow Stevens *Aramis* • Rosamond Pinchot *Queen Anne* • Nigel de Brulier *Cardinal Richelieu* ■ *Dir* Rowland V Lee • *Scr* Dudley Nichols, Rowland V Lee, from the novel by Alexandre Dumas

The Three Musketeers ★★ U

Swashbuckling comedy 1939 · US · BW · 73min

This 1939 effort does almost count as a musical (it was retitled *The Singing Musketeer* in Britain), though Dumas's story remains essentially unchanged. Don Ameche stars as D'Artagnan, Binnie Barnes is Milady and the Ritz Brothers (Fox's answer to the Marxes) are three slapstick lackeys. Songs include *My Lady, Song of the Musketeers* and *Viola*. Veteran director Allan Dwan also directed the 1917 Douglas Fairbanks picture *A Modern Musketeer*. AT

Don Ameche *D'Artagnan* • The Ritz Brothers [Al Ritz] *Lackey* • The Ritz Brothers [Jimmy Ritz] *Lackey* • The Ritz Brothers [Harry Ritz] *Lackey* • Binnie Barnes *Milady de Winter* • Lionel Atwill *De Rochefort* • Gloria Stuart *Queen* • Pauline Moore *Lady Constance* • Joseph Schildkraut *King* • John Carradine *Naveau* • Miles Mander *Cardinal Richelieu* • Douglass Dumbrille *Athos* ■ *Dir* Allan Dwan • *Scr* MM Musselman, William A Drake, Sam Hellman, Sid Kuller, Ray Golden, from the novel by Alexandre Dumas

The Three Musketeers ★★★ U

Swashbuckling adventure
1948 · US · Colour · 120min

Directed in glorious Technicolor by underrated maestro George Sidney, this has a marvellously athletic Gene Kelly as D'Artagnan. The long screen fencing sequences are the highlight of what is a rather overlong and relentlessly Americanised version of the classic tale. In order not to offend American Catholics, Richelieu (endearingly overacted by Vincent Price) is no longer a cardinal and all internecine court wrangling is played down. Nevertheless, Lana Turner is a ravishingly beautiful countess. TS

Lana Turner *Milady, Countess Charlotte de Winter* • Gene Kelly *D'Artagnan* • June Allyson *Constance Bonacieux* • Van Heflin *Athos* • Angela Lansbury *Queen Anne* • Frank Morgan *King Louis XIII* • Vincent Price *Richelieu* ■ *Dir* George Sidney (2) • *Scr* Robert Ardrey, from the novel by Alexandre Dumas

The Three Musketeers ★★★★ U

Swashbuckling comedy adventure
1973 · UK/Sp/Pan · Colour · 102min

This is a sparkling version of the famous duel between the all-for-one quartet and Cardinal Richelieu and his scheming accomplice, Milady. Michael York gives D'Artagnan a clever twist of yokel to contrast him with his more worldly companions, played with wit and charm by Oliver Reed, Richard Chamberlain and Frank Finlay. The action has all the pace and unpredictability one has come to expect from director Richard Lester. The first sequel, *The Four Musketeers*, was filmed at the same time, while fans had to wait a further 15 years for the second sequel, *The Return of the Musketeers*. DP *DVD* *Blu-ray*

Michael York *D'Artagnan* • Raquel Welch *Constance Bonacieux* • Oliver Reed *Athos* • Richard Chamberlain *Aramis* • Frank Finlay *Porthos* • Charlton Heston *Cardinal Richelieu* • Faye Dunaway *Milady de Winter* • Christopher Lee *Rochefort* • Spike Milligan *M Bonancieux* • Roy Kinnear *Planchet* ■ *Dir* Richard Lester • *Scr* George MacDonald Fraser, from the novel by Alexandre Dumas

The Three Musketeers ★★ PG

Swashbuckling comedy adventure
1993 · US · Colour · 101min

Richard Lester's knockabout, anarchic 1973 take on Alexandre Dumas's classic is unlikely to be surpassed, and this version for the grown-up Brat Pack is misconceived from start to finish. Kiefer Sutherland, Charlie Sheen and Oliver Platt are the swashbuckling trio, Chris O'Donnell is the idealistic D'Artagnan who joins their cause and Rebecca De Mornay the sinister Milady. The Americanisation jar and the action set pieces are clumsily handled. JF *DVD*

Charlie Sheen *Aramis* • Kiefer Sutherland *Athos* • Chris O'Donnell *D'Artagnan* • Oliver Platt *Porthos* • Tim Curry *Cardinal Richelieu* • Rebecca De Mornay *Milady* • Gabrielle Anwar *Queen Anne* • Michael Wincott *Rochefort* • Paul McGann *Girad/Jussac* • Julie Delpy *Constance* • Hugh O'Conor *King Louis* ■ *Dir* Stephen Herek • *Scr* David Loughery, from the novel by Alexandre Dumas

The Three Musketeers ★★★ 12

Swashbuckling adventure
2011 · Ger/Fr/UK/US · Colour · 105min

This take on Alexandre Dumas's swashbuckling tale takes steampunk-styled liberties with the story, and features beautiful costumes, stunning Bavarian scenery and terrifically paced stuntwork. The fabled Three – Athos (Matthew Macfadyen), Aramis (Luke Evans) and Porthos (Ray Stevenson) – are joined by the young D'Artagnan (Logan Leman) to thwart a fiendish plot to undermine the young King Louis (Freddie Fox). Clipping along with a snappy script that isn't afraid to be silly, and some perfectly pitched support performances, this rip-snorting swathe of

derring-do is thoroughly enjoyable. KK Some violence. *DVD* *Blu-ray* *3D*

Logan Lerman *D'Artagnan* • Milla Jovovich *Milady* • Matthew Macfadyen *Athos* • Ray Stevenson *Porthos* • Luke Evans *Aramis* • Mads Mikkelsen *Rochefort* • Orlando Bloom *Duke of Buckingham* • Christoph Waltz *Cardinal Richelieu* ■ *Dir* Paul WS Anderson [Paul Anderson (1)] • *Scr* Andrew Davies, Alex Litvak, from the novel by Alexandre Dumas

3 Ninjas ★★ PG

Martial arts adventure
1992 · US/S Kor · Colour · 84min

This was the first of a series of four films featuring Victor Wong's high-kicking grandchildren and youngsters will probably revel in the pre-teen chop-socky adventure. As anyone who's seen *Home Alone* knows, the last thing villains should do is take on resourceful youngsters, especially when their dad is an FBI agent and grandpa is a martial arts master. But that's what the henchmen of an evil arms dealer do here – so they really were asking for trouble. DP

Victor Wong (2) *Grandpa* • Michael Treanor *Rocky* • Max Elliott Slade *Colt* • Chad Power *Tum Tum* • Rand Kingsley *Snyder* • Alan McRae *Sam Douglas* ■ *Dir* Jon Turteltaub • *Scr* Edward Emanuel, from the story *Three Ninja Kids* by Kenny Kim

Three o'Clock High ★★ 15

Comedy 1987 · US · Colour · 85min

Director Phil Joanou here turns his hand to a teen comedy, which is effectively a rip-off of *High Noon* but in a familiar high school setting. Casey Siemaszko is student, facing up to a showdown with a fearsome teen rival in this lightweight fare, which is only slightly redeemed by the sterling performances of the cast. JB

Casey Siemaszko *Jerry Mitchell* • Anne Ryan *Franny Perrins* • Richard Tyson *Buddy Revell* • Stacey Glick *Brei Mitchell* • Jonathan Wise *Vincent Costello* • Jeffrey Tambor *Mr Rice* • Philip Baker Hall *Detective Mulvahill* • John P Ryan *Mr O'Rourke* ■ *Dir* Phil Joanou • *Scr* Richard Christian Matheson, Thomas Szollosi

Three of Hearts ★★ 18

Romantic comedy drama
1992 · US · Colour · 105min

Kelly Lynch and Sherilyn Fenn play a gay couple who contrive to split up by the end of the opening credits. A devastated Lynch then hires stud and gigolo William Baldwin to escort her to a wedding. Baldwin suggests a plan to win Fenn back that involves him wooing her and then breaking her heart. Original and feisty initially, the film descends into more conventional territory when Baldwin falls for Fenn. Watchable, but average. LH *DVD*

William Baldwin *Joe Casella* • Kelly Lynch *Connie* • Sherilyn Fenn *Ellen* • Joe Pantoliano *Mickey* • Gail Strickland *Yvonne* • Cec Verrell *Allison* • Claire Callaway *Isabella* • Marek Johnson *Gail* ■ *Dir* Yurek Bogayevicz • *Scr* Adam Greenman, Mitch Glazer, from a story by Adam Greenman

Three on a Couch ★★★ U

Comedy 1966 · US · Colour · 108min

In an art competition, Jerry Lewis wins prize money and a commission to paint a prestigious mural in Paris. His fiancée, psychiatrist Janet Leigh, is reluctant to go with him, however, as she is in the middle of delicate therapy with three women who have suffered at the hands of thoughtless men. Lewis then tries to cure the women himself. The idiosyncratic Jerry Lewis is more restrained than normal in this clumsy comedy that still moments of genius. DF

Jerry Lewis *Christopher Pride/Warren/Ringo/ Rutherford/Heather* • Janet Leigh *Dr Elizabeth Acord* • Mary Ann Mobley *Susan Manning* • Gila Golan *Anna Jacque* • Leslie Parrish *Mary Lou Mauve* • James Best *Dr Ben Mizer* • Kathleen Freeman *Murphy* • Buddy Lester *Drunk* • Scatman Crothers *Dr Jerry Lewis* ■ *Scr* Bob Ross, Samuel A Taylor, from a story by Arne Sultan, Marvin Worth

Three on a Match ★★★

Drama 1932 · US · BW · 63min

The bizarre title of this tale hides an intelligent little movie about friendships and new rivalries. A suspenseful atmosphere pervades throughout and director Mervyn LeRoy makes good use of external locations to develop the theme of encroaching tragedy. Watch out for Humphrey Bogart, not yet a superstar, in a cast that plays a well honed script to the hilt. Not a masterpiece, but worth the effort. SH

Joan Blondell *Mary Keaton* • Warren William *Henry Kirkwood* • Ann Dvorak *Vivian Revere* • Bette Davis *Ruth Westcott* • Lyle Talbot *Mike Loftus* • Humphrey Bogart *Harve the Mug* • Patricia Ellis *Linda* ■ *Dir* Mervyn LeRoy • *Scr* Lucien Hubbard, Kubec Glasmon, John Bright, from the story by Kubec Glasmon, John Bright

Three on a Spree ★ U

Farce 1961 · UK · BW · 89min

First made as a silent by Oscar Apfel and Cecil B DeMille in 1914, *Brewster's Millions* underwent another reworking in this shoddy British offering. The story lumbers around London as Jack Watling attempts to spend a small fortune in a bid to land a whopping inheritance. Carole Lesley comes along for the ride, without being much to the picnic. Sidney J Furie's leaden, laugh-free direction saps the morale of a willing, but woefully wasted supporting cast. DP

Jack Watling *Michael Brewster* • Carole Lesley *Susan* • Renee Houston *Mrs Gray* • John Slater *Sid Johnson* • Colin Gordon *Mitchell* • John Salew *Mr Monkton* ■ *Dir* Sidney J Furie • *Scr* Siegfried Herzig, Charles Rogers, Wilkie Mahoney, James Kelly, Peter Miller, from the play *Brewster's Millions: a Comedy in Four Acts* by Winchell Smith, Byron Ongley, from the novel *Brewster's Millions* by George Barr McCutcheon

Three Ring Circus ★★

Drama 1954 · US · Colour · 103min

Just what Dean Martin and Jerry Lewis saw in each other is beside the point, it's what audiences at the time saw in them. This film is typical of their routine mix of slapstick and schmaltz, with the pair playing discharged servicemen joining a circus. It's not to everyone's taste, but it was certainly popular with the public in the 1950s, with Martin's role as cynical smoothie more appealing to some than Lewis's rather less sophisticated interpretation of his character. TH

Dean Martin *Pete Nelson* • Jerry Lewis *Jerry Hotchkiss* • Joanne Dru *Jill Brent* • Zsa Zsa Gabor *Saadia* • Wallace Ford *Sam Morley* • Sig Ruman *Fritz Schlitz* • Gene Sheldon *Puffo* • Elsa Lanchester *Bearded lady* ■ *Dir* Joseph Pevney • *Scr* Don McGuire

Three Sailors and a Girl ★★ U

Musical 1953 · US · Colour · 95min

This Warner Bros romp is, amazingly, based on a stage play by Pulitzer Prize-winning author George S Kaufman. There's little trace of its source as likeable Gordon MacRae, hoofer Gene Nelson and winsome Jane Powell get involved in one of those staple musical plots about raising the money to put on a show. Predictable stuff, pleasant but not inspiring. TS

Jane Powell *Penny Weston* • Gordon MacRae *Choir Boy Jones* • Gene Nelson *Twitch* • Sam Levene *Joe Woods* • George Givot *Rossi* • Veda Ann Borg *Faye Foss* • Archer MacDonald *Webster* • Raymond Greenleaf *Morrow* ■ *Dir* Roy Del Ruth • *Scr* Roland Kibbee, Devery Freeman, from the play *The Butter and Egg Man* by George S Kaufman

Three Seasons ★★★ 12

Drama 1999 · US/Viet · Colour · 108min

Striking in its imagery but disappointingly cosy in its themes, Tony Bui's feature debut is the first American film to be made in Vietnam since the war. There's an element of bridge-building here, particularly in the plot strand concerning ex-GI Harvey Keitel's search for the daughter he's never seen. Other threads follow a young woman (Nguyen Ngoc Hiep) who learns to balance

T

tradition and progress while picking flowers in a lotus garden and cyclo driver Don Duong, whose love for prostitute Zoë Bui is an object lesson in forgiving and forgetting the past. DP Vietnamese, English +subtitles. Sexual references, nudity. *DVD*

Don Duong *Hai* • Nguyen Ngoc Hiep *Kien An* • Tran Manh Cuong *Teacher Dao* • Harvey Keitel *James Hager* • Zoe Bui *Lan* • Nguyen Huu Duoc *Woody* • Minh Ngoc *Truck driver* ■ *Dir* Tony Bui • *Scr* Tony Bui, Timothy Linh Bui

Three Secrets ★★★
Drama 1950 · US · BW · 97min

With a less talented director and actresses, this weepie could have drowned in its own tears. But Robert Wise keeps the drama on course and Eleanor Parker, Patricia Neal and Ruth Roman are splendid as the three mothers who wait together in a mountain cabin for news after a plane crash. Considerable emotion is derived from an admittedly contrived situation in which a five-year-old boy is the sole survivor of the crash. The news that the crash happened on his birthday and that he was given up for adoption unites the women, each of whom made a sacrifice years previously and believe the child may be theirs. BB

Eleanor Parker *Susan Chase* • Patricia Neal *Phyllis Horn* • Ruth Roman *Ann Lawrence* • Frank Lovejoy *Bob Duffy* • Leif Erickson *Bill Chase* • Ted De Corsia *Del Prince* • Larry Keating *Mark Harrison* ■ *Dir* Robert Wise • *Scr* Martin Rackin, Gina Kaus, from their story *Rock Bottom*

The Three Sisters ★★
Period drama 1966 · US · BW · 166min

A filmed version of Lee Strasberg's Actors Studio production that ran comfortably on Broadway during the mid-1960s, this version of Chekhov's turn-of-the-century play doesn't quite come off, but it's certainly different. Three unhappy women for whom city life in Moscow is the centre of their universe search for a meaningful life in a Russian village. Though it may be interesting for students of the Method and/or fans of offbeat experiments with the classics, this theatrical transcription may irritate others. JG

Gerald Hiken *Andrei* • Shelley Winters *Natalya* • Geraldine Page *Olga* • Kim Stanley *Masha* • Sandy Dennis *Irina* • Albert Paulsen *Kulygin* • Kevin McCarthy *Vershinin* • James Olson *Baron Tuzenbach* • Robert Loggia *Solyony* • Luther Adler *Chebutikin* ■ *Dir* Paul Bogart • *Scr* from the play by Anton Chekhov

Three Sisters ★★ U
Period drama 1970 · UK · Colour · 155min

Though of value to biographers and theatre historians, this record of Laurence Olivier's National Theatre production is a negligible cinematic experience. Apart from two added sequences, there is no attempt to make this a "movie". Olivier is simply content to have Geoffrey Unsworth's camera rooted to its tripod as it records some admittedly fine performances from the actors portraying the three sisters who grow bored with provincial life and yearn for the glamour of Moscow. AT *DVD*

Jeanne Watts *Olga* • Joan Plowright *Masha* • Louise Purnell *Irina* • Derek Jacobi *Andrei* • Alan Bates *Colonel Vershinin* • Kenneth Mackintosh *Kulighin* • Sheila Reid *Natasha* • Laurence Olivier *Chebutikin* • Ronald Pickup *Tusenbach* ■ *Dir* Laurence Olivier, John Sichel • *Scr* Moura Budber, from the play by Anton Chekhov

Three Sisters ★★★ 12
Drama 1988 · It/Fr/W Ger · Colour · 112min

This reworking of Chekhov's play sees the action transported from Russia to the chilly Italian town of Pavia. The story has been updated, with Greta Scacchi unhappily married to a TV comic and the threat of the arms race hanging over the proceedings. Director Margarethe von Trotta has retained the subtle complexities of the original play, and, in a dual role, Scacchi acquits herself well. But the achingly beautiful visuals can't quite atone for the over-deliberate pacing. DP Italian, French, German +subtitles.

Fanny Ardant *Velia* • Greta Scacchi *Maria/Maria's mother* • Valeria Golino *Sandra* • Peter Simonischek *Massimo* • Sergio Castellitto *Roberto* • Agnes Soral *Sabrina* • Paolo Hendel *Federico* • Jan-Paul Biczycki *Cecchini* ■ *Dir* Margarethe von Trotta • *Scr* Dacia Maraini, Margarethe von Trotta

360 ★★ 15
Drama 2011 · UK/Austria/Fr/Bra · Colour · 105min

This weak portmanteau film from director Fernando Meirelles and *The Queen* writer Peter Morgan hammers home its points that we are all connected and that one thing does indeed lead to another. Many notable actors (including Anthony Hopkins and Rachel Weisz) appear in roles that never add up to anything. The exception is a plot strand involving a battle-weary Russian gangster who is tired of covering for his boss; it's only here that the film reveals something warm and real in a schematic drama that otherwise seems populated by plot-serving automatons. DW English, German, Arabic, French, Portuguese, Russian +subtitles. *DVD* *BL*

Rachel Weisz *Rose* • Jude Law *Michael Daly* • Anthony Hopkins *Older man* • Ben Foster *Tyler* • Moritz Bleibtreu *Salesman* • Marianne Jean-Baptiste *Fran* ■ *Dir* Fernando Meirelles • *Scr* Peter Morgan (1), from the play *Der Reigen* by Arthur Schnitzler

Three Smart Girls ★★★★ U
Romantic musical comedy
1937 · US · BW · 80min

Three young daughters (Nan Grey, Barbara Read and Deanna Durbin) of divorced parents determine to stop the remarriage of their mega-rich Wall Street financier father Charles Winninger to young gold-digger Binnie Barnes, and reunite their parents. The driving force is the youngest sister, a precocious and irrepressible hoyden with an opera singer's voice. This is the comedy that made Durbin a huge star and established the formula for her subsequent clutch of moneymakers. It's complete nonsense and, as played by a splendid cast, is thoroughly delightful. RK *DVD*

Deanna Durbin *Penny Craig* • Binnie Barnes *Donna Lyons* • Alice Brady *Mrs Lyons* • Ray Milland *Lord Michael Stuart* • Charles Winninger *Judson Craig* • Mischa Auer *Count Arisztid* • Nan Grey *Joan Craig* • Barbara Read *Kay Craig* • Franklin Pangborn *Jeweler* ■ *Dir* Henry Koster • *Scr* Adele Comandini, Austin Parker, from a story by Adele Comandini

Three Smart Girls Grow Up ★★★ U
Comedy drama 1939 · US · BW · 83min

Teenage diva Deanna Durbin repeats her role as the youngest of three sisters in her debut feature, *Three Smart Girls*. This time, Deanna devotes her precocious energies to marrying off her two older sisters, in between which she exercises her bright soprano voice on *Because*, which became one of the major hits of her career. It's everything one would expect of a Durbin film. A second sequel, *Hers to Hold*, followed in 1943. RK

Deanna Durbin *Penelope "Penny" Craig* • Nan Grey *Joan Craig* • Helen Parrish *Katherine "Kay" Craig* • Charles Winninger *Judson Craig* • Nella Walker *Mrs Craig* • Robert Cummings *Harry Loren* • William Lundigan *Richard Watkins* ■ *Dir* Henry Koster • *Scr* Bruce Manning, Felix Jackson

The Three Stooges ★★★
Biographical drama
2000 · US · BW and Colour · 88min

This is a fond, TV-movie memoir of the slapstick trio that hurled insult into countless Columbia shorts for little tangible reward. Paul Ben-Victor plays Moe Howard, whose flashbacked recollections chart how he rose through vaudeville to minor Hollywood celebrity in the pratfalling company of his brothers Curly (Michael Chiklis) and Shemp (John Kassir). The studio politics sequences involving monstrous mogul Harry Cohn rarely ring true, but director James Frawley efficiently

explores the physical toll that the Stooges' routines took, as well as their comic legacy. DP

Paul Ben-Victor *Moe Howard* • Evan Handler *Larry Fine* • John Kassir *Shemp Howard* • Michael Chiklis *Jerome "Curly" Howard* • Rachael Blake *Helen Howard* • Anna-Lise Phillips *Mabel Fine* • Jeanette Cronin *Gertrude Howard* ■ *Dir* James Frawley • *Scr* Kirk Ellis, Janet Roach, from the book *From Amalgamated Morons to American Icons: The Three Stooges* by Michael Fleming

The Three Stooges ★★★ PG
Comedy 2012 · US · Colour · 88min

The more you know about the Three Stooges, the more you'll love this peppy homage by the Farrelly Brothers. The film captures the speed and wildness of their 1930s slapstick routines, but updates their antics to the present, allowing them to cause havoc in a world of smartphones and reality TV. This will appeal to all those who like their comedies dumb but well developed. KK *DVD* *BL*

Sean Hayes *Larry* • Will Sasso *Curly* • Chris Diamantopoulos *Moe* • Sofia Vergara *Lydia* • Jane Lynch *Mother Superior* • Jennifer Hudson *Sister Rosemary* • Larry David *Sister Mary-Mengele* ■ *Dir* Bobby Farrelly, Peter Farrelly • *Scr* Mike Cerrone, Bobby Farrelly, Peter Farrelly

The Three Stooges Go around the World in a Daze ★★ U
Adventure farce 1963 · US · BW · 93min

As the epitome of crazed and meaningless slapstick comedy, the Three Stooges are not to everyone's taste. However, this relentlessly silly homage to *Around the World in 80 Days* is chucklesome in spots. Phileas Fogg's great-grandson is challenged by a dastardly conman to re-create his ancestor's famous journey. Alas, he decides to take his servants, the Stooges, along for the ride. JG

Moe Howard • Larry Fine • Joe De Rita • Jay Sheffield *Phileas Fogg III* • Joan Freeman *Amelia* • Walter Burke *Lory Filch* • Peter Forster *Vickers Cavendish* • Maurice Dallimore *Crotchet* ■ *Dir* Norman Maurer • *Scr* Elwood Ullman, from a story by Norman Maurer, loosely based on the novel *Le Tour du Monde en Quatre-vingt Jours* by Jules Verne

The Three Stooges in Orbit ★★ U
Science-fiction comedy 1962 · US · BW · 87min

After many years of tweaking, thumping, poking and brawling, the Stooges were moving into weirder areas. Here they're battling a pair of Martian invaders Ogg (George N Neise) and Zogg (Rayford Barnes) who are plotting to steal the secret plans of a super-vehicle invented by eccentric professor Emil Sitka. Not one of the boys' best efforts, but there's plenty of the usual flesh-slapping antics once so beloved of small boys. DF

Moe Howard • Larry Fine • Joe De Rita • Carol Christensen *Carol* • Edson Stroll *Capt Tom Andrews* • Emil Sitka *Prof Danforth* • George N Neise *Ogg* • Rayford Barnes *Zogg* ■ *Dir* Edward Bernds • *Scr* Elwood Ullman, from a story by Norman Maurer

The Three Stooges Meet Hercules ★★ U
Comedy 1962 · US · BW · 88min

After creating the expected havoc with the soda fountain, drug store clerks Moe, Larry, and "Curly" Joe are accidentally transported back to ancient Greece with their wimpy scientist friend when his new time machine malfunctions. When they meet Hercules (who is a villain here), the Stooges decide to get their friend to stand up for himself and become more of a man. Those who are familiar with the Stooges's brand of humour will pretty much know right away whether they will enjoy the movie. KB

Moe Howard • Larry Fine • Joe De Rita • Vicki Trickett *Diane Quigley* • Quinn Redeker *Schuyler Davis* • Samson Burke *Hercules* ■ *Dir* Edward Bernds • *Scr* Elwood Ullman, from a story by Norman Maurer

Three Strange Loves ★★★ 15
Drama 1949 · Swe · BW · 80min

The most commercially successful of Ingmar Bergman's early films is also something of an artistic watershed, as it weaves flashbacks, dreams and subplots into an engaging dramatic whole, which places a new emphasis on the female perspective. Travelling in a train compartment that symbolises her confinement in a non-communicative marriage, former ballerina Eva Henning recalls the affair that left her unable to conceive. Juxtaposed with this is the sequence of events that drove art historian Birger Malmsten's first wife, Birgit Tengroth, to suicide. (Tengroth also wrote the source stories.) DP Swedish +subtitles. *DVD*

Eva Henning *Rut* • Birger Malmsten *Bertil* • Birgit Tengroth *Viola* • Hasse Ekman *Dr Rosengren* • Mimi Nelson *Valborg* • Bengt Eklund *Raoul* ■ *Dir* Ingmar Bergman • *Scr* Herbert Grevenius, from short stories by Birgit Tengroth

Three Strangers ★★★
Drama 1946 · US · BW · 92min

A New Year's Eve pact between three strangers culminates in each signing a sweepstake ticket that they hope will bring a change in their fortunes. Instead a combination of embezzlement, adultery and murder brings misery to all three. This story was dreamed up by John Huston, who subsequently worked on the screenplay, but Jean Negulesco eventually took over the project. Sydney Greenstreet is his usual imperious self, Peter Lorre is bug-eyed and shifty and the third member of the triumvirate is Geraldine Fitzgerald. AT

Sydney Greenstreet *Arbutney* • Peter Lorre *Johnny West* • Geraldine Fitzgerald *Crystal* • Joan Lorring *Icy* • Robert Shayne *Fallon* • Marjorie Riordan *Janet* • Arthur Shields *Prosecutor* ■ *Dir* Jean Negulesco • *Scr* John Huston, Howard Koch, from the story *Three Men and a Girl* by John Huston

3 Strikes ★ 15
Crime comedy 2000 · US · Colour · 78min

Hip-hop legend DJ Pooh comes seriously unstuck with this, his directorial debut. Pitching two-time loser Brian Hooks into an *After Hours* scenario after he becomes innocently involved in a police shoot-out, the film revels in lowbrow humour and witless misanthropy. An untidy, unfunny and mean-spirited mess. DP

Brian Hooks *Rob* • N'Bushe Wright *Juanita* • David Alan Grier *Jenkins* • Faizon Love *Tone* • George Wallace *Pops* ■ *Dir/Scr* DJ Pooh

3:10 to Yuma ★★★★★ PG
Western 1957 · US · BW · 88min

Unquestionably one of the finest westerns ever made, this is a gripping and truly suspenseful tale. It features consummate performances from Glenn Ford, as the cocksure baddie, and Van Heflin, as the farmer pledged to hold Ford in check until the titular train arrives. Director Delmer Daves makes superior use of camera cranes and bleak horizons, and the screenplay (based on an Elmore Leonard original) is an object lesson in scripting for the screen. The scenes between Ford and bargirl Felicia Farr are exceptionally well crafted and the superb whole is boosted by a marvellous Frankie Laine theme song. TS

Glenn Ford *Ben Wade* • Van Heflin *Dan Evans* • Felicia Farr *Emmy* • Leora Dana *Alice Evans* • Henry Jones *Alex Potter* • Richard Jaeckel *Charlie Prince* • Robert Emhardt *Mr Butterfield* ■ *Dir* Delmer Daves • *Scr* Halsted Welles, from the story by Elmore Leonard

3:10 to Yuma ★★★★ 15
Western 2007 · US · Colour · 117min

This glossy remake of Delmer Daves's low-key 1957 western is powered along by two enthralling star turns. Christian Bale is engagingly understated as the meek rancher who boldly offers to escort a dangerous prisoner to the local train station. It's difficult to take your eyes off him, except to try to figure out what's going on in the mind of Russell Crowe, the passenger booked on a trip to the jailhouse. Although the backstory takes a while to unfold, director James Mangold (*Walk the Line*) pulls no punches when it comes to showing Crowe's dark side. A bond begins to grow between the outlaw and the family man, and the tension mounts as Crowe's gang slowly closes in. Despite getting a little too theatrical in the final showdown, Mangold's film remains an exciting and emotional ride. SP Violence, some swearing. 📀 💿

Russell Crowe *Ben Wade* • Christian Bale *Dan Evans* • Ben Foster *Charlie Prince* • Alan Tudyk *Doc Potter* • Peter Fonda *Byron McElroy* • Gretchen Mol *Alice Evans* ■ *Dir* James Mangold • *Scr* Halsted Welles, Michael Brandt, Derek Haas, from the short story by Elmore Leonard

Three the Hard Way ★★★
Blaxploitation action adventure
1974 · US · Colour · 90min

This above-average blaxploitation flick teams a triumvirate of black action stars – Jim Brown, Fred Williamson and ex-karate champion Jim Kelly. The preposterous plot involves a bunch of neo-Nazis attempting to infect the water supply of several US cities with a serum that kills only black people. Director Gordon Parks Jr just about keeps a straight face amid the numerous shoot-outs and bouts of kung fu fighting. RS

Jim Brown *Jimmy Lait* • Fred Williamson *Jagger Daniels* • Jim Kelly *Mister Keyes* • Sheila Frazier *Wendy Kane* • Jay Robinson *Monroe Feather* • Charles McGregor *Charley* • Howard Platt *Keep* • Richard Angarola *Dr Fortrero* ■ *Dir* Gordon Parks Jr • *Scr* Eric Bercovici, Jerry Ludwig

3000 Miles to Graceland ★★18
Crime comedy thriller
2000 · US · Colour · 120min

In this tired caper, Demian Lichtenstein over-indulges in the camera pyrotechnics that characterised his time as a director of commercials and pop videos. Kurt Russell gets to wear Elvis gear once more, as the leader of a gang planning a raid on a Las Vegas casino, while Kevin Costner attempts to kickstart his flagging career by playing against type as a foul-mouthed sociopath. Crass and excessive. DP Sex scenes, swearing, violence. 📀

Kurt Russell *Michael Zane* • Kevin Costner *Murphy* • Courteney Cox Arquette [Courteney Cox] *Cybil Waingrow* • Christian Slater *Hanson* • Kevin Pollak *Federal Marshal Damitry* • David Arquette *Gus* • Jon Lovitz *Jay Peterson* • Howie Long *Jack* • Thomas Haden Church *Federal Marshal Quigley* ■ *Dir* Demian Lichtenstein • *Scr* Richard Recco, Demian Lichtenstein

Three Times ★★★12
Portmanteau romantic drama
2005 · Tai · Colour · 129min

Taiwanese auteur Hou Hsiao-Hsien's triptych has a visual gloss and dramatic intensity that belies its tight schedule and low budget. It also boasts vivid performances from Shu Qi and Chang Chen, who respectively play a pool hall hostess and a soldier, a courtesan and a client, and an epileptic lesbian singer and a photographer in three stories: *A Time for Love* (set in 1966); *A Time for Freedom* (set in 1911); and *A Time for Youth* (set in 2005). While the pacing is measured and the insights into the socio-cultural forces that shape human behaviour are intriguing, the concluding section has an alienatingly melodramatic pessimism. DP Mandarin +subtitles. 📀

Shu Qi *May/Ah Mei/Jing* • Chang Chen *Chen/Mr Chang/Zhen* ■ *Dir* Hou Hsiao-Hsien • *Scr* Chu Tien-Wen

Three to Tango ★★★12
Romantic comedy   1999 · US · Colour · 94min

This sweet, if somewhat politically incorrect, romantic comedy is worth seeking out for a nice performance from Matthew Perry and a hilarious one from Oliver Platt. The plot is simple. Big businessman Dylan McDermott thinks Perry is gay, so he asks him to watch

over his mistress Neve Campbell, little realising that Perry is falling for her. Cute rather than uproariously funny. JB 📀

Matthew Perry *Oscar Novak* • Neve Campbell *Amy Post* • Dylan McDermott *Charles Newman* • Oliver Platt *Peter Steinberg* • Cylk Cozart *Kevin Cartwright* • John C McGinley *Strauss* • Bob Balaban *Decker* • Deborah Rush *Lenore* ■ *Dir* Damon Santostefano • *Scr* Rodney Vaccaro, Aline Brosh McKenna, from a story by Rodney Vaccaro

Three Tough Guys ★★
Action crime drama
1974 · US/It · Colour · 91min

This unusual Italian buddy movie features a two-fisted renegade ex-con priest, who's in Chicago to investigate a bank robbery. (Give it its due: bet you haven't seen that before). The cleric teams up with Isaac Hayes who, besides turning in a well-judged performance, supplies a pretty listenable soundtrack. The dubbing detracts somewhat from the dialogue, but it's fast moving and efficient. JG Italian dubbed. Some violence.

Lino Ventura *Father Charlie* • Isaac Hayes *Lee Stevens* • Fred Williamson *Joe Snake* • Paula Kelly *Fay Collins* • William Berger *Captain Ryan* • Luciano Salce *Bishop* ■ *Dir* Duccio Tessari • *Scr* Luciano Vincenzoni, Nicola Badalucco

Three Violent People ★★PG
Western   1956 · US · Colour · 95min

They've got a saying in Texas – the Rio Grande changes its course, the Saunders don't." Charlton Heston is the inflexible rancher who marries Anne Baxter's southern woman on an impulse and throws her out on when he learns about her unsavoury past. Tom Tryon is the one-armed brother who falls out with Heston. And then there's the post-Civil War adminstration making iniquitous tax demands. It ought to add up to highly combustible entertainment but the one-dimensional characters means it doesn't. AE 📀

Charlton Heston *Colt Saunders* • Anne Baxter *Lorna Hunter Saunders* • Gilbert Roland *Innocencio* • Tom Tryon *Cinch Saunders* • Forrest Tucker *Cable* • Bruce Bennett *Harrison* • Elaine Stritch *Ruby LaSalle* • Barton MacLane *Yates* ■ *Dir* Rudolph Maté • *Scr* James Edward Grant, from a story by Leonard Praskins, Barney Slater

The Three Weird Sisters★★
Thriller   1948 · UK · BW · 83min

One of two melodramas co-written by Dylan Thomas and directed by Daniel Birt (the other being *No Room at the Inn*), this is set in a Welsh village, where three elderly sisters in need of money plot to murder their wealthy brother. When he changes his will in favour of his secretary Nova Pilbeam, the old maids decide to kill her, too. This boasts a good cast (notably Nancy Price as the dominant sister) and some theatrically sinister moments. BB

Nancy Price *Gertrude Morgan-Vaughan* • Mary Clare *Maude Morgan-Vaughan* • Mary Merrall *Isobel Morgan-Vaughan* • Nova Pilbeam *Claire Prentiss* • Anthony Hulme *David Davies* • Raymond Lovell *Owen Morgan-Vaughan* ■ *Dir* Daniel Birt • *Scr* Louise Birt, David Evans, Dylan Thomas, from the novel *The Case of the Three Weird Sisters* by Charlotte Armstrong

Three Wise Girls ★★
Drama   1932 · US · BW · 66min

Three girls (Mae Clarke, Jean Harlow, and Marie Prevost) leave their one-horse town for jobs, excitement and romance in the Big Apple. One, not so wisely, becomes a kept Park Avenue mistress; another settles happily for an agreeable chauffeur; and a third becomes a store mannequin. The last is Harlow who has to deal with the fact her lover is married – should she go or should she stay? Routine. RK

Jean Harlow *Cassie Barnes* • Mae Clarke *Gladys Kane* • Walter Byron *Jerry Dexter* • Marie Prevost *Dot* • Andy Devine *Chauffeur* • Natalie Moorhead *Ruth* • Jameson Thomas *Arthur Phelps* ■ *Dir* William Beaudine • *Scr* Agnes Christine Johnston, Robert Riskin, from the story *Blonde Baby* by Wilson Collison

Three Wise Guys ★★
Seasonal comedy   2005 · US · Colour · 86min

Three hitmen pursue the mistress of casino boss Tom Arnold in this irreverent, festive crime caper. Judd Nelson stars as one of the bungling trio continually outmanoeuvred by the heavily pregnant woman (Jodi Lyn O'Keefe). Events are neither subtle nor realistic, relying on gangster clichés, pregnancy gags and corny Christmas asides for their humour. Fortunately, a snappy pace and fun performances keep the combination engaging, with Katey Sagal particularly enjoyable as Arnold's gutsy wife. SF

Eddie McClintock *Joey* • Judd Nelson *George* • Nick Turturro [Nicholas Turturro] *Vincent* • Jodi Lyn O'Keefe *Mary Ann Davidson* • Arye Gross *Leo* • Tom Arnold *Murray Crown* • Katey Sagal *Shirley Crown* ■ *Dir* Robert Iscove • *Scr* Lloyd "Lucky" Gold, from the story by Damon Runyon

Three Wishes ★★PG
Fantasy drama   1995 · US · Colour · 110min

Patrick Swayze stars as the stranger who comes into the family fold and changes everyone's life. A tramp with a dog on a string, he may be an angel sent to help them cope with the potential loss of their father, reported missing in action in the Korean War, and with one son's cancer. Clumsily structured as a flashback to the 1950s, this is daft and sentimental. LH

Patrick Swayze *Jack McCloud* • Mary Elizabeth Mastrantonio *Jeanne Holman* • Joseph Mazzello *Tom Holman* • Seth Mumy *Gunny Holman* • David Marshall Grant *Phil* • Jay O Sanders *Coach Schramka* • Michael O'Keefe *Adult Tom* • John Diehl *Leland's dad* ■ *Dir* Martha Coolidge • *Scr* Elizabeth Anderson, from a story by Ellen Green, Clifford Green

3 Women ★★★★PG
Drama   1977 · US · Colour · 118min

This very personal Robert Altman movie based on a dream is as enthralling as it is entertaining, with keen insights into feminine psychology. An enigmatic chamberwork, as opposed to the orchestrations of the original *MASH* or his masterpiece, *Nashville*, this is about the transference of personality. Shelley Duvall is vapidly splendid as the gossip therapist into whose flat moves the adoring Sissy Spacek, while tongue-tied Janice Rule is the painter formulating fears of male aggression into mythic murals. TH Brief violence, nudity. 📀 💿

Shelley Duvall *Millie Lammoreaux* • Sissy Spacek *Pinky Rose* • Janice Rule *Willie Hart* • Robert Fortier *Edgar Hart* • Ruth Nelson *Mrs Rose* • John Cromwell *Mr Rose* • Sierra Pecheur *Mr Bunweill* ■ *Dir/Scr* Robert Altman

Three Women in Love ★★★18
Comedy drama   1988 · W Ger · Colour · 83min

Littered with classical allusions, Rudolf Thome's metaphysical satire provides a sharp insight into the arrogance of even the most unworldly males in setting their expectations of women so low. Totally wrapped up in the minor success of his book on Heraclitus, academic Johannes Herrschmann is vain enough to believe that shopgirls Adriana Altaras, Friederike Tiefenbacher and Claudia Matschulla are adoring acolytes content to minister to his every need, instead of semi-divine agents using him as a messenger for their ethereal thoughts. DP German +subtitles.

Johannes Herrschmann *Georg Hermes* • Adriana Altaras *Franziska* • Friederike Tiefenbacher *Beate* • Claudia Matschulla *Martha* • Jürgen Wink *Franziska's lover* • Werner Gerber *Martha's lover* • Anton Rey *Beate's lover* ■ *Dir/Scr* Rudolf Thome

The Three Worlds of Gulliver ★★★U
Fantasy adventure   1959 · UK · Colour · 94min

Kerwin Mathews spends most of his time among the giants of Brobdingnag and the little people of Lilliput in this loose adaptation of Jonathan Swift's timeless classic novel. Playing down the satire in

favour of family adventure, director Jack Sher benefits from the expertise of his supporting cast, but it's the Superdynamation work of effects maestro Ray Harryhausen that gives the action its fantastical feel. DP 📀

Kerwin Mathews *Dr Lemuel Gulliver* • Jo Morrow *Gwendolyn* • June Thorburn *Elizabeth* • Lee Patterson *Reldresal* • Grégoire Aslan *King Brobdingnag* • Basil Sydney *Emperor of Lilliput* • Charles Lloyd Pack *Makovan* ■ *Dir* Jack Sher • *Scr* Arthur Ross, Jack Sher, from the novel *Gulliver's Travels* by Jonathan Swift • *Music* Bernard Herrmann

The Threepenny Opera ★★★★PG
Musical black comedy
1931 · Ger/US · BW · 104min

That master of early German cinema, GW Pabst, seemed the ideal choice for this reworking of Bertolt Brecht's play, but Brecht was furious with the film's toning down of his play's anti-capitalist content and sued the German production company. Several of Brecht and Kurt Weill's original songs are missing, but Weill's wife, Lotte Lenya, mesmerisingly re-creates her legendary stage role, and Rudolf Forster makes a roguish Mackie Messer. What's more, the film is a triumph of visual stylisation, thanks to Andre Andreiev's evocative sets and Fritz Arno Wagner's superb photography. DP German +subtitles. 📀

Rudolf Forster *Mackie Messer* • Carola Neher *Polly Peachum* • Reinhold Schünzel *Tiger Brown* • Fritz Rasp *Peachum* • Valeska Gert *Mrs Peachum* • Lotte Lenya *Jenny* • Hermann Thimig *Vicar* ■ *Dir* GW Pabst • *Scr* Leo Lania, Ladislaus Vadja, Béla Balász, from the play by Bertolt Brecht, from the play *The Beggar's Opera* by John Gay

Threesome ★★★18
Romantic comedy   1994 · US · Colour · 89min

A clerical error puts student Lara Flynn Boyle in the same digs as jock Stephen Baldwin and sensitive Josh Charles in Andrew Fleming's appealing, if contrived, look at teenage sexual identity. *The* romantic triangle that develops between the three is sometimes handled intelligently, but the writing lacks reality and conviction. This remains a prime example of Hollywood being just too tasteful with "controversial" material, and the end result is mawkish. AJ Swearing, drug abuse, sex scenes, nudity. 📀

Lara Flynn Boyle *Alex* • Stephen Baldwin *Stuart* • Josh Charles *Eddy* • Alexis Arquette *Dick* • Martha Gehman *Renay* • Mark Arnold *Larry* • Michele Matheson *Kristen* ■ *Dir/Scr* Andrew Fleming

Threshold ★★★PG
Drama   1981 · Can · Colour · 92min

American distributors ignored this dramatically persuasive fictional story of the world's first artificial-heart transplant for two years – until speculative fiction became headline fact. This is a surprisingly low-key account of the effect on people of such revolutionary surgery. It's a pity that some strong performances – Donald Sutherland as the surgeon, Jeff Goldblum as the artificial heart's inventor and Mare Winningham as the worried recipient – were left in the dark for so long. TH

Donald Sutherland *Dr Thomas Vrain* • Jeff Goldblum *Dr Aldo Gehring* • Allan Nicholls *Dr Basil Rents* • Sharon Acker *Tilla Vrain* • Jessica Steen *Tracy Vrain* • Michael Lerner *Henry De Vici* • John Marley *Edgar Fine* • Mare Winningham *Carol Severance* ■ *Dir* Richard Pearce • *Scr* James Salter

Thrill of a Romance ★★
Musical   1945 · US · Colour · 103min

Another of the trite, vacuous musical romances dreamed up for MGM's human mermaid, Esther Williams, this one has romance blossoming in a mountain resort between Esther, who swims, and soldier-on-leave Van Johnson, who sings. The numbers include hits *I Should Care* and *Please Don't Say No, Say Maybe*, the latter memorable for being belted out by famous

T

Wagnerian opera tenor Lauritz Melchior, making his film debut in the first of several such frivolities. RK

Esther Williams *Cynthia Glenn* • Van Johnson *Major Thomas Milvaine* • Frances Gifford *Maude Bancroft* • Henry Travers *Hobart Glenn* • Spring Byington *Nona Glenn* • Lauritz Melchior *Nils Knudsen* ■ *Dir* Richard Thorpe • *Scr* Richard Connell, Gladys Lehman

The Thrill of It All ★★★ U
Romantic comedy 1963 · US · Colour · 107min

An enjoyably wacky satire on the world of advertising, this paired Doris Day with the immensely likeable James Garner for the first time. It's the one in which Day becomes a star of soap commercials, much to the annoyance of her gynaecologist husband Garner. There's lots to chuckle over in the clever Carl Reiner screenplay, not least the super cameo he wrote in for himself. It may seem a bit dated now, but back in the 1960s this irreverent comedy was considered strong, anarchic stuff. TS DVD

Doris Day *Beverly Boyer* • James Garner *Dr Gerald Boyer* • Arlene Francis *Mrs Fraleigh* • Edward Andrews *Gardiner Fraleigh* • Reginald Owen *Old Tom Fraleigh* • ZaSu Pitts *Olivia* • Elliott Reid *Mike Palmer* • Carl Reiner ■ *Dir* Norman Jewison • *Scr* Carl Reiner, from a story by Carl Reiner, Larry Gelbart

Throne of Blood ★★★★★ PG
Period drama 1957 · Jpn · BW · 104min

TS Eliot considered this the finest film ever made, though several critics have attacked this loose adaptation of Shakespeare's *Macbeth* for the one-dimensionality of the characters. Whatever faults there may be in the dramatic structure, there's no denying the power of the atmosphere director Akira Kurosawa builds up through his majestic use of camera movement and the eerie sets that earned the film its alternative title, *Cobweb Castle*. At the centre of these Noh tableaux stands Toshiro Mifune, as the villain so much at the mercy of fate and the elements that all you can feel at his death *is* pity. DP Japanese +subtitles. Violence. DVD BL

Toshiro Mifune *Taketoki Washizu* • Isuzu Yamada *Asaji* • Takashi Shimura *Noriyasu Odagura* • Minoru Chiaki *Yoshiaki Miki* ■ *Dir* Akira Kurosawa • *Scr* Hideo Oguni, Shinobu Hashimoto, Ryuzo Kikushima, Akira Kurosawa, from the play *Macbeth* by William Shakespeare

Through a Glass Darkly ★★★★ 15
Drama 1961 · Swe · BW · 85min

Ingmar Bergman's unrelenting drama took the Oscar for best foreign film of 1961. Set on a remote Baltic island, it charts the descent into madness of Harriet Andersson (outstanding), while her father Gunnar Björnstrand and husband Max von Sydow look on with a mix of morbid curiosity and utter helplessness. Gone are the optimistic symbols Bergman usually associates with summer and in their place come some of the bleakest and most searching images of his career. One of the films that earned Bergman his reputation as a harbinger of doom, it is gripping nonetheless. DP Swedish +subtitles. DVD

Harriet Andersson *Karin* • Gunnar Björnstrand *David* • Max von Sydow *Martin* • Lars Passgård *Minus* ■ *Dir/Scr* Ingmar Bergman • *Cinematographer* Sven Nykvist

Through the Olive Trees ★★★★ U
Romantic drama 1994 · Iran/Fr · Colour · 99min

The final part of Abbas Kiarostami's "friendship" trilogy centres on the production of the second episode, *And Life Goes On...*, which was itself a revisitation of the first film, *Where Is My Friend's House?* Blurring the lines between life and art, Kiarostami pokes fun at the filming process, as his *cinéma vérité* project turns into an off-screen melodrama, after orphan student Tahereh Ladanian stops speaking to her leading man, stonemason Hossein Rezai, because she considers his marriage proposal insulting. But besides the self-reflection, this is also a tribute to the hardy

inhabitants of Iran's earthquake-ravaged northlands. DP Farsi +subtitles.

Hossein Rezai *Hossein* • Tahereh Ladanian *Tahereh* • Mohammad Ali Keshavarz *Film Director* • Zarifeh Shiva *Mrs Shiva* • Farhad Kheradmand *Farhad* • Mahbanou Darabi ■ *Dir/Scr* Abbas Kiarostami

Throw Momma from the Train ★★★★ 15
Comedy 1987 · US · Colour · 87min

Danny DeVito made an assured directorial debut with this zany comedy, in which he also stars as the henpecked son of monstrous mother Anne Ramsey. Asked by his writing teacher Billy Crystal to view Hitchcock's *Strangers on a Train*, DeVito is inspired by the murder-swap idea. Chaos and spiky black comedy ensue as DeVito the director focuses on the vitality of his characters and the wonderfully creative dialogue, rather than overheating the barminess of the central situation. DeVito and Crystal give accomplished performances, but both are overshadowed by the marvellous Ramsey. JM DVD

Danny DeVito *Owen Lift* • Billy Crystal *Larry Donner* • Anne Ramsey *Momma* • Kim Greist *Beth* • Kate Mulgrew *Margaret* • Branford Marsalis *Lester* • Rob Reiner *Joel* • Bruce Kirby *Detective DeBenedetto* • Oprah Winfrey ■ *Dir* Danny DeVito • *Scr* Stu Silver

A Throw of Dice ★★★ U
Silent epic 1929 · Ind/Ger/UK · BW · 73min

Inspired by an episode from ancient Hindu epic *The Mahabharata*, this rousing 1929 melodrama from director Franz Osten has been described as a "cross between Chaplin, Cecil B DeMille and an early Bollywood movie" by composer Nitin Sawhney, who has provided a new score for the overlooked silent gem. Chronicling the rivalry between two kings for the heart of a hermit's daughter (Seeta Devi), it's an old-fashioned morality tale about the evils of gambling and the enduring power of love. Filmed on location in Rajasthan to vividly capture its wildlife and breathtaking landscapes, this is not always a subtle experience, but the photography is achingly beautiful. DP DVD

Himansu Rai *Sohan* • Seeta Devi *Sunita* • Charu Roy *Ranjit* • Sarada Gupta *The hermit* ■ *Dir* Franz Osten • *Scr* WA Burton, Max Jungk, from a story by Niranjan Pal • *Cinematographer* Emil Schünemann • *Music* Nitin Sawhney

Thumb Tripping ★ 18
Road movie 1972 · US · Colour · 90min

A strained counterculture road movie that nobody, not even the *Easy Rider* hippies, was aimed at, went to see. That's because its a jangling mess, with Meg Foster and Michael Burns hitching their way to California and coming into contact with various unhinged characters: switchblade-wielding Bruce Dern, lust-crazed trucker Mike Conrad and nymphomaniac Mariana Hill. AJ

Michael Burns *Gary* • Meg Foster *Chay* • Mariana Hill [Marianna Hill] *Lynn* • Burke Burns *Jack* • Mike Conrad *Diesel* • Bruce Dern *Smitty* ■ *Dir* Quentin Masters • *Scr* Don Mitchell (3), from his novel

Thumbelina ★★ U
Animated adventure 1994 · US/Ire · Colour · 63min

This is Don Bluth's cartoon version of Hans Christian Andersen's tale about the tiniest of tots who is parted from her fairy prince to suffer the attentions of Berkeley Beetle, a troupe of toads and an elderly, unsuitable mole. The song *Follow Your Heart*, co-written by Barry Manilow, adds more sweetener to an already saccharine story, while the animation is rather lifeless. TH DVD

Jodi Benson *Thumbelina* • Gino Conforti *Jacquimo* • Barbara Cook *Mother* • Will Ryan *Hero/Reverend Rat* • June Foray *Queen Tabitha* • Kenneth Mars *King Colbert* • Gary Imhoff *Prince Cornelius* • Joe Lynch *Grundel* ■ *Dir* Don Bluth, Gary Goldman • *Scr* Don Bluth, from the fairy tale by Hans Christian Anderson

Thumbsucker ★★ 15
Black comedy drama 2005 · US · Colour · 92min

Keanu Reeves playing an orthodontist is probably the most arresting thing in this meandering, inconclusive drama. Lou Pucci is a troubled teen whose continued thumb-sucking troubles both him and his domineering dad. After taking advice from said orthodontist and a debating coach (Vince Vaughn), Pucci attempts to replace his reliance on the offending digit first with Ritalin and then with the more common adolescent pursuits of pot and sex. Pucci is likeable and convincing, but the screenplay doesn't generate much dramatic heat. AS DVD

Lou Pucci [Lou Taylor Pucci] *Justin Cobb* • Tilda Swinton *Audrey Cobb* • Vince Vaughn *Mr Geary* • Vincent D'Onofrio *Mike Cobb* • Keanu Reeves *Dr Perry Lyman* • Benjamin Bratt *Matt Schramm* • Kelli Garner *Rebecca* • Chase Offerle *Joel Cobb* ■ *Dir* Mike Mills • *Scr* Mike Mills, from the novel by Walter Kirn

Thunder Alley ★★
Sports drama 1967 · US · Colour · 90min

This uninspired drama has one-time heart-throb Fabian as a former driver who joins a low-rent stock-car circus after a blackout destroys his racing career. Tension builds when he get the chance to run a 500-mile race, as his protégé and partner Warren Berlinger tries to take the lead against orders. Car aficionados might enjoy the stock footage of crashes, which pepper the picture. Love interest and songs are provided by Annette Funicello, another fondly remembered teen idol. JG

Annette Funicello *Francie Madsen* • Fabian *Tommy Callahan* • Diane McBain *Annie Blaine* • Warren Berlinger *Eddie Sands* • Jan Murray *Pete Madsen* • Stanley Adams *Mac Lunsford* • Maureen Arthur *Babe* ■ *Dir* Richard Rush • *Scr* Sy Salkowitz

Thunder Bay ★★ U
Adventure drama 1953 · US · Colour · 98min

James Stewart and partner Dan Duryea drill for oil off the Louisiana coast and threaten the local shrimp industry in a disappointing Universal adventure. It's the sort of movie that's made by numbers: a bit of action, a bit of romance, a bit of capitalist conflict and the weather turns bad. AT DVD

James Stewart *Steve Martin* • Joanne Dru *Stella Rigaud* • Dan Duryea *Johnny Gambi* • Gilbert Roland *Teche Bossier* • Marcia Henderson *Francesca Rigaud* • Robert Monet *Phillipe Bayard* • Jay C Flippen *Kermit MacDonald* ■ *Dir* Anthony Mann • *Scr* Gil Doud, John Michael Hayes, from a story by John Michael Hayes, from an idea by George W George, George F Slavin

Thunder in the City ★★★
Satirical comedy drama 1937 · UK · BW · 76min

Seeing Edward G Robinson and Ralph Richardson acting their respective socks off is the juicy prospect offered by this enjoyable comedy proving the old adage of America and England being two countries separated by a common language. Robinson is the Yank who arrives in London aiming to raise a million dollars to finance a mine in Africa; Richardson is the rather staid establishment banker he must win over. AT

Edward G Robinson *Dan Armstrong* • Luli Deste *Lady Patricia* • Nigel Bruce *The Duke of Glenavon* • Constance Collier *The Duchess of Glenavon* • Ralph Richardson *Henry Graham Manningdale* • Annie Esmond *Lady Challoner* • Arthur Wontner *Sir Peter Challoner* • Elizabeth Inglis *Dolly* ■ *Dir* Marion Gering • *Scr* Akos Tolnay, Aben Kandel, Robert E Sherwood, Walter Hackett, from a story by Robert E Sherwood, Aben Kandel

Thunder in the East ★
Period adventure 1953 · US · BW · 97min

During the upheavals following India's independence in 1947, American arms trafficker Alan Ladd turns up in Kandahar to sell arms to pacifist leader Charles Boyer, who doesn't want them. In between times, Ladd falls for Deborah Kerr, the blind daughter of a lovable English missionary. Lavish production values and a grade-A

cast are powerless to rescue a mind-numbingly wordy script that drains the film of any possible excitement or real drama. RK

Alan Ladd *Steve Gibbs* • Deborah Kerr *Joan Willoughby* • Charles Boyer *Singh* • Corinne Calvet *Lizette Damon* • Cecil Kellaway *Dr Willoughby* • Marc Cavell *Moti Lal* ■ *Dir* Charles Vidor • *Scr* Frederick Hazlitt Brennan, Jo Swerling, George Tabori, Lewis Meltzer, from the novel *Rage of the Vulture* by Alan Moorehead

Thunder in the Sun ★★ U
Western 1959 · US · Colour · 80min

Susan Hayward falls for handsome wagon-train scout Jeff Chandler in a movie that can't make up its mind whether it's a western or the true story of the beginning of California's Napa Valley wine industry. Not that anybody cares – the pace is too sluggish, the plot is totally mind-numbing and Hayward is saddled with a ridiculous and almost incomprehensible fake accent as the wife of a Basque leader. Basically this film is an insult to Basques and everyone else. TS

Susan Hayward *Gabrielle Dauphin* • Jeff Chandler *Lon Bennett* • Jacques Bergerac *Pepe Dauphin* • Blanche Yurka *Louise Dauphin* • Carl Esmond *Andre Dauphin* • Fortunio Bonanova *Fernando Christophe* • Bertrand Castelli *Edmond Duquette* • Veda Ann Borg *Marie* ■ *Dir* Russell Rouse • *Scr* Russell Rouse, Stewart Stern, from a story by Guy Trosper, James Hill

Thunder Island ★★ U
Thriller 1963 · US · BW · 64min

This fast-moving thriller finds professional assassin Gene Nelson forcing an American couple to help him murder a dictator exiled on a Latin American island. The job proves more difficult that the hitman intended, leading to an exciting chase in Puerto Rico's El Morro castle. An efficient and occasionally gripping movie, this has Jack Nicholson credited as co-screenwriter. JG

Gene Nelson *Billy Poole* • Fay Spain *Helen Dodge* • Brian Kelly (1) *Vincent Dodge* • Miriam Colon *Anita Chavez* • Art Bedard *Ramon Alou* • Evelyn Kaufman *Jo Dodge* • Antonio Torres Martino *Col Cepeda* • Stephanie Rifkinson *Linda Perez* ■ *Dir* Jack Leewood • *Scr* Don Devlin, Jack Nicholson

Thunder Mountain ★ PG
Western 1947 · US · BW · 60min

This was the first of a new series of B-westerns in which Tim Holt starred for RKO after four years of service in the Second World War. Since he was also in demand for such top-drawer pictures as *My Darling Clementine* and *The Treasure of the Sierra Madre*, it is a shame that the talented star preferred the security of churning out undistinguished formula westerns, such as this re-working of Zane Grey's *To the Last Man* with its background of feuding families. AE DVD

Tim Holt *Marvin Hayden* • Martha Hyer *Ellen Jorth* • Richard Martin (1) *Chito Rafferty* • Steve Brodie *Chick Jorth* • Virginia Owen *Ginger Kelly* • Harry Woods *Trimble Carson* • Jason Robards [Jason Robards Sr] *James Gardner* • Richard Powers [Tom Keene] *Johnny Blue* ■ *Dir* Lew Landers • *Scr* Norman Houston, from the novel *To the Last Man* by Zane Grey

A Thunder of Drums ★★★
Western 1961 · US · Colour · 97min

This well-made western stars Richard Boone, fresh from his TV series *Have Gun Will Travel*, as a growling fort commander, and the dashing George Hamilton as a conscience-stricken lieutenant. *The Big Circus* director Joseph M Newman is clever enough to know how to get the most out of this familiar stuff. TS

Richard Boone *Capt Stephen Maddocks* • George Hamilton *Lt Curtis McQuade* • Luana Patten *Tracey Hamilton* • Arthur O'Connell *Sgt Rodermill* • Charles Bronson *Trooper Hanna* • Richard Chamberlain *Lt Porter* • Duane Eddy *Trooper Eddy* • James Douglas *Lt Gresham* • Slim Pickens *Trooper Erschick* ■ *Dir* Joseph M Newman • *Scr* James Warner Bellah

Thunder on the Hill ★★ PG

Mystery melodrama 1951 · US · BW · 81min

Claudette Colbert, one of Hollywood's most sparkling queens of sophisticated comedy, dons a nun's habit in this dramatic thriller, set in a convent presided over by Mother Superior Glacys Cooper. During a flood, a distraught Ann Blyth - who's accused of murder and under guard - arrives to take refuge from the storm, and Colbert sets out to prove she's innocent. Director Douglas Sirk maintains a sense of atmosphere, but it's uneventful. RK 𝐃𝐕𝐃

Claudette Colbert *Sister Mary Bonaventure* • Ann Blyth *Valerie Carns* • Robert Douglas *Dr Jeffreys* • Anne Crawford *Isabel Jeffreys* • Philip Friend *Sidney Kingham* • Gladys Cooper *Mother Superior* ■ *Dir* Douglas Sirk • *Scr* Oscar Saul, Andrew Solt, from the play *Bonaventure* by Charlotte Hastings

Thunder over Arizona ★★ U

Western 1956 · US · Colour · 74min

George Macready is the town tyrant who evokes the arcane Apex Rule whereby, if a mineral vein runs through his land, the owners of the territory containing the head of the vein have to surrender their rights. Of course, he's not going to get away with that. Unfortunately, he fails to recognise that his hired gun, Skip Homeier, isn't actually the killer he thinks he is. This pacey B-western from Republic was shot in their cheap widescreen process, Naturama. TS

Skip Homeier *Tim Mallory* • Kristine Miller *Fay Warren* • George Macready *Ervin Plummer* • Wallace Ford *Hal Styles* • Jack Elam *Slats* • Nacho Galindo *Pancho* • Gregory Walcott *Mark* • George Keymas *"Shotgun" Kelly* ■ *Dir* Joe Kane [Joseph Kane] • *Scr* Sloan Nibley

Thunder over the Plains ★★ U

Western 1953 · US · Colour · 82min

It's Texas just after the Civil War, as the state comes under the exploitative influence of northern carpetbaggers. Randolph Scott is the native Texan who, as a captain in the Union army of occupation, has the tricky job of enforcing law and order despite his sympathy for Charles McGraw's defiant band of vigilantes. Andre De Toth's direction keeps the complicated story on the move but he can't create any real tension. AE

Randolph Scott *Captain David Porter* • Lex Barker *Captain Bill Hodges* • Phyllis Kirk *Norah* • Charles McGraw *Ben Westman* • Henry Hull *Lt Col Chandler* • Elisha Cook Jr *Standish* • Fess Parker *Kirby* ■ *Dir* Andre De Toth • *Scr* Russell Hughes

Thunder Road ★★★ U

Crime drama 1958 · US · BW · 88min

Robert Mitchum made the plunge into independent production with this pioneering drama of moonshiners brewing illicit whisky. He researched the subject, provided the story, put his son James into a key supporting role, and hired an obscure director with a penchant for surrealism, Arthur Ripley. He even wrote song lyrics for the movie. A cult favourite in Deep South drive-ins, this has obvious technical problems and some inept acting, but is very much one of a kind. AE 𝐃𝐕𝐃

Robert Mitchum *Lucas Doolin* • Gene Barry *Troy Barrett* • Jacques Aubuchon *Carl Kogan* • Keely Smith *Francie Wymore* • Trevor Bardette *Vernon Doolin* • James Mitchum *Robin Doolin* ■ *Dir* Arthur Ripley • *Scr* Robert Mitchum, James Atlee Phillips, Walter Wise, from a story by Robert Mitchum

Thunder Rock ★★★★ PG

Supernatural drama 1942 · UK · BW · 106min

Without ever breaking entirely free from its theatrical origins, this propagandist allegory succeeds in creating an atmosphere that is at once haunting, mournful and inspiring. As the writer disillusioned by the world's complacent response to fascism, Michael Redgrave gives one of his most complex and tormented performances. He regains his crusading spirit as a result of his encounters with the victims of a shipwreck

that occurred years before on the rocks near the lighthouse he now tends. With a bullish contribution from James Mason and truly touching support from Lilli Palmer, this is one of the Boulting brothers' finest achievements. DP 𝐃𝐕𝐃

Michael Redgrave *David Charleston* • Barbara Mullen *Ellen Kirby* • James Mason *Streeter* • Lilli Palmer *Melanie Kurtz* • Finlay Currie *Captain Joshua* • Frederick Valk *Dr Kurtz* • Frederick Cooper *Ted Briggs* ■ *Dir* Roy Boulting • *Scr* Jeffrey Dell, Bernard Miles, from the play by Robert Ardrey

Thunder Run ★ 15

Action thriller 1986 · US · Colour · 86min

A shameless and inferior *Mad Max* rip-off, this amounts to little more than one long and largely unthrilling chase sequence across the Nevada and Arizona deserts, as a veteran trucker battles to bring a cargo of plutonium through in the face of fiendish opposition. Only of interest as the last feature made by Forrest Tucker. PF Swearing, nudity.

Forrest Tucker *Charlie Morrison* • John Ireland *George Adams* • John Shepherd *Chris* • Jill Whitlow *Kim* • Wally Ward *Paul* • Cheryl M Lynn *Jilly* ■ *Dir* Gary Hudson • *Scr* Charles Davis, Carol Heyer, from a story by Carol Lynn, Clifford Wenger Sr

Thunderball ★★★ PG

Spy adventure 1965 · UK · Colour · 130min

The Bond series went well and truly comic strip with this gadget-filled extravaganza that too often cuts plotline corners to squeeze in all the hi-tech hardware. Playing 007 for the fourth time, Sean Connery is still getting a kick out of the part, but he's less the suave spy and more the man of action than in previous outings. Adolfo Celi makes a worthy opponent, but Claudine Auger is one of the least memorable of the Bond girls. Director Terence Young never quite solves the pacing problems posed by filming underwater, but John Stears's Oscar-winning special effects more than compensate. DP 𝐃𝐕𝐃 🅑🅛🅤

Sean Connery *James Bond* • Claudine Auger *Domino Derval* • Adolfo Celi *Emilio Largo* • Luciana Paluzzi *Fiona Volpe* • Rik Van Nutter *Felix Leiter* • Bernard Lee *"M"* • Martine Beswick *Paula Caplan* • Guy Doleman *Count Lippe* • Molly Peters *Patricia Fearing* • Desmond Llewelyn *"Q"* • Lois Maxwell *Moneypenny* ■ *Dir* Terence Young • *Scr* Richard Maibaum, John Hopkins, from the story by Kevin McClory, Jack Whittingham, Ian Fleming, from characters by Ian Fleming

Thunderbird 6 ★★ U

Science-fiction adventure 1968 · UK/US · Colour · 85min

The second big-screen outing (after 1966's *Thunderbirds Are Go!*) for the International Rescue crew is a step down from its predecessor but still diverting entertainment for children and fans of the series. This time Lady Penelope and chauffeur Parker take centre stage as they embark on the round-the-world maiden voyage of *Skyship One*, a new luxury aircraft. A bunch of puppets aren't enough to hold the viewer's attention for 85 minutes, and it turned out to be yet another box office dud. RS 𝐃𝐕𝐃

Peter Dyneley *Jeff Tracy* • Shane Rimmer *Scott Tracy* • Sylvia Anderson *Lady Penelope* • Jeremy Wilkin *Virgil Tracy/Hogarth* • Matt Zimmerman *Alan Tracy/Carter* • David Graham *Gordon Tracy/ Brains/Parker* • Christine Finn *Tin-Tin/Indian fortune teller* • Keith Alexander *John Tracy* ■ *Dir* David Lane • *Scr* Gerry Anderson, Sylvia Anderson

Thunderbirds ★★ PG

Science-fiction adventure 2004 · UK/US/Fr · Colour · 90min

Fans of the original 1960s TV series may well feel short-changed by this pedestrian live-action adventure. Here the focus is on sulky adolescent Brady Corbet, who resents studying at boarding school while his dad (Bill Paxton) and brothers are saving the world. He and his two cutesy pals are left to defeat the Hood (Ben Kingsley) after the dastardly villain deploys the International Rescue team on a fake mission and takes

over Tracy Island. The retro-futuristic design and scenery look great, but style alone can't save a weak script. SF 𝐃𝐕𝐃

Bill Paxton *Jeff Tracy* • Anthony Edwards *Hiram "Brains" Hackenbacker* • Sophia Myles *Lady Penelope Creighton-Ward* • Ben Kingsley *The Hood* • Brady Corbet *Alan Tracy* • Soren Fulton *Fermat Hackenbacker* • Vanessa Anne Hudgens *Tin-Tin* • Ron Cook *Parker* • Philip Winchester *Scott Tracy* • Lex Shrapnel *John Tracy* • Dominic Colenso *Virgil Tracy* • Ben Torgersen *Gordon Tracy* ■ *Dir* Jonathan Frakes • *Scr* William Osborne, Michael McCullers, from a story by Peter Hewitt, William Osborne, from the TV series by Gerry Anderson, Sylvia Anderson

Thunderbirds Are Go! ★★★ U

Science-fiction adventure 1966 · UK/US · Colour · 89min

The first big-screen spin-off from Gerry Anderson's hugely popular TV series is directed with efficient briskness by David Lane. International Rescue is requested to oversee the launch of Zero X, a manned mission to Mars, but saboteur and arch nemesis the Hood (yes, the bald guy with the glowing eyes) is waiting in the wings. As ever the effects and model work are superb, but while the TV stories just about held one's interest for the full hour the novelty ultimately wears thin here. RS 𝐃𝐕𝐃

Peter Dyneley *Jeff Tracy* • Shane Rimmer *Scott Tracy* • Sylvia Anderson *Lady Penelope* • Jeremy Wilkin *Virgil Tracy* • Matt Zimmerman *Alan Tracy* • David Graham *Gordon Tracy/Brains/Parker* • Ray Barrett *John Tracy/The Hood* • Bob Monkhouse *Brad Newman, the Swinging Star compère* ■ *Dir* David Lane • *Scr* Gerry Anderson, Sylvia Anderson

Thunderbolt ★★★★

Crime drama 1929 · US · BW · 91min

Before Josef von Sternberg made Marlene Dietrich into a star, the very different George Bancroft was his favourite actor. In the fourth and last of his films with Sternberg, Bancroft, in the title role, plays a gangster. While on death row he plots to kill his moll's lover, falsely imprisoned in the same jail. Although the quality of the sound recording is primitive -- it was Sternberg's first talkie - the director uses it as atmospherically as he does the camera. RB

George Bancroft *Jim "Thunderbolt" Lang* • Fay Wray *Mary, "Ritzie"* • Richard Arlen *Bob Moran* • Tully Marshall *Warden* • Eugenie Besserer *Mrs Moran* • James Spottswood *"Snapper" O'Shea* ■ *Dir* Josef von Sternberg • *Scr* Jules Furthman, Herman J Mankiewicz, from a story by Jules Furthman, Charles Furthman • *Cinematographer* Henry Gerrard

Thunderbolt and Lightfoot ★★★★ 18

Crime drama 1974 · US · Colour · 109min

This marvellous crime drama marked the directing debut of Michael Cimino, who later distinguished himself with *The Deer Hunter*. Clint Eastwood plays the crook who teams up with drifter Jeff Bridges and, with George Kennedy and Geoffrey Lewis in pursuit, goes on a quest for hidden loot. Eastwood takes a bit of a back seat, letting the other three walk away with the acting honours. Bridges is terrific, but it's the manic Lewis you will remember. The scenery is handsome and, if you can ignore its rather tasteless sense of humour, this is enormously enjoyable. TS Violence, swearing, nudity. 𝐃𝐕𝐃 🅑🅛🅤

Clint Eastwood *John "Thunderbolt" Doherty* • Jeff Bridges *"Lightfoot"* • George Kennedy *Red Leary* • Geoffrey Lewis *Goody* • Catherine Bach *Melody* • Garey Busey [Gary Busey] *Curly* • Burton Gilliam *Welder* ■ *Dir/Scr* Michael Cimino

Thundercrack! ★★★

Sex melodrama 1975 · US · BW · 158min

Underground film-maker George Kuchar – lover of Hollywood melodrama, especially *film noir* – had many acolytes, the best-known of which was Curt McDowell, the director of this insane parody of *The Old Dark House*. It sounds and looks like Kuchar's work because Kuchar wrote it (indulgently) and lit it (often strikingly). He's

also the actor inside the gorilla suit. Strangers seeking shelter from a nasty storm stumble upon an isolated house. The characters lounge and talk (and talk) and eventually get around to (unsimulated) sex. While the mock soap-opera dialogue is banal and the shock of the outlandish sex scenes is insufficient for the running time, this is genuinely a one-off. DM

Marion Eaton *Mrs Gert Hammond* • George Kuchar *Bing* • Melinda McDowell *Sash* • Mookie Blodgett *Chandler* • Moira Benson *Roo* • Rick Johnson (1) *Toydy* • Ken Scudder *Bond* • Maggie Pyle *Willene* ■ *Dir* Curt McDowell • *Scr* George Kuchar, from a story by Mark Ellinger, Curt McDowell

Thunderhead – Son of Flicka ★★★ U

Drama 1945 · US · Colour · 76min

Roddy McDowall, Preston Foster and Rita Johnson return for this eventful sequel to *My Friend Flicka*. Once again the horses are shown in all their glory as Thunderhead overcomes the injury that forced him to quit racing, in order to drive away his own father, a rogue stallion that is troubling the herds of neighbouring ranchers. Pacier and more action-packed than the original, the film's highlight is undoubtedly the ferocious fight sequence. DP

Roddy McDowall *Ken McLaughlin* • Preston Foster *Rob McLaughlin* • Rita Johnson *Nelle* • James Bell *Gus* • Diana Hale *Hildy* • Carleton Young *Major Harris* • Ralph Sanford *Mr Sargent* • Robert Filmer *Tim* ■ *Dir* Louis King • *Scr* Dwight Cummins, Dorothy Yost, from the novel *Thunderhead* by Mary O'Hara

Thunderheart ★★★★ 15

Thriller 1992 · US · Colour · 114min

In this intelligent, gripping thriller, set in the 1970s and loosely based on real events, Val Kilmer stars as an FBI agent with native American roots who's assigned to investigate a murder on a reservation. Director Michael Apted treats the subject matter with some sensitivity and there are powerful supporting turns. This was one of the first projects undertaken by Robert De Niro's production house. JF Violence, swearing. 𝐃𝐕𝐃

Val Kilmer *Ray Levoi* • Sam Shepard *Frank Coutelle* • Graham Greene (2) *Walter Crow Horse* • Fred Ward *Jack Milton* • Fred Dalton Thompson *William Dawes* • Sheila Tousey *Maggie Eagle Bear* • Chief Ted Thin Elk *Grandpa Sam Reaches* ■ *Dir* Michael Apted • *Scr* John Fusco

Thunderpants ★ PG

Fantasy adventure 2002 · UK/Ger · Colour · 83min

This excruciatingly vulgar comedy fantasy is an absolute stinker. Ten-year-old Bruce Cook was born with two stomachs, which cause him to break wind continuously. When his boffin pal Rupert Grint designs a pair of Heath Robinson-like trousers allowing flatulence storage, his power-farting attracts the attention of the US Space Center. AJ 𝐃𝐕𝐃

Simon Callow *Sir John Osgood* • Stephen Fry *Sir Anthony Silk QC* • Celia Imrie *Miss Rapier* • Paul Giamatti *Johnson J Johnson* • Ned Beatty *Ed Sheppard* • Bruce Cook *Patrick Smash* • Rupert Grint *Alan A Allen* • Leslie Phillips *Judge* ■ *Dir* Pete Hewitt [Peter Hewitt] • *Scr* Phil Hughes, from a story by Pete Hewitt [Peter Hewitt]

Thursday ★★★★ 18

Comedy crime drama 1998 · US · Colour · 84min

This Tarantino-esque movie relates the blackly comic tale of ex-criminal Thomas Jane, who has now taken the path of respectability, with all its suburban trappings. Cue 24 hours of hell when old buddy Aaron Eckhart turns up on his doorstep, laden with drugs and looking for a safe place to stash them. A relatively short film, but densely packed, this combines action with luscious dialogue and a first-rate cast. Jane and old buddy Aaron Eckhart are fine, but both are overshadowed by Paulina Porizkova, as the slinky, sexy heroine. Sick and sadistic, but in a fun way. JC Swearing, violence.

T

Thomas Jane *Casey Wells* • Aaron Eckhart *Nick* • Paulina Porizkova *Dallas* • James LeGros *Billy Hilly* • Paula Marshall *Christine Wells* • Michael Jeter *Doctor Jarvis* • Glenn Plummer *Rasta Man* • Mickey Rourke *Kasarov* ■ *Dir/Scr* Skip Woods

Thursday till Sunday ★★★ 12A

Drama 2012 · Chil/Neth · Colour · 95min

This low-key Chilean road movie sees a couple on the cusp of breaking up, as observed from the back seat by their ten-year-old daughter. Santi Ahumada gives a terrific, naturalistic performance as the young girl, who is on a drive north from Santiago with her parents (Francisco Pérez-Bannen and Paola Giannini) and younger brother (Emiliano Freifeld). Writer/director Dominga Sotomayor's feature debut uses the combination of enclosed space, the weather-beaten Chilean terrain and an encounter with an old friend to gradually expose the disintegrating marriage. But don't expect much incident; this is a languid, almost dream-like experience that proceeds at a distinctly art-house pace. JA Spanish, French +subtitles. Swearing.

Francisco Pérez-Bannen *Papá* • Paola Giannini *Ana* • Santi Ahumada *Lucía* • Emiliano Freifeld *Manuel* • Jorge Becker *Jorge* • Axel Dupré *José* ■ *Dir/Scr* Dominga Sotomayor [Dominga Sotomayor Castillo]

Tiara Tahiti ★★ PG

Comedy drama 1962 · UK · Colour · 96min

Director Ted Kotcheff's feature debut is an adequate showcase for the talents of James Mason and John Mills. Nobody can smarm like Mason as he breezes through the picture, as a cultured crook who sees Mills's arrival on Tahiti to negotiate a hotel deal as the chance to pay him back for his being cashiered at the end of the war. Mills occasionally struggles to convince in the more difficult role, not always managing to keep the lid on his histrionics. DP

James Mason *Captain Brett Aimsley* • John Mills *Lt Colonel Clifford Southey* • Claude Dauphin *Henri Farengue* • Herbert Lom *Chong Sing* • Rosenda Monteros *Belle Annie* • Jacques Marin *Marcel Desmoulins* • Libby Morris *Adele Franklin* • Madge Ryan *Millie Brooks* • Roy Kinnear *Captain Tom Enderby* ■ *Dir* William T Kotcheff [Ted Kotcheff] • *Scr* Geoffrey Cotterell, Ivan Foxwell, Mordecai Richler, from the novel by Geoffrey Cotterell • *Cinematographer* Otto Heller

The Tic Code ★★

Drama 1998 · US · Colour · 91min

Polly Draper makes her screenwriting debut with this candid but highly contrived drama. She also stars, as a single mother whose young son (Christopher George Marquette) with Tourette syndrome is helped in his ambition to become a jazz musician by saxophonist Gregory Hines, who shares the boy's affliction. The adults embark on a hesitant romance, Marquette has to learn to stand alone and Hines is forced to confront the emotions he's been avoiding. DP

Gregory Hines *Tyrone* • Polly Draper *Laura* • Christopher George Marquette *Miles* • Desmond Robertson *Todd* • Carlos McKinney *Chester* • Dick Berk *Dick* ■ *Dir* Gary Winick • *Scr* Polly Draper

The Tichborne Claimant ★★ PG

Period drama based on a true story
1998 · UK · Colour · 94min

Based on a true tale of Victorian fortune-hunting, this period piece is more televisual than filmic, and sadly lacking in originality. Manservant John Kani takes to the seas in search of lost aristocrat and heir Sir Roger Tichborne. He returns to Blighty with a coarse alcoholic in Tichborne's place and it all becomes rather ridiculous. The presence of Stephen Fry, Robert Hardy and Sir John Gielgud adds class, but that isn't enough to make this good cinema. LH

John Kani *Andrew Bogle* • Robert Pugh *The claimant* • John Gielgud *Cockburn* • Stephen Fry *Hawkins* • Robert Hardy *Lord Rivers* • Rachael Dowling *Mary Anne* • Paola Dionisotti *Dowager* • Charles Gray *Arundell* ■ *Dir* David Yates • *Scr* Joe Fisher

tick... tick... tick... ★★★

Drama 1969 · US · Colour · 96min

Subtlety was never a hallmark of Ralph Nelson's movies, although occasionally – as here – there are qualities that transcend the bludgeoning. This has the unlikely premise of the black Jim Brown elected to replace white sheriff George Kennedy in a town in the American South during the 1950s. The election turns the formerly peaceful community into the time bomb alluded to in the film's title. What redeems this movie is the sense of atmosphere and the good performances, in particular from Fredric March as the town's mayor. BB

Jim Brown *Jimmy Price* • George Kennedy *John Little* • Fredric March *Mayor Jeff Parks* • Lynn Carlin *Julia Little* • Don Stroud *Bengy Springer* • Janet MacLachlan *Mary Price* ■ *Dir* Ralph Nelson • *Scr* James Lee Barrett

Ticker ★★ 15

Action thriller 2001 · US · Colour · 88min

When it comes to knuckleheaded violence, few can match Albert Pyun's pyrotechnic proficiency. Of course, it always helps to have Dennis Hopper as your deranged bomber, detonating random devices all over San Francisco simply because girlfriend Jaime Pressly has been arrested. It does no harm, either, to have Tom Sizemore as the grizzled cop on the case. But Steven Seagal's best days are way behind him and his cameo as a Zen explosives expert introduces an unintentional comic element that raises more laughs than one of Hopper's rants. DP *DVD*

Steven Seagal *Glass* • Dennis Hopper *Swann* • Tom Sizemore *Ray Nettles* • Nas *Art "Fuzzy" Rice* • Jaime Pressly *Claire* ■ *Dir* Albert Pyun • *Scr* Paul B Margolis

The Ticket of Leave Man ★★

Crime melodrama 1937 · UK · BW · 71min

Villainous Victorians were Tod Slaughter's stock in trade, and this film is no exception. Based on a 1918 silent, it's the story of a murderer who tries to drag criminals even further into a life of crime. Even in the 1930s, Slaughter's films were seen as old-fashioned melodrama, hysterically overacted. Now they're cherished as collector's items in the "so bad, they're good" category. The cast always seems to be having great fun hamming it up but, of course, we're laughing at the film, not with it. SG

Tod Slaughter *Tiger Dalton* • Marjorie Taylor *May Edwards* • John Warwick *Bob Brierly* • Robert Adair *Hawkshaw* • Frank Cochran *Melter Moss* • Peter Gawthorne *Joshua Gibson* ■ *Dir* George King • *Scr* HF Maltby, AR Rawlinson, from the play by Tom Taylor

A Ticket to Tomahawk ★★★ U

Comedy western 1950 · US · Colour · 90min

Western spoofs were rare in the earnest early 1950s, but this colourful 20th Century-Fox romp sends up the old "stagecoach versus incoming railroad" plot to grand effect. It's helped by a witty screenplay by director Richard Sale and his then wife, the novelist and playwright Mary Loos, and superb Technicolor photography from Harry Jackson. Amiable Dan Dailey is

the travelling salesman who teams up with sharp-shootin' Anne Baxter, while slimy Rory Calhoun uses every means he can to stop the railroad from gettin' through to Colorado. Look closely at the actress on Dan Dailey's right-hand side in the big production number: that's Marilyn Monroe. TS

Dan Dailey *Johnny Behind-the-Deuces* • Anne Baxter *Kit Dodge Jr* • Rory Calhoun *Dakota* • Walter Brennan *Terence Sweeney* • Charles Kemper *Chuckity* • Connie Gilchrist *Madame Adelaide* • Arthur Hunnicutt *Sad Eyes* • Will Wright *US Marshal Dodge* • Marilyn Monroe *Clara* ■ *Dir* Richard Sale • *Scr* Mary Loos, Richard Sale

Tickets ★★★★ 15

Portmanteau comedy drama
2005 · It/UK/Iran · Colour · 104min

All three vignettes in this trainbound treatise on what unites and divides modern Europe are accomplished and affecting. There's a wistful melancholy about Ermanno Olmi's first episode, as ageing scientist Carlo Delle Piane ruminates on PA Valeria Bruni Tedeschi's kindness in reorganising his travel arrangements. Abbas Kiarostami's second segment offers a sharp contrast – both in the stridency of war widow Silvana De Santis's tantrums over a booked seat and a mobile phone, and the hesitancy of her reluctant escort Filippo Trojano's corridor encounter with a knowing teenage girl. Yet, these are eclipsed by Ken Loach's finale, which sees a trio of Celtic fans en route to a Champions League game in Rome struggling to reconcile knee-jerk prejudice, underdog self-interest and instinctive social justice as they confront the migrant Albanian family they suspect of stealing one of their tickets. DP English, Albanian, Italian +subtitles. Swearing. *DVD*

Valeria Bruni Tedeschi [Valéria Bruni-Tedeschi] *PR Lady* • Carlo Delle Piane *Professor* • Silvana De Santis *Woman* • Filippo Trojano *Filippo* • Martin Compston *Jamesy* • William Ruane *Frank* • Gary Maitland *Spaceman* • Klajdi Qorraj *Boy, Albanian family* • Blerta Cahani *Girl, Albanian family* • Sanije Dedja *Grandmother, Albanian family* ■ *Dir* Ermanno Olmi, Abbas Kiarostami, Ken Loach • *Scr* Ermanno Olmi, Abbas Kiarostami, Paul Laverty

Tickle Me ★ U

Musical comedy 1965 · US · Colour · 87min

Judging by the improbable situation and silly set pieces, it is unsurprising to discover that a pair of ex-Three Stooges writers scripted this unengaging Elvis Presley vehicle. An ex-rodeo rider falls in love when he gets a job in a health spa (for women only, of course), and becomes involved in a hunt for hidden treasure. Elvis is watchable (just), but it's one for fans of the King only. JG *DVD*

Elvis Presley *Lonnie Beale* • Jocelyn Lane *Pam Merritt* • Julie Adams *Vera Radford* • Jack Mullaney *Stanley Potter* • Merry Anders *Estelle Penfield* • Connie Gilchrist *Hilda* • Edward Faulkner *Brad Bentley* • Bill Williams *Deputy Sturdivant* ■ *Dir* Norman Taurog • *Scr* Elwood Ullman, Edward Bernds

A Ticklish Affair ★★ U

Romantic comedy 1963 · US · Colour · 87min

This pleasant if unadventurous comedy concerns US naval commander Gig Young, who investigates a false alarm set off by a child, and falls in love with the boy's widowed mother Shirley Jones. Initially, she's unwilling to remarry. One of her kids (Billy Mumy, who played Will Robinson in TV's *Lost in Space*) saves the day. JG

Shirley Jones *Amy Martin* • Gig Young *Cmdr Key Weedon* • Red Buttons *Flight Officer Simon Shelley* • Carolyn Jones *Tandy Martin* • Edgar Buchanan *Gramps Martin* • Peter Robbins *Grover Martin* • Billy Mumy [Bill Mumy] *Alex Martin* • Bryan Russell *Luke Martin* ■ *Dir* George Sidney (2) • *Scr* Ruth Brooks Flippen, from the story *Moon Walk* by Barbara Luther

Ticks ★★ 18

Horror 1993 · US · Colour · 81min

This affectionate homage to the big monster movies of the 1950s spoofs the

typical moments of the genre while adding gore and dark humour for the 1990s audience. A marijuana farmer in a mountain village concocts a special fertiliser for his plants, but his leaky machine spills it on to some tick eggs, causing massive mutation and mayhem. Several plot holes and narrative gaps later, the level of gore is so extreme that it becomes comical instead of disgusting. KB Violence, swearing. *DVD*

Peter Scolari *Charles Danson* • Rosalind Allen *Holly Lambert* • Ami Dolenz *Dee Dee Davenport* • Alfonso Ribeiro *Darrel "Panic" Lumley* • Ray Oriel *Rome Hernandez* • Seth Green *Tyler Burns* • Virginya Keehne *Melissa Danson* ■ *Dir* Tony Randel • *Scr* Brent V Friedman

Tideland ★★ 15

Fantasy drama 2005 · Can/UK · Colour · 115min

Director Terry Gilliam's gothic look at a strange and frightening childhood has its moments of charm but mostly is a tale too scary for children and far too odd for adults. Young Jeliza-Rose (Jodelle Ferland) is taken by her rock guitarist father (Jeff Bridges) from the city to an isolated farmhouse after her mother's overdose. Swinging from dreamy to nightmarish, this takes one macabre turn after another to leave nothing but a fanciful, bewildering tale with a shocking sting of reality at its end. KK *DVD*

Jodelle Ferland *Jeliza-Rose* • Brendan Fletcher *Dickens* • Jeff Bridges *Noah* • Janet McTeer *Dell* • Jennifer Tilly *Queen Gunhilda* ■ *Dir* Terry Gilliam • *Scr* Terry Gilliam, Tony Grisoni, from the novel by Mitch Cullin

Tie Me Up! Tie Me Down! ★★ 18

Black comedy drama 1990 · Sp · Colour · 97min

In Pedro Almodóvar's unfocused and lurid tale of kinky sex and bondage, actress and former porn star Victoria Abril is kidnapped by Antonio Banderas, who's recently been released from psychiatric care. He hopes that she'll eventually fall in love with him and start the family he's always wanted. Abril does indeed fall for her captor, making this darkly orgiastic comedy of terrors and errors one of the more controversial entries in the Spanish wunderkind's cult camp canon. AJ Spanish +subtitles. *DVD*

Victoria Abril *Marina* • Antonio Banderas *Ricky* • Francisco Rabal *Maximo Espejo* • Loles Leon *Lola* • Julieta Serrano *Alma* ■ *Dir/Scr* Pedro Almodóvar

The Tie That Binds ★★★ 18

Thriller 1995 · US · Colour · 94min

Debuting director Wesley Strick delivers a double whammy of emotional manipulation in this tug-of-love movie. Julia Devin is abandoned by criminal couple Daryl Hannah and Keith Carradine, and adopted by yuppies Vincent Spano and Moira Kelly. When her parents returns to claim her, the traumatised child is caught between the two families. A gulp-in-the-throat tear-jerker. TH Swearing, violence. *DVD*

Daryl Hannah *Leann Netherwood* • Keith Carradine *John Netherwood* • Moira Kelly *Dana Clifton* • Vincent Spano *Russell Clifton* • Julia Devin *Janie* • Ray Reinhardt *Sam Bennett* • Barbara Tarbuck *Jean Bennett* ■ *Dir* Wesley Strick • *Scr* Michael Auerbach

Tiffany Jones ★ 18

Comedy 1973 · UK · Colour · 86min

Made in the days of dolly birds and psychedelia, this pathetic attempt to produce an *Avengers* clone, but with more nudity, is adapted from a newspaper's comic strip and has Anouska Hempel helping a denim-clad prince regain his throne from a wicked dictator. At least Ray Brooks has the talent to seem embarrassed, but nothing can faze director Pete Walker. TH Swearing, nudity.

Anouska Hempel *Tiffany Jones* • Ray Brooks *Guy* • Susan Sheers *Jo* • Damien Thomas *Salvador* • Eric Pohlmann *President Jabal* • Richard Marner *Vorjak* • Ivor Salter *Karatik* • Lynda Baron *Anna Karekin* ■ *Dir* Pete Walker • *Scr* Alfred Shaughnessy, from the comic strip by Pat Tourret, Jenny Butterworth

Ticket to Heaven ★★★ 15

Drama 1981 · Can · Colour · 102min

Nick Mancuso is on top form as a man on the rebound from a bad relationship, who's brainwashed into becoming a "heavenly child" by a fanatical sect. There's a top-notch supporting cast, but the most memorable performance comes from the obscure RH Thomson as a pragmatic cult deprogrammer. It's no barrel of laughs, but there are flashes of humour to lighten the load. DA

Nick Mancuso *David* • Saul Rubinek *Larry* • Meg Foster *Ingrid* • Kim Cattrall *Ruthie* • RH Thomson *Linc Strunk* • Jennifer Dale *Lisa* • Guy Boyd *Eric* ■ *Dir* Ralph L Thomas • *Scr* Ralph L Thomas, Anne Cameron, from the novel *Moonwebs* by Josh Freed

The Tiger and the Pussycat ★★

Comedy drama   1967 · US/It · Colour · 108min

This US/Italian co-production makes almost nothing of either country's qualities, though it's filmed in Rome. Vittorio Gassman is a 45-year-old engineer and family man experiencing an early midlife crisis. Approaching American art student Ann-Margret to blame her for his spurned son's suicide attempt, he finds himself attracted to her. The film wastes several opportunities, though it has a certain box-office gloss. TH

Vittorio Gassman *Francesco Vincenzini* • Ann-Margret *Carolina* • Eleanor Parker *Esperia* • Caterina Boratto *Delia* • Eleonora Brown *Luisella* • Antonella Steni *Pinella* ■ *Dir* Dino Risi • *Scr* Agenore Incrocci, Furio Scarpelli, from a story by Agenore Incrocci, Furio Scarpelli, Dino Risi

Tiger Bay ★★ PG

Period drama   1934 · UK · BW · 65min

Chinese-American actress Anna May Wong carved out a significant career in the 1920s and early 30s, though Hollywood tended to cast her in stereotypical "Dragon Lady" roles. She received more rewarding parts in Europe, as here where she plays a charismatic Chinese club owner trying to make a living in a lowlife backwater. Beset by a group of brutish layabouts, she's aided by a dapper Englishman Not surprisingly, the film is a bit creaky and its occasional broad humour seems ill placed, but Wong is certainly a shimmering presence. JA DVD

Anna May Wong *Lui Chang* • Henry Victor *Olaf* • Lawrence Grossmith *Whistling Rufus* • Margaret Yarde *Fay* • René Ray *Letty* • Victor Garland *Michael* ■ *Dir* J Elder Wills • *Scr* John Quin, from a story by J Elder Wills

Tiger Bay ★★★ PG

Thriller   1959 · UK · BW · 102min

Hayley Mills gives an astonishing performance in her film debut, playing a young girl who befriends murderous sailor Horst Buchholz and hinders detective John Mills's investigation at every turn. The "kid and the killer" plot cropped up regularly during the 1950s and this variation has nothing new to say, but J Lee Thompson surrounds 12-year-old Hayley with credible characters and faithfully captures the sights and sounds of Cardiff's docklands. DP

DVD

John Mills *Superintendent Graham* • Horst Buchholz *Korchinsky* • Hayley Mills *Gillie* • Yvonne Mitchell *Anya* • Megs Jenkins *Mrs Phillips* • Anthony Dawson *Barclay* • George Selway *Det Sgt Harvey* ■ *Dir* J Lee Thompson • *Scr* John Hawkesworth, Shelley Smith from the novel *Rodolphe et le Revolver* by Noël Calef

Tiger by the Tail ★

Thriller   1955 · UK · BW · 82min

Another trudge through the lowest depths of British movie-making, in the company of quota quickie specialist John Gilling. Larry Parks stars in this, one of his British movies, made after he was driven out of Hollywood at the height of his career during the McCarthy era witch-hunts of the 1950s. He plods through a tatty little tale about a journalist threatened by hoodlums. A thrill-free thriller. DP

Larry Parks *John Desmond* • Constance Smith *Jane Claymore* • Lisa Daniely *Anna Ray* • Cyril Chamberlain *Foster* • Ronan O'Casey *Nick* • Donald Stewart (1) *Macaulay* ■ *Dir* John Gilling • *Scr* John Gilling, Willis Goldbeck, from the novel by John Mair

Tiger by the Tail ★★★

Mystery melodrama   1970 · US · Colour · 99min

This is one of the first melodramas to use the aftermath of Vietnam as a context for its thrills. When veteran Christopher George is wrongly accused of killing his brother, his socialite girlfriend (Tippi Hedren) seeks to help him out. It's a neat little film, which director RG Springsteen contrives to make quite watchable. TH

Christopher George *Steve Michaelis* • Tippi Hedren *Rita Armstrong* • Dean Jagger *Top Polk* • John Dehner *Sheriff Chancey Jones* • Charo

Darlita • Lloyd Bochner *Del Ware* • Glenda Farrell *Sarah Harvey* • Alan Hale [Alan Hale Jr] *Billy Jack Whitehorn* ■ *Dir* RG Springsteen • *Scr* Charles A Wallace

Tiger in the Smoke ★★★

Crime drama   1956 · UK · BW · 92min

Margery Allingham's source novel provides a distinctly offbeat, metaphysical edge to this thriller, in which male lead Donald Sinden spends most of his time gagged and bound. Meanwhile Tony Wright's personification of evil terrorises his fiancée (Muriel Pavlow) and her clergyman father (Laurence Naismith) in his search for a treasure that proves to be worth more than he could ever have imagined. From its opening image of street musicians in the London fog, the film builds up a compelling atmosphere. AE

Donald Sinden *Geoffrey Levett* • Muriel Pavlow *Meg Elgin* • Tony Wright *Jack Havoc* • Bernard Miles *Tiddy Doll* • Alec Clunes *Asst Commissioner Oates* • Laurence Naismith *Canon Avril* • Christopher Rhodes *Chief Inspector Luke* ■ *Dir* Roy Baker [Roy Ward Baker] • *Scr* Anthony Pelissier, from the novel by Margery Allingham • *Cinematographer* Geoffrey Unsworth

The Tiger of Eschnapur ★★★ PG

Adventure drama
1959 · W Ger/Fr/It · Colour · 100min

With his career nearing its end, Fritz Lang returned from Hollywood to Germany and to a script that he had written over 30 years earlier for an adventure directed by Joe May. The first of a two-part story (completed by *The Indian Tomb*, 1959) it uses many real Indian locations and creates a world that is both fabulous and authentic. The story of persecuted lovers fleeing a jealous maharajah has a comic-strip nature, and the acting is rather stilted, but Lang's use of colour and decor provides some pleasure. Both features were brutally re-edited for release as a single 95-minute film in the USA and the UK as *Journey to the Lost City*. RB German +subtitles. DVD

Debra Paget *Seeta* • Walter Reyer *Chandra* • Paul Hubschmid *Harald Berger* • Claus Holm *Dr Walter Rhode* • Sabine Bethmann *Irene Rhode* • Valery Inkijinoff *Yama* • René Deltgen *Prince Ramigani* • Jochen Brockmann *Padhu* ■ *Dir* Fritz Lang • *Scr* Fritz Lang, Werner Jörg Lüddecke, from an idea by Thea von Harbou, from a novel by Richard Eichberg

Tiger Raid ★★★

Thriller   2016 · UK/Ire · Colour · 92min

This modest, desert-set tale follows two bickering Irish mercenaries as they embark on a covert mission in the Middle East. Brian Gleeson is unquestionably loyal to their mysterious boss, while Damien Molony has ambitions of his own. As you might expect, their mission doesn't quite go to plan. Gleeson and Molony are superb in their respective roles, portraying a pair of morally reprehensible killers whose relationship is constantly shifting. Some viewers may find this uneventful (it's based on a stage play), but it is worth a look. SC Violence, swearing. DVD

Brian Gleeson *Joe* • Damien Molony *Paddy* • Sofia Boutella *Shadha* ■ *Dir* Simon Dixon • *Scr* Simon Dixon, Mick Donnellan, Gareth Coulam Evans

Tiger Shark ★★★

Drama   1932 · US · BW · 80min

Rumoured to be an inspiration for *Jaws* and pre-dating that blockbuster by a few decades, this efficient little melodrama features Edward G Robinson as a tuna-fishing Captain Hook – he lost a hand to the sharks – who is involved in a vicious triangle with wife Zita Johann and Richard Arlen. An early film by Howard Hawks, it is, for all its tabloid theatricality, typically well crafted. TH

Edward G Robinson *Mike Mascarena* • Richard Arlen *Pipes Boley* • Zita Johann *Quita Silva* • Leila Bennett *Muggsey* • Vince Barnett *Engineer* • J Carrol Naish *Tony* • William Ricciardi *Manuel Silva* • Edwin Maxwell *Doctor* ■ *Dir* Howard Hawks • *Scr* Wells Root, from the story *Tuna* by Houston Branch

A Tiger Walks ★★ U

Drama   1964 · US · Colour · 84min

A couple of years after making *The Lion* on location in Africa, child actor Pamela Franklin has a go at something similar for Disney, only this time it's an escaped tiger that's loose in small-town America. The tone is unusually downbeat for Disney, with the film's sense of provincial politics owing more to Ibsen than Burbank. The cast also includes one-time "Elephant Boy" Sabu in his last movie role. TS

Brian Keith *Sheriff Pete Williams* • Vera Miles *Dorothy Williams* • Pamela Franklin *Julie Williams* • Sabu *Ram Singh* • Edward Andrews *Governor* • Peter Brown *Vern Goodman* • Kevin Corcoran *Tom Hadley* ■ *Dir* Norman Tokar • *Scr* Lowell S Hawley, from the novel by Ian Niall

Tiger Warsaw ★ 15

Drama   1988 · US · Colour · 88min

Fifteen years after he shot and wounded his father during a violent argument, Patrick Swayze returns to his home town to try to make peace with his family. He finds it a long and slow struggle, as will anyone watching this movie, which is filled with both pointless scenes and no explanation of key details. KB

Patrick Swayze *Chuck "Tiger" Warsaw* • Lee Richardson *Mitchell Warsaw* • Piper Laurie *Frances Warsaw* • Mary McDonnell *Paula Warsaw* • Barbara Williams (2) *Karen* • Bobby DiCicco *Tony* • Jenny Chrisinger *Val* • James Patrick Gillis *Roger* ■ *Dir* Amin Q Chaudhri • *Scr* Roy London

Tigerland ★★★ 18

Wartime drama   2000 · US/Ger · Colour · 96min

Joel Schumacher is obviously revelling in going back to basics with this tale of infantry conscripts undergoing jungle combat training before being shipped out to Vietnam. Colin Farrell plays the charismatic lead, a disruptive dissenter who wants out of the army, and who'll do anything to get his wish. Determinedly low budget and filmed sometimes in an in-your-face, almost documentary style, this is potent screen drama with a genuinely real feel about it. DA Violence, swearing, drug abuse, a sex scene. DVD Blu

Colin Farrell (2) *Roland Bozz* • Matthew Davis *Paxton* • Clifton Collins Jr *Miter* • Thomas Guiry [Tom Guiry] *Cantwell* • Shea Whigham *Wilson* ■ *Dir* Joel Schumacher • *Scr* Ross Klavan, Michael McGruther

The Tiger's Tail ★★ 18

Black comedy thriller
2006 · UK/Ire · Colour · 102min

Brendan Gleeson stars in a double role in this offbeat black comedy, playing both a property developer and his long-lost identical twin. The former's life is sent into a tailspin after his brother steals his identity, his business and even his wife. Director John Boorman used to make muscular moviessuch as *Point Blank* and *Deliverance*, butthis clumsy and whimsical satire never really hits the mark as it tackles the get-rich-quick ethos fuelling Ireland's recent economic boom (the Celtic "tiger's tail" of the title). Although Gleeson has fun with his dual personas, the film's misjudged mix of social commentary and comic buffoonery is risibly ham-fisted. JR Some violence. DVD

Brendan Gleeson *Liam/Double* • Kim Cattrall *Jane* • Sinead Cusack *Oona* • Ciaran Hinds *Father Andy* • Sean McGinley *Declan* • Briain Gleeson [Brian Gleeson] *Connor* • Angeline Ball *Ursula* • Cathy Belton *Sally* ■ *Dir/Scr* John Boorman

A Tiger's Tale ★★ 15

Romantic comedy   1987 · US · Colour · 93min

Another of Kirk Douglas's sons, Peter, made his directorial debut with this self-penned effort, which tries to be too many things at once and ends up being very little at all. The age-gap romance between C Thomas Howell and his girlfriend's mother Ann-Margret, is vaguely credible, especially once she becomes pregnant. But too many other aspects smack of contrivance and the humour is tastelessly patronising. DP

Ann-Margret *Rose Butts* • C Thomas Howell *Bubber Drumm* • Charles Durning *Charlie Drumm* • Kelly Preston *Shirley Butts* • Ann Wedgeworth *Claudine* • William Zabka *Randy* ■ *Dir* Peter Vincent Douglas [Peter Douglas] • *Scr* Peter Vincent Douglas [Peter Douglas], from the novel *Love and Other Natural Disasters* by Allen Hannay III

The Tigger Movie ★★ U

Animated adventure   2000 · US · Colour · 73min

Winnie the Pooh's striped sidekick takes centre stage for the first *Pooh* picture to hit cinemas in nearly two decades. The voice artists have changed, but otherwise it's the same formula as before, with a down-in-the-dumps Tigger bouncing off in search of his family and his pals mounting a rescue mission when he fails to return. This Disney offering is pitched at pre-school, nursery and younger kids. Accompanying adults, however, may yawn at the sluggish pace and simplistic moralising. DA DVD

Jim Cummings *Tigger/Winnie the Pooh* • Nikita Hopkins *Roo* • Ken Sansom *Rabbit* • John Fiedler *Piglet* • Peter Cullen *Eeyore* • Andre Stojka *Owl* • Kath Soucie *Kanga* • Tom Attenborough *Christopher Robin* • John Hurt *Narrator* ■ *Dir* Jun Falkenstein • *Scr* Jun Falkenstein, from a story by Eddie Guzelian, from the characters by AA Milne

Tight Spot ★★★ PG

Film noir   1955 · US · BW · 92min

Ginger Rogers stars as the wisecracking moll who's afraid to give evidence against big-time gangster Lorne Greene. Edward G Robinson co-stars as the attorney seeking her co-operation and Brian Keith is the cop in charge of her safety. This highly capable cast has the benefit of a well worked-out script and of tight direction that makes the most of the confined setting of a hotel room. The result is a gripping thriller, quite the best of Rogers's later films. AE

Ginger Rogers *Sherry Conley* • Edward G Robinson *Lloyd Hallett* • Brian Keith *Vince Striker* • Lorne Greene *Benjamin Costain* • Katherine Anderson *Mrs Willoughby* • Allen Nourse *Marvin Rickles* • Peter Leeds *Fred Packer* • Doye O'Dell *Mississippi Mac* ■ *Dir* Phil Karlson • *Scr* William Bowers, from the play *Dead Pigeon* by Lenard Kantor

Tightrope ★★★★ 18

Thriller   1984 · US · Colour · 109min

Clint Eastwood has always been willing to explore the darker side of his film persona, and in this underrated thriller he once again plays a maverick detective on the trail of a serial killer, only this time he is worried that he and the man he is hunting share the same sexual tastes. Writer/director Richard Tuggle is either unwilling or unable to develop the theme fully, but he does make good use of the New Orleans settings and secures a powerful performance from Geneviève Bujold as a rape counsellor. JF Violence, swearing, sex scenes, nudity. DVD Blu

Clint Eastwood *Wes Block* • Geneviève Bujold *Beryl Thibodeaux* • Dan Hedaya *Detective Molinari* • Alison Eastwood *Amanda Block* • Jennifer Beck (2) *Penny Block* • Marco St John *Leander Rolfe* • Rebecca Perle *Becky Jacklin* ■ *Dir/Scr* Richard Tuggle

Tigrero: a Film That Was Never Made ★★★

Documentary
1994 · Fin/Bra/Ger · Colour · 75min

Hollywood history is littered with failed projects, but the dirt on them rarely sees the light of day – which makes Mika Kaurismäki's documentary all the more revelatory and valuable. Set in Brazil's Mato Grosso, *Tigrero* was a jungle adventure that was slated to star John Wayne, Tyrone Power and Ava Gardner, before 20th Century-Fox mogul Darryl F Zanuck wrote it off as an insurance risk. Escorted by Jim Jarmusch, director Sam Fuller returns to the jungle village of Karaja for the first time since he scouted locations back in the 1950s, offering his attentive protégé a colourful version of the truth. DP

■ *Dir/Scr* Mika Kaurismäki • *Cinematographer* Jacques Cheuiche

T

'Til There Was You ★★ 12

Romantic comedy 1997 · US · Colour · 109min

The woeful miscasting of Jeanne Tripplehorn sabotages this romantic comedy, as two people who are destined to meet contrive to keep missing each other. Tripplehorn fumbles all her attempts at comedy. Dylan McDermott fares better as the man she will one day meet and fall for, and director Scott Winant handles this with a lack of sentimentality. JB Swearing. *DVD*

Jeanne Tripplehorn *Gwen Moss* • Dylan McDermott *Nick Dawkan* • Sarah Jessica Parker *Francesca Lanfield* • Jennifer Aniston *Debbie* • Craig Bierko *Jon* ■ *Dir* Scott Winant • *Scr* Winnie Holzman

'Til We Meet Again ★★★

Romance 1940 · US · BW · 99min

One of the greatest of all shipboard romances, this was definitively filmed in 1932 as *One Way Passage* with Kay Francis and William Powell as the doomed lovers. The remake isn't at all bad, but George Brent's savoir-faire always seemed assumed, and it's hard to care whether Merle Oberon actually succumbs to her fatal disease. Nevertheless, the setting is superb and director Edmund Goulding certainly knows how to keep the romance simmering. TS

Merle Oberon *Joan Ames* • George Brent *Dan Hardesty* • Pat O'Brien *Steve Burke* • Geraldine Fitzgerald *Bonny Coburn* • Binnie Barnes *Countess Liz de Bresac* • Frank McHugh *Rockingham T Rockingham* • Eric Blore *Sir Harold Pinckard* ■ *Dir* Edmund Goulding • *Scr* Warren Duff, from a story by Robert Lord • *Cinematographer* Tony Gaudio

Tilaï ★★★★ PG

Drama
1990 · Burkina Faso/Swi/Fr · Colour · 78min

Set in an isolated village in the scrublands of Burkina Faso, this is a compelling tale of filial disobedience and fraternal loyalty from Idrissa Ouedraogo. Deftly handling the complexities of the plot and making expert use of the colours and vistas of the landscape, Ouedraogo courageously questions an array of tribal customs, including the *tilaï*, the ancient law that insists that incest is punishable by death. The stately pace (so typical of much sub-Saharan cinema) and the glowing photography enhance the power of the drama. DP More +subtitles.

Rasmane Ouedraogo *Saga* • Ina Cisse *Nogma* • Roukietou Barry *Kuilga* • Assane Ouedraogo *Kougri* • Sibidou Sidibe *Poko* • Moumouni Ouedraogo *Tenga* • Mariam Barry *Bore* ■ *Dir/Scr* Idrissa Ouedraogo

Till Death Us Do Part ★★ 12

Comedy 1968 · UK · Colour · 96min

One of the great strengths of the original TV series of *Till Death Us Do Part* was the loose, discursive nature of each episode and the topicality of many of the Alf Garnett character's diatribes about politics, race, religion and royalty. Obviously, the feature format precluded the use of a similar structure and writer Johnny Speight's decision to opt for a *Millions like Us* account of family fortunes from the 1930s to contemporary times only partly comes off. DP *DVD*

Warren Mitchell *Alf Garnett* • Dandy Nichols *Else Garnett* • Anthony Booth *Mike* • Una Stubbs *Rita Garnett* • Liam Redmond *Mike's father* • Bill Maynard *Bert* • Brian Blessed *Sergeant* ■ *Dir* Norman Cohen • *Scr* Johnny Speight, from his TV series

Till the Clouds Roll By ★★★★ U

Musical biography 1946 · US · Colour · 135min

MGM's lush tribute to Jerome Kern was intended as a straightforward biography, but Kern's death in 1945 turned this biopic into a most moving celebration, as the studio's full roster of stars perform the composer's greatest numbers, climaxing with Frank Sinatra crooning *Ol' Man River*. The film has some marvellous highlights, including a sequence featuring Judy Garland as Broadway star Marilyn Miller. The dramatic stuff, though, is heavily handled by former actor Richard Whorf, and Robert Walker is not ideally cast as Kern. Watch this for the MGM talent on display, and the dazzling array of production numbers. TS *DVD*

Robert Walker *Jerome Kern* • Van Heflin *James I Hessler* • Judy Garland *Marilyn Miller* • Lucille Bremer *Sally* • Joan Wells *Sally as a girl* • Paul Langton *Oscar Hammerstein II* • Dorothy Patrick *Mrs Jerome Kern* • Mary Nash *Mrs Muller* • Dinah Shore *Julie Sanderson* • Frank Sinatra ■ *Dir* Richard Whorf • *Scr* Myles Connolly, Jean Holloway, George Wells (adaptation), from a story by Guy Bolton

Till the End of Time ★★★

Romantic drama 1946 · US · BW · 105min

This melodrama about three returning Second World War veterans was a successful vehicle for heart-throb Guy Madison. Dorothy McGuire is sympathetic as a war widow, a role that could have become cloying in other hands, and Robert Mitchum provides a tough contrast to Madison's lightweight leading man. The theme song, adapted from Chopin's *Polonaise in A Flat Major*, was a massive hit in its day for Perry Como. TS

Dorothy McGuire *Pat Ruscomb* • Guy Madison *Cliff Harper* • Robert Mitchum *William Tabeshaw* • Bill Williams *Perry Kincheloe* • Tom Tully *CW Harper* • William Gargan *Sgt Gunny Watrous* • Jean Porter *Helen Ingersoll* • Johnny Sands *Tommy* ■ *Dir* Edward Dmytryk • *Scr* Allen Rivkin, from the novel *They Dream of Home* by Niven Busch

Till We Meet Again ★★★

First World War romantic thriller 1936 · US · BW · 71min

Distinguished Herbert Marshall (who himself lost a leg during the First World War) is quite brilliant as an actor from England who falls in love with German actress Gertrude Michael, only to lose contact with her when war breaks out. Marshall's clever underplaying is extremely moving, with Michael also excellent. This beautifully made, very touching spy romance is luminously photographed by the great Victor Milner. TS

Herbert Marshall *Alan Barclay* • Gertrude Michael *Elsa Durany* • Lionel Atwill *Ludwig* • Rod La Rocque *Carl Schrottle* • Guy Bates Post *Captain Minton* • Vallejo Gantner *Vogel* • Torben Meyer *Kraus* ■ *Dir* Robert Florey • *Scr* Edwin Justus Meyer, Brian Marlow, Alfred Davis, Morton Barteaux, from the play *The Last Curtain* by Alfred Davis

Till We Meet Again ★★

Second World War drama 1944 · US · BW · 88min

Director Frank Borzage has a reputation for being one of the great romantic movie storytellers, but his actual output is rather patchy, ranging from sublime Janet Gaynor silents such as *Seventh Heaven* to sentimental tosh such as this routine wartime drama. B-movie regular Barbara Britton is the French nun who helps flier Ray Milland get back behind Allied lines. This isn't very good, but Milland is worth watching. TS

Ray Milland *John* • Barbara Britton *Sister Clothilde* • Walter Slezak *Mayor Vitrey* • Lucile Watson *Mother Superior* • Konstantin Shayne *Major Krupp* • Vladimir Sokoloff *Cabeau* • Marguerite D'Alvarez [Margarita D'Alvarez] *Madame Sarroux* • Mona Freeman *Elise* ■ *Dir* Frank Borzage • *Scr* Lenore Coffee, from the play by Alfred Maury

Tillie and Gus ★★

Comedy 1933 · US · BW · 58min

The first of four films that infant Baby LeRoy (who retired from the screen aged four) made with on-screen child-hater WC Fields. This rather haphazard comedy, directed by Francis Martin, has Fields as a card-sharp married to a landlady from Alaska (the then 70-year-old Alison Skipworth), who helps to foil a conman who is fleecing Skipworth's niece and her husband. Fields has strong competition from his very funny leading lady, but the plot is somewhat hazy. RK

WC Fields *Augustus Q Winterbottom* • Alison Skipworth *Tillie Winterbottom* • Baby LeRoy *The "King" Sheridan* • Jacqueline Wells [Julie Bishop] *Mary Blake Sheridan* • Clifford Jones [Philip Trent] *Tom Sheridan* • Clarence Wilson *Phineas Pratt* • George Barbier *Capt Fogg* • Barton MacLane *Commissioner McLennan* ■ *Dir* Francis Martin • *Scr* Walter DeLeon, Francis Martin, from a story by Rupert Hughes

Tillie's Punctured Romance ★★★ U

Silent comedy 1914 · US · BW · 74min

America's first feature-length comedy (six reels) had Charles Chaplin in its cast, but Marie Dressler was the lead because she was the star of the stage musical comedy *Tillie's Nightmare*. Dressler is believed to be a recent heiress by Chaplin and Mabel Normand, and he rushes her into marriage. However, she realises love's deception and she and Normand soon regard themselves as victims of male treachery. Directed by Mack Sennett, it now appears crude , but it was a ground-breaker for its time, and it made Chaplin a star. TH *DVD*

Marie Dressler *Tillie Banks, country girl* • Charles Chaplin *Charlie, city slicker* • Mabel Normand *Mabel, his girl friend* • Charles Bennett *Douglas Banks, Tillie's millionaire uncle* • Mack Swain *John Banks, Tillie's father* • Chester Conklin *Mr Whoozis, friend of John Banks* ■ *Dir* Mack Sennett • *Scr* Hampton Del Ruth, from the play *Tillie's Nightmare* by Edgar Smith

Tim ★★★ PG

Romantic drama 1979 · Aus · Colour · 103min

Mel Gibson starred in this low-profile weepie in between the first two *Mad Max* movies. It couldn't be further from the murder and mayhem of those action favourites. Gibson plays a trusting simpleton who tumbles into a relationship with the wary older woman (Piper Laurie) who is teaching him to read. The sexual tensions between this odd couple keep sentiment at bay, and Gibson's performance as the wide-eyed innocent alerted audiences to the fact that there was more to the man than just action movies. JA *DVD*

Piper Laurie *Mary Horton* • Mel Gibson *Tim Melville* • Alwyn Kurts *Ron Melville* • Pat Evison *Emily Melville* • Peter Gwynne *Tom Ainsley* • Deborah Kennedy *Dawn Melville* • David Foster *Mick Harrington* • Margo Lee *Mrs Harrington* • James Condon *John Harrington* ■ *Dir* Michael Pate • *Scr* Michael Pate, from the novel by Colleen McCullough

Tim Burton's Corpse Bride ★★★★ PG

Animated fantasy
2005 · UK/US · Colour · 73min

This exquisitely crafted example of stop-motion animation puts a hip spin on a Russian folk tale, with shy Victor Van Dort (voiced by Johnny Depp) wandering into the woods to practise his marriage vows and ending up spliced to a stiff (Helena Bonham Carter) - a passionate, blue-hued beauty with a maggot living in her eye. She whisks him off to a curiously vibrant subterranean land, but this enchanting world and his new bride's increasingly apparent charms are little comfort to Victor when he'd rather be hitched to his living, breathing fiancée Victoria (Emily Watson). Gothic morbidity is tinged with sweetness, and the often lyrical script is consistently funny. LF *DVD*

Helena Bonham Carter *Corpse Bride* • Johnny Depp *Victor Van Dort* • Albert Finney *Finis Everglot* • Richard E Grant *Lord Barkis Bittern* • Christopher Lee *Pastor Galswells* • Joanna Lumley *Maudeline Everglot* • Emily Watson *Victoria Everglot* • Tracey Ullman *Nell Van Dort/Hildegarde* • Paul Whitehouse *William Van Dort/Mayhew/Paul the head waiter* • Michael Gough *Elder Gutknecht* • Jane Horrocks *Black widow spider/Mrs Plum* • Danny Elfman *Bonejangles* ■ *Dir* Tim Burton, Mike Johnson (2) • *Scr* Pamela Pettler, Caroline Thompson, John August, from characters by Tim Burton, Carlos Grangel

Timber Falls ★★★ 18

Horror thriller 2007 · US · Colour · 100min

A camping trip in the West Virginia backwoods turns nasty in director Tony Giglio's above-average survival horror. There are shades of *Deliverance* as the unwed Mike (Josh Randall) and Sheryl (Brianna Brown) run into some very unfriendly locals. Worse is to follow, when Sheryl's disappearance leads Mike to the home of religious fanatics with unforgiving views on pre-marital sex. The plot may lack any real surprises, but there are plenty of genuinely scary moments in the duo's terrified plight. AJ *DVD*

Josh Randall *Mike* • Brianna Brown *Sheryl* • Nick Searcy *Clyde* • Beth Broderick *Ida* • Sascha Rosemann *Deacon* • TW Leshner *Darryl* ■ *Dir* Tony Giglio • *Scr* Dan Kay [Daniel Kay]

Timberjack ★★ U

Western drama 1955 · US · Colour · 92min

In this average western drama, Sterling Hayden seeks revenge for the murder of his father and pits the family timber business against powerful competitor David Brian, who's also his rival for Vera Ralston's saloon keeper. Some fresh scenery and details count for little against routine plotting and brawling, and, while veteran Adolphe Menjou revels in his flowery dialogue, the songs by a dubbed Ralston and Hoagy Carmichael are dreary. AE

Sterling Hayden *Tim Chipman* • Vera Ralston *Lynne Tilton* • David Brian *Croft Brunner* • Adolphe Menjou *Swiftwater Tilton* • Hoagy Carmichael *Jingles* • Chill Wills *Steve Riika* • Jim Davis (1) *Poole* ■ *Dir* Joseph Kane • *Scr* Allen Rivkin, from the novel by Dan Cushman

Timbuktu ★★★★ 12A

Drama 2014 · Fr/Mauritania · Colour · 95min

Set in 2012 when jihadists occupied the Malian city of the title, *Timbuktu* is particularly timely, especially given subsequent events in Isis-controlled territories. Criss-crossing between different characters, we meet a family of goat and cattle herders, local musicians, fishmongers and imams who are all suddenly compelled to obey sharia laws that prohibit things granted.Mauritanian-born, Malian-reared director Abderrahmane Sissako exposes the cruelty and absurdity of fundamentalist regimes, but with a warm, surprisingly humorous touch. Seldom has a film about a subject as grim as this been so generous in its sympathy for the oppressors, often confused befuddled souls, who know not what they do. LF In Arabic, Bambara, English, French, Songhay, Tamasheq. Some violence, swearing. *DVD* *BL*

Ibrahim aka Pino Ahmed [Ibrahim Ahmed (2)] *Kidane* • Toulou Kiki *Satima* • Abel Jafri *Abdelkrim* • Fatoumata Diawara *Fatou* ■ *Dir* Abderrahmane Sissako • *Scr* Abderrahmane Sissako, Kessen Tall

Time after Time ★★★★ 15

Science-fiction crime thriller 1979 · US · Colour · 107min

In Nicholas Meyer's splendid literary conceit, the novelist HG Wells (Malcolm McDowell) follows Jack the Ripper (David Warner) from Victorian London to contemporary San Francisco in his time machine. It's a sometimes gruesome experience, but it's wittily aware of anachronisms, as the blood-steeped Ripper, warped in nature as well as time, becomes gratefully aware that the present day has many more killing devices. TH Violence, swearing.

Malcolm McDowell *Herbert G Wells* • David Warner *Dr John Lesley Stevenson* • Mary Steenburgen *Amy Robbins* • Charles Cioffi *Lieutenant Mitchell* • Laurie Main *Inspector Gregson* • Andonia Katsaros *Mrs Turner* • Patti D'Arbanville *Shirley* ■ *Dir* Nicholas Meyer • *Scr* Nicholas Meyer, from a story by Karl Alexander, Steve Hayes

Time and Tide ★★★★ 18
Action crime thriller
2000 · HK · Colour · 108min

Tsui Hark's kinetic, hyper-stylised thriller offers both high-velocity action and well-developed characters, as a hitman and a bodyguard are connected via both their work conflicts and impending fatherhood. This touches upon similar themes to many of John Woo's Hong Kong movies and Tsui's visual orchestration is no less impressive, with wild angles, incredible stunt work and audacious editing techniques that give the fast-paced story a dynamic edge. JC Cantonese, English, Spanish +subtitles. DVD

Nicholas Tse *Tyler* • Wu Bai *Jack* • Candy Lo *Ah Hui* • Anthony Wong (1) *Uncle Ji* ■ *Dir* Tsui Hark • *Scr* Hui Koan, Tsui Hark

Time Bandits ★★★★ PG
Fantasy comedy
1981 · UK · Colour · 111min

Before Terry Gilliam found success in the US with *The Fisher King* and *Twelve Monkeys*, he made a series of wondrously inventive fantasies, of which this was one of the best. Its story of a schoolboy accompanying a group of outlaw dwarves on a jolting trip through time has some astonishing sequences, while the marvellous cast includes John Cleese as Robin Hood, Sean Connery as a Greek warrior king and Ralph Richardson as God. TH Violence. DVD ☐ Blu-ray

John Cleese *Robin Hood* • Sean Connery *King Agamemnon* • Craig Warnock *Kevin* • Shelley Duvall *Pansy* • Katherine Helmond *Mrs Ogre* • Ian Holm *Napoleon* • Michael Palin *Vincent* • Ralph Richardson *Supreme Being* • Kenny Baker (2) *Fidget* ■ *Dir* Terry Gilliam • *Scr* Michael Palin, Terry Gilliam

Time Flies ★★★ U
Fantasy comedy
1944 · UK · BW · 84min

ITMA radio series star Tommy Handley takes a trip to Elizabethan England. Handley's regular radio writer Ted Kavanagh is part of the team serving up a generous portion of period gags, such as Handley pipping Sir Walter Raleigh to tobacco and a spot of cloak laying, and George Moon singing a music-hall song at the Globe. Some of the jokes have travelled less well and it falls flat in places, but it's an entertaining romp. DP

Tommy Handley *Tommy* • Evelyn Dall *Susie Barton* • George Moon *Bill Barton* • Felix Aylmer *Professor* • Moore Marriott *Soothsayer* • Graham Moffatt *Nephew* • John Salew *William Shakespeare* • Leslie Bradley *Walter Raleigh* • Olga Lindo *Queen Elizabeth* ■ *Dir* Walter Forde • *Scr* Howard Irving Young, JOC Orton, Ted Kavanagh

A Time for Drunken Horses ★★★★ PG
Drama
2000 · Fr/Iran · Colour · 75min

Refusing to flinch from the harshest of realities about the life of dispossessed Kurds on the Iran-Iraq border, writer/director Bahman Ghobadi focuses on the selfless determination of a couple of orphans to fund an operation for their severely handicapped brother. His juxtaposition of insistent close-ups and forbidding vistas highlights the reckless courage of the contraband smugglers, who resort to dosing their horses with alcohol to get them through the blizzard-blasted mountain passes. DP Farsi +subtitles. DVD

Ayoub Ahmadi *Ayoub* • Nezhad Ekhtiar-Dini *Madi* • Mehdi Ekhtiar-Dini • Ameneh Ekhtiar-Dini *Amaneh* • Rojin Younessi *Rojin* ■ *Dir/Scr* Bahman Ghobadi

A Time for Killing ★★★ 15
Western
1967 · US · Colour · 80min

Confederate soldier George Hamilton escapes from a Union prison and is pursued by Captain Glenn Ford whose fiancée, Inger Stevens, has been taken hostage and is then raped by Hamilton as revenge for the South's defeat. Sadly, a weak performance from Hamilton and a bland one from Ford diminish the story, which otherwise has a startling realism and toughness in its evocation of America after the Civil War. Released on video in the UK as *The Long Ride Home*. AT

Glenn Ford *Major Walcott* • George Hamilton *Capt Bentley* • Inger Stevens *Emily Biddle* • Paul Peterson *Blue Lake* • Max Baer Jr *Sgt Luther Liskell* • Todd Armstrong *Lt Prudessing* • Timothy Carey *Billy Cat* • Harrison Ford *Lt Shaffer* ■ *Dir* Phil Karlson • *Scr* Halsted Welles, from the novel *The Southern Blade* by Nelson Wolford, Shirley Wolford

A Time for Loving ★★
Portmanteau romantic drama
1971 · UK · Colour · 103min

This British-made portmanteau film echoes the structure of the same year's *Plaza Suite* by setting a series of romantic episodes in the same Parisian apartment. Directed by Christopher Miles from a script by French playwright Jean Anouilh and with theme music by Michael Legrand, it features an international cast. Unfortunately, without Neil Simon's comic gifts or a sufficiently skilled or attractive cast, the intended soufflé falls flat more often than it rises. RK

Mel Ferrer *Dr Harrison* • Joanna Shimkus *Joan* • Britt Ekland *Josette* • Philippe Noiret *Marcel* • Susan Hampshire *Patricia* • Mark Burns *Geoff* • Lila Kedrova *Madame Dubillard* • Robert Dhéry *Leonard* ■ *Dir* Christopher Miles • *Scr* Jean Anouilh

Time Gentlemen Please! ★★ U
Comedy
1952 · UK · BW · 85min

One of the few pictures produced by the ill-fated low-budget Group 3 company, this feeble film attempts to reproduce the whimsy of the Ealing comedies and succeeds only in being snobbish, predictable and dull. Eddie Byrne overplays his hand as the rascal who is the blot on a village's 100 per cent employment record and threatens to ruin its chances of national publicity. Sid James scores as the pub landlord, but the plot is contrived and inconsequential. DP

Eddie Byrne *Dan Dance* • Hermione Baddeley *Emma Stebbins* • Raymond Lovell *Sir Digby Montague* • Jane Barrett *Sally* • Dora Bryan *Peggy Stebbins* • Robert Brown *Bill Jordan* • Thora Hird *Alice Crouch* • Sidney James *Eric Hace* ■ *Dir* Lewis Gilbert • *Scr* Peter Blackmore, Val Guest, from the novel *Nothing to Lose* by RJ Minney

The Time Guardian ★★★ PG
Science-fiction action adventure
1987 · Aus · Colour · 83min

This reasonably exciting fantasy set in Australia has a quite complicated plot beginning in the year 4039. Earth has been destroyed by a cyborg master race called the Jen-Diki. Escaping ruler Dean Stockwell sends warriors Carrie Fisher and Tom Burlinson back in time to 1988 to engineer another future battle with the killer robots before they become too strong. In the outback, the two culture-clash soldiers meet loner Nikki Coghill, who helps them fight the corrupt Aussie police. Good special effects and a quick pace disguise plot holes you could fly a spaceship through. AJ

Tom Burlinson *Ballard/The Time Guardian* • Nikki Coghill *Annie* • Dean Stockwell *Boss* • Carrie Fisher *Petra* • Peter Merrill *Zuryk* • Tim Robertson *Sergeant McCarthy* • John Clark (2) • Jimmy James ■ *Dir* Brian Hannant • *Scr* Brian Hannant, John Baxter (2)

Time in the Sun ★★★
Documentary drama
1939 · US/Mex · BW · 60min

In 1931, Sergei Eisenstein spent some months in Mexico shooting his semi-documentary *Que Viva Mexico!*. After fighting bureaucracy and trying to obtain money to keep the film going, the great Russian director had to return to the USSR. However, his producer, the American novelist Upton Sinclair, never sent him the reels to edit. Instead he sold them to producer Sol Lesser, who assembled some of the raw material into a crude film called *Thunder over Mexico* (1933). Later Eisenstein's first biographer Marie Seton edited the reels to make this version, a superior travelogue with banal narration. Though not quite as Eisenstein envisaged, it still retains much of his bizarre humour and homoeroticism, and its magnificent photography. RB

Charles Frederick Lindsley *Narrator* • William Royal *Narrator* • Ponce Espino *Narrator* • Carlos Tarin *Narrator* ■ *Dir* Sergei Eisenstein • *Scr* Grigori Alexandrov, Marie Seton, Paul Burnford, Anita Breener, Franz Blom, Samuel A Datlowe

Time Lapse ★★ 15
Thriller
2001 · US · Colour · 84min

Nowadays, Roy Scheider is often cast as the villain in mediocre genre movies - rather like this one, in which he slips agent William McNamara a dose of amnesia serum and then arranges a nuclear transaction with a Middle Eastern spy. There's a hint of *Memento* about the way in which McNamara pieces together his past, although he's helped by the loyal support of ex-wife Dina Meyer, who seems to buy his story of a major memory lapse a touch too willingly for an ace reporter. DP DVD

Roy Scheider *Agent La Nova* • Dina Meyer *Kate* • William McNamara *Clayton Pierce* • Henry Rollins *Gaines* • Cassandra Hitti *Soozy Li* • Gabriella Bern *Anna* ■ *Dir* David Worth • *Scr* David Keith Miller, Karen Kelly

Time Limit ★★★
Wartime courtroom drama
1957 · US · BW · 96min

An engrossing, if stagey court martial drama, this is the only film to have been directed by actor Karl Malden. It's set during the Korean War and deals with an American major (Richard Basehart) charged with collaboration with the enemy during his time as a PoW. Basehart pleads guilty but the investigating officer digs deeper and discovers a terrible secret. The cast, led by Richard Widmark, is uniformly excellent, especially the undervalued Basehart. AT

Richard Widmark *Colonel William Edwards* • Richard Basehart *Major Harry Cargill* • Dolores Michaels *Corporal Jean Evans* • June Lockhart *Mrs Cargill* • Carl Benton Reid *General Connors* • Martin Balsam *Sergeant Baker* • Rip Torn *Lieutenant George Miller* • Alan Dexter *Mike* ■ *Dir* Karl Malden • *Scr* Henry Denker, from the play by Ralph Berkey, Henry Denker

Time Lock ★★★
Drama
1957 · UK · BW · 72min

Shot on a shoestring at the old Beaconsfield Studios but set in Canada, this nail-biting thriller was based on a TV play by Arthur Hailey, who went on to find huge success as the writer of blockbuster novels such as *Airport* and *Hotel*. It's a race against time to free a small boy from a bank vault before he suffocates. Director Gerald Thomas builds the tension adroitly enough and gets a fine performance out of young Vincent Winter. It provided Sean Connery with his first speaking role, as a welder. DP

Robert Beatty *Peter Dawson* • Betty McDowall *Lucille Walker* • Vincent Winter *Steven Walker* • Lee Patterson *Colin Walker* • Sandra Francis *Evelyn Webb* • Alan Gifford *George Foster* • Robert Ayres *Inspector Andrews* • Victor Wood *Howard Zeeder* • Sean Connery *Welder* ■ *Dir* Gerald Thomas • *Scr* Peter Rogers, from a TV play by Arthur Hailey

The Time Machine ★★★★ PG
Science-fiction fantasy adventure
1960 · UK/US · Colour · 98min

HG Wells's marvellous novel is superbly brought to life in this charming and stylish adaptation by *The War of the Worlds* producer George Pal. Leaving his comfortable Victorian life behind, inventor Rod Taylor hops aboard his ingenious time contraption to explore the horrors of the future. He speeds through two World Wars and atomic destruction (in 1966!) towards the eventual enslavement of the human race by subterranean cannibals. This richly speculative science-fiction classic both stimulates and entertains, and deservedly won an Oscar for special effects. AJ DVD

Rod Taylor *George* • Alan Young *David Filby/James Filby* • Yvette Mimieux *Weena* • Sebastian Cabot *Dr Philip Hillyer* • Tom Helmore *Anthony Bridewell* • Whit Bissell *Walter Kemp* • Doris Lloyd *Mrs Watchett* ■ *Dir* George Pal • *Scr* David Duncan, from the novel by HG Wells • *Special Effects* Gene Warren, Tim Baer, Wah Chang

The Time Machine ★★ PG
Science-fiction fantasy adventure
2002 · US · Colour · 91min

What will this dull, philosophically fudged and digitally dependent remake say about the early 21st-century when seen in the future? Chiefly, that we can't tell a tried and tested yarn - Victorian inventor travels 800,000 years forward in time and finds that a post-apocalyptic civilisation has divided into a two-tier caste system - without recourse to standard action-movie heroics. Guy Pearce tries hard to inhabit the character of the driven professor, but a more experienced director than Simon Wells (the great-grandson of the esteemed author) was needed. AC DVD

Guy Pearce *Professor Alexander Hartdegen* • Samantha Mumba *Mara* • Jeremy Irons *Uber-Morlock* • Orlando Jones *Vox* • Mark Addy *Dr David Philby* • Sienna Guillory *Emma* • Phyllida Law *Mrs Watchit* ■ *Dir* Simon Wells • *Scr* John Logan, from the 1960 film, from the novel by HG Wells

A Time of Destiny ★ 15
Second World War drama
1988 · US · Colour · 112min

The significant talents of William Hurt and Timothy Hutton are diminished by the pseudo-operatic approach in this overblown melodrama. Hurt is the revenge-driven son determined to kill Hutton, whom he believes caused the death of his Basque father. The two become best buddies during the Second World War and find themselves in mortal danger before Hurt hits the vengeance trail again. TH Swearing, violence.

William Hurt *Martin* • Timothy Hutton *Jack* • Melissa Leo *Josie* • Francisco Rabal *Jorge* • Concha Hidalgo *Sebastiana* • Stockard Channing *Margaret* ■ *Dir* Gregory Nava • *Scr* Gregory Nava, Anna Thomas

Time of Favor ★★★ 12
Political drama
2000 · Is · Colour · 102min

Joseph Cedar's directorial debut provides a commendably balanced insight into the intransigence sustaining the violent tensions that dominate life in Jerusalem and the West Bank. Although the military aspect of the story strains credibility, there's much to ponder in the relationship between Assi Dayan, a rabbi who advocates the reclamation of the Temple Mount, and his daughter, Tinkerbell, who resents his attempts to impose favoured student Edan Alterman as her husband when she has designs on his army buddy, Aki Avni. Undeniably melodramatic, but also provocative and emotive. DP Hebrew +subtitles.

Aki Avni *Menachem* • Tinkerbell *Michal Meltzer* • Edan Alterman *Pini* • Assi Dayan *Rabbi Meltzer* • Micha Selektar *Itamar* • Amnon Volf *Mookie* ■ *Dir/Scr* Joseph Cedar

The Time of His Life ★★★ U
Comedy
1955 · UK · BW · 73min

Richard Hearne's enduring creation Mr Pastry delighted audiences for over 25 years. The youthful Hearne's impersonation of an incident-prone old man was popular not just in the UK and the US, but all across Europe. The character made a record number of appearances on *The Ed Sullivan Show* and was a favourite of comedy superstar Buster Keaton. In this film, Mr Pastry is an ex-con paying an unwanted visit to his daughter, who has moved up in society. While not a patch on the TV shows, this is still a nostalgic treat. DF

Richard Hearne *Charles Pastry* • Ellen Pollock *Lady Florence* • Richard Wattis *Edgar* • Robert Moreton *Humphrey* • Frederick Leister *Sir John* • Peter Sinclair *Kane* • John Downing *Simon* • Anne Smith *Penelope* ■ *Dir* Leslie Hiscott • *Scr* Leslie Hiscott, Richard Hearne, from the story by Leslie Hiscott, Brock Williams

T

Time of Indifference ★★

Period drama 1964 · Fr/It · BW · 84min

Adapted from a novel by Alberto Moravia, this 1920s-set drama is dominated by director Francesco Maselli's communist contempt for the bourgeois family paralysed by financial problems and indecision. The dysfunctional group hope for salvation, but their "saviour" turns out to be a conman. Glum stuff, it boasts a trio of formidable American imports, each suffering a dip in their careers. BB

Rod Steiger *Leo* • Claudia Cardinale *Carla Ardengo* • Shelley Winters *Lisa* • Paulette Goddard *Maria Grazia Ardengo* • Tomas Milian *Michele Ardengo* ■ *Dir* Francesco Maselli • *Scr* Suso Cecchi D'Amico, Francesco Maselli, from the novel *Gli Indifferenti* by Alberto Moravia

Time of the Gypsies ★★★★★ 15

Fantasy drama 1988 · Yug · Colour · 136min

This astonishing fantasy drama, inspired by true events, is a blend of romance, realism and raw humour that won the best director prize at Cannes in 1989 for Sarajevo-born Emir Kusturica. Using both trained and non-professional performers, he reveals the divisions, deprivations and dreams of the Romany people, with Milan and the breathtaking but severe countryside of the former Yugoslavia as a backdrop. Davor Dujmovic gives a remarkable performance as the young gypsy with telekinetic powers who is prepared to sacrifice everything to win the hand of his beloved. At once epic and intimate, this is the work of a master film-maker. DP Romany, Serbo-Croat +subtitles. Violence, nudity.

Davor Dujmovic *Perhan* • Bora Todorovic *Ahmed Dzida* • Ljubica Adzovic *Grandmother* • Husnija Hasmovic *Uncle Merdzan* • Elvira Sali *Daca* ■ *Dir* Emir Kusturica • *Scr* Emir Kusturica, Gordan Mihic

Time of the Wolf ★★★ 15

Drama 2003 · Fr/Austria/Ger · Colour · 108min

Set against the bleak backdrop of an unexplained apocalypse, Michael Haneke's feature may despair of society's bestial excesses, but he's clearly not lost faith in humanity. Haneke pitches Isabelle Huppert and her children into a nightmare that begins with the murder of her husband and deepens on their arrival at a railway depot, presided over by Olivier Gourmet. Jürgen Jürges's nocturnal photography is outstanding and the performances painfully intense, but Haneke's dystopian vision won't persuade everyone. DP French +subtitles. Violence, swearing. *DVD*

Isabelle Huppert *Anne Laurent* • Anaïs Demoustier *Eva Laurent* • Lucas Biscombe *Ben Laurent* • Patrice Chéreau *Thomas Brandt* • Béatrice Dalle *Lise Brandt* • Maurice Bénichou *Monsieur Azoulay* • Daniel Duval *Georges Laurent* • Olivier Gourmet *Koslowski* ■ *Dir/Scr* Michael Haneke

The Time of Their Lives ★★ PG

Period comedy fantasy 1946 · US · BW · 78min

Between 1941 and the early 1950s, the comedy duo of Abbott and Costello were a national institution and earned around $800,000 a year – a fantastic sum for actors in black-and-white B-movies. But in 1945, they temporarily fell out over a domestic matter and did not speak for months. Reunited, they made this "thriller" in which they did not work as a team but as individual characters. The plot involved two revolutionary ghosts haunting a country house – a phenomenon investigated with predictably comic results. BB

Bud Abbott *Ralph Greenway/Cuthbert Greenway* • Lou Costello *Horatio Prim* • Marjorie Reynolds *Melody Allen* • Binnie Barnes *Mildred "Millie" Dean* • John Shelton *Sheldon "Shelly" Gage* • Jess Barker *Tom Danbury* • Gale Sondergaard *Emily* ■ *Dir* Charles Barton • *Scr* Val Burton, Walter DeLeon, Bradford Ropes, John Grant

The Time of Your Life ★★★★ U

Comedy drama 1948 · US · BW · 100min

Produced by William Cagney for Cagney Productions and starring brother James, this faithful rendering of William Saroyan's play, for which the author won, but refused, the 1940 Pulitzer Prize, is set entirely in a San Francisco waterfront bar run by gruff but kindly William Bendix. Here, a bunch of eccentrics, failures and wannabes live on dreams, acutely and understandingly observed by a mysterious Cagney, part tough guy, part altruist. Although leisurely, talky, too long and characterised by sentimental philosophising, it's extremely well acted and well directed, with some terrific tap-dancing from Paul Draper. RK *DVD*

James Cagney *Joe* • William Bendix *Nick* • Wayne Morris *Tom* • Jeanne Cagney *Kitty Duval* • Broderick Crawford *Krupp, a bewildered cop* • Ward Bond *McCarthy* • Paul Draper *Harry* ■ *Dir* HC Potter • *Scr* Nathaniel Curtis, from the play by William Saroyan

Time Out ★★★ PG

Drama 2001 · Fr · Colour · 128min

Staged with meticulous care, this solemnly fascinating drama is loosely based on the case of Jean-Claude Romand, the seemingly successful businessman who wove a web of deception to prevent his family discovering he'd lost his job. Choosing not to follow the Romand case to its violent conclusion – Romand eventually murdered his family – director Laurent Cantet here re-creates the routines that occupied the man's empty days. DP French +subtitles. *DVD*

Aurélien Recoing *Vincent* • Karin Viard *Muriel* • Serge Livrozet *Jean-Michel* • Jean-Pierre Mangeot *Vincent's father* • Nicolas Kalsch *Julien* • Marie Cantet *Alice* ■ *Dir* Laurent Cantet • *Scr* Robin Campillo, Laurent Cantet

Time Out for Rhythm ★ U

Comedy drama 1941 · US · BW · 74min

Columbia produced this forgettable and forgotten effort about a couple of theatrical agents locked into an ongoing vendetta. Although jam-packed with speciality acts, orchestras, rhumba bands, crooner Rudy Vallee and the Three Stooges, the only moments able to surmount the dreary plot and pathetic screenplay are those featuring the great Ann Miller. RK

Ann Miller *Kitty Brown* • Rudy Vallee *Daniel Collins* • Rosemary Lane *Frances Lewis* • Allen Jenkins *Off-Beat "One Note" Davis* • Moe Howard • Larry Fine • Curly Howard ■ *Dir* Sidney Salkow • *Scr* Edmund Hartmann [Edmund L Hartmann], Bert Lawrence, from a story by Bert Granet, from the play *Show Business* by Alex Ruben

Time out of Mind ★★

Period drama 1947 · US · BW · 88min

Britain's ladylike Phyllis Calvert, unsuitably cast, made an undistinguished Hollywood debut in this tale of Robert Hutton whose aspirations to become a composer fall foul of his dictatorial seafaring father Leo G Carroll. Hutton seeks refuge in an unhappy marriage and the bottle, but is rescued and returned to music by the unstinting encouragement of housekeeper's daughter Calvert and by his sister Ella Raines. A dull effort. RK

Phyllis Calvert *Kate Fernald* • Robert Hutton *Christopher Fortune* • Ella Raines *Clarissa "Rissa" Fortune* • Eddie Albert *Jack Bullard* • Leo G Carroll *Captain Fortune* • Helena Carter *Dora Drake* ■ *Dir* Robert Siodmak • *Scr* Abem Finkel, Arnold Phillips, from the novel by Rachel Field

Time out of Mind ★★★★ 15

Drama 2014 · US · Colour · 116min

Richard Gere sheds all traces of glamour to portray a homeless man in need in New York, and trying to reconnect with estranged daughter Jena Malone. At first it's a stretch to accept the debonair star in such surroundings, but a drawn, flabby Gere soon disappears into the role of an isolated, long-term alcoholic struggling to accept that he's reached his lowest ebb.

While the documentary-influenced drama's deliberate pace and minimal plotting may prove testing for some viewers, it's ultimately convincing and affecting. TJ Swearing, sexual references. *DVD*

Richard Gere *George* • Ben Vereen *Dixon* • Jena Malone *Maggie* • Kyra Sedgwick *Karen/Fake Sheila* • Jeremy Strong *Jack* • Steve Buscemi *Art* ■ *Dir* Oren Moverman • *Scr* Oren Moverman, from a story by Jeffrey Caine, Moverman

Time Regained ★★★★ 18

Drama 1999 · Fr/It/Por · Colour · 155min

As time elapses from the optimistic 1880s to the depressed 1920s, Chilean director Raúl Ruiz calls on all manner of technical strategies to blend narrative, memory, emotion and dream into a sublime cinematic experience. Surrounded by such luminaries as Catherine Deneuve and John Malkovich, Marcello Mazzarella proves pivotal as Marcel, the writer whose life among the aristocracy becomes his art. Handsomely staged and acutely scripted, this is a triumph of technique and intellect. DP French +subtitles. *DVD*

Catherine Deneuve *Odette* • Emmanuelle Béart *Gilberte* • Vincent Perez *Morel* • Pascal Greggory *Saint-Loup* • Marcello Mazzarella *Marcel Proust* • Chiara Mastroianni *Albertine* • Marie-France Pisier *Madame Verdurin* • John Malkovich *Baron de Charlus* ■ *Dir* Raúl Ruiz • *Scr* Raul Ruiz, Gilles Taurand, from the novel *Le Temps Retrouvé* by Marcel Proust

Time Runner ★ 15

Science-fiction action adventure 1993 · Can · Colour · 92min

How far he has fallen since *Star Wars*. Mark Hamill's 21st-century character travels back to 1992 in order to warn Earth of a future alien invasion, but the invaders are already secretly in place and are out to stop him. Appallingly cheap and dull, with a time-jumping script and dim-witted characters. KB

Mark Hamill *Michael Raynor* • Rae Dawn Chong *Karen* • Brion James *Neila* • Marc Baur *Colonel Freeman* • Gordon Tipple *Arnie* ■ *Dir* Michael Mazo • *Scr* Greg Derochie, Ron Tarrant, Ian Bray, Christopher Hyde, Michael Mazo, from a story by John A Curtis

The Time That Remains: Chronicle of a Present Absentee ★★★★ 15

Political comedy drama 2009 · UK/It/Bel/Fr/UAE · Colour · 109min

Palestinian auteur Elia Suleiman's marvellous and insightful film charts the history of his family in Nazareth from 1948 to the present, and completes the deeply personal trilogy that includes *Chronicle of a Disappearance* (1996) and *Divine Intervention* (2002). Leavening the indignities heaped upon the residents of the occupied territories with mordant humour, Suleiman recalls the participation of his father Fuad in the failed resistance movement and Fuad's marriage to his sweetheart. Even more amusing are the scholastic misadventures of the young Elia. There's genuine pathos in the sequences between Suleiman and his widowed mother after he returns from exile in the present day. DP Arabic, Hebrew, English +subtitles. *DVD*

Elia Suleiman *Elia Suleiman, "ES"* • Saleh Bakri *Fuad* • Zuhair Abu Hanna *"ES" (child)* • Ayman Espanioli *"ES" (teenager)* • Shafika Bajjali *Mother* • Samar Qudha Tanus *Mother (1970)* ■ *Dir/Scr* Elia Suleiman

A Time to Kill ★★★★ 15

Thriller 1996 · US · Colour · 143min

This adaptation of John Grisham's first novel cleaned up at the box office and propelled the then unknown Matthew McConaughey to the front rank of Hollywood stars. McConaughey plays an inexperienced southern lawyer defending a working-class black father (Samuel L Jackson) who publicly murdered the man who abducted and raped his ten-year-old daughter. Sandra Bullock is the enthusiastic law student who offers to help McConaughey. In the redneck corner are

politically ambitious district attorney Kevin Spacey and most of the small town of Clanton, Mississippi. McConaughey makes a pretty good fist of the lead role, but the real strength is in the superb supporting turns. JF Violence, swearing. *DVD*

Matthew McConaughey *Jake Brigance* • Sandra Bullock *Ellen Roark* • Samuel L Jackson *Carl Lee Hailey* • Kevin Spacey *Rufus Buckley* • Oliver Platt *Harry Rex Vonner* • Charles S Dutton *Sheriff Ozzie Walls* • Brenda Fricker *Ethel Twitty* • Donald Sutherland *Lucien Wilbanks* • Kiefer Sutherland *Freddie Cobb* ■ *Dir* Joel Schumacher • *Scr* Akiva Goldsman, from the novel by John Grisham

Time to Leave ★★★ 18

Drama 2005 · Fr · Colour · 77min

Young, handsome and gay, Melvil Poupaud seems to have it all: a glamorous career as a fashion photographer, an affectionate family and a cute boyfriend (Walter Pagano). Then he finds out he has cancer and less than three months to live. He opts to cut off all ties, telling only his grandmother (Jeanne Moreau, in a charming cameo) about his condition. François Ozon's film offers a poignant view of a man coping with mortality, with a charismatic performance from Poupaud. LF French +subtitles. Sex scenes. *DVD*

Melvil Poupaud *Romain* • Jeanne Moreau *Laura, the grandmother* • Valéria Bruni-Tedeschi *Jany* • Christian Sengewald *Sasha* • Daniel Duval *The father* • Marie Rivière *The mother* • Louise-Anne Hippeau *Sophie* • Henri de Lorme *The doctor* • Walter Pagano *Bruno* ■ *Dir/Scr* François Ozon

The Time to Live and the Time to Die ★★★★ PG

Period drama 1985 · Tai · Colour · 136min

Hou Hsiao-Hsien's most autobiographical film is a fond evocation of life in Taiwan after the mainland revolution that offers a shrewd insight into the pain of fumbling towards adolescent understanding. Passing from trusting youth to wannabe delinquent, more interested in acquiring teen-gang street-cred than filial duty, You Anshun gives a fine performance. Hou reinforces the allegorical aspects of the story, which sees the siblings rally round to survive the familial and financial crisis attending the death of their father. Steadily directed, it features typical flashes of gentle wit and deep humanity. DP Mandarin, Hokkien +subtitles.

You Anshun • Tian Feng • Tang Ruyun • Xiao Ai ■ *Dir* Hou Hsiao-Hsien • *Scr* Zhu Tianwen

A Time to Love and a Time to Die ★★ PG

Second World War romance 1958 · US · Colour · 126min

Adapted from the novel by Erich Maria Remarque, this is set during the Second World War and is the tale of young German soldier John Gavin who marries Lilo Pulver during his leave, but still returns to the Russian front. The film fails to convince, with Gavin and his fellow soldiers so strongly American it's impossible to relate to them as Germans. RK *DVD* *BLU*

John Gavin *Ernst Graeber* • Lilo Pulver [Liselotte Pulver] *Elizabeth Kruse* • Jock Mahoney *Immerman* • Don DeFore *Boettcher* • Keenan Wynn *Reuter* • Erich Maria Remarque *Professor Pohlmann* • Dieter Borsche *Captain Rahe* • Thayer David *Oscar Binding* • Klaus Kinski *Gestapo Lieutenant* ■ *Dir* Douglas Sirk • *Scr* Orin Jannings, from the novel by Erich Maria Remarque

Time to Say Goodbye? ★★

Drama 1997 · US · Colour · 91min

Eva Marie Saint and Richard Kiley play a devoted couple whose close-knit family life is torn apart by Alzheimer's disease in this manipulative drama. Dealing with the thorny topic of euthanasia, it sees an ailing doctor's request for assisted suicide disintegrate into a bitter legal battle with his children. Unfortunately, none of the performances is intense enough to really capture the characters' agony, giving increasingly tragic events less impact than they deserve. SF

U SUITABLE FOR ALL   Uc SUITABLE ESPECIALLY FOR YOUNG CHILDREN (DVD ONLY)   PG PARENTAL GUIDANCE   12A UNDER 12s TO BE ACCOMPANIED (CINEMA ONLY)

Eva Marie Saint *Ruth Klooster* • Richard Kiley *Dr Gerald Klooster* • Margaret Colin *Kristen Hamstra* • Rick Roberts *Chip Klooster* • Alex Carter *Craig Klooster* • Kevin Hicks *Curt Klooster* • John Neville *Michigan Judge* ■ *Dir* David Hugh Jones [David Jones (3)] • *Scr* Jacqueline Feather, David Seidler

Time Trackers ★★U
Science-fiction adventure
1989 · US · Colour · 81min

In 2033, evil scientist Lee Bergere commandeers a time tunnel and uses the device to go back in history so he can claim the credit for inventing it. Unfortunately, he ends up in medieval England where a Robin Hood-type hero is the nemesis of villains everywhere. Produced on the cheap by Roger Corman, this sci-fi adventure is most successful on the humour front, thanks to Ned Beatty's sparkling turn as the cop in hot pursuit of Bergere through the centuries. AJ

Ned Beatty *Harry* • Wil Shriner *Charles* • Kathleen Beller *RJ* • Bridget Hoffman *Madeline* • Alex Hyde-White *Edgar* • Lee Bergere *Zandor* ■ *Dir/Scr* Howard R Cohen

The Time Traveler's Wife ★★12
Romantic science-fiction drama
2008 · Ger/US · Colour · 102min

Rachel McAdams stars as the wife of the title, but it's her husband (Eric Bana) who's at the centre of this sci-fi drama. Bana involuntarily slips through time at the most inopportune moments, and can be gone for weeks - often visiting her in childhood - while McAdams pines for his return. In the bestselling novel, the premise allowed author Audrey Niffenegger to explore dysfunctional relationships in a unique fashion. Here, director Robert Schwentke creates intrigue, but also skirts the emotional crux of the matter, and the mundane way the couple treats the time-travel also dampens the mood. A disappointment. SP Brief nudity. *DVD* Blu

Rachel McAdams *Clare Abshire* • Eric Bana *Henry De Tamble* • Ron Livingston *Gomez* • Arliss Howard *Richard DeTamble* • Stephen Tobolowsky *Dr David Kendrick* • Alex Ferris *Young Henry* • Brooklynn Proulx *Young Clare* ■ *Dir* Robert Schwentke • *Scr* Bruce Joel Rubin, from the novel by Audrey Niffenegger • *Cinematographer* Florian Ballhaus

The Time Traveller ★★★PG
Science-fiction drama
1964 · US · Colour · 80min

Conceived by director Ib Melchior as a sequel of sorts to *The Time Machine*, this is popcorn entertainment in the old-fashioned sense. A group of scientists led by Preston Foster hurtle 107 years into Earth's future, only to discover it in post-nuclear ruins and its human android survivors living underground and hiding from mutants who roam the surface. Given its modest budget, the film's ambition must be admired, though tarnished by stilted dialogue. RS *DVD*

Preston Foster *Dr Erik von Steiner* • Philip Carey *Steve Connors* • Merry Anders *Carol White* • John Hoyt *Varno* • Forrest J Ackerman *Technician* ■ *Dir* Ib Melchior • *Scr* Ib Melchior, from a story by Ib Melchior, David L Hewitt • *Cinematographer* William Zsigmond [Vilmos Zsigmond]

Time Will Tell ★★★15
Documentary
1992 · UK · BW and Colour · 85min

Bob Marley died of cancer at the age of 36 in 1981, and this documentary restricts itself largely to what proved to be the Jamaican's final tour. Reggae fans will revel in the footage of concert and rehearsal renditions of such classics as *Could You Be Loved* and *Coming in from the Cold*. But Declan Lowney studiously avoids presenting a rounded portrait of the man who did more than most to bring Rastafarianism to a global audience. Indeed, Marley's pronouncements here tend towards proselytising, but the less laudable aspects of his life are ignored. DP *DVD*

Bob Marley ■ *Dir* Declan Lowney

Time without Pity ★★★
Crime drama
1957 · UK · BW · 89min

After years of dodging the Hollywood blacklist by releasing films under pseudonyms or crediting them to other film-makers, Joseph Losey was able to put his own name to this adaptation of Emlyn Williams's stage play. Although the story of a father trying to save his son from the gallows is supposed to be a thriller, Losey places so much emphasis on the capital punishment angle that the social theme too often swamps the suspense. Michael Redgrave is solid, however, as the alcoholic dad fighting against time. DP

Michael Redgrave *David Graham* • Ann Todd *Honor Stanford* • Leo McKern *Robert Stanford* • Peter Cushing *Jeremy Clayton* • Alec McCowen *Alec Graham* • Renee Houston *Mrs Harker* • Paul Daneman *Brian Stanford* • Lois Maxwell *Vicky Harker* ■ *Dir* Joseph Losey • *Scr* Ben Barzman, from the play *Someone Waiting* by Emlyn William

Timebomb ★★18
Action crime thriller
1991 · US · Colour · 92min

Michael Biehn plays a bookish watch repairer who experiences strange and violent flashbacks, and who is repeatedly attacked by mysterious people trying to kill him. He hires psychiatrist Patsy Kensit to unlock his mind. After this intriguing set-up, Biehn's character quickly becomes grating and unlikeable, and the mystery becomes sillier. Good action sequences keep this watchable. KB Swearing, sex scenes, violence *DVD*

Michael Biehn *Eddie Kay* • Patsy Kensit *Dr Anna Nolmar* • Richard Jordan *Colonel Taylor* • Tracy Scoggins *Ms Blue* • Billy Blanks *Mr Brown* • Jim Maniaci *Mr Grey* • Steven J Oliver *Mr Redd* • Ray "Boom Boom" Mancini [Ray Mancini] *Mr Black* ■ *Dir/Scr* Avi Nesher

Timecode ★★★★15
Experimental drama
1999 · US · Colour · 89min

Shot on cutting-edge digital video, this quirky and innovative comedy thriller from Mike Figgis is a technical tour de force. It offers four separate but intertwined takes on the same series of events, shown simultaneously on a single, quartered screen. Emphasis on one or more of the four soundtracks provides guidance as to what to watch when, while the familiar faces help catch the eye. The sequences, which all feature characters directly or indirectly involved with a Los Angeles film-production company, play out in real time, and were filmed that way, too, in continuous takes with no edits. An intriguing and cleverly realised idea. DA *DVD*

Salma Hayek *Rose* • Jeanne Tripplehorn *Lauren Hathaway* • Saffron Burrows *Emma* • Kyle MacLachlan *Bunny Drysdale* • Stellan Skarsgård *Alex Green* • Holly Hunter *Executive* • Julian Sands *Quentin* • Glenne Headly *Therapist* ■ *Dir/Scr* Mike Figgis

Timecop ★★★18
Science-fiction adventure
1994 · US · Colour · 93min

The Muscles from Brussels encounters his younger self when he's sent back in time to catch a sinister senator who is trying to change the past for his own monetary ends. If you can follow the time-travel logic, then director Peter Hyams's gleaming comic-strip action adventure is dumb fun. Most sci-fi fans, however, will find it desperately outdated. AJ Swearing, violence, sex scenes, nudity. *DVD* Blu

Jean-Claude Van Damme *Max Walker* • Mia Sara *Melissa* • Ron Silver *McComb* • Bruce McGill *Matuzak* • Gloria Reuben *Fielding* • Scott Bellis *Ricky* • Jason Schombing *Atwood* ■ *Dir* Peter Hyams • *Scr* Mark Verheiden, from a story by Mark Verheiden, Mark Richardson, from a comic book series

Timecrimes ★★★
Science-fiction drama
2007 · Sp · Colour · 92min

Director Nacho Vigalondo's low-tech Spanish sci-fi tale is an engaging doodle on that time-travel cliché of someone continually running into himself. That someone here is Karra Elejalde, who must chase doppelgangers of himself in order to stabilise his universe - and save his wife's life. It's an audaciously plotted puzzle-box conceit that nevertheless does seem to make complete sense as the layers unfold. Vigalondo (who also plays a time-research scientist) directs with a subtle dexterity that keeps suspense high as the twists tie the brain into knots. AJ Spanish +subtitles.

Karra Elejalde *Héctor* • Candela Fernández *Clara* • Bárbara Goenaga *Girl* • Nacho Vigalondo *Chico* ■ *Dir/Scr* Nacho Vigalondo

Timeline ★★12
Science-fiction adventure fantasy
2003 · US · Colour · 110min

In this time-travelling fantasy, director Richard Donner presses too heavily on the significance of events in Michael Crichton's source novel, leaving the absurdities to take over. When Billy Connolly, the professor leading an archaeological dig in the Dordogne valley, gets thrust back in time by the shady corporation sponsoring the dig, his son (Paul Walker) and fellow students follow to rescue him and find themselves in a 14th-century war. Featuring clunky dialogue and outrageous situations. TH English, French +subtitles. *DVD*

Paul Walker *Chris Johnston* • Frances O'Connor *Kate Ericson* • Gerard Butler *Andre Marek* • Billy Connolly *Professor Edward Johnston* • Anna Friel *Lady Claire* • Neal McDonough *Frank Gordon* • Ethan Embry *Josh Stern* • David Thewlis *Robert Doniger* • Matt Craven *Steven Kramer* • Michael Sheen *Lord Oliver* ■ *Dir* Richard Donner • *Scr* Jeff Maguire, George Nolfi, from the novel by Michael Crichton

Times and Winds ★★★★15
Drama
2006 · Tur · Colour · 106min

Earthy passions drive the characters in this majestic Turkish drama, a hypnotic meditation on man and nature (as well as man's nature). Told from the perspective of three pre-teen children, it takes a bleak view of humanity: Ozakan Ozen dreams up various schemes to kill his father; Elit Iscan is appalled when she glimpses her parents having sex; Ali Bey Kayali is hopelessly in love with his schoolteacher. Director Reha Erdem follows the children's aimless meandering in the rocky hills as they try to make sense of their growing role in the adult world. Lyrical and unhurried, the film is suffused with deep poetry - goat bells tinkling, the wind in the trees - but what is really moving is the creeping sense of eroded innocence. JR Turkish +subtitles. *DVD*

Ozakan Ozen *Omer* • Ali Bey Kayali *Yakup* • Elit Iscan *Yildiz* • Bulent Emin Yarar *Imam* • Taner Birsel *Zekeriya* • Yigit Ozsener *Yusuf* ■ *Dir/Scr* Reha Erdem • *Music* Arvo Pärt

The Times of Harvey Milk ★★★★15
Documentary
1983 · US · Colour · 34min

Using TV news footage and a host of fascinating interviews, this absorbing Oscar-winning documentary outlines the brief political career of the charismatic Harvey Milk, America's first openly gay politician. Elected as a San Francisco Supervisor in 1977, Milk was assassinated the following year alongside Mayor George Moscone. The murders provoked storms of protest, especially when the killer, an ex-policeman, was given a light sentence (he pleaded temporary insanity induced by junk food!), and a very moving candle-lit vigil. Eloquent, insightful, and narrated by *Torch Song Trilogy*'s Harvey Fierstein. AJ Swearing.

Harvey Fierstein *Narrator* ■ *Dir* Robert Epstein [Rob Epstein]

Times Square ★15
Comedy drama
1980 · US · Colour · 106min

This overblown and laughable attempt by Hollywood to do for punk what *Saturday Night Fever* did for disco came at least three years too late. Poor little rich girl Trini Alvarado runs away to Manhattan. There she meets punkette Robin Johnson, who first inducts her into the New Wave scene and then turns them both into the cult singing sensations The Sleaze Sisters. Fatuous, glossy rubbish. AJ

Tim Curry *Johnny Laguardia* • Trini Alvarado *Pamela Pearl* • Robin Johnson *Nicky Marotta* • Peter Coffield *David Pearl* • Herbert Berghof *Dr Huber* • David Margulies *Dr Zymabsky* • Anna Maria Horsford *Rosie Washington* ■ *Dir* Allan Moyle • *Scr* Jacob Brackman, from a story by Allan Moyle, Leanne Unger

Timeslip ★★12
Science-fiction thriller
1955 · UK · BW · 90min

In this quaint British sci-fi oddity, a radiation overdose propels an atomic scientist seven seconds into the future. Numerous muddled plotlines intertwine, with gangsters and spies trying to exploit his reaction to events before they happen, but nothing too interesting is done with the nifty premise. Ken Hughes slows it down further with conventional direction. AJ *DVD*

Gene Nelson *Mike Delaney* • Faith Domergue *Jill Friday* • Joseph Tomelty *Inspector Cleary* • Donald Gray *Maitland* • Vic Perry *Vasquo* • Peter Arne *Stephen Maitland* • Launce Maraschal *Editor* • Charles Hawtrey *Scruffy* ■ *Dir* Ken Hughes • *Scr* Charles Eric Maine, Ken Hughes, from the novel *The Isotope Man* by Maine

Tim's Vermeer ★★★12A
Documentary
2013 · US · Colour · 79min

Made by magicians Penn and Teller, this intriguing Bafta-nominated documentary chronicles geeky inventor Tim Jenison's obsessive bid to prove that the incredible photorealism of the great Dutch painters - hundreds of years before photography - could only be explained by their use of mirror and glass "tracing aids". It's a mammoth undertaking, which involves him recreating Vermeer's 17th-century masterpiece *The Music Lesson* with the materials available to the artist. Overall, this is fascinating stuff. DA Brief swearing.

Tim Jenison • Penn Jillette ■ *Dir* Teller

Tin Cup ★★★15
Romantic sports comedy
1996 · US · Colour · 129min

This likeable film reunited Kevin Costner with his *Bull Durham* director Ron Shelton. Costner plays a drunken, down-at-heel pro of a driving range in the back of beyond. When Rene Russo, the girlfriend of his long-standing rival, Don Johnson, drops by for golf lessons, Costner is smitten, and since she turns out to be a therapist, she can help rid him of his inner demons. The scene is set for a suspenseful finale at the US Open. AT Swearing, nudity. *DVD*

Kevin Costner *Roy McAvoy* • Rene Russo *Dr Molly Griswold* • Don Johnson *David Simms* • Cheech Marin [Richard "Cheech" Marin] *Romeo Posar* • Linda Hart *Doreen* • Dennis Burkley *Earl* • Rex Linn *Dewey* ■ *Dir* Ron Shelton • *Scr* Ron Shelton, John Norville

The Tin Drum ★★★★15
Wartime drama
1979 · W Ger/Fr/Yug/Pol · Colour · 156min

The winner of the Palme d'Or at Cannes and an Oscar for best foreign film, Volker Schlöndorff's adaptation of Günter Grass's allegorical novel compensates for diminishing the original's thematic complexity with some supreme visual bravado. Even more laudable is the performance of David Bennent, who decides at the age of three to stop growing and express his disgust at the folly of the adults, so casually treading the path to Nazism, by emitting glass-shattering screams and thumping his beloved tin drum. Although occasionally over-reliant on expressionist excess, this is still powerful and memorable. DP German +subtitles. *DVD* Blu

David Bennent *Oskar* • Mario Adorf *Alfred Matzerath* • Angela Winkler *Agnes Matzerath* • Daniel Olbrychski *Jan Bronski* • Katharina Thalbach *Maria Matzerath* • Charles Aznavour *Sigismund Markus* ■ *Dir* Volker Schlöndorff • *Scr* Jean-Claude Carrière, Franz Seitz, Volker Schlöndorff, from the novel by Günter Grass

T

Tin Men ★★★★ 15
Comedy drama 1987 · US · Colour · 107min

Director Barry Levinson is much sought after in Hollywood, but his smaller personal projects remain the most fun. This, along with *Diner*, is one of his best. Danny DeVito and Richard Dreyfuss are the rival aluminium cladding salesmen who fall out after a car accident and become locked in an ever-escalating feud. The 1960s settings are lovingly re-created and Levinson wonderfully captures the hustling banter of the reps. In spite of the laughs, there's a bittersweet undercurrent running throughout. JF Swearing. DVD

Richard Dreyfuss *Bill "BB" Babowsky* · Danny DeVito *Ernest Tilley* · Barbara Hershey *Nora Tilly* · John Mahoney *Moe* · Jackie Gayle *Sam* · Stanley Brock *Gil* · Seymour Cassel *Cheese* · Bruno Kirby *Mouse* · JT Walsh *Wing* ■ Dir/Scr Barry Levinson

Tin Pan Alley ★★★ U
Musical 1940 · US · BW · 94min

In this attractive and popular 20th Century-Fox vehicle, Alice Faye is cast with upcoming starlet Betty Grable, dynamic Jack Oakie and handsome but boring John Payne. This plot is one of those stand-bys about struggling songwriters. There are still plenty of highlights to enjoy, but despite Alfred Newman's Oscar-winning soundtrack, this movie's mainly for nostalgia lovers. TS

Alice Faye *Katie Blane* · Betty Grable *Lily Blane* · Jack Oakie *Harry Calhoun* · John Payne *Skeets Harrigan* · Allen Jenkins *Sergeant Casey* · Esther Ralston *Nora Bayes* · Ben Carter *Boy* · John Loder *Reggie Carstair* ■ Dir Walter Lang · Scr Robert Ellis, Helen Logan, from a story by Pamela Harris

The Tin Star ★★★★★ U
Western 1957 · US · BW · 92min

Here's a *real* western. It's a sturdy, finely wrought work from masters of the genre in their *prime*, with lawman-turned-bounty hunter Henry Fonda helping young sheriff Anthony Perkins to hold down his job in a town ravaged by outlaws. Written by Dudley Nichols (*Stagecoach*) and Oscar-nominated for best story and screenplay, it's directed by maestro Anthony Mann, who takes a linear, classic and deliberately under-emphatic approach, allowing the setting and characters to tell the story. Mann eschews false *High Noon* ethics and really understands the essence of heroism. This is an underrated must-see experience. TS

Henry Fonda *Morg Hickman* · Anthony Perkins *Sheriff Ben Owens* · Betsy Palmer *Nona Mayfield* · Michel Ray *Kip Mayfield* · Neville Brand *Bart Bogardus* · John McIntire *Dr McCord* · Mary Webster *Millie Parker* · Lee Van Cleef *Ed McGaffey* ■ Dir Anthony Mann · Scr Dudley Nichols, from the story *The Tin Badge* by Barney Slater, Joel Kane

Tina: What's Love Got to Do with It ★★★★ 18
Biographical drama 1993 · US · Colour · 112min

As you would expect of a film based on the autobiography *I, Tina* and on which Tina Turner herself acted as on-set adviser, this is hardly the most objective showbiz biopic. While Angela Bassett should be applauded for her beautifully observed portrait of the singing superstar, perhaps greater credit should be given to Laurence Fishburne for his warts-and-all performance as Ike, the man who, for all his faults, did put Tina in the spotlight. Both stars deserved their Oscar nominations for virtually carrying a picture that looks and sounds great, but is a little oversimplified. DP Violence, swearing, drug abuse. DVD

Angela Bassett *Tina Turner* · Laurence Fishburne *Ike Turner* · Vanessa Bell Calloway *Jackie* · Jenifer Lewis *Zelma Bullock* · Phyllis Yvonne Stickney *Alline Bullock* · Khandi Alexander *Darlene* ■ Dir Brian Gibson · Scr Kate Lanier, from the autobiography *I, Tina* by Tina Turner, Kurt Loder

The Tingler ★★★★ 15
Horror 1959 · US · BW · 78min

One of the best examples of the work of the great horror producer/director William Castle, the king of gimmick cinema, whose shockers always shouted "Boo!" with lurid style. Here, doctor Vincent Price discovers that fear creates a parasite, which grows on the spine unless the victim screams. Price isolates one of the large insect-like creatures and it escapes. Immensely enjoyable hokum, it was originally shown with the legendary stunt "Percepto" – selected cinema seats wired to administer mild electric shocks. This mini-classic abounds with bizarre chills and goofy psychedelic imagery. AJ DVD

Vincent Price *Dr William Chapin* · Judith Evelyn *Mrs Higgins* · Darryl Hickman *David Morris* · Patricia Cutts *Isabel Chapin* · Pamela Lincoln *Lucy Stevens* · Philip Coolidge *Ollie Higgins* ■ Dir William Castle · Scr Robb White

Tinker Bell ★★★ U
Animated fantasy adventure 2008 · US · Colour · 74min

Two things strike you about this straight-to-DVD story that centres on Peter Pan's fairy playmate. First, she can actually speak, and second the traditional animation style has been replaced by a digital 3D rendering. Thankfully, that's as far as messing with the character goes, as the hot-headed little madam retains all those very human flaws that make her so likeable. This being an origins story, we see Tinker Bell's dreams of joining the nature fairies dashed when she's chosen for the odd-job brigade. Sentimentality and moralising are largely kept at bay, and there are a few pleasing touches harking back to Disney's 1953 original *Peter Pan*. JH DVD

Mae Whitman *Tinker Bell* · Kristin Chenoweth *Rosetta* · Raven-Symoné *Iridessa* · Lucy Liu *Silvermist* · America Ferrera *Fawn* · Jane Horrocks *Fairy Mary* · Anjelica Huston *Queen Clarion* ■ Dir Bradley Raymond · Scr Jeffrey M Howard, from characters by JM Barrie

Tinker Bell and the Legend of the NeverBeast ★★★ U
Animated fantasy 2014 · US · Colour · 73min

Disney's favourite fairy flies solo for the umpteenth time in a dramatic and rather moving "Beauty and the Beast"-type tale. When fairy Fawn befriends a big furry monster, alarm bells ring for Tinker Bell and the rest of the fairy folk. But after several surprisingly tense misadventures they realise that you can't judge a book by its cover – nor a NeverBeast by its outward appearance. Colourful, bright and brief, this is good, wholesome fun for younger kids. DA DVD

Mae Whitman *Tinker Bell* · Megan Hilty *Rosetta* · Lucy Liu *Silvermist* · Raven-Symoné *Iridessa* · Anjelica Huston *Queen Clarion* · Rosario Dawson *Nyx* · Ginnifer Goodwin *Fawn* ■ Dir Steve Loter

Tinker Tailor Soldier Spy ★★★★ 15
Spy thriller 2011 · UK · Colour · 122min

Admirers of the 1979 BBC mini-series might think it foolish to make a feature film of John le Carré's thriller novel, but this period adaptation features great performances and terrific Cold War detail, as retired spy George Smiley (Gary Oldman) is brought back after the death of a colleague (John Hurt). In the course of two hours the plot points whizz past at a bewildering rate, but the cast and set dressing are first class, superbly capturing a weary lull in British history. DW Violence, swearing, sex scenes. DVD

Gary Oldman *George Smiley* · Colin Firth *Bill Haydon* · Benedict Cumberbatch *Peter Guillam* · Mark Strong *Jim Prideaux* · Toby Jones *Percy Alleline* · Tom Hardy *Ricki Tarr* · John Hurt *Control* ■ Dir Tomas Alfredson · Scr Bridget O'Connor, Peter Straughan, from the novel by John le Carré

TinkerBell and the Pirate Fairy ★★★ U
Animated fantasy adventure 2014 · US · Colour · 77min

A runaway fairy spells trouble for Pixie Hollow in this reassuringly sweet fifth outing for our impish heroine and her friends. *Mad Men*'s Christina Hendricks voices Tinkerbell's wilful and inquisitive friend Zarina, who is forced to flee under a black cloud after her home experiments into alchemy backfire spectacularly. JH DVD

Mae Whitman *Tinkerbell* · Christina Hendricks *Zarina* · Tom Hiddleston *James Hook* · Lucy Liu *Silvermist* · Raven-Symoné *Iridessa* ■ Dir Peggy Holmes

Tinkerbell and the Secret of the Wings ★★★ U
Animated fantasy adventure 2012 · US · Colour · 71min

The petite pixie lands herself in more trouble in another pleasing if inessential entry in the animated series. This time Tinkerbell's nose for adventure takes her to the forbidden Winter Woods, where she befriends a long-lost family member. However, by defying the rules, Tink ends up putting the lives of all the fairies in jeopardy. It's colourfully animated with some moderate thrills and plenty of giggles, while the film's messages of friendship, co-operation and reconciliation are all adeptly handled. JH DVD

Mae Whitman *Tinkerbell* · Lucy Hale *Periwinkle* · Timothy Dalton *Lord Milori* · Raven-Symoné *Iridessa* · Lucy Liu *Silvermist* · Anjelica Huston *Queen Clarion* ■ Dir/Scr Bobs Gannaway [Roberts Gannaway], Peggy Holmes

Tintin and the Lake of Sharks ★★★ U
Animated adventure 1972 · Bel/Fr · Colour · 76min

After numerous books and several TV serials, Tintin finally graduated to feature-length films, including this rousing encounter with his archenemy, Rastapopoulos. Die-hard fans of Hergé's blond-quiffed troubleshooter may not be bowled over by this animated adventure, but the action rattles along nicely, as Tintin, Snowy, Captain Haddock and Thomson and Thompson investigate skulduggery in Syldavia. DP In French.

Jacques Careuil *Tintin* · Micheline Dax *Bianca Castafiore* ■ Dir Raymond Le Blanc · Scr Greg [Michel Régnier], Jos Marissen, Rainer Goksch, Eddie Lateste, Jean-Michel Charlier, from the comic book *Tintin et le Lac aux Requins* by Hergé

Tintin and the Mystery of the Golden Fleece ★★ PG
Adventure 1961 · Fr/Bel · Colour · 97min

When Steven Spielberg directed his 2011 Tintin film using motion-capture, some critics wondered why someone with his talent didn't just make a live-action feature about the inquisitive boy reporter. After watching this 1961 French-Belgian co-production, the first to use live actors, they might feel differently. From a modern standpoint, this smacks more of a travelogue piece, as Tintin and co make their way around beautiful locations in Turkey and Greece in search of lost treasure. A bizarre curiosity rather than a rollicking good yarn. JA Dubbed. DVD

Jean-Pierre Talbot *Tintin* · Georges Wilson *Captain Haddock* · Georges Loriot *Professor Calculus* · Charles Vanel *Father Alexandre* · Marcel Bozzuffi *Angoraapoulos* ■ Dir Jean-Jacques Vierne · Scr André Barret, Rémo Forlani [Remo Forlani], from characters by Hergé

Tintorera ★
Adventure /rama 1977 · UK/Mex · Colour · 88min

This is one of several international rip-offs rushed out following the success of Spielberg's *Jaws*. Several naked starlets (among them Susan George, who must have signed the contract purely for the Mexican holiday) frolic on board a yacht

and in the sea and, almost incidentally, are menaced by a tiger shark. The views are pretty, but the direction is atrocious. DM

Susan George *Gabriella* · Hugo Stiglitz *Esteban* · Andres Garcia *Miguel* ■ Dir Rene Cardona Jr · Scr Ramon Bravo

Tiny Furniture ★★★★ 15
Comedy 2010 · US · Colour · 99min

Lena Dunham demonstrates a keen eye for detail, a sharp ear for dialogue and a nice line in deadpan playing in this, her debut feature. Although clearly influenced by Jerry Seinfeld and Woody Allen, she imposes her own personality as Aura, a middling film student struggling to compete with the overachievements of her photographer mother and precocious teenage sibling. The whip-smart satire is enlivened by Jemima Kirke, who's hilarious as Aura's ditzy pal, Charlotte. The 20-something writer/director also casts her real-life sister, Grace Dunham, and their mother, Laurie Simmons, as her family, lending an intriguingly witty autobiographical element to proceedings. DP Swearing, drug abuse, a sex scene, brief nudity. DVD

Lena Dunham *Aura* · Laurie Simmons *Siri* · Grace Dunham *Nadine* · Alex Karpovsky *Jed* · David Call *Keith* ■ Dir/Scr Lena Dunham

'Tis Autumn: the Search for Jackie Paris ★★★ 15
Documentary 2007 · US · Colour and BW · 99min

In his 1950s heyday, jazz singer Jackie Paris played with the likes of Charlie Parker and Charles Mingus and recorded a version of "Skylark" that drew comparisons with Frank Sinatra and Tony Bennett. But he disappeared after making just a handful of albums and only resurfaced years later in a kitschy double act with singer Anne Marie Moss. Here, director Raymond De Felitta sets out to discover why Paris went so rapidly from bebop icon to obscurity, as the septuagenarian hits the comeback trail in 2004. De Felitta never quite gets to the heart of his subject, but it's fascinating to watch Paris (who died later in 2004) perform for both the camera, as he reinvents his own legend with each recollection, and on stage in a small New York nightclub. DP

Jackie Paris · Anne Marie Moss · Peter Bogdanovich · Harlan Ellison ■ Dir/Scr Raymond De Felitta

The Tit and the Moon ★★ 18
Comedy drama 1994 · Sp/Fr · Colour · 86min

Having set up his central relationships, Bigas Luna becomes so besotted with both Mathilda May's body and his own symbolic imagery that this film about a young Catalan boy searching for a substitute for his mother's breast becomes as tedious as it is unfathomable. The young Biel Duan is appealing enough, while Gérard Darmon makes the impotent *pétomane* (professional farter) surprisingly sympathetic. DP Catalan, Spanish, French +subtitles. Nudity. DVD

Biel Duan *Tete* · Mathilda May *Estrellita "La Gabacha"* · Gérard Darmon *Maurice "El Gabacho"* · Miguel Poveda *Miquel "El Charmego"* · Abel Folk *Father* · Genis Sanchez *Stallone* · Laura Mañá *Mother* · Victoria Lepori *She of the Breasts* ■ Dir Bigas Luna · Scr Cuca Canals, Bigas Luna · Cinematographer José Luis Alcaine

Tit for Tat ★★★★ U
Comedy 1934 · US · BW · 19min

In *Them Thar Hills* (1934) a health trip turned into an escalating battle, as Laurel and Hardy clashed with irascible Charlie Hall over a misunderstanding involving the latter's wife (Mae Busch) and a well full of bootlegged liquor. In this Oscar-nominated sequel, the two factions revive their feud when they find themselves as neighbouring shopkeepers – a situation that gives them plenty of painful props with which to abuse one another. A classic and hilarious example of the team's peculiar brand of patient, methodical aggression. TH DVD

Stan Laurel *Stanley* • Oliver Hardy *Oliver* • Mae Busch *Grocer's wife* • Charlie Hall *Grocer* • James C Morton *Policeman* ■ *Dir* Charles Rogers • *Scr* Stan Laurel

Titan AE ★★★★ PG
Animated science-fiction adventure
2000 · US · Colour · 91min

Talk about starting with a bang. Don Bluth kicks off this animated spectacular with nothing less than the blowing-up of the Earth, forcing survivors Cale (voiced by Matt Damon) and Akima (Drew Barrymore) to put one over on the offending aliens by reactivating a hidden supercraft, The Titan. Three parts *Star Wars* to one part *Star Trek III*, the film imaginatively blends top-quality cel and digital animation, resulting in something well beyond mere eye candy for kids. DA DVD

Matt Damon *Cale* • Drew Barrymore *Akima* • Bill Pullman *Korso* • John Leguizamo *Gune* • Nathan Lane *Preed* • Janeane Garofalo *Stith* • Ron Perlman *Prof Sam Tucker* • Alex D Linz *Young Cale* ■ *Dir* Don Bluth, Gary Goldman • *Scr* Ben Edlund, John August, Joss Whedon, from a story by Hans Bauer, Randall McCormick • *Animation Director* Len Simon

Titanic ★★★ PG
Historical disaster drama
1953 · US · BW · 97min

An impressively staged, all-star account of the great 1912 luxury liner disaster, this is well mounted and well played, despite being markedly inferior to its 1997 namesake and to a superb British version made five years later (Rank's *A Night to Remember*). Barbara Stanwyck and Clifton Webb are top-billed as a couple trapped in a doomed marriage, and a young Robert Wagner romances the couple's daughter, Audrey Dalton. TS DVD Blu

Clifton Webb *Richard Sturges* • Barbara Stanwyck *Julia Sturges* • Robert Wagner *Giff Rogers* • Audrey Dalton *Annette Sturges* • Thelma Ritter *Mrs Maude Young* • Brian Aherne *Captain EJ Smith* ■ *Dir* Jean Negulesco • *Scr* Charles Brackett, Walter Reisch, Richard Breen [Richard L Breen]

Titanic ★★★★ 12
Romantic disaster epic
1997 · US · Colour · 186min

There are two love stories here: one is between James Cameron and a ship; the other is between society girl Kate Winslet and third-class passenger Leonardo DiCaprio. Cameron's script wouldn't have sustained Clark Gable and Vivien Leigh for 80 minutes, but, somehow, he and his magical cast revive that old-style studio gloss for three riveting hours. *Titanic* is a sumptuous assault on the emotions, with a final hour that captures the horror and the freezing, paralysing fear of the moment. Winning 11 Oscars, it also shares - with *Ben-Hur* and *The Lord of the Rings: The Return of the King* - the record haul of Academy Awards. AT Swearing, brief nudity. DVD Blu

Leonardo DiCaprio *Jack Dawson* • Kate Winslet *Rose DeWitt Bukater* • Billy Zane *Cal Hockley* • Kathy Bates *Molly Brown* • Frances Fisher *Ruth DeWitt Bukater* • Gloria Stuart *Old Rose* • Bill Paxton *Brock Lovett* • Bernard Hill *Captain EJ Smith* ■ *Dir/Scr* James Cameron • *Cinematographer* Russell Carpenter • *Music* James Horner • *Editors* Conrad Buff, James Cameron, Richard A Harris

Titanic Town ★★★ 15
Comedy drama
1998 · UK/Ger/Fr · Colour · 97min

Based on a semi-autobiographical novel by Mary Costello, this woman's view of Belfast at the height of the Troubles in 1972 contains broad - sometimes slapstick - humour that is somewhat at odds with its subject matter. Nevertheless, fans of Julie Walters will not be disappointed by her barnstorming performance as Catholic housewife Bernie McPhelimy, who adopts a grassroots approach to bringing peace to the region. DM Swearing.

Julie Walters *Bernie McPhelimy* • Ciaran Hinds *Aidan McPhelimy* • Ciaran McMenamin *Dino/Owen* • Nuala O'Neill *Annie McPhelimy* • Lorcan

Cranitch *Tony* • Oliver Ford Davies *George Whittington* ■ *Dir* Roger Michell • *Scr* Anne Devlin, from a novel by Mary Costello

The Titfield Thunderbolt ★★★ U
Comedy
1952 · UK · Colour · 80min

Although it gives off an undeniably warm glow, this tale of the rescue of a much-loved branch line clearly shows that the Ealing comedy express was beginning to run out of steam. Only in this rather too cosy world could social protest be undertaken on behalf of the forelock-tugging lower classes by squires, bishops, vicars, bumbling town clerks and amiable drunks. Despite a patronising tone and writer TEB Clarke's failure to realise the full potential of the satire, this is still an entertaining piece, thanks to director Charles Crichton's formidable talent and the highly polished playing of the cast. DP DVD Blu

Stanley Holloway *Valentine* • George Relph *Reverend Weech* • Naunton Wayne *Blakeworth* • John Gregson *Gordon* • Godfrey Tearle *Bishop* • Hugh Griffith *Dan* • Gabrielle Brune *Joan* • Sidney James *Hawkins* ■ *Dir* Charles Crichton • *Scr* TEB Clarke

Titicut Follies ★★★★
Documentary
1967 · US · BW · 84min

Banned for almost 25 years, Frederick Wiseman's uncompromising account of life inside the Bridgewater state hospital in Massachusetts remains the only film to be censored in America on grounds other than obscenity. The graphic presentation of the brutal cruelty meted out by guards, social workers and psychiatrists is disturbing enough. But what makes the treatment of the criminally insane inmates all the more shocking is what it reveals about a nation that would tolerate such inhumanity while claiming to be the global champion of social justice. Unbearable to watch, but impossible to forget, this is a landmark in documentary film-making. DP

■ *Dir* Frederick Wiseman • *Editor* Frederick Wiseman • *Cinematographer* John Marshall

Title Shot ★ 15
Crime drama
1979 · Can · Colour · 84min

There have been several classic boxing movies, but this is not one of them. In fact, it's a contender for the title of worst pug picture ever made. Weighing in at well over his matinée idol poundage, Tony Curtis is beaten before he starts with this story of a crooked fight manager whose boxer is too dumb to take a dive. DP

Tony Curtis *Frank Renzetti* • Richard Gabourie *Blake* • Susan Hogan *Sylvia* • Allan Royal *Dunlop* • Robert Delbert *Rufus Taylor* • Natsuko Ohama *Terry* ■ *Dir* Les Rose • *Scr* John Saxton, from a story by Richard Gabourie

Tito and Me ★★★★
Period comedy drama
1992 · Yug/Fr · Colour · 105min

With its blend of proletarian comedy and political allegory, could any film have been more fitting to be the last bearer of the imprint "Made in Yugoslavia" than this one? Exploding the cult of personality and poking fun at the socialist realist style that dominated Eastern Bloc cinema, Goran Markovic's semi-autobiographical rite-of-passage picture is set in 1954 and chronicles ten-year-old foodaholic Dimitrie Vojnov's bid to win the heart of classmate Milena Vukosav. DP In Serbo-Croat.

Dimitrie Vojnov *Zoran* • Lazar Ristovski *Raja* • Anica Dobra *Mother* • Pedrag Manojlovic [Miki Manojlovic] *Father* • Ljiljana Dragutinovic *Aunt* • Milena Vukosav *Jasna* • Vojislav Brajovic *Marshall Tito* ■ *Dir/Scr* Goran Markovic

Titus ★★★ 18
Tragedy
1999 · US/UK · Colour · 155min

Julie Taymor wowed Broadway with her musical version of Disney's *The Lion King* and this epic retelling of Shakespeare's gory tragedy, based on another stage production, has a similar knockout impact. It's a shame the same attention lavished on the visual elements wasn't afforded to the

performances, which range from the gruff (Anthony Hopkins's wronged Roman general) and the camp (Alan Cumming's Hitler-esque emperor) to the downright bizarre (Jessica Lange's Amazonian warrior queen). Still, there are enough jaw-dropping scenes to entertain. NS DVD

Anthony Hopkins *Titus Andronicus* • Jessica Lange *Tamora* • Alan Cumming *Saturninus* • Harry J Lennix [Harry Lennix] *Aaron* • Colm Feore *Marcus* • Angus MacFadyen *Lucius* • Jonathan Rhys Meyers *Chiron* • Matthew Rhys *Demetrius* • Laura Fraser *Lavinia* ■ *Dir* Julie Taymor • *Scr* Julie Taymor, from the play *Titus Andronicus* by William Shakespeare

Tizoc ★★★
Romantic drama
1956 · Mex · Colour · 110min

Having started out singing *rancheras* on Mexican radio, Pedro Infante enjoyed a decade of screen stardom before he was killed in a plane crash. This was his penultimate appearance and it landed him the best actor prize at the Berlin film festival. While Infante's liaison with Maria Felix may be doomed from the start, they generate an electricity that ensured both the film's commercial success and national mourning at Infante's untimely demise. DP Spanish +subtitles.

Maria Felix *Maria* • Pedro Infante *Tizoc* • Eduardo Fajardo *Arturo* • Julio Aldama *Nicuil* • Alicia del Lago *Machinza* ■ *Dir* Ismael Rodriguez • *Scr* Ismael Rodriguez, Manuel R Ojeda, Ricardo Parada Leon, Carlos Orellana

To Be or Not to Be ★★★★★ U
Second World War satire
1942 · US · BW · 94min

"So they call me Concentration Camp Ehrhardt?". There's good taste, and there's this fabulously funny and original comedy from director Ernst Lubitsch, which transcends taste. Witty and cleverly satirical by turns, this movie about a theatre company in Warsaw avoids giving offence by its magnificent casting, with Jack Benny as "that great, great actor Joseph Tura" and the wonderful comedian Carole Lombard, in her final film. There's poignancy, too, and a terrific running joke involving Lombard's admirer, played by the young Robert Stack. Mel Brooks starred in an audacious remake of this story, but the immutable style of this classic proved impossible to re-create. TS

Carole Lombard *Maria* • Jack Benny *Joseph Tura* • Robert Stack *Lt Stanislav Sobinski* • Felix Bressart *Greenberg* • Lionel Atwill *Rawitch* • Stanley Ridges *Professor Siletsky* • Sig Rumann [Sig Ruman] *Colonel Ehrhardt* • Tom Dugan (1) *Bronski* ■ *Dir* Ernst Lubitsch • *Scr* Edwin Justus Mayer, from a story by Ernst Lubitsch (uncredited), Melchior Lengyel

To Be or Not to Be ★★★ U
Second World War satire
1983 · US · Colour · 102min

The coarse-grained humour makes one long for the sublime Ernst Lubitsch 1942 original, but this update is still a cracking comedy. Mel Brooks stars as the hammy head of a theatrical troupe who becomes involved in the Polish resistance's fight against the Nazis and Alan Johnson does well to keep the star in check. Co-starring with husband Brooks for the first time, Anne Bancroft is tremendous fun, but what was the Academy thinking of when it nominated Charles Durning for his shocking performance as "Concentration Camp Erhardt"? DP DVD

Mel Brooks *Frederick Bronski* • Anne Bancroft *Anna Bronski* • Tim Matheson *Lieutenant Andre Sobinski* • Charles Durning *Colonel Erhardt* • José Ferrer *Professor Siletski* • Christopher Lloyd *Captain Schultz* ■ *Dir* Alan Johnson • *Scr* Thomas Meehan, Ronny Graham, from the 1942 film

To Catch a Thief ★★★★ PG
Romantic mystery
1955 · US · Colour · 102min

Alfred Hitchcock devised this witty romantic mystery to team his blonde obsession at the time, Grace Kelly, with his old favourite, Cary Grant. Sandwiched between the director's masterworks *Rear Window* and

The Trouble with Harry, and therefore often overlooked, this box office hit follows a retired jewel thief's attempts to catch a copycat criminal. Adhering to the director's customary droll intentions, Grant and Kelly are on sparkling form, as is Jessie Royce Landis as the latter's formidable and smirky mother, and the French Riviera is beautifully captured by the Oscar-winning cinematography of Robert Burks. RK In English, French. DVD

Cary Grant *John Robie* • Grace Kelly *Frances Stevens* • Jessie Royce Landis *Mrs Jessie Stevens* • John Williams *HH Hughson* • Charles Vanel *Bertani* • Brigitte Auber *Danielle Foussard* • Jean Martinelli *Foussard* ■ *Dir* Alfred Hitchcock • *Scr* John Michael Hayes, from the novel by David Dodge • *Costume Designer* Edith Head • *Cinematographer* Robert Burks

To Die For ★★ 15
Fantasy comedy
1994 · UK · Colour · 96min

The ghost of a drag queen, who has died from an Aids-related illness, returns to haunt his promiscuous boyfriend and to force him to mourn properly. It's a ponderously well-meaning, lightweight, fantasy comedy with a cast of British television personalities including Jean Boht and Tony Slattery. It's heart is in the right place, but nothing else is. AJ

Thomas Arklie *Simon* • Ian Williams *Mark* • Tony Slattery *Terry* • Dillie Keane *Siobhan* • Jean Boht *Mrs Downs* • John Altman *Doctor* • Caroline Munro *Mrs Pignon* • Gordon Milne *Drop Dead Gorgeous* • Nicholas Harrison *Siobhan's first lover* • Ian McKellen *Quilt documentary narrator* • Sinitta *Quilt documentary narrator* ■ *Dir* Peter Mackenzie Litten [Peter Litten] • *Scr* Johnny Byrne, from a story by Paul McEnvoy, Pater Litten

To Die For ★★★★★ 15
Satirical crime drama
1995 · US · Colour · 102min

Nicole Kidman gives a great performance in director Gus Van Sant's brilliantly acerbic satire on fame and the American Dream. She plays a shallow, suburban princess, whose entire life has been devoted to becoming a television celebrity. Trouble is, husband Matt Dillon keeps getting in the way of her grandiose plans, so he has to be eliminated. Sharply scripted by Buck Henry from Joyce Maynard's bestselling novel, which was inspired by true events, this frighteningly funny, razor-sharp anecdote is one of Van Sant's most accessible movies. AJ Violence, swearing, sex scenes, drug abuse. DVD Blu

Nicole Kidman *Suzanne Stone* • Matt Dillon *Larry Maretto* • Joaquin Phoenix *Jimmy Emmett* • Casey Affleck *Russell Hines* • Illeana Douglas *Janice Maretto* • Alison Folland *Lydia Mertz* • Dan Hedaya *Joe Maretto* • Wayne Knight *Ed Grant* • David Cronenberg *Man at lake* ■ *Dir* Gus Van Sant • *Scr* Buck Henry, from the novel by Joyce Maynard

To Die in Madrid ★★★
Documentary
1963 · Fr · BW · 85min

This is an impassioned account of the triumph of fascism in 1930s Spain. Frédéric Rossif makes little attempt to disguise his left-wing sympathies as he champions the cause of the International Brigade over the Condor Legion, with its Italo-German hardware and the remorseless backing of the nobility and the church. Gleaned from contemporary newsreels, the footage reveals the pitiless nature of the conflict and the growing hopelessness of Republican resistance. Complete with a melancholic score by Maurice Jarre, this may not be an impartial record, but it's a powerful one. DP English, French +subtitles.

John Gielgud *Narration* • Irene Worth *Narration* ■ *Dir* Frédéric Rossif

To Die in San Hilario ★★★ 12
Comedy
2005 · Sp · Colour · 95min

Director Laura Mañá imparts a whimsical twist to this cordial comedy of errors, in which an urban exile unexpectedly finds himself at home among the eccentric residents of an Argentinian backwater. But

T

while fugitive mobster Lluís Homar's growing friendships with one-eyed artist Ferran Rañé and widowed seamstress Ana Fernández are touchingly played, the plot is overly dependent upon both San Hilario's utter obscurity and its faded reputation as a popular place to die. **DP** Spanish +subtitles. **DVD**

Lluís Homar *"Piernas" Germán* • Ana Fernández *Esther* • Ferran Rañé *Teodoro* • Ulises Dumont *Mariano* • Juan Echanove *Father Antonio* • Eric Bonicatto *Cándido* • Milton de La Canal *Pablo* • Max Berliner *Cayetano* ■ *Dir/Scr* Laura Mañá

The To Do List ★★★ 15
Comedy   2013 · US · Colour · 103min

Bright, breezy and not a little bawdy, this fun US comedy about a girl's first sexual experiences is a small treat. Aubrey Plaza (of TV's *Parks and Recreation*) plays Brandy, a geeky goody-two-shoes who compiles a sexual to-do list that she wants to complete before she goes to college. The film is a little erratic, and occasionally misjudges its tone, but largely, it's nicely played. It should appeal to anyone who liked *Juno*, *Easy A* or even the early incarnations of *American Pie*. **DA** Swearing, sex scenes, drug abuse.

Aubrey Plaza *Brandy Klark* • Johnny Simmons *Cameron* • Bill Hader *Willy* • Alia Shawkat *Fiona* • Rachel Bilson *Amber* • Clark Gregg *Judge Klark* ■ *Dir/Scr* Maggie Carey

To Dorothy, a Son ★★ U
Comedy   1954 · UK · BW · 88min

Having made her name as both a playwright and screenwriter, Muriel Box turned director in 1952, and she struggles to make something of a story short on credibility and atmosphere. Shelley Winters stars as a vengeful divorcee trying to keep her mitts on a fortune by preventing her successor from producing a male heir. Co-stars John Gregson and Peggy Cummins have more trouble coping with Winters's overplaying. **DP**

Shelley Winters *Myrtle La Mar* • John Gregson *Tony Rapallo* • Peggy Cummins *Dorothy Rapallo* • Wilfrid Hyde White *Mr Starke* • Mona Washbourne *Nurse Appleby* • Hal Osmond *Livingstone Potts* • Hartley Power *Cy Daniel* ■ *Dir* Muriel Box • *Scr* Peter Rogers, from the play by Roger MacDougall

To Each His Own ★★★★
Melodrama   1946 · US · BW · 123min

After two years' absence from the screen, while she conducted – and won – a court case against Warners Bros's draconian contractual regulations, Olivia de Havilland returned to star for Paramount in this example of a "woman's picture" at its best, and won the best actress Oscar. Impeccably directed by Mitchell Leisen, the movie has de Havilland as an unmarried mother haunted by regrets at having given up her baby for adoption during the First World War. A very satisfying contribution to a long and honourable tradition. **RK**

Olivia de Havilland *Jody Norris* • John Lund *Capt Cosgrove/Gregory Piersen* • Mary Anderson *Corinna Sturges Piersen* • Roland Culver *Lord Desham* • Phillip Terry *Alex Piersen* • Bill Goodwin *Mac Tilton* • Virginia Welles *Liz Lorimer* ■ *Dir* Mitchell Leisen • *Scr* Charles Brackett, Jacques Thery, from a story by Charles Brackett

To End All Wars ★★ 15
War drama based on a true story
2001 · UK/US/Thai · Colour · 118min

This is a well-intentioned but leaden adaptation of Ernest Gordon's memoir about the building of the Burma railroad. Allied soldiers Ciaran McMenamin, Robert Carlyle and Kiefer Sutherland are among the PoWs forced to lay the infamous track. The subplots involving Sutherland's illicit still and Mark Strong's bush university only reinforce the aura of cliché. **DP** Swearing, violence. **DVD**

Robert Carlyle *Maj Ian Campbell* • Kiefer Sutherland *Lt Jim Reardon* • Ciaran McMenamin *Capt Ernest Gordon* • Mark Strong *Dusty Miller* • James Cosmo *Lt Col Stuart McLean* • Masayuki Yui *Capt Noguchi* • Sakae Kimura *Ito* • Shu Nakajima *Lt Col Nagatomo* • John Gregg *Dr*

Coates ■ *Dir* David L Cunningham • *Scr* Brian Godawa, from the memoir *Miracle on the River Kwai* by Ernest Gordon

To Gillian on Her 37th Birthday ★★★ 15
Romantic drama   1996 · US · Colour · 88min

Peter Gallagher as a widower still haunted not just by the memory of his dead wife, but by apparitions of her. *Ally McBeal* creator David E Kelley wrote the screenplay and co-produced, while the deceased Gillian is played by his wife, Michelle Pfeiffer. Claire Danes is the daughter Gallagher emotionally neglects, and Kathy Baker and Bruce Altman try to bring him to his senses during a celebration to mark what would have been Gillian's 37th birthday. Sentimental tosh, but it will no doubt appeal to those who enjoy Kelley's unique insights into the female psyche. **DA** Swearing, sexual references.

Peter Gallagher *David Lewis* • Michelle Pfeiffer *Gillian Lewis* • Claire Danes *Rachel Lewis* • Laurie Fortier *Cindy Bayles* • Wendy Crewson *Kevin Dollof* • Bruce Altman *Paul Wheeler* • Kathy Baker *Esther Wheeler* ■ *Dir* Michael Pressman, Michael Pressman • *Scr* David E Kelley, from the play by Michael Brady

To Have and Have Not ★★★★★ PG
Second World War romantic drama
1944 · US · BW · 96min

When producer/director Howard Hawks accepted the drunken challenge of filming Ernest Hemingway's "unfilmable" novel, neither of the two reprobates could have foreseen this as the outcome. One of Hollywood's most satisfying romantic melodramas, this features Humphrey Bogart in one of his best roles, as a reluctant patriot who falls for sultry Lauren Bacall (in her movie debut), and the two leads created an on-screen chemistry that resulted in a lifetime's love affair: "If you want me, just whistle. You know how to whistle, don't you Steve?". This is a gloriously witty, wonderfully enjoyable movie. **TS** **DVD**

Humphrey Bogart *Harry Morgan* • Walter Brennan *Eddie* • Lauren Bacall *Marie Browning "Slim"* • Dolores Moran *Helene De Bursac* • Hoagy Carmichael *Crickett* • Walter Molnar *Paul De Bursac* • Sheldon Leonard *Lieutenant Coyo* ■ *Dir* Howard Hawks • *Scr* Jules Furthman, William Faulkner, from the novel by Ernest Hemingway

To Have & to Hold ★ 18
Romantic thriller   1996 · Aus · Colour · 95min

The second feature film from Australian award-winner John Hillcoat is an uninteresting and unpleasant yarn about the destructive obsession of lovers Tcheky Karyo and Rachel Griffiths in the Papua New Guinea jungle. Great photography can't disguise a feeble plot, in which Karyo's ongoing obsession with his dead wife (Anni Finsterer) threatens his sanity and Griffiths's life. **AJ** Swearing, sex scenes, violence. **DVD**

Tcheky Karyo *Jack* • Rachel Griffiths *Kate Henley* • Steve Jacobs *Sal* • Anni Finsterer *Rose* • David Field *Stevie* ■ *Dir* John Hillcoat • *Scr* Gene Conkie, from a story by John Hillcoat, Gene Conkie

To Hell and Back ★★★ PG
Biographical war drama
1955 · US · Colour · 101min

Cowboy star Audie Murphy was America's most celebrated hero in the Second World War, and this is the movie version of his life, based on his autobiography. A relatively big movie for Murphy and Universal, it was expensively filmed in early CinemaScope with authentically re-created battle scenes. Murphy is a likeable lead, so it's regrettable that his subsequent career was confined almost solely to westerns. After years fighting insomnia and depression that led to an addiction to sleeping pills, Murphy died in an air crash at the age of 47. **TS** **DVD**

Audie Murphy • Marshall Thompson *Johnson* • Charles Drake *Brandon* • Gregg Palmer *Lt Manning* • Jack Kelly *Kerrigan* • Paul Picerni

Valentino • Susan Kohner *Maria* ■ *Dir* Jesse Hibbs • *Scr* Gil Doud, from Audie Murphy's autobiography

To Joy ★★★ PG
Drama   1950 · Swe · BW · 94min

This is only a minor entry in the Ingmar Bergman canon, but no film by him is without interest. Several themes that were to recur throughout his career are touched upon, notably the fragility of marital bliss and the conflict between artistic creativity and personal contentment. Gunnar Fischer's subtle cinematography reinforces the claustrophobia of the chamber drama, which is played with an occasionally overcooked intensity by Stig Olin and Maj-Britt Nilsson, as the musicians whose sterile marriage is torn apart by his affair. Victor Sjöström impresses in a cameo as an orchestra conductor. **DP** Swedish +subtitles. **DVD**

Stig Olin *Stig Ericsson* • Maj-Britt Nilsson *Martha* • Berit Holmström *Child* • Björn Montin *Child* • Victor Sjöström *Sönderby* • John Ekman *Mikael Bro* • Margit Carlqvist *Nelly Bro* • Georg Skarstedt *Anker* ■ *Dir/Scr* Ingmar Bergman

To Kill a King ★★★ 12
Historical drama
2003 · UK/Ger · Colour · 98min

Director Mike Barker's historical drama begins as the English Civil War ends, focusing on the relationship between the Parliamentarians' military commander Thomas Fairfax (Dougray Scott), and his deputy, Oliver Cromwell (Tim Roth). Fairfax finds himself torn between Cromwell and his wife (Olivia Williams). The former seems determined to accept nothing less than the head of King Charles I, the latter refuses to abandon old friends and standards. Despite woefully stilted dialogue, this is a fascinating if controversial history lesson. **BP** Violence. **DVD**

Tim Roth *Oliver Cromwell* • Dougray Scott *Thomas Fairfax* • Rupert Everett *King Charles I* • Olivia Williams *Lady Anne Fairfax* • James Bolam *Denzil Holles, Speaker of the House* • Corin Redgrave *Lord De Vere, Lady Anne's father* • Patricia Kerrigan *Mrs Cromwell* ■ *Dir* Mike Barker • *Scr* Jenny Mayhew

To Kill a Mockingbird ★★★★ PG
Classic drama   1962 · US · BW · 129min

Based on the Pulitzer Prize-winning novel by Harper Lee, this tale of small-town insularity distils the many stories in the novel down to two key strands: the mystery surrounding reclusive Boo Radley (Robert Duvall in his debut) and the defence by lawyer Atticus Finch (Gregory Peck, in a role that defined his career and earned him a best actor Oscar) of a black man accused of rape. The town's lynch-mob reaction to the trial proves an education for the lawyer's two children. A fine, moving period piece that's as much an abiding favourite as the book. **AC** **DVD** **SD**

Gregory Peck *Atticus Finch* • Mary Badham *Scout Finch* • Phillip Alford *Jem Finch* • John Megna *Dill Harris* • Frank Overton *Sheriff Heck Tate* • Rosemary Murphy *Miss Maudie Atkinson* • Brock Peters *Tom Robinson* • Estelle Evans *Calpurnia* • Ruth White *Mrs Dubose* • Robert Duvall *Boo Radley* ■ *Dir* Robert Mulligan • *Scr* Horton Foote, from the novel by Harper Lee

To Kill a Priest ★★ 18
Biographical drama
1988 · Fr/US · Colour · 112min

Christopher Lambert heads a strong cast in this biographical film about a radical priest in Poland in the early 1980s. Ed Harris is the militia man charged with finding and eliminating Solidarity supporter Father Alek (Lambert), before his fervent opposition to the government spreads any further. The film moves from convoluted scene to convoluted scene, and Lambert is bland and miscast, so Harris as his would-be killer becomes (wrongly) more sympathetic. **LH** Violence, swearing, brief nudity.

Christopher Lambert *Father Alek* • Ed Harris *Stefan* • Joanne Whalley *Anna* • Joss Ackland *Colonel* • David Suchet *Bishop* • Tim Roth *Feliks* • Pete Postlethwaite *Joseph* • Timothy Spall *Igor*

Cherie Lunghi *Halina* • Gregor Fisher *Father Irek* • Brian Glover *Minister* ■ *Dir* Agnieszka Holland • *Scr* Agnieszka Holland, Jean-Yves Pitoun, from a story by Agnieszka Holland

To Let ★★★
Horror thriller   2006 · Sp · Colour · 68min

A young couple are thrown into a living nightmare after answering an ad for a vacant flat in this relentless cat-and-mouse chiller from *[Rec]* co-director Jaume Balagueró. Macarena Gómez proves her scream-queen credentials as the pregnant, prospective tenant who battles to find her and her boyfriend (Adrià Collado) an escape when an eerily over-enthusiastic landlady (Nuria González) turns nasty. Made for the Spanish TV anthology series *6 Films to Keep You Awake*, the edge-of-the-seat tale delivers a short, sharp shock of stripped-down horror and fast-paced, moody visuals combine with a frenetic soundtrack to infuse every frame with dread. **SF** Spanish +subtitles.

Macarena Gómez *Clara* • Adrià Collado *Mario* • Nuria González *Caretaker* • Ruth Diaz *Girl* • Roberto Romero *Caretaker's son* • David Sandanya *Boy* ■ *Dir* Jaume Balagueró • *Scr* Jaume Balagueró, Alberto Marini

To Live ★★★★ 12
Epic drama   1994 · Chi · Colour · 126min

While it might lack the visual splendour of *Red Sorghum* or the dramatic intensity of *Raise the Red Lantern*, this is still a superbly realised piece of work, combining the historical sweep of an epic with the finely etched characterisations of a chamber drama. Although it incurred the wrath of the authorities, the film isn't a condemnation of the errors of Mao, but a tribute to the spirit of the Chinese people who survived them. Gong Li seems to be incapable of giving a bad performance, but she's more than matched by Ge You, who won the best actor award at Cannes. **DP** Mandarin +subtitles. Violence.

Ge You *Xu Fugui* • Gong Li *Jiazhen* • Niu Ben *Town Chief Niu* • Guo Tao *Chunsheng* • Wu Jiang *Wan Erxi* ■ *Dir* Zhang Yimou • *Scr* Lu Wei, from the novel *Lifetimes* by Yu Hua

To Live and Die in LA ★★★ 18
Crime thriller   1985 · US · Colour · 110min

Director William Friedkin's cult hi-tech thriller features excitingly kinetic car chases through the City of Angels and high-energy gun battles choreographed to a pounding uptempo rock score. Treasury agents William Petersen and John Pankow go to extraordinary lengths by bending their Federal rule book to crack the operation of sadistic counterfeiter Willem Dafoe. Dafoe is a suitably slimy adversary in the maverick director's exercise in nihilistic *noir*. **AJ** Violence, swearing, nudity. **DVD**

William L Petersen *Richard Chance* • Willem Dafoe *Eric Masters* • John Pankow *John Vukovich* • Debra Feuer *Bianca Torres* • John Turturro *Carl Cody* • Darlanne Fluegel *Ruth Lanier* • Dean Stockwell *Bob Grimes* • Steve James (1) *Jeff Rice* • Robert Downey Sr *Thomas Bateman* • Michael Greene *Jim Hart* ■ *Dir* William Friedkin • *Scr* William Friedkin, Gerald Petievich, from the novel by Gerald Petievich

To Live For ★★ PG
Romantic drama   1999 · US · Colour · 91min

This TV drama is manipulative, heart-tugging stuff, but it's done with some proficiency. Attorney Nancy Travis discovers that she has incurable cancer and has to make decisions for her young daughter, Jamie Renee Smith. Director Michael Schultz's penchant for lighter entertainments hardly suits this weepie. **DP** **DVD**

Nancy Travis *Susan* • Scott Bairstow *Michael Blake* • Jamie Renee Smith *Carson* • James Karen *Phil* • Viveka Davis *Kate* • Holland Taylor *Marnie* ■ *Dir* Michael Schultz • *Scr* Katie Ford

To Our Loves ★★★★ 15
Drama   1984 · Fr · Colour · 99min

Three years after shocking audiences with Isabelle Huppert's adulterous pursuit of the boorish Gérard Depardieu in *Loulou*, Maurice Pialat explored the theme of teenage promiscuity in this equally controversial picture. Pialat draws a disturbingly authentic performance from Sandrine Bonnaire, whose confused relationship with her absentee father (Pialat) prompts her to adopt an increasingly reckless attitude towards sex. The violent slanging matches with her brother are grimly arresting, but less revealing than the still naive 15-year-old's excruciating encounters with the father whose love she craves. DP French +subtitles.

Sandrine Bonnaire *Suzanne* • Dominique Besnéhard *Robert* • Maurice Pialat *The father* • Evelyne Ker *The mother* ■ *Dir* Maurice Pialat • *Scr* Maurice Pialat, Arlette Langmann

To Paris with Love ★★★

Romantic comedy 1954 · UK · Colour · 78min

This amiable, light-hearted exercise in postwar "naughtiness" stars Alec Guinness and Vernon Gray as father and son, each planning amorous adventures for the other. The ensuing complications are enlivened by Guinness's engaging performance. Both the leading lady, Odile Versois, and Paris itself are delightful in mid-1950s Technicolor, and this movie is often shamefully underrated. TS

Alec Guinness *Colonel Sir Edgar Fraser* • Odile Versois *Lisette Marconnet* • Vernon Gray *Jon Fraser* • Jacques François *Victor de Colville* • Elina Labourdette *Sylvia Gilbert* • Austin Trevor *Léon de Colville* ■ *Dir* Robert Hamer • *Scr* Robert Buckner

To Please a Lady ★★★U

Romantic sports drama 1950 · US · BW · 91min

Clark Gable and Barbara Stanwyck star for veteran MGM director Clarence Brown in an efficient, straightforward movie that combines motor-racing action with drama and romance. Gable is a champion midget-car driver, hated by the crowds after the death of another driver in an accident for which he is held responsible. Journalist Stanwyck tries to get his side of the story, but he won't talk. Needless to say, neither the action nor their relationship stops there. RK

Clark Gable *Mike Brannan* • Barbara Stanwyck *Regina Forbes* • Adolphe Menjou *Gregg* • Will Geer *Jack Mackay* • Roland Winters *Dwight Barrington* • William C McGaw *Joie Chitwood* ■ *Dir* Clarence Brown • *Scr* Barré Lyndon, Marge Decker, from their story

To Protect and Serve ★★18

Thriller 1992 · Swi · Colour · 88min

An intriguing spin on the "bent coppers" scenario, this focuses on an investigation into why corrupt lawmen are turning up dead. The evidence points inexplicably to a young policeman (C Thomas Howell) but is he being set up? Although Howell struggles to carry off his leading role, the film does benefit from a strong supporting cast. JF Swearing, violence, sex scenes, drug abuse.

C Thomas Howell *Egan* • Lezlie Deane *Harriet* • Richard Romanus *Captain Maloul* • Joe Cortese *Kazinsky* • Steve Ganon *Lieutenant Burton* • Jessie Lawrence Ferguson *Becker* ■ *Dir* Eric Weston • *Scr* Darren Dalton, Kent Perkins, Eric Weston, Freeman King

To Rome with Love ★★★12

Comedy 2012 · US/It/Sp · Colour · 107min

Woody Allen here continues his extended, and clearly refreshing, European Grand Tour. Having visited London (*Match Point*), Spain (*Vicky Cristina Barcelona*) and the French capital (*Midnight in Paris*), he finally reaches the Eternal City and delivers this fluffily entertaining dispatch composed of four intercut but not intertwining stories. It's at its best with the tales featuring Alec Baldwin as an ageing architect and Penélope Cruz as a brassy call girl, and less successful with the other two stories. But the overall mood of sunny good cheer is difficult to resist. AS In English, Italian. Swearing, sexual references. *DVD*

Woody Allen *Jerry* • Alec Baldwin *John* • Penélope Cruz *Anna* • Roberto Benigni *Leopoldo* • Judy Davis *Phyllis* • Jesse Eisenberg *Jack* • Ellen Page *Monica* ■ *Dir/Scr* Woody Allen

To Sir, with Love ★★★PG

Drama 1967 · UK · Colour · 100min

Sidney Poitier plays a new teacher in London's East End, motivating surly pupils to be responsible citizens. Director James Clavell's adaptation of ER Braithwaite's novel is a soft-centred affair, though Poitier does punch Christ an Roberts just to prove he's boss. This is probably best remembered for Lulu singing the title song, though Judy Geeson gives a credible performance as a lovelorn pupil. Naive it may have been, but it became one of the year's top box-office hits. In 1996, Peter Bogdanovich directed a belated made-for-TV sequel. TH Swearing. *DVD*

Sidney Poitier *Mark Thackeray* • Christian Roberts *Denham* • Judy Geeson *Pamela Dare* • Suzy Kendall *Gillian Blanchard* • Lulu *Barbara Pegg* • Faith Brook *Mrs Evans* • Geoffrey Bayldon *Weston* • Edward Burnham *Florian* • Gareth Robinson *Tich* • Grahame Charles *Fernman* • Roger Shepherd *Buckley* • Patricia Routledge *Clinty* ■ *Dir* James Clavell • *Scr* James Clavell, from the novel by ER Braithwaite

To Sleep with Anger ★★★★12

Drama 1990 · US · Colour · 97min

Charles Burnett's story of a black family settled in Los Angeles from the South is an engrossing study of conflicts in black America. Danny Glover has never been better, playing a seductive charmer from the past whose storytelling moves from the comic to the sinister, a domestic demagogue who stirs up nightmare tensions in the family. TH Swearing. *DVD*

Danny Glover *Harry Mention* • Paul Butler *Gideon* • Mary Alice *Suzie* • Carl Lumbly *Junior* • Vonetta McGee *Pat* • Richard Brooks (2) *Babe Brother* ■ *Dir/Scr* Charles Burnett

To the Devil a Daughter ★★18

Horror 1976 · UK/W Ger · Colour · 88min

This Hammer film is a muddled mixture of post-*Exorcist* shock and the more traditional House of Horror style. Based on Dennis Wheatley's occult bestseller (he hated it), the plot has Satanist Christopher Lee coercing nubile nun Nastassja Kinski into having the Devil's offspring, while Richard Widmark, a writer specialising in the supernatural, tries to foil his plan. Peter Sykes directs with a tendency towards a trendy fragmented narrative and explicit exploitation. AJ Violence, swearing, nudity. *DVD*

Richard Widmark *John Verney* • Christopher Lee *Father Michael Raynor* • Honor Blackman *Anna Fountain* • Denholm Elliott *Henry Beddows* • Michael Goodliffe *George de Grass* • Nastassia Kinski [Nastassja Kinski] *Catherine Beddows* • Anthony Valentine *David* ■ *Dir* Peter Sykes • *Scr* Chris Wicking, from the novel by Dennis Wheatley

To the Ends of the Earth ★★★

Crime drama 1948 · US · BW · 108min

The title refers to the many continents crossed by government agent Dick Powell in his quest for a gang of opium smugglers with fanatical ambitions for world domination. The plot, though complicated, is comprehensible and it's well handled by director Sidney Buchman, ensuring maximum tension and entertainment value. Swedish import Signe Hasso contributes the girl glamour; as almost always, crooner-turned-tough-guy Powell convinces as the action hero. RK

Dick Powell *Mike Barrows* • Signe Hasso *Ann Grant* • Maylia *Shu Pan Wu* • Ludwig Donath *Nicolas Sokim* • Vlad mir Sokoloff *Lum Chi Chow* • Edgar Barrier *Grieg* • John Hoyt *Bennett* ■ *Dir* Robert Stevenson, Sidney Buchman • *Scr* Jay Richard Kennedy, from his story

To the Shores of Tripoli ★★U

Second World War drama 1942 · US · Colour · 85min

This is a salute to the US marines, the title coming from the military song. There isn't much of a plot – merely the training of the blokes, their patriotism, the tough sergeant, the girl back home, winsome nurse – you know the drill. Much of it was shot at the marines' major Pacific base in San Diego, in full Technicolor, a rarity for 1942 since most Second World War movies were in black-and-white, only changing to colour in 1944 when victory was assured. AT

John Payne *Chris Winters* • Maureen O'Hara *Mary Carter* • Randolph Scott *Sgt Dixie Smith* • Nancy Kelly *Helene Hunt* • William Tracy *Johnny Dent* • Maxie Rosenbloom *Okay Jones* • Henry Morgan [Harry Morgan] *Mouthy* ■ *Dir* Bruce Humberstone [H Bruce Humberstone] • *Scr* Lamar Trotti, from a story by Steve Fisher

To the Starry Island ★★★★

Drama 1994 · S Kor · Colour · 99min

A poet returns to his island to discover that the locals are unwilling to bury his friend's father because of past events. Revisiting familiar places, he recalls the characters that inhabited his childhood and the moment when the Korean War turned everybody into strangers. Demonstrating a mastery of flashback and a keen insight into human interaction, Park Kwang-Su excels himself in the scene where the locals betray each other to invading troops. An affecting and superbly observed study of the impact of war on village life. DP Korean +subtitles.

Moon Sung-Keun *Moon Duk-bae/Moon Chae-ku* • Ahn Sung-kee *Kim Senior/Kim Shul* ■ *Dir* Park Kwang-Su • *Scr* Park Kwang-Su, Lee Chang-Dong, Im Chulwoo

To the Wonder ★★12

Romantic drama 2012 · US · Colour · 107min

The Tree of Life earned writer/director Terrence Malick an Oscar nomination for best director in 2012, but the dreaml-ike aesthetic of that ambitious epic doesn't have the same impact when applied to this love triangle involving Ben Affleck, his partner (Olga Kurylenko) and his childhood sweetheart (Rachel McAdams). Kurylenko delivers a voiceover, in French, picking through her feelings and exploring questions of faith without really getting anywhere. Presumably, this is why Javier Bardem picks up the narration halfway through – he plays a priest trying to make sense of the loss of *his* faith. At the centre of the story is Affleck, a man torn between two women, but he is cast adrift and left to merge into beautiful backgrounds – mostly sandy beaches and sunlit fields of wheat. For a film about the most profound human emotion, *To the Wonder* is a bit flighty and beige. SP *DVD* 🅱

Ben Affleck *Neil* • Olga Kurylenko *Marina* • Rachel McAdams *Jane* • Javier Bardem *Father Quintana* • Charles Baker *Charles* ■ *Dir/Scr* Terrence Malick • *Production Designer* Jack Fisk

To Trap a Spy ★★★

Spy adventure 1966 · US · Colour · 92min

The first movie spin-off from the highly successful TV spy show *The Man from UNCLE* also stands as one of the best. Comprising footage from the pilot episode, it contains additional new scenes which focused on turning Napoleon Solo, played with devilish charm by Robert Vaughn, into a playboy about town. Poor old David McCallum as sidekick Illya Kuryakin hardly gets a look in. The *femme fatale* quota was also enhanced to spice up the box office. Never mind the thin plot – UNCLE agents must protect a visiting African diplomat from assassination – just feel the nostalgia. RS Violence.

Robert Vaughn (1) *Napoleon Solo* • David McCallum (1) *Illya Kuryakin* • Patricia Crowley [Pat Crowley] *Elaine May Donaldson* • Fritz Weaver *Vulcan* • Luciana Paluzzi *Angela* • William Marshall (2) *Ashumen* • Will Kuluva *Mr Allison* ■ *Dir* Don Medford • *Scr* Sam Rolfe

To Walk with Lions ★★★★12

Biographical drama 1999 · Can/UK/Ken · Colour · 105min

Grittier and less sentimental than the original, this fine follow-up to *Born Free* stars Richard Harris as an ageing George Adamson, long separated from wife Joy, but still enjoying life with the lions despite the predations of poachers and the grudging tolerance of the Kenyan government. The story is seen through the eyes of an English backpacker (John Michie), who chronicles Adamson's life up to his brutal killing by poachers in 1989. The leonine-looking Harris delivers a towering lead performance. DA Swearing, violence, a sex scene. *DVD*

Richard Harris *George Adamson* • John Michie *Tony Fitzjohn* • Ian Bannen *Terence Adamson* • Kerry Fox *Lucy Jackson* • Hugh Quarshie *Maxwell* • Honor Blackman *Joy Adamson* • Geraldine Chaplin *Victoria Andrecelli* ■ *Dir* Carl Schultz • *Scr* Sharon Buckingham, Keith Ross Leckie

To Wong Foo, Thanks for Everything, Julie Newmar ★★★PG

Comedy 1995 · US · Colour · 103min

America's riposte to *The Adventures of Priscilla, Queen of the Desert* is a good concept in search of a plot. The concept? Dress macho movie stars Patrick Swayze and Wesley Snipes in evening gowns, sit back, and watch the camp laughs roll in. And sometimes they do. The plot? Three New York drag queens on the road to Hollywood get stuck in small-town America. Although sentimentally shallow, Beeban Kidron's frock opera is diverting enough. AJ Violence, swearing. *DVD*

Wesley Snipes *Noxeema Jackson* • Patrick Swayze *Vida Boheme* • John Leguizamo *Chi Chi Rodriguez* • Stockard Channing *Carol Ann* • Blythe Danner *Beatrice* • Arliss Howard *Virgil* • Jason London *Bobby Ray* • Chris Penn *Sheriff Dollard* • Melinda Dillon *Merna* • Beth Grant *Loretta* ■ *Dir* Beeban Kidron • *Scr* Douglas Carter

Toast ★★★★PG

Comedy drama 2010 · UK · Colour · 92min

What a triumph! *Billy Elliot* writer Lee Hall has turned Nigel Slater's best-selling *Toast*, his poignant, funny and unflinching memoir, into an evocative and thoroughly winning film. Newcomer Oscar Kennedy (he's 11, it's his first major role and he's wonderful) is young Nigel, the child of middle-class parents, whose love of food begins to dominate his life. *Toast* never puts a foot wrong; none of the novel's complex undercurrents is lost, the performances are spot on, the re-creation of the deadly, brown 1960s is perfect, and there's even a cameo from the real Nigel Slater. AG Some swearing, sexual references. *DVD*

Helena Bonham Carter *Joan Potter* • Freddie Highmore *Nigel Slater* • Matthew McNulty *Josh* • Oscar Kennedy *Young Nigel Slater* • Victoria Hamilton *Mum* • Clare Higgins *Mavis* • Ken Stott *Dad* ■ *Dir* SJ Clarkson • *Scr* Lee Hall, from the non-fiction book *Toast: the Story of a Boy's Hunger* by Nigel Slater • *Cinematographer* Balazs Bolygo

The Toast of New Orleans ★★★U

Musical drama 1950 · US · Colour · 96min

Tenor Mario Lanza's second starring role (the first was in the previous year's *That Midnight Kiss*) again teams him with glamorous co-star Kathryn Grayson. This was the film that helped him become a household name, belting out the momentous *Be My Love* at every possible opportunity, as he portrays a singing fisherman discovered by suave impresario David Niven. Lanza's next film was the smash hit *The Great Caruso*, and the seeds of both his stardom and his self-destruction were duly sown. TS

Kathryn Grayson *Suzette Micheline* • Mario Lanza *Pepe Abellard Duvalle* • David Niven *Jacques Riboudeaux* • J Carrol Naish *Nicky Duvalle* •

James Mitchell *Pierre* • Richard Hageman *Maestro P Trelini* ■ *Dir* Norman Taurog • *Scr* Sy Gomberg, George Wells

The Toast of New York

★★★ U

Biographical drama   1937 · US · BW · 104min

Rotund character actor Edward Arnold makes a strong fist of the leading role of the American 19th-century entrepreneur John Fisk, but the thunder (and there's quite a lot of that!) is stolen from Arnold by juvenile leads Cary Grant and Frances Farmer. Farmer is exceptionally lively, while Grant glides through the role of Fisk's partner, revealing that graceful quality that would serve him well, but he seems far too contemporary for this biopic, which, as Hollywood has a tendency to do, plays fast and loose with the known facts. TS

Edward Arnold *Jim Fisk* • Cary Grant *Nick Boyd* • Frances Farmer *Josie Mansfield* • Jack Oakie *Luke* • Donald Meek *Daniel Drew* • Thelma Leeds *Fleurique* • Clarence Kolb *Cornelius Vanderbilt* ■ *Dir* Rowland V Lee • *Scr* Dudley Nichols, John Twist, Joel Sayre, from the book *Book of Daniel Drew* by Bouck White, from the story *Robber Barons* by Matthew Josephson

Tobacco Road

★★★

Drama   1941 · US · BW · 84min

Erskine Caldwell's novel was a solid sensation in its day, uncovering the (literal) dirt on a Georgia backwoods community, and went on to become an amazingly long-running Broadway success. When 20th Century-Fox filmed the piece, it wisely retained Charley Grapewin to repeat his role as the head of a clan beset by financial woes and seemingly incapable of sorting out its problems. He's terrific, but the studio settings look phoney today, and Fox's resident beauty Gene Tierney looks strained and out of place. Darkly comic. TS

Charley Grapewin *Jeeter Lester* • Marjorie Rambeau *Sister Bessie* • Gene Tierney *Ellie May Lester* • William Tracy *Duke Lester* • Elizabeth Patterson *Ada Lester* • Dana Andrews *Dr Tim* ■ *Dir* John Ford • *Scr* Nunnally Johnson, from the play by Jack Kirkland, from the novel by Erskine Caldwell

Tobruk

★★★ PG

Second World War adventure
1966 · US · Colour · 104min

Rock Hudson is in a decidedly Hollywood backlot North Africa, surrounded by assorted British war-film veterans, having a go at blowing up Rommel's fuel lines. While director Arthur Hiller makes it heavy going, it's watchable, thanks to the interesting screenplay by actor Leo V Gordon (who also appears in the film). The action scenes were used again in the Richard Burton action adventure *Raid on Rommel*. TS

DVD *BL*

Rock Hudson *Major Donald Craig* • George Peppard *Capt Kurt Bergman* • Nigel Green *Colonel John Harker* • Guy Stockwell *Lt Max Mohnfeld* • Jack Watson *Sgt Major Tyne* • Norman Rossington *Alfie* • Percy Herbert *Dolan* • Leo Gordon *Sgt Krug* ■ *Dir* Arthur Hiller • *Scr* Leo V Gordon

Toby Tyler, or Ten Weeks with a Circus

★★ Uc

Adventure   1960 · US · Colour · 90min

Disney regular Kevin Corcoran is the young lad who succeeds in doing what most children dream of: swap life at home for the excitement of the circus. It's an easy-going if dated adventure, but the performances are pleasing and the youngsters will lap it up. JF

Kevin Corcoran *Toby Tyler* • Henry Calvin *Ben Cotter* • Gene Sheldon *Sam Treat* • Bob Sweeney *Harry Tupper* • Richard Eastham *Colonel Sam Castle* • James Drury *Jim Weaver* • Barbara Beaird *Mademoiselle Jeanette* ■ *Dir* Charles Barton • *Scr* Bill Walsh, Lillie Hayward, from the novel by James Otis Kaler

Today We Live

★★★

First World War romance
1933 · US · BW · 110min

Joan Crawford, deeply attached to her brother Franchot Tone and engaged to her childhood sweetheart Robert Young, falls in love with Gary Cooper. All four end up on active service in France where, between air battles and tragedy, the complicated emotional triangle is played out. Co-scripted by William Faulkner and directed by Howard Hawks, this is surely one of the weirdest films ever made. The plot defies credibility at almost every turn, and the intimate scenes of high drama between the protagonists are written and spoken in a curiously clipped, semi-poetical shorthand. This is a real oddity, but an interesting one. RK

Joan Crawford *Diana Boyce-Smith* • Gary Cooper *Richard Bogard* • Robert Young (1) *Claude* • Franchot Tone *Ronnie Boyce-Smith* • Roscoe Karns *McGinnis* • Louise Closser Hale *Applegate* • Rollo Lloyd *Major* • Hilda Vaughn *Eleanor* ■ *Dir* Howard Hawks • *Scr* Edith Fitzgerald, Dwight Taylor, William Faulkner, from the story *Turn About* by William Faulkner

Today You Die

★★ 18

Action drama   2005 · US · Colour · 87min

One final job predictably leads to betrayal and revenge for Steven Seagal's retiring criminal in this tired action drama. Breaking out of prison with a well-connected gangsta (rapper Anthony "Treach" Criss), the modern-day Robin Hood attempts to wreak violent havoc on his double-crossing associates. Unfortunately, all the requisite gunplay and explosions that follow can't mask the clichéd plot and comically bad performances. SF Violence, swearing.

DVD

Steven Seagal *Harlan Banks* • Anthony "Treach" Criss *Ice Cool* • Sarah Buxton *Rachel* • Mari Morrow *Jada* • Nick Mancuso *Agent Saunders* ■ *Dir* Don E FauntLeRoy • *Scr* Danny Lerner, Kevin Moore, Les Weldon

Together

★★★ 15

Comedy drama
2000 · Swe/Den/It · Colour · 101min

Life on a commune in the mid-1970s may seem like a soft target, but Swedish director Lukas Moodysson isn't interested in the obvious. There's plenty of laissez-faire liberalism in the attitudes of the chunky sweatered leader and his kaftan-wearing acolytes. Yet, amid all the dope-smoking and free-loving permissiveness, there's a real sense of socio-political conflict as human nature intrudes upon the idyll. Exploring the group's self-satisfied moral rectitude and their blithe disregard for how this alternative lifestyle will impact on their children, Moodysson provides a shrewd insight into the era. DP Swedish +subtitles.

DVD

Lisa Lindgren *Elisabeth* • Michael Nyqvist *Rolf* • Gustav Hammarsten *Göran* • Anja Lundqvist *Lena* • Jessica Liedberg *Anna* • Ola Norell *Lasse* ■ *Dir/Scr* Lukas Moodysson

Together Again

★★★

Romantic comedy   1944 · US · BW · 99min

The title unashamedly refers to the reteaming of Irene Dunne and Charles Boyer, the hit duo of *Love Affair* and *When Tomorrow Comes*, but this time eschewing the tempestuous storms of romantic melodrama for the shenanigans of romantic comedy. She plays the widowed mayoress of a New England town; he is a New York sculptor commissioned, at the suggestion of Dunne's cupid-playing father-in-law Charles Coburn, to cast a new statue of her late husband, the former mayor. Featherweight fun. RK

Irene Dunne *Anne Crandall* • Charles Boyer *George Corday* • Charles Coburn *Jonathan Crandall Sr* • Mona Freeman *Diana Crandall* • Jerome Courtland *Gilbert Parker* • Elizabeth Patterson *Jessie* • Charles Dingle *Morton.Buchman* • Walter Baldwin *Witherspoon* ■ *Dir* Charles Vidor • *Scr* Virginia Van Upp, F Hugh Herbert, from a story by Stanley Russell, Herbert J Biberman

Together Again for the First Time

★★

Seasonal comedy   2008 · US · Colour · 85min

In yet another film about the true meaning of Christmas, a warring stepfamily descends into tragicomic meltdown after getting together for the first time in seven years to celebrate the festive season. Cue a hit-and-miss mix of slapstick, pratfalls and acid-tinged bickering, as the stage play-based narrative goes overboard to be energetic and wacky, but ends up largely a puerile drag. Only long-suffering patriarch David Ogden Stiers brings a gentle charm and dry wit to the increasingly far-fetched events. SF

Julia Duffy *Audrey Wolders Frobisher* • David Ogden Stiers *Max Frobisher* • Larisa Oleynik *Brenda* • Joey Lawrence *Carey Krzyznyk* ■ *Dir* Jeff Parkin • *Scr* Reed McColm, Jeff Parkin, from McColm's play

Together with You

★★★ PG

Drama   2002 · Chi · Colour · 113min

Music has been an important feature of Chen Kaige's films since *Life on a String*. Yet, despite this Beijing melodrama turning around a provincial peasant who sacrifices all so that his son can study the violin, the unforced sincerity and acute insight of his early work continues to elude a director caught between China's dramatic socio-economic transformation and his own international art house celebrity. However, Liu Peiqi and Tang Yun are charmingly credible as proud father and teenage prodigy, while Wang Zhiwen and Chen Hong provide genial support as an eccentric genius and a good-time girl. DP Mandarin +subtitles. *DVD*

Liu Peiqi *Liu Cheng* • Tang Yun *Liu Xiaochun* • Chen Hong *Lili* • Wang Zhiwen *Professor Jiang* • Chen Kaige *Professor Yu Shifeng* • Cheng Qian Hui, *Lili's lover* ■ *Dir* Chen Kaige • *Scr* Chen Kaige, Xue Xiaolu

Tokyo Chorus

★★★★

Silent comedy drama   1931 · Jpn · BW · 91min

Yasujiro Ozu was in his 20s and still refining his style when he directed this, so there is slightly more camera movement and overtly "cinematic" technique than in his later, greater sound works. Still, it's recognisably Ozu in its concern with family life – here given an extra dimension since the story tells of a man (Tokihiko Okada) who is sacked when he supports an unfairly treated fellow worker. He's forced to look for work in Depression-tainted Tokyo, so the film, which begins light-heartedly, gradually darkens into a characteristically humane study of a lower middle-class victim of society. BB

Tokihiko Okada *Shinji Okajima* • Emiko Yagumo *Sugao, Okajima's wife* • Hideo Sugawara *Okajima's son* • Hideko Takamine *Miyoko, Okajima's daughter* • Tatsuo Saito *Omura, Okajima's old teacher* • Choko Iida *Omura's wife* ■ *Dir* Yasujiro Ozu • *Scr* Kogo Noda, from the novel *Tokyo no Gassho* by Komatsu Kitamura

Tokyo Cowboy

★★★

Comedy   1994 · Can · Colour and BW · 94min

A festival favourite in its native Canada, this charming tale of movie mania and cross-cultural confusion sees Hiromoto Ida as the Japanese fast-food employee who quits his dead-end existence for a chance to emulate his cowboy heroes in the backwoods home of his Canadian penpal. Neatly played, this warm, funny film owes its greatest debt to director Kathy Garneau and photographer Kenneth Hewlett, who stage Ida's black-and-white western daydreams with considerable skill. DP

Hiromoto Ida *No Ogawa* • Christianne Hirt *Kate Beatty* • Janne Mortil *Shelly* • Alec Willow *Postman* • Anna Ferguson *Kate's mother* ■ *Dir* Kathy Garneau • *Scr* Caroline Anderson

Tokyo Decadence

★★★

Drama   1992 · Jpn · Colour · 112min

The fourth film directed by Japanese novelist Ryu Murakami recalls *In the Realm of the Senses* in its graphic depiction of sex as a symbol for the nation's decay. Its exposé of a prostitute's relentless degradation (linked only by empty ritual to the romanticised image of the geisha) is made all the more powerful by the clinically unerotic sadomasochism in which timid graduate Miho Nikaido participates with yakuza and businessmen alike. Nikaido's performance is undeniably courageous, but the fragmentary detachment of Murakami's direction precludes involvement. DP Japanese +subtitles. *DVD*

Miho Nikaido *Ai* • Sayoko Amano *Saki* • Masahiko Shimada *Mr Ishioka* ■ *Dir* Ryu Murakami • *Scr* Ryu Murakami, from his novel novel *Topaz*

Tokyo Drifter

★★★★ 12

Cult action thriller
1966 · Jpn · Colour and BW · 80min

This deliriously contrived yakuza flick earned director Seijun Suzuki a cult following outside Japan. Combining elements from hard-boiled pulp, the spaghetti western and the Hollywood musical, this cartoon-like parody of the gangster movie also makes spectacular use of colour, stylised decor and an ambiguous narrative. At the centre of the often surreal mayhem is Tetsuya Watari, whose ambition to quit the rackets is frustrated by his inability to shake his dark past. DP Japanese +subtitles. *DVD*

Tetsuya Watari *Tetsuya "Phoenix, Tetsu" Hondo* • Chieko Matsubara *Chiharu* • Hideaki Nitani *Kenji Aizawa* • Ryuji Kita *Kurata* • Tsuyoshi Yoshida *Keiichi* • Hideaki Esumi *Otsuka* ■ *Dir* Seijun Suzuki • *Scr* Yasunori Kawauchi, from his novel

Tokyo Fist

★★★★ 18

Action horror drama   1995 · Jpn · Colour · 83min

This extraordinarily oppressive, raw and gore-drenched tale charts the mental and physical transformation of a wimpy insurance salesman (director Shinya Tsukamoto, who also produced, wrote, shot and edited), his disturbed girlfriend and an old schoolfriend turned rival, a professional boxer. Shot with a darting hand-held camera, Tsukamoto demonstrates mesmerising mastery of light, colour and sound as the trio conflict outside and inside the fight ring in some of the most punishing, bloody fight scenes since *Raging Bull*. JC Japanese +subtitles. Sex scenes, swearing, violence. *DVD* *BL*

Kahori Fujii *Hizuru* • Kohji Tsukamoto *Kojima Takuji* • Shinya Tsukamoto *Tsuda Shinya* • Naoto Takenaka *Ohizumi, trainer* ■ *Dir* Shinya Tsukamoto • *Scr* Shinya Tsukamoto, from a story by Hisashi Saito, Shinya Tsukamoto

Tokyo Joe

★★★

Melodrama   1949 · US · BW · 88min

Humphrey Bogart is running a bar in an exotic location and trying to win back his ex-wife Florence Marly, who's gone off and married dull Alexander Knox. It's as uninvolving as it sounds, and dates from that awkward period in Bogart's career between his public recantation that he had no communist tendencies, and his public and industry return to favour with *The African Queen*. The main weakness is the casting of Marly, a totally uncharismatic Franco-Czech actress, but Bogie is, as ever, watchable. TS

Humphrey Bogart *Joe Barrett* • Alexander Knox *Mark Landis* • Florence Marly *Trina* • Sessue Hayakawa *Baron Kimura* • Jerome Courtland *Danny* • Gordon Jones *Idaho* • Teru Shimada *Ito* ■ *Dir* Stuart Heisler • *Scr* Cyril Hume, Bertram Millhauser, Walter Doniger, from a story by Steve Fisher

Tokyo Olympiad

★★★★

Documentary   1965 · Jpn · Colour · 132min

The Tokyo Games of 1964 were preserved as a tribute to human athleticism and endurance in this lyrical documentary. Employing 164 camera units, many of which were equipped with especially devised telephoto and night-vision lenses, Kon Ichikawa was only interested in winners and losers if they exemplified the spirit of competition. He focused on the last-minute preparations of sprinters, the watering techniques of marathon runners and the progress of the Olympic torch. Inspirational stuff. DP

■ *Dir* Kon Ichikawa • *Scr* Kon Ichikawa, Natto Wada, Yoshio Shiraska, Shuntaro Tanikawa

Tokyo Pop ★★★ 18

Comedy drama 1988 · US · Colour · 98min

This engaging teen romance takes some very gentle pot-shots at the differences between East and West. Carrie Hamilton (daughter of actress Carol Burnett) is the impulsive budding singer who swaps New York for Tokyo and finds romance with band leader Yutaka Tadokoro. Fran Rubel Kuzui breathes fresh life into the clichéd storyline and directs the proceedings with style, while the two leads turn in winning performances. JF

Carrie Hamilton *Wendy Reed* · Yutaka Tadokoro *Hiro Yamaguchi* · Taiji Tonoyama *Grandfather* · Tetsuro Tanba [Tetsuro Tamba] *Dota* · Masumi Harukawa *Mother* · Toki Shiozawa *Mama-san* · Hiroshi Mikami *Seki* ■ *Dir* Fran Rubel Kuzui · *Scr* Fran Rubel Kuzui, Lynn Grossman, from a story by Kuzui

Tokyo Raiders ★★ 12

Martial arts action drama 2000 · HK · Colour · 96min

Set in Japan, this tortuously plotted tale finds jilted bride Kelly Chen travelling to Tokyo to find her fiancé and discovering that he is mixed up with both the Japanese Mob and the CIA. Also along for for the ride are ace private eye Tony Leung and interior decorator Ekin Cheng. There's plenty of inventive martial arts, even if director Jingle Ma does overdo the slow motion a tad. The script, however, is cringe-worthy. JF In Cantonese, Japanese. *DVD*

Tony Leung (2) *Lam* · Ekin Cheng *Yung* · Kelly Chen *Macy* · Cecilia Cheung *Saori* · Toru Nakamura *Takahashi* ■ *Dir* Jingle Ma · *Scr* Susan Chan, Felix Chong

Tokyo Sonata ★★★★ 12

Drama 2008 · Jpn/Neth/HK · Colour · 119min

Japanese director Kiyoshi Kurosawa (*Pulse*) has a rare knack for imbuing seemingly ordinary situations with apocalyptic significance. It's put to good use here as a Tokyo businessman (Teruyuki Kagawa) can't face the shame of telling his family that he's been made redundant. Unable to find new work, he commutes into the city each morning and queues for charity food handouts until his wife discovers his deception. Kagawa is superb as the haggard, droopy-faced breadwinner facing obsolescence, while co-star Kyoko Koizumi has a deceptively passive role as the family's long-suffering mother. Dissecting not just the loss of paternal authority but a global malaise – something underscored by a subplot in which eldest son Yu Koyanagi joins the peacekeeping effort in Iraq – it's a mysterious, multilayered film. JR Japanese +subtitles. Swearing, some violence. *DVD* *BL*

Teruyuki Kagawa *Ryuhei Sasaki* · Kyoko Koizumi *Megumi Sasaki* · Yu Koyanagi *Taka Sasaki* · Kai Inowaki *Kenji Sasaki* · Haruka Igawa *Ms Kaneko* · Kanji Tsuda *Kurosu* ■ *Dir* Kiyoshi Kurosawa · *Scr* Kiyoshi Kurosawa, Sachiko Tanaka, Max Mannix

Tokyo Story ★★★★★ U

Drama 1953 · Jpn · BW · 129min

Yasujiro Ozu was a master film-maker who specialised in the kind of middle-class family melodrama known in Japanese as *shomin-geki*, and this one of his finest achievements. Chishu Ryu and Chieko Higashiyama give performances of great dignity as the parents who are rejected by their thankless children. Setsuko Hara, playing the widow of their favourite son, is the epitome of gentleness as the only relative to show them any kindness. Ryu and Hara were regular members of Ozu's acting troupe, and Hara retired from films when the director died in 1963. DP Japanese +subtitles. *DVD* *BL*

Chishu Ryu *Shukishi Hirayama* · Chieko Higashiyama *Tomi Hirayama* · Setsuko Hara *Noriko* · So Yamamura *Koichi* · Haruko Sugimura *Shige Kaneko* · Kuniko Miyake *Koichi's wife, Fumiko* ■ *Dir* Yasujiro Ozu · *Scr* Kogo Noda, Yasujiro Ozu

Tokyo Tribe ★★★★ 18

Science-fiction musical drama 2014 · Jpn · Colour · 116min

Near future Tokyo is the site of street gang warfare in an all-out exploitation movie that tells much of its story through Japanese rap. A daunting task for the subtitling unit, but a challenge, too, for writer/director Sion Sono, who unleashes gratuitous nudity and violence from the outset, but still manages to keep the mischief fresh and frisky. Evidently, Sono's hyper-kinetic hijinks will not be to all tastes, but this promises and delivers a quintessentially Japanese level of insanity. TJ Japanese +subtitles. Violence, swearing, sex scenes, nudity. *DVD* *BL*

Ryohei Suzuki *Mera* · Young Dais *Kai* · Nana Seino *Sunmi* · Riki Takeuchi *Buppa* ■ *Dir* Sion Sono · *Scr* Sion Sono, from the *manga Tokyo Tribe 2* by Santa Inoue

Tokyo Twilight ★★★★★★

Drama 1957 · Jpn · BW · 139min

Yasujiro Ozu's sublime, unassuming genius concerns itself with lower middle-class family life, as a microcosm of society. Stories may smack of melodrama or "soap," but there is no heightened drama or artificiality, simply snatches of conversation stemming from characters and reflections of the sometimes violent aspects of family relationships. In this intense, naturalistic work, he presents a portrait of two daughters living with their father – one in exile from an abusive husband, the other involved in an unhelpful relationship that has lead to pregnancy. The narrative is complicated by the unanticipated return of the family's mother, who had eloped with another man, resulting in distress and decline. BB Japanese +subtitles. *DVD*

Setsuko Hara *Takako Numata* · Isuzu Yamada *Kisako Soma* · Ineko Arima *Akiko Sugiyama* · Chishu Ryu *Shukichi Sugiyama* · Masami Taura *Kenji Kimura* ■ *Dir* Yasujiro Ozu · *Scr* Yasujiro Ozu, Kogo Noda

Tol'able David ★★★★

Silent melodrama 1921 · US · BW · 118min

One of the best of Henry King's simple, nostalgic evocations of rural and small town America, the film gave 26-year-old Richard Barthelmess his finest role. He plays a gentle mailman living happily in Greenstream Valley until his idyll is disturbed by a family of fugitives from justice. He defends the community, becomes a hero and wins the girl. Beautifully shot on location in the Virginia mountains. RB

Richard Barthelmess *David Kinemon* · Gladys Hulette *Esther Hatburn* · Walter P Lewis *Iscah Hatburn* · Ernest Torrence *Luke Hatburn* · Ralph Yearsley *Luke's brother* · Forrest Robinson *Grandpa Hatburn* ■ *Dir* Henry King · *Scr* Edmund Goulding, Henry King, from the short story by Joseph Hergesheimer · *Cinematographer* Henry Cronjager

Tollbooth ★★★★ 15

Comedy drama 1994 · US · Colour · 104min

This bona-fide "sleeper" of a movie all but disappeared after making quite a splash at Cannes 1994. In this dark, comic fable of Florida roadside life, Fairuza Balk is Doris, who has been waiting 20 years for her father, a cab driver, to return home. Her mother, Louise Fletcher, also awaits his return, though it transpires he was quite an unsavoury character. Balk's boyfriend, Lenny Von Dohlen, is a tollbooth attendant who takes snapshots of every cab to pass through the booth, determined to locate her father. The story, however, is secondary to the quirky style of the piece and director Salome Breziner serves up a sizzling slice of dysfunctional life. DF Swearing, violence. *DVD*

Fairuza Balk *Doris* · Lenny Von Dohlen *Jack* · Will Patton *Dash* · Louise Fletcher *Lillian* · Seymour Cassel *Larry/Leon* · James Wilder *Vic* · William Katt *Waggy* · Roberta Hanley *Twyla* ■ *Dir/Scr* Salome Breziner

Tom and Huck ★★★ PG

Adventure 1995 · US · Colour · 88min

This is yet another adaptation of Mark Twain's classic story of the Missouri scamps who witness a graveyard killing and get caught up in the subsequent wrongful arrest and court case. Brad Renfro is a suitably mischievous Huck, but it's Jonathan Taylor Thomas who makes the better impression as the more responsible Tom Sawyer. Disney take typical care with the trappings, but Norman Taurog's 1938 version (*The Adventures of Tom Sawyer*) remains the best one to date. DP

Jonathan Taylor Thomas *Tom Sawyer* · Brad Renfro *Huck Finn* · Eric Schweig *Injun Joe* · Charles Rocket *Judge Thatcher* · Amy Wright *Aunt Polly* · Micheal McShane *Muff Potter* · Marian Seldes *Widow Douglas* · Rachael Leigh Cook *Becky Thatcher* ■ *Dir* Peter Hewitt · *Scr* Stephen Sommers, David Loughery, from the novel *The Adventures of Tom Sawyer* by Mark Twain

Tom and Jerry: the Movie ★★ U

Animation 1992 · US · Colour · 80min

Having starred in 161 cartoons, won numerous Oscars and danced with Gene Kelly and Esther Williams, surely Tom and Jerry deserved more respect than this. Director Phil Roman and writer Dennis Marks should have Spike the bulldog set upon them for making the now-talking duo become friends in adversity. The whole point of those marvellous shorts was the comic mayhem, not the tacky bonhomie. Children who are not familiar with the original cartoons may find some enjoyment here - if they can get past the ghastly songs. DP

Richard Kind *Tom* · Dana Hill *Jerry* · Anndi Lynn McAfee [Anndi McAfee] *Robyn Starling* · Charlotte Rae *Aunt Figg* · Tony Jay *Lickboot* · Henry Gibson *Dr Applecheek* ■ *Dir* Phil Roman · *Scr* Dennis Marks, from characters by William Hanna, Joseph Barbera

Tom & Thomas ★★ PG

Drama 2002 · Neth/UK · Colour · 106min

With a sinister institution and a case of mistaken identity at its centre, Dutch director Esmé Lammers's movie is pitched somewhere between a Victorian melodrama and a Children's Film Foundation adventure. Aaron Johnson gives an energetic performance as the young son of pre-occupied artist Sean Bean, whose conviction that he has a double is proven when he stumbles upon the child-smuggling ring operating out of Derek de Lint's supposedly respectable orphanage. Cynical teens are going to see through the plot's transparent contrivances, but younger viewers might just get caught up in the nocturnal careerings around an inhospitably wintry London. DP

Sean Bean *Paul Sheppard* · Aaron Johnson *Tom/Thomas* · Inday Ba *Celia Scofield* · Sean Harris *Kevin* · Geraldine James *Miss Tromp* ■ *Dir/Scr* Esmé Lammers

Tom & Viv ★★★ 15

Biographical drama 1994 · US/UK · Colour · 119min

Willem Dafoe stars as Tom, otherwise known as the poet TS Eliot, and Miranda Richardson plays Viv, the society girl who marries him and ends up in a lunatic asylum. While she lets rip with a suitable display of madness, Dafoe behaves quietly and poetically, before locking her up and getting out his pen. Well done, although It often looks and sounds like a play, which it was. AT Swearing. *BL*

Miranda Richardson *Vivienne Haigh-Wood* · Willem Dafoe *TS "Tom" Eliot* · Tim Dutton *Maurice Haigh-Wood* · George Bertrand Russell · Clare Holman *Louise Purdon* · Rosemary Harris *Rose Haigh-Wood* · Philip Locke *Charles Haigh-Wood* · Joanna McCallum *Virginia Woolfe* ■ *Dir* Brian Gilbert · *Scr* Michael Hastings, Adrian Hodges, from the play by Michael Hastings

Tom at the Farm ★★★ 15

Drama 2013 · Can/Fr · Colour · 98min

In this foreboding drama, precocious 24-year-old writer/director Xavier Dolan (*Laurence Anyways*) also plays Tom, a shaggy-haired, confused young man who arrives at the Quebec farm owned by the family of his recently deceased male lover. It's gnarly, intriguing fare, as secrets emerge on all sides, and Dolan makes effective use of a Hitchcockian score by Gabriel Yared to add the brooding atmosphere of a vintage thriller. Yet the direction takes a misstep by withholding information to create a greater sense of mystery. The effect is somewhat exasperating, making the movie less satisfying than it might have been. TJ French +subtitles. Violence, swearing, sexual references, drug abuse. *DVD* *BL*

Xavier Dolan *Tom* · Pierre-Yves Cardinal *Francis* · Lise Roy *Agathe* · Evelyne Brochu *Sara* · Caleb Landry Jones *Guillaume* ■ *Dir* Xavier Dolan · *Scr* Xavier Dolan [Xavier Dolan-Tadros], Michel Marc Bouchard, from Bouchard's play *Tom à la ferme*

Tom Brown's Schooldays ★★ U

Drama 1940 · US · BW · 81min

Rugby School relocates to the Bowery for this RKO adaptation of Thomas Hughes's novel. This is more about taming street urchins than reforming the iniquities of 19th-century public schooling, a fact confirmed by the presence of Dead End Kid Billy Halop as Flashman. Oozing with liberal sentimentality, the script emphasises the saintly deeds of Cedric Hardwicke's Dr Arnold, rather than the suffering of our hero. Of the boys, Freddie Bartholomew is less Fauntleroyish than usual, while Jimmy Lydon is out of his depth as Tom. DP

Cedric Hardwicke *Dr Thomas Arnold* · Freddie Bartholomew *East* · Jimmy Lydon [James Lydon] *Tom Brown* · Josephine Hutchinson *Mrs Arnold* · Billy Halop *Flashman* ■ *Dir* Robert Stevenson · *Scr* Walter Ferris, Frank Cavett, Gene Towne, Graham Baker, Robert Stevenson, from the novel by Thomas Hughes

Tom Brown's Schooldays ★★★ U

Drama 1951 · UK · BW · 94min

Shot on location at Rugby School, this is a reverential, if rather lacklustre, rendition of Thomas Hughes's famous portrait of public school life. Robert Newton gives a performance of almost saintly sincerity as the headmaster intent on ridding his school of class prejudice and bullying. John Howard Davies gives a nice line in smiling through the tears as Tom Brown, but the film belongs squarely to John Forrest, who, as Flashman, is the epitome of vicious snobbery. DP

John Howard Davies *Tom Brown* · Robert Newton *Doctor Arnold* · Diana Wynyard *Mrs Arnold* · Hermione Baddeley *Sally Harrowell* · Kathleen Byron *Mrs Brown* · James Hayter *Old Thomas* · John Charlesworth *East* · John Forrest *Flashman* · Michael Hordern *Wilkes* · Max Bygraves *Coach guard* ■ *Dir* Gordon Parry · *Scr* Noel Langley, from the novel by Thomas Hughes

Tom, Dick and Harry ★★★ U

Comedy 1941 · US · BW · 82min

Ginger Rogers has to choose between the three characters of the title, but her character's rather mercenary nature makes her hard to like. Will she marry for love or money or both. In fact, the bloke we end up rooting for is Phil Silvers's obnoxious ice-cream man, a clear precursor of Sergeant Bilko. With hindsight, perhaps writer Paul Jarrico, was trying to make some pertinent points about capitalism (he was later blacklisted), but director Garson Kanin just keeps the pace fast and the laughter flowing. Remade in 1957 as *The Girl Most Likely*. TS

Ginger Rogers *Janie* · George Murphy *Tom* · Alan Marshal *Dick Hamilton* · Burgess Meredith *Harry* · Joe Cunningham *Pop* · Jane Seymour (1)

T

Ma • Leonore Lonergan *Babs* • Vicki Lester *Paula* • Phil Silvers *Ice Cream Man* ■ *Dir* Garson Kanin • *Scr* Paul Jarrico

Tom Horn ★★★ 15
Biographical western 1980 · US · Colour · 93min

Steve McQueen stars in his penultimate film as the notorious cavalry scout-turned-bounty hunter. Hired by a rancher to put a stop to local rustling, Horn's violent methods soon alienate the cattlemen who decide to take action. This western is a good deal better than it deserves to be, given that McQueen fell out with the credited, relatively inexperienced director William Wiard, and the shoot was ramshackle, with pages of the script discarded daily. Nevertheless, this is well photographed (by John Alonzo), and McQueen captures the grim, realistic mood perfectly. TS Swearing. DVD

Steve McQueen (1) *Tom Horn* • Linda Evans *Glendolene Kimmel* • Richard Farnsworth *John Coble* • Billy Green Bush *Joe Belle* • Slim Pickens *Sam Creedmore* ■ *Dir* William Wiard • *Scr* Thomas McGuane, Bud Shrake

Tom Jones ★★★★ PG
Period comedy adventure 1963 · UK · Colour · 123min

This massively popular period romp carted off four Oscars, including best picture and best director. It was always arch, overlong and uncertain of tone, but nevertheless very funny and extraordinarily bawdy, especially in the notorious eating scene between Albert Finney (as Tom) and Joyce Redman. Technically, the film was massively influential and the desaturated colour, speeded-up action and lewd narration characterised the 1960s "Swinging England" cinema, and attracted all of the Hollywood majors to come and make movies here. TS DVD

Albert Finney *Tom Jones* • Susannah York *Sophie Western* • Hugh Griffith *Squire Western* • Edith Evans *Miss Western* • Diane Cilento *Molly Seagrim* • George Devine *Squire Allworthy* • David Warner *Blifil* • Lynn Redgrave *Susan* ■ *Dir* Tony Richardson • *Scr* John Osborne, from the novel *The History of Tom Jones, a Foundling* by Henry Fielding

Tom Sawyer ★★★
Adventure 1930 · US · BW · 85min

The first of several sound versions of Mark Twain's novel – it was filmed as a silent in 1917 with Mary Pickford's brother, Jack, in the title role. In this version, Jackie Coogan plays Tom and at the age of only 16 it marked his screen comeback, for he had not made a film for three years. Huck Finn is played by Junior Durkin and both lads starred in the sequel, *Huckleberry Finn*, the following year. Off the set they were firm friends, but tragedy struck in 1935 when Durkin was killed in a car crash and Coogan was the only survivor. AT

Jackie Coogan *Tom Sawyer* • Junior Durkin *Huckleberry Finn* • Mitzi Green *Becky Thatcher* • Lucien Littlefield *Teacher* • Tully Marshall *Muff Potter* • Clara Blandick *Aunt Polly* • Mary Jane Irving *Mary* • Ethel Wales *Mrs Harper* • Jane Darwell *Widow Douglass* ■ *Dir* John Cromwell • *Scr* Sam Mintz, Grover Jones, William Slavens McNutt, from the novel *The Adventures of Tom Sawyer* by Mark Twain

Tom Sawyer ★★★★ U
Musical period adventure 1973 · US · Colour · 102min

Co-financed by *Reader's Digest*, this is a simply marvellous children's version of Mark Twain's oft-filmed classic about two orphaned chillun – Tom and his pal, Huckleberry Finn – and life on the Mississippi riverbanks. All the famous scenes – like Tom's painting of the picket fence and the nocturnal body-snatching – are filmed just as they are described in the book. There are some dispensable songs, but what counts is the beautifully evocative photography, two nicely modulated juvenile performances and Warren Oates enjoying himself as the local drunkard. *Reader's Digest* also produced *Huckleberry Finn*, released the following year. AT

Johnny Whitaker *Tom Sawyer* • Celeste Holm *Aunt Polly* • Warren Oates *Muff Potter* • Jeff East *Huckleberry Finn* • Jodie Foster *Becky Thatcher* • Kunu Hank *Injun Joe* • Lucille Benson *Widder Douglas* • Henry Jones *Mr Dobbins* ■ *Dir* Don Taylor • *Scr* Robert B Sherman, Richard M Sherman, from the novel *The Adventures of Tom Sawyer* by Mark Twain • *Cinematographer* Frank Stanley

tom thumb ★★★★ U
Fantasy musical 1958 · US/UK · Colour · 95min

The endearing and enduring MGM musical fantasy version of the Brothers Grimm fairy tale, made by Puppetoon king and special effects wizard George Pal, and partly shot at MGM's British studios. Technically this is a treat, with wonderfully acrobatic dancer Russ Tamblyn perfectly cast as the minuscule hero who brings joy to his elderly parents (Bernard Miles and Jessie Matthews). The production sequences are splendid entertainment for children of all ages, and Peter Sellers and Terry-Thomas make a very hissable pair of pantomime villains. The effects won an Oscar. TS

Russ Tamblyn *Tom Thumb* • Alan Young *Woody the piper* • Terry-Thomas *Ivan* • Peter Sellers *Tony* • Jessie Matthews *Anna* • June Thorburn *Forest Queen* • Bernard Miles *Jonathan* • Ian Wallace *Cobbler* • Peter Butterworth *Kapellmeister* ■ *Dir* George Pal • *Scr* Ladislas Foder, from the story by the Brothers Grimm

Tomahawk ★★★
Western 1951 · US · Colour · 82min

Following the critical acclaim for 1950's *Broken Arrow*, Hollywood sought to present the native American in a more positive light. But, as this tale of betrayal and slaughter shows, old habits die hard and even though director George Sherman emphasises the treachery of various soldiers, traders and politicians, the Sioux are once again depicted as savage warriors. Peace-loving scout Van Heflin reveals a more liberal attitude, but even he is more interested in the firepower of the new breach-loading rifle than race relations. DP

Van Heflin *Jim Bridger* • Yvonne De Carlo *Julie Madden* • Preston Foster *Col Carrington* • Jack Oakie *Sol Beckworth* • Alex Nicol *Lt Rob Dancy* • Tom Tully *Dan Costello* • Ann Doran *Mrs Carrington* • Rock Hudson *Burt Hanna* • Susan Cabot *Monahseetah* ■ *Dir* George Sherman • *Scr* Silvia Richards, Maurice Geraghty, from a story by Daniel Jarrett

The Tomb of Ligeia ★★★★ 12
Horror 1964 · UK · Colour · 78min

Stunningly photographed by Arthur Grant at an ancient Norfolk abbey, the last in Roger Corman's celebrated Edgar Allan Poe cycle is one of the best. Set in England in the 1820s, the film departs somewhat from Poe's original tale, but there's a distinct chill in the air as Vincent Price believes his new bride has been possessed by the evil spirit of his late first wife (both played by Elizabeth Shepherd). With more than a nod in the direction of Hitchcock's *Vertigo* (both in terms of theme and dénouement), this stylish picture also marked Corman's temporary retirement as a horror director until *Frankenstein Unbound* in 1990. DP DVD

Vincent Price *Verden Fell* • Elizabeth Shepherd *Lady Ligeia Fell/Lady Rowena Trevanion* • John Westbrook *Christopher Gough* • Oliver Johnston *Kenrick* • Derek Francis *Lord Trevanion* • Richard Vernon *Dr Vivian* ■ *Dir* Roger Corman • *Scr* Robert Towne, from the story *Ligeia* by Edgar Allan Poe

Tomboy ★★★★ U
Drama 2011 · Fr · Colour · 78min

A little girl decides she'd rather be a little boy in this engrossing French drama from director Céline Sciamma. When ten-year-old Laure (Zoé Héran) and her family move into a new apartment block, she takes advantage of her svelte physique to introduce herself to the neighbourhood kids as "Michaël". Astonishingly natural performances from the young cast are the keynote here, and the androgynous Héran is utterly believable at the centre of a film

that conjures up wit, suspense and pathos from its keenly observed chronicle of the tricky pathway from childhood to adolescence. TJ French +subtitles. DVD

Zoé Héran *Laure/Michaël* • Malonn Lévana *Jeanne* • Jeanne Disson *Lisa* • Sophie Cattani *Mother* • Mathieu Demy *Father* ■ *Dir/Scr* Céline Sciamma

Tombstone ★★★★ 15
Western 1993 · US · Colour and BW · 124min

Right from the dazzling opening of Robert Mitchum narrating over silent, black-and-white western footage accompanied by Bruce Broughton's expectant score, before the screen explodes into colour, this take on the Wyatt Earp legend never shifts out of top gear. This is very much a traditional western and an interesting contrast to the Kevin Costner version, *Wyatt Earp*, released later the same year. Kurt Russell makes a satisfyingly equivocal hero, while Val Kilmer has a field day in the showier role as the consumptive Doc Holliday. The film was sharply scripted by Kevin Jarre, who was sacked as director and replaced by George Pan Cosmatos. AT Swearing, violence. DVD

Kurt Russell *Wyatt Earp* • Val Kilmer *Doc Holliday* • Sam Elliott *Virgil Earp* • Bill Paxton *Morgan Earp* • Powers Boothe *Curly Bill Brocius* • Michael Biehn *Johnny Ringo* • Charlton Heston *Henry Hooker* • Jason Priestley *Deputy Sheriff Billy Breckenridge* • Robert Mitchum *Narrator* ■ *Dir* George Pan Cosmatos • *Scr* Kevin Jarre

Tomcats ★★ 15
Comedy 2000 · US · Colour · 90min

This crude, obnoxious comedy piles on gross-out humour, but mostly leaves a sour taste in the mouth. Heavily in debt to a Las Vegas gangster, Jerry O'Connell resorts to nefarious means to pocket the cash prize that will be awarded to the last single man among his friends. There's lots of surreal, cartoonish slapstick moments and no sick stone is left unturned. However, even with a game cast and a parade of fantasy women, there are far more misses than hits. JC DVD

Jerry O'Connell *Michael Delaney* • Shannon Elizabeth *Natalie Parker* • Jake Busey *Kyle Brenner* • Horatio Hanz *Steve* • Jaime Pressly *Tricia* • Bill Maher *Carlos* • David Ogden Stiers *Dr Crawford* ■ *Dir/Scr* Gregory Poirier

Tommy ★★★ 15
Musical 1975 · UK · Colour · 106min

The Who's rock opera, about "a deaf, dumb and blind kid" who becomes an exploited "pinball wizard", gets the inimitable Ken Russell treatment, which is no more than it deserves. For, while eye-popping excess – what's done to Ann-Margret is unforgivable – keeps us watching, the story is as absurd as the grotesque nature of its telling. Stridency, both vocal and visual, is all, and Roger Daltrey's Tommy is flattened by the weight of celebrity. Elton John has the best of it, thumping away on a piano as though trying to prove something, rather like Ken Russell himself. TH DVD

Roger Daltrey *Tommy Walker* • Oliver Reed *Frank Hobbs* • Ann-Margret *Nora Walker Hobbs* • Elton John *Pinball Wizard* • Eric Clapton *Preacher* • Keith Moon *Uncle Ernie* • Jack Nicholson *Specialist* • Robert Powell *Group Captain Walker* • Paul Nicholas *Cousin Kevin* • Tina Turner *Acid Queen* ■ *Dir* Ken Russell • *Scr* Ken Russell, from the rock opera by Pete Townsend and the Who • *Cinematographers* Dick Bush, Ronnie Taylor

Tommy Boy ★★★ 12
Comedy 1995 · US · Colour · 93min

Chris Farley's tragic career closely mirrored that of John Belushi's: fame on *Saturday Night Live*, an aversion to healthy pursuits and a young death at the age of 33. But he never had the *Blues Brothers* or *Animal House*-style success of his more famous contemporary, and most of his films disappeared quickly from view. This is about the best of the bunch: a big, dumb comedy about Farley's attempts to save the family business from gold-digger Bo Derek. Subtle

it ain't, but there are enough gross moments to raise a few laughs. JF DVD

Chris Farley *Tommy* • David Spade *Richard* • Brian Dennehy *Big Tom* • Bo Derek *Beverly* • Dan Aykroyd *Zalinsky* • Julie Warner *Michelle* • Rob Lowe *Paul* ■ *Dir* Peter Segal • *Scr* Bonnie Turner, Terry Turner, Fred Wolf

The Tommy Steele Story ★★ U
Musical biography 1957 · UK · Colour · 77min

Who else would have been able to carry the life story (such as it was after 21 years) of Britain's first rock 'n' roll star, Tommy Steele, but the Bermondsey boy himself? Following young Tommy Hicks from his humble beginnings, through his days at sea to the contract with Decca and that breakthrough single *Rock with the Caveman*, this is an unremarkable meteoric rise story, not made any easier to swallow by Steele's swaggering performance. DP

Tommy Steele *Tommy* • Patrick Westwood *Brushes* • Hilda Fenemore *Tommy's mother* • Charles Lamb *Tommy's father* • Peter Lewiston *John Kennedy* ■ *Dir* Gerard Bryant • *Scr* Norman Hudis

Tommy the Toreador ★★★ U
Musical comedy 1959 · UK · Colour · 83min

Perky pop star Tommy Steele, a former seaman himself, plays the part of a sailor in this lively and likeable musical comedy. The film concerns Steele's adventures after he saves the life of a bullfighter while on leave in Spain. Comic consequences include Tommy having to take the toreador's place and confronting a bull in the ring. A nice variety of songs intersperse the events. TV

Tommy Steele *Tommy* • Janet Munro *Amanda* • Sidney James *Cadena* • Bernard Cribbins *Paco* • Kenneth Williams *Vice Consul* • Eric Sykes *Martin* • Warren Mitchell *Waiter* • Charles Gray *Gomez* ■ *Dir* John Paddy Carstairs • *Scr* Nicholas Phipps, Sid Colin, Talbot Rothwell, from a story by George H Brown, Patrick Kirwan

Tommy Tricker and the Stamp Traveller ★ U
Fantasy 1988 · Can · Colour · 101min

After classmate Tommy Tricker swindles him into trading his father's rare stamp, a boy sets off on a magical journey halfway around the world to find a replacement using a magic spell that enables him to travel on stamps. More than half of this excruciatingly slow movie goes by before the journey actually starts, and the on-location shooting in China and Australia is remarkably uninspired. Even for such a young cast, the acting is remarkably poor. KB

Lucas Evans *Ralph* • Anthony Rogers *Tommy* • Jill Stanley *Nancy* • Andrew Whitehead *Albert* ■ *Dir/Scr* Michael Rubbo

Tommy's Honour ★★★
Sports drama based on a true story 2016 · UK · Colour · 117min

A strained father-son relationship is at the centre of this modest sporting drama set during the early days of professional golf. Based on a true story, it begins in the 1860s, with Peter Mullan and Jack Lowden as respectively the respectful greenkeeper and the caddie who would really rather be playing himself. With Lowden challenging the established order, this is where the film works best, as the class struggles create more drama than the golf matches. It's a well-acted, perfectly enjoyable film – in golfing terms, it's a par. SC

Peter Mullan *Tom Morris Sr* • Jack Lowden *Tom Morris Jr* • Sam Neill *Alexander Boothby* • Ophelia Lovibond *Meg Drinnen* • Peter Ferdinando *Major Molesworth* ■ *Dir* Jason Connery • *Scr* Pamela Marin, Kevin Cook, from Kevin Cook's non-fiction book

Tomorrow ★★★★
Drama 1972 · US · BW · 103min

Has Robert Duvall ever made a truly bad film? If so, this isn't it. Instead, it's Duvall firing on all cylinders in a fine adaptation of a lesser-known William Faulkner story. He plays a handyman who falls for a pregnant woman who mysteriously turns up at his place of work. The girl is played equally brilliantly by Olga Bellin, who seems to have since vanished without trace. Like her, the film is rarely seen, but worth seeking out. **DA**

Robert Duvall *Jackson Fentry* • Olga Bellin *Sarah Eubanks* • Sudie Bond *Mrs Hulie* • Richard McConnell *Isham Russell* • Peter Masterson *Lawyer* • William Hawley *Papa Fentry* ▪ *Dir* Joseph Anthony • *Scr* Horton Foote, from a story by William Faulkner

Tomorrow at Ten ★★★

Crime drama   1962 · UK · BW · 80min

This modest little thriller managed to secure a grade A cast, but was still released as a B-feature. Rank regular John Gregson is the cop sorting out a nasty child kidnapping case involving a ruthless bomber. The bad guy is *Jaws*'s Robert Shaw (before he became an international star), while theatre actor Alec (father of Martin) Clunes plays the father of the kidnap victim. Veteran British director Lance Comfort expertly translates the workmanlike script, and the support cast contains many familiar faces. **TS**

John Gregson *Inspector Parnell* • Robert Shaw *Marlow* • Alec Clunes *Anthony Chester* • Alan Wheatley *Bewley* • Kenneth Cope *Sergeant Grey* • Ernest Clark *Doctor Towers* • Piers Bishop *Jonathan* • Helen Cherry *Robbie* • William Hartnell *Freddy* ▪ *Dir* Lance Comfort • *Scr* Peter Millar, James Kelly

Tomorrow Is Forever ★★

Drama   1945 · US · BW · 103min

This hackneyed melodrama, directed at a deadly tempo by Irving Pichel, stars Claudette Colbert as a Baltimore chemist who, after her husband Orson Welles is reported killed in the First World War, is taken in by her boss George Brent, whom she eventually marries. Many years later, when Brent imports a limping, heavily-bearded scientist from Austria to work for him, guess who he turns out to be? The most interesting aspect of this below average "woman's picture" is the early appearance of six-year-old Natalie Wood as Colbert's daughter. **RK**

Claudette Colbert *Elizabeth MacDonald Hamilton* • Orson Welles *John MacDonald/Erich Kessler* • George Brent *Larry Hamilton* • Lucile Watson *Aunt Jessie Hamilton* • Richard Long *John Andrew "Drew" Hamilton* • Natalie Wood *Margaret* ▪ *Dir* Irving Pichel • *Scr* Lenore Coffee, from a novel by Gwen Bristow

Tomorrow Never Comes

★★★ 15

Crime drama   1977 · Can/UK · Colour · 102min

In this violent thriller, Stephen McHattie discovers his former girlfriend Susan George is seeing another man and takes her hostage. Oliver Reed is the police lieutenant given the job of breaking the siege. Peter Collinson directs with a sharp eye for the unsavoury detail, while Pinewood writing stalwarts Sydney Banks, David Pursall and Jack Seddon plumb the depths of seediness rather than character. **TH** **DVD**

Oliver Reed *Jim Wilson* • Susan George *Janie* • Raymond Burr *Burke* • John Ireland *Captain* • Stephen McHattie *Frank* • Donald Pleasence *Dr Todd* • Paul Koslo *Willy* • John Osborne *Lyne* ▪ *Dir* Peter Collinson • *Scr* David Pursall, Jack Seddon, Sydney Banks

Tomorrow Never Dies

★★★★ 12

Spy adventure   1997 · US/UK · Colour · 114min

For the first hour or so, this 18th Bond movie is up there with the best of them: it has terrific pace, Pierce Brosnan has romantic and rough-house appeal, Teri Hatcher is a match for him, and the post-Cold War story has grip and even plausibility. Sadly, the second half doesn't quite sustain the momentum: the story moves from Europe to Asia and Jonathan Pryce's media mogul is an unthreatening villain whose motto is "There's no news like bad news". Flaws aside, this is still one of the best Bond movies since the days of

Sean Connery. **AT** Violence, swearing, sex. **DVD** **Blu**

Pierce Brosnan *James Bond* • Jonathan Pryce *Elliot Carver* • Michelle Yeoh *Wai Lin* • Teri Hatcher *Paris Carver* • Ricky Jay *Henry Gupta* • Götz Otto [Gotz Otto] *Stamper* • Joe Don Baker *Jack Wade* • Vincent Schiavelli *Dr Kaufman* • Judi Dench *"M"* • Desmond Llewelyn *"Q"* • Samantha Bond (2) *Miss Moneypenny* • Colin Salmon *Robinson – Chief of Staff* • Geoffrey Palmer *Admiral Roebuck* ▪ *Dir* Roger Spottiswoode • *Scr* Bruce Feirstein, from characters by Ian Fleming

Tomorrow We Live ★★★ U

Spy melodrama   1942 · UK · BW · 87min

In the darkest days of the Second World War, dashing John Clements gets mixed up with French freedom fighters, and two women: Greta Gynt, seemingly pro-Nazi, and waitress Judy Kelly, who actually is hustling for the occupying forces. *Casablanca* this isn't: it is, however, packed with action, and Clements is excellent in what today seems like a rather obvious piece of propaganda – unsurprising, really, since it was produced by British Aviation Films. **TS**

John Clements *Jean Batiste* • Godfrey Tearle *The Mayor* • Hugh Sinclair *Major Von Kleist* • Greta Gynt *Marie Duschen* • Judy Kelly *Germaine* • Yvonne Arnaud *Madame Labouche* • Karel Stepanek *Seitz* • Herbert Lom ▪ *Dir* George King • *Scr* Anatole de Grunwald, from a story by Dorothy Hope

Tomorrow, When the War Began ★★★ 12

Action adventure   2010 · Aus/US · Colour · 99min

This accomplished action flick, based on a bestselling Australian series of young adult novels, riffs on the same premise that drove John Milius's Reagan-era hit *Red Dawn* – teenagers take up arms against foreign invaders – but sensibly ditches the Commie-baiting and overblown flag-waving. Director Stuart Beattie knows his way around the action, and draws believable performances from his young cast. This was the highest-grossing Australian movie of 2010 and a sequel has already been given the green light. **JF** Some swearing, drug abuse. **DVD** **Blu**

Caitlin Stasey *Ellie Linton* • Rachel Hurd-Wood *Corrie McKenzie* • Lincoln Lewis *Kevin Holmes* • Deniz Akdeniz *Homer Yannos* • Phoebe Tonkin *Fiona Maxwell* ▪ *Dir* Stuart Beattie • *Scr* Stuart Beattie, from the novel by John Marsden

Tomorrowland: a World Beyond ★★★★ 12

Science-fiction mystery   2015 · US · Colour · 124min

As well as being a fun rollercoaster ride inspired by the Disney theme park, this totally beguiling, mind-bending trip is also a call to action for kids to take ownership of the future or else inherit a troubled planet. Among them is science buff Casey (Britt Robertson) who has a vision of a Jetsons-style futuristic utopia. There's also a bitter old inventor (a gruff George Clooney) who has had similar experiences. Director Brad Bird peels away the layers of a complex story – taking in time travel, environmental issues and the nature of reality – to reveal the bigger picture with lots of retro-cool stylings and eye-popping set pieces. Enlightening stuff for older children and it's a blast, too. **SP** **DVD** **Blu**

George Clooney *Frank Walker* • Britt Robertson [Brittany Robertson] *Casey Newton* • Raffey Cassidy *Athena* • Hugh Laurie *David Nix* • Thomas Robinson *Young Frank Walker* • Kathryn Hahn *Ursula* ▪ *Dir* Brad Bird • *Scr* Brad Bird, Damon Lindelof, from a story by Bird, Lindelof, Jeff Jensen

Tom's Midnight Garden

★★ PG

Fantasy adventure   1998 · US/UK/Jpn · Colour · 92min

This fantasy is unlikely to sustain the interests of children, while adults are unlikely to see it as anything other than a twee fable. Singer Anthony Way stars as a teenager who, during a summer stay with

his childless aunt and uncle, discovers that at midnight, the ugly area around the building turns into a magical garden inhabited by a lonely orphan from the previous century. Sadly the scenes between the children are unengaging, while the adults add no lustre to an overlong effort. **BB** **DVD**

Greta Scacchi *Aunt Gwen* • James Wilby *Uncle Alan Kitson* • Joan Plowright *Mrs Bartholomew* • Anthony Way *Tom* • David Bradley (2) *Abel* • Penelope Wilton *Aunt Melbourne* • Nigel Le Vaillant *Tom Long, as adult* • Liz Smith *Mrs Willows* • Florence Hoath *Hatty at 12* ▪ *Dir* Willard Carroll • *Scr* Willard Carroll, from the novel by Philippa Pearce

Toni ★★★★ PG

Romantic crime drama   1935 · Fr · BW · 81min

Jean Renoir's fact-based tale of marital angst (Charles Blavette takes the blame for his beloved's crime of passion) was a key influence on neorealism via one of Renoir's assistants, Luchino Visconti. Shooting exclusively on location in the Midi, with a predominantly non-professional cast, Renoir succeeds in marrying character and environment in a way that not only emphasises their nature and authenticity, but also defuses the more melodramatic aspects of the plot. Simple, sensual and woefully undervalued. **DP** In French. **DVD**

Charles Blavette *Antonio "Toni" Canova* • Célia Montalvan *Josepha* • Jenny Hélia *Marie* • Max Dalban *Albert* ▪ *Dir* Jean Renoir • *Scr* Jean Renoir, Carl Einstein, from an incident documented by Jacques Levert [Jacques Mortier]

Tonight and Every Night

★★★ U

Wartime romance   1945 · US · Colour · 88min

This is a tribute to Soho's Windmill Theatre (called the Music Box here), which claimed it never closed during the Blitz. Actually, it was more famous for its nude revues, although here the showgirls, including Rita Hayworth, keep well covered. Hayworth falls for pilot Lee Bowman and Janet Blair for dancer Marc Platt (a weak actor but a good dancer). The title number uses a trick of having the performers walking out of a film onto the stage. **RB**

Rita Hayworth *Rosalind "Roz" Bruce* • Lee Bowman *Paul Lundy* • Janet Blair *Judy Kane* • Marc Platt *Tommy Lawson* • Leslie Brooks *Angela* • Shelley Winters *Bubbles* ▪ *Dir* Victor Saville • *Scr* Lesser Samuels, Abem Finkel, from the play *Heart of the City* by Lesley Storm

Tonight for Sure! ★★

Erotic comedy western   1961 · US · Colour · 75min

Francis Ford Coppola's first movie – made while he was studying at UCLA – is a piece of audacity forgivable because of his youth. Don Kenney spies on women and Karl Schanzer imagines nude women everywhere. Not much evidence of Coppola's later talents, but interesting because of what was to come. **TH**

Don Kenney • Karl Schanzer • Virginia Gordon • Marli Renfro ▪ *Dir/Scr* Francis Coppola [Francis Ford Coppola]

Tonight We Sing ★★ U

Musical biography   1953 · US · Colour · 109min

Sol Hurok used his exceptional appreciation of musical talent to become the most famously dedicated, ambitious and successful of the American impresarios. What possessed 20th Century-Fox to cast the bloodless David Wayne as Hurok in this biopic, though, is something only the studio's late chiefs must know. The script, cobbled together from bits and pieces of Hurok's memoirs, is a similarly feeble affair, and Mitchell Leisen's direction is leaden. Fortunately, however, the film remains a feast of music. **RK**

David Wayne *Sol Hurok* • Ezio Pinza *Feodor Chaliapin* • Roberta Peters *Elsa Valdine* • Tamara Toumanova *Anna Pavlova* • Anne Bancroft *Emma Hurok* • Isaac Stern *Eugene Ysaye* ▪ *Dir* Mitchell Leisen • *Scr* Harry Kurnitz, George Oppenheimer, from a book by Sol Hurok, Ruth Goode

Tonite Let's All Make Love in London ★★★

Documentary   1967 · UK · BW and Colour · 69min

Director Peter Whitehead turns his camera on Swinging London – the era when Carnaby Street was the centre of the universe and even *Time* magazine featured it on the front cover. This documentary features some fascinating interviews with 1960s trendsetters such as Mick Jagger, Julie Christie, Michael Caine and David Hockney. No real conclusions are drawn, apart from Caine's prediction: "All this dolly-bird stuff won't matter a damn in ten years' time. It's on the way out already." **TH**

Michael Caine • Lee Marvin • Vanessa Redgrave • Mick Jagger • Julie Christie • David Hockney ▪ *Dir/Scr* Peter Whitehead

Tonka ★★★ U

Period adventure   1958 · US · Colour · 92min

This adventure set against the Sioux War arrived at a time when Hollywood was trying to make amends for its various injustices. Here Disney reverses a tendency towards negative portrayals of native American Indians, by casting Sal Mineo as a young Sioux tribesman who tames a wild, white horse he calls Tonka, only then for it to be taken away from him and sold to the cavalry, where it is renamed Comanche. **TH**

Sal Mineo *White Bull* • Philip Carey *Captain Miles Keogh* • Jerome Courtland *Lieutenant Henry Nowlan* • Rafael Campos *Strong Bear* • HM Wynant *Yellow Bull* • Joy Page *Prairie Flower* • Britt Lomond *General George Armstrong Custer* ▪ *Dir* Lewis R Foster • *Scr* Lewis R Foster, Lillie Hayward, from the novel *Comanche* by David Appel

Tony ★★★ 18

Thriller   2009 · UK · Colour · 72min

This micro-budget British shocker creates an absolutely convincing portrait of psychosis. Tony (Peter Ferdinando) is just another loner living anonymously in a scuzzy east London flat, but he harbours a dark secret. Driven by rage – and perhaps even sexual self-disgust – he's responsible for a series of brutal slayings on victims every bit as marginalised as himself. Echoing the Dennis Nilsen case and the grimy look of *Henry: Portrait of a Serial Killer*, Gerard Johnson's debut isn't the last word in originality. However, this film clearly has cult potential for those prepared to overlook the slightness of the plot. **TJ**

Peter Ferdinando *Tony* • Ricky Grover *Paul, Davey's dad* • Kerryann White *Lisa, Davey's mum* • Sam Kempster *Davey, boy* • George Russo *Mackey* • Francis Pope *Smudger* ▪ *Dir/Scr* Gerard Johnson

Tony Manero ★★★★ 18

Thriller   2008 · Bra/Chil · Colour · 93min

Set in Chile in 1978, as General Pinochet's reign of terror was plumbing new depths of barbaric depravity, this chilling study of monomania centres on shady 50-something Alfredo Castro's obsession with the character played by John Travolta in *Saturday Night Fever*. The action fluctuates between the bleakly comic and the sickeningly creepy, as director Pablo Larrain uses the grim reality and absurdist fantasy here to establish a metaphorical connection between Castro's dismal sex life, Pinochet's deluded self-image and the grotesque decrepitude of the country's infrastructure. **DP** Spanish +subtitles. Violence, swearing, sex scenes, nudity. **DVD**

Alfredo Castro *Raúl Peralta Paredes O* • Paola Lattus *Pauli* • Héctor Morales *Goyo* • Amparo Noguera *Cony* • Elsa Poblete *Wilma* ▪ *Dir* Pablo Larraín • *Scr* Alfredo Castro, Mateo Iribarren, Pablo Larrain

Tony Rome ★★★ 15

Detective thriller   1967 · US · Colour · 105min

Frank Sinatra always wanted to be Bogart, and here he successfully takes on his mantle of hard-boiled private eye à la Philip Marlowe or Sam Spade. This tough and nasty Miami-set thriller is a classy act, with

T

searing dialogue, a fine Billy May score and top-notch support from the likes of Richard Conte and Gena Rowlands. Director Gordon Douglas cleverly masks the fact that the plot is no great shakes, though it does bear comparison with *The Big Sleep*. Sinatra returned as Tony Rome in *Lady in Cement*. TS *DVD*

Frank Sinatra *Tony Rome* • Jill St John *Ann Archer* • Richard Conte *Lt Santini* • Gena Rowlands *Rita Kosterman* • Simon Oakland *Rudolph Kosterman* • Jeffrey Lynn *Adam Boyd* • Lloyd Bochner *Vic Rood* • Robert J Wilke *Ralph Turpin* • Rocky Graziano *Packy* ■ *Dir* Gordon Douglas • *Scr* Richard L Breen, from the novel *Miami Mayhem* by Anthony Rome [Marvin H Albert]

Tony Takitani ★★★★ U
Drama 2004 · Jpn · Colour · 76min

Issey Ogata impresses alongside Rie Miyazawa (each taking dual roles) in this exquisite study of inhibited passion, misjudged obsession and lamented admonition. Based on Haruki Murakami's beguiling short story, it employs a third-person narration to tell the story of a lonely illustrator who advertises for a lookalike to wear his shopaholic wife's wardrobe. Director Jun Ichikawa makes sublime use of the camera and his leisurely lateral movements not only evoke Japanese scroll art, but also reinforce the titular character's feelings of regret. This melancholic paean to beauty is a bittersweet delight. DP Japanese +subtitles. *DVD*

Issey Ogata *Tony Takitani/Shozaburo Takitani* • Rie Miyazawa *Konuma Eiko/Hisako* • Shinohara Takahumi *Young Tony Takitani* • Hidetoshi Nishijima *Narrator* ■ *Dir* Jun Ichikawa • *Scr* Jun Ichikawa, from the short story by Haruki Murakami

Too Bad She's Bad ★★
Comedy 1955 · It · BW · 103min

Vittorio De Sica is a pickpocket who cajoles his beautiful daughter Sophia Loren into acting as his assistant. Complications arise when Loren, acting as a honey trap for a couple of crooks out to rob an honest cabbie, finds her own feelings start to stir when the taxi driver, Marcello Mastroianni, falls for her. A modest romantic comedy at best, it's notable as the first-time pairing of Loren and Mastroianni, and as the film where Loren first showed a penchant for comedy. DF Italian dubbed.

Sophia Loren *Lina* • Vittorio De Sica *Stroppiani* • Marcello Mastroianni *Paolo* • Umberto Melnati *Man whose wallet is stolen* • Margherita Bagni *His wife* ■ *Dir* Alessandro Blasetti • *Scr* Suso Cecchi D'Amico, Ennio Flaiano, Alessandro Continenza, from a story by Alberto Moravia

Too Big to Fail ★★★
Political drama 2011 · US · Colour · 98min

The US financial crisis of 2008 is put under the spotlight in this quality HBO movie from *LA Confidential* director Curtis Hanson. It charts the battle by US Treasury Secretary Henry Paulson (William Hurt) to save the economy from catastrophe by bailing out investment bank Lehman Brothers. Hanson's examination of the back-room machinations is thoroughly absorbing, even though it's a densely factual affair. Hurt gives a standout performance as the careworn Paulson, at the centre of an economic maelstrom. JA Swearing.

William Hurt *Henry Paulson* • Edward Asner *Warren Buffett* • Billy Crudup *Timothy Geithner* • Paul Giamatti *Ben Bernanke* • Topher Grace *Jim Wilkinson* • Matthew Modine *John Thain* ■ *Dir* Curtis Hanson • *Scr* Peter Gould, from the non-fiction book by Andrew Ross Sorkin

Too Hard to Die ★★18
Crime thriller 1998 · US · Colour · 88min

In the low-budget world of TV movies, you don't get much more of an A-list cast than this. Jeff Fahey, Michael Madsen and Gary Busey are the stars, and they're given fine support by Tim Thomerson and James Russo. The material itself is pretty standard stuff, concerning a plan to rob a Mob boss that goes badly wrong, but the direction from the less famous Travolta, John's brother Joey, is proficient enough, and the

actors can do crime thrillers in their sleep. SuR

Jeff Fahey *Danny Devlin* • Michael Madsen *Burl Rogers* • Gary Busey *Mo Ginsburg* • James Russo *Ziggy Rotella* • Tim Thomerson *Mel Kiner* ■ *Dir* Joey Travolta • *Scr* Raymond Martino, William Stroum

Too Hot to Handle ★★★★
Comedy adventure 1938 · US · BW · 105min

This is a hugely enjoyable three-hander from Clark Gable, Myrna Loy and Walter Pidgeon, in which Gable and Pidgeon play devil-may-care newsreel photographers vying for the attentions of feisty aviatrix Loy. Gable is in his element - charming, wry, raffish and risk-taking - and his spoof bombing raid into China is the film's *pièce de résistance*. Everything gels in this movie: the stars, the action scenes and a stylish, witty script. SH

Clark Gable *Chris Hunter* • Myrna Loy *Alma Harding* • Walter Pidgeon *Bill Dennis* • Walter Connolly *Gabby MacArthur* • Leo Carrillo *Joselito* • Virginia Weidler *Hulda Harding* • Henry Kolker *Pearly Todd* • Marjorie Main *Miss Wayne* ■ *Dir* Jack Conway • *Scr* Laurence Stallings, John Lee Mahin, from a story by Len Hammond

Too Hot to Handle ★★12
Crime thriller 1960 · UK · Colour · 87min

In 1960, British censors would tolerate a film about the new striptease sensation in London's Soho only if it depicted this world as thoroughly sordid. Consequently, in Terence Young's melodramatic thriller, the men are all corrupt, the women jaded or pathetic. Club owner Leo Genn knowingly fixes up underage stripper Barbara Windsor with a slimy patron. What busty blonde Jayne Mansfield is doing here is anyone's guess. This is wholly incredible - though often astonishing - nonsense. DM

Jayne Mansfield *Midnight Franklin* • Leo Genn *Johnny Solo* • Karlheinz Böhm *Robert Jouvel* • Danik Patisson *Lilliane Decker* • Christopher Lee Novak • Barbara Windsor *Pony Tail* ■ *Dir* Terence Young • *Scr* Herbert Kretzmer, from a story by Harry Lee

Too Hot to Handle ★★15
Comedy drama 1991 · US · Colour · 111min

Originally released as *The Marrying Man*, this Kim Basinger/Alec Baldwin comedy is a clunker under any name. The rumours of on-set battles between the leads and the producers were far more interesting than the story itself, which follows the on-off love affair in the 1940s between nightclub singer and gangster's moll Basinger and millionaire playboy Baldwin. Unfortunately, neither lead is a deft hand at comedy, and the humour in the script is not that strong either. JB Violence, swearing. *DVD*

Kim Basinger *Vicki Anderson* • Alec Baldwin *Charley Pearl* • Robert Loggia *Lew Horner* • Elisabeth Shue *Adele Horner* • Armand Assante *Bugsy Siegel* • Paul Reiser *Phil* • Fisher Stevens *Sammy* • Peter Dobson *Tony Madden* ■ *Dir* Jerry Rees • *Scr* Neil Simon

Too Late Blues ★★★12
Musical drama 1961 · US · BW · 100min

Director John Cassavetes, who had struck creative gold with the improvisational *Shadows*, tries to shoehorn his energy into a more conventional, plot-driven film. In this story about jazz pianist John "Ghost" Wakefield (Bobby Darin), notions about artistic commitment aren't fully explored. However, in the musician's brittle relationship with a neurotic aspiring singer (Stella Stevens) and his deteriorating relations with his band are well drawn. The music, blasted out by the likes of Benny Carter and Red Mitchell, is a five-star treat. JM *DVD* Blu

Bobby Darin *John "Ghost" Wakefield* • Stella Stevens *Jess Polanski* • Cliff Carnell *Charlie* • Seymour Cassel *Red* • Bill Stafford *Shelly* • Richard Chambers *Pete* • Nick Dennis *Nick* ■ *Dir* John Cassavetes • *Scr* John Cassavetes, Richard Carr

Too Late the Hero ★★★15
Second World War drama 1970 · US · Colour · 133min

This Second World War tale about male bonding is typical mid-career fare from director Robert Aldrich - exciting and violent, but rather too long - as soldiers Michael Caine and Cliff Robertson are dispatched on a suicide mission in the Pacific arena. This is entertaining, but with a bit of pruning it could have been even more so. TS Violence, swearing. *DVD*

Michael Caine *Private Tosh Hearne* • Cliff Robertson *Lieutenant Lawson* • Ian Bannen *Thornton* • Harry Andrews *Lt Col Thompson* • Denholm Elliott *Captain Hornsby* • Ronald Fraser *Campbell* • Lance Percival *Corporal Mclean* • Percy Herbert *Johnstone* • Henry Fonda *Captain Nolan* • Ken Takakura *Major Yamaguchi* ■ *Dir* Robert Aldrich • *Scr* Robert Aldrich, Lukas Heller, from the story by Robert Aldrich, Robert Sherman

Too Late to Say Goodbye ★★
Drama 2009 · US/Can · Colour · 86min

A deliciously villainous Rob Lowe is the draw for this otherwise undynamic true-crime tale based on Ann Rule's bestseller. Going from cocky and controlling to increasingly temperamental, he plays an Atlanta dentist whose perfect marriage is shown to be a sham when his wife, Jenn, apparently commits suicide. Naturally, the woman's sister (Lauren Holly) insists it was murder, resulting in a flimsy and contrived movie that's a mixture of dry police procedural and flashback-centred melodrama. But though the cops drag their heels, the audience will have solved the case immediately - despite deliberately distracting revelations about Jenn's secret online relationship. Consequently, what keeps you watching is the arrival of Lowe's comeuppance, as the truth finally leads to an emotional day in court. SF

Stefanie von Pfetten *Jenn Corbin* • Rob Lowe *Bart Corbin* • Lauren Holly *Heather* • Mary Ashton *Dolly Hearn* • Yannick Bisson *Bobby Corbin* ■ *Dir* Norma Bailey • *Scr* Fab Filippo, Donald Martin, from the novel by Ann Rule

Too Many Crooks ★★★U
Comedy 1958 · UK · BW · 81min

The cast is a who's who of British comedy and the script is by Michael Pertwee, but this picture never lives up to its billing, largely owing to the cack-handed direction of Mario Zampi. Terry-Thomas gives a priceless performance as the wheeler-dealer unconcerned whether he sees abducted wife Brenda de Banzie ever again, but George Cole, Sid James and the gang overdo the "cor blimey" criminality. DP *DVD*

Terry-Thomas *Billy Gordon* • George Cole *Fingers* • Brenda de Banzie *Lucy* • Bernard Bresslaw *Snowdrop* • Sidney James *Sid* • Joe Melia *Whisper* • Vera Day *Charmaine* • Delphi Lawrence *Beryl, secretary* • John Le Mesurier *Magistrate* • Nicholas Parsons *Tommy* ■ *Dir* Mario Zampi • *Scr* Michael Pertwee, from the story by Jean Nery, Christiane Rochefort

Too Many Girls ★★★U
Musical comedy 1940 · US · BW · 84min

This entertaining version of the hit show retains many of the original cast and is directed for the screen by the grand old man of Broadway himself, George Abbott. It's geared as a vehicle for Lucille Ball, who met future husband and business partner Desi Arnaz on set. Also having fun with what's left of the Rodgers and Hart score are Frances Langford and Ann Miller, and the movie also marks the debuts of stars-to-be Van Johnson and Eddie Bracken. The songs aren't vintage, but there's no denying the sheer verve of the piece. TS

Lucille Ball *Connie Casey* • Richard Carlson *Clint Kelly* • Ann Miller *Pepe* • Eddie Bracken *Jojo Jordan* • Frances Langford *Eileen Eilers* • Desi Arnaz *Manuelito* • Van Johnson *Chorus boy* ■ *Dir* George Abbott • *Scr* John Twist, from the stage musical by George Marion Jr, Richard Rodgers, Lorenz Hart

Too Many Husbands ★★★
Screwball comedy 1940 · US · BW · 81min

Mistakenly believed to have drowned in a shipwreck, Fred MacMurray finds his way home to discover that his wife (Jean Arthur) is now remarried. The two men vie for the right to "their" wife, who encourages and relishes their attentions, until the matter of where she belongs must be decided in court. Slight but neat romantic comedy, tailor-made for its star trio and directed with his habitual flair by Wesley Ruggles. Remade as a musical, *Three for the Show*, with Betty Grable in 1955. RK

Jean Arthur *Vicky Lowndes* • Fred MacMurray *Bill Cardew* • Melvyn Douglas *Henry Lowndes* • Harry Davenport *George* • Dorothy Peterson *Gertrude Houlihan* • Melville Cooper *Peter* • Edgar Buchanan *McDermott* ■ *Dir* Wesley Ruggles • *Scr* Claude Binyon, from the play by W Somerset Maugham

Too Much Johnson ★★★U
Silent comedy 1938 · US · BW · 67min

Three years before Orson Welles shook up the film world with *Citizen Kane*, the then 23-year-old directed this curio, believed lost until 2008. Essentially, it's an unfinished print intended as bridging material for a play by William Gillette (a renowned Sherlock Holmes on stage). A pastiche of silent comedy, it has Joseph Cotten, as the quarry of a moustache-twirling cuckold. What follows is a chase movie shot among the streets, rooftops and tenements of New York, with Cotten a comic revelation. JA *DVD* Blu

Joseph Cotten *Augustus Billings* • Virginia Nicolson *Lenore Faddish* • Edgar Barrier *Leon Dathis* • Arlene Francis *Mrs Clairette Dathis* • Ruth Ford *Mrs Billings* • Mary Wickes *Mrs Upton Battison* • Orson Welles *Keystone Kop* • Judy Holliday *Crowd member* ■ *Dir* Orson Welles • *Scr* Orson Welles, from William Gillette's play

Too Much Sun ★18
Comedy 1990 · US · Colour · 93min

Robert Downey Sr directs Junior in a totally tasteless farce about a multimillionaire, whose offspring must compete to produce an heir and inherit his fortune. The hitch is that the brother and sister are gay - cue much tasteless humour. This is laugh-an-hour stuff despite the best efforts of a cast which, in addition to Downey Jr, also features Ralph Macchio and veteran Howard Duff. DA

Robert Downey Jr *Reed Richmond* • Eric Idle *Sonny Rivers* • Andrea Martin *Bitsy Rivers* • Jim Haynie *Father Seamus Kelly* • Laura Ernst *Susan Connor* • Leo Rossi *George Bianco* • Ralph Macchio *Frank Della Rocca Jr* • Howard Duff *OM Rivers* ■ *Dir* Robert Downey Sr • *Scr* Robert Downey, Laura Ernst, Al Schwartz

Too Much, Too Soon ★★
Biographical drama 1958 · US · BW · 101min

The Barrymores were known as the Royal Family of Broadway, but the second generation did much to tarnish the reputation as this lacklustre biopic of Diana Barrymore reveals. Dorothy Malone is suitably downbeat as the daughter destroyed by the drinking of her famous father John, who is played with disturbing authenticity by Errol Flynn. Flynn makes the most of a disappointing script, but it was a sad farewell to Warners Bros, the studio where he had once been the king of the swashbucklers. DP

Dorothy Malone *Diana Barrymore* • Errol Flynn *John Barrymore* • Efrem Zimbalist Jr *Vincent Bryant* • Ray Danton *John Howard* • Neva Patterson *Michael Strange* • Murray Hamilton *Charlie Snow* • Martin Milner *Lincoln Forrester* ■ *Dir* Art Napoleon • *Scr* Art Napoleon, Jo Napoleon, from the autobiography by Diana Barrymore, Gerold Frank

Too Scared to Scream ★★18
Psychological thriller 1982 · US · Colour · 94min

Actor-turned-director Tony LoBianco's first-time slasher thriller has New York cops Mike Connors and Anne Archer investigate murders in a high-rise apartment block. Prime suspect is doorman Ian McShane, a bitter ex-actor eager to recite Shakespeare at the drop of a knife, who lives with his invalid mother Maureen O'Sullivan. Obvious red herrings defy the slow-building suspense but the cast brings a much needed zing to events. AJ

Mike Connors *Lieutenant Dinardo* • Anne Archer *Kate* • Leon Isaac Kennedy *Frank* • Ian McShane *Hardwick* • Ruth Ford *Irma* • John Heard *Lab technician* • Carrie Nye *Graziella* • Maureen O'Sullivan *Mother* ■ *Dir* Tony LoBianco • *Scr* Glenn Leopold, Neal Barbera

Too Soon to Love ★★★
Drama 1960 · US · BW · 89min

The first film directed by Richard Rush – one of a group of independent film-makers who formed an American version of the *nouvelle vague* – this tale of two teenage sweethearts driven by uncomprehending parents into a saga of unwanted pregnancy, abortion, robbery and attempted suicide, is better than it sounds and a social document of its time. Stars Jennifer West and Richard Evans had less than sparkling careers, but playing the hero's buddy is Jack Nicholson. TV

Jennifer West *Cathy Taylor* • Richard Evans *Jim Mills* • Warren Parker *Mr Taylor* • Ralph Manza *Hughie Wineman* • Jack Nicholson *Buddy* • Jacqueline Schwab *Irene* • Billie Bird *Mrs Jefferson* ■ *Dir* Richard Rush • *Scr* Laszlo Gorog, Richard Rush

The Toolbox Murders ★★18
Horror 1978 · US · Colour · 91min

This deranged "video nasty" gore classic is TV director Dennis Donnelly's only feature film. Cameron Mitchell chews the scenery as a homicidal landlord killing helpless female tenants with an imaginative array of power tools, screwdrivers and hammers. Brutal, prurient stuff, yet still remarkably dull, this is notorious for the sleazy sequence in which adult movie star Marianne Walter gets nail-gunned to death. AJ Violence, nudity. *DVD*

Cameron Mitchell *Kingsley* • Pamelyn Ferdin *Laurie Ballard* • Wesley Eure *Kent* • Nicolas Beauvy *Joey Ballard* • Aneta Corsaut [Aneta Corseaut] *JoAnn Ballard* • Tim Donnelly *Detective Jamison* • Marianne Walter *Dee Ann* ■ *Dir* Dennis Donnelly • *Scr* Robert Easter, Neva Friedenn, Ann N Kindberg [Ann N Kindberg]

Toolbox Murders ★★15
Horror 2003 · US/UK · Colour · 95min

Old-school exploitation gets an old-school reworking in this grimy chiller from director Tobe Hooper. Based on a 1970s slasher flick, this plays like a grindhouse sleaze-fest, with none of the precision or skill of Hooper's seminal classic *The Texas Chain Saw Massacre*. There's plenty of gore but very little else, as a ruthless psychopath picks off the residents of a decaying Hollywood apartment block with the contents of his toolbox. SF Swearing, violence. *DVD*

Angela Bettis *Nell Barrows* • Juliet Landau *Julia Cunningham* • Brent Roam *Steven Barrows* • Rance Howard *Chas "Jazz" Rooker* • Marco Rodriguez *Luis Saucedo* • Adam Gierasch *Ned Lundy* ■ *Dir* Tobe Hooper • *Scr* Jace Anderson, Adam Gierasch

Toomorrow ★★PG
Science-fiction musical 1970 · UK · Colour · 90min

Anthropologist Roy Dotrice is really an Alphoid alien in disguise whose Earth mission is to track down a "tonaliser" causing good vibrations on his planet. The instrument is the invention of Vic Cooper who, with fellow Chelsea art students Benny Thomas, Karl Chambers and Olivia Newton-John, has set up the pop group Toomorrow to earn money for college expenses. The group are whisked to his home planet to add soul to their out-of-tune computerised music. A lightweight musical fantasy, the contrived plot is sweetened enormously by some sophisticated humour, extravagant production design and expert direction by genre doyen Val Guest. AJ *DVD*

Olivia Newton-John *Olivia* • Benny Thomas [Ben Thomas] *Benny* • Vic Cooper *Vic* • Karl Chambers *Karl* • Roy Dotrice *John Williams* • Roy Marsden *Alpha* ■ *Dir/Scr* Val Guest

Tooth ★U
Fantasy adventure 2003 · UK · Colour · 87min

This dreadful adventure about a modern-day tooth fairy is a amateurish and old-fashioned, reliant on weak humour and bumbling performances from a host of minor British stars. Tooth fairy Yasmin Paige teams up with two human children to restore the lost magic to Fairytopia. The paper-thin script and sloppy direction only compound the mess. SF *DVD*

Yasmin Paige *Tooth* • Harry Enfield *Plug* • Sally Phillips *Mom* • Tim Dutton *Dad* • Phyllida Law *Mrs Claus* • Jim Broadbent *Rabbit* • Vinnie Jones *The Extractor* • Stephen Fry *Pedro* • Richard E Grant *Jarvis Jarvis* • Jerry Hall *Bon Bon* ■ *Dir/Scr* Edouard Narmour

Tooth Fairy ★★★PG
Fantasy comedy 2009 · US/Can · Colour · 97min

This energetic vehicle for Dwayne "The Rock" Johnson hardly stretches the former wrestler. He plays a washed-up ice hockey star who tells his girlfriend's young daughter there's no such thing as the tooth fairy. Cue a trip to Fairyland, where he's sentenced to a week as a real-life tooth fairy to make amends. Of course, it does take a while to get going, is ultimately very predictable and lapses into sentimentality towards the end, but Johnson is an eminently likeable lead and the impressive supporting cast, including Ricky Gervais collaborator Stephen Merchant, Julie Andrews and Billy Crystal, makes up for Johnson's lack of acting finesse. A sequel is due in 2012. LB *DVD*

Dwayne Johnson *Derek Thompson/Tooth Fairy* • Ashley Judd *Carly* • Stephen Merchant *Tracy* • Ryan Sheckler *Mick Donnelly* • Seth MacFarlane *Ziggy* • Julie Andrews *Lily* • Chase Ellison *Randy* • Billy Crystal *Jerry* ■ *Dir* Michael Lembeck • *Scr* Joshua Sternin, Jeffrey Ventimilia, Lowell Ganz, Babaloo Mandel, Randi Mayem Singer, from a story by Jim Piddock

Tootsie ★★★★15
Comedy 1982 · US · Colour · 111min

One of the highlights of Dustin Hoffman's illustrious career, this cross-dressing comedy drama avoids all the obvious pitfalls and manages to make some pertinent comments on the role of women within both showbiz and society. Hoffman's Dorothy Michaels is a wonderfully realised creation and testament to the actor's painstaking preparation for a part. Director Sydney Pollack judges the shifts of tone to perfection, but special mention must be made of his clever pastiche of daytime soaps. Nominated for ten Oscars, the film landed only one – a best supporting statuette for Jessica Lange. DP *DVD*

Dustin Hoffman *Michael Dorsey/Dorothy Michaels* • Jessica Lange *Julie* • Teri Garr *Sandy* • Dabney Coleman *Ron* • Charles Durning *Les* • Bill Murray *Jeff* • Sydney Pollack *George Fields* • George Gaynes *John Van Horn* • Geena Davis *April* ■ *Dir* Sydney Pollack • *Scr* Larry Gelbart, Murray Schisgal, Elaine May (uncredited), from a story by Don McGuire, Gelbart

Top Banana ★★★
Musical comedy 1953 · US · Colour · 103min

The immortal Phil Silvers (Sgt Bilko), enjoyed a distinguished career before his small screen triumph. Undoubtedly his biggest pre-Bilko success was in the Tony Award-winning Broadway musical comedy *Top Banana*. Silvers is brilliant as fast-talking TV comic Jerry Biffle, the "Top Banana" of the title (ie headlining comedian of a show) and his performance, along with the authentic burlesque routines on offer, make this rewarding viewing. Originally made in 3D, a gimmick which was undergoing a boom at the time. DF

Phil Silvers *Jerry Biffle* • Rose Marie *Betty Dillon* • Danny Scholl *Cliff Lane* • Judy Lynn *Sally Peters* • Jack Albertson *Vic Davis* • Johnny Coy *Tommy*

Phelps • Joey Faye *Pinky* • Herbie Faye *Moe* ■ *Dir* Alfred E Green • *Scr* Gene Towne, from the musical by Hy Kraft, Johnny Mercer

Top Cat: the Movie ★★★U
Animated action comedy 2011 · Mex/Arg · Colour · 90min

Fifty years after its TV debut, here's a belated movie appearance for the fondly remembered cartoon that's essentially *Sgt Bilko* with cats. It's pleasingly similar to the original in spirit, sound and look, though with the needless addition of indifferent 3D. The plot sees TC and his alley cat pals falling foul of an evil new police chief who plots to replace the whole city police force with robocops. The film isn't always as amusing as it might be, but younger kids will lap up its bright, breezy and undemanding fun, while adults can drift off down TV memory lane as they realise they still remember all the lyrics to the catchy theme song. DA *DVD* ⬅ 🎦

Jason Harris *Top Cat/Griswald/Strickland/Choo-Choo/Brain/Big Gus* • Chris Edgerly *Benny* • Ben Diskin *Spook* • Matthew Piazzi *Fancy-Fancy* • Bill Lobely *Officer Dibble* ■ *Dir* Alberto Mar • *Scr* Kevin Seccia, Tim McKeon

Top Cat Begins ★U
Animated comedy 2016 · Mex · Colour · 89min

The first Top Cat film, *Top Cat: the Movie*, though cute enough for younger kids, hardly set the world on fire. So it comes as some surprise that its Mexican animators and their English-language dubbers have now served up a second feature-length helping of what's basically *Sgt Bilko*, but with cats. They needn't have bothered. Telling the story of how TC first met Officer Dibble and his feline chums, *Top Cat Begins* is loud, unfunny, randomly plotted, and utterly bereft of the roguish charm of the TV original. CW

Jason Harris *Top Cat/Choo Choo/Brain* • David Hoffman *Granny Dibble/Counter Person/Statue* • Chris Edgerly *Benny* • Bill Lobley *Officer Dibble* • Ben Diskin *Spook* • David Boat *Chief Thumbton* ■ *Dir* Andrés Couturier • *Scr* Douglas Langdale, James Krieg, Jorge Ramírez Suárez, from characters by William Hanna, Joseph Barbera

Top Dog ★★12
Action comedy 1995 · US · Colour · 89min

Chuck Norris stars as a tough cop who teams up with the San Diego police force's most cavalier canine to solve the murder of the dog's former partner. Someone should tell Norris not to play alongside actors who are more dynamic than he is – the mutt is superior in every way. Parents should note that there is some violence and innuendo here, although children may love the dog's antics. ST *DVD*

Chuck Norris *Jake Wilder* • Clyde Kusatsu *Captain Callahan* • Michele Lamar Richards *Savannah Boyette* • Peter Savard Moore *Karl Koller* • Erik Von Detten *Matthew Swanson* • Carmine Caridi *Lou Swanson* ■ *Dir* Aaron Norris • *Scr* Ron Swanson, from a story by Aaron Norris, Tim Grayem

Top Five ★★★15
Comedy 2014 · US · Colour · 101min

Chris Rock shows real maturity in his third film as writer/director by offering up his dubious career choices for consideration and ridicule. He plays a successful but critically maligned actor, who's ashamed of his popular *Hammy the Bear* franchise and forthcoming wedding to a reality TV star, and so decides to reinvent himself. Rosario Dawson is the journalist who gets close to him. There's nuance in the acting and bite in the script, but it could have done with a stronger hand behind the camera. EAS

Chris Rock *Andre Allen* • Rosario Dawson *Chelsea Brown* • Gabrielle Union *Erica Long* • Kevin Hart *Charles* • JB Smoove *Silk* • Ben Vereen *Carl Allen* • Adam Sandler • DMX ■ *Dir/Scr* Chris Rock

Top Gun ★★★15
Action drama 1986 · US · Colour · 105min

Quentin Tarantino's vigorous assertion in *Sleep with Me* that this is the ultimate gay

fantasy movie rather pulls the carpet from under the feet of those attempting to appraise this slavish tribute to flash fly boys and their hi-tech toys. There is no denying the quality and entertainment value of the flying sequences, which blend mile-high footage with state-of-the-art modelwork, but the rivalry between Tom Cruise and Val Kilmer, and Cruise's tempestuous affair with Kelly McGillis are pure bunk. Director Tony Scott takes the credit for preventing this mindless macho daydream from nose-diving. DP A sex scene, swearing. *DVD* 🔵

Tom Cruise *Pete "Maverick" Mitchell* • Kelly McGillis *Charlotte "Charlie" Blackwood* • Val Kilmer *Tom "Iceman" Kazansky* • Anthony Edwards *Nick "Goose" Bradshaw* • Tom Skerritt *Commander Mike Metcalf, "Viper"* • Michael Ironside *Dick "Jester" Wetherly* • John Stockwell *Bill "Cougar" Cortell* • Barry Tubb *Henry "Wolfman" Ruth* • Rick Rossovich *Ron "Slider" Kerner* • Tim Robbins *Sam "Merlin" Wills* • Meg Ryan *Carole* ■ *Dir* Tony Scott • *Scr* Jim Cash, Jack Epps Jr

Top Hat ★★★★★U
Classic musical comedy 1935 · US · BW · 93min

The quintessential Fred Astaire-Ginger Rogers movie; *Swing Time* may be more sophisticated, but there's no question that this fabulous production was more popular. The mistaken identity plot actually works, and the casting is simply flawless. Astaire consolidates his image with the title number *Top Hat, White Tie and Tails* and the Irving Berlin score is a constant delight. Good-natured, warm-hearted and very witty (especially the hansom cab scene), this is a movie to treasure for its sumptuous Art-Deco design and the pairing of its principal players. TS *DVD*

Fred Astaire *Jerry Travers* • Ginger Rogers *Dale Tremont* • Edward Everett Horton *Horace Hardwick* • Erik Rhodes *Alberto Beddini* • Eric Blore *Bates* • Helen Broderick *Madge Hardwick* • Donald Meek *Curate* • Florence Roberts *Curate's wife* ■ *Dir* Mark Sandrich • *Scr* Dwight Taylor, Allan Scott, Karl Noti, from the play *The Girl Who Dared* by Alexander Farago, Aladar Laszlo

Top of the Form ★★U
Crime comedy 1953 · UK · BW · 75min

The Will Hay classic *Good Morning, Boys* is the inspiration for this misfiring Ronald Shiner vehicle. Shiner is a racing tipster mistakenly appointed head of a boys' school who discovers his charges have a natural proclivity for gambling, which comes in handy when he escorts them on a cultural trip to Paris. However, they're soon distracted from the tables when they uncover a plot to steal the Mona Lisa. This efficient but underwhelming caper is all too typical of its director, John Paddy Carstairs. DP

Ronald Shiner *Ronnie Fortescue* • Harold Fowler *Albert* • Alfie Bass *Artie Jones* • Jacqueline Pierreux *Yvette* • Anthony Newley *Percy* • Mary Jerrold *Mrs Bagshott* • Richard Wattis *Willoughby-Gore* • Ronnie Corbett *Student* ■ *Dir* John Paddy Carstairs • *Scr* Leslie Arliss, John Paddy Carstairs, Marriott Edgar, Val Guest, Patrick Kirwan, Ted Willis, from a story by Anthony Kimmins

Top of the World ★18
Thriller 1997 · US · Colour · 94min

This bottom-of-the-barrel cop thriller wastes a good cast in a weak heist plot and surrounds them with botched action and bad special effects. Ex-cop Peter Weller leaves prison after serving time for a pension fund scam only to find himself in the centre of a Las Vegas casino robbery planned by stereotypical baddie Dennis Hopper. So sloppy in places it defies belief, this gives new meaning to the word lacklustre. AJ Swearing, violence. *DVD*

Peter Weller *Ray Mercer* • Dennis Hopper *Charles Atlas* • Tia Carrere *Rebecca Mercer* • David Alan Grier *Detective Augustus* • Cary-Hiroyuki Tagawa *Captain Hefter* • Joe Pantoliano *Vince Castor* ■ *Dir* Sidney J Furie • *Scr* Bart Madison

Top Secret! ★★★ 15
Spy spoof 1984 · US · Colour · 86min

The *Airplane!* team is a touch off-form with this Cold War spoof that has an Elvis Presley-style musical grafted on. Part of the problem is the absence of Leslie Nielsen; instead, Val Kilmer makes his feature debut, playing a rock star who becomes involved in a plot to reunite Germany when he plays a gig in East Germany. Not as funny as it should be, but entertaining enough. AT Swearing.

Val Kilmer *Nick Rivers* • Omar Sharif *Cedric* • Jeremy Kemp *General Streck* • Warren Clarke *Colonel von Horst* • Lucy Gutteridge *Hillary Flammond* • Michael Gough *Dr Flammond* • Tristram Jellinek *Major Crumpler* • Peter Cushing *Bookstore proprietor* ■ *Dir* Jim Abrahams, David Zucker, Jerry Zucker • *Scr* Jim Abrahams, David Zucker, Jerry Abrahams, Martyn Burke

Top Secret Affair ★★★ U
Comedy 1957 · US · BW · 99min

The chemistry is missing between stars Kirk Douglas and Susan Hayward in this rather heavy-handed frolic, maybe because they were old buddies in real life who went to school together back in New York before Hollywood beckoned. Comedy was never really Douglas's forte, and his dimpled grimacing doesn't help this adaptation of John P Marquand's satire. Hayward, however, positively sizzles as the publisher who's trying to discredit diplomat Douglas. TS

Kirk Douglas *Maj Gen Melville Goodwin* • Susan Hayward *Dottie Peale* • Paul Stewart *Bentley* • Jim Backus *Colonel Gooch* • John Cromwell *General Grimshaw* • Michael Fox *Lotzie* • Frank Gerstle *Sergeant Kruger* ■ *Dir* HC Potter • *Scr* Roland Kibbee, Allan Scott, from the novel *Melville Goodwin, USA* by John P Marquand

Topaz ★★ PG
Spy thriller 1969 · US · Colour · 120min

Leon Uris adapted his own bestseller for this lacklustre spy story. Alfred Hitchcock, who had no real enthusiasm for the project, eventually asked for a rewrite by Samuel Taylor (who had worked on *Vertigo*), but there was still far too much plot, too many explanations, and not enough character depth to bring this Cold War thriller to life. The action centres on a Cuban revolutionary and double agents in the French Secret Service. DP *DVD* *BL*

John Forsythe *Michael Nordstrom* • Frederick Stafford *André Devereaux* • Dany Robin *Nicole Devereaux* • John Vernon *Rico Parra* • Karin Dor *Juanita de Cordoba* • Michel Piccoli *Jacques Granville* • Philippe Noiret *Henri Jarre* • Claude Jade *Michele Picard* • Michel Subor *François Picard* • Roscoe Lee Browne *Philippe Dubois* ■ *Dir* Alfred Hitchcock • *Scr* Samuel Taylor, from the novel by Leon Uris

Topaze ★★★★
Comedy drama 1933 · US · BW · 78min

John Barrymore's wonderfully timed and sympathetic study as the honest but hugely naive schoolmaster lights up this Ben Hecht version of Marcel Pagnol's play. After losing his job in a private school, Barrymore is inveigled into a scheme to sell designer mineral water, organised by crooked baron Reginald Mason. Myrna Loy plays Mason's lover, who is attracted by Barrymore's transformation from dupe into man of substance. The story was later remade by Peter Sellers as *Mr Topaze* (1961). TH

John Barrymore *Auguste Topaze* • Myrna Loy *Coco* • Albert Conti *Henri* • Luis Alberni *Dr Bomb* • Reginald Mason *Baron de Latour-Latour* • Jobyna Howland *Baroness de Latour-Latour* • Jackie Searle *Charlemagne de Latour-Latour* • Frank Reicher *Dr Stegg* ■ *Dir* Harry d'Abbadie D'Arrast • *Scr* Ben Hecht, Benn W Levy, from the play by Marcel Pagnol

Topaze ★★★
Satire 1951 · Fr · BW · 136min

Proving that behind every cynic there's a lapsed idealist, Fernandel is superb as the bashful schoolmaster unable to declare his feelings for headmaster's daughter Jacqueline Pagnol. However, he is much less convincing as the fast-learning political dupe who outwits his corrupt master, Jacques Morel. Marcel Pagnol directs this version of his own play. DP In French.

Fernandel *Topaze* • Hélène Perdrière *Suzy Courtois* • Jacqueline Pagnol *Ernestine Muche* • Pierre Larquey *Tamise* • Jacques Morel *Régis Castel-Vergnac* • Marcel Vallée *Muche* • Milly Mathis *Baroness Pitar-Vergnolles* • Yvette Etiévant *Secretary* ■ *Dir* Marcel Pagnol • *Scr* Marcel Pagnol, from his play

Topkapi ★★★★ U
Comedy crime caper 1964 · US · Colour · 114min

In spoofing his own intricate heist classic, *Rififi*, Jules Dassin pioneered one of the most popular subgenres of the 1960s, the comic crime caper. Deliciously scripted by one-time Ealing alumnus Monja Danischewsky, it combines sparkling dialogue with moments of unbearable tension, most notably during the prolonged heist in an Istanbul museum in a bid to purloin a priceless dagger. The misfits hired by Melina Mercouri and Maximilian Schell are effectively played, but it was the showy performance of Peter Ustinov that caught the eye and earned him a best supporting actor Oscar. DP *DVD*

Melina Mercouri *Elizabeth Lipp* • Peter Ustinov *Arthur Simon Simpson* • Maximilian Schell *Walter Harper* • Robert Morley *Cedric Page* • Akim Tamiroff *Geven* • Gilles Ségal *Giulio* • Jess Hahn *Hans Fischer* • Titos Wandis [Titos Vandis] *Harback* • Ege Ernart *Major Tufan* ■ *Dir* Jules Dassin • *Scr* Monja Danischewsky, from the novel *The Light of Day* by Eric Ambler

El Topo ★★★ 18
Surreal western 1971 · Mex · Colour · 124min

There's plenty to offend everyone here. Shot in Mexico by the Chilean-born actor/writer/director Alexandro Jodorowsky, *El Topo*, which translates as *The Mole*, is the cult film fan's cult film. A brief description would do scant justice to the bewildering array of images – some witty, some bleak and some so obscure that only Jodorowsky himself can have the foggiest idea what they actually mean. But, given the knowledge that the references range from Fellini and Buñuel to Marcel Marceau and the Bible, you will get a better idea of just how eclectic this western (yes, western!) really is. DP Spanish +subtitles. Violence, sex scenes. *DVD*

Alexandro Jodorowsky *El Topo* • Brontis Jodorowsky *Brontis (as a child)* • Mara Lorenzio *Mara* • David Silva *Colonel* • Paula Romo *Woman in black* ■ *Dir/Scr* Alexandro Jodorowsky

Topper ★★★★
Fantasy screwball comedy 1937 · US · BW · 98min

This excellent whimsical comedy stars Cary Grant and Constance Bennett as the rich couple who drive their streamlined automobile into a tree. Surviving as ghosts, they harass Mr Topper (Roland Young), their starchy, hen-pecked bank manager, who has regarded them as irresponsible and trivial, which is exactly what they are. The movie aims for a soft subversiveness and was a huge hit, with two sequels following. AT

Cary Grant *George Kerby* • Constance Bennett *Marion Kerby* • Roland Young *Cosmo Topper* • Billie Burke *Mrs Topper* • Alan Mowbray *Wilkins* • Eugene Pallette *Casey* • Arthur Lake *Elevator boy* • Hedda Hopper *Mrs Stuyvesant* ■ *Dir* Norman Z McLeod • *Scr* Jack Jevne, Eric Hatch, Eddie Moran, from the novel *The Jovial Ghosts* by Thorne Smith

Topper Returns ★★★ PG
Fantasy screwball comedy 1941 · US · BW · 88min

The spooky slapstick series of three Topper pictures ended with this old dark house spoof. All the ingredients are here, including wall panels, hidden passages and disappearing bodies. The film begins with the killing of Joan Blondell, who then returns in phantom form to solve her own murder. There are quite a few laughs, but the movie is but a ghost of *Topper* (1937) and *Topper Takes a Trip* (1939), although Roland Young was his wonderfully bemused self again in the title role. RB *DVD*

Roland Young *Cosmo Topper* • Joan Blondell *Gail Richards* • Carole Landis *Ann Carrington* • Billie Burke *Mrs Topper* • Dennis O'Keefe *Bob* • Patsy Kelly *Maid* • HB Warner *Henry Carrington/Walter Harberg* ■ *Dir* Roy Del Ruth • *Scr* Jonathan Latimer, Gordon Douglas, from characters by Thorne Smith

Topper Takes a Trip ★★★ U
Fantasy screwball comedy 1939 · US · BW · 80min

The sequel to the original *Topper* (1937), with Roland Young again playing hen-pecked banker Cosmo Topper, now being sued for divorce by Billie Burke. For no real reason, the action shifts to Europe where the spectral Constance Bennett – the reason for the divorce proceedings – works to save the marriage when Burke eyes a Riviera fancy boy. Cary Grant appears only in a flashback to the first film but his role as Constance's constant companion is taken by a yapping dog. It's all very silly, but oddly sophisticated, too. AT

Constance Bennett *Marion Kerby* • Roland Young *Mr Cosmo Topper* • Billie Burke *Mrs Clara Topper* • Alan Mowbray *Wilkins* • Verree Teasdale *Mrs Parkhurst* • Franklin Pangborn *Louis, hotel manager* • Alexander D'Arcy [Alex D'Arcy] *Baron de Rossi* • Paul Hurst *Bartender* • Cary Grant *George Kerby* ■ *Dir* Norman Z McLeod • *Scr* Eddie Moran, Jack Jevne, Corey Ford, from the novel *Topper Takes a Trip* by Thorne Smith

Topsy-Turvy ★★★★★ 12
Biographical comedy drama 1999 · UK/US · Colour · 153min

After Laurel and Hardy, the most notable odd couple in showbusiness is probably British operetta writers Gilbert and Sullivan. Director Mike Leigh here celebrates their collaborative genius, using the construction of *The Mikado* to show that their casual virtuosity was really painstaking craft. The newly-knighted Arthur Sullivan (Allan Corduner), a musician, lecher and dandy, met his literary match in William Schwenck Gilbert (Jim Broadbent), whose taste for the absurd extended to his librettos. Leigh skilfully convinces us that their separate talents spoke with one voice. TH *DVD*

Jim Broadbent *William Schwenck Gilbert* • Allan Corduner *Arthur Sullivan* • Timothy Spall *Richard Temple* • Lesley Manville *Lucy "Kitty" Gilbert* • Ron Cook *Richard D'Oyly Carte* • Wendy Nottingham *Helen Lenoir* • Kevin McKidd *Durward Lely* • Shirley Henderson *Leonora Braham* • Alison Steadman *Madame Leon* ■ *Dir/Scr* Mike Leigh

Tora! Tora! Tora! ★★★ U
Second World War drama 1970 · US/Jpn · Colour · 136min

This is a meticulous account of the preparations for and execution of the Japanese attack on the US naval base at Pearl Harbor on 7 December 1941. With Richard Fleischer staging the American segments and Toshio Masuda and Kinji Fukasaku directing events from the Japanese perspective, the film bends over backwards to show that patriotism, courage and commitment were present on both sides, and therein lies its weakness. The battle sequences are magnificent, but the production's even-handedness makes it impossible to judge the true impact of the happenings on either nation. DP Japanese, English +subtitles. *DVD* *BL*

Martin Balsam *Admiral Husband E Kimmel* • Soh Yamamura [So Yamamura] *Admiral Isoroku Yamamoto* • Jason Robards Jr [Jason Robards] *General Walter C Short* • Joseph Cotten *Henry L Stimson* • Tatsuya Mihashi *Commander Minoru Genda* • EG Marshall *Lt Col Rufus S Bratton* • Takahiro Tamura *Lt Com Fuchida* • James Whitmore *Admiral William F Halsey* ■ *Dir* Richard Fleischer, Toshio Masuda, Kinji Fukasaku • *Scr* Larry Forrester, Hideo Oguni, Ryuzo Kikushima, from the book by Gordon W Prange and the book *The Broken Seal* by Ladislas Farago

Torch Singer ★★
Musical melodrama 1933 · US · BW · 70min

Claudette Colbert, who seldom put a foot wrong in her long and prolific career, is the saving grace of this damp piece of soap that refuses to foam. She plays an unmarried entertainer who gives her baby away, regrets it and transforms herself from torch singer to children's radio show host while searching for the child. Feeble and unconvincing, but Colbert bravely battles against odds that include a dreary, wooden performance by Ricardo Cortez. RK

Claudette Colbert *Sally Trent/Mimi Benton* • Ricardo Cortez *Tony Cummings* • David Manners *Michael Gardner* • Lyda Roberti *Dora Nichols* • Charley Grapewin *Judson* ■ *Dir* Alexander Hall, George Somnes • *Scr* Lenore Coffee, Lynn Starling, from the short story *Mike* in *Liberty* magazine

Torch Song ★★
Romantic drama 1953 · US · Colour · 90min

There's camp, and there's *Torch Song*. Joan Crawford (far too old) is an unhappy Broadway star, and Michael Wilding is a blind pianist who falls in love with her and nearly ruins his Hollywood career. Fortunately, his character can't see Crawford perform *Two-Faced Woman* in blackface, but, alas, we can. Charles Walters, appearing as Crawford's dancing partner in the opening number, directs this cliché-upon-cliché farrago. TS

Joan Crawford *Jenny Stewart* • Michael Wilding *Tye Graham* • Gig Young *Cliff Willard* • Marjorie Rambeau *Mrs Stewart* • Henry Morgan [Harry Morgan] *Joe Denner* • Dorothy Patrick *Martha* • James Todd *Philip Norton* ■ *Dir* Charles Walters • *Scr* John Michael Hayes, Jan Lustig, from the story *Why Should I Cry?* by IAR Wylie

Torch Song Trilogy ★★★★ 15
Drama 1988 · US · Colour · 114min

The driving force behind this splendid gay romantic comedy drama is Harvey Fierstein, who repeats his Tony award-winning stage performance in this screen version of his own hit play. Although it occasionally lapses into soppiness, the script is a finely judged mix of sass and schmaltz. Gravel-voiced, camp and desperately vulnerable, Fierstein is tremendous, while Anne Bancroft does the best of her string of Jewish mama routines. The surprise is Matthew Broderick, who is perfect, playing against type, as Harvey's lover. DP

Harvey Fierstein *Arnold Becker* • Anne Bancroft *Ma* • Matthew Broderick *Alan* • Brian Kerwin *Ed* • Karen Young *Laurel* • Eddie Castrodad *David* • Ken Page *Murray* • Charles Pierce *Bertha Venation* ■ *Dir* Paul Bogart • *Scr* Harvey Fierstein, from his play

Torchlight ★★ 18
Drama 1984 · US · Colour · 88min

This "holier than thou" take on the dangers of cocaine addiction fails to be anything other than black and white. Artist Pamela Sue Martin meets construction boss Steve Railsback and, after a whirlwind romance, they marry. Their domestic bliss is shattered by the arrival of cocaine dealer Ian McShane. Director Tom Wright's morality tale may be a useful deterrent for teenagers, but adult audiences are likely to be unimpressed. LH *DVD*

Pamela Sue Martin *Lillian Gregory* • Steve Railsback *Jake Gregory* • Ian McShane *Sidney* • Al Corley *Al* • Rita Taggart *Rita* • Arnie Moore *Richard* ■ *Dir* Tom Wright [Thomas J Wright] • *Scr* Eliza Moorman, Pamela Sue Martin

Torment ★★★ 12
Drama 1944 · Swe · BW · 96min

This sombre work was the first big international Swedish success for more than two decades. It was rightly acclaimed at the time for its marvellous performances, especially from Mai Zetterling, and the clever sustained direction of Alf Sjöberg. Today, however, this study of schoolboy Alf Kjellin's affair with Zetterling, the mistress of his despised, despotic teacher (Stig Jarrel), is mainly of interest because its screenplay is by Ingmar Bergman, who would go on to become a giant of world cinema. TS Swedish +subtitles. *DVD*

Alf Kjellin *Jan-Erik* • Mai Zetterling *Bertha* • Stig Järrel *Caligula* • Olof Winnerstrand *School principal* • Gosta Cederlund *Pippi* ■ *Dir* Alf Sjöberg • *Scr* Ingmar Bergman

Tormented ★★★ 15
Horror   2009 · UK · Colour · 87min

In director Jon Wright's slick feature debut, a bullied schoolboy returns from the dead to take violent revenge on the classmates who drove him to suicide. But is the "zombie ghost" real or just a figment of the guilty students' consciences? Wright gives a cynical British slant to glossy American high-school horrors such as *Carrie* and *The Faculty*, and is aided by a referential script from Stephen Prentice that's full of sarcastic wit and cruel humour. Alex Pettyfer stands out among the good-looking young cast that also features alumni from TV's *Skins* and *Grange Hill*. A smartly satirical morality tale that's scary but diverting experience. AJ *DVD*

Alex Pettyfer *Bradley* • April Pearson *Tasha* • Dimitri Leonidas *Alexis* • Calvin Dean *Darren Mullett* • Tuppence Middleton *Justine Fielding* • Georgia King *Sophie* ■ *Dir* Jon Wright • *Scr* Stephen Prentice

Torn Apart ★★
Romantic drama   1990 · US · Colour · 95min

So much care has been taken not to offend anyone, that this adaptation of Chayym Zeldis's Romeo and Juliet novel offers few worthwhile insights into the extent to which the Middle East conflict affects everyday life. It also doesn't help casting a couple of photogenic Americans in the key roles of the Israeli soldier and his Arab girlfriend, even though both Adrian Pasdar and Cecilia Peck turn in creditable performances. DP

Adrian Pasdar *Ben Arnon* • Cecilia Peck *Laila Malek* • Barry Primus *Arie Arnon* • Machram Huri *Mahmoud Malek* • Arnon Zadok *Professor Mansour* • Margrit Polak *Ilana Arnon* ■ *Dir* Jack Fisher • *Scr* Marc Kristal, from the novel *A Forbidden Love* by Chayym Zeldis

Torn Apart ★★
Thriller   2004 · US · Colour · 87min

It's hard to take Tia Carrere seriously in writer/director Stuart Alexander's weakly scripted and badly made TV-movie thriller. Wildly miscast, she's unconvincing on every level, playing a surgeon facing a terrible life-or-death choice when a former patient's deranged relative kidnaps her family. But though the clock's ticking down, the film is tension-free and underwhelming: stuffed with boring shots of Carrere in her car, trying to look anxious, or literally running around the hospital achieving almost nothing. Only a generically dramatic score creates a sense of momentum, becoming increasingly intense in direct contrast to the lacklustre events. The absence of punch continues to the convenient climax, where the feature's lack of realism reaches its peak. SF

Tia Carrere *Dr Vicki Westin* • Dale Midkiff *Jerry Bender* • Richard Burgi *Billy Westin* • Michael Arata *Officer Bingham* • Zachary Canon *Scott Horner* ■ *Dir/Scr* Stuart Alexander

Torn Curtain ★★★ 15
Spy thriller   1966 · US · Colour · 122min

What looked in its day to be a failure and a disappointment to fans of Alfred Hitchcock does, at least, contain one of the maestro's most compelling sequences. "I wanted to show how difficult it is to kill someone," Hitch said, and in a prolonged scene involving Paul Newman played without dialogue he certainly does. It's the high spot in a remarkably ridiculous Cold War thriller, very much of its period, with phoney locations, phonier (although admittedly deliberate) back projection, and, phoniest of all, the casting of Newman and Julie Andrews as an alleged American defector and his fiancée. If there was any chemistry between the stars, it certainly doesn't show on the screen. TS *DVD* Blu

Paul Newman *Professor Michael Armstrong* • Julie Andrews *Sarah Sherman* • Lila Kedrova *Countess Kuchinska* • Hansjoerg Felmy [Hansjörg Felmy] *Heinrich Gerhard* • Tamara Toumanova

Ballerina • Ludwig Donath *Professor Gustav Lindt* • Wolfgang Kieling *Hermann Gromek* • Günter Strack *Professor Karl Manfred* ■ *Dir* Alfred Hitchcock • *Scr* Briar Moore, from his story

Tornado! ★★ PG
Action adventure   1996 · US · Colour · 83min

Ernie Hudson plays the scientist looking to perfect a machine that can detect lethal tornados, while Bruce Campbell is his dashing, risk-taking chum. Shannon Sturges provides the love interest as the grumpy accountant who finally succumbs to Campbell's charms. The action breezes along, but this TV movie lacks the budget for any extraordinary visual effects. JF Swearing. *DVD*

Bruce Campbell *Jake Thorne* • Shannon Sturges *Sam Callen* • Ernie Hudson *Dr Branson* ■ *Dir* Noel Nosseck • *Scr* John Logan

Tornado Warning ★ PG
Science-fiction disaster movie
2012 · US · Colour · 99min

Aliens are trying to invade Earth using electrical tornados in this lame disaster movie. Fortunately, farmer Jeff Fahey and blogger Kari Wuhrer are on hand to stop them, after discovering the truth behind the weird weather with ridiculous ease and speed. But then nothing about this made-for-TV project feels realistic, as flat and nonsensical events are rendered doubly unconvincing by stereotyped and badly acted characters, while the pitiful effects only emphasise these flaws further. The film's one saving grace is David Jensen's hilariously exaggerated supporting turn: playing a sinister FBI agent with a campness that's incongruous yet entertaining. SF *DVD* Blu

Kari Wuhrer *Gail Curtis* • Jeff Fahey *Judd Walker* • Terry Kiser *Mike Hardy* • David Jensen *Armstrong* ■ *Dir* Jeff Burr • *Scr* Paul A Birkett

Torpedo Run ★★★ U
Second World War drama
1958 · US · Colour · 95min

Claustrophobically made in CinemaScope, this boasts a tense plot as commander Glenn Ford accidentally blows up a Japanese prison ship with his own family on board. The chase is then on to find the enemy aircraft carrier which used the ship as a shield. This is from the most successful period in Ford's career, and his nervy, tense performance is mesmerising, but director Joseph Pevney's pacing is a shade too slow. TS

Glenn Ford *Lt Cmdr Barney Doyle* • Ernest Borgnine *Lt Archer Sloan* • Diane Brewster *Jane Doyle* • Dean Jones *Lt Jake "Fuzz" Foley* • LQ Jones *"Hash" Benson* • Philip Ober *Admiral Samuel Setton* • Richard Carlyle (2) *Chief Don Adams* ■ *Dir* Joseph Pevney • *Scr* Richard Sale, William Wister Haines, from stories by Richard Sale

Torque ★★★ 15
Action thriller   2003 · US/Aus · Colour · 80min

Tongue-in-cheek trash with flash doesn't get much more enjoyable than the feature debut of music video director Joseph Kahn. This pokes as much fun at the "choppers and chicks" genre as it does its high-gear self. The improbable tale has ace biker Martin Henderson returning from Thailand to clear his name of drug-smuggling charges, only to be framed for murder. The script is dumb and the acting dumber, but it doesn't matter. Kahn knows his audience wants to see mega-octane thrills and he doesn't disappoint. AJ Swearing, violence. *DVD*

Martin Henderson *Cary Ford* • Ice Cube *Trey* • Monet Mazur *Shane* • Adam Scott *McPherson* • Matt Schulze *Henry* • Jaime Pressly *China* • Jay Hernandez *Dalton* • Will Yun Lee *Val* ■ *Dir* Joseph Kahn • *Scr* Matt Johnson

The Torrent ★★★★
Silent romantic drama   1926 · US · BW · 68min

Vicente Blasco Ibañez was one of the most adapted novelists of the silent era, and it was one of his potboilers that provided Greta Garbo with her Hollywood entrance. Starring opposite MGM's very own Latin

lover, Ricardo Cortez, she was somewhat improbably cast as a provincial Spanish girl, who recovers from their parting by becoming a famous Parisian diva. Even at the age of 20, Garbo's genius is apparent in the small, slow, seductive movements that reveal the psychological intensity that would become her trademark. DP

Ricardo Cortez *Don Rafael Brull* • Greta Garbo *Leonora* • Gertrude Olmsted *Remedios* • Edward Connelly *Pedro Moreno* ■ *Dir* Monta Bell • *Scr* Katherine Hilliker (titles), HH Caldwell (titles), from the novel *Entre Naranjos (Among the Orange Trees)* by Vicente Blasco Ibañez, adapted by Dorothy Farnum

Torrents of Spring ★★ PG
Period romantic drama
1989 · Fr/It · Colour · 97min

Jerzy Skolimowski has badly misjudged the tone of Ivan Turgenev's novel and turned a stifling chamber drama into a dreamily sunlit travelogue. Instead of being driven to distraction by his love for German baker's daughter Valeria Golino and his passion for married noblewoman Nastassja Kinski, Timothy Hutton merely looks alternately moon-faced and peevish. DP

Timothy Hutton *Dimitri Sanin* • Nastassja Kinski *Maria Nikolaevna Polozov* • Valeria Golino *Gemma Rosselli* • Francesca De Sapio *Signora Rosselli – Gemma's mother* • William Forsythe *Polozov* • Urbano Barberini *Von Doenhof* • Jacques Herlin *Pantaleone* ■ *Dir* Jerzy Skolimowski • *Scr* Jerzy Skolimowski, Arcangelo Bonaccorso, from the novel *Spring Torrents* by Ivan Turgenev

Torrid Zone ★★★
Adventure   1940 · US · BW · 93min

The combustible James Cagney here sports a pencil-thin moustache and a sneer. Pat O'Brien, Cagney's boss, runs an export business in Central America and saloon singer Ann Sheridan, then known as the "Oomph Girl", competes with Helen Vinson for Cagney's attention. This sweaty piece of tropical torpor was never that torrid, but is still enjoyable. AT

James Cagney *Nick Butler* • Pat O'Brien *Steve Case* • Ann Sheridan *Lee Donley* • Andy Devine *Wally Davis* • Helen Vinson *Gloria Anderson* • George Tobias *Rosario* • Jerome Cowan *Bob Anderson* ■ *Dir* William Keighley • *Scr* Richard Macaulay, Jerry Wald

Tortilla Flat ★★★ U
Drama   1942 · US · Sepia · 105min

Off-screen machinations marked the transition from page to screen of John Steinbeck's novel. John Garfield was keen to star as the newly wealthy Danny, but MGM had to pull out all the stops in their efforts to persuade Warner Bros to release him. Spencer Tracy and Akim Tamiroff have plum roles as a couple of freeloaders talking Garfield into letting them have one of the houses he's inherited. Hedy Lamarr had the best part of her career as the strong-minded object of Garfield's affections in this amiable drama that was a bigger hit with critics than public on release. TH

Spencer Tracy *Pilon* • Hedy Lamarr *Dolores "Sweets" Ramirez* • John Garfield *Danny* • Akim Tamiroff *Pablo* • Frank Morgan *Pirate* • Sheldon Leonard *Tito Ralph* • John Qualen *Jose Maria Corcoran* • Donald Meek *Paul D Cummings* ■ *Dir* Victor Fleming • *Scr* John Lee Mahin, Benjamin Glaser, from the novel by John Steinbeck

Tortilla Soup ★★★ PG
Comedy drama   2001 · US · Colour · 99min

The showboating of a miscast Raquel Welch and an over-abundance of feel-good elements are the only ingredients to sour this flavoursome remake of Ang Lee's *Eat Drink Man Woman*. Transposing the scene to a Los Angeles restaurant, the action turns around Hector Elizondo, a chef with failing taste buds. He has a trio of daughters: sanctimonious teacher Elizabeth Peña, firebrand foodie Jacqueline Obradors and dreamer Tamara Mello. Director Maria Ripoll could have added a pinch more social spice to the scenes of sibling bonding, but the performances are splendid. DP Swearing. *DVD*

Hector Elizondo *Martin Naranjo* • Jacqueline Obradors *Carmen Naranjo* • Elizabeth Peña *Leticia Naranjo* • Tamara Mello *Maribel Naranjo* • Nikolai Kinski *Andy* • Paul Rodriguez *Orlando* • Raquel Welch *Hortensia* • Constance Marie *Yolanda* ■ *Dir* Maria Ripoll • *Scr* Tom Musca, Ramon Menendez, Vera Blasi, from the film *Eat Drink Man Woman* by Ang Lee, James Schamus, Hui-Ling Wang

The Tortoise and the Hare ★★★★★
Animated comedy   1935 · US · Colour · 8min

One of the Disney studio's many landmark cartoons of the 1930s, this Oscar-winning retelling of Aesop's fable marked the first successful animation of speed. Whereas previous cartoons carefully delineated every stage of a character's movement, rendering it sluggish, Max Hare's fast pace in this film is often reduced to a mixture of extreme start-and-finish movements and intermediate blurs, some lasting for only a few frames. This film had a profound influence on the cartoon industry, especially at Warner Bros where speed became essential to Looney Tunes humour. CLP

■ *Dir* Wilfred Jackson

Torture Garden ★★★ 15
Portmanteau horror   1967 · UK · Colour · 96min

A group of fairground visitors are shown their futures by the strange Dr Diabolo (Burgess Meredith) in one of the better compendium chillers from Amicus, Hammer's main British horror rival. Robert (*Psycho*) Bloch's skilful script, which includes cannibal cats, haunted pianos, eternal Hollywood life and the reincarnation of Edgar Allan Poe, gives director Freddie Francis imaginative opportunities to indulge in stylish camerawork for maximum gothic effect. AJ

Jack Palance *Ronald Wyatt* • Beverly Adams *Carla Haynes* • Burgess Meredith *Dr Diabolo* • Peter Cushing *Lancelot Canning* • Michael Bryant *Colin Williams* • Maurice Denham *Colin's uncle* • John Standing *Leo* • Robert Hutton *Paul* ■ *Dir* Freddie Francis • *Scr* Robert Bloch, from his stories *Enoch, Terror Over Hollywood, Mr Steinway, The Man Who Collected Poe*

Toryboy the Movie ★★★★
Documentary   2010 · UK · Colour

Film-maker John Walsh caused something of a stir when his revealing and droll fly-on-the-wall documentary was released after the 2010 General Election. What started out as an exposé of the process of becoming a Member of Parliament took a left turn when he discovered incumbent MP Sir Stuart Bell (in situ since 1983) had not held a surgery for constituents in 15 years. It doesn't matter what party you support – this fascinating odyssey reflects disillusionment with the system, as relevant today as it was then. JA Swearing. *DVD*

■ *Dir/Scr* John Walsh

Tosca ★★ PG
Opera   2001 · Fr/It · Colour and BW · 124min

Benoît Jacquot's rarefied adaptation of Puccini's opera divides its time between lustrous monochrome footage of the cast's studio sessions with the orchestra and chorus of the Royal Opera House, and fragmented scenes meticulously staged on a deliciously artificial set. Ruggero Raimondi impresses as the Machiavellian police chief who tricks singer Angela Gheorghiu into betraying artist Roberto Alagna's sheltering of a fugitive. However, the inconsistent lip-synching proves as distracting from the music as the utterly superfluous video inserts. DP Italian +subtitles.

Angela Gheorghiu *Tosca* • Roberto Alagna *Mario Cavaradossi* • Ruggero Raimondi *Scarpia* • David Cangelosi *Spoletta* • Sorin Coliban *Sciarrone* • Enrico Fissore *Sacristan* • Maurizio Muraro *Angelotti* ■ *Dir* Benoît Jacquot • *Scr* Benoît Jacquot, from the opera by Giacomo Puccini, Luigi Illica, Giuseppe Giacosa, from the play by Victorien Sardou

Total Eclipse ★★ 18

Biographical drama
1995 · UK/Fr/Bel · Colour · 106min

Female *Titanic* fanatics will probably want to catch this film because it features then teen heart-throb Leonardo DiCaprio in the buff. But apart from that they are likely to be disappointed. Director Agnieszka Holland and writer Christopher Hampton have produced a stodgy biopic that focuses on the more lurid aspects of the (sadomasochistic) relationship between 19th-century poets Verlaine (David Thewlis) and Rimbaud (DiCaprio). JB **DVD**

Leonardo DiCaprio *Arthur Rimbaud* • David Thewlis *Paul Verlaine* • Romane Bohringer *Mathilde Verlaine* • Dominique Blanc *Isabelle Rimbaud* • Nita Klein *Rimbaud's mother* • Christopher Hampton *The judge* ■ *Dir* Agnieszka Holland • *Scr* Christopher Hampton

Total Recall ★★★★ 18

Science-fiction thriller
1990 · US · Colour · 108min

Director Paul Verhoeven, armed with a smart script loosely based on a short story by cult novelist Philip K Dick, cuts loose with a gloriously over-the-top mix of black humour, ultra-violence and spectacular effects. Arnold Schwarzenegger stars as the dull construction worker who is drawn into a conspiracy on the planet Mars when a virtual reality holiday awakens long-dormant memories. However, the real find turned out to be Sharon Stone, whose performance led to her star-making role in Verhoeven's next movie, *Basic Instinct*. JF Violence, swearing, nudity. **DVD** **BL**

Arnold Schwarzenegger *Douglas Quaid* • Rachel Ticotin *Melina* • Sharon Stone *Lori Quaid* • Ronny Cox *Cohaagen* • Michael Ironside *Richter* • Marshall Bell *George/Kuato* • Mel Johnson Jr *Benny* • Michael Champion *Helm* • Roy Brocksmith *Dr Edgemar* ■ *Dir* Paul Verhoeven • *Scr* Ronald Shusett, Dan O'Bannon, Gary Goldman, from a story by Shusett, O'Bannon, Jon Povill, from the short story *We Can Remember It for You Wholesale* by Philip K Dick

Total Recall ★★★ 12

Science-fiction action thriller
2012 · US · Colour · 113min

This reboot of Arnie's 1990 hit stars Colin Farrell as a factory worker who, in search of excitement, visits a company that implants false memories. After the procedure goes awry, he learns he's really a spy, his loving wife (Kate Beckinsale) is not who she seems, and his dream woman (Jessica Biel) is real. There's much to enjoy here, but what was once an inventive concept now feels routine, with director Len Wiseman (married to Beckinsale) focusing on overblown effects at the expense of plot or credibility. AJ **DVD** **BL**

Colin Farrell (2) *Douglas Quaid/Hauser* • Kate Beckinsale *Lori Quaid* • Jessica Biel *Melina* • Bryan Cranston *Vilos Cohaagen* • Bokeem Woodbine *Harry* • Bill Nighy *Matthias Lair* ■ *Dir* Len Wiseman • *Scr* Kurt Wimmer, Mark Bomback, from a story by Ronald Shusett, Dan O'Bannon, Jon Povill, Wimmer, from the short story *We Can Remember It for You Wholesale* by Philip K Dick • *Cinematographer* Paul Cameron

Totally F***ed Up ★★★ 18

Comedy drama 1993 · US · Colour · 75min

In 15 numbered chapters, six gay and lesbian LA teenagers divulge every minute detail about how screwed up their disenfranchised lives are. There's the slacker, the would-be film-maker, his artist boyfriend, the skateboarder, and two lesbians who dream of having a baby. Edgy, moody, humorous and containing some immensely powerful moments, this is a penetrating look at what it means to be young, gay and terminally bored. AJ

James Duval *Andy* • Roko Belic *Tommy* • Susan Behshid *Michele* • Jenee Gill *Patricia* • Gilbert Luna *Steven* • Lance May *Deric* • Alan Boyce *Ian* • Craig Gilmore *Brendan* ■ *Dir/Scr* Gregg Araki

Toto Le Héros ★★★★ 15

Drama 1991 · Bel/Fr/Ger · Colour · 87min

Jaco Van Dormael made an outstanding start to his directorial career with this remarkable film that is both a beguiling portrait of childhood and a touching treatise on unrealised dreams. Effortlessly slipping between past and present through a sequence of stylish flashbacks, Van Dormael traces the lifelong resentment of Thomas, who has waited 60 years to avenge himself on Alfred, a business tycoon, with whom Thomas believes he was switched shortly after birth. The three actors who play Toto are all superb, but it's the dark humour, atmosphere and narrative complexity that make this so enthralling. DP French +subtitles. Violence, nudity. **DVD**

Michel Bouquet *Old Thomas* • Jo de Backer *Adult Thomas* • Thomas Godet *Young Thomas* • Gisela Uhlen *Old Evelyne* • Mireille Perrier *Adult Evelyne* • Sandrine Blancke *Alice* • Peter Böhlke *Old Alfred* • Didier Ferney *Adult Alfred* ■ *Dir/Scr* Jaco Van Dormael

The Touch ★★★ 15

Drama 1971 · US/Swe · Colour · 107min

On the surface, this appears to be one of Ingmar Bergman's lesser chamber dramas. In the Swedish master's first English-language film, Elliott Gould appears uncomfortable playing the Jewish archaeologist who embarks on an affair with Bibi Andersson. The film takes on deeper meaning when we realise it is a meditation on the troubled marriage of Bergman's parents, with the photograph Andersson shows Gould of her mother depicting Karin Bergman. DP

Bibi Andersson *Karin Vergerus* • Elliott Gould *David Kovac* • Max von Sydow *Andreas Vergerus* • Sheila Reid *Sara* • Staffan Hallerstram *Anders Vergerus* • Maria Nolgard *Agnes Vergerus* ■ *Dir/Scr* Ingmar Bergman

Touch ★★★ 15

Comedy drama 1996 · US/Fr · Colour · 93min

Director Paul Schrader's first feature after a long lay-off is a quizzical adaptation of bestselling author Elmore Leonard's atypical novel. Deftly skirting supernatural satire, this uncommonly sophisticated and amusing comic fable focuses on Skeet Ulrich, an ex-monk with curative abilities, whose gift is seen by opportunist Christopher Walken as media gold. Loaded with fine performances and acute observations on media manipulation and right wing religious extremists, this is wonderfully eccentric. AJ **DVD**

Bridget Fonda *Lynn Faulkner* • Christopher Walken *Bill Hill* • Skeet Ulrich *Juvenal* • Gina Gershon *Debra Lusanne* • Tom Arnold *August Murray* • Paul Mazursky *Artie* • Janeane Garofalo *Kathy Worthington* • LL Cool J ■ *Dir* Paul Schrader • *Scr* Paul Schrader, from the novel by Elmore Leonard

Touch and Go ★ U

Comedy 1955 · UK · Colour · 81min

This is a depressing wallow in the sort of whimsy that Ealing foisted upon the world as British Realism. The clumsy clash of ancient and modern revolves around the furniture designer Jack Hawkins's decision to emigrate to Australia when his latest efforts are deemed too futuristic by his stick-in-the-mud employer. DP

Jack Hawkins *Jim Fletcher* • Margaret Johnston *Helen Fletcher* • June Thorburn *Peggy Fletcher* • John Fraser *Richard Kenyon* • Roland Culver *Reg Fairbright* • Alison Leggatt *Alice Fairbright* ■ *Dir* Michael Truman • *Scr* William Rose, from a story by Tania Rose, William Rose

Touch and Go ★ 15

Romantic comedy drama 1986 · US · Colour · 97min

Comedian Michael Keaton tries flexing his dramatic muscle for the first time in a formula romance that, despite its violent conclusion, remains grounded in sentiment. He plays a Chicago hockey star who becomes involved with single mother Maria Conchita Alonso after her son has tried to mug him. The usual relationship problems ensue, which never hit any note of truth and stick essentially to sitcom parameters. AJ **DVD**

Michael Keaton *Bobby Barbato* • Maria Conchita Alonso *Denise DeLeon* • Ajay Naidu *Louis DeLeon* • John Reilly *Jerry Pepper* • Maria Tucci *Dee Dee* ■ *Dir* Robert Mandel • *Scr* Alan Ormsby, Bob Sand, Harry Colomby

Touch Me ★★★

Romantic drama 1997 · US · Colour · 104min

Although several films have been made about Aids from the gay perspective, few have explored the prevalence of the condition among heterosexuals. Striving to avoid the preachiness with which Hollywood invests so many of its message movies, this drama has its share of turmoils and betrayals. Amanda Peet may be playing a struggling actress, but her reaction to discovering that she is HIV-positive is both human and understandable. DP Swearing, sex scenes, nudity.

Amanda Peet *Bridgette* • Michael Vartan *Adam* • Peter Facinelli *Bail* • Kari Wuhrer *Margot* • Erica Gimpel *Kareen* ■ *Dir* H Gordon Boos • *Scr* H Gordon Boos, from a story by Boos, Greg H Sims

A Touch of Adultery ★ 15

Romantic comedy 1991 · It · Colour · 98min

The teaming of perennial *Mary Poppins* virgin Julie Andrews with Italian heart-throb Marcello Mastroianni must have looked good on paper. But both stars are ill-served by a vacuous script about two recently divorced strangers finding solace and companionship with each other. Leaden direction by Gene Saks doesn't help. AJ

Julie Andrews *Pamela Picquet* • Marcello Mastroianni *Cesareo Gramaldi* • Ian Fitzgibbon *Bobby Picquet* • Jean-Pierre Castaldi *Marcel* • Jean-Jacques Dulon *Dr Noiret* • Maria Machado *Miss Knudson* ■ *Dir* Gene Saks • *Scr* Ronald Harwood, from the play *Tchin Tchin* by François Billetdoux

A Touch of Class ★★★★★★

Romantic comedy 1973 · UK · Colour · 105min

Glenda Jackson shows her flair for romantic comedy in this classy effort from writer/director Melvin Frank. Playing a divorced fashion designer, she's more than a match for married American businessman George Segal, subjecting him to a series of well-timed barbs during a disastrous holiday in Spain. The script is honed to a cutting edge to ensure that sentimentality doesn't oversweeten the romance, and Frank succeeds in keeping the piece ironically humorous rather than schmaltzily corny. Jackson picked up her second Oscar for this, though Segal's harassed stud deserved something too for his polished performance. TH Swearing.

George Segal *Steve Blackburn* • Glenda Jackson *Vicki Allessio* • Paul Sorvino *Walter Menkes* • Hildegard Neil *Gloria Blackburn* • Cec Linder *Wendell Thompson* • K Callan *Patty Menkes* • Mary Barclay *Martha Thompson* ■ *Dir* Melvin Frank • *Scr* Melvin Frank, Jack Rose

Touch of Evil ★★★★★ 12

Classic crime thriller 1958 · US · BW · 106min

It was star Charlton Heston (improbably cast as a Mexican) who persuaded Universal to hire Orson Welles to direct this crime thriller. In so doing, he secured not only Welles's most magnificent late character creation (as corrupt corpulent cop Hank Quinlan), but also the film that virtually capped a style the great Welles himself had helped create. It's a byzantine and brilliant melodrama that rivets an audience from its now justly-famed opening title sequence to its grisly finale. In composition, in dialogue and character, and in sheer style, this is what cinema can and should be capable of, and it took the genius of Orson Welles to turn the cheap novel *Badge of Evil* into this terrifically entertaining study in depravity. TS **DVD** **BL**

Charlton Heston *Ramon Miguel "Mike" Vargas* • Janet Leigh *Susan Vargas* • Orson Welles *Hank Quinlan* • Joseph Calleia *Pete Menzies* • Akim Tamiroff *"Uncle" Joe Grandi* • Joanna Moore *Marcia Linnekar* • Ray Collins *Adair* • Dennis Weaver *The night man* • Valentin de Vargas *Pancho* • Marlene Dietrich *Tanya* • Zsa Zsa Gabor *Strip club owner* • Joseph Cotten *Coroner* • Mercedes McCambridge *Gang leader* • Keenan Wynn ■ *Dir* Orson Welles • *Scr* Orson Welles, from the novel *Badge of Evil* by Whit Masterson • *Cinematographer* Russell Metty

A Touch of Larceny ★★★ U

Comedy 1959 · UK · BW · 94min

James Mason was never anything less than a suave and sophisticated performer. However, comedy was not really his forte, even when it was as gentle as in this urbane tale of treachery and libel. The film benefits from the polished presence of that other silky screen smoothie, George Sanders, and willing support from Vera Miles. DP

James Mason *Commander Max Easton* • George Sanders *Sir Charles Holland* • Vera Miles *Virginia Killain* • Oliver Johnston *Minister* • Robert Flemyng *Larkin* ■ *Dir* Guy Hamilton • *Scr* Roger MacDougall, Paul Winterton, Ivan Foxwell, Guy Hamilton, from the novel *The Megstone Plot* by Andrew Garve

A Touch of Love ★★★ 12

Drama 1969 · UK · Colour · 102min

Margaret Drabble adapted her novel, *The Millstone*, for this capable and well-made social drama. An unwed student (Sandy Dennis, in one of her most effective performances) loses her virginity and becomes pregnant. The rest of the cast is also strong, including Ian McKellen's sharp television announcer, the unwitting father of the child. JG **DVD**

Sandy Dennis *Rosamund Stacey* • Ian McKellen *George* • Eleanor Bron *Lydia* • John Standing *Roger* • Michael Coles *Joe* • Rachel Kempson *Sister Harvey* • Margaret Tyzack *Sister Bennett* ■ *Dir* Waris Hussein • *Scr* Margaret Drabble, from her novel *The Millstone*

A Touch of Sin ★★★★ 15

Drama 2013 · Chi · Colour · 124min

Overlapping stories of ordinary folk excluded from China's economic transformation build to a blood-splattered portrait of a nation in director Jia Zhang Ke's film. He unleashes gunfire and violent psychosis in four micro-dramas drawn from actual newspaper stories: here's a village blowhard who won't stay quiet about the local bigwig who's prospered while the community stays poor; there's a migrant worker committing armed robbery to grab his piece of the otherwise elusive consumerist dream. While the various sections achieve a balance between art house anomie and Tarantino-esque carnage, the cumulative effect is what's significant - a fierce, angry statement about the state of modern China. TJ Mandarin +subtitles. Violence, swearing. **DVD** **BL**

Wu Jiang *Dahai* • Wang Baoqiang *Zhou San* • Zhao Tao *Xiao Wu* • Lanshan Luo *Xiao Hui* ■ *Dir/Scr* Jia Zhang Ke

A Touch of the Sun ★★ U

Comedy 1956 · UK · BW · 77min

Try as he might, Frankie Howerd just couldn't crack movies. This was his fifth feature after he made his name on radio's *Variety Bandbox*, but the harder he mugged, the less amusing he became. He stars here as a bellboy who uses an unexpected inheritance to buy the hotel where he once worked. He then installs his workmates as satisfied guests in a bid to dupe a cabal of avaricious snobs. DP

Frankie Howerd *William Darling* • Ruby Murray *Ruby* • Dennis Price *Hatchard* • Dorothy Bromiley *Rose* • Katherine Kath *Lucienne* • Gordon Harker *Sid* • Reginald Beckwith *Hardcastle* ■ *Dir* Gordon Parry • *Scr* Alfred Shaughnessy

A Touch of the Sun ★

Comedy 1979 · UK/US · Colour · 93min

This would-be comedy stars Oliver Reed as a bumbling US Army officer and Peter Cushing as a British commissioner who attempt to recover an American spaceship that's being held for ransom by an African emperor. The humour is so strained as to be sieved of all fun. TH Violence, swearing.

Oliver Reed *Captain Nelson* • Sylvaine Charlet *Natasha* • Peter Cushing *Commissioner Potts* • Keenan Wynn *General Spelvin* • Edwin Manda *Emperor Sumumba* • Fred Carter *President P*

Nutts • Hilary Pritchard *Miss Funnypenny* • Wilfrid Hyde White *M1* • *Dir* Peter Curran • *Scr* Alfred Shaughnessy

A Touch of Zen ★★★★12
Martial arts action drama
1969 · Tai · Colour · 169min

Hu King was one of the masters of the *wu xia* or swordplay film, yet this labyrinthine epic is much more than a simple action flick. This is at the same time a study of rural life, a ghost story, a discussion of philosophical ideas and a thrilling fight film, with each element being handled with rare skill by Hu, whose love of Chinese opera and classical art is evident in every frame. DP Mandarin +subtitles. *DVD* 🅑

Hsu Feng *Yang* • Chun Shih *Ku* • Pai Ying *Shih* • Tien Peng *Ou-Yang* • Hsueh Han *Lu* ■ *Dir/Scr* King Hu

Touch the Top of the World ★★
Drama based on a true story
2006 · Can · Colour · 89min

Strength through adversity is taken to the ultimate level in this inspirational biographical drama. Peter Facinelli gives a solid performance as American adventurer Erik Weihenmayer, the first blind man to reach the summit of Mount Everest. Yet while the facts of his life story are astonishing, an average script and excessive sentimentality mean justice is not really done to his exploits here. SF

Peter Facinelli *Erik Weihenmayer* • Bruce Campbell *Ed Weihenmayer* • Sarah Manninen *Ellie Weihenmayer* • Tom Carey *Brad Bull* • Jack Knight *Erik Weihenmayer age 12* • Sean Anthony Olsen *Eddi Weihenmayer* • Brooklynn Proulx *Emma Weihenmayer* ■ *Dir* Peter Winther • *Scr* Peter Silverman, from the non-fiction book by Erik Weihenmayer

Touched by Love ★★★U
Drama based on a true story
1979 · US · Colour · 93min

Also known as *To Elvis, with Love* (a title which tends to give away the plot), this moving if somewhat sentimental drama is based on a true story. It's a tale of a child with cerebral palsy who becomes more open and communicative after a nursing trainee (Deborah Raffin) encourages her to write a letter to Elvis Presley. Raffin gives a competent performance as Lena Canada (she received a Golden Globe nomination) but it is a young Diane Lane who steals the film. JB

Deborah Raffin *Lena Canada* • Diane Lane *Karen* • Michael Learned *Dr Bell* • John Amos *Tony* • Cristina Raines *Amy* • Mary Wickes *Margaret* • Clu Gulager *Don Fielder* ■ *Dir* Gus Trikonis • *Scr* Hesper Anderson, from the book *To Elvis, with Love* by Lena Canada

Touching the Void ★★★★15
Documentary drama
2003 · UK/US · Colour · 101min

This vivid survival docudrama recounts the harrowing story of British climbing buddies Joe Simpson and Simon Yates. When his own life is threatened, Yates is forced to abandon his partner, leaving him for dead high in the Peruvian Andes. But, remarkably, Simpson survives and despite a shattered leg manages to crawl painfully back to base camp. It's impossible not to wince as he makes the incredible journey. The film combines interviews with the climbers with terrific reconstructions of their ordeals, both physical and psychological. Directed by Kevin Macdonald, who made the equally impressive *One Day in September*, about the terrorist attack on the 1972 Munich Olympic Games, this is dramatised documentary-making at its peak. DA Swearing. *DVD* 🅑

Joe Simpson • Simon Yates • Richard Hawking • Brendan Mackey *Joe Simpson* • Nicholas Aaron *Simon Yates* • Ollie Ryall *Richard Hawking* ■ *Dir* Kevin Macdonald • *Scr* from the non-fiction book by Joe Simpson • *Cinematographer* Mike Eley

Touchy Feely ★★★15
Drama
2013 · US · Colour · 84min

Delving once again into the tangled bonds and neuroses of a close-knit circle of friends and family, the latest from Sundance favourite Lynn Shelton centres on an easy-going massage therapist (Rosemarie DeWitt) who develops a pathological fear of touching other people's skin. As her life begins to unravel, the life of her emotionally repressed dentist brother (Josh Pais) takes a considerable turn for the better as he experiences a big uplift in business. The film boasts plenty of quirky charm and the warm, low-key performances from the talented ensemble help make up for a meandering storyline. JF Swearing, sex scenes.

Rosemarie DeWitt *Abby* • Ellen Page *Jenny* • Allison Janney *Bronwyn* • Josh Pais *Paul* • Scoot McNairy *Jesse* ■ *Dir/Scr* Lynn Shelton

Tough Enough ★15
Sports drama
1982 · US · Colour · 101min

This is a forgettable attempt by Richard Fleischer to explore the ugly world of the "Tough Man" fighting circuit in America. Dennis Quaid struggles as the failing singer turned pugilist and the storyline is barely worthy of lasting the first round, let alone going the distance. NF

Dennis Quaid *Art Long* • Carlene Watkins *Caroline Long* • Warren Oates *James Neese* • Stan Shaw *PT Coolidge* • Pam Grier *Myra* • Bruce McGill *Tony Fallon* • Wilford Brimley *Bill Long* • Fran Ryan *Gert Long* ■ *Dir* Richard O Fleischer [Richard Fleischer] • *Scr* John Leone

Tough Guys ★★★15
Comedy
1986 · US · Colour · 99min

To watch Kirk Douglas and Burt Lancaster use their combined star power to rescue a ropey script is to witness celebrity at its most intense and endearing. As the perpetrators of America's last train robbery, they are released from prison, elderly and bewildered, into an ageist world, so they mount their own grey offensive. Douglas's athletic and sexual prowess is a show-off embarrassment, but Lancaster retains a dignity and poise which confronts the dilemma of age with enormous poignancy. Both, though, spark an on-screen magic. TH Violence, swearing. *DVD*

Burt Lancaster *Harry Doyle* • Kirk Douglas *Archie Long* • Charles Durning *Deke Yablonski* • Alexis Smith *Belle* • Dana Carvey *Richie Evans* • Darlanne Fluegel *Skye Foster* • Eli Wallach *Leon B Little* • Monty Ash *Vince* ■ *Dir* Jeff Kanew • *Scr* James Orr, Jim Cruickshank

Tough Guys Don't Dance ★★18
Black comedy
1987 · US · Colour · 104min

This bizarre black comedy with *film noir* flourishes was written and directed by Norman Mailer as an exercise in experimental movie-making. Ryan O'Neal plays a downtrodden would-be writer who may have committed a murder – but can't quite remember. Yes, it's that sort of film, with lots of weird people running around, saying weird things. The movie seeks to send up Raymond Chandler, but only works intermittently. DA

Ryan O'Neal *Tim Madden* • Isabella Rossellini *Madeleine* • Debra Sandlund *Patty Lareine* • Wings Hauser *Regency* • John Bedford Lloyd *Wardley Meeks III* • Clarence Williams III *Bolo* • Lawrence Tierney *Dougy Madden* ■ *Dir/Scr* Norman Mailer

The Tourist ★12
Thriller
2010 · US/Fr · Colour · 98min

This laughably inept thriller finds mystery woman Angelina Jolie and oblivious holidaying maths teacher Johnny Depp being shadowed through Venice by Scotland Yard's Paul Bettany and vicious gangster Steven Berkoff in the hope that she will lead them to her on-the-run lover who has stolen millions from Berkoff. Director Florian Henckel von Donnersmarck (whose debut feature *The Lives of Others* won a best foreign film Oscar) quickly loses control of his convoluted and hackneyed narrative, Depp's character is an uneasy blend of hammy matinée idol and Clouseau-like farceur, while Jolie is in the running for the most annoying and insipid ice maiden in cinema history. TeS Violence, swearing. *DVD* 🅑

Angelina Jolie *Elise Clifton-Ward* • Johnny Depp *Frank Tupelo* • Paul Bettany *Inspector John Acheson* • Timothy Dalton *Chief Inspector Jones* • Steven Berkoff *Reginald Shaw* • Rufus Sewell *The Englishman* • Christian De Sica *Colonnelo Lombardi* ■ *Dir* Florian Henckel von Donnersmarck • *Scr* Florian Henckel von Donnersmarck, Julian Fellowes, Christopher McQuarrie, from the film *Anthony Zimmer* by Jérôme Salle

Tourist Trap ★15
Horror
1979 · US · Colour · 89min

Suspense is a rare commodity in this low-budget horror flick that focuses on a group of teens who get marooned in the desert when their jeep breaks down. Unluckily for them it's near a museum housing a collection of wax models controlled by nutty Chuck Connors. The dummies give the best performances. RS

Chuck Connors *Slausen* • Jon Van Ness *Jerry* • Jocelyn Jones *Molly* • Robin Sherwood *Eileen* • Tanya Roberts *Becky* • Keith McDermott *Woody* ■ *Dir* David Schmoeller • *Scr* David Schmoeller, J Larry Carroll

The Tournament ★★★18
Action drama
2009 · UK · Colour · 91min

Assassins Ving Rhames, Ian Somerhalder and Kelly Hu battle it out in Middlesborough (!) for a $10 million prize, while alcoholic priest Robert Carlyle finds himself an unwilling participant in the tournament after unknowingly swallowing a competitor's tracking device. Scott Mann's slick and surprisingly entertaining debut feature is an action-packed bloodbath on a budget, with sharp doses of black comedy scattered among the unflinching visceral violence and exploding body parts. Best not to dwell on the gaping plot holes or Bulgarian locations masquerading as the Tees Valley. It's a popcorn treat, pure and simple. AJ *DVD* 🅑

Robert Carlyle *Father MacAvoy* • Kelly Hu *Lai Lai Zhen* • Ian Somerhalder *Miles Slade* • Liam Cunningham *Powers* • Ving Rhames *Joshua Harlow* ■ *Dir* Scott Mann • *Scr* Gary Young, Jonathan Frank, Nick Rowntree

Tous les Matins du Monde ★★★★15
Historical drama
1991 · Fr · Colour · 109min

The winner of seven Césars (the French equivalent to the Oscars), this majestic historical costume drama is a delight for both eyes and ears. Jean-Pierre Marielle is outstanding as 17th-century composer Sainte Colombe, while on his debut Guillaume Depardieu is splendidly dashing as his sole pupil, Marin Marais. Guillaume's father Gérard Depardieu has a choice cameo as the older Marais, who becomes Louis XIV's musical director, looking back with regret on his reckless youth. Director Alain Corneau captures the period perfectly and the baroque viola da gamba music is magnificent. DP French +subtitles. Sex scenes, nudity. *DVD*

Jean-Pierre Marielle *Monsieur de Sainte Colombe* • Gérard Depardieu *Marin Marais* • Anne Brochet *Madeleine* • Guillaume Depardieu *Young Marin Marais* • Caroline Sihol *Mme de Sainte Colombe* • Carole Richert *Toinette* • Michel Bouquet *Baugin* ■ *Dir* Alain Corneau • *Scr* Pascal Quignard, Alain Corneau, from the novel by Pascal Quignard

Tout Va Bien ★★★18
Experimental political drama
1972 · Fr/It · Colour · 91min

After four years of making 16mm and video movies, Marxist co-directors Jean-Luc Godard and Jean-Pierre Gorin returned to "commercial" film-making by casting Jane Fonda and Yves Montand in the leading roles. But audiences didn't exactly flock to see this depiction of workers occupying their factory and holding their bosses prisoner. Fonda plays an American journalist and Montand – her lover – a former New Wave director now forced to make TV ads for a living, as Godard himself had done. There is a lot of serious talk, a splendid composite set and a few jokes. RB French +subtitles. *DVD*

Jane Fonda *Susan* • Yves Montand *Jacques* • Vittorio Caprioli *Factory manager* • Pierre Oudrey *Frédéric* • Jean Pignol *CGT delegate* • Elizabeth Chauvin *Geneviève* ■ *Dir/Scr* Jean-Luc Godard, Jean-Pierre Gorin

Tovarich ★★★
Comedy
1937 · US · BW · 92min

Claudette Colbert and Charles Boyer, anticipating the Russian Revolution, are the aristocrats who escape to Paris, where they deposit the tsar's billions in a Paris bank and, unwilling to spend the cash, set themselves up as a maid and butler in a grand French home. Inevitably, they are found out, leading to a farcical comedy of disguise. While not nearly as entertaining or as politically astute as the later *Ninotchka*, Colbert and Boyer make a suave and witty couple, ably supported by an imperious Basil Rathbone. AT

Claudette Colbert *The Grand Duchess Tatiana Petrovna/Tina Dubrovsky* • Charles Boyer *Prince Mikail Alexandrovitch Ouratieff/Michel* • Basil Rathbone *Gorotchenko* • Anita Louise *Helen Dupont* • Melville Cooper *Charles Dupont* • Isabel Jeans *Fernande Dupont* • Maurice Murphy *Georges Dupont* ■ *Dir* Anatole Litvak • *Scr* Casey Robinson, Robert E Sherwood, from the play by Jacques Deval

Tovarisch, I Am Not Dead ★★★12A
Documentary
2007 · UK · Colour and BW · 83min

Garri Urban fled Soviet and Nazi oppression, survived the Holocaust and spent much of his adult life being harassed by the KGB. No wonder, therefore, that his film-maker son Stuart should want to make a documentary about his remarkable experiences. Yet, for all his charisma, Garri is a prickly character and tensions mount as the pair traverse eastern Europe to revisit the people and places that shaped his destiny. Following the lead set by recent filial memoirs like Nathaniel Kahn's *My Architect* and Doug Block's *51 Birch Street*, this is a fascinating insight into the impact of the political upheavals of the 20th century on ordinary citizens. DP In English, Russian.

Garri Urban • Stuart Urban • Anne Applebaum • Noka Kapranova • Menachem Urban ■ *Dir* Stuart Urban • *Scr* Stuart Urban, inspired by the autobiography by Garri Urban

Toward the Unknown ★★U
Drama
1956 · US · Colour · 114min

Stressed pilot William Holden tries to regain the respect of his men in this dour, unexciting film. The flight sequences here probably looked spectacular at the time, but the action grinds to a halt when the planes are on the ground. James Garner makes his film debut. TS

William Holden (2) *Major Lincoln Bond* • Lloyd Nolan *Brig Gen Bill Banner* • Virginia Leith *Connie Mitchell* • Charles McGraw *Colonel "Mickey" McKee* • Murray Hamilton *Major "Bromo" Lee* • Paul Fix *Maj Gen Bryan Shelby* • LQ Jones *Lieutenant Sweeney* • James Garner *Major Joe Craven* ■ *Dir* Mervyn LeRoy • *Scr* Beirne Lay Jr

Towed in a Hole ★★★★U
Comedy
1932 · US · BW · 20min

The best Stan and Ollie movie is the one you are watching, although some masterpieces are so ingenious in their destructive comedy that they linger in the mind. The springboard here is Stanley's suggestion that they should not just sell fish, but catch it as well – thus doubling their income. A boat is found and its refit becomes an orgy of misfortune. Memorable jokes include Stanley, confined below, getting his head stuck behind the mast. Oliver is up a ladder painting it. Stanley finds a saw... Anticipation is more than half the pleasure with this duo – the most endearing and inventive comedians in cinema history. BB *DVD*

Stan Laurel *Stan* • Oliver Hardy *Ollie* • Billy Gilbert *Joe, junkyard owner* ■ *Dir* George Marshall • *Scr* HM Walker, Stan Laurel

Tower Block ★★★★ 15
Thriller 2012 · UK · Colour · 86min

Top-floor residents of a derelict East End tower block come under attack from a psycho sniper in directors James Nunn and Ronnie Thompson's riveting splatter thriller. Helping the nerve-jangling cause enormously are Sheridan Smith, as the accidental Sigourney Weaver-style heroine, and Jack O'Connell, who genially sends up his hard-man persona. Yes, the maniac's motive barely passes muster, but it still makes for a nastily rousing, high-tension ride full of smart twists and turns. AJ *DVD* *Blu*

Sheridan Smith *Becky* • Jack O'Connell (2) *Kurtis* • Ralph Brown *Neville* • Russell Tovey *Paul* • Jill Baker *Violet* • Julie Graham *Carol* • Chris Fulford [Christopher Fulford] *Kevin* ■ *Dir* James Nunn, Ronnie Thompson • *Scr* James Moran

Tower Heist ★★★ 12
Action crime comedy
2011 · US /Jpn · Colour · 100min

Downtrodden workers seek payback from a dodgy Wall Street trader in this topical yet goofy action comedy. Ben Stiller is typically uptight as the manager of a Manhattan hotel who turns on penthouse resident Arthur Shaw (Alan Alda) after he cons the staff out of their savings. Eddie Murphy echoes the rogue he played in *Trading Places*, though he's not quite as charming, as a petty thief that Stiller employs to help take back the millions hidden in Shaw's suite. The film never feels quite as epic as it should, although Brett Ratner (the *Rush Hour* series) directs some impressive action in and around the skyscraper. Overall though, it's the mismatch of criminal minds that raises the entertainment value. SP Swearing, sexual references. *DVD* *Blu*

Ben Stiller *Josh Kovacs* • Eddie Murphy *Slide* • Matthew Broderick *Chase Fitzhugh* • Casey Affleck *Charlie Gibbs* • Alan Alda *Arthur Shaw* • Téa Leoni *Special Agent Claire Denham* • Michael Peña [Michael Pena] *Dev'Reaux* ■ *Dir* Brett Ratner • *Scr* Ted Griffin, Jeff Nathanson, from a story by Bill Collage, Adam Cooper, Griffin

Tower of Evil ★★ 18
Horror 1972 · UK · Colour · 89min

A series of killings and some buried treasure lure detective Bryant Halliday and a group of unusually attractive, pot-smoking, sex-starved archaeologists to the archetypal accursed isle. It isn't long before further frenzied murders start to reduce their number. Terrible dialogue and not much suspense, but the nudity, violence and Robin Askwith are very 1970s, and this has found a new generation of fans. DM

Bryant Halliday *Det Brent* • Jill Haworth *Rose* • Anthony Valentine *Dr Simpson* • Anna Palk *Nora* • Jack Watson *Hamp Gurney* • Mark Edwards *Adam* • Derek Fowlds *Dan* • Robin Askwith *Des* ■ *Dir* Jim O'Connolly • *Scr* Jim O'Connolly, from a story by George Baxt

Tower of London ★★★
Historical drama 1939 · US · BW · 92min

Universal, having hit pay dirt with their fictitious monsters, here turned their attentions to British history, producing a highly fanciful account of the Duke of Gloucester's machinations to seize the throne as Richard III. The Duke of Clarence is drowned in a wine barrel, but most of the rest, involving Gloucester and royal executioner Mord dispatching all and sundry, is fabrication, grim but too often plodding. The chief appeal is the fruity performances. DM

Basil Rathbone *Richard, Duke of Gloucester* • Boris Karloff *Mord* • Barbara O'Neil *Queen Elizabeth* • Ian Hunter *King Edward IV* • Vincent Price *Duke of Clarence* • Nan Grey *Lady Alice Barton* • John Sutton *John Wyatt* • Leo G Carroll *Hastings* ■ *Dir* Rowland V Lee • *Scr* Robert N Lee

Tower of London ★★
Horror 1962 · US · BW · 79min

Roger Corman's film about Richard III keeps the basic structure of the better 1939 film of the same title, as the Duke of Gloucester murders everyone who blocks his path to the throne. This is more of a spook film, as Gloucester is troubled, like Macbeth, by the ghosts of his victims. Vincent Price, who played the Duke of Clarence in the earlier film, makes a formidable if camp Gloucester, and the script is unusually intelligent, but the action is grim without being chilling. DM

Vincent Price *Richard of Gloucester* • Michael Pate *Sir Ratcliffe* • Joan Freeman *Lady Margaret* • Robert Brown *Sir Justin* • Justice Watson *Edward IV* • Sarah Selby *Queen Elizabeth* • Richard McCauly *Clarence* • Eugene Martin *Edward V* ■ *Dir* Roger Corman • *Scr* Leo V Gordon, F Amos Powell, James B Gordon, from a story by Leo V Gordon, F Amos Powell • *Dialogue Director* Francis Ford Coppola

The Towering Inferno ★★★★ 12
Disaster movie 1974 · US · Colour · 158min

It took two major studios – Fox and Warner Bros, pooling resources – and two similar novels – *The Tower* and *The Glass Inferno* – to make this triple-Oscar-winning disaster movie. The fun comes from guessing which superstars will get fried to a crisp in the burning San Francisco skyscraper, ignited during the opening ceremony, and who will be saved by daring fire chief Steve McQueen. The big-name cast plays second fiddle to the blazing special effects, but the mounting suspense and outlandish rescue attempts fan the consistently entertaining flames. AJ Swearing. *DVD* *Blu*

Steve McQueen (1) *Fire Chief Michael O'Hallorhan* • Paul Newman *Doug Roberts* • William Holden *Jim Duncan* • Faye Dunaway *Susan Franklin* • Fred Astaire *Harlee Claiborne* • Susan Blakely *Patty Simmons* • Richard Chamberlain *Roger Simmons* • Jennifer Jones *Lisolette Mueller* • OJ Simpson *Security Chief Jernigan* • Robert Vaughn (1) *Senator Gary Parker* • Robert Wagner *Dan Bigelow* ■ *Dir* John Guillermin, Irwin Allen • *Scr* Stirling Silliphant, from the novels *The Tower* by Richard Martin Stern and *The Glass Inferno* by Thomas N Scortia, Frank M Robinson

The Town ★★★★ 15
Crime thriller 2010 · US · Colour · 119min

In this smart and taut thriller from Ben Affleck, bank robbers are alarmed to discover that the manager they briefly took hostage (Rebecca Hall) lives in their blue collar Boston neighbourhood and may be able to identify them, despite the masks they wore. In addition to directing with flair and confidence, Affleck plays the central conflicted character with admirable subtlety, and there's also fine work by Jon Hamm as an FBI agent and Chris Cooper as Affleck's incarcerated father. But everyone is eclipsed by the intensity of Jeremy Renner as short-fused Jem, driven by loyalty to both his friends and his working-class roots. TeS Violence, swearing, some sex scenes, drug abuse. *DVD* *Blu*

Ben Affleck *Doug MacRay* • Rebecca Hall *Claire Keesey* • Jon Hamm *FBI Special Agent Frawley* • Jeremy Renner *James Coughlin* • Blake Lively *Krista Coughlin* • Titus Welliver *Detective Dino Ciampa* • Pete Postlethwaite *Fergus "Fergie" Colm* • Chris Cooper *Stephen "Mac" MacRay* ■ *Dir* Ben Affleck • *Scr* Ben Affleck, Peter Craig, Aaron Stockard, from the novel *Prince of Thieves* by Chuck Hogan

Town & Country ★★★ 15
Comedy 2001 · US · Colour · 100min

The tittle-tattle about on-set feuds and last-minute recuts has helped ensure that this ensemble farce became one of the biggest money losers of all time. But its only real crimes – a dated sense of humour and a lack of directorial acuity – mean that Peter Chelsom has turned out a movie that feels more Blake Edwards than Woody Allen. The marital shenanigans involving Warren Beatty and Diane Keaton and their buddies Garry Shandling and Goldie Hawn may be midlife and bourgeois, but the acting is always polished. DP *DVD*

Warren Beatty *Porter Stoddard* • Diane Keaton *Ellie Stoddard* • Goldie Hawn *Mona* • Garry Shandling *Griffin* • Andie MacDowell *Eugenie Claybourne* • Charlton Heston *Mr Claybourne* • Marian Seldes *Mrs Claybourne* • Josh Hartnett *Tom Stoddard* • Jenna Elfman *Auburn* • Nastassja Kinski *Alex* • Buck Henry *Suttler* ■ *Dir* Peter Chelsom • *Scr* Michael Laughlin, Buck Henry

A Town Called Hell ★★ 15
Spaghetti western 1971 · UK/Sp · Colour · 97min

This brutal western, also known as *A Town Called Bastard*, is one of the few British ventures into the genre. Set in 1895 in Mexico (but shot in Spain), it follows Stella Stevens as she seeks out those who killed her husband a decade earlier, while Martin Landau threatens to reveal that his brother, Robert Shaw, is not a priest but a ruthless bandit. The interesting cast nearly compensates for a slackness in direction, as the film lurches from tightly shot moments of brooding tension to frantic outbursts of stylised violence. DP *DVD*

Robert Shaw *Priest* • Telly Savalas *Don Carlos* • Stella Stevens *Alvira* • Michael Craig *Paco* • Martin Landau *Colonel* • Dudley Sutton *Spectre* • Fernando Rey *Old blind farmer* ■ *Dir* Robert Parrish • *Scr* Richard Aubrey

A Town Called Panic ★★★★ PG
Animated adventure
2009 · Bel/Fr/Lux · Colour · 75min

Based on a cult French TV series, this stop-motion adventure uses plastic toys to tell a surreal story about two pals, Cowboy and Indian, who are plotting a surprise present for their friend Horse. When their outlandish plans destroy their house, the trio sets off for an underwater world where they are soon in hot pursuit of amphibians who've been stealing the debris of their home. A succession of delightfully bizarre scenarios, full of Tom and Jerry-style slapstick and off-the-wall humour, should appeal to adults as much as children, while the crude animation never lacks invention. TeS French +subtitles. *DVD*

Stéphane Aubier *Cowboy/Max Briquenet/Mr Ernotte* • Nicolas Buysse *Sheep/Jean-Paul* • Bruce Ellison *Indian* • Christelle Mahy *Hen* • Vincent Patar *Horse/Maman Atlante* • David Ricci *Donkey/Michel* ■ *Dir/Scr* Stéphane Aubier, Vincent Patar

The Town Christmas Forgot ★★
Seasonal drama 2010 · Can · Colour · 95min

A dysfunctional yuppie family restores hope to a backwater Colorado town in this far-fetched diversion celebrating unity and the magic of Christmas. Stranded in the appropriately named Nowhere following car trouble, Lauren Holly, Rick Roberts and their two kids inadvertently each become saviours – laughably able to solve all the stereotyped residents' woes with their big-city ways. Naturally, the materialistic clan also gets transformed, with young son Azer Greco (Holly's real-life offspring) bringing genuine sweetness to the otherwise emotionally flat final act. SF

Lauren Holly *Annie Benson* • Rick Roberts *Charles Benson* • Torri Webster *Trish Benson* • Azer Greco *Nolan Benson* ■ *Dir* John Bradshaw • *Scr* Jim Makichuk

A Town like Alice ★★★ PG
Second World War drama
1956 · UK · BW · 111min

Director Jack Lee's documentary background is evident in this earnest adaptation of Nevil Shute's wartime novel about the hardships faced by a group of women route-marched across Malaya by the Japanese. But while he has little difficulty setting the scene, he struggles to prevent some episodes lapsing into overwrought melodrama. Takagi (as a sympathetic guard), Jean Anderson and Renee Houston offer stout support to Virginia McKenna, whose romantic interludes with Peter Finch provide charming relief from the trials of the trek. DP *DVD*

Virginia McKenna *Jean Paget* • Peter Finch *Joe Harman* • Takagi [Kenji Takaki] *Japanese sergeant* • Tran Van Khe *Captain Sugaya* • Jean Anderson *Miss Horsefall* • Marie Lohr *Mrs Dudley Frost* • Maureen Swanson *Ellen* • Renee Houston *Ebbey* ■ *Dir* Jack Lee (2) • *Scr* WP Lipscomb, Richard Mason, from the novel by Nevil Shute

Town of Runners ★★★ PG
Documentary 2012 · Eth/UK · Colour · 88min

In the isolated Ethiopian town of Bekoji, coach Sentayehu Eshetu's remarkable eye for talent has resulted in several of his charges achieving championship greatness (Olympic gold medallists Tirunesh Dibaba and Kenenisa Bekele, among them). Yet, as Jerry Rothwell discovers in this intriguing, but inconsistent documentary, athletic success often owes as much to luck as genuine talent in a country where corruption and incompetence blight progress. Rothwell exposes the shambolic situation by following the fortunes of assorted teenagers as they attempt to better their lives. Rothwell's film raises many pressing issues, but the fragmented structure means it's never as touching or hard-hitting as it should have been. DP *DVD*

■ *Dir* Jerry Rothwell

Town on Trial ★★
Murder mystery 1956 · UK · BW · 96min

In this very British whodunnit, John Mills stars as a Scotland Yard detective who's called in to investigate unsavoury goings-on in an English town. A woman with a dubious reputation has been found dead on club property and there's no shortage of suspects for Mills to grill, all of whom seem to have a dodgy past. It's a modest mystery in the Agatha Christie tradition, and it offers a modicum of tension. AT

John Mills *Supt Mike Halloran* • Charles Coburn *Dr John Fenner* • Barbara Bates *Elizabeth Fenner* • Derek Farr *Mark Roper* • Alec McCowen *Peter Crowley* • Elizabeth Seal *Fiona Dixon* ■ *Dir* John Guillermin • *Scr* Robert Westerby, Ken Hughes

Town Rat, Country Rat ★★★★
Silent animation 1923 · Fr · Tinted · 14min

Ladislaw Starewicz demonstrates his cinematic ingenuity and a fondness for slapstick, as well as his genius for puppetry, in this spicily satirical retelling of the familiar fable of the country rat overwhelmed by city life. Starting with a mischievous use of back projection, as the town rat motors out of Paris, the film also includes iconic cartoon dialogue, and a segment combining live-action and animation (as a curious kitten chases the rodentine revellers at a cabaret soirée) and an intricate superimposition flashback, as the country rat recalls his adventure. DP

■ *Dir* Ladislaw Starewicz • *Scr* Ladislaw Starewicz, from a fable by Jean de La Fontaine

Town without Pity ★★ 15
Courtroom drama
1961 · US/W Ger/Swi · BW · 99min

Kirk Douglas has often been drawn to roles in which he can express self-disgust. Here he stars as an army officer defending four American servicemen on a charge of raping a young girl in Germany (played by Christine Kaufmann). As the case progresses, Douglas reluctantly sullies the girl's reputation to save the men from a death sentence. Filmed in Germany, this is crude, revelling in its sensational aspects. AE

Kirk Douglas *Maj Steve Garrett* • EG Marshall *Maj Jerome Pakenham* • Christine Kaufmann *Karin Steinhof* • Robert Blake *Jim* • Richard Jaeckel *Bidie* • Frank Sutton *Chuck* ■ *Dir* Gottfried Reinhardt • *Scr* Silvia Reinhardt, Georg Hurdalek, Jan Lustig, from the novel *Das Urteil* by Manfred Gregor

U SUITABLE FOR ALL Uc SUITABLE ESPECIALLY FOR YOUNG CHILDREN (DVD ONLY) PG PARENTAL GUIDANCE 12A UNDER 12s TO BE ACCOMPANIED (CINEMA ONLY)

The Toxic Avenger ★★★ 18

Spoof horror 1985 · US · Colour · 75min

After years of churning out teen comedies that weren't very funny, Troma Films hit the big time with this outrageously tacky superhero spoof. Weedy janitor Mark Torgl is transformed into good-guy monster the Toxic Avenger (Mitchell Cohen) after being dumped into a barrel of toxic goo by a gang of thugs. Toxie (as he's known to his friends) is very nice to his blind girlfriend but metes out violent punishment to local criminals. Loaded with infantile slapstick, amateurish acting, teen-orientated erotica and extreme gore (trimmed considerably in the UK) this is B-movie making at its crudest and purest. RS DVD BD

Andree Maranda *Sara* · Mitchell Cohen *Toxic Avenger* · Jennifer Baptist *Wanda* · Cindy Manion *Julie* · Robert Prichard *Slug* · Gary Schneider *Bozo* · Mark Torgl *Melvin* · Marisa Tomei *Health club girl* ■ *Dir* Michael Herz, Samuel Weil · *Scr* Joe Ritter, Lloyd Kaufman, Gay Partington Terry, Stuart Strutin

The Toxic Avenger, Part II
★ 18

Spoof horror 1988 · US · Colour · 90min

Fans of Troma Films' most celebrated creation had to wait three years for the inevitable follow-up. In the meantime their hero had achieved near iconic status, but even his most die-hard fans will have trouble finding anything to enjoy in this debacle which sees Toxie travelling to Japan to save Earth's ecosystem from an evil industrial conglomerate. Shot back-to-back with the even more lamentable *Part III*, and followed in 2000 by a fourth instalment. RS DVD BD

Ron Fazio *The Toxic Avenger* · John Altamura *The Toxic Avenger* · Phoebe Legere *Claire* · Rick Collins *Apocalypse Inc Chairman* · Rikiya Yasuoka *Big Mac* ■ *Dir* Lloyd Kaufman, Michael Herz · *Scr* Gay Partington Terry, from a story by Lloyd Kaufman

The Toy ★★ PG

Comedy 1982 · US · Colour · 97min

Richard Pryor, a journalist fallen on hard times, is working as a janitor at the Bates department store. His slapstick incompetence at dealing with an inflatable toy is watched by nine-year-old Scott Schwartz, the spoiled heir to the Bates empire. Schwartz is allowed to visit his father (Jackie Gleason) at work once every year and to have anything he chooses for that week. He chooses to have Pryor as a human "toy". This has some fine moments (especially at the start) but soon degenerates into a mawkish message movie. DF

Richard Pryor *Jack Brown* · Jackie Gleason *US Bates* · Ned Beatty *Morehouse* · Scott Schwartz *Eric Bates* · Teresa Ganzel *Fancy Bates* · Wilfrid Hyde White *Barkley* ■ *Dir* Richard Donner · *Scr* Carol Sobieski, from the film *Le Jouet* by Francis Veber

Toy Soldiers ★★ 15

Action thriller 1991 · US · Colour · 107min

This dopey movie blends *Animal House* antics with Rambo-ish heroics to risible effect. Sean Astin and Wil Wheaton are the teenage pranksters who lead their classmates in a fight back when nasty South American mobsters take over their school. Louis Gossett Jr and Denholm Elliott provide a few memorable moments, but the sheer silliness of the concept doomed this project right from the start. JF Violence. DVD BD

Sean Astin *Billy Tepper* · Wil Wheaton *Joey Trotta* · Keith Coogan *Snuffy Bradberry* · Andrew Divoff *Luis Cali* · R Lee Ermey *General Kramer* · Mason Adams *Deputy Director Brown* · Denholm Elliott *Headmaster* · Louis Gossett Jr *Dean Parker* ■ *Dir* Daniel Petrie Jr · *Scr* Daniel Petrie Jr, David Koepp, from the novel by William P Kennedy

---

LANDMARK FILM
The world's first feature film to be created entirely within a computer

Toy Story ★★★★★ PG

Animated comedy adventure
1995 · US · Colour · 77min

The first completely computer-generated animation feature is a masterpiece from director John Lasseter, with voiceovers by Tom Hanks, Tim Allen, Don Rickles and others rounding out convincing characterisations. Woody, an old-fashioned pullstring cowboy, is his owner Andy's favourite toy, and lords it benevolently over Mr Potato Head, Bo-Peep and Rex the Dinosaur. Until, that is, the arrival of newcomer Buzz Lightyear, a hi-tech space-ranger. It's a great adventure story that will not only entertain children but can also be enjoyed as a jokey parable by adults. Mention should also be made of Randy Newman's masterly score, which was Oscar nominated along with his song *You've Got a Friend*. Released in 3D in autumn 2009. TH
DVD BD 3D

Tom Hanks *Woody* · Tim Allen *Buzz Lightyear* · Don Rickles *Mr Potato Head* · Jim Varney *Slinky Dog* · Wallace Shawn *Rex* · John Ratzenberger *Hamm* · Annie Potts *Bo Peep* ■ *Dir* John Lasseter · *Scr* Joss Whedon, Andrew Stanton, Joel Cohen, Alec Sokolow, from a story by John Lasseter, Pete Docter Andrew Stanton, Joe Ranft · *Animators* Pete Docter, Rich Quade, Ash Brannon

Toy Story 2 ★★★★★ U

Animated comedy adventure
1999 · US · Colour · 88min

Originally intended as a 60-minute, straight-to-video project, this was a work in progress right up to its release - complete with last-minute additions to the cast. Yet who can be wholly cynical about a film that not only manages to surpass its predecessor, but also restores credibility to that much-debased term "family entertainment"? Buzz's bid to rescue Woody from the clutches of a sleazy toy collector will keep the youngsters on the edge of their seats. However, it's the little touches that will delight the grown-ups, most notably the in-jokes and the charming re-creation of a 1950s TV puppet show. A straight-to-video spin-off, *Buzz Lightyear of Star Command*, led to a TV series. DP DVD BD CS

Tom Hanks *Woody* · Tim Allen *Buzz Lightyear* · Joan Cusack *Jessie* · Kelsey Grammer *Prospector* · Don Rickles *Mr Potato Head* · Jim Varney *Slinky Dog* · Wallace Shawn *Rex* · John Ratzenberger *Hamm* · Annie Potts *Bo Peep* · John Morris *Andy* · Laurie Metcalf *Andy's mom* ■ *Dir* John Lasseter, Lee Unkrich, Ash Brannon · *Scr* Andrew Stanton, Rita Hsiao, Doug Chamberlin, Chris Webb, from a story by John Lasseter, Pete Docter, Ash Brannon, Andrew Stanton

Toy Story 3 ★★★★★ U

Animated comedy adventure
2010 · US · Colour · 98min

The glow of originality may have dimmed, but Pixar's third rummage in the toy box delivers exactly what it's supposed to, with appealing fringe benefits. Director Lee Unkrich (*Monsters, Inc*, *Finding Nemo*) serves up an expert blend of slapstick fun and heartfelt adventure, in which Andy goes to college and his playthings are donated to a day-care centre where the repressive toy regime consigns them to age-inappropriate man-handling. The new characters - including plush teddy bear villain Lotso and his creepy sidekick Big Baby - are a delight, but it's Woody to the rescue in a sweet, thrilling and engrossing take on prison-break movies, with the underlying message about embracing life transitions leading to a tear-inducing finale. AJ DVD BD

Tom Hanks *Woody* · Tim Allen *Buzz Lightyear* · Joan Cusack *Jessie* · Michael Keaton *Ken* · Wallace Shawn *Rex* · John Ratzenberger *Hamm* · Timothy Dalton *Mr Pricklepants* ■ *Dir* Lee Unkrich · *Scr* Michael Arndt, from a story by John Lasseter, Andrew Stanton, Lee Unkrich

---

Toy Story 4

Animated comedy adventure 2018 · US · Colour

This is a preview - no prints were available to review prior to publication: Now due for release in June 2018, this will be one of the most anticipated movie events of the year - and not just because the series to date has taken almost $2 billion at the box office. Woody, Buzz and the gang have captured a place in our hearts, so expectations will be sky high. Original director John Lasseter will direct the story that sees Woody experience a touch of romance in the arms of Bo Peep. Risky, or realistic? We can hardly wait. TF

Tom Hanks *Woody* · Tim Allen *Buzz Lightyear* · John Ratzenberger *Hamm* ■ *Dir* John Lasseter · *Scr* Rashida Jones, Will McCormack, from a story by John Lasseter, Andrew Stanton, Pete Docter, Lee Unkrich · *Music* Randy Newman

The Toy Wife ★★ U

Period romantic drama 1938 · US · BW · 93min

Returned from Europe to the family seat in Louisiana, Luise Rainer throws off her beau Robert Young and steals her sister's fiancé, Melvyn Douglas. They marry and have a child, but she proves incapable of meeting the demands of her position. This overheated period melodrama was considered old-fashioned in its day, and now has little to offer other than high-class sets and costumes. RK

Luise Rainer *Gilberta "Frou Frou" Brigard* · Melvyn Douglas *Georges Sartoris* · Robert Young (1) *André Vallaire* · Barbara O'Neil *Louise Brigard* · HB Warner *Victor Brigard* · Alma Kruger *Mme Vallaire* · Libby Taylor *Suzanne* ■ *Dir* Richard Thorpe · *Scr* Zoë Akins [Zoe Akins], from the play *Frou-frou* by Henri Meilhac, Ludovic Halévy, and the play *Frou Frou* by Augustin Daly

Toys ★★ PG

Comedy fantasy 1992 · US · Colour · 116min

War-addicted Michael Gambon inherits a toy factory, turning it into an assembly line for destructive toys. You'll gasp in sheer amazement at the magnificent sets and decor, which alone make this vainglorious slice of whimsy worth a look - just try to ignore the rather naive and self-indulgent plot. Robin Williams, playing the nephew who tries to stop Gambon manufacturing only war games, tanks and guns, is surprisingly low-key. AJ Violence. DVD

Robin Williams *Leslie Zevo* · Michael Gambon *The General* · Joan Cusack *Alsatia Zevo* · Robin Wright *Gwen* · LL Cool J *Patrick* · Donald O'Connor *Kenneth Zevo* · Arthur Malet *Owens Owens* · Jack Warden *Zevo Sr* ■ *Dir* Barry Levinson · *Scr* Valerie Curtin, Barry Levinson

Toys in the Attic ★★★

Melodrama 1963 · US · BW · 90min

Lillian Hellman's play is the basis for this steamy though softened drama about bizarre goings-on in a fading New Orleans family. Dean Martin is good as the ne'er-do-well who brings his young bride home to visit his poverty-stricken spinster sisters (Wendy Hiller and Geraldine Page), while hiding his ill-gotten riches. Not quite Tennessee Williams, but still engrossing. JG

Dean Martin *Julian Berniers* · Geraldine Page *Carrie Berniers* · Yvette Mimieux *Lily Prine Berniers* · Wendy Hiller *Anna Berniers* · Gene Tierney *Albertine Prine* · Nan Martin *Charlotte Warkins* · Larry Gates *Cyrus Warkins* ■ *Dir* George Roy Hill · *Scr* James Poe, from the play by Lillian Hellman

Traces of a Dragon: Jackie Chan & His Lost Family
★★★

Documentary 2003 · HK · Colour · 96min

Interweaving newsreel footage, interviews and clips from nine Jackie Chan movies, this is a fascinating documentary portrait of Chan's parents' extended family in China. The Hong Kong chop socky star only recently discovered the connection, and director Mabel Cheung wisely focuses on Jackie's octogenarian father, Chan Chi-Long, who relates his past life as a Nationalist spy, Shanghai mobster and embassy handyman with vigour. Yet his wife Lily's experiences as an opium smuggler and glamorous gambler are equally compelling, as are the recollections of the couple's children from previous marriages - Lily's devoted daughters and Chi-Long's sons, a pig farmer and a postman. DP Cantonese, Mandarin +subtitles.

■ *Dir* Mabel Cheung · *Cinematographer* Arthur Wong · *Music* Henry Lai

Traces of Red ★★ 15

Erotic thriller 1992 · US · Colour · 100min

In *Sunset Blvd* fashion, recently killed cop James Belushi narrates the story of a serial killer with a penchant for Yves Saint Laurent lipstick and bad poetry. Unfortunately the similarity ends there, as the convoluted and implausible plot is interspersed with the standard mixture of soft-core porn and violence. The proceedings are elevated a little above the norm by a cast that includes a sexually ravenous Lorraine Bracco. DA DVD

James Belushi *Jack Dobson* · Lorraine Bracco *Ellen Schofield* · Tony Goldwyn *Steve Frayn* · William Russ *Michael Dobson* · Faye Grant *Beth Frayn* · Michelle Joyner *Morgan Cassidy* ■ *Dir* Andy Wolk · *Scr* Jim Piddock

Track of the Cat ★★★

Western drama 1954 · US · Colour · 102min

This strange and brooding western melodrama is distinguished by its unique sense of design. While filmed in CinemaScope and colour, the whole film is art directed, costumed, and lit for black-and-white - only occasional flashes of colour breaking up the wintry landscape. Although rather ponderous, there are fine performances from lead Robert Mitchum and from Beulah Bondi as the family matriarch. TS

Robert Mitchum *Curt Bridges* · Teresa Wright *Grace Bridges* · Diana Lynn *Gwen Williams* · Tab Hunter *Harold "Hal" Bridges* · Beulah Bondi *Ma Bridges* · Philip Tonge *Pa Bridges* · William Hopper *Arthur* · Carl "Alfalfa" Switzer *Joe Sam* ■ *Dir* William A Wellman · *Scr* Al Bezzerides, from a novel by Walter Van Tilburg Clark

Track 29 ★★★ 18

Fantasy melodrama 1988 · UK · Colour · 86min

Surrealist director Nicolas Roeg joins arcane writer Dennis Potter for a well constructed Freudian psychodrama about cloaking sexual unfulfilment behind easy nostalgia. Taking its title from the song *Chattanooga Choo-Choo*, housewife Theresa Russell finds her erotic fantasies triggered by stranger Gary Oldman, while her dowdy husband plays with his model railway in the attic. However, Oldman's multiple-identity crisis means he could also be her adopted son. Shockingly original, amusingly chilling and occasionally inaccessible. AJ Swearing, violence, nudity.

Theresa Russell *Linda Henry* · Gary Oldman *Martin* · Christopher Lloyd *Dr Henry Henry* · Sandra Bernhard *Nurse Stein* · Colleen Camp *Arlanda* · Seymour Cassel *Dr Bernard Fairmont* · Leon Rippy *Trucker* ■ *Dir* Nicolas Roeg · *Scr* Dennis Potter

Tracker ★★★ 12

Period action adventure
2010 · NZ/UK · Colour · 97min

In this New Zealand-set period adventure, an embittered Boer War veteran (Ray Winstone, doing pretty well in the accent stakes) tracks down a Maori seaman (Temuera Morrison, of *Once Were Warriors*) wanted for murdering a British soldier. It's pretty obvious that hunter and hunted will eventually realise they have much in common, but this efficient chase story does well to deliver sundry twists and turns along the way. The drama's more satisfying than exciting, but it's a solid entertainment nonetheless. TJ Some violence, gore. DVD BD

Ray Winstone *Arjan van Diemen* · Temuera Morrison *Kereama* · Gareth Reeves *Major Carlysle* · Andy Anderson *Bryce* · Mark Mitchinson *Sergeant Major Saunders* ■ *Dir* Ian Sharp · *Scr* Nicolas van Pallandt

T

Tracks ★
Drama 1977 · US · Colour · 91min

This is a mess from Hollywood's most pretentious independent director, Henry Jaglom. Dennis Hopper plays a Vietnam veteran with problems, principally the dead body of a buddy he's transporting across the US for burial. Jaglom's slick symbolism and Hopper's "Hey man, like, real heavy" dialogue puts this into a time capsule that should be buried real deep, man. **AT** Swearing, sex scenes, nudity.

Dennis Hopper *Sergeant Jack Falen* · Taryn Power *Stephanie* · Dean Stockwell *Mark* · Topo Swope *Chloe* · Michael Emil *Emile* ■ *Dir/Scr* Henry Jaglom

Tracks ★★★★ 12
Biographical drama 2013 · Aus · Colour · 108min

In 1977 Robyn Davidson became famous by making the 1,700-mile trek from Alice Springs to the Indian Ocean, accompanied by four camels and a dog. Why she did it was a complex matter, fuelled partly by instincts inherited from her naturalist father, but the beauty of her director John Curran's striking film is that it never seeks to explain, treating the event more as a calling than a road trip. Key to its success is a star turn from Mia Wasikowska – and a ringer for the real Robyn – who dives fearlessly into the desert dirt. **DW** Swearing, brief nudity. *DVD* ⓑⓛ

Mia Wasikowska *Robyn Davidson* · Adam Driver *Rick Smolan* · Rolley Mintuma *Eddie* · Rainer Bock *Kurt Posel* · Robert Coleby *Pop* ■ *Dir* John Curran · *Scr* Marion Nelson

Trade ★ 15
Crime thriller 2006 · Ger/US · Colour · 119min

This crime thriller, based on an award-winning US magazine article, presents itself as a hard-hitting exposé of the child sex trade across the Mexican-US border. Such incendiary subject matter surely calls for a cool head, but German director Marco Kreuzpaintner is determined to present hysterical melodrama rather than sobering analysis. Cesar Ramos gives an enthusiastic but merely adequate performance as 17-year-old Jorge, who sees his 13-year-old sister snatched from the streets of Mexico City. A woebegone turn from an ill-cast Kevin Kline, as a Texas police officer with scores of his own to resolve, sets the seal on what is, sadly, a well-meaning stinker. **TJ** In English, Spanish, Polish, Russian, Arabic.

Kevin Kline *Ray* · Cesar Ramos *Jorge* · Alicja Bachleda [Alicja Bachleda-Curus] *Veronica* · Paulina Gaitan *Adriana* · Marco Perez *Manuelo* · Kate del Castillo *Laura* ■ *Dir* Marco Kreuzpaintner · *Scr* José Rivera, from a story by Peter Landesman, Rivera, from the article *The Girls Next Door* by Landesman

Trade Winds ★★
Detective comedy drama 1938 · US · BW · 93min

Director Tay Garnett justified a tax-deductible sailing trip around the world by taking a cinematographer to record the sights and writing a story en route. The footage provided the backdrop for this lightweight tale of detective Fredric March's pursuit of high-class murder suspect Joan Bennett. The stars never had to leave the studio, as the film used a record amount of back projection. Predictably, this contributed to an air of tedium. **AE**

Fredric March *Sam Wye* · Joan Bennett *Kay Kerrigan* · Ralph Bellamy *Ben Blodgett* · Ann Sothern *Jean Livingstone* · Sidney Blackmer *Thomas Bruhme II* · Thomas Mitchell *Commissioner Blackton* · Robert Elliott *Capt George Faulkiner* ■ *Dir* Tay Garnett · *Scr* Dorothy Parker, Alan Campbell, Frank R Adams, from a story by Tay Garnett

Trader Horn ★★★★
Adventure 1931 · US · BW · 123min

The troubles that beset the first film to be made on location in Africa almost outweighed the life-and-death struggle of the title character (Harry Carey) and his young companion (Duncan Renaldo) as they venture among dangerous animals, and even more dangerous tribes, engaged in a search for the white daughter of missionaries abducted 20 years earlier. They find her, of course, in the beautiful, blonde guise of Edwina Booth. The film was almost abandoned when the studio saw the rag-bag of footage assembled by director WS Van Dyke, but another year's work in Hollywood and Mexico eventually earned it a best picture Oscar nomination. The actual filming (especially of animal behaviour) is impressive by any standards, especially those of 1931. **RK**

Harry Carey *Aloysius "Trader" Horn* · Edwina Booth *Nina Trent* · Duncan Renaldo *Peru* · Mutia Omoolu *Renchero* · Olive Golden *Edith Trent* · C Aubrey Smith *Trader* ■ *Dir* WS Van Dyke II [WS Van Dyke] · *Scr* Richard Schayer, Cyril Hume, Dale Van Every, John Thomas Neville, from the novel by Alfred Aloysius Horn, Ethelreda Lewis · *Cinematographer* Clyde De Vinna

Trading Hearts ★★★
Period romantic comedy 1988 · US · Colour · 88min

Raul Julia is the dumped baseball player who hooks up with singer Beverly D'Angelo in this 1950s-set drama that flits between a light-hearted romance and a legal battle when D'Angelo is threatened with court action by her ex-husband who wants custody of their child. It's well played with some nice period details, but it's not exactly original. **JB** Swearing.

Raul Julia *Vinnie* · Beverly D'Angelo *Donna* · Jenny Lewis *Yvonne* · Parris Buckner *Robert* · Robert Gwaltney *Ducky* ■ *Dir* Neil Leifer · *Scr* Frank Deford

Trading Places ★★★★ 15
Comedy 1983 · US · Colour · 111min

This unacknowledged reworking of *The Prince and the Pauper* is a rattling comedy showcase for the talents of Eddie Murphy and Dan Aykroyd. However, there is no question that the acting honours go to the veterans Don Ameche and Ralph Bellamy, as the mischievous business bigwigs whose wager brings about the respective rise and fall of the stars. Director John Landis tends to pull his satirical punches against yuppiedom, and it's a shame he settles for a brash slapstick finale after so many fresh, immaculately timed comic situations. **DP** Swearing, nudity. *DVD*

Eddie Murphy *Billy Ray Valentine* · Dan Aykroyd *Louis Winthorpe III* · Jamie Lee Curtis *Ophelia* · Ralph Bellamy *Randolph Duke* · Don Ameche *Mortimer Duke* · Denholm Elliott *Coleman* · Paul Gleason *Beeks* · Bo Diddley *Pawnbroker* · Jim Belushi [James Belushi] *King Kong* ■ *Dir* John Landis · *Scr* Timothy Harris, Herschel Weingrod

Traffic ★★★★ PG
Comedy 1970 · US · Colour · 97min

Any number of things could go wrong as Monsieur Hulot takes the vehicle of the future to an Amsterdam motor show. The fact that not many did bothered the critics, who wanted something more spectacular than some loosely linked observations on motoring and modernity. But Jacques Tati's final feature is filled with astute musings about, for example, the way owners resemble their cars or have windscreen wipers in tune with their personalities. The nose-picking sequence and the grotesque ballet of the pile-up reinforce his thesis that life is increasingly lived in isolation and that progress is a highly relative term. **DP** French +subtitles. *DVD* ⓑⓛ

Jacques Tati *Monsieur Hulot* · Maria Kimberly *Maria* · Marcel Fravel *Truck driver* ■ *Dir* Jacques Tati · *Scr* Jacques Tati, Jacques Lagrange

Traffic ★★★★ 18
Crime drama 2000 · US · Colour · 140min

Director Steven Soderbergh's brilliantly realised high-tone thriller is shot in scintillating docudrama style, using a broad but involving multi-strand story canvas to give a powerful overview of the complex chain supplying North America's drug culture. On the one hand, there's newly appointed drugs tsar Michael Douglas who is unaware that his teenage daughter has a serious drug habit. On the other is wealthy drug kingpin Steven Bauer whom DEA agents Don Cheadle and Luis Guzman are desperately trying to nail. Wonderfully acted by an amazing cast, the stand-out performances come from a magnetic Benicio Del Toro, playing a Mexican cop torn between morality and temptation, and Catherine Zeta-Jones as Bauer's shell-shocked pregnant wife. **AJ** English, Spanish +subtitles. Drug abuse, violence, swearing. *DVD*

Michael Douglas (1) *Robert Wakefield* · Don Cheadle *Montel Gordon* · Benicio Del Toro *Javier Rodriquez* · Catherine Zeta-Jones *Helena Ayala* · Dennis Quaid *Arnie Metzger* · Steven Bauer *Carlos Ayala* · Luis Guzman *Ray Castro* · Erika Christensen *Caroline Wakefield* · Clifton Collins Jr *Francisco Flores* · Miguel Ferrer *Eduardo Ruiz* · Amy Irving *Barbara Wakefield* · Albert Finney *Chief of Staff* · James Brolin *General Ralph Landry* ■ *Dir* Steven Soderbergh · *Scr* Stephen Gaghan, from the TV series *Traffik* by Simon Moore · *Editor* Stephen Mirrione

Traffic in Souls ★★★★
Silent drama 1913 · US · BW · 74min

A landmark in the history of the American cinema, miraculously preserved for posterity, this was remarkable in its time for both its subject matter and its length. Focusing on the white slave traffic that was obsessing America and its moral reformers, the plot sets a lily-white heroic cop (Matt Moore) against a corrupt organisation of traffickers led by publicly respectable "pillar" of New York society (William Welsh), who kidnap Moore's fiancée's sister (Ethel Grandin) for purposes of prostitution. With its histrionic style, the film raises the occasional giggle, but it's acted with commitment, photographed with wonderful depths of texture and edited for maximum suspense. **RK**

Jane Gail *Mary Barton* · Ethel Grandin *Lorna Barton* · William Turner (1) *Isaac Barton* · Matt Moore *Officer Larry Burke* · William Welsh *William Trubus* · Mrs Hudson Lyston *Mrs Trubus* · Irene Wallace *Alice Trubus* · William Cavanaugh *Bill Bradshaw* ■ *Dir* George Loane Tucker · *Scr* Walter MacNamara, George Loane Tucker

The Tragedy of a Ridiculous Man ★★★
Drama 1981 · It · Colour · 116min

Ugo Tognazzi plays a rich cheese manufacturer who has to decide whether to sell everything to raise a ransom for his kidnapped son. The twist is that his offspring may be one of the gang, radicals dedicated to the overthrow of capitalism. It works as both a thriller and a black comedy, tuning in to then-current topics of kidnapping and Red Brigade terrorism. Interesting rather than exciting, this lacks the stylistic flourishes one expects of its director. **AT** Italian +subtitles.

Ugo Tognazzi *Primo* · Anouk Aimée *Barbara* · Laura Morante *Laura* · Victor Cavallo *Adelfo* · Olimpia Carlisi *Chiromant* · Vittorio Caprioli *Marshal* ■ *Dir/Scr* Bernardo Bertolucci

The Trail Beyond ★★ U
Western 1934 · US · BW · 54min

With a bigger budget than John Wayne was used to at his home-from-home, Monogram Studios, this Lone Star western was the first talkie version of popular cowboy novel *The Wolf Hunters*. The extra cash gave the Duke the benefit of both Noah Beery Sr and Noah Beery Jr in support, plus more location shooting, but the screenplay by future western producer Lindsley Parsons errs seriously on the side of melodrama. **TS** *DVD*

John Wayne *Rod Drew* · Noah Beery Sr [Noah Beery] *George Newsome* · Noah Beery Jr *Wabi* · Verna Hillie *Felice Newsome* · Iris Lancaster *Marie* · Robert Frazer *Jules Larocque* · Earl Dwire *Benoit* · Eddie Parker *Ryan, the Mountie* ■ *Dir* Robert N Bradbury · *Scr* Lindsley Parsons, from the novel *The Wolf Hunters* by James Oliver Curwood · *Cinematographer* Archie Stout

The Trail of '98 ★★★
Silent drama 1929 · US · BW · 87min

Filmed mostly on arduous locations near Denver, this MGM epic was assigned to director Clarence Brown, who gathered 2,000 extras to trudge up a mountain pass in a powerful reconstruction of the Klondike gold rush. Snowfalls and rapids claimed the lives of several crew members. The film looks real enough, but is handicapped by a weak plot about the assorted fortunes of various gold seekers. The film was made as a silent, but also released with a music and effects soundtrack. **AE**

Dolores Del Rio *Berna* · Ralph Forbes *Larry* · Karl Dane *Lars Petersen* · Harry Carey *Jack Locasto* · Tully Marshall *Salvation Jim* · George Cooper (1) *Samuel Foote, the Worm* ■ *Dir* Clarence Brown · *Scr* Benjamin Glazer, Waldemar Young, Joe Farnham [Joseph Farnham] (titles), from the novel by Robert William Service

Trail of Robin Hood ★★ U
Western 1950 · US · Colour · 66min

A seasonal storyline enlivens this Roy Rogers western originally aimed at the Christmas market. Jack Holt is a retired western star intent on supplying Christmas trees to poor kids at a price they can afford, but a wicked commercial outfit obstructs his efforts. Rogers arranges for Holt to receive a helping hand from other western star. There are the usual songs and this one has the dubious bonus of Trucolor. **AE**

Roy Rogers · Penny Edwards *Toby Aldridge* · Gordon Jones *Splinters McGonigle* · Rex Allen *Rex Allen the Arizona Cowboy* · Allan "Rocky" Lane [Allan Lane] *Allan "Rocky" Lane* · Monte Hale · William Farnum · Tom Tyler · Tom Keene · Jack Holt · George Chesebro ■ *Dir* William Witney · *Scr* Gerald Geraghty

The Trail of the Lonesome Pine ★★★
Drama 1936 · US · Colour · 102min

Becky Sharp may have been first but it was this drama that really sold 1930s audiences on the new three-strip Technicolor process through the beauty of outdoor settings filmed on Californian locations by cameraman W Howard Greene. The tale of a long-running feud between two mountain clans was an old favourite, filmed twice before, but a young director and youthful stars give it a fresh look. Henry Fonda's performance is supposed to have been the inspiration for Al Capp's *Li'l Abner*. **AE**

Sylvia Sidney *June Tolliver* · Fred MacMurray *Jack Hale* · Henry Fonda *Dave Tolliver* · Fred Stone *Judd Tolliver* · Nigel Bruce *Mr Thurber* · Beulah Bondi *Melissa* · Robert Barrat *Buck Falin* ■ *Dir* Henry Hathaway · *Scr* Grover Jones, Harvey Thew, Horace McCoy, from the novel by John Fox Jr

Trail of the Pink Panther ★ PG
Comedy 1982 · US · Colour · 92min

This purported tribute to the genius of Peter Sellers is exploitation at its most shameless. Released two years after Sellers's death, the film is a crudely assembled compilation of out-takes and dismally unfunny new footage involving TV reporter Joanna Lumley descending on Clouseau's friends and foes to piece together a picture (if you will) of the Inspector after he vanishes on a case. Director Blake Edwards proceeded to direct *The Curse of the Pink Panther* and *Son of the Pink Panther*, which hit new lows of taste and quality. **DP** *DVD*

Peter Sellers *Inspector Clouseau* · David Niven *Sir Charles Litton* · Herbert Lom *Dreyfus* · Richard Mulligan *Clouseau Sr* · Joanna Lumley *Marie Jouvet* · Capucine *Lady Litton* · Robert Loggia *Bruno* · Harvey Korman *Professor Balls* · Burt Kwouk *Cato* · Graham Stark *Hercule* ■ *Dir* Blake Edwards · *Scr* Frank Waldman, Tom Waldman, Blake Edwards, Geoffrey Edwards, from a story by Blake Edwards

Trail Street ★★ U
Western 1947 · US · BW · 84min

This bustling western has a nicely belated entry by star Randolph Scott as legendary lawman "Bat" Masterson, summoned to a Kansas town to stop the cattlemen from trampling wheat farmers underfoot. Though briskly directed by Ray Enright, it's over-stuffed with familiar ingredients, including the saloon singer played by Anne

Jeffreys and the contrasting nice girl played by Madge Meredith, but its subplot of discovering a heat-resistant strain of wheat is based on fact. **AE**

Randolph Scott *"Bat" Masterson* • Robert Ryan *Allen Harper* • Anne Jeffreys *Ruby Stone* • George "Gabby" Hayes *Billy* • Madge Meredith *Susan Pritchett* • Steve Brodie *Logan Maury* • Billy House *Carmody* • Virginia Sale *Hannah* • Jason Robards *[Jason Robards Sr] Jason* ■ *Dir* Ray Enright • *Scr* Gene Lewis, from the novel *Golden Horizon* by William Corcoran

The Trail to Hope Rose ★★
Western 2004 · US · Colour · 89min

The spirit of the B-western lingers on in this well-told tale, which sees Lou Diamond Phillips's mixed race outlaw become the last hope of the repressed residents of an 1850s mining town. Determined to keep his head down after a stretch for armed robbery, Phillips endures the tyranny of tycoon Warren Stevens and his sadistic sidekick, Richard Tyson. But his love for Tyson's put-upon, pregnant mistress, Marina Black, finally prompts him to take action. **DP**

Lou Diamond Phillips *Keenan Deerfield* • Ernest Borgnine *Eugene Lawson* • Lee Majors *Marshall Luther Toll* • Marina Black *Christine Beckford* • Richard Tyson *Gerald Rutledge* • Warren Stevens *Samuel Drigger* • Jonathan Murphy *Jack Lester* ■ *Dir* David S Cass [David S Cass Sr] • *Scr* Kevin Cutts

The Train ★★★★
Second World War drama
1964 · Fr/It/US · BW · 127min

Burt Lancaster is superb as the railwayman attempting to stop demented Nazi officer Paul Scofield from pillaging art treasures from France in the dying days of the Second World War. The technically flawless direction is by John Frankenheimer, who took over at short notice from Arthur Penn, and the sheer excitement of using real trains is palpable. The French locations are exceptionally well used, and Jeanne Moreau and the great Michel Simon contribute tellingly authentic portrayals. **TS** *DVD*

Burt Lancaster *Labiche* • Paul Scofield *Colonel von Waldheim* • Jeanne Moreau *Christine* • Michel Simon *Papa Boule* • Suzanne Flon *Miss Villard* • Wolfgang Preiss *Herren* • Richard Münch *Von Lubitz* ■ *Dir* John Frankenheimer • *Scr* Franklin Coen, Frank Davis, Walter Bernstein [uncredited], from a story by Franklin Coen, Frank Davis, derived from *Le Front de l'Art; Défense des Collections Françaises 19391945* by Rose Valland

Train of Events ★★★
Portmanteau drama 1949 · UK · BW · 85min

As the night express from Euston to Liverpool is about to career off the rails, the movie also lurches into flashback, showing why various passengers were making the fated journey. There's the engine driver; a philandering orchestra conductor; an actor who's killed his wife; and a girl in love with an escaped German PoW. This portmanteau effort is inevitably uneven, though the cast of stalwarts is worth watching. **AT**

Jack Warner *Jim Hardcastle* • Gladys Henson *Mrs Hardcastle* · Susan Shaw *Doris Hardcastle* • Joan Dowling *Ella* • Laurence Payne *Richard* • Olga Lindo *Mrs Bailey* • Valerie Hobson *Stella* • John Clements *Raymond Hillary* • Irina Baronova *Irina* • Peter Finch *Phillip* • Mary Morris *Louise* • Laurence Naismith *Joe Hunt* ■ *Dir* Sidney Cole, Basil Dearden, Charles Crichton • *Scr* Basil Dearden, TEB Clarke, Ronald Millar, Angus MacPhail

The Train Robbers ★★★
Western 1973 · US · Colour · 88min

This rather overlooked western is a typical example of director Burt Kennedy's rumbustious view of frontier life. John Wayne stars as a no-nonsense old-timer hired by grieving widow Ann-Margret to retrieve the gold stolen by her late husband. Wayne still cuts an imposing figure during the action sequences and shows again that he was a better actor than he gave himself credit for. **DP** *DVD*

John Wayne *Lane* • Ann-Margret *Mrs Lowe* • Rod Taylor *Grady* • Ben Johnson (1) *Wil Jesse* • Christopher George *Calhoun* • Bobby Vinton *Ben*

Young • Jerry Gatlin *Sam Turner* • Ricardo Montalban *Pinkerton man* ■ *Dir/Scr* Burt Kennedy

Train to Pakistan ★★★
Period drama 1997 · Ind/UK · Colour · 107min

This thought-provoking drama is set in the period immediately after the partition of India. The emphasis is on the tensions that arose between the subcontinent's various ethnic groups, with writer/director Pamela Rooks concentrating on the events that spark gang warfare between the dominant Sikhs and the Muslim minority in the small Punjabi town of Mano Majra. The politics aren't always easy to follow, but the cast members, led by Mohan Agashe, turn in committed performances. **DP** Hindi, Punjabi +subtitles. *DVD*

Mohan Agashe *Hukum Chand* • Nirmal Pandey *Jagga* • Rajit Kapur *Jailor* • Smriti Mishra *Nimmo* ■ *Dir* Pamela Rooks • *Scr* Pamela Rooks, from the novel by Khushwant Singh

Training Day ★★★★
Police drama 2001 · US/Aus · Colour · 117min

Arguably the edgiest and most pessimistic release from a major Hollywood studio since *Fight Club*, this is a powerful anti-buddy movie set on the mean streets of LA. Looking to join an elite narcotics squad, rookie cop Ethan Hawke is teamed with the unit's swaggering, streetwise commander Denzel Washington for an educational 24 hours during which he will be expected to prove his mettle. Directed with style and snap by Antoine Fuqua and anchored by highly credible characterisations from its two stars, this striking thriller paints a dark hued portrait of LA law enforcement. **JC** Violence, swearing, drug abuse, brief nudity. *DVD* *BL*

Denzel Washington *Alonzo Harris* • Ethan Hawke *Jake Hoyt* • Scott Glenn *Roger* • Tom Berenger *Stan Gursky* • Harris Yulin *Doug Rosselli* • Raymond J Barry *Lou Jacobs* • Dr Dre *Paul* • Snoop Dogg *Blue* ■ *Dir* Antoine Fuqua • *Scr* David Ayer

Trainspotting ★★★★★
Drama 1995 · UK · Colour · 89min

Irvine Welsh's controversial bestseller is brought to the screen as a dazzling assault on the senses, thanks to director Danny Boyle's cinematic imagination and invention. A fiercely original and provocative shocker, this focuses on the disintegrating friendship of four Edinburgh lads as they embark on an endless drugs and petty-crime bender heading seemingly towards self-destruction. The harrowing and bleak subject matter is presented as a hilariously funny walk on the wild side, with no moral stance taken or punches pulled. Ewan McGregor is absolutely brilliant as the smart-aleck junkie Renton, with high praise, too, for Robert Carlyle, who gives a stunning performance as the violent Begbie. A savagely sophisticated work and a landmark British classic. **AJ** Violence, swearing, sex scenes, drug abuse, nudity. *DVD* *BL*

Ewan McGregor *Mark Renton* • Ewen Bremner *Daniel "Spud"* • Jonny Lee Miller *Simon "Sick Boy"* • Kevin McKidd *Tommy* • Robert Carlyle *Begbie* • Kelly Macdonald *Diane* • Peter Mullan *Swanney* • James Cosmo *Mr Renton* • Eileen Nicholas *Mrs Renton* • Susan Vidler *Allison* • Irvine Welsh *Mikey* ■ *Dir* Danny Boyle • *Scr* John Hodge, from the novel by Irvine Welsh

T2: Trainspotting 2
Drama 2016 · UK · Colour

This is a preview – no prints were available to review prior to publication: Almost two decades after *Trainspotting*, Danny Boyle rounds up the old gang of junkie misfits for this sequel, only loosely based on the novel by Irvine Welsh, as the director has publicly stated that it's "not a great book in the way that *Trainspotting* is genuinely a masterpiece". The final script, by Boyle's frequent collaborator John Hodge, has at least lured back Ewan McGregor, who previously expressed his reluctance to reprise the role of Renton. Set ten years after *Trainspotting*, it features porn, incest,

---

rape and necrophilia, so expect to be shocked. **SP**

Ewan McGregor *Renton* • Jonny Lee Miller *Sick Boy* • Robert Carlyle *Begbie* • Ewen Bremner *Spud* ■ *Dir* Danny Boyle • *Scr* John Hodge, from Irvine Welsh's novel *Porno*

Trainwreck ★★★★
Comedy 2015 · US · Colour · 123min

This wildly funny film from Judd Apatow is the screenwriting debut of stand-up Amy Schumer, who also stars. Her promiscuous and commitment-phobic namesake is a merry mess working at a low-rent men's magazine, under a brassy editor (an excellent Tilda Swinton). The film gets great mileage out of the publication's base impulses, as well as its protagonist's bemusing sexual encounters, the laughs are hearty and Schumer's schtick is so refreshing that it's miles from the disaster the title suggests. **EAS** Swearing, sex scenes. *DVD* *BL*

Amy Schumer *Amy* • Bill Hader *Aaron* • Brie Larson *Kim* • Colin Quinn *Gordon* • Tilda Swinton *Dianna* ■ *Dir* Judd Apatow • *Scr* Amy Schumer

The Traitor ★★
Spy drama 1957 · UK · BW · 81min

Nuance was not Donald Wolfit's strong suit, but he had presence and power in spades. He totally dominates this story with a bluster and conviction that keeps an uninspiring tale of the hunt for a Second World War traitor from falling flat on its face. Writer/director Michael McCarthy had a splendid sense of place, but no talent whatsoever for sustaining suspense. **DP** *DVD*

Donald Wolfit *Colonel Price* • Robert Bray *Major Shane* • Jane Griffiths *Vicki Toller* • Carl Jaffe *Professor Toller* • Anton Diffring *Joseph Brezzini* • Oscar Quitak *Clinton* • John Van Eyssen *Lt Grant* • Christopher Lee *Doctor Neumann* ■ *Dir/Scr* Michael McCarthy

Traitor ★★★
Thriller 2008 · US/Can · Colour · 109min

Don Cheadle stars in this terrorist thriller as Samir Horn, an American Muslim and former Special Forces agent imprisoned in Yemen for moving explosives into the Middle East. Along with fellow inmate and member of the al-Nathir terrorist group Omar (Saïd Taghmaoui), Horn becomes involved in al-Nathir's activities, eventually being asked to lead an operation to blow-up civilian coaches in the US. With an outstanding central performance from Cheadle and a strong supporting cast that includes Guy Pearce as an FBI agent on the group's trail, this solidly directed, intelligent film ends up being quite a nail-biter. **KK** English, Arabic +subtitles. Some violence, brief swearing. *DVD* *BL*

Don Cheadle *Samir Horn* • Guy Pearce *Agent Roy Clayton* • Saïd Taghmaoui *Omar* • Neal McDonough *Max Archer* • Alyy Khan *Fareed* • Archie Panjabi *Chandra Dawkin* ■ *Dir* Jeffrey Nachmanoff • *Scr* Jeffrey Nachmanoff, from a story by Steve Martin, Nachmanoff

The Tramp ★★★★
Silent comedy 1915 · US · BW · 19min

Having saved Edna Purviance from larcenous hobos, Charlie Chaplin is rewarded with a job on her farm. However, any romantic aspirations he has are frustrated by the arrival of her fiancé. Almost halfway through his Essanay contract, Chaplin here began to refine the "Little Fellow" who remains the most recognisable figure of the silent era. The pugnacious approach to bullies, the gentility around women and the balletic feuding with inanimate objects are all present and correct. So, unfortunately, is the pathos that many feel undermines his comic genius, manifesting itself in the first appearance of that trademark sashay down a dusty road. **DP**

Charlie Chaplin *Tramp* • Edna Purviance *Farmer's daughter* • Bud Jamison *Tramp* • Leo White *Tramp* • Lloyd Bacon *Lover* ■ *Dir/Scr* Charlie Chaplin

---

Tramp, Tramp, Tramp ★★★★
Silent comedy 1926 · US · BW · 64min

Whey-faced clown Harry Langdon, known as "The Wonderful Baby", made a number of shorts for Mack Sennett before his first feature, co-written by Frank Capra, who developed Langdon's innocent film persona. Although some of the gags are reminiscent of those performed by Buster Keaton and Harold Lloyd, there are many that belong to Langdon alone – watch how he throws rocks at a cyclone to persuade it to go away. The film is a series of amusing exploits he has while competing in a cross-country walk to win the heart of Joan Crawford. **RB**

Harry Langdon *Harry* • Joan Crawford *Betty Burton* • Edwards Davis *John Burton* • Carlton Griffin *Roger Caldwell* ■ *Dir* Harry Edwards • *Scr* Frank Capra, Tim Whelan, Hal Conklin, J Frank Holliday, Gerald Duffy, Murray Roth

Trance ★★★
Thriller 2013 · US/UK/Aus · Colour · 97min

This densely plotted thriller stars James McAvoy as a fine-art auctioneer involved in an audacious heist. After suffering a blow to the head he forgets where he's hidden the canvas, so mastermind Vincent Cassel enlists hypnotherapist Rosario Dawson to help unlock his memory – but further obstacles and mysteries emerge as she delves into his subconscious. Director Danny Boyle embraces the themes of *film noir*, albeit with a hi-tech edge, but the often confusing layers of plot twists leave the complex story on the verge of collapsing in on itself. McAvoy plays the inside man out of his depth with a neat blend of mischief and wide-eyed innocence, although it's Cassel's ruthless kingpin who makes the strongest impression. **TeS** Violence, swearing, sex scenes, nudity. *DVD* *BL*

James McAvoy *Simon* • Vincent Cassel *Franck* • Rosario Dawson *Elizabeth* • Danny Sapani *Nate* • Matt Cross *Dominic* ■ *Dir* Danny Boyle • *Scr* Joe Ahearne, John Hodge, from a story by Ahearne • *Cinematographer* Anthony Dod Mantle

Trancers ★★★
Science-fiction fantasy thriller
1985 · US · Colour · 76min

Tim Thomerson is a 23rd-century cop who goes back in time to capture his arch-nemesis who is planning to change the past in order to control the future with his zombie henchmen ("trancers"). Thomerson gives a wonderfully high-flying Dirty Harry-goes-cyber-punk portrayal and Helen Hunt makes an early appearance as his sidekick in present day LA. A nail-biting quickie from minor cult director Charles Band. **AJ** *DVD* *BL*

Tim Thomerson *Jack Deth/Philip Dethon* • Helen Hunt *Leena* • Michael Stefani *Martin Whistler/Lt Wiesling* • Art LaFleur *McNulty* • Telma Hopkins *Engineer Raines* • Richard Herd *Chairman Spencer* • Anne Seymour *Chairman Ashe* ■ *Dir* Charles Band • *Scr* Danny Bilson, Paul De Meo

Trancers II: The Return of Jack Deth ★★
Science-fiction action 1991 · US · Colour · 84min

Tim Thomerson returns as the no-nonsense Jack Deth, a cop from the future stuck in modern-day Los Angeles, in Charles Band's belated sequel to his own mid-1980s cult hit. Once again pitted against zombie-like creatures (trancers), Thomerson's engagingly laconic Deth also has to deal with a convoluted love life – two wives in different centuries. Not nearly as much fun as its predecessor, but that didn't stop the makers from churning out four more sequels (to date). **RS** *DVD*

Tim Thomerson *Jack Deth* • Helen Hunt *Lena Deth* • Megan Ward *Alice Stillwell* • Biff Manard *Hap Ashby* • Martine Beswick *Nurse Trotter* • Jeffrey Combs *Doctor Pyle* ■ *Dir* Charles Band • *Scr* Jackson Barr, from a story by Charles Band, Barr

T

Trans ★★★★
Road movie   1998 · US · Colour · 80min

This indie movie marked the debuts of both director Julian Goldberger and his 16-year-old star, Ryan Daugherty. As the dead-end teenager who goes searching for his uncaring mother after escaping from a Florida reformatory, Daugherty manages to charm without compromising his authenticity. It was something of a risk to allow such an inexperienced actor the latitude to improvise. But this is a film of gambles – from the occasionally cockeyed cutting to the cut-price lyricism of the 16mm footage – and most of them pay off, thanks to Goldberger's courage and honesty. DP

Ryan Daugherty *Ryan Kazinski* • Justin Lakes *Justin Mallenkoff* • Michael Gulnac *Mike Gonzales* • Jon Daugherty *Little Brother* • Charles Walker *Inmate/Party rapper* • Elijah Smith *Inmate/Party rapper* ■ *Dir* Julian Goldberger • *Scr* Julian Goldberger, from a story by Michael Robinson, Martin Garner, Julian Goldberger

Trans-Europ-Express ★★★ 15
Experimental drama   1966 · Fr · BW · 94min

The audacious intellectualism of French musicians, novelists and film-makers in the 1950s and 1960s seems self-conscious today, thanks to our relentless trivialisation of the arts. But to anyone wanting to see what the fuss was about, Alain Robbe-Grillet's exhilarating – and irritating – journey on the express train from Paris to Antwerp remains essential viewing. He's cast himself as a movie-maker, writing a story about a sadistic drug dealer (Jean-Louis Trintignant). It's a self-referential parody of the New Wave, a treatise on reality (or what passes for it) with in-jokes and humour that may seem a little arch. But the cool star and the constant provocation make for intriguing viewing. BB French +subtitles. DVD

Jean-Louis Trintignant *Elias/Jean-Louis Trintignant* • Marie-France Pisier *Eva* • Charles Millot *Franck* • Christian Barbier *Lorentz* • Nadine Verdier *Hotel maid* • Alain Robbe-Grillet *Jean, the director* • Catherine Robbe-Grillet *Lucette* ■ *Dir/Scr* Alain Robbe-Grillet

Transamerica ★★★★ 15
Road movie comedy drama   2005 · US · Colour · 99min

This quirky road movie stars an Oscar-nominated Felicity Huffman and charts the emotional and physical journey taken by a pre-op male-to-female transsexual after discovering that she has a 17-year-old son (Kevin Zegers). Having been told that she must face up to her parental responsibilities before having sex-change surgery, Huffman embarks on a cross-country trip to bail the delinquent teen out of jail. Writer/director Duncan Tucker's attempt to combine serious identity issues with the sensibilities of a smart-mouthed buddy flick does have its awkward moments, but it's Huffman's outstanding performance that holds it all together. SF Swearing. DVD

Felicity Huffman *Sabrina/Bree* • Kevin Zegers *Toby* • Fionnula Flanagan *Elizabeth* • Elizabeth Peña *Margaret* • Graham Greene (2) *Calvin* • Burt Young *Murray* • Carrie Preston *Sydney* ■ *Dir/Scr* Duncan Tucker

Transcendence ★★★ 12
Science-fiction action drama   2014 · US · Colour · 114min

This complicated techno fable stars Johnny Depp as scientist Will Caster who, left fighting for his life after a violent attack, has his brain connected to a giant supercomputer. However, as Will's links to the worldwide web allow him to venture beyond his mortal self, his friends and family (including Rebecca Hall as his wife) begin to the question the wisdom of the project. First-time director Wally Pfister's intriguing premise falls prey to muddied philosophical navel-gazing about man playing God, but the disembodied Depp still manages to bring charisma to his role, and Paul Bettany (as Will's conflicted colleague) provides a pivotal moral centre, and the talented cast keeps the film bolstered with that all-important human element. TeS Violence, swearing. DVD ⬭

Johnny Depp *Will Caster* • Rebecca Hall *Evelyn Caster* • Kate Mara *Bree* • Paul Bettany *Max Waters* • Morgan Freeman *Joseph Tagger* • Cillian Murphy *Agent Buchanan* ■ *Dir* Wally Pfister • *Scr* Jack Paglen

The Transfiguration ★★
Horror   2016 · US · Colour

Orphaned teen Eric Ruffin thinks he's undead in director Michael O'Shea's independent first feature, a minimalist anti-horror movie that wears its bleeding heart on its sleeve. To escape his miserable life, Milo has drenched himself in vampire lore gleaned from movie classics and sucks strangers' blood. It's only when he befriends equally troubled Chloe Levine that things really kick off. With only the barest neo-realist approach to the horror, this nihilistic meditation on teenage angst will disappoint genre lovers expecting a gore-fest. AJ

Eric Ruffin *Milo* • Chloe Levine *Sophie* • Larry Fessenden *Drunk man* ■ *Dir/Scr* Michael O'Shea (2)

Transformers – the Movie ★ U
Animated adventure   1986 · US · Colour · 81min

This feature-length version of the cartoon TV series is based on the toys that mutate into hi-tech weaponry and vehicles. The fighting cyborgs must save the universe from the planet Unicron – voiced by Orson Welles – and its intergalactic army, led by the evil Megatron. The mind-numbing blitz of cheap graphics, marginally vulgar dialogue and nasty violence means parents with impressionable children should take heed. AJ DVD ⬭

Leonard Nimoy *Galvatron* • Robert Stack *Ultra Magnus* • Eric Idle *Wreck Gar* • Judd Nelson *Hot Rod/Rodimus Prime* • Lionel Stander *Kup* • John Moschitta *Blurr* • Orson Welles *Planet Unicron* ■ *Dir* Nelson Shin • *Scr* Ron Friedman, based on the toys by Hasbro

Transformers ★★★★ 12
Science-fiction action adventure   2007 · US · Colour · 137min

Shia LaBeouf holds the key to mankind's survival when the long-waged war between alien Autobots and their nemeses the Decepticons crash-lands on Earth. Director Michael Bay's testosterone-fuelled sci-fi action adventure puts Hasbro's ever-popular toy franchise centre stage in a super-sized extravaganza painted in cartoon broad-strokes. It may be a bit overlong and a robotic replay of (executive producer) Steven Spielberg's *ET* with grafted on elements from other popular fantasies. But the wow factor and humorous high-octane thrills are never less than astonishing. The conversion from cars and helicopters into enormously detailed iron giants in seconds is breathtaking. Despite a finale overloaded with spectacle, *Transformers* is truly innovative. AJ Some violence. DVD ⬭ CS

Shia LaBeouf *Sam Witwicky* • Megan Fox *Mikaela Banes* • Josh Duhamel *Captain Lennox* • Rachael Taylor *Maggie Madsen* • Tyrese Gibson *Technical Sgt Epps* • Jon Voight *Defense Secretary John Keller* • Anthony Anderson *Glen Whitmann* • John Turturro *Agent Simmons* ■ *Dir* Michael Bay • *Scr* Roberto Orci, Alex Kurtzman, from a story by Orci, Kurtzman, John Rogers, from a toy range by Hasbro

Transformers: Revenge of the Fallen ★★ 12
Science-fiction action adventure   2009 · US · Colour · 143min

It's a case of diminishing returns as action maestro Michael Bay piles on heavy metal noise and epic explosions in this slick yet soulless sequel. This time Shia LaBeouf and Megan Fox are on a mission to save mankind from the first-ever Decepticon. But neither the silly, fragmented plot nor the proficient acting really matter; the point here is giant robots turning into cars, planes and anything else. Despite being visually impressive, the metal mayhem feels tiresomely synthetic and the robots are just not engaging. AJ DVD ⬭

Shia LaBeouf *Sam Witwicky* • Megan Fox *Mikaela Banes* • Tyrese Gibson *USAF Tech Sergeant Epps* • John Turturro *Agent Simmons* • Kevin Dunn *Ron Witwicky* • Julie White *Judy Witwicky* • John Benjamin Hickey *Galloway* • Ramon Rodriguez *Leo Spitz* • Isabel Lucas *Alice* • Rainn Wilson *Professor Colan* ■ *Dir* Michael Bay • *Scr* Ehren Kruger, Alex Kurtzman, Roberto Orci, from a story by Kurtzman, Orci, from a toy range by Hasbro

Transformers: Dark of the Moon ★★★★ 12
Science-fiction action adventure   2011 · US · Colour · 147min

The screenplay is ragged, the cheap humour is miscalculated, it's far too long and Megan Fox substitute Rosie Huntington-Whiteley sucks the life from every scene – but on the awesome-spectacle front, director Michael Bay raises the action bar to a completely new jaw-dropping level with this second sequel. The story opens by recounting how the 1960s space race turned out to be a Decepticon plot to reshape the universe and enslave humankind. Naturally, it's left to Shia LaBeouf and the Autobots to save the world again. An exhausting, eye-aching watch, this certainly takes your breath away. AJ Violence, swearing. DVD ⬭

Shia LaBeouf *Sam Witwicky* • Josh Duhamel *Major Lennox* • John Turturro *Simmons* • Tyrese Gibson *USAF Tech Sergeant Epps* • Rosie Huntington-Whiteley *Carly* • John Malkovich *Bruce* • Frances McDormand *Charlotte Mearing* • Patrick Dempsey *Dylan* ■ *Dir* Michael Bay • *Scr* Ehren Kruger, from the toy range by Hasbro

Transformers: Age of Extinction ★★★ 12
Science-fiction action adventure   2014 · US · Colour · 165min

The longest and most wearisome *Transformers* sequel yet sees muscular Mark Wahlberg take over as the lead of director Michael Bay's dazzling but bombastically bloated, hi-tech, high-decibel robot fantasy reboot. The star plays a struggling engineer who becomes embroiled in a power struggle between shady CIA operative Kelsey Grammer and tech billionaire Stanley Tucci. The incredible action sequences are hugely impressive, but empty spectacle is all there is to this audio-visual assault on the senses. AJ Some violence, brief swearing. DVD ⬭ 3D

Mark Wahlberg *Cade Yeager* • Nicola Peltz *Tessa Yeager* • Stanley Tucci *Joshua Joyce* • Kelsey Grammer *Harold Attinger* • Sophia Myles *Darcy Tirrel* ■ *Dir* Michael Bay • *Scr* Ehren Kruger

The Transporter ★★★ 15
Action thriller   2002 · Fr/US · Colour · 88min

Jason Statham plays second fiddle to a battery of special effects in this brainless high voltage action thriller. He stars as a cool criminal driver who's paid to transport cargo with no questions asked. When he violates his code by looking in one of the "packages" and discovers a Chinese girl (Shu Qi), he's forced to go on the run. Much posturing macho extravagance follows. AJ Violence, swearing. DVD ⬭

Jason Statham *Frank Martin* • Shu Qi *Lai* • François Berléand *Tarconi* • Matt Schulze *Wall Street* • Ric Young *Mr Kwai* ■ *Dir* Corey Yuen • *Scr* Luc Besson, Robert Mark Kamen

The Transporter 2 ★★★ 15
Action thriller   2005 · Fr/US · Colour · 83min

Jason Statham returns as slick mercenary Frank Martin in this frenetic and more polished sequel. Co-written once again by film-maker Luc Besson, it sees Frank relocating from the French Riviera to Miami, where he unexpectedly bonds with the cute six-year-old (Hunter Clary) he's being paid to drive to and from school. However, it's kick-ass business as usual when the boy is kidnapped, allowing Statham to flaunt his impressive athleticism as his character embarks on a one-man recovery mission. SF In English, French, Italian. Violence, swearing. DVD ⬭

Jason Statham *Frank Martin* • Alessandro Gassman *Gianni* • Amber Valletta *Audrey Billings* • Kate Nauta *Lola* • Matthew Modine *Jefferson Billings* • Jason Flemyng *Dimitri* • Keith David *Stappleton* • Hunter Clary *Jack Billings* ■ *Dir* Louis Leterrier • *Scr* Luc Besson, Robert Mark Kamen, from their characters

Transporter 3 ★★★ 15
Action thriller   2008 · Fr/US · Colour · 99min

Action man Jason Statham shows a softer side here, when he's forced to drive kidnapped Natalya Rudakova around Europe. Statham has to wear a bracelet that's rigged to explode should he wander too far from his car, meaning he and Rudakova have to get closer than expected and inevitably fall in love. The irrelevant plot merely serves to showcase the typically outrageous stunts and provide excuses for Statham to get his kit off. But while the flash, bang, wallop stuff once used to be fun, this is just boring and brainless. AJ DVD ⬭

Jason Statham *Frank Martin* • Natalya Rudakova *Valentina* • François Berléand *Johnson* • Robert Knepper *Johnson* • Jeroen Krabbé *Leonid Vasilev* • Alex Kobold *Leonid's aide* ■ *Dir* Olivier Megaton • *Scr* Luc Besson, Robert Mark Kamen, from their characters

The Transporter Refuelled ★★ 15
Action thriller   2015 · Fr/Chi · Colour · 96min

Game of Thrones star Ed Skrein replaces Jason Statham as Frank Martin in this underwhelming attempt to give the action franchise new life. This time, the plot revolves around vengeful prostitutes plotting to take down their boss, but apart from Ray Stevenson as Skrein's roguish old dad, the ingredients – car chases, punch-ups, female eye candy and scenery-chewing baddies – are more or less the same. It peaks too early, but the major difference is Skrein, who doesn't bring nearly enough charisma to the party. TJ Violence.

Ed Skrein *Frank Martin* • Ray Stevenson *Frank Martin Sr* • Loan Chabanol *Anna* • Gabriella Wright *Gina* • Tatiana Pajkovic *Maria* ■ *Dir* Camille Delamarre • *Scr* Bill Collage, Adam Cooper (1), from characters by Luc Besson, Robert Mark Kamen

Transsiberian ★★★ 15
Thriller   2008 · Ger/Sp/UK/Lith · Colour · 106min

Ben Kingsley's Russian narcotics detective investigates an apparent gang killing in Vladivostok, while an American couple Roy (Woody Harrelson) and Jessie (Emily Mortimer) embark on a lengthy train journey across Siberia. Brad Anderson's thriller has as many twists and turns as a theme-park train ride, as characters disappear and reappear with alarming regularity. With numerous nods to Hitchcock, it is in turn intriguing, clever, implausible and genuinely scary. Though it does perhaps go off the rails towards the end, what is truly original and unsettling is the way the film manages to combine the claustrophobic confines of the train with the vast, chilly nothingness of the surrounding landscape. BP English, Russian +subtitles. Violence, swearing. DVD ⬭

Woody Harrelson *Roy* • Emily Mortimer *Jessie* • Ben Kingsley *Grinko* • Kate Mara *Abby* • Eduardo Noriega (2) *Carlos* • Thomas Kretschmann *Kolzak* ■ *Dir* Brad Anderson • *Scr* Brad Anderson, Will Conroy • *Cinematographer* Xavi Giménez

Transylvania ★★★ 15
Romantic drama   2006 · Fr/Rom · Colour · 97min

French director Tony Gatlif follows a similar path to his 2004 feature *Exiles* with this vibrant and picturesque road-movie romance set in the heart of Romania. A loosely structured account of obsessive love and one woman's hunt for elusive happiness, it's given focus by a spirited lead performance from Asia Argento. She draws on her own strong-willed personality to play an abandoned mother-to-be who embarks on a mission to track down her Romany musician lover (Italian rock star Marco Castoldi – the father of Argento's real-life daughter). Plotwise, the tale displays little logic, choosing to concentrate on the heart rather than the head. However, it comes into its own visually and atmospherically, capturing the country's beauty and cultural extremities with a vivid intensity. SF French, Romanian, English +subtitles. **DVD**

Asia Argento *Zingarina* • Birol Unel *Tchangalo* • Amira Casar *Marie* • Alexandra Beaujard *Luminitsa* • Marco Castoldi *Milan* ■ *Dir* Tony Gatlif • *Scr* Tony Gatlif, Marco Castoldi

Transylvania 6-5000 ★ PG
Comedy horror   1985 · US · Colour · 94min

Jeff Goldblum and Ed Begley Jr are cringingly unfunny as journalists sent to Transylvania, where they encounter a werewolf, a mummy and other classic movie monsters. With a cast of comic notables, you would expect a fair quota of laughs, but the actors tiresomely overplay a surfeit of unoriginal gags. Geena Davis surely won't want reminding of her role as a nymphomaniac vampire. DM

Jeff Goldblum *Jack Harrison* • Joseph Bologna *Dr Malavaqua* • Ed Begley Jr *Gil Turner* • Carol Kane *Lupi* • Jeffrey Jones *Lepscu* • John Byner *Radu* • Geena Davis *Odette* • Michael Richards *Fejos* ■ *Dir/Scr* Rudy DeLuca

Transylvania Twist ★★★ 15
Horror parody   1989 · US · Colour · 78min

Think *Carry On Screaming* meets *Airplane!* and you'll have a pretty good idea of the merits of this better-than-average horror spoof. Terminally silly for sure, but enough of the gags hit their target to keep you watching as youngsters search for a fabled book with the power to raise evil spirits, hidden in a spooky castle. Director Jim Wynorski lampoons genre clichés, institutions such as *The Exorcist* and fright icons Jason and Leatherface. An undiscovered minor treat for horror buffs that's worth catching. RS

Robert Vaughn (1) *Lord Byron Orlock* • Teri Copley *Marissa Orlock* • Steve Altman *Dexter Ward* • Ace Mask *Van Helsing* • Angus Scrimm *Stefan* • Monique Gabrielle *Patricia* ■ *Dir* Jim Wynorski • *Scr* RJ Robertson

The Trap ★
Mystery   1947 · US · BW · 68min

After nine years and 22 films in the role, Sidney Toler was to bow out of the increasingly bankrupt series Charlie Chan series. Better known for his work on William Boyd's Hopalong Cassidy pictures, Howard Bretherton directs with little sense of the genre and resorts to such horror clichés as creeping around in the dark, as Charlie and "Number Two Son" Victor Sen Yung head for Malibu Beach to expose the killer in an acting troupe. DP

Sidney Toler *Charlie Chan* • Mantan Moreland *Birmingham* • Victor Sen Yung *Jimmy Chan* • Tanis Chandler *Adelaide* • Larry Blake [Larry J Blake] *Rick Daniels* • Kirk Alyn *Sgt Reynolds* ■ *Dir* Howard Bretherton • *Scr* Miriam Kissinger, from a character created by Earl Derr Biggers

The Trap ★★★★ 15
Romantic adventure
1966 · UK/Can · Colour · 101min

Made at the height of the Swinging Sixties, this surprisingly moving drama was a distinct change of pace for stars Oliver Reed and Rita Tushingham. Set in Canada in the 1880s, it traces the relationship of fur trapper Reed and the waif-like Tushingham, a mute he purchases at a wife auction. Acting almost solely with her enormous eyes, Tushingham gives a genuinely affecting performance and, as impatience turns to understanding and ultimately affection, Reed also demonstrates a mellow side that he too rarely allows us to see. Director Sidney Hayers makes their adventures believable. DP

Rita Tushingham *Eve* • Oliver Reed *Jean La Bête* • Rex Sevenoaks *Trader* • Barbara Chilcott *Trader's wife* • Linda Goranson *Trader's daughter*

• Blain Fairman *Clerk* ■ *Dir* Sidney Hayers • *Scr* David Osborn, from his story • *Cinematographer* Robert Krasker • *Music* Ron Goodwin

Trap for Cinderella ★★★ 15
Psychological thriller
2011 · UK/US · Colour · 95min

The Wings of the Dove director Iain Softley's twisty thriller about identity and memory is a decent-enough distraction, starring Tuppence Middleton and Alexandra Roach (from TV's *Utopia*) as former best friends who meet again after drifting apart. When a devastating fire leaves one dead, the amnesiac survivor embarks on a tortuous road to recovery. Genre fans may be well ahead of the twists and turns, but good performances and a distinctive European tone maintain the absorbing atmosphere. DA Violence, swearing, sex scenes, drug abuse, nudity. **DVD** **BD**

Tuppence Middleton *Micky* • Alexandra Roach *Do* • Kerry Fox *Julia* • Aneurin Barnard *Jake* • Alex Jennings *Chance* ■ *Dir* Iain Softley • *Scr* Iain Softley, from the novel *Piège pour Cendrillon* by Sébastien Japrisot

Trapeze ★★★ U
Drama   1956 · US · Colour · 101min

Shot at the Cirque d'Hiver in Paris, this simmering melodrama was something of a departure for director Carol Reed after two decades of typically British themes and central European thrillers. However, Reed always knew where to place his camera and he achieves some of the finest ever big-top shots thanks to the high-flying work of cinematographer Robert Krasker. Burt Lancaster, an acrobat before he entered films, is perfectly cast as the only person to have completed the triple somersault, while Tony Curtis gives a good account of himself as both Lancaster's pupil and his rival for the affections of Gina Lollobrigida. DP **DVD**

Burt Lancaster *Mike Ribble* • Tony Curtis *Tino Orsini* • Gina Lollobrigida *Lola* • Katy Jurado *Rosa* • Thomas Gomez *Bouglione* • Johnny Puleo *Max the dwarf* • Minor Watson *John Ringling North* • Gérard Landry *Chikki* • Sidney James *Snake charmer* ■ *Dir* Carol Reed • *Scr* James R Webb, Liam O'Brien, from the novel *The Killing Frost* by Max Catto

Trapped ★★ 15
Crime thriller   2002 · US/Ger · Colour · 101min

This begins with a terrifying jolt as the six-year-old daughter of yuppie parents Stuart Townsend and Charlize Theron is snatched by husband-and-wife extortionists, Kevin Bacon and Courtney Love. At this point, the tension is practically palpable and is given an extra edge by Bacon's superbly reptilian performance. Unfortunately, this soon descends into jaw-dropping stupidity as events become far-fetched. SF **DVD**

Charlize Theron *Karen Jennings* • Courtney Love *Cheryl Hickey* • Stuart Townsend *Will Jennings* • Kevin Bacon *Joe Hickey* • Pruitt Taylor Vince *Marvin* • Dakota Fanning *Abby Jennings* • Colleen Camp *Joan Evans* ■ *Dir* Luis Mandoki • *Scr* Greg Iles, from his novel *24 Hours*

Trapped in Paradise ★★★ PG
Seasonal comedy   1994 · US · Colour · 106min

One from the days before Nicolas Cage reinvented himself as an action star, this is a slight, but engaging festive offering. Cage is the hapless good guy who is roped into a yuletide robbery by his brothers (Dana Carvey and Jon Lovitz), when they find themselves trapped by the weather in possibly the nicest small town in America. Carvey and Lovitz grab the best lines, but Cage is a commendable straight man. Writer/director George Gallo keeps the story moving in amiable fashion. JF Swearing.

Nicolas Cage *Bill Firpo* • Dana Carvey *Alvin Firpo* • Jon Lovitz *Dave Firpo* • Mädchen Amick *Sarah Collins* • Vic Mazzucci *Vic Manni* • Florence Stanley *Ma Firpo* • Richard Jenkins *Shaddus Peyser* • Donald Moffat *Clifford Anderson* • Angela Patton *Hattie Anderson* ■ *Dir/Scr* George Gallo

Traps ★★★
Period drama   1994 · Aus · Colour · 98min

Set in Vietnam in the 1950s, this film makes the disturbances in the nation become a metaphor for the disintegrating marriage of visiting photographer Saskia Reeves and her journalist husband Robert Reynolds. He refuses to see the country's unrest, but Reeves picks up on the volatile political situation, as communist guerrillas protest against French occupation. Their relationship with plantation owner Sami Frey and his daughter brings matters to head. Reeves is excellent, though the film loses its way at the end. LH

Saskia Reeves *Louise Duffield* • Robert Reynolds *Michael Duffield* • Sami Frey *Daniel Renouard* • Jacqueline McKenzie *Viola Renouard* • Kiet Lam *Tuan* ■ *Dir* Pauline Chan • *Scr* Pauline Chan, Robert Carter, from the novel *Dreamhouse* by Kate Grenville

Trash ★★★ 18
Comedy drama   1970 · US · Colour · 103min

This was arguably the first product from the Warhol studio to resemble a mainstream film. It has a conventional narrative, with actors playing parts as opposed to themselves, and it is "properly" edited. The story of a heroin addict rendered impotent carries a clear anti-drugs message, but this did not impress the British censor, who originally cut a shooting up scene. As the junkie, Joe Dallesandro enjoyed his finest hour, although he and others still stumble over their lines and have trouble sustaining their characters. Transvestite Holly Woodlawn, playing Dallesandro's roommate, has the funniest scenes. Too long, but too startling to be boring. DM **DVD**

Joe Dallesandro *Joe* • Holly Woodlawn *Holly* • Jane Forth *Jane* • Michael Sklar *Welfare investigator* • Geri Miller *Go-go dancer* • Andrea Feldman *Rich girl* • Johnny Putnum *Boy from Yonkers* • Bruce Pecheur *Jane's husband* • Bob Dallesandro *Boy on street* ■ *Dir/Scr* Paul Morrissey • *Producer* Andy Warhol

Trash ★★★ 15
Adventure   2014 · UK/Bra · Colour · 109min

City of God meets *Slumdog Millionaire* in director Stephen Daldry's exciting yet gritty tale set in Brazil. Andy Mulligan's young adult novel is given a grown-up if still easy-going tone by scriptwriter Richard Curtis, as street urchins find damning evidence of political corruption on a Rio garbage dump and then must stay one step ahead of the crooked police. Discounting the story's swerves into credibility-straining coincidence, Daldry injects some welcome humour and a palpable rawness into the colourful action, while Martin Sheen and Rooney Mara lend international box-office appeal in their roles as a priest and his assistant. AJ Portuguese, English +subtitles. **DVD** **BD**

Rickson Tevez *Raphael* • Eduardo Luis *Gardo* • Gabriel Weinstein *Rato* • Martin Sheen *Father Juilliard* • Rooney Mara *Olivia* • Wagner Moura *José Angelo* • Selton Mello *Frederico* ■ *Dir* Stephen Daldry • *Scr* Richard Curtis, from Andy Mulligan's novel

Trashed ★★★ 12A
Documentary   2012 · US · Colour · 98min

Candida Brady's indictment of reckless consumerism is backed up by some impressive talent. An opening montage of apocalyptic images is accompanied by an ominous Vangelis score before Jeremy Irons enters the scene to examine the potential ramifications of the planet's burgeoning waste crisis. But, while Brady and Irons provide plentiful evidence of the problems caused by landfills and incinerators and the effects on our oceans of drifting garbage, the recycling solutions they suggest lack similar vigour. Too little is said about how ordinary people can help overcome governmental and industrial resistance to implement these and actually clean up the mess. DP Disturbing images.

Jeremy Irons ■ *Dir/Scr* Candida Brady • *Music* Vangelis

Trauma ★★ 18
Horror thriller   1993 · US/It · Colour · 101min

Even fans of horror director Dario Argento are likely to find this boring. Asia Argento (Dario's daughter) plays a troubled young woman who may have the key to a killer's identity, but her semi-romantic involvement with a journalist slows the movie down. It's still an Argento film, what with the psycho on the loose who shows a fondness for decapitating his victims with an electric saw, but this features less of the fluid camerawork and over-the-top gore effects one expects from his best work. ST Swearing, violence, nudity, drug abuse. **DVD**

Christopher Rydell *David* • Asia Argento *Aura Petrescu* • Laura Johnson *Grace* • James Russo *Captain Travis* • Brad Dourif *Dr Lloyd* • Frederic Forrest *Dr Judd* • Piper Laurie *Adriana Petrescu* ■ *Dir* Dario Argento • *Scr* Dario Argento, TED Klein, from a story by Franco Ferrini, Giovanni Romoli, Argento

Trauma ★ 15
Psychological thriller
2004 · UK/Ire/US · Colour · 90min

Colin Firth awakens from a coma to restart his shattered life after the car crash death of his wife. Haunted by ghostly visions, his grip on reality is further eroded when police also blame him for a famous pop diva's murder. Slow, confusing and ultimately ridiculous, Marc Evans's film is done no favours by a fragmented screenplay over-loaded with enigmatic dialogue. Tiresome and timid. AJ Violence, swearing. **DVD**

Colin Firth *Ben* • Mena Suvari *Charlotte* • Naomie Harris *Elisa* • Tommy Flanagan *Tommy* • Sean Harris *Roland* • Brenda Fricker *Petra* • Kenneth Cranham *Inspector Jackson* ■ *Dir* Marc Evans • *Scr* Richard Smith

The Traveller ★★★★
Drama   1974 · Iran · BW · 75min

Abbas Kiarostami made his feature film debut with this bittersweet story that demonstrates the enduring legacy of neorealism. Footie-mad Hassan Darabi is the epitome of rapscallion innocence, as he wheels, deals and steals his way to the money that buys him a ticket to Teheran for a big World Cup game. But it's the way Kiarostami sees through the boy's wide eyes each petty frustration and perceived injustice, as well as the awe-inspiring city sites, that makes this traveller's tale so shrewd, amusing and, ultimately, heartbreaking. DP Farsi +subtitles.

Hassan Darabi *Ghassem Joulai* ■ *Dir* Abbas Kiarostami • *Scr* Abbas Kiarostami, from a short story by Hassan Rafi'ie

Traveller ★★★ 18
Drama   1997 · US · Colour · 96min

This is a highly watchable buddy movie, set against the backdrop of the US's nomadic Irish-American community, with its rigid rules, intense distrust of outsiders, and almost Mob-style hierarchy. Bill Paxton plays a veteran traveller and scamster. Mark Wahlberg is the young semi-outsider who teams up with him to learn the ropes. The plot switches from character-driven to action-driven when Paxton cons cash from a crook to pay Julianna Margulies's medical bills. Boasting strong performances and a solid plot, this also looks terrific, courtesy of first-time director Jack Green's former incarnation as cinematographer. DA Swearing, violence.

Bill Paxton *Bokky* • Mark Wahlberg *Pat* • Julianna Margulies *Jean* • James Gammon *Double D* • Luke Askew *Boss Jack* • Nikki Deloach *Kate* • Danielle Wiener *Shane* ■ *Dir* Jack Green [Jack N Green] • *Scr* Jim McGlynn

Traveller's Joy ★★
Comedy   1949 · UK · BW · 86min

Married in real life, John McCallum and Googie Withers star as a couple who, having divorced, both find themselves stranded and penniless in Sweden. Joining forces in order to obtain funds the pair are reconciled and their wild schemes cause local havoc. An adaptation of a popular

T

British play, the film seems to have lost much of its comedy in the transfer. The usually excellent stars are frenzied rather than funny, leaving only the mildest of amusements. RK

Googie Withers *Bumble Pelham* • John McCallum *Reggie Pelham* • Yolande Donlan *Lil Fowler* • Maurice Denham *Fowler* • Colin Gordon *Tony Wright* • Gerard Heinz *Helstrom* • Geoffrey Sumner *Lord Tilbrook* • Dora Bryan *Eva* ■ *Dir* Ralph Thomas • *Scr* Allan MacKinnon, Bernard Quayle, from the play by Arthur Macrae

Travelling North ★★★★ 15
Comedy drama   1986 · Aus · Colour · 93min

Film-makers have rarely been able to refrain from revealing the soft centres of grumpy old men. However, David Williamson's splendid adaptation of his stage hit resists the temptation and, by keeping Leo McKern's retired engineer cantankerous to the last, he presents us with a totally believable human being. In his first film in his native Australia, McKern gives an outstanding performance as a short-tempered know-all trying the patience of his new neighbours, and Julia Blake is equally impressive as the middle-aged divorcee who shares his new life. Carl Schultz imaginatively opens out the play and keeps the sentiment in check. DP Swearing.

Leo McKern *Frank* • Julia Blake *Frances* • Graham Kennedy *Freddie* • Henri Szeps *Saul* • Michele Fawdon *Helen* • Diane Craig *Sophie* ■ *Dir* Carl Schultz • *Scr* David Williamson, from his play

The Travelling Players
                                        ★★★★
Epic political drama   1975 · Gr · Colour · 230min

This epic exploration of post-Civil War Greece (which won international acclaim and a number of awards) was partially made in secret during the military junta of 1967–74. Sprawling to nearly four hours, it makes extensive use of lingering long takes as a troupe of itinerant players and their (constantly interrupted) interpretation of a rustic idyll entitled *Golfo the Shepherdess* traverse 12 years of political turmoil from 1939 to 1952. With its stately pace and obscure references to mythology and contemporary events, the film requires patience, but its power and intelligence more than repay the effort. DP Greek +subtitles.

Eva Kotamanidou *Electra* • Aliki Georgoulis *Mother* • Stratos Pachis *Agamemnon* • Maris Vassiliou *Clytemnestra* • Vaneglis Kazan *Aegisthus* • Grigoris Evangelatos *Poet* ■ *Dir/Scr* Theodoros Angelopoulos [Theo Angelopoulos]

Travels with My Aunt ★★★
Comedy   1972 · US · Colour · 109min

This adaptation of Graham Greene's novel had a lot going for it – an Oscar-nominated turn from Maggie Smith, strong support from the likes of Alec McCowen and Robert Stephens, and direction from Hollywood veteran George Cukor. McCowen plays timid bank manager Henry Pulling, who meets his "aunt" (Smith) at his mother's cremation and is persuaded to accompany her on some freewheeling travels. Smith overdoes the eccentricity a bit and the plot obviously strains credibility, but it's colourful fun and one of the lighter and more entertaining screen versions of Greene's work. TH

Maggie Smith *Aunt Augusta* • Alec McCowen *Henry Pulling* • Louis Gossett Jr *Wordsworth* • Robert Stephens *Visconti* • Cindy Williams *Tooley* • Valerie White *Madame Dambreuse* ■ *Dir* George Cukor • *Scr* Jay Presson Allen, from the novel by Graham Greene

La Traversée de Paris ★★★
Second World War comedy drama
1956 · Fr/It · BW · 82min

Jean Gabin, wonderfully cast as a well-off painter, and Bourvil, playing a grasping taxi driver, share the acting honours in a box-office hit that shed new light on life during the Occupation. They are traversing Paris with suitcases full of black-market pork,

with Germans, collaborators and four-legged creatures making life tiresome. Thanks to fine acting, a talented director and a sharp script, the film delivers neat observations on the less heroic aspects of Paris under the Nazis. BB French +subtitles.

Jean Gabin *Grandgil* • Bourvil *Marcel Martin* • Jeanette Batti *Mariette* • Louis De Funès *Jambier* • Georgette Anys *La Patronne du Café Belotte* ■ *Dir* Claude Autant-Lara • *Scr* Jean Aurenche, Pierre Bost, from a novel by Marcel Aymé

La Traviata ★★★★ U
Opera   1982 · It · Colour · 105min

Director Franco Zeffirelli's version of the classic opera with vocal heavyweights Placido Domingo and Teresa Stratas is entirely successful. Unlike most translations, this version of the Verdi opera hammers home the tragedy of the consumptive courtesan Violetta and her doomed love for Alfredo. Sumptuous, indulgent and cinematic, even an opera-resistant audience will find this accessible. LH Italian +subtitles.

Teresa Stratas *Violetta* • Placido Domingo *Alfredo* • Cornell MacNeil *Germont* • Alan Monk *Baron* • Axelle Gall *Flora* ■ *Dir* Franco Zeffirelli

Treacherous Beauties ★★ 12
Crime thriller   1994 · US · Colour · 88min

Harlequin is America's version of Mills and Boon, but this glossy melodrama in the Harlequin TV series has more in common with the "sex and shopping" genre than the British company's chaste romances. In seeking her brother's killer, Emma Samms goes head to head with Catherine Oxenberg, who just might have been his secret lover. Sparks also fly between Samms and Oxenberg's brother, Bruce Greenwood, but is he innocent? DP Sex scenes, nudity. DVD

Emma Samms *Anne Marie Kerr* • Catherine Oxenberg *Simone Hollister* • Bruce Greenwood *Jason Hollister* • Mark Humphrey *Brent Hollister* • Tippi Hedren *Lettie Hollister* ■ *Dir* Charles Jarrott • *Scr* Naomi Janzen, Jim Henshaw

Treacle Jr ★★★ 15
Drama   2010 · UK · Colour · 80min

British film doesn't come any more basic than this ultra-low-budget, self-financed drama shot on the streets of south London. It follows Midlander Tom (Tom Fisher), who walks out on his wife and child and boards a train to London. Following an incident with a gang of hoodies, he meets over-friendly Irishman Aidan (Aidan Gillan), a parrot-voiced loser, whose idiocy allows him to see the best in everyone. This is a nicely ragged and offbeat mismatched-buddy movie that, though it becomes a little predictable, makes an unexpected hero of a profoundly irritating character. DW Swearing, sex scenes. DVD

Aidan Gillen *Aidan* • Tom Fisher *Tom* • Riann Steele *Linda* ■ *Dir/Scr* Jamie Thraves

Tread Softly ★
Musical murder mystery comedy
1952 · UK · BW · 70min

This is an awesomely bad musical comedy thriller, offering only the melancholy spectacle of a once great star on her uppers. American Frances Day, a bubbly singer/comedian in Britain from the 1920s, was fading fast by the time she made this senseless feature about a company of actors trying to stage a revue in a haunted theatre. DM

Frances Day *Madeleine Peters* • Patricia Dainton *Tangye Ward* • John Bentley *Keith Gilbert* • John Laurie *Angus Mcdonald* • Olaf Olsen *Philip Defoe* • Nora Nicholson *Isobel Mayne* ■ *Dir* David MacDonald • *Scr* Gerald Verner, from his radio serial *The Show Must Go On*

Tread Softly Stranger ★ PG
Crime drama   1958 · UK · BW · 91min

The big question here is, what on earth were Diana Dors, Terence Morgan and George Baker doing in such a dreary little film? Director Gordon Parry was capable of making involving pictures, but here he insists on his cast delivering each line as if it had the dramatic weight of a Russian novel,

which is more than a little preposterous for a petty melodrama about criminal brothers falling for the same girl. DP

Diana Dors *Calico* • George Baker *Johnny Mansell* • Terence Morgan *Dave Mansell* • Patrick Allen *Paddy Ryan* • Jane Griffiths *Sylvia* • Maureen Delaney *Mrs Finnegan* • Betty Warren *Flo* ■ *Dir* Gordon Parry • *Scr* George Minter, Denis O'Dell, from the play *Blind Alley* by Jack Popplewell

Treasure Hunt ★★★ U
Comedy   1952 · UK · Colour · 82min

Artist/novelist/screenwriter John Paddy Carstairs adapts MJ Farrell and John Perry's hit stage play, managing to capture much of the eccentric charm of the piece. An extended Irish family has mislaid its fortune and takes in lodgers to make ends meet. Wild chaos ensues. A first class cast is headed by Jimmy Edwards, here turning in another larger than life performance in a dual role. DF

Jimmy Edwards *Hercules Ryall/Sir Roderick* • Martita Hunt *Aunt Anna Rose* • Naunton Wayne *Eustace Mills* • Athene Seyler *Consuelo Howard* • June Clyde *Mrs Cleghorn-Thomas* • Miles Malleson *Mr Walsh* • Susan Stephen *Mary O'Leary* ■ *Dir* John Paddy Carstairs • *Scr* Anatole de Grunwald, from a play by MJ Farrell, John Perry

Treasure Island ★★★ U
Adventure   1934 · US · BW · 98min

The first sound version of Robert Louis Stevenson's ripping yarn is directed by Victor Fleming who later made *Gone with the Wind*. Wallace Beery is well cast as Long John Silver (though not, perhaps, as memorably as Robert Newton in 1950), Lionel Barrymore is Billy Bones and young Jackie Cooper plays "Aaargh, Jim lad". More than 60 years on, a certain amount of woodworm has infested the foremasts, so what was always a rather ponderous adventure may seem even more so today. AT

Wallace Beery *Long John Silver* • Jackie Cooper *Jim Hawkins* • Lionel Barrymore *Billy Bones* • Otto Kruger *Dr Livesey* • Lewis Stone *Capt Alexander Smollett* • Nigel Bruce *Squire Trelawney* • Charles "Chic" Sale *Ben Gunn* • William V Mong *Pew* • Charles McNaughton *Black Dog* ■ *Dir* Victor Fleming • *Scr* John Lee Mahin, Leonard Praskins, John Howard Lawson, from the novel by Robert Louis Stevenson

Treasure Island ★★★ U
Adventure   1950 · UK · Colour · 95min

This live-action Disney adventure owes its reputation to just one thing: Robert Newton's performance as Long John Silver. Here is the original, larger-than-life portrayal of the leering pirate rogue by the extraordinary Newton whose body lurches drunkenly and whose piglet eyes have the twinkle of gin. Newton did not have to act this way; he was pickled much of the time. Apart from some pretty camerawork by Freddie Young, the rest of this production isn't much to shout about, and as Jim Hawkins, Bobby Driscoll is the worst sort of precocious American child star who, in real life, was headed for a very un-Disney future of drug addiction, poverty and an early death. Newton reprised his role in the sequel, *Long John Silver* (1954). AT DVD

Bobby Driscoll *Jim Hawkins* • Robert Newton *Long John Silver* • Basil Sydney *Capt Smollett* • Walter Fitzgerald *Squire Trelawney* • Denis O'Dea *Dr Livesey* • Ralph Truman *George Merry* • Finlay Currie *Billy Bones* • John Laurie *Blind Pew* ■ *Dir* Byron Haskin • *Scr* Lawrence E Watkin, from the novel by Robert Louis Stevenson

Treasure Island ★★★ PG
Adventure
1972 · UK/Sp/Fr/W Ger · Colour · 84min

This reasonably entertaining canter through the oft-filmed pages of Robert Louis Stevenson has Orson Welles delivering a monstrously fat and fruity performance as Long John Silver. Although Welles gets a co-writer's credit, he actually initiated this project in 1966. He wrote the screenplay and started directing it back-to-back with his Shakespearean rumination, *Chimes at Midnight*. But the usual Welles gremlins and

health problems forced him to abandon *Treasure Island* until his Spanish producer brought in another director, John Hough, to take over the reins. AT DVD

Orson Welles *Long John Silver* • Kim Burfield *Jim Hawkins* • Walter Slezak *Squire Trelawney* • Lionel Stander *Billy Bones* • Paul Muller *Blind Pew* • Maria Rohm *Mrs Hawkins* • Angel Del Pozo *Dr Livesey* • Michel Garland *Merry* ■ *Dir* John Hough • *Scr* Wolf Mankowitz, Orson Welles, from the novel by Robert Louis Stevenson

Treasure Island ★
Adventure   1986 · Fr/US · Colour · 115min

Experimental, expatriate Chilean director Raúl Ruiz is far too clever to make your everyday adaptation; he has to make a film about a film about *Treasure Island*. This egg-head non-version, with its in-jokes, allusions and analysis of Stevenson's classic, sometimes looks and sounds like a Godard anti-movie. AT

Vic Tayback *Silver* • Melvil Poupaud *Jonathan* • Martin Landau *Old Captain* • Lou Castel *Doctor/Father* • Jeffrey Kime *Timothy* • Anna Karina *Mother* • Jean-Pierre Léaud *Midas* ■ *Dir* Raúl Ruiz • *Scr* Raúl Ruiz, from the novel by Robert Louis Stevenson

Treasure Island ★★★ PG
Adventure   1990 · US · Colour · 126min

Robert Louis Stevenson's classic adventure gets the lavish telemovie treatment under Fraser C Heston's direction. His father Charlton is Long John Silver and *Empire of the Sun* star Christian Bale is Jim Hawkins. Shot on the same ship used for *Mutiny on the Bounty* (1962), the lush Caribbean locations make the familiar thrills easy on the eye. AJ

Charlton Heston *Long John Silver* • Christian Bale *Jim Hawkins* • Oliver Reed *Capt Billy Bones* • Christopher Lee *Blind Pew* • Richard Johnson *Squire Trelawney* • Julian Glover *Doctor Livesey* • Michael Thoma (2) *Hunter* ■ *Dir* Fraser C Heston • *Scr* Fraser C Heston, from the novel Robert Louis Stevenson

Treasure Island ★★ 12
Adventure   1998 · UK/Can · Colour · 91min

Operating on a modest budget, director Peter Rowe has gone for a highly traditional approach and he's unable to set pulses racing, despite a willing cast and some splendid locations. Kevin Zegers is particularly anaemic as Jim Hawkins, while Jack Palance is given too much to do as Long John Silver. It's careful and reverential, but dull. DP DVD

Jack Palance *Long John Silver* • Patrick Bergin *Billy Bones* • Kevin Zegers *Jim Hawkins* • Walter Sparrow *Ben Gunn* • David Robb *Doctor Livesey* • Christopher Benjamin *Squire Trelawney* ■ *Dir* Peter Rowe • *Scr* Peter Rowe, from the novel by Robert Louis Stevenson

Treasure of Lost Canyon
                                        ★★ U
Adventure   1952 · US · Colour · 81min

After being conned out of his inheritance by a dubious San Francisco attorney, orphaned Tommy Ivo is given a home by kindly small-town doctor William Powell who helps him track down a treasure chest. Directed by former cameraman Ted Tetzlaff and loosely based on a story by Robert Louis Stevenson, this is a mediocre adventure movie for children. RK

William Powell *Doc Brown* • Tommy Ivo *David* • Rosemary DeCamp *Samuella* • Henry Hull *Lucius* • Julia Adams [Julie Adams] *Myra Wade* • Charles Drake *Jim Anderson* • Chubby Johnson *Baltimore Dan* ■ *Dir* Ted Tetzlaff • *Scr* Brainerd Dullfield, Emerson Crocker, from the story *The Treasure of Franchard* by Robert Louis Stevenson

Treasure of Matecumbe
                                        ★★ U
Adventure   1976 · US · Colour · 110min

This movie is a typical example of a well-intentioned Disney family crowd-pleaser. It's an overlong, simplistic tale about two boys looking for treasure, helped by a useless batch of character actors. Location shooting on the Florida Keys is a plus, but

U SUITABLE FOR ALL   Uc SUITABLE ESPECIALLY FOR YOUNG CHILDREN (DVD ONLY)   PG PARENTAL GUIDANCE   12A UNDER 12s TO BE ACCOMPANIED (CINEMA ONLY)

the whole interminable mess looks no better than a TV pilot. DP

Peter Ustinov *Dr Srodgrass* • Robert Foxworth *Jim* • Joan Hackett *Lauriette* • Vic Morrow *Spangler* • Johnny Doran *Davie* • Billy Attmore *Thad* • Jane Wyatt *Aunt Effie* ■ *Dir* Vincent McEveety • *Scr* Dor Tait, from the novel *A Journey to Matecumbe* by Robert Lewis Taylor

The Treasure of Monte Cristo ★★★

Period adventure 1960 · UK · Colour · 79min

An interesting adventure involving buried treasure on the famous island, this has Hollywood exile Rory Calhoun providing the muscle and Italy's Gianna Maria Canale the glamour. It's is really only double-bill material, though there's plenty of action and thrills, plus a certain low-budget style that's rather endearing. The British contingent headed by genteel Patricia Bredin and slimy Peter Arne does what is required efficiently enough. TS

Rory Calhoun *Captain Adam Corbett* • Patricia Bredin *Pauline Jackson* • John Gregson *Renato* • Gianna Maria Canale *Lucetta* • Peter Arne *Count Boldini* • Sam Kydd *Albert* ■ *Dir* Monty Berman, Robert S Baker • *Scr* Leon Griffiths

The Treasure of Pancho Villa ★★

Western 1955 · US · Colour · 95min

Although this western set during the Mexican Revolution of the early 20th century is rather lethargic, it has an interesting premise – cynical mercenary Rory Calhoun clashes with idealists Gilbert Roland and Shelley Winters en route to deliver a shipment of gold to legendary rebel leader Villa. But director George Sherman struggles under the gravitas of his theme and falters, thanks to the war of words. SF

Rory Calhoun *Tom Bryan* • Shelley Winters *Ruth Harris* • Gilbert Roland *Juan Castro* • Joseph Calleia *Pablo Morales* • Carlos Mosquiz *Commandant* ■ *Dir* George Sherman • *Scr* Niven Busch, from a story by J Robert Bren, Gladys Atwater

The Treasure of San Teresa ★★★

Drama 1959 · UK/W Ger · BW · 81min

One of those "hunt for the wartime treasure" movies, cheerfully put together with an attractive international cast, headed by Eddie Constantine at his most rugged and Dawn Addams at her most gorgeous. The eclectic supporting cast includes double-dealing Marius Goring, Christopher Lee, Nadine Tallier and Clive Dunn, no less. Despite the diversity of nationalities, director Alvin Rakoff manages to hold all the accents together (not to mention the complexities of the plot). TS

Eddie Constantine *Larry Brennan* • Dawn Addams *Hedi von Hartmann* • Gaylord Cavallaro *Mike Jones* • Marius Goring *Rudi Siebert* • Nadine Tallier *Zizi* • Willie White *General von Hartmann* • Walter Gotell *Inspector* • Christopher Lee *Jaeger* ■ *Dir* Alvin Rakoff • *Scr* Jack Andrews, from a story by Jeffrey Dell

Treasure of the Golden Condor ★★★

Adventure 1953 · US · Colour · 92min

This has Cornel Wilde seeking his fortune in Central America, with a plot reminiscent of Tyrone Power's *Son of Fury*. To movie fans, the female members of the cast are the most interesting: although the lead is lacklustre Constance Smith, there's also *King Kong's* Fay Wray and a very young Anne Bancroft. TS

Cornel Wilde *Jean-Paul* • Constance Smith *Clara* • Finlay Currie *MacDougal* • Walter Hampden *Pierre* • Anne Bancroft *Marie* • George Macready *Marquis* • Fay Wray *Marquise* • Leo G Carroll *Dondel* ■ *Dir* Delmer Daves • *Scr* Delmer Daves, from the novel *Benjamin Blake* by Edison Marshall

The Treasure of the Sierra Madre ★★★★★ PG

Western adventure 1947 · US · BW · 125min

Humphrey Bogart turns in a memorable performance here as drifter Fred C Dobbs, who, along with Tim Holt's young idealist, latches onto gnarled old Klondike prospector Walter Huston (playing *sans* false teeth) in a search for gold in bandit-infested Mexico. Pitched as an updated biblical fable about greed and human despair, and partly shot in the Mojave Desert, the movie has a superb opening, some portentous passages and a thunderous score by Max Steiner. Much imitated – not least the ending – it proved a historic success for writer/director John Huston, who won Oscars for his direction and screenplay, while his father Walter won as best supporting actor. AT DVD Blu

Humphrey Bogart *Dobbs* • Walter Huston *Howard* • Tim Holt *Curtin* • Bruce Bennett *Cody* • Barton MacLane *McCormick* • Alfonso Bedoya *"Gold Hat"* • A Soto Rangel *Presidente* • Manuel Donde *El Jefe* • José Torvay *Pablo* • John Huston *"White Suit"* ■ *Dir* John Huston • *Scr* John Huston, from the novel by B Traven • *Cinematographer* Ted McCord

Treasure Planet ★★ U

Animated science-fiction adventure 2002 · US · Colour · 91min

Disney continues its literary plundering with an animated take on Robert Louis Stevenson's classic novel. Slickly revamped for today's more sophisticated youngsters, the swashbuckling pirate adventure now unfolds in space. This allows for creative imaginations to run wild, as teen tearaway Jim Hawkins joins the crew of a space galleon to cross the universe in search of a fabled treasure trove, but while such artistic abandon does result in some stunning intergalactic landscapes, it also leads to a hotch-potch of flat alien characters. SF DVD

Joseph Gordon-Levitt *Jim Hawkins* • Brian Murray *John Silver* • David Hyde Pierce *Doctor Doppler* • Emma Thompson *Captain Amelia* • Michael Wincott *Scroop* • Martin Short *BEN* • Laurie Metcalf *Sarah* • Patrick McGoohan *Billy Bones* ■ *Dir* John Musker, Ron Clements • *Scr* Ron Clements, John Musker, Rob Edwards, from a story by Ron Clements, John Musker, Ted Elliott, Terry Rossio, from the novel *Treasure Island* by Robert Louis Stevenson

The Treatment ★★★★ 18

Crime thriller 2014 · Bel · Colour · 130min

A harrowing gut-wrencher based on the thriller by British author Mo Hayder and expertly relocated to Belgium. Haunted by the unsolved disappearance of his brother, for which a known sex offender was released due to insufficient evidence, a cop (Geert Van Rampelberg) faces further anguish investigating a similar case involving another missing juvenile. The intense nature of the crimes concerned will prove disturbing but director Hans Herbots handles the emotionally jarring issues in this gritty shocker with sensitivity. AJ Flemish +subtitles. Violence, swearing, sexual abuse references

Geert Van Rampelberg *Nick Cafmeyer* • Ina Geerts *Danni Petit* • Johan van Assche *Ivan Plettinckx* • Laura Verlinden *Steffi Vankerkhove* ■ *Dir* Hans Herbots • *Scr* Carl Joos, from Mo Hayder's novel

The Tree ★★★ 12A

Drama 2010 · Fr/Aus · Colour · 100min

Since Otar Left director Julie Bertuccelli examines the process of mourning in this contemplative and beautifully shot modern-day fable, set in rural Australia. Combining simple family drama with hints of understated magical realism, the feature sees grief-stricken mum of four Charlotte Gainsbourg struggling to get her life back on track following her husband's sudden death. The situation is complicated by her precocious eight-year-old daughter (impressive newcomer Morgana Davies), who believes that her dad's spirit now inhabits a giant fig tree that's encroaching

on the house. SF A sex scene, brief swearing. DVD

Charlotte Gainsbourg *Dawn O'Neil* • Marton Csokas *George* • Morgana Davies *Simone O'Neil* • Aden Young *Peter* • Gillian Jones *Vonnie* • Penne Hackforth-Jones *Mrs Johnson* ■ *Dir* Julie Bertuccelli • *Scr* Julie Bertuccelli, from the novel *Our Father Who Art in the Tree* by Judy Pascoe • *Cinematographer* Nigel Bluck

A Tree Grows in Brooklyn ★★★★ U

Period drama 1945 · US · BW · 123min

The debut feature of celebrated director Elia Kazan is set in the early 1900s and is a tale of New York tenement life. Dorothy McGuire is excellent as the stoic Ma Nolan, whose efforts to keep her family together are hampered by an alcoholic husband (James Dunn) and the arrival of a third baby. Peggy Ann Garner received a special Academy Award for her role as the daughter, who dreams of a better life, free from grinding poverty, and for whom the titular tree is a symbol of hope. Stick with this one for the initial dull 30 minutes – it will reward your patience. SH DVD

Dorothy McGuire *Katie* • Joan Blondell *Aunt Sissy* • James Dunn *Johnny Nolan* • Lloyd Nolan *McShane* • Peggy Ann Garner *Francie Nolan* • Ted Donaldson *Neeley Nolan* • James Gleason *McGarrity* • Ruth Nelson *Miss McDonough* ■ *Dir* Elia Kazan • *Scr* Tess Slesinger, Frank Davis, from the novel by Betty Smith

Tree of Hands ★★ 18

Thriller 1988 · UK · Colour · 85min

Novelist Ruth Rendell's psychological thriller is turned into a rather messy and underwhelming movie, with Helen Shaver as the woman whose own child dies and who then takes on a child kidnapped by her mother, played by Lauren Bacall. The parents of the kidnapped child bring one set of problems, while Shaver herself is being blackmailed. Lacklustre direction and a schlock script are the major weaknesses. AT

Helen Shaver *Benet Archdale* • Lauren Bacall *Marsha Archdale* • Malcolm Stoddard *Dr Ian Raeburn* • Peter Firth *Terence* • Paul McGann *Barry* • Kate Hardie *Carol* • Tony Haygarth *Kostas* • Phyllida Law *Julia* • David Schofield *Detective Inspector* ■ *Dir* Giles Foster • *Scr* Gordon Williams, from the novel by Ruth Rendell

The Tree of Life ★★★★ 12

Fantasy drama 2010 · US · Colour · 133min

Terrence Malick's film (only his fifth in a career spanning almost 40 years) is the director's most ambitious work to date. The origins of life on Earth are explored and hymned, starting from the framework of a flashback drama set in 1950s Texas. Among the cast, Brad Pitt and Sean Penn, as father and grown-up son, are matched by a compellingly real Hunter McCracken as the young lad. Many will find it ponderous and indulgent, but too often modern cinema is efficient and focus-grouped. The work of Terrence Malick becomes ever more vital as an antidote. AC DVD Blu

Sean Penn *Jack O'Brien* • Brad Pitt *Mr O'Brien* • Jessica Chastain *Mrs O'Brien* • Hunter McCracken *Young Jack* • Fiona Shaw *Grandmother* • Joanna Going *Jack's wife* • Kari Matchett *Jack's ex* • Crystal Mantecon *Elisa* ■ *Dir/Scr* Terrence Malick

The Tree of Wooden Clogs ★★★★ 12

Period drama 1978 · It · Colour · 178min

Ermanno Olmi's sprawling study of peasant life in Lombardy at the end of the 19th century is one of the last great neorealist films. Shot on 16mm and using only non-professional players, this pseudo-documentary epic finds drama in the changing of the seasons and the everyday tasks of the farm. Acting as his own cameraman, Olmi opts for muted colours that suggest both the period and the simplicity of the lifestyle. However, he is somewhat less subtle in emphasising the Marxist message, which he neatly conveys by means of religious, as well as traditional, rural imagery. DP Italian +subtitles. DVD

Luigi Ornaghi *Batisti* • Francesca Moriggi *Batistina* • Omar Brignoli *Minek* • Antonio Ferrari *Tuni* ■ *Dir/Scr* Ermanno Olmi

Treeless Mountain ★★★★ PG

Coming-of-age drama 2008 · US/S Kor · Colour · 89min

Korean-born writer/director So Yong Kim draws on her own childhood for this poignant rite-of-passage tale. When their mother goes off to search for their absentee father, seven-year-old Jin (Kim Hee-yeon) and toddler sister Bin (Kim Song-hee) are foisted upon their hard-drinking, penny-pinching aunt (Kim Mi-hyang). Avoiding sentiment and whimsicality, the director coaxes exquisite performances from her dauntless leads as they bemusedly try to make sense of the grown-ups' aberrant behaviour, while cinematographer Anne Misawa's discreet close-ups help deliver a telling critique of South Korean attitudes to females of all backgrounds and ages. DP Korean +subtitles.

Kim Hee-yeon *Jin* • Kim Song-hee *Bin* • Kim Mi-hyang *Big Aunt* • Lee Soo-ah *Mom* • Park Boon-tak *Grandma* • Lee Byung-yong *Grandpa* ■ *Dir/Scr* So Yong Kim • *Cinematographer* Anne Misawa

Trees Lounge ★★★★ 15

Comedy drama 1996 · US · Colour · 91min

This is indie film-making à la John Cassavetes rather than Quentin Tarantino, with the humour being understated, the drama credible, the dialogue having an everyday ring and the performances ideally suited to a world of regrets and whiskey chasers. If the camerawork is occasionally prone to showiness, the atmosphere of both the neighbourhood Steve Buscemi prowls in his ice-cream van and the Trees Lounge itself is totally authentic. DP Drug abuse, swearing, violence. DVD

Steve Buscemi *Tommy* • Carol Kane *Connie* • Mark Boone Junior *Mike* • Chloë Sevigny *Debbie* • Bronson Dudley *Bill* • Anthony LaPaglia *Rob* • Michael Buscemi *Raymond* • Elizabeth Bracco *Theresa* ■ *Dir/Scr* Steve Buscemi

Trekkies ★★★ PG

Documentary 1997 · US · Colour · 83min

Obsession is the name of the game in this diverting documentary that beams down into the lives of devoted *Star Trek* fans. Naturally, director Roger Nygard has uncovered some of the more eccentric individuals, so we are introduced to the woman who wore a *Star Trek* uniform while on jury service for the Whitewater trial, and the dentist whose surgery ("Star Base Dental") is designed around the franchise. But there's also much to enjoy here for those who pour scorn upon the phenomenon, and also for the more conservative fans who don't want to go the whole hog and have their ears made more pointed. LB DVD

Denise Crosby ■ *Dir* Roger Nygard

Tremors ★★★★★ 15

Comedy horror 1989 · US · Colour · 91min

The spirit of the "Killer Bs" is gloriously resurrected in this, the ultimate story of the worm that turned. Kevin Bacon and Fred Ward are a sort of "Simple and Simpler", an endearingly goofy pair of handymen who discover that huge underground worms have broken through the Earth's surface and are now swallowing up everything in their path. Director Ron Underwood keeps both the action and laughs roaring along at a tremendous pace and there's a string of entertaining cameos, most notably from Michael Gross and country star Reba McEntire as an unlikely pair of survivalists. Add to that a refreshingly tough and intelligent female lead (Finn Carter) and the result is a sharp, very funny monster movie. JF Swearing, violence. DVD Blu

Kevin Bacon *Valentine McKee* • Fred Ward *Earl Bassett* • Finn Carter *Rhonda LeBeck* • Michael Gross *Burt Gummer* • Reba McEntire *Heather Gummer* • Bobby Jacoby *Melvin Plug* • Charlotte Stewart *Nancy* • Tony Genaro *Miguel* • Ariana Richards *Mindy* • Richard Marcus *Nestor* ■

T

Dir Ron Underwood • *Scr* SS Wilson, Brent Maddock, from a story by SS Wilson, Brent Maddock, Ron Underwood

Tremors II: Aftershocks
★★★ 12

Comedy horror   1995 · US · Colour · 95min

This is an entertaining made-for-video sequel to Ron Underwood's monster movie classic. The giant worms are munching in Mexico, so Fred Ward is called in along with Christopher Gartin. Sharply written and engagingly performed, this stays true to the jokey spirit of the original, while adding a new breed of overground "graboids" to chew the scenery, literally. Although it lacks the frantic pace and sprightly camerawork of the original, it's still smart and fun. JC Swearing, violence. **DVD**

Fred Ward *Earl Bassett* • Michael Gross *Burt Gummer* • Helen Shaver *Kate* • Marcelo Tubert *Senor Ortega* • Christopher Gartin *Grady Hoover* ■ *Dir* SS Wilson • *Scr* SS Wilson, Brent Maddock

Tremors 3: Back to Perfection
★★ PG

Horror comedy   2001 · US · Colour · 99min

First came the Graboids, then the Shriekers. Now, amid the theme park razzmatazz that has grown up around the town of Perfection, Nevada, come the Ass Blasters – giant critters that can both fly and detect targets by sensing body heat. Worm-waster Michael Gross is just one of the citizens returning to protect their burgh from the new generation of mutant man-eaters and director Brent Maddock slips in the old faces with almost parodic glee. Passable, if overfamiliar. A further sequel and a TV series followed. DP **DVD Blu**

Michael Gross *Burt Gummer* • Shawn Christian *Desert Jack Sawyer* • Susan Chuang *Jodi Chang* • Charlotte Stewart *Nancy Sterngood* • Ariana Richards *Mindy Sterngood* • Tony Genaro *Miguel* ■ *Dir* Brent Maddock • *Scr* John Whelpley, from a story by SS Wilson, Brent Maddock

The Trench
★★ 15

First World War drama
1999 · UK/Fr · Colour · 94min

William Boyd's directorial debut is a sincere but stagey attempt to explore the psychological pressures weighing on diverse tommies awaiting their first day on the Somme. Although the camera restlessly suggests the cramped, primitive conditions, Tony Pierce-Roberts's glassy photography too often highlights the atmospheric shortcomings of the sets. Similarly, the cast rallies to the colours, but their commitment can't disguise the fact that the script is populated solely by stock combat characters. DP Swearing, violence. **DVD**

Paul Nicholls *Billy MacFarlane* • Daniel Craig *Sgt Telford Winter* • Julian Rhind-Tutt *Ellis Harte* • Danny Dyer *Victor Dell* • James D'Arcy *Colin Daventry* • Tam Williams *Eddie MacFarlane* • Antony Strachan *Horace Beckwith* ■ *Dir/Scr* William Boyd (2)

Trent's Last Case
★★★ U

Crime mystery   1952 · UK · BW · 86min

EC Bentley's diverting detective story was the prototype for the modern whodunnit. Michael Wilding stars as the shrewd sleuth of the title investigating the suspicious death of tycoon Orson Welles, who, in just a few flashbacks, masterfully creates a victim who was simply begging to be bumped off. Herbert Wilcox sprinkles the clues and red herrings with a steady hand, while John McCallum and Margaret Lockwood stand out among the suspects. DP **DVD**

Margaret Lockwood *Margaret Manderson* • Michael Wilding *Philip Trent* • Orson Welles *Sigsbee Manderson* • John McCallum *John Marlowe* • Miles Malleson *Burton Cupples* • Hugh McDermott *Calvin C Bunner* • Sam Kydd *Inspector Murch* • Jack McNaughton *Martin* ■ *Dir* Herbert Wilcox • *Scr* Pamela Bower, from the novel by EC Bentley

36 Quai des Orfèvres
★★★★ 15

Crime drama   2004 · Fr · Colour · 106min

Exploiting his own experiences and a notorious case from the mid-1980s, former cop Olivier Marchal brings a brisk sense of abrasive professionalism to this Paris-set crime drama. As chief André Dussollier prepares to leave, two plain-clothes detectives compete for his job by trying to catch the gang responsible for a spate of armoured-car raids. As the rivals, Daniel Auteuil and Gérard Depardieu convey the ruthless grit required to cope with their stressful jobs. Slick, authentic and credible, this intricate tale represents the *policier* near its best. DP French +subtitles. Swearing, violence. **DVD**

Daniel Auteuil *Léo Vrinks* • Gérard Depardieu *Denis Klein* • André Dussollier *Robert Mancini* • Roschdy Zem *Hugo Silien* • Valeria Golino *Camille Vrinks* • Daniel Duval *Eddy Valence* • Catherine Marchal *Eve Verhagen* • Francis Renaud *Titi Brasseur* ■ *Dir* Olivier Marchal • *Scr* Olivier Marchal, Julien Rappeneau, Franck Mancuso, Dominique Loiseau, from a story by Marchal

Trespass
★★ 15

Crime thriller   1992 · US · Colour · 96min

Here, an unlikely premise (two firemen discover a map that points to a cache of gold in a disued factory) is buoyed up by a merely efficient set of thrills, which are sometimes funny, but veer towards the hysterical as the film approaches its tough finale. JM Violence, swearing. **DVD**

Bill Paxton *Vince* • Ice T [Ice-T] *King James* • William Sadler *Don* • Ice Cube *Savon* • Art Evans *Bradlee* • De'Voreaux White *Lucky* • Bruce A Young *Raymond* • Glenn Plummer *Luther* • Stoney Jackson *Wickey* • TE Russell *Video* • Tiny Lister [Tom "Tiny" Lister Jr] *Cletus* ■ *Dir* Walter Hill • *Scr* Bob Gale, Robert Zemeckis

Trespass
★★ 15

Thriller   2011 · US · Colour · 86min

This unintentionally daft hostage drama stars Nicolas Cage as a diamond broker and Nicole Kidman as his wife. When a gang of vicious thugs breaks into their hi-tech home, what seems at first a straightforward robbery evolves into a complex discovery of personal dynamics, not only between members of the gang, but also between the gang and the couple themselves. *Trespass* is a hysterical riot of craziness, daft plot twists, pointless flashbacks, and characters so cardboard you could make cereal packets from them. But it's also entertaining in a stupid, turn-your-brain-off kind of way. **DVD BA** Violence, swearing, drug abuse. **DVD**

Nicolas Cage *Kyle Miller* • Nicole Kidman *Sarah Miller* • Ben Mendelsohn *Elias* • Liana Liberato *Avery Miller* • Cam Gigandet *Jonah* ■ *Dir* Joel Schumacher • *Scr* Karl Gajdusek

The Trespasser
★★★

Drama   1929 · US · BW · 91min

Silent-screen drama queen Gloria Swanson produced, took a hand in the screenplay, and starred in this, her first talkie, making herself a million at the box office. She plays a secretary whose marriage to Robert Ames, the son of a multi-millionaire, is destroyed by Ames' father. A romantic melodrama on the familiar theme of mother love and self-sacrifice, the movie would not hold much interest now if it were not for the always mesmerising presence of la Swanson, who earned the first of an Oscar nomination. Director/screenwriter Edmund Goulding rewrote and redirected it in 1937 as *That Certain Woman* with Bette Davis. RK

Gloria Swanson *Marion Donnell* • Robert Ames *Jack Merrick* • Purnell Pratt *Hector Ferguson* • Henry B Walthall *Fuller* • Wally Albright Jr [Wally Albright] *Jackie* • William Holden (1) *John Merrick Sr* • Blanche Frederici *Miss Potter* • Kay Hammond *Catherine "Flip" Merrick* ■ *Dir/Scr* Edmund Goulding

Trial
★★★★

Drama   1955 · US · BW · 108min

Scripted by Don Mankiewicz from his own novel, this is a powerful study of courtroom justice, and one of the few movies to deal with the influence of communism on US politics. Here, it's in open discussion as it impinges on the case of a Mexican youth (Rafael Campos) on trial for murder. The film is also the first to feature an African-American judge, played by Juano Hernandez. The Oscar-nominated Arthur Kennedy and the underrated Dorothy McGuire provide excellent support, but this is Glenn Ford's movie, and what a presence he is. TS

Glenn Ford *David* • Dorothy McGuire *Abbe* • Arthur Kennedy *Barney* • John Hodiak *John J. Armstrong* • Katy Jurado *Mrs Chavez* • Rafael Campos *Angel Chavez* • Juano Hernandez *Judge Theodore Motley* • Robert Middleton *AS "Fats" Sanders* ■ *Dir* Mark Robson • *Scr* Don M Mankiewicz, from his novel

The Trial
★★★★ PG

Drama   1962 · Fr/It/W Ger · BW · 114min

Orson Welles's film of Franz Kafka's novel is everything one expects: audacious, weird and impish, filled with references to Welles's own life as well as to *Citizen Kane*. Anthony Perkins is Joseph K, who is arrested and put on trial for no obvious reason in some strange autocratic state. Welles's use of locations (notably the Gare D'Orsay in Paris) is spellbinding, creating a dark labyrinth with the slenderest of resources. While Perkins is brilliantly paranoid, Jeanne Moreau and Romy Schneider are exotic. Welles himself plays the Advocate, the ringmaster of this nightmare comedy. AT **DVD**

Orson Welles *The Advocate* • Anthony Perkins *Joseph K* • Jeanne Moreau *Miss Burstner* • Romy Schneider *Leni* • Elsa Martinelli *Hilda* • Akim Tamiroff *Bloch* • Arnoldo Foà *Inspector A* • William Kearns *First Asst Inspector* • Jess Hahn *Second Asst Inspector* • Suzanne Flon *Miss Pittl* • Michael Lonsdale [Michel Lonsdale] *Priest* ■ *Dir* Orson Welles • *Scr* Orson Welles, from the novel by Franz Kafka

The Trial
★★ 12

Drama   1993 · UK/It · Colour · 115min

Kyle MacLachlan and Anthony Hopkins star in director David Jones's version of Kafka's classic novel about an innocent man accused. Unlike Orson Welles's 1963 version – and despite this version's scripting from Harold Pinter – this is seriously lacking the necessary dramatic darkness. MacLachlan is bland as Josef K, arrested and struggling to uncover the reason why, and Hopkins manages to steal the film completely with his very brief appearance as the priest who helps Josef. LH **DVD**

Kyle MacLachlan *Josef K* • Anthony Hopkins *The Priest* • Jason Robards Jr [Jason Robards] *Dr Huld* • Jean Stapleton *Landlady* • Juliet Stevenson *Fraulein Burstner* • Polly Walker *Leni* • Alfred Molina *Titorelli* ■ *Dir* David Jones (3) • *Scr* Harold Pinter, from the novel by Franz Kafka

Trial and Error
★★★ U

Comedy   1962 · UK · BW · 75min

Also known as *The Dock Brief*, this neat little comedy was adapted from a radio play by John Mortimer (of *Rumpole* fame). The amusing storyline pits failed barrister Peter Sellers against Richard Attenborough's henpecked husband, who confounds all Sellers's ploys to have him acquitted on a charge of murdering his wife. Sellers does a nice line in comic despair, but this is not one of his most memorable characterisations and he is easily outflanked by Attenborough, who has a marvellous time playing the role of a killer. DP **DVD**

Peter Sellers *Morgenhall/Doctor* • Richard Attenborough *Fowle/Judge/Jury foreman/Member of public/Character witness* • Beryl Reid *Doris* • David Lodge *Bateson* • Frank Pettingell *Tuppy Morgan* • Eric Woodburn *Judge Banter* ■ *Dir* James Hill • *Scr* Pierre Rouve, from the radio play by John Mortimer

Trial and Error
★★ 12

Comedy   1997 · US · Colour · 94min

Michael Richards provides a few laughs in this misfiring comedy as the pal of lawyer Jeff Daniels, who agrees to impersonate him in court when Daniels is indisposed, but hilarity is at a premium. Director Jonathan Lynn has shown a deft hand at comedy, but he's let down here by a lumpen script. It's a shame when he has a talented cast that includes Charlize Theron and Rip Torn. JB Swearing.

Michael Richards *Richard "Ricky" Rietti* • Jeff Daniels *Charles "Charlie" Tuttle* • Charlize Theron *Billie Tyler* • Jessica Steen *Elizabeth Gardner* • Austin Pendleton *Judge Paul Z Graff* • Rip Torn *Benny Gibbs* ■ *Dir* Jonathan Lynn • *Scr* Sara Bernstein, Gregory Bernstein, from a story by Cliff Gardner, Sara Bernstein, Gregory Bernstein

Trial by Combat
★★

Black comedy   1976 · UK · Colour · 89min

Initially released as *Choice of Arms*, this is an idiotic fantasy about a secret society calling itself the Knights of Avalon, whose members dress up in medieval armour and act as a lynch mob, murdering dangerous criminals to make up for what they believe is an ineffective justice system. It has some nice touches, though it's not funny, stylish or subversive. AT Violence, swearing.

John Mills *Bertie Cook* • Donald Pleasence *Sir Giles Marley* • Barbara Hershey *Marion Evans* • Margaret Leighton *Ma Gore* • Brian Glover *Sidney Gore* • David Birney *Sir John Gifford* • Peter Cushing *Sir Edward Gifford* ■ *Dir* Kevin Connor • *Scr* Julian Bond, Steve Rossen, Mitchell Smith, from a story by Fred Weintraub, Paul Heller

Trial by Jury
★★ 15

Thriller   1994 · US · Colour · 102min

Joanne Whalley-Kilmer stars as the woman who stands up against mobster Armand Assante, who wants to ensure his court case goes his way. Director Heywood Gould does his best, but the plotting gets sillier by the minute and the performances from the starry cast are erratic. Assante is wildly over the top, William Hurt low key and sleazy as a bent ex-cop. JF Sexual references, swearing, violence.

Joanne Whalley-Kilmer [Joanne Whalley] *Valerie Aston* • Armand Assante *Rusty Pirone* • Gabriel Byrne *Daniel Graham* • William Hurt *Tommy Vesey* • Kathleen Quinlan *Wanda* • Margaret Whitton *Jane Lyle* • Ed Lauter *John Boyle* • Richard Portnow *Leo Greco* ■ *Dir* Heywood Gould • *Scr* Jordan Katz, Heywood Gould

The Trial of the Incredible Hulk
★★ PG

Science-fiction adventure
1989 · US · Colour · 95min

Surely after three TV movies and a four-year series, the Hulk would have vented all his anger and stopped going through his supply of shirts so rapidly? Well, no. Bill Bixby steps behind the camera to bring yet another instalment of the comic-book hero's adventures to the screen, with all the hallmarks of an idea that has run out of steam. Bixby went on to direct yet another helping of this tame action fare. NF **DVD**

Bill Bixby *Dr David Banner* • Lou Ferrigno *The Hulk* • Rex Smith *Matt Murdoch/Daredevil* • John Rhys-Davies *Wilson Fisk* • Marta DuBois *Ellie Mendez* • Nancy Everhard *Christa Klein* • Nicholas Hormann *Edgar* • Joseph Mascolo *Tendelli* • Richard Cummings Jr *Al Pettiman* ■ *Dir* Bill Bixby • *Scr* Gerald DiPego, from characters by Stan Lee, Jack Kirby

The Trials of Oscar Wilde
★★★★

Historical drama   1960 · UK · Colour · 123min

This is a moving account of the fall from grace of the finest playwright of the Victorian era. Although Peter Finch looks nothing like Wilde, he gives an assured, poignant and Bafta-winning performance, excelling particularly during his courtroom jousts with James Mason. John Fraser makes an admirably self-centred Lord Alfred Douglas, while Lionel Jeffries plays impressively against type as the irascible Marquis of Queensberry, who first publicly

   U SUITABLE FOR ALL   **Uc** SUITABLE ESPECIALLY FOR YOUNG CHILDREN (DVD ONLY)   **PG** PARENTAL GUIDANCE   **12A** UNDER 12s TO BE ACCOMPANIED (CINEMA ONLY)

accused Wilde of homosexuality. Gregory Ratoff's black-and-white picture, *Oscar Wilde*, starring Robert Morley, was released almost simultaneously. DP

Peter Finch *Oscar Wilde* • James Mason *Sir Edward Carson* • Yvonne Mitchell *Constance Wilde* • Nigel Patrick *Sir Edward Clarke* • John Fraser *Lord Alfred Douglas* • Lionel Jeffries *Marquis of Queensberry* • Maxine Audley *Ada Leverson* • James Booth *Alfred Wood* ■ *Dir* Ken Hughes • *Scr* Ken Hughes, from the play *The Stringed Lute* by John Furnell and the book by Montgomery Hyde

Triangle ★★★★ 15
Horror mystery thriller
2009 · UK/Aus · Colour · 94min

Melissa George is trapped in a purgatorial Groundhog Day in writer/director Christopher Smith's highly polished chiller. The former *Home and Away* star gives a haunting performance as a single mother who's forced to take refuge on a strangely deserted liner when her yachting party's vessel is overturned in a storm. However, all is not what it seems as events play out like the plot of *Ghost Ship* but with a sophisticated *Twilight Zone* spin. Eschewing the flamboyant violence of *Creep* and *Severance*, Smith effortlessly marries supernatural and slasher elements to create a consistently strange atmosphere that remains intriguing right up to the finale. AJ Violence, swearing. DVD Blu-ray

Melissa George *Jess* • Michael Dorman *Greg* • Rachael Carpani *Sally* • Henry Nixon *Downey* • Emma Lung *Heather* • Liam Hemsworth *Victor* ■ *Dir/Scr* Christopher Smith

The Tribe ★★★ 18
Drama 2014 · Ukr/Neth · Colour · 126min

In one sense, this Ukraine-set drama about a gang of young hoodlums is a lot like hundreds of other gang films, with a story that follows an outsider (Grigoriy Fesenko) rising to the top of the heap through cunning and violence. What makes director Miroslav Slaboshpitsky's feature debut extraordinary is the fact that all the characters (and the actors playing them) are deaf sign-language users, and the movie has no subtitles. The approach sounds disorienting, but after a while the expressiveness of the gestures and the acting is all the viewer needs to understand what's going on. It's a disturbing and extraordinary work. LF In Ukrainian sign language. Violence, sex scenes, nudity. DVD

Grigoriy Fesenko *Sergey* • Yana Novikova *Anya* • Rosa Babiy *Svetka* • Alexander Dsiadevich *Gera* ■ *Dir/Scr* Miroslav Slaboshpitsky

Tribute ★★
Drama 1980 · Can · Colour · 125min

Having enjoyed a Broadway triumph with this over-ripe and tragicomic role in the original play, it was inevitable that Jack Lemmon would be invited to immortalise his character on screen. It comes across as talkative and maudlin with Lemmon – as a glib theatrical press agent – encouraged to give a very mannered performance. Better acting comes from Lee Remick as his estranged wife and Robby Benson as the son who returns to discover his father has a fatal illness. BB

Jack Lemmon *Scottie Templeton* • Robby Benson *Jud Templeton* • Lee Remick *Maggie Stratton* • Colleen Dewhurst *Gladys Petrelli* • John Marley *Lou Daniels* • Kim Cattrall *Sally Haines* • Gale Garnett *Hilary* • Teri Keane *Evelyn* ■ *Dir* Bob Clark • *Scr* Bernard Slade, from his play

Tribute to a Bad Man ★★★★ PG
Western 1956 · US · Colour · 91min

Well directed by Robert Wise and beautifully shot by the great cinematographer Robert Surtees, this fine MGM western has a genuine feel for life on the frontier. It's dominated by a larger-than-life performance from James Cagney as a ruthless cattle baron. Co-star Irene Papas's relationship with gruff Cagney forms the tough centre of the movie. The two leads

are backed up by a knockout cast of western faces, including Lee Van Cleef and Royal Dano. TS

James Cagney *Jeremy Rodock* • Don Dubbins *Steve Miller* • Irene Papas *Jocasta Constantine* • Stephen McNally *McNulty* • Vic Morrow *Lars Peterson* • James Griffith *Barjack* • Lee Van Cleef *Fat Jones* ■ *Dir* Robert Wise • *Scr* Michael Blankfort, from a short story by Jack Schaefer

Les Tricheurs ★★★
Melodrama 1958 · Fr/It · BW · 107min

Marcel Carné's beatnik melodrama has been wrongly dismissed as a fogey's bid to get with the in-crowd. It actually explores the fascination of faddism with a dispassion that ensures the focus remains on the rebellious lovers whose brief encounter ends in tragedy. Pascale Petit and Jacques Charrier's romance is less significant than the attitudes they strike and the ideas they espouse, with Claude Renoir's moody monochrome cinematography helping to capture the atmosphere of Paris's jazz scene. Its sheen has faded, but this remains a valuable snapshot of pre-rock, pre-New Wave culture. DP In French.

Jacques Charrier *Bob Letellier* • Pascale Petit *Mic* • Andréa Parisy *Clo* • Laurent Terzieff *Alain* • Roland Lesaffre *Roger* ■ *Dir* Marcel Carné • *Scr* Marcel Carné, Jacques Sigurd, from an idea by Charles Spaak

Trick ★★★ 15
Romantic comedy 1999 · US · Colour · 85min

Jim Fall's unassuming gay romantic comedy pokes gentle fun at such stereotypes as the bitchy drag queen and the disco stud. Christian Campbell could hardly be more cherubic as the struggling musical composer whose chance to make it with a hunky stripper, JP Pitoc, is frustrated by a lack of privacy and a wealth of conflicting advice. Yet it's the much maligned Tori Spelling's animated performance as a motor-mouthed off-Broadway wannabe that leaves the deepest impression. DP DVD

Christian Campbell *Gabriel* • JP Pitoc *Mark Miranda* • Tori Spelling *Katherine Lambert* • Lorri Bagley *Judy* • Brad Beyer *Rich* • Steve Hayes *Perry* ■ *Dir* Jim Fall • *Scr* Jason Schafer

A Trick of the Mind ★★
Thriller 2006 · Can · Colour

Anyone who's watched a few TV mysteries will swiftly deduce what's happening in this join-the-dots clunker. Coincidence-heavy and full of silly people behaving preposterously, it's yet another take on the *Gaslight* theme, as mentally fragile heiress Alexandra Holden seemingly starts to lose her mind after a female private eye warns her that new husband Paul Johansson isn't what he seems. It's thankfully briskly paced, and there is pleasure in seeing the villain's smug expression finally wiped off his face. SF

Alexandra Holden *Jamie* • Paul Johansson *Michael* • Stacy Grant *Helen* • Wanda Cannon *Dr Hauser* • Ben Cole (2) *Josh* ■ *Dir* Terry Ingram • *Scr* Jeff Barmash, George Erschbamer, Barbara Fixx

Trick or Treat ★★ 18
Comedy horror 1986 · US · Colour · 93min

Evil Kiss-type rock star Tony Fields returns from the dead when one of his biggest fans, Marc Price, plays his last unreleased album backwards. At first Price caters to every murderous whim the spirit demands, until he realises he's being duped by the Devil. A tedious and adolescent heavy metal comedy horror it features head-bangers Ozzie Osbourne and Gene Simmons in cameo roles and is perfunctorily directed by Charles Martin Smith. AJ DVD

Tony Fields *Sammi Curr* • Marc Price *Eddie Weinbauer* • Lisa Orgolini *Leslie Graham* • Doug Savant *Tim Hainey* • Elaine Joyce *Angie Weinbauer* • Ozzy Osbourne *Reverend Aaron Gilstrom* • Gene Simmons *Nuke* ■ *Dir* Charles Martin Smith • *Scr* Rhet Topham, Michael S Murphey, Joel Soisson, from a story by Rhet Topham

Trick 'r Treat ★★★★
Horror 2007 · US · Colour · 82min

The quintessential haunted spirit of the autumn holiday is used with elan not seen since John Carpenter's *Halloween* in writer/director Michael Dougherty's wickedly winning horror anthology. Mirthful, nasty, poignant yet always sinister, terror tales involving vampires, zombies, werewolves and serial killers are given an EC Comic edge complete with mischievous retribution twists as they intermingle during one night of costumed celebration in Smalltown USA. AJ

Brian Cox (1) *Mr Kreeg* • Anna Paquin *Laurie* • Quinn Lord *Sam* • Dylan Baker *Steven* ■ *Dir/Scr* Michael Dougherty

Tricks ★★★★ 12A
Comedy drama 2007 · Pol · Colour · 95min

A little boy's hopes of reuniting his fractured family shape this Polish comedy drama. Six-year-old Stefek (Damian Ul) is convinced that the man he sees on the railway platform each morning is his estranged father and begins his own secret campaign to reshape destiny to his own ends. At first, writer/director Andrzej Jakimowski's film appears almost defiantly low-key, but the unforced portrayal of small-town life and the likeable characters with their believable dilemmas gradually weave their magic. As such, it's a tribute to the cunning and confidence of a film-maker able to invest seemingly mundane everyday details with imaginative resonance and genuine emotional punch. TJ Polish, Italian +subtitles. Swearing, sexual references.

Damian Ul *Stefek* • Ewelina Walendziak *Elka* • Rafal Guzniczak *Jerzy* • Tomasz Sapryk *Father* • Iwona Fornalczyk *Mother* ■ *Dir/Scr* Andrzej Jakimowski

The Trigger Effect ★★★ 15
Thriller 1996 · US · Colour · 90min

A massive power failure causes panic among the inhabitants of a well-to-do US suburb. There's a parallel with *Lord of the Flies* in this stark reminder of the thin veneer that disguises our more savage instincts. Director David Koepp handles the chaos with some aplomb, despite his reduction of most characters to disaster-movie stereotypes. He's helped by a high calibre cast. DA Swearing, sexual references, violence.

Kyle MacLachlan *Matthew* • Elisabeth Shue *Annie* • Dermot Mulroney *Joe* • Richard T Jones *Raymond* • Bill Smitrovich *Steph* • Michael Rooker *Gary* ■ *Dir/Scr* David Koepp

Trigger Happy ★★★★ 15
Crime comedy 1996 · US · Colour · 92min

Originally known as *Mad Dog Time*, this is a quirky gangster comedy featuring hilarious turns from an impressive all-star cast. Richard Dreyfuss is Vic, the Mob boss in a mental institution. Meanwhile, his associates and rivals battle over who takes control of his business and his girlfriend. Jeff Goldblum, Ellen Barkin, Diane Lane, Gabriel Byrne, Kyle MacLachlan and Gregory Hines are just some of the mobsters and their molls scattering Larry Bishop's odd little film, which will delight those with a skewed sense of humour. JB

Larry Bishop *Nick* • Richard Dreyfuss *Vic* • Gabriel Byrne *Ben London* • Ellen Barkin *Rita Everly* • Jeff Goldblum *Mickey Holliday* • Diane Lane *Grace Everly* • Gregory Hines *Jules Flamingo* • Kyle MacLachlan *Jake Parker* • Burt Reynolds *"Wacky" Jacky Jackson* ■ *Dir/Scr* Larry Bishop

Triggermen ★ 15
Crime comedy 2002 · Can/US · Colour · 92min

This ghastly so-called comedy finds chancers Neil Morrissey and Adrian Dunbar getting mistaken for hitmen by Chicago mobsters keen to rub out rival gangster Pete Postlethwaite. Much allegedly comic mayhem ensues when the real hitmen turn up, and one of them falls for Postlethwaite's daughter, Claire Forlani. Duff material, indifferent direction. DA DVD

Neil Morrissey *Pete Maynard* • Donnie Wahlberg *Terry Malloy* • Adrian Dunbar *Andy Jarrett* • Claire Forlani *Emma Cutler* • Amanda Plummer *Penny Archer* • Michael Rapaport *Tommy O'Brian* • Saul Rubinek *Jazzer* • Pete Postlethwaite *Ben Cutler* ■ *Dir* John Bradshaw • *Scr* Tony Johnston

Trilogy ★★★
Portmanteau drama 1969 · US · Colour · 110min

Truman Capote enjoyed a fruitful relationship with the screen via adaptations of his original works - as here - and contributions to classics such as *The Innocents*. This trio of stories is directed with delicacy and wit by Frank Perry. *Miriam*, based on his first published work, and *Among the Paths to Eden* are effective thanks to the fine acting that characterises the project. The longer *A Christmas Memory*, narrated by Capote, is the standout. Geraldine Page is mesmerising as she ritually collects the ingredients and prepares the seasonal cake in this unsentimental evocation of a bygone era. BB

Mildred Natwick *Miss Miller* • Susan Dunfee *Miriam* • Carol Gustafson *Miss Lake* • Robin Ponterio *Emily* • Beverly Ballard *Nina* • Maureen Stapleton *Mary O'Meaghan* • Martin Balsam *Ivor Belli* • Geraldine Page *Woman* • Truman Capote *Narrator* ■ *Dir* Frank Perry • *Scr* Truman Capote, Eleanor Perry, from the Truman Capote stories *Miriam* and *A Christmas Memory* in *Mademoiselle* and *Among the Paths to Eden* in *Esquire*

Trilogy: the Weeping Meadow ★★★ PG
Romantic drama 2004 · Gr/Fr/It/Ger · Colour · 162min

Despite its surfeit of glorious images, the first part of Theo Angelopoulos's projected "Greek exile" trilogy is too superficial to wholly engross. Following Alexandra Aidini, a Greek refugee from Russia who has been orphaned by the Bolshevik revolution, this spans 30 tumultuous years of history. While the plight of the interwar refugee is ably explored, this is swamped by historical events that pass before their significance can be understood. DP Greek +subtitles. DVD

Alexandra Aidini *Eleni* • Nikos Poursanidis *Spyros's son* • Yorgos Armenis *Nikos, the fiddler* • Vasilis Kolovos *Spyros* • Eva Kotamanidou *Cassandra* • Toula Stathopoulou *Woman in coffee house* • Mihalis Yannatos *Zissis, the clarinetist* • Thalia Argyriou *Danae* ■ *Dir* Theo Angelopoulos • *Scr* Theo Angelopoulos, Tonino Guerra, Petros Markaris, Giorgio Silvagni

Trio ★★★ U
Portmanteau drama 1950 · UK/US · BW · 87min

Sandwiched between *Quartet* and *Encore*, this is the second of Gainsborough's Somerset Maugham portmanteau pictures. Considering the writing talent involved and the quality of the performances, it seems slightly strange that the only Oscar nomination the picture received was for best sound. Ken Annakin directs the first two stories, *The Verger*, with James Hayter and Kathleen Harrison on sparkling form, and *Mr Knowall*, with cheeky chappy supreme Nigel Patrick. The final half of the film contains Harold French's sentimental *Sanatorium*, starring Jean Simmons and Michael Rennie. DP DVD

James Hayter *Albert Foreman* • Kathleen Harrison *Emma Brown* • Felix Aylmer *Bank manager* • Michael Hordern *Vicar* • Nigel Patrick *Max Kelada "Mr Know-All"* • Anne Crawford *Mrs Ramsay* • Wilfrid Hyde White *Mr Gray* • Jean Simmons *Evie Bishop* • Roland Culver *Ashenden* • Michael Rennie *George Templeton* ■ *Dir* Ken Annakin, Harold French • *Scr* W Somerset Maugham, RC Sherriff, Noel Langley, from the short stories by W Somerset Maugham • *Sound* Gordon McCallum, CC Stevens, J Mitchell

The Trip ★★★ 18
Drama 1967 · US · Colour · 75min

"Feel Purple, Taste Green" screamed the posters for cult director Roger Corman's highly controversial drugs epic in which hippy Bruce Dern guides confused commercials director Peter Fonda through his first LSD acid trip. After scoring from

T

Dennis Hopper (who else?) it's back to a luxury LA pad where Fonda digs an orange's aura, experiences good and bad vibes, has psychedelic visions of sex, death and dancing girls. Part exploitation flick, part non-preachy message picture, this fractured love-in, scripted by Jack Nicholson and told almost entirely through rapid-fire visuals, is a fascinating period piece. AJ DVD

Peter Fonda *Paul Groves* • Susan Strasberg *Sally Groves* • Bruce Dern *John* • Dennis Hopper *Max* • Salli Sachse *Glenn* • Katherine Walsh *Lulu* • Barboura Morris *Flo* • Caren Bernsen *Alexandra* • Dick Miller *Cash* ■ *Dir* Roger Corman • *Scr* Jack Nicholson • *Cinematographer* Arch R Dalzell

The Trip to Bountiful ★★★★ U

Drama   1985 · US · Colour · 103min

Geraldine Page's superb, Oscar-winning performance is the showpiece of this classy, intelligent, affecting and enjoyable drama, adapted with much skill by Horton Foote from his own stage and TV play. John Heard and Carlin Glynn give fine support as the son and peevish daughter-in-law of an elderly Texan woman (Page), who sets off from Houston on a journey of escape and returns to the small town of Bountiful where she was born. A far from conventional road movie, but one not to be missed. PF DVD

Geraldine Page *Carrie Watts* • John Heard *Ludie Watts* • Carlin Glynn *Jessie Mae* • Richard Bradford *Sheriff* • Rebecca De Mornay *Thelma* • Kevin Cooney *Roy* ■ *Dir* Peter Masterson • *Scr* Horton Foote, from his TV play

Triple Agent ★★★★ U

Period thriller
2003 · Fr/It/Sp/Gr/Rus · Colour · 110min

Inspired by fact, Eric Rohmer's period morality tale explores the notion of cause over country that has a subtle contemporary resonance. Set in Paris in 1936, the story concerns White Russian exile Serge Renko, who is prepared to conspire with democrats and fascists alike to undermine the Communist regime back home. But his duplicitous diplomacy seems to feel like a form of infidelity to his Greek artist wife Katerina Didaskalou. As ever with Rohmer, the literate dialogue is paramount, although he frequently resorts to newsreel footage to put the story into the context of unfolding world events. DP French, Greek, Russian +subtitles. DVD

Katerina Didaskalou *Arsinoé Vorodin* • Serge Renko *Fiodor Vorodin* • Cyrielle Clair [Cyrielle Claire] *Maguy* • Grigori Manoukov [Grigori Manukov] *Boris* • Dimitri Rafalsky *General Dobrinsky* • Nathalia Krougly *General Dobrinsky's wife* • Amanda Langlet *Janine* • Jeanne Rambur *Dany* ■ *Dir/Scr* Eric Rohmer

Triple Bogey on a Par Five Hole ★★★★

Comedy   1991 · US · BW · 88min

The Levys, a pair of married crooks who specialise in robbing people on golf courses, are both shot dead by one of their would-be victims. Thirteen years later, screenwriter Remy Gravelle (played by underground film-maker Eric Mitchell) is hired to research the story of their three children who live off Manhattan on a luxury yacht called the *Triple Bogey*. Mitchell tries to remain dispassionate but gradually gets drawn into their complex world. Mesmerising and haunting. DF

Eric Mitchell *Remy Gravelle* • Daisy Hall *Amanda Levy* • Angela Goethals *Bree Levy* • Jesse McBride *Satch Levy* • Alba Clemente *Nina Baccardi* • Robbie Coltrane *Steffano Baccardi* • Philip Seymour Hoffman *Klutch* ■ *Dir/Scr* Amos Poe

Triple Cross ★★ PG

Biographical Second World War drama
1966 · Fr/UK · Colour · 120min

Stuffed with plot and counterplot, this unexceptional Second World War drama is based on the allegedly true exploits of Eddie Chapman. Christopher Plummer plays Chapman, in jail on Jersey when the Nazis invade. He promptly secures a job in the

Intelligence Service, leaving viewers to wonder if he's a traitor. Plummer makes the most of his enigmatic character. AT DVD

Christopher Plummer *Eddie Chapman* • Romy Schneider *The Countess* • Trevor Howard *Distinguished civilian* • Gert Fröbe *Col Steinhager* • Yul Brynner *Baron von Grunen* • Claudine Auger *Paulette* • Georges Lycan *Leo* ■ *Dir* Terence Young • *Scr* René Hardy, William Marchant, from the autobiography *The Eddie Chapman Story* by Eddie Chapman, Frank Owen

The Triple Echo ★★★

Wartime drama   1972 · UK · Colour · 94min

Adapted from a novel by HE Bates and set on a remote farm in 1942, this unlikely drama might have provoked a few unintentional smirks if it hadn't been so sensitively played by Glenda Jackson and Brian Deacon. Michael Apted's careful direction makes the ruse of disguising deserter Deacon as Jackson's sister seem almost credible, while his re-creation of the tranquil wartime countryside makes the abrupt intrusion of vulgar sergeant Oliver Reed all the more foreboding. DP Swearing, violence.

Glenda Jackson *Alice Charlesworth* • Oliver Reed *Sergeant* • Brian Deacon *Barton* • Anthony May *Subaltern* • Gavin Richards *Stan* • Jenny Lee Wright *Christine* • Ken Colley [Kenneth Colley] *Corporal* • Daphne Heard *Shopkeeper* ■ *Dir* Michael Apted • *Scr* Robin Chapman, from the novel by HE Bates

Triple 9 ★★★ 15

Crime thriller   2015 · US · Colour · 110min

A story of dirty cops and robbers, this sees Chiwetel Ejiofor and his Atlanta gang narrowly escaping the opening bank job only to then end up coerced by Kate Winslet's merciless mob boss into an even riskier heist. By Hillcoat standards, this crime thriller is short on impact and depth, and Winslet fails to bring the requisite menace as she wrestles with an unconvincing accent. But some sporadic directorial swagger – particularly in the tensely handled action sequences – and the rest of the high-calibre cast keep it watchable. EAS Violence, swearing, nudity. DVD Blu

Casey Affleck *Chris Allen* • Chiwetel Ejiofor *Michael Belmont* • Anthony Mackie *Marcus Atwood* • Norman Reedus *Russel Welch* • Aaron Paul *Gabe Welch* • Woody Harrelson *Sergeant Detective Jeffrey Allen* • Kate Winslet *Irina Vlaslov* ■ *Dir* John Hillcoat • *Scr* Matt Cook

The Tripper ★★★ 18

Horror   2006 · US · Colour · 93min

Scream star David Arquette's directorial debut is very much a family affair, as various ex-wives/husbands of the Arquette clan appear on screen, including Courteney Cox and Thomas Jane. In the late 1960s, a young Ronald Reagan fan goes mad with a chainsaw, then at a present-day Free Love festival, a psycho in a Reagan mask starts slaughtering neo-hippies. Arquette's lively gore-fest cleverly encompasses both pointed comment and the usual slice-and-dice savagery, and all on a minuscule budget. AJ DVD

Jaime King *Samantha* • Thomas Jane *Buzz Hall* • David Arquette *Muff* • Courteney Cox Arquette [Courteney Cox] *Dog lover hippie* • Balthazar Getty *Jimmy* • Lukas Haas *Ivan* • Jason Mewes *Joey* ■ *Dir* David Arquette • *Scr* David Arquette, Joe Harris

Trishna ★★★★ 15

Drama   2011 · UK/Swe/Ind · Colour · 113min

Director Michael Winterbottom turns once more to Thomas Hardy - following *Jude* (1996) and *The Claim* (2000) - in this compelling Bollywood makeover of *Tess of the d'Urbervilles*. Audaciously combining the novel's twin suitors into a single character and relocating its fascination with the corrosive nature of class distinction to present-day India, Winterbottom is faithful to the spirit of Hardy while presenting a steamy melodrama and an authentic vision of a rapidly changing globalised society. Riz Ahmed plays the wealthy hotelier, whose offer of a job to country girl Freida Pinto is the seed of her tragedy. DP English, Hindi

+subtitles. Violence, swearing, sex scenes. DVD

Freida Pinto *Trishna* • Riz Ahmed [Rizwan Ahmed] *Jay* • Roshan Seth *Mr Singh* • Meeta Vasisht *Bhaanumathi* • Harish Khanna *Vijay* ■ *Dir* Michael Winterbottom • *Scr* Michael Winterbottom, from the novel *Tess of the d'Urbervilles* by Thomas Hardy

Tristan + Isolde ★★ 12

Period romantic drama
2005 · UK/Ger/US/Cz · Colour · 120min

Sophia Myles and James Franco are the star-crossed lovers prepared to risk everything for their forbidden romance. The Irish princess and English warrior are brought together by fate after she saves his life, but when Tristan later wins Isolde's hand for his lord and surrogate father (a poignantly dignified Rufus Sewell), the duo are unable to sever their relationship. With little visual imagination or overall vitality, the film needs the central stars to carry the drama, but while Myles beautifully captures her character's emotional dilemma, wooden Franco fails. SF Violence, sex scenes. DVD

James Franco *Tristan* • Sophia Myles *Isolde* • Rufus Sewell *Lord Marke* • David Patrick O'Hara [David O'Hara] *King Donnchadh* • Henry Cavill *Melot* • JB Blanc *Leon* • Mark Strong *Wictred* • Bronagh Gallagher *Bragnae* ■ *Dir* Kevin Reynolds • *Scr* Dean Georgaris

Tristana ★★★★★ PG

Period drama   1970 · Sp/It/Fr · Colour · 94min

The last film that Luis Buñuel shot in his native Spain is not only a searing indictment of the Franco regime, but also an attack on the Spanish people as a whole for allowing their country to be consumed by corruption and decay. Set in Toledo in the late 1920s, the film explores the relationship between a depraved nobleman and his ward, who is determined to avenge the seduction that ruined her life. Revelling in his sins, Fernando Rey is superb as the pitiless Don Lope, while Catherine Deneuve is at her chilling best as the victim turned tormentor. Bitter and brilliant. DP Spanish +subtitles. DVD

Catherine Deneuve *Tristana* • Fernando Rey *Don Lope* • Franco Nero *Horacio* • Lola Gaos *Saturna* • Antonio Casas *Don Cosme* • Jesus Fernandez *Saturno* • Vicente Soler *Don Ambrosio* ■ *Dir* Luis Buñuel • *Scr* Luis Buñuel, Julio Alejandro, from the novel by Benito Perez Galdos

The Triumph ★★ 12

Drama based on a true story
2006 · US · Colour · 86min

In this mediocre TV movie, Matthew Perry plays an idealistic, small-town teacher whose innovative methods and sheer tenacity gradually transform the lives of a class of failing 12 year olds when he moves to New York. Perry impresses as the real-life educational hero Ron Clark, but sadly he's let down by a superficial script and lacklustre execution. *Children of a Lesser God* director Randa Haines seems to be merely going through the motions, delivering the cliché-riddled events without achieving much impact or realism. SF DVD

Matthew Perry *Ron Clark* • Ernie Hudson *Principal Turner* • Brandon Mychal Smith [Brandon Smith] *Tayshawn* • Hannah Hodson *Shameika* • Melissa De Sousa *Marissa Vega* • Isabelle Deluce *Alita* ■ *Dir* Randa Haines • *Scr* Annie DeYoung, Max Enscoe

Triumph of the Spirit ★★★ 15

Second World War drama
1989 · US · Colour · 115min

In this powerful fact-based Holocaust drama filmed on location at the Auschwitz-Birkenau death camp, Willem Dafoe portrays a Jewish boxer who's forced, literally, to fight for his life, and for the lives of his family. It's a work of some restraint, preferring to forgo the familiar shock-horror Holocaust imagery, and opting instead to mirror the monstrosities in people's reactions to them. Dafoe shed 20 pounds to play the part, and looks skeletal. Grimly hard-hitting. DA

Willem Dafoe *Salamo Arouch* • Wendy Gazelle *Allegra* • Robert Loggia *Father Arouch* • Edward James Olmos *The Gypsy* • Kelly Wolf *Elena* • Costas Mandylor *Avram Arouch* • Kario Salem *Jacko Levy* ■ *Dir* Robert M Young • *Scr* Laurence Heath, Andrzej Krakowski, Robert M Young, Arthur Coburn, Millard Lampell, Shimon Arama, Zion Haen

Triumph of the Will ★★★★

Classic propaganda   1935 · Ger · BW · 120min

Personally selected by Hitler, Leni Riefenstahl was given unlimited financial resources, the full co-operation of the Nazi hierarchy and a crew of more than a hundred to make a record of the 1934 Nuremberg Party rally. Special ramps, elevators, tracks and platforms were constructed so that every detail of Albert Speer's meticulously choreographed spectacle could be captured and used to convey the might and universality of Nazism and the messianic aura of the Führer. Taking eight months to edit, this remains one of the most potent pieces of propaganda ever produced, with Riefenstahl's mastery of her medium ensuring the total success of a pernicious project. DP German +subtitles. DVD

■ *Dir* Leni Riefenstahl • *Scr* Walter Ruttmann (subtitles) • *Editor* Leni Riefenstahl • *Cinematographers* Sepp Allgeier, Karl Attenberger, Werner Bohne • *Music* Herbert Windt

Triumphs of a Man Called Horse ★ 15

Adventure   1983 · US/Mex · Colour · 85min

Fans of the previous two *Horse* films (*A Man Called Horse* and *The Return of a Man Called Horse*) and will be disappointed by the relatively brief appearance of Richard Harris as the ageing Sioux leader. This lame sequel finds him joining with son Michael Beck and army captain Vaughn Armstrong to protect the tribe against settlers drawn by the gold rush. AT

Richard Harris *Man Called Horse* • Michael Beck *Koda* • Ana De Sade *Redwing* • Vaughn Armstrong *Capt Cummings* • Anne Seymour *Elk Woman* • Buck Taylor *Sgt Bridges* • Simon Andreu *Gance* • Lautaro Murua *Perkins* ■ *Dir* John Hough • *Scr* Ken Blackwell, Carlos Aured, from a story by Jack DeWitt, from characters by Dorothy M Johnson

Trixie ★★ 15

Comedy   2000 · US · Colour · 110min

Ill-disciplined and over-written, this comedic sledgehammer nevertheless has a certain kooky charm, thanks to the gallant efforts of Emily Watson as a malapropping Chicago security guard with a yen to be a detective. Clearly director Alan Rudolph envisaged creating a screwball *noir*. Yet he never comes to terms with either the mystery - senator Nick Nolte's role in the disappearance of gangster's moll Lesley Ann Warren - or with the tone of the humour, which combines slapstick and wordplay with careless abandon. DP DVD

Emily Watson *Trixie Zurbo* • Dermot Mulroney *Dex Lang* • Nick Nolte *Senator Drummond Avery* • Nathan Lane *Kirk Stans* • Brittany Murphy *Ruby Pearli* • Lesley Ann Warren *Dawn Sloane* • Will Patton *RedRafferty* • Stephen Lang *Jacob Slotnick* ■ *Dir* Alan Rudolph • *Scr* Alan Rudolph, from a story by Alan Rudolph, John Binder

Trog ★ 15

Science-fiction horror
1970 · UK · Colour · 87min

This indescribable nonsense sees anthropologist Joan Crawford battling Michael Gough over the fate of a recently discovered prehistoric caveman. Will Crawford teach the Missing Link all about life in the 20th century before Gough calls in the army to destroy him? This painful dud has intercut footage from *The Animal World* serving as Trog's memories in Crawford's last feature film. AJ

Joan Crawford *Dr Brockton* • Michael Gough *Sam Murdock* • Bernard Kay *Inspector Greenham* • Kim Braden *Anne* • David Griffin *Malcolm* • John Hamill *Cliff* • Thorley Walters *Magistrate* • Jack May *Dr Selbourne* ■ *Dir* Freddie Francis • *Scr* Aben Kandel, from a story by Peter Bryan, John Gilling

Trois Chambres à Manhattan ★★★

Drama 1965 · Fr/It · BW · 112min

Marcel Carné specialised in claustrophobic melodramas featuring couples pondering the fate of their tortuous affair. But there's none of that oppressive melancholy in this adaptation of Georges Simenon's novel. Certainly the New York romance between French actor Maurice Ronet and diplomat's wife Annie Girardot (who won best actress at Venice) rarely runs smoothly, but there's a sustainable optimism about their reunion, which reinforces Carné's quaintly old-fashioned belief in love. DP French +subtitles.

Annie Girardot *Kay Larsi* • Roland Lesaffre *Pierre* • OE Hasse *Hourvitch* • Maurice Ronet *François Comte* • Gabriele Ferzetti *Count Larsi* • Geneviève Page [Genevieve Page] *Yolande Combes* • Robert De Niro ■ *Dir* Marcel Carné • *Scr* Jacques Sigurd, Marcel Carné, from the novel by Georges Simenon

Trojan Eddie ★★★ 15

Drama 1996 · Ire/UK · Colour · 99min

The totally different styles of bully-boy Richard Harris and hangdog Stephen Rea mesh to advantage in this slow-moving Irish fable. Rea is a loser, a peddler forced by circumstances to fetch and carry for Harris, godfather to the local travellers. The Irish landscape looks beautiful and there's plenty of time to observe it, but the depiction of the mentality of the people is as idiotic as it is idealistic. As dour as a bog. TH Violence, swearing. DVD

Richard Harris *John Power* • Stephen Rea *Trojan Eddie* • Brendan Gleeson *Ginger Power* • Sean McGinley *Raymie* • Angeline Ball *Shirley* • Brid Brennan *Betty* • Stuart Townsend *Dermot* ■ *Dir* Gillies MacKinnon • *Scr* Billy Roche

The Trojan War ★★ U

Period action adventure
1961 · Fr/It · Colour · 103min

In this routine, but watchable sword-and-sandal epic set a decade into the eponymous conflict, Trojan ruler Paris becomes jealous of people's champion Aeneas (Steve Reeves) and denounces him. Meanwhile, the Greeks plan their wooden horse trick. Very spectacular and the action moves along excitingly enough. JG In Italian.

Steve Reeves *Aeneas* • John Drew Barrymore *Ulysses* • Warner Bentivegna *Paris* • Juliette Mayniel *Creusa* • Lidia Alfonsi *Cassandra* • Arturo Dominici *Achilles* ■ *Dir* Giorgio Ferroni • *Scr* Giorgio Stegani, Ugo Liberatore, Federico Zardi

The Trojan Women ★

Drama 1971 · Gr/US · Colour · 111min

This is as dull as counting sheep in a fog, despite the presence of such luminaries as Katharine Hepburn, Vanessa Redgrave and Irene Papas. Directed by Michael Cacoyannis, it's the story of Helen, Hecuba and that sassy seer Cassandra. Brian Blessed seems to be competing in the Anthony Quinn "River of Life" contest, but loses out to Patrick Magee who seems on the verge of imploding. AT

Katharine Hepburn *Hecuba* • Geneviève Bujold *Cassandra* • Vanessa Redgrave *Andromache* • Irene Papas *Helen* • Brian Blessed *Tathybius* • Patrick Magee *Menelaus* ■ *Dir* Michael Cacoyannis • *Scr* Michael Cacoyannis, from the play by Euripides

Troll ★ 15

Fantasy horror 1986 · US · Colour · 79min

Michael Moriarty and Shelley Hack move into a new apartment building, and a mysterious troll possesses their little girl. The troll in his new guise then starts mutating the building's residents into creatures, or into forests as is the case with resident Sonny Bono. Whatever his actions

---

are, the common factor is cheesiness. A dire, completely unrelated "sequel" followed in 1992. KB DVD

Noah Hathaway *Harry Potter Jr* • Michael Moriarty *Harry Potter Sr* • Shelley Hack *Anne Potter* • Jennifer Beck (2) *Wendy Potter* • Sonny Bono *Peter Dickinson* • Phil Fondacaro *Malcolm Malory/Torok* • Julia Louis-Dreyfus *Jeanette Cooper* ■ *Dir* John Carl Buechler • *Scr* Ed Naha

The Troll Hunter ★★★★ 15

Horror thriller 2010 · Nor · Colour · 99min

This fantastic "found footage" film adds Norwegian folklore to a *Blair Witch* vibe to thrilling effect. The movie is set in the Norse wilds, and it chronicles, via "authenticated" videos, the experiences of a student film crew who come across the sun-hating, Christian-hunting monsters. Trolls are, so we are told, not the stuff of myth, but the Norwegian people don't know it because of a comprehensive government cover-up. The trolls are terrific and the film balances genuine thrills and spills with moments of great humour. DA Norwegian +subtitles. DVD

Otto Jespersen *Hans/Trolljegeren* • Tomas Alf Larsen *Kalle* • Hans Morten Hansen *Finn* • Johanna Morck *Johanna* ■ *Dir/Scr* Andre Ovredal

The Trollenberg Terror ★★

Horror 1958 · UK · BW · 82min

A Swiss ski resort is terrorised by tentacled monsters from outer space in an efficiently suspenseful British cheapie marred by awful special effects. Two bits of cotton wool stuck on a mountain photo make do for the cloudy snowscapes in veteran Hammer scriptwriter Jimmy Sangster's screen version of the BBC TV series. Forrest Tucker is miscast as the hero, but Janet Munro is affecting as the telepathic heroine the aliens seize as their mouthpiece. AJ

Forrest Tucker *Alan Brooks* • Laurence Payne *Philip Truscott* • Janet Munro *Anne Pilgrim* • Jennifer Jayne *Sarah Pilgrim* • Warren Mitchell *Professor Crevett* • Frederick Schiller *Klein* ■ *Dir* Quentin Lawrence • *Scr* Jimmy Sangster, from the BBC TV series by Peter Key

Trolls

Animated musical adventure 2016 · US · Colour

This is a preview – no prints were available to review as we went to press: With *Shrek* and *Kung Fu Panda* their most durable franchises to date, Dreamworks is hoping to get a new money-spinner airborne with this vividly coloured animation whose plot – grumpy troll and cute princess set out on a do-or-die quest – mixes plot elements of both. Justin Timberlake and Anna Kendrick provide the voices, and Timberlake also provides some of the songs, one of which, *Can't Stop the Feeling!*, has already been a number one hit. SvM 3D

Justin Timberlake *Branch* • Anna Kendrick *Princess Poppy* • Zooey Deschanel *Bridget* • Christopher Mintz-Plasse *Prince Gristle* • Christine Baranski *Chef* • John Cleese *King Gristle* • Russell Brand *Creek* ■ *Dir* Mike Mitchell, Walt Dohrn [Walter Dohrn] • *Scr* Jonathan Aibel, Glenn Berger, Erica Rivinoja

Tromeo & Juliet ★ 18

Erotic spoof 1996 · US · Colour · 102min

The Troma team's take on Shakespeare is unremittingly awful. With Motörhead's Lemmy as narrator, this mainly serves as an excuse to string together a series of loathsome and resolutely unfunny set pieces. Quite appalling. JF Swearing, sex scenes, violence. DVD BD

Jane Jensen *Juliet Capulet* • Will Keenan *Tromeo Que* • Valentine Miele *Murray Martini* • Maximillian Shaun *Cappy Capulet* • Steve Gibbons *London Arbuckle* • Sean Gunn *Sammy Capulet* • Lemmy *Narrator* ■ *Dir* Lloyd Kaufman • *Scr* James Gunn, Lloyd Kaufman

---

Tron ★★★ PG

Science-fiction adventure
1982 · US · Colour · 91min

Disney's journey to *Toy Story* began with this dazzling electronic fantasy. Once computer genius Jeff Bridges entered cyberspace to prove himself the rightful inventor of stolen game patents, director Steven Lisberger broke new cinematic ground by using, and inventing, state-of-the-art digital graphics to depict a bizarre video netherworld. The "light cycle" race – where machines create solid walls of colour behind them as they speed around a grid – is the highlight of a complex, but light-hearted, adventure. It's dated already, but video-game enthusiasts will love it. AJ DVD BD

Jeff Bridges *Kevin Flynn/Clu* • David Warner *Ed Dillinger/Sark* • Bruce Boxleitner *Alan Bradley/Tron* • Cindy Morgan *Lora/Yori* • Barnard Hughes *Dr Walter Gibbs/Dumont* • Dan Shor *Ram* • Peter Jurasik *Crom* ■ *Dir* Steven Lisberger • *Scr* Steven Lisberger, from a story by Steven Lisberger, Bonnie MacBird

Tron Legacy ★★★ PG

Science-fiction thriller
2010 · US · Colour · 125min

The game has changed since 1982, when *Tron* broke new ground for the use of computer-generated imagery in movies. But while still ultra-slick and super-shiny, this delayed sequel is derailed by a confusing plot and a blank lead in the form of Garrett Hedlund. The story is basically one of father and son reconciliation, as Hedlund enters the virtual universe known as the Grid to find his missing father (Jeff Bridges), who has been trapped there by his jealous avatar. First-time director Joseph Kosinski's coldly remote CGI world contains no genuine emotional connections, but as an action-packed visual feast, the movie is truly astonishing. AJ Some violence. DVD BD

Jeff Bridges *Kevin Flynn/Clu* • Garrett Hedlund *Sam Flynn* • Olivia Wilde *Quorra* • Bruce Boxleitner *Alan Bradley/Tron* • James Frain *Jarvis* • Beau Garrett *Gem* ■ *Dir* Joseph Kosinski • *Scr* Adam Horowitz, Edward Kitsis, from a story by Brian Klugman, Lee Sternthal, Horowitz, Kitsis, from characters by Steven Lisberger, Bonnie MacBird

Troop Beverly Hills ★★ PG

Comedy 1989 · US · Colour · 101min

In this airy comedy, a bunch of moneyed little misses strive to be hits as Wilderness Girls (a Girl Guide-type group), but a resentful area troop leader resolves to make them fail. Neatly made and hard to hate, stars Shelley Long and Craig T Nelson bring their customary professionalism to the mildly amusing movie. DA

Shelley Long *Phyllis Nefler* • Craig T Nelson *Freddy Nefler* • Betty Thomas *Velda Plendor* • Mary Gross *Annie Herman* • Stephanie Beacham *Vicki Sprantz* • Audra Lindley *Frances Temple* • Edd Byrnes *Ross Coleman* • Ami Foster *Claire Sprantz* ■ *Dir* Jeff Kanew • *Scr* Pamela Norris, Margaret Grieco Oberman, from a story by Ava Ostern Fries

Trooper Hook ★★

Western 1957 · US · BW · 82min

Barbara Stanwyck gives an intelligent performance as the rescued captive of the Apaches who won't give up the son she had by an Indian chief, but Joel McCrea is not quite tough enough as the cavalry sergeant who escorts her back to her rancher husband. There's a fatal lack of subtlety in the supporting characters, while the direction of Charles Marquis Warren is often clumsy, and Tex Ritter's title song soon becomes tiresome. AE

Joel McCrea *Sgt Hook* • Barbara Stanwyck *Cora Sutliff* • Earl Holliman *Jeff Bennett* • Edward Andrews *Charlie Travers* • John Dehner *Fred Sutliff* • Susan Kohner *Consuela* • Royal Dano *Trude* • Terry Lawrence *Quito* ■ *Dir* Charles Marquis Warren • *Scr* Charles Marquis Warren, David Victor, Herbert Little Jr, from a story by Jack Schaefer

---

Trop Belle pour Toi ★★★★ 18

Comedy 1989 · Fr · Colour · 87min

Director Bertrand Blier was accused of sexism in many quarters for this tale of a car dealer who abandons his statuesque wife for a plain, older secretary. Yet, thanks to the wholehearted performances of Gérard Depardieu and Josiane Balasko, this is a touching love story. Blier can't resist mocking the sexual repression and social hypocrisy of the middle classes in a manner that recalls the later satires of Luis Buñuel. A touch short of stamina, but the blend of earthy drama and surrealist fantasy is thrilling. DP French +subtitles. Swearing, nudity. DVD

Gérard Depardieu *Bernard Barthélémy* • Josiane Balasko *Colette Chevassu* • Carole Bouquet *Florence Barthélémy/colette's Neighbour* • Roland Blanche *Marcello* • François Cluzet *Pascal Chevassu* • Didier Benureau *Léonce* • Philippe Loffredo *Tanguy* • Sylvie Orcier *Marie-Catherine* ■ *Dir/Scr* Bertrand Blier

Tropic Thunder ★★★★ 15

Comedy action adventure
2008 · Ger/US/UK · Colour · 102min

Ben Stiller co-writes, directs and stars in this hilarious send-up of "serious" war movies and self-absorbed stars. Stiller plays a fading action hero who's making a Vietnam epic with fellow pampered thespians Jack Black and Robert Downey Jr. When director Steve Coogan resorts to a "guerrilla style" jungle shoot, they are plunged into the middle of a real battle with drug lords. In a great cast, it's Oscar-nominated Downey Jr who steals everybody's thunder as the actor so committed to his craft that he's had his skin dyed to portray an African-American soldier. The gags are sometimes silly but often brilliant, spoofing every cliché without undermining the thrill of the adventure. SP Violence, swearing, sexual references. DVD BD

Ben Stiller *Tugg Speedman* • Jack Black *Jeff Portnoy* • Robert Downey Jr *Kirk Lazarus* • Steve Coogan *Damien Cockburn* • Jay Baruchel *Kevin Sandusky* • Danny McBride (2) *Cody* • Brandon T Jackson *Alpa Chino* • Nick Nolte *John "Four Leaf" Tayback* • Matthew McConaughey *Rick Peck* • Tom Cruise *Les Grossman* ■ *Dir* Ben Stiller • *Scr* Etan Cohen, Justin Theroux, Ben Stiller, from a story by Theroux, Stiller

Trottie True ★★ U

Romantic comedy 1949 · UK · Colour · 92min

This could have been a nostalgic romp through an age when every stage-door johnny was a milord, waiting to sweep a chorus girl off to a life of luxury. However, in the hands of perpetual underachiever Brian Desmond Hurst, it becomes a cheap exercise in gold-digging set against backdrops that, in spite of the rich Technicolor, look second-hand rather than antique. Yet Jean Kent is plucky enough as she falls for trouper Bill Owen, balloonist Andrew Crawford and aristocrat James Donald. DP

Jean Kent *Trottie True* • James Donald *Lord Digby Landon* • Hugh Sinclair *Maurice Beckenham* • Lana Morris *Bouncie Barrington* • Andrew Crawford *Sid Skinner* • Bill Owen *Joe Jugg* • Harcourt Williams *Duke of Wellwater* • Michael Medwin *Marquis Monty* • Hattie Jacques *Daisy Delaware* ■ *Dir* Brian Desmond Hurst • *Scr* C Denis Freeman, from the play by Caryl Brahms, SJ Simon

Le Trou ★★★★ 12

Prison drama 1959 · Fr/It · BW · 125min

Jacques Becker's final feature marks a significant stylistic departure from his previous pictures. Shot with an austerity that reinforces the grimly claustrophobic story of an attempted prison break, and made with a non-professional cast, it has inevitably been compared to Robert Bresson's *A Man Escaped*. But, the influence of Jean Renoir and John Huston ensures that this is more a study in psychology than spirituality, and there's also a painstaking attention to the finger-numbing mechanics of digging a tunnel with makeshift tools.

T

Emotionally searing, yet deeply humanistic. DP French +subtitles. **DVD**

Michel Constantin *Geo* • Philippe Leroy *Manu* • Marc Michel *Gaspard* • Raymond Meunier *Monseigneur* • Jean Keraudy *Roland* ■ *Dir* Jacques Becker • *Scr* Jacques Becker, Jean Aurel, José Giovanni

Trouble along the Way
★★★ U

Comedy drama 1953 · US · BW · 105min

John Wayne stars in this uncharacteristically mawkish vehicle as a divorcee trying to retain custody of his daughter Sherry Jackson. Directed by Michael Curtiz, there's a lot of religiosity on hand, which some may find hard to take, and a school football team makes an uncomfortable metaphor for teamwork at home. Still, Donna Reed shines, and the whole is, if not entirely entertaining, at least quite fascinating. TS

John Wayne *Steve Aloysius Williams* • Donna Reed *Alice Singleton* • Charles Coburn *Father Burke* • Tom Tully *Father Malone* • Sherry Jackson *Carole Williams* • Marie Windsor *Anne McCormick* • Tom Helmore *Harold McCormick* ■ *Dir* Michael Curtiz • *Scr* Melville Shavelson, Jack Rose, from the story *It Figures* by Douglas Morrow, Robert H Andrews

Trouble Bound
★★★ 18

Action crime comedy 1993 · US · Colour · 85min

Underrated Michael Madsen plays an out-of-luck gambler who sets off across country with a dead body in the boot of a car he's just won. But it quickly proves the least of his problems as he then hooks up with winsome waitress Patricia Arquette, who's out to avenge the murder of her Mafia grandfather. Of course, this curious couple end up being pursued. This is tongue-in-cheek, if violent, entertainment. DA Violence, swearing, nudity. **DVD**

Michael Madsen *Harry Talbot* • Patricia Arquette *Kit Califano* • Florence Stanley *Granny* • Seymour Cassel *Santino* • Sal Jenco *Danny* • Paul Ben-Victor *Zand* • Darren Epton *Raphael* • Billy Bob Thornton *Coldface* ■ *Dir* Jeffrey Reiner • *Scr* Darrell Fetty, Francis Delia

Trouble Brewing
★★★ U

Comedy 1939 · UK · BW · 86min

George Formby is a printer with a detective fixation, intent on capturing a gang of counterfeiters to impress journalist Googie Withers. It hardly takes Sherlock Holmes to figure out who is the master criminal, but the red herrings that pad out the story are amusing. Anthony Kimmins keeps the action brisk, but like all Formby directors he makes a stilted hash of the saucy songs. DP

George Formby *George Gullip* • Googie Withers *Mary Brown* • Gus McNaughton *Bill Pike* • Garry Marsh *AG Brady* • Joss Ambler *Lord Redhill* • Martita Hunt *Madame Berdi* ■ *Dir* Anthony Kimmins • *Scr* Anthony Kimmins, Angus MacPhail, Michael Hogan

Trouble Every Day
★★ 18

Horror 2000 · Fr/Ger/Jpn · Colour · 96min

Claire Denis gets out of her depth with this tenebrous horror outing. The opening segments are enacted with scarcely any dialogue, as honeymooners Vincent Gallo and Tricia Vessey arrive in Paris just as doctor Alex Descas imprisons the carnivorous Béatrice Dalle in his mansion. Unfortunately, any sense of foreboding is rapidly frittered away once the characters begin justifying their actions and behaving in an increasingly bizarre manner. DP French, English +subtitles. Violence, nudity. **DVD**

Vincent Gallo *Shane Brown* • Tricia Vessey *June* • Béatrice Dalle *Coré* • Alex Descas *Léo* • Florence Loiret Caille *Christelle* • Nicolas Duvauchelle *Erwan* ■ *Dir* Claire Denis • *Scr* Claire Denis, Jean-Pol Fargeau

Trouble for Two
★★★

Comedy thriller 1936 · US · BW · 75min

You'd never guess from the title, but this is MGM's version of Robert Louis Stevenson's "Suicide Club" stories. It's an expertly made, glossily produced oddity, pairing the excellent Robert Montgomery, playing an

unlikely 19th-century prince, with an unusually mysterious Rosalind Russell. The theme is interesting: members of an anarchic London club set Montgomery a series of life-threatening tasks before he can marry his beloved, Russell. This wayward, off-the-wall product of the studio system deserved greater recognition. TS

Robert Montgomery *Prince Florizel* • Rosalind Russell *Miss Vandeleur* • Frank Morgan *Colonel Geraldine* • Reginald Owen *Dr Franz Noel* • Louis Hayward *Young man with cream tarts* • EE Clive *King* • Walter Kingsford *Malthus* • Ivan Simpson *Collins* ■ *Dir* J Walter Ruben • *Scr* Manuel Seff, Edward E Paramore Jr, from the *Suicide Club* stories by Robert Louis Stevenson

Trouble in Mind
★★★★ 15

Futuristic crime thriller 1985 · US · Colour · 107min

This is an intelligent yet not wholly successful attempt by Alan Rudolph to re-create the kind of futuristic *film noir* pioneered by Jean-Luc Godard in *Alphaville*. Kris Kristofferson stars as an ex-cop just out of jail for murder, whose hopes for a fresh start with diner owner Geneviève Bujold are sidetracked by his involvement with Lori Singer and her violent partner, Keith Carradine, a petty crook whose behaviour and appearance grow increasingly bizarre and violent as he becomes entangled with Rain City crime boss, Divine. It's engrossing stuff and if the romance falls flat, the use of comedy to map Carradine's decline is inspired. DP **DVD**

Kris Kristofferson *John Hawkins* • Keith Carradine *Coop* • Lori Singer *Georgia* • Geneviève Bujold *Wanda* • Joe Morton *Solo* • Divine *Hilly Blue* • George Kirby *Lieutenant Gunther* • John Considine *Nate Nathanson* ■ *Dir/Scr* Alan Rudolph

Trouble in Paradise
★★★★★ U

Romantic comedy 1932 · US · BW · 82min

Two expert European thieves (Miriam Hopkins and Herbert Marshall) masquerading as aristocrats meet in Venice, fall in love and team up professionally. Their elaborate plans almost come unstuck when, in the guise of secretaries, they infiltrate the household of a wealthy and glamorous Parisienne (Kay Francis) whose charms extend beyond her jewellery collection. Made by Ernst Lubitsch, whose famous "touch" is everywhere evident, this is arguably the most highly sophisticated romantic comedy ever to emerge from Hollywood. Brilliantly scripted, flawlessly stylish and faultlessly acted, it's a masterpiece, as well as being wonderfully good fun. RK In English, Italian. **DVD**

Miriam Hopkins *Lily Vautier* • Kay Francis *Mariette Colet* • Herbert Marshall *Gaston Monescu, "LuValle"* • Charlie Ruggles [Charles Ruggles] *Major* • Edward Everett Horton *François Filiba* • C Aubrey Smith *Giron* ■ *Dir* Ernst Lubitsch • *Scr* Grover Jones, Samson Raphaelson, from the play *A Becsuletes Megtalalo (The Honest Finder)* by Aladar Laszlo • *Cinematographer* Victor Milner

Trouble in Store
★★★ U

Comedy 1953 · UK · BW · 82min

This was Norman Wisdom's film debut and, according to some, it was all downhill from here. It's certainly one of his best outings, largely because the sentimentality that became almost unbearable in his later films is rigorously kept in check here by director John Paddy Carstairs. Wisdom is as willing and as hopeless as ever, but he still manages to take time off from his hectic schedule of driving store boss Jerry Desmonde to the brink of distraction to find romance with Lana Morris. DP **DVD**

Norman Wisdom *Norman* • Margaret Rutherford *Miss Bacon* • Moira Lister *Peggy* • Derek Bond *Gerald* • Lana Morris *Sally* • Jerry Desmonde *Freeman* • Megs Jenkins *Miss Gibson* • Joan Sims *Edna* ■ *Dir* John Paddy Carstairs • *Scr* John Paddy Carstairs, Maurice Cowan, Ted Willis

Trouble in the Glen
★ U

Comedy 1954 · UK · Colour · 91min

Margaret Lockwood enjoyed great success as an ingénue, then as Britain's leading actress during much of the 1940s, but films such as this contributed to her virtual retirement from the screen when barely 40. Co-star Orson Welles helps turn it into something nearer tragicomedy with his dodgy wig and even dodgier South American accent. Shot in a terrible process called Trucolor. BB

Margaret Lockwood *Marissa* • Orson Welles *Sanin Mengues/Sanin Menzies* • Forrest Tucker *Jim "Lance" Lancing* • Victor McLaglen *Parlan* • John McCallum *Malcolm* • Eddie Byrne *Dinny Sullivan* • Archie Duncan *Nolly Dukes* • Ann Gudrun *Dandy Dinmont* ■ *Dir* Herbert Wilcox • *Scr* Frank S Nugent, from a story by Maurice Walsh

Trouble Man
★

Blaxploitation crime thriller 1972 · US · Colour · 99min

This crude and violent underworld melodrama hoped to reproduce the success of *Shaft*. In a one-note role as Mr T, a supercool LA private eye drawn into a gangland feud, Robert Hooks is out-acted by Paul Winfield (as a double-crossing racketeer) and Julius Harris (as a rival hood). AE

Robert Hooks *Mr T* • Paul Winfield *Chalky* • Ralph Waite *Pete* • William Smithers *Captain Joe Marks* • Paula Kelly *Cleo* • Julius Harris *Big* • Bill Henderson *Jimmy* ■ *Dir* Ivan Dixon • *Scr* John DF Black

The Trouble with Angels
★★★ U

Comedy drama 1966 · US · Colour · 110min

Best known for her acting in hard-bitten melodramas, Ida Lupino may seem a curious choice to direct this convent comedy. Yet she brings a much-needed hint of steel to what might otherwise have become another predictable journey down the road from rebellion to reformation. Hayley Mills is naughtier than in her Disney days, but much of her thunder is stolen by the debuting June Harding as her mousey friend, while Mother Superior Rosalind Russell walks away with every scene she's in. The sequel *Where Angels Go... Trouble Follows* hit the screen two years later. DP

Rosalind Russell *Mother Superior* • Hayley Mills *Mary Clancy* • June Harding *Rachel Devery* • Binnie Barnes *Sister Celestine* • Camilla Sparv *Sister Constance* • Gypsy Rose Lee *Mrs Phipps* ■ *Dir* Ida Lupino • *Scr* Blanche Hanalis, from the novel *Life with Mother Superior* by Jane Trahey

The Trouble with Girls
★ U

Period comedy drama 1969 · US · Colour · 95min

It's 1927, and Elvis Presley brings his mobile "chautauqua" show (an entertainment born out of the popular adult educational movement of the previous century), to Iowa, where he battles with Marilyn Mason as she tries to organise a performers' union. This love/hate scenario is disrupted when the local chemist is found dead. The support cast is wasted, and this joyless vehicle provides Elvis with only a handful of numbers. JG **DVD**

Elvis Presley *Walter Hale* • Marilyn Mason *Charlene* • Nicole Jaffe *Betty* • Sheree North *Nita Bix* • Edward Andrews *Johnny* • John Carradine *Mr Drewcolt* • Anissa Jones *Carol* • Vincent Price *Mr Morality* ■ *Dir* Peter Tewksbury • *Scr* Arnold Peyser, Lois Peyser, from a story by Mauri Grashin

The Trouble with Harry
★★★★★ PG

Black comedy 1954 · US · Colour · 95min

This delicious black comedy flopped at the box office, but director Alfred Hitchcock always named it among his personal favourites. There's the odd suspenseful moment, but this is primarily a masterpiece of wry humour and dramatic understatement, as John Forsythe, Shirley MacLaine, Edmund Gwenn and Mildred Natwick decide in the most matter-of-fact

way what to do with the body of a man three of them think they might have killed. The acting is perfection, with MacLaine quite wonderful. DP **DVD** **SL**

Edmund Gwenn *Captain Albert Wiles* • John Forsythe *Sam Marlowe* • Shirley MacLaine *Jennifer Rogers* • Mildred Natwick *Miss Graveley* • Mildred Dunnock *Mrs Wiggs* • Jerry Mathers *Arnie Rogers* • Royal Dano *Calvin Wiggs* • Parker Fennelly *Millionaire* ■ *Dir* Alfred Hitchcock • *Scr* John Michael Hayes, from the novel by Jack Trevor Story

The Trouble with Spies
★★ PG

Spy spoof 1987 · US · Colour · 85min

In this cheerful but anorexic spy spoof, Donald Sutherland plays a bumbling agent whose missions are so secret, everyone knows about them. He's sent to Ibiza to obtain the secret recipe for a truth serum but spends the time avoiding numerous attempts on his life. Fortunately for Sutherland, he has a cast of noted actors to support him. Unfortunately, the direction by Burt Kennedy is just inept. TH

Donald Sutherland *Appleton Porter* • Ned Beatty *Harry Lewis* • Ruth Gordon *Mrs Arkwright* • Lucy Gutteridge *Mona Smith* • Michael Hordern *Jason Lock* • Robert Morley *Angus Watkins* ■ *Dir* Burt Kennedy • *Scr* Burt Kennedy, Marc Lovell

Trouble with the Curve
★★★ 12

Sports drama 2012 · US · Colour · 106min

This workmanlike drama stars Clint Eastwood as Gus, an ageing baseball scout in the twilight of his career who sets off on one last recruiting trip to find the game's next golden boy. As his eyes are giving him trouble, his neglected daughter, Mickey (Amy Adams), is persuaded to accompany him. Eastwood's longtime collaborator, Robert Lorenz, directs here, and pushes all the expected dysfunctional family buttons, with Eastwood playing a variation of a character we've seen before: part curmudgeonly war veteran of *Gran Torino*, part awkward parental figure of *Million Dollar Baby*. But while the latter also used sport (boxing) as a backdrop, the baseball motifs here serve a more corny story and predictable plot. TeS **DVD** **SL**

Clint Eastwood *Gus* • Amy Adams *Mickey* • Justin Timberlake *Johnny* • John Goodman *Pete Klein* • Matthew Lillard *Phillip Sanderson* • Robert Patrick *Vince* • Scott Eastwood *Billy Clark* ■ *Dir* Robert Lorenz • *Scr* Randy Brown

The Troublemaker
★★

Crime comedy 1964 · US · BW · 81min

This is a dated and very tame comedy about the adventures of a yokel (Tom Aldredge) at large in New York. It's made no better by being improvised by a group called "The Premise", which included the director Theodore J Flicker and source writer Buck Henry, presumably there to guard the few words he had written. TH

Tom Aldredge *Jack Armstrong* • Joan Darling *Denver James* • Theodore J Flicker *Crime Commissioner* • James Frawley *Sol/Sal/Judge Kelly* • Buck Henry *Tr Kingston* ■ *Dir* Theodore J Flicker • *Scr* Theodore J Flicker, Buck Henry, from a story by Henry

Troy
★★★ 15

Epic period adventure 2004 · UK/US/Malta · Colour · 156min

This attempts to make over Homer's *The Iliad* in gory *Gladiator* style and, for the most part, succeeds. Helen, Queen of Sparta (played by Diane Kruger) is seduced away from her much older husband Menelaus (Brendan Gleeson) by the impulsive Paris, Prince of Troy (Orlando Bloom). The aggrieved Greek forces demanding her return are lead by Brian Cox's Agamemnon, who numbers Achilles (a rather uncomfortable-looking Brad Pitt) among his allies. Director Wolfgang Petersen shows tremendous command of the wide-open spaces and the battle scenes are stupendous. The dialogue is more Hollywood corn than Greek tragedy and the performances are uneven. TH A sex scene, violence. *DVD* *Blu*

Brad Pitt *Achilles* • Eric Bana *Hector* • Orlando Bloom *Paris* • Diane Kruger *Helen* • Brendan Gleeson *Menelaus* • Brian Cox (1) *Agamemnon* • Peter O'Toole *Priam* • Sean Bean *Odysseus* • Rose Byrne *Briseis* • Saffron Burrows *Andromache* • Julie Christie *Thetis* ■ *Dir* Wolfgang Petersen • *Scr* David Benioff, from the poem *The Iliad* by Homer

The Truce ★★★
Biographical drama
1997 · It/Fr/Swi/Ger/UK/Neth · Colour · 145min

A prize-winning director, known initially for his uncompromising social realism, Francesco Rosi gained a reputation in his later career for literary adaptations. This faithful account of Primo Levi's postwar journey from Auschwitz back to Italy still has the power to provoke and move. But John Turturro's need to push through the chaos prevents us from fully empathising with either his tortured memories or his response to freedom. DP Italian +subtitles. Swearing.

John Turturro *Primo* • Massimo Ghini *Cesare* • Rade Serbedzija *The Greek* • Stefano Dionisi *Daniele* • Teco Celio *Colonel Rovi* • *Dir* Francesco Rosi • *Scr* Francesco Rosi, Stefano Rulli, Sandro Petraglia, Tonino Guerra, from the novel by Primo Levi

Truck Stop Women ★★★
Action
1974 · US · Colour · 87min

Here's a cult movie that really delivers in terms of raucous exploitation. Lieux Dressler plays the boss of a robbery and prostitution ring who has to fight off efforts by the Mob to take over her operation, based in a highway truck stop. Director Mark L Lester slams everything at us in terms of action – road crashes, sexual shenanigans, the denting of macho morale – while Dressler, and *Playboy* playmate Claudia Jennings and Gene Drew could be in a Russ Meyer movie. TH

Claudia Jennings *Rose* • Lieux Dressler *Anna* • John Martino *Smith* • Dennis Fimple *Curly* • Dolores Dorn *Trish* • Gene Drew *Mac* ■ *Dir* Mark L Lester • *Scr* Mark L Lester, Paul Deason, from a story by Paul Deason

Truck Turner ★★18
Blaxploitation
1974 · US · Colour · 87min

Apart from providing the voice for *South Park's* Chef, soul brother Isaac Hayes is probably better known for his Oscar-winning *Shaft* theme than for his acting. Here he makes a credible hero in a typical 1970s blaxploitation action movie. Hayes plays the title character, a ruthless bounty hunter whose targets are pimps and pushers. Director Jonathan Kaplan provides the no-frills, in-your-face action, while also eliciting an outrageous performance from Nichelle Nichols. RS *DVD*

Isaac Hayes *Truck Turner* • Yaphet Kotto *Harvard Blue* • Alan Weeks *Jerry* • Annazette Chase *Annie* • Paul Harris *Gator* • Nichelle Nichols *Dorinda* • Sam Laws *Nate* ■ *Dir* Jonathan Kaplan • *Scr* Leigh Chapman, Oscar Williams, Michael Allin, from a story by Jerry Wilkes

Trucker ★★★15
Drama
2009 · US · Colour · 92min

Michelle Monaghan is something of a revelation as the appropriately named truck driver Diane Ford in this otherwise unremarkable drama from writer/director James Mottern. When she's forced to take care of the 11-year-old son she walked out on ten years previously, Diane has no choice but to connect with someone who's as lost as she is, and to look out for someone other than herself. Diane's swearing, drinking and one night stands make her quite unlike the women we're used to from Hollywood fare. But beyond this interesting subversion of gender roles and a likeable turn from Nathan Fillion, *Trucker* never manages to step up a gear and ends up feeling rather conventional. DnM *DVD*

Michelle Monaghan *Diane Ford* • Nathan Fillion *Runner* • Benjamin Bratt *Len Bonner* • Joey Lauren Adams *Jenny Bell* ■ *Dir/Scr* James Mottern

True as a Turtle ★U
Comedy
1956 · UK · Colour · 92min

This tiresome cross-Channel version of *Genevieve* has John Gregson and June Thorburn falling out over juvenile jealousies and petty pomposities while honeymooning on board Cecil Parker's yacht. Then they discover that they have become involved with a counterfeit gaming chip racket centred in a French casino. Crass. DP

John Gregson *Tony Hudson* • June Thorburn *Jane Hudson* • Cecil Parker *Dudley* • Keith Michell *Harry Bell* • Elvi Hale *Anne* • Avice Landone *Valerie* ■ *Dir* Wendy Toye • *Scr* Jack Davies, John Coates, Nicholas Phipps, from the novel by John Coates

True Believer ★★★15
Courtroom drama
1989 · US · Colour · 103min

This underrated courtroom drama gives James Woods a rare good-guy role as a one-time radical lawyer who now scrapes a living defending drug dealers under dubious constitutional arguments. He rediscovers his idealism when he takes up the case of a young Korean, who claims he has been framed for a gangland murder. Woods turns in a edgy, passionate performance and is ably supported by Robert Downey Jr as his assistant. JF Violence, swearing, drug abuse. *DVD*

James Woods *Eddie Dodd* • Robert Downey Jr *Roger Baron* • Margaret Colin *Kitty Greer* • Yuji Okumoto *Shu Kai Kim* • Kurtwood Smith *District Attorney Robert Reynard* • Tom Bower *Cecil Skell* ■ *Dir* Joseph Ruben • *Scr* Wesley Strick

True Blue ★★15
Sports drama based on a true story
1996 · UK · Colour · 110min

There's an intriguing story of macho rivalries and treacheries trying to get out of this account of events leading up to the 1987 Boat Race, when experienced American oarsmen were drafted into the Oxford team. But the potentially fascinating tale of modern sporting endeavour fights a losing battle with director Ferdinand Fairfax's laborious scene-setting and Brian Tufano's painterly photography, while talented young actors get caught in a backwash of bathos. TH Swearing, brief nudity. *DVD*

Johan Leysen *Daniel Topolski* • Dominic West *Donald Macdonald* • Dylan Baker *Michael Suarez* • Geraldine Somerville *Ruth Macdonald* • Josh Lucas *Dan Warren* • Brian McGovern *Rick Ross* • Ryan Bollman *Morrison Black* ■ *Dir* Ferdinand Fairfax • *Scr* Rupert Walters, from the non-fiction book by Daniel Topolski, Patrick Robinson

True Colors ★★15
Drama
1991 · US · Colour · 105min

It's perfectly clear from the outset of this by-the-numbers drama what will happen when two law students graduate and go their own ways, one to the Justice Department where spotless behaviour is seemingly the norm, the other into the moral sewer of politics. True actors John Cusack and James Spader are defeated by the all-too-obvious plot, yet both leads bring enough energy and detail to their roles. JM Swearing.

John Cusack *Peter Burton* • James Spader *Tim Garrity* • Imogen Stubbs *Diana Stiles* • Mandy Patinkin *John Palmeri* • Richard Widmark *Senator James B Stiles* • Dina Merrill *Joan Stiles* • Philip Bosco *Senator Steubens* • Paul Guilfoyle (2) *John Lawry* ■ *Dir* Herbert Ross • *Scr* Kevin Wade

True Confession ★★★
Screwball comedy mystery
1937 · US · BW · 84min

Fred MacMurray and Carole Lombard co-star as a highly moral attorney and his wife, a compulsive liar. When she's had up for murdering her boss, her husband gets her off on grounds of self-defence. A romantic screwball farce, directed by Wesley Ruggles and played with sufficient expertise to disguise some of the weaker aspects of the script, which declines to explain why Lombard is incapable of telling the truth.

The movie spirals from mad to madder and is extremely funny. RK

Carole Lombard *Helen Bartlett* • Fred MacMurray *Kenneth Bartlett* • John Barrymore *Charley Jasper* • Una Merkel *Daisy McClure* • Porter Hall *Prosecutor* • Edgar Kennedy *Darsey* • Hattie McDaniel *Ella* • *Dir* Wesley Ruggles • *Scr* Claude Binyon, from the play *Mon Crime* by Louis Verneuil, Georges Berr

True Crime ★★18
Thriller
1995 · US · Colour · 89min

Alicia Silverstone plays a Catholic school girl who is a bit of a Nancy Drew. Addicted to detective novels, she naturally decides to do her own snooping when some teenage girls are murdered. Kevin Dillon has the thankless job of playing the cop who teams up with and loses her virginity to. This, of course, means he puts himself in danger when the killer decides to make Alicia his next target. JB Violence. *DVD*

Alicia Silverstone *Mary Giordano* • Kevin Dillon *Tony Campbell* • Bill Nunn *Jerry* • Michael Bowen *Earl Parkins* • Ann Devaney *Sherry Tarnley* • Joshua Schaefer *John Giordano* • Marla Sokoloff *Vicki Giordano* • *Dir/Scr* Pat Verducci

True Crime ★★★18
Crime thriller
1999 · US · Colour · 127min

Clint Eastwood directs and stars as a grizzled journalist with just 12 hours to prove a prisoner on San Quentin's death row is innocent. Alternately tautly gripping and ridiculously facile, this thriller at times resembles a big-budget episode of *Murder, She Wrote*, yet retains its "beat the clock" shape because the superstar director accents character and detail above the mechanics of the whodunnit material. AJ Swearing, violence. *DVD*

Clint Eastwood *Steve "Ev" Everett* • Isaiah Washington *Frank Louis Beachum* • Lisa Gay Hamilton *Bonnie Beachum* • James Woods *Alan Mann* • Denis Leary *Bob Findley* • Bernard Hill *Warden Luther Plunkitt* • Diane Venora *Barbara Everett* • Michael McKean *Reverend Shillerman* ■ *Dir* Clint Eastwood • *Scr* Stephen Schiff, Paul Brickman, Larry Gross, from the novel by Andrew Klavan

True Grit ★★★★PG
Western
1969 · US · Colour · 122min

Big John Wayne finally won peer group recognition, taking the best actor Oscar for his portrayal of a cantankerous, one-eyed, drunken old reprobate hired by Kim Darby to avenge her father's death at the hands of thoroughly nasty Jeff Corey. This movie has acquired a reputation for being a rollicking fun western, but actually it is extraordinarily violent for its era and is not really suitable for family viewing, despite its strong moral theme. Glen Campbell is ineffective as a Texas Ranger (a role first offered to Elvis Presley, to whom Wayne wouldn't take second billing). A memorable film. TS *DVD* *Blu*

John Wayne *Reuben J "Rooster" Cogburn* • Glen Campbell *La Boeuf* • Kim Darby *Mattie Ross* • Jeff Corey *Tom Chaney* • Robert Duvall *Ned Pepper* • Jeremy Slate *Emmett Quincy* • Dennis Hopper *Moon* ■ *Dir* Henry Hathaway • *Scr* Marguerite Roberts, from the novel by Charles Portis

True Grit ★★★★15
Western
2010 · US · Colour · 105min

Fans of the Coen brothers could be forgiven for having qualms over the decision to revisit the western that earned John Wayne a best actor Oscar, particularly after the underwhelming reception given to their 2004 take on *The Ladykillers*. But worry not, this is no remake but a faithful dramatisation of the original Charles Portis novel, in which a 14-year-old girl tracks down her father's murderer with the help of a boozy, gnarled one-eyed lawman. Jeff Bridges is a revelation as Rooster Cogburn, comfortably filling the boots of the Duke and then some; Matt Damon also impresses as the pompous but resolute Texas Ranger La Boeuf who's after the killer for his own reasons; and Hailee Steinfeld as spirited, plain-speaking Mattie Ross occasionally outshines her more experienced co-stars. The ending is an abrupt one, after all that

precedes it, but the glorious final shoot-out between Cogburn and the bad guys (a standout scene in the 1969 film) remains wonderfully intact. JA Violence. *DVD* *Blu*

Jeff Bridges *Marshal Reuben J "Rooster" Cogburn* • Matt Damon *La Boeuf* • Josh Brolin *Tom Chaney* • Barry Pepper *"Lucky" Ned Pepper* • Hailee Steinfeld *Mattie Ross* • Domhnall Gleeson *Moon* • Paul Rae *Emmett Quincy* • Dakin Matthews *Colonel Stonehill* ■ *Dir* Ethan Coen, Joel Coen • *Scr* Ethan Coen, Joel Coen, from the novel by Charles Portis • *Cinematographer* Roger Deakins

True Identity ★★★15
Comedy thriller
1991 · US · Colour · 89min

Comic Lenny Henry stars as a struggling actor who crosses the path of mobster Frank Langella, and decides he has to take a different identity so he can't be found. Naturally, Lenny's make-up artist pal turns our hero into a white man so he can avoid the wrath of the Mob. The script doesn't do justice to the star's talent, but the transformation is impressive, and Henry does a good job of turning every duff line and situation into a rib-tickling one. JB Violence, swearing. *DVD*

Lenny Henry *Miles Pope* • Frank Langella *Frank Luchino/Leland Carver* • Charles Lane (3) *Duane* • JT Walsh *Craig Houston* • Anne-Marie Johnson *Kristi Reeves* • Andreas Katsulas *Anthony* • Michael McKean *Harvey Cooper* ■ *Dir* Charles Lane (3) • *Scr* Andy Breckman, Will Osborne, Will Davies, from a sketch by Andy Breckman

True Lies ★★★★15
Action comedy
1994 · US · Colour · 134min

It may be wildly implausible and a trifle misogynistic, but, on the pure excitement level, James Cameron's blockbuster is unbeatable entertainment. Arnold Schwarzenegger is the unshaken, unstirred secret agent, always saving the world in time to get home for dinner with his wife and kids, who are blissfully unaware of his dangerous job. Aside from the truly spectacular action, there's exceptional comedy support from Tom Arnold and a winning performance from Jamie Lee Curtis, who transforms from timid housewife to confident heroine. AJ Swearing, violence. *DVD*

Arnold Schwarzenegger *Harry Tasker* • Jamie Lee Curtis *Helen Tasker* • Tom Arnold *Gib* • Bill Paxton *Simon* • Tia Carrere *Juno* • Art Malik *Aziz* • Eliza Dushku *Dana* • Charlton Heston *Spencer Trilby* ■ *Dir* James Cameron • *Scr* James Cameron, from a screenplay (unproduced) by Claude Zidi, Simon Michael, Didier Kaminka

True Love ★★★★15
Comedy drama
1989 · US · Colour · 100min

All imminent newlyweds should avoid this like the plague, because it's a film about the kind of doubts that can bring that thundering juggernaut known as your wedding day to a screeching halt. Directed with admirable insight by the debuting Nancy Savoca, this is so close to the bone that it's often wincingly painful to watch. Annabella Sciorra is perfectly cast as the Italian-American who suddenly discovers dipsomaniac Ron Eldard isn't the man of her dreams. A witty throwback to the days when Hollywood could do this kind of thing blindfold. DP Swearing.

Annabella Sciorra *Donna* • Ron Eldard *Michael* • Star Jasper *JC* • Aida Turturro *Grace* • Roger Rignack *Dom* • Kelly Cinnante *Yvonne* ■ *Dir* Nancy Savoca • *Scr* Nancy Savoca, Richard Guay

True North ★★★★15
Drama
2006 · Ger/Ire/UK · Colour · 95min

Writer/director Steve Hudson's feature debut is a gut-wrenching tale of people-smuggling and divided loyalties, set aboard a Scottish trawler. Desperate to save his father's ship from repossession, Sean (Martin Compston) enlists the help of roguish deck hand Riley (Peter Mullan) in a plan to smuggle Chinese immigrants. But they end up butting heads when the situation grows increasingly perilous. Compston elegantly portrays his character's struggle to find a balance between helping his unwitting father (Gary

Lewis) and getting the Chinese safely ashore, while Mullan gives a hearty, believable performance as man unused to thinking about consequences. Hudson's script deals in delicate shades of grey, and child actress Angel Li brings a sense of hope to even the darkest parts of the story. SP English, Mandarin +subtitles.

Peter Mullan *Riley* • Martin Compston *Sean* • Gary Lewis *Skipper* • Steven Robertson *Cook* • Angel Li *Su Li* • Pat Kiernan *Henri* ■ *Dir/Scr* Steve Hudson

True Romance ★★★★ 18
Black comedy thriller 1993 · US · Colour · 116min

Movie-obsessed comic-store worker Christian Slater meets hooker Patricia Arquette, gets married and then accidentally steals a fortune in cocaine from her pimp Gary Oldman. Scriptwriter Quentin Tarantino blends Hong Kong gangster movie clichés, *film noir* revisionism, slick but ultra-heavy violence and a host of great star cameos to create an acid cocktail. Director Tony Scott's superb visual style is the icing on the cake. AJ Swearing, drug abuse, nudity, sex scenes. *DVD* 🅑

Christian Slater *Clarence Worley* • Patricia Arquette *Alabama Whitman* • Dennis Hopper *Clifford Worley* • Val Kilmer *Mentor* • Gary Oldman *Drexl Spivey* • Brad Pitt *Floyd* • Christopher Walken *Vincenzo Coccotti* • Bronson Pinchot *Elliot Blitzer* • Samuel L Jackson *Big Don* • Michael Rapaport *Dick Ritchie* • Saul Rubinek *Lee Donowitz* • James Gandolfini *Virgil* • Chris Penn *Nicky Dimes* • Tom Sizemore *Cody Nicholson* • Conchata Ferrell *Mary Louise Ravencroft* ■ *Dir* Tony Scott • *Scr* Quentin Tarantino, Roger Avary (uncredited)

True Stories ★★★ PG
Comedy 1986 · US · Colour · 85min

Not so much a movie as a feature-length rock video held together by a kooky storyline, with former Talking Head David Byrne strolling through the eccentric lives of the common, but secretly colourful, folk of the fictional community of Virgil, Texas, as they prepare for their annual "Celebration of Specialness". Alternately intriguing and condescending, Byrne's ironic detachment ultimately wears out its welcome, though the soundtrack is consistently entertaining, and the ensemble cast is brilliant. AJ

David Byrne *Narrator* • John Goodman *Louis Fyne* • Swoosie Kurtz *Miss Rollings, the laziest woman in the world* • Spalding Gray *Earl Culver* • Alix Elias *Cute woman* • Annie McEnroe *Kay Culver* ■ *Dir* David Byrne • *Scr* David Byrne, Beth Henley, Stephen Tobolowsky

True Story ★★★ 15
Crime drama based on a true story
2015 · US · Colour · 99min

This twisting tale of stolen identity purports to be as good as its title and faithful to the actual events it depicts. But in the circumstances, who knows? Jonah Hill plays a discredited *New York Times* journalist who discovers that arrested family-murderer James Franco has been using his name while on the run. For both personal and professional reasons, he determines to find out why. Hill is nicely cast against type, while Franco is his usual slick self. The film is heavy-handed with the message that there's rarely such a thing as absolute truth, but it's a good story, grippingly told. DA Swearing.

Jonah Hill *Michael Finkel* • James Franco *Christian Longo* • Felicity Jones *Jill Barker* • Robert John Burke [Robert Burke] *Greg Ganley* • Gretchen Mol *Karen* • Ethan Suplee *Pat Frato* ■ *Dir* Rupert Goold • *Scr* Rupert Goold, David Kajganich, from a memoir by Michael Finkel

The True Story of Jesse James ★★ PG
Western 1957 · US · Colour · 88min

This is anything but the "true story" of the notorious outlaw. The movie is seriously undermined by an unnecessary flashback structure and by the crippling use of contemporary Fox contractees. While attractive to watch, juvenile stars Robert Wagner and Jeffrey Hunter are wholly

inadequate as Jesse and Frank James. Director Nicholas Ray quite fails to grasp the tale's potential and, in his own words, made "a very ordinary movie". TS *DVD*

Robert Wagner *Jesse James* • Jeffrey Hunter *Frank James* • Hope Lange *Zee* • Agnes Moorehead *Mrs Samuel* • Alan Hale Jr *Cole Younger* • Alan Baxter *Remington* • John Carradine *Reverend Jethro Bailey* ■ *Dir* Nicholas Ray • *Scr* Walter Newman, from the film *Jesse James* by Nunnally Johnson

The True Story of Lynn Stuart ★★★
Crime thriller 1957 · US · BW · 76min

In this gritty crime drama, dope smugglers are brought to book by a resourceful housewife. Although a minor production, Betsy Palmer gives an intelligent performance as the woman who cuddles up to Jack Lord's hoodlum in order to avenge the death of her dope-addicted nephew. It may sound far-fetched, but it's actually based on real-life events. Burnett Guffey's photography, largely done on location, adds a touch of class to Lewis Seiler's competent direction. AE

Betsy Palmer *Phyllis Carter* • Jack Lord *Willie Down* • Barry Atwater *Hagan* • Kim Spalding *Ralph Carter* • Karl Lukas *Hal Bruck* • Casey Walters *Eddie Dine* • Harry Jackson *Husband Officer* ■ *Dir* Lewis Seiler • *Scr* John H Kneubuhl, from articles by Pat Michaels

True to Life ★★★ U
Comedy 1943 · US · BW · 93min

This is an engaging comedy in which Dick Powell plays a radio writer who looks for a "typical" American family from which he can obtain material for his soap opera, but instead finds a household full of eccentrics. Although these include the irritating comic actor Victor Moore, Mary Martin, in one of her few straight roles, is charming. RB

Mary Martin *Bonnie Porter* • Franchot Tone *Fletcher Marvin* • Dick Powell *Link Ferris* • Victor Moore *Pop Porter* • Mabel Paige *Mom Porter* • William Demarest *Jake* • Clarence Kolb *Mr Huggins* • Yvonne De Carlo *Girl* ■ *Dir* George Marshall • *Scr* Don Hartman, Harry Tugend, from a story by Ben Barzman, Bess Taffel, Sol Barzman

Truly Madly Deeply ★★★★ PG
Romantic drama 1990 · UK · Colour · 102min

It was dubbed the British *Ghost*, but this is a far more witty and incisive affair. It's distinguished by the glorious performances of Alan Rickman as the dearly departed who returns and Juliet Stevenson as his grief-stricken partner struggling to come to terms with her loss. But the strengths of this movie are numerous, most notably an emotional integrity that shines through in every scene and director Anthony Minghella's ability to inject the pathos with well-aimed humour. SH Swearing. *DVD*

Juliet Stevenson *Nina* • Alan Rickman *Jamie* • Bill Paterson *Sandy* • Michael Maloney *Mark* • Deborah Findlay *Claire* • Christopher Rozycki *Titus* • David Ryall *George* • Jenny Howe *Burge* ■ *Dir/Scr* Anthony Minghella

Truman ★★★★ PG
Biographical drama 1995 · US · Colour · 133min

This outstanding Emmy winner, based on the Pulitzer Prize-winning biography by David McCullough, features a tour de force performance from the incomparable Gary Sinise as Harry S Truman, the 33rd President of the United States. Insightful direction by Frank Pierson enlivens the intelligent script by Tom Rickman, while the authentic re-creation of the period adds class to the production. Diana Scarwid and Richard Dysart are standouts in the effective supporting cast. This captivating TV biopic is not just for history buffs, but for all those who enjoy fine film-making. MC *DVD*

Gary Sinise *Harry S Truman* • Diana Scarwid *Bess Wallace Truman* • Richard Dysart *Henry L Stimson* • Colm Feore *Charlie Ross* • James Gammon *Sam Rayburn* • Tony Goldwyn *Clark Clifford* • Pat Hingle *Thomas Joseph*

Pendergast ■ *Dir* Frank Pierson • *Scr* Tom Rickman, from the biography by David McCullough

The Truman Show ★★★★★ PG
Satirical comedy drama
1998 · US · Colour · 98min

From audacious start to poignant finale, this ingenious film is both dazzling and sophisticated. Truman Burbank (Jim Carrey) is the star of the world's most popular television show, only he doesn't know it. Although he thinks he lives in the idyllic island community of Seahaven, it's just an elaborate set housed in a vast studio, and all his family and friends are really actors. How that realisation slowly dawns and spurs him on to find out what's real and what's fake in his emotionally confused universe is the stuff of ambitious cinematic brilliance. With superlative support from Ed Harris (as the programme's creator) and Laura Linney (as Truman's "wife"), Carrey reveals his dramatic range in this compelling fable about media omnipotence. AJ *DVD* 🅑

Jim Carrey *Truman Burbank* • Ed Harris *Christof* • Laura Linney *Meryl* • Noah Emmerich *Marlon* • Natascha McElhone *Lauren/Sylvia* • Holland Taylor *Truman's mother* • Brian Delate *Truman's father* ■ *Dir* Peter Weir • *Scr* Andrew Niccol

Trumbo ★★★ 15
Biographical drama 2015 · US · Colour · 124min

The blacklisting of film-makers for their Communist sympathies in the 1940s and 50s remains a prickly subject for Hollywood. So the makers of this biopic of unrepentant screenwriter Dalton Trumbo should be applauded for getting the finance together. *Breaking Bad* star Bryan Cranston brings stature and eccentricity to the title role, and director Jay Roach (*Meet the Parents*) relishes the Tinseltown milieu, cleverly blending newsreel of the HUAC hearings with dramatisation. Pity John McNamara's script underplays the complex situation. AC Swearing. *DVD* 🅑

Bryan Cranston *Dalton Trumbo* • Elle Fanning *Niki Trumbo* • Diane Lane *Cleo Trumbo* • Alan Tudyk *Ian McLellan Hunter* • Helen Mirren *Hedda Hopper* • John Goodman *Frank King* ■ *Dir* Jay Roach • *Scr* John McNamara, from the non-fiction book *Dalton Trumbo* by Bruce Cook (2)

Trust ★★★ 15
Drama 1990 · UK/US · Colour · 101min

Dangerous things happen in this tragicomedy from independent film-maker Hal Hartley. Teenager Adrienne Shelly breaks the news of her pregnancy to her parents, causing dad to suffer a heart attack. Elsewhere, a baby is abducted and the antihero (Martin Donovan) carries a hand grenade around in case of emergency. This was Hartley's second feature (after 1989's *The Unbelievable Truth*), but such is the deadpan approach that you're never totally involved. TH *DVD*

Adrienne Shelly *Maria Coughlin* • Martin Donovan (2) *Matthew Slaughter* • Merritt Nelson *Jean Coughlin* • John MacKay *Jim Slaughter* • Edie Falco *Peg Coughlin* • Gary Sauer *Anthony* ■ *Dir/Scr* Hal Hartley

Trust ★★★ 15
Drama 2010 · US · Colour · 105min

Just as social-networking sites have proliferated, so, too, have the films about them. This one is directed by former *Friends* star David Schwimmer and, despite a slight tendency towards melodrama, it's one of the best so far. Clive Owen and Catherine Keener play the slightly distant parents of a typically sullen and introvert 14-year-old (the excellent Liana Liberato), whose online boyfriend is not what he seems. It's a thought-provoking film about online sexual predation, teen vulnerability to it, and parental responsibility for it. DA Violence, swearing. *DVD* 🅑

Clive Owen *Will Cameron* • Catherine Keener *Lynn Cameron* • Liana Liberato *Annie Cameron* • Viola Davis *Gail Friedman* • Jason Clarke (2) *Agent Doug Tate* ■ *Dir* David Schwimmer • *Scr* Andy Bellin, Rob Festinger

The Trust ★★★ 15
Crime thriller 2016 · UK · Colour · 87min

In this modestly scaled crime flick from first-time directors Ben and Alex Brewer, Nicolas Cage and Elijah Wood play low-level functionaries in the Las Vegas police force who spot their chance for a life-changing score when they happen upon a drug gang's secret vault. There's not quite enough narrative substance to go round, but the directors' quirkily disarming visuals, and two stars who seem genuinely engaged for a change, make this worth a look. TJ Swearing, violence, sex scenes, drug abuse. *DVD* 🅑

Nicolas Cage *Jim Stone* • Elijah Wood *David Waters* • Sky Ferreira *Woman* • Jerry Lewis *Stone's father* ■ *Dir* Alex Brewer, Benjamin Brewer • *Scr* Benjamin Brewer, Adam Hirsch

Trust Me ★★ 15
Comedy thriller 1989 · US · Colour · 85min

Adam Ant has never managed to shake off his Prince Charming/Dandy Highwayman pop image. Here he stars as an art gallery owner in debt who decides the only way out is to promote a respected artist and then kill him so the work increases in value. A daft idea, and the acting isn't much better as the star moves through each scene looking as if he's in search of a pop interlude. JB Swearing.

Adam Ant *James Callendar* • David Packer *Sam Brown* • Talia Balsam *Catherine Walker* • William Deacutis *Billy Brawthwaite* • Joyce Van Patten *Nettie Brown* • Barbara Bain *Mary Casal* ■ *Dir* Bobby Houston • *Scr* Bobby Houston, Gary Rigdon

Trust the Man ★★★ 15
Romantic comedy drama
2006 · US · Colour · 95min

Relationship angst afflicts a group of Manhattanites in this wry romantic comedy from writer/director Bart Freundlich. As a married couple whose sex life is stagnating, David Duchovny and Julianne Moore revive their chemistry from *Evolution* and are given some memorable scenes. Freundlich evidently wants to reproduce the wisecracking flavour of Woody Allen's best 1970s movies and, though he never steps out from the shadow of the New York maestro, there are some moments of witty invention. It's just a shame that supporting couple Billy Crudup and Maggie Gyllenhaal have such underwritten parts and that a ridiculously overblown ending contrasts so sharply with the urbane, deadpan humour that precedes it. Still, it's pleasantly diverting while it lasts. SP Swearing, sexual references. *DVD*

David Duchovny *Tom* • Julianne Moore *Rebecca* • Billy Crudup *Tobey* • Maggie Gyllenhaal *Elaine* • James LeGros *Dante* • Eva Mendes *Faith* • Ellen Barkin *Norah* • Garry Shandling *Dr Beekman* ■ *Dir/Scr* Bart Freundlich

The Truth ★★ 15
Black comedy drama
2006 · UK · Colour · 118min

An impressive cast is left high and dry by a verbose script and hesitant direction in this would-be scathing assault on contemporary social attitudes. Elizabeth McGovern plays a Californian self-help guru who has gathered a motley bunch of clients at her remote Scottish retreat. Wheelchair-using Elaine Cassidy is sceptical, but reluctantly agrees to give the eccentric group therapy sessions a try. Inconsistent performances and uncertainties of tone render this unbelievable and muddled. DP Swearing.

William Beck *Scott* • Elaine Cassidy *Cardy* • Stephen Lord *Felix* • Elizabeth McGovern *Donna* • Lea Mornar *Mia* • Rachael Stirling *Martha* • Zoe Telford *Blossom* • Karl Theobald *Spud* • Sean Murray *Candy's father* • Amelia Bullmore *Candy's mother* ■ *Dir* George Milton • *Scr* George Milton, Mark Tilton

Truth ★★★ 15
Drama based on a true story
2015 · Aus/US · Colour · 120min

Cate Blanchett and Robert Redford headline as under-fire journalists in this wordy, worthy dramatisation of a true story. Blanchett impresses as Mary Mapes, the sure-footed TV producer who assembled a team to investigate rumours of George W Bush receiving preferential military treatment during the Vietnam War. Her decision that Dan Rather (a careful, nuanced Redford) should report on uncorroborated information shines a light on the dirty tactics used by both sides in the media war over the presidency. KK Swearing, sex/drug references. **DVD** **BD**

Cate Blanchett *Mary Mapes* · Robert Redford *Dan Rather* · Topher Grace *Mike Smith* · Dennis Quaid *Lt Colonel Roger Charles* · Elisabeth Moss *Lucy Scott* ■ *Dir* James Vanderbilt · *Scr* James Vanderbilt, from the non-fiction book *Truth and Duty: the Press, the President and the Privilege of Power* by Mary Mapes

The Truth about Cats and Dogs ★★★★ 15
Romantic comedy 1996 · US · Colour · 96min

This adorable and very funny romantic comedy stars a scene-stealing Janeane Garofalo as the radio talk show vet who charms listener Ben Chaplin. Garofalo is convinced Chaplin will be disappointed when he actually meets her, so she sends lovely but dim Uma Thurman in her place. Numerous romantic complications ensue as both women fall for the lucky fellow. It all zips along merrily, with Thurman showing a previously unseen talent for comedy. JB Swearing. **DVD**

Uma Thurman *Noelle* · Janeane Garofalo *Abby* · Ben Chaplin *Brian* · Jamie Foxx *Ed* · James McCaffrey *Roy* · Richard Coca *Eric* · Stanley DeSantis *Mario* ■ *Dir* Michael Lehmann · *Scr* Audrey Wells

The Truth about Charlie ★ 12
Romantic comedy thriller
2002 · US · Colour · 99min

Expectations are automatically lowered for remakes of Hollywood classics – in this case, Stanley Donen's effervescent Hitchcock-homage *Charade* – but this is far worse than imagined. Director Jonathan Demme at least stays fairly close to the original's Paris-set story about the pursuit of a dead man's hidden fortune. But there isn't a single scene or performance (the pairing of Mark Wahlberg and Thandie Newton is spark free) that doesn't feel awkward or misjudged. JC **DVD**

Mark Wahlberg *Joshua Peters* · Thandie Newton *Regina Lambert* · Tim Robbins *Mr Bartholomew* · Park Joong-Hoon *Il-Sang Lee* · Ted Levine *Emil Zatapec* · Lisa Gay Hamilton *Lola Jansco* · Christine Boisson *Commandant Dominique* · Stephen Dillane *Charles Lambert* ■ *Dir* Jonathan Demme · *Scr* Jonathan Demme, Steve Schmidt, Jessica Bendinger, Peter Joshua [Peter Stone], from the film *Charade* by Peter Stone

The Truth about Demons ★★★ 18
Horror 2000 · NZ · Colour · 86min

With a neo-punk visual edge, this glossy shocker features wonderfully elliptical CGI devils, heart-grabbing gore and numerous plot surprises. Karl Urban is the professor of esoteric cults and mysticism whose life becomes a paranoid nightmare when he becomes the sacrificial target for a Satanic cult. With only reformed black magician Katie Wolfe to help him over the hurdles of disbelief, he must fulfil an ancient prophecy to end the sect's reign of terror. Glenn Standring's creditable chiller consistently fires on all creepy cylinders. AJ **DVD**

Karl Urban *Harry* · Katie Wolfe *Benny* · Sally Stockwell *Celia* · Jonathon Hendry *Le Valliant* · Tony MacIver *Johnny* ■ *Dir/Scr* Glenn Standring · *Cinematographer* Simon Baumfield

The Truth about Love ★★ 15
Romantic comedy 2004 · UK · Colour · 90min

Jennifer Love Hewitt, like Gwyneth Paltrow and Renée Zellweger before her, is thoroughly convincing as a young English lady, though this is no *Bridget Jones's Diary*, nor even a *Sliding Doors*. Hewitt plays a happily married woman who, as a prank, sends an anonymous Valentine to her husband (Jimi Mistry). When he fails to

mention it, she begins to suspect that he has a wandering eye. Further complicating matters is Hewitt's secret admirer, Dougray Scott. The Bristol locations make a pleasant change but, despite the agreeable performances and breezy direction, it's all too contrived. JF Swearing, sexual references. **DVD**

Jennifer Love Hewitt *Alice* · Dougray Scott *Archie* · Jimi Mistry *Sam* · Kate Miles *Felicity* · Emma Noble *Sheena* · Karl Howman *Cliff* · Simon Webbe *Dan* ■ *Dir* John Hay · *Scr* William Johnston (3), Peter Bloore, Rik Carmichael, John Hay, from a story by Bloore

The Truth about Spring ★★ U
Adventure 1964 · UK · Colour · 102min

John Mills teams with daughter Hayley for the third time in this fanciful adventure that might well have passed for children's entertainment in the mid-1960s, but probably won't appeal to today's more sophisticated youngsters. Sir John hams it up as a crusty sea captain whose brush with smugglers lands tomboy Hayley in the arms of a young James MacArthur. Richard Thorpe directs at a fair clip, but too little stirs the imagination. DP

Hayley Mills *Spring Tyler* · John Mills *Tommy Tyler* · James MacArthur *William Ashton* · Lionel Jeffries *Cark* · Harry Andrews *Sellers* · Niall MacGinnis *Cleary* · Lionel Murton *Simmons* · David Tomlinson *Skelton* ■ *Dir* Richard Thorpe · *Scr* James Lee Barrett, from the story *Satan: a Romance of the Bahamas* by Henry de Vere Stacpoole

The Truth about Women ★★ 12
Comedy 1958 · UK · Colour · 99min

In a bizarre charade, Laurence Harvey plays a sort of Don Juan character, recalling his amorous, exotic adventures in Arabia, Paris, London, New York, the First World War and beyond. The moral is that one's first love is the only love that matters – aaah! – but the problem here is that Harvey is also something of a cold fish, not overly furnished with charm. The women make the most of their extended cameos, and pose in their Cecil Beaton costumes. AT **DVD**

Laurence Harvey *Sir Humphrey Tavistock* · Julie Harris (2) *Helen Cooper* · Diane Cilento *Ambrosine Viney* · Mai Zetterling *Julie* · Eva Gabor *Louise* · Michael Denison *Rollo* ■ *Dir* Muriel Box · *Scr* Sydney Box, Muriel Box

The Truth Game ★★ 18
Drama 2000 · UK · Colour · 75min

Simon Rumley's second feature is a claustrophobic character study that suffers from an over-reliance on improvisation and too many unnecessary camera movements. Three unsympathetic couples clash over dinner, but the cast's inexperience means they're always consciously acting, rather than role-playing. DP **DVD**

Paul Blackthorne *Dan* · Tania Emery *Charlotte* · Thomas Fisher [Tom Fisher] *Alan* · Selina Giles *Lilly* · Stuart Laing *Eddy* · Wendy Wason *Kate* · Jennifer White *Alex* ■ *Dir/Scr* Simon Rumley

Truth or Consequences, NM ★★★ 18
Crime thriller 1997 · US · Colour · 102min

For his feature directing debut, Kiefer Sutherland might have chosen something just a little bit more original than this routine heist-goes-wrong scenario. Vincent Gallo plays an ex-con setting up one last robbery with former cell-mate Sutherland, a trigger-happy sociopath. Naturally things don't go to plan and the gang ends up taking hostages and falling foul of Rod Steiger's Las Vegas mobster and fruitcake Martin Sheen. Violently played out among the scenic mountains and deserts of Utah, this is expertly played by a solid cast, while Sutherland proves a safe pair of hands behind the lens. RS **DVD**

Kiefer Sutherland *Curtis Freley* · Vincent Gallo *Raymond Lembecke* · Mykelti Williamson *Marcus Weans* · Kevin Pollak *Gordon Jacobson* · Kim

Dickens *Addy Monroe* · Grace Phillips *Donna Moreland* · Martin Sheen *Sir* · Rod Steiger *Tony Vago* ■ *Dir* Kiefer Sutherland · *Scr* Brad Mirman

Truth or Dare ★★★ 15
Horror 2011 · UK · Colour · 91min

In this brutal, efficient British horror a group of teenagers is invited to a party in a remote cottage. Within minutes, they're in the clutches of a psychopathic former soldier who's seeking the truth about the suicide of his younger brother, a friend of the luckless party animals. The sadistic scheme used to extract that truth is a deadly game of spin-the-bottle. *Truth or Dare* is slickly made and decently acted. It has its bloody horror film moments, but director Robert Heath wisely puts equal emphasis on the psychology of its hostage situation. DA Violence, swearing, sex scenes, drug abuse. **DVD** **BD**

Liam Boyle *Paul* · Jack Gordon *Chris* · Florence Hall *Gemma* · Nicky Henson *Mr Hautbois* ■ *Dir* Robert Heath · *Scr* Matthew McGuchan

The Trygon Factor ★★ 15
Crime drama 1967 · UK · Colour · 83min

Fake nuns set up a million-dollar heist in this farcical British crime drama. Stewart Granger is the Scotland Yard detective called in to investigate a convent situated on the grounds of Cathleen Nesbitt's stately home; Susan Hampshire is her photographer daughter. Blackly comic at best, the film boasts a cast of British stalwarts, but they just end up milling around in the hope of being directed by Cyril Frankel. TH

Stewart Granger *Supt Cooper-Smith* · Susan Hampshire *Trudy Emberday* · Robert Morley *Hubert Hamlyn* · Cathleen Nesbitt *Livia Emberday* · Brigitte Horney *Sister General/Mrs Hamlyn* · Sophie Hardy *Sophie* · James Robertson-Justice *Sir John* ■ *Dir* Cyril Frankel · *Scr* Derry Quinn, Stanley Munro, from a story by Derry Quinn

Tsotsi ★★★★ 15
Crime drama 2005 · UK/S Afr · Colour · 90min

Winner of the Oscar for best foreign language film, this is the story of a violent and disaffected young South African nicknamed Tsotsi, which means "thug" in township patois. The drama pivots on his theft of a car and the discovery of a baby on the back seat. Tsotsi takes the infant home and its presence begins to have a humanising effect on the hitherto cold-blooded sociopath. In the title role, Presley Chweneyagae delivers a wonderfully underplayed performance. Director Gavin Hood's film was shot on location in Johannesburg and vibrates with the rhythms of township life. BP Zulu, Xhosa, Afrikaans +subtitles. Swearing, violence. **DVD**

Presley Chweneyagae *Tsotsi* · Terry Pheto *Miriam* · Kenneth Nkosi *Aap* · Mothusi Magano *Boston* · Zenzo Ngqobe *Butcher* · Zola Fela *Ndlovu* · Rapulana Seiphemo *John* · Nambitha Mpumlwana *Pumla* ■ *Dir* Gavin Hood · *Scr* Gavin Hood, from the novel by Athol Fugard

Tsui Hark's Vampire Hunters ★★ 15
Action horror
2002 · HK/Jpn/Neth · Colour · 85min

You might get some fun from this slapdash Hong Kong horror, but only if you can negotiate the labyrinthine plot, vacuous script and wooden acting. Four fairly fearless hunters of the undead searching for their lost master come across a creepy mansion inhabited by an expert embalmer, and must prevent hopping zombies from being made into vampires by an over-made-up vampire king. SuR Cantonese +subtitles. Violence. **DVD**

Ken Chang *Hei (Wind)* · Michael Chow *Fat (Thunder)* · Lam Suet *Kung (Rain)* · Chan Kwok Kwan *Choi (Lightning)* · Anya Sasa · Yu Rong Guang *Master Jiang* ■ *Dir* Wellson Chin · *Scr* Tsui Hark

Tuck Everlasting ★★★★
Animated fantasy 1980 · US · Colour · 114min

In an utterly beguiling fable, a woods-dwelling family who are impervious to pain, ageing and death are stumbled upon by an inquisitive 12-year-old girl. Based on Natalie Babbitt's award-winning novel, this independently-produced animation is almost as well-kept a secret as the family's immortality. But hunt it out: family entertainment doesn't come much better than this. DA

Fred A Keller *Angus Tuck* · James McGuire *Man in yellow suit* · Paul Flessa *Jesse Tuck* · Margaret Chamberlain *Winnie* · Sonia Raimi *Mary Tuck* · Bruce D'Aurio *Miles Tuck* ■ *Dir* Frederick King Keller · *Scr* Stratton Rawson, Fred A Keller, Frederick King Keller, from the novel by Natalie Babbitt

Tuck Everlasting ★★★ PG
Period fantasy drama
2002 · US · Colour · 86min

This Disney adaptation of Natalie Babbitt's intelligent children's story is beautifully shot without the rose-tinted glasses that might alienate older audiences. In upstate New York at the beginning of the 20th century, teenager Alexis Bledel runs away from her restrictive parents, discovering a woodland fountain of youth and the Tuck family. The innocent romance between her and Jonathan Jackson is well handled, and the supporting cast is strong. Tinged with both humour and melancholy, this holds a captivating affection for its period, characters and story. JC **DVD**

Alexis Bledel *Winnie Foster* · William Hurt *Angus Tuck* · Sissy Spacek *Mae Tuck* · Jonathan Jackson *Jesse Tuck* · Scott Bairstow *Miles Tuck* · Ben Kingsley *Man in the Yellow Suit* · Amy Irving *Mother Foster* · Victor Garber *Robert Foster* · Elisabeth Shue *Narrator* ■ *Dir* Jay Russell · *Scr* Jeffrey Lieber, James V Hart, from the novel by Natalie Babbitt

Tucker and Dale vs Evil ★★★★ 15
Comedy horror 2009 · Can · Colour · 84min

This likeable marriage of buddy comedy and horror spoof sees good-hearted backwoodsmen Tucker (Alan Tudyk) and Dale (Tyler Labine) head to their new cabin in the forest, a ramshackle hut eerily reminiscent of the one in Sam Raimi's *The Evil Dead*. But after they attempt to save a young college girl from drowning, the duo are mistaken for murderous rural lunatics à la *Deliverance*, and in a neat reversal of the slasher status quo, the preppy college kids spend most of the movie trying to kill the hapless hillbillies. It's a silly idea, but the central pair are so appealing and the nods to the "slaughter in the woods" genre so well judged that it can be forgiven its very occasional comic longueurs. AS **DVD** **BD**

Tyler Labine *Dale* · Alan Tudyk *Tucker* · Katrina Bowden *Allison* · Jesse Moss *Chad* · Brandon Jay McLaren *Jason* · Christie Laing *Naomi* ■ *Dir* Eli Craig · *Scr* Eli Craig, Morgan Jurgenson

Tucker: the Man and His Dream ★★ PG
Biographical drama 1988 · US · Colour · 105min

Under the directorial auspices of Francis Ford Coppola, Jeff Bridges stars as Preston Tucker, a real-life innovative car designer whose career was gunned down by his big business competitors. Also a loyal family man, the portrayal of his home life with wife Joan Allen just plays like a bad sitcom. Beautiful to look at, though, thanks to the scintillating work of master cameraman Vittorio Storaro. LH

Jeff Bridges *Preston Tucker* · Joan Allen *Vera Tucker* · Martin Landau *Abe Karatz* · Frederic Forrest *Eddie Dean* · Mako *Jimmy Sakuyama* · Dean Stockwell *Howard Hughes* · Lloyd Bridges *Senator Homer Ferguson* · Elias Koteas *Alex Tremulis* · Christian Slater *Junior* ■ *Dir* Francis Ford Coppola · *Scr* Arnold Schulman, David Seidler · *Executive Producer* George Lucas

T

Tudor Rose ★★★
Historical drama   1936 · UK · BW · 80min

The short life and even shorter reign of Lady Jane Grey is given some poignancy by Nova Pilbeam, and heraldic significance and atmosphere by director Robert Stevenson. This is a Tudor story in which Elizabeth scarcely makes an appearance, but a mainly British cast make the "prithees" sound convincing. The American title, *Nine Days a Queen*, was an adequate description of the film's storyline. **TH**

John Mills *Lord Guildford Dudley* · Sir Cedric Hardwicke [Cedric Hardwicke] *Earl of Warwick* · Felix Aylmer *Edward Seymour* · Leslie Perrins *Thomas Seymour* · Frank Cellier *Henry VIII* · Desmond Tester *Edward VI* · Sybil Thorndike *Ellen* ■ *Dir* Robert Stevenson · *Scr* Robert Stevenson, Miles Malleson

Tu£sday ★★ 15
Heist action thriller   2007 · UK · Colour · 78min

Released hot on the heels of *The Bank Job* and *Daylight Robbery*, this comedy-tinged thriller offers little variation on the British heist-movie formula. The set-up sees three different parties (a gang of professional thieves, two opportunistic female bank clerks and a disgruntled customer) independently deciding to rob the same bank at the same time on the same day. Chaos, of course, ensues. John Simm and Philip Glenister (stars of TV's *Life on Mars*) certainly lend lustre to the ensemble cast, but writer/director Sacha Bennett's feature debut is let down by its confusing flashback structure. You can't help feeling that this is just one blag too far. **DA** _DVD_

Philip Glenister *Earp* · John Simm *Silver* · Kevin R McNally [Kevin McNally] *Jerry* · Ashley Walters *Billy* · Cristian Solimeno *Butch* · Kate Magowan *Angie* · Kirsty Mitchell *Samantha* · Linal Haft *William* ■ *Dir/Scr* Sacha Bennett

Tuesdays with Morrie ★★★★ PG
Drama based on a true story
1999 · US · Colour · 89min

Mitch Albom's memoir of his afternoons spent chewing the fat with his old college professor became a fixture on the US bestseller lists. It's not an easy book to adapt and there are moments in this TV movie when the fortune-cookie philosophy threatens to take over. But thanks to Mick Jackson's sensitive handling and Theo van de Sande's nostalgically shot Boston vistas, this is an old-fashioned, heart-warming delight. Hank Azaria impresses as the workaholic sports writer who regains a sense of perspective through his mentor's bons mots. But this is Jack Lemmon's show, as he dexterously portrays both Morrie Schwartz's physical decline and his zest for life. **DP** _DVD_

Jack Lemmon *Morrie Schwartz* · Hank Azaria *Mitch Albom* · Wendy Moniz *Janine* · Caroline Aaron *Connie* · Bonnie Bartlett *Charlotte* ■ *Dir* Mick Jackson · *Scr* Tom Rickman, from the non-fiction book by Mitch Albom

Tugboat Annie ★★★
Comedy drama   1933 · US · BW · 87min

A ramshackle vehicle (in all senses of the word) reuniting the popular star team of the 1930 hit *Min and Bill*, lovable Marie Dressler and gruff Wallace Beery. It was based on Norman Reilly Raine's *Saturday Evening Post* stories about Annie Brennan and her no-good hubby Terry, who never hit Annie "'cept in self-defence". When this was made, Oscar winner Dressler was number one at the box office; a year later she was dead from cancer. **TS**

Marie Dressler *Annie Brennan* · Wallace Beery *Terry Brennan* · Robert Young (1) *Alec Brennan* · Maureen O'Sullivan *Pat Severn* · Willard Robertson *Red Severn* · Tammany Young *Shif'less* ■ *Dir* Mervyn LeRoy · *Scr* Zelda Sears, Eve Green, Norman Reilly Raine, from stories by Raine

Tulpan ★★★★ 12
Comedy drama
2008 · Ger/Kaz/Pol/Rus/Swi/It · Colour · 98min

Anyone enchanted by *The Story of the Weeping Camel* will warm to this quirkily charming comedy drama set on the steppes of Kazakhstan. Returning from Russian naval service, Asa (Askhat Kuchinchirekov) moves into a cramped yurt with his sister and her family. Asa wants to become a shepherd, but he needs a wife and sets off to meet the only marriageable girl in the district. Drawing on his documentary experience, director Sergey Dvortsevoy unflinchingly depicts the harshness (and occasional beauty) of a nomadic life in the central Asian wilderness. But he also includes an irresistible mix of whimsical and raucous humour that leavens the bleakness of that environment. **DP** Kazakh, Russian +subtitles. _DVD_

Askhat Kuchinchirekov *Asa* · Samal Yeslyamova *Samal, Asa's sister* · Ondasyn Besikbasov *Ondas, Samal's husband* · Tulepbergen Baisakalov *Boni* · Bereke Turganbayev *Beke* · Nurzhigit Zhapabayev *Nuka* ■ *Dir* Sergey Dvortsevoy · *Scr* Sergey Dvortsevoy, Gennady Ostrovski

Tulsa ★★ U
Drama   1949 · US · Colour · 87min

Leading lady Susan Hayward is building an empire based on oil, the black gold, with the help of Robert Preston's geologist, but enters into an unholy partnership with oil baron Lloyd Gough. There's a conservation angle thrown into this otherwise formula-bound drama as oil pollutes the traditional grazing lands of her native American friend, Pedro Armendáriz. **AE** _DVD_

Susan Hayward *Cherokee "Cherry" Lansing* · Robert Preston *Brad "Bronco" Brady* · Pedro Armendáriz *Jim Redbird* · Chill Wills *Pinky Jimpson* · Harry Shannon *Nelse Lansing* · Ed Begley *"Crude" Johnny Brady* · Jimmy Conlin *Homer Triplette* ■ *Dir* Stuart Heisler · *Scr* Frank Nugent, Curtis Kenyon, from a story by Richard Wormser

Tumbleweed ★★ U
Western   1953 · US · Colour · 78min

This very average Universal western stars its resident cowboy, Audie Murphy, who this time out is accused of deserting a wagon train during an Indian raid. There are lots of familiar western faces on hand, including Chill Wills and Lee Van Cleef, but perhaps it's worth mentioning that the title role goes to a horse. **TS**

Audie Murphy *Jim Harvey* · Lori Nelson *Laura* · Chill Wills *Sheriff Murchoree* · Roy Roberts *Nick Buckley* · Russell Johnson *Lam* · KT Stevens *Louella Buckley* · Lee Van Cleef *Marv* ■ *Dir* Nathan Juran · *Scr* John Meredyth Lucas, from the novel *Three Were Renegades* by Kenneth Perkins

Tumbleweeds ★★★
Silent western epic   1925 · US · BW · 82min

The first real cowboy star – just a gallop ahead of Tom Mix – and a major influence on the development of the western during the silent era, William S Hart made his final appearance in what is probably the best-known of his films. The plot has Hart vanquishing the lawless with the aid of his sharpshooting and playing protector to pioneer settler Barbara Bedford. Simple, formula stuff to be sure, but with an authentic flavour of the Old West and a famous land-rush action sequence. In 1939, the star reissued *Tumbleweeds* with sound effects and a prologue, spoken by himself, about how the West had changed. **RK**

William S Hart *Don Carver* · Barbara Bedford *Molly Lassiter* · Lucien Littlefield *Kentucky Rose* · J Gordon Russell *Noll Lassiter* · Richard R Neill *Bill Freel* · Jack Murphy *Bart Lassiter* ■ *Dir* King Baggot · *Scr* C Gardner Sullivan, from a story by Hal G Evarts

Tumbleweeds ★★★ 12
Drama   1999 · US · Colour · 98min

Janet McTeer gives an Oscar-nominated performance as a free spirit who drags her 12-year-old daughter (newcomer Kimberley J Brown) out west in search of a better life. This funny, tender and predictably tear-stained slice of life echoes other parent-and-child road movies, yet it has a sassy charm all its own. McTeer's unselfconscious sexuality provides a vivid contrast to Brown's unaffected innocence. Writer/director Gavin O'Connor (whose ex-wife Angela Shelton based the story on her own mother) also appears as McTeer's truck-driving lover. **AME** _DVD_

Janet McTeer *Mary Jo Walker* · Kimberly J Brown *Ava Walker* · Jay O Sanders *Dan* · Gavin O'Connor *Jack Ranson* · Michael J Pollard *Mr Cummings* · Laurel Holloman *Laurie Pendleton* ■ *Dir* Gavin O'Connor · *Scr* Gavin O'Connor, Angela Shelton

The Tune ★★★ PG
Animated musical comedy
1992 · US · Colour · 66min

Bill Plympton's feature debut pays homage to the collages of image and rhythm from the 1930s avant-garde, as a failed songwriter tries his hand at a variety of musical styles in order to relaunch his career. The action occasionally becomes a little mushy, as the inhabitants of the fantasy world of Flooby Nooby try to teach their guest to write from the heart, but there is undoubted beauty in the 30,000 pencil-and-watercolour drawings that comprise this entertaining film. **DP**

Daniel Nieden *Del* · Maureen McElheron *Didi* · Marty Nelson *Mayor/Mr Mega/Mrs Mega* · Emily Bindiger *Dot* ■ *Dir* Bill Plympton · *Scr* Bill Plympton, Maureen McElheron, PC Vey

Tunes of Glory ★★★★ PG
Drama   1960 · UK · Colour · 102min

John Mills won best actor at the Venice film festival for his priggish performance in this stiff-upper-lipped military drama, but few critics would have had any complaints had he shared the prize with his co-star Alec Guinness. Mills is the blue-blooded Pacific veteran who's determined to make his new regiment fit for the demands of peacetime, while Guinness is the time-serving Alamein hero who remains stubbornly obsessed with past glories. James Kennaway's rather bombastic script was Oscar nominated, and, if Ronald Neame's direction is occasionally stodgy, the conflict between Mills and Guinness remains as compelling as its resolution is shocking. **DP** _DVD_

Alec Guinness *Lt Col Jock Sinclair* · John Mills *Lt Col Basil Barrow* · Dennis Price *Major Charlie Scott* · Susannah York *Morag Sinclair* · John Fraser *Corporal Piper Fraser* · Allan Cuthbertson *Captain Eric Simpson* · Kay Walsh *Mary* · John MacKenzie (2) *Pony Major* · Gordon Jackson *Captain Jimmy Cairns* ■ *Dir* Ronald Neame · *Scr* James Kennaway, from his novel

The Tunnel of Love ★★
Comedy   1958 · US · BW · 98min

This film marked the first time Gene Kelly had directed a picture which he was not in, and though he makes an efficient job of transcribing a Broadway comedy, it comes out as one of those plays that convulsed theatre audiences in New York and London but seems only mildly amusing on screen. Doris Day and Richard Widmark (the latter in a rare comedy role) play a married couple forced to battle through all sorts of bureaucratic formalities in order to adopt a child. Shot in only three weeks on virtually one set, the film still lost money. **TV**

Doris Day *Isolde Poole* · Richard Widmark *Augie Poole* · Gig Young *Dick Pepper* · Gia Scala *Estelle Novick* · Elisabeth Fraser *Alice Pepper* · Elizabeth Wilson *Miss MacCracken* · Vikki Dougan *Actress* ■ *Dir* Gene Kelly · *Scr* Joseph Fields, Jerome Chodorov (uncredited), Peter De Vries, from their play

Tunnel Vision ★★ 18
Thriller   1994 · Aus · Colour · 90min

Patsy Kensit and Robert Reynolds play two detectives on the trail of an artistically minded serial killer. To complicate things further, Reynolds finds himself a suspect in a separate case when the man he suspects of sleeping with his wife turns up dead. The leads are no more than competent, but at least Kensit doesn't make any wince-inducing attempts at an accent, and there are some nifty twists in the plot. **JF** Swearing, nudity. _DVD_

Patsy Kensit *Kelly Wheatstone* · Robert Reynolds *Frank Yanovitch* · Rebecca Rigg *Helena Martelli* · Gary Day *Steve Docherty* · Shane Briant *Kevin Bosey* ■ *Dir/Scr* Clive Fleury

Tupac: Resurrection ★★★★ 15
Documentary
2003 · US · Colour and BW · 108min

This powerful documentary charts the life and sudden death of the rap superstar. Told in Tupac's own words, it's a compelling story of "ambition, violence, redemption and love". The film's strength lies in its wealth of archive material and Tupac's voiceover – culled from interviews – which is used to good effect. Unsurprisingly the soundtrack is packed with excellent tunes, but these are sometimes used a little too literally to illustrate key points. Tupac himself comes across as a charismatic yet deeply conflicted man, and it's this constant battle between the public *Thug Life* version of himself and the private, intelligent, politically savvy man that gives the film depth. It's a little overlong and highly subjective, but as a reverential portrait of an influential figure in American popular culture, it's hard to beat. **GM** _DVD_

■ *Dir* Lauren Lazin · *Cinematographer* Jon Else

Turbo ★★★★ U
Animated comedy adventure
2013 · US · Colour · 91min

The common or garden snail of the title finds himself imbued with blistering super speed, courtesy of a freak accident involving a racing car and some supercharging nitrous oxide. Cleverly calling time on too much slime, *Turbo*'s creators manage to make snails both cute and cuddly. Add a sharp script, top-notch voicing (Ryan Reynolds, Paul Giamatti, Samuel L Jackson), and race sequences with a genuine feel-of-the-wheel about them, and you have a family film that's fun, fast and furious. **DA** _DVD_ _Blu_ _SD_ _CS_

Ryan Reynolds *Turbo* · Paul Giamatti *Chet* · Michael Peña [Michael Pena] *Tito* · Samuel L Jackson *Whiplash* · Luis Guzmán [Luis Guzman] *Angelo* · Snoop Dogg *Smoove Move* · Maya Rudolph *Burn* ■ *Dir* David Soren · *Scr* Darren Lemke, Robert D Siegel, David Soren

Turbo: a Power Rangers Adventure ★ PG
Science-fiction adventure
1997 · US · Colour · 95min

Viewers who have never seen the *Mighty Morphin Power Rangers* TV show will be absolutely lost in this second big-screen adaptation. Painfully bad dialogue and technical incompetence rule here as the Power Rangers face a new alien menace. At least the previous movie had some ambition to entertain beyond being a toy commercial. **KB** _DVD_

Nakia Burrise *Tanya* · Jason David Frank *Tommy* · Catherine Sutherland *Kat* · Johnny Yong Bosch *Adam* · Blake Foster *Justin* · Paul Schrier *Bulk* · Jason Narvy *Skull* · Richard Genelle *Ernie* · Hilary Shepard Turner [Hilary Shepard] *Divatox* ■ *Dir* David Winning, Shuki Levy · *Scr* Shuki Levy, Shell Danielson

Turbo Kid ★★★★ 15
Science-fiction action adventure
2014 · Can/NZ · Colour · 88min

A lovingly made sci-fi yarn that will go down a storm with fans of 1980s home video. Teenager the Kid (Munro Chambers) roams the post-apocalypse wasteland, evading local tyrant Zeus (scenery-chewer Michael Ironside), to eventually hook up for adventures with infectiously cheery child-woman Apple (Laurence Laboeuf). Made with an affection for 80s flicks like *BMX Bandits*, and violent slice-and-dice carnage recalling Peter Jackson in his *Bad Taste* days, this is a delightful homage that will have you smiling... and wincing. **JA** Violence, swearing. _DVD_ _Blu_

Munro Chambers *The Kid* • Laurence Leboeuf *Apple* • Michael Ironside *Zeus* • Edwin Wright *Skeletron* ■ Dir/Scr François Simard, Anouk Whissell, Yoann-Karl Whissell

Turbulence ★★★ 18
Action thriller   1997 · US · Colour · 96min

Ray Liotta stars as a psycho who hijacks a Christmas Eve flight transporting him to prison. Lauren Holly plays the plucky flight attendant who has to beat off Liotta's advances and attempt to land the aircraft safely. This is far from sophisticated adult entertainment, but it's so ludicrously overblown that it's hard not to enjoy the sheer enthusiasm and abandonment of logic and credibility. Two sequels followed. JC Swearing, violence. *DVD*

Ray Liotta *Ryan Weaver* • Lauren Holly *Teri Halloran* • Brendan Gleeson *Stubbs* • Hector Elizondo *Detective Aldo Hines* • Rachel Ticotin *Rachel Taper* • Jeffrey DeMunn *Brooks* • John Finn *Sinclair* • Ben Cross *Captain Bowen* • Dir Robert Butler • Scr Jonathan Brett

Turbulence II: Fear of Flying ★ 15
Action thriller   2000 · US · Colour · 96min

Director David Mackay assembles a passenger list straight out of Stereotype Central for this tiresome, unrelated sequel to an action thriller that was itself riddled with clichés and caricatures. It's almost as if *Airplane!* hadn't happened, as the lovers with mile-high ambitions, the assured stewardess and the widower coping with grief join a flight from Seattle to Los Angeles. The result is more likely to provoke suppressed smirks than gasps of suspense. DP *DVD*

Craig Sheffer *Martin Messerman* • Jennifer Beals *Jessica* • Tom Berenger *Robert Sikes* • Jeffrey Nordling *Elliott Stephenson* • Jay Brazeau *Harold* • Daryl Shuttleworth *Captain Lloyd Reynolds* • Paul Jarrett *Vaclav* ■ Dir David Mackay • Scr Kevin Bernhardt, Brendan Broderick, Rob Kerchner

The Turin Horse ★★★★ 15
Drama   2011 · Hun/Fr/Ger/Swi · BW · 154min

The film that regrettably brings down the curtain on the remarkable career of director Bela Tarr opens with a telling anecdote about philosopher Friedrich Nietzsche and proceeds to focus for an unrelenting 150 minutes on the daily activities of a Hungarian coachman and his morose daughter inside their wind-blasted cottage. For some, this may sound like a nightmare, but anyone with an appreciation of the intricacies of screen composition will relish this compelling psychological study. Capturing the "action" in just 30 takes, and expertly photographed in stunning monochrome, this tale is open to multiple interpretations. But its genius lies in its compassion, control and cinematic purity. DP Hungarian +subtitles. Swearing. *DVD* Blu

Janos Derzsi *Ohlsdorfer* • Erika Bok *Ohlsdorfer's daughter* • Mihaly Kormos *Bernhard* ■ Dir Bela Tarr, Agnes Hranitzky • Scr Laszlo Krasznahorkai, Bela Tarr

Turk 182! ★★ 15
Drama   1985 · US · Colour · 92min

Timothy Hutton plays a New York graffiti artist who uses his talent to shame mayor Robert Culp after the city fathers fail to compensate his fireman brother, injured in an off-duty rescue. Hutton is seriously miscast as the spray-can vigilante, while Peter Boyle, Darren McGavin and Paul Sorvino are wasted in minor roles. The presence of Robert Urich as Hutton's brother and Kim Cattrall as his girlfriend tips us off that this is B-movie fare. DP

Timothy Hutton *Jimmy Lynch* • Robert Urich *Terry Lynch* • Kim Cattrall *Danny Boudreau* • Robert Culp *Mayor Tyler* • Darren McGavin *Detective Kowalski* • Steven Keats *Jockamo* • Paul Sorvino • Peter Boyle *Detective Ryan* ■ Dir Bob Clark • Scr James Gregory Kingston, Denis Hamill, John Hamill, from a story by James Gregory Kingston

Turkey Shoot ★★★ 18
Futuristic action thriller   1981 · Aus · Colour · 89min

Set in the Australian outback of the future, when social deviants (freedom fighter Steve Railsback, good girl Olivia Hussey, prostitutes et al) are sent to barbaric concentration camps, supposedly for re-education. But in reality it's to provide human prey for warden Michael Craig to indulge his sadistic predilection for extreme blood sports. Convincingly mounted and violent, this cynical political allegory may be exploitation, but it does deliver a high shock quotient. AJ Violence, swearing, nudity. *DVD*

Steve Railsback *Paul Anders* • Olivia Hussey *Chris Walters* • Michael Craig *Charles Thatcher* • Carmen Duncan *Jennifer* • Noel Ferrier *Mallory* • Lynda Stoner *Rita Daniels* • Roger Ward *Ritter* • Michael Petrovitch *Tito* • Gus Mercurio *Red* ■ Dir Brian Trenchard-Smith • Scr Jon George, Neill Hicks, from a story by George Schenck, Robert Williams, David Lawrence

Turkish Delight ★★★★ 18
Erotic drama   1973 · Neth · Colour · 103min

Dutch director Paul Verhoeven burst onto the international film scene with this truly bizarre and shocking romance featuring unprecedented amounts of frontal nudity, graphic sex and scatological behaviour. It also shot star Rutger Hauer to fame. He plays a sex-obsessed artist/sculptor whose exhibitionism is fuelled by an intense relationship with suburban Monique van de Ven. But whereas his carnal conduct is more about affronting respectable society with revolutionary values, hers has a darker base in mental imbalance due to a brain tumour. A surprisingly tender and touching tale. AJ Dutch dubbed. *DVD*

Monique van de Ven *Olga* • Rutger Hauer *Eric* • Tonny Huurdeman *Mother* • Dolf de Vries *Paul* ■ Dir Paul Verhoeven • Scr Gerard Soeteman, from the novel *Turks Fruit* by Jan Wolkers

The Turn of the Screw ★ 18
Supernatural horror   1992 · UK/US/Fr · Colour · 91min

Yet another adaptation of Henry James's classic horror novella, and yet another adaptation which falls short of the original 1961 film version *The Innocents*. Director Rusty Lemorande has gone at the material and stripped it of all subtlety, which includes adding superfluous narration from Marianne Faithful and updating the context to 1960s England. Patsy Kensit is also sadly inadequate as the young governess whose charges appear possessed by their former manservant and governess. LH

Patsy Kensit *Jenny* • Julian Sands *Mr Cooper* • Stéphane Audran *Mrs Grose* • Clare Szekeres *Flore* • Olivier Debray *Quint* • Joseph England *Miles* • Bryony Brind *Miss Jessel* • Marianne Faithfull *Narrator* ■ Dir Rusty Lemorande • Scr Rusty Lemorande, from the novella by Henry James

Turn the Key Softly ★★
Drama   1953 · UK · BW · 81min

Worthy intentions are still discernible beneath this superficial social melodrama essaying 24 hours in the lives of three women (played by Yvonne Mitchell, Joan Collins and Kathleen Harrison) released from Holloway prison. In her first starring role, Mitchell makes a silk purse out of a sow's ear, but the rest of the cast go with the caricatures they're given. Extensive location work shows London in the grip of postwar austerity. DM

Joan Collins *Stella Jarvis* • Yvonne Mitchell *Monica Marsden* • Kathleen Harrison *Mrs Quilliam* • Terence Morgan *David* • Thora Hird *Landlady* • Dorothy Alison *Joan* • Glyn Houston *Bob* • Geoffrey Keen *Gregory* ■ Dir Jack Lee (2) • Scr Maurice Cowan, Jack Lee, John Brophy, from a novel by John Brophy

Turner & Hooch ★★★ PG
Comedy   1989 · US · Colour · 95min

In this enjoyable comedy, Tom Hanks stars as a dapper California detective who teams up with slobbering dog Hooch to solve a drug-related murder. While the script is sometimes short on laughs, British director Roger Spottiswoode keeps the action jogging along, giving Hanks room to display the kind of comic timing that established his Hollywood reputation. Hanks is well-served by his canine co-star, but Mare Winningham is sadly wasted. DP *DVD*

Tom Hanks *Scott Turner* • Mare Winningham *Emily Carson* • Craig T Nelson *Police Chief Hyde* • Reginald VelJohnson *Detective David Sutton* • Scott Paulin *Zack Gregory* • JC Quinn *Walter Boyett* • John McIntire *Amos Reed* ■ Dir Roger Spottiswoode • Scr Dennis Shryack, Michael Blodgett, Daniel Petrie Jr, Jim Cash, Jack Epps Jr, from a story by Dennis Shryack, Michael Blodgett, Daniel Petrie Jr

The Turning ★ 18
Drama   1992 · US · Colour · 87min

A 20-year old skinhead returns to his rural home town to torment his parents, who have recently decided to divorce. In an attempt to reconcile the family, he takes his dad's new girlfriend hostage. This movie, based on a stage play, would have deservedly languished in total obscurity if not for the fact that Gillian Anderson of *The X Files* fame made her motion picture debut here. Other than that, there's no reason to watch. ST

Karen Allen *Glory* • Raymond J Barry *Mark Harnish* • Michael Dolan *Cliff Harnish* • Tess Harper *Martha Harnish* • Gillian Anderson *April Cavanaugh* ■ Dir Lou Puopolo • Scr Lou Puopolo, from the play *Home Fires Burning* by Chris Ceraso

The Turning ★★★ 15
Portmanteau drama   2013 · Aus · Colour · 106min

Although quite a few famous Australian faces (Cate Blanchett, Hugo Weaving) pepper this ambitious attempt to translate Tim Winton's book of short stories into an experimental collage of short films, it was first conceived as an art project, and is perhaps best viewed that way. It's also worth noting that, to those unfamiliar with the book, certain characters recur, to be reinterpreted by different directors and actors. The result is only fitfully interesting. DW Violence, swearing, sex scenes.

Cate Blanchett *Gail Lang* • Rose Byrne *Raelene* • Hugo Weaving *Bob Lang* • Miranda Otto *Sherry* • Richard Roxburgh *Vic Lang* • Harrison Gilbertson *Vic Lang* ■ Dir Jonathan auf der Heide, Tony Ayres, Jub Clerc, Robert Connolly, Shaun Gladwell, Rhys Graham, Justin Kurzel, Yaron Lifschitz, Anthony Lucas, Claire McCarthy, Ian Meadows, Ashlee Page, Stephen Page, Simon Stone, Warwick Thornton, Marieka Walsh, Mia Wasikowska, David Wenham • Scr From the short stories by Tim Winton

The Turning Point ★★★
Crime   1952 · US · BW · 85min

This powerful, well-cast Hollywood crime drama was one of several suggested by the Kefauver hearings on organised crime in the early 1950s. It builds considerable tension as Edmond O'Brien's crimebusting lawyer heads an investigation into a city's racketeering and is slowly exposed to the depth of corruption and villainy involved. William Holden is astutely cast as the cynical reporter who finds himself helping O'Brien. Director William Dieterle creates a visual style to convey a dark world in which a villain will burn down an occupied tenement block to cover his tracks. AE

William Holden (2) *Jerry McKibbon* • Edmond O'Brien *John Conroy* • Alexis Smith *Amanda Waycross* • Tom Tully *Matt Conroy* • Ed Begley *Eichelberger* • Dan Dayton *Ackerman* ■ Dir William Dieterle • Scr Warren Duff, from the story *Storm in the City* by Horace McCoy

The Turning Point ★★★ PG
Drama   1977 · US · Colour · 114min

This woman's movie was nominated for 11 Oscars but astonishingly won none. The American Ballet Theatre stops off in Oklahoma reuniting two former colleagues: Anne Bancroft, now prima ballerina in the company, and Shirley MacLaine, who opted for marriage and children. In the course of the movie both wonder whether they made the right decision, finally coming to terms with their lives and futures through the fate of MacLaine's daughter Leslie Browne. The dancing is relegated to second place behind the drama, but is still splendid and intoxicating, featuring many of the stars of the day. FL *DVD*

Shirley MacLaine *Deedee Rodgers* • Anne Bancroft *Emma Jacklin* • Mikhail Baryshnikov *Kopeikine* • Leslie Browne *Emilia* • Tom Skerritt *Wayne* • Martha Scott *Adelaide* • Antoinette Sibley *Sevilla* • Alexandra Danilova *Dahkarova* • Starr Danias *Carolyn* ■ Dir Herbert Ross • Scr Arthur Laurents

Turtle Beach ★ 15
Political drama   1992 · US · Colour · 84min

A strong subject – the plight of the Vietnamese boat people – is squandered by this movie in which everything except the scenery looks shoddy. Greta Scacchi plays an Australian journalist who heads for Malaysia to cover events as the locals hack the refugees to pieces. Preview responses were so bad that the film was drastically shortened, though it still bombed everywhere. AT Violence, sex scenes.

Greta Scacchi *Judith Wilkes* • Joan Chen *Lady Minou Hobday* • Jack Thompson *Ralph Hamilton* • Art Malik *Kanan* • Norman Kaye *Sir Adrian Hobday* • Victoria Longley *Sancha Hamilton* • Martin Jacobs *Richard* ■ Dir Stephen Wallace • Scr Ann Turner, from the novel by Blanche d'Alpuget

Turtle Diary ★★★ PG
Comedy drama   1985 · UK · Colour · 91min

This odd two-hander stars Glenda Jackson and Ben Kingsley as a pair of lonely liberals desperate to liberate the turtles in a zoo from what they see as their cruel plight. As you would expect, the acting is subtle and intelligent, with John Irvin's direction giving the film a stately but oversimplified pace. The movie's main problem is that it fails to bring out the great insights on Britain and the Brits that distinguish Russell Hoban's insightful novel. SH

Glenda Jackson *Neaera Duncan* • Ben Kingsley *William Snow* • Richard Johnson *Mr Johnson* • Michael Gambon *George Fairbairn* • Rosemary Leach *Mrs Inchcliff* • Eleanor Bron *Miss Neap* • Harriet Walter *Harriet* • Jeroen Krabbé *Sandor* • Nigel Hawthorne *Publisher* ■ Dir John Irvin • Scr Harold Pinter, Bill Darrid, from the novel by Russell Hoban

Turtles Can Fly ★★★★ 15
Black comedy drama   2004 · Iraq/Iran · Colour · 93min

Set in a camp on the Iraqi-Turkish border shortly before coalition forces launched their attack on Saddam Hussein, Bahman Ghobadi's hellish drama makes an unlikely vehicle for absurdist comedy. But it's impossible not to be amused by Kurdish teenager Soran Ebrahim's wheeler-dealing or his liberal translations for various US satellite news broadcasts. Similarly, the plight of the countless orphans who survive by collecting landmines and the despair of demure refugee Avaz Latif bring home the reality of shattered childhoods. DP Kurdish +subtitles. *DVD*

Soran Ebrahim *Kak Satellite* • Hiresh Feyssal Rahman *Henkov* • Avaz Latif *Agrin* • Saddam Hossein Feysal *Pasheo* • Abdol Rahman Karim Riga ■ Dir/Scr Bahman Ghobadi

A Turtle's Tale: Sammy's Adventures ★★★ U
Animated adventure   2010 · Bel · Colour · 85min

If you're a 3D sceptic, this is a film you must see. The underwater world of little Sammy the turtle and his friends jumps out of the screen in a riot of colour and excitement. It's just a pity that more care was not taken in translating and voicing this Belgian production for an English-speaking audience, with John Hurt an exception. The film begins in the present day: as grandfather Sammy watches over hatchling turtles struggling from their nest to the sea, he remembers his own battle for survival against a backdrop of 20th-century historical highlights. SuR *DVD* Blu

Dominic Cooper *Sammy* • Gemma Arterton *Shelly* • John Hurt *Old Sammy* • Christine Bleakley *Sandra* • Robert Sheehan *Ray* • Melanie Cooper *Snow* ■ *Dir* Ben Stassen • *Scr* Domonic Paris, from a story by Ben Stassen, Paris

The Tuskegee Airmen

★★★★ PG

Wartime drama based on a true story
1995 · US · Colour · 101min

In the tradition of *Glory*, this TV movie recalls the exploits of the first black aerial combat unit sent into action during the Second World War. Billeted at the Tuskegee air base, the "Fighting 99th" was formed to boost the civil rights cause, although the recruits were subjected to racial abuse from the top brass down. While the emphasis is on Hannibal Lee (played with distinction by Laurence Fishburne), this is very much an ensemble piece. DP

Laurence Fishburne *Hannibal Lee* • Cuba Gooding Jr *Billy Roberts* • Allen Payne *Walter Peoples* • Malcolm-Jamal Warner *Leroy Cappy* • Courtney B Vance *Lieutenant Jeffrey Glenn* • André Braugher *Lt Col Benjamin O Davis* • John Lithgow *Senator Conyers* ■ *Dir* Robert Markowitz • *Scr* Paris H Qualles, Ron Hutchinson, Trey Ellis, from a story by Robert Williams, TS Cook

The Tuttles of Tahiti

★★★ U

Comedy   1942 · US · BW · 91min

This South Seas island comedy starring Charles Laughton is based on a novel by the authors of *Mutiny on the Bounty*. Laughton's performance here is far removed from his memorable Captain Bligh, but he has fun as the idler who engages in a verbal battle with the formidable Florence Bates, while Bates's daughter Peggy Drake makes eyes at Laughton's son Jon Hall. Mindless nonsense, but skilfully handled by director Charles Vidor, and the literate screenplay makes this eminently watchable. TS

Charles Laughton *Jonas* • Jon Hall *Chester* • Peggy Drake *Tamara* • Victor Francen *Dr Blondin* • Florence Bates *Emily* • Gene Reynolds *Ru* • Curt Bois *Jensen* • Adeline De Walt Reynolds *Mama Ruau* ■ *Dir* Charles Vidor • *Scr* S Lewis Meltzer, Robert Carson, James Hilton, from the novel *No More Gas* by Charles Nordhoff, James Norman Hall

The Tuxedo

★★ 12

Action comedy   2002 · US · Colour · 94min

Jackie Chan stars as the chauffeur to millionaire superspy Jason Isaacs, whose hospitalisation leads Chan to try on his boss's hi-tech dinner jacket. Our hero finds it imbues him with acrobatic powers that confusingly lead to his involvement in an international espionage plot. Sadly, the mechanical gadgets are given precedence over his physical talent, leaving the martial arts maestro with little to do. Jennifer Love Hewitt as an inept CIA agent provides the best moments. TH Swearing, violence.
DVD

Jackie Chan *Jimmy Tong* • Jennifer Love Hewitt *Delilah "Del" Blaine* • Jason Isaacs *Clark Devlin* • Debi Mazar *Steena* • Ritchie Coster *Diedrich Banning* • Peter Stormare *Dr Simms* • Mia Cottet *Cheryl* ■ *Dir* Kevin Donovan • *Scr* Michael J Wilson, Michael Leeson, from a story by Phil Hay, Matt Manfredi, Michael J Wilson

Tweety's High Flying Adventure

★★ U

Animated comedy adventure
2000 · US · Colour · 68min

No one watched the Sylvester and Tweety Pie cartoons for the canary. So why did Warner Bros deem him worthy of a solo feature? There are dozens of puddy tats in this slapdash reworking of *Around the World in 80 Days*, but only Sylvester is the cat's miaow. Seriously missing the vocal subtlety of the great Mel Blanc, this musical misfire fails primarily because Tweety has become too smart and too cynical for his own good. DP

Joe Alaskey *Tweety/Sylvester* • June Foray *Granny* ■ *Dir* James T Walker, Karl Toerge, Charles Visser • *Scr* Tom Minton, Tim Cahill, Julie McNally

Twelfth Night

★★★ U

Comedy   1996 · UK/US · Colour · 128min

Beautifully designed in a pre-Raphaelite sort of way by Sophie Becher and with rich autumnal photography by Clive Tickner, this is a handsome version of Shakespeare's cruellest comedy. The film skirts around virtually all of the social and sexual themes raised by the various misunderstandings and alliances that follow the storm-tossed arrival of Imogen Stubbs and brother Steven Mackintosh on the shores of Illyria. Notwithstanding the conservative direction, the performances are highly polished. DP
DVD

Helena Bonham Carter *Olivia* • Imogen Stubbs *Viola* • Nigel Hawthorne *Malvolio* • Richard E Grant *Sir Andrew Aguecheek* • Ben Kingsley *Feste* • Mel Smith *Sir Toby Belch* • Imelda Staunton *Maria* • Toby Stephens *Orsino* • Steven Mackintosh *Sebastian* • Nicholas Farrell *Antonio* ■ *Dir* Trevor Nunn • *Scr* Trevor Nunn, from the play by William Shakespeare

Twelve and Holding ★★★ 15

Coming-of-age drama
2005 · US · Colour · 90min

Three 12-year-olds struggle to deal with the complexities of the adult world in this moving drama. Early in the film, an act of arson kills the twin brother of Jacob (Conor Donovan) and leaves him and his friends, precocious Malee (Zoë Weizenbaum) and overweight Leonard (Jesse Camacho), reassessing their barely lived lives. Despite the script's somewhat familiar coming-of-age themes, director Michael Cuesta (*LIE*) coaxes strong performances from his young cast, adding unexpected weight to a tender story of children old beyond their years but not quite ready for the responsibilities of adulthood. JR

Linus Roache *Jim Carges* • Annabella Sciorra *Carla Chuang* • Jayne Atkinson *Ashley Carges* • Jeremy Renner *Gus Maitland* • Marcia DeBonis *Grace Fisher* • Tom McGowan *Patrick Fisher* • Conor Donovan *Jacob/Rudy Carges* • Jesse Camacho *Leonard Fisher* • Zoë Weizenbaum *Malee Chuang* ■ *Dir* Michael Cuesta • *Scr* Anthony S Cipriano

12 Angry Men

★★★★★ U

Classic courtroom drama
1957 · US · BW · 96min

Based on a television play by Reginald Rose about a lone juror holding out for a not guilty verdict with the remaining 11 ready to convict, this marvellous movie has become part of life's currency. Henry Fonda stars as juror eight (no characters have names), and he also co-produced the movie. Although acclaimed as an instant classic, the film made no money on release, and Fonda wasn't able to pay himself his deferred acting fee. His integrity illuminates the film, which benefits immeasurably from debut director Sidney Lumet's masterly sense of cinema: the action takes place on a single claustrophobic set (an actual New York jury room), yet Lumet finds an infinite variety of visual set-ups and angles within the confines. TS DVD

Henry Fonda *Juror eight* • Lee J Cobb *Juror three* • Ed Begley *Juror ten* • EG Marshall *Juror four* • Jack Warden *Juror seven* • Martin Balsam *Juror one* • John Fiedler *Juror two* • Jack Klugman *Juror five* • Edward Binns *Juror six* • Joseph Sweeney *Juror nine* • George Voskovec *Juror eleven* • Robert Webber *Juror twelve* ■ *Dir* Sidney Lumet • *Scr* Reginald Rose, from his TV play

12 Angry Men ★★★★ 12

Courtroom drama
1997 · US · Colour · 112min

Writer Reginald Rose updated his original 1954 Emmy-winning TV play and 1957 feature screenplay for this classy made-for-cable remake. An all-star cast including George C Scott and Jack Lemmon headlines this absorbing drama that centres around 12 jurors who, having been charged by the judge to deliver a verdict, retire to the jury room to deliberate. It seems to be an open-and-shut case of an inner-city boy accused of murdering his father, but one juror (Lemmon) believes the youth is innocent on grounds of "reasonable doubt". Under William Friedkin's skilful direction, Lemmon gives a brilliant performance, as does the strong supporting cast. MC

Jack Lemmon *Juror No 8* • Courtney B Vance *Juror No 1* • Ossie Davis *Juror No 2* • George C Scott *Juror No 3* • Armin Mueller-Stahl *Juror No 4* • Dorian Harewood *Juror No 5* • James Gandolfini *Juror No 6* • Tony Danza *Juror No 7* • Hume Cronyn *Juror No 9* • Mykelti Williamson *Juror No 10* • Edward James Olmos *Juror No 11* • William L Petersen *Juror No 12* ■ *Dir* William Friedkin • *Scr* Reginald Rose, from his TV play

The Twelve Chairs ★★★ U

Black comedy   1970 · US · Colour · 89min

Russian bureaucrat Ron Moody learns that his mother is dying and races home, only to be told that she has hidden the family fortune in one of 12 dining chairs left in their ancestral home. He hurries home, only to find the chairs have gone to the Ministry of Housing to be relocated. Moody teams up with young conman Frank Langella and the pair go off in search of the chairs. Mel Brooks's second feature is a sustained laugh-fest with a much more disciplined plot than his later works. DF DVD

Ron Moody *Ippolit Vorobyaninov* • Frank Langella *Ostap Bender* • Dom DeLuise *Father Fyodor* • Mel Brooks *Tikon* • Bridget Brice *Young woman* • Robert Bernal *Curator* • David Lander *Engineer Bruns* • Diana Coupland *Madame Bruns* ■ *Dir* Mel Brooks • *Scr* Mel Brooks, from the play by Ilya Ilf, Yevgeny Petrov

12 Dates of Christmas ★★

Romantic fantasy comedy   2011 · US · Colour

Amy Smart gets stuck on repeat for the sake of true love and redemption in this sweet but extremely simple yuletide spin on *Groundhog Day*. As perky as the fluffy tale's jolly pop soundtrack, Smart plays an egocentric 20-something who winds up having a dozen first dates with likeable Mark-Paul Gosselaar when she's magically forced to re-live the same Christmas Eve until she becomes a better person. The end result is a series of bitty though warmly engaging episodes that go from playful to increasingly sentimental as the moral of her predicament becomes clear. SF

Amy Smart *Kate Stanton* • Mark-Paul Gosselaar *Miles Dufine* • Jayne Eastwood *Margine Frumkin* • Benjamin Ayres *Jack Evans* ■ *Dir* James Hayman • *Scr* Janet Brownell, Aaron Mendelsohn, from a story by Blake J Harris, Mendelsohn

The Twelve Days of Christmas Eve ★★

Seasonal fantasy comedy
2004 · US · Colour · 88min

In this seasonal comedy from Martha Coolidge (*The Prince & Me*), a successful businessman who neglects his nearest and dearest is given 12 days to change his ways, or else. Steven Weber stars as the errant mogul and Molly Shannon plays his guardian angel. It's pleasantly free from the sugary sentimentality of other seasonal confections, but you'll recognise elements from just about every other Christmas movie in the plot. SuR

Steven Weber *Calvin Carter* • Molly Shannon *Angie* • Patricia Velasquez *Isabel Frias* • Teryl Rothery *Marilyn Carter* • Stefanie von Pfetten *Rhianna* ■ *Dir* Martha Coolidge • *Scr* JB White, from a story by White, Jean Abounader

12 in a Box ★★ 12

Comedy   2007 · UK · Colour · 95min

Writer/director John McKenzie can thank the popularity of Miranda Hart (in only a minor role) for helping his affable ensemble comedy to receive a belated release, six years after it was completed. Shot on a shoestring in splendid Palladian surroundings, it chronicles the efforts of a dozen former pupils from an eccentric millionaire's alma mater to win £1 million each by spending 96 hours isolated from the outside world. Belle Hithersay stands out as a hypocritical God-botherer and the punch line is a doozie, but otherwise the farce is forced, the gags grate and the standard of playing varies wildly. DP Some swearing, sexual references. DVD

Miranda Hart *Rachel* • Katy Wix *Andrea* • Ed Bennett *PC Willis* • Kenneth Collard *Barry* • Robert Cargill *Alan Hayward* • Lucy Chalkley *Samantha* ■ *Dir* John McKenzie • *Scr* John McKenzie, from his story

Twelve Monkeys ★★★★ 15

Science-fiction thriller
1995 · US/UK/Ger/Jpn/Fr · Colour · 129min

Inspired by Chris Marker's acclaimed 1962 short film *La Jetée*, this labyrinthine sci-fi thriller was penned by the co-writer of *Blade Runner*, David Webb Peoples, and his wife, Janet. Yet it's very much the work of Monty Python alumnus Terry Gilliam, who imposes his own pseudo-poetic vision on to a world that is doomed to viral annihilation unless time traveller Bruce Willis can prevent the disaster. Although it was Brad Pitt who landed the Oscar nomination for his twitchy performance as an asylum inmate, it is Willis's anguished introvert who holds this gripping, hauntingly atmospheric film together. DP Swearing, violence, nudity. DVD BD

Bruce Willis *James Cole* • Madeleine Stowe *Dr Kathryn Railly* • Brad Pitt *Jeffrey Goines* • Christopher Plummer *Dr Goines* • Joseph Melito *Young Cole* • Jon Seda *Jose* • David Morse *Dr Peters* • Frank Gorshin *Dr Fletcher* • *Dir* Terry Gilliam • *Scr* David Peoples, Janet Peoples, from the film *La Jetée* by Chris Marker • *Cinematographer* Roger Pratt

12:08 East of Bucharest

★★★★ 15

Comedy drama   2005 · Rom · Colour · 85min

Chaos descends upon a TV show celebrating the anniversary of dictator Nicolae Ceausescu's overthrow in this mischievous satire, which earned writer/director Corneliu Porumboiu the Camera d'Or at Cannes in 2006. Neither drunken history teacher Teo Corban nor testy old timer Mircea Andreescu has prospered under democracy, yet they agree to reminisce about the 1989 revolution. However, Corban's recollections of his rabble-rousing patriotism are challenged by phone-in callers and it transpires that their town stumbled towards freedom rather than marching in the vanguard. Porumboiu keeps the focus firmly on Corban's fake heroics and the prejudices from the Communist era, suggesting a country preoccupied with its past. DP Romanian +subtitles. DVD

Mircea Andreescu *Piscoci* • Teo Corban [Teodor Corban] *Manescu* • Ion Sapdaru *Virgil Jderescu* ■ *Dir/Scr* Corneliu Porumboiu • *Cinematographer* Marius Panduru

12:01

★★★★ 15

Science-fiction thriller
1993 · US · Colour · 90min

Whereas *Groundhog Day* used the idea of living the same day over and over again for laughs, director Jack Sholder takes the same premise (from Richard Lupoff's 1973 novella) and goes for dynamic action to craft a clever thriller. Engaging Jonathan Silverman is the clerk caught in a time-loop involving an associate's murder, who tries to prevent the killing from taking place by changing incidental details each time the same day dawns. A neatly cut and highly polished gem, the tale is continuously engrossing and never contrived. AJ

Jonathan Silverman *Barry Thomas* • Helen Slater *Lisa Fredericks* • Martin Landau *Dr Thadius Moxley* • Jeremy Piven *Howard Richter* • Robin Bartlett *Ann Jackson* • Nicholas Surovy [Nicolas Surovy] *Robert Denk* ■ *Dir* Jack Sholder • *Scr* Philip Morton, from a short film by Jonathan Heap, Hillary Ripps, from the novella *12:01 PM* by Richard Lupoff

Twelve o'Clock High

★★★★ U

Second World War drama
1949 · US · BW · 126min

To watch Gregory Peck crack under the strain of high command (he's in charge of a pressure-cooked American bomber unit based in England during the Second World War) is as alarming as the collapse of the Statue of Liberty: he's such a monument to liberal integrity. However, although he was nominated for an Oscar for his performance here, it was Dean Jagger who won the award for best supporting actor. It's all a wonderful example of ensemble acting, so any trophies are a bit redundant, though no doubt they were gratefully received. TH *DVD*

Gregory Peck *General Frank Savage* • Hugh Marlowe *Lt Col Ben Gately* • Gary Merrill *Colonel Keith Davenport* • Dean Jagger *Major Harvey Stovall* • Millard Mitchell *General Pritchard* • Robert Arthur (1) *Sergeant McIllhenny* • Paul Stewart *Captain "Doc" Kaiser* • John Kellogg *Major Cobb* ■ *Dir* Henry King • *Scr* Sy Bartlett, Beirne Lay Jr, from their novel

Twelve plus One ★★
Comedy 1969 · It/Fr · Colour · 95min

There are 13 salon chairs, one of which contains a hidden fortune in jewels. Mel Brooks made a movie out of this Russian story in the same year. This version is watchable due to the chocolate-box assortment of stars on show, including the positively sofa-like Orson Welles, ageing Italian heart-throb Vittorio Gassman and eccentric Englishman Terry-Thomas. Hollywood starlet Sharon Tate makes her final appearance before her murder. AT

Vittorio Gassman *Mike* • Orson Welles *Markau* • Mylène Demongeot *Judy* • Sharon Tate *Pat* • Terry-Thomas *Albert* • Tim Brooke-Taylor *Jackie* • Vittorio De Sica *Di Seta* • *Dir* Luciano Lucignani • *Scr* Nicolas Gessner, Marc Benham, from a story by Ilya Ilf, Yevgeny Petrov

12 Rounds ★★15
Action thriller 2008 · US · Colour · 103min

New Orleans cop Danny Fisher (John Cena) plays cat-and-mouse with a ruthless, grudge-holding terrorist in this conventional and clichéd action fest from director Renny Harlin (*Die Hard 2*). Unsurprisingly, this provides the opportunity for Fisher to leave an escalating trail of destruction, while typically tight-lipped FBI agents struggle to uncover the bad guy's ulterior motive. Harlin aims for the tension-cranking thrills of a *Die Hard* or *Speed*, but his bombs 'n' bullets set pieces lack originality. It also doesn't help that wrestling star Cena is a fairly uncharismatic leading man. TeS *DVD* *Blu-ray*

John Cena *Danny Fisher* • Aidan Gillen *Miles Jackson* • Ashley Scott *Molly Porter* • Steve Harris *George Aiken* • Brian White *Hank Carver* • Gonzalo Menendez *Ray Santiago* ■ *Dir* Renny Harlin • *Scr* Daniel Kunka

The 12 Tasks of Asterix ★★★★U
Animated adventure 1975 · Fr · Colour · 78min

Written especially for the screen by René Goscinny and Albert Uderzo, this is the best of the Asterix cartoons, if only because something of the wit and ingenuity of the original books shines through. Determined to rid himself of the indomitable Gauls once and for all, Caesar sets Asterix and Obelix a Herculean quota of seemingly impossible tasks. But crocodiles, ghosts, Greek sprinters, German wrestlers, Egyptian sorcerers and even Rome's bureaucrats prove no match for our intrepid heroes. Graphically it's on the conservative side, but otherwise this is brisk, slick and hugely entertaining. There also comes in a French language version. DP

■ *Dir/Scr* René Goscinny, Albert Uderzo

12 Years a Slave ★★★★★15
Period drama based on a true story
2013 · US · Colour · 128min

Aside from the milestone 1970s mini-series *Roots*, Quentin Tarantino's puerile revenge fantasy *Django Unchained*, and a handful of others, there have been precious few films about slavery in the US told from the point of view of the enslaved. At the very least, director Steve McQueen's adaptation of Solomon Northup's memoir (which was previously adapted for TV in 1984, starring Avery Brooks) represents essential viewing for correcting that imbalance. It's also a tremendously powerful piece of cinema, a tale of suffering, endurance, courage and abiding humanity about a freeborn man kidnapped and sold into slavery, which packs all the more wallop for the elegance with which it's made. Chiwetel Ejiofor's restrained, finely modulated lead performance fully deserves all the praise that's been heaped upon it, but the supports, especially Lupita Nyong'o and Michael Fassbender, are no less impressive. LF Violence, racist language, sex scenes, nudity. *DVD* *Blu-ray*

Chiwetel Ejiofor *Solomon Northup* • Benedict Cumberbatch *Ford* • Michael Fassbender *Edwin Epps* • Sarah Paulson *Mistress Epps* • Paul Dano *Tibeats* • Paul Giamatti *Freeman* • Adepero Oduye *Eliza* • Brad Pitt *Bass* • Alfre Woodard *Mistress Shaw* ■ *Dir* Steve McQueen (2) • *Scr* John Ridley, from the autobiography *Twelve Years a Slave* by Solomon Northup • *Cinematographer* Sean Bobbitt • *Music* Hans Zimmer • *Costume Designer* Patricia Norris

Twentieth Century ★★★★★U
Screwball comedy 1934 · US · BW · 88min

The title refers to the express train that ran between New York and Chicago, where movie producers and stars changed for the connection to Los Angeles. Aboard this deliriously enjoyable trip is a Broadway impresario (John Barrymore) and a recalcitrant Hollywood star (Carole Lombard). She is his protégé, but after several flops he's trying to lure her back to Broadway. Directed at supersonic speed by Howard Hawks, this is a stream of acidic barbs, offering the stars ample scope for grandiose caricature. In fact, the arch theatricality of the piece functions as a comment on movie-making and the edgy relationship between Hollywood and Broadway in the early years of the talkies. First class all the way. AT

John Barrymore *Oscar Jaffe* • Carole Lombard *Lily Garland* • Walter Connolly *Webb* • Roscoe Karns *O'Malley* • Charles Levison [Charles Lane (2)] *Jacobs* • Etienne Girardot *Clark* • Dale Fuller *Sadie* ■ *Dir* Howard Hawks • *Scr* Charles MacArthur, Ben Hecht, from their play, from the play *Napoleon on Broadway* by Charles Bruce Millholland

28 Days ★★15
Drama 2000 · US · Colour · 99min

Sandra Bullock is the Manhattan wild child forced into rehab after hijacking a limo at her sister's wedding and driving it into a house. Refusing to admit she has a drink problem, Bullock comes to terms with her addiction with help from tough-but-fair guidance counsellor Steve Buscemi and the usual round of kooky Hollywood misfits. This is the kind of sentimental hogwash that's more likely to drive people to drink than keep them off it. NS Violence, swearing, sex scenes, drug abuse, nudity. *DVD*

Sandra Bullock *Gwen Cummings* • Viggo Mortensen *Eddie Boone* • Dominic West *Jasper* • Diane Ladd *Bobbie Jean* • Elizabeth Perkins *Lily* • Steve Buscemi *Cornell* • Alan Tudyk *Gerhardt* • Michael O'Malley [Mike O'Malley] *Oliver* • Marianne Jean-Baptiste *Roshanda* ■ *Dir* Betty Thomas • *Scr* Susannah Grant

28 Days Later... ★★★★18
Horror 2002 · UK/US/Neth · Colour · 108min

This Dogme-driven apocalyptic nightmare from director Danny Boyle is a tense, exciting and terrifying horror. As a highly contagious virus spreads across the country, locking its victims into a permanent state of homicidal rampage, four individuals who have so far escaped infection have to fight off the deranged hordes. This triumphantly executed piece of contemporary horror (written by *The Beach*'s slave labour) generates genuine shocks with its down-and-dirty violence and disturbing authenticity. Shot on digital video for a documentary feel, Garland's story grips on every level. AJ Swearing, sex scenes. *DVD* *Blu-ray*

Cillian Murphy *Jim* • Naomie Harris *Selena* • Christopher Eccleston *Major Henry West* • Megan Burns *Hannah* • Brendan Gleeson *Frank* • Noah Huntley *Mark* ■ *Dir* Danny Boyle • *Scr* Alex Garland

Twenty8k ★★15
Thriller 2012 · UK · Colour · 101min

Set against the backdrop of the 2012 Olympics, this convoluted, uninspired thriller is strewn with clichés and caricatures, which is surprising and disappointing given that it was co-written by Paul Abbott (*Shameless*, *State of Play*). Parminder Nagra works hard as the fashion executive who returns from Paris when brother Sebastian Nanena is arrested for murder. But her investigation lacks suspense and her encounters with a surfeit of sketchy secondary characters are perfunctory. DP Violence, swearing, sex scenes. *DVD* *Blu-ray*

Parminder Nagra *Deeva Jani* • Jonas Armstrong *Clint O'Connor* • Kaya Scodelario *Sally Weaver* • Nichola Burley *Andrea Patterson* • Stephen Dillane *DCI Edward Stone* • Kierston Wareing *Francesca Marchetto* ■ *Dir* David Kew, Neil Thompson (2) • *Scr* Jimmy Dowdall, Paul Abbott, from a story by David Kew, Ian & Neil Thompson

28 Weeks Later ★★★★18
Horror thriller
2007 · UK/US/Sp · Colour · 95min

Intacto director Juan Carlos Fresnadillo's sequel to Danny Boyle's *28 Days Later...* retains the grim tone and sense of dread but on a more epic scale. Survivors of the rage virus that devastated Britain are now quarantined on London's Isle of Dogs, as the US army tries to oversee the resettlement of the city. Among them is Robert Carlyle, whose wife (Catherine McCormack) is presumed dead. Evoking terror imagery from George A Romero's *The Crazies* and his *Dead* movies, Fresnadillo expertly orchestrates the gory action as Canary Wharf goes up in flames. AJ *DVD* *Blu-ray*

Robert Carlyle *Don* • Rose Byrne *Scarlet* • Jeremy Renner *Sgt Doyle* • Harold Perrineau *Flynn* • Catherine McCormack *Alice* • Mackintosh Muggleton *Andy* • Imogen Poots *Tammy* ■ *Dir* Juan Carlos Fresnadillo • *Scr* Rowan Joffe, Juan Carlos Fresnadillo, Jesus Olmo, EL Lavigne [Enrique López Lavigne]

Twenty Feet from Stardom ★★★★12
Music documentary 2013 · US · Colour · 87min

This Oscar-winning documentary turns the spotlight on the backing vocalists who've added harmonies to some of the best-known pop songs in history but still remain largely anonymous. The likes of Merry Clayton and Phil Spector stalwart Darlene Love recall tales of struggle between engagements and acceptance of life in the shadows when solo fame eludes them, while superstars Bruce Springsteen, Mick Jagger and Stevie Wonder sing the praises of their less heralded employees. Director Morgan Neville skilfully blends modern-day interviews with reams of archive footage, although he occasionally tries too hard to make his subjects' circumstances fit a tidy Cinderella template. That said, the eye-opening anecdotes come thick and fast, as he celebrates the vital components of some truly great music. TeS Some swearing. *DVD* *Blu-ray*

Darlene Love • Merry Clayton • Lisa Fischer • Táta Vega • Judith Hill • Mick Jagger • Bette Midler • Sting • Bruce Springsteen ■ *Dir* Morgan Neville

The 25th Hour ★★
Second World War drama
1967 · Fr/It/Yug · Colour · 118min

This lavishly made, episodic war epic stars Anthony Quinn as a Romanian peasant who is accused of being Jewish and condemned to slave labour. Shunned by the Jewish prisoners he becomes essentially stateless and thus a walking, talking metaphor. He changes sides and becomes a German soldier, all the time searching for his wife, Virna Lisi. AT In French.

Anthony Quinn *Johann Moritz* • Virna Lisi *Suzanna Moritz* • Grégoire Aslan *Nicolai Dobresco* • Michael Redgrave *Defense counsel* • Serge Reggiani *Trajan Koruga* • Marcel Dalio *Strul* • Marius Goring *Col Müller* • Alexander Knox *Prosecutor* • John Le Mesurier *Magistrate* ■ *Dir* Henri Verneuil • *Scr* Henri Verneuil, François Boyer, Wolf Mankowitz, from the novel *La Vingt-Cinquieme Heure* by Constantin Virgil Gheorghiu

25th Hour ★★★15
Drama 2002 · US · Colour · 129min

Fine ensemble acting and the frisson of this being the first film to use post-11 September Manhattan as a bleak character mirror make this edgy version of David Benioff's novel one of director Spike Lee's better dramas. Due to begin a seven-year prison sentence, drug dealer Edward Norton spends his last day of freedom taking stock of his life and weighing up his choices. Despite Lee's pace being a little too leisurely at times, the sense of human aimlessness and desolation is powerfully conveyed. AJ Violence, swearing, sex scenes, drug abuse, nudity. *DVD*

Edward Norton *Monty Brogan* • Philip Seymour Hoffman *Jacob Elinsky* • Barry Pepper *Francis Xavier Slaughtery* • Rosario Dawson *Naturelle Rivera* • Anna Paquin *Mary D'Annunzio* • Brian Cox (1) *James Brogan* • Tony Siragusa *Kostya Novotny* ■ *Dir* Spike Lee • *Scr* David Benioff, from his novel

24 Hour Party People ★★★★18
Comedy drama based on a true story
2001 · UK · Colour · 112min

Prolific director Michael Winterbottom is unafraid of mythologising a slice of recent musical/cultural history in this comedy drama, which tells the story of the rise and fall of Manchester's Factory Records and the world-famous Hacienda nightclub. Tony Wilson, played with relish by Steve Coogan, is in real life a self-publicist of gigantic proportions, so when he compares shambolic Happy Mondays singer Shaun Ryder (an uncanny impersonation by Danny Cunningham) to WB Yeats, you take it with a pinch of salt but buy into it anyway. This is a well-cast blend of evocative energy, fine vintage music and irreverent humour. AC Swearing, drug abuse, nudity. *DVD*

Steve Coogan *Tony Wilson* • Lennie James *Alan Erasmus* • Shirley Henderson *Lindsay Wilson* • Paddy Considine *Rob Gretton* • Andy Serkis *Martin Hannett* • Sean Harris *Ian Curtis* • Danny Cunningham *Shaun Ryder* ■ *Dir* Michael Winterbottom • *Scr* Frank Cottrell Boyce

The 24 Hour Woman ★★
Comedy drama 1999 · US · Colour · 93min

There are shades of the Diane Keaton vehicle *Baby Boom* in this comedy about a morning television show producer (Rosie Perez) who attempts to juggle career and baby. While the film does have some funny moments, it's mainly due to a bitchy supporting turn from Patti LuPone (as Perez's calculating boss) rather than Perez's screechy performance or the script from director Nancy Savoca. A disappointment. JB

Marianne Jean-Baptiste *Madeline Labelle* • Rosie Perez *Grace Santos* • Patti LuPone *Joan Marshall* • Margo Lynn *Karen Duffy* • Diego Serrano *Eddie Diaz* • Wendell Pierce *Roy Labelle* ■ *Dir* Nancy Savoca • *Scr* Nancy Savoca, Richard Guay

TwentyFourSeven ★★★15
Comedy drama 1997 · UK · BW · 92min

The first full-length feature from British director Shane Meadows provides the often under-used Bob Hoskins with his best role in years. Hoskins plays an amiable former boxer who sets up a council-estate fight club as a focus for the unharnessed energies of local youth. The performances, many of them from first-time actors, pack a punch, and Meadows brings a gritty feel to proceedings through his decision to shoot it all in black and white. DA Violence, swearing, drug abuse. *DVD*

Bob Hoskins *Alan Darcy* • Danny Nussbaum *Tim* • Justin Brady *Gadget* • James Hooton *Knighty* • Darren Campbell *Daz* • Karl Collins *Stuart* ■ *Dir* Shane Meadows • *Scr* Shane Meadows, Paul Fraser

20 Million Miles to Earth
★★★ **PG**

Science-fiction horror 1957 · US · BW · 79min

A spaceship returning from an expedition to Venus crashes near Sicily, releasing a fast-growing reptilian beast that rampages through Rome in one of animation master Ray Harryhausen's best fantasy films, and his own personal favourite. The snake-tailed giant Ymir monster is also one of Harryhausen's finest creations: it has a well-defined personality and evokes sympathy for its plight. The Ymir's fight with an elephant and the Roman locations add unique touches to this minor classic. **AJ**
DVD

William Hopper *Calder* • Joan Taylor *Marisa* • Frank Puglia *Dr Leonardo* • John Zaremba *Dr Judson Uhl* • Thomas B Henry *Thomas Browne Henry*] *General AD McIntosh* • Tito Vuolo *Police commissioner* ■ *Dir* Nathan Juran • *Scr* Bob Williams, Christopher Knopf, from a story by Charlott Knight, Ray Harryhausen

29 Acacia Avenue
★★★

Comedy 1945 · UK · BW · 84min

The film version of the West End success about a couple who return home unexpectedly after a holiday and surprise their teenage offspring fails to fully disguise its theatrical origins. It nevertheless makes for pleasant period entertainment, with particularly likeable performances from British veterans Gordon Harker and Betty Balfour as the parents. Today, though, the problems encountered seem relatively trivial, but it's nice to see stars Jimmy Hanley and Dinah Sheridan (once husband and wife) in their youth. **TS**

Gordon Harker *Mr Robinson* • Betty Balfour *Mrs Robinson* • Jimmy Hanley *Peter* • Carla Lehmann *Fay* • Hubert Gregg *Michael* • Jill Evans *Joan* • Henry Kendall *Mr Wilson* • Dinah Sheridan *Pepper* ■ *Dir* Henry Cass • *Scr* Muriel and Sydney Box, from the play by Denis Constanduros, Mabel Constanduros

29th Street
★★★ **15**

Comedy drama based on a true story
1991 · US · Colour · 97min

Frank Pesce Jr is a remarkable character. Cursed with a lucky streak that constantly seems to work against him, the garrulous New Yorker crops up in a cameo and also had a hand in the writing of this breezy comedy based on his win on the state lottery that ended up being more trouble than it was worth. Speaking Brooklynese like a native, Australian-born Anthony LaPaglia gives a spirited performance as Pesce, while Danny Aiello makes a splendid sparring partner as his opinionated father. But it's Lainie Kazan as Pesce's dotty mother who steals the show. **DP** **DVD**

Danny Aiello *Frank Pesce Sr* • Lainie Kazan *Mrs Pesce* • Anthony LaPaglia *Frank Pesce Jr* • Robert Forster *Sergeant Tartaglia* • Frank Pesce *Vito Pesce* • Donna Magnani *Madeline Pesce* • Ron Karabatsos *Philly the Nap* ■ *Dir* George Gallo • *Scr* George Gallo, from a story by Frank Pesce Jr, James Franciscus

Twenty-One
★★★ **15**

Drama 1991 · UK · Colour · 97min

Patsy Kensit has a long list of movies to her name, but it must to be said that most were forgettable. This, though, is one of her more commendable efforts: a brave, breezy 20-something comedy drama, with Kensit discovering the dating game is not all that it is cracked up to be. With her straight-to-camera observations, Kensit has a lot of weight to carry, but generally convinces as a sparky, independent young woman. **JF** Swearing, sex scenes, drug abuse, nudity.

Patsy Kensit *Katie* • Jack Shepherd *Kenneth* • Patrick Ryecart *Jack* • Maynard Eziashi *Baldie* • Rufus Sewell *Bobby* • Sophie Thompson *Francesca* • Susan Wooldridge *Janet* ■ *Dir* Don Boyd • *Scr* Don Boyd, Zoe Heller, from a story by Don Boyd

21
★★★ **12**

Drama based on a true story
2008 · US · Colour · 117min

In what must be the ultimate "revenge of the nerds" story, six maths students crunch numbers at the gaming tables of Las Vegas – and nearly break the bank. British actor Jim Sturgess brings a winning charm to the role of Ben, the lead player who agrees to the card-counting scam proposed by his professor (a menacing Kevin Spacey) in order to fund his education. Although based on Ben Mezrich's bestselling non-fiction account, the film plays fast and loose with the facts, adding a clichéd romance and an over-plotted revenge thriller element. Sturgess keeps the story anchored, however, and director Robert Luketic should get credit for the tense and exciting gaming scenes. **SP** Violence, sexual references, brief nudity. **DVD** **BL**

Jim Sturgess *Ben Campbell* • Kevin Spacey *Mickey Rosa* • Kate Bosworth *Jill Taylor* • Laurence Fishburne *Cole Williams* • Aaron Yoo *Choi* • Josh Gad *Miles* ■ *Dir* Robert Luketic • *Scr* Peter Steinfeld, Allan Loeb, from the non-fiction book *Bringing Down the House* by Ben Mezrich

21 and Over
★★ **15**

Comedy 2012 · US · Colour · 89min

In this loud and brash comedy, straight-A student Justin Chon's fun-loving buddies persuade him to go for a birthday drink the night before an important interview. Predictably, one beer leads to another and to ever-escalating high jinks, as the innocent young man is corrupted by loose women and wild parties. Writer/directors Jon Lucas and Scott Moore penned the original *Hangover* movie, but here liberally plunder a slew of broad frat-boy comedies, from *National Lampoon's Animal House* to *American Pie* and all points in between. Chon portrays the descent from golden boy to booze hound with vigour, but there's little on offer that hasn't been seen before. **TeS** **DVD** **BL**

Miles Teller *Miller* • Sarah Wright *Nicole* • Skylar Austin *Casey* • Justin Chon *Jeff Chang* • Jonathan Keltz *Randy* • François Chau *Dr Chang* ■ *Dir/Scr* Jon Lucas, Scott Moore

21 Days
★★★ **PG**

Melodrama 1937 · UK · BW · 71min

Here's a classy pedigree: Graham Greene co-wrote the screenplay of this Alexander Korda production based on a John Galsworthy West End hit. The story, about two lovers who spend precious time together before the man is tried for murder, features a well-cast Laurence Olivier making a dashing leading man, but it's his later real-life wife, the top-billed Vivien Leigh, who positively sparkles. Rather wordy, but still worthy. **TS**

Vivien Leigh *Wanda* • Laurence Olivier *Larry Durrant* • Leslie Banks *Keith Durrant* • Francis L Sullivan *Mander* • Hay Petrie *John Aloysius Evans* • Esme Percy *Henry Walenn* • Robert Newton *Tolly* • Victor Rietti *Antonio* ■ *Dir* Basil Dean • *Scr* Graham Greene, Basil Dean, from the play *The First and the Last* by John Galsworthy

21 Grams
★★★★ **15**

Drama 2003 · US/Ger · Colour · 119min

Showcasing some of the finest screen acting, Mexican director Alejandro González Iñárritu has created an astonishing account of faith and redemption. As with Iñárritu's first film, the acclaimed *Amores Perros*, an auto accident links three disparate lives: Naomi Watts's husband and two daughters have been killed by Benicio Del Toro's drunk-turned-Jesus freak; Sean Penn's professor receives the husband's heart and is drawn into an affair with his widow. Iñárritu again uses a non-linear, mosaic narrative technique to lure us into a maze of contradictions that eventually lead to revelation. An extraordinary vision. **TH** Swearing, violence, sex scenes, drug abuse. **DVD** **BL**

Sean Penn *Paul Rivers* • Benicio Del Toro *Jack Jordan* • Naomi Watts *Cristina Peck* • Charlotte Gainsbourg *Mary Rivers* • Melissa Leo *Marianne Jordan* • Eddie Marsan *Rev John* • Clea DuVall *Claudia* • Danny Huston *Michael* • Paul Calderon

21 Jump Street
★★★★ **15**

Action comedy 2012 · US · Colour · 105min

Though it shares the same title and basic premise as the cheesy 1980s TV show, there's not much else that this update drawn from *Cloudy with a Chance of Meatballs* co-directors Phil Lord and Christopher Miller has in common with the series that rocketed Johnny Depp to stardom. Channing Tatum and Jonah Hill play the dimwit cop duo who are sent back to their high school to pose as students in order to root out a drugs ring. While Jonah Hill is certainly a lot of fun as the needy nerd, it's pin-up Channing Tatum who really shines, and Depp appears in a cameo. **AS** Violence, swearing, sex scenes, drug abuse. **DVD** **BL**

Channing Tatum *Jenko* • Jonah Hill *Schmidt* • Dave Franco *Eric* • Ice Cube *Captain Dickson* • Brie Larson *Molly* • Rob Riggle *Mr Walters* • Johnny Depp *Tom Hanson* ■ *Dir* Phil Lord, Christopher Miller [Chris Miller] • *Scr* Michael Bacall, from a story by Bacall, Jonah Hill, from the TV series by Patrick Hasburgh, Stephen J Cannell

22 Jump Street
★★★★ **15**

Action comedy 2014 · US · Colour · 107min

Channing Tatum and Jonah Hill return for duty in this sequel to the 2012 cop comedy *21 Jump Street*. The big surprise here is that the partnership has lost none of its charm and, arguably, this outing is even funnier than the first. Here the duo is sent under cover in college by their hilariously hot-headed police captain (Ice Cube) in order to identify a drug dealer. But when Tatum gets pally with a suspect, Hill descends into jealousy and angst. Directors Phil Lord and Christopher Miller treat all the familiar elements of action sequels with a knowing wink, which might be overbearing were it not for Tatum and Hill, who send themselves up mercilessly. Explosive stunts aside, it's the chemistry between the guys that really sets the screen alight. **SP** Violence, swearing, sexual references. **DVD** **BL** **CS**

Jonah Hill *Schmidt* • Channing Tatum *Jenko* • Ice Cube *Captain Dickson* • Peter Stormare *Big Meat* • Amber Stevens *Maya* ■ *Dir* Phil Lord, Christopher Miller • *Scr* Michael Bacall, Oren Uziel, Rodney Rothman, from a story by Bacall, Jonah Hill, from the TV series *21 Jump Street* by Patrick Hasburgh, Stephen J Cannell

27 Dresses
★★★ **12**

Romantic comedy 2008 · US · Colour · 106min

In this fluffy, New York-set romantic comedy, Katherine Heigl (*Knocked Up*) plays a woman who is always the bridesmaid, never the bride – and she has 27 bridesmaid dresses in her wardrobe to prove it. Her story attracts the attention of newspaper wedding columnist James Marsden. He falls for Heigl, but she only has eyes for her oddly oblivious boss, Edward Burns) whose interest lies with her sister, Malin Akerman. The target audience for Anne Fletcher's film is unashamedly feminine and there's something oddly reassuring about the lack of surprises – it's like the cinematic equivalent of an old comfort blanket. **DA** Some swearing, sexual references. **DVD** **BL**

Katherine Heigl *Jane Nichols* • James Marsden *Kevin Doyle* • Malin Akerman *Tess* • Judy Greer *Casey* • Melora Hardin *Maureen* • Brian Kerwin *Hal* ■ *Dir* Anne Fletcher • *Scr* Aline Brosh McKenna

The 27th Day
★★★ **U**

Science fiction 1957 · US · BW · 75min

This quite extraordinary anti-communist tract masquerades as naïve science fiction. An alien gives five people from five different countries a box of capsules capable of destroying life on their continent if opened. The capsules become harmless after 27 days or on the owner's death. Suicide or destruction is the choice until the Russian emissary is ordered to annihilate the western world. A real Cold War curio

with a bizarre payoff despite pedestrian direction. **AJ**

Gene Barry *Jonathan Clark* • Valerie French *Eve Wingate* • George Voskovec *Professor Klaus Bechner* • Arnold Moss *The Alien* • Stefan Schnabel *Leader* • Ralph Clanton *Mr Ingram* • Friedrich Ledebur *Dr Karl Neuhaus* • Paul Birch *Admiral* ■ *Dir* William Asher • *Scr* John Mantley, from his novel

20,000 Days on Earth
★★★★★ **15**

Documentary 2014 · UK · Colour · 93min

This documentary about one day in the life of Nick Cave brilliantly encapsulates what makes the writer/musician tick, and does so in bravura style. Placing him against the backdrop of his adopted home town of Brighton, the Aussie singer holds forth on love, drugs, religion and the transformative power of performance. This is a man who has lived a life and has stories to share (including the funniest Nina Simone anecdote you're ever likely to hear), and the film is as intelligent, articulate and subtly mischievous as its subject. **JH** Swearing. **DVD** **BL**

Nick Cave • Warren Ellis • Ray Winstone • Kylie Minogue *Kylie Minogue* • Blixa Bargeld ■ *Dir* Iain Forsyth, Jane Pollard • *Scr* Iain Forsyth, Jane Pollard, Nick Cave

20,000 Leagues under the Sea
★★★ **U**

Silent adventure 1916 · US · BW · 83min

Captain Nemo (Allan Holubar) and his crew of the submarine *Nautilus* journey through the ocean depths to a tropical island to rescue Nemo's daughter, encountering challenges such as a fight with an octopus. Written and directed by Stuart Paton, this is an impressive achievement for so early a film. The pioneering Williamson brothers built an underwater camera for the production, which cost Universal founder Carl Laemmle such a fortune that even the film's popularity was unable to yield a profit. **RK**

Allan Holubar *Captain Nemo/Prince Daaker* • Jane Gail *A child of nature/Princess Daaker* • Dan Hanlon *Professor Aronnax* • Edna Pendleton *Aronnax's daughter* • Curtis Benton *Ned Land* • Matt Moore *Lt Bond* ■ *Dir* Stuart Paton • *Scr* Stuart Paton, from the novel by Jules Verne

20,000 Leagues under the Sea
★★★★ **U**

Adventure 1954 · US · Colour · 121min

James Mason is marvellous as submariner Captain Nemo in this beautifully designed (Oscars for art direction and special effects) and fabulously cast cinema retelling of Jules Verne's fantasy saga. Also on board the *Nautilus* is Kirk Douglas, who gives a bravura performance as harpoonist Ned Land, even using his own voice for the song *A Whale of a Tale*. Peter Lorre adds comic relief, while Paul Lukas and the underrated Robert J Wilke bring dignity to the proceedings. Director Richard Fleischer makes the most of the action sequences, notably a sensational battle with a giant squid. **TS** **DVD**

Kirk Douglas *Ned Land* • James Mason *Captain Nemo* • Paul Lukas *Professor Aronnax* • Peter Lorre *Conseil* • Robert J Wilke *Mate on the Nautilus* • Carleton Young *John Howard* • Ted De Corsia *Captain Farragut* ■ *Dir* Richard Fleischer • *Scr* Earl Felton, from the novel by Jules Verne

20,000 Leagues under the Sea
★★

Adventure 1997 · US · Colour · 95min

Condensed from a two-part mini-series, this ponderously scripted TV-movie dramatisation of Jules Verne's sci-fi classic has little to recommend it. Despite advances in techniques, the special effects can't hold a candle to the Oscar-winning art direction and effects work in Disney's 1954 version, and Ben Cross has none of the charismatic menace of James Mason as Captain Nemo. However, where it really falls down is in the decision to give Professor Aronnax (Richard Crenna) a daughter (Julie Cox), whose romantic dithering between

Nemo and Ned Land (Paul Gross) is somehow allowed to sideline the underwater adventure. **DP**

Richard Crenna *Professor Aronnax* • Ben Cross *Captain Nemo* • Paul Gross *Ned Land* • Julie Cox *Sophie Aronnax* • Michael Jayston *Admiral Sellings* • Jeff Harding *Captain Farragut* • David Henry *Scotia Captain* • Nicholas Hammond *Saxon* ■ *Dir* Michael Anderson • *Scr* Joe Wiesenfeld, from the novel by Jules Verne

20,000 Years in Sing Sing
★★★
Prison drama   1933 · US · Colour · 81min

One of Warner Bros' torrid crime melodramas, allegedly "torn from today's headlines", this is filmed in a quasi-documentary style and provides gutsy entertainment in the guise of moral enlightenment. Spencer Tracy is a jailed gangster taking on the prison authorities, and Bette Davis is his moll. The movie wears its social conscience on its sleeve, but it also remains solid enough, with good performances from the two stars and sleek direction from Michael Curtiz. **AT**

Spencer Tracy *Tom Connors* • Bette Davis *Fay* • Lyle Talbot *Bud* • Arthur Byron *Warden Long* • Grant Mitchell *Dr Ames* • Warren Hymer *Hype* • Louis Calhern *Joe Finn* ■ *Dir* Michael Curtiz • *Scr* Courtney Terrett, Robert Lord, Wilson Mizner, Brown Holmes, from the book by Warden Lewis E Lawes

23 Paces to Baker Street
★★★★ PG
Thriller   1956 · US · Colour · 98min

Former musical star Van Johnson confirms his acting versatility in this cracking London-set thriller, starring as a blind playwright who overhears dastardly doings. Londoners will enjoy seeing director Henry Hathaway's skew-whiff city geography, and there's a fair amount of on-screen fog. However, despite the clichés, the suspense is kept taut, the English support cast is faultless, and American import Vera Miles is sympathetic. **TS DVD**

Van Johnson *Philip Hannon* • Vera Miles *Jean Lennox* • Cecil Parker *Bob Matthews* • Patricia Laffan *Miss Alice MacDonald* • Maurice Denham *Inspector Grovening* • Estelle Winwood *Barmaid* • Liam Redmond *Mr Murch/Joe* ■ *Dir* Henry Hathaway • *Scr* Nigel Balchin, from the novel *A Warrant for X* by Philip MacDonald

22 Bullets
★★★ 18
Crime thriller based on a true story
2010 · Fr · Colour · 112min

Jean Reno stars in this decent French crime thriller, which is based on a true story. Reno plays a former Marseille crime boss who has decided to go straight. His former partner has 22 bullets pumped into him but Reno miraculously survives, and sets out for brutal and bloody vengeance. *22 Bullets* is neatly acted, nicely made and boasts complex characters that have depth. It hits the target, too, by portraying good and bad guys on both sides of the law. **DA** French +subtitles. Violence. **DVD** Blu-ray

Jean Reno *Charly Mattei* • Kad Merad *Tony Zacchia* • Jean-Pierre Darroussin *Martin Beaudinard* • Marina Foïs [Marina Fois] *Marie Goldman* • Luc Palu *Pascal Vasetto* • Richard Berry *Aurelio Rampoli* ■ *Dir* Richard Berry • *Scr* Richard Berry, Matthieu Delaporte, Alexandre de la Patellière, Eric Assous, from the novel *L'Immortel* by Franz-Olivier Giesbert

Twice in a Lifetime
★★★★ 15
Drama   1985 · US · Colour · 106min

The cast and production team use their considerable experience to good effect in this fine drama. Colin Welland, who won an Oscar for his *Chariots of Fire* screenplay, was responsible for the script, which tells an all-too-common story of a family being torn apart when the husband strays, in this case with a local barmaid on the eve of his 50th birthday. The well-judged performances by Gene Hackman as the blue-collar husband, Ellen Burstyn as his quietly despairing wife and Ann-Margret as the other woman help make Bud Yorkin's film a moving, and at times riveting, experience. **NF**

Twice round the Daffodils
★★ PG
Comedy   1962 · UK · BW · 85min

This is a watered-down *Carry On Nurse* set (tastefully) in a male tuberculosis ward, with nurse Juliet Mills running the show. The *Carry On* producer/director team of Peter Rogers and Gerald Thomas would occasionally make these forays away from their popular series, but would invariably use a similar cast. Here's Joan Sims and Kenneth Williams again, plus Donalds Sinden and Houston, chasing nurses Jill Ireland and Nanette Newman. Followed by *Nurse on Wheels*. **TS DVD**

Juliet Mills *Catty* • Donald Sinden *Ian Richards* • Donald Houston *John Rhodes* • Kenneth Williams *Harry Halfpenny* • Ronald Lewis *Bob White* • Joan Sims *Harriet Halfpenny* • Andrew Ray *Chris Walker* • Lance Percival *George Logg* • Jill Ireland *Janet* • Sheila Hancock *Dora* • Nanette Newman *Joyce* ■ *Dir* Gerald Thomas • *Scr* Norman Hudis, from the play *Ring for Catty* by Patrick Cargill, Jack Beale

Twice Told Tales
★★
Portmanteau horror   1963 · US · Colour · 119min

This crudely creepy anthology failed to give horror writer Nathaniel Hawthorne the same box-office cred already achieved by Edgar Allan Poe. Given the sparse production values and varying degrees of horror and atmosphere, it's not difficult to see why, despite the fine source material. Vincent Price discovers the elixir of eternal youth, tragically injects his beloved offspring with a potion that makes her lethal to the touch and tangles with warlocks and ancestral karma, in three different tales. **AJ**

Vincent Price *Alex Medbourne/Dr Rappaccini/Gerald Pyncheon* • Sebastian Cabot *Dr Carl Heidegger* • Mari Blanchard *Sylvia Ward* • Brett Halsey *Giovanni Guastconti* • Abraham Sofaer *Prof Pietro Baglioni* • Joyce Taylor *Beatrice Rappaccini* • Beverly Garland *Alice Pyncheon* • Richard Denning *Jonathan Maulle* • Jacqueline de Wit *Hannah* ■ *Dir* Sidney Salkow • *Scr* Robert E Kent, from stories by Nathaniel Hawthorne

Twice Two
★★★ U
Comedy   1933 · US · BW · 20min

Laurel and Hardy reached their creative peak in the 1930s with films that ranged from the sublime (*The Music Box*) to the ordinary. This oddity falls in between and revives a gimmick from *Brats* (1930), where they played their own sons. That film used elaborate sets and trick photography, but here they tackle four roles utilising clever editing. Stanley and Oliver have each married the other's twin sisters. They share a house and the "boys" work together. The nub of the story is a dinner during which the "girls" chaotically fall out. **BB DVD**

Stan Laurel *Stan/Mrs Hardy* • Oliver Hardy *Ollie/Mrs Laurel* • Baldwin Cooke *Soda jerk* • Charlie Hall *Delivery boy* • Ham Kinsey *Passer-by outside store* • Carol Tevis *Mrs Hardy* • Mae Wallace *Mrs Laurel* ■ *Dir* James Parrott • *Scr* Stanley Laurel

Twilight
★★★ 15
Detective drama   1998 · US · Colour · 90min

Gene Hackman, Susan Sarandon and Paul Newman star in this low-key detective drama that harks back to the heyday of *film noir*. Newman stars as a private eye who lives with cancer-stricken actor Hackman and his wife Sarandon. Asked to deliver blackmail money, Newman finds himself resurrecting a 20-year-old murder case involving Sarandon's ex-husband. Newman as a 70-something is still convincing in both action and love scenes, but the overall pace of the film tends towards the sluggish and reflective. **LH** Swearing, violence, sex scenes. **DVD**

Paul Newman *Harry Ross* • Susan Sarandon *Catherine Ames* • Gene Hackman *Jack Ames* • Stockard Channing *Verna* • Reese Witherspoon *Mel Ames* • Giancarlo Esposito *Reuben* • James Garner *Raymond Hope* • Liev Schreiber *Jeff Willis* ■ *Dir* Robert Benton • *Scr* Robert Benton, Richard Russo

Twilight
★★★ 12
Romantic horror fantasy
2008 · US/UK · Colour · 116min

A teenage girl falls for a vampire in the first film to be adapted from Stephenie Meyer's bestselling series of fantasy novels. Kristen Stewart is suitably enigmatic as the heroine, Bella, who's been sent to a small town in Washington state to live with her dad (Billy Burke). There she struggles to fit in at school, until a mutual attraction to handsome Edward (played by British actor Robert Pattinson) blossoms into a relationship that's fraught with danger. Pattinson (Cedric Diggory in the *Harry Potter* films) does tend to ham it up with his James Dean pose, but his chemistry with Stewart more than makes amends, and teenage audiences will no doubt forgive some overwrought moments in what is a charming tale. A sequel, *New Moon*, was released in 2009. **SP DVD** Blu-ray

Kristen Stewart *Bella Swan* • Robert Pattinson *Edward Cullen* • Taylor Lautner *Jacob Black* • Billy Burke *Charlie Swan* • Peter Facinelli *Dr Carlisle Cullen* • Elizabeth Reaser *Esme Cullen* • Nikki Reed *Rosalie Hale* • Ashley Greene *Alice Cullen* ■ *Dir* Catherine Hardwicke • *Scr* Melissa Rosenberg, from the novel by Stephenie Meyer

Twilight in the Sierras
★★
Western   1950 · US · Colour · 66min

One of the few varying elements in Roy Rogers's series of westerns was the type of criminal activity he thwarted. Here he's up against counterfeiting when a gang kidnaps a paroled practitioner of the art and force him to create plates for printing gold certificates. There's a shocking moment when Roy's steed, Trigger, takes a bullet in the neck. To fill out the running time, the film has a subplot about a mountain lion on the rampage, in addition to the usual handful of songs. **AE**

Dale Evans *Deputy Patricia Callahan* • Estelita Rodriguez *Lola Chavez* • Pat Brady *Dr Sparrow Biffle* • Russ Vincent *Ricardo Chavez* • George Meeker *Matt Brunner* ■ *Dir* William Witney • *Scr* Sloan Nibley

Twilight of Honor
★★★
Courtroom drama   1963 · US · BW · 104min

This is something of a *déjà vu* melodrama. Richard Chamberlain - on sabbatical from *Dr Kildare* - plays a small-town, small-time lawyer who takes on the defence of a young hooligan (Oscar nominee Nick Adams) aided by the sage advice of veteran attorney Claude Rains. Not exactly a star-making turn for Chamberlain but it's directed with some style. **TH**

Richard Chamberlain *David Mitchell* • Joey Heatherton *Laura Mae Brown* • Nick Adams *Ben Brown* • Claude Rains *Art Harper* • Joan Blackman *Susan Harper* • James Gregory *Norris Bixby* • Pat Buttram *Cole Clinton* • Jeanette Nolan *Amy Clinton* ■ *Dir* Boris Sagal • *Scr* Henry Denker, from the novel by Al Dewlen

Twilight People
★★ 15
Horror   1973 · Phil · Colour · 75min

This film from Filipino fright-master Eddie Romero has John Ashley transported to a remote South Pacific island where a crazed doctor is creating the usual half human/half animal rebellious menagerie. The nice line in crude monsters includes a flying bat man, an antelope man and blaxploitation icon Pam Grier as the Panther woman. A silly yet quite gory exploiter. **AJ**

John Ashley *Matt Farrell* • Pat Woodell *Neva Gordon* • Pam Grier *Panther woman* ■ *Dir* Eddie Romero • *Scr* Eddie Romero, Jerome Small • *Executive Producer* Roger Corman

The Twilight Samurai
★★★★ 12
Period drama   2002 · Jpn · Colour · 129min

Director Yoji Yamada adds a touch of family circumstance to ratchet up the tension in this period drama. There is a class-conscious desperation about the samurai hero, Hiroyuki Sanada, which makes the setting of the 19th century even more credible. Sanada holds a lowly position within his clan, and he's nicknamed Twilight Samurai (Tasogore Seibei) because he doesn't join them for after-work drinks, but heads home to look after his motherless daughters and their elderly grandmother. Then Rie Miyazawa, a battered wife, finds shelter in their home, brightening up their poverty-stricken existence. Yamada's film looks into the hearts of the men wielding the lethal weapons, and so achieves an inspirational quality. **TH** Japanese +subtitles. **DVD**

Hiroyuki Sanada *Iguchi Seibei* • Rie Miyazawa *Tomoe* • Ren Osugi *Kouda Toyotarou* • Mitsuru Fukikoshi *Michinojo Iinuma* • Min Tanaka *Yogo Zenemon* ■ *Dir* Yoji Yamada • *Scr* Yoji Yamada, Yoshitaka Asama, from novels by Shuhei Fujisawa

Twilight Zone: the Movie
★★★ 15
Portmanteau supernatural drama
1983 · US · Colour · 96min

Despite the involvement of Hollywood major league directors Steven Spielberg, John Landis and Joe Dante, it was Australian George Miller, responsible for cult hit *Mad Max* and its sequels, who produced the one truly scary section of this feature-length stab at Rod Serling's classic TV series. In Miller's tale, paranoid passenger John Lithgow is the only person on a plane who can see a creature gnawing away at the wings. The rest of the stories are a mixed bag, with Landis's contribution overshadowed by the controversial death of star Vic Morrow during filming. **JF** Violence, swearing.

Burgess Meredith *Narrator* • Dan Aykroyd *Passenger* • Albert Brooks *Driver* • Vic Morrow *Bill* • Doug McGrath *Larry* • Charles Hallahan *Ray* • Bill Quinn *Conroy* ■ *Dir* John Landis, Steven Spielberg, Joe Dante, George Miller (2) • *Scr* John Landis, George Clayton Johnson, Josh Rogan, Richard Matheson

Twilight's Last Gleaming
★★★★★ 15
Political thriller
1977 · US/W Ger · Colour · 137min

If Colonel Kurtz from *Apocalypse Now* had survived, he might have ended up like Burt Lancaster in this absolutely riveting thriller. Lancaster, a brilliant, medal-heavy war hero, decides to force the US government to come clean about why it fought in Vietnam. He does this by hijacking a nuclear missile silo and periodically raises the temperature by pushing the right buttons. While President Charles Durning sweats, Richard Widmark and the army gathers outside Lancaster's underground bunker. This is a clever, plausible and subversive movie that capitalised on President Carter's avowed policy of open government. **AT** Swearing, violence.

Burt Lancaster *Lawrence Dell* • Richard Widmark *Martin MacKenzie* • Charles Durning *President Stevens* • Melvyn Douglas *Zachariah Guthrie* • Paul Winfield *Willis Powell* • Burt Young *Augie Garvas* • Joseph Cotten *Arthur Renfrew* ■ *Dir* Robert Aldrich • *Scr* Ronald M Cohen, Edward Huebsch, from the novel *Viper Three* by Walter Wager

Twin Detectives
★★
Thriller   1976 · US · Colour · 78min

The whole point of this TV movie was to persuade executives to award a series to Lillian Gish, the veteran actress who began her career with pioneering director DW Griffith back in 1912. However, this tale of twin detectives who take on the gang behind a fake psychic racket lacks the invention to sustain its intriguing premise. More to the point, real-life twins Jim and Jon Hager simply don't have the screen presence to carry the action, despite the valiant efforts of director Robert Day to hide their inadequacies. **DP**

Jim Hager *Tony Thomas* • Jon Hager *Shep Thomas* • Lillian Gish *Billy Jo Haskins* • Patrick O'Neal (1) *Leonard Ranier* ■ *Dir* Robert Day • *Scr* Robert Specht, from a story by Robert Specht, Robert Carrington, Everett Chambers

Twin Dragons ★★★ PG
Action comedy 1992 · HK · Colour · 99min

This sprightly chopsocky comedy once again has Jackie Chan combining the styles of Bruce Lee and Charlie Chaplin to entertaining effect. As twins separated at birth, Chan keeps both girlfriends Maggie Cheung and Nina Chi Li and a gangster's gormless henchmen guessing through a series of slick set pieces. Such is the pace of the action that it's impossible to detect the seams between the scenes handled by co-directors Tsui Hark and Ringo Lam. DP Cantonese dubbed. *DVD*

Jackie Chan *Boomer/John Ma* · Cheung Man-Yuk [Maggie Cheung] *Barbara* · Nina Chi Li *Tammy* · Anthony Chan *Hotel staffer* · Philip Chan *Hotel manager* · John Wu [John Woo] *Priest* ■ *Dir* Lam Ling-Tung [Ringo Lam], Tsui Hark · *Scr* Barry Wong, Tsui Hark, Cheung Tung Jo, Yik Wong, Val Kuklowsky, Rod Dean

Twin Falls Idaho ★★ 15
Drama 1999 · US · Colour · 110min

Screenwriters and real-life brothers Mark and Michael Polish take a page from David Lynch in this bizarre movie. They also play the parts of Siamese twins holed up in a seedy hotel who are eventually befriended by hooker Michele Hicks. It starts off well, promising to be darkly funny, tragic and a fascinating look at the nature of twins. After Hicks's initially shocked character takes an active interest in the two, the movie's momentum comes to a dead halt and doesn't revive until the last 20 minutes. KB *DVD*

Michele Hicks *Penny* · Teresa Hill *Sissy* · Robert Beecher *D'Walt* · Michael Polish *Francis Falls* · Mark Polish *Blake Falls* · Patrick Bauchau *Miles* · Lesley Ann Warren *Francine* ■ *Dir* Michael Polish · *Scr* Michael Polish, Mark Polish

Twin Peaks: Fire Walk with Me ★★★★ 18
Cult drama 1992 · US · Colour · 134min

The exploding TV set at the beginning is the tip-off that David Lynch's deeply disturbing descent into Laura Palmer's private hell, which begins seven days before she's found wrapped in plastic, will pursue dark introspective themes that his landmark pseudo-psychic series dared only hint at. Undervalued on cinema release, the Sultan of Strange's Rubik cube glorification of the terror-filled magic of life is a spaced-out odyssey of extraordinary obsession and power. As one hypnotic sequence follows another, Lynch's startling contemplation on our unfair universe is a must for *Twin Peaks* freaks. AL Drug abuse, swearing, nudity. *DVD* BL

Sheryl Lee *Laura Palmer* · Ray Wise *Leland Palmer* · Moira Kelly *Donna Hayward* · David Bowie *Phillip Jeffries* · Chris Isaak *Special agent Chester Desmond* · Harry Dean Stanton *Carl Rodd* · Kyle MacLachlan *Special agent Dale Cooper* · Mädchen Amick *Shelly Johnson* ■ *Dir* David Lynch · *Scr* David Lynch, Robert Engels · *Cinematographer* Ronald Victor Garcia · *Music* Angelo Badalamenti

Twin Sisters of Kyoto ★★★★
Melodrama 1963 · Jpn · Colour · 107min

This Oscar-nominated class drama concerns sisters who were abandoned at birth because twins were reputed to bring bad luck. Now the daughter of a wealthy merchant, Chieko goes in search of her sibling, only for their contentment to be short-lived as she becomes convinced Naeko is attempting to steal her beau. Appearing in over 100 films, Shima Iwashita worked many times with Yasujiro Ozu and her husband, Masahiro Shinoda. But nothing surpasses her dual performance in this affecting study of identity and self-image which is handled with tact and insight by Noboru Nakamura. DP Japanese +subtitles.

Shima Iwashita *Chieko/Naeko* · Seiji Miyaguchi *Takichiro Sada* · Teruo Yoshida *Ryusuke Mizuki* · Tamotsu Hayakawa *Shinichi Mizuki* ■ *Dir* Noboru Nakamura · *Scr* Toshihide Gondo, from the novel *Koto* by Yasunari Kawabata

Twin Town ★★ 18
Black comedy 1997 · UK · Colour · 95min

Described by some as a Welsh *Trainspotting*, this muddled, Swansea-set black comedy does share some superficial similarities, but has none of the style, energy or invention of that movie. Real-life brothers Llyr Evans and Rhys Ifans (*Notting Hill*) are manic, moral-free young criminals who exact revenge when their builder father is refused compensation for an accident at work. There's no shortage of candid sex, drugs and rock 'n' roll, but the fun soon drains away and the tone turns really nasty. JC Sex scenes, drug abuse. *DVD*

Llyr Evans *Julian Lewis* · Rhys Ifans *Jeremy Lewis* · Dorien Thomas *Greyo* · Dougray Scott *Terry Walsh* · Biddug Williams *Mrs Mort* · Ronnie Williams *Mr Mort* ■ *Dir* Kevin Allen · *Scr* Kevin Allen, Paul Durden

Twin Warriors ★★ 15
Martial arts action drama 1993 · HK · Colour · 89min

The first and so far only pairing of two of the biggest names in Hong Kong film, Jet Li and Michelle Yeoh, this boasts enough astonishing martial arts action to allow you to overlook the clumsy storyline. Friends Li and Chin Siu-hou are monks and martial arts experts who part ways after a clash with their temple's leaders. Faced with an oppressive ruler the ambitious Chin is quickly won over to the dark side, leaving Li and new love Yeoh to lead a small group of rebels JF Cantonese dubbed. *DVD*

Jet Li *Zhang Junbao* · Michelle Yeoh *Siu Lin* · Chin Siu-hou *Chin Bo* · Fennie Yuen *Miss Li* · Yuen Chueng-Yan *Rev Ling* ■ *Dir* Yuen Woo-Ping · *Scr* Kwong Kim Yip

The Twinkle in God's Eye ★★ U
Western 1955 · US · BW · 72min

In this personally produced project, Mickey Rooney plays a former wild boy who turns over a new leaf to become a parson and brings religion to a frontier mining town. Rooney was so keen on the project he also wrote the title song (but refrains from singing it). In actual fact, Rooney's self-assurance suits the part and he converts the toughest of hombres as well as the dancing girls in the saloon. Coleen Gray co-stars as one of the floozies with Hugh O'Brian as the gambling hall proprietor. AE

Mickey Rooney *Reverend Macklin* · Coleen Gray *Laura* · Hugh O'Brian *Marty* · Joey Forman *Ted* ■ *Dir* George Blair · *Scr* PJ Wolfson

Twinky ★ 12
Romantic drama 1969 · UK/It · Colour · 87min

Richard Donner directs this abysmal relic from Swinging London that not even its distinguished supporting cast can salvage. Susan George plays a 16-year-old schoolgirl who elopes with an American novelist played by Charles Bronson. Both sets of parents are appalled. The audience is, too. AT *DVD*

Charles Bronson *Scott Wardman* · Susan George *Lola Twinky Londonderry* · Trevor Howard *Grandfather* · Honor Blackman *Mrs Londonderry* · Michael Craig *Mr Londonderry* · Robert Morley *Judge Roxburgh* · Jack Hawkins *Judge Millington-Draper* · Lionel Jeffries *Mr Creighton* · Orson Bean *Hal* ■ *Dir* Richard Donner · *Scr* Norman Thaddeus Vane

Twins ★★★★ PG
Comedy 1988 · US · Colour · 102min

Here's one of those rare things: a one-joke comedy that actually works. Danny DeVito plays the dim-witted scuzzball who discovers naive, intelligent Arnold Schwarzenegger is his genetically engineered brother. Comic moments abound as the odd couple team up to find their long-lost mom – Arnie's first awkward attempt at romance with Kelly Preston is a highlight. DeVito is on form and Arnie shows that he can handle comedy. JB Swearing. *DVD*

Arnold Schwarzenegger *Julius Benedict* · Danny DeVito *Vincent Benedict* · Kelly Preston *Marnie Mason* · Chloe Webb *Linda Mason* · Bonnie Bartlett *Mary Ann Benedict* · Marshall Bell *Webster* · Trey Wilson *Beetroot McKinley* · David Caruso *Al Greco* ■ *Dir* Ivan Reitman · *Scr* William Davies, William Osborne, Timothy Harris, Herschel Weingrod

Twins of Evil ★★★ 15
Horror 1971 · UK · Colour · 83min

Hammer ransacked J Sheridan Le Fanu's classic terror tale *Carmilla* for the last time in this completion of its trilogy following *The Vampire Lovers* and *Lust for a Vampire*. Mary and Madelaine Collinson, *Playboy* magazine's first twin centrefolds, play "which one's the vampire?" in a streamlined, if predictable, period piece laced with the usual quota of heaving bosoms, blood-red lipstick, lesbianism and gory decapitations. Touches of ethereal gothic atmosphere and a neat funereal flamboyancy lift this slick shock package. AJ *DVD* BL

Peter Cushing *Gustav Weil* · Kathleen Byron *Katy Weil* · Dennis Price *Dietrich* · Madelaine Collinson *Frieda Gellhorn* · Mary Collinson *Maria Gellhorn* · Damien Thomas *Count Karnstein* · David Warbeck *Anton Hoffer* · Isobel Black *Ingrid Hoffer* ■ *Dir* John Hough · *Scr* Tudor Gates, from the story *Carmilla* by J Sheridan Le Fanu

The Twist ★★
Comedy 1976 · Fr · Colour · 105min

When he's good he's exceptional, but when he's off form even the most devoted fan is hard pressed to explain the appeal of Claude Chabrol. Although at his best with thrillers, he has produced a number of incisive character studies, but he struggles to separate the poignant from the pretentious in this languid study of the infidelities and prejudices of diverse bourgeois couples. DP

Bruce Dern *William Brandeis* · Stéphane Audran *Claire Brandeis* · Sydne Rome *Nathalie* · Jean-Pierre Cassel *Jacques Lalovet* · Ann-Margret *Charlie Minerva* · Curd Jürgens [Curt Jurgens] *Jeweller* · Charles Aznavour *Dr Lartigue* ■ *Dir* Claude Chabrol · *Scr* Claude Chabrol, Norman Enfield, Ennio De Concini, Maria Pafusto, from Lucie Faure's novel *Le Malheur Fou*

A Twist of Sand ★★ U
Adventure 1967 · UK · Colour · 91min

Dubious opportunist Jeremy Kemp persuades Second World War submarine skipper Richard Johnson to make for the Skeleton Coast of Africa to retrieve some hidden diamonds in this lacklustre aquatic adventure. This sort of B-movie plotline was long past its sell-by date by 1967, and director Don Chaffey rather goes through the motions as his cast encounters some decidedly unspectacular storms and the usual underwater dangers. Honor Blackman just looks bored. DP

Richard Johnson *Geoffrey Peace* · Honor Blackman *Julie Chambois* · Jeremy Kemp *Harry Riker* · Peter Vaughan *Johann* · Roy Dotrice *David Carland* · Guy Doleman *Patrol boat commander* ■ *Dir* Don Chaffey · *Scr* Marvin H Albert, from the novel by Geoffrey Jenkins

Twisted ★★ 15
Crime thriller 2003 · US · Colour · 92min

Ashley Judd stars in this monotonous thriller from *Quills* director Philip Kaufman. Joined by Andy Garcia as her cop partner, she plays a newly-promoted police inspector hunting for a serial killer who's murdering her casual lovers. There are so many red herrings and so little real action that it all becomes tiresome, especially when Judd's contribution is a repeated cycle of drinking, passing out and waking up to find another corpse. SF Swearing, violence. *DVD*

Ashley Judd *Jessica Shepard* · Samuel L Jackson *John Mills* · Andy Garcia *Mike Delmarco* · David Strathairn *Dr Melvin Frank* · Russell Wong *Lieutenant Tong* · Camryn Manheim *Lisa* · Mark Pellegrino *Jimmy Schmidt* · Titus Welliver *Dale Becker* · DW Moffett *Ray Porter* · Richard T Jones *Wilson Jefferson* ■ *Dir* Philip Kaufman · *Scr* Sarah Thorp

Twisted Nerve ★★★ 18
Thriller 1968 · UK · Colour · 117min

In its day, this was a highly controversial and, to some, tasteless thriller. One would expect nothing less from Leo Marks, writer of *Peeping Tom*. But this time round, the story of a seemingly nice young man, who is in fact a homicidal maniac, went too far by implying a link between Down's syndrome and psychosis. Film-makers the Boulting Brothers had to add a disclaimer to the front of the film. Hayley Mills and Hywel Bennett, are ludicrously miscast, and suspense is not comedy director Roy Boulting's forte, but the bizarre story is still gripping, and the murders, though a long time coming, provide a suitably ghastly climax. DM *DVD*

Hayley Mills *Susan Harper* · Hywel Bennett *Martin Durnley/Georgie Clifford* · Billie Whitelaw *Joan Harper* · Phyllis Calvert *Enid Durnley* · Frank Finlay *Henry Durnley* · Barry Foster *Gerry Henderson* · Timothy West *Superintendent Dakin* ■ *Dir* Roy Boulting · *Scr* Leo Marks, Roy Boulting, from a story by Roger Marshall, from an idea by Roger Marshall, Jeremy Scott

Twister ★★★ PG
Action adventure 1996 · US · Colour · 108min

Speed director Jan De Bont takes destruction to new levels in this daft but breathtaking adventure, a salute to the daredevil meteorologists who chase the tornados that plague America's Midwest. Here, Bill Paxton stars as a TV weatherman who is drawn back to his dangerous former profession as a storm chaser to help estranged wife Helen Hunt place a tornado-measuring invention in the eye of a storm. Don't worry about the laboured storyline or the lack of chemistry between the leads; just enjoy the wondrous effects. JF Swearing. *DVD* BL

Bill Paxton *Bill Harding* · Helen Hunt *Jo Harding* · Jami Gertz *Melissa* · Cary Elwes *Dr Jonas Miller* · Lois Smith *Aunt Meg* · Alan Ruck *Rabbit* · Philip Seymour Hoffman *Dustin Davis* ■ *Dir* Jan De Bont · *Scr* Michael Crichton, Anne-Marie Martin

Twixt ★★★ 15
Horror thriller 2011 · US · Colour · 84min

Francis Ford Coppola returns to his B-movie roots with a playful and simply plotted horror whodunnit. Feeling like a mash-up of David Lynch and latter-day Tobe Hooper, this divisive and sometimes pretentious mix of gothic horror clichés, goofy humour and thinly veiled references is Coppola at his slightest and yet most liberated. Ultimately, it's pure fun that drives the events, a fact emphasised by the mischievous in-jokes, and Bruce Dern is marvellously exaggerated as an eccentric sheriff. SF *DVD*

Val Kilmer *Hall Baltimore* · Bruce Dern *Bobby LaGrange* · Ben Chaplin *Edgar Allan Poe* · Elle Fanning *V* · Joanne Whalley *Denise* · David Paymer *Sam Malkin* · Tom Waits *Narrator* ■ *Dir/Scr* Francis Ford Coppola

Two a Penny ★★★
Drama 1968 · UK · Colour · 99min

In 1966, while searching for a new direction, Cliff Richard found God via evangelist Billy Graham and this film followed shortly after. It is surprisingly well balanced – offering both pro and con viewpoints – and contains some fine performances from Dora Bryan, Avril Angers and other well-known character actors of the time. The obstacle is Cliff himself, who was already a popular family entertainer but is awkwardly miscast as a hoodlum who would rather push drugs than marry his Bible-thumping girlfriend. Today, of course, the film has considerable curiosity value. DM

Cliff Richard *Jamie Hopkins* · Dora Bryan *Ruby Hopkins* · Avril Angers *Mrs Burry* · Ann Holloway *Carol Turner* · Geoffrey Bayldon *Alec Fitch* · Peter Barkworth *Vicar* ■ *Dir* James F Collier · *Scr* Stella Linden

Two against the Law ★★★★
Crime drama 1973 · Fr/It · Colour · 100min

Trying to go straight after serving ten years for robbery, Alain Delon falls back on the support of Jean Gabin's social worker when his wife is killed in a car crash. However, a new romance with bank clerk Mimsy Farmer coincides with the escape of his former buddy, Victor Lanoux, and suspicious cop Michel Bouquet begins to turn up the heat. With its unforgettable final scene, the third and last collaboration between the iconic Gabin and young pretender Delon not only makes for a fascinating contrast between their acting styles, but also provides some penetrating insights into the problems facing released prisoners. DP French, Italian dubbed.

Alain Delon *Gino* • Mimsy Farmer *Lucy* • Michel Bouquet *Goitreau* • Victor Lanoux *Mariel* • Ilaria Occhini *Sophie* • Jean Gabin *Germain* ■ *Dir/Scr* José Giovanni

Two and Two Make Six
★★ U

Romantic comedy   1961 · UK · BW · 50min

Ace cinematographer Freddie Francis made his directorial debut with this trifle about a US Air Force deserter who rides off on his motorbike and falls in love with his pillion passenger. George Chakiris takes a leading film role for the first time and Janette Scott co-stars. Francis seemed happier with later horror fare and eventually went back behind the camera for such movies as *The Elephant Man.* TS

George Chakiris *Larry Curado* • Janette Scott *Irene* • Alfred Lynch *Tom* • Jackie Lane *[Jocelyn Lane] Julie* • Athene Seyler *Aunt Phoebe* • Bernard Braden *Sgt Sokolow* • Malcolm Keen *Harry Stoneham* • Ambrosine Philpotts *Lady Smith-Adams* ■ *Dir* Freddie Francis • *Scr* Monja Danischewsky

Two Arabian Knights ★★★

Silent romantic comedy   1927 · US · BW · 92min

Relative newcomer Lewis Milestone won an Oscar for best comedy direction (the only time this award was given) at the first Academy Awards ceremony. It tells of the rivalry between a tough sergeant (Louis Wolheim) and a smart private (William Boyd, the future Hopalong Cassidy) who seem to hate each other more than the enemy. But when they are captured by the Germans, they make their escape disguised as Arabs, and rescue a maiden (Mary Astor) from an evil bey. This profitable and amusing farce was only the second production of the 22-year-old Howard Hughes. RB

William Boyd (I) *Pte W Daingerfield Phelps* • Mary Astor *Anis Bin Adham* • Louis Wolheim *Sgt Peter McGaffney* • Michael Vavitch *Emir of Jaffa* • Boris Karloff *Purser* ■ *Dir* Lewis Milestone • *Scr* James T O'Donohue, Wallace Smith, George Marion Jr (titles)

Two Bits ★★★ 12

Period drama   1995 · US · Colour · 80min

Displaying ingenuity in adversity, a Depression-era kid concocts all manner of schemes to make the money he needs to attend the opening of a new movie theatre. Newcomer Jerry Barone is terrific as the tyke. Al Pacino is as excellent as ever as the kid's inspirational but dying grandad, and there's good support from Mary Elizabeth Mastrantonio as Barone's mum. With a crack cast and crew, this is solid entertainment. DA *DVD*

Mary Elizabeth Mastrantonio *Luisa* • Al Pacino *Grandpa* • Jerry Barone *Gennaro* • Patrick Borriello *Tullio* • Andy Romano *Dr Bruna* • Donna Mitchell *Mrs Bruna* ■ *Dir* James Foley • *Scr* Joseph Stefano

Two-Bits and Pepper ★★ PG

Comedy   1995 · US · Colour · 88min

This is a rather dire, though quirky, *Home Alone* rip-off, with Joe Piscopo starring in a dual role as a pair of burglars who kidnap a couple of girls and decide to hold them for ransom. It gets decidedly weird when the girls outwit their captors with the help of two Mr Ed-like talking horses. While funny in places, this is too uneven and downright silly to work for its entire running time, despite the presence of deft comedian Piscopo. JB *DVD*

Joe Piscopo *Spider/Zike* • Lauren Eckstrom *Tyler* • Rachel Crane *Katie* • Perry Stephens *Roger* • Kathrin Lautner *Carla* • Dennis Weaver *Sheriff Pratt* • Shannon Gallant *Monica* • Ethan Erickson *Boyfriend* ■ *Dir/Scr* Corey Michael Eubanks

Two Brothers ★★★ U

Period adventure drama
2004 · Fr/UK · Colour · 100min

As he proved with *The Bear* (1988), Jean-Jacques Annaud has always had a way with animals, and the tigers Kumal and Sangha are the undoubted stars of this uneven melodrama set in French Indochina during the 1920s. The opening sequences in which the parents mate and the cubs find their feet are enchanting. But once big-game hunter Guy Pearce stumbles across the family and captures the adorably clumsy Kumal, the action is hijacked by the humans, who are not as engaging. DP
DVD

Guy Pearce *Aidan McRory* • Jean-Claude Dreyfus *Eugène Normandin* • Philippine Leroy-Beaulieu *Mathilde Normandin* • Freddie Highmore *Young Raoul* • Vincent Scarito *Zerbino* • Stéphanie Lagarde *Miss Paulette* • Le Mai Anh *Nai-Rea* • Moussa Maaskri *Saladin* • Oanh Nguyen *Prince* ■ *Dir* Jean-Jacques Annaud • *Scr* Jean-Jacques Annaud, Alain Godard, from an idea by Jean-Jacques Annaud

Two by Two ★★★ U

Animated comedy adventure
2015 · Ger/Bel/Lux/Ire · Colour · 86min

This animated, all-animal take on the Noah's Ark tale isn't the most original film you'll ever see, referencing *Ice Age* and *Rio*, but it's still fast-paced fun for kids. A couple of colourful creatures, Finny and Leah, are accidentally left behind as the ark sails, and they have to team up to fight both rising flood waters and flying predators. Although derivative, *Two by Two* is bright and breezy, and will captivate youngsters without offering much for accompanying adults. DA

Callum Maloney *Finny* • Ava Connolly *Leah* • Tara Flynn *Hazel* • Paul Tylak *Obesey* • Dermot Magennis *Dave/Mr Griffin* • Aileen Mython *Mrs Griffin* ■ *Dir* Toby Genkel, Sean McCormack • *Scr* Toby Genkel, Richard Conroy, Mark B Hodkinson, Marteinn Thorisson

Two Can Play That Game ★★★ 15

Romantic comedy   2001 · US · Colour · 87min

Mark Brown makes a sharply observed directorial debut with this likeable and intelligent movie about relationships. It's as perky and attractive as its female protagonists – a group of sassy African-Americans who turn to their best friend Shanté (a delightful Vivica A Fox) whenever man trouble dampens their spirits. However, when Fox's boyfriend Morris Chestnut is caught with his arch rival, it's time for the love guru to follow her own "Ten Day Plan" to get him back in line. Spiked with astute observations, this is a well-acted and funny battle of the sexes. SF Swearing. *DVD*

Vivica A Fox *Shanté Smith* • Morris Chestnut *Keith Fenton* • Anthony Anderson *Tony* • Gabrielle Union *Conny* • Wendy Raquel Robinson *Karen* • Tamala Jones *Tracye Edwards* • Mo'Nique *Diedre* • Ray Wise *Bill Parker* ■ *Dir/Scr* Mark Brown

2 Days in New York ★★ 15

Comedy drama
2011 · Ger/Fr/Belize · Colour · 95min

Actress Julie Delpy goes back behind the camera for this fractured follow-up to her 2007 romantic comedy *2 Days in Paris*. Delpy once again stars as the neurotic Marion, however, Adam Goldberg (her boyfriend in the first film) is no longer on the scene. Marion now lives with radio host Mingus, played by motormouth comic Chris Rock. Mingus has got a few of his own issues to work out, which come to the fore when Marion's vulgar French family come to stay. On the surface, this has the look of a Woody Allen film, but it lacks his sharp insights or really scathing one-liners. Rock has the best scene: an improvised skit with a cardboard cut-out of President Obama.

It's just a shame that all the other characters are equally two-dimensional. SP

Julie Delpy *Marion* • Chris Rock *Mingus* • Alexia Landeau *Rose* • Albert Delpy *Jeannot* • Alexandre Nahon [Alex Nahon] *Manu* • Julie Delpy • *Scr* Julie Delpy, Alexia Landeau, from a story by Alexandre Nahon, Landeau, Delpy, from characters by Delpy

2 Days in Paris ★★★ 15

Romantic comedy drama
2006 · Fr/Ger · Colour · 96min

Paris may be known as the city of lovers and romance, but in Julie Delpy's second directorial outing it's turned into a place of heartache and recrimination. This acerbic comedy of errors follows a New York couple Marion (Delpy) and Jack (Adam Goldberg) as they stop off in Paris to visit Marion's parents (played by the director's real-life mother and father, Marie Pillet and Albert Delpy). Pretty soon Parisian life is taking its toll, as racist cabbies, undersized French condoms and Marion's seemingly endless parade of ex-lovers drive their relationship onto the rocks. Shot on a limited budget, the joy of Delpy's film lies in the smart, occasionally offbeat dialogue, while the two leads manage to hold the slight story together and invest it with surprising poignancy. JR English, French +subtitles. *DVD*

Julie Delpy *Marion* • Adam Goldberg *Jack* • Daniel Brühl *Lukas* • Marie Pillet *Anna* • Albert Delpy *Jeannot* • Alexia Landeau *Rose* • Adan Jodorowsky *Mathieu* • Alex Nahon *Manu* ■ *Dir/Scr* Julie Delpy

2 Days in the Valley ★★★ 18

Comedy crime thriller
1996 · US · Colour · 104min

This interestingly quirky and occasionally steamy comedy tips its hat at Tarantino's *Pulp Fiction* and Robert Altman's *Short Cuts*. Danny Aiello, James Spader, Teri Hatcher, Jeff Daniels and then-unknown Charlize Theron play just some of the unusual characters who inhabit the strange environs of LA in this amoral and often bizarre tale. Writer/director John Herzfeld is better known for less hip fare, including a number of TV movies. JB Swearing, violence, sex scenes. *DVD*

Danny Aiello *Dosmo Pizzo* • Greg Cruttwell *Allan Hopper* • Jeff Daniels *Alvin Strayer* • Teri Hatcher *Becky Foxx* • Glenne Headly *Susan Parish* • Peter Horton *Roy Foxx* • Marsha Mason *Audrey Hopper* • Paul Mazursky *Teddy Peppers* • Charlize Theron *Helga Svelgen* • James Spader *Lee Woods* ■ *Dir/Scr* John Herzfeld

Two Days, One Night ★★★★ 15

Drama   2014 · Bel/It/Fr · Colour · 91min

Costumed with a scrunchie and cheap vests so as to look convincingly like an ordinary working-class woman, Marion Cotillard gives her formidable all as Sandra, a woman on the verge of losing her job in this urgent, humanist drama from the Dardennes brothers. As the hours tick away, the film-makers work up a great head of tension, but some viewers may have the feeling that they've seen this sort of high-minded drama from the Dardennes before. LF French +subtitles. Some violence, swearing. *DVD* ⊞

Marion Cotillard *Sandra* • Fabrizio Rongione *Manu* • Pili Groyne *Estelle* • Simon Caudry *Maxime* • Catherine Salée *Juliette* ■ *Dir/Scr* Jean-Pierre Dardenne, Luc Dardenne

Two Deaths ★★★ 18

Drama   1994 · UK · Colour · 98min

Director Nicolas Roeg and screenwriter Allan Scott have shifted the scene from Chile to Romania for this adaptation of Stephen Dobyns's novel. This set-bound drama could be situated anywhere, however, and it would still have the same resonance. There's no escaping the theatricality of the piece, but the story that unfolds over dinner is both compelling and disturbing. Michael Gambon effortlessly conveys pride and regret as he reveals how he has mistreated his housekeeper, Sonia Braga, whose statuesque dignity masks a

burning desire for revenge. Far from Roeg's best, but still solid. DP Violence, a sex scene, nudity.

Michael Gambon *Daniel Pavenic* • Sonia Braga *Ana Puscasu* • Patrick Malahide *George Buscan* • Ion Caramitru *Carl Dalakis* • Nickolas Grace *Marius Vernescu* • Lisa Orgolini *Young Ana* • Niall Refoy *Young Pavenic* ■ *Dir* Nicolas Roeg • *Scr* Allan Scott, from the novel *The Two Deaths of Senora Puccini* by Stephen Dobyns

Two Evil Eyes ★★★ 18

Horror   1990 · It/US · Colour · 114min

Masters of horror George A Romero and Dario Argento joined forces to create this double bill based on a pair of Edgar Allan Poe stories. Romero's contribution is *The Facts in the Case of M Valdemar*, in which a man is mesmerised at the moment of death but with awful consequences. Poe's slim story is stretched to no avail, and the new material is handled in a conventional TV style. Argento's version of *The Black Cat* is more successful. The adaptation, a radical update involving Harvey Keitel as a photographer who goes mad and murders his girlfriend, is again overlong but builds to a mad and bloody climax. DM *DVD*

Adrienne Barbeau *Jessica Valdemar* • EG Marshall *Steven Pike* • Bingo O'Malley *Ernest Valdemar* • Harvey Keitel *Rod Usher* • Madeleine Potter *Annabel* • John Amos *Legrand* • Sally Kirkland *Eleonora* • Martin Balsam *Mr Pym* • Kim Hunter *Mrs Pym* ■ *Dir* George A Romero, Dario Argento • *Scr* George A Romero, Dario Argento, Franco Ferrini, from the stories *The Facts in the Case of M Valdemar* and *The Black Cat* by Edgar Allan Poe • *Music* Pino Donaggio

Two-Faced Woman ★★★

Screwball comedy   1941 · US · BW · 93min

Greta Garbo's last movie is nowhere near as bad as contemporary reviews would have you believe, and certainly didn't warrant the most fabulous female screen face of all opting for a retirement that would last until her death almost 50 years later. There's much to enjoy in this sophisticated comedy, especially Garbo dancing the "Chica-Chocka". The risqué material led to the Catholic League of Decency condemning the movie, and it was actually banned in Australia. Today we can appreciate it for what it is: a very well-performed piece of froth. TS

Greta Garbo *Karin Borg Blake/Katherine Borg* • Melvyn Douglas *Larry Blake* • Constance Bennett *Griselda Vaughn* • Roland Young *OO Miller* • Robert Sterling *Dick Williams* • Ruth Gordon *Miss Ellis* ■ *Dir* George Cukor • *Scr* SH Behrman, Salka Viertel, George Oppenheimer, from the play by Ludwig Fulda

The Two Faces of Dr Jekyll ★★ 15

Erotic horror   1960 · UK · Colour · 84min

Hammer's flop version of the overworked Robert Louis Stevenson classic grafts on Oscar Wilde's *The Picture of Dorian Gray* for extra literacy amid the tired gothic chills. This time the old and weak Jekyll (Paul Massie) transforms into a dashing and virile playboy with an eye for London's cancan girls. Christopher Lee lends his usual excellent support as the lecherous best friend. AJ *DVD*

Paul Massie *Dr Henry Jekyll/Mr Edward Hyde* • Dawn Addams *Kitty Jekyll* • Christopher Lee *Paul Allen* • David Kossoff *Ernest Litauer* • Francis De Wolff *Inspector* • Norma Marla *Maria* • Joy Webster *Sphinx girl* • Magda Miller *Sphinx girl* • Oliver Reed *Bouncer* ■ *Dir* Terence Fisher • *Scr* Wolf Mankowitz, from the novel by Robert Louis Stevenson

The Two Faces of January ★★★★ 12

Thriller   2013 · Fr/UK/US/Lux · Colour · 92min

Drive scriptwriter Hossein Amini makes an admirable directing debut with this atmospheric 1960s-set thriller based on Patricia Highsmith's 1964 novel. Viggo Mortensen plays an American conman on the run, who arrives in Athens with his wife (Kirsten Dunst). When he accidentally kills a private detective, he persuades their scam-artist tour guide (Oscar Isaac) to help and the trio enter a high-stakes game as they attempt flee the country. True, it shares plenty with *The Talented Mr Ripley* – sun, superb scenery and sexual tension – but it's also an enticing, intelligent and well-crafted minor gem in its own right. AJ English, Greek, Turkish +subtitles. Swearing, some violence. DVD BL

Viggo Mortensen *Chester MacFarland* • Kirsten Dunst *Colette MacFarland* • Oscar Isaac *Rydal* • Daisy Bevan *Lauren* • Yigit Ozsener *Yahya* ■ *Dir* Hossein Amini • *Scr* Hossein Amini, from Patricia Highsmith's novel

2 Fast 2 Furious ★★★ 12

Action thriller   2003 · US/Ger · Colour · 102min

You'll miss Vin Diesel – model-turned-actor Tyrese is no substitute – but director John Singleton's splashily shallow sequel provides enough revved-up cheap thrills to make the grade. Paul Walker is back as the discredited cop, who is trying to infiltrate the evil empire of Miami drugs baron Cole Hauser. Just about on his side are his old pal Tyrese and Hauser's mistress (Eva Mendes). How they halt Hauser's escape into wealthy exile without help from the apparently inept FBI is entertaining if standard-issue stuff (clue: it involves lots of cars). A second sequel followed in 2006. AJ Violence, swearing. DVD BL

Paul Walker *Brian O'Conner* • Tyrese [Tyrese Gibson] *Roman Pearce* • Eva Mendes *Monica Fuentes* • Cole Hauser *Carter Verone* • Chris "Ludacris" Bridges *Tej* • James Remar *Agent Markham* • Thom Barry *Agent Bilkins* • Michael Ealy *Slap Jack* • Mark Boone Junior *Detective Whitworth* ■ *Dir* John Singleton • *Scr* Michael Brandt, Derek Haas, from a story by Michael Brandt, Derek Haas, Gary Scott Thompson, from characters by Gary Scott Thompson

Two Flags West ★★★ U

Wartime western   1950 · US · BW · 91min

It took a lot of nerve for anyone but John Ford to make cavalry westerns, but writer/producer Casey Robinson and director Robert Wise gave it a good try with this dramatic story built on the fact that Confederate prisoners were allowed to serve in Union army posts out west during the Civil War. Jeff Chandler makes a strong impression as an embittered commanding officer; Joseph Cotten is the Confederate leader plotting to escape. There's more talk and less action than in most westerns, but director Wise brings the fort setting to life and stages the final Apache attack with considerable vigour. AE

Joseph Cotten *Col Clay Tucker* • Linda Darnell *Elena Kenniston* • Jeff Chandler *Maj Henry Kenniston* • Cornel Wilde *Capt Mark Bradford* • Dale Robertson *Lem* • Jay C Flippen *Sgt Terrance Duffy* • Noah Beery [Noah Beery Jr] *Cy Davis* • Harry Von Zell *Ephraim Strong* ■ *Dir* Robert Wise • *Scr* Casey Robinson, from a story by Frank S Nugent, Curtis Kenyon

Two for Texas ★★★ 15

Western   1998 · US · Colour · 92min

Going over familiar historical territory, this made-for-cable western is a high quality, pacey retelling of the war between the fledgling United States and Mexico over who gets to own Texas. This time around, though, the valiant last stand of Davy Crockett and company at the Alamo is only one part of the story, with director Rod Hardy opting to look at the aftermath as well. The story itself is seen from the perspective of two escaped convicts, Kris Kristofferson and Scott Bairstow, who inadvertently find themselves caught up in the making of history. JF Violence.

Kris Kristofferson *Hugh Allison* • Scott Bairstow *Son Holland* • Tom Skerritt *Sam Houston* • Peter Coyote *Jim Bowie* • Irene Bedard *Sana* • Victor Rivers *Emile Landry* ■ *Dir* Rod Hardy • *Scr* Larry Brothers, from the novel by James Lee Burke

Two for the Money ★★ 15

Comedy drama   2005 · US · Colour · 117min

Al Pacino proffers yet another variant on his patented crazy-but-charismatic mentor routine in this morality tale set in the world of high-stakes betting. After an injury ends his football career, former college quarterback Matthew McConaughey gets a

job dishing out sporting tips on a dial-up advice line. He's recruited into the big time by a shady entrepreneur and TV personality (Pacino). It's business as usual for a shouty Pacino and the rest of the competent but unstretched cast. LF Swearing, sex scenes, violence. DVD BL

Al Pacino *Walter Abrams* • Matthew McConaughey *Brandon Lang/John Anthony* • Rene Russo *Toni Morrow* • Armand Assante *Novian* • Jeremy Piven *Jerry* • Jaime King *Alexandria* ■ *Dir* DJ Caruso • *Scr* Dan Gilroy

Two for the Road ★★★★ PG

Comedy drama   1967 · UK/US · Colour · 106min

The relationship of Audrey Hepburn and Albert Finney, from the youthful idyll of their love affair and early years of marriage through the stages of disillusion to the brink of collapse, is told in a series of sometimes confusing flashbacks and flash-forwards. Directed by Stanley Donen with his customary flair, the comedy drama is played out in glossy French locations as the couple make a series of road trips across the country over a period of 12 years. Frederic Raphael's Oscar-nominated screenplay is a quintessentially Swinging Sixties piece, reflecting both the strengths and weakness of the period. Hepburn evinces a range of emotions with controlled subtlety, while Finney is also excellent. RK DVD BL

Audrey Hepburn *Joanna Wallace* • Albert Finney *Mark Wallace* • Eleanor Bron *Cathy Manchester* • William Daniels (2) *Howard Manchester* • Claude Dauphin *Maurice Dalbret* • Nadia Gray *Françoise Dalbret* ■ *Dir* Stanley Donen • *Scr* Frederic Raphael

Two for the Seesaw ★★ PG

Romantic comedy drama
1962 · US · BW · 114min

Jewish dancer Shirley MacLaine befriends Robert Mitchum, a sultry out-of-towner who arrives in New York after his marriage breaks up. Based on a 1950s Broadway play, it's really an extended conversation piece about the moral climate of the time, with the camera anchored to the spot while the stars wade through the reams of dialogue. It looks tame today, but the British censor thought all this "adult" talk worthy of an X-rating. AT DVD

Robert Mitchum *Jerry Ryan* • Shirley MacLaine *Gittel Mosca* • Edmon Ryan *Taubman* • Elisabeth Fraser *Sophie* • Eddie Firestone *Oscar* • Billy Gray *Mr Jacoby* ■ *Dir* Robert Wise • *Scr* Isobel Lennart, from the play by William Gibson

Two Gentlemen Sharing ★★

Drama   1969 · UK · Colour · 106min

One of the many daring, if trendy attacks on racial prejudice and class barriers that 1960s television and cinema specialised in. Ted Kotcheff's film focuses on the love lives of a white, aristocratic advertising executive and a black Jamaican lawyer – both Oxford graduates – sharing a flat in London. There are few surprises on offer, but the film is competently acted, particularly by flatmates Robin Philips and Hal Frederick and love interest Judy Geeson. JG

Robin Phillips *Roddy* • Judy Geeson *Jane* • Hal Frederick *Andrew* • Esther Anderson *Caroline* • Norman Rossington *Phil* • Hilary Dwyer *Ethne* • Rachel Kempson *Mrs Ashby-Kydd* ■ *Dir* Ted Kotcheff • *Scr* Evan Jones, from the novel by David Stuart Leslie

Two Girls and a Guy ★★★★ 18

Comedy drama   1997 · US · Colour · 82min

Robert Downey Jr gives a superb performance as the egotistical struggling actor who is confronted by his two girlfriends – neither of whom knew the other existed – when he returns to his New York home following a trip. The film takes place almost entirely in the apartment, as Heather Graham and Natasha Gregson Wagner battle it out for the man both believed was perfect but whom they've discovered is anything but. More like a riveting performance piece than a narrative film, writer/director James Toback's darkly comic story of infidelity is every actor's

dream and a fascinating experiment. JB Swearing, a sex scene.

Robert Downey Jr *Blake Allen* • Natasha Gregson Wagner *Lou* • Heather Graham *Carla* • Angel David *Tommy* • Frederique Van Der Wal *Carol* ■ *Dir/Scr* James Toback

Two Girls and a Sailor ★★★ U

Musical   1944 · US · Colour · 124min

This overlong MGM extravaganza is rewarding if you feel inclined to stick with it. Highlights include Jimmy Durante in his bizarre prime and Lena Horne singing *Paper Doll*. As for the two girls of the title, who are a wartime nightclub song-and-dance act, June Allyson seems too knowing, but the always underrated Gloria DeHaven charms, while Van Johnson gives a delightful, easy-going performance of great charisma. Look for a very young Ava Gardner in support. TS

June Allyson *Patsy Deyo* • Gloria DeHaven *Jean Deyo* • Van Johnson *John "Johnny" Dyckman Brown III* • Tom Drake *Sgt Frank Miller* • Henry Stephenson *John Dyckman Brown I* • Henry O'Neill *John Dyckman Brown II* • Jimmy Durante *Billy Kipp/"Junior" Kipp* • Ava Gardner *Canteen dancer* ■ *Dir* Richard Thorpe • *Scr* Richard Connell, Gladys Lehman

2 Guns ★★★★ 15

Action crime drama   2013 · US · Colour · 104min

Denzel Washington and Mark Wahlberg headline a smart and zesty thriller as agents embedded in a Mexican narcotics syndicate, unaware of each other's true identity. That is until they're hung out to dry by their respective bureaus and a botched bank raid puts a price on their heads. Director Baltasar Kormakur, who worked with Wahlberg a year previously on *Contraband*, delivers a well-paced and action-packed adventure confidently marshalling the myriad plot twists without ever losing sight of the storyline. TeS Violence, swearing. DVD

Denzel Washington *Robert "Bobby" Trench* • Mark Wahlberg *Michael "Stig" Stigman* • Paula Patton *Deb Rees* • Bill Paxton *Earl* • James Marsden *Quince* • Edward James Olmos *Papi Greco* ■ *Dir* Baltasar Kormakur • *Scr* Blake Masters, from a comic book by Steven Grant

Two Hands ★★★ 15

Crime comedy   1999 · Aus · Colour · 99min

Heath Ledger and Bryan Brown star in this stylish, slyly scripted urban crime caper, with a neat twist that makes amends for some failed gambits. The decision to have the proceedings narrated by Ledger's dead brother is unfortunate, as is a contrivance involving a street urchin. Moreover, the storyline, in which a routine courier job on behalf of Mob boss Brown goes wrong, is doggedly predictable. Yet, the bank raid sequence has a pleasing knockabout quality and Ledger's attempt to seduce country girl Rose Byrne is winningly awkward. DP Violence. DVD

Heath Ledger *Jimmy* • Bryan Brown *Pando* • David Field *Acko* • Rose Byrne *Alex* • Susie Porter *Deirdre* • Steven Vidler *Michael/The Man* ■ *Dir/Scr* Gregor Jordan

200 Cigarettes ★★ 15

Romantic comedy   1999 · US · Colour · 97min

What looks very promising – a 20-something comedy starring top Hollywood young guns – is disappointing. Ben Affleck and brother Casey, Courtney Love, Jay Mohr and Christina Ricci are all angst-ridden young adults trying to get their lives in gear. But we've seen these relationship and insecurity problems played out ad infinitum and sadly this has a feel of a sitcom not worthy of the silver screen. LH Swearing, sex scenes.

Ben Affleck *Bartender* • Casey Affleck *Tom* • Angela Featherstone *Caitlyn* • Janeane Garofalo *Ellie* • Kate Hudson *Cindy* • Courtney Love *Lucy* • Jay Mohr *Jack* • Martha Plimpton *Monica* • Christina Ricci *Val* • Paul Rudd *Kevin* ■ *Dir* Risa Bramon Garcia • *Scr* Shana Larsen

200 Motels ★★★

Music documentary   1971 · US · Colour · 95min

Taking a leaf out of the cute anarchy of *A Hard Day's Night*, directors Frank Zappa and Tony Palmer invest Zappa's own music (performed by the Mothers of Invention) with animation, sketches and jokes, much of it skewed towards a comic critique of touring, rock-band style. As with Zappa's own brand of guitar hysteria, many of the interludes are imaginative, funny or mad and depend on the viewer having some knowledge of the fab world of pop. His libretto was declared obscene, and so what was conceived as a live show became this film instead. JM DVD

Ringo Starr *Larry the dwarf* • Frank Zappa • Theodore Bikel *Rance Muhammitz* • Don Preston *Bif Debris* • Jimmy Carl Black *Cowboy Burtram* • Keith Moon *Hot Nun* ■ *Dir* Frank Zappa, Tony Palmer • *Scr* Frank Zappa, Tony Palmer, from a story by Zappa

Two in the Wave ★★★ 12A

Documentary   2010 · Fr · BW and Colour · 96min

François Truffaut and Jean-Luc Godard were the driving forces behind the French New Wave in the late 1950s and 60s. As critics on the influential journal *Cahiers du Cinéma*, they demanded that directors became auteurs with personal styles and fiercely denounced the polished brand of film-making that they mockingly labelled "cinéma du papa". Unfortunately, director Emmanuel Laurent barely scratches the surface of this fascinating relationship in a documentary that contains some exceptional clips and archive footage, but lacks consistency of focus and tone. Nevertheless, it's a passable introduction to a compelling topic. DP French +subtitles. Brief violence, sexual references. DVD

■ *Dir* Emmanuel Laurent • *Scr* Antoine de Baecque

The Two Jakes ★★★ 15

Detective thriller   1990 · US · Colour · 131min

If Robert Towne and Roman Polanski fell out over *Chinatown*, worse happened during this sequel. With Towne directing, shooting was cancelled after the first day when Robert Evans – the producer of the first film – was fired in the role of the villain, the other Jake. Shooting resumed four years later with Jack Nicholson as director/star and Harvey Keitel as his co-star, and Towne and Nicholson haven't spoken since. The second in Towne's planned trilogy about land deals in Los Angeles in the late 1940s, it evokes eerie echoes of the first story, but is muddled. AT Violence, swearing. DVD

Jack Nicholson *Jake Gittes* • Harvey Keitel *Jake Berman* • Meg Tilly *Kitty Berman* • Madeleine Stowe *Lillian Bodine* • Eli Wallach *Cotton Weinberger* • Rubén Blades *Mickey Nice* • Frederic Forrest *Chuck Newty* • David Keith *Loach* • Richard Farnsworth *Earl Rawley* ■ *Dir* Jack Nicholson • *Scr* Robert Towne

Two-Lane Blacktop ★★★ 15

Road movie drama   1971 · US · Colour · 98min

This existential road movie takes its cue from *Easy Rider* and features Beach Boys' drummer Dennis Wilson and 1970s singer/songwriter James Taylor in their first straight leading roles. They play drifters cruising the American Southwest in their souped-up 1955 Chevrolet, who challenge old-timer Warren Oates (a career-best performance) and his GTO Pontiac to a cross-country race with car ownership as the prize. Monte Hellman's intense direction and the quirky charm compensate for a low-key script, and there are nice supporting turns from Laurie Bird and Harry Dean Stanton as hitch-hikers. RS DVD BL

James Taylor *Driver* • Dennis Wilson *Mechanic* • Warren Oates *GTO* • Laurie Bird *Girl* • HD Stanton [Harry Dean Stanton] *Oklahoma hitchhiker* • David Drake *Needles station attendant* • Richard Ruth *Needles station mechanic* • Jaclyn Hellman *Driver's girl* ■ *Dir* Monte Hellman • *Scr* Rudy Wurlitzer, Will Corry, from a story by Will Corry

Two Left Feet ★★★ 15

Comedy　　　　1963 · UK · BW · 89min

In this adult comedy about adolescent sexual complications, Michael Crawford is an unworldly 19-year-old who goes out on a date to a jazz club with older waitress Nyree Dawn Porter. At the club Porter ignores him, instead flirting with two other guys. Crawford in turn meets Julia Foster with whom he seems far happier. This stark look at 1960s sexual mores has fine performances, especially from Crawford and Porter. DF

Michael Crawford *Alan Crabbe* • Nyree Dawn Porter *Eileen* • Julia Foster *Beth Crowley* • Michael Craze *Ronnie* • David Hemmings *Brian* • Dilys Watling *Mavis* • David Lodge *Bill* • Bernard Lee *Mr Crabbe* ■ *Dir* Roy Baker [Roy Ward Baker] • *Scr* Roy Baker [Roy Ward Baker], John Hopkins, from the novel *In My Solitude* by David Stuart Leslie

Two Living, One Dead ★★ U

Psychological crime drama
1961 · UK/Swe · BW · 101min

One postal clerk dies in an armed robbery, another resists and is acclaimed as a hero, the third hands over the cash and is branded a coward. This study of small-town attitudes is based on a Swedish novel and filmed on location there by director Anthony Asquith with a strong British cast. It becomes an awkward hybrid, abandoning social critique for a melodramatic conclusion and never finding the right tone. AE

Virginia McKenna *Helen Berger* • Bill Travers *Anderson* • Patrick McGoohan *Berger* • Dorothy Alison *Esther Kester* • Alf Kjellin *Rogers* • Noel Willman *Inspector Johnson* • Pauline Jameson *Miss Larsen* ■ *Dir* Anthony Asquith • *Scr* Lindsay Galloway, from the novel *Två Levande och en Död* by Sigurd Wesley Christiansen

Two Lovers ★★★ 15

Romantic drama
2008 · US/Fr · Colour · 105min

Joaquin Phoenix delivers a heart-rending performance in this drama about a troubled man tortured by desire. Leonard (Phoenix) is living with his parents and under his mother's thumb when he catches sight of Michelle (Gwyneth Paltrow), the blonde who's just moved into the building. She befriends him, but the path to romance has several stumbling blocks, including his married lover (Elias Koteas) and the "nice Jewish girl" (Vinessa Shaw) Leonard's parents are trying to foist upon him. Paltrow's role is a little too thinly drawn and the film's ending is rather questionable, but writer/director James Gray's feel for nuance is expertly employed throughout. SP Swearing, sexual references, brief drug abuse. DVD BLU

Joaquin Phoenix *Leonard Kraditor* • Gwyneth Paltrow *Michelle Rausch* • Vinessa Shaw *Sandra Cohen* • Isabella Rossellini *Ruth Kraditor* • Elias Koteas *Ronald Blatt* • Moni Moshonov *Reuben Kraditor* ■ *Dir* James Gray • *Scr* James Gray, Richard Menello

Two Loves ★

Drama　　　　1961 · US · Colour · 99min

This bizarre melodrama stars Shirley MacLaine as a teacher in New Zealand who drinks brandy for breakfast, burns on a short fuse and is probably bonkers. Her pupils love her. So does teaching colleague Laurence Harvey, a bit mad himself, but his amorous attentions are snubbed. MGM bungles everything about this hotbed of emotion in prim, middle-class New Zealand and makes it laughable in quite the wrong way. AT

Shirley MacLaine *Anna Vorontosov* • Laurence Harvey *Paul Lathrope* • Jack Hawkins *WWJ Abercrombie* • Nobu McCarthy *Whareparita* • Ronald Long *Headmaster Reardon* • Norah Howard *Mrs Cutter* • Juano Hernandez *Rauhuia* • Edmund Vargas *Matawhero* ■ *Dir* Charles Walters • *Scr* Ben Maddow, from the novel *Spinster* by Sylvia Ashton-Warner

Two Men in Manhattan ★★★

Crime　　　　1959 · Fr · BW · 100min

Having been forced to abandon two projects following *Bob Le Flambeur*, Jean-Pierre Melville somewhat understandably took a hands-on approach to this study in journalistic ethics. In addition to scripting, directing and starring, he also shot a good deal of the New York location footage himself, capturing the seedy underside of the city, while still giving it an irresistible allure. Melville's reporter teams with scoop-chasing photographer Pierre Grasset to track down a missing UN diplomat, only to fall out when they discover his corpse. A hard-nosed, cynical film with an unexpectedly poetic heart. DP English, French +subtitles.

Jean-Pierre Melville *Moreau* • Pierre Grasset *Delmas* • Michèle Bailly • Jean Darcante ■ *Dir/Scr* Jean-Pierre Melville

Two Men Went to War ★★★ PG

Second World War comedy drama
2002 · UK · Colour · 104min

Had it been made 50 years ago, with Roger Livesey as the Great War veteran and Ian Carmichael as his young charge, setting off together for occupied France with a knapsack of grenades, hellbent on taking a pop at Hitler, this fact-based story would have evolved into a much-loved tribute to British eccentricity. Even now, with Kenneth Cranham and Leo Bill as the ill-matched duo who go AWOL from the dental corps, it has considerable period feel and comic charm. But, as with *Dad's Army*, the humour also belies a shrewd social analysis that gives the combat finale that vital ring of authenticity. DP DVD

Kenneth Cranham *Sergeant Peter King* • Leo Bill *Private Leslie Cuthbertson* • Rosanna Lavelle *Emma Fraser* • Derek Jacobi *Major Merton* • Phyllida Law *Faith* • James Fleet *Major Bates* • Julian Glover *Colonel Hatchard* • Anthony Valentine *Sergeant Major Dudley* ■ *Dir* John Henderson • *Scr* Richard Everett, Christopher Villiers

Two-Minute Warning ★★ 15

Thriller　　　　1976 · US · Colour · 110min

The recipient of an Oscar nomination for its editing, this interminable drama has all the character sophistication of a disaster movie. In a cast littered with guest stars, everyone is a loser of sorts, unlike the sniper at the NFL play-off and his police pursuer, who are both psychopaths. While the acting styles of John Cassavetes and Charlton Heston clash like cymbals, director Larry Peerce preoccupies himself with grandstanding camerawork that does little to heighten tension. DP Violence, swearing. DVD

Charlton Heston *Captain Peter Holly* • John Cassavetes *Sergeant Chris Button* • Martin Balsam *Sam McKeever* • Beau Bridges *Mike Ramsay* • Marilyn Hassett *Lucy* • David Janssen *Steve* • Jack Klugman *Stu Sandman* • Gena Rowlands *Janet* • Walter Pidgeon *Pickpocket* ■ *Dir* Larry Peerce • *Scr* Edward Hume, from the novel by George La Fountaine • *Editors* Walter Hanneman, Eve Newman

The Two Mr Kissels ★★

Crime drama based on a true story
2008 · US · Colour · 86min

Secrets, lies and resentments destroy the affluent lives of two businessmen brothers in this undynamic melodrama. Rushed and episodic, the sketchy TV movie turns a fascinating rise-and-fall story into a dull time-waster, in which many juicy events are talked about but never shown. Ineffective performances compound the poor script and uneven direction, with neither John Stamos nor Anson Mount bringing any depth to their title characters. Robin Tunney provides the film's only highlight as a money-grabbing wife. SF

John Stamos *Andrew Kissel* • Robin Tunney *Nancy Kissel* • Anson Mount *Robert Kissel* • Gretchen Egolf *Hayley Wolff* • Chuck Shamata *Bill Kissel* ■ *Dir* Ed Bianchi • *Scr* Maria Nation

Two Moon Junction ★★ 18

Erotic drama　　　　1988 · US · Colour · 100min

In a soft-porn flick from the stable of director Zalman King, a poor plot forms an excuse for various pornographic encounters, but it's naff fun nevertheless. Sherilyn Fenn rejects her educated past to run off with hunk Richard Tyson. The couple are chased by her family and local law enforcers intent on stopping their adventures. Watch out for supermodel and future *Joan of Arc* star Milla Jovovich in one of her first acting attempts. A sequel, *Return to Two Moon Junction*, followed six years later. LH DVD

Sherilyn Fenn *April Delongpre* • Kristy McNichol *Patti-Jean* • Richard Tyson *Perry* • Louise Fletcher *Belle* • Burl Ives *Sheriff Earl Hawkins* • Martin Hewitt *Chad Douglas Fairchild* • Millie Perkins *Mrs Delongpre* • Don Galloway *Senator Delongpre* ■ *Dir* Zalman King • *Scr* Zalman King, from a story by Zalman King, MacGregor Douglas

The Two Mrs Carrolls ★★★ PG

Crime drama　　　　1945 · US · BW · 94min

The only teaming of two great movie icons, Humphrey Bogart and Barbara Stanwyck, this sordid tale about a wife-killer leaves much to be desired. Today, this nasty old tosh is resolutely entertaining, though you can still understand why Warners kept it on the shelf for a couple of years after it was filmed in 1945. Bogie is seriously miscast as the psychopathic artist murderer, Stanwyck is equally under-used as his intended victim, and the whole betrays its stage origins. TS

Humphrey Bogart *Geoffrey Carroll* • Barbara Stanwyck *Sally Morton Carroll* • Alexis Smith *Cecily Latham* • Nigel Bruce *Dr Tuttle* • Isobel Elsom *Mrs Latham* • Pat O'Moore *[Patrick O'Moore] Charles Fennington* ■ *Dir* Peter Godfrey • *Scr* Thomas Job, from the play by Martin Vale

Two Much ★ PG

Romantic comedy
1995 · Sp/US · Colour · 113min

Making a good screwball comedy is an exact science, but director Fernando Treuba fumbles every aspect of this one. Antonio Banderas comes off worst as the art dealer who romances socialite Melanie Griffith but then falls for her sister Daryl Hannah, causing him to pretend he actually has an identical twin. Cue lots of ridiculous situations and Banderas looking increasingly ill-at-ease. JB DVD

Antonio Banderas *Art Dodge* • Melanie Griffith *Betty Kerner* • Daryl Hannah *Liz Kerner* • Danny Aiello *Gene Paletto* • Joan Cusack *Gloria* • Eli Wallach *Sheldon* • Gabino Diego *Manny* ■ *Dir* Fernando Treuba • *Scr* Fernando Treuba, David Trueba, from the novel by Donald E Westlake

Two Mules for Sister Sara ★★★★ 15

Western　　　　1970 · US · Colour · 100min

Clint Eastwood plays a quizzical, slightly bemused cowboy in this immensely enjoyable Don Siegel caper, saving nun Shirley MacLaine from a fate worse than death in the Mexican desert. The two leads are perfectly paired, and MacLaine in particular turns in a great comic performance as her ill-fitting habit begins to slip. Siegel keeps the tension and pace roaring along as he pitches them into the middle of the Mexican Revolution, though some may find the final, gory battle scene out of kilter with the light-hearted tone of the rest of the movie. SH Violence, swearing. DVD BLU

Clint Eastwood *Hogan* • Shirley MacLaine *Sister Sara* • Manolo Fabregas *Colonel Beltran* • Alberto Morin *General LeClaire* • Armando Silvestre *1st American* • John Kelly (3) *2nd American* • Enrique Lucero *3rd American* • David Estuardo *Juan* ■ *Dir* Don Siegel • *Scr* Albert Maltz, from a story by Budd Boetticher

Two Night Stand ★★ 15

Romantic comedy　　　2013 · US · Colour · 82min

The directorial debut of the late Mike Nichols's son Max, this indie romantic comedy almost gets by on the charms of its talented leads, Miles Teller (*Whiplash*) and Analeigh Tipton. A freak snowstorm traps them in Teller's flat for a night so, with most of the action constrained to one set, the film was always going to stand or fall on the strength of the writing. But while there is plenty of rude banter and a good few laughs, Mark Hammer's script is neither witty nor insightful enough to carry the load. JF DVD

Analeigh Tipton *Megan* • Miles Teller *Alec* • Jessica Szohr *Faiza* • Scott Mescudi *Cedric* • Josh Salatin *Chris* • Michael Showalter *Rick Raines* ■ *Dir* Max Nichols • *Scr* Mark Hammer (2)

Two o'Clock Courage ★

Murder mystery　　　1945 · US · BW · 66min

It starts promisingly, with a bloodied Tom Conway staggering forward to lean on a signpost at a deserted city crossroads. But it goes downhill rapidly and stays there after Ann Rutherford's wisecracking cabbie picks him up and improbably decides to help Conway solve his case of amnesia. Anthony Mann's alert staging tries to bring some life to the verbose story, but it's beyond resuscitation. AE

Tom Conway *Man* • Ann Rutherford *Patty Mitchell* • Richard Lane *Haley* • Lester Matthews *Mark Evans* • Roland Drew *Steve Maitland* • Emory Parnell *Inspector Bill Brenner* • Bettejane Greer [Jane Greer] *Helen Carter* ■ *Dir* Anthony Mann • *Scr* Robert E Kent, from a novel by Gelett Burgess

Two of a Kind ★★ PG

Fantasy romantic comedy
1983 · US · Colour · 83min

Five years on from *Grease*, John Travolta and Olivia Newton-John re-teamed for a fantasy romance about a couple used as guinea pigs by God in an experiment to prove that not all mortals are irredeemably corrupt. Played as a screwball comedy, it has its stupid moments, and its endearing ones, but not enough of them. True fans of the stars will probably quite like it. DA DVD

John Travolta *Zach Melon* • Olivia Newton-John *Debbie Wylder* • Charles Durning *Charlie* • Oliver Reed *Beazley* • Beatrice Straight *Ruth* • Scatman Crothers *Earl* • Richard Bright *Stuart* ■ *Dir/Scr* John Herzfeld

The Two of Us ★★★★ U

Second World War comedy drama
1967 · Fr · BW · 86min

Michel Simon won the best actor prize at Berlin for his work in Claude Berri's autobiographical tale about a Catholic, Pétain-supporting anti-Semite who unknowingly forms a close friendship with a young Jewish refugee. This is a superlative performance, as Simon humanises the fascist who never lets up for a second in his attempt to indoctrinate the boy with his hideous views. It's also a courageous and selfless piece of acting, as he allows young Alain Cohen to steal scene after scene as the irrepressible eight year-old who delights in deflating his host. DP French +subtitles.

Michel Simon *Pépé* • Alain Cohen *Claude* • Luce Fabiole *Granny Mémé* • Roger Carel *Victor* • Paul Preboist *Maxime* ■ *Dir* Claude Berri • *Scr* Claude Berri, Gérard Brach, Michel Rivelin

Two of Us ★★

Drama　　　　2000 · US · Colour · 90min

Having spent time with the Beatles while shooting *Let It Be*, Michael Lindsay-Hogg is better placed than most to speculate on what might have been said when John Lennon and Paul McCartney met up for the first time after the band's acrimonious split. Everything in this TV movie is pure supposition and pretty uninspired it is, too, as it trades on Nice Paul, Nasty John clichés. However, Aidan Quinn and Jared Harris's impersonations are impressively observant. DP

Aidan Quinn *Paul McCartney* • Jared Harris *John Lennon* • Ric Reid *TV interviewer* ■ *Dir* Michael Lindsay-Hogg • *Scr* Mark Stanfield

Two on a Guillotine ★★

Mystery   1964 · US · BW · 107min

To claim her magician father's estate, Connie Stevens (who also plays her deceased mother) has to spend a week in his scary mansion. A quintessential haunted house picture, produced and directed by TV's *Cannon* William Conrad. Cesar Romero has a lot of camp fun with better than average material. JG

Connie Stevens *Melinda Duquesne/Cassie Duquesne* • Dean Jones *Val Henderson* • Cesar Romero *John "Duke" Duquesne* • Parley Baer *"Buzz" Sheridan* • Virginia Gregg *Dolly Bast* • Connie Gilchrist *Ramona Ryerdon* ■ *Dir* William Conrad • *Scr* Henry Slesar, John Kneubuhl, from a story by Slesar

Two or Three Things I Know about Her ★★★★15

Experimental drama   1966 · Fr · Colour · 83min

Inspired by an article on high-rise prostitution and shot simultaneously with *Made in USA*, this is, according to Jean-Luc Godard, "a sociological essay in the form of a novel, written not with words, but with notes of music". Marina Vlady stars as the housewife hooker who turns tricks to survive in an increasingly consumerist society. But the real "Her" of the title is Paris, which cinematographer Raoul Coutard captures with a symphonic energy that matches Godard's audacious combination of ideas, images and sounds. A tad dated, but still daring, dazzling and dynamic. DP French +subtitles. *DVD*

Marina Vlady *Juliette Janson* • Anny Duperey *Marianne* • Roger Montsoret *Robert Janson* • Jean Narboni *Roger* • Christophe Bourseiller *Christophe* • Marie Bourseiller *Solange* • Raoul Lévy *The American* • Jean-Luc Godard *Narrator* ■ *Dir* Jean-Luc Godard • *Scr* Jean-Luc Godard, suggested by the article *Les Etoiles Filantes* by Catherine Vimenet in *Le Nouvel Observateur*

Two Pennyworth of Hope ★★★

Romantic comedy drama   1952 · It · BW · 102min

Having established himself as perhaps the finest exponent of "calligraphism" or the literary period picture, Renato Castellani proved he was capable of tackling contemporary concerns with his rose-tinted trilogy of young love. Set on the slopes of Vesuvius, the shamelessly optimistic story, in which Maria Fiore determines to persuade her parents that the hapless Vincenzo Musolino is worthy of her affection, stands in cosy contrast to the fading gloom of the neorealist era. DP Italian +subtitles.

Vincenzo Musolino *Antonio* • Maria Fiore *Carmela* • Filomeno Russo *Antonio's mother* • Luigi Astarita *Carmela's father* • Luigi Barone *Priest* ■ *Dir* Renato Castellani • *Scr* Renato Castellani, Titina de Filippo, from a story by Castellani, M [Ettore Maria] Margadonna

Two People ★

Romance   1973 · US · Colour · 100min

Robert Wise unwisely dives into the "youth market" with this romance between guilt-ridden draft dodger Peter Fonda and unhappy fashion model Lindsay Wagner. There's far too much "hey man" soul-searching and a rush of domestic crises that would occupy a TV soap for months. Wise's direction also seems to have been influenced by the worst excesses of the French New Wave and the intellectualism of Michelangelo Antonioni. AT

Peter Fonda *Evan Bonner* • Lindsay Wagner *Deirdre McCluskey* • Estelle Parsons *Barbara Newman* • Alan Fudge *Fitzgerald* • Philippe March *Gilles* • Frances Sternhagen *Mrs McCluskey* • Brian Lima *Marcus McCluskey* ■ *Dir* Robert Wise • *Scr* Richard DeRoy

Two Rode Together ★★★PG

Western   1961 · US · Colour · 104min

This rather slow-moving late John Ford western stars James Stewart and Richard

---

Widmark, who both seem slightly ill at ease in underwritten roles as a cynical sheriff and a gallant cavalry officer out to rescue victims of Comanche raids. The Stewart character has most of the dialogue but none of the answers, and neither, one suspects, has Ford. TS *DVD*

James Stewart *Guthrie McCabe* • Richard Widmark *Lt Jim Gary* • Shirley Jones *Marty Purcell* • Linda Cristal *Elena de la Madriaga* • Andy Devine *Sgt Darius P Posey* • John McIntire *Major Frazer* • Paul Birch *Edward Purcell* ■ *Dir* John Ford • *Scr* Frank Nugent, from the novel *Comanche Captives* by Will Cook

Two Seconds ★★★

Crime drama   1932 · US · BW · 68min

The greatest decade for Warner Bros, the 1930s, was characterised by realist dramas and gangster movies, showing particular sympathy for blue-collar workers and the oppressed. Mervyn Le Roy's brisk and powerful adaptation stars Edward G Robinson as one such victim - a construction worker whose life during the Depression flashes before him in the seconds prior to his dying by execution. A sap tricked into marriage by a "taxi-dancer" who then betrays him, he accidentally kills his best friend and later shoots his wife. But he is shown accepting the consequences of a life at once pathetic yet decent in its simple humanity. BB

Edward G Robinson *John Allen* • Vivienne Osborne *Shirley Day* • Guy Kibbee *Bookie* • Preston Foster *Bud Clark* • J Carrol Naish *Tony* ■ *Dir* Mervyn LeRoy • *Scr* Harvey Thew, from the play by Elliott Lester

Two Sisters from Boston ★★★

Musical romantic comedy
1946 · US · BW · 112min

Boston blue-blood Kathryn Grayson works as the belle of a Bowery nightspot to finance her opera studies. She conceals the fact from her family with the help of her initially outraged younger sister June Allyson and her boss Jimmy Durante, and achieves her ambitions. Sometimes very funny, and with some cute touches - along with famous tenor Lauritz Melchior strutting his stuff, and a very young and pretty Peter Lawford contributing to the romance - it's a charming dose of heavenly nonsense. RK

Kathryn Grayson *Abigail Chandler* • June Allyson *Martha Canford Chandler* • Lauritz Melchior *Olstrom* • Jimmy Durante *"Spike"* • Peter Lawford *Lawrence Patterson Jr* • Ben Blue *Wrigley* • Isobel Elsom *Aunt Jennifer* • Harry Hayden *Uncle Jonathan* ■ *Dir* Henry Koster • *Scr* Myles Connolly, James O'Hanlon, Harry Crane, Charles Previn, William Wymetal

Two Stage Sisters ★★★★★

Period melodrama   1964 · Chi · Colour · 114min

Denounced for a formalism that supposedly undermined its political value, Xie Jin's period musical drama is one of the glories of pre-Cultural Revolution cinema. Rarely have colour, camera movement and composition been so harmoniously combined for what is, essentially, a backstage melodrama. Showgirls Xie Fang and Cao Yindi drift apart in wartime Shanghai, with the latter marrying in pursuit of material comfort, while the former begins to see the political light. Feminist tract, political thesis and nationalist paean it may be, but this is also an impeccably realised film that succeeds equally as art, propaganda and entertainment. DP in Mandarin.

Xie Fang *Chunhua* • Cao Yindi *Yuehong* • Feng Ji *Xing* • Gao Yuansheng *Jiang Bo* • Shen Fengjuan *Xiao Xiang* ■ *Dir* Xie Jin • *Scr* Lin Gu, Xu Jin, Xie Jin

The Two Tars ★★★★★U

Silent comedy   1928 · US · BW · 21min

As an example of what Stan called "reciprocal destruction", this is one of the greatest of Laurel and Hardy's early silents. It features them as two sailors on leave from the USS *Oregon*, doing the kind of comic damage only they are capable of -

---

from wrecking a gum machine to causing a traffic jam of mutilated cars. The girls they pick up on the way - Thelma Hill and Ruby Blaine - are only too happy to get a lift in the rented Model T, but they sneak off quickly when things get tough and bad-tempered characters such as Edgar Kennedy appear. This has the classic final shot in which Stan and Ollie's tin lizzie has an argument with a train and slims down considerably. "Everybody follow them sailors," shouts an irate traffic cop. For years audiences have delighted in following that order. TH *DVD*

Stan Laurel *Stan* • Oliver Hardy *Ollie* • Thelma Hill *Brunette coquette* • Ruby Blaine *Blonde coquette* • Charley Rogers *Man whose fenders are ripped back* • Edgar Kennedy *Family motorist* ■ *Dir* James Parrott • *Scr* Leo MacCarey, HM Walker (titles)

LANDMARK FILM
Science fiction grows up

2001: a Space Odyssey ★★★★★U

Science-fiction epic
1968 · UK/US · Colour · 135min

Stanley Kubrick's seminal sci-fi work is now considered by some to be less a supreme piece of cinema than an interesting, innovative product of the 1960s. But the memorable celluloid images still strongly resonate, like the giant Starchild floating through space and the tribe of apes painfully putting two and two together. It is Kubrick's haunting, stylised combination of music and visuals that gives *2001* its eerie, mesmerising quality, but even its most devoted disciples are hard pressed to tell you what it's actually about, and, as a slice of philosophy on how we all got started and where we ultimately go, the movie has little credence. Still, it's a must-see. SH *DVD*

Keir Dullea *David "Dave" Bowman* • Gary Lockwood *Frank Poole* • William Sylvester *Dr Heywood Floyd* • Daniel Richter *Moonwatcher* • Leonard Rossiter *Smyslov* • Margaret Tyzack *Elena* • Robert Beatty *Halvorsen* • Sean Sullivan *Michaels* • Douglas Rain *HAL 9000* ■ *Dir* Stanley Kubrick • *Scr* Stanley Kubrick, Arthur C Clarke, from the short story *The Sentinel* by Arthur C Clarke in *Ten Story Fantasy*

The 2006 FIFA World Cup Film: the Grand Finale ★★

Sports documentary
2006 · UK · Colour · 108min

This official chronicle of the 2006 World Cup certainly has some pedigree behind the camera in the form of pioneering documentarian Michael Apted. But it's still a pretty straightforward work that tends to skim through the group games before getting down to the business end with the knockout stages. England's quarter-final against Portugal is covered and, of course, French genius Zinédine Zidane's moment of madness in the final against Italy is a particularly dramatic segment. However, the talking heads offer very little insight and the football fan is merely left with unadulterated match footage to maintain interest. JA

Pierce Brosnan *Narrator* • Thierry Henry ■ *Dir* Michael Apted

2010 ★★★PG

Science-fiction drama
1984 · US · Colour · 111min

Based on the novel by Arthur C Clarke, writer/director Peter Hyams's earnest script unites Soviets and Americans to discover why astronaut Bowman vanished. Some spectacular special effects (the space walk transference) are the highlights of this unnecessary sequel to the monumental *2001: a Space Odyssey*, which quickly runs out of rocket fuel after a bright start. The Black Monolith is back, but there is little of Stanley Kubrick's epic sense or masterfully ambiguous myths and mysteries. Instead, director Peter Hyams replaces them with banal over-explicitness. AJ *DVD*

Roy Scheider *Heywood Floyd* • John Lithgow *Walter Curnow* • Helen Mirren *Tanya Kirbuk* • Bob Balaban *R Chandra* • Keir Dullea *Dave Bowman* •

Douglas Rain *Voice of Hal 9000* • Madolyn Smith *Caroline Floyd* • Dana Elcar *Dimitri Moisevitch* ■ *Dir* Peter Hyams • *Scr* Peter Hyams, from the novel *2010: Odyssey Two* by Arthur C Clarke

2012 ★★★12

Disaster movie   2009 · US · Colour · 151min

Writer/director Roland Emmerich (*Independence Day*, *The Day after Tomorrow*) is firmly in his comfort zone for this disaster movie, but this time it's solar flares that are to blame, as the planet gets microwaved. Cue some expensive, dramatic and genuinely awesome CGI as Yellowstone goes supervolcano, entire cities are destroyed and giant tsunamis romp across the globe. John Cusack stars as the failed author who is told the truth about the end of the world by Woody Harrelson's conspiracy theory nut, and attempts to save his kids and ex-wife (Amanda Peet). The script is nonsensical, and the actors are, inevitably, dwarfed by what can only be described as breathtaking visual effects. JR Swearing. *DVD* *Blu*

John Cusack *Jackson Curtis* • Chiwetel Ejiofor *Adrian Helmsley* • Amanda Peet *Kate Curtis* • Oliver Platt *Carl Anheuser* • Thandie Newton *Laura Wilson* • Danny Glover *President Thomas Wilson* • Woody Harrelson *Charlie Frost* • Tom McCarthy [Thomas McCarthy] *Gordon* ■ *Dir* Roland Emmerich • *Scr* Roland Emmerich, Harald Kloser

2046 ★★12

Romantic science-fiction drama
2004 · HK/Fr/It/Chi · Colour · 123min

Tony Leung once again stars as a writer living in a seedy Hong Kong hotel in the 1960s in this disappointing quasi-sequel to *In the Mood for Love*. Still obsessed with his earlier unconsummated love for married woman Maggie Cheung, his dreamy dalliances with three other women (Zhang Ziyi, Carina Lau, Gong Li) who move into room 2046 next door inspire him to write sci-fistories that, although set in the year 2046, detail his desire to recapture past memories. AJ Cantonese +subtitles. Sex scenes. *DVD*

Tony Leung Chiu-Wai [Tony Leung (2)] *Chow Mo-Wan* • Gong Li *Su Lizhen* • Zhang Ziyi *Bai Ling* • Maggie Cheung *slz 1960* • Takuya Kimura *Tak* • Faye Wong *Wang Jingwen/wjw 1967* • Carina Lau *Lulu/Mimi cc 1966* • Wang Sum *Mr Wang/Train captain* ■ *Dir/Scr* Wong Kar-Wai

Two Thousand Maniacs! ★★18

Horror   1964 · US · Colour · 87min

Just outside the southern town of Pleasant Valley, whose citizens were massacred by Union troops during the Civil War, the dead villagers reappear to wreak horrific revenge on six northern tourists. While as badly acted and technically inept as any Herschell G Lewis drive-in exploiter, the cheaply graphic effects still carry a potent charge and this was the nearest the agony auteur ever got to a crossover success. AJ *DVD*

Connie Mason *Terry Adams* • Thomas Wood [William Kerwin] *Tom White* • Jeffrey Allen *Mayor Buckman* • Ben Moore *Lester* • Shelby Livingston *Bea Miller* ■ *Dir* Herschell G Lewis [Herschell Gordon Lewis] • *Scr* Herschell G Lewis [Herschell Gordon Lewis], from his story

Two Thousand Women ★★★PG

Second World War drama
1944 · UK · BW · 92min

This is an effective piece of propaganda, with an uplifting plot (co-written by Frank Launder and Sidney Gilliat) about women at a German-run detention centre in France helping three RAF airmen to escape. A celebration of British pluck, a healthy spot of Nazi bashing and a dash of gallows humour: it's just what Churchill ordered in 1944, but today it weighs a little heavily. Fortunately, among the two thousand of the title are some of the finest actresses of the time, whose appeal remains undiminished. DP *DVD*

Phyllis Calvert *Freda Thompson* • Flora Robson *Miss Manningford* • Patricia Roc *Rosemary Brown* • Renee Houston *Maud Wright* • Anne Crawford

---

Margaret Long • Jean Kent *Bridie Johnson* • Reginald Purdell *Alec Harvey* ■ *Dir* Frank Launder • *Scr* Frank Launder, Sidney Gilliat, from a story by Frank Launder, Michael Pertwee

Two Tickets to Broadway
★★★ U

Musical comedy 1951 · US · Colour · 106min

There's a super cast and a nice line in satire in this immensely likeable Technicolor musical that sends up the then-new medium of television. Bob Crosby gives a superb mickey-take of his famous brother Bing, the girls are particularly scintillating and the Busby Berkeley-choreographed routines are all you'd expect. Tony Martin is a bit of a pudding in the lead, but amiable sidekick Eddie Bracken more than compensates. Lawyer-turned-director James V Kern wisely stands back and lets the musical numbers and comedy skits work for themselves. TS

Tony Martin (1) *Dan Carter* • Janet Leigh *Nancy Peterson* • Gloria DeHaven *Hannah Holbrook* • Eddie Bracken *Lew Conway* • Ann Miller *Joyce Campbell* • Barbara Lawrence "*Foxy*" *Rogers* • Bob Crosby • Joe Smith *Harry* • Charles Dale *Leo* ■ *Dir* James V Kern • *Scr* Sid Silvers, Hal Kanter, from a story by Sammy Cahn

[Two] Un Couple Epatant
★★★ PG

Romantic comedy
2002 · Fr/Bel · Colour · 93min

This French farce is an abrupt shift in tone from the shadowy pessimism of the first part of Lucas Belvaux's trilogy (*[One] Cavale*). But while it serves as pleasing comic relief between its two weightier companions, their intensity only emphasises this tale's triviality and over-reliance on unlikely contrivance. That said, Ornella Muti revels in the role of the suspicious bourgeoise whose conviction that husband François Morel is sleeping with his secretary and/or her teaching colleague (Dominique Blanc), prompts her to hire smitten cop Gilbert Melki to tail him. Followed by *[Three] Après la Vie*. DP French +subtitles. Swearing, violence. *DVD*

Ornella Muti *Cécile Costes* • François Morel *Alain Costes* • Dominique Blanc *Agnès Manise* • Gilbert Melki *Pascal Manise* • Valérie Mairesse *Claire* • Catherine Frot *Jeanne Rivet* • Lucas Belvaux *Pierre* ■ *Dir/Scr* Lucas Belvaux

Two Way Stretch
★★★★ U

Prison comedy 1960 · UK · BW · 83min

Fans of Peter Sellers rate this British venture, made before he started to believe his own publicity, as one of the best things he did. It's a prison comedy with a snarling stand-off between cocky convict Sellers, his cellmates Bernard Cribbins and David Lodge, and paranoid warden Lionel Jeffries. The plot – about a group of prisoners trying to break back into jail after a heist – is wonderfully developed and there are delightful cameos along the way. TH *DVD*

Peter Sellers *Dodger Lane* • Wilfrid Hyde White *Reverend Basil "Soapy" Fowler* • David Lodge *Jelly Knight* • Bernard Cribbins *Lennie Price* • Maurice Denham *Cmdr Horatio Bennet, the prison governor* • Lionel Jeffries *Sidney Crout* • Irene Handl *Mrs Price* • Liz Fraser *Ethel* • Beryl Reid *Miss Pringle* ■ *Dir* Robert Day • *Scr* John Warren, Len Heath, Alan Hackney, from the story by John Warren

Two Weeks in Another Town
★★★★

Melodrama 1962 · US · Colour · 106min

If you think film-makers are unstable, this overwrought but convincing fable about Hollywood has-beens will confirm it. Kirk Douglas is the on-the-skids actor in Rome for a small part in a low-budget movie directed by the equally struggling Edward G Robinson, but he's hampered by ex-wife Cyd Charisse and jet-set corruption. This examines the soul-destroying insecurity that goes with celebrity, and is extraordinarily well acted. TH

Kirk Douglas *Jack Andrus* • Edward G Robinson *Maurice Kruger* • Cyd Charisse *Carlotta* • George Hamilton *Davie Drew* • Dahlia Lavi *Veronica* • Claire Trevor *Clara Kruger* • James Gregory *Brad*

Byrd • Rosanna Schiaffino *Barzelli* • Joanna Roos *Janet Bark* ■ *Dir* Vincente Minnelli • *Scr* Charles Schnee, from the novel by Irwin Shaw

Two Weeks Notice
★★ 12

Romantic comedy
2002 · US/Aus · Colour · 96min

Sandra Bullock plays a liberal lawyer who fights for environmental causes; Hugh Grant is a real estate tycoon who plans to knock down her local community centre in Coney Island to build condominiums – she agrees to work for him if he doesn't go ahead with the demolition. So, the pair are thrown together in true romantic comedy tradition: opposites fighting an attraction. The formulaic plot is not the main problem here: it's Bullock and Grant. They're just trying too hard and with little result. StH *DVD* *CS*

Sandra Bullock *Lucy Kelson* • Hugh Grant *George Wade* • Alicia Witt *June Carter* • Dana Ivey *Ruth Kelson* • Robert Klein *Larry Kelson* • Heather Burns *Meryl* • David Haig *Howard Wade* ■ *Dir/Scr* Marc Lawrence (2)

Two Women
★★★ 15

Second World War drama
1960 · It/Fr · BW · 99min

Two Women marked the graduation of Sophia Loren from pouting sex-kitten to major league actress as she and her daughter experience the ravages of war, the desolation of being refugees and the horror of rape following the Allied bombing of Rome. Filmed in the neorealist style of Vittorio De Sica's earlier classic, *Bicycle Thieves*, the picture earned Loren an Oscar – the first ever awarded to a non-American actor or actress performing in a foreign language. It was a feat not repeated until Roberto Benigni won in 1999 for *Life is Beautiful*. AT Italian +subtitles. Violence, some swearing.

Sophia Loren *Cesira* • Jean-Paul Belmondo *Michele* • Raf Vallone *Giovanni* • Eleanora Brown *Rosetta* • Renato Salvatori *Florindo* • Carlo Ninchi *Michele's father* • Andrea Checchi *Fascist* ■ *Dir* Vittorio De Sica • *Scr* Cesare Zavattini, Vittorio De Sica, Alberto Moravia

Two Years before the Mast
★★★

Drama 1946 · US · BW · 97min

They say worse things happen at sea, and they don't come any worse than serving under Howard Da Silva's martinet of a captain in this grim saga of 19th-century seafaring based on a classic book which aimed at reforming sailors' working conditions. Alan Ladd is the shipowner's son, shanghaied into serving under Da Silva and soon stripped to the waist for a flogging. Director John Farrow had a real-life passion for the sea and this lavishly staged and strongly cast production (with William Bendix, Barry Fitzgerald and Brian Donlevy as members of the crew) is the best of his several maritime adventures. AE

Alan Ladd *Charles Stewart* • Brian Donlevy *Richard Henry Dana* • William Bendix *Amazeen* • Howard Da Silva *Captain Francis Thompson* • Barry Fitzgerald *Dooley* • Esther Fernandez *Maria Dominguez* • Albert Dekker *Brown* ■ *Dir* John Farrow • *Scr* Seton I Miller, George Bruce, from the novel by Richard Henry Dana Jr

Twogether
★★ 18

Drama 1994 · US · Colour · 117min

This wry look at modern love is not quite as trite as the title suggests. It's a twist on the old "morning after the night before" story, as artist Nick Cassavetes and environmental activist Brenda Bakke get drunk, get married, conceive and get divorced – although not necessarily in that order. Poking none-too-subtle fun at 1990s hedonism, this could have done with less lust and more laughs. DP

Nick Cassavetes *John Madler* • Brenda Bakke *Allison McKenzie* • Jeremy Piven *Arnie* • Jim Beaver *Oscar* • Tom Dugan (2) *Paul* • Damian London *Mark Saffron* ■ *Dir/Scr* Andrew Chiaramonte

Tycoon
★★★ U

Adventure 1947 · US · Colour · 123min

John Wayne may seem unlikely casting as a railroad engineer in this epic saga, but he's actually very good at conveying steely determination required of his character. It's certainly entertaining enough, though a stronger director than Richard Wallace may well have got more out of the romance between the Duke and mine-owner's daughter Laraine Day. Nevertheless, there's a very distinguished supporting cast and it's shot in exceptionally fine Technicolor. TS *DVD*

John Wayne *Johnny Munroe* • Laraine Day *Maura Alexander* • Cedric Hardwicke *Frederick Alexander* • Judith Anderson *Miss Braithwaite* • James Gleason *Pop Mathews* • Anthony Quinn *Ricky* • Grant Withers *Fog Harris* ■ *Dir* Richard Wallace • *Scr* Borden Chase, John Twist, from a novel by CE Scoggins

Tyler Perry's Why Did I Get Married Too?
★★ 12

Relationship comedy 2010 · US · Colour · 115min

Hugely successful African-American director, writer, producer and star Tyler Perry's sequel to his 2007 stateside hit *Why Did I Get Married?* carries on the intertwined relationship stories of a group of old college friends. Shot in practical fashion, the film features unremarkable performances from the ensemble cast, which includes Perry and Janet Jackson. Poor production values also stress the simplistic storyline, which is crammed with hurt, discovery and disaster. All of modern trauma is here – infidelity, unemployment, loss of self-respect and lack of communication – and it's all conveniently spelled out. KK Some violence, swearing, sexual references. *DVD*

Tyler Perry *Terry* • Janet Jackson *Patricia* • Jill Scott *Sheila* • Sharon Leal *Dianne* • Malik Yoba *Gavin* ■ *Dir/Scr* Tyler Perry

Typhoon
★★

Romantic adventure 1940 · US · Colour · 70min

After Sam Goldwyn borrowed Dorothy Lamour and had a huge hit with *The Hurricane*, the star's contract studio, Paramount, tried to go one better with *Typhoon*, photographing their famous "Sarong Girl" in glorious Technicolor. It's set on an island in the Pacific and the irretrievably silly plot has Lamour as a castaway since childhood who's discovered by a couple of sailors. The rest of the action involves the stock ingredients of a South Seas romantic adventure, with Robert Preston as Lamour's amour. RK

Dorothy Lamour *Dea* • Robert Preston *Johnny Potter* • Lynne Overman *Skipper Joe* • J Carrol Naish *Mekaike* ■ *Dir* Louis King • *Scr* Allen Rivkin, from a story by Steve Fisher

Typhoon
★★ 15

Action thriller 2005 · S Kor · Colour · 103min

If *Typhoon* was remade as an American action movie, it would undoubtedly be directed by Michael Bay and star Tom Cruise. It's another entry in South Korean cinema's continuing attempt to play Hollywood at its own game, with a blockbuster plot about a North Korean terrorist (Jang Dong-kun) who's trying to launch a nuclear weapon over the peninsula during a typhoon. Hopping restlessly from Korea to Russia to Thailand, the film searches for an epic, international scope. But a turgid lack of action means that it blows itself out before it's started. JR Korean, English, Thai, Russian, Mandarin +subtitles. *DVD*

Jang Dong-kun *Sin/Choi Myung-shin* • Lee Jung-jae *Gang Se-jong* • Lee Mi-yeon *Choi Myung-ju* • David McInnis *Somchai* • David No *Leather Jacket* • Chatthapong Phantan-Angkul *Toto* ■ *Dir/Scr* Kwak Kyung-taek

Tyrannosaur
★★★★★ 18

Drama 2010 · UK · Colour · 88min

British actor Paddy Considine's directorial debut is not for the faint-hearted. Considine is known for a variety of roles (*Dead Man's Shoes*, *Submarine*), but this bleak but

brilliant tale would rival Gary Oldman's *Nil by Mouth* for grimness. Peter Mullan plays a lonely drunk who one day staggers into the charity shop run by middle-class housewife Olivia Colman. Over time he gains a begrudging respect for her, but what he doesn't know is that this sweet, caring woman has demons of her own. Mullan plays this unsympathetic lead with power and magnetism, but it is Colman's terrific performance that sticks in the mind. DW Violence, swearing. *DVD* *BD*

Peter Mullan *Joseph* • Olivia Colman *Hannah* • Ned Dennehy *Tommy* • Sally Carman *Marie* • Samuel Bottomley *Samuel* • Paul Popplewell *Bod* ■ *Dir/Scr* Paddy Considine

Tyson
★★★★ 15

Sports documentary 2008 · US · Colour · 90min

The plot twists of Mike Tyson's all-too-real soap opera of a life have been well documented, but rarely has the former heavyweight boxing champion spoken on camera about his troubled past. Longtime friend James Toback's brutally revealing film intersperses archive fight footage and newsreel with candid confessionals, as Tyson confronts the inner demons that cost him his marriage, his livelihood and – for three years – his liberty. What emerges is a sad portrait of a broken man unable to come to terms either with his sporting worth or his astronomical wealth. A cautionary tale of the perils of a life in the spotlight. TeS Swearing, some violence, sexual references. *DVD* *BD*

Mike Tyson ■ *Dir* James Toback

T

U-Carmen eKhayelitsha
★★★ 12

Romantic musical drama
2004 · S Afr · Colour · 121min

This contemporary South African reworking of Bizet's opera *Carmen* was a curious choice to win the Golden Bear at the Berlin film festival. The music's majestic, the township setting ambitious and the performances boldly vibrant, yet the action doesn't always escape its stage origins. Performed in the Xhosa language, this opens with a scene-setting montage that captures the harshness of life on South Africa's margins. As the temptress who drives a lawman to his doom, Pauline Malefane makes an imposing Carmen, although Andile Tshoni is less persuasive as Jongikhaya, the lovesick cop. DP Xhosa +subtitles. Swearing. **DVD**

Pauline Malefane *Carmen* • Andries Mbali *Bra Nkomo* • Andiswa Kedama *Amanda* • Ruby Mthethwa *Pinki* • Andile Tshoni *Jongikhaya* • Lungelwa Blou *Nomakhaya* • Zamile Gantana *Captain Gantana* ■ *Dir* Mark Dornford-May • *Scr* Mark Dornford-May, Andiswa Kedama, Pauline Malefane, from the opera *Carmen* by Georges Bizet

UFO
★★★ 18

Science-fiction comedy
1993 · UK · Colour · 75min

Ultra-blue comedian Roy "Chubby" Brown made his screen debut in this raucous, very British sci-fi comedy. (Not since Sid Field had a comic gone direct from stage to film without doing TV in between.) When Brown is being his cheekily offensive self, it is often hard to suppress a smile. But when he is abducted by female extraterrestrials, who punish him for his sexism, the plot goes to pieces, entire scenes make no sense and the laughs are few. A pity that a live act of undoubted talent was not better coached for films. ("Contains swearing" is putting it mildly.) DM

Roy "Chubby" Brown • Sara Stockbridge *Zoe* • Amanda Symonds *Ava* • Roger Lloyd Pack *Solo* • Shirley Anne Field *Supreme commander* • Sue Lloyd *Judge* • Kiran Shah *Genghis Khan* • Kenny Baker (2) *Casanova* ■ *Dir* Tony Dow • *Scr* Richard Hall, Simon Wright, Roy "Chubby" Brown

U-571
★★★ 12

Second World War action thriller
2000 · US · Colour · 111min

This rip-roaring throwback to the wartime adventures of old finds Matthew McConaughey as a rookie submarine skipper in charge of a crippled U-boat after a secret plot to steal an Enigma code machine from the Nazis goes pear-shaped in the middle of the Atlantic. Since it was British sailors who got hold of the Enigma, it's a tad galling to see the likes of Bill Paxton, Harvey Keitel and Jon Bon Jovi take the credit. Not a patch on Wolfgang Petersen's seminal *Das Boot*, Jonathan Mostow's film does at least deliver its fair share of undemanding popcorn entertainment. NS Swearing. **DVD BLU**

Matthew McConaughey *Lt Andrew Tyler* • Bill Paxton *Lt Commander Mike Dahlgren* • Harvey Keitel *Chief Klough* • Jon Bon Jovi *Lt Peter Emmett* • David Keith *Marine Major Coonan* ■ *Dir* Jonathan Mostow • *Scr* Jonathan Mostow, Sam Montgomery, David Ayer, from a story by Jonathan Mostow

UHF
★★ PG

Comedy
1989 · US · Colour · 92min

Comic musician "Weird Al" Yankovic (who co-wrote the script) plays a slacker who takes over the management of a failing TV station, and is soon producing bizarre yet top-rated shows, raising the ire of rival TV station manager Kevin McCarthy. Michael Richards gives a side-splittingly funny performance as a simple-minded janitor, and the occasional laughs found in the samples of the TV programming make this fun for those willing to put their brain in neutral. KB **DVD BLU**

"Weird Al" Yankovic *George Newman* • Victoria Jackson *Teri* • Kevin McCarthy *RJ Fletcher* • Michael Richards *Stanley Spadowski* • David Bowe *Bob* • Stanley Brock *Uncle Harvey* • Anthony Geary *Philo* • Trinidad Silva *Raul Hernandez* ■ *Dir* Jay Levey • *Scr* Al Yankovic ["Weird Al" Yankovic], Jay Levey

US Marshals
★★ 15

Action thriller
1998 · US · Colour · 125min

This is not so much a belated sequel to *The Fugitive* as a rehash, with Tommy Lee Jones reprising his Oscar-winning role. In place of Harrison Ford we have Wesley Snipes, and in place of a murdered wife we have a corkscrew plot about the CIA. Former editor Stuart Baird keeps the action rolling along in a monotonous manner and characterisation is limited to the odd one-liner before the next big bang. AT Violence, swearing. **DVD**

Tommy Lee Jones *Chief Deputy Marshal Samuel Gerard* • Wesley Snipes *Mark Sheridan* • Robert Downey Jr *John Royce* • Joe Pantoliano *Deputy Marshal Cosmo Renfro* • Daniel Roebuck *Deputy Marshal Biggs* • Tom Wood *Deputy Marshal Newman* • LaTanya Richardson *Deputy Marshal Cooper* • Irène Jacob *Marie* • Kate Nelligan *US Marshal Walsh* ■ *Dir* Stuart Baird • *Scr* John Pogue, from the characters by Roy Huggins

The US vs John Lennon
★★★ 12

Documentary
2006 · US · Colour and BW · 95min

Despite being vetted by Yoko Ono and overlooking some of the ex-Beatle's less savoury antics, this is anything but a portrait of a victimised saint. It's a compelling account of John Lennon's politicisation and his struggle to beat a 1972 extradition order from the US government. The film also suggests that he was duped by the very people he sought to promote, who set him up as a high-profile decoy for the Nixon administration. There's a lack of balance in loading the talking heads with anti-establishment veterans such as Noam Chomsky and Gore Vidal, but the thesis that he was a naive peacenik whose conviction in his own legend enabled him to be exploited is both original and intriguing. DP **DVD**

John Lennon • Yoko Ono Lennon [Yoko Ono] *Yoko Ono* • Carl Bernstein • Noam Chomsky • Walter Cronkite • Ron Kovic • Gore Vidal ■ *Dir/Scr* David Leaf, John Scheinfeld

U Turn
★★★★ 18

Black comedy thriller
1997 · US/Fr · Colour · 119min

After the information overload of *Nixon* and the controversy of *Natural Born Killers*, Oliver Stone directed this low-budget, compact thriller. It's a rarity from the normally serious director – a surreal black comedy, starring Sean Penn as the mysterious drifter who arrives in Superior, Arizona, and becomes embroiled in a small-town conspiracy involving local flirt Jennifer Lopez and her husband Nick Nolte. As a sustained mood piece, the movie is a triumph. AT Swearing, violence, sex scenes.

Sean Penn *Bobby Cooper* • Jennifer Lopez *Grace McKenna* • Nick Nolte *Jake McKenna* • Powers Boothe *Sheriff Potter* • Claire Danes *Jenny* • Joaquin Phoenix *Toby N Tucker* • Billy Bob Thornton *Darrell* • Jon Voight *Blind man* • Julie Hagerty *Flo* • Bo Hopkins *Ed* • Liv Tyler *Girl in bus station* ■ *Dir* Oliver Stone • *Scr* John Ridley, from his novel *Stray Dogs*

U2 Rattle and Hum ★★★ 15

Concert documentary
1988 · US · Colour and BW · 94min

After the very wonderful *This Is Spinal Tap*, it's hard to take any "rockumentary" seriously these days, particularly one about the ever sincere U2. In fact, the Irish band even make a very moving visit to Gracelands during their 1987–88 North American tour. That said, this is stylishly shot in a mixture of grainy black and white and colour by Phil Joanou, there's a scene-stealing performance from blues legend BB King and the concert footage is stunning. JF

Bono • Adam Clayton • BB King ■ *Dir* Phil Joanou • *Cinematographers* Robert Brinkmann, Jordan Cronenweth

U23D
★★★ U

Music documentary
2007 · Ire/US · Colour · 84min

This splendid digital 3D concert movie was filmed during several shows given by rock band U2 in Buenos Aires, and mined from around 100 hours of footage. Eschewing the "hurl things at your face" approach of classic 3D, this is a sophisticated experience – even the glasses are different, the red-and-green cardboard type having been superseded by clear plastic – though first and foremost one for dedicated U2 fans. (Aficionados should note that the "Vertigo" tour playlist covers everything from *New Year's Day* to *Beautiful Day*.) But this also amply demonstrates the potential of the digital 3D format. Some day, all concert films may be made like this. DA

Bono • The Edge • Adam Clayton • Larry Mullen Jr ■ *Dir* Catherine Owens, Mark Pellington • *Cinematographer* Tom Krueger

UFOria
★★★ PG

Science-fiction comedy
1980 · US · Colour · 89min

Grocery store cashier and born-again Christian Cindy Williams awaits the appearance of a flying saucer, which she believes will bring salvation. Her boyfriend Fred Ward works for phoney evangelist Harry Dean Stanton who intends to exploit the "God is an astronaut" phenomenon for all that it's worth. Made in 1980 but shelved until the mid-1980s, this is an amiable, oddball movie that, on its eventual release, picked up quite a few admirers. The acting is fine and the piece has charm. DF

Cindy Williams *Arlene* • Harry Dean Stanton *Brother Bud* • Fred Ward *Sheldon* • Robert Gray *Emile* • Darrell Larson *Toby* • Harry Carey Jr *George Martin* • Hank Worden *Colonel* ■ *Dir/Scr* John Binder

Ugetsu Monogatari

★★★★★ PG

Period melodrama
1953 · Jpn · BW · 101min

Drawing on two stories by Akinari Ueda and one by Guy de Maupassant, this ethereal *jidai-geki* (Japanese period drama) won a top prize at Venice and confirmed Kenji Mizoguchi's reputation in the west. Set during the 16th-century civil wars, the story concerns two peasants whose weakness spells disaster for their wives. Farmer Sakae Ozawa's dream of becoming a samurai precipitates the rape of Mitsuko Mito, while potter Masayuki Mori's obsession with the ghostly Machiko Kyo results in the death of Kinuyo Tanaka. In exploring the transience of happiness and the injustice of patriarchal society, Mizoguchi makes lyrical use of gliding long takes that reinforce his material and mystical themes. Sheer genius. DP In Japanese. **DVD BLU**

Machiko Kyo *Lady Wakasa* • Masayuki Mori *Genjuro* • Kinuyo Tanaka *Miyagi* • Sakae Ozawa [Eitaro Ozawa] *Tobei* • Mitsuko Mito *Ohama* ■ *Dir* Kenji Mizoguchi • *Scr* Matsutaro Kawaguchi, Yoshikata Yoda, from the stories *Asaji Ga Yado* and *Jasei No In* from *Ugetsu Monogatari* by Akinari Ueda and from the story *Décoré!* by Guy de Maupassant • *Cinematographer* Kazuo Miyagawa

The Ugly American ★★★ PG

Political drama
1963 · US · Colour · 115min

Marlon Brando stars in one of his least known roles, as the American ambassador to Sarkhan, an Asian state divided between north and south, capitalist and communist. Brando intended this as a hard-hitting critique of American foreign policy and a movie that supported the work of the UN – he even cast his sister, Jocelyn, as a UN aid worker. But as usual with Brando, things got rather muddled, the studio interfered and no one could make a decision about anything. But despite its obvious flaws and bungled scenes, it's eerily prophetic about the Vietnam War. TS

Marlon Brando *Harrison Carter MacWhite* • Eiji Okada *Deong* • Sandra Church *Marion MacWhite* • Pat Hingle *Homer Atkins* • Arthur Hill *Grainger* • Jocelyn Brando *Emma Atkins* • Kukrit Pramoj *Prime Minister Kwen Sai* ■ *Dir* George Englund • *Scr* Stewart Stern, from the novel by William J Lederer, Eugene Burdick

The Ugly Dachshund ★★★ U

Comedy
1966 · US · Colour · 89min

Ideal entertainment for dog lovers everywhere, this Disney story is about a Great Dane called Brutus who's brought up with dachshunds and thinks he's one of them – however tall he gets. Dean Jones and Suzanne Pleshette are the human stars having to face up to the havoc caused in this charming family fare. Barking mad, but delightfully so. TH **DVD**

Dean Jones *Mark Garrison* • Suzanne Pleshette *Fran Garrison* • Charlie Ruggles [Charles Ruggles] *Dr Pruitt* • Kelly Thordsen *Officer Carmody* • Parley Baer *Mel Chadwick* • Robert Kino *Mr Toyama* • Mako *Kenji* • Charles Lane (2) *Judge* ■ *Dir* Norman Tokar • *Scr* Albert Aley, from the book *Dogs in an Omnibus* by Gladys Bronwyn Stern

The Ugly Duckling and Me
★★ U

Animated comedy
2006 · Fr/Ger/Ire/UK/Den · Colour · 85min

Younger children will lap up Michael Hegner and Karsten Kiilerich's breezy update of Hans Christian Andersen's beloved fable. The story follows the misadventures of rodent Ratso, a wannabe showbiz entrepreneur who sees a chance to make his fortune promoting Ugly the duckling as a carnival attraction. However, he doesn't count on being followed by an old flame bent on marriage or on his increasing fondness for his new feathered friend. The dialogue is frequently uncouth and self-consciously colloquial, while the action too often descends into broad farce. Despite these shortcomings the tale does keep moving at a cracking pace and unfussily peddles the age-old message that it's OK to be different. DP **DVD**

Morgan C Jones *Ratso/Frank* • Paul Tylack *Wesley* • Anna Olson *Phyllis* • Gary Hetzler *Stan* • *Scr* Mark Hodkinson, from a story by Michael Hegner, Karsten Kiilerich, inspired by the fairy tale by Hans Christian Andersen

The Ugly Truth
★★ 15

Romantic comedy
2009 · US · Colour · 91min

Perfectionist TV producer Katherine Heigl is horrified when chauvinist mouthpiece Gerard Butler is hired to increase ratings on her morning show. In spite of their antagonism, Butler persuades Heigl to follow his dating advice to land a handsome doctor. The two leads are alluring solo performers despite a lack of on-screen chemistry, and both enjoy exploring the deep flaws of their characters. Uneven though the script is, it still supplies a steadyish stream of prickly if hardly memorable banter and stirs up just enough trouble to amuse. Yet as a battle of the sexes, this isn't insightful or surprising. KK Swearing, sexual references. **DVD BLU**

Gerard Butler *Mike Chadway* • Katherine Heigl *Abby Richter* • Eric Winter *Dr Colin Anderson* • Cheryl Hines *Georgia* • Bree Turner *Joy* • Vicki Lewis *Saleswoman* • Nate Corddry [Nathan Corddry] *Josh* ■ *Dir* Robert Luketic • *Scr* Nicole Eastman, Karen McCullah Lutz, Kirsten Smith, from a story by Eastman

Ulee's Gold
★★★★ 15

Drama
1997 · US · Colour · 112min

The winner of a Golden Globe (though denied a best actor Oscar), Peter Fonda returned from years in the cinematic wilderness to give the best performance of his career in this slow-burning southern drama. Fonda meticulously builds up the character of the Florida beekeeper and Vietnam veteran who has to interrupt his strict routine to rescue his estranged daughter-in-law and tackle the villains double-crossed by his jailed son. Wisely, director Victor Nunez lets the pace roll as languorously as Tupelo honey dripping off a comb. A rare treat. **DP** Violence, swearing, drug abuse. **DVD**

Peter Fonda *Ulysses "Ulee" Jackson* • Patricia Richardson *Connie Hope* • Jessica Biel *Casey Jackson* • J Kenneth Campbell *Sheriff Bill Floyd* • Christine Dunford *Helen Jackson* • Steven Flynn *Eddie Flowers* • Dewey Weber *Ferris Dooley* ■ *Dir/Scr* Victor Nunez

The Ultimate Warrior ★★★★ 15
Science-fiction thriller
1975 · US · Colour · 89min

Ecological catastrophes have left New York in ruins and under Max von Sydow's ruthless leadership. Yul Brynner is the "street fighter" who guides his own posse of survivors to a better life away from such post-Armageddon tyranny. This is exciting, intelligent stuff from Robert Clouse, with loads of ingenious details and chilling moments. The final chase is a model of gripping suspense. **AJ** Swearing. **DVD**

Yul Brynner *Carson* • Max von Sydow *The Baron* • Joanna Miles *Melinda* • William Smith *Carrot* • Richard Kelton *Cal* • Stephen McHattie *Robert* • Darrell Zwerling *Silas* ■ *Dir/Scr* Robert Clouse

Ultraviolet ★★ 15
Science-fiction action thriller
2005 · US · Colour · 83min

Set at the end of the 21st century, the film depicts a world in which a botched biological weapons experiment has created a subclass of vampiric humans that the government is now trying to wipe out. One of these mutants, Milla Jovovich, is determined not to go down without a fight. Nick Chinlund hams it up dreadfully as the villain of the piece, while Cameron Bright pouts as the mysterious boy that Jovovich ends up protecting. This looks just like a shoot-'em-up computer game. **JF** English, Vietnamese +subtitles. Violence. **DVD** **BD**

Milla Jovovich *Violet* • Cameron Bright *Six* • Nick Chinlund *Daxus* • Sébastien Andrieu *Nerva* • William Fichtner *Garth* • Ida Martin *Young Violet* • David Collier *BF-1* ■ *Dir/Scr* Kurt Wimmer

Ulysses ★★★ U
Adventure
1954 · It · Colour · 99min

Several Italians plus classy Hollywood hacks Ben Hecht and Irwin Shaw laboured on this film of Homer's *Odyssey*, but whenever the actors open their mouths the movie loses its credibility (and the dubbing doesn't help). However, Kirk Douglas has tremendous presence – even barefoot and in a mini-skirt – on the long commute home from the Trojan wars and going in to battle with the Cyclops, sultry Sirens and Anthony Quinn. The special effects are cheap and wonky but the movie has an élan that makes it hard to resist. **AT** Italian dubbed.

Kirk Douglas *Ulysses* • Silvana Mangano *Penelope/Circe* • Anthony Quinn *Antinous* • Rossana Podesta *Nausicaa* • Sylvie Euriclea • Daniel Ivernel *Euriloco* • Jacques Dumesnil *Alicinous* ■ *Dir* Mario Camerini • *Scr* Franco Brusati, Mario Camerini, Ennio De Concini, Hugh Gray, Ben Hecht, Ivo Perilli, Irwin Shaw, from the poem *The Odyssey* by Homer

Ulysses ★★★ 15
Fantasy drama
1967 · US/UK · Colour · 119min

If ever a great novel was unfilmable, this is it – James Joyce's sublime chronicle of Dublin Jew Leopold Bloom's long night's journey into day. Milo O'Shea is poignant as everyman Bloom and Barbara Jefford is superb as his rancid, randy wife Molly, but the enthusiasm of producer/director/co-writer Joseph Strick just isn't enough to lift Joyce's classic work from the pages and bring it to life. A flawed enterprise, the film is partly salvaged by the use of genuine Dublin locations and the marvellous performances of the mainly Irish cast. **TH** **DVD**

Barbara Jefford *Molly Bloom* • Milo O'Shea *Leopold Bloom* • Maurice Roëves *Stephen Dedalus* • TP McKenna *Buck Mulligan* • Martin Dempsey *Simon Dedalus* • Sheila O'Sullivan *May Goulding Dedalus* ■ *Dir* Joseph Strick • *Scr* Joseph Strick, Fred Haines, from the novel by James Joyce

Ulysses' Gaze ★★★★ PG
Epic drama
1995 · Gr/Fr/It · Colour · 169min

Harvey Keitel stars as a Greek film-maker who goes in search of his Balkan roots in director Theodorus Angelopoulos's lengthy and haunting political fable. Clearly based on Angelopoulos's own experiences, the film slips between past and present, with both classical and personal allusions, until, by the end of a bleak odyssey of self-discovery, the film-maker has learned more than he ever wanted to know about his former home. This gently unfolding epic drama has an assurance that's matched by its audacious courage. **AJ** English, Greek +subtitles.

Harvey Keitel *A* • Maia Morgenstern *Woman* • Erland Josephson *Preserver* • Thanassis Vengos *Chauffeur* • Yorgos Michalakopoulos *Correspondent* • Dora Volonaki *Old woman (Athens)* ■ *Dir* Theodoros Angelopoulos [Theo Angelopoulos] • *Scr* Theodoros Angelopoulos, Tonino Guerra, Petro Markaris

Ulzana's Raid ★★★★ 18
Western
1972 · US · Colour · 96min

This was attacked by some for being a reactionary return to the depiction of native Americans as bloodthirsty savages and mocked by others for its attempts to combine violent action with diatribes about racial prejudice. Yet Robert Aldrich's powerful 1970s western also has many champions, who see it as both a bold Vietnam allegory and an attempt to restore a semblance of historical accuracy to events coloured by decades of horse-opera exploitation and liberal revisionism. Burt Lancaster is superb as the scout saddened by conflict, while Alan Sharp's script and Joseph Biroc's cinematography are first class. **AT** Violence, some swearing, brief nudity. **DVD**

Burt Lancaster *McIntosh* • Bruce Davison *Lt Garnett DeBuin* • Jorge Luke *Ke-Ni-Tay* • Richard Jaeckel *Sergeant* • Joaquin Martinez *Ulzana* • Lloyd Bochner *Captain Gates* • Karl Swenson *Rukeyser* ■ *Dir* Robert Aldrich • *Scr* Alan Sharp

Umberto D ★★★★★ PG
Drama
1952 · It · BW · 85min

The ideal film," wrote Cesare Zavattini, the theoretical father of neorealism, "would be 90 minutes in the life of a man to whom nothing happens." Shot on location, with a non-professional cast and an attention to detail that allows the viewer to discover the emotional or dramatic content of a scene, Vittorio De Sica's poignant study of an ageing civil servant, ostracised by the society he'd so faithfully served, comes close to fulfilling that vision. Fighting despair with dignity, Carlo Battisti is outstanding, whether coddling his devoted dog, Flike, or relishing his chats with pregnant maid, Maria-Pia Casilio. A sublime piece of humanist, observational cinema. **DP** Italian +subtitles.. **DVD**

Carlo Battisti *Umberto Domenico Ferrari* • Maria-Pia Casilio *Maria* • Lina Gennari *Landlady* • Alberto Albani Barbieri *Fiancé* • Elena Rea *Sister* • Ileana Simova *Surprised woman in the bedroom* • Memmo Carotenuto *Voice of light for Umberto in hospital* ■ *Dir* Vittorio De Sica • *Scr* Cesare Zavattini, Vittorio De Sica, from a story by Cesare Zavattini

The Umbrellas of Cherbourg ★★★★★ U
Musical
1964 · Fr/W Ger · Colour · 87min

Everything is sung – even the most mundane dialogue – in director Jacques Demy's enchanting French throwback to the Hollywood musicals of the late 1920s. The stunning design (Cherbourg citizens allowed their buildings to be painted pink and red) and Catherine Deneuve's ethereal performance add to the fairy-tale qualities of the haunting love story between a shop girl and a garage attendant. It's when he

leaves her pregnant to fight in the Algerian War that Demy's tuneful heartbreaker reaches the dizzy romantic heights. Michel Legrand's gorgeous score includes the standard *I Will Wait for You* and *Watch What Happens*. Absolutely beguiling. **AJ** French +subtitles. **DVD** **BD**

Catherine Deneuve *Geneviève Emery* • Nino Castelnuovo *Guy Foucher* • Anne Vernon *Madame Emery* • Ellen Farner *Madeleine* • Marc Michel *Roland Cassard* • Mireille Perrey *Aunt Elise* • Jean Champion *Aubin* • Harald Wolff *Dubourg* ■ *Dir/Scr* Jacques Demy

The Unbearable Lightness of Being ★★★ 18
Romantic political drama
1988 · US · Colour · 165min

The problem of coming to terms with reality is the simplest explanation for this blatant, European-style art film directed by American Philip Kaufman. Lengthily elaborated from Milan Kundera's bestseller, it concerns a womanising surgeon (Daniel Day-Lewis) whose main loves are sacred (Juliette Binoche) and profane (Lena Olin), and how their involvement collides with the communist authorities in Czechoslovakia. Some wonderful atmospherics of a besieged culture don't make up for the fact that it runs out of important things to say. **TH** Swearing, sex scenes. **DVD**

Daniel Day-Lewis *Tomas* • Juliette Binoche *Tereza* • Lena Olin *Sabina* • Derek De Lint *Franz* • Erland Josephson *The Ambassador* • Pavel Landovsky *Pavel* • Donald Moffat *Chief Surgeon* ■ *Dir* Philip Kaufman • *Scr* Philip Kaufman, Jean-Claude Carrière, from the novel by Milan Kundera

The Unbeatables ★★★ U
Animated sports adventure
2013 · Arg/Sp · Colour · 97min

The Unbeatables is the computer animated story of Amadeo (voiced by Rupert Grint), a table football expert whose pint-size players come to life to help him take on arrogant football superstar striker Flash (Anthony Head) in an actual match to save his village. While the plot may wander at times, the English-language version of this Argentinian film benefits greatly from the comedy trio of Ralf Little, Peter Serafinowicz and Rob Brydon as the voices of Amadeo's diminutive team-mates. The witty script and banter between the three makes for some very funny moments. **JL** **3D**

Rupert Grint *Amadeo* • Rob Brydon *Rico* • Anthony Head *Flash* • Ralf Little *Skip* • Alex Norton *Gregor* ■ *Dir* Juan José Campanella • *Scr* Michael Smith, Richard Smith, David Burgess, Victor Glynn, Juan José Campanella, from a story by Gastón Gorali, Eduardo Sacheri, Campanella, Axel Kuschevatzky, from the short story *The Memoirs of a Right-winger* by Roberto Fontanarrosa

The Unbelievable Truth ★★★ 15
Drama
1989 · US · Colour · 86min

Although it has echoes of a popular soap opera in its celebration of the mundane, Hal Hartley's feature debut (shot in just 11 days) is the closest thing yet to a suburban western – a sort of *Shane* on Long Island. Robert Burke is suitably terse and mysterious as the man in black who gives discontented Adrienne Shelly something more to think about than parental suffocation, nuclear holocaust and teenage romance. Full of quirky conversations and eccentric characters, but with occasionally overintrusive direction. **DP** Swearing. **DVD** **BD**

Adrienne Shelly *Audry Hugo* • Robert John Burke [Robert Burke] *Josh Hutton* • Christopher Cooke [Chris Cooke] *Vic Hugo* • Julia McNeal *Pearl* • Katherine Mayfield *Liz Hugo* • Gary Sauer *Emmet* • Mark Bailey *Mike* • David Healy *Todd Whitbread* • Edie Falco *Jane, a waitress* ■ *Dir/Scr* Hal Hartley

The Unborn ★ 15
Horror thriller
2008 · US · Colour · 84min

Writer/director David S Goyer gives some well-worn exorcism conventions a tasteless Jewish spin in this lazy, laughable

possession horror. Student Casey (*Cloverfield's* Odette Yustman) suffers from terrifying visions linked to her twin brother, who died in the womb. Worse, the evil kaballah spirit haunting her is a "dybbuk", a soul in limbo denied entrance to the afterlife. It's left to bored-looking rabbi Gary Oldman to expunge it and halt the family curse in a tame crash-bang finale. Monstrous apparitions include pensioners walking crab-style and dogs with upside-down heads, but the few jolts on offer here are largely the result of sudden loud noises on the soundtrack. **AJ** **DVD** **BD**

Odette Yustman *Casey Beldon* • Gary Oldman *Rabbi Sendak* • Meagan Good *Romy Marshall* • Cam Gigandet *Mark Hardigan* • James Remar *Gordon Beldon* • Jane Alexander *Sofi Kozma* ■ *Dir/Scr* David S Goyer

Unbreakable ★★★★ 12
Fantasy drama
2000 · US · Colour · 106min

Director M Night Shyamalan's follow-up to *The Sixth Sense* also stars Bruce Willis and deals with a paranormal phenomenon. While not quite as good, it does have much going for it, moving the supernatural genre to a thought-provoking and surreal new level. After becoming the sole survivor of a train crash, security guard Willis is told by brittle-boned comic-art gallery owner Samuel L Jackson that he's an invincible superhero in disguise. What's more, Jackson believes that comic books are the only way this heroic tradition has been kept alive. This is an assured, enthralling and subtle fantasy. **AJ** **DVD** **BD**

Bruce Willis *David Dunn* • Samuel L Jackson *Elijah Price* • Robin Wright Penn [Robin Wright] *Audrey Dunn* • Spencer Treat Clark *Joseph Dunn* • Charlayne Woodard *Elijah's mother* ■ *Dir/Scr* M Night Shyamalan

Unbroken ★★★★ 15
Drama based on a true story
2014 · US · Colour · 131min

Angelina Jolie takes a conventional but confident approach to directing the amazing life story of Louis Zamperini, with Jack O'Connell as the self-proclaimed regular guy who competed in the Berlin Olympics in 1936. But Zamperini's life took some terrible turns: after crashing in the Pacific and spending days adrift, he was saved only to be thrown into a Japanese PoW camp. If Jolie denies us a more complex portrayal, she makes up for it with visceral scenes of struggle, which are well balanced with Zamperini's bright, unrelenting optimism. **SP** **DVD** **BD**

Jack O'Connell (2) *Louis Zamperini* • Domhnall Gleeson *Russell Allen "Phil" Phillips* • Garrett Hedlund *John Fitzgerald* • Miyavi [Takamasa Ishihara] *Mutsuhiro Watanabe* • Alex Russell *Pete Zamperini* • Finn Wittrock *Francis "Mac" McNamara* • Luke Treadaway *Miller* • Jai Courtney *Hugh "Cup" Cuppernell* ■ *Dir* Angelina Jolie • *Scr* Ethan Coen, Joel Coen, Richard LaGravenese, William Nicholson, from Laura Hillenbrand's non-fiction book

The Uncanny ★ 15
Portmanteau horror
1977 · Can/UK · Colour · 84min

Petrified Peter Cushing has written a book proving that cats are planning world domination and tries to persuade Ray Milland to publish it on the strength of a trio of creepy tales. In the first, Simon Williams and Susan Penhaligon try to cheat Joan Greenwood's cats out of their inheritance, while in the second an orphan shrinks her evil cousin and uses her as a cat toy. But Donald Pleasence and Samantha Eggar put some vim into their *Pit and the Pendulum* pastiche. Overall, however, this dismal picture induces cringes rather than chills. **DP** **DVD**

Peter Cushing *Wilbur Gray* • Ray Milland *Frank Richards* • Susan Penhaligon *Janet* • Joan Greenwood *Miss Malkin* • Alexandra Stewart *Mrs Joan Blake* • Donald Pleasence *Valentine De'Ath* • Samantha Eggar *Edina Hamilton* ■ *Dir* Denis Héroux • *Scr* Michel Parry

U

Uncensored ★★ U
Second World War drama
1942 · UK · BW · 106min

The problem with this wartime movie is that it's too polite. There's no sense of menace or danger in the Belgian setting, where the Nazis are in occupation. That's partly the fault of the screenplay and of director Anthony Asquith, who hadn't the temperament for such a story. Eric Portman and Phyllis Calvert revive a patriotic underground newspaper, only to be betrayed. BB

Eric Portman *Andre Delange* · Phyllis Calvert *Julie Lanvin* · Griffith Jones *Father de Gruyte* · Raymond Lovell *Von Koerner* · Peter Glenville *Charles Neels* · Frederick Culley *Victor Lanvin* · Irene Handl *Frau von Koerner* ■ *Dir* Anthony Asquith · *Scr* Wolfgang Wilhelm, Terence Rattigan, Rodney Ackland

Uncertain Glory ★★★ U
Second World War drama
1944 · US · BW · 97min

Only too obviously typecast, Errol Flynn plays a philandering criminal in Second World War-ravaged Europe who gives his life, hoping to redeem himself. Though rather talky for a Raoul Walsh-directed movie, it features fine performances by Flynn, Paul Lukas and Jean Sullivan. TH

Errol Flynn *Jean Picard* · Paul Lukas *Marcel Bonet* · Jean Sullivan *Marianne* · Lucile Watson *Mme Maret* · Faye Emerson *Louise* · James Flavin *Captain of the Guard Mobile* · Douglas Dumbrille [Douglas Dumbrille] *Police commissioner* ■ *Dir* Raoul Walsh · *Scr* Laszlo Vadnay, Max Brand, from a story by Joe May, Laszlo Vadnay

The Uncle ★★★★ PG
Drama
1964 · UK · BW · 86min

This little charmer caused controversy by being denied a release for two years, during which time the film was slightly re-edited against its director's wishes. But *The Uncle* is one of the cinema's most inventive and perceptive portraits of childhood. It's about a seven-year-old boy (Robert Duncan) who becomes an uncle rather suddenly. The shock of the birth catapults him into an emotional crisis, leading to isolation from his family and schoolfriends. Filmed in and around Plymouth, it's a touching story, and beautifully performed. AT DVD

Rupert Davies *David* · Brenda Bruce *Addie* · Robert Duncan *Gus* · William Marlowe *Wayne* · Ann Lynn *Sally* · Barbara Leake *Emma* · Helen Fraser *Mary* ■ *Dir* Desmond Davis · *Scr* Desmond Davis, Margaret Abrams, from the novel by Abrams

Uncle Benjamin ★★★
Swashbuckling comedy
1969 · Fr · Colour · 91min

The name of Edouard Molinaro will forever be associated with *La Cage aux Folles*. All the good taste and restraint that made that picture an Oscar winner for best foreign language film is gleefully absent in this rollicking piece of costume bawdiness, which comes over as a cross between a Henry Fielding novel and a Hollywood swashbuckler. Jacques Brel is solid enough as the 18th-century country doctor of the title, but veteran actor Bernard Blier steals the picture as a coarse, cruel aristocrat. DP French dubbed.

Jacques Brel *Benjamin Rathery* · Claude Jade *Manette* · Rosy Varte *Bettine* · Robert Dalban *Aubergiste* · Bernard Blier *Cambyse* · Armand Mestral *Machecourt* ■ *Dir* Edouard Molinaro · *Scr* André Couteaux, Jean-François Hauduroy, from a story by Claude Tillier

Uncle Boonmee Who Can Recall His Past Lives ★★★ 12
Fantasy drama
2010 · UK/Thai/Fr/Ger/Sp/Neth/US · Colour · 108min

Thai director Apichatpong Weerasethakul once more exercises his unique gift for finding the extraordinary in the everyday in 2010's surprise Cannes Palme d'Or winner. Very much an acquired taste, this strange tale of a dying man visited by family ghosts

will hardly convert the uninitiated from dull bewilderment to a praised state of ethereal serenity. Get on Weerasethakul's mystical wavelength, however, and the rewards are a genuinely haunted atmosphere and keen emotional resonance. But, even with broad humour and local politics thrown in, this film's stark approach won't be easily digestible for the mainstream majority. AJ Thai +subtitles. A sex scene. DVD Blu

Jenjira Pongpass *Jen* · Sakda Kaewbuadee *Tong* ■ *Dir/Scr* Apichatpong Weerasethakul

Uncle Buck ★★★ 12
Comedy
1989 · US · Colour · 95min

This movie marked writer/director John Hughes's move away from adolescence, after films such as *The Breakfast Club* and *Ferris Bueller's Day Off*, and return to childhood. Despite the fact that this was also the film that unleashed Macaulay Culkin on to the world at large, there is still much to enjoy. John Candy makes the most of his starring role as the lovable slob who is pressed into looking after his brother's children and Hughes stages some neat comic set pieces. Only the sentimental moralising strikes a false note. JF Swearing. DVD Blu

John Candy *Buck Russell* · Macaulay Culkin *Miles Russell* · Jean Louisa Kelly *Tia Russell* · Gaby Hoffman [Gaby Hoffmann] *Maizy Russell* · Amy Madigan *Chanice Kobolowski* · Elaine Bromka *Cindy Russell* · Garrett M Brown *Bob Russell* · Laurie Metcalf *Marcie Dahlgren-Frost* · Jay Underwood *Bug* ■ *Dir/Scr* John Hughes

Uncle Silas ★★★
Period thriller
1947 · UK · BW · 102min

Though dated, this melodrama is distinguished by a glowing performance from the lovely Jean Simmons as the teenage waif sent to live with creepy old Uncle Silas (Derrick de Marney) in his ramshackle mansion. Atmospherics abound, with the nightmarish feel superbly sustained by the cinematography of Robert Krasker and Nigel Huke, and helped by the over-the-top performances of de Marney and Greek actress Katina Paxinou. TS

Jean Simmons *Caroline Ruthyn* · Katina Paxinou *Madame de la Rougierre* · Derrick de Marney *Uncle Silas* · Derek Bond *Lord Richard Ilbury* · Sophie Stewart *Lady Monica Waring* · Manning Whiley *Dudley Ruthyn* · Esmond Knight *Dr Bryerly* · Reginald Tate *Austin Ruthyn* ■ *Dir* Charles Frank · *Scr* Ben Travers, from the novel by Sheridan Le Fanu

Uncommon Valor ★★★ 15
Action drama
1983 · US · Colour · 100min

Gene Hackman brings an unusual psychological depth to the part of an embittered father leading a hand-picked platoon into Laos to find his son, reported missing in action ten years before in Vietnam. Joe Gayton's script wins no prizes for originality or political correctness and the direction of Ted Kotcheff only just passes muster, but co-producer John Milius knows how to put on a show. DP Violence, swearing. DVD

Gene Hackman *Colonel Rhodes* · Robert Stack *MacGregor* · Fred Ward *Wilkes* · Reb Brown *Blaster* · Randall "Tex" Cobb *Sailor* · Patrick Swayze *Scott* · Harold Sylvester *Johnson* · Tim Thomerson *Charts* ■ *Dir* Ted Kotcheff · *Scr* Joe Gayton

Unconditional Love ★★ 15
Comedy mystery
2001 · US · Colour · 116min

Alternating between laugh-out-loud hilarious and cringingly bad, this contrived comedy is both wildly unconventional and totally traditional. Kathy Bates is an obsessed American housewife who treks off to Britain for the funeral of her favourite crooner (Jonathan Pryce), only to become embroiled in a hunt for his murderer with the star's lover, Rupert Everett. Though this odd-couple pairing has charm, it's the sharp tongue of Bates's dwarf daughter-in-law, Meredith Eaton, that's the real delight. SF Swearing, violence. DVD

Kathy Bates *Grace Beasley* · Rupert Everett *Dirk Simpson* · Jonathan Pryce *Victor Fox* · Jake Noseworthy *Andrew* · Meredith Eaton *Maudey* ·

Peter Sarsgaard *Window washer* · Lynn Redgrave *Nola Fox* · Stephanie Beacham *Harriet Fox-Smith* · Richard Briers *Barry Moore* · Marcia Warren *Lynette Fox-Moore* ■ *Dir* PJ Hogan · *Scr* Jocelyn Moorhouse, PJ Hogan

Unconquered ★★★
Period adventure
1947 · US · Colour · 146min

Cecil B DeMille's vast western epic stars Paulette Goddard as a cockney murderess transported to slavery in colonial America, where Gary Cooper saves her from the clutches of fur trapper Howard Da Silva. As if that weren't enough, there's savage tribesmen, shooting the rapids and being burned at the stake to contend with, too. Fortunately, DeMille keeps the moralising to a minimum and packs as much passion, drama, and colour into it as the budget will allow. A real galumpher of a movie. AT

Paulette Goddard *Abby Hale* · Gary Cooper *Capt Chris Holden* · Howard Da Silva *Martin Garth* · Boris Karloff *Guyasuta* · Cecil Kellaway *Jeremy Love* · Ward Bond *John Fraser* · Katherine DeMille *Hannah* · Henry Wilcoxon *Capt Steele* · C Aubrey Smith *Lord Chief Justice* ■ *Dir* Cecil B DeMille · *Scr* Charles Bennett, Frederic M Frank, Jesse Lasky Jr, from the novel *The Judas Tree* by Neil H Swanson

Unconquered ★★★★ PG
Drama based on a true story
1989 · US · Colour · 113min

This TV movie combines an uplifting true story of individual sporting success against the odds with an illuminating study of racial hatred in the American South at the time of Martin Luther King. The worthy cast is headed by Peter Coyote as a progressive senator and Dermot Mulroney as his athlete son, coping with both the prejudice against his father and his own physical disabilities. The result is an above-average effort that could be described as *Chariots of Fire* with a social conscience. PF

Peter Coyote *Richmond Flowers Sr* · Dermot Mulroney *Richmond Flowers Jr* · Tess Harper *Mary Flowers* · Jenny Robertson *Cindy Shiver* · Frank Whaley *Arnie Woods* · Bob Gunton *George Wallace* · Larry Riley *Martin Luther King* · RD Call *Floyd Petrie* · Noble Willingham *Bear Bryant* ■ *Dir* Dick Lowry · *Scr* Pat Conroy, from a story by Martin Chitwood

Uncorked ★★
Romantic drama
2008 · US · Colour · 102min

In this routine romance, Julie Benz (from TV's *Dexter*) plays a high-flying executive who finds true love during a work conference at a vineyard. Scott Elrod is well cast as the handsome widower and celebrity chef whose charm leaves the enamoured Benz torn between her career and a serious relationship, and there's quality support from JoBeth Williams and Elliott Gould as Elrod's financially strapped parents. Naturally, happy endings are guaranteed; it's just a pity that the many business scenes are so stagnant, slowing down the pace and reducing the film's emotional impact. SF

Julie Benz *Johnetta "Johnny" Prentis* · Scott Elrod *Andrew Browning* · Elliott Gould *Paul* · JoBeth Williams *Sophia* · Anne-Marie Johnson *Debra* ■ *Dir* David S Cass Sr · *Scr* Jim Head

Uncovered: the War on Iraq ★★★★
Documentary
2004 · US · Colour · 83min

Robert Greenwald's authoritative documentary is an uncompromising assessment of George W Bush's "war on terror". More considered and less self-congratulatory than *Fahrenheit 9/11*, this nevertheless shares Michael Moore's incredulity that the president was able to use the September 11 terrorist attacks to justify the invasion of Iraq. Intelligence and diplomatic experts, including former chief weapons inspector Dr David Kay, analyse and pour scorn over the arguments for going to war, backing up their revelations with damning evidence. It's impossible to watch this clinical exposé without harbouring grave misgivings about the way the modern world is run. DP DVD

■ *Dir* Robert Greenwald

The Undead ★★★ 15
Horror
1957 · US · BW · 71min

Cult director Roger Corman's first "real" horror movie – albeit one with sci-fi overtones – was this quickie reincarnation tale that cashed in on the "previous existence" craze of the 1950s. Filmed in a derelict supermarket (hence the strangely effective claustrophobic atmosphere), the film has Pamela Duncan as a hapless hooker hypnotised by her psychiatrist back to medieval times where she's condemned as a witch. Textbook Corman. AJ DVD

Pamela Duncan *Helene/Diana* · Richard Garland *Pendragon* · Allison Hayes *Livia* · Val Dufour *Quintus* · Mel Welles *Smolkin* · Dorothy Neuman *Meg Maud* · Billy Barty *The Imp* ■ *Dir* Roger Corman · *Scr* Charles Griffith, Mark Hanna

Undead ★★ 15
Horror
2002 · Aus · Colour · 104min

Every gory moment of note from the past four decades of zombie horror ends up present and politically incorrect in this low-budget feature debut from twins Peter and Michael Spierig. Set in rural Queensland, it begins with a meteor shower that soon has the effect of turning the population of a small fishing village into brain-munching zombies. A badly paced mess, this becomes increasingly repetitive and incomprehensible as it meanders on. AJ DVD

Felicity Mason *Rene* · Mungo McKay *Marion* · Rob Jenkins *Wayne* · Lisa Cunningham *Sallyanne* · Dirk Hunter *Harrison* · Emma Randall *Molly* · Steve Grieg *Agent* · Noel Sheridan *Chip* ■ *Dir/Scr* Michael Spierig, Peter Spierig

The Undeclared War ★★★★
Documentary
1992 · Fr · Colour · 240min

Gleaned from 50-odd hours of interviews with 28 conscripted veterans of the battle for Algeria (1954-62), Bertrand Tavernier's documentary broke a silence that had existed since a divided France ceded what to many was less a colony than an integral part of *La Patrie*. Employing personal photos and establishing shots of the north African desert and the city of Grenoble (home to the interviewees and site of one of the most ferocious anti-war demonstrations), Tavernier allows the men to explore their own memories and emotions. While some deliver impenitent diatribes, others simply break down. Harrowing and revelatory. DP French +subtitles.

■ *Dir* Bertrand Tavernier

The Undefeated ★★ PG
Western
1969 · US · Colour · 113min

This western is undistinguished but beautifully photographed by veteran cameraman William Clothier. A toupeed, paunchy John Wayne is the Union colonel on his way to Mexico, who confronts mustachioed Confederate colonel Rock Hudson. The theme of post-Civil War reconciliation ensures that no sparks fly between the two main characters, nor is there any real chemistry between the stars. Director Andrew V McLaglen seems to have had problems establishing the right tone for this tale. TS DVD

John Wayne *Colonel John Henry Thomas* · Rock Hudson *Colonel James Langdon* · Tony Aguilar *General Rojas* · Roman Gabriel *Blue Boy* · Marian McCargo *Ann Langdon* · Lee Meriwether *Margaret Langdon* · Michael Vincent [Jan-Michael Vincent] *Bubba Wilkes* · Ben Johnson (1) *Short Grub* · Harry Carey Jr *Webster* ■ *Dir* Andrew V McLaglen · *Scr* James Lee Barrett, from a story by Stanley L Hough

Undefeated ★★★★★ 12A
Sports documentary
2011 · US · Colour · 113min

In a run-down corner of Tennessee, a volunteer football coach battles to help a high school team better themselves and overcome over 100 years of underachievement. It sounds like the stuff of too many sports dramas, but this wonderful, Oscar-winning documentary is the real thing. The big games, injury crises and personality conflicts are all present, but

U SUITABLE FOR ALL   Uc SUITABLE ESPECIALLY FOR YOUNG CHILDREN (DVD ONLY)   PG PARENTAL GUIDANCE   12A UNDER 12s TO BE ACCOMPANIED (CINEMA ONLY)

the effect is so much more powerful because film-makers Dan Lindsay and TJ Martin understand that what we're watching is more about building character than it is about winning games. TJ **DVD**

■ *Dir* Daniel Lindsay, TJ Martin

Under California Stars ★★ U

Western 1948 · US · Colour · 69min

In this minor late entry in the career of self-styled "king of the cowboys" Roy Rogers, much of the pleasure is provided by B-musical star Jane Frazee, a former radio singer. She provides a watchable alternative to Trigger, as Rogers once again manages to avoid damage to his cowboy outfits, despite fisticuffs and some hard riding. TS

Roy Rogers *Roy Rogers* • Jane Frazee *Caroline Maynard* • Andy Devine *Cookie Bullfincher* • George H Lloyd [George Lloyd] *Jonas "Pop" Jordan* • Wade Crosby *Lye McFarland* • Michael Chapin *Ted Conover* • House Peters Jr *Ed* ■ *Dir* William Witney • *Scr* Sloan Nibley, Paul Gangelin, from a story by Gangelin

Under Capricorn ★★★ PG

Period melodrama 1949 · UK · Colour · 117min

Although this is one of Alfred Hitchcock's oddest movies, the master's hand is firmly in evidence. It's a melodrama set in 19th-century Australia starring Ingrid Bergman as a rich woman coming to terms with her marriage to stablehand and transported convict Joseph Cotten. The production was troubled by the start of Bergman's infamous love affair with Roberto Rossellini and by Hitchcock's eagerness to finish the film quickly to avoid paying British taxes. You may notice some shots that run for more than five minutes without a cut, contributing to the film's heady romanticism. AT **DVD**

Ingrid Bergman *Lady Henrietta Flusky* • Joseph Cotten *Sam Flusky* • Michael Wilding *Charles Adare* • Margaret Leighton *Milly* • Cecil Parker *Governor* • Denis O Dea *Corrigan* • Jack Watling *Winter* ■ *Dir* Alfred Hitchcock • *Scr* James Bridie, Hume Cronyn, from the play by John Colton, Margaret Linden and from the novel by Helen Simpson

Under Fire ★★★★ 15

Political drama 1983 · US · Colour · 122min

This exceptional political thriller, part morality tale and part action adventure, has three journalists (Nick Nolte, Gene Hackman and Joanna Cassidy) covering the Nicaraguan revolution and becoming involved in the violent struggle. Director Roger Spottiswoode has brilliantly realised the electric atmosphere generated by rubble-strewn streets, above which snipers lurk and in which people die just because they get in the way. Jean-Louis Trintignant is credibly creepy as a double agent. TH Swearing. **DVD**

Nick Nolte *Russell Price* • Ed Harris *Oates* • Gene Hackman *Alex Grazier* • Joanna Cassidy *Claire Stryder* • Alma Martinez *Isela* • Holly Palance *Journalist* • Jean-Louis Trintignant *Marcel Jazy* ■ *Dir* Roger Spottiswoode • *Scr* Ron Shelton, Clayton Frohman, from a story by Frohman

Under Great White Northern Lights ★★★

Music documentary 2009 · US · Colour and BW · 93min

Rock duo the White Stripes embark on a tour visiting out-of-the-way towns in every Canadian province and territory in director Emmett Malloy's low-key documentary. Part concert movie, part travelogue, this demonstrates little insight into what makes the band tick, owing in no small part to drummer Meg White's discomfort in front of the camera. Jack White, however, is a garrulous presence - whether jamming with the elders of an Inuit tribe, sampling raw caribou or hobnobbing with small-town dignitaries - and the live footage electrifies. TeS

Jack White • Meg White ■ *Dir* Emmett Malloy • *Cinematographer* Giles Dunning

Under Milk Wood ★★★ 15

Drama 1971 · UK · Colour · 87min

Dylan Thomas's celebrated 1954 radio play was a complex blend of dream, reality and poetry, which dealt with life, love and liquid refreshment in the mythical Welsh fishing village of Llareggub. Richard Burton, who plays "First Voice" - the narrator - knew Thomas well and had performed the play on radio. He's joined here by his then-wife Elizabeth Taylor as the childhood sweetheart of Captain Cat, the blind seafarer played by Peter O'Toole. There's a fascinating cast and Thomas's dialogue remains exceptionally vivid - especially with Burton's voice driving much of it. Andrew Sinclair's direction sensibly avoids any fireworks. AT **DVD**

Richard Burton *First Voice* • Elizabeth Taylor *Rosie Probert* • Peter O'Toole *Captain Cat* • Glynis Johns *Myfanwy Price* • Vivien Merchant *Mrs Pugh* • Sian Phillips *Mrs Ogmore-Pritchard* • Victor Spinetti *Mog Edwards* ■ *Dir* Andrew Sinclair • *Scr* Andrew Sinclair, from the radio play by Dylan Thomas

Under Milk Wood ★★ 15

Drama 2015 · UK · Colour · 86min

Under Milk Wood is a surreal, dream-like experience. Adapted from Dylan Thomas's celebrated radio play, it takes place in a small fishing village on the coast of Wales, where residents are preoccupied with their dreams and fantasies. The film plays out as a succession of abstract sequences that jump from character to character, accompanied by Thomas's lyrical, evocative prose poetry, most of which is narrated to us by Rhys Ifans. Every scene is filled with striking imagery and rich, descriptive language, and the result is a fairly unusual film that can be difficult to follow. SC English, Welsh +subtitles. Sex scenes, nudity. **DVD** **BLU**

Rhys Ifans *Captain Cat* • Charlotte Church *Polly Garter* • Aneirin Hughes *Organ Morgan* • Boyd Clack *Mr Pugh* • Sue Roderick *Mrs Pugh* • Bradley Freegard *Sinbad Sailors* ■ *Dir* Kevin Allen • *Scr* Kevin Allen, Michael Breen, Murray Lachlan Young, from Dylan Thomas's radio play

Under Pressure ★★★ 15

Thriller 1997 · US · Colour · 84min

Charlie Sheen - here billed as Charles - plays a fireman who wins a bravery medal. But because his wife leaves him he turns into the neighbour from hell, menacing little kids, killing repair men and generally behaving badly. Sheen gives a fine performance, the direction is too mild-mannered to make this TV thriller as chilling as it should have been. AT **DVD**

Charles Sheen [Charlie Sheen] *Lyle Wilder* • Mare Winningham *Catherine Braverton* • David Andrews (2) *Reese Braverton* • Noah Fleiss *Zach Braverton* • Chelsea Russo *Marcie Braverton* • John Ratzenberger *Al Calavito* • Dawnn Lewis *Sandy Tierra* ■ *Dir* Craig R Baxley • *Scr* Betsy Giffen Nowrasteh

Under Siege ★★★★ 15

Action adventure 1992 · US · Colour · 98min

Steven Seagal struck gold with this slick nautical spin on the *Die Hard* concept. Portraying possibly the unlikeliest cook in the history of cinema, Seagal is the US Navy's only hope when a crack squad of terrorists, led by Tommy Lee Jones, hijacks his ship. Seagal lacks natural charisma, but a flamboyant performance from Jones, plus some sterling work from fellow baddies Gary Busey and Colm Meaney, more than compensate for his deficiencies. Director Andrew Davis never misses a beat and stages some awesome set pieces. JF Violence, swearing, nudity. **DVD** **BLU**

Steven Seagal *Casey Ryback* • Tommy Lee Jones *William Strannix* • Gary Busey *Commander Krill* • Erika Eleniak *Jordan Tate* • Patrick O'Neal (2) *Captain Adams* • Damian Chapa *Tackman* • Troy Evans *Granger* • David McKnight *Flicker* • Colm Meaney *Daumer* ■ *Dir* Andrew Davis • *Scr* JF Lawton

Under Siege 2 ★★ 18

Action thriller 1995 · US · Colour · 93min

The original was a hugely entertaining affair, thanks mainly to the sheer scale of the destruction and its top-drawer cast of cartoon villains. This sequel sadly falls down in both departments. Basically, it's the same story but this time set on a train. Steven Seagal is a chef who finds himself up against another gang of international terrorists, led by the faintly ludicrous mad professor Eric Bogosian. JF Swearing, violence. **DVD**

Steven Seagal *Casey Ryback* • Eric Bogosian *Travis Dane* • Katherine Heigl *Sarah Ryback* • Morris Chestnut *Bobby Zachs* • Everett McGill *Penn* • Kurtwood Smith *General Stanley Cooper* • Nick Mancuso *Tom Breaker* • Andy Romano *Admiral Bates* ■ *Dir* Geoff Murphy • *Scr* Richard Hatem, Matt Reeves, from the character created by JF Lawton

Under Suspicion ★★★ 18

Thriller 1991 · US/UK · Colour · 95min

This intriguing if not entirely successful attempt to create a home-grown *noir* thriller stars Liam Neeson as a cynical private eye caught up in a tortuous murder plot involving *femme fatale* Laura San Giacomo. The 1950s Brighton setting is suitably seedy and, as with other films of its ilk, there are plenty of twists and turns. However the story is a little far-fetched and Neeson never really convinces as the hard-boiled investigator. JF

Liam Neeson *Tony Aaron* • Laura San Giacomo *Angeline* • Kenneth Cranham *Frank* • Maggie O'Neill *Hazel* • Alan Talbot *Powers* • Malcolm Storry *Waterston* • Martin Grace *Colin* • Kevin Moore *Barrister* ■ *Dir/Scr* Simon Moore

Under Suspicion ★★★ 15

Murder mystery thriller 2000 · US/Fr · Colour · 110min

Gene Hackman and Morgan Freeman star in director Stephen Hopkins's absorbing remake of the 1981 French thriller *Garde à Vue*, now relocated to Puerto Rico. Following the rape and murder of two young girls, police captain Freeman questions lawyer Hackman, who discovered one of the bodies. What starts as a friendly chat escalates into a thought-provoking battle as Freeman's suspicions are fuelled by inconsistencies in Hackman's story. LH Swearing, sex scenes. **DVD**

Morgan Freeman *Capt Victor Benezet* • Gene Hackman *Henry Hearst* • Thomas Jane *Detective Felix Owens* • Monica Bellucci *Chantal Hearst* • Nydia Caro *Isabella* • Miguel Angel Suarez *Superintendent* ■ *Dir* Stephen Hopkins • *Scr* Tom Provost, W Peter Iliff, from the film *Garde à Vue* by Claude Miller, Jean Herman, from the novel *Brainwash* by John Wainwright

Under Ten Flags ★★ U

Second World War drama 1960 · US/It · BW · 113min

Produced in Italy by Dino De Laurentiis with an Italian director and crew, this stars Charles Laughton as a British bulldog admiral and Van Heflin as a German skipper, playing cat and mouse with each other. While Van Heflin is not your usual card-carrying Nazi, just a clever tactician, Laughton goes for the full Churchillian effect. A derisory love story with French import Mylène Demongeot is thrown in but just slows things down. AT

Van Heflin *Reger* • Charles Laughton *Adm Russell* • Mylène Demongeot *Zizi* • John Ericson *Krueger* • Liam Redmond *Windsor* • Alex Nicol *Knoche* • Grégoire Aslan *Master of Abdullah* • Cecil Parker *Col Howard* ■ *Dir* Duilio Coletti • *Scr* Vittoriano Petrilli, Duilio Coletti, Ulrich Mohr, Leonardo Bercovici (uncredited), William Douglas Home, from the diaries of Bernhard Rogge

Under the Boardwalk ★ 15

Comedy 1988 · US · Colour · 98min

This update of Shakespeare's *Romeo and Juliet* is set on the beaches of California. Here members of rival surf teams fall in love during a weekend of fierce competition at an annual surf-off. Weirdly, this teen romance is narrated by a character from the future, but even this oddity fails to add

spark to what is a lucklustre story and a cheap production. DF

Keith Coogan *Andy* • Danielle Von Zerneck *Allie* • Richard Joseph Paul *Nick Rainwood* • Steve Monarque *Reef* • Roxana Zal *Gitch* • Brian Avery (2) *Hap Jordan* • Hunter Von Leer *Midas* ■ *Dir* Fritz Kiersch • *Scr* Robert King, from a story by Matthew Irmas, King Robert

Under the Bombs ★★★ 15

Romantic drama 2007 · UK/Fr/Leb/Bel · Colour · 94min

Philippe Aractingi's romantic drama follows a Christian cabby ferrying a Shia Muslim mother around Lebanon in search of her son who's gone missing in a bombing raid. Blown bridges cause diversions that allow the improvising Georges Khabbaz and Nada Abou Farhat to get to know each other, adding an extra human dimension to the catalogue of savagery and suffering. With moments of broad humour relieving the horror, this offers fascinating insights into the region's politics of race, religion, gender and class, while the denouement is genuinely poignant. DP Arabic +subtitles. **DVD**

Nada Abou Farhat *Zeina* • Georges Khabbaz *Tony* • Rawya El Chab *The receptionist* • Bshara Atallah *The journalist* ■ *Dir* Philippe Aractingi • *Scr* Michel Léviant, Philippe Aractingi, Anjo Rihane

Under the Cherry Moon ★ 15

Musical romance 1986 · US · BW · 100min

Even Prince's ardent fans will scoff at this monumentally pretentious ego trip, in which His Purpleness plays a piano-playing gigolo on the French Riviera, wooing rich Kristin Scott Thomas against her father's wishes. In a gobsmacking black-and-white exercise in narcissistic posturing, Prince endlessly compares wardrobes with Jerome Benton, makes love on a bed of rose petals, and finally dies (thank goodness!). Not even worth watching for kitsch value. AJ Some violence, swearing. **DVD**

Prince *Christopher Tracy* • Jerome Benton *Tricky* • Kristin Scott Thomas *Mary Sharon* • Steven Berkoff *Mr Sharon* • Francesca Annis *Mrs Wellington* • Emmanuelle Sallet *Katy* • Alexandra Stewart *Mrs Sharon* ■ *Dir* Prince • *Scr* Becky Johnston

Under the Doctor ★ 18

Comedy 1976 · UK · Colour · 83min

Such was the state of British screen comedy in the 1970s that even its stalwarts were reduced to accepting roles as nudie cuties. Indeed, Liz Fraser did nothing but peek-a-boo fluff in the middle of the decade, managing to retain her dignity while all else were losing their clothes. She's joined here by Barry Evans, who gets to play four different roles, the most significant being an amorous psychiatrist coping with a clientele made up exclusively of sexually frustrated females. DP

Barry Evans *Colin/Dr Boyd/Mr Johnson/Lt Cranshaw* • Liz Fraser *Sandra* • Hilary Pritchard *Lady Victoria* • Penny Spencer *Marion* • Jonathan Cecil *Rodney Harrington-Harrington/Lord Woodbridge* ■ *Dir* Gerry Poulson • *Scr* Ron Bareham

Under the Hula Moon ★★★

Comedy thriller 1995 · US · Colour · 96min

This is an eccentric film about a trailer-park couple who have only their dream of moving to Hawaii to sustain them. Their dream is put on the backburner when the husband's convict brother escapes from prison and comes a-calling. Stephen Baldwin and Chris Penn play the male leads, while the film's leading lady is the watchable Emily Lloyd. DA Violence, swearing.

Stephen Baldwin *Buzz* • Emily Lloyd *Betty* • Chris Penn *Turk* • Musetta Vander *Maya Gundinger* • Pruitt Taylor Vince *Bob* ■ *Dir* Jeff Celentano • *Scr* Jeff Celentano, Gregory Webb

Under the Mud ★★★ 12

Comedy 2006 · UK · Colour · 85min

This truly independent British comedy, with funding from a mishmash of sources, was written by 14 inexperienced youngsters

U

from the Garston area of Liverpool, under the tutelage of director Sol Papadopoulos and producer Roy Boulter. Cast using local unknowns – and Andrew Schofield (of 1980s TV show *Scully*) – it's a magical-realist social farce about a Liverpool family's ups and down on the first Holy Communion day of eight-year-old "angel" Olivia (Jasmine Mubery). It's as broad as the accents, with scouse sentimentality and silly slapstick jarring occasionally, but the sheer do-it-yourself energy of the piece, which recalls earliest Shane Meadows, counts for much. **AC** Swearing, some drug abuse. **DVD**

Andrew Schofield *Joe Potts* • Keith Carter *Chill* • Mick Colligan *DJ Worm* • Kate Fitzgerald *Nan* • James McMartin *One Dig* ■ *Dir* Sol Papadopoulos

Under the Piano ★★★ 15
Drama based on a true story
1995 · Can · Colour · 87min

One of the world's leading opera stars takes centre stage in this heart-rending melodrama. As the faded diva who is too wrapped up in her own woes to recognise the talent of her autistic savant daughter, Teresa Stratas sweeps through every scene with imperious disdain. Strong performances from Megan Follows and Amanda Plummer maintain the balance, however, with Follows particularly impressive as she battles her domineering mother to fulfil her musical potential. Based on the true story of sisters Dolly and Henrietta Giardini, this TV movie is thoughtful and powerfully played. **DP DVD**

Amanda Plummer *Franny* • Megan Follows *Rosetta* • Teresa Stratas *Regina* • James Carroll *Nick* • John Juliani *Frank* • Jackie Richardson *Mrs Syms* • Richard Blackburn *Dr Banman* • Dan Lett *Dr Harkness* ■ *Dir* Stefan Scaini • *Scr* Blair Ferguson

Under the Rainbow ★ PG
Comedy
1981 · US · Colour · 93min

Despite the presence of the great Eve Arden, a former Ziegfeld girl and put-down queen of screwball comedies, this strange attempt at a comedy set in Hollywood's golden era is a grotesque misfire. Chevy Chase and Carrie Fisher are a talent scout and FBI agent respectively who uncover a Nazi plot in a hotel over-run with scores of oddball eccentrics from the cast of *The Wizard of Oz*. A yellow brick road to nowhere. **TH**

Chevy Chase *Bruce Thorpe* • Carrie Fisher *Annie Clark* • Billy Barty *Otto Kriegling* • Eve Arden *Duchess* • Joseph Maher *Duke* • Robert Donner *Assassin* • Mako *Nakamuri* • Cork Hubbert *Rollo Sweet* ■ *Dir* Steve Rash • *Scr* Pat McCormick, Harry Hurwitz, Martin Smith, Pat Bradley, Fred Bauer, from a story by Pat Bradley, Fred Bauer

Under the Rainbow ★★ 15
Romantic comedy
2013 · Fr · Colour · 112min

In this ensemble comedy, Cinderella-like Agathe Bonitzer meets and loses the man of her dreams (Arthur Dupont) at a ball. However, he's no regal catch but a struggling student with a tightwad father (Jean-Pierre Bacri). Digital effects intermittently turn Paris into a fantastical setting, but as the story threads multiply to include a scatty third-rate actress (director Agnès Jaoui) rehearsing a school play, the whole affair becomes ill-focused and ponderous, even if the story's occasional wit is undeniable. **TJ** French +subtitles. Some swearing, drug abuse.

Agathe Bonitzer *Laura* • Arthur Dupont *Sandro* • Valerie Crouzet *Eleonore* • Jean-Pierre Bacri *Pierre* • Dominique Valadié [Dominique Valadie] *Jacqueline* • Benjamin Biolay *Maxime* • Agnès Jaoui *Marianne* ■ *Dir* Agnès Jaoui • *Scr* Jean-Pierre Bacri, Agnès Jaoui

Under the Red Robe ★★
Swashbuckling drama
1937 · UK · BW · 80min

Victor Sjöström was the director of many silent classics in his native Sweden and, most famously, *The Wind*, made in Hollywood, and *The Divine Woman*, the sole Garbo film lost to history. Also a fine actor, he retired from directing in 1930, then

returned to the megaphone for this final movie, made for Alexander Korda. It's set in 17th-century France, with Conrad Veidt as a gambler condemned to be executed, who's then given a deadly mission by Cardinal Richelieu (Raymond Massey). It has the odd moment, but is not a high point in Sjöström's career. **AT**

Conrad Veidt *Gil de Berault* • Annabella *Lady Marguerite* • Raymond Massey *Cardinal Richelieu* • Romney Brent *Marius* • Sophie Stewart *Elise, Duchess of Foix* • Wyndham Goldie *Edmond, Duke of Foix* • Lawrence Grant *Father Joseph* ■ *Dir* Victor Seastrom [Victor Sjöström] • *Scr* Lajos Biró, Philip Lindsay, JL Hodson, Arthur Wimperis, from the play by Edward E Rose and the novel by Stanley J Weyman

Under the Sand ★★★★ 15
Drama
2000 · Fr/Jpn · Colour · 92min

Charlotte Rampling turns in the finest performance of her career in this sensitively relentless study of melancholy delusion. Convinced she still sees him every day, a sophisticated Parisienne teacher (Rampling) simply refuses to accept that her husband (Bruno Cremer) drowned on their seaside holiday and treats her liaison with Jacques Nolot as a deliciously reckless adultery. Reducing dialogue to essentials and making exemplary use of cool, reflective surfaces, François Ozon finds poetry and optimism in the depths of grief. **DP** French +subtitles. Swearing, sex scenes. **DVD**

Charlotte Rampling *Marie Drillon* • Bruno Cremer *Jean Drillon* • Jacques Nolot *Vincent* • Alexandra Stewart *Amanda* • Pierre Vernier *Gérard* ■ *Dir* François Ozon • *Scr* Ozon François, Emmanuèle Bernheim, Marina de Van, Marcia Romano

Under the Skin ★★★★ 18
Drama
1997 · UK · Colour · 79min

When their mother (Rita Tushingham) dies, two Liverpool sisters react differently to the bereavement. Claire Rushbrook, who is pregnant, cries a lot but gets on with her life, whereas the younger, wilder Samantha Morton starts a downward moral spiral of sordid sex and alcohol binges. This quest for emotional fulfilment in tragic times may lack overall polish, but with its *cinéma vérité* style, this is wrenching, thanks to Morton's raw and riveting portrayal. **AJ** Swearing, sex scenes. **DVD**

Samantha Morton *Iris Kelley* • Claire Rushbrook *Rose* • Rita Tushingham *Mum* • Christine Tremarco *Veronica/"Vron"* • Stuart Townsend *Tom* • Matthew Delamere *Gary* • Mark Womack *Frank* • Clare Francis *Elana* ■ *Dir/Scr* Carine Adler

Under the Skin ★★★★ 15
Science-fiction drama
2013 · UK/US/Swi · Colour · 103min

Director Jonathan Glazer's third feature in 14 years (after heist thriller *Sexy Beast* and New York psychodrama *Birth*) is, ostensibly, the darkly esoteric tale of a mysterious, English-accented *femme fatale* (Scarlett Johansson) who preys on unsuspecting local men in Scotland. But the tale opens with a jaw-dropping cosmic sequence that sets an otherworldly tone sharply at odds with the hidden-camera footage of grey, rainy Glasgow and its unwitting inhabitants. Johansson is truly mesmerising as the rouge-lipped siren who lures her suitors to a nondescript van to meet a horrific fate worse than death. Like Johansson's unearthly visitor, the film loses its way occasionally, but it's an experience you'll not forget in a hurry. **AC** Violence, sex scenes, nudity. **DVD** SL

Scarlett Johansson *The Female* • Jeremy McWilliams *The Bad Man* • Paul Brannigan *Andrew* ■ *Dir* Jonathan Glazer • *Scr* Walter Campbell, Jonathan Glazer, from Michel Faber's novel

Under the Sun ★★★
Period drama
1998 · Swe · Colour · 118min

The theme of mistrust within a close-knit community that informed director Colin Nutley's acclaimed *House of Angels* is also evident in this Oscar-nominated adaptation. Nutley's wife, Helena Bergström, is once again the star, on this occasion playing the

housekeeper who arrives at Rolf Lassgård's isolated farm and immediately drives a wedge between the middle-aged illiterate oaf and his scheming buddy, Johan Widerberg. Nutley directs with a focused, but unforced maturity that not only captures the gentler pace of 1950s life, but also the tension underpinning this enthralling battle of wits. **DP** Swedish +subtitles.

Rolf Lassgard *Olof* • Helena Bergström *Ellen* • Johan Widerberg *Erik* • Gunilla Röör *Newspaper receptionist* • Jonas Falk *Preacher* ■ *Dir* Colin Nutley • *Scr* Johanna Hald, David Neal, Colin Nutley, from the short story *The Little Farm* by HE Bates

Under the Tuscan Sun ★ 12
Romantic comedy drama
2003 · US · Colour · 108min

Diane Lane stars in this corny, old-fashioned slushfest as a successful writer who journeys to Italy after a messy divorce and impulsively buys a broken-down villa in Tuscany. It's the cue for encounters with every kind of local stereotype, from cutely rustic repairmen to lusty Latin lotharios. Lane looks ravishing. So does the scenery. But the whole thing has the depth of a puddle. **DA DVD**

Diane Lane *Frances* • Sandra Oh *Patti* • Lindsay Duncan *Katherine* • Raoul Bova *Marcello* • Vincent Riotta [Vincenzo Ricotta] *Martini* • Giulia Steigerwalt *Chiara* • Pawel Szajda *Pawel* • Mario Monicelli *Old man with flowers* ■ *Dir* Audrey Wells • *Scr* Audrey Wells, from a story by Audrey Wells, from the memoirs by Frances Mayes

Under the Volcano ★★★ 15
Drama
1984 · UK · Colour · 107min

Malcolm Lowry's 1947 novel is a cult classic about an alcoholic British consul adrift in Mexico with his unfaithful ex-wife and his half-brother, a journalist just back from the Spanish Civil War. John Huston long cherished a movie version and – as with *Moby Dick* – it proved to be a daunting task, since the novel is a stream of consciousness, a river of booze and a mountain of poetic symbolism. Albert Finney gives the drunk act to end all drunk acts and rather overshadows the beautiful Jacqueline Bisset. **AT DVD**

Albert Finney *Geoffrey Firmin* • Jacqueline Bisset *Yvonne Firmin* • Anthony Andrews *Hugh Firmin* • Ignacio Lopez Tarso *Dr Vigil* • Katy Jurado *Señora Gregoria* • James Villiers *Brit* • Dawson Bray *Quincey* ■ *Dir* John Huston • *Scr* Guy Gallo, from the novel by Malcolm Lowry • *Cinematographer* Gabriel Figueroa

Under the Yum Yum Tree ★★
Comedy
1963 · US · Colour · 109min

With *The Apartment*, Jack Lemmon defined the urbanised, neurotic, sexually insecure American male. Thus typecast, Lemmon drifted through a series of movies including this "sex comedy". Lemmon plays a lecherous landlord who starts to lust after one of his tenants, Carol Lynley, who is living with her boyfriend Dean Jones. Lemmon always has his precious moments and those make this comedy worth watching – just. **AT**

Jack Lemmon *Hogan* • Carol Lynley *Robin* • Dean Jones *David* • Edie Adams *Irene* • Imogene Coca *Dorkus* • Paul Lynde *Murphy* • Robert Lansing *Charles* ■ *Dir* David Swift • *Scr* Lawrence Roman, David Swift, from the play by Lawrence Roman

Under Two Flags ★★★
Action adventure
1936 · US · BW · 110min

This Foreign Legion saga, already filmed twice in the silent era, stars Ronald Colman and Victor McLaglen as the desert-based soldiers, and Claudette Colbert and Rosalind Russell as zee women in zee kasbah. Frank Lloyd directed the talkie bits, Otto Brower the battles, which look like afterthoughts since the real battle is between the sexes and between two Oxford graduates, Colman and Arab chieftain Onslow Stevens. It's *Boys' Own* stuff, with Colman often caught posing for the camera and Colbert tossing

aside her usual chic and letting her hair down. **AT**

Ronald Colman *Corporal Victor* • Claudette Colbert *Cigarette* • Victor McLaglen *Major Doyle* • Rosalind Russell *Lady Venetia* • J Edward Bromberg *Colonel Ferol* • Nigel Bruce *Captain Menzies* • Herbert Mundin *Rake* • Gregory Ratoff *Ivan* ■ *Dir* Frank Lloyd, Otto Brower • *Scr* WP Lipscomb, Walter Ferris, from the novel by Ouida

Under Western Skies ★★ U
Musical western
1945 · US · BW · 56min

A programme filler about a vaudeville singer, played by Martha O'Driscoll, who fetches up in an Arizona town and gets involved in all sorts of trouble. There are some funny moments, but this is very slight indeed, though the songs are pleasant enough. **TS**

Martha O'Driscoll *Katie* • Noah Beery Jr *Tod* • Leo Carrillo *King Randall* • Leon Errol *Willie* • Irving Bacon *Sheriff* • Ian Keith *Prof Moffet* • Jennifer Holt *Charity* ■ *Dir* Jean Yarbrough • *Scr* Stanley Roberts, Clyde Bruckman, from a story by Stanley Roberts

Under Your Hat ★ U
Musical comedy
1940 · UK · BW · 76min

You really needed to have been there at the time to appreciate the humour in this woeful comedy of errors. Wartime audiences were so grateful to see just about anything that they were willing to forgive even the most dismal movies – particularly morale-boosting flag-wavers. The lowest of many dips below zero is the scene in which Cicely Courtneidge poses as a French maid to catch hubby Jack Hulbert with Leonora Corbett. **DP DVD**

Jack Hulbert *Jack Millett* • Cicely Courtneidge *Kay Millett* • Austin Trevor *Boris Vladimir* • Leonora Corbett *Carole Markoff* • Cecil Parker *Sir Geoffrey Arlington* • Tony Hayes *George* • Charles Oliver *Carl* • HF Maltby *Colonel Sheepshanks* ■ *Dir* Maurice Elvey • *Scr* Rodney Ackland, Anthony Kimmins, L Green, Jack Hulbert, from the play by Hulbert, Archie Menzies, Geoffrey Kerr, Arthur Macrae

Underclassman ★★ 12
Action comedy thriller
2004 · US · Colour · 89min

Working from a script that is as clunky as its title, fresh-faced star Nick Cannon makes an unwelcome grab for the *Beverly Hills Cop* audience in this lazy crime caper. He plays an ambitious cop who goes undercover to investigate the murder of a reporter on a school paper. Cannon co-executive produced so he has to accept some of the blame for the lack of laughs and thrills, leaving Hugh Bonneville to ham it up for all he's worth as the school's snobbish headmaster. **JF DVD**

Nick Cannon *Tracy "Tre" Stokes* • Shawn Ashmore *Rob Donovan* • Roselyn Sanchez *Karen Lopez* • Kelly Hu *Lisa Brooks* • Ian Gomez Detective *Gallecki* • Hugh Bonneville *Headmaster Powers* • Richard "Cheech" Marin *Captain Delgado* ■ *Dir* Marcos Siega • *Scr* David T Wagner, Brent Goldberg

Undercover ★
Second World War drama
1943 · UK · BW · 88min

This Ealing Resistance drama aims for a docudramatic feel, but realism was outside the range of such starchy actors as John Clements, Michael Wilding and Tom Walls. The result is, frankly, embarrassing. **DP**

John Clements *Milosh Petrovitch* • Tom Walls *Kossan Petrovitch* • Mary Morris *Anna Petrovitch* • Godfrey Tearle *General Von Staengel* • Michael Wilding *Constantine* • Niall MacGinnis *Dr Jordan* • Robert Harris *Colonel Von Brock* • Rachel Thomas *Maria Petrovitch* ■ *Dir* Sergei Nolbandov • *Scr* John Dighton, Monja Danischewsky, Sergei Nolbandov, Milos Sokulich, from a story by George Slocombe

Undercover Blues ★★★ 15
Comedy thriller
1993 · US · Colour · 86min

Dennis Quaid and Kathleen Turner are super spies on leave in New Orleans with their infant, who are called back into service to help foil a plot to sell off top secret weapons. Quaid and Turner make charismatic leads and are surrounded by a talented support cast. Herbert Ross's direction is suitably light and, while it isn't as amusing as it should be, it's still undemanding fun. JF Swearing. **DVD**

Kathleen Turner *Jane Blue* • Dennis Quaid *Jeff Blue* • Fiona Shaw *Movacek* • Stanley Tucci *Muerte* • Larry Miller *Detective Sergeant Halsey* • Tom Arnold *Vern Newman* ■ *Dir* Herbert Ross • *Scr* Ian Abrams

Undercover Brother ★★ 12

Blaxploitation spoof 2002 • US • Colour • 82min

The first major feature film to be adapted from an internet cartoon, this satire-cum-spoof stars comedian Eddie Griffin as a leather-clad, afro-sporting secret agent who's recruited by an organisation called The Brotherhood. His archenemy is The Man, a white racist megalomaniac. This attempts to poke fun at white perceptions of black culture while celebrating the glories of blaxploitation movies and 1970s fashions and music. But many of the jokes are stale. BP **DVD**

Eddie Griffin *Undercover Brother* • Chris Kattan *Mr Feather* • Denise Richards *White She Devil* • Aunjanue Ellis *Sistah Girl* • Dave Chappelle *Conspiracy Brother* • Chi McBride *Chief* • Neil Patrick Harris *Lance* • Billy Dee Williams *General Boutwell* ■ *Dir* Malcolm D Lee • *Scr* John Ridley, Michael McCullers, from a story by John Ridley, from characters by John Ridley

Undercover Girl ★★★

Crime 1950 • US • BW • 82min

Policewoman Alexis Smith joins forces with plain-clothes policeman Scott Brady and is sent undercover to pose as a drug buyer in order to nail a narcotics ring. This is a routine 1950s programme filler, but no less entertaining for that, and it's refreshing to have a glamorous woman at the centre of the rough stuff. RK

Alexis Smith *Christine Miller/"Sal Willis"* • Scott Brady *Lt Mike Trent* • Richard Egan *Jess Taylor* • Gladys George *Liz Crow* • Edmon Ryan *Doc Holmes* • Gerald Mohr *Reed Menig* • Royal Dano *Moocher* ■ *Dir* Joseph Pevney • *Scr* Harry Essex, from a story by Robert Hardy Andrews, Francis Rosenwald

Undercover Girl ★★

Crime drama 1957 • UK • BW • 76min

This cheap British B-movie has the regulation "glamour" leading lady and the obligatory American (in this case Canadian) leading man. Former band crooner Paul Carpenter is an amiable star of sorts and co-star Kay Callard has a passable second-string leading lady quality. The real interest lies in the appearance in an "acting" role of Jackie Collins, now better known for writing raunchy novels. TS

Paul Carpenter *Johnny Carter* • Kay Callard *Joan Foster* • Monica Grey *Evelyn King* • Bruce Seton *Ted Austin* • Jackie Collins *Peggy Foster* • Maya Koumani *Miss Brazil* ■ *Dir* Francis Searle • *Scr* Bernard Lewis, Bill Luckwell, from a story by Bernard Lewis

The Undercover Man ★★★

Crime thriller 1949 • US • BW • 84min

This is an entertaining co-feature from cult director Joseph H Lewis, best known for his remarkable thriller *Gun Crazy*. It's based on the real-life entrapment of gangster Al Capone for tax evasion, a tale beloved of Hollywood scriptwriters. The story is economically filmed and driven at a fine pace, and there are terrific performances by leads Glenn Ford, Nina Foch and James Whitmore, making his screen debut. The crisp images of *Bonnie and Clyde* cinematographer Burnett Guffey are also a major plus. TS

Glenn Ford *Frank Warren* • Nina Foch *Judith Warren* • James Whitmore *George Pappas* • Barry Kelley *Edward O'Rourke* • David Wolfe *Stanley Weinburg* • Frank Tweddell *Inspector Herzog* • Howard St John *Joseph S Horan* • Leo Penn *Sidney Gordon* ■ *Dir* Joseph H Lewis • *Scr* Sydney Boehm, Malvin Wald, Jerry Rubin, from the article *Undercover Man: He Trapped Capone* by Frank J Wilson

Undercurrent ★★★ 15

Spy drama 1946 • US • BW • 115min

With a knockout cast (Katharine Hepburn, Robert Taylor, Robert Mitchum), a director (Vincente Minnelli) hitting his creative stride and MGM (the Rolls-Royce of studios near its prime), how can you go wrong? Easy. By having a moth-eaten cardboard script, obvious studio interiors, a cast that doesn't care and a director plagued by domestic problems. It's over-written, overwrought and overlong, but sheer star power saves the day, and the three principals make this mesmerisingly watchable. TS

Katharine Hepburn *Ann Hamilton* • Robert Taylor (1) *Alan Garroway* • Robert Mitchum *Michael Garroway* • Edmund Gwenn *Prof Dink Hamilton* ■ *Dir* Vincente Minnelli • *Scr* Edward Chodorov, Marguerite Roberts, George Oppenheimer, from the novel *You Were There* by Thelma Strabel

Underdog ★★ U

Action comedy adventure
2007 • US • Colour • 78min

This innocuous live-action Disney movie stars a cute beagle pup (voiced by Jason Lee) who becomes a reluctant crime-fighter after a laboratory explosion gives him super powers. Going heavy on the CGI, it sets up some cartoonish thrills as Underdog talks, flies and flexes his super-muscles in pursuit of evil scientist Peter Dinklage. Five-year-olds will doubtless appreciate the silliness as Underdog tries out a variety of home-made superhero costumes and chases "cat" burglars; long-suffering adults may wish someone had kept this talking-dog movie on a tighter leash. JR **DVD** **Blu-ray**

Jason Lee *Underdog* • Peter Dinklage *Dr Simon Barsinister* • James Belushi *Dan Unger* • Patrick Warburton *Cad* • Alex Neuberger *Jack* • Taylor Momsen *Molly* • Amy Adams *Polly* ■ *Dir* Frederik Du Chau • *Scr* Adam Rifkin, Joe Piscatella, Craig A Williams, from a story by Rifkin, Piscatella, Williams, from the TV series by W Watts Biggers

Underground ★★★★ PG

Silent drama 1928 • UK • BW • 89min

Anthony Asquith, the son of First World War prime minister Herbert Henry Asquith, proved to have the common touch with this intriguing drama. He reveals his familiarity with prevailing continental approaches to silent cinema in a working-class saga that chronicles the romantic tug-of-war between London Underground attendant Brian Aherne, power station electrician Cyril McLaglen, perky shop girl Elissa Landi and McLaglen's devoted neighbour, Norah Baring. Asquith's eye for location detail (whether shooting in confined or open spaces) most impresses, as the everyday lyricism makes the artier modernism seem less conspicuous. The result is something of a neglected gem. DP **DVD** **Blu-ray**

Brian Aherne *Bill* • Elissa Landi *Nell* • Norah Baring *Kate* • Cyril McLaglen *Bert* ■ *Dir/Scr* Anthony Asquith

Underground ★★★ 15

Epic Second World War comedy
1995 • Fr/Ger/Hun • Colour • 163min

Although it won Emir Kusturica a second Palme d'Or at Cannes, this bittersweet dramatisation of the decline of Yugoslavia so angered critics in his native Bosnia (for failing to condemn Serbian aggression) that he threatened to abandon cinema altogether. Beneath the black farce – Second World War partisans take refuge in a cellar, which becomes their home for decades – there are traces of nostalgia for the illusory union of Tito's Yugoslavia. With much of the action taken at a frantic pace, to the accompaniment of brass or gypsy bands, this is as breathless as it is perplexing. DP Serbian, German +subtitles. **DVD**

Miki Manojlovic *Marko* • Lazar Ristovski *Petar "Blacky" Popara* • Mirjana Jokovic *Natalija* • Slavko Stimac *Ivan* • Ernst Stotzner *Franz* • Srdjan Todorovic *Jovan* • Mirjana Karanovic *Vera* ■ *Dir* Emir Kusturica • *Scr* Emir Kusturica, from a story by Dusan Kovacevic

Underground ★★★★ 18

Crime thriller 1998 • UK • Colour • 93min

This gritty, ultra-low-budget, British thriller is about teen drug-dealer Billy Smith, who makes deliveries around the clock. When he wanders into another supplier's patch, the film follows him as he spends a long night of hide and seek. Writer/director Paul Spurrier (who also performed just about every technical role) does an exceptional job. The naturalistic performances are good and the music soundtrack is comparable to most major releases. Amazingly, it was shot in a fortnight and the climactic car chase was filmed entirely without permission or stunt drivers. JC Swearing. **DVD**

Billy Smith *Rat* • Zoe Smale *Skye* • Ian Dury *Rat's dad* • Chrissie Cotterill *Rat's mum* • Nick Sutton *Raymond* • Alison Lintott *Debbie* ■ *Dir/Scr* Paul Spurrier

The Underneath ★★★ 15

Crime thriller 1995 • US • Colour • 94min

In director Steven Soderbergh's intriguing remake of the 1949 film noir *Criss Cross*, Peter Gallagher takes on the Burt Lancaster role of the black sheep who returns to his Texas home town for his mother's wedding and gets caught up with former lover Alison Elliott and her crooked husband, William Fichtner. Soderbergh mixes erotic duplicity, sibling rivalry and sizzling suspense into an increasingly corkscrew plot with a surprise payoff. A few style inconsistencies and a rather slow build-up aside, this is a tautly constructed thriller. AJ Swearing, violence.

Peter Gallagher *Michael Chambers* • Alison Elliott (2) *Rachel* • William Fichtner *Tommy Dundee* • Adam Trese *David Chambers* • Joe Don Baker *Clay Hinkle* • Paul Dooley *Ed Dutton* • Elisabeth Shue *Susan* ■ *Dir* Steven Soderbergh • *Scr* Sam Lowry [Steven Soderbergh], Daniel Fuchs, from the film *Criss Cross* by Daniel Fuchs, from the novel *Criss Cross* by Don Tracy

Undertow ★★

Crime drama 1949 • US • BW • 71min

Although he's better known for gimmicky horror movies, William Castle makes the most of this muted B-feature crime drama, which marked the second screen appearance of one Rock Hudson. Star Scott Brady plays a war hero with a criminal past, whose hopes of opening a ski lodge seem dashed when he's framed for the murder of a mobster while stopping off in Chicago to collect girlfriend Dorothy Hart. A passable diversion. DP

Scott Brady *Tony Reagan* • John Russell *Danny Morgan* • Dorothy Hart *Sally Lee* • Peggy Dow *Ann McKnight* • Charles Sherlock *Cooper* • Rock Hudson *Detective* ■ *Dir* William Castle • *Scr* Lee Loeb, Arthur T Horman, from the story *The Big Frame* by Arthur T Horman

Undertow ★★★ 15

Crime drama 2004 • US • Colour • 103min

Jamie Bell's first American film has the *Billy Elliot* boy pursued by a psychopathic uncle (Josh Lucas) who's after the gold coins that he and his younger brother have fled with after the killing of their father (Dermot Mulroney). Set among the backwater hamlets of Georgia, it's a strange and quirky chase thriller that chronicles the offbeat characters and situations the brothers encounter while running for their lives. This warped fairy tale's concerns are as much symbolic as they are realistic. Bell's "Americanisation" is convincing. DA Violence. **DVD**

Jamie Bell *Chris Munn* • Josh Lucas *Deel Munn* • Devon Alan *Tim Munn* • Dermot Mulroney *John Munn* • Shiri Appleby *Violet* • Pat Healy *Grant the mechanic* • Bill McKinney *Grandfather* ■ *Dir* David Gordon Green • *Scr* David Gordon Green, Joe Conway, from a story by Lingard Jervey

Undertow ★★★ 15

Drama 2009 • Peru/Col/Fr/Ger • Colour • 96min

The debut feature from director Javier Fuentes-León appears to address contentious issues. However, it's actually as duplicitous as fisherman and father-to-be Cristian Mercado, who is cheating on wife Tatiana Astengo with openly gay painter Manolo Cardona. The performances are admirable and the intentions sincere. But Mauricio Vidal's glossy visuals push this closer to magic realism than neorealism, while the plot twists owe less to real life than the telenovelas that Astengo makes Mercado watch instead of football. DP Spanish +subtitles. Violence, sex scenes. **DVD**

Cristian Mercado *Miguel* • Tatiana Astengo *Mariela* • Manolo Cardona *Santiago* ■ *Dir/Scr* Javier Fuentes-León

Underwater! ★★★ U

Adventure 1955 • US • Colour • 94min

The most remarkable thing about this Jane Russell movie was not that it was the first film in Superscope, nor that it was started by cult director Nicholas Ray, but that its world premiere was held underwater in a headline-grabbing stunt organised by ace publicist Russell Birdwell (the man who once engineered the search for Scarlett O'Hara). The film itself is an interesting enough adventure about the search for lost treasure in the Caribbean. John Sturges eventually took over the directorial reins, but not even he could do much with the routine plot. TS

Jane Russell *Theresa* • Richard Egan *Johnny* • Gilbert Roland *Dominic* • Lori Nelson *Gloria* • Robert Keith (1) *Father Cannon* • Joseph Calleia *Rico* • Eugene Iglesias *Miguel* ■ *Dir* John Sturges • *Scr* Walter Newman, from the story *The Big Rainbow* by Hugh King, Robert B Bailey

Underworld ★★★★

Silent crime melodrama 1927 • US • BW • 75min

Considered by some critics to be the first gangster picture, the model for a prolific genre, this silent film was based on an original story by Ben Hecht who, as a reporter, had witnessed several of the elements incorporated into the film. However, Hecht wanted his name taken off the credits because he felt that director Josef von Sternberg had distorted his intentions – though that didn't prevent him picking up his Oscar. It was only Sternberg's third solo feature and already his strong visual sense and eye for detail was evident. The plot involves a racketeer (George Bancroft), his moll (Evelyn Brent) and an alcoholic lawyer (Clive Brook), but it's less important than the atmosphere. RB

George Bancroft *"Bull" Weed* • Clive Brook *"Rolls Royce"* • Evelyn Brent *"Feathers"* • Larry Semon *"Slippy" Lewis* • Fred Kohler *"Buck" Mulligan* • Helen Lynch *Mulligan's girl* ■ *Dir* Josef von Sternberg • *Scr* Robert N Lee, Charles Furthman, from a story by Ben Hecht, George Marion Jr • *Cinematographer* Bert Glennon • *Set Designer* Hans Dreier

Underworld ★★ 15

Horror
2003 • US/Ger/Hun/UK • Colour • 116min

Debut director Len Wiseman has crafted the most stylistically derivative and monotonously plotted horror film possible. The casting is equally defective, with Kate Beckinsale unconvincing as a sullen vampire and Michael Sheen lacking stature as her werewolf enemy. Set against a hackneyed melancholy gothic backdrop, the story piles on scene after scene of portentous, humourless exposition. The film's final battle is faintly enjoyable, but only Bill Nighy makes any sort of real impression. JC Swearing, violence. **DVD** **Blu-ray**

Kate Beckinsale *Selene* • Scott Speedman *Michael Corvin* • Michael Sheen *Lucian* • Bill Nighy *Viktor* • Shane Brolly *Kraven* • Erwin Leder *Singe* • Sophia Myles *Erika* • Robbie Gee *Kahn* ■ *Dir* Len Wiseman • *Scr* Danny McBride, from a story by Kevin Grevioux, Len Wiseman, Danny McBride

Underworld: Evolution ★★ 18

Horror 2006 • US • Colour • 101min

In this confusing and sloppy sequel, vampire warrior Kate Beckinsale and her hybrid werewolf lover Scott Speedman must unlock the secrets of their respective bloodlines. New addition Derek Jacobi hams it up as the immortal cause of the monster

feud. Director Len Wiseman disregards plot in favour of incident. AJ Violence, a sex scene, nudity DVD BL
Kate Beckinsale *Selene* • Scott Speedman *Michael Corvin* • Bill Nighy *Viktor* • Michael Sheen *Lucian* • Derek Jacobi *Alexander Corvinus* • Steven Mackintosh *Tannis* • Shane Brolly *Kraven* • Scott McElroy *Soren* ■ *Dir* Len Wiseman • *Scr* Danny McBride, from a story by McBride, Len Wiseman, from characters by Kevin Grevioux, Wiseman, McBride

Underworld: Rise of the Lycans ★★★ 18
Horror   2009 · US · Colour · 88min

This prequel to the previous two *Underworld* movies explores the origins of the vampire/werewolf conflict and is the best of the saga. In a nod to *Spartacus*, enslaved Lycan Lucian (Michael Sheen at his buff and charismatic best) incites his wolf/man species to rebel. Patrick Tatopoulos – the designer of the creatures in the series – makes his directorial debut here and enhances the gloom and goth look of the franchise with fantasy flair and captivating fairy-tale atmosphere. The final battle even gives *The Lord of the Rings* a run for its money in epic quality. AJ DVD BL
Michael Sheen *Lucian* • Bill Nighy *Viktor* • Rhona Mitra *Sonja* • Steven Mackintosh *Arnaud Tannis* • Kevin Grevioux *Raze* • Craig Parker *Sabas* ■ *Dir* Patrick Tatopoulos • *Scr* Danny McBride (1), Dirk Blackman, Howard McCain, from a story by Len Wiseman, Robert Orr, McBride, from characters by Wiseman, McBride, Kevin Grevioux

Underworld: Awakening ★★ 18
Horror   2012 · US · Colour · 84min

From its opening montage of old footage to the open-ended finale, this third sequel feels slapdash. The undercover Lycans are after Kate Beckinsale's hybrid daughter, so they can become immune to lethal silver weapons in an unspectacular hodge-podge of bloody action and empty thrills. The returning Beckinsale wears her dominatrix duds with hauteur, yet is clearly going through the motions. Charles Dance's cowardly vampire lifts the gloom slightly, but even franchise fans will spot the stretch marks here. AJ Violence. DVD BL
Kate Beckinsale *Selene* • Stephen Rea *Dr Lane* • Charles Dance *Thomas* • India Eisley *Eve* • Michael Ealy *Sebastian* • Theo James *David* ■ *Dir* Mans Marlind, Bjorn Stein • *Scr* Len Wiseman, John Hlavin, J Michael Straczynski, Allison Burnett, from a story by Wiseman, Hlavin, from characters by Kevin Grevioux, Wiseman, Danny McBride

The Underworld Story ★★★
Crime drama   1950 · US · BW · 90min

This tough-as-nails crime drama from director Cy Endfield was made before he fell foul of the Hollywood blacklist and moved to Britain. A co-feature about a crusading reporter who uncovers small-town corruption, it's given muscle by rugged Dan Duryea as the hero and suave Herbert Marshall as the villain, while Gale Storm is intriguingly cast as a *femme fatale*. TS
Dan Duryea *Mike Reese* • Herbert Marshall *Stanton* • Gale Storm *Cathy* • Howard Da Silva *Durham* • Michael O'Shea (1) *Munsey* • Mary Anderson *Molly* • Gar Moore *Clark* • Melville Cooper *Major Radford* ■ *Dir* Cy Endfield • *Scr* Henry Blankfort, Cy Endfield, from a story by Craig Rice

Underworld USA ★★★★
Crime drama   1961 · US · BW · 98min

What sets this apart from other revenge movies is Cliff Robertson's brooding, stricken presence as a man seeking vengeance upon the four gangsters who, when he was young, killed his father. Sam Fuller's writing and direction substantiate the authenticity of the theme of sin without salvation and – unusually for a Fuller movie – women get a look in in this macho world. Dolores Dorn is a sympathetic girlfriend and Beatrice Kay a pillar of compassion. TH

Cliff Robertson *Tolly Devlin* • Dolores Dorn *Cuddles* • Beatrice Kay *Sandy* • Paul Dubov *Gela* • Robert Emhardt *Conners* • Larry Gates *Driscoll* • Richard Rust *Gus* ■ *Dir* Samuel Fuller • *Scr* Samuel Fuller, from articles in the *The Saturday Evening Post* by Joseph F Dinneen

Undisputed ★★★ 15
Prison sports drama   2002 · US · Colour · 89min

Walter Hill's boxing drama exemplifies the director's predilection for studies of no-nonsense tough guys taking care of business. He rattles through the preamble, which witnesses both the sentencing of heavyweight champion Ving Rhames for rape and lifer Wesley Snipes attracting the attention of wily mobster Peter Falk after whupping a white supremacist in Sweetwater Prison's "combat cage". When the inevitable rumble arrives, it's unrivalled in its brutality. Rhames excels as the cocky champ. DP Violence, swearing. DVD
Wesley Snipes *Monroe Hutchens* • Ving Rhames *Iceman Chambers* • Peter Falk *Mendy Ripstein* • Michael Rooker *AJ Mercker* • Jon Seda *Jesus "Chuy" Campos* • Wes Studi *Mingo Pace* • Fisher Stevens *Ratbag Dolan* ■ *Dir* Walter Hill • *Scr* David Giler, Walter Hill

The Undying Monster ★★★
Monster horror   1942 · US · BW · 62min

This Holmesian affair about a cursed English family places the emphasis on brooding atmosphere rather than horrific effects. Director John Brahm made his name with shadowy costume melodramas such as *Hangover Square*, and this thoughtful, if stolid, outing is one of his best – particularly for the brilliant striking-clock opening, which sets the gloomy tone. AJ DVD
James Ellison *Bob Curtis* • Heather Angel *Helga Hammond* • John Howard (1) *Oliver Hammond* • Bramwell Fletcher *Dr Geoffrey Covert* • Heather Thatcher *Christy* • Aubrey Mather *Inspector Craig* ■ *Dir* John Brahm • *Scr* Lillie Hayward, Michael Jacoby, from the play by Jessie Douglas Kerruish

The Unearthly ★
Horror   1957 · US · BW · 68min

Mad scientist John Carradine and his assistant Marilyn Buferd discover a new gland containing the secret of youth and, in their crazed efforts to achieve immortality, end up with a cellar full of grotesque monsters. Poorly scripted, crudely directed and overacted by Carradine, this is cheap fear fodder. AJ
John Carradine *Professor Charles Conway* • Allison Hayes *Grace Thomas* • Myron Healey *Mark Houston* • Sally Todd *Natalie* • Marilyn Buferd *Dr Sharon Gilchrist* • Arthur Batanides *Danny Green* • Tor Johnson *Lobo* • Harry Fleer *Harry Jedrow* ■ *Dir* Brook L Peters • *Scr* Geoffrey Dennis [John DF Black], Jane Mann, from a story by Jane Mann

The Unexpected Journey ★★★
Drama based on a true story   2004 · US · Colour · 90min

Mary-Louise Parker gives a moving performance as a single mother battling to get her seven-year-old autistic twins a mainstream education. Yet while Parker adds consistency and heart to events in this true story-based drama, key issues remain frustratingly unexplored and an abrupt leap forward to the boys as teens is jarring, missing out the mechanics of their remarkable development. Nonetheless, the two adolescent actors are excellent, with *High School Musical's* Zac Efron a standout. SF
Mary-Louise Parker *Corrine Morgan-Thomas* • Aidan Quinn *Douglas Thomas* • Zac Efron *Steven Morgan* • Thomas Lewis [Bubba Lewis] *Phillip Morgan* • Jacob Cherry [Jake Cherry] *Young Steven* • Jeremy Shada *Young Phillip* • Michael Arata *Brian* • Lenore Banks *Kate* ■ *Dir* Gregg Champion • *Scr* Mike Maples

The Unexpected Mrs Pollifax ★★★
Spy drama   1999 · US · Colour · 90min

Venerable stage and screen actress Angela Lansbury gives a plucky performance as the silver-haired secret agent Emily Pollifax, who, recently widowed, pursues her lifelong ambition to become a spy. In a case of mistaken identity, she is hired by the CIA and sent to Morocco to pick up a book containing an encrypted message. Filmed on location in Ireland, Paris and Morocco, this diverting TV movie is fast-paced and fun. MC
Angela Lansbury *Mrs Pollifax* • Thomas Ian Griffith *Farrell* • Ed Bishop *Carstairs* • Joseph Long *Alekseiyagoda* • Paul Birchard *Bishop* ■ *Dir* Anthony Pullen Shaw • *Scr* Robert T Megginson, from the novel *A Palm for Mrs Pollifax* by Dorothy Gilman

The Unfaithful ★★★
Melodrama   1947 · US · BW · 108min

Seven years after Bette Davis and Herbert Marshall starred so effectively in an adaptation of Somerset Maugham's *The Letter* for Warner Bros, the studio returned to the material, rearranging it, but retaining the central plot. Ann Sheridan is the woman who, having been unfaithful to her husband (Zachary Scott) during his absence on war duty, suffers genuine remorse over her infidelity and finds herself implicated in the murder of her erstwhile lover. Director Vincent Sherman, well in control, elicits a strong central performance from Sheridan and delivers an altogether respectable remake of a classic of stage and screen. RK
Ann Sheridan *Chris Hunter* • Lew Ayres *Larry Hannaford* • Zachary Scott *Bob Hunter* • Eve Arden *Paula* • Jerome Cowan *Prosecuting attorney* • Steven Geray *Martin Barrow* • John Hoyt *Detective-Lt Reynolds* • Peggy Knudsen *Claire* ■ *Dir* Vincent Sherman • *Scr* David Goodis, James Gunn, from the play *The Letter* by W Somerset Maugham (uncredited)

Unfaithful ★★ 15
Erotic thriller   2002 · US · Colour · 118min

Director Adrian Lyne made a big impact in the 1980s with slick but enjoyable erotic dramas and he returns to familiar territory with this tale of adultery and its violent aftermath. Diane Lane is flung into the path of French super stud Olivier Martinez and embarks on a steamy affair that jeopardises her happy marriage to Richard Gere. Gere smells a rat and hires a private detective. It's stylishly executed, but is let down by an ambiguous ending. LH DVD BL
Richard Gere *Edward Sumner* • Diane Lane *Constance "Connie" Sumner* • Olivier Martinez *Paul Martel* • Chad Lowe *Bill Stone* • Kate Burton *Tracy* • Margaret Colin *Sally* ■ *Dir* Adrian Lyne • *Scr* Alvin Sargent, William Broyles Jr, from the film *La Femme Infidèle* by Claude Chabrol

Unfaithfully Yours ★★★★ PG
Screwball comedy   1948 · US · BW · 100min

In this highly amusing look at suspicion and revenge, Rex Harrison plays a celebrated conductor who believes his wife, Linda Darnell, is having an affair. Laced with director Preston Sturges's customary acidic humour, it has great wit and flair, and the scenes in which Harrison attempts to humiliate Darnell add a dash of strychnine in the mix. Darnell is sublime and the dramatic swathes of Rossini, Tchaikovsky and Wagner add to the dark atmosphere. This beautifully crafted black comedy was remade in 1984. SH DVD
Rex Harrison *Sir Alfred de Carter* • Linda Darnell *Daphne de Carter* • Rudy Vallee *August Henschler* • Barbara Lawrence *Barbara Henschler* • Kurt Kreuger *Anthony Windborn* • Lionel Stander *Hugo Standoff* • Edgar Kennedy *Detective Sweeney* ■ *Dir/Scr* Preston Sturges

Unfaithfully Yours ★★★ 15
Comedy   1983 · US · Colour · 92min

Dudley Moore gives one of his better performances in this gently diverting and broadly satisfactory remake of the 1948 Preston Sturges comedy about a symphony orchestra conductor who suspects his

young wife of making beautiful music with a handsome violinist. Indeed, as both a comedian and musician, Moore could hardly have better credentials for the role of a jealous conductor, originally played by Rex Harrison, while Nastassja Kinski is coquettish as his flirting spouse. A slighter film than the original, this is also a pacier one. PF
Dudley Moore *Claude Eastman* • Nastassja Kinski *Daniella Eastman* • Armand Assante *Maximillian Stein* • Albert Brooks *Norman Robbins* • Cassie Yates *Carla Robbins* • Richard Libertini *Giuseppe* • Richard B Shull *Jess Keller* ■ *Dir* Howard Zieff • *Scr* Valerie Curtin, Barry Levinson, Robert Klane, from the 1948 film by Preston Sturges

Unfinished Business ★★★ U
Romantic comedy drama   1941 · US · BW · 95min

En route to the big city, small-town girl Irene Dunne enjoys a trainboard romance with Preston Foster, but is later taken up by his brother, Robert Montgomery, whom she marries. The path of matrimony fails to run smoothly and Dunne runs off and joins the chorus of an opera house. This vapid romantic comedy, neither particularly romantic nor especially amusing, s elevated by the 18-carat direction of Gregory La Cava and the stylish performances of Dunne and Montgomery. RK
Irene Dunne *Nancy Andrews Duncan* • Robert Montgomery *Tommy Duncan* • Preston Foster *Steve Duncan* • Eugene Pallette *Elmer* • Esther Dale *Aunt Mathilda* • Dick Foran *Frank* ■ *Dir* Gregory La Cava • *Scr* Eugene Thackrey, Vicki Baum, from a story by Gregory La Cava

Unfinished Business ★★ 15
Comedy   2015 · US · Colour · 90min

This wild comedy sees Vince Vaughn, Dave Franco and Tom Wilkinson play three businessmen who go to extreme lengths to land the contract of their dreams and defeat their former boss (Sienna Miller). Numerous R-rated shenanigans and aspirations towards a movie in the style of *The Hangover* cover up a plot that really has very little to offer. Taking the outline of almost every Vince Vaughn is as dry and fast-talking as you would expect, although he is met with likeable co-stars in Wilkinson and Franco, and the bumbling trio have a certain underdog charm in dealing with all manner of mishaps. JL In English, German.
Vince Vaughn *Daniel Trunkman* • Tom Wilkinson *Timothy McWinters* • Dave Franco *Mike Pancake* • Sienna Miller *Chuck Portnoy* • James Marsden *Jim Spinch* • Nick Frost *Bill Whitney* ■ *Dir* Ken Scott (2) • *Scr* Steve Conrad • *Cinematographer* Oliver Stapleton

The Unfinished Dance ★★
Dance drama   1947 · US · Colour · 100min

Keen to break with her goodie image, Margaret O'Brien is superficially petulant as the trainee ballerina who sabotages Karin Booth's career to protect her idol Cyd Charisse. But she mugs less fiercely than comedian Danny Thomas, who is clearly out to make an impact in his film debut. The musical interludes are intrusive, but David Lichine's *Holiday for Strings* will please dance fans. DP
Margaret O'Brien *Margaret "Meg" Merlin* • Cyd Charisse *Mlle Ariane Bouchet* • Karin Eooth *Anna La Darina* • Danny Thomas *Mr Paneros* • Esther Dale *Olga* • Thurston Hall *Mr Ronsell* ■ *Dir* Henry Koster • *Scr* Myles Connolly, from the novel *La Mort du Cygne* by Paul Morand

An Unfinished Life ★ 12
Drama   2005 · Ger/US · Colour · 103min

Robert Redford plays a curmudgeonly Rocky Mountain rancher, whose routines are interrupted by the arrival of his dead son's widow (Jennifer Lopez) and a granddaughter he never knew he had. With its appallingly mawkish and turgid script, saccharine score and over-egged performances this must rank as the worst film that Lasse Hallström has made for production company Miramax. LF DVD
Robert Redford *Einar Gilkyson* • Jennifer Lopez *Jean Gilkyson* • Morgan Freeman *Mitch Bradley* • Josh Lucas *Crane Curtis* • Damian Lewis *Gary Winston* • Camryn Manheim *Nina* • Becca

Gardner *Griff Gilkyson* ■ *Dir* Lasse Hallström • *Scr* Mark Spragg, Virginia Korus Spragg, from the novel by Mark Spragg

An Unfinished Piece for Mechanical Piano ★★★★ U
Period romantic drama
1976 · USSR · Colour · 97min

The cryptic title refers to Anton Chekhov's early unfinished play *Platanov*, which director Nikita Mikhalkov, who also plays the drunken doctor, has skilfully adapted for the screen. Set in 1910 and at times a tragic farce, the film beautifully captures the atmosphere of the lazy summer's day at widow Antonina Shuranova's country estate. The leisurely pace reflects the lethargy of the characters, who are superbly portrayed by the ensemble cast. RB In Russian.

Aleksandr Kalyagin *Platonov* • Elena Solovei *Sophia* • Evgenia Glushenko *Sasha* • Antonina Shuranova *Anna Petrovna* • Yuri Bogatyrev *Sergei* ■ *Dir* Nikita Mikhalkov • *Scr* Nikita Mikhalkov, Aleksander Adabashyan, from the play *Platonov* by Anton Chekhov

Unforgettable ★★ 15
Thriller
1996 · US · Colour · 112min

In order to find his wife's killer, police medical examiner Ray Liotta injects himself with the secret memory-transfer formula of researcher Linda Fiorentino, together with the brain fluid of his wife, in order to "see" her last memories. Amazingly, this outrageous premise never comes across as the least bit goofy, but that's where the problem lies. The film is so solemn and serious that it never gets a chance to be exciting and mysterious. KB Swearing.

Ray Liotta *Dr David Krane* • Linda Fiorentino *Dr Martha Briggs* • Peter Coyote *Don Bresler* • Christopher McDonald *Stewart Gleick* • David Paymer *Curtis Avery* • Duncan Fraser *Michael Stratton* • Caroline Elliott *Cara Krane* ■ *Dir* John Dahl • *Scr* Bill Geddie

An Unforgettable Summer ★★★★
Period political drama
1994 · Fr/Rom · Colour · 80min

Directed with the unflinching honesty that has characterised Lucian Pintilie's canon, this adaptation may be set in the mid-1920s but it packs a powerful contemporary punch. Dispatched to an isolated garrison on Romania's border with Bulgaria, Claudiu Bleont is ordered to shoot local Bulgarian-speaking peasants as a reprisal for an ambush by Macedonian bandits. However, his judgement is clouded by the compassion of his wife, Kristin Scott Thomas. Exposing the racial hatred that blights this tinder-box region, Pintilie's impeccably performed picture is not so much a plea for tolerance as an anguished cry to stop the insanity. DP Romanian, French, English +subtitles.

Kristin Scott Thomas *Marie-Therese Von Debretsy* • Claudiu Bleont *Captain Dumitriu* • Olga Tudorache *Mme Vorvoreanu* • George Constantin *General Tchilibia* • Ion Pavlescu *Serban Lascari* ■ *Dir* Lucian Pintilie • *Scr* Lucian Pintilie, from the short story *La Salade* by Petru Dumitriu

The Unforgiven ★★★★ PG
Western
1960 · US · Colour · 116min

This handsome Texas-set western from director John Huston is based on a novel by Alan LeMay, whose more famous *The Searchers* tells the flipside of this tale. Huston is particularly well served by Burt Lancaster and an interesting support cast. Only Audrey Hepburn, unusually, lacks credibility. Superbly photographed on location by Franz Planer, with a fine Dimitri Tiomkin score, this film deserves to be better known. The racial issues it deals with are no less comfortable now than they were at both the time of the historical events and when the movie was made. TS *DVD*

Burt Lancaster *Ben Zachary* • Audrey Hepburn *Rachel Zachary* • Audie Murphy *Cash Zachary* • John Saxon *Johnny Portugal* • Charles Bickford *Zeb Rawlins* • Lillian Gish *Mattilda Zachary* • Albert Salmi *Charlie Rawlins* ■ *Dir* John Huston • *Scr* Ben Maddow, from the novel by Alan LeMay

Unforgiven ★★★★★ 15
Western
1992 · US · Colour · 125min

Winner of four Oscars, including best picture and best director, Clint Eastwood's western is one of the finest films made in the genre. Exploring the harsh realities of frontier life, he depicts the west as an unforgiving place. It's clear from the fevered manner in which Saul Rubinek's dime novelist gathers his Wild West stories that an era is about to pass into legend. Eastwood's own world-weary performance as the retired gunslinger, forced to strap on the six-shooters one last time to feed his children, is exemplary. The support playing of Morgan Freeman as his former partner, Richard Harris as a vain killer and Oscar-winning Gene Hackman as the vicious sheriff is unsurpassable. DP Violence, swearing. *DVD* *Blu*

Clint Eastwood *William Munny* • Gene Hackman *Sheriff "Little Bill" Daggett* • Morgan Freeman *Ned Logan* • Richard Harris *English Bob* • Jaimz Woolvett *Schofield Kid* • Saul Rubinek *WW Beauchamp* • Frances Fisher *Strawberry Alice* • Anna Thomson [Anna Levine] *Delilah Fitzgerald* ■ *Dir* Clint Eastwood • *Scr* David Webb Peoples

Unforgiven ★★★ 15
Period action drama
2014 · Jpn · Colour · 135min

More than 50 years after Hollywood remade *The Seven Samurai* as *The Magnificent Seven*, Japanese director Lee Sang-il returns the favour by re-imagining Clint Eastwood's revenge western as a samurai film. Famed ex-samurai Jubei the Killer (Ken Watanabe) is now a farmer and facing tough times. So, when he's offered reward money for hunting down the men who disfigured prostitute Shiori Kutsuna, he takes the job. The storyline transfers so comfortably from west to east that Sang-il gets away with an almost scene-for-scene reconstruction of the original. It's nicely made and beautifully acted, but what really fascinates is the culture shift to a Japan where swords and samurais are becoming things of the past. DA Japanese +subtitles. Violence. *DVD* *Blu*

Ken Watanabe *Jubei Kamata* • Koichi Sato *Ichizo Oishi* • Akira Emoto *Kingo Baba* • Yuya Yagira *Goro Sawada* ■ *Dir* Lee Sang-il • *Scr* Lee Sang-il, from the 1992 film

Unfriended ★★★ 15
Horror
2014 · US · Colour · 79min

Revenge finds its way online in this "found footage" horror. A group of teens are terrorised by an online presence seeking vengeance for the death of a classmate they shamed into suicide a year earlier. Told through a series of quickly shifting chat windows and social-media screens, our troupe of believable (and slightly unbearable) teens are picked off one by one. It's a ludicrous concept and there's not much about the film that won't seem predictable, but the enjoyment and terror comes in the execution. JL Violence, swearing, sex scenes, suicide theme. *DVD* *Blu*

Shelley Hennig *Blaire* • Moses Storm *Mitch* • Renee Olstead *Jess* • Jacob Wysocki *Ken* • Will Peltz *Adam* ■ *Dir* Leo Gabriadze [Levan Gabriadze] • *Scr* Nelson Greaves

The Unguarded Moment ★★ U
Crime drama
1956 · US · Colour · 94min

Actress Rosalind Russell provided the story on which this unusual study in sexism was based. But it's even more noteworthy for providing aqua-musicals star Esther Williams with a rare non-swimming role, as the teacher whose attempts to understand the spoilt son of an arrogant misogynist result in her being suspended for inappropriate behaviour. Williams acquits herself well in a rather lurid role, but the direction is decidedly pedestrian. DP

Esther Williams *Lois Conway* • George Nader *Harry Graham* • John Saxon *Leonard Bennett* • Edward Andrews *Mr Bennett* • Les Tremayne *Mr Pendleton* • Jack Albertson *Professor* • Dani

Crayne *Josie Warren* • John Wilder *Sandy* ■ *Dir* Harry Keller • *Scr* Herb Meadow, Larry Marcus, from a story by Marcus, Rosalind Russell

The Unholy ★ 18
Horror
1988 · US · Colour · 97min

In a misguided and ultimately tedious attempt at a theologically-themed horror movie, Ben Cross is the priest who, after surviving a drop from a five-storey building, becomes the "Chosen One" and is assigned to rid a church of a demonic presence that's seducing and killing clergymen. Good location work in New Orleans, but Camilo Vila's slow-paced direction kills this stone dead. RS *DVD*

Ben Cross *Father Michael* • Ned Beatty *Lieutenant Stern* • William Russ *Luke* • Jill Carroll *Millie* • Hal Holbrook *Archbishop Mosley* • Trevor Howard *Father Silva* • Peter Frechette *Claude* ■ *Dir* Camilo Vila • *Scr* Philip Yordan, Fernando Fonseca

The Unholy Garden ★★ U
Crime drama
1931 · US · BW · 71min

This decidedly creaky Samuel Goldwyn production stars Ronald Colman and Fay Wray in a tale of desert intrigue. It was the first original screenplay written for Hollywood by the New York theatre team of Ben Hecht and Charles MacArthur, who quickly devised the plot (a den of thieves, a beautiful girl, etc) in return for an astronomical $25,000 and a slice of the profits. Slightly unfairly trashed by the critics and ended up losing $200,000. AT

Ronald Colman *Barrington Hunt* • Fay Wray *Camille de Jonghe* • Estelle Taylor *Eliza Mowbray* • Tully Marshall *Baron de Jonghe* • Ulrich Haupt [Ullrich Haupt] *Colonel Von Axt* • Henry Armetta *Nick the Goose* • Lawrence Grant *Dr Shayne* ■ *Dir* George Fitzmaurice • *Scr* Ben Hecht, Charles MacArthur

Unholy Partners ★★
Crime drama
1941 · US · BW · 94min

Edward G Robinson and Mervyn LeRoy made one of the first of the crusading newspaper movies, *Five Star Final*, in 1931. But this similarly themed story, set just after the First World War, isn't in the same league – though Robinson is incapable of delivering any bravura performance. He plays an idealistic editor whose paper is bankrolled by racketeeer Edward Arnold. The story of their feud features too many contrivances and melodramatics. AT

Edward G Robinson *Bruce Corey* • Edward Arnold *Merrill Lambert* • Laraine Day *Miss Cronin* • Marsha Hunt *Gail Fenton* • William T Orr *Tommy Jarvis* • Don Beddoe *Michael Z Reynolds* • Walter Kingsford *Managing editor* • Charles Dingle *Clyde Fenton* ■ *Dir* Mervyn LeRoy • *Scr* Earl Baldwin, Bartlett Cormack, Lesser Samuels

The Unholy Rollers ★★★
Sports action drama
1972 · US · Colour · 88min

A funky and very funny cult classic from the Roger Corman production line, this stars the wonderful Claudia Jennings, the *Playboy* model-turned-action heroine. She hits the *Rocky* road to fame as a single-minded factory worker desperate for glory in the roller-derby ring. How she overcomes the usual slew of obstacles – vicious rivals, bitchy opponents and domestic problems – is brilliantly marshalled with zip, zing and charm by director Vernon Zimmerman. AJ

Claudia Jennings *Karen* • Louis Quinn *Stern* • Betty Anne Rees *Mickey* • Roberta Collins *Jennifer* • Alan Vint *Greg* • Candice Roman *Donna* ■ *Dir* Vernon Zimmerman • *Scr* Howard R Cohen, from a story by Vernon Zimmerman, Howard R Cohen

The Unholy Three ★★★★
Silent crime drama
1925 · US · BW · 86min

A midget who masquerades as a baby, a giant strongman and a cross-dressing ventriloquist (Lon Chaney) become a crime syndicate in miniature in director Tod Browning's strangely affecting silent melodrama. This is a serious and imaginative presentation of diabolical deeds, cruel vindictiveness and ghoulish humour. Genre creator Browning fashions unique thrills from the sheer novelty value

of the freak-show outlaw story and highlights the twisted scenario with a wealth of deft narrative touches. This sensational shocker is one of his, and Chaney's, finest achievements. AJ

Lon Chaney *Professor Echo/Granny O'Grady* • Harry Earles *Tweedledee* • Victor McLaglen *Hercules* • Mae Busch *Rosie O'Grady* • Matt Moore *Hector McDonald* • Matthew Betz *Regan* • William Humphreys *Defense attorney* ■ *Dir* Tod Browning • *Scr* Waldemar Young, from the story *The Terrible Three* by Clarence Aaron "Tod" Robbins

The Unholy Three ★★
Crime drama
1930 · US · BW · 75min

The success of the 1925 version of Clarence Aaron "Tod" Robbins's story about a triumvirate of circus exiles becoming master criminals led to this remake, cashing in on the novelty of sound. It's Lon Chaney's first talkie and his last picture ever as he died from throat cancer straight afterwards. Director Jack Conway is clearly not in the same class as auteur Tod Browning and his quick refit is far inferior to the original. AJ

Lon Chaney *Prof Echo* • Lila Lee *Rosie O'Grady* • Elliott Nugent *Hector McDonald* • Harry Earles *Midget* • John Miljan *Prosecuting attorney* • Ivan Linow *Hercules* • Clarence Burton *Regan* • Crauford Kent *Defense attorney* ■ *Dir* Jack Conway • *Scr* JC Nugent, Elliott Nugent, from the story *The Terrible Three* by Clarence Aaron "Tod" Robbins

The Unholy Wife ★★
Crime drama
1957 · US · Colour · 94min

Diana Dors's Hollywood sojourn yielded two RKO programme fillers, this crime melodrama and the dreadful *I Married a Woman*. Unfortunately for Dors, there were just too many starlets in the studio system, and she couldn't compete with the likes of Marilyn Monroe and Jayne Mansfield. Rod Steiger manages to chew less scenery than usual in his role as Dors's cuckolded husband, but overall this has few memorable moments. TS

Rod Steiger *Paul Hochen* • Diana Dors *Phyllis Hochen* • Tom Tryon *San* • Beulah Bondi *Emma Hochen* • Marie Windsor *Gwen* • Arthur Franz *Reverend Stephen Hochen* • Luis Van Rooten *Ezra Benton* • Joe De Santis *Gino Verdugo* ■ *Dir* John Farrow • *Scr* Jonathan Latimer, from a story by William Durkee

Unhook the Stars ★★★ 15
Comedy drama
1996 · Fr · Colour · 100min

Nick Cassavetes (son of actor/director John) directs his mother Gena Rowlands in this comedy drama. Marisa Tomei gives a nice performance as the young mother who disrupts the life of neighbour Rowlands while looking for a babysitter for her son. However, Rowlands unsurprisingly steals the film from not only Tomei, but also male co-star Gérard Depardieu, who seems slightly ill at ease throughout. JB Swearing, sexual references.

Gena Rowlands *Mildred* • Marisa Tomei *Monica* • Gérard Depardieu *Big Tommy* • Jake Lloyd *JJ* • Moira Kelly *Ann Mary Margaret* • David Sherrill *Ethan* ■ *Dir* Nick Cassavetes • *Scr* Nick Cassavetes, Helen Caldwell

The Uninvited ★★★★★ PG
Horror
1944 · US · BW · 95min

The *Casablanca* of horror, this is a programme filler in which all the elements came together to produce a classic of the genre. Brother and sister Ray Milland and Ruth Hussey buy a house in Cornwall and find it haunted. Though containing what are now narrative clichés (a mysterious room, sinister housekeeper) and strained humour, this is an ingenious ghost story. Aided by Charles Lang's photography and Victor Young's score, it still sends shivers up the spine. This was the first film by Lewis Allen, who failed to re-create the formula in his follow-up, *The Unseen*. DM *DVD*

Ray Milland *Roderick "Rick" Fitzgerald* • Ruth Hussey *Pamela Fitzgerald* • Donald Crisp *Commander Beech* • Cornelia Otis Skinner *Miss Holloway* • Dorothy Stickney *Miss Bird* • Barbara Everest *Lizzie Flynn* • Alan Napier *Dr Scott* • Gail

U

Russell *Stella Meredith* ■ *Dir* Lewis Allen • *Scr* Dodie Smith, Frank Partos, from the novel *Uneasy Freehold* by Dorothy Macardle

The Uninvited ★★15

Horror thriller
2008 · US/Can/Ger · Colour · 83min

This American remake of the 2003 Korean hit *A Tale of Two Sisters* loses the psychological complexities and subtle art house stylings of the original to become a straightforward thriller mystery. Grief-stricken over her mother's tragic death, teenager Anna (Emily Browning) is haunted by ghosts that reveal dark secrets about stepmother-to-be Rachel (Elizabeth Banks). The debut film of the Guard brothers (Thomas and Charles) is more heightened-reality family drama than flat-out horror and, despite polished production values, once again the refined dread of a popular Asian legend gets lost in translation. AJ
DVD *SL*

Emily Browning *Anna* • Elizabeth Banks (2) *Rachel* • Arielle Kebbel *Alex* • David Strathairn *Steven* • Maya Massar *Mom* • Kevin McNulty *Sheriff Emery* ■ *Dir* Guard Brothers [Charles Guard], Guard Brothers [Thomas Guard] • *Scr* Craig Rosenberg, Doug Miro, Carlo Bernard, from the film *A Tale of Two Sisters* by Kim Ji-woon

Union City ★★12

Drama
1980 · US · Colour · 81min

Blondie singer Debbie Harry plays the plain, frustrated wife of a meek businessman (Dennis Lipscomb) whose obsession with catching a petty thief leads to murder. Director Mark Reichert plays it too offbeat, arty and tricksy for it to emerge as another classic from Cornell Woolrich's work. Most of the opportunities for smart black comedy are blown by the relentlessly downbeat tone and Reichert's fudged aim for Fassbinder-esque European irony. AJ
DVD

Dennis Lipscomb *Harlan* • Deborah Harry *Lillian* • Irina Maleeva *Mrs Gofka - the Contessa* • Everett McGill *Larry Longacre* • Sam McMurray *Young vagrant* • Terina Lewis *Evelyn - secretary* • Pat Benatar *Jeanette* ■ *Dir* Mark Reichert • *Scr* Mark Reichert, from the story *The Corpse Next Door* by Cornell Woolrich

Union Depot ★★★

Comedy drama
1932 · US · BW · 75min

Completely overshadowed by MGM's *Grand Hotel* to which it is often compared, this modest offering from First National, set amid the bustle of a major train station, is a snappy and appealing entertainment. Douglas Fairbanks Jr stars as a young hobo who finds some money, decks himself out as a gentleman, and falls for a broke dancer (Joan Blondell) who needs $64 to get to Salt Lake City. Quite silly, but the stars are charming and attractive and the supporting players excellent. RK

Douglas Fairbanks Jr *Chic Miller* • Joan Blondell *Ruth* • Guy Kibbee *Scrap Iron* • Alan Hale *Baron* • Frank McHugh *Drunk* • George Rosener *Bernardi* • Dickie Moore *Little Boy* ■ *Dir* Alfred E Green • *Scr* Kenyon Nicholson, Walter DeLeon, John Bright, Kubec Glasmon, from the play by Gene Fowler, Douglas Durkin, Joe Laurie

Union Pacific ★★★U

Western
1939 · US · BW · 134min

This epic about the construction of the first transcontinental railroad was a smash hit in 1939. It stars Joel McCrea as the overseer for Union Pacific, fighting local tribesman and saboteurs on the way to linking up with the Central Pacific line. Barbara Stanwyck is a tomboy postmistress and Robert Preston (in his first big role) impresses as a likeable gambler. As usual, producer/director Cecil B DeMille stages too many scenes in the comfort of a sound stage, relying on obvious back projection, and it is the outdoor footage, including the raid on the train, that provides the film's most memorable moments. AE

Barbara Stanwyck *Mollie Monahan* • Joel McCrea *Jeff Butler* • Akim Tamiroff *Fiesta* • Robert Preston *Dick Allen* • Lynne Overman *Leach Overmile* • Brian Donlevy *Sid Campeau* • Lon Chaney Jr *Dollarhide* ■ *Dir* Cecil B DeMille • *Scr*

Walter DeLeon, C Gardner Sullivan, Jesse Lasky Jr, Jack Cunningham, from the novel *Trouble Shooters* by Ernest Haycox

Union Station ★★★

Crime thriller
1950 · US · BW · 80min

Considered a real nail-biter in its day, this competent police thriller benefits from the real location of the concourse, platforms and threatening bowels of a bustling Art Deco station. Here, a millionaire is instructed to deliver the ransom for his kidnapped blind daughter. William Holden, tight-jawed and efficient, is in charge of the on-the-spot manhunt, Barry Fitzgerald is the kindly police chief and Nancy Olson the necessary feminine interest. Ace cinematographer-turned-director Rudolph Maté extracts maximum mileage from the settings, and wrings tension from the simple plot. RK

William Holden (2) *Lt William Calhoun* • Nancy Olson *Joyce Willecombe* • Barry Fitzgerald *Insp Donnelly* • Lyle Bettger *Joe Beacom* • Jan Sterling *Marge Wrighter* • Allene Roberts *Lorna Murcall* • Herbert Heyes *Henry Murcall* • Don Dunning *Gus Hadder* ■ *Dir* Rudolph Maté • *Scr* Sydney Boehm, from the story *Nightmare in Manhattan* by Thomas Walsh

A United Kingdom

Romantic drama based on a true story
2017 · UK · Colour

This is a preview - no prints were available to review as we went to press: Still basking in the glow from his success as Martin Luther King Jr in *Selma*, David Oyelowo steps into the shoes of another visionary leader, though less well known this time. Seretse Khama, a Bechuanaland (later Botswana) prince, returned home from London in the late 1940s accompanied by a white wife (Rosamund Pike), infuriating the newly apartheid regime in South Africa. Director Amma Asante's 2013 film *Belle* scored her a hit, so a crafty melding of human drama and political intrigue is highly likely. SvM

David Oyelowo *Seretse Khama* • Rosamund Pike *Ruth Williams* • Jack Davenport *Alistair Canning* • Terry Pheto *Naledi Khama* • Tom Felton *Rufus Lancaster* • Jack Lowden *Tony Benn* ■ *Dir* Amma Asante • *Scr* Guy Hibbert, from the non-fiction book *Colour Bar* by Susan Williams

United 93 ★★★★15

Drama based on a true story
2006 · UK/US/Fr · Colour · 106min

The first major film to be released about the events of 9/11 is no hackneyed disaster movie, but a fittingly sober and dignified affair. For this re-telling of the events aboard the only hijacked plane that didn't reach its intended target that day, writer/director Paul Greengrass adopts a dialogue-light, almost documentary approach. The sense of reality is heightened by the casting of relative unknowns and the use of varying perspectives. Blending known facts with educated guesswork, Greengrass crafts a credible and moving film about ordinary folk forced into one extraordinary act of courage. DA Violence, swearing. *DVD* *SL*

Lewis Alsamari *Saeed Al Ghamdi* • JJ Johnson *Captain Jason M Dahl* • Gary Commock *First Officer LeRoy Homer* • Trish Gates *Sandra Bradshaw* • Polly Adams *Deborah Welsh* • Cheynne Jackson *Mark Bingham* • Opal Alladin *CeeCee Lyles* • Starla Benford *Wanda Anita Green* • David Alan Basche *Todd Beamer* ■ *Dir/Scr* Paul Greengrass

The United States of Leland ★★★15

Crime drama
2002 · US · Colour · 104min

When moody but intelligent teenager Ryan Gosling murders a learning disabled youngster, juvenile detention teacher Don Cheadle is bent on discovering what provoked such a senseless act. However, like most of the characters in this thoughtful indie drama, he also has an ulterior motive. While it's a little contrived at times, writer/director Matthew Ryan Hoge's impressive debut feature offers an unsettling portrait of alienated youth. JF
DVD

Ryan Gosling *Leland P Fitzgerald* • Don Cheadle *Pearl Madison* • Chris Klein *Allen Harris* • Jena Malone *Becky Pollard* • Lena Olin *Marybeth Fitzgerald* • Kevin Spacey *Albert T Fitzgerald* • Michelle Williams *Julie Pollard* • Martin Donovan (2) *Harry Pollard* ■ *Dir/Scr* Matthew Ryan Hoge

United We Fall ★15

Sports comedy
2014 · UK · Colour · 89min

The story of how Manchester United blew three trophies in 2010 is related in a mockumentary that will appeal more to ABUs (Anyone But United) than Old Trafford fans. The performances are willing and vaguely spoof the talking heads in Benjamin and Gabe Turner's *The Class of '92*. But the anecdotes simply aren't funny, while secondary interviews with a David Cameron-like Prime Minister and a corrupt (and dismayingly unPC) Arab FIFA official are as embarrassing as the WAGs' climactic dinner party. DP Swearing, sexual references, nudity.

Matthew Avery *Kwasi Abdullah Amoako* • Jonathan Broke *Kurt Kurtz* • Jack Donnelly *Olly Hunter* • Ryan Pope *Danny Keegan* • James Rastall *Stevo Fallis* • Robert Portal *Prime Minister* ■ *Dir/Scr* Gary Sinyor

Unity ★★15

Documentary
2015 · US · Colour · 99min

Shaun Monson's disappointing follow-up to 2005's *Earthlings* is a plea for compassion for animals. Monson divides his tract into five sections - Cosmic, Mind, Body, Heart and Soul - and divides sound bites between 100 celebrity narrators. These stars deliver their lines with a reverence that matches the intensity of the sometimes harrowing montage. If everything is ostensibly designed to provoke thought, the dogmatic tone only stifles it. DP

Joaquin Phoenix • Jennifer Aniston • Dr Dre • Ben Kingsley • Helen Mirren • Tom Hiddleston • Kevin Spacey • Susan Sarandon • Ben Whishaw • Michael Gambon ■ *Dir/Scr* Shaun Monson

Universal Horror ★★★★PG

Documentary
1998 · UK · Colour and BW · 95min

Kevin Brownlow ranks alongside Henri Langlois as one of cinema's most significant archivists, and here he has compiled a fascinating insight into the working methods of the production unit that made Universal the biggest name in horror. Recalling the achievements of such craftsmen as Karl Freund, James Whale and Jack Pierce (who created the now legendary bolt-necked Frankenstein make-up), this documentary explores the German expressionist influence on 1930s Hollywood horror and the debt owed to such European actors as Boris Karloff and Bela Lugosi. Combining clips, archive interviews and the reminiscences of stalwarts such as Fay Wray, it is both hugely informative and highly entertaining. DP

Kenneth Branagh *Narrator* ■ *Dir* Kevin Brownlow

Universal Soldier ★★★18

Futuristic action thriller
1992 · US · Colour · 99min

This sci-fi potboiler from director Roland Emmerich is a by-the-numbers affair, with dialogue you'd swear appears in comic balloons. But as no one takes the ultimate warrior premise seriously, the unpretentious pandering to the action-plus brigade is a likeable strength, not a jarring weakness. The Muscles from Brussels (Jean-Claude Van Damme) has the edge over the Swedish Meatball (Dolph Lundgren) in every respect, from his showcase kick boxing to his send-up nude scene, in this OTT jeopardy jackpot. AJ Violence, swearing *DVD* *SL*

Jean-Claude Van Damme *Luc Deveraux* • Dolph Lundgren *Andrew Scott* • Ally Walker *Veronica Roberts* • Ed O'Ross *Colonel Perry* • Jerry Orbach *Dr Gregor* • Leon Rippy *Woodward* • Tico Wells *Garth* • Ralph Moeller *GR76* ■ *Dir* Roland Emmerich • *Scr* Richard Rothstein, Christopher Leitch, Dean Devlin

Universal Soldier 2: Brothers in Arms ★★18

Futuristic action thriller
1998 · Can · Colour · 89min

Although Jean-Claude Van Damme eventually returned for a big-screen follow-up to *Universal Soldier*, this is the official sequel, even though it's a TV movie with a totally different cast. Having been starved of funds to develop his army of undead warriors, UnSol supremo Gary Busey sets out to teach Washington a lesson. However, he hasn't counted on journalist Chandra West and her combat-hardened boyfriend, Matt Battaglia. Undemanding. DP Violence, swearing, nudity.

Matt Battaglia *Luc Devreaux* • Jeff Wincott *Eric* • Chandra West *Veronica Roberts* • Gary Busey *Mazur* • Burt Reynolds *Mentor* ■ *Dir* Jeff Woolnough • *Scr* Peter M Lenkov

Universal Soldier 3: Unfinished Business ★★18

Futuristic action thriller
1998 · US · Colour · 91min

Having been less than enthralled with the results of reconstructing an army from the dead in part two, those fiendish UnSol boffins set out to create test-tube troopers in this follow-up TV movie. Although it starts tiresomely with a lengthy resumé of previous events, the new adventure eventually kicks in, with Matt Battaglia and reporter sidekick Chandra West being challenged with halting the dangerous research. DP

Matt Battaglia *Luc Devreaux* • Jeff Wincott *Eric* • Chandra West *Veronica Roberts* • Gary Busey *Mazur* • Burt Reynolds *Mentor* ■ *Dir* Jeff Woolnough • *Scr* Peter M Lenkov

Universal Soldier - the Return ★18

Futuristic action thriller
1999 · US · Colour · 83min

This is an insultingly awful big-screen follow-up to the 1992 Jean-Claude Van Damme hit. His nice guy terminator is now a technical adviser on the secret government project that turns dead soldiers into killing machines. Thinly plotted and painfully clichéd even by genre standards, this is a moronic mess. JC Violence, swearing, nudity. *DVD* *SL*

Jean-Claude Van Damme *Luc Devreaux* • Michael Jai White *SETH* • Heidi Schanz *Erin* • Xander Berkeley *Dylan Cotner* • Justin Lazard *Captain Blackburn* • Kiana Tom *Maggie* • Daniel Von Bargen *General Radford* • James Black (2) *Sergeant Morrow* ■ *Dir* Mic Rodgers • *Scr* William Malone, John Fasano, from characters by Richard Rothstein, Christopher Leitch, Dean Devlin

Universal Soldier: Regeneration ★★18

Futuristic action thriller
2009 · US · Colour · 92min

Jean-Claude Van Damme returns to one of his best-known roles in this ambitious but flimsy reboot. Ageing yet agile, he demonstrates he's still got the moves, as his reanimated warrior is forcibly re-commissioned to help stop stereotypical terrorists from blowing up the crippled Chernobyl nuclear plant, SF *DVD*

Andrei "The Pit Bull" Arlovski [Andrei Arlovski] *NGU* • Jean-Claude Van Damme *Luc Deveraux* • Dolph Lundgren *Andrew Scott* ■ *Dir* John Hyams • *Scr* Victor Ostrovsky, from characters by Richard Rothstein, Christopher Leitch, Dean Devlin • *Cinematographer* Peter Hyams

The Unknown ★★★★PG

Silent drama
1927 · US · BW · 49min

Single-minded in its brutality, perversity and odd shock value, Tod Browning's Freudian nightmare is the most accomplished and morbid melodrama Master of Silent Macabre ever directed. Lon Chaney straps his arms down with a painful harness as Alonzo the Armless Wonder, a circus performer who throws knives with his feet. It's when he falls in love with Joan Crawford who has a fear of being touched that murder, amputation and obsession come under the dark carnival spotlight. A fascinating silent classic, it still appals because of its sadomasochistic and devious tone. AJ **DVD**

Lon Chaney *Alonzo* • Norman Kerry *Malabor* • Joan Crawford *Estrellita* • Nick De Ruiz *Zanzi* • John George *Cojo* • Frank Lanning *Costra* ■ *Dir* Tod Browning • *Scr* Waldemar Young, from a story by Tod Browning

The Unknown ★★15
Horror action adventure
2005 · US · Colour · 83min

Supposedly based on real events, this suffers from poor creature make-up and an uncertain tone, mixing genuine scares with offbeat humour as grisly murders in a Pacific Northwest community are attributed to a marauding grizzly – but is it something more sinister? Shown on DVD as *Clawed: the Legend of Sasquatch*, it pays its dues to *Jaws* as the local mayor attempts to make light of the killings to save the tourist industry. One-time Tarzan Miles O'Keeffe surfaces here as a hunter who is sole survivor of the initial attack. But the rest of the cast takes after the title. SuR **DVD**

Dylan Purcell *Richard Winslow* • Brandon Henschel *Jay Kelter* • Miles O'Keeffe *Ed Janzer* • Jack Conley *Sheriff Chuck Kassel* • Chelsea Hobbs *Jenny Ackers* • Casey LaBow *Shea Landers* • Nathaniel Arcand *Ranger John Eagleheart* ■ *Dir* Karl Kozak • *Scr* Don J Rearden, Karl Kozak

Unknown ★★15
Mystery thriller 2006 · US · Colour · 81min

Collective amnesia blurs the line between the good guys and the bad in this clunky indie thriller from former music-video director Simon Brand. Boasting a solid ensemble cast (including Jim Caviezel, Greg Kinnear and Barry Pepper), the tale sees five men wake up in a locked, deserted warehouse à la *Saw*, with no idea who they are or how they got there. With each of them in varying states of injury, it's obvious that their lives are at risk, resulting in the onset of *Reservoir Dogs*-style paranoia as the group rush to unravel the mystery. Unfortunately, this intriguing set-up rapidly falls flat thanks to a threadbare plot and a tension-killing mix of cutaways and *Memento*-type flashbacks. SF Violence, swearing. **DVD** 🔵

Jim Caviezel *Jean Jacket* • Greg Kinnear *Broken Nose* • Joe Pantoliano *Bound Man* • Barry Pepper *Rancher Shirt* • Jeremy Sisto *Handcuffed Man* • Bridget Moynahan *Eliza Coles* • Peter Stormare *Snakeskin Boots* ■ *Dir* Simon Brand • *Scr* Matthew Waynee

Unknown ★★★12
Thriller
2011 · Can/Fr/US/UK/Ger/Jpn · Colour · 108min

American botanist Liam Neeson awakens after a Berlin car accident to find no one recognises him in *Orphan* director Jaume Collet-Serra's solid Euro thriller. Shifting between identity-theft mystery and geo-political intrigue before propelling headlong into an assassination-bureau conspiracy plot, this well-maintained puzzler remains tautly suspenseful even through some preposterous moments. Neeson makes for a likeable everyman hero, January Jones (TV's *Mad Men*) is ice-cool as his Hitchcock-blonde wife and Diane Kruger plays his taxi-driver saviour. AJ Violence. **DVD** 🔵

Liam Neeson *Dr Martin Harris* • Diane Kruger *Gina* • January Jones *Elizabeth Harris* • Frank Langella *Rodney Cole* • Aidan Quinn *Martin B* • Bruno Ganz *Ernst Jürgen* ■ *Dir* Jaume Collet-Serra • *Scr* Oliver Butcher, Stephen Cornwell, from the novel *Out of My Head* by Didier Van Cauwelaert

The Unknown Guest ★★ U
Mystery drama 1943 · US · BW · 64min

A script by Philip Yordan and a score by Dmitri Tiomkin (although hardly their best work) add to the unnerving atmosphere of this curious country chiller in which the arrival of renegade Victor Jory coincides with the disappearance of his aged aunt and uncle from their hotel. Director Kurt

Neumann puts an interesting slant on small-town life. DP

Victor Jory *Chuck Williams* • Pamela Blake *Julie* • Veda Ann Borg *Helen* • Harry Hayden *Nadroy* • Nora Cecil *Martha Williams* • Lee White [Lee "Lasses" White] *Joe Williams* • Paul Fix *Fats* ■ *Dir* Kurt Neumann • *Scr* Philip Yordan, from a story by Maurice Franklin

The Unknown Known
★★★★
Documentary
2013 · US · Colour and BW · 102min

Under scrutiny here by *Fog of War* director Errol Morris is the disturbingly ebullient Donald Rumsfeld, US Secretary of Defense under President George W Bush. His involvement with major events of the 21st century (9/11, the Iraq War, the War on Terror) is at the heart of the movie, but what's equally fascinating is his proximity to the previous century's history, too: Watergate, US withdrawal from Vietnam, the Iraq-Iran War. Rumsfeld is certainly an enigmatic figure: unrepentant, evasive, with a Cheshire Cat grin, and Morris skilfully allows his target to revel in his own doublespeak. JA Violence, nudity. **DVD**

Donald Rumsfeld ■ *Dir* Errol Morris • *Music* Danny Elfman

Unknown Pleasures ★★★12
Comedy drama
2002 · Chi/Jpn/Fr/S Kor · Colour · 107min

Shooting on digital video in the run-down industrial town of Datong, director Jia Zhang Ke offers a wry look at the flip side of China's much-vaunted consumer boom. Wu Qiong and Zhao Wei Wei are persuasively indolent as the unemployed teenagers latching on to anything to occupy their time, with Wu's obsession with Zhao Tao (a self-deluded dancer with a brewery road show) providing much of the comic incident. But it's his fellow slacker's more considered approach to the future that proves more poignant, especially once he's diagnosed with hepatitis. DP Mandarin +subtitles. **DVD**

Zhao Tao *Qiao Qiao* • Zhao Wei Wei *Bin Bin* • Wu Qiong *Xiao Ji* • Zhou Qing Feng *Yuan Yuan* • Wang Hong Wei *Xiao Wu* ■ *Dir/Scr* Jia Zhang Ke

Unknown White Male
★★★12
Documentary
2005 · UK · Colour and BW · 88min

In July 2003, Doug Bruce found himself riding a subway train to Coney Island with no idea how he got there or who he was. Some convenient clues eventually led to his identity being established and, with the help of mates and medics, the British stockbroker-turned-photographer slowly began to piece together his past. However, since Rupert Murray released this documentary account of his friend's struggle to rediscover himself, doubts have been cast over its veracity and some suggest the entire enterprise may well be a hoax. Whether the participation of eminent Harvard psychologist Daniel Schacter is part of the ruse or not, this is still a visually striking exercise, in which cinematographer Orlando Stuart and colourist Richard Shadick ingeniously approximate Bruce's confusion with a series of dazzling abstract images. DP **DVD**

■ *Dir* Rupert Murray

Unknown World ★ U
Science-fiction adventure
1951 · US · BW · 74min

Scientists bore into the Earth aboard a half tank/half submarine mole ship, dubbed a "cyclotram", to find a subterranean safe haven from atomic war. Unfortunately, the peaceful centre proves harmful to human reproduction in a highly moral sci-fi quickie containing a wordy script, plodding direction, dinky special effects and not even an occasional thrill. AJ

Unlawful Entry ★★★18
Thriller 1992 · US · Colour · 106min

Meet the psychotic cop - so unbalanced that you see him unravelling before your eyes. He's portrayed with credibility by Ray Liotta, who never reduces his character to caricature. As he targets innocent couple Kurt Russell and Madeleine Stowe, his insecurities become unnervingly mixed in with his charm. Sadly, there are yawning gaps in the plot, and the climax is overcooked. JM Violence, swearing, nudity. **DVD**

Kurt Russell *Michael Carr* • Ray Liotta *Officer Pete Davis* • Madeleine Stowe *Karen Carr* • Roger E Mosley *Officer Roy Cole* • Ken Lerner *Roger Graham* • Deborah Offner *Penny* • Carmen Argenziano *Jerome Lurie* ■ *Dir* Jonathan Kaplan • *Scr* Lewis Colick, from a story by George D Putnam, John Katchner, Lewis Colick

Unleashed ★★★18
Martial arts action thriller
2005 · Fr/US/UK · Colour · 97min

Martial arts star Jet Li plays a sort of human Rottweiler, raised and kept caged like an animal, who is only unleashed when gangster Bob Hoskins needs some fighting done. Set in Glasgow, this sees Li rediscovering his humanity, courtesy of the relationship he builds with blind piano tuner Morgan Freeman. The fight scenes are fast, brutal and with a feel of the real about them, but this is also Li's most interesting non-Hong Kong work to date. DA Violence, swearing, nudity. **DVD**

Jet Li *Danny* • Morgan Freeman *Sam* • Bob Hoskins *Bart* • Kerry Condon *Victoria* ■ *Dir* Louis Leterrier • *Scr* Luc Besson • *Music* Neil Davidge

The Unloved ★★★15
Social drama 2009 · UK · Colour · 103min

Actress Samantha Morton's powerful directorial debut is an often painfully sad account of a young girl's experiences of a children's home. Drawing on Morton's own troubled childhood, *The Unloved* follows 11-year-old Lucy (played by young Molly Windsor, in an astonishing performance), abandoned by her mother and beaten by her father (Susan Lynch and Robert Carlyle), as she becomes swallowed by the care system. The events at the heart of the drama, scripted by Tony Grisoni with Morton, are seen entirely from Lucy's perspective as she is buffeted from one place to another with barely a murmur. The result is gut-wrenching. AG **DVD**

Molly Windsor *Lucy* • Robert Carlyle *Lucy's father* • Susan Lynch *Lucy's mother* • Craig Parkinson *Ben* • Andrea Lowe *Vicky* • Karl Collins *Karl* ■ *Dir* Samantha Morton • *Scr* Tony Grisoni, from original material by Samantha Morton

Unmade Beds ★★★15
Comedy drama 2009 · UK/Fr · Colour · 93min

Rootless young bohemians search for emotional anchors in London's trendy East End in Argentine writer/director Alexis Dos Santos's sweet though slight mood piece. Demonstrating an idealism that matches that of its characters, this intimate indie traces the meandering fortunes of two angsty European expats (Fernando Tielve and Déborah François) whose paths briefly cross in an overtly stylised squat. Colour-saturated visuals and an eclectic soundtrack enhance the film's energy, creating an impression of freshness, despite the loose narrative's well-trodden themes and frequent clichés. Occasionally the material gets too self-indulgently arty but the way it lingers over the small moments of human interaction more than compensates. SF English, French, Spanish +subtitles. Swearing, sex scenes, nudity. **DVD**

Déborah François *Vera* • Fernando Tielve *Axl* • Michiel Huisman *X-ray man* • Iddo Goldberg *Mike* • Richard Lintern *Anthony* • Katia Winter *Hannah* ■ *Dir/Scr* Alexis Dos Santos

Unman, Wittering and Zigo
★★★★
Mystery 1971 · UK · BW · 101min

No surprise that this creepy script by Giles Cooper moved from medium to medium (a radio play in 1957, then a TV play in 1965, and then this 1971 film) as it is a truly nightmarish scenario. Teacher David Hemmings is informed by his pupils at a boys' public school that they murdered his predecessor and will bump him off as well if he doesn't follow orders. Hemmings conveys very well the terror of being at the mercy of a class of delinquents, and the suspense is marred only by occasionally fussy camerawork. DM

David Hemmings *John Ebony* • Douglas Wilmer *Headmaster* • Anthony Haygarth [Tony Haygarth] *Cary Farthingale* • Carolyn Seymour *Silvia Ebony* • Hamilton Dyce *Mr Winstanley* • Barbara Lott *Mrs Winstanley* • Michael Cashman *Terhew* ■ *Dir* John Mackenzie (1) • *Scr* Simon Raven, from the play by Giles Cooper

An Unmarried Woman
★★★★18
Romantic comedy 1978 · US · Colour · 119min

Jill Clayburgh produces an assured and sensitive portrayal of wounded Big Apple womanhood when her privileged Manhattan lifestyle is undermined by her husband leaving her. Director Paul Mazursky has a sharp eye for New York detail – lots of vacuous parties, sweaty aerobics and a perceptive parade of Clayburgh's self-obsessed beaus. As her character inches towards feminism, Clayburgh truly comes into her own as the movie's second half gains neat pace and momentum. It doesn't matter that it all looks a little dated at times. SH

Jill Clayburgh *Erica* • Alan Bates *Saul* • Michael Murphy (1) *Martin* • Cliff Gorman *Charlie* • Pat Quinn [Patricia Quinn] *Sue* • Kelly Bishop *Elaine* • Lisa Lucas *Patti* • Linda Miller *Jeannette* • Andrew Duncan *Bob* ■ *Dir/Scr* Paul Mazursky

The Unnamable ★18
Horror 1988 · US · Colour · 87min

This tedious haunted house tale ransacks the ingeniously twisted work of HP Lovecraft to little horrific effect. A demon pursues four university students through an old mansion sealed years before by a priest. Lots of annoying false scares, fake tree monsters and bloody decapitations lead to a daft climax. Unwatchable. JF Violence. **DVD**

Charles King (3) *Howard Damon* • Mark Kinsey Stephenson *Randolph Carter* • Alexandra Durrell *Tanya Heller* • Katrin Alexandre *The Creature* • Laura Albert *Wendy Barnes* • Delbert Spain *Joshua Winthrop* ■ *Dir* Jean-Paul Ouellette • *Scr* Jean-Paul Ouellette, from the story by HP Lovecraft

The Unnamable Returns
★18
Horror 1992 · US · Colour · 100min

...but whatever for? Literally picking up the story on exactly the same night the uninspired original ended, this sequel features Maria Ford as an ancient monster's beautiful alter ego who can't stop her beastly half gorily killing off more Arkham County inhabitants. While marginally better than its predecessor (this one actually has a budget), this is not only unnamable, but unnecessary. AJ Swearing. **DVD**

Mark Kinsey Stephenson *Randolph Carter* • Charles Klausmeyer *Eliot Damon Howard* • Maria Ford *Alyda Winthrop* • John Rhys-Davies *Professor Harley Warren* • David Warner *Chancellor Thayer* • Richard Domeier *Officer Malcolm Bainbridge* • Siobhan McCafferty *Officer Debbie Lesh* ■ *Dir* Jean-Paul Ouellette • *Scr* Jean-Paul Ouellette, from the stories *The Statement of Randolph Carter* and *The Unnamable* by HP Lovecraft

Unpublished Story ★★PG
Second World War drama
1942 · UK · BW · 79min

Richard Greene was seconded from the Army to star in this flag-waver, in which a peace organisation is at the centre of some disreputable dealings until it's exposed by a reporter. Greene is captured by Nazi spies using their privileged position to snoop with impunity. Luckily, plucky Valerie Hobson is on hand to bail him out – though this requires plenty of noble sacrifice. DP DVD

Richard Greene *Bob Randall* • Valerie Hobson *Carol Bennett* • Basil Radford *Lamb* • Roland Culver *Stannard* ■ *Dir* Harold French • *Scr* Anatole de Grunwald, Patrick Kirwan, Sidney Gilliat, Lesley Storm, from a story by Anthony Havelock-Allan, Allan MacKinnon

Unrelated ★★15

Drama 2007 · UK · Colour · 96min

Writer/director Joanna Hogg uses the setting of a Tuscan holiday to explore a range of gender, generational and class issues. Anna (Kathryn Worth) is a childless 40-something who's struggling to hold her life together. Leaving her husband at home, she joins an old schoolfriend's family at an idyllic Italian villa, where she's drawn to another (much younger) guest. Cinematographer Oliver Curtis makes magnificent use of the gorgeous scenery and Hogg stages occasional scenes with filmic ingenuity. But, like an over-written hybrid of Mary Wesley and Eric Rohmer, this degenerates into a rather contemptuous treatise on self-centred Brits abroad. DP DVD

Kathryn Worth *Anna* • Tom Hiddleston *Oakley* • Mary Roscoe *Verena* • David Rintoul *George* • Henry Lloyd-Hughes *Jack* • Harry Kershaw *Archie* • Emma Hiddleston *Badge* ■ *Dir/Scr* Joanna Hogg • *Cinematographer* Oliver Curtis

Les Uns et les Autres ★★★

Historical drama 1981 · Fr · Colour · 173min

As a bloated, all-stops-out melodrama this effort from Claude Lelouch takes some beating, though an hour may be enough for the majority of viewers. Starting in 1936, it chronicles the lives of four couples (played by actors in multiple roles) – American, Russian, French and German – and takes them through the obstacle race and marathon that is that thing called life. The music links everyone together in a sort of hey-ho, let's-go medley. Exhausting yet somehow amazing. AT French +subtitles.

James Caan *Glenn Sr/Glenn Jr* • Robert Hossein *Simon Meyer/Robert Prat* • Nicole Garcia *Anne* • Geraldine Chaplin *Suzan/Sarah Glenn* • Daniel Olbrychski *Karl* • Jacques Villeret *Jacques* ■ *Dir/Scr* Claude Lelouch

The Unseen ★★★

Murder mystery 1945 · US · BW · 81min

Although co-scripted by Raymond Chandler, this has none of the sawn-off dialogue for which he was famous. Nevertheless, it's full of an atmosphere of foreboding as governess Gail Russell starts to believe that dark deeds were done in a neighbouring house and Joel McCrea's children had something to do with them. There is a mood of authentic creepiness that was obviously meant to follow in the same shuddery footfalls as the previous year's *The Uninvited*, which was also directed by Lewis Allen. TH

Joel McCrea *David Fielding* • Gail Russell *Elizabeth Howard* • Herbert Marshall *Dr Charles Evans* • Richard Lyon *Barnaby Fielding* • Nona Griffith *Ellen Fielding* • Phyllis Brooks *Maxine* • Isobel Elsom *Marian Tygarth* • Norman Lloyd *Jasper Goodwin* ■ *Dir* Lewis Allen • *Scr* Raymond Chandler, Hagar Wilde, Ken Englund, from the novel *Her Heart in Her Throat* by Ethel Lina White

The Unsinkable Molly Brown ★★★★ U

Musical 1964 · US · Colour · 123min

This has much to recommend it, particularly the leading performance of the Oscar-nominated Debbie Reynolds. Despite marrying well, the once-impoverished Molly Brown (Reynolds) still craves acceptance by Denver's high society. Director Charles Walters does what he can with a substandard score by *The Music Man*'s Meredith Willson, but is helped by a sparkling cast, especially Jack Kruschen

and *grande dame* Martita Hunt, revelling in their roles. The Colorado scenery is splendid, as is leading man Harve Presnell. TS DVD

Debbie Reynolds *Molly Brown* • Harve Presnell *Johnny Brown* • Ed Begley *Shamus Tobin* • Jack Kruschen *Christmas Morgan* • Hermione Baddeley *Mrs Grogan* • Vassili Lambrinos *Prince Louis de Laniere* • Fred Essler *Baron Karl Ludwig von Ettenburg* • Martita Hunt *Grand Duchess Elise Lupovinova* • Harvey Lembeck *Polak* ■ *Dir* Charles Walters • *Scr* Helen Deutsch, from the musical by Meredith Willson, Richard Morris

Unstable ★★

Mystery thriller 2009 · Can · Colour

An emotionally damaged woman struggles to prove her sanity in this predictable, *Gaslight*-style psychological thriller. Shiri Appleby swings between affectingly insecure and childishly petulant as the delicate newlywed who's convinced by her too-good-to-be-true husband (David Alpay) that she's losing her mind once again. But a weak, initially uneventful script and awkwardly unnatural dialogue make this apparent mental relapse rather dull to watch, despite the cast's earnest performances. When the penny drops for both Appleby and the audience – which it does very quickly – events become slightly more dramatic and engaging, in the hope there will be a thoroughly climactic confrontation. Unfortunately, this potential treat is undermined by heavy visual hints that compound the transparent storytelling. SF

Shiri Appleby *Megan Walker* • David Alpay *Woody Monroe* • Charlotte Sullivan *Samantha Walker* • John Bourgeois *Dan Walker* • Kathy Baker *Betty Walker* ■ *Dir* Don McBrearty • *Scr* Charles Bohl

Unstoppable ★★15

Action thriller 2004 · US · Colour · 92min

The clock's ticking for traumatised ex-soldier Wesley Snipes after he's inadvertently injected with a deadly mind-control drug in this flat and farcical straight-to-DVD tale. Ineffective villains (particularly pantomimic henchman Kim Coates) destroy all sense of tension, but it's the lazy action scenes that ultimately do the most damage, mirroring Snipes's lack of spark and making even the climactic shoot-'em-up forgettable. SF Violence, swearing. DVD

Wesley Snipes *Dean Cage* • Jacqueline Obradors *Detective Amy Knight* • Stuart Wilson (1) *Sullivan* • Kim Coates *Peterson* ■ *Dir* David Carson • *Scr* Tom Vaughan (2)

Unstoppable ★★★12

Action thriller 2010 · US · Colour · 94min

This edge-of-your-seat yarn finds veteran railwayman Denzel Washington and rookie conductor Chris Pine racing against the clock to stop an unmanned runaway train loaded with toxic chemicals derailing near a densely populated town. Known for the over-the-top bluster of his action fests, director Tony Scott shows considerable restraint, focusing as much on the lives of his characters as their white-knuckle predicament. The high-octane train sequences are staged with increasingly nail-biting tension, admirably shot without reverting to computer-generated trickery. But the never-ending faux news footage does get a bit tiresome. TeS Some violence, swearing. DVD

Denzel Washington *Frank* • Chris Pine *Will* • Rosario Dawson *Connie* • Kevin Dunn *Galvin* • Jessy Schram *Darcy* • Paul Vasquez ■ *Dir* Tony Scott • *Scr* Mark Bomback

Unstrung Heroes ★★★★PG

Comedy drama based on a true story 1995 · US · Colour · 89min

This is a charming film from actress/director Diane Keaton (who remains behind the camera for this one). Nathan Watt plays the little boy who grows up under the influence of his quirky father John Turturro (superb) and his even wackier uncles (Maury Chaykin and Michael Richards) when his mother Andie MacDowell (in her best performance to date) becomes seriously ill. Keaton capably handles the mix

of humour and sadness, delivering a superbly performed, moving and very funny tale about growing up and the weirdness of families. JB DVD

Andie MacDowell *Selma Lidz* • John Turturro *Sid Lidz* • Michael Richards *Danny Lidz* • Maury Chaykin *Arthur Lidz* • Nathan Watt *Steven/Franz Lidz* • Kendra Krull *Sandy Lidz* ■ *Dir* Diane Keaton • *Scr* Richard LaGravenese, from the book by Franz Lidz

An Unsuitable Job for a Woman ★★★15

Mystery 1981 · UK · Colour · 90min

This is the original film adaptation of PD James's bestseller, later made into a TV series starring Helen Baxendale. Pippa Guard is quietly efficient as Cordelia Gray, who takes over a detective agency after her partner commits suicide. There's certainly nothing straightforward about her first case: she's hired to investigate the "suicide" of a businessman's son in a picturesque cottage. Director Christopher Petit casts a moody pall over traditional whodunnit country and scatters clues with skill. DP

Billie Whitelaw *Elizabeth Leaming* • Pippa Guard *Cordelia Gray* • Paul Freeman *James Callender* • Dominic Guard *Andrew Lunn* • Elizabeth Spriggs *Miss Markland* • David Horovitch *Sergeant Maskell* • Dawn Archibald *Isobel* • James Gilbey *Boy* ■ *Dir* Christopher Petit • *Scr* Elizabeth McKay, Brian Scobie, Christopher Petit, from the novel by PD James

The Unsuspected ★★★★

Crime drama 1947 · US · BW · 102min

This virtually unknown but highly underrated suspense thriller is impeccably directed by the great Michael Curtiz and features the urbane Claude Rains as a radio star performer specialising in spine-shivering broadcasts. This was actually intended as a starring vehicle for one Michael North, a Curtiz discovery who didn't work out, and the subsequent revoicing of North and the minimising of his role creates a truly unsettling feeling throughout the film. The period insights into the workings of radio are deftly done, as are the action sequences, but the clever scripting is the real bonus. TS

Claude Rains *Victor Grandison* • Joan Caulfield *Matilda Frazier* • Audrey Totter *Althea Keane* • Constance Bennett *Jane Moynihan* • Hurd Hatfield *Oliver Keane* • Michael North [Ted North] *Steven Francis Howard* • Fred Clark *Richard Donovan* • Jack Lambert *Mr Press* ■ *Dir* Michael Curtiz • *Scr* Ranald MacDougall, Bess Meredyth, from a novel by Charlotte Armstrong

Untamed ★★★

Romantic adventure 1955 · US · Colour · 108min

This is a splendid early CinemaScope melodrama, with the then-new widescreen process deployed effectively in a South Africa-located tale of a trek across the veldt. Passions flare and Zulus attack the wagon train in this lusty adaptation of a bodice-ripper of a novel. Featuring two of 20th Century-Fox's finest (handsome Tyrone Power and fiery redhead Susan Hayward), this is one of the last examples of this type of imperialist tosh. There's some fine support, but the real star here is the stunning photography. TS

Tyrone Power *Paul Van Riebeck* • Susan Hayward *Katie O'Neill* • Richard Egan *Kurt Hout* • John Justin *Shawn Kildare* • Agnes Moorehead *Aggie* • Rita Moreno *Julia* • Hope Emerson *Maria De Groot* ■ *Dir* Henry King • *Scr* Talbot Jennings, Frank Fenton, William A Bacher, Michael Blankfort, from the novel by Helga Moray • *Cinematographer* Leo Tover

Untamed Frontier ★★

Western 1952 · US · Colour · 75min

This is a routine range war western, despite talented Argentinian director Hugo Fregonese's attempts to make something more of the territorial theme. Joseph Cotten and Shelley Winters star, but there's certainly nothing in the script worthy of attention. Cotten finds himself in the middle of a conflict when his cattle baron uncle refuses to allow settlers to travel across his land. As much of a chore to watch as the

cast and crew obviously felt it was to make. TS

Joseph Cotten *Kirk Denbow* • Shelley Winters *Jane Stevens* • Scott Brady *Glenn Denbow* • Suzan Ball *Lottie* • Minor Watson *Matt Denbow* • Katherine Emery *Camilla Denbow* • Lee Van Cleef *Dave Chittun* ■ *Dir* Hugo Fregonese • *Scr* Gerald Drayson Adams, John Bagni, Polly James, Gwen Bagni, from a story by Houston Branch, Eugenia Night

Untamed Heart ★★★15

Romantic drama 1993 · US · Colour · 97min

Marisa Tomei and Christian Slater both work hard to wring every ounce of emotion from director Tony Bill's well-meaning, if slightly contrived, romance. Slater is the shy kitchen guy with a congenital heart defect who saves waitress Tomei from some thugs, an event that leads the bruised souls to embark on a hesitant relationship. Everyone says it can't last, especially delicious Rosie Perez in another of her trademark sassy, wisecracking roles but, although the outcome is fairly predictable, there's enough here to engage. AJ Violence, swearing, nudity. DVD

Christian Slater *Adam* • Marisa Tomei *Caroline* • Rosie Perez *Cindy* • Kyle Secor *Howard* • Willie Garson *Patsy* • Claudia Wilkens *Mother Camilla* ■ *Dir* Tony Bill • *Scr* Tom Sierchio

Unthinkable ★★★18

Psychological thriller 2010 · US · Colour · 93min

Michael Sheen takes a break from real-life characters to play an American Muslim terrorist in this thought-provoking, if occasionally clumsy, psychological thriller. The British star gives a powerful performance as a former military man who claims to have placed nuclear bombs in three US cities; it's up to by-the-book FBI agent Carrie-Anne Moss and cheerfully brutal black ops interrogator Samuel L Jackson to find out where the explosives are before they go off. It goes off the rails in the final act, but it's an intriguing thriller all the same. JF Violence. DVD

Samuel L Jackson *H* • Carrie-Anne Moss *Agent Helen Brody* • Michael Sheen *Younger* • Stephen Root *Charlie* • Lora Kojovic *Rina* • Martin Donovan *Jack Saunders* • Gil Bellows *Agent Vincent* • Brandon Routh *Agent Jackson* ■ *Dir* Gregor Jordan • *Scr* Peter Woodward

Until Death ★★15

Action thriller 2007 · US · Colour · 96min

"*Bad Lieutenant* meets *Regarding Henry* and starring Jean-Claude Van Damme" must have been the pitch for this unusual but not very competent addition to the Belgian's CV. Van Damme plays a corrupt, heroin-addicted New Orleans cop who ends up in a coma after being shot in the head. Spending some time in a vegetative state does wonders for his sense of morality and it's not long before he's back on his feet and looking for redemption. JR Violence, swearing, nudity, drug abuse. DVD

Jean-Claude Van Damme *Anthony Stowe* • Selina Giles *Valerie* • Mark Dymond *Mark Rossini* • William Ash *Serge* • Stephen Lord *Jimmy Medina* • Gary Beadle *Mac* ■ *Dir* Simon Fellows • *Scr* Dan Harris [Daniel P Harris], James Portolese

Until September ★★15

Romantic drama 1984 · US · Colour · 92min

Richard Marquand directs this ill-conceived romantic drama. Karen Allen is the Yank visiting France who misses her flight home and then falls for dashing Thierry Lhermitte (*Le Cop*). The international cast does its best, but no one's heart is in it. JF Swearing, nudity.

Karen Allen *Mo Alexander* • Thierry Lhermitte *Xavier de la Perouse* • Christopher Cazenove *Philip* • Marie Catherine Conti *Isabelle* • Hutton Cobb *Andrew* • Michael Mellinger *Colonel Viola* ■ *Dir* Richard Marquand • *Scr* Janice Lee Graham

Until the End of the World ★★15

Science-fiction road movie 1991 · Ger/Fr/Aus · Colour · 151min

This misbegotten epic shows how an art house director can blow $23 million and still emerge with a three-hour film that's less than perfect. Thus Wim Wenders took William Hurt, Max von Sydow, Sam Neill and others to eight countries without a script, assuming that sheer genius was enough. All they had was an idea about a nuclear satellite crashing to Earth in 1999 and a cluster of unrelated subplots. Nicely shot, though. AT Violence, swearing, nudity.

William Hurt *Trevor McPhee/Sam Farber* • Solveig Dommartin *Claire Tourneur* • Sam Neill *Eugene Fitzpatrick* • Max von Sydow *Henry Farber* • Rüdiger Vogler *Philip Winter* • Ernie Dingo *Burt* • Jeanne Moreau *Edith Farber* ■ *Dir* Wim Wenders • *Scr* Wim Wenders, Peter Carey, from the story by Wim Wenders, Solveig Dommartin

Until They Sail ★★★
Second World War drama
1957 · US · BW · 94min

This marvellously overwrought war drama is brought to the screen with a superb cast: Joan Fontaine, Jean Simmons, Piper Laurie and Sandra Dee as sisters, getting emotionally wrapped up with American servicemen, with murder and melodrama as the result. Superbly directed by ace craftsman Robert Wise, this also features Paul Newman and a pre-Disney Dean Jones. No great shakes, but a jolly good matinée weepie. TS

Jean Simmons *Barbara Leslie Forbes* • Joan Fontaine *Anne Leslie* • Paul Newman *Captain Jack Harding* • Piper Laurie *Delia Leslie* • Charles Drake *Captain Richard Bates* • Sandra Dee *Evelyn Leslie* • Wally Cassell *"Shiner" Phil Friskett* • Alan Napier *Prosecution* • Dean Jones ■ *Dir* Robert Wise • *Scr* Robert Anderson, from a story by James A Michener

Untouchable ★★★★ 15
Comedy drama based on a true story
2011 · Fr · Colour · 107min

The very epitome of feel-good, this uplifting comedy drama is one of the most successful French films ever made. Philippe (François Cluzet) is a billionaire businessman who's been left paralysed from the neck down in a paragliding accident. He advertises for a live-in carer, and winds up with young offender Driss (Omar Sy), a Senegalese immigrant whose cocky, carefree attitude may not be what the doctor ordered, but is exactly what Philippe needs. Their very amusing chalk-and-cheese relationship forms the core of a big-hearted movie and is excellently played by both leads. CA French +subtitles. Swearing, drug abuse. DVD Blu

François Cluzet *Palippe* • Omar Sy *Driss* • Anne Le Ny *Yvonne* • Audrey Fleurot *Magalie* • Clotilde Mollet *Marcelle* ■ *Dir/Scr* Olivier Nakache, Eric Toledano

The Untouchables
★★★★★ 15
Crime drama
1987 · US · Colour · 114min

In Brian De Palma's riveting take on the old TV show, Kevin Costner gives a star-making performance as Eliot Ness, the quiet Treasury agent and family man who picks up a pump-action rifle in order to rid Chicago of bootlegger Al Capone. Always a showman, De Palma lets loose with a barrage of bloody set pieces, notably the climax at the railway station – a nod to the famous Odessa steps sequence in *The Battleship Potemkin*. David Mamet's dialogue crackles, Ennio Morricone's music soars and the production design sparkles. Andy Garcia joins the team, and a plumped-up Robert De Niro plays Capone, yet for many the main attraction is Sean Connery's Oscar-winning performance as the veteran cop who shows Costner the ropes. AT Violence, swearing. DVD Blu

Kevin Costner *Eliot Ness* • Sean Connery *Jim Malone* • Andy Garcia *George Stone* • Robert De Niro *Al Capone* • Charles Martin Smith *Oscar Wallace* • Richard Bradford *Mike* • Jack Kehoe *Payne* • Brad Sullivan *George* • Billy Drago *Frank Nitti* ■ *Dir* Brian De Palma • *Scr* David Mamet, suggested by the TV series and from the works of Oscar Fraley, with Eliot Ness, Paul Robsky • *Cinematographer* Stephen H Burum • *Production Designer* Patrizia von Brandenstein

Untraceable ★★ 18
Horror thriller
2008 · US · Colour · 96min

This downbeat serial-killer thriller has an intriguing premise: a tech-savvy psycho sets up the killwithme.com website where the more people view, the quicker his victims die. FBI cyber crimes agent Jennifer Marsh (the ever-reliable Diane Lane) has to identify the maniac who's turning inquisitive webheads into snuff movie accomplices. Its *Se7en* by way of *Hostel*, with just enough horrifying imagery to ensure that the social issue it raises doesn't tip into exploitative voyeurism. But, as plot inconsistencies arise and clues to the killer's identity conveniently fall into place, believability evaporates and clichés begin to pile up, turning *Untraceable* into something quite unremarkable. AJ DVD Blu

Diane Lane *Jennifer Marsh* • Billy Burke *Detective Eric Box* • Colin Hanks *Griffin Dowd* • Joseph Cross *Owen Reilly* • Mary Beth Hurt *Stella Marsh* • Peter Lewis *Richard Brooks* • Tyrone Giordano *Tim Wilks* • Perla Haney-Jardine *Annie Haskins* ■ *Scr* Mark R Brinker [Mark Brinker], Allison Burnett, Robert Fyvolent, from a story by Brinker, Fyvolent

The Unwinking Gaze
★★★ PG
Documentary
2008 · UK · Colour · 69min

Exiled since 1959, the 14th Dalai Lama has been celebrated in a number of film profiles that have been blatantly hagiographic. Here, however, Joshua Dugdale captures the pressures placed upon this deeply spiritual but sanely pragmatic man, as he strives to adopt a position of strength without giving his subjects false hope or provoking Beijing. Accorded unprecedented access to the Dalai and his inner circle over three years, Dugdale manages some intriguing insights into the man's diplomatic acuity, and his awareness that the ultimate accomplishment of his mission increasingly depends upon finding a worthy successor. DP

Dalai Lama ■ *Dir* Joshua Dugdale • *Cinematographers* Jonathan Jenkins, Scot Openshaw • *Editor* Scot Openshaw

Unzipped ★★★★ 15
Documentary
1995 · US · Colour and BW · 73min

This hugely enjoyable documentary follows New York fashion designer Isaac Mizrahi as he plans his 1994 show around an "Eskimo" look inspired by another documentary, 1922's *Nanook of the North*. Mizrahi performs very amusingly for the camera, and his supermodels (Naomi Campbell, Cindy Crawford, Kate Moss et al) also seem to know exactly how to behave for maximum effect; and yet, despite the artifice, this is a far truer portrait of the world of haute couture than Altman's farcical *Pret-a-Porter*. Not surprisingly, director Douglas Keeve is a fashion photographer, and his mostly black-and-white footage contrasts strikingly with colour for the clothes sequences. DM

Isaac Mizrahi • Cindy Crawford • Naomi Campbell • Kate Moss • Linda Evangelista • Christy Turlington • Eartha K tt ■ *Dir* Douglas Keeve

Up ★★★ 18
Sex comedy
1976 · US · Colour · 78min

The penultimate movie from the notorious Russ Meyer stars the inexplicably named Raven De La Croix as a woman who revenges herself against the man who raped her. It's one of his best and most outrageous, typically overflowing with outsize bosoms, cartoon violence and Bible-thumping morality that ensures wrongdoers get their just deserts. The Meyer sense of humour is also intact, one shot takes place inside a man's trousers as his flies are unzipped. From a story co-written by celebrated US film critic Roger Ebert, this is likely to offend most fragile sensibilities, feminists especially. RS Sex scenes, violence.

Robert McLane *Paul* • Edward Schaaf *Adolph Schwartz* • Mary Gavin *Headsperson* • Elaine Collins *Ethiopian chief* • Su Ling *Limehouse* •

Linda Sue Ragsdale *Gwendolyn* • Janet Wood *Sweet Li'l Alice* • Raven De La Croix *Margo Winchester* ■ *Dir* Russ Meyer • *Scr* B Callum [Russ Meyer], from a story by Russ Meyer, Reinhold Timme [Roger Ebert], Jim Ryan

Up ★★★★★ U
Animated fantasy adventure
2009 · US · Colour · 92min

The tenth Pixar animated masterwork sees a grumpy old widower (effectively growled by Ed Asner) fulfil a lifelong dream of great adventure when he attaches thousands of balloons to his house and floats it away to a South American lost world. But he has company in the shape of an accidental stowaway – an eight-year-old scout (Jordan Nagai). The pair then attempts to save a rare bird of paradise from the clutches of an eccentric explorer (Christopher Plummer). Funny, thrilling, startling and moving by turns, the film weaves pure entertainment magic into its seamlessly created world. Aimed at adults – the near-silent prelude charting the passing of married life is wonderfully poignant – but with enough action to entertain the kids, *Up* is breathtaking in its imaginative detail and astonishing in its emotional range. AJ DVD Blu

Ed Asner [Edward Asner] *Carl Fredricksen* • Christopher Plummer *Charles Muntz* • Jordan Nagai *Russell* • John Ratzenberger *Construction foreman Tom* • Elie Docter *Young Ellie* • Delroy Lindo *Beta* • Bob Peterson *Dug/Alpha* • Jerome Ranft *Gamma* ■ *Dir* Pete Docter • *Scr* Bob Peterson, Pete Docter, from their story

Up at the Villa ★★★★ 12
Period romantic thriller
1998 · US · Colour · 110min

The dark forces of fascism intrude upon idyllic Tuscany in this stylishly shot drama set in the 1930s. Kristin Scott Thomas, a penniless aristocrat on the verges of colonial society, is befriended by countess Anne Bancroft and pursued by a stalwart Edward Fox. In a matter of hours her world is turned upside down by two chance encounters: one with a refugee that results in murder, the other with a rakish Sean Penn whose appearance sparks mutual passion. The chemistry between the two leads is tangible, while Philip Haas directs with an energy that makes his film very compelling indeed. LH

Kristin Scott Thomas *Mary Panton* • Sean Penn *Rowley Flint* • Anne Bancroft *Princess San Ferdinando* • James Fox *Sir Edgar Swift* • Jeremy Davies *Karl Richter* • Derek Jacobi *Lucky Leadbetter* • Dudley Sutton *Harold Atkinson* ■ *Dir* Philip Haas • *Scr* Belinda Haas, from a novella by W Somerset Maugham

Up Close & Personal ★★★ 15
Romantic drama
1996 · US · Colour · 119min

Robert Redford and Michelle Pfeiffer star in this romantic drama set in a Miami television newsroom. Redford plays the veteran former White House correspondent who takes small-town girl Pfeiffer under his wing, helping her overcome stage fright and seeing her career as a television journalist take off as his idles. It's all tosh, of course, but its *Star Is Born* theme of male self-sacrifice is finely manipulated by director Jon Avnet so, as a three-hankie movie, it's not to be sniffed at. TH Swearing, violence, sexual references. DVD

Robert Redford *Warren Justice* • Michelle Pfeiffer *Tally "Sallyanne" Atwater* • Stockard Channing *Marcia McGrath* • Joe Mantegna *Bucky Terranova* • Kate Nelligan *Joanna Kennelly* • Glenn Plummer *Ned Jackson* • James Rebhorn *John Merino* • Scott Bryce *Rob Sullivan* • Dedee Pfeiffer *Luanne Atwater* ■ *Dir* Jon Avnet • *Scr* Joan Didion, John Gregory Dunne, from the book *Golden Girl* by Alanna Nash

Up for Love ★★ 12A
Romantic comedy
2016 · Fr · Colour · 98min

French director Laurent Tirard was drawn to this story when he lost weight during a difficult illness. He casts Jean Dujardin as an architect who has to cope with people not taking him seriously because he is only 4ft 5in tall. After Dujardin finds his lost phone, lawyer Virginie Efira struggles with the fact

that he's 16 inches shorter than herself (without heels), but, this being a romantic comedy, love will find a way. The leads are charming, although there's no spark between them, perhaps because of the amount of green-screen work involved. DP In French. Some swearing, sexual references.

Jean Dujardin *Alexandre* • Virginie Efira *Diane* • Cédric Kahn *Bruno* • Stéphanie Papanian *Coralie* ■ *Dir* Laurent Tirard • *Scr* Laurent Tirard, Grégoire Vigneron, from the film *Corazon de Leon* by Marcos Carnevale

Up from the Beach ★★★ U
Second World War drama
1965 · US · BW · 98min

Cliff Robertson gives his usual distinguished performance as an American army sergeant who becomes involved with Resistance civilians after the D-Day landings. Slow-moving, but it has its gripping moments, especially with Françoise Rosay playing an elderly peasant-woman whom you just don't know whether to trust or not. Director Robert Parrish just about controls the action, but takes it all at too steady a pace. TH

Cliff Robertson *Sgt Edward Baxter* • Red Buttons *Pfc Harry Devine* • Irina Demick *Lili Rolland* • Marius Goring *German Commandant* • Slim Pickens *Artillery Colonel* • James Robertson-Justice *British Beachmaster* • Broderick Crawford *US MP Major* • Françoise Rosay *Lili's grandmother* ■ *Dir* Robert Parrish • *Scr* Stanley Mann, Claude Brulé, Howard Clewes, from the novel *Epitaph For an Enemy* by George Barr

Up in Arms ★★★ U
Musical comedy
1944 · US · Colour · 105min

A remake of the 1930 Eddie Cantor vehicle *Whoopee!*, this first starring vehicle for Danny Kaye has dated badly, its wartime theme about a hypochondriac who's drafted into the army seeming faintly distasteful today, and the obvious studio settings aren't enhanced by the garish 1940s Technicolor. Nevertheless, former Broadway comedian Kaye proves to be far superior to his surroundings, aided by some wonderful material. Dinah Shore and Constance Dowling both look ravishing in 1940s get-up. TS

Danny Kaye *Danny Weems* • Constance Dowling *Mary Morgan* • Dinah Shore *Virginia Merrill* • Dana Andrews *Joe Nelson* • Louis Calhern *Colonel Ashley* • George Mathews *Blackie* • Benny Baker *Butterball* • Elisha Cook Jr *Info Jones* ■ *Dir* Elliott Nugent • *Scr* Don Hartman, Allen Boretz, Robert Pirosh, from the play *The Nervous Wreck* by Owen Davis

Up in Central Park ★★★ U
Musical comedy
1948 · US · BW · 83min

This disappointing adaptation of the Broadway success deals with the unlikely subject of city hall corruption, revolving around New York's notoriously crooked statesman Boss Tweed, played effectively by Vincent Price. Turned here into a vehicle for Deanna Durbin, the film loses most of the original Sigmund Romberg score, though Dick Haymes makes a likeable enough leading man. The film needed a more expensive production, but Durbin fans will cherish this, her penultimate movie before her retirement. TS DVD

Deanna Durbin *Rosie Moore* • Dick Haymes *John Matthews* • Vincent Price *Boss Tweed* • Albert Sharpe *Timothy Moore* • Tom Powers *Regan* • Hobart Cavanaugh *Mayor Oakley* • Thurston Hall *Governor Motley* ■ *Dir* William A Seiter • *Scr* Karl Tunberg, from the play by Dorothy Fields, Herbert Fields, Sigmund Romberg

Up in Mabel's Room ★★
Farce
1944 · US · BW · 76min

The marital bliss of newly married Dennis O'Keefe and Marjorie Reynolds is shattered when O'Keefe's friendship with glamorous Gail Patrick, the fiancée of his business partner Lee Bowman, is misinterpreted. A standard bedroom farce, it's directed by Allan Dwan and is good-natured but uninterestingly tame. RK

Dennis O'Keefe *Gary Ainsworth* • Marjorie Reynolds *Geraldine Ainsworth* • Gail Patrick *Mabel Essington* • Mischa Auer *Boris* • Charlotte

U

Greenwood *Martha* • Lee Bowman *Arthur Weldon* • John Hubbard *Jimmy Larchmont* • Binnie Barnes *Alicia Larchmont* ■ *Dir* Allan Dwan • *Scr* Tom Reed, Isobel Dawn, from a play by Wilson Collison, Otto Harbach, from the story *Oh Chemise* by Wilson Collison

Up in the Air ★★★★ 15
Romantic comedy drama 2009 · US · Colour · 104min

George Clooney uses his matinee-idol image to maximum effect in this often superb adult comedy. He plays sophisticated "downsizing executive" Ryan Bingham, a smooth-talking hired gun who fires people for a living. Bingham lives his life in aircraft cabins and hotels. This rarefied lifestyle comes under threat when new colleague Natalie (Anna Kendrick) dreams up a business plan that will literally ground him, and prevent him seeing his on/off lover, the flighty and equally rootless Alex (Vera Farmiga). Wonderfully sharp and flirty banter ensues, and though the film strains credibility in its final stretches, it stays clear of genre clichés, offering a satisfying hybrid of 1950s glamour, 70s realism and 21st-century attitude. **DW** Swearing, sexual references, nudity. *DVD* Blu

George Clooney *Ryan Bingham* • Vera Farmiga *Alex Goran* • Anna Kendrick *Natalie Keener* • Jason Bateman *Craig Gregory* • Danny McBride (2) *Jim Miller* • Melanie Lynskey *Julie Bingham* • Amy Morton *Kara Bingham* • Sam Elliott *Maynard Finch* ■ *Dir* Jason Reitman • *Scr* Jason Reitman, Sheldon Turner, from the novel by Walter Kirn

Up in the Cellar ★★★★
Comedy 1970 · US · Colour · 93min

Wes Stern is a hapless student whose life is turned upside down when his poetry scholarship is annulled by a rogue computer. He finds himself a puppet in a battle between David Arkin, a wealthy student with ideas of revolution, and the monstrous college president Larry Hagman. Using sex as a weapon, Stern tries to get at Hagman through the women in his life. Director Theodore J Flicker's follow-up to his magnificent satire *The President's Analyst* is another effervescent comedy overflowing with great ideas and cunning twists. **DF**

Wes Stern *Colin Slade* • Joan Collins *Pat Camber* • Larry Hagman *Maurice Camber* • Nira Barab *Tracy Camber* • Judy Pace *Harlene Jones* • David Arkin *Hugo* ■ *Dir* Theodore J Flicker • *Scr* Theodore J Flicker, from the novel *The Late Wonder Boy* by Angus Hall

Up in the World ★★ U
Comedy 1956 · UK · BW · 86min

This tacky comedy gave notice that Norman Wisdom's winning formula was beginning to wear thin. The slapstick centres around ladders and broken windows, as window cleaner Wisdom becomes friends with a lonely boy millionaire (Michael Caridia), much to the annoyance of sniffy guardian Jerry Desmonde. The worst aspect of this maudlin mishmash is that Wisdom gets to warble so often. **DP** *DVD*

Norman Wisdom *Norman* • Maureen Swanson *Jeannie* • Jerry Desmonde *Major Willoughby* • Ambrosine Philpotts *Lady Banderville* • Colin Gordon *Fletcher Hetherington* • Michael Caridia *Sir Reginald Banderville* ■ *Dir* John Paddy Carstairs • *Scr* Jack Davies, Henry E Blyth, Peter Blackmore

Up 'n' Under ★★ 12
Sports comedy 1997 · UK · Colour · 98min

A top line-up of British sitcom stars takes to the rugby field in a mildly diverting by-the-numbers sports comedy. Gary Olsen bets his house on a ridiculous wager with smug rival Tony Slattery. Naturally, Olsen's team is the least enthusiastic and skilful in the land. Very, very predictable fare, but it pushes some of the right buttons. **JC** Swearing.

Gary Olsen *Arthur Hoyle* • Neil Morrissey *Steve* • Samantha Janus *Hazel Scott* • Richard Ridings *Frank* • Ralph Brown (2) *Phil* • Adrian Hood *Tommy* • David MacCreedy *Tony* • Tony Slattery

Reg Welch • Griff Rhys Jones *Ray Mason* ■ *Dir* John Godber • *Scr* John Godber, from his play

Up on the Roof ★★ 15
Musical drama 1997 · UK · Colour · 95min

It's difficult to identify with the dreams and disappointments of a group of Hull University buddies, despite the best efforts of a bullish cast of British newcomers. The trouble is that Adrian Lester's pop wannabe, Daniel Ryan's garden-centre boss, Clare Cathcart's singing waitress and Billy Carter's children's television star have been designed to fit their slots in the storyline. They don't click as people, whether as 1970s students or their older selves reuniting for Amy Robbins's wedding and for a 15-year-anniversary of their graduation. **DP** A sex scene, swearing.

Billy Carter *Tim* • Clare Cathcart *Angela* • Adrian Lester *Scott* • Amy Robbins *Bryony* • Daniel Ryan *Keith* • Lavinia Bertram *Bryony's mother* • Robin Herford *Gavin* ■ *Dir* Simon Moore • *Scr* Simon Moore, Jane Prowse

Up Periscope ★★★ U
Second World War drama 1959 · US · Colour · 99min

Warner Bros knew the box-office value of a good submarine flick, having produced *Destination Tokyo*. Here the ever-economic studio reworked the sets from the previous year's Alan Ladd vehicle *The Deep Six* to showcase its new star, TV's *Maverick* James Garner, in a nail-biting Second World War drama. This also benefits from the skill of veteran director Gordon Douglas, and from stalwart Edmond O'Brien in support. **TS**

James Garner *Ken Braden* • Edmond O'Brien *Stevenson* • Andra Martin *Sally* • Alan Hale Jr *Malone* • Carleton Carpenter *Carney* • Frank Gifford *Mount* • William Leslie *Doherty* ■ *Dir* Gordon Douglas • *Scr* Richard Landau, from the novel by Robb White

Up Pompeii ★★ 15
Comedy 1971 · UK · Colour · 86min

Frankie Howerd dons a toga for a film version of his TV series based on the life of Roman slave Lurcio. Unfortunately, the blatantly obvious *Carry On*-style formula (the cast even features *Carry On* regular Bernard Bresslaw) only works sporadically. There's more interest in trying to put names to the plethora of familiar British faces in the cast, among them Patrick Cargill as the Emperor Nero and Michael Hordern as the unfortunate Ludicrus Sextus. **NF** Nudity. *DVD*

Frankie Howerd *Lurcio* • Patrick Cargill *Nero* • Michael Hordern *Ludicrus* • Barbara Murray *Ammonia* • Lance Percival *Bilius* • Bill Fraser *Prosperus* • Adrienne Posta *Scrubba* • Julie Ege *Voluptua* • Bernard Bresslaw *Gorgo* • Roy Hudd *MC* ■ *Dir* Bob Kellett • *Scr* Sid Colin, from an idea by Talbot Rothwell

Up the Chastity Belt ★★ PG
Period comedy 1971 · UK · Colour · 89min

A glance at the credits – produced by Ned Sherrin, script by Sid Colin, Ray Galton and Alan Simpson, score by Carl Davis – raises one's hopes for this medieval incarnation of Frankie Howerd's TV hit *Up Pompeii*. But, sadly, expectations are soon dashed as it becomes clear that Lurkalot is a pale imitation of his ancient ancestor Lurcio. Howerd looks very ordinary beside the infinitely more versatile supporting cast of top character comics. **DP** *DVD*

Frankie Howerd *Lurkalot/King Richard The Lionheart* • Graham Crowden *Sir Coward de Custard* • Bill Fraser *Sir Braggart de Bombast* • Roy Hudd *Nick the Pick* • Hugh Paddick *Robin Hood* • Anna Quayle *Lady Ashfodel* • Lance Percival *Reporter* • Godfrey Winn *Archbishop of all England* • Eartha Kitt *Scheherazade* ■ *Dir* Bob Kellett • *Scr* Sid Colin, Ray Galton, Alan Simpson

Up the Creek ★★★ U
Comedy 1958 · UK · BW · 79min

Veteran writer/director Val Guest and an experienced cast of *farceurs* enliven this British naval farce with its timeworn story of an incompetent officer pitted against the wily lower ranks. Silly, accident-prone David

Tomlinson is given the command of an ancient destroyer, where Peter Sellers controls the rackets. The chaos when admiral Wilfrid Hyde White arrives for an inspection is extremely funny. The film's success inspired a sequel, *Further up the Creek*. **DM** *DVD*

David Tomlinson *Lt Humphrey Fairweather* • Peter Sellers *Bosun Docherty* • Wilfrid Hyde White *Admiral Foley* • Vera Day *Lily* • Liliane Sottane *Susanne* • Tom Gill *Flag Lieutenant* • Michael Goodliffe *Nelson* • Reginald Beckwith *Publican* ■ *Dir* Val Guest • *Scr* Val Guest, Len Heath, John Warren

Up the Down Staircase ★★
Drama 1967 · US · Colour · 123min

Sandy Dennis plays a young, novice teacher who has her ideals severely tested in an underfunded, bureaucratic inner-city school. Much of the movie is shot on location but, even though the kids perform well, the adult characters are a little too pat for the film to be totally convincing. **JG**

Sandy Dennis *Sylvia Barrett* • Patrick Bedford *Paul Barringer* • Eileen Heckart *Henrietta Pastorfield* • Ruth White *Beatrice Schracter* • Jean Stapleton *Sadie Finch* • Sorrell Booke *Dr Bester* ■ *Dir* Robert Mulligan • *Scr* Tad Mosel, from the novel by Bel Kaufman

Up the Front ★ PG
First World War comedy 1972 · UK · Colour · 84min

The final film to be spun off from TV's *Up Pompeii* leaves Frankie Howerd stranded in the middle of no man's land with nothing more than a tattoo to cover his blushes. Not even Morecambe and Wise's regular writer Eddie Braben could do anything to pep up Sid Colin's desperate script, while the lacklustre performances really merit reproach. **DP** *DVD*

Frankie Howerd *Lurk* • Zsa Zsa Gabor *Mata Hari* • Bill Fraser *Groping* • Lance Percival *Von Gutz* • Stanley Holloway *Vincento* • Madeline Smith *Fanny* • Hermione Baddeley *Monique* • William Mervyn *Lord Twithampton* • Dora Bryan *Cora Crumpington* • Bob Hoskins *Recruiting sergeant* ■ *Dir* Bob Kellett • *Scr* Sid Colin, Eddie Braben

Up the Junction ★★
Drama 1967 · UK · Colour · 118min

When Ken Loach adapted Nell Dunn's provocative novel *Up the Junction* for TV in the 1960s, it shocked the nation. Director Peter Collinson's big screen version was more polished, and therein lay its undoing. Loach's semi-documentary style gave Battersea the suitably bleak look that made the central character's decision to move there from Chelsea seem both politically significant and socially courageous. Collinson, however, offers a working-class wonderland and has Suzy Kendall play the girl as a cross between a 1960s supermodel and a melodramatic sob sister. **DP**

Suzy Kendall *Polly* • Dennis Waterman *Peter* • Adrienne Posta *Rube* • Maureen Lipman *Sylvie* • Liz Fraser *Mrs McCarthy* • Hylda Baker *Winny* • Alfie Bass *Charlie* ■ *Dir* Peter Collinson • *Scr* Roger Smith, from the novel by Nell Dunn

Up the River ★★
Prison comedy 1930 · US · BW · 92min

This is a major movie for collectors of screen debuts since Spencer Tracy and Humphrey Bogart made their start in features right here. It began as a prison drama but when MGM's *The Big House* cornered that market it was quickly transformed into a comedy. Bogart plays an upper-class convict who is in love with fellow jailbird, Claire Luce. Tracy is an escaped con who voluntarily returns to help his prison win a crucial ball game. Director John Ford called it "a piece of junk", but you can't deny the novelty of two of Hollywood's finest beginning their careers in such an offbeat comedy. **AT**

Spencer Tracy *St Louis* • Warren Hymer *Dannemora Dan* • Humphrey Bogart *Steve* • Claire Luce *Judy* • William Collier Sr *Pop* • Joan Lawes *Jean* • Sharon Lynn [Sharon Lynne] *Edith La Verne* ■ *Dir* John Ford • *Scr* Maurine Watkins, John Ford, William Collier Sr

Up the Sandbox ★★★ 15
Comedy 1972 · US · Colour · 93min

A genuinely charming performance by Barbra Streisand redeems this awkward yet fitfully touching theatrical account of being alone in a crowded and thoughtless New York. Streisand has any number of fantasies – including one that involves being seduced by Fidel Castro! – and director Irvin Kershner cleverly manages to integrate them into the main narrative. Not a success at the time, this now has more than a little period appeal. **TS** Some violence, swearing, nudity, a sex scene. *DVD*

Barbra Streisand *Margaret Reynolds* • David Selby *Paul Reynolds* • Jane Hoffman *Mrs Yussim* • John C Becher *Mr Yussim* • Jacobo Morales *Fidel Castro* • Ariane Heller *Elizabeth* ■ *Dir* Irvin Kershner • *Scr* Paul Zindel, from the novel by Anne Richardson Roiphe

Up There ★★★ 15
Comedy drama 2011 · UK · Colour · 79min

Zam Salim here expands his award-winning short *Laid Off* into a droll feature that equates death with unemployment and re-imagines purgatory as a restart centre. Burn Gorman plays a carer who welcomes arrivals to the afterlife, but when his garrulous partner (Aymen Hamdouchi) scares away a newcomer, the pair have to trek to the sleepy Scottish community of Newport to retrieve him. Smartly scripted and deftly played, this is engaging and intriguing, despite losing its edge and momentum in the final third. **DP** Swearing

Burn Gorman *Martin* • Kate O'Flynn *Liz* • Aymen Hamdouchi *Rash* • Kulvinder Ghir *Ali* • Jo Hartley *Margaret* ■ *Dir/Scr* Zam Salim

Up to His Ears ★★★ U
Comedy adventure 1965 · Fr/It · Colour · 96min

An updated version of a Jules Verne novel, this is one of several comic adventure movies Philippe de Broca made with the energetic Jean-Paul Belmondo in a daredevil role. Belmondo is a millionaire, bored with life, who hires a hitman to assassinate him, but changes his mind after meeting the statuesque Ursula Andress, who is as easy on the eye as the Far Eastern locations. But, filmed at a frenzied pace, it loses much of its initial humour and impetus along the way. **RB** In French.

Jean-Paul Belmondo *Arthur Lempereur* • Ursula Andress *Alexandrine* • Maria Pacôme *Suzy* • Valérie Lagrange *Alice Ponchabert* • Valery Inkijinoff *M Goh* • Jean Rochefort *Léon* ■ *Dir* Philippe de Broca • *Scr* Philippe de Broca, Daniel Boulanger, from the novel *Les Tribulations d'un Chinois en Chine* by Jules Verne

Upper World ★★★
Crime drama 1934 · US · BW · 72min

This fine Warner Bros melodrama is based on a Ben Hecht story about a romance across the tracks between dancer Ginger Rogers and married businessman Warren William, whose socialite ("upper world") wife is impeccably played by Mary Astor. When the burlesque girl is found dead, the cops are loathe to incriminate William, and thereby hangs a terrific tale, unhindered in its day by the new censorship code that movies like this one encouraged. Look out for a very young Mickey Rooney. **TS**

Warren William *Alexander Stream* • Mary Astor *Hettie Stream* • Ginger Rogers *Lilly Linder* • Theodore Newton *Rocklen* • Andy Devine *Oscar, the Chauffeur* • Dickie Moore *Tommy Stream* • J Carrol Naish *Lou Colima* • Robert Barrat *Commissioner Clark* • Mickey Rooney *Jerry* ■ *Dir* Roy Del Ruth • *Scr* Ben Markson, from a story by Ben Hecht

Ups and Downs of a Handyman ★★ 18
Sex comedy 1975 · UK · Colour · 85min

Barry Stokes brings a certain cheeky charm to the title role, but what little comedy there is comes from Benny Hill stalwart Bob Todd, as the local magistrate, and Chic Murray, as a harassed bobby. Derrick Slater's script is one long smutty gag, while the direction is perfunctory at best. **DP** Nudity.

U SUITABLE FOR ALL Uc SUITABLE ESPECIALLY FOR YOUNG CHILDREN (DVD ONLY) PG PARENTAL GUIDANCE 12A UNDER 12s TO BE ACCOMPANIED (CINEMA ONLY)

Barry Stokes *Bob* • Gay Soper *Maisie* • Sue Lloyd *The blonde* • Bob Todd *Squire Bullsworthy* • Chic Murray *PC Knowles* • Robert Dorning *Newsagent* • Valerie Leon *Redhead* • Penny Meredith *Margaretta* ■ *Dir* John Sealey • *Scr* Derrick Slater

Upside Down: the Creation Records Story ★★★ 15

Music documentary
2010 · UK · Colour and BW · 100min

This overpopulated but evocative chronicle of the rise and fall of Creation Records – which, between 1983 and 1999, gave the world The Jesus and Mary Chain, My Bloody Valentine, Primal Scream and, more lucratively, Britpop superstars Oasis – is guilty of the same self-mythologising as the independent label itself. A garrulous and entertaining Alan McGee, who founded the label in the fertile aftermath of punk, dominates the documentary, but contributions from key players, including Oasis kingpin Noel Gallagher, add colour and wry humour. Director Danny O'Connor captures the hedonistic mood of a particular time – although anyone who wasn't there might find it a bit impenetrable. AC Swearing. *DVD* *BL*

Alan McGee • Bobby Gillespie • Noel Gallagher • Irvine Welsh ■ *Dir* Danny O'Connor

The Upside of Anger ★★★ 15

Comedy drama 2005 · US · Colour · 111min

This comedy drama from writer/director Mike Binder is a funny, sympathetic account of a middle-aged woman facing up to being dumped by her husband. Joan Allen gives a superb performance as the abandoned wife who seeks solace in the bottle while venting her bitterness on her four teenage daughters. But it's to her credit that, for all her character's faults, Allen still manages to make you care for her. Binder also elicits a terrific performance from Kevin Costner as a former baseball star who becomes Allen's drinking buddy, eventual lover and a surrogate father to her children. As for Binder himself, he has a lot of fun as the most appalling character in the movie: a 40-something producer who preys on younger women. JF *DVD*

Joan Allen *Terry Wolfmeyer* • Kevin Costner *Denny* • Erika Christensen *Andy Wolfmeyer* • Evan Rachel Wood *Popeye Wolfmeyer* • Keri Russell *Emily Wolfmeyer* • Alicia Witt *Hadley Wolfmeyer* • Mike Binder *Shep* • Dane Christensen *Gordon* ■ *Dir/Scr* Mike Binder • *Cinematographer* Richard Greatrex

Upstairs and Downstairs ★★★

Comedy 1959 · UK · Colour · 100min

It must have been very frustrating for the cast of accomplished British performers, let alone for stars Claudia Cardinale and Mylène Demongeot, to have watched all their efforts being frittered away by such dull leads as Michael Craig and Anne Heywood. As the newlyweds searching for the perfect servant, they are the weak link in every scene. But you can still enjoy seeing Cardinale as a man-mad maid, Joan Hickson as a secret tippler, Joan Sims as a timid Welsh nanny, Sid James as a put-upon bobby and Demongeot as a Pollyanna-like au pair. DP

Michael Craig *Richard Barry* • Anne Heywood *Kate Barry* • Mylène Demongeot *Ingrid Gunnar* • James Robertson-Justice *Mansfield* • Claudia Cardinale *Maria* • Sidney James *PC Edwards* • Joan Hickson *Rosemary* • Joan Sims *Blodwen* • Joseph Tomelty *Arthur Farringdon* • Nora Nicholson *Mrs Edith Farringdon* • Daniel Massey *Wesley Cotes* ■ *Dir* Ralph Thomas • *Scr* Frank Harvey, from the novel by Ronald Scott Thorne

Upstream Color ★★★ 12

Science-fiction drama
2013 · US · Colour · 96min

The second feature from Shane Carruth, the director of *Primer*, is an abstract, experimental science-fiction thriller shot in a spare, stark style that will get under your skin, one way or another. It hinges on a mysterious figure (Thiego Martins) who infects a young woman (Amy Seimetz) with a parasitic worm that makes her susceptible to a form of hypnosis. Oddly beguiling, sometimes beautiful and always enigmatic, the movie was a hit at the 2013 Sundance Film Festival, but it will divide viewers. KK A sex scene, some swearing. *DVD* *BL*

Amy Seimetz *Kris* • Shane Carruth *Jeff* • Andrew Sensenig *The Sampler* • Thiago Martins *Thief* • Kathy Carruth *Orchid Mother* • Meredith Burke *Orchid Daughter* ■ *Dir/Scr* Shane Carruth • *Cinematographer* Shane Carruth

Uptight ★★★

Drama 1968 · US · Colour · 104min

Although it misfires on many levels, this is still an ambitious attempt to rework John Ford's 1935 Oscar-winning drama, *The Informer*. In shifting the scene away from Dublin in the 1920s to Cleveland in the aftermath of Martin Luther King's assassination, director Jules Dassin attempts to explore both the impact the event had on the African-American community and on the divisions that existed within its ranks. The performances now seem strained, but the power of the film's messages is undimmed. DP

Raymond St Jacques *BG* • Ruby Dee *Laurie* • Frank Silvera *Kyle* • Roscoe Lee Browne *Clarence* • Julian Mayfield *Tank* • Janet MacLachlan *Jeannie* ■ *Dir* Jules Dassin • *Scr* Jules Dassin, Ruby Dee, Julian Mayfield, from the novel *The Informer* by Liam O'Flaherty

Uptown Girls ★★ 12

Comedy 2003 · US · Colour · 88min

Newly broke "It Girl" Brittany Murphy takes a job as nanny to precocious youngster Dakota Fanning in this predictable comedy. A frothy tale of trust and responsibility, it buries the strong performances of its leads under a nauseating script and an embarrassing romantic subplot. Fanning is remarkably sophisticated as an uptight eight-year-old, while the always quirky Murphy fits the bill perfectly as a dead rock star's immature daughter. SF Some swearing. *DVD*

Brittany Murphy *Molly Gunn* • Dakota Fanning *Ray Schleine* • Marley Shelton *Ingrid* • Donald Faison *Huey* • Jesse Spencer *Neal* • Austin Pendleton *Mr McConkey* • Heather Locklear *Roma Schleine* ■ *Dir* Boaz Yakin • *Scr* Julia Dahl, Mo Ogrodnik, Lisa Davidowitz, from a story by Allison Jacobs

Uptown Saturday Night ★★★ PG

Comedy 1974 · US · Colour · 99min

Sidney Poitier directs and stars in this comedy about a pair of buddies (Poitier and Bill Cosby) who become involved with the criminal underworld when they try to retrieve a stolen winning lottery ticket. There's a very funny Harry Belafonte as a black godfather – Brando-style – and such comic talents as Richard Pryor and Flip Wilson. Sociologists might argue that these amiable romps did nothing to advance African-American cinema, but audiences at the time didn't care. The film generated two sequels: *Let's Do It Again* and *A Piece of the Action*. TS Swearing.

Sidney Poitier *Steve Jackson* • Bill Cosby *Wardell Franklin* • Harry Belafonte *Geechie Dan Beauford* • Flip Wilson *The Reverend* • Richard Pryor *Sharp Eye Washington* • Rosalind Cash *Sarah Jackson* • Roscoe Lee Browne *Congressman Lincoln* ■ *Dir* Sidney Poitier • *Scr* Richard Wesley

The Upturned Glass ★★★

Crime drama 1947 · UK · BW · 86min

In his last British film before taking off for Hollywood, James Mason returned to the kind of brooding figure that female audiences had adored in *The Seventh Veil* and *Odd Man Out*. He's the brain surgeon who concocts an elaborate revenge on the shrewish figure responsible for the death of the married woman he loved. Pamela Kellino (Mason's wife, who co-scripted) plays the murderess. Heavily contrived, but Mason's performance and Lawrence Huntington's directorial flair keep you hooked. AE

James Mason *Michael Joyce* • Rosamund John *Emma Wright* • Pamela Kellino *Kate Howard* • Ann Stephens *Ann Wright* • Morland Graham *Clay* ■ *Dir* Lawrence Huntington • *Scr* John P Monaghan, Pamela Kellino, from a story by John P Monaghan

Upworld ★★ PG

Comedy thriller 1992 · US · Colour · 87min

Another variation on the mismatched cops scenario sees a detective paired with a leftover from *The Lord of the Rings*. Detective Anthony Michael Hall discovers that the only witness to an undercover assignment that goes wrong is a furry little creature from the depths of the Earth who has been sent to the surface to recharge a magical stone that provides power for his subterranean world. Kids would love the Ewok-style capers; most parents will probably marvel at the sheer stupidity of the concept. JF

Anthony Michael Hall *Casey Gallagher* • Claudia Christian *Samantha Kennedy* • Jerry Orbach *Stan Walton* • Mark Harelik *Derek Kaminsky* • Eli Danker *Zadar* • Robert Z'Dar *Reggie* • Joseph R Sicari *Lou Ferril* ■ *Dir* Stan Winston • *Scr* Pen Densham, John Watson, from a story by Densham

Urban Cowboy ★★★ 12

Drama 1980 · US · Colour · 129min

A steamy romance between Texas oil worker John Travolta and strong-willed Debra Winger is played out against the backdrop of honky-tonk dancing and mechanical rodeos in an uneven country-and-western soap opera. Packed with music from the likes of the Eagles, the Charlie Daniels Band and Linda Ronstadt, director James Bridges' overlong portrait of American manhood in the early 1980s was an effort to re-promote Travolta as the nightclub macho man. AJ Violence, swearing. *DVD*

John Travolta *Bud Davis* • Debra Winger *Sissy Davis* • Scott Glenn *Wes Hightower* • Madolyn Smith *Pam* • Barry Corbin *Uncle Bob* • Brooke Alderson *Aunt Corene* • Cooper Huckabee *Marshall* ■ *Dir* James Bridges • *Scr* James Bridges, Aaron Latham, from a story by Aaron Latham

Urban Ghost Story ★★★ 15

Supernatural horror 1998 · UK · Colour · 84min

This low-budget – yes – urban ghost story has a 12-year-old girl (newcomer Heather Ann Foster) in a Glasgow tenement, who starts to detect supernatural rumblings while recovering from an ecstasy-linked near-death experience. Jason Connery plays against type as a tabloid reporter seeking to exploit the story, as ghostbusters and spiritualists descend on the council flat. Original and naturalistic film-makers, Genevieve Jolliffe and Chris Jones certainly have the promise to back up their vision and the constraints of a £220,000 budget prove the mother of invention. AC *DVD*

Jason Connery *John Fox* • Stephanie Buttle *Kate Fisher* • Heather Ann Foster *Lizzie Fisher* • Nicola Stapleton *Kerrie* • James Cosmo *Minister* ■ *Dir* Genevieve Jolliffe • *Scr* Chris Jones, Genevieve Jolliffe

Urban Legend ★★ 18

Horror thriller 1998 · US/Fr · Colour · 95min

One of the weaker examples of the late 1990s resurgence in stalk 'n' slash movies, this shows attractive teenagers being dispatched in the form of – you've guessed it – urban legends. The gimmicky murders are the film's sole stab at innovation, although some of the later "legends" seem made up for the purposes of the plot. The pedestrian direction, bland cast and a ludicrous final unmasking don't add up to much. JC Violence, swearing. *DVD* *BL*

Alicia Witt *Natalie* • Jared Leto *Paul* • Rebecca Gayheart *Brenda* • Michael Rosenbaum *Parker* • Loretta Devine *Reese* • Joshua Jackson *Damon* • Robert Englund *Professor Wexler* • Brad Dourif *Gas station attendant* ■ *Dir* Jamie Blanks • *Scr* Silvio Horta

Urban Legends: Final Cut ★★ 15

Horror thriller 2000 · US/Fr · Colour · 94min

As with the original, this sequel doesn't deliver the promise of its premise. The first film maintained the storyline about a serial killer murdering in the style of notorious folk-myths until about the half-way mark: here it's ditched after the first few minutes. Then it turns into son-of-*Scream*, complete with movie in-jokes, as the serial slayer dices his way through the students at a film school. This underachieves in the scare department. DA *DVD*

Jennifer Morrison *Amy Mayfield* • Matthew Davis *Travis/Trevor* • Hart Bochner *Professor Solomon* • Loretta Devine *Reese* • Joseph Lawrence [*Joey* Lawrence] *Graham Manning* • Anson Mount *Toby* ■ *Dir* John Ottman • *Scr* John Harris Boardman, Scott Derrickson, from characters by Silvio Horta

Urga ★★★★ PG

Drama 1990 · Fr/USSR · Colour · 114min

The winner of the Golden Lion at the Venice film festival, this is a visually stunning parable on the dubious benefits of progress. Alternating between the rolling expanses of the steppe and the homely clutter of a shepherd's tent, director Nikita Mikhalkov manages to make both the traditional lifestyle of the Mongolian family and the trappings of consumerism seem attractive, while at the same time pointing out their pitfalls. Vladimir Gostukhin is superb as the coarse Russian truck driver, while Badema and Bayaertu are quietly impressive as the couple who give him shelter. DP Russian, Mongolian +subtitles.

Badema *Pagma* • Bayaertu *Gombo* • Vladimir Gostukhin *Sergei* • Babushka *Grandma* • Larissa Kuznetsova *Marina* • Jon Bochinski *Stanislas* ■ *Dir* Nikita Mikhalkov • *Scr* Roustam Ibraguimbekov, from a short story by Roustam Ibraguimbekov, Nikita Mikhalkov

Urotsukidoji: Legend of the Overfiend ★★★ 18

Animated fantasy horror
1987 · Jpn · Colour · 102min

This was one of the first Japanese *anime* to gain widespread attention in the UK, no doubt due to the novelty value of the insane levels of splattery violence and extremely graphic sexual content. The plot (something about a search for a super fiend who can unite the three worlds of humans, beasts and demons) isn't easy to follow. But, although the animation is simplistic, the story does provide some genuinely disturbing imagery. What's more, the English dubbing is first-rate. Continued in *Legend of the Demon Womb*. JC Japanese dubbed. *DVD*

Christopher Courage *Amano* • Rebel Joy *Akemi* • Danny Bush *Nagumo* • Lucy Morales *Megumi* ■ *Dir* Hideki Takayama • *Scr* Noboru Aikawa, Michael Lawrence (2), from the comic strip by Toshio Maeda

Used Cars ★★★★ 15

Comedy 1980 · US · Colour · 107min

Tasteless, risqué, outrageous and amoral, this early offering from director Robert Zemeckis is all these things and more. But it's also an extremely funny rumination on American values, as the car showroom becomes a warped microcosm of society. Revealing Kurt Russell's under-utilised talent as a first-rate comedian, it's a good-natured if highly eccentric wisecracker, finding amusement in the misfortunes and embarrassment of others. AJ Swearing. *DVD*

Kurt Russell *Rudy Russo* • Jack Warden *Roy L Fuchs/Luke Fuchs* • Gerrit Graham *Jeff* • Frank McRae *Jim the Mechanic* • Deborah Harmon *Barbara Fuchs* • Joseph P Flaherty *Sam Slaton* • David L Lander *Freddie Paris* • Michael McKean *Eddie Winslow* ■ *Dir* Robert Zemeckis • *Scr* Robert Zemeckis, Bob Gale

Used People ★★★ 15

Comedy drama 1992 · US · Colour · 111min

This is one of those huge feel-good ensemble pieces where the sheer size and quality of the cast help disguise the lack of substance. The fact that this was Italian star Marcello Mastroianni's first true Hollywood movie was the main talking point on the film's release, and he delivers a typically charming performance as he courts the recently widowed Shirley MacLaine. British director Beeban Kidron, also making her Hollywood debut, orchestrates the proceedings with confidence. JF Sex scenes, swearing.

Shirley MacLaine *Pearl Berman* • Marcello Mastroianni *Joe Meledandri* • Kathy Bates *Bibby* • Jessica Tandy *Frieda* • Sylvia Sidney *Becky* • Marcia Gay Harden *Norma* • Bob Dishy *Jack Berman* ■ *Dir* Beeban Kidron • *Scr* Todd Graff, from his play *The Grandma Plays*

A Useful Life ★★★★ U
Drama 2010 · Urug/Sp/Neth · BW · 63min

An ageing cineaste discovers that though movies may be sublime, they will never be a substitute for real life in this charming paean to cinema from director Federico Veiroj. Jorge Jellinek plays the Montevideo art-house cinema employee who learns from his boss that the venue is to close. Thus he is forced into the wider world, where everyday events become the stuff of screen heroics. Exquisitely photographed by Arauco Hernández, and converted from colour to monochrome, the movie's deceptively simple action evokes the heyday of Italian neorealism. But Veiroj also channels slapstick, screwball comedy and MGM musicals in charting Jellinek's amusing transformation, making it utterly irresistible. DP Spanish +subtitles. *DVD*

Jorge Jellinek *Jorge* • Manuel Martínez Carril *Martínez* • Paola Venditto *Paola* • Gonzalo Delgado *Director* ■ *Dir* Federico Veiroj • *Scr* Inés Bortagaray, Gonzalo Delgado, Arauco Hernández, Federico Veiroj

Ushpizin ★★★ PG
Comedy 2004 · Is · Colour · 92min

Taking its title from the Aramaic for "holy guests", Gidi Dar's comedy is the first filmic collaboration between Israel's religious and secular communities. Screenwriter Shuli Rand works hard as the ultra-Orthodox Jew whose poverty prevents him and childless wife Michal Bat Sheva Rand from celebrating the Succoth festival, until a friend from his wild past (Shaul Mizrahi) shows up seeking sanctuary from the law with his hair-trigger sidekick (Ilan Ganani). This is an essentially genial outing and, even though the proselytising polemic is far from subtle, it provides a serio-comic insight into life within a strict ultra-Orthodox Jewish society. DP Hebrew +subtitles.

Shuli Rand *Moshe Bellanga* • Michal Bat Sheva Rand *Malli Bellanga* • Shaul Mizrahi *Eliyahu Scorpio* • Ilan Ganani *Yossef* • Avraham Abutbul *Ben Baruch* • Yonathan Danino *Gabai* • Daniel Dayan *Rabbi* ■ *Dir* Gidi Dar • *Scr* Shuli Rand

The Usual Suspects ★★★★★ 18
Crime thriller 1995 · US · Colour · 101min

What made this audacious but unheralded thriller the must-see film of 1995? Maybe it was the intricacy of the flashback-packed script and the deft sleights of hand executed by its fledgling director. Perhaps everyone admired the outstanding ensemble acting. Yes, Kevin Spacey stole the show and fully merited the best supporting actor Oscar for his mesmerising performance, but everyone in that rogues' gallery played their part to perfection, not to mention the mysterious Pete Postlethwaite and confused cops Dan Hedaya and Chazz Palminteri. Or was it simply that noticeboard that kept coming back to haunt everyone? Whatever the reason, this is a film that demands to be watched repeatedly – a good old-fashioned pulp fiction told in the slickest 1990s style. DP Violence, swearing. *DVD* Blu

Gabriel Byrne *Dean Keaton* • Kevin Spacey *Roger "Verbal" Kint* • Chazz Palminteri *Dave Kujan* • Benicio Del Toro *Fred Fenster* • Stephen Baldwin *Michael McManus* • Kevin Pollak *Todd Hockney* • Pete Postlethwaite *Kobayashi* • Suzy Amis *Edie Finneran* • Giancarlo Esposito *Jack Baer* • Dan

Hedaya *Sergeant Jeff Rabin* • Paul Bartel (1) *Smuggler* ■ *Dir* Bryan Singer • *Scr* Christopher McQuarrie

Utopia ★★ U
Comedy 1950 · Fr/It · BW · 82min

Sadly, Laurel and Hardy's last film, unavailable for many years, is as mediocre as we had been led to believe – not badly made, just ill-conceived and dull. The boys are shipwrecked on an atoll while en route to a desert island, after which most of the action focuses on Suzy Delair, who is fleeing a jealous boyfriend. Stan and Ollie become supporting players in an increasingly bizarre tale involving the discovery of uranium. Also known as *Atoll K*. DM French dubbed. *DVD*

Stan Laurel *Stanley* • Oliver Hardy *Oliver* • Suzy Delair *Cherie Lamour* • M Elloy [Max Elloy] *Antoine* • M Dalmatoff *Alecto* ■ *Dir* Leo Joannon [Léo Joannon], John Berry • *Scr* Monty Collins [Monte Collins], Piero Tellini, R Wheeler, from an idea by Léo Joannon

Utopia ★★★★
Documentary 2013 · UK/Aus · Colour and BW · 114min

Here Australian-born journalist John Pilger deals with a subject close to his heart – the racism and poor treatment meted out to his homeland's Aboriginal people. His relentless indictment of past and present Australian governments is sustained by clips from his TV reports of the 1980s and 90s, which show there's been little, if any, improvement. When one elder says his people are "refugees in our own country", it's difficult to disagree. Critics of the esteemed journalist may round on him for his lack of neutrality, but this is definitely one axe that requires grinding. JA Swearing. *DVD*

John Pilger ■ *Dir* John Pilger, Alan Lowery • *Scr* John Pilger

Utu ★★★ 15
Action drama 1983 · NZ · Colour · 99min

This is a powerful drama that plays like a New Zealand western. A Maori serving with the colonial British Army finds his family massacred by some of its rogue elements and vows *utu*, Maori for "retribution". He then raises a rebel army and goes in for a spot of payback. Action-packed yet poignant, the film was made by Geoff Murphy, director of the equally competent *The Quiet Earth*. DA

Anzac Wallace *Te Wheke* • Bruno Lawrence *Williamson* • Wi Kuki Kaa *Wiremu* • Tim Elliott *Colonel Elliott* • Ilona Rodgers *Emily Williamson* • Tania Bristowe *Kura* • Maerata Mita *Matu* ■ *Dir* Geoff Murphy • *Scr* Geoff Murphy, Keith Aberdein

Utz ★★★ 12
Mystery drama 1992 · UK /Ger/It · Colour · 93min

With an award-winning performance from Armin Mueller-Stahl, this is a complex character study of an obsessive Czech collector of fine porcelain figures who's understandably distraught when the country's then-communist government decrees his collection actually belongs to the State. A top-notch cast features in a film that's as fine and detailed as the figures Utz collects, though it may be too dry for some tastes. DA

Armin Mueller-Stahl *Baron Kaspar Joachim von Utz* • Brenda Fricker *Marta* • Peter Riegert *Marius Fischer* • Paul Scofield *Doctor Vaclav Orlik* • Miriam Karlin *Grandmother Utz* ■ *Dir* George Sluizer • *Scr* Hugh Whitemore, from the novel by Bruce Chatwin

Uzak ★★★★ 15
Drama 2003 · Tur/Neth · Colour · 106min

Mehmet Emin Toprak and Muzaffer Ozdemir shared the best actor prize at Cannes for their work in Nuri Bilge Ceylan's meticulous insight into the disintegration of traditional ties and the crisis of masculinity in modern Turkey. Making evocative use of snow, Ceylan conveys both the isolation and the alienation of Ozdemir's disillusioned Istanbul photographer and Toprak's

optimistically indolent country cousin. Indeed, his emphasis on their inability to communicate is reinforced by his studied pacing and mastery of environment. Not an easy film, but a deeply moving one. DP Turkish +subtitles. Swearing, nudity. *DVD*

Muzaffer Ozdemir *Mahmut* • Mehmet Emin Toprak *Yusuf* • Zuhal Gencer Erkaya *Nazan* • Nazan Kirilmis *Lover* • Feridun Koc *Janitor* • Fatma Ceylan *Mother* • Ebru Ceylan *Young girl* ■ *Dir/Scr* Nuri Bilge Ceylan

Uzumasa Limelight ★★★★ 15
Action drama 2014 · Jpn · Colour · 104min

Inspired by Chaplin's *Limelight*, this is a poignant paean to the *jidai-geki* period picture. Seizo Fukumoto plays the stuntman whose long-running TV show has just been cancelled. Though Fukumoto is reduced to giving swordplay displays to tourists, aspiring actress Chihiro Yamamoto remains eager to learn from him before his craft is lost. Affectionately made, this manages to be both critical and nostalgic without being mawkish, and Fukumoto (a real-life *kirareyaku* who's perished 50,000 times on screen) excels as the twilight warrior. DP Japanese +subtitles. Violence. Blu

Seizo Fukumoto *Seiichi* • Chihiro Yamamoto *Satsuki Iga* • Masashi Goda *Kawashima* • Hirotaro Honda *Kenichi Naganuma* • Hisako Manda *Mitsuru Tamura* ■ *Dir* Ken Ochiai • *Scr* Hiroyuki Ono

V for Vendetta ★★★ 15
Futuristic action thriller
2005 · UK/Ger · Colour · 127min

This adaptation of a graphic novel is set in a near-future totalitarian Britain, where an enigmatically masked vigilante called V (Hugo Weaving) ignites a revolution with the help of unlikely ally Evey (Natalie Portman). It's by turns audaciously risk-taking and clunky, featuring banned Muslim texts, avian flu, Tube-bomb terrorism and pro-gay manifestos. But debuting director James McTeigue's preachy, over-serious polemic still delivers a stunningly executed and movingly relevant ending. AJ Swearing, violence. *DVD* Blu

Natalie Portman *Evey Hammond* • Hugo Weaving *V* • Stephen Rea *Chief Inspector Finch* • John Hurt *Chancellor Adam Sutler* • Stephen Fry *Deitrich* • Tim Pigott-Smith *Creedy* • Rupert Graves *Dominic* • Roger Allam *Lewis Prothero* • Ben Miles *Dascomb* • Sinead Cusack *Delia Surridge* ■ *Dir* James McTeigue • *Scr* The Wachowski brothers, from the comic book by Alan Moore (uncredited), David Lloyd

V/H/S ★★★★ 18
Horror anthology 2012 · US · Colour · 111min

Demons and ghouls come out to play in this 21st-century spin on the portmanteau horror. The mayhem begins when a gang of roughnecks is hired to steal a videotape from a derelict house. With only a dead man on site, it appears to be a simple enough task, until they become distracted by other tapes, so unleashing a killer collection of short, sharp found-footage shockers. Gruesome, creepy and unnerving, this set of tales lingers long after the lights go up. A sequel was released in 2013. JA Violence, swearing, drug abuse, sex scenes, nudity.

Adam Wingard *Brad* • Hannah Fierman *Lily* • Joe Swanberg *Sam* • Norma C Quinones *Wendy* • Helen Rogers *Emily* • Chad Villella *Chad* ■ *Dir* Adam Wingard, David Bruckner, Ti West, Glenn McQuaid, Joe Swanberg, Radio Silence [Matt Bettinelli-Olpin], Radio Silence [Tyler Gillett], Radio Silence [Justin Martinez], Radio Silence [Chad Villella]

V/H/S/2 ★★★★ 18
Horror anthology 2013 · US · Colour · 91min

More tales of terror are unearthed from dusty old videos in this slick sequel to the 2012 horror anthology. On this occasion, it's two private investigators on a missing-persons case who come across the cassettes. But whereas the first film's quintet of stories were of varying quality, the calibre of the four shorts here is consistently higher. It's terrifyingly terrific stuff. Part 3, *V/H/S: Viral*, didn't live up to its promise, however, and went straight to DVD. JA Violence, swearing, sex scenes, nudity. *DVD*

Lawrence Michael Levine *Larry* • Kelsy Abbott *Ayesha* • Adam Wingard *Herman* • Jay Saunders *Biker* • Fachry Albar *Adam* • Hannah Al-Raschid *Lena* • Riley Eisener *Tank* ■ *Dir* Simon Barrett, Adam Wingard, Gregg Hale, Edúardo Sanchez [Eduardo Sanchez], Timo Tjahjanto, Gareth Huw Evans [Gareth Evans], Jason Eisener • *Scr* Simon Barrett, Jamie Nash, Timo Tjahjanto, Gareth Huw Evans, Jason Eisener, John Davies, from a concept by Brad Miska

The VIPs ★★
Drama 1963 · UK · Colour · 119min

Made principally to cash in on the Richard Burton/Elizabeth Taylor romance, this is a glossy but tedious drama set in the VIP lounge of the then London Airport. Only Margaret Rutherford's deliriously dotty, Oscar-winning duchess and Orson Welles's

---

U SUITABLE FOR ALL   Uc SUITABLE ESPECIALLY FOR YOUNG CHILDREN (DVD ONLY)   PG PARENTAL GUIDANCE   12A UNDER 12s TO BE ACCOMPANIED (CINEMA ONLY)

movie mogul fleeing the taxman breathe life into the bottomless pit of clichés. **AT**

Elizabeth Taylor *Frances Andros* • Richard Burton *Paul Andros* • Louis Jourdan *Marc Champselle* • Elsa Martinelli *Gloria Gritti* • Margaret Rutherford *Duchess of Brighton* • Maggie Smith *Miss Mead* • Rod Taylor *Les Mangrum* • Linda Christian *Miriam Marshall* • Orson Welles *Max Buda* • Dennis Price *Commander Millbank* ■ *Dir* Anthony Asquith • *Scr* Terence Rattigan

VI Warshawski ★★ 15
Crime mystery 1991 · US · Colour · 85min

A rasping, sassy Kathleen Turner stars as Sara Paretsky's spiky, difficult, liberal-feminist private eye VI "Vic" Warshawski. But in this film the investigator becomes a man-fearing, baseball-obsessed pain in the rear, in a film that's sunk by its plot – a lame piece of fluff about a 13-year-old and a dodgy inheritance. Only worth watching for Turner, who desperately attempts to inject some grit into the proceedings. **SH** Violence, swearing. *DVD*

Kathleen Turner *Victoria I Warshawski* • Jay O Sanders *Murray Ryerson* • Charles Durning *Lieutenant Mallory* • Angela Goethals *Kat Grafalk* • Nancy Paul *Paige Grafalk* • Frederick Coffin *Horton Grafalk* • Charles McCaughan *Trumble Grafalk* ■ *Dir* Jeff Kanew • *Scr* Edward Taylor, David Aaron Cohen, Nick Thiel, from a story by Edward Taylor, from novels by Sara Paretsky

Va Savoir ★★★★ PG
Romantic comedy drama 2001 · Fr/Ger/It · Colour · 147min

Jacques Rivette again demonstrates his skills as a director of nuance and pace in this literate charade. Set in present-day Paris, the old French master explores the love affairs that emerge between three men and three women during a theatrical troupe's production of Pirandello's *As You Desire Me*. No one puts a foot wrong in an exemplary ensemble cast headed by Jeanne Balibar and Sergio Castellitto. Rivette's exploration of the relationship between art and life is so precisely staged and performed, it seems almost effortless. **DP** French, Italian +subtitles. *DVD*

Jeanne Balibar *Camille Renard* • Sergio Castellitto *Ugo Bassani* • Jacques Bonnaffé *Pierre Mauduit* • Marianne Basler *Sonia* • Hélène de Fougerolles *Dominique "Do" Desprez* • Bruno Todeschini *Arthur Delamarche* ■ *Dir* Jacques Rivette • *Scr* Pascal Bonitzer, Christine Laurent, Jacques Rivette

Vacancy ★★★★ 15
Horror thriller 2007 · US · Colour · 81min

Avoiding gore in favour of throat-grabbing tension, *Kontroll* director Nimrod Antal's scare show is a superior shocker. Forced to stay in a seedy motel after their car breaks down, estranged couple Luke Wilson and Kate Beckinsale fight for their lives against a snuff movie operation. Well-sustained suspense separates this chic *Psycho* for the multi-media age from the rest of the Splat Pack. Hitchcock's shadow looms large over this lean, mean, technically impressive nightmare, and credibility is stretched yet never undermines the sense of dread lurking in squalid rooms and underground tunnels. **AJ** *DVD* *BL*

Luke Wilson *David Fox* • Kate Beckinsale *Amy Fox* • Frank Whaley *Mason* • Ethan Embry *Mechanic* • Scott G Anderson *Killer* • Mark Cassella *Truck driver* • David Doty *Highway patrol* ■ *Dir* Nimrod Antal • *Scr* Mark L Smith • *Cinematographer* Andrzej Sekula

Vacas ★★★ 15
Period drama 1991 · Sp · Colour · 92min

Described as a "negative comedy", Julio Medem's directorial debut is a difficult film to like. Yet the standard of its imaginative camerawork, its playful shifts from reality to fantasy and the assuredness with which the narrative strands have been woven together have to be admired. Following the fortunes of two Basque families through the civil wars of 1875 and 1936, the four stories have something of a fairy-tale quality and are interesting enough, but the

lack of character depth prevents total involvement. **DP** Spanish +subtitles. *DVD*

Emma Suarez *Cristina* • Carmelo Gomez *Manuel/Ignacio/Peru* • Ana Torrent *Catalina* • Karra Elejalde *Ilegorri/Lucas* • Klara Badiola *Madalen* • Txema Blasco *Manuel* • Kandido Uranga *Carmelo/Juan* • Pilar Bardem *Paulina* ■ *Dir* Julio Medem • *Scr* Julio Medem, Michel Gaztambide, from a story by Julio Medem

Vacation ★★ 15
Comedy adventure 2015 · US · Colour · 94min

A reboot of the beloved National Lampoon comedies, this sees Ed Helms takes his family on a disaster-packed road trip to Walley World. The film desperately tries to re-create the charm of the original films, but too often gets sidelined by jokes that are either too obvious or downright crude. There's an attempt to force a message about family unity, but when one of the film's signature gags is tied to Chris Hemsworth's "nether regions", that message becomes diluted. A drab, juvenile misfire. **JL** Swearing, sexual references, nudity. *DVD*

Ed Helms *Rusty Griswold* • Christina Applegate *Debbie Griswold* • Beverly D'Angelo *Ellen Griswold* • Chris Hemsworth *Stone Crandall* • Leslie Mann *Audrey Criswold* • Chevy Chase *Clark Griswold* ■ *Dir* John Francis Daley, Jonathan M Goldstein • *Scr* John Francis Daley, Jonathan M Goldstein, from characters by John Hughes

The Vagabond ★★★ U
Silent comedy drama 1916 · US · BW · 21min

This short fully confirmed Charlie Chaplin as the Little Tramp – with tarnished bowler hat, holey baggy pants and jaunty cane. He plays a fiddling busker who rescues Edna Purviance from the clutches of the ever-villainous and even-more-mountainous Eric Campbell. Shameless sentiment in a timeless world, this effort prefers straight drama to belly laughs, but that's not to say it doesn't entertain. **TH** *DVD*

Charles Chaplin *Street musician* • Edna Purviance *Girl stolen by gypsies* • Eric Campbell *Gypsy chieftain* • Leo White *Old Jew/Gypsy woman* ■ *Dir* Charles Chaplin • *Scr* Charles Chaplin, Vincent Bryan

Vagabond ★★★★ 15
Mystery drama 1985 · Fr · Colour · 101min

Opening with the discovery of Sandrine Bonnaire's body, this is less an investigation into the personality and problems of the teenage drifter than a penetrating examination of the society that was culpable for her demise. Combining eyewitness testimonies with reconstructions of Bonnaire's peripatetic final days, director Agnès Varda reveals a cold, alienated individual who reflects the prejudices and fears of those she encounters, including liberal academic Macha Méril, who finds herself uncomfortably fascinated by her. Shot with spartan poetry and solemnly played by a largely non-professional cast, this is a cheerless study of displacement, waste and collective responsibility. **DP** French +subtitles.

Sandrine Bonnaire *Mona Bergeron* • Macha Méril *Madame Landier* • Yolande Moreau *Yolande* • Stéphane Freiss *Jean-Pierre* • Marthe Jarnais *Aunt Lydie* • Joël Fosse *Paulo* ■ *Dir/Scr* Agnès Varda

The Vagabond King ★★★ U
Musical 1956 · US · Colour · 87min

Maltese baritone Oreste "Kirkop" stars as the beggar-rogue poet François Villon in this screen outing of Rudolf Friml's operetta. Sadly, though a pleasant personality and singer, both the star's name and voice have been forgotten, as this was his only movie. It was also the last film appearance of soprano Kathryn Grayson. Familiar and old-fashioned, it has some good songs such as *Love Me Tonight*, as well as new ones composed by Friml. **RB**

Kathryn Grayson *Catherine de Vaucelles* • Oreste "Kirkop" *Francois Villon* • Rita Moreno *Huguette* • Sir Cedric Hardwicke [Cedric Hardwicke] *Tristan* • Walter Hampden *King Louis XI* • Leslie Nielsen *Thibault* • William Prince *Rene* • Jack Lord

Ferrebone ■ *Dir* Michael Curtiz • *Scr* Ken Englund, Noel Langley, from the musical by Rudolf Friml, Brian Hooker, William H Post, from the play *If I Were King* by Justin Huntly McCarthy, from a novel by RH Russell

The Vagrant ★★ 18
Comedy horror 1992 · US/Fr · Colour · 87min

Bill Paxton, unwisely cast against type, is the ordinary middle-class professional who finds himself the target for homeless derelict Marshall Bell, who proceeds to make his life a living hell. Chris Walas directs with flamboyance and the cast, including Michael Ironside as an investigating police officer, certainly hams it up enthusiastically. However, the film is undone by a script lacking in depth and bite. **JF** Swearing, violence, sex scenes.

Bill Paxton *Graham Krakowski* • Michael Ironside *Lieutenant Ralf Barfuss* • Marshall Bell *The vagrant* • Mitzi Kapture *Edie Roberts* • Colleen Camp *Judy Dansig* • Patrika Darbo *Doatti* • Marc McClure *Chuck* ■ *Dir* Chris Walas • *Scr* Richard Jeffries

The Valachi Papers ★★ 18
Crime drama 1972 · It/Fr · Colour · 119min

Based on the true story of famed Mob informant Joe Valachi, and with Charles Bronson playing Valachi, this study of early 20th-century gangster life should have had more of an impact. Instead, it views Valachi's rise and fall, and the intricacies of rules and roles in the Mafia in a rather casual fashion. The almost European look of the movie also dilutes the gritty feel of the movie tries to generate. The 50-year-old Bronson is good, but isn't convincing in the flashback scenes of his character as a young man. **KB** *DVD*

Charles Bronson *Joseph Valachi* • Lino Ventura *Vito Genovese* • Jill Ireland *Maria Valachi* • Walter Chiari *Dominic "The Gap" Petrilli* • Joseph Wiseman *Salvatore Maranzano* • Gerald S O'Loughlin *Ryan* • Amedeo Nazzari *Gaetano Reina* • Fausto Tozzi *Albert Anastasia* ■ *Dir* Terence Young • *Scr* A Maiuri [Dino Maiuri], Massimo De Rita, Stephen Geller, from the book by Peter Maas

The Valdez Horses ★★★ 15
Western 1973 · It/Sp/Fr · Colour · 92min

Charles Bronson gives one of his best performances in this little-known European western. He stars as a mixed-race cowboy who takes in young runaway Vincent Van Patten on his small ranch. Bronson's character is more complex than the typical western loner; he's not always sympathetic and handles the local racists in an atypical way for both the genre and for the star. **KB** *DVD*

Charles Bronson *Chino Valdez* • Jill Ireland *Louise* • Vincent Van Patten *Jamie Wagner* • Marcel Bozzuffi *Maral* • Melissa Chimenti *Indian Girl* • Fausto Tozzi *Cruz* ■ *Dir* John Sturges • *Scr* Dino Maiuri, Massimo De Rita, Clair Haffaker, from the novel by Lee Hoffman

Valdez Is Coming ★★ 15
Western 1971 · US · Colour · 86min

This western is notable only for a performance of immense dignity from the great Burt Lancaster as a Mexican-American lawman bent on justice. It's an unlikely debut for Broadway theatre director Edwin Sherin, who fails to get the most out of the material and quite clearly has no cinema technique. The film is crucially undercast, with a far stronger screen presence than Jon Cypher required as Lancaster's adversary. **TS** Violence, swearing, sex scenes. *DVD*

Burt Lancaster *Bob Valdez* • Susan Clark *Gay Erin* • Jon Cypher *Frank Tanner* • Barton Heyman *El Segundo* • Richard Jordan *RI Davis* • Frank Silvera *Diego* • Hector Elizondo *Mexican rider* • Phil Brown *Malson* ■ *Dir* Edwin Sherin • *Scr* Ronald Kibbee, David Rayfiel, from the novel by Elmore Leonard

Valentín ★★★ PG
Period drama 2002 · Arg/Neth/Fr/Sp · Colour · 79min

Argentinian director Alejandro Agresti draws on his own childhood memories for this delightful tale of a eight-year-old

outsider discovering his place in a world that consistently bemuses him. Occasionally, the nuggets of insight contained in young Rodrigo Noya's narration don't chime with his presentation as a space-obsessed innocent who mooches round the backstreets of 1960s Buenos Aires torn between affection for the mother who abandoned him and loyalty towards his violent father (Agresti). But Noya's rapport with his grumbling grandmother (Carmen Maura) gives the film charm. **DP** Spanish +subtitles. *DVD*

Carmen Maura *Grandmother* • Rodrigo Noya *Valentín* • Julieta Cardinali *Leticia* • Jean Pierre Noher *Uncle Chiche* • Alejandro Agresti *Vicente, Valentín's father* ■ *Dir/Scr* Alejandro Agresti

Valentina ★★★
Romantic wartime drama 1982 · Sp · Colour · 85min

This appealing account of the making of a hero is told from a French prison camp at the end of the Spanish Civil War by a defeated Republican volunteer. Set in a small north-eastern Spanish town in 1911, it follows eight-year-old Jorge Sanz, as he is inspired in his pursuit of his pretty neighbour, Paloma Gomez, by the local priest's tales of the champions, saints and poets of days past. Drawing fine performances from both his young cast and Hollywood veteran Anthony Quinn, writer/director Antonio J Betancor bathes the action in an uplifting nostalgic glow. Betancor continued the story in *1919* (1983). **DP** Spanish dubbed.

Anthony Quinn *Mosen Joaquin* • Jorge Sanz *Jose Garces* (boy) • Paloma Gomez *Valentina* • Saturno Cerra *Don Jose* • Conchita Leza *Dona Luisa* • Alfredo Lucchetti *Don Arturo* ■ *Dir* Antonio J Betancor [Antonio Jose Betancor] • *Scr* Antonio J Betancor, Carlos Escobedo, Antonio José, Javier Moro, Lautano Murua, from the novel *Days of Dawn* by Ramon J Sender

Valentine ★ 15
Horror 2001 · US/Aus · Colour · 92min

A handful of girls who were spiteful to a schoolboy when they were young find themselves the target of a brutal killer 13 years later. This lame chiller contains all the horror clichés and dumb moves (girls wandering off on their own while a killer is on the loose) you can fit into an hour and a half, plus a handful of inexcusable plot holes. **JB** Violence, swearing. *DVD*

David Boreanaz *Adam Carr* • Denise Richards *Paige Prescott* • Marley Shelton *Kate Davies* • Katherine Heigl *Shelley* • Jessica Capshaw *Dorothy Wheeler* • Jessica Cauffiel *Lily* ■ *Dir* Jamie Blanks • *Scr* Donna Powers, Wayne Powers, Gretchen J Berg, Aaron Harberts, from a novel by Tom Savage

Valentine's Day ★★★ 12
Romantic comedy 2010 · US · Colour · 119min

A wealth of stars old and new are dovetailed into stories in director Garry Marshall's latest romantic comedy, which has a plot that looks at love from a number of different angles during a very American Valentine's Day. The movie centres on Ashton Kutcher's florist who, on the busiest day of the year, finds his love life agitated by his fiancée (Jessica Alba) and his best friend (Jennifer Garner). Julia Roberts appears as an army captain flying home for one day, while Taylor Swift is ditsy and enchanting in her debut role as the high-school sweetheart of then real-life boyfriend Taylor Lautner. Light, breezy, sentimental and amusing, *Valentine's Day* is delightful and cringe-making by turns. Marshall's all-star follow-up, *New Year's Eve*, is due at the end of 2011. **KK** Sexual references. *DVD* *BL*

Anne Hathaway *Liz* • Jessica Alba *Morley Clarkson* • Julia Roberts *Kate Hazeltine* • Taylor Lautner *Willy* • Bradley Cooper *Holden* • Ashton Kutcher *Reed Bennett* • Jessica Biel *Kara Monahan* • Jennifer Garner *Julia Fitzpatrick* • Taylor Swift *Felicia* ■ *Dir* Garry Marshall • *Scr* Katherine Fugate, from a story by Fugate, Abby Kohn, Marc Silverstein

Valentino ★★
Romantic drama 1951 · US · Colour · 104min

It probably seemed a good idea to film the life of Hollywood's most famous Latin lover, but unfortunately the tale proved impossible to cast. Newcomer Anthony Dexter was unveiled in a welter of publicity, hair brilliantined and duly parted in the middle, but unfortunately he had no personal charisma whatsoever. Despite being paired with ravishing Eleanor Parker, the screen refused to ignite. **TS**

Anthony Dexter *Rudolph Valentino* • Eleanor Parker *Joan Carlisle* • Richard Carlson *William King* • Patricia Medina *Lila Reyes* • Joseph Calleia *Luigi Verducci* • Dona Drake *Maria Torres* • Otto Kruger *Mark Towers* ■ *Dir* Lewis Allen • *Scr* George Bruce

Valentino ★★★ 18
Biographical drama 1977 · UK · Colour · 122min

Director Ken Russell seems to have approached the life story of Rudolph Valentino with no particular aim, and structures it simply as a series of flashbacks spinning out of the silent star's funeral. Much of what is depicted is probably far from the truth. Valentino's conflicts with power-crazy moguls and totally crazy actresses are irresistibly entertaining. There is also the endless fascination of watching Rudolf Nureyev (in his screen acting debut) attempt the role of the Great Lover. **DM**
DVD **BLU**

Rudolf Nureyev *Rudolph Valentino* • Leslie Caron *Alla Nazimova* • Michelle Phillips *Natasha Rambova* • Carol Kane *"Fatty"'s girl* • Felicity Kendal *June Mathis* • Seymour Cassel *George Ullman* • Peter Vaughan *Rory O'Neil* • Huntz Hall *Jesse Lasky* • Ken Russell *Rex Ingram* ■ *Dir* Ken Russell • *Scr* Ken Russell, Mardik Martin, from the book *Valentino: An Intimate Exposé of the Sheik* by Brad Steiger, Chaw Mank

Valérian and the City of a Thousand Planets
Science-fiction action adventure 2017 · Fr · Colour

This is a preview – no prints were available to review as we went to press: If nothing else, you're promised a visual feast in this comic-book sci-fi adventure from Luc Besson – the man who brought us *The Fifth Element* and, more recently, *Lucy*. Up-and-comers Dane DeHaan and Cara Delevingne are secret agents sent to keep the peace at an intergalactic city, which is home to multiple alien breeds. Time travel chaos is also thrown into the mix, so expect big action set pieces to distract you from the plot holes. **SP** **Usp**

Dane DeHaan *Valerian* • Cara Delevingne *Laureline* • John Goodman • Ethan Hawke ■ *Dir* Luc Besson • *Scr* Luc Besson, from a comic book by Pierre Christin, Jean-Claude Mézières

Valerie ★★★
Western courtroom drama 1957 · US · BW · 82min

With the ghost of *Rashomon* hovering over its approach, this mix of western and courtroom drama, although manoeuvred in and out of flashback skilfully enough by director Gerd Oswald, inevitably suffers by comparison. Sterling Hayden, a former Civil War hero and now a respected member of a ranching community, is on trial for murdering wife Anita Ekberg's parents and violently assaulting her. A curious little drama with a melodramatic and unconvincing climax, but not without interest. **RK**

Sterling Hayden *John Garth* • Anita Ekberg *Valerie* • Anthony Steel *Reverend Blake* • Peter Walker (1) *Herb Garth* • John Wengraf *Louis Horvat* • Iphigenie Castiglioni *Mrs Horvat* • Jerry Barclay *Mingo* ■ *Dir* Gerd Oswald • *Scr* Leonard Heideman, Emmett Murphy

Valerie and Her Week of Wonders ★★★ 15
Fantasy horror 1970 · Cz · Colour · 72min

Writer Angela Carter was apparently impressed by this barmy slice of fairy-tale fantasy and you can see elements of the surreal yarn in her *The Company of Wolves*. As a teenage girl is pursued by all manner of nastiness, directors such as Luis Buñuel or Ken Russell could have had a ball with the material, including incest, witch-burning and religious hypocrisy. But, somehow, the constant rush of memorably striking images, all in glistening soft-focus, makes the experience a strangely watchable one. **JA** Czech +subtitles. **DVD**

Jaroslava Schallerova *Valerie* • Helena Anyzova *Babicka/Elsa/Matka/Rusovlaska* • Petr Kopriva *Orlik* ■ *Dir* Jaromil Jires • *Scr* Jaromil Jires, Ester Krumbachova, Jiri Musil, from a novel by Vitezslav Nezval

Valhalla Rising ★★★ 15
Period action adventure 2009 · Den/UK/Nor/Fr · Colour · 88min

Nicolas Winding Refn's atmospheric action movie is a far cry from Hollywood's Viking epics, eschewing any notion of romance to present man as just one short evolutionary grunt away from the beasts. Mads Mikkelsen (*Casino Royale*) plays a mute slave who is kept chained and caged, and who is used by his captors for rudimentary gladiatorial contests. The accents and a passing reference to Sutherland reveal the initial setting to be Scotland, and from there the story sees Mikkelsen join a boatload of warriors bound for the Holy Land. The tone of the film is impressive, and the small cast, slow pace and sense of a journey into the heart of darkness are reminiscent of Werner Herzog's *Aguirre, Wrath of God*. **BP** Violence, nudity. **DVD** **BLU**

Mads Mikkelsen *One-Eye* • Jamie Sives *Gorm* • Gary Lewis *Kare* • Ewan Stewart *Eirik* • Alexander Morton *Barde* ■ *Dir* Nicolas Winding Refn • *Scr* Nicolas Winding Refn, Roy Jacobsen

The Valiant ★★★
Crime drama 1929 · US · BW · 66min

Paul Muni earned an Oscar nomination on debut for his work in this adaptation of a celebrated one-act play. The problems inherent in filming in the early sound era largely explain director William K Howard's stilted staging. But Muni surpasses these limitations in his sensitive portrayal of the drifter who conceals his true identity to avoid bringing shame on his well-to-do family after he's sentenced to death for the accidental killing of a police witness. The sequence in which he convinces mother Edith Yorke and sister Marguerite Churchill that he is a stranger is particularly affecting. **DP**

Paul Muni *James Dyke* [*Johnny Mack Brown*] • John Mack Brown *Robert Ward* • Edith Yorke *Mrs Douglas* • Richard Carlyle (1) *Chaplain* • Marguerite Churchill *Mary Douglas* • DeWitt Jennings *Warden* • Henry Kolker *Judge* ■ *Dir* William K Howard • *Scr* Tom Barry, John Hunter Booth, from the play by Robert Middlemass, Holworthy Hall

Valiant ★★ U
Animated comedy adventure 2005 · UK/US · Colour · 72min

This old-fashioned CGI adventure draws on historical fact about the crucial role played by homing pigeons during the Second World War. Valiant (voiced by Ewan McGregor) is a country wood pigeon who follows his dream to join the Royal Homing Pigeon Service. When Nazi falcon General Von Talon (Tim Curry) captures a number of his comrades, Valiant's courage is put to the test. Nothing more than technically adequate, the film never really takes off due to its clichéd, stiff-upper-lip story and lack of visual invention. **AJ** **DVD**

Ewan McGregor *Valiant* • Ricky Gervais *Bugsy* • Tim Curry *General Von Talon* • John Cleese *Mercury* • John Hurt *Felix* • Jim Broadbent *Sergeant* • Hugh Laurie *Gutsy* • Rik Mayall *Cufflingk* • Olivia Williams *Victoria* • Pip Torrens *Lofty* ■ *Dir* Gary Chapman • *Scr* Jordan Katz, George Melrod, George Webster, from a story by George Webster

Valiant Is the Word for Carrie ★★★
Melodrama 1936 · US · BW · 109min

The undervalued actress Gladys George was nominated for a best actress Oscar for her performance in this uninhibited melodrama, a quintessential four-handkerchief weepie. As the town trollop who selflessly devotes herself to caring for two orphans, George suffers with style and was unlucky to lose the Oscar to Luise Rainer for *The Great Ziegfeld*. **TV**

Gladys George *Carrie Snyder* • Arline Judge *Lady* • John Howard (1) *Paul Darnley* • Dudley Digges *Dennis Ringrose* • Harry Carey *Phil Yonne* • Isabel Jewell *Lili Eipper* ■ *Dir* Wesley Ruggles • *Scr* Claude Binyon, from the novel by Barry Benefield

Valkyrie ★★★ 12
Second World War drama based on a true story 2008 · US/Ger · Colour · 115min

In 1944 a group of disillusioned German officers led by the aristocratic Claus von Stauffenberg hatched a plot to assassinate Adolf Hitler and forge a truce with the Allies. *X-Men*'s Bryan Singer turns this footnote in German history into a predictable wartime drama, which is somewhat overwhelmed by the sheer star power of Tom Cruise and by Singer's breakneck direction. Cruise is supported by the cream of British acting talent (including Terence Stamp, Kenneth Branagh and a top-notch Bill Nighy) as his co-conspirators. However, character shading and subtlety is largely sacrificed in an attempt to ratchet up the suspense and keep the action epic. Taken as a straightforward assassination thriller though, *Valkyrie* is a reasonably satisfying effort. **AJ** **DVD** **BLU**

Tom Cruise *Claus von Stauffenberg* • Kenneth Branagh *Henning von Tresckow* • Bill Nighy *Friedrich Olbricht* • Tom Wilkinson *Friedrich Fromm* • Carice van Houten *Nina von Stauffenberg* • Thomas Kretschmann *Otto Ernst Remer* • Terence Stamp *Ludwig Beck* • Eddie Izzard *Erich Fellgiebel* • David Bamber *Adolf Hitler* ■ *Dir* Bryan Singer • *Scr* Christopher McQuarrie, Nathan Alexander

The Valley ★★★ 15
Erotic road movie 1972 · Fr · Colour · 101min

The second movie by Barbet Schroeder to use the music of Pink Floyd (the first was *More*), this hippy epic has dropout Bulle Ogier and friends travelling through New Guinea looking for a mythical Eden-like valley where they can freely indulge their alternative lifestyles. The professional actors interact with the primitive tribesmen, and even join in with their stripped-down rituals to fascinating and effect, highlighted by the trance-like Floyd score. Strangely compelling. **AJ** French +subtitles. **DVD** **BLU**

Jean-Pierre Kalfon *Gaetan* • Bulle Ogier *Viviane* • Michael Gothard *Olivier* • Valérie Lagrange *Hermine* • Jerome Beauvarlet *Yann* ■ *Dir/Scr* Barbet Schroeder

Valley Girl ★★★★ 15
Romantic comedy 1983 · US · Colour · 98min

This bright and breezy teen film features the barrier-crossing romance between an upscale San Fernando Valley suburbanite (Deborah Foreman) and an out-there Hollywood punk (the out-there Nicolas Cage). Funny, sexy and almost impossible to dislike, this is widely rated as one of the top teen romances of the 1980s. Director Martha Coolidge brings some much-needed class to the normally male-made genre. **DA**

Nicolas Cage *Randy* • Deborah Foreman *Julie* • Elizabeth Daily *Loryn* • Michael Bowen *Tommy* • Cameron Dye *Fred* • Heidi Holicker *Stacey* • Michelle Meyrink *Suzie* ■ *Dir* Martha Coolidge • *Scr* Wayne Crawford, Andrew Lane

The Valley of Decision ★★★
Period drama 1945 · US · BW · 118min

Greer Garson is the daughter of Irish steel worker Lionel Barrymore in Pittsburgh, who goes to work as a maid in the household of mill owner Donald Crisp and becomes indispensable to his family. Although loved by one of the mill owner's sons (Gregory Peck), the possibility of their marriage is thwarted by industrial strife between Barrymore and Crisp that ends in tragedy. The winning warmth of Garson won the actress her fifth consecutive Oscar nomination and Peck climbed higher in the star stakes, while the film grossed nearly $6 million on its first release. **RK**

Gregory Peck *Paul Scott* • Greer Garson *Mary Rafferty* • Donald Crisp *William Scott* • Lionel Barrymore *Pat Rafferty* • Preston Foster *Jim Brennan* • Gladys Cooper *Clarissa Scott* • Marsha Hunt *Constance Scott* • Reginald Owen *McCready* ■ *Dir* Tay Garnett • *Scr* John Meehan, Sonya Levien, from the novel by Marcia Davenport

Valley of Eagles ★★ PG
Crime drama 1951 · UK · BW · 78min

There are really three films here: a wildlife adventure, a Cold War thriller and a standard issue cop yarn complete with Jack Warner. The story concerns a boffin's wife who absconds to Lapland with her husband's invention and his assistant, played by Anthony Dawson. The husband, the policeman and two children set off in pursuit and, after being attacked by bears en route, meet the Laplanders who hunt with eagles. Ambitious for what is really a B-movie. **AT** **DVD**

Jack Warner *Inspector Petersen* • John McCallum *Dr Nils Ahlen* • Nadia Gray *Kara Niemann* • Anthony Dawson *Sven Nystrom* • Mary Laura Wood *Helga Ahlen* • Christopher Lee *First detective* ■ *Dir/Scr* Terence Young

The Valley of Gwangi ★★ U
Fantasy adventure 1969 · US · Colour · 91min

An unsuccessful touring circus encounters a forbidden valley full of prehistoric animals, and captures its massive allosaurus leader. Guess what? It escapes to terrorise the cast. A very watchable fantasy adventure, though as with other films Ray Harryhausen had a hand in, the stop-motion special effects put the flat characters and routine plot in the shade. **JG** Some violence. **DVD**

James Franciscus *Tuck Kirby* • Gila Golan *TJ Breckenridge* • Richard Carlson *Champ Connors* • Laurence Naismith *Prof Horace Bromley* • Freda Jackson *Tia Zorina* ■ *Dir* James O'Connolly [Jim O'Connolly] • *Scr* William Bast, Julian More, from the story by Willis O'Brien (uncredited)

Valley of Love ★★★ 15
Drama 2015 · Fr/Bel · Colour · 92min

The searing heat of Death Valley is the setting for this mystery drama bringing together French screen icons Gérard Depardieu and Isabelle Huppert, essentially playing themselves. True, they were never married and then divorced like the couple here, yet in what's surprisingly their first pairing since 1980's *Loulou*, they project a telling, lived-in intimacy as French parents brought together by the suicide of their son. Probably too enigmatic for some, this is still distinctive thanks to mesmerising work from the stars. **TJ** In English, French.

Isabelle Huppert *Isabelle* • Gérard Depardieu *Gérard* • Dan Warner *Paul* • Aurelia Thierrée *The woman* ■ *Dir/Scr* Guillaume Nicloux

Valley of Mystery ★
Adventure 1967 · US · Colour · 93min

This lacklustre effort contains a bunch of second division film stars trying to salvage what's left of their careers by appearing in a plane-crash drama originally made for television. Ending up in the South American jungle, the survivors are made up of familiar screen characters – has-been comedian, escaped killer, famous singer, novelist on a quest. Like the plane after the crash, it's a pile of junk though it still managed to get a cinema release. **JA**

Richard Egan *Wade Cochran* • Peter Graves (2) *Ben Barstow* • Joby Baker *Pete Patton* • Lois Nettleton *Rita Brown* • Harry Guardino *Danny O'Neill* • Julie Adams *Joan Simon* • Fernando Lamas *Fidel Rivera* ■ *Dir* Joseph Leytes • *Scr* Richard Neal, Lowell Barrington, from a story by Lawrence B Marcus, Richard Neal

Valley of Song ★★ U

Comedy 1953 · UK · BW · 71min

War breaks out among a bickering group of Welsh choristers preparing for a major concert in this engaging little comedy, scripted by Phil Park and Cliff Gordon from the latter's radio play. There's no Harry Secombe but look out for Rachel Roberts and Kenneth Williams in early roles. JF **DVD**

Mervyn Johns *Minister Griffiths* • Clifford Evans *Geraint Llewellyn* • Maureen Swanson *Olwen Davies* • John Fraser *Cliff Lloyd* • Rachel Thomas *Mrs Lloyd* • Betty Cooper *Mrs Davies* • Rachel Roberts (1) *Bessie Lewis* • Hugh Pryse *Lloyd, the undertaker* • Edward Evans *Davies, the shopkeeper* • Kenneth Williams *Lloyd, the haulage man* ■ *Dir* Gilbert Gunn • *Scr* Cliff Gordon, Phil Park, from the radio play *Choir Practice* by Gordon

Valley of the Dolls ★★★★ 15

Melodrama 1967 · US · Colour · 118min

Based on Jacqueline Susann's landmark mega-bestseller, this rags-to-bitches exposé of how Broadway singer Patty Duke, sex starlet Sharon Tate and demure model Barbara Parkins claw their way to Hollywood success on the boozy, pill-popping fame express heading for inevitable derailment is one of the all-time great, and most beloved, trash movies. Every backstabbing line is a classic and every glitzy showbiz second is an over-the-top hyper-cliché in director Mark Robson's fabulously camp extravaganza. AJ **DVD**

Barbara Parkins *Anne Welles* • Patty Duke *Neely O'Hara* • Sharon Tate *Jennifer North* • Paul Burke *Lyon Burke* • Tony Scotti *Tony Polar* • Martin Milner *Mel Anderson* • Charles Drake *Kevin Gilmore* • Alexander Davion *Ted Casablanca* • Lee Grant *Miriam* • Susan Hayward *Helen Lawson* • Jacqueline Susann *Reporter* ■ *Dir* Mark Robson • *Scr* Helen Deutsch, Dorothy Kingsley, from the novel by Jacqueline Susann

Valley of the Kings ★★ U

Romantic adventure 1954 · US · Colour · 85min

Apart from the majestic musical score by Miklos Rozsa, there's not much to recommend this archaeological adventure. Set in 1900, Robert Taylor is the rough, tough treasure hunter who's persuaded by old flame Eleanor Parker to go on an expedition to the ancient tombs of Egypt. Of course, feelings are rekindled but Parker is now married to Carlos Thompson. Into this romantic mix can be added a band of tomb robbers and some attractive locations but that's all there is to this tomb with a view. TH

Robert Taylor (1) *Mark Brandon* • Eleanor Parker *Ann Mercedes* • Carlos Thompson *Philip Mercedes* • Kurt Kasznar *Hamed Bachkour* • Victor Jory *Taureg chief* • Leon Askin *Valentine Arko* ■ *Dir* Robert Pirosh • *Scr* Robert Pirosh, Karl Tunberg, from the book *Gods, Graves and Scholars* by CW Ceram

Valley of the Sun ★★ U

Western 1942 · US · BW · 78min

Director George Marshall, who had made a great job of combining the conventions of comedy with those of the western in *Destry Rides Again*, was hauled in to repeat the trick here but clearly mislaid his magic wand. The story concerns rivalry and conflict between army scout James Craig and nasty Indian agent Dean Jagger, both after Lucille Ball. The former also objects to the latter's treatment of the Indians. Violent action and imbecilic farce fail to mix here. RK

Lucille Ball *Christine Larson* • James Craig *Jonathan Ware* • Sir Cedric Hardwicke [Cedric Hardwicke] *Warrick* • Dean Jagger *Jim Sawyer* • Tom Tyler *Geronimo* • Antonio Moreno *Chief Cochise* ■ *Dir* George Marshall • *Scr* Horace McCoy, from a story by Clarence Budington Kelland

Valmont ★★★★ 15

Period drama 1989 · Fr/UK · Colour · 136min

Coming hot on the heels of *Dangerous Liaisons*, this opulent reworking of the notorious Choderlos de Laclos novel plays on the emotions in the same way that Stephen Frears's film teased the intellect. Director Milos Forman is more concerned with the perils of pursuing your desires than in the machinations of the indolent and, consequently, the characters take as much pleasure in the act of seduction as in its art. It's impossible to resist comparing the two productions, but while Frears's is truer to the calculating spirit of the book and has the showier cast, Forman's has greater human interest and the more heartfelt performances. DP

Colin Firth *Vicomte de Valmont* • Annette Bening *Marquise de Merteuil* • Meg Tilly *Madame de Tourvel* • Fairuza Balk *Cécile de Volanges* • Sian Phillips *Madame de Volanges* • Jeffrey Jones *Gercourt* • Henry Thomas *Danceny* • Fabia Drake *Madame de Rosemonde* • TP McKenna *Baron* • Isla Blair *Baroness* ■ *Dir* Milos Forman • *Scr* Jean-Claude Carrière, from the novel *Les Liaisons Dangereuses* by Choderlos de Laclos

Les Valseuses ★★★★ 18

Drama 1974 · Fr · Colour · 112min

Bertrand Blier's often shocking film was named after the French slang word for "testicles". As the grotesque, joy-riding delinquents who tend to think with that part of their anatomy, Gérard Depardieu and Patrick Dewaere are the personification of ignorance, indulgence and insensitivity. Their sexual encounters with newly sprung jailbird Jeanne Moreau and drifting thrill-seeker Miou-Miou manage to be both repellent and compelling. But the film loses its bite after Depardieu and Dewaere go on the run, although the sequence with a young Isabelle Huppert has a dark fascination. DP French +subtitles. **DVD**

Gérard Depardieu *Jean-Claude* • Patrick Dewaere *Pierrot* • Miou-Miou *Marie-Ange* • Jeanne Moreau *Jeanne* • Jacques Chailieux *Jacques* • Michel Peyrelon *Surgeon* • Brigitte Fossey *Young mother* • Isabelle Huppert *Jacqueline* ■ *Dir* Bertrand Blier • *Scr* Bertrand Blier, Philippe Dumarcay, from the novel by Bertrand Blier

Value for Money ★★

Comedy 1955 · UK · Colour · 93min

Take one bluff, penny-wise Yorkshireman and a blowsy, blonde showgirl, exaggerate every regional characteristic and then whisk them together into a romantic froth. Season with a couple of quaint cameos and you have this. The on-screen antics of John Gregson and Diana Dors (neither of whom are on form) are mediocre in this featherweight comedy. DP

John Gregson *Chayley Broadbent* • Diana Dors *Ruthine West* • Susan Stephen *Ethel* • Derek Farr *Duke Popplewell* • Frank Pettingell *Higgins* • Jill Adams *Joy* • Charles Victor *Lumm* • James Gregson *Oldroyd* • Ernest Thesiger *Lord Dewsbury* • Donald Pleasence *Limpy* ■ *Dir* Ken Annakin • *Scr* RF Delderfield, William Fairchild, from Derrick Boothroyd's novel

Vamp ★★ 18

Horror comedy 1986 · US · Colour · 90min

Grace Jones oozes animal sexuality and danger as the sensual vampire of the title, but even she can't save this botched attempt to mix *Animal House* laughs with kinky horror. Chris Makepeace and Robert Rusler are the college students who stumble upon a den of strippers with serious dental problems, but the one good gag is lifted directly from the far superior *An American Werewolf in London*. JF **DVD** **BD**

Grace Jones *Katrina* • Chris Makepeace *Keith* • Robert Rusler *AJ* • Sandy Baron *Vic* • Dedee Pfeiffer *Amaretto* • Gedde Watanabe *Duncan* ■ *Dir* Richard Wenk • *Scr* Richard Wenk, from a story by Donald P Borchers, Wenk

Vampira ★★ 15

Comedy horror 1975 · UK · Colour · 84min

David Niven dons the cloak of Dracula in this long-in-the-tooth vampire comedy well past its Swinging Sixties sell-by-date. The Count, who has turned his castle into a Playboy-style tourist resort, is searching for a rare blood type donor to revive his wife Vampira. The stale gag is that she's eventually reincarnated as black babe Teresa Graves. Niven adds a touch of class to the ridiculously old-fashioned proceedings and is the only reason for watching this dire farce from director Clive Donner. AJ

David Niven *Count Dracula* • Teresa Graves *Countess Vampira* • Peter Bayliss *Maltravers* • Jennie Linden *Angela* • Nicky Henson *Marc* • Linda Hayden *Helga* ■ *Dir* Clive Donner • *Scr* Jeremy Lloyd

The Vampire Bat ★ PG

Horror 1933 · US · BW · 60min

A series of small-town murders turn out to be the work of scientist Lionel Atwill who drains his victims of blood in order to nourish a flesh parasite he has created. A standard-issue mad doctor tale, it was evidently made to cash-in on the success of Universal's *Dracula* with frightened Fay Wray and hero Melvyn Douglas lending limp support to the hopelessly outdated proceedings. AJ

Lionel Atwill *Dr Otto von Niemann* • Fay Wray *Ruth Bertin* • Melvyn Douglas *Karl Brettschneider* • Maude Eburne *Gussie Schnappmann* • George E Stone *Kringen* • Dwight Frye *Herman Gleib* ■ *Dir* Frank R Strayer • *Scr* Edward T Lowe

Vampire Circus ★★★ 18

Horror 1971 · UK · Colour · 83min

This isn't the freak show its title might suggest, but a fast-moving, imaginative Hammer vampire tale of punishment and revenge. It's set in an isolated plague-ridden town in 19th-century central Europe that welcomes the arrival of a circus, until the vampire count's revenge becomes clear. Adrienne Corri's intense beauty shines like a beacon in the murky atmosphere, but the delicacy of mood collapses into blood-spurting horrifics towards the end. TH **DVD**

Adrienne Corri *Gypsy woman* • Laurence Payne *Professor Mueller* • Thorley Walters *Burgermeister* • John Moulder-Brown *Anton Kersh* • Lynne Frederick *Dora Mueller* ■ *Dir* Robert William Young [Robert Young (2)] • *Scr* Judson Kinberg, from a story by George Baxt, Wilbur Stark

Vampire Hunter D ★★★ 15

Animated science-fiction horror 1985 · Jpn · Colour · 80min

This is an adventurous *manga* melange of JRR Tolkien, Sergio Leone, Hammer horror and mainstream sci-fi. Far off in the 13th millennium, D is hired by village beauty Doris to save her from Count Magnus Lee's clutches. Having sampled her jugular, the ancient giant now wants Doris for his bride and D must infiltrate his mountain fortress in order to halt his plans. Director Toyoo Ashida uses a wildly eclectic palate of styles and astonishing depth to achieve his helter-skelter imagery in one of the best Japanese cartoons in the *Akira* tradition. AJ Japanese dubbed. Violence. **DVD**

■ *Dir* Toyoo Ashida, Carl Macek • *Scr* Yasuhi Hirano

Vampire in Brooklyn ★★★ 15

Horror 1995 · US · Colour · 97min

Eddie Murphy's streetwise persona is often at odds here with director Wes Craven's more explicit, doom-laden beastliness, and the intended comedy becomes lost in the horror. Murphy stars as suave vampire Maximillian, a master of disguise, who comes to America to find his soulmate – cop Angela Bassett, who is unaware that she is Murphy's bride-to-be. There are some good moments, but too often Craven puts on the frighteners so heavily that the chuckles get squeezed out. TH **DVD**

Eddie Murphy *Maximillian/Preacher Pauley/Guido* • Angela Bassett *Rita* • Allen Payne *Justice* • Kadeem Hardison *Julius* • John Witherspoon *Silas* • Zakes Mokae *Dr Zeko* • Joanna Cassidy *Dewey* • Simbi Khali *Nikki* ■ *Dir* Wes Craven • *Scr* Charles [Charlie] Murphy, Christopher Parker, Michael Lucker, from a story by Charles and Eddie Murphy, Vernon Lynch Jr

Vampire in Venice ★★ 18

Horror 1987 · It · Colour · 89min

Returning to the role of Dracula, Klaus Kinski is here confronted with vampire hunter Christopher Plummer as he wearily inducts a princess and her eager sister into the ranks of the undead. Kinski gives a demonstration of melancholic malevolence that is every bit as impressive as his performance in Werner Herzog's *Nosferatu*. But Augusto Caminito relies too much on Venetian splendour and close-ups of Kinski's eyes to conjure up atmosphere and the result is languor, not horror. DP Italian dubbed. Violence, sexual content.

Klaus Kinski *Nosferatu* • Barbara De Rossi *Helietta Canins* • Christopher Plummer *Paris Catalano* • Yorgo Voyagis *Giuseppe Barnabo* • Clara Colosimo *Medium* • Maria C Cumani *Matilde Canins* • Donald Pleasence *Don Alvise* ■ *Dir* Augusto Caminito • *Scr* Augusto Caminito, Leandro Lucchetti, from a story by Alberto Alfieri

The Vampire Lovers ★★ 15

Horror 1970 · UK · Colour · 90min

The first of Hammer's three Karnstein chillers (based on Sheridan LeFanu's *Carmilla*) is an atmospheric and erotic undead tale detailing the life of lesbian vampire Mircalla, voluptuously played by Ingrid Pitt. Peter Cushing lends a greater credibility to the sensuality-heavy production than the repetitious script warrants. Inventive direction by Roy Ward Baker conspires to make this brazenly exploitative horror hokum better than it deserves to be. *Lust for a Vampire* and *Twins of Evil* followed. AJ **DVD** **BD**

Ingrid Pitt *Mircalla/Marcilla/Carmilla Karnstein* • Peter Cushing *General Spielsdorf* • Madeline Smith *Emma* • Jon Finch *Carl* • Pippa Steele *Laura Spielsdorf* • George Cole *Morton* • Dawn Addams *Countess* • Douglas Wilmer *Baron Hartog* • Kate O'Mara *Mme Perrodot* • Ferdy Mayne *Doctor* ■ *Dir* Roy Ward Baker • *Scr* Tudor Gates, from the story *Carmilla* by J Sheridan Le Fanu, adapted by Harry Fine, Michael Style

Vampires ★★★ 18

Horror 1998 · US · Colour · 107min

James Woods gives a wonderfully laconic performance as a vampire slayer on the Vatican payroll in director John Carpenter's rip-roaring western horror flick. Woods is out to destroy a 600-year-old bloodsucker before the evil creature gets his hands on an ancient relic that will enable him to appear during daylight hours. Carpenter laces the suspense and splatter with agreeable humour and arty special effects, and there's smart support from Sheryl Lee as the psychic link to the undead leader. Followed in 2001 by a sequel, *Vampires: los Muertos*. AJ Violence, sex scenes. **DVD**

James Woods *Jack Crow* • Daniel Baldwin *Montoya* • Sheryl Lee *Katrina* • Thomas Ian Griffith *Valek* • Maximilian Schell *Cardinal Alba* • Tim Guinee *Father Adam Guiteau* • Mark Boone Junior *Catlin* • Gregory Sierra *Father Giovanni* ■ *Dir* John Carpenter • *Scr* Don Jakoby, from the novel by John Steakley • *Cinematographer* Gary B Kibbe

Vampires in Havana ★★

Animated horror comedy 1985 · Cub · Colour · 80min

Vampirism is equated to the Mafia in a delightfully stylised if sometimes crudely drawn Cuban cartoon feature combining Hammer horror, gangster movies, James Bond and Latin American history. Professor Von Dracula and his nephew Joseph Amadeus become the focus of a war between the undead of Chicago and Düsseldorf, thanks to Vampisol, a sun-block drug that allows vampires to walk around in daylight. Light-hearted fun with little political comment. AJ Spanish +subtitles.

■ *Dir/Scr* Juan Padron

Vampire's Kiss ★ 18

Horror comedy 1988 · US · Colour · 99min

Yuppie Nicolas Cage gets bitten by sexy vampire Jennifer Beals, but when he doesn't turn into a vampire, he fakes it and becomes a mixed-up psycho wearing plastic fangs and prowling discos for victims. Falling between horror comedy and a serious study of mental illness, director Robert Bierman's farrago is hideously unfunny, witless and offensively stupid. AJ Violence. DVD

Nicolas Cage *Peter Loew* • Maria Conchita Alonso *Alva Restrepo* • Jennifer Beals *Rachel* • Elizabeth Ashley *Dr Glaser* • Kasi Lemmons *Jackie* • Bob Lujan *Emilio* • Jessica Lundy *Sharon* • John Walker *Donald* ■ *Dir* Robert Bierman • *Scr* Joseph Minion

Vampires: los Muertos

★★ 18

Horror   2002 · US · Colour · 89min

An insipid Jon Bon Jovi swaps soft rock for slaying in this weak, straight-to-video sequel to John Carpenter's 1998 action horror *Vampires*. Heading a ragtag team that includes pumped-up priest Cristian De La Fuente and an annoying, bitten-though-still-human Natasha Gregson Wagner, he's out to stake the devious bloodsucker (*Blade's* Arly Jover) who's causing carnage in Mexico. Unconvincing performances compound the unimaginative plotting, with Jover in particular lacking the seductiveness and malevolence that her pivotal role requires. SF DVD

Jon Bon Jovi *Derek Bliss* • Cristian De La Fuente [Christian De La Fuente] *Father Rodrigo* • Natasha Wagner [Natasha Gregson Wagner] *Zoey* • Arly Jover *Una* • Darius McCrary *Ray Collins* • Diego Luna *Sancho* ■ *Dir/Scr* Tommy Lee Wallace

Vampires Suck

★★ 15

Comedy spoof   2010 · US · Colour · 78min

The men behind *Date Movie* and *Meet the Spartans* are behind this spoof on the *Twilight* series. While it is spot-on with its costumes, set design and characters, the script is erratic and barely humorous, while Jason Friedberg and Aaron Seltzer's direction is patchy, to say the least. Jenn Proske does an uncanny take of *Twilight's* Bella Swann, and Matt Lanter has the ability to be both amusing and alluring as vampire Edward Sullen, but the high production values are wasted. KK Violence, swearing, sexual references. DVD BL

Matt Lanter *Edward Sullen* • Jenn Proske *Becca Crane* • Christopher N Riggi [Chris Riggi] *Jacob White* • Ken Jeong *Daro* ■ *Dir/Scr* Jason Friedberg, Aaron Seltzer

Vamps

★★ 15

Comedy horror   2012 · US · Colour · 88min

Nearly two decades after *Clueless*, Alicia Silverstone and director Amy Heckerling attempt to recapture that old magic. Sadly, despite some winning gags and perky performances, this supernatural comedy lacks the same bite. Silverstone and Krysten Ritter play best friends who happen to be vampires and feed only on rats' blood, but their cosy lifestyle is threatened when Ritter falls for the son of vampire hunter Van Helsing. The gentle quirkiness here feels too tame to make a lasting impression. JF DVD

Alicia Silverstone *Goody* • Krysten Ritter *Stacy* • Dan Stevens *Joey* • Sigourney Weaver *Cisserus* • Malcolm McDowell *Vlad Tepish* ■ *Dir/Scr* Amy Heckerling

Vampyr

★★★★★ PG

Horror   1932 · Fr/Ger · BW · 62min

Based on *Carmilla*, Carl Th Dreyer's hypnotic psychological chiller also borrows from other stories contained in J Sheridan Le Fanu's collection, *In a Glass Darkly*. The film's visual ethereality was an accident caused by the fogging of a lens, but the dream-like structure (with its shifting perspectives, unexpected juxtapositions and defiance of logic) was a conscious attempt to keep the viewer disorientated. Shot on location in France, this was Dreyer's first talkie, although dialogue was subordinate to the way his eerily poetic, almost erotic, imagery probes the links between good and evil, imagination and reality, faith and the supernatural. A singular masterwork. DO German +subtitles. DVD

Julian West *David Gray* • Maurice Schutz *Lord of the Manor* • Rena Mandel *Gisèle* • Sybille Schmitz *Léone* • Jan Hieronimko *Village doctor* • Henriette Gérard *Marguerite Chopin* • Albert Bras *Old servant* ■ *Dir* Carl Th Dreyer • *Scr* Carl Th

Dreyer, Christen Jul, from the story *Carmilla* by J Sheridan Le Fanu • *Cinematographers* Rudolph Maté, Louis Née

Vampyros Lesbos

★ 18

Cult erotic horror
1970 · Sp/W Ger · Colour · 85min

Maverick Spanish film-maker Jesus Franco strikes out again with this abysmal erotic horror. The count's descendant Soledad Miranda entices women via striptease dreams to her isolated Mediterranean island so she can suck their blood and live for ever. To Franco lovers, this one's a surreal melancholic poem about vampire loneliness. It will strike everyone else as nothing more than a slow, trivial and irritating slice of sleazy "Horrotica". AJ German +subtitles. DVD

Soledad Miranda *Countess Nadine Carody* • Dennis Price *Dr Alwin Seward* • Paul Muller *Dr Steiner* • Ewa Stromberg *Linda Westinghouse* ■ *Dir* Franco Manera [Jesus Franco] • *Scr* Jesus Franco, Jaime Chavarri, from their story

The Van

★★ 15

Comedy drama   1996 · Ire/UK · Colour · 95min

It's been a case of diminishing returns as far as the cinematic adaptations of Roddy Doyle's Barrytown trilogy are concerned. Following the soulful success of Alan Parker's *The Commitments*, Stephen Frears struggled to bring much bite to *The Snapper*, and in this concluding episode he never gets out of first gear. The flashes of the Republic of Ireland's achievements at the 1990 World Cup are wonderfully evocative, but the tale of unemployed scalliwags Colm Meaney and Donal O'Kelly feels forced. DP Swearing.

Colm Meaney *Larry* • Donal O'Kelly *Bimbo* • Ger Ryan *Maggie* • Caroline Rothwell *Mary* • Neili Conroy *Diane* • Ruaidhri Conroy *Kevin* • Brendan O'Carroll *Weslie* • Stuart Dunne *Sam* ■ *Dir* Stephen Frears • *Scr* Roddy Doyle, from his novel

Van Gogh

★★★★ 15

Biographical drama   1991 · Fr · Colour · 151min

Maurice Pialat's superbly photographed account of Van Gogh's last few months is by far the most compelling of the number of films about the tortured artist. Creating the atmosphere of Auvers-sur-Oise with great care, he builds up his portrait through a wealth of tiny details. Gaunt, withdrawn and acting on impulses that are terrifying in their suddenness and ferocity, Jacques Dutronc is magnificent in the title role, whether ranting against his brother Theo, seeking consolation in women or drink, or simply painting. DP French +subtitles. DVD BL

Jacques Dutronc *Vincent van Gogh* • Alexandra London *Marguerite Gachet* • Gérard Séty *Doctor Gachet* • Bernard Le Coq *Theo van Gogh* • Corinne Bourdon *Jo* • Elsa Zylberstein *Cathy* ■ *Dir/Scr* Maurice Pialat • *Cinematographers* Gilles Henry, Emmanuel Machuel

Van Helsing

★★★ 12

Action fantasy horror
2004 · US · Colour · 126min

Writer/director Stephen Sommers delivers an exciting, effects-driven romp that combines the pulling power of Dracula, the Wolf Man and Frankenstein's Monster. Gabriel Van Helsing (Hugh Jackman) is dispatched by a secret, Vatican-based organisation to 19th-century Transylvania where he comes to the aid of Kate Beckinsale in her long-running battle against the vampire Count and his evil allies. The CGI could have been better – as could the dialogue – but viewed solely as escapism, this is an exhilarating ride. SF Violence. DVD BL

Hugh Jackman *Gabriel Van Helsing* • Kate Beckinsale *Anna Valerious* • Richard Roxburgh *Count Dracula* • David Wenham *Carl* • Shuler Hensley *Frankenstein's Monster* • Elena Anaya *Aleera* • Kevin J O'Connor *Igor* • Will Kemp *Velkan Valerious* • Alun Armstrong *Cardinal Jinette* • Samuel West *Dr Victor Frankenstein* ■ *Dir/Scr* Stephen Sommers

Van Wilder: Party Liaison

★ 15

Comedy   2002 · US/Ger · Colour · 88min

A spiritless melting pot of fratboy high jinks and syrupy sentimentality, director Walt Becker's first film doesn't seem to know whether it's a cheeky romance or a moralistic farce. This tale of world-shy student Van Wilder (Ryan Reynolds), who will do anything to maintain his indefinite college stay, is a pitiful failure. SF Swearing, drug abuse, sex scenes. DVD

Ryan Reynolds *Van Wilder* • Tara Reid *Gwen Pearson* • Tim Matheson *Vance Wilder Sr* • Kal Penn *Taj Mahal Badalandabad* • Teck Holmes *Hutch* • Daniel Cosgrove *Richard Bagg* ■ *Dir* Walt Becker • *Scr* Brent Goldberg, David T Wagner

Vanessa, Her Love Story ★

Melodrama   1935 · US · BW · 74min

Unaware that her husband is suffering from inherited insanity, unhappily married Helen Hayes takes a lover (Robert Montgomery), who later loses an arm while on military duty with the British army in Egypt. Although the film features a quality supporting cast, this is a really deathly soap opera that belongs on the bottom of the heap. RK

Helen Hayes *Vanessa* • Robert Montgomery *Benjie* • Otto Kruger *Ellis* • May Robson *Judith* • Lewis Stone *Adam* • Henry Stephenson *Barney* • Violet Kemble-Cooper *Lady Herries* ■ *Dir* William K Howard • *Scr* Lenore Coffee, Hugh Walpole, from the novel by Walpole

Vanilla Sky

★★ 15

Romantic fantasy thriller
2001 · US · Colour · 130min

Writer/director Cameron's Crowe's disappointing remake of Alejandro Amenábar's off-kilter Spanish thriller *Open Your Eyes* makes the fatal error of jettisoning the original's potent psychological suspense. Crowe has turned a disquieting and disorientating murder mystery into a superficial showcase for star Tom Cruise. There's no chemistry between Cruise and Penélope Cruz (reprising her role from the original), and both look uncomfortable. JC Violence, swearing, sex scenes, nudity. DVD

Tom Cruise *David Aames* • Penélope Cruz *Sofia Serrano* • Cameron Diaz *Julie Gianni* • Kurt Russell *McCabe* • Jason Lee *Brian Shelby* • Noah Taylor *Edmund Ventura* • Timothy Spall *Thomas Tipp* • Tilda Swinton *Rebecca Dearborn* • Alicia Witt *Libby* ■ *Dir* Cameron Crowe • *Scr* Cameron Crowe, from the film *Abre los ojos (Open Your Eyes)* by Alejandro Amenábar, Mateo Gil

Vanished without a Trace

★★★ PG

Drama based on a true story
1993 · US · Colour · 89min

When it comes to TV movies based on true stories, Hollywood relishes the chance to exploit the unsettling and horrid goings-on in the trim gardens of small-town America. Here, a rather imaginative kidnapping involving 26 children, their bus driver and three rich-kid criminals causes ructions in the setting of Chowchilla, California. The suspense is ably sustained by director Vern Gillum, and Karl Malden, as the driver, enlivens the proceedings with his trademark mix of doggedness and decency. JM DVD

Karl Malden *Edward Ray* • Tim Ransom *Fred Woods IV* • Travis Fine *Rick Schoenfeld* • Tom Hodges *Jim Schoenfeld* • Julie Harris (2) *Odessa Ray* • Bobby Zameroski *Tim Pearson* ■ *Dir* Vern Gillum • *Scr* David Eyre Jr, from the book *Why Have They Taken Our Children* by Jack W Baugh, Jefferson Morgan

The Vanishing

★★★★ 15

Psychological thriller
1988 · Neth/Fr · Colour · 101min

George Sluizer's chilling tale of premeditation, abduction and obsession stars Bernard-Pierre Donnadieu as the unassuming family man infatuated with the perfect kidnap. He emerges as one of the screen's most chilling, calculating and conceited psychopaths, and the quiet satisfaction with which he explains his

technique to the victim's boyfriend, Gene Bervoets, is unnerving in the extreme. From the moment we realise Johanna Ter Steege is in danger to the final shocking twist, Sluizer inexorably and expertly draws us deeper into the mystery, exposing our own morbid curiosity in the process. DP Dutch, French +subtitles. Violence. DVD

Bernard-Pierre Donnadieu *Raymond Lemorne* • Gene Bervoets *Rex Hofman* • Johanna Ter Steege *Saskia Wagter* • Gwen Eckhaus *Lienexe* • Simone Lemorne [Bernadette Le Saché] *Simone Lemorne* • Tania Latarjet *Denise* ■ *Dir* George Sluizer • *Scr* Tim Krabbé, George Sluizer (adaptation), from the novel *The Golden Egg* by Tim Krabbé

The Vanishing

★★ 15

Thriller   1993 · US · Colour · 105min

George Sluizer directs this Hollywood remake of his outstanding original European version. Kiefer Sutherland is the troubled holidaymaker whose girlfriend vanishes without a trace at a service station. His obsessive search for her leads him to eccentric teacher Jeff Bridges. Sluizer fails to sustain the icy air of menace of the first film, and the movie is further unhinged by a bizarre, over-the-top performance from the normally reliable Bridges. JF Swearing, violence. DVD

Jeff Bridges *Barney Cousins* • Kiefer Sutherland *Jeff Harriman* • Nancy Travis *Rita Baker* • Sandra Bullock *Diane Shaver* • Park Overall *Lynn* • Maggie Linderman *Denise Cousins* • Lisa Eichhorn *Helene* • George Hearn *Arthur Bernard* ■ *Dir* George Sluizer • *Scr* Todd Graff, from the novel *The Golden Egg* by Tim Krabbé

The Vanishing Corporal

★★★★ PG

Second World War comedy drama
1962 · Fr · BW · 101min

Jean-Pierre Cassel is the vanishing corporal, a prisoner of war who dedicates himself to escape, but all his attempts fail and he is sent to detention camps for punishment. Finally, he and his buddy (Claude Brasseur) get back to Paris where they vow to join the Resistance. Set in a German PoW camp, like his masterpiece *La Grande Illusion*, though this time in the Second World War, Jean Renoir approaches the subject as comedy but he manages to suggest the grimmer reality beneath the surface. RB In French. DVD

Jean-Pierre Cassel *The Corporal* • Claude Brasseur *Dad* • Claude Rich *Ballochet* • Jean Carmet *Emile* • Jacques Jouanneau *Penche à gauche* • Conny Froboess [Cornelia Froboess] *Erika* ■ *Dir* Jean Renoir • *Scr* Jean Renoir, Guy Lefranc, from the novel *Le Caporal Epinglé* by Jacques Perret

Vanishing of the Bees

★★★ U

Documentary   2009 · US/UK · Colour · 96min

Taking an impassioned look at the effect of colony collapse disorder (CCD) on beekeepers in the US and abroad, this film interviews the Pennsylvania apiarist who brought the mysterious bee disappearances to the attention of the scientific community. With a look at the bees' place in history and their key pollination role in agriculture today, this is more an entertaining and moving love letter to the honeybee than a serious scientific study of the reasons behind CCD. SuR DVD

Emilia Fox *Narrator* ■ *Dir* George Langworthy, Maryam Henein

Vanishing Point

★★★ 18

Cult road movie   1971 · US · Colour · 94min

Car delivery boy Barry Newman takes a bet that he can't drive a Dodge Challenger from Denver to San Francisco in 15 hours in this gritty cult road movie. Newman switches on the ignition, puts his foot down and, stopping only for fuel (petrol for the Dodge, amphetamines for him), follows in the wake of *Easy Rider* and sets out to be a similar essay in alienation, but has little of that film's low-budget magic. AT DVD BL

Barry Newman *Kowalski* • Cleavon Little *Super Soul* • Dean Jagger *Prospector* • Victoria Medlin *Vera* • Paul Koslo *Young cop* • Robert Donner

Older cop ■ *Dir* Richard C Sarafian · *Scr* Guillermo Cain, from a story outline by Malcolm Hart

The Vanishing Virginian ★★★ U

Biographical comedy drama
1941 · US · BW · 96min

Life in the happy and comfortably off family of dedicated public prosecutor, husband and father of five Robert Yancey (Frank Morgan), as lived down South between 1918 and 1929 is the subject of this affectionate drama. Fewer spoonfuls of sugar would have helped this somewhat rambling exercise in nostalgia, but it's a good-hearted, well-characterised and enjoyable excursion into an era when the mere idea of votes for women was enough to cause consternation. Newcomer Kathryn Grayson gets to exercise her vocal chords with a handful of songs. RK

Frank Morgan *Robert "Cap'n Bob" Yancey* · Kathryn Grayson *Rebecca Yancey* · Spring Byington *Rosa Yancey* · Natalie Thompson *Margaret Yancey* · Douglass Newland *Jim Shirley* · Mark Daniels *Jack Holden* · Louise Beavers *Aunt Emmeline Preston* ■ *Dir* Frank Borzage · *Scr* Jan Fortune, from the biography by Rebecca Yancey Williams

Vanity Fair ★★★ PG

Period comedy drama
2004 · US/UK · Colour · 135min

It can't have been easy condensing William Makepeace Thackeray's sprawling, dense novel into a movie. Small wonder, then, that Mira Nair's film is a little lacking in linear plot, being more a series of bitty scenes than a coherent narrative. But there's still much to admire in this nicely written and handsomely mounted adaptation. Reese Witherspoon is good as Becky Sharp, Thackeray's calculating, ambitious heroine. James Purefoy, as the gambler she marries during her no-holds-barred bid for a better life, stands out in a starry supporting cast. DA *DVD*

Reese Witherspoon *Becky Sharp* · Eileen Atkins *Miss Matilda Crawley* · Jim Broadbent *Mr Osborne* · Gabriel Byrne *The Marquess of Steyne* · Romola Garai *Amelia Sedley* · Bob Hoskins *Sir Pitt Crawley* · Rhys Ifans *William Dobbin* · Geraldine McEwan *Lady Southdown* · James Purefoy *Rawdon Crawley* · Jonathan Rhys Meyers *George Osborne* ■ *Dir* Mira Nair · *Scr* Matthew Faulk, Mark Skeet, Julian Fellowes, from the novel by William Makepeace Thackeray

The Vanquished ★★★ U

Portmanteau drama
1953 · It · BW · 86min

This collection of stories explores the moral turpitude of postwar Europe. In the opening episode, French pupils kill a classmate for cash; an Italian college student becomes involved with the black market in the second, while an English poet seeks to profit from the death of an apparently respectable woman in the third. Censorship problems dogged the picture, but Michelangelo Antonioni's genius for linking the inner self and environment is well established. DP In Italian.

Jean-Pierre Mocky *Pierre* · Etchika Choureau *Simone* · Franco Interlenghi *Claudio* · Anna-Maria Ferrero *Marina* · Evi Maltagliati *Claudio's Mother* · Eduardo Ciannell *Claudio's Father* · Peter Reynolds *Aubrey* · Fay Compton *Mrs Pinkerton* · Patrick Barr *Kent Watton* ■ *Dir* Michelangelo Antonioni · *Scr* Michelangelo Antonioni, Suso Cecchi D'Amico, Giorgio Bassani, Diego Fabbri, Turi Vasile, Roger Nimier

Vantage Point ★★ 12

Thriller
2008 · US · Colour · 86min

When US President Ashton (William Hurt) arrives in Salamanca, Spain, for a historic summit on terrorism, everyone is on high alert. Yet, as violence erupts, none of his staff could have predicted what unfolds in this risible thriller that's told from the differing viewpoints of eight characters. They include two Secret Service agents (Dennis Quaid and Matthew Fox), a TV producer (Sigourney Weaver) who thinks she caught the suspect on film, and a tourist (Forest Whitaker) with a video camera who saw more than he realises.

Director Pete Travis (terrorist drama *Omagh*) aims for a post-9/11 *Rashomon* but delivers a surprisingly silly thriller that's full of ridiculous plot twists. JR English, Spanish +subtitles. Some violence, brief swearing. *DVD* Blu-ray

Dennis Quaid *Thomas Barnes* · Matthew Fox *Kent Taylor* · Forest Whitaker *Howard Lewis* · Edgar Ramirez *Javier* · Ayelet Zurer *Veronica* · Sigourney Weaver *Rex Brooks* · William Hurt *President Ashton* · Saïd Taghmaoui *Suarez* ■ *Dir* Pete Travis · *Scr* Barry L Levy [Barry Levy] · *Cinematographer* Amir Mokri

Vanya on 42nd Street ★★★ U

Drama
1994 · US · Colour · 115min

Three directors on different continents took on Anton Chekhov's *Uncle Vanya* within the space of two years. Michael Blakemore staged his version of the play *Country Life* in the Australian outback, while Anthony Hopkins located his interpretation called *August* in North Wales. But only Louis Malle could have thought of setting the play in a dilapidated New York theatre, with the action being performed by a rehearsing cast sitting around a table in their day clothes. Wallace Shawn is excellent in the title role, but, while Malle's approach allows us to concentrate on the text and offers an insight into the acting process, his final film marks a slightly disappointing end to an exceptional career. DP

Wallace Shawn *Vanya* · Julianne Moore *Yelena* · Andre Gregory · George Gaynes *Serebryakov* · Brooke Smith *Sonya* · Larry Pine *Dr Astrov* · Phoebe Brand *Nanny* · Lynn Cohen *Maman* · Jerry Mayer *Waffles* · Madhur Jaffrey *Mrs Chao* ■ *Dir* Louis Malle · *Scr* David Mamet, from the play *Uncle Vanya* by Anton Chekhov

Varian's War ★★★

Wartime drama based on a true story
2000 · Can/US/UK · Colour · 122min

This is an earnest, if unquestioning made-for-TV tribute to a selfless individual who risked all to counter the effects of the Holocaust. Having failed to alert Americans to the imminent plight of European Jews, journalist Varian Fry returned to France during the early days of the war with the aim of rescuing some of the continent's leading intellectuals. William Hurt and Julia Ormond perform admirably. DP

William Hurt *Varian Fry* · Julia Ormond *Miriam* · Matt Craven *Beamish* · Maury Chaykin *Marcello* · Alan Arkin *Freier* · Lynn Redgrave *Alma Werfel-Mahler* ■ *Dir/Scr* Lionel Chetwynd

Variety Girl ★★ U

Comedy musical
1947 · US · BW and Colour · 86min

This is yet another entry in the seemingly interminable string of studio star cavalcades of which Paramount seemed to be particularly fond. The characteristic non-plot has two hopefuls (Mary Hatcher, Olga San Juan) arriving at the studio in search of a future. Here, they encounter a starry roster of names. RK

Mary Hatcher *Catherine Brown Variety Sheridan* · Olga San Juan *Amber La Vonne* · DeForest Kelley *Bob Kirby* · Bing Crosby · Bob Hope · Gary Cooper · Ray Milland · Alan Ladd · Barbara Stanwyck · Paulette Goddard · Dorothy Lamour · Sonny Tufts · William Holden (2) ■ *Dir* George Marshall · *Scr* Edmund Hartmann [Edmund L Hartmann], Frank Tashlin, Robert Welch, Monte Brice

Variety Jubilee ★★★ U

Musical
1942 · UK · BW · 92min

This simple, nostalgic tribute to the British music hall tradition begins with two former variety artists who become partners in running a vaudeville venue at the dawn of the 20th century. One of their sons is then killed in the First World War, before a grandson takes over the family enterprise and makes it a success again. The film consists largely of musical variety acts performed by numerous forgotten old-timers of a bygone era. Wonderful! RK

Reginald Purdell *Joe Swan* · Ellis Irving *Kit Burns* · Lesley Brook *Evelyn Vincent* · Marie Lloyd Jr *Marie Lloyd* · Tom E Finglass *Eugene Stratton* · John Rorke *Gus Elen* · Betty Warren *Florrie*

Forde · Charles Coborn ■ *Dir* Maclean Rogers · *Scr* Kathleen Butler, from a story by Mabel Constanduros

Varsity Blues ★★★ 15

Comedy drama
1999 · US · Colour · 104min

James Van Der Beek is the high-school football player who challenges the authority of his control-freak coach Jon Voight (giving another hilariously over-the-top performance) when he becomes the team's star quarterback. This teenage drama is basically a 1990s throwback to 1980s sports movies such as *Youngblood* and *All the Right Moves* with the usual mix of sports action, drinking and girls and the odd moral tale thrown in. Predictable stuff. JB Swearing, nudity.

James Van Der Beek *Jonathan "Mox" Moxon* · Jon Voight *Coach Bud Kilmer* · Paul Walker *Lance Harbor* · Ron Lester *Billy Bob* · Scott Caan *Tweeter* · Richard Lineback *Joe Harbor* · Tiffany C Love *Collette Harbor* ■ *Dir* Brian Robbins · *Scr* W Peter Iliff

Vassa ★★★★ PG

Drama
1983 · USSR · Colour · 136min

Gleb Panfilov directed Maxim Gorky's play as a vehicle for his wife Inna Churikova and depicts her as the last bastion of strength in a morass of corruption, indolence and perversion. Her husband is charged with child molestation, her drunken brother is accused of impregnating the maid, her daughters are insane and nymphomaniac, and then her detested daughter-in-law arrives with news of her son's terminal illness. It's soap operatic, but the pre-Revolutionary trappings are sumptuous. DP Russian +subtitles.

Inna Churikova *Vassa Zheleznova* · Vadim Medvedev *Sergei* · Nikolai Skorobogatov *Prokhor, Vassa's brother* · Valentina Telichkina *Anna, Vassa's secretary* · Valentina Yakunina *Rachel* ■ *Dir* Gleb Panfilov · *Scr* Gleb Panfilov, from the play *Vassa Zheleznova* by Maxim Gorky

Vatel ★★

Period comedy drama
2000 · Fr/US · Colour · 117min

All the ingredients seem right – a screenplay co-written by Tom Stoppard, an Ennio Morricone score and Gérard Depardieu as François Vatel, the backstreet urchin whose culinary expertise and genius for baroque entertainments enchanted the court of Louis XIV. But under Roland Joffé's undistinguished direction, what emerges is a disappointing romp, where sexual and political intrigue intersperse with misfiring spectacle and inconsequential banter. DP

Gérard Depardieu *François Vatel* · Uma Thurman *Anne de Montausier* · Tim Roth *Marquis de Lauzun* · Julian Glover *Prince de Conde* · Julian Sands *King Louis XIV* · Timothy Spall *Gourville* ■ *Dir* Roland Joffé · *Scr* Jeanne Labrune, Tom Stoppard (English adaptation)

The Vatican Tapes ★★ 15

Supernatural horror
2015 · US · Colour · 87min

Crank co-director Mark Neveldine flies solo for the first time (from regular partner Brian Taylor) with this serviceable if derivative tale of demonic possession. Olivia Taylor Dudley (*Chernobyl Diaries*, *Paranormal Activity: the Ghost Dimension*) stars as the wide-eyed innocent, whose life goes awry after a car accident puts her in a coma for 40 days. Local Catholic priest Michael Peña suspects something supernatural is brewing. Neveldine is blessed with a decent budget and cast, but his movie too often points towards better movies that have more devilish thrills. This is just too tame to terrify. JA Violence, swearing, sexual references. *DVD*

Olivia Taylor Dudley [Olivia Dudley] *Angela* · Michael Peña [Michael Pena] *Father Lozano* · Dougray Scott *Roger Holmes* · Djimon Hounsou *Vicar Imani* · Peter Andersson *Cardinal Mattias Bruun* ■ *Dir* Mark Neveldine · *Scr* Christopher Borrelli, Michael C Martin, from a story by Borrelli, Chris Morgan

Vaudeville ★★★★

Silent melodrama
1925 · Ger · BW · 57min

EA Dupont was handed this assignment after producer Erich Pommer felt FW Murnau was approaching it with too little enthusiasm. However, the dazzling display of visual artistry that transformed this otherwise humdrum showbiz melodrama was fashioned not by the director, but by his cinematographer Karl Freund. His bravura use of chiaroscuro lighting, subjective camera, overlapping dissolves and expressionist montage is quite masterly and demonstrates the pictorial sublimity of silent cinema. The story of the trapeze artist who murders his rival in love was much butchered for its US release to remove its moral ambiguities, although both versions have their merits. DP

Emil Jannings *Boss Huller* · Lya de Putti *Bertha-Marie* · Warwick Ward *Artinelli* · Charles Lincoln *Actor* ■ *Dir* EA Dupont · *Scr* EA Dupont, Leo Birinksi, from the novel *Der Eid des Stephan Huller* by Felix Holländer

The Vault of Horror ★★★ 15

Portmanteau horror
1973 · UK · Colour · 83min

Five men trapped in a mysterious basement room following a trip in a lift tell each other their recurring nightmares in this ghoulish companion piece to *Tales from the Crypt*. Based on another terror title from EC comics, the fiendish anthology features vampires, voodoo and grave-robbers in stories with such titles as *This Trick'll Kill You*. The cast has a touch of class, too, with a pre-*Doctor Who* Tom Baker as a vengeful painter and Terry-Thomas and Glynis Johns in a tale of domestic bliss that goes savagely and horribly wrong. If you like your fright fables darkly droll, then this will do the trick. JA *DVD*

Daniel Massey *Rogers* · Anna Massey *Donna* · Terry-Thomas *Critchit* · Glynis Johns *Eleanor* · Marianne Stone *Jane* · Curt Jurgens *Sebastian* · Dawn Addams *Inez* · Michael Craig *Maitland* · Edward Judd *Alex* · Tom Baker *Alex Moore* · Denholm Elliott *Diltant* ■ *Dir* Roy Ward Baker · *Scr* Milton Subotsky, from the comic magazines *The Vault of Horror* and *Tales from the Crypt* by Al Feldstein, William Gaines

Veer-Zaara ★★★★ U

Epic romantic drama
2004 · Ind · Colour · 192min

Yash Chopra's politically hard-hitting romantic drama stars Bollywood's alternative to Tom Cruise, Shahrukh Khan. It's a big, stylish and deeply enjoyable melodrama that uses an unlikely romance to tackle the continuing cross-border conflict between India and Pakistan. Khan plays a principled rescue pilot with the Indian air force who becomes obsessed with Preity Zinta, a provincial Pakistani girl he befriends after a bus accident strands her in India. Khan is suitably heroic, while Zinta gives a persuasive portrayal of a complex woman. OA Hindi, Urdu, Punjabi +subtitles. *DVD*

Shahrukh Khan [Shah Rukh Khan] *Veer Pratap Singh* · Preity Zinta *Zaara Hayaat Khan* · Rani Mukerji [Rani Mukherji] *Saamiya Siddiqui* · Amitabh Bachchan *Mr Singh* ■ *Dir* Yash Chopra · *Scr* Aditya Chopra

Vegas Vacation ★★ PG

Comedy
1997 · US · Colour · 90min

The hapless Chevy Chase and long-suffering wife Beverly D'Angelo head for Las Vegas and get mixed up in a series of unamusing misadventures, in yet another *National Lampoon* venture. Randy Quaid, as Chase's trailer trash cousin, fares the best, but laughs are pretty much thin on the ground. Not even a talented supporting cast (Wallace Shawn, Sid Caesar) can do much to rescue this. JF *DVD*

Chevy Chase *Clark W Griswold* · Beverly D'Angelo *Ellen Griswold* · Randy Quaid *Cousin Eddie* · Ethan Embry *Rusty Griswold* · Marisol Nichols *Audrey Griswold* · Wayne Newton ■ *Dir* Stephen Kessler · *Scr* Elisa Bell, from a story by Bob Ducsay

V

Vehicle 19 ★★★ 12
Thriller 2013 · US · Colour · 81min

The Fast and the Furious star Paul Walker is back behind the wheel for this man-on-the-run thriller. Shot entirely within the confines of a rental car, the story follows Walker's American ex-con as he arrives in Johannesburg to patch things up with his ex-partner. But he's the wrong man in the wrong place at the wrong time, as the vehicle he hires involves him in kidnapping and police corruption, making him a wanted man. The novel conceit of shooting the whole film from inside an automobile is certainly intriguing and adds to the pressure-cooker nature of the story. Short, taut and with decent car chases, Michael Mukunda Dewil's film proves that low budget doesn't always mean low quality. JA
Violence, swearing. DVD BL

Paul Walker *Michael Woods* • Naima McLean *Rachel Shabangu* • Gys de Villiers *Detective Smith* • Leyla Haidarian *Angelica Moore* ■ *Dir/Scr* Mukunda Michael Dewil

The Velocity of Gary ★★ 15
Drama 1998 · US · Colour · 96min

Exploring the critical issue of sexual responsibility in the Aids era, James Still's play is translated to the screen with calculating theatricality by director Dan Ireland. The set-up itself is highly contrived, as country boy Thomas Jane arrives in the big city and intrudes upon bisexual porn star Vincent D'Onofrio's on-off relationship with mouthy doughnut waitress Salma Hayek. The melodramatics are enacted at such a furious pitch, particularly by a near-hysterical Hayek, that the story has already passed several emotional peaks before the real revelations begin. DP DVD

Vincent D'Onofrio *Valentino* • Salma Hayek *Mary Carmen* • Thomas Jane *Gary* • Olivia D'Abo *Veronica* • Chad Lindberg *Kid Joey* • Lucky Luciano *The King* ■ *Dir* Dan Ireland • *Scr* James Still, from his play *The Velocity of Gary (Not His Real Name)*

Velvet Goldmine ★★ 15
Drama 1998 · UK/US · Colour · 118min

Todd Haynes is an imaginative and original director, and he employs both these qualities here but, sadly, they fail to make this mishmash of a movie work. Ewan McGregor and Jonathan Rhys Meyers star as a couple of cultish singers over-indulging on sex, drugs and rock'n'roll, and failing to make their lives function. It looks great and has tons of atmosphere, but this is a soulless, unstructured piece of film-making. LH Swearing, nudity, sex scenes, violence. DVD

Ewan McGregor *Curt Wild* • Jonathan Rhys Meyers *Brian Slade* • Toni Collette *Mandy Slade* • Christian Bale *Arthur Stuart* • Eddie Izzard *Jerry Devine* • Emily Woof *Shannon* • Janet McTeer *Female narrator* ■ *Dir* Todd Haynes • *Scr* Todd Haynes, from a story by James Lyons, Todd Haynes

The Velvet Touch ★★ PG
Crime drama 1948 · US · BW · 96min

Rosalind Russell and her husband, producer Frederick Brisson played safe with this mechanical and lifeless melodrama, for which she specially hired top cinematographer Joseph Walker to ensure she looked her best in dresses by Travis Banton. She plays the Broadway star who kills her former lover in an argument and lets another actress, take the blame. AE
DVD

Rosalind Russell *Valerie Stanton* • Leo Genn *Michael Morrell* • Claire Trevor *Marion Webster* • Sydney Greenstreet *Captain Danbury* • Leon Ames *Gordon Dunning* • Frank McHugh *Ernie Boyle* • Walter Kingsford *Peter Gunther* • Dan Tobin *Jeff Trent* • Lex Barker *Paul Banton* ■ *Dir* John Gage • *Scr* Leo Rosten, Walter Reilly, from a story by William Mercer, from a story by Annabel Ross

Vendetta ★★ 18
Action thriller 2013 · UK · Colour · 101min

Danny Dyer returns to London after going AWOL from the Royal Marines in Afghanistan to track down the vicious gang who immolated his parents in their own garage. It's easy to dismiss Brit-crime movies for their Mockney clichés and caricatures, but although this is packed with plenty of both, it also exhibits a grim efficiency, as Dyer uses his killer instincts to dispatch his foes. The vigilante slayings have a cheap horror gimmickiness to them, while the action lacks menace and macabre wit. But Dyer is credibly lethal and Reynolds makes solid use of his urban locales. DP
Violence, swearing, sex scenes, drug abuse. DVD

Danny Dyer *Jimmy Vickers* • Josef Altin *Rob* • Roxanne McKee *Morgan* • Alistair Petrie *DCI Spencer Holland* • Bruce Payne *Rooker* • Tony Denham *George Vickers* • Emma Samms *Sandra Vickers* ■ *Dir/Scr* Stephen Reynolds (2)

Vendredi Soir ★★★★ 15
Drama 2002 · Fr · Colour · 85min

Both an unconventional love story and a piercing study of urban dislocation, this chance encounter on a chilly Parisian night says a good deal about modern society with the minimum of dialogue. Whether in the snarled traffic that compounds Valérie Lemercier's doubts about committing to her partner or the spartan hotel room where her tentative relationship with hitcher Vincent Lindon develops into liberating passion, director Claire Denis and cinematographer Agnès Godard capture character and emotion with the utmost discretion. But it's the impressionistic use of hazy lights and jumbled sounds to re-create the trappings and pitfalls of city life that most impresses. DP French +subtitles.
Swearing, sex scenes. DVD

Valérie Lemercier *Laure* • Vincent Lindon *Jean* • Hélène de Saint Père *Marie* • Hélène Fillières *Woman in pizzeria* • Florence Loiret Caille *Girl playing pinball* • Grégoire Colin *Passer-by in parka* ■ *Dir* Claire Denis • *Scr* Emmanuèle Bernheim, Claire Denis, from the novel by Emmanuèle Bernheim

The Venetian Affair ★★
Spy thriller 1966 · US · Colour · 92min

Evidently made by MGM to cash in on the popularity of Robert Vaughn in *The Man from UNCLE*, this thriller is a gritty exploration of the murky world of espionage. Vaughn is an ex-agent who's brought in from the cold to investigate the death of a diplomat at a Venetian peace conference. The involvement of Elke Sommer – his ex-wife and the reason he was sacked in the first place – only complicates matters further. An unremarkable affair apart from a welcome bit of menace from Boris Karloff. TH

Robert Vaughn (1) *Bill Fenner* • Elke Sommer *Sandra Fane* • Felicia Farr *Claire Connor* • Karlheinz Böhm *Robert Wahl* • Luciana Paluzzi *Giulia Almeranti* • Boris Karloff *Dr Pierre Vaugiroud* • Roger C Carmel *Mike Ballard* • Edward Asner *Frank Rosenfeld* ■ *Dir* Jerry Thorpe • *Scr* E Jack Neuman, from the novel by Helen MacInnes

Venetian Bird ★★ PG
Crime drama 1952 · UK · BW · 91min

Borrowing liberally from *The Third Man*, this is a tolerable time-passer, although a little lightweight in the suspense department. Director Ralph Thomas offers some pretty postcard views of Venice, but he only fully exploits this fascinating location during the ingenious final chase sequence, which culminates in a Hitchcockian use of a famous landmark. Richard Todd is below par as the detective dispatched to uncover information about an air-raid victim who might be a war hero, a master criminal or both. DP DVD

Richard Todd *Edward Mercer* • Eva Bartok *Adriana* • John Gregson *Cassana* • George Coulouris *Spadoni* • Margot Grahame *Rosa Melitus* • Walter Rilla *Count Boria* • Sidney James *Bernardo* ■ *Dir* Ralph Thomas • *Scr* Victor Canning, from his novel

Vengeance ★ 15
Spaghetti western 1968 · It/W Ger · Colour · 96min

Years after Clint Eastwood had hung up his holsters and ridden back to his home turf, the Italians were still cranking out spaghetti westerns and this is the usual mix of bad dubbing, stylish visuals and violence. Director Antonio Margheriti (here working under the name Anthony Dawson) has since cashed in on all the big movie trends: when the westerns dried up, he concentrated on horror. JF Italian dubbed.

Richard Harrison *Joko* • Claudio Camaso *Mendoza* • Werner Pochath *Riky* • Paolo Gozlino *Domingo* • Guido Lollobrigida *Lee Burton* ■ *Dir* Anthony Dawson [Antonio Margheriti] • *Scr* Antonio Margheriti, Renato Savino

Vengeance Is Mine ★★★ 18
Biographical crime drama 1979 · Jpn · Colour · 140min

A constant sense of uneasiness pervades this crime drama, based on the true story of Iwao Enokizu (Ken Ogata), a Japanese serial killer who went on a murder and robbery spree lasting over two months. Director Shohei Imamura offers no easy explanations (if any) for Enokizu's actions, simply showing his life and actions. The film also highlights aspects of the Japanese psyche – citizens are seen recognising the wanted Enokizu, but doing nothing. Less successful are the interludes focusing on supporting characters, which seem both distracting and pointless. KB Japanese +subtitles. DVD BL

Ken Ogata *Iwao Enokizu* • Rentaro Mikuni *Shizuo Enokizu* • Chocho Mikayo *Kayo Enokizu* • Mitsuko Baisho *Kazuko Enokizu* ■ *Dir* Shohei Imamura • *Scr* Masaru Baba, from a book by Ryuzo Saki

The Vengeance of Fu Manchu ★★ PG
Crime drama 1967 · UK/W Ger/HK/Ire · Colour · 87min

The inscrutable Oriental arch villain forces a surgeon to create a killer clone of his Scotland Yard nemesis, Nayland Smith, in the third Fu Manchu tale starring Christopher Lee. Don Sharp's light direction in the original *The Face of Fu Manchu* is sorely missed here, and director Jeremy Summers half-heartedly trys to patch a lacklustre affair together out of plodding material. AJ DVD

Christopher Lee *Fu Manchu* • Tony Ferrer *Inspector Ramos* • Tsai Chin *Lin Tang* • Douglas Wilmer *Nayland Smith* • Wolfgang Kieling *Dr Lieberson* • Suzanne Roquette *Maria Lieberson* • Howard Marion-Crawford *Dr Petrie* ■ *Dir* Jeremy Summers • *Scr* Peter Welbeck [Harry Alan Towers], from characters by Sax Rohmer

The Vengeance of She ★★ PG
Fantasy adventure 1968 · UK · Colour · 96min

Czechoslovakian beauty Olinka Berova is taken for the reincarnation of novelist H Rider Haggard's Ayesha (as immortalised by Ursula Andress) in this mediocre sequel to *She* (1965). Director Cliff Owen piles on the close-ups of Berova in a Lost City fantasy adventure with reliable Hammer production values and colourful exotica. AJ DVD

John Richardson *King Killikrates* • Olinka Berova [Olga Schoberova] *Carol* • Edward Judd *Philip Smith* • Colin Blakely *George Carter* • Derek Godfrey *Men-Hari* • Jill Melford *Sheila Carter* • George Sewell *Harry Walker* ■ *Dir* Cliff Owen • *Scr* Peter O'Donnell, from characters by H Rider Haggard

Vengeance Valley ★★★ PG
Western 1951 · US · Colour · 82min

In this decent psychological western, Burt Lancaster plays a rancher's adopted son who always takes the rap for his foster-brother, played by snivelling, sneering Robert Walker. A woman comes between them – gets pregnant – and we're into Eugene O'Neill territory or a Wild West spin on Cain and Abel, nicely shot in the Rocky Mountains. AT DVD

Burt Lancaster *Owen Daybright* • Robert Walker *Lee Strobie* • Joanne Dru *Jen Strobie* • Ray Collins *Arch Strobie* • Sally Forrest *Lily Fasken* • John Ireland *Hub Fasken* • Hugh O'Brian *Dick Fasken* • Carleton Carpenter *Hewie* ■ *Dir* Richard Thorpe • *Scr* Irving Ravetch, from the novel by Luke Short

Venice/Venice ★
Comedy drama 1992 · US · Colour · 108min

This is an exasperating and self-indulgent exercise from director Henry Jaglom. After taking his latest movie to Venice, Italy, for the annual film festival and baring his soul to journalists (while being annoyingly ignored by John Landis, his friend on the critics' jury), it's back to Venice, California, for some embarrassing sexual guru posturing. Nothing more than an elaborate home movie and, despite some scathing showbiz truths and a neat turn by David Duchovny (as the star of Jaglom's festival offering), just as intolerable to watch. AJ

Nelly Alard *Jeanne* • Henry Jaglom *Dean* • Suzanne Bertish *Carlotta* • Daphna Kastner *Eve* • David Duchovny *Dylan* • Suzanne Lanza *Dylan's girlfriend* • Vernon Dobtcheff *Alexander* • John Landis ■ *Dir/Scr* Henry Jaglom

Venom ★★★ 15
Thriller 1981 · UK · Colour · 88min

This ridiculously enjoyable thriller looks as though it was dreamed up during an extremely drunken weekend. Kidnappers plus child (with asthma) are holed up in a house, together with (for reasons not worth going into) a deadly black mamba snake. The script may be weak in places, but be prepared to shriek when the serpent slithers up wicked Oliver Reed's trouser leg. DM Violence, swearing. DVD

Klaus Kinski *Jacmel* • Oliver Reed *Dave* • Nicol Williamson *Commander William Bulloch* • Sarah Miles *Dr Marion Stowe* • Sterling Hayden *Howard Anderson* • Cornelia Sharpe *Ruth Hopkins* • Lance Holcomb *Philip Hopkins* • Susan George *Louise* ■ *Dir* Piers Haggard • *Scr* Robert Carrington, from the novel by Alan Scholefield

Le Vent de la Nuit ★★★
Romantic drama 1999 · Fr · Colour · 95min

Desire, doubt and disillusion dominate this intense character study from the underrated Philippe Garrel. Art student Xavier Beauvois vacillates between an unsatisfactory liaison with a possessive housewife and a dream job with a celebrated architect Daniel Duval. Catherine Deneuve gives a brittle performance as the mistress racked by fears that Beauvois is only interested in her money. However, she is matched all the way by Duval's blend of professionalism and pain, as he remains haunted by both his wife's suicide and the electroshock therapy he endured after his participation in the 1968 Paris riots. DP French +subtitles.

Catherine Deneuve *Hélène* • Daniel Duval *Serge* • Xavier Beauvois *Paul* • Jacques Lasalle *Hélène's husband* ■ *Dir* Philippe Garrel • *Scr* Xavier Beauvois, Marc Cholodenko, Arlette Lagmann

Vent d'Est ★★★
Political documentary drama 1969 · Fr/It/W Ger · Colour · 92min

Hailed as the first Marxist western, this is the fourth of the six anti-movies that Jean-Luc Godard made under the auspices of the Dziga-Vertov Group. He sought to bring down what he considered to be the crumbling edifice of traditional filmic language by constructing a political argument out of pure sounds and images. However, as this resolutely non-narrative essay reveals, the very act of articulating a statement or creating an impression is impossible without betraying a degree of subjectivity. DP French +subtitles.

Gian Maria Volonté *Soldier* • Anne Wiazemsky *Whore* ■ *Dir* Jean-Luc Godard • *Scr* Jean-Luc Godard, Daniel Cohn-Bendit

Venus ★★★ 15
Romantic comedy drama 2006 · UK/US · Colour · 90min

Peter O'Toole leaps off the screen (arthritic knees and all) as a septuagenarian rebel without a cause in this whimsical tale from *Notting Hill* director Roger Michell. O'Toole stars as Maurice Russell, an ageing actor who's reduced to playing corpses on TV hospital dramas, and who spends his spare time with fellow veteran thespian Ian (an endearing Leslie Phillips). But when Maurice

U SUITABLE FOR ALL Uc SUITABLE ESPECIALLY FOR YOUNG CHILDREN (DVD ONLY) PG PARENTAL GUIDANCE 12A UNDER 12s TO BE ACCOMPANIED (CINEMA ONLY)

meets Ian's parochial but pretty grandniece Jessie (the amusingly brash Jodie Whittaker), a complex relationship develops. O'Toole and Phillips's early scenes are brilliantly funny, but sadly the story eventually bows to the conventions of melodrama. SP Swearing. **DVD**

Peter O'Toole *Maurice Russell* • Leslie Phillips *Ian* • Jodie Whittaker *Jessie* • Richard Griffiths *Donald* • Vanessa Redgrave *Valerie* ■ *Dir* Roger Michell • *Scr* Hanif Kureishi

Venus and Serena ★★★ 12A
Sports documentary   2012 · US · Colour · 99min

This fly-on-the-wall portrait of the all-conquering Williams sisters goes on and off the court for an intimate if straightforward exploration of the dominant force in female tennis for a generation. The African-American siblings are front and centre of an absorbing rags-to-riches tale about talented athletes who overcome illness, injury, scepticism and personal tragedy to become the outstanding sportswomen of their age. They are refreshingly frank and outspoken, particularly younger sister Serena, and though the film does meander on occasion, it's still a useful reflection on two players who have changed the game of tennis. JA Swearing.

Venus Williams • Serena Williams • Anna Wintour • Billie Jean King • John McEnroe ■ *Dir* Maiken Baird, Michelle Major

Venus Beauty Institute
★★★ 15
Comedy drama   1998 · Fr · Colour · 106min

Nathalie Baye is a beautician who seeks casual sex to numb the sense of loneliness she feels when not working at prudish Bulle Ogier's Paris salon. But, while Baye's brittle performance holds the film together, the eccentric collection of clients and co-workers adds intrigue to Tonie Marshall's disarmingly frank study of modern woman and what she'll do to remain true to her self-image. DP French +subtitles. Swearing, nudity.

Nathalie Baye *Angèle Piana* • Bulle Ogier *Nadine* • Samuel LeBihan [Samuel Le Bihan] *Antoine Dumont* • Jacques Bonnaffé *Jacques* • Mathilde Seigner *Samantha* • Audrey Tautou *Marie* ■ *Dir* Tonie Marshall • *Scr* Tonie Marshall, Jacques Audiard, Marion Vernoux

Venus in Fur ★★★ 15
Drama   2013 · Fr/Pol · Colour · 91min

David Ives's hit play is the basis for Roman Polanski's psychodrama exploring the gender politics of dominance and submission. On a claustrophobic theatre stage, an unknown actress (Emmanuelle Seigner, Mrs Polanski, in an ultra showy turn) arrives late to audition for an adaptation of Sacher-Masoch's 1870 novel *Venus in Furs*. This is similar to his other stage transfer *Death and the Maiden*, but it's the uneven shifts in tone and perspective that Polanski can't quite capture, making everything feel flatter than it should. AJ French +subtitles. **DVD** **BD**

Emmanuelle Seigner *Vanda* • Mathieu Amalric *Thomas* ■ *Dir* Roman Polanski • *Scr* Roman Polanski, from David Ives's play *Venus in Fur*, from the novel *Venus in Furs* by Leopold von Sacher-Masoch

Venus Peter ★★ 12
Drama   1989 · UK · Colour · 92min

After many fine performances, Ray McAnally deserved a more distinguished swan song than this muddled piece of mysticism and malarkey. This view of Orkneys' life in the late 1940s brims o'er with eccentric characters and meaningless dialogue. Debuting director Ian Sellar throws in some haunting seascapes, but little of interest happens to disturb the flow of words. DP Nudity.

Ray McAnally *Grandfather* • David Hayman *Kinnear* • Sinead Cusack *Miss Balsilbie* • Gordon R Strachan *Peter* • Sam Hayman *Baby Peter* • Caroline Paterson *Mother* • Alex McAvoy *Beadle* ■ *Dir* Ian Sellar • *Scr* Ian Sellar, Christopher Rush from the book *A Twelvemonth and a Day* by Christopher Rush

Vera Cruz ★★★★ PG
Western   1954 · US · Colour · 89min

Gary Cooper headlines but co-star Burt Lancaster is the man to watch in this terrific Mexico-set western in which a former Confederate soldier and an outlaw join forces to escort a shipment of gold. Produced by Lancaster's own company, it's directed by Robert Aldrich, who would collaborate out west once more with Lancaster in *Ulzana's Raid*. The movie has a rattling pace (thanks to editor Alan Crosland Jr) and a fine sense of style that's hard to top, plus a great supporting cast. TS **DVD** **BD**

Gary Cooper *Benjamin Trane* • Burt Lancaster *Joe Erin* • Denise Darcel *Countess Marie Duvarre* • Cesar Romero *Marquis de Labordere* • Sarita Montiel *Nina* • George Macready *Emperor Maximilian* • Ernest Borgnine *Donnegan* • Morris Ankrum *General Aguilar* • Henry Brandon *Danette* • Charles Buchinsky [Charles Bronson] *Pittsburgh* ■ *Dir* Robert Aldrich • *Scr* Roland Kibbee, James R Webb, from the story by Borden Chase

Vera Drake ★★★★ 12
Period drama   2004 · UK/Fr · Colour · 119min

Set in the repressed and repressive Britain of 1950, director Mike Leigh's drama hinges on a stunning lead performance from Imelda Staunton. She plays an altruistic but naive cleaning lady who secretly helps out unfortunate girls by performing backstreet abortions. But when her actions are discovered, the law reprimands her severely. Staunton is nothing less than superb; equally fine are the support performances, plus Leigh's impeccable re-creation of both place and period. If there's one small criticism to be made of the film, it's perhaps a touch too relentlessly dark and dour. Otherwise, this is as good, if as grim, as it gets. DA **DVD**

Imelda Staunton *Vera Drake* • Phil Davis [Philip Davis] *Stan Drake* • Peter Wight *Det Inspector Webster* • Adrian Scarborough *Frank* • Heather Craney *Joyce* • Daniel Mays *Sid Drake* • Alex Kelly *Ethel Drake* • Sally Hawkins *Susan Wells* • Eddie Marsan *Reg* • Ruth Sheen *Lily* • Helen Coker *WPC Best* ■ *Dir/Scr* Mike Leigh

Verboten! ★★ PG
Thriller   1959 · US · BW · 86min

This high-flown melodrama is much beloved by fans of maverick director Samuel Fuller, though other viewers may think it's hardly worth passing the time of day with. James Best brings dignity to a rare leading role as the GI uncovering a neo-Nazi conspiracy in postwar Germany, but Susan Cummings is woefully inadequate as his romantic interest. There's a naive subtext that's either quite disturbing, or enjoyable, depending on your point of view. TS

James Best *Sgt David Brent* • Susan Cummings *Helga Schiller* • Tom Pittman *Bruno Eckart* • Paul Dubov *Capt Harvey* • Harold Daye *Franz Schiller* • Dick Kallman *Helmuth* ■ *Dir/Scr* Samuel Fuller

The Verdict ★★★
Crime mystery   1946 · US · BW · 86min

Dirty Harry director Don Siegel's first feature marked the last reteaming of Sydney Greenstreet and Peter Lorre, the dynamic duo from *The Maltese Falcon*, where Scotland Yard superintendent Greenstreet is forced to resign, only to become embroiled in another murder case. A little dusty maybe, but still enjoyable. AJ

Sydney Greenstreet *George Edward Grodman* • Peter Lorre *Victor Emmric* • Joan Lorring *Lottie* • George Coulouris *Superintendent Buckley* • Rosalind Ivan *Mrs Benson* • Paul Cavanagh *Clive Russell* • Arthur Shields *Reverend Holbrook* • Morton Lowry *Arthur Kendall* ■ *Dir* Don Siegel • *Scr* Peter Milne, from the novel *The Big Bow Mystery* by Israel Zangwill

Verdict ★★★
Courtroom thriller   1974 · Fr/It · Colour · 97min

In his penultimate picture, the great Jean Gabin gives a typically gutsy performance as a judge whose diabetic wife is abducted by a besotted mother, determined to have her student son acquitted when he's charged with rape and murder. Less sure-

footed is Sophia Loren, who overdoes the eye-rolling as the kidnapper, and director André Cayatte also betrays his limitations in the scenes outside the courtroom. DP French +subtitles. Violence.

Sophia Loren *Térésa Léoni* • Jean Gabin *Président Leguen* • Henri Garcin *Maître Lannelonge* • Julien Bertheau *Advocate General Verlac* • Michel Albertini *André Léoni* • Gisèle Casadesus *Nicole Leguen* • Muriel Catala *Annie Chartier* ■ *Dir* André Cayatte • *Scr* André Cayatte, Henri Coupon, Pierre Dumayet, Paul Andreota

The Verdict ★★★ 15
Courtroom drama   1982 · US · Colour · 123min

This is a return to court for Sidney Lumet, director of the masterly *12 Angry Men*. Paul Newman was widely (and wrongly) tipped to win his first Oscar for his portrayal of an alcoholic lawyer on the skids, who fights to redeem himself when a medical malpractice case pits him against the power of the Catholic Church. Scripted by David Mamet, it's a compelling, if wordy, piece, rooted in liberalism and stubbornly refusing to deliver the promised fireworks. Charlotte Rampling and James Mason are in the fine supporting cast. AT Swearing. **DVD**

Paul Newman *Frank Galvin* • Charlotte Rampling *Laura Fischer* • Jack Warden *Mickey Morrissey* • James Mason *Ed Concannon* • Milo O'Shea *Judge Hoyle* • Lindsay Crouse *Kaitlin Costello Price* • Edward Binns *Bishop Brophy* ■ *Dir* Sidney Lumet • *Scr* David Mamet, from the novel by Barry Reed

La Vérité ★★★
Thriller   1960 · Fr/It · BW · 125min

Henri-Georges Clouzot had a reputation as one of the darkest French film-makers, but here he strays into the courtroom territory usually associated with André Cayatte and rather loses his way in a maze of flashbacks. Brigitte Bardot digs deep into her acting resources as the young girl accused of murdering her sister's trendy boyfriend, but, although she breezes through certain scenes, it's hard to escape the suspicion that the role is beyond her talents. DP French +subtitles.

Brigitte Bardot *Dominique Marceau* • Charles Vanel *Maître Guerin, defence attorney* • Paul Meurisse *Eparvier, prosecuting attorney* • Sami Frey *Gilbert Tellier* • Marie-José Nat *Annie Marceau* • Louis Seigner *President of the Court* ■ *Dir* Henri-Georges Clouzot • *Scr* Henri-Georges Clouzot, Simone Drieu, Michèle Perrein, Jérôme Géronimi, Christiane Rochefort, Simone Marescat, Vera Clouzot

Verity's Summer ★★
Drama   2012 · UK · Colour

With his feature film debut, writer/director Ben Crowe shows great ambition, but his reach exceeds his grasp in trying to examine a wide range of social issues through the eyes of sulkily precocious teenager Verity (Indea Barbe-Willson). She falls for a Polish cabby (Cristi Hogas) while her academic mother (Nicola Wright) and policeman father (James Doherty) bicker about his involvement with a homeless war veteran (Martin McGlade). Although the views of the Northumberland coast are sublime this is self-consciously arty and a little stultifying. DP

Indea Barbe-Wilson *Verity* • James Doherty *Jim* • Martin McGlade *Castle* • Nicola Wright *Anne* • Cristi Hogas *Karol* ■ *Dir/Scr* Ben Crowe

Veronica Guerin ★★★★ 18
Biographical drama   2003 · US/UK/Ire · Colour · 94min

The age of the newspaper reporter as crusading hero is given an excellent treatment in this real-life drama. Veronica Guerin (emphatically played by Cate Blanchett) was assassinated after writing a series of revelatory stories exposing the drug overlords who battled for control of Dublin in the mid-1990s. Her courageous story has already provided the inspiration for the 2000 film *When the Sky Falls*, but director Joel Schumacher's reconstruction of events works thanks to Blanchett's star appeal. Colin Farrell also offers a sly portrait of a druggie informer and Brenda Fricker

has a poignant cameo as Veronica's mother. TH Violence, swearing, drug abuse, sex scenes, nudity. **DVD**

Cate Blanchett *Veronica Guerin* • Gerard McSorley *John Gilligan* • Ciaran Hinds *John Traynor* • Brenda Fricker *Bernadette Guerin* • Barry Barnes *Graham Turley* • Joe Hanley *Holland* • David Murray Bowden *Spanky* Peter "Fatso" Mitchell • Colin Farrell (2) *Spanky McSpank* ■ *Dir* Joel Schumacher • *Scr* Carol Doyle, Mary Agnes Donoghue, from a story by Carol Doyle

Veronica Mars ★★★ 12
Murder mystery   2014 · US · Colour · 103min

Made after an online appeal by creator Rob Thomas and star Kristen Bell raised nearly $6 million from fans of the original TV series, this feature spin-off is class act. Bell returns the former teen private eye, now in her 20s and working as a lawyer in New York, who's compelled to return to her Californian home town when an ex-boyfriend is charged with murder. The film is well written and nicely pitched between soft- and hard-boiled, though the plot occasionally goes astray, and it patently resonates more if you're familiar with the original TV show. But there's enough charm, wit and mystery to make it well worth watching. DA Violence, swearing, a sex scene. **DVD**

Kristen Bell *Veronica Mars* • Jason Dohring *Logan Echolls* • Krysten Ritter *Gia Goodman* • Ryan Hansen *Dick Casablancas* • Francis Capra *Eli "Weevil" Navarro* • Tina Majorino *Cindy "Mac" Mackenzie* ■ *Dir* Rob Thomas • *Scr* Rob Thomas, Diane Ruggiero, from Thomas's story and original characters

Veronika Voss ★★★ 12
Period drama   1982 · W Ger · BW · 100min

Rainer Werner Fassbinder's film is inspired by the tragic life of Sybille Schmitz, "the German Garbo", whose death eerily presages the director's own later in the year. As ever, exploiting the conventions of Hollywood melodrama, Fassbinder draws parallels between the worlds promised by politicians and film-makers alike, as he sets sports writer Hilmar Thate the impossible task of saving faded Nazi star Rosel Zech from herself and her coterie. The piercing monochrome conveys both the period and a shadowy sense of doom. DP German +subtitles.

Rosel Zech *Veronika Voss* • Hilmar Thate *Robert Krohn* • Cornelia Froboess *Henriette* • Annemarie Düringer *Dr Marianne Katz* • Doris Schade *Josefa* • Erik Schumann *Dr Edel* ■ *Dir* Rainer Werner Fassbinder • *Scr* Rainer Werner Fassbinder, Peter Marthesheimer, Pea Fröhlich

Versus: The Life and Films of Ken Loach ★★★★ 12A
Documentary   2016 · UK · Colour and BW · 93min

Veteran left-wing agitator-turned-national treasure Ken Loach came out of retirement in 2016 for one more modest social drama about life at the sharp end – *I, Daniel Blake* – and won his second Cannes Palme d'Or. Louise Osmond's substantial documentary features interviews and illuminating on-set footage showing the then 79-year-old at work. It's left to early collaborator Tony Garnett to offer candid observations about Loach's determination and self-belief. In all, it makes for a unique portrait of a one-off film-maker. AC Swearing.

Ken Loach • Tony Garnett ■ *Dir* Louise Osmond

Vertical Limit ★★ 12
Action adventure thriller   2000 · US/Ger · Colour · 119min

Snapped ropes, dislodged boulders and crumbling ledges are just some of the perils facing mountaineer Chris O'Donnell in this predictable but watchable adventure. Now working as a photographer, O'Donnell is still haunted by memories of the harrowing climb that ended in his father's death. O'Donnell is an uncharismatic hero, but some enjoyable action sequences almost make up for the clichéd characterisations. DA Swearing, violence. **DVD** **BD**

Chris O'Donnell *Peter Garrett* • Bill Paxton *Elliot Vaughn* • Robin Tunney *Annie Garrett* • Scott Glenn *Montgomery Wick* • Izabella Scorupco *Monique Aubertina* ■ *Dir* Martin Campbell • *Scr* Robert King, Terry Hayes, from a story by Robert King

LANDMARK FILM

Hitchcock invents the "dolly-out, zoom-in" effect, later copied by Spielberg for the shot of Roy Scheider on the beach in *Jaws*

Vertigo ★★★★★ PG

Classic psychological thriller
1958 · US · Colour · 128min

In one of the truly great later Hitchcocks, James Stewart plays a retired cop with a terror of heights who's hired by Tom Helmore to follow his suicidal wife, Kim Novak. Stewart falls in love with the enigmatic blonde, but can't prevent tragedy from occurring. Some months later he spots a woman (also played by Novak) who bears an uncanny resemblance to the dead woman, and is drawn into a complex web of deceit and obsession. Novak gives her greatest performance, while Stewart presents a disturbingly dark and layered characterisation. A hallucinatory movie – the glistening San Francisco locations give both place and events a dream-like quality – this remains one of the most painful depictions of romantic fatalism in all of cinema. TH *DVD* ꞏ

James Stewart *John "Scottie" Ferguson* • Kim Novak *Madeleine/Judy* • Barbara Bel Geddes *Midge* • Tom Helmore *Gavin Elster* • Henry Jones *Coroner* • Raymond Bailey *Doctor* • Ellen Corby *Manageress* • Konstantin Shayne *Pop Leibel* • Paul Bryar *Captain Hansen* ■ *Dir* Alfred Hitchcock • *Scr* Alec Coppel, Samuel Taylor, from the novel *D'entre les Morts* by Pierre Boileau, Thomas Narcejac • *Cinematographer* Robert Burks

Very Annie-Mary ★★★ 15

Musical comedy 2000 · UK/Fr · Colour · 99min

Rhyl-born Sara Sugarman's film – a quirky tragicomedy about the healing powers of song – seeks to meet the clichés about Wales head on. The village of Ogw is determined to win the prize money in a Cardiff talent contest so that a local, terminally ill girl can go to Disneyland. Can gangling Rachel Griffiths find her voice in time? That's the simple plot, but it's told with a Dylan Thomas-like attention to local colour, made more authentic through the use of non-actors. AC *DVD*

Rachel Griffiths *Annie-Mary* • Jonathan Pryce *Father* • Ruth Madoc *Mrs Ifans* • Matthew Rhys *Nob* • Ioan Gruffudd *Hob* ■ *Dir/Scr* Sara Sugarman

Very Bad Things ★★★★ 18

Black comedy 1998 · US · Colour · 100min

Peter Berg's directorial debut is a very black comedy that is certainly not for the easily offended. Berg brings together a cool cast for a twisted and hilarious tale of mayhem that begins when bridegroom Jon Favreau and his pals embark on a stag weekend in Las Vegas, before his marriage to the beautiful but ruthless Cameron Diaz. Their booze and drug-fuelled party goes awry, however, when an unfortunate accident leaves them with a dead stripper on their hands. This gruesome tale is propelled by a sharp script and top-notch performances. JB *DVD*

Christian Slater *Robert Boyd* • Cameron Diaz *Laura Garrety* • Daniel Stern *Adam Berkow* • Jeanne Tripplehorn *Lois Berkow* • Jon Favreau *Kyle Fisher* • Jeremy Piven *Michael Berkow* • Leland Orser *Charles Moore* • Lawrence Pressman *Mr Fisher* ■ *Dir/Scr* Peter Berg

A Very Brady Sequel ★★★ 12

Comedy 1996 · US · Colour · 86min

One of the rare occasions when a sequel works better than the original, this follow-up to the big-screen adaptation of TV's *The Brady Bunch* not only pokes more fun at the Bradys, but mocks them more savagely. Yet the movie still has great affection for the characters, who are wonderfully played by the cast, especially Shelley Long and Gary Cole as parents Carol and Mike Brady.

Still stuck in a 1970s time warp in the 1990s, the Bradys are stunned by the appearance of a man claiming to be Carol's former husband, who was previously believed to have been dead. KB *DVD*

Shelley Long *Carol Brady* • Gary Cole *Mike Brady* • Christopher Daniel Barnes *Greg Brady* • Christine Taylor *Marcia Brady* • Paul Sutera *Peter Brady* • Jennifer Elise Cox *Jan Brady* • Jesse Lee *Bobby Brady* • Olivia Hack *Cindy Brady* • Henriette Mantel *Alice* ■ *Dir* Arlene Sanford • *Scr* Harry Elfont, Deborah Kaplan, James Berg, Stan Zimmerman, from a story by Harry Elfont, Deborah Kaplan, from the characters by Sherwood Schwartz

A Very British Gangster ★★★ 15

Documentary
2006 · UK · Colour and BW · 97min

Undercover reporter Donal MacIntyre's first documentary feature is a fly-on-the wall account of the Noonan family, a clan of Manchester gangsters who have been the bane of the police for nearly two decades. The focus of MacIntyre's three-year investigation is rotund chief hood Dominic, whose long record includes convictions for armed robbery and fraud. With snappy editing and a relentless contemporary soundtrack, but little in the way of testimony from the gang's victims, some may regard this as a skewed, even romanticised, view of a bunch of provincial thugs. But in the quieter moments, MacIntyre does reveal some of the complexities of Dominic's personality, as well as an undeniable Manchester wit. AS *DVD*

Dominic Noonan • Donal MacIntyre ■ *Dir* Donal MacIntyre

The Very Edge ★

Drama 1962 · UK · Colour · 89min

This is another British cheapie that hoped to lure audiences into auditoriums with the sort of sensationalist story found in their Sunday papers. Here, we have sexual pervert Jeremy Brett's obsession with pregnant Anne Heywood passing from harassment to assault, with the result that she loses her baby. Husband Richard Todd takes the law into his own hands, basing his dispirited perfomance in his stock quality of stuffy indignance. DP

Anne Heywood *Tracey Lawrence* • Richard Todd *Geoffrey Lawrence* • Jack Hedley *McInnes* • Nicole Maurey *Helen* • Jeremy Brett *Mullen* • Barbara Mullen *Dr Shaw* • Maurice Denham *Crawford* ■ *Dir* Cyril Frankel • *Scr* Elizabeth Jane Howard, from a story by Vivian Cox, Leslie Bricusse, Raymond Stross

A Very Harold & Kumar 3D Christmas ★★★ 18

Comedy 2011 · US · Colour · 96min

More unashamedly vulgar mayhem pops up – in eye-blowing 3D – in this bromance threequel, as the endearing stoner duo attempt a holiday reconciliation, having drifted apart since the events of *Harold & Kumar Escape from Guantanamo Bay*. But when Harold's father-in-law's beloved Christmas tree goes up in smoke, ignited by a giant joint, the pair must find a replacement. It all remains on the light-hearted, harmless and inoffensive side despite bad-taste gags and gory yuletide violence. It's fast-paced and the special effects are top-notch. It seems *Bad Santa* has a festive cult rival. AJ Drug abuse.
DVD ꞏ ᴽᴰ

John Cho *Harold Lee* • Kal Penn *Kumar Patel* • Paula Garcés *Maria* • Danneel Harris *Vanessa* • Elias Koteas *Sergei Katsov* • Danny Trejo *Mr Perez* ■ *Dir* Todd Strauss-Schulson • *Scr* Hayden Schlossberg, Jon Hurwitz, from their characters

Very Important Person ★★★ U

Comedy 1961 · UK · BW · 93min

The key to this winning comedy is a witty script by Jack Davies and Henry Blyth, which cleverly lampoons many of the conventions and stereotypes of the prisoner-of-war pictures that had been a staple of the British film industry for over a

decade. Stanley Baxter gives one of his best film performances as a PoW posing as a high-ranking Nazi in a bid to spring scientist James Robertson-Justice, while the deft comic support from Leslie Phillips, Eric Sykes and the deadpan Richard Wattis is of a high order. DP *DVD*

James Robertson-Justice *Sir Ernest Pease* • Leslie Phillips *Jimmy Cooper* • Stanley Baxter *Everett/Major Stampfel* • Eric Sykes *Willoughby* • Richard Wattis *Woodcock* ■ *Dir* Ken Annakin • *Scr* Jack Davies, Henry Blyth

A Very Long Engagement ★★★★ 15

Period romantic drama
2004 · Fr/US · Colour · 127min

Jean-Pierre Jeunet's lyrical treat for the eye and heart is grittier in tone than his international hit *Amélie*, containing unflinching scenes of battlefield carnage, but still has whimsical charm to spare. The gorgeously gamine Audrey Tautou stars as the fiancée of a First World War soldier who was abandoned to face an ignominious death in no-man's land as punishment for a self-inflicted wound. Tatou refuses to believe he has been killed and begins an investigation into her lover's fate. This sweeping saga is fabulous looking, beautifully performed and, though overlong, remains an engaging, utterly involving portrait of unswerving devotion. AJ French +subtitles. Violence, sex scenes. *DVD*

Audrey Tautou *Mathilde* • Gaspard Ulliel *Manech* • Jean-Pierre Becker *Lieutenant Esperanza* • Dominique Bettenfeld *Ange Bassignano* • Clovis Cornillac *Benoît Notre Dame* • Marion Cotillard *Tina Lombardi* • Jean-Pierre Darroussin *Benjamin Gordes* • Jodie Foster *Elodie Gordes* • Jean-Claude Dreyfus *Commandant Lavrouye* • Ticky Holgado *Germain Pire* • Tcheky Karyo *Captain Favourier* ■ *Dir* Jean-Pierre Jeunet • *Scr* Jean-Pierre Jeunet, Guillaume Laurant, from the novel *Un Long Dimanche de Fiançailles* by Sébastien Japrisot

A Very Private Affair ★★★

Drama 1962 · Fr/It · Colour · 93min

Brigitte Bardot plays a movie star, an idolised sex symbol, suffering from the pressures of stardom and seeking love. She finds it in Marcello Mastroianni, an intellectual theatre director. There is some fascination in seeing Bardot playing a role that is modelled on herself, but both she and Mastroianni cannot overcome the shallowness of the screenplay. One of Louis Malle's least distinguished movies, it does have some superb camerawork by Henri Decaë. RB French +subtitles.

Brigitte Bardot *Jill* • Marcello Mastroianni *Fabio* • Gregor von Rezzori *Gricha* • Eléonore Hirt *Cecile* ■ *Dir* Louis Malle • *Scr* Louis Malle, Jean-Paul Rappeneau, Jean Ferry

The Very Thought of You ★★

Drama 1944 · US · BW · 98min

Very much of its period, not just in title but also in wartime content, this tale of romance and marriage falls flat due to bland Dennis Morgan. He is seriously undercast as the male lead opposite volatile (and ever underrated) Eleanor Parker, whose hairstyle alone makes this worth watching. Skilled director Delmer Daves, almost as well known for his melodramas as he was for his westerns, doesn't seem to bring too much to the table here. TS

Dennis Morgan *Sgt Dave Stewart* • Eleanor Parker *Janet Wheeler* • Dane Clark *"Fixit"* • Faye Emerson *Cora* • Beulah Bondi *Mrs Wheeler* ■ *Dir* Delmer Daves • *Scr* Alvah Bessie, Delmer Daves, from a story by Lionel Wiggam

Vessel of Wrath ★★★★

Comedy drama 1938 · UK · BW · 86min

The story (by Somerset Maugham) of a spinster missionary and her attempts to reform a drunken beach bum, has obvious similarities to *The African Queen*, and happily this is nearly in the same league as that classic. Elsa Lanchester and Charles Laughton are delightful as the mismatched pair, the quirky Lanchester having her

largest (and favourite) screen role. The only film directed by the legendary European producer Erich Pommer, it was a box-office failure, but is a real gem. Robert Newton, who has a supporting role in this version, starred with Glynis Johns in a fair remake titled *The Beachcomber* in 1954. TV

Charles Laughton *Ginger Ted* • Elsa Lanchester *Martha Jones* • Tyrone Guthrie *Owen Jones, M D* • Robert Newton *Controleur* • Dolly Mollinger *Lia* • Rosita Garcia *Kati* ■ *Dir* Erich Pommer, Bartlett Cormack • *Scr* Bartlett Cormack, B Van Thal, from the short story by W Somerset Maugham

The Veteran ★★ 15

Thriller 2011 · UK · Colour · 94min

A brooding former para returns to London from Afghanistan to find himself in another kind of war zone in this low-budget thriller. Exuding apparent calm and repressed rage, Toby Kebbell impresses as the ex-soldier whose attempts to adjust to civvy street see him opposing a local drugs lord on his run-down estate while becoming involved with some shady spooks (Brian Cox, Tony Curran) as they try to thwart a jihadi plot. Kebbell dominates the film, but the writers can't decide on a vigilante or conspiracy angle, so satisfy neither. JA Violence, swearing. *DVD* ᴽᴰ

Toby Kebbell *Robert Miller* • Brian Cox (1) *Gerry Langdon* • Tony Curran *Chris Turner* • Adi Bielski *Alayna Wallace* • Ashley Thomas [Ashley "Bashy" Thomas] *Tyrone Jones* • Tom Brooke *Danny Turner* ■ *Dir* Matthew Hope • *Scr* Matthew Hope, Robert Henry Craft

La Veuve de Saint-Pierre ★★★ 15

Period romantic drama
2000 · Fr/Can · Colour · 107min

Set in 1850, Patrice Leconte's sombre tragedy unfolds against the austere backdrop of Saint-Pierre, a small French island off the Canadian coast. A drunken drifter (played by Yugoslavian film director Emir Kusturica) is found guilty of murder and is sentenced to death. There being neither guillotine nor executioner on the isle, the condemned man is placed in the custody of captain Daniel Auteuil and his wife, Juliette Binoche, who become attached to their prisoner and plot his escape. It's an unusual story, told with empathy and precision, while Binoche and Auteuil are well-matched as the couple who risk all in an act of compassion. NS French +subtitles. *DVD*

Juliette Binoche *Madame La* • Daniel Auteuil *The Captain* • Emir Kusturica *Neel Auguste* • Michel Duchaussoy *The Governor* • Philippe Magnan *President Venot* ■ *Dir* Patrice Leconte • *Scr* Claude Faraldo

Vexille ★★★ 12

Animated science-fiction adventure
2007 · Jpn · Colour · 109min

The creative minds behind 2004's hit *anime Appleseed* re-team for this stunning blend of traditional animation and CGI. Events unfold in 2077, where Japan has isolated itself behind an electromagnetic field to enable the continued development of outlawed biomechanical technology. An American special forces unit led by tough female agent Vexille is sent in to investigate, paving the way for a series of explosive set pieces. Though there are cinematic nods to other sci-fi movies from *Dune* to *The Matrix*, the inventiveness and energy of director/co-writer Fumihiko Sori's vision keep the feature feeling fresh, despite some clunky exposition and bland characters. SF Japanese +subtitles. Some violence. *DVD* ꞏ

Meisa Kuroki *Vexille* • Shosuke Tanihara *Leon* • Yasuko Matsuyuki *Maria* • Takahiro Sakurai *Ryo* • Romi Pak *Takashi* ■ *Dir* Sori [Fumihiko Sori] • *Scr* Fumihiko Sori, Haruka Handa

Vibes ★ PG

Adventure comedy 1988 · US · Colour · 95min

This attempt to launch an acting career for singer Cyndi Lauper, of *Girls Just Want to Have Fun* fame, was a disaster. Lauper and Jeff Goldblum play rent-a-psychics hired by Peter Falk to find a legendary lost city of

U SUITABLE FOR ALL   Uc SUITABLE ESPECIALLY FOR YOUNG CHILDREN (DVD ONLY)   PG PARENTAL GUIDANCE   12A UNDER 12s TO BE ACCOMPANIED (CINEMA ONLY)

gold. Goldblum survived the debacle. Lauper made *Life with Mikey* and *Off and Running*, but has rarely been seen on screen since. DA

Cyndi Lauper *Sylvia Pickel* • Jeff Goldblum *Nick Deezy* • Julian Sands *Dr Harrison Steele* • Googy Gress *Ingo Swedlin* • Peter Falk *Harry Buscafusco* • Michael Lerner *Burt Wilder* • Ramon Bieri *Eli Diamond* • Elizabeth Peña *Consuela* ■ *Dir* Ken Kwapis • *Scr* Lowe l Ganz, Babaloo Mandel, from a story by Babaloo Mandel, Deborah Blum, Lowell Ganz

The Vicar of Bray ★★
Period drama 1937 · UK · BW · 66min

Making extravagantly expansive gestures and projecting to hit the rear of the music hall stalls, Stanley Holloway shows why it took so long for him to establish himself as a screen performer. Here he plays the Irish clergyman who is hired to tutor the future Charles II and finds himself matchmaking in an English Civil War version of *Romeo and Juliet*. The songs are ghastly and the period trappings cheap and inaccurate, but Felix Aylmer and Garry Marsh go some way to atoning. DP

Stanley Holloway *Bray* • Hugh Miller *King Charles I* • K Hamilton Price *Prince Charles Stuart* • Felix Aylmer *Earl of Brendon* • Margaret Vines *Lady Norah Brendon* • Garry Marsh *Sir Richard Melross* • Esmond Knight *Dennis Melross* • Martin Walker *Sir Patrick Condon* • Eve Gray *Meg Clancy* • Kitty Kirwan *Molly* ■ *Dir* Henry Edwards • *Scr* H Fowler Mear, from the story by Anson Dyer

Vice Squad ★★
Crime drama 1953 · US · BW · 88min

This is a day in the life of a Los Angeles cop, played by Edward G Robinson, and co-starring Paulette Goddard as the owner of an escort agency. Semi-documentary in style, it lurches from one murder to the next. It's serious and slightly dull, and Robinson and Goddard have few opportunities to display their talents. Spaghetti weste~n fans should watch for Lee Van Cleef as a heavy. AT

Edward G Robinson *Captain Barnaby* • Paulette Goddard *Mona* • KT Stevens *Ginny* • Porter Hall *Jack Hartrampf* • Adam Williams *Marty Kusalich* • Edward Binns *Al Barkis* • Lee Van Cleef *Pete* ■ *Dir* Arnold Laven • *Scr* Lawrence Roman, from the novel *Harness Bull* by Leslie T White

Vice Squad ★★★ 18
Crime thriller 1982 · US · Colour · 86min

This is the movie that made Wings Hauser a star, deservedly bringing him critical raves as a psychotic pimp who brutally murders one of his prostitutes when she tries to walk out on him. When hooker Season Hubley is forced by police into taking part in a sting operation that results in Hauser's arrest, he plans to kill her when he escapes custody. It's unusual that an exploitation movie set in the world of prostitution has no nudity or real sex, with more chitchat than action in or out of the bedroom. KB

Season Hubley *Princess* • Gary Swanson *Tom Walsh* • Wings Hauser *Ramrod* • Pepe Serna *Pete Mendez* • Beverly Todd *Louise Williams* • Joseph DiGiroloma *Kowalski* • Maurice Emmanuel Edwards ■ *Dir* Gary A Sherman [Gary Sherman] • *Scr* Sandy Howard, Robert Vincent O'Neil, Kenneth Peters

Vice Versa ★★★ U
Comedy 1947 · UK · BW · 97min

This is quite a treat, even funnier now than when it first came out and better than its 1988 Judge Reinhold remake. Under Peter Ustinov's nimble direction, father and son Roger Livesey and Anthony Newley swap places, and succeed in outraging all and sundry. There are some lovely supporting performances, especially from a bemused, schoolmasterly James Robertson-Justice. TS 📀

Roger Livesey *Paul Bultitude* • Kay Walsh *Mrs Verlayne* • David Hutcheson *Marmaduke Paradine* • Anthory Newley *Dick Bultitude* • James Robertson-Justice *Dr Grimstone* • Petula Clark *Dulcie Grimstone* • Patricia Raine *Alice* • Joan Young *Mrs Grimstone* • Vida Hope *First nanny* ■ *Dir* Peter Ustinov • *Scr* Peter Ustinov, from the novel by F Anstey

Vice Versa ★★★ PG
Comedy 1988 · US · Colour · 94min

Although it lacks the charm of the 1947 British film of the same name, this is a better-than-average body-swap movie. Most of it is down to the inspired playing of Judge Reinhold and Fred Savage, who learn that their respective lives are not quite as enjoyable as they imagine when they switch bodies. The two leads are fresh and convincing in both their personae, and, although sentimentality occasionally raises its head, director Brian Gilbert keeps the action flowing at a pleasing rate. JF Swearing. 📀

Judge Reinhold *Marshall Seymour* • Fred Savage *Charlie Seymour* • Corinne Bohrer *Sam* • Swoosie Kurtz *Tina* • David Proval *Turk* • Jane Kaczmarek *Robyn* • Gloria Gifford *Marcie* • William Prince *Avery* • Beverly Archer *Mrs Luttrell* • James Hong *Kwo* ■ *Dir* Brian Gilbert • *Scr* Dick Clement, Ian La Frenais

The Vicious Circle ★★ PG
Crime drama 1957 · UK · BW · 80min

Adapting his own serial, *My Friend Charles*, Francis Durbridge was evidently over-attached to his material as there is simply too much plot. John Mills has a fair stab at the Hitchcockian "wrong man", playing a respectable London doctor desperate to discover who is trying to frame him for the murder of an actress whose body has fetched up in his flat. *Carry On* stalwart Gerald Thomas directs with an affinity for the whodunnit. DP

John Mills *Dr Howard Latimer* • Derek Farr *Ken Palmer* • Noelle Middleton *Laura James* • Wilfrid Hyde White *Robert Brady* • Roland Culver *Inspector Dane* • Mervyn Johns *Dr George Kimber* • René Ray *M*r*s Amber* • Lionel Jeffries *Geoffrey Windsor* ■ *Dir* Gerald Thomas • *Scr* Francis Durbridge, from his TV series *My Friend Charles*

Vickery's Wild Ride ★★
Adventure 2009 · US · Colour

High-achieving city dwellers learn to reassess their priorities in this predictable fish-out-of-water tale. Jonathan Silverman heads up the gadget-addicted clan who get a taste of old-fashioned family values when they reluctantly holiday at a no-frills mountain cabin left to them by an uncle. As the unsubtle script hammers home messages about personal happiness and the evils of mobile-phone culture, it's all very idealistic. But, contrary to the title's suggestion, it's also rather bland. SF

Jonathan Silverman *Jack Vickery* • Peter Strauss *"Wild" Bill Cohen* • Dedee Pfeiffer *Emily Vickery* • Linsey Godfrey *Charlotte* ■ *Dir* Bradford May • *Scr* Alex Greenfield

Vicky Cristina Barcelona ★★★★ 12
Romantic comedy drama 2008 · US/Sp · Colour · 92min

After the ill-conceived *Cassandra's Dream*, Woody Allen rediscovers his sense of humour with this warm, witty and surprisingly sexy comedy. A narrator tells the misadventures of young American women Vicky (British actress Rebecca Hall) and Cristina (Scarlett Johansson) during a visit to Barcelona. The two friends catch the eye of painter Juan Antonio (Javier Bardem), whose brazen proposition elicits different responses from the footloose Cristina and the soon-to-be-wed Vicky. Couplings and conflicts of loyalty unfold against picturesque locations, with the return of Juan Antonio's fiery ex-wife (Penélope Cruz) leading to further upheavals. In depicting the culture clash between Americans and Europeans, Allen largely steers clear of stereotypes, with Bardem both seductive and sympathetic without being overly macho. But it's Cruz who makes the biggest dramatic and comic impact. SS English, Spanish +subtitles. 📀 💿

Rebecca Hall *Vicky* • Scarlett Johansson *Cristina* • Javier Bardem *Juan Antonio* • Penélope Cruz *Maria Elena* • Christopher Evan Welch *Narrator* • Chris Messina *Doug* • Patricia Clarkson *Judy*

Nash • Kevin Dunn *Mark Nash* ■ *Dir/Scr* Woody Allen • *Cinematographer* Javier Aguirresarobe

LANDMARK FILM
Dirk Bogarde's ground-breaking depiction of a gay man influences the UK's partial decriminalisation of homosexuality in 1967

Victim ★★★ 12
Drama 1961 · UK · BW · 95min

A ground-breaker in its depiction of homosexuality, this film marks Dirk Bogarde's brave bid to break free of his matinée idol image. He plays a homosexual barrister whose former lover is arrested and commits suicide to protect Bogarde's name. This tragic death leads Bogarde to a blackmail ring targeting gay men, which he decides to pursue at the risk of his marriage (to Sylvia Syms) and his career. Although director Basil Dearden insisted that homosexuals should be called "inverts", the movie nevertheless refuses to pigeonhole or patronise its subject, depicting homosexuality in every class and every walk of life. AT Swearing. 📀 💿

Dirk Bogarde *Melville Farr* • Sylvia Syms *Laura Farr* • Dennis Price *Calloway* • Anthony Nicholls *Lord Fullbrook* • Peter Copley *Paul Mandrake* • Norman Bird *Harold Doe* • Peter McEnery *Jack Barrett* • Donald Churchill *Eddy Stone* ■ *Dir* Basil Dearden • *Scr* Janet Green, John McCormick

Victim ★★ 15
Crime drama 2011 · UK · Colour · 82min

Director Alex Pillai's disappointing crime drama follows Tyson (Ashley Chin), a young Londoner who funds the upbringing of his younger sister by means of clever robberies involving his friends and unfortunate wealthy men. The movie is not without heart and good intentions, and there are some strong supporting turns, but the unconvincing central performances and a cliché-ridden script fail to conjure enough grit and steel to elevate this urban drama above the ordinary. MF Violence, swearing, drug abuse, sexual references. 📀

Ashley Chin *Tyson* • Ashley Madekwe *Tia* • Jason Maza *Mannie* • Anna Nightingale *Davina* • Michael Maris *Jason* • Letitia Wright *Nyla* ■ *Dir* Alex Pillai • *Scr* Ashley Chin, Michael Maris

Victim of Love ★★★ 15
Thriller 1991 · US · Colour · 88min

A pre-007 Pierce Brosnan stars in a role that's far removed from that of the suave and sophisticated secret agent. He plays a British professor who, following the recent death of his wife, charms his way into the life of psychologist JoBeth Williams, who is unaware that he has a rather sinister side. This TV movie has a fair quota of tense moments, and Brosnan is perfect as the villian. JB Swearing, nudity. 📀

Pierce Brosnan *Paul Tomlinson* • JoBeth Williams *Tess Palmer* • Virginia Madsen *Carla Simmons* • Georgia Brown *Emma Walters* • Murphy Cross *Roz Fleisher* ■ *Dir* Jerry London • *Scr* James J Desmarais, Alison Rosenfeld Desmarais

Victim of Rage ★★ 18
Drama based on a true story 1994 · US · Colour · 90min

This made-for-TV movie is based on the true story of a Los Angeles woman for whom a blind date is the start of a nightmare. Jaclyn Smith suffers glamorously, while Brad Johnson chews the scenery as the husband whose body-building pills turn him into a maniac. More proof that the truth doesn't always make great drama. DP Violence. 📀

Jaclyn Smith *Donna Yaklich* • Brad Johnson *Dennis Yaklich* • David Lascher *Denny Yaklich* • Hilary Swank *Patty* ■ *Dir* Armand Mastroianni • *Scr* Christopher Canaan

Victor ★★
Biographical drama 2008 · Can · Colour · 96min

The life and legacy of Canadian Olympic swimmer Victor Davis are laid bare in this candid TV-movie drama. Working from his own script, Mark Lutz (himself a former international swimmer) delivers a striking lead performance as the mercurial sporting hero, who courted controversy and

overcame many challenges in his ferocious pursuit of athletic excellence. But the film's confusing and unfocused narrative structure means that even his tragic demise lacks the full impact it deserves. SF

Mark Lutz *Victor Davis* • Ron Lea *Cliff Barry* • Peter MacNeill *Mel Davis* • Polly Shannon *Donna Clavel* • Sasha Roiz *Alex Baumann* • Chris Owens *Dave Stubbs* ■ *Dir* Jerry Ciccoritti • *Scr* Mark Lutz

Victor Frankenstein ★★
Horror 1977 · Ire/Swe · Colour · 92min

This elegantly photographed, but dull co-production of Mary Shelley's classic tale of terror was promoted as being the most faithful version ever committed to film. Too melodramatic and psychologically straightforward to qualify as authentic, Per Oscarsson plays the Creature as a juvenile delinquent, brutally railing against his experimental creator, Leon Vitali, and society in general. This pretentious reading was a festival favourite, but not an audience one. AJ

Leon Vitali *Victor Frankenstein* • Per Oscarsson *Monster* • Nicholas Clay *Henry* • Stacy Dorning *Elisabeth* • Jan Ohlsson *William* • Olof Bergström *Father* ■ *Dir* Calvin Floyd • *Scr* Calvin Floyd, Yvonne Floyd, from the novel *Frankenstein* by Mary Shelley • *Cinematographer* Tony Forsberg

Victor Frankenstein ★★ 12
Horror 2015 · US · Colour · 109min

The Frankenstein legend through the eyes of Igor (Daniel Radcliffe), a circus clown who becomes physician Victor Frankenstein's assistant. Radcliffe tries to provide the moral centre of the story but is drowned out by a maniacal and occasionally amusing James McAvoy as Frankenstein. Andrew Scott works hard as the puritanical detective on the case, but like love interest Jessica Brown Findlay, the character is underdeveloped. What starts out as a bold re-imagining soon feels more like just another clone. JL Violence. 📀 💿

Daniel Radcliffe *Igor* • James McAvoy *Victor Frankenstein* • Jessica Brown Findlay *Lorelei* • Andrew Scott *Roderick Turpin* • Charles Dance *Frankenstein* ■ *Dir* Paul McGuigan • *Scr* Max Landis, from Mary Shelley's novel

Victor/Victoria ★★★ 15
Period musical screwball comedy 1982 · UK · Colour · 128min

Julie Andrews as a bloke? Although this decision earns it an honourable mention in the hall of fame for monumental pieces of miscasting, this typically crude Blake Edwards comedy remains quite a hoot. Andrews is the struggling singer who leaps to fame and fortune in 1930s Paris when she decides to impersonate a man impersonating a woman. James Garner is the very heterosexual American troubled by his attraction to him/her. There are a few songs to keep Andrews fans happy, plus an outrageously camp turn from Robert Preston. JF 📀

Julie Andrews *Victor/Victoria* • James Garner *King Marchan* • Robert Preston *Carroll "Toddy" Todd* • Lesley Ann Warren *Norma* • Alex Karras *Squash* • John Rhys-Davies *André Cassell* • Graham Stark *Waiter* ■ *Dir* Blake Edwards • *Scr* Blake Edwards, from the play *Viktor und Viktoria* by Reinhold Schünzel • *Music* Henry Mancini

V

Victoria ★★★★ 15
Crime thriller 2015 · Ger · Colour · 132min

A night of clubbing in Berlin has unexpected consequences for Spanish girl Victoria (Laia Costa) in this German drama which, remarkably, unfolds in a single 130-minute shot. Victoria finds herself drawn into a bank job after falling for, and falling in with, a likely Berlin lad and his streetwise mates. For all the seeming gimmickry of the edit-free camerawork, it's the spontaneity of the lead performances that draw you into director Sebastian Schipper's daringly ambitious thriller. A captivating ride. TJ In German, English, Spanish. Swearing, drug abuse. 📀 💿

Laia Costa *Victoria* • Frederick Lau *Sonne* • Franz Rogowski *Boxer* • Burak Yiğit *Blinker* ■ *Dir* Sebastian Schipper • *Scr* Sebastian Schipper, Olivia Neergaard-Holm, Eike Frederik Schulz

Victoria the Great ★★★ U
Historical biographical drama
1937 · UK · BW and Colour · 105min

Laurence Housman's play *Victoria Regina* was banned by the Lord Chamberlain as, in 1935, the royal family could not be shown on the British stage. But the play was a hit on Broadway and such was the enthusiasm of King Edward VIII, he commissioned producer/director Herbert Wilcox to make it into a film to commemorate the centenary of Victoria's accession to the throne. Anna Neagle takes Victoria from girlhood to old age, and the drama concentrates on her relationship with Prince Albert (Anton Walbrook). Her sympathy for the monarch shines through, and the final reel, which bursts into glorious Technicolor for the Diamond Jubilee, is a delightful piece of patriotic pomp. **SuR**

Anna Neagle *Queen Victoria* • Anton Walbrook *Prince Albert* • Walter Rilla *Prince Ernest* • Mary Morris *Duchess of Kent* • HB Warner *Lord Melbourne* • Grete Wegener *Baroness Lehzen* • CV France *Archbishop of Canterbury* ■ *Dir* Herbert Wilcox • *Scr* Miles Malleson, Charles de Grandcourt, from the play *Victoria Regina* by Laurence Housman

The Victors ★★★ 12
War epic   1963 · US/UK · BW · 146min

Carl Foreman's film is one of the most ambitious war movies ever made, shot in black and white with an all-star cast and designed to show how war degrades people on all sides. A shot of victors and vanquished – both exhausted and looking like vagrants – rams home the point. Subtlety was never on Foreman's agenda and three hours of episodic hectoring and ironic twists of fate do get a bit wearisome. However, there are some stunning sequences. **AT** In English, German.

George Hamilton *Cpl Trower* • George Peppard *Cpl Chase* • Eli Wallach *Sgt Craig* • Jeanne Moreau *Frenchwoman* • Romy Schneider *Regine* • Melina Mercouri *Magda* • Vincent Edwards [Vince Edwards] *Baker* • Rosanna Schiaffino *Maria* • Maurice Ronet *French Lt Cohn* • Peter Fonda *Weaver* • Senta Berger *Trudi* • Elke Sommer *Helga* • Albert Finney *Russian soldier* ■ *Dir* Carl Foreman • *Scr* Carl Foreman, from the novel *The Human Kind: a Sequence* by Alexander Baron

Victory ★★
Drama   1940 · US · BW · 78min

Fredric March is the perpetual exile who lives on an island in the Malay archipelago, contentedly detached from life until he rescues an English girl and has to cope with three rogues sent by local strongman Sig Ruman. Time and time again, Joseph Conrad's deeply metaphysical dramas prove tough nuts to crack, though in this case the studio-imposed restriction on length doomed everyone to failure before the cameras started rolling. **AT**

Fredric March *Hendrik Heyst* • Betty Field *Alma* • Sir Cedric Hardwicke [Cedric Hardwicke] *Mr Jones* • Jerome Cowan *Martin Ricardo* • Sig Rumann [Sig Ruman] *Mr Schomberg* • Margaret Wycherly *Mrs Schomberg* ■ *Dir* John Cromwell • *Scr* John L Balderston, from the novel by Joseph Conrad

Victory ★★ 15
Period romance
1995 · UK/Fr/Ger · Colour · 94min

This sluggish screen version of the Joseph Conrad novel focuses on a Dutch East Indies recluse who rescues a woman from bothersome baddies and offers her refuge on his remote island. Unfortunately, the island obviously isn't remote enough, and their troubles soon come looking for them. The attractive cast is given little to get their teeth into by a film that's long on steamy languor, but short on characterisation. **DA** Violence, nudity.

Willem Dafoe *Axel Heyst* • Sam Neill *Mr Jones* • Irène Jacob *Alma* • Rufus Sewell *Martin Ricardo* • Jean Yanne *Schomberg* • Ho Yi *Wang* • Bill

Paterson *Captain Davidson* ■ *Dir* Mark Peploe • *Scr* Mark Peploe, from the novel by Joseph Conrad

Victory at Entebbe ★★
Drama based on a true story
1976 · US · Colour · 118min

In June 1976, Palestinian and German terrorists hijacked an Air France airbus and flew to Idi Amin's Uganda. After six days, an Israeli commando unit stormed the airport at Entebbe to free the hostages. Within five months two lousy movies had been made – *Raid on Entebbe* and this one, both for American TV, but released in cinemas elsewhere. The movie reduces everything to the level of a soap opera, but with an all-star cast. **AT**

Kirk Douglas *Hershel Vilnofsky* • Burt Lancaster *Shimon Peres* • Elizabeth Taylor *Edra Vilnofsky* • Anthony Hopkins *Yitzhak Rabin* • Richard Dreyfuss *Colonel Yonatan "Yonni" Netanyahu* • Helen Hayes *Mrs Wise* • Theodore Bikel *Yakov Shlomo* • Julius Harris *President Idi Amin* • Linda Blair *Chana Vilnofsky* • Harris Yulin *General Dan Shomron* • Helmut Berger *German terrorist* ■ *Dir* Marvin J Chomsky • *Scr* Ernest Kinoy

The Victory of Women ★★★
Drama   1946 · Jpn · Colour · 84min

Returning to the director's chair for the first time after the Second World War, Kenji Mizoguchi's tender sympathy for the plight of women in Japanese society again came to the fore in this indictment of the prejudicial legal system and the sinister legacy of old-style militarism. Kinuyo Tanaka gives a typically feisty performance as the lawyer defending a poverty-stricken mother who killed her baby in a desperate fit of grief following the death of her husband. **DP** Japanese +subtitles.

Kinuyo Tanaka *Hiroko Hosokawa* • Michiko Kuwano *Michiko* • Mitsuko Miura *Moto Asakura* • Shin Tokudaiji *Keita Yamaoka* • Toyoko Takahashi *Mother* • Yoshihira Matsumoto [Katsuhira Matsumoto] *Prosecutor Kono* ■ *Dir* Kenji Mizoguchi • *Scr* Kogo Noda, Kaneto Shindo

Victory through Air Power ★★★ U
Part-animated wartime documentary
1943 · US · Colour · 65min

This is one of the best known of the many propaganda and training films produced by the Disney studio during the Second World War. Although it begins with a comic history of aviation, the real purpose of the picture was to convince the top brass of the viability of Major Alexander de Seversky's theories on strategic long-range bombing and how it could disrupt enemy weapons production and supply lines, as well as demoralise the civilian population. The mix of live action, knockabout cartooning and serious graphics worked on wartime audiences and remains powerful today. **DP**

■ *Dir* Clyde Geronimi, Jack Kinney, James Algar • *Scr* Perce Pearce, from the non-fiction book by Major Alexander de Seversky

Vidal Sassoon ★★★ PG
Documentary
2010 · US · Colour and BW · 93min

The name Vidal Sassoon conjures up images of iconic sculpted hairstyles from the Swinging Sixties, beauty bibles from the 1970s and some guy hawking hair products on TV in the 1980s. Craig Teper's pleasant if fluffy documentary takes in all of the hairdresser extraordinaire's self-reinvention, with talking heads filling the gaps where it wouldn't be fitting for Vidal himself to say how wonderful he is. Even if you're not into fashion, this film will have you casting your eye over every hairdo to look for the revolutionary influence of Sassoon's five-point cut. **KK** Some swearing, sexual references. **DVD Blu-ray**

Vidal Sassoon • Ronnie Sassoon • Mary Quant ■ *Dir* Craig Teper • *Scr* Craig Teper, Heather Campbell Gordon

Videocracy ★★
Documentary
2009 · UK/Swe/Den/Fin · Colour · 84min

Italian prime minister Silvio Berlusconi has been the subject of several scathing satires, often targeting his media empire, which has been blamed for the country's cultural decline. Sadly, film-maker Erik Gandini misses an opportunity to follow suit in this documentary that sets out to explore the links between Berlusconi's business interests and his political standing. Instead, Gandini becomes fascinated by a trio of wannabes whose hopes of fleeting fame are exploited by Berlusconi's Mediaset organisation. **DP** In English, Italian. **DVD**

Silvio Berlusconi • Flavio Briatore ■ *Dir* Erik Gandini

Videodrome ★★★★ 18
Horror thriller   1982 · Can · Colour · 88min

With its subject matter of screen violence, this remains one of David Cronenberg's most personal, complex and disturbing films, even if it doesn't always make a lot of sense. James Woods is the amoral cable programmer who gets drawn to a sickening sadomasochistic channel called "Videodrome", which turns out to have a much more sinister purpose. Cronenberg uses this framework to explore his favourite themes (new technology fusing with the human body, voyeurism, the links between sex and violence) and, although the plot begins to unravel, the startling imagery and Woods's fierce performance make for a deeply unsettling experience. **JF** Violence, swearing, nudity. **DVD Blu-ray**

James Woods *Max Renn* • Sonja Smits *Bianca O'Blivion* • Deborah Harry *Nicki Brand* • Peter Dvorsky *Harlan* • Les Carlson *Barry Convex* • Jack Creley *Brian O'Blivion* • Lynne Gorman *Masha* ■ *Dir/Scr* David Cronenberg

LANDMARK FILM
The first time a feature is shot entirely on high-definition digital video

Vidocq ★★
Period detective thriller
2001 · Fr · Colour · 98min

The adventures of the eponymous 19th-century Parisian detective were first screened in the silent era. However, they've never received such a shock-tactic makeover as in this eye-popping thriller, which was the first theatrical feature to be shot entirely in high-resolution digital video. Opening with the hero's death, the action then flashes back through Vidocq's various battles with his arch nemesis, The Alchemist. Special effects maestro Pitof's directorial debut is a fussy, flashy, furiously edited farrago, which is sustained solely by the hulkingly assured presence of Gérard Depardieu. **DP** French +subtitles.

Gérard Depardieu *Vidocq* • Guillaume Canet *Etienne Boisset* • Inés Sastre *Préah* • André Dussollier *Lautrennes* • Edith Scob *Sylvia* • Moussa Maaskri *Nimier* ■ *Dir* Pitof • *Scr* Jean-Christophe Grange, Pitof

La Vie de Château ★★★★ U
Wartime comedy drama   1965 · Fr · BW · 89min

This gripping and extremely evocative comedy drama about the French Resistance is set in the crumbling Normandy manor house owned by the staid Philippe Noiret and his beautiful wife Catherine Deneuve. Into their midst arrives a Free French agent on a mission from England to prepare for D-Day. Deneuve falls in love with him and things are further complicated when the Germans suddenly take over the château. Part wartime thriller, part marital drama, it's about the bravery and heroism that lies dormant in everyone. **AT** French +subtitles. **DVD**

Catherine Deneuve *Marie* • Philippe Noiret *Jérôme* • Pierre Brasseur *Dimanche* • Mary Marquet *Charlotte* • Henri Garcin *Julien* • Carlos Thompson *Klopstock* ■ *Dir* Jean-Paul Rappeneau • *Scr* Jean-Paul Rappeneau, Alain Cavalier, Claude Sautet, Daniel Boulanger

La Vie de Jésus ★★★ 18
Drama   1996 · Fr · Colour · 91min

This pseudo-Bressonian study of teenage ennui by debuting director Bruno Dumont is based on his time as a teacher of disaffected small-town kids. Despite looking older, David Douche is the skinheaded 19-year-old leader of a scooter gang in Bailleul, northern France. His relationship with cashier Marjorie Cottreel is based on perfunctory sex and he responds to her interest in Arab teenager Kader Chaatouf with a violence that's both proprietorial and racist. As surly a study of spiritual humanism as cinema has seen. **DP** French +subtitles. Violence. **DVD**

David Douche *Freddy* • Marjorie Cottreel *Marie* • Kader Chaatouf *Kader* • Sébastien Delbaere *Gégé* • Samuel Boidin *Michou* • Steve Smagghe *Robert* • Sébastien Bailleul *Quinquin* • Geneviève Cottreel *Yvette, Freddy's mother* ■ *Dir/Scr* Bruno Dumont

La Vie en Rose ★★★ 12
Period biographical drama
2007 · Fr/UK/Cz Rep · Colour · 134min

This is a biopic of legendary French chanteuse Edith Piaf – she of *Non, Je Ne Regrette Rien* fame. But her fascinating story could have been better told here. The fractured structure of Olivier Dahan's film is often confusing, with the tale flitting about all over the place. And there are incidents in the "Little Sparrow's" life that are skated over, such as her involvement with the French underworld and the sudden appearance of a child. It's as if this already lengthy drama had been cut down from a much longer film. But none of these quibbles should detract from a stunning lead performance by Marion Cotillard. She doesn't just *act* Piaf – she *is* Piaf. The result is a flawed diamond, but a diamond nonetheless. **DA** French +subtitles. Swearing, drug abuse, brief nudity. **DVD Blu-ray**

Marion Cotillard *Edith Piaf* • Sylvie Testud *Mômone* • Pascal Greggory *Louis Barrier* • Emmanuelle Seigner *Titine* • Jean-Paul Rouve *Louis Gassion* • Gérard Depardieu *Louis Leplée* • Clotilde Courau *Anetta* ■ *Dir* Olivier Dahan • *Scr* Olivier Dahan, Isabelle Sobelman

La Vie Est à Nous ★★★
Propaganda   1936 · Fr · BW · 62min

Although Jean Renoir was never a member of the French Communist Party, he was asked by them to supervise this propaganda film of sketches, newsreels and political speeches. Despite the fact that there were eight directors on the project, including the great still photographer Henri Cartier-Bresson, with the styles ranging from French naturalism to Russian Socialist Realism, the collaborative effort has the stamp of Renoir on it. An interesting and uneven document of the day, it glows with enthusiasm and optimism (the Popular Front had just won a victory in the Spanish election). Banned soon after, it resurfaced after May 1968. **RB** French +subtitles.

Julien Bertheau *Unemployed worker* • Marcel Duhamel *Garage owner* • O'Brady [Frédéric O'Brady] *Washer* • Jean Dasté *Schoolteacher* • Emile Drain *Worker* • Jean Renoir *Bistro owner* ■ *Dir* Jean Renoir, Jean-Paul Le Chanois, Jacques Becker, André Zwobada, Pierre Unik, Henri Cartier-Bresson, P Vaillant-Couturier, Jacques Brunius • *Scr* Jean Renoir, Jean-Paul Le Chanois, Jacques Becker, André Zwobada, Pierre Unik, P Vaillant-Couturier, Henri Cartier-Bresson, Jacques Brunius

La Vie Est Belle ★★★ PG
Comedy musical
1987 · Bel/Fr/Zaire · Colour · 82min

Papa Wemba leaves his village for Kinshasa to pursue his ambition to become a recording star, only to have to work as a houseboy. He falls in love with Bibi Krubwa, but her mother forces an end to the relationship until a witch doctor intervenes. Co-written and co-directed by Belgian-born Benoît Lamy and Zaire's Ngangura Mweze, this is an interesting insight into an unfamiliar culture. It's charming, cheerful

V

and well-played, particularly by Wemba, a Paris-based pop star. **RK** French +subtitles.

Papa Wemba *Kourou* • Bibi Krubwa *Kabibi* • Landu Nzunzimbu Matshia *Mamou* • Kanku Kasongo *Nvouandou* • Lokinda Mengi Feza *Nzazi* • Kalimazi Lombume *Mongali* ■ *Dir* Benoît Lamy, Ngangura Mweze • *Scr* Benoît Lamy, Maryse Léon, Ngangura Mweze

A View from Here ★★
Drama 2009 · US · Colour · 100min

A simple film sends out simple messages, as investigative TV reporter Laura Leighton puts her journalism skills to good use in a return to her Nevada home town. Assisted by her gothy teen daughter, she not only tackles the rift between her and her ailing mother (an unconvincing Angie Dickinson) but also uncovers a local conspiracy. Events unfold exactly as expected, and clichéd characters and behaviour add to the predictability, though the tale's warmth makes it a pleasant enough diversion. **SF**

Laura Leighton *Kelly Faraday* • Angie Dickinson *Ruth Hanson* • Peter Jason *Hank Bentley* • David Lee Smith *Walt Mitchell* ■ *Dir* Stephen Bridgewater • *Scr* Donald Martin, Mitchell Gabourie

View from the Top ★ PG
Romantic comedy 2003 · US · Colour · 83min

Even an over-used and under-funny Mike Myers can't salvage this flight-attendant comedy that never leaves the terminal, let alone gets off the ground. It's hard to see what first attracted Myers and Gwyneth Paltrow to this mediocre tale of a small-town stewardess who wants to fly with a major airline. **DA** DVD

Gwyneth Paltrow *Donna Jensen* • Christina Applegate *Christine Montgomery* • Mark Ruffalo *Ted Stewart* • Candice Bergen *Sally Weston* • Kelly Preston *Sherry* • Rob Lowe *Pilot Steve Bench* • Mike Myers *John Whitney* • Josh Malina [Joshua Malina] *Randy Jones* ■ *Dir* Bruno Barreto • *Scr* Eric Wald

A View to a Kill ★★ PG
Spy adventure 1985 · UK · Colour · 125min

This below-average Bond movie has Roger Moore as 007 for the seventh and final time. His smoothness is now a bit tired, but there's still some action and excitement to be had. The baddies are headed by Christopher Walken and his accomplice, girlfriend Grace Jones, and, while both can look pretty scary, you don't get the impression that they're particularly evil. Tanya Roberts does what Bond girls do pretty well, but the plot doesn't really convince. **AT** Violence. DVD BL

Roger Moore *James Bond* • Christopher Walken *Max Zorin* • Tanya Roberts *Stacey Sutton* • Grace Jones *May Day* • Patrick Macnee *Tibbett* • David Yip *Chuck Lee* • Fiona Fullerton *Pola Ivanova* • Desmond Llewelyn *"Q"* • Robert Brown *"M"* • Lois Maxwell *Miss Moneypenny* • Walter Gotell *General Gogol* ■ *Dir* John Glen • *Scr* Richard Maibaum, Michael G Wilson, from characters by Ian Fleming

Vigil ★★★ 15
Drama 1984 · NZ · Colour · 86min

This is an early film from Vincent Ward, director of the excellent *The Navigator - a Medieval Odyssey* and *Map of the Human Heart*, and the ghastly *What Dreams May Come*. Ward is noted for his visual style, and there's plenty on which to feast the eyes in this attractive tale of a New Zealand farm girl struggling to adapt when a young drifter fills the family place vacated by her recently dead dad. Absorbing viewing. **DA**

Penelope Stewart *Elizabeth Peers* • Frank Whitten *Ethan Ruir* • Fiona Kay *Lisa Peers, "Toss"* • Bill Kerr *Birdie* • Gordon Shields *Justin Peers* ■ *Dir* Vincent Ward • *Scr* Vincent Ward, Graeme Tetley

Vigil in the Night ★★★
Medical melodrama 1940 · US · BW · 95min

This exciting melodrama features the marvellous Carole Lombard as a committed nurse who takes the blame for a fatal mistake made by her sister Anne Shirley. The RKO studio's re-creation of England is, unusually for a Hollywood film of this period, remarkably convincing, and the British support cast headed by handsome doctor Brian Aherne is also excellent. (Watch out for a very young Peter Cushing.) Director George Stevens's no-nonsense cinematic style makes this very satisfying. **TS**

Carole Lombard *Anne Lee* • Anne Shirley *Lucy Lee* • Brian Aherne *Dr Prescott* • Julien Mitchell *Matthew Bowley* • Robert Coote *Dr Caley* • Rita Page *Glennie* • Peter Cushing *Joe Shand* ■ *Dir* George Stevens • *Scr* Fred Guiol, PJ Wolfson, Rowland Leigh, from the novel by AJ Cronin

Vigilante Force ★★★ 18
Action drama 1975 · US · Colour · 85min

Kris Kristofferson is the Vietnam vet brought in by his brother (Jan-Michael Vincent) to fight off lawless oil workers in a booming California town in this awkward combination of western and war genres from director George Armitage. Highlighting male bonding and nasty violence above a cohesive story, at heart it's a self-conscious retelling of the Cain and Abel saga. But Kristofferson acquits himself well, as does Bernadette Peters in a barnstorming portrayal as a down-at-heel cabaret artist. **AJ** Violence, swearing.

Kris Kristofferson *Aaron Arnold* • Jan-Michael Vincent *Ben Arnold* • Victoria Principal *Linda Christopher* • Bernadette Peters *Little Dee* • Brad Dexter *Mayor Bradford* • Judson Pratt *Harry Lee* ■ *Dir/Scr* George Armitage

The Vigilantes Return ★★ U
Western 1947 · US · Colour · 66min

This pretty average western has marshal Jon Hall hiding his true identity to trap villain Robert Wilcox, whose saloon is the front for an outlaw lair. Nothing special, but efficiently done. Watch for terrific baddie Jack Lambert in one of his earliest roles. **TS**

Jon Hall *Johnnie Taggart* • Margaret Lindsay *Kitty* • Paula Drew *Louise Holden* • Andy Devine *Andy* • Robert Wilcox *Clay Curtwright* • Jonathan Hale *Judge Holden* • Arthur Hohl *Sheriff* ■ *Dir* Ray Taylor • *Scr* Roy Chanslor

Vigo: Passion for Life ★★ 15
Biographical drama
1997 · UK/Jpn/Fr/Sp/Ger · Colour · 98min

Sadly, this filmic essay on the tragic life of 1930s French film director Jean Vigo fails to improve on director Julien Temple's earlier efforts. Though imaginatively shot, this is ultimately a depressing, dragging tale of Vigo and his wife Lydu's terminal tuberculosis and how the couple live under feelings of acute mortality. Though lifted by earnest and endearing performances from leads James Frain and Romane Bohringer, the film fails to convey the revolutionary legacy Vigo left behind him; he died at 29, having already made classics *Zéro de Conduite* and *L'Atalante*. **LH** Swearing, sex scenes. DVD

Romane Bohringer *Lydu Lozinska* • James Frain *Jean Vigo* • Diana Quick *Emily* • William Scott-Masson *Marcel* • James Faulkner *Dr Gerard* • Jim Carter *Bonaventure* • Paola Dionisotti *Marie* • Lee Ross *Oscar Levy* ■ *Dir* Julien Temple • *Scr* Peter Ettedgui, Anne Devlin, Julien Temple, from the play *Love's a Revolution* by Chris Ward, from the biography *Jean Vigo* by Paulo Emilio Salles Gomes

The Viking Queen ★
Period adventure 1967 · UK · Colour · 91min

There's only one reason for catching this risible offering from Hammer and that's the chance to spot the Viking wearing a wristwatch! Otherwise, there's little pleasure to be gained from watching seasoned performers making fools of themselves in a story that would struggle to get a pass grade in GCSE English. **DP**

Don Murray *Justinian* • Carita *Salina* • Donald Houston *Maelgan* • Andrew Keir *Octavian* • Adrienne Corri *Beatrice* • Niall MacGinnis *Tiberion* • Wilfrid Lawson *King Priam* • Nicola Pagett *Talia* • Patrick Troughton *Tristram* ■ *Dir* Don Chaffey • *Scr* Clarke Reynolds, from a story by John Temple-Smith

Viking Women and the Sea Serpent ★ PG
Period adventure 1957 · US · BW · 65min

This is an attempt to set a standard escape story in a distinct historical time period. Unfortunately the paltry budget meant all Norse fact had finally to be ignored and enough cheap fantasy tossed in to please the horror crowd. Hence the last minute appearance of the cheesy sea monster. Badly lit and ultra-phoney (the cast members all wear blond wigs), this is a seldom-seen Roger Corman quickie. You'll soon realise why. **AJ** DVD

Abby Dalton *Desir* • Susan Cabot *Enger* • Brad Jackson *Vedric* • June Kenney *Asmild* • Richard Devon *Stark* ■ *Dir* Roger Corman • *Scr* Lawrence Goldman, from a story by Irving Block

The Vikings ★★★★★ PG
Epic adventure 1958 · US · Colour · 110min

This tremendously exciting, if gory, adventure epic was a huge hit for independent producer/star Kirk Douglas, who generously changed the title of Edison Marshall's novel *The Viking* in order to include his friends Tony Curtis, Janet Leigh and Ernest Borgnine. Jack Cardiff's location photography is superb, and Harper Goff's splendid art direction gives a remarkably authentic sense of period. There is a fine feel of lusty enjoyment pervading this movie, and it's hard to see how it could have been made any better. The uncredited title narration is by Orson Welles. **TS** DVD

Tony Curtis *Eric* • Kirk Douglas *Einar* • Ernest Borgnine *Ragnar* • Janet Leigh *Morgana* • James Donald *Egbert* • Alexander Knox *Father Godwin* • Frank Thring *Aella* ■ *Dir* Richard Fleischer • *Scr* Calder Willingham, Dale Wasserman, from the novel *The Viking* by Edison Marshall

Viktor und Viktoria ★★★
Period comedy musical 1933 · Ger · BW · 100min

This delightful German original (filmed concurrently in French as *Georges et Georgette*) went on to inspire the 1936 British remake *First a Girl* and, more famously, *Victor/Victoria* in 1982. It's the story of struggling female impersonator Renate Müller who is persuaded to pretend she's a man cross-dressing as a woman. Müller then becomes the talk of the town, but complications soon arise from the merry-go-round of gender swapping. Light-hearted and atmospheric. **BB** German +subtitles.

Renate Müller *Susanne Lohr* • Hermann Thimig *Viktor Hempel* • Hilde Hildebrand *Ellinor* • Friedel Pisetta *Lilian* • Adolf Wohlbruck [Anton Walbrook] *Robert* ■ *Dir* Reinhold Schünzel • *Scr* Reinhold Schünzel, from the play by Reinhold Schünzel

Villa Amalia ★★★★ PG
Drama 2009 · Fr/Swi · Colour · 94min

Adapted from a novel by Pascal Quignard, Benoît Jacquot's film is a contrived but utterly compelling study in seizing back one's life. Isabelle Huppert stars as a musician who decides to sell everything and quit her career on witnessing her partner (Xavier Beauvois) with another woman. However, a chance encounter with Georges (Jean-Hugues Anglade), a long-lost friend from her childhood, enables her to make the break and she embarks on a tortuous continental odyssey. Jacquot's fractured editing reinforces both Huppert's emotional turmoil and the forward momentum of her flight, and Jacquot adds emotional resonance by punctuating the shifting vistas with enigmatic close-ups of the typically exceptional actress. **DP** French, Italian +subtitles.

Isabelle Huppert *Ann* • Jean-Hugues Anglade *Georges* • Xavier Beauvois *Thomas* • Maya Sansa *Giula* • Clara Bindi *Marion* • Viviana Aliberti *Veri* ■ *Dir* Benoît Jacquot • *Scr* Benoît Jacquot, Julien Boivent, from the novel by Pascal Quignard

Villa des Roses ★★ 12
Period romantic drama
2002 · Bel/UK/Neth/Lux · Colour · 114min

Despite looking suitably gaunt, Julie Delpy fails to convey the emotional fragility of the provincial widow who accepts work as a maid in Harriet Walter and Timothy West's crumbling Parisian guest house, only to fall under the spell of a shiftless German artist (Shaun Dingwall). Director Frank Van Passel makes moody use of the dingy interiors, but his use of anachronistic camera effects proves intrusive, while he leaves intriguing minor characters in the shadows. **DP** DVD

Julie Delpy *Louise Créteur* • Shaun Dingwall *Richard Grünewald* • Shirley Henderson *Ella* • Harriet Walter *Olive Burrell* • Timothy West *Hugh Burrell* • Frank Vercruyssen *Aasgaard* ■ *Dir* Frank Van Passel • *Scr* Christophe Dirickx, from the novel by Willem Elsschot

The Village ★★★ 12
Horror thriller 2004 · US · Colour · 103min

Set in an unspecified time and place, this beautifully photographed tale concerns an isolated rural community that seems idyllic, except for the mysterious creatures that inhabit the surrounding woods. The villagers respect the territory of these rarely seen beings, but the uneasy truce is challenged when Joaquin Phoenix steps across the boundary line. Director M Night Shyamalan uses just about every trick in the book to create a sense of unease and his cast performs admirably, particularly newcomer Bryce Dallas Howard (daughter of director Ron Howard). However, Shyamalan piles on the twists till the story buckles. **BP** Violence. DVD

Joaquin Phoenix *Lucius Hunt* • Bryce Dallas Howard *Ivy Walker* • Adrien Brody *Noah Percy* • William Hurt *Edward Walker* • Sigourney Weaver *Alice Hunt* • Brendan Gleeson *August Nicholson* • Cherry Jones *Mrs Clack* • Jayne Atkinson *Mrs Walker* • Judy Greer *Kitty Walker* ■ *Dir/Scr* M Night Shyamalan • *Cinematographer* Roger Deakins • *Music* James Newton Howard

Village at the End of the World ★★★★ 12A
Documentary 2012 · Den/UK · Colour · 81min

Co-director Sarah Gavron and David Katznelson's compelling movie follows the 59 residents of the Greenland fishing village of Niaqornat who are striving to prevent their own ecological and economic extinction. The focus falls on four quirky individuals: Lars, a rap-loving Manchester United fan; his estranged father Karl; Ilannguaq, an outsider who met his wife online; and 76-year-old Ane, who recalls the times when artificial light came from burning whale blubber. It's a superbly photographed study of a community harnessing tradition and progress to bring hope and prosperity. **DP** Greenlandic +subtitles. Swearing.

■ *Dir* Sarah Gavron, David Katznelson

Village in the Mist ★★★
Drama 1983 · S Kor · Colour · 90min

Im Kwon-taek had already directed more than 70 films by the time he made this startlingly graphic success, which many critics have cited as a South Korean *Straw Dogs*. Dark secrets lurk beneath the surface calm of the remote village to which Chong Yun-hee is dispatched as a supply teacher, but they begin to emerge after she's raped by a sinister outsider, Ahn Sung-kee. The main focus of this technically dazzling film is on the status of women within the Confucian morality system. **DP** Korean +subtitles.

Ahn Sung-kee *Sinister outsider* • Chong Yun-hee *Teacher* ■ *Dir* Im Kwon-taek • *Scr* Song Kil-han, from the book *Island without a Name* by I Mun-yol

Village of Daughters ★★ U
Comedy 1961 · UK · BW · 90min

Eric Sykes rarely landed leading roles and he struggles to make an impact in this slight Sicilian farce. Travelling salesman Sykes arrives in a village that's so short of eligible men that a letter from London requesting a bride for an exile's son is a cause for commotion. He is invited by local priest John Le Mesurier to select the most suitable candidate. However, he's soon abusing his position. Corrupt mayor Grégoire Aslan has his moments, but, essentially, this is a mediocre one-gag film. DP

Eric Sykes *Herbert Harris* • Scilla Gabel *Angelina Vimercati* • Yvonne Romain *Annunziata Gastoni* • Jill Carson *Lucia Puccelli* • Talitha Pol *Gioia Spartaco* • Bettine Le Beau *Alisa Marcio* • Carol White *Natasha Passoti* • Grégoire Aslan *Gastoni* • John Le Mesurier *Don Calogero* ■ *Dir* George Pollock • *Scr* David Pursall, Jack Seddon

Village of the Damned
★★★★ 12

Science-fiction horror   1960 · UK · BW · 74min

Twelve women give birth to blond alien offspring after a strange force puts their community into a 24-hour trance, in this remarkably faithful adaptation of John Wyndham's novel *The Midwich Cuckoos*. In a film that is compelling, creepy and often unbearably tense, an icy George Sanders becomes their teacher and then tries to halt their world domination plans. Superbly acted, with the human/family side of the horror unusually explored more than the fantasy elements, this British near-classic is a sci-fi treat and remains so. A less satisfying sequel, *Children of the Damned*, followed in 1964. AJ Violence. **DVD**

George Sanders *Gordon Zellaby* • Barbara Shelley *Anthea Zellaby* • Martin Stephens *David* • Michael Gwynn *Major Alan Bernard* • Laurence Naismith *Dr Willers* • Richard Warner *Harrington* • Jenny Laird *Mrs Harrington* • Sarah Long *Evelyn Harrington* ■ *Dir* Wolf Rilla • *Scr* Wolf Rilla, Stirling Silliphant, George Barclay [Ronald Kinnoch], from the novel *The Midwich Cuckoos* by John Wyndham

Village of the Damned ★★ 15

Science-fiction horror
1995 · US · Colour · 93min

Those blond alien youngsters return to wreak havoc in a small town in cult director John Carpenter's update of the 1960 British sci-fi near-classic. Despite the setting being transferred to California, superior special effects heightening the nastiness and Christopher Reeve giving a nicely heroic performance, the end result forgoes the touches and stylish atmosphere you might expect from Carpenter for a bland sheen. AJ Violence. **DVD**

Christopher Reeve *Alan Chaffee* • Kirstie Alley *Dr Susan Verner* • Linda Kozlowski *Jill McGowan* • Michael Paré *Frank McGowan* • Meredith Salenger *Melanie Roberts* • Mark Hamill *Reverend George* • Pippa Pearthree *Mrs Sarah Miller* ■ *Dir* John Carpenter • *Scr* David Himmelstein, from the 1960 film, from the novel *The Midwich Cuckoos* by John Wyndham

Village of the Giants ★★ PG

Science-fiction comedy drama
1965 · US · Colour · 77min

Producer Bert I Gordon was a master of crude productions with gimmicky titles, and this improbable but fun tale about a boy genius (Ron Howard) who invents a food that causes growth to gigantic proportions is down to his usual standard. However, it's enjoyable hokum, supposedly based on an HG Wells original, which gets by on pure brio. JG

Tommy Kirk *Mike* • Johnny Crawford *Horsey* • Beau Bridges *Fred* • Ronny Howard [Ron Howard] *Genius* • Joy Harmon *Merrie* • Bob Random *Rick* • Tisha Sterling *Jean* ■ *Dir* Bert I Gordon • *Scr* Alan Caillou, by Bert I Gordon, from the novel *The Food of the Gods* by HG Wells

Village Tale ★★★

Drama   1935 · US · BW · 80min

The dark side of human nature is to the fore in this tale of bitter rivalry between wealthy Randolph Scott and local landowning nonentity Arthur Hohl for the affections of Hohl's wife, Kay Johnson. The simmering feud in a small rural community becomes the focus for the collected pettiness and malice of the townspeople. A somewhat static drama, steeped in unpleasantness, but interesting and well acted, particularly by the supporting players. RK

Randolph Scott *TN "Slaughter" Somerville* • Kay Johnson *Janet Stevenson* • Arthur Hohl *Elmer Stevenson* • Robert Barrat *Drury Stevenson* • Janet Beecher *Amy Somerville* • Edward Ellis *Old*

Ike • Dorothy Burgess *Lulu Stevenson* • Donald Meek *Charlie* • Guinn Williams [Guinn "Big Boy" Williams] *Ben Roberts* ■ *Dir* John Cromwell • *Scr* Allan Scott, from the novel *Village Tale* by Phil Stong

Villain ★★★ 18

Crime drama   1971 · UK · Colour · 93min

Richard Burton stars as a vicious East End gangster, who rules by fear and the cut-throat razor. Clearly inspired, if that's the word, by the career of the Kray twins, the picture is one of unrelieved ugliness, from the run-down locations to the run-down bulk of Burton himself: overweight, shabby, self-loathing. Adored by his mother, he's a homosexual with a toy-boy lover, and a Labour voter who worries about OAPs. Wavering uneasily between horror, black comedy and sentimentality, it's held together by Burton's performance. AT Violence, swearing.

Richard Burton *Vic Dakin* • Ian McShane *Wolfe Lissner* • Nigel Davenport *Bob Matthews* • Donald Sinden *Gerald Draycott* • Fiona Lewis *Venetia* • TP McKenna *Frank Fletcher* • Joss Ackland *Edgar Lowis* ■ *Dir* Michael Tuchner • *Scr* Dick Clement, Ian La Frenais, Al Lettieri, from the novel *The Burden of Proof* by James Barlow

Villain ★★★ 15

Drama   2010 · Jpn · Colour · 139min

On the surface, Lee Sang-il's dramatisation of Shuichi Yoshida's novel is a murder mystery that evolves into a doomed romance forged on the run between an outsider (Satoshi Tsumabuki) and a lonely girl (Eri Fukatsu). But it is also a reflection on the generational chasm that is opening up in Japan, as the young disregard the notions of honour, loyalty and politeness that once typified their society. In trying to cover so much thematic ground, Lee occasionally allows the action to drift, but, fortunately, the performances make as big an impact as the sweeping seascapes and the lyrical score. DP Japanese +subtitles. Sex scenes. **DVD**

Satoshi Tsumabuki *Yuichi Shimizu* • Eri Fukatsu *Mitsuyo Magome* • Kirin Kiki *Fusae Shimizu* • Masaki Okada *Keigo Masuo* ■ *Dir* Sang-il Lee • *Scr* Shûichi Yoshida, Lee Sang-il, from the novel by Yoshida

The Villain Still Pursued Her ★★

Comedy   1940 · US · BW · 65min

Ham abounds in this spoof on old-time melodrama, directed by Edward Cline, former creative aide to Buster Keaton and other silent clowns. Keaton makes a guest appearance in this tale of villainous landlord Alan Mowbray, who terrorises the sweet-natured Margaret Hamilton and her attractive daughter Anita Louise. Boos and hisses are encouraged but it doesn't work as it should and audiences generally sit silent and baffled. TH

Hugh Herbert *Frederick Healy* • Anita Louise *Mary Wilson* • Alan Mowbray *Cribbs* • Buster Keaton *William Dalton* • Joyce Compton *Hazel Dalton* • Richard Cromwell *Edward Middleton* • Billy Gilbert *Announcer* • Margaret Hamilton *Mrs Wilson* ■ *Dir* Edward F Cline [Edward Cline] • *Scr* Elbert Franklin, from the play *The Fallen Saved*

La Ville Est Tranquille ★★★★ 18

Drama   2000 · Fr · Colour · 127min

Robert Guédiguian directs this multilayered portrait of everyday life among the lower-class denizens of Marseille. As ever, he receives excellent service from his trusted ensemble cast in their depiction of numerous interlocking stories. Jean-Pierre Darroussin exhibits genuine pain as the lonely cab driver whose good intentions towards part-time prostitute Ariane Ascaride and her drug-addled daughter fail to alleviate an increasingly desperate situation. Awash with drugs, vice, violence, poverty and racial tension, Guédiguian's beloved Marseille is very much a city on a knife edge, yet he commends the spirit of her inhabitants as they battle on against

---

insurmountable odds. DP French +subtitles. **DVD**

Ariane Ascaride *Michèle* • Jean-Pierre Darroussin *Paul* • Gérard Meylan *Gérard* • Jacques Boudet *Paul's father* • Pascale Roberts *Paul's mother* • Christine Brücher *Viviane Froment* • Jacques Pieiller *Yves Froment* ■ *Dir* Robert Guédiguian • *Scr* Robert Guédiguian, Jean-Louis Milesi

Vincent and Theo ★★★ 15

Biographical drama
1990 · UK/Fr/US · Colour · 134min

Outlining the last years of painter Vincent van Gogh (Tim Roth), as seen through the eyes of his brother Theodore (Paul Rhys), this is a haunting study in loneliness, obsession and the tough quest for validation in the blinkered art world. Unusual direction by Robert Altman and an intense performance by Roth as the tortured genius make this a thought-provoking look at the nature of the creative impulse as it impacts on family life. AJ **DVD**

Tim Roth *Vincent van Gogh* • Paul Rhys *Theodore van Gogh* • Bernadette Giraud *Marguerite Gachet* • Adrian Brine *Uncle Cent* • Jip Wijngaarden *Sien Hoornik* • Wladimir Yordanoff *Paul Gauguin* ■ *Dir* Robert Altman • *Scr* Julian Mitchell

Vincent, François, Paul and the Others ★★★

Comedy drama   1974 · It/Fr · Colour · 118min

The lives, loves and midlife crises of a group of middle-class Parisians, principally a doctor, a writer and a factory owner who are all 50-somethings and looking for something better. Surrounding them are the "others" – friends, wives, mistresses – and they all interact with ingenious timing and often witty results. As in all authentically French movies, coffee is sipped, cigarettes smoked and philosophy explored, but Claude Sautet's film is really just an extremely glossy soap opera made watchable by its heavyweight cast. AT In French.

Yves Montand *Vincent* • Michel Piccoli *François* • Serge Reggiani *Paul* • Gérard Depardieu *Jean* • Stéphane Audran *Catherine* • Marie Dubois *Lucie* • Antonella Lualdi *Julia* ■ *Dir* Claude Sautet • *Scr* Jean-Loup Dabadie, Claude Néron, Claude Sautet, from the novel *La Grande Marrade* by Claude Néron

Vincent: the Life and Death of Vincent Van Gogh
★★★ PG

Biographical documentary
1987 · Austria · Colour · 95min

This is a film closer in spirit to documentary than Vincente Minnelli's *Lust for Life* or Robert Altman's *Vincent and Theo*. Paul Cox's essay uses the artist's letters (sensitively read by John Hurt) to both examine the sources of his creative inspiration and reassess his mental state during those tormented final years, when he not only painted at a furious rate, but also suffered an anguish that finally crushed his ferocious resolve to remain sane. The film also traces the development of Van Gogh's style from the earliest line drawings to the powerfully emotive canvases of his Arles period. Enthralling. DP

John Hurt *Reader* ■ *Dir* Paul Cox • *Scr* Paul Cox, from the letters of Vincent van Gogh

Vincere ★★★ 15

Historical biographical drama
2009 · It/Fr · Colour and BW · 119min

Good Morning, Night director Marco Bellocchio again delves into the murkier aspects of Italian history with this stylish, almost operatic historical drama. The subject here is the little known story of Ida Dalser (Giovanna Mezzogiorno), the secret lover of Benito Mussolini (Filippo Timi) and mother of his child. Timi is a powerful presence and Mezzogiorno is mesmerising as she moves from obsessive lover to scorned mother, doomed to exile from her son in various rural asylums. But though the subject matter is undoubtedly of interest,

---

there are some meandering longueurs. JA Italian, German +subtitles. **DVD** **BD**

Giovanna Mezzogiorno *Ida Dalser* • Filippo Timi *Benito Mussolini/Benito Albino* • Fausto Russo Alesi *Riccardo Paicher* • Michela Cescon *Rachele Mussolini* • Corrado Invernizzi *Doctor Cappelletti* • Pier Giorgio Bellocchio [Piergiorgio Bellocchio] *Pietro Fedele* ■ *Dir* Marco Bellocchio • *Scr* Marco Bellocchio, Daniela Ceselli, from a story by Bellocchio

Vinegar Hill ★★

Drama   2004 · US · Colour · 93min

Although it's set in the early 1970s, the storyline of this melodramatic TV movie has the ring of a 19th-century penny-dreadful. With painter husband Tim Guinee out of work, Mary-Louise Parker agrees to stay with his parents in small-town Wisconsin until their prospects improve. But, no sooner has she bumped into her old flame (who is now the sheriff) and Guinee has fallen for a lingerie store clerk, than father-in-law Tom Skerritt begins delivering brimstone diatribes reflecting his hypocritical belief in a vengeful God. The cast does a decent enough job, but too little is left to the imagination. DP

Mary-Louise Parker *Ellen Grier* • Tom Skerritt *Fritz Grier* • Betty Buckley *Mary Margaret Grier* • Tim Guinee *Jake Grier* ■ *Dir* Peter Werner • *Scr* Suzette Couture, from the novel by A Manette Ansay

Vinyan ★★★ 18

Horror thriller
2008 · Fr/Bel/UK/Aus · Colour · 92min

This atmospheric horror thriller from director Fabrice du Welz (*Calvaire*) stars Emmanuelle Béart and Rufus Sewell as a couple devastated by the disappearance of their son in the 2004 tsunami. Six months after that catastrophe, Béart is convinced she has spotted her son in a charity worker's video of a village in Burma, and persuades the sceptical Sewell to get them into the country to rescue him. Du Welz's second feature is an ambitious attempt to fuse Thai cinema's ghost genre with Joseph Conrad's *Heart of Darkness*, and Nicolas Roeg's *Don't Look Now*. The photography is striking, but the plotline is cluttered with implausibilities. DP In English, Thai. Violence, swearing, sex scenes, nudity. **DVD** **BD**

Emmanuelle Béart *Jeanne Bellmer* • Rufus Sewell *Paul Bellmer* • Petch Osathanugrah *Thaksin Gao* • Julie Dreyfus *Kim* • Ampon Pankratok *Sokghaï* • Josse De Pauw *Matthias* ■ *Dir/Scr* Fabrice du Welz

Vinyl ★★

Satire   1965 · US · BW · 70min

One of several films Andy Warhol made with playwright Ronald Tavel during 1965. The quasi-script, reputedly based on Anthony Burgess's novel *A Clockwork Orange*, focuses on sadomasochism and features a lot of bondage and torture. The dialogue in the second reel is inaudible because there are records playing in another part of the studio. Finally the cast get stoned on amyl nitrate, and an orgy begins. Dedicated cineastes may retain a modicum of interest. DM

Gerard Malanga *Victor* • Edie Sedgwick *Woman on trunk* • John MacDermott *Detective* • Ondine ■ *Dir* Andy Warhol • *Scr* Ronald Tavel, from the novel *A Clockwork Orange* by Anthony Burgess

Vinyl ★★★ 15

Comedy based on a true story
2012 · US · Colour · 81min

In 2004, Mike Peters, frontman of 1980s Welsh rock band the Alarm, convinced young unknowns the Wayriders to call themselves the Poppy Field and pass off the Alarm's *45 RPM* as their own song. Peters then exposed the hoax after the song entered the Top 30. Co-writer/director Sara Sugarman uses the story as a basis for this enjoyable comedy. Phil Daniels keeps things on track as a washed-up rocker who is convinced that his old band can return to the spotlight. But a stinging introduction to juvenile tastes and soulless showbiz prompts him to put together a photogenic

---

U SUITABLE FOR ALL   Uc SUITABLE ESPECIALLY FOR YOUNG CHILDREN (DVD ONLY)   PG PARENTAL GUIDANCE   12A UNDER 12s TO BE ACCOMPANIED (CINEMA ONLY)

band of stooges, led by busker Jamie Blackley. There's not much in the way of acerbic industry satire or poignant character development – and the song *Free Rock 'n' Roll* – is nobody's idea of an instant punk anthem, but this is still a spirited swipe at designer pop. DP Swearing, sexual references, drug abuse.

Phil Daniels *Johnny Jones* • Perry Benson *Robbie* • Jamie Blackley *Drainpipe* • Keith Allen *Minto* • Chris Turner [Christopher Roy Turner] *Griff* • Julia Ford *Jules* ■ *Dir* Sara Sugarman • *Scr* Sara Sugarman, Jim Cooper (2), from Cooper's story

The Violators ★★★ 15

Drama 2015 · UK · Colour · 96min

Acclaimed novelist Helen Walsh makes an accomplished directorial debut with this twisting rites-of-passage tale set against Birkenhead's decaying docklands. Excellent newcomer Lauren McQueen plays the 15-year-old dropout who seeks the protection of pawnbroker Stephen Lord when she discovers that her abusive father is to be released from prison. Walsh conveys the predatory nature of Lord's relationship with McQueen with acuity, but the dénouement is overstated. DP Sexual abuse, swearing

DVD

Lauren McQueen *Shelly* • Brogan Ellis *Rachel* • Derek Barr *Andy* • Stephen Lord *Mikey* ■ *Dir/Scr* Helen Walsh

Violent Cop ★★★★ 18

Thriller 1989 · Jpn · Colour · 98min

Although he was already a massive star in Japan, this brooding thriller made actor/first-time director Takeshi "Beat" Kitano the hip name to drop in film circles in the UK. The plot itself could have come from any mainstream blockbuster: a tough, unconventional cop (Kitano) and his new, inexperienced partner find themselves up against their fellow officers when investigating a drugs case. However, the usual Hollywood clichés are turned on their head by Kitano's highly stylised direction, the splashes of quirky black humour and sudden jolts of extreme violence. On the screen, Kitano's charismatic performance is riveting. JF Japanese +subtitles. *DVD*

"Beat" Takeshi [Takeshi Kitano] *Detective Azuma* • Maiko Kawakami *Akari* • Haku Ryu *Kiyohiro, hit man* • Makoto Ash kawa *Kikuchi, rookie* • Shiro Sano *Police Chief Yoshinari* • Shigeru Hiraizumi *Detective Iwaki* ■ *Dir* Takeshi Kitano • *Scr* Hisashi Nozawa

The Violent Enemy ★★ U

Political thriller 1969 · UK · Colour · 93min

This downbeat thriller stars Tom Bell as an IRA man on the run, who is reluctantly recruited to blow up a British-owned power station. It's efficiently made, if unsurprising, and familiar American actor Ed Begley is worth watching as the fanatical Irish mastermind behind the scheme. JG

Tom Bell *Sean Roçan* • Susan Hampshire *Hannah Costello* • Ed Begley *Colum O'More* • Jon Laurimore *Austin* • Michael Standing *Fletcher* • Noel Purcell *John Michael Leary* ■ *Dir* Don Sharp • *Scr* Edmund Ward, from the novel *A Candle For The Dead* by Hugh Marlowe [Jack Higgins]

The Violent Men ★★★ PG

Western 1955 · US · Colour · 91min

This well-cast but under-scripted western has Edward G Robinson as a disabled land baron, who discovers that his venal wife Barbara Stanwyck is in love with his own brother, played by the ever-excellent Brian Keith. Into this positively seething morass of emotion walks rancher Glenn Ford, intent on pacifying the townsfolk who've turned against the unscrupulous empire-building Robinson. There's real star power on display here, and Ford is superb, but the whole isn't quite as good as the sum of its parts. TS *DVD*

Glenn Ford *John Farrish* • Barbara Stanwyck *Martha Wilkison* • Edward G Robinson *Lew Wilkison* • Dianne Foster *Judith Wilkison* • Brian Keith *Cole Wilkison* • May Wynn *Caroline Vail* • Warner Anderson *Jim McCloud* ■ *Dir* Rudolph Maté • *Scr* Harry Kleiner, from the novel *Rough Company* by Donald Hamilton

The Violent Ones ★★★

Crime drama 1967 · US · Colour · 87min

Actor Fernando Lamas directed himself stylishly in this grim drama about three Anglo-American strangers implicated in the rape and murder of a girl in a small Mexican town. Lamas plays the sheriff who has to protect the Mexican-hating suspects from a lynch mob spurred on by the dead girl's father. Not particularly original in its examination of prejudice, the movie nevertheless does all it needs to convince and contains an exciting desert-chase climax. TH

Fernando Lamas *Manuel Vega* • Aldo Ray *Joe Vorzyck* • Tommy Sands *Mike Marain* • David Carradine *Lucas Barnes* • Lisa Gaye *Dolores* • Melinda Marx *Juanita* ■ *Dir* Fernando Lamas • *Scr* Doug Wilson, Charles Davis, from a story by Fred Freiberger, Herman Miller

Violent Playground ★★ PG

Crime drama 1958 · UK · BW · 101min

From the producing/directing team of Michael Relph and Basil Dearden comes a drearily predictable but well-handled slice of dour realism, set in Liverpool. Stanley Baker is a policeman who, after unsuccessfully investigating an outbreak of arson, is transferred to the job of juvenile liaison officer in a depressed area. He falls in love with Anne Heywood, only to discover that her young brother David McCallum is the arsonist. RK *DVD*

Stanley Baker *Sgt Truman* • Anne Heywood *Cathie Murphy* • David McCallum (1) *Johnny Murphy* • Peter Cushing *Priest* • John Slater *Sgt Walker* • Clifford Evans *Heaven Evans* • Moultrie Kelsall *Superintendent* • George A Cooper (2) *Chief Inspector* ■ *Dir* Basil Dearden • *Scr* James Kennaway, from his novel

Violent Road ★★ U

Drama 1958 · US · BW · 77min

This ordinary Hollywood picture shows three pairs of drivers taking trucks full of dangerous rocket fuel along a rough mountain road. The journey is full of contrived incidents and, naturally, not everyone makes it – but it's hard to care one way or the other. AE

Brian Keith *Mitch* • Dick Foran *Sarge* • Efrem Zimbalist Jr *George Lawrence* • Merry Anders *Carrie* • Sean Garrison *Ken Farley* • Joanna Barnes *Peg Lawrence* • Perry Lopez *Manuelo* • Ann Doran *Edith* ■ *Dir* Howard W Koch • *Scr* Richard Landau, from a story by Don Martin

Violent Saturday ★★★★ 12

Crime drama 1955 · US · Colour · 89min

A well-made, tense and exciting study of the preparations for a bloody and daring bank raid in a small Arizona town, this was filmed on actual locations in early CinemaScope, a process favoured by talented director Richard Fleischer. The assembled cast is impressive, but the real star of the film is its superb climax, as the gripping robbery unfolds. TS *DVD* *Blu-ray*

Victor Mature *Shelley Martin* • Richard Egan *Boyd Fairchild* • Stephen McNally *Harper* • Virginia Leith *Linda* • Tommy Noonan *Harry Reeves* • Lee Marvin *Dill* • Margaret Hayes *Emily* • J Carrol Naish *Chapman* • Sylvia Sidney *Elsie* • Ernest Borgnine *Stadt* ■ *Dir* Richard Fleischer • *Scr* Sydney Boehm, from the novel by William L Heath

Violets Are Blue ★★★ PG

Romantic drama 1986 · US · Colour · 82min

There are some great performances in this strong film, with Kevin Kline and Sissy Spacek leading the way playing former high-school sweethearts. Since graduation Kline has settled down and become a family man and Spacek is now a world famous photographer. When she returns to her home town and encounters him, he welcomes her into his family fold. This is a subtle and sophisticated handling of difficult choices that avoids being trite and schmaltzy. The result makes for compelling and mature viewing. LH

Sissy Spacek *Gussie Sawyer* • Kevin Kline *Henry Squires* • Bonnie Bedelia *Ruth Squires* • John Kellogg *Ralph Sawyer* • Jim Standiford *Addy Squires* • Augusta Dabney *Ethel Sawyer* ■ *Dir* Jack Fisk • *Scr* Naomi Foner

Violette ★★★★ 15

Biographical drama 2013 · Fr/Bel · Colour · 138min

Violette Leduc was never admitted to French literature's inner sanctum, and her struggle to get her voice heard is limned with intelligence and insight in this stylish biopic. Leduc (Emmanuelle Devos) is first seen operating as a black marketeer in the wartime provinces, but everything changes when she moves to Paris and is encouraged to write by Simone de Beauvoir (Sandrine Kiberlain), who willingly acts as her mentor while resisting the bisexual Leduc's amorous advances. Director Martin Provost ably conveys the agonies of the creative process but it's Devos's outstanding performance that ensures this compels as both cultural history and human drama. DP French +subtitles.

Emmanuelle Devos *Violette Leduc* • Sandrine Kiberlain *Simone de Beauvoir* • Olivier Gourmet *Jacques Guérin* • Catherine Hiegel *Berthe Dehous* • Jacques Bonnaffé *Jean Genet* ■ *Dir* Martin Provost • *Scr* Martin Provost, Marc Abdelnour, Renéde Ceccatty

Violette Nozière ★★★

Historical crime drama 1977 · Fr · Colour · 123min

Based on a sensational 1930s murder case, this film is every bit as mixed-up as its heroine; for while Claude Chabrol teases us with extravagant ellipses, he actually tells the story of the Parisienne who murdered her father in a highly traditional, typically sub-Hitchcockian manner. Isabelle Huppert won the best actress prize at Cannes for her work as the demure teenager whose wild nights in the Latin Quarter result in syphilis and the opportunity to poison Jean Carmet and the more durable Stéphane Audran. DP In French.

Isabelle Huppert *Violette Nozière* • Stéphane Audran *Germaine Nozière* • Jean Carmet *Baptiste Nozière* ■ *Dir* Claude Chabrol • *Scr* Odile Barski, Herve Bromberger, Frederic Grendel, from a non-fiction book by Jean-Marie Fitere

The Violin ★★★★ 15

Drama 2005 · Mex · BW · 94min

An imperious display of dignified fury by 80-something Don Angel Tavira and Martin Boege Pare's austere monochrome photography are the keys to writer/director Francisco Vargas's compelling debut feature, which remains taut throughout. Having been driven from his village in the inhospitable Guerrero region during the Mexican peasant revolts of the 1970s, one-armed violinist Tavira seeks to use his talents to charm sadistic army captain Dagoberto Gama and recover the weapons stashed by his son on their smallholding. The contrast between Tavira's duplicitious ingratiation and Gama's urbane brutality makes their encounters endlessly fascinating, especially as Vargas keeps us guessing as to who has the upper hand. Consequently, this grips and provokes right up to its harrowing climax. DP In Spanish. *DVD*

Don Angel Tavira *Don Plutarco* • Dagoberto Gama *The Captain* • Fermin Martinez *The Lieutenant* • Gerardo Taracena *Genaro* • Mario Garibaldi *Lucio* ■ *Dir/Scr* Francisco Vargas • *Cinematographer* Martin Boege Pare

Virgil Bliss ★★★ 15

Drama 2001 · US · Colour · 93min

Joe Maggio strives to emulate the improvisational style of John Cassavetes, Mike Leigh and Ken Loach throughout his feature debut, which makes it all the more disappointing that he settles for so melodramatic a finale. Shot on grainy digital video and set in New York's less salubrious neighbourhoods, it follows the tortuous relationship between paroled crook Clint Jordan and crack-addicted hooker Kirsten

Russell. This has some shaky moments, but also a certain rough charm. DP

Clint Jordan *Virgil Bliss* • Kirsten Russell *Ruby* • Anthony Gorman *Manny* • Marc Romeo *Devo* • Greg Amici *Gillette* • Tom Brangle *Captain* • Rich Bierman *Prison guard* ■ *Dir/Scr* Joe Maggio

The Virgin and the Gypsy ★★★

Period drama 1970 · UK · Colour · 95min

Published posthumously, DH Lawrence's novella explored many of the sexual and social themes that recurred so often in his work. In this film version, Joanna Shimkus plays the curious innocent, whose strict upbringing drives her to sample the forbidden temptations offered by traveller Franco Nero. Both give decent performances, while the supporting cast is accomplished, but the film smoulders when it should catch fire. DP Nudity.

Joanna Shimkus *Yvette Saywell* • Franco Nero *Gypsy* • Honor Blackman *Mrs Fawcett* • Mark Burns *Major Eastwood* • Maurice Denham *Rector* • Fay Compton *Grandma* • Kay Walsh *Aunt Cissie* • Harriet Harper *Lucille Saywell* ■ *Dir* Christopher Miles • *Scr* Alan Plater, from the novella by DH Lawrence

Virgin Island ★★ U

Romantic drama 1958 · UK · Colour · 98min

Perfect English rose Virginia Maskell is cruising the Virgin Islands when archaeologist John Cassavetes sweeps her off her feet. Within a few days they are married, and they subsequently have a baby and become tediously contented. Even Maskell's mum, Isabel Dean, seems happy, despite the fact that Cassavetes, an inwardly seething Method actor, is hardly romantic leading man material. Nothing more than a travelogue with silly dialogue, it's bland. AT

John Cassavetes *Evan* • Virginia Maskell *Tina* • Sidney Poitier *Marcus* • Isabel Dean *Mrs Lomax* • Colin Gordon *The Commissioner* • Howard Marion-Crawford *Prescott* • Edric Connor *Captain Jason* ■ *Dir* Pat Jackson • *Scr* Philip Rush, Pat Jackson, from the novel *Our Virgin Island* by Robb White

The Virgin Queen ★★ U

Historical drama 1955 · US · Colour · 88min

Bette Davis stars as the last Tudor in this colourful but rather tepid melodrama. She gets to chew a little scenery as she realises that Richard Todd's Walter Raleigh is in love with lady-in-waiting Joan Collins, but the history lesson script keeps her on a short leash. Todd comes across as a sulky boy who isn't allowed to play in the Americas rather than an ambitious man of action, and his romance with the demure Collins is soggier than a cloak over a puddle. DP *DVD*

Bette Davis *Queen Elizabeth I* • Richard Todd *Sir Walter Raleigh* • Joan Collins *Beth Throgmorton* • Jay Robinson *Chadwick* • Herbert Marshall *Lord Leicester* • Dan O'Herlihy *Lord Derry* ■ *Dir* Henry Koster • *Scr* Harry Brown, Mindret Lord

The Virgin Soldiers ★★★ 15

War comedy drama 1969 · UK · Colour · 90min

Leslie Thomas's first novel went straight to the top of the bestseller charts in 1966 and this movie version quickly tried to capitalise on its success. Thomas wrote about his national service experiences in Singapore, where manhood was discovered through "sex" and military action during the Malayan Emergency. In one sense the movie is just *Private's Progress* with a touch of *Carry On Sergeant*, but the vivid action scenes and the probability of getting shot give it a blacker dramatic edge. *Stand Up Virgin Soldiers* arrived eight years later. AT

Hywel Bennett *Private Brigg* • Lynn Redgrave *Phillipa Raskin* • Nigel Davenport *Sergeant Driscoll* • Nigel Patrick *Regimental Sergeant Major Raskin* • Rachel Kempson *Mrs Raskin* • Jack Shepherd *Sergeant Wellbeloved* • Tsai Chin *Juicy Lucy* • Christopher Timothy *Corporal Brook* ■ *Dir* John Dexter • *Scr* John Hopkins, John McGrath, Ian La Frenais, from the novel by Leslie Thomas

V

The Virgin Spring ★★★★ 15
Period drama 1960 · Swe · BW · 85min

Winner of the 1960 Oscar for best foreign film, Ingmar Bergman's stark study of the cruelty and superstition of the Middle Ages positively drips with symbolism. However, it also works as a powerful revenge tragedy, as Max von Sydow encounters the men who raped and murdered his daughter after she'd been cursed by her half-sister. Often considered one of Bergman's bleakest films, the story has a miraculous ending that dispels his doubts about the presence of God. The acting has a rare intensity and the photography of Sven Nykvist (working with Bergman for the first time) is a joy to behold. DP Swedish +subtitles. *DVD*

Max von Sydow *Herr Tore* • Birgitta Valberg *Mareta Tore* • Gunnel Lindblom *Ingeri* • Birgitta Pettersson *Karin Tore* • Axel Duberg *Thin herdsman* • Tor Isedal *Mute herdsman* ■ *Dir* Ingmar Bergman • *Scr* Ulla Isaksson, from the 14th-century ballad *Tores Dotter I Vange*

The Virgin Suicides
★★★★ 15
Drama 1999 · US · Colour · 92min

Sofia Coppola's directorial debut confirmed real talent behind the camera. It's based on the 1970s-set Jeffrey Eugenides novel about five sisters in an affluent Michigan suburb who obsess the local adolescent males and eventually kill themselves. Coppola (who also wrote the screenplay) captures a melancholic truth about the awkwardness of blooming adolescent sexuality without jeopardising an otherworldly, backlit lyricism. Kirsten Dunst, as the eldest sister, and Josh Harnett, as the cocky stud, are exceptional, as is the music by French duo Air. But the secret of the film lies in the quiet symbolism and the evocative splendour. AC *DVD*

James Woods *Mr Lisbon* • Kathleen Turner *Mrs Lisbon* • Kirsten Dunst *Lux Lisbon* • Josh Hartnett *Trip Fontaine* • Hanna Hall *Cecilia Lisbon* • Chelse Swain *Bonnie Lisbon* • AJ Cook *Mary Lisbon* • Leslie Hayman *Therese Lisbon* • Danny DeVito *Dr Hornicker* ■ *Dir* Sofia Coppola • *Scr* Sofia Coppola, from the novel by Jeffrey Eugenides

Virginia City ★★★ U
Western 1940 · US · Sepia · 120min

A badly miscast Warner Bros western, set during the American Civil War, this features Humphrey Bogart, on the cusp of stardom, playing the most unlikely snarling Mexican bandit you'll ever see. It's hard to believe in prissy Miriam Hopkins, not a hair out of place, as a Confederate spy posing as a dance-hall girl. Nevertheless, the scale is lavish, the camerawork is professional, and Errol Flynn and Randolph Scott are very watchable. TS

Errol Flynn *Kerry Bradford* • Miriam Hopkins *Julia Hayne* • Randolph Scott *Vance Irby* • Humphrey Bogart *John Murrell* • Frank McHugh *Mr Upjohn* • Alan Hale *Olaf "Moose" Swenson* • Guinn "Big Boy" Williams *"Marblehead"* • John Litel *Marshal* ■ *Dir* Michael Curtiz • *Scr* Robert Henry Buckner [Robert Buckner], Norman Reilly Raine (uncredited), Howard Koch (uncredited)

The Virginian ★★★★
Western 1929 · US · BW · 92min

This early talkie retains its bite even though so many of its details have since become clichés. Gary Cooper is splendid as the Virginian, a ranch foreman forced into a romantic rivalry with his weak friend Richard Arlen. The object of their affection is Mary Brian's priggish schoolmarm who tries to restrain Cooper from shooting it out with Walter Huston's rustler villain. Besides its celebrated line, "If you want to call me that... smile!", there's also the first voicing of "This town ain't big enough for the both of us". Victor Fleming's direction is assured and imaginative. AE

Gary Cooper *The Virginian* • Walter Huston *Trampas* • Richard Arlen *Steve* • Mary Brian *Molly Wood* • Chester Conklin *Uncle Hughey* • Eugene Pallette *Honey Wiggin* • EH Calvert *Judge Henry* • Helen Ware *Ma Taylor* • Victor Potel *Nebrasky* ■ *Dir* Victor Fleming • *Scr* Howard Estabrook, Edward E Paramore Jr, Grover Jones,

Keene Thompson, Joseph L Mankiewicz, from the play by Owen Wister, Kirk La Shelle, from the novel by Wister

The Virginian ★★ U
Western 1946 · US · Colour · 83min

This version of Owen Wister's classic western has poker-faced Joel McCrea warning off villain Brian Donlevy. The Technicolor helps the aged tale, but overall there's nothing particularly special about the story of two cowboys competing for the affections of a school teacher. Sonny Tufts delivers one of his best performances as a good guy-turned-rustler, but you'll still find this wanting. TS *DVD*

Joel McCrea *The Virginian* • Brian Donlevy *Trampas* • Sonny Tufts *Steve Andrews* • Barbara Britton *Molly Wood* • Fay Bainter *Mrs Taylor* • Henry O'Neill *Mr Taylor* • Bill Edwards *Sam Bennett* ■ *Dir* Stuart Gilmore • *Scr* Frances Goodrich, Albert Hackett, Edward E Paramore Jr, Howard Estabrook, from the play by Owen Wister, Kirk La Shelle, from the novel by Owen Wister

The Virginian ★★ PG
Western 2000 · US · Colour · 90min

Owen Wister's much-filmed novel may have lost little of its romanticised toughness, but Bill Pullman is more Joel McCrea than Gary Cooper in the title role in this TV movie. Moreover, Pullman's direction lacks the punch required to sustain the story of the upright cowboy fighting to prevent a range war. Nice to see 1960s TV Virginian James Drury make an appearance, though. DP

Bill Pullman *The Virginian* • Diane Lane *Molly Stark* • John Savage *Steve* • Dennis Weaver *Sam Balaam* • James Drury *Rider* • Colm Feore *Trampas* ■ *Dir* Bill Pullman • *Scr* Larry Gross, from the novel *The Virginian; a Horseman of the Plains* by Owen Wister

Viridiana ★★★★★ 15
Satirical drama 1961 · Mex/Sp · BW · 86min

Luis Buñuel's most scathing attack on the Catholic Church and the depravity of the modern world was filmed with the uncompromising approval of Franco's fascist cinema supremos. Later they unsuccessfully tried to withdraw the picture after nominating it as Spain's official entry at Cannes. *Viridiana* traces the moral decline of a saintly girl who inadvertently drives her lascivious uncle to suicide and is then brutally exploited by the outcasts she shelters on his estate. The apex of Buñuel's satire is a mocking pastiche of Leonardo da Vinci's *Last Supper*. The Vatican censured the film as "an insult to Christianity" but it still won the Cannes Palme d'Or. DP Spanish +subtitles. *DVD*

Silvia Pinal *Viridiana* • Francisco Rabal *Jorge* • Fernando Rey *Don Jaime* • Margarita Lozano *Ramona* • Victoria Zinny *Lucia* • Teresa Rabal *Rita* ■ *Dir* Luis Buñuel • *Scr* Luis Buñuel, Julio Alajandro, from a story by Luis Buñuel

Virtual Girl ★ 18
Erotic science-fiction thriller 1998 · US · Colour · 83min

In this daft erotic thriller, a computer programmer creates the eponymous girl (the alluring Charlie Curtis), while developing a new game. Director Richard Gabai (who also stars) made *Assault of the Party Nerds*, *Virgin High* and many more of this ilk, which gives you a good indication of how awful this is. Followed by a sequel, but this is exclusively for collectors of straight-to-video trash. DM *DVD*

Charlie Curtis *Virtuality/Cynthia Lee* • Richard Gabai *Fred Renfield* • Max Dixon *John Lewis* • Warren Draper *Charlie R Poppy* ■ *Dir* Richard Gabai • *Scr* Richard Gabai, LA Maddox

Virtual Nightmare ★★ 12
Science-fiction action fantasy 2000 · Aus · Colour · 85min

There are shades of *The Matrix* in this modest but rewarding sci-fi thriller, which, like the latter, was shot in Australia. Michael Muhney is the ad man who starts losing his grip on reality when he discovers that he may have been living in a virtual world all along. There are no big names in the cast

but the performances are solid and director Michael Pattinson works well with a limited budget. JF

Michael Muhney *Dale Hunter* • Tasma Walton *Wendy* • Jennifer Congram *Natalie* • Paul Gleeson *Sanford* • John Noble *Dad* ■ *Dir* Michael Pattinson • *Scr* Dan Mazur, David Tausik

Virtual Sexuality ★★★ 15
Fantasy comedy 1999 · UK · Colour · 88min

Laura Fraser is the lovelorn teenage girl who uses a virtual reality makeover machine to create her ideal man in this *Weird Science*-style British comedy scripted by former agony uncle Nick Fisher. Smartly written and aimed firmly at young girls, this has an attractive cast and zips along merrily to a fun conclusion. Possibly a bit slight for anyone over the age of 18, but perfect low-budget fun for *Just Seventeen* readers. JB *DVD*

Laura Fraser *Justine* • Rupert Penry-Jones *Jake* • Luke de Lacey *Chas* • Kieran O'Brien *Alex* • Marcelle Duprey *Fran* • Natasha Bell *Hoover* • Steve John Shepherd *Jason* ■ *Dir* Nick Hurran • *Scr* Nick Fisher

Virtuosity ★★★ 15
Science-fiction thriller 1995 · US · Colour · 101min

If disgraced cop-turned-convict Denzel Washington can eliminate the computer-generated serial killer SID 6.7, he'll be gratefully pardoned in director Brett Leonard's spasmodically entertaining hi-tech fantasy adventure. Problem is, SID 6.7 (played by Russell Crowe) has 183 separate homicidal tendencies – including those of Hitler and Charles Manson – to his personality. Cyberspace wizardry covers the yawning gaps in this soulless thriller and the loose ends mount up faster than the body count, despite expert performances by the two commanding leads. AJ *DVD*

Denzel Washington *Parker Barnes* • Kelly Lynch *Madison Carter* • Russell Crowe *Sid 6.7* • Stephen Spinella *Lindenmeyer* • William Forsythe *William Cochran* • Louise Fletcher *Elizabeth Deane* ■ *Dir* Brett Leonard • *Scr* Eric Bernt

The Virtuous Sin ★★
Romantic drama 1930 · US · BW · 80min

This drawn-out drama revolves around the efforts of Kay Francis in 1917 Russia to save her bacteriologist husband Kenneth MacKenna, a military misfit, from having to go to war by seducing his commanding officer Walter Huston. Matters are complicated when she falls in love with the officer. The Russian setting and characters are of no visible benefit to this forgotten offering from Paramount, which marked George Cukor's second directing effort, shared with Louis Gasnier and giving no indication of his future prominence. RK

Walter Huston *Gen Gregori Platoff* • Kay Francis *Marya Ivanovna* • Kenneth MacKenna *Lt Victor Sablin* ■ *Dir* George Cukor, Louis Gasnier • *Scr* Martin Brown, Louise Long, from the novel *A Tábornok (The General)* by Lajos Zilahy

Virus ★★ PG
Disaster fantasy 1980 · Jpn · Colour · 102min

It seems more of the cash went to the all-star cast than on the special effects in this big-budget movie. Not content to focus on the few survivors of a worldwide plague, it also packs in forced prostitution and nuclear holocaust. The results don't completely make sense, especially in prints that cut about an hour from the running time. Some striking visuals and badly cast stars provide the curious points of interest. KB

Sonny Chiba *Dr Yamauchi* • Chuck Connors *Captain MacCloud* • Stephanie Faulkner *Sarah Baker* • Glenn Ford *Richardson* • Stuart Gillard *Dr Mayer* • Olivia Hussey *Marit* • George Kennedy *Admiral Conway* • Ken Ogata *Professor Tsuchiya* • Edward James Olmos *Captain Lopez* • Henry Silva *Garland* • Sonny Chiba *Dr Koji Takada*, Gregory Knapp, Kinji Fukasaku, from a novel by Sakyo Komatsu

Virus ★★ 18
Science-fiction horror 1998 · US · Colour · 95min

A sinking tugboat crew takes refuge on a deserted Russian science vessel during a typhoon only to find it harbouring an alien energy force. John Bruno's hybrid mass of genre clichés only entertains on a schlock level, with Jamie Lee Curtis, William Baldwin and Donald Sutherland giving undistinguished performances. AJ Violence, swearing. *DVD*

Jamie Lee Curtis *Kit Foster* • William Baldwin *Steve Baker* • Donald Sutherland *Captain Everton* • Joanna Pacula *Nadia* • Marshall Bell *JW Woods Jr* • Julio Oscar Mechoso *Squeaky* • Sherman Augustus *Richie* • Cliff Curtis *Hiko* ■ *Dir* John Bruno • *Scr* Chuck Pfarrer, Dennis Feldman, from the comic books by Chuck Pfarrer

Vision Quest ★★ 15
Sports drama 1985 · US · Colour · 107min

Matthew Modine stars as an overly thin high school wrestling champ, whose obsession with his sport is confused by a growing infatuation with his father's lodger Linda Fiorentino. Wrestling is a strange sport and, as a subject, makes for an even stranger movie. Fiorentino is as strong as ever and Modine just about holds his own, given the risible storyline. LH

Matthew Modine *Louden Swain* • Linda Fiorentino *Carla* • Michael Schoeffling *Kuch* • Ronny Cox *Loudon's father* • Harold Sylvester *Tanneran* • Charles Hallahan *Coach* • JC Quinn *Elmo* • Daphne Zuniga *Margie Epstein* • Forest Whitaker *Bulldozer* ■ *Dir* Harold Becker • *Scr* Darryl Ponicsan, from a novel by Terry Davis

Visions ★★★ 15
Horror 2014 · US · Colour · 78min

In this spooky yarn from Kevin Greutert (a graduate of the *Saw* franchise), Isla Fisher's mother-to-be finds herself plagued by terrifying hallucinations when she moves to an idyllic vineyard with her hunky husband (Anson Mount). A hooded figure and some mobile mannequins provide a few scary moments while a decent cast including Joanna Cassidy (a psychic), Eva Longoria (her vampy pal) and *Big Bang Theory's* Jim Parsons (her doctor) are eminently watchable. Not vintage horror, but still entertaining. JA English, Spanish +subtitles. Violence. *DVD*

Isla Fisher *Eveleigh Maddox* • Anson Mount *David Maddox* • Gillian Jacobs *Sadie* • Joanna Cassidy *Helena* • Eva Longoria *Eileen* • Jim Parsons *Dr Mathison* ■ *Dir* Kevin Greutert • *Scr* Lucas Sussman ■ *Music* Anton Sanko

Visions of Eight ★★
Sports documentary 1973 · US · Colour · 109min

It was hoped that having eight directors from different nationalities working on the official film of the 1972 Munich Olympics would be symbolic of the internationalism of the sportsmen and women themselves. However, the result was a spoiled broth that gave neither statistics nor expressed any of the excitement of the events. Instead we are given a series of arty, tricksy and often spectacular moments created in a vacuum. The killing of 11 members of the Israeli team by Palestinian guerrillas is touched upon only with the memorial service. RB

■ *Dir* Yuri Ozerov, Mai Zetterling, Arthur Penn, Michael Pfleghar, Kon Ichikawa, Claude Lelouch, Milos Forman, John Schlesinger • *Scr* Deliara Ozerova, David Hughes, Arthur Penn, Michael Pfleghar, Shuntaro Tanikawa, Claude Lelouch, John Schlesinger

Visions of Light ★★★★ PG
Documentary 1992 · US/Jpn · Colour and BW · 90min

This fascinating documentary pays handsome tribute to the forgotten artists of film, the cinematographers. Passing with regrettable speed over silent geniuses like Billy Bitzer, who truly sculpted with light, the film sings the praises of black-and-white photography and reveals how some of the most memorable images ever shot in Hollywood were achieved. The work of such

V

master craftsmen as George Barnes, Gregg Toland, William Daniels and John Alton is illustrated with well-chosen clips and heartfelt praise from the leading lighting cameramen of today. If you've ever marvelled at an image and wondered how they did it, this is for you. DP **DVD**

Todd McCarthy *Narrator* ■ *Dir* Arnold Glassman, Todd McCarthy, Stuart Samuels • *Scr* Todd McCarthy

The Visit ★★
Drama 1964 · W Ger/Fr/It/US · BW · 100min

Ingrid Bergman is the richest woman in the world who returns to her impoverished home village. On arriving she promises the peasants riches but only if they execute Anthony Quinn – her former lover and the father of her dead child who, to save his own skin, forced her into exile and prostitution. This is a good dramatic story that might have made a western, though the original play was set in Switzerland, as is this movie version. Even Bergman can't quite bring this stodgy Euro-pudding to life. AT

Ingrid Bergman *Karla Zachanassian* • Anthony Quinn *Serge Miller* • Irina Demick *Anya* • Paolo Stoppa *Doctor* • Hans Christian Blech *Capt Dobrick* • Romolo Valli *Town painter* • Valentina Cortese *Mathilda Miller* ■ *Dir* Bernhard Wicki • *Scr* Ben Barzman, from the play by Maurice Valency, from the play *Der Besuch der alten Dame* by Friedrich Dürrenmatt

The Visit ★★★ 15
Black comedy horror 2015 · US · Colour · 93min

Two youngsters (Olivia DeJonge and Ed Oxenbould) are sent by their mother to spend time with her estranged parents. By day, Nana (Deanna Dunagan) and Pop Pop (Peter McRobbie) are nice as pie. But come nightfall, things get very, very weird indeed. Writer/director M Night Shyamalan has had his ups and downs and this sits somewhere mid-spectrum. A contrived and cockamamy "explanation" could have been cut, but there is some genuinely scary stuff, too, and if you're a lover of the weird, it's a must-see. DA Violence. **DVD Blu**

Deanna Dunagan *Nana* • Peter McRobbie *Pop Pop* • Kathryn Hahn *Mom* • Ed Oxenbould *Tyler* • Olivia DeJonge *Becca* ■ *Dir/Scr* M Night Shyamalan • *Cinematographer* Maryse Alberti

Les Visiteurs ★★★★ 15
Fantasy comedy 1993 · Fr · Colour · 102min

A bawdy riposte to French cinema's propensity for intellectual navel-gazing, this time-travelling farce smashed box-office records on its original release. The slapstick adventures of a medieval nobleman and his squire who wind up in 1990s France will strike many as a sort of *Carry On Blackadder*. But there's also a mischievous social subtext here, as Jean Reno and Christian Clavier's search for a book of spells brings them into contact with various bourgeois caricatures. A sequel, plus a disappointing Hollywood remake, *Just Visiting* (2001), followed. DP French +subtitles. Swearing. **DVD**

Christian Clavier *Jacquouille La Fripouille/Jacquart* • Jean Reno *Godefroy de Montmirail* • Valérie Lemercier *Frénégonde de Pouille/Béatrice* • Marie-Anne Chazel *Ginette la clocharde* ■ *Dir* Jean-Marie Poiré • *Scr* Jean-Marie Poiré, Christian Clavier

Les Visiteurs 2: Les Couloirs du Temps ★★★
Fantasy comedy 1998 · Fr · Colour · 116min

The French have never been particularly prone to sequel tis, but Jean-Marie Poiré succumbed on this occasion and made a pretty fair job of re-creating both the madcap comedy and commercial success of the original. Opening with a neat illuminated manuscript reprise, the action darts back and forth through time, as 12th-century knight Jean Reno returns to the future to avert a curse or his forthcoming marriage. Patchy, but energetically played and anarchic. DP In French.

Jean Reno *Godefroy de Montmirail* • Christian Clavier *Jacquouille/Jacquart* • Muriel Robin *Béatrice/Frénégonde* • Marie-Anne Chazel

---

Ginette • Christian Bujeau *Jean-Pierre* ■ *Dir* Jean-Marie Poiré • *Scr* Jean-Marie Poiré, Christian Clavier

Les Visiteurs du Soir ★★★
Romantic fantasy 1942 · Fr · BW · 122min

Forced by the German Occupation to make "escapist" films, the team of Marcel Carné and Jacques Prévert went back to the 15th century for this rather stilted and whimsical fairy tale. Alain Cuny and Arletty play servants of the Devil disguised as minstrels. They arrive at a wedding of a baron's daughter with the intention of causing mischief. It was seen by many of the French audiences at the time as an allegory of their situation with the Devil (Jules Berry) as Hitler. Today we can enjoy the performances and the superb art design and photography. RB French +subtitles.

Arletty *Dominique* • Alain Cuny *Gilles* • Jules Berry *The Devil* • Marie Déa *Anne* • Fernand Ledoux *Baron Hughes* • Marcel Herrand *Renaud* • Simone Signoret • Alain Resnais ■ *Dir* Marcel Carné • *Scr* Jacques Prévert, Pierre Laroche • *Art Directors* Alexandre Trauner, Georges Wakhevitch • *Cinematographer* Roger Hubert

The Visitor ★ 18
Horror 1980 · It/US · Colour · 97min

From opportunist producer Ovidio G Assonitis comes the Italian *Omen*, souped up with reheated sci-fi and horror leftovers from every success in the genre. A rich occultist tries to father a devil child in this incoherent mess, complete with odd special effects, weird camera angles and religious mumbo jumbo. Directors Sam Peckinpah and John Huston also appear in baffling cameo roles in this triumph of bad taste. AJ

Mel Ferrer *Dr Walker* • John Huston *Jersey Colsowitz, the visitor* • Glenn Ford *Jake* • Lance Henriksen *Raymond* • Paige Conner *Katie Collins* • Joanne Nail *Barbara Collins* • Shelley Winters *Jane Phillips* • Sam Peckinpah *Sam* ■ *Dir* Michael J Paradise [Giulio Paradisi] • *Scr* Luc Comici, Robert Mundi, from a story by Michael J Paradise [Giulio Paradisi], Ovidio G Assonitis

The Visitor ★★★★ 15
Drama 2007 · US · Colour · 99min

Writer/director Thomas McCarthy's follow-up to *The Station Agent* is a timely meditation on what it means to be an immigrant in the United States. Key to this is the superb Richard Jenkins as Walter Vale, an uptight university professor whose visit to new York to cover an academic conference is thrown into turmoil when he finds his long-unattended apartment inhabited by Arab musician Tarek (Haaz Sleiman) and his African girlfriend. Vale is angry at first but soon becomes fascinated with Tarek's exotic djembe drum. These opening scenes are wry and rich in comic nuance, but the mood becomes darker when Tarek is arrested and Walter is drawn into his deportation trial. Fortunately, Jenkins is a more than good enough actor to carry the film through this drastic tonal shift, to leave the audience with an affecting view of America's legal system and the people it dehumanises. DW Swearing. **DVD**

Richard Jenkins *Walter Vale* • Hiam Abbass *Mouna* • Haaz Sleiman *Tarek* • Danai Gurira *Zainab* ■ *Dir/Scr* Tom McCarthy [Thomas McCarthy] • *Cinematographer* Oliver Bokelberg

The Visitors ★★★ 15
Drama 1972 · US · Colour · 102min

Elia Kazan self-financed this drama on a shoestring, shooting it in and around his own New England home from a script by his son, Chris. It deals with Vietnam, showing how a GI accuses two of his confrères of raping and murdering a Vietnamese girl. After the war, the two ex-GIs show up looking for vengeance. Barely released anywhere – it had a controversial screening at Cannes, mainly because jury president Joseph Losey had a long-standing feud with Kazan over the McCarthy witch-hunts – it has many flaws, but should be seen for its treatment of a complex theme and for the feature-film debut of James Woods. AT

Patrick McVey *Harry Wayne* • Patricia Joyce *Martha Wayne* • James Woods *Bill Schmidt* • Chico Martinez *Tony Rodriguez* • Steve Railsback *Mike Nickerson* ■ *Dir* Elia Kazan • *Scr* Chris Kazan

Vital ★★★ 18
Supernatural romantic drama 2004 · Jpn · Colour · 85min

The fleshy mysteries of a female cadaver hold the key to unlocking buried memories in this intriguing and stylish drama from Shinya Tsukamoto. Tadanobu Asano plays an amnesiac medical student who's forced to confront his past when he begins his dissection course. Studying a young woman's corpse, he makes a disturbing discovery that unleashes a mix of forgotten truths and disorientating fantasy. With its unconventional take on obsessive love and emotion, this boldly experimental film may be too strange for many. SF Japanese +subtitles. **DVD**

Tadanobu Asano *Hiroshi Takagi* • Nami Tsukamoto *Ryoko* • Kiki (2) *Ikumi* • Ittoku Kishibe *Dr Kashiwabuchi* • Kazumi Kushida *Hiroshi's father* • Lily *Hiroshi's mother* • Jun Kunimura *Ryoko's father* • Hana Kino *Ryoko's mother* ■ *Dir/Scr* Shinya Tsukamoto

Vital Signs ★★ 15
Drama 1990 · US · Colour · 98min

A bunch of third-year med students live and love their way through training. Packed with all the usual medical clichés, from ward emergencies to quickies in the linen cupboard, the film is flattered by a cast that includes Adrian Pasdar, Diane Lane and Laura San Giacomo. Jimmy Smits is especially good as the instructing surgeon, but this is routine and unmemorable. DA

Adrian Pasdar *Michael Chatham* • Diane Lane *Gina Wyler* • Jack Gwaltney *Kenny Rose* • Laura San Giacomo *Lauren Rose* • Jane Adams (2) *Suzanne Maloney* • Jimmy Smits *Dr David Redding* • Tim Ransom *Bobby Hayes* ■ *Dir* Marisa Silver • *Scr* Larry Ketron, Jeb Stuart, from a story by Larry Ketron

I Vitelloni ★★★★ PG
Drama 1953 · It/Fr · BW · 103min

Federico Fellini was trying to greenlight *La Strada* when he devised this portrait of the reckless *vitelloni* (literally "overgrown calves") he'd known during his youth in Rimini. Sketched with satirical insight, this tale focuses on five boys who are gradually forced to confront their bleak futures. At the centre of the action is a carnival, in which the buddies' costumes, masks and pranks are symbolically linked to the alienation and sexual frustration rife in early 1950s Italy. DP Italian +subtitles. **DVD**

Franco Interlenghi *Moraldo* • Franco Fabrizi *Fausto* • Alberto Sordi *Alberto* • Leopoldo Trieste *Leopoldo* • Riccardo Fellini *Riccardo* • Elenora Ruffo *Sandra* ■ *Dir* Federico Fellini • *Scr* Federico Fellini, Ennio Flaiano, Tullio Pinelli, from a story by Federico Fellini, Ennio Flaiano, Tullio Pinelli

Viva Italia! ★★★
Portmanteau black comedy 1978 · It · Colour · 115min

This portmanteau black comedy is made up of nine episodes designed to show that the typical Italian male is a monster. Some segments run less than five minutes while others last nearly 15, linked by a surprise ending. Three of Italy's biggest stars – Vittorio Gassman, Alberto Sordi and Ugo Tognazzi – seize their chances, either tossing food all over the kitchen, giving a lift to a crime victim in a Rolls-Royce and then chucking him out after he bleeds over the leather, or breaking a wife's legs to try to revive her fading singing career. AT Italian +subtitles.

Ugo Tognazzi *The Husband* • Vittorio Gassman *The Cardinal* • Ornella Muti *The Hitchhiker* • Orietta Berti *The Singer* ■ *Dir* Mario Monicelli, Dino Risi, Ettore Scola • *Scr* Agenore Incrocci, Ruggero Maccari, Giuseppe Moccia, Ettore Scola, Bernardino Zapponi

Viva Knievel! ★★ PG
Action thriller 1977 · US · Colour · 99min

This amazingly kitsch one-off stars the man himself – Evel Knievel, a non-actor if ever

---

there was one – in a movie so absurd it simply has to be seen to be believed. Directed by veteran Gordon Douglas, this is vanity cinema with a vengeance: the opening sequence involving Knievel and a group of orphans is truly amazing. However, there is a real and perverse pleasure to be gained from watching the work of true professionals such as Douglas and Gene Kelly, as they manage to save this from becoming a complete laughing stock. TS

Evel Knievel • Gene Kelly *Will Atkins* • Lauren Hutton *Kate Morgan* • Red Buttons *Ben Andrews* • Leslie Nielsen *Stanley Millard* • Frank Gifford • Sheila Allen *Sister Charity* • Cameron Mitchell *Barton* ■ *Dir* Gordon Douglas • *Scr* Antonio Santillan, Norman Katkov, from a story by Santillan

Viva Las Vegas ★★★★ U
Musical 1964 · US · Colour · 81min

This is one of the last great MGM musicals, in which, for once, the fabulous Elvis Presley found himself in the hands of a good director, George Sidney, and teamed with a worthy co-star, the vivacious Ann-Margret. He plays a young racing driver with ambitions to win the city's grand prix. Choreography is by *West Side Story*'s David Winters, there's wonderful Panavision cinematography by Joseph Biroc (who was camera operator on all the Astaire/Rogers musicals) and the whole glossy package is Elvis's best post-*Blue Hawaii* movie. TS **DVD**

Elvis Presley *Lucky Jackson* • Ann-Margret *Rusty Martin* • Cesare Danova *Count Elmo Mancini* • William Demarest *Mr Martin* • Nicky Blair *Shorty Farnsworth* • Robert B Williams *Swanson* • Bob Nash *Big Gus Olson* ■ *Dir* George Sidney (2) • *Scr* Sally Benson

Viva Maria! ★★★ 12
Comedy 1965 · Fr/It · Colour · 111min

The pairing of Brigitte Bardot and Jeanne Moreau created enough excitement in 1965 for this to be an art house blockbuster. Bardot was France's reigning sex symbol and so was Moreau, but in artier movies. Here they're singers who tussle with a typically disorganised Mexican revolution. Both actresses seem to be enjoying the occasion, as does a perfectly cast George Hamilton. Georges Delerue's songs are pleasing, and the photography is ravishingly beautiful, but the picture's length has it running out of steam. AT French, German +subtitles. **DVD**

Brigitte Bardot *Maria II* • Jeanne Moreau *Maria I* • George Hamilton *Florès* • Gregor von Rezzori *Diogène* • Paulette Dubost *Mme Diogène* • Carlos Lopez Moctezuma *Rodriguez* ■ *Dir* Louis Malle • *Scr* Louis Malle, Jean-Claude Carrière

Viva Max! ★★★ U
Comedy 1969 · US · Colour · 92min

It's impossible to ignore Peter Ustinov, but try to let your eye drift away from the master scene-stealer and on to John Astin (Gomez in TV's *The Addams Family*), who gives an understated comic performance as his doltish sidekick. His twitchy idiocy stands in stark contrast to Ustinov's heavily-accented showboating as the Mexican general who leads a ramshackle band across the border in a bid to retake the Alamo. Buoyantly played, but sloppily directed. DP

Peter Ustinov *General Maximilian Rodrigues de Santos* • Pamela Tiffin *Paula Whitland* • Jonathan Winters *General Billy Joe Hallson* • John Astin *Sgt Valdez* • Keenan Wynn *General Barney LaComber* • Harry Morgan *Chief of Police George Sylvester* • Alice Ghostley *Hattie Longstreet Daniel* • Kenneth Mars *Dr Sam Gillison* ■ *Dir* Jerry Paris • *Scr* Elliot Baker, from a novel by James Lehrer

Viva Riva! ★★★ 15
Action crime drama 2010 · Congo/Fr/Bel/Aus · Colour · 93min

Cinema in the Democratic Republic of Congo came of age with this rousing thriller by Djo Tunda Wa Munga. In the midst of societal mayhem, opportunist Patsha Bay Mukana simply seeks to make a fast buck. His troubles start when his illicit fuel racket

---

V

is uncovered and mobster Diplome Amekindra learns he has been flirting with his feisty mistress. The odd gag misfires and the glut of minor characters sometimes confuses things. But this is uncomplicated, occasionally UnPc and invariably explosive escapism. DP French, Lingala +subtitles.

DVD

Patsha Bay *Riva* • Manie Malone *Nora* • Hoji Fortuna *Cesar* • Alex Herabo *JM* ■ *Dir/Scr* Djo Tunda Wa Munga [Jo Munga]

Viva Villa!   ★★★
Biographical drama   1934 · US · BW · 115min

This is an intelligently crafted, David O Selznick-produced MGM adventure epic, credited to director Jack Conway, but actually started by Howard Hawks. Some obvious studio-bound sequences mar enjoyment, and the whole thing is a tad overlong, but with some excellent supporting performances. Beery plays Villa, the Mexican revolutionary, as scripted by Ben Hecht, warts and all. The crowd scenes are particularly well handled (the assistant director, John Waters, received an Oscar) and the scale is undeniably epic. TS

Wallace Beery *Pancho Villa* • Fay Wray *Teresa* • Stuart Erwin *Johnny Sykes* • Leo Carrillo *Sierra* • Donald Cook *Don Felipe* • George E Stone *Chavito* • Joseph Schildkraut *General Pascal* ■ *Dir* Jack Conway • *Scr* Ben Hecht, from the non-fiction book by Edgcumb Pinchon, OB Stade

Viva Zapata!   ★★★ PG
Biographical drama   1952 · US · BW · 108min

Marlon Brando stars as Mexican revolutionary leader Emiliano Zapata in director Elia Kazan's celebrated drama. When the movie was first planned, producer Darryl Zanuck wanted Tyrone Power for the lead, but Kazan, who had just made *A Streetcar Named Desire*, persuaded him to go with Brando. This is a strong, exciting and heavily politicised picture, with a script by John Steinbeck, and Anthony Quinn won an Oscar, playing Brando's brother and revolutionary colleague. AT *DVD*

Marlon Brando *Emiliano Zapata* • Jean Peters *Josefa Espejo* • Anthony Quinn *Eufemio Zapata* • Joseph Wiseman *Fernando Aguirre* • Arnold Moss *Don Nacio* • Alan Reed *Pancho Villa* • Margo *La Soldadera* • Harold Gordon *Don Francisco Madero* ■ *Dir* Elia Kazan • *Scr* John Steinbeck, from the novel *Zapata the Unconquered* by Edgcumb Pichon

Viva Zapatero!   ★★★ 15
Documentary   2005 · It · Colour · 76min

Although this soberingly amusing documentary is not quite the "Italian *Fahrenheit 9/11*", as some have claimed, it still captures a fascinating duel between a feisty satirist and an establishment hell-bent on controlling its image. In 2003, Sabina Guzzanti had her topical show pulled by the state broadcaster RAI for fear that her impression of Silvio Berlusconi would prompt the-then Prime Minister into a costly slander suit. However, Guzzanti was convinced that the media was dangerously in Berlusconi's thrall and her transcontinental odyssey explores how much freedom of speech actually exists across western Europe. With Rory Bremner among her interviewees, this is a provocative and incisively intelligent insight into the impact that comedy has on politics. DP Italian +subtitles. Swearing.

DVD

Rory Bremner ■ *Dir/Scr* Sabina Guzzanti

Vivacious Lady   ★★★ U
Screwball comedy   1938 · US · BW · 89min

Professor James Stewart tries to tell his conservative dad, the wonderfully irascible Charles Coburn, that he has married showgirl Ginger Rogers in this sparkling screwball comedy, directed by the great George Stevens. It's a funny idea, and you don't really notice that it's a one-joke movie. Super support actors include Beulah Bondi, playing slightly against type as Stewart's mum, and lovable Hattie McDaniel. TS

DVD

Ginger Rogers *Frances Brent* • James Stewart *Peter Morgan* • James Ellison *Keith Beston* • Charles Coburn *Doctor Morgan* • Beulah Bondi *Mrs Morgan* • Frances Mercer *Helen* • Phyllis Kennedy *Jenny* • Alec Craig *Joseph* • Franklin Pangborn *Apartment manager* • Grady Sutton *Culpepper* • Hattie McDaniel *Hattie, the maid* • Jack Carson *Charlie, the waiter captain* ■ *Dir* George Stevens • *Scr* PJ Wolfson, Ernest Pagano, from a story by IAR Wylie

Vive L'Amour   ★★★★ 15
Drama   1994 · Tai · Colour · 117min

Virtually silent, yet saying more about urban alienation than the most eloquent of screenplays, this is a saturnine study of life in modern Taipei. Director Tsai Ming-liang is admirably served by a sensitive cast, led by Yang Kuei-Mei as the estate agent who begins a passionless relationship with street vendor Chen Chao-jung, unaware that they are being observed by Lee Kang-sheng, a gay suicidal cemetery salesman squatting in one of Yang's properties. DP Mandarin +subtitles.

Yang Kuei-Mei *May* • Chen Chao-jung *Ah-jung* • Lee Kang-sheng *Hsiao-kang* ■ *Dir* Tsai Ming-liang • *Scr* Tsai Ming-liang, Tsai Yi-chun, Yang Pi-ying

Vivre pour Vivre   ★
Romantic drama   1967 · Fr · Colour · 130min

Despite the talents of Yves Montand and Candice Bergen, this sun-saturated, overstylised and poorly scripted film couldn't be worse. Montand plays a TV reporter who is married to Annie Girardot, but is unable to resist the charms of super-glamorous model Bergen. Cue an all too familiar love triangle with lashings of sex and tears, accompanied by a terrible soundtrack. LH French +subtitles.

Yves Montand *Robert Colomb* • Candice Bergen *Candice* • Annie Girardot *Catherine Colomb* • Irène Tunc *Mireille* • Anouk Ferjac *Jacqueline* ■ *Dir* Claude Lelouch • *Scr* Claude Lelouch, Pierre Uytterhoeven

Vivre Sa Vie   ★★★★★ 15
Drama   1962 · Fr · BW · 79min

Jean-Luc Godard's New Wave masterpiece concerns a prostitute who maintains a sort of spiritual integrity before falling victim to gangsters. Abandoning conventional narrative, Godard offers the story as 12 chapters and names his heroine Nana, after Zola's heroine; he also has her go to the cinema to see Carl Th Dreyer's legendary silent classic about another martyr, Joan of Arc. The then frank depiction of sex earned the film a certain notoriety, not to mention the application of the British censor's scissors. Now, though, what's most noticeable is Godard's technique and the luminous filming of Anna Karina, who had just become the director's wife and here gives a marvellous performance. AT French +subtitles. *DVD* ⃝

Anna Karina *Nana Kleinfrankenheim* • Sady Rebbot *Raoul* • André S Labarthe *Paul* • Guylaine Schlumberger *Yvette* • Jean-Luc Godard *Voice* ■ *Dir* Jean-Luc Godard • *Scr* Jean-Luc Godard, with additional narrative from *Où en Est la Prostitution* by Judge Marcel Sacotte and from the short story *The Oval Portrait* by Edgar Allen Poe

Vixen!   ★★★★ 18
Cult sex satire   1968 · US · Colour · 72min

A huge box-office hit, the one genuinely erotic movie made by cult director Russ Meyer led him to mainstream Hollywood and his stunning trash satire *Beyond the Valley of the Dolls*. Pneumatic Erica Gavin is the Canadian nymphomaniac of the title, a pun on the then popular lesbian drama *The Fox*. Meyer got his explosive sexual cocktail past the censors of the day (not in Britain, though!) by cleverly incorporating the hot contemporary issues of racism, communism and Vietnam into his histrionic mix. Gavin rises to the occasion with a truthful abandon and conviction rarely seen in the soft-core genre. AJ Swearing, sex scenes.

DVD

Erica Gavin *Vixen Palmer* • Harrison Page *Niles* • Garth Pillsbury *Tom Palmer* • Michael Donovan O'Donnell *O'Bannion* • Vincene Wallace *Janet King* • Jon Evans *Jud* • Robert Aitken *Dave*

King ■ *Dir* Russ Meyer • *Scr* Robert Rudelson, from a story by Russ Meyer, Anthony James Ryan

Vizontele   ★★★ 15
Comedy   2001 · Tur · Colour · 110min

A huge hit in its native Turkey, this is a genial, but slyly barbed social comedy, set in a tightly knit community divided by the intrusion of the outside world. The bone of contention is the first TV set to arrive in a small southern village in 1974. The mayor, Altan Erkekli, sees it as a symbol of progress, but outdoor cinema owner Cezmi Baskin considers it a threat to his business and tries to convince patrons the "vison-tele" is an affront to Islam. DP Turkish +subtitles. Swearing.

Yilmaz Erdogan *Deli Emin* • Demet Akbag *Siti Ana* • Altan Erkekli *Nazmi* • Cem Yilmaz *Sitki* • Cezmi Baskin *Latif* ■ *Dir* Yilmaz Erdogan, Omer Faruk Sorak • *Scr* Yilmaz Erdogan

Vladimir et Rosa   ★★★
Experimental political drama   1970 · Fr/W Ger/US · Colour · 103min

Ostensibly, this is one of Jean-Luc Godard and Jean-Pierre Gorin's Dziga-Vertov experiments is a reconstruction of the Chicago Seven conspiracy trial. But Godard's main purpose is to explore the film-making process, from the technical and artistic choices involved to the compromises that inevitably have to be made. Comprising peeks at the off-stage lives of the characters and tactical discussions between the directors, the film alights on everything from the Black Panthers to radical feminism. DP French +subtitles.

Jean-Luc Godard *Jean-Luc Godard/Vladimir Lenin* • Jean-Pierre Gorin *Jean-Pierre Gorin/Karl Rosa (after Rosa Luxemburg)* • Anne Wiazemsky *Ann, women's liberation militant* • Juliet Berto *Juliet/Weatherwoman/Hippie* • Yves Alfonso *Yves, revolutionary student from Berkeley* ■ *Dir/Scr* Jean-Luc Godard, Jean-Pierre Gorin

Vodka Lemon   ★★★★ PG
Comedy drama   2003 · Fr/It/Swi/Arm · Colour · 86min

Kurdish director Hiner Saleem evokes the wry observational humour of Otar Iosseliani in this gentle take on life in post-Soviet Armenia. The story of elderly Romen Avinian's cemetery encounters with widow Lala Sarkissian is consistently charming and proves more engaging than sub-plots involving Avinian's sons and his granddaughter's wedding. But it's the community that Saleem assembles around the reticent couple – including such eccentrics as a bed-ridden flautist, a singing bus driver and a galloping horseman – that gives the comedy its satirical edge and keeps justifiable despair at bay. DP Armenian +subtitles. *DVD*

Romen Avinian *Hamo* • Lala Sarkissian *Nina* • Ivan Franek *Dilovan* • Armen Marouthian *Romik* • Astrik Avaguian *Avin* ■ *Dir* Hiner Saleem • *Scr* Hiner Saleem, Lei Dinety, Pauline Gouzenne

Vogues of 1938   ★★★
Musical comedy   1937 · US · Colour · 108min

A breathtaking and, unusually, blonde Joan Bennett stars as an impoverished debutante who ditches hateful millionaire Alan Mowbray at the altar and goes to work as a model at New York's top fashion house, only to fall for its owner, Warner Baxter. However, the plot – involving dirty tricks from rival designer Mischa Auer and romantic complications – is totally unimportant to a film whose *raison d'être* is high fashion. And what fashion it is – an extravaganza of magnificent clothes donned by America's top models of the time. RK

Warner Baxter *George Curson* • Joan Bennett *Wendy Van Klettering* • Helen Vinson *Mary Curson* • Mischa Auer *Prince Muratov* • Alan Mowbray *Henry Morgan* • Jerome Cowan *Mr Brockton* • Alma Kruger *Sophie Miller* • Marjorie Gateson *Mrs Lemke* • Hedda Hopper *Mrs Van Klettering* ■ *Dir* Irving Cummings • *Scr* Bella Spewack, Samuel Spewack • *Costume Designer* Helen Taylor

Voice in the Mirror   ★★★
Drama   1958 · US · BW · 102min

This second cousin to the screen's classic study of alcoholism, *The Lost Weekend* (1945), charts the decline of successful LA commercial artist Richard Egan who, after his daughter dies, takes refuge in the bottle, despite the support and sympathy of his wife Julie London and his doctor Walter Matthau. Rather wafty and sentimental, but this modest and non-starry movie does fine in the wake of its hard-hitting predecessor. RK

Richard Egan *Jim Burton* • Julie London *Ellen Burton* • Walter Matthau *Dr Leon Karnes* • Arthur O'Connell *William Tobin* • Ann Doran *Mrs Devlin* • Bart Bradley *Gene Devlin* • Hugh Sanders *Mr Hornsby* ■ *Dir* Harry Keller • *Scr* Larry Marcus

Voice of Merrill   ★★
Mystery   1952 · UK · BW · 81min

This complex and rather dull suspenser has Valerie Hobson and James Robertson-Justice as a husband and wife under suspicion for murdering a blackmailer. A talent much stronger than John Gilling's (who both wrote and directed this tosh) was needed to bring off this tale of murder among the plummy voices, but these days there's pleasure to be gained just from watching the elegant cast go through their preposterous paces. TS

Valerie Hobson *Alycia Roach* • Edward Underdown *Hugh Allen* • James Robertson-Justice *Jonathan Roach* • Henry Kendall *Ronald Parker* ■ *Dir* John Gilling • *Scr* John Gilling, from a story by Gerald Landeau, Terence Austin

Voice of the Turtle   ★★★
Comedy drama   1947 · US · BW · 102min

During the Second World War, a lonely soldier on leave in New York meets an actress suffering from a broken love affair and falls for her. The synopsis belies a tender, sophisticated, witty Broadway romantic comedy hit, which was still running when the movie opened. Ronald Reagan, in one of his more distinguished outings, is excellent, although outshone by his co-stars Eleanor Parker and the brilliantly acerbic, wisecracking Eve Arden as her friend. The original three-handed play was opened out slightly and some characters added for the movie. RK

Ronald Reagan *Sgt Bill Page* • Eleanor Parker *Sally Middleton* • Eve Arden *Olive Lashbrooke* • Wayne Morris *Cmdr Ned Burling* • Kent Smith *Kenneth Bartlett* ■ *Dir* Irving Rapper • *Scr* John Van Druten, Charles Hoffman, from the play by John Van Druten

The Voices   ★★★★ 15
Comedy crime thriller   2014 · US/Ger · Colour · 99min

Ryan Reynolds is endearing and utterly terrifying all at once in this blackly comic portrait of a serial killer. Iranian director Marjane Satrapi (*Persepolis*), skilfully veers between comedy and tragedy, portraying the world through the gently rose-tinted spectacles of Jerry, her psychotic antihero. He seems happy enough in his small-town existence until an unfortunate series of events leads him to decapitate the girl he fancies. Gemma Arterton sparkles in that role, even when reduced to a talking head in Jerry's fridge, and Anna Kendrick is on form, too, as the girl who takes a shine to him. The plot is a little too tailored to draw sympathy for Jerry, but the overall approach is daring and Reynolds offers a wonderfully funny, vivid and harrowing portrayal of insanity. He talks to his pets and they talk back – Reynolds does some brilliant voice work, especially for his Scottish tabby cat – and when he's finally forced to confront reality, it comes as a hard and palpable blow. The unusual mix of laughs, lunacy and a touch of melancholy ensures *The Voices* will stick in your head. SP *DVD* ⃝

Ryan Reynolds *Jerry Hickfang/Mr Whiskers/ Bosco/Deer/Bunny Monkey* • Gemma Arterton *Fiona* • Anna Kendrick *Lisa* • Jacki Weaver *Dr Warren* • Ella Smith *Alison* • Paul Chahidi *Dennis Kowalski* ■ *Dir* Marjane Satrapi • *Scr* Michael R Perry

Volcano ★★★ 12
Disaster thriller 1997 · US · Colour · 99min

Emergency chief Tommy Lee Jones has to save Los Angeles from being covered by molten lava in this taut, effects-laden disaster movie. Director Mick Jackson uses the simple suspense device of cross-cutting as the cast members go about their daily activities with magma bubbling menacingly just under LA's threatened streets. The digital special effects come into their own when the city is awash with rivers of fire and the urban destruction goes into overdrive. Gripping and spectacular. AJ Swearing, violence. *DVD* *BL*

Tommy Lee Jones *Mike Roark* · Anne Heche *Dr Amy Barnes* · Gaby Hoffman [Gaby Hoffmann] *Kelly Roark* · Don Cheadle *Emmit Reese* · Jacqueline Kim *Dr Jaye Calder* · Keith David *Lieutenant Ed Fox* · John Corbett *Norman Calder* · Michael Rispoli *Gator Harris* ■ *Dir* Mick Jackson · *Scr* Jerome Armstrong, from a story by Billy Ray

Volere, Volare ★★★★ 15
Part-animated romantic fantasy 1991 · It · Colour · 91min

Even though Maurizio Nichetti and Guido Manuli ingeniously combine live-action and animated footage in this endlessly inventive comedy, it's the noises that linger in the memory. As the exacting sound editor who begins to turn into a cartoon on encountering kinky hooker Angela Finocchiaro, Nichetti combines slapstick and psychological humour to great effect. Things get off to a sluggish start, but once animated animals and Nichetti's pornographer brother start interfering in his love life, the action becomes increasingly amusing and audacious. DP Italian +subtitles. Nudity.

Angela Finocchiaro *Martina* · Maurizio Nichetti *Maurizio* · Mariella Valentini *Loredana* · Patrizio Roversi *Patrizio* · Remo Remotti *Professor Bambino* ■ *Dir* Maurizio Nichetti, Guido Manuli · *Scr* Maurizio Nichetti, Guido Manuli

Les Voleurs ★★ 18
Thriller 1996 · Fr · Colour · 111min

By shuffling perspectives and alternating time frames, André Téchiné makes a bold assault here on the structure of the traditional police drama. But in seeking to show that truth is often fragmentary, he concentrates too much on technique, with too little emotion expended on his characters. The action centres primarily on the relationship between tomboy shoplifter Laurence Côte, Daniel Auteuil (a cop in a family of thieves) and lesbian philosophy teacher Catherine Deneuve. DP French +subtitles. Sex scenes, swearing, violence.

Catherine Deneuve *Marie* · Daniel Auteuil *Alex* · Laurence Côte *Juliette* · Benoît Magimel *Jimmy* · Fabienne Babe *Mireille* · Didier Bezace *Ivan* · Julien Rivière *Justin* ■ *Dir* André Téchiné · *Scr* André Téchiné, Gilles Taurand, Michel Alexandre, Pascal Bonitzer

Volpone ★★★
Comedy 1941 · Fr · BW · 98min

Made before the outbreak of war, this handsome version of Ben Jonson's classic comedy was released during the occupation of France. It starred the great French actor Harry Baur in the title role, who had a Jewish wife and had played Jewish roles since the silent days. In 1943 after the film was shown, he was arrested, strenuously tortured by the Gestapo and died a few days later. Directed by Maurice Tourneur, the film altered the central characterisation but otherwise acknowledged its origins with stylish visuals and memorable performances. BB French +subtitles.

Harry Baur *Volpone* · Louis Jouvet *Mosca* · Fernand Ledoux *Corvino* · Marion Dorian *Canina* · Jean Temerson *Voltore* · Alexandre Rignault *Leone* ■ *Dir* Maurice Tourneur · *Scr* Jules Romains, from the play by Ben Jonson

Volunteers ★★ 15
Comedy 1985 · US · Colour · 102min

Tom Hanks is reunited with his *Splash* co-star John Candy for this clumsy, but occasionally amusing outing. Hanks plays the arrogant heir running away from his gambling debts who joins the Peace Corps in the early 1960s and gets caught up with Asian warlords, communist guerrillas and the CIA. Candy steals the show playing an earnest patriot brainwashed into becoming a Maoist revolutionary, but director Nicholas Meyer plays down the satirical opportunities of the plot in the search for easy laughs. JF Violence, swearing. *DVD*

Tom Hanks *Lawrence Bourne III* · John Candy *Tom Tuttle From Tacoma* · Rita Wilson *Beth Wexler* · Tim Thomerson *John Reynolds* · Gedde Watanabe *At Toon* · George Plimpton *Lawrence Bourne Jr* · Ernest Harada *Chung Mee* ■ *Dir* Nicholas Meyer · *Scr* Ken Levine, David Isaacs, from a story by Keith Critchlow

Volver ★★★★★ 15
Comedy drama 2006 · Sp · Colour · 121min

Penélope Cruz is simply mesmerising in Pedro Almodóvar's celebration of motherhood, his La Mancha roots and how the dead hold sway over the living. Cruz covers up the accidental killing of her abusive husband by her daughter while her "dead" mother (Carmen Maura) takes up residence with her timid sister (Lola Dueñas) to unearth family skeletons. Devoid of the usual flashiness and vibrant colour palette, Almodóvar's signature style still remains intact during the slow burn towards a subdued yet intensely touching finale in this flawlessly cast mix of farce, melodrama and emotional crescendos. AJ Spanish +subtitles. *DVD*

Penélope Cruz *Raimunda* · Carmen Maura *Irene* · Lola Dueñas *Sole* · Blanca Portillo *Agustina* · Yohana Cobo *Paula* · Chus Lampreave *Aunt Paula* ■ *Dir/Scr* Pedro Almodóvar

Von Ryan's Express ★★★ PG
Second World War drama 1965 · US · Colour · 112min

This rattlingly exciting Second World War escape adventure has a well cast Frank Sinatra as a tough PoW who seizes a German train delivering Allied prisoners. Sinatra's character is unusually uncompromising, even for him, and the star delivers one of his best performances. Director Mark Robson uses his camera skilfully, and the support cast, including Trevor Howard, is exceptionally well chosen. The film was a major commercial success in its day. TS English, German +subtitles. *DVD*

Frank Sinatra *Col Joseph L Ryan* · Trevor Howard *Major Eric Fincham* · James Brolin *Private Ames* · Raffaela Carra *Gabriella* · Brad Dexter *Sergeant Bostick* · Sergio Fantoni *Captain Oriani* · John Leyton *Orde* · Edward Mulhare *Costanzo* · Wolfgang Preiss *Major von Klemment* ■ *Dir* Mark Robson · *Scr* Wendell Mayes, Joseph Landon, from a novel by David Westheimer

Voodoo Man ★
Horror 1944 · US · BW · 62min

Bela Lugosi continued his downward career trend in this Monogram mediocrity as the lunatic occultist who kidnaps women to transfer their souls into his comatose wife, who has been in a permanent trance for over 20 years. Viewing this chronic schlock ordeal would make anyone equally catatonic. AJ

Bela Lugosi *Dr Richard Marlowe* · John Carradine *Toby* · George Zucco *Nicolas* · Michael Ames [Tod Andrews] *Ralph Dawson* · Wanda McKay *Betty Benton* · Ellen Hall *Mrs Evelyn Marlowe* ■ *Dir* William Beaudine · *Scr* Robert Charles

Voodoo Woman ★ PG
Horror 1957 · US · BW · 76min

A mad professor carries out horrible experiments on a young and beautiful woman. The stilted acting and dialogue may raise a laugh for some fans of this sort of cult nonsense, but one thing is for sure, no one will be remotely frightened by it. JF *DVD*

Marla English *Marilyn Blanchard* · Tom Conway *Dr Roland Gerard* · Touch Connors [Mike Connors] *Ted Bronson* · Lance Fuller *Rick/Harry*

· Mary Ellen Kaye *Susan* · Paul Dubov *Marcel the Innkeeper* ■ *Dir* Edward L Cahn · *Scr* Russell Bender, VI Voss

Vote for Huggett ★★ U
Comedy 1948 · UK · BW · 81min

The endearing Huggett family first appeared as characters in *Holiday Camp*. After *Here Come the Huggetts*, this was the second of three films following their progress. Later a long-running radio series ensured their popularity. Here, Joe is standing for election as a councillor but runs into trouble when he proposes a war memorial site on land part-owned by his wife. Jack Warner and Kathleen Harrison are wonderful as mum and dad and young Diana Dors plays the troublesome niece. BB

Jack Warner *Joe Huggett* · Kathleen Harrison *Ethel Huggett* · Susan Shaw *Susan Huggett* · Petula Clark *Pet Huggett* · David Tomlinson *Harold Hinchley* · Diana Dors *Diana* · Peter Hammond *Peter Hawtrey* · Amy Veness *Grandma* ■ *Dir* Ken Annakin · *Scr* Mabel Constanduros, Denis Constanduros, Allan MacKinnon, from characters by Godfrey Winn

The Vow ★★ 12
Romantic drama 2012 · US/Bra/Fr/Aus/UK/Ger · Colour · 99min

Action man Channing Tatum revisits *Dear John* territory here to once again show off his more sensitive side. The GI Joe star plays Leo, whose wife Paige (Rachel McAdams) suffers severe head trauma in a car crash and loses all memory of her time with her husband. So he resolves to woo her again, despite opposition from Paige's parents (Jessica Lange and Sam Neill, both under-used). This tear-jerker is slickly made and pushes all the right emotional buttons, but the more cynical may baulk at its schmaltzy manipulativeness, pretentious voice-over and, truth to tell, innate dullness. But for anyone who's easily pleased and likes a good old sob, it's just the ticket. DA *DVD* *BL*

Rachel McAdams *Paige* · Channing Tatum *Leo* · Sam Neill *Bill Thornton* · Scott Speedman *Jeremy* · Jessica Lange *Rita Thornton* · Lucas Bryant *Kyle* ■ *Dir* Michael Sucsy · *Scr* Jason Katims, Abby Kohn, Marc Silverstein, Michael Sucsy, from a story by Stuart Sender

The Voyage ★★
Drama 1974 · It · Colour · 101min

This dreary and ill-cast commercial disaster is based upon Pirandello's tale of two lovers – not allowed to marry – who find themselves destroyed by fate. Neither Sophia Loren nor Richard Burton seem comfortable here, and it's depressing to discover that it was directed by the once-great neorealist genius Vittorio De Sica. There's effective support from Ian Bannen, but the dubbing of the Italian supports leaves much to be desired. TS Italian dubbed.

Sophia Loren *Adriana* · Richard Burton *Cesar* · Ian Bannen *Antonio* · Renato Pinciroli *Doctor* · Daniele Pitani *Notary* · Barbara Pilavin *Mother* · Sergio Bruni *Armando Gill* ■ *Dir* Vittorio De Sica · *Scr* Diego Fabbri, Massimo Franciosa, Luisa Montagnana, from a play by Luigi Pirandello

LANDMARK FILM
Georges Méliès's masterwork lays the foundations of movie storytelling

Le Voyage dans la Lune ★★★★★ U
Silent science-fiction 1902 · Fr · BW · 14min

A cornerstone of narrative cinema – and probably celluloid's first foray into science fiction – Georges Méliès's beautifully designed space adventure about an exploratory trip to the moon comprises 31 scenes – each one a *tableau vivant* shot front-on from a stationary camera – whose most famous shot depicts a rocket landing in the Man in the Moon's eye. Drawing from the writings of Jules Verne and HG Wells, this early treasure offers much more in the way of a league of swimsuited beauties waving off the intrepid (and rather aged) members of the Astronomic Club followed by a lunar encounter with the hostile

Selenites. An inspired masterwork from a true visionary. DP *DVD*

Georges Méliès *Professor Barbenfouillis* · Bleuette Bernon *La lune* ■ *Dir* Georges Méliès · *Scr* Georges Méliès, from the works of Jules Vernes, HG Wells · *Cinematographers* Lucien Tainguy, Michaut

Voyage of the Damned ★★ PG
Drama based on a true story 1976 · UK · Colour · 174min

This drama from director Stuart Rosenberg is based on the real-life voyage of the SS *St Louis*, which set sail for Cuba in 1939 with 937 Jewish refugees on board, only to be forced back to Europe when it was refused a berth. As the ship's captain, Max von Sydow brings some much needed gravitas to the proceedings, but the script is desperate and the direction unbearably ponderous. The odds against so many star names giving such bad performances in the same film are incalculable. A miserable memorial to a tragic event. DP

Faye Dunaway *Denise Kreisler* · Max von Sydow *Captain Gustav Schroeder* · Oskar Werner *Dr Egon Kreisler* · Malcolm McDowell *Max* · James Mason *Dr Juan Remos* · Orson Welles *Jose Estedes* · Katharine Ross *Mira Hauser* · Ben Gazzara *Morris Troper* · Lee Grant *Lili Rosen* · Sam Wanamaker *Carl Rosen* · Lynne Frederick *Anna Rosen* · Julie Harris (2) *Alice Feinchild* ■ *Dir* Stuart Rosenberg · *Scr* Steve Shagan, David Butler, from the non-fiction book by Max Morgan-Witts, Gordon Thomas

Voyage to Cythera ★★★★
Drama 1984 · Gr · Colour · 120min

Returning home after 32 years exiled in the Soviet Union, Manos Katrakis refuses to discuss his past regrets or hopes for the future. But rather than settle into ennui, he follows the example of Odysseus in pre-Homeric legend and makes for Cythera, the island of dreams and domain of Aphrodite, to continue his lifelong pursuit of happiness. Dispirited by the depoliticisation of Greek society – what he called "the silence of history" – Theo Angelopoulos sets out to contrast the truths inherent in myth and reality in this complex, but always fascinating drama that makes densely symbolic use of the landscape. DP Greek +subtitles.

Manos Katrakis *Old man* · Mary Chronopoulou *Voula* · Dora Volanaki *Old woman* · Giulio Brogi *Alexandros* ■ *Dir* Theo Angelopoulos · *Scr* Theo Angelopoulos, Thanassis Valtinos, Tonino Guerra

Voyage to the Bottom of the Sea ★★★ U
Science-fiction adventure 1961 · US · Colour · 100min

Walter Pidgeon and Joan Fontaine are top billed in this entertaining sci-fi outing, but the real star is the submarine *Seaview*. Accounting for $400,000 of the picture's budget, the glass-fronted nuclear sub went on to star in its own TV series following its exploits here, as admiral Pidgeon fires its missiles into the Van Allen radiation belt and saves Earth from meltdown. Fontaine is totally out of her depth, but Peter Lorre and the rest of the cast are splendid. Irwin Allen went on to become the king of the disaster movie in the early 1970s. DP *DVD* *BL*

Walter Pidgeon *Admiral Harriman Nelson* · Joan Fontaine *Dr Susan Hiller* · Barbara Eden *Cathy Connors* · Peter Lorre *Commodore Lucius Emery* · Robert Sterling *Capt Lee Crane* · Michael Ansara *Miguel Alvarez* · Frankie Avalon *Chip Romano* · Regis Toomey *Dr Jamieson* ■ *Dir* Irwin Allen · *Scr* Irwin Allen, Charles Bennett, from a story by Allen

Voyage to the Planet of Prehistoric Women ★
Science-fiction fantasy 1966 · US · Colour · 78min

Following *Voyage to the Prehistoric Planet*, this also recycles special effects highlights from the 1962 Russian science-fiction spectacle *Planeta Burg*. A disorientating dog's dinner of a movie with new footage shot by Peter Bogdanovich, it features 1950s sex bomb Mamie Van Doren as the

V

leader of a tribe of bikini-clad alien maidens. None of the new scenes really match in this tortuously repackaged exploiter. AJ

Mamie Van Doren *Moana* • Mary Mark • Paige Lee ■ *Dir* Derek Thomas [Peter Bogdanovich] • *Scr* Henry Ney

Voyage to the Prehistoric Planet ★
Fantasy   1965 · US · Colour · 80min

Roger Corman used cannibalised footage from the 1962 Russian space epic *Planeta Burg* and incorporated new material shot by director Curtis Harrington. A spaceship crew crash-land on a planet and relay their encounters with robot men and dinosaurs to a space platform orbiting above them. As was often the case with Corman quickies of the 1960s, the story behind the movie is more interesting than the movie itself. AJ

Basil Rathbone *Professor Hartman* • Faith Domergue *Marcia* ■ *Dir/Scr* John Sebastian [Curtis Harrington]

Voyager ★★★ 15
Drama
1991 · Ger/Fr/Gr · Colour and BW · 108min

The always impressive Sam Shepard stars as a Unesco worker and traveller who drifts through Europe and across the Atlantic on an ocean liner in search of love and the meaning of life. He's haunted by an affair from his past and a new romance with a young woman only takes him further back in time. Director Volker Schlöndorff cleverly conveys the mood of postwar Europe, and, even though the locations veer far and wide, the main aim of the story is to journey inside Shepard's head. AT Sex scenes.

Sam Shepard *Walter Faber* • Julie Delpy *Sabeth* • Barbara Sukowa *Hannah* • Dieter Kirchlechner *Herbert Hencke* • Deborra-Lee Furness *Ivy* • Traci Lind *Charlene* • August Zirner *Joachim* ■ *Dir* Volker Schlöndorff • *Scr* Rudy Wurlitzer, from the novel *Homo Faber* by Max Frisch

Vroom ★★ 15
Road movie drama   1988 · UK · Colour · 84min

David Thewlis and Clive Owen hope to fulfil their dreams by hitting the open road in a classic American car they have lovingly restored. Unfortunately, they also take along a sultry divorcee, and soon the libidos and tensions begin to rise. Although nothing more than a formulaic road movie with a few quirky twists, the acting from the leads makes it worthwhile. AJ

Clive Owen *Jake* • David Thewlis *Ringe* • Diana Quick *Susan* • Jim Broadbent *Donald* • Philip Tan *Shane* ■ *Dir* Beeban Kidron • *Scr* Jim Cartwright

W. ★★ 15
Biographical drama
2008 · US/Aus/HK/Swi/Chi · Colour · 124min

Considering Oliver Stone's filmography (*JFK*, *Nixon*), it's probably not too much of a surprise that the first biopic of a sitting US President would be directed by him. It's a well-cast portrait of George W Bush (Josh Brolin) that mixes *West Wing*-like, behind-the-scenes re-enactments of the lead-up to the 2003 invasion of Iraq, with more fancifully imagined scenes from Bush's early pre-politics life. While Stone's *Nixon* set a high standard with its humanising reappraisal of a past president, *W.* serves only to reinforce the popular public image of the latterly unpopular incumbent. Brolin sidesteps caricature with an even-handed, even warm portrayal yet, as a cinematic exercise, Stone's film feels rather pointless. AC *DVD* *Blu-ray*

Josh Brolin *George W Bush* • Elizabeth Banks (2) *Laura Bush* • Ellen Burstyn *Barbara Bush* • Thandie Newton *Condoleezza Rice* • Richard Dreyfuss *Dick Cheney* • James Cromwell *George Herbert Walker Bush* • Jeffrey Wright *General Colin Powell* • Scott Glenn *Donald Rumsfeld* • Toby Jones *Karl Rove* • Ioan Gruffudd *Tony Blair* ■ *Dir* Oliver Stone • *Scr* Stanley Weiser

WC Fields and Me ★★★
Biographical drama   1976 · US · Colour · 111min

Lambasted on release for taking liberties with the truth, Arthur Hiller's biopic of famed tippler comedian WC Fields (Rod Steiger) is still impressive. Covering the life of the vaudevillian-turned-film-star from the perspective of his lover Carlotta Monti, there's a feel of the real in its re-creation of the Hollywood of long ago. Like Fields, Steiger never lets you forget he's the star, but there are sterling support performances from Valerie Perrine and Bernadette Peters among others. DA

Rod Steiger *WC Fields* • Valerie Perrine *Carlotta Monti* • John Marley *Studio Head Bannerman* • Jack Cassidy *John Barrymore* • Bernadette Peters *Melody* • Dana Elcar *Agent Dockstedter* • Paul Stewart *Florenz Ziegfeld* • Billy Barty *Ludwig* ■ *Dir* Arthur Hiller • *Scr* Bob Merrill, from the book by Carlotta Monti, Cy Rice • *Music* Henry Mancini

W.E. ★★★ 15
Romantic drama   2011 · UK · Colour · 114min

The second film by pop diva Madonna is an intriguing, if overlong romantic curio that benefits from some terrific performances and a style-icon's eye for detail. It takes place in two timeframes, the first involving a modern-day woman, Wally (Abbie Cornish), who becomes obsessed with the love affair that led to the abdication of Edward VIII in 1936. But *W.E.* excels mostly in the period scenes, which reconstruct the relationship between the besotted king (James D'Arcy) and the brash American socialite Wallis Simpson (Andrea Riseborough). In its clearer moments, this handsomely staged film cleverly defies the history books with some provocative points about the price Simpson "really" paid for her notoriety. DW Violence, swearing.

DVD *Blu-ray*

Andrea Riseborough *Wallis* • James D'Arcy *Edward VIII* • Abbie Cornish *Wally Winthrop* • Oscar Isaac *Evgeni* • Richard Coyle *William Winthrop* • David Harbour *Ernest* • James Fox *King George V* • Natalie Dormer *Elizabeth Bowes-Lyon* • Laurence Fox *Bertie* ■ *Dir* Madonna • *Scr* Madonna, Alek Keshishian

WR – Mysteries of the Organism ★★★ 18
Experimental documentary drama
1971 · Yug · Colour · 79min

The WR of the title is Wilhelm Reich, the Austrian-born sexologist whose theories on the correlation between erogenous satisfaction and political freedom inspired this anarchic, almost stream-of-imagery dissertation from Dusan Makavejev. Achieving cult status on its release, the film is beginning to betray its age, although the clips of Stalin in the 1946 propaganda feature, *The Vow*, remain as amusing as the footage from the Nazi documentary advocating euthanasia is horrifying. But Makavejev's allegorical fiction involving the romance between a Yugoslav girl and an inhibited Russian skater is clumsy. DP Serbian, English +subtitles. Sex scenes, swearing.

Milena Dravic *Milena* • Jagoda Kaloper *Jagoda* • Zoran Radmilovic *Radmilovic* • Ivica Vidovic *Vladimir Ilyich* ■ *Dir/Scr* Dusan Makavejev

WUSA ★★★★
Drama   1970 · US · Colour · 114min

Anthony Perkins upstages a clutch of famous faces in this dark drama. Paul Newman stars as a cynical disc jockey at a right-wing New Orleans radio station; Perkins is the liberal conscience whose confrontations with the station are so raw and relevant they sideline the brittle affair between Joanne Woodward and Newman. Despite such dramatic imbalance, there are enough insights here to make this one of the more important movies about the state of America in the 1970s. TH

Paul Newman *Rheinhardt* • Joanne Woodward *Geraldine* • Anthony Perkins *Rainey* • Laurence Harvey *Farley* • Pat Hingle *Bingamon* • Cloris Leachman *Philomene* • Don Gordon *Bogdanovich* ■ *Dir* Stuart Rosenberg • *Scr* Robert Stone, from his novel *A Hall of Mirrors*

WW and the Dixie Dancekings ★★★
Comedy   1975 · US · Colour · 90min

This amiable redneck dirt-kickin' romp comes from the days when genial Burt Reynolds could do no wrong, and when John G Avildsen was a director of promise. The "Dixie Dancekings" of the title are a hokey country-and-western outfit fronted by genuine country star Jerry Reed. Reynolds's attempts to propel the band onwards and upwards are amusing and the easy charm that became his trademark makes this pleasant viewing. SH Violence, swearing.

Burt Reynolds *WW Bright* • Conny Van Dyke *Dixie* • Jerry Reed *Wayne* • Ned Beatty *Country Bull* • James Hampton *Junior* • Don Williams *Leroy* • Richard D Hurst *Butterball* • Art Carney *Deacon Gore* ■ *Dir* John G Avildsen • *Scr* Thomas Rickman [Tom Rickman]

Wabash Avenue ★★★
Period musical   1950 · US · Colour · 92min

One of Betty Grable's most popular and well-remembered musical vehicles, this Technicolor frolic is the one where she sings *I Wish I Could Shimmy like My Sister Kate* among the 26 song standards propping up the soundtrack, and where hunk Victor Mature and casino owner Phil Harris vie for her favours in 1890s Chicago. Director Henry Koster injects pace and overall brightness into a likeable and quaintly vulgar venture. TS

Betty Grable *Ruby Summers* • Victor Mature *Andy Clark* • Phil Harris *Uncle Mike* • Reginald Gardiner *English Eddie* • James Barton *Hogan* • Barry Kelley *Bouncer* • Margaret Hamilton *Tillie Hutch* ■ *Dir* Henry Koster • *Scr* Harry Tugend, Charles Lederer

The Wackiest Ship in the Army ★★ U
Comedy   1961 · US · Colour · 95min

A broken-down boat is used as a decoy in the Second World War, but the tone is uncertain: is it meant to be funny, or isn't it? As a screenwriter, Richard Murphy

worked on some interesting films, but here, he proves not to be the ideal director of his own material, despite a cast headed by the genial Jack Lemmon and teen idol Ricky Nelson, for whom underplaying is no real substitute for acting ability. Even though it later spawned a TV series, the film simply doesn't work. TS

Jack Lemmon *Lt Rip Crandall* • Ricky Nelson *Ensign Tommy Hanson* • John Lund *Commander Vandewater* • Chips Rafferty *Patterson* • Tom Tully *Capt McClung* • Joby Baker *Josh Davidson* • Warren Berlinger *Sparks* • Patricia Driscoll *Maggie* ■ *Dir* Richard Murphy (1) • *Scr* Richard Murphy, Herbert Margolis, William Raynor, from a story by Herbert Carlson

The Wackness ★★★★ 15
Comedy drama   2008 · US · Colour · 94min

In a pre-9/11 New York, Josh Peck is Luke, a high-school graduate whose life is stretching out before him and who makes ends meet by selling marijuana from an ice-cream trolley. One of his best clients is his psychiatrist, ageing hippie Jeff Squires (Ben Kingsley), and when the older man's marriage to his bored trophy wife breaks down, they join forces to embark on a drug-influenced graffiti campaign. The serious side of things is ably handled and thankfully never too maudlin, but the comedy is where *The Wackness* wins out, with Kingsley on superb form as the daffy Squires. Like the film itself, it's an off-kilter performance that flirts with eccentricity but stays just the right side of human. DW *DVD* *Blu-ray*

Ben Kingsley *Dr Squires* • Josh Peck *Luke Shapiro* • Famke Janssen *Kristin Squires* • Olivia Thirlby *Stephanie* • Mary-Kate Olsen *Union* • Aaron Yoo *Justin* • Talia Balsam *Mrs Shapiro* • David Wohl *Mr Shapiro* ■ *Dir/Scr* Jonathan Levine

Wacko ★★★
Spoof horror   1981 · US · Colour · 80min

This is a sloppy but lively and funny *Airplane!*-style spoof of *Halloween* and other famous horror movies. Whoever had the idea of casting Joe Don Baker as the world's sloppiest and most dirty-minded cop deserves a medal for his brilliance. His policeman character is in pursuit of the "Lawnmower Killer", who has left signs that he'll strike again 13 years to the day from when he first appeared. The best gags involve the skewering of the countless clichés found in slasher movies. KB

Joe Don Baker *Dick Harbinger* • Stella Stevens *Marg Graves* • George Kennedy *Dr Graves* • Julia Duffy *Mary Graves* • Scott McGinnis *Norman Bates* • Andrew Clay [Andrew Dice Clay] *Tony* • Elizabeth Daily *Bambi* • Michele Tobin *Rosie* • Anthony James *Zeke* ■ *Dir* Greydon Clark • *Scr* Dana Olsen, Michael Spound, M James Kauf Jr, David Greenwalt

Waco ★★
Western   1966 · US · Colour · 71min

While the local citizenry is being terrorised by a gang of lawless thugs, Howard Keel – a gunslinger with a hot reputation – is cooling his heels behind bars until somebody has the bright idea that he is the man to drive out the desperados. Released for the purpose, he does what's expected of him, with glamorous Jane Russell on hand for encouragement. A run-of-the-mill, second-rung western. RK

Howard Keel *Waco* • Jane Russell *Jill Stone* • Brian Donlevy *Ace Ross* • Wendell Corey *Preacher Sam Stone* • Terry Moore *Dolly* • John Smith *Joe Gore* • John Agar *George Gates* • Gene Evans *Deputy Sheriff O'Neill* • DeForest Kelley *Bill Rile* ■ *Dir* RG Springsteen • *Scr* Steve Fisher, from the novel *Emporia* by Harry Sanford, Max Lamb

Wadi 1981–1991 ★★★
Documentary   1991 · Is · Colour · 97min

In 1981, Amos Gitai explored the daily reality of the Arab-Israeli conflict in *Wadi*, a revealing talking-head documentary. Returning to the scrubland of Wadi Rushmia, near Haifa, Gitai discovers that much has changed in the decade since his original documentary about the difficulties of co-existence in Israel's disputed territories. The main focus this time is on a

couple of Russian immigrants, one of whom has fallen in love with a Galilean woman, while the other lives in isolation with his animals, having been shunned by this tinderbox of a community. DP
■ *Dir/Scr* Amos Gitai

Wadjda ★★★★ PG
Drama   2012 · Saudi Arab a/Ger/US/UAE · Colour · 92min

Haifaa Al Mansour's beguiling rite-of-passage tale is the first feature filmed entirely within Saudi Arabia. A sly study of the status of women in a rigid patriarchy, its potent points are tempered by some disarming humour and the sheer charm of Waad Mohammed's performance as a ten-year-old tomboy. Behind the simple storyline, Al Mansour examines such contentious topics as marital law, the place of the Koran in daily life, the restrictions placed on female travel and the hypocrisy of the conservative elite. With the cast displaying a winning naturalism, this entertains as much as it intrigues and perturbs. DP Arabic +subtitles. *DVD* Bl

Reem Abdullah *Mother* • Waad Mohammed *Wadjda* • Abdullrahman Al Gohani *Abdullah* • Ahd *Ms Hussa* ■ *Dir/Scr* Haifaa Al Mansour

Wag the Dog ★★★★ 15
Satirical comedy   1997 · US · Colour · 92min

Shot by Barry Levinson in a mere 29 days, this satire on the media and politics is a joy from start to finish. Just before an election, the US President is accused of molesting a teenage girl in the Oval Office. To divert interest away from the scandal, he orders his spin doctors to come up with something quickly. In consultation with a Hollywood producer, they invent a war against Albania. Robert De Niro is creepily effective as the spin doctor hired by White House PR woman Anne Heche, but best of all is Dustin Hoffman, who gives a hilarious performance as a Hollywood mogul. AT Swearing. *DVD*

Dustin Hoffman *Stanley Motss* • Robert De Niro *Conrad Brean* • Anne Heche *Winifred Ames* • Denis Leary *Fad King* • Willie Nelson *Johnny Green* • Andrea Martin *Liz Butsky* • Kirsten Dunst *Tracy Lime* • William H Macy *Mr Young* • Craig T Nelson *Senator Neal* • Woody Harrelson *Sergeant William Schumann* • Jim Belushi [James Belushi] ■ *Dir* Barry Levinson · *Scr* David Mamet, Hilary Henkin, from the novel *American Hero* by Larry Beinhart

The Wages of Fear ★★★★★ PG
Adventure thriller   1953 · Fr · BW · 130min

The tension is unbearable as two trucks full of nitroglycerin are driven over 300 miles of inhospitable Latin American terrain in order to help extinguish an oilfield fire. But, for all it says about courage and endurance, this is also a grindingly cynical study of human nature, with each member of the quartet willing to sacrifice the others for a bigger payoff. In bringing Georges Arnaud's novel to the screen, Henri-Georges Clouzot wisely spends time shading in the background detail that intensifies the excitement of the action by drenching it in a sweaty spirit of rivalry. This is cinema's most suspenseful condemnation of capitalism. DP French, English, German, Italian +subtitles. *DVD* Bl

Yves Montand *Mario* • Charles Vanel *Jo* • Vera Clouzot *Linda* • Folco Lulli *Luigi* • Peter Van Eyck *Bimba* • William Tubbs *O'Brien* • Dario Moreno *Hernandez* ■ *Dir* Henri-Georges Clouzot · *Scr* Henri-Georges Clouzot, Jérome Géronimi, from the novel *Le Salaire de la Peur* by Georges Arnaud

Wagner ★★ 15
Epic biographical drama   1983 · UK/Hun/Austria · Colour · 488min

This biopic of the composer was conceived by maverick director Tony Palmer on a very grand scale indeed. It was shot in six countries with Richard Burton in the title role; Olivier, Gielgud and Richardson on screen together; and a supporting cast of thousands. Wagner's music is played by three orchestras, conducted by Georg Solti.

The first cut, nine hours long, premiered in London in 1983 to mixed reviews. Wagnerians hoping for new insight into the obsessions of a highly complex mind will find instead an epic folly of the old school. DM

Richard Burton *Richard Wagner* • Vanessa Redgrave *Cosima* • Gemma Craven *Minna Wagner* • Laszlo Galffi *Ludwig II* • John Gielgud *Pfistermeister* • Ralph Richardson *Pfordten* • Laurence Olivier *Pfeufer* • Ekkehard Schall *Franz Liszt* ■ *Dir* Tony Palmer · *Scr* Charles Wood · *Cinematographer* Vittorio Storaro

Wagonmaster ★★★★ PG
Western   1950 · US · BW · 86min

This is one of the greatest and most warmly human films in the series of westerns made by the master of the genre, John Ford. Its simple plot follows two young itinerant cowboys helping lead a Mormon wagon train to Utah. As the youths, Harry Carey Jr and Ben Johnson reveal a callow expectancy of what life has in store and are profoundly moving as they play off each other when deciding to "fall in 'hind the wagon train". Many sequences are beautifully filmed, and it is interesting to see Ward Bond, who would later play the lead in *Wagon Train*, the successful TV series inspired by the movie. TS

Ben Johnson (1) *Travis* • Ward Bond *Wiggs* • Joanne Dru *Denver* • Harry Carey Jr *Sandy* • Charles Kemper *Uncle Shiloh* • Alan Mowbray *Dr Locksley Hall* • Jane Darwell *Sister Ledeyard* • James Arness *Floyd Clegg* ■ *Dir* John Ford · *Scr* Frank S Nugent [Frank Nugent], Patrick Ford, from a story by John Ford · *Cinematographer* Bert Glennon

Wagons East! ★ PG
Comedy western   1994 · US · Colour · 102min

It's always a shame when a star dies young, but it seems doubly unfair that someone as likeable and talented as John Candy should have bowed out part-way through the production of this stinker. The idea of having a bunch of lily-livered pioneers quit the Wild West and head home is essentially a good one. But writer/director Peter Markle buries it in a quagmire of comic incompetence and dismal slapstick. Quite dreadful. DP Swearing. *DVD*

John Candy *James Harlow* • Richard Lewis *Phil Taylor* • John C McGinley *Julian* • Ellen Greene *Belle* • Robert Picardo *Ben Wheeler* • Ed Lauter *John Slade* • William Sanderson *Zeke* • Rodney A Grant *Little Feather* ■ *Dir* Peter Markle · *Scr* Matthew Carlson, from a story by Jerry Abrahamson

The Wagons Roll at Night ★★
Crime drama   1941 · US · BW · 83min

Humphrey Bogart is the owner of a seedy carnival, intent on protecting his convent-educated young sister, Joan Leslie, from his rough life. Meanwhile, when a lion escapes, he fires his tamer (Sig Ruman) and takes on Eddie Albert instead, who proceeds to fall for Leslie. A melodramatic farrago that ill-befits its star. RK

Humphrey Bogart *Nick Coster* • Sylvia Sidney *Flo Lorraine* • Eddie Albert *Matt Varney* • Joan Leslie *Mary Coster* • Sig Ruman [Sig Ruman] *Hoffman the Great* • Cliff Clark *Doc* ■ *Dir* Ray Enright · *Scr* Fred Niblo Jr, Barry Trivers, from the novel *Kid Galahad* by Francis Wallace

Wah-Wah ★★★ 15
Period coming-of-age drama   2005 · UK/Fr/S Afr · Colour · 95min

Actor Richard E Grant makes his debut as writer/director with this affectionate and poignant coming-of-age drama. Loosely based on his own childhood in late 1960s Swaziland, the handsome film juxtaposes the death throes of British rule in Africa with the disintegration of a colonial family. Young Ralph Compton's idealised world is destroyed when his adulterous mother (an icy Miranda Richardson) runs off, leaving bureaucrat dad Harry (Gabriel Byrne) a broken alcoholic. Despite this tragic core, the tale remains warm and spirited, infused with charm and humanity. SF Swearing. *DVD*

Gabriel Byrne *Harry Compton* • Emily Watson *Ruby Compton* • Julie Walters *Gwen Traherne* • Nicholas Hoult *Ralph Compton, aged 14* • Miranda Richardson *Mrs Lauren Compton* • Fenella Woolgar *June* • Zac Fox [Zachary Fox] *Ralph Compton, aged 11* • Olivia Grant *Monica* • Celia Imrie *Lady Riva Hardwick* ■ *Dir/Scr* Richard E Grant

Waikiki Wedding ★★★
Musical comedy   1937 · US · BW · 88min

This good-natured sun-drenched musical, characteristic of the period, is set in a Paramount studio version of Hawaii. Here, amid the grass skirts and exotic scenery, pineapple growers PR man Bing Crosby is masterminding a Miss Pineapple beauty contest. Bing, of course, falls for the winner, Shirley Ross, and croons his way through several "South Seas" numbers, including Oscar-winning mega-hit *Sweet Leilani*, while his sidekick Bob Burns tangles with motormouthed Martha Raye to supply the comedy. RK

Bing Crosby *Tony Marvin* • Bob Burns (2) *Shad Buggle* • Martha Raye *Myrtle Finch* • Shirley Ross *Georgia Smith* • George Barbier *JP Todhunter* • Leif Erickson *Dr Victor Quimby* • Anthony Quinn *Kimo* ■ *Dir* Frank Tuttle · *Scr* Frank Butler, Don Hartman, Walter DeLeon, Frances Martin, from a story by Frank Butler, Don Hartman · *Choreographer* LeRoy Prinz

Waist Deep ★★ 15
Action crime drama   2006 · US · Colour · 92min

After the disaster that was the Mariah Carey vehicle *Glitter*, actor-turned-director Vondie Curtis-Hall (*Gridlock'd*) is back in more familiar territory with this formulaic but taut urban thriller. Tyrese Gibson plays an ex-con trying to go straight whose son ends up in the hands of a vicious gangster (The Game) after a carjacking goes wrong. Needing $100,000 to free him, he teams up with initially reluctant hustler Coco (Meagan Good), to raise the money through some ingeniously staged robberies. Although Curtis-Hall doesn't succeed in avoiding all the clichéd machismo that typifies the genre, it looks great, and Gibson and Good make for a charismatic pair of leads. JF *DVD* Bl

Tyrese Gibson *O2* • Meagan Good *Coco* • Larenz Tate *Lucky* • The Game *Meat* • H Hunter Hall [Henry Hunter Hall] *Junior* • Kimora Lee Simmons *Fencing House Lady* ■ *Dir* Vondie Curtis-Hall [Vondie Curtis-Hall] · *Scr* Vondie Curtis-Hall, Darin Scott, from a story by Michael Mahern

The Wait ★★★ 12A
Drama   2015 · It/Fr · Colour · 100min

An unlikely scenario proves surprisingly poignant in this dolorous drama from the debuting Piero Messina. Set during Holy Week in a lakeside villa on the edge of a small Sicilian town, the action turns around the relationship that develops when grieving mother Juliette Binoche decides not to break the news of her son's death to his Parisian girlfriend (Lou de Laâge). The performances are deeply affecting, with the emotionally taut Binoche striving to keep her child alive through de Laâge, who hopes she can impress her lover's mother and atone for a past infidelity. DP In Italian, French. Nudity.

Juliette Binoche *Anna* • Lou de Laâge *Jeanne* • Giorgio Colangeli *Pietro* • Domenico Diele *Giorgio* • Giovanni Anzaldo *Giuseppe* ■ *Dir* Piero Messina · *Scr* Giacomo Bendotti, Ilaria Macchia, Andrea Paolo Massara, Piero Messina, from a play by Luigi Pirandello

Wait 'til the Sun Shines, Nellie ★★★ U
Drama   1952 · US · Colour · 107min

Produced by vaudeville legend George Jessel, this is a polished and thoroughly professional piece of period melodrama that demonstrates the virtue of that old-fashioned concept – a story with a beginning, a middle and an end. David Wayne gives his finest screen performance as the homely small-town barber who accepts the joys and trials of life with equal grace. Directed by Henry King with a sure

grasp of bygone America, this is finely crafted entertainment. DP

David Wayne *Ben Halper* • Jean Peters *Nellie* • Hugh Marlowe *Ed Jordan* • Albert Dekker *Lloyd Slocum* • Helene Stanley *Eadie Jordan* • Tommy Morton [Tom Morton] *Ben Halper Jr, aged 20* • Joyce MacKenzie *Bessie Jordan* • Alan Hale Jr *George Oliphant* ■ *Dir* Henry King · *Scr* Allan Scott, Maxwell Shane, from the novel *I Heard Them Sing* by Ferdinand Reyher

Wait until Dark ★★★★ 12
Thriller   1967 · US · Colour · 103min

A powerful piece of theatre can often seem very flat on film because the screen distances the viewer from the immediacy and intimacy of the stage performance. Terence Young's version of Frederick Knott's Broadway hit is a magnificent exception. Oscar-nominated Audrey Hepburn is quite superb as the blind woman who keeps her wits about her when drug dealers break into her apartment to recover a doll full of heroin. Alan Arkin pulls out all the terror stops as the leader of the gang, and Young never lets the suspense drop. DP *DVD*

Audrey Hepburn *Susy Hendrix* • Alan Arkin *Roat* • Richard Crenna *Mike Talman* • Efrem Zimbalist Jr *Sam Hendrix* • Jack Weston *Carlino* • Samantha Jones *Lisa* • Julie Herrod *Gloria* • Frank O'Brien *Shatner* ■ *Dir* Terence Young · *Scr* Robert Carrington, Jane-Howard Carrington, from the play by Frederick Knott · *Cinematographer* Charles Lang

Wait until Spring, Bandini ★★
Period drama   1989 · Bel/Fr/It/US · Colour · 100min

Too little is asked of a fine cast in this handsome but uninspiring adaptation. Belgian director Dominique Deruddere brings a keen outsider's eye to the Colorado setting, but his grasp of the 1920s atmosphere is less assured. Joe Mantegna offers a bullish performance, as the unemployed bricklayer with a penchant for gambling and a loathing of his mother-in-law. But neither Ornella Muti, as his put-upon wife, nor Faye Dunaway, as a seductive neighbour, make much of an impact. DP

Joe Mantegna *Svevo Bandini* • Ornella Muti *Maria Bandini* • Faye Dunaway *Mrs Effie Hildegarde* • Burt Young *Rocco Saccone* • Michael Bacall *Arturo Bandini* • Renata Vanni *Donna Toscana, Maria's mother* ■ *Dir* Dominique Deruddere · *Scr* Dominique Deruddere, from the novel by John Fante

Waiting ★★★ 15
Drama   1990 · Aus · Colour · 93min

An artist agrees to be a surrogate mum to a childless couple's baby. This domestic drama follows the girl and her friends through the pregnancy, with events taking a dramatic turn when she starts having second thoughts about giving the baby up. Noni Hazlehurst plays the lady who waits while her co-stars include Deborra-Lee Furness. DA CS

Noni Hazlehurst *Clare* • Deborra-Lee Furness *Diane* • Frank Whitten *Michael* • Helen Jones *Sandy* • Denis Moore *Bill* • Fiona Press *Therese* • Ray Barrett *Frank* • Noga Bernstein *Rosie* ■ *Dir/Scr* Jackie McKimmie

Waiting... ★ 15
Comedy   2005 · US/Aus · Colour · 90min

Ryan Reynolds stars in this crude ensemble comedy about the puerile antics of the staff of a tacky small-town restaurant. Reynolds is on autopilot as the wisecracking chief troublemaker, while the talents of a decent supporting cast are wasted by a script that is well past its sell-by date. JF Swearing. *DVD*

Ryan Reynolds *Monty* • Anna Faris *Serena* • Justin Long *Dean* • Kaitlin Doubleday *Amy* • Andy Milonakis *Nick* • Dane Cook *Floyd* • Chi McBride *Bishop* • Luis Guzman *Raddimus* ■ *Dir/Scr* Rob McKittrick

W

Waiting for Guffman★★★ 15

Satire   1996 · US · Colour · 80min

This straight-faced "mockumentary" sends up am-dram pretentiousness and middle American values in equal measure. Directed by and starring Christopher Guest (*Spinal Tap*), the film's spot-on spoofery focuses on a small-town "auteur" and his ambitious plan to stage a musical review to mark the town's 150th anniversary. The results are far funnier than the film's inability to secure UK distribution might suggest, and there's a strong supporting cast. DA DVD

Christopher Guest *Corky St Clair* • Eugene Levy *Dr Allan Pearl* • Fred Willard *Ron Albertson* • Catherine O'Hara *Sheila Albertson* • Parker Posey *Libby Mae Brown* • Bob Balaban *Lloyd Miller* • Lewis Arquette *Clifford Wooley* ■ *Dir* Christopher Guest • *Scr* Christopher Guest, Eugene Levy • *Music/lyrics* Michael McKean, Harry Shearer, Christopher Guest

Waiting for Happiness
                                  ★★★★ U

Drama   2002 · Fr/Swi/Neth/Cz · Colour · 91min

The clash between tradition and progress is a familiar theme in African cinema. But rarely has it been explored with such poignancy as in this collection of characters from Mauritanian director Abderrahmane Sissako. The coastal town of Nouadhibou serves as a microcosm for a continent whose menfolk are leaving in search of work, whose women have few rights and many responsibilities, and whose children are increasingly exposed to cultures the elderly regard with disdain. The largely improvised performances of the non-professional cast convey the moods and attitudes with conviction. DP Hassianya, French +subtitles. DVD

Khatra Ould Abdel Kader *Khatra* • Maata Ould Mohamed Abeid *Maata* • Mohamed Mahmoud Ould Mohamed *Abdallah* • Fatimetou Mint Ahmeda *Soukeyna* • Nana Diakite *Nana* • Makanfing Dabo *Makan* ■ *Dir/Scr* Abderrahmane Sissako

Waiting for "Superman"
                                  ★★★ PG

Documentary   2010 · US · Colour · 106min

Prompted by fatherhood to investigate the quality of America's schools, director Davis Guggenheim looks at the Catch-22 situation - too few good schools for too many pupils - facing parents in the matter of their child's education. Following several disparate families at various stages in the school system, the film perhaps spends too long on the disappointments (eg weeping children clutching lottery tickets that will determine their educational future). There's also not enough time given to the highs, notably inspirational guest speakers such as educational activist Geoffrey Canada, who relates the sad tale that gives the film its title (steeped in irony). DW DVD

■ *Dir* Davis Guggenheim • *Scr* Davis Guggenheim, Billy Kimball

Waiting for the Light
                                  ★★★ PG

Comedy drama   1989 · US · Colour · 90min

In her later years Shirley MacLaine has specialised in portrayals of eccentric ladies of a certain age. This is one of her best - a former circus performer, now children's entertainer, whose behaviour brings trouble to her niece Teri Garr, who has taken on a diner in a small town in Washington State. It's pleasant enough, but director Chris Monger's debut feature has little rhyme or reason. MacLaine gives a polished performance and the surface sheen makes for enjoyable viewing. TH Some swearing.

Shirley MacLaine *Aunt Zena* • Teri Garr *Kay Harris* • Colin Baumgartner *Eddie Harris* • Hillary Wolf *Emily Harris* • Clancy Brown *Joe* • Vincent Schiavelli *Mullins* • John Bedford Lloyd *Reverend Stevens* • Jeff McCracken *Charlie* ■ *Dir/Scr* Christopher Monger

Waiting for the Moon   ★★

Biographical drama
1987 · US/Fr · Colour · 88min

Linda Bassett and Linda Hunt play one of the 20th century's most interesting couples, author Gertrude Stein and cookery writer Alice B Toklas. The infamous pair lived together in Paris for more than 20 years and played host to artists from Hemingway to Picasso. Sadly, this great story is still waiting to be told well, as Jill Godmilow's film only skims the surface and there is no depth to the relationship between the women, despite the talent of the two actresses. LH

Linda Hunt *Alice B Toklas* • Linda Bassett *Gertrude Stein* • Andrew McCarthy *Henry Hopper* • Bernadette Lafont *Fernande Olivier* • Bruce McGill *Ernest Hemingway* • Jacques Boudet *Guillaume Apollinaire* ■ *Dir* Jill Godmilow • *Scr* Mark Magill, from a story by Jill Godmilow, Mark Magill

The Waiting Room   ★★ 15

Romantic drama   2007 · UK · Colour · 101min

Writer/director Roger Goldby's rather dull romantic drama attempts to examine the role that fate can play in relationships. Elderly Roger (Frank Finlay) spends his days down at the local railway station, hanging around for his wife, who may or may not exist. While waiting one day, he plays Cupid to two complete strangers - Stephen (Ralf Little), one of Roger's care-home workers, who is agonising over committing to his girlfriend, and Anna (Anne-Marie Duff), a single parent who is having an ill-advised affair. Sparks fly between Stephen and Anna, but the pair leave without speaking and then spend the rest of the film attempting to find each other. The performances are uniformly good, but you are left with the distinct feeling that you've seen it all before. DA DVD

Anne-Marie Duff *Anna* • Ralf Little *Stephen* • Rupert Graves *George* • Frank Finlay *Roger* • Zoe Telford *Jem* • Phyllida Law *Helen* • Christine Bottomley *Fiona* ■ *Dir/Scr* Roger Goldby

Waiting to Exhale   ★★★ 15

Drama   1995 · US · Colour · 118min

No matter what problems confront the female quartet in this crowd-pleasing melodrama, the most pressing concern always seems to be the shortage of good men. Like that woman's picture extraordinaire *Thelma & Louise*, it's directed by a man - marking the directorial debut of Forest Whitaker. There's a patronising tone of indulgence pervading the film that manifests itself in the smart one-liners, the minor triumphs designed to elicit high-fives among the audience and the tear-jerking feel-good of the finale. Expertly acted, this owes little to life and a bit too much to glossy magazine aspirations. DP

Whitney Houston *Savannah* • Angela Bassett *Bernadine* • Loretta Devine *Gloria* • Lela Rochon *Robin* • Gregory Hines *Marvin* • Dennis Haysbert *Kenneth* • Mykelti Williamson *Troy* • Michael Beach *John Sr* ■ *Dir* Forest Whitaker • *Scr* Terry McMillan, Ronald Bass, from the novel by Terry McMillan

Waiting Women   ★★★ 12

Comedy   1952 · Swe · BW · 103min

This episodic drama from Ingmar Bergman continued his fascination with exploring the battle of the sexes from the female perspective. Waiting for their partners to join them for the summer, three sisters-in-law describe key moments in their relationships. Anita Björk talks about an extramarital affair and the effect it had on her husband; Maj-Britt Nilsson recalls the pregnancy that led her to marry painter Birger Malmsten; and Eva Dahlbeck alights on a night stuck in a lift with her pompous spouse, Gunnar Björnstrand. It's a patchy anthology, but the comic finale is splendid. DP Swedish +subtitles. DVD

Anita Björk *Rakel* • Eva Dahlbeck *Karin* • Maj-Britt Nilsson *Marta* • Karl Arne Holmsten *Eugen* • Jarl Kulle *Kaj* • Birger Malmsten *Martin* • Gunnar Björnstrand *Fredrik* ■ *Dir/Scr* Ingmar Bergman

Waitress   ★★★★ 12

Romantic comedy   2007 · US · Colour · 103min

This warm and engaging film deals with issues of motherhood, abusive relationships and female empowerment - adding some sly and welcome twists along the way. Small-town diner waitress Jenna (Keri Russell) is distressed to find herself pregnant. Married to a violent lout, she bakes her famed pies (such as the "I Hate My Husband" pie) for comfort and dreams of escaping her stifling marriage. During a routine trip to the medical centre, Jenna meets new locum Dr Pomatter (*Serenity's* Nathan Fillion) and they begin a torrid, if not entirely ethical, affair. Fillion makes a likeable romantic interest, and the camera clearly loves Russell, but ultimately *Waitress* is a testament to the promise of its writer/director/co-star Adrienne Shelly, who was tragically murdered in November 2006, just weeks after the film was finished. DW DVD

Keri Russell *Jenna* • Nathan Fillion *Dr Pomatter* • Cheryl Hines *Becky* • Adrienne Shelly *Dawn* • Jeremy Sisto *Earl* • Andy Griffith *Old Joe* • Eddie Jemison *Ogie* ■ *Dir/Scr* Adrienne Shelly

Wake in Fright   ★★★★★ 18

Thriller   1970 · Aus/UK · Colour · 108min

Lost for over 30 years, this startling outback odyssey - a sort of Aussie *Deliverance* - is a breathtaking experience. Gary Bond stars as the young teacher whose attempts to get home at Christmas are thwarted when a stopover in a mining town plunges him into the gambling, carousing and drinking culture that passes for everyday life there. His descent into madness is darkly comic and shocking, but this simmering drama is also scathing critique of antipodean machismo from director Ted Kotcheff, with Donald Pleasence outstanding as an alcoholic doctor-cum-bar-room philosopher. JA Violence, swearing, sex scenes, nudity, scenes of kangaroo hunting/slaughter. DVD Blu

Donald Pleasence *"Doc" Tydon* • Gary Bond *John Grant* • Chips Rafferty *Jock Crawford* • Sylvia Kay *Janette Hynes* • Al Thomas *Tim Hynes* ■ *Dir* Ted Kotcheff • *Scr* Evan Jones, from Kenneth Cook's novel

Wake Island   ★★★★

Second World War drama
1942 · US · BW · 87min

Director John Farrow achieves an almost documentary-style realism, even though the film is relentlessly Hollywood in style and features that well-known studio platoon consisting entirely of stereotypes. News of the heroic December 1941 defence of Wake, a Pacific island lost to the Japanese, was barely off the presses when filming began, and a grim gung-ho mood is apparent throughout the feature. It received four Oscar nominations, including best picture, best director and best supporting actor for William Bendix, who, along with Brian Donlevy, gives a particularly fine performance. The ending is very moving and patriotic. TS

Brian Donlevy *Major Geoffrey Caton* • Macdonald Carey *Lieutenant Cameron* • Robert Preston *Joe Doyle* • William Bendix *Smacksie Randall* • Albert Dekker *Shad McClosky* • Walter Abel *Commander Roberts* • Mikhail Rasumny *Probenzky* • Don Castle *Private Cunkel* ■ *Dir* John Farrow • *Scr* WR Burnett, Frank Butler

Wake of the Red Witch
                                  ★★★ PG

Adventure   1949 · US · BW · 102min

This John Wayne seafaring action adventure would have benefited from colour, but still provides reasonable entertainment. Gail Russell is the girl Wayne and rival ship owner Luther Adler are fighting over, and the South Seas setting is very studio-bound. The *Red Witch* herself was used again in 1953's *Fair Wind to Java*, and now resides in the Hollywood Wax Museum on Hollywood Boulevard. Incidentally, Wayne named his film production company, Batjac, after the

fictional shipping line in this movie. TS DVD

John Wayne *Captain Ralls* • Gail Russell *Angelique Desaix* • Gig Young *Sam Rosen* • Luther Adler *Mayrant Ruysdaal Sidneye* • Adele Mara *Teleia Van Schreeven* • Paul Fix *Antonio "Ripper" Arrezo* • Eduard Franz *Harmenszoon Van Schreeven* ■ *Dir* Edward Ludwig • *Scr* Harry Brown, Kenneth Gamet, from the novel by Garland Roark

Wake Up and Live   ★★★

Musical comedy   1937 · US · BW · 91min

Alice Faye's beautiful rendition here of *There's a Lull in My Life* should be more than enough for most of her fans. But this Faye vehicle (one of four she made the same year) also has a plot involving a feud between band leader Ben Bernie and arch-columnist and broadcaster Walter Winchell, no less. There's some nice clowning, too, from Jack Haley as a performer with a phobia about microphones. Former jazz musician Sidney Lanfield provides the pacey direction for this fine example of Hollywood taking revenge on its then-current rival, radio. TS

Walter Winchell • Ben Bernie • Alice Faye *Alice Huntley* • Patsy Kelly *Patsy Kane* • Ned Sparks *Steve Cluskey* • Jack Haley *Eddie Kane* • Grace Bradley *Jean Roberts* ■ *Dir* Sidney Lanfield • *Scr* Harry Tugend, Jack Yellen, from a story by Curtis Kenyon, from the non-fiction book by Dorothea Brande

Wake Wood   ★★★ 18

Horror   2010 · Ire/UK/Swe · Colour · 86min

The bleak realities of grief infuse co-writer/director David Keating's grim but oddly moving modern chiller, which is filled with all the classic horror elements you'd expect from a movie sporting the revamped Hammer brand. Aidan Gillen and Eva Birthistle star as a couple heartbroken over their young daughter's tragic death who relocate to a remote Irish village to start afresh. There they learn of an ancient pagan ceremony that will revive her for three days, allowing them to seek proper closure. The result is a compelling twist on the Faustian pact that builds to a truly memorable, if starkly horrifying, ending. AJ Violence. DVD

Eva Birthistle *Louise* • Aidan Gillen *Patrick* • Timothy Spall *Arthur* • Ella Connolly *Alice* • Ruth McCabe *Peggy O'Shea* ■ *Dir* David Keating • *Scr* David Keating, Brendan McCarthy, from a story by McCarthy

Waking Life   ★★★ 15

Animated drama   2001 · US · Colour · 96min

Intellectually acute viewers may occasionally be alienated by the sophomoric posturings in director Richard Linklater's dazzlingly innovative attempt to provoke audience introspection, as an array of characters voice their philosophies of life to Wiley Wiggins's latter-day Candide during a series of dream-like perambulations. It's impossible not to be impressed by Linklater's inspired imagery. Created by a 31-strong animation team, the hybrid visuals consist of live-action digital video footage that has been "painted" over, frame by frame, using software developed by art director Bob Sabiston. This provides a striking graphic diversity that perfectly complements the conflicting philosophical reflections. DP DVD Blu

Wiley Wiggins *Main Character* • Ethan Hawke *Jesse* • Julie Delpy *Celine* • Steven Soderbergh ■ *Dir/Scr* Richard Linklater

Waking Ned   ★★★ PG

Comedy   1998 · UK/Fr · Colour · 87min

This charming film from first-time director Kirk Jones was a surprise hit stateside thanks to an imaginative marketing effort. Set on a tiny Irish island, two old men become hysterical when they discover an anonymous local has won the lottery. Their attempts to uncover the lucky so-and-so involve bribery and much false nicety until success results in them orchestrating a complex lie which involves the entire community. Ian Bannen stars with David Kelly as the avaricious OAPs in a tale that is both laugh-out-loud funny and touching. LH Nudity. *DVD*

Ian Bannen *Jackie O'Shea* • David Kelly *Michael O'Sullivan* • Fionnula Flanagan *Annie O'Shea* • Susan Lynch *Maggie* • James Nesbitt *Pig Finn* • Maura O'Malley *Mrs Kennedy* • Robert Hickey *Maurice* • Paddy Ward *Brendy* ■ *Dir/Scr* Kirk Jones

Waking the Dead ★★15

Romantic mystery drama
2000 · US · Colour · 100min

A fine supporting cast props up this sometimes uncomfortable combination of *The Way We Were* and *The Sixth Sense*. Achieving little of the intrigue generated by *Mother Night*, director Keith Gordon pulls together an ambiguous plotline, but it's hard to believe in the passion between budding politician Billy Crudup and radical activist Jennifer Connelly, which seems to survive her death a decade earlier in a car bombing. DP *DVD*

Billy Crudup *Fielding Pierce* • Jennifer Connelly *Sarah Williams* • Janet McTeer *Caroline Pierce* • Molly Parker *Juliet Beck* • Sandra Oh *Kim* • Hal Holbrook *Isaac Green* • Ed Harris *Jerry Carmichael* ■ *Dir* Keith Gordon • *Scr* Robert Dillons, from the novel by Scott Spencer

Waking Up in Reno ★★15

Romantic comedy 2000 · US · Colour · 87min

An ill-advised redneck variation on the slick 1969 couples comedy *Bob & Carol & Ted & Alice*, this stubbornly refuses to flicker into life, despite the quirky casting. Billy Bob Thornton plays a used-car dealer who is betraying spouse Natasha Richardson with Charlize Theron, the wife of his best buddy Patrick Swayze. When the infidelity is discovered on a road trip to Reno, Nevada, all hell breaks loose. Badly acted and resolutely unfunny, this has curio value only. DP Swearing. *DVD*

Billy Bob Thornton *Lonnie Earl Dodd* • Charlize Theron *Candy Kirkendall* • Natasha Richardson *Darlene Dodd* • Patrick Swayze *Roy Kirkendall* • Holmes Osborne *Doc Tuley* • Chelcie Ross *Fred Bush* • Pénélope Cruz *Brenda* (Spanish woman) ■ *Dir* Jordan Brady • *Scr* Brent Briscoe, Mark Fauser

Wakolda ★★★12

Drama based on a true story
2013 · Arg/Fr/Sp/Nor · Colour · 90min

Writer/director Lucía Puenzo clearly wants viewers to be in on the identity of the German doctor who arrives in a Patagonian village in 1960 - but she also wants to keep them in suspense. So, she tells the story through the eyes of a 12-year-old girl whose mother allows the doctor to administer growth hormones. Further clues to the sinister doctor's identity come courtesy of his fascination with the mother's unborn twins. The performances are solid and the use of the mountainous locale exemplary, but Puenzo overdoes the symbolism and edges into fairy-tale territory when the material would be more suited to a low-key horror. DP Spanish, German, Hebrew +subtitles. Some violence. *DVD*

Alex Brendemühl *Josef Mengele* • Natalia Oreiro *Eva* • Diego Perett *Enzo* • Elena Roger *Nora Eldoc* ■ *Dir/Scr* Lucía Puenzo

Wal-Mart: the High Cost of Low Price ★★PG

Documentary 2005 · US · Colour · 99min

Like Michael Moore's controversial polemic *Fahrenheit 9/11*, this documentary takes a blunderbuss approach to its subject matter - in this case the allegedly malign influence of American superstore chain Wal-Mart. Interviewing ex-employees, customers and rival store-owners, director Robert Greenwald takes a scattergun approach to his attack on the company, never staying long enough with any one topic to make his case effectively. AS *DVD*

James Cromwell *Bob Whitebread* • Frances Fisher *Wendy Whitebread* ■ *Dir* Robert Greenwald • *Cinematographer* Kristy Tully

Walesa: Man of Hope ★★★★12A

Biographical drama
2013 · Pol · Colour and BW · 124min

In his dramas *Man of Marble* and *Man of Iron*, director Andrzej Wajda chronicled the end of Polish communist domination and the rise of the Solidarity trade union. This biopic of Lech Walesa, the labourer whose name became synonymous with those changes, can be seen, therefore, as wrapping up a loose historical trilogy. But, while Wajda is ready to acknowledge Walesa's mistakes, he also readily recognises how crucial his charm and negotiating skills were to the uprising in the Gdansk shipyard following the 1979 visit of Polish pope John Paul II. Making exceptional use of archive footage and dramatic reconstruction, Wajda stops short of hagiography. But this is a fulsome and often jubilant tribute to a man who helped change the course of European history. DP Polish, Italian +subtitles. Swearing, some violence. *DVD*

Robert Wieckiewicz *Lech Walesa* • Agnieszka Grochowska *Danuta Walesa* • Maria Rosaria Omaggio *Oriana Fallaci* • Zbigniew Zamachowski *Nawislak* ■ *Dir* Andrzej Wajda • *Scr* Janusz Glowacki

The Walk ★★★PG

Drama based on a true story
2015 · US · Colour · 123min

Frenchman Philippe Petit's 1974 tightrope walk between the Twin Towers gets a caper-like workout at the hands of *Back to the Future* director Robert Zemeckis. He brings that perilous task to nerve-jangling life with technical savvy, while Joseph Gordon-Levitt captures the charisma of the likeable Petit and looks every inch the wirewalker. The re-creation is a genuinely sweat-inducing experience. But for all the virtuosity here, James Marsh's 2008 film on the same subject, *Man on Wire*, just can't be topped. JA In English, French. Swearing, brief nudity. *DVD* *Blu* *3D*

Joseph Gordon-Levitt *Philippe Petit* • Ben Kingsley *Papa Rudy* • Charlotte Le Bon *Annie Allix* • James Badge Dale *Jean-Pierre/JP* ■ *Dir* Robert Zemeckis, Christopher Browne

Walk a Crooked Path ★★★

Drama 1969 · UK · Colour · 85min

Tenniel Evans is an embittered boarding school housemaster who, passed over for promotion, plans to murder his rich, alcoholic wife Faith Brook and live with his mistress Patricia Haynes. Bizarrely, he does this by paying student Clive Endersby to claim that he was homosexually abused by Evans, thus humiliating Brook so badly that she commits suicide. The plot is quite clever, revealed in flashbacks and sudden twists and revelling in the rather risqué elements. AT

Tenniel Evans *John Hemming* • Faith Brook *Elizabeth Hemming* • Christopher Coll *Bill Colman* • Patricia Haines *Nancy Colman* • Clive Endersby *Philip Dreaper* • Georgina Simpson *Elaine* • Georgina Cookson *Imogen Dreaper* ■ *Dir* John Brason • *Scr* Barry Perowne

A Walk among the Tombstones ★★15

Action crime thriller 2014 · US · Colour · 108min

Liam Neeson resumes his craggy hero guise in writer/director Scott Frank's moody, misjudged thriller. Neeson (looking more fed up and delivering less conviction than ever) plays a former police officer with a chequered, alcoholic past who, when investigating the murder of the wife of a drug dealer (a shifty, goateed Dan Stevens), finds out that she wasn't the first to die and she won't be the last. It's a film that's wearyingly unoriginal, and the pulpy, poorly thought through dialogue is likely to raise titters. EAS Violence, swearing, brief nudity. *DVD* *Blu*

Liam Neeson *Matt Scudder* • Dan Stevens *Kenny Kristo* • Sebastian Roché *Yuri Landau* • Whitney Able *Denise* ■ *Dir* Scott Frank • *Scr* Scott Frank, from Lawrence Block's novel

Walk, Don't Run ★★★U

Romantic comedy 1966 · US · Colour · 109min

Cary Grant is as magically urbane as ever in his final movie, but, sadly, leaves the romance to the youngsters. It's a so-so comedy set during the 1964 Tokyo Olympic Games, with Samantha Eggar as the embassy secretary with whom British industrialist Grant lodges, and Jim Hutton as the member of the American Olympic squad he introduces into her life. A remake of the 1943 film *The More the Merrier*, it's lower on laughs but notable for Grant's sleek charm as the matchmaker. TH *DVD*

Cary Grant *Sir William Rutland* • Samantha Eggar *Christine Easton* • Jim Hutton *Steve Davis* • John Standing *Julius P Haversack* • Miiko Taka *Aiko Kurawa* • Ted Hartley *Yuri Andreyovitch* • Ben Astar *Dimitri* • George Takei *Police captain* ■ *Dir* Charles Walters • *Scr* Sol Saks, from the film *The More the Merrier* by Robert Russell, Frank Ross, Richard Flournoy, Lewis R Foster • *Cinematographer* Harry Stradling

Walk East on Beacon ★U

Spy thriller 1952 · US · BW · 97min

In a typically inept "red scare" thriller, George Murphy trails communist agents across a paranoid free world. The script is based on a *Reader's Digest* article written by the then head of the FBI, J Edgar Hoover. The whole picture (and many others of its ilk) seems to be bankrolled by the FBI as both a recruitment advertisement and a dire warning to ordinary Americans about the dangers of communism. AT

George Murphy *Inspector Belden* • Finlay Currie *Professor Kafer* • Virginia Gilmore *Millie* • Karel Stepanek *Alex* • Louisa Horton *Elaine* • Peter Capell *Gino* • Bruno Wick *Danzig* ■ *Dir* Alfred Werker • *Scr* Leo Rosten, Virginia Shaler, Emmett Murphy, Leonard Heidemann, from the magazine article *The Crime of the Century* by J Edgar Hoover

Walk Hard: the Dewey Cox Story ★★★★15

Musical comedy 2007 · US · Colour · 92min

John C Reilly showed his comic prowess as Will Ferrell's sidekick in *Talladega Nights: the Ballad of Ricky Bobby* and here he gets the opportunity to go it alone. Jake Kasdan's spoof biopic tells the story of singer Dewey Cox (Reilly), whose stratospheric rise through the music industry takes in teenyboppers, 1960s flower power (Dewey writes protest songs for midgets) and his eventual decline as drugs, sex and old age take their toll. Co-written by Kasdan and Judd Apatow (*Knocked Up, The 40 Year Old Virgin*) this is a hilarious pastiche of musical movies like *Walk the Line* and *Ray*. Teeming with skits and some very funny songs, the film also features cameos from the likes of Jason Schwartzman, Jack White and Paul Rudd. JR *DVD* *Blu*

John C Reilly *Dewey Cox* • Jenna Fischer *Darlene* • Tim Meadows *Sam* • Kristen Wiig *Edith Cox* • Raymond J Barry *Pa Cox* • Harold Ramis *L'Chai'm* • Margo Martindale *Ma Cox* • Chris Parnell *Theo* • Paul Rudd *John Lennon* • Justin Long *George Harrison* ■ *Dir* Jake Kasdan • *Scr* Judd Apatow, Jake Kasdan

A Walk in the Clouds ★★PG

Period romantic drama
1995 · US · Colour · 98min

Keanu Reeves stars in this cliché-ridden, 1940s-set romantic drama - the American debut of Mexican director Alfonso Arau. Returning from the Second World War to be reunited with his unfaithful wife, travelling salesman Reeves meets a pregnant girl during a business trip and agrees to pose as her husband to protect her from the wrath of her strict, vineyard-owning family in California. Grandpa Anthony Quinn overacts as if only he can make up for Reeves's wooden performance. TH Violence, nudity. *DVD* *Blu*

Keanu Reeves *Paul Sutton* • Aitana Sanchez-Gijon *Victoria Aragon* • Anthony Quinn *Don Pedro Aragon* • Giancarlo Giannini *Alberto Aragon* • Angélica Aragón *Marie Jose Aragon* • Evangelina Elizondo *Guadelupe Aragon* • Freddy Rodriguez *Pedro Aragon Jr* • Debra Messing *Betty Sutton* ■ *Dir* Alfonso Arau • *Scr* Robert Mark Kamen, Mark Miller, Harvey Weitzman, from the 1942 film *Four Steps in the Clouds* by Piero Tellini, Giuseppe Amato, Cesare Zavattini, Vittorio De Benedetti

A Walk in the Spring Rain ★

Romantic melodrama 1970 · US · Colour · 98min

The bored, middle-aged wife (Ingrid Bergman) of a bored, middle-aged college professor (Fritz Weaver), while vacationing in Tennessee mountain country, meets a local farmer (Anthony Quinn) who is the polar opposite of her husband. One of far too many films which marked the nadir of Bergman's post-Rossellini career, this is turgid rubbish, whose stars make a frankly incredible duo. RK

Anthony Quinn *Will Cade* • Ingrid Bergman *Libby Meredith* • Fritz Weaver *Roger Meredith* • Katherine Crawford *Ellen Meredith* • Tom Fielding *Boy Cade* • Virginia Gregg *Ann Cade* • Mitchell Silberman *Bucky* ■ *Dir* Guy Green • *Scr* Stirling Silliphant, from the novella by Rachel Maddux

A Walk in the Sun ★★★★12

Second World War drama
1945 · US · BW · 116min

The story is simple: a ragbag of foot-slogging GIs are part of the invasion force in Italy and chase the Germans north to eventual defeat. The excellent but unstarry cast means no John Wayne or Clark Gable-style heroics, but they all "talk the talk" in a way that seems completely authentic and most of the time they are just coping with boredom, exhaustion and the probability of sudden death. There are mercifully no overt "war is hell" messages in Lewis Milestone's prototype platoon picture. AT *DVD*

Dana Andrews *Sgt Tyne* • Richard Conte *Rivera* • John Ireland *Windy* • George Tyne *Friedman* • Lloyd Bridges *Sgt Ward* • Sterling Holloway *McWilliams* • Herbert Rudley *Sgt Porter* • Norman Lloyd *Archimbeau* • Steve Brodie *Judson* • Huntz Hall *Carraway* ■ *Dir* Lewis Milestone • *Scr* Robert Rossen, from a story by Harry Brown

A Walk in the Woods ★★★★15

Adventure based on a true story
2015 · US · Colour · 99min

A witty addition to the *mature movie* genre sees Robert Redford as travel writer Bill Bryson, who fancies a trek on the arduous Appalachian Trail. Citing gruesome headlines, his wife forbids him until Bryson's libidinous old pal (Nick Nolte), whose red face and crazy hair belies a blunt but no less lively intellect, offers himself as a trail buddy. Based on Bryson's memoirs, the story is amusing and, although Kwapis's style is conventional, he traps lightning in a bottle: Redford and Nolte are genuinely hilarious together. KK Swearing, sexual references. *DVD* *Blu*

Robert Redford *Bill Bryson* • Nick Nolte *Stephen Katz* • Emma Thompson *Catherine Bryson* • Mary Steenburgen *Jeannie* • Kristen Schaal *Mary Ellen* ■ *Dir* Ken Kwapis • *Scr* Bill Holderman, Rick Kerb, from the non-fiction book by Bill Bryson

Walk like a Dragon ★★

Western 1960 · US · BW · 94min

James Clavell was known primarily as a writer but also produced and directed a couple of his screenplays including this well-intentioned western drama with a central theme of racial conflict. Jack Lord (later of *Hawaii Five-O* fame) plays an American who rescues a young Chinese woman (Nobu McCarthy) from slavery and the prospect of enforced prostitution. When he takes her to his home in San Francisco, he is faced by prejudice. BB

Jack Lord *Line Bartlett* • Nobu McCarthy *Kim Sung* • James Shigeta *Cheng Lu* • Mel Tormé *The Deacon* • Josephine Hutchinson *Ma Bartlett* ■ *Dir* James Clavell • *Scr* James Clavell, Daniel Mainwaring

W

Walk like a Man ★ PG
Comedy 1987 · US · Colour · 82min

Howie Mandel has never quite made the transition to the big screen, and this one-joke comedy is a good example why. He plays a man raised by wolves who returns to civilisation just in time to make life difficult for his brother, Christopher Lloyd. Most of the jokes revolve around slobbering and other social faux pas, and it's painful to watch. JB

Howie Mandel *Bobo Shand* • Christopher Lloyd *Reggie Henry* • Cloris Leachman *Margaret Shand* • Colleen Camp *Rhonda Shand* • Amy Steel *Penny* • Stephen Elliott (1) *Walter Welmont* • George DiCenzo *Bub Downs* • John McLiam *HP Truman* ■ *Dir* Melvin Frank • *Scr* Robert Klane

A Walk on the Moon ★★ 15
Drama 1999 · US · Colour · 107min

Woodstock and "one giant leap for mankind" form a life-changing backdrop to this run-of-the-mill holiday of discovery. Diane Lane and Anna Paquin are on great form, as an unfulfilled wife succumbing to a campsite affair and her confused teenage daughter respectively. The script is very mundane, though, and is hampered by predictable plotting and meagre dramatic moments that never really catch fire. JC Swearing, sex scenes.

Diane Lane *Pearl Kantrowitz* • Viggo Mortensen *Walker Jerome* • Liev Schreiber *Marty Kantrowitz* • Anna Paquin *Alison Kantrowitz* • Tovah Feldshuh *Lilian Kantrowitz* • Bobby Boriello *Daniel Kantrowitz* • Stewart Bick *Neil Leiberman* • Jess Platt *Herb Fogler* ■ *Dir* Tony Goldwyn • *Scr* Pamela Gray

Walk on the Wild Side ★★★ 15
Melodrama 1962 · US · BW · 109min

Although purporting to be a frank exploration of prostitution and lesbianism, Edward Dmytryk's adaptation of Nelson Algren's racy novel pulls its punches in virtually every scene. Too much time is spent in the company of dull Texan Laurence Harvey as he searches for his runaway lover, Capucine, and helps Anne Baxter and Jane Fonda to see the error of their ways. Far more interesting is madam Barbara Stanwyck's obsession with Capucine, but both script and direction keep the action at a gentle simmer rather than pressing on to boiling point. Saul Bass's title credits are rightly renowned as classic examples of the art. DP

Laurence Harvey *Dove Linkhorn* • Capucine *Hallie* • Jane Fonda *Kitty Twist* • Anne Baxter *Teresina Vidaverri* • Barbara Stanwyck *Jo Courtney* • Joanna Moore *Miss Precious* • Richard Rust *Oliver* • Karl Swenson *Schmidt* • Donald Barry *Dockery* • Juanita Moore *Mama* ■ *Dir* Edward Dmytryk • *Scr* John Fante, Edmund Morris, from the novel by Nelson Algren

Walk on Water ★★★ 15
Thriller 2004 · Is/Swe · Colour · 103min

This Israeli political thriller grabs the attention and only rarely relaxes its grip. It tells the story of Mossad hitman Lior Ashkenazi, who is tailing a German brother and sister whose grandfather was a high-ranking Nazi. Spending time with the siblings (Knut Berger and Caroline Peters) exposes the Arab-hating, homophobic assassin to their liberal views, and Ashkenazi soon begins to lose interest in his real mission – to find and kill the old man. Deftly spelling out what it feels like to live in modern-day Israel, the story is an enlightening experience. KK Hebrew +subtitles. DVD

Lior Ashkenazi *Eyal* • Knut Berger *Axel Himmelman* • Caroline Peters *Pia Himmelman* • Gidon Shemer *Menachem* • Carola Regnier *Axel's mother* • Hanns Zischler *Axel's father* • Ernest Lenart *Alfred Himmelman* • Eyal Rozales *Jello* ■ *Dir* Eytan Fox • *Scr* Gal Uchovsky

Walk Softly, Stranger ★★
Drama 1949 · US · BW · 81min

Filmed before Joseph Cotten and Alida Valli teamed up for *The Third Man*, but released afterwards, this marked the end of RKO's collaboration with David O Selznick's Vanguard Films. It proved the studio's biggest flop of the year, losing $775,000. The fault lies less with Robert Stevenson's unimaginative direction than with Frank Fenton's melodramatic screenplay, in which Cotten's charming fugitive hides out in a Midwestern backwater where he falls for Valli's disabled heiress. DP

Joseph Cotten *Chris Hale* • Alida Valli *Elaine Corelli* • Spring Byington *Mrs Brentman* • Frank Puglia *AJ Corelli* • Paul Stewart *Whitey* • Jeff Donnell *Gwen* • Howard Petrie *Bowen* • Jack Paar *Ray Healey* ■ *Dir* Robert Stevenson • *Scr* Frank Fenton, from a story by Manuel Seff, Paul Yawitz

Walk the Line ★★★★ 12
Musical biographical drama 2005 · US/Ger · Colour · 123min

Joaquin Phoenix gives a remarkable performance as country-rock legend Johnny Cash in director James Mangold's impressive biopic. The film begins with Cash's legendary live recording at Folsom Prison in 1968, flashing back to his childhood and feelings of guilt over the accidental death of his brother, then picks up the story with Cash writing songs in the air force, falling in love with and marrying Sun recording artists Elvis and Jerry Lee Lewis. Joining them on tour is June Carter (Reese Witherspoon), the woman whom Cash pursued for years despite the fact that both were already married. Phoenix and Witherspoon convincingly bring the relationship between Johnny and June to life without lapsing into impersonation. BP Swearing, drug abuse. DVD

Joaquin Phoenix *John R Cash* • Reese Witherspoon *June Carter* • Ginnifer Goodwin *Vivian Cash* • Robert Patrick *Ray Cash* • Dallas Roberts *Sam Phillips* • Dan John Miller *Luther Perkins* • Larry Bagby [Larry Bagby III] *Marshall Grant* • Shelby Lynne *Carrie Cash* • Tyler Hilton *Elvis Presley* ■ *Dir* James Mangold • *Scr* James Mangold, Gill Dennis, from the autobiographies *Man in Black* and *Cash: the Autobiography* by Johnny Cash

Walk the Proud Land ★★ U
Biographical western 1956 · US · Colour · 84min

Baby-faced war hero Audie Murphy stars as John Philip Clum, the Indian agent who was responsible for liaising with the captured Apache warrior Geronimo. This potentially powerful story of conflict is rather spoiled by the emphasis on Clum's domestic troubles, which nullifies the original premise. Nevertheless, Murphy is convincing, and both Pat Crowley and Anne Bancroft are excellent in supporting roles. TS

Audie Murphy *John P Clum* • Anne Bancroft *Tianay* • Pat Crowley *Mary Dennison* • Charles Drake *Tom Sweeney* • Tommy Rall *Taglito* • Robert Warwick *Eskiminzin* • Jay Silverheels *Geronimo* ■ *Dir* Jesse Hibbs • *Scr* Gil Doud, Jack Sher, from the biography *Apache Agent* by Woodworth Clum

A Walk to Remember ★★ PG
Romantic drama 2002 · US · Colour · 97min

Based on Nicholas Sparks's bestseller and featuring MTV pop singer Mandy Moore in her first leading movie role, this type of love story might have worked back in the 1970s, but it's far too cloying and contrived to seduce today's teenagers. Peter Coyote and Daryl Hannah cope well in their atypical roles as a preacher and a single mother. However, Moore barely convinces as the ultra-demure daughter of a small-town Baptist minister who falls for rebellious Shane West. DP DVD

Shane West *Landon Carter* • Mandy Moore *Jamie Sullivan* • Peter Coyote *Reverend Sullivan* • Daryl Hannah *Cynthia Carter* • Lauren German *Belinda* • Clayne Crawford *Dean* • Al Thompson *Eric* • Paz de la Huerta *Tracie* ■ *Dir* Adam Shankman • *Scr* Karen Janszen, from the novel by Nicholas Sparks

A Walk with Love and Death ★ 15
Period drama 1969 · US · Colour · 86min

John Huston got the worst notices of his long career for this fiasco and he was vilified for casting his own daughter, Anjelica, in the leading role of the nobleman's daughter caught up in the Hundred Years' War. As her suitor, Huston rejected actors and cast Assaf Dayan, the son of Moshe Dayan, the defence minister of Israel. It was a crazy project from the start, born of nepotism, egotism and the flower-power movement of the 1960s. AT DVD

Anjelica Huston *Lady Claudia* • Assaf Dayan *[Assi Dayan] Heron of Foix* • Anthony Corlan *[Anthony Higgins] Robert* • John Hallam *Sir Meles of Bohemia* • Eileen Murphy *Gypsy girl* • Anthony Nicholls *Father Superior* ■ *Dir* John Huston • *Scr* Dale Wasserman, from the novel by Hans Koningsberger • *Music* Georges Delerue

Walkabout ★★★★★ 12
Drama 1970 · Aus · Colour · 96min

Nicolas Roeg's second film as director is an atmospheric masterpiece of sexual tension. Jenny Agutter and Luc Roeg (the director's son, here credited as Lucien John) play the children stranded in the outback when their father commits suicide. As they are guided by an Aborigine youth (David Gulpilil), who teaches them how to live off the seemingly arid land, Roeg successfully conjures up a tale that is as dazzling as the shimmering landscape against which it is set. TH Nudity, violence. DVD BD

Jenny Agutter *Girl* • Lucien John [Luc Roeg] *Brother* • David Gulpilil *Aborigine* • John Meillon *Father* • Peter Carver *No-hoper* • John Illingsworth *Husband* ■ *Dir* Nicolas Roeg • *Scr* Edward Bond, from the novel *The Children* by James Vance Marshall • *Music* John Barry (1)

Walker ★★ 18
Period biographical drama 1987 · US · Colour · 90min

This highly stylised film from director Alex Cox is the stiffly told story of US mercenary William Walker who, backed by a tycoon, took over as President of Nicaragua in the mid-19th century. Ed Harris is bombastically charismatic, though the anti-American rant, which may have been justified, proves too one-sided for real drama. TH Swearing. DVD

Ed Harris *William Walker* • Peter Boyle *Cornelius Vanderbilt* • Richard Masur *Ephraim Squier* • René Auberjonois *Major Siegfried Henningson* • Marlee Matlin *Ellen Martin* • Sy Richardson *Captain Hornsby* ■ *Dir* Alex Cox • *Scr* Rudy Wurlitzer

The Walker ★★★ 15
Drama 2006 · UK/Ger · Colour · 103min

Paul Schrader is on familiar ground with this atmospheric but underdeveloped society drama. It stars Woody Harrelson as the titular "walker" – a gay, Washington-based charmer who escorts the wives of the rich and powerful. But when he tries to protect one of his circle (Kristin Scott Thomas) from scandal, his world starts to crumble. Schrader's dialogue sparkles with cynical wit, and his cast adds depth, with Harrelson particularly pitch perfect without resorting to caricature. Unfortunately, the slack narrative can't match the fine performances. SF Swearing, some violence, nudity. DVD

Woody Harrelson *Carter Page III* • Kristin Scott Thomas *Lynn Lockner* • Lauren Bacall *Natalie Van Miter* • Lily Tomlin *Abigail Delorean* • Ned Beatty *Jack Delorean* • Willem Dafoe *Larry Lockner* ■ *Dir/Scr* Paul Schrader

Walking across Egypt ★★★ 12
Drama 1999 · US · Colour · 96min

This is yet another eloquent showcase for the talents of Ellen Burstyn. Abandoned by her grown-up children, Judge Reinhold and Gail O'Grady, the small-town God-fearing busybody sets out to reform dogcatcher Mark Hamill and his delinquent orphan nephew, Jonathan Taylor Thomas. This could easily have lapsed into liberal sentimentality, but quadruple Emmy-winning director Arthur Allan Seidelman brings a shabby Deep Southern charm to proceedings that are brimful of gently comic set pieces and wry wisdom. DP DVD

Ellen Burstyn *Mattie Rigsbee* • Jonathan Taylor Thomas *Wesley Benfield* • Mark Hamill *Lamar* • Edward Herrmann *Reverend Vernon* • Judge Reinhold *Robert Rigsbee* • Gail O'Grady *Elaine Rigsbee* • Dana Ivey *Beatrice Vernon* ■ *Dir* Arthur Allan Seidelman • *Scr* Paul Tamasy, from the novel by Clyde Edgerton

Walking and Talking ★★★ 15
Comedy drama 1996 · UK/US · Colour · 82min

Writer/director Nicole Holofcener makes an impressive debut with this New York-based tale of fantasy, angst and desire, which had her somewhat cynically dismissed as a young Woody Allen. Sharply scripted and smartly cast, this comedy of discontent is inhabited by credible characters who have something approximating real conversations. As the longtime friends whose lives begin to unravel when marriage rears its head, Catherine Keener and Anne Heche are both fresh and funny. However, they do have nearly all the best lines, as the chaps are less well defined, although Kevin Corrigan's geeky video clerk is hilarious. DP Swearing.

Catherine Keener *Amelia* • Anne Heche *Laura* • Todd Field *Frank* • Liev Schreiber *Andrew* • Kevin Corrigan *Bill* • Randall Batinkoff *Peter* ■ *Dir/Scr* Nicole Holofcener

The Walking Dead ★★★
Horror 1936 · US · BW · 66min

Boris Karloff is framed for murder and sent to the electric chair. A mad doctor electronically revives him, however, to wreak vengeance on the gangsters responsible for his fate, in a surprisingly moving and macabre variation on the *Frankenstein* theme. Benefiting enormously from Karloff's first-rate turn as the hollow-eyed zombie with a penchant for the piano, director Michael Curtiz keeps predictability at bay with a slick style and some marvellously expressionistic lighting. AJ

Boris Karloff *John Ellman* • Ricardo Cortez *Nolan* • Warren Hull *Jimmy* • Robert Strange *Merritt* • Joseph King (1) *Judge Shaw* • Edmund Gwenn *Dr Evan Beaumont* • Marguerite Churchill *Nancy* • Barton MacLane *Loder* • Henry O'Neill *Warner* • Paul Harvey *Blackstone* ■ *Dir* Michael Curtiz • *Scr* Ewart Adamson, Peter Milne, Robert Andrews, Lillie Hayward, from a story by Adamson, Joseph Fields

The Walking Hills ★★★
Western 1949 · US · BW · 78min

Nine men and one woman look for buried treasure in the desert. Partly filmed in Death Valley, it's an old story with the usual assortment of incompatible characters but cleverly written by western novelist Alan LeMay, smartly directed by a young John Sturges, and ably cast. The setting is made to count and there's a memorable sandstorm in which a fight with shovels occurs. AE

Randolph Scott *Jim Carey* • Ella Raines *Chris Jackson* • William Bishop *Shep* • Edgar Buchanan *Old Willy* • Arthur Kennedy *Chalk* • John Ireland *Frazee* ■ *Dir* John Sturges • *Scr* Alan LeMay, Virginia Roddick

Walking on Sunshine ★★★ 12
Romantic musical comedy 2014 · UK · Colour · 93min

Hannah Arterton returns to the Italian resort where she had a memorable holiday romance to attend her sister's wedding, only to discover that her former lover, Giulio Berruti, is her future brother-in-law. Aiming for the same feel-good camp factor that made *Mamma Mia!* a hit, the familiar farcical shenanigans are peppered here with 1980s karaoke favourites belted out by a cast who bound about picturesque streets with gay abandon. There is something charming and infectious about the film's unashamedly cheesy outlook, even if the obvious but effective gags, provided by Katy Brand as the sisters' best friend, merely fill the spaces in-between energetic musical numbers. JL Some swearing, sexual references. DVD BD

Hannah Arterton *Taylor* • Annabel Scholey *Maddie* • Greg Wise *Doug* • Leona Lewis *Elena* • Giulio Berruti (2) *Raf* ■ *Dir* Max [Max Giwa], Dania [Dania Pasquini] • *Scr* Joshua St Johnston

The Walking Stick ★★★★
Drama 1970 · UK · Colour · 101min

In this charming bittersweet romance set in lovely Hampstead, disabled businesswoman Samantha Eggar is courted by mysterious artist David Hemmings. The love story is old-fashioned for its time (with bedroom scenes dissolving to the next morning), but gradually switches gear into another genre with surprising ease. Director Eric Till has a fine eye for detail, and the supporting cast is distinguished. DM

David Hemmings *Leigh Hartley* • Samantha Eggar *Deborah Dainton* • Emlyn Williams *Jack Foil* • Phyllis Calvert *Erica Dainton* • Ferdy Mayne *Douglas Dainton* • Francesca Annis *Arabella Dainton* • Bridget Turner *Sarah Dainton* ■ *Dir* Eric Till • *Scr* George Bluestone, from the novel by Winston Graham

Walking Tall ★★15
Action drama 2004 · US · Colour · 82min

Former wrestling star The Rock takes on an ambitious role in a film that requires him to flex his acting muscles. Like the 1973 movie of the same name, this is inspired by the story of Tennessee sheriff Buford Pusser. The Rock returns to his home town after years in the US Special Forces to discover it changed for the worse. The town's lumber mill has been closed by villain Neal McDonough, who's opened a casino. The star becomes sheriff and with the help of best friend Johnny Knoxville and a large hunk of wood batters small-town values into the corrupted citizens. TH violence, swearing, drug abuse DVD Blu

The Rock [Dwayne Johnson] *Chris Vaughn* • Johnny Knoxville *Ray Templeton* • Neal McDonough *Jay Hamilton Jr* • Kristen Wilson *Michelle Vaughn* • Ashley Scott *Deni* • Khleo Thomas *Pete Vaughn* • John Beasley *Chris Vaughn Sr* • Barbara Tarbuck *Connie Vaughn* • Michael Bowen *Sheriff Stan Watkins* • Kevin Durand *Booth* ■ *Dir* Kevin Bray • *Scr* David Klass, Channing Gibson, David Levien, Brian Koppelman, from the 1973 film by Mort Briskin

Walking with Dinosaurs: the 3D Movie ★★U
Animated wildlife adventure 2013 · US/UK/Ind/Aus · Colour · 87min

Inspired by the BBC TV series that first aired in 1999, this is the feature-length story of Patchi the pachyrhinosaurus (voiced by Justin Long), who experiences the perils and joys of life during the Cretaceous period. No problems arise with the brilliantly animated prehistoric creatures, but what completely ruins any naturalness is the jarring voiceovers and a script full of poop and butt gags. A jarring combo of lecturing and inanity, this has little to do with the ground-breaking series. AJ 3D

John Leguizamo *Alex* • Justin Long *Patchi* • Karl Urban *Uncle Zack* • Charlie Rowe *Ricky* ■ *Dir* Neil Nightingale, Barry Cook • *Scr* John Collee

Wall ★★★★12
Documentary 2004 · Fr/Is/US · Colour · 95min

The tragic folly of the construction of a barrier between Israel and the Palestinian territories is exposed in this mournfully laconic documentary by Moroccan-born Jewish director, Simone Bitton. The genius of her approach is that it's never obviously apparent on which side of the wall she's filming, nor which cause is being espoused by the faceless voices on the soundtrack. Contradictions abound everywhere, as impoverished Palestinians take jobs building the wall, while Israelis find irony in the comparisons to the European ghettos of the past. But hardline attitudes are also displayed by the unrepentant settlers and the youths prepared to martyr themselves for freedom. A courageous, revealing and dispiriting film. DP Hebrew, Arabic +subtitles. DVD

■ *Dir/Scr* Simone Bitton

The Wall ★★★12
Drama 2012 · Austria/Ger · Colour · 103min

Accepting the metaphorical premise is half the battle with this adaptation of Marlen Haushofer's 1962 novel, which plays a Kafka-esque riff on *Robinson Crusoe*. While staying in a remote hunting lodge with friends, a 40-something woman (Martina Gedeck) finds herself alone and unable to leave an Alpine enclave that appears to have been enveloped by an invisible barrier. Gedeck gives a typically imposing performance, but director Julian Roman Pölsler relies far too heavily on her voiceover to convey ideas and emotions, and the dénouement proves every bit as problematic as the set-up. DP German +subtitles. Some violence. DVD

Martina Gedeck *Women* • Karl Heinz Hackl [Karlheinz Hackl] *Hugo* • Ulrike Beimpold *Luise* • Hans-Michael Rehberg *Cottager* • Julia Gschnitzer *Cottager* ■ *Dir* Julian Roman Pölsler [Julian Pölsler] • *Scr* Julian Roman Pölsler, from the novel *Die Wand* by Marlen Haushofer

WALL-E ★★★★★U
Animated science-fiction comedy 2008 · US · Colour · 94min

Finding Nemo writer/director Andrew Stanton serves up another treat with this enchanting, animated tale about a lonely robot. WALL-E (Waste Allocation Load Lifter Earth-class) is programmed to continually compress rubbish, a job that remains unfinished several hundred years after the human race has left the Earth. But when WALL-E falls for EVE (Extraterrestrial Vegetation Evaluator), which is on Earth looking for signs of life, he follows the probe-droid back to her mother ship where humans once again threaten to spoil the mood. Classic moments abound here, such as a zero-gravity dance and WALL-E hitching a ride through space. Stanton also produces a haunting sense of WALL-E's isolation in the early scenes on an eerie, unpopulated Earth and is well served by a voice cast that includes Sigourney Weaver and Pixar regular John Ratzenberger. SP DVD Blu CS

Ben Burtt *WALL-E/M-O* • Elissa Knight *EVE* • Fred Willard *Shelby Forthright, BnL CEO* • John Ratzenberger *John* • Jeff Garlin *Captain* • Kathy Najimy *Mary* • Sigourney Weaver *Ship's computer* • Kim Kopf *Hover chair mother* • Garrett Palmer *Hover chair son* ■ *Dir* Andrew Stanton • *Scr* Andrew Stanton, Jim Reardon, from a story by Stanton, Pete Docter

Wall Street ★★★★15
Drama 1987 · US · Colour · 125min

Oliver Stone co-wrote and directed this stylish morality tale about insider trading – a topical subject at the time. Charlie Sheen gives a believable performance as the gullible broker who's prepared to break the law in pursuit of riches, and he's matched by his father Martin (also playing his screen father) as the blue-collar union representative who takes a dim view of his son's wheeler-dealing. Stealing the show, however, is Oscar winner Michael Douglas, who is memorable as ruthless corporate raider Gordon Gekko. JM DVD Blu

Michael Douglas (1) *Gordon Gekko* • Charlie Sheen *Bud Fox* • Daryl Hannah *Darien Taylor* • Martin Sheen *Carl Fox* • Terence Stamp *Sir Larry Wildman* • Hal Holbrook *Lou Mannheim* • Sean Young *Kate Gekko* • James Spader *Roger Barnes* • Sylvia Miles *Sylvie Drimmer* • Saul Rubinek *Harold Salt* ■ *Dir* Oliver Stone • *Scr* Oliver Stone, Stanley Weiser

Wall Street: Money Never Sleeps ★★★12
Drama 2010 · US · Colour · 127min

Oliver Stone's 1987 film *Wall Street* was a devastating critique of the go-go 80s and at its dark heart was Gordon Gekko, played to Oscar-winning effect by Michael Douglas. Here, Gekko has served his jail time for illegal wheeler-dealing and sets about promoting his writing career and attempting a reconciliation with his daughter (Carey Mulligan), who is dating a young swashbuckling trader (Shia LaBeouf). But has he really changed? Stone directs

with propulsive efficiency and draws effective performances from his cast. But the strength of the original was in Gekko and his ruthless personification of 80s greed. And though Douglas does his best, a conflicted, ambivalent Gekko just isn't as much fun. AS Swearing. DVD Blu

Michael Douglas (1) *Gordon Gekko* • Shia LaBeouf *Jacob "Jake" Moore* • Carey Mulligan *Winnie Gekko* • Frank Langella *Louis Zabel* • Josh Brolin *Bretton James* • Susan Sarandon *Sylvia, Jacob's mother* • Eli Wallach *Julie Steinhardt* ■ *Dir* Oliver Stone • *Scr* Allan Loeb, Stephen Schiff, from characters by Oliver Stone, Stanley Weiser

Wallace & Gromit in The Curse of the Were-Rabbit ★★★★U
Animated comedy adventure 2005 · UK · Colour · 81min

Aardman Animation's claymation heroes Wallace and Gromit make their feature-length debut in this witty, imaginative film. The enterprising inventor (voiced, as ever, by Peter Sallis) and his faithful dog cash in on the approaching Giant Vegetable Competition by offering a humane pest-control service to rid the neighbourhood of rabbits. However, business is jeopardised when a mysterious monster begins destroying local gardens. Despite being peppered slightly too heavily with modern innuendo, the tale retains its charm, gaining plenty of comic mileage from its quaint depiction of northern life. SF DVD CS

Peter Sallis *Wallace* • Ralph Fiennes *Victor Quartermaine* • Helena Bonham Carter *Lady Tottington* • Peter Kay *PC Mackintosh* • Liz Smith *Mrs Mulch* • Nicholas Smith *Reverend Clement Hedges* ■ *Dir* Nick Park, Steve Box • *Scr* Nick Park, Bob Baker, Steve Box, Mark Burton, from characters by Nick Park, Steve Rushton

Walls of Glass ★★★15
Drama 1985 · US · Colour · 82min

As odd as its title, this likeable independent one-off gives the opportunity of a lifetime to character actor Philip Bosco, a face you'll certainly recognise even if the name doesn't ring any bells. He plays a Shakespeare-spouting New York cabbie, but this quirky drama failed to turn Bosco into a star, and, despite a distinguished cast, the public didn't respond to this winning tale. TS Swearing.

Philip Bosco *James Flanagan* • Geraldine Page *Mama* • Linda Thorson *Andrea* • William Hickey *Papa* • Olympia Dukakis *Mary* • Brian Bloom *Danny* • Steven Weber *Sean* ■ *Dir* Scott Goldstein [Scott D Goldstein] • *Scr* Edmond Collins, Scott Goldstein

Walpurgis Night ★★★★
Drama 1935 · Swe · BW · 82min

Hailed on its release as one of the best films ever made in Sweden, this sensationalist melodrama packed a powerful social punch of the kind that few pictures made anywhere else in the world could match. Tackling both adultery and abortion, Gustaf Edgren's film focuses on the unhappy marriage between Lars Hanson and his vain wife Karin Kavli. While both give earnest performances, the film belongs to Ingrid Bergman as Hanson's devoted lover and to Victor Sjöström as her father, a crusading editor leading a campaign to boost the birth rate. DP Swedish +subtitles.

Lars Hanson *Johan Borg* • Karin Kavli *Clary Borg* • Victor Seastrom [Victor Sjöström] *Fredrik Bergstrom* • Ingrid Bergman *Lena* • Erik Berglund *Gustav Palm* • Sture Lagerwall *Svenson* ■ *Dir* Gustaf Edgren • *Scr* Oscar Rydqvist, Gustaf Edgren

Waltz of the Toreadors ★★★★15
Comedy 1962 · UK · Colour · 100min

In one of his most impressive performances, Peter Sellers plays a retired general, unhappily married to Margaret Leighton and given a second chance at fulfilment with old flame Dany Robin. French playwright Jean Anouilh, from whose comedy the movie is derived, made despair glossily fashionable in the 1960s and director John Guillermin and writer

Wolf Mankowitz transform bleak emotional undercurrents into a seductively bittersweet proposition. TH DVD

Peter Sellers *General Leo Fitzjohn* • Dany Robin *Ghislaine* • Margaret Leighton *Emily Fitzjohn* • John Fraser *Robert* • Cyril Cusack *Doctor Grogan* • Prunella Scales *Estella* • Denise Coffey *Sidonia* • Jean Anderson *Agnes* • John Le Mesurier *Vicar* ■ *Dir* John Guillermin • *Scr* Wolf Mankowitz, from the play *La Valse des Toréadors* by Jean Anouilh

Waltz with Bashir ★★★★18
Animated documentary 2008 · Is/Ger/Fr/US/Jpn/Fin/Swi/Bel/Aus · Colour · 86min

During the first Lebanon War in 1982, film-maker Ari Folman served with the Israel Defense Force in Beirut. More than 25 years later, an encounter with a troubled former comrade prompts him to interview the men he fought alongside. Presenting the live-action footage of meetings as a mix of Flash animation and 3D, the film's seductive visuals give the resulting war stories a surreal edge in which guilt and post-traumatic stress intertwine. For all its talk of dreams and memory, though, the heart of this powerful documentary concerns a very real war crime: the massacre of Palestinians in the Sabra and Shatila refugee camps by Christian militia gunmen. Instead of excusing the Israeli Army's role in the atrocity, Folman offers a harrowing portrait of a generation of young soldiers forever scarred by the horrors of war. JR Hebrew, German +subtitles. DVD Blu

■ *Dir/Scr* Ari Folman

Waltzes from Vienna ★
Musical drama 1933 · UK · BW · 80min

There's discord in the Strauss household as composer Johann senior (Edmund Gwenn) resents the competition from his son. Johann junior (Esmond Knight) gets his big break with a commission from a wealthy countess (Fay Compton) and, hey presto, comes up with *The Blue Danube* waltz. This tedious period drama, laced with the Waltz King's music, was an unsuitable and uncharacteristic assignment for Alfred Hitchcock and is completely devoid of his signature trademarks. RK

Jessie Matthews *Rasi* • Esmond Knight *"Shani", Johann Strauss the Younger* • Frank Vosper *The Prince* • Fay Compton *Countess Von Stahl* • Edmund Gwenn *Johann Strauss the Elder* • Robert Hale *Ebezeder* ■ *Dir* Alfred Hitchcock • *Scr* Guy Bolton, Alma Reville, from a play by Guy Bolton

Wanda ★★★★15
Crime drama 1971 · US · Colour · 97min

The winner of the International Critics' Prize at Venice, Barbara Loden's charming film also earned her the distinction of being the first woman director to have her debut feature awarded a cinema release since Ida Lupino's *Not Wanted* in 1949. Based on a true story and shot in 16mm, it is an unsentimental hard luck tale, in which Loden also stars as an outsider who agrees to act as a getaway driver for her neurotic lover, Michael Higgins. Loden, who was married to Elia Kazan, is totally believable. DP

Barbara Loden *Wanda* • Michael Higgins *Mr Dennis* • Charles Dosinan *Dennis's father* • Frank Jourdano *Soldier* • Valerie Manches *Girl in roadhouse* ■ *Dir/Scr* Barbara Loden

Wanda Nevada ★★
Western 1979 · US · Colour · 105min

Notable solely for being the only film to feature father and son Henry and Peter Fonda together, this western, set in the 1950s, has Fonda Jr as a poker-faced poker player who wins orphaned Brooke Shields as his jackpot and takes her gold prospecting in the Grand Canyon. The whimsicality of the piece is sometimes hard to take and Shields, then aged 14, lacks the quirkiness of, say, Tatum O'Neal in *Paper Moon*. Fonda Sr appears late in the picture as a prospector. AT

W

Peter Fonda *Beaudray Demerille* • Brooke Shields *Wanda Nevada* • Fiona Lewis *Dorothy Deerfield* • Luke Askew *Ruby Muldoon* • Ted Markland *Strap Pangburn* • Severn Darden *Merlin Bitterstix* • Paul Fix *Texas Curly* • Henry Fonda *Old Prospector* • Fred Ashley *Barber* ■ *Dir* Peter Fonda • *Scr* Dennis Hackin

The Wanderers ★★★ 18
Drama   1979 · US/Neth · Colour · 112min

Though less lauded than the broadly similar *American Graffiti*, and more variable in its tone and quality (it's a bit episodic), this tale of the high-school life of a bunch of Italian-American kids in New York's Bronx in the early 1960s remains thoroughly entertaining. Indeed, in some quarters it has become a retro cult fave. AT **DVD**

Ken Wahl *Richie* • John Friedrich *Joey* • Karen Allen *Nina* • Toni Kalem *Despie Galasso* • Alan Rosenberg *"Turkey"* • Jim Youngs *Buddy* • Tony Ganios *Perry* • Linda Manz *"Peewee"* ■ *Dir* Philip Kaufman • *Scr* Rose Kaufman, Philip Kaufman, from the novel by Richard Price • *Cinematographer* Michael Chapman

Wandering Eye ★★
Thriller   2011 · Can · Colour

In yet another ham-fisted TV movie about the evils of the internet, neglected doctor's wife Amanda Righetti is targeted by a serial killer, after using the titular networking site designed to facilitate extramarital affairs. But her marked-woman status proves largely uninspiring to watch, thanks to insubstantial plotting and an absence of tension and realism that makes even the climactic confrontation seem disappointingly benign. SF

Amanda Righetti *Maren Abbott* • Krista Bridges *Jacqueline Fitzpatrick* • Andrew Shaver *Kyle Solomon* • Allen Altman *Will Atherton* • Amy Sobol *Zooey* ■ *Dir* François Dompierre • *Scr* JB White

The Wandering Jew ★★
Fantasy drama   1933 · UK · BW · 111min

Between 1913 and 1957, Maurice Elvey directed some 300 features, including many comedies and two versions of this work – the first a silent treatment in 1923. Ten years later this starry version of E Temple Thurston's once famous play emerged to mixed reviews and a bemused public. It stars the mesmeric Conrad Veidt as the eponymous figure who demands the release of Barabbas and is condemned to everlasting life. BB

Conrad Veidt *Matathias/The Unknown Knight/Matteos Battadios/Dr Matteos Battadios* • Marie Ney *Judith* • Cicely Oates *Rachel* • Basil Gill *Pontius Pilate* • Anne Grey *Joanne de Beaudricourt/* • Bertram Wallis *Boemund, Prince of Tarentum* • Jack Livesey *Godfrey, Duke of Normandy* • Hay Petrie *Merchant* • Peggy Ashcroft *Olalla Quintana* ■ *Dir* Maurice Elvey • *Scr* H Fowler Mear, from the play by E Temple Thurston

Wanderlust ★★ 15
Comedy   2011 · US · Colour · 93min

Jennifer Aniston and Paul Rudd headline this lame comedy, playing stressed-out city folk who quit New York and stumble upon a rural retreat called Elysium, the sort of retro commune full of lovable eccentrics that only exists in Hollywood films. Elysium initially seems idyllic, but soon proves to be anything but. Aniston and Rudd are attractive leads, and certainly have chemistry, but they deserve better than this largely unfunny film that relies on explicitness and pottymouth dialogue to whip up a few cheap laughs. DA **DVD** **Blu**

Paul Rudd *George* • Jennifer Aniston *Linda* • Justin Theroux *Seth* • Malin Akerman *Eva* • Kathryn Hahn *Karen* • Alan Alda *Carvin* ■ *Dir* David Wain • *Scr* David Wain, Ken Marino

Wanted ★★★ 18
Action adventure   2008 · US · Colour · 105min

The first Hollywood movie from Timur Bekmambetov (*Night Watch*, *Day Watch*) is a high-octane action adventure adapted from the cult comic book of the same name. James McAvoy does a sterling job as office drone Wesley Gibson who goes from zero to super-skilled hitman when he's

recruited by a guild of assassins led by Morgan Freeman. Among his fellow killers is a smoulderingly cool Angelina Jolie, who acts as the callow youth's mentor as he tries to accept his destiny as the son of the world's greatest assassin. Bekmambetov brings his unique eye for hyper-kinetic action to the chase sequences, and there's plenty of understated mordant humour to leaven the inevitable ludicrousness of the violent mayhem. JA Violence, swearing, sex scenes, nudity. **DVD** **Blu**

James McAvoy *Wesley Gibson* • Morgan Freeman *Sloan* • Angelina Jolie *Fox* • Terence Stamp *Pekwarsky* • Thomas Kretschmann *Cross* • Common *The Gunsmith* • David Patrick O'Hara [David O'Hara] *Mr X* • Chris Pratt *Barry* ■ *Dir* Timur Bekmambetov • *Scr* Michael Brandt, Derek Haas, Chris Morgan, from the comic book by Mark Millar, JG Jones • *Cinematographer* Mitchell Amundsen • *Music* Danny Elfman

Wanted Dead or Alive ★★ 18
Action adventure   1986 · US · Colour · 101min

Rutger Hauer stars as a former CIA agent turned bounty hunter – referred to as the grandson of Steve McQueen's character from the identically named 1950s TV show – with a reputation for hauling in the toughest criminals. However he has his hands full when Arab terrorists, led by Kiss frontman Gene Simmons, start a bombing campaign in LA. Hauer excels as an action man, but the daft plot and excessive violence do him no favours. RS **DVD**

Rutger Hauer *Nick Randall* • Robert Guillaume *Philmore Walker* • Gene Simmons *Malak Al Rahim* • Mel Harris *Terry* • William Russ *Danny Quintz* • Susan MacDonald *Louise Quintz* • Jerry Hardin *John Lipton* ■ *Dir* Gary Sherman • *Scr* Michael Patrick Goodman, Brian Taggert, Gary Sherman

Wanted for Murder ★★★
Crime thriller   1946 · UK · BW · 102min

Eric Portman is on fine form in this chilling thriller as the descendant of a public hangman who strangles young women in London's open spaces, creating a tragic figure of a man who can't help his inherited impulses. Roland Culver is a skilful adversary as the Scotland Yard inspector who slowly and patiently closes in on his man. This makes superb use of London backgrounds and has a memorable climax near the Serpentine in Hyde Park, which has the cold grip of nightmare about it. AE

Eric Portman *Victor Colebrooke* • Dulcie Gray *Anne Fielding* • Derek Farr *Jack Williams* • Roland Culver *Inspector Conway* • Stanley Holloway *Sgt Sullivan* • Barbara Everest *Mrs Colebrooke* • Kathleen Harrison *Florrie* • Bonar Colleano *Corporal Mappolo* ■ *Dir* Lawrence Huntington • *Scr* Emeric Pressburger, Rodney Ackland, Maurice Cowan, from the play by Percy Robinson, Terence de Marney

Waqt ★★★★ 15
Drama   1965 · Ind · Colour · 163min

A major box-office success, this lavish melodrama is so full of plot that there is scarcely room for the songs, many of which went on to become popular hits. Beginning with an earthquake and a family tragedy, the film ends with a nail-biting courtroom sequence, when a lawyer has to defend his thief brother, who has been framed for murder. Superstar Sunil Dutt is splendid as the lawyer and there is sterling support from Raaj Kumar and Sadhana as the girl for whose affections they both vie. Director Yash Chopra juggles drama, comedy and spectacle with great aplomb. DP Hindi +subtitles. **DVD**

Sunil Dutt *Raja Kumar* • Sadhana • Sharmila Tagore • Shashi Kapoor ■ *Dir* Yash Chopra • *Scr* Akhtar-ul-Iman

WAQT: the Race against Time ★★★ PG
Drama   2005 · Ind · Colour · 147min

In this intense family saga, Akshay Kumar plays the layabout son who refuses to shoulder his responsibilities and persistently tries the patience of his wealthy tycoon father (Amitabh Bachchan, giving another powerhouse performance). The storyline is awash with sentiment and emotion and it is

matched perfectly by Kumar's unflinching performance. The melodrama is at times overwhelming but on the whole this is neatly polished and skilfully assembled. OA Hindi +subtitles. **DVD**

Amitabh Bachchan *Ishwar* • Akshay Kumar *Aditya* • Shefali Shah [Shefali Shetty] *Sumi* • Priyanka Chopra *Pooja* ■ *Dir* Vipul Amrutlal Shah • *Scr* Aatish Kapadia, from a story by Kapadia

The War ★★ 12
Drama   1994 · US · Colour · 119min

Had this slender tale of childhood in the 1970s simply focused on the feud between neighbourhood kids from different sides of the tracks, it would have engrossed viewers of all ages. But no one bought the heavy-handed pacifism and morality that Jon Avnet felt were essential. With both Kevin Costner and Mare Winningham straying on the wrong side of earnestness, it's left to Elijah Wood and the rest of the junior cast to provide the dramatic impetus. DP **DVD**

Elijah Wood *Stu* • Kevin Costner *Stephen* • Mare Winningham *Lois* • Lexi Randall *Lidia* • LaToya Chisholm *Elvadine* • Christopher Fennell *Billy* • Donald Sellers *Arliss* • Leon Sills *Leo* • Will West *Lester Lucket* ■ *Dir* Jon Avnet • *Scr* Kathy McWorter

War ★★ 15
Action drama   2002 · Rus · Colour · 119min

Sergei Bodrov Jr's cynical captain helps British actor Ian Kelly deliver Danish fiancée Ingeborga Dapkunaite from the clutches of Chechen warlord Georgi Gurgulia. At times resembling a Russian Rambo, this also has some suitably acerbic comments to make on the opportunism of the media (with Channel 4 stumping up part of the ransom money in return for Kelly's video diary). However, its scarcely concealed racism renders this an unworthy swan song for Bodrov, who was killed on location shortly afterwards. DP Russian, English, Chechen +subtitles. **DVD**

Alexei Chadov *Ivan Yermakov* • Ian Kelly *John* • Sergei Bodrov Jr *Captain Medvedev* • Ingeborga Dapkunaite *Margaret* ■ *Dir/Scr* Alexei Balabanov

War ★★ 18
Action thriller   2007 · US · Colour · 98min

Hong Kong martial artist Jet Li and British bruiser Jason Statham last starred together in sci-fi oddity *The One* (2001), in which Statham played second fiddle to not one but two Jet Lis. Six years on things have changed: Li's Hollywood career has faltered somewhat, while Statham has carved out an action-man niche for himself. Here he plays an FBI agent chasing a mysterious hitman (Li) who's murdering the members of rival Yakuza and Triad gangs. It's a set-up ripe for brainless action, if only director Philip G Atwell (a veteran of music videos for Xzibit and 50 Cent) could cope with the convoluted screenplay's reams of plot exposition. Sporadic fight scenes involving samurai swords and the odd ninja prove disappointingly perfunctory. JR **DVD** **Blu**

Jet Li *Rogue/Victor Shaw* • Jason Statham *Crawford* • John Lone *Chang* • Devon Aoki *Kira* • Luis Guzman *Benny* • Saul Rubinek *Dr Sherman* • Andrea Roth *Jenny Crawford* ■ *Dir* Philip G Atwell • *Scr* Lee Anthony Smith, Gregory J Bradley

A War ★★★★ 15
War drama   2015 · Den · Colour · 115min

For a Danish commander (Pilou Asbaek) facing the Taliban in Afghanistan, missing his family only adds to the stresses in this topical drama from the team behind 2012's potent pirate saga *A Hijacking*. A mid-point twist puts the focus on Asbaek's decision-making and reveals the film's underlying purpose – asking whether it's viable for Western troops to adhere to moral standards ignored by their ruthless opponents. There are few easy answers here, just strong performances, and a gripping approach to thorny issues. TJ Danish +subtitles. Swearing.

Pilou Asbaek *Claus Pedersen* • Tuva Novotny *Maria Pedersen* • Dar Salim *Najib Bisma* • Soren Malling *Martin R Olsen* • Charlotte Munck *Lisbeth Danning* ■ *Dir/Scr* Tobias Lindholm

The War against Mrs Hadley ★★★ U
Second World War drama   1942 · US · BW · 85min

When the Second World War comes to America with the bombing of Pearl Harbor, the spoiled, wealthy, snobbish and stubborn Fay Bainter, widow of a Washington newspaper magnate, regards it as a personal affront that her needs are ignored, and learns a lot of hard lessons about life and herself. This is a cunning mix of family drama, psychological study, moral fable and patriotic wartime propaganda. RK

Edward Arnold *Elliott Fulton* • Fay Bainter *Stella Hadley* • Richard Ney *Theodore Hadley* • Jean Rogers *Patricia Hadley* • Sara Allgood *Mrs Michael Kirkpatrick* • Spring Byington *Cecilia Talbot* • Van Johnson *Michael Fitzpatrick* ■ *Dir* Harold S Bucquet • *Scr* George Oppenheimer

War and Peace ★★★ U
Historical epic   1956 · It/US · Colour · 199min

No less than four versions of Tolstoy's epic novel were planned by Hollywood in the mid-1950s, but producer Dino De Laurentiis moved faster than anyone else: he hired King Vidor to direct, he hired the Italian army and, crucially, he hired Audrey Hepburn. As a spectacle, it's still impressively humane, though not particularly Russian, and the casting is decidedly odd: Henry Fonda as Pierre, Mel Ferrer (Hepburn's then husband) as Prince Andrei, plus John Mills, Herbert Lom and the amazing Anita Ekberg. The vast battle scenes were later dwarfed by the six-hour Soviet version. AT **DVD**

Audrey Hepburn *Natasha Rostov* • Henry Fonda *Pierre Bezukhov* • Mel Ferrer *Prince Andrei Bolkonsky* • Vittorio Gassman *Anatole Kuragin* • John Mills *Platon Karatayev* • Herbert Lom *Napoleon* • Oscar Homolka *General Mikhail Kutuzov* • Anita Ekberg *Helene* • Helmut Dantine *Dolokhov* ■ *Dir* King Vidor • *Scr* Bridget Boland, Robert Westerby, King Vidor, Mario Camerini, Ennio De Concini, Ivo Perilli, Irwin Shaw, from the novel by Leo Tolstoy • *Cinematographer* Jack Cardiff

War and Peace ★★★★ PG
Historical epic   1966 · USSR · Colour · 399min

All the resources of the Soviet film industry and the Red Army were put at Sergei Bondarchuk's disposal to make what was intended to be an expression of Soviet pride – designed to be premiered in instalments at international film festivals – and to dwarf anything turned out by capitalist Hollywood. The sumptuous ballroom scenes match those in Visconti's *The Leopard* while the battle scenes are awesome in their scope and filmed with overhead cameras which glide over thousands of extras as they fight Napoleon's army at Austerlitz and Borodino. Just how Sergei Bondarchuk directed all this while also playing the major role of Pierre is anyone's guess. Avoid the edited English-dubbed version; the original version, though extremely patchy, is masterly in parts and fascinating to watch. AT In Russian. **DVD**

Lyudmila Savelyeva *Natasha Rostov* • Sergei Bondarchuk *Pierre Bezukhov* • Vyacheslav Tikhonov *Prince Andrei Bolkonsky* • Viktor Stanitsyn *Ilya Andreyevich Rostov* • Kira Golovko *Countess Rostova* • Oleg Tabakov *Nikolay Rostov* • Norman Rose *Narrator* ■ *Dir* Sergei Bondarchuk • *Scr* Sergei Bondarchuk, Vasily Solovyov, from the novel by Leo Tolstoy

War Arrow ★★ U
Western   1953 · US · Colour · 78min

Jeff Chandler and Maureen O'Hara make a spirited pair in this innocuous western. He's the cavalry major who overrides the opposition of fort commander John McIntire and recruits friendly native American Seminoles to help defeat hostile Kiowas, while O'Hara plays the feisty wife of a missing captain. Handsomely photographed in Technicolor and adequately directed by George Sherman, it's assembly line stuff. AE

Maureen O'Hara *Elaine Corwin* • Jeff Chandler *Major Howell Brady* • Suzan Ball *Avis* • John McIntire *Colonel Jackson Meade* • Charles Drake

Luke Schermerhorn • Dennis Weaver *Pino* • Noah Beery Jr *Augustus Wilks* • Henry Brandon *Maygro* ■ *Dir* George Sherman • *Scr* John Michael Hayes

The War at Home ★★ 18
Drama   1996 · US · Colour · 118min

Emilio Estevez directs and stars in this leaden tale of a young Vietnam vet finding it impossible to readjust to family life. Its trump cards are the always brilliant Kathy Bates and real-life dad Martin Sheen, but James Duff's script is long on clichés, short on characterisation and becomes less plausible as it goes along. Estevez's embittered, one-note performance is less than believable and his direction never more than workmanlike. JC Swearing, violence.

Emilio Estevez *Jeremy Collier* • Kathy Bates *Maurine Collier* • Martin Sheen *Bob Collier* • Kimberly Williams *Karen Collier* • Corin Nemec *Donald* • Ann Hearn *Music teacher* • Carla Gugino *Melissa* ■ *Dir* Emilio Estevez • *Scr* James Duff, from his play *Homefront*

The War between Men and Women ★★★
Comedy drama   1972 · US · Colour · 105min

Based on the cartoons of James Thurber, this sounds like a comedy but it's more of a mawkish drama with funny bits about cynical cartoonist Jack Lemmon who is going blind and the divorced mother of three (Barbara Harris) whom he marries. Then her ex-husband shows up – the excellent Jason Robards as a war photographer. Lemmon does his usual neurotic schtick but Harris matches him scene for scene. However, the real embodiment of Thurber's sense of the ridiculous is their pregnant dog which all but steals the show. AT

Jack Lemmon *Peter Wilson* • Barbara Harris *Terry Kozlenko* • Jason Robards *Stephen Kozlenko* • Herb Edelman *Howard Mann* • Lisa Gerritsen *Linda Kozlenko* • Moosie Drier *David Kozlenko* ■ *Dir* Melville Shavelson • *Scr* Melville Shavelson, Danny Arnold, from writings and drawings by James Thurber

The War between Us ★★★
Wartime drama   1995 · Can · Colour · 93min

Surprisingly few films have been made about the experiences of Japanese people in North America during the Second World War. Rather than exploring the subject in any great depth, this film from Canadian director Anne Wheeler uses it as the backdrop for the friendship that develops between a Japanese woman who has to leave behind everything she has worked for in the city and a housewife who knows little of life beyond her mining town in the wastes of British Columbia. Sensibly directed and undoyingly played. DP

Shannon Lawson *Peg Parnham* • Mieko Ouchi *Aya Kawashima* • Robert Wisden *Ed Parnham* • Ian Tracey *Jig Parnham* • Juno Ruddell *Marg Parnham* • Edmond Kato *Masaru Kawashima* • Robert Ito *Mr Kawashima* ■ *Dir* Anne Wheeler • *Scr* Sharon Gibbon

War Book ★★★ 15
Political drama   2014 · UK · Colour · 92min

An intense drama that reveals how little power this country wields. As UK government officials rehearse how to respond to calamitous circumstances, director Tom Harper uses claustrophobic use of the single-room setting. But this is really about the performances, as chair Sophie Okonedo tries to balance clashing personalities – Treasury aide Antony Sher, special adviser Ben Chaplin – with their political priorities. Some of the speeches are overly deliberate, but this is still an intelligent speculation on a chillingly plausible scenario. DP Swearing

Sophie Okonedo *Philippa* • Ben Chaplin *Gary* • Nathan Stewart-Jarrett *Austin* • Shaun Evans *Tom* • Kerry Fox *Maria* ■ *Dir* Tom Harper (3) • *Scr* Jack Thorne • *Cinematographer* Zac Nicholson

The War Bride ★★ PG
Second World War romantic drama
2001 · UK/Can · Colour · 103min

Anna Friel has problems nailing good movies and this doesn't change her run of duff luck. Ringing of TV rather than film, this details the experiences of two London lasses who marry Canadian soldiers during the Blitz. Friel and her daughter are then shipped over to Canada to live with husband Aden Young's family until his return. Disparate performances and a lightweight plot make this wash over you. LH *DVD*

Anna Friel *Lily* • Molly Parker *Sylvia* • Brenda Fricker *Betty* • Loren Dean *Joe* • Julie Cox *Sophie* • Aden Young *Charlie Travis* ■ *Dir* Lyndon Chubbuck • *Scr* Angela Workman

War Dogs ★★★★★ 15
Comedy thriller based on a true story
2016 · US · Colour · 114min

One of those stranger-than-fiction true stories provides the basis for a cracking comedy thriller. Jonah Hill and Miles Teller (*Whiplash*) are surely the unlikeliest gunrunners of the lot, as 20-something stoners who win contracts supplying arms to George W Bush's US military through the mid-to-late noughties. Their dealings with a terror suspect (Bradley Cooper) add to an ominous mood that builds between shots of wry humour. It's a skilful balancing act by *Hangover* director Todd Phillips and whenever you think it can't get any crazier, it blows your mind. SP

Miles Teller *David Packouz* • Jonah Hill *Efraim Diveroli* • Ana de Armas *Iz* • Shaun Toub *Marlboro* ■ *Dir* Todd Phillips • *Scr* Todd Phillips, Stephen Chin, Jason Smilovic

War for the Planet of the Apes
Science-fiction action adventure
2017 · US · Colour

This is a preview – no prints were available to review as we went to press: Having directed *Cloverfield* and *Dawn of the Planet of the Apes*, Matt Reeves's undoubted feel for action and character has won him a second crack at this reborn franchise. In the revolving door of cast members, Woody Harrelson arrives as a baddie called The Colonel, a fitting adversary for Andy Serkis's Caesar, the ape who according to Reeves is going to become a "mythic figure, like Moses" by the end of this sequel. SvM

Woody Harrelson *Colonel* • Andy Serkis *Caesar* • Judy Greer *Cornelia* • Steve Zahn ■ *Dir* Matt Reeves • *Scr* Mark Bomback, Matt Reeves, from the novel *Monkey Planet* by Pierre Boulle

The War Game ★★★★ 12
Documentary drama   1965 · UK · BW · 46min

Such was the power of this documentary drama that the BBC refused to transmit Peter Watkins's film, leaving it to sit on the shelf, gathering dust and notoriety, before a cinema release in 1966. Watkins uses documentary-style techniques to create an image of England in the moments before a nuclear attack. It's a nightmarish blend of Ealing comedy, *Dad's Army* and wartime Ministry of Information. View it in the context of 1965 when the Cold War was at its hottest and when the youth of the world awoke each day thinking they would be vaporised at any minute. AT *DVD*

Michael Aspel *Commentator* • Dick Graham *Commentator* ■ *Dir/Scr* Peter Watkins • *Cinematographer* Peter Bartlett

War Horse ★★★★ 12
First World War drama
2011 · UK/US · Colour · 140min

Although lacking the puppet theatricality of the acclaimed stage production, Steven Spielberg's adaptation of Michael Morpurgo's 1982 novel emerges as an old-fashioned crowd-pleaser. It's a moving odyssey that outlines the suffering of the First World War and the loss of life while remaining family-friendly. Sold to the cavalry, thoroughbred Joey is captured by Germans and hidden by a French peasant, while tracked by the Devon farmer's son

(Jeremy Irvine) who trained and nurtured him. Full of stirring spectacle and poignant moments, much of the story is knowingly designed to induce tears, but there's still no doubting Spielberg's sincerity. AJ *DVD* *Blu-ray*

Emily Watson *Rosie Narracott* • David Thewlis *Lyons* • Jeremy Irvine *Albert Narracott* • Peter Mullan *Ted Narracott* • Niels Arestrup *Grandfather* • Tom Hiddleston *Captain Jim Nicholls* • Benedict Cumberbatch *Major Stewart* • Toby Kebbell *Colin* ■ *Dir* Steven Spielberg • *Scr* Lee Hall, Richard Curtis, from the play by Nick Stafford and novel by Michael Morpurgo • *Cinematographer* Janusz Kaminski • *Music* John Williams

War Hunt ★★
War drama   1962 · US · BW · 82min

One of the most enduring actor-director partnerships has been that of Robert Redford and Sydney Pollack. This is where they first met, both making their screen debuts as actors in this low-budget, rapidly shot platoon drama set in the Korean War. Redford is a private and Pollack a sergeant and they are both disturbed by the psychotic behaviour of John Saxon, a knife-wielding private who has an adoring, orphaned Korean boy as some sort of mascot. AT *DVD*

John Saxon *Pte Raymond Endore* • Robert Redford *Pte Roy Loomis* • Charles Aidman *Capt Wallace Pratt* • Sydney Pollack *Sgt Van Horn* • Gavin Macleod *Pte Crotty* • Tommy Matsuda *Charlie* • Tom Skerritt *Corporal Showalter* ■ *Dir* Denis Sanders • *Scr* Stanford Whitmore

War, Inc ★★ 15
Satirical drama   2008 · US · Colour · 102min

Playing a superannuated version of his *Grosse Pointe Blank* character, John Cusack is the conscience-stricken hitman visiting "Turaqistan" to assassinate an oil minister on the site of "the first war ever to be 100 per cent outsourced to private enterprise". In a classic case of a satire underestimating its audience, some scenes in this polemic against US involvement in Iraq and Afghanistan hit their targets but many simply do not. The performances, on the other hand, really work, with the ever cool Cusack making his mark, as does Dan Aykroyd as the assassin's Dick Cheney-esque boss. *Strangelove* it ain't, but there are jewels hidden within, and Cusack and company certainly cannot be accused of not nailing their colours to the mast. SvM *DVD*

John Cusack *Hauser* • Hilary Duff *Yonica Babyyeah* • Marisa Tomei *Natalie Hegalhuzen* • Joan Cusack *Marsha Dillon* • Ben Kingsley *Walken* • Dan Aykroyd *Mr Vice President* • Lyubomir Neikov *Omar Sharif* ■ *Dir* Joshua Seftel • *Scr* Mark Leyner, Jeremy Pikser, John Cusack

The War Lord ★★★★ PG
Period epic   1965 · US · Colour · 115min

In this sombre, beautifully photographed historical epic, Charlton Heston plays a feudal warlord who exerts his *droit du seigneur* – the knight's right to spend the night with any new wife-to-be he chooses. He selects blushing bride Rosemary Forsyth but Heston only takes her reluctantly since he's delirious from a wound and – against all reason – he seems influenced by pagan tradition and the druid fertility symbols that litter the landscape of 11th-century Normandy. This is fascinating, literate and rather disturbing. AT *DVD* *Blu-ray*

Charlton Heston *Chrysagon* • Richard Boone *Bors* • Rosemary Forsyth *Bronwyn* • Maurice Evans *Priest* • Guy Stockwell *Draco* • Niall MacGinnis *Odins* • James Farentino *Marc* ■ *Dir* Franklin Schaffner [Franklin J Schaffner] • *Scr* John Collier, Millard Kaufman, from the play *The Lovers* by Leslie Stevens • *Cinematographer* Russell Metty

The War Lover ★★★ PG
War drama   1962 · US/UK · BW · 101min

Steve McQueen stars as a US bomber pilot based in East Anglia whose recklessness in the air over Germany is mirrored by his disregard for the feelings of the women who share his bed. But it's McQueen's

sensitive friend, Robert Wagner, who wins Shirley Anne Field's heart and their love affair is set beside McQueen's love for war. Philip Leacock twists McQueen's charisma to bring out the nastier qualities of his character. AT *DVD*

Steve McQueen (1) *Buzz Rickson* • Robert Wagner *Ed Bolland* • Shirley Ann Field [Shirley Anne Field] *Daphne Caldwell* • Gary Cockrell *Lynch* • Michael Crawford *Junior Sailen* • Billy Edwards [Bill Edwards] *Brindt* • Chuck Julian *Lamb* ■ *Dir* Philip Leacock • *Scr* Howard Koch, from the novel by John Hersey

A War of Children ★★★★
Political drama   1972 · US/UK · Colour · 87min

George Schaefer, a former stage and occasional film director, was at his best with television drama, usually dealing with intimate, serious topics and this made-for-TV movie about the conflict in Northern Ireland is typical of his best work. Set contemporaneously to its production, this docudrama was – and sadly remains – timely in its story of two families, the Catholic Tomeltys and the Protestant McCullums trying to remain friends against all the odds. When Jenny Agutter, the young daughter of the Tomelty family, falls in love with Anthony Andrews, a British soldier, an already tense situation leads to inevitable heartache. BB

Jenny Agutter *Maureen Tomelty* • Vivien Merchant *Nora Tomelty* • John Ronane *Frank Tomelty* • Danny Figgis *Donal Tomelty* • Anthony Andrews *Reg Hogg* • Aideen O'Kelly *Meg McCullum* • David G Meredith *Robbie McCullum* ■ *Dir* George Schaefer • *Scr* James Costigan

War of the Buttons ★★★
Comedy drama   1962 · Fr · BW · 93min

Louis Pergaud's novel is brought to the screen with an irresistible mix of nostalgia, satire and adolescent high jinks. But there's a pronounced sentimental streak undermining Yves Robert's account of the rivalry between two gangs of French schoolboys which results in their leaders, André Treton and Michel Isella, being sent to a reformatory. The most famous sequence is undoubtedly the nude attack made by Treton's gang to prevent their buttons and belts being captured as war trophies. DP French +subtitles.

Martin Lartigue *Tigibus* • André Treton *Lebrac* • Michel Isella *Aztec* • Jacques Dufilho *Aztec's father* • Pierre Trabaud *Teacher* ■ *Dir* Yves Robert • *Scr* François Boyer, Yves Robert, from the novel *La Guerre des Boutons* by Louis Pergaud

War of the Buttons ★★ PG
Comedy drama   1993 · UK/Fr · Colour · 90min

Producer David Puttnam and writer Colin Welland, both Oscar winners for *Chariots of Fire*, teamed up again for this remake of the 1962 French movie in which gangs of boys from rival villages stalk the forests and steal each other's buttons, forcing them to fight stark naked. Transplanted to Ireland, the story retains its whimsy as well as its hints at allegory. Sadly, energetic performances from the kids and well-paced direction from debutant John Roberts didn't prevent a box-office disaster. AT

Gregg Fitzgerald *Fergus* • Gerard Kearney *Big Con* • Daragh Naughton *Boffin* • Brenda McNamara *Tim* • Kevin O'Malley *Fishy* • John Cleere *Peter* • John Coffey *Geronimo* • Colm Meaney *Geronimo's dad* ■ *Dir* John Roberts • *Scr* Colin Welland, from the novel *La Guerre des Boutons* by Louis Pergaud

W

War of the Colossal Beast ★ PG
Cult science-fiction
1958 · US · BW and Colour · 68min

The Amazing Colossal Man didn't die! He turned up in Mexico with a disfigured face and a gigantic appetite in a "what have we done to deserve this" sequel from trashmaster supremo, Bert I Gordon. The producer/director's initials are the only thing that is BIG about this fourth division dud, though. AJ *DVD*

Sally Fraser *Joyce Manning* • Dean Parkin *Colonel Glenn Manning* • Roger Pace *Major Baird* • Russ Bender *Dr Carmichael* • Charles Stewart *Captain Harris* • George Becwar *Swanson* ■ *Dir* Bert I Gordon • *Scr* George Worthing Yates, from a story by Bert I Gordon

War of the Gargantuas ★★
Science-fiction monster horror
1970 · Jpn/US · Colour · 93min

Intended as the sequel to *Frankenstein Conquers the World*, the American re-edited version of director Inoshiro Honda's wackily conceived continuation obscures all reference to the original only to emerge as one of the funniest monster extravaganzas ever. No point trying to make sense of the deconstructed plot - scientist Russ Tamblyn blaming himself for an epic battle between a furry brown giant monster and his evil green-hued twin which destroys Tokyo - just thrill along to the spectacular effects. AJ

Russ Tamblyn *Dr Paul Stewart* • Kumi Mizuno *His assistant* • Kipp Hamilton *Singer* • Yu Fujiki *Army commander* ■ *Dir* Inoshiro Honda • *Scr* Inoshiro Honda, Kaoru Mabuchi

The War of the Roses
★★★★ 15
Black comedy   1989 · US · Colour · 111min

This blistering black comedy from Danny DeVito is less an assault on marriage than on the acquisitiveness of Reaganite America. Suggesting that hell is not other people, but other people's possessions, the film rapidly escalates into a frenzy of comic viciousness. Michael Douglas and Kathleen Turner hurl themselves into their parts, tainting expressions of vengeful glee with real bile. The scene in which Douglas seasons the fish stew is a standout among several wickedly excessive incidents that raise laughs as well as hackles thanks to DeVito's bravura direction. DP Violence, swearing. *DVD*

Michael Douglas (1) *Oliver Rose* • Kathleen Turner *Barbara Rose* • Danny DeVito *Gavin D'Amato* • Marianne Sägebrecht *Susan* • Peter Donat *Larrabee* • Sean Astin *Josh, aged 17* • Heather Fairfield *Carolyn, aged 17* • GD Spradlin *Harry Thurmont* ■ *Dir* Danny DeVito • *Scr* Michael Leeson, from the novel by Warren Adler

War of the Satellites ★ U
Science fiction   1958 · US · BW · 66min

Within months of the first Russian Sputnik being launched into space, cult director Roger Corman released this cash-in. Aliens threaten the destruction of Earth unless the space programme is terminated. Scientist Richard Devon's dead body is taken over by the aliens to sabotage further intergalactic explorations in this excruciatingly dull exploiter. AJ

Dick Miller *Dave Royer* • Susan Cabot *Sybil Carrington* • Richard Devon *Dr Van Pander* • Eric Sinclair *Dr Lazar* • Michael Fox *Akad* • Roger Corman *Ground control* ■ *Dir* Roger Corman • *Scr* Lawrence Louis Goldman, from the story by Irving Block, Jack Rabin • *Special Effects* Jack Rabin, Irving Block, Louis DeWitt

War of the Wildcats ★★ U
Western   1943 · US · BW · 97min

John Wayne drills for oil and tries to win the hand of Martha Scott from rival Albert Dekker. Political matters enter the fray when Wayne starts fighting for the rights of American Indians - the "little fellers" as he calls them. Reputedly, this caused consternation in Washington where it was thought the implication that native Americans had been treated badly by the government could be exploited by the Nazis. Republic made the changes asked of them and made a box-office hit, too. AT
DVD

John Wayne *Daniel Somers* • Martha Scott *Catherine Allen* • Albert Dekker *James E Gardner* • George "Gabby" Hayes *Desprit Dean* • Marjorie Rambeau *Bessie Baxter* • Dale Evans *Cuddles Walker* • Grant Withers *Richardson* • Sidney Blackmer *Teddy Roosevelt* ■ *Dir* Albert S Rogell • *Scr* Ethel Hill, Eleanor Griffin, from a story by Thomson Burtis

The War of the Worlds
★★★★ PG
Science-fiction adventure
1953 · US · Colour · 81min

Although it never comes close to reproducing the panic generated by Orson Welles's famous 1938 radio broadcast, this is a splendid version of HG Wells's sci-fi classic. When the "meteor" that lands in southern California turns out to be the mothership of a Martian invasion, the governments of the world unleash their most potent weapons in an attempt to stem the tide of destruction. Director Byron Haskin enhances the impact of the Oscar-winning special effects by ensuring that his extras convey a genuine sense of terror as civilisation collapses around them. DP
DVD

Gene Barry *Dr Clayton Forrester* • Ann Robinson *Sylvia Van Buren* • Les Tremayne *General Mann* • Robert Cornthwaite *Doctor Pryor* • Sandro Giglio *Doctor Bilderbeck* • Lewis Martin *Pastor Collins* • William Phipps *Wash Perry* • Paul Birch *Alonzo Hogue* • Cedric Hardwicke *Narrator* ■ *Dir* Byron Haskin • *Scr* Barré Lyndon, from the novel by HG Wells • *Cinematographer* George Barnes • *Special Effects* Gordon Jennings

War of the Worlds ★★★★ 12
Science-fiction thriller
2005 · US · Colour · 111min

Steven Spielberg's mega-upgrade of the science-fiction landmark is a spectacular disaster epic of two halves. The first (and much the superior) hour is a masterclass in escalating tension, with grandiose and brilliantly executed sequences following in rapid succession. The human drama (though admittedly clichéd in construction) is transfixing, as divorced dockworker Tom Cruise flees the invasion with his two estranged children (played by Justin Chatwin and Dakota Fanning). It's in the second hour that the story begins to wilt, petering out until a rather abrupt ending in which Hollywood schmaltz wins the day. AJ Violence. *DVD* *Blu*

Tom Cruise *Ray Ferrier* • Dakota Fanning *Rachel Ferrier* • Miranda Otto *Mary Ann Ferrier* • Justin Chatwin *Robbie Ferrier* • Tim Robbins *Harlan Ogilvy* • David Alan Basche *Tim* • Yul Vazquez *Julio* • Gene Barry *Grandfather* • Ann Robinson *Grandmother* • Morgan Freeman *Narrator* ■ *Dir* Steven Spielberg • *Scr* David Koepp, from the novel by HG Wells

The War on Democracy
★★★ 12
Political documentary
2007 · Aus/UK · Colour · 93min

This provocative documentary from John Pilger offers a startling reading of modern history and American imperialism. According to Pilger, the United States has spent the last 50 years interfering in the affairs of sovereign states, particularly in Latin America. Giving us a brisk lesson in modern history, Pilger draws stark conclusions about the American empire and its willingness to undermine and sometimes overthrow democratically elected governments to suit its own interests. Pilger is an incisive, passionate commentator and his argument is forceful; however, his willingness to abandon objectivity to deliver tub-thumping speeches about the march of people power robs this otherwise compelling documentary of some of its weight. JR *DVD*

Hugo Chávez • Howard Hunt • Duane Clarridge • John Pilger ■ *Dir* John Pilger, Chris Martin [Christopher Martin (3)] • *Scr* John Pilger • *Cinematographers* Preston Clothier, Rupert Binsley

War Paint ★★★
Western   1953 · US · Colour · 89min

Boasting a strong leading performance by Robert Stack, a tense and involving plot, and stark desert locations in Death Valley, this is a notch above average among cavalry and Indian westerns. The grim drama centres on the efforts of Stack's lieutenant to deliver an urgent peace treaty to an Indian chief. He finds himself up against sabotage within his patrol, lack of

water, and a rebellion over gold. The steady pace is disrupted only by a campfire song interlude. AE

Robert Stack *Lt Billings* • Joan Taylor *Wanima* • Charles McGraw *Sgt Clarke* • Keith Larsen *Taslik* • Peter Graves (2) *Tolson* ■ *Dir* Lesley Selander • *Scr* Martin Berkeley, Richard Alan Simmons, from a story by Fred Freiberger, William Tunberg

War Party ★★★ 18
Action drama   1988 · US · Colour · 93min

In an alternative take on the western, modern-day white folk and native Americans take opposite sides for a town's centennial re-creation of an old cowboy/Indian fight. But old wounds are reopened, and old prejudices reignited, when someone starts using live ammunition. A potentially intriguing idea, but it's exhausted in the first 20 minutes; the film then becomes just a variant on the traditional western. There are good performances, though. DA

Billy Wirth *Sonny Crowkiller* • Kevin Dillon *Skitty Harris* • Tim Sampson *Warren Cutfoot* • Jimmy Ray Weeks [Jimmie Ray Weeks] *Jay Stivic* • Kevyn Major Howard *Calvin Morrisey* ■ *Dir* Franc Roddam • *Scr* Spencer Eastman

War Requiem ★★★★ 12
Experimental documentary drama
1988 · UK · BW and Colour · 88min

Benjamin Britten's *War Requiem*, written in 1962 for the dedication of the new Coventry Cathedral, is visualised as an elongated music video by director Derek Jarman. Laurence Olivier, in his last work on film before his death, plays a disabled veteran Second World War soldier whose memories and reflections accompany the highly acclaimed Britten opus. Newsreel footage of the Great War and atomic explosions are intercut with sequences featuring Owen Teale (as the Unknown Soldier) and Tilda Swinton (a battlefield nurse) looking powerlessly on at all the devastation and wasted lives. Jarman's ultimately inspiring, negative statement on war matches the intense emotions of Britten's music to perfection. AJ *DVD*

Nathaniel Parker *Wilfred Owen* • Tilda Swinton *Nurse* • Laurence Olivier *Old soldier* • Patricia Hayes *Mother* • Rohan McCullough *Enemy mother* • Nigel Terry *Abraham* • Owen Teale *Unknown Soldier* • Sean Bean *German soldier* ■ *Dir* Derek Jarman • *Scr* Derek Jarman, from the oratorio *War Requiem* by Benjamin Britten (music), Wilfred Owen (libretto) • *Cinematographer* Richard Greatrex

The War Room ★★★★
Political documentary
1993 · US · Colour · 90min

DA Pennebaker hit the campaign trail in this Oscar-nominated account of the 1992 election. The focus is less on Bill Clinton than the contrasting temperaments of his chief spin-doctors - plain-speaking campaign boss James Carville and suave press spokesman George Stephanopoulos - as they seek to counter allegations of adultery, dope-smoking and draft dodging. There are also fascinating insights into the in-fighting within the Democratic camp and the romantic liaison between Carville and George Bush's senior aide, Mary Matalin. DP

■ *Dir* DA Pennebaker, Chris Hegedus • *Cinematographers* Nick Doob, DA Pennebaker, Kevin Rafferty

The War Wagon ★★★ U
Western   1967 · US · Colour · 96min

Westerns starring John Wayne and Kirk Douglas approached the genre from very different directions. It's not surprising, therefore, that there's an uneasy tension behind the pair's bonhomie in this rugged comedy adventure about a plan to steal some gold. Yet nobody was better at directing this kind of romp than Burt Kennedy, who not only exploits the rivalry between his stars, but also gets superior supporting performances the supporting cast. The action might have been a little more robust, but the wagon itself (with its swivelling turret and machine gun) is a real scene-stealer. DP *DVD* *Blu*

John Wayne *Taw Jackson* • Kirk Douglas *Lomax* • Howard Keel *Levi Walking Bear* • Robert Walker [Robert Walker Jr] *Billy Hyatt* • Keenan Wynn *Wes Catlin* • Bruce Cabot *Frank Pierce* • Valora Noland *Kate Catlin* • Joanna Barnes *Lola* • Bruce Dern *Hammond* • Gene Evans *Hoag* ■ *Dir* Burt Kennedy • *Scr* Clair Huffaker, from his novel *Badman*

The War Zone ★★★★ 18
Drama   1999 · UK/It · Colour · 98min

Actor Tim Roth makes a stunning directorial debut with a distressingly believable story of incest within a close-knit family. Adapted by Alexander Stuart from his acclaimed novel, this bleak drama elicits supremely natural performances from young newcomers Freddie Cunliffe and Lara Belmont, while Ray Winstone portrays their abusive father as no *Nil by Mouth* monster, but as a loving parent. Roth also makes inspired, emotive use of the stark, jagged Devon landscapes, whose grey-hued coldness seems to mirror Belmont's pain and turns an already uncomfortable experience into a devastating one. JC Swearing, nudity. *DVD*

Ray Winstone *Dad* • Lara Belmont *Jessie* • Freddie Cunliffe *Tom* • Tilda Swinton *Mum* • Annabelle Apsion *Nurse* • Kate Ashfield *Lucy* • Colin J Farrell [Colin Farrell (2)] *Nick* ■ *Dir* Tim Roth • *Scr* Alexander Stuart, from his novel

Warcraft: the Beginning
★★ 12A
Fantasy adventure   2016 · US · Colour · 122min

Director Duncan Jones's long-gestating adaptation of video game *World of Warcraft* centres on a war between the land of Azeroth and an Orc army. Using computer effects astoundingly, Jones clearly understands his source material. However, an enormous number of characters means the film is very dense, which can be a trying experience for newcomers and experts alike. Ben Foster's wizard and Toby Kebbell as Orc warrior Durotan stand out but another hour might have lifted this potential franchise-starter. JL Some violence. 3p

Travis Fimmel *Sir Anduin Lothar* • Paula Patton *Garona Halforcen* • Toby Kebbell *Durotan* • Ben Foster *Medivh* • Dominic Cooper *King Llane Wrynn* ■ *Dir* Duncan Jones • *Scr* Duncan Jones, Charles Leavitt, from a story by Chris Metzen

The Ware Case ★★ PG
Mystery drama   1938 · UK · BW · 73min

Opening with an Old Bailey jury deliberating on the fate of Clive Brook, the action flashes back to show the baronet living the high life to the disapproval of wife Jane Baxter and her wealthy brother Peter Bull. But then the latter is found drowned at the ancestral home. Roland Pertwee's screenplay feels bitty and, while the performances are as solid as Robert Stevenson's direction, this is most memorable for cinematographer Ronald Neame's experiments with deep focus. DP
DVD

Clive Brook *Sir Hubert Ware* • Jane Baxter *Lady Margaret "Meg" Ware* • Barry K Barnes *Michael Adye* • CV France *Judge* • Francis L Sullivan *Attorney General* ■ *Dir* Robert Stevenson • *Scr* Roland Pertwee, Robert Stevenson, from GP Bancroft's play

WarGames ★★★★ PG
Thriller   1983 · US · Colour · 108min

Whizzkid Matthew Broderick accidentally hacks into a Pentagon computer and starts playing what he thinks is a game called Global Thermonuclear War, only to discover he's pushing the world toward destruction for real. This is an inventive nail-biter that's consistently entertaining and worryingly thought-provoking, laced by director John Badham with just the right amount of invigorating humour. Great edge-of-the-seat suspense is generated as defence specialist Dabney Coleman desperately tries to avert the impending holocaust, while preachy sentiment is kept to a minimum. AJ Swearing. *DVD* *Blu*

Matthew Broderick *David Lightman* • Dabney Coleman *John McKittrick* • John Wood (2) *Professor Falken* • Ally Sheedy *Jennifer Mack* •

Barry Corbin *General Beringer* • Juanin Clay *Pat Healy* • Dennis Lipscomb *Lyle Watson* ■ *Dir* John Badham • *Scr* Lawrence Lasker, Walter F Parkes

Warlock ★★★★ 🄿
Western 1959 · US · Colour · 116min

This impressive psychological western has Henry Fonda on magnificent form as a former gunfighter, aching with regret for a passing age and a wasted life, whose success as a lawman means that his corrupt regime is tolerated by the locals. The gradual disintegration of Fonda's friendship with gambler Anthony Quinn is deftly handled by director Edward Dmytryk, allowing the stars' contrasting acting styles to define their characters. This deserves to be better known. DP *DVD*

Richard Widmark *Johnny Gannon* • Henry Fonda *Clay Blaisdell* • Anthony Quinn *Tom Morgan* • Dorothy Malone *Lily Dollar* • Dolores Michaels *Jessie Marlow* • Wallace Ford *Judge Holloway* • Tom Drake *Abe McQuown* • Richard Arlen *Bacon* • DeForest Kelley *Curley Burne* • Regis Toomey *Skinner* ■ *Dir* Edward Dmytryk • *Scr* Robert Alan Aurthur, from Oakley Hall's novel

Warlock ★★★ 🄸🄵
Horror 1989 · US · Colour · 97min

Richard E Grant's great central performance as a witchfinder elevates this gory "bell, book and candle" tale to convincing heights. He's hunting warlock Julian Sands who, having escaped through a 1691 time portal to present-day LA, is looking for a Satanic bible to help him destroy the world. Slasher veteran Steve Miner's assured direction keeps everything exciting while an unusual plot twists maintain a level of constant surprise. It spawned a couple of less successful sequels. AJ

Richard E Grant *Giles Redferne* • Julian Sands *The Warlock* • Lori Singer *Kassandra* • Kevin O'Brien *Chas* • Mary Woronov *Channeller* • Richard Kuss *Mennonite* ■ *Dir* Steve Miner • *Scr* David Twohy • *Music* Jerry Goldsmith

Warlock: the Armageddon ★★🄸🄴
Horror 1993 · US · Colour · 94min

Julian Sands returns for the second time as the titular warlock, emerging fully grown, if you please, from a woman recently impregnated. He's on a quest to track down six magical stones that hold the power to herald the second coming of his satanic master, or dad as he likes to call him. Horror veteran Anthony Hickox knows it's a load of old tosh so directs with total disregard for the boundaries of taste or style. RS Violence, swearing. *DVD*

Julian Sands *The Warlock* • Chris Young *Kenny Travis* • Paula Marshall *Samantha Ellison* • Joanna Pacula *Paula Dare* • Steve Kahan *Will Travis* • RG Armstrong *Franks* • Charles Hallahan *Ethan Larson* • Bruce Glover *Ted Ellison* ■ *Dir* Anthony Hickox • *Scr* Kevin Rock, Sam Bernard

Warlock III: the End of Innocence ★★🄸🄴
Horror 1999 · US · Colour · 90min

Better than the first sequel, but not a patch on the original black magic frightener, director Eric Freiser's effort generates a fair amount of atmosphere and chills thanks to its unpretentious story that embroiders on haunted house conventions. Art student Ashley Laurence takes possession of a family home she never knew existed and, with several of her schoolfriends, takes up residence to stop it being demolished. Enter architect Bruce Payne (slicing the theatrical ham thickly) who is really the Devil's disciple and wants to sacrifice Laurence. AJ *DVD*

Ashley Laurence *Kris Miller* • Bruce Payne *Warlock/Philip Covington* • Paul Francis Michael • Jan Schweiterman *Jerry* • Boti Ann Bliss *Robin* ■ *Dir* Eric Freiser • *Scr* Eric Freiser, Bruce David Eisen

The Warlords ★★★🄸🄵
Period action drama 2008 · Chi/HK · Colour · 108min

Jet Li proves there is more to him than martial arts prowess in this violent, epic tale of blood-brotherhood, ambition and conflicting loyalties, set against the backdrop of political turmoil in 19th-century China. Li is excellent as General Pang, an idealistic military leader who convinces a group of bandits to fight alongside him to quash a rebellion. But as the conflict continues and worsens, he becomes corrupted by power, which strains his friendship with the other men. It's not always easy to work out which warlord is doing what to whom, or why, but the underlying theme of betrayal and the spectacular battle scenes more than compensate. DA Mandarin +subtitles. *DVD* 🅱

Jet Li *Pang Qing-yun* • Xu Jinglei *Lian* • Andy Lau *Zhao Er-hu* • Takeshi Kaneshiro *Jiang Wu-yang* ■ *Dir* Peter Ho-Sun Chan • *Scr* Xu Lan, Chun Tin-nam, Aubrey Lam, Huang Jianxin, Hui Jojo [Jojo Yuet-Chun Hui], He Jiping, Guo Junli, James Yuen

Warlords of Atlantis ★★★🄿🄶
Action adventure 1978 · UK · Colour · 92min

It may be small beer compared with the monster movies of the computer age, but this is still a decent romp from director Kevin Connor. Doug McClure is the clean-cut Hollywood hero (and about as Victorian as skateboards) who discovers the fabled city (ruled, would you believe, by Cyd Charisse and Daniel Massey) and its monstrous menagerie of sundry sea beasties – including a giant octopus. The sets and the creatures are as wobbly as the script and the performances, but that's just part of the charm. AT *DVD*

Doug McClure *Greg Collinson* • Peter Gilmore *Charles Aitken* • Shane Rimmer *Captain Daniels* • Lea Brodie *Delphine Briggs* • Michael Gothard *Atmir* • Hal Galili *Grogan* • John Ratzenberger *Fenn* • Cyd Charisse *Atsil* • Daniel Massey *Atraxon* ■ *Dir* Kevin Connor • *Scr* Brian Hayles

Warm Bodies ★★★🄸🄴
Romantic comedy horror 2012 · US · Colour · 93min

Nicholas Hoult feels dead inside at the start of this offbeat romantic comedy, mainly because he's a zombie. But writer/director Jonathan Levine breaks the rules of the genre by delivering an undead hero, R, who is able to think deeply about his life (or lack of it) and conveys this in a rib-tickling voiceover. That residual spark of humanity is then fanned into something warmer thanks to a meeting with mortal blonde Julie (Teresa Palmer). The plot does lumber a bit, but the interplay between the couple is surprisingly tender and witty, with a shot of adrenaline later on when R faces off with Julie's zombie hunter dad (a rabid John Malkovich) and an army of lethal skeleton zombies. It's not seamless, but Hoult carries the burden gracefully, even with a lopsided gait. SP Violence, swearing. *DVD* 🅱

Nicholas Hoult *R* • Teresa Palmer *Julie* • John Malkovich *General Grigio* • Rob Corddry *M* • Analeigh Tipton *Nora* ■ *Dir* Jonathan Levine • *Scr* Jonathan Levine, from Isaac Marion's novel

A Warm December ★★
Romantic drama 1973 · UK · Colour · 100min

This mawkish affair begins as a thriller and ends up as a romance. Sidney Poitier (making his second film as director) stars as an American widower, a doctor who falls for the supposedly hounded niece (Esther Anderson) of an African diplomat, only to discover that the people who are following her are doing it for her own good. Tough all round, especially for audiences. TH

Sidney Poitier *Doctor Matt Younger* • Esther Anderson *Catherine* • Yvette Curtis *Stefanie Younger* • George Baker *Henry Barlow* • Earl Cameron *Ambassador George Oswandu* • Johnny Sekka *Myomo* ■ *Dir* Sidney Poitier • *Scr* Lawrence Roman

Warm Nights on a Slow Moving Train ★★★🄸🄴
Drama 1986 · Aus · Colour · 87min

This intriguing Australian tale of dual personality was withheld from release after its completion in 1986. However, director Bob Ellis's simmering thriller deserves a wider showing. As the mousey Catholic school art teacher who works as a train-board prostitute by night to help her morphine-addicted, paraplegic brother, Wendy Hughes gives a performance that is as subtle and sensitive as it is dark and disturbing. Colin Friels also does well as the client who draws her into a dangerous liaison. DP

Wendy Hughes *Girl* • Colin Friels *Man* • Norman Kaye *Salesman* • John Clayton *Football coach* • Lewis Fitz-Gerald *Girl's brother* • Rod Zuanic *Soldier* • Steve J Spears *Singer* • Grant Tilly *Politician* ■ *Dir* Bob Ellis • *Scr* Bob Ellis, Denny Lawrence

Warm Water under a Red Bridge ★★★🄸🄵
Comedy 2001 · Jpn/Fr · Colour · 114min

Shohei Imamura's adaptation of Henmi Yo's fantastical novel – about a young woman who expels torrents of water during sex – seems more like an over-elaborate anecdote than a profound meditation on female sensuality. Hisao Inagaki's designs are exquisite, and are captured in all their glory by cinematographer Shigeru Komatsubara, but the film lacks the philosophical depth to complement its gleeful physicality. DP Japanese +subtitles. *DVD*

Koji Yakusho *Yosuke Sasano* • Misa Shimizu *Saeko Aizawa* • Mitsuko Baisho *Mitsu Aizawa* • Kazuo Kitamura *Taro* • Mansaku Fuwa *Gen* ■ *Dir* Shohei Imamura • *Scr* Shohei Imamura, Motofumi Tomikawa, Daisuke Tengan, from a novel by Henmi Yo

Warning Shot ★★★
Crime thriller 1967 · US · Colour · 99min

David Janssen was at the height of his fame from playing the title role in TV's long-running series *The Fugitive* when he starred in this pacey and entertaining thriller about a policeman's bid to clear his name – not unlike the Fugitive himself – of killing an apparently unarmed and upstanding medic. In the process, he encounters plenty of drama, excitement and an all-star cast. PF

David Janssen *Sergeant Tom Valens* • Ed Begley *Captain Roy Klodin* • Keenan Wynn *Sergeant Ed Musso* • Sam Wanamaker *Frank Sanderman* • Lillian Gish *Alice Willows* • Stefanie Powers *Liz Thayer* • Eleanor Parker *Mrs Doris Ruston* • George Grizzard *Walt Cody* • George Sanders *Calvin York* • Steve Allen *Perry Knowland* • Carroll O'Connor *Paul Jerez* • Joan Collins *Joanie Valens* • Walter Pidgeon *Orville Ames* ■ *Dir* Buzz Kulik • *Scr* Mann Rubin, from the novel *711 – Officer Needs Help* by Whit Masterson

Warning Sign ★★★🄸🄵
Science-fiction thriller 1985 · US · Colour · 94min

Although derivative of a dozen other mind-melt movies, Hal Barwood's thriller is engrossing action all the way with its bacterial twists and brain-damaged turns. The excellent acting lifts it way above the norm, although mouth-foaming maniac Richard Dysart delivers some stupidly inspired dialogue about rage being beautiful. You'll be sorry when the curtain falls on this exciting tale. AJ

Sam Waterston *Cal Morse* • Kathleen Quinlan *Joanie Morse* • Yaphet Kotto *Major Connolly* • Jeffrey DeMunn *Dan Fairchild* • Richard Dysart *Dr Nielsen* • GW Bailey *Tom Schmidt* • Jerry Hardin *Vic Flint* ■ *Dir* Hal Barwood • *Scr* Hal Barwood, Matthew Robbins

Warpath ★★🄿
Western 1951 · US · Colour · 95min

A sobering pre-revisionist western and a reminder of a Hollywood where American Indians were treated like dirt, this Paramount caper is actually dedicated to the Seventh Cavalry. Using events leading up to the Battle of Little Bighorn as a background for a stark revenge plot, Edmond O'Brien (too chubby for a western hero) rides out to avenge his slaughtered fiancée. In the hands of director Byron Haskin, it's a time-passer. TS

Edmond O'Brien *John Vickers* • Dean Jagger *Sam Quade* • Charles Stevens *Courier* • Forrest Tucker *Sergeant O'Hara* • Harry Carey Jr *Captain Gregson* • Polly Bergen *Molly Quade* • James Millican *General Custer* • Wallace Ford *Private*

Potts • Paul Fix *Private Fiore* ■ *Dir* Byron Haskin • *Scr* Frank Gruber • *Cinematographer* Ray Rennahan

The Warrior ★★★🄸🄶
Period drama 2001 · UK/Fr/Ger/Ind · Colour · 82min

Writer/director Asif Kapadia draws on both eastern and western cultural and cinematic influences for his inspiration for this languorous odyssey. But while this retains its visual splendour, the story quickly loses its focus, as Irfan Khan renounces violence and quits his life as head of a warlord's private army, only to be pursued through the Himalayan foothills by his master's enforcer, Sheikh Annuddin. Dealing in types not characters, and situations rather than psychology, Kapadia's debut feature is auspicious yet aloof. DP Hindi +subtitles. Violence. *DVD*

Irfan Khan *Lafcadia, the warrior* • Puru Chibber *Katiba, Lafcadia's son* • Sheikh Annuddin *Biswas* ■ *Dir* Asif Kapadia • *Scr* Asif Kapadia, Tim Miller

Warrior ★★★★🄸🄶
Action drama 2011 · US · Colour · 134min

Tommy Conlon (Tom Hardy) cuts a dark and brooding figure, bubbling with pent up anger at his estranged father (Nick Nolte) who divided him from his brother. Reconciliation seems impossible, with bitterness on both sides, until the brothers enter a martial arts tournament. The pace is thrilling, brought to a head in a tremendous finale that rivals the impact of Sylvester Stallone's *Rocky*. Such an emotional investment in the characters makes this film as powerful as one of Tommy Conlon's knock-out punches. AIS *DVD* 🅱

Tom Hardy *Tommy Conlon* • Joel Edgerton *Brendan Conlon* • Nick Nolte *Paddy Conlon* • Jennifer Morrison *Tess Conlon* ■ *Dir* Gavin O'Connor • *Scr* Gavin O'Connor, Anthony Tambakis, Cliff Dorfman

The Warrior and the Sorceress ★★🄸🄴
Martial arts action adventure 1983 · US · Colour · 77min

Part samurai movie, part western and part fantasy, in the end this fumbling affair comes across as nothing more than a blatant rip-off of Akira Kurosawa's *Yojimbo*. David Carradine plays a holy warrior, in all but name his television *Kung Fu* character, who arrives in an impoverished village where two rival gangs vie for control over a water well. Exotic Maria Socas, cast as the sorceress, spends the entire movie topless. Maybe the budget was so small they could only afford half her costume! RS *DVD*

David Carradine *Kain* • Luke Askew *Zeg* • Maria Socas *Naja* • Anthony De Longis *Kief* • Harry Townes *Bludge* ■ *Dir* John C Broderick • *Scr* John C Broderick, from a story by William Stout, John C Broderick

Warrior King ★★★🄸🄴
Martial arts crime thriller 2005 · Thai · Colour · 105min

Asiaphiles won't disappointed by muay thai martial arts star Tony Jaa's follow-up to 2003's *Ong-Bak*. But, while the fight sequences are outstanding, the plotline is slender and Jaa lacks the charisma of his Hong Kong counterparts. Fortunately, transsexual Jin Xing contributes some scene-stealing support as the Sydney-based former Shanghai Ballet star who seems to be behind the theft of the Thai country boy's prized elephants. DP Thai, English +subtitles. *DVD*

Tony Jaa *Kham* • Petchthai Wongkamlao *Mark* • Bongkod Kongmalai *Pla* • David Asavanond *Officer Rick* • Jin Xing *Madame Rose* • Johnny Tri Nguyen *Johnny* • Nathan B Jones *TK* ■ *Dir* Prachya Pinkaew • *Scr* Napalee, Piyaros Thongdee, Joe Wannapin, Kongdej Jaturanrasmee, from a story by Prachya Pinkaew

Warrior Queen ★🄸🄴
Period sex drama 1986 · US · Colour · 67min

Silliness, thy name is *Warrior Queen*. Sybil Danning stars as the titular Queen Berenice, an attractive but deadly woman who arrives in Pompeii for a festival and to negotiate with the city's ruler, Clodius. Donald Pleasence leaves no bit of scenery unchewed as the self-indulgent mayor, so it's no wonder his wife wants to hook up with an attractive young gladiator. **ST**

Sybil Danning *Berenice* • Donald Pleasence *Clodius* • Richard Hill *Marcus* • Josephine Jacqueline Jones *Chloe* • Tally Chanel *Vespa* • Stasia Micula [Samantha Fox] *Philomena/Augusta* • Suzanna Smith *Veneria* ■ *Dir* Chuck Vincent • *Scr* Rick Marx, from a story by Harry Alan Towers

The Warriors ★★★★ 15
Action drama   1979 · US · Colour · 89min

This vivid and violent gangland thriller from director Walter Hill is, essentially, an urban western. It centres on a New York gang whose members battle their way back to home turf following the murder of a rival gang leader during a ceasefire meeting. Despite the gritty storyline and locations, there's a doomed, romantic feel to the film and a poetic quality to the exhilarating fight scenes. Hill sketches the characters with some sympathy and is rewarded with excellent performances from his cast. **JF** Swearing, drug abuse. **DVD** **Blu**

Michael Beck *Swan* • James Remar *Ajax* • Thomas Waites [Thomas G Waites] *Fox* • Dorsey Wright *Cleon* • Brian Tyler (2) *Snow* • David Harris *Cochise* • Tom McKitterick *Cowboy* • Mercedes Ruehl *Policewoman* ■ *Dir* Walter Hill • *Scr* Walter Hill, David Shaber, from the novel by Sol Yurick • *Cinematographer* Andrew Laszlo

Warriors of Virtue ★★ PG
Fantasy action adventure
1996 · US/Chi · Colour · 98min

The warriors are plentiful, but there's very little virtue in this children's fantasy about a boy who's sucked down a kind of intergalactic plughole to a planet where the kangaroo-style natives are battling an evil overlord. While youngsters may appreciate the imaginative sets and director Ronny Yu's well staged fight scenes, the feebleness of the acting and the cod new-age treatment make this a sub-standard effort. A poor sequel followed. **DA** **DVD**

Angus MacFadyen *Komodo* • Mario Yedidia *Ryan Jeffers* • Marley Shelton *Elysia* • Chi Chao-Li *Master Chung* • Tom Towles *General Grillo* ■ *Dir* Ronny Yu • *Scr* Michael Vickerman, Hugh Kelley, from characters by Dennis Law, Ronald Law, Christopher Law, Jeremy Law

The Warrior's Way ★ 15
Action fantasy western
2010 · S Kor/US/Aus · Colour · 96min

A Korean warrior flees a centuries-old clan conflict for America's Old West, in this unsuccessful blend of Asian martial arts and rootin'-tootin' frontier gunplay. Korean poster-boy Jang Dong-gun looks good waving a blade around but is defeated by the demands of emotional expression or comic timing. Kate Bosworth puts in a lot of effort as the tomboyish gal who befriends him, but as the brooding new arrival helps her take on the marauders who killed her folks, there's a striking absence of tension or culture-clash humour. The climactic bout of digitally manicured carnage is tedious and uninvolving. For the viewer, however, the real battle is sticking it out to the end. **TJ** Violence. **DVD** **Blu**

Jang Dong-gun *Yang* • Kate Bosworth *Lynne* • Danny Huston *The Colonel* • Geoffrey Rush *Ron* • Tony Cox *Eight-Ball* • Ti Lung *Saddest Flute* ■ *Dir/Scr* Sngmoo Lee

The Wash ★★ 15
Comedy   2001 · US · Colour · 92min

Rappers Snoop Dogg and Dr Dre head the cast in this shipshod comedy as a couple of losers who briefly sideline their fixation with getting high and pursuing foxy females in order to rescue car-wash boss George Washington from a gang of incompetent kidnappers. Utterly reliant on the kind of African-American stereotypes and clichés that writer/director Robert Townsend lamented in *Hollywood Shuffle*, this is a lazy film that trades cynically on supposedly

subversive chic and the notoriety of its leads. **DP** **DVD**

Dr Dre *Sean* • Snoop Dogg *Dee Loc* • George Wallace *Mr Washington* • Angell Conwell *Antoinette* • Tommy "Tiny" Lister Jr [Tom "Tiny" Lister Jr] *Bear* • Bruce Bruce *DeWayne* ■ *Dir/Scr* DJ Pooh

Washington Merry-Go-Round ★★
Political melodrama   1932 · US · BW · 78min

Lee Tracy finds himself on the trail of corruption in high places in this creaky ode to the American way. Although it touches on many of the points later raised in *Mr Smith Goes to Washington*, James Cruze's half-hearted picture lacks the sharpness of the Frank Capra classic, and Tracy (more at home in his familiar role as a fast-talking reporter) is no James Stewart. The enthusiastic Constance Cummings is given too little to do as Tracy's Girl Friday. **DP**

Lee Tracy *Button Gwinnett Brown* • Constance Cummings *Alice Wylie* • Alan Dinehart *Norton* • Walter Connolly *Senator Wylie* • Clarence Muse *Clarence, the Valet* • Arthur Vinton *Beef Brannigan* • Frank Sheridan *Kelleher* ■ *Dir* James Cruze • *Scr* Jo Swerling, from a story by Maxwell Anderson

Washington Square ★★★ PG
Period romantic drama
1997 · US · Colour · 111min

Jennifer Jason Leigh is the dowdy spinster in 19th-century America, whose chance of marriage is cruelly denied her by her domineering father Albert Finney. It starts promisingly as director Agnieszka Holland sets the scene with a breathtaking camera swoop from above the treetops to a bedroom where a beautiful woman has just died, bloodily, in childbirth. From then on, however, Holland is less assured and this Henry James adaptation ultimately fails to live up to its early promise. **TH**

Jennifer Jason Leigh *Catherine Sloper* • Albert Finney *Dr Austin Sloper* • Ben Chaplin *Morris Townsend* • Maggie Smith *Aunt Lavinia Penniman* • Judith Ivey *Aunt Elizabeth Almond* • Betsy Brantley *Mrs Montgomery* • Jennifer Garner *Marian Almond* • Peter Maloney *Jacob Webber/Notary* • Robert Stanton *Arthur Townsend* • Arthur Laupus *Mr Almond* ■ *Dir* Agnieszka Holland • *Scr* Carol Doyle, from the novel by Henry James

The Wasp Woman ★★ PG
Science-fiction horror   1959 · US · BW · 72min

Cosmetics boss Susan Cabot uses wasp enzymes for a rejuvenation formula and turns into a blood-lusting bug-eyed monster in cult director Roger Corman's ironic rip-off of *The Fly*. It's pretty slow, and more ridiculous than frightening, but Cabot's coolly professional performance makes up for the cheapness of the production (the first to be made by Corman's own company, Filmgroup) and helps paper over the weak scripting. **AJ** **DVD**

Susan Cabot *Janice Starlin* • Fred Eisley [Anthony Eisley] *Bill Lane* • Barboura Morris *Mary Dennison* • Michael Mark *Dr Eric Zinthrop* • Frank Gerstle *Hellman* ■ *Dir* Roger Corman • *Scr* Leo Gordon

Waste Land ★★★★ PG
Documentary   2009 · Bra/UK · Colour · 98min

A film about extreme poverty, in which men and women are forced to make a living by foraging in the rubbish dumps of Rio de Janeiro, might seem to be a hard sell. But Lucy Walker's Oscar-nominated documentary doesn't dwell on the misery it finds in the worst slums of Brazil; instead it focuses on the work of artist Vik Muniz, who literally creates his incredible artworks from trash. Walker follows Muniz as he selects some of the workers to be his subjects, and the results are surprising. Not only does the film confirm the old maxim about not judging a book by its cover, it also here sidesteps the serious issues of exploitation that arise, ending on a seriously uplifting moment of optimism. **DW**

Portuguese, English +subtitles. Some swearing. **DVD**

Vik Muniz ■ *Dir* Lucy Walker, Joao Jardim, Karen Harley • *Music* Moby

The Watch ★★★ 15
Science-fiction comedy
2012 · US · Colour · 97min

This crude but often funny comedy stars Ben Stiller as a store manager who decides to form a neighbourhood watch group after his night security guard is murdered. Unfortunately, his call to action attracts only misfits: boorish sports fan Vince Vaughn, angry police reject Jonah Hill and oddball Richard Ayoade (*The IT Crowd*). The overall premise is a little on the flimsy side – think a smutty *Ghost Busters* set in the suburbs – but director Akiva Schaffer piles on the set pieces to keep things moving. **TeS** Violence, swearing, sex scenes. **DVD** **Blu**

Ben Stiller *Evan* • Vince Vaughn *Bob* • Jonah Hill *Franklin* • Richard Ayoade *Jamarcus* ■ *Dir* Akiva Schaffer • *Scr* Evan Goldberg, Seth Rogen, from a story by Jared Stern

Watch on the Rhine ★★★★★ U
Drama   1943 · US · BW · 107min

Lillian Hellman's hit 1941 play came to the screen directed by Herman Shumlin, responsible for the Broadway production, and retained much of its original stage cast. One of the most powerful and impassioned pleas for resistance to fascism in modern drama, the action takes place before the outbreak of the Second World War and involves German Paul Lukas, his American wife Bette Davis and their children, who, while staying with Davis's mother Lucille Watson, encounter dispossessed Romanian count George Coulouris. The film combines politics, heroism, poignancy, suspense and sophisticated wit to gripping effect. Lukas won the best actor Oscar, with picture, screenplay and Watson nominated. **RK**

Bette Davis *Sara Muller* • Paul Lukas *Kurt Muller* • Geraldine Fitzgerald *Marthe de Brancovis* • Lucile Watson *Fanny Farrelly* • Beulah Bondi *Anise* • George Coulouris *Teck de Brancovis* • Donald Woods *David Farrelly* ■ *Dir* Herman Shumlin • *Scr* Dashiell Hammett, Lillian Hellman, from the play by Lillian Hellman • *Music* Max Steiner • *Cinematographer* Hal Mohr

Watch the Birdie ★★ U
Comedy   1950 · US · BW · 70min

Although red-haired comic Red Skelton was one of MGM's top comedians, the studio executives never quite knew what to do with him, as this dreary remake of Buster Keaton's *The Cameraman* (1928) shows. In it, photographer Skelton inadvertently films a private conversation revealing a crooked scam and saves rich girl Arlene Dahl from financial ruin. Skelton insisted on also playing the roles of his father and grandfather, which was not a good idea. **TH**

Red Skelton *Rusty Cammeron/Pop Cammeron/Grandpop Cammeron* • Arlene Dahl *Lucia Corlane* • Ann Miller *Miss Lucky Vista* • Leon Ames *Grantland D Farns* • Pam Britton [Pamela Britton] *Mrs Shanway* • Richard Rober *Mr Shanway* ■ *Dir* Jack Donohue • *Scr* Ivan Tors, Devery Freeman, Harry Ruskin, from a story by Marshall Neilan Jr

Watch Your Stern ★★ PG
Comedy   1960 · UK · BW · 84min

Gerald Thomas's nautical comedy may be full of *Carry On* names on both sides of the camera, but it's a disappointing affair. There aren't all that many laughs as twitchy tar Connor assumes a range of disguises to cover up a blunder over torpedo plans. But the by-play between the characters is slick and there's some amusing slapstick. **DP** **DVD**

Kenneth Connor *Ordinary Seaman Blissworth* • Eric Barker *Captain David Foster* • Leslie Phillips *Lieutenant Commander Fanshawe* • Joan Sims *Ann Foster* • Hattie Jacques *Agatha Potter* • Spike Milligan *Dockyard mate* • Eric Sykes *Dockyard mate* • Sid James *Chief Petty Officer Mundy* • Ed Devereaux *Commander Phillips* • David Lodge *Security sergeant* ■

Dir Gerald Thomas • *Scr* Alan Hackney, Vivian A Cox, from the play *Something about a Sailor* by Earle Couttie

The Watcher ★★ 15
Psychological thriller
2000 · US · Colour · 92min

In this dismal thriller, Keanu Reeves portrays an FBI-taunting serial killer. Reeves plays the strangler who's relocated to Chicago to continue his game of psychological warfare with James Spader's troubled agent. There are a few creepy sequences, but pop video-maker and first-time director Joe Charbanic never manages to sustain a credible air of menace. **JF** Violence, swearing. **DVD**

James Spader *Joel Campbell* • Marisa Tomei *Polly* • Keanu Reeves *David Allen Griffin* • Ernie Hudson *Ibby* • Chris Ellis *Hollis* ■ *Dir* Joe Charbanic • *Scr* David Elliot, Clay Ayers, from a story by Darcy Meyers, David Elliot

The Watcher in the Woods ★★ PG
Supernatural drama
1982 · US/UK · Colour · 79min

Disney attempted to shake off its popcorn image with this tale of a composer's family moving into a mysterious cottage owned by sinister Bette Davis. But the psychic alien time-warp plot is too silly for adults and not daft enough to make it a proper children's treat. Director John Hough sustains the atmosphere quite well, despite ex-ice skater Lynn-Holly Johnson's bland central performance. Disney changed the climax after a disastrous test screening. **AJ** **DVD**

Bette Davis *Mrs Aylwood* • Carroll Baker *Helen Curtis* • David McCallum (1) *Paul Curtis* • Lynn-Holly Johnson *Jan Curtis* • Kyle Richards *Ellie Curtis* • Ian Bannen *John Keller* • Richard Pasco *Tom Colley* ■ *Dir* John Hough, Vincent McEveety • *Scr* Brian Clemens, Harry Spalding, Rosemary Anne Sisson, from the novel by Florence Engel Randall

Watchers ★ 18
Science-fiction horror
1988 · Can · Colour · 86min

Horror novelist Dean R Koontz was extremely unhappy with this adaptation of his work, though he had plenty of warning with bargain-basement producers Roger Corman and Damian Lee attaching themselves to the project. Corey Haim is cast as the teen hero who finds an extremely intelligent dog, not knowing that it is the result of a government experiment. **KB** **DVD**

Corey Haim *Travis* • Barbara Williams (2) *Nora* • Michael Ironside *Lem* • Lala Sloatman *Tracey* • Duncan Fraser *Sheriff Gaines* ■ *Dir* Jon Hess • *Scr* Bill Freed, Damian Lee, from the novel by Dean R Koontz

The Watchmaker of St Paul ★★★★ 12
Crime drama   1973 · Fr · Colour · 100min

Bertrand Tavernier made his feature debut with this reworking of Georges Simenon's US-set novella. The fact that it was co-scripted by veterans Jean Aurenche and Pierre Bost betrays Tavernier's desire to produce a literate picture in the "Tradition of Quality" mode. But there's no studio-bound realism here, as Tavernier captures the authentic Lyonnais atmosphere and uses his own birthplace as the setting for several key scenes. Philippe Noiret is superb as the watchmaker questioning both his bourgeois beliefs and his paternal value on learning of his son's involvement in a political killing. **DP** French +subtitles. **DVD**

Philippe Noiret *Michel Descombes* • Jean Rochefort *Inspector Guiboud* • Jacques Denis *Antoine* • Yves Afonso *Inspector Bricard* • Sylvain Rougerie *Bernard* • Christine Pascal *Liliane Torrini* ■ *Dir* Bertrand Tavernier • *Scr* Bertrand Tavernier, Jean Aurenche, Pierre Bost, from the novel *L'Horloger d'Everton* by Georges Simenon

Watchmen ★★★★ 18
Action fantasy thriller
2009 · US · Colour · 155min

This long-awaited adaptation of Alan Moore and Dave Gibbons's seminal comic-book

W

1376   **U** SUITABLE FOR ALL   **Uc** SUITABLE ESPECIALLY FOR YOUNG CHILDREN (DVD ONLY)   **PG** PARENTAL GUIDANCE   **12A** UNDER 12s TO BE ACCOMPANIED (CINEMA ONLY)

series is less faithful than totally obsessive – a fanboy's love letter to a complex, adult work that deconstructed the American superhero myth. Lifting whole frames from the source material, director Zack Snyder (*Man of Steel*) delivers a dark, violent epic set in an alternative 1980s in which America was victorious in Vietnam, Nixon remains president and masked crime fighters have been outlawed. It's here that a brutal mystery man investigates a "mask" murder and unravels a complex conspiracy. Hyper-stylised visuals capture the *noir*-like seediness of Moore's world brilliantly, with the opening credits a tour-de-force scene-setter for the events that follow. JR **DVD**

Malin Akerman *Laurie Jupiter/"Silk Spectre II"* • Billy Crudup *"Dr Manhattan"/Jon Osterman* • Matthew Goode *Adrian Veidt/"Ozymandias"* • Jackie Earle Haley *Rorschach* • Jeffrey Dean Morgan *Edward Blake/"Comedian"* • Patrick Wilson *Dan Dreiberg/"Nite Owl" II* • Carla Gugino *Sally Jupiter/"Silk Spectre"* • Matt Frewer *Edgar Jacobi/Moloch the Mystic* ■ *Dir* Zack Snyder • *Scr* David Hayter, Alex Tse, from the graphic novel by Alan Moore (uncredited), Dave Gibbons

Water ★ 15
Comedy   1985 · UK · Colour · 93min

One of the disasters that sank HandMade Films, this stars Michael Caine as a British diplomat on a West Indian island awash with communist insurrection and Americans dredging mineral water. Intended as a satire on the Falklands and Grenada, it falls flat in all departments. AT Swearing. **DVD**

Michael Caine *Baxter Thwaites* • Valerie Perrine *Pamela* • Brenda Vaccaro *Dolores* • Leonard Rossiter *Sir Malcolm Leveridge* • Billy Connolly *Delgado* • Dennis Duggan *Rob* • Fulton Mackay *Eric* • Jimmie Walker *Jay Jay* • Dick Shawn *Deke Halliday* • Fred Gwynne *Spender* • Maureen Lipman *Prime minister* • Ruby Wax *Spenco executive* ■ *Dir* Dick Clement • *Scr* Dick Clement, Ian La Frenais, Bill Persky, from a story by Bill Persky

Water ★★★ 12
Period drama   2005 · Can/US · Colour · 117min

The final film in controversial director Deepa Mehta's loosely themed "elemental" trilogy – following *Fire* (1996) and *Earth* (1998) – is a lush weepie that shines an unflattering light on certain aspects of traditional Hindu culture. The subject is the treatment of widows, who, according to custom, were often forbidden from remarrying and were instead housed together in segregated communities. Set in the 1930s, this drama focuses on eight-year-old child bride Chuyia (the captivating if a little precocious Sarala), who is quickly widowed and must adapt to a strange new life with a group of older women in the same boat. It's overly melodramatic at times, but it looks gorgeous and ultimately offers a moving indictment of what was a deplorable practice. JF Hindi +subtitles.

Seema Biswas *Shakuntala* • Lisa Ray *Kalyani* • John Abraham *Narayan* • Sarala *Chuyia* • Manorma [Manorama] *Madhumati* • Dr Vidula Javalgekar [Vidula Javalgekar] *Patiraji/Auntie* ■ *Dir/Scr* Deepa Mehta

The Water Babies ★ U
Part-animated fantasy adventure
1978 · UK/Pol · Colour · 81min

Combining cartoon and live action, this is a ghastly adaptation of the Charles Kingsley classic. Admitted y, director Lionel Jeffries had to revert to animation to tell the tale of a young chimney sweep who rescues a group of underwater children from a tyrannical shark. But the cartooning is bland, the voicing of the sea creatures and the water babies too cute and the songs are a disgrace. DP **DVD**

James Mason *Grimes* • Billie Whitelaw *Mrs Doasyouwouldbedoneby* • Tommy Pender *Tom* • Bernard Cribbins *Masterman* • Joan Greenwood *Lady Harriet* • David Tomlinson *Sir John* • Samantha Gates *Ellie* • Paul Luty *Sladd* ■ *Dir* Lionel Jeffries • *Scr* Michael Robson, from the novel by Charles Kingsley

The Water Diviner ★★★ 15
Period drama   2014 · Aus/US · Colour · 106min

Russell Crowe makes a sure-footed if unadventurous debut as director with this tale of a father in search of the bodies of his three sons, all of whom were lost during the bloody and futile battle at Gallipoli. Crowe has had the good sense to surround himself with top drawer technical talent: the cinematography by Andrew Lesnie (*Lord of the Rings*) is positively luminous, and David Hirschfelder's score is haunting and subtle. But, although it is sometimes moving, the film takes few risks, while the screenplay's sudden hairpin-turn into Hollywood happy ending territory uncoes more than a little of what's gone before. AS **DVD**

Russell Crowe *Joshua Connor* • Olga Kurylenko *Ayshe* • Yilmaz Erdogan *Major Hasan* • Cem Yilmaz *Sergeant Jemel* • Jai Courtney *Lt Col Hughes* • Ryan Corr *Arthur "Art" Connor* • Dan Wyllie *Captain Brindley*

Water Drops on Burning Rocks ★★★ 18
Drama   1999 · Fr/Jpn · Colour · 85min

Written when he was 19 yet unperformed in his lifetime, Rainer Werner Fassbinder's first full-length play is here artfully translated to the screen by iconoclastic director François Ozon. The highly charged action chronicles bisexual Bernard Girardeau's relationships with a callow youth, the youth's naive girlfriend and his own transsexual ex-wife. The film is made notable by Ozon's fidelity to Fassbinder's cinematic style and in his treatment of the characters as marionettes at the mercy of the story's twists and turns. DP French, German +subtitles. Swearing. **DVD**

Bernard Giraudeau *Léopold Blum* • Malik Zidi *Franz Meister* • Ludivine Sagnier *Anna* • Anna Thomson [Anna Levine] *Véra* ■ *Dir* François Ozon • *Scr* François Ozon, from the play *Tropfen auf Heisse Steine* by Rainer Werner Fassbinder

Water for Elephants ★★ 12
Period romantic drama
2011 · US · Colour · 115min

This romantic melodrama in the mould of *The Greatest Show on Earth* – but with digital effects – is pitched at a tween audience with its sly casting of Robert Pattinson. (You can imagine the pitch: "The kid from *Twilight* – on an elephant!") Told in flashback to the Depression, it finds Pattinson's student landing a job as a vet with a circus where he falls for Reese Witherspoon's horsewoman, wife of cruel owner Christoph Waltz, and torrid events ensue. Director Francis Lawrence assembles the material well enough, but the stars talents are wasted in what is a wishy-washy attempt at old-school entertainment. AC Some violence, brief nudity. **DVD**

Reese Witherspoon *Marlena* • Robert Pattinson *Jacob* • Christoph Waltz *August* • Paul Schneider (2) *Charlie* • Jim Norton *Camel* • Hal Holbrook *Old Jacob* • Mark Povinelli *Kinko/Walter* • James Frain *Rosie's caretaker* ■ *Dir* Francis Lawrence • *Scr* Richard LaGravenese, from the novel by Sarah Gruen

The Water Horse ★★★★ PG
Fantasy adventure
2007 · US/UK · Colour · 107min

The myth of the Loch Ness Monster is the starting point for this charming fantasy adventure. Set in the Scottish Highlands during the Second World War, it's the story of a lonely young boy called Angus (Alex Etel), who discovers a mysterious egg near the local loch. He takes it home and it hatches into a cute little monster that soon outgrows the house. There are similarities here to *ET* – particularly as Angus attempts to conceal the beastie from his mum (Emily Watson). But Jay Russell's film also treats its audience with a degree of sophistication, particularly in the boy's growing realisation that his father may not be coming home from the war. A few sequences here may be too alarming for very young children, but otherwise this is almost perfect family entertainment. AS **DVD**

Emily Watson *Anne MacMorrow* • Alex Etel *Angus MacMorrow* • Ben Chaplin *Lewis Mowbray* • David Morrissey *Captain Hamilton* • Brian Cox (1) *Old Angus* • Marshall Napier *Sgt Strunk* • Joel Tobeck *Sgt Walker* • Bruce Allpress *Jock McGowan* ■ *Dir* Jay Russell • *Scr* Robert Nelson Jacobs, from the novel by Dick King-Smith • *Cinematographer* Oliver Stapleton

Water Lilies ★★★★ 15
Coming-of-age drama
2007 · Fr · Colour · 80min

The debut feature of director Céline Sciamma captures the agonies of first love with a perceptive charm that cleverly exploits the teenage protagonists' obsession with synchronised swimming. Blonde beauty Adèle Haenel is not only the star of the swim team, but she's also dating handsome Warren Jacquin. However, she comes to rely upon adoring waif Pauline Acquart, whose sudden sense of importance to another causes her to neglect podgy pal Louise Blachère. Whether bitching or flirting, pursuing their desires or exposing their vulnerability, the female leads are superb. But it's Sciamma's insights into adolescent angst that infuse this offbeat rite-of-passage tale with such emotional depth and unassuming wit. DP French +subtitles. **DVD**

Pauline Acquart *Marie* • Louise Blachère *Anne* • Adèle Haenel *Floriane* • Warren Jacquin *François* • Barbara Renard *Natacha* • Christel Baras [Christelle Baras] *The inspector* ■ *Dir/Scr* Céline Sciamma

The Waterboy ★★★ 12
Sports comedy   1998 · US · Colour · 86min

Incredibly dumb but equally endearing, this stars Adam Sandler as a lowly, put-upon dispenser of water to sweaty college footballers. One day, their abuse (this time about his beloved Cajun mum, Kathy Bates) is just too much and he strikes back by charging one of the players, so impressing the coach that he ends up on the team. Featuring great performances from Bates and Henry Winkler, this popular hit allows Sandler to put his modest comedic talent to good use. JB Swearing, nudity. **DVD**

Adam Sandler *Bobby Boucher* • Kathy Bates *Mama Boucher* • Henry Winkler *Coach Klein* • Fairuza Balk *Vicki Vallencourt* • Jerry Reed *Red Beaulieu* • Larry Gilliard Jr *Derek Wallace* • Blake Clark *Farmer Fran* • Peter Dante *Gee Grenouille* ■ *Dir* Frank Coraci • *Scr* Tim Herlihy, Adam Sandler

The Waterdance ★★★ 15
Drama   1991 · US · Colour · 102min

This gritty, syrup-free movie is about a disparate group of young men attempting to come to terms with the fact that they will be paralysed for the rest of their lives. As a young novelist who has an accident on a hiking holiday and slowly puts his life back together, Eric Stoltz is excellent in the lead, with Wesley Snipes and William Forsythe equally good as two fellow paraplegics. A well-acted, moving and often witty tour through a variety of fears and neuroses. JF Violence, swearing, nudity.

Eric Stoltz *Joel Garcia* • Wesley Snipes *Raymond Hill* • William Forsythe *Bloss* • Helen Hunt *Anna* • Elizabeth Peña *Rosa* • William Allen Young *Les* • Henry Harris *Mr Gibson* ■ *Dir* Neal Jimenez, Michael Steinberg • *Scr* Neal Jimenez

Waterfront ★★★ PG
Drama   1950 · UK · BW · 77min

Having co-directed *Private Angelo*, Michael Anderson went solo with this sobering portrait of Liverpool in the Depression. The film is undeniably melodramatic, yet it has a surprisingly raw naturalism that suggests the influence of both Italian neorealism and the proud British documentary tradition. As the seaman whose drunken binges mean misery for his family and trouble for his shipmates, Robert Newton reins in his tendency for excess, and he receives solid support from the ever-dependable Kathleen Harrison and a young Richard Burton, in his third feature. DP **DVD**

Robert Newton *Peter McCabe* • Kathleen Harrison *Mrs McCabe* • Richard Burton *Ben Satterthwaite* • Avis Scott *Nora McCabe* • Susan Shaw *Connie McCabe* • Robin Netscher *George Alexander* • Kenneth Griffith *Maurice Bruno* ■ *Dir* Michael Anderson • *Scr* John Brophy, Paul Soskin, from the novel by John Brophy

Waterhole #3 ★★★ 15
Comedy western   1967 · US · Colour · 91min

Where else would you expect a western about deception, ambition and naked greed to be set but in Integrity, Arizona? James Coburn becomes the hero of this comedy tale by dint of the fact that he is marginally less repellent than his rivals, all scouring this particular desert watering hole for the proceeds of a gold robbery. The ever-vivacious Joan Blondell is on sparkling form as an avaricious madam, while Carroll O'Connor hams up a storm as a sheriff with some personal views on upholding the law. DP **DVD**

James Coburn *Lewton Cole* • Carroll O'Connor *Sheriff John Copperud* • Margaret Blye [Maggie Blye] *Billee Copperud* • Claude Akins *Sgt Henry Foggers* • Timothy Carey *Hilb* • Joan Blondell *Lavinia* • Robert Cornthwaite *George* • Bruce Dern *Deputy Sheriff* • James Whitmore *Captain Shipley* ■ *Dir* William Graham [William A Graham] • *Scr* Joseph T Steck, Robert R Young

Waterland ★★ 15
Drama   1992 · UK · Colour · 89min

Based on Graham Swift's Booker short-listed novel, this was very much a pet project of Jeremy Irons who stars with his wife Sinead Cusack. The story charts the emotional collapse of a teacher and his wife who grew up on the flat marshlands of the East Anglian fens. This landscape, superbly captured, serves to underline the characters as they flash back and forward through the bleak wreckage of their lives, all for the benefit of Irons's American students. Earnest, unpleasant and tedious. AT Swearing, nudity. **DVD**

Jeremy Irons *Tom Crick* • Sinead Cusack *Mary Crick* • Ethan Hawke *Mathew Price* • Grant Warnock *Young Tom* • Lena Headey *Young Mary* • David Morrissey *Dick Crick* • John Heard *Lewis Scott* • Callum Dixon *Freddie Parr* ■ *Dir* Stephen Gyllenhaal • *Scr* Peter Prince, from Graham Swift's novel

Waterloo ★★★★ U
Historical epic   1970 · It/USSR · Colour · 128min

Rod Steiger gives a magnificent performance as Napoleon - all hot rages and cool calculation - as he heads for his destiny in Belgium in Ukrainian director Sergei Bondarchuk's epic history lesson. Steiger even manages to upstage the thousands of Soviet soldiers recruited as extras for the battle scenes, yet he's nearly outshone by Christopher Plummer as the Duke of Wellington, whose arrogance shows his contempt for cannon-fodder. Bondarchuk filmed in Italy and the Ukraine, and the result is a mightily credible reconstruction of a crunch-point that changed the course of history. TH **DVD**

Rod Steiger *Napoleon Bonaparte* • Christopher Plummer *Duke of Wellington* • Orson Welles *Louis XVIII* • Jack Hawkins *General Thomas Picton* • Virginia McKenna *Duchess of Richmond* • Dan O'Herlihy *Marshal Michel Ney* • Michael Wilding *Sir William Ponsonby* • Donald Donnelly [Donal Donnelly] *Private O'Connor* • Terence Alexander *Lord Uxbridge* ■ *Dir* Sergei Bondarchuk • *Scr* HAL Craig, Sergei Bondarchuk, Vittorio Bonicelli

Waterloo Bridge ★★
Romantic war melodrama
1931 · US · BW · 72min

The first screen version of Robert Sherwood's play about the doomed love affair between an army officer and a young woman of questionable morals sits respectably in the canon of early 1930s woman's weepie melodramas, but it isn't a patch on the truly heart-rending MGM remake nine years later. It does, however, feature a strong performance from Mae Clarke as the tragic heroine, and a very early role for Bette Davis. RK

Mae Clarke *Myra Deauville* • Kent Douglass [Douglass Montgomery] *Roy Cronin* • Doris Lloyd *Kitty* • Frederick Kerr *Major Wetherby* • Enid Bennett *Mrs Wetherby* • Bette Davis *Janet Cronin*

W

• Ethel Griffies *Mrs Hobley* ▪ *Dir* James Whale • *Scr* Tom Reed, from the play by Robert E Sherwood

Waterloo Bridge ★★★★ PG
Romantic war melodrama
1940 · US · BW · 104min

This was the second version of Robert E Sherwood's celebrated stage play of star-crossed lovers to make it to the screen, and MGM director Mervyn LeRoy went for an unashamedly tear-jerking approach, even though the Hollywood prudishness of the day forced him to draw some of the sting from the story. Vivien Leigh gives a heartbreaking performance as the ballerina who falls in love with army captain Robert Taylor during a First World War air raid, only to be driven on to the streets after she is misinformed of his death. Taylor was never more handsome, and there's sterling support from Hollywood's British colony. DP

Vivien Leigh *Myra Lester* • Robert Taylor (1) *Captain Roy Cronin* • Lucile Watson *Lady Margaret Cronin* • Virginia Field *Kitty* • Maria Ouspenskaya *Madame Olga Kirowa* • C Aubrey Smith *Duke* • Janet Shaw *Maureen* • Janet Waldo *Elsa* ▪ *Dir* Mervyn LeRoy • *Scr* SN Behrman, Hans Rameau, George Froeschel, from the play by Robert E Sherwood

Waterloo Road ★★ PG
Wartime drama
1944 · UK · BW · 72min

This is best remembered today as the wartime movie with a terrific fist-fighting climax as tiny John Mills beats up his wife's lover, six-foot-plus spiv Stewart Granger. If you believe that, you'll probably believe in the rest of this atypically stodgy Sidney Gilliat production. Told in a rather woolly flashback structure by Alastair Sim's kindly philosophising doctor, the plot is extremely realistic for its day, but Arthur Crabtree's stark photography fails to disguise the cramped studio interiors used for much of the film. TS

John Mills *Jim Colter* • Stewart Granger *Ted Purvis* • Alastair Sim *Dr Montgomery* • Joy Shelton *Tillie Colter* • Beatrice Varley *Mrs Colter* • Alison Leggatt *Ruby* • Leslie Bradley *Mike Duggan* ▪ *Dir* Sidney Gilliat • *Scr* Val Valentine, from a story by Sidney Gilliat

Watermelon Man ★★★
Comedy drama
1970 · US · Colour · 99min

Bigoted white insurance salesman Godfrey Cambridge wakes up one morning to find he has turned black overnight. The transformation, which baffles doctors, sees Cambridge being ostracised by his friends and family, and having to seek a new life in the black community. Melvin Van Peebles's savage satire may have dated but its message (hammered home in Herman Raucher's script) is still potent. Comedian Godfrey Cambridge is marvellous in the lead. DF

Godfrey Cambridge *Jeff Gerber* • Estelle Parsons *Althea Gerber* • Howard Caine *Mr Townsend* • D'Urville Martin *Bus driver* • Mantan Moreland *Counterman* • Kay Kimberly *Erica* • Kay E Kuter *Dr Wainwright* • Scott Garrett *Burton Gerber* • Erin Moran *Janice Gerber* ▪ *Dir* Melvin Van Peebles • *Scr* Herman Raucher • *Music* Melvin Van Peebles

The Watermelon Woman ★★ 15
Comedy drama
1996 · US · Colour · 80min

It might have won the Teddy Bear for the best gay film at the 1996 Berlin festival, but Cheryl Dunye's fictional documentary is too inward-looking for its own good. Hollywood's denial of opportunity to black (let alone gay and lesbian) performers in the 1930s and 40s is certainly a topic worthy of discussion. But Dunye's pursuit of the "watermelon woman", a character actress she keeps spotting in old movies, gets tangled up too often in her relationships with her friend and a new white lover. DP

Cheryl Dunye *Cheryl* • Guinevere Turner *Diana* • Valerie Walker *Tamara* • Lisa Marie Bronson *Fae "The Watermelon Woman" Richards* • Irene Dunye • Brian Freeman *Lee Edwards* • Ira Jeffries *Shirley Hamilton* • Camille Paglia ▪ *Dir/Scr* Cheryl Dunye

Watership Down ★★★ U
Animation
1978 · UK · Colour · 87min

This animated version of Richard Adams's bestselling novel about a group of rabbits searching for a new home was a box-office success, despite the difficulty of being pigeonholed as a "kids' movie" but released with a PG certificate (for several genuinely scary scenes). In fact, its faithful retelling of the story gives the movie a dark sophistication that will attract older children and their parents. The visual style is ambitious, and the voice cast is truly impressive, with telling contributions from John Hurt, Ralph Richardson, Denholm Elliott, Richard Briers and a bonkers Zero Mostel as the seagull Kehaar. TF

John Hurt *Hazel* • Richard Briers *Fiver* • Michael Graham-Cox *Bigwig* • John Bennett *Captain Holly* • Ralph Richardson *Chief Rabbit* • Simon Cadell *Blackberry* • Terence Rigby *Silver* • Roy Kinnear *Pipkin* • Hannah Gordon *Hyzenthlay* • Zero Mostel *Kehaar* • Michael Hordern *Frith* ▪ *Dir* Martin Rosen • *Scr* Martin Rosen, from the novel by Richard Adams

Waterworld ★★★★ 12
Futuristic adventure 1995 · US · Colour · 129min

Declared dead in the water owing to escalating costs, nightmarish production problems and clashing egos, Kevin Reynolds's lavish *Mad Max* on jet-skis emerged as a spectacular and thrilling sci-fi fantasy. In the far future, the polar icecaps have melted, covering the entire planet in water and making dirt the most valuable commodity. Only the enigmatic loner Kevin Costner offers a ray of hope to Jeanne Tripplehorn and Tina Majorino. He battles bandits led by Dennis Hopper and continues his search to find the one piece of mythical Dryland. Costner gives one of his finest performances and holds the epic adventure together. AJ Violence, swearing, nudity.

Kevin Costner *Mariner* • Dennis Hopper *Deacon* • Jeanne Tripplehorn *Helen* • Tina Majorino *Enola* • Michael Jeter *Gregor* • Gerard Murphy *Nord* • RD Call *Enforcer* ▪ *Dir* Kevin Reynolds • *Scr* Peter Rader, David Twohy, Joss Whedon (uncredited) • *Cinematographer* Dean Semler

Wattstax ★★★
Documentary 1972 · US · Colour · 101min

This is a filmed record of the 1972 benefit concert held at the Los Angeles Coliseum to raise money for the Watts community on the seventh anniversary of the violent riots. Amusingly emceed by Richard Pryor, the impressive roster of black soul and R&B acts includes the Dramatics, the Staple Singers, Carla Thomas, William Bell, Kim Weston and the Bar-Kays. The highlights are Isaac Hayes belting out *Shaft*, Rufus Thomas doing the *Funky Chicken* and the Reverend Jesse Jackson singing *I Am Somebody*. AJ

▪ *Dir* Mel Stuart

The Wave ★★★★ 15
Psychological drama
2008 · Ger · Colour · 102min

Dennis Gansel's film transposes the extraordinary story of an American high-school experiment to contemporary Germany. In 1967, a teacher in the Californian city of Palo Alto gave his class a demonstration of how the will of the individual gave way to collective discipline in Nazi Germany by transforming them into an unquestioningly obedient unit known as "The Third Wave". Revisiting that controversial and not exactly scientific project, here teacher Rainer Wenger (Jürgen Vogel) is put in charge of a bored class of kids studying autocracy as part of a history course. DW German +subtitles. Violence, swearing.

Frederick Lau *Tim* • Max Riemelt *Marco* • Jennifer Ulrich *Karo* • Christiane Paul *Anke Wenger* • Elyas M'Barek *Sinan* • Cristina Do Rego *Lisa* • Jacob Matschenz *Dennis* ▪ *Dir* Dennis Gansel • *Scr* Dennis Gansel, Peter Thorwarth, from the 1981 film

The Way ★★★ 12
Drama 2010 · US/Sp/UK · Colour · 123min

Emilio Estevez directs his real-life father, Martin Sheen, in this uplifting film about journeys both physical and spiritual. Sheen stars as an American doctor who backpacks the world-famous Camino de Santiago pilgrimage route in memory of his son (played by Estevez), who died while walking it. In the process, and with the help of a motley bunch of fellow pilgrims (including

Waveriders ★★★ PG
Sports documentary
2008 · UK/Ire · Colour · 75min

This documentary traces the surprising Irish influence on surfing, starting with the pioneering George Freeth, the Hawaiian-born son of an Irish immigrant who helped popularise the sport in the early 20th century. The film then follows the sport to its modern-day incarnation, as practised along the spectacular Northern Irish coast near Mullaghmore. As with all surfing documentaries since the grandaddy of them all, 1964's *The Endless Summer*, this relies on stunning cinematography together with a mounting anticipation of catching the really big breaks - which here are generated by 50-foot swells, the biggest ever ridden in Ireland. AS

Cillian Murphy *Narrator* ▪ *Dir* Joel Conroy • *Scr* Joel Conroy, Lauren Davies

Wax Mask ★★ 18
Horror 1997 · It · Colour · 94min

A nostalgic salute to vintage Hammer horror by way of *House of Wax* and souped up with extra gore and kinky sex, this car-boot-sale chiller is a luridly engaging if shoddy shocker. Robert Hossein is the Roman wax museum owner hiding dark secrets and a scarred face behind masks that allow him to masquerade as every other cast member in the convoluted whodunnit plot. AJ In Italian. Violence, sex scenes, swearing.

Robert Hossein *Boris* • Romina Mondello *Sonia* • Riccardo Serventi Longhi *Andrea* • Gabriella Giogelli *Francesca* • Umberto Balli *Alex* ▪ *Dir* Sergio Stivaletti • *Scr* Lucio Fulci, Daniele Stroppa, from a story by Dario Argento, from the novel *The Wax Museum* by Gaston Leroux

Waxwork ★★ 18
Horror 1988 · US · Colour and BW · 93min

When a mysterious waxworks museum appears overnight in a small town, its sinister owner invites a group of teens to a special midnight showing. The youngsters are then sucked into the wax tableaux to meet a grisly doom. Director Anthony Hickox certainly has tongue firmly in cheek, but his pastiches of old-time movie monsters such as Dracula and the Mummy lack wit and soon become repetitive. A sequel followed in 1992. RS Violence

Zach Galligan *Mark* • Deborah Foreman *Sarah* • Michelle Johnson *China* • Dana Ashbrook *Tony* • Miles O'Keeffe *Count Dracula* • Patrick Macnee *Sir Wilfred* • David Warner *Mr Lincoln* • John Rhys-Davies *Werewolf* ▪ *Dir/Scr* Anthony Hickox

Waxworks ★★★★
Silent gothic horror 1924 · Ger · BW · 93min

Paul Leni's last film in Germany before continuing on his chilly way to America is also one of his best, and gives us a chance to see four of Germany's finest actors in their earlier days. Wilhelm Dieterle, who was to become a renowned Hollywood director, plays a young poet who tells three stories behind three exhibits in a wax museum: Haroun-al-Raschid (Emil Jannings), Ivan the Terrible (Conrad Veidt) and Jack the Ripper (Werner Krauss). The expressionist designs are symbolic of character and plot, creating a haunting atmosphere. RB

Wilhelm Dieterle [William Dieterle] *Young poet/Assad/Groom* • Emil Jannings *Haroun-al-Raschid* • Conrad Veidt *Ivan the Terrible* • Werner Krauss *Jack the Ripper, "Spring Heeled Jack"* • Olga Belajeff *Showman's daughter/Zarah/Bride* • John Gottowt *Showman* ▪ *Dir* Paul Leni • *Scr* Henrik Galeen • *Cinematographer* Helmar Lerski • *Art Directors* Paul Leni, Fritz Maurischat

James Nesbitt as an Irish writer), he rediscovers his own sense of identity and reconnects with the son he lost. Like its pilgrims, the film does rather plod, but Sheen is on good form, the Basque-country locations look great, and the gentle, meditative messages put out make this hard to dislike. DA Some drug abuse.

Martin Sheen *Tom* • Emilio Estevez *Daniel* • Deborah Kara Unger *Sarah* • James Nesbitt *Jack* • Tcheky Karyo *Captain Henri* ▪ *Dir/Scr* Emilio Estevez

The Way Ahead ★★★★ U
Second World War drama
1944 · UK · BW · 109min

This is one of the finest flag-wavers produced in Britain during the Second World War. From Eric Ambler and Peter Ustinov's script, director Carol Reed, who had earned a reputation for social realism in the mid-1930s and had spent part of the war making army documentaries, creates a totally believable world in which a squad of raw recruits becomes an integral part of the local community as they go through basic training. David Niven is top-billed, but he enters into the ensemble spirit that makes this beautifully observed drama as uplifting today as it was in 1944. DP

David Niven *Lieutenant Jim Perry* • Raymond Huntley *Davenport* • Billy Hartnell [William Hartnell] *Sergeant Fletcher* • Stanley Holloway *Brewer* • James Donald *Lloyd* • John Laurie *Luke* • Leslie Dwyer *Beck* • Hugh Burden *Parsons* • Jimmy Hanley *Stainer* • Renee Ascherson [Renée Asherson] *Marjorie Gillingham* ▪ *Dir* Carol Reed • *Scr* Eric Ambler, Peter Ustinov, from a story by Eric Ambler

The Way Back ★★ 12
Second World War drama based on a true story
2010 · US · Colour · 127min

Peter Weir's grim but beautifully photographed drama is based on the true story of a group of prisoners who broke out of a Siberian gulag during the Second World War and faced a relentless journey over thousands of miles to find safety. Jim Sturgess, Ed Harris and Colin Farrell are among the motley crew whose survival instincts develop into a powerful bond as they cross the harshest of terrain - picking up a young female refugee (Saoirse Ronan) on the way. But as extraordinary as the real-life source material may be, Weir stumbles into too many cinematic triumph-over-adversity clichés and the film loses pace over its lengthy running time. TeS Violence.

Jim Sturgess *Janusz* • Ed Harris *Mr Smith* • Colin Farrell (2) *Valka* • Saoirse Ronan *Irena* • Mark Strong *Khabarov* • Gustaf Skarsgard *Voss* ▪ *Dir* Peter Weir • *Scr* Peter Weir, Keith Clarke, from the memoir *The Long Walk: the True Story of a Trek to Freedom* by Slavomir Rawicz

Way Down East ★★★★★ U
Silent melodrama
1920 · US · BW Tinted · 144min

Lillian Gish, at her most lovely and moving, is the innocent and trusting young country girl tricked into a fake marriage by wealthy, womanising wastrel Lowell Sherman, who leaves her pregnant. The baby dies and the destitute girl finds employment with fanatically religious farmer Burr McIntosh, whose son Richard Barthelmess falls in love with Gish. DW Griffith's film is a miracle of visual composition, brilliantly acted, with Gish giving one of the most eloquent performances of the silent screen. Justly celebrated for the climactic sequence where Gish, drifting unconscious on a raft of ice in a storm, is rescued by Barthelmess, the film offers many moments just as memorable. RK DW

Lillian Gish *Anna Moore* • Richard Barthelmess *David Bartlett* • Mrs David Landau *Anna's mother* • Lowell Sherman *Lennox Sanderson* • Burr McIntosh *Squire Bartlett* • Josephine Bernard *Mrs Tremont* • Norma Shearer *Barn dancer* ▪ *Dir* DW Griffith • *Scr* Anthony Paul Kelly, from the play *Annie Laurie* by Lottie Blair Parker • *Cinematographers* GW Bitzer [Billy Bitzer], Hendrik Sartov, Paul H Allen

Way Down East ★★

Melodrama   1935 · US · BW · 84min

Fifteen years after the silent collaboration of DW Griffith and Lillian Gish, Fox handed a sound version to Henry King and Rochelle Hudson, with Henry Fonda in the Richard Barthelmess role. King's work is all right, especially his re-creation of the ice-river climax, but Hudson is no match for Gish, leaving the honours to Fonda in a much smaller role. The major problem though, is the material, which, by the mid-1930s, played as outmoded melodrama. RK

Rochelle Hudson *Anna Moore* · Henry Fonda *David Bartlett* · Slim Summerville *Constable Seth Holcomb* · Edward Trevor *Lennox Sanderson* · Margaret Hamilton *Martha Perkins* · Russell Simpson *Squire Bartlett* · Spring Byington *Mrs Bartlett* ■ *Dir* Henry King · *Scr* Howard Estabrook, William Hurlbut, from the 1920 film by Anthony Paul Kelly

Way of a Gaucho ★★★ U

Western   1952 · US · Colour · 90min

Director Jacques Tourneur was a dab hand at many styles of film-making. Out West, he responded to the landscape with a natural eye, turning out this clever but forgotten Argentinian-set western. Although not ideally cast, Rory Calhoun does well as the disaffected gaucho of the title, who greets the arrival of civilisation on the pampas by organising outlaw resistance. It's an interesting concept, and Tourneur's direction is striking. TS

Rory Calhoun *Martin* · Gene Tierney *Teresa* · Richard Boone *Salinas* · Hugh Marlowe *Miguel* · Everett Sloane *Falcon* ■ *Dir* Jacques Tourneur · *Scr* Philip Dunne, from the novel by Herbert Childs

The Way of All Flesh ★★★★

Silent melodrama   1927 · US · BW · 90min

The great German actor Emil Jannings, in his first American film, stars as a respectable bank clerk - a model husband and father of six - who, en route to delivering a package of bonds in Chicago, is conned by a girl and her criminal boyfriend. The latter is killed by a passing train. Jannings changes places with the dead man and then disappears, an act which leads to his steady descent into the gutter. Jannings won the first ever Oscar jointly for his full-blooded performances in this and *The Last Command*. RK

Emil Jannings *August Schiller* · Belle Bennett *Mrs Schiller* · Phyllis Haver *Mayme* · Donald Keith *August Jr* · Fred Kohler *The Tough* ■ *Dir* Victor Fleming · *Scr* Jules Furthman, Lajos Biró, Julian Johnson (titles)

The Way of All Flesh ★★

Melodrama   1940 · US · BW · 85min

Louis King directs and Akim Tamiroff stars in this pointless remake of the 1927 film. Stripped of the more awesomely melodramatic aspects that proved effective in the silent version, this tale of a respectable bank cashier who goes to the dogs in the big city, leaving his wife (the wonderful Gladys George) and family to nurse their memories, is competent, but dated and all-too predictable. RK

Akim Tamiroff *Paul Kriza Sr* · Gladys George *Anna Kriza* · William Henry *Paul Jr* · John Hartley *Victor Kriza* · Marilyn Knowlden *Julie Kriza* · Betty McLaughlin *Mitzi Kriza* ■ *Dir* Louis King · *Scr* Lenore Coffee, from the 1927 film by Jules Furthman, Lajos Biró

A Way of Life ★★★ 15

Drama   2004 · UK · Colour · 87min

This is a relentlessly dispiriting portrait of life among the underprivileged in Britain from debuting director Amma Asante. Newcomer Stephanie James delivers a blistering performance as the teenage single mum on a South Wales estate who blames everyone for her destitution while refusing to accept responsibility for any of her actions. By stressing the desperation and irrationality of James's crimes, Asante draws attention to the creeping resentment that is fuelling racism in so many deprived environments in 21st-century Britain. DP Swearing, violence, sex scenes. *DVD*

Brenda Blethyn *Annette* · Stephanie James *Leigh-Anne Williams* · Nathan Jones *Gavin Williams* · Gary Sheppeard *Robbie Matthews* · Dean Wong *Stephen Rajan* · Sara Gregory *Julie Osman* · Oliver Haden *Hassan Osman* ■ *Dir/Scr* Amma Asante

The Way of the Dragon ★★★ 18

Martial arts adventure   1973 · HK · Colour · 94min

This was the only film martial arts icon Bruce Lee had complete control over, being director, writer and fight choreographer. In a desperately thin tale, Lee arrives in Rome to help out at a Chinese restaurant that's at the mercy of local gangsters. It's typical of its genre; the dubbing is lousy, the characters are mere ciphers, and there are too many clumsy comedy routines. However, the action more than compensates: Lee's face-off with Chuck Norris inside the Colosseum is one of the best two-man scraps in movie history. RS Cantonese dubbed. Violence. *DVD* *Blu-ray*

Bruce Lee *Tang Lung* · Nora Miao *Chen Ching Hua* · Chuck Norris *Colt* · Wang Chung Hsin *Uncle Wang* · Tong Liu *Tony* · Ti Chin *Ah K'ung* · Jon T Benn *Boss* · Robert Wall *Robert, Colt's pupil* ■ *Dir/Scr* Bruce Lee

The Way of the Gun ★★★ 18

Crime drama   2000 · US · Colour · 114min

Outrageous, unrelenting and blood-soaked, the directorial debut of Christopher McQuarrie - the Oscar-winning screenwriter of *The Usual Suspects* - is a quirky crime thriller. McQuarrie's visceral ode to contemporary cowboys is an edgy and smartly cynical treat for those who like raw action and provocative themes. Small-time villains Ryan Phillippe and Benicio Del Toro abduct flaky surrogate mother Juliette Lewis in order to hold the wealthy parents-to-be to ransom. Unfortunately for the crooked duo, the expectant father has underworld connections. AJ *DVD*

Ryan Phillippe *Parker* · Benicio Del Toro *Longbaugh* · Juliette Lewis *Robin* · James Caan *Sarno* · Taye Diggs *Jeffers* · Nicky Katt *Obecks* · Scott Wilson *Hale Chidduck* ■ *Dir/Scr* Christopher McQuarrie

Way of the Morris ★★★ 12A

Documentary   2011 · UK · Colour · 70min

Morris dancing is often more the stuff of mockery than a serious folk tradition. But, as actor/writer/director Tim Plester discovers in this affectionate documentary, there's more to prancing around in bells, baldrics and black top hats than meets the eye. Having resisted the urge to follow a family tradition, Plester is persuaded to dance with the Adderbury Village Morris Men after their pilgrimage to the Somme to pay tribute to the locals whose demise during the Great War helped curtail a centuries-old tradition. Plester's growing realisation of the cultural and communal significance of Morris make this as affecting as grandfather Harold Plester's old home movies. DP *DVD*

Billy Bragg · MyAnna Buring *Will-O'-Wisps* · Chris Leslie · Donald Sumpter *Creation* ■ *Dir* Rob Curry, Tim Plester · *Scr* Tim Plester

Way Out West ★★★★★ U

Classic comedy western   1937 · US · BW · 63min

Stan Laurel and Oliver Hardy get to sing their hit song *Trail of the Lonesome Pine* as they go west to deliver a mine-deed inheritance to prospector's daughter Rosina Lawrence. However they are waylaid by crooked saloon owner James Finlayson and his moll, Sharon Lynne. This inspired western parody contains some of the duo's most memorable routines, making it one of those films you can watch umpteen times and still come back for more. DP *DVD*

Stan Laurel *Stan* · Oliver Hardy *Ollie* · James Finlayson *Mickey Finn* · Sharon Lynne *Lola Marcel* · Rosina Lawrence *Mary Roberts* · Stanley Fields *Sheriff* ■ *Dir* James W Horne · *Scr* Charles Rogers, Felix Adler, James Parrott, from a story by Jack Jevne, Charles Rogers

The Way to the Stars ★★★★ U

Second World War drama   1945 · UK · BW · 104min

This well-judged tale concerns the stiff-upper-lipped activities of an RAF squadron, and its members' relationships with their loved ones and the flashy flyboys who have recently arrived from America. The first joint project of director Anthony Asquith, producer Anatole de Grunwald and writer Terence Rattigan, this perfectly captures the spirit of Britain at a moment when loss was perhaps even more agonising, simply because victory was so close at hand. Michael Redgrave and Rosamund John are straight out of the Noël Coward school of British bourgeoisie, but John Mills and Renée Asherson are closer to reality as the couple dallying over a wartime wedding. DP *DVD*

Michael Redgrave *David Archdale* · John Mills *Peter Penrose* · Rosamund John *Miss Toddy Todd* · Douglass Montgomery *Johnny Hollis* · Stanley Holloway *Mr Palmer* · Trevor Howard *Squadron Leader Carter* · Renée Asherson *Iris Winterton* · Felix Aylmer *Rev Charles Moss* · Bonar Colleano *Joe Friselli* · Jean Simmons *Singer* ■ *Dir* Anthony Asquith · *Scr* Terence Rattigan, Anatole de Grunwald, from a story by Rattigan, Richard Sherman

The Way Way Back ★★ 12

Coming-of-age comedy   2013 · US · Colour · 99min

Teenager Liam James is taken to the seaside by his ditzy mother (Toni Collette) and her resentful boyfriend (Steve Carell), where he strikes up an unlikely friendship with a theme park's maverick manager (Sam Rockwell). Rockwell gives it his best shot, but whenever he's not on screen, the film sinks into a torpor. Carell's spiteful asides are darkly funny on occasion but otherwise they stand out like a sore thumb in a movie that feels like a decade of indie comedy mashed down into an hour and 45 minutes. DW

Steve Carell *Trent* · Toni Collette *Pam* · Allison Janney *Betty* · AnnaSophia Robb *Susanna* · Sam Rockwell *Owen* · Maya Rudolph *Caitlin* · Liam James *Duncan* ■ *Dir/Scr* Nat Faxon, Jim Rash

The Way We Were ★★★★ PG

Romantic drama   1973 · US · Colour · 113min

Barbra Streisand and Robert Redford play the ideal odd couple: she's poor, jittery, Jewish and a radical; he's rich, self-assured, Gentile and conservative. Set against the backdrop of a changing America, including the McCarthy-era witch-hunts, every scene seems dreamed up by a dating-agency computer, though the sheer professionalism of the picture and the performances can't fail to touch you. Redford, as a character seemingly hewn from the pages of F Scott Fitzgerald, is perfectly cast and Streisand is simply Streisand. AT Swearing. *DVD*

Barbra Streisand *Katie Morosky* · Robert Redford *Hubbell Gardiner* · Bradford Dillman *JJ* · Lois Chiles *Carol Ann* · Patrick O'Neal (1) *George Bissinger* · Viveca Lindfors *Paula Reisner* · Allyn Ann McLerie *Rhea Edwards* · Murray Hamilton *Brooks Carpenter* · Herb Edelman *Bill Verso* · Diana Ewing *Vicki Bissinger* · James Woods *Frankie McVeigh* ■ *Dir* Sydney Pollack · *Scr* Arthur Laurents, from his novel

The Way West ★★★★

Western   1967 · US · Colour · 122min

Directed by Andrew V McLaglen from the Pulitzer Prize-winning novel by AB Guthrie Jr, this spectacular western boasts a magnificent leading trio of Kirk Douglas, Robert Mitchum and Richard Widmark in roles they were born to play. The scale is impressive as politician Douglas leads a wagon train west along the hazardous Oregon Trail to California. Mitchum is remarkably good as a scout and watch out for a young Sally Field in her movie debut. Bronislau Kaper's outstanding score is a splendid accompaniment to the action and deserves to be better known. TS

Kirk Douglas *Senator William J Tadlock* · Robert Mitchum *Dick Summers* · Richard Widmark *Lije Evans* · Lola Albright *Rebecca Evans* · Michael Witney *Johnnie Mack* · Michael McGreevey *Brownie Evans* · Sally Field *Mercy McBee* · Katherine Justice *Amanda Mack* · Stubby Kaye *Sam Fairman* · Jack Elam *Preacher Wetherby* ■ *Dir* Andrew V McLaglen · *Scr* Ben Maddow, Mitch Lindemann, from the novel by AB Guthrie Jr

waydowntown ★★★★

Comedy   2000 · Can · Colour · 87min

Set in the Canadian city of Calgary, where a central commercial complex has been linked together by a series of glass tunnels, this is a compelling investigation into the modern tendency to cocoon ourselves, whether by architecture, technology or apathy. Taking sly pot shots at office politics and mall culture, Gary Burns's cracklingly tense comedy centres on a bet between four colleagues to see who can stay indoors the longest. But while the increasingly desperate competition enthrals, it's Burns's use of space, place and colour that creates the sinisterly satirical atmosphere. DP

Fab Filippo *Tom* · Don McKellar *Brad* · Marya Delver *Sandra West* · Gordon Currie *Curt Schwin* · Jennifer Clement *Vicki* · Tobias Godson *Randy* ■ *Dir* Gary Burns · *Scr* Gary Burns, James Martin

Wayne's World ★★★★ PG

Comedy   1992 · US · Colour · 90min

This spin-off from the TV show *Saturday Night Live* brought "teen speak" to a new level. Mike Myers and Dana Carvey play Wayne and Garth, whose low-budget public access cable show is transformed into a national TV phenomenon by sleazy producer Rob Lowe. Along the way, Myers falls in love with rock chick Tia Carrere and, along with Carvey, gets to meet their idol Alice Cooper. Aiming for the unashamedly moronic, director Penelope Spheeris still sneaks in some sly satirical jibes and it benefits from inspired casting. JF Swearing, sex scenes. *DVD* CS

Mike Myers *Wayne Campbell* · Dana Carvey *Garth Algar* · Rob Lowe *Benjamin Oliver* · Tia Carrere *Cassandra* · Brian Doyle-Murray *Noah Vanderhoff* · Lara Flynn Boyle *Stacy* · Michael DeLuise *Alan* ■ *Dir* Penelope Spheeris · *Scr* Mike Myers, Bonnie Turner, Terry Turner, from characters by Mike Myers

Wayne's World 2 ★★★ PG

Comedy   1993 · US · Colour · 90min

Wayne and Garth return for another goofy pop culture delve into suburban Americana. This time Mike Myers's cleverly conceived alter ego is searching for meaning in his life and decides to mount a "Waynestock" rock concert. The gleeful party atmosphere conjured up by the first and funnier movie continues here with silly gags, daft catchphrases and hip in-jokes. But it's a sloppy affair despite the odd hysterical highlight. AJ Swearing. *DVD* CS

Mike Myers *Wayne Campbell* · Dana Carvey *Garth Algar* · Tia Carrere *Cassandra* · Christopher Walken *Bobby Cahn* · Ralph Brown (2) *Del Preston* · Olivia D'Abo *Betty Jo* · Kim Basinger *Honey Hornée* · James Hong *Mr Wong* · Heather Locklear ■ *Dir* Stephen Surjik · *Scr* Mike Myers, Terry Turner, Bonnie Turner, from characters by Myers

The Wayward Bus ★★

Drama   1957 · US · BW · 88min

A *Grand Hotel* type story from a novel by John Steinbeck about a group of people whose lives are changed on a bus trip in California, this is a patchy affair with an interesting cast that deserved a better script. Jayne Mansfield gives a touching performance as a stripper who wants to become a "real actress", and there are good performances by Dan Dailey as a travelling salesman and Joan Collins as the driver's tipsy wife, but the characterisation is superficial and situations pat. TV

Joan Collins *Alice* · Jayne Mansfield *Camille* · Dan Dailey *Ernest Horton* · Rick Jason *Johnny Chicoy* · Betty Lou Keim *Norma* · Dolores

Michaels *Mildred Pritchard* • Larry Keating *Pritchard* ■ *Dir* Victor Vicas • *Scr* Ivan Moffat, from the novel by John Steinbeck

WAZ ★★18

Horror thriller 2006 · UK · Colour · 99min

British director Tom Shankland displays a promising neo-*noir* style in the early stages of this film, plus the sort of menace and moral degradation evinced in the likes of *Se7en*. World-weary detective Stellan Skarsgård and his idealistic new partner Melissa George are on the trail of a serial killer who dispatches victims two at a time. It soon becomes clear, however, that one death is inflicted by the other victim to save themselves from further torture. Both the twists and the violence become more difficult to take as the film progresses, and the gaping plot-holes mean that it soon loses its tentative grip on any sort of narrative credibility. **BP** *DVD*

Stellan Skarsgård *Eddie Argo* • Melissa George *Helen Westcott* • Selma Blair *Jean Lerner* • Ashley Walters *Daniel Leone* • John Sharian *Jack Corelli* • Paul Kaye *Doctor Gelb* ■ *Dir* Tom Shankland • *Scr* Clive Bradley

We All Loved Each Other So Much ★★★★

Romantic drama
1974 · It · BW and Colour · 136min

With guest appearances by Vittorio De Sica and Federico Fellini, a wealth of clips from the likes of Rossellini, Visconti and Antonioni, and impudent pastiches of some classic scenes, this cinematic rattlebag will prove an endless delight for fans of postwar Italian film. However, the casual viewer is also catered for, as Ettore Scola chronicles the 30-year friendship between political activist Nino Manfredi, radical cinéaste Stefano Satta Flores and self-made bourgeois, Vittorio Gassman, who not only share a common history, but also a mutual passion for the ravishing Stefania Sandrelli. Alternately broad and sentimental, inspired and contrived, but always sympathetic and amusing. **DP** In Italian.

Nino Manfredi *Antonio* • Vittorio Gassman *Gianni* • Stefania Sandrelli *Luciana* • Stefano Satta Flores *Nicola* • Vittorio De Sica • Federico Fellini • Giovanna Ralli *Elide* ■ *Dir* Ettore Scola • *Scr* Age [Agenore Incrocci], Furio Scarpelli, Ettore Scola

We Are Many ★★★★12

Documentary 2014 · UK · Colour · 103min

The Stop the War march on 15 February 2003 now seems a mere historical footnote, particularly as the Iraq War went ahead regardless. However, director Amir Amirani's rousing chronicle of the global outcry to stop the US/UK-led conflict is an inspiring experience, thanks to spot-on archive and incisive contributions from speakers ranging from Damon Albarn and John le Carré to the indefatigable Tony Benn and weapons inspector Hans Blix. A valuable tribute to protest, it's a film that should be seen by the many. **JA** *DVD*

Mark Rylance • Danny Glover • Ken Loach • Richard Branson • Noam Chomsky • Damon Albarn • Ron Kovic ■ *Dir/Scr* Amir Amirani

We Are Monster ★★15

Psychological drama based on a true story
2014 · UK · Colour · 84min

With just five hours of his 90-day sentence left to serve, British Asian teenager Zahin Mubarek was bludgeoned to death by Robert Stewart, his cellmate at Feltham Young Offenders' Institution. Actor/writer Leeshon Alexander has purportedly based his screenplay on the facts of the 2000 case, examining Stewart's mental instability by using confrontations between his alter egos. The film succeeds in generating a mood of claustrophobic menace, but the dramatic elements are too often clumsily realised. **DP** Violence, swearing. *DVD*

Leeshon Alexander *Robert Stewart* • Aymen Hamdouchi *Zahid Mubarek* • Gethin Anthony *Maurice Travis* • Justin Salinger *Chief Officer Dean* • Doug Allen *Officer Poll* • Shazad Latif *Officer Shah* • Drew Edwards *Officer Hart* ■ *Dir* Antony Petrou • *Scr* Leeshon Alexander

We Are Not Alone ★★

Drama 1939 · US · BW · 105min

This Hollywood melodrama is set in one of those quiet English villages where dark passions flow just as strongly as the Earl Grey. Paul Muni is the local doctor, Flora Robson is his fearsome wife and Jane Bryan the dancer with whom he falls in love. The story seldom rises above Mills and Boon levels of cliché and predictability, but the setting at the outbreak of the First World War meant much to audiences in 1939. **AT**

Paul Muni *Dr David Newcome* • Jane Bryan *Leni-Krafft* • Flora Robson *Jessica Newcome* • Raymond Severn *Gerald Newcome* • Una O'Connor *Susan* • Alan Napier *Archdeacon* • James Stephenson *Sir William Clintock* • Montagu Love *Major Millman* • Henry Daniell *Sir Ronald Dawson* ■ *Dir* Edmund Goulding • *Scr* James Hilton, Milton Krims, from the novel by Hilton

We Are the Best! ★★★★15

Drama 2013 · Swe · Colour · 97min

It's 1982, and two Stockholm-reared 13-year-old girls, shy bespectacled Bobo (Mira Barkhammar) and more confident Klara (Mira Grosin), refuse to accept that punk is dead. They decide to form a band, blithely undeterred by their inability to play. What they do have is passion and attitude to spare. And after recruiting a third member, Hedvig (Liv LeMoyne), a willowy 15-year-old Christian who can actually play guitar, it soon looks like they have the makings of Sweden's first Riot Grrrl outfit. The film has its darker moments – like the spot-on exploration of how resentment and jealousy can fester within the fondest friendship – but you'd have to have a heart of Arctic ice to finish the film not smiling with joy. **LF** Swedish +subtitles. Swearing. *DVD*

Mira Barkhammar *Bobo* • Mira Grosin *Klara* • Liv LeMoyne *Hedvig* • Johan Liljemark *Kenneth* • Mattias Wiberg *Roger* • Jonathan Salomonsson *Elis* ■ *Dir* Lukas Moodysson • *Scr* Lukas Moodysson, from a comic book by Coco Moodysson

We Are the Freaks ★★★15

Comedy 2013 · UK · Colour · 71min

The Midlands, 1990, and this coming-of-age comedy sees misfit teen Jamie Blackley sleepwalking his way through an admin job, while what passes for excitement in his life involves gatecrashing a Young Conservatives soirée with his equally maladjusted pals. Justin Edgar breeds an air of unpredictability as the lads' big night careens out of control – he brought a similar rebel spirit to *Special People*, and this is slight in comparison, yet it remains frisky and likeable for the duration. **TJ** Swearing, sexual references, drug abuse. *DVD*

Jamie Blackley *Jack* • Sean Teale *Chunks* • Mike Bailey *Parsons* • Michael Smiley *Killer Colin* • Amber Anderson *Elinor* ■ *Dir/Scr* Justin Edgar

We Are the Giant ★★★★15

Documentary
2014 · US/UK · BW and Colour · 92min

This documentary about the Arab Spring has the terrifying immediacy of first-hand footage and is a harrowing exercise in citizen reportage that leaves an indelible impression. It also explains why so many have been prepared to risk all for the passionately held causes that have shaken the Arab world from the Maghreb to the Gulf. Director Greg Barker name-checks every subversive from Jesus Christ to Nelson Mandela, but even so, his film lacks political context. With a bit more trust in the audience's intelligence and a lot more directorial humility, this unflinching record might have been even more unforgettable. **DP** In English, Arabic.

Osama Bensadik • Ghassan Yassin • Motaz Murad • Maryam Al Khawaja • Zainab Al Khawaja ■ *Dir* Greg Barker

We Are the Night ★★★15

Horror 2010 · Ger · Colour · 95min

This German vampire flick stars Karoline Herfurth as a pickpocket who attracts the attention of immortal Nina Hoss and her two gal pals. She's soon one of the gang and embarks on a hedonistic lifestyle of fast cars, shopping, clubbing and quaffing the red stuff. Problem is, a young cop is also on Herfurth's trail and the smitten Hoss is not too chuffed with the romantic competition. Director Dennis Gansel adds little that is original to the undead movie canon, but this is a stylish, elegant film, which benefits from distinctive locations, snappily edited action scenes and some nifty special effects. **JA** German +subtitles. Violence, swearing, brief nudity. *DVD*

Karoline Herfurth *Lena* • Nina Hoss *Louise* • Jennifer Ulrich *Charlotte* • Anna Fischer *Nora* • Max Riemelt *Tom* ■ *Dir* Dennis Gansel • *Scr* Jan Berger, from the story *The Dawn* by Dennis Gansel

We Are Together ★★★★PG

Documentary
2006 · UK/S Afr /US · Colour · 86min

Paul Taylor's inspirational documentary about the children of the Agape orphanage in KwaZulu Natal, South Africa, finds hope even in the midst of tragedy. Following 12-year-old Aids orphan Slindile, the film charts three years in the life of Agape, where the young residents are encouraged to join the orphanage's choir. Slindile watches her older brother Sifiso die a slow death from an Aids-related illness and she and her fellow orphans prepare for a series of fundraising concerts. Contrasting the childlike play of these kids with the harshness of their lives and the soulful tenderness of their singing, this tear-jerking documentary illuminates the realities of the pandemic in Africa with great humanity. **JR** Zulu, English +subtitles.

Slindile Moya • "Grandma" Zodwa Mqadi • Swaphiwe Moya • Alicia Keys • Lorraine Bracco • Paul Simon ■ *Dir* Paul Taylor • *Scr* Paul Taylor, Slindile Moya

We Are What We Are ★★★★15

Horror drama 2010 · Mex · Colour · 85min

Jorge Michel Grau's accomplished debut begins with an impoverished nobody dying in a Mexico City shopping mall. However, the discovery of a woman's finger in his stomach during the autopsy hints at the shocking reality of the nature of this man, and the wife and three adult children he has left behind. Without him to provide for them, his cannibalistic brood are forced to go out into the world to hunt for flesh. Echoes of *Let the Right One In* and *Dogtooth* reverberate around this atmospheric study of desperate survival, whose exceptional performances are complemented by Enrico Chapela's forbidding score. But it's Grau's social commentary, rather than the gore, that makes this so compelling. **DP** Spanish +subtitles. Violence, swearing. *DVD*

Francisco Barreiro *Alfredo* • Alan Chávez *Julián* • Paulina Gaitán [Paulina Gaitan] *Sabina* • Carmen Beato *Patricia* • Jorge Zárate *Owen* • Esteban Soberanes *Octavio* ■ *Dir/Scr* Jorge Michel Grau • *Music* Enrico Chapela • *Cinematographer* Santiago Sánchez

We Are What We Are ★★★★18

Horror drama 2013 · US · Colour · 101min

Jim Mickle's savvy re-imagining of the 2010 Mexican horror marks a quantum leap forward in maturity and style for the *Stake Land* director. Following their mother's death, two teenage sisters are ordered by their stern father to continue a macabre ancestral ritual. But when torrential storms hit upstate New York and the river overflows, local authorities start uncovering long-buried clues leading them closer to the family's cannibalistic secret. A bold, satisfyingly restrained shocker with remarkable performances and a bold artistic integrity. **AJ** *DVD*

Bill Sage *Frank Parker* • Ambyr Childers *Iris Parker* • Julia Garner *Rose Parker* • Kelly McGillis *Marge* • Michael Parks *Doc Barrow* • Odeya Rush *Alyce Parker* ■ *Dir* Jim Mickle • *Scr* Jim Mickle, Nick Damici, from the film by Jorge Michel Grau

We Are Your Friends ★★★15

Music drama 2015 · US/Fr/UK · Colour · 91min

This won't catapult Zac Efron's career to the next level, but it's a well-made, vibrant music-scene drama that's well targeted at a hip audience. Efron plays an ambitious LA dance-party DJ and writer of rave music. But his plans are set back by some boorish buddies, having to make ends meet, and by falling for his DJ-mentor's girlfriend (Emily Ratajkowski). Efron's climactic killer dance track is a mite underwhelming, and attempts to visualise the scene's sounds and styles are a little lame. But this is still one of the better recent music-scene films. **DA** Violence, swearing, sexual references, nudity, drug abuse. *DVD* *BD*

Zac Efron *Cole* • Emily Ratajkowski *Sophie* • Jonny Weston *Mason* • Shiloh Fernandez *Ollie* • Alex Shaffer *Squirrel* • Wes Bentley *James* ■ *Dir* Max Joseph • *Scr* Max Joseph, Meaghan Oppenheimer, from a story by Richard Silverman

We Bought a Zoo ★★★PG

Comedy drama 2011 · US · Colour · 118min

Matt Damon stars in this cute comedy drama inspired by a true story. He plays newly widowed Benjamin Mee, who moves with his two children from the city to a wildlife park in rural California. His young daughter (Maggie Elizabeth Jones) immediately takes to the animals but for teenage son Dylan (Colin Ford), it's another traumatic upheaval. This prickly relationship gives the film a pulse and Ford's quiet intensity also tempers director Cameron Crowe's gushing sentiment. Damon's wry performance has a similar effect, though his slow-burning romance with zookeeper Scarlett Johansson has less traction than Ford's hesitant courtship of Elle Fanning. **SP** *DVD* *BD*

Matt Damon *Benjamin Mee* • Scarlett Johansson *Kelly Foster* • Thomas Haden Church *Duncan Mee* • Patrick Fugit *Robin Jones* • Elle Fanning *Lily Miska* • John Michael Higgins *Walter Ferris* ■ *Dir* Cameron Crowe • *Scr* Cameron Crowe, Aline Brosh McKenna, from memoirs by Benjamin Mee

We Dive at Dawn ★★★U

Second World War drama
1943 · UK · BW · 92min

This tense British study of submarine warfare, directed by Anthony Asquith, is packed with incident (as a determined crew pursues a Nazi battleship across the Baltic) and credible characters, played by the likes of John Mills and Eric Portman, who remain human for all their quiet heroism. **DP** *DVD*

Eric Portman *James Hobson* • John Mills *Lt Freddie Taylor* • Reginald Purdell *CPO Dicky Dabbs* • Niall MacGinnis *PO Mike Corrigan* • Joan Hopkins *Ethel Dabbs* • Josephine Wilson *Alice Hobson* ■ *Dir* Anthony Asquith • *Scr* JP Williams, Frank Launder, Val Valentine

We Don't Live Here Anymore ★★★★15

Relationship drama
2003 · US/Can · Colour · 94min

In this autumnal chamber piece, the four libidinous characters are motivated less by pleasure or love than by loneliness and revenge. Rumpled academic Mark Ruffalo is married to alcoholic Laura Dern but having an affair with elegant Naomi Watts who's married to his best friend Peter Krause, a teacher who sleeps mostly with his students. Painfully poignant at times, the misery quotient is cut by stabs of humour, while the superb acting nails through looks and gestures what the characters can't say in words. **LF** Swearing, sex scenes. *DVD*

Mark Ruffalo *Jack Linden* • Laura Dern *Terry Linden* • Peter Krause *Hank Evans* • Naomi Watts *Edith Evans* • Sam Charles *Sean Linden* • Haili Page *Natasha Linden* • Jennifer Bishop (2) *Sharon Evans* ■ *Dir* John Curran • *Scr* Larry Gross, from the short stories *We Don't Live Here Anymore* and *Adultery* by Andre Dubus

We Don't Want to Talk about It ★★★★ PG
Period drama 1993 · Arg/It · Colour · 93min

This is essentially a touching parable on the blindness of love, though some will find the romance between an ageing Casanova and a fabulously cultured dwarf rather hard to take. Yet the only dubious character in this intriguing flashback to an imaginary Latin American town in the 1930s is scheming widow Luisina Brando, whose motives for pairing Marcello Mastroianni with her daughter, Alejandra Podesta, are not exactly selfless. Flirting occasionally with lapses in taste and the lazy deceits of magic realism, this is kept on track by the excellence of the performances. DP Spanish +subtitles. Nudity.

Marcello Mastroianni *Ludovico D'Andrea* · Luisina Brando *Leonor* · Alejandra Podesta *Charlotte* · Betiana Blum *Madama* · Roberto Carnaghi *Padre Aurelio* · Alberto Segado *Dr Blanes* · Jorge Luz *Alcalde* ■ *Dir* Maria Luisa Bemberg · *Scr* Maria Luisa Bemberg, Jorge Goldenberg, from a short story by Julio Llinas

We Have a Pope ★★★ PG
Drama 2011 · It/Fr · Colour · 100min

Having satirised the Italian system of government in 2006's *The Caiman*, Nanni Moretti here turns his attention to the Catholic Church. It's a mild but witty critique of an institution that seems more bound to tradition than serving the faithful. When the newly elected pope (Michel Piccoli) is struck by self-doubt, Moretti's snarky, non-believing psychiatrist is summoned to analyse him. But he's left to organise a volleyball tournament for cardinals and clerics, while the Pope goes soul-searching across Rome and his spokesman (Jerzy Stuhr) tries to fend off the media. Moretti loses his way in having the pontiff befriended by a Chekhovian theatre troupe, but there are several amusing moments and Piccoli is typically superb. DP Italian +subtitles. DVD

Michel Piccoli *Cardinal Melville* · Jerzy Stuhr *The Spokesman* · Renato Scarpa *Cardinal Gregori* · Franco Graziosi *Cardinal Bollati* · Camillo Milli *Cardinal Pescardona* · Roberto Nobile *Cardinal Cevasco* ■ *Dir* Nanni Moretti · *Scr* Nanni Moretti, Francesco Piccolo, Federica Pontremoli

We Joined the Navy ★★ PG
Comedy 1962 · UK · Colour · 101min

Kenneth More stars as a blithering idiot ordered to train navy cadets at Dartmouth College. Making a hash of that billet, More is transferred to the American fleet in the Med, thus allowing Hollywood hero Lloyd Nolan to help the film at the box-office in America. It's really little more than *Doctor in the House* in uniform, but is modestly amusing. AT DVD

Kenneth More *Lt Cmdr "Bodger" Badger* · Lloyd Nolan *Admiral Ryan* · Joan O'Brien *Carol Blair* · Mischa Auer *Colonel/President* · Jeremy Lloyd *Dewberry* · Dinsda e Landen *Bowles* · Derek Fowlds *Carson* · Denise Warren *Collette* · John Le Mesurier *Dewberry Senior* · Lally Bowers *Mrs Dewberry* · Laurence Naismith *Admiral Blake* · Andrew Cruickshank *Admiral Filmer* · Brian Wilde *Petty Officer Gibbons* · Esma Cannon *Consul's Wife* · Dirk Bogarde *Dr Simon Sparrow* · Michael Bentine *Psychologist* · Sidney James *Dancing instructor* ■ *Dir* Wendy Toye · *Scr* Arthur Dales [Howard Dimsdale], from a novel by John Winton

We Live Again ★★★ PG
Melodrama 1934 · US · BW · 78min

The Russian answer to the Swedish Garbo, Anna Sten was exceptionally well cast opposite dashing Fredric March in this uncredited adaptation of Tolstoy's *Resurrection*, but the public never really warmed to her. Today, this movie is an impressive work, beautifully photographed by Gregg Toland and impressively condensed into 80-odd minutes, in part by newcomer Preston Sturges. Director Rouben Mamoulian's sense of scale is awesome, from the opening scenes on the steppes, and including a detailed Russian Orthodox Easter Mass. TS

Fredric March *Prince Dmitri* · Anna Sten *Katusha Maslova* · Jane Baxter *Missy Kortchagin* · C Aubrey Smith *Prince Kortchagin* · Sam Jaffe *Gregory Simonson* · Ethel Griffies *Aunt Maria* · Gwendolyn Logan *Aunt Sophia* · Mary Forbes *Mrs Kortchagin* ■ *Dir* Rouben Mamoulian · *Scr* Maxwell Anderson, Leonard Praskins, Preston Sturges, from the novel *Resurrection* by Leo Tolstoy

We Live in Public ★★ 15
Documentary 2009 · US/UK · Colour · 89min

This watchable documentary charts the strange, mercurial career of internet entrepreneur and conceptual artist Josh Harris who made millions in the 1990s from early dot-com companies. However, he then squandered it all on a series of "art projects" including the eponymous Weliveinpublic.com, in which he rigged his apartment with numerous cameras to broadcast his and his girlfriend's lives on the web 24/7. In the end, Harris's experiments seem to be an extension of a narcissistic personality conveying nothing more profound than an episode of *Gilligan's Island*, the 1960s US sitcom with which he was also weirdly obsessed. AS

Josh Harris · Tanya Corrin · Ondi Timoner *Narrator* ■ *Dir/Scr* Ondi Timoner

We Need to Talk about Kevin ★★★★ 15
Drama 2011 · UK/US · Colour · 107min

Lionel Shriver's 2003 novel took the form of a series of letters from a mother to her husband, trying to fathom how their teenage son became a sociopathic killer. This beautifully crafted but disturbing film takes a more traditional approach, flashing backwards and forwards through the story of Eva (Tilda Swinton), a former travel writer whose love-hate relationship with her child has made her life a living hell. Swinton is excellent as the worn-down Eva, equalled by newcomer Ezra Miller as the conniving Kevin. However, the director is the real star - Lynne Ramsay, with only her third feature, has fashioned a dazzling drama with a suffocating, dream-like atmosphere. DW Swearing, sex scenes, nudity. DVD BL

Tilda Swinton *Eva* · John C Reilly *Franklin* · Ezra Miller *Kevin, teenager* · Ashley Gerasimovich *Celia* · Siobhan Fallon Hogan [Siobhan Fallon] *Wanda* ■ *Dir* Lynne Ramsay · *Scr* Lynne Ramsay, Rory Stewart Kinnear, from the novel by Lionel Shriver

We of the Never Never ★★★ U
Adventure drama 1982 · Aus · Colour · 128min

This is an influential Aussie drama, one of the first to really register in the UK, and based on a true story. Angela Punch McGregor packs her middle name as a gutsy high-society girl who marries a cattle-station manager, and leaves for an outback life among macho men who regard women as a liability. Handsomely mounted and impeccably played. DA DVD

Angela Punch McGregor *Jeannie Gunn* · Arthur Dignam *Aeneas Gunn* · Tony Barry *Mac* · Tommy Lewis *Jackeroo* · Lewis Fitz-Gerald *Jack* · Martin Vaughan *Dan* · John Jarratt *Dandy* ■ *Dir* Igor Auzins · *Scr* Peter Schreck, from an autobiography by Jane Taylor Gunn

We Own the Night ★★★ 15
Crime drama 2007 · US · Colour · 112min

The title of James Gray's murky thriller was a motto used by the New York police in the 1980s. In this film's ambiguous moral world, though, it's uncertain who the night really belongs to. Bobby Green (Joaquin Phoenix) is the manager of a Brooklyn nightclub owned by a Russian family with criminal connections. His bosses are unaware that Bobby's father (Robert Duvall) and brother (Mark Wahlberg) are cops leading the operation against a drug dealer operating out of the club. But it's not long before Bobby is forced to abandon his neutral stance - a decision that also rebounds on his girlfriend Amada (Eva Mendes). Like the director's earlier work, *The Yards* and *Little Odessa*, this ambitious thriller largely avoids the expected clichés and concentrates instead on the price of familial loyalties. JR DVD BL

Joaquin Phoenix *Robert "Bobby" Green* · Mark Wahlberg *Joseph Grusinsky* · Eva Mendes *Amada Juarez* · Robert Duvall *Burt Grusinsky* · Danny Hoch *Jumbo Falsetti* · Alex Veadov *Vadim Nezhinski* · Dominic Colon *Freddie* · Tony Musante *Jack Shapiro* ■ *Dir/Scr* James Gray

We Steal Secrets: the Story of WikiLeaks ★★★★ 15
Documentary 2013 · US · Colour · 124min

This film from Alex Gibney (*Mea Maxima Culpa*) affords a fresh and fascinating insight into internet phenomenon WikiLeaks and its founder, Julian Assange. Analysing key events in the story - from the leak of classified information about US foreign policy to the rape scandal that led Assange to seek political asylum - Gibney succeeds in creating a real-life spy thriller. The greatest intrigue is derived from a probing dissection of Assange, whose idealism and egotism are both laid bare in a complex, intimate portrait, despite his refusal to be interviewed. This isn't the whole story by any means, but it does fill in some of the gaps in the news coverage with startling impact. SP

Julian Assange ■ *Dir* Alex Gibney

We Still Kill the Old Way ★ 18
Crime drama 2014 · UK · Colour · 94min

This grubby British gangland drama does nothing to enhance the reputations of such stars as Ian Ogilvy and Steven Berkoff. It's the film that taste forgot, rooted in the spurious notion that there was a Golden Age of gangsterdom. Ogilvy plays the Costa-del-criminal who vows revenge when his old-school-baddie brother is kicked to death. Factor in duff dialogue, duffer action scenes and an overall ambience akin to a bad smell and you have a thoroughly vile film. DA Violence, swearing, sexual references. DVD BL

Ian Ogilvy *Richie* · Alison Doody *Susan Taylor* · Danny-Boy Hatchard *Aaron* · Lysette Anthony *Lizzie Davis* · Nicky Henson *Houghton* ■ *Dir* Sacha Bennett · *Scr* Sacha Bennett, Dougie Brimson, Gary Lawrence

We the Living ★★★★
Political drama 1942 · It · BW · 270min

Director Goffredo Alessandrini's splendid film version of Ayn (*The Fountainhead*) Rand's novel stars Alida Valli and Rossano Brazzi, both first-class and at the peak of their youthful beauty, as a student in love with an anti-Communist aristocrat in 1920s Russia. To help Brazzi, who is suffering from TB but being denied medical treatment, Valli engages in an affair with an influential member of the secret police (Fosco Giachetti), setting the rest of the action in motion. After a successful run in Italy, the film was withdrawn on political grounds by the Mussolini-era authorities and disappeared until 1986, when Rand's legal advisers tracked down a copy and restored it. RK Italian +subtitles.

Alida Valli *Kira Argounova* · Rossano Brazzi *Leo Kovalensky* · Fosco Giachetti *Andrei Taganov* · Giovanni Grasso *Tishenko* · Emilio Cigoli *Pavel Syerov* · Cesrina Gheraldi *Comrade Sonia* ■ *Dir* Goffredo Alessandrini · *Scr* Anton Giulio Majano, from the novel by Ayn Rand, adapted by Corrado Alvaro, Orio Vergani

We Think the World of You ★★★ PG
Comedy drama 1988 · UK · Colour · 94min

Tackling homosexual prejudice in 1950s Britain, Alan Bates is a civil servant with an ongoing passion for bad boy Gary Oldman. In return, Oldman plays Bates for his money and when he is sent to prison, Oldman's wife continues the scrounging. Aware he is being taken for a ride but helpless in his unrequited passion, Bates projects all his feelings about the younger man onto Oldman's alsatian dog. Not an easy film, this is masterfully intelligent and understated with spot-on performances from Oldman and Bates. LH

Alan Bates *Frank Meadows* · Gary Oldman *Johnny Burney* · Frances Barber *Megan* · Liz Smith *Millie Burney* · Max Wall *Tom Burney* · Kerry Wise *Rita* · Ivor Roberts *Harry* ■ *Dir* Colin Gregg · *Scr* Hugh Stoddart, from the novel by Joseph R Ackerley [JR Ackerley]

We 3 ★★★
Drama 2011 · Bra · Colour · 80min

Three Sao Paulo flatmates have their relationship further complicated by participation in a reality show in this handsomely shot but emotionally timid love-triangle tale from Brazil. Once they start to live a largely scripted home life, pals Gabriel Godoy, Victor Mendes and Juliana Schalch find the laid-back intimacy of their student days replaced by superficiality and fakeness that gradually threaten the bond they're so desperate to maintain. Initially, there's a gentle humour in the trio's activities, but by the final third of the film, even supposedly honest moments seem insincere, while the excessively languid pacing and bland ending exacerbate the sense of a plot that's run out of steam. SF Portuguese +subtitles.

Juliana Schalch *Camila* · Gabriel Godoy *Cazé* · Victor Mendes *Rafael* · Rafael Maia *Guilherme* · Sophia Reis *Bárbara* ■ *Dir* Nando Olival · *Scr* Nando Olival, Thiago Dottori

We Went to War ★★★★
Documentary 2012 · UK · Colour and BW · 77min

This remarkable documentary revisits the lives of three US veterans of the Vietnam War over 40 years after British director Michael Grigsby had first captured their testimony in his 1970 TV film *I Was a Soldier*. Black-and-white footage of the men taken just after their return home to Texas weaves in and out of newly shot interviews, where they explain how the outrage and abandonment they felt at being left alone to deal with the horrific memories of combat has only intensified with time. And with its unadorned approach and slow-building intensity, it makes for a fitting tribute to Grigsby himself, who died shortly before the film's completion. TJ

■ *Dir* Michael Grigsby · *Cinematographer* Jonas Mortensen

We Were Soldiers ★★ 15
War drama based on a true story 2002 · US · Colour · 132min

This is an overlong account of how Lt General Harold G Moore's men stood their ground against overwhelming numbers of North Vietnamese soldiers in the first major confrontation of the Vietnam War in November 1965. The film earnestly treads familiar ground as director Randall Wallace manipulates the audience between violent action, sentimental pep talks and scenes from the home front. Devoid of political comment and historical background, with no real characterisation. AJ DVD BL

Mel Gibson *Lt Col Harold G Moore* · Madeleine Stowe *Julie Moore* · Greg Kinnear *Maj Bruce Crandall* · Sam Elliott *Sgt Maj Basil Plumley* · Chris Klein *Second Lt Jack Geoghegan* · Keri Russell *Barbara Geoghegan* · Barry Pepper *Joseph L Galloway* ■ *Dir* Randall Wallace · *Scr* Randall Wallace, from the non-fiction book *We Were Soldiers Once... and Young* by Lt Gen Harold G Moore Moore, Joseph L Galloway

We Were Strangers ★★★
Adventure drama 1949 · US · BW · 105min

The charismatic John Garfield, nearing the end of a career destroyed by the McCarthy blacklist, stars in this sombre political drama set in the early 1930s and well directed by John Huston. Garfield plays a Cuban-born American who returns to the country of his birth to help with a revolutionary group's elaborate plan to assassinate some government ministers. There's also time for an obligatory romance (with Jennifer Jones). Even though it dissipates its serious political theme with too much mechanical detail, the film is still tense and atmospheric. RK

Jennifer Jones *China Valdes* • John Garfield *Tony Fenner* • Pedro Armendáriz *Armando Ariete* • Gilbert Roland *Guillermo Mantilla* • Ramon Novarro *Chief* • Wally Cassell *Miguel* ■ *Dir* John Huston • *Scr* Peter Viertel, John Huston, from the novel *China Valdez* in the novel *Rough Sketch* by Robert Sylvester

The Weak and the Wicked ★★★ PG

Prison drama | 1953 · UK · BW · 83min

This is one of those riveting women's prison pictures full of sneering warders and snarling, sulky inmates that alternates alarmingly between enlightening social comment and overloaded melodrama. A robust cast that contains all the usual suspects (there's a fine performance from Diana Dors) acts out the story, which provides a meaty glimpse behind the clanging doors. **SH**

Glynis Johns *Jean Raymond* • Diana Dors *Betty* • John Gregson *Michael* • Jane Hylton *Babs* • Sidney James *Sid Baden* • AE Matthews *Harry Wicks* • Anthony Nicholls *Chaplain* ■ *Dir* J Lee Thompson • *Scr* J Lee Thompson, Anne Burnaby, Joan Henry, from the book *Who Lie in Gaol* by Joan Henry

Weak at Denise ★ 18

Black comedy | 2000 · UK · Colour · 83min

Harking back to the unlamented days of the British sex comedy, this cataclysm of a movie marks the directorial debut of Julian Nott. Nott assaults mild-mannered Bill Thomas with a domineering mum, a gold-digging wife, a lesbian punk stepdaughter and a plot to bump him off for his money. Outdated and unfunny. **DP** *DVD*

Bill Thomas *Colin* • Chrissie Cotterill *Denise* • Craig Fairbrass *Roy* • Tilly Blackwood *Wendy* • Claudine Spiteri *Sharon* • Edna Doré *Iris* ■ *Dir* Julian Nott • *Scr* Graham Williams, Julian Nott, from a novel by Graham Williams

The Weaker Sex ★★ U

Second World War drama
1948 · UK · BW · 84min

A marvellous British cast plays out this nostalgic and very human story of the latter war years, leading up to D-Day. Ursula Jeans adds to her housewife duties with stints as a canteen worker and fire watcher. Her son is away fighting and her two daughters are Wrens living at home. With two navy men billeted at the house, Jeans's life is full as she waits for the war's end and a family reunion. Based on a successful play, *No Medals*, this gentle film was given a nicely ironic title for the screen version. **BB**

Ursula Jeans *Martha Dacre* • Cecil Parker *Geoffrey Radcliffe* • Joan Hopkins *Helen Dacre* • Derek Bond *Nigel* • Lana Morris *Lolly Dacre* • John Stone (1) *Roddy* • Thora Hird *Mrs Gaye* ■ *Dir* Roy Baker [Roy Ward Baker] • *Scr* Esther McCracken, Paul Soskin, from the play *No Medals* by Esther McCracken

The Weather Man ★★ 15

Black comedy drama 2005 · US · Colour · 97min

Nicolas Cage plays the title role of the slick, handsome broadcaster who has no real knowledge of his subject in this black comedy drama from *Pirates of the Caribbean* director Gore Verbinski. He is separated from his wife (Hope Davis) and has trouble communicating with his distant son, overweight daughter and intimidating father. Michael Caine is excellent in the latter role of a Pulitzer Prize-winning novelist who's struggling with both serious illness and disappointment in his offspring. But Cage presents a character who simply seems muddled, indecisive and self-indulgent. **BP** Swearing, sex scenes. *DVD*

Nicolas Cage *Dave Spritz* • Michael Caine *Robert Spritz* • Hope Davis *Noreen Spritz* • Michael Rispoli *Russ* • Gil Bellows *Don* ■ *Dir* Gore Verbinski • *Scr* Steven Conrad

The Web ★★★

Film noir thriller | 1947 · US · BW · 87min

In an exceptionally well-scripted thriller, Vincent Price stands out as the wealthy New York businessman who twice uses Edmond O'Brien's young bodyguard to dispose of his adversaries. Ella Raines

makes a spirited secretary who helps O'Brien clear himself while William Bendix is the police lieutenant who's not as dumb as he looks. **AE**

Ella Raines *Noel Faraday* • Edmond O'Brien *Bob Regan* • William Bendix *Lt Damico* • Vincent Price *Andrew Colby* • Maria Palmer *Martha Kroner* • John Abbott *Murdock, Charles* • Fritz Leiber *Leopold Kroner* • Howland Chamberlin *James Nolan* ■ *Dir* Michael Gordon • *Scr* William Bowers, Bertram Milhauser, from a story by Harry Kurnitz

Web of Passion ★★★

Mystery drama | 1959 · Fr · Colour · 108min

This adaptation of Stanley Ellin's novel marked Claude Chabrol's entry into the full-colour, big-budget mainstream. Yet the detachment that would undermine several future projects is already in evidence, as he prioritises technique over dialogue and character. However, the influence of Hitchcock and Lang is also felt in this astute blend of thriller and social drama, in which Chabrol takes savage delight in dissecting Jacques Dacqmine's dysfunctional bourgeois household. Madeleine Robinson won the best actress prize at Venice as Dacqmine's shrewish wife, but it's Jean-Paul Belmondo's coarse Hungarian catalyst who catches the eye. **DP** In French.

Madeleine Robinson *Thérèse Marcoux* • Jacques Dacqmine *Henri Marcoux* • Jean-Paul Belmondo *Laszlo Kovacs* • Bernadette Lafont *Julie* • Antonella Lualdi *Léda* ■ *Dir* Claude Chabrol • *Scr* Paul Gégauff, from the novel *The Key to Nicholas Street* by Stanley Ellin

A Wedding ★★★★ 15

Comedy drama | 1978 · US · Colour · 119min

Robert Altman sets his sights on a high-society wedding, employing his trademark scattershot technique, and the result is a marital massacre rather than a nuptial mass. As two families collide, booze floats Sunday-best appearances out of the window, and skeletons rattle out of cupboards. The performances – by Carol Burnett, Paul Dooley, Mia Farrow, Vittorio Gassman and Lillian Gish among them – are marvellous enough in isolation, but Altman's splintering style slides them into a mosaic as comic as it is dramatic and poignant. **TH** Swearing. *DVD*

Carol Burnett *Tulip Brenner, mother of the bride* • Paul Dooley *Snooks Brenner, father of the bride* • Amy Stryker *Muffin Brenner, the bride* • Mia Farrow *Buffy Brenner, the bride's sister* • Dennis Christopher *Hughie Brenner, the bride's brother* • Lillian Gish *Nettie Sloan, the groom's grandmother* • Geraldine Chaplin *Rita Billingsley, wedding co-ordinator* • Desi Arnaz Jr *Dino Corelli, the groom* • Nina Van Pallandt *Regina Corelli, the groom's mother* • Vittorio Gassman *Luigi Corelli, the groom's father* ■ *Dir* Robert Altman • *Scr* John Considine, Patricia Resnick, Allan Nicholls, Robert Altman, from a story by John Considine, Robert Altman

The Wedding ★★ PG

Drama | 1998 · US · Colour · 162min

Race and class issues collide in this soap opera-style melodrama adapted from Dorothy West's bestselling novel. Edited down from a two-part mini-series executive-produced by Oprah Winfrey, it stars Halle Berry as a mixed-race girl in a prosperous, 1950s black family who stirs up a hornets' nest when she decides to marry a poor white musician. It never really has the impact its subject matter demands; instead, handsome visuals and an attractive cast sugar-coat the serious moral messages, and Berry carries the film on charm rather than depth of performance. **SF**

Halle Berry *Shelby Coles* • Lynn Whitfield *Corinne Coles* • Shirley Knight *Gram* • Eric Thal *Meade Howell* • Carl Lumbly *Lute* • Michael Warren *Clark Coles* • Cynda Williams *Liz* • Richard Brooks (1) *Lincoln* ■ *Dir* Charles Burnett • *Scr* Lisa Jones, from the novel by Dorothy West

The Wedding Banquet ★★★★ 15

Comedy | 1993 · Tai/US · Colour · 103min

The clash between eastern and western cultures is adeptly wrung for marvellously rich comedy and pathos in Ang Lee's

refreshing look at the marriage-go-round that occurs when gay Winston Chao decides to wed for convenience. Unfortunately, his thrilled parents decide to hop over from Taiwan for the ceremony and that's when the hilarious complications really start in the absorbing efforts to hide his real sexuality, nonconformist lifestyle and boyfriend. Sharply observed and never once striking a false note, this sweet-and-sour rib-tickler is a real treat. **AJ** English, Mandarin +subtitles. Sex scenes, nudity. *DVD*

Winston Chao *Gao Wai-Tung* • May Chin *Wei-Wei* • Gua Ah-Leh *Mrs Gao* • Lung Sihung *Mr Gao* • Mitchell Lichtenstein *Simon* • Neal Huff *Steve* • Ang Lee *Wedding guest* ■ *Dir* Ang Lee • *Scr* Ang Lee, Neil Peng, James Schamus

Wedding Crashers ★★ 15

Romantic comedy 2005 · US · Colour · 121min

Paired in this lowbrow comedy as buddies who spend their free time gate-crashing weddings to pick up women, Owen Wilson and Vince Vaughn enjoy an easy chemistry that's difficult to dislike. There are some funny moments as their season-end event is a weekend with Christopher Walken and his dysfunctional family, after Wilson falls for engaged daughter Rachel McAdams. Sadly, the leads can't sustain the humour and struggle with an over-stretched storyline and stale, contrived material. **SF** Swearing, sex scenes. *DVD* *Blu*

Owen Wilson *John Beckwith* • Vince Vaughn *Jeremy Grey* • Christopher Walken *William Cleary* • Rachel McAdams *Claire Cleary* • Isla Fisher *Gloria Cleary* • Jane Seymour (2) *Kathleen Cleary* ■ *Dir* David Dobkin • *Scr* Steve Faber, Bob Fisher

The Wedding Date ★★ 12

Romantic comedy
2004 · US/UK · Colour · 85min

Tying the knot proves a messy business here, but it's British director Clare Kilner who winds up in a tangle. *Will & Grace* star Debra Messing is left to coast on charm alone as a lonely New York-based singleton who employs professional escort Dermot Mulroney to hang off her arm at her half-sister's posh English wedding. Matters are complicated by the fact that her former fiancé (Jeremy Sheffield) is the best man. Both leads struggle with the thin script. **SP** Swearing, sexual references. *DVD*

Debra Messing *Kat Ellis* • Dermot Mulroney *Nick Mercer* • Amy Adams *Amy* • Jack Davenport *Edward Fletcher-Wooten* • Sarah Parish *TJ* • Jeremy Sheffield *Jeffrey* • Peter Egan *Victor Ellis* • Holland Taylor *Bunny Ellis* • Jolyon James Woody ■ *Dir* Clare Kilner • *Scr* Dana Fox, from the novel *Asking for Trouble* by Elizabeth Young

Wedding Daze ★★

Comedy | 2004 · US · Colour · 88min

John Larroquette does his best Steve Martin impression in this inoffensive *Father of the Bride*-style comedy, in which the hapless Larroquette is thrown into emotional and financial chaos when his three adult daughters decide they want to marry in an extravagant triple ceremony. Though the film lacks freshness, the gentle laughs and amiable performances keep events ticking along – even if the characters are all stereotypes. **SF**

John Larroquette *Jack Landry* • Karen Valentine *Audrey Landry* • Kelly Overton *Dahlia Landry* • Marina Black *Nora Landry* • Jaime Ray Newman *Teri Landry* ■ *Dir* Georg Stanford Brown • *Scr* Marc Herson

Wedding Daze ★★ 15

Romantic comedy 2006 · US · Colour · 87min

Black comedy is a tough tightrope to walk, and *Wedding Daze* falls off after just a couple of steps. *American Pie* star Jason Biggs is back in familiar territory here as a lovable loser whose "perfect" girlfriend drops dead from shock when he proposes. A year later, in an effort to conquer his depression, he spontaneously proposes to waitress Isla Fisher, a girl he's never met before. Inexplicably, she says "I do". But, of course, the path of new love never runs smooth. Despite some wild and wacky

moments, *Wedding Daze* never recovers from its unfunny opening, nor the improbability of its premise. Biggs is a likeable leading man but he deserves better than this - as does the audience. **DA** Sexual references. *DVD*

Jason Biggs *Anderson* • Isla Fisher *Katie* • Joe Pantoliano *Smitty* • Joanna Gleason *Lois* • Matt Malloy *Stuart* • Edward Herrmann *Lyle* • Margo Martindale *Betsy* • Michael Weston *Ted* ■ *Dir/Scr* Michael Ian Black • *Cinematographer* Daniel J Stoloff [Daniel Stoloff]

Wedding in Galilee ★★★ 12

Drama | 1987 · Bel/Fr · Colour · 111min

Set in the occupied West Bank at a time of martial law, Palestinian director Michel Khleifi's debut feature is an impassioned, if naive, plea for tolerance. An elder is intent on giving his son a traditional Arab wedding, and must enlist the help of the local Israeli governor. Maintaining a documentarist's distance, Khleifi concentrates on the human interaction of these implacable foes. Performed by a largely non-professional cast, the film successfully contrasts political tension with the undeniable sexual *frisson* between the guests. **DP** In Arabic, Hebrew, Turkish. Some nudity.

Ali Mohammed El Akili *The Mukhtar* • Nazih Akleh *The Groom* • Bushra Karaman *The mother* • Anna Achdian *Bride* ■ *Dir/Scr* Michel Khleifi

The Wedding March ★★★★★

Silent melodrama
1928 · US · BW and Colour · 113min

This is a silent masterpiece by the great Erich von Stroheim, who also stars as a dissolute Viennese aristocrat falling in love with a peasant girl. The complex combination of cynicism, irony and genuine romanticism elevates this work to great cinematic art, and it contains many truly startling sequences, not least of which is the astounding scene in which Stroheim's mother virtually seduces her own son into marrying for money, or the one where the respective fathers seal the wedding pact in a brothel. There is a remarkable pageant scene in early Technicolor, replete with robust reds, and the whole is enhanced by a new score by Carl Davis. But the real glory is in the casting - to watch Stroheim and the lovely Fay Wray flirt and fall in love is transcendental. An uncredited Josef von Sternberg edited the film. **TS**

Erich von Stroheim *Prince Nicki* • Fay Wray *Mitzi Schrammell* • Matthew Betz *Schani Eberle* • ZaSu Pitts *Cecelia Schweisser* • Hughie Mack *Anton Eberle, Schani's father* • George Fawcett *Prince Ottokar von Wildeliebe-Rauffenburg* • Maude George *Princess Maria von Wildeliebe-Rauffenburg* • George Nichols *Fortunat Schweisser* • Dale Fuller *Katerina Schrammell* • Cesare Gravina *Martin Schrammel* ■ *Dir* Erich von Stroheim • *Scr* Erich von Stroheim, Harry Carr • *Cinematographers* Hal Mohr, B Sorenson, Ben Reynolds • *Set Designers* Richard Day, Erich von Stroheim

The Wedding Night ★★ PG

Drama | 1935 · US · BW · 79min

The third, and last, of producer Samuel Goldwyn's attempts to turn his Russian protégée Anna Sten into a new Garbo. Although charismatic in her European films, Sten seemed hard and unlikeable in English. Here, she's well cast as a Polish tobacco-grower's daughter in an interesting and original story, and supported by an endearing Gary Cooper performance, but the public didn't take to her at all. The moody photography by Gregg Toland is first-rate, though. **TS**

Gary Cooper *Tony Barrett* • Anna Sten *Manya Novak* • Ralph Bellamy *Fredrik* • Helen Vinson *Dora Barrett* • Siegfried Rumann [Sig Ruman] *Jan Novak* • Esther Dale *Mrs Kaise Novak* • Walter Brennan *Bill Jenkins* ■ *Dir* King Vidor • *Scr* Edith Fitzgerald, from a story by Edwin Knopf

The Wedding Party ★★

Comedy | 1966 · US · BW · 90min

Brian De Palma's directorial first was actually shot in 1964, completed in 1966 and released, even then only briefly, in 1969. It's a comedy drama about an impending wedding, with the groom getting cold feet once he discovers what boors his fiancée and her family are. Made wholly in collaboration with a teacher and fellow student from De Palma's college days, the film is a curiosity for its debutante appearances by both Jill Clayburgh and Robert De Niro. DA

Jill Clayburgh *Josephine Fish* • Charles Pfluger *Charlie* • Valda Setterfield *Mrs Fish* • Jennifer Salt *Phoebe* • Raymond McNally *Mr Fish* • John Braswell *Reverend Oldfield* • Judy Thomas *Celeste, organist* • Robert DeNero [Robert De Niro] *Cecil* ■ *Dir/Scr* Cynthia Munroe, Brian De Palma, Wilford Leach

The Wedding Planner ★★PG
Romantic comedy 2001 · US/UK/Ger · Colour · 99min

Jennifer Lopez strays into Julia Roberts territory with another romantic comedy that explores the rocky road to matrimony and true love. Lopez plays a wedding organiser who spends her free time playing Scrabble. Charged with arranging the nuptials for Bridgette Wilson-Sampras, Lopez commits the sin of falling for the groom-to-be, Matthew McConaughey. The star makes an implausible spinster. LH **DVD**

Jennifer Lopez *Mary Fiore* • Matthew McConaughey *Steve Edison* • Bridgette Wilson-Sampras [Bridgette Wilson] *Fran Donolly* • Justin Chambers *Massimo* • Judy Greer *Penny* ■ *Dir* Adam Shankman • *Scr* Pamela Falk, Michael Ellis

Wedding Present ★★★
Screwball comedy 1936 · US · BW · 80min

Two attractive, devil-may-care newspaper reporters fall in love with each other, only to have their romance turn sour when he is promoted to editor and she decides to marry a more conventionally reliable man. That, of course, is not the end of the story which, though it starts promisingly, degenerates into somewhat heavy-handed farce in an attempt to pep up rather thin formula fair. Three stars though, for the pleasure of keeping company with Cary Grant and Joan Bennett. RK

Joan Bennett *Monica "Rusty" Fleming* • Cary Grant *Charlie Mason* • George Bancroft *Pete Stagg* • Conrad Nagel *Roger Dodacker* • Gene Lockhart *Archduke Gustav Ernest* • William Demarest *"Smiles" Benson* ■ *Dir* Richard Wallace • *Scr* Joseph Anthony, from the short story by Paul Gallico in *The Saturday Evening Post*

Wedding Rehearsal ★★U
Romantic comedy 1932 · UK · BW · 75min

Grandmother Kate Cutler is going to curtail bachelor marquis Roland Young's allowance if he doesn't marry one of her chosen wedding candidates, but he falls for his mother's secretary, who believe it or not turns out to be beautiful without her glasses. Unsurprising, since she's lovely Merle Oberon. Unfortunately, no one in this creaky comedy, except for leading man Young, seems able to act their way out of a paper bag. As a period piece, though, this is fascinating. TS

Roland Young *Reggie, Marquis of Buckminster* • George Grossmith *Lord Stokeshire* • John Loder *"Bimbo"* • Maurice Evans *"Tootles"* • Wendy Barrie *Lady Mary Rose Wroxbury* • Joan Gardner *Lady Rosemary Wroxbury* • Merle Oberon *Miss Hutchinson* • Lady Tree *Lady Stokeshire* ■ *Dir* Alexander Korda • *Scr* Arthur Wimperis, Helen Gordon, from a story by Lajos Biró, George Grossmith

The Wedding Ringer ★★15
Comedy 2015 · US · Colour · 97min

Worried that he'll look like a chump at his forthcoming nuptials without a best man to give a speech, fat, friendless Josh Gad takes on the services of a fast-talking wedding "fixer". This situation comedy with a touch of "bromance" stars Kevin Hart as the resourceful wheeler-dealer posing as the groom's best mate from way back, with inevitable comedic consequences. The movie does well enough by its promising central conceit but it's a shame that the cast and film-makers don't make more of

their material. TJ Swearing, sexual references, drug abuse. **DVD** **Blu**

Kevin Hart *Jimmy Calahan/Bic* • Josh Gad *Doug Harris* • Kaley Cuoco-Sweeting [Kaley Cuoco] *Gretchen Palmer* • Jorge Garcia *Lurch/Garvey* • Dan Gill *Bronstein/Dickerson* ■ *Dir* Jeremy Garelick • *Scr* Jeremy Garelick, Jay Lavender

The Wedding Singer
★★★★12
Romantic comedy 1998 · US · Colour · 92min

Adam Sandler is pitch-perfect in his role here as hopelessly romantic cabaret wedding singer Robbie Hart, who falls in love with a waitress (Drew Barrymore) at a nuptial function only to discover that she's engaged to someone else. The chemistry between the two stars works like a charm and director Frank Coraci has enormous fun with the music, fashions and fads of the mid-1980s setting. This good-natured romp has a knowing sense of the ridiculous and a great pop soundtrack. AJ Sexual references, swearing. **DVD**

Adam Sandler *Robbie Hart* • Drew Barrymore *Julia* • Christine Taylor *Holly* • Allen Covert *Sammy* • Matthew Glave *Glenn* • Ellen Albertini Dow *Rosie* • Angela Featherstone *Linda* • Alexis Arquette *George* ■ *Dir* Frank Coraci • *Scr* Tim Herlihy

The Wedding Tackle ★★15
Comedy 2000 · UK · Colour · 89min

Take a comedy of errors, toss in some soap-opera crises and lace with innuendo, and the result is this glorified British sitcom. The ensemble cast gives it everything, but the characters feel like dismally uncool outcasts from *This Life*, with each infantile, groin-motivated male trying to squirm out of (or wriggle into) the affections of their marginally more mature female counterparts. Skeletons fall out of the stag-night cupboard with alarming regularity, and Rami Dvir's film is difficult to warm to. DP Swearing. **DVD**

Adrian Dunbar *Mr Mac* • James Purefoy *Hal* • Tony Slattery *Little Ted* • Neil Stuke *Salty* • Leslie Grantham *George* • Victoria Smurfit *Clodagh* • Susan Vidler *Vinni* • Amanda Redman *Petula* • Sara Stockbridge *Felicity* ■ *Dir* Rami Dvir • *Scr* Nigel Horne

The Wedding Video ★★★15
Comedy 2012 · UK · Colour · 90min

This fresh take on mockumentaries follows the build-up to an over-the-top wedding, all filmed by best man Rufus Hound. A familiar love-triangle plot takes shape, as bride-to-be Lucy Punch is an old school crush of Hound's, while the groom (Robert Webb) is his brother. Webb gives a sly, amusing performance, but the real stars of the show are Punch - an underrated comedy talent - and Harriet Walter as her excitable mother. Except for a silly ending, *Calendar Girls* director Nigel Cole's film goes down as easily as a glass of bubbly. SP Swearing, nudity. **DVD** **Blu**

Rufus Hound *Raif* • Lucy Punch *Saskia* • Robert Webb *Tim* • Harriet Walter *Alex* • Miriam Margolyes *Patricia* • Angus Barnett *Reverend Dobbs* ■ *Dir* Nigel Cole • *Scr* Tim Firth

Wedding Wars ★★
Romantic comedy drama 2006 · US/Can · Colour · 87min

Gay marriage is explored in this warm and well-intentioned TV movie that uses froth instead of force to convey its positive messages. But though the uneven hybrid of comedy and seriousness ends up a little too playful at times, it's held together by charming performances. Stereotypes are both pandered to and turned on their heads with unsubtle, occasionally silly humour, but the powerful splash of poignancy that's employed to emphasise the universal issues here make for a contrived yet engaging story. SF

John Stamos *Shel Grandy* • Eric Dane *Ben Grandy* • Bonnie Somerville *Maggie Welling* • James Brolin *Governor Conrad Welling* ■ *Dir* Jim Fall • *Scr* Stephen Mazur

The Wee Man ★★★15
Crime drama based on a true story 2013 · UK · Colour · 101min

Writer/director Ray Burdis's solid, serious-minded crime drama wheels out a lot of gangster movie clichés - psychotic killers, bent coppers, criminals trying to go straight - but he has the excuse that it's all true. In 1970s Glasgow, Paul Ferris (Martin Compston) is a bullied kid whose dad (Denis Lawson) advises him to keep his head down. Paul wholeheartedly rejects that advice, taking bloody revenge on his tormentors and going on to become an enforcer for gang boss Arthur Thompson (Patrick Bergin) through the 80s and 90s. The script may lack spark, and the performances are patchy. But Compston is a compelling antihero and Stephen McCole impresses as his foolhardy nemesis, while the cinematography and direction are striking, belying the film's low budget. LB Violence, swearing, drug abuse. **DVD** **Blu**

Martin Compston *Paul Ferris* • John Hannah *Tam McGraw* • Patrick Bergin *Arthur Thompson* • Stephen McCole *Junior Thompson* • Denis Lawson *Willie Ferris* • Clare Grogan *Jenny Ferris* ■ *Dir/Scr* Ray Burdis

Wee Willie Winkie ★★★
Comedy drama 1937 · US · Sepia · 103min

Shirley Temple stars as yet another cute moppet in this sickly sweet reworking of Rudyard Kipling's vigorous tale of military life during the Raj. It is prevented from lapsing into unbearable sentimentality by the firm but sympathetic hand of western maestro John Ford, the polished reserve of C Aubrey Smith as Temple's malleable grandpa and the gruff good nature of Victor McLaglen. DP

Shirley Temple *Priscilla Williams* • Victor McLaglen *Sergeant MacDuff* • C Aubrey Smith *Colonel Williams* • June Lang *Joyce Williams* • Michael Whalen *Lieutenant "Coppy" Brandes* • Cesar Romero *Khoda Khan* ■ *Dir* John Ford • *Scr* Ernest Pascal, Julien Josephson, from the story by Rudyard Kipling

Weeds ★★18
Drama 1987 · US · Colour · 113min

Nick Nolte is the prisoner at San Quentin who forms a theatre group with his fellow convicts in this drama, loosely based on a true story. While Nolte and his worthy co-stars (William Forsythe, Joe Mantegna) give strong performances, they are bogged down by a script that can't decide whether to be light-hearted or serious. JB Violence, swearing.

Nick Nolte *Lee Umstetter* • Lane Smith *Claude* • William Forsythe *Burt the Booster* • John Toles-Bey *Navarro* • Joe Mantegna *Carmine* • Ernie Hudson *Bagdad* • Rita Taggart *Lillian Bingington, newspaper critic* ■ *Dir* John Hancock • *Scr* Dorothy Tristan, John Hancock

Le Week-end ★★★15
Comedy drama 2013 · UK · Colour · 89min

This bookish relationship drama finds spiky couple Jim Broadbent and Lindsay Duncan off to Paris to visit the haunts of honeymoon, 30 years previously. After many turbulent years together, a chance reunion with urbane college friend Jeff Goldblum offers a momentary distraction. The performances are terrific, especially the waspish, unfathomable Duncan, while Goldblum steals every scene as the unctuous ghost of all the ideals that the downtrodden Broadbent has long since abandoned. DW English, French +subtitles. Swearing, sexual references, drug abuse. **DVD** **Blu**

Jim Broadbent *Nick Burrows* • Lindsay Duncan *Meg Burrows* • Jeff Goldblum *Morgan* • Olly Alexander *Michael* • Judith Davis *Eve* • Xavier de Guillebon *Jean-Pierre* ■ *Dir* Roger Michell • *Scr* Hanif Kureishi

Week-End at the Waldorf ★★★
Portmanteau comedy drama 1945 · US · BW · 129min

Borrowing the idea from its more famous *Grand Hotel*, MGM came up with this star-

studded portmanteau movie covering nefarious goings-on and various romances during a weekend at Manhattan's glitzy Waldorf Astoria. Robert Benchley provides a narrative link between the stories, which feature Edward Arnold, Lana Turner, Van Johnson, Keenan Wynn and, centrally, the romantic comedy entanglement between Ginger Rogers as a famous movie star and Walter Pidgeon as a famous war correspondent. Diverting, but slightly heavy-handed. RK

Ginger Rogers *Irene Malvern, the actress* • Lana Turner *Bunny Smith, the stenographer* • Walter Pidgeon *Chip Collyer, the war correspondent* • Van Johnson *Capt James Hollis, the flyer* • Edward Arnold *Martin X Edley, the promoter* • Keenan Wynn *Oliver Webson, the cub reporter* • Robert Benchley *Randy Morton, the columnist* • Phyllis Thaxter *Cynthia Drew* ■ *Dir* Robert Z Leonard • *Scr* Sam Spewack, Bella Spewack, Guy Bolton (adaptation, from the play *Menschen im Hotel* (*Grand Hotel*) by Vicki Baum

Weekend ★★★★★18
Drama 1967 · Fr · Colour · 98min

Jean-Luc Godard's nightmare vision of the collapse of western capitalism has lost none of its blistering power. Hurling traditional narrative methods to the winds, Godard sends Mireille Darc and Jean Yanne on a journey to her mother's during the course of which they encounter such diverse characters as Emily Brontë dressed as Alice in Wonderland, the French Revolutionary Saint-Just and a cell of Maoist cannibals who persuade Darc to join them. The most audacious moment in this film of ceaseless invention is the lengthy traffic jam tracking shot, in which increasingly disturbing images are recorded with a lack of passion. DP French +subtitles. **DVD**

Mireille Darc *Corinne* • Jean Yanne *Roland* • Jean-Pierre Kalfon *Leader of the FLSO* • Valérie Lagrange *His moll* • Jean-Pierre Léaud *Saint-Just/Young man in phone booth* • Yves Beneyton *Member of FLSO* • Paul Gégauff *Pianist* ■ *Dir/Scr* Jean-Luc Godard

Weekend ★★★★18
Romantic drama 2011 · UK · Colour · 92min

After a casual Friday night pick-up, introverted lifeguard Russell (Tom Cullen) is forced outside his comfort zone by art gallery assistant Glen (Chris New), and quickly finds himself becoming more deeply attracted to the garrulous stranger. Indeed, Glen's own commitment phobia comes increasingly under strain as the pair do drugs, have sex and reveal their secrets. Writer/director Andrew Haigh breathes new life into the old adage that opposites attract in this beautifully shot and engaging love story. It's splendidly played with an understated intensity that deftly captures the shifting emotional tone of the relationship. DP Drug abuse, sex scenes, sexual references. **DVD** **Blu**

Tom Cullen *Russell* • Chris New *Glen* • Jonathan Race *Jamie* • Laura Freeman *Jill* • Jonathan Wright (2) *Johnny* • Loretto Murray *Cathy* ■ *Dir/Scr* Andrew Haigh

Weekend at Bernie's ★★★12
Comedy 1989 · US · Colour · 97min

OK, it's a one-joke movie and, yes, the gags are largely moronic, but this is still pretty good fun. Andrew McCarthy and Jonathan Silverman are the two junior executives who are forced to pretend their crooked boss (Terry Kiser) is still alive over a weekend in which he is to host a swinging party at the beach. It's a lot more tasteless than you would expect, and Kiser makes it all worthwhile in a scene-stealing performance as the much put-upon corpse. JF Violence, swearing **DVD** **Blu**

Andrew McCarthy *Larry Wilson* • Jonathan Silverman *Richard Parker* • Catherine Mary Stewart *Gwen Saunders* • Terry Kiser *Bernie Lomax* • Don Calfa *Paulie, the "Iceman"* • Catherine Parks *Tina* • Eloise Broady *Tawny* ■ *Dir* Ted Kotcheff • *Scr* Robert Klane

W

Weekend at Bernie's II ★ PG
Comedy   1992 · US · Colour · 85min

The central idea – 101 uses for a corpse – was barely substantial enough to sustain the first movie, but, unbelievably, most of the original team were talked into this foolish sequel. The now jobless Andrew McCarthy and Jonathan Silverman use the hapless Bernie (Terry Kiser), who's been turned into a walking zombie through voodoo, in a bid to locate some stolen money. JF

Andrew McCarthy *Larry Wilson* • Jonathan Silverman *Richard Parker* • Terry Kiser *Bernie Lomax* • Troy Beyer *Claudia* • Barry Bostwick *Hummel* • Tom Wright *Charles* • Steve James (1) *Henry* ■ *Dir/Scr* Robert Klane

Weekend in Havana ★★★
Comedy musical   1941 · US · Colour · 80min

This characteristic entry in the series of anodyne, colourful Fox musicals of the period packs Alice Faye off to Havana as a department store assistant who goes on a trip to the Cuban hot spot and falls in love with John Payne. As in all these movies, Carmen Miranda is on hand as a nightclub entertainer, showcasing her outrageously ebullient Latin-American flavoured dance routines and camp, exotic headgear. RK

Alice Faye *Nan Spencer* • Carmen Miranda *Rosita Rivas* • John Payne *Jay Williams* • Cesar Romero *Monte Blanca* • Cobina Wright Jr *Terry McCracken* • George Barbier *Walter McCracken* • Sheldon Leonard *Boris* • Leonid Kinskey *Rafael* • Billy Gilbert *Arbolado* ■ *Dir* Walter Lang • *Scr* Karl Tunberg, Darrell Ware

Weekend of a Champion ★★★★ PG
Documentary   1971 · UK · Colour · 89min

Formula One fans musn't miss this excellent and sometimes quirky profile of Jackie Stewart as he prepares for the Monaco Grand Prix in 1971, the year he won his second World Championship. The film was produced by Roman Polanski – like Stewart, one of the smart set and a racing fanatic who wanders around the pits and the track, getting the inside story. Way above the standard of the usual sports documentary, it probes the mind and the frayed nervous system of a racing driver, and vividly captures the mad F1 circus at its most glamorous venue. AT

Jackie Stewart (1) *Jackie Stewart* ■ *Dir/Scr* Frank Simon

Weekend Pass ★ 18
Comedy   1984 · US · Colour · 85min

In this inane sex comedy, four navy men fresh out of boot camp go wild on leave in Los Angeles. There they have the usual drunken brawls and meet a bevy of strippers. Their weekend comes to an end sooner for them than this mild exploitation picture does for the viewer. AJ

DW Brown *Paul Fricker* • Peter Ellenstein *Lester Gidley* • Patrick Hauser *Webster Adams* • Chip McAllister *Bunker Hill* ■ *Dir* Lawrence Bassoff • *Scr* Lawrence Bassoff, from a story by Mark Tenser

Weekend with Father ★★★
Romantic comedy   1951 · US · BW · 83min

Van Heflin and Patricia Neal, usually unsmiling in downbeat dramas, manage to display a lighter touch in this modest family romantic comedy directed by Douglas Sirk, before he gained his reputation for rich and ripe Technicolor melodramas. Heflin plays a widower with two daughters, and Neal is a widow with two sons. They meet while taking their respective children to summer camp, and naturally fall in love. Predictable and cosy it may be, but it's harmless and amusing. RB

Van Heflin *Brad Stubbs* • Patricia Neal *Jean Bowen* • Gigi Perreau *Anne Stubbs* • Virginia Field *Phyllis Reynolds* • Richard Denning *Don Adams* • Jimmy Hunt *Gary Bowen* • Janine Perreau *Patty Stubbs* • Tommy Rettig *David Bowen* ■ *Dir* Douglas Sirk • *Scr* Joseph Hoffman, from a story by George F Slavin, George W George

Weekender ★★ 15
Comedy drama   2011 · UK · Colour · 86min

Everything about Karl Golden's low-budget British drama seems familiar, from the charismatic young Manchester rogues who sweet-talk their way to the theft of a cigarette machine to the illegal raves run in disused warehouses that make a fortune for the organisers. The acting and direction are stylish and brash, with a confidence that teeters dangerously close to smugness, and there's also the perennial problem with party films that the audience is left in the position of wallflower, standing on the sidelines looking on. BP Swearing, drug abuse. *DVD* *Blu-ray*

Jack O'Connell (2) *Dylan* • Henry Lloyd-Hughes *Matt* • Emily Barclay *Claire* • Stephen Wight *Gary Mac* • Ben Batt *John Anderson* • Tom Meeten *Captain Acid* ■ *Dir* Karl Golden • *Scr* Chris Coghill

The Weight of Water ★★ 15
Thriller   2000 · Fr/US/Can · Colour · 109min

Kathryn Bigelow's downbeat, character-driven drama bypassed British cinemas and went straight to video. It's better than it sounds, despite its mild delusions of grandeur and confused and confusing ending. The split-level plotline involves a grisly murder 100 years earlier of two young girls that has a resonance and ramifications for two couples on a present-day yacht trip. Sean Penn, Catherine McCormack and Sarah Polley head a quality cast. DA Violence, swearing, sex scenes, nudity. *DVD*

Catherine McCormack *Jean Janes* • Sarah Polley *Maren Hontvedt* • Sean Penn *Thomas Janes* • Josh Lucas *Rich Janes* • Elizabeth Hurley *Adaline Gunne* • Ciaran Hinds *Louis Wagner* • Ulrich Thomsen *John Hontvedt* • Anders W Berthelsen *Evan Christenson* • Katrin Cartlidge *Karen Christenson* ■ *Dir* Kathryn Bigelow • *Scr* Alice Arlen, Christopher Kyle, from the novel *The Weight of Water* by Anita Shreve

Weiner ★★★ 15
Documentary   2016 · US · Colour · 95min

An authorised account of congressman Anthony Weiner's bid to become New York mayor after coming back from a sexting scandal. All is going relatively well… and then lewd photos come to light. It's here that Josh Kriegman and Elyse Steinberg's intimate documentary becomes excruciating farce and a grimly fascinating case study in narcissism, as Weiner fights masochistically on. The real story is his spouse, however, who admits on camera that it's "like living a nightmare". You couldn't make it up. AC *DVD*

Anthony Weiner ■ *Dir/Scr* Josh Kriegman, Elyse Steinberg

Weird Science ★★ 12
Comedy fantasy   1985 · US · Colour · 89min

This is the worst of John Hughes's early comedies, but still a cut above most teen fodder of the time. Hughes regular Anthony Michael Hall and Ilan Mitchell-Smith are the sex-obsessed hi-tech anoraks who summon up the computer-generated woman of their dreams (Kelly LeBrock). Hughes remains a sharp observer of teenage woes but this time around there is a crassness to much of the humour. The best performance comes from Bill Paxton as Mitchell-Smith's fascist brother, and look out, too, for an early role for Robert Downey Jr. JF Swearing, nudity. *DVD* *Blu-ray*

Anthony Michael Hall *Gary* • Ilan Mitchell-Smith *Wyatt* • Kelly LeBrock *Lisa* • Bill Paxton *Chet* • Suzanne Snyder *Deb* • Judie Aronson *Hilly* • Robert Downey Jr *Ian* • Robert Rusler *Max* ■ *Dir/Scr* John Hughes

Weird Woman ★★
Horror   1944 · US · BW · 63min

This *Inner Sanctum* series entry was adapted from Fritz Leiber Jr's novel *Conjure Wife*, also the inspiration for *Night of the Eagle* and *Witches' Brew*. Although Lon Chaney Jr was the series mainstay, this film firmly belongs to scream queen Evelyn Ankers, who becomes deliriously jealous when Chaney's college professor returns from an exotic holiday with new bride Anne Gwynne. In dealing with her rival, whose past is steeped in voodoo mystery, Ankers resorts to insinuation and murder. DP

Lon Chaney [Lon Chaney Jr] *Prof Norman Reed* • Anne Gwynne *Paula Reed* • Evelyn Ankers *Ilona Carr* • Ralph Morgan *Prof Millard Sawtelle* • Elisabeth Risdon *Grace Gunnison* ■ *Dir* Reginald Le Borg • *Scr* Brenda Weisberg, W Scott Darling [Scott Darling], from the novel *Conjure Wife* by Fritz Leiber Jr

Weirdsville ★★ 15
Black comedy drama   2006 · Can · Colour · 87min

Weird is the word for this B-movie from maverick Canadian director Allan Moyle, in which a pair of stoners (played by Scott Speedman and Wes Bentley) concoct a plan to clear their debt to a local drugs kingpin. However, before they can enact the questionable scheme, they have to bury the body of a girlfriend (Taryn Manning) who has apparently overdosed on their stash, disturbing some preppy Satanists in the process. This frenetic black comedy is the sort of experience that will either be rated a cult classic in 20 years time, or completely forgotten. In either case, its low-budget feel and scattershot approach make it best suited to viewing on DVD. DA *DVD*

Scott Speedman *Dexter* • Wes Bentley *Royce* • Taryn Manning *Matilda* • Greg Bryk *Abel* • Maggie Castle *Treena* • Dax Ravina *Seamus* • Joe Dinicol *Jeremy* • Raoul Bhaneja *Omar* ■ *Dir* Allan Moyle • *Scr* Willem Wennekers

Welcome ★★★ 15
Drama   2009 · Fr/Bel · Colour · 109min

Vincent Lindon excels at playing the everyman who draws on untapped resources to meet unexpected challenges. However, not even his committed turn as an altruistic Calais swimming coach can atone for the contrivances in this otherwise well-meaning migrant melodrama. Director Philippe Lioret passes incisive comment on French immigration laws and the cynicism of the local gendarmerie, as well as making evocative use of forbidding images of the docks and beaches to suggest the harshness of a transient's existence, in what turns out to be a fitfully engrossing yet frustrating tale. DP French, Kurdish, English +subtitles. Violence, swearing.

Vincent Lindon *Simon* • Firat Ayverdi *Bilal* • Audrey Dana *Marion* • Derya Ayverdi *Mina* • Thierry Godard *Bruno* • Selim Akgul *Zoran* ■ *Dir* Philippe Lioret • *Scr* Philippe Lioret, Olivier Adam, Emmanuel Courcol, Serge Frydman

Welcome Home ★★★ 15
Drama   1989 · US · Colour · 88min

Or not, as the case may be, when Kris Kristofferson, a Vietnam veteran, is shipped home after 17 years living contentedly with his Cambodian wife and children. His American wife, JoBeth Williams, is now remarried and cut the yellow ribbon years ago. This is a partially successful attempt to examine the consequences of rising from the dead, but it's exceptionally mushy stuff. Sam Waterston, as Williams's husband number two, gives a sterling portrayal of compassion. SH Swearing, nudity. *DVD*

Kris Kristofferson *Jake* • JoBeth Williams *Sarah* • Sam Waterston *Woody* • Brian Keith *Harry* • Thomas Wilson Brown *Tyler* • Trey Wilson *Colonel Barnes* • Ken Pogue *Senator Camden* • Kieu Chinh *Leang* • Matthew Beckett *Kim* • Jessica Ramien *Siv* ■ *Dir* Franklin J Schaffner • *Scr* Maggie Kleinman

Welcome Home Roscoe Jenkins ★★ 12
Comedy   2008 · US · Colour · 109min

Sibling rivalry delivers plenty of hard knocks in this Georgia-set homecoming comedy. Martin Lawrence plays an A-list Hollywood talk-show host who returns to the Deep South to celebrate the 50th wedding anniversary of his parents (James Earl Jones and Margaret Avery), only to have his comic pretensions ruthlessly mocked by his family. Heavy on high jinks, the film is fatally short on heart, with its bickering characters so over-the-top, they're virtually caricatures. JR Sex scenes, brief swearing. *DVD*

Martin Lawrence *RJ* • Margaret Avery (2) *Mamma Jenkins* • Joy Bryant *Bianca Kittles* • Louis CK *Marty* • Michael Clarke Duncan *Otis* • Mike Epps *Reggie* • Mo'Nique *Betty* • Cedric the Entertainer *Clyde* • James Earl Jones *Papa Jenkins* ■ *Dir/Scr* Malcolm D Lee

Welcome Home, Roxy Carmichael ★★★ 15
Comedy   1990 · US · Colour · 91min

This subtle comedy starring Winona Ryder relies heavily on her performance and that of co-star Jeff Daniels. Ryder plays a 15-year-old misfit who is awaiting the return to the town of legendary local Roxy Carmichael, whom she believes is her real mother. Predictable in places, the plot hasn't been fully developed, but once again Ryder gives a winning performance. JB Some nudity. *DVD*

Winona Ryder *Dinky Bossetti* • Jeff Daniels *Denton Webb* • Laila Robins *Elizabeth Zaks* • Thomas Wilson Brown *Gerald Howells* • Joan McMurtrey *Barbara Webb* • Graham Beckel *Leo Bossetti* • Frances Fisher *Rochelle Bossetti* • Robby Kiger *Beannie Billings* ■ *Dir* Jim Abrahams • *Scr* Leigh Hopkins

Welcome Stranger ★★
Medical comedy drama   1947 · US · BW · 107min

Paramount scored a massive box-office hit with *Going My Way* (1944), in which Barry Fitzgerald and Bing Crosby co-starred as a crusty old priest and a new young assistant. In this flagrant rerun of the formula, the pair are doctors, running a clinic and adored by their patients. Crosby bursts into song on several occasions, romances blonde schoolteacher Joan Caulfield, and saves curmudgeonly old Fitzgerald's life, much as he saved his church in the earlier film. RK

Bing Crosby *Dr Jim Pearson* • Joan Caulfield *Trudy Mason* • Barry Fitzgerald *Dr Joseph McRory* • Wanda Hendrix *Emily Walters* • Frank Faylen *Bill Walters* • Elizabeth Patterson *Mrs Gilley* ■ *Dir* Elliott Nugent • *Scr* Arthur Sheekman, Richard Nash [N Richard Nash], from a story by Frank Butler

Welcome to Arrow Beach ★ 18
Horror   1974 · US · Colour · 80min

What on earth drew Laurence Harvey to such lurid material? This exploration of cannibalism was an all the more regrettable choice when it proved to be his swan song. Harvey directs and also stars as a Korean War veteran who developed a taste for human flesh when his bomber crashed on a deserted island and he was forced to live off his comrades. Now living with his sister (Joanna Pettet) his unusual table manners attract the attention of local cops. Inept and distasteful. RS

Laurence Harvey *Jason Henry* • Joanna Pettet *Grace Henry* • Stuart Whitman *Deputy Rakes* • John Ireland *Sheriff H "Duke" Bingham* • Gloria LeRoy *Ginger* • David Macklin *Alex Heath* ■ *Dir* Laurence Harvey • *Scr* Wallace C Bennett, Jack Gross Jr, from a story by Wallace C Bennett

Welcome to Collinwood ★★★ 15
Crime caper   2002 · US/Ger · Colour · 82min

Film-making siblings Joe and Anthony Russo display cinematic verve and a keen eye for sleaze in this Cleveland-set remake of the much-loved 1958 Italian heist comedy *Big Deal on Madonna Street*. Petty crook Luis Guzman is given details of the perfect crime (a "Bellini" – the script is full of enjoyable made-up slang) and a ragtag band of lowlifes is assembled for the job. There's little suspense, but it's diverting watching them fail. AC Violence, swearing. *DVD*

Sam Rockwell *Pero* • William H Macy *Riley* • Michael Jeter *Toto* • Luis Guzman *Cosimo* • Isaiah Washington *Leon* • Andrew Davoli *Basil* • Patricia Clarkson *Rosalind* • Gabrielle Union *Michelle* • George Clooney *Jerzy* ■ *Dir* Anthony Russo, Joe Russo • *Scr* Anthony Russo, Joe

U SUITABLE FOR ALL   Uc SUITABLE ESPECIALLY FOR YOUNG CHILDREN (DVD ONLY)   PG PARENTAL GUIDANCE   12A UNDER 12s TO BE ACCOMPANIED (CINEMA ONLY)

Russo, from the film *Big Deal on Madonna Street* by Suso D'Amico Cecchi, Mario Monicelli, Agenore Incrocci, Furio Scarpelli.

Welcome to Hard Times ★★
Western   1967 · US · Colour · 102min

This hard-to-watch, grim and slow allegorical western is somewhat of a surprise coming from director Burt Kennedy, better known for his comedy westerns. Aldo Ray is a vicious killer, forced into confrontation with mayor Henry Fonda, and the supporting cast is marvellous, with great performances from western regulars Warren Oates, Edgar Buchanan and Elisha Cook Jr. But the whole leaves a very nasty taste in the mouth, and the symbolism doesn't really come off. **TS**

Henry Fonda *Will Blue* • Janice Rule *Molly Riordan* • Keenan Wynn *Zar* • Janis Page *Adah* • Aldo Ray *Man from Bodie* • John Anderson *Ezra/Isaac Maple* • Warren Oates *Jenks* • Fay Spain *Jessie* • Edgar Buchanan *Brown* • Denver Pyle *Alfie* ■ *Dir* Burt Kennedy • *Scr* Burt Kennedy, from the novel by EL Doctorow

Welcome to LA   ★★★ 15
Drama   1976 · US · Colour · 89min

Produced by Robert Altman, this early Alan Rudolph picture is clearly modelled after *Nashville* and centres on cynical songwriter Keith Carradine arriving in LA to work on an album and sleeping around with a number of women. Rudolph blends together sour social satire, musical numbers, improvisational scenes and jaundiced views on marriage for a compelling whole, sharply summing up Tinseltown attitudes. **AJ**

Keith Carradine *Carroll Barber* • Sally Kellerman *Ann Goode* • Geraldine Chaplin *Karen Hood* • Harvey Keitel *Ken Hood* • Lauren Hutton *Nona Bruce* • Viveca Lindfors *Susan Moore* • Sissy Spacek *Linda Murray* • Denver Pyle *Carl Barber* ■ *Dir/Scr* Alan Rudolph

Welcome to Leith ★★★★ 15
Documentary   2015 · US · Colour · 82min

The remote North Dakota community of Leith finds itself vulnerable to the machinations of a white supremacist, in this utterly absorbing documentary. And as tensions escalate, uniformed neo-Nazis turn up at a town meeting. The film-makers capture all this vividly on the hoof, but remain scrupulously even-handed, recording both the distress of the residents and the resentment of the supremacists. The result is a thought-provoking offering that looks at the legal status of those espousing unpalatable ideologies. **TJ** Swearing, offensive language.

■ *Dir* Michael Beach Nichols, Christopher K Walker • *Cinematographer* Michael Beach Nichols

Welcome to Me   ★★★ 15
Comedy drama   2014 · US · Colour · 83min

Taking a swing at the cultural climate that rewards self-obsession, this is the second feature from Shira Piven. The title refers to a TV show devised by a lottery-winning "emotional exhibitionist" (Kristen Wiig), who's suffering from borderline personality disorder and has come off her meds. More successful at the surreal than the satirical, this terrific platform for Wiig's deadpan comedic skills never quite goes for the jugular, so fails to draw out the cynicism of the enterprise. It does dabble with the dark side, but it feels a little lightweight. **EAS** Swearing, sex scenes. *DVD* *BL*

Kristen Wiig *Alice Klieg* • Wes Bentley *Gabe Ruskin* • Linda Cardellini *Gina Selway* • Joan Cusack *Dawn Hurley* • Jennifer Jason Leigh *Deb Moseley* ■ *Dir* Shira Piven • *Scr* Eliot Laurence

Welcome to Mooseport   ★★ PG
Comedy   2004 · US · Colour · 105min

American TV star Ray Romano fails to transfer successfully to the big screen in this flaccid, by-the-numbers comedy. It's all about a mayoral race between an ex-president (played by the dependable Gene Hackman) and an average Joe (Romano) in small-town America. This is a toothless satire that relies on clichéd characterisation

as it lurches from one predictable scene to another. **GM** *DVD*

Gene Hackman *Monroe Cole* • Ray Romano *Handy Harrison* • Marcia Gay Harden *Grace Sutherland* • Maura Tierney *Sally Mannis* • Christine Baranski *Charlotte Cole* • Fred Savage *Bullard* • Rip Torn *Bert Langdon* • June Squibb *Irma* ■ *Dir* Donald Petrie • *Scr* Tom Schulman, from a story by Doug Richardson

Welcome to New York
           ★★★★ 18
Drama based on a true story
2014 · US · Colour · 125min

Gérard Depardieu is simultaneously compelling and repulsive in this slow-burning orgy of sex, money and power from Abel Ferrara (*Bad Lieutenant*). Depardieu plays Devereaux, a thinly fictionalised version of disgraced finance mogul Dominique Strauss-Kahn, who lives a life of hedonistic excess until he is arrested for sexual assault on a trip to New York. Ferrara's unflinching direction results in several absorbing sequences, while Depardieu offers a brave performance as the self-confessed sex addict. **SC** Violence, sex scenes. *DVD* *BL*

Gérard Depardieu *Devereaux* • Jacqueline Bisset *Simone* • Marie Mouté *Sophie Devereaux* • Pamela Afesi *Chambermaid* • Nikki James *Judge* • Paul Calderon *Pierre* ■ *Dir* Abel Ferrara • *Scr* Abel Ferrara, Christ Zois

Welcome to Sarajevo   ★★★ 15
Drama based on a true story
1997 · UK/US · Colour · 97min

This is a vigorously unsentimental treatment of love in a time of war – the Bosnian conflict – based on a true story in which ITN TV reporter Michael Henderson (played by Stephen Dillane) decides to smuggle a young refugee girl out to Britain. The seedy hotel-based world of foreign correspondents is expertly evoked by director Michael Winterbottom, though Woody Harrelson's tough-talking American journalist manages to upstage even the conflict itself. **TH** Violence, swearing. *DVD*

Stephen Dillane *Michael Henderson* • Woody Harrelson *Flynn* • Marisa Tomei *Nina* • Emira Nusevic *Emira* • Kerry Fox *Jane Carson* • Goran Visnjic *Risto* • James Nesbitt *Gregg* • Emily Lloyd *Annie McGee* ■ *Dir* Michael Winterbottom • *Scr* Frank Cottrell Boyce, from the non-fiction book *Natasha's Story* by Michael Nicholson

Welcome to the Dollhouse
           ★★★★ 15
Comedy drama   1995 · US · Colour · 87min

Before he made his name with the controversial *Happiness* (1998), Todd Solondz also raised a few eyebrows with this truthful look at the nightmares of growing up. Eleven-year-old New Jersey misfit Dawn Wiener (a superb performance from young Heather Matarazzo) has all the problems of an average schoolgirl: she has an unrequited crush on her brother's friend, is being threatened by the school tough guy and is overlooked by her mother in favour of her ballet-dancing younger sister. Thanks to Solondz's original ideas, no-holds-barred script and determination never to stray into sentimentality, plus an impressive young cast, this is both fascinating and ironic. **JB** *DVD*

Heather Matarazzo *Dawn Wiener* • Victoria Davis *Lolita* • Christina Brucato *Cookie* • Christina Vidal *Cynthia* • Siri Howard *Chrissy* • Brendan Sexton Jr [Brendan Sexton III] *Brandon McCarthy* • Daria Kalinina *Missy Wiener* ■ *Dir/Scr* Todd Solondz

Welcome to the Jungle   ★★★ 15
Action comedy adventure
2003 · US · Colour · 99min

Former wrestler The Rock vies for the 21st-century action man crown in this energetic comedy adventure, in which he demonstrates acting prowess to match his physical strength. He plays a Mob "retrievals expert" who's eager to go straight and become a chef, but he's given the final job of recovering his boss's double-

dealing son (the wisecracking Seann William Scott) from the Brazilian jungle. The frenetically paced film delivers exciting set pieces and quick-hit humour. **SF** Violence. *DVD* *BL*

The Rock [Dwayne Johnson] *Beck* • Seann William Scott *Travis* • Rosario Dawson *Mariana* • Christopher Walken *Hatcher* • Ewen Bremner *Declan* • Jon Gries [Jonathan Gries] *Harvey* • William Lucking *Walker* • Ernie Reyes Jr *Manito* ■ *Dir* Peter Berg • *Scr* RJ Stewart, James Vanderbilt, from a story by RJ Stewart

Welcome to the Punch
           ★★★★ 15
Crime thriller   2012 · UK · Colour · 95min

James McAvoy and Mark Strong are on a collision course in this slick London-set action thriller inspired by Michael Mann's *Heat* and Hong Kong cop films. It doesn't quite hit the same levels of intensity, but it's still an exhilarating ride, confidently handled by director Eran Creevy. While in pursuit of serial robber Jacob Sternwood (Strong), cop Max Lewinsky (McAvoy) takes a bullet. Three years later, Max is a shell of a man, crippled emotionally and physically, but he gets a shot at redemption when Sternwood breaks cover to see his critically injured son. The aesthetic is cool steel (it was shot mostly in the financial heart of the city), but the morality is painted in shades of grey. There's also top-notch support from the likes of Andrea Riseborough, David Morrissey and Peter Mullan in a story that is played with great swagger. **SP** Violence, swearing. *DVD* *BL*

James McAvoy *Max Lewinsky* • Mark Strong *Jacob Sternwood* • Andrea Riseborough *Sarah Hawks* • Peter Mullan *Roy Edwards* • David Morrissey *Thomas Geiger* • Daniel Mays *Nathan Bartnick* • Jason Flemyng *Harvey Crown* ■ *Dir/Scr* Eran Creevy

Welcome to the Rileys   ★★★ 15
Drama   2009 · US · Colour · 110min

The crushing effect of grief is the main theme of this well-acted drama from director Jake Scott (son of Ridley). James Gandolfini and Melissa Leo play an Indianapolis husband and wife struggling to come to terms with the loss of their teenage daughter. But when Gandolfini decides to stay in New Orleans after a business trip and befriends a volatile, foul-mouthed stripper (Kristen Stewart, in a role that's a million miles from *Twilight's* Bella Swan), it's the catalyst for change in the lives of these emotionally bereft people. This will win no prizes for originality, but it benefits greatly from the subtle performances of the two leads, particularly Leo, who is by turns irritating, sweet, funny and insightful in a part that could easily have turned into caricature. **JA** *DVD*

James Gandolfini *Doug Riley* • Melissa Leo *Lois Riley* • Kristen Stewart *Mallory* • Joe Chrest *Jerry* • Ally Sheedy *Harriet* • Tiffany Coty *Tara* ■ *Dir* Jake Scott • *Scr* Ken Hixon

Welcome II the Terrordome
           ★★ 18
Science-fiction thriller
1994 · UK · Colour · 89min

This semi-futuristic thriller certainly has more than its fair share of heavy-handed messages to the detriment of any discernible entertainment value. Its starting point, the hounding into the sea of black slaves in 17th-century North Carolina, is powerfully drawn and provides a thumpingly dramatic opening that director Ngozi Onwurah fails to build on. A bit of a yawn. **SH** Violence.

Suzette Llewellyn *Angela McBride/African woman #1* • Saffron Burrows *Jodie* • Felix Joseph *Black Rad/African leader* • Valentine Nonyela *Spike/African Man #1* • Ben Wynter *Hector/African boy* • Sian Martin *Chrisele/African woman #2* • Jason Traynor *Jason/Assistant overseer* ■ *Dir/Scr* Ngozi Onwurah

The Well   ★★★
Drama   1951 · US · BW · 85min

The disappearance of a young black girl leads to the wrongful arrest of a white man

(Harry Morgan) on a kidnapping charge. When the girl is discovered to have fallen down a deep well, the arrested man is released and eventually helps with the digging operation to rescue her. Leo Popkin and Russell Rouse direct this suspenseful race relations drama from an Oscar-nominated screenplay by Rouse and Clarence Greene, drawing excellent performances from a non-star cast, and mining the rescue action for maximum tension. **RK**

Harry Morgan *Claude Packard* • Gwendolyn Laster *Carolyn Crawford* • Richard Rober *Sheriff Ben Kellogg* • Maidie Norman *Mrs Crawford* • George Hamilton *Grandfather* • Ernest Anderson *Mr Crawford* • Barry Kelley *Sam Packard* • Tom Powers *Mayor* ■ *Dir* Leo C Popkin, Russell Rouse • *Scr* Russell Rouse, Clarence Greene

The Well Digger's Daughter
           ★★★★ PG
Period romantic drama
2010 · Fr · Colour · 109min

For his directorial debut, Daniel Auteuil remakes a 1940 film written by Marcel Pagnol. But Auteuil (star of the Pagnol-sourced *Jean de Florette* and *Manon des Sources*) avoids bathing the action in a nostalgic glow. A widowed father summons his 18-year-old daughter (Astrid Bergès-Frisbey) from Paris to care for her younger sisters. However, her youthful charms enchant bourgeois would-be pilot Nicolas Duvauchelle, and it falls to Auteuil's faithful retainer (Kad Merad) to attempt to reunite father and daughter after he disowns her. Relishing Auteuil's literate script, the stellar ensemble cast excels, while the camerawork of Jean-François Robin captures time and place with unfussy fidelity. **DP** French +subtitles. *DVD*

Daniel Auteuil *Pascal Amoretti* • Astrid Bergès-Frisbey *Patricia Amoretti* • Kad Merad *Félipe Rambert* • Nicolas Duvauchelle *Jacques Mazel* • Jean-Pierre Darroussin *Mr Mazel* • Sabine Azéma *Mrs Mazel* ■ *Dir* Daniel Auteuil • *Scr* Daniel Auteuil, from the film *La Fille du Puisatier* by Marcel Pagnol • *Cinematographer* Jean-Francois Robin

Well Done Abba   ★★
Comedy drama   2009 · Ind · Colour · 144min

Veteran director Shyam Benegal follows up the socially conscious high jinks of *Welcome to Sajjanpur* with another vibrantly shot, though overlong, Hindi comedy about Indian village life. Following Mumbai driver Boman Irani's attempts to get a well built for his rural-dwelling daughter, the satire is at its strongest when dealing with the humorous desperation accompanying his situation, but the issue-stuffed story meanders excessively, introducing too many characters and subplots. **SF** Hindi +subtitles.

Boman Irani *Armaan Ali/Rehman Ali* • Minissha Lamba *Muskaan Ali* • Sammir Dattani [Sameer Dattani] *Arif Ali* • Ila Arun *Salma Ali* ■ *Dir* Shyam Benegal • *Scr* Jayut Kripilani, Ashok Mishra, from short story *Phulwa Ka Pul* by Sanjeev and short story *Narsayya Ki Bavdi* by Jeelani Bano

The Well Groomed Bride
           ★★★ U
Romantic comedy   1946 · US · BW · 75min

There's a severe champagne shortage in San Francisco. Naval officer Ray Milland needs some to launch a ship. Bride-to-be Olivia de Havilland has some, but insists on keeping it for her wedding to ex-footballer Sonny Tufts. Why only one bottle of the stuff is available remains a mystery in a plot so slight as to border on the invisible, but Milland's efforts to wrest the precious liquid from de Havilland bubble along merrily enough. **RK**

Olivia de Havilland *Margie* • Ray Milland *Lt Dudley Briggs* • Sonny Tufts *Torchy McNeil* • James Gleason *Capt Hornby* • Constance Dowling *Rita Sloane* • Percy Kilbride *Mr Dawson* ■ *Dir* Sidney Lanfield • *Scr* Claude Binyon, Robert Russell, from a story by Robert Russell

W

We'll Meet Again ★★★ U
Musical 1942 · UK · BW · 81min

No prizes for guessing who's the star of this British wartime flag-waver. Based on what remains to this day her signature tune, Vera Lynn shows in this sugary confection why you can count her film appearances on the fingers of one hand. However, nostalgia nuts will not be disappointed as she keeps smiling through even though her best pal, Patricia Roc, has clouded her blue skies by eloping with her soldier boyfriend. This is a pretty amateurish affair, but tune in for a sing-song with Dame Vera, and Geraldo and his orchestra. DP *DVD*

Vera Lynn *Peggy Brown* • Geraldo *Gerry* • Patricia Roc *Ruth* • Ronald Ward *Frank* • Donald Gray *Bruce McIntosh* • Frederick Leister *Mr Hastropp* • Betty Jardine *Miss Bohne* ■ *Dir* Phil Brandon • *Scr* James Seymour, Howard Thomas, from a story by Derek Sheils

We'll Never Have Paris ★★ 15
Romantic comedy 2014 · US · Colour · 91min

This lacklustre romantic comedy seems a little like a lost episode in the life of Simon Helberg's *Big Bang Theory* character, Howard Wolowitz. Purportedly inspired by the courtship of Helberg and his wife Jocelyn Towne (who co-directs), this also feels like a discarded draft of an early Woody Allen picture, as Helberg dumps longtime girlfriend Melanie Lynskey for Maggie Grace, then tries to get Lynskey back. No one will be in any doubt how this will end, but what will most disappoint *Big Bang* fans is the chauvinism on display. DP In English, French. Swearing, sex scenes. *DVD*

Simon Helberg *Quinn* • Melanie Lynskey *Devon* • Alfred Molina *Terry* • Zachary Quinto *Jameson* • Maggie Grace *Kelsey* ■ *Dir* Jocelyn Towne, Simon Helberg • *Scr* Simon Helberg

We'll Smile Again ★★★ U
Second World War musical comedy
1942 · UK · BW · 93min

Unlike many stage, radio or television double acts who flounder when put on the big screen, Bud Flanagan and Chesney Allen fared rather well as movie stars, and this is a typical effort, combining bright comedy with songs and human interest. Flanagan (who had a hand in the script) plays a down-and-out hired by stage star Allen to be his dresser, but his actions are misunderstood when he tries to rout Nazi spies who are using Allen's act to send coded messages. Directed with no pretension by John Baxter, it is an engaging showcase for one of Britain's best-loved song-and-comedy teams. TV

Bud Flanagan *Bob Parker* • Chesney Allen *Gordon Maxwell* • Meinhart Maur *Herr Steiner* • Phyllis Stanley *Gina Cavendish* • Peggy Dexter *Googie* • Horace Kenney *George* • Gordon McLeod *MacNaughton* • Alexander Kardan *Holtzman* ■ *Dir* John Baxter • *Scr* Bud Flanagan, Austin Melford, Barbara K Emary

Wells Fargo ★★★
Western 1937 · US · BW · 115min

Oscar-winning director Frank Lloyd is virtually forgotten today, his epic style and passionate narrative sense well out of fashion. This is the story of America's famous freight carrier, unfolding as we follow the screen marriage of leads Joel McCrea and Francis Dee (a married couple in real life). Regrettably, their tortuous relationship gets in the way of the truly epic saga of Wells Fargo itself. This was McCrea's first substantial leading role, and he underplays in the style of the great silent western stars. Stirring entertainment. TS

Joel McCrea *Ramsay MacKay* • Bob Burns (2) *Hank York* • Frances Dee *Justine* • Lloyd Nolan *Del Slade* • Porter Hall *James Oliver* • Ralph Morgan *Mr Pryor* • Mary Nash *Mrs Pryor* • Robert Cummings *Trimball* • Henry O'Neill *Henry Wells* ■ *Dir* Frank Lloyd • *Scr* Paul Schofield, Gerald Geraghty, Frederick Jackson, from a story by Stuart N Lake

Wendigo ★★ 15
Horror thriller 2001 · US · Colour · 88min

Devoid of any sense of terror or even tension, this snail's pace horror tale barely features the ravenous, mythological spirit of its title. Instead, writer/director Larry Fessenden creates a kind of low budget *Deliverance*, in which a haughty New York couple and their overly sensitive son get on the wrong side of the redneck locals in the snowy Catskill Mountains. Fessenden relies on creaky doors and obscure camera angles to create atmosphere. SF *DVD*

Patricia Clarkson *Kim* • Jake Weber *George* • Erik Per Sullivan *Miles* • John Speredakos *Otis* • Christopher Wynkoop *Sheriff* ■ *Dir/Scr* Larry Fessenden

Wendy and Lucy ★★★★ 15
Social drama 2008 · US · Colour · 76min

Director Kelly Reichardt's heartbreaking drama recalls the spirit of writer John Steinbeck and film-maker Vittorio De Sica, particularly his 1952 drama *Umberto D*. Already impoverished, Wendy (Michelle Williams) breaks down in a small Oregon town as she heads towards Alaska in hope of a job at a cannery. Unable to afford food for herself and her faithful dog Lucy, let alone the garage bill, she's arrested for shoplifting and later finds that her sole companion in the world has disappeared. It says much for Williams's poignantly understated performance that she is not upstaged by her photogenic canine sidekick. But it's the evocation of the Great Depression, with its train tracks, hobos and gnawing sense of defeat, decay and despair, that leaves the most indelible impression. DP *DVD*

Michelle Williams *Wendy* • Will Patton *Mechanic* • John Robinson (3) *Andy* • Larry Fessenden *Man in Park* ■ *Dir* Kelly Reichardt • *Scr* Jon Raymond [Jonathan Raymond], Kelly Reichardt, from the story *Train Choir* by Raymond

Went the Day Well? ★★★★★ PG
Second World War drama
1942 · UK · BW · 88min

This is without question the finest Home Front picture made during the Second World War. Adapted from Graham Greene's short story, it depicts the seizure of a quiet English village by disguised Nazi soldiers in league with local quislings with such plausibility that it must have chilled contemporary audiences to the bone. Those watching today will be similarly struck by the steel beneath the quintessential Englishness of the villagers. What makes this such compelling cinema for viewers decades later is the realism and restraint with which director Alberto Cavalcanti tells his tale and the naturalistic playing of his splendid cast. DP *DVD* *BL*

Leslie Banks *Oliver Wilsford* • Elizabeth Allan *Peggy* • Frank Lawton *Tom Sturry* • Basil Sydney *Ortler* • Valerie Taylor *Nora Ashton* • Mervyn Johns *Sims* • Edward Rigby *Poacher* • Marie Lohr *Mrs Frazer* • CV France *Vicar* • David Farrar *Jung* • Muriel George *Mrs Collins* • Thora Hird *Land girl* • Harry Fowler *George Truscott* • Patricia Hayes *Daisy* ■ *Dir* Alberto Cavalcanti • *Scr* Angus MacPhail, Diana Morgan, John Dighton, from the short story *The Lieutenant Died Last* by Graham Greene

Werckmeister Harmonies ★★★★ 12
Drama
2000 · Hun/Fr/Ger/It/Swi · BW · 139min

This confirms Bela Tarr's status as a director of extraordinary vision. Set in a town about to implode into anarchy, it's a terrifying study of the helplessness of the individual in the face of cowardly repression and mob rule. Yet there's a bleak beauty about the monochrome imagery (credited to cinematographer Gabor Medvigy, among others), whether it's capturing the growing tension on the windswept streets, the pathos of a stuffed whale exhibited in the main square or the brutality of the climactic assault on a hospital. Densely symbolic, yet never inaccessible, this is artistically unique and overwhelmingly powerful. DP Hungarian +subtitles. *DVD*

Lars Rudolph *Janos Valuska* • Peter Fitz *Gyorgy Eszter* • Hanna Schygulla *Tunde Eszter* • Janos Derzsi *Man in broad-cloth coat* • Djoko Rossich *Man in western boots* • Tamas Wichmann *Man in the sailor cap* • Ferenc Killai *Director* ■ *Dir* Bela Tarr • *Scr* Laszlo Krasznahorkai, Bela Tarr, from the novel *Melancholy of Resistance* by Laszlo Krasznahorkai

We're Back! A Dinosaur's Story ★★★ U
Animated fantasy 1993 · US · Colour · 67min

This animated tale wasn't widely shown in the UK – a shame since it's a jolly enough affair, well designed and featuring a literate script from Oscar-winning writer John Patrick Shanley. The story revolves around four dinosaurs who travel through time to New York and get mixed up in a series of adventures. Children will adore the dino-antics while adults will recognise some familiar voices. JF *DVD*

John Goodman *Rex* • Blaze Berdahl *Buster* • Rhea Perlman *Mother Bird* • Jay Leno *Vorb* • Rene Levant *Woo* • Felicity Kendal *Elsa* • Charles Fleischer *Dweeb* • Walter Cronkite *Captain Neweyes* • Julia Child *Doctor Bleeb* • Martin Short *Stubbs, the Clown* ■ *Dir* Dick Zondag, Ralph Zondag, Phil Nibbelink, Simon Wells • *Scr* John Patrick Shanley, from the book *We're Back* by Hudson Talbott

We're Going to Be Rich ★★
Musical drama 1938 · UK · BW · 80min

Made for 20th Century-Fox, this attempt to launch Gracie Fields as an international star was a failure outside England. This is hardly surprising, given the feebleness of the material which finds Gracie as a 19th-century singer married to feckless Victor McLaglen. They go to South Africa where he has invested their savings in a gold mine, and find they have lost the money. She sings in a saloon, becomes romantically involved with its owner Brian Donlevy and parts from hubby, but not irrevocably... RK

Gracie Fields *Kit Dobson* • Victor McLaglen *Dobbie Dobson* • Brian Donlevy *Yankee Gordon* • Coral Browne *Pearl* • Ted Smith *Tim Dobson* • Gus McNaughton *Broderick* • Charles Carson *Keeler* ■ *Dir* Monty Banks • *Scr* Sam Hellman, Rohama Siegel, from a story by James Edward Grant

We're No Angels ★★ U
Comedy 1955 · US · Colour · 101min

Humphrey Bogart, Peter Ustinov and Aldo Ray are the three cons who escape from Devil's Island and intend to rip off French shopkeeper, Leo G Carroll, and his alluring wife, Joan Bennett, in this unruly caper. Reunited with the director of *Casablanca*, Bogart isn't well matched with his co-stars or best suited to this sort of farce. And when the script turns all moralistic and gooey (with Bogart dressing up as Santa Claus and singing carols) you start looking around for Bing Crosby. A misjudgement. AT *DVD*

Humphrey Bogart *Joseph* • Joan Bennett *Amelie Ducotel* • Peter Ustinov *Jules* • Aldo Ray *Albert* • Leo G Carroll *Felix Ducotel* • Basil Rathbone *André Trochard* • Gloria Talbott *Isabelle Ducotel* ■ *Dir* Michael Curtiz • *Scr* Ranald MacDougall, from the play *La Cuisine des Anges* by Albert Husson

We're No Angels ★★ 15
Comedy thriller 1989 · US · Colour · 101min

Neil Jordan's film, while not that bad, is a disappointing waste of an impressive array of talent. The script is by David Mamet, and the cast includes Robert De Niro, Sean Penn and Demi Moore. Yet the result is a leaden, only fitfully funny farce in which escaped cons De Niro and Penn pose as priests as they attempt to cross the border to Canada. Moore's role is mainly decorative and the best performances come from a wily support cast. JF Violence, swearing, brief nudity.

Robert De Niro *Ned* • Sean Penn *Jim* • Demi Moore *Molly* • Hoyt Axton *Father Levesque* • Bruno Kirby *Deputy* • Ray McAnally *Warden* • James Russo *Bobby* • Wallace Shawn *Translator*

• Jay Brazeau *Sheriff* • Elizabeth Lawrence *Mrs Blair* ■ *Scr* Neil Jordan • *Scr* David Mamet, from the play *La Cuisine des Anges* by Albert Husson

We're Not Dressing ★★★
Musical comedy 1934 · US · BW · 74min

Culled without credit from JM Barrie's *The Admirable Crichton*, this gives the plum role to Bing Crosby and, accordingly, supplies a handful of songs for him to croon. Crosby is the deck hand on millionairess Carole Lombard's luxury yacht, cruising with a bunch of disparate, sometimes eccentric, friends and her pet bear in the South Seas. Shipwrecked on a desert island, none are able to cope except Crosby, who takes charge of the situation – and of spoiled heiress Lombard. Inconsequential, but madcap and enjoyable. RK

Bing Crosby *Stephen Jones* • Carole Lombard *Doris Worthington* • George Burns *George* • Gracie Allen *Gracie* • Ethel Merman *Edith* • Leon Errol *Hubert* • Raymond Milland [Ray Milland] *Prince Michael* ■ *Dir* Norman Taurog • *Scr* Horace Jackson, Francis Martin, George Marion Jr, from a story by Benjamin Glazer • *Music/lyrics* Mack Gordon, Harry Revel

We're Not Married ★★★ U
Portmanteau comedy 1952 · US · BW · 82min

This portmanteau movie is delightful froth, all about five couples who discover they're not legally married in a clever, censor-circumventing series of tales. The major attraction for today's audience, however, is not in the witty Nunnally Johnson/Dwight Taylor screenplay, but in the fourth-billed presence of Marilyn Monroe. Ginger Rogers is top-billed, but there's much pleasure to be gained from watching the sparkling cast. Don't blink or you'll miss an uncredited Lee Marvin. TS *DVD*

Ginger Rogers *Ramona* • Fred Allen (2) *Steve Gladwyn* • Victor Moore *Justice of the Peace* • Marilyn Monroe *Annabel Norris* • David Wayne *Jeff Norris* • Eve Arden *Katie Woodruff* • Paul Douglas *Hector Woodruff* • Eddie Bracken *Willie Fisher* • Mitzi Gaynor *Patsy Fisher* • Louis Calhern *Freddie Melrose* • Zsa Zsa Gabor *Eve Melrose* • Lee Marvin ■ *Dir* Edmund Goulding • *Scr* Nunnally Johnson, Dwight Taylor, from a story by Gina Kaus, Jay Dratler

We're the Millers ★★★ 15
Comedy 2013 · US · Colour · 105min

Jason Sudeikis is the small-time pot dealer who has his stash stolen, leaving him owing thousands to buddy Ed Helms, now a major drug kingpin. To settle the debt he agrees to smuggle a large shipment from Mexico, recruiting a stripper (Jennifer Aniston) and two surly teens to pose as his holidaying family. While Sudeikis and Aniston make a good pairing as the would-be spouses, the stand-out performance in this broad comedy comes from Will Poulter as their nerdy fake son. TeS Swearing, sexual references. *DVD* *BL*

Jennifer Aniston *Rose O'Reilly* • Jason Sudeikis *David Clark* • Emma Roberts *Casey Mathis* • Ed Helms *Brad Gurdlinger* • Will Poulter *Kenny Rossmore* ■ *Dir* Rawson Marshall Thurber • *Scr* Bob Fisher, Steve Faber, Sean Anders, John Morris (2), from a story by Fisher, Faber

The Werewolf ★★
Horror 1956 · US · BW · 79min

Scientists S John Launer and George Lynn experiment on tormented family man Steven Ritch to find a cure for radiation poisoning and turn him into a werewolf in the process. A competent and timely marriage of horror with science fiction just as the latter form was going out of favour in the 1950s. Clever trick photography and Ritch's sympathetic performance make this up a few notches from routine. AJ

Steven Ritch *Duncan Masch/The Werewolf* • Don Megowan *Jack Haines* • Joyce Holden *Amy Standish* • Eleanore Tanin *Helen Marsh* • Harry Lauter *Clovey* • Ken Christy *Dr Gilchrist* • S John Launer *Dr Emery Forrest* • George Lynn *Dr Morgan Chambers* ■ *Dir* Fred F Sears • *Scr* Robert E Kent, James B Gordon

Werewolf of Washington ★★ 15

Comedy horror   1973 · US · Colour · 84min

Conceived at the height of the Watergate scandal, this odd blend of horror and political satire has lost much of its counterculture bite. Dean Stockwell stars as the journalist who asks to be posted to Hungary when a First Family affair is uncovered. Bitten by a werewolf, he returns to the Washington as a White House press aide and terrorises the capital. This is as technically erratic as it is now terminally dated, but does have a social history value. AJ *DVD*

Dean Stockwell *Jack Whittier* • Biff McGuire *President* • Clifton James *Attorney General* • Beeson Carroll *Commander Salmon* • Jane House *Marion* • Michael Dunn *Dr Kiss* • Nancy Andrews *Mrs Captree* • Ben Yaffee *Judge Captree* ■ *Dir/Scr* Milton Moses Ginsberg

Wes Craven's Don't Look Down ★★ 12

Horror thriller   1998 · US · Colour · 86min

Despite the presence of *Scream* director Wes Craven as co-executive producer, this TV movie struggles to make an impression. After her sister falls off a cliff in a freak accident, Megan Ward joins a controversial support group to overcome her fear of heights. When the members of the group start getting killed one by one, the weak terror begins. AJ *DVD*

Megan Ward *Carla Engel* • Billy Burke *Mark Engel* • Terry Kinney *Dr Paul Sadowski* • Angela Moore *Jocelyn* • William MacDonald *Ben* • Kate Robbins (1) *Hallie* • Aaron Smolinski *Zak* ■ *Dir* Larry Shaw • *Scr* Gregory Goodell

Wes Craven's New Nightmare ★★★ 18

Horror   1994 · US · Colour · 107min

Before director Wes Craven came back big time with *Scream*, he took a stab at the intellectual horror film, adding this semi-documentary style sequel to the *Nightmare on Elm Street* series. The terrorised teen from the original, Heather Langenkamp, plays herself, an actress troubled by (a real?) Freddy Krueger. There's a healthy dose of shocks, a look behind the scenes of the horror flick, and, although the project occasionally reeks of self-indulgence, you have to credit Craven (who also appears as himself) with trying something new. AJ Violence, swearing. *DVD* *Blu*

Robert Englund *Freddy Krueger/Robert Englund* • Heather Langenkamp • Miko Hughes *Dylan* • David Newsom *Chase Porter* • Jeffrey John Davis *Freddy's hand double* • Matt Winston *Chuck* • Rob LaBelle *Terry* • Wes Craven • Marianne Maddalena ■ *Dir* Wes Craven • *Scr* Wes Craven, from his characters

West ★★★ 15

Drama   2013 · Ger · Colour · 102min

Writer/director Christian Schwochow does a decent job of adapting Julia Franck's novel about the plight of East Germans crossing the Berlin Wall. Jördis Triebel stars as single mother Nelly, who in 1978 gets across the border with her son to escape Stasi surveillance after the death of her partner. But her true identity is quickly discovered at the refugee centre, where Nelly is torn between trusting a longtime inmate or the interrogator who believes her other half is a spy now living in Moscow. Despite conveying a sense of Cold War paranoia and dread, this is a rather routine melodrama that lacks the intrigue of similarly themed pictures. DP German, English, Russian, Polish +subtitles. Violence, sex scenes

Jördis Triebel *Nelly Senff* • Tristan Göbel *Alexei Senff* • Alexander Scheer *Hans Pischke* • Jacky Ido *John Bird* • Stefan Lampadius *Jürgen* ■ *Dir* Christian Schwochow • *Scr* Heide Schwochow, from the novel *Lagerfeuer* by Julia Franck

West Beirut ★★★★ 15

Drama   1998 · Fr/Leb/Bel/Nor · Colour · 105min

Having served as assistant cameraman on Quentin Tarantino's first three features, Ziad Doueiri makes his directorial debut with this autobiographical account of growing up in war-torn Lebanon in the 1970s. Capturing the exuberance of youth and the vicarious thrill of the situation without ever losing sight of the seriousness of the conflict, Doueiri draws an outstanding performance from his younger brother, Rami, as the Muslim teenager whose passion for movies prompts him to travel across the barricaded city in search of adventure. A real eye-opener. DP French, Arabic +subtitles. Swearing.

Rami Doueiri *Tarek* • Mohamad Chamas *Omar* • Rola Al Amin *May* • Carmen Lebbos *Hala* • Joseph Bou Nassar *Riad* ■ *Dir/Scr* Ziad Doueiri

West 11 ★★ 15

Crime drama   1963 · UK · BW · 93min

Michael Winner's skirmish with British social realism shows what life was like in the bedsits of Notting Hill, years before Julia Roberts showed up. Among the cast are Alfred Lynch as a drifter, Eric Portman as a cashiered officer and Diana Dors as a lonely heart. The script is mostly a series of loosely connected sketches, though the film's sole virtue nowadays is the location camerawork of Otto Heller that captures the then peeling and shabbily converted Regency houses that were riddled with dry rot and Rachmanism, which exchanged squalor for extortionate rents. AT *DVD*

Alfred Lynch *Joe Beckett* • Kathleen Breck *Ilsa Barnes* • Eric Portman *Richard Dyce* • Diana Dors *Georgia* • Kathleen Harrison *Mrs Beckett* • Finlay Currie *Mr Cash* • Patrick Wymark *Father Hogan* • Freda Jackson *Mrs Hartley* ■ *Dir* Michael Winner • *Scr* Keith Waterhouse, Willis Hall, from the novel *The Furnished Room* by Laura del Rivo

West Is West ★★ 15

Comedy drama   2010 · UK · Colour · 98min

In this sequel to 1999's popular multicultural romp *East Is East*, stern Salford dad George Khan (Om Puri) decides his youngest son needs to get back in touch with his Pakistani roots, prompting a return to the country, and the family, that he left 30 years before. Writer Ayub Khan Din offers a change of scenery that also brings a change of tone, but director Andy DeEmmony struggles to create the air of mystery and magic that the exotic milieu lends itself to. Puri does work wonders revealing the vulnerability behind George's bluff exterior, but by trying to do something different with the characters, the film omits much of the good-hearted yet slightly edgy laughter we enjoyed so much the first time round. TJ English, Punjabi +subtitles. Swearing. *DVD* *Blu*

Om Puri *George Khan* • Aqib Khan *Sajid Khan* • Linda Bassett *Ella Khan* • Emil Marwa *Maneer Kahn* • Jimi Mistry *Tariq Khan* • Ila Arun *Basheera Khan* ■ *Dir* Andy DeEmmony • *Scr* Ayub Khan Din

West of Memphis ★★★★ 15

Documentary   2012 · US/NZ · Colour · 141min

The case of the "West Memphis Three", an alleged miscarriage of justice in which a trio of teenagers was convicted for the brutal murder of three eight-year-old boys in 1993, has already been the subject of a number of excellent documentaries. So it may be a surprise that there is anything left to say. But this rigorously researched film does indeed add to the account, not least in challenging the accepted version of events and in its shocker of an ending, which points the finger of blame in a direction that is both surprising and convincing. AS Swearing. *DVD*

■ *Dir* Amy Berg • *Scr* Amy Berg, Billy McMillin

West of the Divide ★★★ U

Western   1934 · US · BW · 52min

Monogram studio fans insist that this is the best of John Wayne's "Lone Star" series; it melds two familiar western plots, the revenge for the death of the hero's father and the cowboy masquerading as an outlaw to avenge the said death, and Wayne proves himself at ease with such material. TS *DVD*

John Wayne *Ted Hayden* • Virginia Brown Faire *Fay Winters* • Lloyd Whitlock *Gentry* • George Hayes [George "Gabby" Hayes] *Dusty Rhodes* • Yakima Canutt *Hank* • Billy O'Brien (1) *Spud* ■ *Dir/Scr* Robert N Bradbury

West of Zanzibar ★★★

Silent melodrama   1928 · US · BW · 63min

Lon Chaney gives his most twisted performance in silent genius Tod Browning's bitterly grim morality fable that proved to be another bizarre and amazing signpost in the evolution of modern horror. Paralysed in an altercation with his wife's lover, sadistic magician "Dead Legs" Flint (Chaney) takes their offspring to Africa, leaves her in a whorehouse and plots a terrible ritual revenge after becoming the wheelchaired god to the local natives. The ultimate Browning/Chaney freak show is an extreme depiction of parent-child alienation and as sordid a slice of atrocity exotica as 1920s censors would allow. AJ

Lon Chaney *Flint* • Lionel Barrymore *Crane* • Warner Baxter *Doc* • Mary Nolan *Maizie* ■ *Dir* Tod Browning • *Scr* Elliott Clawson, Waldemar Young, Joe Farnham [Joseph Farnham] (titles), from a story by Chester De Vonde, Kilbourne Gordon • *Set Designer* Cedric Gibbons

West of Zanzibar ★★ U

Adventure   1954 · UK · Colour · 90min

The sequel to *Where No Vultures Fly* again features Anthony Steel as African wildlife conservationist and game warden Bob Payton. Payton's wife is now played by Sheila Sim, replacing Dinah Sheridan but perfectly transferring the social graces of Tunbridge Wells to the African bush. The emphasis is on travelogue material and shots of animals, most of which were rehashed from the earlier film. Drama is trumped up by ivory poachers and the ravages of drought. It all seems simplistic and racist today, and it was banned by the Kenyan government, then in the grip of the Mau Mau uprising, who felt the film was patronising. AT *DVD*

Anthony Steel *Bob Payton* • Sheila Sim *Mary Payton* • William Simons *Tim Payton* • Orlando Martins *M'Kwongwi* • Edric Connor *Chief Ushingo* • David Osieli *Ambrose* • Bethlehem Sketch *Bethlehem* • Martin Benson *Lawyer Dhofar* ■ *Dir* Harry Watt • *Scr* Max Catto, Jack Whittingham, from a story by Harry Watt

The West Point Story ★★ U

Musical comedy   1950 · US · BW · 106min

James Cagney is in *Yankee Doodle Dandy* mode here, putting on a musical show for the cadets at West Point military academy. Cagney displays plenty of energy but struggles to shine, while co-stars Virginia Mayo, Doris Day and Gordon MacRae sing and strut their way through a roster of songs that badly needs a showstopper. Roy Del Ruth, a veteran of the *Broadway Melody* movies, could direct this sort of thing with his eyes closed, and probably did. AT

James Cagney *Elwin Bixby* • Virginia Mayo *Eve Dillon* • Doris Day *Jan Wilson* • Gordon MacRae *Tom Fletcher* • Gene Nelson *Hal Courtland* • Alan Hale Jr *Bull Gilbert* • Roland Winters *Harry Eberhart* • Raymond Roe *Bixby's "wife"* ■ *Dir* Roy Del Ruth • *Scr* John Monks Jr, Charles Hoffman, Irving Wallace, from the story *Classmates* by Irving Wallace

West Side Story ★★★★★ PG

Musical romantic drama   1961 · US · Colour · 145min

Ten well-deserved Oscars – plus a special award for Jerome Robbins's dynamic choreography – adorned this electrifying version of the magnificent Leonard Bernstein-Stephen Sondheim musical. It's an update of *Romeo and Juliet*, here turned into a New York gang parable set in the turbulent late 1950s. And surely the only Oscar ever given to an actor for merely looking good went to the elegant George Chakiris. Natalie Wood is touching as the tragic Maria and Richard Beymer – criticised at the time as Tony – now seems the very quintessence of adolescent yearning. TS *DVD* *Blu*

Natalie Wood *Maria* • Richard Beymer *Tony* • Russ Tamblyn *Riff* • Rita Moreno *Anita* • George Chakiris *Bernardo* • Simon Oakland *Lieutenant Schrank* • Ned Glass *Doc* • Tucker Smith *Ice* • Tony Mordente *Action* • Jose De Vega *Chino* • Jay Norman *Pepe* ■ *Dir* Robert Wise, Jerome Robbins • *Scr* Ernest Lehman, from the stage play by Arthur Laurents, from an idea by Jerome Robbins, from Shakespeare's *Romeo and Juliet* • *Costume Designer* Irene Sharaff • *Cinematographer* Daniel L Fapp • *Editor* Thomas Stanford • *Art Director* Boris Leven

The West Side Waltz ★★★

Comedy drama   1995 · US · Colour · 90min

Ernest Thompson, Oscar-winning screenplay writer of *On Golden Pond*, wrote and directed this starry, if slightly sudsy, TV-movie drama. Shirley MacLaine and Liza Minnelli play the grumpy older women whose lives are opened up when they encounter aspiring young actress Jennifer Grey. The two stars give sterling performances – Minnelli in particular is cast effectively against type – and they're well backed by classy supporting turns from the likes of Robert Pastorelli and Kathy Bates. SuR

Shirley MacLaine *Margaret Mary Elderdice* • Liza Minnelli *Cara Varnum* • Jennifer Grey *Robin Ouiseau* • Kathy Bates *Mrs Goo* • Robert Pastorelli *Sookie Cerullo* • August Schellenberg *Serge* ■ *Dir/Scr* Ernest Thompson

Westbound ★★★ U

Western   1959 · US · Colour · 68min

This decent Civil War western stars genre stalwart Randolph Scott as a Union officer transporting gold from California to finance the war effort and running into Confederate sympathisers and old flame Virginia Mayo along the way. While not breaking any new ground, this re-ploughs the old furrows with consummate professionalism, pacing and style. SH

Randolph Scott *John Hayes* • Virginia Mayo *Norma Putnam* • Karen Steele *Jeannie Miller* • Michael Dante *Rod Miller* • Andrew Duggan *Clay Putnam* • Michael Pate *Mace* ■ *Dir* Budd Boetticher • *Scr* Berne Giler, from the story *The Great Divide No 2* by Berne Giler, Albert Shelby LeVino

Western ★★ 15

Romantic comedy road movie   1997 · Fr · Colour · 128min

This quirky French road movie won the Grand Jury Prize at Cannes in 1997. Two rootless men, Sergi Lopez and Sacha Bourdo meet, fight and become firm friends, both falling on French female hospitality in their search of hearth, love and home-made bread. With its thin storyline and some very questionable moral commentary, this treads a fine line between good and bad taste. LH French +subtitles. Swearing, sex scenes.

Sergi Lopez *Paco Cazale* • Sacha Bourdo *Nino* • Elisabeth Vitali *Marinette* • Marie Matheron *Nathalie* • Basile Siekoua *Baptiste* ■ *Dir* Manuel Poirier • *Scr* Manuel Poirier, Jean-François Goyet, from an idea by Manuel Poirier

Western Union ★★★ U

Western   1941 · US · Colour · 91min

German émigré director Fritz Lang seemed comfortable out west, and this movie followed quickly on the heels of his *The Return of Frank James*. Today these films seem a little tame, and this tale of the building of the telegraph line between Omaha, Nebraska, and Salt Lake City, Utah, suffers from being undercast – there's a particularly uncharismatic lead in Robert Young, but the set pieces are done with bravura and the cinematography is ravishing. TS *DVD*

Robert Young (1) *Richard Blake* • Randolph Scott *Vance Shaw* • Dean Jagger *Edward Creighton* • Virginia Gilmore *Sue Creighton* • John Carradine *Doc Murdoch* • Chill Wills *Homer* • Barton MacLane *Jack Slade* ■ *Dir* Fritz Lang • *Scr* Robert Carson, from the novel by Zane Grey • *Cinematographers* Edward Cronjager, Allen M Davey

W

The Westerner ★★★★ U
Western   1940 · US · BW · 95min

Director William Wyler cut his teeth on westerns and here brings all his professional skills to bear in a fine example of the genre. In the lead is the star who always looked at home in the West, lanky Gary Cooper, in a tale based on the life of the notorious Judge Roy Bean, played by Walter Brennan, who won a third best supporting actor Oscar for his ferocious performance. The story itself may be fable, but Bean's celebrated obsession with Lillie Langtry was real enough, and the clever screenplay makes good use of it, particularly at the climax. TS

Gary Cooper *Cole Hardin* • Walter Brennan *Judge Roy Bean* • Doris Davenport *Jane-Ellen Mathews* • Fred Stone *Caliphet Mathews* • Paul Hurst *Chickenfoot* • Chill Wills *Southeast* • Forrest Tucker *Wade Harper* ■ *Dir* William Wyler • *Scr* Jo Swerling, Niven Busch, from a story by Stuart N Lake • *Cinematographer* Gregg Toland

Westfront 1918 ★★★★
First World War drama   1930 · Ger · BW · 98min

Released in the same year as Lewis Milestone's *All Quiet on the Western Front*, GW Pabst's film on the same subject, the Great War, caught the anti-war mood of the times. The film captures the horror of trench warfare, something audiences were only then becoming familiar with 12 years after the event. The story of how it effects four soldiers is rather simple, and the plea for universal brotherhood is expressed in a naive manner, but Pabst, using sound for the first time, and low tracking shots over the battleground, gives one of the most vivid impressions of what it was actually like on the spot. RB In German.

Fritz Kampers *The Bavarian* • Gustav Diessl *Karl* • Hans Joachim Moebis *The Student* • Claus Clausen *The Lieutenant* ■ *Dir* GW Pabst • *Scr* Ladislaus Vajda, Peter Martin Lampel, from the novel *Vier von der Infanterie* by Ernst Johannsen

Westward Ho ★★
Western   1935 · US · BW · 61min

This is a B-western with John Wayne before he was worth watching. It does rate a footnote in film history as the first release of Republic, a newly-formed amalgamation of several small outfits, though there is little difference between this effort and those he was making beforehand. Wayne plays the vigilante leader hunting badmen with a vengeance. Be warned that the Duke warbles a love song (dubbed, of course!) in the moonlight. AE

John Wayne *John Wyatt* • Sheila Mannors [Sheila Bromley] *Mary Gordon* • Frank McGlynn Jr *Jim Wyatt* • James Farley *Lafe Gordon* • Jack Curtis (1) *Walt Ballard* • Yakima Canutt *Red* ■ *Dir* RN Bradbury [Robert N Bradbury] • *Scr* Lindsley Parsons, Robert Emmett [Robert Emmett Tansey]

Westward Passage ★★
Romantic comedy   1932 · US · BW · 72min

Laurence Olivier is the vain but blocked writer who believes his wife, Ann Harding, is responsible. They bicker all day long, get divorced and she marries Irving Pichel until realising it's Olivier she loves truly, madly, deeply. The tone is decidedly Shaftesbury Avenue rather than Hollywood because Olivier, under contract to RKO, was being touted as the toast of the London stage. The title implied a western which is perhaps why it flopped. AT

Ann Harding *Olivia Van Tyne* • Laurence Olivier *Nick Allen* • ZaSu Pitts *Mrs Truedale* • Juliette Compton *Henriette* • Irving Pichel *Harry Lenman* • Irene Purcell *Diane Van Tyne* ■ *Dir* Robert Milton • *Scr* Bradley King, Humphrey Pearson, from the novel by Margaret Ayer Barnes

Westward the Women ★★
Western   1951 · US · BW · 116min

Frank Capra had wanted to make this western but his story was purchased by MGM and assigned to director William A Wellman. Its novelty is that Robert Taylor recruits over a hundred women in Chicago to start a new life as the wives of men out west and they make up his wagon train –

learning to shoot, fight hostile tribes and endure various hardships en route to their new life. It's something of an ensemble piece, with Denise Darcel as the standout. AE

Robert Taylor (1) *Buck Wyatt* • Denise Darcel *Fifi Danon* • Hope Emerson *Patience Hawley* • John McIntire *Roy Whitman* • Julie Bishop *Laurie Smith* • Beverly Dennis *Rose Meyers* • Marilyn Erskine *Jean Johnson* ■ *Dir* William A Wellman • *Scr* Charles Schnee, from a story by Frank Capra

Westworld ★★★★ 15
Futuristic thriller   1973 · US · Colour · 85min

The seeds of *Jurassic Park* and its sequel *The Lost World* can easily be recognised in this futuristic suspense thriller from writer/director Michael Crichton about a resort where people go to live out their fantasies. But Richard Benjamin and James Brolin's dream cowboy vacation turns into a nightmare when the android population malfunctions and robot gunslinger Yul Brynner pursues them relentlessly. This is a fun scare flick that puts its clever gimmicks to imaginative use, with the inspired casting of chilling Brynner, good special effects and an incisive message about the dark side of male fantasies adding extra resonance. The less successful *Futureworld* followed in 1976. AJ Violence, swearing. **DVD** **Blu**

Yul Brynner *Gunslinger* • Richard Benjamin *Peter Martin* • James Brolin *John Blane* • Norman Bartold *Medieval Knight* • Alan Oppenheimer *Chief Supervisor* • Victoria Shaw *Medieval Queen* • Dick Van Patten *Banker* ■ *Dir/Scr* Michael Crichton

The Wet Parade ★★
Period drama   1932 · US · BW · 118min

This self-important MGM production is a real oddity that condemns demon drink while also criticising Prohibition, trying to be hard-hitting while not giving offence to any point of view. Despite fine production and a strong cast, it is heavy going. The first half depicts Southern patriarch Lewis Stone being destroyed by alcohol, while the second half focuses on the thankless work of Prohibition agents. The casting of Jimmy Durante as a government agent is just one of the film's perverse qualities. TV

Dorothy Jordan *Maggie May Chilcote* • Lewis Stone *Roger Chilcote* • Neil Hamilton *Roger Chilcote Jr* • Emma Dunn *Mrs Sally Chilcote* • Frederick Burton *Judge Brandon* • Reginald Barlow *Major Randolph* • Robert Young (1) *Kip Tarleton* • Walter Huston *Pow Tarleton* • Jimmy Durante *Abe Shilling* • Wallace Ford *Jerry Tyler* • Myrna Loy *Eileen Pinchon* ■ *Dir* Victor Fleming • *Scr* John Lee Mahin, from the novel by Upton Sinclair

Wetherby ★★★★ 15
Drama   1985 · UK · Colour · 98min

Written and directed by playwright David Hare, this subtle, suddenly shocking, story set in Wetherby, a cold, bleak town in Yorkshire, where unmarried local teacher Vanessa Redgrave gives a small dinner party. The next day she is visited by one of the guests, Tim McInnerny, who suddenly takes out a gun and kills himself. The reasons are not at all explicable at first, but as they gradually emerge, the apparently innocuous party is seen again in a whole new light. An intriguing British movie, underrated in its day. TH **DVD**

Vanessa Redgrave *Jean Travers* • Ian Holm *Stanley Pilborough* • Judi Dench *Marcia Pilborough* • Marjorie Yates *Verity Braithwaite* • Tom Wilkinson *Roger Braithwaite* • Tim McInnerny *John Morgan* • Suzanna Hamilton *Karen Creasy* • Joely Richardson *Young Jean* ■ *Dir/Scr* David Hare

Whale Music ★★★
Romance   1994 · Can · Colour · 110min

Maury Chaykin won the best actor Genie (the Canadian equivalent of an Oscar) for his performance as a washed-up rock star in this touching but rather low-key drama. The song *Claire* also took an award, but the musical centrepiece is a symphony for whales that Chaykin hopes will be his lasting memorial. However, life seems to be conspiring against his completing the piece. Chaykin is convincing, as is Cyndy Preston

as the teenage runaway who befriends him. DP Swearing, sex scenes, nudity.

Maury Chaykin *Desmond Howl* • Cyndy Preston *Claire Lowe* • Jennifer Dale *Fay Ginzburg-Howl* • Kenneth Walsh *Kenneth Sexston* • Paul Gross *Daniel Howl* • Blu Mankuma *Mookie Saunders* • Alan Jordan *Sal Goneau* ■ *Dir* Richard J Lewis • *Scr* Paul Quarrington, Richard J Lewis, from the novel by Quarrington

Whale Rider ★★★ PG
Drama   2002 · NZ/Ger · Colour · 97min

If you want a family drama that takes in such weighty issues as spirituality, destiny and the role of women in Maori culture, then this unsentimental drama from director Niki Caro fits the bill. Can schoolgirl Paikea (Oscar-nominated Keisha Castle-Hughes) prove her ancestral worth and leadership qualities to her old-fashioned grandfather, a believer in upholding masculine tribal traditions? The stern character of the patriarchal Koro (Rawiri Paratene), the stunning scenery of the New Zealand coastline, the often sharply funny and well-observed script and the uniformly solid acting ensure any cloying worthiness is well disguised. AJ **DVD**

Keisha Castle-Hughes *Paikea* • Rawiri Paratene *Koro* • Vicky Haughton *Flowers* • Cliff Curtis *Porourangi* • Grant Roa *Uncle Rawiri* • Mana Taumaunu *Hemi* ■ *Dir* Niki Caro • *Scr* Niki Caro, from the novel by Witi Ihimaera

The Whales of August ★★★★ U
Drama   1987 · US · Colour · 90min

While Lindsay Anderson is chiefly remembered for classic and explosive movies such as *if...*, he was also in love with the theatre and with stage actors, so he naturally jumped at the chance to make this autumnal showcase for Bette Davis and Lillian Gish. It's chiefly a battle of wits between two curmudgeonly stars. Gish, then aged 91, nurses her sister Davis who is blind. Gish – in her last film – is still the delicate actress from the silent days. Fans of Old Hollywood will adore it. AT

Lillian Gish *Sarah Webber* • Bette Davis *Libby Strong* • Vincent Price *Mr Nikolai Maranov* • Ann Sothern *Tisha Doughty* • Harry Carey Jr *Joshua Brackett* • Frank Grimes *Mr Beckwith* ■ *Dir* Lindsay Anderson • *Scr* David Berry, from his play

What? ★ 18
Drama   1973 · It/Fr/W Ger · Colour · 108min

Roman Polanski said this showed the absurdity and extravagance of the outgoing 1960s, dealing with an American flower child (Sydne Rome) who arrives at a Mediterranean villa, strips off and indulges in sex and power games with Marcello Mastroianni and non-acting jet-set types. A self-indulgent mess. AT Italian dubbed. **DVD** **Blu**

Marcello Mastroianni *Alex* • Sydne Rome *The Girl* • Romolo Valli *Administrator* • Hugh Griffith *Owner of Villa* • Guido Alberti *Priest* • Giancarlo Piacentini *Stud* • Carlo Delle Piane *The Boy* • Roman Polanski *Zanzara* ■ *Dir* Roman Polanski • *Scr* Roman Polanski, Gérard Brach

What a Carve Up! ★★★ U
Comedy horror   1961 · UK · BW · 84min

An old dark house comedy, co-written by that master of the *double entendre*, Ray Cooney. *Carry On* regulars Sid James and Kenneth Connor are among those gathering at a musty mansion in the hope of inheriting a fortune, but, as anyone who has seen *The Cat and the Canary* can tell you, the chances of a will being read without blood being shed are pretty slim. The cast works wonders with a script that too often settles for a cheap laugh. DP **DVD**

Kenneth Connor *Ernie Broughton* • Sidney James *Syd Butler* • Shirley Eaton *Linda Dickson* • Dennis Price *Guy Broughton* • Donald Pleasence *Mr Sloane, solicitor* • Michael Gough *Fisk, the butler* • Valerie Taylor *Janet Broughton* • Esma Cannon *Aunt Emily* ■ *Dir* Pat Jackson • *Scr* Ray Cooney, Tony Hilton, Leonard J Hines, from the novel and play *The Ghoul* by Dr Frank King, Leonard J Hines

What a Crazy World ★★ 12
Musical drama   1963 · UK · BW · 85min

With Tommy Steele and Cliff Richard making movies, it was only a matter of time before Joe Brown would have a go. The result is an amiable but outdated musical that is still worth catching to see Brown and the Bruvvers, Freddie and the Dreamers, Susan Maughan and Marty Wilde at the height of their powers. The longueurs between the musical numbers, which the more generous might call the plot, are distinctly dodgy. DP **DVD**

Joe Brown (2) *Alf Hitchens* • Susan Maughan *Marilyn* • Marty Wilde *Herbie Shadbolt* • Harry H Corbett *Sam Hitchens* • Avis Bunnage *Mary Hitchens* • Michael Ripper *Common Man* • Grazina Frame *Doris Hitchens* ■ *Dir* Michael Carreras • *Scr* Alan Klein, Michael Carreras, from the play by Klein

What a Girl Wants ★★ PG
Comedy   2003 · US · Colour · 100min

Previously filmed as *The Reluctant Debutante* with Sandra Dee and Rex Harrison in 1958, this lightweight comedy stars Amanda Bynes as the love child of American Kelly Preston and titled Brit Colin Firth, who leaves her home in New York to go in search of her father in England. There are the usual fish-out-of-water calamities, as Firth and Bynes learn to like as well as love each other. JA **DVD**

Amanda Bynes *Daphne Reynolds* • Colin Firth *Henry Dashwood* • Kelly Preston *Libby Reynolds* • Eileen Atkins *Jocelyn Dashwood* • Anna Chancellor *Glynnis Payne* • Jonathan Pryce *Alistair Payne* • Oliver James *Ian Wallace* • Sylvia Syms *Princess Charlotte* ■ *Dir* Dennie Gordon • *Scr* Jenny Bicks, Elizabeth Chandler, from the film *The Reluctant Debutante* by William Douglas Home, from the play by William Douglas Home

What a Way to Go! ★★★ U
Comedy   1964 · US · Colour · 106min

This lavish, frantic comedy has Shirley MacLaine as a serial wife, marrying one of the best casts ever assembled: Dick Van Dyke's humble storekeeper turned zillionaire; Paul Newman's American artist in Paris; Robert Mitchum's Howard Hughes-type tycoon; and Gene Kelly's matinée idol. Occasionally the movie falls flat, but the script comes up with some clever demises for the husbands and mercilessly satirises the egotism of Kelly. In 1964 the visual style was a knockout; today one might need sunglasses to watch. AT **DVD**

Shirley MacLaine *Louisa* • Paul Newman *Larry Flint* • Robert Mitchum *Rod Anderson* • Dean Martin *Leonard Crawley* • Gene Kelly *Jerry Benson* • Bob Cummings [Robert Cummings] *Dr Stephanson* • Dick Van Dyke *Edgar Hopper* ■ *Dir* J Lee Thompson • *Scr* Betty Comden, Adolph Green, from a story by Gwen Davis • *Cinematographer* Leon Shamroy

What a Whopper! ★★ U
Comedy   1961 · UK · BW · 89min

Adam Faith stars in this whimsical tale about a struggling writer who fakes photographs of the Loch Ness monster and then heads for the Highlands to convince the locals so that they'll back his book. Just about every comedy stalwart you can think of crops up in support, and even Spike Milligan has a cameo as a tramp, but the laughs are as elusive as Nessie. DP

Adam Faith *Tony Blake* • Sidney James *Harry* • Charles Hawtrey *Arnold* • Freddie Frinton *Gilbert Pinner* • Terry Scott *Sergeant* • Marie France *Marie* • Carole Lesley *Charlie* • Spike Milligan *Tramp* ■ *Dir* Gilbert Gunn • *Scr* Terry Nation, from a story by Trevor Peacock, Jeremy Lloyd

What a Widow! ★★
Romantic comedy   1930 · US · BW · 90min

Gloria Swanson lives up to the exclamation mark as the wealthy widow who changes her men as often as the attractive costumes she wears. Among the many beaus to her string are a lawyer, a violinist, a Spanish baritone and a nightclub dancer. Allan Dwan directs swiftly, as if unwilling to dwell on the unfunny sequences, and Swanson sings a couple of songs. Its box-office failure caused a rift between

Swanson and her patron Joseph P Kennedy, father of John F. RB

Gloria Swanson *Tamarind* • Owen Moore *Gerry* • Lew Cody *Victor* • Margaret Livingston *Valli* • William Holden (1) *Mr Lodge* ■ *Dir* Allan Dwan • *Scr* James Gleason, James Seymour, from a story by Josephine Lovett

What a Woman! ★★
Romantic comedy 1943 · US · BW · 93min

Rosalind Russell stars as an all-powerful literary agent in this silly and plot-starved romantic comedy. While busily attempting to persuade author Willard Parker, whose novel she has just sold to Hollywood, that he should star in the film version, she is interviewed by journalist Brian Aherne, who gets caught up in the general mayhem. Despite its failings, the movie is kept bubbling along by Russell, a powerhouse of comedic accomplishment; Shelley Winters makes her debut in a bit part. RK

Rosalind Russell *Carol Ainsley* • Brian Aherne *Henry Pepper* • Willard Parker *Professor Michael Cobb aka Andrew Street* • Alan Dinehart *Pat O'Shea* • Edward Fielding *Senator Ainsley* • Ann Savage *Jane Hughes* • Shelley Winter [Shelley Winters] *Actress* ■ *Dir* Irving Cummings • *Scr* Therese Lewis, Barry Trivers, from a story by Erik Charell

What about Bob? ★★★★PG
Comedy 1991 · US · Colour · 99min

Richard Dreyfuss and Bill Murray make a dynamic comedy duo in this amiably manic satire on the therapy business directed by ex-Muppeteer Frank Oz. Murray is especially funny as the annoying multi-phobic patient who follows psychiatrist Dreyfuss on holiday and totally ruins his control-freak life. His carefree schizo slobbishness contrasts with Dreyfuss's Freudian posing, and the frenzied laughs come thick and fast without losing their welcome sharp edge or delightfully twisted compassion. AJ Swearing. *DVD*

Bill Murray *Bob Wiley* • Richard Dreyfuss *Dr Leo Marvin* • Charlie Korsmo *Siggy Marvin* • Julie Hagerty *Fay Marvin* • Kathryn Erbe *Anna Marvin* • Tom Aldredge *Mr Guttman* • Susan Willis *Mrs Guttman* ■ *Dir* Frank Oz • *Scr* Tom Schulman, from a story by Alvin Sargent, Laura Ziskin

What Becomes of the Broken Hearted? ★★18
Drama 1999 · NZ/Aus · Colour · 98min

Once Were Warriors was a frighteningly believable account of domestic violence and did a lot to overturn the cosy picture postcard view of modern New Zealand. It was a lot to live up to and sadly this belated sequel has to go down as a disappointment despite the return of star Temuera Morrison and writer Alan Duff. Morrison still spends his time drinking himself – and beating other people – senseless. However, when his son Julian Arahanga is killed in a gang shooting, he is forced to re-evaluate his life. JF *DVD*

Temuera Morrison *Jake Heke* • Clint Eruera *Sonny Heke* • Nancy Brunning *Tania Rogers* • Pete Smith *Apeman* • Lawrence Makoare *Grunt* • Rawiri Paratene *Mulla Rota* • Julian Arahanga *Nig Heke* • Edna Stirling *Rita* ■ *Dir* Ian Mune • *Scr* Alan Duff, from his novel

What Changed Charley Farthing? ★
Comedy adventure 1974 · UK · Colour · 100min

This British attempt at a featherweight frolic by regular writing partners Jack Seddon and David Pursall sinks with scarcely a ripple of loss. Toothsome Doug McClure tries to escape a Cuba-style republic, while L ovel Jeffries, Warren Mitchell and Hayley Mills attempt to make some impact on the resolutely flabby plot. That they do not succeed is partly their fault: they should have read the script before they agreed to take part. TH

Doug McClure *Charley Farthing* • Lionel Jeffries *Henry Houlihan* • Hayley Mills *Jenny* • Warren Mitchell *MacGregor* • Alberto de Mendoza *Jumbo De Santos* • Dilys Hamlett *Miss Parchment* ■ *Dir* Sidney Hayers • *Scr* David Pursall, Jack Seddon, from a novel by Mark Hebdon

What Did You Do in the War, Daddy? ★★
Second World War comedy 1966 · US · Colour · 115min

You start wishing Peter Sellers had agreed to star in this silly Blake Edwards war comedy about a Sicilian village whose inhabitants will only surrender to the US Army if they can hold their annual soccer match and wine festival first. Edwards's *Pink Panther* collaborator might have breathed life into William Peter Blatty's ponderous script. As it is, James Coburn, Dick Shawn, Aldo Ray and Sergio Fantoni are just too heavy-handed for this kind of comedy. TH

James Coburn *Lieutenant Christian* • Dick Shawn *Captain Cash* • Sergio Fantoni *Captain Oppo* • Giovanna Ralli *Gina Romano* • Aldo Ray *Sergeant Rizzo* • Harry Morgan *Major Pott* • Carroll O'Connor *General Bolt* ■ *Dir* Blake Edwards • *Scr* William Peter Blatty, from a story by Blake Edwards, Maurice Richlin

What Dreams May Come ★★15
Fantasy romantic drama 1998 · US · Colour · 108min

This ghastly love-after-death fantasy has Annabella Sciorra as a suicide consigned to her own private hell. Robin Williams is her dead hubby, a car-crash victim consigned to his own painterly paradise, who forsakes it to be reunited with the love of his life – and death. Vincent Ward brings his usual visual style to this tosh and as a result the film looks wonderful. But that's all that is wonderful about it as, visuals aside, this is slow and sentimental slush. DA Swearing, violence, nudity. *DVD*

Robin Williams *Chris Nielsen* • Cuba Gooding Jr *Albert* • Annabella Sciorra *Annie Nielsen* • Max von Sydow *The Tracker* • Jessica Brooks Grant *Marie Nielsen* • Josh Paddock *Ian Nielsen* • Rosalind Chao *Leona* ■ *Dir* Vincent Ward • *Scr* Ron Bass [Ronald Bass], from the novel by Richard Matheson

What Ever Happened to...? ★★
Psychological drama 1991 · US · Colour · 100min

This TV-movie remake of the *Grand Guignol* masterpiece *What Ever Happened to Baby Jane?* is most interesting aspect for the first screen pairing of Lynn and Vanessa Redgrave as the showbiz sisters fallen on hard times. Lynn goes right over the top in the Bette Davis role of Baby Jane, leaving Vanessa little space to improve on Joan Crawford's rendition of the wheelchair-using Blanche. However, TV-movie specialist David Greene lacks Robert Aldrich's genius for the grotesque. DP Violence, some swearing.

Vanessa Redgrave *Blanche Hudson* • Lynn Redgrave *Jane Hudson* • John Glover *Billy Cork* • Bruce A Young *Dominick* • Amy Steel *Connie Trotter* • John Scott Clough *Frank Trotter* ■ *Dir* David Greene • *Scr* Brian Taggert, from the novel *What Ever Happened to Baby Jane?* by Henry Farrell

What Ever Happened to Baby Jane? ★★★★★12
Gothic drama 1962 · US · BW · 128min

This innovative and much imitated chiller set the trend for ageing Hollywood divas to revive their careers by playing unhinged maniacs – but no one beats Bette Davis or Joan Crawford in the snarl-and-shriek department. Here the former queens of Hollywood play actress sisters divided by age-old resentments, with Davis's grotesquely made-up former child star torturing her paralysed sister (Crawford). The on-screen fireworks were reportedly fuelled by off-screen hatred, but the chemistry between the stars is hair-raising and upped the gothic stakes to camp shock levels. This deals with the frightening decay of illusions by cleverly incorporating both actresses' earlier work into the psychodrama. AJ *DVD*

Bette Davis *Jane Hudson* • Joan Crawford *Blanche Hudson* • Victor Buono *Edwin Flagg* • Anna Lee *Mrs Bates* • Maidie Norman *Elvira Stitt* •

Marjorie Bennett *Della Flagg* ■ *Dir* Robert Aldrich • *Scr* Lukas Heller, from the novel by Henry Farrell • *Costume Designer* Norma Koch • *Cinematographer* Ernest Haller

What Every Woman Knows ★★★
Political comedy drama 1934 · US · BW · 90min

This charts the rise of a poverty-stricken but brilliant and ambitious young Scottish socialist (Brian Aherne) from humble beginnings to becoming a Member of Parliament. His success is made possible by financial help from the brothers of a mousy spinster (Helen Hayes) on condition that he will later marry her. Adapted from JM Barrie's sentimental play, the movie has a tedious first 25 minutes or so. It's worth persevering, though, for the charming tale that follows, and for Aherne's performance. RK

Helen Hayes *Maggie Wylie* • Brian Aherne *John Shand* • Madge Evans *Lady Sybil Tenterden* • Lucile Watson *La Comtesse* • Dudley Digges *James Wylie* • Donald Crisp *David Wylie* • David Torrence *Alick Wylie* ■ *Dir* Gregory La Cava • *Scr* Monckton Hoffe, John Meehan, James K McGuinness, Marian Ainslee, from the play by JM Barrie

What Happens in Vegas ★★12
Romantic comedy 2008 · US · Colour · 94min

This romantic comedy starring Cameron Diaz and Ashton Kutcher is a bit like a night in Vegas: loud, flashy and difficult to recall the next day. Slacker and party animal Jack (Kutcher) is out to let off steam in "Sin City" when he meets Joy (Diaz), a control freak trying hard to let her hair down after being dumped. A few drinks later and they're saying "I do". But things get really complicated when he hits the jackpot on the casino floor – using her coin. A game of one-upmanship quickly grows tiresome as each party seeks to claim the cash, but the two leads have good chemistry and at least Kutcher keeps the mugging to a minimum. SP Swearing, sexual references. *DVD* *Blu-ray*

Cameron Diaz *Joy McNally* • Ashton Kutcher *Jack Fuller* • Queen Latifah *Dr Twitchell* • Krysten Ritter *Kelly* • Lake Bell *Tipper* • Dennis Farina *Banger* • Zach Galifianakis *Dave the Bear* • Rob Corddry *Steve "Hater" Hader* ■ *Dir* Tom Vaughan (1) • *Scr* Dana Fox

What Have I Done to Deserve This? ★★★18
Black comedy 1984 · Sp · Colour · 97min

This typical "kitsch 'n' think" mixture of tragedy and comedy from director Pedro Almodóvar stars Carmen Maura as an unhappy Madrid housewife. She rebels against the pressures of modern life with drugs and manslaughter when her family's myriad problems drag her deeper into depression. Using the language of Italian neorealism, sexual taboos, fake commercials for bogus products and his skewed sense of social conscience, Almodóvar mines this spiky black farce for all its allegorical worth. AJ Spanish +subtitles. *DVD*

Carmen Maura *Gloria* • Luis Hostalot *Polo* • Angel De Andrés-López *Antonio* • Gonzalo Suarez *Lucas Villalba* • Verónica Forqué *Cristal* • Juan Martinez *Toni* • Chus Lampreave *Grandmother* ■ *Dir/Scr* Pedro Almodóvar

What I Did for Love ★★
Comedy 2006 · US · Colour · 88min

Stereotypes abound in this gentle, fish-out-of-water comedy in which slick LA lawyer Jeremy London tries to charm the backwater rancher family of doctor girlfriend Dorie Barton after asking her to marry him. But in predictable, *Meet the Parents*-type fashion, nothing goes according to plan – a situation that's worsened when Barton's cowboy ex also tries to undermine her new beau. Although the low-key laughs are grounded in clichés rather than reality, there's sufficient harmless fun to keep events engaging. The Sierra Nevada mountain scenery is particularly impressive, detracting from

some of the cheesier plot elements, while the expected lessons-learned finale is warm enough not to nauseate. SF Some violence.

Jeremy London *James White* • Dorie Barton *Sadie Ryder* • James Gammon *Karl Ryder* • Sally Struthers *Aunt Trudy* • John Littlefield *Clint* • Jonny Acker *Travis* ■ *Dir* Mark Griffiths • *Scr* Marjorie A Sweeney

What If ★★★15
Romantic comedy drama 2013 · Can/Ire · Colour · 97min

Daniel Radcliffe headlines a cute, quintessentially indie romantic comedy that thinks it's a bit cleverer than it actually is. It's the opposite for the character he plays, Wallace, a medical school dropout who's lost his faith in love after a break-up. So he takes solace in his friendship with animator Chantry, played with familiar kookiness by Zoe Kazan.Director Michael Dowse relies on the witty banter between his leads to keep the formulaic action zipping along, but Radcliffe isn't quite as comfortable as his co-star with this screwball approach. SP Swearing, sexual references, brief nudity. *DVD* *Blu-ray*

Daniel Radcliffe *Wallace* • Zoe Kazan *Chantry* • Megan Park *Dalia* • Adam Driver *Allan* • Rafe Spall *Ben* • Amanda Crew *Lisa* ■ *Dir* Michael Dowse • *Scr* Elan Mastai, from the play *Toothpaste and Cigars* by TJ Dawe, Michael Rinaldi

What Just Happened? ★★15
Satirical comedy drama 2007 · US · Colour · 99min

Comparisons with Robert Altman's *The Player* are inevitable, as real-life producer Art Linson scripts the fictionalised version of his own memoir. Robert De plays Ben, a powerful "suit" beset with professional problems – one of his movies is being sabotaged by its star (Bruce Willis, playing himself), the other by its intransigent director. Ben tries to mollify his paymasters while also juggling the demands of his ex-wives and estranged children. De Niro gives his character a surprisingly sympathetic, low-key charm, but unlike in Altman's film, the trials of a Tinseltown player soon wear thin in this lame, self-indulgent satire. DW *DVD*

Robert De Niro *Ben* • Catherine Keener *Lou Tarnow* • Sean Penn • John Turturro *Dick Bell* • Robin Wright Penn [Robin Wright] *Kelly* • Stanley Tucci *Scott Solomon* • Kristen Stewart *Zoe* • Bruce Willis ■ *Dir* Barry Levinson • *Scr* Art Linson, from his memoir *What Just Happened: Bitter Hollywood Tales from the Front Line*

What Lies Beneath ★★★15
Supernatural thriller 2000 · US · Colour · 124min

Harrison Ford and Michelle Pfeiffer star in this formulaic but highly enjoyable supernatural thriller from director Robert Zemeckis. Scientist Ford and his wife Pfeiffer have renovated their idyllic Vermont lakeside house, but their domestic bliss is disturbed when she starts seeing and hearing ghostly apparitions. A creaking cocktail of light suspense and implausible plotting that pushes every tried-and-tested scare button, this shocker is illuminated by Pfeiffer's believable performance as the traumatised wife. AJ Violence, swearing. *DVD*

Harrison Ford *Norman Spencer* • Michelle Pfeiffer *Claire Spencer* • Diana Scarwid *Jody* • Joe Morton *Dr Drayton* • James Remar *Warren Feur* • Miranda Otto *Mary Feur* • Amber Valletta *Madison Elizabeth Frank* ■ *Dir* Robert Zemeckis • *Scr* Clark Gregg, from a story by Sarah Kernochan, Gregg

What Love Sees ★★PG
Drama based on a true story 1996 · US · Colour · 91min

This fantastically syrupy TV movie is about a romance between two blind people from different sides of the tracks in the 1930s. Annabeth Gish stars as a wealthy woman who finds true love with farmer Richard Thomas, much to the distress of her city-based family who worry that he won't be able to look after her out West. The performances from the two leads are pretty good, but the treacle's a little too thick. JF

Richard Thomas *Gordon Holly* • Annabeth Gish *Jean Treadway* • Edward Herrmann *Morton Treadway* • Kathleen Noone *Sarah Treadway* • August Schellenberg *Earl* • Romy Rosemont *Lucy Treadway* ■ *Dir* Michael Switzer • *Scr* Robert L Freedman, from the book by Susan Vreeland

What Maisie Knew ★★★★ 15
Drama   2013 · US · Colour · 94min

Henry James's classic novel about feckless high-society parents in 1890s London is transposed to modern-day New York in this drama retaining the book's central thrust and tracing the emotional effect of acrimonious divorce on their small daughter. Onata Aprile is utterly believable as the child, Julianne Moore absolutely committed to a largely unsympathetic part as her rock singer mother, and Steve Coogan quite superb as the father singularly unequipped for his role. Astute, classy and very affecting. TJ Swearing.
DVD Blu

Julianne Moore *Susanna* • Alexander Skarsgård *Lincoln* • Steve Coogan *Beale* • Onata Aprile *Maisie* • Emma Holzer *Holly* ■ *Dir* Scott McGehee, David Siegel • *Scr* Carroll Cartwright, Nancy Doyne, from Henry James's novel • *Cinematographer* Giles Nuttgens

What – No Beer? ★★
Comedy   1933 · US · BW · 65min

Yoked together by MGM for several comedies, Buster Keaton and Jimmy Durante here play dopey friends who put their money into a run-down brewery in the hope that Prohibition will soon be lifted. It isn't and the duo find themselves in trouble with the police and gangsters. Little of the old Keaton magic is in evidence while the rasp-voiced Durante abrades the soundtrack with unsubtle gags. TH

Buster Keaton *Elmer J Butts* • Jimmy Durante *Jimmy Potts* • Rosco Ates [Roscoe Ates] *Schultz* • Phyllis Barry *Hortense* • John Miljan *Butch Lorado* • Henry Armetta *Tony* • Edward Brophy *Spike Moran* • Charles Dunbar *Mulligan* ■ *Dir* Edward Sedgwick • *Scr* Carey Wilson, Jack Cluett, from a story by Robert E Hopkins

What Planet Are You From? ★★ 15
Science-fiction comedy
2000 · US · Colour · 100min

When is Greg Kinnear going to tire of playing smarmy love rats? He's at it again in Gary Shandling's hugely disappointing big screen debut, but at least he provides a welcome distraction from the film's only joke – a humming penis. Clearly uneasy with Shandling's screenplay, director Mike Nichols resorts to stuffing the action with cameos, but there's just no escaping Shandling's timid alien and his bid to seduce recovering alcoholic Annette Bening in order to repopulate his planet. DP Swearing, sex scenes. *DVD*

Garry Shandling *Harold Anderson* • Annette Bening *Susan* • Greg Kinnear *Perry Gordon* • Ben Kingsley *Graydon* • Linda Fiorentino *Helen Gordon* • John Goodman *Roland Jones* ■ *Dir* Mike Nichols • *Scr* Garry Shandling, Michael Leeson, Ed Solomon, Peter Tolan, from a story by Garry Shandling, Michael Leeson

What Price Glory ★★★
Silent war comedy   1926 · US · BW · 122min

Considered very daring in its day for its mix of pathos and jokes, director Raoul Walsh's depiction of the First World War as a slapstick farrago is still a feat of arms. Rivalling US marines Captain Flagg and Sergeant Quirk (Victor McLaglen and Edmund Lowe) squabble over women (Dolores Del Rio in particular) on the front line. The film juxtaposes some very realistic battle scenes with boisterous comedy. The stars reprised their characters in 1929's *The Cock-Eyed World*. TH

Victor McLaglen *Captain Flagg* • Edmund Lowe *Sergeant Quirt* • Dolores Del Rio *Charmaine de la Cognac* • William V Mong *Cognac Pete* • Phyllis Haver *Hilda of China* ■ *Dir* Raoul Walsh • *Scr* James T O'Donohoe, Malcolm Stuart Boylan (titles), from the play by Laurence Stallings, Maxwell Anderson

What Price Glory? ★★★ U
First World War comedy
1952 · US · Colour · 109min

This is a slightly misguided attempt to remake the 1926 silent hit. The garish Technicolor and Robert Wagner's brilliantined hairstyle are quite wrong for such a tale. Even so, director John Ford seems to regard the whole enterprise as a lark, with a past-his-prime James Cagney and a likeable Dan Dailey performing as though this were a musical without songs. Still enjoyable. TS *DVD*

James Cagney *Captain Flagg* • Corinne Calvet *Charmaine* • Dan Dailey *Sergeant Quirt* • William Demarest *Corporal Kiper* • Craig Hill *Lieutenant Aldrich* • Robert Wagner *Lewisohn* ■ *Dir* John Ford • *Scr* Phoebe Ephron, Henry Ephron, from the play by Laurence Stallings, Maxwell Anderson

What Price Hollywood? ★★★★
Drama   1932 · US · BW · 88min

George Cukor's sophisticated and still appealing Hollywood story features Constance Bennett as a waitress at the famous Brown Derby restaurant who becomes a star. Meanwhile, her discoverer and mentor, played by real-life director Lowell Sherman, slips into drunken obscurity. Sherman, it is said, modelled his alcoholism on observing his then brother-in-law, John Barrymore. The picture offers an atmospheric and authentic portrait of Hollywood at the time and gave producers a cast-iron storyline which they have recycled as *A Star Is Born* three times. AT

Constance Bennett *Mary Evans* • Lowell Sherman *Maximilian Carey* • Neil Hamilton *Lenny Borden* • Gregory Ratoff *Julius Saxe* • Brooks Benedict *Muto* • Louise Beavers *Bonita, the maid* • Eddie "Rochester" Anderson *James* ■ *Dir* George Cukor • *Scr* Jane Murfin, Ben Markson, Gene Fowler, Rowland Brown, from a story by Adela Rogers St Johns

What Rats Won't Do ★★
Romantic comedy   1998 · UK · Colour · 84min

From the producers of *Four Weddings and a Funeral*, this movie crams in elements from that hit plus a sprinkling of *A Fish Called Wanda*. It's a romantic farce about two barristers falling in love while contesting a case. Natascha McElhone is fun and Charles Dance in a leopard-skin G-string could be considered a visual bonus. Don't let the ghastly title put you off, as there is an oddly Swinging Sixties vibe here that's quite charming. AT

James Frain *Jack* • Natascha McElhone *Kate* • Charles Dance *Gerald* • Parker Posey *Mirella* • Samantha Bond (2) *Jane* • Peter Capaldi *Tony* ■ *Dir* Alastair Reid • *Scr* Steve Coombes, Dave Robinson, William Osborne

What Richard Did ★★★★ 15
Drama based on a true story
2012 · Ire · Colour · 83min

A Dublin student puts his bright future at risk when jealousy over his girlfriend's old flame gets out of hand on one fateful night in this engrossing Irish drama. Newcomer Jack Reynor is highly impressive in the demanding central role, displaying the charisma that makes protagonist Richard the alpha male in his circle of middle-class achievers, yet also conveying genuine depth to his soul-searching when the full implications of his actions hit home. A compelling, haunting portrayal of one young man at a moral crossroads. TJ Swearing, sex scenes, some violence, sexual references. *DVD* Blu

Jack Reynor *Richard Karlsen* • Roisin Murphy *Lara Hogan* • Sam Keeley *Conor Harris* • Lars Mikkelsen *Peter Karlsen* • Lorraine Pilkington *Katherine Karlsen* ■ *Dir* Lenny Abrahamson • *Scr* Malcolm Campbell

What the Butler Saw ★ U
Comedy   1950 · UK · BW · 61min

Elderly Edward Rigby leads a B-movie cast in this impoverished (one set), stiffly directed comedy, an early product from the Hammer studio. The plot, about a

Polynesian princess who follows her lover, a butler, home to England and causes consternation in a country house, has a pre-war feel. DM

Edward Rigby *The Earl* • Henry Mollison *Bembridge* • Mercy Haystead *Lapis* • Michael Ward *Gerald* • Eleanor Hallam *Lady Mary* • Peter Burton *Bill Fenton* ■ *Dir* Godfrey Grayson • *Scr* AR Rawlinson, Edward J Mason, from a story by Roger Good, Donald Good

What the #$*! Do We Know!? ★★ 12
Drama documentary
2004 · US · Colour · 108min

This hybrid purports to unravel the mysteries of quantum physics, but actually serves as a facile recruiting advert for the Ramtha School of Enlightenment. The three film-makers are students of Ramtha, a 35,000-year-old philosopher from the lost continent of Atlantis, whose voice is "channelled" through former saleswoman JZ Knight. Exemplifying the hokey arguments about how each individual can create their own reality is a hearing-impaired photographer (played by Marlee Matlin), who's wondering what the "bleep" life's all about after a divorce. JR *DVD*

Marlee Matlin *Amanda* • Elaine Hendrix *Jennifer* • Robert Bailey Jr *Reggie* • Armin Shimerman *Older man* • Barry Newman *Frank* • John Ross Bowie *Elliot* • Larry Brandenburg *Bruno* ■ *Dir* Mark Vicente, Betsy Chasse, William Arntz • *Scr* Betsy Chasse, William Arntz, Matthew Hoffman

What to Expect When You're Expecting ★★★ 12
Romantic comedy drama
2012 · US · Colour · 105min

The lives of five couples with parenthood problems are tenuously linked in this star-studded comedy inspired by the bestselling pregnancy book. Expectant mothers include Cameron Diaz's celebrity fitness coach, Jennifer Lopez's keen-to-adopt photographer and a hysterical Elizabeth Banks as a baby-obsessive married to the son of a rich racing-car driver (Dennis Quaid) with a trophy wife. Director Kirk Jones (*Nanny McPhee, Everybody's Fine*) keeps the reproductive tale on the right side of light, so it could be just the movie for exhausted parents. For others, it may be a little too laboured. KK Swearing, sexual references. *DVD* Blu

Cameron Diaz *Jules* • Jennifer Lopez *Holly* • Elizabeth Banks (2) *Wendy* • Ben Falcone *Gary* • Dennis Quaid *Ramsey* • Chris Rock *Vic* • Cheryl Cole ■ *Dir* Kirk Jones • *Scr* Shauna Cross, Heather Hach, from a book by Heidi Murkoff

What We Did on Our Holiday ★★★★ 12
Comedy drama   2014 · UK · Colour · 91min

David Tennant and Rosamund Pike are the names, playing a divorcing British couple in this disarming British film, but it's the kids (Emilia Jones, Bobby Smalldridge and the hilarious little Harriet Turnbull) who are the stars. *Outnumbered* creators Andy Hamilton and Guy Jenkin write and direct, as Tennant and Pike pack the kids up for a visit to their sick grandpa. The tonal shifts can be a touch jarring, but the thin line between comedy and tragedy is all the more poignant seen through innocent eyes. SP Some swearing, sexual references. *DVD* Blu

David Tennant *Doug McLeod* • Rosamund Pike *Abi McLeod* • Ben Miller *Gavin McLeod* • Billy Connolly *Gordie McLeod* • Celia Imrie *Agnes Chisholm* ■ *Dir/Scr* Andy Hamilton, Guy Jenkin

What We Do in the Shadows ★★★★ 15
Horror comedy
2014 · NZ · Colour and BW · 81min

This delightfully deadpan spoof about a ragtag bunch of Kiwi vampires breathes new life into the mockumentary. A documentary crew follows the dandyish Viago and the rampant Vladislav as they argue about the washing-up, hit the clubs, and suck the life from virgins (but try to

remember to put a towel down first). There are some hilarious riffs on undead mythology, while the script cunningly plays with your expectations, and Rhys Darby, as the unfailingly polite werewolf leader, is a fantastic treat. LB In English, German. Violence, swearing. *DVD* Blu

Jemaine Clement *Vladislav* • Taika Waititi *Viago* • Jonathan Brugh *Deacon* • Cori Gonzalez-Macuer *Nick* • Stuart Rutherford *Stu* • Rhys Darby *Anton, werewolf* ■ *Dir/Scr* Jemaine Clement, Taika Waititi

What Women Want ★★★★ 12
Romantic comedy   2001 · US · Colour · 121min

Mel Gibson stars as a chauvinistic advertising executive who accidentally suffers an electric shock, and suddenly finds himself able to hear women's thoughts. His unique gift sometimes proves to be a mixed blessing, but gradually his insights into how women think, and what they want, bring out his feminine side. Despite the daft premise, this is wittily written and sharply directed, with Gibson effortlessly running the gamut from sheer obnoxiousness to utter charm. Helen Hunt is great, too, as his far-from-perfect love match. DA Swearing. *DVD* Blu

Mel Gibson *Nick Marshall* • Helen Hunt *Darcy Maguire* • Marisa Tomei *Lola* • Mark Feuerstein *Morgan Farwell* • Lauren Holly *Gigi* • Ashley Johnson *Alex Marshall* • Alan Alda *Dan Wanamaker* • Judy Greer *Erin* • Bette Midler *Therapist* ■ *Dir* Nancy Meyers • *Scr* Josh Goldsmith, Cathy Yuspa, from a story by Goldsmith, Yuspa, Diane Drake

Whatever ★★ 15
Drama   1998 · US/Fr · Colour · 108min

Debuting director Susan Skoog, who also wrote and produced this, presents a portrait of teenage disillusion in the early 1980s that never rings true. Dismissive of her gold-digging mother and odious brother, Liza Weil allows her passion for art to be diluted by her sexual curiosity and a self-destructive streak. The main focus is on those old adolescent chestnuts – conformity and rebellion – but Skoog's views are as predictable as her choices on the post-punk soundtrack. DP

Liza Weil *Anna Stockard* • Chad Morgan *Brenda Talbot* • Frederic Forrest *Mr Chaminsky* • Gary Wolf *Eddie* • Dan Montano *Zak* ■ *Dir/Scr* Susan Skoog

Whatever Happened to Aunt Alice? ★★★★ 15
Mystery thriller   1969 · US · Colour · 96min

Produced by Robert Aldrich, who directed Bette Davis and Joan Crawford in the classic gothic drama *What Ever Happened to Baby Jane?*, this scary story isn't quite in the same class. Ruth Gordon poses as a housekeeper to Geraldine Page, who's got into the unpleasant habit of disposing of her domestic help. Director Lee H Katzin contrives a baleful bitches' brew of women at war with each other, and he maintains the suspense with skill. TH *DVD*

Geraldine Page *Mrs Claire Marrable* • Ruth Gordon *Mrs Alice Dimmock* • Rosemary Forsyth *Harriet Vaughn* • Robert Fuller *Mike Darrah* • Mildred Dunnock *Miss Tinsley* • Joan Huntington *Julia Lawson* ■ *Dir* Lee H Katzin • *Scr* Theodore Apstein, from the novel *The Forbidden Garden* by Ursula Curtiss

Whatever Happened to Harold Smith? ★★★ 15
Comedy   1999 · UK · Colour · 92min

Veteran British star Tom Courtenay makes a magnificent comeback as Harold Smith, whose magical powers stop three pacemakers at an old people's home in 1970s Sheffield. While his son Michael Legge dithers between punk and disco, Courtenay becomes a scandalous celebrity thanks to his occult powers. Peter Hewitt's comedy offers a quirky account of the times. This is a home-grown product that, like *The Full Monty*, proves regional ideas can have a powerful metropolitan impact. TH

U SUITABLE FOR ALL   Uc SUITABLE ESPECIALLY FOR YOUNG CHILDREN (DVD ONLY)   PG PARENTAL GUIDANCE   12A UNDER 12s TO BE ACCOMPANIED (CINEMA ONLY)

Tom Courtenay *Harold Smith* • Michael Legge *Vince Smith* • Laura Fraser *Joanna Robinson* • Stephen Fry *Doctor Peter Robinson* • Charlotte Roberts *Lucy Robinson* • Amanda Root *Margaret Robinson* • Lulu Irene Smith *Keith Nesbitt* ■ *Dir* Peter Hewitt • *Scr* Ben Steiner

Whatever It Takes ★ 12
Romantic comedy   2000 · US · Colour · 90min

Shane West and Marla Sokoloff are high school neighbours, friends who don't fancy each other. But in order to start dating the school bimbo Jodi Lyn O'Keefe, West feels he must make his best mate woo Sokoloff to get her out of the way. Cue a crass Cyrano pastiche of West in the bushes whispering words of wonder to his dumb buddy. LH DVD

Jodi Lyn O'Keefe *Ashley " Ash " Grant* • Shane West *Ryan Woodman/Brian Ryan* • Marla Sokoloff *Maggie Carter* • Manu Intiraymi *Dunleavy* • Aaron Faul *Floyd* • Julia Sweeney *Kate Woodman* ■ *Dir* David Raynr • *Scr* Mark Schwahn

Whatever Works ★★★ 12
Romantic comedy
2009 · US/Fr · Colour · 87min

Woody Allen and Larry David team up for this engaging hybrid of Allen's 1979 classic *Manhattan* and David's hit TV show *Curb Your Enthusiasm*, which serves as a spiky denunciation of the fanaticism of conservative America. David's quantum physicist recalls his brief marriage to a Mississippi pageant queen (Evan Rachel Wood) and how this impacted upon the couple and the young woman's staid parents (Patricia Clarkson and Ed Begley Jr). There's an abundance of incisive one-liners, with David bringing a new caustic flavour to Allen's nebbish alter ego, and if the action is occasionally contrived, it's mostly amusing and assured. DP DVD

Larry David *Boris Yellnikoff* • Evan Rachel Wood *Melody* • Patricia Clarkson *Marietta* • Ed Begley Jr *John* • Michael McKean *Joe* • Henry Cavill *Randy James* • John Gallagher Jr *Perry* ■ *Dir/Scr* Woody Allen

What's Cooking? ★★★ 12
Seasonal drama
2000 · US/UK · Colour · 109min

Gurinder Chadha turns to the great melting pot society of the United States to see how an African-American, Hispanic, Vietnamese and Jewish family each celebrates Thanksgiving Day. As the narrative threads intertwine, secondary themes such as patriarchy, homophobia, adultery, delinquency, age-gap tension and class snobbery have their moment under the microscope. Yet while Chadha handles each storyline with creditable dexterity, she overseasons with life/food metaphors and melodramatic revelations. However, the sizeable ensemble largely succeeds in avoiding caricature. DP Swearing.

Joan Chen *Trinh Nguyen* • Julianna Margulies *Carla* • Mercedes Ruehl *Elizabeth Avila* • Kyra Sedgwick *Rachel Seelig* • Alfre Woodard *Audrey Williams* • Maury Chaykin *Herb Seelig* • Victor Rivers *Javier Avila* • Dennis Haysbert *Ronald Williams* ■ *Dir* Gurinder Chadha • *Scr* Gurinder Chadha, Paul Mayeda Berges

What's Eating Gilbert Grape ★★★ 12
Comedy drama   1993 · US · Colour · 112min

Johnny Depp takes the title role in this gentle oddity, playing the sensitive but level-headed teenager who has his hands full coping with his enormously obese mother (Darlene Cates), who won't leave the house, and a mentally disabled younger brother (Leonardo DiCaprio). The latter steals the show, but the entire cast turns in winning performances. Director Lasse Hallström lets sentiment creep in, but still demonstrates a sharp outsider's eye for the quirkiness of Americana. JF Swearing, sex scenes. DVD

Johnny Depp *Gilbert Grape* • Juliette Lewis *Becky* • Mary Steenburgen *Betty Carver* • Leonardo DiCaprio *Arnie Grape* • John C Reilly *Tucker Van Dyke* • Darlene Cates *Bonnie Grape* • Laura Harrington *Amy Grape* • Mary Kate Schellhardt *Ellen Grape* • Crispin Glover *Bobby*

McBurney* • Kevin Tighe *Mr Carver* ■ *Dir* Lasse Hallström • *Scr* Peter Hedges, from his novel • *Cinematographer* Sven Nykvist

What's Good for the Goose ★ PG
Comedy   1969 · UK · Colour · 98min

With a contrived title and a simply appalling script (co-written by Norman Wisdom himself), this is one of the biggest blots on the British movie copybook. Directed with no feel for Wisdom's unique brand of comedy, it is jam-packed with cringeworthy moments. Norman the sexy banker? No wonder he didn't make another film for three years. DP

Norman Wisdom *Timothy Bartlett* • Sally Geeson *Nikki* • Sarah Atkinson *Meg* • Terence Alexander *Frisby* • Sally Bazely *Margaret Bartlett* • Derek Francis *Harrington* • David Lodge *Hotel porter* ■ *Dir* Menahem Golan • *Scr* Norman Wisdom, Menahem Golan, Christopher Gilmore

What's New, Pussycat? ★★★ 15
Comedy   1965 · US/Fr · Colour · 104min

Woody Allen has never had much time for this frantic farce, which marked his debut as both writer and performer. Originally planned as a low-key black-and-white affair, it snowballed into a freewheeling star vehicle over which director Clive Donner was not always in total control. Even though the film was a box-office smash, Allen complained that unchecked ad-libbing and a disinclination to excise the mediocre had swamped his material, with Peter Sellers particularly guilty as the psychiatrist jealous of patient Peter O'Toole's success with women. Glossy and often hilarious. DP DVD

Peter Sellers *Doctor Fritz Fassbender* • Peter O'Toole *Michael James* • Romy Schneider *Carol Werner* • Capucine *Renée Lefèbvre* • Paula Prentiss *Liz* • Woody Allen *Victor Shakapopolis* • Ursula Andress *Rita* • Richard Burton ■ *Dir* Clive Donner • *Scr* Woody Allen

What's Opera, Doc? ★★★★★ U
Animated classic   1957 · US · Colour · 6min

In spite of the many excellent contributions from such directors as Friz Freleng and Bob Clampett, Chuck Jones remains Bugs Bunny's best-known director. This is partly owing to his penchant for placing the star in rarified cultural circumstances, and this justly celebrated short marks the culmination of Jones's interest in classical music as a context for comedy: the familar Bugs and Elmer rabbit hunt is played out as opera, with dialogue sung to music from Wagner's *Ring Cycle* and *Tannhäuser*. With over a hundred striking designs by Maurice Noble, and the Warner studio orchestra's magnificent condensation of Wagner's epic, the result is a milestone in Hollywood animation. CLP

Mel Blanc *Bugs Bunny* • Arthur Q Bryan *Elmer Fudd* ■ *Dir* Chuck Jones • *Scr* Michael Maltese • *Layout* Maurice Noble • *Music Director* Milt Franklyn

What's So Bad about Feeling Good? ★★
Comedy   1968 · US · Colour · 93min

In a quintessential 1960s film, a toucan infected with a happiness virus that spreads the "disease" throughout Manhattan. Among the grouchy New Yorkers whose personalities are transformed are advertising executive turned artist George Peppard, his hippy girlfriend Mary Tyler Moore and guest star Thelma Ritter, whose acerbity is most welcome. The studio East Village backlot, period clothes and garish Universal-style Technicolor make it strangely watchable. TS

George Peppard *Pete* • Mary Tyler Moore *Liz* • Dom DeLuise *J Gardner Monroe* • John McMartin *The Mayor* • Nathaniel Frey *Conrad* • Charles Lane (1) *Dr Shapiro* • Thelma Ritter *Mrs Schwartz* • Cleavon Little *Phil* ■ *Dir* George Seaton • *Scr* George Seaton, Robert Pirosh, from the novel *I Am Thinking of My Darling* by Vincent McHugh

What's the Matter with Helen? ★★★
Thriller   1971 · US · Colour · 100min

Answer: nothing a good bout of killing wouldn't cure. Strong female stars pull this number though a hedge of campy production, set in the 1930s as Debbie Reynolds and Shelley Winters try to forget their sordid past by setting up a school for talented youngsters in Hollywood. Curtis Harrington directs with an acute feel for the period and personalities, which include Dennis Weaver and Agnes Moorehead. TH

Debbie Reynolds *Adelle Bruckner* • Shelley Winters *Helen Hill* • Dennis Weaver *Lincoln Palmer* • Agnes Moorehead *Sister Alma* • Michael MacLliammoir *Hamilton Starr* • Sammee Lee Jones *Winona Palmer* • Robbi Morgan *Rosalie Greenbaum* • Helene Winston *Mrs Greenbaum* ■ *Dir* Curtis Harrington • *Scr* Henry Farrell • *Cinematographer* Lucien Ballard

What's the Worst That Could Happen? ★ 15
Crime comedy   2001 · US · Colour · 94min

This is trite, unfunny and shockingly mediocre, and one wonders what lead actors Danny DeVito and Martin Lawrence could have been thinking. Lawrence is a professional thief who steals his way into the affections of sweet English actress, Carmen Ejogo. But her attempts to straighten him out go belly up when he robs crooked mogul DeVito and starts a vendetta, that puts each actor at the end of a very large ego bone. LH DVD

Martin Lawrence *Kevin Caffery* • Danny DeVito *Max Fairbanks* • John Leguizamo *Berger* • Glenne Headly *Gloria* • Carmen Ejogo *Amber Belhaven* • Bernie Mac *Uncle Jack* • Larry Miller *Earl Radburn* ■ *Dir* Sam Weisman • *Scr* Matthew Chapman, from a novel by Donald E Westlake

What's Up, Doc? ★★★★★ U
Screwball comedy   1972 · US · Colour · 89min

Barbra Streisand stars as the zany dropout with her eyes on absent-minded professor Ryan O'Neal in director Peter Bogdanovich's hilarious homage to the screwball comedies of the 1930s by Howard Hawks and Preston Sturges. The tone is set by the wacky title, a reference to the scene when Streisand meets O'Neal for the first time – she's chomping on a carrot à la Bugs Bunny. There's also brilliant support from Madeline Kahn as O'Neal's fiancée, and beautiful photography from Laszlo Kovacs. It's a shame that Bogdanovich has never again touched these heights of cartoonish wit. TH DVD

Barbra Streisand *Judy Maxwell* • Ryan O'Neal *Professor Howard Bannister* • Madeline Kahn *Eunice Burns* • Kenneth Mars *Hugh Simon* • Austin Pendleton *Frederick Larrabee* • Michael Murphy (1) *Mr Smith* • Phil Roth *Mr Jones* • Sorrell Booke *Harry* • Stefan Gierasch *Fritz* • Mabel Albertson *Mrs Van Hoskins* • Liam Dunn *Judge Maxwell* • Randall R "Randy" Quaid [Randy Quaid] *Professor Hosquith* ■ *Dir* Peter Bogdanovich • *Scr* Buck Henry, David Newman, from a story by Peter Bogdanovich

What's Up, Tiger Lily? ★★★ PG
Spoof action comedy
1966 · US/Jpn · Colour · 76min

A year after the sex farce *What's New, Pussycat?* which Woody Allen both appeared in and wrote came this even more questionable comedy, in which he spoofs a Japanese James Bond-style thriller by re-dubbing it with English voices at variance to the action. It's a single-track joke, which soon runs out of steam, but some of the mismatched words work wonderfully well. TH Violence, swearing. DVD

Woody Allen *Narrator/Host/Voice* • Tatsuya Mihashi *Phil Moscowitz* • Mie Hama *Terri Yaki* • Akiko Wakabayashi *Suki Yaki* • Tadao Nakamaru *Shepherd Wong* • Susumu Kurobe *Wing Fat* • China Lee • Frank Buxton • Len Maxwell • Louise Lasser ■ *Dir* Senkichi Taniguchi • *Scr* Woody Allen, Frank Buxton, Len Maxwell, Louise Lasser, Mickey Rose, Bryna Wilson, Julie Bennett, from a film by Kazuo Yamada

What's Your Number? ★★★★ 15
Romantic comedy   2011 · US · Colour · 112min

Anna Faris (the *Scary Movie* franchise) stars in this fast-paced, snarky and sometimes shocking romantic comedy. Faris plays Ally Darling, who frantic to find the right man, hunts down all of her ex-beaus to see which of them was the one that got away. The set-up may sound like your average no-brainer chick flick, but laid on top of its standard storyline is some terrific dialogue and some genuinely sassy scenes, not least between Faris and co-star Chris Evans (Captain America). Like *Bridesmaids* before it, *What's Your Number* is a wonderfully funny comedy that shows young women in their real environment, competing with themselves. KK Swearing, sexual references. DVD BD

Anna Faris *Ally Darling* • Chris Evans *Colin Shea* • Joel McHale *Roger* • Blythe Danner *Ava Darling* • Andy Samberg *Gerry Perry* • Chill Wills *Jay Rick* ■ *Dir* Mark Mylod • *Scr* Gabrielle Allan, Jennifer Crittenden, from the novel *20 Times a Lady* by Karyn Bosnak

The Wheeler Dealers ★★★ U
Comedy caper   1963 · US · Colour · 104min

James Garner goes to Wall Street. More than just a shrewd hick from the sticks, he's in his most likeable mode as a Texas tycoon showing New York businesswoman Lee Remick how to make a bundle from a non-existent product. There's a whole lot of chicanery going on, but director Arthur Hiller manoeuvres his comedy options with a shrewd hand. TH

James Garner *Henry Tyroon* • Lee Remick *Molly Thatcher* • Phil Harris *Ray Jay* • Chill Wills *Jay Ray* • Charles Watts *JR* • Jim Backus *Bullard Bear* • Patricia Crowley [Pat Crowley] *Eloise* • John Astin *Hector Vanson* ■ *Dir* Arthur Hiller • *Scr* George JW Goodman, Ira Wallach, from the novel by Goodman

Wheels on Meals ★★★ 15
Martial arts comedy thriller
1984 · HK · Colour · 103min

Swinging wildly from full-speed action to dozy interludes, this is an extremely strange mix of comedy, romance and kung fu. Jackie Chan plays one of two brothers who run a fast-food business in Spain. It reaches a witty high by spoofing *The Three Musketeers*, yet even during the longueurs there is a sense of the weird that keeps the film ticking. JM Cantonese dubbed. Violence, some swearing. DVD

Jackie Chan *Thomas* • Sammo Hung *Moby* • Yuen Biao *David* • Lola Forner *Sylvia* • Susanna Sentis *Gloria* • Pepe Sancho *Mondale* ■ *Dir* Sammo Hung • *Scr* Edward Tang, Antonio Llorens

When a Man Loves ★★★
Silent period romance   1926 · US · BW · 110min

Following the success of *Don Juan*, Warners reteamed director Alan Crosland and the mercurial John Barrymore for its third feature to benefit from a synchronised Vitaphone soundtrack. But it wasn't the prospect of a score and some sound effects that prompted audiences to flock to this reworking of Abbé Prevost's classic novel. It was Barrymore's French aristocrat wielding his sword in defence of Dolores Costello, who'd been exploited as a courtesan by her wicked brother Warner Oland. DP

John Barrymore *Chevalier Favien des Grieux* • Dolores Costello *Manon Lescaut* • Warner Oland *André Lescaut* • Sam De Grasse *Comte Guillot de Morfontaine* • Helmes Herbert *Jean Tiberge* • Stuart Holmes *Louis XV, King of France* ■ *Dir* Alan Crosland • *Scr* Bess Meredyth, from the opera *Manon Lescaut* by Giacomo Puccini, from the novel *L'Histoire du Chevalier des Grieux et de Manon Lescaut* by Abbé Prevost

When a Man Loves a Woman ★★ 15
Drama   1994 · US · Colour · 120min

In this sobering drama, Meg Ryan proves no more adept portraying a drunk than she was playing an action heroine in 1996's

W

Courage under Fire. As a wife and mother attempting to face life without the consolation of a bottle, she's guilty of trying too hard to convince. Andy Garcia is hardly more impressive as her insensitive husband, while Ellen Burstyn is as Ryan's mother. DP Swearing. **DVD**

Andy Garcia *Michael Green* • Meg Ryan *Alice Green* • Ellen Burstyn *Emily* • Tina Majorino *Jess Green* • Mae Whitman *Casey Green* • Lauren Tom *Amy* • Philip Seymour Hoffman *Gary* ■ *Dir* Luis Mandoki • *Scr* Ronald Bass, Al Franken

When a Stranger Calls ★★ 15

Horror thriller   1979 · US · Colour · 93min

Don't watch the opening of this suspense shocker alone. The build-up of claustrophobic tension is near-masterly, as a babysitter, alone in a dark house, is terrorised by a crank call from a homicidal maniac lurking in a room upstairs! But after that blistering beginning, Fred Walton's film stalls badly – with the killer escaping years later to wreak havoc upon the same woman – and only truly comes alive again in the last reel. RS

Charles Durning *John Clifford* • Carol Kane *Jill Johnson* • Tony Beckley *Curt Duncan* • Colleen Dewhurst *Tracy* • Rachel Roberts (1) *Dr Monk* • Ron O'Neal *Lt Garber* • Bill Boyett *Sgt Sacker* • Kirsten Larkin *Nancy* ■ *Dir* Fred Walton • *Scr* Steve Feke, Fred Walton

When a Stranger Calls ★ 15

Horror thriller   2006 · US · Colour · 83min

Fred Walton's 1979 movie about a babysitter terrorised by crank phone calls from inside the house gets an ill-advised remake. This time it's colourless Camilla Belle who is forced to babysit in a remote lakeside house as punishment for mobile phone misuse. Suspense and interest hit rock bottom fast as the film cranks up the sound effects while lowering the gore factor to the point where there's no sense of real dread. AJ Swearing, violence. **DVD**

Camilla Belle *Jill Johnson* • Tommy Flanagan *Stranger* • Tessa Thompson *Scarlet* • Brian Geraghty *Bobby* • Clark Gregg *Mr Johnson* • Derek de Lint [Derek De Lint] *Dr Mandrakis* • Kate Jennings Grant *Mrs Mandrakis* ■ *Dir* Simon West • *Scr* Jake Wade Wall, from the 1979 film by Steve Feke, Fred Walton

When a Woman Ascends the Stairs ★★★★ PG

Drama   1960 · Jpn · BW · 110min

Following the career of an ageing bar hostess as she struggles to stay out of debt in 1950s Tokyo, this moving film from director Mikio Naruse ranks among his best. Hideko Takamine's graceful heroine, a widowed hostess in her 30s, faces a stark choice between a marriage of convenience or opening her own bar. Full of intimate intensity and stark pessimism, this is a heartbreaking drama. JR Japanese +subtitles.

Hideko Takamine *Keiko Yashiro* • Daisuke Kato *Matsukichi Sekine* • Masayuki Mori *Nobuhiko Fujisaki* • Reiko Dan *Junko Inchihashi* ■ *Dir* Mikio Naruse • *Scr* Ryuzo Kikushima • *Cinematographer* Masao Tamai

When Billie Beat Bobby ★★★

Sports drama based on a true story
2001 · Can/US · Colour · 90min

Holly Hunter teams with writer/director Jane Anderson for this made-for-TV reconstruction of the famous tennis match between crusading women's champion Billie Jean King and chauvinist showman, Bobby Riggs. Sporting biopics rarely convince on an action level, but both Hunter and Ron Silver give a good account on themselves on court. However, Anderson's emphasis is firmly placed on the wider gender political issues at stake and the vastly differing motives that persuaded a committed feminist to risk her reputation to participate in a media circus. DP

Holly Hunter *Billie Jean King* • Ron Silver *Bobby Riggs* • Matt Letscher *Larry King* • Bob Gunton *Jerry Perenchio* ■ *Dir/Scr* Jane Anderson

When Brendan Met Trudy ★★★ 15

Romantic comedy
2000 · Ire/UK · Colour · 90min

Roddy Doyle's first work written directly for the screen is a romantic comedy, with, unsurprisingly, a very Irish flavour. Flora Montgomery is a star in the making as the brash, foul-mouthed Dubliner who steamrolls her way into the life of timid teacher Peter McDonald. While their romance is very unlikely – he's a stay-at-home film buff and singer in the local choir – watching her completely obliterate his quiet life is often great fun, aided by Doyle's sparkling script. JB Swearing, sex scenes, nudity. **DVD**

Peter McDonald *Brendan* • Flora Montgomery *Trudy* • Marie Mullen *Mother* • Pauline McLynn *Nuala* • Don Wycherley *Niall* ■ *Dir* Kieron J Walsh • *Scr* Roddy Doyle

When Dinosaurs Ruled the Earth ★★★ PG

Prehistoric adventure
1969 · UK · Colour · 92min

Hammer's sequel to *One Million Years BC* doesn't star Raquel Welch or Ray Harryhausen's marvellous special effects, but it's still pretty solid entertainment. *Playboy* playmate Victoria Vetri wears the fur bikini this time and American stop-motion animation expert Jim Danforth supplies the prehistoric monster battles. With no more than 27 words of dialogue between them, rival tribe members Vetri and Robin Hawdon fall in love, escape death and cope with the harsh elements. Dotty, endearing and exotic fun. AJ

Victoria Vetri *Sanna* • Robin Hawdon *Tara* • Patrick Allen *Kingsor* • Drewe Henley *Khaku* • Sean Caffrey *Kane* ■ *Dir* Val Guest • *Scr* Val Guest, from a treatment by JG Ballard

When Eight Bells Toll ★★★ 15

Adventure   1971 · UK · Colour · 90min

Made at an early stage in Anthony Hopkins's film career, this Alistair MacLean adventure gave him one of his rare opportunities to play an action hero. In a story about piracy (adapted by MacLean himself), he plays his naval agent as a single-minded professional, intent on doing the job without falling for the high-life distractions that other spies are prone to. Consequently, he comes across as rather charmless and we find ourselves longing for more of Robert Morley's delicious turn as a spymaster. DP Violence. **DVD**

Anthony Hopkins *Philip Calvert* • Robert Morley *Sir Arthur Arnold-Jones* • Jack Hawkins *Sir Anthony Skouras* • Nathalie Delon *Charlotte Skouras* • Corin Redgrave *Hunslett* • Derek Bond *Lord Charnley* • Ferdy Mayne *Lavorski* • Maurice Roëves *Helicopter pilot* ■ *Dir* Étienne Périer • *Scr* Alistair MacLean, from his novel

When Father Was Away on Business ★★★★ 15

Period drama   1985 · Yug · Colour · 130min

Written by Bosnian poet Abdulah Sidran, this Oscar-nominated drama was the surprise winner of the Palme d'Or at Cannes. In 1950s Sarajevo, no one is safe from wagging tongues and spiteful vendettas and Miki Manojlovic is arrested by his own brother-in-law. Told from the half-comprehending perspective of his son, Moreno D'e Bartolli, this naturalistic insight into Tito's Yugoslavia in the last days of Stalinism compels thanks to Emir Kusturica's assured blend of satire, whimsy and harsh historical comment. The harrowing circumcision, whoring and rape scenes stand as startling metaphors for the corruption, brutality and treachery of the period. DP Serbo-Croat +subtitles. **DVD**

Moreno D'e Bartolli *Malik* • Miki Manojlovic *Mesa* • Mirjana Karanovic *Senija* ■ *Dir* Emir Kusturica • *Scr* Abdulah Sidran

When Harry Met Sally... ★★★★★ 15

Romantic comedy   1989 · US · Colour · 91min

This romantic comedy argues the question of whether men and women can ever have friendship without sex. The teaming of Meg Ryan and Billy Crystal is perfect, while supporting stars Carrie Fisher and Bruno Kirby are outstanding and add a welcome suggestion of edge. With its glitzy New York locations and beguiling soundtrack of popular standards, the movie offers a glamorised excursion into Woody Allen territory, and is a triumph of expert and irresistible escapist entertainment. The fake-orgasm-in-a-deli set piece propelled Ryan into stardom, but there are numerous other pleasures to be found in Nora Ephron's Oscar-nominated screenplay and Rob Reiner's astute direction. RK Swearing. **DVD Blu**

Billy Crystal *Harry Burns* • Meg Ryan *Sally Albright* • Carrie Fisher *Marie* • Bruno Kirby *Jess* • Steven Ford *Joe* • Lisa Jane Persky *Alice* ■ *Dir* Rob Reiner • *Scr* Nora Ephron

When in Rome ★★ PG

Romantic comedy   2009 · US · Colour · 87min

This yawnsome romantic comedy sees newly-dumped New York museum curator Beth (Kristen Bell) travel to Rome for her sister's wedding. While there she takes some coins from a magical fountain and finds herself hotly pursued by the now-spellbound men who threw them in there. True love seems to lie with relatively normal sports journalist Nick (Josh Duhamel) – or does it? *When in Rome* is watchable enough but is far less magical than its storyline. DA **DVD**

Kristen Bell *Beth* • Josh Duhamel *Nick* • Anjelica Huston *Celeste* • Danny DeVito *Al Russo* • Will Arnett *Antonio* • Jon Heder *Lance* ■ *Dir* Mark Steven Johnson • *Scr* David Diamond, David Weissman

When Knights Were Bold ★★

Musical comedy   1936 · UK · BW · 57min

This film version of a (then) famous play teams Jack Buchanan with Fay Wray. A satire on the British aristocracy, it has Buchanan as a soldier in India who inherits a vast English estate and returns there only to dream he is the chain-mailed reincarnation of an ancestor, a medieval warlord who, being Buchanan, can also sing and tap dance. It's dated, of course. AT

Jack Buchanan *Sir Guy De Vere* • Fay Wray *Lady Rowena* • Garry Marsh *Brian Ballymote* • Kate Cutler *Aunt Agatha* • Martita Hunt *Aunt Esther* • Robert Horton *Cousin Bertie* • Aubrey Mather *Canon* ■ *Dir* Jack Raymond • *Scr* Austin Parker, Douglas Furber, from the play by Charles Marlowe

When Ladies Meet ★★★★

Romantic comedy drama   1933 · US · BW · 73min

Successful lady novelist Myrna Loy falls desperately in love with her publisher, Frank Morgan, and spurns her devoted suitor, newspaper reporter Robert Montgomery. However, when she meets Morgan's wife, Ann Harding, without knowing who she is, matters come to a head. Adapted from a stage play and directed by Harry Beaumont, this is an intelligent, sophisticated romantic comedy drama of the highest level, exquisitely played – especially by the sublime and undeservedly forgotten Harding – marvellously designed and dressed. RK

Ann Harding *Claire Woodruf* • Robert Montgomery *Jimmy Lee* • Myrna Loy *Mary Howard* • Alice Brady *Bridget Drake* • Frank Morgan *Rogers Woodruf* • Martin Burton *Walter Manning* • Sterling Holloway *Jerome* ■ *Dir* Harry Beaumont • *Scr* John Meehan, Leon Gordon, from the play by Rachel Crothers • *Art Director* Cedric Gibbons • *Costume Designer* Adrian

When Ladies Meet ★★

Romantic comedy drama
1941 · US · BW · 105min

Directed by Robert Z Leonard and sticking more or less to the original 1933 version, this updated remake of what was a stylish look at the consequences of a lady novelist's love for her married publisher coarsens the bitingly sharp original, even vulgarising the settings. Joan Crawford makes a decent fist of the leading character, Greer Garson is probably the best substitute for Ann Harding, and Robert Taylor is fine as the newsman who loves Crawford. Only the usually impeccable Herbert Marshall as the publisher lover fails to convince. RK

Joan Crawford *Mary Howard* • Robert Taylor (1) *Jimmy Lee* • Greer Garson *Claire Woodruff* • Herbert Marshall *Rogers Woodruff* • Spring Byington *Bridget Drake* • Rafael Storm *Walter Del Canto* • Max Willenz *Pierre* ■ *Dir* Robert Z Leonard • *Scr* SK Lauren, Anita Loos, from the play by Rachel Crothers

When London Sleeps ★★

Crime drama   1932 · UK · BW · 70min

Well, it probably didn't take the city's residents long to nod off when they were watching this creaky old British thriller. Leslie Hiscott is often cited as the director who brought "quota quickies" into disrepute. The seventh of the ten films he churned out in 1932, this is a trashy tale in which only gambler Harold French can save wealthy heiress René Ray from the clutches of her villainous cousin, Francis L Sullivan. The action rattles along, but it's poor stuff. DP

Harold French *Tommy Blythe* • Francis L Sullivan *Rodney Haines* • René Ray *Mary* • A Bromley Davenport *Colonel Grahame* • Alexander Field *Sam* • Diana Beaumont *Hilda* • Ben Field *Lamberti* • Barbara Everest *Mme Lamberti* • Herbert Lomas *Pollard* ■ *Dir* Leslie Hiscott • *Scr* Bernard Merivale, H Fowler Mear, from a play by Charles Darrell

When Love Comes ★★ 18

Romantic drama   1998 · NZ · Colour · 91min

Tired of the US cabaret circuit, Reno Owen's 1970s pop icon returns to Auckland to get her head together and draws strength from her gay buddy Simon Prast, whose own life is in crisis thanks to songwriter Dean O'Gorman's sexual confusion. Throw in a grungy girl band, an unexpected pregnancy and a crunch weekend at the beach and you have a melodrama packed with resistible characters and obsessed with its own trivialities. A dull diva drama. DP **DVD**

Rena Owen *Katie* • Dean O'Gorman *Mark* • Simon Prast *Stephen* • Nancy Brunning *Fig* ■ *Dir* Garth Maxwell • *Scr* Garth Maxwell, Rex Pilgrim, Peter Wells

When Magoo Flew ★★★★ U

Animated comedy   1955 · US · Colour · 6min

Since the animation studio United Productions of America grew out of the ashes of the Disney strike of 1941, it was probably inevitable that it should sport a conscious attempt to break away from the traditional Disney approach. The most obvious manifestation of this was in its use of stylised, staccato design. Abandoning animals for human characters, they created Mr Magoo, who quickly became a star and eventually won two Oscars, the first for this, UPA's first CinemaScope cartoon. The simple plot has the myopic, mood-swinging gent boarding a plane in the belief that he's entering a cinema. When a potential hijack takes place, he thinks it's part of a film that's playing. CLP

Jim Backus *Mr Magoo* • Jerry Hausner *Waldo* ■ *Dir* Pete Burness • *Scr* Barbara Hammer, Tedd Pierce [Ted Pierce]

When Marnie Was There ★★★ U

Animated mystery   2014 · Jpn · Colour · 102min

The latest animation from Studio Ghibli is an affecting but somewhat queer ghost story revolving around a shy, short-haired tomboy who forms an intense bond with a mysterious blonde moppet. Tonally, it's much closer to the realism of Hayao Miyazaki's wartime drama *The Wind Rises*, rather than the whimsy of *Spirited Away*. However, the painterly, old-school aesthetic brings an aptly nostalgic feel to this examination of how the past can haunt the present and the rapturous intensity of young friendship. **LF** In Japanese.

Hailee Steinfeld *Anna Sasaki* • Kiernan Shipka *Marnie* • Geena Davis *Yoriko Sasaki, "Auntie"* • John C Reilly *Kiyomasa Oiwa* • Catherine O'Hara *Old lady* • Ellen Burstyn *Nanny* ■ *Dir* Hiromasa Yonebayashi • *Scr* Keiko Niwa, Masashi Ando, Hiromasa Yonebayashi, from Joan G Robinson's novel

When My Baby Smiles at Me ★★★★
Musical 1948 · US · Colour · 97min

Though largely forgotten nowadays, Dan Dailey was nominated as best actor at the 1948 Academy Awards for his performance in this film about a married vaudevillian couple. He is magnificent in this remake of a hoary old Broadway play, and, while top-billed Betty Grable isn't Dailey's equal in the drama stakes, she tries hard. Director Walter Lang knows well enough when to sit back and let the actors get on with it. A very satisfying movie. **TS**

Betty Grable *Bonny* • Dan Dailey *Skid* • Jack Oakie *Bozo* • June Havoc *Gussie* • Richard Arlen *Harvey* • James Gleason *Lefty* • Vanita Wade *Bubbles* ■ *Dir* Walter Lang • *Scr* Elizabeth Reinhardt, Lamar Trotti, from the play *Burlesque* by George Manker Watters, Arthur Hopkins

When Night Is Falling ★★★18
Drama 1995 · Can · Colour · 89min

A companion piece to *I've Heard the Mermaids Singing*, this is a less obviously comic and far more sensual study of lesbian awakening from Patricia Rozema. From its contrived beginning, the romance follows along overly familiar lines, but the performances of tempestuous circus artist Rachael Crawford and prissy Protestant academic Pascale Bussières give it a truth to match its rising passion. Henry Czerny is also impressive as Bussières's colleague and confused lover. Dreamily photographed but gushingly scripted and symbolically clumsy. **DP**

Pascale Bussières *Camille* • Rachael Crawford *Petra* • Henry Czerny *Martin* • David Fox *Reverend DeBoer* • Don McKellar *Timothy* • Tracy Wright *Tory* • Clare Coulter *Tillie* ■ *Dir/Scr* Patricia Rozema

When Santa Fell to Earth ★★★U
Fantasy comedy 2011 · Ger · Colour · 107min

German director Oliver Dieckmann dismisses the big-business mentality of Christmas in this amiable tale by Cornelia Funke (author of the *Inkheart* trilogy). The story sees Niklas Goodfellow (Alexander Scheer) enlisting the help of a couple of youngsters to regain control of the Christmas Palace, after villainous Gerold Geronimus Goblynch (Volker Lechtenbrink) has replaced festive traditions with new customs revolving around expensive presents. There is the odd slow patch, and the CGI isn't quite Hollywood standard, but it's a sweet tale that finds room to touch upon trust, loyalty, neighbourliness and even the global recession. **DP** German dubbed.

Alexander Scheer *Santa Claus/Niklas Goodfellow* • Volker Lechtenbrink *Gerold Geronimus Goblynch* • Noah Kraus *Ben* • Jessica Schwarz *Ben's mother* • Fritz Karl *Ben's father* • Mercedes Jadea Diaz *Charlotte* ■ *Dir* Oliver Dieckmann • *Scr* Benjamin Biehn, Robin Getrost, Uschi Reich, from Cornelia Funke's novel

When Saturday Comes ★★★15
Sports drama 1995 · UK · Colour · 94min

Football and cinema have never been the best of bedfellows. However, anyone who can look back nostalgically at *Roy of the*

Rovers will lap up this unashamedly clichéd rags-to-riches tale. Sean Bean obviously relishes every minute of his role here as the working-class lad who is plucked from obscurity by wise old talent scout Pete Postlethwaite to play in the big time. Along the way he wins and loses his mentor's niece (Emily Lloyd) and even gets the chance to indulge in some *Rocky*-style training. **JF** A sex scene, swearing, nudity. **DVD** **Blu**

Sean Bean *Jimmy Muir* • Emily Lloyd *Annie Doherty* • Pete Postlethwaite *Ken Jackson* • Craig Kelly (2) *Russell Muir* • John McEnery *Joe Muir* • Ann Bell *Sarah Muir* • Melanie Hill *Mary Muir* • Chris Walker *Mac* ■ *Dir/Scr* Maria Giese

When the Bough Breaks ★★★
Drama 1947 · UK · BW · 80min

Gainsborough turned from costume melodrama to contemporary problem picture with this story aimed firmly at female picturegoers. Patricia Roc is the working-class woman who allows her child to be adopted by middle-class Rosamund John and years later wants the boy back. Should he be plucked from his comfortable existence and promising future to live with his real mother in poverty? Either way, it's a tear-jerker, made on the cheap but forcefully acted and ably directed by Lawrence Huntington. **AE**

Patricia Roc *Lily Bates* • Rosamund John *Frances Norman* • Bill Owen *Bill* • Brenda Bruce *Ruby Chapman* • Patrick Holt *Robert Norman* • Cavan Malone *Jimmy* • Leslie Dwyer *George* ■ *Dir* Lawrence Huntington • *Scr* Peter Rogers, Muriel Box, Sydney Box, from a story by Moie Charles, Herbert Victor

When the Bough Breaks ★★★18
Thriller 1993 · US · Colour · 102min

It's a stunning, shocking premise: after heavy rainfall, the drains in an American town throw up a gruesome find – a bag containing the severed hands of children. And although writer/director Michael Cohn doesn't quite manage to sustain the chilling horror of the opening scenes, this remains a gripping serial killer thriller, as psychological expert Ally Walker follows the murderer's trail to an autistic child who may hold the key to the case. Cohn draws out a fine central performance from Walker in this underrated gem. **JF** **DVD**

Ally Walker *Audrey MacLeah* • Martin Sheen *Swaggert* • Ron Perlman *Dr Eben* • Tara Subkoff *Jordan/Jenny* • Robert Knepper *Creedmore* ■ *Dir/Scr* Michael Cohn

When the Bough Breaks 2: Perfect Prey ★★18
Thriller 1998 · US · Colour · 99min

The original was a genuinely chilling affair. This sequel is not in the same league – none of the original cast is on hand, either – but it is still a creepy affair, with Kelly McGillis stepping into Ally Walker's shoes as the Texas Ranger tracking a serial killer who's preying on successful career women, torturing them and then dumping their suffocated bodies in a series of bizarre poses around the state. **JF** **DVD**

Kelly McGillis *Audrey MacLeah* • Bruce Dern *Captain Swaggert* • David Keith *Dwayne Alan Clay* • DW Moffett *Jimmy Cerullo* • Joely Fisher *Elizabeth Crane* ■ *Dir* Howard McCain • *Scr* Robert McDonnell

When the Cat's Away... ★★★★15
Romantic comedy 1996 · Fr · Colour · 90min

Cédric Klapisch's witty and stylish urban comedy is as much about the changing face of Paris as it is the romantic fortunes of make-up artist Garance Clavel. This is something of a wild cat chase in terms of plot, but the search for missing moggy Gris Gris serves as an excellent excuse for some character study and conversations that are refreshingly authentic. Providing a sparkling slant on the familiar theme of love in the city, Klapisch draws vibrant performances

from his cast. **DP** French +subtitles. Swearing, sex scenes.

Garance Clavel *Chloé* • Zinedine Soualem *Djamel* • Olivier Py *Michel* • Renée Lecalm *Madame Renée* • Simon Abkarian *Carlos* ■ *Dir/Scr* Cédric Klapisch

When the Daltons Rode ★★★
Biographical western 1940 · US · BW · 80min

One of the classy big-budget westerns of its time, this rousing adventure pays little heed to historic truth as it re-creates the lives and times of the notorious Dalton gang, taking its leads, Randolph Scott and Brian Donlevy, from the previous year's big hit *Jesse James*. The elegant Kay Francis is stunning, and Scott is sturdy as the lawyer out to give the outlaws a fair trial, but the real treats in this movie are the superb stunts which have seldom, if ever, been equalled. **TS**

Randolph Scott *Tod Jackson* • Kay Francis *Julie King* • Brian Donlevy *Grat Dalton* • George Bancroft *Caleb Winters* • Broderick Crawford *Bob Dalton* • Stuart Erwin *Ben Dalton* • Andy Devine *Ozark* • Frank Albertson *Emmett Dalton* ■ *Dir* George Marshall • *Scr* Harold Schumate, Lester Cole, Stuart Anthony, from the non-fiction book by Emmett Dalton, Jack Jungmeyer Sr

When the Dragon Swallowed the Sun ★★★15
Documentary 2010 · US · Colour · 113min

Most documentaries about Tibet are staunchly anti-Chinese. But Dirk Simon allows Beijing to put its case in this well-balanced summary of the arguments for and against Tibetan autonomy. Following a brief resumé of events since the 1950 Communist invasion, Simon concentrates on the future and pays due deference to the Dalai Lama's call for a Middle Way that would see Tibet achieve self-rule within the People's Republic. Celebrity champions like Richard Gere and Archbishop Desmond Tutu have their say, while Damien Rice and Thom Yorke contribute songs to Philip Glass's score. A serious-minded bid to understand an intractable problem. **DP** In English, Tibetan.

■ *Dir* Dirk Simon • *Scr* Dirk Simon, Kristen Riordan

When the Last Sword Is Drawn ★★★★15
Period martial arts drama 2003 · Jpn · Colour · 137min

While exploring the same period as *The Last Samurai*, Yojiro Takita's *chambara* (Japanese swordplay film) is far less ostentatious in its assessment of the transition between the warrior tradition of the Tokugawa Shogunate and the firearmed might of the Meiji Restoration. Comprised of a series of flashbacks, the story charts Koichi Sato's relationship with Kiichi Nakai, a celebrated swordsman whose loyalty to both his clan and the cause earns him the enmity of those who once admired him. Takita stages several striking set pieces and allows some occasional comic relief, but his primary concern is the effect on individuals of the decline of the bushido code. **DP** Japanese +subtitles. **DVD**

Kiichi Nakai *Kanichiro Yoshimura* • Koichi Sato *Hajime Saito* • Yui Natsukawa *Shizu* • Takehiro Murata *Chiaki Ono* • Miki Nakatani *Nui* • Yuji Miyake *Jiroemon Ono* ■ *Dir* Yojiro Takita • *Scr* Takehiro Nakajima, from a story by Jiro Asada

When the Legends Die ★★★★
Western drama 1972 · US · Colour · 105min

This fly-blown modern western is so full of atmosphere that you can almost smell the apple pie on the empty diner's counter. But this beautifully constructed piece is far more than mere effective staging and the central performances from Richard Widmark and Frederic Forrest are quite superb. In a complex web of conflicting desires and loyalties, Widmark's dissolute drunk stands out as a man riven by emotional pain, while Forrest's talented

young Indian rodeo rider is the perfect foil. **SH**

Richard Widmark *Red Dillon* • Frederic Forrest *Tom Black Bull* • Luana Anders *Mary* • Vito Scotti *Meo* • Herbert Nelson *Dr Wilson* • John War Eagle *Blue Elk* • John Gruber *Tex Walker* ■ *Dir* Stuart Millar • *Scr* Robert Dozier, from the novel by Hal Borland

When the Lights Went Out ★★★15
Horror based on a true story 2010 · UK · Colour · 82min

Inspired by a real-life case, this 1970s-set horror finds a young Yorkshire family plagued by a malevolent spirit in their new home, with daughter Sally the focus of the ghostly goings-on. Writer/director Pat Holden delivers a low-key but fright-filled movie rich in period detail (this must be the only poltergeist in cinema history who plays Buckaroo and communicates through an Etch A Sketch), opting for unseen terrors in the shadows rather than full-on apparitions. Among a host of uniformly subtle and reserved performances, Tasha Connor stands out as the misunderstood adolescent. **TeS** Swearing. **DVD** **Blu**

Kate Ashfield *Jenny* • Steven Waddington *Len* • Craig Parkinson *Brian* • Andrea Lowe *Rita* • Martin Compston *Mr Price* ■ *Dir/Scr* Pat Holden

When the Party's Over ★★15
Drama 1992 · US · Colour · 110min

There's something here, but you have to wade through an awful lot of 20-something angst to find it. Three women and a gay man share a house in LA, and through the various flashbacks to which we are subjected, it's established that none of them are very nice people. Sandra Bullock and Rae Dawn Chong lend some limited class to this tale of desperation and manipulation, but in the end it's too confusing, petty, and exploitative to maintain interest. **ST** **DVD**

Elizabeth Berridge *Frankie* • Rae Dawn Chong *MJ* • Sandra Bullock *Amanda* • Kris Kamm *Banks* • Brian McNamara *Taylor* • Fisher Stevens *Alexander* • Michael Landes *Willie* ■ *Dir* Matthew Irmas • *Scr* Ann Wycoff, from a story by Matthew Irmas, Ann Wycoff

When the Sky Falls ★★★18
Biographical drama 2000 · Ire/US · Colour · 102min

This thinly disguised biography of Veronica Guerin, the crusading Irish journalist shot dead by the Dublin criminals she sought to expose, marks a return to form for director John Mackenzie (*The Long Good Friday*). Joan Allen stars as a wife and mother whose single-minded determination to bring the city's gangsters to justice becomes increasingly perilous for both herself and her family. Despite having an American lead, Mackenzie resists the temptation to Hollywood things up, while Allen brings conviction and depth to her performance. **NS** **DVD**

Joan Allen *Sinead Hamilton* • Patrick Bergin *Mackey* • Jimmy Smallhorne *Mickey O'Fagan* • Liam Cunningham *The Runner* • Kevin McNally *Tom Hamilton* • Pete Postlethwaite *Martin Shaughnessy* • Jason Barry *Dempsey* ■ *Dir* John Mackenzie (1) • *Scr* Michael Sheridan, Ronan Gallagher, Colum McCann

When the Whales Came ★★★U
Drama 1989 · UK · Colour · 95min

In this modest but touching drama set in the Scilly Isles at the start of the First World War, Paul Scofield plays an elderly loner, hiding away from the world, who is befriended by two curious children. The story is slight, but it is attractively directed by Clive Rees, who draws refreshingly natural performances from young leads Helen Pearce and Max Rennie. A galaxy of familiar British faces lends solid support. **JF**

Paul Scofield *The Birdman* • Helen Mirren *Clemmie Jenkins* • Helen Pearce *Gracie Jenkins* • Max Rennie *Daniel Pender* • David Suchet *Will* • Kerra Spowart *Margaret Pender* • Barbara Ewing *Mary Pender* • John Hallam *Treve Pender* •

W

Barbara Jefford *Auntie Mildred* • David Threlfall *Jack Jenkins* • *Dir* Clive Rees • *Scr* Michael Morpurgo, from his novel

When the Wind Blows

★★★★ PG

Animation   1986 · UK · Colour · 80min

With the threat of Armageddon now, hopefully, behind us, this adaptation of Raymond Briggs's chilling cartoon book seems rather quaint. However, the fact that few of us know how to conduct ourselves should there be a nuclear winter is powerfully brought home in the superbly told story. Animator Jimmy T Murakami's decision to use flat figures against three-dimensional backgrounds hauntingly begs the question, "It can't happen here, can it?", while the disarming voiceovers of John Mills and Peggy Ashcroft add poignancy to the proceedings. Clever, credible and heartbreaking. DP *DVD*

Peggy Ashcroft *Hilda Bloggs* • John Mills *Jim Bloggs* • Robin Houston *Announcer* • *Dir* Jimmy T Murakami • *Scr* Raymond Briggs, from his comic book

When Time Ran Out   ★ PG

Disaster adventure   1980 · US · Colour · 104min

Irwin Allen, the producer of *The Poseidon Adventure* and *The Towering Inferno*, rehashed the disaster formula yet again with this stinker about a volcano that threatens to trash a luxury holiday resort. Paul Newman leads his co-stars and their associated subplots to possible safety, while William Holden is the tycoon who owns the hotel. The eruption, when it finally comes, is a wonderfully cheesy amalgam of wobbly back projection, bathtub tidal wave and scared expressions from the cast. AT *DVD*

Paul Newman *Hank Anderson* • Jacqueline Bisset *Kay Kirby* • William Holden (2) *Shelby Gilmore* • Edward Albert *Brian* • Red Buttons *Francis Fendly* • Barbara Carrera *Iolani* • Burgess Meredith *Rene Valdez* • Ernest Borgnine *Tom Conti* • James Franciscus *Bob Spangler* • *Dir* James Goldstone • *Scr* Carl Foreman, Stirling Silliphant, from the novel *The Day the World Ended* by Gordon Thomas, Max Morgan Witts • *Music* Lalo Schifrin

When Tomorrow Comes

★★★

Romantic melodrama   1939 · US · BW · 91min

Irene Dunne and Charles Boyer, after their phenomenal success in RKO's *Love Affair* earlier in the year, reunite for this tale of a waitress and a concert pianist who meet when she serves him in a restaurant. Friendship turns to love when they're stranded in a Long Island church during a hurricane. Boyer, however, turns out to have a wife (Barbara O'Neil) who has lost her mind. A clichéd weepie, but impeccably assembled and irresistible. It was badly remade in 1957 as *Interlude*. RK

Irene Dunne *Helen* • Charles Boyer *Philip André Chagal* • Barbara O'Neil *Madeleine* • Onslow Stevens *Holden* • Nydia Westman *Lulu* • Nella Walker *Madame Dumont* • *Dir* John M Stahl • *Scr* Dwight Taylor, from a story by James M Cain

When Trumpets Fade

★★★★★ 15

Second World War drama
1998 · US · Colour · 92min

This made-for-cable film based on a true story plays like a fine art house feature, with some genuinely gripping and novel situations. During the winter of 1944, in western Germany, an emotionally and physically exhausted American private (Ron Eldard) is promoted against his will when he serendipitously survives as the rest of his comrades die around him. Whether or not he's a hero, coward or pure victim of circumstance is the point of this searingly affecting film, which dramatises one of the most senseless battles of the Second World War. Given both intelligence and power by the sure-handed direction of John Irvin, this is wise, affecting television that should not be missed. MC Swearing, violence, nudity. *DVD*

Ron Eldard *Private David Manning* • Frank Whaley *Medic Chamberlain* • Zak Orth *Warren Sanderson* • Dylan Bruno *Sergeant Talbot* •

Martin Donovan (2) *Captain Pritchett* • Dwight Yoakam *Lieutenant Colonel* • *Dir* John Irvin • *Scr* WW Vought

When We Were Kings

★★★★★ PG

Sports documentary   1996 · US · Colour · 83min

The experts had Muhammad Ali out for the count even before he stepped into the ring against George Foreman in Zaire in 1974. But the "Rumble in the Jungle" turned out to be anything but a "Disaster in Kinshasa", as Ali fought his way to a remarkable victory. Leon Gast's Oscar-winning documentary not only focuses on Ali the athlete, but also examines his importance to the African-American community at large. With telling contributions from Norman Mailer, George Plimpton and Spike Lee, and footage from the soul concerts that accompanied the big bout, this exceptional film proves that Ali was indeed "The Greatest". DP *DVD*

Muhammad Ali • George Foreman • Don King • James Brown (2) *James Brown* • BB King • Spike Lee • Norman Mailer • *Dir* Leon Gast

When Willie Comes Marching Home   ★★★

Comedy   1950 · US · BW · 82min

John Ford may be remembered best for making westerns, but he also made dramas, war movies and, though it is sometimes forgotten, comedies, of which this is a prime example. It wasn't his most natural genre, but this is still a competent, likeable and even funny movie about the ups and downs of a small-town boy during the Second World War. Dan Dailey does well in the title role, while an intelligent screenplay by Mary Loos and Richard Sale has some thoughtful things to say about wartime patriotism. PF

Dan Dailey *Bill Kluggs* • Corinne Calvet *Yvonne* • Colleen Townsend *Marge Fettles* • William Demarest *Herman Kluggs* • James Lydon *Charles Fettles* • Lloyd Corrigan *Mayor Adams* • Evelyn Varden *Gertrude Kluggs* • *Dir* John Ford • *Scr* Mary Loos, Richard Sale, from the story *When Leo Comes Marching Home* by Sy Gomberg

When Worlds Collide ★★★ U

Science-fiction adventure
1951 · US · Colour · 78min

From *War of the Worlds* producer George Pal, this paranoid parable about Earth's imminent collision with a runaway planet – the only hope of survival being a Noah's Ark expedition to a satellite moon – is a prime example of 1950s science fiction. Compensating for the bland script and uninspired cast are the Oscar-winning special effects and Rudolph Maté's arresting direction. AJ *DVD*

Richard Derr *David Randall* • Barbara Rush *Joyce Hendron* • Larry Keating *Dr Cole Hendron* • Peter Hanson *Dr Tony Drake* • John Hoyt *Sydney Stanton* • Stephen Chase (1) *Dean Frye* • Judith Ames *Julie Cummings* • *Dir* Rudolph Maté • *Scr* Sydney Boehm, Philip Wylie, from the novel *When Worlds Collide* by Edwin Balmer

When You Come Home ★ U

Comedy   1947 · UK · BW · 97min

Director John Baxter, once Britain's most uncompromising disciple of social realism, hit his cinematic nadir with this desperate flashback comedy. Rarely able to project his popular music-hall persona into movies, Frank Randle comes across as a colossal bore in this nostalgic wallow as he regales his granddaughter with tall tales about his chequered past. Adding to the torment are the songs. For movie masochists only. DP

Frank Randle • Leslie Sarony *First songwriter* • Leslie Holmes *Second songwriter* • Diana Decker *Paula Ryngelbaum* • Fred Conyngham *Mike O'Flaherty* • *Dir* John Baxter • *Scr* David Evans, Geoffrey Orme, Frank Randle

When You're in Love

★★★ U

Musical romantic comedy
1937 · US · BW · 98min

Robert Riskin was Columbia's ace screenwriter, responsible for such Frank Capra hits as *It Happened One Night* and *Mr*

Deeds Goes to Town, and Columbia boss Harry Cohn rewarded him with the direction of this vehicle for opera star Grace Moore, believing it to be director-proof. Cohn wasn't wrong. Grace Moore was an immensely likeable soprano, sexy and talented, and an ideal partner for screen "hubby" Cary Grant. Fun, in its period sort of way. TS

Grace Moore *Louise Fuller* • Cary Grant *Jimmy Hudson* • Aline MacMahon *Marianne Woods* • Henry Stephenson *Walter Mitchell* • Thomas Mitchell *Hank Miller* • Catherine Doucet *Jane Summers* • Luis Alberni *Luis Perugini* • Gerald Oliver Smith *Gerald Meeker* • *Dir* Robert Riskin • *Scr* Robert Riskin, from an idea by Ethel Hill, Cedric Worth

When You're Strange   ★★

Music documentary
2009 · US · Colour and BW · 85min

The music of the Doors, one of the most influential groups of the 1960s, continues to cast a hypnotic spell over subsequent generations of fans. However, director Tom DiCillo's documentary barely scratches the surface of the band's enduring appeal. The main difficulty here is the overly simplistic narration, delivered by Johnny Depp, which veers between standard biographical detail and laughably fawning statements. TeS *DVD* Blu

Jim Morrison • Robby Krieger • Ray Manzarek • John Densmore • Johnny Depp *Narrator* • *Dir/Scr* Tom DiCillo

When Zachary Beaver Came to Town   ★★ PG

Drama   2003 · US · Colour · 81min

Adapted from Kimberly Willis Holt's award-winning novel, this is a typical "summer in the life" family film that serves as an admirable vehicle for the former *Jerry Maguire* and *Stuart Little* moppet, Jonathan Lipnicki. Here, he's having to face the twin agonies of his singer mother abandoning him for a tilt at fame in Nashville and an unrequited crush on classmate Amanda Alch. Fun but far too sentimental. DP *DVD*

Jonathan Lipnicki *Toby Wilson* • Eric Stoltz *Otto Wilson* • Jane Krakowski *Heather Wilson* • Sasha Neulinger *Zachary Beaver* • Cody Linley *Cal McKnight* • *Dir* John Schultz • *Scr* John Schultz, from the novel by Kimberly Willis Holt

Where Angels Fear to Tread   ★★★ PG

Drama   1991 · UK · Colour · 107min

This adaptation of EM Forster's novel, brought to the screen by the team responsible for the *Brideshead Revisited* TV drama, is a classy story about earthy passion and xenophobia, with Helen Mirren as the strong-willed, widowed Englishwoman, who falls in love with Tuscany and acquires a young Italian lover. Back home, her frosty family sinks in shame and sends Rupert Graves to sort things out. The lashings of dappled Tuscan sunlight and some strong performances by the cast add up to the movie equivalent of high tea. AT *DVD*

Helena Bonham Carter *Caroline Abbott* • Judy Davis *Harriet Herriton* • Rupert Graves *Philip Herriton* • Helen Mirren *Lilia Herriton* • Giovanni Guidelli *Gino Carella* • Barbara Jefford *Mrs Herriton* • Thomas Wheatley *Mr Kingcroft* • *Dir* Charles Sturridge • *Scr* Tim Sullivan, Derek Granger, Charles Sturridge, from the novel by EM Forster

Where Angels Go... Trouble Follows   ★★ U

Comedy   1968 · US · Colour · 93min

Although nun films are generally neither funny nor clever, this sequel to *The Trouble with Angels* (1966) is a pleasant culture clash comedy with Rosalind Russell returning to her role as the Mother Superior, this time trying to keep her young rebellious charges on the straight and narrow on a convent school trip. Look out for Susan Saint James as one of the teenage tearaways. JG

Rosalind Russell *Mother Simplicia* • Stella Stevens *Sister George* • Binnie Barnes *Sister Celestine* • Mary Wickes *Sister Clarissa* • Dolores Sutton *Sister Rose Marie* • Susan Saint James *Rosabelle* • Milton Berle *Film director* • Van Johnson *Father Chase* • Robert Taylor (1) *Mr Farriday* • *Dir* James Neilson • *Scr* Blanche Hanalis, from characters by Jane Trahey

Where Are My Children?

★★

Drama based on a true story   1994 · US · Colour

One of those heart-tuggers so beloved of American TV movie-makers and, yes, it's based on a true story. Marg Helgenberger stars as the unfortunate woman who is not only falsely imprisoned, but discovers on her release that her three children have disappeared into foster care, thus sparking an epic search to recover them. JF

Marg Helgenberger *Vanessa Myer* • Corbin Bernsen *Tom Scott* • Christopher Noth *Cliff Vernon* • Cynthia Martells *Terry Hill* • Jerry Hardin *TK Macready* • *Dir* George Kaczender • *Scr* Michael Zagor

Where Danger Lives   ★★★

Film noir   1950 · US · BW · 80min

This minor-league but effective *film noir* is directed by John Farrow. Robert Mitchum stars as a doctor, Faith Domergue is a mentally unstable temptress and the open road to Mexico is their refuge, until she thinks maybe she should kill him – after all, it wouldn't be the first time. This doomed romance is well worth watching, not least for the way that Mitchum's physical presence is constantly undermined by the plot. AT *DVD*

Robert Mitchum *Jeff Cameron* • Faith Domergue *Margo Lannington* • Claude Rains *Frederick Lannington* • Maureen O'Sullivan *Julie Dawn* • Charles Kemper *Police chief* • Ralph Dumke *Klauber* • Billy House *Mr Bogardus* • *Dir* John Farrow • *Scr* Charles Bennett, from a story by Leo Rosten

Where Do We Go from Here?   ★★★ U

Musical fantasy   1945 · US · Colour · 77min

This unfairly forgotten musical fantasy is very much of its time, its satirical barbs numbed by the aftermath of the Second World War. Nevertheless, sympathetically viewed today, it remains a genuinely engaging period piece, and features a clever and neglected score by composing greats Kurt Weill and Ira Gershwin. The main theme involving a genie sending Fred MacMurray back through time is quite affecting, and certainly original. MacMurray and the lovely June Haver (MacMurray's future wife) play sweetly together. The superb 1940s Technicolor is especially effective. TS

Fred MacMurray *Bill* • Joan Leslie *Sally* • June Haver *Lucilla* • Gene Sheldon *Ali* • Anthony Quinn *Indian Chief* • Carlos Ramírez *Benito* • Alan Mowbray *General George Washington* • Fortunio Bonanova *Christopher Columbus* • Otto Preminger *General Rahl* • *Dir* Gregory Ratoff • *Scr* Morrie Ryskind, from a story by Morrie Ryskind, Sig Herzig

Where Do We Go Now?

★★★ 12

Comedy drama
2011 · Fr/Leb/Egy/It · Colour · 97min

Nadine Labaki's laudable but lightweight tale falls short of the high standards set by her excellent directorial debut, *Caramel* (2007). It's set in an unnamed Middle-Eastern village, where Amale (Labaki) and her female friends strive to distract the men from the war situation occurring in the outside world. But a killing sees the mood darken, leaving little room for genial subplots like Amale's cross-faith romance with Julien Farhat's Muslim handyman. Labaki acts and directs with spirit, but the slender storyline simply cannot support the tonal shifts, musical interludes and excess of sketchy secondary characters. DP Arabic, Russian, English +subtitles. *DVD*

Claude Baz Moussawbaa *Takla* • Layla Hakim *Afaf* • Nadine Labaki *Amale* • Yvonne Maalouf *Yvonne* • Antoinette Noufaily *Saydeh* • Julien

Farhat *Rabin* ■ *Dir* Nadine Labaki • *Scr* Rodney al Haddad, Thomas Bidegain, Jihad Hojeily, Nadine Labaki

Where Does It Hurt? ★
Black comedy 1971 · US · Colour · 87min

Crooked administrator Peter Sellers runs his hospital stictly for profit, with the willing help of his motley, under-qualified staff. But patient Rick Lenz sees through the charade and is determined to bring Sellers down. If it were a patient, this mess would be on the critical list. DF

Peter Sellers *Albert T Hopfnagel* • Jo Ann Pflug *Alice Gilligan* • Rick Lenz *Lester Hammond* • Eve Bruce *Nurse Lamarr* • Harold Gould *Dr Zerny* • William Elliott *Oscar* • Norman Alden *Katzen* • Keith Allison *Hinkley* ■ *Dir* Rod Amateau • *Scr* Rod Amateau, Budd Robinson, from their novel *The Operator*

Where Eagles Dare ★★★★ PG
Second World War action thriller
1969 · UK · Colour · 148min

Clint Eastwood called this wartime frolic "Where Doubles Dare", in view of the army of stuntmen who performed the acrobatics in the Austrian Alps. His co-star, Richard Burton, was paid a million dollars plus a big percentage of what turned out to be a hugely profitable picture. It's the usual espionage hokum, with Burton and Eastwood infiltrating a Nazi stronghold to discover a hornets' nest of spies. There are so many double- and triple-crosses that the plot is at times incomprehensible. But this is a picture about big bangs, James Bond-style fights on cable cars and body counts. It's hilarious and exciting, often at the same time. AT DVD BL

Richard Burton *Major John Smith* • Clint Eastwood *Lieutenant Morris Schaffer* • Mary Ure *Mary Ellison* • Michael Hordern *Vice Admiral Rolland* • Patrick Wymark *Colonel Wyatt Turner* • Robert Beatty *Cartwright Jones* • Anton Diffring *Colonel Kramer* • Donald Houston *Olaf Christiansen* ■ *Dir* Brian G Hutton • *Scr* Alistair MacLean, from his novel

Where in the World Is Osama Bin Laden? ★★★ 12
Documentary 2008 · US/Fr · Colour · 89min

Writer/director Morgan Spurlock risked his health with a daily diet of MacDonald's meals for his Oscar-nominated documentary *Super-Size Me*. Such a willingness to risk death has deserted him, however, for this amiable but blunt-edged follow-up, in which he tries to locate the most famous terrorist in the world. The trouble is, he coesn't try very hard, visiting Egypt, the Middle East, Afghanistan and finally Pakistan, but eschewing hard facts in favour of vox pops with the locals. The main point – we're all the same deep down, so let's be friends – may seem astoundingly glib to war-sceptic Europeans, but Spurlock's an engaging host, and if his film lacks bite, it certainly gets by on warmth and charm. DW Swearing. DVD

Morgan Spurlock ■ *Dir* Morgan Spurlock • *Scr* Morgan Spurlock, Jeremy Chilnick • *Cinematographer* Daniel Marracino

Where Is My Friend's House? ★★★★
Drama 1987 · Iran · Colour · 90min

The first part of the "friendship" trilogy (completed by *And Life Goes On...* and *Through the Olive Trees*) was made under the auspices of Iran's Institute for the Intellectual Development of Children and Young Adults and provides a deceptively simple account of conscientious schoolboy Babek Ahmed Poor's quest to the neighbouring village to spare a classmate from being expelled by returning a missing notebook. Abbas Kiarostami explores innocent notions of loyalty and everyday heroics with a mixture of realism, touching earnestness and gentle humour. DP Farsi +subtitles.

Babek Ahmed Poor *Ahmed* • Ahmed Ahmed Poor *Mahamed Reda Nematzadeh* • Kheda Barech Defai *Teacher* • Iran Outari *Mother* • Ait Ansari *Father* ■ *Dir/Scr* Abbas Kiarostami

Where Is Parsifal? ★ 15
Comedy 1983 · UK · Colour · 86min

Orson Welles plays a rich Romany who is interested in the laser skywriter patented by hypochondriac eccentric Tony Curtis. But he faces stiff competition from both millionaire Erik Estrada and Donald Pleasence, who is trying to gain access to Curtis's castle to seize goods equivalent to his debts. The chaotic approach overshoots madcap and crash-lands in a mess. DP

Tony Curtis *Parsifal Katzenellenbogen* • Erik Estrada *Henry Board II* • Peter Lawford *Montague Chippendale* • Orson Welles *Klingsor* • Berta Dominguez D *Elba* • Ron Moody *Beersbohm* • Donald Pleasence *Mackintosh* ■ *Dir* Henri Helman • *Scr* Berta Dominguez D

Where Love Has Gone ★★★
Melodrama 1964 · US · Colour · 114min

The pot of venomous passions boils over in this lurid melodrama as mother and daughter Bette Davis and Susan Hayward act out their mutual hatred with all stops out. The temperature rises further when Hayward's own daughter (Joey Heatherton) kills Hayward's lover. Adapted from the bestselling novel by Harold Robbins, who drew on the Lana Turner-Cheryl Crane-Johnny Stompanato scandal for his material, the film was slaughtered by critics while audiences flocked. Fans of the genre are guaranteed a richly entertaining wallow. RK

Susan Hayward *Valerie Hayden Miller* • Bette Davis *Mrs Gerald Hayden* • Michael Connors [Mike Connors] *Luke Miller* • Joey Heatherton *Danielle Valerie "Dani" Miller* • Jane Greer *Marian Spicer* • DeForest Kelley *Sam Corwin* • George Macready *Gordon Harris* • Anne Seymour *Dr Sally Jennings* ■ *Dir* Edward Dmytryk • *Scr* John Michael Hayes, from the novel by Harold Robbins

Where No Vultures Fly ★★★★ U
Adventure 1951 · UK · Colour · 103min

Chosen for the Royal film performance of its year, this is a splendid semi-documentary shot on exotic African locations, with an ecological message still potently relevant today. Anthony Steel plays a game warden on the lookout for evil ivory hunters in the shadow of Mount Kilimanjaro. The suspense is exceptionally well maintained, with a stunning fight sequence between Steel and Harold Warrender, and the Technicolor matching of studio material and location footage is particularly clever. So successful was this film that it led to a sequel, the equally popular *West of Zanzibar*. TS

Anthony Steel *Robert Payton* • Dinah Sheridan *Mary Payton* • Harold Warrender *Mannering* • Meredith Edwards *Gwil Davies* • William Simons *Tim Payton* ■ *Dir* Harry Watt • *Scr* Ralph Smart, WP Lipscomb, from a story by Leslie Norman Watt • *Cinematographer* Geoffrey Unsworth

Where Sleeping Dogs Lie ★ 15
Psychological thriller 1991 · US · Colour · 87min

Dylan McDermott plays a self-absorbed author who moves into a run-down house in which an entire family was once murdered in this dreadful thriller. Tom Sizemore is his twitchy tenant, taking an active interest in the author's portrait of the killer with grisly consequences. Disjointed, predictable and leaden-paced, with surprisingly unconvincing performances from the decent cast. JC

Dylan McDermott *Bruce Simmons* • Tom Sizemore *Eddie Hale* • Sharon Stone *Serena Black* • Joan Chen *Sara* • Kristen Hocking *Marlee* ■ *Dir* Charles Finch • *Scr* Charles Finch, Yolande Turner

Where the Boys Are ★★★ PG
Romantic comedy 1960 · US · Colour · 95min

The boys are at a Fort Lauderdale resort, invaded by college kids in search of romance during the Easter vacation. Against this background of youthful sun-seeking and partying, the action focuses on the contrasting relationships that develop between four girls and guys, of whom Paula Prentiss (her debut) and Jim Hutton are the most charming. Good-natured, nostalgic stuff with an interesting moral take on virginity. RK DVD

Dolores Hart *Merritt Andrews* • George Hamilton *Ryder Smith* • Yvette Mimieux *Melanie* • Jim Hutton *TV Thompson* • Barbara Nichols *Lola* • Paula Prentiss *Tuggle Carpenter* • Connie Francis *Angie* • Chill Wills *Police Captain* ■ *Dir* Henry Levin • *Scr* George Wells, from a story by Glendon Swarthout

Where the Buffalo Roam ★★★ 18
Comedy 1980 · US · Colour · 94min

Through the eyes of the pioneer of "gonzo journalism", Hunter S Thompson, we see various facets of US political life in the late 1960s and early 1970s. The underrated Bill Murray is Thompson while Peter Boyle plays his outrageous legal acquaintance, Lazlo. This movie was "based on the twisted legend of Hunter S Thompson" according to its title sequence. It was panned on release in the US but it's actually an interesting and savage little piece that deserved better. DF DVD BL

Peter Boyle *Lazlo* • Bill Murray *Dr Hunter S Thompson* • Bruno Kirby *Marty Lewis* • René Auberjonois *Harris* • RG Armstrong *Judge Simpson* • Danny Goldman *Porter* • Rafael Campos *Rojas* • Leonard Frey *Desk clerk* ■ *Dir* Art Linson • *Scr* John Kaye, from writings by Hunter S Thompson • *Music* Neil Young (1)

Where the Bullets Fly ★★★
Spy spoof 1966 · UK · Colour · 88min

The British have the Spurium Apparatus, a small nuclear device for powering aircraft. The Russians want it and enlist the aid of Michael Ripper and his clandestine international crime organisation to steal it. To succeed he has to clash with super secret agent Charles Vine (Tom Adams), on his second outing following 1965's *Licensed to Kill*. One of a huge number of Bond spoofs about at the time, none of which seemed to realise that the 007 movies themselves were spoofs. A jaunty enough romp. A third and final segment *Somebody's Stolen Our Russian Spy* followed. DF

Tom Adams *Charles Vine* • Dawn Addams *Felicity "Fiz" Moonlight* • Sidney James *Mortuary attendant* • Wilfrid Brambell *Train guard* • Joe Baker *Minister* • Tim Barrett *Seraph* • Michael Ripper *Angel* • John Arnatt *Rockwell* • Ronald Leigh-Hunt *Thursby* ■ *Dir* John Gilling • *Scr* Michael Pittock

Where the Green Ants Dream ★★★ 15
Drama 1984 · W Ger · Colour · 100min

Imbued with the romanticism that has characterised Werner Herzog's film-making exploits around the globe, this study of the clash between tradition and progress in the Australian outback is one of his least memorable accomplishments. Jörg Schmidt-Reitwein's vistas are suitable evocative and the ethnographic and environmental messages are essentially sound. But, despite the eloquent championing of a wholly fictitious 40,000 year-old Aboriginal tradition that green ants will wreak havoc if their dreaming ground is disturbed by Bruce Spence's mining company, Herzog fails to sustain the dramatic tension. DP

Bruce Spence *Lance Hackett* • Wandjuk Marika *Miliritbi* • Roy Marika *Dayipu* • Ray Barrett *Cole* • Norman Kaye *Baldwin Ferguson* ■ *Dir/Scr* Werner Herzog

Where the Heart Is ★ 15
Comedy drama 1990 · US/Can · Colour · 102min

Seeing that director John Boorman's prior effort was *Hope and Glory* one expected more of him than this dreadful comedy. Under the auspices of Disney, Boorman has produced an unfunny, unappealing movie about demolition expert Dabney Coleman who chucks his children (Uma Thurman, David Hewlett and Suzy Amis) into squalor in downtown Brooklyn. Written by Boorman and his daughter Telsche, this might have worked on the page but it sure is a turkey on screen. LH DVD

Dabney Coleman *Stewart McBain* • Uma Thurman *Daphne* • Christopher Plummer *Homeless gent* • Joanna Cassidy *Jean* • Suzy Amis *Chloe* • Crispin Glover *Lionel* • David Hewlett *Jimmy* ■ *Dir* John Boorman • *Scr* John Boorman, Telsche Boorman

Where the Heart Is ★★ 12
Comedy drama 2000 · US · Colour · 115min

Natalie Portman stars in what could be seen as a paean to product placement, playing a heavily pregnant teenager who's dumped by her no-good boyfriend outside a Wal-Mart store in Oklahoma. Secretly setting up home inside, she gives birth to what the media immediately dubs the "Wal-Mart Baby". The film lacks pace and purpose, and Portman is a little lightweight in her first leading role, but there are some memorable moments courtesy of her scene-stealing co-stars. DA Swearing. DVD

Natalie Portman *Novalee Nation* • Ashley Judd *Lexie Coop* • Stockard Channing *Sister Husband* • Joan Cusack *Ruth Meyers* • James Frain *Forney Hull* • Dylan Bruno *Willy Jack Pickens* • Keith David *Moses Whitecotten* • Sally Field *Mama Lil* ■ *Dir* Matt Williams • *Scr* Lowell Ganz, Babaloo Mandel, from a novel by Billie Letts

Where the Lilies Bloom ★★★ U
Drama 1974 · US · Colour · 97min

This is the old story of the loving kids who can't bear the thought of being parted and so hide the death of their parents from the authorities by putting on a show of business as usual. But don't give up on this movie as just another chunk of family values mush. Scriptwriter Earl Hamner Jr (*The Waltons*) has not only produced a sensitive and well-observed portrait of backwoods American life, but he has also come up with flesh-and-blood children who don't seem to have been born on Walton's Mountain. DP

Julie Gholson *Mary Call* • Jan Smithers *Devola* • Matthew Burrill *Romey* • Helen Harmon *Ima Dean* • Harry Dean Stanton *Kiser Pease* • Rance Howard *Roy Luther* ■ *Dir* William A Graham • *Scr* Earl Hamner Jr, from a novel by Vera Cleaver, Bill Cleaver

Where the Money Is ★★★ 15
Comedy crime thriller
2000 · Ger/US/UK · Colour · 84min

Paul Newman proves his star quality hasn't dimmed in this lively crime caper. He plays a jailed bank robber who is transferred to a convalescent home after suffering a stroke that seemingly leaves him near paralysed. One of the home's nurses, played by Linda Fiorentino, suspects Newman might be faking, and it's not long before she has seen through his very impressive act. In return for keeping his secret, she persuades him to help her and her husband (Dermot Mulroney) commit a robbery of their own. It's a witty adventure, made enjoyable by the three central performances. JB Swearing. DVD

Paul Newman *Henry Manning* • Linda Fiorentino *Carol* • Dermot Mulroney *Wayne* • Susan Barnes *Mrs Foster* • Anne Pitoniak *Mrs Tetlow* • Bruce MacVittie *Karl* ■ *Dir* Marek Kanievska • *Scr* E Max Frye, Topper Lilien, Carroll Cartwright, from a story by E Max Frye

Where the Red Fern Grows ★★★ U
Adventure 1974 · US · Colour · 96min

In this entertaining family movie, a 12-year-old boy (Stewart Petersen) living in 1930s Oklahoma finds caring for his two hounds helps him overcome the trials and tribulations of the Depression era. Directed by children's adventure specialist Norman Tokar, it stars James Whitmore as the boy's grandfather and former Roger Corman ingénue Beverly Garland as his mother. This was successful enough to lead to a straight-to-video sequel nearly two decades later, 1992's *Where the Red Fern Grows II*. TH

James Whitmore *Grandpa* • Beverly Garland *Mother* • Jack Ging *Father* • Lonny Chapman *Sheriff* • Stewart Petersen *Billy* • Jill Clark *Alice* •

W

Jeanne Wilson *Sara* ■ *Dir* Norman Tokar • *Scr* Douglas Day Stewart, Eleanor Lamb, from the novel by Wilson Rawls

Where the Rivers Flow North ★★★ 15

Period drama   1993 · US · Colour · 106min

In 1920s Vermont, a stubborn logger and landowner (a suitably ursine Rip Torn) is refusing to sell his property to the government-backed power company about to build a dam. It's not as dull as it sounds, as director Jay Craven concentrates on the relationship between Torn and his long-suffering native American housekeeper Tantoo Cardinal. The two central performances are both excellent and moving, elevating an overused premise and making this a very watchable film. LH

Rip Torn *Noel Lord* • Tantoo Cardinal *Bangor* • Bill Raymond *Wayne Quinn* • Michael J Fox *Clayton Farnsworth* • Treat Williams *Champ's Manager* • Amy Wright *Loose Woman* ■ *Dir* Jay Craven • *Scr* Jay Craven, Don Bredes, from the novel *Where the Rivers Run North* by Howard Frank Mosher

Where the Sidewalk Ends ★★★★ 12

Film noir   1950 · US · BW · 92min

A superb example of 20th Century-Fox *film noir* at its finest, this is a clearly plotted thriller, impeccably directed by the great Otto Preminger, which creates a nightmare world of guilt and corruption. Brutal cop Dana Andrews tries to hide the fact that, while searching for a murderer, he himself has killed Craig Stevens. The beautiful Gene Tierney is excellent in an enigmatic role as Stevens's estranged wife – a part that manages to keep her acting limitations well concealed – and watch for Neville Brand's chilling portrayal of a homosexual criminal in some censor-circumventing scenes well ahead of their time. TS *DVD*

Dana Andrews *Mark Dixon* • Gene Tierney *Morgan Taylor* • Gary Merrill *Tommy Scalise* • Bert Freed *Paul Klein* • Tom Tully *Jiggs Taylor* • Karl Malden *Lieutenant Bill Thomas* • Ruth Donnelly *Martha* • Oleg Cassini ■ *Dir* Otto Preminger • *Scr* Ben Hecht, from a treatment by Frank P Rosenberg, Victor Trivas, Robert E Kent, from a novel by William L Stuart • *Cinematographer* Joseph LaShelle

Where the Spies Are ★★

Spy adventure   1965 · UK · Colour · 112min

One of the many dozens of Bond send-ups and rip-offs, this spoofy affair is distinguished by a typically suave and disarming performance from David Niven, who in 1967 played Bond himself in *Casino Royale*. Niven is recruited by MI6 and sent to the Middle East to defend Britain's vital oil interests. The usual scrapes, escapes, explosions, lethal gadgets and bedroom seductions ensue, all treated in a rather obvious satirical style by co-writer/director Val Guest. AT

David Niven *Dr Jason Love* • Françoise Dorléac *Vikki* • John Le Mesurier *Col Douglas MacGillivray* • Cyril Cusack *Peter Rosser* • Eric Pohlman [Eric Pohlmann] *Farouk* • Richard Marner *Josef* • Paul Stassino *Simmias* • Noel Harrison *Jackson* • Geoffrey Bayldon *Lecturer* ■ *Dir* Val Guest • *Scr* Wolf Mankowitz, Val Guest, James Leasor

Where the Truth Lies ★★ 18

Mystery thriller
2005 · Can/UK · Colour · 105min

The almost impenetrable plot of director Atom Egoyan's 1970s-set thriller follows Alison Lohman, a feisty journalist investigating the suspicious death of a young woman, whose body was found in a New York hotel room in 1957. The focus of her enquiries is a pair of popular nightclub entertainers of that era (Colin Firth and Kevin Bacon), who appear to be implicated in the tragedy. Bacon is excellent as a supercilious entertainer whose "real" personality is a world away from his polished stage persona. The flashbacks and shifting perspectives are confusing and frustrating. AS Sex scenes, drug abuse. *DVD*

Kevin Bacon *Lanny Morris* • Colin Firth *Vince Collins* • Alison Lohman *Karen O'Connor* • Rachel Blanchard *Maureen O'Flaherty* • David Hayman *Reuben* • Maury Chaykin *Sally Sanmarco* • Kristin Adams *Alice* • Sonja Bennett *Bonnie Trout* ■ *Dir* Atom Egoyan • *Scr* Atom Egoyan, from the novel by Rupert Holmes

Where the Wild Things Are ★★★ PG

Fantasy drama
2009 · Ger/US/Aus · Colour · 96min

Spike Jonze's take on Maurice Sendak's children's book does offer plenty of the *Being John Malkovich* director's customary wildness and wackiness, although it's also unusually sombre. Young hero Max (Max Records) is a bit of a terror – he's introduced wrestling his dog and generally driving mum (Catherine Keener) crazy. But Jonze has a Spielberg-like ability to engage us with a child's point of view, so Max is never overbearing. The same can't be said for Carol (voiced by James Gandolfini), a bad-tempered beast who befriends Max after he runs away to a magical realm. The story of their friendship is handled rather subtly, meaning this is more likely to appeal to older children than those who the book is really aimed at. But the fantastical creatures (produced by Jim Henson's Creature Shop) look great. SP *DVD* *Blu-ray*

Max Records *Max* • Catherine Keener *Mom* • Lauren Ambrose *KW* • James Gandolfini *Carol* • Chris Cooper *Douglas* • Forest Whitaker *Ira* • Catherine O'Hara *Judith* • Mark Ruffalo *Boyfriend* • Paul Dano *Alexander* ■ *Dir* Spike Jonze • *Scr* Spike Jonze, Dave Eggers, from the illustrated children's book by Maurice Sendak • *Music* Carter Burwell, Karen O [Karen Orzolek]

Where There's a Will ★★★ PG

Comedy   1936 · UK · BW · 76min

Will Hay created wonderful comic characters, incompetent because they were masquerading in their work or were not up to the job. Here the latter is true, as he plays an unsuccessful solicitor whose office happens to be over a bank that a gang decides to rob. Hay is knocked out but later, as he sponges off wealthy relatives at a party, the same gang turn up for a repeat performance. Can the master of the supercilious sniff save the day? It's notable as the first collaboration between the devious Hay and his regular sidekick, Graham Moffatt, here playing an office boy. BB *DVD*

Will Hay *Benjamin Stubbins* • Gina Malo *Goldie Kelly* • Hartley Power *Duke Wilson* • Graham Moffatt *Willie* • HF Maltby *Sir Roger Wimpleton* • Norma Varden *Lady Margaret Wimpleton* • Peggy Simpson *Barbara Stubbins* • Gibb McLaughlin *Martin* ■ *Dir* William Beaudine • *Scr* William Beaudine, Will Hay, Ralph Spence, Robert Edmunds, from a story by Leslie Arliss, Sidney Gilliat

Where There's Life ★★★★

Comedy   1947 · US · BW · 75min

Bob Hope is a small-time New York DJ who discovers he is the heir to a mysterious European kingdom. He is then chased through New York by not only those wish to take him back to the country to take up the throne but also anti-royalists who are out to kill him. This is from the golden era of Hope's work, with the fast-talking comedy actor on top wisecracking form. Satisfaction is guaranteed with this combination and at the time there was no one better than Hope at blending thrills and comedy. DF

Bob Hope *Michel Valentine* • Signe Hasso *Katrina Grimovitch* • William Bendix *Victor O'Brien* • George Coulouris *Premier Krivoc* • Vera Marshe *Hazel O'Brien* • George Zucco *Paul Stertorius* • Dennis Hoey *Minister of War Grubitch* • John Alexander (1) *Mr Herbert Jones* ■ *Dir* Sidney Lanfield • *Scr* Allen Boretz, Melville Shavelson, Barney Dean, Frank Tashlin, from a story by Melville Shavelson

Where to Invade Next ★★★ 15

Documentary   2015 · US · Colour · 120min

Down-home polemicist Michael Moore's latest leftist provocation is less of a *Fahrenheit 9/11* state-of-the-nation address and closer in tone and approach to *Sicko*, his scattershot hymn to universal healthcare. *Where to Invade Next* similarly attacks American social policy by looking outward to schemes around the world. The gimmick of an increasingly unkempt-looking Moore "invading" these countries is thin, but the upbeat content, resourcefully filmed across three continents with a small crew, and gently cajoled testimony from Italian CEOs and Portuguese cops, speaks for itself. AC In English, Italian, French, German, Finnish, Norwegian, Portuguese, Arabic. Violence, swearing, drug abuse, nudity.

Michael Moore (2) *Michael Moore* ■ *Dir* Michael Moore (2)

Where Were You When the Lights Went Out? ★★ PG

Comedy   1968 · US · Colour · 89min

Doris Day's penultimate picture is notable only for the fact that she spent much of its production in traction, having pinched a nerve in her back, and for an excruciating in-joke that had her character starring in a play called *The Constant Virgin*. It's a contrived affair from start to finish, relying on blackouts, sleeping pills, embezzled funds and sexual jealousy to bring Doris and husband Patrick O'Neal to a happy ending. DP

Doris Day *Margaret Garrison* • Robert Morse *Waldo Zane* • Terry-Thomas *Ladislau Walichek* • Patrick O'Neal (1) *Peter Garrison* • Lola Albright *Roberta Lane* • Steve Allen *Radio announcer* • Jim Backus *Tru-Blue Lou* ■ *Dir* Hy Averback • *Scr* Everett Freeman, Karl Tunberg, from the play *Monsieur Masure* by Claude Magnier

Where's Jack? ★★ U

Period drama   1969 · UK · Colour · 119min

The damaging flaw in this 18th-century account of highway skulduggery is the miscasting of pop-singer Tommy Steele as ruffian Jack Sheppard, who is pursued – and, to an extent, manipulated by – the venal Stanley Baker (who also co-produced). But director James Clavell, who would go on to write blockbuster novels such as *Shogun*, makes a brave attempt at re-creating the bawdy, squalid times. TH

Tommy Steele *Jack Sheppard* • Stanley Baker *Jonathan Wild* • Fiona Lewis *Edgworth Bess Lyon* • Alan Badel *The Lord Chancellor* • Dudley Foster *Blueskin* • Noel Purcell *Leatherchest* • William Marlowe *Tom Sheppard* • Sue Lloyd *Lady Darlington* • Michael Elphick *Hogarth* ■ *Dir* James Clavell • *Scr* David Newhouse, Rafe Newhouse

Where's Poppa? ★★★★

Black comedy   1970 · US · Colour · 83min

Successful lawyer George Segal lives with his sometimes senile, widowed mother Ruth Gordon. Whenever he brings a girl home his mother undergoes a remarkable change, springing to life and scuppering his chances. When he falls for his mother's new nurse Trish Van Devere, Segal is driven to try to kill Gordon. A fast-paced, jet black comedy with fine performances all around. DF

George Segal *Gordon Hocheiser* • Ruth Gordon *Mrs Hocheiser* • Trish Van Devere *Louise Callan* • Ron Leibman *Sidney Hocheiser* • Rae Allen *Gladys Hocheiser* • Florence Tarlow *Miss Morgiani* • Paul Sorvino *Owner of "Gus and Grace's Home"* • Rob Reiner *Roger* • Vincent Gardenia *Coach Williams* ■ *Dir* Carl Reiner • *Scr* Robert Klane, from his novel

Where's That Fire? ★★★ U

Comedy   1939 · UK · BW · 73min

In this comic gem, Will Hay creates another variant in his gallery of incompetents – this time he's a fireman in a small village. His regular sidekicks Graham Moffatt and Moore Marriott help form what was once described as "the holy trinity of the [British] studio system". They stumble across a gang of thieves, who reassure them that they are making an historical film, when in fact they are after the crown jewels. As usual, things turn out for the best in the slightly askew world created by these three wonderful comedians. BB

Will Hay *Capt Benjamin Viking* • Moore Marriott *Jerry Harbottle* • Graham Moffatt *Albert Brown* • Peter Gawthorne *Chief Officer* • Eric Clavering *Hank Sullivan* • Hugh McDermott *Jim Baker* • Charles Hawtrey *Youth* ■ *Dir* Marcel Varnel • *Scr* Marriott Edgar, Val Guest, JOC Orton, from a story by Maurice Braddell

Which Way Is Up? ★★★

Comedy   1977 · US · Colour · 94min

Richard Pryor is a simple migrant orange picker who is manipulated into management by the boss of the large agricultural concern that employs him. But this is just the start of his seduction. This US version of Lina Wertmüller's 1972 Italian comedy *The Seduction of Mimi* doesn't match the original despite some fine work from Pryor in a triple role. AB

Richard Pryor *Leroy Jones/Rufus Jones/Reverend Thomas* • Lonette McKee *Vanetta* • Margaret Avery (2) *Annie Mae* • Morgan Woodward *Mr Mann* • Marilyn Coleman *Sister Sarah* ■ *Dir* Michael Schultz • *Scr* Carl Gottlieb, Cecil Brown, from the film *The Seduction of Mimi* by Lina Wertmüller

Which Way to the Front? ★ U

Comedy   1970 · US · Colour · 92min

Few things in showbusiness are sadder to see than a comedian deserted by his muse. Jerry Lewis hits rock bottom with some untenable and tasteless material (a group of misfits deciding to wage their own war against Hitler), appallingly assembled and perfunctorily put together. Jerry himself mugs unwatchably, and John Wood and Jan Murray offer futile support. TS

Jerry Lewis *Brendan Byers III* • Jan Murray *Sid Hackle* • John Wood (2) *Finkel* • Steve Franken *Peter Bland* • Willie Davis *Lincoln* • Dack Rambo *Terry Love* • Paul Winchell *Schroeder* • Sidney Miller *Adolf Hitler* • Robert Middleton *Colonico* ■ *Dir* Jerry Lewis • *Scr* Gerald Gardner, Dee Caruso, from a story by Gerald Gardner, Dee Caruso, Richard Miller

Whiffs ★ 15

Crime comedy   1975 · US · Colour · 88min

Soldier Elliott Gould is pensioned out of the army due to the disabling effects of the toxins he has encountered on behalf of the military. He teams up with Harry Guardino and the two form a criminal partnership, using their knowledge of chemicals to rob banks. This is a tired caper comedy, which tries to capture the style of *MASH* but fails ignominiously, despite the presence of Gould. DP

Elliott Gould *Dudley Frapper* • Eddie Albert *Colonel Lockyer* • Harry Guardino *Chops* • Godfrey Cambridge *Dusty* • Jennifer O'Neill *Scottie* • Alan Manson *Sgt Poultry* ■ *Dir* Ted Post • *Scr* Malcolm Marmorstein

While I Live ★★ PG

Drama   1947 · UK · BW · 80min

Veteran movie-goers might just remember seeing this excitable melodrama under the title *The Dream of Olwen*, under which it was re-released to exploit the success of Charles Williams's theme tune. Sonia Dresdel dominates the proceedings with a Mrs Danvers-like display of neurotic malice, playing a Cornish spinster who becomes convinced that amnesiac Carol Raye is her reincarnated sister. DP *DVD*

Sonia Dresdel *Julia Trevelyan* • Tom Walls *Nehemiah* • Clifford Evans *Peter* • Carol Raye *Sally Warwick* • Patricia Burke *Christine* • John Warwick *George Warwick* ■ *Dir* John Harlow • *Scr* John Harlow, Doreen Montgomery, from the play *This Same Garden* by Robert Bell

While I Was Gone ★★

Suspense drama
2004 · US/Can · Colour · 110min

The past comes back to haunt Boston veterinarian Kirstie Alley in this TV movie adaptation of Sue Miller's novel. Alley's stuck in a turgid marriage with minister Bill Smitrovich, and temptation crosses her path when a seriously ill dog that she's treating turns out to belong to old flame Peter Horton. His appearance stirs up memories of her hippy youth in the 1960s, but also precipitates the revelation of a shocking secret. The shift in tone is neatly done, but the dénouement is disappointing. DP

Kirstie Alley *Jo Beckett* • Bill Smitrovich *Daniel Beckett* • Janaya Stephens *Cass* • Peter Horton *Eli Mayhew* • Rebecca Benson *Jo (in flashbacks)* ■ *Dir* Mike Robe • *Scr* Alan Sharp, from the novel by Sue Miller

While the City Sleeps
★★★PG

Thriller 1956 · US · BW · 95min

This thriller about the battle for control of a newspaper is quite intriguing and boasts a starry cast. It's compulsively watchable, even if Vincent Price and Ida Lupino, in particular, have little to do. Revered director Fritz Lang, making one of his final American movies, filmed this in Superscope, which means on TV you'll see a lot of ceilings and floors. TS 📀

Dana Andrews *Edward Mobley* • Rhonda Fleming *Dorothy Kyne* • Vincent Price *Walter Kyne Jr* • George Sanders *Mark Loving* • Thomas Mitchell *John Day Griffith* • Sally Forrest *Nancy* • Ida Lupino *Mildred* • Howard Duff *Lt Kaufman* • John Barrymore Jr *[John Drew Barrymore] Manners* ■ *Dir* Fritz Lang • *Scr* Casey Robinson, from the novel *The Bloody Spur* by Charles Einstein

While the Sun Shines
★★

Drama 1946 · UK · BW · 83min

A boisterous American and a suave young Frenchman both pursue the daughter of an impoverished aristocrat. This causes some upheavals in her relationship with her wealthy and titled fiancé, who is serving in the navy as a humble sailor. This light romantic comedy, based on a play by Terence Rattigan, fails to translate adequately to the screen. The leads lack the necessary sparkle, being stalwart rather than starry, and it's left to a top-notch supporting cast of famous British character actors to flavour a bland concoction. RK

Barbara Miller *Lady Elisabeth Randall* • Ronald Squire *Duke of Ayr and Stirling* • Brenda Bruce *Mabel Crum* • Bonar Colleano *Joe Mulvaney* • Michael Allan *Colbert* • Ronald Howard *Earl of Harpenden* • Miles Malleson *Horton* • Margaret Rutherford *Dr Winifred Frye* • Joyce Grenfell *Daphne* • Wilfrid Hyde White *Male receptionist* ■ *Dir* Anthony Asquith • *Scr* Terence Rattigan, Anatole de Grunwald, from the play by Terence Rattigan

While We're Young
★★★★15

Comedy drama 2014 · US · Colour · 93min

Middle-aged anxieties are explored to amusing effect in this insightful tale from indie film-maker Noah Baumbach. The story follows the exploits of 40-something couple Ben Stiller and Naomi Watts whose lives have become rather stale, but things change as friendship blossoms with free-spirited new arrivals Adam Driver and Amanda Seyfried. One or two scenes feel like they've wandered in from a broader comedy, yet Stiller, in particular, has never been better and the film is filled with witty exchanges. SC Swearing, drug abuse. 📀
🔵

Ben Stiller *Josh Srebnik* • Naomi Watts *Cornelia Srebnik* • Amanda Seyfried *Darby* • Adam Driver *Jamie* • Charles Grodin *Leslie* • Adam Horovitz *Fletcher* ■ *Dir/Scr* Noah Baumbach

While You Were Sleeping
★★★★★PG

Romantic comedy 1995 · US · Colour · 98min

This warmly engaging and winning romantic comedy has plenty of novel twists and witty turns. Sandra Bullock is nothing short of sensational as the lonely Chicago subway clerk, who poses as the fiancée of coma victim Peter Gallagher after saving his life, much to the thrilled amazement of his family and the yearning of his sceptical brother Bill Pullman. This smartly scripted Cinderella love story is crammed with charm and Jon Turteltaub's expert direction hits all the right emotional buttons. AJ Some swearing. 📀

Sandra Bullock *Lucy Moderatz* • Bill Pullman *Jack Callaghan* • Peter Gallagher *Peter Callaghan* • Peter Boyle *Ox* • Jack Warden *Saul* • Glynis Johns *Elsie* • Michael Rispoli *Joe Jr* • Jason Bernard *Jerry* • Micole Mercurio *Midge* ■ *Dir* Jon Turteltaub • *Scr* Daniel G Sullivan, Fredric Lebow

The Whip Hand
★★★

Thriller 1951 · US · BW · 81min

This taut thriller may lack star names, but it is masterfully directed and designed by William Cameron Menzies. Elliott Reid plays the photojournalist on vacation in Wisconsin who stumbles on a village of unfriendly inhabitants, a lake where the fish have vanished and a mysterious, heavily guarded lodge. The original ending involved Adolf Hitler plotting a comeback, but RKO studio boss Howard Hughes, who was virulently anti-communist, opted for a Red threat instead. AE

Elliott Reid *Matt Corbin* • Raymond Burr *Steve Loomis* • Carla Balenda *Janet Koller* • Edgar Barrier *Dr Edward Koller* • Otto Waldis *Dr Bucholtz* • Michael Steele *Chick* • Lurene Tuttle *Molly Loomis* ■ *Dir* William Cameron Menzies • *Scr* George Bricker, Frank L Moss, from a story by Roy Hamilton

Whip It
★★★12

Comedy drama 2009 · US · Colour · 106min

Drew Barrymore's directorial debut is an exuberant and heart-warming coming-of-age tale. *Juno*'s Ellen Page is utterly believable as a small-town girl looking for a way out of her dull life. Then she discovers Roller Derby, and it's not long before she becomes a member of the league's underdog team and starts to make her dreams come true. What follows is often predictable, but Barrymore excels at capturing the strength of female friendships and the sense of empowerment that doing something you love brings, making it hard not to be moved by the irrepressible sense of fun and optimism on display here. LB
📀 🔵

Ellen Page *Bliss Cavendar* • Marcia Gay Harden *Brooke Cavendar* • Kristen Wiig *Maggie Mayhem* • Drew Barrymore *Smashley Simpson* • Juliette Lewis *Iron Maven* • Jimmy Fallon *"Hot Tub" Johnny Rocket* • Alia Shawkat *Pash* • Daniel Stern *Earl Cavendar* • Landon Pigg *Oliver* ■ *Dir* Drew Barrymore • *Scr* Shauna Cross, from her novel *Derby Girl*

Whiplash
★★★★★15

Drama 2014 · US · Colour · 102min

A hugely entertaining, refreshingly subversive take on the well-worn "inspirational teacher" theme, this is the blisteringly told tale of an aspiring drum soloist and his bullying mentor. Miles Teller is the student jazz drummer who's promoted to the elite school band run by foul-mouthed maestro JK Simmons (winner of the best supporting actor Oscar). The more minor players don't stand a chance against a brace of storming performances from the two leads, but the barnstorming, perfectly judged ending is truly satisfying. AS Violence, swearing. 📀
🔵

Miles Teller *Andrew Neiman* • JK Simmons *Terence Fletcher* • Paul Reiser *Jim* • Melissa Benoist *Nicole* • Austin Stowell *Ryan* • Chris Mulkey *Uncle Frank* • Damon Gupton *Mr Kramer* ■ *Dir/Scr* Damien Chazelle

Whipped
★18

Comedy 1999 · US · Colour · 78min

Peter M Cohen clearly rates his directorial debut as a marvel of cutting-edge technique depicting a riotous lads' night out. It's stuffed with wiseacre dialogue and cocksure incorrectness, and there's nothing amusing about the way in which Brian Van Holt, Zorie Barber and Jonathan Abrahams stalk the supposedly enigmatic Amanda Peet. Coarse, crass and abysmally acted. DP
📀

Amanda Peet *Mia* • Brian Van Holt *Brad* • Jonathan Abrahams *Jonathan* • Zorie Barber *Zeke* ■ *Dir/Scr* Peter M Cohen

Whipsaw
★★★

Crime drama 1935 · US · BW · 78min

A trio of crooks, one of whom is Myrna Loy, steals some valuable jewels in Europe. Back in New York, where the booty is lifted by rival thieves, G-man Spencer Tracy is assigned to find the gems. He courts Loy, who believes he is also a thief, and they fall in love before the truth is revealed. The felicitous pairing of Loy with Tracy (replacing the intended but unavailable William Powell) and Sam Wood's direction, which has enough pace and spirit to hide the holes in a basically unconvincing script, result in an entertaining romantic crime drama. RK

Myrna Loy *Vivian Palmer* • Spencer Tracy *Ross McBride* • Harvey Stephens *Ed Dexter* • William Harrigan *Doc Evans* • Clay Clement *Harry Ames* • Robert Gleckler *Steve Arnold* • Robert Warwick *Wadsworth* • Georges Renavent *Monetta* ■ *Dir* Sam Wood • *Scr* Howard Emmett Rogers, from the story by James Edward Grant

Whirlpool
★★★PG

Crime drama 1949 · US · BW · 93min

This is a chunk of pure 20th Century-Fox late 1940s *film noir*, a highly entertaining melodrama directed by one of the past masters, Otto Preminger. He even manages to make ace ham José Ferrer credible as a dubious hypnotist treating vivacious kleptomaniac Gene Tierney. The screenplay is by a group of left-wing intellectuals, including a blacklisted Ben Hecht using the pseudonym Lester Barstow. The subtext about mind control is, therefore, by no means accidental. TS 📀 🔵

Gene Tierney *Ann Sutton* • Richard Conte *Dr William Sutton* • José Ferrer *David Korvo* • Charles Bickford *Lieutenant Colton* • Barbara O'Neil *Theresa Randolph* • Eduard Franz *Martin Avery* • Constance Collier *Tina Cosgrove* • Fortunio Bonanova *Feruccio di Ravallo* • Ruth Lee *Miss Hall* ■ *Dir* Otto Preminger • *Scr* Lester Barstow [Ben Hecht], Andrew Solt, from the novel by Guy Endore • *Cinematographer* Arthur Miller

Whiskey Tango Foxtrot
★★★15

War comedy based on a true story
2016 · US · Colour · 111min

Based on the memoir of American war reporter Kim Barker, this dramedy from Glenn Ficarra and John Requa sees a professionally dissatisfied news producer (Tina Fey) sent to Afghanistan. Arriving in Kabul, she's inducted into the precarious, hard-partying lifestyle by fellow journalist Margot Robbie. It's rare to see a war story told from a female perspective, and screenwriter Robert Carlock takes aim at the cynicism of modern news output. But it never feels sufficiently scathing, and the trite conclusions don't help, making the movie come across as a touch cowardly for a story that's all about taking the plunge. EAS Swearing, sexual references, drug abuse.

Tina Fey *Kim Barker* • Margot Robbie *Tanya Vanderpoel* • Martin Freeman *Iain MacKelpie* • Alfred Molina *Ali Massoud Sadiq* • Christopher Abbott *Fahim Ahmadzai* • Billy Bob Thornton *Colonel Walter Hollanek* ■ *Dir* Glenn Ficarra, John Requa • *Scr* Robert Carlock, from the memoirs *The Taliban Shuffle: Strange Days in Afghanistan and Pakistan* by Kim Barker (2)

Whisky
★★★★15

Romantic comedy drama
2004 · Urug/Arg/Sp/Ger · Colour · 95min

Juan Pablo Rebella and Pablo Stoll put Uruguayan cinema on the map with this deliciously deadpan study of sibling envy, unrequited loyalty and late-life disappointment. The opening sequences at Andrés Pazos's Montevideo sock factory smack of Aki Kaurismäki. The film develops its own quirky charm, though, as the scene shifts to the coastal resort of Piriapolis, where dowdy assistant Mirella Pascual unexpectedly blossoms as she poses as Pazos's wife in order impress his younger, more successful brother, Jorge Bolani. Full of small smiles and wise insights, this is a little gem. DP Spanish +subtitles. 📀

Andrés Pazos *Jacobo Koller* • Mirella Pascual *Marta Acuña* • Jorge Bolani *Herman Koller* • Ana Katz *Graciela* • Daniel Hendler *Martín* ■ *Dir* Juan Pablo Rebella, Pablo Stoll • *Scr* Juan Pablo Rebella, Pablo Stoll, Gonzalo Delgado Galiana

Whisky Galore!
★★★★★PG

Classic comedy 1949 · UK · BW · 80min

Alexander Mackendrick's sublime film is one of the jewels in the Ealing crown. At the centre of this droll story of whisky smuggling in the Hebrides during the Second World War stands Basil Radford, who gives the performance of his career as the despised Sassenach commanding the local Home Guard. The Todday islanders are played to perfection by such accomplished actors as Gordon Jackson, Wylie Watson and Joan Greenwood, while Catherine Lacey is a delight as Radford's wife, who greets his posturing and humiliation with equal detachment. *Rockets Galore* (1958) followed. DP 📀

Basil Radford *Captain Paul Waggett* • Catherine Lacey *Mrs Waggett* • Bruce Seton *Sergeant Odd* • Joan Greenwood *Peggy Macroon* • Gordon Jackson *George Campbell* • Wylie Watson *Joseph Macroon* • Gabrielle Blunt *Catriona Macroon* • Jean Cadell *Mrs Campbell* • James Robertson-Justice *Dr MacLaren* ■ *Dir* Alexander Mackendrick • *Scr* Compton Mackenzie, Angus MacPhail, from the novel by Compton Mackenzie

Whisky Galore!
★★★

Comedy 2016 · UK · Colour · 98min

It was always going to be a tough challenge to remake an Ealing classic that is widely regarded as one of the best comedies of all time. The new version is not the misconstrued effort that the Coens produced when they relocated *The Ladykillers* from London to the American Deep South. But while there is whisky, whimsy and charm galore, laughs are a rarer commodity. However, Eddie Izzard is excellent as the pompous Home Guard officer, as is Fenella Woolgar as his wife. Probably best enjoyed by those unfamiliar with the original. BP

Gregor Fisher *Macroon* • Eddie Izzard *Captain Waggett* • Sean Biggerstaff *Sergeant Odd* • Naomi Battrick *Peggy Macroon* • James Cosmo *Macalister* ■ *Dir* Gillies MacKinnon • *Scr* Peter McDougall, from Compton Mackenzie's novel

Whisper of the Heart
★★★U

Animated romantic drama
1995 · Jpn · Colour · 110min

This is the only feature that Japanese animator Hayao Miyazaki's long-time assistant Yoshifumi Kondo managed to complete before his tragically early death at 47. Fans of *The Cat Returns* (2002) will note the introduction of The Baron in this curious mix of feline fantasy and *shoujo* (girl-orientated) romance. But the ethereal interludes never feel fully integrated into the story of the bookish Shizuku's crush on the grandson of an eccentric shopkeeper and, while this is consistently charming, it's not always compelling. DP Japanese dubbed. 📀 🔵

Brittany Snow *Shizuku Tsukishima* • David Gallagher *Seiji* • Jean Smart *Asako Tsukishima* • Cary Elwes *The Baron* ■ *Dir* Yoshifumi Kondo • *Scr* Hayao Miyazaki, Cindy Davis Hewitt (English version), Donald H Hewitt (English version), from a comic book by Aoi Hiragi

The Whisperers
★★★★

Drama 1967 · UK · BW · 105min

One of writer/director Bryan Forbes's most admired films, this is essentially an effective and moving study of loneliness, which has as its subject an old lady teetering on the edge of senility. One does feel a little sidetracked by the plot development involving the poor old dear being exploited by her criminal son (Ronald Fraser) and husband (Eric Portman), but there is still the constant pleasure of Dame Edith Evans at her finest, moving us to laughter and tears. DM

Edith Evans *Mrs Maggie Ross* • Eric Portman *Archie Ross* • Nanette Newman *Girl upstairs* • Gerald Sim *Mr Conrad* • Avis Bunnage *Mrs Noonan* • Ronald Fraser *Charlie Ross* • Leonard

Rossiter *National Assistance official* • Kenneth Griffith *Mr Weaver* • Sarah Forbes *Mrs Ross as a child* ■ *Dir* Bryan Forbes • *Scr* Bryan Forbes, from the novel *Mrs Ross* by Robert Nicolson

Whispering Corridors ★★★ 15

Supernatural horror
1998 · S Kor · Colour · 105min

More an allegory on the rigidity of the Korean education system than a gory chiller, Park Ki-hyung's debut feature is an assured amalgam of generic tropes and populist snipes. Its setting in an all-girls' school briefly evokes Dario Argento's *Suspiria*. But as various sadistic teachers meet their grisly ends, it's clear that Park is more interested in the militarisation of youth than graphic displays of gothic blood-letting. Lee Mi-Youn impresses as the resourceful heroine, although Kim Kyu-Li has more fun as the teen possessed by a suicide's spirit. DP Korean +subtitles. *DVD*

Lee Mi-yeon *Kim Kyu-li* • Kim Yong-su • Lee Yong-nyuh • Kim Yu-seok ■ *Dir* Park Ki-hyung • *Scr* In Jung-Ok, Park Ki-Hyung

Whispering Pages ★★★

Experimental drama
1993 · Rus/Ger · BW and Colour · 80min

Aleksandr Sokurov sets himself a near impossible task here in seeking to create a visual equivalent to the bleak spirit of 19th-century Russian literature. But, to his credit, he comes close to pulling it off by allowing wisps of colour to permeate the resolutely monochrome and virtually silent world inhabited by antihero Aleksandr Cherednik and his female companion, Elizaveta Korolyova. Indeed, such is the hallucinatory texture of the visuals that the lower depths experienced by the various beggars and lunatics (as described by the likes of Dostoyevsky, Gogol and Gorky) become manifest in the city's forbidding buildings and labyrinthine passageways. DP Russian +subtitles.

Aleksandr Cherednik *Hero* • Sergei Barkovsky *Official* • Elizaveta Korolyova *Girl* • Galina Nikulina ■ *Dir/Scr* Aleksandr Sokurov

Whispering Smith ★★★

Western
1948 · US · Colour · 88min

Alan Ladd hit his peak during the 1940s, mainly in thrillers, with his slightly glacial good looks suiting *noir* films. Towards the end of the decade he made this, his first starring western, which works more as a detective story with Ladd playing an undercover agent on the trail of train wreckers. It was his first film in colour, made just five years before he achieved immortality as Shane. The film is briskly handled by journeyman director Leslie Fenton, who brings the story to a rousing climax. BB

Alan Ladd *Luke "Whispering" Smith* • Robert Preston *Murray Sinclair* • Donald Crisp *Barney Rebstock* • Brenda Marshall *Marian Sinclair* • William Demarest *Bill Dansing* • Fay Holden *Emmy Dansing* • Murvyn Vye *Blake Barton* • Frank Faylen *Whitey Du Sang* ■ *Dir* Leslie Fenton • *Scr* Frank Butler, Karl Kamb, from the novel by Frank H Spearman

Whispers ★★ 18

Thriller
1990 · Can · Colour · 89min

Based on a novel by Dean R Koontz, this Canadian-made thriller puts Victoria Tennant into a real jam – she thinks she has murdered her assailant, Jean Leclerc, until he inconveniently shows up at the police station. The unfortunate cop on duty is Chris Sarandon. Tennant sometimes tends to act as if English is not her first language. Here she just needs to look scared and guilty. AT

Victoria Tennant *Hilary Thomas* • Jean LeClerc *Bruno* • Chris Sarandon *Sgt Clemenza* • Linda Sorenson *Kayla* • Peter MacNeill *Frank* ■ *Dir* Douglas Jackson • *Scr* Anita Doohan, from a novel by Dean R Koontz

Whispers: an Elephant's Tale ★★

Wildlife adventure
2000 · US · Colour · 72min

This Disney real-life adventure merely highlights the difficulties of combining wildlife footage with an invented storyline. The film was shot over 18 months in Botswana, but the action doesn't gel with the screenplay, which feels like a rush job. There's no novelty in the story of a calf that gets separated from its mother, and the dialogue is undistinguished. DP

Angela Bassett *Groove* • Joanna Lumley *Half Tusk* • Anne Archer *Gentle Heart* • Debi Derryberry *Whispers* • Kevin Michael Richardson *Adult Whispers* • Alice Ghostley *Tuskless* • Betty White *Round* • Kat Cressida *Princess* • Joan Rivers *Spike* • Tone Loc *Macho Bull* ■ *Dir* Dereck Joubert • *Scr* Dereck Joubert, Jordan Moffet, Holly Goldberg Sloan

Whispers in the Dark ★★★ 18

Erotic thriller
1992 · US · Colour · 98min

This pacey little thriller overextends a thin plot, but still grips agreeably from the start. Annabella Sciorra is convincing as the psychiatrist who's perturbed by her response to a female patient – and gets herself and everyone else into extremely hot water by not grasping the Freudian nettle firmly enough. The high spots are Alan Alda as Sciorra's psychiatrist guru and Anthony LaPaglia as a tough cop who will have no truck with all this "talkie feelie" stuff. SH Swearing, sex scenes, nudity.

Annabella Sciorra *Ann Hecker* • Jamey Sheridan *Doug McDowell* • Anthony LaPaglia *Morgenstern* • Jill Clayburgh *Sarah Green* • Alan Alda *Leo Green* • John Leguizamo *Johnny C* • Deborah Unger [Deborah Kara Unger] *Eve Abergray* ■ *Dir/Scr* Christopher Crowe

The Whistle Blower ★★★ PG

Spy thriller
1986 · UK · Colour · 99min

In a low-key but satisfying thriller, Michael Caine investigates the mysterious death of his son, Nigel Havers, who worked as a Russian translator at GCHQ. Caine is tremendously convincing as the Korean war veteran who now feels betrayed by his country. Eschewing the usual thrills, the picture creates a plausible world of whispers and a seemingly impenetrable wall of class privilege and secrecy. AT *DVD*

Michael Caine *Frank Jones* • James Fox *Lord* • Nigel Havers *Robert Jones* • John Gielgud *Sir Adrian Chapple* • Felicity Dean *Cynthia Goodburn* • Barry Foster *Charles Greig* • Gordon Jackson *Bruce* • Kenneth Colley *Bill Pickett* ■ *Dir* Simon Langton • *Scr* Julian Bond, from the novel by John Hale

Whistle down the Wind ★★★★ PG

Drama
1961 · UK · BW · 94min

In this daring allegory, Alan Bates plays a dishevelled murderer on the run who's confronted by three Lancashire children who think he's the persecuted Jesus Christ deserving of their protection. First-time director Bryan Forbes treats his material with heart-touching gravity and delicacy, and the symbolism only starts to come to pieces when the grown-up need for justice intrudes. Young Hayley Mills – her mother wrote the novel on which this film is based – is wonderfully wide-eyed, while Bates, as the ambiguous stranger, gives one of his most involving performances. TH *DVD*

Hayley Mills *Kathy* • Alan Bates *The man* • Bernard Lee *Mr Bostock* • Norman Bird *Eddie* • Diane Holgate *Nan* • Alan Barnes *Charles* • Roy Holder *Jackie* • Barry Dean *Raymond* ■ *Dir* Bryan Forbes • *Scr* Keith Waterhouse, Willis Hall, from the novel by Mary Hayley Bell

Whistle Stop ★★

Crime melodrama
1946 · US · BW · 83min

One of three American films made by the Paris-based Russian Léonide Moguy, this is a complicated crime farrago involving George Raft, Tom Conway, Victor McLaglen and – as the catalyst that sets cross and double-cross in motion – Ava Gardner. Having left gambler-lover Raft for the big city, Gardner returns and takes up with club owner Conway, whereupon McLaglen enlists Raft in a scheme to bump off Conway. Formula crime fodder. RK

George Raft *Kenny Veech* • Ava Gardner *Mary* • Victor McLaglen *Gitlo* • Tom Conway *Lew* • Jorja Curtright *Fran* ■ *Dir* Léonide Moguy • *Scr* Philip Yordan, from the novel by Maritta Wolff • *Music* Dimitri Tiomkin [Dmitri Tiomkin]

The Whistleblower ★★★ 15

Drama based on a true story
2010 · US · Colour · 107min

This grim and gruelling biopic follows Kathy Bolkovac (Rachel Weisz), a real-life Nebraska cop who joined the UN peacekeeping mission in Bosnia in 1999 and uncovered an underground network of underage sex trafficking. As the crusading whistleblower, Weisz gives a measured performance, while Canadian director Larysa Kondracki (making her feature film debut) shoots the harrowing scenes of abuse with an unflinching refusal to compromise. JR In English, Ukrainian, Russian, Bosnian. *DVD Blu*

Rachel Weisz *Kathryn Bolkovac* • David Strathairn *Peter Ward* • Vanessa Redgrave *Madeleine Rees* • Monica Bellucci *Laura Levin* • Benedict Cumberbatch *Nick Kaufman* • Liam Cunningham *Bill Hynes* ■ *Dir* Larysa Kondracki • *Scr* Larysa Kondracki, Eilis Kirwan

The Whistler ★★★

Mystery
1944 · US · BW · 60min

This is the first instalment in Columbia's B-movie series, culled from a long-running radio show in which a whistling omniscient narrator introduced the weekly mystery. A doughty star of the silent era, Richard Dix eked out his twilight years in seven of the eight films (with Michael Duane taking over for the final entry). Here Dix hires killer Don Costello to finish him off after his wife drowns – only for the missus to turn up and the unreachable J Carrol Naish to inherit responsibility for the hit after Costello is killed. Director William Castle keeps the story rattling along. DP

Richard Dix *Earl Conrad* • J Carrol Naish *The killer* • Gloria Stuart *Alice Walker* • Alan Dinehart *Gorman* • Don Costello (1) *Lefty Vigran* • Joan Woodbury *Toni Vigran* • Otto Forrest *The Whistler* ■ *Dir* William Castle • *Scr* Eric Taylor, from a story by J Donald Wilson, from the radio series by J Donald Wilson

Whistling in the Dark ★★★

Crime comedy
1941 · US · BW · 77min

Red Skelton gets his first starring role playing a writer and star of a radio series in which his character, "The Fox", unravels seemingly unsolveable crimes. Skelton is kidnapped by an unscrupulous religious cult, headed by Conrad Veidt, and forced into concocting a perfect murder for them so they can get their hands on a million-dollar inheritance. Gripping, clever and funny, the film was a surprise success for MGM and spawned two sequels, *Whistling in Dixie* (1942) and *Whistling in Brooklyn* (1943). RT

Red Skelton *Wally Benton* • Conrad Veidt *Joseph Jones* • Ann Rutherford *Carol Lambert* • Virginia Grey *"Fran" Post* • Rags Ragland *Sylvester* • Henry O'Neill *Philip Post* • Eve Arden *"Buzz" Baker* ■ *Dir* S Sylvan Simon • *Scr* Robert MacGonigle, Harry Clork, Albert Mannheimer, from the play by Laurence Gross, Edward Childs Carpenter

The White Angel ★★★

Biographical drama
1936 · US · BW · 75min

This is an old-fashioned, thoroughly workmanlike and somewhat sentimentally idealised biopic of Florence Nightingale, heroine of the Crimean War. The casting of beautiful, sophisticated Kay Francis, more at home in the drawing rooms of Park Avenue than the bloody field hospitals of Scutari, is an initial impediment to credibility, but the star makes a noble effort, and the distressing war scenes are powerfully effective. RK

Kay Francis *Florence Nightingale* • Ian Hunter *Fuller* • Donald Woods *Charles Cooper* • Nigel Bruce *Dr West* • Donald Crisp *Dr Hunt* • Henry O'Neill *Dr Scott* ■ *Dir* William Dieterle • *Scr* Mordaunt Shairp

The White Balloon ★★★★ U

Drama
1995 · Iran · Colour · 80min

Scripted by Abbas Kiarostami, who shared the Palme d'Or at Cannes for *The Taste of Cherries* in 1997, this delightful picture from director Jafar Panahi won the Caméra d'Or at the same festival in 1995 for the best newcomer. Told in real time, this is a journey of discovery. As the seven-year-old experiencing the mysteries of the bazaar for the first time, Aida Mohammadkhani gives a remarkable performance, but it's Panahi's ability to convey both what she sees and what she feels that makes this deceptively simple film so miraculous. DP Farsi +subtitles.

Aida Mohammadkhani *Razieh* • Mohsen Kafili *Ali* • Fereshteh Sadr Orfani *Mother* • Anna Bourkowska *Old woman* ■ *Dir* Jafar Panahi • *Scr* Abbas Kiarostami

White Banners ★★★

Drama
1938 · US · BW · 88min

This earnest morality tale seems less impressive today than it did to audiences on release, despite fine direction by Edmund Goulding and an Oscar-nominated star performance by Fay Bainter (who also won in the supporting category the same year for *Jezebel*). She plays a mystic figure who comes into the home of inventor Claude Rains and his family, and has a profound effect on their lives. TV

Claude Rains *Paul Ward* • Fay Bainter *Hannah Parmalee* • Jackie Cooper *Peter Trimble* • Bonita Granville *Sally Ward* • Henry O'Neill *Sam Trimble* • Kay Johnson *Marcia Ward* • James Stephenson *Thomas Bradford* • J Farrell MacDonald *Dr Thompson* ■ *Dir* Edmund Goulding • *Scr* Lenore Coffee, Cameron Rogers, Abem Finkel, from the novel by Lloyd C Douglas

White Bird in a Blizzard ★★★ 15

Mystery thriller
2014 · Fr/US · Colour · 91min

A chilly suburban mystery lies at the centre of this dreamy, sexually charged teen drama from indie film-maker Gregg Araki. Opening in 1988, it tells the story of Kat Connors (Shailene Woodley), a hormonal teenager who is gradually coming to terms with her burgeoning sexuality. One day, Kat's life is suddenly changed forever, as she returns home to discover that her mother (Eva Green) has disappeared. On the plus side, the retro soundtrack is cool and the central performances are solid, with Woodley proving typically impressive in the lead role. The film is uneven, but it's fairly effective as a portrait of sexual awakenings during adolescence, even if there's nothing in it that you haven't seen before. SC

Shailene Woodley *Kat Connors* • Eva Green *Eve Connors* • Christopher Meloni *Brock Connors* • Shiloh Fernandez *Phil* • Gabourey Sidibe *Beth* ■ *Dir* Gregg Araki • *Scr* Gregg Araki, from a novel by Laura Kasischke

The White Buffalo ★

Western
1977 · US · Colour · 97min

This attempt at an allegorical western features Charles Bronson as Wild Bill Hickok, returning to the plains in search of the white buffalo that he dreams of every night. Deep, deep down there is the potential for a meditative and mythical western but almost everything about this doesn't work. A real clinker. AT

Charles Bronson *James Otis/Wild Bill Hickok* • Jack Warden *Charlie Zane* • Will Sampson *Chief Crazy Horse/"Worm"* • Kim Novak *Poker Jenny Schermerhorn* • Clint Walker *Whistling Jack Kileen* • Stuart Whitman *Winifred Coxy* • Slim Pickens *Abel Pickney* • John Carradine *Amos Briggs* ■ *Dir* J Lee Thompson • *Scr* Richard Sale, from his novel

White Cargo ★★

Drama
1942 · US · BW · 87min

Walter Pidgeon runs a British government rubber plantation in the heart of the Congo, with only drink-sodden doctor Frank Morgan, disillusioned clergyman Henry O'Neill, and his newly-arrived assistant Richard Carlson for company. Emotions boil over when Carlson falls for Hedy Lamarr, a dangerously devious native sexpot. Although the atmosphere is strong and the film's early sequences are quite interesting, the descent into absurdity is total, making the result unintentionally hilarious. RK

Hedy Lamarr *Tondelayo* • Walter Pidgeon *Harry Witzel* • Frank Morgan *Doctor* • Richard Carlson *Langford* • Reginald Owen *Skipper* • Henry O'Neill *Rev Roberts* • Bramwell Fletcher *Wilbur Ashley* ■ *Dir* Richard Thorpe • *Scr* Leon Gordon, from his play, from the novel *Hell's Playground* by Ida Vera Simonton

White Cargo ★ 15
Comedy 1973 · UK · Colour · 73min

A rare feature film appearance from TV star David Jason, this is a daft comedy in which a dithering civil servant becomes overinvolved in the plight of a Soho stripper. It's a lacklustre strike at "fish out of water" territory that soon descends into ludicrous farce. SH

David Jason *Albert Toddey* • Hugh Lloyd *Chumley* • Imogen Hassall *Stella* • Tim Barrett *Fosdyke* • Dave Prowse *Harry* • Raymond Cross *Dudley* • John Barber *Special agent* ■ *Dir* Ray Selfe • *Scr* Ray Selfe, David McGillivray, from a story by Ray Selfe

White Chicks ★ 15
Comedy 2004 · US · Colour · 110min

In this terminally lowbrow comedy, real-life siblings Marlon and Shawn Wayans play FBI agents and brothers. To save their jobs after messing up a drugs bust, the dim-witted duo are forced to don latex masks, flesh-tight miniskirts and receive a full-body blanching in to impersonate and protect a pair of spoilt, brattish socialites. The central interracial, cross-dressing idea might have provided a clever engine for risk-taking humour, but doesn't come close. LF *DVD*

Shawn Wayans *Kevin Copeland* • Marlon Wayans *Marcus Copeland* • Jaime King *Heather Vandergeld* • Frankie Faison *Section Chief Elliott Gordon* • Lochlyn Munro *Agent Jake Harper* • John Heard *Warren Vandergeld* • Busy Philipps *Karen* • Terry Crews *Latrell Spencer* • Brittany Daniel *Megan Vandergeld* ■ *Dir* Keenen Ivory Wayans • *Scr* Keenen Ivory Wayans, Marlon Wayans, Shawn Wayans, Andy McElfresh, Michael Anthony Snowden, Xavier Cook, from a story by Keenen Ivory Wayans, Marlon Wayans, Shawn Wayans

White Christmas ★★★★ U
Seasonal musical 1954 · US · Colour · 115min

This partial remake of the 1942 film *Holiday Inn* - the Bing Crosby movie that gave the world the Irving Berlin song *White Christmas* - provided Paramount with an opportunity to introduce its new screen process Vistavision. Crosby's *Holiday Inn* partner Fred Astaire wasn't available, and Donald O'Connor pulled out, so Danny Kaye reluctantly agreed to second billing to co-star with Crosby, in what proved to be a fortuitous move. Kaye is superb, especially in his knockout dance routine with Vera-Ellen. Veteran Michael Curtiz directed, rightly embracing the sentiment rather than keeping it at bay. TS *DVD* *BL*

Bing Crosby *Bob Wallace* • Danny Kaye *Phil Davis* • Rosemary Clooney *Betty* • Vera-Ellen *Judy* • Dean Jagger *General Waverly* • Mary Wickes *Emma* • John Brascia *Joe* • Anne Whitfield *Susan* • Sig Rumann [Sig Ruman] *Landlord* ■ *Dir* Michael Curtiz • *Scr* Norman Krasna, Norman Panama, Melvin Frank

The White Cliffs of Dover ★★★ U
Wartime drama 1944 · US · BW · 124min

This is a long, lavish, starry, and tear-jerkingly sentimental account of a woman's courage through the First World War, in which her husband is killed, and the Second World War, during which her dying soldier son (Peter Lawford) is brought in to the hospital where she works as a Red Cross nurse. One of several admiring, pro-British

flag-wavers from MGM, the film stars Irene Dunne as the indestructible heroine. RK

Irene Dunne *Lady Susan Dunn Ashwood* • Alan Marshal *Sir John Ashwood* • Roddy McDowall *John Ashwood II, as a boy* • Frank Morgan *Hiram Porter Dunn* • Van Johnson *Sam Bennett* • C Aubrey Smith *Colonel Walter Forsythe* • Gladys Cooper *Lady Jean Ashwood* • Peter Lawford *John Ashwood II, as a young man* • Elizabeth Taylor *Betsy Kenney, aged 10* ■ *Dir* Clarence Brown • *Scr* Claudine West, Jan Lustig, George Froeschel, from the poem by Alice Duer Miller, with additional poetry by Robert Nathan

White Comanche ★★ 12
Spaghetti western 1968 · Sp · Colour · 90min

Unless the prospect of seeing William Shatner in dual roles has you running for the hills, this much-maligned euro western doesn't really deserve its rubbished reputation. The actor took time out between shooting series of *Star Trek* to play Notah and Johnny Moon, twin brothers born on a reservation to a white father and Comanche mother, who have each followed different paths, setting them on a collision course. Joseph Cotten adds a touch of class as the lawman whose town plays host to the showdown. JH Some violence

Joseph Cotten *Sheriff Logan* • William Shatner *Johnny Moon/Notah* • Rossana Yanni *Kelly* • Perla Cristal *White Fawn* • Vidal Molina *General Garcia* ■ *Dir* Gilbert Lee Kay [José Briz Méndez] • *Scr* Robert I Holt, Frank Gruber

White Corridors ★★★ U
Medical drama 1951 · UK · BW · 101min

This Midlands-set medical tale charts the various comings and goings of doctors and patients. The central plot involves doctor James Donald who, perfecting a serum for treating a blood disease, infects himself - thus requiring the intervention of the doctor who loves him (Googie Withers). While it may sound like a hokey soap opera, it is actually a well-made British A-feature, realistically played by a large and excellent cast that includes a number of well-known faces. RK *DVD*

James Donald *Neil Marriner* • Googie Withers *Sophie Dean* • Godfrey Tearle *Groom Sr* • Jack Watling *Dick Groom* • Petula Clark *Joan Shepherd* • Moira Lister *Dolly Clark* • Barry Jones *Shoesmith* ■ *Dir* Pat Jackson • *Scr* Pat Jackson, Jan Read, from the novel *Yeoman's Hospital* by Helen Ashton

The White Countess ★★★ PG
Period romantic drama
2005 · UK/US/Ger/Chi · Colour · 130min

The final Merchant Ivory collaboration, following the death of producer Ismail Merchant during production, is an elegant but uneven affair. Scripted by novelist Kazuo Ishiguro, this charts the relationship that forms between blind former US diplomat Ralph Fiennes and Russian refugee Natasha Richardson in late 1930s Shanghai. With the city on the brink of Japanese invasion, the drama ripples with political intrigue and underworld corruption, but while the events look wonderful, they're too sanitised to ring true. SF *DVD*

Ralph Fiennes *Todd Jackson* • Natasha Richardson *Countess Sofia Belinskya* • Vanessa Redgrave *Princess Vera Belinskya* • Hiroyuki Sanada *Matsuda* • Lynn Redgrave *Olga Belinskya* • Allan Corduner *Samuel Feinstein* • Ying Da *Kao* • Madeleine Daly *Katya* ■ *Dir* James Ivory • *Scr* Kazuo Ishiguro

The White Dawn ★★★★
Period adventure drama
1974 · US · Colour and BW · 109min

A group of whalers are shipwrecked and left stranded among an Inuit tribe in 1896. It's a study of cultural collision, done with an almost wordless script, and a paean to the beauties of the Arctic. Part Herman Melville, part Jack London and part "new-age" San Francisco, this stirring drama knocks spots off most other films of the genre. Never condescending and remarkably open-minded about the conflict between nature's and capitalism's hunters, it's superbly filmed on Frobisher Bay and well acted by a cast that must have endured a lot of discomfort. AT Inuktitut, English +subtitles.

Warren Oates *Billy* • Timothy Bottoms *Daggett* • Louis Gossett Jr *Portagee* • Simonie Kopapik *Sarkak* • Joanasie Salomonie *Kangiak* • Pilitak *Neevee* ■ *Dir* Philip Kaufman • *Scr* James Houston, Tom Rickman, Martin Ransohoff, from the novel by James Houston • *Cinematographer* Michael Chapman

White Dog ★★★★ 15
Drama 1981 · US · Colour · 85min

In his first Hollywood movie in years, director Sam Fuller tackled the controversial subject of racism in a story about a German shepherd dog that has been trained to kill black people. Kristy McNichol plays an actress who adopts the ostensibly docile dog and uncovers its terrible history after it attacks a rapist in her home. This was never released theatrically in the US and eventually found its way on to cable in a watered down version. Fuller turned his back on Hollywood, taking the complete version to Europe where it was hailed as a masterpiece by some critics. TH Violence, swearing. *DVD* *BL*

Kristy McNichol *Julie Sawyer* • Paul Winfield *Keys* • Burl Ives *Carruthers* • Jameson Parker *Roland Gray* • Lynne Moody *Molly* • Marshall Thompson *Director* • Bob Minor *Joe* ■ *Dir* Samuel Fuller • *Scr* Samuel Fuller, Curtis Hanson, from the novella and *Life* magazine article by Romain Gary • *Cinematographer* Bruce Surtees • *Music* Ennio Morricone

White Elephant ★★★ 15
Drama 2012 · Arg/Sp/Fr · Colour · 100min

Argentinian director Pablo Trapero considers the challenge of keeping the faith in the face of suffering and injustice in this impeccably performed drama. The title actually refers to the massive shell of an unfinished hospital building - a real-life monument to Argentina's turbulent political past - which towers over a shantytown that's home to the poverty-stricken flock of a dedicated priest (Ricardo Darín). Caught between the city council, the church hierarchy and the local drug barons, he's learned to be pragmatic, but the arrival of a Belgian missionary is to prove the tipping point in various neighbourhood conflicts. Trapero's film does spend too long on a low simmer, and never quite ignites as drama, but it certainly offers food for thought in exploring the conundrums involved in trying to make a difference. TJ Spanish +subtitles. Violence, swearing, sex scenes, drug abuse. *DVD*

Ricardo Darín [Ricardo Darin] *Father Julián* • Jérémie Renier *Father Nicolás* • Martina Gusman *Luciana* • Federico Benjamín Barga *Monito* • Walter Alfredo Jakob *Lisandro* ■ *Dir* Pablo Trapero • *Scr* Pablo Trapero, Alejandro Fadel, Martin Mauregui, Santiago Mitre • *Music* Michael Nyman

White Fang ★★
Adventure 1936 · US · BW · 70min

The novel *White Fang* was Jack London's sequel to his hugely popular *Call of the Wild*, filmed by Fox in 1935 with Clark Gable and Loretta Young. Writer Gene Fowler scripted both movies as outdoor adventures aimed at the family audience, though this second movie doesn't boast the same fine cast or the same primitive flair. Michael Whalen makes a pallid hero and Jean Muir is the love interest, her only rival the wolf of the title. AT

Michael Whalen *Gordon Scott/Scotty* • Jean Muir *Sylvia Burgess* • Slim Summerville *Slats Magee* • Charles Winninger *Doc McFane* • John Carradine *Beauty Smith* • Jane Darwell *Maud Mahoney* • Thomas Beck *Hal Burgess* • Joseph Herrick *Kobi* ■ *Dir* David Butler • *Scr* Gene Fowler, Hal Long, SG Duncan, from the novel by Jack London

White Fang ★★★ PG
Adventure 1991 · US · Colour · 104min

Jack London's ferocious story about the half-wolf in the Klondike is tamed *Lassie*-style by Disney, with most of the savagery squeezed out. Ethan Hawke, with dubious partners Klaus Maria Brandauer and Seymour Cassel, is the young gold prospector who seeks to establish a

prosperous claim. The film may be a bit of a letdown for previously Oscar-nominated Brandauer, but he turns a minor role into a memorable one. TH *DVD*

Klaus Maria Brandauer *Alex* • Ethan Hawke *Jack* • Seymour Cassel *Skunker* • Susan Hogan *Belinda* • James Remar *Beauty* • Bill Moseley *Luke* • Clint B Youngreen *Tinker* • Pius Savage *Grey Beaver* ■ *Dir* Randal Kleiser • *Scr* Jeanne Rosenberg, Nick Thiel, David Fallon, from the novel by Jack London

White Fang 2: Myth of the White Wolf ★★ U
Adventure 1994 · US · Colour · 101min

Ethan Hawke puts in an uncredited appearance at the start of this handsome Disney adventure, which, unlike its predecessor, owes little or nothing to the much loved novel by Jack London. Scott Bairstow steps into Hawke's shoes as he abandons the Alaskan gold fields and, along with his beautiful canine companion, searches for a herd of lost caribou for a tribe of starving native Americans. The soppy romance won't do much for the majority of younger viewers, but they should find the tribal mythology and mysticism fascinating. DP *DVD*

Scott Bairstow *Henry Casey* • Charmaine Craig *Lily Joseph* • Al Harrington *Moses Joseph* • Anthony Michael Ruivivar *Peter* • Victoria Racimo *Katrin* • Alfred Molina *Reverend Leland Drury* • Ethan Hawke *Jack* • Geoffrey Lewis *Heath* ■ *Dir* Ken Olin • *Scr* David Fallon

White Feather ★★ PG
Western 1955 · US · Colour · 98min

Gauche Robert Wagner is the government surveyor trying to persuade the Cheyenne that living on a reservation is their best option, but they find his resolutely 1950s cool bravado as hard to take as we do. Jeffrey Hunter looks equally uncomfortable as an American Indian brave and cavalryman John Lund acts throughout as though he'd rather be somewhere else. Yet, despite the poor casting, Lucien Ballard's handsome CinemaScope photography gives this film some dignity. TS

Robert Wagner *Josh Tanner* • John Lund *Colonel Lindsay* • Debra Paget *Appearing Day* • Jeffrey Hunter *Little Dog* • Eduard Franz *Chief Broken Hand* • Noah Beery Jr *Lieutenant Ferguson* • Virginia Leith *Ann Magruder* • Emile Meyer *Magruder* ■ *Dir* Robert Webb [Robert D Webb] • *Scr* Delmer Daves, Leo Townsend, from a story by John Prebble

White God ★★★★ 15
Drama 2014 · Hun/Ger/Swe · Colour · 116min

From its audacious opening of an enormous pack of dogs chasing a girl on a bicycle through deserted Budapest streets, it's clear that *White God* is a strange beast. Director Kornel Mundruczo has created a beautiful and bizarre film that veers between gritty realism and haunting fantasy, as a dog searches for his owner and finds both kindness and cruelty along the way, giving rise to some scenes of violence that are hard to watch. It's a unique film, proving that working with children and animals can be a risk worth taking. LB Hungarian +subtitles. Swearing. *DVD* *BL*

Zsofia Psotta *Lili* • Sandor Zsoter *Daniel* • Szabolcs Thuroczy *Old man* • Lili Monori *Bev* ■ *Dir* Kornel Mundruczo • *Scr* Kornel Mundruczo, Viktoria Petranyi, Kata Weber

White Heat ★★★★★ 15
Classic crime drama 1949 · US · BW · 109min

"Made it, Ma! Top of the world!" shrieks a demented James Cagney from the top of an oil tank before going out in a blaze of vainglory. Directed by Raoul Walsh, this is one of the greatest of all gangster pictures, a nightmarish excursion into the maladjusted mind of Arthur Cody Jarrett, a thug who sits on his mother's knee, steals and kills for pure pleasure, and probably sucks his thumb in private. All the major gangster heroes of the 1930s had their psychological problems, but here Cagney is a whole library of Freudian theory put through the blender, and the poor lad

W

suffers from epilepsy to boot. Operatic, sinisterly funny and utterly compelling. **AT** *DVD*

James Cagney *Arthur Cody Jarrett* • Virginia Mayo *Verna Jarrett* • Edmond O'Brien *Hank Fallon/Vic Pardo* • Margaret Wycherly *Ma Jarrett* • Steve Cochran *"Big Ed" Somers* • John Archer *Philip Evans* • Wally Cassell *Giovanni "Cotton" Valetti* • Mickey Knox *Het Kohler* ■ *Dir* Raoul Walsh • *Scr* Ivan Goff, Ben Roberts, from a story by Virginia Kellogg • *Cinematographer* Sid Hickox

White House Down ★★★ 12
Action thriller   2013 · US · Colour · 126min

On paper, *White House Down* and *Olympus Has Fallen* seem identical, but where *Olympus* plays it straight, this is more an all-action romp. Channing Tatum is the John McClane-type hero of this *Die Hard in the White House* and Jamie Foxx the president who turns action hero to help him thwart the terrorists. They're both capable enough, but they play second fiddle to the spectacularly staged stunts. Only director Roland Emmerich could manage to wrest a car chase out of a film set entirely in the White House. **DA** Some violence, brief swearing. *DVD Blu-ray*

Channing Tatum *John Cale* • Jamie Foxx *President James Sawyer* • Maggie Gyllenhaal *Carol Finnerty* • Jason Clarke (2) *Emil Stenz* • Richard Jenkins *Eli Raphelson, Speaker of the House* • James Woods *Martin Walker* • Garcelle Beauvais *The First Lady* ■ *Dir* Roland Emmerich • *Scr* James Vanderbilt

White Hunter, Black Heart
★★★★ PG
Adventure drama   1990 · US · Colour · 107min

Clint Eastwood's ambitious film is a thinly veiled account of the making of John Huston's *The African Queen*, already well documented in books by Katharine Hepburn and screenwriter Peter Viertel. As "Huston", Eastwood is just marvellous – aristocratic, bombastic and so obsessed with hunting and killing an elephant that his movie-making is left on the back burner. Beautifully filmed on location in Zimbabwe, the movie has pace, drama, a genuine sense of adventure and an astutely critical eye for the dying vestiges of British imperialism. **AT** Violence, swearing.

Clint Eastwood *John Wilson* • Jeff Fahey *Pete Verrill* • George Dzundza *Paul Landers* • Alun Armstrong *Ralph Lockhart* • Marisa Berenson *Kay Gibson* • Timothy Spall *Hodkins* • Catherine Neilson *Irene Saunders* • Norman Lumsden *Butler George* ■ *Dir* Clint Eastwood • *Scr* Peter Viertel, James Bridges, Burt Kennedy, from the novel by Peter Viertel • *Cinematographer* Jack N Green

The White King ★★
Science-fiction drama   2016 · UK · Colour

A dystopian drama set in an unspecified nation where the populace are constantly monitored. Main character Djata (Lorenzo Allchurch) is a 12-year-old boy whose father is taken away by the authorities. There are a couple of effective scenes as Djata's mother (Agyness Deyn) tries to free her husband, including a tense sequence where Djata's grandfather (Jonathan Pryce) pressures Djata to shoot a cat. Unfortunately, though, *The White King* only springs to life when Pryce is on screen, which isn't often enough. **SC** Violence.

Lorenzo Allchurch *Djata* • Agyness Deyn *Hannah* • Jonathan Pryce *Colonel Fitz* • Olafur Darri Olafsson *Pickaxe* • Greta Scacchi *General Meade* • Olivia Williams *Sophia* ■ *Dir* Alex Helfrecht, Jörg Tittel • *Scr* Alex Helfrecht, Jörg Tittel, from Gyorgy Dragoman's novel

White Lightnin' ★★ 18
Biographical fantasy
2008 · UK/US/Cro · Colour · 92min

As grim and unrelenting as its subject, this fictionalised biopic of Appalachian folk dancer Jesco White explores the darkest corners of American society without ever shedding any light on what it finds there. Despite an outstanding lead performance from star Edward Hogg and the startling sight of Carrie Fisher as his much older, glassy-eyed boozy floozy, there's a grubbiness here that doesn't wash off

easily. Jesco flies off the rails at an early age, and from sniffing petrol to ingesting amphetamines and psychedelics, his life unfurls in a downward spiral of increasingly harsh vignettes, all scored with an equally abrasive rockabilly soundtrack. **DW** Violence, swearing, drug abuse.

Edward Hogg *Jesco White* • Carrie Fisher *Cilla White* • Muse Watson *D-Ray White* • Owen Campbell *Young Jesco* • Wallace Merck *Hudd* • Stephanie Astalos-Jones *Birty Mae* ■ *Dir* Dominic Murphy • *Scr* Eddy Moretti, Shane Smith, from a story by Smith, Dominic Murphy

White Lightning ★★★ 15
Action crime thriller   1973 · US · Colour · 97min

One of the best of Burt Reynolds's good ol' boy movies, in which he's a moonshiner whose manufacture of illicit liquor puts him up against crooked sheriff Ned Beatty. As the corrupt lawman was responsible for the death of Burt's brother, revenge is also on the menu. Director Joseph Sargent makes good use of some interesting swampland locations and keeps the drama from being too formulaic. A sequel, *Gator*, followed in 1976. **TH** *DVD*

Burt Reynolds *Gator McKlusky* • Jennifer Billingsley *Lou* • Ned Beatty *Sheriff Connors* • Bo Hopkins *Roy Boone* • Matt Clark *Dude Watson* • Louise Latham *Martha Culpepper* • Diane Ladd *Maggie* • RG Armstrong *Big Bear* ■ *Dir* Joseph Sargent • *Scr* William Norton

White Line Fever ★★★ 15
Action drama   1975 · US · Colour · 85min

Back on civvy street after a stint in the air force, Jan-Michael Vincent buys a truck, marries his sweetheart Kay Lenz and gets started in the hauling business, only to learn that it is run by racketeers and smugglers. Refusing to bow to the system, he endangers himself by fighting corruption. The movie, convincingly played by Vincent and the supporting cast, marked a step up for director Jonathan Kaplan who handles the material well. **RK**

Jan-Michael Vincent *Carrol Jo Hummer* • Kay Lenz *Jerri Hummer* • Slim Pickens *Duane Haller* • LQ Jones *Buck Wessle* • Don Porter *Josh Cutler* • Sam Laws *Pops* • Johnny Ray McGhee *Carnell* ■ *Dir* Jonathan Kaplan • *Scr* Ken Friedman, Jonathan Kaplan

The White Lions ★★★
Adventure   1980 · US · Colour · 96min

Directed by Mel Stuart (*Willy Wonka and the Chocolate Factory*), this location-shot safari movie in the *Born Free* mould stars Michael York as the naturalist who takes his wife and daughter with him when he goes out to Africa to study endangered wildlife. It's too twee for comfort, but children who love natural-history TV programmes should like it. **TH**

Michael York *Chris McBride* • Glynnis O'Connor *Mrs McBride* • Donald Moffat *Vreeland* • Lauri Lynn Myers *Laura McBride* ■ *Dir* Mel Stuart • *Scr* Corey Blechman, Peter Dixon

White Mane ★★★★ PG
Adventure drama   1952 · Fr · BW · 38min

Winner of the Prix Jean Vigo, Albert Lamorisse's third film may not be as well known as *The Red Balloon*, but it is still a charming study of the all-too-fleeting wonder of childhood. Young Alain Emery gives a spirited performance as the kid whose daily routine of fishing and poaching with his grandfather is interrupted by the appearance of a proud white stallion, which defies all attempts by the local ranchers to capture it. With the Camargue marshlands emphasising the wildness of both the horse and his boy, this is a poetic and truly inspiring tribute to the beauty of nature. **DP** In French.

Alain Emery *Folco* • Pascal Lamorisse • Frank Silvera ■ *Dir/Scr* Albert Lamorisse

White Man's Burden ★★★ 15
Fantasy drama   1995 · US · Colour · 85min

This reversed-reality drama is set in an alternate Los Angeles where blacks hold all the positions of power and influence, and

where whites do all the menial work. John Travolta plays a blue-collar worker who, more by default than design, winds up kidnapping black boss Harry Belafonte when he calls at his mansion to protest at being unfairly fired. It's a neat idea, less fully realised than it might have been. There are good performances from the two stars, though. **DA** Swearing, some violence.

John Travolta *Louis Pinnock* • Harry Belafonte *Thaddeus Thomas* • Kelly Lynch *Marsha Pinnock* • Margaret Avery (2) *Megan Thomas* • Tom Bower *Stanley* • Carrie Snodgress *Josine* ■ *Dir/Scr* Desmond Nakano

White Material ★★★ 15
Drama   2009 · Fr/Cameroon · Colour · 113min

Director Claire Denis returns to Africa for this elliptical tale about an indomitable woman attempting to survive the destruction of her livelihood. Set in an unnamed country, the picture is dominated by Isabelle Huppert as the French owner of a coffee plantation, who's determined to harvest her crop despite an increasingly violent civil war that threatens to engulf the area. Huppert is a magnetic presence in this atmospheric film in which primal, almost elemental forces seem to bear down upon its protagonists. Unfortunately, the disconnected narrative leaves a lot to be desired when it comes to figuring out when and where events are occurring. **JA** French +subtitles. Violence, nudity, drug abuse. *DVD Blu-ray*

Isabelle Huppert *Maria Vial* • Christophe Lambert [Christopher Lambert] *André Vial* • Nicolas Duvauchelle *Manuel* • Michel Subor *Henri Vial, the landlord* • Isaach de Bankole *The Boxer* ■ *Dir* Claire Denis • *Scr* Claire Denis, Marie N'Diaye

White Men Can't Jump
★★★★ 15
Sports comedy drama
1992 · US · Colour · 115min

Writer/director Ron Shelton is that rare beast: someone who can make movies with wit, warmth and perception about American sports. This is a marvellous tale of two basketball players (Wesley Snipes and Woody Harrelson) who make their living hustling fellow street players around Los Angeles. The plot is fairly simplistic, but the pleasure comes from Shelton's fizzing foul-mouthed dialogue, the charismatic performances and the superbly choreographed basketball sequences. Rosie Perez, as Harrelson's girlfriend, stays on the right side of irritating. **JF** Violence, swearing, nudity. *DVD*

Wesley Snipes *Sidney Deane* • Woody Harrelson *Billy Hoyle* • Rosie Perez *Gloria Clemente* • Tyra Ferrell *Rhonda Deane* • Cylk Cozart *Robert* • Kadeem Hardison *Junior* • Ernest Harden Jr *George* • John Marshall Jones *Walter* ■ *Dir/Scr* Ron Shelton

White Mile ★★★ 15
Drama based on a true story
1994 · US · Colour · 95min

In this TV movie Alan Alda plays the hard-as-nails boss of a company who refuses to accept any responsibility when a white-water rafting trip he has organised for his staff ends in tragedy. Peter Gallagher is the tormented executive wondering whether he should fall into line. Director Robert Butler's direction is unobtrusive, but he nonetheless brings considerable drama to the central action sequence, and he is well served by a better-than-average cast. **JF** Violence, swearing.

Alan Alda *Dan Cutler* • Peter Gallagher *Jack Robbins* • Robert Loggia *Nick Karas* ■ *Dir* Robert Butler • *Scr* Michael Butler

White Mischief ★★★ 18
Historical drama   1987 · UK · Colour · 103min

The less-than-wholesome traits of Kenya's scandal-ridden "Happy Valley" crowd in the 1940s are nicely delineated, in all their dissolute, gin-swilling, expat glory, by director Michael Radford. Based on a true story about the murder of a promiscuous aristocrat who was servicing half of the valley's bored ladies, this over-egged drama has no one who elicits any sympathy.

Charles Dance makes a believable stud, however, and Greta Scacchi is gorgeous, even if Joss Ackland overacts as her cuckolded husband. **SH** Violence, swearing, sex scenes, nudity. *DVD*

Charles Dance *Josslyn Hay, Earl of Erroll* • Greta Scacchi *Diana* • Joss Ackland *Sir John "Jock" Delves Broughton* • Sarah Miles *Alice de Janze* • John Hurt *Gilbert Colvile* • Geraldine Chaplin *Nina Soames* • Ray McAnally *Morris* • Trevor Howard *Jack Soames* • Hugh Grant *Hugh* ■ *Dir* Michael Radford • *Scr* Michael Radford, Jonathan Gems, from the book by James Fox

White Nights ★★★ U
Drama   1957 · It/Fr · BW · 98min

Based on a Dostoyevsky story, this touching fantasy concerns a meek and lonely clerk who falls deeply in love with a girl on a bridge – she goes there every night to meet her own lover, a sailor, who has promised to return but never does. This movie marked a radical departure for the arch neorealist and communist Luchino Visconti, who treats it rather like a Fellini film. It was staged on deliberately artificial sets and has the ambience of a dream. Marcello Mastroianni gives one of his best performances of the 1950s as the doomed clerk. **AT** Italian +subtitles.

Maria Schell *Natalia* • Marcello Mastroianni *Mario* • Jean Marais *Lodger* • Clara Calamai *Prostitute* • Marcella Rovena *Housewife* • Maria Zanolli *Housekeeper* ■ *Dir* Luchino Visconti • *Scr* Luchino Visconti, Suso Cecchi D'Amico, from the story *Belye Nochi* by Fyodor Mikhailovich Dostoyevsky

White Nights ★★★ 15
Political thriller   1985 · US · Colour · 130min

This entertaining blend of ballet and bullets stars dancer Mikhail Baryshnikov as a bolshy Bolshoi-er who defected to America eight years previously but finds himself back in the USSR when the plane he's defecting on is forced to make a (spectacular) crash-landing. Fellow hoofer Gregory Hines co-stars as an American tap-star who relocated to Russia, and is charged with helping Baryshnikov to re-defect. Not the world's most credible plot, but Baryshnikov is good and there are stunning dance and action sequences. **DA** *DVD*

Mikhail Baryshnikov *Nikolai "Kolya" Rodchenko* • Gregory Hines *Raymond Greenwood* • Jerzy Skolimowski *Colonel Chaiko* • Helen Mirren *Galina Ivanova* • Geraldine Page *Anne Wyatt* • Isabella Rossellini *Darya Greenwood* • John Glover *Wynn Scott* ■ *Dir* Taylor Hackford • *Scr* James Goldman, Eric Hughes, from a story by James Goldman

White Noise ★★ 15
Supernatural thriller
2004 · UK/Can/US · Colour · 93min

Michael Keaton obsessively communicates with his deceased wife via paranormal messages in this slow-moving supernatural thriller. Captured as "white noise" on his TV and other electronic devices, the eerie snippets appear to be guiding him to save others from death. What unfolds is a dangerous race against time that is meant to be twisting and dramatic but is actually rather dull. **SF** *DVD*

Michael Keaton *Jonathan Rivers* • Deborah Kara Unger *Sarah Tate* • Chandra West *Anna Rivers* • Ian McNeice *Raymond Price* • Sarah Strange *Jane* • Nicholas Elia *Mike Rivers* • Mike Dopud *Detective Smits* ■ *Dir* Geoffrey Sax • *Scr* Niall Johnson

White Noise: the Light
★★ 15
Horror thriller   2006 · US/Can · Colour · 94min

White Noise was about electronic voice phenomena and starred Michael Keaton as a man being contacted by the dead. Despite its title, this decent follow-up bears little connection to the first film – it's about the killer consequences of near-death experience, and Keaton has been replaced by *Serenity* and *Slither* star Nathan Fillion. He plays a man whose own close call leaves him with the ability not only to sense imminent death in others, but also to avert it. It's a furrow that's been better ploughed by such shockers as *Final Destination*, but the special effects are OK, and the storyline entertains despite its tendency to go increasingly over the top. DA DVD

Nathan Fillion *Abe Dale* • Katee Sackhoff *Sherry Clarke* • Craig Fairbrass *Henry Caine* • Adrian Holmes *Marty Bloom* • Kendall Cross *Rebecca Dale* • Teryl Rothery *Julia Caine* • William MacDonald *Dr Karras* ■ *Dir* Patrick Lussier • *Scr* Matt Venne

White of the Eye ★★★ 18
Psychological thriller
1986 · UK · Colour · 106min

Donald Cammell ended a decade-long exile from the director's chair with this bizarre, yet decidedly disturbing thriller. The Indian mysticism is pretty half-baked, the symbolism is anything but subtle and the Steadicam work is overly intrusive. But Cammell creates an atmosphere of real menace as he delves beneath the surface calm of a sleepy former mining town in Arizona. He's well served by a cast that never quite made the front rank. DP Violence, swearing.

David Keith *Paul White* • Cathy Moriarty *Joan White* • Art Evans *Detective Charles Mendoza* • Alan Rosenberg *Mike Desantos* • Alberta Watson *Ann Mason* • Michael Green *Phil Ross* • Danko Gurovich *Arnold White* • William G Schilling *Harold Gideon* • China Cammell [China Kong] *Ruby Hoy* ■ *Dir* Donald Cammell • *Scr* China Cammell [China Kong], Donald Cammell, from the novel *Mrs White* by Margaret Tracy

White Oleander ★★★ 12
Drama 2002 · US · Colour · 104min

It would have been easy to rework Janet Fitch's bestseller – a teenager is fostered out after her artist mother is jailed for murdering her lover – as a stellar TV movie, but director Peter Kosminsky rejects the melodrama-by-numbers option and uses attention-grabbing imagery to convey much of the confusion Alison Lohman feels after Michelle Pfeiffer's arrest. His assured grasp of structure and pacing, and some accomplished acting, ensure that we only gradually come to appreciate the shifting nature of their relationship. DP Swearing, sex scenes, nudity. DVD

Alison Lohman *Astrid Magnussen* • Robin Wright Penn [Robin Wright] *Starr Thomas* • Michelle Pfeiffer *Ingrid Magnussen* • Renée Zellweger *Claire Richards* • Billy Connolly *Barry Kolker* • Svetlana Efremova *Rena Grushenka* • Patrick Fugit *Paul Trout* • Cole Hauser *Ray* • Noah Wyle *Mark Richards* ■ *Dir* Peter Kosminsky • *Scr* Mary Agnes Donoghue, from the novel by Janet Fitch

White Palace ★★★★ 18
Romantic drama 1990 · US · Colour · 98min

James Spader plays a youngish middle-class ad man who falls for 40-something waitress Susan Sarandon, much to the dismay of his peers. Spader and Sarandon spark off each other superbly, making the most of a mature script that intelligently explores class and sexuality in modern America. Luis Mandoki's direction is admirably level-headed, and he sidesteps the usual clichés and melodramatics. JF Swearing, sex scenes. DVD

Susan Sarandon *Nora Baker* • James Spader *Max Baron* • Jason Alexander *Neil Horowitz* • Kathy Bates *Rosemary Powers* • Eileen Brennan *Judy* • Steven Hill *Sol Horowitz* • Corey Parker *Larry Klugman* ■ *Dir* Luis Mandoki • *Scr* Ted Tally, Alvin Sargent, from the novel by Glenn Savan

The White Parade ★★★
Medical drama 1934 · US · BW · 83min

Set in a school for trainee nurses in the American Midwest, the focus is on Loretta Young, whose dedication to her calling is challenged by romantic involvement with wealthy Bostonian John Boles, who forces her to choose between him and her career. Young is excellent in a film that combines an almost documentary approach with old-fashioned romantic soap opera. Directed by Irving Cummings, it's entertaining enough and was a big box-office success on release, but its Oscar nomination as best picture is something of a surprise. RK

Loretta Young *June Arden* • John Boles *Ronald Hall III* • Dorothy Wilson *Zita Scofield* • Muriel Kirkland *Glenda Farley* • Astrid Allwyn *Gertrude*

Mack • Frank Conroy *Doctor Thorne* • Jane Darwell *Sailor Roberts* ■ *Dir* Irving Cummings • *Scr* Sonya Levien, Ernest Pascal, from the novel by Rian James, adapted by Rian James, Jesse Lasky Jr

The White Ribbon ★★★★ 15
Period mystery drama
2009 · Austria/Fr/Ger/It · BW · 137min

Director Michael Haneke won the Palme d'Or for this immaculate monochrome mystery set in the bucolic north German village of Eichwald on the eve of the Great War. There's a hint of *Heimat* about the narrated, linear action that links the fates of baron Ulrich Tukur, pastor Burghart Klaussner and the increasingly disaffected underlings in their care. There's also a sense of the first buds of Nazism flourishing in the populace's unquestioning adherence to aristocratic authoritarianism and Protestant patriarchy. The ensemble performances are outstanding, and Haneke's vision and control imbues the ever-more suspenseful and harrowing events with an oppressive sense of psychological and historical significance. DP German +subtitles. Child abuse references. DVD Blu

Christian Friedel *The schoolteacher* • Ernst Jacobi *The narrator* • Leonie Benesch *Eva* • Ulrich Tukur *The Baron* • Ursina Lardi *Marie-Louise, the Baroness* • Fion Mutert *Sigmund* ■ *Dir/Scr* Michael Haneke

White Sands ★★★ 15
Thriller 1992 · US · Colour · 97min

In this New Mexico-set thriller, deputy sheriff Willem Dafoe becomes involved in mega-black doings when he discovers half-a-million mysterious dollars in a suitcase belonging to a dead FBI agent. Roger Donaldson's direction loses focus when Dafoe meets up with arms dealer Mickey Rourke and his society girlfriend Mary Elizabeth Mastrantonio, while the plot's twists and turns become entangled, but there's still enough intriguing action to keep us involved. AT Swearing, violence, brief nudity. DVD

Willem Dafoe *Ray Dolezal* • Mary Elizabeth Mastrantonio *Lane Bodine* • Mickey Rourke *Gorman Lennox* • Sam Jackson [Samuel L Jackson] *Greg Meeker* • M Emmet Walsh *Bert Gibson* • Mimi Rogers *Molly Dolezal* ■ *Dir* Roger Donaldson • *Scr* Daniel Pyne

White Savage ★★★
Adventure 1943 · US · Colour · 75min

Following the success of *Arabian Nights* (1942), Universal realised the appeal of undemanding Technicolor escapism to war-weary audiences and dispatched the reunited quartet of Jon Hall, Maria Montez, Sabu and Turhan Bey to a South Pacific island for this gloriously camp island adventure. A variety of insurmountable obstacles (including a showstopping earthquake) litter the path to true love, but no one really doubts that Sabu will eventually persuade princess Montez that villain Thomas Gomez is the rogue after the treasure in her temple pool and not Hall's rugged shark fisherman. DP

Jon Hall *Kaloe* • Maria Montez *Princess Tahia* • Sabu *Orano* • Don Terry *Gris* • Turhan Bey *Tamara* • Thomas Gomez *Sam Miller* • Sidney Toler *Wong* ■ *Dir* Arthur Lubin • *Scr* Richard Brooks, from a story by Peter Milne

White Shadows in the South Seas ★★★
Drama 1928 · US · BW · 88min

MGM sent acclaimed documentary director Robert Flaherty and rising outdoor action director WS Van Dyke to shoot a South Seas adventure on location at a time when real exotic settings held huge box-office appeal. Flaherty resigned early on and Van Dyke made his reputation with this pictorially magnificent, sombre story of a white trader corrupting pagan. The studio then decided to launch the film as its first sound release, adding some crude dialogue, sound effects and music score, and these now have a quaint charm although

criticised for their technical shortcomings at the time. AE

Monte Blue *Lloyd* • Raquel Torres *Faraway* • Robert Anderson (1) *Sebastian* ■ *Dir* WS Van Dyke • *Scr* Jack Cunningham, John Colton, Ray Doyle, from the novel by Frederick O'Brien • *Cinematographers* Clyde De Vinna • *Cinematographers* George Nagle, Bob Roberts

The White Sheik ★★★ U
Romantic comedy drama 1951 · It · BW · 83min

Originally devised by Michelangelo Antonioni (who retained a story credit), Federico Fellini's first solo outing not only lampoons bourgeois sensibilities, but also the photo-romance magazines that did a roaring trade in the 1950s. Arriving in Rome for her honeymoon, Brunella Bovo ditches husband Leopoldo Trieste's carefully planned itinerary in order to meet both her favourite fumetti star, Alberto Sordi, and the Pope. Vital to this sympathetic study of shattered illusions is Fellini's mischievous sense of fantasy, but Sordi's performance as the dissolute, hen-pecked idol is also top drawer. A key cinematic stepping-stone. DP Italian +subtitles. DVD

Alberto Sordi *Fernando Rivoli, "The White Sheik"* • Brunella Bovo *Wanda Cavalli* • Leopoldo Trieste *Ivan Cavalli* • Giulietta Masina *Cabiria* ■ *Dir* Federico Fellini • *Scr* Federico Fellini, Tullio Pinelli, Ennio Flaiano, from a story by Federico Fellini, Tullio Pinelli, from an idea by Michelangelo Antonioni

The White Sister ★★★
Silent romantic drama 1923 · US · BW · 143min

After the death of her father, Italian aristocrat Lillian Gish is thrown out of the ancestral home and cheated of her inheritance by her vindictive sister. Hearing that Italian army officer Ronald Colman, whom she loves, has been killed, she becomes a nun, only for Colman to reappear and attempt to prise her out of the convent. An impressive silent drama, unusual for its time in dealing with religion against a contemporary background, and well-directed by Henry King (with help from the Vatican) on location in Italy. RK

Lillian Gish *Angela Chiaromonte* • Ronald Colman *Capt Giovanni Severini* • Gail Kane *Marchesa di Mola* • J Barney Sherry *Monsignor Saracinesca* • Charles Lane (1) *Prince Chiaromonte* ■ *Dir* Henry King • *Scr* George V Hobart, Charles E Whittaker, Will M Ritchey, Don Bartlett, from the novel by F Marion Crawford

The White Sister ★★
Melodrama 1933 · US · BW · 105min

This so-called "woman's picture", shot by Garbo's cameraman William H Daniels, is directed by Clark Gable's macho hunting pal, Victor Fleming. Gable and Helen Hayes play the lovelorn couple, he a soldier and she his beloved who believes he has been killed in combat. But Gable returns and is totally gutted to discover that Hayes has married someone else, namely God, for she has taken her vows as a nun. Because of its profoundly religious theme, this load of tosh is wisely located in Italy. The story had been a major success as a silent film ten years earlier. AT

Helen Hayes *Angela Chiaromonte* • Clark Gable *Lt Giovanni Severi* • Lewis Stone *Prince Guido Chiaromonte* • Louise Closser Hale *Mina* • May Robson *Mother Superior* • Edward Arnold *Father Saracinesca* • Alan Edwards *Ernesto Traversi* ■ *Dir* Victor Fleming • *Scr* Donald Ogden Stewart, from the play by F Marion Crawford, Walter Hackett, from the novel by F Marion Crawford

White Squall ★★★ 12
Adventure based on a true story
1996 · US · Colour · 123min

Neither Jeff Bridges's quiet authority nor the "in-your-face" dramatics of a killer storm can lift director Ridley Scott's attempt to remake *Top Gun* (which was directed by brother Tony) at sea. School-ship skipper Bridges gathers a group of undisciplined students aboard the brigantine *Albatross* for a voyage of self-discovery to South America. This undemanding but entertaining rites-of-passage adventure takes a sudden lurch

into disaster with the arrival of the storm of the title. TH Swearing, brief nudity. DVD

Jeff Bridges *"Skipper" Christopher Sheldon* • Caroline Goodall *Dr Alice Sheldon* • John Savage *McCrea* • Scott Wolf *Chuck Gieg* • Jeremy Sisto *Frank Beaumont* • Ryan Phillippe *Gil Martin* • David Lascher *Robert March* ■ *Dir* Ridley Scott • *Scr* Todd Robinson

The White Stripes: Under Blackpool Lights ★★★ 12A
Concert documentary
2004 · UK/US · Colour · 80min

Despite playing two nights at the cavernous Alexandra Palace in London, Jack and Meg White ultimately decided to release the gig from Blackpool's Empress Ballroom as the official record of their 2004 tour since it was both more intimate and immediate. The musicianship is occasionally as shaky as Dick Carruthers's agitated, atmospherically grainy camerawork, but the sheer energy of the band burns through. Some will be disappointed that the 26-song set doesn't include *Fell in Love with a Girl*, but this still amounts to a rousing resumé for the garage rockers, with White Stripes originals jostling alongside Robert Johnson blues standards and treats such as Dolly Parton's *Jolene*. DP

■ *Dir* Dick Carruthers

The White Tower ★★★ U
Adventure 1950 · US · Colour · 97min

In this mountaineering drama, Glenn Ford joins a climb in the Swiss Alps. A lot of emotional baggage is carried along with the mountaineers: Ford falls for fellow climber Alida Valli, whose father was killed on the same peak; Lloyd Bridges is an arrogant former Nazi army officer; Cedric Hardwicke is an ageing British botanist; Claude Rains is a self-destructive French writer who is drunk most of the time. Despite the predictability of the symbolism and some wooden performances, there is some excellent location photography. AT

Glenn Ford *Martin Ordway* • Valli [Alida Valli] *Carla Alton* • Claude Rains *Paul Delambre* • Oscar Homolka *Andreas* • Sir Cedric Hardwicke [Cedric Hardwicke] *Nicholas Radcliffe* • Lloyd Bridges *Mr Hein* ■ *Dir* Ted Tetzlaff • *Scr* Paul Jarrico, from the novel by James Ramsay Ullman

The White Warrior ★★★ U
Period adventure 1959 · It/Yug · Colour · 85min

This rousing rendition of the classic 19th-century adventure is elegantly directed by Italian horror maestro Riccardo Freda and ravishingly photographed by future genre genius, Mario Bava. Delivering some low-budget epic thrills, Steve Reeves plays a rebel chief who clashes with the Tsar's army over Caucasian land rights. The full Italian print features scenes of sadistic erotica and torture, but deleted in the edited US version. A mini-*War and Peace*, spaghetti style. AJ Italian dubbed.

Steve Reeves *Hadji Murad* • Georgia Moll [Giorgia Moll] *Sultanet* • Renato Baldini *Akmet Khan* • Scilla Gabel *Princess Maria* • Gerard Herter *Prince Sergei/General Vorontzov* ■ *Dir* Riccardo Freda • *Scr* Gino De Santis, Akos Tolnay, from the novel *Khadzhi-Murat* by Leo Tolstoy

White Water Summer ★★★ 15
Action adventure 1987 · US · Colour · 85min

This superior outdoor adventure stars Kevin Bacon as a bullyboy wilderness guide and Sean Astin as one of four kids he hikes off into the middle of nowhere to make men of them. The plot kicks in when Bacon is badly injured and finds himself dependent on Astin, previously the main target for his bullying. Good performances bolster the proceedings and the scenery is great. DA

Kevin Bacon *Vic* • Sean Astin *Alan* • Jonathan Ward *Mitch* • KC Martel *George* • Matt Adler *Chris* • Caroline McWilliams *Virginia Block* • Charles Siebert *Jerry Block* ■ *Dir* Jeff Bleckner • *Scr* Manya Starr, Ernest Kinoy

White Witch Doctor ★★★ U
Romantic adventure 1953 · US · Colour · 93min

Nurse Susan Hayward arrives in the Congo and is taken in hand by treasure hunter Robert Mitchum. Black water fever, tribal dancing, skirmishes with the Bakuba tribe and a man-eating lion persuade them to dedicate the rest of their lives to helping the Africans. This blend of old-fashioned adventure and post-Imperial politics has the advantage of two appealing stars, some striking location work and an evocative score. **AT**

Susan Hayward *Ellen Burton* • Robert Mitchum *Lonni Douglas* • Walter Slezak *Huysman* • Mashood Ajala *Jacques* • Joseph C Narcisse *Utembo* • Elzie Emanuel *Kapuka* • Timothy Carey *Jarrett* • Otis Greene *Bakuba boy* ■ *Dir* Henry Hathaway • *Scr* Ivan Goff, Ben Roberts, from the novel by Louise A Stinetorf • *Cinematographer* Leon Shamroy • *Music* Bernard Herrmann

White Woman ★★★
Romantic melodrama 1933 · US · BW · 73min

A torrid melodrama, this steamy vehicle can only be enjoyed if approached in the right spirit. Carole Lombard is a penniless showgirl, stranded in Malaya, who marries plantation owner Charles Laughton to get out of her predicament and is soon seeking true love in younger arms while her husband takes it out on the natives. The men all sweat a lot and grow designer stubble while Lombard remains expertly gowned and coiffured in this totally artificial but irresistible slice of hokum. **TV**

Carole Lombard *Judith Denning* • Charles Laughton *Horace H Prin* • Charles Bickford *Ballister* • Kent Taylor *David von Elst* • Percy Kilbride *Jakey* ■ *Dir* Stuart Walker • *Scr* Samuel Hoffenstein, Gladys Lehman, from the play *Hangman's Whip* by Norman Reilly Raine, Frank Butler

White Zombie ★★★ PG
Horror 1932 · US · BW · 64min

The first feature about Haiti's undead, this was a bold attempt by director Victor Halperin to break away from the endless chat of the early talkies. The long wordless passages allow an eerie atmosphere to develop as the camera glides menacingly around the jungle to the unnerving accompaniment of distant wailing. And who could be more at home in such sinister surroundings than Bela Lugosi as the evil voodoo sorcerer. **DP**

Bela Lugosi *"Murder" Legendre* • Madge Bellamy *Madeline Short* • John Harron *Neil Parker* • Joseph Cawthorn *Dr Bruner, Missionary* • Robert Frazer *Charles Beaumont* • Clarence Muse *Coach Driver* ■ *Dir* Victor Halperin • *Scr* Garnett Weston

Whiteboys ★★ 15
Comedy 1999 · US · Colour and BW · 84min

Lacking the cultural empathy and social insight of *Slam*, Marc Levin's wannabe comedy is little more than a long-playing promo. Performance artist Danny Hoch headlines as the Iowa teen who's a rapper at heart and heads for Chicago with homies Dash Mihok and Trevor Webber to lay some tracks, score some blow and dig some chicks. In other words, it's a white boy's hip-hop daydream (complete with fantasy sequences featuring a bewildered Snoop Dogg). **DP** Swearing, violence.

Danny Hoch *Flip* • Dash Mihok *James* • Mark Webber *Trevor* • Piper Perabo *Sara* • Eugene Byrd *Khalid* • Bonz Malone *Darius* • Snoop Dogg *Snoop Dog* ■ *Dir* Marc Levin • *Scr* Garth Belcon, Danny Hoch, Marc Levin, Richard Stratton, from a story by Garth Belcon, Danny Hoch

Whiteout ★★ 15
Crime action thriller
2009 · US/Fr · Colour · 96min

This rather ordinary adaptation of an award-winning graphic novel has some impressive snowy vistas and isolated landscapes, but essentially it's a bog-standard stolen-cargo thriller enlivened only by some blizzard-buffeted set pieces. Investigating Antarctica's first ever homicide, US Marshal Carrie Stetko (Kate Beckinsale) is caught between the cold and a cold-blooded killer when the murder trail

leads to a buried Russian plane that crashed in 1957. Beckinsale isn't commanding enough to be credible and, with the vague slasher and blurred sci-fi plot contortions adding nothing of a suspenseful nature to the lackadaisical narrative, this muddle is more wipeout than whiteout. **AJ** Violence, swearing, nudity. DVD BL

■ *Dir* Dominic Sena • *Scr* Jon & Erich Hoeber, Chad & Carey W Hayes, from the graphic novel by Greg Rucka

Whity ★★★
Melodrama 1970 · W Ger · Colour · 95min

Shot on a spaghetti western set in Spain by Rainer Werner Fassbinder, this Deep South plantation melodrama has all the laconic intensity of Sergio Leone, the narrative rigour of classical Hollywood and the thematic resonance of Fassbinder's literary bible, Theodor Fontane's *Effi Briest*. Handsomely photographed by Michael Ballhaus and played with deliberation, the story focuses on Günther Kaufmann, a slave who acquiesces in Ron Randell's tyranny until he learns of its murderous immorality from prostitute Hanna Schygulla. **DP** German +subtitles.

Günther Kaufmann *Whity* • Hanna Schygulla *Hanna* • Ulli Lommel *Frank* • Harry Baer *Davy* • Katrin Schaake *Katherine* • Ron Randell *Mr Nicholson* • Rainer Werner Fassbinder *Guest in saloon* ■ *Dir/Scr* Rainer Werner Fassbinder

Who? ★★
Science-fiction thriller
1974 · UK/W Ger · Colour · 93min

This intriguing but not wholly successful sci-fi thriller attempts to probe somewhat seriously into the nature of identity. The narrative isn't helped by being told in flashback, and Elliott Gould is perhaps a little too laid-back in the lead. There is a stunning performance, however, from third-billed actor Joseph Bova as the scientist Martino, whose face has been restructured following an alleged car crash in Russia, and he alone makes this curious mix of sci-fi and spy drama worth watching. **TS** Some swearing, sex scenes.

Elliott Gould *Rogers* • Trevor Howard *Azarin* • Joseph Bova *Martino* • Ed Grover [Edward Grover] *Finchley* • John Lehne *Haller* • James Noble *Deptford* • Lyndon Brook *Barrister* ■ *Dir* Jack Gold • *Scr* John Gould, from the novel by Algis Budrys

Who Dares Wins ★★ 15
Action adventure 1982 · UK · Colour · 119min

Lewis Collins, managing to look stern-faced throughout, lives up to his tough-guy image in a British action movie inspired by the 1980 storming of the Iranian Embassy in London by the SAS. This is not much more than a glamorised episode of *The Professionals*, but at least it benefits from the presence of Judy Davis. **NF** Violence, swearing. DVD BL

Lewis Collins *Captain Peter Skellen* • Judy Davis *Frankie Leith* • Richard Widmark *Secretary of State Curry* • Edward Woodward *Commander Powell* • Robert Webber *General Ira Potter* • Tony Doyle *Colonel Hadley* • John Duttine *Rod* • Kenneth Griffith *Bishop Crick* ■ *Dir* Ian Sharp • *Scr* Reginald Rose

Who Done It? ★★ U
Comedy mystery 1942 · US · BW · 78min

Part of the abiding success of Abbott and Costello was that there were few – if any – surprises in their films. Familiarity lent contentment and Lou was always going to be put upon (but emerge triumphant) and Bud was always going to be surly. Their characters are equally familiar as two not-very-bright soda jerks with ambitions to write for radio. When they go to the station with an idea for a mystery series, the duo find themselves mixed up in a real case. Cue action and mild comedy. **BB**

Bud Abbott *Chick Larkin* • Lou Costello *Mervyn Milgrim* • Patric Knowles *Jimmy Turner* • Louise Allbritton *Jane Little* • Thomas Gomez *Col JR Andrews* • Mary Wickes *Juliet Collins* ■ *Dir* Erle C Kenton • *Scr* Stanley Roberts, Edmund Joseph, John Grant, from a story by Stanley Roberts

Who Done It? ★★ U
Comedy 1956 · UK · BW · 78min

Considering he was then one of Britain's most important directors, Basil Dearden might have seemed a peculiar choice for TV comic Benny Hill's sole starring venture. But Dearden adeptly judges the slapstick content of this amiable caper, in which Hill's hapless gumshoe bungles along in pursuit of eastern bloc spies David Kossoff and George Margo. Belinda Lee shows to advantage as Benny's sidekick, but this was all a bit of a come down for TEB Clarke, who had penned some of Ealing's best-known comedies. **DP**

Benny Hill *Hugo Dill* • Belinda Lee *Frankie Mayne* • David Kossoff *Zacco* • Garry Marsh *Inspector Hancock* • George Margo *Barakov* • Ernest Thesiger *Sir Walter Finch* • Denis Shaw *Otto Stumpf* • Irene Handl *Customer* • Charles Hawtrey *Disc jockey* ■ *Dir* Basil Dearden • *Scr* TEB Clarke

Who Framed Roger Rabbit ★★★★★ PG
Part-animated detective comedy
1988 · US · Colour · 99min

This whizz-bang breakthrough in mixing live action with cartoon characters won a special achievement Oscar for animator Richard Williams. It follows the adventures of private eye Bob Hoskins, who ventures into Toontown – where the cartoon personalities live – to help animated superstar Roger Rabbit, who suspects his wife of adultery. Guest appearances by a wealth of cartoon favourites adorn the tale as Hoskins's investigation leads to villain Christopher Lloyd, who's planning to cleanse Toontown of its animated inhabitants. Highlights include Hoskins's encounter with Roger's seductive wife Jessica (voiced by Kathleen Turner) and the fantastic opening sequence. **TH** DVD BL

Bob Hoskins *Eddie Valiant* • Christopher Lloyd *Judge Doom* • Joanna Cassidy *Dolores* • Charles Fleischer *Roger Rabbit/Benny the Cab/Greasy/Psycho* • Kathleen Turner *Jessica* • Amy Irving *Jessica (singing voice)* • Stubby Kaye *Marvin Acme* • Alan Tilvern *RK Maroon* • Mel Blanc *Daffy Duck/Tweety Pie/Bugs Bunny/Sylvester/Porky Pig* ■ *Dir* Robert Zemeckis • *Scr* Jeffrey Price, Peter S Seaman, from the novel *Who Censored Roger Rabbit?* by Gary K Wolf • *Cinematographer* Dean Cundey

Who Has Seen the Wind ★★
Drama 1977 · Can · Colour · 100min

This fictional tale, based on a much loved Canadian novel about two children growing up in Depression-hit Saskatchewan, is concerned with the psychology of juveniles but lacks the punch of director Allan King's earlier *Warrendale* (1967). However, there's a strong supporting cast, including Gordon Pinsent and José Ferrer, who gives a great performance as a silver-tongued bootlegger. Ultimately, though, it's rather dreary. **TH**

Brian Painchaud *Brian* • Douglas Junor *Young Ben* • Gordon Pinsent *Gerald O'Connal* • Chapelle Jaffe *Maggie* • José Ferrer *The Ben* ■ *Dir* Allan King • *Scr* Patricia Watson, from a novel by WO Mitchell

Who Is Dayani Cristal? ★★★★ 12A
Documentary 2013 · UK/Mex · Colour · 84min

After a body is discovered in the Arizona desert, a forensics team immediately goes to work to find out who the dead man was and how he got there. But this isn't a traditional whodunnit, it's a socially conscious documentary asking profound questions about the plight of migrants trying to cross into the United States. Director Marc Silver follows Gael García Bernal in re-creating the journey of the man with the name "Dayani Cristal" tattooed on his chest, elevating him from victim to hero en route. It's a story with a number of twists, which leads to a powerful conclusion, but the fact that is so commonplace makes it all the more shocking. **SP** Spanish, English +subtitles.

Gael García Bernal *Bernal, Gael García* ■ *Dir* Marc Silver (2)

Who Is Harry Kellerman, and Why Is He Saying Those Terrible Things about Me? ★
Comedy drama 1971 · US · Colour · 107min

This is one of those weird, vaguely experimental, sub-culture self-indulgences that got made into movies in the 1960s and early 1970s. Dustin Hoffman plays a pop musician driven to despair by anonymous phone calls and by sessions with his shrink, Jack Warden. Woody Allen turned this sort of material into satirical gold but here it's just a dollop of American psychobabble about life, art, ageing and all that stuff. **AT**

Dustin Hoffman *Georgie Soloway* • Jack Warden *Dr Moses* • Barbara Harris *Allison* • David Burns *Leon Soloway* • Gabriel Dell *Sid* • Betty Walker *Margot Soloway* • Dom DeLuise *Irwin* ■ *Dir* Ulu Grosbard • *Scr* Herb Gardner, from his short story

Who Is Killing the Great Chefs of Europe? ★★
Murder mystery comedy
1978 · US/W Ger · Colour · 112min

When food connoisseur Robert Morley publishes his list of the world's greatest chefs, he inadvertently sets in motion a stream of jealousy, anger and eventually murder. George Segal, ex-husband of Jacqueline Bisset, who's on the list, finds himself in the midst of the murder spree. It's a promising premise with a soupçon of good jokes, a sprinkle of bad puns and more than a dash of bad taste. But the recipe just doesn't gel and this good looking dish could have been much tastier. **DF**

George Segal *Robby Ross* • Jacqueline Bisset *Natasha O'Brien* • Robert Morley *Max Vandervere* • Jean-Pierre Cassel *Louis Kohner* • Philippe Noiret *Jean-Claude Moulineau* ■ *Dir* Ted Kotcheff • *Scr* Peter Stone, from the novel *Someone Is Killing the Great Chefs of Europe* by Nan Lyons, Ivan Lyons

Who Killed Nancy? The True Story... ★★
Documentary 2009 · UK · Colour · 93min

More than 30 years after punk groupie Nancy Spungen was killed in New York's Chelsea Hotel (allegedly by her Sex Pistols' boyfriend Sid Vicious), his biographer Alan G Parker delves into the iconic couple's drug-addled history to explore one of rock's greatest mysteries. Unfortunately, while this routine documentary extensively dissects Sid and Nancy's romance, it barely tackles its central question until the throwaway final reel. Instead of tenacious investigation and hard facts, this cheap-looking exposé relies on time-tainted, personal remembrances. These will undoubtedly fascinate fans, but they lack the visual dynamism to hook casual viewers. **SF**

■ *Dir* Alan G Parker

Who Killed the Electric Car? ★★★ U
Documentary 2006 · US · Colour · 88min

During the 1990s, automobile giant General Motors launched its first electric vehicle; cheaper and more environmentally friendly than petrol-powered cars, it also drove well. Why, then, has it been sent to the scrapyard? Although the single-issue focus prevents director Chris Paine from asking wider questions about America's addiction to gasoline, this documentary whodunnit is never less than intriguing. Hearing testimony from scientists, industrialists, enthusiasts and several celebrities (including Mel Gibson), Paine delivers his verdict with brisk efficiency and the extent of corporate doublethink that Paine uncovers in US boardrooms is deeply unsettling. **JR** DVD

Martin Sheen *Narrator* • Ed Begley Jr • Mel Gibson • Phyllis Diller ■ *Dir/Scr* Chris Paine • *Cinematographer* Thaddeus Wadleigh

U SUITABLE FOR ALL   Uc SUITABLE ESPECIALLY FOR YOUNG CHILDREN (DVD ONLY)   PG PARENTAL GUIDANCE   12A UNDER 12s TO BE ACCOMPANIED (CINEMA ONLY)

W

Who Says I Can't Ride a Rainbow? ★★★
Adventure   1971 · US · Colour · 85min

This is an offbeat children's adventure about a battle to preserve an urban zoo. It stars likeable Jack Klugman as a man who believes that children hold the key to the world's future. This movie also marked Morgan Freeman's debut. **TS**

Jack Klugman *Barney Marcovitz* • Norma French *Mary Lee* • Ruben Figueroa [Reuben Figueroa] *Angel* • David Mann *David* • Kevin Riou *Kevin* • Morgan Freeman *Afro* ■ *Dir* Edward Mann • *Scr* Edward Mann, Daniel Hauer

Who Shot Patakango? ★★
Drama   1989 · US · Colour · 104min

More serious, and thus more insightful, than the usual high-school romp, this peek at events at a Brooklyn school was a labour of love for director Robert Brooks. He not only scripted and edited the film along with his wife Halle (who produced), he even worked the camera. As the director homes in on a group of final-year pupils, he proves more skilled at documentary-style detail than at building sustained drama. Even though the film is knocked off course on more than one occasion, it does possess a convincing sense of time and place. **JM** Swearing, violence.

David Knight *Bic Bickham* • Sandra Bullock *Devlin Moran* • Kevin Otto *Mark Bickham* • Aaron Ingram *Cougar* • Brad Randall *Patakango* ■ *Dir* Robert Brooks • *Scr* Robert Brooks, Halle Brooks

Who Slew Auntie Roo? ★★ 15
Satirical horror   1971 · US/UK · Colour · 87min

This is an oddball update of the Hansel and Gretel fairy tale, with a frenetic Shelley Winters menacing two orphan children (Mark Lester and Chloe Franks). What begins as a well-intentioned fantasy becomes a crass nightmare of *Grand Guignol*, maybe because it's co-written by Jimmy Sangster, maestro of so many Hammer horrors. **TH**

Shelley Winters *Rosie Forrest* • Mark Lester (2) *Christopher* • Ralph Richardson *Mr Benton* • Lionel Jeffries *Inspector Willoughby* • Judy Cornwell *Clarine* • Michael Gothard *Albie* • Hugh Griffith *The Pigman/mr Harrison* • Chloe Franks *Katy* • Rosalie Crutchley *Miss Henley* ■ *Dir* Curtis Harrington • *Scr* Robert Blees, James [Jimmy] Sangster, Gavin Lambert, from a story by David Osborn

Who Was That Lady? ★★ U
Comedy   1960 · US · BW · 115min

This is a strained romantic comedy that has already outstayed its welcome before it turns into a Cold War farce. Caught in flagrante with one of his students, professor Tony Curtis persuades his TV writer buddy, Dean Martin, to concoct an excuse to assuage his jealous wife, Janet Leigh (then Mrs Curtis off screen, too). However, their story about the FBI and a nest of Russian spies is closer to the truth than they suspect. It's polished enough, but there's more to screwball than just pace. **DP**

Tony Curtis *David Wilson* • Dean Martin *Michael Haney* • Janet Leigh *Ann Wilson* • James Whitmore *Harry Powell* • John McIntire *Bob Doyle* • Barbara Nichols *Gloria Coogle* • Larry Keating *Parker* • Larry Storch *Orenov* ■ *Dir* George Sidney (2) • *Scr* Norman Krasna, from his play *Who Was That Lady I Saw You With?* • *Music* André Previn

Who Will Love My Children? ★★ PG
Drama based on a true story
1983 · US · Colour · 90min

A Golden Globe-winning Ann-Margret is diagnosed with terminal cancer in 1950s Iowa, and embarks on an agonising mission – to find good homes for her ten children before she dies. But what should be a relentless hard-hitter is instead too sanitised for modern tastes, with director John Erman (who bagged an Emmy) never finding the drama in the superficially scripted events. It's actually Frederic

Forrest as the troubled husband who comes closest to showing the gut-wrenching trauma of the situation. **SF**

Ann-Margret *Lucy Fray* • Frederic Forrest *Ivan Fray* • Cathryn Damon *Hazel Anderson* • Donald Moffat *Dick Thomas* ■ *Dir* John Erman • *Scr* Michael Bortman

The Whole Nine Yards ★★ 15
Black comedy   2000 · US · Colour · 94min

Friends star Matthew Perry makes another stab at big-screen stardom in this limp black comedy from British director Jonathan Lynn. Perry is the humble, hen-pecked dentist, none too chuffed to discover that Mafia iceman Bruce Willis has just bought a house in his dull Montreal neighbourhood. The farce is too forced, the humour too broad and the end result a far cry from such superior hitman comedies as *Prizzi's Honor* and *Grosse Pointe Blank*. **NS** Violence, sex scenes, swearing, nudity. *DVD*

Bruce Willis *Jimmy "The Tulip" Tudeski* • Matthew Perry *"Oz" Oseransky* • Rosanna Arquette *Sophie* • Michael Clarke Duncan *Frankie Figs* • Natasha Henstridge *Cynthia* ■ *Dir* Jonathan Lynn • *Scr* Mitchell Kapner

The Whole Ten Yards ★★ 12
Crime comedy   2004 · US · Colour · 94min

This sequel to *The Whole Nine Yards* reunites Matthew Perry and Bruce Willis, reprising their roles of nervy dentist and retired Mafia hitman respectively. Willis comes to the rescue when Perry's wife Natasha Henstridge is kidnapped by a Hungarian mob led by Kevin Pollak. Bruce Willis's usually reliable comic timing is nowhere to be seen and the actresses seem bored by the contrivances haphazardly put together by director Howard Deutch. The only real winner is Perry. **TH** *DVD*

Bruce Willis *Jimmy "The Tulip" Tudeski* • Matthew Perry *"Oz" Oseransky* • Amanda Peet *Jill* • Kevin Pollak *Laszlo* • Natasha Henstridge *Cynthia* • Frank Collison *Strabo* • Johnny Messner *Zevo* • Silas Weir Mitchell *Yermo* • Tallulah Belle Willis *Buttercup Scout* ■ *Dir* Howard Deutch • *Scr* George Gallo, from a story by Mitchell Kapner, from characters by Mitchell Kapner

The Whole Town's Talking ★★★★
Crime comedy   1935 · US · BW · 92min

There's a double helping of Edward G Robinson in this crime comedy as he plays the dual role of a gangster and a meek little clerk. The clerk is the spitting image of a notorious hoodlum and is mistakenly arrested. He's eventually released and issued with an identity card, so police won't confuse the two again – that is, until the gangster turns up and demands a loan of the card. This is a rare pure comedy effort from John Ford, but with a script co-written by Frank Capra favourite Robert Riskin, there's also a certain Capra-esque element to this comedy of mistaken identity. **RB**

Edward G Robinson *Arthur Ferguson Jones/ "Killer" Manion* • Jean Arthur *Wilhelmina "Bill" Clark* • Arthur Hohl *Det Sgt Mike Boyle* • Wallace Ford *Healy* • Arthur Byron *Spencer* • Donald Meek *Hoyt* ■ *Dir* John Ford • *Scr* Jo Swerling, Robert Riskin, from the story *Jail Breaker* by WR Burnett

The Whole Truth ★★★
Thriller   1958 · UK · BW · 84min

Former A-list stars who had had their day in Hollywood looked to Britain for an honest bob. Thus, Stewart Granger plays a movie producer whose affair with an Italian starlet leads to him covering up her imagined murder and then being arrested when she's found dead for real. George Sanders makes a suitably creepy villain and Donna Reed appears as Granger's wife. The over-the-top performances and overwrought direction ensure it's never boring. **AT**

Stewart Granger *Max Poulton* • Donna Reed *Carol Paulton* • George Sanders *Carliss* • Gianna Maria Canale *Gina Bertini* • Michael Shillo

Inspector Simon • Peter Dyneley *Willy Reichel* ■ *Dir* John Guillermin • *Scr* Jonathan Latimer, from the stage and TV play by Philip Mackie

The Whole Truth 15
Thriller   2016 · US · Colour · 93min

This is a preview – no prints were available to review as we went to press: Keanu Reeves stars here as an attorney working to defend a teenage boy (Gabriel Basso, *Super 8*) accused of killing his wealthy father. In shades of Julia Roberts in *The Pelican Brief*, British actress Gugu Mbatha-Raw (*Belle*) co-stars in the slightly patronising role of a young lawyer determined to seek out the truth. It's not John Grisham, but Nicholas (son of Elia) Kazan wrote the script, so if pedigree is anything to go by it promises much. **TP**

Keanu Reeves *Richard Ramsey* • Gugu Mbatha-Raw *Janelle* • Gabriel Basso *Mike Lassiter* • James Belushi *Boone Lassiter* • Renée Zellweger ■ *Dir* Courtney Hunt • *Scr* Nicholas Kazan

The Whole Wide World ★★★
Biographical romantic drama
1996 · US · Colour · 111min

In 1933, Novalyne Price (Renee Zellweger) began a stormy relationship with Robert E Howard (Vincent D'Onofrio), a morose author prone to sudden psychotic acts, who became a pulp fantasy icon as creator of *Conan the Barbarian*. This engrossing biopic reveals a tender portrait of the man she loved, who could never reciprocate her feelings, as well as a telling insight into his imaginative writing philosophy. Director Dan Ireland's poignant character study is greatly enhanced by the two wonderful central performances and is an affecting appreciation of the man and the myth that overtook him after he died of a self-inflicted gunshot wound. **AJ**

Vincent D'Onofrio *Robert E Howard* • Renee Zellweger [Renée Zellweger] *Novalyne Price* • Ann Wedgeworth *Mrs Howard* • Harve Presnell *Dr Howard* • Benjamin Mouton *Clyde Smith* • Helen Cates *Enid* ■ *Dir* Dan Ireland • *Scr* Michael Scott Myers, from the novel *One Who Walked Alone* by Novalyne Price Ellis

Who'll Stop the Rain? ★★★★★ 18
Crime drama   1978 · US · Colour · 120min

Nick Nolte stars as a disillusioned Vietnam veteran who is roped into a drug deal organised by traumatised former Vietnam journalist Michael Moriarty. Directed by Karel Reisz, it's a powerful study of alienation, a story about outsiders and a country that has turned its back on heroism and patriotism. It's bleak but gripping, with terrific performances from Nolte, Moriarty and Tuesday Weld as the latter's drug-addict wife. The film was a flop on release, but its reputation is growing all the time. **AT** Swearing, drug abuse. *DVD*

Nick Nolte *Ray Hicks* • Tuesday Weld *Marge Converse* • Michael Moriarty *John Converse* • Anthony Zerbe *Antheil* • Richard Masur *Danskin* • Ray Sharkey *Smitty* • Gail Strickland *Charmian* • Charles Haid *Eddie Peace* ■ *Dir* Karel Reisz • *Scr* Judith Rascoe, Robert Stone, from Stone's novel *Dog Soldiers*

Whom the Gods Love ★★ U
Biographical drama   1936 · UK · BW · 79min

This Mozart biopic is filled with unintentionally hilarious dialogue, but director Basil Dean seemed too busy showcasing new wife Victoria Hopper to care. He also appears indifferent to the fact that the debuting Stephen Haggard is wholly out of his depth as Wolfgang, whose relationship with Constance is under threat from the machinations of Prince Lobkowitz (John Loder) and the need to finish the score for *The Marriage of Figaro* in time for its premiere. The music conducted by Sir Thomas Beecham is, of course, sublime, while Russian production designer Andrej Andrejew and Czechoslovak cinematographer Jan Stallich make fine use of the locations in Salzburg and Vienna. But, for all its laudable ambition, this superficial spectacle can't hold a candle to

Milos Forman's multiple Oscar winner, *Amadeus*. DP *DVD*

Stephen Haggard *Wolfgang Amadeus Mozart* • Victoria Hopper *Constance Mozart* • John Loder *Prince Lobkowitz* • Liane Haid *Aloysia* • Jean Cadell *Frau Mozart* ■ *Dir* Basil Dean • *Scr* Margaret Kennedy, Gordon Wellesley

Whoopee! ★★★
Musical comedy   1930 · US · Colour · 94min

It may look awfully stagebound now, but this inane early Eddie Cantor vehicle was a huge hit in its day, and was cinematically important for being one of the first movies in Technicolor, albeit only two-strip. The theme of a hypochondriac at large – reused in several later films, including the remake of this one, Danny Kaye's *Up in Arms* – is enhanced here by the sumptuous early Busby Berkeley-choreographed production numbers. Watch very closely; the lead chorus girl is a young Betty Grable. **TS**

Eddie Cantor *Henry Williams* • Eleanor Hunt *Sally Morgan* • Paul Gregory (1) *Wanenis* • John Rutherford *Sheriff Bob Wells* • Ethel Shutta *Mary Custer* • Spencer Charters *Jerome Underwood* ■ *Dir* Thornton Freeland • *Scr* William Conselman, from the musical by William Anthony McGuire, Walter Donaldson, Gus Kahn, from the play *The Nervous Wreck* by Owen Davis, from the story *The Wreck* by EJ Rath

Whoops Apocalypse ★★ 15
Comedy   1986 · UK · Colour · 87min

The four-year gap between the often hilarious TV original and this inconsistent feature seems to have sapped the inspiration from writers Andrew Marshall and David Renwick. The need to introduce a degree of narrative logic precludes much of the wackiness that made the series so biting and fresh. Even though it dissects sombre subjects like the Cold War and a Falklands-style invasion, the satire has mostly been toned down, with only the swipes at the Royals, Peter Cook's performance as a doltish prime minister and a wonderful clown funeral hitting the mark. DP Swearing, nudity. *DVD*

Loretta Swit *Barbara Adams* • Peter Cook *Sir Mortimer Chris* • Michael Richards *Lacrobat* • Rik Mayall *Specialist Catering Commander* • Ian Richardson *Rear Admiral Bendish* • Alexei Sayle • Herbert Lom *General Mosquera* ■ *Dir* Tom Bussmann • *Scr* Andrew Marshall, David Renwick

Whore ★ 18
Drama   1991 · US · Colour · 81min

Largely talking directly to camera, Theresa Russell is an inner-city prostitute who tells of and acts out the humiliations of her job and the viciousness of her pimp, Benjamin Mouton. The movie offensively wallows in misogyny, exuding an excited air whenever Russell suffers abuse and giving the swaggering Mouton powerful centre stage, which at times borders on admiration. Ken Russell directs it all with a staggeringly inappropriate and jokey approach. **SH** Violence, swearing, nudity. *DVD*

Theresa Russell *Liz* • Benjamin Mouton *Blake* • Antonio Fargas *Rasta* • Sanjay Indian • Elizabeth Morehead *Katie* • Michael Crabtree *Man in car* • John Diehl *Derelict* ■ *Dir* Ken Russell • *Scr* Ken Russell, Deborah Dalton, from the play *Bondage* by David Hines

Who's Afraid of Virginia Woolf? ★★★★ 12
Drama   1966 · US · BW · 125min

Should your front room be in need of redecoration, then Elizabeth Taylor's performance here is guaranteed to strip the paint off the walls with just one verbal volley. In tandem with her screen husband (played by then real-life husband Richard Burton), she spits malicious barbs across their abode, often hitting their dinner guests en route. The ebb and flow of the full-blown arguments are acutely judged by director Mike Nichols, who typically laces his film with juicy psychological and social pointers. The winner of five Oscars, this was regarded as punishingly honest in its day, though it seems a tad more muted now. **JM** Swearing. *DVD*

Elizabeth Taylor *Martha* • Richard Burton *George* • George Segal *Nick* • Sandy Dennis *Honey* ■ *Dir* Mike Nichols • *Scr* Ernest Lehman, from the play by Edward Albee • *Costume Designer* Irene Sharaff • *Cinematographer* Haskell Wexler

Who's Been Sleeping in My Bed? ★★

Comedy　　　　1963 · US · Colour · 103min

Dean Martin plays a TV matinée idol who is a smoothie male sex symbol, but not slick enough to avoid amorous shenanigans with the wives of various friends. It's up to girlfriend Elizabeth Montgomery to persuade him to abandon his loose living and settle down with her. A nudge-nudge, wink-wink bedroom farce, superficially glossy, but largely boring except for a handful of laughs and Carol Burnett in the supporting cast. RK

Dean Martin *Jason Steel* • Elizabeth Montgomery *Melissa Morris* • Martin Balsam *Sanford Kaufman* • Jill St John *Toby Tobler* • Richard Conte *Leonard Ashley* • Macha Méril *Jacqueline Edwards* • Louis Nye *Harry Tobler* ■ *Dir* Daniel Mann • *Scr* Jack Rose

Who's Got the Action? ★★

Comedy　　　　1962 · US · Colour · 94min

Dean Martin and Lana Turner are a married couple in a comedy whose humour resides in a lot of stock but quite amusing clichés about bookies and gamblers. Martin is a lawyer who bets compulsively on the horses, to the increasing detriment of his bank balance and the despair of his wife. She finally takes matters into her own hands, colludes with a bookie in handling his bets and turns him into a winner. The supporting cast offers a stand-out performance from Walter Matthau as a Mr Big. RK

Dean Martin *Steve Flood* • Lana Turner *Melanie Flood* • Eddie Albert *Clint Morgan* • Nita Talbot *Saturday Knight* • Walter Matthau *Tony Gagoots* • Paul Ford *Judge Boatwright* • Margo Roza ■ *Dir* Daniel Mann • *Scr* Jack Rose, from the novel *Four Horse-Players Are Missing* by Alexander Rose

Who's Harry Crumb? ★ PG

Comedy　　　　1989 · US · Colour · 86min

The question on most people's lips before this lacklustre comedy is over will be, "Who cares?" The late John Candy was quite funny when he allowed a director to control his unrestrained manic mugging. Unfortunately, here Paul Flaherty just lets him get away with farcical murder as a bungling private detective assigned to solve a kidnapping case. Heavy going with very little wit and a great deal of slapstick. AJ *DVD*

John Candy *Harry Crumb* • Jeffrey Jones *Eliot Draisen* • Annie Potts *Helen Downing* • Tim Thomerson *Vince Barnes* • Barry Corbin *PJ Downing* • Shawnee Smith *Nikki Downing* ■ *Dir* Paul Flaherty • *Scr* Robert Conte, Peter Martin Wortmann

Who's Minding the Mint?

★★★ U

Comedy　　　　1967 · US · Colour · 96min

This comedy has a superb cast and a truly daft premise, in which a group of crooks help US mint employee Jim Hutton replace money he has accidentally disposed of, with wonderfully funny results. This is an overlooked gem, shrewdly directed by Sid Caesar associate Howard Morris with a baleful eye for the absurd. The cast is uniformly excellent, but special praise should go to the pompously demented Victor Buono. Sadly, the production values are only average. TS

Jim Hutton *Harry Lucas* • Dorothy Provine *Verna Baxter* • Milton Berle *Luther Burton* • Walter Brennan *Pop Gillis* • Joey Bishop *Ralph Randazzo* • Bob Denver *Willie Owens* • Victor Buono *Captain* • Jamie Farr *Mario* ■ *Dir* Howard Morris • *Scr* RS Allen, Harry Bullock

Who's Minding the Store?

★★★ U

Comedy　　　　1963 · US · Colour · 89min

Jerry Lewis relaxes under the direction of one of Hollywood's cleverest and wittiest craftsmen, former cartoonist Frank Tashlin, whose Lewis movies resembled a series of manic sketches strung together, and this is one of the funniest. It's wildly inventive, and peppered with a gallery of fabulously eccentric character actors, used in the most simple of ideas: Lewis let loose in a department store. The 1960s Technicolor and prop designs are super. TS

Jerry Lewis *Raymond Phiffier* • Jill St John *Barbara Tuttle* • Agnes Moorehead *Phoebe Tuttle* • John McGiver *Mr Tuttle* • Ray Walston *Mr Quimby* • Francesca Bellini *Shirley* ■ *Dir* Frank Tashlin • *Scr* Frank Tashlin, Harry Tugend, from a story by Harry Tugend

Who's That Girl ★★ PG

Screwball comedy　　1987 · US · Colour · 89min

With Griffin Dunne hot off the back of his triumph in Martin Scorsese's *After Hours* and Madonna in dire need of a hit after the *Shanghai Surprise* fiasco, you would have thought the two stars would have plumped for something more substantial than this woeful attempt at screwball comedy. Slouching and mistiming wisecracks with the nonchalance of a rock star convinced her presence is a favour to the producer, Madonna is a shadow of the sassy star of *Desperately Seeking Susan*. DP *DVD*

Madonna *Nikki Finn* • Griffin Dunne *Loudon Trott* • Haviland Morris *Wendy Worthington* • John McMartin *Simon Worthington* • Bibi Besch *Mrs Worthington* • John Mills *Montgomery Bell* ■ *Dir* James Foley • *Scr* Andrew Smith, Ken Finkleman, from a story by Andrew Smith

Who's That Knocking at My Door

★★★ 15

Drama　　　　1968 · US · BW · 86min

This is the first film not just for director Martin Scorsese, but also actor Harvey Keitel (if you overlook his uncredited appearance in *Reflections in a Golden Eye* the previous year). Displaying early indications of all Scorsese's trademark concerns, this autobiographical film is crude but compelling, with Keitel as a strict but streetwise Catholic taking a guilt trip through his relationship with free-thinking Zina Bethune. It's essential viewing as an early example of two masters learning their respective crafts. DA *DVD*

Harvey Keitel *JR* • Zina Bethune *The girl* • Lennard Kuras *Joey* • Ann Colette *Girl in dream* • Michael Scala *Sally* • Wendy Russell *Sally's girl friend* • Philip Carlson *Mountain guide* • Robert Uricola *Gunman at stag party* ■ *Dir/Scr* Martin Scorsese

Who's the Man? ★★ 15

Comedy　　　　1993 · US · Colour · 85min

Ted Demme (nephew of famed director Jonathan Demme) brings his *Yo! MTV Raps* stars Ed Lover and Dr Dre to the big screen for this undistinguished hip-hop effort. The makers clearly wanted to say something pertinent about exploitative inner-city landlords, but a farce built around a couple of nitwit barbers who accidentally become cops is hardly the best way to go about it. The leads are amiable enough and the presence of Denis Leary and cameos by several rappers is most welcome, but they don't atone for the shortage of gags and the clumsiness of Demme's approach. DP Violence, swearing.

Dr Dre • Ed Lover • Jim Moody *Nick Crawford* • Badja Djola *Lionel Douglas* • Denis Leary *Sergeant Cooper* • Richard Bright *Demetrius* • Ice-T *Nighttrain/Chauncey* ■ *Dir* Ted Demme • *Scr* Seth Greenland, from a story by Seth Greenland, Dr Dre, Ed Lover

Whose Life Is It Anyway?

★★★ 15

Drama　　　　1981 · US · Colour · 118min

Brian Clark's award-winning play is well transposed to the screen by director John Badham and stars Richard Dreyfuss as the artist who is rendered immobile from the neck down after a terrible car accident. The crux of the narrative is his persistent demand to the hospital chief of staff (John Cassavetes) to be allowed the right to die. Meanwhile he's cared for and develops relationships with doctor Christine Lahti and nurse Kaki Hunter. Amazingly funny given the circumstances, this is both touching and relevant. LH

Richard Dreyfuss *Ken Harrison* • John Cassavetes *Dr Michael Emerson* • Christine Lahti *Dr Clare Scott* • Bob Balaban *Carter Hill* • Kenneth McMillan *Judge of staff* • Kaki Hunter *Mary Jo Sadler* • Thomas Carter *Orderly John* ■ *Dir* John Badham • *Scr* Brian Clark, Reginald Rose, from the play by Brian Clark

Why Change Your Wife? ★★★

Silent comedy　　1920 · US · BW · 100min

The name of director Cecil B DeMille has become synonymous with the historical and Biblical epic. However, this mighty Hollywood pioneer and starmaker was responsible for dozens of sparkling and successful bedroom farces during his long and influential association with Paramount, of which this is just one. The soufflé plot, concerning the complications of extramarital flirtations, serves as an excuse the delightful cast going through their risqué paces, cleverly manipulated by DeMille. RK

Thomas Meighan *Robert Gordon* • Gloria Swanson *Beth Gordon* • Bebe Daniels *Sally Clark* • Theodore Kosloff *Radinoff* • Clarence Geldart *The doctor* • Sylvia Ashton *Aunt Kate* ■ *Dir* Cecil B DeMille • *Scr* Olga Printzlau, Sada Cowan, from a story by William C de Mille

Why Do Fools Fall in Love? ★★★ 15

Biographical musical drama
1998 · US · Colour · 111min

This is a fun, if not exactly deeply probing, look at the short life of 1950s teenage singer Frankie Lymon (Larenz Tate) who left three wives (he never got around to divorcing any of them) behind when he died in 1968 at the age of 25. Because there are so many conflicting opinions about what Frankie was actually like, Tate isn't given a great deal to work with, but the wives are better drawn and well played by a cast of talented actresses. Ben Vereen and Little Richard add some history to the snappily directed proceedings. JB Swearing, violence.

Ben Vereen *Richard Barrett* • Larenz Tate *Frankie Lymon* • Halle Berry *Zola Taylor* • Lela Rochon *Emira Eagle* • Vivica A Fox *Elizabeth Waters* • Little Richard • Miguel A Nunez Jr *Young Little Richard* • Paul Mazursky *Morris Levy* ■ *Dir* Gregory Nava • *Scr* Tina Andrews

Why Does Herr R Run Amok? ★★★

Drama　　　　1970 · W Ger · Colour · 88min

This film is brutal in its story and in its unwillingness to come to conclusions, since the murderous Herr R of the title is not presented as a villain but as a victim of emotional exploitation, unhappy in his family and work. Director Rainer Werner Fassbinder takes no sides, but presents his central character, played by Kurt Raab, in his comfortable home, enjoying the fruits of a decent job. Why then does all this lead to shocking violence? This is a sombre work of undeniable power and pessimism. BB German +subtitles.

Kurt Raab *Kurt Raab, "Herr R"* • Lilith Ungerer *Frau Raab* • Amadeus Fengler *Amadeus, their son* • Franz Maron *Boss* • Hanna Schygulla *Schoolfriend* • Peter Raben *Schoolfriend* ■ *Dir/Scr* Rainer Werner Fassbinder, Michael Fengler

Why Has Bhodi-Dharma Left for the East? ★★★

Drama　　　　1989 · S Kor · Colour · 137min

South Korean painter Bae Yong-Kyun devoted several years of his life to making this debut feature. His genius for a telling image is readily apparent, notably in a stunning silhouetted sequence framed against some gnarled trees and a glorious sunset. But the pacing of his story is also impeccable, reflecting the contrast between life in the town and the mountain hermitage in which a Zen master imparts his wisdom to a wavering acolyte and a mischievous orphan. Intellectually and artistically rewarding. DP Korean +subtitles.

Yi Pan-Yong *Hyegok* • Sin Won-Sop *Kibong* • Huang Hae-Jin *Haejin* ■ *Dir/Scr* Bae Yong-Kyun

Why Him?

Comedy　　　　2016 · US · Colour

This is a preview – no prints were available to review as we went to press: Bryan Cranston earned plaudits for his role in TV comedy *Malcolm in the Middle*, and here gets to show his funny side in a seasonal spin on the *Meet the Parents* formula. He plays the proud dad who's invited to meet his daughter's boyfriend, a megabucks-rich tech entrepreneur played by James Franco. But despite all Franco's success, Cranston decides this oddball is not good enough for his girl, prompting an awkward holiday for one and all. JH

Bryan Cranston *Ned Fleming* • James Franco *Laird Mayhew* • Zoey Deutch *Stephanie Fleming* • Megan Mullally *Barb Fleming* ■ *Dir* John Hamburg • *Scr* John Hamburg, Ian Helfer

Why Me? ★ 15

Comedy　　　　1990 · US · Colour · 84min

Christopher Lambert has little flair for comedy, but that didn't stop him from being cast in this excruciatingly unfunny caper movie. Lambert's jewel thief character unknowingly steals a very valuable ruby belonging to the Turkish government, and soon finds himself pursued by not only them, but also the police, the CIA and Armenian terrorists. Not even Christopher Lloyd can generate a single laugh. KB

Christopher Lambert *Gus Cardinale* • Christopher Lloyd *Bruno* • Kim Greist *June Cardinale* • JT Walsh *Inspector Mahoney* • Michael J Pollard *Ralph* • Tony Plana *Benjy* • John Hancock *Tiny* ■ *Dir* Gene Quintano • *Scr* Donald E Westlake, Leonard Mass Jr [Leonard Mass], from the novel by Donald E Westlake

Why Shoot the Teacher

★★★ PG

Period drama　　1976 · Can · Colour · 95min

Canadian director Silvio Narizzano came to fame with *Georgy Girl*, but this altogether more attractive work found him back on home ground with an adaptation of a novel set in the mid-1930s. Bud Cort plays a young teacher whose only offer of a job is in the depressed prairie lands of Saskatchewan. He moves there but proves unpopular because of his youth and eastern manners. Not particularly original, but the central story is nicely set against a picturesque background. BB

Bud Cort *Max Brown* • Samantha Eggar *Alice Field* • Chris Wiggins *Lyle Bishop* • Gary Reineke *Harris Montgomery* • John Friesen *Dave McDougall* • Michael J Reynolds *Bert Field* ■ *Dir* Silvio Narizzano • *Scr* James DeFelice, from the novel by Max Braithwaite

Wichita ★★★ U

Western　　　　1955 · US · Colour · 81min

This is an excellent, intelligent and moving study of US marshal Wyatt Earp. As Earp, Joel McCrea is superbly cast, his rugged middle-aged features creating instant empathy for the troubled lawman. Jacques Tourneur's direction is exemplary, as ever, and if certain incidents seem to presage later westerns such as Sam Peckinpah's *The Wild Bunch*, perhaps that's because Peckinpah himself worked on this movie as dialogue director. TS

Joel McCrea *Wyatt Earp* • Vera Miles *Laurie* • Lloyd Bridges *Gyp* • Wallace Ford *Whiteside* • Edgar Buchanan *Doc Black* • Peter Graves (2) *Morgan Earp* • Keith Larsen *Bat Masterson* • Carl Benton Reid *Mayor* • John Smith *Jim Earp* ■ *Dir* Jacques Tourneur • *Scr* Daniel Ullman [Daniel B Ullman]

Wicked ★★ 15
Black comedy thriller 1998 · US · Colour · 85min

Julia Stiles plays a mature teenager who tries to take the place of her murdered mother in this mediocre thriller. Director Michael Steinberg employs some expressive camerawork to try to pep things up, but fails to make the telegraphed twists feel anything more than second-hand, particularly in the climactic stages. However, Stiles still brings a reasonable air of menace to her role of shrewd manipulator. JC *DVD*

Julia Stiles *Ellie Christianson* · Chelsea Field *Karen Christianson* · Patrick Muldoon *Lawson Smith* · Vanessa Zima *Inger Christianson* · William R Moses *Ben Christianson* · Michael Parks *Detective Boland* ■ *Dir* Michael Steinberg · *Scr* Eric A Weiss

The Wicked Lady ★★★★ PG
Period drama 1945 · UK · BW · 99min

This period drama struck a resounding chord with the public and gave British cinema one of its most striking images: that of highway robber Margaret Lockwood's beauty-spotted bosom heaving as she sneered at some poor male victim. Despite its popularity at the time, this is a fairly predictable costume affair, with a large selection of B-movie regulars striding about in thigh-length boots. Yet, seen from the distance of time, it is wonderful entertainment, with James Mason catching the swaggering heart of the movie and Lockwood giving a marvellous portrayal of villainy. SH *DVD*

Margaret Lockwood *Barbara Worth/Lady Skelton* · James Mason *Captain Jackson* · Patricia Roc *Caroline* · Griffith Jones *Sir Ralph Skelton* · Enid Stamp-Taylor *Henrietta Kingsclere* · Michael Rennie *Kit Locksby* · Felix Aylmer *Hogarth* · David Horne *Martin Worth* · Martita Hunt *Cousin Agatha* ■ *Dir* Leslie Arliss · *Scr* Leslie Arliss, Aimee Stuart, Gordon Glennon, from the novel *The Life and Death of the Wicked Lady Skelton* by Magdalen King-Hall

The Wicked Lady ★★★ 18
Adventure 1983 · UK · Colour · 94min

Michael Winner's Technicolor remake of the effective 1945 hokum that made Margaret Lockwood a star has Faye Dunaway as the amoral "lady" who takes up with a highwayman. Winner's version is in dubious taste, frankly exploitative and trashy in its unashamed injection of sex and violence, and famously caused a furore with the censors over a scene in which Dunaway takes a whip to another woman, ripping her clothes to shreds. Questionable though it may be, however, the movie is enjoyable high camp and efficiently made. RK

Faye Dunaway *Lady Barbara Skelton* · Alan Bates *Captain Jerry Jackson* · John Gielgud *Hogarth* · Denholm Elliott *Sir Ralph Skelton* · Prunella Scales *Lady Henrietta Kingsclere* · Glynis Barber *Caroline* · Oliver Tobias *Kit Locksby* · Joan Hickson *Aunt Agatha Trimble* ■ *Dir* Michael Winner · *Scr* Leslie Arliss, Michael Winner, from the novel *The Life and Death of the Wicked Lady Skelton* by Magdalen King-Hall

Wicked Stepmother ★ PG
Comedy horror 1989 · US · Colour · 89min

This was catastrophic end to Bette Davis's glittering career. The actress who took on the Hollywood studio system and won in the 1930s was equally prepared to fight her corner in what turned out to be her last movie. Her disgust with director Larry Cohen's work led to her walking out, and her part as the stepmother who uses her paranormal powers to torment her family was drastically reduced. One hopes her atrocious performance was a poisonous act of revenge. DP Violence, swearing.

Bette Davis *Miranda* · Barbara Carrera *Priscilla* · Colleen Camp *Jenny* · David Rasche *Steve* · Lionel Stander *Sam* · Tom Bosley *Lieutenant MacIntosh* · Shawn Donahue *Mike* · Richard Moll *Nat* ■ *Dir/Scr* Larry Cohen

The Wicker Man ★★★★ 15
Classic horror 1973 · UK · Colour · 84min

Edward Woodward stars as the devoutly Christian policeman who finds his beliefs tested to the limit when he investigates the disappearance of a young girl on the pagan shores of Summerisle in this cult horror classic. With a literate script by Anthony Shaffer and a memorable Scottish folk score, director Robin Hardy's fascinating mixture of horror, eroticism and religion is a thoughtful, challenging and highly provocative experience. Christopher Lee, who plays the lord of the island, thinks it's the finest film he's ever made – and he's right. Do seek out the director's cut, which in 2002 restored the studio-cut original print to something like its original glory. AC Violence, swearing, nudity. *DVD* *Blu-ray*

Edward Woodward *Sergeant Neil Howie* · Christopher Lee *Lord Summerisle* · Diane Cilento *Miss Rose* · Britt Ekland *Willow MacGregor* · Ingrid Pitt *Librarian/Clerk* · Lindsay Kemp *Alder MacGregor* ■ *Dir* Robin Hardy · *Scr* Anthony Shaffer · *Cinematographer* Harry Waxman

The Wicker Man ★★★★ 15
Classic horror 1973 · UK · Colour · 84min

Edward Woodward stars as the devoutly Christian policeman who finds his beliefs tested to the limit when he investigates the disappearance of a young girl on the pagan shores of Summerisle in this cult horror classic. With a literate script by Anthony Shaffer and a memorable Scottish folk score, director Robin Hardy's fascinating mixture of horror, eroticism and religion is a thoughtful, challenging and provocative experience. Christopher Lee, who plays the lord of the island, thinks it's the finest film he's ever made – and he's right. Do seek out the director's cut, which in 2002 restored the studio-cut original print to something like its original glory. AC Violence, swearing, nudity. *DVD* *Blu-ray*

Edward Woodward *Sergeant Neil Howie* · Christopher Lee *Lord Summerisle* · Diane Cilento *Miss Rose* · Britt Ekland *Willow MacGregor* · Ingrid Pitt *Librarian/Clerk* · Lindsay Kemp *Alder MacGregor* ■ *Dir* Robin Hardy · *Scr* Anthony Shaffer · *Cinematographer* Harry Waxman

The Wicker Man ★ 15
Horror 2006 · Ger/US · Colour · 97min

The 1973 British cult classic gets a glossy, expensive and utterly pointless remake courtesy of writer/director Neil LaBute. The action is shifted from Scotland to America's Pacific Northwest coast, as traumatised cop Nicolas Cage is lured by ex-lover Kate Beahan to the remote island of Summersisle to look for her missing daughter. There he stumbles upon a matriarchal society of bee-keepers, led by Ellen Burstyn, that's engaged in some disturbing pagan May Day rituals. No longer a chaste Christian, instead Cage's character is allergic to bees – a meaningless plot change if ever there was one. Adapting Anthony Shaffer's screenplay, LaBute both dumbs and dulls down, and offers a laughable finale. AJ *DVD*

Nicolas Cage *Edward Malus* · Ellen Burstyn *Sister Summersisle* · Kate Beahan *Sister Willow* · Frances Conroy *Dr Moss* · Molly Parker *Sister Rose/Sister Thorn* · Leelee Sobieski *Sister Honey* ■ *Dir* Neil LaBute · *Scr* Neil LaBute, from the 1973 film

Wicker Park ★★★ 12
Romantic thriller 2004 · US · Colour · 110min

On the eve of a business trip, Josh Hartnett catches a fleeting glimpse of old flame Diane Kruger, who mysteriously disappeared from his life a few years earlier. Postponing his trip and abandoning his fiancée, Hartnett determines to track her down, only to discover the woman he saw is really someone else (Rose Byrne). But this lady has her own agenda, and is on the point of starting a relationship with Hartnett's friend (played by a scene-stealing Matthew Lillard). This American take on Gilles Mimouni's *L'Appartement* retains the Hitchcock-inspired thrills of the original. BP Swearing. *DVD*

Josh Hartnett *Matthew* · Rose Byrne *Alex* · Matthew Lillard *Luke* · Diane Kruger *Lisa* · Jessica Paré *Rebecca* ■ *Dir* Paul McGuigan · *Scr* Brandon Boyce, from the film *L'Appartement* by Gilles Mimouni

The Wicker Tree ★ 15
Horror drama 2010 · UK · Colour · 92min

From the makers of the 1973 classic *The Wicker Man* comes a companion piece so misjudged it beggars belief. A gospel singer and her boyfriend touring Scotland to spread the word of God are invited to take part in an ancient pagan custom by the laird of a remote border village. Anyone who has seen the original will be expecting something much better than this virtual retread, which lacks any sense of style and features dreadful special effects. Adding insult to injury, Christopher Lee cameos. AJ *DVD* *Blu-ray*

Brittania Nicol *Beth Boothby* · Henry Garrett *Steve Thomson* · Graham McTavish *Sir Lachlan Morrison* · Honeysuckle Weeks *Lolly* · Clive Russell *Beame* ■ *Dir* Robin Hardy · *Scr* Robin Hardy, from his novel *Cowboys for Christ*

Wide Awake ★★★ PG
Drama 1998 · US · Colour · 83min

M Night Shyamalan made this drama before writing and directing the smash hit *The Sixth Sense*. It's the story of a Catholic schoolboy who starts to question his faith after his grandfather dies, and devotes a whole school year to reassuring himself that grandad is spending eternity in good hands. The film is intriguing enough, but is a little let down by a sugary script. DA *DVD*

Denis Leary *Mr Beal* · Rosie O'Donnell *Sister Terry* · Dana Delany *Mrs Beal* · Robert Loggia *Grandpa Beal* · Joseph Cross *Joshua Beal* · Timothy Reifsnyder *Dave O'Hara* ■ *Dir/Scr* M Night Shyamalan

Wide Eyed and Legless ★★★★
Drama 1993 · UK · Colour · 90min

Originally made for TV but given a limited theatrical release, this was the first of two films based on Deric Longden's own life story (the other was *Lost for Words* which won a TV Bafta for Thora Hird). Julie Walters is superb as Diana, a woman suffering from a mysterious illness (now known as ME or chronic fatigue syndrome) for which the doctors have no answer. As she deteriorates, her frustration and fury are sublimated for the sake of her husband Deric (Jim Broadbent) until she can tolerate her poor quality of life no longer. Never maudlin, always convincing and with perfect performances from the two leads. FL

Julie Walters *Diana Longden* · Jim Broadbent *Deric Longden* · Thora Hird *Deric's mother* · Sian Thomas *Aileen Armitage* · Andrew Lancel *Nick Longden* · Anastasia Mulroney *Sally Longden* ■ *Dir* Richard Loncraine · *Scr* Jack Rosenthal, from the non-fiction books *Diana's Story* and *Lost for Words* by Deric Longden

Wide Sargasso Sea ★ 18
Period drama 1992 · Aus · Colour · 94min

This adaptation of the Jean Rhys novel explores the story behind *Jane Eyre* by telling the history of the future Mrs Rochester. Set in 19th-century Jamaica, Rochester (Nathaniel Parker) encounters the passionate and erotic Creole heiress Antoinette (Karina Lombard) and, after marrying her, discovers a family history of insanity. Unlike the novel, this is pure melodrama and poorly disguised erotica. What was an interesting literary tale is lost in a sea of sweaty sheets and bad acting. LH

Karina Lombard *Antoinette Cosway* · Nathaniel Parker *Rochester* · Rachel Ward *Annette Cosway* · Michael York *Paul Mason* · Martine Beswicke [Martine Beswick] *Aunt Cora* ■ *Dir* John Duigan · *Scr* Jan Sharp, Carole Angier, John Duigan, from the novel by Jean Rhys · *Music* Stewart Copeland

The Widow Couderc ★★★★
Romantic drama 1971 · Fr · Colour · 90min

With such an idyllic canal-side setting and an overwhelming sense of well-being, Simone Signoret's rural idyll can only turn sour, as it so often does in the world of novelist Georges Simenon. Initially, the canker comes from her scheming in-laws seizing upon her relationship with fugitive Alain Delon as a pretext for reclaiming her late husband's farm. But just as sinister is the rise of fascism, which underpins the family's skulduggery. Pierre Granier-Deferre judges the tone to perfection, but it's the inspired pairing of Signoret and Delon that gives the film its heart. DP French dubbed.

Alain Delon *Jean* · Simone Signoret *Widow Couderc* · Ottavia Piccolo *Félicie* · Jean Tissier *Henri* ■ *Dir* Pierre Granier-Deferre · *Scr* Pierre Granier-Deferre, Pascal Jardin, from a story by Georges Simenon

Widow on the Hill ★★
Drama based on a true story 2005 · US/Can · Colour · 120min

Natasha Henstridge plays social-climbing nurse Linda Dupree, who marries the wealthy widower of one of her former patients. When the widower dies, Dupree is accused of not just his murder, but his first wife's, too. Everything is proficiently assembled, and James Brolin and Henstridge smoulder effectively, but stories like this, whether true or not, are two-a-penny. SF Sex scenes.

Natasha Henstridge *Linda Dupree Cavanaugh* · James Brolin *Hank Cavanaugh* · Jewel Staite *Jenny Cavanaugh* · Roman Podhora *Ransom* · Michelle Duquet *Felicia Cavanaugh* · Marcia Bennett *Dottie* ■ *Dir* Peter Svatek · *Scr* Stephen Harrigan, from an article by Michael Shnayerson

Widows' Peak ★★★ PG
Black comedy drama 1993 · UK · Colour · 97min

The malicious, delicious old biddies of a picturesque Irish village declare war when their ranks are infiltrated by a wealthy and attractive new widow. It's tea-and-biscuits at 20 paces as hostilities prompt shameless behaviour, de-closeted skeletons and maybe even murder. Mia Farrow, Joan Plowright and Natasha Richardson play the black widows; Jim Broadbent and Adrian Dunbar are the menfolk desperate to avoid being eaten alive by them. DP *DVD*

Mia Farrow *Catherine O'Hare* · Joan Plowright *Mrs "DC" Doyle Counihan* · Natasha Richardson *Edwina Broome* · Adrian Dunbar *Godfrey* · Jim Broadbent *Clancy* · Anne Kent *Miss Grubb* · John Kavanagh *Canon* ■ *Dir* John Irvin · *Scr* Hugh Leonard, from his story

Wiener-Dog ★★★★ 15
Comedy 2016 · US · Colour · 88min

While misfit auteur Todd Solondz's seventh feature further mines the same suburban misanthropy minted in 1998 breakout film *Happiness*, *Wiener-Dog* might be his most optimistic work yet. Its quartet of stories representing four life stages are linked by the serene dachshund of the title, passed between owners like a parcel. The humans don't come out of it well, but Wiener-Dog herself surely offers uncomplicated hope. AC Swearing, sexual/drug references.

Greta Gerwig *Dawn Wiener* · Ellen Burstyn *Nana* · Kieran Culkin *Brandon* · Julie Delpy *Dina* · Danny DeVito *Schmerz* · Tracy Letts *Danny* ■ *Dir/Scr* Todd Solondz

Wife, Doctor and Nurse ★★★
Comedy 1937 · US · BW · 85min

Loretta Young made five movies for Fox in 1937, and this was the only one in which she didn't co-star with either Tyrone Power or Don Ameche. However, she did manage to change her wardrobe for virtually every scene; even the *New York Times* commented on her changes of outfit in their normally austere review. The plot's a wisp: Young is married to doctor Warner Baxter, who is also loved by his nurse, Virginia Bruce. The ending's daring, and Walter Lang directs with skill, helped by a cast that contains many well-loved faces. TS

Loretta Young *Ina* · Warner Baxter *Dr Judd Lewis* · Virginia Bruce *Steve, nurse* · Jane Darwell *Mrs Krueger, the Housekeeper* · Sidney Blackmer *Dr Therberg* · Maurice Cass *Pomout* ■ *Dir* Walter Lang · *Scr* Kathryn Scola, Darrell Ware, Lamar Trotti

Wife, Husband and Friend ★★★

Musical comedy   1939 · US · BW · 75min

This classy comedy from 20th Century-Fox was produced and written for the screen by that laconic southerner Nunnally Johnson, who would remake it to greater success ten years later as *Everybody Does It* with a more sophisticated cast. Loretta Young looks lovely, but never really convinces as the would-be singer whose husband really has the tuneful voice. Binnie Barnes as a prima donna and Helen Westley as Young's supportive mother get the most out of two splendidly written roles. TS

Loretta Young *Doris Blair Borland* · Warner Baxter *Leonard Borland/Logan Bennett* · Binnie Barnes *Cecil Carver* · Cesar Romero *Hugo* · George Barbier *Major Blair* · J Edward Bromberg *Rossi* · Eugene Pallette *Mike Craig* ■ *Dir* Gregory Ratoff · *Scr* Nunnally Johnson, from the story *Career in C Major* by James M Cain in *American Magazine*

Wife vs Secretary ★★★★

Comedy drama   1936 · US · BW · 85min

Clark Gable, Myrna Loy and Jean Harlow are the gold-plated stars in this snappy, intelligent comedy drama about marital misunderstanding. Harlow's personal secretary has a close, demanding but entirely innocent working relationship with Gable's magazine publisher; Loy is the wife who almost loses Gable through jealous suspicion of Harlow. The on-screen empathy of the familiar Gable-Harlow team, devoid of the usual sexual pull, is wonderful to watch. James Stewart, pre-leading man stardom, is Harlow's boyfriend. RK

Clark Gable *Van Stanhope/Jake* · Jean Harlow *Helen "Whitey" Wilson* · Myrna Loy *Linda Stanhope* · May Robson *Mimi Stanhope* · George Barbier *JD Underwood* · James Stewart *Dave* · Hobart Cavanaugh *Joe* · Tom Dugan (1) *Finney* ■ *Dir* Clarence Brown · *Scr* Norman Krasna, John Lee Mahin, Alice Duer Miller, from the short story by Faith Baldwin

Wilbur (Wants to Kill Himself) ★★★★

Black comedy drama   2002 · Den/UK/Swe/Fr · Colour · 104min

Danish director Lone Scherfig examines the unpredictability of love in her English-language debut. The consequences of single mother Shirley Henderson's encounter with second-hand bookshop owner Adrian Rawlins and his suicidal sibling Jamie Sives are melodramatic. But the misfits' romantic triangle is so deftly underplayed that an unfussy realism seeps into proceedings, which are further authenticated by the Glaswegian mix of hard-knock compassion and deadpan humour. The supporting cast also catches the mood, with Julia Davis splendid as an insensitive nurse. DP

Jamie Sives *Wilbur North* · Adrian Rawlins *Harbour North* · Shirley Henderson *Alice* · Lisa McKinlay *Mary* · Mads Mikkelsen *Dr Horst* · Julia Davis *Moira* · Susan Vidler *Sophie* ■ *Dir* Lone Scherfig · *Scr* Anders Thomas Jensen, Lone Scherfig

The Wilby Conspiracy ★★★

Political thriller   1975 · UK · Colour · 101min

In this drama set at the height of apartheid in South Africa, Sidney Poitier plays a political activist who drags unwilling Michael Caine on a cross-country flight from law and order, represented by the bigoted figure of Nicol Williamson. Villainous Williamson bides his time in the hope that the two fugitives will lead him to a rebel leader. Although the South African milieu is significant, Ralph Nelson's apparent return to the anti-racist controversy of *Soldier Blue* is merely a chase thriller. TH

Sidney Poitier *Shack Twala* · Michael Caine *Keogh* · Nicol Williamson *Horn* · Prunella Gee *Rina Van Nierkirk* · Persis Khambatta *Dr Persis Ray* · Saeed Jaffrey *Dr Mukerjee* · Rutger Hauer *Blaine Van Niekirk* ■ *Dir* Ralph Nelson · *Scr* Rod Amateau, Harold Nebenzal, from the novel by Peter Driscoll

The Wild ★★

Animated comedy adventure   2006 · US · Colour · 78min

If you get a sense of déjà vu watching this computer animated adventure, it's because you have indeed seen it all before. This tale of captive animals let loose in the wild is as derivative as they come. Yet while innovation is scarce, there's plenty of colour and humour for youngsters to enjoy, as Samson the New York Zoo lion (nicely voiced by Kiefer Sutherland) leads a mission to rescue his son, who's been mistakenly shipped to the jungle. SF

Kiefer Sutherland *Samson* · Jim Belushi [James Belushi] *Benny* · Greg Cipes *Ryan* · Eddie Izzard *Nigel* · Janeane Garofalo *Bridget* · William Shatner *Kazar* · Richard Kind *Larry* ■ *Dir* Steve "Spaz" Williams · *Scr* Ed Decter, John J Strauss, Mark Gibson, Philip Halprin

Wild ★★★

Biographical drama   2014 · US · Colour · 110min

In 1995, a troubled young woman decided to hike over a 1,000 miles along the Pacific Crest Trail in order to find herself. On the way, she encountered a variety of setbacks and obstacles, many of which are re-created by Jean-Marc Vallée (*Dallas Buyers Club*) in this episodic wilderness drama. The problem is the movie lacks emotional weight – despite a committed performance from Reese Witherspoon. As a result, *Wild* isn't quite able to achieve the profound impact that it's evidently aiming for. SC

Reese Witherspoon *Cheryl Strayed* · Laura Dern *Bobbi Lambrecht* · Gaby Hoffmann *Aimee Hurt* ■ *Dir* Jean-Marc Vallée · *Scr* Nick Hornby, from Cheryl Strayed's memoirs *Wild: from Lost to Found on the Pacific Crest Trail*

Wild about Harry ★★★★

Romantic comedy   2000 · UK/Ger/Ire · Colour · 87min

This is like *Regarding Henry* with heart, humour and no schmaltz. Brendan Gleeson is the naffest of Irish TV chefs, whose serial womanising is tabloid news. In the midst of divorce proceedings from his long-suffering wife Amanda Donohoe, Gleeson slips into a coma. Awakening with amnesia he gradually wins back the hearts of his wife and family, but old habits die hard. *Father Ted* director Declan Lowney handles this emotional merry-go-round with a deft touch, and the performances are excellent. LH

Brendan Gleeson *Harry McKee* · Amanda Donohoe *Ruth McKee* · James Nesbitt *Walter Adair* · Adrian Dunbar *JJ MacMahon* · Bronagh Gallagher *Miss Boyle* · George Wendt *Frankie* ■ *Dir* Declan Lowney · *Scr* Colin Bateman, Adrian Dunbar, George Wendt, James Nesbitt

The Wild Affair ★★★

Comedy drama   1963 · UK · BW · 84min

Before her wedding, secretary Nancy Kwan decides to have a final fling, taking advantage of the opportunities offered by an office party. Kwan was not the best choice for the lead and, this being the early 1960s, the affair is not as wild as it pretends to be. But after a slow start, the party atmosphere becomes infectious, mainly because of a wealth of comedy talent. Wonderful Terry-Thomas plays the boss and his staff includes some giants of the British music-hall (Bud Flanagan, Jimmy Logan, Gladys Morgan). DM

Nancy Kwan *Marjorie Lee* · Terry-Thomas *Godfrey Dean* · Jimmy Logan *Craig* · Bud Flanagan *Sergeant Bletch* · Gladys Morgan *Mrs Tovey* · Betty Marsden *Mavis Cook* · Paul Whitsun-Jones *Tiny Hearst* · Victor Spinetti *Quentin* · Frank Finlay *Drunk* ■ *Dir* John Krish · *Scr* John Krish, from the novel *The Last Hours of Sandra Lee* by William Sansom

Wild America ★★

Adventure based on a true story   1997 · US · Colour · 101min

Teen heart-throbs Devon Sawa and Jonathan Taylor Thomas star in this clunky eco-tale about a group of children who embark on a trans-American trek to photograph their country's fast-disappearing wildlife. This has its heart in the right place, but director William Dear relies a little too much on a series of staged encounters with animals. DA

Jonathan Taylor Thomas *Marshall* · Devon Sawa *Mark* · Scott Bairstow *Marty* · Frances Fisher *Agnes* · Jamey Sheridan *Marty Senior* · Tracey Walter *Leon* ■ *Dir* William Dear · *Scr* David Michael Wieger

The Wild and the Innocent ★★

Comedy western   1959 · US · Colour · 84min

Audie Murphy and Sandra Dee play a couple of innocents from the mountains who find themselves out of their depth in an unruly town. Also on hand are tough and sexy Joanne Dru, whose experience of character roles in John Ford and Howard Hawks westerns is put to good use here, and the always watchable Gilbert Roland. Not one of Murphy's best efforts, but not unwatchable and nicely shot in CinemaScope. TS

Audie Murphy *Yancey* · Joanne Dru *Marcy Howard* · Gilbert Roland *Sheriff Paul Bartell* · Jim Backus *Cecil Forbes* · Sandra Dee *Rosalie Stocker* · George Mitchell *Uncle Hawkes* ■ *Dir* Jack Sher · *Scr* Sy Gomberg, Jack Sher, from a story by Jack Sher

The Wild and the Willing ★★★

Drama   1962 · UK · BW · 113min

An unsuccessful play is the source of this exposé of British student life. Once shocking, it has aged badly, but now has curiosity value, not least because of early appearances by Ian McShane, Samantha Eggar, John Hurt and others. McShane shines as the scholarship boy who vents his wrath on privileged society by having a fling with a professor's wife. Relatively explicit bedroom scenes are disconcertingly combined with student japes. DM

Virginia Maskell *Virginia* · Paul Rogers *Professor Chown* · Ian McShane *Harry* · John Hurt *Phil* · Samantha Eggar *Josie* · Catherine Woodville *Sarah* · Jeremy Brett *Gilby* ■ *Dir* Ralph Thomas · *Scr* Nicholas Phipps, Mordecai Richler, from the play *The Tinker* by Laurence Dobie, Robert Sloman

Wild and Wonderful ★★

Comedy   1964 · US · Colour · 87min

Tony Curtis and his then wife Christine Kaufmann team in this frippery that is more notable for the performance of a poodle called Monsieur Cognac than for the efforts of its human stars. Curtis plays yet another American in Paris, who allows his music to suffer once he hits the right note with movie star Kaufmann. The leads are clearly in love, but it gets in the way of their acting, which is as unconvincing as the fake Paris sets. DP

Tony Curtis *Terry Williams* · Christine Kaufmann *Giselle Ponchon* · Larry Storch *Rufus Gibbs* · Pierre Olaf *Jacquot* · Mary Ingels *Doc Bailey* · Jacques Aubuchon *Papa Ponchon* ■ *Dir* Michael Anderson · *Scr* Larry Markes, Michael Morris, Waldo Salt, from a treatment by Richard M Powell, Phillip Rapp, from a short story by Dorothy Crider

The Wild Angels ★★★★

Action drama   1966 · US · Colour · 82min

The first and most controversial Hell's Angel shocker from cult director Roger Corman kick-started a whole cycle of biker movies. None were better than this brutal tale of leather-clad punks taking drugs, gang-raping women, beating up priests and having a drunken orgy at the church funeral of chapter member Bruce Dern. Shot documentary-style for added realism, it's based on true incidents as related to Corman by Californian Angels. Super cool Peter Fonda heads a hip cast of B-movie stalwarts, anti-establishment icons and pop singers. Graphic violence and the final message "There's nowhere to go" caused Corman's counterculture portrait to be banned in many countries. AJ

Peter Fonda *Heavenly Blues* · Nancy Sinatra *Mike* · Bruce Dern *Loser* · Marc Cavell *Frankenstein* · Michael J Pollard *Pigmy* · Lou Procopio *Joint* · Coby Denton *Bull Puckey* · Buck Taylor *Dear John* · Norman Alden *Medic* ■ *Dir* Roger Corman · *Scr* Charles Griffith

Wild at Heart ★★★★

Drama   1990 · US · Colour · 119min

Director David Lynch goes over the top, over people's heads and somewhere over the psychedelic rainbow in another ultra-violent and sleazily sexy pulp art attack. Forget the story; Lynch clearly has. Just follow convict and Elvis fan Nicolas Cage and his trailer trash girlfriend Laura Dern as they are pursued through the Deep South by her crazed mother's gumshoe lover. Stuffed with the Sultan of Strange's transfixing brand of deranged visuals, haunting weirdness and exuberant camp, it's another hypnotic ride through the twin peaks of pretentiousness and exhilaration. AJ

Nicolas Cage *Sailor Ripley* · Laura Dern *Lula Pace Fortune* · Diane Ladd *Marietta Pace* · Willem Dafoe *Bobby Peru* · Isabella Rossellini *Perdita Durango* · Harry Dean Stanton *Johnnie Farragut* · Crispin Glover *Dell* · Grace Zabriskie *Juana* ■ *Dir* David Lynch · *Scr* David Lynch, from the novel by Barry Gifford · *Music* Angelo Badalamenti

Wild Beauty ★★

Western   1946 · US · BW · 61min

This desperately over-complicated Universal programme filler is ostensibly about an Indian boy and his horse called Wild Beauty, but also contains an unsavoury subplot about capturing mustangs and turning their hides into shoe leather. There's relief from the tedium in producer/director Wallace Fox's deathless combination of earnestness and cheapskate production values. TS

Don Porter *Dave Morrow* · Lois Collier *Linda Gibson* · Jacqueline de Wit *Sissy* · George Cleveland *Barney* · Robert Wilcox *Gordon Madison* ■ *Dir* Wallace W Fox [Wallace Fox] · *Scr* Adele Buffington

Wild Bill ★★★★

Western   1995 · US · Colour · 93min

This is a flawed but fascinating look at an American legend. Starring a superbly cast Jeff Bridges as William "Wild Bill" Hickok, the movie opens with the killing of a dozen or so men over the course of a decade, then focuses on the ageing gunslinger's quest for old flame Calamity Jane (Ellen Barkin) while setting up a confrontation with a vengeful youngster who may be Hickok's bastard son. Walter Hill paints a far from pretty picture of the West and of Hickok: he's a drug addict, a killer and a monster haunted by his past. It oozes period atmosphere and is an epic of disillusionment. AT

Jeff Bridges *James Butler "Wild Bill" Hickok* · Ellen Barkin *Calamity Jane* · John Hurt *Charley Prince* · Diane Lane *Susannah Moore* · David Arquette *Jack McCall* · Keith Carradine *Buffalo Bill Cody* · Christina Applegate *Lurline* · Bruce Dern *Will Plummer* ■ *Dir* Walter Hill · *Scr* Walter Hill, from the play *Fathers and Sons* by Thomas Babe and the novel *Deadwood* by Pete Dexter

Wild Bill ★★★

Drama   2011 · UK · Colour · 94min

Family drama meets crime thriller on the streets of East London in the bleakly entertaining directorial debut by actor Dexter Fletcher. Just released from an eight-year prison stretch, Bill (Charlie Creed-Miles) discovers his two sons (Will Poulter, Sammy Williams) fending for themselves in the family's Newham council flat and is blackmailed into hanging around until social services are appeased. Held together by engaging performances from stalwart Creed-Miles and his junior co-stars, this uneven offering works well when it sticks to its filial bonding story, but falters when it brings on unconvincing neighbourhood drug dealers. TJ

Charlie Creed-Miles *Bill* • Will Poulter *Dean* • Liz White *Roxy* • Sammy Williams *Jimmy* • Leo Gregory *Terry* • Neil Maskell *Dicky* • Andy Serkis *Glen* ■ *Dir* Dexter Fletcher • *Scr* Dexter Fletcher, Danny King

The Wild Blue Yonder ★★★
Science-fiction fantasy
2005 · Ger/UK/Fr · BW and Colour · 81min

Described by its director as a "sci-fi fantasy", Werner Herzog's docudrama is an ingenious, occasionally frustrating attempt to craft a lo-fi sci-fi movie out of archive footage. Brad Dourif plays an alien stuck on Earth who recounts the story of his arrival and mankind's attempt to colonise his planet. Using archive footage of NASA expeditions and deep-sea diving in the Arctic, Herzog has made a sci-fi movie with just one actor and no special effects. It doesn't really work, not least because the archive footage isn't quite epic enough. But that doesn't stop Herzog offering a melancholy take on the fragility of human (and alien) aspirations. JR

Brad Dourif *The alien* • Donald Williams *Commander* • Ellen Baker *Physician* • Franklin Chang-Diaz *Plasma physicist* • Shannon Lucid *Biochemist* ■ *Dir/Scr* Werner Herzog

The Wild Bunch ★★★★★ 18
Classic western 1969 · US · Colour · 138min

Arguably, one of the greatest westerns ever made. And argument is what Sam Peckinpah's masterpiece has always caused, with its slow-motion spurting of blood, its surrealistically choreographed gunfights and its portrayal of Pike Bishop's amoral Texas outlaws as heroes. Yet William Holden's laconic Bishop, however violent, is of a truly romantic breed as he leads his bunch to their deaths. Lucien Ballard's photography gives a funereal hue to this elegy to the passing of a certain breed of chivalry. You can see why John Wayne is said to have hated the film; Peckinpah was practically reinventing a genre, with no place left for false nobility. TH Violence, nudity. DVD BL

William Holden (2) *Pike Bishop* • Ernest Borgnine *Dutch Engstrom* • Robert Ryan *Deke Thornton* • Edmond O'Brien *Sykes* • Warren Oates *Lyle Gorch* • Jaime Sanchez *Angel* • Ben Johnson (1) *Tector Gorch* • Emilio Fernandez *Mapache* ■ *Dir* Sam Peckinpah • *Scr* Walon Green, Sam Peckinpah, from a story by Walon Green, Roy N Sickner

Wild Card ★★ 15
Crime thriller 2014 · US · Colour · 98min

There's a melancholy vibe to this sun-bleached neon-noir, which finds hardman Jason Statham in more reflective mode than usual. Sadly, Statham – like director Simon West, who gave us the rabble-rousing *Con Air* – is better suited to kick-ass action, which punctuates *Wild Card* less frequently than it ought to. Vegas minder Statham is solicited by sometime girlfriend Sofia Vergara to get revenge on the Mafia hoods who beat and raped her. The fight scenes are electric, but the attempts at comedy and pathos are sorely misjudged. DW DVD BL

Jason Statham *Nick Wild* • Sofia Vergara *DD* • Stanley Tucci *Baby* • Anne Heche *Roxy* • Michael Angarano *Cyrus Kinnick* • Milo Ventimiglia *Danny DeMarco* ■ *Dir* Simon West • *Scr* William Goldman, from his novel *Heat*

Wild Child ★★★ 12
Comedy 2008 · US/UK/Fr · Colour · 94min

Emma Roberts stars as Poppy, a spoilt California "princess", in this cross between *St Trinian's* and *Mean Girls*. Roberts is dispatched by exasperated dad Aidan Quinn to a posh English boarding school ruled by acid-tongued headmistress Natasha Richardson. The school has a regime of decorum and discipline, but Poppy's obnoxious, spoilt-brat ways soon earn the enmity of all – in particular the school's upstaged head girl. No prizes for guessing, though, that life lessons are learned and that Poppy emerges a perfect poppet from the experience. Debut director Nick Moore's film hasn't an original bone in its body, yet it treads well-worn territory with a bright and

breezy aplomb that even the odd super-wooden performance can't spoil. DA DVD BL

Emma Roberts *Poppy* • Natasha Richardson *Mrs Kingsley* • Shirley Henderson *Matron* • Alex Pettyfer *Freddie* • Nick Frost *Mr Christopher* • Aidan Quinn *Gerry* • Daisy Donovan *Miss Rees-Withers* ■ *Dir* Nick Moore • *Scr* Lucy Dahl

Wild Country ★★★ 15
Horror 2005 · UK · Colour · 72min

Writer/director Craig Strachan's feature debut, a horror with a lycanthropic twist, begins with a nod to the sensibilities of Ken Loach, as teenager Samantha Shields gives birth and then hands the baby over for adoption. A few weeks later she is off tramping through the Scottish countryside with a bunch of other maladjusted Glasgow teens, including Martin Compston. But the film veers off in a different direction when they find themselves menaced by something very nasty in the undergrowth. Poor camerawork sometimes obscures the action, but overall this film represents a refreshing change from slick American teen horror product. BP Violence, swearing.

Samantha Shields *Kelly Ann* • Martin Compston *Lee* • Peter Capaldi *Father Steve* • Alan McHugh *Shepherd* • Kevin Quinn *David* • Nicola Muldoon *Louise* • Jamie Quinn *Mark* • Karen Fraser *Missy* • Tracey Robertson *Elaine* ■ *Dir/Scr* Craig Strachan

The Wild Duck ★★★
Drama 1983 · Aus · Colour · 95min

Henri Safran makes so little capital out of relocating Henrik Ibsen's play to turn-of-the-century Australia that one wonders why he bothered. Yet the structure and brooding atmosphere of this fiercely melodramatic story remain intact and, apart from name changes, so do the characters. Thus Arthur Dignam is wilfully pompous as he hauls family skeletons before the bemused Jeremy Irons, who can scarcely believe that his timid wife, Liv Ullmann, bore him another man's child. This highly symbolic piece ends on a note of shocking tragedy, which nowadays seems grotesque. DP

Liv Ullmann *Gina Ackland* • Jeremy Irons *Harold* • Lucinda Jones *Henrietta Ackland* • John Meillon *Major Ackland* • Arthur Dignam *Gregory Wardle* • Michael Pate *George Wardle* • Colin Croft *Mollison* ■ *Dir* Henri Safran • *Scr* Peter Smalley, John Lind, Henri Safran, from the play by Henrik Ibsen

The Wild Geese ★★★ 15
Action adventure 1978 · UK · Colour · 128min

Richards Burton and Harris, plus Roger Moore and Hardy Kruger, are evidently enjoying themselves in this all-action adventure. They play mercenaries hired by Stewart Granger to rescue a deposed African president and put him back in power, all for the sake of big-business interests. Politically it's a dog's dinner of woolly liberalism and right-wing rhetoric – it was filmed in South Africa during the height of apartheid – but, as a firework display, the movie is often exciting. DVD BL Drug abuse, violence, swearing.

Richard Burton *Col Allen Faulkner* • Roger Moore *Shawn Fynn* • Richard Harris *Rafer Janders* • Hardy Kruger *Pieter Coetzee* • Stewart Granger *Sir Edward Matherson* • Jack Watson *Sandy Young* • Winston Ntshona *President Julius Limbani* • Frank Finlay *Priest* ■ *Dir* Andrew V McLaglen • *Scr* Reginald Rose, from the novel by Daniel Carney

Wild Geese II ★ 18
Action adventure 1985 · UK · Colour · 120min

This infantile follow-up to *The Wild Geese* hinges on a gang of mercenaries trying to get the ageing Rudoph Hess (Laurence Olivier in a positively embarrassing performance) out of Spandau Prison. It revamps the original in having a brutal and tedious training sequence before the actual mission. The film is cobbled together with leaden predictability and absolutely no narrative flow whatsoever. BB Violence. DVD

Scott Glenn *John Haddad* • Barbara Carrera *Kathy Lukas* • Edward Fox *Alex Faulkner* • Laurence Olivier *Rudolf Hess* • Robert Webber *Robert McCann* • Robert Freitag *Stroebling* • Kenneth Haigh *Col Reed-Henry* • Stratford Johns *Mustapha El Ali* ■ *Dir* Peter Hunt • *Scr* Reginald Rose, from the novel *The Square Circle* by Daniel Carney

Wild Geese Calling ★★
Drama 1941 · US · BW · 78min

Restless lumberjack Henry Fonda, in search of excitement, tracks down old pal and gambler Warren William in Seattle. There he meets and marries saloon dancer Joan Bennett who, unbeknown to him, is William's old flame and gets involved in William's dangerous dispute with big Barton MacLane. With a top-notch cast and enough plot to fill two movies, one could have expected more of this adventure drama. For all its incident, however, the script is not sharp enough, and is further flattened by John Brahm's laboured direction. RK

Henry Fonda *John Murdock* • Joan Bennett *Sally Murdock* • Warren William *Blackie Bedford* • Ona Munson *Clarabella* • Barton MacLane *Pirate Kelly* • Russell Simpson *Len Baker* • Iris Adrian *Mazie* • James C Morton *Mack* ■ *Dir* John Brahm • *Scr* Horace McCoy, Sam Hellman, Jack Andrews, Robert Carson, from the novel by Stewart Edward White

The Wild Girl ★★
Period adventure 2010 · Can · Colour · 100min

Former *Beverly Hills 90210* star Brian Austin Green makes a bland hero in this bitty, book-based period adventure. He plays a valet-turned-aspiring news photographer who joins a 1932 expedition to find a young boy kidnapped by Apaches. But with most of the group treating the venture like a casual hunting trip rather than a serious rescue mission, the film's first hour feels plodding and uneventful. Only the capture of the titular native American orphan adds interest. A flurry of dramatic activity in the last third is therefore very welcome, although rushed pacing means proceedings lack their intended emotional impact. SF

Brian Austin Green *Ned Giles* • Kathleen Munroe *Margaret Hawkins* • Matthew Edison *Tolley Phillips* • Andrew Gillies *Mr Browning* ■ *Dir* Don McBrearty • *Scr* Ronald Parker, from the novel by Jim Fergus

Wild Grass ★★★ 12A
Romantic drama 2008 · Fr/It · Colour · 103min

Veteran director Alain Resnais here crafts a playful piece of whimsy with a dark undertow. Georges (André Dussollier) is a middle-aged man with an increasingly weak grip on reality, who finds a wallet that belongs to glamorous Marguerite (Sabine Azéma), but in attempting to return it to her, has to navigate the tricky social protocols of giving and receiving thanks. There are some strange shifts in tone, and Resnais inserts his trademark visual style, but this is a film that's mildly diverting without lingering too long in the memory. DA French +subtitles.

André Dussollier *Georges Palet* • Sabine Azéma *Marguerite Muir* • Emmanuelle Devos *Josépha Bellotch* • Mathieu Amalric *Bernard de Bordeaux* • Anne Consigny *Suzanne Palet* • Michel Vuillermoz *Lucien d'Orange* ■ *Dir* Alain Resnais • *Scr* Alex Reval, Laurent Herbiet, from the novel *L'Incident* by Christian Gailly

A Wild Hare ★★★★
Animated comedy 1940 · US · Colour · 8min

Before he made his debut in this cartoon, Bugs Bunny had been through many development stages. Two years earlier, Bob Clampett used Tex Avery's rejected Daffy Duck gags to create a similarly daffy rabbit. Later, animator Charles Thorson redesigned him and named him after director Bugs Hardaway while Chuck Jones subdued his crazy ways. It wasn't until Tex Avery combined these elements with his own revolutionary ideas that a rabbit recognisable as Bugs Bunny appeared. Bugs is the antithesis of his zany origins, as well as his real-life counterparts, as he resists dopey Elmer Fudd's attempts to shoot him

("What's up, Doc" being his first line of dialogue). CLP

Mel Blanc *Bugs Bunny* • Arthur Q Bryan *Elmer Fudd* ■ *Dir* Fred Avery [Tex Avery] • *Scr* Rich Hogan

Wild Hearts ★★
Drama 2006 · US · Colour · 90min

Still best known for playing John-Boy in the long-running TV series *The Waltons*, Richard Thomas returns to the great outdoors for this plot-heavy melodrama. He's typically decent as the LA cop who arrives in Hope, Montana, to take up the post of interim sheriff that was bequeathed to him, along with a mustang ranch, by his estranged father. However, he's soon struggling to cope with rebellious daughter Hallee Hirsh's disillusion with her new surroundings, the attentions of genial vet Nancy McKeon and the machinations of sinister property developer Joseph Culp. It's undemanding pulp, but entertaining enough. DP

Richard Thomas *Bob Hart* • Nancy McKeon *Emily Benson* • Hallee Hirsh *Madison Hart* • Geoffrey Lewis *Hank Hughes* • AJ Trauth *Tim Carter* • Joseph Culp *Cody McMichael* ■ *Dir* Steve Boyum • *Scr* Mitchell Gabourie, Donald Martin

Wild Hearts Can't Be Broken ★★★ U
Romantic drama 1991 · US · Colour · 85min

A lovingly re-created Depression-era America provides the setting for this beautifully mounted Disney drama about the life of legendary stunt diver Sonora Webster, who overcame personal tragedy to become a star attraction with her horse-diving act. Gabrielle Anwar gives a gutsy performance in the lead role, while veteran actor Cliff Robertson provides the necessary eccentricity as her cranky employer. SH DVD

Gabrielle Anwar *Sonora Webster* • Cliff Robertson *Doctor Carver* • Dylan Kussman *Clifford* • Michael Schoeffling *Al Carver* • Kathleen York *Marie* • Frank Renzulli *Mr Slater* • Nancy Moore Atchison *Arnette* • Lisa Norman *Aunt Helen* ■ *Dir* Steve Miner • *Scr* Matt Williams, Oley Sassone

Wild Heritage ★★★ U
Western 1958 · US · Colour · 78min

This absorbing saga made on the cheap involves a brace of pioneer families and their trials and tribulations, mainly associated with their teenage offspring. Appearing among the youngsters are such icons as folksie composer Rod McKuen and teen idol Troy Donahue. Newly widowed Maureen O'Sullivan presides over the gunplay, and gnarly Will Rogers Jr makes a fair bid at his real-life father's style of homespun wisdom. The teenagers gang together and blast the baddies. TS

Will Rogers Jr *Judge Copeland* • Maureen O'Sullivan *Emma Breslin* • Rod McKuen *Dirk Breslin* • Casey Tibbs *Rusty* • Troy Donahue *Jesse Bascomb* • Judy Meredith [Judi Meredith] • Callie Bascomb • Gigi Perreau *Missouri Breslin* • George "Foghorn" Winslow [George Winslow] • Talbot Breslin ■ *Dir* Charles Haas • *Scr* Paul King, Joseph Stone, from a story by Steve Frazee

Wild Hogs ★★ 12
Road movie comedy adventure
2007 · US · Colour · 95min

The combined comic talents of John Travolta, Tim Allen, Martin Lawrence and William H Macy deserve rather better than this mediocre road movie, which was probably much more fun to make than it is to watch. Travolta and company play middle-aged "weekend" bikers who hit the road on their Harley-Davidsons (nicknamed "hogs") in a desperate bid to recapture their lost youth. But instead they fall foul of rabid Ray Liotta and his badass biker gang. *Wild Hogs* has its chucklesome moments, and the four stars are unquestionably a class act. But the film consistently underachieves, opting for dumbed-down crassness when it had the potential to be altogether sharper. DA DVD BL

W

Tim Allen *Doug Madsen* • John Travolta *Woody Stevens* • Martin Lawrence *Bobby Davis* • William H Macy *Dudley Frank* • Ray Liotta *Jack* • Marisa Tomei *Maggie* • Kevin Durand *Red* • MC Gainey *Murdock* • Peter Fonda *Damien Blade* ■ *Dir* Walt Becker • *Scr* Brian Copeland • *Cinematographer* Robbie Greenberg

Wild Horses ★★★ PG
Western drama 1985 · US/NZ · Colour · 90min

Country singer Kenny Rogers takes a break from warbling to star in this entertaining, contemporary cowboy TV flick. He plays an ex-rodeo star who finds his new blue-collar life boring, and turns his back on it to take part in a wild-horse roundup. Rogers has an easy charm, and fans will appreciate his songs that have slipped in. **DA**

Kenny Rogers *Matt Cooper* • Pam Dawber *Daryl Reese* • Richard Farnsworth *Chuck Reese* • Ben Johnson (1) *Bill Ward* • David Andrews (2) *Dean Ellis* • Richard Masur *Bob* • Jack Rader *Dick Post* ■ *Dir* Dick Lowry • *Scr* Daniel Vining, Roderick Taylor

Wild in the Country ★★ PG
Musical drama 1961 · US · Colour · 109min

This drama about a backwoods delinquent on parole, who ends up going to college to become a great writer, represents an attempt to unveil Elvis Presley as a straight dramatic actor. He makes a respectable attempt but is not quite good enough, and has no help from an unconvincing plot and script. Strangely, this unlikely piece is based on the true story of a Kentucky hillbilly who became a successful writer. **RK** *DVD*

Elvis Presley *Glenn Tyler* • Hope Lange *Irene Sperry* • Tuesday Weld *Noreen* • Millie Perkins *Betty Lee Parsons* • Rafer Johnson *Davis* • Christina Crawford *Monica George* • John Ireland *Phil Macy* • Gary Lockwood *Cliff Macy* • Jason Robards Jr [Jason Robards] *Judge Parker* ■ *Dir* Philip Dunne • *Scr* Clifford Odets, from the novel *The Lost Country* by JR Salamanca

Wild in the Streets ★★ 15
Drama 1968 · US · Colour · 92min

Christopher Jones, a world-famous pop megastar with a mother complex, starts a political campaign buoyed by Barry Mann and Cynthia Weil protest songs. When several states lower the voting age, the door is open for the first teenager to win the presidency, and Jones helps the political process along by putting LSD in the Washington water supply. When this modish satire of teenage rebellion was released at the fag-end of the 1960s, it must have seemed a lot more cutting then. However, the film is well made, lively and often funny. **JG**

Shelley Winters *Mrs Flatow* • Christopher Jones *Max Frost* • Diane Varsi *Sally LeRoy* • Ed Begley *Senator Allbright* • Millie Perkins *Mary Fergus* • Hal Holbrook *John Fergus* • Richard Pryor *Stanley X* ■ *Dir* Barry Shear • *Scr* Robert Thom, from his article *The Day It All Happened, Baby*

Wild Is the Wind ★★
Melodrama 1957 · US · BW · 114min

This gloomy, po-faced melodrama features Anthony Quinn as a widowed Italian shepherd farming in Nevada. Needing a new wife, he imports his sister-in-law (Anna Magnani) from Italy and marries her. The sparks start to fly when she makes off with Quinn's adopted son, Anthony Franciosa. George Cukor came on board when John Sturges was diverted to *The Old Man and the Sea*. It was apparently a turbulent production thanks to an uncomfortable relationship with prima donna Magnani. **AT**

Anna Magnani *Gioia* • Anthony Quinn *Gino* • Anthony Franciosa *Bene* • Dolores Hart *Angie* • Joseph Calleia *Alberto* • Lili Valenty *Teresa* ■ *Dir* George Cukor • *Scr* Arnold Schulman, from the novel *Furia* by Vittorio Nino Novarese

The Wild Life ★ 18
Comedy 1984 · US · Colour · 90min

Like *Fast Times at Ridgemont High*, this is a collection of vignettes concerning eccentric teenagers as they embark on entering the adult world. Not only does the movie frequently forget to be funny, it is executed without any energy or passion in front of or

behind the camera; aside from the golden oldie/Eddie Van Halen soundtrack, the only thing wild about it is its title. **KB**

Chris Penn *Tom Drake* • Ilan Mitchell-Smith *Jim Conrad* • Eric Stoltz *Bill Conrad* • Jenny Wright *Eileen* • Lea Thompson *Anita* • Rick Moranis *Harry* • Randy Quaid *Charlie* ■ *Dir* Art Linson • *Scr* Cameron Crowe

Wild Man Blues ★★★★ 12
Music documentary 1997 · US · Colour · 105min

Music is low on director Barbara Kopple's list of priorities in this account of Woody Allen's 1996 European tour with his jazz band. Instead, she tags along as he's hurtled from pillar to post by civic and cultural dignitaries to receive awards and greet the great and the good (with a priceless mix of embarrassment and irritation). But it's the private moments with his then girlfriend – now his wife – Soon-Yi Previn that make this compelling portrait of a highly complex man so intriguing. Completely at home in the limelight, she comes across as the guiding light of their relationship. Yet, if you think she's overbearing, wait until you see Allen's parents in action during a hilarious coda. **DP** Swearing. *DVD*

Woody Allen • Soon-Yi Previn ■ *Dir* Barbara Kopple

The Wild North ★★ U
Adventure 1952 · US · Colour · 97min

A first-rate cast figures in this below-standard adventure in which Stewart Granger kills a man in self-defence and is forced to flee into the Canadian wilderness. Hotly following is Mountie Wendell Corey, but trapper Granger knows every inch of the harsh countryside and leads him on a perilous trail. Andrew Marton directs with some pace, but with Cyd Charisse also featuring, it's the stars who are of main interest here. **TH**

Stewart Granger *Jules Vincent* • Wendell Corey *Constable Pedley* • Cyd Charisse *Indian girl* • Morgan Farley *Father Simon* • JM Kerrigan *Callahan* • Howard Petrie *Brody* • Houseley Stevenson *Old man* • John War Eagle *Indian chief* ■ *Dir* Andrew Marton • *Scr* Frank Fenton

Wild on the Beach ★★
Musical comedy 1965 · US · BW · 77min

Sherry Jackson and singer Frankie Randall (being hailed as a new Sinatra at the time) head the cast in this tale of a group of teenagers who take over a beach house when there is a housing shortage on their campus. Their wrangling and romantic entanglements take up most of the screen time, and the film would be totally forgettable were it not for the presence of Sonny and Cher. The couple had just become pop sensations, and the film marked Cher's screen debut. **TV**

Frankie Randall *Adam* • Sherry Jackson *Lee Sullivan* • Sonny Bono • Cher ■ *Dir* Maury Dexter • *Scr* Harry Spalding, from a story by Hank Tani

The Wild One ★★★★ PG
Drama 1953 · US · BW · 75min

"What are you rebelling against, Johnny?" asks a female admirer. "What've you got?" snarls Marlon Brando, his leather-clad biker entering the iconography of the decade. Long-banned in Britain, this is the first, the best, the quintessential motorbike movie, actually based on a 1947 incident when a cycle gang terrorised the small town of Hollister, California one desperate Fourth of July. OK, the back projection is a joke, Lee Marvin's far too old and the direction's often inadequate (as is the budget), but Brando is simply brilliant and the film still retains its unique power to astound. **TS** *DVD*

Marlon Brando *Johnny* • Mary Murphy (1) *Kathie* • Robert Keith (1) *Harry Bleeker* • Lee Marvin *Chino* • Jay C Flippen *Sheriff Singer* • Peggy Maley *Mildred* • Hugh Sanders *Charlie Thomas* • Ray Teal *Frank Bleeker* ■ *Dir* Laslo Benedek • *Scr* John Paxton, from a story by Frank Rooney • *Cinematographer* Hal Mohr

Wild Orchid ★ 18
Erotic drama 1990 · US · Colour · 106min

In a ghastly piece of soft-pore corn from trashmaster Zalman King, Carré Otis plays a lawyer who courts trouble when she falls for earring-wearing, super-bronzed Mickey Rourke during the carnival celebrations in Rio de Janeiro. Silly girl! It's the cue for much simulated sex, and precious little else. **DA** Swearing, sex scenes, nudity *DVD* *Blu*

Mickey Rourke *James Wheeler* • Jacqueline Bisset *Claudia* • Carré Otis *Emily Reed* • Assumpta Serna *Hanna* • Bruce Greenwood *Jerome* ■ *Dir* Zalman King • *Scr* Zalman King, Patricia Louisianna Knop

Wild Orchid 2: Two Shades of Blue ★★ 18
Erotic drama 1992 · US · Colour · 103min

Nina Siemaszko is the young girl who is lured into working for brothel madam Wendy Hughes, while mourning her jazz drifter dad Tom Skerritt. As usual with Zalman King productions, this looks terrific, but the plotting and dialogue are risible. Still, it's marginally better than the largely unconnected original. Followed by *The Red Shoe Diaries*, starring David Duchovny, which spawned a long-running series of its own. **JF** *DVD*

Nina Siemaszko *Blue* • Tom Skerritt *Ham* • Robert Davi *Sully* • Brent Fraser *Josh* • Christopher McDonald *Senator Dixon* • Wendy Hughes *Elle* • Joe Dallesandro *Jules* ■ *Dir* Zalman King • *Scr* Zalman King, Patricia Louisiana Knop

Wild Orchids ★★★
Silent romantic drama 1929 · US · BW · 100min

On a boat to Java, the beautiful young wife (Greta Garbo) of a middle-aged, unemotional business tycoon (Lewis Stone), twice her age, is lusted after by a foreign prince (Nils Asther) who invites them to stay at his opulent Javanese palace. There, the tension mounts and the situation reaches its climax during a tiger shoot. This little-known Garbo silent, lavishly mounted and directed with excellent judgement by Sidney Franklin, is out of the school of exotic, erotic, fantasy melodrama. Garbo is good, Asther is perfectly cast as the scheming lover, and Stone is superb as the husband. **RK**

Greta Garbo *Lili Sterling* • Lewis Stone *John Sterling* • Nils Asther *Prince De Gace* ■ *Dir* Sidney Franklin • *Scr* Hans Kräly, Richard Schayer, Willis Goldbeck, Marian Ainslee, Ruth Cummings, from the story *Hunt* by John Colton

The Wild Pair ★★ 18
Action crime drama 1987 · US · Colour · 91min

This thoroughly routine action movie outing features Beau Bridges and Bubba Smith as, respectively, a yuppie FBI agent and a streetwise cop who team up to track down a bunch of drug-dealing killers. Bridges directs, his first time for the big screen, while dad Lloyd Bridges makes it something of a family affair by taking one of the chunkier supporting roles. **DA**

Beau Bridges *Joe Jennings* • Bubba Smith *Benny Avalon* • Lloyd Bridges *Colonel Hester* • Raymond St Jacques *Ivory* • Gary Lockwood *Captain Kramer* • Danny De La Paz *Tucker* • Lela Rochon *Debby* ■ *Dir* Beau Bridges • *Scr* Joseph Gunn, from a story by John Crowther, Joseph Gunn

The Wild Party ★★★
Comedy drama 1929 · US · BW · 77min

Clara Bow's first talking picture has the original "It Girl" as a larky student who develops a crush on her tutor, played by Fredric March. Gossip, pranks, insubordination and 1920s sophomore slang all play their part in a fascinating period piece that is hard to watch today due to its forgivable technical limitations, yet which retains enough of its original energy to be entertaining. Bow acquits herself well here, and it is more likely that scandal (including her elopement with screen cowboy Rex Bell) was the main reason for her subsequent obscurity rather than the advent of sound. **RB**

Clara Bow *Stella Ames* • Fredric March *Gil Gilmore* • Shirley O'Hara (1) *Helen Owens* • Marceline Day *Faith Morgan* • Joyce Compton *Eva Tutt* ■ *Dir* Dorothy Arzner • *Scr* E Lloyd Sheldon, John VA Weaver, from a story by Warner Fabian

The Wild Party ★★★
Drama 1975 · US · Colour · 100min

In an impressive re-creation of silent-era Hollywood, James Coco plays a fading film funnyman whose hopes are pinned on a comeback movie hit. Raquel Welch plays the girlfriend who hosts a wild party for Tinseltown's moviebiz movers and shakers to promote it. It's a grim film that's based on the story of Fatty Arbuckle, the silent-era comic whose fan following vanished like mist when he was charged with killing a girl during a sex romp gone wrong. Welch is actually very good in this Merchant Ivory production. **DA**

James Coco *Jolly Grimm* • Raquel Welch *Queenie* • Perry King *Dale Sword* • Tiffany Bolling *Kate* • Royal Dano *Tex* • David Dukes *James* • Dena Dietrich *Mrs Murchison* ■ *Dir* James Ivory • *Scr* Walter Marks, from a poem by Joseph Moncure March • *Producer* Ismail Merchant • *Cinematographer* Walter Lassally

The Wild Racers ★★
Action drama 1968 · US · Colour · 83min

Although he'd been script doctoring for several years and had already directed a couple of features, Francis Ford Coppola had to be content with a second-unit credit on this typically effusive exploitation offering from B feature maestro, Roger Corman. The story of an ambitious racing driver who jeopardises his chances by living in the fast lane is classic Corman, with its achingly unhip dialogue and surfeit of inserted stock footage. **DP**

Fabian *Jo-Jo Quillico* • Mimsy Farmer *Katherine* • Alan Haufrect *Virgil* • Judy Cornwell *Pippy* • David Landers *Manager* • Talia Coppola [Talia Shire] *First girlfriend* ■ *Dir* Daniel Haller • *Scr* Max House

The Wild Ride ★★ PG
Drama 1960 · US · BW · 61min

In one of Jack Nicholson's earliest films, the future superstar plays a homicidal hot-rodder fed up with a former pal who's given up the wild life to settle down with girlfriend Georgianna Carter. Kidnapping the girl, he takes her on a high-speed rampage pursued by the local constabulary. It's a cheap quickie, but it has its own exploitative charm. **AT** *DVD*

Jack Nicholson *Johnny Varron* • Georgianna Carter *Nancy* • Robert Bean *Dave* ■ *Dir* Harvey Berman • *Scr* Ann Porter, Marion Rothman • *Editor* Monte Hellman

Wild River ★★★★ PG
Drama 1960 · US · Colour · 105min

This was a commercial failure for Elia Kazan, one of the key directors of postwar American cinema. But today this study of an old woman's intransigence when faced by the Tennessee Valley Authority's need to buy up her property in order to build a dam proves to be an intelligent and moving film, graced by a superbly tender performance from Montgomery Clift in one of his last and most tortured roles. Lee Remick is touching as his confidante, and there's a sharply-etched portrait by Jo Van Fleet in the role of the old woman. Watch out too for Bruce Dern in his movie debut. **TS** *DVD* *Blu*

Montgomery Clift *Chuck Glover* • Lee Remick *Carol Baldwin* • Jo Van Fleet *Ella Garth* • Albert Salmi *FJ Bailey* • Jay C Flippen *Hamilton Garth* • James Westerfield *Cal Garth* • Big Jeff Bess *Joe John Garth* • Bruce Dern *Jack Roper* ■ *Dir* Elia Kazan • *Scr* Paul Osborn, from the novels *Mud on the Stars* by William Bradford Huie and *Dunbar's Cove* by Borden Deal

Wild Rovers ★★★★ 15
Western 1971 · US · Colour · 125min

This fine western stars William Holden, Ryan O'Neal and Karl Malden. It's very much a film made in the wake of *The Wild Bunch* (in which Holden also starred), telling the story of an ageing cowboy and his adoring younger partner who dream of getting rich by robbing a bank. Beautifully shot and with a fine Jerry Goldsmith score, this is an exciting and often touching study of honour, heroism and changing times. O'Neal is perfectly cast, for once, and Holden is as craggy as the Rocky Mountains scenery. AT

William Holder (2) *Ross Bodine* • Ryan O'Neal *Frank Post* • Karl Malden *Walter Buckman* • Lynn Carlin *Sada Billings* • Tom Skerritt *John Buckman* • Joe Don Baker *Paul Buckman* • James Olson *Joe Billings* • Leora Dana *Nell Buckman* • Moses Gunn *Ben* • Victor French *Sheriff* ■ *Dir/Scr* Blake Edwards • *Cinematographer* Philip Lathrop

Wild Search ★★ 15
Crime thriller 1989 · UK · Colour · 94min

One of Hong Kong star Chow Yun-Fat's more obscure films, this is a more than able crime thriller, expertly choreographed by director Ringo Lam. While this lacks the bravura of the best Hong Kong thrillers, it still bears comparison with most Hollywood fodder. JF Cantonese +subtitles. Violence.

Chow Yun-Fat *Mickey Lau* • Cherie Chung *Cher* • Paul Chin *Mr Hung* • Chan Cheuk-yan *Ka-ka* • Lau Kong *Leung* • Tommy Wong *Lam* • Roy Cheung *Tiger* ■ *Dir* Ringo Lam • *Scr* Nam Yin

Wild Side ★★★ 18
Erotic thriller 1995 · US · Colour · 110min

Anne Heche stars as a banker who also works as a call girl to make ends meet. But an encounter with infamous money launderer Christopher Walken leads to an affair with his wife (Joan Chen) and involvement in an undercover FBI operation. The fourth and final film made by director Donald Cammell, this was re-cut without his permission and released on cable in a severely truncated form (Cammell was credited as Franklin Brauner). Cammell committed suicide shortly afterwards, and his widow China Kong and longtime editor Frank Mazzola have here reconstructed a seemingly improvised pulp thriller thats closer to the director's original vision. It won't be to everyone's taste – there's a brutal rape scene – yet it stands as a compelling piece of cinema from a sadly underused talent. JA DVD

Christopher Walken *Bruno Buckingham* • Anne Heche *Alex Lee* • Joan Chen *Virginia Chow* • Steven Bauer *Tony* • Allen Garfield *Dan Rackman* • Adam Novack *Lyle Litvak* ■ *Dir* Donald Cammell • *Scr* Donald Cammell, China Kong • *Music* Ryuichi Sakamoto

Wild Side ★★★ 18
Drama 2004 · Fr/Bel/UK · Colour · 90min

This is a thoughtful treatise on individuality and the courage needed to make difficult choices. Having established the humiliation that transsexual prostitute Stéphanie (played by Stéphanie Michelini) endures in Paris, director Sébastien Lifshitz reveals the true extent of her vulnerability when she returns to her childhood home in northern France to nurse her dying mother (Josiane Stoleru). However, the arrival of Michelini's bisexual Russian over (Edouard Nikitine) and an Arab hustler (Yasmine Belmadi) further complicates her attempt to reconcile herself to her past. DP French, Russian +subtitles. Swearing, sex scenes. DVD

Stéphanie Michelini *Stéphanie* • Edouard Nikitine *Mikhail* • Yasmine Belmadi *Djamel* • Josiane Stoleru *Mother* • Antony Hegarty *Café singer* ■ *Dir* Sébastien Lifshitz • *Scr* Sébastien Lifshitz, Stéphane Bouquet

Wild Strawberries ★★★★★ 15
Drama 1957 · Swe · BW · 87min

Contrasting the innocent expectancy of youth with the bitter regret of old age, this is Ingmar Bergman's warmest and most accessible film. Sweden's greatest silent director, Victor Sjöström, gives a magisterial performance as the frosty, vain professor who seizes the chance for redemption offered to him in the dreams and nightmares he experiences while travelling to a degree ceremony with his daughter-in-law, Ingrid Thulin. The symbolism of the nightmares (including

handless clocks and runaway hearses) is occasionally overpowering, but the memories of idyllic summers spent with cousin Bibi Andersson rank among the finest moments of the director's career. DP Swedish +subtitles. DVD

Victor Sjöström *Professor Isak Borg* • Bibi Andersson *Sara* • Ingrid Thulin *Marianne Borg* • Gunnar Björnstrand *Evald Borg* ■ *Dir/Scr* Ingmar Bergman

Wild Target ★★★★ 15
Comedy thriller 1993 · Fr · Colour · 84min

Jean Rochefort, one of the finest character actors currently working in French cinema, has rarely been better than in this scorching debut from writer/director Pierre Salvadori. Rochefort is quite superb as a meticulous hitman whose ordered existence begins to disintegrate when he takes on impetuous accomplice Guillaume Depardieu – son of Gérard – and falls in love with his next hit, glamorous art forger and petty thief Marie Trintignant (daughter of Jean-Louis and Nadine). The scenes at the hotel and Rochefort's country house are executed with great flair and a delicious black wit. DP French +subtitles.

Jean Rochefort *Victor Meynard* • Marie Trintignant *Renée* • Guillaume Depardieu *Antoine* • Patachou *Madame Meynard* • Charlie Nelson *Dremyan* • Wladimir Yordanoff *Casa Bianca* • Serge Riaboukine *Manu* • Philippe Girard *Tony* ■ *Dir/Scr* Pierre Salvadori

Wild Target ★★ 12
Action comedy drama 2009 · UK/Fr · Colour · 93min

Bill Nighy and Emily Blunt melted hearts as a father and daughter in TV drama *Gideon's Daughter*, but their relationship in this black comedy will more likely turn stomachs. Nighy is initially very charming as a hitman having an identity crisis, but when he fails to pull the trigger on a pretty thief (Blunt doing kooky) who has defrauded an effortlessly sinister Rupert Everett, events become contrived – Nighy serves as Blunt's bodyguard and winds up mentoring Rupert Grint (in a completely extraneous role). Martin Freeman has a few shining moments as a rival assassin, but the budding romance between the young free spirit and the crotchety old triggerman really kills it. SP DVD Blu-ray

Bill Nighy *Victor Maynard* • Emily Blunt *Rose* • Rupert Grint *Tony* • Rupert Everett *Ferguson* • Eileen Atkins *Mother* • Martin Freeman *Dixon* • Gregor Fisher *Mike* ■ *Dir* Jonathan Lynn • *Scr* Lucinda Coxon, from the film *Cible Emouvante* by Pierre Salvadori

Wild Things ★★★ 18
Thriller 1998 · US · Colour · 103min

Things are certainly steamy in Florida in this eyebrow-raising thriller. Neve Campbell and Denise Richards star as high-school students who falsely accuse teacher Matt Dillon of rape in a preposterous tale that's more notable for its X-rated scenes than for its great acting or script. There are a few nice twists, however, and the handsome cast clearly enjoys vamping it up in what is essentially a sexed-up, feature-length MTV video. Popular enough to produce a sequel in 2004. JB Violence, swearing, sex scenes, nudity. DVD CS

Kevin Bacon *Ray Duquette* • Matt Dillon *Sam Lombardo* • Neve Campbell *Suzie Toller* • Theresa Russell *Sandra Van Ryan* • Denise Richards *Kelly Van Ryan* • Daphne Rubin-Vega *Gloria Perez* • Robert Wagner *Tom Baxter* • Bill Murray *Ken Bowden* ■ *Dir* John McNaughton • *Scr* Stephen Peters

The Wild Thornberrys Movie ★★ U
Animated comedy 2003 · US · Colour · 81min

Bespectacled, brace-wearing Eliza Thornberry and her eccentric nature documentary-making family are given the feature-length treatment in Nickelodeon's small-screen spin-off. But while this is more than palatable in bite-sized servings, stretched over 85 minutes it rapidly loses its verve. There's not enough plot, or indeed

action, to engage young minds for the movie's duration. SF DVD

Lacey Chabert *Eliza Thornberry* • Tom Kane *Darwin* • Tim Curry *Nigel Thornberry/Col Thornberry* • Lynn Redgrave *Cordelia Thornberry* • Jodi Carlisle *Marianne Thornberry* • Danielle Harris *Debbie Thornberry* • Flea *Donnie Thornberry* • Rupert Everett *Sloan Blackburn* • Marisa Tomei *Bree Blackburn* • Brenda Blethyn *Mrs Fairgood* ■ *Dir* Jeff McGrath, Cathy Malkasian • *Scr* Katie Boutilier, from characters by Arlene Klasky, Gabor Csupo, Steve Pepoon, David Silverman, Stephen Sustarsic

Wild West ★★★ 15
Comedy 1992 · UK · Colour · 80min

In this rip-roaring tale of the old west (old west London, that is), a bunch of country music-loving Pakistani "outlaws" from Southall want to make music – but instead find themselves facing it when their band leader falls for an Asian girl who's unhappily wed to a villainous "gringo". Naveen Andrews and Sarita Choudhury star in this enjoyable romp. DA Swearing. DVD

Naveen Andrews *Zaf Ayub* • Sarita Choudhury *Rifat* • Ronny Jhutti *Kay Ayub* • Ravi Kapoor *Ali Ayub* • Ameet Chana *Gurdeep* • Bhasker *Jagdeep* • Lalita Ahmed *Mrs Ayub* ■ *Dir* David Attwood • *Scr* Harwant Bains

Wild Wheels ★★★
Documentary 1992 · US · Colour · 64min

This highly engaging, witty and touching documentary is all about unconventional car owners and the way they customise their vehicles to reflect their personalities or important moments in their lives. Written and directed by Harrod Blank, whose own Volkswagen is lovingly covered in plastic globes and sunflowers with a huge black fly on the hood, his tribute shows other cars decorated with buttons, beads, huge crucifixes, taps and even plastic flamingos. The drivers come from all walks of life and ethnic groups and, although Blank's focus is goofy eccentricity, there is frequently a meaningful motivation behind the decor. Unusual and quirky. AJ

■ *Dir/Scr* Harrod Blank • *Cinematographers* Harrod Blank, Paul Cope, Les Blank

Wild Wild West ★★ 12
Western adventure fantasy 1999 · US · Colour · 101min

Superficial and predictable, with special effects bloated out of all proportion, director Barry Sonnenfeld's big screen adaptation of the cult 1960s TV series may have an invisible script, but it's still fun thanks to the charisma of Will Smith and some fabulous gadgetry. Smith and Kevin Kline star as mismatched US Secret Service agents using anachronistic contraptions and fancy disguises to stop mad genius Kenneth Branagh from assassinating President Grant (Kline again). The one-liners are below average. AJ Violence, sexual references. DVD

Will Smith *James West* • Kevin Kline *Artemus Gordon/President Ulysses S Grant* • Kenneth Branagh *Dr Arliss Loveless* • Salma Hayek *Rita Escobar* • M Emmet Walsh *Coleman* • Ted Levine *General McGrath* • Frederique Van Der Wal *Amazonia* • Musetta Vander *Munitia* ■ *Dir* Barry Sonnenfeld • *Scr* SS Wilson, Brent Maddock, Jeffrey Price, Peter S Seaman, from a story by Jim Thomas, John Thomas • *Music* Elmer Bernstein

The Wild Women of Wongo ★ U
Fantasy comedy 1958 · US · Colour · 52min

This is one of several films that were voted the worst ever made and consequently gained a new lease of life among camp followers in the 1980s. A prehistoric comedy, closer in spirit to a burlesque sketch than parody, it is about the romance between the Princess of Wongo, where the women are beautiful and the men are ugly, and the Prince of Goona, where it's vice versa. The unspeakable dialogue and risible performances are fun for a while, although the joke wears thin pretty quickly. DM

Jean Hawkshaw *Omoo* • John Walsh *Engor* • Mary Ann Webb *Mona* • Cande Gerrard *Ahtee* • Adrienne Bourbeau *Wana* • Ed Fury *Gahbo* ■ *Dir* James L Wolcott • *Scr* Cedric Rutherford

Wildcats ★★ 15
Comedy 1986 · US · Colour · 101min

Most of the interest in this routine Goldie Hawn comedy is generated by the sight of some familiar faces in the supporting cast who were making their first steps on the way to stardom. Hawn is the fledgling American football coach who sets about transforming a terrible college side, much to the disbelief of the macho team members, who include a young Wesley Snipes and Woody Harrelson. There are some amusing moments, and, as usual, Hawn's comic timing can't be faulted. In the end, however, it remains one for die-hard fans only. JF Swearing, nudity.

Goldie Hawn *Molly McGrath* • Swoosie Kurtz *Verna* • Robyn Lively *Alice McGrath* • Brandy Gold *Marian McGrath* • James Keach *Frank McGrath* • Jan Hooks *Stephanie* • Nipsey Russell *Ben Edwards* • M Emmet Walsh *Coes* • Wesley Snipes *Trumaine* • Woody Harrelson *Krushinski* ■ *Dir* Michael Ritchie • *Scr* Ezra Sacks

The Wildcats of St Trinian's ★
Comedy 1980 · UK · Colour · 91min

In truth, there was only one genuinely funny entry – *The Belles of St Trinian's* – in this five-film series, with each instalment failing more dismally than the last to match the comic anarchy of the original movie. Why Frank Launder felt the need to return to the old place after a 14-year hiatus is hard to fathom, especially as he could only come up with this lame story about kidnapping and strikes, which is essentially an excuse for scantily clad sixth-formers and dodgy gags. DP

Sheila Hancock *Olga Vandemeer* • Michael Hordern *Sir Charles Hackforth* • Joe Melia *Flash Harry* • Thorley Walters *Hugo Culpepper-Brown* • Rodney Bewes *Peregrine Butters* • Deborah Norton *Miss Brenner* • Maureen Lipman *Katy Higgs* • Julia McKenzie *Dolly Dormancott* ■ *Dir* Frank Launder • *Scr* Frank Launder, from the drawings by Ronald Searle

Wilde ★★★★ 15
Biographical period drama 1997 · UK · Colour · 111min

Once you've seen Stephen Fry in the title role of Oscar Wilde it's difficult to imagine anyone better suited. Playing to the myth of the giant of wit, restraint and wisdom, Fry conveys the strain of a public figure tied to a false marriage (with Jennifer Ehle) while besieged by his love for another man (a bitingly excellent Jude Law as the rich and spoilt Lord Alfred Douglas). Assertive in its graphic exploration of male love, this may not suit all tastes, but is beautifully written with spot-on attention to period detail. LH Swearing, sex scenes, nudity. DVD Blu-ray

Stephen Fry *Oscar Wilde* • Jude Law *Lord Alfred Douglas* • Vanessa Redgrave *Lady Speranza Wilde* • Jennifer Ehle *Constance Wilde* • Gemma Jones *Lady Queensberry* • Judy Parfitt *Lady Mount-Temple* • Michael Sheen *Robert Ross* • Zoë Wanamaker *Ada Leverson* • Tom Wilkinson *Marquess of Queensberry* • Ioan Gruffudd *John Gray* ■ *Dir* Brian Gilbert • *Scr* Julian Mitchell, from the biography *Oscar Wilde* by Richard Ellman

Wilde Salomé ★★ 15
Drama documentary 2011 · US · Colour and BW · 95min

Directed by Al Pacino, this is a companion documentary to his *Salomé*, the filmed version of the powerful, no-frills 2006 theatre staging of the Oscar Wilde play. Part "making of" and part exploration of Pacino's obsession with Wilde, it's a solid but unsensational documentary, best watched in conjunction with *Salomé*... but not too closely in conjunction, for so extended are the extracts that, seen too closely together, you may feel you've just sat through the same film twice. DA Swearing, nudity.

Al Pacino *Al Pacino/King Herod* • Jessica Chastain *Salome* • Kevin Anderson *John the Baptist/Jokanaan* • Roxanne Hart *Herodias* • Estelle Parsons ■ *Dir* Al Pacino • *Scr* Al Pacino, from Oscar Wilde's play

Wilder ★★★ 18
Detective suspense thriller   2000 · Can · Colour · 88min

This pairing of Pam Grier and straight-to-video specialist Rutger Hauer doesn't promise great things, yet this is a tough, amusing and eventfully plotted police thriller. Grier is a formidable presence as a spirited Chicago cop unravelling a deep big business conspiracy with amiable doctor Hauer, the prime suspect in a murder investigation. Although the opening section suggests routine police procedural clichés, this develops into an enjoyable, funky thriller, with pleasing chemistry between the stars and a commendable balance of brutal action and light comedy. JC *DVD*

Pam Grier *Det Della Wilder* • Rutger Hauer *Dr Sam Charney* • Luccio Romano Orzari *Det Harlan Lee* • John Dunn-Hill *Capt Jerry Crandall* • Eugene Clark *Attorney Marlowe King* • Richard Robitaille *Ricky Harwell* ■ *Dir* Rodney Gibbons • *Scr* Terry Abrahamson

Wilder Napalm ★ 15
Comedy   1993 · US · Colour · 104min

Debra Winger stars in this lamentable comedy (to use the word in its loosest sense). She is caught up in the feud between brothers Dennis Quaid and Arliss Howard, who can't decide how best to exploit their fire-starting genius. It rapidly becomes almost unbearable to watch otherwise talented performers getting so badly burned. DP Violence, swearing, sex scenes.

Debra Winger *Vida* • Dennis Quaid *Wallace Foudroyant* • Arliss Howard *Wilder Foudroyant* • M Emmet Walsh *Fire chief* • Jim Varney *Rex* • Mimi Lieber *Snake lady* • Marvin J McIntyre *Deputy Sheriff Spivey* ■ *Dir* Glenn Gordon Caron • *Scr* Vince Gilligan

Wilderness ★★ 15
Horror   2006 · UK · Colour · 90min

A bunch of violent young offenders go on a team-building exercise to a deserted island in director Michael J Bassett's brutal survival horror. But far from enjoying a holiday from their harsh regime, the group comes under sustained attack from a malevolent figure who is seeking vicious vengeance for a past crime. Bassett efficiently orchestrates the carnage – involving nasty dog attacks, decapitation and man-traps – within the film's obvious *Lord of the Flies*-meets-*Deliverance* parameters. But it's predictable stuff, with inane dialogue and no room for sympathy or humour. AJ *DVD*

Toby Kebbell *Callum* • Sean Pertwee *Jed* • Alex Reid *Louise* • Ben McKay *Lindsay* • Stephen Wight *Steve* • Lenora Crichlow *Mandy* • Luke Neal *Lewis* • Karly Greene *Jo* ■ *Dir* Michael J Bassett • *Scr* Dario Poloni

The Wildest Dream ★★★ PG
Documentary   2009 · UK/US · Colour · 88min

British climber George Mallory's fatal 1924 attempt to conquer Everest is the subject of this variable documentary, in which US climber Conrad Anker, who discovered Mallory's body in 1999, retraces the route he took. He tests out replicas of Mallory's equipment and attempts to shed light on one of mountaineering's enduring mysteries: could Mallory and his partner Andrew "Sandy" Irvine have reached the summit decades before Edmund Hillary and Sherpa Tensing did in 1953? The photography is suitably spectacular but, despite a starry voice cast, the romantic element seems tacked on. AS *DVD* *BLU*

Liam Neeson *Narrator* • Ralph Fiennes *George Mallory* • Natasha Richardson *Ruth Mallory* • Hugh Dancy *Andrew "Sandy" Irvine* • Alan Rickman *Noel Odell* • Conrad Anker ■ *Dir* Anthony Geffen • *Scr* Mark Halliley

Wildflower ★★★ 15
Period drama   1991 · US · Colour · 90min

Directed by actress Diane Keaton, this moving TV drama is set in 1930s Georgia and follows the experiences of Patricia Arquette, a partially deaf epileptic imprisoned by her stepfather, who is convinced she is possessed by the Devil. Adapted by Sara Flanigan from her own book, this is subtly handled by Keaton, and her direction is complemented by involving performances. JB *DVD*

Patricia Arquette *Alice Guthrie* • Beau Bridges *Jack Perkins* • Susan Blakely *Ada Guthrie* • Reese Witherspoon *Ellie Perkins* • William McNamara *Sammy Perkins* ■ *Dir* Diane Keaton • *Scr* Sara Flanigan, from her non-fiction book *Alice*

Will ★★ PG
Drama   2011 · UK · Colour · 101min

This family-friendly story of a young football fan's solo trek to Turkey is not only corny, but unintentionally funny at times. However, the wide-eyed innocence of 11-year-old Will (Perry Eggleton, rather good) makes it hard to hate. He's a rabid Liverpool fan and over the moon when his estranged dad (Damian Lewis) secures tickets to see the team play in the 2005 Champions League final in Istanbul. Due to unforeseen circumstances, Will runs away to make the trip alone. But this isn't a tale of war zones or child slavers. Instead, you'll giggle at the helpfulness of folk that he meets, including a former Yugoslavian football star (Kristian Kiehling). DA

Damian Lewis *Gareth* • Bob Hoskins *Davey* • Kristian Kiehling *Alek* • Perry Eggleton *Will* • Alice Krige *Sister Carmel* • Brandon Robinson *Richie* ■ *Dir* Ellen Perry • *Scr* Zack Anderson, Ellen Perry

Will & Testament ★★★★ 12
Documentary   2014 · UK · Colour · 91min

Mention great postwar British parliamentarians and Tony Benn will probably be near the top of any list. A peer who famously renounced his title to become a Labour MP, he was controversial, forthright, the doughtiest of debaters, "the most dangerous man in Britain" according to the tabloids. Skip Kite's elegiac film is a scrapbook of the man's life (elegantly narrated by Benn shortly before his death) rather than the usual talking-heads documentary. Highly personal and poignant, it's a fabulous tribute to a formidable political personality. JA

Tony Benn ■ *Dir/Scr* Skip Kite

Will Any Gentleman...? ★★ U
Comedy   1953 · UK · Colour · 79min

Michael Anderson directs this over-literal adaptation of Vernon Sylvaine's stage success. However, even laying aside the clumsiness of much of the comedy, a fair proportion of modern viewers won't be particularly well disposed towards a story in which a hypnotist turns a timid bank clerk into a swaggering lothario. As the entranced enchanter, George Cole makes the most of his awkward charm, but his enthusiasm too often gets the better of him. DP *DVD*

George Cole *Henry Sterling* • Veronica Hurst *Mrs Sterling* • Jon Pertwee *Charlie Sterling* • James Hayter *Dr Smith* • Heather Thatcher *Mrs Whittle* • William Hartnell *Inspector Martin* • Sidney James *Mr Hobson* • Joan Sims *Beryl* ■ *Dir* Michael Anderson • *Scr* Vernon Sylvaine, from his play

Will It Snow for Christmas? ★★★ 12
Drama   1996 · Fr · Colour · 86min

Sandrine Veysett won a César for this, her directorial debut. It's an oblique, slow-moving tribute to farm labour and a universal commentary on the nature of dysfunctional family. Dominique Reymond is a mother with seven illegitimate children who rents and works a farm. Her life is punctuated by the periodic visits of her wayward lover, Daniel Duval. Married with a family elsewhere, he continues returning to bed Reymond. However, when Duval makes advances on their eldest daughter, Reymond is forced into making a crucial decision about their lives. LH French +subtitles.

Dominique Reymond *Mother* • Daniel Duval *Father* • Jessica Martinez *Jeanne* • Alexandre Roger *Bruno* • Xavier Colonna *Pierrot* • Fanny Rochetin *Marie* ■ *Dir/Scr* Sandrine Veysset

Will Penny ★★★★ 12
Western   1967 · US · Colour · 105min

Charlton Heston gives a fine performance as the grizzled lone rider of the title, confronting the memorable Joan Hackett and uncertain of how to break the tough habits of a lifetime: "I'm a cowboy. I don't know nuthin' else." Director Tom Gries never hit these heights again: this is one of the great westerns, invariably overlooked, and marred only by the florid performance of an ill-cast Donald Pleasence. The photography by Lucien Ballard is particularly outstanding, as is the fine score from David Raksin. TS Violence, swearing. *DVD*

Charlton Heston *Will Penny* • Joan Hackett *Catherine Allen* • Donald Pleasence *Preacher Quint* • Lee Majors *Blue* • Bruce Dern *Rafe Quint* • Ben Johnson (1) *Alex* • Slim Pickens *Ike Wallerstein* ■ *Dir/Scr* Tom Gries

Will Success Spoil Rock Hunter? ★★★ U
Satirical drama   1957 · US · Colour · 88min

Fresh from her Broadway success, Jayne Mansfield reprises her role as the pouting movie star with voluptuous glee in Frank Tashlin's film version of George Axelrod's hit play. However, it's Tony Randall, as the meek advertising agent who is forced to play the fame game to keep a prestigious lipstick account, who keeps this ambitious satire on track. Tashlin was never going to land all his punches, but this glossy, rather hollow enterprise, while very much a hit-and-miss affair, still has charm. DP *BLU*

Tony Randall *Rockwell Hunter* • Jayne Mansfield *Rita Marlowe* • Betsy Drake *Jenny* • Joan Blondell *Violet* • John Williams *Le Salle Jr* • Henry Jones *Rufus* • Lili Gentle *April* • Mickey Hargitay *Bobo* • Groucho Marx *Surprise guest* ■ *Dir* Frank Tashlin • *Scr* Frank Tashlin, from the play by George Axelrod

Willard ★★★
Horror   1971 · US · Colour · 95min

In this hugely successful story of violent vermin, oppressed office boy Bruce Davison turns the tables on his tormentors by training his two pet rats, Socrates and Ben, and their sewer pals, to attack on command. But when he neglects them after falling in love with Sondra Locke, hell hath no fury like rodents scorned! Solid direction by Daniel Mann and Davison's creepily introverted performance turned this horror revenge tale into a huge box-office hit. A sequel, *Ben*, followed. AJ

Bruce Davison *Willard Stiles* • Ernest Borgnine *Al Martin* • Elsa Lanchester *Henrietta Stiles* • Sondra Locke *Joan* • Michael Dante *Brandt* • Jody Gilbert *Charlotte Stassen* ■ *Dir* Daniel Mann • *Scr* Gilbert A Ralston, from the novel *Ratman's Notebooks* by Stephen Gilbert [Gilbert A Ralston]

Willard ★★★ 15
Horror   2003 · US · Colour · 96min

Hollywood eccentric Crispin Glover is perfectly cast in this quirky reinterpretation of the 1971 horror classic. All tics and emotional insecurities, he shines as the downtrodden office boy who uses his two pet rats and their furry pals to wreak violent revenge on his tormentors. The film is more gothic fantasy fable than outright chiller and, despite a sinister core, its childlike imagination and visual strangeness make the barbed tale as weird and whimsical as it is creepy. SF *DVD*

Crispin Glover *Willard* • R Lee Ermey *Mr Martin* • Laura Elena Harring [Laura Harring] *Catherine* • Jackie Burroughs *Mrs Stiles* • Kimberly Patton [Kim McKamy] *Ms Leach* • William S Taylor *Mr Garter* ■ *Dir* Glen Morgan • *Scr* Glen Morgan, from the film by Gilbert A Ralston, from the novel *Ratman's Notebooks* by Stephen Gilbert [Gilbert A Ralston]

William & Kate ★★ PG
Biographical romance   2011 · US/UK · Colour · 87min

Aiming to satisfy the appetites of royal watchers everywhere, this fictionalised and clearly inaccurate account of the relationship between Prince William and Kate Middleton stars New Zealander Nico Evers-Swindell and Berkshire-born Camilla Luddington as the royal couple. Ben Cross attempts Prince Charles's accent and mannerisms, but his lines are pure pantomime, and the central love affair is rather tepid with only the odd watchable moment. A shameless cash-in if ever there was one. SuR Some swearing, sexual references. *DVD*

Camilla Luddington *Kate Middleton* • Nico Evers-Swindell *Prince William* • Ben Cross *Prince Charles* • Justin Hanlon *Prince Harry* • Serena Scott Thomas *Carole Middleton* • Christopher Cousins *Mike Middleton* • Mary Elise Hayden *Pippa Middleton* ■ *Dir* Mark Rosman • *Scr* Nancey Silvers

William at the Circus ★★ U
Comedy   1948 · UK · BW · 92min

No devotee of Richmal Crompton's creation would be satisfied by a screen version of William. However, Val Guest captures a little of the exuberant antics of the original and William Graham is nicely cast as the ever questioning boy. His parents have promised him an outing to the circus – if he's good. Not the most likely of outcomes then. BB

William Graham *William Brown* • Garry Marsh *Mr Brown* • Jane Welsh *Mrs Brown* • AE Matthews *Minister* • Muriel Aked *Emily* • Hugh Cross *Robert Brown* • Kathleen Stuart *Ethel Brown* • Brian Roper *Ginger* ■ *Dir* Val Guest • *Scr* Val Guest, from the stories by Richmal Crompton

William Shakespeare's Romeo + Juliet ★★★★ 12
Romantic tragedy   1996 · US/Aus/Can · Colour · 115min

Baz Luhrmann's flamboyantly hip, achingly modern and unashamedly teen-targeted update of Shakespeare's enduring romantic tragedy relocates star-crossed lovers Leonardo DiCaprio and Claire Danes from 15th-century Italy to MTV-era "Verona Beach" – a place of gang warfare, raves, motorbikes and party drugs. The dialogue is true to the text, but delivered as if it were modern parlance, while the soundtrack (a mix of alt-rock, dance and orchestral) keeps the narrative pumping along. A closer cousin of *West Side Story* than Franco Zeffirelli's lush 1968 classic, it couldn't be more palatable to younger audiences, while Pete Postlethwaite, Paul Sorvino and Miriam Margoyles add adult thespian gravitas. It's a bold, infectious and courageous entry to the canon of Shakespeare adaptations. AC Some violence, a sex scene. *DVD* *BLU*

Leonardo DiCaprio *Romeo* • Claire Danes *Juliet* • Brian Dennehy *Ted Montague* • John Leguizamo *Tybalt* • Pete Postlethwaite *Father Laurence* • Paul Sorvino *Fulgencio Capulet* • Diane Venora *Gloria Capulet* • Harold Perrineau *Mercutio* • Paul Rudd *Dave Paris* • Jesse Bradford *Balthasar* • Dash Mihok *Benvolio* • Miriam Margoyles *Nurse* ■ *Dir* Baz Luhrmann • *Scr* Craig Pearce, Baz Luhrmann, from the play by William Shakespeare

William Shakespeare's The Merchant of Venice ★★★ PG
Period drama   2004 · UK/It · Colour · 126min

Al Pacino stars in this sumptuous production of one of the Bard's more controversial plays, which is often regarded as being anti-Semitic. As Jewish moneylender Shylock, Pacino gives a subtle performance, but he's obviously having to work hard just to keep up with Jeremy Irons's quietly noble merchant Antonio, whose flesh Shylock demands as recompense for an unpaid loan, and Lynn Collins's hugely impressive Portia. Michael Radford's direction is straightforward and unflashy, while the film benefits from shooting scenes on location in Venice itself. DA *DVD*

Al Pacino *Shylock* • Jeremy Irons *Antonio* • Lynn Collins *Portia* • Joseph Fiennes *Bassanio* • Zuleikha Robinson *Jessica* • Kris Marshall *Gratiano* • Charlie Cox *Lorenzo* • John Sessions *Salerio* • Mackenzie Crook *Lancelot Gobbo* ■ *Dir* Michael Radford • *Scr* Michael Radford, from the play by William Shakespeare

Willie and Phil ★★★ 18

Drama 1980 · US · Colour · 111min

Paul Mazursky was on a hiding to nothing when he embarked on this updating of François Truffaut's classic *Jules et Jim*. The *joie de vivre* that made the original so beguiling is clearly missing from this episodic drama that is more about Mazursky's perception of the 1970s than it is about the relationships between teacher Michael Ontkean, photographer Ray Sharkey and the girl they both love, Margot Kidder. The performances are fine considering the shallowness of all the characters, but the lifestyle satire has dated badly. DP Swearing, nudity.

Michael Ontkean *Willie Kaufman* • Margot Kidder *Jeanette Sutherland* • Ray Sharkey *Phil D'Amico* • Jan Miner *Mrs Kaufman* • Tom Brennan *Mr Kaufman* • Julie Bovasso *Mrs D'Amico* • Louis Guss *Mr D'Amico* • *Dir/Scr* Paul Mazursky

Willow ★★ PG

Fantasy adventure 1988 · US · Colour · 120min

This rare misfire from director Ron Howard takes too long mating the Saturday-morning-pictures wonderment of *Raiders* with the Tolkienesque elfin-twaddle of *Lord of the Rings*. Val Kilmer and Joanne Whalley look uncomfortable in this tale of a baby whose safekeeping will overthrow an evil empire. Forced, formulaic and sadly lacking in that sense of magic that's at the root of all successful fantasy. DA DVD

Val Kilmer *Madmartigan* • Joanne Whalley *Sorsha* • Warwick Davis *Willow Ufgood* • Jean Marsh *Queen Bavmorda* • Patricia Hayes *Fin Raziel* • Billy Barty *High Aldwin* • Pat Roach *General Kael* ■ *Dir* Ron Howard • *Scr* Bob Dolman, from a story by George Lucas

Willow Creek ★★★ 15

Horror 2013 · US · Colour · 79min

Comic-turned-director Bobcat Goldthwait spins the Bigfoot myth into a winning found-footage horror that also works as a sly commentary on the urban legend business. Amateur documentarian Bryce Johnson and his supportive if sceptical girlfriend, Alexie Gilmore, head to Willow Creek, California (where the famed 1967 film of the beast was shot) to hopefully capture Sasquatch on camera. The film is clearly influenced by *The Blair Witch Project*, but Goldthwait ratchets up the suspense in an eccentric mixture of reality and fiction that consistently engages against all odds. AJ Swearing. DVD

Alexie Gilmore *Kelly* • Bryce Johnson *Jim* ■ *Dir/Scr* Bobcat Goldthwait

Willy/Milly ★★★ 15

Comedy 1986 · US · Colour · 83min

Years before Hilary Swank produced her Oscar-winning cross-gender performance in *Boys Don't Cry*, Pamela Segall gave an equally sterling turn in *Willy/Milly*, albeit in a comedy. Segall is a girl who longs to be a boy and gets her wish (sort of) when she takes a magic potion during an eclipse. Overnight she develops an additional set of genitals. Segall then has to decide whether to spend her life as a girl or as a boy. Patty Duke Astin is good as the mother. DF

Pamela Segall *Milly/Willy* • Eric Gurry *Alfie* • Mary Tanner *Stephanie* • Patty Duke *Mrs Niceman* • John Glover *Mr Niceman* • Seth Green *Malcolm* • John David Cullum *Tom* • Jeb Ellis-Brown *Harry* ■ *Dir* Paul Schneider (1) • *Scr* Walter Carbone, Carla Reuben, from the story by Alan Friedman

Willy Wonka and the Chocolate Factory ★★★★ U

Fantasy 1971 · US · Colour · 99min

In this fabulous musical adaptation of Roald Dahl's evergreen story, Gene Wilder parks his buffoonish comic persona to bring a pinch of the macabre to the wide-eyed candy-maker. Dahl wrote the script and though he had misgivings about the finished film, this vibrant, imaginative fantasy still reveals a layer of grimness beneath the confection, despite tuneful ditties like *The Candy Man*, *Pure Imagination* and the Oompa-Loompa song. JA DVD BL

Gene Wilder *Willy Wonka* • Jack Albertson *Grandpa Joe* • Peter Ostrum *Charlie Bucket* • Michael Bollner *Augustus Gloop* • Ursula Reit *Mrs Gloop* • Denise Nickerson *Violet Beauregarde* • Leonard Stone *Mr Beauregarde* • Roy Kinnear *Mr Salt* ■ *Dir* Mel Stuart • *Scr* Roald Dahl, from his illustrated children's book *Charlie and the Chocolate Factory* • *Music/lyrics* Anthony Newley, Leslie Bricusse

Wilson ★★ U

Biographical drama 1944 · US · Colour · 153min

This was to be 20th Century-Fox chief Darryl F Zanuck's finest hour: he personally produced this lengthy biopic about Woodrow Wilson, America's 28th president, who founded the League of Nations. But, despite his idealism, the great man is a boring subject for a movie. Apart from winning five Oscars, the only thing really impressive about *Wilson* is that it was made at all. Alexander Knox is a resolutely uncharismatic lead, and, despite the award-winning Technicolor photography of Leon Shamroy, there's precious little to look at. TS

Alexander Knox *Woodrow Wilson* • Charles Coburn *Professor Henry Holmes* • Geraldine Fitzgerald *Edith Wilson* • Thomas Mitchell *Joseph Tumulty* • Ruth Nelson *Ellen Wilson* • Cedric Hardwicke *Henry Cabot Lodge* • Vincent Price *William G McAdoo* ■ *Dir* Henry King • *Scr* Lamar Trotti

Wilt ★★ 15

Comedy 1989 · UK · Colour · 88min

Tom Sharpe's brilliantly comic novel is about a liberal studies lecturer (Griff Rhys Jones) pursued for the murder of his wife (Alison Steadman) by police inspector Mel Smith, a copper incompetent enough to make Clouseau seem like Sherlock Holmes. The story kicks in with a hint of lesbianism, a life-sized sex doll and the kind of smut-tinged humour you might have thought British comedies had grown out of. Steadman and Rhys Jones make their characters as authentic as possible with an expertise missing in the rest of the film. TH Swearing, nudity. DVD

Griff Rhys Jones *Henry Wilt* • Mel Smith *Inspector Flint* • Alison Steadman *Eva Wilt* • Diana Quick *Sally* • Jeremy Clyde *Hugh* • Roger Allam *Dave* • David Ryall *Reverend Froude* • Roger Lloyd Pack *Dr Pittman* ■ *Dir* Michael Tuchner • *Scr* Andrew Marshall, David Renwick, from the novel by Tom Sharpe

Wimbledon ★★★ 12

Romantic sports comedy 2004 · US/UK/Fr · Colour · 93min

Paul Bettany takes on the role of a fading British tennis player who's facing his last Wimbledon but gets fuel-injected when he falls for US tennis prodigy Kirsten Dunst. Richard Loncraine's movie is great on the loser mentality of British sport, and the actual matches are thrillingly souped up by some decent CGI effects. However, away from tennis, this doesn't really nail either the comedic or romantic spots. It's amusing rather than hilarious, sweet as opposed to heartfelt; still, Bettany and Dunst have appealing charm. IF Swearing, brief nudity. DVD BL

Kirsten Dunst *Lizzie Bradbury* • Paul Bettany *Peter Colt* • Sam Neill *Dennis Bradbury* • Jon Favreau *Ron Roth* • Bernard Hill *Edward Colt* • Eleanor Bron *Augusta Colt* • Nikolaj Coster-Waldau *Dieter Prohl* • Austin Nichols *Jake Hammond* • Robert Lindsay *Ian Frazier* • James McAvoy *Carl Colt* • John McEnroe • Chris Evert ■ *Dir* Richard Loncraine • *Scr* Adam Brooks, Jennifer Flackett, Mark Levin • *Cinematographer* Darius Khondji

Win a Date with Tad Hamilton! ★★★ PG

Romantic comedy 2004 · US · Colour · 92min

This pleasing romantic comedy may break no new ground, but it treads old territory with surprising sweetness. Kate Bosworth plays a small-town supermarket checkout girl who enters a competition to win a date with dreamboat Hollywood superstar Tad (Josh Duhamel). And, of course, she wins, much to the chagrin of her co-worker Topher Grace, who's secretly in love with her. The star finds himself falling head over heels for the girl's simple charms. Next thing you know, he's off to Hicksville to woo and win her. Nicely underplayed, with likeably credible leads. DA Swearing. DVD

Kate Bosworth *Rosalee Futch* • Topher Grace *Pete Monash* • Josh Duhamel *Tad Hamilton* • Gary Cole *Henry Futch* • Ginnifer Goodwin *Cathy Feely* • Kathryn Hahn *Angelica* • Octavia Spencer *Janine* • Sean Hayes *Richard Levy the Shameless* • Nathan Lane *Richard Levy the Driven* • Amy Smart *Nurse* ■ *Dir* Robert Luketic • *Scr* Victor Levin

Win Win ★★★ 15

Comedy drama 2011 · US · Colour · 101min

Despite the title, Paul Giamatti plays another lovable loser in co-writer/director Tom McCarthy's comedy drama. He stars as Mike Flaherty, who coaches a hopeless school wrestling team while also running an unprofitable New Jersey legal practice. Flaherty seeks to improve his finances by offering to house an elderly client with dementia, only to put him in a home and collect the monthly benefit payments. While another actor might lose your sympathy, Giamatti effectively portrays the quiet desperation of a decent man on the edge, and it's his soul-searching turn that keeps you pinned to your seat. SP Swearing. DVD BL

Paul Giamatti *Mike Flaherty* • Amy Ryan *Jackie Flaherty* • Bobby Cannavale *Terry Delfino* • Jeffrey Tambor *Stephen Vigman* • Burt Young *Leo Poplar* • Melanie Lynskey *Cindy* ■ *Dir* Tom McCarthy [Thomas McCarthy] • *Scr* Tom McCarthy, from a story by McCarthy, Joe Tiboni

Winchester '73 ★★★★ U

Western 1950 · US · BW · 92min

The first of a marvellous series of movies pairing star James Stewart and director Anthony Mann, this western doesn't really tell the tale of "the gun that won the West". Instead, it focuses on the legendary "one in a thousand" perfect Winchester, first seen here as a prize in a Dodge City shooting contest where Will Geer, as Wyatt Earp, presides over sharpshooters Stewart and a brilliantly sneering Stephen McNally. This is a fine, mature work, creating a laconic new persona for the admirable Stewart. The brilliant black-and-white camerawork is by Garbo's favourite, William Daniels, and director Mann's use of transition (dissolves, fades to black) is exemplary. TS DVD

James Stewart *Lin McAdam* • Shelley Winters *Lola Manners* • Dan Duryea *Waco Johnny Dean* • Stephen McNally *Dutch Henry Brown* • Millard Mitchell *Johnny "High Spade" Williams* • Charles Drake *Steve Miller* • John McIntire *Joe Lamont* • Will Geer *Wyatt Earp* • Jay C Flippen *Sergeant Wilkes* • Rock Hudson *Young Bull* • Steve Brodie *Wesley* • Anthony Curtis [Tony Curtis] *Doan* ■ *Dir* Anthony Mann • *Scr* Robert L Richards, Borden Chase, from the story by Stuart N Lake • *Cinematographer* William Daniels (1)

Winchester '73 ★★★

Western 1967 · US · Colour · 97min

This remake of the 1950 James Stewart western was one of the first movies made for TV after the US networks began their concerted commissioning policy in the mid-1960s. While less accomplished than the original, the battle between brothers Tom Tryon and John Saxon for the rifle of the title still has its moments of drama. But what raises it above conveyor-belt TV fare are the supporting turns of veterans Joan Blondell and Dan Duryea (who featured in the Stewart version), as well as such B-movie stalwarts as Jack Lambert and John Hoyt. DP

Tom Tryon *Lin McAdam* • John Saxon *Dakin McAdam* • Dan Duryea *Bart McAdam* • John Drew Barrymore *Preacher* • Joan Blondell *Larouge* • John Dehner *High-Spade Johnny Dean* • Jack Lambert *Scots* • John Hoyt *Sunrider* ■ *Dir* Herschel Daugherty • *Scr* Richard L Adams, Stephen Kandel, from the 1950 film by Borden Chase, Robert L Richards

The Wind ★★★★★

Silent drama 1928 · US · BW · 94min

Swedish émigré Victor Sjöström made this stunning antidote to the western just prior to sound. In one of the greatest screen performances in history, Lillian Gish plays the fragile Virginian girl who heads for the Texas panhandle to share a wooden shack with her cousin and his family. Not only does she cause an emotional earthquake, the weather seems to conspire against her as well, resulting in a sandstorm of Biblical proportions. Filmed under the most arduous conditions in the Mojave Desert, the film is marred only by the unconvincing ending which was added when preview audiences found the original conclusion too bleak. AT

Lillian Gish *Letty* • Lars Hanson *Lige* • Montagu Love *Roddy Wirt* • Dorothy Cumming *Cora* • Edward Earle *Beverly* • William Orlamond *Sourdough* ■ *Dir* Victor Seastrom [Victor Sjöström] • *Scr* Frances Marion, from the novel by Dorothy Scarborough

Wind ★★ PG

Sports drama 1992 · US · Colour · 120min

Carroll Ballard brings his usual visual flair to this tale of ocean racing; it's just a shame the story is so hackneyed. Matthew Modine is the sailor, haunted by a mistake that cost his country the America's Cup, who gets another shot at wresting the trophy back from the Australians. While the story remains on water, Ballard doesn't put a foot wrong and there is some breathtaking racing footage; however, on dry land the clichéd film flounders. JF DVD

Matthew Modine *Will Parker* • Jennifer Grey *Kate Bass* • Cliff Robertson *Morgan Weld* • Jack Thompson *Jack Neville* • Stellan Skarsgård *Joe Heiser* • Rebecca Miller *Abigail Weld* • Ned Vaughn *Charley Moore* ■ *Dir* Carroll Ballard • *Scr* Rudy Wurlitzer, Mac Gudgeon, Larry Gross, from a story by Jeff Benjamin, Howard Chelsey, Kimball Livingston, Roger Vaughan

Wind across the Everglades ★★★

Period drama 1958 · US · Colour · 84min

A strange eco-melodrama, scripted by Budd Schulberg of *On the Waterfront* fame, this is about an alcoholic game warden intent on chasing poachers out of the swamps in turn-of-the-century Florida. Cult director Nicholas Ray fails to control his eclectic scenery-chewing cast, headed by Burl Ives and Christopher Plummer. Watch out, however, for a promising screen debut from Peter Falk. Despite its many faults, there are memorable moments in this unusual effort. TS DVD

Burl Ives *Cottonmouth* • Christopher Plummer *Walt Murdock* • Gypsy Rose Lee *Mrs Bradford* • George Voskovec *Aaron Nathanson* • Tony Galento *Beef* • Howard I Smith [Howard Smith] *George* • Emmett Kelly *Bigamy Bob* • Peter Falk *Writer* ■ *Dir* Nicholas Ray • *Scr* Budd Schulberg, from his story *Across the Everglades*

The Wind and the Lion ★★★★ PG

Period adventure 1975 · US · Colour · 113min

In this stunning desert adventure, Sean Connery stars as the Berber chieftain who kidnaps Candice Bergen (in a role intended for Katharine Hepburn) and incurs the wrath of US President Teddy Roosevelt, who sends the "big stick" into Morocco. This brilliant satire on colonialism, written and directed by John Milius, pays due tribute to such diverse movies as *Lawrence of Arabia* and the samurai epics and is both funny and thrilling. Add to this a soaring Jerry Goldsmith score and some marvellous locations and you have one of the most enjoyable movies of the 1970s. AT DVD

W

Sean Connery *Mulay El Raisuli* • Candice Bergen *Eden Pedecaris* • Brian Keith *Theodore Roosevelt* • John Huston *John Hay* • Geoffrey Lewis *Gummere* • Steve Kanaly *Captain Jerome* • Roy Jenson *Admiral Chadwick* • Vladek Sheybal *Bashaw* • Darrell Fetty *Dreighton* • Nadim Sawalha *Sherif of Wazan* ■ *Dir/Scr* John Milius

The Wind Cannot Read ★★ U

Second World War romantic drama
1958 · UK · Colour · 108min

Dirk Bogarde's fifth film in just over a year, as the Rank Organisation relentlessly paraded its biggest box-office attraction before an adoring public. But the strain shows in his tired portrayal of an RAF officer who falls for Japanese teacher Yoko Tani. Director Ralph Thomas certainly knows how to make the most of his star's looks and charm, and wrings every drop of sentiment out of this four-hankie weepie, but neither plot nor performances really convince. DP

Dirk Bogarde *Flight Lt Michael Quinn* • Yoko Tani *"Sabby" Suzuki San* • Ronald Lewis *Squadron Leader Fenwick* • John Fraser *Flying Olfficer Peter Munroe* • Anthony Bushell *Brigadier* • Henry Okawa *Lt Nakamura* • Marne Maitland *Bahadur* ■ *Dir* Ralph Thomas • *Scr* Richard Mason, from his novel

Wind Chill ★★★ 15

Horror thriller　2007 · US/UK · Colour · 87min

College student Emily Blunt gets a lot more than she bargained for when she accepts a ride home for Christmas from geeky outsiderAshton Holmes. They crash on a remote country road and an intense relationship develops between the pair as they're forced to brave both the harsh winter elements and a ghoulish legacy. Nasty cop Martin Donovan is the clue to their supernatural nightmare, yet the most disturbing chills come when Holmes reveals his stalker-like crush on Blunt. Director Gregory Jacobs (*Criminal*) uses the bleakest of landscapes to create some icy scares. Both actors give fine performances in what is basically a two-hander, etching a believable connection in the face of death. AJ **DVD**

Emily Blunt *Girl* • Ashton Holmes *Guy* • Martin Donovan *Highway patrolman* • Ned Bellamy *Snowplow driver* • Ian Wallace [Ian A Wallace] *Priest* • Chelan Simmons *Blonde girl* ■ *Dir* Gregory Jacobs • *Scr* Joe Gangemi, Steven Katz

The Wind in the Willows ★★ U

Adventure　1996 · UK · Colour · 83min

This clumsy live-action version of Kenneth Grahame's timeless classic by writer/director Terry Jones has captured little of the magic of the book. Jones's rendition of Toad is suitably ebullient, while fellow Python Eric Idle and Steve Coogan are pleasing enough as Rat and Mole. However, the addition of a dog-meat factory subplot to supplement Toad's brushes with the law is a major misjudgement, as is the decision to pack the supporting cast with cameoing celebrities. Not as much fun as it should be. DP **DVD**

Steve Coogan *Mole* • Eric Idle *Rat* • Terry Jones *Toad* • Antony Sher *Chief Weasel* • Nicol Williamson *Badger* • John Cleese *Mr Toad's lawyer* • Stephen Fry *Judge* • Bernard Hill *Engine driver* • Michael Palin *The Sun* • Nigel Planer *Car salesman* • Julia Sawalha *Jailer's daughter* • Victoria Wood *Tea lady* ■ *Dir* Terry Jones • *Scr* Terry Jones, from the novel by Kenneth Grahame

The Wind of Change ★★ 12

Crime drama　1961 · UK · BW · 61min

Vernon Sewell's attempt at depicting gang racial hatred and its effect on a family fails mainly because of its overly simplistic approach to a complex problem. Donald Pleasence appears in an unusual role as the father of a troubled gang teenager, who is played by none other than a young Johnny Briggs, who became better known as Mike Baldwin of *Coronation Street*. NF **DVD**

Donald Pleasence *Pop* • Johnny Briggs *Frank* • Antonita Dias *Sylvia* • Ann Lynn *Josie* • Hilda Fenemore *Gladys* • Glyn Houston *Sgt Parker* • Norman Gunn Ron • Bunny May *Smithy* • David Hemmings *Ginger* ■ *Dir* Vernon Sewell • *Scr* Alexander Doré, John McLaren

The Wind Rises ★★★ PG

Animated wartime drama
2013 · Jpn · Colour · 126min

A boy who dreams of flight grows up to become an aircraft designer in acclaimed Japanese animator Hayao Miyazaki's Oscar-nominated movie. It's based on the life of Jiro Horikoshi, designer of the Mitsubishi A6M Zero, who is presented as a dreamer (which doesn't sit too well with the film's later scenes of wartime devastation). But older viewers and fans will be enchanted by this modest entry in Miyazaki's canon and appreciate the more personal elements of what he has declared to be his final film. DW Japanese, German, Italian dubbed.

Joseph Gordon-Levitt *Jiro Horikoshi* • John Krasinski *Honjo* • Emily Blunt *Nahoko Satomi* • Martin Short *Kurokawa* • Stanley Tucci *Caproni* • Mandy Patinkin *Hattori* ■ *Dir* Hayao Miyazaki • *Scr* Hayao Miyazaki, from his comic book

The Wind That Shakes the Barley ★★★ 15

Historical drama
2006 · UK/Ire/Ger/It/Sp/Swi · Colour · 121min

Ken Loach and regular writer Paul Laverty tackle the Irish Question with passion in their surprise Cannes Palme d'Or winner. It's 1920 and Cillian Murphy is set to take up a post as a doctor in London. However British military atrocities force him to reconsider his priorities, and he opts to join the Republican movement. Loach approaches the action sequences with gusto, but politics are never far away, and a lengthy debate about the merits of the Anglo-Irish Treaty is a prelude to an awkward third act. What should be an emotionally devastating climax is diluted by mixed sympathies and ambiguity over what the director is trying to say. BP **DVD**

Cillian Murphy *Damien* • Liam Cunningham *Dan* • Padraic Delaney *Teddy* • Orla Fitzgerald *Sinead* • Mary Riordan *Peggy* • Mary Murphy (2) *Bernadette* • Laurence Barry *Micheail* • Gerard Kearney *Donacha* • Damien Kearney *Finbar* • William Ruane *Gogan* ■ *Dir* Ken Loach • *Scr* Paul Laverty

The Wind Will Carry Us ★★★★ U

Drama　1999 · Fr/Iran · Colour · 113min

A stranger arrives in a Kurdish village on a mission he conducts with eccentric secrecy. The winner of the Golden Lion at Venice, Abbas Kiarostami's enigmatic anti-drama challenges the spectator to speculate about withheld information and, thus, to play an active role in the action unfolding before a distant, largely static camera. Melding character and location, he maintains an emotional detachment in passing subtle social comment on the suppression of all things beautiful and the indolence of the intelligentsia. A masterly film from a cinematic original. DP Farsi +subtitles. **DVD**

Behzad Dourani *Engineer* ■ *Dir* Abbas Kiarostami • *Scr* Abbas Kiarostami, from an idea by Mahmoud Ayedin • *Editor* Abbas Kiarostami

Wind with the Gone ★★★★

Surreal comedy drama
1998 · Sp/Fr/Arg/Neth · Colour · 90min

Set in a small village in Patagonia, Alejandro Agresti's fable is filled with lovable eccentrics, from the scientist whose inventions already have patents, to the cinema projectionist who keeps showing films in the wrong order – which goes some way to explaining this isolated community's cockamamie worldview. However, everything changes with the arrival of two unsuspecting intruders, Buenos Aires cab-driver Vera Fogwill, and fading French movie-star, Jean Rochefort. Testament to the enduring power of cinema, this is

deliciously eccentric, yet cuttingly acute. DP Spanish +subtitles.

Vera Fogwill *Soledad* • Angela Molina *Dona Maria* • Fabian Vena *Pedro* • Jean Rochefort *Edgar Wexley* • Ulises Dumont *Antonio* • Carlos Roffe *Amalfi* ■ *Dir/Scr* Alejandro Agresti

Windbag the Sailor ★★★ U

Comedy　1936 · UK · BW · 81min

Even though he had a hand in the script, Will Hay is a shade below par in this patchy comedy that is significant only for his first teaming with those much loved stooges Moore Marriott and Graham Moffatt. After a promising start, the film is all too quickly blown off course once we're at sea, before finally running aground. Yet Hay's always watchable and still raises a few chuckles as a blustering sea dog whose bluff is called by a crooked tycoon bent on scuttling his ship for the insurance. DP **DVD**

Will Hay *Capt Ben Cutlet* • Moore Marriott *Jeremiah Harbottle* • Graham Moffatt *Albert* • Norma Varden *Olivia Potter-Porter* • Dennis Wyndham *Maryatt* ■ *Dir* William Beaudine • *Scr* Marriott Edgar, Will Hay, Stafford Dickens, Robert Edmunds, Val Guest, from a story by Robert Stevenson, Leslie Arliss

Windom's Way ★★★★ PG

Drama　1957 · UK · Colour · 103min

This neglected gem stars a charismatic Peter Finch at the height of his heart-throb powers. He plays Alec Windom, a doctor full of confident dedication, toiling away in a remote Malayan village and helping the locals to resist a rebellious takeover. It's a very powerful, tightly directed film with some stunning supporting performances. What could have been a cliché-ridden outing and a one-man demonstration of star ego emerges as a simply great movie. SH **DVD**

Peter Finch *Dr Alec Windom* • Mary Ure *Lee Windom* • Michael Hordern *Patterson* • Natasha Parry *Anna* • John Cairney *Jan Vidal* • Robert Flemyng *George Hasbrook* ■ *Dir* Ronald Neame • *Scr* Jill Craigie, from the novel by James Ramsey Ullman

The Window ★★★★

Thriller　1949 · US · BW · 73min

In this superior B-movie, based on Cornell Woolrich's short novel, a youngster (the excellent Bobby Driscoll) witnesses a killing but can't get anyone to take him seriously because he has a reputation for telling tales. Despite its age-old plot, this film made a huge impression on audiences of the day, and has since been relentlessly rehashed and remade. The adults are well cast, while Driscoll was awarded a special miniature Oscar for his performance. TS

Barbara Hale *Mrs Woodry* • Arthur Kennedy *Mr Woodry* • Bobby Driscoll *Tommy Woodry* • Paul Stewart *Mr Kellerton* • Ruth Roman *Mrs Kellerton* • Anthony Ross *Ross* ■ *Dir* Ted Tetzlaff • *Scr* Mel Dinelli, from the novelette *The Boy Cried Murder* by Cornell Woolrich

A Window in London ★★★

Thriller　1939 · UK · BW · 76min

From the window of a train, Michael Redgrave sees what appears to be somebody strangling a woman in a house. He goes to the police, but the couple in question (Paul Lukas, Sally Gray) turn out to be an illusionist and his wife rehearsing their act. Some weeks later, Redgrave and his wife (Patricia Roc), again from a train, witness a repeat performance of the incident. A short, modest but intriguing thriller which offers a good cast and a satisfyingly neat twist. RK

Michael Redgrave *Peter Thompson* • Sally Gray *Vivienne* • Paul Lukas *Louis Zoltini* • Hartley Power *Max Preston* • Patricia Roc *Pat Thompson* • Glen Alyn *Andrea* ■ *Dir* Herbert Mason • *Scr* Ian Dalrymple, Brigid Cooper, from the story *Metropolitain* by Herbert Maret

Windprints ★★★ 15

Political crime drama 1989 · UK · Colour · 95min

Set in Namibia during the apartheid regime, David Wicht's drama approaches this complexities of southern African politics from a white liberal, rather than a rebel,

perspective. Sent to track down a notoriously elusive killer (played by Lesley Fong), Sean Bean's Afrikaner cameraman is caught between ethnic loyalty and professional ethics, as he comes to suspect that Fong is in league with Marius Weyers's supremacist landowner. DP

John Hurt *Charles Rutherford* • Sean Bean *Anton Van Heerden* • Marius Weyers *Henning* • Eric Nobbs *"Platvoet" Du Plessis* • Lesley Fong *Nhadiep* ■ *Dir/Scr* David Wicht

Windrider ★★★ 15

Romantic drama　1986 · Aus · Colour · 88min

Buried beneath a mass of curly hair, Nicole Kidman is suitably perky as the pop singer pursued by beach bum Tom Burlinson, who needs her to tell his mates that she witnessed his perfect 360-degree surf turn. The usual round of squabbles and misunderstandings ensues, with former cinematographer Vincent Monton demonstrating a good grasp of soundbite storytelling. DP Swearing, sex scenes.

Tom Burlinson *PC Simpson* • Nicole Kidman *Jade* • Charles Tingwell *Simpson Sr* • Jill Perryman *Miss Dodge* ■ *Dir* Vincent Monton • *Scr* Everett De Roche, Bonnie Harris

Winds of the Wasteland ★★ U

Western　1936 · US · Colour · 53min

John Wayne stars in this pre-*Stagecoach* B-western. He is a Pony Express rider put out of work by the arrival of the telegraph. Wayne competes for a new government mail-hauling contract against the dirty tricks of Douglas Cosgrove's stage line owner. Attractive scenery, a friendly skunk and a brief running time are in its favour. AE **DVD**

John Wayne *John Blair* • Phyllis Fraser *Barbara Forsythe* • Douglas Cosgrove *Cal Drake* • Lane Chandler *Larry Adams* • Sam Flint *Dr William Forsythe* • Lew Kelly *Rocky O'Brien* ■ *Dir* Mack V Wright • *Scr* Joseph Poland

Windtalkers ★★ 15

Second World War action drama
2001 · US · Colour · 128min

John Woo's booming and bloody drama had the potential for a fresh perspective on the war epic, chronicling the real-life contribution of native Americans, responsible for a military code that couldn't be cracked by the Japanese. Yet this is explored with the heaviest of hands, as the nicely performed relationship between genial Navajo Adam Beach and cynical sergeant Nicolas Cage is buried beneath a barrage of explosions and melodramatic skirmishes. JC Violence, swearing. **DVD** **Blu-ray**

Nicolas Cage *Joe F Enders* • Adam Beach *Ben Yahzee* • Christian Slater *Pete "Ox" Anderson* • Peter Stormare *Gunnery Sergeant Hjelmstad* • Noah Emmerich *Chick* • Mark Ruffalo *Pappas* ■ *Dir* John Woo • *Scr* John Rice, Joe Batteer

Windwalker ★★★★

Western　1980 · US · Colour · 108min

Trevor Howard is the only star in this ground-breaking independent movie by director Kieth Merrill. He plays a Cheyenne chief recounting his life story on his deathbed, including how his wife was killed and one of his twin sons kidnapped by enemy Crow Indians. Set before the forked-tongued white man took over, this stunningly shot drama uses English subtitles for the Crow and Cheyenne dialogue spoken by the amateur cast. TH In English, Crow, Cheyenne.

Trevor Howard *Windwalker* • Nick Ramus *Narration* • James Remar *Windwalker, as a young man* • Serene Hedin *Tashina* • Dusty "Iron Wing" McCrea *Dancing Moon* • Silvana Gallardo *Little Feather* • Billy Drago *Crow Scout* • Rudy Diaz *Crow Eyes* ■ *Dir* Kieth Merrill • *Scr* Ray Goldrup, from a novel by Blaine M Yorgason

Windy City ★★★ 15

Romantic drama　1984 · US · Colour · 102min

Yuppies are caught on the downbeat in a world where heartbreak and disillusion are happy bedfellows. John Shea, Kate

Capshaw and Josh Mostel look back in regretful nostalgia as a marriage and illness threaten to alter their friendship. Director Armyan Bernstein makes it moody and melancholy and Shea gives a moving portrayal of a man about to lose everything. TH

John Shea *Danny Morgan* • Kate Capshaw *Emily Ruebens* • Josh Mostel *Sol* • Jim Borrelli *Mickey* • Jeffrey DeMunn *Bobby* • Eric Pierpoint *Pete* ■ *Dir/Scr* Armyan Bernstein

Wing and a Prayer ★★★PG

Second World War drama
1944 · US · BW · 93min

Don Ameche (familiar as the septuagenarian from *Cocoon*) is here seen in an earlier incarnation as a versatile leading man in the 1930s and 40s. He plays the stern commander on a Pacific-bound aircraft carrier, leading Dana Andrews and fellow US Navy pilots in a plot to lure the Japanese just prior to the Battle of Midway. It's rousing stuff, directed with an accent on joshing camaraderie and an eye for operational detail by Henry Hathaway. SuR DVD

Don Ameche *Flight Commander Bingo Harper* • Dana Andrews *Squadron Commander Edward Moulton* • William Eythe *Oscar Scott* • Charles Bickford *Captain Waddell* • Cedric Hardwicke *Admiral* • Kevin O'Shea *Cookie Cunningham* • Richard Jaeckel *Beezy Bessemer* ■ *Dir* Henry Hathaway • *Scr* Jerome Cady, from his story

Wing Commander ★PG

Science-fiction action drama
1999 · US · Colour · 96min

Based on a popular computer game, this movie plays like a pale rip-off of *Star Wars*. Most of the Gen-X actors playing pilots are atrocious and neither the game's space battles, nor its fun feline aliens – who have been drained of all their personality and now look like seals – are well transposed. ST Swearing. DVD

Freddie Prinze Jr *Christopher " Maverick" Blair* • Matthew Lillard *Todd "Maniac" Marshall* • Saffron Burrows *Jeanette "Angel" Deveraux* • Jürgen Prochnow *Commander Gerald* • Tcheky Karyo *Commander James "Paladin" Taggart* • David Warner *Admiral Geoffrey Tolwyn* • David Suchet *Captain Sansky* • Ginny Holder *Rosie Forbes* ■ *Dir* Chris Roberts • *Scr* Kevin Droney, from characters by Chris Roberts, from the computer game by Electronic Arts

Winged Migration ★★★★U

Documentary
2001 · Fr/Ger/Sp/It/Swi · Colour · 85min

The production statistics for Jacques Perrin's visually stunning avian documentary speak for themselves. Five film crews comprising 14 cinematographers and 17 aircraft pilots laboured for three years following dozens of species of birds as they made their lengthy seasonal journeys. What emerges is a breathtaking visual experience, with shot after seemingly impossible shot of birds in flight: to achieve this the crew raised some of the birds to be oblivious to aircraft noise. Sadly a pretentious, uninformative commentary and a truly noxious new-age soundtrack intrude on the exquisite images occasionally, but they only slightly spoil what is an otherwise astonishing piece of lyrical film-making. AS In English, French. DVD

Jacques Perrin *Narrator* ■ *Dir* Jacques Perrin, Jacques Cluzaud, Michel Debats • *Scr* Stéphane Durand, Jacques Perrin, from an idea by Valentine Perrin

Winged Victory ★★U

Second World War drama
1944 · US · BW · 130min

George Cukor's contribution to the war effort is about the training of fighter pilots with a pathetic leading man (Lon McCallister), a pretty but vacuous heroine (Jeanne Crain) and an interesting supporting cast. With the full resources of the Army Air Force at his disposal, Cukor revelled in his power: "All I had to say was, it would be nice to have some movement in the background and next thing there were hundreds of men, planes landing and taking off. But the story was silly, full of patriotism and nothing else." AT

Lon McCallister *Frankie Davis* • Jeanne Crain *Helen* • Edmond O'Brien *Irving Miller* • Jane Ball *Jane Preston* • Judy Holliday *Ruth Miller* ■ *Dir* George Cukor • *Scr* Moss Hart, from his play

Wings ★★★PG

Silent war drama
1927 · US · BW · 142min

Winner of the very first best picture Oscar, this silent epic about fighter pilots in the First World War is still exciting aloft but terribly sentimental and cliché-ridden on the ground. The director, William A "Wild Bill" Wellman, had himself been a highly decorated fighter pilot with the Lafayette Flying Corps, so he brought to the project much of his own experience, giving the thrilling action sequences their excitement and veracity. But the story – devised by former pilot John Monk Saunders – switches between a lame love affair and the friendship between two pilots who join up together. AT DVD

Clara Bow *Mary Preston* • Charles "Buddy" Rogers *Jack Powell* • Richard Arlen *David Armstrong* • Jobyna Ralston *Sylvia Lewis* • Gary Cooper *Cadet White* • Arlette Marchal *Celeste* • El Brendel *Patrick O'Brien* • Hedda Hopper *Mrs Powell* ■ *Dir* William A Wellman • *Scr* Hope Loring, Louis D Lighton, from a story by John Monk Saunders

Wings in the Dark ★★★

Romantic drama
1935 · US · BW · 68min

The wings are those of flier Cary Grant's plane, the dark is the fact that he has been blinded in an accident but nonetheless manages to pilot his aircraft to the rescue when his stunt-flier girlfriend gets into trouble during her Moscow to New York run. She, incredibly, is Myrna Loy, who was borrowed from MGM by Paramount for what one would expect to be a romantic comedy but is in fact a romantic drama. Bizarre casting and an unbelievable storyline, but played with such conviction and polish by its two gleaming stars under the well-judged direction of James Flood that it's easy to suspend disbelief. RK

Myrna Loy *Sheila Mason* • Cary Grant *Ken Gordon* • Roscoe Karns *Nick Williams* • Hobart Cavanaugh *Mac* • Dean Jagger *Tops Harmon* • Russell Hopton *Jake Brasheer* ■ *Dir* James Flood • *Scr* Jack Kirkland, Frank Partos, from the story *Eyes of the Eagle* by Nell Shipman, Philip D Hurn, adapted by Dale Van Every, EH Robinson

Wings of Desire ★★★★12

Fantasy drama
1987 · W Ger · Colour and BW · 122min

Wim Wenders's elegiac fantasy is shot in crisp, sepia-tinged monochrome (and at key points, warm colour) around an austere, brutalist West Berlin, where angels Bruno Ganz and Otto Sander move about the city – invisible, eternal observers of everyday lives. They listen beatifically in on people's thoughts, including those of an elderly poet, a lonely circus performer (Solveig Dommartin) and a suicidal young man on a factory roof, their inability to intervene eventually causing a crisis of conscience for Ganz. Peter Falk appears as a tactile, English-speaking ex-angel researching the past, but the cumulative, atmospheric and philosophical whole is more important than individual narratives. Achingly trendy at the time, not least for the contributions of suitably gothic musician Nick Cave, it abides as an important meditative document from the time of the Berlin Wall. AC German +subtitles. DVD

Bruno Ganz *Damiel* • Solveig Dommartin *Marion* • Otto Sander *Cassiel* • Curt Bois *Homer* • Peter Falk ■ *Dir* Wim Wenders • *Scr* Wim Wenders, Peter Handke, Richard Reitinger • *Cinematographer* Henri Alekan

The Wings of Eagles ★★★U

Biographical drama
1957 · US · Colour · 105min

This is a ramshackle but enjoyable biopic of tragic screenwriter/flying ace Frank "Spig" Wead. A strangely subdued John Wayne plays Wead, actually appearing in the later scenes without his characteristic toupee. Dan Dailey is fun as Wead's buddy, but Maureen O'Hara is wasted with little more than two good scenes as the navy wife. The film's greatest delight is Ward Bond as movie director "John Dodge", in other words, John Ford, (Ford's study was authentically duplicated here using real props, including his Oscars). But there's a smug feel to the whole piece. TS

John Wayne *Frank W "Spig" Wead* • Maureen O'Hara *Minnie Wead* • Dan Dailey *"Jughead" Carson* • Ward Bond *John Dodge* • Ken Curtis *John Dale Price* • Edmund Lowe *Admiral Moffett* • Kenneth Tobey *Captain Herbert Allen Hazard* • James Todd *Jack Travis* ■ *Dir* John Ford • *Scr* Frank Fenton, William Wister Haines, from the life and writings of Commander Frank W Wead USN and the biography *Wings of Men*

Wings of Fame ★★15

Fantasy
1990 · Neth · Colour · 109min

In this fantasy tale, spirits of the dead end up at a huge offshore hotel, a sort of halfway house for the famous. Peter O'Toole is a movie star, murdered by writer Colin Firth, who himself has died in an accident. The pair meet at the hotel and talk about what happened and why. And, oh yes, Albert Einstein, the kidnapped Lindbergh child and even Lassie are there as well. It's Agatha Christie meets *Last Year in Marienbad*. The performances have some gusto, but it's very weird indeed. AT Swearing, nudity.

Peter O'Toole *Valentin* • Colin Firth *Smith* • Marie Trintignant *Bianca* • Andréa Ferréol *Theresa* • Maria Becker *Dr Frisch* • Gottfried John *Zlatogorski* ■ *Dir* Otakar Votocek • *Scr* Otakar Votocek, Herman Koch

The Wings of Honneamise ★★★★15

Animated adventure 1987 · Jpn · Colour · 119min

Made the year before *Akira* introduced western audiences to the *anime* movies based on Japanese *manga* comics, this is one of the most costly examples. Yet the budget has clearly been well spent, with a superb Ryuichi Sakamoto score, the feuding nations convincingly futuristic and the camera movements and lighting effects worthy of a Hollywood blockbuster. But, although our hero is a member of the Royal Space Force, his journey is more one of self-discovery than all-conquering bravado. For all his ingenuity, 23-year-old writer/director Hiroyuki Yamaga overdoes the religious symbolism, while revealing a political naivety akin to his hero's. A a classic of its kind. DP Japanese +subtitles. Violence.

■ *Dir/Scr* Hiroyuki Yamaga • *Music* Ryuichi Sakamoto • *Art Director* Hiromasa Ogura

Wings of the Apache ★★15

Action drama
1990 · US · Colour · 83min

Nicolas Cage's heart doesn't seem to be in his role of a maverick helicopter pilot, while Sean Young is even less convincing as a fellow flier/former girlfriend. In the end, it is left to the reliable Tommy Lee Jones to mop up the acting honours as the hard-nosed commander preparing his troops for the war against the drug dealers. JF Swearing, violence. DVD

Nicolas Cage *Jake Preston* • Tommy Lee Jones *Brad Little* • Sean Young *Billie Lee Guthrie* • Bryan Kestner *Breaker* • Dale Dye *AK McNeil* • Mary Ellen Trainor *Janet Little* • JA Preston *General Olcott* • Peter Onorati *Rice* ■ *Dir* David Green • *Scr* Nick Thiel, Paul F Edwards, from a story by Step Tyner, John K Swensson, Dale Dye

The Wings of the Dove ★★★★15

Period romantic drama
1997 · US · Colour · 97min

Newcomer Hossein Amini was Oscar nominated for his adaptation of one of Henry James's most difficult novels, and director Iain Softley also succeeds in doing James justice in this visually arresting, lyrical and dark film. Helena Bonham Carter gives her best performance to date as a modern miss who encourages her rough lover Linus Roache to fall for dying heiress Alison Elliott. The friendship that develops between the women and the genuine love that Elliott arouses in Roache complicate the callous scheme and threaten to destroy them all. LH Sex scenes, nudity. DVD BL

Helena Bonham Carter *Kate Croy* • Linus Roache *Merton Densher* • Alison Elliott (2) *Millie Theale* • Charlotte Rampling *Aunt Maude* • Elizabeth McGovern *Susan Stringham* • Michael Gambon *Lionel Croy* • Alex Jennings *Lord Mark* ■ *Dir* Iain Softley • *Scr* Hossein Amini, from the novel by Henry James

Wings of the Morning ★★★

Romantic sports drama
1937 · UK · Colour · 87min

Henry Fonda and Annabella co-star with beautiful soft-toned colour, lush Irish and English scenery and a racehorse in Britain's first Technicolor feature. A prologue set in the 1890s has Irish aristocrat Leslie Banks defying convention to marry beautiful Spanish gypsy Annabella. After his death in a riding accident, she goes back to Spain, returning many years later (and played by Irene Vanbrugh) with her granddaughter (who Annabella now plays) and a horse to train for the Derby. Initially disguised as a boy, Annabella meets Canadian race trainer Fonda and both fall in love. Gentle and charming. RK

Annabella *Maria/Marie* • Henry Fonda *Kerry Gilfallen* • Stewart Rome *Sir Valentine MacFarland* • Irene Vanbrugh *Marie* • Harry Tate *Paddy* • Helen Haye *Jenepher* • Leslie Banks *Lord Clontarf* ■ *Scr* Tom Geraghty, from short stories by Donn Byrne

The Winner ★★★15

Black comedy thriller
1996 · US/Aus · Colour · 87min

One of the more coherent films from the maverick independent director Alex Cox, of *Sid and Nancy* fame. Vincent D'Onofrio plays a Las Vegas man who can't lose. Rebecca DeMornay, Billy Bob Thornton and Michael Madsen are among the losers who latch on to him, in the hope of grabbing a share of his pot. A strange little story, nicely played and compellingly told. DA Swearing, violence.

Vincent D'Onofrio *Philip* • Richard Edson *Frankie* • Saverio Guerra *Paulie* • Delroy Lindo *Kingman* • Michael Madsen *Wolf* • Billy Bob Thornton *Jack* • Frank Whaley *Joey* • Alex Cox *Gaston* ■ *Dir* Alex Cox • *Scr* Wendy Riss, from her play *A Darker Purpose*

A Winner Never Quits ★★★

Sports drama based on a true story
1986 · US · Colour · 96min

Keith Carradine impresses as one-armed 1940s baseball star Pete Gray in this no-frills fictionalisation of the US sporting hero's life and career. Capturing the obstinacy and resilience of Grey's relentlessly driven character, Carradine fittingly elicits admiration and never sympathy, as Grey fights prejudice and ridicule to overcome his disability and gradually achieve his dream of major league success. It's an inspiring story, unsentimentally told, but underwhelming baseball scenes dilute the impact of some key moments. SF

Keith Carradine *Pete Gray* • Mare Winningham *Annie* • Huckleberry Fox *Nelson Gary Jr* • Ed O'Neill *Whitey Wyshner* • Dennis Weaver *Mr Wyshner* • Fionnula Flanagan *Mrs Wyshner* ■ *Dir* Mel Damski • *Scr* Burt Prelutsky

Winnie the Pooh ★★★U

Animated comedy 2011 · US · Colour · 60min

Disney revisits an old favourite for a new generation of youngsters with this, the first big-screen outing in 35 years for AA Milne's most famous creation. And a real honey this Winnie is, too: bright, breezy and blissfully 2D. It's narrated by John Cleese and the voice cast is led by Jim Cummings, who has provided the voices of Pooh and Tigger on video and DVD since 1990. However, at barely an hour long, perhaps it doesn't represent the best value in moviegoing money. Still, it's thoroughly traditional and, like Pooh himself, it's warm, whimsical - and short. DA DVD CS

W

Jim Cummings *Pooh/Tigger* • Craig Ferguson *Owl* • Tom Kenny *Rabbit* • John Cleese *Narrator* • Bud Luckey *Eeyore* • Travis Oates *Piglet* ■ *Dir* Stephen J Anderson, Don Hall (2) • *Scr* From stories by AA Milne

Winnie the Pooh: Springtime with Roo ★★U
Animated adventure 2004 · US · Colour · 62min

Rabbit and Roo learn a few things about fun and friendship in this cute but over-stretched Disney adventure for undiscerning pre-schoolers. Simply animated in attractive candy colours, the made-for-DVD tale sees the uptight bunny upset his young kangaroo pal by cancelling the Hundred Acre Wood's annual Easter egg hunt in favour of spring cleaning. One massive life lesson follows, as Tigger and the soothingly voiced Narrator (David Ogden Stiers) show crabby Rabbit the error of his ways in *A Christmas Carol*-style visits to the past and the future. Gentle humour – including a sly Dickens reference – and a stream of sweetly silly songs maintain the lively pace, while padding out the slight plotline that celebrates the traditional holiday's social, rather than religious, significance. SF **DVD**

Jim Cummings *Winnie the Pooh/Tigger* • Ken Sansom *Rabbit* • Jimmy Bennett *Roo* • David Ogden Stiers *Narrator* • Kath Soucie *Kanga* • John Fiedler *Piglet* ■ *Dir* Saul Andrew Blinkoff, Elliot M Bour • *Scr* Tom Rogers, based on characters by AA Milne

Winnie the Pooh's Most Grand Adventure ★★U
Animated adventure 1997 · US · Colour · 72min

As *The Tigger Movie* proved, searching is what the residents of the Hundred Acre Wood do best. The end of this quest is Christopher Robin, who doesn't have the heart to tell Pooh he is off to school, so leaves a note that the bear of little brain interprets as a plea for help. Devotees of the original Disney cartoons will probably mourn the absence of Kanga and Roo and will find the songs as trite as the story's theme of self-reliance. DP **DVD**

Jim Cummings *Winnie the Pooh/Skullasaurus* • John Fiedler *Piglet* • Ken Sansom *Rabbit* • Andre Stojka *Owl* • Peter Cullen *Eeyore* • Brady Bluhm *Christopher Robin* • Paul Winchell *Tigger* • David Warner *Narrator* ■ *Dir* Karl Geurs • *Scr* Karl Geurs, Carter Crocker, from characters by AA Milne

Winning ★★★PG
Motor racing drama 1969 · US · Colour · 117min

Paul Newman and Steve McQueen, the two biggest male stars of the 1960s, loved to race cars in their spare time and both made their own motor-racing movies. Newman's was *Winning*, followed two years later by McQueen's *Le Mans*. Both were flops because no one had figured out what to do with the cast during pit stops, but this is the better movie. Newman plays a driver who values racing more than his wife (Joanne Woodward), and stepson (callow Richard Thomas), and Robert Wagner is the rival racer who steps into the romantic breach. It's all very macho stuff, with predictably exciting racing sequences. AT

Paul Newman *Frank Capua* • Joanne Woodward *Elora* • Richard Thomas *Charley* • Robert Wagner *Luther Erding* • David Sheiner *Crawford* • Clu Gulager *Larry* • Barry Ford *Les Bottineau* ■ *Dir* James Goldstone • *Scr* Howard Rodman

Winning London ★★U
Comedy adventure 2001 · US · Colour · 93min

The American pre-teen marketing phenomenon that is the Olsen twins makes for Europe in this twee teenybop adventure. The result is more travelogue than drama, although it could also be mistaken for a feature-length exercise in product placement. Amid the landmarks and labels, Mary-Kate falls for charming Jesse Spencer, while Ashley gets cosy with Brandon Tyler, a fellow US member of the Model United Nations. DP **DVD**

Mary-Kate Olsen *Chloe Lawrence* • Ashley Olsen *Riley Lawrence* • Eric Jungmann *Dylan* • Brandon Tyler *Brian* • Rachel Roth *Rachel* • Paul Ridley

Lord Browning • Jesse Spencer *James Browning* ■ *Dir* Craig Shapiro • *Scr* Karol Ann Hoeffner

The Winning of Barbara Worth ★★★★
Silent romantic western 1926 · US · BW · 83min

After playing extras and bit parts in two-reelers, Gary Cooper was suddenly cast as a last minute replacement for one of the supporting players here. Cooper plays a local Arizona boy and rival of eastern engineer Ronald Colman for the hand of Vilma Banky (the eponymous Barbara). Shot in the Nevada desert, the film, about the harnessing of the Colorado river, offers sandstorms, floods and romance. There is some fine camerawork by George Barnes and his 22-year-old assistant Gregg Toland, who would later shoot *Citizen Kane*. RB

Ronald Colman *Willard Holmes* • Vilma Banky *Barbara Worth* • Charles Lane (1) *Jefferson Worth* • Paul McAllister *The Seer* • EJ Ratcliffe *James Greenfield* • Gary Cooper *Abe Lee* ■ *Dir* Henry King • *Scr* Frances Marion, from the novel by Harold Bell Wright

The Winslow Boy ★★★★U
Drama 1948 · UK · BW · 113min

An object lesson in how to transfer stage to screen, this proves it *can* be done well. Terence Rattigan's tightly wound text is left largely untouched, but the scenes are broadened out to give the original play room to breathe. Robert Donat is wonderful as the celebrated barrister defending a naval cadet charged with theft, and Rattigan's insights into class and hypocrisy are sharpened by Anthony Asquith's assured direction. Primarily a cinematic experience, but the play is left unscarred. SH **DVD**

Robert Donat *Sir Robert Morton* • Margaret Leighton *Catherine Winslow* • Cedric Hardwicke *Arthur Winslow* • Basil Radford *Esmond Curry* • Kathleen Harrison *Violet* • Francis L Sullivan *Attorney General* • Marie Lohr *Grace Winslow* • Jack Watling *Dickie Winslow* • Frank Lawton *John Watherstone* • Neil North *Ronnie Winslow* • Wilfrid Hyde White *Wilkinson* ■ *Dir* Anthony Asquith • *Scr* Terence Rattigan, Anatole de Grunwald, from the play by Terence Rattigan

The Winslow Boy ★★★★U
Period drama 1999 · US · Colour · 100min

David Mamet adapts and directs Terence Rattigan's play about a father's unwavering and potentially destructive love for his son. When Guy Edwards is expelled from the Royal Naval Academy for theft, Nigel Hawthorne believes in the boy's virtue so much he nearly bankrupts his family trying to prove it. Suffragette daughter Rebecca Pidgeon falls for barrister Jeremy Northam, while mother Gemma Jones cannot understand her husband's obsessive pursuit of justice. Mamet and his remarkable cast reveal the truth behind the motives. TH **DVD**

Nigel Hawthorne *Arthur Winslow* • Jeremy Northam *Sir Robert Morton* • Rebecca Pidgeon *Catherine Winslow* • Gemma Jones *Grace Winslow* • Guy Edwards *Ronnie Winslow* • Matthew Pidgeon *Dickie Winslow* • Aden Gillett *John Watherstone* ■ *Dir* David Mamet • *Scr* David Mamet, from the play by Terence Rattigan

Winstanley ★★★★PG
Historical drama 1975 · UK · BW · 91min

Kevin Brownlow and Andrew Mollo's second film is set in Cromwellian England and deals with a disparate group of people, united in their disillusion, poverty and landlessness who create a commune and call themselves Diggers. Their leader is Gerrard Winstanley, a man with a utopian dream of social equality. Based on David Caute's novel *Comrade Jacob*, it fits into the world of 1960s agitprop, riding the anti-everything, drop-out tide of student protest, but Brownlow and Mollo are not firebrand radicals, much less flower power hippies. They are, first and foremost, serious historians who shot the film for over a year, often in harsh conditions. As a period reconstruction it has few equals. AT **DVD**

Miles Halliwell *Gerrard Winstanley* • Jerome Willis *General Lord Fairfax* • Terry Higgins *Tom Haydon* • Phil Oliver *Will Everard* • David Bramley *Parson John Platt* • Allison Halliwell *Mrs Platt* • Dawson France *Captain Gladman* ■ *Dir* Kevin Brownlow, Andrew Mollo • *Scr* Kevin Brownlow, Andrew Mollo, from the novel *Comrade Jacob* by David Caute

Winter Carnival ★★U
Romantic drama 1939 · US · BW · 90min

Although he's not credited, F Scott Fitzgerald had a hand in scripting this lacklustre comedy that co-scenarist Budd Schulberg (who was fired by producer Walter Wanger) used as the backdrop for his 1950 novel, *The Disenchanted*. Ann Sheridan takes the lead as a divorced countess returning to Dartmouth College for the annual ice fest to see if baby sister Helen Parrish can follow in her footsteps as carnival queen. However, she spends much of her time flirting with alumnus Richard Carlson who is now a penniless professor. DP

Ann Sheridan *Jill Baxter* • Richard Carlson *Professor John Weldon* • Helen Parrish *Ann Baxter* • James Corner *Mickey Allen* • Alan Baldwin *Don Reynolds* • Robert Armstrong *Tiger Reynolds* ■ *Dir* Charles F Reisner [Charles Reisner] • *Scr* Lester Cole, Bud Schulberg, Maurice Rapf, from a story by Bud Schulberg, Maurice Rapf, from the short story *Echoes That Old Refrain* by Corey Ford in *The Saturday Evening Post*

The Winter Guest ★★★15
Drama 1996 · US/UK · Colour · 104min

Alan Rickman's directorial debut stars Emma Thompson as a mother grieving over the death of her husband, unable to support and nurture their son and also unable to see her own mother's ill health. As family events unfold, Rickman introduces other elements from the isolated Scottish village setting: two old dears get their kicks out of going to funerals and two small boys play on the always-blustery beach. It's a brave attempt to open up Sharman MacDonald's play, but overall the film never quite escapes from its theatrical roots. LH **DVD**

Emma Thompson *Frances* • Phyllida Law *Elspeth* • Sheila Reid *Lily* • Sandra Voe *Chloe* • Arlene Cockburn *Nita* • Gary Hollywood *Alex* • Sean Biggerstaff *Tom* • Douglas Murphy *Sam* ■ *Dir* Alan Rickman • *Scr* Alan Rickman, Sharman MacDonald, from the play by Sharman MacDonald

Winter in Wartime ★★★15
Second World War drama 2008 · Neth/Bel · Colour · 104min

This is an accomplished if predictable attempt to present the Second World War occupation of the Netherlands from a teenage perspective. Martijin Lakemeier longs to join his uncle (Yorick van Wageningen) in the Resistance. But dreams of heroism prove very different from reality when Lakemeier has to rely on his nurse sister (Melody Klaver) to help a wounded RAF pilot (Jamie Campbell Bower) reach safety. It's always more visually striking than dramatically convincing, but by confining events to Lakemeier's viewpoint, director Martin Koolhoven is able to convey the confusion and treachery of warfare. DP Dutch, English, German +subtitles. **DVD** **Blu-ray**

Martijin Lakemeier *Michiel* • Yorick van Wageningen *Oom Ben* • Jamie Campbell Bower *Jack* • Raymond Thiry *Johan* ■ *Dir* Martin Koolhoven • *Scr* Mieke de Jong, Martin Koolhoven, Paul Jan Nelissen, from the novel by Jan Terlouw

Winter Kills ★★★18
Political black comedy 1979 · US · Colour · 87min

This genuine collector's item is based on the remarkable satirical novel about the Kennedys by Richard Condon, who also wrote *The Manchurian Candidate* and *Prizzi's Honor*. Jeff Bridges, playing the son of patriarch John Huston, tries to discover who was responsible for killing his brother, the US President. In the starry cast, the likes of Anthony Perkins, Sterling Hayden, Dorothy Malone and Toshiro Mifune make

telling contributions, while Elizabeth Taylor appears in a cameo, and it's all held together by William Richert's assured direction. TS Swearing, nudity. **DVD**

Jeff Bridges *Nick Kegan* • John Huston *Pa Kegan* • Anthony Perkins *John Ceruti* • Sterling Hayden *ZK Dawson* • Eli Wallach *Joe Diamond* • Dorothy Malone *Emma Kegan* • Tomas Milian *Frank Mayo* • Belinda Bauer *Yvette Malone* • Ralph Meeker *Gameboy Baker* • Toshiro Mifune *Keith* • Richard Boone *Keifitz* • Elizabeth Taylor *Lola Comante* ■ *Dir* William Richert • *Scr* William Richert, from the novel by Richard Condon

Winter Light ★★★PG
Drama 1962 · Swe · BW · 77min

Tormented by doubts about his own faith and tempted by an offer of marriage from schoolteacher Ingrid Thulin, pastor Gunnar Björnstrand is also aware of the duty he owes to parishioner Max von Sydow, who is contemplating suicide in the face of a nuclear crisis. Composed for the most part in close-ups, Ingmar Bergman's film is a powerful and pessimistic look at God's relationship with humanity, but, in spite of exceptional performances, it won't be for all tastes. DP Swedish +subtitles. **DVD**

Ingrid Thulin *Marta Lundberg* • Gunnar Björnstrand *Tomas Ericsson* • Max von Sydow *Jonas Persson* • Gunnel Lindblom *Karin Persson* • Allan Edwall *Algot Frovik* ■ *Dir/Scr* Ingmar Bergman

Winter Meeting ★
Drama 1948 · US · BW · 104min

Even Bette Davis, characteristically accomplished and uncharacteristically restrained, can't save audiences from the mind-numbing tedium of this bleak and ponderously verbose drama. Davis is a repressed spinster poetess who becomes involved with naval officer James Davis (no relation - and little talent) who really wants to become a Catholic priest. The movie is one of Bette's last duds before finally leaving Warner Bros to freelance. RK

Bette Davis *Susan Grieve* • Janis Paige *Peggy Markham* • James Davis [Jim Davis (1)] *Lt Slick Novak* • John Hoyt *Stacy Grant* • Florence Bates *Mrs Castle* • Walter Baldwin *Mr Castle* • Ransom Sherman *Mr Moran* ■ *Dir* Bretaigne Windust • *Scr* Catherine Turney, from the novel by Ethel Vance

Winter of Discontent ★★★15
Drama 2012 · Egy · Colour · 96min

Released in Britain in the midst of social and political upheaval in Egypt, Ibrahim El Batout's earnest drama strikingly reveals how the mood of the nation oscillated in the days surrounding the resignation of President Mubarak. On the eve of the 2011 Tahrir Square demonstrations, activist Amr uploads politicised videos and thinks back two years to the pitiless torture he endured at the hands of the chief of the secret police. Meanwhile, his ex-girlfriend Farah agonises over her own less-than-worthy behaviour during the upheaval. El Batout ably conveys the brutality of the ousted tyranny but he also insinuates that the triumph of the masses isn't the end of the story. DP Arabic +subtitles. Some violence.

Amr Waked *Amr* • Salah Al Hanafy *Adel* • Farah Youssef *Farah* ■ *Dir* Ibrahim El Batout • *Scr* Ibrahim El Batout, Ahmed Amer, Yasser Naim, Habi Seoud

Winter Sleep ★★★★★15
Drama 2014 · Tur/Fr/Ger · Colour · 188min

This Turkish 2014 Cannes Palme d'Or winner comes with a lot of baggage, not least its 196-minute running time. But for those willing to commit the time to check in - the lead character, Aydin (Haluk Bilginer), runs a remote hotel in central Anatolia - *Winter Sleep* is not only a fantastically well-scripted and performed comment on the rifts in modern society, it also looks stunning, capturing the strange rock formations of the region to captivating effect. DW Turkish, English +subtitles. **DVD** **Blu-ray**

Haluk Bilginer *Aydin* • Melisa Sözen *Nihal* • Demet Akbag *Necla* • Ayberk Pekcan *Hidayet, driver* ■ *Dir* Nuri Bilge Ceylan • *Scr* Nuri Bilge Ceylan, Ebru Ceylan • *Cinematographer* Gokhan Tiryaki

Winterhawk ★★★
Western   1975 · US · Colour · 86min

In this cowboys and Indians film, the whites are the baddies. Michael Dante plays a Blackfoot brave who comes to a white settlement for a smallpox serum, only to be attacked. The Indian then takes revenge by abducting two white kids. It's good to see genre conventions being broken down, but the film is still clichéd, even if the clichés are inverted. It's watchable, though, and notable for a panoply of familiar "cowboy" faces. DA

Leif Erickson *Guthrie* • Woody Strode *Big Rude* • Denver Pyle *Arkansas* • LQ Jones *Gates* • Michael Dante *Winterhawk* • Elisha Cook Jr *Reverend Will Finley* ■ *Dir* Charles B Pierce • *Scr* Charles B Pierce, Earl E Smith

Winter's Bone ★★★★ 15
Thriller   2010 · US · Colour · 95min

The dilapidated American shanty towns of the Ozarks region provide the setting for this excellent, award-winning thriller. Jennifer Lawrence (so good in 2008's *The Burning Plain*) gives a superb performance in her first starring role as Ree Dolly, an older-than-her-years teenager who is forced to take charge of her flaky mother and much younger siblings when her drug-dealing father jumps bail and goes on the run. The film never flinches from the ugliness of its details – Ree guts and cooks squirrel for her starving family – but Lawrence's inspiring determination makes this much, much more than a grim skid-row whodunnit. DW Violence, swearing, drug abuse. *DVD* *BL*

Jennifer Lawrence (2) *Ree Dolly* • John Hawkes *Teardrop* • Kevin Breznahan *Little Arthur* • Dale Dickey *Merab* • Garret Dillahunt *Sheriff Baskin* • Lauren Sweetser *Gail* ■ *Dir* Debra Granik • *Scr* Debra Granik, Anne Rosellini, from the novel by Daniel Woodrell

The Winter's Tale ★★ U
Romantic comedy   1966 · UK · Colour · 150min

Frank Dunlop's theatre production, which presumably wowed audiences at the 1966 Edinburgh Festival, transfers unconvincingly to celluloid, and the usual faults of cine-theatre, such as over-frequent close-ups, are here in all their vainglory. Nevertheless, the film has its moments. Laurence Harvey makes a competent Leontes, the king who for little apparent reason develops a jealous streak which threatens to destroy all around him. However, he's nearly upstaged by Jim Dale, who makes a fine Autolycus as well as composing the score. JG

Laurence Harvey *Leontes* • Jane Asher *Perdita* • Diana Churchill *Paulina* • Moira Redmond *Hermione* • Jim Dale *Autolycus* • Esmond Knight *Camillo* ■ *Dir* Frank Dunlop • *Scr* from the play by William Shakespeare

A Winter's Tale ★★★★ 15
Romantic drama   1992 · Fr · Colour · 109min

Eric Rohmer is unique in his ability to fashion fully fleshed characters to persuade us to become utterly absorbed in the petty problems that beset lives that are every bit as ordinary as our own. Exploring the emotions, confusions and contradictions attendant on romance, this witty adult fairy tale, set in the heart of the callous city, is a joy to behold thanks to the naturalism of its performances and the sublime subtlety of its direction. DP French +subtitles. *DVD*

Charlotte Very *Félicie* • Frédéric Van Den Driessche *Charles* • Michel Voletti *Maxence* • Hervé Furic *Loïc* • Ava Loraschi *Elise* ■ *Dir/Scr* Eric Rohmer

Winterset ★★★
Drama   1936 · US · BW · 75min

Burgess Meredith, repeating his Broadway role, is the star of this adaptation of Maxwell Anderson's once-famous play, originally written in blank verse and inspired by the Sacco and Vanzetti case. Very much

---

a prestige production in its day, hailed by the critics and the cognoscenti but ignored by the customers, this account of a man seeking to clear the name of his wrongfully executed, liberal father is stagey, talky, and now dated, but its passionate arguments against intolerance and mob hysteria have a powerful ring. RK

Burgess Meredith *Mio Romagna* • Margo *Miriamne Esdras* • Eduardo Ciannelli *Trock Estrella* • Maurice Moscovitch [Maurice Moscovici] *Esdras* • Paul Guilfoyle (1) *Garth Esdras* • Mischa Auer *Radical* • John Carradine *Bartolomeo Romagna* ■ *Dir* Alfred Santell • *Scr* Anthony Veiller, from the play by Maxwell Anderson

Wintersleepers ★★★ 15
Melodrama   1997 · Ger · Colour · 122min

German director Tom Tykwer revives the long-dormant "mountain film" with this cool take on heroism and the formidability of nature. After a superbly controlled opening that culminates in a shocking road accident, the pace drops – a tad too deliberately – to allow the snowball of coincidence to gather momentum. Yet there's a ghoulish fascination in watching the links emerge between amnesiac projectionist Ulrich Matthes and the family of his victim. Tykwer doesn't always keep the lid on the more extreme emotions, but this is still tense and beautifully filmed. DP German +subtitles. Swearing, sex scenes.

Ulrich Matthes *Rene* • Marie-Lou Sellem *Laura* • Floriane Daniel *Rebecca* • Heino Ferch *Marco* • Josef Bierbichler *Theo* ■ *Dir* Tom Tykwer • *Scr* Tom Tykwer, Anne-Françoise Pyszora, from the novel *Expense of the Spirit* by Pyszora

Wintertime ★★ U
Musical comedy   1943 · US · BW · 82min

Norwegian skating star Sonja Henie, in a triumph of scriptwriting imagination, plays a Norwegian skating star in this last of her Fox musicals. She turns up at the declining Canadian resort hotel owned by her dear old uncle, SZ "Cuddles" Sakall, where her mere presence puts the place back on the tourist map. And that, as well as her romance with Cornel Wilde, is it – aside from the skating, that is. RK

Sonja Henie *Nora* • Jack Oakie *Skip Hutton* • Cesar Romero *Brad Barton* • Carole Landis *Flossie Fouchere* • SZ Sakall *Hjalmar Ostgaard* • Cornel Wilde *Freddy Austin* ■ *Dir* John Brahm • *Scr* E Edwin Moran, Jack Jevne, Lynn Starling, from a story by Arthur Kober

Wired ★ 18
Biographical drama   1989 · US · Colour · 104min

As if the death of comedian John Belushi wasn't tragic enough, this dreadful biopic purports to tell the truth about his career and the drugged-out events leading up to his fatal heroin and cocaine overdose in LA's Chateau Marmont hotel in 1982. Michael Chiklis fails to convince as the doomed Blues Brother, and this crude low-budget exploiter is a grotesque character assassination. JM Swearing, drug abuse.

Michael Chiklis *John Belushi* • Ray Sharkey *Angel Velasquez* • JT Walsh *Bob Woodward* • Patti D'Arbanville *Cathy Smith* • Lucinda Jenney *Judy Belushi* • Gary Groomes *Dan Aykroyd* • Alex Rocco *Arnie Fromson* ■ *Dir* Larry Peerce • *Scr* Earl Mac Rauch, from the book *Wired: the short life and fast times of John Belushi* by Bob Woodward

Wisdom ★ 18
Crime drama   1986 · US · Colour · 104min

If only director Emilio Estevez would demonstrate a little wisdom by quitting directing and sticking to acting. Here he directs himself for the first time as a high school dropout who turns into a local Robin Hood and, with girlfriend Demi Moore at his side, begins bombing banks to help his debt-ridden neighbours. There is nothing to recommend this except an exhilarating car chase but it's unlikely that you'll be awake long enough. LH

Emilio Estevez *John Wisdom* • Demi Moore *Karen Simmons* • Tom Skerritt *Lloyd Wisdom* • Veronica Cartwright *Samantha Wisdom* • William Allen Young *Williamson* • Richard Minchenberg *Cooper* • Bill Henderson *Theo* ■ *Dir/Scr* Emilio Estevez

---

The Wisdom of Crocodiles ★★★ 18
Horror romance   1998 · UK · Colour · 94min

By day a medical researcher, by night a vampire, Jude Law stars as the undead preying on women in the hope of finding the true love that will bring about his redemption. Rescuing Kerry Fox from a suicide attempt, he then beds and bloods her. However, his subsequent encounter with the beautiful Elina Lowensohn becomes a complex love affair when he can't bring himself to bite her jugular. Over-stylised by director Po Chih Leong, realism is on hand in Timothy Spall's characterisation of the downbeat detective who soon gets on Law's case. LH Violence, sex scenes, swearing.

Jude Law *Steven Griscz* • Elina Lowensohn *Anne Levels* • Timothy Spall *Inspector Healey* • Kerry Fox *Maria Vaughan* • Jack Davenport *Sergeant Roche* • Colin Salmon *Martin* ■ *Dir* Po Chih Leong • *Scr* Paul Hoffman

Wise Blood ★★★ 15
Gothic fantasy drama 1979 · US/W Ger · Colour · 101min

A greatly admired and critically acclaimed film in many quarters, this blood-and-salvation southern gothic fantasy seems to cry out for a more outré approach than that of director John Huston, who clearly relished (since he also appears in) this virtually blasphemous and undeniably strange version of Flannery O'Connor's obsessive fable about the disillusioned former soldier who starts a godless chuch. Brad Dourif is mightily effective as the leader of "The Church of Truth without Jesus Christ" but, while the movie's taste becomes highly questionable, there's no denying its powerful appeal and subversive humour. TS Swearing. *DVD*

Brad Dourif *Hazel Motes* • Harry Dean Stanton *Asa Hawks* • Ned Beatty *Hoover Shoates* • Daniel Shor [Dan Shor] *Enoch Emery* • Amy Wright *Sabbath Lily Hawks* • John Huston *Hazel's grandfather* • William Hickey *Preacher* ■ *Dir* John Huston • *Scr* Benedict Fitzgerald, Michael Fitzgerald, from the novel by Flannery O'Connor

Wise Guys ★ 15
Black comedy   1986 · US · Colour · 87min

Comedy is not Brian De Palma's forte, as most people who saw his supposed satire *The Bonfire of the Vanities* will confirm. Conclusive evidence that De Palma can't tell a joke is provided by this woeful effort in which Danny DeVito plays a Mafia messenger boy and Harvey Keitel is a hotelier. The comedy is pitched so low you need a mechanical digger to find it. AT

Danny DeVito *Harry Valentini* • Joe Piscopo *Moe Dickstein* • Harvey Keitel *Bobby Dilea* • Ray Sharkey *Marco* • Dan Hedaya *Anthony Castelo* • Captain Lou Albano *Frank the Fixer* • Julie Bovasso *Lil Dickstein* • Patti LuPone *Wanda Valentini* ■ *Dir* Brian De Palma • *Scr* George Gallo

Wisecracks ★★★★
Documentary   1991 · Can · Colour · 91min

Gail Singer's impressive documentary provides a valuable insight into the careers of some of comedy's most important female stars. It combines film footage of Mae West, Gracie Allen, Lucille Ball and the like with contemporary clips from and interviews with Whoopi Goldberg, Phyllis Diller, Jenny Lecoat and others. Liberal chunks of the participants' comedy routines ensure a high level of humour throughout this excellent production. Shorter versions turn up occasionally but the original 91-minute cut is the one to see. DF

■ *Dir* Gail Singer • *Cinematographers* Zoe Dirse, Bob Fresco • *Editor* Gordon McClellan

Wisegirls ★★★ 15
Crime thriller   2001 · US/UK/Can · Colour · 92min

The gangster thriller gets a feminine twist in this well-executed feature from director David Anspaugh. Mira Sorvino stars as a woman trying to forget her past, who takes

---

on a restaurant waitressing job, only to become embroiled with its Mafia clientele. Centred on a trio of strong performances, from Sorvino and her co-worker friends Mariah Carey and Melora Walters, it's a gripping tale of sisterhood that's as warm as it is brutal. Essentially a chick flick in mobster clothing, this benefits from an above average script and plenty of meaty drama. SF Swearing, violence, drug abuse. *DVD*

Mira Sorvino *Meg Kennedy* • Mariah Carey *Raychel* • Melora Walters *Kate* • Arthur Nascarella *Mr Santalino* • Saul Stein *Umberto* • Joseph Siravo *Gio* • Christian Maelen *Frankie* • Anthony Alessandro *Lorenzo* ■ *Dir* David Anspaugh • *Scr* John Meadows

The Wiser Sex ★★
Crime drama   1932 · US · BW · 72min

Berthold Viertel's penultimate Hollywood picture before he relocated to the UK is pretty racy for its day, with sophisticate Claudette Colbert posing as a woman of easy virtue to deliver her lawyer lover, Melvyn Douglas, from a murder rap. Sadly, there's not a shred of conviction about either her performance or the storyline, in which her dealings with mobster William "Stage" Boyd are complicated by his vengeful mistress, Lilyan Tashman. DP

Claudette Colbert *Margaret Hughes/Ruby Kennedy* • Melvyn Douglas *District Attorney David Rolfe* • Lilyan Tashman *Claire Foster* • William "Stage" Boyd *Harry Evans* • Ross Alexander (1) *Jimmie O'Neill* • Franchot Tone *Phil Long* ■ *Dir* Berthold Viertel • *Scr* Harry Hervey, Caroline Francke, from the play *The Woman in the Case* by Clyde Fitch

Wish I Was Here ★★★ 15
Comedy drama   2014 · US · Colour · 106min

Scrubs lead Zach Braff directs and stars as a married man, father of two young children, and a jobbing actor whose life is thrown into crisis when his father (Mandy Patinkin) reveals he has been diagnosed with terminal cancer. The personal awakening story is enjoyable and self-deprecatingly honest, but what isn't so much fun is Braff's decision to add religion to the mix, which leads to some ponderous stretches. DW Swearing, sexual references.

Zach Braff *Aidan Bloom* • Kate Hudson *Sarah Bloom* • Mandy Patinkin *Gabe Bloom* • Joey King *Grace Bloom* • Pierce Gagnon *Tucker Bloom* ■ *Dir* Zach Braff • *Scr* Zach Braff, Adam J Braff

The Wish List ★★
Romantic comedy drama 2010 · US · Colour · 88min

In this energetic TV movie, super-efficient human resources executive Jennifer Esposito learns that love and life rarely go according to a master plan. It's a simple and clichéd lesson, though enjoyably delivered, as she compiles an elaborate profile of her ideal man, only to find herself torn between her theoretical Mr Right and a coffee-shop manager who meets none of her criteria. Split screens, swipes and other visual tricks jazz up the playful atmosphere that is at its best whenever the career girl and barista banter. Ultimately, this is a romantic comedy that preaches risk-taking without following its own advice, but Esposito's so engaging that it scarcely matters. SF

Jennifer Esposito *Sarah* • David Sutcliffe *Fred* • Mark Deklin *Erik* • Sydney Penny *Chloe* ■ *Dir* Kevin Connor • *Scr* Gary Goldstein

Wish You Were Here
★★★★ 15
Comedy drama   1987 · UK · Colour · 88min

Emily Lloyd's startling debut as a sexually defiant seaside teenager prevents writer/director David Leland's 1950s-set comedy drama from being just another rebellious youngster movie. Her vibrant performance as the 16-year-old intent on shocking everyone begs the question: why has her career since failed to make any impact? There's also strong support from Tom Bell in a decidedly unsympathetic role as a lecherous family friend. SuR Swearing, sex scenes, nudity. *DVD*

Emily Lloyd *Lynda* • Tom Bell *Eric* • Clare Clifford *Mrs Parfitt* • Barbara Durkin *Valerie* • Geoffrey Hutchings *Hubert* • Charlotte Barker *Gillian* • Chloe Leland *Margaret* • Jesse Birdsall *Dave* • Pat Heywood *Aunt Millie* ■ *Dir/Scr* David Leland

Wish You Were Here ★★★ 15

Mystery thriller   2012 · Aus · Colour · 88min

Kieran Darcy-Smith's atmospheric feature debut follows four Australians on a hedonistic holiday to Cambodia – from which only three return. The film alternates between the booze, pills and beachside raves of over there and the silences, suspicions and recriminations of back home. Setting aside the dark thriller dynamics, what the director is really interested in is the relationship between Joel Edgerton, his pregnant wife and her younger hotter sister in this solid exercise in slow-build tension. SvM English, Vietnamese +subtitles. Violence, swearing, sex scenes. *DVD*

Joel Edgerton *Dave Flannery* • Felicity Price *Alice Flannery* • Teresa Palmer *Steph McKinney* ■ *Dir* Kieran Darcy-Smith · *Scr* Kieran Darcy-Smith, Felicity Price

Wishful Thinking ★ 15

Romantic comedy drama
1997 · US · Colour and BW · 85min

You will wishfully be thinking of anything else while watching this so-called romantic comedy, which fails to either raise laughs or lay on love. Cinema projectionist and commitment-phobe James LeGros can't say "I do" to girlfriend Jennifer Beals and instead accuses her of infidelity. Meanwhile the cinema's overly quirky cashier Drew Barrymore harbours a hidden love for LeGros which she restricts to *Brief Encounter*-esque black-and-white daydreams. Told separately from these three characters' points of view, you care little for them or their fates. LH

Drew Barrymore *Lena* • Jennifer Beals *Elizabeth* • James LeGros *Max* • Jon Stewart *Henry* • Mel Gorham *Lourdes* • Eric Thal *Jack* ■ *Dir/Scr* Adam Park

The Wishing Tree ★★

Seasonal drama   2012 · US · Colour · 94min

An unconventional teacher and a small-town charity event change the lives of three boarding-school students in this formulaic though heart-warming seasonal tale. Jason Gedrick gives a likeable turn as the widowed educator whose task of supervising the pupils remaining for Christmas is complicated when one of the trio (Richard Harmon) causes trouble at the site of a special fundraiser tree. The bad-boy teen's punishment has major consequences for everybody, in a movie that remains engaging thanks to the uplifting themes of hope and self-belief. SF

Jason Gedrick *Evan Farnsworth* • Richard Harmon *Drew* • Emmalyn Estrada *Juliet* ■ *Dir* Terry Ingram · *Scr* Michael J Murray

The Wishing Well ★★

Romantic fantasy   2009 · US · Colour · 90min

Reality is a minor consideration in this far-fetched romantic fantasy. Slight yet innocuous, it sees slick reporter Jordan Ladd experience a surprising turnabout in her shallow existence when she's assigned to write an article on a small-town wishing well that is reputed to have magical qualities. A slew of life lessons offers sugary food for thought, with 92-year-old Ernest Borgnine among the open-hearted townsfolk sharing their wisdom. Ultimately, neither the events nor the acting are particularly convincing, but the film's simple warmth makes it a painless experience. SF

Ernest Borgnine *Big Jim* • Jordan Ladd *Cynthia Tamerline* • Jason London *Mark Jansen* • Charles Shaughnessy *Bosley* • Yeardley Smith *Mary* • Sally Kellerman *Donette* ■ *Dir* David Jackson · *Scr* Steven H Berman

Wishman ★★★

Romantic fantasy   1991 · US · Colour · 90min

Paul Le Mat delivers a typically astute performance as a Hollywood hustler whose talent for smooth talking fails him whenever he sees his heart's desire, Quin Kessler. But Le Mat is totally upstaged by a quirky turn from Geoffrey Lewis, as a two million-year-old genie who agrees to grant Le Mat's wishes providing he helps locate Lewis's stolen bottle. Paul Gleason and Brion James head a seasoned supporting cast that stands aside and lets Lewis steal every scene. DP

Paul Le Mat *Basie* • Geoffrey Lewis *Hitchcock the genie* • Paul Gleason *Silverstein* • Quin Kessler *Lily Andon* • Nancy Parsons *Miss Crabbe* • Brion James *Staten Jack Rose* ■ *Dir/Scr* Mike Marvin

Wishmaster ★★★ 18

Horror   1997 · US · Colour · 86min

This is an oddly comforting throwback to the early 1980s slasher glory days, directed by former special-effects genius Robert Kurtzman and executive produced by Wes Craven. Los Angeles gem specialist Tammy Lauren must stop the evil 12th-century Persian Djinn (genie), played by Andrew Divoff, wreaking havoc after he tries to trick her into making three wishes when she discovers him trapped in an enchanted opal. The one-jolt premise does get stretched out to vanishing point, yet the casting, plus all the exploding body parts, make for a nostalgic tonic for splatter addicts. Three listless straight-to-video sequels followed. AJ Violence, swearing. *DVD*

Tammy Lauren *Alexandra Amberson* • Andrew Divoff *The Djinn/Nathaniel Demerest* • Kane Hodder *Merritt's guard* • Tony Todd *Johnny Valentine* • Robert Englund *Raymond Beaumont* • Angus Scrimm *Narrator* • Ari Barak *Zoroaster* ■ *Dir* Robert Kurtzman · *Scr* Peter Atkins

Wit ★★★★

Drama   2001 · US · Colour · 98min

In seeking suitably cinematic solutions to the considerable problems posed by Margaret Edson's Pulitzer Prize-winning play, director Mike Nichols places the greatest emphasis in this TV movie on the text, with its wealth of allusions, rhythms and insights. He's not intimidated by its intellectual discussion of the religious poetry of John Donne and the emotions experienced by scholar Emma Thompson, as she takes a leap of faith in battling ovarian cancer. Such is the intensity and honesty of Thompson's performance that the occasional contrivance can be forgiven. DP

Emma Thompson *Vivian Bearing* • Christopher Lloyd *Dr Harvey Kelekian* • Eileen Atkins *EM Ashford* • Audra McDonald *Susie Monahan* • Jonathan M Woodward *Dr Jason Posner* • Harold Pinter *Mr Bearing* ■ *Dir* Mike Nichols · *Scr* Emma Thompson, Mike Nichols, from the play by Margaret Edson

The Witch ★★★★ 15

Period supernatural horror
2015 · US/UK/Can/Bra · Colour · 88min

The wilderness of 1630s New England proves a terrifying place for one Puritan family in this spellbinding horror that drips with dread. Ralph Ineson and Kate Dickie play the God-fearing settlers living on the edge of a forest with their five children whose peaceful existence is ripped asunder when a child vanishes from under their noses. Unknown to the locals, there's a sorceress lurking in the woods. First-time director Robert Eggers creates an authentic-looking chiller seamed with oppressive atmosphere and impending doom. JA Violence, nudity *DVD* *BL*

Ralph Ineson *William* • Kate Dickie *Katherine* • Anya Taylor-Joy *Thomasin* • Harvey Scrimshaw *Caleb* • Ellie Grainger *Mercy* • Lucas Dawson *Jonas* ■ *Dir/Scr* Robert Eggers

Witchboard ★ 15

Supernatural horror   1987 · US · Colour · 93min

A group of young people play around with a Ouija board at a party, indirectly leading to an evil spirit possessing Tawny Kitaen. This

is bad news for those around her as they get killed off one by one. The worst part of the entire ordeal is that hardly anything (horrible or otherwise) happens, while the special effects are of the quality and scale you'd expect from a high school production. Two equally bad sequels followed. KB *DVD*

Todd Allen *Jim Morar* • Tawny Kitaen *Linda Brewster* • Stephen Nichols *Brandon Sinclair* • Kathleen Wilhoite *Zarabeth* • Burke Byrnes *Lieutenant Dewhurst* ■ *Dir/Scr* Kevin S Tenney

Witchcraft ★★ 18

Horror   1988 · US · Colour · 85min

New mother Anat Topol-Barzilai reluctantly moves in with her strange mother-in-law and starts having demonic visions of witch-burnings and decapitations. Slow-moving occult nonsense grafting the *Nightmare on Elm Street* dreams-within-false-dreams concept into a basic *Rosemary's Baby* scenario. Plenty of bogus scares and very little sense keep this half-hearted horror dud grounded. AJ *DVD*

Anat Topol-Barzilai *Grace* • Gary Sloan *John* • Mary Shelley *Elizabeth* • Alexander Kirkwood *Priest* ■ *Dir* Robert Spera [Rob Spera] · *Scr* Jody Savin

Witchcraft ★ 18

Horror   1989 · It · Colour · 92min

German actress Hildegarde Knef came out of retirement to play a witch holding demonic sway over a New England island in this nasty slice of Italian exploitation. Stranded visitors fall foul to *Omen*-style murders thanks to her black magic and suffer assorted fates including crucifixion, grotesque rape, mouth-stitching and being hung upside down in a fireplace. So much graphic unpleasantness and still so boring. AJ *DVD*

Linda Blair *Jane Brooks* • David Hasselhoff *Gary* • Hildegarde Knef [Hildegarde Neff] *Lady in Black* • Annie Ross *Rose Brooks* • Catherine Hickland *Linda Sullivan* • Leslie Cummings *Leslie* ■ *Dir* Fabrizio Laurenti · *Scr* Danielle Stroppa

The Witches ★★★ 12

Horror   1966 · UK · Colour · 87min

Hollywood stars never faded, they simply made films in Britain. Joan Fontaine here reprises her "frightened lady" turn, first seen in *Rebecca*, as the cursed schoolmistress discovering devil worship in rural parts. It's a Hammer that never quite makes contact with your nerves, even though it's written by Nigel Kneale, who created *Quatermass*. At least director Cyril Frankel treats it as though it mattered, but for Fontaine it signalled her big screen career's end. TH *DVD* *BL*

Joan Fontaine *Gwen Mayfield* • Kay Walsh *Stephanie Bax* • Alec McCowen *Alan Bax* • Ann Bell *Sally* • Ingrid Brett *Linda* • John Collin *Dowsett* • Michele Dotrice *Valerie* • Gwen Ffrangcon-Davies *Granny Rigg* • Duncan Lamont *Bob Curd* • Leonard Rossiter *Dr Wallis* ■ *Dir* Cyril Frankel · *Scr* Nigel Kneale, from the novel *The Devil's Own* by Peter Curtis

The Witches ★★★

Surreal portmanteau drama
1966 · Fr/It · Colour · 105min

This portmanteau picture, featuring work by some of Italy's most celebrated directors, gave Clint Eastwood a rare opportunity to appear in a European art movie. He features in Vittorio De Sica's bookend segment as a banker being forced to compete with comic book characters for the love of his bored wife Silvana Mangano. Mangano also stars in the other four stories: as a holidaying movie star in Luchino Visconti's opener; a woman driver whose dithering spells trouble for injured trucker Alberto Sordi; a spinster with a short-fused father in Franco Rossi and Luigi Magni's Sicilian comedy; and an imaginary maid in Pier Paolo Pasolini's silent gem. The movie is inconsistent, but intriguing. DP Italian dubbed.

Silvana Mangano *Gloria/Lady/Giovanna* • Annie Girardot *Valeria* • Francisco Rabal *Valeria's husband* • Alberto Sordi *Truck driver* • Clint Eastwood *Husband* ■ *Dir* Luchino Visconti,

Mauro Bolognini, Pier Paolo Pasolini, Franco Rossi, Vittorio De Sica · *Scr* Giuseppe Patroni-Griffi, Cesare Zavattini, Agenore Incrocci, Furio Scarpelli, Bernardino Zapponi, Pier Paolo Pasolini, Franco Rossi, Luigi Magni, Fabio Carpi, Enzio Muzii

The Witches ★★★ PG

Fantasy adventure   1989 · UK · Colour · 87min

Roald Dahl's book about a little boy on a seaside holiday who discovers a witches' convention plotting to annihilate children is brilliantly brought to life in this fantasy adventure by director Nicolas Roeg. As chief witch, Anjelica Huston gets a gruesome Jim Henson's Creature Shop makeover, while Mai Zetterling is transformed into lavender and old lace as the boy's granny. Memorable sequences include the one in which the boy is turned into a mouse. TH *DVD*

Anjelica Huston *Miss Ernst/Grand High Witch* • Mai Zetterling *Helga* • Bill Paterson *Mr Jenkins* • Brenda Blethyn *Mrs Jenkins* • Rowan Atkinson *Mr Stringer* • Jasen Fisher *Luke* • Charlie Potter *Bruno Jenkins* • Jane Horrocks *Miss Irvine* ■ *Dir* Nicolas Roeg · *Scr* Allan Scott, from Roald Dahl's illustrated children's book

Witches' Brew ★★ 15

Fantasy comedy   1979 · US · Colour · 93min

File under "Bad Weird Oddity One Ought to See". Originally made in 1979 as *Which Witch Is Which?*, but not released until 1985 with additional footage, this is an uncredited version of Fritz Leiber Jr's classic novel *Conjure Wife*. The story concerns Richard Benjamin forcing his witch wife Teri Garr to forsake her spell-casting ways, thus allowing super-witch Lana Turner to meddle in their lives. Sadly, neither the gags nor the special effects are up to much. AJ

Richard Benjamin *Joshua Lightman* • Teri Garr *Margaret Lightman* • Lana Turner *Vivian Cross* • Kathryn Leigh Scott *Susan Carey* • James Winker *Linus Cross* • Bill Sorrels *Nick Carey* • Kelly Jean Peters *Linda Reynolds* • Jordan Charney *Charlie Reynolds* ■ *Dir* Richard Shorr · *Scr* Syd Dutton, Richard Shorr

The Witches of Eastwick ★★★★ 18

Comedy drama   1987 · US · Colour · 113min

This raunchy metaphor for the battle between the sexes from *Mad Max* director George Miller soars with inspired lunacy, as three romance-starved suburban women dabble in off-white magic and some offbeat chandelier swinging. While Jack Nicholson dominates this spellbinding adaptation of John Updike's ironic bestseller as the horny little devil, the luminous female talent (Cher, Susan Sarandon and Michelle Pfeiffer) almost matches him in a charming sensual fantasy that's slightly overloaded with needless special effects. AJ Swearing, violence. *DVD*

Jack Nicholson *Daryl Van Horne* • Cher *Alexandra Medford* • Susan Sarandon *Jane Spofford* • Michelle Pfeiffer *Sukie Ridgemont* • Veronica Cartwright *Felicia Alden* • Richard Jenkins *Clyde Alden* • Keith Jochim *Walter Neff* • Carel Struycken *Fidel* • Helen Biddie *Mrs Biddie* ■ *Dir* George Miller (2) · *Scr* Michael Cristofer, from the novel by John Updike

The Witches of Salem ★★★

Period drama   1957 · Fr/E Ger · BW · 147min

Belgian actor-turned-director Raymond Rouleau proved an uninspired choice for this first screen version of Arthur Miller's compelling play, *The Crucible*. In spite of star performances from real-life husband and wife Yves Montand and Simone Signoret, playing the persecuted Proctors, the play's intense commitment and political conviction are weakened by Jean-Paul Sartre's stodgy adaptation and Rouleau's flat direction. Still, nothing could ruin the story of a young woman in 1692 Massachusetts, who vengefully accuses Signoret of witchcraft. BB French +subtitles.

Yves Montand *John Proctor* • Simone Signoret *Elisabeth Proctor* • Mylène Demongeot *Abigail* • Jean Debucourt *Reverend Parris* • Raymond Rouleau *Danforth, the governor* • Françoise

Lugagne *Mrs Putnam* ■ *Dir* Raymond Rouleau • *Scr* Jean-Paul Sartre, from the play *The Crucible* by Arthur Miller

Witchfinder General
★★★★★ 15

Horror 1968 · UK · Colour · 81min

Condemned on first release as extremely bloody and sadistic, Michael Reeves's penetrating chronicle of the social evils at large during the English Civil War is now an acknowledged horror classic. Vincent Price plays it straight for once as the cynical religious maniac instigating torture and degradation for pleasure and profit in an intense study of pathological cruelty. With non-gratuitous violent imagery crucial to the brutal history lesson, Reeves's final work (he died of an overdose shortly after) is a thematically fascinating and gruesomely incisive look at the lust for and abuse of power. AJ Violence, nudity. *DVD*

Vincent Price *Matthew Hopkins* • Ian Ogilvy *Richard Marshall* • Rupert Davies *John Lowes* • Hilary Dwyer *Sara* • Robert Russell *John Stearne* • Patrick Wymark *Oliver Cromwell* • Wilfrid Brambell *Master Coach* • Nicky Henson *Trooper Swallow* ■ *Dir* Michael Reeves • *Scr* Michael Reeves, Tom Baker, from the novel by Ronald Bassett

With a Song in My Heart
★★★★ U

Musical biographical drama
1952 · US · Colour · 116min

Some of the greatest song standards ever written turn up in this fine Technicolor wallow, purportedly the true, tragic (but inspiring) life story of singer Jane Froman who rose from radio commercials to universal acclaim in the 1930s, but was then badly injured in a wartime plane crash. It's Froman's voice on the soundtrack, and lip-synching the vocals with credible conviction is Susan Hayward, here displaying character-steel as only she can, earning a best actress Oscar nomination in the process. An Oscar did go to brilliant musical director Alfred Newman, and mention should also be made of the notable star-making performance from a very young Robert Wagner as a shell-shocked soldier. This is finely performed and intelligently crafted. TS

Susan Hayward *Jane Froman* • Rory Calhoun *John Burns* • Davic Wayne *Don Ross* • Thelma Ritter *Clancy* • Robert Wagner *GI Paratrooper* • Helen Westcott *Jennifer March* • Una Merkel *Sister Marie* ■ *Dir* Walter Lang • *Scr* Lamar Trotti

With Honors
★★ PG

Comedy drama 1994 · US · Colour · 96min

This patchy campus comedy has homeless Joe Pesci trading the pages of student Brendan Fraser's dissertation for food. The problem here is predictability. We know Pesci can't just be any old tramp, and soon the wit and wisdom come tumbling out for the benefit of Fraser and his undeserving roommates. Pesci trots out his familiar tricks and wipes the floor with his juvenile co-stars. DP

Joe Pesci *Simon Wilder* • Brendan Fraser *Monty Kessler* • Moira Kelly *Courtney Blumenthal* • Patrick Dempsey *Everett Calloway* • Josh Hamilton *Jeff Hawkes* • Gore Vidal *Professor Philip Hayes* ■ *Dir* Alek Keshishian • *Scr* William Mastrosimone

With or without You ★★★ 18

Romantic comedy drama
1999 · UK · Colour · 87min

Originally titled *Old New Borrowed Blue*, this low-key, Belfast-based drama from director Michael Winterbottom has Dervla Kirwan and Christopher Eccleston as a young couple desperate to start a family. When an old French pen pal of hers (Yvan Attal) turns up out of the blue, the tension that has been building between them threatens to capsize their marriage. Writer John Forte does not shy away from Ulster's age-old sectarian divisions, but neither does he let them interfere with the refreshing seam of optimism that runs through this gentle gem. NS *DVD*

Christopher Eccleston *Vincent Boyd* • Dervla Kirwan *Rosie Boyd* • Yvan Attal *Benoit* • Julie Graham *Cathy* • Alun Armstrong *Sammy* • Lloyd Hutchinson *Neil* • Michael Liebman *Brian* • Doon Mackichan *Neil* • Gordon Kennedy *Ormonde* • Fionnula Flanagan *Irene* ■ *Dir* Michael Winterbottom • *Scr* John Forte

With Six You Get Eggroll
★★ U

Comedy 1968 · US · Colour · 90min

Doris Day's last movie is this amiable trifle, in which she plays a widow with three sons who marries convenient widower Brian Keith, father of teenage daughter Barbara Hershey, hence the arch title. The offspring naturally object to the relationship. There's a tired 1960s gloss to the whole thing, and it's easy to see why Doris called it a Day. TS *DVD*

Doris Day *Abby McClure* • Brian Keith *Jake Iverson* • Pat Carroll *Maxine Scott* • Barbara Hershey *Stacey Iverson* • George Carlin *Herbie Fleck* • Alice Ghostley *Housekeeper* • John Findlater *Flip McClure* • Jimmy Bracken *Mitch McClure* • Richard Steele *Jason McClure* ■ *Dir* Howard Morris • *Scr* Gwen Bagni, Paul Dubov, Harvey Bullock, RS Allen, from a story by Gwen Bagni, Paul Dubov

Withnail & I
★★★★ 15

Cult black comedy 1986 · UK · Colour · 102min

Those born before 1950 will regard this cult classic about two dissolute 1960s hippies (Richard E Grant and Paul McGann) with unbridled horror. There are empty bottles and dirty underwear everywhere, along with half-finished joints and fag ends stubbed out in congealing boiled eggs. But this is in fact a glorious rites-of-passage movie, as the lads decamp to a cottage in the Lake District where they struggle to survive the weather and a lecherous Uncle Monty. Written and directed by Bruce Robinson, based on his own experiences in London's Camden Town. SH Swearing, drug abuse. *DVD* *Blu-ray*

Richard E Grant *Withnail* • Paul McGann *... and I* • Richard Griffiths *Monty* • Ralph Brown (2) *Danny* • Michael Elphick *Jake* • Daragh O'Malley *Irishman* • Michael Wardle *Isaac Parkin* • Una Brandon-Jones *Mrs Parkin* • Noel Johnson *General* ■ *Dir/Scr* Bruce Robinson

Without a Clue
★★★ PG

Comedy mystery 1988 · UK · Colour · 101min

The real brains behind Sherlock Holmes belonged to Dr Watson, according to this hit-and-miss, hammy Baker Street farce; in fact, the shy doctor (Ben Kingsley) invented the fictitious sleuth as a front for his own brilliant crime detection skills. As Holmes captured the public's imagination, Kingsley is forced to hire actor Michael Caine to impersonate him. How they fare while investigating a plot to undermine the British Empire with forged five pound notes is the comedy basis for this mismatched buddy movie. Good fun despite the patchy laughs. AJ *DVD*

Michael Caine *Sherlock Holmes/Reginald Kincaid* • Ben Kingsley *Dr John Watson* • Jeffrey Jones *Inspector Lestrade* • Lysette Anthony *Leslie Giles* • Paul Freeman *Professor Moriarty* • Nigel Davenport *Lord Smithwick* • Pat Keen *Mrs Hudson* • Peter Cook *Greenhough* ■ *Dir* Thom Eberhardt • *Scr* Gary Murphy, Larry Strawther

Without a Paddle
★ 12

Comedy 2004 · US · Colour · 94min

This truly awful buddy comedy features Matthew Lillard, Seth Green and Dax Shepard, who embark on a whitewater rafting adventure in memory of a recently deceased childhood friend, only to be pursued by insane backwoodsmen. The trio are a thoroughly unappealing and boorish lot and the asinine screenplay is irritating, tedious and tasteless. AS *DVD*

Seth Green *Dr Dan Mott* • Matthew Lillard *Jerry Conlaine* • Dax Shepard *Tom Marshall* • Ethan Suplee *Elwood* • Burt Reynolds *Del Knox* • Abraham Benrubi *Dennis* • Rachel Blanchard *Flower* • Christina Moore *Butterfly* ■ *Dir* Steven Brill • *Scr* Jay Leggett, Mitch Rouse, from a story by Fred Wolf, Harris Goldberg, Tom Nursall

Without a Trace
★★★ 15

Drama based on a true story
1983 · US · Colour · 115min

This impressive drama sadly falls down thanks to a rather ludicrous conclusion. Kate Nelligan is the mother who continues to believe her six-year-old son will return after he vanishes, though everyone around her loses faith. Nelligan is very watchable as the overwrought mother, while Judd Hirsch and stage and screen actress Stockard Channing both match her scene for scene. JB

Kate Nelligan *Susan Selky* • Judd Hirsch *Al Menetti* • David Dukes *Graham Selky* • Stockard Channing *Jocelyn Norris* • Jacqueline Brookes *Margaret Mayo* • Keith McDermott *Phillipe* • Kathleen Widdoes *Ms Hauser* ■ *Dir* Stanley R Jaffe • *Scr* Beth Gutcheon, from her novel *Still Missing*

Without Limits
★★★ 15

Sports biography 1998 · US · Colour · 118min

Co-produced by Tom Cruise, this is the tragic tale of American runner Steve Prefontaine, who came close to winning gold at the 1972 Munich Olympics, only to die in a car crash three years later. The rather uninteresting Billy Crudup stars as Prefontaine, and it's Donald Sutherland who steals the show playing coach Bill Bowerman, known for the running shoes he designed for his team and as the man who invented Nike trainers. The cast is upstaged by the lovingly filmed athletic scenes. JB Some swearing.

Billy Crudup *Steve Prefontaine* • Donald Sutherland *Bill Bowerman* • Monica Potter *Mary Marckx* • Jeremy Sisto *Frank Shorter* • Matthew Lillard *Roscoe Devine* • Billy Burke *Kenny Moore* ■ *Dir* Robert Towne • *Scr* Robert Towne, Kenny Moore • *Producers* Paula Wagner, Tom Cruise

Without Love
★★★

Romantic comedy 1945 · US · BW · 110min

Spencer Tracy and Katharine Hepburn survive the long arm of coincidence in Donald Ogden Stewart's screenplay, as well as the pedestrian direction of Harold S Bucquet, in this tale of a weary scientist who lodges himself and his work in the home of a woman who, under her cool exterior, longs for love. *Adam's Rib* it isn't, but the stars are on form, and there is added zest from Keenan Wynn and a wisecracking Lucille Ball. RK

Spencer Tracy *Pat Jamieson* • Katharine Hepburn *Jamie Rowan* • Lucille Ball *Kitty Trimble* • Keenan Wynn *Quentin Ladd* • Carl Esmond *Paul Carrell* • Patricia Morison *Edwina Collins* • Felix Bressart *Professor Grinza* • Emily Massey *Anna* • Gloria Grahame *Flower girl* ■ *Dir* Harold S Bucquet • *Scr* Donald Ogden Stewart, from the play by Philip Barry

Without Malice
★★

Thriller 2000 · US · Colour · 89min

The only thing puzzling about this thriller is why such a competent cast was attracted to it. Perhaps the Canadian locations tempted Craig Sheffer and Corey Haim, who play prospective brothers-in-law whose "get-to-know-you" hunting trip turns sour when they accidentally shoot a forest ranger and cover up the deed. A real patience-tester. DP

Craig Sheffer *Dr Paul Venters* • Jennifer Beals *Samantha Wilkes* • Gabrielle Anwar *Susan* • Corey Haim *Marty* • Ian Black *Nick* ■ *Dir* Rob W King • *Scr* Peter Layton

Without Reservations
★★★ U

Comedy 1946 · US · BW · 102min

This deft and underrated Hollywood-on-Hollywood comedy has the irresistible Claudette Colbert as a wacky author searching for a leading man to play the screen hero in the movie of her book. She settles on marine flier John Wayne and won't let him out of her sight. Director Mervyn LeRoy knows this territory well and calls on some personal friends to prop up the story: Cary Grant's surprise appearance is very funny, and keep your eyes open, too, for guest star Jack Benny. TS *DVD*

Claudette Colbert *Christopher "Kit" Madden/Kit Klotch* • John Wayne *Captain Rusty Thomas* • Don DeFore *Lt Dink Watson* • Anne Triola *Consuela "Connie" Callaghan* • Phil Brown *Soldier* • Frank Puglia *Ortega* • Thurston Hall *Baldwin* • Dona Drake *Dolores Ortega* • Louella Parsons • Cary Grant • Jack Benny • Raymond Burr *Paul Gill* ■ *Dir* Mervyn LeRoy • *Scr* Andrew Solt, from the novel *Thanks, God, I'll Take It from Here* by Jane Allen, Mae Livingston

Without Warning
★ 15

Horror 1980 · US · Colour · 89min

This absolute turkey is derailed by the outrageous ham acting from two of its all-tarnished-star cast, Jack Palance and Martin Landau. An alien lands in a remote rural area and starts flinging pizza-shaped, flesh-sucking parasites around in order to decorate his spaceship with human trophies gleaned from hapless campers and redneck locals. Totally inept. AJ

Jack Palance *Taylor* • Martin Landau *Fred* • Tarah Nutter *Sandy* • Christopher S Nelson *Greg* • Cameron Mitchell *Hunter* • Neville Brand *Leo* • Sue Ann Langdon [Sue Ane Langdon] *Aggie* ■ *Dir* Greydon Clark • *Scr* Lyn Freeman, Daniel Grodnik, Ben Nett, Steve Mathis

Without Warning: Terror in the Towers
★★ 15

Drama based on a true story
1993 · US · Colour · 92min

This is a predictable but involving TV movie, dramatising the heroic efforts and individual crises surrounding the 1993 terrorist bombing of New York City's World Trade Center. The large cast includes George Clooney and Fran Drescher; thanks to their solid performances, along with effective special effects, this delivers enough melodrama to be an enjoyable, reasonably absorbing entertainment. MC

George Clooney *Kevin Shea* • Scott Plank *Gary Geidel* • John Karlen *Jack McAllister* • James Avery *Fred Ferby* • Susan Ruttan *Anne Marie Tesoriero* • Fran Drescher *Rosemarie Russo* ■ *Dir* Alan J Levi • *Scr* Stephen Downing, Duane Poole

Without Warning: the James Brady Story ★★★★

Drama based on a true story
1991 · US · Colour · 85min

James Brady was the Presidential press secretary shot in the head during John Hinckley's assassination attempt on Ronald Reagan in 1981. The film is a deeply moving tribute to the way that Brady and his wife (Joan Allen) fought his disabilities and campaigned for tighter gun control - the so-called Brady Bill. Produced by David Puttnam for American cable TV, it is notable for a truly astonishing performance by Beau Bridges, and for its literate script by Robert Bolt, who was himself disabled by a stroke in 1979. AT Swearing.

Beau Bridges *James Brady* • Joan Allen *Sarah Brady* • David Strathairn *Dr Kobrine* • Christopher Bell *Scotty* • Christine Healy *Ruth* • Timothy Landfield *Bob* • Bryan Clark *Ronald Reagan* • Susan Brown *Nancy Reagan* • Steven Flynn *John W Hinckley Jr* ■ *Dir* Michael Toshiyuki Uno • *Scr* Robert Bolt, from the book *Thumbs Up: the Life and Courageous Comeback of White House Press Secretary Jim Brady* by Mollie Dickenson

Without You I'm Nothing
★★★ 15

Comedy 1990 · US · Colour · 89min

This filmed record of bisexual comedian Sandra Bernhard's off-Broadway show features her on full-throttle assault. As uncomfortably mean-spirited as she is funny, Bernhard makes mincemeat of such pop icons as Diana Ross, Barbra Streisand, Andy Warhol and Prince, and also explores Jewish envy, her attraction to black culture and decries the male gender. Director John Boskovich cuts from Bernhard's edgy routines to shocked audience members, conjuring up the sense of flirtatious danger that makes her brand of abrasive comedy work. Hilarious, offensive and true. AJ

W

Sandra Bernhard • John Doe • Steve Antin • Lu Leonard *Sandra's manager* • Cynthia Bailey *Roxanne* • Denise Vlasis *Shoshanna* • Ken Foree *Emcee* ■ *Dir* John Boskovich • *Scr* Sandra Bernhard, John Boskovich

Witness ★★★★★ 15
Romantic thriller 1985 · US · Colour · 107min

Directed by Peter Weir, this is partly a love story and partly a thriller, but mainly a study of cultural collision. A murder at a city railway station is witnessed by a small boy, Lukas Haas, who is a member of the Amish community, a religious sect living in rural Pennsylvania that eschews as much of modern life – notably machinery – as they can. Pursued by the bad guys, the boy and his widowed mother (Kelly McGillis) are protected by cop Harrison Ford, who takes them back to their village and awaits the killers' arrival. The performances are immaculate, yet it's Weir's delicacy of touch that impresses the most. He juggles the various elements of the story and makes the violence seem even more shocking when played out on the fields of Amish denial. JF Swearing, nudity. *DVD*

Harrison Ford *John Book* • Kelly McGillis *Rachel Lapp* • Josef Sommer *Deputy Commissioner Schaeffer* • Lukas Haas *Samuel Lapp* • Jan Rubes *Eli Lapp* • Alexander Godunov *Daniel Hochleitner* • Danny Glover *McFee* • Brent Jennings *Carter* • Patti LuPone *Elaine* • Viggo Mortensen *Moses Hochleitner* ■ *Dir* Peter Weir • *Scr* Earl W Wallace, William Kelley, from a story by Kelley, Wallace, Pamela Wallace • *Cinematographer* John Seale • *Music* Maurice Jarre • *Editor* Thom Noble

Witness for the Prosecution ★★★★★ U
Courtroom drama 1957 · US · BW · 111min

Director Billy Wilder's gleefully enjoyable film version of Agatha Christie's play stars Tyrone Power (in his last completed role) as the husband on trial for murder and Marlene Dietrich as his wife testifying against him. The whole plot is an intricate, slightly leaky bag of tricks, with a trademark "surprise" ending. But to conceal the cracks, Wilder throws up a variety of smokescreens and provides the broadest stage imaginable for Charles Laughton's barrister – a performance of epic extravagance, invention and downright hamminess. Ralph Richardson, Deborah Kerr and Diana Rigg assumed the key parts for an enjoyable but less accomplished TV remake 25 years later. AT *DVD*

Tyrone Power *Leonard Stephen Vole* • Marlene Dietrich *Christine Helm Vole* • Charles Laughton *Sir Wilfrid Robarts* • Elsa Lanchester *Miss Plimsoll* • John Williams *Brogan-Moore* • Henry Daniell *Mayhew* • Ian Wolfe *Carter* • Torin Thatcher *Mr Myers* • Norma Varden *Mrs Emily French* • Una O'Connor *Janet McKenzie* • Francis Compton *Judge* ■ *Dir* Billy Wilder • *Scr* Billy Wilder, Harry Kurnitz, Larry Marcus, from the play by Agatha Christie, from her short story • *Art Director* Alexandre Trauner

Witness for the Prosecution ★★★ PG
Courtroom drama 1982 · US · Colour · 97min

Although not the Billy Wilder version, this TV movie of Agatha Christie's audacious courtroom whodunnit isn't bad, either. When it came to eccentric characterisations, Ralph Richardson could match Laughton twitch for twitch and he is wonderful as barrister Sir Wilfred Robarts, ably supported by Deborah Kerr (making her TV movie debut) as his fussy nurse. But it's Diana Rigg whom you'll be raving about afterwards, out-Dietriching Marlene with a wicked performance that surely ranks among her best. DP

Ralph Richardson *Sir Wilfred Robarts* • Deborah Kerr *Miss Plimsoll* • Beau Bridges *Leonard Vole* • Donald Pleasence *Mr Myers* • Wendy Hiller *Janet MacKenzie* • Diana Rigg *Christine Vole* • David Langton *Mayhew* • Richard Vernon *Brogan Moore* • Peter Sallis *Carter* • Frank Mills *Chief Inspector Hearne* ■ *Dir* Alan Gibson • *Scr* John Gay, Lawrence B Marcus (adaptation), from the film by Billy Wilder, Harry Kurnitz, from the play by Agatha Christie

Witness in the War Zone ★★★ 15
Political drama 1986 · UK/W Ger/Is · Colour · 95min

This stars Christopher Walken as an American reporter covering the war in Lebanon. The excellent Walken can play a cynical newshound as well as anyone, but the plot starts to unravel when Walken falls for nurse Marita Marschall and finds himself making news instead of simply covering it. Tighter direction would have heightened the suspense. DP Violence, swearing, nudity.

Christopher Walken *Don Stevens* • Marita Marschall *Linda Larson* • Hywel Bennett *Mike Jessop* • Arnon Zadok *Hamdi Abu-Yussuf* • Amos Lavie *Yessin Abu-Riadd* • Etti Ankri *Samira* • Martin Umbach *Bernard* ■ *Dir* Nathaniel Gutman • *Scr* Hanan Peled

Witness Protection ★★★ 15
Crime drama 1999 · US · Colour · 96min

The underrated Tom Sizemore landed a Golden Globe nomination for his performance in this compelling, made-for-TV insight into life within the federal witness protection programme. Forced to abjure his wealth and power, Sizemore agrees to accept a new identity after his associates turn against him. However, the combined pressures of enduring high-security confinement and having to start again in a strange town soon begin to undermine his marriage to Mary Elizabeth Mastrantonio. Both tense and intense. DP *DVD*

Tom Sizemore *Bobby Batton* • Mary Elizabeth Mastrantonio *Cindy Batton* • Forest Whitaker *Steven Beck* • Shawn Hatosy *Sean Batton* • Skye McCole Bartusiak *Suzie Batton* • William Sadler *Sharp* ■ *Dir* Richard Pearce • *Scr* Daniel Therriault, from a story by Daniel Therriault, Robert Sabbag, from the article *The Invisible Family* by Robert Sabbag

Witness to Murder ★★★
Crime thriller 1954 · US · BW · 81min

Barbara Stanwyck is the unfortunate witness who sees George Sanders murdering a girl in the apartment across the way. But, since he cannily disposes of the corpse and all the evidence, detective Gary Merrill simply doesn't believe her. A run-of-the-mill script and a plot idea as old as the hills is turned into a gripping little thriller, thanks to the all-stops-out performances and direction by Roy Rowland. He milks the material for every possible element of nail-biting tension as silky ex-Nazi Sanders closes in on a terrified Stanwyck. RK

Barbara Stanwyck *Cheryl Draper* • George Sanders *Albert Richter* • Gary Merrill *Lawrence Mathews* • Jesse White *Eddie Vincent* • Harry Shannon *Captain Donnelly* • Claire Carleton *The Blonde* • Lewis Martin *Psychiatrist* ■ *Dir* Roy Rowland • *Scr* Chester Erskine

The Witnesses ★★★ 15
Drama 2006 · Fr/Sp · Colour · 109min

The sense of time and place is impeccable in this soapy French drama from André Téchiné that expertly evokes the reckless hedonism and growing paranoia that dominated 1980s sexual politics. The story shifts from the intoxicating emancipation felt by doctor Adrien (Michel Blanc), as he embarks on a relationship with free spirit Manu (Johan Libéreau), to dismay and mistrust on discovering Manu has been cheating on him and has developed an Aids-related illness. Manu's fling with Mehdi (Sami Bouajila), a bisexual vice cop, also impacts upon Mehdi's writer wife Sarah (Emmanuelle Béart). The themes of love and loss and absolution and acceptance are subtly explored. Ultimately, however, too much emphasis is placed on plot at the expense of character depth, meaning Sarah and Manu's opera-singing sister Julie (Julie Depardieu) are reduced to ciphers. DP French +subtitles. *DVD*

Michel Blanc *Adrien* • Emmanuelle Béart *Sarah* • Sami Bouajila *Mehdi* • Julie Depardieu *Julie* • Johan Libéreau *Manu* • Constance Dollé *Sandra* • Lorenzo Balducci *Steve* • Alain Cauchi *Chief of* police ■ *Dir* André Téchiné • *Scr* André Téchiné, Laurent Guyot, Viviane Zingg • *Cinematographer* Julien Hirsch

Wittgenstein ★★★ 12
Biographical drama 1993 · UK · Colour · 133min

With his health and eyesight failing from Aids-related complications, avant-garde director Derek Jarman somehow managed to shoot this lucid and glowingly vibrant portrait of the tormented 20th-century gay philosopher Ludwig Wittgenstein on a minuscule budget in two weeks. Karl Johnson plays the man searching for intellectual self-development, while struggling with alienation because of his sexual preferences, in a starkly realised series of bleakly amusing and acid-coloured vignettes. One of Jarman's best, although still of a typically rarefied nature. AJ *DVD*

Karl Johnson (2) *Ludwig Wittgenstein* • Tilda Swinton *Lady Morrell* • Michael Gough *Bertrand Russell* • John Quentin *John Maynard Keynes* • Clancy Chassay *Young Ludwig* • Kevin Collins *Johnny* • Jill Balcon *Leopoldine Wittgenstein* • Sally Dexter *Hermine Wittgenstein* • Nabil Shaban *Martian* ■ *Dir* Derek Jarman • *Scr* Derek Jarman, Terry Eagleton, Ken Butler

Wives under Suspicion ★★
Courtroom drama 1938 · US · BW · 68min

Warren William stars as a tough-minded, morally upright and obsessively dedicated district attorney. In prosecuting a man who has murdered his faithless wife in a fit of jealousy, William comes to realise that the case is a mirror of his own life in which his neglected wife (Gail Patrick) is seeking solace with William Lundigan. A modest and mildly interesting drama, directed by James Whale who made a more stylish job of *The Kiss before the Mirror* in 1933, of which this is a remake. RK

Warren William *District Attorney Jim Stowell* • Gail Patrick *Lucy Stowell* • Constance Moore *Elizabeth* • William Lundigan *Phil* • Ralph Morgan *Professor Shaw MacAllen* • Cecil Cunningham *"Sharpy"* • Samuel S Hinds *David Marrow* ■ *Dir* James Whale • *Scr* Myles Connolly, from the play *The Kiss before the Mirror* by Ladislaus Fodor [Ladislas Fodor]

The Wiz ★★ U
Musical fantasy 1978 · US · Colour · 128min

A 34-year-old Diana Ross plays Dorothy in this all-black version of *The Wizard of Oz*, which casts a pall over memories of the 1939 classic. It's easy to see why director Sidney Lumet's clunker ranks as one of the most expensive movie flops of all time. While the Tony Walton sets are fabulous, the famous plot is immersed in a dark inner-city impressionism, the quasi-rocker songs are lacklustre, and diva Ross is just ludicrous in the Judy Garland role. Michael Jackson is good as the Scarecrow, though. AJ *DVD*

Diana Ross *Dorothy* • Michael Jackson (3) *Scarecrow* • Nipsey Russell *Tin Man* • Ted Ross *Lion* • Mabel King *Evillene* • Theresa Merritt *Aunt Em* • Thelma Carpenter *Miss One* • Lena Horne *Glinda the Good* • Richard Pryor *The Wiz* • Stanley Greene *Uncle Henry* ■ *Dir* Sidney Lumet • *Scr* Joel Schumacher, from the musical by William F Brown, Charlie Smalls, from the novel *The Wonderful Wizard of Oz* by L Frank Baum

The Wizard of Baghdad ★★ U
Fantasy comedy 1960 · US · Colour · 92min

After all the cardboard cutout Oriental fantasies that have masqueraded as movies over the years, at last comes a parody of the genre, though it's of little consequence. Dick Shawn, playing a lazy genie threatened with being turned human for not completing any duties, gives a performance that ensures indolence will affect the amount of laughs as well. The special effects – including a rather frayed flying carpet – are as dodgy as the plotline which, of course, involves the uniting of a prince and princess in wedded bliss. TH

Dick Shawn *Ali Mahmud, Genie* • Diane Baker *Princess Yasmin* • Barry Coe *Prince Husan* • John Van Dreelen *Jullnar* • Robert F Simon *Shamadin* •

Vaughn Taylor *Norodeen* ■ *Dir* George Sherman • *Scr* Jesse L Lasky Jr [Jesse Lasky Jr], Pat Silver, from a story by Samuel Newman

The Wizard of Gore ★★★ 18
Horror 1970 · US · Colour · 95min

Slasher pioneer Herschell Gordon Lewis could never be accused of pretension or artifice in his unashamedly fuctional approach to slaughter. Taking his own nickname for its title, this hilarious offering follows the demented Montag the Magician (Ray Sager) on a mesmeric killing spree. The eviscerations Montag performs before a mind-numbed audience are schlock of the most gloriously silly variety and Sager's performance is 5 per cent inspiration, 95 per cent ineptitude. DP *DVD*

Ray Sager *Montag the Magnificent* • Judy Cler *Sherry Carson* • Wayne Ratay *Jack* • Phil Laurenson *Greg* • Jim Rau *Steve* ■ *Dir* Herschell Gordon Lewis • *Scr* Allen Kahn

The Wizard of Loneliness ★★★ 15
Period drama 1988 · US · Colour · 106min

Lukas Haas gives one of the best performances of his career in this rites-of-passage drama set in New England during the Second World War. This is an engaging tale in which Haas finds himself at the centre of a family crisis when the shady past of aunt Lea Thompson comes to light. Director Jenny Bowen does a good job of creating the period atmosphere, but she might have tightened up the action in places. DP Violence, swearing.

Lukas Haas *Wendall Olet* • Lea Thompson *Sybil* • Lance Guest *John T* • John Randolph *Doc* • Dylan Baker *Duffy* • Anne Pitoniak *Cornelia* • Jeremiah Warner *Tom* ■ *Dir* Jenny Bowen • *Scr* Nancy Larson, from the novel by John Nichols

The Wizard of Oz ★★★ U
Silent fantasy 1925 · US · BW · 85min

It's fascinating to compare the classic movie we all love with this earlier version. It was created by comedian Larry Semon as a vehicle for himself – even Dorothy (played by Semon's real-life wife Dorothy Dwan) is a supporting character to Semon's Scarecrow. Dorothy gets blown to Oz in a tornado, but there are no witches and no Munchkins. Instead the people of Oz hail Dorothy as their ruler. The farm-hand who briefly becomes the Tin Man is a very young Oliver Hardy. The Lion is a substantial role for a young, black acrobat named G Howe Black, who is subjected to some awesomely racist humour. The ending is startlingly abrupt. DM *DVD*

Larry Semon *Scarecrow* • Bryant Washburn *Prince Kynde* • Dorothy Dwan *Dorothy* • Virginia Pearson *Countess Vishuss* • Charles Murray *Wizard* • Oliver Hardy *Tin Woodsman* • G Howe Black *Rastus* ■ *Dir* Larry Semon • *Scr* Larry Semon, L Frank Baum Jr, Leon Lee, from Baum's novel *The Wonderful Wizard of Oz*

The Wizard of Oz ★★★★★ U
Classic musical fantasy 1939 · US · Colour and sepia · 98min

One of Hollywood's quintessential productions, this musical adaptation of L Frank Baum's classic fable is probably the most beloved fantasy film of all time and the ultimate family picture. It has something for everyone: wonderfully strange lands, fun-scary moments, a dazzling assortment of fairy-tale characters, fabulous songs to take us all somewhere over the rainbow, a peerless Judy Garland performance, and meaningful messages in abundance. Continuously enthralling, this is one hardy perennial you can never tire of watching. Uncredited King Vidor directed some of the sequences. AJ *DVD* *Blu* *Sp*

Judy Garland *Dorothy Gale* • Ray Bolger *Scarecrow/"Hunk"* • Bert Lahr *Cowardly Lion/"Zeke"* • Jack Haley *Tin Man/"Hickory"* • Billie Burke *Glinda* • Margaret Hamilton *Wicked Witch of the West/Miss Almira Gulch* • Frank Morgan *Prof Marvel/Wizard of Oz/Doorkeeper of the Emerald City/Coachman/Wizard's doorkeeper* • Charley Grapewin *Uncle Henry* • Clara Blandick *Auntie Em* ■ *Dir* Victor Fleming • *Scr* Noel Langley, Florence Ryerson, Edgar Allan Woolf, from the novel *The Wonderful Wizard of Oz* by L

Frank Baum • *Cinematographer* Harold Rosson • *Art Directors* Cedric Gibbons, William A Horning • *Music/lyrics* Harold Arlen, EY Harburg

Wolf ★★★ 15
Horror   1994 · US · Colour · 120min

Everything is right about this film apart from the direction. Jack Nicholson and Michelle Pfeiffer are suitably stellar – he as the middle-aged book editor, she as his boss's daughter whose burgeoning romance is cursed by the fangs of a werewolf. Giuseppe Rotunno's glossy photography lends a sinister sophistication, Ennio Morricone's eerie score plays on our unease and make-up maestro Rick Baker's transformations combine ingenuity with a real sense of agony. But director Mike Nichols is so interested in the romantic entanglements that he forgets to make the horror horrific. DP Sex scenes, violence, swearing. *DVD* 🔵

Jack Nicholson *Will Randall* • Michelle Pfeiffer *Laura Alden* • James Spader *Stewart Swinton* • Kate Nelligan *Charlotte Randall* • Richard Jenkins *Detective Bridger* • Christopher Plummer *Raymond Alden* • Eileen Atkins *Mary* • David Hyde Pierce *Roy* • Om Puri *Dr Vijay Alezias* • Ron Rifkin *Doctor* • Prunella Scales *Maude* ■ *Dir* Mike Nichols • *Scr* Jim Harrison, Wesley Strick

The Wolf at the Door ★★★ 18
Biographical drama
1986 · Fr/Den · Colour · 86min

Danish director Henning Carlsen found an international audience with this biopic of the artist Paul Gauguin. In a far cry from Anthony Quinn's portrayal in *Lust for Life*, Donald Sutherland plays Gauguin as a man at the crossroads, caught between the need to support his mistresses and the desire to fulfil his artistic destiny. Intelligently scripted by Christopher Hampton and beautifully shot by Mikael Salomon, this is a laudable attempt to understand a complex personality. DP Nudity.

Donald Sutherland *Paul Gauguin* • Valerie Morea *Annah-la-Javanaise* • Max von Sydow *August Strindberg* • Sofie Grabol *Judith Molard* • Merete Voldstedlund *Mette Gauguin* • Jørgen Reenberg *Edward Brandes* • Yves Barsack *Edgar Degas* ■ *Dir* Henning Carlsen • *Scr* Christopher Hampton, from a story by Henning Carlsen, Jean-Claude Carriere

Wolf Children ★★★ PG
Animated fantasy   2012 · Jpn · Colour · 117min

Mamoru Hosoda's intriguing *anime* tale of a mother rearing her half-lupine kids in the Japanese countryside explores the primitive aspects of the rural idyll with handsome, largely hand-drawn visuals. Hosoda's visual style and mixing of fantasy and the everyday has elicited comparisons with Hayao Miyazaki, though here he allows sentimental anthropomorphism to creep in. Hosoda chronicles their upbringing with plenty of gentle humour, and it is only when one decides to take the human route and the other opts to embrace his transformational nature that the real drama begins. Hosoda cogently tackles themes of identity, prejudice and the nature vs nurture debate but, while his metaphorical message is astute, the movie sometimes feels as twee as it is poetic. DP Japanese +subtitles.

Aoi Miyazaki *Hana* • Haru Kuroki *Yuki* • Yukito Nishii *Ame* ■ *Dir* Mamoru Hosoda • *Scr* Mamoru Hosoda, Satoko Okudera, from Hosoda's story

Wolf Creek ★★★★ 18
Horror   2005 · Aus · Colour · 94min

Inspired by the horrific backpacker murders of the 1990s, this is arguably the best horror flick to come out of Australia yet. Local lad Nathan Phillips teams up with British tourists (Cassandra Magrath and Kestie Morassi) to visit the site of a meteor strike. Things start to go wrong when their car breaks down and they meet a friendly local hunter (John Jarratt), who offers to tow them to his camp. First-time director Greg McLean is not afraid to subvert the usual genre rules and is confident enough to take his time in setting up the story, which makes the shockingly raw explosion

of violence in the final half truly disturbing. A straight-to-DVD sequel was released in 2013. JF *DVD* 🔵

John Jarratt *Mick Taylor* • Nathan Phillips *Ben Mitchell* • Cassandra Magrath *Liz Hunter* • Kestie Morassi *Kristy Earl* ■ *Dir/Scr* Greg McLean

Wolf Lake ★★ 18
Thriller   1979 · US · Colour · 83min

Further evidence of Rod Steiger's declining fortunes was obvious in this depressing movie (also known as *Honor Guard*), laden with Vietnam overtones. When four ex-marines meet a deserter while staying in a Canadian hunting lodge, one of them decides to avenge his son's death in Vietnam. Steiger's usual heavyweight presence only adds to the grim nature of the story. However, if writer/director Burt Kennedy was trying to get a message about Vietnam across, he fails to make it clear here. NF

Rod Steiger *Charlie* • David Huffman *David* • Robin Mattson *Linda* • Jerry Hardin *Wilbur* • Richard Herd *George* • Paul Mantee *Sweeney* ■ *Dir/Scr* Burt Kennedy

The Wolf Man ★★★★ PG
Classic horror   1941 · US · BW · 69min

This Universal movie not only established Lon Chaney Jr as a horror star but it also instigated most of the cinematic werewolf lore concerning pentagrams, the Moon and the fatality of silver. Chaney returns home to Wales and, after being warned of life-threatening danger by gypsy Maria Ouspenskaya, is attacked by her werewolf son Bela Lugosi and cursed to transform into a wolf man himself whenever the moon is full. An intelligent, literate script, fine direction by George Waggner, convincing make-up by Jack Pierce and a sympathetic performance by Chaney put this chiller in the top rank. AJ *DVD* 🔵

Lon Chaney [Lon Chaney Jr] *Lawrence "Larry" Talbot/The Wolf Man* • Claude Rains *Sir John Talbot* • Evelyn Ankers *Gwen Conliffe* • Ralph Bellamy *Captain Paul Montford* • Warren William *Dr Lloyd* • Patric Knowles *Frank Andrews* • Maria Ouspenskaya *Maleva* • Bela Lugosi *Bela* ■ *Dir* George Waggner • *Scr* Curt Siodmak • *Makeup* Jack P Pierce [Jack Pierce] • *Cinematographer* Joseph Valentine

The Wolf of Wall Street ★★★★★ 18
Black comedy drama based on a true story
2013 · US · Colour · 172min

Martin Scorsese's fifth collaboration with Leonardo DiCaprio is the closest the director has come so far to duplicating the career-defining highs of the eight films he made with his former favourite collaborator, Robert De Niro. Charting the rise and fall of high-flying New York finance executive Jordan Belfort, who became a multimillionaire in the 1990s through fraudulent share trading and stock-price manipulation, this is an exhilarating story of decadence and debauchery. DiCaprio gives a charismatic and physical lead performance and is notably supported by Jonah Hill as Belfort's larger-than-life sidekick. Unusually for a Scorsese movie, the tone is flat-out black comedy, with farcical X-rated laughs that perfectly offset the savagely funny, *Sopranos*-style dialogue. DW Violence, swearing, sex scenes, drug abuse, nudity. *DVD* 🔵

Leonardo DiCaprio *Jordan Belfort* • Jonah Hill *Donnie Azoff* • Margot Robbie *Naomi Lapaglia* • Kyle Chandler *Patrick Denham* • Rob Reiner *Max Belfort* • Matthew McConaughey *Mark Hanna* • Jean Dujardin *Jean-Jacques Saurel* • Jon Favreau *Manny Riskin* • Joanna Lumley *Aunt Emma* ■ *Dir* Martin Scorsese • *Scr* Terence Winter, Ted Griffin, from Jordan Belfort's memoirs • *Music* Howard Shore • *Editor* Thelma Schoonmaker • *Costume Designer* Sandy Powell

WolfCop ★★ 15
Comedy horror   2014 · Can · Colour · 75min

Expanded from the winning entry in a competition, writer/director Lowell Dean's comedy horror turns on the brilliant idea of having a badass cop become a werewolf. However, he fails to follow it up with

enough other good ideas, so the film quickly runs out of inspiration. Leo Fafard snarls gamely as the small-town deputy whose maverick policing style acquires a lycanthropic edge after he is targeted by a sinister cult. There's gore aplenty, but as far as the actual story goes, the *Scooby-Doo* mysteries throw up more suspects and red herrings than this flimsy romp. DP Violence, swearing, nudity. *DVD* 🔵

Leo Fafard *WolfCop/Lou Garou* • Amy Matysio *Tina* • Jonathan Cherry *Willie* • Sarah Lind *Jessica* ■ *Dir/Scr* Lowell Dean

Wolfen ★★★ 18
Horror   1981 · US · Colour · 109min

Michael Wadleigh directs this classy, thoughtful, gory, but not in the least bit scary horror movie about a mutant breed of killer wolf with super-intelligent tracking abilities running wild in the Bronx. New York cop Albert Finney investigates, and, in a typical Wadleigh eco-addition to Whitley Strieber's so-so supernatural novel, links the plight of the American Indian to the wolves' brutally violent acts. Subjective camerawork, denoting the wolves' point of view, features extensive optical special effects so the prowling always makes for galvanising viewing, while Finney makes the most of his tart dialogue. AJ Violence, swearing, nudity. *DVD*

Albert Finney *Dewey Wilson* • Diane Venora *Rebecca Neff* • Edward James Olmos *Eddie Holt* • Gregory Hines *Whittington* • Tom Noonan *Ferguson* • Dick O'Neill *Warren* ■ *Dir* Michael Wadleigh • *Scr* David Eyre, Michael Wadleigh, from the novel by Whitley Strieber

The Wolfman ★★★ 15
Horror thriller   2009 · US · Colour · 102min

Universal lets its hairy horror icon loose in the digital era in this enjoyable remake. For the most part, director Joe Johnston (*Jurassic Park III*) ensures that his $100-million makeover remains faithful to the spirit of the 1941 original, while updating its skin-stretching, bone-clacking special effects. Benicio Del Toro plays it straight as Lawrence Talbot, who becomes the victim of a family curse. Less convincing are Anthony Hopkins as Talbot Sr and Emily Blunt as the anaemic damsel in distress. Despite some erratic pacing and an occasional lack of emotion, the curse of the film's notoriously troubled production (change of director, reshoots, delayed release date) is held at bay. JR Violence. *DVD* 🔵

Benicio Del Toro *Lawrence Talbot* • Anthony Hopkins *Sir John Talbot* • Emily Blunt *Gwen Conliffe* • Hugo Weaving *Detective Aberline* • Geraldine Chaplin *Maleva* • Art Malik *Singh* • Antony Sher *Dr Hoenegger* • David Schofield *Constable Nye* ■ *Dir* Joe Johnston • *Scr* Andrew Kevin Walker, David Self, from the 1941 film *The Wolf Man* • *Make-up* Rick Baker • *Cinematographer* Shelly Johnson

The Wolfpack ★★★ 15
Documentary   2015 · US · Colour · 89min

Home-schooled by their mother and ostensibly kept under lock and key by their father, the long-haired, close-knit Angulo brothers happily shun the outside world, staying in their family apartment in Manhattan to painstakingly re-create their favourite films from their DVD collection. The creativity on display makes for compelling viewing, but the bigger picture isn't quite so satisfying: questions go unasked, important details are skimmed or even skipped and, most frustrating of all, the Angulos' set-up isn't really what it seems. DW Swearing.

■ *Dir* Crystal Moselle

The Wolverine ★★★ 12
Action adventure   2013 · US · Colour · 120min

The second solo outing for Hugh Jackman's clawed mauler is a definite improvement on *X-Men Origins: Wolverine*. This time Logan is drawn out of self-imposed exile in the hope of being relieved of the burden of immortality, but he's soon caught up in a turf war in Tokyo. Director James Mangold makes great play of the fish-out-of-water

element of the story, while a beefed-up Jackman rises to the occasion with a powerful but restrained performance. It makes for an intriguing curtain-raiser for the next big X-fest, *Days of Future Past*. JA Violence, swearing. *DVD* 🔵 🔵 CS

Hugh Jackman *Logan/Wolverine* • Tao Okamoto *Mariko Yashida* • Rila Fukushima *Yukio* • Hiroyuki Sanada *Shingen Yashida* • Svetlana Khodchenkova *Viper* • Famke Janssen *Jean Grey* ■ *Dir* James Mangold • *Scr* Mark Bomback, Scott Frank

Wolverine 3
Action adventure   2017 · US · Colour

This is a preview – no prints were available to review prior to publication: With seven appearances as Logan under his belt, Hugh Jackman's decision to make this movie his last as the sabre-clawed superhero will have made fans hope that he goes out with a bang. So if he is going to save his kind in this final episode, we can expect the claws to be out, and the fur to fly. TF 🔵

Hugh Jackman *Logan/Wolverine* • Patrick Stewart *Charles Xavier/Professor X* • Boyd Holbrook • Stephen Merchant • Richard E Grant • Eriq La Salle ■ *Dir* James Mangold • *Scr* Michael Green, David James Kelly

The Wolves ★★★ 15
Period crime drama   1971 · Jpn · Colour · 130min

Set against the backdrop of the nascent Showa era, this is a bruising insight into the unforgiving underworld of 1920s Japan. Pardoned during an amnesty, Tatsuya Nakadai returns to discover his ambitious brother, Noboru Ando, has not only arranged a merger between their Enokiya gang and their deadly Kannon rivals, but has also planned a Manchurian railroad takeover that could spell disaster for his partners in crime. Although it ends with a ferocious moonlight swordfight, the emphasis in this stylish thriller is more on the bushido influence on yakuza culture, with its sense of clan loyalty and honour. DP Japanese +subtitles. *DVD*

Tatsuya Nakadai *Iwahashi* • Noboru Ando *Ozeki* • Komaki Kurihara *Asakura* • Kyoko Enami *Oyu* ■ *Dir/Scr* Hideo Gosha

Wolves ★★ 15
Action horror   2013 · Fr/Can · Colour · 87min

A high-school jock discovers his inner werewolf and heads off to find his roots in a coming-of-age horror that has its moments. Lucas Till (Havoc in *X-Men: First Class*) plays the tortured teen who goes on the run (after apparently eating his parents) and ends up in a backwoods town where age-old lycanthrope dynasties struggle to get along. Debuting director David Hayter does a decent job of keeping the action pacey, but there aren't enough scary bits or gore here to sate the hardened horror-hound. JA Violence, swearing. *DVD*

Jason Momoa *Connor* • Lucas Till *Cayden Richards* • Merritt Patterson *Angelina Timmins* • Stephen McHattie *John Tollerman* • John Pyper-Ferguson *Wild Joe* ■ *Dir/Scr* David Hayter

The Wolves of Willoughby Chase ★★★ PG
Period adventure   1988 · UK · Colour · 88min

Based on Joan Aiken's children's novel, this is a fun romp set in a snowy Yorkshire overrun by wolves during the Industrial Revolution. Emily Hudson and Aleks Darowska are the two girls trying to foil a plot by their evil governess, who is played with bitchy glee by Stephanie Beacham. Grown-up viewers may find parts of the film tedious, but it is brightened up by the over-the-top performances from Mel Smith, Geraldine James and Richard O'Brien. JB

Stephanie Beacham *Letitia Slighcarp* • Mel Smith *Mr Grimshaw* • Geraldine James *Mrs Gertrude Brisket* • Richard O'Brien *James* • Emily Hudson *Bonnie Willoughby* • Aleks Darowska *Sylvia* • Jane Horrocks *Pattern* • Eleanor David *Lady Willoughby* • Jonathan Coy *Lord Willoughby* • Lynton Dearden *Simon* ■ *Dir* Stuart Orme • *Scr* William M Akers, from the novel by Joan Aiken

W

The Woman ★★★ 18

Horror　　2011 · US · Colour · 98min

Dysfunctional families are a horror staple but few are as twisted as the one in this controversial shocker by horror stalwart Lucky McKee. Labelled as both a misogynistic outrage and a dark, feminist satire, the sequel to 2009's *Offspring* sees an outwardly upstanding lawyer (a gleefully vile Sean Bridgers) capture the sole survivor of a feral clan in backwoods America and then force his psychologically damaged wife and kids to help "civilise" her. Irony-laden dialogue and an incongruous alt-rock soundtrack add upbeat contrast to heighten viewer discomfort, as McKee and his co-writer, novelist Jack Ketchum, take the occasionally sluggish narrative from matter-of-fact realism to all-out nastiness. SF Violence. DVD SD

Pollyanna McIntosh *The Woman* • Sean Bridgers *Chris Cleek* • Angela Bettis *Belle Cleek* • Lauren Ashley Carter *Peggy Cleek* • Zach Rand *Brian Cleek* ■ *Dir* Lucky McKee • *Scr* Lucky McKee, Jack Ketchum

The Woman and the Hunter ★★

Drama　　1957 · US · BW · 89min

As a child actor, Paris-born George Breakston appeared in several high-profile pictures before taking on the recurring role of Beezy Anderson in MGM's Andy Hardy series. But his attention turned to directing after he launched his own production company in Kenya in the late 1940s. This is more a melodrama than an adventure, although it still contains plenty of local scenery. However, being torn between John Loder and David Farrar proved a disappointing swan song for one-time "Oomph Girl" Ann Sheridan. DP

Ann Sheridan *Laura Dodds* • David Farrar *David Kirby* • John Loder *Robert Gifford* ■ *Dir* George Breakston • *Scr* Maurice Conn, from his story

Woman Chases Man ★★★ U

Screwball comedy　　1937 · US · BW · 66min

This screwball comedy about money, booze and property is fairly typical of its genre, and is played with ineffable skill by the sparkling trio of Miriam Hopkins, Charles Winninger and a very young Joel McCrea. Unfortunately crippled by a screenplay that runs out of ideas about three-quarters of the way through, the film leaves its principal characters quite literally up a tree! TS

Miriam Hopkins *Virginia Travis* • Joel McCrea *Kenneth Nolan* • Charles Winninger *BJ Nolan* • Erik Rhodes *Henri Saffron* • Ella Logan *Judy Williams* • Leona Maricle *Nina Tennyson* • Broderick Crawford *Hunk Williams* • Charles Halton *Mr Judd* ■ *Dir* John Blystone [John G Blystone] • *Scr* Joseph Anthony, Mannie Seff, David Hertz, from the story *The Princess and the Pauper* by Lynn Root, Frank Fenton

The Woman Eater ★

Horror　　1957 · UK · BW · 70min

Fans of mad scientists and killer vegetables should on no account miss this little-known Z-grade affair, a British studio's successful attempt to match trash coming out of Hollywood in the late 1950s. Boffin George Coulouris propagates a tree that eats young women in the belief that the sap excreted will make him immortal. DM

George Coulouris *Dr James Moran* • Vera Day *Sally* • Joy Webster *Judy Ryan* • Peter Wayn *Jack Venner* • Jimmy Vaughan *Tanga* • Sara Leighton *Susan Curtis* ■ *Dir* Charles Saunders • *Scr* Brandon Fleming

The Woman for Joe ★★ U

Drama　　1955 · UK · BW · 91min

A slow and rather disappointing Rank production, this is the old "hunchback of Notre Dame" chestnut, about fairground owner George Baker who hires a midget, only for him to turn into a Napoleon figure, lusting for power and lusting, too, for Diane Cilento, who's in love with Baker. It's pretty nasty, in fact, with none of the poetry of Victor Hugo's story, let alone Tod Browning's similarly themed masterpiece, *Freaks*. AT

Diane Cilento *Mary* • George Baker *Joe Harrap* • Jimmy Karoubi *George Wilson* • David Kossoff *Max* • Earl Cameron *Lemmie* • Sydney Tafler *Butch* • Violet Farebrother *Ma Gollatz* ■ *Dir* George More O'Ferrall • *Scr* Neil Paterson, from his story *And Delilah*

Woman Hater ★★ U

Romantic comedy　　1948 · UK · BW · 96min

A French film star, played by legendary French star and beauty Edwige Feuillère, retreats into seclusion in an English country house, claiming she has given up men and wants to be alone. Landed gentleman Stewart Granger, suspecting a publicity stunt, sets out to prove it by courting her. Creaky, tedious and witless, this totally squanders the talents of an excellent cast. RK

Stewart Granger *Terence, Lord Datchett* • Edwige Feuillère *Colette Marly* • Jeanne de Casalis *Claire* • Ronald Squire *Jameson* • David Hutcheson *Robert* • Mary Jerrold *Dowager Lady Datchett* ■ *Dir* Terence Young • *Scr* Robert Westerby, Nicholas Phipps, from a story by Alec Coppel

The Woman I Love ★★★

Wartime melodrama　　1937 · US · BW · 85min

European director Anatole Litvak was brought to RKO to make his Hollywood debut with this tale, set in France during the First World War. Paul Muni stars as a fighter pilot whose safety record is questionable until he is joined by new man Louis Hayward. They form a successful partnership in the air and close friendship on the ground, until Hayward falls in love with Miriam Hopkins, unaware that she is Muni's wife. This solid romantic melodrama features some good aerial action. RK

Paul Muni *Lt Claude Maury* • Miriam Hopkins *Denise LaValle/Hélène Maury* • Louis Hayward *Lt Jean Herbillion* • Colin Clive *Capt Thelis* • Minor Watson *Deschamps* • Elisabeth Risdon *Mme Herbillion* • Paul Guilfoyle (1) *Berthier* ■ *Dir* Anatole Litvak • *Scr* Ethel Borden, from the film *L'Equipage* by Joseph Kessel, Anatole Litvak, from the novel *L'Equipage* by Joseph Kessel

Woman in a Dressing Gown ★★★★ PG

Drama　　1957 · UK · BW · 89min

This painfully honest drama, based on a play by Ted Willis, was light years ahead of its time in its treatment of women and their place in marriage. Yvonne Mitchell stars in a role that should have seen her showered in awards. Her portrayal of clinical depression is stunning in its depth and understanding, and director J Lee Thompson pulls no punches in his exploration of a partnership gone sour with the intrusion of a younger woman. In many ways this movie heralded a new dawn in gritty British film-making which culminated in the "kitchen sink" social dramas of the 1960s. SH DVD

Yvonne Mitchell *Amy Preston* • Anthony Quayle *Jim Preston* • Sylvia Syms *Georgie Harlow* • Andrew Ray *Brian Preston* • Carole Lesley *Hilda* • Michael Ripper *Pawnbroker* • Nora Gordon *Mrs Williams* ■ *Dir* J Lee Thompson • *Scr* Ted Willis, from his play

The Woman in Black ★★★ 12

Supernatural horror　　2011 · UK · Colour · 91min

This classy if cliché-ridden ghost story from Hammer is a full-throated reminder of the studio's Gothic horror heyday. Efficiently adapted by Jane (*Kick-Ass*) Goldman from Susan Hill's popular novel (basis for the long-running West End stage hit), it follows grieving solicitor Arthur Kipps (Daniel Radcliffe acquitting himself nicely) as he uncovers the dark secret of a remote community haunted by rampant child mortality. *Eden Lake* director James Watkins does a fine job chasing shadowy scares via sudden loud noises and close-up shock cuts. The melodrama creaks as much as the nursery rocking chair, but the grim resolution adds an unexpectedly uplifting and bittersweet twist. AJ DVD SD

Daniel Radcliffe *Arthur Kipps* • Ciarán Hinds [Ciaran Hinds] *Mr Daily* • Janet McTeer *Mrs Daily* • Shaun Dooley *Fisher* • Roger Allam *Mr Bentley* •

Sophie Stuckey *Stella Kipps* • David Burke *PC Collins* ■ *Dir* James Watkins • *Scr* Jane Goldman, from the novel by Susan Hill

The Woman in Black: Angel of Death ★★★ 15

Horror thriller　　2014 · UK · Colour · 98min

Based on a story outline by Susan Hill, author of the original novel, this sequel is set four decades after events in the 2011 film. A group of schoolchildren and their troubled teacher (a capable Phoebe Fox) are evacuated from Blitz-era London to the now derelict Eel Marsh House, where their presence awakens its spectral inhabitant. Director Tom Harper relies heavily on the creepy potency of the watery causeway and misty visuals to develop a sense of dread, leading to a dénouement that's unexpectedly satisfying. AJ

Jeremy Irvine *Harry Burnstow* • Phoebe Fox *Eve Parkins* • Helen McCrory *Jean Hogg* • Adrian Rawlins *Dr Rhodes* • Leanne Best *Woman in Black* • Oaklee Pendergast *Edward* • Leilah de Meza *Ruby* ■ *Dir* Tom Harper (3) • *Scr* Jon Croker, from a story by Susan Hill

Woman in Gold ★★★ 12

Drama based on a true story　　2015 · UK/US · Colour · 104min

Helen Mirren stars in a sentimental true-life drama, playing Maria Altmann, a proud Jewish woman who fled Austria during the Nazi invasion and made headlines decades later, in 2000, when she sought to reclaim a Gustav Klimt portrait of her aunt – Klimt's muse, Adele Bloch-Bauer – from the Belvedere Gallery in Vienna. There are shades of *Philomena* as the older woman teams up with a lawyer (Ryan Reynolds) seeking justice on her behalf. Altmann is a source of mild humour, with her brittle exactitude, even if director Simon Curtis isn't sure how to approach her – the flashbacks to her escape from Austria are the tensest scenes of the film, and that surely isn't as it should be. SP Swearing DVD SD

Helen Mirren *Maria Altmann* • Ryan Reynolds *Randol Schoenberg* • Daniel Brühl *Hubertus Czernin* • Katie Holmes *Pam* • Tatiana Maslany *Young Maria* • Max Irons *Fritz* ■ *Dir* Simon Curtis • *Scr* Alexi Kaye Campbell, Alex Campbell, from the life story by E Randol Schoenberg, Maria Altmann

The Woman in Green ★★★ PG

Mystery　　1945 · US · BW · 66min

This is one of the weirdest films in Universal's series of mysteries based on Sir Arthur Conan Doyle's characters. It pits Sherlock Holmes (Basil Rathbone) against the evil Professor Moriarty (Henry Daniell) and a beautiful hypnotist (Hillary Brooke) as he investigates the murders of women who are found with their right forefingers severed. The grindingly eerie music used to mesmerise the victims sounds a note of real unease, which not even the bumbling banalities of Nigel Bruce (as Dr Watson) can dispel. TH DVD

Basil Rathbone *Sherlock Holmes* • Nigel Bruce *Dr John H Watson* • Hillary Brooke *Lydia Marlow* • Henry Daniell *Professor Moriarty* • Paul Cavanagh *Sir George Fenwick* • Matthew Boulton *Inspector Gregson* • Eve Amber *Maude Fenwick* ■ *Dir* Roy William Neill • *Scr* Bertram Millhauser, from characters by Sir Arthur Conan Doyle

The Woman in Question ★★★

Crime mystery　　1950 · UK · BW · 99min

One of Dirk Bogarde's earlier pictures, this inventive thriller is directed by Anthony Asquith and co-stars Jean Kent as a fortune teller whose death leads to a serious case of flashback syndrome during which we try to spot her killer. Kent has a juicy role here, since all her acquaintances have a different view of her ranging from kindly neighbour to drunken bitch. AT

Jean Kent *Madame Astra* • Dirk Bogarde *Bob Baker* • John McCallum *Murray* • Susan Shaw *Catherine* • Hermione Baddeley *Mrs Finch* • Charles Victor *Pollard* • Duncan Macrae

Superintendent Lodge • Lana Morris *Lana* • Joe Linnane *Inspector Butler* ■ *Dir* Anthony Asquith • *Scr* John Cresswell

The Woman in Red ★★

Melodrama　　1935 · US · BW · 68min

Barbara Stanwyck struggles valiantly against an uninspired script and an irritating leading man in this thankfully short tale of a professional horsewoman who, to the ire of her mega-rich employer Genevieve Tobin, marries Gene Raymond, the man Tobin wants for herself. John Eldredge is good in support, but the only honours in this dreary little film go to Tobin, who plays with relish and polish. RK

Barbara Stanwyck *Shelby Barrett* • Gene Raymond *Johnny Wyatt* • Genevieve Tobin *Nicko Nicholas* • John Eldredge *Eugene Fairchild* • Russell Hicks *Clayton* • Philip Reed *Dan McCall* • Nella Walker *Aunt Bettina* • Dorothy Tree *Olga* ■ *Dir* Robert Florey • *Scr* Mary McCall Jr, Peter Milne, from the novel *North Shore* by Wallace Irwin

The Woman in Red ★★★ 15

Comedy　　1984 · US · Colour · 82min

One of the enduring cinema images of the 1980s is Kelly LeBrock dancing over an air vent in her flame-red dress à la Marilyn Monroe in *The Seven Year Itch*, hypnotising an awe-struck Gene Wilder. The rest of this warm-hearted and amusing story of obsession and extramarital longings doesn't quite live up to this promising opening, but it's a movie that just about holds the attention. Wilder is at his fretful best, ably supported by the likes of real-life wife Gilda Radner and Charles Grodin. Stevie Wonder's hit single *I Just Called to Say I Love You* features on the soundtrack. SH Violence, swearing, nudity. DVD

Gene Wilder *Theodore Pierce* • Kelly LeBrock *Charlotte* • Charles Grodin *Buddy* • Joseph Bologna *Joe* • Judith Ivey *Didi* • Michael Huddleston *Michael* • Gilda Radner *Ms Milner* ■ *Dir* Gene Wilder • *Scr* Gene Wilder, from the film *Pardon Mon Affaire* by Jean-Loup Dabadie, Yves Robert

The Woman in the Fifth ★★ 15

Psychological mystery thriller　　2011 · Fr/Pol/UK · Colour · 80min

Writer Ethan Hawke arrives in Paris to find his estranged wife and daughter and seek literary inspiration, only to be entangled in underworld intrigue, in this adaptation of Douglas Kennedy's 2007 novel. "The Fifth" is a geographical reference to the city's Latin Quarter, where alluring translator Kristin Scott Thomas holds court and the shambling Hawkes falls under her spell. Technically, you would call this a mystery thriller, but it's heavy on the mystery, light on thrills and is more perplexing as it goes along. TJ English, French +subtitles. DVD SD

Ethan Hawke *Tom Ricks* • Kristin Scott Thomas *Margit* • Joanna Kulig *Ania* • Samir Guesmi *Sezer* • Delphine Chuillot *Nathalie* • Julie Papillon *Chloé* ■ *Dir* Pawel Pawlikowski • *Scr* Pawel Pawlikowski, from Douglas Kennedy's novel

The Woman in the Moon ★★★ U

Silent fantasy　　1929 · Ger · BW · 162min

One of the last silent films made in Germany, Fritz Lang's comic-strip fantasy concerns scientist Klaus Pohl who believes the moon is rich in gold and, with the help of rocket designer Willy Fritsch, organises the first flight there. However melodramatic and farcical the plot, the takeoff is portrayed using dramatic montage and camera angles, and there are a few sinister Langian touches. Despite the quaintness of the technology, the Nazis took the film out of distribution because they felt the rocket was too close to one they were creating on the V2 programme at the time. RB DVD SD

Gerda Maurus *Friede Velten* • Willy Fritsch *Wolf Helius* • Fritz Rasp *Walter Turner* • Gustav von Wangenheim *Hans Windegger* • Klaus Pohl (1)

U SUITABLE FOR ALL　Uc SUITABLE ESPECIALLY FOR YOUNG CHILDREN (DVD ONLY)　PG PARENTAL GUIDANCE　12A UNDER 12s TO BE ACCOMPANIED (CINEMA ONLY)

W

Prof Georg Manfeldt ▪ *Dir* Fritz Lang • *Scr* Thea von Harbou, Fritz Lang, from a story by von Harbou

The Woman in the Window
★★★★**PG**

Film noir   1945 · US · BW · 94min

This clever melodrama, written and produced by Nunnally Johnson, is directed with just the right amount of moody atmosphere by expressionist master Fritz Lang. Edward G Robinson is marvellous as the academic who makes that fatal 1940s error of falling for the subject of a portrait and then finds himself swept up in a convoluted web of murder and deception. Joan Bennett is an ideal "ideal" in one of her four fine performances for Lang. The famous ending is still controversial, but whatever conclusion you come to there's no denying the power of this nightmare. TS

Edward G Robinson *Professor Richard Wanley* • Joan Bennett *Alice Reed* • Raymond Massey *Frank Lalor* • Edmond Breon [Edmund Breon] *Dr Michael Barkstone* • Dan Duryea *Heidt/Doorman* • Thomas E Jackson *Inspector Jackson* • Arthur Loft *Claude Mazard* ▪ *Dir* Fritz Lang • *Scr* Nunnally Johnson, from the novel *Once Off Guard* by JH Wallis

The Woman in White   ★★★

Period mystery drama   1948 · US · BW · 108min

Based on the classic Victorian gothic thriller by Wilkie Collins, the film stars an effectively histrionic Sydney Greenstreet as the evil Count Fosco, plotting to get his hands on Eleanor Parker's fortune. He has her twin sister (also Parker) committed to an insane asylum from where she escapes, returning in the guise of a ghostly apparition to foil Greenstreet's plans. The descent of Agnes Moorehead, Greenstreet's already somewhat mad wife, into murderous insanity is one of the high points of a film which, though atmospheric, is hampered by over-respectful restraint and a dull Parker. RK

Alexis Smith *Marian Halcombe* • Eleanor Parker *Laura Fairlie/Ann Catherick* • Sydney Greenstreet *Count Alesandro Fosco* • Gig Young *Walter Hartright* • Agnes Moorehead *Countess Fosco* • John Abbott *Frederick Fairlie* • John Emery *Sir Percival Glyde* • Curt Bois *Louis* ▪ *Dir* Peter Godfrey • *Scr* Stephen Morehouse Avery, from the novel by Wilkie Collins

The Woman Next Door   ★★★**12**

Drama   1981 · Fr · Colour · 101min

This study of provincial infidelity is both suspenseful and romantic thanks to François Truffaut's affinity for characters trapped in an obsession they're powerless to abandon. Contemporary critics weren't convinced by Fanny Ardant (who was Truffaut's lover), as the neighbour who rekindles a long-suppressed passion in contented Grenoble bourgeois Gérard Depardieu. But they both generate a *frisson* that explains their commitment to a relationship that each knows to be ruinous. DP French +subtitles. **DVD** **BD**

Gérard Depardieu *Bernard Coudray* • Fanny Ardant *Mathilde Bauchard* • Henri Garcin *Philippe Bauchard* • Michèle Baumgartner *Arlette Courdray* • Véronique Silver *Madame Jouve* ▪ *Dir* François Truffaut • *Scr* Jean Aurel, Suzanne Schiffman, François Truffaut

Woman Obsessed   ★★

Romantic adventure   1959 · US · Colour · 102min

This is a star vehicle for tempestuous redhead Susan Hayward and, alas, little else. Hayward is a "widder-woman" who marries rugged Stephen Boyd, and there's plenty of cussin' and feudin', but no real dramatic force. Director Henry Hathaway and his star fail to rise above the puerile material. TS

Susan Hayward *Mary Sharron* • Stephen Boyd *Fred Carter* • Barbara Nichols *Mayme Radzevitch* • Dennis Holmes *Robbie Sharron* • Theodore Bikel *Dr Gibbs* • Ken Scott (1) *Sergeant Le Moyne* • Arthur Franz *Tom Sharron* ▪ *Dir* Henry Hathaway • *Scr* Sydney Boehm, from the novel *The Snow Birch* by John Mantley

A Woman of Affairs   ★★★

Silent melodrama   1928 · US · BW · 92min

Prevented from marrying John Gilbert, whom she loves, rich and beautiful young English society woman Greta Garbo (with alcoholic brother Douglas Fairbanks Jr) finds her reputation tarnished by circumstance. She then goes from man to man in Europe, but meets her only love again with tragic consequences. This over-the-top romantic melodrama is absolute rubbish, but a characteristic silent Garbo vehicle with a starry cast. RK

Greta Garbo *Diana* • John Gilbert (1) *Neville* • Lewis Stone *Hugh* • John Mack Brown [Johnny Mack Brown] *David* • Douglas Fairbanks Jr *Jeffrey* ▪ *Dir* Clarence Brown • *Scr* Bess Meredyth, Marian Ainslee (titles), Ruth Cummings (titles), from the novel *The Green Hat* by Michael Arlen

A Woman of Distinction
★★**U**

Romantic comedy   1950 · US · BW · 84min

With its focus on middle-aged protagonists, this idiotic romantic comedy is part farce and occasionally embarrassing but still manages to be quite entertaining. Rosalind Russell is the uptight college dean, who has devoted her mind and her life to higher things than love and marriage. When visiting professor Ray Milland is installed, a journalist on the local paper runs a story which, to Russell's horror and Milland's bewilderment, suggests they're having an affair. RK

Rosalind Russell *Susan Manning Middlecott* • Ray Milland *Alec Stevenson* • Edmund Gwenn *Mark Middlecott* • Janis Carter *Teddy Evans* • Mary Jane Saunders *Louisa Middlecott* • Francis Lederer *Paul Simone* • Jerome Courtland *Jerome* ▪ *Dir* Edward Buzzell • *Scr* Charles Hoffman, Frank Tashlin, from a story by Ian McLellan Hunter, Hugo Butler

A Woman of Paris   ★★★★**U**

Silent drama   1923 · US · BW · 78min

This silent rags-to-riches drama from Charles Chaplin marked a breakthrough in romantic realism in its day. Chaplin makes only a brief appearance as a railway porter and devotes most of his energies to directing his favoured actress, Edna Purviance. She plays a country girl who retains her illusions about love, despite being seduced by the big city and a suave Adolphe Menjou. The idea may be very dated, but it's Chaplin's near-Dickensian insights that make the tale still relevant. Enchanting and spellbinding. TH **DVD**

Edna Purviance *Marie St Clair* • Adolphe Menjou *Pierre Revel* • Carl Miller *Jean Millet* • Lydia Knott *Jean's mother* • Charles French [Charles K French] *Jean's father* • Clarence Geldert *Marie's stepfather* • Betty Morrissey *Fifi* • Malvina Polo *Paulette* • Charles Chaplin *Station Porter* ▪ *Dir/Scr* Charles Chaplin

Woman of Straw   ★★

Mystery thriller   1964 · UK · Colour · 121min

Sean Connery stars in this set-bound thriller, which sets off at a lively pace, but gets bogged down once wheelchair-using tyrant Ralph Richardson has been found dead and gold-digging nephew Connery finds himself among the murder suspects. Revelling in Richardson's wonderfully cantankerous performance, director Basil Dearden seems to lose interest after his demise, leaving Connery and Gina Lollobrigida, as the old devil's nurse, somewhat in the lurch. DP

Gina Lollobrigida *Maria* • Sean Connery *Anthony Richmond* • Ralph Richardson *Charles Richmond* • Alexander Knox *Lomer* • Johnny Sekka *Thomas* • Laurence Hardy *Baines* • Danny Daniels *Fenton* ▪ *Dir* Basil Dearden • *Scr* Robert Muller, Stanley Mann, Michael Relph, from the novel *La Femme de Paille* by Catherine Arley

Woman of the Dunes
★★★★★**15**

Drama   1963 · Jpn · BW · 118min

Adapted by Kobo Abe from his own novel, this stark human condition parable was denounced by some critics for its photographic neutrality. But director Hiroshi Teshigahara and cinematographer Hiroshi Segawa achieve a rich diversity of visual textures that adds to the sensual atmosphere of this intense drama, in which entomologist Eiji Okada finds himself trapped in the deep-dune home of social outcast, Kyoko Kishida. Even the editorial technique (shifting from languid dissolves to sharp cuts) reflects the environment and the state of the couple's relationship, which Teshigahara further explores through his use of symbolic imagery. DP Japanese +subtitles. **DVD**

Eiji Okada *Jumpei Niki* • Kyoko Kishida *Widow* • Koji Mitsui • Sen Yano • Hiroko Ito ▪ *Dir* Hiroshi Teshigahara • *Scr* Kobo Abe, from his novel *Suna No Onna*

Woman of the Year
★★★★**U**

Romantic comedy   1942 · US · BW · 114min

The first teaming of one of Hollywood's greatest couples: the inimitable Katharine Hepburn and laconic, rugged Spencer Tracy. They're beautifully matched, she a columnist wishing to ban baseball until the end of the Second World War, he a reporter defending the sport in print. They meet, wed and generally provide a high old time for audiences everywhere. This is close to the apex of sophisticated romantic comedy, today marred slightly by its wartime conventions and a subplot involving the adoption of a young refugee. Nevertheless, adroit director George Stevens doesn't let the fun get bogged down. TS **DVD**

Spencer Tracy *Sam Craig* • Katharine Hepburn *Tess Harding* • Minor Watson *William Harding* • Fay Bainter *Ellen Whitcomb* • Reginald Owen *Clayton* • William Bendix *Pinkie Peters* • Gladys Blake *Flo Peters* ▪ *Dir* George Stevens • *Scr* Ring Lardner Jr, Michael Kanin

The Woman on Pier 13   ★★

Drama   1949 · US · BW · 72min

When mogul Howard Hughes seized control of RKO, one of his credos was to use the studio and its product as an anti-communist tool, and this moody and suspenseful thriller was the first fruit of his labours. The film ostensibly concerns a shipyard boss being blackmailed over past affiliations, with, interestingly, real-life liberal Robert Ryan playing the "hero". The mercifully short movie was plagued by Hughes's predilection for constant reshoots, so don't blame director Robert Stevenson for what is, or isn't, on the screen. The film leaves a genuinely nasty taste in the mouth today, but is interesting as a social document of its time. TS

Laraine Day *Nan Collins* • Robert Ryan *Brad Collins* • John Agar *Don Lowry* • Thomas Gomez *Vanning* • Janis Carter *Christine* • Richard Rober *Jim Travis* • William Talman *Bailey* • Paul E Burns *Arnold* • Paul Guilfoyle (1) *Ralston* ▪ *Dir* Robert Stevenson • *Scr* Charles Grayson, Robert Hardy Andrews, from a story by George W George, George F Slavin

The Woman on the Beach
★★★★

Film noir   1947 · US · BW · 70min

Jean Renoir regarded his seven-year sojourn in America as wasted time. Yet, in spite of the harmful cuts ordered by studio bosses at RKO, there is no denying the quality of his parting shot to Hollywood. Joan Bennett, in the title role, reinforced her reputation as one of *film noir*'s finest *femmes fatales*. By focusing on her highly charged interaction with blind husband Charles Bickford and shell-shocked lifeguard Robert Ryan, Renoir produces a smouldering and gripping melodrama. DP

Joan Bennett *Peggy Butler* • Robert Ryan *Lt Scott Burnett* • Charles Bickford *Ted Butler* • Nan Leslie *Eve Geddes* • Jay Norris *Jimmy* • Walter Sande *Otto Wernecke* • Irene Ryan *Mrs Wernecke* ▪ *Dir* Jean Renoir • *Scr* Frank Davis, Jean Renoir, Michael Hogan [JR Michael Hogan], from the novel *None So Blind* by Mitchell Wilson

Woman on Top   ★★**15**

Romantic comedy   2000 · US · Colour · 87min

Penélope Cruz is the young wife with a knack for creating hot, tasty dishes who flees from Brazil to San Francisco when she discovers husband Murilo Benicio has been cheating on her. Her talents in the kitchen are soon discovered and she ends up hosting a TV cookery show. There are a few insights into the power of food and the sensuality of cooking before everyone ends up living happily ever after. Slight stuff. JB **DVD**

Penélope Cruz *Isabella Oliveira* • Murilo Benicio *Toninho Oliveira* • Harold Perrineau Jr [Harold Perrineau] *Monica Jones* • Mark Feuerstein *Cliff Lloyd* • John de Lancie *Alex Reeves* • Anne Ramsay *TV director* • Ana Gasteyer *Claudia Hunter* ▪ *Dir* Fina Torres • *Scr* Vera Blasi

A Woman Rebels   ★★

Historical drama   1936 · US · BW · 88min

Katharine Hepburn, her popularity in decline after a series of misconceived failures, is perfectly cast as Pamela Thistlewaite, a non-conformist, asserting women's rights and her own independence in Victorian England. Her fight against the rigid constraints of society, embodied by her unbending father (Donald Crisp), makes for an interesting film, but it degenerates into soft-centred melodrama when she has an illegitimate child. RK

Katharine Hepburn *Pamela Thistlewaite* • Herbert Marshall *Thomas Lane* • Elizabeth Allan *Flora Thistlewaite* • Donald Crisp *Judge Thistlewaite* • Doris Dudley *Young Flora* • David Manners *Alan* • Van Heflin *Gerald* ▪ *Dir* Mark Sandrich • *Scr* Anthony Veiller, Ernest Vajda, from the novel *Portrait of a Rebel* by Netta Syrett

A Woman Scorned   ★★★**15**

Drama based on a true story   1992 · US · Colour · 89min

Meredith Baxter stars as Betty Broderick, the San Diego housewife who resorted to murder after the husband, for whom she had sacrificed everything in order to support him through college, left her for his young assistant. Having given a credible impression of a devoted wife, Baxter throws restraint to the wind in the second half of this TV movie, which promptly falls apart as her jealousy turns to revenge. The story continued in the sequel, A Woman Deceived. DP Some swearing.

Meredith Baxter *Elizabeth "Betty" Broderick* • Stephen Collins *Dan Broderick* • Michelle Johnson *Linda Kolkena* • Kelli Williams *Kate Broderick* • Stephen Root *Kevin McDonald* • Lori Hallier *Joan* • Christine Jansen *Susan McDonald* ▪ *Dir* Dick Lowry • *Scr* Joe Cacaci, from the newspaper article *Till Murder Do Us Part* in the *LA Times* by Amy Wallace

The Woman They Almost Lynched   ★★★**U**

Western   1953 · US · BW · 90min

Women take over the action in this delightfully ludicrous Republic western, set in an outlaw-ridden town trying to preserve neutrality during the Civil War. Joan Leslie and Audrey Totter strap on six-guns for a shoot-out on main street while Leslie, the good girl of the two, is almost strung up on the orders of lady mayor Nina Varela when she is thought to be a Confederate spy. Totter's worst crime is to attempt two song numbers. AE

John Lund *Lance Horton* • Brian Donlevy *William Quantrill* • Audrey Totter *Kate Quantrill* • Joan Leslie *Sally Maris* • Ben Cooper *Jesse James* • Nina Varela *Mayor Delilah Courtney* • James Brown (1) *Frank James* ▪ *Dir* Allan Dwan • *Scr* Steve Fisher, from the story by Michael Fessier

Woman Times Seven   ★★★**15**

Portmanteau comedy drama   1967 · US/Fr/It · Colour · 103min

Shirley MacLaine stars in seven vignettes, paired with or pitted against seven different men, ranging from Peter Sellers to Rossano Brazzi to Michael Caine who appears in the final episode as a mysterious stranger who never says a word. As with all portmanteau

W

movies, some segments work better than others and much depends on one's tolerance for MacLaine's mannerisms and trademark kookiness. AT

Shirley MacLaine *Paulette (Funeral Procession)/Maria Terese (Amateur Night)/Linda (Two Against One)/Edith (The Super-Simone)/Eve Minou (At the Opera)/Marie (The Suicides)/Jeanne (Snow)* • Alan Arkin *Fred* • Peter Sellers *Jean* • Rossano Brazzi *Giorgio* • Vittorio Gassman *Cenci* • Lex Barker *Rik* • Robert Morley *Dr Xavier* • Michael Caine *Handsome stranger* • Anita Ekberg *Claudie* • Philippe Noiret *Victor* ■ *Dir* Vittorio De Sica • *Scr* Cesare Zavattini

A Woman under the Influence ★★★ 15

Drama 1974 · US · Colour · 140min

Gena Rowlands, wife of blue-collar worker Peter Falk and mother of three children, falls prey to increasingly erratic behaviour, slipping in and out of reality until her devoted but distressed family are forced to institutionalise her. Discharged some months later, not much has changed. Written and directed by John Cassavetes as a vehicle for his wife, the magnificent Rowlands, this was two years in the making, financed by friends and family. Despite an awesome tour de force from Rowlands, and sterling support, the film is disadvantaged by its length. Still, it should be seen for its brilliant elements. RK DVD Blu-ray

Peter Falk *Nick Longhetti* • Gena Rowlands *Mabel Longhetti* • Matthew Cassel *Tony Longhetti* • Matthew Laborteaux *Angelo Longhetti* • Christina Grisantii *Maria Longhetti* • Katherine Cassaveтes *Mama Longhetti* • Lady Rowlands *Martha Mortensen* ■ *Dir/Scr* John Cassavetes

Woman Wanted ★★

Crime drama 1935 · US · BW · 65min

In this desperately routine, seen-it-all-before mix of crime and romance, good-hearted lawyer Joel McCrea gives refuge to Maureen O'Sullivan who is wanted on a murder charge. The bulk of the running time is taken up with McCrea's efforts to prove her innocence, which involves him in searching for the real culprit. RK

Maureen O'Sullivan *Ann Gray* • Joel McCrea *Tony Baxter* • Lewis Stone *District Attorney Martin* • Louis Calhern *Smiley* • Edgar Kennedy *Sweeney* • Adrienne Ames *Betty Randolph* ■ *Dir* George B Seitz • *Scr* Leonard Fields, Dave Silverstein, from the story or play *Get That Girl* by Wilson Collison

A Woman without Love ★★

Drama 1951 · Mex · BW · 90min

Luis Buñuel considered this rudimentary and overblown melodrama the worst film he ever made – shot in just 30 days and edited in three. Paternal tyranny and sibling rivalry dominate the action, as inseparable half-brothers Tito Junco and Joaquin Cordero fall out over the inheritance of their respective fathers, a vulgar antique dealer and a kindly engineer. DP Spanish +subtitles.

Rosario Granados *Rosario Jiménez de Montero* • Tito Junco *Julio Mistral* • Julio Villarreal *Don Carlos Montero* • Joaquin Cordero *Carlos, hijo* • Xavier Loyà *Miguel* • Elda Peralta *Luisa Asúnsolo* • Niño Jaime Calpe *Carlitos* ■ *Dir* Luis Buñuel • *Scr* Luis Buñuel, Jaime Salvador (adaptation), Rodolfo Usigli (dialogue), from the novel *Pierre et Jean* by Guy de Maupassant

A Woman's Face ★★★★

Melodrama 1938 · Swe · BW · 100min

Grotesquely disfigured in an accident during childhood, Ingrid Bergman has grown into a hard and bitter woman, but her vengeful nature is transformed, along with her face, after an operation restores her beauty. However, further distress is just around the corner when she becomes involved in a murder plot. The young Bergman gives a brilliant performance in this high-toned melodrama, adapted from a French play and made in Sweden before Hollywood adopted her. RK In Swedish.

Ingrid Bergman *Anna Holm* • Tore Svennberg *Magnus Barring* • Georg Rydeberg *Torsten Barring* • Goran Bernhard *Lars-Erik Barring* • Anders Henrikson *Dr Wegert* • Karin Kavli *Fru Vera Wegert* ■ *Dir* Gustaf Molander • *Scr* Gösta

Stevens, Ragnhild Prim, Stina Bergman, from the play *Il Etait une Fois* by Francis de Croisset [François Wiener]

A Woman's Face ★★★★

Melodrama 1941 · US · BW · 106min

This melodrama about a woman whose plastic surgery changes her looks but not, it would appear, her soul was a major MGM vehicle for Joan Crawford. Previously filmed in Sweden with Ingrid Bergman, this version is a stirring and exciting reminder of Crawford's heyday and still manages to hold an audience. Co-stars Melvyn Douglas as the surgeon and Conrad Veidt as the scheming love interest give consummate performances, and it's superbly directed by George Cukor, but this is Crawford's movie through and through. Her embittered and scarred blackmailer is one of her all-time great creations. TS

Joan Crawford *Anna Holm* • Melvyn Douglas *Dr Gustav Segert* • Conrad Veidt *Torsten Barring* • Osa Massen *Vera Segert* • Reginald Owen *Bernard Dalvik* • Albert Basserman *Consul Magnus Barring* • Marjorie Main *Emma Kristiansdotter* • Donald Meek *Herman Rundvik* • Connie Gilchrist *Christina Dalvik* ■ *Dir* George Cukor • *Scr* Donald Ogden Stewart, Elliott Paul, from the play *Il Etait une Fois* by Francis de Croisset [François Wiener]

A Woman's Secret ★★

Crime drama 1949 · US · BW · 84min

Fans of Nicholas Ray will find little to satisfy them here. As one of the famed director's apprentice works, there's little indication of the glories to come, even for the most die-hard members of his cult following. This is a daft-as-a-brush, turgid melodrama, told in contrived and unnecessary flashback. Gloria Grahame, Ray's wife at the time, has her moments, as does suave Victor Jory, but the whole is a very minor piece. TS

Maureen O'Hara *Marian Washburn* • Melvyn Douglas *Luke Jordan* • Gloria Grahame *Susan Caldwell* • Bill Williams *Lee* • Victor Jory *Brook Matthews* • Jay C Flippen *Detective Fowler* • Mary Philips *Mrs Fowler* • Robert Warwick *Roberts* ■ *Dir* Nicholas Ray • *Scr* Herman J Mankiewicz, from the novel by Vicki Baum

A Woman's Tale ★★★

Drama 1991 · Aus · Colour · 93min

Writer/director Paul Cox continues examining eccentric individuals with this touching tale of old age, independence and undying friendship. Sheila Florance takes centre stage as the terminally ill woman determined to die on her own terms, against the wishes of her uncomprehending son. Cox lays on the sentiment a bit thickly and offers few original insights, but it's still pleasingly offbeat. DP

Sheila Florance *Martha* • Gosia Dobrowolska *Anna* • Norman Kaye *Billy* • Chris Haywood *Johnathan* • Ernest Gray *Peter* ■ *Dir* Paul Cox • *Scr* Paul Cox, Barry Dickins

Woman's World ★★★ U

Drama 1954 · US · Colour · 94min

This is a credible and entertaining look at how a giant corporation operated in the 1950s, with particular reference to the treatment of its executives' wives. Clifton Webb turns in a neat portrayal as a business tycoon and has some able support from the likes of June Allyson and Van Heflin. The problem is that a great opportunity is partially thrown away to concentrate on theatrical trifles. Pretty impressive in its day, but now dated. SH

Lauren Bacall *Elizabeth* • June Allyson *Katie* • Clifton Webb *Gifford* • Van Heflin *Jerry* • Fred MacMurray *Sid* • Arlene Dahl *Carol* • Cornel Wilde *Bill Baxter* ■ *Dir* Jean Negulesco • *Scr* Claude Binyon, Mary Loos, Howard Lindsay, Russel Crouse, Richard Sale, from a story by Mona Williams

Wombling Free ★ U

Comedy musical 1977 · UK · Colour · 92min

The litter-gathering Wombles of Wimbledon Common turned into movie stars after their first conquering television and having a number of Top 20 hits. But director Lionel Jeffries's silly and charmless musical confection came

far too late to revive the careers of the adult-sized furry creations or make them as globally popular as the Muppets. Here the creatures, invisible to mankind unless they believe, lead a protest against pollution. AJ DVD

David Tomlinson *Roland Frogmorton* • Frances de la Tour *Julia Frogmorton* • Bonnie Langford *Kim Frogmorton* • Bernard Spear *Arnold Takahashi* • Yasuko Nagazumi *Doris Takahashi* • Lionel Jeffries *Womble* • David Jason *Womble* • Jon Pertwee *Womble* ■ *Dir* Lionel Jeffries • *Scr* Lionel Jeffries, from characters by Elisabeth Beresford

The Women ★★★★ U

Comedy 1939 · US · BW and Colour · 133min

"There's a name for you ladies, but it's not used in high society outside of kennels." This enjoyable and witty MGM special is immaculately cast without any men, even down to the sex of the featured animals. The complicated plot, from Clare Boothe Luce's Broadway comedy, centres around divorce and infidelity, with star Norma Shearer upstaged by the magnificent Joan Crawford and the utterly superb Rosalind Russell. George Cukor was in his element with such material and such a cast, and there is a famous fashion sequence in Technicolor. The 1956 musical remake entitled *The Opposite Sex* introduced men and was markedly inferior. TS

Norma Shearer *Mary, Mrs Stephen Haines* • Joan Crawford *Crystal Allen* • Rosalind Russell *Sylvia, Mrs Howard Fowler* • Mary Boland *Flora, the Countess De Lave* • Paulette Goddard *Miriam Aarons* • Joan Fontaine *Peggy, Mrs John Day* • Lucile Watson *Mrs Moorehead* • Phyllis Povah *Edith, Mrs Phelps Potter* • Virginia Weidler *Little Mary Haines* • Marjorie Main *Lucy* • Hedda Hopper *Dolly DePuyster* ■ *Dir* George Cukor • *Scr* Anita Loos, Jane Murfin, from the play by Clare Boothe Luce • *Costume Designer* Adrian

The Women ★★ 12

Comedy drama 2008 · US/UK · Colour · 109min

George Cukor's 1939 satire was ahead of its time with its scathing depiction of Manhattan society wives, but this remake from Diane English swaps bitching for self-indulgent blubbing. Meg Ryan is rather bland as Mary Haines, a woman who seems to have everything until she discovers that her successful husband is being unfaithful with local gold-digger Eva Mendes. Unfortunately, and in stark contrast to Joan Crawford's portrayal of the scarlet woman in the original film, there is no depth to Mendes's character. Everything feels contrived and out of step, with the exception of a wisecracking turn by Candice Bergen as Mary's mother. SP DVD Blu-ray

Meg Ryan *Mary Haines* • Annette Bening *Sylvie Fowler* • Eva Mendes *Crystal Allen* • Debra Messing *Edie Cohen* • Jada Pinkett Smith *Alex Fisher* • Bette Midler *Leah Miller* • Candice Bergen *Catherine Frazier* • Carrie Fisher *Bailey Smith* ■ *Dir* Diane English • *Scr* Diane English, from the 1939 film, from the play by Clare Boothe Luce

Women and Men: Stories of Seduction ★★★ 15

Portmanteau comedy drama 1990 · US · Colour · 83min

This is a classy, starry made-for-TV compendium based on three short stories by Mary McCarthy, Dorothy Parker and Ernest Hemingway. The latter fares the best, with director Tony Richardson's elegiac, moving take on *Hills Like White Elephants*, boasting a typically mesmerising performance from James Woods alongside Melanie Griffith. Novelist Frederic Raphael's version of McCarthy's *The Man in the Brooks Brothers Shirt* is a witty and surprisingly accomplished piece, nicely acted by Beau Bridges and Elizabeth McGovern. Only Ken Russell lets the side down with his overblown version of Parker's story *Dusk before Fireworks*, featuring Peter Weller and Molly Ringwald. JF

Elizabeth McGovern *Vicki* • Beau Bridges *Gerry Breen* • Peter Weller *Hobie* • Molly Ringwald *Kit* • James Woods *Robert* • Melanie Griffith *Madley* ■ *Dir* Frederic Raphael, Ken Russell, Tony Richardson • *Scr* Frederic Raphael, Valerie Curtin, Joan Didion, John Gregory Dunne, from

the short stories *The Man in the Brooks Brothers Shirt* by Mary McCarthy, *Dusk before Fireworks* by Dorothy Parker, *Hills Like White Elephants* by Ernest Hemingway

Women in Cages ★★ 18

Prison drama 1972 · US · Colour · 74min

This Roger Corman co-produced sexploitation movie ups the sadism quotient, lowers the humour and softens the political feminist stance prevalent in other examples of the chicks-in-chains genre from the same era. Black icon Pam Grier is the whip-cracking, lesbian warden of a Filipino women's prison who has it in for inmates Roberta Collins and Judy Brown. Little gore, copious topless nudity and lip-smacking direction give this a vile vitality. AJ

Jennifer Gan *Jeff* • Judy Brown [Judith Brown] *Sandy* • Roberta Collins *Stoke* • Pam Grier *Alabama* ■ *Dir* Gerardo De Leon • *Scr* Jim Watkins

Women in Love ★★★★★ 18

Period drama 1969 · UK · Colour · 125min

This is one of Ken Russell's most successful and, for its time, sensational forays into literature, and works so well because it is cohesively respectful of its source, besides allowing its stars acting leeway. Set in the mining community of Nottinghamshire, it stars Oliver Reed (never better) and Alan Bates who woo Glenda Jackson (an Oscar winner) and Jennie Linden, in the process bringing love and tragedy upon them all. The nude male wrestling scene gave the film notoriety but there's more to this scintillating offering than that. TH Sex scenes. DVD

Glenda Jackson *Gudrun Brangwen* • Alan Bates *Rupert Birkin* • Oliver Reed *Gerald Crich* • Jennie Linden *Ursula Brangwen* • Eleanor Bron *Hermione Roddice* • Alan Webb *Thomas Crich* • Vladek Sheybal *Loerke* • Catherine Willmer *Mrs Crich* • Sarah Nicholls [Phoebe Nicholls] *Winifred Crich* • Michael Gough *Tom Brangwen* ■ *Dir* Ken Russell • *Scr* Larry Kramer, from the novel by DH Lawrence

Women in Revolt ★★★ 18

Comedy drama 1971 · US · Colour · 94min

The last feature film from Andy Warhol's Factory may be the only one on which the artist genuinely collaborated with film-maker Paul Morrissey. (The early static films were created by Warhol alone, but after Morrissey arrived, his was the sole presence behind the camera.) The result is a satire of women's liberation, in which the leading female roles are played by Warhol's transvestite superstars (Jackie Curtis, Candy Darling and Holly Woodlawn). On the one hand, it's a tiresomely sustained joke, pulled in different directions. On the other, it's strangely moving to see the performers strutting their stuff for the last time under the King of Pop Art's direct influence. DM

Jackie Curtis *Jackie* • Candy Darling *Candy* • Holly Woodlawn *Holly* • Marty Kove [Martin Kove] *Marty* • Maurice Braddell *Candy's father* • Duncan MacKenzie *Duncan, Candy's brother* ■ *Dir/Scr* Paul Morrissey

Women of Twilight ★

Drama 1952 · UK · BW · 91min

The worst aspect of this tawdry example of tabloid film-making is that it was penned by Anatole de Grunwald, who wrote and/or produced some of the most impressive features made in postwar Britain. The twilight women are single mothers who are lured to the boarding house run by Freda Jackson as a front for her baby-farming operation. Clichéd and tasteless. DP

Freda Jackson *Helen Allistair* • René Ray *Vivianne Bruce* • Lois Maxwell *Christine Ralston* • Joan Dowling *Rosie Gordon* • Dora Bryan *Olga Lambert* • Vida Hope *Jess Smithson* • Laurence Harvey *Jerry Nolan* ■ *Dir* Gordon Parry • *Scr* Anatole de Grunwald, from the play by Sylvia Rayman

The Women on the 6th Floor ★★ 12
Comedy 2010 · Fr · Colour · 101min

In 1960s Paris, stuffy middle-class couple Fabrice Luchini and Sandrine Kiberlain hire a wholesome and attractive Spanish maid (Natalia Verbeke), only to find their lives permanently changed by her friends, who all live and work in the same apartment building. But what starts out as a lively interchange between cultures, sexes and classes quickly degrades into stereotype, suspicion and infidelity. Despite some charming moments and a burgeoning sense of fun, this social comedy is really nothing more than your common-or-garden middle-aged sex fantasy. KK French, Spanish +subtitles. *DVD*

Fabrice Luchini *Jean-Louis Joubert* • Sandrine Kiberlain *Suzanne Joubert* • Natalia Verbeke *Maria Gonzalez* • Carmen Maura *Concepción Ramirez* • Lola Dueñas *Carmen* ■ *Dir* Philippe Le Guay • *Scr* Philippe Le Guay, Jérôme Tonnerre

Women on the Verge of a Nervous Breakdown
★★★★★ 15
Comedy 1988 · Sp · Colour · 85min

A classic comedy of treachery, lust and drugged gazpacho, this is the glorious summation of the themes and visual devices of Pedro Almodóvar's early career. The pace is unrelenting, as actress Carmen Maura tries to cope with the emotional and human fallout after she is dumped by her married lover. Immaculately designed and edited, and deliciously filmed in a riot of colour by José Luis Alcaine, this is art house at its most accessible. It seems almost unfair to select key moments from such a bewilderingly busy and uproariously funny film, but the sight of Julieta Serrano speeding along on a motorbike will stay with you for ever. DP Spanish +subtitles. Swearing, sex scenes. *DVD*

Carmen Maura *Pepa* • Antonio Banderas *Carlos* • Fernando Guillen [Fernando Guillen-Cuervo] *Ivan* • Julieta Serrano *Lucia* • Maria Barranco *Candela* • Rossy de Palma *Marisa* • Kiti Manver *Paulina* ■ *Dir/Scr* Pedro Almodóvar • *Cinematographer* José Luis Alcaine

Women Talking Dirty ★★ 15
Comedy drama 1999 · UK/US · Colour · 93min

Set in Edinburgh, this female buddy movie has Helena Bonham Carter and Gina McKee as friends who share everything. Drawn together by their bad experiences with the opposite sex (in particular the dastardly James Purefoy), they wail on each other's shoulder, paddle in the Scottish sea and relish their differences. Not surprisingly, a dark secret threatens their relationship – the problem is that you don't really care. The excellent McKee is criminally misused, and the direction is uneven. LH *DVD*

Helena Bonham Carter *Cora* • Gina McKee *Ellen* • James Purefoy *Daniel* • James Nesbitt *Stanley* • Richard Wilson (3) *Ponald* • Kenneth Cranham *George* • Eileen Atkins *Emily Boyle* ■ *Dir* Coky Giedroyc • *Scr* Isla Dewar, from her novel

Women without Men
★★★ 15
Drama 2009 · Ger/Aus/Fr/It · Colour · 96min

This first feature by Shirin Neshat (in collaboration with her partner, fellow artist Shoja Azari) is set in the build-up to the 1953 military coup in Iran, where four women play out their own drama of rebellion and repression. The struggles of a general's estranged wife, a young prostitute, a sister affronted by her brother's matchmaking, and the latter's religious friend, all unfold in period settings, though are obviously intended as a comment on today's Iran. The script proves an overly didactic affair, but the film's sheer beauty and the passion it conveys certainly grab the attention. TJ Farsi +subtitles. *DVD*

Arita Shahrzad *Fakhri* • Orsi Toth *Zarin* • Shabnam Tolouei *Munis* • Pegah Ferydoni *Faezeh* ■ *Dir* Shirin Neshat, Shoja Azari • *Scr* Shoja Azari, Shirin Neshat, Steven Henry Madoff, from the novel by Shahrnush Parsipur

Women's Prison ★★★
Drama 1955 · US · BW · 79min

Yesterday's thick-ear melodrama becomes today's camp trash, as the enjoyable elements in this Columbia programme filler include Ida Lupino, described in the movie as a "borderline psychopath", supervisor in a jail full of 1950s blondes, including forger Jan Sterling, killer Phyllis Thaxter and a clever stripper played by the now-forgotten Vivian Marshall. The men don't get much of a look-in, and it disappoints overall because of its lack of surprises. TS

Ida Lupino *Amelia Van Zant* • Jan Sterling *Brenda Martin* • Cleo Moore *Mae* • Audrey Totter *Joan Burton* • Phyllis Thaxter *Helene Jensen* • Howard Duff *Dr Clark* • Warren Stevens *Glen Burton* ■ *Dir* Lewis Seiler • *Scr* Crane Wilbur, Jack DeWitt

Won Ton Ton, the Dog Who Saved Hollywood ★
Period parody 1976 · US · Colour · 91min

In this dismal spoof of the Golden Age of Hollywood, Michael Winner mistakes fast for fun and excess for success, as he ploughs haphazardly through a Rin Tin Tin-type plot about a dog that becomes a movie star. Star-spotting is the film's only abiding appeal. DA

Bruce Dern *Grayson Potchuck* • Madeline Kahn *Estie Del Ruth* • Art Carney *JJ Fromberg* • Ron Leibman *Rudy Montague* • Teri Garr *Fluffy Peters* ■ *Dir* Michael Winner • *Scr* Arnold Schulman, Cy Howard

Wonder Bar ★★★★
Musical romance 1934 · US · BW · 84min

This "La Ronde" of romances serves as an excuse for Busby Berkeley's choreography, which notably includes a production showstopper done with mirrors and an embarrassing blackface number. Plotwise, nightclub owner Al Jolson and his band singer Dick Powell are both in love with dancer Dolores Del Rio, while she has her sights set on her dance partner Ricardo Cortez, who is also the choice of wealthy socialite Kay Francis. Dirty old man comedy native to the genre is provided by Guy Kibbee and Hugh Herbert, who play married men pursuing the chorus girls. Terrific entertainment. RK

Al Jolson *Al Wonder* • Kay Francis *Liane Renaud* • Dolores Del Rio *Ynez* • Ricardo Cortez *Harry* • Dick Powell *Tommy* • Guy Kibbee *Simpson* ■ *Dir* Lloyd Bacon • *Scr* Earl Baldwin, from the play *Die Wunderbar* (book by Geza Herczeg, Karl Farkas, music by Robert Katscher) • *Director (musical Numbers)* Busby Berkeley

Wonder Boys ★★★★ 15
Comedy drama 2000 · US/Ger/UK/Jpn · Colour · 106min

Director Curtis Hanson followed the marvellous *LA Confidential* with this quirky, dark and unforgettable comedy drama. Michael Douglas is an ageing, pot-smoking college professor whose life is on shaky ground – his young third wife has left him, he's having an affair with the (married) college chancellor (Frances McDormand) and she's pregnant, he's struggling with the follow-up to his celebrated first novel, and he also has to deal with an odd, but potentially talented, student Tobey Maguire. Hanson expertly weaves all of these threads into a mesmerising drama complete with fascinating characters and a wicked sense of humour. JB Swearing, drug abuse. *DVD*

Michael Douglas (1) *Grady Tripp* • Tobey Maguire *James Leer* • Frances McDormand *Sara Gaskell* • Robert Downey Jr *Terry Crabtree* • Katie Holmes *Hannah Green* • Richard Thomas *Walter Gaskell* • Rip Torn *Quentin "Q" Morewood* • Philip Bosco *Hank Winters* ■ *Dir* Curtis Hanson • *Scr* Steve Kloves, from the novel by Michael Chabon

Wonder Man ★★★ U
Musical comedy 1945 · US · Colour · 94min

In a splendidly Technicolored fantasy, the talented Danny Kaye plays two roles, a mild-mannered academic and his brother, a nightclub performer bumped off by gangsters, enabling his spirit to enter his brother's body. Producer Samuel Goldwyn spared no expense in surrounding Kaye with good-looking co-stars and a fine supporting cast, and the whole enterprise ended up taking that year's Oscar for best special effects. Kaye's verve and genial madness keep this endeavour buoyantly afloat. TS

Danny Kaye *Buzzy Bellew/Edwin Dingle* • Virginia Mayo *Ellen Shanley* • Vera-Ellen *Midge Mallon* • Donald Woods *Monte Rossen* • SZ Sakall *Schmidt* • Allen Jenkins *Chimp* • Steve Cochran *Ten-Grand Jackson* • Otto Kruger *DA O'Brien* ■ *Dir* Bruce Humberstone [H Bruce Humberstone] • *Scr* Don Hartman, Melville Shavelson, Philip Rapp, Jack Jevne, Eddie Moran, from a story by Arthur Sheekman

Wonder Woman
Action adventure 2017 · US · Colour

This is a preview – no prints were available to review prior to publication: Kate Beckinsale, Sandra Bullock, Eva Green, Christina Hendricks and your mum – it's hard to find a woman that hasn't been linked to this role over the years. Finally director Patty Jenkins, who has mainly made episodes of TV series *Arrested Development* and *Entourage* has landed the gig for a story that spins-off from the *Batman v Superman* film, while Israeli actress Gal Gadot (who proved her action credentials by performing her own stunts in three of the *Fast and Furious* movies) is the one finally chosen to don the iconic costume. TP

Gal Gadot *Wonder Woman* • Chris Pine *Steve Trevor* • Robin Wright *General Antiope* • Connie Nielsen *Hippolyta* • David Thewlis ■ *Dir* Patty Jenkins • *Scr* Allan Heinberg, Geoff Johns, from a story by Heinberg, Zack Snyder, from characters by William M Marston

The Wonderful Country
★★★★ U
Western 1959 · US · Colour · 97min

Westerns usually offer positive leading men with a purpose, but here Robert Mitchum makes a very passive figure as the gunman for hire, an American who has adopted Mexican ways, slowly learning on which side of the Rio Grande he really belongs. Made by the star's own production company, this introspective journey of discovery has little conventional action (a broken leg sidelines Mitchum for quite a while) but presents an absorbing range of well-detailed characters that are far from the usual western stereotypes. Deftly scripted by Robert Ardrey from the novel by Tom Lea (who appears briefly as the barber), it is always superbly photographed, slow but ultimately most rewarding. AE

Robert Mitchum *Martin Brady* • Julie London *Ellen Colton* • Gary Merrill *Major Stark Colton* • Pedro Armendáriz *Governor Cipriano Castro* • Jack Oakie *Travis Hight* • Albert Dekker *Captain Rucker* • Victor Mendoza [Victor Manuel Mendoza] *General Castro* • Charles McGraw *Doc Stovall* ■ *Dir* Robert Parrish • *Scr* Robert Ardrey, from the novel by Tom Lea

The Wonderful, Horrible Life of Leni Riefenstahl
★★★★
Biographical documentary 1993 · Ger · Colour and BW · 182min

How can you possibly hope to sustain a reputation as the finest female film-maker of all time when your sponsor was Adolf Hitler? No one can watch either *Triumph of the Will* or *Olympiad* without being repulsed by their fascist overtones. But it's equally impossible to deny that Leni Riefenstahl had an unrivalled eye for a telling image and a supreme sense of visual rhythm. Celebrating her acting career and her post-Nazi achievements as a stills photographer, cultural anthropologist and underwater documentarist, Ray Muller attempts a rounded portrait that balances Riefenstahl's anti-propagandist claims with some pretty damning evidence. Riveting, revealing, but rarely irrefutable. DP English, German +subtitles. *DVD*

Leni Riefenstahl ■ *Dir/Scr* Ray Muller

The Wonderful Lie of Nina Petrovna ★★★★
Silent romantic melodrama 1929 · Ger · BW · 92min

Originally screened with a lyrical orchestral score by Maurice Jaubert, Hanns Schwarz's silent melodrama was restored to something approaching its pristine glory in the late 1980s. Brigitte Helm revealed herself to be a sensitive and soulful actress with this affecting display of self-sacrificing love. Francis Lederer also impresses as the impoverished lieutenant in the Tsarist army who steals her heart, although he's made to look a little fey by Warwick Ward, as the jilted colonel, who duplicitously suggests they play poker for her affections. Pure melodrama, but tinged with art. DP

Brigitte Helm *Nina Petrowna* • Franz Lederer [Francis Lederer] *Lt Michael Rostoff* • Warwick Ward *Colonel Beranoff* ■ *Dir* Hanns Schwarz • *Scr* Hans Székely

Wonderful Life ★★ U
Musical comedy 1964 · UK · Colour · 108min

The happy-clappy pop musical had been dealt a fatal blow in 1964 by the release of the Beatles' endlessly innovative and iconoclastic *A Hard Day's Night*. Yet the winsome formula continued to rear its sweetly smiling head throughout the decade. Here, Cliff Richard and the Shadows rescue timid actress Susan Hampshire from tyrannical director Walter Slezak. The highlight, if that's the right word, is a song-and-dance history of the movies. DP *DVD*

Cliff Richard *Johnnie* • Susan Hampshire *Jenny* • Walter Slezak *Lloyd Davis* • Hank Marvin • Bruce Welch • Brian Bennett • John Rostill • Melvyn Hayes *Jerry* • Richard O'Sullivan *Edward* • Una Stubbs *Barbara* • Derek Bond *Douglas Leslie* ■ *Dir* Sidney J Furie • *Scr* Peter Myers, Ronald Cass

The Wonderful World of the Brothers Grimm ★★ U
Musical fantasy 1962 · US · Colour · 130min

Fantasy producer George Pal followed up his *tom thumb* with another fairy-tale picture, only this time it was inflated for the giant screen Cinerama process, losing most of its potential lightness and charm. Two rather humourless actors, Laurence Harvey and Karlheinz Böhm, play the writer brothers in a framing story for three of their tales. Some excellent puppetry and animation are featured in the imaginary fables, while Mary Wills won an Oscar for her costumes. AE

Laurence Harvey *Wilhelm Grimm* • Karl Boehm [Karlheinz Böhm] *Jacob Grimm* • Claire Bloom *Dorothea Grimm* • Walter Slezak *Stossel* • Barbara Eden *Greta Heinrich* • Oscar Homolka *The Duke* • Arnold Stang *Rumpelstiltskin* • Yvette Mimieux *The Princess* • Russ Tamblyn *The Woodsman* • Jim Backus *The King* • Beulah Bondi *The Gypsy* • Terry-Thomas *Ludwig* • Martita Hunt *Story-teller* ■ *Dir* Henry Levin, George Pal • *Scr* David P Harmon, Charles Beaumont, William Roberts, from a story by Harmon, from the non-fiction book *Die Brüder Grimm* by Hermann Gerstner and from stories by Jacob and Wilhelm Grimm

Wonderland ★★★★ 15
Drama 1999 · UK · Colour · 104min

Though the title may seem odd for a film depicting the harsh reality of London life, this celebrates the ordinary people who have found the capital isn't paved with the gold of opportunity. Chekhovian in form, Laurence Coriat's screenplay tells the intertwined stories of three sisters and their bickering parents (Kika Markham and Jack Shepherd). Lonely Gina McKee seeks love and sex via a dating agency; pregnant Molly Parker is having trouble with her husband John Simm; while good-time-girl Shirley Henderson neglects her 11-year-old son. The narrative seems to be in free fall, but the film resolves its issues in dramatic fashion. TH Swearing, sex scenes, nudity.

Gina McKee *Nadia* • Molly Parker *Molly* • Shirley Henderson *Debbie* • Ian Hart *Dan* • Stuart Townsend *Tim* • John Simm *Eddie* • Jack Shepherd *Bill* • Kika Markham *Eileen* ■ *Dir* Michael Winterbottom • *Scr* Laurence Coriat

Wonderland ★★ 18

Crime drama based on a true story
2003 · US · Colour · 100min

The life story of porn legend John Holmes has already been brought to the screen in fictionalised form in *Boogie Nights*, but this true-crime saga takes up where Paul Thomas Anderson's film left off. It charts the performer's descent into a drug-addled hell, during which he is implicated in a quadruple homicide. Val Kilmer's portrayal of Holmes as a doe-eyed dope leavens what could have been an intolerably sleazy tale, but James Cox's direction is distractingly bombastic. **AS** Violence, drug abuse. *DVD*

Val Kilmer *John Holmes* • Kate Bosworth *Dawn Schiller* • Lisa Kudrow *Sharon Holmes* • Josh Lucas *Ron Launius* • Tim Blake Nelson *Billy Deverell* • Dylan McDermott *David Lind* • Christina Applegate *Susan Launius* • Eric Bogosian *Eddie Nash* • Carrie Fisher *Sally Hansen* • Franky G *Louis Cruz* • MC Gainey *Bill Ward* • Janeane Garofalo *Joy Miller* • Ted Levine *Sam Nico* • Faizon Love *Greg Diles* • Natasha Gregson Wagner *Barbara Richardson* ■ *Dir* James Cox • *Scr* James Cox, Captain Mauzner, Todd Samovitz, D Loriston Scott

The Wonders ★★★ 15

Drama   2014 · It/Swi/Ger · Colour · 111min

Winner of the Cannes Grand Prix, Alice Rohrwacher's story about beekeepers in Italy is, refreshingly, not a sentimental hymn to peasant culture, more a debate about tradition versus modernity. The focus is quasi-hippies who have come to the area seeking self-sufficiency but find themselves butting heads with EU regulations and pesticide-using neighbours. The drama is a bit episodic, but the performances are nuanced, and there's incisive observation about family dynamics, as well as bonus tips on beekeeping. **LF** Italian, French, German +subtitles. Swearing. *DVD*

Maria Alexandra Lungu *Gelsomina* • Sam Louwyck *Wolfgang* • Alba Rohrwacher *Angelica* • Sabine Timoteo *Coco* ■ *Dir/Scr* Alice Rohrwacher

Wonderwall ★★★ 15

Drama   1968 · UK · Colour · 74min

This is one of the quintessential (and now forgotten) Swinging London films of the late 1960s. Eccentric professor Jack MacGowran peers through his hole in the wall at disturbed model Jane Birkin amid psychedelic butterfly effects and swirling sitars. Though Joe Massot is the movie's credited director, its real inspiration comes from its four superb collaborators: cameraman Harry Waxman, art director Assheton Gorton, editor Rusty Coppleman, and composer, Beatle George Harrison. **TS** Sex scenes, drug abuse. *DVD* *Blu*

Jack MacGowran *Oscar Collins* • Jane Birkin *Penny* • Irene Handl *Mrs Peurofoy* • Richard Wattis *Perkins* • Iain Quarrier *Young Man* • Beatrix Lehmann *Mother* ■ *Dir* Joe Massot • *Scr* Guillermo Cain, from a story by Gérard Brach

Wondrous Oblivion ★★ PG

Period comedy drama
2003 · UK/Ger · Colour · 101min

The problem with this rite-of-passage tale is that writer/director Paul Morrison can't decide whether to focus on 11-year-old Sam Smith's desire to silence bullying schoolboys by improving his cricket batting skills or on his Jewish parents Emily Woof's crush on Caribbean neighbour Delroy Lindo. Moreover, instead of tackling racial prejudice in suburban London in the early 1960s, Morrison opts for a cosy feel-good approach that neither charms nor convinces. **DP** *DVD*

Delroy Lindo *Dennis Samuels* • Emily Woof *Ruth Wiseman* • Stanley Townsend *Victor Wiseman* • Angela Wynter *Grace Samuels* • Leonie Elliott *Judy Samuels* • Sam Smith *David Wiseman* • Naomi Simpson *Dorothy Samuels* ■ *Dir/Scr* Paul Morrison

Won't Back Down ★★★ PG

Drama   2012 · US · Colour · 120min

This cheesily heart-warming tale of American parent power stars Maggie Gyllenhaal and Viola Davis as chalk-and-cheese mums who team up to take on the entrenched and toxic bureaucracy at their kids' failing inner-city elementary school. Their plan: to assume control of the establishment, give it a revamp, then run it themselves along more enlightened lines. The film is a little heavy-handed, more than a little corny and a touch too long, not to mention being rooted in an education system that is very different to ours this side of the pond. But it has its heart in the right place and is passionately acted, while the themes explored are universal enough to make this worth the watch. **DA** Some swearing.

Maggie Gyllenhaal *Jamie Fitzpatrick* • Viola Davis *Nona Alberts* • Oscar Isaac *Michael Perry* • Holly Hunter *Evelyn Riske* • Rosie Perez *Breena Harper* • Ving Rhames *Principal Thompson* ■ *Dir* Daniel Barnz • *Scr* Daniel Barnz, Brin Hill

Woo ★ 15

Romantic comedy   1998 · US · Colour · 81min

Jada Pinkett Smith is the stuck-up girl who proves a nightmare for date Tommy Davidson in this unfunny and hugely irritating comedy that's slightly redeemed by a decent hip-hop soundtrack. Pinkett Smith overacts ridiculously, while the rest of the cast stands on the sidelines watching this disaster of a movie plod to its predictable conclusion. **JB** Violence, swearing, drug abuse, sex scenes, nudity.

Jada Pinkett Smith *Woo/Off the wall babe* • Tommy Davidson *Tim* • Duane Martin *Frankie* • Michael Ralph *Romaine* • Darrel M Heath *Hop* • Dave Chappelle *Lenny* • Paula Jai Parker *Claudette* • LL Cool J *Darryl* • Aida Turturro *Tookie* ■ *Dir* Daisy von Scherler Mayer • *Scr* David C Johnson

The Woo Woo Kid ★★ PG

Biographical romantic comedy
1987 · US · Colour · 94min

This is a documentary-style nostalgia film about the shenanigans of 15-year-old Ellsworth "Sonny" Wisecarver, who was put on trial in 1944 for being utterly irresistible after two affairs with older women – one of whom he married. The film is simply an excuse for a lingering look at a Waltonesque lifestyle with Patrick Dempsey playing the seducer, Talia Balsam as his love interest and the real Wisecarver putting in a cameo amid some fake newsreel footage. **LH**

Patrick Dempsey *Ellsworth "Sonny" Wisecarver* • Talia Balsam *Judy Cusimano* • Beverly D'Angelo *Francine Glatt* • Michael Constantine *Mr Wisecarver* • Ellsworth "Sonny" Wisecarver *Mailman* ■ *Dir* Phil Alden Robinson • *Scr* Phil Alden Robinson, from a story by Bob Kosberg, David Simon, Robinson

The Wood ★★★ 15

Comedy   1999 · US · Colour · 102min

A trio of middle-class African-Americans use one of their number's impending nuptials as an excuse to recall their early experiences in the LA suburb of Inglewood. Cue a series of extended flashbacks that show the friends dealing with school, bullies and girls. Wedding day jitters are a comedy staple, and Rick Famuyiwa's debut feature adds no new spins to the formula. What does impress is the way he steers clear of the usual gangsta/ghetto clichés while wittily revisiting the sights, sounds and outrageous fashions of the 1980s. **NS** *DVD*

Taye Diggs *Roland* • Omar Epps *Mike* • Richard T Jones *Slim* • Sean Nelson *Young Mike* • Trent Cameron *Young Roland* • Duane Finley *Young Slim* • Malinda Williams *Young Alicia* • De'Aundre Bonds *Stacey* ■ *Dir* Rick Famuyiwa • *Scr* Rick Famuyiwa, from a story by Famuyiwa, Todd Boyd

The Wooden Horse ★★★ U

War drama based on a true story
1950 · UK · BW · 98min

This is one of the most famous escape stories of the Second World War in which PoWs use a vaulting horse to hide their tunnel. Scripted by Eric Williams (from his own bestseller) and directed by ex-documentary maker Jack Lee, it has a ring of authenticity that is reinforced by a splendid cast led by Leo Genn and David Tomlinson. However, the action only really becomes compelling outside Stalag Luft III as the escapees make for the coast. **DP** *DVD*

Leo Genn *Peter* • David Tomlinson *Phil* • Anthony Steel *John* • David Greene *Bennett* • Peter Burton *Nigel* • Patrick Waddington *Commanding Officer* • Michael Goodliffe *Robbie* • Anthony Dawson *Pomfret* ■ *Dir* Jack Lee (2) • *Scr* Eric Williams, from his book *The Tunnel Escape*

The Woodlanders ★★ U

Period romantic drama
1997 · UK · Colour · 93min

Phil Agland's feature debut is this Thomas Hardy tale of fickle passion and betrayed devotion. Yet, while Agland admirably captures the atmosphere of the woodlands, he struggles to bring the drama to life. Much of the problem stems from the length and pacing of the scenes, although a hesitant cast, cinematographer Ashley Rowe's gloomy interiors and George Fenton's glutinous score don't help. **DP**

Emily Woof *Grace Melbury* • Rufus Sewell *Giles Winterbourne* • Cal MacAninch *Dr Fitzpiers* • Tony Haygarth *Melbury* • Jodhi May *Marty South* • Polly Walker *Mrs Charmond* • Walter Sparrow *Old Creedle* • Sheila Burrell *Grandma Oliver* ■ *Dir* Phil Agland • *Scr* David Rudkin, from the novel by Thomas Hardy

The Woods ★★ 15

Psychological horror 2006 · US · Colour · 87min

Director Lucky McKee's long-delayed follow-up to his 2001 cult horror *May* is a slow-burning witchcraft tale. Patricia Clarkson adds class playing an icy headmistress whose sinister connection to the spooky woods surrounding her school throws troubled new student Agnes Bruckner into a supernatural tizzy. Much strangeness ensues – most of it enjoyably daft – as McKee creates a movie that's more about atmosphere than actual scares. The plot may be underdeveloped nonsense, but do keep watching for a small but colourful turn by genre icon Bruce Campbell. **SF** *DVD*

Agnes Bruckner *Heather Fasulo* • Patricia Clarkson *Ms Traverse* • Bruce Campbell *Joe Fasulo* • Rachel Nichols *Samantha Wise* • Gordon Currie *The Sheriff* • Jane Gilchrist *Ms Cross* ■ *Dir* Lucky McKee • *Scr* David Ross

The Woodsman ★★★★ 15

Drama   2004 · US · Colour · 83min

It's a brave actor who plays a paedophile and attempts to invest the role with some humanity. Kevin Bacon, long one of Hollywood's underappreciated talents, pulls it off magnificently in this sombre, disturbing tale of a convicted child molester trying to make a life for himself after parole. He finds himself living within sight of a primary school, being harassed by a local cop (rapper Mos Def) and falling in love with a co-worker (played by Bacon's wife Kyra Sedgwick) who's unaware of his past. It's never comfortable to watch, but it's also an intelligent and humane film. **AS** Swearing. *DVD*

Kevin Bacon *Walter Rossworth* • Kyra Sedgwick *Vickie* • Eve *Mary-Kay* • Mos Def *Sgt Lucas* • David Alan Grier *Bob* • Benjamin Bratt *Carlos* • Michael Shannon *Rosen* • Hannah Pilkes *Robin* ■ *Dir* Nicole Kassell • *Scr* Nicole Kassell, Steven Fechter, from the play by Fechter

Woodstock ★★★★★ 15

Music documentary 1970 · US · Colour · 177min

Some three decades on, Woodstock the event is more ridiculed than revered. Yet, as Michael Wadleigh's vibrant documentary demonstrates, this concert in some muddy fields in upstate New York was much more than a simple moment in time – it was the last hurrah of hippy idealism. Wadleigh and assistant directors Thelma Schoonmaker and Martin Scorsese waded through untold miles of footage, using split-screen techniques to do justice to the goings-on both on stage and in the audience. Time may not have been kind to some of the views espoused here, but this is a dazzling piece of film-making and an invaluable insight into what late-1960s youth was trying to achieve. **DP** Drug abuse, swearing, nudity. *DVD* *Blu*

Joan Baez • Jefferson Airplane • Joe Cocker • Sly and the Family Stone • Jimi Hendrix ■ *Dir* Michael Wadleigh

Woody Allen: a Documentary ★★★ 15

Documentary
2012 · US · Colour and BW · 192min

Robert B Weide has managed to interview everyone that matters (with the notable exceptions of former flame Mia Farrow and current spouse Soon-Yi Previn) to provide this intelligent insight into both the man and his movies. Woody Allen himself is amusingly self-deprecating in assessing his achievements, although he is more forthcoming about his childhood and early stand-up career than he is about his approach to film-making. Weide's analysis of Allen's films is also shrewdly handled, as he explores the refinement of the film-maker's comic style. The original two-part television film was never shown in the UK, and one wonders what gems were lost in the edit to this shorter version, but it remains an engaging documentary. **DP** Sexual references, some swearing. *DVD* *Blu*

■ *Dir/Scr* Robert B Weide

The Words ★★ 15

Drama   2012 · US · Colour · 102min

If you found a brilliant manuscript in an old satchel, would you pass it off as your own? That's what failed writer Bradley Cooper does in this tale-within-a-tale meditation on integrity and ambition. Cooper's involvement in the project began over ten years ago, when he was helping his childhood friends, co-writers/directors Brian Klugman and Lee Sternthal, out on their first project. It's a lush-looking literary drama, but it has more acting power than it can use, including Jeremy Irons as a mysterious old man and Zoe Saldana as Cooper's wife. Sadly, any promising ethical issues the film raises end up frittered away by its damp-squib ending. **KK** Swearing.

Bradley Cooper *Rory Jansen* • Jeremy Irons *The old man* • Dennis Quaid *Clay Hammond* • Zoe Saldana [Zoë Saldana] *Dora Jansen* • Olivia Wilde *Daniella* • JK Simmons *Mr Jansen* • Ben Barnes *The young man* ■ *Dir/Scr* Brian Klugman, Lee Sternthal

Words and Music ★★★ U

Musical biography 1948 · US · Colour · 121min

This engaging MGM extravaganza purports to tell the story of brilliant songsmiths Richard Rodgers and Lorenz Hart through their music – and, to a degree, it does. Trouble is, Tom Drake is such a colourless Rodgers and Mickey Rooney such a bumptious, unsympathetic Hart that you don't give two hoots for the men behind the songs. It's a major flaw, even allowing for the fact that in 1948 Hart's homosexuality and Rodgers's ice-cold business deals couldn't really be dealt with on film at all. Still, there are many pleasures to be had. **TS**

Mickey Rooney *Lorenz "Larry" Hart* • Tom Drake *Richard "Dick" Rodgers* • Marshall Thompson *Herbert Fields* • Janet Leigh *Dorothy Feiner* • Betty Garrett *Peggy Lorgan McNeil* • Ann Sothern *Joyce Harmon* • Perry Como *Eddie Lorrison Anders* • Judy Garland • Mel Tormé • Gene Kelly • Vera-Ellen ■ *Dir* Norman Taurog • *Scr* Fred Finklehoffe, Ben Feiner Jr, from a story by Guy Bolton, Jean Holloway

Words and Pictures ★★ 12

Romantic comedy drama
2013 · US · Colour · 110min

For a film about the redemptive power of art and literature, this romance lacks creative spark. Clive Owen, once a promising poet, is now a boozy English teacher at a posh US private school. The arrival of a feisty new art teacher, Juliette Binoche, prompts a good-natured feud between the pair. Reframing *Dead Poets Society* as a romantic comedy is an intriguing concept but, despite likeable leads, writer Gerald DiPego's words and director Fred Schepisi's pictures too often descend into cliché. JF **DVD**

Clive Owen *Jack Marcus* • Juliette Binoche *Dina Delsanto* • Bruce Davison *Walt* • Navid Negahban *Will Rashid* • Amy Brenneman *Elspeth* • Valerie Tian *Emily* ■ *Dir* Fred Schepisi • *Scr* Gerald DiPego

Work ★★★ U
Silent comedy drama   1915 · US · BW · 24min

Usually screened with another two-reeler, *Police*, Charlie Chaplin's silent short is about a family that hires him to re-paper their home. Adapted from a music-hall sketch that was created during Chaplin's early days with Fred Karno, it has lost little of its slapstick hilarity and moves at a terrifically jocular pace. TH **DVD**

Charles Chaplin *Paperhanger's assistant* • Charles Insley *Paperhanger* • Edna Purviance *Maid* • Billy Armstrong *Husband* • Marta Golden *Wife* • Leo White *Secret lover* ■ *Dir/Scr* Charles Chaplin

The Working Class Goes to Heaven ★★★
Drama   1971 · It · Colour · 126min

The joint winner of the Palme d'Or at Cannes, Elio Petri's uncompromising study of politics in the workplace may seem a little strident at times. Factory worker Gian Maria Volonté's transformation from capitalist lackey to impassioned unionist might take some swallowing. But, viewed as a portrait of a man unable to temper his convictions, the story takes on a greater universal significance by virtue of the discomforting realism of Volonté's domestic disputes with girlfriend, Mariangela Melato. DP Italian +subtitles.

Gian Maria Volonté *Ludovico Massa, "Lulu"* • Mariangela Melato *Lidia* • Mietta Albertini *Adalgisa* • Salvc Randone *Militina* • Gino Pernice *Union politician* ■ *Dir* Elio Petri • *Scr* Ugo Pirro, Elio Petri

Working Girl ★★★★ 15
Comedy   1988 · US · Colour · 108min

This appealing executive-suite comedy sees Melanie Griffith climbing the corporate ladder to success by stepping on Sigourney Weaver's fingers, falling for Harrison Ford in the process. Griffith is the exploited and bossed-about secretary to Weaver, taking over from her in her absence and getting Ford as the main prize. This secretary's wish-fulfillment comedy is an easy-going treat for all in director Mike Nichols's assured hands. Carly Simon's Oscar-winning song, *Let the River Run*, makes the soundtrack one to treasure. TH Swearing, nudity. **DVD**

Harrison Ford *Jack Trainer* • Sigourney Weaver *Katharine Parker* • Melanie Griffith *Tess McGill* • Alec Baldwin *Mick Dugan* • Joan Cusack *Cyn* • Oliver Platt *Lutz* • Kevin Spacey *Bob Speck* • Olympia Dukakis *Personnel Director* ■ *Dir* Mike Nichols • *Scr* Kevin Wade

Working Girls ★★★ 18
Drama   1986 · US · Colour · 89min

Director Lizzie Borden has made a movie about prostitution that is interesting, empathic and intelligent. Set within a Manhattan brothel, the film depicts men as seeking individuality and reassurance by acting out their sexual fantasies. Not a great film by any means, it is nevertheless a refreshing take on an industry that is usually portrayed with cliché and prejudice. LH

Louise Smith *Molly* • Ellen McElduff *Lucy* • Amanda Goodwin *Dawn* • Marusia Zach *Gina* • Janne Peters *April* • Helen Nicholas *Mary* ■ *Dir* Lizzie Borden • *Scr* Lizzie Borden, Sandra Kay, from a story by Borden

Working Miracles ★★
Drama   2010 · US · Colour · 100min

Former *CSI: Miami* star Eddie Cibrian fails to convince as a school janitor who acquires healing powers in this badly executed family drama. However, his gift predictably becomes a curse, turning the bitty events into a heavy-handed commentary on the

exploitative nature of human beings. A surfeit of religious talk and Biblical metaphors compounds the clumsiness, but it's the intrusive soundtrack that really damages the film. Consequently, what should have been an affecting little fable barely captures the magic and tragedy of Cibrian's miraculous abilities. SF

Eddie Cibrian *Buddy Hoyt* • Lisa Sheridan *Alice* • Patrick Duffy *Uncle Norman* • Megan Fay *Aunt Beth* • Kali Majors *Callie Boxby* ■ *Dir* Bradford May • *Scr* Steven H Berman

The World According to Garp ★★★ 15
Drama   1982 · US · Colour · 130min

This magical mystery tour of a New England writer's life – based on John Irving's sprawling and virtually unfilmable satirical novel – involves the mind but never engages the heart. Robin Williams stars as Garp, a writer married to Mary Beth Hurt, who's forever at the mercy of lethal modern contraptions and overshadowed by his domineering mum (brilliantly played by Glenn Close in her feature debut). Director George Roy Hill contrives some felicitous moments, but felicity doesn't resolve into clarity despite good intentions. AT Violence, swearing, nudity.

Robin Williams *TS Garp* • Mary Beth Hurt *Helen Holm* • Glenn Close *Jenny Fields* • John Lithgow *Roberta Muldoon* • Hume Cronyn *Mr Fields* • Jessica Tandy *Mrs Fields* • Swoosie Kurtz *Hooker* ■ *Dir* George Roy Hill • *Scr* Steve Tesich, from the novel by John Irving

A World Apart ★★★★ PG
Drama based on a true story
1987 · UK · Colour · 108min

This very well received anti-apartheid drama is based on the true story of a white South African mother who was jailed for her support of the African National Congress. Barbara Hershey is excellent as the woman torn between the love of her family and her political beliefs, and the underused Jodhi May gives an unforgettable performance as the daughter through whose eyes the story unfolds. Stirring stuff from director Chris Menges. LH

Jodhi May *Molly Roth* • Barbara Hershey *Diana Roth* • Jeroen Krabbé *Gus Roth* • David Suchet *Muller* • Paul Freeman *Kruger* • Tim Roth *Harold* • Linda Mvusi *Elsie* • Carolyn Clayton-Cragg *Miriam Roth* • Yvonne Bryceland *Bertha* ■ *Dir* Chris Menges • *Scr* Shawn Slovo

The World Changes ★★★★
Drama   1933 · US · BW · 90min

This dynastic saga begins in uncharted 1850s Dakota and ends with the 1929 Wall Street crash. Paul Muni stars as a farm lad who becomes Chicago's leading meat industry tycoon. He is forced to watch helplessly as his wealth corrupts the values of his wife (Mary Astor), his children and grandchildren, bringing misery and destruction in its wake. At once a hymn to American enterprise and progress, and a pointed morality tale, the film, directed by Mervyn LeRoy, brings a striking central performance from 38-year-old Muni, who ages from early 20s to late 70s. RK

Paul Muni *Orin Nordholm Jr* • Aline MacMahon *Anna Nordholm* • Mary Astor *Virginia* • Donald Cook *Richard Nordholm* • Patricia Ellis *Natalie* • Jean Muir *Selma Peterson* • Margaret Lindsay *Jennifer* • Guy Kibbee *Claflin* ■ *Dir* Mervyn LeRoy • *Scr* Edward Chodorov, from the story *America Kneels* by Sheridan Gibney

World for Ransom ★★★
Crime drama   1953 · US · BW · 81min

Robert Aldrich's second feature, shot in just 11 days in a Hollywood studio, is set Singapore. Dan Duryea is a private eye involved in a convoluted scenario that leads at first to the underworld, then to Cold War intrigue and atomic meltdown, while the lady in the case proves to be the biggest mystery of all. AT

Dan Duryea *Mike Callahan* • Gene Lockhart *Alexis Pederas* • Patric Knowles *Julian March* • Reginald Denny *Major Bone* • Nigel Bruce *Governor Coutts* • Marian Carr *Frennessey March* • Arthur Shields

Sean O'Connor • Douglass Dumbrille *Inspector McCollum* ■ *Dir* Robert Aldrich • *Scr* Lindsay Hardy (front for Hugo Butler)

World Gone Wild ★★ 18
Science-fiction action adventure
1988 · US · Colour · 90min

This undistinguished post-holocaust action adventure has a few imaginative riffs along the way to keep interest maintained. It's 2087, water is a precious commodity, and hippy clan leader Bruce Dern is looking for mercenaries to protect the Lost Wells oasis from an attack by power-mad Adam Ant. Guru Dern acts everybody else off the screen as this drifts into predictability. AJ

Bruce Dern *Ethan* • Adam Ant *Derek Abernathy* • Michael Paré *George Landon* • Catherine Mary Stewart *Angie* • Rick Podell *Exline* • Julius J Carry III *Nitro* • Alan Autry *Hank* • Anthony James *Ten Watt* ■ *Dir* Lee H Katzin • *Scr* Jorge Zamacona

The World in His Arms ★★★ U
Romantic adventure   1952 · US · Colour · 104min

In a corny but enjoyable romantic adventure, Gregory Peck plays an illegal sealskin trader who sails into San Francisco from Alaska, falls for a Russian countess (Ann Blyth) and has to use his fists and his sailing savvy to keep her. Directed by action expert Raoul Walsh, it's macho stuff, professionally done, with the high point an exciting race on the high seas. And way down the cast list, before he abandoned his acting career, is writer/director Bryan Forbes, with sideburns and an American accent. AT

Gregory Peck *Captain Jonathan Clark* • Ann Blyth *Countess Marina Selanova* • Anthony Quinn *Portuges* • John McIntire *Deacon Greathouse* • Andrea King *Mamie* • Carl Esmond *Prince Semyon* • Eugenie Leontovich *Madame Selanova* • Sig Ruman *General Ivan Vorashilov* • Bryan Forbes *William Cleggett* ■ *Dir* Raoul Walsh • *Scr* Borden Chase, Horris McCoy, from the novel by Rex Beach

The World Is Full of Married Men ★★ 18
Melodrama   1979 · UK · Colour · 102min

With a title like this, it comes as no surprise that this film is based on a sex 'n' shopping novel by Jackie Collins. Anthony Franciosa and Carroll Baker star in this tale of a faithful wife who reassesses her life when her husband begins an affair. This is typical British 1970s titillation (lots of make-up, jewellery and low-cut tops and that's just the men), with a cast of actors who would probably now choose to leave this opus off their CVs. JB Swearing, nudity.

Anthony Franciosa *David Cooper* • Carroll Baker *Linda Cooper* • Sherrie Cronn *Claudia Parker* • Gareth Hunt *Jay Grossman* • Georgina Hale *Lori Grossman* • Paul Nicholas *Gem Gemini* • Anthony Steel *Conrad Lee* ■ *Dir* Robert William Young [Robert Young (2)] • *Scr* Jackie Collins, from her novel

The World Is Not Enough ★★★★ 12
Spy adventure   1999 · US/UK · Colour · 122min

In a welcome return to the gritty glamour of such early outings as *From Russia with Love*, this 19th James Bond adventure effortlessly juggles a topical plot about the global domination of oil pipelines with all the expected "super spy" embellishments for maximum suspense and thrills. Pierce Brosnan is clearly comfortable as 007, both in the dramatic sequences and during the spectacular stunts. (The opening speedboat chase along the River Thames gets things moving in turbo drive.) Matching him every step of the way are Sophie Marceau, the best Bond girl in ages, and Robert Carlyle, who is perfect as a vicious villain. AJ Violence, swearing. **DVD** **Blu-ray**

Pierce Brosnan *James Bond* • Sophie Marceau *Elektra* • Robert Carlyle *Renard* • Denise Richards *Christmas Jones* • Robbie Coltrane *Valentin Zukovsky* • Judi Dench *"M"* • Desmond Llewelyn *"Q"* • John Cleese *"R"* ■ *Dir* Michael Apted • *Scr*

Neal Purvis, Robert Wade, Bruce Fierstein, from a story by Purvis, Wade, from characters by Ian Fleming

The World Moves On ★★★
Period drama   1934 · US · BW · 104min

The least-known of the three times John Ford directed in 1934 is a saga charting the fortunes of two New Orleans families from the 1800s to the 1920s. Along the way, it depicts the acquisition of their wealth across continents, the collapse of their commercial empires through war and the subsequent Depression, and the promise of renewal by a new generation. Ford directs this sometimes lumbering but ambitious film with impressive battlefront sequences, a strong pacifist message, and a solid cast. RK

Madeleine Carroll *Mary Warburton* • Franchot Tone *Richard Girard* • Reginald Denny *Erik von Gerhardt* • Siegfried Rumann [Sig Ruman] *Baron von Gerhardt* • Louise Dresser *Baroness von Gerhardt* • Raul Roulien *Carlos Girard/Henri Girard* • Lumsden Hare *Sir John Warburton* ■ *Dir* John Ford • *Scr* Reginald Berkeley, from his story

The World of Apu ★★★★★ U
Drama   1959 · Ind · BW · 100min

Concluding the "Apu" trilogy that began with *Pather Panchali* and *Aparajito*, this confirmed Satyajit Ray as the natural heir to both Jean Renoir and the neorealist tradition. Adapted from Bibhutibhushan Bannerjee's semi-autobiographical novel, the unexpectedly linear narrative focuses on Soumitra Chatterjee's bid to become a writer and his struggle to accept Alok Chakravarty, the son whose birth caused the death of his beloved wife, Sharmila Tagore. Shooting on location in detail-packed long takes (pausing only for the delightfully comic father /son montage sequence), Ray coaxes heartfelt performances from his largely non-professional cast to ensure a fittingly humanist conclusion to this sublimely cinematic masterpiece. DP Bengali +subtitles. **DVD**

Soumitra Chatterjee *Apurba Kumar Ray (Apu)* • Sharmila Tagore *Aparna* • Alok Chakravarty *Kajal* ■ *Dir* Satyajit Ray • *Scr* Satyajit Ray, from the novel *Aparajito* by Bibhutibhushan Bannerjee

The World of Henry Orient ★★★★ U
Comedy   1964 · US · Colour · 104min

This is a charming and neglected rite-of-passage comedy, centring on the obsession of two teenage girls with a womanising concert pianist. Although Peter Sellers and his mistress Paula Prentiss turn in broadly amusing performances, it's the fantasising innocents, Tippy Walker and Merrie Spaeth, who catch the eye. Nora and Nunnally Johnson's playful script (based on the former's novel) also provides showy supporting roles for Tom Bosley and Angela Lansbury as Walker's parents. If only someone had told director George Roy Hill to stop mucking about with the film speeds, this might have garnered the attention it deserves. DP **DVD**

Peter Sellers *Henry Orient* • Paula Prentiss *Stella* • Tippy Walker *Valerie Boyd* • Merrie Spaeth *Marion "Gil" Gilbert* • Angela Lansbury *Isabel Boyd* • Tom Bosley *Frank Boyd* • Phyllis Thaxter *Mrs Gilbert* ■ *Dir* George Roy Hill • *Scr* Nora Johnson, Nunnally Johnson, from the novel by Nora Johnson

The World of Suzie Wong ★★
Romantic drama   1960 · UK · Colour · 128min

William Holden plays an American artist who becomes involved with a Hong Kong prostitute, played by Nancy Kwan. Unbeknown to Holden, Kwan has a baby son whom she hides in a slum. When Holden rejects her offer to become his "steady girlfriend", Kwan turns her attention to playboy Michael Wilding. Seriously hampered by censorship restrictions, Richard Quine treats it as a comic travelogue that exploits the heroine in its own way. AT

William Holden (2) *Robert Lomax* • Nancy Kwan *Suzie Wong* • Sylvia Syms *Kay O'Neill* • Michael Wilding *Ben* • Laurence Naismith *Mr O'Neill* • Jacqui Chan *Gwenny Lee* • Bernard Cribbins *Otis* ■ *Dir* Richard Quine • *Scr* John Patrick, from the play by Paul Osborn and the novel by Richard Mason

The World Ten Times Over
★★ 12

Melodrama 1963 · UK · BW · 89min

When it appeared, this gloomy stylised melodrama struck some as a failed British attempt to emulate the French *nouvelle vague* cinema of the likes of Godard and Truffaut. Nowadays, it seems more interesting for its offbeat central situation: two over-the-hill nightclub hostesses (Sylvia Syms and June Ritchie) live together happily as long as they keep men at bay. A depressing but intelligent movie. JG

Sylvia Syms *Billa* • Edward Judd *Bob* • June Ritchie *Ginnie* • William Hartnell *Dad* • Sarah Lawson *Elizabeth* • Francis De Wolff *Shelbourne* • Davy Kaye *Compere* • Linda Marlowe *Penny* ■ *Dir/Scr* Wolf Rilla

The World, the Flesh and the Devil
★★

Science-fiction drama 1959 · US · BW · 94min

A passionate, earnest and totally daft post-holocaust racial allegory. Miner Harry Belafonte lives through an atomic attack and meets two other survivors – gorgeous Inger Stevens and bigoted Mel Ferrer – when he arrives in devastated New York City. Aside from a few impressively mounted sequences on the deserted Manhattan streets where the two men stalk each other, this eternal triangle plea for harmony is condescending and unbelievable. AJ

Harry Belafonte *Ralph Burton* • Inger Stevens *Sarah Crandall* • Mel Ferrer *Benson Thacker* ■ *Dir* Ranald MacDougall • *Scr* Ranald MacDougall, from the story *End of the Wall* by Ferdinand Reyher and the novel *The Purple Cloud* by Matthew Phipps Shiel

World Trade Center ★★★ 12

Drama based on a true story
2006 · US · Colour · 123min

While *United 93* dramatised the events of 9/11 in hand-held, documentary style, here Oliver Stone uses broad brush strokes to convey the enormity of the attacks on New York. With four times the budget of Paul Greengrass's film, Stone employs disaster-movie effects to take us deep into the rubble of the collapsed buildings, where two Port Authority cops (Nicolas Cage, mercifully subdued, and Michael Peña) await rescue. Though based on the real-life experiences of the McLoughlin and Jimeno families, the story's resolution seems convenient and hokey. It's certainly well made, but anyone hoping for political context or comment will be disappointed by a film that – in the main – avoids controversy and focuses on heroism. AC
DVD **Blu**

Nicolas Cage *John McLoughlin* • Michael Peña [Michael Pena] *Will Jimeno* • Maggie Gyllenhaal *Allison Jimeno* • Maria Bello *Donna McLoughlin* • Stephen Dorff *Scott Strauss* • Jay Hernandez *Dominick Pezzulo* • Michael Shannon *Dave Karnes* ■ *Dir* Oliver Stone • *Scr* Andrea Berloff, suggested by the experiences of John McLoughlin, Donna McLoughlin, William Jimeno, Allison Jimeno

W

World War Z ★★★ 15

Action horror thriller
2013 · US/Malta · Colour · 115min

In Marc Forster's curiously bloodless zombie yarn, Brad Pitt stars as the former UN troubleshooter who must scour the globe in an attempt to find the cause of the cataclysmic pandemic that's transforming Earth's population into swarms of the undead. Pitt oozes (a bit too much) serenity in the face of deadly encounters in Philadelphia (played here by Glasgow), Korea, Israel and Wales, particularly as the safety of his family is dependent on

whether he survives to report his findings. But there are one or two jump-out-of-your-skin moments here, and the epic dimension of the tale (including masses of undead scaling the walled city of Jerusalem like an army of ants) is jaw-dropping at times. JA Violence, some swearing. **DVD** **Blu** **3D**

Brad Pitt *Gerry Lane* • Mireille Enos *Karin Lane* • Daniela Kertesz *Segen* • James Badge Dale *Captain Speke* • Ludi Boeken *Jurgen Warmbrunn* • Matthew Fox *Parajumper* • David Morse *Ex-CIA agent* • John Gordon-Sinclair *Navy SEAL commander* ■ *Dir* Marc Forster • *Scr* Matthew Michael Carnahan, Drew Goddard, Damon Lindelof, from a story by Carnahan, J Michael Straczynski, from the novel *World War Z: an Oral History of the Zombie War* by Max Brooks • *Music* Marco Beltrami

World without End ★★

Science fiction 1955 · US · Colour · 80min

Returning from a Mars mission, an American spaceship enters a time warp and ends up on Earth in the 26th century. Unfortunately, it's after a nuclear war has left the planet's surface inhabited by mutant cavemen, giant spiders and a superior, if listless, race forced to live underground. This colourful and very loose unofficial adaptation of HG Wells's *The Time Machine* is tacky and fast-paced fun, if a little moralistic. The subterranean fairy-tale-style costumes were designed by famed pin-up artist Vargas. AJ

Hugh Marlowe *John Borden* • Nancy Gates *Garnet* • Rod Taylor *Herbert Ellis* • Nelson Leigh *Dr Galbraithe* • Christopher Dark *Henry Jaffe* ■ *Dir/Scr* Edward Bernds

A World without Pity ★★★ 15

Romantic drama 1989 · Fr · Colour · 84min

Eric Rochant's directorial debut is a French equivalent of the American slacker movie. Rochant won the César (France's Oscar equivalent) for best first film, while Yvan Attal took the best newcomer prize for his performance. His co-star, Hippolyte Girardot, is the waster who comes to realise there might be more to life than scamming and partying after he falls for the ultra-respectable and brilliant Mireille Perrier. Rochant hurries through the action with a restless energy that reflects the pace of the young Parisians' lifestyle. DP French +subtitles. Swearing.

Hippolyte Girardot *Hippo* • Mireille Perrier *Nathalie* • Yvan Attal *Halpern* • Jean-Marie Rollin *Xavier* • Cécile Mazan *Francine* • Aline Still *Mother* ■ *Dir/Scr* Eric Rochant

World without Sun ★★★★

Documentary 1964 · Fr · Colour · 90min

Eight years after he won the best documentary Oscar for *The Silent World*, which he co-directed with Louis Malle, Captain Jacques-Yves Cousteau landed a second statuette for this account of his mission to the bottom of the Red Sea. Living one thousand feet below the surface in a prefabricated house, Cousteau and his oceanauts conducted a thorough investigation into the region's highly diverse plant life and encountered all manner of friendly and potentially lethal creatures. DP French +English commentary. **DVD** **Blu**

■ *Dir* Jacques-Yves Cousteau • *Scr* James Dugan, Al Ramrus, Jim Schmerer

The World's End ★★★ 15

Science-fiction comedy
2013 · UK · Colour · 104min

After tackling zombie horrors (*Shaun of the Dead*) and action thrillers (*Hot Fuzz*), director Edgar Wright goes sci-fi for this spoof. Simon Pegg and Nick Frost are joined by three other old friends (Eddie Marsan, Paddy Considine, Martin Freeman) to complete a pub crawl started during their suburban school days. But pesky robot replicas wanting to bring Earth into intergalactic line just keep getting in the way! Once more, Wright cleverly remoulds a beloved genre, producing many laugh-out-loud moments and only a few juvenile clunkers. The barmaggedon scenario treads familiar ground and overdoes the action

spectacle, but there's an engaging chemistry between the five boozers, while the surprise cameos, early 1990s indie soundtrack, zany violence and visual effects add to a self-aware, matey romp that slips down a treat. AJ Swearing, sexual references. **DVD** **Blu**

Simon Pegg *Gary King* • Nick Frost *Andy Knightley* • Paddy Considine *Steven Prince* • Martin Freeman *Oliver Chamberlain* • Eddie Marsan *Peter Page* • Rosamund Pike *Sam Chamberlain* ■ *Dir* Edgar Wright • *Scr* Edgar Wright, Simon Pegg

The World's Fastest Indian
★★★★ 12

Adventure based on a true story
2005 · NZ/US/Jpn/Swi · Colour · 121min

Centring on an endearingly eccentric performance from Anthony Hopkins, this uplifting biopic is an inspirational portrait of ageing New Zealander Burt Munro who, in 1967, followed his dreams and became a motorcycle legend. After a lifetime of perfecting his classic Indian Twin Scout bike, the plucky pensioner travelled to the US, where he set a still unbroken, world land-speed record on Utah's famous Bonneville Salt Flats. Unusually for modern cinema, the film is devoid of cynicism – remaining as open-hearted as its protagonist and the colourful characters he encounters. SF **DVD**

Anthony Hopkins *Burt Munro* • Diane Ladd *Ada* • Aaron Murphy *Tom* • Paul Rodriguez *Fernando* • Annie Whittle *Fran* • Chris Williams *Tina* • Chris Lawford [Christopher Lawford] *Jim Moffet* ■ *Dir/Scr* Roger Donaldson

The World's Greatest Athlete ★★★ U

Comedy 1973 · US · Colour · 88min

In this hugely enjoyable nonsense from Disney, beleaguered coaches John Amos and Tim Conway return from a trip to Africa with jungle dweller Jan-Michael Vincent and his pet tiger. Vincent does a nice line in bewilderment and athletic prowess, but the main fun comes when one of the coaches is shrunk by witch doctor Roscoe Lee Browne and stumbles around some giant props. DP

Jan-Michael Vincent *Nanu* • Tim Conway *Milo* • John Amos *Coach Sam Archer* • Roscoe Lee Browne *Gazenga* • Dayle Haddon *Jane Douglas* • Nancy Walker *Mrs Petersen* • Danny Goldman *Leopold Maxwell* ■ *Dir* Robert Scheerer • *Scr* Gerald Gardner, Dee Caruso • *Music* Marvin Hamlisch

World's Greatest Dad
★★★ 15

Black comedy drama
2009 · US · Colour · 98min

Comedian-turned-director Bobcat Goldthwait scores a direct hit with this darkest of dark comedies about a born loser. Robin Williams plays a talented writer who fritters away his skill teaching poetry at a small high school, and is ridden roughshod over by his girlfriend and abused by his crude son (Daryl Sabara). But when the latter dies in unexpected circumstances, the opportunity for a new life arises. Bitter, twisted and full of witty dialogue, this is a film for everyone who thinks American movies are too nice, and always have a predictable ending. KK Swearing, sexual references. **DVD**

Robin Williams *Lance Clayton* • Alexie Gilmore *Claire* • Daryl Sabara *Kyle* • Geoff Pierson *Prinicipal Anderson* • Henry Simmons *Mike Lane* • Mitzi McCall *Bonnie* ■ *Dir/Scr* Bobcat Goldthwait

The Worst Woman in Paris? ★

Drama 1933 · US · BW · 75min

In Paris, pretty American art student Benita Hume is dubbed the city's "worst woman" by gossips because of her association with wealthy shipping tycoon Adolphe Menjou. She leaves for home, becomes the heroine of a train crash in Kansas, and gets involved in various other situations before returning to Paris. A series of jarringly different events make for a most peculiar plot in an odd, under-characterised movie. RK

Benita Hume *Peggy Vane* • Adolphe Menjou *Adolphe Ballou* • Harvey Stephens *John Strong* • Helen Chandler *Mary Dunbar* • Margaret Seddon *Mrs Strong* ■ *Dir* Monta Bell • *Scr* Monta Bell, Marion Dix

Woyzeck ★★★★ 15

Drama 1978 · W Ger · Colour · 76min

Georg Büchner's famous anti-militarist play has never been more perceptively staged than by Werner Herzog and his on-screen alter ego, Klaus Kinski. Revisiting the expressionist tropes he had so recently employed on *Nosferatu, the Vampire*, Herzog conveys the mental and spiritual disintegration of Kinski's impoverished soldier, as he endures not only the dietary experiments of a local quack and the bullying of his commanding officers, but also the humiliation of being cuckolded by his wife Eva Mattes. The heavy stylisation also reinforces the sense of socio-political and sexual suppression. DP In German.
DVD

Klaus Kinski *Woyzeck* • Eva Mattes *Marie* • Wolfgang Reichmann *Captain* • Willy Semmelrogge *Doctor* ■ *Dir* Werner Herzog • *Scr* Werner Herzog, from the play by Georg Büchner

The Wraith ★ 18

Supernatural action horror
1986 · US · Colour · 88min

Charlie Sheen stars as a leather-clad avenging angel who returns to wreak revenge upon the gang of car thieves responsible for his death. It's a plot boring enough to make you play "spot the famous sibling in the cast", which should keep you busy for most of the picture. RS **DVD**

Charlie Sheen *Jake Kesey/The Wraith* • Nick Cassavetes *Packard Walsh* • Sherilyn Fenn *Keri Johnson* • Randy Quaid *Loomis* • Matthew Barry *Billy Hankins* • Clint Howard *Rughead* • David Sherrill *Skank* • James Bozian *Gutterboy* • Griffin O'Neal *Oggie Fisher* ■ *Dir/Scr* Mike Marvin

The Wrath of God ★★

Satirical western 1972 · US · Colour · 111min

A certain sadness hangs over this banana republic epic since it marked the final screen appearance of Rita Hayworth, one of Hollywood's legendary sex goddesses who had developed Alzheimer's disease. She plays the mother of Frank Langella, a warlord in Central America in the 1920s, while Robert Mitchum is cast as a defrocked priest who carries a gun in his Bible and ends up wired to a crucifix. It's hard to tell if the aim was to make a surrealist drama, a black comedy or merely a post-Peckinpah exercise in violence. AT

Robert Mitchum *Father Van Horne* • Frank Langella *Tomas De La Plata* • Rita Hayworth *Senora De La Plata* • John Colicos *Colonel Santilla* • Victor Buono *Jennings* • Ken Hutchison *Emmet* • Paula Pritchett *Chela* ■ *Dir* Ralph Nelson • *Scr* Ralph Nelson, from the novel by James Graham

Wrath of the Titans ★★ 12

Fantasy action adventure
2012 · US · Colour · 99min

This routine sequel to 2010's *Clash of the Titans* is more about looking epic than telling an interesting story, as it piles on the empty spectacle and one-note action. The Cyclops, the Minotaur and the prison abyss of Tartarus are among the Greek myths plundered this time around, as Perseus (Sam Worthington) races to the Underworld to save his father, Zeus (Liam Neeson), from the mighty Kronos. Despite some edge-of-the seat excitement, this adventure is strictly off the Hollywood assembly line. AJ Some violence, swearing. **DVD** **Blu** **3D**

Liam Neeson *Zeus* • Ralph Fiennes *Hades* • Sam Worthington *Perseus* • Rosamund Pike *Andromeda* • Bill Nighy *Hephaestus* • Danny Huston *Poseidon* • Edgar Ramirez *Ares* ■ *Dir* Jonathan Liebesman • *Scr* Dan Mazeau, David Leslie Johnson, from a story by Mazeau, Johnson, Greg Berlanti

Wreck-It Ralph ★★★ PG

Animated adventure 2012 · US · Colour · 97min

Disney's variant on *Toy Story* themes is a mixed bag of frantic action, humorous antics and blunted satire pitched squarely at the juvenile. Tired of playing the same role in an arcade game, the Donkey Kong-style villain of the piece (voiced with winning gruff vulnerability by John C Reilly) abandons his destructive day job and decides to become a hero, inadvertently wreaking havoc as he travels through other games in search of meaning to his pixellated existence. Ultimately, it's all rather exhausting, though it is a colourfully cute romp for kids and appearances from videogame legends like Sonic the Hedgehog and Pac-Man add to the chaotic fun. AJ DVD BL

John C Reilly *Wreck-It Ralph* • Sarah Silverman *Vanellope von Schweetz* • Jack McBrayer *Fix-It Felix Jr* • Jane Lynch *Sergeant Calhoun* • Alan Tudyk *King Candy* • Rich Moore • *Dir* • *Scr* Phil Johnston, Jennifer Lee (3)

The Wreck of the Mary Deare ★★★ U
Adventure drama 1959 · US · Colour · 104min

In a richly entertaining mystery adventure, Gary Cooper stars as the only man left on a freighter drifting in the English Channel when it is boarded by Charlton Heston's salvage expert. This MGM picture has some spectacular scenes at sea and is lavishly staged with a strong supporting cast in the later scenes. Cooper gives his co-star Heston a lesson in underplaying, while Michael Anderson's unshowy direction helps make this a fine late example of a highly polished studio product. AE

Gary Cooper *Gideon Patch* • Charlton Heston *John Sands* • Michael Redgrave *Mr Nyland* • Emlyn Williams *Sir Wilfred Falcett* • Cecil Parker *Chairman* • Alexander Knox *Petrie* • Virginia McKenna *Janet Taggart* • Richard Harris *Higgins* ■ *Dir* Michael Anderson • *Scr* Eric Ambler, from the novel by Hammond Innes

Wreckers ★★ 15
Drama 2010 · UK · Colour · 81min

In this low-key British domestic drama, Benedict Cumberbatch and Claire Foy play newlyweds renovating a house in the former's home town in the Fens, and trying to start a family. Cumberbatch's wayward younger brother (Shaun Evans) turns up. His arrival revives old memories, reveals family lies, and arouses new passions. *Wreckers* is nicely acted and decently made, but earnest, rather dull, and a touch too full of itself. DA Swearing, sex scenes. DVD

Claire Foy *Dawn* • Benedict Cumberbatch *David* • Shaun Evans *Nick* • Peter McDonald *Gary* ■ *Dir/Scr* DR Hood [Dictynna Hood]

The Wrecking Crew ★★★ PG
Action spy comedy 1969 · US · Colour · 100min

For the fourth and last of the Matt Helm spy spoofs starring Dean Martin, Phil Karlson, director of the original movie (*The Silencers*), was dragooned back into service. Helm has to locate tons of hijacked American bullion before its theft leads to economic meltdown. Needless to say, Helm's investigation involves the seduction of several women (including Sharon Tate), a trek across Europe and a lot of gadgets. Fans of Austin Powers will lap up its sexism, groovy styling and general lack of subtlety. AT

Dean Martin *Matt Helm* • Elke Sommer *Linka Karensky* • Sharon Tate *Freya Carlson* • Nancy Kwan *Yu-Rang* • Nigel Green *Count Massimo Contini* • Tina Louise *Lola Medina* • John Larch *MacDonald* • Chuck Norris *Garth* ■ *Dir* Phil Karlson • *Scr* William P McGivern, from the novel by Donald Hamilton • *Karate Advisor* Bruce Lee

The Wrecking Crew ★★★
Music documentary 2008 · US · Colour · 101min

This heartfelt documentary reveals the story of the 20 or so key session musicians (nicknamed "The Wrecking Crew") who were responsible for playing classic TV themes and backing famous names during a vintage era. Everyone from Sinatra and Sonny & Cher to The Beach Boys and Simon and Garfunkel used members of the crew, including drummer Hal Blaine and bassist Carol Kaye, huge, undervalued talents who now have their moment in the limelight. TJ

Hal Blaine • Tommy Tedesco • Carol Kaye • Al Casey ■ *Dir* Denny Tedesco

The Wrestler ★★★★★ 15
Sports drama 2008 · US/Fr · Colour · 104min

Mickey Rourke is simply perfect for the role of Randy "The Ram" Robinson in this remarkable, visceral tale of a washed-up wrestling star. Comparisons to Rourke's own spectacular fall from grace are unavoidable: he turned away from a promising Hollywood career to become a pro-boxer, which resulted in facial injuries, poor plastic surgery and regular bouts of unemployment. All perfect research then for Darren Aronofsky's low-key, almost documentary-style film. The plot sees Robinson taking bouts on the local circuit to pay the rent, then having to reach out to the few women in his empty life (Marisa Tomei, Evan Rachel Wood) after a heart attack forces him to retire from the ring. And still he keeps alive the hope of a final, redemptive comeback bout. It may sound dour, but Rourke gives the role a lovely, flaky humanity. DW DVD BL

Mickey Rourke *Randy "The Ram" Robinson* • Marisa Tomei *Pam "Cassidy"* • Evan Rachel Wood *Stephanie Robinson* • Ernest Miller (2) *The Ayatollah* • Todd Barry *Wayne* • Wass Stevens *Nick Volpe* • Judah Friedlander *Scott Brumberg* • Dylan Summers *Necro Butcher* ■ *Dir* Darren Aronofsky • *Scr* Robert Siegel

Wrestling Ernest Hemingway ★★★ 12
Drama 1993 · US · Colour · 117min

The most startling fact about this good-natured study of growing old in Florida is that it was actually written by a 23-year-old. Young screenwriter Steve Conrad provides meaty roles that are seized on with relish by Robert Duvall, as a lonely Cuban barber, and the sublime Richard Harris, as a flamboyant old sea dog. Extra spice is provided by the excellent supporting cast, and only Shirley MacLaine grates. Overall, however, this is poignant and likeable. TS Swearing, nudity.

Robert Duvall *Walt* • Richard Harris *Frank* • Shirley MacLaine *Helen* • Sandra Bullock *Elaine* • Micole Mercurio *Bernice* • Marty Belafsky *Ned Ryan* • Harold Bergman *Sleeper* • Piper Laurie *Georgia* ■ *Dir* Randa Haines • *Scr* Steve Conrad

Wrestling with Alligators ★★★
Period romantic drama 1998 · US/UK · Colour · 95min

Even though rock 'n' roll was breaking down barriers, it's sometimes easy to forget just how many taboos survived into the late 1950s. Writer/director Laurie Weltz perhaps tries to tackle too many of them in this small-town melodrama, but her insights into teenage first love, abortion, matrimonial breakdown and faded glory are thoughtful and unhurried. Aleksa Palladino holds things together, as the runaway who befriends abandoned French war bride Joely Richardson. However, the standout is Claire Bloom, as an embittered silent movie star reduced to running a boarding house. DP

Aleksa Palladino *Maddy Hawkins* • Joely Richardson *Claire* • Claire Bloom *Lulu Fraker* • Sam Trammell *Will* • Jay O Sanders *Rick* • Adrienne Shelly *Mary* • Tom Guiry *Pete* ■ *Dir* Laurie Weltz • *Scr* Laurie Weltz, Scott Kraft

Wrinkles ★★★ 15
Animated drama 2011 · Sp · Colour · 89min

In this animation for grown-ups, retired bank manager Emilio (voiced by Martin Sheen), feeling betrayed by his son and daughter-in-law, is placed in a care home. He takes out his frustrations on his bullish roommate Miguel (George Coe), but becomes increasingly dependent upon him as the symptoms of Alzheimer's Disease become more apparent. Emilio and Miguel are believable and empathetic, and despite the odd self-consciously whimsical moment, director Ignacio Ferreras tackles issues of rejection, isolation, illness and mortality with gentle humour and sensitivity. DP Swearing.

Martin Sheen *Emilio* • Matthew Modine *Juan* • George Coe *Miguel* • Casey E Lewis *Doctor* • Mallory Moye *Ana* ■ *Dir* Ignacio Ferreras • *Scr* Ignacio Ferreras, Rosanna Cecchini, Paco Roca, Angel de la Cruz, from the comic book *Arrugas* by Roca

Wristcutters: a Love Story ★★★ 15
Comedy fantasy drama 2006 · US · Colour · 84min

Croatian-born director Goran Dukic makes an affecting feature debut with this ingeniously conceived and cleverly designed afterlife fantasy adapted from the novella *Kneller's Happy Campers*. Having decided life is pointless without girlfriend Leslie Bibb, Patrick Fugit wakes in a limbo for suicides, where he works at Kamikaze Pizza and hangs out with Russian rock star Shea Whigham. However, he hits the road on learning that Bibb has also topped herself and hooks up with spiky Shannyn Sossamon on an Oz-like odyssey that culminates in a showdown at Messiah Will Arnett's citadel. The dénouement is a bit of a disappointment. But the banter between Fugit and Sossamon is disarmingly deadpan, and few films have so wittily envisaged an eternity that is so much more relentlessly grim than life itself. DP DVD

Patrick Fugit *Zia* • Shannyn Sossamon *Mikal* • Shea Whigham *Eugene* • Tom Waits *Kneller* • Will Arnett *Messiah* • Leslie Bibb *Desiree* • Mikal P Lazarev *Nanuk* ■ *Dir* Goran Dukic • *Scr* Goran Dukic, from the novella *Kneller's Happy Campers* by Etgar Keret

Written on the Wind ★★★★ PG
Melodrama 1956 · US · Colour · 95min

For all its flaunting of wealth and power, Douglas Sirk's movie is a brutal indictment of the way the American Dream plunges spiritual values down-market. Rock Hudson and Lauren Bacall are the "normals" sucked into the hysterical paranoia of a Texas oil millionaire's spoilt offspring, played by Robert Stack and Oscar-winning Dorothy Malone, who are outstanding in their portrayals of unleashed anger and arousal. It could have been trashy, but in Sirk's masterful hands this becomes riveting. TH DVD

Rock Hudson *Mitch Wayne* • Lauren Bacall *Lucy Moore* • Robert Stack *Kyle Hadley* • Dorothy Malone *Marylee Hadley* • Robert Keith (1) *Jasper Hadley* • Grant Williams *Biff Miley* • Harry Shannon *Hoak Wayne* • Robert J Wilke *Dan Willis* ■ *Dir* Douglas Sirk • *Scr* George Zuckerman, from the novel by Robert Wilder • *Cinematographer* Russell Metty

The Wrong Arm of the Law ★★★★ U
Crime comedy 1962 · UK · BW · 90min

Peter Sellers is at his funniest as a cockney criminal mastermind who uses a West End dress salon as a front for the illegal activities of his inept gang. He's up against inspector Lionel Jeffries, whose bungling would give the future Inspector Clouseau a run for his money. Cliff Owen directs the marvellously inventive script with due care as Scotland Yard and Sellers decide to co-operate to apprehend a bunch of Australian crooks posing as policemen. TH DVD

Peter Sellers *Pearly Gates* • Lionel Jeffries *Inspector Parker* • Bernard Cribbins *Nervous O'Toole* • Davy Kaye *Trainer King* • Nanette Newman *Valerie* • Bill Kerr *Jack Coombes* • John Le Mesurier *Assistant Commissioner* • Michael Caine ■ *Dir* Cliff Owen • *Scr* John Warren, Len Heath, Ray Galton, Alan Simpson, John Antrobus, from a story by Ivor Jay, William Whistance Smith

The Wrong Box ★★★ U
Period comedy 1966 · UK · Colour · 101min

Shambolic and slackly directed, Bryan Forbes's overlong period comedy is based on a novel co-authored by Robert Louis Stevenson, about family shenanigans involving an inheritance. A veritable cornucopia of British comedy talent is featured in a film that owes more to the freewheeling Swinging Sixties than to the Victorian era in which it is set. The daft plot involves John Mills trying to bump off Ralph Richardson, and, among all the vintage talent, then-new boy Michael Caine more than holds his own. TS DVD

John Mills *Masterman Finsbury* • Ralph Richardson *Joseph Finsbury* • Michael Caine *Michael Finsbury* • Peter Cook *Morris Finsbury* • Dudley Moore *John Finsbury* • Nanette Newman *Julia Finsbury* • Tony Hancock *Detective* • Peter Sellers *Dr Pratt* • Wilfrid Lawson *Peacock* ■ *Dir* Bryan Forbes • *Scr* Larry Gelbart, Burt Shevelove, from the novel by Robert Louis Stevenson, Lloyd Osbourne

The Wrong Man ★★★★ PG
Crime drama based on a true story 1956 · US · BW · 101min

This murky and unpopular film in the Alfred Hitchcock canon sees the maestro of suspense opting for a grim and stark style, almost documentary in nature, as he relates the true story of New York musician Manny Balestrero, arrested for a crime he did not commit. Henry Fonda is superbly believable in the title role, suggesting genuine puzzlement and dismay, and Vera Miles is a revelation as the wife who can't handle the situation. Only distinguished English thespian Anthony Quayle seems out of place in a role that needed an American actor. A fine and disturbing work that deserves to be better known. TS DVD

Henry Fonda *Christopher Emmanuel "Manny" Balestrero* • Vera Miles *Rose Balestrero* • Anthony Quayle *Frank O'Connor* • Harold J Stone *Lieutenant Bowers* • Esther Minciotti *Mrs Balestrero* • Charles Cooper *Detective Matthews* • Nehemiah Persoff *Gene Conforti* • Laurinda Barrett *Constance Willis* ■ *Dir* Alfred Hitchcock • *Scr* Maxwell Anderson, Angus MacPhail, from the non-fiction book *The True Story of Christopher Emmanuel Balestrero* by MacPhail • *Cinematographer* Robert Burks • *Music* Bernard Herrmann

Wrong Turn ★★★ 18
Horror 2003 · US/Ger/Can · Colour · 80min

Director Rob Schmidt pays tribute to 1970s exploitation cinema with this simplistic but satisfying horror feature. Mutant hillbillies are turning the woods of West Virginia into their personal (human) hunting ground, but the grisly extent of their "sport" only becomes clear when five campers and a stranded doctor fall prey to their cannibalistic urges. While Desmond Harrington and Eliza Dushku deliver the heroics, it's producer Stan Winston's special effects that steal the show. Pretension-free but derivative, this really packs a punch. SF DVD CS

Desmond Harrington *Chris Finn* • Eliza Dushku *Jessie Burlingame* • Emmanuelle Chriqui *Carly* • Jeremy Sisto *Scott* • Kevin Zegers *Evan* • Lindy Booth *Francine* • Julian Richings *Three Finger* • Garry Robbins *Saw-Tooth* • Ted Clark *One-Eye* ■ *Dir* Rob Schmidt • *Scr* Alan B McElroy

Wrong Turn 2: Dead End ★★★ 18
Horror thriller 2007 · US/Can · Colour · 92min

First-time director Joe Lynch cuts straight to the chase in this solid sequel to 2003's hillbilly horror *Wrong Turn*. Laying out his gory intentions with a gruesomely outrageous opening, he delivers a quick-hit succession of shocks and kills, as contestants in a survival reality show fall victim to backwoods cannibal inbreds. Henry Rollins is particularly well cast as the TV programme's tough-as-nails, ex-marine host, while *The Texas Chain Saw Massacre* is plundered to fun, if unimaginative, effect with the skin-crawling fate of heroine Erica Leerhsen. SF Violence. DVD

Erica Leerhsen *Nina* • Henry Rollins *Dale Murphy* • Texas Battle *Jake Washington* • Daniella Alonso *Amber* • Steve Braun *Jonesy* ■ *Dir* Joe Lynch • *Scr* Turi Meyer, Al Septien, from characters by Alan McElroy

Wrong Turn at Tahoe ★★ 18

Crime thriller 2009 · US · Colour · 86min

Quentin Tarantino has a lot to answer for. This gangster thriller isn't the first film to copy his style, but it's all the poorer for imitating instead of innovating. Cuba Gooding Jr stars as the loyal right-hand man to vicious Washington State mafioso Miguel Ferrer. When his boss finds himself locked in a bloody war with a rival (Harvey Keitel), Gooding Jr begins to question his commitment to "the life". Aping Tarantino's penchant for stomach-churning violence and pop-culture laden banter, this forgettable effort struggles to make its mark. JR *DVD*

Cuba Gooding Jr *Joshua* · Miguel Ferrer *Vincent* · Harvey Keitel *Nino* · Noel G [Noel Guglielmi] *Frankie Tahoe* · Johnny Messner *Mickey* ■ *Dir* Franck Khalfoun · *Scr* Eddie Nickerson

The Wrong Woman ★★ 15

Thriller 1996 · US/Can · Colour · 90min

In this TV movie, we see Nancy McKeon get framed, get arrested, go to court and then confront the real killer (who we see do the dirty deed and then bump off anyone who can expose her) without ever once feeling a pang of sympathy for her plight. Tame stuff, indeed. DP Some violence.

Nancy McKeon *Melanie Brooke* · Michele Scarabelli *Christine Henley* · Chelsea Field *Margaret Bateman* · Gary Hudson *Lt Nagel* ■ *Dir* Douglas Jackson · *Scr* Douglas Soesbe

Wrongfully Accused ★ PG

Crime spoof 1998 · US/Ger · Colour · 82min

A nonstop assault of lame verbal and visual gags fails to elevate this second-rate spoof. Leslie Nielsen spreads himself alarmingly thin playing a superstar classical violinist accused of murder and on the run to find the real culprit, a one-armed, one-legged, one-eyed man. Pat Proft's rough-and-ready hotch-potch misses practically every single target it tries so desperately to hit. AJ Swearing, sexual references.

Leslie Nielsen *Ryan Harrison* · Kelly LeBrock *Lauren Goodhue* · Michael York *Hibbing Goodhue* · Richard Crenna *Marshal Fergus Falls* · Sandra Bernhard *Doctor Fridley* ■ *Dir/Scr* Pat Proft

Wuthering Heights ★★★★★ U

Classic romantic drama 1939 · US · BW · 99min

Laurence Olivier's Heathcliff is even more handsome than the Yorkshire moors across which he howls his doomed love for Cathy (Merle Oberon) in this stirring melodrama of seething and brooding passion set in England in the 19th century. Produced by Sam Goldwyn, directed by William Wyler, this is still the best by some way of the five big screen versions of Emily Brontë's novel (including Spanish and Egyptian productions). It garnered eight Oscar nominations, including best picture, but only won one, for Gregg Toland's black-and-white cinematography. PF *DVD*

Merle Oberon *Cathy Linton* · Laurence Olivier *Heathcliff* · David Niven *Edgar Linton* · Donald Crisp *Dr Kenneth* · Flora Robson *Ellen Dean* · Geraldine Fitzgerald *Isabella Linton* · Hugh Williams *Hindley Earnshaw* · Leo G Carroll *Joseph* · Cecil Humphreys *Judge Linton* ■ *Dir* William Wyler · *Scr* Ben Hecht, Charles MacArthur, from the novel by Emily Brontë

Wuthering Heights ★★★

Romantic drama 1953 · Mex · BW · 91min

Luis Buñuel first set out to film Emily Brontë's classic novel in 1934, but lost interest in the idea. The same diminution of enthusiam occurred in 1953, but this time he found he could not withdraw and shot the film with a script in which he had little confidence. The Mexican uplands could not be more different from the Yorkshire moors, but they still provide a suitable backdrop for this intense drama of bitterness and revenge. Notable for the ferocity of Jorge Mistral, Irasema Dilian's passion and the cruelty inflicted on animals, the film clearly captures the book's glowering mood. DP In Spanish.

Irasema Dilian *Catalina* · Jorge Mistral *Alejandro* · Lilia Prado *Isabel* · Ernesto Alonso *Eduardo* ■ *Dir* Luis Buñuel · *Scr* Luis Buñuel, Dino Maiuri [Arduino Maiuri], Julio Alejandro, from the novel by Emily Brontë

Wuthering Heights ★★★ U

Romantic drama 1970 · UK · Colour · 80min

In this atmospheric adaptation of Emily Brontë's famous novel Timothy Dalton smoulders to good effect as Heathcliff and Anna Calder-Marshall makes an appealing Cathy. Obviously aiming for a little cultural respectability, producers Samuel Z Arkoff and James H Nicholson (co-founders of B-movie factory AIP) were rewarded with striking images from cinematographer John Coquillon and steady direction from Robert Fuest. DP *DVD*

Anna Calder-Marshall *Catherine Earnshaw* · Timothy Dalton *Heathcliff* · Harry Andrews *Mr Earnshaw* · Pamela Brown *Mrs Linton* · Judy Cornwell *Nellie* · James Cossins *Mr Linton* · Rosalie Crutchley *Mrs Earnshaw* · Hilary Dwyer *Isabella Linton* ■ *Dir* Robert Fuest · *Scr* Patrick Tilley, from the novel by Emily Brontë

Wuthering Heights ★ PG

Romantic drama 1992 · UK · Colour · 101min

Why there was a need for another adaptation of the Emily Brontë novel is one question. And then why adapt it so badly is the other. Ralph Fiennes and Juliette Binoche are poorly directed in this tepid tale of Heathcliff, the wild child orphan, and his lover Cathy. Binoche struggles with her English while they both fail to raise any sexual chemistry. LH *DVD*

Juliette Binoche *Cathy/Catherine* · Ralph Fiennes *Heathcliff* · Janet McTeer *Ellen Dean* · Sinead O'Connor *Emily Brontë* · Sophie Ward *Isabella Linton* · Simon Shepherd *Edgar Linton* · Jeremy Northam *Hindley Earnshaw* · Jason Riddington *Hareton* ■ *Dir* Peter Kosminsky · *Scr* Anne Devlin, from the novel by Emily Brontë

Wuthering Heights ★★★ 15

Romantic drama 2011 · UK · Colour · 123min

Writer/director Andrea Arnold (*Red Road*, *Fish Tank*) effects a brave leap from the urban, contemporary setting of her previous films, to Emily Brontë's beloved rural 19th-century love story. It's an earthy, elemental dramatisation: you can almost smell the Yorkshire moors in the weather-beaten locations. With detailed natural sound design, no score and a young, unknown cast – Shannon Beer and Solomon Glave are particularly striking as the young Cathy and Heathcliff (who, in this provocative version, is black) – Arnold chases the action, handheld, like a *Bourne* movie. It's a boldly modernist approach, and although it's pleasingly tactile, it's perhaps too avant garde; its fractured narrative and glimpses of lens flare constantly break the spell of the period fiction. AC *DVD* *BD*

Kaya Scodelario *Catherine Earnshaw* · James Howson *Heathcliff* · Solomon Glave *Young Heathcliff* · Shannon Beer *Young Cathy* · Steve Evets *Joseph* · Oliver Milburn *Mr Linton* ■ *Dir* Andrea Arnold · *Scr* Olivia Hetreed, Andrea Arnold, from the novel by Emily Brontë

Wyatt Earp ★★★★ 12

Epic western drama 1994 · US · Colour · 182min

Director Lawrence Kasdan's epic journey to the notorious shoot-out at the OK Corral is a monumental western that works both as a serious history lesson and as a quietly understated drama. Beautifully filmed, it portrays the man not the legend, tracing Earp's move from boyhood innocence to knowing cynicism. Kevin Costner has seldom been better as the older Earp, yet he still leaves plenty of room for Dennis Quaid to steal the show as the tuberculosis-ridden dentist Doc Holliday. AJ Violence, swearing. *DVD* *BD*

Kevin Costner *Wyatt Earp* · Dennis Quaid *John "Doc" Holliday* · Gene Hackman *Nicholas Earp* · Michael Madsen *Virgil Earp* · Linden Ashby *Morgan Earp* · Jeff Fahey *Ike Clanton* · Mare Winningham *Mattie Blaylock* · Joanna Going *Josie Marcus* · Mark Harmon *Sheriff Johnny Behan* · Catherine O'Hara *Allie Earp* · David Andrews (2) *James Earp* · Bill Pullman *Ed Masterson* · Isabella Rossellini *Big Nose Kate* ■ *Dir* Lawrence Kasdan · *Scr* Lawrence Kasdan, Dan Gordon · *Cinematographer* Owen Roizman

Wyatt Earp: Return to Tombstone ★★

Western 1994 · US · Colour and tinted · 94min

This TV movie is an ill-conceived attempt to wring the last drop out of *The Life and Legend of Wyatt Earp* series that ran on American TV between 1955 and 1961, and uses colourised clips from the black-and-white original. Hugh O'Brian returns in the role that made his name, searching for a gravestone inscription and confronting a cocky young sureshot. He pluckily attempts to roll back the years, but the story would have worked better as one of the original half-hour shows. DP

Hugh O'Brian *Wyatt Earp* · Jay Underwood *Zack* · Harry Carey Jr *Digger Phelps* · Bruce Boxleitner *Sheriff Darling* · Alex Hyde-White *Editor Clum* ■ *Dir* Frank McDonald, Paul Landres · *Scr* Frederick Hazlitt Brennan, Dan Ullman

Wyoming Mail ★★ U

Western 1950 · US · Colour · 86min

This routine Universal western is made more interesting today by the fact that the supporting cast became more famous than unremarkable stars Stephen McNally and Alexis Smith. Future leading man Richard Egan steals the scenes he's in, while James Arness, the bargain-basement John Wayne, makes a strong impression in his pre-Matt Dillon days. Dull as ditchwater, thanks to Reginald LeBorg's turgid direction. TS

Stephen McNally *Steve Davis* · Alexis Smith *Mary Williams* · Howard Da Silva *Cavanaugh* · Ed Begley *Haynes* · Dan Riss *George Armstrong* · Roy Roberts *Charles DeHaven* · Whit Bissell *Sam Wallace* · James Arness *Russell* ■ *Dir* Reginald LeBorg [Reginald Le Borg] · *Scr* Harry Essex, Leonard Lee, from a story by Robert Hardy Andrews

Wyoming Outlaw ★★ U

Western 1939 · US · BW · 57min

This is a routine *Three Mesquiteers* B-western which John Wayne made before Republic recognised that his loan-out for *Stagecoach* had turned him into a major star. He puts a professional face on having to team up with Ray Corrigan and Raymond Hatton in another trite story, about helping an outlaw expose a crooked politician. Playing the outlaw is future western lead Don Barry. Silent star Elmo Lincoln came out of retirement for the small role of a US marshal. AE

John Wayne *Stony Brooke* · Ray "Crash" Corrigan *Tucson Smith* · Raymond Hatton *Rusty Joslin* · Yakima Canutt *Ed Sims* ■ *Dir* George Sherman · *Scr* Betty Burbridge, Jack Natteford, from a story by Natteford, from characters by William Colt MacDonald

Wyoming Renegades ★★ U

Western 1955 · US · Colour · 72min

Scotching the cosy myths peddled by Paul Newman and Robert Redford in *Butch Cassidy and the Sundance Kid*, this routine B-movie western reveals a very different side of the two outlaws. Philip Carey plays the former Hole in the Wall Gang member who is blamed for a bank robbery that Gene Evans's greedy Cassidy has done, and decides to ride with the gang again until he can clear his name. Carey is better known for his dependable support in the likes of *Calamity Jane*. He works hard at this rare lead, but lacks heroic presence. DP

Phil Carey [Philip Carey] *Brady Sutton* · Gene Evans *Butch Cassidy* · Martha Hyer *Nancy Warren* · William Bishop *Sundance Kid* · Douglas Kennedy *Charlie Veer* · Roy Roberts *Sheriff McVey* ■ *Dir* Fred F Sears · *Scr* David Lang

X-15 ★ U

Drama 1961 · US · Colour · 106min

Charles Bronson climbs into X-15, a rocket that will take man into space. On the ground, meanwhile, various boffins and military types bombard us with technobabble. James Stewart's narration is intended to give this gravitas, but it nose-dived at the box office, though it did mark the debut of director Richard Donner. AT

David McLean *Matt Powell* · Charles Bronson *Lt Colonel Lee Brandon* · Ralph Taeger *Major Ernest Wilde* · Brad Dexter *Major Anthony Rinaldi* · Kenneth Tobey *Colonel Craig Brewster* · Mary Tyler Moore *Pamela Stewart* · James Stewart *Narrator* ■ *Dir* Richard Donner · *Scr* Tony Lazzarino, James Warner Bellah, from a story by Lazzarino

The X-Files ★★★★ 15

Science-fiction thriller 1998 · US · Colour · 117min

The TV phenomenon of the 1990s makes an effortless transition to the big screen, and, while the plot remains firmly grounded in the themes of the series, it plays equally well as a classy conspiracy thriller. Here, intrepid FBI duo Mulder and Scully (David Duchovny and Gillian Anderson) investigate an explosion at a federal building and stumble across the biggest alien cover-up in the world's history. Director Rob Bowman (who has also worked on the series) is faithful to the show's paranoiac roots, but gleefully opens the action out to stage some spectacular set pieces. JF Violence, swearing. *DVD*

David Duchovny *Special Agent Fox Mulder* · Gillian Anderson *Special Agent Dana Scully* · John Neville *Well-Manicured Man* · William B Davis *Cigarette-Smoking Man* · Martin Landau *Dr Alvin Kurtzweil* · Mitch Pileggi *FBI Assistant Director Walter Skinner* · Armin Mueller-Stahl *Strughold* ■ *Dir* Rob Bowman · *Scr* Chris Carter, from a story by Chris Carter, Frank Spotnitz

The X-Files: I Want to Believe ★★ 15

Science-fiction thriller 2008 · US/Can · Colour · 103min

Series creator Chris Carter is behind the camera for this second film spin-off, which comes a full ten years after the first. Sadly, legions of *X-Files* fans will be dispirited. It's less fast-paced thriller, more plodding melodrama as former FBI spooks Mulder (David Duchovny) and Scully (Gillian Anderson) become distracted from their investigation of the mysterious abduction of a young agent and grapple with their own personal demons. Billy Connolly provides the only real intrigue as a psychic paedophile priest who has visions of the crime. However, conspiracy-philes will be most disappointed by the fact that the dynamic duo don't have a sinister system and the Cigarette-Smoking Man to pit their wits against. Compared to the TV series, it all feels so small. SP *DVD* *BD*

David Duchovny *Fox Mulder* · Gillian Anderson *Dana Scully* · Amanda Peet *ASAC Dakota Whitney* · Billy Connolly *Father Joseph Crissman* · Callum Keith Rennie *Janke Dacyshyn* · Alvin "Xzibit" Joiner [Xzibit] *Agent Mosley Drummy* · Adam Godley *Father Ybarra* ■ *Dir* Chris Carter · *Scr* Chris Carter, Frank Spotnitz, from the TV series by Carter

The X from Outer Space ★

Science fiction 1967 · Jpn · Colour · 89min

X doesn't mark the entertainment spot in the first Shochiku Studio entry in the Japanese monster sweepstakes. Guilala, a spear-spitting stegosaurus-cum-chicken creature, grows from a single cell into a behemoth after being brought back from a Moon-to-Mars mission attached to the spaceship hull. And Tokyo is destroyed yet again. Hiroshi Ikeda's special effects aren't up to the usual standard and Kazui Nihonmatsu's direction borders on the disinterested. AJ In Japanese.

Eiji Okada *Dr Kato* • Toshiya Wazaki *Sano* • Peggy Neal *Liza* • Itoko Harada *Michiko* ■ *Dir* Kazui Nihonmatsu

X-Men ★★★ 12
Fantasy action adventure
2000 · US · Colour · 104min

Directed and co-written by Bryan Singer, this is set in the not-too-distant future and follows the power struggle between two factions of a new breed of humans with assorted strange powers – the good led by disabled professor Patrick Stewart and the bad led by Ian McKellen. The Marvel Comics characters are well realised and Singer mixes the classic values of good storytelling with liberal amounts of digital magic. On the down side, this plays a little too much like the beginning of a franchise and – with the exception of Stewart and McKellen – star quality is in rather short supply. AC Violence. *DVD* 🔵

Hugh Jackman *Logan/Wolverine* • Patrick Stewart *Professor Charles Xavier* • Ian McKellen *Erik Magnus Lehnsherr/Magneto* • Famke Janssen *Jean Grey* • James Marsden *Scott Summers/Cyclops* • Halle Berry *Ororo Munroe/Storm* • Anna Paquin *Marie/Rogue* • Tyler Mane *Sabretooth* • Ray Park *Toad* • Rebecca Romijn-Stamos *Mystique* • Bruce Davison *Senator Robert Frank Kelly* ■ *Dir* Bryan Singer • *Scr* David Hayter, from a story by Tom DeSanto, Bryan Singer, from the characters by Stan Lee, Jack Kirby

X2 ★★★★ 12
Fantasy action adventure
2003 · US · Colour · 128min

This sequel to *X-Men* capitalises on the original's groundwork and pays the audience back in spades. This is what a mega-budget comic book action movie should be and the pace never lets up. Former nemesis Magneto (played with relish by Ian McKellen) is now allied with the X-Men against Brian Cox's ruthless military scientist. Our Marvel heroes, again led by Hugh Jackman's cigar-chomping Wolverine and augmented by Alan Cumming's camp shape-shifter and a handsome new intake of students, are pleasingly human and a sharp script leavens the dark melancholy at the tale's core with soap-opera romance and comic one-liners. AC *DVD* 🔵

Patrick Stewart *Professor Charles Xavier* • Hugh Jackman *Wolverine/Logan* • Ian McKellen *Magneto/Erik Magnus Lehnsherr* • Halle Berry *Storm/Ororo Munroe* • Famke Janssen *Dr Jean Grey* • James Marsden *Cyclops/Scott Summers* • Rebecca Romijn-Stamos *Mystique/Raven Darkholme* • Anna Paquin *Rogue/Marie D'Ancanto* • Alan Cumming *Nightcrawler/Kurt Wagner* • Brian Cox (1) *General William Stryker* • Bruce Davison *Senator Robert Kelly* ■ *Dir* Bryan Singer • *Scr* Dan Harris, Michael Dougherty, David Hayter, from a story by Hayter, Bryan Singer, Zak Penn, from the graphic novel *God Lives, Man Kills* by Chris Claremont, Brent Anderson, from the characters by Stan Lee, Jack Kirby

X-Men – the Last Stand ★★★ 12
Fantasy action adventure
2006 · US · Colour · 99min

Director Brett Ratner takes over the reins of the Marvel Comics franchise for this underwhelming but still enjoyable episode. War looms when a cure for mutants is invented and the future of their kind is cast into doubt. The faction led by Prof Xavier (Patrick Stewart) stands for choice, while Magneto (Ian McKellen) believes in the survival of the fittest. But Magneto gains a powerful ally in the form of the resurrected Dr Jean Grey (Famke Janssen). The script suffers from a mass of storylines, but Ratner's blockbuster is technically spectacular to a fault. AJ *DVD* 🔵 CS

X-Men Origins: Wolverine ★★ 12
Fantasy action adventure
2009 · US · Colour · 102min

With his indestructible claws and growling demeanour, Logan aka Wolverine (Hugh Jackman) was undeniably the most charismatic character in the *X-Men* franchise. This spin-off prequel capitalises on his crowd-pleasing appeal by revealing his origins and filling out his backstory – he's recruited along with the ferocious Sabretooth (Liev Schreiber) to join an elite mutant special forces team led by William Stryker (the deliciously villainous Danny Huston). A robustly enjoyable opening section lets Jackman breathe real life into the character's attempt to live a normal existence, but then revenge draws him back and the empty pyrotechnics take over. JR Some violence, brief swearing, nudity. *DVD* 🔵

Hugh Jackman *Logan/Wolverine* • Liev Schreiber *Victor Creed/Sabretooth* • Danny Huston *William Stryker* • Dominic Monaghan *Chris Bradley/Bolt* • Ryan Reynolds *Wade Wilson/Deadpool* • Taylor Kitsch *Remy LeBeau/Gambit* • Will i am *John Wraith* ■ *Dir* Gavin Hood • *Scr* David Benioff, Skip Woods, from a character by Len Wein, John Romita

X-Men: First Class ★★★★ 12
Fantasy action adventure
2011 · US · Colour · 126min

Answering all questions about the early relationship between Professor Xavier (the superb James McAvoy) and Magneto (a top-notch Michael Fassbender) and the origins of their mutant factions, Matthew Vaughn's prequel is a terrific reboot of the series. Beginning in Nazi Germany and ending with the 1962 Cuban Missile Crisis, this grandiose globetrotting fantasy boasts plentiful action spectacle and effective character-based drama set in an age of civil unrest and Cold War paranoia. Bent on world domination, Kevin Bacon makes for a great villain, first uniting then dividing the nicely defined assortment of mutants. AJ Some violence, swearing. *DVD* 🔵

James McAvoy *Professor Charles Xavier* • Michael Fassbender *Erik Lehnsherr/Magneto* • Kevin Bacon *Sebastian Shaw/Dr Schmidt* • Rose Byrne *Dr Moira MacTaggert* • January Jones *Emma Frost* • Oliver Platt *Man in black* • Jennifer Lawrence (2) *Raven Darkholme/Mystique* • Nicholas Hoult *Hank McCoy/Beast* • Hugh Jackman *Logan/Wolverine* ■ *Dir* Matthew Vaughn • *Scr* Ashley Edward Miller, Zack Stentz, Jane Goldman, Matthew Vaughn, from a story by Bryan Singer, Sheldon Turner, from the comic book/characters *The X-Men* by Stan Lee, Jack Kirby

X-Men: Days of Future Past ★★★★ 12
Fantasy action adventure
2014 · US · Colour · 126min

Having kicked the whole *X-Men* series off, director Bryan Singer triumphantly returns here, as a grizzled Wolverine (Hugh Jackman) is sent back to 1973 by old sparring partners Professor X (Patrick Stewart) and Magneto (Ian McKellen) to save the future from mechanoid mutant killers called Sentinels. There are plenty of memorable action sequences – not least a terrific *Mission: Impossible*-style rescue that introduces mutant speedster Quicksilver (Evan Peters). Plaudits should go to Singer for making the franchise fit for purpose, and his rip-roaring recalibration of past and current X-teams should provide these characters with a bright new future. JA Swearing, violence, brief nudity. *DVD* 🔵 CS

Hugh Jackman *Logan/Wolverine* • James McAvoy *Charles Xavier* • Michael Fassbender *Erik Lehnsherr* • Jennifer Lawrence (2) *Raven/Mystique* • Patrick Stewart *Professor X* • Ian McKellen *Magneto* • Nicholas Hoult *Hank/Beast* • Halle Berry *Storm* • Ellen Page *Kitty Pryde* • Anna Paquin *Rogue* • Evan Peters *Peter/Quicksilver* ■ *Dir* Bryan Singer • *Scr* Jane Goldman, Simon Kinberg, Matthew Vaughn, from a comic book by John Byrne (artist), Chris Claremont (writer)

X-Men: Apocalypse ★★★ 12A
Fantasy action adventure
2016 · US · Colour · 143min

Time-spanning X-teams may have stopped the apocalypse in *Days of Future Past* (2014), but director Bryan Singer ups the challenge here by pitting Professor X's student mutants against a god-like immortal called Apocalypse (Oscar Isaac). Singer's fourth film in the franchise smacks of handing over the baton to a new generation but it's a decent all-action adventure, if below the fabulous standards of its two predecessors. JA Violence, swearing. 3D CS

James McAvoy *Professor Charles Xavier* • Michael Fassbender *Erik Lensherr/Magneto* • Jennifer Lawrence (2) *Raven/Mystique* • Oscar Isaac *En Sabah Nur/Apocalypse* • Nicholas Hoult *Hank McCoy/Beast* • Channing Tatum *Gambit* ■ *Dir* Bryan Singer • *Scr* Simon Kinberg, from a story by Michael Dougherty, Dan Harris, Bryan Singer

X+Y ★★★ 12
Comedy drama
2014 · UK · Colour · 106min

Films that portray people with autism often give them compensatory "superpowers", and on the surface this British comedy drama is no exception. The young hero here is the socially awkward Nathan (Asa Butterfield), who is a maths whizz. A maths contest improves Nathan's confidence and this emotional connection also has an effect on Nathan's relationships with his maths mentor (Rafe Spall) and his widowed mum (Sally Hawkins). The debut feature from Morgan Matthews may lack a climax and, at approaching two hours, outstays its welcome. But it is nicely feel-good, is less manipulative than it could have been, and is well played by the high-calibre cast. DA English, Mandarin +subtitles. *DVD*

Asa Butterfield *Nathan Ellis* • Sally Hawkins *Julie Ellis* • Rafe Spall *Martin Humphreys* • Eddie Marsan *Richard Grieve* • Martin McCann *Michael Ellis* ■ *Dir* Morgan Matthews • *Scr* James Graham

X the Unknown ★★ PG
Science-fiction horror
1956 · UK · BW · 75min

In the wilds of Scotland there are some baffling deaths at an atomic research establishment. It could be bog-standard radiation leaks and poisoning but maybe something else is going on, some alien slime on the loose? A typical product of the Cold War, it's all jolly polite as British boffins are led by US import Dean Jagger. AT *DVD*

Dean Jagger *Dr Adam Royston* • Edward Chapman *Elliott* • Leo McKern *McGill* • Marianne Brauns *Zena, nurse* • William Lucas *Peter Elliott* • John Harvey *Major Cartwright* • Peter Hammond *Lt Bannerman* ■ *Dir* Leslie Norman • *Scr* Jimmy Sangster

xXx ★★★ 12
Spy action thriller
2002 · US · Colour · 118min

Vin Diesel cements his action-star status as "a new breed of secret agent", but, in every other respect, director Rob Cohen's film is just pure, turbo-driven exploitation. Diesel plays an extreme-sports hero who is coerced by US government agent Samuel L Jackson into infiltrating a Prague-based terrorist organisation. The movie lacks wit and consistency, but the stunts are overblown and outrageous enough to produce sheer adrenaline-pumping excitement. AJ Violence, swearing. *DVD* 🔵

Vin Diesel *Xander Cage*, *"X"* • Asia Argento *Yelena* • Marton Csokas *Yorgi* • Samuel L Jackson *Agent Augustus Gibbons* • Danny Trejo *El Jefe* • Michael Roof *Toby Lee Shavers* • Tom Everett *Senator Dick Hotchkiss* ■ *Dir* Rob Cohen • *Scr* Rich Wilkes

xXx: the Next Level ★★ 12
Spy action thriller
2005 · US · Colour · 96min

Ice Cube replaces Vin Diesel for this sequel, playing an imprisoned special ops soldier who's sprung by Samuel L Jackson's shadowy agent to thwart Willem Dafoe's military coup against the US President. Not as good as the first film, it's entertaining enough for the video game generation. DA Violence, swearing. *DVD* 🔵

Ice Cube *"XXX", Darius Stone* • Willem Dafoe *Secretary of Defense General George Octavius Deckert* • Samuel L Jackson *Augustus Gibbons* • Scott Speedman *Agent Kyle Steele* • Xzibit *Zeke* • Peter Strauss *President James Sanford* • Nona Gaye *Lola* Jackson • Sunny Mabrey *Charlie Mayweather* ■ *Dir* Lee Tamahori • *Scr* Simon Kinberg, from characters by Rich Wilkes

xXx: the Return of Xander Cage
Spy action thriller
2017 · US · Colour

This is a preview – no prints were available to review prior to publication: In 2002, the first *xXx* film added extreme sports to an old formula. At the time, Vin Diesel was doing similar favours for the road-race movie (with the first of *The Fast and the Furious* series) and the space adventure (in *Pitch Black*). To say his return to the series that made his name is eagerly awaited is an understatement. Helping Diesel hit the ground running are Samuel L Jackson as his old handler, and some true giants of martial arts, including Donnie Yen and Tony Jaa. SvM

Vin Diesel *Xander Cage* • Samuel L Jackson *Augustus Gibbons* • Nina Dobrev *Becky* • Toni Collette • Tony Jaa *Talon* ■ *Dir* DJ Caruso • *Scr* John D Brancato, Michael Ferris, F Scott Frazier, from characters by Rich Wilkes

XX/XY ★★ 15
Drama
2001 · US · Colour · 86min

Superficially, Austin Chick's debut feature is a spicy slice of indie chic, but beneath the stylish veneer is an implausible world of narcissism and female immaturity. Fledgeling animator Mark Ruffalo gets embroiled in a complicated three-way relationship with college girls Maya Stange and Kathleen Robertson. Ten years later a chance encounter sets the sexual sparks flying again. Only Ruffalo's vulnerable charm has any sort of appeal. Meandering and plodding. SF Swearing, sex scenes, drug abuse.

Mark Ruffalo *Coles Burroughs* • Kathleen Robertson *Thea* • Maya Stange *Sam* • Petra Wright *Claire* • Kel O'Neill *Sid* • Joshua Spafford *Jonathon* • Zach Shaffer *Nick* • David Thornton *Miles* ■ *Dir/Scr* Austin Chick

XXY ★★★★ 15
Romantic drama
2007 · Arg/Fr/Sp · Colour · 87min

Writer/director Lucía Puenzo's compelling debut is adapted from a short story by Sergio Bizzio. Set on a small island off Uruguay, it centres on the crisis of identity blighting Alex (Inés Efron). A teenage hermaphrodite who lives as a girl, Alex is being coerced into making a decision about her future by her parents, but is unwilling to be rushed, even though she's being bullied and at one point is nearly gang raped. Eschewing easy solutions and delicately played by a fine cast, this pulsating drama is beautifully photographed by Natasha Braier in languorous long shots that allow the various dilemmas to simmer in their emotional intensity. DP Spanish +Engish subtitles. Violence, swearing, a sex scene. *DVD*

Ricardo Darín [Ricardo Darin] *Kraken* • Valeria Bertuccelli *Suli* • Germán Palacios *Ramiro* • Carolina Peleritti *Erika* • Martín Piroyansky *Alvaro* • Inés Efron *Alex* • Luciano Angelelli *Juan* • César Troncoso *Washington* ■ *Dir* Lucía Puenzo • *Scr* Lucía Puenzo, from the short story *Cinismo* by Sergio Bizzio

X

Xala ★★★★ 12

Satirical comedy drama
1974 · Sen · Colour · 117min

This savage attack on the Senegal bourgeoisie and their eagerness to indulge in the vices of their former colonial masters is couched in terms of a hilarious sex comedy, in which Thierno Leye's political promotion coincides with his third marriage and the onset of impotence. His status and dignity crumble in the face of traditional curses and cures, and Leye becomes a symbol for outdated patriarchy. His wives, on the other hand, embrace diverse historical and contemporary influences, standing for the future. Ousmane Sembene confirmed his reputation as a key sub-Saharan film-maker. DP Senegalese, French +subtitles.

Thierno Leye *El Hadji Aboukader Beye* · Seune Samb *Adja Assatou* · Miriam Niang *Rama* ■ *Dir* Ousmane Sembene · *Scr* Ousmane Sembene, from his novel

Xanadu ★ PG

Musical
1980 · US · Colour · 91min

Olivia Newton-John stars as a muse, who's descended from her heavenly seat to inspire artist Michael Beck, in a veritable cult classic of camp and glitter, roller-skating dance numbers and Gene Kelly in his final feature film role. Unfortunately, it's also an excuse for dreadful song and dance numbers, a nonexistent plot and a dose of 1980s disco. A laugh, if only for its mind-boggling awfulness. LH *DVD* *BL*

Olivia Newton-John *Kira* · Gene Kelly *Danny McGuire* · Michael Beck *Sonny Malone* · James Sloyan *Simpson* · Dimitra Arliss *Helen* · Katie Hanley *Sandra* · Fred McCarren *Richie* ■ *Dir* Robert Greenwald · *Scr* Richard Christian Danus, Marc Reid Rubel, Michael Kane · *Music/lyrics* Jeff Lynne, John Farrar

XChange ★★★ 18

Futuristic action thriller
2000 · Can · Colour · 105min

In this smart, swiftly paced futuristic thriller, a corporate executive is "floated" into another man's body to attend an important meeting (there wasn't time for air travel), then finds his own stand-in is a terrorist with a plan. More creative than the premise suggests, this is nicely performed by Kyle MacLachlan as the initial body swap and Stephen Baldwin as the short-life clone acquired as a means of escape. Although the action scenes are unremarkable, there's some clever ideas mined from the body-swap scenario, as well as a droll injection of black humour. JC *DVD*

Stephen Baldwin *Clone No 1/Toffler 3* · Pascale Bussières *Madeleine Ranard* · Kim Coates *Toffler/Fisk 2* · Kyle MacLachlan *Fisk/Toffler 2* · Tom Rack *Mr Finerman* · Arnold Pinnock *Dickerson* ■ *Dir* Allan Moyle · *Scr* Christopher Pelham

Xiao Wu ★★★

Drama
1997 · Chi/HK · Colour · 113min

Shot on 16mm and set in the provincial town of Fenyang, Jia Zhang Ke's directorial debut is a frank portrait of a society as much in the thrall of consumerism and the black market as rigid Beijing rhetoric. Non-professional Wang Hong Wei excels as the petty thief whose world falls apart because he has neither the resolve nor the resources to move with the times. With its ultra-naturalistic style, this is a blend of uncompromising social comment and sly wit. DP Mandarin +subtitles.

Wang Hong Wei *Xiao Wu* ■ *Dir/Scr* Jia Zhang Ke

Xiu Xiu: The Sent Down Girl ★★★

Political drama
1999 · US/Tai/Chi · Colour · 110min

Joan Chen makes an accomplished debut as director with this haunting tale of unconventional love in the dying days of the Cultural Revolution. Pretty tailor's daughter Lu Lu is sent to the countryside to share her big city smarts with the peasantry. Though painfully slow in parts,

Chen's powerful drama shows her to have great promise. NS Mandarin +subtitles.

Lu Lu *Xiu Xiu* · Qian Zheng *Li Chuanbei* · Gao Jie *Mother* · Lopsang *Lao Jin* · Li Zhizhen *Headquarters Chief* ■ *Dir* Joan Chen · *Scr* Yan Geling, Joan Chen, from the story *Tian Yu* by Yan

Xtro ★ 18

Science-fiction horror
1983 · UK · Colour · 82min

British family man Philip Sayer is abducted by a UFO. Three years later, he returns to his family, claiming to remember nothing of what happened to him in the intervening years. Soon his wife and son begin to notice some odd behavior, like his penchant for eating snake eggs, and the string of horribly mutilated bodies he leaves in his wake. Released a year after *ET* with the tagline "Not all aliens are friendly", it's only memorable now for its incredibly graphic violence and for Maryam D'Abo's first film role (and her first nude scene). Surprisingly, this spawned two sequels. ST

Philip Sayer *Sam Phillips* · Bernice Stegers *Rachel Phillips* · Danny Brainin *Joe Daniels* · Simon Nash *Tony Phillips* · Maryam D'Abo *Analise* · David Cardy *Michael* ■ *Dir* Harry Bromley Davenport · *Scr* Robert Smith, Iain Cassie, Jo Ann Kaplan, from a screenplay (unproduced) by Harry Bromley Davenport, Michel Parry

Xtro 2: the Second Encounter ★ 18

Science-fiction horror
1990 · Can · Colour · 89min

Scientists at a secret facility discover a way to send people to an alternate dimension, and, after doing so, act really surprised when slimy killer aliens come through from the other side and infest the lab. Familiar scenes of people with guns edging down darkened corridors follow. A third Xtro film followed in 1995. ST

Jan-Michael Vincent *Dr Ron Sheperd* · Paul Koslo *Dr Alex Summerfield* · Tara Buckman *Dr Julie Casserly* · Jano Frandsen *McShane* · Nicholas Lea *Baines* · WF Wadden *Jedburg* ■ *Dir* Harry Bromley Davenport · *Scr* John A Curtis, Edward Kovach, Robert Smith, Steven Lister

YSL: Yves Saint Laurent ★★ 15

Biographical drama
2014 · Fr · Colour · 100min

Was the life of the French fashion icon really this bland? The subject matter should be riveting, yet it fails to hold the attention, even with the addition of some spurious mother issues, and a random flashback voiceover. As YSL, Pierre Niney captures the demeanour of the petulant bipolar designer well, and his signature looks – the Mondrian mini, the woman's tuxedo – are superbly re-created. But this is essentially a dull frock opera accessorised with way too much window dressing. AJ In French. Sex scenes, drug abuse. *DVD*

Pierre Niney de la Comédie-Française [Pierre Niney] *Yves Saint Laurent* · Guillaume Gallienne de la Comédie-Française [Guillaume Gallienne] *Bergé, Pierre* · Charlotte Le Bon *Victoire Doutreleau* · Laura Smet *Loulou de la Falaise* · Marie de Villepin *Betty Catroux* · Nikolai Kinski *Karl Lagerfeld* ■ *Dir* Jalil Lespert · *Scr* Jacques Fieschi, Marie-Pierre Huster, Jalil Lespert, from the biography by Laurence Benaïm

Y Tu Mamá También ★★★ 18

Road movie comedy 2001 · Mex · Colour · 101min

This road movie became the biggest home-grown box-office hit in Mexican history. There's more to it than sex as two high-school graduates (played by Diego Luna and superstar-in-waiting Gael García Bernal) borrow a car and head off for the mythical "Heaven's Mouth" beach with unhappily married older woman Maribel Verdú. Throughout the journey, director Alfonso Cuarón highlights the economic rift between Mexico's middle classes and poor with comments by a deadpan narrator. AC Spanish +subtitles. Swearing, sex scenes, drug abuse, nudity. *DVD* *BL*

Maribel Verdú *Luisa Cortés* · Gael García Bernal *Julio Zapata* · Diego Luna *Tenoch Iturbide* · Marta Aura *Enriqueta "Queta" Allende* · Diana Bracho *Silvia Allende de Iturbide* ■ *Dir* Alfonso Cuarón · *Scr* Carlos Cuarón, Alfonso Cuarón

Yaaba ★★★ PG

Drama tragedy
1989 · Burkina Faso · Colour · 89min

Inspired by the folk tales he heard as a child and played with finesse by a non-professional cast, Idrissa Ouedraogo's delicately paced, neorealist study of life in rural Burkina Faso returns to the familiar sub-Saharan themes of superstition, patriarchal arrogance and the need to strike a balance between tradition and progress. Young Noufou Ouedraogo is torn between personal feelings and communal responsibility as he tries to remain loyal to Fatima Sanga, a wizened yaaba, or grandmother, who has been ostracised by the village. DP Burkinabé +subtitles.

Fatima Sanga *Yaaba* · Noufou Ouedraogo *Bila* · Roukietou Barry *Nopoko* · Adama Ouedraogo *Kougri* ■ *Dir/Scr* Idrissa Ouedraogo

Yaadein ★★★ PG

Romantic musical drama
2001 · Ind · Colour · 182min

Hrithik Roshan is teamed for the first time with Kareena Kapoor in this sprawling melodrama from master showman Subhash Ghai. This explores the problems facing emigrant parents whose children don't see the relevance of traditional Indian values. The focus is on the young lovers, but Jackie Shroff and Anang Desai turn in nuanced performances as the restaurant owner and

business tycoon, whose class rivalry stands in the way of true love. DP Hindi +subtitles. *DVD*

Jackie Shroff *Raj Singh Puri* · Hrithik Roshan *Ronit Malhotra* · Kareena Kapoor *Isha Singh Puri* · Kiran Rathod *Monishka Rai* · Anang Desai *LK Mahotra* ■ *Dir/Scr* Subhash Ghai

Yahudi ★★★ U

Romantic melodrama 1958 · Ind · BW · 162min

Bimal Roy's movie is a version of the classic story, *The Jew's Daughter*, about a Jewish woman and a Roman prince. Set in Rome at a time of Jewish persecution, it portrays the tragic love affair between a couple separated by religion. The story offers both Shakespearean echoes and universal truths, but still has room for many popular songs. PF Urdu +subtitles.

Dilip Kumar *Prince Marcus* · Sohrab Modi *Ezra, the Jew* · Meena Kumari *Hannah* ■ *Dir* Bimal Roy · *Scr* Nabendu Ghosh, from the play *The Jew's Daughter* by Agha Hashar

The Yakuza ★★★★ 15

Thriller 1975 · US/Jpn · Colour · 107min

Robert Mitchum gives a brilliant performance as an ex-serviceman taking on the might of the Japanese underworld when the daughter of his best friend is kidnapped by gangsters. Writers Robert Towne (*Chinatown*) and Paul Schrader (*Taxi Driver*), working from a story by Schrader's brother Leonard, transform this simple idea into a complex and compelling thriller. Director Sydney Pollack sweeps the action along at a fast pace, allowing his cast plenty of room for manoeuvre and making the most of his Japanese locations. A must-see. TH Violence, swearing. *DVD*

Robert Mitchum *Harry Kilmer* · Ken Takakura *Ken Tanaka* · Brian Keith *George Tanner* · Herb Edelman *Oliver Wheat* · Richard Jordan *Dusty* · Keiko Kishi *Tanaka Eiko* · James Shigeta *Goro* ■ *Dir* Sydney Pollack · *Scr* Paul Schrader, Robert Towne, from a story by Leonard Schrader

Yakuza Apocalypse ★★★ 18

Martial arts action horror
2015 · Jpn · Colour · 115min

Takashi Miike's vampire yakuza revenge movie is a hyperactive mash-up of plotlines. Its scattershot plot features malodorous demons, a plague of vampirism that turns people into clichéd Japanese gangsters, and an ass-kicking frog monster. Non-Japanese viewers will probably struggle to catch all the straight-to-video V-cinema references, but the presence in the cast of Yayan Ruhian, the Indonesian star of *The Raid*, means that the martial arts action hits home. WI In Japanese, English. Violence, swearing.

Yayan Ruhian *Kyoken* · Riri Furanki *Genyo Kamiura* · Hayato Ichihara *Kagayama* ■ *Dir* Takashi Miike · *Scr* Yoshitaka Yamaguchi

The Yakuza Papers ★★★★ 18

Crime drama 1973 · Jpn · Colour · 98min

The opening instalment of the crime series that forged Kinji Fukasaku's reputation is a fearless indictment of the Japanese underworld and the descent of the bushido code into an excuse for brutality. The violence appalled contemporaries, yet there's no attempt to glorify the part played by Bunta Sugawara in Nobuo Kaneko's clan victory over Hiroshi Nawa. But he's accorded a shred of honour by the fact his fury is partly inspired by the death of his friend. DP Japanese +subtitles. *DVD*

Bunta Sugawara *Hirono Shoz* · Hiroki Matsukata *Sakai Tetsuya* · Nobuo Kaneko · Tatsuo Umemiya *Wakasugi Hiroshi* · Hiroshi Nawa ■ *Dir* Kinji Fukasaku · *Scr* Kazuo Kasahara, from a story by Koichi Iiboshi

Yam Daabo ★★★

Drama 1986 · Burkina Faso · Colour · 80min

This is a harrowing picture of the impact of drought and famine on Idrissa Ouedraogo's homeland, Burkina Faso. Just as the later *Yaaba* would rework the rites-of-passage picture, this is a sub-Saharan variation on the road movie, as a desperate family heads south in the hope of a fresh start. Some of the symbolism is heavy-handed, but the film concludes on a note of optimism. DP Burkinabé +subtitles.

Auoa Guiraud *Mother* • Moussa Bologo *Bintou* • Assita Ouedraogo *Tipoko* ■ *Dir/Scr* Idrissa Ouedraogo

Yangtse Incident ★★★ PG
War drama based on a true story
1956 · UK · BW · 88min

This adventure is a fact-based yarn about a British warship, HMS *Amethyst*, which sails up the Yangtse in 1949 intending to relieve the British embassy at Nanking. Instead, it comes under massive bombardment from Chinese communists, who blockade the river and trap the ship. Made less than ten years after Mao's revolution, one shouldn't expect an analysis of Chinese politics. What we get are standard British heroics from a crew commanded by Richard Todd, courtesy of an Eric Ambler script, efficiently handled by Michael Anderson. AT DVD

Richard Todd *Lieutenant Commander Kerans* • William Hartnell *Leading Seaman Frank* • Akim Tamiroff *Colonel Peng* • Keye Luke *Captain Kuo Tai* • Donald Houston *Lieutenant Weston* • Robert Urquhart *Flight Lieutenant Fearnley* • Sophie Stewart *Charlotte Dunlap* ■ *Dir* Michael Anderson • *Scr* Eric Ambler, from the non-fiction book *Escape of the Amethyst* by Laurence Earl

A Yank at Eton ★★ U
Comedy drama 1942 · US · BW · 88min

This is as much a wartime treatise on Anglo-American relations as adolescent entertainment, yet it amuses, thanks to Mickey Rooney's well-honed blend of bluster and sentiment. Arriving in Blighty with a sizeable chip on his shoulder, following his mother's remarriage to horse-breeding landowner Ian Hunter, Rooney embarks on bucking the system, until he comes to appreciate its values and traditions. Pure corn. DP

Mickey Rooney *Timothy Dennis* • Edmund Gwenn *Justin* • Ian Hunter *Roger Carlton* • Freddie Bartholomew *Peter Carlton* • Marta Linden *Winifred Dennis Carlton* • Juanita Quigley *Jane "The Runt" Dennis* • Peter Lawford *Ronnie Kenvil* ■ *Dir* Norman Taurog • *Scr* George Oppenheimer, Lionel Houser, Thomas Phipps, from a story by Oppenheimer

A Yank at Oxford ★★★
Comedy 1938 · US/UK · BW · 100min

Designed to foster good relationships between Britain and America as Nazi stormclouds were gathering in Europe, this is the movie that marked the moment when Hollywood star factory MGM set up production in the heart of Ye Olde England. Robert Taylor plays a brash American student at Oxford who shines at athletics and gains the envy of his fellow students while Maureen O'Sullivan goes weak at the knees at the very sight of him. It's still good fun, especially for the Hollywood view of the way we were then. AT

Robert Taylor (1) *Lee Sheridan* • Lionel Barrymore *Dan Sheridan* • Maureen O'Sullivan *Molly Beaumont* • Vivien Leigh *Elsa Craddock* • Edmund Gwenn *Dean of Cardinal College* • Griffith Jones *Paul Beaumont* • CV France *Dean Snodgrass* • Edward Rigby *Scatters* ■ *Dir* Jack Conway • *Scr* Malcolm Stuart Boylan, Walter Ferris, George Oppenheimer, Roland Pertwee, F Scott Fitzgerald, Frank Wead, Angus MacPhail, from a story by Leon Gordon, Sidney Gilliat, Michael Hogan, from an idea by John Monk Saunders

A Yank in Ermine ★★ U
Comedy 1955 · UK · Colour · 84min

As there had already been a Yank at Oxford and in the RAF, it was only a matter of time before one was elevated to the peerage. Unfortunately, he came in the shape of Peter Thompson, a particularly charmless specimen of American manhood. Admittedly, he's not helped by a damp squib of a script. DP

Peter M Thompson *Joe Turner* • Jon Pertwee *"Slowburn" Jenks* • Noelle Middleton *Angela* • Harold Lloyd Jr *"Butch" Halliday* • Diana Decker *Gloria* • Reginald Beckwith *Kimp* • Edward Chapman *Duke of Fontenham* • Richard Wattis

Boone • Guy Middleton *Bertram Maltravers* • Harry Locke *Clayton* ■ *Dir* Gordon Parry • *Scr* John Paddy Carstairs, from his novel *Solid, Said the Earl*

A Yank in the RAF ★★ U
Second World War romance
1941 · US · BW · 93min

The need for a patriotic lift was often enough to get audiences into the threepenny fleapits. Here, aside from Betty Grable giving it her all-singing, all-dancing all in a couple of numbers, this is a bit of a damp squib. The stars look good, however, with Tyrone Power as a cocky American pilot and Grable as the girlfriend. JM DVD

Tyrone Power *Tim Baker* • Betty Grable *Carol Brown* • John Sutton *Wing Commander Morley* • Reginald Gardiner *Roger Pillby* • Donald Stuart *Corporal Harry Baker* • John Wilde *Graves* • Richard Fraser *Thorndyke* • Morton Lowry *Squadron Leader* ■ *Dir* Henry King • *Scr* Darrell Ware, Karl Tunberg, from a story by Melville Crossman [Darryl F Zanuck]

Yankee Doodle Dandy ★★★★ U
Musical biography 1942 · US · BW · 125min

The great James Cagney gives the performance of his life as Broadway's George M Cohan. The film needs to be viewed in context today; it is fearsomely patriotic, overlong to a degree and extremely sentimental, but it was geared to serve a major purpose. It reminded Americans that there was a war going on in Europe and, in saluting the composer of *Over There*, Warner Bros effectively fashioned a celluloid recruiting poster. Bear with it for Cagney's classic dance routines: if you only know him as a gangster, here's the reminder that he was a match for both Gene Kelly and Fred Astaire. TS DVD

James Cagney *George M Cohan* • Joan Leslie *Mary* • Walter Huston *Jerry Cohan* • Richard Whorf *Sam Harris* • George Tobias *Dietz* • Irene Manning *Fay Templeton* • Rosemary DeCamp *Nellie Cohan* • Jeanne Cagney *Josie Cohan* • SZ Sakall *Schwab* ■ *Dir* Michael Curtiz • *Scr* Robert Buckner, Edmund Joseph, from a story by Buckner

Yanks ★★★ 15
Second World War romantic drama
1979 · UK · Colour · 133min

This pleasing effort from director John Schlesinger glows with a homely period charm, but never descends into sentimentality. Richard Gere stars in this story that is about GIs stationed in Britain during the Second World War, and Schlesinger gives a nice touch to the juxtaposition of British working-class morality on a collision course with young adult hormones. The strong ensemble cast interplays well, and the scene where the lads march off for D-Day is moving. SH DVD

Richard Gere *Sergeant Matt Dyson* • Vanessa Redgrave *Helen* • William Devane *John* • Lisa Eichhorn *Jean Moreton* • Chick Vennera *Sergeant Danny Ruffelo* • Rachel Roberts (1) *Clarrie Moreton* • Tony Melody *Jim Moreton* • Wendy Morgan *Mollie* ■ *Dir* John Schlesinger • *Scr* Walter Bernstein, Colin Welland, from his story

The Yards ★★★ 15
Crime drama 2000 · US · Colour · 110min

New York's mass transit train yards provide the backdrop for this brooding tale of murder and union corruption. The top-notch cast includes Mark Wahlberg as a newly sprung con, Joaquin Phoenix as his hair-trigger buddy and James Caan as his grafting uncle. But director James Gray wastes what could have been the film's greatest asset – the atmospheric marshalling yards – while the strong female contingent is underemployed. A tough, workmanlike drama, but lacking pace and personality. DP Violence, swearing, nudity. DVD

Mark Wahlberg *Leo Handler* • Joaquin Phoenix *Willie Gutierrez* • Charlize Theron *Erica Stoltz* • James Caan *Frank Olchin* • Ellen Burstyn *Val Handler* • Faye Dunaway *Kitty Olchin* • Steve Lawrence *Arthur Mydanick* ■ *Dir* James Gray • *Scr* James Gray, Matt Reeves

YatterMan ★★ 15
Action fantasy adventure
2009 · Jpn · Colour · 111min

Genre-hopping cult director Takashi Miike brings a 1970s Japanese cartoon series to vibrant life in this great-looking if perplexingly pitched live-action fantasy. "YatterMan" are actually a duo, girlfriend and boyfriend Ai and Gad, and the story sees them and their old foes, the Doronbo gang, competing to find the lost pieces of a wish-granting skull. With plenty of CGI-fuelled action, cute robot sidekicks and the huge animal "mecha" transports, you'd imagine this would be ideal kid-friendly fare, but don't be fooled. Quirkiness and colourful production design alone cannot sustain the interest for something that is too adult for kids, yet too childish for grown-ups. JH Japanese +subtitles. Sexual references. DVD

Sho Sakurai *Gan Takada* • Saki Fukuda *Ai* • Kyoko Fukada *Lady Doronjo* ■ *Dir* Takashi Miike • *Scr* Masashi Sogo, from Tatsuo Yoshida's TV series

The Year My Voice Broke ★★★★ 15
Drama 1987 · Aus · Colour · 100min

One of those rare movies about teenagers that doesn't treat them as an alien species, this neither patronises nor exploits. That's because writer/director John Duigan constructs his piece with understanding and insight, while the young actors in the lovesick triangle – Noah Taylor, Loene Carmen, Ben Mendelsohn – bring their characters to life with subtle authority. The story continues in the even better *Flirting*. TH Swearing.

Noah Taylor *Danny Embling* • Loene Carmen *Freya Olson* • Ben Mendelsohn *Trevor* • Graeme Blundell *Nils Olson* • Lynette Curran *Anne Olson* • Malcolm Robertson *Bruce Embling* • Judi Farr *Sheila Embling* ■ *Dir/Scr* John Duigan

The Year of Living Dangerously ★★★★ PG
Romantic political thriller
1982 · Aus/US · Colour · 109min

This atmospheric thriller sees Aussie radio journalist Mel Gibson on assignment in Indonesia in the mid-1960s, where the dictatorship is shaky and Sigourney Weaver is working as an attaché at the British embassy. Peter Weir's film wanders at times, but also offers plenty of spectacle and colour, a steamy romance between Gibson and Weaver, and its share of excitement when Gibson discovers more than it is safe for him to know. But the highlight is Linda Hunt's performance as a male Chinese-Australian photographer, for which she won an Oscar. PF Swearing.

Mel Gibson *Guy Hamilton* • Sigourney Weaver *Jill Bryant* • Linda Hunt *Billy Kwan* • Bembol Roco *Kumar* • Domingo Landicho *Hortono* • Hermino De Guzman *Immigration officer* • Michael Murphy (1) *Pete Curtis* • Noel Ferrier *Wally O'Sullivan* ■ *Dir* Peter Weir • *Scr* David Williamson, Peter Weir, CJ Koch, from the novel by Koch • *Cinematographer* Russell Boyd

Year of the Comet ★★★ PG
Romantic comedy adventure
1992 · US · Colour · 86min

This sardonic screwball adventure is set around the Scottish Highlands and the French Riviera. Wine merchant Penelope Ann Miller discovers a rare bottle of wine worth $1 million and plans to escort it to auction. But bon viveur villain Louis Jourdan wants it because written on the label is a formula for the elixir of life. Tim Daly is the suave action man hero who accidentally gets sucked into the *Boys' Own* adventure complete with offbeat action and sassy one-liners. An underrated black comedy romp with many fun moments. AJ DVD

Penelope Ann Miller *Maggie Harwood* • Timothy Daly *Oliver Plexico* • Louis Jourdan *Philippe* • Art Malik *Nico* • Ian Richardson *Sir Mason Harwood* • Ian McNeice *Ian* • Timothy Bentinck *Richard Harwood* • Julia McCarthy *Landlady* ■ *Dir* Peter Yates • *Scr* William Goldman

Year of the Dog ★★★ PG
Black comedy drama 2007 · US · Colour · 92min

The directorial debut of *Nacho Libre* co-writer Mike White proves to be more than just a wilfully zany comedy. Starring *Saturday Night Live* alumnus Molly Shannon, this story of a lonely single woman who takes her canine obsession a step too far is a midlife crisis movie that leaves a slightly sour aftertaste. The loss of her beloved pooch is unbearable but the chain of events it kick-starts is absurd, as Peggy becomes increasingly radicalised by the animal rights movement. This uneven and dryly funny film retains a solid comedic core thanks to a fearless and sympathetic turn from Shannon. DW DVD

Molly Shannon *Peggy* • Laura Dern *Bret* • Regina King *Layla* • Thomas McCarthy *Pier* • Josh Pais *Robin* • John C Reilly *Al* • Peter Sarsgaard *Newt* ■ *Dir/Scr* Mike White

Year of the Dragon ★★ 18
Crime drama 1985 · US · Colour · 128min

Michael Cimino's violent crime thriller is unexceptional in every respect, barring some accusations of inherent Asian racism. With a script co-written by Oliver Stone, this sour-tasting tale of highly decorated cop Mickey Rourke cleaning up corrupt Chinatown features some incredibly intense action and one of Rourke's more believable characterisations. Trouble is, there's not a likeable character in sight, the tone is absurdly melodramatic and it seems to go on forever. JC DVD

Mickey Rourke *Stanley White* • John Lone *Joey Tai* • Ariane *Tracy Tzu* • Leonard Termo *Angelo Rizzo* • Raymond Barry *Raymond J Barry* • Louis Bukowski • Caroline Kava *Connie White* • Eddie Jones *William McKenna* ■ *Dir* Michael Cimino • *Scr* Oliver Stone, Michael Cimino, from the novel by Robert Daley

Year of the Gun ★★★ 15
Political thriller 1991 · US · Colour · 107min

Set in Rome in 1978, when the Red Brigades terrorist group was active, this reasonably gripping and intriguing thriller follows the fortunes of two journalists. Andrew McCarthy is writing a novel that features a fictitious terrorist mission; Sharon Stone is a photographer whose efforts to gatecrash McCarthy's project and his love life lead to mayhem. While Stone looks good and looks the part, too, the main problem is the bland McCarthy. AT Violence, swearing, nudity. DVD

Andrew McCarthy *David Raybourne* • Sharon Stone *Alison King* • Valeria Golino *Lia Spinelli* • John Pankow *Italo Bianchi* • George Murcell *Pierre Bernier* • Mattia Sbragia *Giovanni* • Roberto Posse *Lucio Spinelli* • Thomas Elliot *Marco Spinelli* ■ *Dir* John Frankenheimer • *Scr* David Ambrose, from the novel by Michael Mewshaw

The Year of the Horse ★ 15
Musical documentary
1997 · US · BW · Colour · 107min

Even fans of folk rocker Neil Young and his band Crazy Horse will find this arch rockumentary tedious. Filmed in Europe and America during the group's 1996 tour, cult director Jim Jarmusch combines new concert footage with archive material of Young when he was at the height of his popularity. Jarmusch's minimalist style and the band's boring musings provide little insight into the Crazy Horse universe and many will be left wondering why they even bothered. AJ Swearing, drug abuse.

■ *Dir* Jim Jarmusch • *Cinematographers* Jim Jarmusch, LA Johnson

A Year of the Quiet Sun ★★★★ 15
Romantic drama
1984 · Pol/US/W Ger · Colour · 108min

The winner of the Golden Lion at Venice, Krzysztof Zanussi's gentle love story, involving an emotionally fractured GI and a fatalistic Polish widow, is set in 1946 against a backdrop of political transformation, war-crimes trials and lingering psychological trauma. Scott Wilson and Maja Komorowska

Y

excel as the diverse couple, while Zanussi's direction has a keen sense of place and poetry. DP Polish, English +subtitles.

Maja Komorowska *Emilia* • Scott Wilson *Norman* • Hanna Skarzanka *Emilia's mother* • Ewa Dalkowska *Stella* • Vadiln Glowna *Niemiec* • Daniel Webb [Danny Webb] *David* ■ *Dir/Scr* Krzysztof Zanussi

Year One ★★ 12
Prehistoric comedy adventure
2009 • US • Colour • 92min

Primitive hunter Jack Black and his gatherer sidekick Michael Cera are banished from paradise and left to fend for themselves in *Groundhog Day* director Harold Ramis's knockabout comedy. As the hapless pair journey through the ancient world, they encounter numerous Biblical figures (Cain and Abel, Abraham) and unwittingly find themselves at the centre of an assassination plot. The lampooning of religion makes *Life of Brian* comparisons unavoidable, although the at times puerile gags are generally broader. As Black is on autopilot throughout, it's Cera's deadpan delivery that gets the most laughs, but even they are few and far between. TeS Some swearing, sexual references. *DVD* ◼

Jack Black *Zed* • Michael Cera *Oh* • Olivia Wilde *Princess Ianna* • June Raphael [June Diane Raphael] *Maya* • David Cross (2) *Cain* • Juno Temple *Eema* • Oliver Platt *High Priest* • Christopher Mintz-Plasse *Isaac* • Hank Azaria *Abraham* ■ *Dir* Harold Ramis • *Scr* Harold Ramis, Gene Stupnitsky, Lee Eisenberg, from a story by Ramis

The Yearling ★★★★ U
Drama
1946 • US • Colour • 122min

This lovely and loving story of a boy and his pet fawn, based on Marjorie Kinnan Rawlings's Pulitzer Prize-winning novel, takes its strength from an understatement of dramatic events and the underplaying of the actors (Gregory Peck and Jane Wyman as poor crop farmers; special Oscar-winning Claude Jarman Jr as their son). Veteran director Clarence Brown shapes it into a tale that touches the heart while never patronising the mind. Sentiment without sentimentality. TH

Gregory Peck *Pa Baxter* • Jane Wyman *Ma Baxter* • Claude Jarman Jr *Jody Baxter* • Chill Wills *Buck Forrester* • Clem Bevans *Pa Forrester* • Margaret Wycherly *Ma Forrester* • Henry Travers *Mr Boyles* • Forrest Tucker *Lem Forrester* • Donn Gift *Fodderwing* ■ *Dir* Clarence Brown • *Scr* Paul Osborn, from the novel by Marjorie Kinnan Rawlings

The Years Between ★★
Drama
1946 • UK • BW • 108min

Marital harmony and political ambition are severely challenged when an MP, supposed killed in the war, turns up alive to find his wife has taken over his seat in parliament and is about to remarry. She gives him back his seat but determines to pursue her own career in politics. This poorly scripted adaptation verges on the unsuitably melodramatic, but the glamorous casting of Michael Redgrave and Valerie Hobson as the couple renders it watchable. RK

Michael Redgrave *Colonel Michael Wentworth* • Valerie Hobson *Diana Wentworth* • Flora Robson *Nanny* • James McKechnie *Richard Llewellyn* • Felix Aylmer *Sir Ernest Foster* • Dulcie Gray *Jill* ■ *Dir* Compton Bennett • *Scr* Muriel Box, Sydney Box, from the play by Daphne du Maurier

Yeelen ★★★★ PG
Fantasy
1987 • Mali • Colour • 104min

The timeless significance of ancient custom to the Bambara peoples of Mali is explored in this haunting political fable from Souleymane Cissé. Having been threatened with death by his shaman father, Issiaka Kane goes into exile, where he learns the power and value of the magical gifts he will need to succeed in his Oedipal struggle. Although much of the symbolism is as obscure to non-Malian viewers as the story's historical background, there's no denying the simple poetry of the landscape or Cissé's technical mastery, as he explores in minute detail the secret Komo rituals that

will ensure prosperity through self-sacrifice. DP Bambara +subtitles.

Issiaka Kane *Nianankoro* • Aova Sangere *Attu* • Niamanto Sanogo *Soma* • Balla Moussa Keita *Peul King* ■ *Dir/Scr* Souleymane Cissé

The Yellow Balloon ★★ PG
Crime drama
1952 • UK • BW • 76min

This is typical of the many dour dramas churned out by postwar British cinema. Writer/director, J Lee Thompson would have done better to focus on the relationship between timid pre-teen Andrew Ray and fugitive killer William Sylvester, but he can't resist throwing in a social message and a family crisis that slows the action and dilutes the suspense. Kenneth More flops as the doting dad, but Kathleen Ryan makes a monstrously shrewish mother. DP *DVD*

Andrew Ray *Frankie* • Kathleen Ryan *Em* • Kenneth More *Ted* • Bernard Lee *Constable Chapman* • Stephen Fenemore *Ron* • William Sylvester *Len* • Marjorie Rhodes *Mrs Stokes* • Peter Jones *Spiv* • Eliot Makeham *Pawnbroker* • Sidney James *Barrow boy* ■ *Dir* J Lee Thompson • *Scr* Anne Burnaby, J Lee Thompson, from the story by Burnaby

The Yellow Cab Man ★★★ U
Comedy
1950 • US • BW • 84min

Three years after he stole the show from Cary Grant and Loretta Young in *The Bishop's Wife*, that unsung character actor James Gleason was back behind the wheel of a cab for this knockabout Red Skelton vehicle. Indeed, it's the supporting cast that keeps this scatterbrained comedy on the road, as Skelton mugs along in typical fashion as an eccentric inventor who causes chaos wherever he goes. Walter Slezak is a standout as the unscrupulous villain desperate to get his hands on the secret of unbreakable glass. DP

Red Skelton *Augustus "Red" Pirdy* • Gloria DeHaven *Ellen Goodrich* • Walter Slezak *Doctor Byron Dokstedder* • Edward Arnold *Martin Creavy* • James Gleason *Mickey Corkins* ■ *Dir* Jack Donohue • *Scr* Devery Freeman, Albert Beich, from a story by Freeman

Yellow Canary ★★ U
Second World War spy drama
1943 • UK • BW • 98min

Anna Neagle stars as an improbable British spy, pretending to be a Nazi sympathiser in Canada. Director Herbert Wilcox hasn't a clue how to build the thrills inherent in this kind of material, and as Neagle and her intelligence shadow Richard Greene sabotage the Nazi plot to blow up a Nova Scotia harbour, the whole thing becomes gently risible. TS

Anna Neagle *Sally Maitland* • Richard Greene *Jim Garrick* • Margaret Rutherford *Mrs Towcester* • Nova Pilbeam *Betty Maitland* • Albert Lieven *Jan Orlock* • Lucie Mannheim *Madame Orlock* • Marjorie Fielding *Lady Maitland* ■ *Dir* Herbert Wilcox • *Scr* Miles Malleson, DeWitt Bodeen, from a story by Pamela Bower

The Yellow Canary ★★
Thriller
1963 • US • BW • 92min

Pop star Pat Boone and his wife Barbara Eden are experiencing marriage difficulties. But their differences are forgotten when they return home one night to find their nursemaid murdered and their baby son missing. The kidnappers have left a note citing "canary" as a code word in future dealings and soon a $200,000 ransom demand is made. A by-numbers thriller with sadly few twists and turns en route. DF

Pat Boone *Andy Paxton* • Barbara Eden *Lissa* • Steve Forrest *Hub Wiley* • Jack Klugman *Lieutenant Bonner* • Jesse White *Ed Thornburg* ■ *Dir* Buzz Kulik • *Scr* Rod Serling, from the novel *Evil Come, Evil Go* by Whit Masterson

Yellow Earth ★★★★★ U
Period drama
1984 • Chi • Colour • 90min

This adaptation of Ke Lan's novel was a key film in the evolution of Fifth Generation Chinese cinema. Set in 1939, the story concerns the hopes of emancipation raised in a peasant girl by a soldier on a mission to collect folk songs. Inspired by the compositional values of traditional art,

debuting director Chen Kaige and cinematographer Zhang Yimou firmly root the characters in their desolate Shaanxi environment and use space, colour and nuance to suggest the contrast between communist zeal and rural complacency. More philosophical than political, this is also a provocative treatise on the need for a balance between tradition and progress. DP

Xue Bai • Wang Xueqi • Tan Tuo • Liu Qiang ■ *Dir* Chen Kaige • *Scr* Zhang Ziliang from the novel by Ke Lan

The Yellow Mountain ★★ U
Western
1954 • US • Colour • 78min

The "yellow" in the mountain is gold, of course, and it leads to some pretty unremarkable sparring between former Tarzan Lex Barker and former radio actor Howard Duff in a very average Universal western. Produced by Ross Hunter before he got into his stride as the purveyor of gloss 'n' froth. TS

Lex Barker *Andy Martin* • Mala Powers *Nevada Wray* • Howard Duff *Pete Menlo* • William Demarest *Jackpot Wray* • John McIntire *Bannon* • Leo Gordon *Drake* ■ *Dir* Jesse Hibbs • *Scr* George Zuckerman, Russell Hughes, Robert Blees, from a story by Harold Channing Wire

Yellow Pages ★★ 15
Spoof thriller
1984 • UK/US • Colour • 87min

This uneven comedy was made in 1984, but for some odd reason (because it was a clunker, perhaps?) remained unseen for four years. Lea Thompson is the spoilt brat on a trip to Europe who is kept under surveillance by Chris Lemmon, a private eye so unskilled that she gets kidnapped right under his nose. Incredibly silly stuff, it's notable only for the supporting performances of Jean Simmons and Viveca Lindfors, who manage to rise above the otherwise poor material. JB

Chris Lemmon *Henry Brilliant* • Jean Simmons *Maxine De La Hunt* • Lea Thompson *Marigold De La Hunt* • Viveca Lindfors *Mrs Bellinger* • Mills Watson *Billy O'Shea* • Nancy Cartwright *Stephanie* ■ *Dir/Scr* James Kenelm Clarke

The Yellow Rolls-Royce ★★
Drama
1964 • UK • Colour • 121min

A typically British trilogy of thin anecdotes about the owners of a Rolls-Royce Phantom II – four wheels, famous radiator, painted yellow, three careful owners. The writer and director have a similar pedigree, though Terence Rattigan and Anthony Asquith's readiness to recycle their previous excursion into jet-set gloss, *The VIPs*, seemed a foolish idea in the first place. The European locations match poorly with the kitsch sets and the whole thing seems all dressed up with nowhere to go. AT

Rex Harrison *Marquess of Frinton* • Jeanne Moreau *Marchioness of Frinton* • Edmund Purdom *John Fane* • Michael Hordern *Harmsworth* • Shirley MacLaine *Mae Jenkins* • George C Scott *Paolo Maltese* • Alain Delon *Stefano* • Art Carney *Joey* • Ingrid Bergman *Gerda Millett* • Omar Sharif *Davich* • Joyce Grenfell *Hortense Astor* • Wally Cox *Ferguson* ■ *Dir* Anthony Asquith • *Scr* Terence Rattigan

The Yellow Rose of Texas ★★ U
Western
1944 • US • BW • 69min

There's a showboat setting for this otherwise routine Roy Rogers western in which Dale Evans plays opposite him: more than two dozen further co-starring roles and off-screen marriage would follow. Here Evans runs the showboat and gives Rogers a singing job on board, not knowing he's an insurance investigator after money supposedly stolen by her father. AE

Roy Rogers • Dale Evans *Betty Weston* • Grant Withers *Lukas* • Harry Shannon *Sam Weston* • George Cleveland *Captain Joe* ■ *Dir* Joseph Kane • *Scr* Jack Townley

The Yellow Sea ★★★ 18
Crime thriller
2010 • S Kor • Colour • 140min

This intense thriller reunites writer/director Na Hong-jin with the stars of his excellent debut, *The Chaser*. Ha Jung-woo is Gu-nam,

a man driven to drink and gambling after his wife disappears. He's then left with no choice but to accept an offer from a local crimelord to carry out a hit in order to clear his debts. In a disorienting sequence, Gu-nam is smuggled into Korea, where he prepares to bump off a wealthy businessman – only to discover that he's not the only would-be assassin on the block. This first hour of plot makes for a slow and suspenseful build-up, at which point the film explodes into violence, as the pursuer suddenly becomes the pursued. The ensuing carnage is punctuated by some exhilarating chase scenes, but the endless stabbing, hacking and bludgeoning does become a little wearisome. JH Korean +subtitles. Violence, sex scenes. *DVD* *BL*

Ha Jung-woo *Gu-nam* • Kim Yoon-suk *Myun Jung-hak* • Cho Seong-ha *Kim Tae-won* • Lee Chul-min *Choi Sung-nam* • Kwak Byoung-kyu *Professor Kim Seung-hyun* • Lim Ye-won *Professor Kim's wife* ■ *Dir* Na Hong-jin • *Scr* Na Hong-jin, Hong Won-chan

Yellow Sky ★★★
Western
1948 • US • BW • 96min

Highly regarded in many critical quarters, this bleak western owes much to superb location photography by Joe MacDonald, and to the confrontational leading roles played by two of 20th Century-Fox's best stars – Gregory Peck and Richard Widmark – in their glorious early years. But the pace is often staggeringly slow and the story, inspired by Shakespeare's *The Tempest*, sits awkwardly in its Death Valley setting. TS *DVD*

Gregory Peck *Stretch* • Anne Baxter *Mike* • Richard Widmark *Dude* • Robert Arthur (1) *Bull Run* • John Russell *Lengthy* • Henry Morgan [Harry Morgan] *Half Pint* • James Barton *Grandpa* • Charles Kemper *Walrus* • Robert Adler *Jed* ■ *Dir* William A Wellman • *Scr* Lamar Trotti, from the novel by WR Burnett

Yellow Submarine ★★★★ U
Animated musical fantasy
1968 • UK • Colour • 86min

The Beatles had little to do with this amazing animated feature (although they do crop up at the end). Directed by George Dunning and boasting *Love Story*'s Erich Segal among the screenwriters, this is an endlessly inventive picture that blends 1960s psychedelia with such diverse styles as pop art and Art Deco to create the fantastical world of Pepperland and its bizarre inhabitants. The mix of new songs and old favourites works a treat, but George Martin's superb score is also worth a listen. DP *DVD* *BL*

John Clive *John* • Geoffrey Hughes *Paul* • Peter Batten *George* • Paul Angelis *Ringo/Chief Blue Meanie* • Dick Emery *Lord Mayor/Nowhere Man/Max* • Lance Percival *Old Fred* ■ *Dir* George Dunning • *Scr* Lee Minoff, Al Brodax, Erich Segal, Jack Mendelsohn, from a story by Minoff, from the song by John Lennon, Paul McCartney

Yellowbeard ★ 15
Comedy adventure
1983 • US • Colour • 92min

What a way to go! Surely Marty Feldman deserved a better screen swan song than this diabolical comedy. Co-stars Graham Chapman and Peter Cook should have been made to walk the plank for their contributions to a sloppy script, and they can count themselves lucky that the cast was made up of old friends, otherwise they might have had a mutiny on their hands. Awful is charitable. DP Violence, swearing, nudity. *DVD*

Graham Chapman *Yellowbeard* • Peter Boyle *Moon* • Richard "Cheech" Marin *El Segundo* • Tommy Chong *El Nebuloso* • Peter Cook *Lord Lambourn* • Marty Feldman *Gilbert* • Michael Hordern *Dr Gilpin* • Eric Idle *Commander Clement* • James Mason *Captain Hughes* • John Cleese *Blind Pew* • Spike Milligan *Flunkie* • Susannah York *Lady Churchill* • Beryl Reid *Lady Lambourn* ■ *Dir* Mel Damski • *Scr* Graham Chapman, Peter Cook, Bernard McKenna

Yellowstone Kelly ★★★ U
Western
1959 • US • Colour • 92min

Veteran Warner Bros director Gordon Douglas is in charge as buckskin-clad Clint

Walker attempts to quell a Sioux uprising, supported by other TV names of the time such as Edward Byrnes (77 Sunset Strip) and John Russell (The Lawman). The Technicolor exteriors are superb, but the monosyllabic Walker never cut it as a movie star, becoming a useful supporting player and occasional lead in programme fillers. TS **DVD**

Clint Walker "Yellowstone' Kelly • Edward Byrnes [Edd Byrnes] Anse • John Russell Gall • Ray Danton Sayap' • Claude Akins Sergeant • Warren Oates Corporal ∎ Dir Gordon Douglas • Scr Burt Kennedy, from the novel by Clay Fisher [Heck Allen]

Yentl ★★ PG
Musical drama 1983 · UK/US · Colour · 127min

Based on a story by Isaac Bashevis Singer and set in 1904 in central Europe, Barbra Streisand's first film as a director is about a Jewish girl who dresses as a boy to receive a religious education. Streisand approaches this seriously, but, despite the obvious pains taken with the period setting, it rather lumbers along. The film won the Oscar for best original score and two songs were nominated. AT Brief nudity. **DVD**

Barbra Streisand Yentl • Mandy Patinkin Avigdor • Amy Irving Hadass ∎ Dir Barbra Streisand • Scr Jack Rosenthal Streisand, from the short story Yentl, the Yeshiva Boy by Isaac Bashevis • Music/Lyrics Michel Legrand, Marilyn Bergman, Alan Bergman

Yes ★★★ 15
Romantic drama 2004 · UK/US · Colour · 99min

Joan Allen and Sam Neill are a long-married couple whose relationship is as cold and sterile as their home. Their intimate life is exposed to their cleaning lady (Shirley Henderson), who reads deeper meanings into stains and rubbish. At a formal dinner, Allen catches the eye of a Lebanese chef (Simon Abkarian) and so begins a torrid affair. The cadenced dialogue (the characters often begin speaking in rhyming couplets) brings a lyricism to their love affair. While this may not be for everyone, it is a beautiful, bold adventure into the psyche of modern life. KK Swearing. **DVD**

Joan Allen She • Simon Abkarian He • Sam Neill Anthony • Shirley Henderson Cleaner • Sheila Hancock Aunt • Samantha Bond (2) Kate • Stephanie Leonidas Grace • Gary Lewis Billy ∎ Dir/Scr Sally Potter

Yes, Giorgio ★ PG
Romantic musical 1982 · US · Colour · 106min

Alp-sized tenor Luciano Pavarotti's film debut ended up as a contrived star vehicle, with the singing mountain (as an opera star (surprise, surprise) who falls for the woman throat specialist called in to cure him when his voice fails during a US tour. It's just about as bad as it sounds. But add an extra star to the rating if you're potty about Pav, and have to see anything he sings in. DA

Luciano Pavarotti Giorgio Fini • Kathryn Harrold Dr Pamela Taylor • Eddie Albert Henry Pollack • Paola Borboni Sister Teresa • James Hong Kwan • Beulah Quo Mei Ling ∎ Dir Franklin J Schaffner • Scr Norman Steinberg, from the novel by Anne Piper

Yes Man ★★★ 12
Comedy 2008 · US/Aus/UK · Colour · 99min

The intriguing concept of this freewheeling Jim Carrey comedy – what would happen if you answered every question with a "yes"? – has been lifted from the non-fiction book by British TV presenter Danny Wallace. The action relocates to LA, where Carrey is a depressed, antisocial, single, divorced loan adviser whose response to every invite is "no". However, after an unconvincing quasi-religious seminar converts him to the affirmative, life takes unexpectedly random turns. Carrey is likeable rather than annoying and generously allows New Zealander Rhys Darby (The Flight of the Conchords) to steal every scene he's in as a geeky, Harry Potter-obsessed bank manager. AC **DVD** **Blu-ray**

Jim Carrey Carl Allen • Zooey Deschanel Allison • Bradley Cooper Peter • John Michael Higgins Nick • Rhys Darby Norman • Terence Stamp Terrence Bundley ∎ Dir Peyton Reed • Scr Nicholas Stoller, Jarrad Paul, Andrew Mogel, from the non-fiction book by Danny Wallace

Yesterday, Today and Tomorrow ★★★ 15
Portmanteau comedy drama 1963 · Fr/It · Colour · 118min

Notwithstanding its superstar backstage credentials, this Oscar-winning portmanteau only occasionally delivers on the screen. In spite of story credits for Alberto Moravia, screenwriting nods for playwright Eduardo De Filippo and neorealist guru Cesare Zavattini and the directorial elegance of Vittorio De Sica, only the first tale Adelina, about Neapolitan husband-and-wife smugglers who exploit a law forbidding the arrest of pregnant women, is consistently amusing. In Mara, a Roman prostitute ends a week-long vow of chastity with a striptease that was to garner all the film's headlines. DP In Italian. **DVD**

Sophia Loren Adelina/Anna/Mara • Marcello Mastroianni Carmine/Renzo/Augusto Rusconi • Tina Pica Grandmother ∎ Dir Vittorio De Sica • Scr Eduardo DeFilippo, Isabella Quarantotti, Cesare Zavattini, Billa Billa Zanuso, from the story Troppo Ricca by Alberto Moravia

Yesterday's Enemy ★★★
Second World War drama 1959 · UK · BW · 95min

This Val Guest-directed tough war movie was one of a group that introduced a note of cynicism and irony, replacing the slightly softer, almost nostalgic war films of the late 1940s. It's set in 1942 and tells of the unexpected consequences when a group of British soldiers take over a Burmese village. The absence of music and the widescreen black-and-white photography lend a gritty feel to this well-acted film. BB **DVD**

Stanley Baker Capt Langford • Guy Rolfe Padre • Leo McKern Max • Gordon Jackson Sgt MacKenzie • David Oxley Doctor • Richard Pasco 2nd Lt Hastings • Russell Waters Brigadier ∎ Dir Val Guest • Scr Peter R Newman, from his TV play

Yesterday's Hero ★
Sports drama 1979 · UK · Colour · 94min

Ian McShane is the George Best-inspired footballer aiming for a comeback after beating a booze problem. Will he make it to the cup final? Paul Nicholas (playing an Elton John-type rock star chairman) and Adam Faith (as McShane's manager) help him achieve his goal. But the end result of this Jackie Collins-scripted effort is strictly fourth division. AJ

Ian McShane Rod Turner • Suzanne Somers Cloudy Martin • Adam Faith Jake Marsh • Paul Nicholas Clint Simon • Sandy Ratcliff Rita • Sam Kydd Sam Turner • Glynis Barber Susan ∎ Dir Neil Leifer • Scr Jackie Collins

Yield to the Night ★★★ 15
Crime drama 1956 · UK · BW · 95min

Directed with a grim sense of purpose by J Lee Thompson, this sincere plea for the abolition of capital punishment was based on the case of Ruth Ellis, the last woman in Britain to be hanged and whose story was retold some 30 years later with a good deal more style by Mike Newell in Dance with a Stranger. Diana Dors gives one of the best performances of her career as the murderess recalling the circumstances that drove her to kill while waiting to hear if she will be reprieved. DP **DVD**

Diana Dors Mary Hilton • Yvonne Mitchell MacFarlane • Michael Craig Jim Lancaster • Geoffrey Keen Chaplain • Olga Lindo Hill • Mary Mackenzie Maxwell • Joan Miller Barker ∎ Dir J Lee Thompson • Scr Joan Henry, John Cresswell, from the novel by Henry

Yoga Hosers ★
Fantasy comedy horror 2016 · US · Colour · 88min

A silly horror-comedy from writer/director Kevin Smith. Colleen C (Lily-Rose Depp, daughter of Johnny) and Colleen M (Harley Quinn Smith, daughter of Kevin) are schoolgirls whose shift at a convenience store is upset by an invasion of sausage men who look like Adolf Hitler. After disposing of them, the girls team up with a legendary man-hunter (Johnny Depp), and go Nazi-hunting. Lazy and amateurish as it is, Depp and Smith do show promise as the heroines. But, all in all, it's a chore. SC In English, French, German.

Harley Quinn Smith Colleen McKenzie • Lily-Rose Melody Depp Colleen Collette • Johnny Depp Guy Lapointe • Kevin Smith (2) Bratzi • Haley Joel Osment Adrien Arcand • Austin Butler Hunter Calloway • Adam Brody Ichabod • Justin Long Yogi Bayer • Natasha Lyonne Tabitha • Stan Lee Dispatcher ∎ Dir/Scr Kevin Smith (2)

Yogi Bear ★★ U
Part-animated comedy adventure 2010 · US/NZ · Colour · 80min

Hanna-Barbera cartoon character Yogi Bear is dragged kicking and screaming into the 21st century with this uncomfortable blend of live-action, CGI and 3D. The voice talents of Dan Aykroyd as Yogi and Justin Timberlake as Boo Boo are lost amid the frenetic action of a story about corrupt politicians and environmental threat. There is one impressive white-water rafting ride down the river, but the rest will only appeal to youngsters who haven't seen it quite so many times before. If the writers had produced something that was smarter than the average script, then perhaps we would have been in business. SuR **DVD** **Blu-ray** **3D**

Dan Aykroyd Yogi Bear • Justin Timberlake Boo Boo • Tom Cavanagh Ranger Smith • Anna Faris Rachel Johnson • Andrew Daly Mayor Brown • Nate Corddry [Nathan Corddry] Chief of Staff ∎ Dir Eric Brevig • Scr Brad Copeland, Joshua Sternin, Jeffrey Ventimilia

Yojimbo ★★★★★ PG
Period action drama 1961 · Jpn · BW · 105min

Such was the influence of the Hollywood western on Akira Kurosawa's superb samurai action adventure that it seems only fair that it, in turn, inspired Sergio Leone's A Fistful of Dollars, the film that launched the Italian "spaghetti" western. Combining moments of comedy, intrigue and sudden, shocking violence, Kurosawa celebrates the samurai genre at the same time as he is subtly subverting it. Toshiro Mifune is tremendous as the wandering warrior who sells his sword skills to both sides in a divided village only to dupe them into mutual slaughter. He returned in the sequel, Sanjuro, the following year. DP Japanese +subtitles. **DVD** **Blu-ray**

Toshiro Mifune Sanjuro Kuwabatake • Eijiro Tono Gonji • Seizaburo Kawazu Seibei • Isuzu Yamada Orin • Hiroshi Tachikawa Yoichiro • Susumu Fujita Homma ∎ Dir Akira Kurosawa • Scr Akira Kurosawa, Ryuzo Kikushima, Hideo Oguni, from the novel Red Harvest by Dashiell Hammett • Music Masaru Sato

Yol ★★★★★ 15
Drama 1982 · Tur · Colour · 109min

Anger and sadness lie at the heart of this treatise on the perpetuation of the patriarchal prejudices underpinning Turkish society. The film was written by Yilmaz Guney, while in prison for so-called political offences, and directed from explicit instructions by his longtime assistant, Serif Goren. The negative was then smuggled to Switzerland, where Guney edited it following his escape. The winner of the Palme d'Or at Cannes, it testifies to the courage of Turkey's greatest-ever film-maker. But, perhaps more significantly, the story of the five parolees who must face up to personal calamity also highlights the tragedy of a nation whose future is so hidebound by its past. DP Turkish +subtitles.

Tarik Akan Seyit Ali • Halil Ergun Mehmet Salih • Necmettin Cobanoglu Omer • Serif Sezer Ziné ∎ Dir Serif Goren • Scr Yilmaz Guney

Yolanda and the Thief ★★★ U
Romantic fantasy musical 1945 · US · Colour · 107min

Fred Astaire, more balletic than usual, and Lucille Bremer, an expressionless red-haired dancer, play the title roles in an MGM musical which gave Vincente Minnelli ample scope to express his taste for decorative fantasy with some stunning dream sequences. These numbers, drenched in exotic colours, burst forth when Astaire dreams himself into a surrealistic landscape and are the best parts of the film. Set in a mythical Latin American country, the whimsical story has Astaire as a confidence trickster, who pretends to be the guardian angel (literally) of the convent-educated heroine, and her millions. RB

Fred Astaire Johnny Parkson Riggs • Lucille Bremer Yolanda Aquaviva • Frank Morgan Victor Budlow Trout • Mildred Natwick Aunt Amarilla • Mary Nash Duenna • Leon Ames Mr Candle ∎ Dir Vincente Minnelli • Scr Ludwig Bemelmans, Irving Brecher, from a short story by Jacques Thery, Bemelmans

Yom Yom ★★★
Period drama 1998 · Fr/Is/It · Colour · 105min

Amos Gitai directs this family comedy set in Haifa about the clash between personal destiny and national identity – one that is more prevalent than many outsiders would assume. Moshe Ivgi stars as the middle-aged mommy's boy, of mixed Arab-Jewish stock, who is forced to rethink his fatalistic approach to life, when his family bakery is threatened by plans for a shopping mall. Exposing the intransigence that makes compromise in the region a near impossibility, Gitai gently satirises the traditions that stand in the way of progress. DP Hebrew +subtitles.

Moshe Ivgi Moshe • Hanna Maron Hanna • Juliano Merr Jules • Dalit Kahan Didi • Yussef Abu Warda Yussef • Nataly Atiya Grisha ∎ Dir Amos Gitai • Scr Jacky Cukier, Amos Gitai

Yossi ★★★ 15
Drama 2012 · Is · Colour · 80min

A decade after Yossi (Ohad Knoller) watched his soldier lover perish in action in Yossi & Jagger, Israeli director Eytan Fox catches up with the character, now a paunchy cardiologist who lives alone. After a botched operation, he is urged to take a sabbatical from his hospital and get out of Tel Aviv. Having shocked conservative compatriots with his original drama, Fox is keen to show how attitudes have changed and, consequently, is less combative in allowing Yossi to move on with his life. The movie is deftly played, sensitively photographed, thoughtfully empathetic and encouragingly reflective. DP Hebrew +subtitles. Sex scenes, nudity. **DVD**

Ohad Knoller Yossi • Oz Zehavi Tom • Orly Silbersatz [Orly Silbersatz Banai] Varda • Ola Schur-Selektar Nina • Lior Ashkenazi Moti • Meir Golan Nimrod ∎ Dir Eytan Fox • Scr Itay Segal

You Again ★★ U
Comedy 2010 · US · Colour · 101min

This virtually mirthless family comedy sees Kristen Bell returning home for her brother's wedding, only to discover he's marrying the bitchy cheerleader (Odette Yustman) who ruined her high-school years. It's a convoluted set-up that combines vindictive yet scarcely believable characters with regular doses of queasy sentiment. Thankfully, Jamie Lee Curtis (Bell's mom, one-time prom queen) and Sigourney Weaver (Yustman's aunt, and Curtis's competitive former best pal) are on hand with a few scores of their own to settle, and their presence makes the movie moderately tolerable. TJ **DVD**

Kristen Bell Marni • Jamie Lee Curtis Gail • Sigourney Weaver Aunt Ramona • Odette Yustman Joanna • Victor Garber Mark • Betty White Grandma Bunny • Kristin Chenoweth Georgia • Dwayne Johnson Air marshal ∎ Dir Andy Fickman • Scr Moe Jelline

You and Me ★★★
Crime drama 1938 · US · BW · 90min

In a department store whose humane owner employs ex-convicts on parole, a love affair blossoms, but goes horribly wrong because of a misguided deceit practised by one of the sweethearts. George Raft and Sylvia Sidney star in this very curious mixture of crime melodrama, moral message and feel-good love story, directed by Fritz Lang who injects some equally curious stylistic devices, as well as his characteristic gift for creating tension. Much reviled by critics at the time, seen now it's actually very entertaining. RK

Sylvia Sidney *Helen* • George Raft *Joe Dennis* • Harry Carey *Mr Morris* • Barton MacLane *Mickey* • Warren Hymer *Gimpy* • Roscoe Karns *Cuffy* ■ *Dir* Fritz Lang • *Scr* Virginia Van Upp, from a story by Norman Krasna • *Music* Kurt Weill • *Lyrics* Sam Coslow

You & Me Forever ★★★★ 15
Coming-of-age drama
2012 · Den · Colour · 82min

Few can match the Scandinavians when it comes to depicting adolescent angst, and Danish director Kaspar Munk follows up 2010's estimable peer-pressure saga *Hold Me Tight* with another sensitive study of the perils of acting on impulse and surrendering one's identity to a bad influence. In truth, the plot is a touch prosaic and contrived, but Munk expertly captures the reckless spirit of youth and coaxes achingly authentic displays of vivacity and vulnerability from his leads. DP English subtitles.

Julie Andersen *Laura* • Frederikke Dahl Hansen *Maria* • Emilie Kruse *Christine* • Benjamin Wandschneider *Jonas* • Allan Hyde *Tobias* ■ *Dir* Kaspar Munk • *Scr* Kaspar Munk, Jannik Tai Mosholt

You and the Night ★★★ 18
Romantic comedy drama
2013 · Fr · Colour · 88min

The eccentric debut of French writer/director Yann Gonzalez, in which a young couple (Kate Moran, Niels Schneider) and their transvestite maid (Nicolas Maury) host an orgy, combines dreams and extraordinary histories with a rather fluid reality. Love, sex and death come crashing together as the strangers bond by sharing their stories, though sex sits on the backburner at first. The film's prurient philosophising can be frustratingly pithy but there's a cheeky gag around every corner. EAS French +subtitles.

Kate Moran *Ali* • Niels Schneider *Matthias* • Nicolas Maury *Udo* • Eric Cantona *Stud* • Fabienne Babe *Star* • Alain Fabien Delon *Teen* ■ *Dir/Scr* Yann Gonzalez

You Belong to Me ★★★
Romantic comedy 1941 · US · BW · 94min

Barbara Stanwyck is a successful doctor married to wealthy Henry Fonda. He doesn't need to work so, with time on his hands, develops an obsessive jealousy of her male patients from which springs both the humorous situations and the more sober moments. The stars are a dream, superseding the otherwise one-dimensional material. RK

Barbara Stanwyck *Dr Helen Hunt* • Henry Fonda *Peter Kirk* • Edgar Buchanan *Billings* • Roger Clark *"Van" Vandemer* • Ruth Donnelly *Emma* • Melville Cooper *Moody* • Ralph Peters *Joseph* • Maude Eburne *Ella* ■ *Dir* Wesley Ruggles • *Scr* Claude Binyon, from the story *You Belong to Me* by Dalton Trumbo

You Can Count on Me ★★★★ 15
Drama 1999 · US · Colour · 106min

Laura Linney deserved her Oscar nomination for a fine performance in this humour-tinged drama. She plays a strong-minded single mum who still lives in the small town where she and her brother (Mark Ruffalo) were orphaned as children. The return of her sibling – a drifter with a chequered past – initially suggests that Linney's character is the smart and stable

one, and Ruffalo is the black sheep. But perceptions shift as she embarks on an ill-judged fling with her bank manager boss (Matthew Broderick), and Ruffalo tries to rebuild the relationship between her son (Rory Culkin) and his estranged dad. Writer/director Kenneth Lonergan delivers a sharp script, with acute observations. DA Swearing, drug abuse, sex scenes. *DVD*

Laura Linney *Sammy Prescott* • Mark Ruffalo *Terry Prescott* • Matthew Broderick *Brian* • Rory Culkin *Rudy* • Bob Tenney *Bob* • J Smith-Cameron *Mabel* ■ *Dir/Scr* Kenneth Lonergan

You Can Thank Me Later ★★★
Comedy drama 1998 · Can · Colour · 110min

As the Cooperberg family anxiously waits in a hospital ward for news of their beloved patriarch, they each flash back to black-and-white confessionals outlining some of the more unsavoury moments in their lives. Jewish director Shimon Dotan takes the dysfunctional family concept to new theatrical heights in a melodramatic comedy rich in character if not in plot. The superlative ensemble cast revels in acting out the home truths and dark secrets. AJ

Geneviève Bujold *Joelle* • Ellen Burstyn *Shirley Cooperberg* • Amanda Plummer *Susan Cooperberg* • Ted Levine *Eli Cooperberg* • Mark Blum *Edward Cooperberg* ■ *Dir* Shimon Dotan • *Scr* Oren Safdie, from his play *Hyper-Allergenic*

You Can't Cheat an Honest Man ★★
Comedy 1939 · US · BW · 76min

Devised by WC Fields, this comedy had a fraught production involving two directors besides the credited George Marshall. A double had to be used in some of Fields's scenes, thanks to on-set arguments and his penchant for drinking doubles. Although not one of his classics, the film allows Fields considerable rein as an impecunious circus owner whose daughter is prepared to marry a wealthy toff to help her father, even though she's in love with someone else. Some of the best moments come when Fields turns up at the proposed wedding. BB

WC Fields *Larson E Whipsnade* • Edgar Bergen *The Great Edgar* • Constance Moore *Victoria Whipsnade* • John Arledge *Phineas Whipsnade* • James Bush *Roger Bel-Goodie* ■ *Dir* George Marshall • *Scr* George Marion Jr, Richard Mack, Everett Freeman, Henry Johnson, Lew Lipton, from a story by Charles Bogle [WC Fields]

You Can't Get Away with Murder ★★
Prison crime drama 1939 · US · BW · 75min

The unwieldy but graphically accurate title of this movie says it all: a formula second-rung crime tale that demands the death of both protagonists. Humphrey Bogart recycles the standard gangster he played 11 times in four years, co-starring with Dead End Kid Billy Halop. Bogart is an irredeemable, conscience-free thug who seduces the youngster into a life of crime, with Halop's disillusion and repentance coming too late to save him. Unoriginal and ponderous. RK

Humphrey Bogart *Frank Wilson* • Gale Page *Madge Stone* • Billy Halop *Johnnie Stone* • John Litel *Attorney Carey* • Henry Travers *Pop* • Harvey Stephens *Fred Burke* ■ *Dir* Lewis Seiler • *Scr* Robert Buckner, Don Ryan, Kenneth Gamet, from the play *Chalked Out* by Lewis E Lawes, Jonathan Finn

You Can't Have Everything ★★★
Musical comedy 1937 · US · BW · 89min

Would you believe Alice Faye as the descendant of Edgar Allan Poe? And that she despises musical comedy? An unlikely peg on which to hang the appearance of a lot of vaudeville troupers, but this movie's got a cast-and-a-half for connoisseurs: the Ritz Brothers, Louis Prima, Tony Martin, and Tip, Tap and Toe. And watch out for featured Louise Hovick – better known as Gypsy Rose Lee. Faye is her usual self, and sings the title with style, but the plot

eventually defeats her. It doesn't matter, though: it's all expertly done. TS

Alice Faye *Judith Poe Wells* • Harry Ritz • Al Ritz • Jimmy Ritz • Don Ameche *George Macrea* • Charles Winninger *Sam Gordon* • Louise Hovick [Gypsy Rose Lee] *Lulu Riley* • David Rubinoff • Tony Martin (1) *Bobby Walker* • Arthur Treacher *Bevins* ■ *Dir* Norman Taurog • *Scr* Harry Tugend, Jack Yellen, Karl Tunberg, from a story by Gregory Ratoff

You Can't Run Away from It ★★ U
Musical 1956 · US · Colour · 94min

A remake of the Oscar-winning classic *It Happened One Night*, this has June Allyson as the runaway heiress and Jack Lemmon as the newsman she runs into on a Greyhound bus. Some sequences, including the famous "Walls of Jericho" and hitch-hiking sketches are transferred from 1934 almost shot-for-shot, but there are also some musical numbers, including a cringe-making song from Stubby Kaye on the bus. Allyson has a dance sequence that is a showstopper in quite the wrong way. AT

June Allyson *Ellie Andrews* • Jack Lemmon *Peter Warne* • Charles Bickford *AA Andrews* • Paul Gilbert *George Shapely* • Jim Backus *Danker* • Stubby Kaye *Fred Toten* ■ *Dir* Dick Powell • *Scr* Claude Binyon, from the film *It Happened One Night* by Robert Riskin, from the short story *Night Bus* by Samuel Hopkins Adams

You Can't Take It with You ★★★★★ U
Comedy 1938 · US · BW · 120min

Frank Capra won a third, well-deserved Oscar in five years for this sparkling comedy (it also won best picture). Based on the George S Kaufman and Moss Hart play and scripted by Oscar winner Robert Riskin, it's about the eccentric Vanderhof family, New Yorkers whose wealth belies a vast range of eccentricity and political opinion. It's also a fable about individualism and everyone's need to resist corporate or group control. The movie contains wonderful performances from a cast that includes bubbly Jean Arthur and James Stewart as her drawling fiancé, and, if it is a touch overlong, that is a minor fault considering the vast comic talent on display. AT *DVD*

Jean Arthur *Alice Sycamore* • Lionel Barrymore *Martin Vanderhof* • James Stewart *Tony Kirby* • Edward Arnold *Anthony P Kirby* • Mischa Auer *Kolenkhov* • Ann Miller *Essie Carmichael* • Spring Byington *Penny Sycamore* • Samuel S Hinds *Paul Sycamore* ■ *Dir* Frank Capra • *Scr* Robert Riskin, from the play by George S Kaufman, Moss Hart • *Cinematographer* Joseph Walker • *Music* Dimitri Tiomkin [Dmitri Tiomkin]

You Can't Win 'Em All ★★★ PG
Comedy adventure 1970 · UK · Colour · 95min

During the collapse of the Ottoman Empire in 1920s Turkey, former American soldiers Tony Curtis and Charles Bronson are hired to protect the Sultan's three daughters and a shipment of gold. Leo V Gordon's poor script is given vitality by Peter Collinson's zippy direction and the repartee of the stars. TH

Tony Curtis *Adam Dyer* • Charles Bronson *Josh Corey* • Michèle Mercier *Aila* • Grégoire Aslan *Osman Bey* • Fikret Hakan *Colonel Elci* • Salih Guney *Captain Enver* • Patrick Magee *General* • Tony Bonner *Reese* ■ *Dir* Peter Collinson • *Scr* Leo V Gordon

You Don't Know Jack ★★★
Biographical drama 2010 · US · Colour · 135min

Dr Death is the name the media tagged to Jack Kevorkian, the retired pathologist who assisted in the suicides of more than 130 terminally ill people during the 1990s. This classy HBO biopic details his almost messianic battle with the authorities in Michigan to establish euthanasia as a civil right. In the hands of director Barry Levinson, the issue-heavy script gains a cinematic sheen and flashes of black humour. For star Al Pacino, in a rare TV

role, it provides plenty of meat, and bagged him both an Emmy and a Golden Globe. PM

Al Pacino *Jack Kevorkian* • Brenda Vaccaro *Margo Janus* • John Goodman *Neal Nicol* • Deirdre O'Connell *Linda* ■ *Dir* Barry Levinson • *Scr* Adam Mazer

You Don't Mess with the Zohan ★★ 12
Comedy 2008 · US · Colour · 108min

In this ludicrous comedy, Adam Sandler puts on a dodgy accent as "The Zohan", an Israeli super-agent who heads for New York to pursue a career in hairdressing. It's every bit as crass as you might expect, but what makes the film doubly grating is the lame attempt to demonstrate its liberal idealism by having Zohan fall for a Palestinian salon owner (Emmanuelle Chriqui). However, while Zohan struggles with these feelings, Salim (Rob Schneider) reinforces every stereotype of the immigrant Arab by driving a cab by day and making bombs by night. John Turturro is vaguely amusing as a terrorist with a fast-food franchise, but Sandler trades mostly in gross-out gags, such as Zohan's love of houmous and his affairs with old ladies. SP Sexual references, nudity, brief swearing. *DVD* *Blu*

Adam Sandler *Zohan "The Zohan" Dvir* • Rob Schneider *Salim* • John Turturro *Phantom* • Emmanuelle Chriqui *Dalia* • Nick Swardson *Michael* • Lainie Kazan *Gail* • Chris Rock *Taxi driver* ■ *Dir* Dennis Dugan • *Scr* Judd Apatow, Adam Sandler, Robert Smigel

You Got Served ★★ PG
Dance drama 2004 · US · Colour · 90min

This is a lively but formulaic teen drama, featuring members of top hip-hop groups. The story is a simple-minded one involving street-dance clashes between rival "crews", with two friends falling out over a girl but reconciling to whup their opponents. The dance sequences are dynamic, the acting serviceable and the production values decent enough. But there's little here to appeal beyond the film's young core audience, and even they might find film too safe and too predictable. DA *DVD*

Marques Houston *Elgin* • Omari Grandberry *David* • Jarell Houston *Rico* • DeMario Thornton *Vick* • Dreux Frederic *Rashaan* • Jennifer Freeman *Liyah* • Lil' Kim • Michael "Bear" Taliferro *Emerald* ■ *Dir/Scr* Christopher B Stokes

You Gotta Stay Happy ★★ U
Romantic comedy 1948 · US · BW · 100min

Joan Fontaine stars in this attempt at screwball romantic comedy. She plays a runaway bride who persuades flyer James Stewart and his buddy Eddie Albert to spirit her off to California. The plane crashes in Oklahoma farmland en route, Stewart and Fontaine fall in love, and you can guess the rest. It's amiable, and Stewart is perfect for his role. RK

Joan Fontaine *Diana "Dee Dee" Dillwood Benson aka Dottie Blucher* • James Stewart *Marvin Payne* • Eddie Albert *Bullets Baker* • Roland Young *Ralph Tutwiler* • Willard Parker *Henry Benson* ■ *Dir* HC Potter • *Scr* Karl Tunberg, from the story by Robert Carson

You Instead ★★ 15
Romantic comedy 2011 · UK · Colour · 76min

This British romantic comedy is more interesting for the manner of its making than for anything that actually happens in it. Guerrilla-filmed at the T in the Park music festival in Scotland, its use of the occasion is clever and convincing. Less convincing, though, is the contrived plot, which sees Luke Treadaway and Natalia Tena in an electro-pop star and punk singer who find themselves handcuffed together after an encounter with a new-age preacher. DA Swearing.

Luke Treadaway *Adam* • Natalia Tena *Morello* • Mathew Baynton *Tyko* • Ruta Gedmintas *Lake* • Gilly Gilchrist *Bruce The Roadie* ■ *Dir* David Mackenzie • *Scr* Thomas Leveritt

You Kill Me ★★★ 15
Crime comedy thriller 2007 · US · Colour · 88min

Ben Kingsley gives a witty portrayal of a hitman who joins Alcoholics Anonymous in this black comedy from *The Last Seduction* director John Dahl. Dahl thankfully sees no point in trying to redeem his (anti)hero, and the dark laughs arise from Kingsley's blasé approach to killing. A love interest in the form of Téa Leoni appears, but this doesn't signal a softening of the film's edges. She plays it just as cool as Kingsley, though it's a pity that her character is treated merely as a sounding board for his often warped philosophy. As the relationship deepens, the gags tail off and the plot becomes harder to swallow. But even then, it's impossible to take your eyes off Kingsley, who delivers the goods with lethal precision. SP Swearing. **DVD**

Ben Kingsley *Frank Falenczyk* · Téa Leoni *Laurel* · Luke Wilson *Tom* · Philip Baker Hall *Roman* · Dennis Farina *O'Leary* · Bill Pullman *Dave* · Marcus Thomas *Stef* · Alison Sealy-Smith *Doris* ■ *Dir* John Dahl · *Scr* Christopher Markus, Stephen McFeely

You Know What Sailors Are ★★ U
Comedy 1954 · UK · Colour · 89min

This is one of Ken Annakin's lesser outings, with too many cheap jibes, but there is some fun to be had as drunken sailor Donald Sinden plants a pawnbroker's sign and a pram on top of a ship and tries to pass it off as "Secret Weapon 998". Akim Tamiroff does what he can with one of his few leading roles, but the mediocre Cold War jokes eventually force him to surrender. DP

Donald Sinden *Lieutenant Sylvester Green* · Akim Tamiroff *President of Agraria* · Sarah Lawson *Betty* · Naunton Wayne *Captain Owbridge* · Bill Kerr *Lieutenant Smart* · Dora Bryan *Gladys* · Michael Hordern *Captain Hamilton* ■ *Dir* Ken Annakin · *Scr* Peter Rogers, from the novel *Sylvester* by Edward Hyams

You Light Up My Life ★ PG
Musical 1977 · US · Colour · 86min

Having made such a good impression as Frenchy in *Grease*, Didi Conn looked set for stardom. But this schmaltzy showbiz melodrama virtually put paid to her movie prospects. Even though the title song won an Oscar (in a very slow year), Joseph Brooks's story of the comedian's daughter with ambitions to become a singer-actress creaks under the weight of its clichés. For tackaholics only. DP

Didi Conn *Laurie Robinson* · Joe Silver *Si Robinson* · Michael Zaslow *Chris Nolan* · Stephen Nathan *Ken Rothenberg* · Melanie Mayron *Annie Gerrard* · Jerry Keller *Conductor* ■ *Dir/Scr* Joseph Brooks

You May Not Kiss the Bride ★★ 12
Romantic comedy adventure 2011 · US · Colour · 94min

A surprisingly starry supporting cast makes this low-on-laughs romantic farce more watchable than it deserves to be. Kathy Bates, Rob Schneider and Vinnie Jones are the familiar faces keeping the predictable events afloat, after an American pet photographer (Dave Annable) is forced to marry a Croatian crime boss's daughter (Katharine McPhee). It's solely for green card purposes, but you know true love will ultimately blossom. Before the slushy ending, though, comes a weak mix of slapstick, sight gags and hit-and-miss banter. SF Violence, sexual references.

Dave Annable *Bryan Lighthouse* · Katharine McPhee *Masha Nikitin* · Rob Schneider *Ernesto* · Mena Suvari *Tonya* · Kathy Bates *Bryan's mother* · Vinnie Jones *Brick* ■ *Dir/Scr* Rob Hedden

You, Me and Dupree ★★ 12
Comedy 2006 · US · Colour · 104min

Owen Wilson's laid-back slacker charm isn't enough to carry this flimsy, contrived comedy vehicle from director brothers Anthony and Joe Russo (*Welcome to Collinwood*). He plays the newly unemployed loser best friend of recently married Matt Dillon, who's allowed to move into the marital home – much to the annoyance of Dillon's wife Kate Hudson. A subplot involving Dillon's conflict with his father-in-law and boss (played by Michael Douglas) seems to belong in a different movie. Wilson has successfully sparked off the comic strengths of co-star Ben Stiller in previous collaborations. But without an effective foil, he's clearly struggling, and the bland direction makes the whole exercise feel annoyingly undercooked. JF Swearing, sexual references. **DVD** ⬆ **CS**

Owen Wilson *Randy Dupree* · Kate Hudson *Molly Peterson* · Matt Dillon *Carl Peterson* · Michael Douglas (1) *Mr Thompson* · Seth Rogen *Neil* · Amanda Detmer *Annie* · Lance Armstrong ■ *Dir* Anthony Russo, Joe Russo · *Scr* Michael LeSieur · *Cinematographer* Charles Minsky

You Must Be Joking! ★★ U
Farce 1965 · UK · BW · 102min

This scattershot comedy from Michael Winner has a sound premise: give five soldiers various unlikely tasks to assess their initiative. The trouble is, there are too many different tests and the slapstick solutions to them soon try the patience. Denholm Elliott and Lionel Jeffries go flat out for laughs, but with a little more gag selectivity on the part of Winner, they would not have had to work quite so hard. DP

Michael Callan *Lieutenant Tim Morton* · Lionel Jeffries *Sergeant Major McGregor* · Denholm Elliott *Captain Tabasco* · Wilfrid Hyde White *General Lockwood* · Bernard Cribbins *Sergeant Clegg* · James Robertson-Justice *Librarian* · Leslie Phillips *Young husband* · Terry-Thomas *Major Foskett* ■ *Dir* Michael Winner · *Scr* Alan Hackney, form a story by Michael Winner, Alan Hackney

You Only Live Once ★★★★★ 12
Classic crime drama 1937 · US · BW · 82min

This ironic masterpiece set in the Depression era borrows from the real-life Bonnie and Clyde saga, as Sylvia Sidney and Henry Fonda play small-timers caught up in an escalation of violence. Fonda has never been better, while Sidney is just wonderful: tender, poignant, vulnerable, scared. Director Fritz Lang creates a bleak half-world of sheer greyness, and, apparently, during the 46-day shoot, forced his actors and production team to stay awake so they'd look and be suitably tired. It's a brilliant, stunning classic you'll remember for ever. TS **DVD**

Henry Fonda *Eddie Taylor* · Sylvia Sidney *Joan Graham* · Barton MacLane *Stephen Whitney* · Jean Dixon *Bonnie Graham* · William Gargan *Father Dolan* · Warren Hymer *Muggsy* · Charles "Chic" Sale *Ethan* · Margaret Hamilton *Hester* ■ *Dir* Fritz Lang · *Scr* Gene Towne, Graham Baker, from a story by Towne · *Cinematographer* Leon Shamroy · *Music* Alfred Newman

You Only Live Twice ★★★★★ PG
Spy adventure 1967 · UK · Colour · 116min

This is one of the best of the Sean Connery Bond films, despite the actor's desire to quit the franchise. Here, 007 is sent to Japan where, having faked his own death, he goes native, "marries" a local girl and, in his quest to discover why spaceships are disappearing, finds a volcano with a false crater. It also has one of the all-time great screen villains in Donald Pleasence's scarred, cat-stroking Blofeld. Director Lewis Gilbert keeps the pace up, and the script (co-written by Roald Dahl) is suitably arch. But it is surely production designer Ken Adam's triumph: the secret base, where the film's explosive climax unfolds, remains definitive and much parodied. AC **DVD** ⬇

Sean Connery *James Bond* · Donald Pleasence *Ernst Stavro Blofeld* · Akiko Wakabayashi *Aki* · Tetsuro Tamba *Tiger Tanaka* · Mie Hama *Kissy Suzuki* · Teru Shimada *Osato* · Karin Dor *Helga Brandt* · Lois Maxwell *Miss Moneypenny* · Desmond Llewelyn "*Q*" · Bernard Lee "*M*" ■ *Dir* Lewis Gilbert · *Scr* Roald Dahl, Harry Jack Bloom, from the novel by Ian Fleming · *Cinematographer* Freddie Young

You Pay Your Money ★ U
Crime drama 1957 · UK · BW · 66min

The much maligned Butcher's Film Service mostly churned out dismal offerings such as this tale of kidnap and rare book smuggling, given only the merest modicum of respectability by the presence of Hugh McDermott and Honor Blackman. Maclean Rogers's adaptation of Michael Cronin's novel is as flat as his direction. DP

Hugh McDermott *Bob Westlake* · Jane Hylton *Rosemary Delgardo* · Honor Blackman *Susie Westlake* · Hugh Moxey *Tom Cookson* · Ivan Samson *Steve Mordaunt* ■ *Dir* Maclean Rogers · *Scr* Maclean Rogers, from the novel by Michael Cronin

You, the Living ★★★★ 15
Comedy drama 2007 · Swe/Ger/Fr/Den/Nor/Jpn · Colour · 89min

Swedish writer/director Roy Andersson's slice-of-Stockholm-life comedy drama introduces us, through a series of tragicomic vignettes, to a gallery of pitiable grotesques: a depressive wife and her frustrated husband; a young woman with a crush on a musician; and an Arab barber who has had enough of racial abuse. The film exposes the farcical reality of existence and the gloomy inevitability of these mundane lives, flitting between the inconsequential occurrences that blight people who have no idea they're interconnected. With musical interludes and dream sequences laying bare the futility of the characters' aspirations, this brilliant cry of despair is as bleak and savage as the best surrealism is supposed to be. DP Swedish +subtitles. A sex scene. **DVD**

Elisabet Helander *Mia* · Jessika Lundberg *Anna* · Bjorn Englund *Tuba player* · Eric Backman *Micke Larsson* · Leif Larsson *Workman* · Ollie Olson [Olle Olson] *Consultant* · Birgitta Persson *Tuba player's wife* · Kemal Sener *Hairdresser* · Hakan Angser *Psychiatrist* · Gunnar Ivarsson *Businessman* ■ *Dir/Scr* Roy Andersson

You Were Meant for Me ★★★
Musical 1948 · US · BW · 91min

A good example of the kind of musical made to use up contracts of personable stars. Jeanne Crain and Dan Dailey play smoothly together as the nice girl and the bandleader she marries in America during the Depression years. Dailey's stock was rising, and the same year he was nominated for the best actor Oscar for *When My Baby Smiles at Me*. Not bad for a song-and-dance man. TS

Jeanne Crain *Peggy Mayhew* · Dan Dailey *Chuck Arnold* · Oscar Levant *Oscar Hoffman* · Barbara Lawrence *Louise Crane* · Selena Royle *Mrs Cora Mayhew* · Percy Kilbride *Mr Andrew Mayhew* ■ *Dir* Lloyd Bacon · *Scr* Elick Moll, Valentine Davies

You Were Never Lovelier ★★★ U
Musical 1942 · US · BW · 93min

The second wartime pairing (after *You'll Never Get Rich*) of the marvellous Rita Hayworth and the ineffable Fred Astaire is a delight, as they dance to a superb Jerome Kern score with Johnny Mercer lyrics. The plot is silly and the budget skimpy, but the two stars are radiant, possibly owing to the fact that they were "an item" on this movie. They also happened to have known each other all their dancing lives, since Fred was half of Fred and Adele Astaire and the young Hayworth, as Margarita Carmen Cansino, was part of the Dancing Cansinos. TS **DVD**

Fred Astaire *Robert Davis* · Rita Hayworth *Maria Acuna* · Adolphe Menjou *Eduardo Acuno* · Leslie Brooks *Cecy Acuna* · Adele Mara *Lita Acuna* · Isobel Elsom *Mrs Maria Castro* ■ *Dir* William A Seiter · *Scr* Michael Fessier, Ernest Pagano, Delmer Daves, from a story and screenplay (unproduced) by Carlos Olivari, Sixto Pondal Rios · *Costume Designer* Irene

You Will Be My Son ★★★★ 15
Drama 2012 · Fr · Colour · 97min

This gripping study of dynastic continuity and class envy is played to perfection by a superior ensemble, as a vineyard owner decides to overlook his plodding heir for the high-flying son of his right-hand man. The script is ponderous in patches and events do teeter on the edge of melodrama. But the landscape contrasts atmospherically with the cool, dark cellars at the chateau. DP French +subtitles. Swearing, a sex scene, sexual references. **DVD**

Niels Arestrup *Paul de Marseul* · Lorànt Deutsch [Lorant Deutsch] *Martin de Marseul* · Patrick Chesnais *François Amelot* · Anne Marivan *Alice* · Nicolas Bridet *Philippe Amelot* ■ *Dir* Gilles Legrand · *Scr* Gilles Legrand, Delphine de Vigan

You Will Meet a Tall Dark Stranger ★★ 12
Romantic comedy drama 2010 · Sp/UK/US · Colour · 94min

Writer/director Woody Allen is on familiar but increasingly stale territory in this multilayered London-set story of dysfunctional relationships. Ageing businessman Anthony Hopkins leaves Gemma Jones, his wife of 40 years, for flighty young call girl Lucy Punch – outraging his daughter Naomi Watts. Watts, meanwhile, is growing restless in her own marriage to struggling novelist Josh Brolin and develops a crush on her dashing gallery-owner boss (Antonio Banderas). Punch provides most of what few laughs there are as the gold-digging Essex girl, but it's hard to escape the feeling that Allen has told this story so many times before – and so much better. TeS Some violence, swearing, sexual references. **DVD**

Naomi Watts *Sally* · Josh Brolin *Roy* · Anthony Hopkins *Alfie* · Gemma Jones *Helena* · Antonio Banderas *Greg* · Freida Pinto *Dia* · Lucy Punch *Charmaine* · Pauline Collins *Cristal* ■ *Dir/Scr* Woody Allen

You'll Find Out ★★
Horror spoof 1940 · US · BW · 96min

Murderous plotters Boris Karloff, Bela Lugosi and Peter Lorre encounter band leader Kay Kyser (with his Kollege of Musical Knowledge) in an apparently haunted house. This odd slice of 1940s popular music history also showcased Dennis O'Keefe and musician Ish Kabibble. Advertised as "A Seance In Swing with the Ha-Ha Horror Boys", it's crammed with enough thriller devices (despite the terror trio being criminally wasted) and good clean fun to qualify as a lightweight nostalgia binge. AJ

Kay Kyser · Peter Lorre *Professor Fenninger* · Bela Lugosi *Prince Saliano* · Boris Karloff *Judge Mainwaring* · Dennis O'Keefe *Chuck Deems* · Helen Parrish *Janis Bellacrest* ■ *Dir* David Butler · *Scr* James V Kern, Monte Brice, Andrew Bennison, RTM Scott, from a story by Kern, David Butler

You'll Like My Mother ★★★
Thriller 1972 · US · Colour · 92min

This refreshingly low-key psycho thriller eschews all the obvious horror trappings to deliver a nail-biting climax. Pregnant widow Patty Duke stumbles on some dark family secrets when she arrives at mother-in-law Rosemary Murphy's house for the first time to grieve over her husband's death in Vietnam. Murphy is not only keeping a mentally disabled girl locked in the attic, she's also hiding her rapist son in the cellar! Trapped in the house by a snowstorm, Duke gives birth and Murphy tells her the baby has died, which sets the scene for unnerving suspense. Despite a few lapses in logic and a certain sloppiness on director Lamont Johnson's part, this is scare show with finesse. AJ

Patty Duke *Francesca Kinsolving* · Rosemary Murphy *Mrs Kinsolving* · Richard Thomas *Kenny* · Sian Barbara Allen *Kathleen Kinsolving* · Dennis Rucker *Red Cooper* · James Neumann *Joey* · James Glazman *Breadman* ■ *Dir* Lamont Johnson · *Scr* Jo Heims, from the novel by Naomi A Hintze

Y

You'll Never Get Rich
★★★ U
Musical comedy 1941 · US · BW · 88min

The only co-star Fred Astaire became romantically involved with in real life was, allegedly, the lovely Rita Hayworth, herself a skilled and trained dancer. They made two movies together at Columbia (this was followed by *You Were Never Lovelier* in 1942) and their dancing together is simply exquisite: it's quite clear that there's something extra-special going on between these two extraordinary talents. Ignore the dumb wartime plot about Fred being caught in the draft, or the relentlessly pedestrian direction by Sidney Lanfield, and just revel in the Cole Porter songs. TS **DVD**

Fred Astaire *Robert Curtis* · Rita Hayworth *Sheila Winthrop* · John Hubbard *Tom Barton* · Robert Benchley *Martin Cortland* · Osa Massen *Sonya* · Frieda Inescort *Mrs Cortland* · Guinn Williams [Guinn "Big Boy" Williams] *Kewpie Blain* ■ *Dir* Sidney Lanfield · *Scr* Michael Fessier, Ernest Pagano

Young Adam
★★★★ 18
Period drama 2003 · UK/Fr · Colour · 93min

In 1950s Glasgow, rootless drifter Ewan McGregor becomes employed as a barge hand on the local canals. Haunted by his past after fishing a drowned woman out of the water, he's thrown into an existential crisis that leads to a series of unfulfilling sexual encounters. Combining *film noir* and kitchen sink melodrama, director David Mackenzie's moody and intimate picture is a superbly crafted performance piece. The movie smoulders with sensuality and raw emotion, thanks in part to a brilliant McGregor's brooding masculinity, but it's Tilda Swinton who is most mesmerising, boldly baring all as his boss's intimacy-hungry wife. SF Swearing, nudity, sex scenes. **DVD**

Ewan McGregor *Joe Taylor* · Tilda Swinton *Ella Gault* · Peter Mullan *Les Gault* · Emily Mortimer *Cathie Dimly* · Jack McElhone *Jim Gault* · Therese Bradley *Gwen* · Ewan Stewart *Daniel Gordon* · Stuart McQuarrie *Bill* · Pauline Turner *Connie* · Alan Cooke (2) *Bob M'bussi* ■ *Dir* David Mackenzie · *Scr* David Mackenzie, from the novel by Alexander Trocchi

Young Adult
★★★ 15
Comedy drama 2011 · US · Colour · 93min

Immature teen-fiction author Mavis (Charlize Theron) returns to her Minnesota home town, intent on luring away her now happily married high-school boyfriend (Patrick Wilson), in this caustic and self-consciously quirky satire that reunites director Jason Reitman with *Juno* writer Diablo Cody. Razor-sharp putdowns and Theron's fearlessly unrestrained performance provide car-crash entertainment as, back on her old stomping ground, the delusional Mavis's barely hidden neuroses come spewing out in a barrage of amusingly monstrous banter. Patton Oswalt provides the scene-stealing heart of the movie as Matt, the crippled ex-classmate and sardonic voice of reason. SF Swearing. **DVD** **BL**

Charlize Theron *Mavis Gary* · Patton Oswalt *Matt Freehauf* · Patrick Wilson *Buddy Slade* · Elizabeth Reaser *Beth Slade* · Jill Eikenberry *Hedda Gary* · Richard Bekins *David Gary* ■ *Dir* Jason Reitman · *Scr* Diablo Cody

The Young Americans
★★★ 18
Thriller 1993 · UK · Colour · 98min

Hard-bitten New York cop Harvey Keitel arrives in London to nail the drug racketeers terrorising the capital's hip night spots in this flashy movie, which landed newcomer Danny Cannon the job of directing 1995's big budget flop *Judge Dredd*. Visually impressive on all fronts, with designer violence being Cannon's forte, this glossily graphic drama at times plays as a tough documentary. AJ Violence, swearing, drug abuse.

Harvey Keitel *John Harris* · Iain Glen *Edward Foster* · Thandie Newton *Rachael Stevens* · Viggo Mortensen *Carl Fraser* · Craig Kelly (2) ·

Christian O'Neill · Nigel Clauzel *Lionel Stevens* · James Duggan *Dermott O'Neill* · Keith Allen *Jack Doyle* ■ *Dir* Danny Cannon · *Scr* Danny Cannon, David Hilton

Young and Dangerous ★★ 18
Action 1996 · HK · Colour · 95min

This violent Hong Kong crime thriller is about a bunch of inexperienced thugs climbing the ladder of the Hung Hing Society Triads. Based on a popular series of graphic novels, this has an unusually youthful cast, who are supposed to be intimidating, although it's hard to believe from what's on show. It certainly captures the brutality of the Triad gangs, but most of the major action scenes are wrecked by the misjudged use of a gimmicky blurring effect. A host of sequels followed. JC Cantonese +subtitles. **DVD**

Cheng Yee-kin *Ho Nam* · Jordan Chan *Chicken* · Gigi Lai *Smartie* ■ *Dir* Andrew Lau · *Scr* Manfred Wong, Sharon Hui, from a story by Dickey Yau, Cow Man

Young and Innocent
★★★★ U
Murder mystery 1937 · UK · BW · 82min

This may be a minor entry in the Hitchcock canon, but, as it boasts one of the most stunning sequences he ever executed – the audacious travelling shot to the murderer's twitching eye – this film still proves him to be the master of technique, as well as suspense. One of Hitch's many "wrong man" thrillers, it takes viewers on a breathless pursuit, pausing only for a nerve-jangling children's party and a mine-shaft cliffhanger, that will leave you as frayed and exhausted as the imperilled Derrick de Marney and Nova Pilbeam. DP **DVD** **BL**

Derrick de Marney *Robert Tisdall* · Nova Pilbeam *Erica* · Percy Marmont *Colonel Burgoyne* · Edward Rigby *Old Will* · Mary Clare *Erica's aunt* · John Longden *Kent* · George Curzon *Guy* · Basil Radford *Uncle Basil* ■ *Dir* Alfred Hitchcock · *Scr* Charles Bennett, Alma Reville, from the novel *A Shilling for Candles* by Josephine Tey

The Young and Prodigious TS Spivet
★★★ 12
Adventure 2013 · Fr/Can · Colour · 100min

Based on a bestselling book, this whimsical adventure is a feast for the eyes but only a light snack for the soul. Pint-sized hero TS Spivet (endearingly played by Kyle Catlett) has still to reach puberty and yet he's just invented a perpetual motion machine, leading him to be invited to accept an award in Washington DC – a world away from his Montana home. As TS sets out alone, *Amélie* director Jean-Pierre Jeunet goes off on a wild tangent, but the real point of the journey – which takes the youngster across the heartland of America – is to come to terms with the death of his brother. Flights of imagination are vividly drawn (and even more breathtaking in 3D), helping to roll over the bumpier parts, while Helena Bonham Carter adds a touch of gravitas as the boy's mum. SP Some swearing. **DVD** **BL** **3D**

Helena Bonham Carter *Dr Clair* · Kyle Catlett *TS Spivet* · Judy Davis *Jibsen* · Callum Keith Rennie *Father* · Niamh Wilson *Gracie* · Jakob Davies *Layton* ■ *Dir* Jean-Pierre Jeunet · *Scr* Jean-Pierre Jeunet, Guillaume Laurant, from the novel *The Selected Works of TS Spivet* by Reif Larsen

Young and Willing ★★ U
Comedy drama 1942 · US · BW · 83min

A bunch of penurious aspiring young actors share a small New York apartment, as well as their hopes, dreams, squabbles and romances, as they wait for the big break on Broadway. A forgettable, lightweight comedy, it whiles away the time pleasantly enough. It also showcases the youthful pre-stardom talents of William Holden, Susan Hayward, and Eddie Bracken, helped along by humorist, writer and actor Robert Benchley. RK

William Holden (2) *Norman Reese* · Eddie Bracken *George Bodell* · Robert Benchley *Arthur Kenny* · Susan Hayward *Kate Benson* · Martha O'Driscoll *Dottie Coburn* · Barbara Britton *Marge*

Benson · Mabel Paige *Mrs Garnet* ■ *Dir* Edward H Griffith · *Scr* Virginia Van Upp, from the play *Out of the Frying Pan* by Francis Swann

Young at Heart ★★★ U
Romantic drama 1955 · US · Colour · 112min

A well-crafted remake from Warner Bros of *Four Daughters*, this features a surly Frank Sinatra, finely cast in the role that made John Garfield a star in the original. Playing opposite Sinatra is Doris Day, who offers a performance of great warmth and sensitivity. Although not a musical (it's a drama with songs), the film still offers plenty of precious moments for the audience to savour. The supporting cast is exemplary, but the tacked-on ending is an unnecessary sop. TS **DVD**

Frank Sinatra *Barney Sloan* · Doris Day *Laurie Tuttle* · Gig Young *Alex Burke* · Ethel Barrymore *Aunt Jessie* · Dorothy Malone *Fran Tuttle* · Robert Keith (1) *Gregory Tuttle* · Elisabeth Fraser *Amy Tuttle* · Alan Hale Jr *Robert Neary* ■ *Dir* Gordon Douglas · *Scr* Liam O'Brien, from the film *Four Daughters* by Julius J Epstein, Lenore Coffee, from the novel *Sister Act* by Fannie Hurst

Young@Heart ★★★ PG
Documentary 2006 · US/UK · Colour · 107min

Young@Heart is a choir from Northampton, Massachusetts, that's comprised entirely of senior citizens, and has played to packed houses around the world. Stephen Walker's documentary about the group starts off fairly predictably, focusing on maverick conductor Bob Cilman as he teaches the members some new songs. But Walker soon drops the fondly derisory tone and what emerges is a deeply moving study of coping with age and loss. Despite the irksome narration and melodramatic tendencies, it's impossible not to be moved by the choristers' enthusiasm, geniality and courage. DP

Stephen Walker *Narrator* · Bob Cilman ■ *Dir* Stephen Walker

Young Bess ★★★ U
Historical drama 1953 · US · Colour · 111min

Hollywood journeyman director George Sidney did an admirable job in preventing this historical drama from toppling over into an unintentional laugh fest. With characters endlessly explaining (in a welter of thous and dosts) who they are to people they've known all their lives, the story of Elizabeth I's relationship with Thomas Seymour is told with a disregard for fact that ultimately becomes endearing. Bygone age, indeed. DP

Jean Simmons *Young Bess* · Stewart Granger *Thomas Seymour* · Deborah Kerr *Catherine Parr* · Charles Laughton *King Henry VIII* · Kay Walsh *Mrs Ashley* · Guy Rolfe *Ned Seymour* · Kathleen Byron *Anne Seymour* ■ *Dir* George Sidney (2) · *Scr* Jan Lustig, Arthur Wimperis, from the novel by Margaret Irwin

Young Billy Young ★★★ PG
Western 1969 · US · Colour · 85min

Not Robert Mitchum's finest hour, but a serviceable western nonetheless, this has a convoluted plot enlivened by strong performances from Mitchum, Angie Dickinson and David Carradine as a nasty villain. The Billy Young of the title (Robert Walker Jr) is a gunman on the run, picked up by lawman Mitchum during the search for the killer of his son (played by Mitchum's own offspring, Chris). JA

Robert Mitchum *Ben Kane* · Angie Dickinson *Lily Beloit* · Robert Walker Jr *Billy Young* · David Carradine *Jesse Boone* · Jack Kelly *John Behan* · John Anderson *Frank Boone* ■ *Dir* Burt Kennedy · *Scr* Burt Kennedy, from the novel *Who Rides with Wyatt?* by Will Henry [Heck Allen]

Young Cassidy ★★
Biographical drama 1965 · US/UK · Colour · 110min

Rod Taylor plays Irish writer Sean O'Casey who for unfathomable reasons is called John Cassidy in this screen treatment. John Ford directed barely 20 minutes of it before illness forced him to be replaced by Jack Cardiff. Taylor sees the prettified poverty and violence of Dublin and falls in and out

of love – perfect preparation for his plays and poetry. The women in the cast make this just about worth watching, but Michael Redgrave is frankly unconvincing as WB Yeats. AT

Rod Taylor *John Cassidy* · Maggie Smith *Nora* · Julie Christie *Daisy Battles* · Flora Robson *Mrs Cassidy* · Sian Phillips *Ella* · Michael Redgrave *William Butler Yeats* · Edith Evans *Lady Gregory* ■ *Dir* Jack Cardiff, John Ford · *Scr* John Whiting, from the autobiography *Mirror in My House* by Sean O'Casey

Young Dillinger ★
Crime drama 1965 · US · BW · 104min

Not simply *Dillinger*, but *Young Dillinger*, in an attempt to lure the teen audience to a dime-budget gangster picture made principally for the drive-in theatres. More of a beach party than a gangster movie, it stops short of seeing our heroes die beneath a hail of FBI bullets because that happened when they were old. AT

Nick Adams *John Dillinger* · Robert Conrad *Pretty Boy Floyd* · John Ashley *Baby Face Nelson* · Dan Terranova *Homer Van Meter* · Victor Buono *Professor Hoffman* ■ *Dir* Terry Morse · *Scr* Arthur Hoerl, Don Zimbalist, from a story by Zimbalist

Young Dr Kildare ★★★
Medical drama 1938 · US · BW · 81min

After the success of the Hardy Family series, MGM was looking for another series to equal it. They developed it from the hospital stories of Max Brand, immediately establishing the magic formula and cast. Lew Ayres plays the idealistic young Kildare who decides to reject a country practice with his father and takes up an offer from a big city hospital. Lionel Barrymore, playing his mentor Dr Gillespie, had recently found himself unable to walk because of a crippling hip disease, but continued his acting career in a wheelchair. The sparky relationship between the pair is one of the delights of the series. Followed by *Calling Dr Kildare*. RB

Lew Ayres *Dr James Kildare* · Lionel Barrymore *Dr Leonard Gillespie* · Lynne Carver *Alice Raymond* · Nat Pendleton *Joe Wayman* · Jo Ann Sayers *Barbara Chanler* · Samuel S Hinds *Dr Stephen Kildare* · Emma Dunn *Mrs Martha Kildare* · Walter Kingsford *Dr Walter Carew* · Monty Woolley *Dr Lane Porteus* ■ *Dir* Harold S Bucquet · *Scr* Willis Goldbeck, Harry Ruskin, from a story by Max Brand

The Young Doctors ★★★
Drama 1961 · US · BW · 102min

Some heavyweight actors lend their personalities and expertise to this standard hospital soap. There are no surprises as new young pathologist (Ben Gazzara) clashes with venerable Fredric March about correct procedure on a couple of cases, or in the romantic entanglements between medics and nurses. Eddie Albert is a senior doctor and George Segal makes his debut in a supporting role. RK

Fredric March *Dr Joseph Pearson* · Ben Gazzara *Dr David Coleman* · Dick Clark *Dr Alexander* · Ina Balin *Cathy Hunt* · Eddie Albert *Dr Charles Dornberger* · George Segal *Dr Howard* ■ *Dir* Phil Karlson · *Scr* Joseph Hayes, from the novel *The Final Diagnosis* by Arthur Hailey

Young Doctors in Love ★★★ 15
Comedy 1982 · US · Colour · 91min

The first film from *Pretty Woman* director Garry Marshall is a wacky comedy that applies the *Airplane!* approach to a laugh-a-minute look at the wilder side of life in a big-city hospital. As ever with such scattergun tactics, some jokes stick, and some don't. But even when they don't, there's a crack cast to keep you interested. DA

Michael McKean *Dr Simon August* · Sean Young *Dr Stephanie Brody* · Harry Dean Stanton *Dr Oliver Ludwig* · Patrick Macnee *Dr Jacobs* · Hector Elizondo *Angelo/Angela Bonafetti* · Dabney Coleman *Dr Joseph Prang* · Demi Moore *New intern* ■ *Dir* Garry Marshall · *Scr* Michael Elias, Rich Eustis · *Music* Maurice Jarre

Y

Young Einstein ★★★ PG
Comedy   1988 · Aus · Colour · 87min

The deliciously named Yahoo Serious, the Australian one-man band who co-wrote, directed, co-produced and stars in this oddity, has more gifts as an actor than a director. Based on the notion that Einstein not only came from Tasmania, but also invented rock 'n' roll, the film is let down by Serious's flat direction and a frantic approach to gags. However, its sheer inventiveness grabs the attention, and its eccentricity and innocence are endearing. **JM** Swearing.

Yahoo Serious *Albert Einstein* • Odile Le Clezio *Marie Curie* • John Howard (2) *Preston Preston* • Pee Wee Wilson *Mr Einstein* • Su Cruickshank *Mrs Einstein* • Basil Clarke *Charles Darwin* • Esben Storm *Wilbur Wright* ■ *Dir* Yahoo Serious • *Scr* David Roach, Yahoo Serious

Young Frankenstein ★★★★★ PG
Horror spoof   1974 · US · BW · 101min

This loopy send-up of classic chiller clichés from Universal's monster heyday is one of director Mel Brooks's best comedies and it's also one of the genre's most thorough and successful fright-film parodies. Gene Wilder plays the infamous baron's grandson, who copies his ancestor's experiments only to create the singularly inane Peter Boyle. Filmed in sumptuous black and white, and shot on sets used in the 1931 original *Frankenstein*, Brooks's ingenious tribute is often hysterically funny and always a scream. Madeleine Kahn's "bride", Gene Hackman's blind hermit, Marty Feldman's hunchbacked Igor and the marvellous "Putting on the Ritz" musical number give this loving homage real staying power. **AJ** Violence, swearing. *DVD* *BL*

Gene Wilder *Doctor Frederick Frankenstein* • Peter Boyle *Monster* • Marty Feldman *Igor* • Madeline Kahn *Elizabeth* • Cloris Leachman *Frau Blücher* • Teri Garr *Inga* • Kenneth Mars *Inspector Kemp* • Gene Hackman *Blindman* • Richard Haydn *Herr Falkstein* ■ *Dir* Mel Brooks • *Scr* Gene Wilder, Mel Brooks, from characters by Mary Shelley

The Young Girls of Rochefort ★★★ PG
Musical comedy   1967 · Fr · Colour · 126min

Jacques Demy failed to charm the critics with this fond tribute to the Hollywood musical. Not even Gene Kelly as an American in Rochefort could entrance in this fairy tale about the caprices of love and the showbiz ambitions of twin sisters, Catherine Deneuve and Françoise Dorléac (in the last film before her car-crash death). Michel Legrand's songs ingeniously propel the narrative, the performances are spirited and the atmosphere is all pastel shades and sunshine. But, apart from the opening number, the choreography is undistinguished. **DP** French +subtitles. *DVD*

Catherine Deneuve *Delphine Garnier* • Françoise Dorléac *Solange Garnier* • George Chakiris *Etienne* • Gene Kelly *Andy Miller* • Danielle Darrieux *Yvonne Garnier* ■ *Dir/Scr* Jacques Demy

The Young Guns ★★
Western   1956 · US · BW · 83min

The juvenile delinquency cycle of the mid-1950s looks rather out of place transposed to the Old West in this story about the offspring of notorious outlaws being tempted to follow in their fathers' footsteps. Russ Tamblyn is too lightweight playing the victim of small-town prejudice, who becomes the leader of a gang but wavers over launching a criminal career. Too much debate, too little action. **AE**

Russ Tamblyn *Tully* • Gloria Talbott *Nora* • Scott Marlowe *Knox Cutler* • Wright King *Jonesy* ■ *Dir* Albert Band • *Scr* Louis Garfinkle

Young Guns ★★★ 18
Western   1988 · US · Colour · 102min

Emilio Estevez plays Billy the Kid in this attempt to breath new life into the western. The movie's casual violence, breakneck pace and relentless hard-rock score offended purists, though, at 26, Estevez was closer in age to the real Billy (who died aged 22) than most previous actors. Estevez chooses to play him as a social bandit, a Robin Hood figure, in a film that also pays much attention to the look, broad racial mix and eccentric characters of the Old West. It's a western that shows both box-office calculation and respect for American history. **AT** Swearing, violence. *DVD* *BL*

Emilio Estevez *"Billy the Kid"* • Kiefer Sutherland *Josiah "Doc" Scurlock* • Lou Diamond Phillips *Chavez* • Charlie Sheen *Dick Brewer* • Dermot Mulroney *"Dirty Steve" Stephens* • Casey Siemaszko *Charley Bowdre* • Terence Stamp *John Henry Tunstall* • Jack Palance *Lawrence G Murphy* ■ *Dir* Christopher Cain • *Scr* John Fusco

Young Guns II ★★ 15
Western   1990 · US · Colour · 99min

More western romping with a modern spin in the company of Billy the Kid who, as played by Emilio Estevez with scene-stealing shamelessness, seems to have been little more than a violent show-off. Kiefer Sutherland and Lou Diamond Phillips also return from the first film, but this time the tone is less certain, wavering uneasily between a serious appreciation of the western and an in-joke with the audience. **JM** Violence, swearing, brief nudity. *DVD*

Emilio Estevez *William H Bonney/Brushy Bill Roberts* • Kiefer Sutherland *Josiah "Doc" Scurlock* • Lou Diamond Phillips *Chavez Y Chavez* • Christian Slater *Arkansas Dave Rudabaugh* • William L Petersen *Pat Garrett* • Alan Ruck *Hendry French* • RD Call *DA Ryerson* • James Coburn *John Chisum* • Balthazar Getty *Tom O'Folliard* • Jack Kehoe *Ashmun Upson* ■ *Dir* Geoff Murphy • *Scr* John Fusco

Young Guns of Texas ★★ U
Western   1962 · US · Colour · 77min

Leads James Mitchum, Alana Ladd and Jody McCrea lack the charisma of their fathers, Robert, Alan and Joel. Still, this is an OK western, which opens with a fight involving McCrea and Gary Conway and soon has a quartet of youngsters on the run after a shooting. It's routine. **BB**

James Mitchum *Morgan Coe* • Alana Ladd *Lily Glendenning* • Jody McCrea *Jeff Shelby* • Chill Wills *Preacher Sam Shelby* • Gary Conway *Tyler Duane* ■ *Dir* Maury Dexter • *Scr* Henry Cross [Harry Spalding]

The Young in Heart ★★★★
Comedy drama   1938 · US · BW · 90min

A family of charming and scatty con tricksters is hounded out of the Riviera where the parents (Roland Young, Billie Burke), masquerading as aristocrats, have been trying to marry their offspring (warm and loving Janet Gaynor, and devil-may-care idler Douglas Fairbanks Jr) to rich spouses. En route to England and penniless, they befriend a lonely, very rich old lady (Minnie Dupree) who takes them in. Their intentions to fleece her and become her heirs slowly disappear as their affection for her grows and brings unexpected changes to their lives. A gloriously funny, original and thoroughly beguiling comedy. **RK**

Janet Gaynor *George-Anne* • Douglas Fairbanks Jr *Richard, her brother* • Paulette Goddard *Leslie Saunders* • Roland Young *"Sahib", their father* • Billie Burke *"Marmy", their mother* • Minnie Dupree *Miss Ellen Fortune* ■ *Dir* Richard Wallace • *Scr* Paul Osborn, Charles Bennett (adaptation), from the novel *The Gay Banditti* by IAR Wylie

The Young Ladies of Wilko ★★★★
Drama   1979 · Pol/Fr · Colour · 115min

Andrzej Wajda demonstrates an elegiac side with this melancholic adaptation, set in the late 1920s. The story follows Daniel Olbrychski on a convalescent return to the rural estate where he enjoyed an idyllic summer before the First World War, only to discover that the object of his youthful affection has died, while her five sisters (like himself disillusioned and jaded by the passage of time) have always adored him from afar. Superbly played and exquisitely bittersweet. **DP** In Polish.

Daniel Olbrychski *Wiktor Ruben* • Anna Seniuk *Julia* • Christine Pascal *Tunia* • Maja Komorowska *Yola* ■ *Dir* Andrzej Wajda • *Scr* Zbigniew Kaminski, from the novella *Panny Z Wilka* by Jaroslaw Iwaszkiewicz

The Young Land ★★ PG
Western   1959 · US · Colour · 86min

A rare example of a minor sub-genre, the western courtroom drama, this attempts historical accuracy in its exploration of racial tension in 1840s California. When a young Anglo murders a Mexican, sheriff Patrick Wayne and judge Dan O'Herlihy must tread carefully while the largely Hispanic population watches to see if America's justice system is as unbiased as it claims. Unfortunately this is not the best made of films; its one saving grace is the charismatic Dennis Hopper as the villain. **SuR** *DVD*

Patrick Wayne *Jim Ellison* • Yvonne Craig *Elena de la Madrid* • Dennis Hopper *Hatfield Carnes* • Dan O'Herlihy *Judge Isham* • Roberto De La Madrid *Don Roberto* ■ *Dir* Ted Tetzlaff • *Scr* Norman Shannon Hall, from the story *Frontier Frenzy* by John Reese

The Young Lions ★★★ PG
Second World War drama   1958 · US · BW · 160min

Adapted by Edward Anhalt from the doorstop novel by Irwin Shaw, this oozes self-importance in every scene. The action leapfrogs from Paris to America and from North Africa to Bavaria, taking nearly three hours to unravel. But, while the script is turgid, and Edward Dmytryk's direction often slows to a crawl, the picture succeeds for three reasons: Marlon Brando as a nice guy who becomes a Nazi and ends up a martyr, Montgomery Clift as a Jewish GI and Dean Martin as a cowardly Broadway star. **AT**

Marlon Brando *Christian Diestl* • Montgomery Clift *Noah Ackerman* • Dean Martin *Michael Whiteacre* • Hope Lange *Hope Plowman* • Barbara Rush *Margaret Freemantle* • May Britt *Gretchen Hardenberg* • Maximilian Schell *Captain Hardenberg* • Lee Van Cleef *Sergeant Rickett* ■ *Dir* Edward Dmytryk • *Scr* Edward Anhalt, from the novel by Irwin Shaw

The Young Lovers ★★ U
Romantic drama   1954 · UK · BW · 92min

For all his technical proficiency and fidelity to the written word, Anthony Asquith had a detached style that all too frequently diluted the dramatic impact of his pictures. With its soulless core and its slickly constructed chase finale, this Cold War tale of star-crossed lovers is a case in point, suffering as it does from that very style. The romance between an American Romeo (David Knight) and an Eastern European Juliet (Odile Versois) lacks both the passion and the sense of danger that might have raised the temperature. **DP** *DVD*

Odile Versois *Anna Szobeck* • David Knight *Ted Hutchens* • Joseph Tomelty *Moffatt* • Paul Carpenter *Gregg Pearson* • David Kossoff *Geza Szobeck* • Theodore Bikel *Joseph* • Jill Adams *Judy* • Betty Marsden *Mrs Forrester* • Joan Sims *Operator* ■ *Dir* Anthony Asquith • *Scr* Robin Estridge, George Tabori

Young Man with a Horn ★★★★ PG
Musical drama   1950 · US · BW · 107min

When Isodore Demsky and Betty Perske dated in New York, they little dreamed they'd one day co-star in a movie biopic of their hero, jazz cornetist Bix Beiderbecke. But here they are on the Warner Bros lot, now rechristened Kirk Douglas and Lauren Bacall respectively, he dubbed by the great Harry James on trumpet, and she playing a daring-for-its-day society closet lesbian. Warners softened the source novel substantially, but enough of the sordid drama gets through, and this is a finely wrought melodrama of its time, with Douglas particularly outstanding as the self-absorbed horn player. **TS** *DVD*

Kirk Douglas *Rick Martin* • Lauren Bacall *Amy North* • Doris Day *Jo Jordan* • Hoagy Carmichael *Smoke Willoughby* • Juano Hernandez *Art Hazzard* • Jerome Cowan *Phil Morrison* • Mary Beth Hughes *Margo Martin* ■ *Dir* Michael Curtiz • *Scr* Carl Foreman, Edmund H North, from the novel by Dorothy Baker

Young Man with Ideas ★★★ U
Comedy   1952 · US · BW · 84min

Glenn Ford is the eponymous hero of this MGM production – a small-time lawyer from a small town, trying to break into the Los Angeles legal circuit, at the insistence of his ambitious wife Ruth Roman. Director Mitchell Leisen approaches what could be called camp in the treatment, but pulls it back securely to make it a likeable, if modest, comedy. **TH**

Glenn Ford *Maxwell Webster* • Ruth Roman *Julie Webster* • Denise Darcel *Dorianne Gray* • Nina Foch *Joyce Laramie* • Donna Corcoran *Caroline Webster* • Ray Collins *Edmund Jethrow* • Mary Wickes *Mrs Gilpin* ■ *Dir* Mitchell Leisen • *Scr* Arthur Sheekman

Young Man's Fancy ★★★ U
Comedy   1939 · UK · BW · 73min

This curious early entry on the CV of Mary Poppins director Robert Stevenson feels like a dry run for one of Anna Neagle and Michael Wilding's postwar period romances. The action takes place in 1870 and opens with aristocratic heir Griffith Jones being browbeaten by impecunious parents Seymour Hicks and Martita Hunt into a betrothal to wealthy Merial Forbes. The setting feels odd, but Wilfred Shingleton's production design and Ronald Neame's photography are splendid, and Hunt and Hicks make the most of the script's plentiful quips. **DP** *DVD*

Griffith Jones *Lord Alban* • Anna Lee *Ada* • Seymour Hicks *Duke of Beaumont* • Billy Bennett *Captain Boumphray* • Edward Rigby *Gray* ■ *Dir* Robert Stevenson • *Scr* Roland Pertwee, from a story by Robert Stevenson

Young Mr Lincoln ★★★★ U
Biographical drama   1939 · US · BW · 95min

If ever a movie could be said to encapsulate the attitudes and ideals of its director, it is this study by John Ford of the early life of Abraham Lincoln, when the future president was a lawyer in Springfield, Illinois. A statesmanlike Henry Fonda is perfectly cast as Lincoln, portraying the man as a truly romantic and heroic figure despite being lumbered with a quite unnecessary false nose. Some may find this pure hagiography, but it is a mighty fine slice of Americana, and Ford keeps up the tension in the courtroom scenes. **TS** *DVD*

Henry Fonda *Abraham Lincoln* • Alice Brady *Abigail Clay* • Marjorie Weaver *Mary Todd* • Arleen Whelan *Hannah Clay* • Eddie Collins *Efe Turner* • Pauline Moore *Ann Rutledge* ■ *Dir* John Ford • *Scr* Lamar Trotti • *Cinematographer* Bert Glennon

The Young Mr Pitt ★★★★ U
Biographical drama   1942 · UK · BW · 118min

This underrated film was designed to show how Britain would always triumph over tyranny providing there was a born war leader at the helm. Yet director Carol Reed's account of how Pitt the Younger simultaneously resisted domestic disquiet and tamed Napoleon rises far above its flag-waving objectives. Reed handles the passing parade of political luminaries with an assurance that has rarely been surpassed. The period detail is nearly perfect and the parliamentary sequences are highly impressive. Leading a fine cast, Robert Donat is a model of embattled dignity, while Robert Morley is suitably flamboyant as Charles James Fox. **DP**

Robert Morley *Charles James Fox* • Robert Donat *William Pitt/Earl of Chatham* • Phyllis Calvert *Eleanor Eden* • Raymond Lovell *George III* • Max Adrian *Richard Brinsley Sheridan* • Felix Aylmer *Lord North* ■ *Dir* Carol Reed • *Scr* Frank Launder, Sidney Gilliat

Y

The Young One ★★★ 15

Drama   1960 · US/Mex · BW · 91min

"This film was made with love, but American morality just couldn't accept it," said Luis Buñuel about this tale of racial hatred, corruption and seduction. The controversial subject concerns the rape of a 14-year-old orphan girl on an isolated island by her guardian. The Lolita-like girl is played rather amateurishly by Key Meersman, while Zachary Scott does his usual nasty bit. Rather turgid, but it does have a rough poetry. RB *DVD*

Zachary Scott *Miller* • Key Meersman *Evalyn* • Bernie Hamilton *Traver* • Crahan Denton *Jackson* • Claudio Brook *Reverend Fleetwood* ■ *Dir* Luis Buñuel • *Scr* Luis Buñuel, HB Addis [Hugo Butler], from the story *Travellin' Man* in *Harper's* by Peter Matthiessen

The Young Ones ★★★ U

Musical comedy drama
1961 · UK · Colour · 103min

This is the epitome of the "it's trad, dad" musical. The "putting on a show" format was as old as the talkies, but Sidney J Furie spruces it up with the help of a sprightly Cliff Richard, the Shadows and Robert Morley, on top form as the millionaire father who refuses to cough up the dough needed to save a youth club. The songs are a hit-and-miss bunch, but it's still amiable. DP *DVD*

Cliff Richard *Nicky Black* • Robert Morley *Hamilton Black* • Carole Gray *Toni* • Richard O'Sullivan *Ernest* • Melvyn Hayes *Jimmy* • Teddy Green *Chris* • Hank Marvin • Bruce Welch • Jet Harris • Tony Meehan ■ *Dir* Sidney J Furie • *Scr* Ronald Cass, Peter Myers, from their story

Young People ★★ U

Musical drama
1940 · US · BW · 79min

With her startlingly successful star career already on the downward slide at age 12, Shirley Temple's seven-year Fox contract ended here, and saw her playing second fiddle to Jack Oakie and Charlotte Greenwood. They are a pair of married vaudevillians who retire, briefly, to a farm; she's their adopted daughter. Standard cosy, innocent musical hokum, delivered with vigour, and fans will enjoy the briefly interpolated clips from some of Temple's early hits. RK

Shirley Temple *Wendy* • Jack Oakie *Joe Ballantine* • Charlotte Greenwood *Kit Ballantine* • Arleen Whelan *Judith* • George Montgomery *Mike Shea* • Kathleen Howard *Hester Appleby* ■ *Dir* Allan Dwan • *Scr* Edwin Blum, Don Ettlinger

The Young Philadelphians ★★★ PG

Melodrama
1959 · US · BW · 136min

A polished example of the "poor boy who'll stop at nothing to succeed" melodrama – much in vogue in the late 1950s – gets a charisma boost from a devastatingly handsome Paul Newman. He plays a hungry young lawyer conniving his way to success. Barbara Rush is fine, too, as the society girl he craves, but it was Robert Vaughn who won an Oscar nomination for his performance as the army buddy on trial for murder for whom Newman risks everything to defend. AME

Paul Newman *Tony Lawrence* • Barbara Rush *Joan Dickinson* • Alexis Smith *Carol Wharton* • Brian Keith *Mike Flanagan* • Diane Brewster *Kate Judson* • Billie Burke *Mrs J Arthur Allen* • Robert Vaughn (1) *Chester "Chet" Gwynn* • Otto Kruger *John M Wharton* ■ *Dir* Vincent Sherman • *Scr* James Gunn, from the novel *The Philadelphian* by Richard Powell

The Young Poisoner's Handbook ★★★★ 15

Black comedy
1994 · UK/Ger · Colour · 95min

Hugh O'Conor is frightfully wonderful in this controversial, fact-based crime drama as the teen chemist who poisons his family and co-workers as part of a warped series of experiments to satisfy his morbid curiosity. Director Benjamin Ross expertly balances black humour, morbidity and heightened reality, and along the creepy way perfectly captures the atmosphere of

1960s London suburbia. This witty delight is extraordinary if disturbing entertainment. AJ Swearing.

Hugh O'Conor *Graham* • Antony Sher *Dr Zeigler* • Ruth Sheen *Molly* • Roger Lloyd Pack *Fred* • Charlotte Coleman *Winnie* • Paul Stacey *Dennis* • Samantha Edmonds *Sue* • Vilma Hollingbery *Aunt Panty* ■ *Dir* Benjamin Ross • *Scr* Jeff Rawle, Benjamin Ross

The Young Savages ★★★

Crime drama
1961 · US · BW · 103min

A typical slice of New York liberal drama stars Burt Lancaster as the DA who prosecutes three delinquents accused of murdering a blind Puerto Rican youth. The story is spiced up by Lancaster's love life as well as his own background in the city slums – he sees in the three kids a mirror image of himself. It's taut, literate and forcefully directed by John Frankenheimer – his second feature. The eagle-eyed may spot Lee Grant in long shots – she walked off the picture and was replaced by Shelley Winters. AT

Burt Lancaster *Hank Bell* • Dina Merrill *Karin Bell* • Shelley Winters *Mary Di Pace* • Edward Andrews *Dan Cole* • Vivian Nathan *Mrs Escalante* • Larry Gates *Randolph* • Telly Savalas *Lt Richard Gunnison* • Pilar Seurat *Louisa Escalante* ■ *Dir* John Frankenheimer • *Scr* Edward Anhalt, JP Miller, from the novel *A Matter of Conviction* by Evan Hunter

Young Sherlock Holmes ★★★ PG

Mystery adventure
1985 · US · Colour · 104min

Director Barry Levinson, working for Steven Spielberg's production company Amblin, gives a sensational, even supernatural, slant to this supposed biography of the young sleuth, which is hardly surprising considering the film's pedigree. As an account of the detective team's first meeting at school, it's quite commendable – Nicholas Rowe is a dashing Holmes, Alan Cox a solid Watson – but it's rather deficient in the proper atmosphere of hansom cabs and ugly deeds. TH *DVD* CS

Nicholas Rowe *Sherlock Holmes* • Alan Cox *John Watson* • Anthony Higgins *Rathe* • Freddie Jones *Chester Cragwitch* • Sophie Ward *Elizabeth* • Susan Fleetwood *Mrs Dribb* • Nigel Stock *Waxflatter* ■ *Dir* Barry Levinson • *Scr* Chris Columbus, from the characters by Sir Arthur Conan Doyle

Young Soul Rebels ★ 18

Drama
1991 · UK · Colour · 100min

There's no soul whatsoever in Isaac Julien's inept social drama set during the Queen's Silver Jubilee year of 1977. Heavily promoted as the first movie from a British-born gay black director, Julien throws everything into his unsubtle appraisal of how both minority groups blossomed during the punk era. Valentine Nonyela and Mo Sesay, as the two pirate radio disc jockeys out to solve the violent death of a gay friend, just don't have the presence to focus attention away from the embarrassment of glitches they're surrounded by. AJ Swearing, drug abuse. *DVD*

Valentine Nonyela *Chris* • Mo Sesay *Caz* • Dorian Healy *Ken* • Frances Barber *Ann* • Sophie Okonedo *Tracy* • Jason Durr *Billibud* ■ *Dir* Isaac Julien • *Scr* Isaac Julien, Paul Hallam, Derrick Saldaan McClintock

The Young Stranger ★★★ U

Drama
1957 · US · BW · 84min

James MacArthur is the young son whose film-executive father James Daly and mother Kim Hunter are too busy with their lives to support his. Resentful of this neglect, he eventually bursts out and assaults a cinema manager and a cop. Self-therapy of the worst kind. This was director John Frankenheimer's first movie after working in TV, a fact betrayed by the small-screen style of the segmented narrative, but the acting is true and touching, with MacArthur's performance – unlike his role – marvellously mature. TH

James MacArthur *Hal Ditmar* • Kim Hunter *Helen Ditmar* • James Daly *Tom Ditmar* • James Gregory *Sgt Shipley* • Whit Bissell *Grubbs, theatre manager* • Jeff Silver *Jerry* • Jack Mullaney *Confused boy* ■ *Dir* John Frankenheimer • *Scr* Robert Dozier, from his TV play *Deal a Blow*

Young Tom Edison ★★★ U

Biographical drama
1940 · US · BW · 85min

MGM's attempt to make a genius seem like the kid next door, though Mickey Rooney acquits himself more than adequately as the American inventor in his early days as a small-town lad with brilliant thoughts. This was the first of a two-parter for MGM's best-known redheads, with Spencer Tracy following hot on Rooney's heels in the *Edison, the Man*. TH

Mickey Rooney *Tom Edison* • Fay Bainter *Mrs Samuel Nancy Edison* • George Bancroft *Samuel Edison* • Virginia Weidler *Tannie Edison* • Eugene Pallette *Mr Nelson* • Bobbie Jordan [Bobby Jordan] *Joe Dingle* • JM Kerrigan *Mr McCarney* • Jack Mintz *Mr Dingle* ■ *Dir* Norman Taurog • *Scr* Bradbury Foote, Dore Schary, from material assembled by H Alan Dunn

Young Toscanini ★★

Biographical drama
1988 · Fr/It/Tur · Colour · 120min

This is an all-too-easily overlooked period biopic from director Franco Zeffirelli. Facts are at a premium and soap operatic excess is very much to the fore in this handsome, sincere, but painfully overwrought melodrama, in which acting styles clash more loudly than the cymbals. C Thomas Howell is hopelessly miscast as the 18-year-old Arturo Toscanini, touring Latin America under the baton of John Rhys-Davies. But his over-exuberance pales beside the grande dame antics of Elizabeth Taylor, as the mistress of Brazilian emperor Philippe Noiret. DP

C Thomas Howell *Arturo Toscanini* • Elizabeth Taylor *Nadina Bulichoff* • Sophie Ward *Margherita* • John Rhys-Davies *Claudio Rossi* • Pat Heywood *Mother Allegri* • Philippe Noiret *Dom Pedro II* ■ *Dir* Franco Zeffirelli • *Scr* William Stadiem, Meno Menjes, from a story by Franco Zeffirelli, Ennio De Concini

The Young Victoria ★★★ PG

Historical biographical drama
2008 · US · Colour · 100min

Britain's longest-reigning monarch gets a vivacious new screen image in this handsome biographical drama. Emily Blunt mixes charm with steely determination as the teenage princess, chafing at the restrictions of life in Kensington Palace in the year leading up to her accession to the throne. But when she becomes queen in 1837, it's the young monarch's courtship of Prince Albert (Rupert Friend) and her dependence on wily Prime Minister Lord Melbourne (Paul Bettany) that take centre stage. Sumptuous royal palaces and gorgeous costumes dominate every scene, and Jim Broadbent has a memorable cameo as the irascible King William. But in choosing to concentrate on the romance in Victoria's life, director Jean-Marc Vallée's treatment feels rather perfunctory. Maybe a case of too much costume and not enough drama. SS *DVD* BL

Emily Blunt *Queen Victoria* • Rupert Friend *Prince Albert* • Paul Bettany *Lord Melbourne* • Miranda Richardson *Duchess of Kent* • Jim Broadbent *King William IV* • Thomas Kretschmann *King Leopold* • Mark Strong *Sir John Conroy* • Harriet Walter *Queen Adelaide* ■ *Dir* Jean-Marc Vallée • *Scr* Julian Fellowes

The Young Warriors ★★

Second World War drama
1967 · US · Colour · 93min

Universal made a number of standard programme filler to break in a string of contract players. This one stars James Drury, who at the time was appearing in the popular TV series *The Virginian*. Nobody in the supporting cast is worthy of note, but what is somewhat surprising is that this compendium of clichés is scripted by the estimable Richard Matheson. TS

James Drury *Sergeant Cooley* • Steve Carlson (1) *Hacker* • Jonathan Daly *Guthrie* • Robert Pine *Foley* • Jeff Scott *Lippincott* • Michael Stanwood *Riley* ■ *Dir* John Peyser • *Scr* Richard Matheson, from his novel *The Beardless Warriors*

Young Warriors ★★ 18

Crime drama
1983 · US · Colour · 102min

When his sister is raped and murdered, student James Van Patten won't wait for justice to take its course like his cop father, Ernest Borgnine, and rounds up some college friends to get revenge on the gang responsible. As the vigilante group roam the neighbourhood looking for the culprits, they viciously punish any other criminals they come across. The rule-of-law message of this brutal exploitation movie is swamped by the one-man-above-all action, making it all the more unpleasant. TH

Ernest Borgnine *Lieutenant Bob Carrigan* • Richard Roundtree *Sergeant John Austin* • Lynda Day George *Beverly Carrigan* • James Van Patten *Kevin Carrigan* • Anne Lockhart *Lucy* • *Dir* Lawrence D Foldes • *Scr* Lawrence D Foldes, Russell W Colgin

Young Winston ★★★ PG

Biographical drama
1972 · UK · Colour · 146min

Richard Attenborough's account of Winston Churchill's early years follows him from school at Harrow to the Boer War to his first major parliamentary speech as MP for Oldham. Lavishly mounted but often lifeless, this is stodgily scripted by producer Carl Foreman. Robert Shaw and Anne Bancroft are excellent as Churchill's parents, and there's an impressive array of British talent in supporting roles, while young Simon Ward makes a fair stab at playing the budding British bulldog. AT *DVD*

Simon Ward *Young Winston Churchill/Sir Winston Churchill's voice* • Robert Shaw *Lord Randolph Churchill* • Anne Bancroft *Lady Jennie Churchill* • John Mills *General Herbert Kitchener* • Ian Holm *George Buckle* • Anthony Hopkins *Lloyd George* ■ *Dir* Richard Attenborough • *Scr* Carl Foreman, from the autobiography *My Early Life: A Roving Commission* by Sir Winston Churchill

Young Wives' Tale ★★

Comedy
1951 · UK · BW · 78min

This comedy of domestic chaos suffers from the problem that blights so many theatrical transfers – the inability to re-create the breathlessly contrived precision of a stage farce on the screen. To his credit, director Henry Cass keeps the action brisk, but the story of two respectable couples who share their house with a man-mad minx lacks the frantic danger that clearly made the live renditions so appealing. A flirtatious Audrey Hepburn steals every scene. DP

Joan Greenwood *Sabina Pennant* • Nigel Patrick *Rodney Pennant* • Derek Farr *Bruce Banning* • Guy Middleton *Victor Manifold* • Athene Seyler *Nanny Gallop* • Helen Cherry *Mary Banning* • Audrey Hepburn *Eve Lester* ■ *Dir* Henry Cass • *Scr* Ann Burnaby, from the play by Ronald Jeans

Youngblood ★★ 15

Sports drama
1986 · US · Colour · 105min

This routine sports drama features Rob Lowe as an up-and-coming hockey player who joins a small-town team, and falls for the daughter of its stereotypically tough-nut coach. The film toddles along, but never really gets its skates on. If you've seen any *Rocky* or *Karate Kid* films, then the "plot" will have a familiar ring, so to stay awake, try to spot Keanu Reeves. It's his feature debut. DA

Rob Lowe *Dean Youngblood* • Cynthia Gibb *Jessie Chadwick* • Patrick Swayze *Derek Sutton* • Ed Lauter *Coach Murray Chadwick* • Keanu Reeves *Heaver* ■ *Dir* Peter Markle • *Scr* Peter Markle, from a story by John Whitmore, Markle

Youngblood Hawke ★★

Drama
1964 · US · BW · 136min

James Franciscus may be the centre of attention as the Kentucky trucker who flirts with literary fame, but it's his female co-stars who contribute the more telling performances. Suzanne Pleshette is elegantly vulnerable as the editor he spurns, but she's given a lesson in scene-stealing from Mary Astor as a self-seeking actress and Genevieve Page as a man-mad socialite. Veteran director Delmer Daves does his best to imbue this potboiler with artistic significance. **DP**

James Franciscus *Youngblood Hawke* • Suzanne Pleshette *Jeanne Greene* • Genevieve Page *Frieda Winter* • Eva Gabor *Fannie Prince* • Mary Astor *Irene Perry* • Lee Bowman *Jason Prince* • Edward Andrews *Quentin Judd* ■ *Dir* Delmer Daves • *Scr* Delmer Daves, from the novel by Herman Wouk

Younger and Younger ★★ 15

Comedy　　1993 · Ger/Fr/Can · Colour · 93min

In another quirky story from German director Percy Adlon, a wife drops dead when she overhears her husband having his latest fling. But her image returns to haunt him and grows younger with every visit, ultimately resulting in him being aptly punished for his misdeeds. The film strives for an offbeat charm, but there's an air of desperation about it; the main interest resides in the strong cast. **DA**

Donald Sutherland *Jonathan Younger* • Lolita Davidovich *Penelope Younger* • Brendan Fraser *Winston Younger* • Sally Kellerman *Zig Zag Lilian* • Julie Delpy *Melodie* • Linda Hunt *Frances* ■ *Dir* Percy Adlon • *Scr* Percy Adlon, Felix O Adlon

The Younger Brothers

**　　　　　　　　　　　　　★★ U**

Western　　1949 · US · Colour · 77min

This utterly routine Technicolor western casts Wayne Morris, Bruce Bennett and James Brown as brothers and former outlaws hoping to make a fresh start as farmers. Only two weeks of parole are left before their pardon, but that's enough time for a revenge-seeking detective to try to involve them in a bank robbery. This is just about worth seeing for Janis Paige's turn as the bandit out to lure the boys back to their old ways. **AE**

Wayne Morris *Cole Younger* • Janis Paige *Kate Shepherd* • Bruce Bennett *Jim Younger* • Geraldine Brooks *Mary Hathaway* • Robert Hutton *Johnny Younger* • Alan Hale *Sheriff Knudson* • James Brown (1) *Bob Younger* • Monte Blue *Joe* ■ *Dir* Edwin L Marin • *Scr* Edna Anhalt, from a story by Morton Grant

The Younger Generation

**　　　　　　　　　　　　　★★ U**

Drama　　　　1929 · US · BW · 80min

An early sound entry, directed by Frank Capra, this melodrama concerns the emotional upheavals and moral conflicts that beset a poor New York Jewish family when their son makes a mint of money and leaves tradition behind for a Park Avenue life. Not without interest, and fielding a good cast headed by Jewish actors Jean Hersholt and the now-forgotten Rosa Rosanova, but it's woolly-minded, contrived, and over-sentimental. **RK**

Jean Hersholt *Julius Goldfish* • Lina Basquette *Birdie Goldfish* • Rosa Rosanova *Tildie Goldfish* • Ricardo Cortez *Morris* • Rex Lease *Eddie Lesser* • Martha Franklin *Mrs Lesser* ■ *Dir* Frank R Capra [Frank Capra] • *Scr* Sonya Levien, Howard J Green, from a story by Fannie Hurst

The Youngest Profession ★★★ U

Comedy　　　1943 · US · BW · 81min

This innocent teens' frolic stars Virginia Weidler as the leader of an autograph collector's club at her girls' school, whose dedication gets her meetings with MGM stars Greer Garson, Walter Pidgeon and Robert Taylor. Parallel with her celebrity-seeking activities, Weidler acts as Little Miss Fixit at home, sorting out various misunderstandings involving her father and the governess. Bright and breezy, cute, and old-fashioned family entertainment. **RK**

Virginia Weidler *Joan Lyons* • Edward Arnold *Burton V Lyons* • John Carroll *Dr Hercules* • Ann Ayars *Susan Thaye* • Marta Linden *Edith Lyons* • Agnes Moorehead *Miss Featherstone* ■ *Dir* Edward Buzzell • *Scr* George Oppenheimer, Charles Lederer, Leonard Spigelgass, from the novel by Lillian Day

Your Beating Heart ★★★ 15

Romantic drama　　1991 · Fr · Colour · 99min

Making stylishly symbolic use of his Parisian locations, director François Dupeyron has succeeded in fashioning a Rohmeresque romance for 40-somethings. Unwilling to risk her marriage to an antique dealer, Dominique Faysse, nevertheless, can't resist Thierry Fortineau, the stranger who seduced her in a trance and now offers her a passion that is absent from her ordered houseboat existence. Faysse gives a marvellous display of disarranged dignity, which is given space to develop by Dupeyron's use of leisurely takes and gentle humour. **DP** In French.

Dominique Faysse *Mado* • Thierry Fortineau *Yves* • Jean-Marie Winling *Jean* • Christophe Pichon *Stéphane* • Steve Kalfa *Luc* • Coralie Seyrig *Jeanne* ■ *Dir/Scr* François Dupeyron

Your Cheatin' Heart

**　　　　　　　　　　　　　★★★ U**

Musical biography　　1964 · US · BW · 98min

George Hamilton turns in one of his most memorable performances as country singer Hank Williams, whose work is probably more famous in the hands of artists as diverse as The Carpenters (*Jambalaya*) and Ray Charles (*Your Cheatin' Heart*). Williams died young in 1953, after alcoholism put paid to a swift and packed career. His son, Hank Jr, who's a respected country star in his own right, provides the vocals. **JG**

George Hamilton *Hank Williams* • Susan Oliver *Audrey Williams* • Red Buttons *Shorty Younger* • Arthur O'Connell *Fred Rose* • Shary Marshall *Ann Younger* • Rex Ingram (2) *Teetot* • Chris Crosby *Sam Priddy* ■ *Dir* Gene Nelson • *Scr* Stanford Whitmore

Your Friends & Neighbors

**　　　　　　　　　　　　　★★★ 18**

Black comedy drama　1998 · US · Colour · 95min

Neil LaBute's follow-up to his stirring, nasty debut, *In the Company of Men*, is a slightly tamer affair that suffers somewhat from an imbalance of unlikeable characters. Jason Patric finds his niche in the role of an insensitive macho man who has no problem bedding the wives and girlfriends of the men he hangs out with. Ben Stiller - unhappy in his domesticated relationship with Catherine Keener - lusts after pal Aaron Eckhart's missus (Amy Brenneman), while she has given up on having a fulfilling sex life with anyone. Troubling, twisted stuff. **JB** Swearing, sex scenes, nudity.

Amy Brenneman *Mary* • Aaron Eckhart *Barry* • Catherine Keener *Terri* • Nastassja Kinski *Cheri* • Jason Patric *Cary* • Ben Stiller *Jerry* ■ *Dir/Scr* Neil LaBute

Your Highness　　　　★★ 15

Fantasy comedy　　2010 · US · Colour · 98min

Director David Gordon Green applies the same rowdy appeal of his *Pineapple Express* to this mock medieval romp. Natalie Portman stars as a feisty princess who helps pot-smoking slacker prince Danny McBride and his heroic brother (James Franco) after the latter's ditsy fiancée (Zooey Deschanel) is whisked off by a wizard. The daft adventure follows a predictable course, although the dialogue is amusing (albeit heavy on the expletives). With a terrific supporting cast that includes Charles Dance, Justin Theroux and Toby Jones, *Your Highness* is well made but lowbrow, and has limited appeal. **KK** Violence, swearing, sexual references.

Danny McBride (2) *Thadeous* • James Franco *Fabious* • Natalie Portman *Isabel* • Zooey Deschanel *Belladonna* • Justin Theroux *Leezar* • Toby Jones *Julie* • Charles Dance *King Tallious* • Damian Lewis *Boremont* ■ *Dir* David Gordon Green • *Scr* Danny R McBride, Ben Best

Your Money or Your Wife ★

Comedy　　　1960 · UK · BW · 90min

Nice title, shame about the movie. This is a farce in every sense of the word, as blissfully married Peggy Cummins and Donald Sinden have to divorce in order to come into an inheritance. Both screenwriter Ronald Jeans and director Anthony Simmons seemed to think that an abundance of slapstick, a little innuendo and bags of mugging would be enough to have the audience in convulsions. Wrong. **DP**

Donald Sinden *Pelham Butterworth* • Peggy Cummins *Gay Butterworth* • Richard Wattis *Hubert Fry* • Peter Reynolds *Theodore Malek* • Georgina Cookson *Thelma Cressingdon* ■ *Dir* Anthony Simmons • *Scr* Ronald Jeans

Your Sister's Sister ★★★ 15

Comedy drama　　2011 · US · Colour · 90min

An unexpected encounter at a lakeside cabin proves fateful in this serio-comic indie. Grieving Mark Duplass is dispatched to the rural retreat by his ever-supportive best friend Emily Blunt in order to clear his head following the loss of his brother. But Blunt's lesbian vegan half-sister (Rosemarie DeWitt) also happens to be there coping with the break-up of her previous relationship. Two emotionally vulnerable people, a stray bottle of tequila and you can guess the rest. There's an element of farce as the scenario plays out, yet thanks to sharply observed performances by all three principals (who largely improvised the dialogue), the results are fresh, funny and believable. **TJ** Swearing, a sex scene. **DVD**

Emily Blunt *Iris* • Rosemarie DeWitt *Hannah* • Mark Duplass *Jack* • Mike Birbiglia *Al* ■ *Dir/Scr* Lynn Shelton

You're a Big Boy Now ★★★

Comedy drama　　1966 · US · Colour · 97min

This laid-back coming-of-age tale is probably most important nowadays as an example of the early work of director Francis Ford Coppola. As such, it is easy enough to overlook the quality cast, as teenager Peter Kastner, the pampered son of parents Geraldine Page and Rip Torn, discovers sex and drugs in the big wide world of New York when he falls for disco-dancer Elizabeth Hartman. Coppola's style and insight are already apparent in the range of characters and situations offered by this entertaining movie. And, as a bonus, there's music by the Lovin' Spoonful. **TH**

Elizabeth Hartman *Barbara Darling* • Geraldine Page *Margery Chanticleer* • Julie Harris (2) *Miss Thing* • Rip Torn *IH Chanticleer* • Michael Dunn *Richard Mudd* • Karen Black *Amy* ■ *Dir* Francis Ford Coppola • *Scr* Francis Ford Coppola, from the novel by David Benedictus

You're Dead　　　　　★ 15

Crime comedy　　1999 · US/Ger · Colour · 92min

This is supposed to be a darkly surreal exploration of how civilised people can descend into savagery under pressure. Yet what emerges is a crass crime caper, in which a bungled bank raid goes nowhere near as badly wrong as the film itself. **DP** **DVD**

John Hurt *Michael Maitland* • Rhys Ifans *Eddie Hayderhall* • Claire Skinner *Jo Simpson* • Barbara Flynn *Professor Corner* • John Benfield *Inspector Dick Badger* • David Schneider (1) *Ian Jeffries* ■ *Dir/Scr* Andy Hurst

You're in the Army Now

**　　　　　　　　　　　　　★ U**

Comedy　　　1936 · UK · BW · 79min

Surprisingly enough, this turgid slab of British melodrama was directed by the great Raoul Walsh. But this picture predates his glory years at Warner Bros and so it can be explained away as the kind of assignment a journeyman director was forced to accept in order to eat. Wallace Ford also made the trip across the Atlantic to give a dreadful performance as a New York gangster lying low in Blighty to avoid a murder rap. **DP**

Wallace Ford *Jim Tracey* • John Mills *Corporal Bert Dawson* • Anna Lee *Sally Bridges* • Grace Bradley *Jean Burdett* • Frank Cellier *Sergeant Major Briggs* ■ *Dir* Raoul Walsh • *Scr* Bryan Edgar Wallace, Austin Melford, AR Rawlinson, from a story by Lesser Samuels, Ralph Gilbert Bettinson

You're in the Navy Now

**　　　　　　　　　　　　　★★ U**

Comedy　　　1951 · US · BW · 92min

The gag in this weary comedy is that the ship's running on steam (hence the original title *USS Teakettle*), but the tone is extremely uncertain, and the comedic intentions misfire as often as the ship's engine. Cooper has the good grace to look uncomfortable, but always in character. Watch very closely for a couple of major movie debuts: Lee Marvin and Charles Bronson (then known as Buchinsky) made their screen bows here. **TS**

Gary Cooper *Lieutenant John Harkness* • Jane Greer *Ellie* • Millard Mitchell *Larrabee* • Eddie Albert *Lieutenant Bill Barron* • John McIntire *Commander Reynolds* • Ray Collins *Admiral Tennant* • Charles Buchinski [Charles Bronson] *Wascylewski* • Lee Marvin ■ *Dir* Henry Hathaway • *Scr* Richard Murphy, from a magazine article in the *New Yorker* by John W Hazard

You're My Everything ★★ U

Musical　　　1949 · US · Colour · 94min

This rose-tinted slice of 20th Century-Fox nostalgia is set at the beginning of the talkie era, a time that producer George Jessel (who also wrote the original story) had more than a passing interest in, since he was once a star of early sound films. Hard-working Dan Dailey is in the lead, but the pace is leaden, the plotline cliché-ridden, and leading lady Anne Baxter inadequate. The unexpected bonus is the great Buster Keaton, in the re-creation of a silent movie. **TS**

Dan Dailey *Timothy O'Connor* • Anne Baxter *Hannah Adams* • Anne Revere *Aunt Jane* • Stanley Ridges *Mr Mercer, producer* • Shari Robinson *Jane O'Connor* • Buster Keaton ■ *Dir* Walter Lang • *Scr* Lamar Trotti, Will H Hays Jr, from a story by George Jessel

You're My Hero　　★★★ 15

Comedy drama　　2003 · Sp · Colour · 98min

Spanish director Antonio Cuadri uses his country's transition from fascist dictatorship to constitutional monarchy to mirror the confusion felt by teenager Manuel Lozano as he arrives at yet another new school. Cuadri cleverly coats the political subtext with nostalgia for the trappings of the mid-1970s, reinforced by the Euro-pop soundtrack. Lozano's dealings with bully Alfonso Mena, tousled pretty boy Félix López and spiky Carmen Navarro are spiritedly enacted, but the contrast between liberal teacher Toni Cantó and martinet priest Juan Fernández, could have been more shaded and Lozano's heart-to-hearts with a fantasy comic book native American feel forced. **DP** Spanish +subtitles. Swearing. **DVD**

Manuel Lozano *Ramón* • Toni Cantó *Mateo* • Félix López *David* • Antonio Dechent *Water cloud* • Carmen Navarro *Paloma* • Juan Fernández [Juan Fernandez] *Don Félix* • Alfonso Mena *Rafa* • Pablo Acosta *Ortega* ■ *Dir* Antonio Cuadri • *Scr* Antonio Cuadri, Miguel Angel Pérez, Carlos Asorey

You're Never Too Young

**　　　　　　　　　　　　　★★★ U**

Comedy　　　1955 · US · Colour · 102min

Dean Martin and Jerry Lewis were in their prime for this funny movie, though the personal cracks were starting to appear in their relationship after six years on screen together. If the plot seems a mite familiar, that's because it's a Sidney Sheldon reworking of Billy Wilder's directing debut *The Major and the Minor*, only this time with the great Lewis masquerading as the 12-year-old Ginger Rogers - don't ask! The film looks stunning in rich Technicolor and trivia buffs might care to note that Diana Lynn appeared in both film versions of this plot. **TS**

Dean Martin *Bob Miles* • Jerry Lewis *Wilbur Hoolick* • Diana Lynn *Nancy Collins* • Nina Foch *Gretchen Brendan* • Raymond Burr *Noonan* • Mitzi McCall *Skeets* • Veda Ann Borg *Mrs Noonan* ■ *Dir* Norman Taurog • *Scr* Sidney Sheldon, from the play *Sunny Goes Home* by

Y

Edward Childs Carpenter, from the story *Connie Goes Home* by Fannie Kilbourne • *Cinematographer* Daniel L Fapp

You're Next ★★★★ 18
Horror   2011 · US · Colour · 90min

The family that dines together dies together in this ferociously entertaining home-invasion horror. Hostilities have barely surfaced between siblings at an anniversary family dinner before masked maniacs lay siege to their mansion. But little do the tooled-up attackers know that one of their prospective victims is a dab hand at do-it-yourself defence. This adds an innovative frisson to a terrific film that's suspenseful, gory and very droll, and announces director Adam Wingard as a talent to watch. JA Violence. DVD ⬅

Sharni Vinson *Erin* • Nicholas Tucci *Felix* • Wendy Glenn *Zee* • AJ Bowen *Crispian* • Joe Swanberg *Drake* ■ *Dir* Adam Wingard • *Scr* Simon Barrett

You're Only Young Once ★★
Comedy drama   1938 · US · BW · 77min

The second of the Andy Hardy films has Lewis Stone taking over the role of Mickey Rooney's dad from Lionel Barrymore who played him in the first film, *A Family Affair*. Adored by studio boss Louis B Mayer, a Jewish émigré who wished to extol the virtues of small-town American life and childhood, the films struck a chord with American audiences on the brink of war. If *A Family Affair* was a try-out, this was the full dress rehearsal for a series that spawned 14 more movies between 1938 and 1958. AT

Lewis Stone *Judge James K Hardy* • Cecilia Parker *Marian Hardy* • Mickey Rooney *Andy Hardy* • Fay Holden *Mrs Emily Hardy* • Frank Craven *Frank Redman* • Ann Rutherford *Polly Benedict* • Eleanor Lynn *"Jerry" Lane* ■ *Dir* George B Seitz • *Scr* Kay Van Riper, from characters by Aurania Rouverol

You're Only Young Twice ★★ U
Comedy   1952 · UK · BW · 84min

This theatrical comedy was shakily brought to the screen by an unlikely alliance of producers, including documentary pioneer John Grierson, then involved in a publicly funded outfit called Group 3, based at studios in Southall. Dealing with various shenanigans at a Scottish university, the story involves mistaken identity, Celtic poetry, horse racing and the rigging of Rectorial elections. AT

Duncan Macrae *Professor Hayman* • Joseph Tomelty *Dan McEntee* • Patrick Barr *Sir Archibald Asher* • Diane Hart *Ada Shore* • Charles Hawtrey *Adolphus Hayman* • Robert Urquhart *Sheltie* • Ronnie Corbett *Bishop* ■ *Dir* Terry Bishop • *Scr* Terry Bishop, Reginald Beckwith, Lindsay Galloway, from the play *What Say They* by James Bridie

You're Telling Me! ★★★
Comedy   1934 · US · BW · 67min

This sound remake of his silent vehicle, *So's Your Old Man*, gave WC Fields the chance to trot out his legendary golf course sketch one last time. But there's plenty to enjoy before this classic finale, as Fields's failed small-town inventor receives some unexpected support from holidaying royal Adrienne Ames. The highlights are the demonstration of his puncture-proof car tyre and the merciless repartee he shares with his shrewish wife, Louise Carter, and snobbish daughter, Joan Marsh, whose boyfriend is played by a pre-*Flash Gordon* Larry "Buster" Crabbe. DP

WC Fields *Sam Bisbee* • Larry "Buster" Crabbe *Bob Murchison* • Joan Marsh *Pauline Bisbee* • Adrienne Ames *Princess Marie Lescaboura* • Louise Carter *Mrs Bessie Bisbee* • Kathleen Howard *Mrs Edward Quimby Murchison* ■ *Dir* Erle C Kenton • *Scr* Walter DeLeon, Paul M Jones, JP McEvoy, from the short story *Mr Bisbee's Princess* by Julian Leonard Street

You're Ugly Too ★★★ 15
Comedy   2015 · Ire · Colour · 80min

A feelgood kitchen sinker sounds like a contradiction in terms, but debuting Mark Noonan pulls it off with this fairly short Irish drama about a released convict (Aiden Gillen) trying to re-connect with his gobby niece (Lauren Kinsella). The arcs on both sides are punishingly familiar – Gillen is going to try to go straight, Kinsella's going to learn to trust an adult again after the death of her mother. And in the hands of lesser actors, it might have seemed simplistic. But Gillen and Kinsella make it work, while Noonan's locations, largely a deadbeat trailer park, perfectly match his low budget, and he's not averse to a bit of sunshine and flare in the lens, either. All in all, a lovely wee film. SvM

Aidan Gillen *Will* • Lauren Kinsella *Stacey* • Erika Sainte *Emilie* ■ *Dir/Scr* Mark Noonan • *Cinematographer* Tom Comerford

Yours, Mine and Ours ★★★ PG
Comedy   1968 · US · Colour · 106min

Widower Henry Fonda has ten children. When he starts dating nurse Lucille Ball he neglects to tell her of his huge family just as she doesn't tell him about her own eight children. Eventually they come clean, marry and amalgamate their offspring – then their troubles really start. Based on the story of a real-life household, this is a slick and professional bit of fluff. Some of Ball's wilder antics seem out of step with the rest of the film but it certainly works as an undemanding family comedy. DF DVD

Lucille Ball *Helen North* • Henry Fonda *Frank Beardsley* • Van Johnson *Darrel Harrison* • Tom Bosley *Doctor* • Louise Troy *Frank's Date* • Ben Murphy *Larry* • Jennifer Leak *Colleen* ■ *Dir* Melville Shavelson • *Scr* Melville Shavelson, Mort Lachman, from a story by Madelyn Davis, Bob Carroll Jr, from the autobiography *Who Gets the Drumstick?* by Helen Beardsley

Yours, Mine & Ours ★ PG
Romantic comedy   2005 · US · Colour · 84min

Dennis Quaid and Rene Russo star in this tiresome remake of the 1968 Lucille Ball/Henry Fonda comedy. They play two widowed high-school sweethearts who reunite after some 30 years and get hitched. The trouble is the mismatched couple have 18 children between them who refuse to live as one, big happy family. What follows is a repetitive procession of slapstick sequences, but no amount of chaos can disguise the minuscule plot or give substance to lazy, stereotypical characters. SF DVD

Dennis Quaid *Frank Beardsley* • Rene Russo *Helen North* • Rip Torn *Commandant Sherman* • Linda Hunt *Mrs Munion* • Jerry O'Connell *Max* • David Koechner *Darrell* ■ *Dir* Raja Gosnell • *Scr* Ron Burch, David Kidd, from the 1968 film

Youth ★★★★ 15
Drama   2015 · It/Fr/Swi/UK · Colour · 118min

In his early 80s, Sir Michael Caine makes the first and possibly only true arthouse movie of his career. He stars as Fred Ballinger, a veteran conductor who is confronted by his past – notably via his daughter, Rachel Weisz, and best friend, Harvey Keitel. Caine's soulful role brings his world-weary charm to the fore, but this is really a playground for Italian maestro Paolo Sorrentino, whose ear for music is quite extraordinary and whose visual genius effortlessly takes us from the absurd to the profound. DW DVD ⬅

Michael Caine *Fred Ballinger* • Harvey Keitel *Mick Boyle* • Rachel Weisz *Lena Ballinger* • Paul Dano *Jimmy Tree* • Jane Fonda *Brenda Morel* • Poppy Corby-Tuech *Spy woman* ■ *Dir/Scr* Paolo Sorrentino

Youth in Revolt ★★★ 15
Romantic comedy drama
2009 · US · Colour · 89min

In this sharp, often crude, comedy Michael Cera stars as timid teen Nick, who's desperate to lose his virginity. However, when he falls for Sheeni, the girl of his dreams (Portia Doubleday), he realises he'll need to develop a rebellious streak to win her heart. Enter Francois Dillinger (Cera again), a bad-boy alter ego who leads Nick on a trail of destruction. Cera plays Nick with a deadpan bewildered charm, and there's a hilarious cameo from Fred Willard as a peacenik neighbour. TeS Swearing, sexual references, drug abuse. DVD Blu

Michael Cera *Nick Twisp/Francois Dillinger* • Steve Buscemi *George Twisp* • Portia Doubleday *Sheeni Saunders* • Jean Smart *Estelle Twisp* • Zach Galifianakis *Jerry* • Justin Long *Paul Saunders* • Ray Liotta *Lance Westcott* • Fred Willard *Mr Ferguson* ■ *Dir* Miguel Arteta • *Scr* Gustin Nash, from the novel by CD Payne

Youth Runs Wild ★
Second World War drama
1944 · US · BW · 66min

The working class community of a town is changed by war. With parents working in the local munitions factory, kids are neglected, misunderstandings arise, and teenagers get into trouble. A misjudged programmer produced by RKO's horror specialist, Val Lewton, who intended a "social conscience" drama but ended up with an earnest, preachy, unfocused mess. All involved are hamstrung by a simplistic, cliché-ridden and heavy-handed script. RK

Bonita Granville *Toddy* • Kent Smith *Danny* • Jean Brooks *Mary* • Glenn Vernon *Frank* • Tessa Brind *Sarah Taylor* • Ben Bard *Mr Taylor* • Mary Servoss *Mrs Hauser* • Arthur Shields *Mr Dunlop* • Lawrence Tierney *Duncan* ■ *Dir* Mark Robson • *Scr* John Fante, Ardel Wray, from a story by Fante, Herbert Klein

Youth without Youth ★★ 15
Period romantic thriller
2007 · US/It/Fr/Ger/Rom · Colour and BW · 119min

Francis Ford Coppola's return to directing after a ten-year break is by turns clumsy and visually extraordinary, confusing and stunningly old-fashioned. Beginning in Romania in 1938, the film opens with ageing linguistics professor Dominic Matei (Tim Roth) getting struck by lightning. But instead of dying, he has his youth miraculously restored, and his intellect becomes highly evolved. He attracts unwanted Nazi attention, so escapes Romania and travels the world incognito for the next 30 or so years to complete his research on the origins of language. Roth appears in many guises, including Matei's doppelganger, and his performance grounds the movie. But with its heavy imagery and overreaching academic tone, Coppola's conceit baffles more than it enlightens. AJ In English, German, Sanskrit, Italian. Sex scenes. DVD

Tim Roth *Dominic Matei* • Alexandra Maria Lara *Laura/Veronica/Rupini* • Bruno Ganz *Professor Stanciulescu* • Andre M Hennicke [Andre Hennicke] *Dr Josef Rudolf* • Marcel Iures *Professor Tucci* • Adrian Pintea *Pandit* • Alexandra Pirici *Woman in room six* ■ *Dir* Francis Ford Coppola • *Scr* Francis Ford Coppola, from the novella by Mircea Eliade

You've Got a Friend ★★
Drama   2007 · US · Colour · 98min

In a drama rich with life lessons, a reclusive Vietnam veteran (John Schneider) is persuaded to help a 12-year-old orphan boy build a race-ready go-cart. But although youngster Dylan McLaughlin has the right sort of puppy-eyed expression, his bland performance ultimately robs the predictable film of its much-needed emotional core. The climactic soap-box derby is not that exciting to watch, either. SF

John Schneider *Jim Kliekan* • Dylan McLaughlin *Bobby Graham* • Jason Brooks *Jeff* • Kate Connor *Aunt Gayle* ■ *Dir* James A Contner • *Scr* Oliver Robins

You've Got Mail ★★★ PG
Romantic comedy   1998 · US · Colour · 114min

Reworking director Ernst Lubitsch's classic *The Shop around the Corner*, and billed as the screen's first internet love story, this frail but winsome comedy reunited Tom Hanks with his *Sleepless in Seattle* co-star Meg Ryan and its director Nora Ephron. Rarely as amusing as it should be, this is frustratingly unromantic, with the stars coming together more like merged files than infatuated lovers. However, this latter-day screwball tale is certainly slickly staged and played with consummate ease, and Ryan and her bookshop staff exude a pleasant feeling of cosiness. DP Swearing. DVD

Meg Ryan *Kathleen Kelly* • Tom Hanks *Joe Fox* • Greg Kinnear *Frank Navasky* • Parker Posey *Patricia Eden* • Steve Zahn *George Pappas* • Dave Chappelle *Kevin Scanlon* • Dabney Coleman *Nelson Fox* ■ *Dir* Nora Ephron • *Scr* Nora Ephron, Delia Ephron, from the film *The Shop around the Corner* by Samson Raphaelson, from the play *Parfumerie* by Miklos Laszlo

Yu-Gi-Oh! The Movie ★★ PG
Animated fantasy adventure
2004 · Jpn/US/S Kor · Colour · 86min

Like *Pokémon* and *Digimon* before it, popular Japanese animation *Yu-Gi-Oh!* seems to exist solely in order to sell its tie-in merchandise. Hero Yugi, the master of a Top Trumps-style game called Duel Monsters, discovers that his hobby has a mysterious (and dangerous) past. Yugi has to battle an evil ancient Egyptian spirit called Anubis. Only fans of the TV series will be able to follow the largely incomprehensible plot and the bog-standard animation won't win it any new ones. LB Japanese dubbed. DVD

Dan Green *Yugi Moto/Yami Yugi* • Amy Birnbaum *Tea Garnder* • Wayne Grayson *Joey Wheeler* • Eric Stuart *Seto Kaiba* ■ *Dir* Hatsuki Tsuji • *Scr* Matthew Drdek, Lloyd Goldfine, Norman J Grossfeld, Michael Pecoriello, from a story by Junki Takegami, Masahiro Hikokubu, from a comic book by Kazuki Takahashi

Yuma ★★★ 15
Crime drama   2012 · Cz Rep/Pol · Colour · 112min

Polish director Piotr Mularuk's debut feature centres on "yuma", the smuggling of stolen goods from the reunified Germany into Poland during the early 1990s. The film also references Delmer Daves's 1957 western *3:10 to Yuma*. Jakub Gierszal leads a spirited ensemble as a young man who strikes it rich in cahoots with his brothel-owning aunt (Katarzyna Figura) but finds his new status grates with his childhood-buddy-turned-cop and a local mobster. The movie doesn't know if it's a gangster movie, a social satire or a doomed love story, but Mularuk captures the look and amoral feel of the period. DP In Polish, German. Violence, swearing, sex scenes.

Jakub Gierszal *Zyga* • Krzysztof Skonieczny *Kula* • Jakub Kamienski *Mlot* • Tomasz Kot *Opat* • Katarzyna Figura *Halinka* ■ *Dir* Piotr Mularuk

Z ★★★★ 15

Political drama   1968 · Fr/Alg · Colour · 121min

Two of Europe's finest actors – Yves Montand and Jean-Louis Trintignant – star in this Oscar-winning political thriller about corruption in high places. Though shot in Algeria and serving as a universal condemnation of totalitarianism, Costa-Gavras's film is in fact based on the murder of a prominent liberal opponent of the military regime in Greece in 1963. As the investigating magistrate, Trintignant uncovers a vicious betrayal surrounding the death of Montand and, as his inquiry progresses and links to the government are established, he is increasingly under pressure to discontinue his probe. This is a landmark, eye-opening movie for its depiction of government depravity; unsurprisingly, it was banned in Greece until the military government was overthrown in 1974. TH French +subtitles.

Yves Montand *The Deputy* · Jean-Louis Trintignant *Examining Magistrate* · Irene Papas *Hélène* · Charles Denner *Manuel* · Georges Géret [Georges Geret] *Nick* · Jacques Perrin *Journalist* · François Périer *Attorney* · Pierre Dux *General* ■ *Dir* Costa-Gavras · *Scr* Costa-Gavras, Jorge Semprun, from the novel by Vassilis Vassilikos · *Cinematographer* Raoul Coutard · *Music* Mikis Theodorakis

ZPG: Zero Population Growth ★★

Science fiction   1971 · US · Colour · 96min

With thought outlawed in *Nineteen Eighty-Four* and age prohibited in *Logan's Run*, it was only a matter of time before reproduction would find itself outside the law. In a smog-bound, overpopulated future a tyrannical regime has launched a line of robot-children and made birth a death penalty offence. Oliver Reed and Geraldine Chaplin play the parents in peril in this dreary hide-and-seek saga. DP Violence.

Oliver Reed *Russ McNeil* · Geraldine Chaplin *Carole McNeil* · Don Gordon *George Borden* · Diane Cilento *Edna Borden* · David Markham *Dr Herrick* · Sheila Reed *Dr Mary Herrick* · Aubrey Woods *Dr Mallory* ■ *Dir* Michael Campus · *Scr* Max Ehrlich, Frank De Felitta

Zabriskie Point ★★★ 15

Drama   1970 · US · Colour · 109min

Michelangelo Antonioni's US debut is a sprawling and often unconvincing examination of American decadence. Made when the radical activism of the 1960s had begun to wane, it has student Mark Frechette and pot-smoking secretary Daria Halprin start a Death Valley love affair. The endless billboards, the carefree frolics in the sand and the psychedelic painting of Frechette's stolen plane all drip with significance, but you can't help feeling that Antonioni hadn't really got to grips with the States. Cracking last shot, though. DP Swearing, drug abuse, nudity. DVD

Mark Frechette *Mark* · Daria Halprin *Daria* · Rod Taylor *Lee Allen* · Paul Fix *Cafe owner* · GD Spradlin *Lee Allen's associate* · Bill Garaway *Morty* · Kathleen Cleaver *Kathleen* ■ *Dir* Michelangelo Antonioni · *Scr* Michelangelo Antonioni, Fred Gardner, Sam Shepard, Tonino Guerra, Clare Peplce, from a story by Antonioni · *Cinematographer* Alfio Contini

Zack and Miri Make a Porno ★★★ 18

Romantic comedy drama   2008 · US · Colour · 97min

Although it's written and directed by Kevin Smith of *Clerks* fame, the shadow of comedy maestro Judd Apatow (*Knocked Up*) looms large over this enthusiastically non-PC mix of filth and fun. Apatow regular Seth Rogen and Elizabeth Banks (*The 40 Year Old Virgin*) play a couple of cash-strapped housemates who've been best friends since childhood. When they can't pay their bills, they decide to raise some cash by starring in and marketing a home-made porno movie. Funniest when it's filthiest, but less successful when it slips into generic romantic comedy slush, this is an intermittently hilarious smut-fest, and most definitely not for the less broad-minded. DA DVD ◗⬋

Seth Rogen *Zack* · Elizabeth Banks (2) *Miri Linky* · Traci Lords *Bubbles* · Jason Mewes *Lester* · Ricky Mabe *Barry* · Craig Robinson *Delaney* ■ *Dir/Scr* Kevin Smith (2)

Zandalee ★★ 18

Romantic thriller   1991 · US · Colour · 99min

In sultry New Orleans, feisty Erika Anderson tires of poet husband Judge Reinhold and starts an affair with his best friend, painter Nicolas Cage. Standard love-tangle stuff, which is notable mainly for its steamy sex scenes and daft dialogue ("I want to shake you naked and eat you alive"). AJ DVD

Nicolas Cage *Johnny Collins* · Judge Reinhold *Thierry Martin* · Erika Anderson *Zandalee Martin* · Joe Pantoliano *Gerri* · Viveca Lindfors *Tatta* · Aaron Neville *Jack* · Steve Buscemi *OPP Man* · Marisa Tomei *Remy* ■ *Dir* Sam Pillsbury · *Scr* Mari Kornhauser

Zandy's Bride ★★

Western drama   1974 · US · Colour · 115min

Even though it's set in the Old West, don't expect stampedes and shoot-outs, for the only showdowns at high noon in what is actually a domestic drama are between a coarse rancher and his feisty mail-order bride. Swedish director Jan Troell is so preoccupied with scenery, mood and period detail that he has left his cast with precious little to do. In the circumstances, Gene Hackman and Liv Ullmann's over-the-top performances are excusable. DP

Gene Hackman *Zandy Allan* · Liv Ullmann *Hannah Lund* · Eileen Heckart *Ma Allan* · Harry Dean Stanton *Songer* · Joe Santos *Frank Gallo* · Frank Cady *Pa Allan* · Sam Bottoms *Mel Allan* ■ *Dir* Jan Troell · *Scr* Marc Norman, from the novel *The Stranger* by Lillian Bos Ross

Zapped! ★★★ 15

Comedy   1982 · US · Colour · 93min

Scott Baio is a nerdy high-school kid who gets zapped in a chem-lab explosion, and finds he has the power to move objects by thought alone. Cue lots of teen high jinks, such as telekinetically divesting the busty local girls of their blouses, and taking control of the ball during a baseball game. Madcap, and surprisingly amusing. DA

Scott Baio *Barney Springboro* · Willie Aames *Peyton Nichols* · Robert Mandan *Walter Johnson* · Felice Schachter *Bernadette* · Scatman Crothers *Dexter Jones* ■ *Dir* Robert J Rosenthal · *Scr* Bruce Rubin, Robert J Rosenthal

Zarak ★★

Adventure   1956 · UK · Colour · 88min

Victor Mature, in full Afghan mode, leads his gang of cut-throats against the might of the British army, headed by Michael Wilding, in a trashy adventure yarn set in the halcyon days of Empire. Apart from a belly dance by Anita Ekberg – which should have earned the movie an X-rating – it's notable only as one of producer "Cubby" Broccoli's pre-Bond collaborations with director Terence Young, writer Richard Maibaum and cameraman Ted Moore, all of whom went on to make *Dr No*. AT

Victor Mature *Zarak Khan* · Anita Ekberg *Salma* · Michael Wilding *Major Ingram* · Bonar Colleano *Biri* · Finlay Currie *The Mullah* · Bernard Miles *Hassu* · Frederick Valk *Haji Khan* · Eunice Gayson *Cathy Ingram* · Patrick McGoohan *Moor Larkin* ■ *Dir* Terence Young · *Scr* Richard Maibaum, from the novel *The Story of Zarak Khan* by AJ Bevan

Zardoz ★★ 15

Science-fiction adventure   1973 · UK · Colour · 101min

Poor Sean Connery – Burt Reynolds obviously knew what he was doing when he said no to this naive futuristic hokum. Yet, thanks to Geoffrey Unsworth's stunning photography, this patently silly story, set in 2293 and telling of a rebellion against sexless intellectualism and soulless technology, has become one of those "risible but unmissable" cult movies, whose main attraction now is the unintentional comedy. The title is a contraction of "Wizard of Oz". DP Swearing, nudity. DVD ◗⬋

Sean Connery *Zed* · Charlotte Rampling *Consuella* · Sara Kestelman *May* · Sally Anne Newton *Avalow* · John Alderton *Friend* · Niall Buggy *Zardoz/Arthur Frayn* · Bosco Hogan *George Saden* · Jessica Swift *Apathetic* · Bairbre Dowling *Star* · Christopher Casson *Old scientist* · Reginald Jarman *Death* ■ *Dir/Scr* John Boorman

Zathura: a Space Adventure ★★★★ PG

Fantasy adventure   2005 · US · Colour · 96min

In this intergalactic *Jumanji*, brothers Jonah Bobo and Josh Hutcherson are taught life lessons when they play a dusty board game found in the cellar that thrusts them into outer space to face meteor showers, a defective robot and lizard-like aliens. Having the entire universe just outside their front door creates huge imaginative scope, while the terrific retro *Dan Dare*-style design matches the film's refreshing reliance on old-fashioned special effects. Director Jon Favreau brings a delightful sense of childlike wonder to this witty comic book adventure that offers fun and scares for all age groups. AJ DVD

Josh Hutcherson *Walter* · Jonah Bobo *Danny* · Dax Shepard *The astronaut* · Kristen Stewart *Lisa* · Tim Robbins *Dad* · Frank Oz *Robot (voice)* ■ *Dir* Jon Favreau · *Scr* David Koepp, John Kamps, from the novel by Chris Van Allsburg

Zatoichi ★★★

Action adventure   1962 · Jpn · Colour · 96min

This is the first of the 26 features about an itinerant blind masseur with a samurai's instinctive sword skills that would star Shintaro Katsu, not to mention more than 100 television episodes. Setting the series' scene, much of the story is taken up with establishing Zatoichi's low social status, his penchant for gambling and the acuity of his remaining senses. Yet considerable emphasis is also placed on his respect for Shigeru Amachi, the ronin with whom he will eventually have to duel to settle a clan turf war. It's B-movie-making at its most meticulous. No wonder a cult was born. DP In Japanese.

Shintaro Katsu *Zatoichi* · Masayo Banri *Otane* · Ryuzu Shimada *Sasagawa boss* · Hajime Mitamura *Hanji of Matsugishi* · Shigeru Amachi *Hirate* · Chitose Maki *Yoshi* · Michio Minami *Tatekichi* ■ *Dir* Kenji Misumi · *Scr* Minoru Inuzuka, from a short story by Kan Shimozawa

Zatoichi ★★★★ 18

Period action adventure   2003 · Jpn · Colour · 110min

Shintaro Katsu may have starred as Zatoichi the blind swordsman in 26 B-movie adventures, but none of those can match the cinematic panache of Takeshi Kitano's thrilling variation on the traditional themes of duty, honour and championing the cause of the oppressed. Kitano takes on the iconic role of the itinerant masseur/swordsman, but his inevitable showdown with the warring clans terrorising the residents of a small town in 19th-century Japan isn't simply a homage to a cult hero. It's a glorious visual scrapbook referencing the greats of Japanese film-making who have influenced Kitano's unique blend of pitiless violence, slapstick comedy and sensitive social detail. DP Japanese +subtitles. Violence. DVD ◗⬋

"Beat" Takeshi [Takeshi Kitano] *Zatoichi* · Tadanobu Asano *Hattori, the bodyguard* · Michiyo Ogusu *Aunt O-Ume* · Yui Natsukawa

Hattori's wife · Guadalcanal Taka *Shinkichi* · Daigoro Tachibana *O-Sei, the geisha* · Yuko Daike *O-Kinu, the geisha* ■ *Dir* Takeshi Kitano · *Scr* Takeshi Kitano, from a short story by Kan Shimozawa

Zatoichi Meets Yojimbo ★★★ 12

Action adventure   1970 · Jpn · Colour · 115min

This is one of the more engaging entries in the Blind Swordsman series, largely because director Kihachi Okamoto is so clearly attempting to duplicate the tone of Akira Kurosawa's 1961 classic *Yojimbo*. Shintaro Katsu again headlines as the one-time masseur who returns to his favourite village and finds it in the thrall of a ruthless merchant. The merchant's feud with his son has prompted the arrival of a couple of sinister samurai, Toshiro Mifune and sword-for-hire Shin Kishida. There's explosive action, but also cerebral strategising. DP Japanese +subtitles. DVD

Shintaro Katsu *Zatoichi* · Toshiro Mifune *Yojimbo* · Mori Kishida *Kuzuryu* · Kanjuro Arashi *Hyoroku* ■ *Dir* Kihachi Okamoto · *Scr* Tetsuro Yoshida, Kihachi Okamoto, from a story by Kan Shimozawa

Zaytoun ★★★ 15

Drama   2012 · UK/Is/Fr · Colour · 105min

With echoes of Tony Curtis and Sidney Poitier in *The Defiant Ones*, director Eran Riklis's follow-up to *Lemon Tree* pitches together a downed Israeli airman and a bereaved Palestinian boy as they try to escape the violence of Lebanon in the early 1980s. Stephen Dorff plays the pilot, but his character never quite gels, the story seems contrived at times and the viewer is left with several uncomfortable questions. Still, Abdallah El Akal delivers such a winning turn as the boy, it more than compensates. BP English, Arabic, Hebrew +subtitles. DVD

Stephen Dorff *Yoni* · Abdallah El Akal *Fahed* · Alice Taglioni *Leclair* · Loai Noufi *Aboudi* ■ *Dir* Eran Riklis · *Scr* Nader Rizq

Zaza ★

Drama   1939 · US · BW · 83min

Claudette Colbert stars as a touring vaudeville singer in the French provinces who falls in love with classy, middle-aged Parisian businessman Herbert Marshall and temporarily abandons her career until she discovers that he is married. Marshall looks uncomfortable and Colbert substitutes stridency for vivacity. RK

Claudette Colbert *Zaza* · Herbert Marshall *Dufresne* · Bert Lahr *Cascart* · Helen Westley *Anais* · Constance Collier *Nathalie* · Genevieve Tobin *Florianne* · Walter Catlett *Malaidot* · Ann E Todd *Toto* ■ *Dir* George Cukor · *Scr* Zoë Akins [Zoe Akins], from the play *Zaza* by Pierre Breton, Charles Simon, adapted by David Belasco

Zazie dans le Métro ★★★ 12

Surreal comedy   1960 · Fr · Colour · 88min

Although he is often spoken of in the same breath as Jean-Luc Godard and François Truffaut, Louis Malle was always on the periphery of the French New Wave rather than an integral part of it. Here, however, he employs all the paraphernalia of his more iconoclastic contemporaries – jump cuts, games with film speed, rapid editing and movie in-jokes – to fashion an exhilarating comic fantasy, which follows the adventures of a young girl and her female impersonator uncle. Demonstrating ridiculous precocity, Catherine Demongeot almost blows the brilliant Philippe Noiret and the city of Paris off the screen. DP French +subtitles. DVD

Catherine Demongeot *Zazie* · Philippe Noiret *Uncle Gabriel* · Hubert Deschamps *Turnadot* · Antoine Roblot *Charles* · Annie Fratellini *Mado* · Carla Marlier *Albertine* ■ *Dir* Louis Malle · *Scr* Louis Malle, Jean-Paul Rappeneau, from the novel *Zazie dans le Métro* by Raymond Queneau · *Cinematographer* Henri Raichi

Zebra Crossing ★★★ 18

Drama   2010 · UK · BW · 91min

A troubled teenager on a rough south London estate comes to a crossroads in his life in writer/director Sam Holland's stylish first feature. Lee Turnbull plays a teen tearaway with a wretched home life who is tired of gang fights, drug dealing and police confrontations, and yearns for something better than a life of endless ducking and diving. Holland's debut has a lot going for it (including magnificent sound design), and Turnbull's anguished and moving portrayal gives the film real heart. JA *DVD*

Lee Turnbull *Justin* • Greg Wakeham *Tommy* • Aaron White *Sean* • Kyle Treslove *Billy* • Kathryn O'Reilly *Suzanne* ■ *Dir/Scr* Sam Holland

Zebrahead ★★ 15
Romantic drama   1992 · US · Colour · 97min

Made with the backing of Robert Redford's Sundance Institute and executive produced by Oliver Stone, this interracial romance boldly attempts to tackle a number of controversial themes. But such is the uncertainty of debutant Anthony Drazan's direction that the action all-too-rapidly becomes entangled in the knot of loose ends. Somewhere in the middle of the protests against their relationship, Michael Rapaport and N'Bushe Wright turn in touchingly honest performances. DP

Michael Rapaport *Zack Glass* • Kevin Corrigan *Dominic* • Lois Bendler *Dominic's mother* • Dan Ziskie *Mr Cimino* • DeShonn Castle *Dee Wimms* • N'Bushe Wright *Nikki* • Marsha Florence *Mrs Wilson* • Shula Van Buren *Michelle* • Ron Johnson *Nut* • Ray Sharkey *Richard Glass* ■ *Dir/Scr* Anthony Drazan

A Zed & Two Noughts ★★ 15
Surreal drama   1985 · UK/Neth · Colour · 111min

British director Peter Greenaway is one of those cinematic luminaries who provoke extreme reactions in people. Some fervently regard his highly stylised, elliptical films as works of deep and majestic genius while others think Greenaway is a classic case of the Emperor's New Celluloid Clothes. This is a perfect example of the latter. Concerned with the behaviour of two zoologist brothers after the bizarre demise of their wives, it looks wonderful, but is so painfully slow and visually driven that this is merely a painting on a cinema screen. SH Nudity. *DVD*

Andréa Ferréol *Alba Bewick* • Brian Deacon *Oswald Deuce* • Eric Deacon *Oliver Deuce* • Frances Barber *Venus de Milo* • Joss Ackland *Van Hoyten* • Jim Davidson *Joshua Plate* • Agnes Brulet *Beta Bewick* • David Attenborough *Narrator of wild-life footage* ■ *Dir/Scr* Peter Greenaway • *Cinematographer* Sacha Vierny • *Music* Michael Nyman

Zee and Co ★★
Drama   1971 · UK · Colour · 110min

They might have called this *Who's Afraid of Elizabeth Taylor?* Scripted by Edna O'Brien, this preposterous marital malarkey should raise a few smirks as Taylor, Michael Caine (as her husband), Susannah York (as his lover) and Margaret Leighton (as a society hostess) play it close to the edge. Taylor slashes her wrists, York's earlier affair with a nun comes to the surface and before long the pair are in bed together. Pity poor Mr Caine. But pity everyone except the costume designer who works wonders with see-through materials. AT Swearing, nudity.

Elizabeth Taylor *Zee Blakeley* • Michael Caine *Robert Blakeley* • Susannah York *Stella* • Margaret Leighton *Gladys* • John Standing *Gordon* • Michael Cashman *Gavin* ■ *Dir* Brian G Hutton • *Scr* Edna O'Brien

Zelig ★★★★ PG
Spoof documentary
1983 · US · BW and Colour · 78min

Shot as a mock 1930s documentary in scratchy black and white, this defiantly uncommercial film from Woody Allen is not just technically ground-breaking - inserting "human chameleon" Leonard Zelig (Allen) into newsreel footage of Hitler and archive photos of Jack Dempsey and President Coolidge - but laugh-out-loud funny, too. In assimilating the characteristics of those around him, whether physical, religious or ethnic, Zelig speaks of a human desire to fit in, and it is apt that the thrust of the

documentary is one of doctors (including the sympathetic Mia Farrow) trying to "cure" him, while the media fêtes him. A poignant, beautifully realised hymn to individualism. AC *DVD*

Woody Allen *Leonard Zelig* • Mia Farrow *Dr Eudora Fletcher* • John Buckwalter *Dr Sindell* • Garrett Brown [Garrett M Brown] *Actor Zelig* • Stephanie Farrow *Sister Meryl* • Will Holt *Rally Chancellor* • Sol Lomita *Martin Geist* ■ *Dir/Scr* Woody Allen • *Cinematographer* Gordon Willis • *Editor* Susan E Morse • *Production Designer* Mel Bourne

Zelly and Me ★★★ 15
Drama   1988 · US · Colour · 88min

This is a graceful film that deals with an ungraceful subject: psychological violence visited on the young. Alexandra Johnes is an orphaned eight-year-old who goes to live with her grandmother Glynis Johns, a lonely woman who jealously tries to keep Johnes for herself. The young girl is attached to her nanny Isabella Rossellini, but her grandmother tries to separate the two by banishing Rossellini for a violation of trust. Johns is excellent at evincing selfish cruelty just as Tina Rathborne's fine direction adds that extra dimension to the turn of the screw. Watch out for Rossellini's then partner, film director David Lynch, in a supporting role. FL

Isabella Rossellini *Zelly* • Glynis Johns *Co-Co* • Alexandra Johnes *Phoebe* • Kaiulani Lee *Nora* • David Lynch *Willie* • Joe Morton *Earl* ■ *Dir/Scr* Tina Rathborne

Zenobia ★★★ U
Comedy   1939 · US · BW · 69min

Known in Britain as *Elephants Never Forget*, this gentle comedy would be forgettable except for the fact that Oliver Hardy starred without Stan Laurel (who was having contract difficulties with the Hal Roach Studios). So Ollie has it all his own way as a doctor in a small town who is given an elephant to look after by showman Harry Langdon. The pesky pachyderm then follows Ollie everywhere. Amiable stuff. TH

Oliver Hardy *Dr Henry Tibbett* • Harry Langdon *Prof McCrackle* • Billie Burke *Mrs Bessie Tibbett* • Alice Brady *Mrs Carter* • James Ellison *Jeff Carter* • Jean Parker *Mary Tibbett* • Step'n Fetchit [Stepin Fetchit] *Zero* • Hattie McDaniel *Dehlia* ■ *Dir* Gordon Douglas • *Scr* Corey Ford, from a story by Walter DeLeon, Harold Belgard, from the short story *Zenobia's Infidelity* by Henry C Bunner

Zeppelin ★★ PG
First World War drama
1971 · UK · Colour · 97min

Warner Bros threw money at this drama, but it simply failed to take off with audiences. Michael York admirably conveys the dilemma facing a Scottish-German soldier who's unsure where his true loyalties lie, but his spying mission for the Admiralty is hamstrung by an over-abundance of civilised chat and a lack of tension. However, the finale is breathtaking. DP Swearing.

Michael York *Geoffrey Richter-Douglas* • Elke Sommer *Erika Altschul* • Marius Goring *Professor Christian Altschul* • Peter Carsten *Major Alfred Tauntler* • Anton Diffring *Colonel Johann Hirsch* • Andrew Keir *Lt Cmdr Horst von Gorian* • Rupert Davies *Captain Whitney* • Alexandra Stewart *Stephanie Ross* ■ *Dir* Etienne Périer • *Scr* Arthur Rowe, Donald Churchill, from a story by Owen Crump

Zero: an Investigation into 9-11 ★★★ 12A
Documentary   2008 · It · Colour · 104min

Despite the echoes of TV's *Brass Eye*, with its smug presentation, garish graphics and blaring musical motifs, this aggressive Italian documentary does a decent job of collating the conspiracy theories surrounding the attacks on the World Trade Center and the Pentagon on 11 September 2001. Celebrity sceptics like Dario Fo and Gore Vidal join eyewitnesses and respected scientific, political and military experts to question the official version of what happened on that day. But while much of the testimony sounds persuasive, this

fascinating but flawed piece is presented more as informed speculation than incontrovertible fact. DP Italian, English +subtitles.

■ *Dir* Franco Fracassi, Francesco Trento

Zero Dark Thirty ★★★★ 15
Action thriller based on a true story
2012 · US · Colour · 150min

The hunt for Osama Bin Laden is catalogued in forensic detail in this wordy but well-paced thriller from the makers of *The Hurt Locker*. Driven CIA operative Maya (Jessica Chastain) follows every small lead across the globe while attempting to track down the al-Qaeda figurehead, frequently locking horns with her superiors back in the United States. Director Kathryn Bigelow skilfully manages to present a cohesive narrative out of potentially confusing material, which includes scenes of torture that provoked widespread controversy. Chastain's performance occasionally veers towards the histrionic, but her character gives the film a strong human centre as events lead up to the thrilling assault on Bin Laden's hideout. TeS Violence, swearing. *DVD* Blu

Jessica Chastain *Maya* • Jason Clarke (2) *Dan* • Joel Edgerton *Patrick, squadron team leader* • Jennifer Ehle *Jessica* • Mark Strong *George* • Kyle Chandler *Joseph Bradley* • James Gandolfini *CIA director* • Stephen Dillane *National security advisor* ■ *Dir* Kathryn Bigelow • *Scr* Mark Boal • *Editors* Dylan Tichenor, William Goldenberg • *Music* Alexandre Desplat

Zéro de Conduite ★★★★★ PG
Classic comedy drama   1933 · Fr · BW · 41min

Comical, lyrical, surreal and packed with references to animator Emile Cohl, Abel Gance and Charlie Chaplin, this savage satire on public school life was considered so inflammatory by the French authorities that it was banned until 1945. Reflecting the militancy of his anarchist father and a loathing of the institutions that blighted his sickly childhood, Jean Vigo abandoned traditional narrative and formal principles and experimented with angles, perspectives and space to convey the psychological state of the rebellious students. However, the film's elliptical poetry was something of an accident, as Vigo was forced to abbreviate the action to fit the agreed running time. DP French +subtitles. *DVD*

Jean Dasté *Superintendent Huguet* • Robert Le Flon *Superintendent Parrain, "Pête-Sec"* • Delphin *Principal* • Blanchar *Superintendent Général aka "Bec de gaz"* • Larive [Léon Larive] *Chemistry professor* • Mme Emile *Madame Colin, "Mère Haricot"* • Louis de Gonzague-Frick *Le Préfet* ■ *Dir/Scr* Jean Vigo • *Cinematographer* Boris Kaufman

Zero Effect ★★★★ 15
Detective comedy thriller
1997 · US · Colour · 111min

Bill Pullman is the world's greatest private detective, but he's also a recluse who only ventures out when on a case, relying the rest of the time on frontman Ben Stiller. The pair are hired by tycoon Ryan O'Neal to solve a quirky mystery, and we're taken on a *Moonlighting*-style ride of comedy, romance and sleuthing as the reclusive Pullman tangles with paramedic Kim Dickens, who seems to have found a way through his defences. Packed with wickedly wacky moments and a terrific performance from Pullman, this is decidedly offbeat, but also smart, witty and entertaining. JB Swearing, violence, sex scenes.

Bill Pullman *Daryl Zero* • Ben Stiller *Steve Arlo* • Ryan O'Neal *Gregory Stark* • Kim Dickens *Gloria Sullivan* • Angela Featherstone *Jess* • Hugh Ross *Bill* • Sara Devincentis *Daisy* ■ *Dir/Scr* Jake Kasdan

Zero Hour! ★★★ U
Drama   1957 · US · BW · 81min

Watching this 1950s airborne drama now, you can see what a wonderful template it was for the spoof *Airplane!* Passengers and crew on a jetplane suffer from food poisoning leaving stressed-out former pilot Dana Andrews as the man of the hour. He's

forced to take over the controls - more than director Hall Bartlet does - much to the joy of wife Linda Darnell and the sneers of ground controller Sterling Hayden. TH

Dana Andrews *Ted Stryker* • Linda Darnell *Elena Stryker* • Sterling Hayden *Capt Treleaven* • Peggy King *Stewardess* • Raymond Ferrell *Joey Stryker* • Elroy "Crazylegs" Hirsch *Capt Wilson* • Jerry Paris *Tony Decker* • Geoffrey Toone *Dr Baird* ■ *Dir* Hall Bartlett • *Scr* Arthur Hailey, Hall Bartlett, John C Champion, from a story by Hailey, from his teleplay *Flight into Danger*

Zero Patience ★★ 18
Musical   1993 · Can · Colour · 100min

Out of the glut of Aids awareness movies, this stands alone for treating the subject in a light-hearted and irreverent manner. Normand Fauteux is the promiscuous airline steward supposedly responsible for introducing the virus into the Northern Hemisphere. Through his ghostly visitations to Victorian anthropologist Richard Burton (don't ask!), we're taken on an outrageous musical odyssey through aspects of gay life. Tasteless and trivial. AJ Swearing, nudity. *DVD*

John Robinson (2) *Sir Richard Francis Burton* • Normand Fauteux *Patient Zero* • Dianne Heatherington *Mary* • Richardo Keens-Douglas *George* • Bernard Behrens *Doctor Placebo* ■ *Dir/Scr* John Greyson

The Zero Theorem ★★★ 15
Science-fiction drama
2013 · US/Rom · Colour · 106min

Though it doesn't come close to his dark fantasy *Brazil*, which remains a milestone in its field, Terry Gilliam's return to the dystopian-future sci-fi genre just about passes muster as an oddball, absurdist comedy, albeit one with no jokes or punchlines. A deadpan Christoph Waltz stars as a technical genius who slaves away at a computer interface and longs to be able to work from home. As with *Brazil*, the storyline is more a series of encounters than a plot, and follows the forlorn Waltz as he's bullied by his employers into proving life itself is futile. Though the more blatant attempts at comedy don't work, Waltz brings a delicate sadness to the role, one that works in perfect counterpoint to Gilliam's overly busy window-dressing. DW Swearing, sexual references, nudity. *DVD* Blu

Christoph Waltz *Qohen Leth* • David Thewlis *Joby* • Mélanie Thierry *Bainsley* • Matt Damon *Management* • Tilda Swinton *Dr Shrink-Rom* ■ *Dir* Terry Gilliam • *Scr* Pat Rushin • *Music* George Fenton

Zeus and Roxanne ★★ U
Comedy adventure   1997 · US · Colour · 94min

In this adequate family film, neighbouring kids play Cupid in a bid to bring their respective single parents together - the mother's a marine biologist, the father's a rock composer. Meanwhile, his pet dog strikes up a special relationship with her research dolphin, leading to much talk about inter-species communication, and even more about inter-human communication. DA

Steve Guttenberg *Terry* • Kathleen Quinlan *Mary Beth* • Arnold Vosloo *Claude Carver* • Dawn McMillan *Becky* ■ *Dir* George Miller (1) • *Scr* Tom Benedek

Zhang Yimou's Blood Simple ★★★ 12
Black comedy thriller
2009 · Chi/HK · Colour · 86min

The Coen brothers' feature debut is reimagined to period China in this blackly comic thriller from director Zhang Yimou. It's the visual touch of the director of *Raise the Red Lantern* that's the saving grace of this intentionally farcical retelling, which sees a policeman bribed by a noodle shop owner to bump off his wife and her lover. Some may find the comic playing too broad and a final-act shift into darker territory jarring, but this remains an interesting experiment. JH Mandarin +subtitles. *DVD*

Sun Honglei *Zhang* • Xiao Shenyang *Li* • Yan Ni *Wang's wife* • Ni Dahong *Wang* ■ *Dir* Zhang Yimou • *Scr* Shi Jianquan, Shang Jing, from Ethan & Joel Coen's 1983 film

Zidane: a 21st Century Portrait ★★★★ PG
Sports documentary
2006 • Fr/Ice • Colour • 91min

This audacious documentary tracks footballer Zinédine Zidane for the duration of a 2005 game between Real Madrid and Villareal. Technically, the film draws attention to itself far too often, with its tricksy shifts between camera angles (courtesy of *Se7en* cinematographer Darius Khondji) and distances. But, as a study in sporting concentration, it's as compelling as it is impressive. Particularly striking is the unswerving intensity that seems to isolate Zidane from his team-mates, as he rarely calls for the ball or issues instructions throughout the match. Revealing the flaws as well as the genius, this is clearly a portrait of an artist at work. DP French, Spanish +subtitles. Some swearing. *DVD*

Zinédine Zidane • Antonio Esteva • Celia Ramirez • Alfonso Villar • Pierre Cangioni ■ *Dir* Douglas Gordon, Philippe Parreno • *Cinematographer* Darius Khondji

Ziegfeld Follies ★★★★ U
Musical
1944 • US • Colour • 104min

In this completely plotless musical, William Powell is in heaven reprising his persona in the title role of 1936's *The Great Ziegfeld* and dreaming of the kind of show he could produce in the gloriously Technicolored 1940s. This potpourri of a music fest, started in 1944 but not properly released until 1946, contains some of the most brilliant examples of MGM's finest: here's *This Heart of Mine* with the inimitable Fred Astaire and Lucille Bremer in their heart-stopping *pas de deux*; here's the witty Judy Garland mercilessly imitating Greer Garson in a devastating lavender-hued parody; and here's a rarity: Astaire and Gene Kelly stepping out with each other for the first time on screen. A real one-off to treasure. TS

Fred Astaire • Lucille Ball • Lena Horne • Judy Garland • Fanny Brice • Cyd Charisse • Kathryn Grayson • Virginia O'Brien • Gene Kelly • Esther Williams • William Powell *Florenz Ziegfeld* ■ *Dir* Vincente Minnelli, George Sidney (2), Robert Lewis (1), Charles Walters, Roy Del Ruth, Lemuel Ayres, Norman Taurog • *Scr* Peter Barry, Harry Tugend, George White, Al Lewis, Robert Alton, David Freedman, Irving Brecher

Ziegfeld Girl ★★★ U
Musical
1941 • US • Sepia • 126min

It looks lavish, it's fabulously cast, and it wears all the production hallmarks of an MGM classic, but closer inspection reveals that this high-octane melodrama is really an excuse to utilise those leftover stock shots from 1936's *The Great Ziegfeld*. But this is MGM, and the three Ziegfeld recruits couldn't be more glamorous: Hedy Lamarr and the young Lana Turner emote to the manner born, but Judy Garland steals the show. TS *DVD*

James Stewart *Gilbert Young* • Judy Garland *Susan Gallagher* • Hedy Lamarr *Sandra Kolter* • Lana Turner *Sheila Regan* • Tony Martin (1) *Frank Merton* • Jackie Cooper *Jerry Regan* • Ian Hunter *Geoffrey Collis* • Charles Winninger *Pop Gallagher* • Edward Everett Horton *Noble Sage* • Eve Arden *Patsy Dixon* ■ *Dir* Robert Z Leonard • *Scr* Marguerite Roberts, Sonya Levien, from a story by William Anthony McGuire

Ziggy Stardust and the Spiders from Mars ★★★ PG
Concert movie
1982 • UK • Colour • 85min

As the director of the Bob Dylan documentary *Don't Look Back* and the concert film *Monterey Pop*, DA Pennebaker was the ideal person to capture the Hammersmith Odeon gig that saw David Bowie bid farewell to his most famous alter ego. The sight of Bowie and his band in full glam regalia is likely to induce more chuckles than nostalgic longing, and

Pennebaker's *cinéma-vérité* style is often too intrusive. But there are some cracking songs on offer, notably the glorious *All the Young Dudes*, the Bowie-penned anthem made famous by Mott the Hoople. DP

David Bowie *David Bowie/Ziggy Stardust* ■ *Dir* DA Pennebaker

Zigzag ★★★ PG
Thriller
1970 • US • Colour • 99min

Though he usually plays the heavy, George Kennedy here has a sympathetic starring role as a dying insurance investigator who confesses to a murder he didn't commit in order to ensure a hefty payoff for his family. This intriguingly complex drama may seem far-fetched, but Kennedy makes it work by the sheer weight of his personality. Released on video as *False Witness*. TH

George Kennedy *Paul R Cameron* • Anne Jackson *Jean Cameron* • Eli Wallach *Mario Gambretti* • Steve Ihnat *Assistant District Attorney Gates* • William Marshall (2) *Morrie Bronson* • Joe Maross *Lt Max Hines* • Dana Elcar *Harold Tracey* • Walter Brooke *Adam Mercer* ■ *Dir* Richard A Colla • *Scr* John T Kelley, from a story by Robert Enders

Zina ★★★ 15
Biographical drama
1985 • UK • BW and Colour • 88min

Skipping around from Berlin to Blackpool to Lanzarote, this intellectually static but emotionally volatile drama draws an analogy between the disturbed mind of Zina (Domiziana Giordano) and the gathering forces of Nazism and communism in the 1930s. It's a connection made more relevant because she's the daughter of Leon Trotsky, arch rival to Stalin. Psychiatrist Ian McKellen sees her divided nature as a symbol of a divided Europe; fatiguing, but intriguing. TH *DVD*

Domiziana Giordano *Zina Bronstein* • Ian McKellen *Professor Kronfeld* • Philip Madoc *Trotsky* • Rom Anderson *Maria* • Micha Bergese *Molanov* • Gabrielle Dellal *Stenographer* • Paul Geoffrey *Lyova* • William Hootkins *Walter Adams* ■ *Dir* Ken McMullen • *Scr* Ken McMullen, Terry James

Zodiac ★★★★ 15
Crime drama based on a true story
2007 • US • Colour • 151min

In real life, the Zodiac Killer terrorised San Francisco in the late 1960s and early 70s, his murders supported by a correspondence with the city's newspapers. He was the inspiration for *Dirty Harry's* Scorpio Killer, yet in David Fincher's intricate drama, the focus is on the police and press investigation into the murders, as a cartoonist (Jake Gyllenhaal), a flamboyant reporter (Robert Downey Jr) and a grizzled police inspector (Mark Ruffalo) try to crack the still-unsolved case. It's over two-and-a-half hours of obsessively gritty procedure that really finds the drama in the details. And, refreshingly, Fincher allows the murders (re-created with disturbing brutality) to take second place to the toll the investigation takes on the protagonists. JR Violence, swearing *DVD*

Jake Gyllenhaal *Robert Graysmith* • Mark Ruffalo *Inspector David Toschi* • Robert Downey Jr *Paul Avery* • Anthony Edwards *Inspector William Armstrong* • Brian Cox (1) *Melvin Belli* • Charles Fleischer *Bob Vaughn* • Zach Grenier *Mel Nicolai* • Philip Baker Hall *Sherwood Morrill* • Dermot Mulroney *Captain Marty Lee* • Chloë Sevigny *Melanie* ■ *Dir* David Fincher • *Scr* James Vanderbilt, from the non-fiction books *Zodiac* and *Zodiac Unmasked: the Identity of America's Most Elusive Serial Killer* by Robert Graysmith

Zoltan... Hound of Dracula ★ 18
Horror
1977 • US • Colour • 83min

Russian soldiers discover Dracula's crypt and unwittingly resurrect the Count's undead pet dog in this barking mad horror howler. It gets even worse when the fanged fido travels to the USA and finds his master's descendant on a lakeside holiday. José Ferrer slums it as the bargain basement Van Helsing-style investigator on

the scent of zombie Zoltan, who is about as scary as Lassie! AJ *DVD*

Michael Pataki *Michael Drake/Count Dracula* • Jan Shutan *Marla Drake* • Libbie Chase *Linda Drake* • John Levin *Steve Drake* • Reggie Nalder *Veidt Smit* • José Ferrer *Inspector Branco* ■ *Dir* Albert Band • *Scr* Frank Ray Perilli, from characters by Bram Stoker

Zombie Flesh Eaters ★★★ 18
Horror
1979 • It • Colour • 87min

Voodoo causes an army of cannibal zombies to leave their tropical island paradise and head for New York in this ultra-gory rip-off of *Dawn of the Dead*, which put Italian director Lucio Fulci on the cult map. Although the movie is extremely silly (a crusty underwater zombie battling a shark) and extremely violent, with several watershed special effects, Fulci often creates a chilling atmosphere amid the hard-core splatter. Tisa Farrow (Mia's sister) had a mini career as a starlet in Italy and heads the cast here. AJ Violence, nudity. *DVD*

Tisa Farrow *Anne* • Ian McCulloch *Peter* • Richard Johnson *Dr Menard* • Al Cliver [Pier Luigi Conti] *Brian* • Auretta Gay *Susan* • Olga Karlatos *Mrs Menard* • Stefania D'Amario *Nurse* ■ *Dir* Lucio Fulci • *Scr* Elisa Briganti

Zombie High ★★ 15
Horror thriller
1987 • US • Colour • 86min

When female students are admitted to a formerly all-male prep school for the first time, they discover their new classmates are walking zombies, the results of experiments carried out by teachers who crave immortal life. The title suggests a kind of camp teen horror flick, but what you get plays more like a masculine version of *The Stepford Wives* – albeit one that's in turn tedious and unintentionally hilarious. RS

Virginia Madsen *Andrea* • Richard Cox *Philo* • James Wilder *Barry* • Sherilyn Fenn *Suzi* • Paul Feig *Emerson* • Kay E Kuter *Dean Eisner* ■ *Dir* Ron Link • *Scr* Elizabeth Passerelli, Tim Doyle, Aziz Ghazal

Zombie Holocaust ★★ 18
Horror
1979 • It • Colour • 80min

Hack director Marino Girolami's legendary Italian exploitation item is a gory mess in more ways than one. Doctor Alexandra Delli Colli and scientist Ian McCullough go to a tiny Pacific island to investigate native rites involving human sacrifice and encounter mad surgeon Donald O'Brien who is experimenting with zombie transplants to extend human life. Combining the cannibal and living dead genres for extra shock value, Girolami then briskly piles on the gratuitous carnage and extreme splatter with little time for logic. AJ Italian dubbed. *DVD*

Ian McCulloch *Dr Peter Chandler* • Sherry Buchanan *Susan Kelly* • Alexandra Delli Colli *Lori Ridgway* • Peter O'Neal *George* ■ *Dir* Frank Martin [Marino Girolami] • *Scr* Romano Scandariato, Fabrizio De Angelis

Zombie Strippers! ★★ 18
Comedy horror
2007 • US • Colour • 90min

George A Romero's living dead meet Russ Meyer's brand of soft-core cartoon titillation in a cheap, cheesy yet cheerfully trashy schlock horror. The plot involves a virus that's been developed by the US military to reanimate its fallen men so they can fight again. But when an infected soldier hides out in a Nebraska strip club, the pneumatic star attraction (a credible turn from porn icon Jenna Jameson) is turned into a super-strong man-eater. Despite the acting and make-up limitations, there's enough here to satisfy the raunchy expectations raised by that no-brainer title. AJ *DVD*

Robert Englund *Ian Essko* • Jenna Jameson *Kat* • Roxy Saint *Lillith* • Penny Drake *Sox* • Whitney Anderson *Gaia* • Jennifer Holland *Jessy* ■ *Dir/Scr* Jay Lee

Zombieland ★★★ 15
Horror comedy
2009 • US • Colour • 84min

In director Ruben Fleischer's fitfully funny and splatter-filled road movie, fearful neurotic Columbus (Jesse Eisenberg), gung-ho cowboy Tallahassee (Woody Harrelson) and two con-artist sisters (Emma Stone, Abigail Breslin) form a reluctant alliance on a post-apocalypse Earth overrun by zombies. Their blackly comic story is padded out with flashbacks while they head for the refuge of a Californian amusement park. It's slick, glossy and engaging, if nowhere near as clever as *Shaun of the Dead*. AJ Violence, swearing, nudity. *DVD* *Blu-ray*

Woody Harrelson *Tallahassee* • Jesse Eisenberg *Columbus* • Emma Stone *Wichita* • Abigail Breslin *Little Rock* • Amber Heard *406* • Bill Murray ■ *Dir* Ruben Fleischer • *Scr* Rhett Reese, Paul Wernick

La Zona ★★★ 15
Crime drama
2007 • Sp/Mex • Colour • 91min

Rodrigo Plá's compelling crime drama shows the residents of an exclusive Mexico City community meting out violent justice after three teenagers from the surrounding slums break into the "zone" and murder a female householder. After shooting dead two of the trio, the inhabitants begin an armed manhunt to catch the terrified, remaining youth (Alan Chávez). The dark tone and striking visuals complement the matter-of-fact performances, capturing the moral decay and primitive brutality beneath the community's idealised perfection. Plá's film is let down only by a rather protracted conclusion. SF Spanish +subtitles.

Daniel Giménez Cacho [Daniel Gimenez Cacho] *Daniel* • Maribel Verdú *Mariana* • Carlos Bardem *Gerardo* • Daniel Tovar *Alejandro* • Alan Chávez *Miguel* ■ *Dir* Rodrigo Plá • *Scr* Rodrigo Plá, Laura Santullo

Zoo ★★★ 18
Drama documentary
2007 • US • Colour • 72min

Documentary maker Robinson Devor here takes an artful look at a fatal incident of bestiality that occurred in America's Washington State in July 2005. A man dies from internal injuries after having sex with a stallion, leading to the investigation of a farm where a group of equine zoophiles congregate. Showing nothing untoward (save for a brief black and white clip of taped evidence), *Zoo* eases away from graphic detail, presenting the disturbing story with detached curiosity rather than prurience. In this mix of reconstruction and documentary, Devor is tactful and respectful; while not condoning what happened, he does attempt to show us how this hidden margin of humanity thinks. KK

John Paulsen *"Mr Hands"* • Russell Hodgkinson *"H"* • Richard Carmen *Brother of "Mr Hands"* ■ *Dir* Robinson Devor • *Scr* Robinson Devor, Charles Mudede • *Cinematographer* Sean Kirby

Zoo in Budapest ★★★
Romantic drama
1933 • US • BW • 85min

This must rank as one of the cinema's most romantic movies, thanks to the sublime technique of cinematographer Lee Garmes. Framed by the highly stylised zoo sets, his subtle, misty compositions enhance the natural beauty of lovely Loretta Young, creating a look unique to this over-whimsical film and making it a rare collector's item. Sadly, director Rowland V Lee fails to extract an acceptable performance from his fey leading man or convey the Hungarian atmosphere. Nevertheless, this is a real one-off. TS

Loretta Young *Eve* • Gene Raymond *Zani* • OP Heggie *Dr Grunbaum* • Wally Albright *Paul Vandor* • Paul Fix *Heine* • Murray Kinnell *Garbosh* • Ruth Warren *Katrina* • Roy Stewart (1) *Karl* ■ *Dir* Rowland V Lee • *Scr* Dan Totheroh, Louise Long, Rowland V Lee, from a story by Melville Baker, John Kirkland

Zookeeper ★★ PG
Romantic comedy
2011 • US • Colour • 97min

This patchy comedy stars Kevin James as a lovelorn zookeeper who decides he needs a better job to attract a mate. When the animals learn of it, they reveal a secret ability to talk and give him dating tips from the wild. Director Frank Coraci assembles a top-notch voice cast (Sylvester Stallone, Nick Nolte, Adam Sandler and Cher) only to come up short on gags. James is true to type as the downtrodden everyman previously seen in *Paul Blart: Mall Cop* and *Grown Ups*, but the script too often falls back on crude slapstick. **TeS** *DVD* ⬚

Kevin James *Griffin Keyes* • Rosario Dawson *Kate* • Nick Nolte *Bernie the gorilla* • Leslie Bibb *Stephanie* • Sylvester Stallone *Joe the lion* • Cher *Janet the lioness* • Adam Sandler *Donald the capuchin monkey* • Jon Favreau *Jerome the grizzly bear* ■ *Dir* Frank Coraci • *Scr* Nick Bakay, Rock Reuben, Kevin James, Jay Scherick, David Ronn, from a story by Scherick, Ronn

Zoolander ★★★★ 12

Satirical comedy
2001 · US/Ger/Aus · Colour · 85min

Director/star Ben Stiller's rapier-sharp satire on the fashion industry balances hipness and endearing stupidity with expert precision. Stiller is the king of the male-modelling world thanks to the "blue steel" stare that's been the key to his cover-boy fortune. However, when the hilariously self-absorbed oaf loses his title to new boy Owen Wilson and decides to retire, furtive fashion mogul Will Ferrell comes to his rescue but only to brainwash the foolish fop into assassinating the Prime Minister of Malaysia. Brilliantly conceived and executed, this mercilessly exposes the shallow and bitchy world of haute couture, and is loaded with fun cameos. A sequel is due in 2016. **AJ** *DVD* ⬚

Ben Stiller *Derek Zoolander* • Owen Wilson *Hansel* • Will Ferrell *Mugatu* • Christine Taylor *Matilda Jeffries* • Milla Jovovich *Katinka* • Jerry Stiller *Maury Ballstein* • Jon Voight *Larry Zoolander* • David Duchovny *JP Prewitt* • Anne Meara *Protestor* ■ *Dir* Ben Stiller • *Scr* Drake Sather, Ben Stiller, John Hamburg, from a story by Sather, Stiller

Zoolander 2 ★★ 12A

Comedy 2016 · US · Colour · 101min

Killing Justin Bieber in the first scene may ingratiate movie-goers old enough to remember the first *Zoolander*, but sadly, the rest of this sequel will also have fans of the 2001 film mourning the ruin of Ben Stiller's original poufy-haired poseur. Fifteen years on, he again directs himself as catwalk superstar Derek Zoolander and is joined by his old partner in fashion crime, Hansel (Owen Wilson), in a hopelessly muddled plot about the investigation surrounding Bieber's murder. Will Ferrell's manic energy is a late but welcome shot in the arm when the action starts to sag, but he's awkwardly shoehorned into the story. **SP** Swearing, some violence

Ben Stiller *Derek Zoolander* • Owen Wilson *Hansel* • Will Ferrell *Mugatu* • Christine Taylor *Matilda Jeffries* • Penélope Cruz *Valentina* • Kristen Wiig *Alexanya Atoz* ■ *Dir* Ben Stiller • *Scr* Justin Theroux, Ben Stiller, Nicholas Stoller, John Hamburg, from a character by Drake Sather, Ben Stiller

Zoom ★ PG

Comedy adventure 2006 · US · Colour · 84min

Imagine a mix of *Sky High* and *The Incredibles* with all the fun, laughs and clever adventure taken out and you've got director Peter Hewitt's atrocious comic-book fiasco. Washed-up superhero Tim Allen is coerced into half-heartedly training Team Phoenix – four "gifted" youngsters – for battle. What the former Captain Zoom doesn't know is the villain about to re-visit Earth is his long-lost brother turned evil by experimental government gamma rays. All of this is mirthless to a mind-numbing degree with the focus on juvenile fart, snot and burp gags. The acting is also terrible, and even the poor special effects-driven action is lame. **AJ** *DVD*

Tim Allen *Jack Shepard/Captain Zoom* • Courteney Cox *Marsha Holloway* • Chevy Chase *Dr Grant* • Spencer Breslin *Tucker Williams/Mega-Boy* • Kevin Zegers *Connor Shepard/Concussion* • Kate Mara *Summer Jones/Wonder* • Michael

Cassidy *Dylan West/Houdini* • Rip Torn *General Larraby* ■ *Dir* Peter Hewitt • *Scr* Adam Rifkin, David Berenbaum, from a story by Rifkin, from the novel *Zoom's Academy for the Super Gifted* by Jason Lethcoe

Zoot Suit ★★ 15

Musical drama 1981 · US · Colour · 99min

Luis Valdez directed this film adaptation of his hit stage musical, which is loosely based on the 1940s Sleepy Lagoon murder trial that unfairly convicted several Mexican-American zoot suit gang members. Except for the spirited musical numbers and an arresting performance by Edward James Olmos, the movie largely fails to bring the impact it had on stage. **KB** Swearing, violence. *DVD*

Daniel Valdez *Henry Reyna* • Edward James Olmos *El Pachuco* • Charles Aidman *George* • Tyne Daly *Alice* • John Anderson *Judge* • Abel Franco *Enrique* • Mike Gomez *Joey* ■ *Dir* Luis Valdez • *Scr* Luis Valdez, from his stage musical

Zootropolis ★★★★★ PG

Animated comedy 2016 · US · Colour · 104min

All the best family movies can be unpeeled, layer after onion layer, to reveal complex ideas within. This, the latest film in a run of unusually high quality from Disney, is no exception. Ostensibly a comedy set in a world of talking animals that coexist in harmony, this perceptive and elegantly structured film is also a commentary on cultural sensitivity and political correctness. When a spate of missing animal cases hits the city, their first ever bunny police officer (Ginnifer Goodwin) is forced to team up with her natural enemy, a wily fox (Jason Bateman). The animation is packed with deft sight gags, but the real vitality is in the smart and funny writing. **WI** *DVD* ⬚ ⬚

Ginnifer Goodwin *Judy Hopps* • Jason Bateman *Nick Wilde* • Idris Elba *Chief Bogo* • JK Simmons *Mayor Lionheart* • Tommy Chong *Yax* ■ *Dir* Byron Howard, Rich Moore, Jared Bush • *Scr* Jared Bush, Phil Johnston, from a story by Byron Howard, Rich Moore, Josie Trinidad, Jim Reardon, Jennifer Lee (3), Bush, Johnston

Zorba the Greek ★★★★ PG

Drama 1964 · US/Gr · BW · 135min

This is a marvellously emotive and perfectly cast film version of the novel about the salt-of-the-earth peasant who teaches an uptight Englishman the secret of life. As Zorba, Anthony Quinn plays the part of a lifetime, so much so that the role greatly impinged on the actor both in real life and in all his movies ever since. Also adding to the film's unusual grace are wonderful Oscar-winning black-and-white photography by Walter Lassally, a haunting Mikis Theodorakis score and a glowingly warm portrayal (also Oscar-rewarded) by Lila Kedrova as an aged prostitute. It's a shade too long for its own good, though. **TS** *DVD*

Anthony Quinn *Alexis Zorba* • Alan Bates *Basil* • Irene Papas *Widow* • Lila Kedrova *Madame Hortense* • George Foundas *Mavrandoni* • Eleni Anousaki *Lola* • Sotiris Moustakas *Mimithos* • Takis Emmanuel *Manolakas* ■ *Dir* Michael Cacoyannis • *Scr* Michael Cacoyannis, from the novel by Nikos Kazantzakis

Zorro ★★

Action adventure 1975 · Fr/It · Colour · 120min

Dashing French star Alain Delon takes on the black cape and rapier of the legendary swordsman, although the province governed by Spanish hardman Stanley Baker is more banana republic than old California. Unfortunately, that isn't the only liberty taken with Johnston McCulley's immortal man in black. Pitched as a children's film, it's probably a bit too long and might well test youthful patience. **AT** French, Italian dubbed.

Alain Delon *Diego/Zorro* • Stanley Baker *Colonel Huerta* • Ottavia Piccolo *Hortensia* • Giampiero Albertini *Brother Francisco* ■ *Dir* Duccio Tessari • *Scr* Giorgio Alorio, from characters by Johnston McCulley

Zorro, the Gay Blade ★ PG

Swashbuckling spoof 1981 · US · Colour · 89min

George Hamilton hams it up shamelessly playing the legendary Zorro's twin sons – one a dashing, macho swordfighter, the other a limp-wristed queen – in a witless swashbuckling parody. When villainous Ron Liebman threatens the peace of a Mexican village, both brothers swish into action and the cheap laughs come thin and slow. **AJ**

George Hamilton *Don Diego Vega/Bunny Wigglesworth* • Lauren Hutton *Charlotte Taylor Wilson* • Brenda Vaccaro *Florinda* • Ron Liebman *Esteban* • Donovan Scott *Paco* • James Booth *Velasquez* • Helen Burns *Consuela* • Clive Revill *Garcia* ■ *Dir* Peter Medak • *Scr* Hal Dresner

Zu Warriors ★★★★ PG

Fantasy 1983 · HK · Colour · 93min

In the distant past all humanity is at war with itself. Evil beings from the netherworld see their opportunity to take over the Earth while its inhabitants are divided. A young warrior hiding out on a magical mountain embarks on a quest through a mythological realm to find the two swords that, when brought together, form the only weapon powerful enough to repel the evil hordes. A truly mind-blowing action fantasy with director Tsui Hark creating a state-of-the-art adventure. **DF** Cantonese +subtitles. Some violence. *DVD*

Adam Cheng *Ting Ying* • Chung Yan Lau *Spellbinder* • Yuen Biao *Ti Ming-chi (virgin boy)* • Meng Hai *I-chen* • Brigitte Lin *Ice Countess* • Tsui Siu Keung *Heaven's Blade* • Judy Ongg *Lil-chi* • Samo Hung *[Sammo Hung] Long Brows* ■ *Dir* Tsui Hark • *Scr* Hong Sze To Chuck

Zubeidaa ★★★ PG

Biographical romantic drama 2000 · Ind · Colour · 143min

Zubeidaa was already a popular silent icon before she headlined the subcontinent's earliest talkie, *Alam Ara*. That 1931 melodrama co-starred Prithviraj Kapoor, whose great-granddaughter, Karishma Kapoor, takes the title role in this *Citizen Kane*-like study of the actress's turbulent private life. Whether resisting the dictates of her bullying father (Amrish Puri), enduring a loveless marriage or competing for the affections of a maharajah (Manoj Bajpai), Karishma effectively balances glamour with realism, although she's outshone by Rekha as Bajpai's first wife. **DP** Hindi, Urdu +subtitles. *DVD*

Karishma Kapoor *Zubeidaa* • Rekha *Mandira* • Manoj Bajpai *Maharaja Vijayendra Singh* • Amrish Puri *Suleman Seth* • Rajit Kapoor *Riyaz* ■ *Dir* Shyam Benegal • *Scr* Khalid Mohamed

Zulu ★★★★★ PG

Historical war drama 1963 · UK · Colour · 138min

This superb re-creation of the 1879 battle of Rorke's Drift is a personal triumph for producer/director Cy Endfield and Welsh producer/star Stanley Baker. Baker heads a remarkable cast, including Michael Caine in a star-making performance playing against type as a toffee-nosed lieutenant. Technically the movie is a revelation, with stunning Technirama photography, brilliant picture editing and a wonderfully evocative soundtrack – who could ever forget the approaching sound of the 4,000 Zulu warriors before we see them, while Richard Burton's narration is genuinely moving. **TS** *DVD*

Stanley Baker *Lieutenant John Chard, RE* • Michael Caine *Lieutenant Gonville Bromhead* • Jack Hawkins *Reverend Otto Witt* • Ulla Jacobsson *Margareta Witt* • James Booth *Private Henry Hook* • Nigel Green *Colour-Sergeant Bourne* • Ivor Emmanuel *Private Owen* • Paul Daneman *Sergeant Maxfield* • Glynn Edwards *Corporal Allen* • Neil McCarthy *Private Thomas* • David Kernan *Private Hitch* ■ *Dir* Cy Endfield • *Scr* John Prebble, Cy Endfield, from an article by Prebble • *Cinematographer* Stephen Dade • *Editor* John Jympson • *Music* John Barry (1)

Zulu ★★ 18

Crime drama 2013 · Fr · Colour · 102min

Orlando Bloom delivers what is arguably his best performance to date in this violent yet

largely underwhelming crime thriller. The setting is South Africa, where the Serious Violent Crime Unit is called in to investigate the grisly murder of a young white girl. After a toxic narcotic is found in her system, two detectives (Bloom, Forest Whitaker) follow the trail to a dangerous and heavily armed gang who are involved with the production of an experimental drug. The gritty thrills that ensue are punctuated by generous helpings of intense violence and gratuitous nudity, yet the film (which is adapted from Caryl Ferey's novel) generates little drama or excitement along the way. **SC** In English, Afrikaans. Violence, nudity. *DVD*

Orlando Bloom *Brian Epkeen* • Forest Whitaker *Ali Sokhela* • Tanya van Graan *Tara* • Natasha Loring *Marjorie* ■ *Dir* Jérôme Salle • *Scr* Jérôme Salle, Julien Rappeneau, from Caryl Ferey's novel

Zulu Dawn ★★ PG

Historical drama 1979 · UK · Colour · 112min

Zulu plonked us down in the heat of battle and didn't have the time to tell us why Britain and the Zulus were arguing so violently. But because the 1963 epic was such a big hit, star Stanley Baker and writer/director Cy Endfield conceived this prequel, although by the time it came out in 1979 Baker had died and Endfield was sidelined. There's spectacle in abundance here but little of the characterisation that made *Zulu* so memorable. **AT**

Burt Lancaster *Colonel Anthony Durnford* • Peter O'Toole *Lord Chelmsford* • Simon Ward *William Vereker* • John Mills *Sir Henry Bartle Frere* • Nigel Davenport *Colonel Hamilton-Brown* • Denholm Elliott *Lt Col Pulleine* • Freddie Jones *Bishop Colenso* • Bob Hoskins *Sgt Major Williams* ■ *Dir* Douglas Hickox • *Scr* Cy Endfield, Anthony Storey, from a story by Endfield

Directors

A

Aaron, Paul (1943-) *A Force of One* 1979; *Maxie* 1985

Abashidze, Dodo (1924-1990) *The Legend of the Suram Fortress* 1984; *Ashik Kerib* 1988

Abbas *Baazigar* 1993; *Aitraaz* 2004

Abbott, George (1887-1995) *Manslaughter* 1930; *My Sin* 1931; *Too Many Girls* 1940; *The Pajama Game* 1957; *Damn Yankees* 1958

Abel, Dominique *Rumba* 2008; *The Fairy* 2011

Abel, Robert (1937-2001) *Elvis on Tour* 1972; *Let the Good Times Roll* 1973

Abraham, Marc *Flash of Genius* 2008; *I Saw the Light* 2015

Abrahams, Jim (1944-) *Airplane!* 1980; *Top Secret!* 1984; *Ruthless People* 1986; *Big Business* 1988; *Welcome Home, Roxy Carmichael* 1990; *Hot Shots!* 1991; *Hot Shots! Part Deux* 1993; *First Do No Harm* 1997; *Jane Austen's Mafia* 1998

Abrahamson, Lenny aka **Abrahamson, Leonard** (1966-) *Adam & Paul* 2004; *Garage* 2007; *What Richard Did* 2012; *Frank* 2013; *Room* 2015

Abrams, J J (1966-) *Mission: Impossible III* 2006; *Star Trek* 2009; *Super 8* 2011; *Star Trek into Darkness* 2013; *Star Wars Episode VII: the Force Awakens* 2015

Abu-Assad, Hany *Paradise Now* 2005; *Omar* 2013

Ackerman, Robert Allan (1944-) *David's Mother* 1994; *Safe Passage* 1994; *Double Platinum* 1999; *Forget Me Never* 1999

Adams, Jamie *Benny & Jolene* 2014; *Black Mountain Poets* 2015

Adams, Marcus *Long Time Dead* 2001; *Octane* 2003

Adamson, Al (1929-1995) *Blood of Dracula's Castle* 1967; *The Female Bunch* 1969; *Dracula vs Frankenstein* 1970

Adamson, Andrew (1966-) *Shrek* 2001; *Shrek 2* 2004; *The Chronicles of Narnia: The Lion, the Witch and the Wardrobe* 2005; *The Chronicles of Narnia: Prince Caspian* 2008; *Cirque du Soleil: Worlds Away* 2012

Adler, Lou *Cheech & Chong's Up in Smoke* 1978; *Ladies and Gentlemen, the Fabulous Stains* 1981

Adlon, Percy (1935-) *Sugarbaby* 1985; *Bagdad Café* 1987; *Rosalie Goes Shopping* 1989; *Salmonberries* 1991; *Younger and Younger* 1993

Adolfi, John G (1888-1933) *The Show of Shows* 1929; *The Man Who Played God* 1932; *A Successful Calamity* 1932

Advani, Nikhil *Kal Ho Naa Ho* 2003; *Salaam E Ishq* 2007

Affleck, Ben (1972-) *Gone Baby Gone* 2007; *The Town* 2010; *Argo* 2012; *Live by Night* 2016

Agresti, Alejandro (1961-) *Secret Wedding* 1989; *Wind with the Gone* 1998; *Valentín* 2002; *The Lake House* 2006

Aja, Alexandre (1978-) *Switchblade Romance* 2003; *The Hills Have Eyes* 2006; *Mirrors* 2008; *Piranha* 2010; *Horns* 2013

Akerlund, Jonas *Spun* 2002; *Horsemen* 2009; *Small Apartments* 2012

Akerman, Chantal (1950-2015) *Je, Tu, Il, Elle* 1974; *Jeanne Dielman, 23 Quai du Commerce, 1080 Bruxelles* 1975; *Les Rendez-vous d'Anna* 1978; *Golden Eighties* 1986; *Night and Day* 1991; *The Captive* 2000; *No Home Movie* 2015

Akin, Fatih *Head-On* 2007; *The Edge of Heaven* 2007; *New York, I Love You* 2009; *The Cut* 2014

Akomfrah, John (1957-) *Testament* 1988; *The Nine Muses* 2010

Alda, Alan (1936-) *The Four Seasons* 1981; *Sweet Liberty* 1986; *A New Life* 1988; *Betsy's Wedding* 1990

Aldrich, Robert (1918-1983) *Big Leaguer* 1953; *World for Ransom* 1953; *Apache* 1954; *Vera Cruz* 1954; *The Big Knife* 1955; *Kiss Me Deadly* 1955; *Attack!* 1956; *Autumn Leaves* 1956; *The Angry Hills* 1959; *Ten Seconds to Hell* 1959; *The Last Sunset* 1961; *Sodom and Gomorrah* 1962; *What Ever Happened to Baby Jane?* 1962; *4 for Texas* 1963; *Hush, Hush, Sweet Charlotte* 1964; *The Flight of the Phoenix* 1965; *The Dirty Dozen* 1967; *The Killing of Sister George* 1968; *The Legend of Lylah Clare* 1968; *Too Late the Hero* 1970;

The Grissom Gang 1971; *Ulzana's Raid* 1972; *Emperor of the North* 1973; *The Mean Machine* 1974; *Hustle* 1975; *The Choirboys* 1977; *Twilight's Last Gleaming* 1977; *The Frisco Kid* 1979; *The California Dolls* 1981

Alea, Tomás Gutiérrez (1928-1996) *Death of a Bureaucrat* 1966; *Memories of Underdevelopment* 1968; *The Last Supper* 1976; *Strawberry and Chocolate* 1993; *Guantanamera* 1995

Aleksandrov, Grigori V (1903-1984) *October* 1928; *The General Line* 1929

Alexander, Lexi *Green Street* 2004; *Punisher: War Zone* 2008

Alfredson, Daniel *The Girl Who Played with Fire* 2009; *The Girl Who Kicked the Hornet's Nest* 2009; *Go with Me* 2015; *Kidnapping Freddy Heineken* 2015

Alfredson, Tomas *Let the Right One In* 2008; *Tinker Tailor Soldier Spy* 2011

Algar, James (1912-1998) *Fantasia* 1940; *Victory through Air Power* 1943; *The Adventures of Ichabod and Mr Toad* 1949; *The Living Desert* 1953; *Jungle Cat* 1959; *Fantasia 2000* 1999

Algrant, Daniel aka **Algrant, Dan** *Naked in New York* 1994; *People I Know* 2002

Allégret, Marc (1900-1973) *Fanny* 1932; *Blanche Fury* 1948; *The Loves of Three Queens* 1954

Allégret, Yves (1905-1987) *The Seven Deadly Sins* 1952; *The Proud Ones* 1953

Allen, Elizabeth (1929-2006) *Aquamarine* 2006; *Ramona and Beezus* 2010

Allen, Irwin (1916-1991) *The Story of Mankind* 1957; *The Lost World* 1960; *Voyage to the Bottom of the Sea* 1961; *Five Weeks in a Balloon* 1962; *City beneath the Sea* 1971; *The Towering Inferno* 1974; *The Swarm* 1978; *Beyond the Poseidon Adventure* 1979

Allen, Kevin (1962-) *Twin Town* 1997; *The Big Tease* 1999; *Agent Cody Banks 2: Destination London* 2003; *Under Milk Wood* 2015

Allen, Lewis (1905-2000) *The Uninvited* 1944; *Those Endearing Young Charms* 1945; *The Unseen* 1945; *Desert Fury* 1947; *The Imperfect Lady* 1947; *Appointment with Danger* 1950; *Sons of the Musketeers* 1951; *Valentino* 1951; *Suddenly* 1954; *A Bullet for Joey* 1955; *Illegal* 1955; *Another Time, Another Place* 1958

Allen, Woody (1935-) *Take the Money and Run* 1969; *Bananas* 1971; *Everything You Always Wanted to Know about Sex ... but Were Afraid to Ask* 1972; *Sleeper* 1973; *Love and Death* 1975; *Annie Hall* 1977; *Interiors* 1978; *Manhattan* 1979; *Stardust Memories* 1980; *A Midsummer Night's Sex Comedy* 1982; *Zelig* 1983; *Broadway Danny Rose* 1984; *The Purple Rose of Cairo* 1985; *Hannah and Her Sisters* 1986; *Radio Days* 1987; *September* 1987; *Another Woman* 1988; *Crimes and Misdemeanors* 1989; *New York Stories* 1989; *Alice* 1990; *Shadows and Fog* 1991; *Husbands and Wives* 1992; *Manhattan Murder Mystery* 1993; *Bullets over Broadway* 1994; *Don't Drink the Water* 1994; *Mighty Aphrodite* 1995; *Everyone Says I Love You* 1996; *Deconstructing Harry* 1997; *Celebrity* 1998; *Sweet and Lowdown* 1999; *Small Time Crooks* 2000; *The Curse of the Jade Scorpion* 2001; *Hollywood Ending* 2002; *Anything Else* 2003; *Melinda and Melinda* 2004; *Match Point* 2005; *Scoop* 2006; *Cassandra's Dream* 2007; *Vicky Cristina Barcelona* 2008; *Whatever Works* 2009; *You Will Meet a Tall Dark Stranger* 2010; *Midnight in Paris* 2011; *To Rome with Love* 2012; *Blue Jasmine* 2013; *Magic in the Moonlight* 2014; *Irrational Man* 2015; *Café Society* 2016

Allers, Roger *The Lion King* 1994; *Open Season* 2006

Almereyda, Michael (1960-) *Nadja* 1995; *The Eternal* 1998; *Hamlet* 2000; *Cymbeline* 2014; *Experimenter: the Stanley Milgram Story* 2014

Almodóvar, Pedro (1951-) *Pepi, Luci, Bom...* 1980; *Labyrinth of Passion* 1982; *Dark Habits* 1983; *What Have I Done to Deserve This?* 1984; *Matador* 1986; *The Law of Desire* 1987; *Women on the Verge of*

a Nervous Breakdown 1988; *Tie Me Up! Tie Me Down!* 1990; *High Heels* 1991; *Kika* 1993; *The Flower of My Secret* 1995; *Live Flesh* 1997; *All about My Mother* 1999; *Talk to Her* 2001; *Bad Education* 2004; *Volver* 2006; *Broken Embraces* 2009; *The Skin I Live In* 2011; *I'm So Excited* 2013; *Julieta* 2016

Altman, Robert (1925-2006) *The Delinquents* 1957; *The James Dean Story* 1957; *Countdown* 1967; *Nightmare in Chicago* 1968; *MASH* 1969; *That Cold Day in the Park* 1969; *Brewster McCloud* 1970; *McCabe and Mrs Miller* 1971; *Images* 1972; *The Long Goodbye* 1973; *California Split* 1974; *Thieves like Us* 1974; *Nashville* 1975; *Buffalo Bill and the Indians, or Sitting Bull's History Lesson* 1976; *3 Women* 1977; *A Wedding* 1978; *A Perfect Couple* 1979; *Quintet* 1979; *HEALTH* 1980; *Popeye* 1980; *Come Back to the Five and Dime, Jimmy Dean, Jimmy Dean* 1982; *Streamers* 1983; *Secret Honor* 1984; *Fool for Love* 1985; *Aria* 1987; *Beyond Therapy* 1987; *OC and Stiggs* 1987; *The Caine Mutiny Court-Martial* 1988; *Vincent and Theo* 1990; *The Player* 1992; *Short Cuts* 1993; *Pret-a-Porter* 1994; *Kansas City* 1995; *Robert Altman's Jazz '34: Remembrances of Kansas City Swing* 1996; *The Gingerbread Man* 1997; *Cookie's Fortune* 1999; *Dr T & the Women* 2000; *Gosford Park* 2001; *The Company* 2003; *A Prairie Home Companion* 2006

Alvarez, Kyle Patrick *Easier with Practice* 2009; *The Stanford Prison Experiment* 2015

Alvart, Christian *Antibodies* 2005; *Case 39* 2008; *Pandorum* 2009

Amateau, Rod (1923-2003) *Where Does It Hurt?* 1971; *The Garbage Pail Kids Movie* 1987

Amelio, Gianni (1945-) *The Stolen Children* 1992; *The Keys to the House* 2004

Amenábar, Alejandro (1972-) *Tesis* 1996; *Open Your Eyes* 1997; *The Others* 2001; *The Sea Inside* 2004; *Agora* 2009; *Regression* 2015

Amiel, Jon (1948-) *Queen of Hearts* 1989; *Aunt Julia and the Scriptwriter* 1990; *Sommersby* 1993; *Copycat* 1995; *The Man Who Knew Too Little* 1997; *Entrapment* 1999; *The Core* 2002; *Creation* 2009

Amurri, Franco (1958-) *Flashback* 1990; *Monkey Trouble* 1994

Amyes, Julian (1917-1992) *A Hill in Korea* 1956; *Miracle in Soho* 1957

Anciano, Dominic *Final Cut* 1998; *Love, Honour and Obey* 2000

Anders, Allison (1954-) *Gas, Food, Lodging* 1992; *Mi Vida Loca* 1993; *Four Rooms* 1995; *Grace of My Heart* 1996; *Sugar Town* 1999

Anders, Sean *Sex Drive* 2008; *That's My Boy* 2012; *Horrible Bosses 2* 2014; *Daddy's Home* 2015

Anderson, Brad (1964-) *Next Stop Wonderland* 1998; *Session 9* 2001; *The Machinist* 2003; *Transsiberian* 2008; *The Call* 2013; *Stonehearst Asylum* 2014

Anderson, Jane (1954-) *If These Walls Could Talk 2* 2000; *When Billie Beat Bobby* 2001; *Normal* 2002

Anderson, Laurie (1947-) *Home of the Brave* 1986; *Heart of a Dog* 2015

Anderson, Lindsay (1923-1994) *This Sporting Life* 1963; *if...* 1968; *O Lucky Man!* 1973; *In Celebration* 1974; *Britannia Hospital* 1982; *The Whales of August* 1987

Anderson, Michael (1920-) *Waterfront* 1950; *Night Was Our Friend* 1951; *Will Any Gentleman...?* 1953; *The Dam Busters* 1954; *1984* 1955; *Around the World in 80 Days* 1956; *Yangtse Incident* 1956; *Chase a Crooked Shadow* 1957; *Shake Hands with the Devil* 1959; *The Wreck of the Mary Deare* 1959; *All the Fine Young Cannibals* 1960; *The Naked Edge* 1961; *Flight from Ashiya* 1963; *Wild and Wonderful* 1964; *Operation Crossbow* 1965; *The Quiller Memorandum* 1966; *The Shoes of the Fisherman* 1968; *Pope Joan* 1972; *Conduct Unbecoming* 1975; *Doc Savage: The Man of Bronze* 1975; *Logan's Run* 1976; *Orca... Killer Whale* 1977; *Dominique* 1978; *Murder by Phone* 1982; *Millennium* 1989; *The Sea Wolf* 1993; *20,000 Leagues under the Sea* 1997; *The New Adventures of Pinocchio* 1999

Anderson (1), Paul aka **Anderson, Paul W S** (1965-) *Shopping* 1993; *Mortal Kombat* 1995; *Event Horizon* 1997; *Soldier* 1998; *Resident Evil*

2002; AVP: Alien vs Predator 2004; *Death Race* 2008; *Resident Evil: Afterlife* 2010; *The Three Musketeers* 2011; *Resident Evil: Retribution* 2012; *Pompeii* 2014; *Resident Evil: the Final Chapter* 2017

Anderson, Paul Thomas (1970-) *Hard Eight* 1996; *Boogie Nights* 1997; *Magnolia* 1999; *Punch-Drunk Love* 2002; *There Will Be Blood* 2007; *The Master* 2012; *Inherent Vice* 2014

Anderson (1), Steve aka **Anderson, Stephen M** aka **Anderson, Stephen Milburn** *South Central* 1992; *Dead Men Can't Dance* 1997; *Ca$h!* 2010

Anderson, Wes (1969-) *Bottle Rocket* 1996; *Rushmore* 1998; *The Royal Tenenbaums* 2001; *The Life Aquatic with Steve Zissou* 2004; *The Darjeeling Limited* 2007; *Fantastic Mr Fox* 2009; *Moonrise Kingdom* 2012; *The Grand Budapest Hotel* 2014

Andersson, Roy (1943-) *Songs from the Second Floor* 2000; *You, the Living* 2007; *A Pigeon Sat on a Branch Reflecting on Existence* 2014

Andrea, Jean-Baptiste *Dead End* 2003; *Big Nothing* 2006

Angelo, Robert *Forbidden Sins* 1998; *Dead Sexy* 2001

Angelopoulos, Theo aka **Angelopoulos, Theodoros** (1935-2012) *The Travelling Players* 1975; *Voyage to Cythera* 1984; *The Bee Keeper* 1986; *Landscape in the Mist* 1988; *Ulysses' Gaze* 1995; *Eternity and a Day* 1998; *Trilogy: the Weeping Meadow* 2004

Anger, Kenneth (1927-) *Fireworks* 1947; *Eaux d'Artifice* 1953; *Inauguration of the Pleasure Dome* 1954; *Scorpio Rising* 1963; *Invocation of My Demon Brother* 1969; *Lucifer Rising* 1981

Annakin, Ken (1914-2009) *Holiday Camp* 1947; *Miranda* 1947; *Broken Journey* 1948; *Here Come the Huggetts* 1948; *Quartet* 1948; *Vote for Huggett* 1948; *The Huggetts Abroad* 1949; *Landfall* 1949; *Trio* 1950; *Hotel Sahara* 1951; *The Planter's Wife* 1952; *The Story of Robin Hood and His Merrie Men* 1952; *The Sword and the Rose* 1952; *The Seekers* 1954; *You Know What Sailors Are* 1954; *Value for Money* 1955; *Loser Takes All* 1956; *Three Men in a Boat* 1956; *Across the Bridge* 1957; *Nor the Moon by Night* 1958; *Swiss Family Robinson* 1960; *Very Important Person* 1961; *Crooks Anonymous* 1962; *The Longest Day* 1962; *The Fast Lady* 1963; *The Informers* 1963; *Battle of the Bulge* 1965; *Those Magnificent Men in Their Flying Machines* 1965; *The Long Duel* 1967; *The Biggest Bundle of Them All* 1968; *Monte Carlo or Bust!* 1969; *Call of the Wild* 1972; *Paper Tiger* 1974; *The 5th Musketeer* 1979; *The New Adventures of Pippi Longstocking* 1988

Annaud, Jean-Jacques (1943-) *Black and White in Color* 1976; *Quest for Fire* 1981; *The Name of the Rose* 1986; *The Bear* 1988; *The Lover* 1992; *Seven Years in Tibet* 1997; *Enemy at the Gates* 2004; *Two Brothers* 2004; *Black Gold* 2011

Anspaugh, David (1946-) *Hoosiers* 1986; *Fresh Horses* 1988; *Rudy* 1993; *Moonlight and Valentino* 1995; *Swing Vote* 1999; *Wisegirls* 2001

Antal, Nimród (1973-) *Kontroll* 2003; *Vacancy* 2007; *Armored* 2009; *Predators* 2010; *Metallica: Through the Never* 2013

Anthony, Joseph (1912-1993) *The Rainmaker* 1956; *The Matchmaker* 1958; *Career* 1959; *All in a Night's Work* 1960; *Captive City* 1962; *Tomorrow* 1972

Antonio, Lou (1934-) *Something for Joey* 1977; *The Gypsy Warriors* 1978; *Between Friends* 1983; *Thirteen at Dinner* 1985

Antonioni, Michelangelo (1912-2007) *Chronicle of a Love* 1950; *Love in the City* 1953; *La Signora senza Camelie* 1953; *The Vanquished* 1953; *Le Amiche* 1955; *Il Grido* 1957; *L'Avventura* 1960; *La Notte* 1961; *The Eclipse* 1962; *Red Desert* 1964; *Blowup* 1966; *Zabriskie Point* 1970; *The Passenger* 1975; *The Oberwald Mystery* 1980; *Identification of a Woman* 1982; *Beyond the Clouds* 1995; *Eros* 2004

Apatow, Judd (1967-) *The 40 Year Old Virgin* 2005; *Knocked Up* 2007; *Funny People* 2009; *This Is 40* 2012; *Trainwreck* 2015

Apted, Michael (1941-) *The Triple Echo* 1972; *Stardust* 1974; *The*

Squeeze 1977; *Agatha* 1978; *Coal Miner's Daughter* 1980; *Continental Divide* 1981; *P'Tang, Yang, Kipperbang* 1982; *Gorky Park* 1983; *Firstborn* 1984; *Bring On the Night* 1985; *Critical Condition* 1987; *Gorillas in the Mist* 1988; *Class Action* 1991; *Thunderheart* 1992; *Blink* 1994; *Nell* 1994; *Extreme Measures* 1996; *The World Is Not Enough* 1999; *Me & Isaac Newton* 2000; *Enigma* 2001; *Enough* 2002; *Amazing Grace* 2006; *The 2006 FIFA World Cup Film: the Grand Finale* 2006; *The Chronicles of Narnia: The Voyage of the Dawn Treader* 2010; *Chasing Mavericks* 2012

Araki, Gregg (1959-) *The Living End* 1992; *Totally F***ed Up* 1993; *Doom Generation* 1995; *Nowhere* 1997; *Splendor* 1999; *Mysterious Skin* 2004; *Kaboom* 2010; *White Bird in a Blizzard* 2014

Aranda, Vicente (1926-2015) *Lovers* 1991; *Carmen* 2003

Arau, Alfonso (1932-) *Like Water for Chocolate* 1993; *A Walk in the Clouds* 1995; *Picking Up the Pieces* 2000; *The Magnificent Ambersons* 2001; *A Painted House* 2003

Arcady, Alexandre (1947-) *Le Grand Pardon* 1981; *Hold-Up* 1985

Arcand, Denys (1941-) *The Decline of the American Empire* 1986; *Jesus of Montreal* 1989; *Love and Human Remains* 1993; *Stardom* 2000; *The Barbarian Invasions* 2003

Arcel, Nikolaj *King's Game* 2004; *A Royal Affair* 2012; *The Dark Tower* 2017

Archainbaud, George (1890-1959) *The Lost Squadron* 1932; *The Penguin Pool Murder* 1932; *After Tonight* 1933; *Murder on the Blackboard* 1934; *Some Like It Hot* 1939; *The Devil's Playground* 1946; *Fool's Gold* 1946; *The Dead Don't Dream* 1948; *Silent Conflict* 1948; *Blue Canadian Rockies* 1952; *On Top of Old Smoky* 1953

Archibugi, Francesca (1960-) *Mignon Has Left* 1988; *Shooting the Moon* 1998

Ardolino, Emile (1943-1993) *Dirty Dancing* 1987; *Chances Are* 1989; *Three Men and a Little Lady* 1990; *Sister Act* 1992; *George Balanchine's The Nutcracker* 1993; *Gypsy* 1993

Argento, Dario (1940-) *The Bird with the Crystal Plumage* 1969; *Cat o'Nine Tails* 1971; *Deep Red* 1975; *Suspiria* 1976; *Inferno* 1980; *Tenebrae* 1982; *Opera* 1987; *Two Evil Eyes* 1990; *Trauma* 1993; *The Stendhal Syndrome* 1996; *The Phantom of the Opera* 1998; *The Card Player* 2004

Argott, Don *Rock School* 2004; *As the Palaces Burn* 2014

Arkin, Alan (1934-) *Little Murders* 1971; *Fire Sale* 1977

Arkush, Allan (1948-) *Hollywood Boulevard* 1976; *Deathsport* 1978; *Rock 'n' Roll High School* 1979; *Heartbeeps* 1981; *Get Crazy* 1983; *Caddyshack II* 1988; *Shake, Rattle and Rock* 1994; *Prince Charming* 2001

Arliss, Leslie (1901-1987) *The Night Has Eyes* 1942; *The Man in Grey* 1943; *Love Story* 1944; *The Wicked Lady* 1945; *A Man about the House* 1947

Armfield, Neil *Candy* 2005; *Holding the Man* 2015

Armitage, George *Hit Man* 1972; *Vigilante Force* 1975; *Miami Blues* 1990; *Grosse Pointe Blank* 1997; *The Big Bounce* 2004

Armstrong, Franny *McLibel* 2005; *The Age of Stupid* 2008

Armstrong, Gillian (1950-) *My Brilliant Career* 1979; *Mrs Soffel* 1984; *High Tide* 1987; *Fires Within* 1991; *The Last Days of Chez Nous* 1992; *Little Women* 1994; *Oscar and Lucinda* 1997; *Charlotte Gray* 2001; *Death Defying Acts* 2007

Armstrong, Michael (1944-) *The Haunted House of Horror* 1969; *Mark of the Devil* 1970

Arnold, Andrea *Red Road* 2006; *Fish Tank* 2009; *Wuthering Heights* 2011; *American Honey* 2016

Arnold, Jack (1916-1992) *The Glass Web* 1953; *It Came from Outer Space* 1953; *Creature from the Black Lagoon* 1954; *The Man from Bitter Ridge* 1955; *Revenge of the Creature* 1955; *Tarantula* 1955; *Red Sundown* 1956; *The Incredible Shrinking Man* 1957; *Man in the Shadow* 1957; *The Tattered Dress* 1957; *High School Confidential* 1958; *The Lady Takes a Flyer* 1958; *The Mouse That Roared*

1959; No Name on the Bullet 1959; Bachelor in Paradise 1961; A Global Affair 1964; Hello Down There 1969; The Swiss Conspiracy 1975

Aronofsky, Darren (1969-) Pi 1997; Requiem for a Dream 2000; The Fountain 2005; The Wrestler 2008; Black Swan 2010; Noah 2014

Arteta, Miguel (1970-) Chuck & Buck 2000; The Good Girl 2001; Youth in Revolt 2009; Cedar Rapids 2011; Alexander and the Terrible, Horrible, No Good Very Bad Day 2014

Arthur, Karen (1941-) The Rape of Richard Beck 1985; Lady Beware 1987

Arzner, Dorothy (1900-1979) The Wild Party 1929; Anybody's Woman 1930; Paramount on Parade 1930; Sarah and Son 1930; Honor among Lovers 1931; Merrily We Go to Hell 1932; Christopher Strong 1933; Nana 1934; Craig's Wife 1936; The Bride Wore Red 1937; Dance, Girl, Dance 1940

Asante, Amma A Way of Life 2004; Belle 2013; A United Kingdom 2017

Asbury, Kelly Spirit: Stallion of the Cimarron 2002; Shrek 2 2004; Gnomeo & Juliet 2011

Ashby, Hal (1929-1988) The Landlord 1970; Harold and Maude 1972; The Last Detail 1973; Shampoo 1975; Bound for Glory 1976; Coming Home 1978; Being There 1979; Let's Spend the Night Together 1982; The Slugger's Wife 1985; 8 Million Ways to Die 1986

Asher, Robert (1915-1979) Follow a Star 1959; The Bulldog Breed 1960; Make Mine Mink 1960; She'll Have to Go 1961; On the Beat 1962; A Stitch in Time 1963 ; The Early Bird 1965; The Intelligence Men 1965; Press for Time 1966

Asher, William (1919-) The 27th Day 1957; Beach Party 1963; Johnny Cool 1963; Bikini Beach 1964; Muscle Beach Party 1964; Beach Blanket Bingo 1965; How to Fill a Wild Bikini 1965; Fireball 500 1966; Movers and Shakers 1985

Ashida, Toyoo Vampire Hunter D 1985; Fist of the North Star 1986

Asquith, Anthony (1902-1968) Underground 1928; A Cottage on Dartmoor 1929; Moscow Nights 1935; Pygmalion 1938; French without Tears 1939; Freedom Radio 1940; Quiet Wedding 1940; Cottage to Let 1941; Uncensored 1942; The Demi-Paradise 1943; We Dive at Dawn 1943; Fanny by Gaslight 1944; The Way to the Stars 1945; While the Sun Shines 1946; The Winslow Boy 1948; The Woman in Question 1950; The Browning Version 1951; The Importance of Being Earnest 1952; The Final Test 1953; The Net 1953; Carrington VC 1954; The Young Lovers 1954; The Doctor's Dilemma 1958; Orders to Kill 1958; Libel 1959; The Millionairess 1960; Two Living, One Dead 1961; Guns of Darkness 1962; The VIPs 1963; The Yellow Rolls-Royce 1964

Assayas, Olivier (1955-) L'Eau Froide; Irma Vep 1996; Late August, Early September 1998; Les Destinées Sentimentales 2000; Demonlover 2002; Clean 2004; Paris, Je T'Aime 2006; Summer Hours 2008; Carlos 2010; Something in the Air 2012; Clouds of Sils Maria 2014

Atkins, Chris Taking Liberties 2007; Starsuckers 2009

Attal, Yvan (1965-) Ma Femme Est une Actrice 2001; New York, I Love You 2009

Attenborough, Richard (1923-2014) Oh! What a Lovely War 1969; Young Winston 1972; A Bridge Too Far 1977; Magic 1978; Gandhi 1982; A Chorus Line 1985; Cry Freedom 1987; Chaplin 1992; Shadowlands 1993; Grey Owl 1999; Closing the Ring 2006

Auburtin, Frédéric The Bridge 1999; Paris, Je T'Aime 2006

Audiard, Jacques (1952-) See How They Fall 1993; A Self-Made Hero 1995; Read My Lips 2001; The Beat That My Heart Skipped 2005; A Prophet 2009; Rust and Bone 2012; Dheepan 2015

Auer, John H (1906-1975) A Man Betrayed 1941; Music in Manhattan 1944; City That Never Sleeps 1953; Johnny Trouble 1957

August, Bille (1948-) Buster's World 1984; Pelle the Conqueror 1987; Best Intentions 1992; The House of the Spirits 1993; Jerusalem

1996; Smilla's Feeling for Snow 1996; Les Misérables 1997; Goodbye Bafana 2007; Night Train to Lisbon 2013

Auster, Paul (1947-) Blue in the Face 1995; Lulu on the Bridge 1998

Austin, Michael Killing Dad 1989; Princess Caraboo 1994

Autant-Lara, Claude (1903-2000) Devil in the Flesh 1947; The Seven Deadly Sins 1952; The Ripening Seed 1953; Le Rouge et le Noir 1954; Marguerite de la Nuit 1955; La Traversée de Paris 1956

Auteuil, Daniel (1950-) The Well Digger's Daughter 2010; Marius 2012; Fanny 2013

Avakian, Aram (1926-1987) End of the Road 1970; Cops and Robbers 1973; 11 Harrowhouse 1974

Avary, Roger (1965-) Killing Zoe 1993; The Rules of Attraction 2002

Avati, Pupi (1938-) Noi Tre 1984; The Best Man 1998

Averback, Hy (1920-1997) Chamber of Horrors 1966; I Love You, Alice B Toklas 1968; Where Were You When the Lights Went Out? 1968; The Great Bank Robbery 1969; Suppose They Gave a War and Nobody Came? 1970

Avery, Tex aka **Avery, Fred** (1908-1980) A Wild Hare 1940; King-Size Canary 1947

Avildsen, John G aka **Mulroon, Danny** (1935-) Joe 1970; Save the Tiger 1973; WW and the Dixie Dancekings 1975; Rocky 1976; Slow Dancing in the Big City 1978; The Formula 1980; Neighbors 1981; A Night in Heaven 1983; The Karate Kid 1984; The Karate Kid Part II 1986; For Keeps 1987; Happy New Year 1987; The Karate Kid III 1989; Lean on Me 1989; Rocky V 1990; The Power of One 1991; 8 Seconds 1994; Desert Heat 1999

Avnet, Jon (1949-) Fried Green Tomatoes at the Whistle Stop Cafe 1991; The War 1994; Up Close & Personal 1996; Red Corner 1997; 88 Minutes 2007; Righteous Kill 2008

Axel, Gabriel (1918-2014) Babette's Feast 1987; Prince of Jutland 1994

Ayer, David (1968-) Harsh Times 2005; Street Kings 2008; End of Watch 2012; Sabotage 2013; Fury 2014; Suicide Squad 2016; Bright 2017

Ayoade, Richard (1977-) Submarine 2010; The Double 2013

Azzopardi, Mario (1950-) Nowhere to Hide 1987; Bone Daddy 1998

B

Babbit, Jamie (1970-) But I'm a Cheerleader 1999; Addicted to Fresno 2015

Babenco, Hector (1946-2016) Pixote 1981; Kiss of the Spider Woman 1985; Ironweed 1987; At Play in the Fields of the Lord 1991; Carandiru 2003

Babluani, Gela 13 (Tzameti) 2005; Legacy 2007; 13 2010

Bacon, Lloyd (1890-1955) The Singing Fool 1928; Say It with Songs 1929; Moby Dick 1930; Kept Husbands 1931; Footlight Parade 1933; 42nd Street 1933; Picture Snatcher 1933; He Was Her Man 1934; Here Comes the Navy 1934; Wonder Bar 1934; Devil Dogs of the Air 1935; Frisco Kid 1935; In Caliente 1935; The Irish in Us 1935; Cain and Mabel 1936; Gold Diggers of 1937 1936; Marked Woman 1937; San Quentin 1937; Boy Meets Girl 1938; Racket Busters 1938; A Slight Case of Murder 1938; Invisible Stripes 1939; The Oklahoma Kid 1939; Brother Orchid 1940; Knute Rockne - All American 1940; Affectionately Yours 1941; Footsteps in the Dark 1941; Larceny, Inc 1942; Action in the North Atlantic 1943; The Fighting Sullivans 1944; Sunday Dinner for a Soldier 1944; Capt Eddie 1945; Home Sweet Homicide 1946; I Wonder Who's Kissing Her Now 1947; Give My Regards to Broadway 1948; You Were Meant for Me 1948; It Happens Every Spring 1949; Miss Grant Takes Richmond 1949; Mother Is a Freshman 1949; The Fuller Brush Girl 1950; Call Me Mister 1951; The Frogmen 1951; Golden Girl 1951; The I Don't Care Girl 1952; The Great Sioux Uprising 1953; Beautiful but Dangerous 1954; The French Line 1954

Badger, Clarence (1880-1964) Hands Up! 1926; It 1927

Badham, John (1939-) The Bingo Long Travelling All-Stars and Motor Kings 1976; Saturday Night Fever 1977; Dracula 1979; Whose Life Is It Anyway? 1981; Blue Thunder 1983; WarGames 1983; American Flyers 1985; Short Circuit 1986; Stakeout 1987; Bird on a Wire 1990; The Hard Way 1991; Another Stakeout 1993; The Assassin 1993; Drop Zone 1994; Nick of Time 1995; Incognito 1997; The Jack Bull 1999; The Last Debate 2000; Evel Knievel 2004

Bahrani, Ramin Man Push Cart 2005; Goodbye Solo 2008; At Any Price 2012; 99 Homes 2014

Bail, Chuck Cleopatra Jones and the Casino of Gold 1975; The Gumball Rally 1976; On Dangerous Ground 1986

Bailey, Fenton The Eyes of Tammy Faye 2000; Party Monster 2003; Inside Deep Throat 2005; Mapplethorpe: Look at the Pictures 2016

Bailey (2), John The Search for Signs of Intelligent Life in the Universe 1991; China Moon 1994

Bailey, Norma (1949-) Bordertown Cafe 1991; Too Late to Say Goodbye 2009; The Devil's Teardrop 2010

Baird, Jon S Cass 2008; Filth 2013

Baird, Stuart (1948-) Executive Decision 1996; US Marshals 1998; Star Trek: Nemesis 2002

Baker, Graham Omen III: the Final Conflict 1980; Impulse 1984; Alien Nation 1988

Baker, Robert S (1916-2009) Blackout 1950; Passport to Treason 1956; Jack the Ripper 1958; The Siege of Sidney Street 1960; The Treasure of Monte Cristo 1960; The Hellfire Club 1961

Baker, Roy Ward aka **Baker, Roy** (1916-2010) The October Man 1947; The Weaker Sex 1948; Highly Dangerous 1950; Morning Departure 1950; Don't Bother to Knock 1952; Inferno 1953; Passage Home 1955; Jacqueline 1956; Tiger in the Smoke 1956; The One That Got Away 1957; A Night to Remember 1958; The Singer Not the Song 1960; Flame in the Streets 1961; Two Left Feet 1963; Quatermass and the Pit 1967; The Anniversary 1968; Moon Zero Two 1969; The Scars of Dracula 1970; The Vampire Lovers 1970; Dr Jekyll & Sister Hyde 1971; Asylum 1972; And Now the Screaming Starts! 1973; The Vault of Horror 1973; The Legend of the 7 Golden Vampires 1974; The Monster Club 1980

Bakshi, Ralph (1938-) Fritz the Cat 1972; The Lord of the Rings 1978; Fire and Ice 1983; Cool World 1992

Balaban, Bob (1945-) Parents 1988; My Boyfriend's Back 1993; Subway Stories: Tales from the Underground 1997; Bernard and Doris 2006; Georgia O'Keeffe 2009

Balaban, Burt (1922-1965) Stranger from Venus 1954; Mad Dog Coll 1961; The Gentle Rain 1966

Balabanov, Alexei (1959-2013) Brother 1997; Of Freaks and Men 1998; War 2002; The Stoker 2010

Balagueró, Jaume (1968-) Darkness 2002; Fragile 2005; To Let 2006; [Rec] 2007; [Rec]² 2009; Sleep Tight 2011; [REC] 4: Apocalypse 2014

Balda, Kyle Dr Seuss' The Lorax 2012; Minions 2015; Despicable Me 3 2017

Baldi, Ferdinando (1927-2007) Texas Adios 1966; Django, Prepare a Coffin 1968; Blind Man 1971

Ball, Wes The Maze Runner 2014; Maze Runner: The Scorch Trials 2015

Ballard, Carroll (1937-) The Black Stallion 1979; Never Cry Wolf 1983; Nutcracker 1986; Wind 1992; Fly Away Home 1996; Duma 2005

Band, Albert (1924-2002) The Young Guns 1956; Zoltan... Hound of Dracula 1977; Prehysteria! 1993; Robot Wars 1993

Band, Charles (1951-) Crash! 1977; The Alchemist 1981; Parasite 1982; Trancers 1985; Trancers II: The Return of Jack Deth 1991; Prehysteria! 1993

Banks (2), Elizabeth (1974-) Movie 43 2013; Pitch Perfect 2 2015; Pitch Perfect 3 2017

Banks, Monty (1897-1950) No Limit 1935; Keep Your Seats, Please 1936; We're Going to Be Rich 1938; Shipyard Sally 1939; Great Guns 1941

Barba, Norberto (1963-) Blue Tiger 1994; Solo 1996

Barbarash, Ernie Rock the House 2011; Six Bullets 2012

Barbash, Uri Beyond the Walls 1984; One of Us 1989

Barbato, Randy The Eyes of Tammy Faye 2000; Party Monster 2003; Inside Deep Throat 2005; Mapplethorpe: Look at the Pictures 2016

Barber, Daniel Harry Brown 2009; The Keeping Room 2014

Barbera, Joseph (1911-2006) The Cat Concerto 1947; Jetsons: the Movie 1990

Barbier, Eric Le Serpent 2006; The Last Diamond 2014

Barboni, Enzo aka **Clucher, E B** (1922-) They Call Me Trinity 1970; Man of the East 1972; Renegade 1987

Bare, Richard L aka **Bare, Richard** (1913-2015) Prisoners of the Casbah 1953; Shoot-Out at Medicine Bend 1957; This Rebel Breed 1960

Barker, Clive (1952-) Hellraiser 1987; Nightbreed 1990; Lord of Illusions 1995

Barker, Mike aka **Barker, Michael** (1966-) The James Gang 1997; Best Laid Plans 1999; To Kill a King 2003; A Good Woman 2004; Butterfly on a Wheel 2007

Barker, Reginald (1886-1937) Civilization 1916; The Moonstone 1934

Barnard, Clio The Arbor 2010; The Selfish Giant 2013

Barney, Matthew (1967-) Cremaster 4 1994; Cremaster 1 1995; Cremaster 5 1997; Cremaster 2 1999; Cremaster 3 2002; Destricted 2006

Barnz, Daniel Beastly 2010; Won't Back Down 2012; Cake 2015

Barr (2), Douglas (1949-) Perfect Romance 2004; Confessions of an American Bride 2005; Taking a Chance on Love 2009

Barreto, Bruno (1955-) Gabriela 1983; A Show of Force 1990; The Heart of Justice 1992; Acts of Love 1995; Four Days in September 1997; View from the Top 2003; Reaching for the Moon 2013

Barron, Steve (1956-) Electric Dreams 1984; Teenage Mutant Ninja Turtles 1990; Coneheads 1993; The Adventures of Pinocchio 1996; Rat 2000; Mike Bassett: England Manager 2001; Choking Man 2006

Barros D'Sa, Lisa Cherrybomb 2008; Good Vibrations 2012

Barry, Ian The Chain Reaction 1980; The Christmas Wish 1998

Barrymore, Lionel (1878-1954) Madame X 1929; The Rogue Song 1930

Bartel, Paul (1938-2000) Death Race 2000 1975; Cannonball 1976; Eating Raoul 1982; Lust in the Dust 1984; Not for Publication 1984; Scenes from the Class Struggle in Beverly Hills 1989; Shelf Life 1993

Barthes, Sophie Cold Souls 2008; Madame Bovary 2014

Bartkowiak, Andrzej (1950-) Romeo Must Die 2000; Exit Wounds 2001; Cradle 2 the Grave 2003; Doom 2005

Bartlett, Hall (1922-1993) Zero Hour! 1957; All the Young Men 1960; The Caretakers 1963; Jonathan Livingston Seagull 1973; The Children of Sanchez 1978

Barton, Charles aka **Barton, Charles T** (1902-1981) The Last Outpost 1935; Hell Town 1937; Reveille with Beverly 1943; The Time of Their Lives 1946; Buck Privates Come Home 1947; Abbott and Costello Meet Frankenstein 1948; The Noose Hangs High 1948; Abbott and Costello Meet the Killer, Boris Karloff 1949; Africa Screams 1949; Double Crossbones 1951; Dance with Me Henry 1956; The Shaggy Dog 1959; Toby Tyler, or Ten Weeks with a Circus 1960

Bass, Jules (1935-) Mad Monster Party 1966; The Last Unicorn 1980

Bassett, Michael J Deathwatch 2002; Wilderness 2006; Solomon Kane 2009; Silent Hill: Revelation 2012

Bassoff, Lawrence Weekend Pass 1984; Hunk 1987

Batmanglij, Zal Sound of My Voice 2011; The East 2013

Baumbach, Noah (1969-) Mr Jealousy 1997; The Squid and the Whale 2005; Margot at the Wedding 2007; Greenberg 2009; Frances Ha 2012; While We're Young 2014; Mistress America 2015

Bava, Mario aka **Lion, Mickey** (1914-1980) The Mask of Satan 1960; Black Sabbath 1963; Blood and Black

Lace 1964; Planet of the Vampires 1965; Dr Goldfoot and the Girl Bombs 1966; Danger: Diabolik 1967; Hatchet for the Honeymoon 1969; Bay of Blood 1971; Baron Blood 1972; Lisa and the Devil 1974

Baxley, Craig R (1949-) Action Jackson 1988; Dark Angel 1989; Stone Cold 1991; Under Pressure 1997; Aces 'n' Eights 2008

Baxter, John (1896-1975) Doss House 1933; Song of the Road 1937; Crooks' Tour 1940; The Common Touch 1941; Love on the Dole 1941; We'll Smile Again 1942; Dreaming 1944; Here Comes the Sun 1945; When You Come Home 1947

Bay, Michael (1965-) Bad Boys 1995; The Rock 1996; Armageddon 1998; Pearl Harbor 2001; Bad Boys II 2003; The Island 2005; Transformers 2007; Transformers: Revenge of the Fallen 2009; Transformers: Dark of the Moon 2011; Pain & Gain 2013; Transformers: Age of Extinction 2014; 13 Hours: the Secret Soldiers of Benghazi 2016

Bayona, Juan Antonio aka **Bayona, J A** The Orphanage 2006; The Impossible 2011; A Monster Calls 2016; Jurassic World 2 2018

Beaird, David (1952-) My Chauffeur 1986; Scorchers 1991

Beattie, Stuart Tomorrow, When the War Began 2010; I, Frankenstein 2013

Beatty, Warren (1937-) Heaven Can Wait 1978; Reds 1981; Dick Tracy 1990; Bulworth 1998; Rules Don't Apply 2016

Beaudin, Jean (1939-) Being at Home with Claude 1992; Nouvelle-France 2004

Beaudine, William (1892-1970) Little Annie Rooney 1925; Sparrows 1926; Make Me a Star 1932; Three Wise Girls 1932; The Old-Fashioned Way 1934; Boys Will Be Boys 1935; Where There's a Will 1936; Windbag the Sailor 1936; Ghosts in the Night 1943; Bowery Champs 1944; Voodoo Man 1944; Come Out Fighting 1945; Kidnapped 1948; Bela Lugosi Meets a Brooklyn Gorilla 1952; Pride of the Blue Grass 1954; Ten Who Dared 1960; Lassie's Great Adventure 1963; Billy the Kid vs Dracula 1966

Beaumont, Gabrielle (1942-) The Godsend 1980; He's My Girl 1987

Beaumont, Harry (1888-1966) Our Dancing Daughters 1928; The Broadway Melody 1929; Dance, Fools, Dance 1931; Laughing Sinners 1931; Faithless 1932; When Ladies Meet 1933; Enchanted April 1935

Beck, Steve Thir13en Ghosts 2001; Ghost Ship 2002

Becker, Harold (1950-) The Ragman's Daughter 1972; The Onion Field 1979; The Black Marble 1980; Taps 1981; Vision Quest 1985; The Boost 1988; Sea of Love 1989; Malice 1993; City Hall 1996; Mercury Rising 1998; Domestic Disturbance 2001

Becker, Jacques (1906-1960) La Vie Est à Nous 1936; Casque d'Or 1952; Honour among Thieves 1954; Montparnasse 19 1958; Le Trou 1959

Becker, Jean (1938-) One Deadly Summer 1983; The Children of the Marshland 1999; Strange Gardens 2003; Conversations with My Gardener 2006; My Afternoons with Marguerite 2010

Becker, Walt (1968-) Buying the Cow 2000; Van Wilder: Party Liaison 2002; Wild Hogs 2007; Old Dogs 2009; Alvin and the Chipmunks: the Road Chip 2015

Beebe, Ford (1888-1978) Laughing at Life 1933; Fantasia 1940; The Reluctant Dragon 1941; Frontier Badmen 1943; Enter Arsene Lupin 1944; The Invisible Man's Revenge 1944; Challenge to Be Free 1972

Beeman, Greg (1962-) License to Drive 1988; Mom and Dad Save the World 1992; Bushwhacked 1995

Beineix, Jean-Jacques (1946-) Diva 1981; The Moon in the Gutter 1983; Betty Blue 1986; Roselyne and the Lions 1989; IP5 1992

Bekmambetov, Timur (1961-) Night Watch 2004; Day Watch 2006; Wanted 2008; Abraham Lincoln: Vampire Hunter 2012; Ben-Hur 2016

Bell, Martin Streetwise 1985; American Heart 1992

Bell, Monta (1891-1958) The Torrent 1926; The Worst Woman in Paris? 1933

Bell, William Brent Stay Alive 2006; The Devil Inside 2011; The Boy 2016

Bellamy, Earl (1917-2003) Stagecoach to Dancer's Rock 1962;

Fluffy 1965; *Gunpoint* 1966; *Incident at Phantom Hill* 1966; *Munster, Go Home!* 1966; *Three Guns for Texas* 1968; *Backtrack* 1969

Bellocchio, Marco (1939-) *Fists in the Pocket* 1965; *Good Morning, Night* 2003; *Vincere* 2009

Belvaux, Lucas (1961-) *[One] Cavale* 2002; *[Three] Après la Vie* 2002; *[Two] Un Couple Epatant* 2002; *Rapt* 2009

Bemberg, Maria Luisa (1922-1995) *Camila* 1984; *Miss Mary* 1986; *I, the Worst of All* 1990; *We Don't Want to Talk about It* 1993

Bendelack, Steve *The League of Gentlemen's Apocalypse* 2005; *Mr Bean's Holiday* 2007; *The Harry Hill Movie* 2013

Benedek, Laslo (1905-1992) *The Kissing Bandit* 1949; *Port of New York* 1949; *Death of a Salesman* 1951; *The Wild One* 1953; *Moment of Danger* 1960; *Namu, the Killer Whale* 1966; *The Night Visitor* 1970

Benegal, Dev (1960-) *English, August* 1994; *Split Wide Open* 1999

Benegal, Shyam (1934-) *Ankur* 1974; *Nishant* 1975; *Junoon* 1978; *Zubeidaa* 2000; *Well Done Abba* 2009

Benigni, Roberto (1952-) *Johnny Stecchino* 1991; *Life Is Beautiful* 1997; *Pinocchio* 2002

Benjamin, Richard (1938-) *My Favorite Year* 1982; *City Heat* 1984; *Racing with the Moon* 1984; *The Money Pit* 1985; *Little Nikita* 1988; *My Stepmother Is an Alien* 1988; *Downtown* 1990; *Mermaids* 1990; *Made in America* 1993; *Milk Money* 1994; *Mrs Winterbourne* 1996; *The Pentagon Wars* 1998; *Laughter on the 23rd Floor* 2000; *The Shrink Is In* 2000; *The Sports Pages* 2001; *Marci X* 2003

Bennett, Bill (1953-) *A Street to Die* 1985; *Stolen Hearts* 1996; *Tempted* 2001

Bennett, Compton (1900-1974) *The Seventh Veil* 1945; *Daybreak* 1946; *The Years Between* 1946; *The Forsyte Saga* 1949; *King Solomon's Mines* 1950; *Gift Horse* 1951; *It Started in Paradise* 1952; *Desperate Moment* 1953; *The Flying Scot* 1957; *That Woman Opposite* 1957; *Beyond the Curtain* 1960

Bennett, Sacha (1971-) *Tu£sday* 2007; *Bonded by Blood* 2010; *Outside Bet* 2011; *We Still Kill the Old Way* 2014

Bentley, Thomas (1880-1953) *Scotland Yard Mystery* 1933; *Those Were the Days* 1934; *Music Hath Charms* 1935; *The Old Curiosity Shop* 1935

Benton, Robert (1932-) *Bad Company* 1972; *The Late Show* 1977; *Kramer vs Kramer* 1979; *Still of the Night* 1982; *Places in the Heart* 1984; *Nadine* 1987; *Billy Bathgate* 1991; *Nobody's Fool* 1994; *Twilight* 1998; *The Human Stain* 2003; *Feast of Love* 2007

Bercovici, Luca (1957-) *Ghoulies* 1985; *Luck of the Draw* 2000

Beresford, Bruce (1940-) *The Adventures of Barry McKenzie* 1972; *Barry McKenzie Holds His Own* 1974; *Side by Side* 1975; *Don's Party* 1976; *The Getting of Wisdom* 1977; *Breaker Morant* 1979; *The Club* 1980; *Puberty Blues* 1981; *Tender Mercies* 1982; *The Fringe Dwellers* 1985; *King David* 1985; *Crimes of the Heart* 1986; *Aria* 1987; *Driving Miss Daisy* 1989; *Her Alibi* 1989; *Black Robe* 1991; *Mister Johnson* 1991; *A Good Man in Africa* 1993; *Silent Fall* 1994; *Last Dance* 1996; *Double Jeopardy* 1999; *Bride of the Wind* 2001; *Evelyn* 2002; *The Contract* 2006; *Peace, Love & Misunderstanding* 2011

Berg, Amy aka **Berg, Amy J** *Deliver Us from Evil* 2006; *West of Memphis* 2012; *Janis: Little Girl Blue* 2015

Berg, Peter (1964-) *Very Bad Things* 1998; *Welcome to the Jungle* 2003; *Friday Night Lights* 2004; *The Kingdom* 2007; *Hancock* 2008; *Battleship* 2012; *Lone Survivor* 2013

Bergeron, Eric "Bibo" aka **Bergeron, Bibo** *The Road to El Dorado* 2000; *Shark Tale* 2004; *A Monster in Paris* 2011

Bergman, Andrew (1945-) *So Fine* 1981; *The Freshman* 1990; *Honeymoon in Vegas* 1992; *It Could Happen to You* 1994; *Striptease* 1996; *Isn't She Great* 1999

Bergman, Ingmar (1918-2007) *Crisis* 1945; *It Rains on Our Love* 1946; *A Ship to India* 1947; *Night Is My Future* 1948; *Port of Call* 1948; *The*

Devil's Wanton 1949; *Three Strange Loves* 1949; *Summer Interlude* 1950; *To Joy* 1950; *Summer with Monika* 1952; *Waiting Women* 1952; *Sawdust and Tinsel* 1953; *Lesson in Love* 1954; *Dreams* 1955; *Smiles of a Summer Night* 1955; *The Seventh Seal* 1957; *So Close to Life* 1957; *Wild Strawberries* 1957; *The Magician* 1958; *The Devil's Eye* 1960; *The Virgin Spring* 1960; *Through a Glass Darkly* 1961; *Winter Light* 1962; *The Silence* 1963; *All These Women* 1964; *Persona* 1966; *The Hour of the Wolf* 1967; *Shame* 1968; *A Passion* 1969; *The Rite* 1969; *The Touch* 1971; *Cries and Whispers* 1972; *Scenes from a Marriage* 1973; *The Magic Flute* 1974; *Face to Face* 1976; *The Serpent's Egg* 1977; *Autumn Sonata* 1978; *From the Life of the Marionettes* 1980; *Fanny and Alexander* 1982; *After the Rehearsal* 1984; *Saraband* 2003

Berke, William aka **Berke, William A** (1903-1958) *The Falcon in Mexico* 1944; *Betrayal from the East* 1945; *Dick Tracy* 1945; *The Falcon's Adventure* 1946; *Jungle Jim* 1948

Berkeley, Busby (1895-1976) *Gold Diggers of 1935* 1935; *Stage Struck* 1936; *Hollywood Hotel* 1937; *Babes in Arms* 1939; *Fast and Furious* 1939; *They Made Me a Criminal* 1939; *Strike Up the Band* 1940; *Babes on Broadway* 1941; *For Me and My Gal* 1942; *The Gang's All Here* 1943; *Cinderella Jones* 1946; *Take Me Out to the Ball Game* 1949

Berlanti, Greg (1972-) *The Broken Hearts Club: a Romantic Comedy* 2000; *Life as We Know It* 2010

Berliner, Alain (1963-) *Ma Vie en Rose* 1997; *Passion of Mind* 2000

Berlinger, Joe (1961-) *Book of Shadows: Blair Witch 2* 2000; *Metallica: Some Kind of Monster* 2004; *Crude* 2009

Berman, Monty (1913-2006) *Jack the Ripper* 1958; *The Siege of Sidney Street* 1960; *The Treasure of Monte Cristo* 1960; *The Hellfire Club* 1961

Berman, Shari Springer (1963-) *American Splendor* 2003; *The Nanny Diaries* 2007; *Cinema Verite* 2011; *Girl Most Likely* 2012

Berman, Ted (1919-2001) *The Fox and the Hound* 1981; *The Black Cauldron* 1985

Bernard, Raymond (1891-1977) *The Chess Player* 1927; *Les Misérables* 1934

Bernds, Edward (1905-2000) *The Bowery Boys Meet the Monsters* 1954; *World without End* 1955; *Reform School Girl* 1957; *Quantrill's Raiders* 1958; *Queen of Outer Space* 1958; *Space Master X 7* 1958; *Return of the Fly* 1959; *The Three Stooges in Orbit* 1962; *The Three Stooges Meet Hercules* 1962

Bernhard, Jack (1914-1997) *Appointment with Murder* 1948; *Search for Danger* 1949

Bernhardt, Curtis aka **Bernhardt, Kurt** (1899-1981) *Three Loves* 1929; *Million Dollar Baby* 1941; *Happy Go Lucky* 1943; *Conflict* 1945; *Devotion* 1946; *My Reputation* 1946; *A Stolen Life* 1946; *High Wall* 1947; *Possessed* 1947; *The Doctor and the Girl* 1949; *The Blue Veil* 1951; *Payment on Demand* 1951; *Sirocco* 1951; *The Merry Widow* 1952; *Miss Sadie Thompson* 1953; *Beau Brummell* 1954; *Interrupted Melody* 1955; *Gaby* 1956; *Kisses for My President* 1964

Bernstein, Armyan *Windy City* 1984; *Cross My Heart* 1987

Berri, Claude (1934-2009) *The Two of Us* 1967; *Marry Me! Marry Me!* 1968; *Un Moment d'Egarement* 1977; *Je Vous Aime* 1980; *Jean de Florette* 1986; *Manon des Sources* 1986; *Germinal* 1993; *Lucie Aubrac* 1997

Berry, John (1917-1999) *Miss Susie Slagle's* 1945; *From This Day Forward* 1946; *Casbah* 1948; *Tension* 1949; *Utopia* 1950; *He Ran All the Way* 1951; *Claudine* 1974; *The Bad News Bears Go to Japan* 1978; *Boesman & Lena* 2000

Bertolucci, Bernardo (1940-) *La Commare Secca* 1962; *Before the Revolution* 1964; *Partner* 1968; *The Conformist* 1970; *The Spider's Stratagem* 1970; *Last Tango in Paris* 1972; *1900* 1976; *La Luna* 1979; *The Tragedy of a Ridiculous Man* 1981; *The Last Emperor* 1987; *The Sheltering Sky* 1990; *Little Buddha* 1993; *Stealing Beauty* 1995; *Besieged* 1998; *Ten Minutes Older: the Cello* 2002; *The Dreamers* 2003; *Me and You* 2012

Bertuccelli, Julie *Since Otar Left* 2003; *The Tree* 2010

Besson, Luc (1959-) *The Last Battle* 1983; *Subway* 1985; *The Big Blue* 1988; *Nikita* 1990; *Atlantis* 1991; *Leon* 1994; *The Fifth Element* 1997; *Joan of Arc* 1999; *Angel-A* 2005; *Arthur and the Invisibles* 2006; *The Extraordinary Adventures of Adèle Blanc-Sec* 2010; *The Lady* 2011; *The Family* 2013; *Lucy* 2014; *Valérian and the City of a Thousand Planets* 2017

Betancor, Antonio Jose aka **Betancor, Antonio J** (1944-) *Valentina* 1982; *1919* 1983

Bettinelli-Olpin, Matt aka **Radio Silence** *V/H/S* 2012; *Devil's Due* 2014; *Southbound* 2015

Betuel, Jonathan (1949-) *My Science Project* 1985; *Theodore Rex* 1995

Bezucha, Thomas *Big Eden* 2000; *The Family Stone* 2005; *Monte Carlo* 2011

Bhansali, Sanjay Leela *Hum Dil De Chuke Sanam* 1999; *Devdas* 2002; *Black* 2004

Bharadwaj, Radha *Closet Land* 1991; *Basil* 1998

Bhatt, Vikram *Raaz* 2001; *Awara Paagal Deewana* 2002

Biberman, Abner (1909-1977) *Gun for a Coward* 1957; *The Night Runner* 1957

Biberman, Herbert J aka **Biberman, Herbert** (1900-1971) *Meet Nero Wolfe* 1936; *The Master Race* 1944; *Salt of the Earth* 1954; *Slaves* 1969

Bielinsky, Fabian (1959-2006) *Nine Queens* 2000; *El Aura* 2005

Bier, Susanne (1960-) *Open Hearts* 2002; *Brothers* 2004; *After the Wedding* 2006; *Things We Lost in the Fire* 2007; *In a Better World* 2010; *Love Is All You Need* 2012; *Serena* 2013; *A Second Chance* 2014

Bierman, Robert *Vampire's Kiss* 1988; *Keep the Aspidistra Flying* 1997

Bigelow, Kathryn (1951-) *The Loveless* 1981; *Near Dark* 1987; *Blue Steel* 1990; *Point Break* 1991; *Strange Days* 1995; *The Weight of Water* 2000; *K-19: the Widowmaker* 2002; *The Hurt Locker* 2008; *Zero Dark Thirty* 2012

Bill, Tony (1940-) *My Bodyguard* 1980; *Six Weeks* 1982; *Five Corners* 1987; *Crazy People* 1990; *A Home of Our Own* 1993; *Untamed Heart* 1993; *Beyond the Call* 1996; *Flyboys* 2006

Billington, Kevin (1934-) *Interlude* 1968; *The Rise and Rise of Michael Rimmer* 1970; *The Light at the Edge of the World* 1971

Binder, Mike (1958-) *Indian Summer* 1993; *Blankman* 1994; *The Sex Monster* 1998; *Londinium* 1999; *The Search for John Gissing* 2001; *The Upside of Anger* 2005; *Reign over Me* 2007

Binder, Steve *The TAMI Show* 1964; *Give 'Em Hell, Harry!* 1975

Binyon, Claude (1905-1978) *The Saxon Charm* 1948; *Stella* 1950; *Dreamboat* 1952; *Here Come the Girls* 1953

Bird, Antonia (1951-2013) *Priest* 1994; *Mad Love* 1995; *Face* 1997; *Ravenous* 1999

Bird, Brad (1957-) *The Iron Giant* 1999; *The Incredibles* 2004; *Ratatouille* 2007; *Mission: Impossible - Ghost Protocol* 2011; *Tomorrowland: a World Beyond* 2015

Birkin, Andrew (1945-) *Burning Secret* 1988; *The Cement Garden* 1992; *Salt on Our Skin* 1992

Birt, Daniel (1907-1955) *No Room at the Inn* 1948; *The Three Weird Sisters* 1948; *The Interrupted Journey* 1949; *Background* 1953

Bishop, Terry (1917-1981) *Cover Girl Killer* 1959; *Life in Danger* 1959

Bixby, Bill (1934-1993) *The Trial of the Incredible Hulk* 1989; *The Death of the Incredible Hulk* 1990

Black, Noel (1937-2014) *Pretty Poison* 1968; *Jennifer on My Mind* 1971; *A Man, a Woman and a Bank* 1979

Black, Shane (1961-) *Kiss Kiss Bang Bang* 2005; *Iron Man Three* 2013; *The Nice Guys* 2016

Blair (4), David *Best Laid Plans* 2011; *The Messenger* 2015; *Away* 2016

Blair, Les (1941-) *Number One* 1984; *Bad Behaviour* 1992

Blakeley, John E (1889-1958) *Somewhere on Leave* 1942; *It's a Grand Life* 1953

Blakemore, Michael (1928-) *Privates on Parade* 1982; *Country Life* 1994

Blakeson, J *The Disappearance of Alice Creed* 2009; *The 5th Wave* 2016

Blanc, Michel (1952-) *The Escort* 1999; *Summer Things* 2002

Blank, Les (1935-2013) *A Poem Is a Naked Person* 1974; *Burden of Dreams* 1982

Blanks, Jamie (1971-) *Urban Legend* 1998; *Valentine* 2001; *Long Weekend* 2008

Blasetti, Alessandro (1900-1987) *Four Steps in the Clouds* 1942; *Lucky to Be a Woman* 1955; *Too Bad She's Bad* 1955

Blatty, William Peter (1928-) *The Ninth Configuration* 1979; *The Exorcist III* 1990

Blaustein, Barry W (1955-) *Beyond the Mat* 1999; *The Ringer* 2005

Bleckner, Jeff (1943-) *Do You Remember Love* 1985; *White Water Summer* 1987; *My Father, My Son* 1988; *Rear Window* 1998; *Flowers for Algernon* 2000; *Beyond the Blackboard* 2011

Blier, Bertrand (1939-) *Les Valseuses* 1974; *Get Out Your Handkerchiefs* 1977; *Buffet Froid* 1979; *Tenue de Soirée* 1986; *Trop Belle pour Toi* 1989; *Merci la Vie* 1991; *Mon Homme* 1996

Blinkoff, Saul Andrew *Winnie the Pooh: Springtime with Roo* 2004; *Kronk's New Groove* 2005

Blitz, Jeffrey aka **Blitz, Jeff** *Spellbound* 2002; *Rocket Science* 2007

Blomkamp, Neill (1979-) *District 9* 2009; *Elysium* 2013; *Chappie* 2015

Bloom, Jason *Bio-Dome* 1996; *Overnight Delivery* 1997

Bloom, Jeffrey *Dogpound Shuffle* 1974; *Blood Beach* 1981; *Flowers in the Attic* 1987

Bluth, Don (1938-) *The Secret of NIMH* 1982; *An American Tail* 1986; *The Land before Time* 1988; *All Dogs Go to Heaven* 1989; *Stanley's Magic Garden* 1994; *Thumbelina* 1994; *The Pebble and the Penguin* 1995; *Anastasia* 1997; *Titan AE* 2000; *Bartok the Magnificent* 1999; *Titan AE* 2000

Blystone, John G aka **Blystone, John** (1892-1938) *Our Hospitality* 1923; *Shanghai Madness* 1933; *Change of Heart* 1934; *Great Guy* 1936; *Woman Chases Man* 1937; *Blockheads* 1938; *Swiss Miss* 1938

Bobin, James *The Muppets* 2011; *Muppets Most Wanted* 2014; *Alice through the Looking Glass* 2016

Bochner, Hart (1956-) *PCU* 1994; *High School High* 1996

Boden, Anna *Sugar* 2008; *It's Kind of a Funny Story* 2010; *Mississippi Grind* 2015

Bodrov, Sergei (1948-) *Prisoner of the Mountains* 1996; *Running Free* 1999; *Mongol* 2007; *Seventh Son* 2014

Boe, Christoffer *Reconstruction* 2003; *Allegro* 2005

Boetticher, Budd (1916-2001) *The Bullfighter and the Lady* 1951; *The Cimarron Kid* 1951; *Horizons West* 1952; *Red Ball Express* 1952; *City beneath the Sea* 1953; *East of Sumatra* 1953; *The Man from the Alamo* 1953; *Seminole* 1953; *The Killer Is Loose* 1956; *Seven Men from Now* 1956; *Decision at Sundown* 1957; *The Tall T* 1957; *Buchanan Rides Alone* 1958; *Ride Lonesome* 1959; *Westbound* 1959; *Comanche Station* 1960; *The Rise and Fall of Legs Diamond* 1960

Bogart, Paul (1919-2012) *The Three Sisters* 1966; *Marlowe* 1969; *Skin Game* 1971; *Cancel My Reservation* 1972; *Class of '44* 1973; *Mr Ricco* 1975; *Oh, God! You Devil* 1984; *Torch Song Trilogy* 1988; *Broadway Bound* 1991

Bogayevicz, Yurek (1948-) *Anna* 1987; *Three of Hearts* 1992

Bogdanovich, Peter aka **Thomas, Derek** (1939-) *Voyage to the Planet of Prehistoric Women* 1966; *Targets* 1968; *The Last Picture Show* 1971; *What's Up, Doc?* 1972; *Paper Moon* 1973; *Daisy Miller* 1974; *At Long Last Love* 1975; *Nickelodeon* 1976; *Saint Jack* 1979; *They All Laughed* 1981; *Mask* 1985; *Illegally Yours* 1988; *Texasville* 1990; *Noises Off* 1992; *The Thing Called Love* 1993; *The Cat's Meow* 2001; *The Mystery of Natalie Wood* 2004; *She's Funny That Way* 2014

Boisset, Yves (1939-) *The Purple Taxi* 1977; *The Lady Cop* 1979

Boleslawski, Richard aka **Boleslavsky, Richard** (1889-1937) *The Gay Diplomat* 1931; *Rasputin and*

the Empress 1932; *Hollywood Party* 1934; *Men in White* 1934; *Operator 13* 1934; *The Painted Veil* 1934; *Clive of India* 1935; *Les Misérables* 1935; *The Garden of Allah* 1936; *Theodora Goes Wild* 1936; *The Last of Mrs Cheyney* 1937

Bollain, Iciar (1967-) *Take My Eyes* 2003; *Even the Rain* 2010

Bolognini, Mauro (1922-2001) *Le Bambole* 1965; *The Witches* 1966; *Arabella* 1967; *The Inheritance* 1976

Bolotin, Craig *That Night* 1992; *Light It Up* 1999

Bondarchuk, Fyodor *9th Company* 2005; *Stalingrad* 2013

Bondarchuk, Sergei (1920-1994) *Destiny of a Man* 1959; *War and Peace* 1966; *Waterloo* 1970

Bonello, Bertrand (1968-) *The Pornographer* 2001; *House of Tolerance* 2011; *Saint Laurent* 2014

Bong Joon-ho (1969-) *Memories of Murder* 2003; *The Host* 2006; *Mother* 2009; *Snowpiercer* 2013

Bonitzer, Pascal (1946-) *Rien sur Robert* 1998; *Petites Coupures* 2002; *Looking for Hortense* 2012

Boone, Josh *Stuck in Love* 2012; *The Fault in Our Stars* 2014

Boorman, John (1933-) *Catch Us If You Can* 1965; *Point Blank* 1967; *Hell in the Pacific* 1968; *Leo the Last* 1970; *Deliverance* 1972; *Zardoz* 1973; *Exorcist II: The Heretic* 1977; *Excalibur* 1981; *The Emerald Forest* 1985; *Hope and Glory* 1987; *Where the Heart Is* 1990; *Beyond Rangoon* 1995; *The General* 1998; *The Tailor of Panama* 2000; *In My Country* 2004; *The Tiger's Tail* 2006; *Queen and Country* 2014

Boos, H Gordon (1958-2004) *Red Surf* 1990; *Touch Me* 1997

Booth, Harry *On the Buses* 1971; *Go for a Take* 1972; *Mutiny on the Buses* 1972

Borden, Lizzie (1954-) *Born in Flames* 1983; *Working Girls* 1986; *Love Crimes* 1991; *Erotique* 1994

Boris, Robert (1945-) *Oxford Blues* 1984; *Buy & Cell* 1988; *Frank and Jesse* 1995

Bornedal, Ole (1959-) *Nightwatch* 1994; *Nightwatch* 1997; *Just Another Love Story* 2007; *The Possession* 2012

Borowczyk, Walerian (1923-2006) *Goto, I'lle d'Amour* 1968; *Blanche* 1971; *Immoral Tales* 1974; *La Bête* 1975

Borsos, Phillip (1953-1995) *The Grey Fox* 1982; *The Mean Season* 1985; *One Magic Christmas* 1985; *Bethune: the Making of a Hero* 1990; *Far from Home: the Adventures of Yellow Dog* 1994

Borthwick, Dave *The Secret Adventures of Tom Thumb* 1993; *The Magic Roundabout* 2005

Borzage, Frank (1894-1962) *7th Heaven* 1927; *Street Angel* 1928; *They Had to See Paris* 1929; *Song o' My Heart* 1930; *Bad Girl* 1931; *A Farewell to Arms* 1932; *Man's Castle* 1933; *Secrets* 1933; *Flirtation Walk* 1934; *Little Man, What Now?* 1934; *No Greater Glory* 1934; *Shipmates Forever* 1935; *Desire* 1936; *Big City* 1937; *Green Light* 1937; *History Is Made at Night* 1937; *Mannequin* 1937; *The Shining Hour* 1938; *Three Comrades* 1938; *Flight Command* 1940; *The Mortal Storm* 1940; *Strange Cargo* 1940; *Smilin' Through* 1941; *The Vanishing Virginian* 1941; *His Butler's Sister* 1943; *Stage Door Canteen* 1943; *Till We Meet Again* 1944; *The Spanish Main* 1945; *Magnificent Doll* 1946; *That's My Man* 1947; *Moonrise* 1948; *China Doll* 1958; *The Big Fisherman* 1959

Boucareb, Rachid (1953-) *Days of Glory* 2006; *London River* 2009

Boulting, John (1913-1985) *Journey Together* 1944; *Brighton Rock* 1947; *Seven Days to Noon* 1950; *The Magic Box* 1951; *Seagulls over Sorrento* 1954; *Private's Progress* 1956; *Lucky Jim* 1957; *I'm All Right Jack* 1959; *Suspect* 1960; *Heavens Above!* 1963; *Rotten to the Core* 1965

Boulting, Roy (1913-2001) *Pastor Hall* 1940; *Thunder Rock* 1942; *Fame Is the Spur* 1947; *The Guinea Pig* 1948; *Seven Days to Noon* 1950; *Sailor of the King* 1953; *Seagulls over Sorrento* 1954; *Josephine and Men* 1955; *Brothers in Law* 1956; *Run for the Sun* 1956; *Happy Is the Bride* 1957; *Carlton-Browne of the FO* 1958; *A French Mistress* 1960; *Suspect* 1960; *The Family Way* 1966; *Twisted Nerve* 1968; *There's a Girl in*

My Soup 1970; *Soft Beds, Hard Battles* 1973

Bour, Elliot M *Winnie the Pooh: Springtime with Roo* 2004; *Kronk's New Groove* 2005

Bourguignon, Serge (1928-) *Sundays and Cybèle* 1962; *The Reward* 1965; *The Picasso Summer* 1969

Bousman, Darren Lynn (1979-) *Saw II* 2005; *Saw III* 2006; *Saw IV* 2007; *Mother's Day* 2010; *The Barrens* 2012

Bowen, Jenny *aka Riley, H Anne* *The Wizard of Loneliness* 1988; *Animal Behavior* 1989

Bowers, David *Flushed Away* 2006; *Astro Boy* 2009; *Diary of a Wimpy Kid: Rodrick Rules* 2011; *Diary of a Wimpy Kid 3: Dog Days* 2012

Bowers, George (1944-2012) *Body and Soul* 1981; *My Tutor* 1983; *Private Resort* 1985

Bowman, Rob (1960-) *Airborne* 1993; *The X-Files* 1998; *Reign of Fire* 2001; *Elektra* 2005

Bowser, Kenneth *In a Shallow Grave* 1988; *Easy Riders, Raging Bulls* 2003

Box, Muriel (1905-1991) *The Lost People* 1949; *The Happy Family* 1952; *The Beachcomber* 1954; *To Dorothy, a Son* 1954; *Simon and Laura* 1955; *Eyewitness* 1956; *The Passionate Stranger* 1957; *Subway in the Sky* 1958; *The Truth about Women* 1958; *This Other Eden* 1959; *The Piper's Tune* 1962; *Rattle of a Simple Man* 1964

Boyd, Don (1948-) *East of Elephant Rock* 1976; *Twenty-One* 1991; *Lucia* 1998; *My Kingdom* 2001; *Andrew & Jeremy Get Married* 2004

Boyle, Danny (1956-) *Shallow Grave* 1994; *Trainspotting* 1995; *A Life Less Ordinary* 1997; *The Beach* 2000; *28 Days Later...* 2002; *Millions* 2004; *Sunshine* 2007; *Slumdog Millionaire* 2008; *'27 Hours* 2011; *Trance* 2013; *Steve Jobs* 2015; *T2: Trainspotting 2* 2016

Boyum, Steve (1952-) *Meet the Deedles* 1998; *Wild Hearts* 2006

Brabin, Charles (1883-1957) *Sporting Blood* 1931; *The Beast of the City* 1932; *The Mask of Fu Manchu* 1932; *The Secret of Madame Blanche* 1933

Bracewell, Richard *The Gigolos* 2006; *Cuckoo* 2009; *Bill* 2014

Bradbury, Robert N *aka Bradbury, Robert North aka Bradbury, R N* (1886-1949) *Riders of Destiny* 1933; *Blue Steel* 1934; *The Lucky Texan* 1934; *The Man from Utah* 1934; *The Star Packer* 1934; *The Trail Beyond* 1934; *West of the Divide* 1934; *The Dawn Rider* 1935; *The Lawless Frontier* 1935; *Texas Terror* 1935; *Westward Ho* 1935

Bradshaw, John (1952-) *Lethal Tender* 1996; *Killing Moon* 1999; *Triggermen* 2002; *They Come Back* 2007; *Family Gathering* 2010; *The Town Christmas Forgot* 2010; *The Christmas Consultant* 2012

Braff, Zach (1975-) *Garden State* 2003; *Wish I Was Here* 2014

Brahm, John (1893-1982) *Broken Blossoms* 1936; *Wild Geese Calling* 1941; *The Undying Monster* 1942; *Wintertime* 1943; *Guest in the House* 1944; *The Lodger* 1944; *Hangover Square* 1945; *The Locket* 1946; *Singapore* 1947; *Face to Face* 1952; *The Miracle of Our Lady of Fatima* 1952; *The Diamond Queen* 1953; *The Mad Magician* 1954; *Bengazi* 1955; *Special Delivery* 1955

Brambilla, Marco (1960-) *Demolition Man* 1993; *Excess Baggage* 1997; *Destricted* 2006

Branagh, Kenneth (1960-) *Henry V* 1989; *Dead Again* 1991; *Peter's Friends* 1992; *Much Ado about Nothing* 1993; *Mary Shelley's Frankenstein* 1994; *In the Bleak Midwinter* 1995; *Hamlet* 1996; *Love's Labour's Lost* 1999; *As You Like It* 2006; *The Magic Flute* 2006; *Sleuth* 2007; *Thor* 2011; *Jack Ryan: Shadow Recruit* 2013; *Cinderella* 2015

Brandstrom, Charlotte (1959-) *Sweet Revenge* 1990; *Road to Ruin* 1992; *A Business Affair* 1993

Brannon, Ash *Toy Story 2* 1999; *Surf's Up* 2007

Brass, Tinto *aka Tinto Brass, Giovanni* (1933-) *Salon Kitty* 1976; *Caligula* 1979

Bray, Kevin *Walking Tall* 2004; *Linewatch* 2008

Breathnach, Paddy (1964-) *I Went Down* 1997; *Blow Dry* 2000; *Shrooms* 2006; *Red Mist* 2008

Breillat, Catherine (1948-) *Romance* 1998; *À Ma Soeur!* 2001; *Sex Is Comedy* 2002; *The Last Mistress* 2007; *Bluebeard* 2009

Brenon, Herbert (1880-1958) *Beau Geste* 1926; *Laugh, Clown, Laugh* 1928; *Beau Ideal* 1931; *Housemaster* 1938

Bresson, Robert (1907-1999) *Les Affaires Publiques* 1934; *Les Anges du Péché* 1943; *Les Dames du Bois de Boulogne* 1946; *Diary of a Country Priest* 1950; *A Man Escaped* 1956; *Pickpocket* 1959; *Le Procès de Jeanne d'Arc* 1962; *Au Hasard, Balthazar* 1966; *Mouchette* 1966; *A Gentle Creature* 1969; *Four Nights of a Dreamer* 1971; *Lancelot du Lac* 1974; *The Devil, Probably* 1977; *L'Argent* 1983

Brest, Martin (1951-) *Going in Style* 1979; *Beverly Hills Cop* 1984; *Midnight Run* 1988; *Scent of a Woman* 1992; *Meet Joe Black* 1998; *Gigli* 2003

Bretherton, Howard (1896-1969) *Hills of Kentucky* 1927; *Ladies They Talk About* 1933; *The Trap* 1947; *The Prince of Thieves* 1948

Brevig, Eric *Journey to the Center of the Earth* 2008; *Yogi Bear* 2010

Brewer, Craig *Hustle & Flow* 2005; *Black Snake Moan* 2006; *Footloose* 2011

Brickman, Marshall (1941-) *Simon* 1980; *Lovesick* 1983; *The Deadly Game* 1986

Brickman, Paul (1949-) *Risky Business* 1983; *Men Don't Leave* 1990

Bridges, Alan (1927-2014) *Invasion* 1965; *The Hireling* 1973; *Brief Encounter* 1974; *Out of Season* 1975; *The Return of the Soldier* 1982; *The Shooting Party* 1984

Bridges, Beau (1941-) *The Wild Pair* 1987; *Seven Hours to Judgment* 1988

Bridges, James (1936-1993) *The Paper Chase* 1973; *September 30, 1955* 1977; *The China Syndrome* 1979; *Urban Cowboy* 1980; *Mike's Murder* 1984; *Perfect* 1985; *Bright Lights, Big City* 1988

Bridgewater, Stephen *aka Bridgewater, Stephen W* (1953-) *Out of the Woods* 2005; *The Christmas Card* 2006; *Prairie Fever* 2008; *A View from Here* 2009

Bright, Matthew (1952-) *Freeway* 1996; *Confessions of a Trickbag* 1999; *Bundy* 2002

Brill, Steven (1962-) *Heavyweights* 1995; *Little Nicky* 2000; *Mr Deeds* 2002; *Without a Paddle* 2004; *Drillbit Taylor* 2007; *Movie 43* 2013

Brinckerhoff, Burt (1936-) *Dogs* 1976; *The Cracker Factory* 1979

Brisseau, Jean-Claude (1944-) *Secret Things* 2002; *The Exterminating Angels* 2006

Britten, Tony *In Love with Alma Cogan* 2011; *Benjamin Britten: Peace and Conflict* 2013; *Chicklit* 2016

Brizé, Stéphane *Not Here to Be Loved* 2005; *Mademoiselle Chambon* 2009; *The Measure of a Man* 2015

Brizzi, Gaetan *Asterix vs Caesar* 1985; *Fantasia 2000* 1999

Brizzi, Paul *Asterix vs Caesar* 1985; *Fantasia 2000* 1999

Broderick, John C (1942-2001) *Sam's Song* 1969; *The Warrior and the Sorceress* 1983

Brodie, Kevin (1952-) *Delta Pi* 1985; *A Dog of Flanders* 1999

Brook, Peter (1925-) *The Beggar's Opera* 1953; *Lord of the Flies* 1963; *Marat/Sade* 1967; *Tell Me Lies* 1967; *King Lear* 1970; *Meetings with Remarkable Men* 1979

Brooks, Adam (1956-) *Almost You* 1984; *The Invisible Circus* 2000; *Definitely, Maybe* 2008

Brooks, Albert (1947-) *Real Life* 1979; *Modern Romance* 1981; *Lost in America* 1985; *Defending Your Life* 1991; *Mother* 1996; *The Muse* 1999

Brooks, James L (1940-) *Terms of Endearment* 1983; *Broadcast News* 1987; *I'll Do Anything* 1994; *As Good as It Gets* 1997; *Spanglish* 2004; *How Do You Know* 2010

Brooks, Joseph (1938-2011) *You Light Up My Life* 1977; *Invitation to the Wedding* 1983

Brooks, Mel (1926-) *The Producers* 1968; *The Twelve Chairs* 1970; *Blazing Saddles* 1974; *Young Frankenstein* 1974; *Silent Movie* 1976; *High Anxiety* 1977; *History of the World Part 1* 1981; *Spaceballs* 1987; *Life Stinks* 1991; *Robin Hood:*

Men in Tights 1993; *Dracula: Dead and Loving It* 1995

Brooks, Richard (1912-1992) *Crisis* 1950; *The Light Touch* 1951; *Deadline - USA* 1952; *Battle Circus* 1953; *Take the High Ground* 1953; *The Last Time I Saw Paris* 1954; *The Blackboard Jungle* 1955; *The Catered Affair* 1956; *The Last Hunt* 1956; *Something of Value* 1957; *The Brothers Karamazov* 1958; *Cat on a Hot Tin Roof* 1958; *Elmer Gantry* 1960; *Sweet Bird of Youth* 1962; *Lord Jim* 1965; *The Professionals* 1966; *In Cold Blood* 1967; *Dollars* 1971; *Bite the Bullet* 1975; *Looking for Mr Goodbar* 1977; *The Man with the Deadly Lens* 1982; *Fever Pitch* 1985

Broomfield, Nick (1948-) *Diamond Skulls* 1989; *Monster in a Box* 1991; *Aileen Wuornos: the Selling of a Serial Killer* 1992; *Fetishes* 1996; *Kurt & Courtney* 1997; *Biggie & Tupac* 2001; *Aileen: Life and Death of a Serial Killer* 2003; *Ghosts* 2006; *Battle for Haditha* 2007; *Tales of the Grim Sleeper* 2014

Bross, Eric (1964-) *Stranger than Fiction* 1999; *On the Line* 2001

Brower, Otto (1895-1946) *Paramount on Parade* 1930; *Fighting Caravans* 1931; *Under Two Flags* 1936; *Suez* 1938; *The Gay Caballero* 1940

Brown, Bruce (1937-) *Slippery When Wet* 1958; *Surf Crazy* 1959; *Barefoot Adventure* 1960; *The Endless Summer* 1964; *On Any Sunday* 1971; *The Endless Summer II* 1994

Brown, Clarence (1890-1987) *The Last of the Mohicans* 1920; *The Eagle* 1925; *The Goose Woman* 1925; *Flesh and the Devil* 1926; *A Woman of Affairs* 1928; *The Trail of '98* 1929; *Anna Christie* 1930; *Romance* 1930; *A Free Soul* 1931; *Inspiration* 1931; *Possessed* 1931; *Emma* 1932; *Night Flight* 1933; *Chained* 1934; *Sadie McKee* 1934; *Ah, Wilderness!* 1935; *Anna Karenina* 1935; *The Gorgeous Hussy* 1936; *Wife vs Secretary* 1936; *Conquest* 1937; *Of Human Hearts* 1938; *Idiot's Delight* 1939; *The Rains Came* 1939; *Edison, the Man* 1940; *Come Live with Me* 1941; *They Met in Bombay* 1941; *The Human Comedy* 1943; *National Velvet* 1944; *The White Cliffs of Dover* 1944; *The Yearling* 1946; *Song of Love* 1947; *Intruder in the Dust* 1949; *To Please a Lady* 1950; *Angels in the Outfield* 1951; *It's a Big Country* 1951; *Plymouth Adventure* 1952

Brown, Georg Stanford (1943-) *Angel in the Family* 2004; *The Long Shot* 2004; *Wedding Daze* 2004; *The Reading Room* 2005

Brown, Harry Joe (1890-1972) *Sitting Pretty* 1933; *Knickerbocker Holiday* 1944

Browning, Tod (1882-1962) *The Unholy Three* 1925; *The Black Bird* 1926; *The Road to Mandalay* 1926; *London after Midnight* 1927; *The Unknown* 1927; *West of Zanzibar* 1928; *Dracula* 1931; *The Iron Man* 1931; *Freaks* 1932; *Mark of the Vampire* 1935; *The Devil-Doll* 1936; *Miracles for Sale* 1939

Brownlow, Kevin (1938-) *It Happened Here* 1963; *Winstanley* 1975; *Universal Horror* 1998

Bruckman, Clyde (1894-1955) *The General* 1927; *Feet First* 1930; *Movie Crazy* 1932; *Man on the Flying Trapeze* 1935

Bruckner, David *The Signal* 2007; *V/H/S* 2012; *Southbound* 2015

Brunel, Adrian (1892-1958) *The Constant Nymph* 1928; *An Old Spanish Custom* 1935; *The Lion Has Wings* 1939

Brunt, Dominic *Before Dawn* 2012; *Bait* 2015

Buck, Chris *Tarzan* 1999; *Surf's Up* 2007; *Frozen* 2013

Bucquet, Harold S *aka Bucquet, Harold* (1891-1946) *Young Dr Kildare* 1938; *Calling Dr Kildare* 1939; *The Secret of Dr Kildare* 1939; *Dr Kildare's Strange Case* 1940; *Dr Kildare Goes Home* 1940; *Dr Kildare's Crisis* 1940; *Dr Kildare's Wedding Day* 1941; *The Penalty* 1941; *The People vs Dr Kildare* 1941; *Calling Dr Gillespie* 1942; *The War against Mrs Hadley* 1942; *The Adventures of Tartu* 1943; *Dragon Seed* 1944; *Without Love* 1945

Buechler, John Carl *Troll* 1986; *Friday the 13th Part VII: the New Blood* 1988

Bugajski, Ryszard *aka Bugajski, Richard* (1943-) *Interrogation* 1982; *Clearcut* 1992

Buitenhuis, Penelope *Cheating Fate* 2007; *Client Seduction* 2014

Bujalski, Andrew *Funny Ha Ha* 2002; *Mutual Appreciation* 2005; *Computer Chess* 2013; *Results* 2015

Buñuel, Luis (1900-1983) *Un Chien Andalou* 1928; *L'Age d'Or* 1930; *Land without Bread* 1933; *The Great Madcap* 1949; *Los Olvidados* 1950; *La Hija del Engaño* 1951; *Mexican Bus Ride* 1951; *A Woman without Love* 1951; *The Adventures of Robinson Crusoe* 1952; *El Bruto* 1952; *El* 1953; *Wuthering Heights* 1953; *The River and Death* 1954; *The Criminal Life of Archibaldo de la Cruz* 1955; *Celà S'Appelle l'Aurore* 1956; *Death in the Garden* 1956; *Nazarín* 1958; *La Fièvre Monte à el Pao* 1959; *The Young One* 1960; *Viridiana* 1961; *The Exterminating Angel* 1962; *The Diary of a Chambermaid* 1964; *Simon of the Desert* 1965; *Belle de Jour* 1967; *The Milky Way* 1968; *Tristana* 1970; *The Discreet Charm of the Bourgeoisie* 1972; *Le Fantôme de la Liberté* 1974; *That Obscure Object of Desire* 1977

Burdis, Ray (1958-) *Final Cut* 1998; *Love, Honour and Obey* 2000; *The Wee Man* 2013

Burge, Stuart (1918-2002) *There Was a Crooked Man* 1960; *Othello* 1965; *Julius Caesar* 1970

Burger, Neil *The Illusionist* 2005; *Limitless* 2011; *Divergent* 2014

Burke, Martyn *Power Play* 1978; *Pirates of Silicon Valley* 1999; *Avenging Angelo* 2002

Burnett, Charles (1944-) *Killer of Sheep* 1977; *To Sleep with Anger* 1990; *The Glass Shield* 1995; *The Wedding* 1998; *The Blues, a Musical Journey: Warming by the Devil's Fire* 2003; *Relative Stranger* 2009

Burns, Edward (1968-) *The Brothers McMullen* 1995; *She's the One* 1996; *No Looking Back* 1998; *Sidewalks of New York* 2000; *Ash Wednesday* 2002

Burns, Gary *waydowntown* 2000; *Cool Money* 2005

Burr, Jeff (1963-) *Stepfather II* 1989; *Leatherface: the Texas Chainsaw Massacre III* 1990; *The Revenge of Pumpkinhead - Blood Wings* 1994; *Tornado Warning* 2012

Burrowes, Geoff (1945-) *Return to Snowy River* 1988; *Run* 1991

Burstall, Tim (1929-2004) *Attack Force Z* 1981; *The Naked Country* 1985; *Kangaroo* 1986

Burstein, Nanette *The Kid Stays in the Picture* 2001; *American Teen* 2008; *Going the Distance* 2010

Burton (1), David (1877-1963) *Fighting Caravans* 1931; *Lady by Choice* 1934; *The Man Who Wouldn't Talk* 1940

Burton, Tim (1958-) *Pee-wee's Big Adventure* 1985; *Beetle Juice* 1988; *Batman* 1989; *Edward Scissorhands* 1990; *Batman Returns* 1992; *Ed Wood* 1994; *Mars Attacks!* 1996; *Sleepy Hollow* 1999; *Planet of the Apes* 2001; *Big Fish* 2003; *Charlie and the Chocolate Factory* 2005; *Tim Burton's Corpse Bride* 2005; *Sweeney Todd: the Demon Barber of Fleet Street* 2007; *Alice in Wonderland* 2010; *Dark Shadows* 2012; *Frankenweenie* 2012; *Big Eyes* 2014; *Miss Peregrine's Home for Peculiar Children* 2016

Buscemi, Steve (1957-) *Trees Lounge* 1996; *Animal Factory* 2000; *Lonesome Jim* 2005; *Interview* 2007

Butler, David (1894-1979) *Sunny Side Up* 1929; *A Connecticut Yankee* 1931; *Delicious* 1931; *Bright Eyes* 1934; *The Little Colonel* 1935; *The Littlest Rebel* 1935; *Captain January* 1936; *Pigskin Parade* 1936; *White Fang* 1936; *Kentucky* 1938; *Kentucky Moonshine* 1938; *East Side of Heaven* 1939; *That's Right - You're Wrong* 1939; *You'll Find Out* 1940; *Playmates* 1941; *Road to Morocco* 1942; *Thank Your Lucky Stars* 1943; *They Got Me Covered* 1943; *The Princess and the Pirate* 1944; *Shine On, Harvest Moon* 1944; *San Antonio* 1945; *My Wild Irish Rose* 1947; *It's a Great Feeling* 1949; *Look for the Silver Lining* 1949; *The Daughter of Rosie O'Grady* 1950; *Tea for Two* 1950; *Lullaby of Broadway* 1951; *Painting the Clouds with Sunshine* 1951; *April in Paris* 1952; *By the Light of the Silvery Moon* 1953; *Calamity Jane* 1953; *The Command* 1954; *King*

Butler, George *Pumping Iron* 1976; *Pumping Iron II: the Women* 1984; *The Endurance: Shackleton's Legendary Antarctic Expedition* 2000

Butler, Robert (1927-) *The Computer Wore Tennis Shoes* 1969; *Guns in the Heather* 1969; *The Barefoot Executive* 1971; *Scandalous John* 1971; *The Blue Knight* 1973; *Dark Victory* 1976; *Hot Lead and Cold Feet* 1978; *Night of the Juggler* 1980; *White Mile* 1994; *Turbulence* 1997

Butoy, Hendel *The Rescuers Down Under* 1990; *Fantasia 2000* 1999

Butterworth, Jez (1969-) *Mojo* 1998; *Birthday Girl* 2001

Buzzell, Edward *aka Buzzell, Edward N* (1895-1985) *Fast Company* 1938; *Paradise for Three* 1938; *At the Circus* 1939; *Honolulu* 1939; *Go West* 1940; *Ship Ahoy* 1942; *Best Foot Forward* 1943; *The Youngest Profession* 1943; *Keep Your Powder Dry* 1945; *Easy to Wed* 1946; *Song of the Thin Man* 1947; *Neptune's Daughter* 1949; *A Woman of Distinction* 1950; *Ain't Misbehavin'* 1955

Bye, Ed *Kevin & Perry Go Large* 2000; *Fat Slags* 2004; *Round Ireland with a Fridge... a True Story* 2010

Byrum, John (1947-) *Inserts* 1975; *Heart Beat* 1979; *The Razor's Edge* 1984

C

Cabanne, Christy (1888-1950) *The Last Outlaw* 1936; *Criminal Lawyer* 1937; *The Mummy's Hand* 1940; *Scared to Death* 1947

Cacoyannis, Michael (1922-2011) *Stella* 1955; *A Matter of Dignity* 1957; *Zorba the Greek* 1964; *The Day the Fish Came Out* 1967; *The Trojan Women* 1971; *Iphigenia* 1976; *The Cherry Orchard* 1998

Cadiff, Andy *Leave It to Beaver* 1997; *Chasing Liberty* 2004; *A Bunch of Amateurs* 2008

Caesar, David *Idiot Box* 1996; *Dirty Deeds* 2002

Caffrey, David (1969-) *Divorcing Jack* 1998; *Grand Theft Parsons* 2003

Cahill, Mike *Another Earth* 2011; *I Origins* 2014

Cahn, Edward L (1899-1963) *Law and Order* 1932; *Confidential* 1935; *Death Drives Through* 1935; *Destination Murder* 1950; *Creature with the Atom Brain* 1955; *The She-Creature* 1956; *Dragstrip Girl* 1957; *Invasion of the Saucer Men* 1957; *Motorcycle Gang* 1957; *Shake, Rattle and Rock!* 1957; *Voodoo Woman* 1957; *It! The Terror from beyond Space* 1958; *Jet Attack* 1958; *Suicide Battalion* 1958; *Beauty and the Beast* 1962

Cain, Christopher *aka Cain, Chris* (1943-) *The Stone Boy* 1984; *That Was Then... This Is Now* 1985; *The Principal* 1987; *Young Guns* 1988; *Pure Country* 1992; *The Next Karate Kid* 1994; *The Amazing Panda Adventure* 1995; *Gone Fishin'* 1997

Camerini, Mario (1895-1981) *Ulysses* 1954; *The Miller's Wife* 1955

Cameron, Cody *Open Season 3* 2010; *Cloudy with a Chance of Meatballs 2* 2013

Cameron, James (1954-) *Piranha II: the Spawning* 1981; *The Terminator* 1984; *Aliens* 1986; *The Abyss* 1989; *Terminator 2: Judgment Day* 1991; *True Lies* 1994; *Titanic* 1997; *Avatar* 2009; *Avatar 2* 2018

Cameron, Ken (1946-) *The Good Wife* 1986; *Payback* 1997

Cammell, Donald (1934-1996) *Performance* 1970; *Demon Seed* 1977; *White of the Eye* 1986; *Wild Side* 1995

Camp, Joe (1939-) *Benji* 1974; *For the Love of Benji* 1977; *Benji the Hunted* 1987

Campanella, Juan José *aka Campanella, Juan José* (1959-) *The Boy Who Cried Bitch* 1991; *Love Walked In* 1997; *Son of the Bride* 2001; *The Secret in Their Eyes* 2009; *The Unbeatables* 2013

Campanile, Pasquale Festa (1927-1986) *The Girl and the General* 1967; *On My Way to the Crusades, I Met a Girl Who...* 1967

Campbell, Doug (1922-) *Killer Flood* 2003; *Accused at 17* 2009

Campbell, Graeme (1954-) Nico the Unicorn 1998; Guilt by Association 2002; An Old-Fashioned Thanksgiving 2008; The National Tree 2009

Campbell, Martin (1940-) Criminal Law 1988; Defenseless 1991; No Escape 1994; GoldenEye 1995; The Mask of Zorro 1998; Vertical Limit 2000; Beyond Borders 2003; The Legend of Zorro 2005; Casino Royale 2006; Edge of Darkness 2009; Green Lantern 2011

Campion, Jane (1954-) Sweetie 1989; An Angel at My Table 1990; The Piano 1993; The Portrait of a Lady 1996; Holy Smoke 1999; In the Cut 2003; Bright Star 2009

Campos, Antonio Buy It Now 2005; Afterschool 2008; Simon Killer 2012

Camus, Mario (1935-) Los Santos Inocentes 1984; The House of Bernarda Alba 1987

Canet, Guillaume (1973-) Tell No One 2006; Little White Lies 2010; Blood Ties 2013

Cannon, Danny (1968-) The Young Americans 1993; Judge Dredd 1995; I Still Know What You Did Last Summer 1998; Phoenix 1998; Goal! 2005

Cantet, Laurent (1961-) Human Resources 1999; Time Out 2001; Heading South 2006; The Class 2008; Foxfire: Confessions of a Girl Gang 2012; 7 Days in Havana 2012

Cappello, Frank aka **Cappello, Frank A** American Yakuza 1994; No Way Back 1996; He Was a Quiet Man 2007

Capra, Frank aka **Capra, Frank R** (1897-1991) The Strong Man 1926; For the Love of Mike 1927; Long Pants 1927; The Matinee Idol 1928; Flight 1929; The Younger Generation 1929; Ladies of Leisure 1930; Rain or Shine 1930; Dirigible 1931; The Miracle Woman 1931; Platinum Blonde 1931; American Madness 1932; The Bitter Tea of General Yen 1932; Forbidden 1932; Lady for a Day 1933; Broadway Bill 1934; It Happened One Night 1934; Mr Deeds Goes to Town 1936; Lost Horizon 1937; You Can't Take It with You 1938; Mr Smith Goes to Washington 1939; Meet John Doe 1941; The Battle of Russia 1943; Arsenic and Old Lace 1944; It's a Wonderful Life 1946; State of the Union 1948; Riding High 1950; Here Comes the Groom 1951; Pocketful of Miracles 1961

Carax, Leos (1960-) Boy Meets Girl 1984; Mauvais Sang 1986; Les Amants du Pont-Neuf 1990; Pola X 1999; Holy Motors 2012

Cardiff, Jack (1914-2009) Intent to Kill 1958; Beyond This Place 1959; Scent of Mystery 1960; Sons and Lovers 1960; The Lion 1962; My Geisha 1962; The Long Ships 1963; Young Cassidy 1965; The Liquidator 1966; Dark of the Sun 1967; The Girl on a Motorcycle 1968; The Mutations 1973; Penny Gold 1973

Cardone, J S Shadowzone 1990; A Row of Crows 1991; The Forsaken 2001

Cardos, John "Bud" (1929-) The Female Bunch 1969; Kingdom of the Spiders 1977; The Dark 1979; The Day Time Ended 1980; Mutant 1984

Carion, Christian (1963-) The Girl from Paris 2001; Merry Christmas 2005; Farewell 2010

Carlei, Carlo (1960-) Fluke 1995; Romeo & Juliet 2012

Carlino, Lewis John (1932-) The Sailor Who Fell from Grace with the Sea 1976; The Great Santini 1979; Class 1983

Carlsen, Henning (1927-2014) Hunger 1966; The Wolf at the Door 1986

Carlson, Richard (1912-1977) The Saga of Hemp Brown 1958; Kid Rodelo 1966

Carnahan, Joe (1969-) Narc 2001; Smokin' Aces 2006; The A-Team 2010; The Grey 2012

Carné, Marcel (1909-1996) Drôle de Drame 1937; Hôtel du Nord 1938; Le Quai des Brumes 1938; Le Jour Se Lève 1939; Les Visiteurs du Soir 1942; Les Enfants du Paradis 1945; Les Portes de la Nuit 1946; Thérèse Raquin 1953; Les Tricheurs 1958; Trois Chambres à Manhattan 1965

Carney, John Once 2006; Begin Again 2013; Sing Street 2015

Caro, Marc (1956-) Delicatessen 1990; The City of Lost Children 1995

Caro, Niki (1967-) Whale Rider 2002; North Country 2005; McFarland, USA 2015

Caron, Glenn Gordon (1954-) Clean and Sober 1988; Wilder Napalm 1993; Love Affair 1994; Picture Perfect 1997

Carpenter, John (1948-) Dark Star 1973; Assault on Precinct 13 1976; Halloween 1978; Someone's Watching Me! 1978; Elvis - the Movie 1979; The Fog 1980; Escape from New York 1981; The Thing 1982; Christine 1983; Starman 1984; Big Trouble in Little China 1986; Prince of Darkness 1987; They Live 1988; Memoirs of an Invisible Man 1992; In the Mouth of Madness 1994; Village of the Damned 1995; Escape from LA 1996; Vampires 1998; John Carpenter's Ghosts of Mars 2001; John Carpenter's The Ward 2010

Carpenter, Stephen aka **Carpenter, Steve** The Kindred 1986; Soul Survivors 2001

Carr, Steve Next Friday 1999; Dr Dolittle 2 2001; Daddy Day Care 2003; Rebound 2005; Are We Done Yet? 2007; Paul Blart: Mall Cop 2009; Movie 43 2013

Carr, Thomas (1907-1997) Captain Scarlett 1953; The Tall Stranger 1957; Cast a Long Shadow 1959

Carré, Jean-Michel Kursk: a Submarine in Troubled Waters 2004; The Putin System 2007

Carreras, Michael (1927-1994) The Steel Bayonet 1957; Maniac 1962; What a Crazy World 1963; The Curse of the Mummy's Tomb 1964; The Lost Continent 1968; Blood from the Mummy's Tomb 1971; Shatter 1974

Carroll, Willard Playing by Heart 1998; Tom's Midnight Garden 1998; Marigold 2007

Carruth, Shane Primer 2004; Upstream Color 2013

Carson, David Star Trek: Generations 1994; Unstoppable 2004

Carstairs, John Paddy (1910-1970) The Saint in London 1939; Spare a Copper 1940; Dancing with Crime 1946; Sleeping Car to Trieste 1948; The Chiltern Hundreds 1949; Fools Rush In 1949; Made in Heaven 1952; Treasure Hunt 1952; Top of the Form 1953; Trouble in Store 1953; One Good Turn 1954; Jumping for Joy 1955; Man of the Moment 1955; The Big Money 1956; Up in the World 1956; Just My Luck 1957; The Square Peg 1958; Tommy the Toreador 1959; Sands of the Desert 1960

Carter, Thomas (1953-) Swing Kids 1993; Metro 1997; Save the Last Dance 2000; Coach Carter 2005; Gifted Hands: the Ben Carson Story 2009

Caruso, D J (1965-) The Salton Sea 2002; Taking Lives 2004; Two for the Money 2005; Disturbia 2007; Eagle Eye 2008; I Am Number Four 2011; xXx: the Return of Xander Cage 2017

Carver, Steve (1945-) Big Bad Mama 1974; Capone 1975; Drum 1976; An Eye for an Eye 1981; Lone Wolf McQuade 1983; Jocks 1986; Bulletproof 1987; River of Death 1989

Cass Sr, David S aka **Cass, Dave** aka **Cass, David S** (1942-) Straight from the Heart 2003; The Hollywood Mom's Mystery 2004; Life on Liberty Street 2004; The Trail to Hope Rose 2004; Back to You and Me 2005; Family Plan 2005; Thicker than Water 2005; Desolation Canyon 2006; Avenging Angel 2007; Spring Thaw 2007; Bound by a Secret 2008; Lone Rider 2008; Prairie Fever 2008; Uncorked 2008; The Christmas Gift 2009; Class 2010; Oliver's Ghost 2011; The Christmas Pageant 2011; Shadow on the Mesa 2013

Cass, Henry (1902-1989) 29 Acacia Avenue 1945; The Glass Mountain 1949; No Place for Jennifer 1949; Last Holiday 1950; Young Wives' Tale 1951; Father's Doing Fine 1952; No Smoking 1954; Booby Trap 1957; The Crooked Sky 1957; Blood of the Vampire 1958

Cassavetes, John (1929-1989) Shadows 1959; Too Late Blues 1961; A Child Is Waiting 1962; Faces 1968; Husbands 1970; Minnie and Moskowitz 1971; A Woman under the Influence 1974; The Killing of a Chinese Bookie 1976; Opening Night 1977; Gloria 1980; Big Trouble 1985

Cassavetes, Nick (1959-) Unhook the Stars 1996; She's So Lovely 1997; John Q 2001; The Notebook 2003; Alpha Dog 2006; My Sister's Keeper 2009; The Other Woman 2014

Castellani, Renato (1913-1985) Two Pennyworth of Hope 1952; Romeo and Juliet 1954; Ghosts - Italian Style 1967

Castellari, Enzo G (1938-) Keoma 1976; Inglorious Bastards 1978; Extralarge: Moving Target 1990

Castle, Nick (1947-) The Last Starfighter 1984; The Boy Who Could Fly 1986; Tap 1989; Dennis 1993; Mr Wrong 1996

Castle, William (1914-1977) Betrayed 1944; The Whistler 1944; Undertow 1949; Cave of Outlaws 1951; Serpent of the Nile 1953; The Iron Glove 1954; The Americano 1955; House on Haunted Hill 1958; Macabre 1958; 13 Ghosts 1959; The Tingler 1959; Homicidal 1961; Mr Sardonicus 1961; The Old Dark House 1963; Strait-Jacket 1963; The Night Walker 1964; I Saw What You Did 1965; The Busy Body 1967

Cates, Gilbert (1934-2011) I Never Sang for My Father 1970; The Affair 1973; Summer Wishes, Winter Dreams 1973; One Summer Love 1975; The Last Married Couple in America 1980; Oh God! Book II 1980; Backfire 1987

Caton-Jones, Michael (1957-) Scandal 1988; Memphis Belle 1990; Doc Hollywood 1991; This Boy's Life 1993; Rob Roy 1995; The Jackal 1997; City by the Sea 2002; Shooting Dogs 2005; Basic Instinct 2: Risk Addiction 2006

Cattaneo, Peter (1964-) The Full Monty 1997; Lucky Break 2001; Opal Dream 2005; The Rocker 2008

Cattet, Hélène The ABCs of Death 2012; The Strange Colour of Your Body's Tears 2013

Cavalcanti, Alberto (1897-1982) Went the Day Well? 1942; Champagne Charlie 1944; Dead of Night 1945; Nicholas Nickleby 1947; They Made Me a Fugitive 1947; The Monster of Highgate Ponds 1961

Cavalier, Alain (1931-) La Chamade 1968; Thérèse 1986

Cavani, Liliana (1936-) The Night Porter 1973; La Pelle 1981; Francesco 1989; Ripley's Game 2002

Cavayé, Fred Anything for Her 2008; Point Blank 2010; Mea Culpa 2012; The Players 2012

Cayatte, André (1909-1989) Nous Sommes Tous des Assassins 1952; Verdict 1974

Cedar, Joseph (1968-) Time of Favor 2000; Beaufort 2007

Celentano, Jeff Under the Hula Moon 1995; Primary Suspect 2000

Cellan Jones, Simon Some Voices 2000; The One and Only 2001

Ceylan, Nuri Bilge (1959-) Uzak 2003; Climates 2006; Three Monkeys 2008; Once upon a Time in Anatolia 2011; Winter Sleep 2014

Chabrol, Claude (1930-2010) Le Beau Serge 1958; Les Cousins 1959; Web of Passion 1959; Les Bonnes Femmes 1960; The Seven Deadly Sins 1961; Bluebeard 1962; Ophélia 1962; The Beautiful Swindlers 1964; Paris Vu Par... 1965; The Champagne Murders 1966; The Road to Corinth 1967; Les Biches 1968; La Femme Infidèle 1968; Le Boucher 1969; Que la Bête Meure 1969; La Rupture 1970; Juste avant la Nuit 1971; Ten Days' Wonder 1971; Les Noces Rouges 1973; Nada 1974; Une Partie de Plaisir 1974; Les Innocents aux Mains Sales 1975; The Twist 1976; Blood Relatives 1977; Violette Nozière 1977; Le Cheval d'Orgueil 1980; The Blood of Others 1984; Cop au Vin 1984; Inspecteur Lavardin 1986; Le Cri du Hibou 1987; Masques 1987; Une Affaire de Femmes 1988; Dr M 1989; Madame Bovary 1991; L'Enfer 1993; La Cérémonie 1995; Rien Ne Va Plus 1997; The Colour of Lies 1999; Merci pour le Chocolat 2000; The Flower of Evil 2002; The Bridesmaid 2004; A Comedy of Power 2006; La Fille Coupée en Deux 2007

Chadha, Gurinder (1960-) Bhaji on the Beach 1993; What's Cooking? 2000; Bend It like Beckham 2001; Bride & Prejudice 2004; Paris, Je T'Aime 2006; Angus, Thongs and Perfect Snogging 2008; It's a Wonderful Afterlife 2010

Chadwick, Justin The Other Boleyn Girl 2008; The First Grader 2010; Mandela: Long Walk to Freedom 2013

Chaffey, Don (1917-1990) The Girl in the Picture 1956; Danger Within 1958; The Man Upstairs 1958; Dentist in the Chair 1960; Greyfriars Bobby 1961; Nearly a Nasty Accident 1961; The Prince and the Pauper 1962; Jason and the Argonauts 1963; The Three Lives of Thomasina 1963; The Crooked Road 1964; A Jolly Bad Fellow 1964; One Million Years BC 1966; A Twist of Sand 1967; The Viking Queen 1967; Creatures the World Forgot 1971; Persecution 1974; Ride a Wild Pony 1976; Pete's Dragon 1977; The Magic of Lassie 1978; CHOMPS 1979

Chahine, Youssef (1926-2008) Cairo Station 1958; Alexandria Why? 1979; Alexandria Encore 1990; Silence... We're Rolling 2001; 11'09"01 - September 11 2002

Chambers Lynch, Jennifer aka **Lynch, Jennifer** Boxing Helena 1993; Surveillance 2007; Chained 2012

Champion, Gower (1919-1980) My Six Loves 1962; Bank Shot 1974

Champion, Gregg (1956-) Short Time 1990; The Cowboy Way 1994; The Simple Life of Noah Dearborn 1999; The Unexpected Journey 2004; Amish Grace 2010

Chan, Benny Jackie Chan's Who Am I? 1998; New Police Story 2004; Shaolin 2011

Chan, Gordon aka **Chan Ka-Seung, Gordon** (1960-) Fist of Legend 1994; Beast Cops 1998; The Medallion 2003

Chan, Jackie (1954-) Project A 1983; Police Story 1985; The Armour of God 1986; Police Story 2 1986; Project A: Part II 1987; Operation Condor: the Armour of God II 1990; Jackie Chan's Who Am I? 1998; Chinese Zodiac 2012

Chan, Peter Ho-Sun The Love Letter 1999; The Warlords 2008; Dragon 2011

Chandon, Alex Cradle of Fear 2001; Inbred 2011

Chandor, J C Margin Call 2011; All Is Lost 2013; A Most Violent Year 2014

Chandrasekhar, Jay (1966-) Super Troopers 2001; Broken Lizard's Club Dread 2004; The Dukes of Hazzard 2005; Beerfest 2006

Chang Cheh One-Armed Swordsman 1967; Five Deadly Venoms 1978

Chapiron, Kim Sheitan 2006; Dog Pound 2009; Smart Ass 2014

Chaplin, Charles aka **Chaplin, Charlie** (1889-1977) His New Job 1915; The Tramp 1915; Work 1915; Behind the Screen 1916; The Floorwalker 1916; The Pawnshop 1916; The Rink 1916; The Vagabond 1916; The Cure 1917; The Immigrant 1917; A Dog's Life 1918; Shoulder Arms 1918; A Day's Pleasure 1919; Sunnyside 1919; The Idle Class 1921; The Kid 1921; Pay Day 1922; The Pilgrim 1923; A Woman of Paris 1923; The Gold Rush 1925; The Circus 1928; City Lights 1931; Modern Times 1936; The Great Dictator 1940; Monsieur Verdoux 1947; Limelight 1952; A King in New York 1957; A Countess from Hong Kong 1967

Chapman, Brenda The Prince of Egypt 1998; Brave 2012

Chapman, Matthew (1950-) Strangers Kiss 1983; Heart of Midnight 1988

Chapman, Michael (1935-) All the Right Moves 1983; The Clan of the Cave Bear 1986

Chappelle, Joe Halloween 6: the Curse of Michael Myers 1995; Phantoms 1998; Dark Prince - the Legend of Dracula 2000

Charell, Erik (1894-1974) Congress Dances 1931; Caravan 1934

Charles, Larry (1956-) Masked and Anonymous 2003; Borat: Cultural Learnings of America for Make Benefit Glorious Nation of Kazakhstan 2006; Religulous 2008; Brüno 2009; The Dictator 2012

Chatiliez, Etienne (1952-) Life Is a Long Quiet River 1988; Tatie Danielle 1990; Le Bonheur Est dans le Pré 1995

Chaumeil, Pascal (1961-2015) Heartbreaker 2010; A Perfect Plan 2012; A Long Way Down 2013

Chazelle, Damien Whiplash 2014; La La Land 2016

Chechik, Jeremiah aka **Chechik, Jeremiah** National Lampoon's Christmas Vacation 1989; Benny & Joon 1993; Tall Tale 1994; Diabolique 1996; The Avengers 1998

Chelsom, Peter (1956-) Hear My Song 1991; Funny Bones 1994; The Mighty 1998; Serendipity 2001; Town & Country 2001; Shall We Dance 2004; Hannah Montana: the Movie 2009; Hector and the Search for Happiness 2014

Chen Kaige (1952-) Yellow Earth 1984; The Big Parade 1986; King of the Children 1987; Life on a String 1991; Farewell My Concubine 1993; Temptress Moon 1996; The Emperor and the Assassin 1999; Killing Me Softly 2001; Ten Minutes Older: the Trumpet 2002; Together with You 2002

Chen, Joan (1961-) Xiu Xiu: The Sent Down Girl 1999; Autumn in New York 2000

Chen, Teddy The Accidental Spy 2001; Kung Fu Killer 2014

Chenal, Pierre (1903-1990) Crime and Punishment 1935; Clochemerle 1948; Native Son 1951

Chéreau, Patrice (1944-2013) The Flesh of the Orchid 1974; La Reine Margot 1994; Those Who Love Me Can Take the Train 1998; Intimacy 2000; Son Frère 2003; Gabrielle 2005

Cherry III, John R aka **Cherry, John** (1948-) Ernest Goes to Camp 1987; Ernest Saves Christmas 1988; Ernest Goes to Jail 1990; Ernest Scared Stupid 1991; Ernest Rides Again 1993; Slam Dunk Ernest 1995

Ching Siu-Tung aka **Ching Siu-tung, Tony** (1953-) A Chinese Ghost Story 1987; Belly of the Beast 2003

Cholodenko, Lisa (1964-) High Art 1998; Laurel Canyon 2002; The Kids Are All Right 2010

Chomet, Sylvain Belleville Rendez-vous 2003; Paris, Je T'Aime 2006; The Illusionist 2010; Attila Marcel 2013

Chomsky, Marvin J (1929-) Evel Knievel 1971; Victory at Entebbe 1976; My Body, My Child 1982

Chong, Tommy aka **Chong, Thomas** (1938-) Cheech and Chong's Next Movie 1980; Cheech and Chong's Nice Dreams 1981; Cheech & Chong's Still Smokin' 1983; Cheech & Chong's The Corsican Brothers 1984

Chopra, Aditya (1971-) Dilwale Dulhania Le Jayenge 1995; Mohabbatein 2000

Chopra, B R (1914-2008) Ek Hi Rasta 1956; Naya Daur 1957; Kanoon 1960

Chopra, Joyce (1938-) Smooth Talk 1985; The Lemon Sisters 1989; Murder in New Hampshire 1991; The Lady in Question 1999; Murder in a Small Town 1999; The Last Chance 2003

Chopra, Vidhu Vinod 1942: a Love Story 1994; Eklavya: the Royal Guard 2007; Broken Horses 2015

Chopra, Yash (1932-2012) Waqt 1965; Veer-Zaara 2004

Chouraqui, Elie (1950-) Love Songs 1984; Man on Fire 1987; Harrison's Flowers 2000

Chow, Stephen (1962-) Shaolin Soccer 2001; Kung Fu Hustle 2004; CJ7 2008; Mermaid 2016

Christian-Jaque (1904-1994) Fanfan la Tulipe 1951; Madame du Barry 1954; Madame 1961; The Black Tulip 1963; The Dirty Game 1965; Dead Run 1967

Christian, Roger (1944-) The Sender 1982; Lorca and the Outlaws 1985; Nostradamus 1993; Masterminds 1997; Battlefield Earth 2000

Chu, Jon M (1979-) Step Up 2 the Streets 2008; Step Up 3 2010; Justin Bieber: Never Say Never 2011; GI Joe: Retaliation 2013; Jem and the Holograms 2015; Now You See Me 2 2016

Chubbuck, Lyndon Naked Souls 1995; The War Bride 2001

Chudnow, Byron Ross (1926-) The Doberman Gang 1972; The Amazing Dobermans 1976

Cianfrance, Derek Blue Valentine 2010; The Place beyond the Pines 2012

Ciccoritti, Jerry aka **Ciccoritti, Gerard** (1955-) Graveyard Shift 1986; The Life before This 1999; Million Dollar Murder 2004; Victor 2008

Cimber, Matt aka **Ottaviano, Matteo** Single Room Furnished 1968; Butterfly 1982

Cimino, Michael (1943-2016) Thunderbolt and Lightfoot 1974; The Deer Hunter 1978; Heaven's Gate 1980; Year of the Dragon 1985; The Sicilian 1987; Desperate Hours 1990; Sunchaser 1996

Clair, René aka **Clair, Rene** (1898-1981) Paris Qui Dort 1923;

Entr'Acte 1924; An Italian Straw Hat 1927; Sous les Toits de Paris 1930; A Nous la Liberté 1931; Le Million 1931; The Ghost Goes West 1935; The Flame of New Orleans 1941; I Married a Witch 1942; Forever and a Day 1943; It Happened Tomorrow 1944; And Then There Were None 1945; Man about Town 1947; La Beauté du Diable 1949; Les Belles de Nuit 1952; Les Grandes Manoeuvres 1955; Gates of Paris 1957

Clark, Bob (1941-2007) Dead of Night 1972; Black Christmas 1974; Breaking Point 1973; Murder by Decree 1978; Tribute 1980; Porky's 1981; A Christmas Story 1983; Rhinestone 1984; Turk 182! 1985; From the Hip 1987; Loose Cannons 1990; Arthur Miller's The American Clock 1993; It Runs in the Family 1994; Baby Geniuses 1999; I'll Remember April 1999

Clark, Greydon (1943-) Without Warning 1980; Wacko 1981; Lambada! The Forbidden Dance 1990

Clark, James B (1908-2000) The Sad Horse 1959; One Foot in Hell 1960; The Big Show 1961; Flipper 1963; Island of the Blue Dolphins 1964

Clark, Jim (1931-) Every Home Should Have One 1970; Rentadick 1972; Madhouse 1974

Clark, Larry (1943-) kids 1995; Another Day in Paradise 1998; Bully 2001; Destricted 2006

Clarke, Alan (1935-1990) Scum 1979; Rita, Sue and Bob Too 1986

Clarke, James Kenelm (1941-) Exposé 1975; Hardcore 1977; Let's Get Laid 1977; Yellow Pages 1984

Clarke, Noel (1975-) Adulthood 2008; 4.3.2.1 2010; The Anomaly 2014; Brotherhood 2016

Claudel, Philippe I've Loved You So Long 2008; Before the Winter Chill 2013

Clavell, James (1925-1994) Walk like a Dragon 1960; To Sir, with Love 1967; Where's Jack? 1969; The Last Valley 1971

Clayton, Jack (1921-1995) The Bespoke Overcoat 1955; Room at the Top 1958; The Innocents 1961; The Pumpkin Eater 1964; Our Mother's House 1967; The Great Gatsby 1974; Something Wicked This Way Comes 1983; The Lonely Passion of Judith Hearne 1987

Clegg, Tom Sweeney 2 1978; McVicar 1980; The Inside Man 1984

Clemens, William (1905-1980) The Case of the Velvet Claws 1936; The Case of the Stuttering Bishop 1937; Nancy Drew - Detective 1938; Devil's Island 1940; The Falcon and the Co-Eds 1943; The Falcon in Danger 1943; The Falcon Out West 1944

Clement, Dick (1937-) Otley 1968; A Severed Head 1970; Catch Me a Spy 1971; Porridge 1979; Bullshot 1983; Water 1985

Clément, René (1913-1996) La Bataille du Rail 1946; La Belle et la Bête 1946; Jeux Interdits 1952; Knave of Hearts 1954; Gervaise 1956; This Angry Age 1957; Plein Soleil 1960; The Love Cage 1964; Is Paris Burning? 1966; Rider on the Rain 1970; The Deadly Trap 1971; And Hope to Die 1972

Clements, Ron (1953-) Basil the Great Mouse Detective 1986; The Little Mermaid 1989; Aladdin 1992; Hercules 1997; Treasure Planet 2002; The Princess and the Frog 2009

Clifford, Graeme (1942-) Frances 1982; Burke and Wills 1985; Gleaming the Cube 1988; Ruby Cairo 1992; Profoundly Normal 2003; Family Sins 2004; And She Was 2007

Cline, Edward aka Cline, Eddie aka Cline, Edward F (1892-1961) Neighbors 1920; One Week 1920; The Scarecrow 1920; The Paleface 1921; Day Dreams 1922; Three Ages 1923; Million Dollar Legs 1932; The Bank Dick 1940; My Little Chickadee 1940; The Villain Still Pursued Her 1940; Never Give a Sucker an Even Break 1941

Cloche, Maurice (1907-1990) Monsieur Vincent 1947; Never Take No for an Answer 1951

Clooney, George (1961-) Confessions of a Dangerous Mind 2002; Good Night, and Good Luck. 2005; Leatherheads 2007; The Ides of March 2011; The Monuments Men 2013

Clouse, Robert (1928-1997) Darker than Amber 1970; Enter the Dragon 1973; Black Belt Jones 1974; Golden Needles 1974; The Ultimate Warrior 1975; The Pack 1977; The Amsterdam Kill 1978; Game of Death 1978; The Big Brawl 1980; China O'Brien 1988

Clouzot, Henri-Georges (1907-1977) The Raven 1943; Quai des Orfèvres 1947; The Wages of Fear 1953; Les Diaboliques 1954; Le Mystère Picasso 1956; Les Espions 1957; La Vérité 1960

Cochran, Stacy My New Gun 1992; Boys 1995

Cocteau, Jean (1889-1963) The Blood of a Poet 1930; La Belle et la Bête 1946; The Eagle Has Two Heads 1948; Les Parents Terribles 1948; Orphée 1950; Le Testament d'Orphée 1960

Coen, Ethan (1957-) The Ladykillers 2004; Paris, Je T'Aime 2006; No Country for Old Men 2007; Burn after Reading 2008; A Serious Man 2009; True Grit 2010; Inside Llewyn Davis 2013; Hail, Caesar! 2016

Coen, Joel (1954-) Blood Simple 1983; Raising Arizona 1987; Miller's Crossing 1990; Barton Fink 1991; The Hudsucker Proxy 1994; Fargo 1995; The Big Lebowski 1997; O Brother, Where Art Thou? 2000; The Man Who Wasn't There 2001; Intolerable Cruelty 2003; The Ladykillers 2004; Paris, Je T'Aime 2006; No Country for Old Men 2007; Burn after Reading 2008; A Serious Man 2009; True Grit 2010; Inside Llewyn Davis 2013; Hail, Caesar! 2016

Coffin, Pierre Despicable Me 2010; Despicable Me 2 2013; Minions 2015; Despicable Me 3 2017

Cohen, Howard R (1942-1999) Saturday the 14th 1981; Saturday the 14th Strikes Back 1988; Time Trackers 1989

Cohen, Larry (1938-) Bone 1972; Black Caesar 1973; Hell Up in Harlem 1973; It's Alive 1974; The Private Files of J Edgar Hoover 1977; It Lives Again 1978; Full Moon High 1982; Q - the Winged Serpent 1982; The Stuff 1985; It's Alive III: Island of the Alive 1987; A Return to Salem's Lot 1987; Wicked Stepmother 1989; The Ambulance 1990; Original Gangstas 1996

Cohen, Norman (1936-1983) Till Death Us Do Part 1968; Dad's Army 1971; Adolf Hitler - My Part in His Downfall 1972; Confessions of a Pop Performer 1975; Confessions of a Driving Instructor 1976; Confessions from a Holiday Camp 1977; Stand Up Virgin Soldiers 1977

Cohen, Rob (1949-) Scandalous 1983; Dragon: the Bruce Lee Story 1993; Daylight 1996; DragonHeart 1996; The Rat Pack 1998; The Skulls 2000; The Fast and the Furious 2001; xXx 2002; Stealth 2005; The Mummy: Tomb of the Dragon Emperor 2008; Alex Cross 2012; The Boy Next Door 2015

Cohn, Michael When the Bough Breaks 1993; Snow White: a Tale of Terror 1996

Coixet, Isabel (1960-) My Life without Me 2002; Paris, Je T'Aime 2006; Elegy 2008; Learning to Drive 2014

Cokliss, Harley (1945-) Battletruck 1982; Black Moon Rising 1985; Malone 1987; Dream Demon 1988

Cole, Nigel (1959-) Saving Grace 2000; Calendar Girls 2003; A Lot like Love 2005; Made in Dagenham 2010; All in Good Time 2012; The Wedding Video 2012

Colizzi, Giuseppe (1925-1978) God Forgives... I Don't! 1967; Ace High 1968; Boot Hill 1969

Colla, Richard A (1918-) Zigzag 1970; Fuzz 1972; Battlestar Galactica 1978; The Great Balloon Adventure 1978; Danielle Steel's Zoya 1995; Swearing Allegiance 1997; Blue Valley Songbird 1999

Collet-Serra, Jaume (1974-) House of Wax 2005; Goal II: Living the Dream 2007; Orphan 2009; Unknown 2011; Non-Stop 2014; Run All Night 2015; The Shallows 2016

Collier, James F (1929-1991) Two a Penny 1968; China Cry 1990

Collinson, Peter (1936-1980) The Penthouse 1967; Up the Junction 1967; The Italian Job 1969; You Can't Win 'Em All 1970; Fright 1971; And Then There Were None 1974; Open Season 1974; The Sellout 1975; Tomorrow Never Comes 1977; The Earthling 1980

Collyer, Laurie Sherrybaby 2006; The Secret Life of Marilyn Monroe 2015

Columbus, Chris (1958-) A Night on the Town 1987; Heartbreak Hotel 1988; Home Alone 1990; Only the Lonely 1991; Home Alone 2: Lost in New York 1992; Mrs Doubtfire 1993; Nine Months 1995; Stepmom 1998; Bicentennial Man 1999; Harry Potter and the Philosopher's Stone 2001; Harry Potter and the Chamber of Secrets 2002; Rent 2005; I Love You, Beth Cooper 2009; Percy Jackson & the Lightning Thief 2010; Pixels 2015

Comencini, Luigi (1916-2007) Bread, Love & Dreams 1953; Le Bambole 1965

Comerford, Joe (1949-) Reefer and the Model 1988; High Boot Benny 1993

Comfort, Lance (1908-1966) Hatter's Castle 1941; Great Day 1944; Hotel Reserve 1944; Bedelia 1946; Daughter of Darkness 1948; Silent Dust 1948; Portrait of Clare 1950; Eight o'Clock Walk 1953; Bang! You're Dead 1954; Man from Tangier 1957; The Man in the Road 1957; Make Mine a Million 1959; The Breaking Point 1961; The Painted Smile 1961; Pit of Darkness 1961; The Break 1962; Tomorrow at Ten 1962; Live It Up 1963; Devils of Darkness 1964; Be My Guest 1965

Compton, Richard (1938-2007) Macon County Line 1973; Return to Macon County 1975; Maniac 1977

Condon, Bill (1957-) Candyman: Farewell to the Flesh 1995; The Man Who Wouldn't Die 1995; Gods and Monsters 1998; Kinsey 2004; Dreamgirls 2006; Breaking Dawn Part One 2011; Breaking Dawn Part Two 2012; The Fifth Estate 2013; Mr Holmes 2014; Beauty and the Beast 2017

Connolly, Robert (1967-) The Bank 2001; The Turning 2013; Paper Planes 2014

Connor, Kevin (1937-) From beyond the Grave 1973; The Land That Time Forgot 1974; At the Earth's Core 1976; Trial by Combat 1976; The People That Time Forgot 1977; Warlords of Atlantis 1978; Arabian Adventure 1979; Motel Hell 1980; The House Where Evil Dwells 1982; Sunset Grill 1992; Jack Reed: Badge of Honor 1993; The Little Riders 1996; Murder without Conviction 2004; Fielder's Choice 2005; Always and Forever 2008; Farewell Mr Kringle 2010; The Wish List 2010; Honeymoon for One 2011

Conrad, William (1920-1994) Two on a Guillotine 1964; Brainstorm 1965; My Blood Runs Cold 1965

Contner, James A (1947-) You've Got a Friend 2007; Ladies of the House 2008

Conway, Jack (1887-1952) Our Modern Maidens 1929; The Unholy Three 1930; Arsene Lupin 1932; Red-Headed Woman 1932; The Gay Bride 1934; The Girl from Missouri 1934; Viva Villa! 1934; A Tale of Two Cities 1935; Libeled Lady 1936; Saratoga 1937; Too Hot to Handle 1938; A Yank at Oxford 1938; Lady of the Tropics 1939; Boom Town 1940; Honky Tonk 1941; Love Crazy 1941; Crossroads 1942; Dragon Seed 1944; High Barbaree 1947; The Hucksters 1947; Julia Misbehaves 1948

Conyers, Darcy (1919-1973) The Night We Dropped a Clanger 1959; The Night We Got the Bird 1960; In the Doghouse 1961

Coogler, Ryan (1986-) Fruitvale Station 2013; Creed 2015; Black Panther 2018

Cook, Barry Mulan 1998; Walking with Dinosaurs: the 3D Movie 2013

Cook, Fielder (1923-2003) Patterns 1956; A Big Hand for a Little Lady 1966; Prudence and the Pill 1968; Eagle in a Cage 1971; The Hideaways 1973; The Member of the Wedding 1997

Coolidge, Martha (1946-) Valley Girl 1983; The City Girl 1984; Joy of Sex 1984; Real Genius 1985; Plain Clothes 1988; Rambling Rose 1991; Crazy in Love 1992; Lost in Yonkers 1993; Angie 1994; Three Wishes 1995; Introducing Dorothy Dandridge 1999; If These Walls Could Talk 2 2000; The Prince & Me 2004; The Twelve Days of Christmas Eve 2004; Material Girls 2006; Nora Roberts' Tribute 2009

Cooney, Ray (1932-) Not Now Darling 1972; Not Now, Comrade 1976; Run for Your Wife 2015

Cooper, Jackie (1922-2011) Perfect Gentlemen 1978; Rainbow 1978; Leave 'Em Laughing 1981

Cooper, Merian C aka Cooper, Merian (1893-1973) Grass: a Nation's Battle for Life 1925; Chang 1927; The Four Feathers 1929; King Kong 1933

Cooper, Scott Crazy Heart 2009; Out of the Furnace 2013; Black Mass 2015

Cooper, Stuart (1942-) Overlord 1975; The Disappearance 1977; The Hunted 1998

Coppola, Christopher (1962-) Dracula's Widow 1988; Palmer's Pick-Up 1999; G-Men from Hell 2000

Coppola, Francis Ford aka Coppola, Francis (1939-) Tonight for Sure! 1961; Dementia 13 1963; You're a Big Boy Now 1966; Finian's Rainbow 1968; The Rain People 1969; The Godfather 1972; The Conversation 1974; The Godfather Part II 1974; Apocalypse Now 1979; One from the Heart 1982; The Outsiders 1983; Rumble Fish 1983; The Cotton Club 1984; Peggy Sue Got Married 1986; Gardens of Stone 1987; Tucker: the Man and His Dream 1988; New York Stories 1989; The Godfather Part III 1990; Bram Stoker's Dracula 1992; Jack 1996; John Grisham's The Rainmaker 1997; Youth without Youth 2007; Tetro 2009; Twixt 2011

Coppola, Sofia (1971-) The Virgin Suicides 1999; Lost in Translation 2003; Marie Antoinette 2005; Somewhere 2010; The Bling Ring 2013

Coraci, Frank (1965-) The Waterboy 1998; The Wedding Singer 1998; Around the World in 80 Days 2004; Click 2006; Zookeeper 2011; Here Comes the Boom 2012; Blended 2014

Corbiau, Gérard (1941-) The Music Teacher 1988; Farinelli il Castrato 1994; Le Roi Danse 2000

Corbijn, Anton (1955-) Control 2007; The American 2010; A Most Wanted Man 2013; Life 2015

Corbucci, Sergio (1926-1990) Duel of the Titans 1961; Django 1966; Navajo Joe 1966; The Great Silence 1967; A Professional Gun 1968; The Con Artists 1976

Corcoran, Bill Mary Higgins Clark's Let Me Call You Sweetheart 1997; Atomic Twister 2002

Core, Ericson Invincible 2006; Point Break 2015

Corman, Roger (1926-) Apache Woman 1955; The Day the World Ended 1956; It Conquered the World 1956; Not of This Earth 1956; The Oklahoma Woman 1956; Attack of the Crab Monsters 1957; Rock All Night 1957; The Undead 1957; Viking Women and the Sea Serpent 1957; Machine Gun Kelly 1958; The Mobster 1958; Teenage Caveman 1958; War of the Satellites 1958; A Bucket of Blood 1959; The Wasp Woman 1959; Atlas 1960; The Fall of the House of Usher 1960; The Last Woman on Earth 1960; The Little Shop of Horrors 1960; Creature from the Haunted Sea 1961; The Intruder 1961; Pit and the Pendulum 1961; The Premature Burial 1962; Tales of Terror 1962; Tower of London 1962; The Haunted Palace 1963; The Man with the X-Ray Eyes 1963; The Raven 1963; The Terror 1963; The Masque of the Red Death 1964; The Secret Invasion 1964; The Tomb of Ligeia 1964; The Wild Angels 1966; The St Valentine's Day Massacre 1967; The Trip 1967; Bloody Mama 1970; Gas-s-s-s, or It Became Necessary to Destroy the World in Order to Save It 1970; Frankenstein Unbound 1990

Corneau, Alain (1943-2010) Choice of Arms 1981; Fort Saganne 1984; Tous les Matins du Monde 1991; Les Enfants de Lumière 1995; Fear and Trembling 2003; Love Crime 2010

Cornelius, Henry (1913-1958) Passport to Pimlico 1949; Genevieve 1953; I Am a Camera 1955; Next to No Time 1958

Cornell, John (1941-) "Crocodile" Dundee II 1988; Almost an Angel 1990

Cornfield, Hubert (1929-2006) Plunder Road 1957; The Third Voice 1960; Pressure Point 1962; The Night of the Following Day 1968

Corrente, Michael (1960-) Federal Hill 1994; American Buffalo 1995; Outside Providence 1999; A Shot at Glory 2000; Brooklyn Rules 2007

Corrigan, Lloyd (1900-1969) No One Man 1932; Murder on a Honeymoon 1935

Corsini, Catherine La Nouvelle Eve 1998; Leaving 2008; Summertime 2015

Cortés, Rodrigo Buried 2009; Red Lights 2012

Coscarelli, Don (1954-) Phantasm 1978; The Beastmaster 1982; Phantasm II 1988; Bubba Ho-tep 2002; John Dies at the End 2012

Cosmatos, George Pan (1941-2005) Sin 1972; Massacre in Rome 1973; The Cassandra Crossing 1976; Escape to Athena 1979; Of Unknown Origin 1983; Rambo: First Blood, Part II 1985; Cobra 1986; Leviathan 1989; Tombstone 1993; Shadow Conspiracy 1996

Costa-Gavras aka Costa-Gavras, Constantin (1933-) The Sleeping Car Murders 1965; Z 1968; The Confession 1970; State of Siege 1972; Missing 1981; Betrayed 1988; Music Box 1989; Mad City 1997; Amen. 2002

Costa, Mario (1904-1995) The Barber of Seville 1946; Pagliacci 1948; Gordon the Black Pirate 1961

Costanzo, Saverio Private 2004; In Memory of Myself 2007

Costner, Kevin (1955-) Dances with Wolves 1990; The Postman 1997; Open Range 2003

Coto, Manny Dr Giggles 1992; Star Kid 1997

Couffer, Jack (1922-) Ring of Bright Water 1969; The Darwin Adventure 1972; Living Free 1972

Coulter, Allen Hollywoodland 2006; Remember Me 2010

Cousins, Mark The First Movie 2009; A Story of Children and Film 2014

Cousteau, Jacques-Yves (1910-1997) Le Monde du Silence 1956; World without Sun 1964

Couturie, Bill Dear America: Letters Home from Vietnam 1987; Ed 1996

Cox, Alex (1954-) Repo Man 1984; Sid and Nancy 1986; Straight to Hell 1987; Walker 1987; Highway Patrolman 1991; The Winner 1996; Revengers Tragedy 2002; Searchers 2.0 2007; Repo Chick 2009

Cox, Paul (1940-2016) Lonely Hearts 1981; Man of Flowers 1984; My First Wife 1984; Cactus 1986; Vincent: the Life and Death of Vincent Van Gogh 1987; Golden Braid 1991; A Woman's Tale 1991; Erotic Tales 1994; Innocence 2000

Cozzi, Luigi aka Coates, Lewis (1947-) Hercules 1983; Hercules II 1984

Crabtree, Arthur (1900-1975) Madonna of the Seven Moons 1944; They Were Sisters 1945; Caravan 1946; Dear Murderer 1947; The Calendar 1948; Quartet 1948; Don't Ever Leave Me 1949; Hindle Wakes 1952; Fiend without a Face 1957; Horrors of the Black Museum 1959

Craven, Wes (1939-2015) Last House on the Left 1972; The Hills Have Eyes 1977; Deadly Blessing 1981; Swamp Thing 1982; A Nightmare on Elm Street 1984; Chiller 1985; Deadly Friend 1986; The Serpent and the Rainbow 1987; Shocker 1989; The People under the Stairs 1991; Wes Craven's New Nightmare 1994; Vampire in Brooklyn 1995; Scream 1996; Scream 2 1997; Music of the Heart 1999; Scream 3 1999; Cursed 2005; Red Eye 2005; Paris, Je T'Aime 2006; My Soul to Take 2010; Scre4m 2011

Crawford, Curtis The Boy She Met Online 2010; My Family's Secret 2010; The Girl He Met Online 2014

Creevy, Eran Shifty 2008; Welcome to the Punch 2013

Crialese, Emanuele Respiro 2002; Golden Door 2006

Crichton, Charles (1910-1999) For Those in Peril 1943; Dead of Night 1945; Painted Boats 1945; Against the Wind 1947; Hue and Cry 1947; Another Shore 1948; Train of Events 1949; Dance Hall 1950; The Lavender Hill Mob 1951; Hunted 1952; The Titfield Thunderbolt 1952; The Love Lottery 1953; The Divided Heart 1954; The Man in the Sky 1956; Floods of Fear 1958; Law and Disorder 1958; The Battle of the Sexes 1960; The Boy Who Stole a Million 1960; The Third Secret 1964; He Who Rides a Tiger 1965; A Fish Called Wanda 1988

Crichton, Michael (1942-2008) Westworld 1973; Coma 1977; The

First Great Train Robbery 1978; *Looker* 1981; *Physical Evidence* 1988

Crisp, Donald (1880-1974) *The Navigator* 1924; *Don Q, Son of Zorro* 1925

Cristofer, Michael (1945-) *Gia* 1998; *Body Shots* 1999; *Original Sin* 2001

Croghan, Emma-Kate (1972-) *Love and Other Catastrophes* 1996; *Strange Planet* 1999

Crombie, Donald (1942-) *Caddie* 1976; *The Irishman* 1978; *Rough Diamonds* 1994

Cromwell, John (1888-1979) *The Texan* 1930; *Tom Sawyer* 1930; *Ann Vickers* 1933; *The Silver Cord* 1933; *Of Human Bondage* 1934; *Spitfire* 1934; *This Man Is Mine* 1934; *I Dream Too Much* 1935; *Village Tale* 1935; *Banjo on My Knee* 1936; *Little Lord Fauntleroy* 1936; *The Prisoner of Zenda* 1937; *Algiers* 1938; *In Name Only* 1939; *Made for Each Other* 1939; *Spirit of the People* 1940; *Victory* 1940; *So Ends Our Night* 1941; *Son of Fury* 1942; *Since You Went Away* 1944; *The Enchanted Cottage* 1945; *Anna and the King of Siam* 1946; *Dead Reckoning* 1947; *Night Song* 1947; *Caged* 1950; *The Company She Keeps* 1950; *The Racket* 1951; *The Goddess* 1958

Cronenberg, David (1943-) *Crimes of the Future* 1970; *Shivers* 1975; *Rabid* 1976; *The Brood* 1979; *Scanners* 1980; *Videodrome* 1982; *The Dead Zone* 1983; *The Fly* 1986; *Dead Ringers* 1988; *Naked Lunch* 1991; *M Butterfly* 1993; *Crash* 1996; *eXistenZ* 1999; *Spider* 2002; *A History of Violence* 2005; *Eastern Promises* 2007; *A Dangerous Method* 2011; *Cosmopolis* 2012; *Maps to the Stars* 2014

Crosland, Alan (1894-1936) *Don Juan* 1926; *When a Man Loves* 1926; *The Jazz Singer* 1927; *The Case of the Howling Dog* 1934

Crowe, Cameron (1957-) *Say Anything...* 1989; *Singles* 1992; *Jerry Maguire* 1996; *Almost Famous* 2000; *Vanilla Sky* 2001; *Elizabethtown* 2005; *Pearl Jam Twenty* 2011; *We Bought a Zoo* 2011; *Aloha* 2015

Crowe, Christopher (1948-) *Saigon* 1988; *Whispers in the Dark* 1992

Crowley, John (1969-) *interMission* 2003; *Is Anybody There?* 2008; *Closed Circuit* 2013; *Brooklyn* 2015

Cruze, James (1884-1942) *Terror Island* 1920; *The Covered Wagon* 1923; *Ruggles of Red Gap* 1923; *The Pony Express* 1925; *The Great Gabbo* 1929; *If I Had a Million* 1932; *Washington Merry-Go-Round* 1932; *I Cover the Waterfront* 1933

Crystal, Billy (1947-) *Mr Saturday Night* 1992; *Forget Paris* 1995; *61** 2001

Csupo, Gabor *Bridge to Terabithia* 2006; *The Secret of Moonacre* 2008

Cuarón, Alfonso (1961-) *A Little Princess* 1995; *Great Expectations* 1997; *Y Tu Mamá También* 2001; *Harry Potter and the Prisoner of Azkaban* 2004; *Children of Men* 2006; *Paris, Je T'Aime* 2006; *Gravity* 2013

Cuesta, Michael *LIE* 2001; *Twelve and Holding* 2005; *Kill the Messenger* 2014

Cukor, George (1899-1983) *Grumpy* 1930; *The Royal Family of Broadway* 1930; *The Virtuous Sin* 1930; *Tarnished Lady* 1931; *A Bill of Divorcement* 1932; *Rockabye* 1932; *What Price Hollywood?* 1932; *Dinner at Eight* 1933; *Little Women* 1933; *Our Betters* 1933; *David Copperfield* 1935; *Romeo and Juliet* 1936; *Sylvia Scarlett* 1936; *Camille* 1937; *Holiday* 1938; *The Women* 1939; *Zaza* 1939; *The Philadelphia Story* 1940; *Susan and God* 1940; *Two-Faced Woman* 1941; *A Woman's Face* 1941; *Her Cardboard Lover* 1942; *Keeper of the Flame* 1942; *Gaslight* 1944; *Winged Victory* 1944; *A Double Life* 1947; *Adam's Rib* 1949; *Edward, My Son* 1949; *Born Yesterday* 1950; *A Life of Her Own* 1950; *The Model and the Marriage Broker* 1951; *The Marrying Kind* 1952; *Pat and Mike* 1952; *The Actress* 1953; *It Should Happen to You* 1954; *A Star Is Born* 1954; *Bhowani Junction* 1956; *Les Girls* 1957; *Wild Is the Wind* 1957; *Heller in Pink Tights* 1960; *Let's Make Love* 1960; *Song without End* 1960; *The Chapman Report* 1962; *My Fair Lady* 1964; *Justine* 1969; *Travels with My Aunt* 1972; *Love among the Ruins* 1975; *The Blue Bird* 1976; *Rich and Famous* 1981

Cummings, Irving (1888-1959) *In Old Arizona* 1929; *The Cisco Kid* 1931; *The Mad Game* 1933; *The White Parade* 1934; *Curly Top* 1935; *Poor Little Rich Girl* 1936; *Vogues of 1938* 1937; *Just around the Corner* 1938; *Little Miss Broadway* 1938; *Hollywood Cavalcade* 1939; *The Story of Alexander Graham Bell* 1939; *Down Argentine Way* 1940; *Lillian Russell* 1940; *Belle Starr* 1941; *Louisiana Purchase* 1941; *That Night in Rio* 1941; *My Gal Sal* 1942; *Springtime in the Rockies* 1942; *Sweet Rosie O'Grady* 1943; *What a Woman!* 1943; *The Dolly Sisters* 1945; *Double Dynamite* 1951

Cundieff, Rusty (1965-) *Fear of a Black Hat* 1992; *Movie 43* 2013

Cunningham, David L *To End All Wars* 2001; *The Dark Is Rising* 2007

Cunningham, Sean S (1941-) *Friday the 13th* 1980; *DeepStar Six* 1989

Curran, John *We Don't Live Here Anymore* 2004; *The Painted Veil* 2006; *Stone* 2010; *Tracks* 2013

Curry, Marshall *Racing Dreams* 2009; *If a Tree Falls: a Story of the Earth Liberation Front* 2011; *Point and Shoot* 2014

Curry, Rob *Way of the Morris* 2011; *Tempest* 2012

Curtis-Hall, Vondie aka *Curtis Hall, Vondie* (1956-) *Gridlock'd* 1996; *Glitter* 2001; *Waist Deep* 2006

Curtis, Dan (1927-2006) *House of Dark Shadows* 1970; *Night of Dark Shadows* 1971; *Dracula* 1974; *Burnt Offerings* 1976; *Me and the Kid* 1993

Curtis, Richard (1956-) *Love Actually* 2003; *The Boat That Rocked* 2009; *About Time* 2013

Curtis, Simon *My Week with Marilyn* 2011; *Woman in Gold* 2015; *Goodbye Christopher Robin* 2017

Curtiz, Michael (1886-1962) *Mammy* 1930; *God's Gift to Women* 1931; *The Mad Genius* 1931; *Cabin in the Cotton* 1932; *Doctor X* 1932; *The Strange Love of Molly Louvain* 1932; *Female* 1933; *The Kennel Murder Case* 1933; *Mystery of the Wax Museum* 1933; *20,000 Years in Sing Sing* 1933; *British Agent* 1934; *Jimmy the Gent* 1934; *The Key* 1934; *Mandalay* 1934; *Black Fury* 1935; *Captain Blood* 1935; *Front Page Woman* 1935; *The Charge of the Light Brigade* 1936; *The Walking Dead* 1936; *Kid Galahad* 1937; *The Perfect Specimen* 1937; *The Adventures of Robin Hood* 1938; *Angels with Dirty Faces* 1938; *Four Daughters* 1938; *Four's a Crowd* 1938; *Gold Is Where You Find It* 1938; *Daughters Courageous* 1939; *Dodge City* 1939; *Four Wives* 1939; *The Private Lives of Elizabeth and Essex* 1939; *Santa Fe Trail* 1940; *The Sea Hawk* 1940; *Virginia City* 1940; *Dive Bomber* 1941; *The Sea Wolf* 1941; *Captains of the Clouds* 1942; *Casablanca* 1942; *Yankee Doodle Dandy* 1942; *Mission to Moscow* 1943; *This Is the Army* 1943; *Passage to Marseille* 1944; *Mildred Pierce* 1945; *Roughly Speaking* 1945; *Night and Day* 1946; *Life with Father* 1947; *The Unsuspected* 1947; *Romance on the High Seas* 1948; *Flamingo Road* 1949; *My Dream Is Yours* 1949; *The Breaking Point* 1950; *Bright Leaf* 1950; *Young Man with a Horn* 1950; *Force of Arms* 1951; *I'll See You in My Dreams* 1951; *Jim Thorpe - All-American* 1951; *The Jazz Singer* 1952; *Trouble along the Way* 1953; *The Boy from Oklahoma* 1954; *The Egyptian* 1954; *White Christmas* 1954; *We're No Angels* 1955; *The Best Things in Life Are Free* 1956; *The Vagabond King* 1956; *The Helen Morgan Story* 1957; *King Creole* 1958; *The Proud Rebel* 1958; *The Hangman* 1959; *The Adventures of Huckleberry Finn* 1960; *A Breath of Scandal* 1960; *The Comancheros* 1961; *Francis of Assisi* 1961

Cutler, R J *The September Issue* 2009; *If I Stay* 2014

Cutts, Graham (1885-1958) *Looking on the Bright Side* 1931; *The Sign of Four* 1932; *Car of Dreams* 1935; *Over She Goes* 1937; *Just William* 1939

Czinner, Paul (1890-1972) *Ariane* 1931; *The Rise of Catherine the Great* 1934; *Escape Me Never* 1935; *As You Like It* 1936; *Stolen Life* 1939; *Romeo and Juliet* 1966

D

Da Costa, Morton (1914-1989) *Auntie Mame* 1958; *The Music Man* 1962; *Island of Love* 1963

Dahan, Olivier (1967-) *La Vie en Rose* 2007; *Grace of Monaco* 2014

Dahl, John (1956-) *Kill Me Again* 1989; *Red Rock West* 1992; *The Last Seduction* 1993; *Unforgettable* 1996; *Rounders* 1998; *Road Kill* 2001; *You Kill Me* 2007

Daldry, Stephen (1960-) *Billy Elliot* 2000; *The Hours* 2002; *The Reader* 2008; *Extremely Loud & Incredibly Close* 2012; *Trash* 2014

Dalrymple, Ian (1903-1989) *Storm in a Teacup* 1937; *Old Bill and Son* 1940; *Esther Waters* 1948

Daly, Lance *Kisses* 2008; *Life's a Breeze* 2013

Damiani, Damiano (1922-2013) *The Empty Canvas* 1963; *A Bullet for the General* 1966; *Amityville II: the Possession* 1982

Damski, Mel (1946-) *Yellowbeard* 1983; *Badge of the Assassin* 1985; *A Winner Never Quits* 1986; *Happy Together* 1989

Daniel, Rod (1942-2016) *Teen Wolf* 1985; *Like Father, like Son* 1987; *K-9* 1989; *The Super* 1991; *Beethoven's 2nd* 1993; *Home Alone 4* 2002

Daniels, Lee *Precious (Base on Nol by Saf) (Based on the Novel "Push" by Sapphire)* 2008; *The Paperboy* 2012; *The Butler* 2013

Dante, Joe (1946-) *Hollywood Boulevard* 1976; *Piranha* 1978; *The Howling* 1981; *Twilight Zone: the Movie* 1983; *Gremlins* 1984; *Explorers* 1985; *Amazon Women on the Moon* 1987; *Innerspace* 1987; *The 'Burbs* 1989; *Gremlins 2: the New Batch* 1990; *Matinee* 1993; *Small Soldiers* 1998; *Looney Tunes: Back in Action* 2003; *The Hole* 2009

Darabont, Frank (1959-) *Buried Alive* 1990; *The Shawshank Redemption* 1994; *The Green Mile* 1999; *The Majestic* 2001; *The Mist* 2007

Darby, Jonathan *The Enemy Within* 1994; *Hush* 1998

Dardenne, Jean-Pierre (1951-) *La Promesse* 1996; *Rosetta* 1999; *The Son* 2002; *L'Enfant* 2005; *The Silence of Lorna* 2008; *The Kid with a Bike* 2011; *Two Days, One Night* 2014

Dardenne, Luc (1954-) *La Promesse* 1996; *Rosetta* 1999; *The Son* 2002; *L'Enfant* 2005; *The Silence of Lorna* 2008; *The Kid with a Bike* 2011; *Two Days, One Night* 2014

Darnell, Eric (1961-) *Antz* 1998; *Madagascar* 2005; *Madagascar: Escape 2 Africa* 2008; *Madagascar 3: Europe's Most Wanted* 2012; *Penguins of Madagascar* 2014

D'Arrast, Harry d'Abbadie (1893-1968) *Laughter* 1930; *Raffles* 1930; *Topaze* 1933

Dash, Julie (1952-) *Daughters of the Dust* 1991; *Subway Stories: Tales from the Underground* 1997

Dassin, Jules (1911-2008) *The Affairs of Martha* 1942; *Reunion in France* 1942; *The Canterville Ghost* 1944; *Brute Force* 1947; *The Naked City* 1948; *Thieves' Highway* 1949; *Night and the City* 1950; *Rififi* 1955; *Celui Qui Doit Mourir* 1957; *Never on Sunday* 1960; *Phaedra* 1962; *Topkapi* 1964; *10:30 PM Summer* 1966; *Uptight* 1968; *A Dream of Passion* 1978; *Circle of Two* 1980

Daugherty, Herschel (1910-1993) *The Light in the Forest* 1958; *Winchester '73* 1967

Davaa, Byambasuren (1971-) *The Story of the Weeping Camel* 2003; *Cave of the Yellow Dog* 2005

Daves, Delmer (1904-1977) *Destination Tokyo* 1943; *Hollywood Canteen* 1944; *The Very Thought of You* 1944; *Pride of the Marines* 1945; *Dark Passage* 1947; *The Red House* 1947; *A Kiss in the Dark* 1949; *Task Force* 1949; *Broken Arrow* 1950; *Bird of Paradise* 1951; *Never Let Me Go* 1953; *Treasure of the Golden Condor* 1953; *Demetrius and the Gladiators* 1954; *Drum Beat* 1954; *Jubal* 1956; *The Last Wagon* 1956; *3:10 to Yuma* 1957; *The Badlanders* 1958; *Cowboy* 1958; *The Hanging Tree* 1959; *A Summer Place* 1959; *Susan Slade* 1961; *Rome Adventure* 1962; *Spencer's Mountain* 1963; *Youngblood Hawke* 1964; *The Battle of the Villa Fiorita* 1965

Davidson, John-Paul *The Grotesque* 1995; *Seve* 2014

Davidson, Martin (1939-) *The Lords of Flatbush* 1974; *Almost Summer* 1977; *Hero at Large* 1980; *Eddie and the Cruisers* 1983; *Heart of Dixie* 1989; *Hard Promises* 1991

Davies, Terence (1945-) *The Terence Davies Trilogy* 1984; *Distant Voices, Still Lives* 1988; *The Long Day Closes* 1992; *The Neon Bible* 1995; *The House of Mirth* 2000; *Of Time and the City* 2008; *The Deep Blue Sea* 2011; *Sunset Song* 2015

Davis, Andrew (1946-) *Code of Silence* 1985; *Nico* 1988; *The Package* 1989; *Under Siege* 1992; *The Fugitive* 1993; *Steal Big, Steal Little* 1995; *Chain Reaction* 1996; *Collateral Damage* 2001; *Holes* 2003; *The Guardian* 2006

Davis, Desmond (1927-) *Girl with Green Eyes* 1963; *The Uncle* 1964; *I Was Happy Here* 1966; *Smashing Time* 1967; *A Nice Girl like Me* 1969; *Clash of the Titans* 1981; *The Country Girls* 1983; *The Sign of Four* 1983

Davis, John A *Jimmy Neutron: Boy Genius* 2001; *The Ant Bully* 2006

Davis (3), Michael (1961-) *Eight Days a Week* 1996; *Monster Man* 2003; *Shoot 'Em Up* 2007

Davis, Ossie (1917-2005) *Cotton Comes to Harlem* 1970; *Black Girl* 1972; *Gordon's War* 1973

Davis, Philip aka **Davis, Phil** (1953-) *ID* 1994; *Hold Back the Night* 1999

Davis, Tamra (1962-) *Guncrazy* 1992; *CB4* 1993; *Billy Madison* 1995; *Best Men* 1997; *Half-Baked* 1998; *Crossroads* 2002

Day, Robert (1922-) *The Green Man* 1956; *First Man into Space* 1958; *Grip of the Strangler* 1958; *Bobbikins* 1959; *Life in Emergency Ward 10* 1959; *The Rebel* 1960; *Tarzan the Magnificent* 1960; *Two Way Stretch* 1960; *Corridors of Blood* 1962; *Operation Snatch* 1962; *Tarzan's Three Challenges* 1963; *She* 1965; *Tarzan and the Valley of Gold* 1966; *Tarzan and the Great River* 1967; *Las Vegas Roundabout* 1975; *Twin Detectives* 1976; *The Man with Bogart's Face* 1980; *Cook & Peary: the Race to the Pole* 1983; *The Quick and the Dead* 1987

Dayton, Jonathan *Little Miss Sunshine* 2006; *Ruby Sparks* 2012; *Battle of the Sexes* 2017

De Bont, Jan (1943-) *Speed* 1994; *Twister* 1996; *Speed 2: Cruise Control* 1997; *The Haunting* 1999; *Lara Croft, Tomb Raider: the Cradle of Life* 2003

de Broca, Philippe (1933-2004) *Cartouche* 1961; *The Seven Deadly Sins* 1961; *That Man from Rio* 1964; *Up to His Ears* 1965; *King of Hearts* 1966; *Le Bossu* 1997

De Cordova, Frederick (1910-2001) *The Countess of Monte Cristo* 1948; *For the Love of Mary* 1948; *The Gal Who Took the West* 1949; *Bedtime for Bonzo* 1951; *Column South* 1953; *I'll Take Sweden* 1965; *Frankie & Johnny* 1966

de Courville, Albert (1887-1960) *Seven Sinners* 1936; *Crackerjack* 1938

De Felitta, Raymond *'Tis Autumn: the Search for Jackie Paris* 2007; *City Island* 2009

De Heer, Rolf aka **de Heer, Rolf** (1951-) *Encounter at Raven's Gate* 1988; *Dingo* 1991; *Bad Boy Bubby* 1993; *The Old Man Who Read Love Stories* 2000; *Ten Canoes* 2006; *Charlie's Country* 2013

De Jarnatt, Steve *Cherry 2000* 1988; *Miracle Mile* 1989

De Jong, Ate (1953-) *Drop Dead Fred* 1991; *Highway to Hell* 1992; *All Men Are Mortal* 1995

de la Iglesia, Alex (1965-) *Acción Mutante* 1993; *The Day of the Beast* 1995; *Perdita Durango* 1997; *La Comunidad* 2000; *The Baby's Room* 2006; *The Oxford Murders* 2008

de Lautour, Charles *Impulse* 1955; *Child in the House* 1956

De Micco, Kirk *Space Chimps* 2008; *The Croods* 2013

De Niro, Robert (1943-) *A Bronx Tale* 1993; *The Good Shepherd* 2006

de Oliveira, Manoel (1908-2015) *Aniki-Bóbó* 1942; *The Divine Comedy* 1992; *Abraham Valley* 1993; *The Convent* 1995; *Journey to the Beginning of the World* 1997; *I'm Going Home* 2001; *Un Filme Falado* 2003; *Belle Toujours* 2006; *Eccentricities of a Blonde-Haired Girl* 2009

De Palma, Brian (1940-) *The Wedding Party* 1966; *Greetings* 1968; *Murder à la Mod* 1968; *Dionysus in '69* 1970; *Hi, Mom!* 1970; *Get to Know Your Rabbit* 1972; *Sisters* 1973; *Phantom of the Paradise* 1974; *Carrie* 1976; *Obsession* 1976; *The Fury* 1978; *Home Movies* 1979; *Dressed to Kill* 1980; *Blow Out* 1981; *Scarface* 1983; *Body Double* 1984; *Wise Guys* 1986; *The Untouchables* 1987; *Casualties of War* 1989; *The Bonfire of the Vanities* 1990; *Raising Cain* 1992; *Carlito's Way* 1993; *Mission: Impossible* 1996; *Snake Eyes* 1998; *Mission to Mars* 1999; *Femme Fatale* 2002; *The Black Dahlia* 2006; *Redacted* 2007; *Passion* 2012

De Rakoff, Alex (1970-) *The Calcium Kid* 2003; *Dead Man Running* 2009

de Rycker, Piet *The Little Polar Bear* 2001; *Laura's Star* 2004; *The Little Polar Bear: the Mysterious Island* 2005

De Sica, Vittorio (1902-1974) *The Children Are Watching Us* 1943; *Shoeshine* 1946; *Bicycle Thieves* 1948; *Miracle in Milan* 1950; *Umberto D* 1952; *Gold of Naples* 1954; *Indiscretion of an American Wife* 1954; *Two Women* 1960; *Yesterday, Today and Tomorrow* 1963; *Marriage - Italian Style* 1964; *After the Fox* 1966; *The Witches* 1966; *Woman Times Seven* 1967; *A Place for Lovers* 1968; *Sunflower* 1969; *The Garden of the Finzi-Continis* 1971; *The Voyage* 1974

de Souza, Steven E *Street Fighter* 1994; *Possessed* 2000

De Toth, Andre (1913-2002) *Passport to Suez* 1943; *Dark Waters* 1944; *None Shall Escape* 1944; *The Other Love* 1947; *Ramrod* 1947; *Pitfall* 1948; *Slattery's Hurricane* 1949; *Man in the Saddle* 1951; *Carson City* 1952; *Last of the Comanches* 1952; *Springfield Rifle* 1952; *House of Wax* 1953; *Thunder over the Plains* 1953; *The Bounty Hunter* 1954; *The City Is Dark* 1954; *Riding Shotgun* 1954; *Tanganyika* 1954; *The Indian Fighter* 1955; *Day of the Outlaw* 1959; *Morgan the Pirate* 1960; *The Mongols* 1961; *Play Dirty* 1969

Dean, Basil (1888-1978) *Birds of Prey* 1930; *Escape* 1930; *Looking on the Bright Side* 1931; *The Impassive Footman* 1932; *The Constant Nymph* 1933; *Lorna Doone* 1934; *Sing as We Go* 1934; *Look Up and Laugh* 1935; *Whom the Gods Love* 1936; *The Show Goes On* 1937; *21 Days* 1937

Dear, William (1944-) *Bigfoot and the Hendersons* 1987; *Teen Agent* 1991; *Angels in the Outfield* 1994; *Wild America* 1997; *Santa Who?* 2000

Dearden, Basil (1911-1971) *The Black Sheep of Whitehall* 1941; *The Goose Steps Out* 1942; *The Bells Go Down* 1943; *The Halfway House* 1943; *My Learned Friend* 1943; *Dead of Night* 1945; *The Captive Heart* 1946; *Frieda* 1947; *Saraband for Dead Lovers* 1948; *The Blue Lamp* 1949; *Train of Events* 1949; *Cage of Gold* 1950; *Pool of London* 1950; *The Gentle Gunman* 1952; *I Believe in You* 1952; *The Square Ring* 1953; *Out of the Clouds* 1954; *The Rainbow Jacket* 1954; *The Ship That Died of Shame* 1955; *Who Done It?* 1956; *The Smallest Show on Earth* 1957; *Violent Playground* 1958; *Sapphire* 1959; *The League of Gentlemen* 1960; *Man in the Moon* 1960; *All Night Long* 1961; *The Secret Partner* 1961; *Victim* 1961; *Life for Ruth* 1962; *The Mind Benders* 1963; *A Place to Go* 1963; *Woman of Straw* 1964; *Masquerade* 1965; *Khartoum* 1966; *Only When I Larf* 1968; *The Assassination Bureau* 1969; *The Man Who Haunted Himself* 1970

Dearden, James (1949-) *Pascali's Island* 1988; *A Kiss before Dying* 1991; *Rogue Trader* 1998

DeBello, John *Attack of the Killer Tomatoes* 1978; *Return of the Killer Tomatoes* 1988

DeBlois, Dean (1970-) *Lilo & Stitch* 2002; *How to Train Your Dragon* 2010; *How to Train Your Dragon 2* 2014

Decoin, Henri (1890-1969) *Secrets d'Alcove* 1954; *Le Masque de Fer* 1962

DeCoteau, David (1962-) *Skeletons* 1996; *I've Been Watching You* 2000

Dehlavi, Jamil *Immaculate Conception* 1991; *Jinnah* 1998; *Infinite Justice* 2006

Deitch, Donna (1945-) *Desert Hearts* 1985; *The Devil's Arithmetic* 1999

Dekker, Fred *The Monster Squad* 1987; *RoboCop 3* 1993

Del Ruth, Roy (1895-1961) *The Desert Song* 1929; *Gold Diggers of Broadway* 1929; *Blonde Crazy* 1931; *Dangerous Female* 1931; *Blessed Event* 1932; *Taxi!* 1932; *Bureau of Missing Persons* 1933; *Employees' Entrance* 1933; *Lady Killer* 1933; *The Little Giant* 1933; *The Mind Reader* 1933; *Bulldog Drummond Strikes Back* 1934; *Kid Millions* 1934; *Upper World* 1934; *Broadway Melody of 1936* 1935; *Folies Bergère* 1935; *Thanks a Million* 1935; *Born to Dance* 1936; *Broadway Melody of 1938* 1937; *On the Avenue* 1937; *Happy Landing* 1938; *My Lucky Star* 1938; *The Star Maker* 1939; *The Chocolate Soldier* 1941; *Topper Returns* 1941; *DuBarry Was a Lady* 1943; *Barbary Coast Gent* 1944; *Broadway Rhythm* 1944; *Ziegfeld Follies* 1944; *It Happened on Fifth Avenue* 1947; *The Babe Ruth Story* 1948; *Always Leave Them Laughing* 1949; *Red Light* 1949; *The West Point Story* 1950; *On Moonlight Bay* 1951; *Stop, You're Killing Me* 1952; *Three Sailors and a Girl* 1953; *The Alligator People* 1959

del Toro, Guillermo (1964-) *Cronos* 1992; *Mimic* 1997; *The Devil's Backbone* 2001; *Blade II* 2002; *Hellboy* 2004; *Pan's Labyrinth* 2006; *Hellboy II: the Golden Army* 2008; *Pacific Rim* 2013; *Crimson Peak* 2015

Delamarre, Camille *Brick Mansions* 2014; *The Transporter Refuelled* 2015

Delannoy, Jean (1908-2008) *Eternal Love* 1943; *La Symphonie Pastorale* 1946; *Secrets d'Alcove* 1954; *The Hunchback of Notre Dame* 1956; *Marie Antoinette* 1956; *Maigret Sets a Trap* 1957; *Imperial Venus* 1963

Delépine, Benoît *Louise-Michel* 2008; *Mammuth* 2010

Dell, Jeffrey (1904-1985) *Don't Take It to Heart* 1944; *Carlton-Browne of the FO* 1958

Delpy, Julie (1969-) *2 Days in Paris* 2006; *2 Days in New York* 2011

DeMille, Cecil B aka **De Mille, Cecil B** (1881-1959) *Carmen* 1915; *The Cheat* 1915; *A Romance of the Redwoods* 1917; *Male and Female* 1919; *Why Change Your Wife?* 1920; *The Ten Commandments* 1923; *The Road to Yesterday* 1925; *The King of Kings* 1927; *The Godless Girl* 1928; *Dynamite* 1929; *Madam Satan* 1930; *The Sign of the Cross* 1932; *This Day and Age* 1933; *Cleopatra* 1934; *Four Frightened People* 1934; *The Crusades* 1935; *The Plainsman* 1936; *The Buccaneer* 1938; *Union Pacific* 1939; *North West Mounted Police* 1940; *Reap the Wild Wind* 1942; *The Story of Dr Wassell* 1944; *Unconquered* 1947; *Samson and Delilah* 1949; *The Greatest Show on Earth* 1952; *The Ten Commandments* 1956

Demme, Jonathan (1944-) *Caged Heat* 1974; *Crazy Mama* 1975; *Fighting Mad* 1976; *Citizens Band* 1977; *Last Embrace* 1979; *Melvin and Howard* 1980; *Stop Making Sense* 1984; *Swing Shift* 1984; *Something Wild* 1986; *Swimming to Cambodia* 1987; *Married to the Mob* 1988; *The Silence of the Lambs* 1991; *Cousin Bobby* 1992; *Philadelphia* 1993; *Subway Stories: Tales from the Underground* 1997; *Beloved* 1998; *Storefront Hitchcock* 1998; *The Truth about Charlie* 2002; *The Agronomist* 2003; *The Manchurian Candidate* 2004; *Neil Young: Heart of Gold* 2006; *Rachel Getting Married* 2008; *Neil Young Journeys* 2011; *Ricki and the Flash* 2015

Demme, Ted (1963-2002) *Who's the Man?* 1993; *Hostile Hostages* 1994; *Beautiful Girls* 1996; *Noose* 1997; *Subway Stories: Tales from the Underground* 1997; *Life* 1999; *Blow* 2001

DeMonaco, James *Staten Island* 2009; *The Purge* 2013; *The Purge: Anarchy* 2014

Demy, Jacques (1931-1990) *Lola* 1960; *The Seven Deadly Sins* 1961; *Bay of the Angels* 1963; *The Umbrellas of Cherbourg* 1964; *The Young Girls of Rochefort* 1967; *Model Shop* 1969; *The Magic Donkey* 1970

Denham, Reginald (1894-1983) *The Silent Passenger* 1935; *Calling the*

Tune 1936; *The House of the Spaniard* 1936; *Flying 55* 1939

Denis, Claire (1948-) *Chocolat* 1988; *Beau Travail* 1999; *Trouble Every Day* 2000; *Ten Minutes Older: the Cello* 2002; *Vendredi Soir* 2002; *The Intruder* 2004; *35 Shots of Rum* 2008; *White Material* 2009; *Bastards* 2013

Densham, Pen *The Kiss* 1988; *Moll Flanders* 1995

Deodato, Ruggero (1939-) *Cannibal Holocaust* 1979; *Phantom of Death* 1988

Depardieu, Gérard (1948-) *The Bridge* 1999; *Paris, Je T'Aime* 2006

Depardon, Raymond (1942-) *Captive of the Desert* 1990; *Modern Life* 2008

Deray, Jacques (1929-2003) *That Man George* 1965; *The Swimming Pool* 1968; *Borsalino* 1970; *The Outside Man* 1973; *Borsalino and Co* 1974; *Police Story* 1975; *Three Men to Destroy* 1980; *The Outsider* 1983

Dercourt, Denis *The Page Turner* 2006; *En Equilibre* 2015

Derek, John (1926-1998) *Once before I Die* 1965; *Tarzan, the Ape Man* 1981; *Bolero* 1984; *Ghosts Can't Do It* 1990

Derrickson, Scott (1966-) *The Exorcism of Emily Rose* 2005; *The Day the Earth Stood Still* 2008; *Sinister* 2012; *Deliver Us from Evil* 2014; *Doctor Strange* 2016

Deruddere, Dominique (1957-) *Wait until Spring, Bandini* 1989; *Suite 16* 1994

Deschanel, Caleb (1944-) *The Escape Artist* 1982; *Crusoe* 1988

DeSimone, Tom *Hell Night* 1981; *Reform School Girls* 1986

Desmond Hurst, Brian aka **Desmond-Hurst, Brian** (1900-1986) *The Lion Has Wings* 1939; *Dangerous Moonlight* 1941; *Hungry Hill* 1946; *The Mark of Cain* 1947; *Trottie True* 1949; *Scrooge* 1951; *Malta Story* 1953; *Simba* 1955; *The Black Tent* 1956; *Dangerous Exile* 1957; *Behind the Mask* 1958; *His and Hers* 1960; *The Playboy of the Western World* 1962

Desplechin, Arnaud (1960-) *Ma Vie Sexuelle* 1996; *Esther Kahn* 2000; *Kings & Queen* 2004; *A Christmas Tale* 2008

Detiege, David (1926-) *The Man from Button Willow* 1965; *Bugs Bunny 1001 Rabbit Tales* 1982

Deutch, Howard (1950-) *Pretty in Pink* 1986; *Some Kind of Wonderful* 1987; *The Great Outdoors* 1988; *Article 99* 1992; *Getting Even with Dad* 1994; *Grumpier Old Men* 1996; *The Odd Couple II* 1998; *The Replacements* 2000; *The Whole Ten Yards* 2004; *My Best Friend's Girl* 2008

Deville, Michel (1931-) *Death in a French Garden* 1985; *Le Paltoquet* 1986; *La Lectrice* 1988; *Almost Peaceful* 2002

DeVito, Danny (1944-) *Throw Momma from the Train* 1987; *The War of the Roses* 1989; *Hoffa* 1992; *Matilda* 1996; *Death to Smoochy* 2002; *Our House* 2003

Dewolf, Patrick *Lapse of Memory* 1992; *Innocent Lies* 1995

Dexter, John (1925-1990) *The Virgin Soldiers* 1969; *I Want What I Want* 1971

Dexter, Maury (1927-) *Young Guns of Texas* 1962; *Wild on the Beach* 1965

Dey, Tom *Shanghai Noon* 2000; *Showtime* 2002; *Failure to Launch* 2006; *Marmaduke* 2010

Dhalia, Heitor *Adrift* 2009; *Gone* 2012

Dhawan, David *Mujhse Shaadi Karogi* 2004; *Partner* 2007

Di Gregorio, Gianni *The Ferragosto Dinner* 2008; *The Salt of Life* 2011

Diamond, Matthew *These Old Broads* 2001; *Camp Rock* 2008

Dibb, Saul *Bullet Boy* 2004; *The Duchess* 2008; *Suite Française* 2014

DiBlasi, Anthony *Dread* 2009; *Cassadaga* 2011

DiCillo, Tom (1954-) *Johnny Suede* 1991; *Living in Oblivion* 1995; *Box of Moonlight* 1996; *The Real Blonde* 1997; *Double Whammy* 2001; *When You're Strange* 2009

Dick, Kirby *Sick: the Life and Death of Bob Flanagan, Supermasochist* 1997; *This Film Is Not Yet Rated* 2006

Dick, Nigel (1953-) *Private Investigations* 1987; *Final Combination* 1993; *Seeing Double* 2003

Dickerson, Ernest R aka **Dickerson, Ernest** (1952-) *Juice* 1991; *Surviving the Game* 1994; *Tales from the Crypt: Demon Knight* 1995; *Bulletproof* 1996; *Futuresport* 1998; *Strange Justice* 1999; *Bones* 2001; *Never Die Alone* 2004; *For One Night* 2006

Dickinson, Thorold (1903-1984) *Calling the Tune* 1936; *The Arsenal Stadium Mystery* 1939; *Gaslight* 1940; *The Prime Minister* 1940; *Next of Kin* 1942; *The Queen of Spades* 1948; *The Secret People* 1951

Dieterle, William aka **Dieterle, Wilhelm** aka **Dieterle, William S** (1893-1972) *Her Majesty Love* 1931; *The Last Flight* 1931; *Jewel Robbery* 1932; *Lawyer Man* 1932; *Scarlet Dawn* 1932; *Fashions of 1934* 1934; *Madame Du Barry* 1934; *The Secret Bride* 1934; *Dr Socrates* 1935; *A Midsummer Night's Dream* 1935; *Satan Met a Lady* 1936; *The Story of Louis Pasteur* 1936; *The White Angel* 1936; *Another Dawn* 1937; *The Great O'Malley* 1937; *The Life of Emile Zola* 1937; *Blockade* 1938; *The Hunchback of Notre Dame* 1939; *Juarez* 1939; *A Dispatch from Reuters* 1940; *Dr Ehrlich's Magic Bullet* 1940; *The Devil and Daniel Webster* 1941; *Syncopation* 1942; *Tennessee Johnson* 1942; *I'll Be Seeing You* 1944; *Kismet* 1944; *Love Letters* 1945; *This Love of Ours* 1945; *The Searching Wind* 1946; *Portrait of Jennie* 1948; *The Accused* 1949; *Rope of Sand* 1949; *Dark City* 1950; *Paid in Full* 1950; *September Affair* 1950; *Boots Malone* 1951; *Peking Express* 1951; *Red Mountain* 1951; *The Turning Point* 1952; *Salome* 1953; *Elephant Walk* 1954; *Magic Fire* 1956; *Omar Khayyam* 1957; *Quick, Let's Get Married* 1964

Dindal, Mark *Cats Don't Dance* 1998; *The Emperor's New Groove* 2000; *Chicken Little* 2005

Dinner, Michael *Catholic Boys* 1985; *Off Beat* 1986; *Hot to Trot* 1988

Dippé, Mark A Z (1958-) *Spawn* 1997; *Frankenfish* 2004; *Garfield Gets Real* 2007

Ditter, Christian *Love, Rosie* 2014; *How to Be Single* 2016

Dmytryk, Edward (1908-1999) *The Devil Commands* 1941; *Sweetheart of the Campus* 1941; *Seven Miles from Alcatraz* 1942; *The Falcon Strikes Back* 1943; *Hitler's Children* 1943; *Tender Comrade* 1943; *Farewell My Lovely* 1944; *Back to Bataan* 1945; *Cornered* 1945; *Till the End of Time* 1946; *Crossfire* 1947; *So Well Remembered* 1947; *Obsession* 1948; *Mutiny* 1952; *The Sniper* 1952; *The Juggler* 1953; *Broken Lance* 1954; *The Caine Mutiny* 1954; *The End of the Affair* 1954; *The Left Hand of God* 1955; *Soldier of Fortune* 1955; *The Mountain* 1956; *Raintree County* 1957; *The Young Lions* 1958; *The Blue Angel* 1959; *Warlock* 1959; *The Reluctant Saint* 1962; *Walk on the Wild Side* 1962; *The Carpetbaggers* 1964; *Where Love Has Gone* 1964; *Mirage* 1965; *Alvarez Kelly* 1966; *Anzio* 1968; *Shalako* 1968; *Bluebeard* 1972; *The Human Factor* 1975

Dobkin, David (1969-) *Clay Pigeons* 1998; *Shanghai Knights* 2003; *Wedding Crashers* 2005; *Fred Claus* 2007; *The Change-Up* 2011; *The Judge* 2014

Docter, Pete *Monsters, Inc* 2001; *Up* 2009; *Inside Out* 2015

Doillon, Jacques (1944-) *Le Jeune Werther* 1992; *Ponette* 1996

Dolan, Xavier (1989-) *I Killed My Mother* 2009; *Heartbeats* 2010; *Laurence Anyways* 2012; *Tom at the Farm* 2013; *Mommy* 2014

Domaradzki, Jerzy (1943-) *Legend of the White Horse* 1985; *Struck by Lightning* 1990

Dominik, Andrew *Chopper* 2000; *The Assassination of Jesse James by the Coward Robert Ford* 2007; *Killing Them Softly* 2012

Donaldson, Roger (1945-) *Smash Palace* 1981; *The Bounty* 1984; *Marie: a True Story* 1985; *No Way Out* 1986; *Cocktail* 1988; *Cadillac Man* 1990; *White Sands* 1992; *The Getaway* 1994; *Species* 1995; *Dante's Peak* 1997; *Thirteen Days* 2000; *The Recruit* 2002; *The World's Fastest Indian* 2005; *The Bank Job* 2008; *Justice* 2011; *The November Man* 2014

Done, Harris (1963-) *Storm* 1999; *Firetrap* 2001

Donehue, Vincent J (1915-1966) *Lonelyhearts* 1958; *Sunrise at Campobello* 1960

Donen, Stanley (1924-) *On the Town* 1949; *Love Is Better than Ever* 1951; *Royal Wedding* 1951; *Singin' in the Rain* 1952; *Give a Girl a Break* 1953; *Deep in My Heart* 1954; *Seven Brides for Seven Brothers* 1954; *It's Always Fair Weather* 1955; *Funny Face* 1957; *Kiss Them for Me* 1957; *The Pajama Game* 1957; *Damn Yankees* 1958; *Indiscreet* 1958; *The Grass Is Greener* 1960; *Surprise Package* 1960; *Charade* 1963; *Arabesque* 1966; *Bedazzled* 1967; *Two for the Road* 1967; *Staircase* 1969; *The Little Prince* 1974; *Lucky Lady* 1975; *Movie Movie* 1978; *Saturn 3* 1980; *Blame It on Rio* 1984; *Love Letters* 1999

Donner, Clive (1926-2010) *Some People* 1962; *The Caretaker* 1963; *Nothing but the Best* 1963; *What's New, Pussycat?* 1965; *Here We Go round the Mulberry Bush* 1967; *Luv* 1967; *Alfred the Great* 1969; *Vampira* 1975; *The Thief of Baghdad* 1978; *The Nude Bomb* 1980; *Charlie Chan and the Curse of the Dragon Queen* 1981; *Oliver Twist* 1982; *The Scarlet Pimpernel* 1982; *A Christmas Carol* 1984; *Babes in Toyland* 1986; *Dead Man's Folly* 1986; *Stealing Heaven* 1988

Donner, Richard (1930-) *X-15* 1961; *Salt & Pepper* 1968; *Twinky* 1969; *The Omen* 1976; *Superman* 1978; *Inside Moves: the Guys from Max's Bar* 1980; *The Toy* 1982; *The Goonies* 1985; *Ladyhawke* 1985; *Lethal Weapon* 1987; *Scrooged* 1988; *Lethal Weapon 2* 1989; *Lethal Weapon 3* 1992; *Radio Flyer* 1992; *Maverick* 1994; *Assassins* 1995; *Conspiracy Theory* 1997; *Lethal Weapon 4* 1998; *Timeline* 2003; *16 Blocks* 2006

Donohue, Jack (1908-1984) *Watch the Birdie* 1950; *The Yellow Cab Man* 1950; *Lucky Me* 1954; *Babes in Toyland* 1961; *Marriage on the Rocks* 1965; *Assault on a Queen* 1966

Donovan, Paul (1954-) *Def-Con 4* 1984; *George's Island* 1991

Doremus, Drake *Like Crazy* 2011; *Breathe In* 2013

Dorfmann, Jacques *Shadow of the Wolf* 1992; *Druids* 2001

Dornhelm, Robert (1947-) *The Children of Theatre Street* 1977; *She Dances Alone* 1981; *Echo Park* 1985; *Cold Feet* 1989; *Requiem for Dominic* 1990; *Identity Theft: the Michelle Brown Story* 2004; *Suburban Madness* 2004; *La Bohème* 2008

Dos Santos, Alexis *Glue* 2006; *Unmade Beds* 2009

Dotan, Shimon (1949-) *The Finest Hour* 1991; *You Can Thank Me Later* 1998

Dougherty, Michael *Trick 'r Treat* 2007; *Krampus* 2015

Douglas, Bill (1934-1991) *My Childhood* 1972; *My Ain Folk* 1973; *My Way Home* 1978; *Comrades: a Lanternist's Account of the Tolpuddle Martyrs and What Became of Them* 1986

Douglas, Gordon aka **Douglas, Gordon M** (1907-1993) *Zenobia* 1939; *Saps at Sea* 1940; *Road Show* 1941; *The Falcon in Hollywood* 1944; *Girl Rush* 1944; *Dick Tracy vs Cueball* 1946; *The Black Arrow* 1948; *Kiss Tomorrow Goodbye* 1950; *Only the Valiant* 1950; *Rogues of Sherwood Forest* 1950; *Come Fill the Cup* 1951; *I Was a Communist for the FBI* 1951; *The Iron Mistress* 1952; *Mara Maru* 1952; *The Charge at Feather River* 1953; *So This Is Love* 1953; *Them!* 1954; *The McConnell Story* 1955; *Sincerely Yours* 1955; *Young at Heart* 1955; *Santiago* 1956; *The Big Land* 1957; *Bombers B-52* 1957; *Up Periscope* 1959; *Yellowstone Kelly* 1959; *The Sins of Rachel Cade* 1960; *Follow That Dream* 1962; *Call Me Bwana* 1963; *Rio Conchos* 1964; *Robin and the 7 Hoods* 1964; *Sylvia* 1964; *Harlow* 1965; *Stagecoach* 1966; *In like Flint* 1967; *Tony Rome* 1967; *The Detective* 1968; *Lady in Cement* 1968; *Skullduggery* 1969; *Barquero* 1970; *They Call Me Mister Tibbs!* 1970; *Slaughter's Big Rip-Off* 1973; *Viva Knievel!* 1977

Douglas, Kirk (1916-) *Scalawag* 1973; *Posse* 1975

Dowdle, John Erick *Quarantine* 2008; *Devil* 2010; *As Above, So Below* 2014; *No Escape* 2014

Dower, John *Live Forever* 2002; *Once in a Lifetime: the Extraordinary*

Story of the New York Cosmos 2006; *My Scientology Movie* 2015

Dowling, Kevin *The Sum of Us* 1995; *Mojave Moon* 1996; *Last Rites* 1998; *The Last Dance* 2000

Dowse, Michael (1973-) *It's All Gone Pete Tong* 2004; *Goon* 2011; *Take Me Home Tonight* 2011; *What If* 2013

Dragoti, Stan (1932-) *Dirty Little Billy* 1972; *Love at First Bite* 1979; *Mr Mom* 1983; *The Man with One Red Shoe* 1985

Drake, Jim *Police Academy 4: Citizens on Patrol* 1987; *Cannonball Fever* 1989

Drazan, Anthony (1955-) *Zebrahead* 1992; *Imaginary Crimes* 1994; *Hurlyburly* 1998

Dreifuss, Arthur (1908-1993) *Baby Face Morgan* 1942; *The Last Blitzkrieg* 1958; *Juke Box Rhythm* 1959; *The Quare Fellow* 1962

Dréville, Jean (1906-1997) *A Cage of Nightingales* 1945; *The Seven Deadly Sins* 1952; *La Reine Margot* 1954

Dreyer, Carl Th (1889-1968) *Leaves from Satan's Book* 1919; *The President* 1919; *Master of the House* 1925; *The Passion of Joan of Arc* 1928; *Vampyr* 1932; *Day of Wrath* 1943; *Ordet* 1955; *Gertrud* 1964

Drury, David *Defence of the Realm* 1985; *Hostile Waters* 1996

Du Chau, Frederik *The Magic Sword: Quest for Camelot* 1997; *Racing Stripes* 2004; *Underdog* 2007

du Welz, Fabrice *Calvaire* 2004; *Vinyan* 2008; *Alleluia* 2014

Ducastel, Olivier (1962-) *Drôle de Félix* 2000; *Ma Vraie Vie à Rouen* 2002; *Cockles & Muscles* 2004; *Born in 68: We'll Love Each Other until Death Do Us Part* 2008

Duffell, Peter (1924-) *The House That Dripped Blood* 1970; *England Made Me* 1973; *Inside Out* 1975; *King of the Wind* 1989

Duffy, Martin *The Boy from Mercury* 1996; *The Testimony of Taliesin Jones* 2000

Dugan, Dennis (1946-) *Problem Child* 1990; *Brain Donors* 1992; *Happy Gilmore* 1996; *Beverly Hills Ninja* 1997; *Big Daddy* 1999; *Evil Woman* 2001; *National Security* 2002; *The Benchwarmers* 2006; *I Now Pronounce You Chuck & Larry* 2007; *You Don't Mess with the Zohan* 2008; *Grown Ups* 2010; *Jack and Jill* 2011; *Just Go with It* 2011; *Grown Ups 2* 2013

Dugowson, Martine *Mina Tannenbaum* 1993; *Portraits Chinois* 1996

Duguay, Christian (1957-) *Scanners II: The New Order* 1991; *Live Wire* 1992; *Scanners III: the Takeover* 1992; *Screamers* 1995; *The Assignment* 1997; *The Art of War* 2000; *Extreme Ops* 2003; *Lies My Mother Told Me* 2005; *Belle and Sebastian - the Adventure Continues* 2015

Duigan, John (1949-) *The Year My Voice Broke* 1987; *Flirting* 1989; *Romero* 1989; *Wide Sargasso Sea* 1992; *Sirens* 1994; *The Journey of August King* 1995; *The Leading Man* 1996; *Lawn Dogs* 1997; *Molly* 1999; *The Parole Officer* 2001; *Head in the Clouds* 2004

Duke, Bill (1943-) *The Killing Floor* 1984; *A Rage in Harlem* 1991; *Deep Cover* 1992; *The Cemetery Club* 1993; *Sister Act 2: Back in the Habit* 1993; *Hoodlum* 1997; *Not Easily Broken* 2009

Duke, Daryl (1929-2006) *Payday* 1972; *I Heard the Owl Call My Name* 1973; *The Silent Partner* 1978; *Tai-Pan* 1986

Dumont, Bruno (1958-) *La Vie de Jésus* 1996; *L'Humanité* 1999; *Flanders* 2005; *Hadewijch* 2009; *Hors Satan* 2011; *Camille Claudel 1915* 2013

Duncan, Peter *Children of the Revolution* 1996; *Passion* 1999

Dunham, Duwayne *Homeward Bound: the Incredible Journey* 1993; *Little Giants* 1994

Dunn, Jan *Gypo* 2005; *Ruby Blue* 2007; *The Calling* 2009

Dunn, Sam *Metal: a Headbanger's Journey* 2005; *Iron Maiden: Flight 666* 2009; *Rush: Beyond the Lighted Stage* 2010

Dunne, Griffin (1955-) *Addicted to Love* 1997; *Practical Magic* 1998; *The Accidental Husband* 2008; *Movie 43* 2013

Dunne, Philip (1908-1992) *Prince of Players* 1955; *Hilda Crane* 1956; *In*

Love and War 1958; Ten North Frederick 1958; Blue Denim 1959; Wild in the Country 1961; The Inspector 1962; Blindfold 1966
Dunstan, Marcus The Collector 2009; The Collection 2011
Dunye, Cheryl (1966-) The Watermelon Woman 1996; Stranger Inside 2001
Dupeyron, François (1950-2016) Your Beating Heart 1991; La Machine 1994; The Officers' Ward 2001; Monsieur Ibrahim and the Flowers of the Koran 2003
Duplass, Jay The Puffy Chair 2005; Cyrus 2010; Jeff, Who Lives at Home 2011
Duplass, Mark (1976-) Cyrus 2010; Jeff, Who Lives at Home 2011
Dupont, E A (1891-1956) Vaudeville 1925; Moulin Rouge 1928; Piccadilly 1929; Hell's Kitchen 1939; The Scarf 1951; Return to Treasure Island 1954
Dutt, Guru (1925-1964) Mr and Mrs '55 1955; Pyaasa 1957; Kaagaz Ke Phool 1959
Dutton, Charles S (1951-) Against the Ropes 2003; Racing for Time 2008
Duvivier, Julien (1896-1967) Poil de Carotte 1932; La Belle Equipe 1936; The Golem 1936; Un Carnet de Bal 1937; Pépé le Moko 1937; The Great Waltz 1938; Marie Antoinette 1938; The End of the Day 1939; Lydia 1941; Tales of Manhattan 1942; Flesh and Fantasy 1943; The Impostor 1944; Anna Karenina 1947; The Little World of Don Camillo 1951; Black Jack 1952; Marianne de Ma Jeunesse 1955; Diabolically Yours 1967
Dwan, Allan (1885-1981) Robin Hood 1922; Stage Struck 1925; The Big Noise 1928; The Iron Mask 1929; What a Widow! 1930; Hollywood Party 1934; Black Sheep 1935; Human Cargo 1936; Heidi 1937; Rebecca of Sunnybrook Farm 1938; Suez 1938; Frontier Marshal 1939; The Three Musketeers 1939; Young People 1940; Look Who's Laughing 1941; Abroad with Two Yanks 1944; Up in Mabel's Room 1944; Brewster's Millions 1945; Driftwood 1946; Rendezvous with Annie 1946; Angel in Exile 1948; Sands of Iwo Jima 1949; The Woman They Almost Lynched 1953; Cattle Queen of Montana 1954; Silver Lode 1954; Escape to Burma 1955; Pearl of the South Pacific 1955; Slightly Scarlet 1956; The Restless Breed 1957; The River's Edge 1957; The Most Dangerous Man Alive 1961
Dylan, Jesse (1966-) American Pie: the Wedding 2003; Kicking & Screaming 2005

E

Eady, David (1924-) Three Cases of Murder 1953; The Man Who Liked Funerals 1959; Faces in the Dark 1960
Eagles, Bill Beautiful Creatures 2000; The Riverman 2004
Eastman, Allan (1950-) Crazy Moon 1986; Danger Zone 1996
Eastwood, Clint (1930-) Play Misty for Me 1971; Breezy 1973; High Plains Drifter 1973; The Eiger Sanction 1975; The Outlaw Josey Wales 1976; The Gauntlet 1977; Bronco Billy 1980; Firefox 1982; Honkytonk Man 1982; Sudden Impact 1983; Pale Rider 1985; Heartbreak Ridge 1986; Bird 1988; The Rookie 1990; White Hunter, Black Heart 1990; Unforgiven 1992; A Perfect World 1993; The Bridges of Madison County 1995; Absolute Power 1996; Midnight in the Garden of Good and Evil 1997; True Crime 1999; Space Cowboys 2000; Blood Work 2002; The Blues, a Musical Journey: Piano Blues 2003; Mystic River 2003; Million Dollar Baby 2004; Flags of Our Fathers 2006; Letters from Iwo Jima 2006; Changeling 2008; Gran Torino 2008; Invictus 2009; Hereafter 2010; J Edgar 2011; American Sniper 2014; Jersey Boys 2014; Sully 2016
Eberhardt, Thom (1947-) Night of the Comet 1984; The Night Before 1988; Without a Clue 1988; A Cut Above 1989; Captain Ron 1992
Edel, Uli aka **Edel, Ulrich** (1947-) Christiane F 1981; Last Exit to Brooklyn 1989; Body of Evidence 1992; Rasputin 1996; Purgatory 1999; The Little Vampire 2000; King of Texas 2002; Sword of Xanten 2004; The Baader Meinhof Complex 2008

Edgar, Justin (1971-) Large 2000; Special People 2007; We Are the Freaks 2013
Edwards, Blake (1922-2010) Bring Your Smile Along 1955; He Laughed Last 1956; Mister Cory 1957; The Perfect Furlough 1958; This Happy Feeling 1958; Operation Petticoat 1959; High Time 1960; Breakfast at Tiffany's 1961; Days of Wine and Roses 1962; The Pink Panther 1963; A Shot in the Dark 1964; The Great Race 1965; What Did You Do in the War, Daddy? 1966; The Party 1968; Darling Lili 1970; Wild Rovers 1971; The Carey Treatment 1972; The Return of the Pink Panther 1974; The Tamarind Seed 1974; The Pink Panther Strikes Again 1976; Revenge of the Pink Panther 1978; 10 1979; SOB 1981; Trail of the Pink Panther 1982; Victor/Victoria 1982; The Curse of the Pink Panther 1983; The Man Who Loved Women 1983; Micki & Maude 1984; A Fine Mess 1986; That's Life 1986; Blind Date 1987; Sunset 1988; Skin Deep 1989; Switch 1991; Son of the Pink Panther 1993
Edwards, Gareth Monsters 2010; Godzilla 2014; Rogue One: a Star Wars Story 2016
Edwards, Henry (1882-1952) D'Ye Ken John Peel? 1934; Lord Edgware Dies 1934; The Lad 1935; Scrooge 1935; Squibs 1935; The Vicar of Bray 1937
Edzard, Christine (1945-) Little Dorrit 1987; The Fool 1990; As You Like It 1992; The Children's Midsummer Night's Dream 2001
Eggleston, Colin (1941-2002) Long Weekend 1977; Sky Pirates 1986; Cassandra 1987
Egleson, Jan (1946-) A Shock to the System 1990; Hard Evidence 1994
Egoyan, Atom (1960-) Family Viewing 1987; Speaking Parts 1989; The Adjuster 1991; Calendar 1993; Exotica 1994; The Sweet Hereafter 1997; Felicia's Journey 1999; Ararat 2002; Where the Truth Lies 2005; Adoration 2008; Chloe 2009; Devil's Knot 2013; The Captive 2014; Remember 2015
Eimbcke, Fernando Duck Season 2004; Lake Tahoe 2008
Eisener, Jason Hobo with a Shotgun 2011; The ABCs of Death 2012; V/H/S/2 2013
Eisenstein, Sergei (1898-1948) Strike 1924; The Battleship Potemkin 1925; October 1928; The General Line 1929; Alexander Nevsky 1938; Time in the Sun 1939; Ivan the Terrible, Part I 1944; Ivan the Terrible, Part II 1946
Eisner, Breck Sahara 2005; The Crazies 2010; The Last Witch Hunter 2015
El Mechri, Mabrouk JCVD 2008; The Cold Light of Day 2012
Eldridge, John (1904-1961) Brandy for the Parson 1951; Conflict of Wings 1953; Laxdale Hall 1953
Elfont, Harry (1968-) Can't Hardly Wait 1998; Josie and the Pussycats 2001
Elgood, Rick Dancehall Queen 1996; One Love 2003
Elikann, Larry (1923-2004) One against the Wind 1991; Out of Darkness 1994
Ellin, Doug Kissing a Fool 1998; Entourage 2015
Elliott, Lang (1950-) The Private Eyes 1980; Cage 1989
Elliott, Stephan (1964-) Frauds 1992; The Adventures of Priscilla, Queen of the Desert 1994; Eye of the Beholder 1999; Easy Virtue 2008; A Few Best Men 2011
Ellis, David R (1952-2013) Homeward Bound II: Lost in San Francisco 1996; Final Destination 2 2002; Cellular 2004; Snakes on a Plane 2006; The Final Destination 2009; Shark Night 3D 2011
Ellis, Sean Cashback 2005; The Broken 2008; Metro Manila 2013
Eltringham, Billie aka **Eltringham, Bille** The Darkest Light 1999; Mrs Ratcliffe's Revolution 2007
Elvey, Maurice (1887-1967) Hindle Wakes 1927; A Honeymoon Adventure 1931; Sally in Our Alley 1931; The Wandering Jew 1933; The Clairvoyant 1934; Love, Life and Laughter 1934; The Man in the Mirror 1936; Sons of the Sea 1939; For Freedom 1940; Under Your Hat 1940; The Gentle Sex 1943; The Lamp Still Burns 1943; Beware of Pity 1946; The Late Edwina Black 1951; My Wife's Lodger 1952; House

of Blackmail 1953; Is Your Honeymoon Really Necessary? 1953; Dry Rot 1956
Emlyn, Endaf (1945-) One Full Moon 1991; Leaving Lenin 1993
Emmerich, Roland (1955-) Making Contact 1985; Moon 44 1990; Universal Soldier 1992; Stargate 1994; Independence Day 1996; Godzilla 1997; The Patriot 2000; The Day after Tomorrow 2004; 10,000 BC 2008; 2012 2009; Anonymous 2011; White House Down 2013; Stonewall 2015; Independence Day: Resurgence 2016
Endfield, Cy aka **Endfield, Cyril** aka **Raker, Hugh** aka **Endfield, C Raker** (1914-1995) The Sound of Fury 1950; The Underworld Story 1950; Tarzan's Savage Fury 1952; Colonel March Investigates 1953; The Master Plan 1954; Impulse 1955; Child in the House 1956; Hell Drivers 1957; Sea Fury 1958; Jet Storm 1959; Mysterious Island 1961; Hide and Seek 1963; Zulu 1963; Sands of the Kalahari 1965; De Sade 1969
English, John (1903-1969) Riders in the Sky 1949; Riders of the Whistling Pines 1949; Mule Train 1950
English, Jonathan Ironclad 2010; Ironclad 2 2014
Englund, George (1926-) The Ugly American 1963; Signpost to Murder 1964; Snow Job 1972
Enright, Ray aka **Enright, Raymond** (1896-1965) Havana Widows 1933; Dames 1934; China Clipper 1936; Slim 1937; Swing Your Lady 1937; Going Places 1938; Hard to Get 1938; Angels Wash Their Faces 1939; Naughty but Nice 1939; The Wagons Roll at Night 1941; Men of Texas 1942; Sin Town 1942; The Spoilers 1942; Gung Ho! 1943; China Sky 1945; Trail Street 1947; Coroner Creek 1948; Return of the Bad Men 1948; South of St Louis 1949; Kansas Raiders 1950; Montana 1950; Flaming Feather 1952; The Man from Cairo 1953
Ephron, Nora (1941-2012) This Is My Life 1992; Sleepless in Seattle 1993; Mixed Nuts 1994; Michael 1996; You've Got Mail 1998; Bewitched 2005; Julie & Julia 2009
Epstein, Rob aka **Epstein, Robert** (1955-) The Times of Harvey Milk 1983; Common Threads: Stories from the Quilt 1989; The Celluloid Closet 1995; Paragraph 175 1999; Howl 2010; Lovelace 2013
Erice, Victor (1940-) The Spirit of the Beehive 1973; El Sur 1983; The Quince Tree Sun 1991; Ten Minutes Older: the Trumpet 2002
Erman, John aka **Sampson, Bill** (1935-) Ace Eli and Rodger of the Skies 1973; Who Will Love My Children? 1983; An Early Frost 1985; The Attic: the Hiding of Anne Frank 1988; Stella 1990; Breathing Lessons 1994; The Boys Next Door 1996; The Sunshine Boys 1997
Erskine, Chester (1905-1986) Midnight 1934; The Egg and I 1947; Androcles and the Lion 1952; A Girl in Every Port 1952
Erskine, James EMR 2004; One Night in Turin 2010; From the Ashes 2011; The Battle of the Sexes 2013; Shooting for Socrates 2014
Espinosa, Daniel Easy Money 2010; Child 44 2014
Espinoza, Ernesto Díaz (1978-) The ABCs of Death 2012; Bring Me the Head of the Machine Gun Woman 2013
Estevez, Emilio (1962-) Wisdom 1986; Men at Work 1990; The War at Home 1996; Rated X 2000; Bobby 2006; The Way 2010
Esway, Alexander (1947-) Music Hath Charms 1935; Conquest of the Air 1936
Eubank, William Love 2011; The Signal 2014
Evans, Bruce A Kuffs 1991; Mr Brooks 2007
Evans, David Fever Pitch 1996; My Nazi Legacy 2015
Evans, David Mickey aka **Evans, David M** aka **David M Evans** (1962-) The Sandlot 1993; First Kid 1996; Beethoven's 3rd 2000; Barely Legal 2003
Evans, Gareth aka **Evans, Gareth Huw** The Raid 2011; The Raid 2 2013; V/H/S/2 2013
Evans, Marc (1959-) House of America 1996; Resurrection Man 1997; My Little Eye 2002; Trauma 2004; Snow Cake 2005; In Prison My Whole Life 2008; Patagonia 2010; Hunky Dory 2011

Eyre, Richard (1943-) Loose Connections 1983; The Ploughman's Lunch 1983; Iris 2001; Stage Beauty 2004; Notes on a Scandal 2006; The Other Man 2008

F

Fabri, Zoltan (1917-1994) Merry-Go-Round 1956; The Boys of Paul Street 1968
Faenza, Roberto (1943-) Order of Death 1983; The Bachelor 1990; The Lost Lover 1999
Faiman, Peter "Crocodile" Dundee 1986; Driving Me Crazy 1991
Fairchild, William (1918-2000) John and Julie 1955; The Extra Day 1956; The Silent Enemy 1958
Fairfax, Ferdinand (1944-) Savage Islands 1983; The Rescue 1988; Spymaker: the Secret Life of Ian Fleming 1990; True Blue 1996
Falardeau, Philippe Monsieur Lazhar 2011; The Good Lie 2014
Falcone, Ben Tammy 2014; The Boss 2015
Fall, Jim Trick 1999; The Lizzie McGuire Movie 2003; Wedding Wars 2006
Famuyiwa, Rick (1973-) The Wood 1999; Brown Sugar 2002; Our Family Wedding 2010; Dope 2015
Färberböck, Max Aimée and Jaguar 1999; Anonyma: a Woman in Berlin 2008
Fargo, James (1938-) The Enforcer 1976; Every Which Way but Loose 1978; A Game for Vultures 1979
Farhadi, Asghar The Beautiful City 2004; About Elly 2009; Nader and Simin, a Separation 2011; The Past 2013
Farino, Julian The Last Yellow 1999; The Oranges 2011
Faris, Valerie Little Miss Sunshine 2006; Ruby Sparks 2012; Battle of the Sexes 2017
Farrelly, Bobby (1958-) Kingpin 1996; There's Something about Mary 1998; Me, Myself & Irene 2000; Osmosis Jones 2001; Shallow Hal 2001; Stuck on You 2003; The Perfect Catch 2005; The Heartbreak Kid 2007; Hall Pass 2011; The Three Stooges 2012; Dumb and Dumber To 2014
Farrelly, Peter (1956-) Dumb and Dumber 1994; Kingpin 1996; There's Something about Mary 1998; Me, Myself & Irene 2000; Osmosis Jones 2001; Shallow Hal 2001; Stuck on You 2003; The Perfect Catch 2005; The Heartbreak Kid 2007; Hall Pass 2011; The Three Stooges 2012; Movie 43 2013; Dumb and Dumber To 2014
Farrow, John (1904-1963) The Invisible Menace 1938; Five Came Back 1939; The Saint Strikes Back 1939; A Bill of Divorcement 1940; The Commandos Strike at Dawn 1942; Wake Island 1942; China 1943; California 1946; Two Years before the Mast 1946; Blaze of Noon 1947; Calcutta 1947; The Big Clock 1948; Night Has a Thousand Eyes 1948; Alias Nick Beal 1949; Copper Canyon 1950; Where Danger Lives 1950; His Kind of Woman 1951; Submarine Command 1951; Botany Bay 1952; Hondo 1953; Ride, Vaquero! 1953; A Bullet Is Waiting 1954; The Sea Chase 1955; Back from Eternity 1956; The Unholy Wife 1957
Fassbinder, Rainer Werner (1945-1982) Gods of the Plague 1969; Love Is Colder than Death 1969; The American Soldier 1970; Beware of a Holy Whore 1970; Whity 1970; Why Does Herr R Run Amok? 1970; The Merchant of Four Seasons 1971; The Bitter Tears of Petra von Kant 1972; Jail Bait 1972; Fear Eats the Soul 1973; Martha 1973; Effi Briest 1974; Fox and His Friends 1975; Mother Küsters Goes to Heaven 1975; Chinese Roulette 1976; Fear of Fear 1976; I Only Want You to Love Me 1976; Satan's Brew 1976; Bolwieser 1977; Despair 1978; In a Year of 13 Moons 1978; The Marriage of Maria Braun 1978; The Third Generation 1979; Berlin Alexanderplatz 1980; Lili Marleen 1980; Lola 1982; Querelle 1982; Veronika Voss 1982
FauntLeRoy, Don E (1953-) Today You Die 2005; Mercenary for Justice 2006; Renegade Justice 2007
Favreau, Jon (1966-) Made 2001; Elf 2003; Zathura: a Space Adventure 2005; Iron Man 2008; Iron Man 2 2010; Cowboys & Aliens

2011; Chef 2014; The Jungle Book 2016
Fawcett, John (1968-) Ginger Snaps 2000; The Dark 2005
Fearnley, Neill (1953-) A Passion for Murder 1992; A Decent Proposal 2006; I Dream of Murder 2006; Stolen Innocence 2007; The Boy Next Door 2008; Christmas in Canaan 2009; Christmas Comes Home to Canaan 2011
Feig, Paul (1962-) Grounded 2006; Bridesmaids 2011; The Heat 2013; Spy 2015; Ghostbusters 2016
Feist, Felix aka **Feist, Felix E** (1906-1965) Deluge 1933; Every Sunday 1936; The Devil Thumbs a Ride 1947; The Big Trees 1952; This Woman Is Dangerous 1952; Donovan's Brain 1953
Feldman, Marty (1933-1982) The Last Remake of Beau Geste 1977; In God We Trust 1980
Fell, Sam Flushed Away 2006; The Tale of Despereaux 2008; ParaNorman 2012
Fellini, Federico (1920-1993) The White Sheik 1951; Love in the City 1953; I Vitelloni 1953; La Strada 1954; The Swindle 1955; Nights of Cabiria 1957; La Dolce Vita 1960; 8½ 1963; Juliet of the Spirits 1965; Histoires Extraordinaires 1967; Satyricon 1969; The Clowns 1970; Fellini's Roma 1972; Amarcord 1973; Casanova 1976; Orchestra Rehearsal 1978; City of Women 1980; And the Ship Sails On 1983; Ginger & Fred 1986; Intervista 1987
Fellowes, Julian (1949-) Separate Lies 2004; From Time to Time 2009
Fellows, Simon 7 Seconds 2005; Second in Command 2006; Until Death 2007; Malice in Wonderland 2009
Feng Xiaogang Big Shot's Funeral 2001; The Banquet 2006; Assembly 2007
Fenton, Leslie (1902-1978) Tell No Tales 1939; The Man from Dakota 1940; The Saint's Vacation 1941; Pardon My Past 1945; Lulu Belle 1948; On Our Merry Way 1948; Saigon 1948; Whispering Smith 1948; Streets of Laredo 1949; The Redhead and the Cowboy 1950
Ferguson, Norman aka **Ferguson, Norm** (1902-1957) Fantasia 1940; The Three Caballeros 1944
Ferland, Guy (1966-) The Babysitter 1995; Telling Lies in America 1997; Our Guys: Outrage in Glen Ridge 1999; After the Storm 2001; Dirty Dancing 2 2003
Ferrante, Anthony C Sharknado 2013; Sharknado 2: the Second One 2014
Ferrara, Abel (1952-) The Driller Killer 1979; Ms 45 1981; Fear City 1984; China Girl 1987; Cat Chaser 1989; King of New York 1989; Bad Lieutenant 1992; Body Snatchers 1993; Dangerous Game 1993; The Addiction 1994; The Funeral 1996; The Blackout 1997; Subway Stories: Tales from the Underground 1997; New Rose Hotel 1998; Pasolini 2014; Welcome to New York 2014
Ferrer, José (1909-1992) The Cockleshell Heroes 1955; The Great Man 1956; The High Cost of Loving 1958; I Accuse! 1958; Return to Peyton Place 1961; State Fair 1962
Ferreri, Marco (1928-1997) La Grande Bouffe 1973; Bye Bye Monkey 1978; Tales of Ordinary Madness 1981; Storia di Piera 1983
Ferroni, Giorgio aka **Padget, Calvin Jackson** (1908-1981) The Trojan War 1961; The Battle of El Alamein 1968
Feste, Shana The Greatest 2009; Country Strong 2010; Endless Love 2014
Feyder, Jacques (1885-1948) Faces of Children 1925; The Kiss 1929; Daybreak 1931; Carnival in Flanders 1935; Knight without Armour 1937
Ficarra, Glenn I Love You Phillip Morris 2009; Crazy, Stupid, Love 2011; Focus 2015; Whiskey Tango Foxtrot 2016
Fickman, Andy She's the Man 2006; The Game Plan 2007; Race to Witch Mountain 2009; You Again 2010; Parental Guidance 2012; Paul Blart: Mall Cop 2 2015
Field, Todd (1964-) In the Bedroom 2001; Little Children 2006
Fiennes, Martha Onegin 1999; Chromophobia 2005
Fiennes, Ralph (1962-) Coriolanus 2010; The Invisible Woman 2013
Fiennes, Sophie Hoover Street Revival 2002; Over Your Cities Grass Will Grow 2010

Figgis, Mike (1950-) *Stormy Monday* 1987; *Internal Affairs* 1990; *Liebestraum* 1991; *Mr Jones* 1993; *The Browning Version* 1994; *Leaving Las Vegas* 1995; *One Night Stand* 1997; *The Loss of Sexual Innocence* 1999; *Miss Julie* 1999; *Timecode* 1999; *Hotel* 2001; *Ten Minutes Older: the Cello* 2002; *The Blues, a Musical Journey: Red, White & Blues* 2003; *Cold Creek Manor* 2003; *Suspension of Disbelief* 2012

Finch, Charles *Where Sleeping Dogs Lie* 1991; *Circle of Passion* 1996

Fincher, David (1962-) *Alien3* 1992; *Se7en* 1995; *The Game* 1997; *Fight Club* 1999; *Panic Room* 2002; *Zodiac* 2007; *The Curious Case of Benjamin Button* 2008; *The Social Network* 2010; *The Girl with the Dragon Tattoo* 2011; *Gone Girl* 2014

Findlay, Roberta *Snuff* 1976; *Prime Evil* 1988

Finkleman, Ken *Airplane II: the Sequel* 1982; *Head Office* 1986

Finlay, Jeanie *Sound It Out* 2011; *The Great Hip Hop Hoax* 2013; *Orion: the Man Who Would Be King* 2015

Finn, Will *Home on the Range* 2004; *Legends of Oz: Dorothy's Return* 2013

Firstenberg, Sam (1950-) *Breakdance 2 - Electric Boogaloo* 1984; *American Ninja* 1985; *Avenging Force* 1986; *Cyborg Cop* 1993; *Operation Delta Force* 1996; *Motel Blue* 1997

Fisher, Terence (1904-1980) *Portrait from Life* 1948; *The Astonished Heart* 1949; *So Long at the Fair* 1950; *Home to Danger* 1951; *Mantrap* 1952; *Stolen Face* 1952; *Blood Orange* 1953; *Four Sided Triangle* 1953; *Spaceways* 1953; *Children Galore* 1954; *Face the Music* 1954; *Final Appointment* 1954; *The Flaw* 1954; *Mask of Dust* 1954; *The Stranger Came Home* 1954; *The Curse of Frankenstein* 1957; *Kill Me Tomorrow* 1957; *Dracula* 1958; *The Revenge of Frankenstein* 1958; *The Hound of the Baskervilles* 1959; *The Man Who Could Cheat Death* 1959; *The Mummy* 1959; *The Brides of Dracula* 1960; *Sword of Sherwood Forest* 1960; *The Two Faces of Dr Jekyll* 1960; *The Curse of the Werewolf* 1961; *The Phantom of the Opera* 1962; *Sherlock Holmes and the Deadly Necklace* 1962; *The Earth Dies Screaming* 1964; *The Gorgon* 1964; *Dracula - Prince of Darkness* 1965; *Frankenstein Created Woman* 1966; *Island of Terror* 1966; *Night of the Big Heat* 1967; *The Devil Rides Out* 1968; *Frankenstein Must Be Destroyed* 1969; *Frankenstein and the Monster from Hell* 1973

Fisk, Jack (1945-) *Raggedy Man* 1981; *Violets Are Blue* 1986; *Daddy's Dyin'... Who's Got the Will?* 1990

Fitzgerald, Thom (1968-) *The Hanging Garden* 1997; *Beefcake* 1998

Fitzmaurice, George (1885-1940) *The Son of the Sheik* 1926; *The Barker* 1928; *Lilac Time* 1928; *The Devil to Pay* 1930; *Mata Hari* 1931; *One Heavenly Night* 1931; *Strangers May Kiss* 1931; *The Unholy Garden* 1931; *As You Desire Me* 1932; *Rockabye* 1932; *Suzy* 1936; *The Emperor's Candlesticks* 1937; *Live, Love and Learn* 1937; *Arsene Lupin Returns* 1938

Fjeldmark, Stefan *Help, I'm a Fish!* 2000; *Asterix and the Vikings* 2006; *Terkel in Trouble* 2006

Flaherty, Paul *IL Again!* 1988; *Who's Harry Crumb?* 1989

Flaherty, Robert aka **Flaherty, Robert J** (1884-1951) *Nanook of the North* 1922; *Moana* 1926; *Man of Aran* 1934; *Elephant Boy* 1937; *Prelude to War* 1943; *Louisiana Story* 1948

Flanagan, Mike *Absentia* 2011; *Oculus* 2013; *Before I Wake* 2015

Fleck, Ryan *Half Nelson* 2006; *Sugar* 2008; *It's Kind of a Funny Story* 2010; *Mississippi Grind* 2015

Fleder, Gary (1965-) *Things to Do in Denver When You're Dead* 1995; *Kiss the Girls* 1997; *Don't Say a Word* 2001; *Impostor* 2001; *Runaway Jury* 2003; *The Express* 2008; *Homefront* 2013

Fleischer, Dave aka **Fleischer, David** (1894-1979) *Gulliver's Travels* 1939; *Hoppity Goes to Town* 1941

Fleischer, Richard aka **Fleischer, Richard O** (1916-2006) *Child of Divorce* 1946; *Bodyguard* 1948; *So This Is New York* 1948; *The Clay Pigeon* 1949; *Armored Car Robbery* 1950; *The Happy Time* 1952; *The Narrow Margin* 1952; *Arena* 1953; *20,000 Leagues under the Sea* 1954; *The Girl in the Red Velvet Swing* 1955; *Violent Saturday* 1955; *Bandido* 1956; *Between Heaven and Hell* 1956; *The Vikings* 1958; *These Thousand Hills* 1959; *Crack in the Mirror* 1960; *Barabbas* 1961; *Fantastic Voyage* 1966; *Doctor Dolittle* 1967; *The Boston Strangler* 1968; *Che!* 1969; *10 Rillington Place* 1970; *Tora! Tora! Tora!* 1970; *Blind Terror* 1971; *The Last Run* 1971; *The New Centurions* 1972; *Soylent Green* 1973; *Mr Majestyk* 1974; *The Spikes Gang* 1974; *Mandingo* 1975; *The Prince and the Pauper* 1977; *Ashanti* 1979; *The Jazz Singer* 1980; *Tough Enough* 1982; *Amityville III: the Demon* 1983; *Conan the Destroyer* 1984; *Red Sonja* 1985

Fleischer, Ruben *Zombieland* 2009; *30 Minutes or Less* 2011; *Gangster Squad* 2012

Fleming, Andrew (1963-) *Threesome* 1994; *The Craft* 1996; *Dick* 1999; *The In-Laws* 2003; *Nancy Drew* 2007; *Hamlet 2* 2008

Fleming, Victor (1889-1949) *Mantrap* 1926; *The Way of All Flesh* 1927; *Abie's Irish Rose* 1928; *The Virginian* 1929; *Renegades* 1930; *Red Dust* 1932; *The Wet Parade* 1932; *Blonde Bombshell* 1933; *The White Sister* 1933; *Treasure Island* 1934; *The Farmer Takes a Wife* 1935; *Reckless* 1935; *Captains Courageous* 1937; *Test Pilot* 1938; *Gone with the Wind* 1939; *The Wizard of Oz* 1939; *Dr Jekyll and Mr Hyde* 1941; *Tortilla Flat* 1942; *A Guy Named Joe* 1944; *Adventure* 1945; *Joan of Arc* 1948

Flemyng, Gordon (1934-1995) *Dr Who and the Daleks* 1965; *Daleks - Invasion Earth 2150 AD* 1966; *Great Catherine* 1968; *The Split* 1968; *The Last Grenade* 1970

Fletcher, Anne (1966-) *Step Up* 2006; *27 Dresses* 2008; *The Proposal* 2009; *The Guilt Trip* 2013; *Hot Pursuit* 2015

Fletcher, Dexter (1966-) *Wild Bill* 2011; *Sunshine on Leith* 2013; *Eddie the Eagle* 2016

Fletcher, Mandie *Deadly Advice* 1993; *Absolutely Fabulous: the Movie* 2016

Flicker, Theodore J (1930-2014) *The Troublemaker* 1964; *The President's Analyst* 1967; *Up in the Cellar* 1970

Flood, James (1895-1953) *Life Begins* 1932; *Wings in the Dark* 1935

Florentine, Isaac *Bridge of Dragons* 1999; *The Shepherd* 2008

Florey, Robert (1900-1975) *The Cocoanuts* 1929; *Murders in the Rue Morgue* 1932; *Ex-Lady* 1933; *The Woman in Red* 1935; *Till We Meet Again* 1936; *The Face behind the Mask* 1941; *Meet Boston Blackie* 1941; *Dangerously They Live* 1942; *The Desert Song* 1944; *The Beast with Five Fingers* 1946; *Tarzan and the Mermaids* 1948; *Outpost in Morocco* 1949

Flynn, John (1932-2007) *The Sergeant* 1968; *The Jerusalem File* 1972; *The Outfit* 1973; *Rolling Thunder* 1977; *Defiance* 1979; *Best Seller* 1987; *Lock Up* 1989; *Out for Justice* 1991; *Brainscan* 1994; *Absence of the Good* 1999

Foley, James (1953-) *Reckless* 1984; *At Close Range* 1985; *Who's That Girl* 1987; *After Dark, My Sweet* 1990; *Glengarry Glen Ross* 1992; *Two Bits* 1995; *The Chamber* 1996; *Fear* 1996; *The Corruptor* 1999; *Confidence* 2002; *Perfect Stranger* 2007; *Fifty Shades Darker* 2017

Folman, Ari *Waltz with Bashir* 2008; *The Congress* 2013

Fonda, Peter (1940-) *The Hired Hand* 1971; *Wanda Nevada* 1979

Fontaine, Anne (1959-) *Comment J'ai Tué Mon Père* 2001; *Nathalie...* 2003; *Coco avant Chanel* 2009; *Adore* 2013; *Gemma Bovery* 2014

Forbes, Bryan (1926-2013) *Whistle down the Wind* 1961; *The L-Shaped Room* 1962; *Seance on a Wet Afternoon* 1964; *King Rat* 1965; *The Wrong Box* 1966; *The Whisperers* 1967; *Deadfall* 1968; *The Madwoman of Chaillot* 1969; *The Raging Moon* 1970; *The Stepford Wives* 1975; *The Slipper and the Rose* 1976; *International Velvet* 1978; *Better Late than Never* 1983; *The Naked Face* 1984

Ford, John aka **Ford, Jack** (1894-1973) *Straight Shooting* 1917; *The Iron Horse* 1924; *3 Bad Men* 1926; *Four Sons* 1928; *Hangman's House* 1928; *Born Reckless* 1930; *Men without Women* 1930; *Up the River* 1930; *Arrowsmith* 1931; *Air Mail* 1932; *Flesh* 1932; *Dr Bull* 1933; *Pilgrimage* 1933; *Judge Priest* 1934; *The Lost Patrol* 1934; *The World Moves On* 1934; *The Informer* 1935; *Steamboat round the Bend* 1935; *The Whole Town's Talking* 1935; *Mary of Scotland* 1936; *The Plough and the Stars* 1936; *The Prisoner of Shark Island* 1936; *The Hurricane* 1937; *Wee Willie Winkie* 1937; *Four Men and a Prayer* 1938; *Submarine Patrol* 1938; *Drums along the Mohawk* 1939; *Stagecoach* 1939; *Young Mr Lincoln* 1939; *The Grapes of Wrath* 1940; *The Long Voyage Home* 1940; *How Green Was My Valley* 1941; *Tobacco Road* 1941; *The Battle of Midway* 1942; *They Were Expendable* 1945; *My Darling Clementine* 1946; *The Fugitive* 1947; *Fort Apache* 1948; *Three Godfathers* 1948; *She Wore a Yellow Ribbon* 1949; *Rio Grande* 1950; *Wagonmaster* 1950; *When Willie Comes Marching Home* 1950; *The Quiet Man* 1952; *What Price Glory?* 1952; *Mogambo* 1953; *The Sun Shines Bright* 1953; *The Long Gray Line* 1955; *Mister Roberts* 1955; *The Searchers* 1956; *The Rising of the Moon* 1957; *The Wings of Eagles* 1957; *Gideon's Day* 1958; *The Last Hurrah* 1958; *The Horse Soldiers* 1959; *Sergeant Rutledge* 1960; *Two Rode Together* 1961; *How the West Was Won* 1962; *The Man Who Shot Liberty Valance* 1962; *Donovan's Reef* 1963; *Cheyenne Autumn* 1964; *Young Cassidy* 1965; *7 Women* 1966

Ford, Tom (1961-) *A Single Man* 2009; *Nocturnal Animals* 2016

Forde, Eugene (1894-1986) *Charlie Chan in London* 1934; *Charlie Chan at Monte Carlo* 1937; *Charlie Chan on Broadway* 1937; *Step Lively, Jeeves* 1937; *Michael Shayne, Private Detective* 1940; *Berlin Correspondent* 1942

Forde, Walter (1896-1984) *The Ghost Train* 1931; *Rome Express* 1932; *Bulldog Jack* 1934; *Chu Chin Chow* 1934; *Jack Ahoy!* 1934; *Forever England* 1935; *Land without Music* 1936; *The Gaunt Stranger* 1938; *Cheer Boys Cheer* 1939; *The Four Just Men* 1939; *Let's Be Famous* 1939; *Charley's (Big Hearted) Aunt* 1940; *Sailors Three* 1940; *Saloon Bar* 1940; *The Ghost Train* 1941; *It's That Man Again* 1942; *Time Flies* 1944; *The Master of Bankdam* 1947; *Cardboard Cavalier* 1949

Forestier, Frederic aka **Forestier, Frédéric** *The Peacekeeper* 1997; *Asterix at the Olympic Games* 2008

Forman, Milos (1932-) *Peter and Pavla* 1964; *A Blonde in Love* 1965; *The Firemen's Ball* 1967; *Taking Off* 1971; *Visions of Eight* 1973; *One Flew over the Cuckoo's Nest* 1975; *Hair* 1979; *Ragtime* 1981; *Amadeus* 1984; *Valmont* 1989; *The People vs Larry Flynt* 1996; *Man on the Moon* 1999; *Goya's Ghosts* 2006

Forster, Marc (1969-) *Monster's Ball* 2001; *Finding Neverland* 2004; *Stay* 2005; *Stranger than Fiction* 2006; *The Kite Runner* 2007; *Quantum of Solace* 2008; *Machine Gun Preacher* 2011; *World War Z* 2013

Forsyth, Bill (1946-) *That Sinking Feeling* 1979; *Gregory's Girl* 1980; *Local Hero* 1983; *Comfort and Joy* 1984; *Housekeeping* 1987; *Breaking In* 1989; *Being Human* 1994; *Gregory's Two Girls* 1999

Fortenberry, John *Jury Duty* 1995; *A Night at the Roxbury* 1998

Forzani, Bruno *The ABCs of Death* 2012; *The Strange Colour of Your Body's Tears* 2013

Fosse, Bob (1927-1987) *Sweet Charity* 1968; *Cabaret* 1972; *Lenny* 1974; *All That Jazz* 1979; *Star 80* 1983

Foster, Giles *Consuming Passions* 1988; *Tree of Hands* 1988

Foster, Jodie (1962-) *Little Man Tate* 1991; *Home for the Holidays* 1995; *The Beaver* 2010; *Money Monster* 2016

Foster, Lewis R (1898-1974) *Men o' War* 1929; *Jamaica Run* 1953; *Crashout* 1955; *The Bold and the Brave* 1956; *Dakota Incident* 1956; *Tonka* 1958

Foster, Norman (1900-1976) *Fair Warning* 1937; *Thank You, Mr Moto* 1937; *Think Fast, Mr Moto* 1937; *Mr Moto Takes a Chance* 1938; *Mr Moto's Last Warning* 1938; *Mysterious Mr Moto* 1938; *Charlie Chan at Treasure Island* 1939; *Charlie Chan in Reno* 1939; *Mr Moto Takes a Vacation* 1939; *Journey into Fear* 1942; *Blood on My Hands* 1948; *Rachel and the Stranger* 1948; *Tell It to the Judge* 1949; *Sombrero* 1952; *Davy Crockett, King of the Wild Frontier* 1955; *Davy Crockett and the River Pirates* 1956

Fothergill, Alastair *Deep Blue* 2003; *Earth* 2007; *African Cats* 2011; *Chimpanzee* 2012

Fowler Jr, Gene (1917-1998) *I Was a Teenage Werewolf* 1957; *Gang War* 1958; *I Married a Monster from Outer Space* 1958; *Showdown at Boot Hill* 1958

Fox, Eytan *Walk on Water* 2004; *Yossi* 2012; *Cupcakes* 2013

Fox, Wallace aka **Fox, Wallace W** (1895-1958) *Block Busters* 1944; *Docks of New York* 1945; *Pillow of Death* 1945; *Wild Beauty* 1946

Foy, Ciaran *Citadel* 2012; *Sinister 2* 2015

Fraker, William A (1923-2010) *Monte Walsh* 1970; *A Reflection of Fear* 1973; *The Legend of the Lone Ranger* 1981

Frakes, Jonathan (1952-) *Star Trek: First Contact* 1996; *Star Trek: Insurrection* 1998; *Clockstoppers* 2002; *Thunderbirds* 2004

Francis, Freddie (1917-2007) *Two and Two Make Six* 1961; *The Brain* 1962; *Nightmare* 1963; *Paranoiac* 1963; *Dr Terror's House of Horrors* 1964; *Evil of Frankenstein* 1964; *Hysteria* 1964; *The Skull* 1965; *The Psychopath* 1966; *The Deadly Bees* 1967; *They Came from beyond Space* 1967; *Torture Garden* 1967; *Dracula Has Risen from the Grave* 1968; *Mumsy, Nanny, Sonny & Girly* 1970; *Trog* 1970; *The Creeping Flesh* 1972; *Tales from the Crypt* 1972; *Craze* 1973; *Legend of the Werewolf* 1974; *The Ghoul* 1975; *The Doctor and the Devils* 1985; *Dark Tower* 1989

Francis, Karl (1943-) *Giro City* 1982; *Rebecca's Daughters* 1991; *One of the Hollywood Ten* 2000

Franco, Jesus aka **Moutier, Norbert** aka **Franco, Jess** aka **Manera, Franco** (1930-2013) *The Awful Dr Orlof* 1962; *The Blood of Fu Manchu* 1968; *The Castle of Fu Manchu* 1968; *The Girl from Rio* 1968; *The Bloody Judge* 1969; *Count Dracula* 1970; *Vampyros Lesbos* 1970; *Dracula, Prisoner of Frankenstein* 1972; *The Female Vampire* 1973

Franco, Michel *After Lucia* 2012; *Chronic* 2015

Franju, Georges (1912-1987) *Eyes without a Face* 1959; *Thérèse Desqueyroux* 1962; *Judex* 1963; *Thomas the Imposter* 1964

Frank, Melvin (1913-1988) *Callaway Went Thataway* 1951; *Above and Beyond* 1952; *Knock on Wood* 1954; *The Court Jester* 1956; *That Certain Feeling* 1956; *The Jayhawkers* 1959; *Li'l Abner* 1959; *The Facts of Life* 1960; *Strange Bedfellows* 1965; *Buona Sera, Mrs Campbell* 1968; *A Touch of Class* 1973; *The Prisoner of Second Avenue* 1974; *The Duchess and the Dirtwater Fox* 1976; *Lost and Found* 1979; *Walk like a Man* 1987

Frank, Robert *Pull My Daisy* 1959; *Candy Mountain* 1987

Frank, Scott *The Lookout* 2007; *A Walk among the Tombstones* 2014

Frankel, Cyril (1921-) *Devil on Horseback* 1954; *Man of Africa* 1954; *It's Great to Be Young* 1956; *No Time for Tears* 1957; *Alive and Kicking* 1958; *Never Take Sweets from a Stranger* 1960; *Don't Bother to Knock* 1961; *On the Fiddle* 1961; *The Very Edge* 1962; *The Witches* 1966; *The Trygon Factor* 1967; *Permission to Kill* 1975

Frankel, David (1959-) *Miami Rhapsody* 1995; *The Devil Wears Prada* 2006; *Marley & Me* 2008; *The Big Year* 2011; *Hope Springs* 2012; *One Chance* 2013; *Collateral Beauty* 2016

Frankenheimer, John (1930-2002) *The Young Stranger* 1957; *The Young Savages* 1961; *All Fall Down* 1962; *Birdman of Alcatraz* 1962; *The Manchurian Candidate* 1962; *Seven Days in May* 1964; *The Train* 1964; *Grand Prix* 1966; *Seconds* 1966; *The Extraordinary Seaman* 1969; *The Gypsy Moths* 1969; *The Horsemen* 1971; *Story of a Love Story* 1973; *99 and 44/100% Dead* 1974; *French Connection II* 1975; *Black Sunday* 1976; *Prophecy* 1979; *The Challenge* 1982; *The Holcroft Covenant* 1985; *52 Pick-Up* 1986; *Dead-Bang* 1989; *The Fourth War* 1990; *Year of the Gun* 1991; *Against the Wall* 1994; *The Burning Season* 1994; *The Island of Dr Moreau* 1996; *Ronin* 1998; *Deception* 2000; *Path to War* 2002

Franklin, Carl (1949-) *Full Fathom Five* 1990; *One False Move* 1992; *Devil in a Blue Dress* 1995; *One True Thing* 1998; *High Crimes* 2002; *Out of Time* 2003

Franklin, Howard *Quick Change* 1990; *The Public Eye* 1992; *Larger than Life* 1996

Franklin, Richard (1948-2007) *Patrick* 1978; *Road Games* 1981; *Psycho II* 1983; *Cloak and Dagger* 1984; *Link* 1986; *FX 2* 1991; *Hotel Sorrento* 1994

Franklin, Sidney (1893-1972) *The Last of Mrs Cheyney* 1929; *Wild Orchids* 1929; *A Lady's Morals* 1930; *Private Lives* 1931; *Smilin' Through* 1932; *Reunion in Vienna* 1933; *The Barretts of Wimpole Street* 1934; *The Dark Angel* 1935; *The Good Earth* 1937; *The Barretts of Wimpole Street* 1956

Fraser, Harry (1889-1974) *'Neath the Arizona Skies* 1934; *Randy Rides Alone* 1934

Fraser, Toa *Dean Spanley* 2008; *The Dead Lands* 2014

Frawley, James (1937-) *The Christian Licorice Store* 1971; *Kid Blue* 1971; *The Big Bus* 1976; *The Muppet Movie* 1979; *Fraternity Vacation* 1985; *The Shamrock Conspiracy* 1995; *The Three Stooges* 2000

Frears, Stephen (1941-) *Gumshoe* 1971; *Bloody Kids* 1979; *The Hit* 1984; *My Beautiful Laundrette* 1985; *Prick Up Your Ears* 1987; *Sammy and Rosie Get Laid* 1987; *Dangerous Liaisons* 1988; *The Grifters* 1990; *Accidental Hero* 1992; *The Snapper* 1993; *Mary Reilly* 1995; *The Van* 1996; *The Hi-Lo Country* 1998; *Fail Safe* 2000; *High Fidelity* 2000; *Dirty Pretty Things* 2002; *Mrs Henderson Presents* 2005; *The Queen* 2006; *Chéri* 2009; *Tamara Drewe* 2010; *Lay the Favorite* 2012; *Philomena* 2013; *The Program* 2015; *Florence Foster Jenkins* 2016

Freda, Riccardo (1909-1999) *Les Misérables* 1946; *Lust of the Vampire* 1956; *The White Warrior* 1959

Freedman, Jerrold (1919-) *Kansas City Bomber* 1972; *Borderline* 1980; *Native Son* 1986

Freeland, Thornton (1898-1987) *Whoopee!* 1930; *Six Cylinder Love* 1931; *Love Affair* 1932; *Flying down to Rio* 1933; *George White's Scandals* 1934; *Accused* 1936; *Jericho* 1937; *Over the Moon* 1937; *The Gang's All Here* 1939; *Meet Me at Dawn* 1946; *The Brass Monkey* 1948; *Dear Mr Prohack* 1949

Freeman, Morgan J (1969-) *Hurricane Streets* 1997; *Desert Blue* 1998; *American Psycho II: All American Girl* 2002

Fregonese, Hugo (1908-1987) *Saddle Tramp* 1950; *Apache Drums* 1951; *Untamed Frontier* 1952; *Blowing Wild* 1953; *Decameron Nights* 1953; *Man in the Attic* 1953; *The Raid* 1954; *Seven Thunders* 1957; *Harry Black and the Tiger* 1958

Freleng, Friz (1906-1995) *Birds Anonymous* 1957; *Looney Looney Looney Bugs Bunny Movie* 1981; *Bugs Bunny 1001 Rabbit Tales* 1982; *Daffy Duck's Movie: Fantastic Island* 1983

French, Harold (1897-1997) *Jeannie* 1941; *Major Barbara* 1941; *The Day Will Dawn* 1942; *Secret Mission* 1942; *Unpublished Story* 1942; *English without Tears* 1944; *Quiet Weekend* 1946; *My Brother Jonathan* 1947; *The Blind Goddess* 1948; *Quartet* 1948; *Adam and Evelyne* 1949; *The Dancing Years* 1949; *Trio* 1950; *Encore* 1951; *The Hour of 13* 1952; *Isn't Life Wonderful!* 1952; *The Man Who Watched Trains Go By* 1952; *Rob Roy, the Highland Rogue* 1953; *Forbidden Cargo* 1954; *The Man Who Loved Redheads* 1954

Frend, Charles (1909-1977) *The Foreman Went to France* 1941; *The Big Blockade* 1942; *San Demetrio London* 1943; *Johnny Frenchman* 1945; *The Loves of Joanna Godden* 1947; *Scott of the Antarctic* 1948; *A*

Run for Your Money 1949; The Magnet 1950; The Cruel Sea 1952; Lease of Life 1954; The Long Arm 1956; Barnacle Bill 1957; Cone of Silence 1960; Girl on Approval 1962

Fresnadillo, Juan Carlos (1967-) Intacto 2001; 28 Weeks Later 2007; Intruders 2011

Freudenthal, Thor Hotel for Dogs 2008; Diary of a Wimpy Kid 2010; Percy Jackson: Sea of Monsters 2013

Freund, Karl (1890-1969) The Mummy 1932; Mad Love 1935

Freundlich, Bart (1970-) The Myth of Fingerprints 1996; Catch That Kid 2004; Trust the Man 2006; The Rebound 2009

Fridriksson, Fridrik Thor (1954-) Cold Fever 1994; Falcons 2002

Friedberg, Jason Epic Movie 2007; Disaster Movie 2008; Meet the Spartans 2008; Vampires Suck 2010

Friedenberg, Richard Mr and Mrs Loving 1993; The Education of Little Tree 1997

Friedkin, William (1935-) Good Times 1967; The Birthday Party 1968; The Night They Raided Minsky's 1968; The Boys in the Band 1970; The French Connection 1971; The Exorcist 1973; The Brink's Job 1978; Deal of the Century 1983; To Live and Die in LA 1985; Rampage 1987; The Guardian 1990; Blue Chips 1994; Jade 1995; 12 Angry Men 1997; Rules of Engagement 2000; The Hunted 2002; Bug 2006; Killer Joe 2011

Friedman, Jeffrey Common Threads: Stories from the Quilt 1989; The Celluloid Closet 1995; Paragraph 175 1999; Howl 2010; Lovelace 2013

Friedman, Seymour (1917-) Escape Route 1952; Khyber Patrol 1954

Frost, Harvey aka Frost, F Harvey Single Santa Seeks Mrs Claus 2004; Meet the Santas 2005; All I Want for Christmas 2007; A Grandpa for Christmas 2007; Battle of the Bulbs 2010; A Soldier's Love Story 2010

Frost, Lee aka Frost, R L (1935-2007) House on Bare Mountain 1962; The Thing with Two Heads 1972; Dixie Dynamite 1976

Fuest, Robert (1927-2012) Just like a Woman 1966; And Soon the Darkness 1970; Wuthering Heights 1970; The Abominable Dr Phibes 1971; Dr Phibes Rises Again 1972; The Final Programme 1973; The Devil's Rain 1975

Fukasaku, Kinji (1930-2003) Tora! Tora! Tora! 1970; The Yakuza Papers 1973; Virus 1980; Battle Royale 2000; Battle Royale 2: Requiem 2003

Fukuda, Jun (1924-2000) Ebirah, Horror of the Deep 1966; Son of Godzilla 1967; Godzilla vs Gigan 1972; Godzilla vs Megalon 1973; Godzilla vs Mechagodzilla 1974

Fukunaga, Cary aka Fukunaga, Cary Joji aka Fukunaga, Cary Joji Sin Nombre 2009; Jane Eyre 2011; Beasts of No Nation 2015

Fulci, Lucio (1927-1996) Beatrice Cenci 1969; Zombie Flesh Eaters 1979; The Black Cat 1981; The House by the Cemetery 1981

Fuller, William (1911-1997) I Shot Jesse James 1949; The Baron of Arizona 1950; Fixed Bayonets! 1951; The Steel Helmet 1951; Park Row 1952; Pickup on South Street 1953; Hell and High Water 1954; House of Bamboo 1955; China Gate 1957; Forty Guns 1957; Run of the Arrow 1957; The Crimson Kimono 1959; Verboten! 1959; Underworld USA 1961; Merrill's Marauders 1962; Shock Corridor 1963; The Naked Kiss 1964; Shark! 1969; Dead Pigeon on Beethoven Street 1972; The Big Red One 1980; White Dog 1981; Street of No Return 1989

Fulton, Keith Lost in La Mancha 2002; Brothers of the Head 2005

Fuqua, Antoine (1966-) The Replacement Killers 1998; Training Day 2001; Tears of the Sun 2003; King Arthur 2004; Lightning in a Bottle 2004; Shooter 2007; Brooklyn's Finest 2009; Olympus Has Fallen 2013; The Equalizer 2014; Southpaw 2015; The Magnificent Seven 2016

Furie, Sidney J (1933-) Doctor Blood's Coffin 1960; The Boys 1961; During One Night 1961; Three on a Spree 1961; The Young Ones 1961; The Leather Boys 1964; Wonderful Life 1964; The Ipcress File 1965; The Appaloosa 1966; The Naked Runner 1967; The Lawyer 1969; Lady Sings

the Blues 1972; Hit! 1973; Gable and Lombard 1976; The Boys in Company C 1978; The Entity 1981; Purple Hearts 1984; Iron Eagle 1985; Superman IV: the Quest for Peace 1987; Iron Eagle II 1988; Ladybugs 1992; Iron Eagle IV 1995; Hollow Point 1996; Top of the World 1997; In Her Defense 1998; Hide and Seek 2000

Furman, Brad The Lincoln Lawyer 2011; Runner Runner 2013; The Infiltrator 2016

Fywell, Tim (1941-) Norma Jean & Marilyn 1996; I Capture the Castle 2002; Ice Princess 2005

G

Gabai, Richard (1964-) Virtual Girl 1998; Imaginary Friend 2012

Gabriel, Mike The Rescuers Down Under 1990; Pocahontas 1995

Gadhvi, Sanjay Dhoom 2004; Dhoom: 2 2006

Gaghan, Stephen Syriana 2005; Gold 2016

Gallenberger, Florian City of War: the Story of John Rabe 2009; Colonia 2015

Gallo, George (1956-) 29th Street 1991; Trapped in Paradise 1994; My Spy 2008

Gallo, Vincent (1961-) Buffalo '66 1998; The Brown Bunny 2003

Gance, Abel (1889-1981) J'Accuse 1919; La Roue 1923; Napoléon 1927; Beethoven 1936; J'Accuse 1938; The Battle of Austerlitz 1960

Gannaway, Roberts aka Gannaway, Bobs Tinkerbell and the Secret of the Wings 2012; Planes: Fire and Rescue 2014

Gans, Christophe (1960-) Necronomicon 1993; Crying Freeman 1995; Brotherhood of the Wolf 2001; Silent Hill 2006

Gansel, Dennis The Wave 2008; We Are the Night 2010; Mechanic: Resurrection 2016

Garant, Robert Ben Balls of Fury 2007; Reno 911!: Miami 2007

Garbus, Liz The Farm: Angola, USA 1996; Bobby Fischer against the World 2011; Love, Marilyn 2012

Garcia, Rodrigo aka Garcia, Rodrigo (1959-) Things You Can Tell Just by Looking at Her 2000; Mother and Child 2009; Albert Nobbs 2011

Gardner, Cyril (1898-1942) Grumpy 1930; The Royal Family of Broadway 1930

Garnett, Tay (1894-1977) Bad Company 1931; One Way Passage 1932; China Seas 1935; Love Is News 1937; Slave Ship 1937; Stand-In 1937; Joy of Living 1938; Trade Winds 1938; Eternally Yours 1939; Slightly Honorable 1939; Seven Sinners 1940; Cheers for Miss Bishop 1941; My Favorite Spy 1942; Bataan 1943; The Cross of Lorraine 1943; Mrs Parkington 1944; The Valley of Decision 1945; The Postman Always Rings Twice 1946; A Connecticut Yankee in King Arthur's Court 1949; The Fireball 1950; Cause for Alarm 1951; Soldiers Three 1951; One Minute to Zero 1952; Main Street to Broadway 1953; The Black Knight 1954; A Terrible Beauty 1960; Cattle King 1963; The Delta Factor 1970; Challenge to Be Free 1997

Garrel, Philippe (1948-) Le Vent de la Nuit 1999; Regular Lovers 2005; Jealousy 2013

Garris, Mick (1951-) Psycho IV: the Beginning 1990; Sleepwalkers 1992

Garrone, Matteo Gomorrah 2008; Reality 2012; Tale of Tales 2015

Gasnier, Louis (1882-1963) The Virtuous Sin 1930; The Last Outpost 1935; Reefer Madness 1936

Gatlif, Tony (1948-) Les Princes 1982; Latcho Drom 1993; Gadjo Dilo 1997; Exiles 2004; Transylvania 2006

Gaup, Nils (1955-) Pathfinder 1987; Shipwrecked 1990; North Star 1996; The Last King 2016

Gavron, Sarah Brick Lane 2007; Village at the End of the World 2012; Suffragette 2015

Gee, Grant Joy Division 2008; Patience (After Sebald) 2011

Gens, Xavier Frontier(s) 2007; Hitman 2007; The Divide 2011; The ABCs of Death 2012

George, Terry Some Mother's Son 1996; Hotel Rwanda 2004

Gerber, Fred Rent-a-Kid 1992; Family Plan 1997

Gerber, Tony Side Streets 1998; The Notorious Mr Bout 2014

Gering, Marion (1901-1977) Devil and the Deep 1932; Madame Butterfly 1932; Jennie Gerhardt 1933; Thirty-Day Princess 1934; Rumba 1935; Thunder in the City 1937

German, Alexei aka German, Aleksei (1938-2013) My Friend Ivan Lapshin 1982; Hard to Be a God 2013

Germi, Pietro (1904-1974) Divorce - Italian Style 1961; The Birds, the Bees, and the Italians 1965; Alfredo Alfredo 1971

Geronimi, Clyde (1901-1989) Victory through Air Power 1943; The Three Caballeros 1944; Make Mine Music 1946; Melody Time 1948; The Adventures of Ichabod and Mr Toad 1949; Cinderella 1950; Alice in Wonderland 1951; Peter Pan 1953; Lady and the Tramp 1955; Sleeping Beauty 1959; One Hundred and One Dalmatians 1960

Gervais, Ricky (1961-) The Invention of Lying 2009; Cemetery Junction 2010; Life on the Road 2016

Gervasi, Sacha Anvil: the Story of Anvil 2008; Hitchcock 2012

Gessner, Nicolas (1931-) Someone behind the Door 1971; The Little Girl Who Lives Down the Lane 1976

Ghai, Subhash (1943-) Pardes 1997; Taal 1999; Yaadein 2001; Kisna - the Warrior Poet 2004

Ghatak, Ritwik (1925-1976) The Cloud Capped Star 1960; E Flat 1961; The Golden Thread 1962

Ghobadi, Bahman (1968-) A Time for Drunken Horses 2000; Turtles Can Fly 2004; No One Knows about Persian Cats 2009

Giannoli, Xavier The Singer 2006; Marguerite 2015

Gibbins, Duncan (1952-1993) Fire with Fire 1986; Eve of Destruction 1991

Gibney, Alex (1953-) Enron: the Smartest Guys in the Room 2005; Taxi to the Dark Side 2007; Gonzo: the Life and Work of Dr Hunter S Thompson 2008; Client-9: the Rise and Fall of Eliot Spitzer 2010; Magic Trip: Ken Kesey's Search for a Kool Place 2011; Mea Maxima Culpa: Silence in the House of God 2012; The Armstrong Lie 2013; We Steal Secrets: the Story of WikiLeaks 2013; Going Clear 2015

Gibson, Alan (1938-1987) Crescendo 1970; Goodbye Gemini 1970; Dracula AD 1972 1972; The Satanic Rites of Dracula 1973; Witness for the Prosecution 1982; Martin's Day 1984

Gibson, Brian (1944-2004) Breaking Glass 1980; Poltergeist II: the Other Side 1986; Tina: What's Love Got to Do with It 1993; The Juror 1996; Still Crazy 1998

Gibson, Mel (1956-) The Man without a Face 1993; Braveheart 1995; The Passion of the Christ 2004; Apocalypto 2006

Giedroyc, Coky Stella Does Tricks 1997; Women Talking Dirty 1999

Giglio, Tony Chaos 2006; Timber Falls 2007

Gil, Mateo Spectre 2006; Blackthorn 2011

Gilbert, Brian (1960-) The Frog Prince 1984; Vice Versa 1988; Not without My Daughter 1990; Tom & Viv 1994; Wilde 1997; The Gathering 2002

Gilbert, Lewis (1920-) Scarlet Thread 1951; There Is Another Sun 1951; Cosh Boy 1952; Emergency Call 1952; Time Gentlemen Please! 1952; Albert, RN 1953; The Good Die Young 1954; The Sea Shall Not Have Them 1954; Reach for the Sky 1956; The Admirable Crichton 1957; Cast a Dark Shadow 1957; A Cry from the Streets 1957; Carve Her Name with Pride 1958; Ferry to Hong Kong 1958; Light Up the Sky 1960; Sink the Bismarck! 1960; The Greengage Summer 1961; HMS Defiant 1962; The 7th Dawn 1964; Alfie 1966; You Only Live Twice 1967; The Adventurers 1970; Paul and Michelle 1974; Operation Daybreak 1975; Seven Nights in Japan 1976; The Spy Who Loved Me 1977; Moonraker 1979; Educating Rita 1983; Not Quite Jerusalem 1985; Shirley Valentine 1989; Stepping Out 1991; Haunted 1995; Before You Go 2002

Gilbey, Julian Rollin with the Nines 2005; Rise of the Footsoldier 2006; A Lonely Place to Die 2011; Plastic 2014

Gillard, Stuart (1950-) Teenage Mutant Ninja Turtles III 1992; Rocketman 1997

Gillespie, Craig (1967-) Lars and the Real Girl 2007; Mr Woodcock 2007; Fright Night 2011; Million Dollar Arm 2014; The Finest Hours 2015

Gillespie, Jim I Know What You Did Last Summer 1997; D-Tox 2001

Gillett, Burt (1891-1971) Flowers and Trees 1932; The Three Little Pigs 1933

Gillett, Tyler aka Radio Silence V/H/S 2012; Devil's Due 2014; Southbound 2015

Gilliam, Terry (1940-) Monty Python and the Holy Grail 1975; Jabberwocky 1977; Time Bandits 1981; Brazil 1985; The Adventures of Baron Munchausen 1988; The Fisher King 1991; Twelve Monkeys 1995; Fear and Loathing in Las Vegas 1998; The Brothers Grimm 2005; Tideland 2005; The Imaginarium of Doctor Parnassus 2009; The Zero Theorem 2013

Gilliat, Sidney (1908-1994) Millions like Us 1943; Waterloo Road 1944; The Rake's Progress 1945; Green for Danger 1946; London Belongs to Me 1948; State Secret 1950; The Story of Gilbert and Sullivan 1953; The Constant Husband 1955; Fortune Is a Woman 1956; Left, Right and Centre 1959; Only Two Can Play 1961; The Great St Trinian's Train Robbery 1966; Endless Night 1971

Gilling, John (1912-1985) No Trace 1950; The Quiet Woman 1950; The Frightened Man 1952; Voice of Merrill 1952; Deadly Nightshade 1953; Escape by Night 1953; The Gilded Cage 1954; Tiger by the Tail 1955; Interpol 1957; The Man Inside 1958; The Bandit of Zhobe 1959; The Flesh and the Fiends 1959; The Challenge 1960; Fury at Smugglers Bay 1961; The Pirates of Blood River 1961; The Shadow of the Cat 1961; The Scarlet Blade 1963; The Night Caller 1965; The Plague of the Zombies 1965; The Mummy's Shroud 1966; The Reptile 1966; Where the Bullets Fly 1966

Gilmore, Stuart (1909-1971) The Virginian 1946; The Half-Breed 1952

Gilroy, Frank D (1925-2015) Desperate Characters 1971; The Gig 1985

Gilroy, Tony (1956-) Michael Clayton 2007; Duplicity 2009; The Bourne Legacy 2012

Giraldi, Bob (1939-) National Lampoon's Movie Madness 1981; Hiding Out 1987; Dinner Rush 2000

Girard, Bernard (1918-1997) Dead Heat on a Merry-Go-Round 1966; The Mind Snatchers 1972; Little Moon & Jud McGraw 1978

Girard, François (1963-) Thirty Two Short Films about Glenn Gould 1993; The Red Violin 1998; Silk 2007; The Choir 2014

Girdler, William (1947-1978) Grizzly 1976; Day of the Animals 1977; The Manitou 1978

Gitai, Amos (1950-) Berlin Jerusalem 1989; Wadi 1981-1991 1991; Yom Yom 1998; Kadosh 1999; Kippur 2000; 11'09"01 - September 11 2002

Giwa, Max aka Max StreetDance 2010; StreetDance 2 2012; Walking on Sunshine 2014

Glaser, Paul Michael aka Glaser, Paul M (1943-) The Running Man 1987; The Cutting Edge 1992; The Air Up There 1993; Kazaam 1996

Glatter, Lesli Linka Now and Then 1995; The Proposition 1998

Glatzer, Richard (1952-2015) The Fluffer 2001; Echo Park LA 2005; Still Alice 2014

Glazer, Jonathan (1966-) Sexy Beast 2000; Birth 2004; Under the Skin 2013

Glebas, Francis Fantasia 2000 1999; Piglet's Big Movie 2003

Glen, John (1932-) For Your Eyes Only 1981; Octopussy 1983; A View to a Kill 1985; The Living Daylights 1987; Licence to Kill 1989; Aces: Iron Eagle III 1992; Christopher Columbus: the Discovery 1992; The Point Men 2000

Glenville, Peter (1913-1996) The Prisoner 1955; Me and the Colonel 1958; Summer and Smoke 1961; Term of Trial 1962; Becket 1964; Hotel Paradiso 1966; The Comedians 1967

Glickenhaus, James (1950-) The Exterminator 1980; The Protector 1985; Blue Jean Cop 1988

Glimcher, Arne (1938-) The Mambo Kings 1992; Just Cause 1995

Gluck, Will Fired Up! 2009; Easy A 2010; Friends with Benefits 2011; Annie 2014

Godard, Jean-Luc (1930-) A Bout de Souffle 1959; Le Petit Soldat 1960; Une Femme Est une Femme 1961; The Seven Deadly Sins 1961; RoGoPaG 1962; Vivre Sa Vie 1962; Les Carabiniers 1963; Le Mépris 1963; Bande à Part 1964; The Married Woman 1964; Alphaville 1965; Paris Vu Par... 1965; Pierrot le Fou 1965; Made in USA 1966; Masculine Feminine 1966; Two or Three Things I Know about Her 1966; La Chinoise 1967; Far from Vietnam 1967; Weekend 1967; Le Gai Savoir 1968; Sympathy for the Devil 1968; Vent d'Est 1969; Vladimir et Rosa 1970; Tout Va Bien 1972; Number Two 1975; Slow Motion 1980; Passion 1982; First Name: Carmen 1983; Je Vous Salue, Marie 1984; Detective 1985; Grandeur et Décadence d'un Petit Commerce de Cinéma 1986; Soigne Ta Droite 1986; Aria 1987; King Lear - Fear and Loathing 1987; Nouvelle Vague 1990; Hélas pour Moi 1993; JLG/JLG - Self Portrait in December 1994; Eloge de l'Amour 2001; Ten Minutes Older: the Cello 2002; Notre Musique 2004; Film Socialisme 2010; Goodbye to Language 2014

Godfrey, Peter (1899-1970) The Lone Wolf Spy Hunt 1939; Christmas in Connecticut 1945; Hotel Berlin 1945; The Two Mrs Carrolls 1945; Cry Wolf 1947; Escape Me Never 1947; The Woman in White 1948; Barricade 1950

Golan, Menahem (1929-2014) What's Good for the Goose 1969; Diamonds 1975; Lepke 1975; The Magician of Lublin 1979; The Apple 1980; Enter the Ninja 1981; Over the Brooklyn Bridge 1983; The Delta Force 1986; Over the Top 1987; Hanna's War 1988; Mack the Knife 1989

Gold, Jack (1930-2015) The Bofors Gun 1968; The Reckoning 1969; The National Health 1973; Who? 1974; Man Friday 1975; Aces High 1976; The Medusa Touch 1978; The Chain 1984; Escape from Sobibor 1987; Stones for Ibarra 1988; The Tenth Man 1988

Goldbacher, Sandra The Governess 1997; Me without You 2001

Goldbeck, Willis (1898-1979) Dr Gillespie's New Assistant 1942; Dr Gillespie's Criminal Case 1943; Three Men in White 1944; Love Laughs at Andy Hardy 1946; Ten Tall Men 1951

Goldberg, Dan aka Goldberg, Danny No Nukes 1980; Feds 1988

Goldberg, Eric (1955-) Pocahontas 1995; Fantasia 2000 1999

Goldberg, Evan This Is the End 2013; The Interview 2014

Goldberg, Gary David (1944-2013) Dad 1989; Must Love Dogs 2005

Goldblatt, Mark Dead Heat 1988; The Punisher 1989

Golden, Karl The Honeymooners 2003; Weekender 2011

Goldenberg, Rachel Escape from Polygamy 2013; A Deadly Adoption 2015

Goldman, Gary (1945-) Stanley's Magic Garden 1994; Thumbelina 1994; Anastasia 1997; Bartok the Magnificent 1999; Titan AE 2000

Goldman, Paul The Night We Called It a Day 2003; Suburban Mayhem 2006

Goldschmidt, John (1943-) She'll Be Wearing Pink Pyjamas 1984; A Song for Europe 1985

Goldstein, Allan A aka Goldstein, Allan Chaindance 1991; Death Wish V: the Face of Death 1994; Memory Run 1995; Home Team 1998; One Way Out 2002

Goldstein, Scott D aka Goldstein, Scott Walls of Glass 1985; Ambition 1991

Goldstone, James (1931-1999) Jigsaw 1968; A Man Called Gannon 1969; Winning 1969; Brother John 1970; The Gang That Couldn't Shoot Straight 1971; Red Sky at Morning 1971; They Only Kill Their Masters 1972; Swashbuckler 1976; Rollercoaster 1977; When Time Ran Out 1980; Dreams of Gold: the Mel Fisher Story 1986

Goldthwait, Bobcat (1962-) Shakes the Clown 1991; Sleeping Dogs Lie. 2006; World's Greatest Dad 2009; God Bless America 2011; Willow Creek 2013

Goldwyn, Tony (1960-) A Walk on the Moon 1999; Animal Attraction 2001; The Last Kiss 2006; Conviction 2010

Gomer, Steve Sunset Park 1996; Barney's Great Adventure 1998; The Miracle of Dommatina 2009
Gomez, Nick (1963-) Laws of Gravity 1992; illtown 1996; Drowning Mona 2000
Gondry, Michel (1963-) Human Nature 2001; Eternal Sunshine of the Spotless Mind 2003; Dave Chappelle's Block Party 2005; The Science of Sleep 2005; Be Kind Rewind 2007; The Thorn in the Heart 2009; The Green Hornet 2011; Is the Man Who Is Tall Happy? 2013; Mood Indigo 2013; Microbe & Gasoline 2015
Goodhew, Philip Intimate Relations 1995; Another Life 2000
Goodwins, Leslie (1899-1969) The Girl from Mexico 1939; Let's Make Music 1940; Mexican Spitfire 1940; The Mummy's Curse 1944; The Singing Sheriff 1944; Fireman Save My Child 1954
Gorak, Chris Right at Your Door 2006; The Darkest Hour 2011
Gordon, Bert I (1922-) The Amazing Colossal Man 1957; Beginning of the End 1957; The Cyclops 1957; Earth vs the Spider 1958; War of the Colossal Beast 1958; The Magic Sword 1962; Village of the Giants 1965; The Food of the Gods 1976; Empire of the Ants 1977
Gordon, Bryan Career Opportunities 1991; Pie in the Sky 1995
Gordon, Daniel 9.79* 2012; The Fall 2016
Gordon, Dennie Joe Dirt 2001; What a Girl Wants 2003; New York Minute 2004
Gordon, Fiona Rumba 2008; The Fairy 2011
Gordon, Josh Blades of Glory 2007; The Switch 2010
Gordon, Keith (1961-) The Chocolate War 1988; A Midnight Clear 1991; Mother Night 1996; Waking the Dead 2000; The Singing Detective 2003
Gordon, Michael (1911-1993) Crime Doctor 1943; The Web 1947; Another Part of the Forest 1948; The Lady Gambles 1949; Cyrano de Bergerac 1950; I Can Get It for You Wholesale 1951; The Secret of Convict Lake 1951; Pillow Talk 1959; Portrait in Black 1960; Boys' Night Out 1962; For Love or Money 1963; Move Over, Darling 1963; Texas across the River 1966; How Do I Love Thee? 1970
Gordon, Robert (1895-1971) It Came from beneath the Sea 1955; Black Zoo 1963; Tarzan and the Jungle Boy 1968; Best o' Enemies 1955
Gordon, Seth (1976-) The King of Kong: a Fistful of Quarters 2007; Four Christmases 2008; Horrible Bosses 2011; Identity Thief 2013; Baywatch 2017
Gordon, Stuart (1947-) Re-Animator 1985; From Beyond 1986; Dolls 1987; Robot Jox 1989; The Pit and the Pendulum 1991; Fortress 1992; Space Truckers 1996; King of the Ants 2003; Edmond 2005; Stuck 2007
Goretta, Claude 1929-) The Lacemaker 1977; The Death of Mario Ricci 1983
Gorin, Jean-Pierre Vladimir et Rosa 1970; Tout Va Bien 1972
Gorris, Marleen (1948-) A Question of Silence 1982; The Last Island 1990; Antonia's Line 1995; Mrs Dalloway 1997; The Luzhin Defence 2000
Goscinny, René (1926-1978) Asterix the Gaul 1967; Asterix and Cleopatra 1968; The 12 Tasks of Asterix 1975
Goslar, Jürgen (1927-) Death in the Sun 1975; Slavers 1977
Gosnell, Raja (1968-) Home Alone 3 1997; Never Been Kissed 1999; Big Momma's House 2000; Scooby-Doo 2002; Scooby-Doo 2: Monsters Unleashed 2004; Yours, Mine & Ours 2005; Beverly Hills Chihuahua 2008; The Smurfs 2011; The Smurfs 2 2013
Gottlieb, Carl (1938-) Caveman 1981; Amazon Women on the Moon 1987
Gottlieb, Michael (1945-2014) Mannequin 1987; Mr Nanny 1992
Gould, Heywood One Good Cop 1991; Trial by Jury 1994
Goulding, Alfred (1896-1972) A Chump at Oxford 1940; The Dark Road 1948
Goulding, Edmund (1891-1959) Sally, Irene and Mary 1925; Love 1927; The Trespasser 1929; The Devil's Holiday 1930; Paramount on Parade 1930; Blondie of the Follies 1932; Grand Hotel 1932; Riptide 1934; That

---

Certain Woman 1937; The Dawn Patrol 1938; White Banners 1938; Dark Victory 1939; The Old Maid 1939; We Are Not Alone 1939; 'Til We Meet Again 1940; The Great Lie 1941; Claudia 1943; The Constant Nymph 1943; Forever and a Day 1943; Of Human Bondage 1946; The Razor's Edge 1946; Nightmare Alley 1947; Everybody Does It 1949; Mister 880 1950; We're Not Married 1952; Teenage Rebel 1956; Mardi Gras 1958
Goursaud, Anne Embrace of the Vampire 1994; Poison Ivy 2 1995; Another 9½ Weeks 1997
Gowariker, Ashutosh Lagaan: Once upon a Time in India 2001; Swades 2004; Jodhaa Akbar 2008
Goyer, David S Blade: Trinity 2004; The Invisible 2007; The Unborn 2008
Graef, Roger (1936-) Pleasure at Her Majesty's 1976; The Secret Policeman's Ball 1980; The Secret Policeman's Other Ball 1982
Graff, Todd (1959-) Camp 2003; Bandslam 2009; Joyful Noise 2012
Graham, Scott Shell 2012; Iona 2015
Graham, William A aka **Graham, William** (1930-) Submarine X-1 1967; Waterhole #3 1967; Change of Habit 1969; The Intruders 1970; Cry for Me Billy 1972; Where the Lilies Bloom 1974; Calendar Girl Murders 1984; Gore Vidal's Billy the Kid 1989; Return to the Blue Lagoon 1991; Death of a Cheerleader 1994; The Man Who Captured Eichmann 1996
Granier-Deferre, Pierre (1927-2007) The Widow Couderc 1971; The Last Train 1972; A Strange Affair 1981
Grant, Brian Complex of Fear 1993; Gladiatress 2002
Grant, Lee (1927-) Tell Me a Riddle 1980; Nobody's Child 1986; Staying Together 1989; Seasons of the Heart 1994
Grau, Jorge Michel We Are What We Are 2010; The ABCs of Death 2012
Grauman, Walter aka **Grauman, Walter E** (1922-2015) Lady in a Cage 1964; 633 Squadron 1964; The Last Escape 1970
Graves, Alex The Crude Oasis 1995; Casualties 1997
Gray, F Gary (1970-) Friday 1995; Set It Off 1996; The Negotiator 1998; The Italian Job 2003; A Man Apart 2003; Be Cool 2005; Law Abiding Citizen 2009; Straight Outta Compton 2015
Gray, James (1969-) Little Odessa 1994; The Yards 2000; We Own the Night 2007; Two Lovers 2008; The Immigrant 2013; The Lost City of Z 2016
Gray, John aka **Gray, John E** Billy Galvin 1986; A Place for Annie 1994; Born to Be Wild 1995; The Glimmer Man 1996; The Day Lincoln Was Shot 1998; The Hunley 1999; Martin and Lewis 2002
Grayson, Godfrey (1913-1998) Dr Morelle - the Case of the Missing Heiress 1949; Room to Let 1949; What the Butler Saw 1950; The Pursuers 1961
Green, Adam Hatchet 2006; Frozen 2009
Green, Alfred E (1889-1960) Little Lord Fauntleroy 1921; Disraeli 1929; Smart Money 1931; The Rich Are Always with Us 1932; Union Depot 1932; Baby Face 1933; Dangerous 1935; The Girl from 10th Avenue 1935; Colleen 1936; The League of Frightened Men 1937; Thoroughbreds Don't Cry 1937; The Duke of West Point 1938; The Gracie Allen Murder Case 1939; East of the River 1940; South of Pago Pago 1940; Mr Winkle Goes to War 1944; A Thousand and One Nights 1945; The Jolson Story 1946; Copacabana 1947; The Fabulous Dorseys 1947; The Girl from Manhattan 1948; They Passed This Way 1948; Sierra 1950; The Eddie Cantor Story 1953; Top Banana 1953
Green, Dave Earth to Echo 2014; Teenage Mutant Ninja Turtles - Out of the Shadows 2016
Green, David (1948-) Car Trouble 1985; Buster 1988; Wings of the Apache 1990
Green, David Gordon (1975-) George Washington 2000; All the Real Girls 2003; Undertow 2004; Pineapple Express 2008; Your Highness 2010; The Sitter 2011; Prince Avalanche 2012; Joe 2013;

Manglehorn 2014; Our Brand Is Crisis 2015
Green, Guy (1913-2005) River Beat 1954; Lost 1955; House of Secrets 1956; Sea of Sand 1958; SOS Pacific 1959; The Angry Silence 1960; Light in the Piazza 1961; The Mark 1961; Diamond Head 1962; A Patch of Blue 1965; Pretty Polly 1967; The Magus 1968; A Walk in the Spring Rain 1970; Luther 1974; Once Is Not Enough 1975; The Devil's Advocate 1977
Greenaway, Peter (1942-) The Falls 1980; The Draughtsman's Contract 1982; A Zed & Two Noughts 1985; The Belly of an Architect 1987; Drowning by Numbers 1988; The Cook, the Thief, His Wife and Her Lover 1989; Prospero's Books 1991; The Baby of Macon 1993; The Pillow Book 1995; 8½ Women 1999; Goltzius and the Pelican Company 2012; Eisenstein in Guanajuato 2014
Greene, David (1921-2003) The Shuttered Room 1967; Sebastian 1968; The Strange Affair 1968; I Start Counting 1970; Madame Sin 1972; Godspell 1973; The Count of Monte Cristo 1974; Gray Lady Down 1978; Friendly Fire 1979; Hard Country 1981; Guilty Conscience 1985; Miles to Go 1986; The Betty Ford Story 1987; Inherit the Wind 1988; What Ever Happened to...? 1991
Greene, Max (1918-1985) Hotel Reserve 1944; The Man from Morocco 1944
Greenfield, Luke The Animal 2001; The Girl Next Door 2004; Something Borrowed 2011; Let's Be Cops 2014
Greengrass, Paul (1955-) Resurrected 1989; The Theory of Flight 1998; Bloody Sunday 2001; The Bourne Supremacy 2004; United 93 2006; The Bourne Ultimatum 2007; Green Zone 2010; Captain Phillips 2013; Jason Bourne 2016
Greenwald, Maggie (1955-) The Kill-Off 1989; The Ballad of Little Jo 1993; Songcatcher 1999; Returning Lily 2003
Greenwald, Robert (1945-) Xanadu 1980; The Burning Bed 1984; Sweet Hearts Dance 1988; Hear No Evil 1993; Breaking Up 1996; Uncovered: the War on Iraq 2004; Wal-Mart: the High Cost of Low Price 2005
Greenwalt, David Secret Admirer 1985; Rude Awakening 1989
Gregg, Colin (1947-) Lamb 1985; We Think the World of You 1988
Greggio, Ezio (1954-) The Silence of the Hams 1993; Screw Loose 1999
Gregoretti, Ugo (1930-) RoGoPaG 1962; The Beautiful Swindlers 1964
Greutert, Kevin Saw VI 2009; Saw: the Final Chapter 2010; Visions 2014
Gréville, Edmond T (1906-1966) Brief Ecstasy 1937; Noose 1948; The Romantic Age 1949; Beat Girl 1960; The Hands of Orlac 1960
Grewal, Shani S aka **Grewal, Shani** After Midnight 1990; Double X: the Name of the Game 1991; Guru in Seven 1997
Gries, Tom (1922-1977) Will Penny 1967; Number One 1969; Fools 1970; The Hawaiians 1970; The Glass House 1972; Journey through Rosebud 1972; Breakout 1975; Breakheart Pass 1976; The Greatest 1977
Griffith, Charles B (1928-2007) Eat My Dust! 1976; Dr Heckyl & Mr Hype 1980
Griffith, D W (1875-1948) The Musketeers of Pig Alley 1912; The Battle of Elderbush 1914; The Battle of the Sexes 1914; The Escape 1914; Home, Sweet Home 1914; The Birth of a Nation 1915; Intolerance 1916; Hearts of the World 1918; Broken Blossoms 1919; The Fall of Babylon 1919; Way Down East 1920; Dream Street 1921; Orphans of the Storm 1921; America 1924; Isn't Life Wonderful 1924; Sally of the Sawdust 1925; Abraham Lincoln 1930; The Struggle 1931
Griffith, Edward H (1894-1975) Holiday 1930; The Animal Kingdom 1932; Lady with a Past 1932; Ladies in Love 1936; Next Time We Love 1936; Café Metropole 1937; I'll Take Romance 1937; Young and Willing 1942; The Sky's the Limit 1943
Griffiths, Mark Tactical Assault 1998; Our House 2006; What I Did for Love 2006
Griffiths, Megan Eden 2012; Lucky Them 2013

Grimaldi, Antonello Il Cielo è Sempre Più Blu 1995; Calm Chaos 2008
Grinde, Nick aka **Grindé, Nicholas** aka **Grinde, Nicholas** (1893-1979) This Modern Age 1931; Shopworn 1932; The Man They Could Not Hang 1939; Million Dollar Legs 1939; Before I Hang 1940
Grint, Alan The Secret Garden 1987; The Man in the Brown Suit 1989
Grosbard, Ulu (1929-2012) The Subject Was Roses 1968; Who Is Harry Kellerman, and Why Is He Saying Those Terrible Things about Me? 1971; Straight Time 1978; Falling in Love 1984; Georgia 1995; The Deep End of the Ocean 1999
Gross, Terence Hotel Splendide 1999; The Day the World Ended 2001
Grossman, Adam Sometimes They Come Back... Again 1996; Carnival of Souls 1999
Guadagnino, Luca I Am Love 2009; A Bigger Splash 2015
Guédiguian, Robert (1953-) Marius et Jeannette 1997; A la Place du Coeur 1998; La Ville Est Tranquille 2000; The Last Mitterrand 2005; The Army of Crime 2009; The Snows of Kilimanjaro 2011
Guerra, Ruy (1931-) Sweet Hunters 1969; Opera do Malandro 1986
Guest, Christopher (1948-) The Big Picture 1989; Attack of the 50 Ft Woman 1993; Waiting for Guffman 1996; Almost Heroes 1998; Best in Show 2000; A Mighty Wind 2003; For Your Consideration 2006
Guest, Val (1911-2006) Bees in Paradise 1943; Miss London Ltd 1943; Give Us the Moon 1944; I'll Be Your Sweetheart 1945; Just William's Luck 1947; William at the Circus 1948; Mr Drake's Duck 1950; Penny Princess 1952; Life with the Lyons 1953; Dance Little Lady 1954; Men of Sherwood Forest 1954; The Runaway Bus 1954; Break in the Circle 1955; The Lyons in Paris 1955; The Quatermass Xperiment 1955; They Can't Hang Me 1955; It's a Wonderful World 1956; The Abominable Snowman 1957; Carry On Admiral 1957; Quatermass II 1957; The Camp on Blood Island 1958; Further up the Creek 1958; Up the Creek 1958; Expresso Bongo 1959; Hell Is a City 1959; Yesterday's Enemy 1959; The Day the Earth Caught Fire 1961; The Full Treatment 1961; Jigsaw 1962; 80,000 Suspects 1963; The Beauty Jungle 1964; Where the Spies Are 1965; Casino Royale 1967; When Dinosaurs Ruled the Earth 1969; Toomorrow 1970; Confessions of a Window Cleaner 1974; Killer Force 1975; The Boys in Blue 1983
Guggenheim, Davis (1963-) Gossip 1999; An Inconvenient Truth 2006; It Might Get Loud 2008; Waiting for "Superman" 2010; He Named Me Malala 2015
Guillermin, John (1925-2015) Miss Robin Hood 1952; Adventure in the Hopfields 1954; Town on Trial 1956; I Was Monty's Double 1958; The Whole Truth 1958; Tarzan's Greatest Adventure 1959; The Day They Robbed the Bank of England 1960; Never Let Go 1960; Tarzan Goes to India 1962; Waltz of the Toreadors 1962; Guns at Batasi 1964; Rapture 1965; The Blue Max 1966; House of Cards 1968; The Bridge at Remagen 1969; El Condor 1970; Skyjacked 1972; Shaft in Africa 1973; The Towering Inferno 1974; King Kong 1976; Death on the Nile 1978; Sheena 1984; King Kong Lives 1986
Guitry, Sacha (1885-1957) Bonne Chance 1935; The Story of a Cheat 1936; Royal Affairs in Versailles 1953; Napoléon 1955
Gunn, Gilbert (1912-1967) Valley of Song 1953; The Strange World of Planet X 1957; Operation Bullshine 1959; What a Whopper! 1961
Gunn (2), James (1970-) Slither 2006; Super 2010; Movie 43 2013; Guardians of the Galaxy 2014; Guardians of the Galaxy Vol 2 2017
Gupta, Amit Resistance 2011; Jadoo 2013
Guterman, Lawrence Cats & Dogs 2001; Son of the Mask 2004
Gutierrez, Sebastian Judas Kiss 1998; She Creature 2001
Guzmán, Patricio Nostalgia for the Light 2010; The Pearl Button 2015
Gyllenhaal, Stephen (1949-) Certain Fury 1985; Promised a Miracle 1988; Evidence of Love 1990; Paris Trout 1991; Waterland 1992; A

Dangerous Woman 1993; Losing Isaiah 1995; Homegrown 1998; Grassroots 2012

H

Haas, Charles aka **Haas, Charles F** (1913-) Showdown at Abilene 1956; Star in the Dust 1956; Tarzan and the Trappers 1958; Wild Heritage 1958; The Beat Generation 1959; The Big Operator 1959; Girls' Town 1959; Platinum High School 1960
Haas, Philip (1954-) The Music of Chance 1993; Angels and Insects 1995; Up at the Villa 1998
Hackford, Taylor (1944-) The Idolmaker 1980; An Officer and a Gentleman 1982; Against All Odds 1984; White Nights 1985; Hail! Hail! Rock 'n' Roll! 1987; Everybody's All-American 1988; Blood In Blood Out 1992; Dolores Claiborne 1995; The Devil's Advocate 1997; Proof of Life 2000; Ray 2004; Parker 2013
Hadzihalilovic, Lucile Innocence 2004; Evolution 2015
Hafstrom, Mikael (1960-) Evil 2003; Derailed 2005; 1408 2007; The Rite 2011; Escape Plan 2013
Haggard, Piers (1944-) Blood on Satan's Claw 1970; The Quatermass Conclusion 1979; The Fiendish Plot of Dr Fu Manchu 1980; Venom 1981; A Summer Story 1987; The Fulfillment of Mary Gray 1989
Haggis, Paul (1953-) Crash 2004; In the Valley of Elah 2007; The Next Three Days 2010; Third Person 2013
Haid, Charles (1943-) Cooperstown 1993; Iron Will 1994; Buffalo Soldiers 1997
Haigh, Andrew Weekend 2011; 45 Years 2015
Haines, Randa (1945-) Children of a Lesser God 1986; The Doctor 1991; Wrestling Ernest Hemingway 1993; Dance with Me 1998; The Outsider 2001; The Triumph 2006
Hajaig, Hadi Puritan 2004; Cleanskin 2012
Hale, Sonnie (1902-1959) Gangway 1937; Head over Heels in Love 1937; Sailing Along 1938
Hale, William (1937-) Gunfight in Abilene 1967; How I Spent My Summer Vacation 1967; Journey to Shiloh 1967; SOS Titanic 1979
Haley Jr, Jack (1934-) The Love Machine 1971; That's Entertainment! 1974; That's Dancing! 1985
Hall, Alexander (1894-1968) Sinners in the Sun 1932; Torch Singer 1933; Little Miss Marker 1934; Goin' to Town 1935; I Am the Law 1938; There's Always a Woman 1938; The Amazing Mr Williams 1939; The Doctor Takes a Wife 1940; This Thing Called Love 1940; Here Comes Mr Jordan 1941; Bedtime Story 1942; My Sister Eileen 1942; They All Kissed the Bride 1942; The Heavenly Body 1943; Once upon a Time 1944; Down to Earth 1947; The Great Lover 1949; Because You're Mine 1952; Let's Do It Again 1953; Forever, Darling 1956
Hall (2), Don Winnie the Pooh 2011; Big Hero 6 2014
Hall, Peter (1930-) A Midsummer Night's Dream 1969; Three into Two Won't Go 1969; Perfect Friday 1970; The Homecoming 1973; Akenfield 1974
Haller, Daniel (1928-) Die, Monster, Die! 1965; The Wild Racers 1968; The Dunwich Horror 1970; Pieces of Dreams 1970; Buck Rogers in the 25th Century 1979
Hallström, Lasse (1946-) A Lover and His Lass 1975; ABBA the Movie 1977; Father to Be 1979; Happy We 1983; My Life as a Dog 1985; Once Around 1991; What's Eating Gilbert Grape 1993; Something to Talk About 1995; The Cider House Rules 1999; Chocolat 2000; The Shipping News 2001; Casanova 2005; An Unfinished Life 2005; The Hoax 2006; Hachi: a Dog's Tale 2008; Dear John 2010; Salmon Fishing in the Yemen 2011; Safe Haven 2013; The Hundred-Foot Journey 2014
Halperin, Victor (1895-1983) Party Girl 1930; White Zombie 1932; Supernatural 1933
Hamburg, John (1970-) Safe Men 1998; Along Came Polly 2004; I Love You, Man 2008; Why Him? 2016
Hamer, Bent (1956-) Kitchen Stories 2003; Factotum (A Man Who Preforms Many Jobs) 2005; O'Horten 2007
Hamer, Robert (1911-1963) Dead of Night 1945; Pink String and Sealing

Wax 1945; It Always Rains on Sunday 1947; Kind Hearts and Coronets 1949; The Spider and the Fly 1949; His Excellency 1952; The Long Memory 1952; Father Brown 1954; To Paris with Love 1954; The Scapegoat 1959; School for Scoundrels 1960

Hamilton, Guy (1922-2016) The Intruder 1953; The Colditz Story 1954; An Inspector Calls 1954; Charley Moon 1956; Manuela 1957; A Touch of Larceny 1959; The Best of Enemies 1961; Goldfinger 1964; The Party's Over 1965; Funeral in Berlin 1966; Battle of Britain 1969; Diamonds Are Forever 1971; Live and Let Die 1973; The Man with the Golden Gun 1974; Force 10 from Navarone 1978; The Mirror Crack'd 1980; Evil under the Sun 1982; Remo - Unarmed and Dangerous 1985

Hamilton, Strathford (1952-) The Set Up 1995; The Proposition 1996

Hamilton, William (1893-1942) Murder on a Bridle Path 1936; Call Out the Marines 1941

Hamm, Nick Martha - Meet Frank, Daniel and Laurence 1997; Talk of Angels 1998; The Hole 2001; Godsend 2003; Killing Bono 2010

Hampton, Christopher (1946-) Carrington 1995; The Secret Agent 1996; Imagining Argentina 2003

Hamri, Sanaa Something New 2006; The Sisterhood of the Traveling Pants 2 2008; Acceptance 2009; Just Wright 2010

Hanbury, Victor (1897-1954) The Avenging Hand 1936; Return of a Stranger 1937; Hotel Reserve 1944

Hancock, John (1942-1992) Bang the Drum Slowly 1973; Weeds 1987; Prancer 1989

Hancock, John Lee (1956-) The Rookie 2002; The Alamo 2004; The Blind Side 2009; Saving Mr Banks 2013; The Founder 2016

Hand, David aka Hand, David D (1900-1986) Snow White and the Seven Dwarfs 1937; Bambi 1942

Handley, Jim Fantasia 1940; The Reluctant Dragon 1941

Haneke, Michael (1942-) The Seventh Continent 1989; Benny's Video 1992; 71 Fragments of a Chronology of Chance 1994; Funny Games 1997; Code Unknown 2000; The Piano Teacher 2001; Time of the Wolf 2003; Hidden 2005; Funny Games US 2008; The White Ribbon 2009; Amour 2012

Hanks, Tom (1956-) That Thing You Do! 1996; Larry Crowne 2011

Hanna, William (1910-2001) The Cat Concerto 1947; Jetsons: the Movie 1990

Hänsel, Marion (1949-) Dust 1985; Il Maestro 1989

Hansen-Løve, Mia The Father of My Children 2009; Goodbye First Love 2011; Eden 2014; Things to Come 2016

Hanson, Curtis (1945-) Losin' It 1983; The Bedroom Window 1987; Bad Influence 1990; The Hand That Rocks the Cradle 1992; The River Wild 1994; LA Confidential 1997; Wonder Boys 2000; 8 Mile 2002; In Her Shoes 2005; Lucky You 2007; Too Big to Fail 2011; Chasing Mavericks 2012

Hardwicke, Catherine (1955-) Thirteen 2003; Lords of Dogtown 2005; The Nativity Story 2006; Twilight 2008; Red Riding Hood 2011; Miss You Already 2015

Hardy, Justin (1964-) A Feast at Midnight 1994; Captain Webb 2014

Hardy, Robin (1929-2016) The Wicker Man 1973; The Fantasist 1986; The Wicker Man 2002; The Wicker Tree 2010

Hardy, Rod (1949-) Thirst 1979; Sad Inheritance 1993; Daniel Defoe's Robinson Crusoe 1996; Two for Texas 1998; High Noon 2000; December Boys 2007

Hare, David (1947-) Wetherby 1985; Paris by Night 1988; Strapless 1988; The Designated Mourner 1997

Harlin, Renny (1959-) Prison 1987; A Nightmare on Elm Street 4: The Dream Master 1988; The Adventures of Ford Fairlane 1990; Die Hard 2: Die Harder 1990; Cliffhanger 1993; CutThroat Island 1995; The Long Kiss Goodnight 1996; Deep Blue Sea 1999; Driven 2001; Mindhunters 2003; Exorcist: the Beginning 2004; The Covenant 2006; Cleaner 2007; 12 Rounds 2008; 5 Days of War 2011; The Dyatlov Pass Incident 2013; The Legend of Hercules 2014

Harlow, John (1896-?) While I Live 1947; The Blue Parrot 1953

Harmon, Robert (1953-) The Hitcher 1986; Eyes of an Angel 1991; Nowhere to Run 1992; They 2002; Highwaymen 2003; Ike: Countdown to D-Day 2004; Stone Cold 2005; November Christmas 2010

Haroun, Mahamat-Saleh Abouna 2002; Daratt 2006; A Screaming Man 2010

Harper (3), Tom The Scouting Book for Boys 2009; War Book 2014; The Woman in Black: Angel of Death 2014

Harrington, Curtis aka **Sebastian, John** (1926-2007) Voyage to the Prehistoric Planet 1965; Planet of Blood 1966; Games 1967; What's the Matter with Helen? 1971; Who Slew Auntie Roo? 1971; The Killing Kind 1973; Ruby 1977; Mata Hari 1985

Harris, Damian (1960-) The Rachel Papers 1989; Deceived 1991; Bad Company 1995; Mercy 2000

Harris, Ed (1950-) Pollock 2000; Appaloosa 2008

Harris, James B (1928-) The Bedford Incident 1965; Fast-Walking 1982; Cop 1988; Boiling Point 1993

Harris, Mark Jonathan The Long Way Home 1996; Into the Arms of Strangers: Stories of the Kindertransport 2000

Harris, Trent (1952-) Rubin & Ed 1991; Plan 10 from Outer Space 1995

Harrison, John Kent Beautiful Dreamers 1990; Old Man 1997; A House Divided 2000; In Love and War 2001; The Courageous Heart of Irena Sendler 2009

Harron, Mary (1953-) I Shot Andy Warhol 1995; American Psycho 2000; The Notorious Bettie Page 2005; The Moth Diaries 2011

Hart, Harvey (1928-1989) Bus Riley's Back in Town 1965; Dark Intruder 1965; The Sweet Ride 1967; Fortune and Men's Eyes 1971; The High Country 1981

Hartford-Davis, Robert aka **Burrowes, Michael** (1923-1977) Saturday Night Out 1963; The Black Torment 1964; The Sandwich Man 1966; Corruption 1968; The Smashing Bird I Used to Know 1969; Incense for the Damned 1970; The Fiend 1971

Hartley, Hal (1959-) The Unbelievable Truth 1989; Trust 1990; Simple Men 1992; Amateur 1994; Henry Fool 1997; The Book of Life 1998

Hartley, Mark Not Quite Hollywood 2008; Electric Boogaloo: the Wild, Untold Story of Cannon Films 2014

Hartman, Don (1900-1958) It Had to Be You 1947; Every Girl Should Be Married 1948; Holiday Affair 1949; It's a Big Country 1951; Mr Imperium 1951

Harvey, Anthony (1931-) Dutchman 1966; The Lion in Winter 1968; They Might Be Giants 1971; The Abdication 1974; The Disappearance of Aimee 1976; Eagle's Wing 1978; Players 1979; The Patricia Neal Story 1981; Grace Quigley 1984

Harvey, Laurence (1928-1973) The Ceremony 1963; Welcome to Arrow Beach 1974

Haskin, Byron (1899-1984) I Walk Alone 1947; Treasure Island 1950; Tarzan's Peril 1951; Warpath 1951; Denver & Rio Grande 1952; His Majesty O'Keefe 1953; The Naked Jungle 1953; The War of the Worlds 1953; Long John Silver 1954; Conquest of Space 1955; The First Texan 1956; From the Earth to the Moon 1958; Captain Sindbad 1963; Robinson Crusoe on Mars 1964; The Power 1968

Hathaway, Henry (1898-1985) Now and Forever 1934; The Lives of a Bengal Lancer 1935; Peter Ibbetson 1935; Go West, Young Man 1936; The Trail of the Lonesome Pine 1936; Souls at Sea 1937; Spawn of the North 1938; The Real Glory 1939; Brigham Young 1940; Johnny Apollo 1940; The Shepherd of the Hills 1941; Sundown 1941; China Girl 1942; Ten Gentlemen from West Point 1942; Home in Indiana 1944; Wing and a Prayer 1944; The House on 92nd Street 1945; Nob Hill 1945; The Dark Corner 1946; 13 Rue Madeleine 1946; Kiss of Death 1947; Call Northside 777 1948; Down to the Sea in Ships 1949; The Black Rose 1950; The Desert Fox 1951; Fourteen Hours 1951; Rawhide 1951; You're in the Navy Now 1951; Diplomatic Courier 1952; O Henry's Full House 1952;

Niagara 1953; White Witch Doctor 1953; Garden of Evil 1954; Prince Valiant 1954; The Racers 1955; Beyond the River 1956; 23 Paces to Baker Street 1956; Legend of the Lost 1957; From Hell to Texas 1958; Woman Obsessed 1959; North to Alaska 1960; Seven Thieves 1960; How the West Was Won 1962; The Magnificent Showman 1964; The Sons of Katie Elder 1965; Nevada Smith 1966; The Last Safari 1967; 5 Card Stud 1968; True Grit 1969; Airport 1970; Raid on Rommel 1971; Shoot Out 1971

Hatton, Maurice (?-1997) Praise Marx and Pass the Ammunition 1968; Long Shot 1978

Hausner, Jessica (1972-) Lourdes 2009; Amour Fou 2014

Hawks, Howard (1896-1977) Fazil 1928; A Girl in Every Port 1928; The Criminal Code 1930; The Dawn Patrol 1930; The Crowd Roars 1932; Scarface 1932; Tiger Shark 1932; Today We Live 1933; Twentieth Century 1934; Barbary Coast 1935; Ceiling Zero 1935; Come and Get It 1936; The Road to Glory 1936; Bringing Up Baby 1938; His Girl Friday 1939; Only Angels Have Wings 1939; Ball of Fire 1941; Sergeant York 1941; Air Force 1943; To Have and Have Not 1944; The Big Sleep 1946; Red River 1948; A Song Is Born 1948; I Was a Male War Bride 1949; The Big Sky 1952; Monkey Business 1952; O Henry's Full House 1952; Gentlemen Prefer Blondes 1953; Land of the Pharaohs 1955; Rio Bravo 1958; Hatari! 1962; Man's Favorite Sport? 1964; Red Line 7000 1965; El Dorado 1967; Rio Lobo 1970

Hay, John The Steal 1994; There's Only One Jimmy Grimble 2000; The Truth about Love 2004

Hay, Will (1888-1949) The Black Sheep of Whitehall 1941; The Goose Steps Out 1942; My Learned Friend 1943

Haydn, Richard (1905-1985) Miss Tatlock's Millions 1948; Dear Wife 1949; Mr Music 1950

Hayers, Sidney (1921-2000) Circus of Horrors 1960; Night of the Eagle 1961; Payroll 1961; This Is My Street 1963; Three Hats for Lisa 1965; Finders Keepers 1966; The Trap 1966; Mister Jerico 1969; The Southern Star 1969; Assault 1970; Diagnosis: Murder 1974; What Changed Charley Farthing? 1974

Hayes, Derek The Miracle Maker 1999; Otherworld 2003

Hayes, John (1930-2000) Mama's Dirty Girls 1974; End of the World 1977

Hayman, David (1950-) Silent Scream 1989; The Hawk 1992; The Near Room 1995

Hayman, James Sorority Wars 2009; Revenge of the Bridesmaids 2010; 12 Dates of Christmas 2011

Haynes, Todd (1961-) Superstar: the Karen Carpenter Story 1987; Poison 1990; [Safe] 1995; Velvet Goldmine 1998; Far from Heaven 2002; I'm Not There. 2007; Carol 2015

Hayward, Jimmy Dr Seuss' Horton Hears a Who! 2008; Jonah Hex 2010; Free Birds 2013

Hazan, Jack A Bigger Splash 1974; Rude Boy 1980

Hazanavicius, Michel OSS 117: Cairo - Nest of Spies 2006; OSS 117: Lost in Rio 2009; The Artist 2011; The Players 2012

Headland, Leslye Bachelorette 2012; Sleeping with Other People 2015

Heap, Jonathan Benefit of the Doubt 1993; Greenmail 2001

Heath, Robert Out on a Limb 2005; Sus 2009; Truth or Dare 2011

Hecht, Ben (1894-1964) Crime without Passion 1934; The Scoundrel 1935; Angels over Broadway 1940; Specter of the Rose 1946; Actors and Sin 1952

Heckerling, Amy (1954-) Fast Times at Ridgemont High 1982; Johnny Dangerously 1984; National Lampoon's European Vacation 1985; Look Who's Talking 1989; Look Who's Talking Too 1990; Clueless 1995; Loser 2000; Vamps 2012

Hedden, Rob (1954-) Friday the 13th Part VIII: Jason Takes Manhattan 1989; You May Not Kiss the Bride 2011

Hedges, Peter Pieces of April 2002; Dan in Real Life 2007; The Odd Life of Timothy Green 2012

Heerman, Victor (1892-1977) Animal Crackers 1930; Paramount on Parade 1930

Heery, Niall Small Engine Repair 2006; Gold 2014

Heffron, Richard T aka **Heffron, Richard** (1930-2007) Newman's Law 1974; The Rockford Files 1974; Futureworld 1976; Outlaw Blues 1977; Foolin' Around 1980; Danielle Steel's No Greater Love 1996

Hegedus, Chris (1952-) The War Room 1993; Startup.com 2001

Heisler, Stuart (1894-1979) The Biscuit Eater 1940; Among the Living 1941; The Glass Key 1942; Along Came Jones 1945; Blue Skies 1946; Smash Up - the Story of a Woman 1947; Tokyo Joe 1949; Tulsa 1949; Chain Lightning 1950; Dallas 1950; Storm Warning 1950; Island of Desire 1952; The Star 1953; This Is My Love 1954; I Died a Thousand Times 1955; The Burning Hills 1956; The Lone Ranger 1956; Hitler 1962

Helander, Jalmari Rare Exports from the Land of the Original Santa Claus 2010; Big Game 2014

Helgeland, Brian (1961-) Payback 1998; A Knight's Tale 2001; The Sin Eater 2002; 42 2013; Legend 2015

Hellman, Monte (1932-) Beast from Haunted Cave 1959; Back Door to Hell 1964; Flight to Fury 1966; The Shooting 1967; Two-Lane Blacktop 1971; Shatter 1974; China 9, Liberty 37 1978

Hemecker, Ralph American Dragons 1997; Nora Roberts' Midnight Bayou 2009; Skyrunners 2009

Hemmings, David (1941-2003) Just a Gigolo 1978; Race for the Yankee Zephyr 1981; The Survivor 1981; Dark Horse 1992

Henderson, John Loch Ness 1995; Bring Me the Head of Mavis Davis 1997; Two Men Went to War 2002; Greyfriars Bobby 2005; Mee-Shee: the Water Giant 2005

Hendricks, Bruce Hannah Montana & Miley Cyrus: Best of Both Worlds Concert 2008; Jonas Brothers: the 3D Concert Experience 2009

Henenlotter, Frank (1950-) Basket Case 1982; Brain Damage 1988; Basket Case 2 1990; Frankenhooker 1990; Basket Case 3: the Progeny 1992

Henley, Hobart (1887-1964) Sinners in Silk 1924; The Big Pond 1930; Bad Sister 1931

Henreid, Paul (1908-1992) Battle Shock 1956; Ballad in Blue 1964; Dead Ringer 1964

Henry, Buck (1930-) Heaven Can Wait 1978; First Family 1980

Hensleigh, Jonathan The Punisher 2004; Kill the Irishman 2011

Henson, Brian (1963-) The Muppet Christmas Carol 1992; Muppet Treasure Island 1996

Henson, Jim (1936-1990) The Great Muppet Caper 1981; The Dark Crystal 1982; Labyrinth 1986

Herek, Stephen (1958-) Critters 1986; Bill & Ted's Excellent Adventure 1988; Don't Tell Mom the Babysitter's Dead 1991; The Mighty Ducks 1992; The Three Musketeers 1993; Mr Holland's Opus 1995; 101 Dalmatians 1996; Holy Man 1998; Rock Star 2001; Life or Something like It 2002; Man of the House 2005

Herman-Wurmfeld, Charles (1966-) Kissing Jessica Stein 2001; Legally Blonde 2: Red, White & Blonde 2003

Herman, Mark (1954-) Blame It on the Bellboy 1992; Brassed Off 1996; Little Voice 1998; Purely Belter 2000; Hope Springs 2002; The Boy in the Striped Pyjamas 2008

Hernández, Antonio (1953-) Lisboa 1999; The City of No Limits 2002

Herrington, Rowdy (1951-) Jack's Back 1988; Road House 1989; Gladiator 1992; Striking Distance 1993; A Murder of Crows 1998; The Stickup 2001; I Witness 2003; Bobby Jones: Stroke of Genius 2004

Herskovitz, Marshall (1952-) Jack the Bear 1993; Dangerous Beauty 1997

Herz, Michael (1949-) The Toxic Avenger 1986; The Toxic Avenger, Part II 1988; Sgt Kabukiman NYPD 1991

Herzfeld, John Two of a Kind 1983; 2 Days in the Valley 1996; Don King: Only in America 1997; 15 Minutes 2001

Herzog, Werner (1942-) Signs of Life 1968; Even Dwarfs Started Small 1970; Land of Silence and Darkness

1971; Aguirre, Wrath of God 1972; The Enigma of Kaspar Hauser 1974; Heart of Glass 1976; Stroszek 1977; Woyzeck 1978; Nosferatu, the Vampyre 1979; Fitzcarraldo 1982; Where the Green Ants Dream 1984; Cobra Verde 1988; Scream of Stone 1991; Little Dieter Needs to Fly 1997; My Best Fiend 1999; Invincible 2001; Ten Minutes Older: the Trumpet 2002; Grizzly Man 2005; The Wild Blue Yonder 2005; Rescue Dawn 2006; Encounters at the End of the World 2007; The Bad Lieutenant - Port of Call: New Orleans 2009; My Son, My Son, What Have Ye Done 2009; Cave of Forgotten Dreams 2010; Into the Abyss: a Tale of Death, a Tale of Life 2011; Queen of the Desert 2015

Hess, Jared Napoleon Dynamite 2004; Nacho Libre 2006; Gentlemen Broncos 2009; Masterminds 2015

Hess, Jon Watchers 1988; Alligator II: the Mutation 1991; Excessive Force 1993

Hessler, Gordon (1925-2014) The Oblong Box 1969; Scream and Scream Again 1969; Cry of the Banshee 1970; Murders in the Rue Morgue 1971; The Golden Voyage of Sinbad 1973; Shogun Warrior 1991

Heston, Charlton (1923-2008) Antony and Cleopatra 1972; A Man for All Seasons 1988

Heston, Fraser C (1955-) Treasure Island 1990; Needful Things 1993; Alaska 1996

Hewitt, Peter aka **Hewitt, Pete** (1965-) Bill & Ted's Bogus Journey 1991; Tom and Huck 1995; The Borrowers 1997; Whatever Happened to Harold Smith? 1999; Thunderpants 2002; Garfield 2004; Zoom 2006; The Heist 2009

Hibbs, Jesse (1906-1985) The All American 1953; Black Horse Canyon 1954; Rails into Laramie 1954; Ride Clear of Diablo 1954; The Yellow Mountain 1954; The Spoilers 1955; To Hell and Back 1955; Walk the Proud Land 1956; Ride a Crooked Trail 1958

Hickenlooper, George (1964-2010) Hearts of Darkness: a Film-Maker's Apocalypse 1991; The Low Life 1995; Persons Unknown 1996; The Man from Elysian Fields 2001; Factory Girl 2006

Hickox, Anthony aka **Hickox, Tony** (1959-) Waxwork 1988; Hellraiser III: Hell on Earth 1992; Full Eclipse 1993; Warlock: the Armageddon 1993; Prince Valiant 1997; Storm Catcher 1999; Contagion 2000; Jill Rips 2000; Federal Protection 2002

Hickox, Douglas (1929-1988) Entertaining Mr Sloane 1969; Sitting Target 1972; Theatre of Blood 1973; Brannigan 1975; Zulu Dawn 1979; The Hound of the Baskervilles 1983

Hickox, James aka **Hickox, James D R** Children of the Corn III: Urban Harvest 1995; Blood Surf 2000

Hicks, Scott (1953-) Shine 1996; Snow Falling on Cedars 1999; Hearts in Atlantis 2001; No Reservations 2007; The Boys Are Back 2009; The Lucky One 2012

Higgin, Howard (1891-1938) High Voltage 1929; The Leatherneck 1929; The Painted Desert 1931; Hell's House 1932

Higgins, Colin (1941-1988) Foul Play 1978; Nine to Five 1980; The Best Little Whorehouse in Texas 1982

Hill, George aka **Hill, George W** (1895-1934) The Big House 1930; Min and Bill 1930; The Secret Six 1931; Hell Divers 1932

Hill, George Roy (1921-2002) Period of Adjustment 1962; Toys in the Attic 1963; The World of Henry Orient 1964; Hawaii 1966; Thoroughly Modern Millie 1967; Butch Cassidy and the Sundance Kid 1969; Slaughterhouse-Five 1972; The Sting 1973; The Great Waldo Pepper 1975; Slap Shot 1977; A Little Romance 1979; The World According to Garp 1982; The Little Drummer Girl 1984; Funny Farm 1988

Hill, Jack (1933-) Spider Baby 1964; House of Evil 1968; Alien Terror 1969; The Big Bird Cage 1972; Coffy 1973; Foxy Brown 1974; Switchblade Sisters 1975

Hill, James (1919-1994) The Kitchen 1961; Lunch Hour 1962; Trial and Error 1962; Every Day's a Holiday 1964; A Study in Terror 1965; Born Free 1966; The Corrupt Ones 1966; Captain Nemo and the Underwater City 1969; An Elephant Called Slowly

1969; *Black Beauty* 1971; *The Belstone Fox* 1973
Hill, Jody *The Foot Fist Way* 2006; *Observe and Report* 2009
Hill, Sinclair *Command Performance* 1937; *Take a Chance* 1937
Hill, Tim *Muppets from Space* 1999; *Max Keeble's Big Move* 2001; *Garfield 2* 2006; *Alvin and the Chipmunks* 2007; *Hop* 2011
Hill, Walter aka **Lee, Thomas** (1942-) *Hard Times* 1975; *The Driver* 1978; *The Warriors* 1979; *The Long Riders* 1980; *Southern Comfort* 1981; *48 HRS* 1982; *Streets of Fire* 1984; *Brewster's Millions* 1985; *Crossroads* 1986; *Extreme Prejudice* 1987; *Red Heat* 1988; *Johnny Handsome* 1989; *Another 48 HRS* 1990; *Trespass* 1992; *Geronimo: an American Legend* 1993; *Wild Bill* 1995; *Last Man Standing* 1996; *Supernova* 2000; *Undisputed* 2002; *Bullet to the Head* 2012
Hillcoat, John (1961-) *Ghosts... of the Civil Dead* 1988; *To Have & to Hold* 1996; *The Proposition* 2004; *The Road* 2009; *Lawless* 2012; *Triple 9* 2015
Hiller, Arthur aka **Smithee, Alan** (1923-2016) *The Careless Years* 1957; *Miracle of the White Stallions* 1963; *The Wheeler Dealers* 1963; *The Americanization of Emily* 1964; *Penelope* 1966; *Promise Her Anything* 1966; *Tobruk* 1966; *Love Story* 1970; *The Out of Towners* 1970; *The Hospital* 1971; *Plaza Suite* 1971; *Man of La Mancha* 1972; *Silver Streak* 1976; *WC Fields and Me* 1976; *The In-Laws* 1979; *Nightwing* 1979; *Author! Author!* 1982; *Making Love* 1982; *Romantic Comedy* 1983; *The Lonely Guy* 1984; *Teachers* 1984; *Outrageous Fortune* 1987; *See No Evil, Hear No Evil* 1989; *Taking Care of Business* 1990; *The Babe* 1992; *Carpool* 1996; *Burn Hollywood Burn* 1997
Hills, Paul *Boston Kickout* 1995; *Do Elephants Pray?* 2009
Hillyer, Lambert (1889-1969) *Dracula's Daughter* 1936; *The Invisible Ray* 1936; *Girls Can Play* 1937
Hirschbiegel, Oliver (1957-) *The Experiment* 2000; *Downfall* 2004; *The Invasion* 2007; *Five Minutes of Heaven* 2009; *Diana* 2013; *13 Minutes* 2015
Hiscott, Leslie (1894-1968) *When London Sleeps* 1932; *A Fire Has Been Arranged* 1935; *The Time of His Life* 1955
Hitchcock, Alfred aka **Hitchcock, Alfred J** (1899-1980) *The Pleasure Garden* 1925; *The Lodger* 1926; *Downhill* 1927; *Easy Virtue* 1927; *The Ring* 1927; *Champagne* 1928; *The Farmer's Wife* 1928; *Blackmail* 1929; *The Manxman* 1929; *Elstree Calling* 1930; *Juno and the Paycock* 1930; *Murder* 1930; *The Skin Game* 1931; *Number Seventeen* 1932; *Rich and Strange* 1932; *Waltzes from Vienna* 1933; *The Man Who Knew Too Much* 1934; *The 39 Steps* 1935; *Sabotage* 1936; *Secret Agent* 1936; *Young and Innocent* 1937; *The Lady Vanishes* 1938; *Jamaica Inn* 1939; *Foreign Correspondent* 1940; *Rebecca* 1940; *Mr and Mrs Smith* 1941; *Suspicion* 1941; *Saboteur* 1942; *Shadow of a Doubt* 1942; *Aventure Malgache* 1944; *Bon Voyage* 1944; *Lifeboat* 1944; *Spellbound* 1945; *Notorious* 1946; *The Paradine Case* 1947; *Rope* 1948; *Stage Fright* 1949; *Under Capricorn* 1949; *Strangers on a Train* 1951; *I Confess* 1953; *Dial M for Murder* 1954; *Rear Window* 1954; *The Trouble with Harry* 1954; *To Catch a Thief* 1955; *The Man Who Knew Too Much* 1956; *The Wrong Man* 1956; *Vertigo* 1958; *North by Northwest* 1959; *Psycho* 1960; *The Birds* 1963; *Marnie* 1964; *Torn Curtain* 1966; *Topaz* 1969; *Frenzy* 1972; *Family Plot* 1976
Hitzig, Rupert *Never Cry Devil* 1989; *Backstreet Dreams* 1990
Hively, Jack (1910-1995) *Anne of Windy Poplars* 1940; *The Saint Takes Over* 1940; *The Saint's Double Trouble* 1940; *The Saint in Palm Springs* 1941; *Are You with It?* 1948
Ho Yim (1952-) *The Day the Sun Turned Cold* 1994; *Kitchen* 1997
Hoblit, Gregory (1944-) *Roe vs Wade* 1989; *Primal Fear* 1996; *Fallen* 1998; *Frequency* 2000; *Hart's War* 2002; *Fracture* 2007
Hodges, Mike aka **Hodges, Michael** (1932-) *Get Carter* 1971; *Pulp* 1972;

The Terminal Man 1974; *Flash Gordon* 1980; *And the Ship Sails On* 1983; *Morons from Outer Space* 1985; *A Prayer for the Dying* 1987; *Black Rainbow* 1989; *Croupier* 1998; *I'll Sleep When I'm Dead* 2003
Hoen, Paul *Jump In!* 2007; *The Mistle-Tones* 2012
Hoffman, Michael (1957-) *Restless Natives* 1985; *Promised Land* 1988; *Some Girls* 1988; *Soapdish* 1991; *Restoration* 1995; *One Fine Day* 1996; *A Midsummer Night's Dream* 1999; *The Emperor's Club* 2002; *The Last Station* 2009; *Gambit* 2012; *The Best of Me* 2014
Hofmeyr, Gray aka **Hofmyer, Gray** *Jock of the Bushveld* 1988; *Out of Darkness* 1990
Hogan, David aka **Hogan, David Glenn** *Barb Wire* 1995; *Most Wanted* 1997
Hogan, James (1891-1943) *Bulldog Drummond Escapes* 1937; *The Last Train from Madrid* 1937; *Bulldog Drummond's Peril* 1938; *The Texans* 1938; *Bulldog Drummond's Bride* 1939
Hogan, P J (1962-) *Muriel's Wedding* 1994; *My Best Friend's Wedding* 1997; *Unconditional Love* 2001; *Peter Pan* 2003; *Confessions of a Shopaholic* 2009; *Mental* 2012
Hogg, Joanna *Unrelated* 2007; *Archipelago* 2010; *Exhibition* 2013
Holcomb, Rod *Captain America* 1979; *The A-Team* 1983; *The Cartier Affair* 1984; *Chains of Gold* 1989; *Songs in Ordinary Time* 2000; *CodeBreakers* 2005
Holden Jones, Amy aka **Jones, Amy** (1953-) *The Slumber Party Massacre* 1982; *Love Letters* 1983; *Maid to Order* 1987; *The Rich Man's Wife* 1996
Holden, Pat *Awaydays* 2009; *When the Lights Went Out* 2010
Holland, Agnieszka (1948-) *To Kill a Priest* 1988; *Europa Europa* 1991; *Olivier Olivier* 1991; *The Secret Garden* 1993; *Total Eclipse* 1995; *Washington Square* 1997; *Copying Beethoven* 2006; *A Girl like Me* 2006; *In Darkness* 2011
Holland, Savage Steve (1960-) *Better Off Dead* 1985; *One Crazy Summer* 1986; *How I Got Into College* 1989; *Legally Blondes* 2008
Holland, Todd *Krippendorf's Tribe* 1998; *Firehouse Dog* 2006
Holland (1), Tom (1943-) *Fright Night* 1985; *Fatal Beauty* 1987; *Child's Play* 1988; *The Temp* 1993; *Stephen King's Thinner* 1996
Holmes, Ben (1890-1943) *The Plot Thickens* 1936; *Maid's Night Out* 1938; *The Saint in New York* 1938
Holmes, Peggy *Tinkerbell and the Secret of the Wings* 2012; *TinkerBell and the Pirate Fairy* 2014
Holofcener, Nicole (1960-) *Walking and Talking* 1996; *Lovely & Amazing* 2001; *Friends with Money* 2006; *Please Give* 2010; *Enough Said* 2013
Holst, Marius *Dragonflies* 2001; *King of Devil's Island* 2010
Holt, Seth (1923-1971) *Nowhere to Go* 1958; *Taste of Fear* 1961; *Station Six-Sahara* 1962; *The Nanny* 1965; *Danger Route* 1967; *Blood from the Mummy's Tomb* 1971
Honda, Inoshiro aka **Honda, Ishiro** (1911-1993) *Godzilla* 1954; *The H-Man* 1954; *Rodan* 1956; *King Kong vs Godzilla* 1962; *Mothra* 1962; *Frankenstein Conquers the World* 1964; *Godzilla vs Mothra* 1964; *Ghidrah, the Three-Headed Monster* 1965; *Invasion of the Astro-Monster* 1965; *Destroy All Monsters* 1968; *Godzilla's Revenge* 1969; *Latitude Zero* 1969; *War of the Gargantuas* 1970; *Terror of Mechagodzilla* 1975
Honoré, Christophe (1970-) *Ma Mère* 2004; *Inside Paris* 2006; *Love Songs* 2007; *Beloved* 2011
Hood, Gavin (1963-) *A Reasonable Man* 1999; *Tsotsi* 2005; *Rendition* 2007; *X-Men Origins: Wolverine* 2009; *Ender's Game* 2013; *Eye in the Sky* 2015
Hook, Harry (1960-) *The Kitchen Toto* 1987; *Lord of the Flies* 1990; *All for Love* 1999
Hooks, Kevin (1958-) *Heat Wave* 1990; *Passenger 57* 1992; *Fled* 1996; *Black Dog* 1998
Hooper, Tobe (1943-) *The Texas Chain Saw Massacre* 1974; *Eaten Alive* 1976; *Salem's Lot* 1979; *The Funhouse* 1981; *Poltergeist* 1982; *Lifeforce* 1985; *Invaders from Mars* 1986; *The Texas Chainsaw Massacre Part 2* 1986; *The Mangler* 1994;

Crocodile 2000; *Toolbox Murders* 2003
Hooper, Tom (1972-) *Red Dust* 2004; *The Damned United* 2009; *The King's Speech* 2010; *Les Misérables* 2012; *The Danish Girl* 2015
Hopkins, Ben (1959-) *Simon Magus* 1998; *The Nine Lives of Tomas Katz* 1999; *Lost in Karastan* 2014
Hopkins, Duane *Better Things* 2007; *Bypass* 2014
Hopkins, Joel *Jump Tomorrow* 2001; *Last Chance Harvey* 2008; *The Love Punch* 2013
Hopkins, Stephen (1959-) *A Nightmare on Elm Street 5: The Dream Child* 1989; *Predator 2* 1990; *Judgment Night* 1993; *Blown Away* 1994; *The Ghost and the Darkness* 1996; *Lost in Space* 1998; *Under Suspicion* 2000; *The Life and Death of Peter Sellers* 2003; *The Reaping* 2006; *Race* 2016
Hopper, Dennis aka **Smithee, Alan** (1936-2010) *Easy Rider* 1969; *The Last Movie* 1971; *Out of the Blue* 1980; *Colors* 1988; *Catchfire* 1989; *The Hot Spot* 1990; *Chasers* 1994
Hopper, Jerry (1907-1988) *Hurricane Smith* 1952; *Pony Express* 1953; *Naked Alibi* 1954; *Secret of the Incas* 1954; *Never Say Goodbye* 1955; *The Private War of Major Benson* 1955; *Smoke Signal* 1955; *The Square Jungle* 1955; *Madron* 1970
Horne, James W aka **Horne, James** (1880-1942) *College* 1927; *Big Business* 1929; *Bonnie Scotland* 1935; *Thicker than Water* 1935; *The Bohemian Girl* 1936; *All over Town* 1937; *Way Out West* 1937
Horner, Harry (1910-1994) *Beware, My Lovely* 1952; *Red Planet Mars* 1952; *New Faces* 1954; *A Life in the Balance* 1955
Horton, Peter (1953-) *Amazon Women on the Moon* 1987; *The Cure* 1995
Hoskins, Bob (1942-2014) *The Raggedy Rawney* 1987; *Rainbow* 1995
Hosoda, Mamoru *Digimon the Movie* 1999; *Summer Wars* 2009; *Wolf Children* 2012
Hou Hsiao-Hsien aka **Hou Xiaoxian** (1947-) *A Summer at Grandpa's* 1984; *The Time to Live and the Time to Die* 1985; *Daughter of the Nile* 1987; *Dust in the Wind* 1987; *A City of Sadness* 1989; *The Puppetmaster* 1993; *Flowers of Shanghai* 1998; *Café Lumière* 2003; *Three Times* 2005; *The Flight of the Red Balloon* 2007; *The Assassin* 2015
Hough, John (1941-) *Eyewitness* 1970; *Twins of Evil* 1971; *Treasure Island* 1972; *The Legend of Hell House* 1973; *Escape to Witch Mountain* 1975; *Brass Target* 1978; *Return from Witch Mountain* 1978; *The Watcher in the Woods* 1982; *Triumphs of a Man Called Horse* 1983; *Biggles* 1986; *American Gothic* 1987; *A Ghost in Monte Carlo* 1990; *Something to Believe In* 1997; *Bad Karma* 2001
Howard, Byron *Bolt* 2008; *Tangled* 2010; *Zootropolis* 2016
Howard, Cy (1915-1993) *Lovers and Other Strangers* 1970; *Every Little Crook and Nanny* 1972
Howard, Leslie (1893-1943) *Pygmalion* 1938; *Pimpernel Smith* 1941; *The First of the Few* 1942; *The Gentle Sex* 1943
Howard, Ron (1954-) *Grand Theft Auto* 1977; *Night Shift* 1982; *Splash* 1984; *Cocoon* 1985; *Gung Ho* 1986; *Willow* 1988; *Parenthood* 1989; *Backdraft* 1991; *Far and Away* 1992; *The Paper* 1994; *Apollo 13* 1995; *Ransom* 1996; *Edtv* 1999; *The Grinch* 2000; *A Beautiful Mind* 2001; *The Missing* 2003; *Cinderella Man* 2005; *The Da Vinci Code* 2006; *Frost/Nixon* 2008; *Angels & Demons* 2009; *The Dilemma* 2011; *Rush* 2013; *In the Heart of the Sea* 2015; *Inferno* 2016
Howard, William K (1899-1954) *The Valiant* 1929; *The First Year* 1932; *Sherlock Holmes* 1932; *The Power and the Glory* 1933; *The Cat and the Fiddle* 1934; *Evelyn Prentice* 1934; *This Side of Heaven* 1934; *Rendezvous* 1935; *Vanessa, Her Love Story* 1935; *The Princess Comes Across* 1936; *Fire over England* 1937; *The Squeaker* 1937; *Back Door to Heaven* 1939; *Johnny Come Lately* 1943
Howitt, Peter aka **Croudins, Peter P** (1957-) *Sliding Doors* 1997;

Antitrust 2000; *Johnny English* 2003; *Laws of Attraction* 2003; *Dangerous Parking* 2007; *Reasonable Doubt* 2014
Howson, Frank (1952-) *Hunting* 1992; *Flynn* 1995
Huda, Menhaj *Kidulthood* 2005; *Everywhere + Nowhere* 2011
Hudlin, Reginald (1961-) *House Party* 1990; *Boomerang* 1992; *The Great White Hype* 1996; *The Ladies Man* 2000; *Serving Sara* 2002
Hudson, Hugh (1936-) *Chariots of Fire* 1981; *Greystoke: the Legend of Tarzan, Lord of the Apes* 1984; *Revolution* 1985; *The Road Home* 1989; *My Life So Far* 1999; *I Dreamed of Africa* 2000
Hughes, Albert aka **The Hughes Brothers** (1972-) *Menace II Society* 1993; *Dead Presidents* 1995; *From Hell* 2001; *The Book of Eli* 2009
Hughes, Allen aka **The Hughes Brothers** (1972-) *Menace II Society* 1993; *Dead Presidents* 1995; *From Hell* 2001; *Knights of the South Bronx* 2005; *The Book of Eli* 2009; *New York, I Love You* 2009; *Broken City* 2013
Hughes, Bronwen *Harriet the Spy* 1996; *Forces of Nature* 1998; *Stander* 2003
Hughes, Howard (1905-1976) *Hell's Angels* 1930; *The Outlaw* 1943
Hughes, John (1950-2009) *Sixteen Candles* 1984; *The Breakfast Club* 1985; *Weird Science* 1985; *Ferris Bueller's Day Off* 1986; *Planes, Trains and Automobiles* 1987; *She's Having a Baby* 1988; *Uncle Buck* 1989; *Curly Sue* 1991
Hughes, Ken (1922-2001) *The Brain Machine* 1954; *Confession* 1955; *Joe Macbeth* 1955; *Little Red Monkey* 1955; *Timeslip* 1955; *The Trials of Oscar Wilde* 1960; *The Small World of Sammy Lee* 1963; *Of Human Bondage* 1964; *Drop Dead Darling* 1966; *Casino Royale* 1967; *Chitty Chitty Bang Bang* 1968; *Cromwell* 1970; *The Internecine Project* 1974; *Alfie Darling* 1975; *Sextette* 1978
Hughes (2), Patrick *Red Hill* 2010; *The Expendables 3* 2014
Hughes, Terry *Monty Python Live at the Hollywood Bowl* 1982; *The Butcher's Wife* 1991; *Mrs Santa Claus* 1996
Humberstone, H Bruce aka **Humberstone, Bruce** (1903-1984) *If I Had a Million* 1932; *Charlie Chan at the Opera* 1936; *Charlie Chan at the Olympics* 1937; *Checkers* 1937; *Pack Up Your Troubles* 1939; *I Wake Up Screaming* 1941; *Sun Valley Serenade* 1941; *Tall, Dark and Handsome* 1941; *To the Shores of Tripoli* 1942; *Hello, Frisco, Hello* 1943; *Pin Up Girl* 1944; *Wonder Man* 1945; *Three Little Girls in Blue* 1946; *Fury at Furnace Creek* 1948; *Happy Go Lovely* 1950; *She's Working Her Way through College* 1952; *The Desert Song* 1953; *The Purple Mask* 1955; *Ten Wanted Men* 1955; *Tarzan and the Lost Safari* 1956; *Tarzan's Fight for Life* 1958; *Madison Avenue* 1962
Hunebelle, André (1896-1985) *Le Bossu* 1959; *The Captain* 1960; *The Mysteries of Paris* 1962
Hung, Sammo (1952-) *The Prodigal Son* 1983; *Wheels on Meals* 1984; *Mr Nice Guy* 1996
Hunsinger, Tom *Boyfriends* 1996; *The Lawless Heart* 2001; *Sparkle* 2006
Hunt, Courtney *Frozen River* 2008; *The Whole Truth* 2016
Hunt, Peter (1928-2002) *On Her Majesty's Secret Service* 1969; *Gold* 1974; *Shout at the Devil* 1976; *Gulliver's Travels* 1977; *Death Hunt* 1981; *Wild Geese II* 1985; *Assassination* 1986
Hunter, Neil *Boyfriends* 1996; *The Lawless Heart* 2001; *Sparkle* 2006
Hunter, Simon (1969-) *Lighthouse* 1999; *Mutant Chronicles* 2008
Hunter, Tim (1947-) *Tex* 1982; *Sylvester* 1985; *River's Edge* 1987; *The Saint of Fort Washington* 1993; *The Maker* 1997
Huntington, Lawrence (1900-1968) *Night Boat to Dublin* 1946; *Wanted for Murder* 1946; *The Upturned Glass* 1947; *When the Bough Breaks* 1947; *Mr Perrin and Mr Traill* 1948; *The Franchise Affair* 1951; *Contraband Spain* 1955; *Death Drums along the River* 1963
Hurran, Nick *Remember Me?* 1996; *Girls' Night* 1997; *Virtual Sexuality* 1999; *Little Black Book* 2004; *It's a Boy/Girl Thing* 2006

Hurwitz, Jon *Harold & Kumar Escape from Guantanamo Bay* 2008; *American Reunion* 2012
Hüseyin, Metin *It Was an Accident* 2000; *Anita & Me* 2002
Hussein, Waris (1938-) *A Touch of Love* 1969; *Quackser Fortune Has a Cousin in the Bronx* 1970; *Melody* 1971; *The Possession of Joel Delaney* 1971; *Henry VIII and His Six Wives* 1972; *Surviving* 1985; *Murder between Friends* 1993; *The Face on the Milk Carton* 1995; *Sixth Happiness* 1997
Huston, Danny (1962-) *Mr Corbett's Ghost* 1986; *Mr North* 1988; *Becoming Colette* 1991; *The Maddening* 1995
Huston, John (1906-1987) *The Maltese Falcon* 1941; *Across the Pacific* 1942; *In This Our Life* 1942; *The Treasure of the Sierra Madre* 1947; *Key Largo* 1948; *We Were Strangers* 1949; *The Asphalt Jungle* 1950; *The African Queen* 1951; *The Red Badge of Courage* 1951; *Moulin Rouge* 1952; *Beat the Devil* 1953; *Moby Dick* 1956; *Heaven Knows, Mr Allison* 1957; *The Barbarian and the Geisha* 1958; *The Roots of Heaven* 1958; *The Unforgiven* 1960; *The Misfits* 1961; *Freud* 1962; *The List of Adrian Messenger* 1963; *The Night of the Iguana* 1964; *The Bible... in the Beginning* 1966; *Casino Royale* 1967; *Reflections in a Golden Eye* 1967; *Sinful Davey* 1969; *A Walk with Love and Death* 1969; *Fat City* 1972; *The Life and Times of Judge Roy Bean* 1972; *The Mackintosh Man* 1973; *The Man Who Would Be King* 1975; *Wise Blood* 1979; *Phobia* 1980; *Escape to Victory* 1981; *Annie* 1982; *Under the Volcano* 1984; *Prizzi's Honor* 1985; *The Dead* 1987
Hutton, Brian G (1935-2014) *Where Eagles Dare* 1969; *Kelly's Heroes* 1970; *Zee and Co* 1971; *Night Watch* 1973; *High Road to China* 1983
Huyck, Willard *French Postcards* 1979; *Best Defense* 1984; *Howard, a New Breed of Hero* 1986
Hyams, Peter (1943-) *Busting* 1974; *Capricorn One* 1978; *Hanover Street* 1979; *Outland* 1981; *The Star Chamber* 1983; *2010* 1984; *Running Scared* 1986; *The Presidio* 1988; *Narrow Margin* 1990; *Stay Tuned* 1992; *Timecop* 1994; *Sudden Death* 1995; *The Relic* 1996; *End of Days* 1999; *The Musketeer* 2001; *Beyond a Reasonable Doubt* 2009; *Enemies Closer* 2013
Hyett, Paul *The Seasoning House* 2012; *Howl* 2015
Hytner, Nicholas (1956-) *The Madness of King George* 1995; *The Crucible* 1996; *The Object of My Affection* 1998; *Center Stage* 2000; *The History Boys* 2006; *The Lady in the Van* 2015

I

Ichaso, Leon (1948-) *Sugar Hill* 1993; *Execution of Justice* 1999; *Piñero* 2001; *El Cantante* 2006; *Left to Die: the Sandra and Tammi Chase Story* 2012
Ichikawa, Kon (1915-2008) *The Burmese Harp* 1956; *Conflagration* 1958; *Fires on the Plain* 1959; *The Key* 1959; *An Actor's Revenge* 1963; *Alone on the Pacific* 1963; *Tokyo Olympiad* 1965; *Visions of Eight* 1973; *The Makioka Sisters* 1983; *The Burmese Harp* 1985
Im Kwon-taek (1936-) *Village in the Mist* 1983; *Chihwaseon (Drunk on Women and Poetry)* 2002
Imamura, Shohei (1926-2006) *The Profound Desire of the Gods* 1968; *Vengeance Is Mine* 1979; *The Ballad of Narayama* 1983; *Black Rain* 1988; *The Eel* 1997; *Warm Water under a Red Bridge* 2001; *11'09"01 - September 11* 2002
Iñárritu, Alejandro González aka **Iñárritu, Alejandro G** (1963-) *Amores Perros* 2000; *11'09"01 - September 11* 2002; *21 Grams* 2003; *Babel* 2006; *Biutiful* 2009; *Birdman or (The Unexpected Virtue of Ignorance)* 2014; *The Revenant* 2015
Ingram (1), Rex (1892-1950) *The Four Horsemen of the Apocalypse* 1921; *The Prisoner of Zenda* 1922; *Scaramouche* 1923; *The Arab* 1924; *Mare Nostrum* 1926; *The Garden of Allah* 1927
Ingram, Terry *A Trick of the Mind* 2006; *Concrete Canyons* 2010; *The Wishing Tree* 2012

Ingster, Boris (1913-1978) *Stranger on the Third Floor 1940; The Judge Steps Out 1949*

Iosseliani, Otar (1934-) *Les Favoris de la Lune 1984; Monday Morning 2002; Gardens in Autumn 2006*

Ireland, Dan (1958-) *The Whole Wide World 1996; The Velocity of Gary 1998; Mrs Palfrey at The Claremont 2005; Living Proof 2008*

Irmas, Matthew *When the Party's Over 1992; Desert Gamble 1996; A Carol Christmas 2003*

Irvin, John (1940-) *The Dogs of War 1980; Ghost Story 1981; Champions 1983; Turtle Diary 1985; Raw Deal 1986; Hamburger Hill 1987; Next of Kin 1989; Robin Hood 1990; Widows' Peak 1993; A Month by the Lake 1994; City of Industry 1996; When Trumpets Fade 1998; Shiner 2000; The Fourth Angel 2001; The Boys & Girl from County Clare 2003*

Irving, David *Rumpelstiltskin 1986; CHUD II: Bud the Chud 1989; Perfume of the Cyclone 1989*

Irving, Richard (1917-1990) *Prescription: Murder 1968; Ransom for a Dead Man 1971; The Six Million Dollar Man 1973*

Isaac, James aka **Isaac, Jim** (1960-2012) *House III: The Horror Show 1989; Jason X 2001; Skinwalkers 2006*

Iscove, Robert (1947-) *Rodgers & Hammerstein's Cinderella 1997; She's All That 1999; Boys and Girls 2000; Three Wise Guys 2005*

Isitt, Debbie *Nasty Neighbours 2000; Confetti 2006; Nativity! 2009; Nativity 2: Danger in the Manger! 2012; Nativity 3: Dude Where's My Donkey 2014*

Israel, Neal (1945-) *Americathon 1979; Bachelor Party 1984; Moving Violations 1985; Surf Ninjas 1993*

Itami, Juzo (1933-1997) *Death Japanese Style 1984; Tampopo 1986; A Taxing Woman 1987*

Ivory, James (1928-) *The Householder 1963; Shakespeare Wallah 1965; The Guru 1969; Bombay Talkie 1970; Savages 1972; Autobiography of a Princess 1975; The Wild Party 1975; Roseland 1977; The Europeans 1979; Hullabaloo over Georgie and Bonnie's Pictures 1979; Jane Austen in Manhattan 1980; Quartet 1981; Heat and Dust 1982; The Bostonians 1984; A Room with a View 1985; Maurice 1987; Slaves of New York 1989; Mr and Mrs Bridge 1990; Howards End 1992; The Remains of the Day 1993; Jefferson in Paris 1995; Surviving Picasso 1996; A Soldier's Daughter Never Cries 1998; The Golden Bowl 2000; Le Divorce 2003; The White Countess 2005*

Izzard, Bryan *Holiday on the Buses 1973; Julie and the Cadillacs 1997*

J

Jackson, David S *Death Train 1993; Night Watch 1995*

Jackson, Douglas aka **Jackson, Doug** (1940-) *Whispers 1990; Midnight in St Petersburg 1995; The Ghost 2000; The Perfect Marriage 2006; A Nanny's Secret 2008; The Perfect Assistant 2008*

Jackson, Mick (1943-) *Chattahoochee 1989; LA Story 1991; The Bodyguard 1992; Clean Slate 1994; Indictment: the McMartin Trial 1995; Volcano 1997; Tuesdays with Morrie 1999; Live from Baghdad 2002; The Memory Keeper's Daughter 2008; Denial 2016; Temple Grandin 2010*

Jackson, Pat (1916-2011) *Encore 1951; White Corridors 1951; The Feminine Touch 1956; The Birthday Present 1957; Virgin Island 1958; What a Carve Up! 1961; Don't Talk to Strange Men 1962*

Jackson, Peter (1961-) *Bad Taste 1987; Meet the Feebles 1989; Braindead 1992; Heavenly Creatures 1994; The Frighteners 1996; The Lord of the Rings: The Fellowship of the Ring 2001; The Lord of the Rings: The Two Towers 2002; The Lord of the Rings: The Return of the King 2003; King Kong 2005; The Lovely Bones 2009; The Hobbit: an Unexpected Journey 2012; The Hobbit: the Desolation of Smaug 2013; The Hobbit: the Battle of the Five Armies 2014*

Jackson, Wilfred (1906-1988) *The Tortoise and the Hare 1935; The Old Mill 1937; Fantasia 1940; Saludos*

Amigos 1943; Song of the South 1946; Melody Time 1948; Cinderella 1950; Alice in Wonderland 1951; Peter Pan 1953; Lady and the Tramp 1955

Jacobs, Alan *Nina Takes a Lover 1993; Diary of a Serial Killer 1997; American Gun 2002*

Jacobs, Gregory *Criminal 2004; Wind Chill 2007; Magic Mike XXL 2015*

Jacobs, Steve (1967-) *La Spagnola 2001; Disgrace 2008*

Jacobson, David *Dahmer 2002; Down in the Valley 2004*

Jacquet, Luc *March of the Penguins 2005; The Fox and the Child 2007; Ice and the Sky 2015*

Jacquot, Benoît (1947-) *Tosca 2001; Villa Amalia 2009*

Jaeckin, Just (1940-) *Emmanuelle 1974; The Story of O 1975; Lady Chatterley's Lover 1981*

Jaglom, Henry (1941-) *A Safe Place 1971; Tracks 1977; Sitting Ducks 1979; National Lampoon's Movie Madness 1981; Can She Bake a Cherry Pie? 1983; Always 1985; Someone to Love 1987; Eating 1990; Venice/ Venice 1992; Babyfever 1994; Last Summer in the Hamptons 1995; Déjà Vu 1997; Festival in Cannes 2001*

James (2), Steve *Hoop Dreams 1994; Prefontaine 1997; Joe and Max 2002; The Interrupters 2011*

Jameson, Jerry (1934-) *Airport '77 1977; Raise the Titanic 1980; Starflight One 1983; Taken Away 1996; Safe Harbor 2009; Captive 2015*

Jancso, Miklos (1921-2014) *The Round-Up 1966; The Red and the White 1967*

Jankel, Annabel *DOA 1988; Super Mario Bros 1993*

Jaoui, Agnès (1964-) *Le Goût des Autres 1999; Look at Me 2004; Let's Talk about the Rain 2008; Under the Rainbow 2013*

Jarecki, Andrew *Capturing the Friedmans 2003; All Good Things 2010*

Jarman, Derek (1942-1994) *Sebastiane 1976; Jubilee 1978; The Tempest 1979; The Angelic Conversation 1985; Caravaggio 1986; Aria 1987; The Last of England 1987; War Requiem 1989; The Garden 1990; Edward II 1991; Blue 1993; Wittgenstein 1993*

Jarmusch, Jim (1953-) *Permanent Vacation 1982; Stranger than Paradise 1984; Down by Law 1986; Mystery Train 1989; Night on Earth 1992; Dead Man 1995; The Year of the Horse 1997; Ghost Dog: the Way of the Samurai 1999; Ten Minutes Older: the Trumpet 2002; Coffee and Cigarettes 2003; Broken Flowers 2005; The Limits of Control 2008; Only Lovers Left Alive 2013*

Jarrold, Julian (1960-) *Kinky Boots 2005; Becoming Jane 2006; Brideshead Revisited 2008; A Royal Night Out 2015*

Jarrott, Charles (1927-2011) *Anne of the Thousand Days 1969; Mary, Queen of Scots 1971; Lost Horizon 1973; The Dove 1974; The Littlest Horse Thieves 1976; The Other Side of Midnight 1977; The Last Flight of Noah's Ark 1980; The Amateur 1981; Condorman 1981; The Boy in Blue 1986; Treacherous Beauties 1994*

Jarvilaturi, Ilkka (1961-) *Darkness in Tallinn 1993; History Is Made at Night 1999*

Jason, Leigh (1904-1979) *The Bride Walks Out 1936; New Faces of 1937 1937; The Mad Miss Manton 1938; Lady for a Night 1942; Out of the Blue 1947*

Jean, Mark *Homecoming 1996; Finding a Family 2011; Finding Mrs Claus 2012*

Jean, Vadim (1966-) *Leon the Pig Farmer 1992; Beyond Bedlam 1993; Clockwork Mice 1994; The Real Howard Spitz 1998; One More Kiss 1999; In the Land of the Free... 2009; Breaking the Bank 2014*

Jeffries, Lionel (1926-2010) *The Railway Children 1970; The Amazing Mr Blunden 1972; Baxter 1973; Wombling Free 1977; The Water Babies 1978*

Jeffs, Christine (1963-) *Rain 2001; Sylvia 2003; Sunshine Cleaning 2008*

Jenkins, Michael (1946-) *Rebel 1985; The Heartbreak Kid 1993*

Jenkins, Patty *Monster 2003; Five 2011; Wonder Woman 2017*

Jenkins, Tamara (1963-) *Slums of Beverly Hills 1998; The Savages 2007*

Jennings, Garth *The Hitchhiker's Guide to the Galaxy 2005; Son of Rambow 2007; Sing 2016*

Jensen, Anders Thomas *The Green Butchers 2003; Men & Chicken 2015*

Jenson, Vicky *Shrek 2001; Shark Tale 2004; Post Grad 2009*

Jessua, Alain (1932-) *Shock Treatment 1973; Les Chiens 1978*

Jeunet, Jean-Pierre (1955-) *Delicatessen 1990; The City of Lost Children 1995; Alien: Resurrection 1997; Amélie 2001; A Very Long Engagement 2004; Micmacs 2009; The Young and Prodigious TS Spivet 2013*

Jewison, Norman (1926-) *Forty Pounds of Trouble 1962; The Thrill of It All 1963; Send Me No Flowers 1964; Art of Love 1965; The Cincinnati Kid 1965; The Russians Are Coming, the Russians Are Coming 1966; In the Heat of the Night 1967; The Thomas Crown Affair 1968; Gaily, Gaily 1969; Fiddler on the Roof 1971; Jesus Christ Superstar 1973; Rollerball 1975; FIST 1978; ...And Justice for All 1979; Best Friends 1982; A Soldier's Story 1984; Agnes of God 1985; Moonstruck 1987; In Country 1989; Other People's Money 1991; Only You 1994; Bogus 1996; The Hurricane 1999; Dinner with Friends 2001; The Statement 2003*

Jia Zhang Ke (1970-) *Xiao Wu 1997; Platform 2000; Unknown Pleasures 2002; A Touch of Sin 2013*

Jiang Wen (1963-) *Devils on the Doorstep 2000; New York, I Love You 2009*

Jires, Jaromil (1935-2001) *The Joke 1968; Valerie and Her Week of Wonders 1970; Labyrinth 1991*

Joannon, Léo aka **Joannon, Leo** (1904-1969) *Utopia 1950; Le Défroqué 1953*

Joanou, Phil (1961-) *Three o'Clock High 1987; U2 Rattle and Hum 1988; State of Grace 1990; Final Analysis 1992; Heaven's Prisoners 1996; Gridiron Gang 2006*

Jobson, Richard *16 Years of Alcohol 2003; New Town Killers 2009*

Jodorowsky, Alexandro (1929-) *El Topo 1971; The Holy Mountain 1973; Santa Sangre 1989; The Rainbow Thief 1990; The Dance of Reality 2013*

Joffe, Mark (1956-) *Nightmaster 1987; Spotswood 1991; Cosi 1996; The Matchmaker 1997; The Man Who Sued God 2001*

Joffé, Roland (1945-) *The Killing Fields 1984; The Mission 1986; Shadow Makers 1989; City of Joy 1992; The Scarlet Letter 1995; Goodbye Lover 1997; Vatel 2000; Captivity 2006*

Joffe, Rowan *Brighton Rock 2010; Before I Go to Sleep 2014*

Johar, Karan (1972-) *Kabhi Khushi Kabhie Gham... 2001; My Name Is Khan 2010*

Johnson, Clark (1954-) *Boycott 2001; SWAT 2003; The Sentinel 2006*

Johnson, Gerard *Tony 2009; Hyena 2014*

Johnson, Kenneth (1942-) *The Incredible Hulk 1977; Short Circuit 2 1988; Sherlock Holmes Returns 1993; Steel 1997*

Johnson, Lamont (1922-2010) *The McKenzie Break 1970; A Gunfight 1971; The Groundstar Conspiracy 1972; You'll Like My Mother 1972; The Last American Hero 1973; The Execution of Private Slovik 1974; Fear on Trial 1975; Lipstick 1976; Somebody Killed Her Husband 1978; Cattle Annie and Little Britches 1980; Spacehunter: Adventures in the Forbidden Zone 1983*

Johnson, Liza *Return 2011; Elvis & Nixon 2016*

Johnson, Mark Steven (1964-) *Simon Birch 1998; Daredevil 2003; Ghost Rider 2007; When in Rome 2009; Killing Season 2013*

Johnson, Niall *The Ghost of Greville Lodge 2000; Keeping Mum 2005*

Johnson, Nunnally (1897-1977) *Black Widow 1954; Night People 1954; How to Be Very, Very Popular 1955; The Man in the Gray Flannel Suit 1956; Oh, Men! Oh, Women! 1957; The Three Faces of Eve 1957; The Man Who Understood Women 1959; The Angel Wore Red 1960*

Johnson, Patrick Read (1964-) *Baby's Day Out 1994; Angus 1995*

Johnson, Rian (1973-) *Brick 2005; The Brothers Bloom 2008; Looper 2012; Star Wars Episode VIII 2017*

Johnson, Tim *Antz 1998; Sinbad: Legend of the Seven Seas 2003; Over the Hedge 2006; Home 2014*

Johnston, Joe (1950-) *Honey, I Shrunk the Kids 1989; Rocketeer 1991; The Pagemaster 1994; Jumanji 1995; October Sky 1999; Jurassic Park III 2001; Hidalgo 2003; The Wolfman 2009; Captain America: the First Avenger 2011*

Jolie, Angelina aka **Jolie Pitt, Angelina** (1975-) *Unbroken 2014; By the Sea 2015*

Jones, Chuck aka **Jones, Charles M** (1912-2002) *Duck Dodgers in the 24½ Century 1953; One Froggy Evening 1955; What's Opera, Doc? 1957; The Dot and the Line 1965; The Phantom Tollbooth 1969; The Bugs Bunny/ Road Runner Movie 1979*

Jones (3), David aka **Jones, David Hugh** (1934-2008) *Betrayal 1982; 84 Charing Cross Road 1986; Jacknife 1988; The Trial 1993; Time to Say Goodbye? 1997; A Christmas Carol 1999; The Confession 1999; Custody of the Heart 2000*

Jones, Duncan (1971-) *Moon 2008; Source Code 2011; Warcraft: the Beginning 2016*

Jones, F Richard (1894-1930) *The Gaucho 1927; Bulldog Drummond 1929*

Jones, Harmon (1911-1972) *As Young as You Feel 1951; Bloodhounds of Broadway 1952; The Pride of St Louis 1952; Gorilla at Large 1954; Princess of the Nile 1954; A Day of Fury 1956; Bullwhip 1958*

Jones, Kirk (1964-) *Waking Ned 1998; Nanny McPhee 2005; Everybody's Fine 2009; What to Expect When You're Expecting 2012; My Big Fat Greek Wedding 2 2016*

Jones, Terry (1942-) *Monty Python and the Holy Grail 1975; Monty Python's Life of Brian 1979; Monty Python's The Meaning of Life 1983; Personal Services 1987; Erik the Viking 1989; The Wind in the Willows 1996; Absolutely Anything 2015*

Jones, Tommy Lee (1946-) *The Good Old Boys 1995; The Three Burials of Melquiades Estrada 2005; The Sunset Limited 2010; The Homesman 2014*

Jonze, Spike (1969-) *Being John Malkovich 1999; Adaptation. 2002; Where the Wild Things Are 2009; Her 2013*

Joost, Henry *Catfish 2010; Paranormal Activity 3 2011; Paranormal Activity 4 2012; Nerve 2016*

Jordan, Glenn (1936-) *Les Misérables 1978; Only When I Laugh 1981; The Buddy System 1984; Mass Appeal 1984; Promise 1986; The Boys 1991; Barbarians at the Gate 1993; My Brother's Keeper 1995; Legalese 1998; The Long Way Home 1998; Midwives 2001; Lucy 2003*

Jordan, Gregor (1968-) *Two Hands 1999; Buffalo Soldiers 2001; Ned Kelly 2003; The Informers 2009; Unthinkable 2010*

Jordan, Neil (1950-) *Angel 1982; The Company of Wolves 1984; Mona Lisa 1986; High Spirits 1988; We're No Angels 1989; The Miracle 1990; The Crying Game 1992; Interview with the Vampire: the Vampire Chronicles 1994; Michael Collins 1996; The Butcher Boy 1997; In Dreams 1998; The End of the Affair 1999; The Good Thief 2002; Breakfast on Pluto 2005; The Brave One 2007; Ondine 2009; Byzantium 2012*

Judge, Mike (1962-) *Beavis and Butt-head Do America 1996; Office Space 1999; Idiocracy 2006; Extract 2009*

Julien, Isaac (1960-) *Young Soul Rebels 1991; Frantz Fanon: Black Skin White Mask 1996*

July, Miranda *Me and You and Everyone We Know 2005; The Future 2011*

Junger, Gil (1954-) *10 Things I Hate about You 1999; Black Knight 2001; If Only 2004; My Fake Fiancé 2009*

Juran, Nathan aka **Hertz, Nathan** aka **Juran, Nathan H** (1907-2002) *The Black Castle 1952; The Golden Blade 1953; Gunsmoke 1953; Law and Order 1953; Tumbleweed 1953; Drums across the River 1954; The Deadly Mantis 1957; 20 Million Miles to Earth 1957; Attack of the 50 Foot Woman 1958; The Brain from Planet Arous 1958; The 7th Voyage of Sinbad 1958; Jack the Giant Killer 1962; The Siege of the Saxons 1963;*

East of Sudan 1964; First Men in the Moon 1964; Land Raiders 1969

Jutra, Claude (1930-1986) *My Uncle Antoine 1971; Kamouraska 1973*

K

Kachyna, Karel (1924-2004) *The Ear 1969; The Last Butterfly 1990*

Kaczender, George (1933-) *In Praise of Older Women 1978; Agency 1981; Chanel Solitaire 1981; Where Are My Children? 1994*

Kadar, Jan (1918-1979) *The Shop on the High Street 1965; The Angel Levine 1970; Lies My Father Told Me 1975*

Kafka, John *Cinderella II: Dreams Come True 2002; Dino Time 2012*

Kagan, Jeremy Paul aka **Kagan, Jeremy** (1945-) *Scott Joplin 1977; The Big Fix 1978; The Chosen 1981; The Sting II 1983; The Journey of Natty Gann 1985; By the Sword 1992; Roswell 1994; The Ballad of Lucy Whipple 2001*

Kahn, Cédric (1966-) *L'Ennui 1998; Roberto Succo 2000; Red Lights 2003*

Kalatozov, Mikhail aka **Kalatozov, Mikhail K** (1903-1973) *The Cranes Are Flying 1957; I Am Cuba 1964; The Red Tent 1969*

Kalin, Tom *Swoon 1992; Savage Grace 2007*

Kammerud, Jim *The Little Mermaid II: Return to the Sea 2000; The Fox and the Hound 2 2007*

Kane, David *This Year's Love 1999; Born Romantic 2000*

Kane, Joseph aka **Kane, Joe** (1897-1975) *Shine On, Harvest Moon 1938; The Arizona Kid 1939; Days of Jesse James 1939; The Yellow Rose of Texas 1944; The Cheaters 1945; Dakota 1945; Flame of the Barbary Coast 1945; The Plunderers 1948; Hoodlum Empire 1952; Fair Wind to Java 1953; The Road to Denver 1955; Timberjack 1955; Accused of Murder 1956; Thunder over Arizona 1956*

Kaneko, Shusuke aka **Kaneko, Shu** (1955-) *Summer Vacation: 1999 1988; Necronomicon 1993*

Kanew, Jeff (1944-) *Eddie Macon's Run 1983; Revenge of the Nerds 1984; Gotcha! 1985; Tough Guys 1986; Troop Beverly Hills 1989; VI Warshawski 1991*

Kang Je-gyu (1962-) *Shiri 1999; Brotherhood 2004*

Kanganis, Charles T *Intent to Kill 1992; Race the Sun 1996; Dennis the Menace Strikes Again 1998; K-911 1999*

Kanievska, Marek (1952-) *Another Country 1984; Less than Zero 1987; Where the Money Is 2000*

Kanin, Garson (1912-1999) *Bachelor Mother 1939; The Great Man Votes 1939; My Favorite Wife 1940; They Knew What They Wanted 1940; Tom, Dick and Harry 1941*

Kanter, Hal (1918-2011) *Loving You 1957; I Married a Woman 1958*

Kapadia, Asif (1973-) *The Warrior 2001; The Return 2006; Far North 2007; Senna 2010; Amy 2015*

Kaplan, Deborah *Can't Hardly Wait 1998; Josie and the Pussycats 2001*

Kaplan, Jonathan (1947-) *Truck Turner 1974; White Line Fever 1975; Mr Billion 1977; Over the Edge 1979; Heart like a Wheel 1983; Project X 1987; The Accused 1988; Immediate Family 1989; Love Field 1992; Unlawful Entry 1992; Bad Girls 1994; Brokedown Palace 1999*

Kaplan, Mike *Luck, Trust & Ketchup 1994; Never Apologize 2007*

Kapoor, Raj (1924-1988) *Barsaat 1949; Awara 1951; Shree 420 1955; Sangam 1964; Bobby 1973*

Kapur, Shekhar (1945-) *Bandit Queen 1994; Elizabeth 1998; The Four Feathers 2002; Elizabeth: the Golden Age 2007; New York, I Love You 2009*

Karbelnikoff, Michael *Mobsters 1991; FTW 1994*

Karlson, Phil (1908-1985) *The Shanghai Cobra 1945; Dark Alibi 1946; Black Gold 1947; Ladies of the Chorus 1949; Lorna Doone 1951; Kansas City Confidential 1952; 99 River Street 1953; They Rode West 1954; The Phenix City Story 1955; Tight Spot 1955; The Brothers Rico 1957; Gunman's Walk 1958; Hell to Eternity 1960; Key Witness 1960; The Secret Ways 1961; The Young Doctors 1961; Kid Galahad 1962; The Silencers 1966; A Time for Killing*

1967; The Wrecking Crew 1969; Ben 1972; Framed 1975

Karson, Eric The Octagon 1980; Hell Camp 1986; Black Eagle 1988

Kasdan, Jake (1975-) Zero Effect 1997; Orange County 2001; Walk Hard: the Dewey Cox Story 2007; Bad Teacher 2011; Sex Tape 2014

Kasdan, Lawrence (1949-) Body Heat 1981; The Big Chill 1983; Silverado 1985; The Accidental Tourist 1988; I Love You to Death 1990; Grand Canyon 1991; Wyatt Earp 1994; French Kiss 1995; Mumford 1999; Dreamcatcher 2003

Kashyap, Anurag Gangs of Wasseypur 2012; Gangs of Wasseypur II 2012

Kassell, Nicole The Woodsman 2004; A Little Bit of Heaven 2011

Kassovitz, Mathieu (1967-) La Haine 1995; The Crimson Rivers 2000; Gothika 2003; Babylon AD 2008; Rebellion 2011

Katselas, Milton (1933-) Butterflies Are Free 1972; 40 Carats 1973; Report to the Commissioner 1975

Katzin, Lee H (1935-2002) Whatever Happened to Aunt Alice? 1969; Le Mans 1971; World Gone Wild 1988

Kaufman, Charlie (1958-) Synecdoche, New York 2008; Anomalisa 2015

Kaufman, Lloyd aka Weil, Samuel (1945-) Class of Nuke 'Em High 1986; The Toxic Avenger, Part II 1988; Sgt Kabukiman NYPD 1991; Tromeo & Juliet 1996; Terror Firmer 1999

Kaufman, Paul A Run the Wild Fields 2000; Honeymoon with Mom 2006; Little Girl Lost: the Delimar Vera Story 2008; Magic beyond Words: the JK Rowling Story 2011

Kaufman, Philip (1936-) The Great Northfield Minnesota Raid 1972; The White Dawn 1974; Invasion of the Body Snatchers 1978; The Wanderers 1979; The Right Stuff 1983; The Unbearable Lightness of Being 1988; Henry & June 1990; Rising Sun 1993; Quills 2000; Twisted 2003

Kaurismäki, Aki (1957-) Crime and Punishment 1983; Hamlet Goes Business 1987; Ariel 1988; Leningrad Cowboys Go America 1989; I Hired a Contract Killer 1990; The Match Factory Girl 1990; Take Care of Your Scarf, Tatjana 1994; Drifting Clouds 1996; Juha 1999; The Man without a Past 2002; Ten Minutes Older: the Trumpet 2002; Lights in the Dusk 2006; Le Havre 2011

Kaurismäki, Mika (1955-) Tigrero: a Film That Was Never Made 1994; LA without a Map 1998; The Girl King 2015

Käutner, Helmut aka Kautner, Helmut (1908-1980) The Devil's General 1955; The Restless Years 1958; A Stranger in My Arms 1959

Kawalerowicz, Jerzy (1922-2007) The Shadow 1956; The Devil and the Nun 1960

Kay, Stephen aka Kay, Stephen T The Last Time I Committed Suicide 1996; Get Carter 2000; Boogeyman 2005

Kaye, Tony American History X 1998; Detachment 2011

Kazan, Elia (1909-2003) A Tree Grows in Brooklyn 1945; Boomerang! 1947; Gentleman's Agreement 1947; The Sea of Grass 1947; Pinky 1949; Panic in the Streets 1950; A Streetcar Named Desire 1951; Viva Zapata! 1952; Man on a Tightrope 1953; On the Waterfront 1954; East of Eden 1955; Baby Doll 1956; A Face in the Crowd 1957; Wild River 1960; Splendor in the Grass 1961; America, America 1963; The Arrangement 1969; The Visitors 1972; The Last Tycoon 1976

Keach, James (1948-) False Identity 1990; The Stars Fell on Henrietta 1995; Blind Dating 2005

Keating, David Last of the High Kings 1996; Wake Wood 2010

Keaton, Buster (1895-1966) Neighbors 1920; One Week 1920; The Scarecrow 1920; The Paleface 1921; Day Dreams 1922; Our Hospitality 1923; Three Ages 1923; The Navigator 1924; Sherlock Junior 1924; Go West 1925; Seven Chances 1925; Battling Butler 1926; The General 1927

Keaton, Diane (1946-) Heaven 1987; Wildflower 1991; Unstrung Heroes 1995; Hanging Up 2000

Kechiche, Abdel aka Kechiche, Abdellatif Couscous 2007; Blue Is the Warmest Colour 2013

Keen, Bob (1960-) Proteus 1995; Shepherd on the Rock 1995

Keighley, William (1889-1972) Ladies They Talk About 1933; "G" Men 1935; Special Agent 1935; Bullets or Ballots 1936; The Singing Kid 1936; God's Country and the Woman 1937; The Prince and the Pauper 1937; The Adventures of Robin Hood 1938; Each Dawn I Die 1939; The Fighting 69th 1940; No Time for Comedy 1940; Torrid Zone 1940; The Bride Came COD 1941; Four Mothers 1941; The Man Who Came to Dinner 1941; George Washington Slept Here 1942; The Street with No Name 1948; Rocky Mountain 1950; Close to My Heart 1951; The Master of Ballantrae 1953

Keiller, Patrick (1950-) London 1994; Robinson in Space 1997; Robinson in Ruins 2010

Keller, Harry (1913-1987) Rose of Cimarron 1952; The Unguarded Moment 1956; Quantez 1957; Day of the Bad Man 1958; The Female Animal 1958; Voice in the Mirror 1958; Seven Ways from Sundown 1960; Tammy Tell Me True 1961; Six Black Horses 1962; Tammy and the Doctor 1963; The Brass Bottle 1964; In Enemy Country 1968

Kellett, Bob (1927-2012) Up Pompeii 1971; Up the Chastity Belt 1971; Our Miss Fred 1972; Up the Front 1972; Don't Just Lie There, Say Something! 1973; Spanish Fly 1975; Are You Being Served? 1977

Kelljan, Bob (1930-1982) Count Yorga, Vampire 1970; The Return of Count Yorga 1971

Kellogg, David (1952-) Cool as Ice 1991; Inspector Gadget 1999

Kellogg, Ray (1919-1981) The Giant Gila Monster 1959; The Killer Shrews 1959; The Green Berets 1968

Kelly, Gene (1912-1996) On the Town 1949; Singin' in the Rain 1952; It's Always Fair Weather 1955; The Happy Road 1956; Invitation to the Dance 1956; The Tunnel of Love 1958; Gigot 1962; A Guide for the Married Man 1967; Hello, Dolly! 1969; The Cheyenne Social Club 1970; That's Entertainment, Part II 1976

Kelly, Richard (1975-) Donnie Darko 2001; Southland Tales 2005; The Box 2008

Kemp, Julian House! 2000; My Last Five Girlfriends 2009

Kenan, Gil Monster House 2006; City of Ember 2008; Poltergeist 2015

Kennedy, Burt (1923-2001) Mail Order Bride 1963; The Rounders 1965; Return of the Seven 1966; The War Wagon 1967; Welcome to Hard Times 1967; The Good Guys and the Bad Guys 1969; Support Your Local Sheriff! 1969; Young Billy Young 1969; Dirty Dingus Magee 1970; The Deserter 1971; Hannie Caulder 1971; Support Your Local Gunfighter 1971; The Train Robbers 1973; The Killer inside Me 1975; Wolf Lake 1979; The Trouble with Spies 1987; Once upon a Texas Train 1988; Suburban Commando 1991

Kentis, Chris Open Water 2004; Silent House 2011

Kenton, Erle C (1896-1980) Island of Lost Souls 1932; You're Telling Me! 1934; The Ghost of Frankenstein 1942; Pardon My Sarong 1942; Who Done It? 1942; House of Frankenstein 1944; House of Dracula 1945

Kern, James V (1909-1966) The Doughgirls 1944; Never Say Goodbye 1946; The Second Woman 1951; Two Tickets to Broadway 1951

Kerrigan, Justin Human Traffic 1999; I Know You Know 2008

Kerrigan, Lodge H aka Kerrigan, Lodge (1964-) Claire Dolan 1998; Keane 2004

Kershner, Irvin (1923-2010) Stakeout on Dope Street 1958; The Hoodlum Priest 1961; The Luck of Ginger Coffey 1964; A Fine Madness 1966; The Flim-Flam Man 1967; Loving 1970; Up the Sandbox 1972; The Return of a Man Called Horse 1976; Raid on Entebbe 1977; Eyes of Laura Mars 1978; Star Wars Episode V: the Empire Strikes Back 1980; Never Say Never Again 1983; RoboCop 2 1990

Kervern, Gustave Louise-Michel 2008; Mammuth 2010

Keshishian, Alek In Bed with Madonna 1991; With Honors 1994

Kesteloot, Vincent Sammy's Great Escape 2012; Robinson Crusoe 2015

Keusch, Michael (1955-) Lena's Holiday 1990; Huck and the King of Hearts 1993; Attack Force 2006; Shadow Man 2006; Flight of Fury 2007

Khalfoun, Franck P2 2006; Wrong Turn at Tahoe 2009; Maniac 2012

Khan, Mehboob (1908-1964) Andaz 1949; Mother India 1957

Khleifi, Michel Wedding in Galilee 1987; Canticle of the Stones 1990

Khouri, Callie (1957-) Divine Secrets of the Ya-Ya Sisterhood 2002; Mad Money 2008

Kiarostami, Abbas (1940-2016) The Traveller 1974; Where Is My Friend's House? 1987; Close-Up 1989; Homework 1989; And Life Goes On... 1991; Through the Olive Trees 1994; A Taste of Cherry 1997; The Wind Will Carry Us 1999; ABC Africa 2001; Ten 2002; Five 2003; Tickets 2005; Shirin 2008; Certified Copy 2009; Like Someone in Love 2012

Kidron, Beeban (1961-) Vroom 1988; Used People 1992; To Wong Foo, Thanks for Everything, Julie Newmar 1995; Amy Foster 1997; Bridget Jones: the Edge of Reason 2004; InRealLife 2013

Kiersch, Fritz Children of the Corn 1984; Gor 1987; Under the Boardwalk 1988; Into the Sun 1992

Kieslowski, Krzysztof (1941-1996) The Scar 1976; Camera Buff 1979; No End 1984; Blind Chance 1987; A Short Film about Killing 1988; A Short Film about Love 1988; The Double Life of Véronique 1991; Three Colours Blue 1993; Three Colours White 1993; Three Colours Red 1994

Kikoine, Gérard (1946-) Dragonard 1987; Edge of Sanity 1989; Buried Alive 1990

Killy, Edward (1903-1981) Murder on a Bridle Path 1936; Along the Rio Grande 1941; Nevada 1944

Kilner, Clare Janice Beard 45 WPM 1999; The Wedding Date 2004

Kim Ji-woon aka Kim Jee-woon (1964-) The Quiet Family 1998; A Tale of Two Sisters 2003; A Bittersweet Life 2005; The Good the Bad the Weird 2008; I Saw the Devil 2010; The Last Stand 2013

Kim Ki-Duk (1960-) Bad Guy 2001; Spring, Summer, Autumn, Winter ... and Spring 2003; Samaritan Girl 2004; 3-iron 2004; Arirang 2011; Pieta 2012; Moebius 2013

Kimmins, Anthony (1901-1964) Keep Fit 1937; I See Ice 1938; It's in the Air 1938; Come On George 1939; Trouble Brewing 1939; Mine Own Executioner 1947; Bonnie Prince Charlie 1948; Mr Denning Drives North 1951; The Captain's Paradise 1953; Smiley 1956; Smiley Gets a Gun 1959; The Amorous Prawn 1962

King, Allan (1930-2009) Who Has Seen the Wind 1977; Silence of the North 1981

King, George (1899-1966) The Crimes of Stephen Hawke 1936; Sweeney Todd, the Demon Barber of Fleet Street 1936; The Ticket of Leave Man 1937; Sexton Blake and the Hooded Terror 1938; Crimes at the Dark House 1939; The Face at the Window 1939; Tomorrow We Live 1942; Candlelight in Algeria 1943; Gaiety George 1946; The Shop at Sly Corner 1946

King, Henry (1888-1982) Tol'able David 1921; Fury 1923; The White Sister 1923; Stella Dallas 1925; The Winning of Barbara Worth 1926; State Fair 1933; Marie Galante 1934; Way Down East 1935; The Country Doctor 1936; Lloyd's of London 1936; In Old Chicago 1937; Alexander's Ragtime Band 1938; Jesse James 1939; Stanley and Livingstone 1939; Chad Hanna 1940; Little Old New York 1940; Maryland 1940; Remember the Day 1941; A Yank in the RAF 1941; The Black Swan 1942; The Song of Bernadette 1943; Wilson 1944; A Bell for Adano 1945; Margie 1946; Captain from Castile 1947; Prince of Foxes 1949; Twelve o'Clock High 1949; The Gunfighter 1950; David and Bathsheba 1951; I'd Climb the Highest Mountain 1951; O Henry's Full House 1952; The Snows of Kilimanjaro 1952; Wait 'til the Sun Shines, Nellie 1952; King of the Khyber Rifles 1953; Love Is a Many-Splendored Thing 1955; Untamed 1955; Carousel 1956; The Sun Also Rises 1957; The Bravados 1958; Beloved Infidel 1959; This Earth Is Mine 1959; Tender Is the Night 1961

King, Jeff aka King, Jeff F Kill Switch 2008; Driven to Kill 2009

King, Louis (1898-1962) Charlie Chan in Egypt 1935; Bulldog Drummond Comes Back 1937; Bulldog Drummond's Revenge 1937; Bulldog Drummond in Africa 1938; Typhoon 1940; The Way of All Flesh 1940; Thunderhead - Son of Flicka 1945; Smoky 1946; Bob, Son of Battle 1947; Green Grass of Wyoming 1948; Mrs Mike 1949; Frenchie 1950; Powder River 1953; Dangerous Mission 1954

King, Michael Patrick Sex and the City: the Movie 2008; Sex and the City 2 2010

King (2), Paul Bunny & the Bull 2009; Paddington 2014

King, Rick Hot Shot 1986; The Killing Time 1987; Forced March 1989; Prayer of the Rollerboys 1990; Kickboxer III: the Art of War 1992; Quick 1993; Rules of Obsession 1994

King, Rob W (1959-) Without Malice 2000; Mary Higgins Clark's The Cradle Will Fall 2004

King, Zalman (1942-2012) Two Moon Junction 1988; Wild Orchid 1990; Wild Orchid 2: Two Shades of Blue 1992; Delta of Venus 1995; In God's Hands 1998

Kinney, Jack (1909-1992) Saludos Amigos 1943; Victory through Air Power 1943; The Three Caballeros 1944; Make Mine Music 1946; Melody Time 1948; The Adventures of Ichabod and Mr Toad 1949

Kinugasa, Teinosuke (1896-1982) A Page of Madness 1926; Gate of Hell 1953

Kiriya, Kazuaki Casshern 2004; Goemon 2009; The Last Knights 2015

Kirkpatrick, Karey Over the Hedge 2006; Imagine That 2009

Kitamura, Ryuhei (1969-) The Midnight Meat Train 2008; No One Lives 2012

Kitano, Takeshi (1947-) Violent Cop 1989; Boiling Point 1990; A Scene at the Sea 1991; Sonatine 1993; Kids Return 1996; Hana-Bi 1997; Kikujiro 1999; Brother 2000; Dolls 2002; Zatoichi 2003

Kizer, R J (1952-) The Return of Godzilla 1984; Hell Comes to Frogtown 1988

Klane, Robert Thank God It's Friday 1978; Weekend at Bernie's II 1992

Klapisch, Cédric (1962-) Un Air de Famille 1996; When the Cat's Away... 1996; Pot Luck 2002; Russian Dolls 2005; Paris 2007; Chinese Puzzle 2013

Klein, William (1929-) Far from Vietnam 1967; Muhammad Ali, the Greatest 1974

Kleiser, Randal (1946-) The Boy in the Plastic Bubble 1976; Grease 1978; The Blue Lagoon 1980; Summer Lovers 1982; Grandview, USA 1984; Flight of the Navigator 1986; Big Top Pee-wee 1988; Getting It Right 1989; White Fang 1991; Honey, I Blew Up the Kid 1992; It's My Party 1996; Shadow of Doubt 1998; Love Wrecked 2005

Klenhard, Walter Mystery Woman 2003; My Neighbor's Keeper 2007

Klimov, Elem (1933-2003) Agony 1975; Come and See 1985

Klooss, Reinhard Animals United 2010; Tarzan 2013

Kloves, Steve (1960-) The Fabulous Baker Boys 1989; Flesh and Bone 1993

Knight, Steven Hummingbird 2013; Locke 2014

Knopf, Edwin H (1899-1981) Paramount on Parade 1930; The Law and the Lady 1951

Knowles, Bernard (1900-1975) A Place o' One's Own 1944; The Magic Bow 1946; Easy Money 1947; Jassy 1947; The Man Within 1947; The Lost People 1949; The Perfect Woman 1949; The Reluctant Widow 1950

Kobayashi, Masaki (1916-1996) The Thick-Walled Room 1953; The Human Condition 1958; Harakiri 1962; Kwaidan 1964; Rebellion 1967; The Empty Table 1985

Koch, Chris Snow Day 2000; A Guy Thing 2002

Koch, Howard W (1916-2001) Big House, USA 1955; The Girl in Black Stockings 1957; Andy Hardy Comes Home 1958; Frankenstein - 1970 1958; Violent Road 1958; Born Reckless 1959; The Last Mile 1959

Koepp, David (1964-) The Trigger Effect 1996; Stir of Echoes 1999;

Secret Window 2004; Ghost Town 2008; Premium Rush 2012; Mortdecai 2015

Kokkinos, Ana (1959-) Head On 1997; The Book of Revelation 2006

Kollek, Amos Forever Lulu 1987; Double Edge 1992

Koller, Xavier (1944-) Journey of Hope 1990; Squanto: the Last Great Warrior 1994

Kon, Satoshi (1963-2010) Perfect Blue 1998; Paprika 2006

Konchalovsky, Andrei aka Mikhalkov-Konchalovsky, Andrei (1937-) The First Teacher 1965; Asya's Happiness 1967; Sibiriada 1979; Maria's Lovers 1984; Runaway Train 1985; Duet for One 1986; Shy People 1987; Homer and Eddie 1989; Tango & Cash 1989; The Inner Circle 1991; The Odyssey 1997; The Nutcracker in 3D 2010

Koppelman, Brian Knockaround Guys 2001; Solitary Man 2009

Kopple, Barbara (1946-) Harlan County, USA 1976; Wild Man Blues 1997; Havoc 2005; Shut Up & Sing: Dixie Chicks 2006

Korda, Alexander (1893-1956) The Private Life of Helen of Troy 1927; Marius 1931; Wedding Rehearsal 1932; The Private Life of Henry VIII 1933; The Private Life of Don Juan 1934; Rembrandt 1936; The Thief of Bagdad 1940; That Hamilton Woman 1941; Perfect Strangers 1945; An Ideal Husband 1947

Korda, Zoltan (1895-1961) Sanders of the River 1935; Conquest of the Air 1936; Elephant Boy 1937; The Drum 1938; The Four Feathers 1939; The Thief of Bagdad 1940; Jungle Book 1942; Sahara 1943; Counter-Attack 1945; The Macomber Affair 1947; Cry, the Beloved Country 1951; Storm over the Nile 1955

Koreeda, Hirokazu aka Kore-eda, Hirokazu (1962-) After Life 1998; Nobody Knows 2003; Still Walking 2008; I Wish 2011; Like Father, like Son 2013; Our Little Sister 2015

Korine, Harmony (1974-) Gummo 1997; julien donkey-boy 1999; Mister Lonely 2007; Spring Breakers 2012

Kormakur, Baltasar (1966-) 101 Reykjavik 2000; Jar City 2006; Contraband 2012; The Deep 2012; 2 Guns 2013; Everest 2015

Korty, John (1936-) The Autobiography of Miss Jane Pittman 1974; Alex and the Gypsy 1976; Oliver's Story 1978; Resting Place 1986

Kosinski, Joseph Tron Legacy 2010; Oblivion 2013

Kosminsky, Peter (1956-) Wuthering Heights 1992; White Oleander 2002

Koster, Henry (1905-1988) One Hundred Men and a Girl 1937; Three Smart Girls 1937; The Rage of Paris 1938; First Love 1939; Three Smart Girls Grow Up 1939; It Started with Eve 1941; Music for Millions 1944; Two Sisters from Boston 1946; The Bishop's Wife 1947; The Unfinished Dance 1947; Come to the Stable 1949; The Inspector General 1949; Harvey 1950; My Blue Heaven 1950; Wabash Avenue 1950; Mr Belvedere Rings the Bell 1951; No Highway 1951; My Cousin Rachel 1952; O Henry's Full House 1952; Stars and Stripes Forever 1952; The Robe 1953; Desiree 1954; Good Morning, Miss Dove 1955; A Man Called Peter 1955; The Virgin Queen 1955; D-Day the Sixth of June 1956; The Power and the Prize 1956; My Man Godfrey 1957; The Naked Maja 1959; The Story of Ruth 1960; Flower Drum Song 1961; Mr Hobbs Takes a Vacation 1962; Take Her, She's Mine 1963; Dear Brigitte 1966; The Singing Nun 1966

Kotcheff, Ted aka Kotcheff, William T (1931-) Tiara Tahiti 1962; Life at the Top 1965; Two Gentlemen Sharing 1969; Wake in Fright 1970; Billy Two Hats 1973; The Apprenticeship of Duddy Kravitz 1974; Fun with Dick and Jane 1977; Who Is Killing the Great Chefs of Europe? 1978; North Dallas Forty 1979; First Blood 1982; Split Image 1982; Uncommon Valor 1983; Joshua Then and Now 1985; Switching Channels 1987; Weekend at Bernie's 1989; Folks! 1992; The Shooter 1994

Kötting, Andrew Gallivant 1996; This Filthy Earth 2001; By Our Selves 2015

Kouf, Jim (1951-) Miracles 1985; Disorganized Crime 1989; Gang Related 1997

Kounen, Jan (1964-) Dobermann 1997; Blueberry 2004; Coco Chanel & Igor Stravinsky 2009

Kozintsev, Grigori (1905-1973) The New Babylon 1929; Don Quixote 1957; Hamlet 1964; King Lear 1970

Kragh-Jacobsen, Søren (1947-) The Island on Bird Street 1997; Mifune 1999; The Hour of the Lynx 2013

Kramer, Lloyd Before Women Had Wings 1997; David and Lisa 1998; Liz & Dick 2012

Kramer, Stanley (1913-2001) Not as a Stranger 1955; The Pride and the Passion 1957; The Defiant Ones 1958; On the Beach 1959; Inherit the Wind 1960; Judgment at Nuremberg 1961; It's a Mad Mad Mad Mad World 1963; Ship of Fools 1965; Guess Who's Coming to Dinner 1967; The Secret of Santa Vittoria 1969; RPM - Revolutions per Minute 1970; Oklahoma Crude 1973; The Domino Principle 1977; The Runner Stumbles 1979

Kramer, Wayne The Cooler 2002; Running Scared 2005; Crossing Over 2008

Krasna, Norman (1909-1984) Princess O'Rourke 1943; The Big Hangover 1950; The Ambassador's Daughter 1956

Kreuzpaintner, Marco Summer Storm 2004; Trade 2006

Krieger, Lee Toland Celeste & Jesse Forever 2012; The Age of Adaline 2015

Krish, John (1923-) The Wild Affair 1963; Decline and Fall... of a Birdwatcher 1968; The Man Who Had Power over Women 1970

Krishnamma, Suri A Man of No Importance 1994; New Year's Day 1999

Kubrick, Stanley (1928-1999) Day of the Fight 1951; Flying Padre 1951; Fear and Desire 1953; The Seafarers 1953; Killer's Kiss 1955; The Killing 1956; Paths of Glory 1957; Spartacus 1960; Lolita 1961; Dr Strangelove, or How I Learned to Stop Worrying and Love the Bomb 1963; 2001: a Space Odyssey 1968; A Clockwork Orange 1971; Barry Lyndon 1975; The Shining 1980; Full Metal Jacket 1987; Eyes Wide Shut 1999

Kulik, Buzz (1923-1999) The Yellow Canary 1963; Warning Shot 1967; Sergeant Ryker 1968; Riot 1969; Brian's Song 1971; Shamus 1973; The Lindbergh Kidnapping Case 1976; Kill Me If You Can 1977; The Hunter 1980

Kull, Edward (1886-1946) The New Adventures of Tarzan 1935; Tarzan and the Green Goddess 1938

Kumble, Roger (1966-) Cruel Intentions 1999; Cruel Intentions 2 2000; The Sweetest Thing 2002; Just Friends 2005; College Road Trip 2008; Furry Vengeance 2010

Kümel, Harry (1940-) Daughters of Darkness 1970; Malpertuis 1971

Kurosawa, Akira (1910-1998) Sanshiro Sugata 1943; No Regrets for Our Youth 1946; Drunken Angel 1948; Stray Dog 1949; Rashomon 1950; Scandal 1950; The Idiot 1951; Ikiru 1952; Seven Samurai 1954; I Live in Fear 1955; The Lower Depths 1956; Throne of Blood 1957; The Hidden Fortress 1958; The Bad Sleep Well 1960; Yojimbo 1961; Sanjuro 1962; High and Low 1963; Red Beard 1965; Dodes'ka-Den 1970; Dersu Uzala 1975; Kagemusha 1980; Ran 1985; Akira Kurosawa's Dreams 1990; Rhapsody in August 1990; No, Not Yet 1993

Kurosawa, Kiyoshi (1955-) Tokyo Sonata 2008; Journey to the Shore 2015

Kurtzman, Alex (1973-) People like Us 2012; The Mummy 2017

Kurys, Diane (1948-) Diabolo Menthe 1977; Entre Nous 1983; A Man in Love 1987; C'est la Vie 1990; Après l'Amour 1992; Six Days, Six Nights 1994; Les Enfants du Siècle 1999

Kurzel, Justin (1974-) Snowtown 2011; The Turning 2013; Macbeth 2015; Assassin's Creed 2016

Kusama, Karyn (1968-) Girlfight 2000; Aeonflux 2005; Jennifer's Body 2009

Kusturica, Emir (1954-) When Father Was Away on Business 1985; Time of the Gypsies 1988; Arizona Dream 1991; Underground 1995; Black Cat, White Cat 1998; Super 8 Stories 2001; Life Is a Miracle 2004

Kuzui, Fran Rubel Tokyo Pop 1988; Buffy the Vampire Slayer 1992

Kwan, Stanley (1957-) Rouge 1987; The Actress 1992

Kwapis, Ken (1957-) Follow That Bird 1985; Vibes 1988; He Said, She Said 1991; Dunston Checks In 1996; The Beautician and the Beast 1997; The Sisterhood of the Traveling Pants 2005; License to Wed 2007; He's Just Not That into You 2008; Big Miracle 2012; A Walk in the Woods 2015

Kwietniowski, Richard (1957-) Love and Death on Long Island 1998; Owning Mahowny 2002

Kyung Ho Lee The Reef 2006; Garfield Gets Real 2007

L

La Cava, Gregory (1892-1952) Big News 1929; The Half Naked Truth 1932; Symphony of Six Million 1932; Gabriel over the White House 1933; The Affairs of Cellini 1934; Gallant Lady 1934; What Every Woman Knows 1934; Private Worlds 1935; She Married Her Boss 1935; My Man Godfrey 1936; Stage Door 1937; 5th Ave Girl 1939; Primrose Path 1940; Unfinished Business 1941; Lady in a Jam 1942; Living in a Big Way 1947

Labaki, Nadine Caramel 2007; Where Do We Go Now? 2011

LaBute, Neil (1963-) In the Company of Men 1997; Your Friends & Neighbors 1998; Nurse Betty 2000; Possession 2002; The Shape of Things 2003; The Wicker Man 2006; Lakeview Terrace 2008; Death at a Funeral 2010

Lachman, Harry (1886-1975) Baby, Take a Bow 1934; George White's Scandals 1934; Dante's Inferno 1935; Charlie Chan at the Circus 1936; The Man Who Lived Twice 1936; Our Relations 1936; Charlie Chan in Rio 1941

Lacombe, Georges (1902-1990) Martin Roumagnac 1946; The Seven Deadly Sins 1952; The Light across the Street 1956

Lado, Aldo aka **Lewis, George B** (1934-) The Short Night of the Glass Dolls 1971; The Humanoid 1979

LaDuca, Rob The Lion King II: Simba's Pride 1998; Joseph: King of Dreams 2000

Lafia, John The Blue Iguana 1988; Child's Play 2 1990; Man's Best Friend 1993

Lafosse, Joachim Private Property 2006; Our Children 2012

LaGravenese, Richard (1959-) Living Out Loud 1998; Freedom Writers 2006; Paris, Je T'Aime 2006; PS I Love You 2007; Beautiful Creatures 2013; The Last 5 Years 2014

Lahiff, Craig (1947-) Heaven's Burning 1997; Black and White 2002

LaLoggia, Frank (1954-) Fear No Evil 1980; Lady in White 1988; The Haunted Heart 1995

Laloux, René (1929-2004) Fantastic Planet 1973; Light Years 1988

Lam, Ringo aka **Lam Ling-Tung** (1954-) City on Fire 1987; Wild Search 1989; Full Contact 1992; Twin Dragons 1992; Maximum Risk 1996; Full Alert 1997; Replicant 2001; In Hell 2003

Lambert, Mary (1951-) Siesta 1987; Pet Sematary 1989; Pet Sematary II 1992; The In Crowd 2000

Lamont, Charles (1898-1993) Hit the Ice 1943; The Merry Monahans 1944; Frontier Gal 1945; Salome, Where She Danced 1945; Slave Girl 1947; Ma and Pa Kettle 1949; Abbott and Costello in the Foreign Legion 1950; I Was a Shoplifter 1950; Abbott and Costello Meet the Invisible Man 1951; Abbott and Costello Meet Captain Kidd 1952; Abbott and Costello Go to Mars 1953; Abbott and Costello Meet Dr Jekyll and Mr Hyde 1953; Abbott and Costello Meet the Keystone Cops 1955; Abbott and Costello Meet the Mummy 1955; Francis in the Haunted House 1956

Lamorisse, Albert (1922-1970) White Mane 1952; The Red Balloon 1956

Lamprell, Mark My Mother Frank 2000; Goddess 2013

Landers, Lew aka **Friedlander, Louis** (1901-1962) The Raven 1935; Stormy 1935; Danger Patrol 1937; Flight from Glory 1937; Annabel Takes a Tour 1938; Condemned Women 1938; Smashing the Rackets 1938; The Boogie Man Will Get You 1942; The Return of the Vampire

1943; Thunder Mountain 1947; Captain Kidd and the Slave Girl 1954

Landesman, Peter Parkland 2013; Concussion 2015

Landis, John (1950-) Schlock 1971; The Kentucky Fried Movie 1977; National Lampoon's Animal House 1978; The Blues Brothers 1980; An American Werewolf in London 1981; Trading Places 1983; Twilight Zone: the Movie 1983; Into the Night 1985; Spies like Us 1985; Three Amigos! 1986; Amazon Women on the Moon 1987; Coming to America 1988; Oscar 1991; Innocent Blood 1992; Beverly Hills Cop III 1994; The Stupids 1995; Blues Brothers 2000 1998; Susan's Plan 1998; Burke & Hare 2010

Landres, Paul (1912-2001) Last of the Badmen 1957; The Return of Dracula 1958; Go, Johnny, Go! 1959; Son of a Gunfighter 1964

Lane (3), Charles (1953-) Sidewalk Stories 1989; True Identity 1991

Lane, David Thunderbirds Are Go! 1966; Thunderbird 6 1968

Lanfield, Sidney (1900-1972) Red Salute 1935; King of Burlesque 1936; One in a Million 1936; Sing, Baby, Sing 1936; Thin Ice 1937; Wake Up and Live 1937; Always Goodbye 1938; The Hound of the Baskervilles 1939; Second Fiddle 1939; Swanee River 1939; You'll Never Get Rich 1941; My Favorite Blonde 1942; Let's Face It 1943; The Meanest Man in the World 1943; Standing Room Only 1944; Bring On the Girls 1945; The Well Groomed Bride 1946; Where There's Life 1947; Station West 1948; Sorrowful Jones 1949; Follow the Sun: the Ben Hogan Story 1951; The Lemon Drop Kid 1951; Skirts Ahoy! 1952

Lang, Fritz (1890-1976) The Spiders 1919; Destiny 1921; Dr Mabuse, the Gambler 1922; The Nibelungen 1924; Metropolis 1926; Spies 1928; The Woman in the Moon 1929; M 1931; The Testament of Dr Mabuse 1932; Fury 1936; You Only Live Once 1937; You and Me 1938; The Return of Frank James 1940; Man Hunt 1941; Western Union 1941; Hangmen Also Die! 1943; Ministry of Fear 1945; Scarlet Street 1945; The Woman in the Window 1945; Cloak and Dagger 1946; Secret beyond the Door 1948; An American Guerrilla in the Philippines 1950; House by the River 1950; Clash by Night 1952; Rancho Notorious 1952; The Big Heat 1953; The Blue Gardenia 1953; Human Desire 1954; Moonfleet 1955; Beyond a Reasonable Doubt 1956; While the City Sleeps 1956; The Indian Tomb 1959; The Tiger of Eschnapur 1959; The Thousand Eyes of Dr Mabuse 1960

Lang, Walter (1898-1972) Meet the Baron 1933; The Mighty Barnum 1934; Love before Breakfast 1936; Wife, Doctor and Nurse 1937; The Baroness and the Butler 1938; The Little Princess 1939; The Blue Bird 1940; Star Dust 1940; Tin Pan Alley 1940; Moon over Miami 1941; Weekend in Havana 1941; The Magnificent Dope 1942; Song of the Islands 1942; Coney Island 1943; Greenwich Village 1944; State Fair 1945; Claudia and David 1946; Sentimental Journey 1946; Mother Wore Tights 1947; Sitting Pretty 1948; When My Baby Smiles at Me 1948; You're My Everything 1949; Cheaper by the Dozen 1950; The Jackpot 1950; On the Riviera 1951; With a Song in My Heart 1952; Call Me Madam 1953; There's No Business like Show Business 1954; The King and I 1956; Desk Set 1957; But Not for Me 1959; Can-Can 1960; The Marriage-Go-Round 1960

Langley, Noel (1911-1980) The Pickwick Papers 1952; Our Girl Friday 1953

Langton, Simon (1941-) Anna Karenina 1985; The Whistle Blower 1986; Forbidden Territory: Stanley's Search for Livingstone 1997

Lanoff, Lawrence Indecent Behavior 1993; Temptress 1995

Lanskaya, Yelena Hidden Places 2006; Hybrid 2007

Lanthimos, Yorgos Dogtooth 2009; Alps 2011; The Lobster 2015

Lanzmann, Claude (1925-) Shoah 1985; Sobibor: 14 October 1943, 16:00 2001; The Last of the Unjust 2013

Lapine, James (1949-) Impromptu 1991; Life with Mikey 1993; Passion 1996; Earthly Possessions 1999

Larkin, John (1912-1965) Quiet Please, Murder 1942; Circumstantial Evidence 1945

Larraín, Pablo Tony Manero 2008; Post Mortem 2010; No 2012; The Club 2015

Larry, Sheldon (1949-) Terminal Choice 1983; Revenge of the Middle-Aged Woman 2004

Lartigau, Eric I Do 2006; The Big Picture 2010; The Players 2012; La Famille Bélier 2014

Lasseter, John (1957-) Toy Story 1995; A Bug's Life 1998; Toy Story 2 1999; Cars 2006; Ponyo 2008; Cars 2 2011; Toy Story 4 2017

Lattuada, Alberto (1914-2005) Love in the City 1953; Tempest 1959; Fraulein Doktor 1968

Lau, Andrew (1960-) Young and Dangerous 1996; A Man Called Hero 1999; Infernal Affairs 2002; Infernal Affairs II 2003; Infernal Affairs 3 2003; Initial D - Drift Racer 2005; The Flock 2007; Legend of the Fist: the Return of Chen Zhen 2010; Revenge of the Green Dragons 2013

Laughlin, Michael Strange Invaders 1983; Mesmerized 1984

Laughlin, Tom aka **Frank, T C** aka **Laughlin, Frank** (1931-2013) Born Losers 1967; The Master Gunfighter 1975

Launder, Frank (1907-1997) Millions like Us 1943; Two Thousand Women 1944; I See a Dark Stranger 1946; Captain Boycott 1947; The Blue Lagoon 1949; The Happiest Days of Your Life 1950; Lady Godiva Rides Again 1951; Folly to Be Wise 1952; The Belles of St Trinian's 1954; Geordie 1955; Blue Murder at St Trinian's 1957; The Bridal Path 1959; The Pure Hell of St Trinian's 1960; Joey Boy 1965; The Great St Trinian's Train Robbery 1966; The Wildcats of St Trinian's 1980

Lautner, Georges (1926-2013) Man in the Trunk 1973; Someone Is Bleeding 1974; No Problem! 1975; Double Dare 1981; The Professional 1981; La Cage aux Folles III: "Elles" Se Marient 1985

Lauzon, Jean-Claude (1953-1997) Night Zoo 1987; Léolo 1992

Laven, Arnold (1922-) Vice Squad 1953; Down Three Dark Streets 1954; The Rack 1956; The Monster That Challenged the World 1957; Slaughter on Tenth Avenue 1957; Anna Lucasta 1958; Geronimo 1962; The Glory Guys 1965; Rough Night in Jericho 1967; Sam Whiskey 1969

Law, Clara (1954-) Autumn Moon 1992; Erotique 1994

Lawlor, Joe Helen 2008; Mister John 2013

Lawrence, Francis (1971-) Constantine 2005; I Am Legend 2007; Water for Elephants 2011; The Hunger Games: Catching Fire 2013; The Hunger Games: Mockingjay Part 1 2014; The Hunger Games: Mockingjay Part 2 2015

Lawrence (2), Marc (1959-) Two Weeks Notice 2002; Music and Lyrics 2007; Did You Hear about the Morgans? 2009; The Rewrite 2014

Lawrence, Quentin (1920-1979) The Trollenberg Terror 1958; Cash on Demand 1961; The Man Who Finally Died 1962

Lawrence, Ray Bliss 1985; Lantana 2001; Jindabyne 2006

Lawton, J F (1960-) Cannibal Women in the Avocado Jungle of Death 1989; The Hunted 1995

Laxton, Richard Life & Lyrics 2006; Grow Your Own 2007; Effie Gray 2014

Le Borg, Reginald aka LeBorg, Reginald (1902-1989) Calling Dr Death 1943; Dead Man's Eyes 1944; The Mummy's Ghost 1944; Weird Woman 1944; Wyoming Mail 1950; The Black Sleep 1956; Diary of a Madman 1963

Le Chanois, Jean-Paul (1909-1985) La Vie Est à Nous 1936; The Case of Dr Laurent 1957; Les Misérables 1957

Le Guay, Philippe (1956-) Nightshift 2000; The Women on the 6th Floor 2010; Cycling with Molière 2013

Leach, Wilford (1929-1988) The Wedding Party 1966; The Pirates of Penzance 1983

Leacock, Philip (1917-1990) Appointment in London 1952; The Brave Don't Cry 1952; The Kidnappers 1953; The Spanish Gardener 1956; High Tide at Noon 1957; Innocent Sinners 1957; Take a Giant Step 1959; Let No Man Write My Epitaph 1960; Reach for Glory

1962; 13 West Street 1962; The War Lover 1962; Tamahine 1963; Adam's Woman 1970

Lean, David (1908-1991) Major Barbara 1941; In Which We Serve 1942; This Happy Breed 1944; Blithe Spirit 1945; Brief Encounter 1945; Great Expectations 1946; Oliver Twist 1948; The Passionate Friends 1948; Madeleine 1949; The Sound Barrier 1952; Hobson's Choice 1953; Summertime 1955; The Bridge on the River Kwai 1957; Lawrence of Arabia 1962; Doctor Zhivago 1965; Ryan's Daughter 1970; A Passage to India 1984

Leconte, Patrice (1947-) Monsieur Hire 1989; The Hairdresser's Husband 1990; Le Parfum d'Yvonne 1994; Ridicule 1996; The Girl on the Bridge 1999; La Veuve de Saint-Pierre 2000; L'Homme du Train 2002; Confidences Trop Intimes 2004; My Best Friend 2006; A Promise 2013

Leder, Herbert J The Frozen Dead 1966; It! 1966; The Candy Man 1969

Leder, Mimi (1952-) The Peacemaker 1997; Deep Impact 1998; Pay It Forward 2000

Lederer, Charles (1906-1976) Fingers at the Window 1942; Never Steal Anything Small 1959

Lee Thompson, J (1914-2002) Murder without Crime 1950; The Yellow Balloon 1952; The Weak and the Wicked 1953; For Better, for Worse 1954; An Alligator Named Daisy 1955; As Long as They're Happy 1955; The Good Companions 1956; Yield to the Night 1956; Woman in a Dressing Gown 1957; Ice Cold in Alex 1958; No Trees in the Street 1958; North West Frontier 1959; Tiger Bay 1959; I Aim at the Stars 1960; The Guns of Navarone 1961; Cape Fear 1962; Taras Bulba 1962; Kings of the Sun 1963; John Goldfarb, Please Come Home 1964; What a Way to Go! 1964; Return from the Ashes 1965; Eye of the Devil 1966; Before Winter Comes 1968; The Chairman 1969; Mackenna's Gold 1969; Country Dance 1970; Conquest of the Planet of the Apes 1972; Battle for the Planet of the Apes 1973; Huckleberry Finn 1974; The Reincarnation of Peter Proud 1975; St Ives 1976; The White Buffalo 1977; The Greek Tycoon 1978; The Passage 1978; Happy Birthday to Me 1981; 10 to Midnight 1983; The Ambassador 1984; The Evil That Men Do 1984; King Solomon's Mines 1985; Firewalker 1986; Murphy's Law 1986; Death Wish 4: the Crackdown 1987; Messenger of Death 1988; Kinjite: Forbidden Subjects 1989

Lee, Ang (1954-) Pushing Hands 1991; The Wedding Banquet 1993; Eat Drink Man Woman 1994; Sense and Sensibility 1995; The Ice Storm 1997; Ride with the Devil 1999; Crouching Tiger, Hidden Dragon 2000; Hulk 2003; Brokeback Mountain 2005; Lust, Caution 2007; Taking Woodstock 2009; Life of Pi 2012

Lee, Damian (1950-) Food of the Gods II 1989; Agent Red 2000; A Dark Truth 2012

Lee, Daniel Black Mask 1996; Dragon Blade 2015

Lee (2), Jack (1913-2002) Once a Jolly Swagman 1948; The Wooden Horse 1950; South of Algiers 1952; Turn the Key Softly 1953; A Town like Alice 1956; Robbery under Arms 1957; The Captain's Table 1958; Circle of Deception 1960

Lee, Malcolm D (1970-) The Best Man 1999; Undercover Brother 2002; Soul Men 2008; Welcome Home Roscoe Jenkins 2008; The Best Man Holiday 2013; Scary Movie V 2013; Barbershop: a Fresh Cut 2016

Lee, Rowland V (1891-1975) Paramount on Parade 1930; The Return of Dr Fu Manchu 1930; The Sign of Four 1932; Zoo in Budapest 1933; The Count of Monte Cristo 1934; Cardinal Richelieu 1935; The Three Musketeers 1935; Love from a Stranger 1936; One Rainy Afternoon 1936; The Toast of New York 1937; Son of Frankenstein 1939; Tower of London 1939; Son of Monte Cristo 1940; Captain Kidd 1945

Lee, Spike (1957-) She's Gotta Have It 1986; School Daze 1988; Do the Right Thing 1989; Mo' Better Blues 1990; Jungle Fever 1991; Malcolm X 1992; Crooklyn 1994; Clockers 1995; Get on the Bus 1996; Girl 6 1996; 4

Little Girls 1997; *He Got Game* 1998; *Summer of Sam* 1999; *Bamboozled* 2000; *The Original Kings of Comedy* 2000; *Ten Minutes Older: the Trumpet* 2002; *25th Hour* 2002; *She Hate Me* 2004; *Inside Man* 2006; *Old Boy* 2013

Leeds, Herbert I (1900-1984) *The Cisco Kid and the Lady* 1939; *Mr Moto in Danger Island* 1939; *The Return of the Cisco Kid* 1939

Lefler, Doug *Dragonheart: a New Beginning* 1999; *The Last Legion* 2006

Lefresne, Anthony *A Sister's Secret* 2009; *The Girl He Met Online* 2014

Lehmann, Michael (1957-) *Heathers* 1989; *Hudson Hawk* 1991; *Meet the Applegates* 1991; *Airheads* 1994; *The Truth about Cats and Dogs* 1996; *My Giant* 1998; *40 Days and 40 Nights* 2002; *Because I Said So* 2007

Leifer, Neil *Yesterday's Hero* 1979; *Trading Hearts* 1988

Leigh, Mike (1943-) *Bleak Moments* 1971; *Abigail's Party* 1977; *High Hopes* 1988; *Life Is Sweet* 1990; *Naked* 1993; *Secrets & Lies* 1995; *Career Girls* 1997; *Topsy-Turvy* 1999; *All or Nothing* 2002; *Vera Drake* 2004; *Happy-Go-Lucky* 2007; *Another Year* 2010; *Mr Turner* 2014

Leiner, Danny *Dude, Where's My Car?* 2000; *Harold & Kumar Get the Munchies* 2004

Leisen, Mitchell (1898-1972) *Death Takes a Holiday* 1934; *Hands across the Table* 1935; *The Big Broadcast of 1937* 1936; *The Big Broadcast of 1938* 1937; *Easy Living* 1937; *Swing High, Swing Low* 1937; *Midnight* 1939; *Arise, My Love* 1940; *Remember the Night* 1940; *Hold Back the Dawn* 1941; *I Wanted Wings* 1941; *The Lady Is Willing* 1942; *Take a Letter, Darling* 1942; *No Time for Love* 1943; *Frenchman's Creek* 1944; *Lady in the Dark* 1944; *Practically Yours* 1944; *Kitty* 1945; *To Each His Own* 1946; *Golden Earrings* 1947; *Suddenly It's Spring* 1947; *Dream Girl* 1948; *Bride of Vengeance* 1949; *Captain Carey, USA* 1950; *No Man of Her Own* 1950; *Darling, How Could You!* 1951; *The Mating Season* 1951; *Young Man with Ideas* 1952; *Tonight We Sing* 1953; *Bedevilled* 1955; *The Girl Most Likely* 1957

Leitch, Christopher *Teen Wolf Too* 1987; *Courage Mountain* 1989; *A Christmas Visitor* 2002; *Secrets in the Walls* 2010

Leland, David (1947-) *Wish You Were Here* 1987; *Checking Out* 1988; *The Big Man* 1990; *The Land Girls* 1997; *Concert for George* 2003

Lelouch, Claude (1937-) *Un Homme et une Femme* 1966; *Far from Vietnam* 1967; *Vivre pour Vivre* 1967; *Visions of Eight* 1973; *And Now My Love* 1974; *Second Chance* 1976; *Another Man, Another Chance* 1977; *Robert et Robert* 1978; *An Adventure for Two* 1979; *Les Uns et les Autres* 1981; *Edith et Marcel* 1983; *A Man and a Woman: 20 Years Later* 1986; *Les Misérables* 1995; *Men, Women: a User's Manual* 1996; *Chance or Coincidence* 1999; *And Now... Ladies and Gentlemen* 2002; *11'09"01 - September 11* 2002

Lembeck, Michael (1948-) *The Santa Clause 2* 2002; *Connie and Carla* 2004; *The Santa Clause 3: the Escape Clause* 2006; *Tooth Fairy* 2009; *Sharpay's Fabulous Adventure* 2011

Lemmons, Kasi (1961-) *Eve's Bayou* 1997; *Talk to Me* 2007

Lemont, John (1914-2004) *The Shakedown* 1959; *And Women Shall Weep* 1960; *Konga* 1960; *The Frightened City* 1961

Lemorande, Rusty *Journey to the Center of the Earth* 1989; *The Turn of the Screw* 1992

Leni, Paul (1885-1929) *Waxworks* 1924; *The Cat and the Canary* 1927; *The Last Warning* 1928; *The Man Who Laughs* 1928

Lenzi, Umberto aka **Milestone, Hank** (1931-) *Sandokan the Great* 1963; *From Hell to Victory* 1979

Leonard, Brett *The Lawnmower Man* 1992; *Hideaway* 1995; *Virtuosity* 1995; *Feed* 2005; *Highlander: the Source* 2007

Leonard, Herbert B (1922-) *The Perils of Pauline* 1967; *Going Home* 1971

Leonard, Robert Z (1889-1968) *The Divorcee* 1930; *The Bachelor Father* 1931; *Susan Lenox: Her Fall and Rise* 1931; *Strange Interlude* 1932; *Dancing Lady* 1933; *Peg o' My Heart* 1933;

After Office Hours 1935; *Escapade* 1935; *The Great Ziegfeld* 1936; *Piccadilly Jim* 1936; *The Firefly* 1937; *Maytime* 1937; *The Girl of the Golden West* 1938; *Broadway Serenade* 1939; *New Moon* 1940; *Pride and Prejudice* 1940; *Third Finger, Left Hand* 1940; *When Ladies Meet* 1941; *Ziegfeld Girl* 1941; *Stand by for Action* 1942; *The Man from Down Under* 1943; *Marriage Is a Private Affair* 1944; *Week-End at the Waldorf* 1945; *The Secret Heart* 1946; *Cynthia* 1947; *BF's Daughter* 1948; *The Bribe* 1949; *In the Good Old Summertime* 1949; *Duchess of Idaho* 1950; *Nancy Goes to Rio* 1950; *The Clown* 1952; *Her Twelve Men* 1954; *Beautiful but Dangerous* 1955; *The King's Thief* 1955

Leone, Sergio (1929-1989) *The Colossus of Rhodes* 1961; *Sodom and Gomorrah* 1962; *A Fistful of Dollars* 1964; *For a Few Dollars More* 1965; *The Good, the Bad and the Ugly* 1966; *Once upon a Time in the West* 1968; *A Fistful of Dynamite* 1971; *Once upon a Time in America* 1984

Leonetti, John R *Mortal Kombat: Annihilation* 1997; *Annabelle* 2014

Leong, Po Chih *The Wisdom of Crocodiles* 1998; *Out of Reach* 2004; *The Detonator* 2006

Lepage, Robert (1957-) *The Confessional* 1995; *Possible Worlds* 2000

Lerner, Dan *Shame* 1992; *Hit and Run* 1999

Lerner, Irving (1909-1976) *Murder by Contract* 1958; *City of Fear* 1959; *The Royal Hunt of the Sun* 1969

Lerner, Murray *Festival* 1967; *From Mao to Mozart: Isaac Stern in China* 1980; *Message to Love* 1995

LeRoy, Mervyn (1900-1987) *Five Star Final* 1931; *Little Caesar* 1931; *High Pressure* 1932; *I Am a Fugitive from a Chain Gang* 1932; *Three on a Match* 1932; *Two Seconds* 1932; *Gold Diggers of 1933* 1933; *Hard to Handle* 1933; *Tugboat Annie* 1933; *The World Changes* 1933; *Hi, Nellie!* 1934; *I Found Stella Parish* 1935; *Page Miss Glory* 1935; *Sweet Adeline* 1935; *Anthony Adverse* 1936; *They Won't Forget* 1937; *Fools for Scandal* 1938; *Escape* 1940; *Waterloo Bridge* 1940; *Blossoms in the Dust* 1941; *Johnny Eager* 1941; *Unholy Partners* 1941; *Random Harvest* 1942; *Madame Curie* 1943; *Thirty Seconds over Tokyo* 1944; *Without Reservations* 1946; *Homecoming* 1948; *Any Number Can Play* 1949; *East Side, West Side* 1949; *Little Women* 1949; *Quo Vadis* 1951; *Lovely to Look At* 1952; *Million Dollar Mermaid* 1952; *Latin Lovers* 1953; *Rose Marie* 1954; *Mister Roberts* 1955; *Strange Lady in Town* 1955; *The Bad Seed* 1956; *Toward the Unknown* 1956; *Home before Dark* 1958; *No Time for Sergeants* 1958; *The FBI Story* 1959; *The Devil at Four o'Clock* 1961; *A Majority of One* 1961; *Gypsy* 1962; *Mary, Mary* 1963; *Moment to Moment* 1966

Lester, Mark L (1946-) *Truck Stop Women* 1974; *Class of 1984* 1982; *Firestarter* 1984; *Commando* 1985; *Armed and Dangerous* 1986; *Class of 1999* 1990; *Showdown in Little Tokyo* 1991; *Night of the Running Man* 1994; *Blowback* 1999; *Hitman's Run* 1999

Lester, Richard aka **Lester, Dick** (1932-) *The Running, Jumping and Standing Still Film* 1959; *It's Trad, Dad* 1961; *The Mouse on the Moon* 1963; *A Hard Day's Night* 1964; *Help!* 1965; *The Knack... and How to Get It* 1965; *A Funny Thing Happened on the Way to the Forum* 1966; *How I Won the War* 1967; *Petulia* 1968; *The Bed Sitting Room* 1969; *The Three Musketeers* 1973; *The Four Musketeers* 1974; *Juggernaut* 1974; *Royal Flash* 1975; *The Ritz* 1976; *Robin and Marian* 1976; *Butch and Sundance: the Early Days* 1979; *Cuba* 1979; *Superman II* 1980; *Superman III* 1983; *Finders Keepers* 1984; *The Return of the Musketeers* 1989; *Get Back* 1991

Leterrier, Louis (1973-) *The Transporter 2* 2005; *Unleashed* 2005; *The Incredible Hulk* 2008; *Clash of the Titans* 2010; *Now You See Me* 2013; *Grimsby* 2016

Leth, Asger *Ghosts of Cité Soleil* 2005; *Man on a Ledge* 2012

Letterman, Rob *Shark Tale* 2004; *Monsters vs Aliens* 2009; *Gulliver's Travels* 2010; *Goosebumps* 2015

Lettich, Sheldon (1962-) *AWOL* 1990; *Double Impact* 1991; *Only the Strong* 1993; *The Order* 2001; *The Hard Corps* 2006

Letts, Don *The Punk Rock Movie* 1978; *Dancehall Queen* 1996; *One Love* 2003

Levant, Brian (1952-) *Problem Child 2* 1991; *Beethoven* 1992; *The Flintstones* 1994; *Little Giants* 1994; *Jingle All the Way* 1996; *The Flintstones in Viva Rock Vegas* 2000; *Snow Dogs* 2002; *Are We There Yet?* 2005; *The Spy Next Door* 2009

Levey, William A (1943-) *The Happy Hooker Goes to Washington* 1977; *Skatetown, USA* 1979

Levien, David *Knockaround Guys* 2001; *Solitary Man* 2009

Levin, Henry (1901-1980) *Cry of the Werewolf* 1944; *The Bandit of Sherwood Forest* 1946; *The Guilt of Janet Ames* 1947; *The Man from Colorado* 1948; *And Baby Makes Three* 1949; *Jolson Sings Again* 1949; *Convicted* 1950; *The Petty Girl* 1950; *Belles on Their Toes* 1952; *The Farmer Takes a Wife* 1953; *The President's Lady* 1953; *The Dark Avenger* 1955; *April Love* 1957; *The Lonely Man* 1957; *A Nice Little Bank That Should Be Robbed* 1958; *Holiday for Lovers* 1959; *Journey to the Center of the Earth* 1959; *The Remarkable Mr Pennypacker* 1959; *Where the Boys Are* 1960; *Come Fly with Me* 1962; *If a Man Answers* 1962; *The Wonderful World of the Brothers Grimm* 1962; *Honeymoon Hotel* 1964; *Kiss the Girls and Make Them Die* 1966

Levin, Marc *The Last Party* 1993; *Slam* 1998; *Whiteboys* 1999; *The Blues, a Musical Journey: Godfathers and Sons* 2003

Levin, Mark *Little Manhattan* 2005; *Nim's Island* 2008

Levin, Peter *A Doctor's Story* 1984; *Death in the Shadows: the Sam Sheppard Story* 1998; *Homeless to Harvard: the Liz Murray Story* 2003; *A Perfect Day* 2006

Levine, Jonathan *All the Boys Love Mandy Lane* 2006; *The Wackness* 2008; *50/50* 2011; *Warm Bodies* 2012; *The Night Before* 2015

Levinson, Barry (1942-) *Diner* 1982; *The Natural* 1984; *Young Sherlock Holmes* 1985; *Good Morning, Vietnam* 1987; *Tin Men* 1987; *Rain Man* 1988; *Avalon* 1990; *Bugsy* 1991; *Toys* 1992; *Disclosure* 1994; *Jimmy Hollywood* 1994; *Sleepers* 1996; *Wag the Dog* 1997; *Sphere* 1998; *Liberty Heights* 1999; *An Everlasting Piece* 2000; *Bandits* 2001; *Envy* 2003; *Man of the Year* 2006; *What Just Happened?* 2007; *You Don't Know Jack* 2010; *The Bay* 2012; *Rock the Kasbah* 2015

Levitow, Abe (1922-1975) *Gay Purr-ee* 1962; *The Phantom Tollbooth* 1969

Levring, Kristian (1957-) *The King Is Alive* 2000; *The Salvation* 2014

Levy, Eugene (1946-) *Once upon a Crime* 1992; *Sodbusters* 1994

Levy, Ralph (1920-2001) *Bedtime Story* 1964; *Do Not Disturb* 1965

Levy, Shawn (1968-) *Big Fat Liar* 2002; *Cheaper by the Dozen* 2003; *Just Married* 2003; *Night at the Museum* 2006; *The Pink Panther* 2006; *Night at the Museum 2* 2009; *Date Night* 2010; *Real Steel* 2011; *The Internship* 2013; *Night at the Museum: Secret of the Tomb* 2014; *This Is Where I Leave You* 2014

Lewin, Albert (1916-1996) *The Moon and Sixpence* 1942; *The Picture of Dorian Gray* 1945; *The Private Affairs of Bel Ami* 1947; *Pandora and the Flying Dutchman* 1950; *Saadia* 1953; *The Living Idol* 1955

Lewin, Ben (1946-) *Georgia* 1988; *The Favour, the Watch and the Very Big Fish* 1991; *The Sessions* 2012

Lewis, Brad *Ponyo* 2008; *Cars 2* 2011

Lewis, Herschell Gordon aka **Lewis, Herschell G** (1926-) *Blood Feast* 1963; *Two Thousand Maniacs!* 1964; *Color Me Blood Red* 1965; *The Gruesome Twosome* 1967; *She-Devils on Wheels* 1968; *The Wizard of Gore* 1970; *The Gore-Gore Girls* 1972

Lewis, Jay (1914-1969) *The Baby and the Battleship* 1956; *Invasion Quartet* 1961; *Live Now - Pay Later* 1962

Lewis, Jerry (1926-) *The Bellboy* 1960; *The Errand Boy* 1961; *The Ladies' Man* 1961; *The Nutty*

Professor 1963; *The Patsy* 1964; *The Family Jewels* 1965; *Three on a Couch* 1966; *The Big Mouth* 1967; *One More Time* 1970; *Which Way to the Front?* 1970

Lewis, Joseph H aka **Lewis, Joseph** (1907-2000) *Boys of the City* 1940; *Invisible Ghost* 1941; *Pride of the Bowery* 1941; *The Mad Doctor of Market Street* 1942; *The Falcon in San Francisco* 1945; *My Name Is Julia Ross* 1945; *So Dark the Night* 1946; *The Return of October* 1948; *Gun Crazy* 1949; *The Undercover Man* 1949; *A Lady without Passport* 1950; *Desperate Search* 1952; *Retreat, Hell!* 1952; *Cry of the Hunted* 1953; *The Big Combo* 1955; *A Lawless Street* 1955; *7th Cavalry* 1956; *The Halliday Brand* 1957; *Terror in a Texas Town* 1958

Lewis, Mark T aka **Lewis, Mark** *Cane Toads - an Unnatural History* 1987; *Cane Toads: the Conquest* 2010

Lewis, Richard J *Whale Music* 1994; *Barney's Version* 2010

Lewis (1), Robert (1909-1997) *Ziegfeld Follies* 1944; *Anything Goes* 1956

Lewis, Robert Michael aka **Lewis, Robert** (1934-) *The Invisible Man* 1975; *Agatha Christie's A Caribbean Mystery* 1983; *Agatha Christie's Sparkling Cyanide* 1983; *Don't Talk to Strangers* 1994

Leyburn, Glenn *Cherrybomb* 2008; *Good Vibrations* 2012

Leytes, Joseph aka **Leytes, Josef** *Valley of Mystery* 1967; *The Counterfeit Killer* 1968

L'Herbier, Marcel (1888-1979) *L'Inhumaine* 1923; *La Nuit Fantastique* 1942

Liapis, Peter *Captured* 1998; *Alone with a Stranger* 2000

Lieberman, Jeff *Squirm* 1976; *Blue Sunshine* 1977; *Just before Dawn* 1980; *Remote Control* 1988

Lieberman, Robert (1941-) *Table for Five* 1983; *All I Want for Christmas* 1991; *Fire in the Sky* 1993; *D3: the Mighty Ducks* 1996; *Eve of Destruction* 2013

Liebesman, Jonathan (1976-) *Darkness Falls* 2003; *The Texas Chainsaw Massacre: the Beginning* 2006; *Battle Los Angeles* 2011; *Wrath of the Titans* 2012; *Teenage Mutant Ninja Turtles* 2014

Lifshitz, Sébastien (1968-) *Presque Rien* 2000; *Wild Side* 2004

Lima, Kevin (1962-) *A Goofy Movie* 1995; *Tarzan* 1999; *102 Dalmatians* 2000; *Eloise at the Plaza* 2003; *Enchanted* 2007

Liman, Doug (1965-) *Getting In* 1994; *Swingers* 1996; *Go* 1999; *The Bourne Identity* 2002; *Mr & Mrs Smith* 2005; *Jumper* 2008; *Fair Game* 2010; *Edge of Tomorrow* 2014; *Mena* 2017

Lin, Justin (1971-) *Better Luck Tomorrow* 2001; *Annapolis* 2005; *The Fast and the Furious: Tokyo Drift* 2006; *Fast & Furious* 2009; *Fast Five* 2011; *Fast & Furious 6* 2013; *Star Trek Beyond* 2016

Lindholm, Tobias *R* 2010; *A Hijacking* 2012; *A War* 2015

Lindsay-Hogg, Michael (1940-) *Let It Be* 1970; *Nasty Habits* 1976; *Nazi Hunter: the Beate Klarsfeld Story* 1986; *The Object of Beauty* 1991; *Frankie Starlight* 1995; *The Rolling Stones Rock and Roll Circus* 1995; *Guy* 1996; *Two of Us* 2000

Linfield, Mark *Earth* 2007; *Chimpanzee* 2012

Linklater, Richard (1961-) *Slacker* 1989; *Dazed and Confused* 1993; *Before Sunrise* 1995; *subUrbia* 1996; *The Newton Boys* 1998; *Tape* 2001; *Waking Life* 2001; *The School of Rock* 2003; *Before Sunset* 2004; *Bad News Bears* 2005; *Fast Food Nation* 2006; *A Scanner Darkly* 2006; *Me and Orson Welles* 2008; *Bernie* 2011; *Before Midnight* 2013; *Boyhood* 2014; *Everybody Wants Some!!* 2016

Linson, Art (1942-) *Where the Buffalo Roam* 1980; *The Wild Life* 1984

Lisberger, Steven (1951-) *Animalympics* 1979; *Tron* 1982; *Hot Pursuit* 1987; *Slipstream* 1989

Little, Dwight H aka **Little, Dwight** (1956-) *Halloween 4: the Return of Michael Myers* 1988; *The Phantom of the Opera* 1989; *Marked for Death* 1990; *Rapid Fire* 1992; *Free Willy 2: the Adventure Home* 1995; *Murder at 1600* 1997; *Anacondas: the Hunt for the Blood Orchid* 2004

Litvak, Anatole aka **Litvak, Major Anatole** (1902-1974) *Mayerling* 1936; *Tovarich* 1937; *The Woman I Love* 1937; *The Amazing Dr Clitterhouse* 1938; *The Sisters* 1938; *Confessions of a Nazi Spy* 1939; *All This, and Heaven Too* 1940; *Castle on the Hudson* 1940; *City for Conquest* 1940; *Blues in the Night* 1941; *Out of the Fog* 1941; *This above All* 1942; *The Battle of Russia* 1943; *Prelude to War* 1943; *The Long Night* 1947; *The Snake Pit* 1948; *Sorry, Wrong Number* 1948; *Decision before Dawn* 1951; *Act of Love* 1953; *The Deep Blue Sea* 1955; *Anastasia* 1956; *Goodbye Again* 1961; *Five Miles to Midnight* 1963; *The Night of the Generals* 1966

Lively, Gerry *Darkness Falls* 1998; *Dungeons & Dragons: Wrath of the Dragon God* 2005

Lizzani, Carlo aka **Beaver, Lee W** (1922-2013) *Love in the City* 1953; *The Dirty Game* 1965; *The Hills Run Red* 1966; *Requiescant* 1967; *The Last Days of Mussolini* 1974

Llosa, Luis *Hour of the Assassin* 1987; *Sniper* 1992; *800 Leagues down the Amazon* 1993; *The Specialist* 1994; *Anaconda* 1997

Lloyd, Frank (1886-1960) *Oliver Twist* 1922; *The Sea Hawk* 1924; *The Divine Lady* 1928; *East Lynne* 1931; *Berkeley Square* 1933; *Cavalcade* 1933; *Mutiny on the Bounty* 1935; *Under Two Flags* 1936; *Wells Fargo* 1937; *If I Were King* 1938; *Rulers of the Sea* 1939; *The Howards of Virginia* 1940; *Forever and a Day* 1943; *Blood on the Sun* 1945; *The Last Command* 1955

Lloyd, Phyllida *Mamma Mia!* 2008; *The Iron Lady* 2011

Lo Wei (1918-1996) *The Big Boss* 1971; *Fist of Fury* 1972

López-Gallego, Gonzalo *King of the Hill* 2007; *Apollo 18* 2011

Loach, Ken aka **Loach, Kenneth** (1936-) *Poor Cow* 1967; *Kes* 1969; *Family Life* 1971; *Black Jack* 1979; *Looks and Smiles* 1981; *Fatherland* 1986; *Hidden Agenda* 1990; *Riff-Raff* 1991; *Raining Stones* 1993; *Ladybird Ladybird* 1994; *Land and Freedom* 1995; *Carla's Song* 1996; *My Name Is Joe* 1998; *Bread and Roses* 2000; *The Navigators* 2001; *11'09"01 - September 11* 2002; *Sweet Sixteen* 2002; *Ae Fond Kiss...* 2004; *McLibel* 2005; *Tickets* 2005; *The Wind That Shakes the Barley* 2006; *It's a Free World...* 2007; *Looking for Eric* 2009; *Route Irish* 2010; *The Angels' Share* 2012; *The Spirit of '45* 2013; *Jimmy's Hall* 2014

Locke, Sondra (1944-) *Ratboy* 1986; *Impulse* 1990

Logan, Joshua (1908-1988) *I Met My Love Again* 1938; *Picnic* 1955; *Bus Stop* 1956; *Sayonara* 1957; *South Pacific* 1958; *Fanny* 1961; *Ensign Pulver* 1964; *Camelot* 1967; *Paint Your Wagon* 1969

Loncraine, Richard (1946-) *Slade in Flame* 1974; *Full Circle* 1977; *Brimstone and Treacle* 1982; *The Missionary* 1982; *Bellman & True* 1987; *Wide Eyed and Legless* 1993; *Richard III* 1995; *My House in Umbria* 2002; *Wimbledon* 2004; *Firewall* 2006; *Ruth & Alex* 2014

London, Jerry (1937-) *The Scarlet and the Black* 1983; *Rent-a-Cop* 1988; *Victim of Love* 1991; *A Mother's Gift* 1995; *As Time Runs Out* 1999; *Take Me Home: the John Denver Story* 2000

Lonergan, Kenneth (1963-) *You Can Count on Me* 1999; *Margaret* 2008

Long, Stanley aka **Long, Stanley A** (1933-2012) *Adventures of a Taxi Driver* 1975; *Adventures of a Private Eye* 1977; *Adventures of a Plumber's Mate* 1978

Longinotto, Kim *Sisters in Law* 2005; *Love Is All* 2014; *Dreamcatcher* 2015

Lord, Jean-Claude (1943-) *Eddie and the Cruisers II: Eddie Lives!* 1989; *Summer House* 2008

Lord, Peter (1953-) *Chicken Run* 2000; *The Pirates! in an Adventure with Scientists!* 2012

Lord, Phil *Cloudy with a Chance of Meatballs* 2009; *21 Jump Street* 2012; *The Lego Movie* 2014; *22 Jump Street* 2014; *Han Solo: a Star Wars Story* 2018

Lorentz, Pare (1905-1992) *The Plow That Broke the Plains* 1934; *The River* 1937

Losey, Joseph aka **Hanbury, Victor** aka **Walton, Joseph** (1909-1984)

Makhmalbaf, Hana Joy of Madness 2003; Buddha Collapsed out of Shame 2007

Makhmalbaf, Mohsen (1952-) Gabbeh 1995; A Moment of Innocence 1996; Kandahar 2001; The President 2014

Makhmalbaf, Samira (1980-) The Apple 1998; Blackboards 2000; 11'09"01 - September 11 2002; At Five in the Afternoon 2003

Makin, Kelly (1961-) National Lampoon's Senior Trip 1995; Kids in the Hall: Brain Candy 1996; Mickey Blue Eyes 1999

Makk, Karoly (1925-) Love 1971; Lily in Love 1985; The Gambler 1997

Malick, Terrence (1945-) Badlands 1973; Days of Heaven 1978; The Thin Red Line 1998; The New World 2005; The Tree of Life 2010; To the Wonder 2012; Knight of Cups 2015

Malle, Louis (1932-1995) Le Monde du Silence 1956; Lift to the Scaffold 1957; Les Amants 1958; Zazie dans le Métro 1960; A Very Private Affair 1962; Le Feu Follet 1963; Viva Maria! 1965; Histoires Extraordinaires 1967; The Thief of Paris 1967; Phantom India 1968; Le Souffle au Coeur 1971; Black Moon 1974; Lacombe Lucien 1974; Pretty Baby 1978; Atlantic City, USA 1980; My Dinner with Andre 1981; Alamo Bay 1985; God's Country 1985; Au Revoir les Enfants 1987; Milou en Mai 1989; Damage 1992; Vanya on 42nd Street 1994

Malmuth, Bruce (1934-2005) Nighthawks 1981; Hard to Kill 1989

Malone, Mark Killer 1994; Hoods 1998; Dead Heat 2002

Malone, William House on Haunted Hill 1999; FearDotCom 2002

Mamet, David (1947-) House of Games 1987; Things Change 1988; Homicide 1991; Oleanna 1994; The Spanish Prisoner 1997; The Winslow Boy 1999; State and Main 2000; Heist 2001; Spartan 2004; Redbelt 2007; Phil Spector 2013

Mamoulian, Rouben (1897-1987) Applause 1929; City Streets 1931; Dr Jekyll and Mr Hyde 1931; Love Me Tonight 1932; Queen Christina 1933; The Song of Songs 1933; We Live Again 1934; Becky Sharp 1935; High, Wide and Handsome 1937; Golden Boy 1939; The Mark of Zorro 1940; Blood and Sand 1941; Rings on Her Fingers 1942; Summer Holiday 1948; Silk Stockings 1957

Manchevski, Milcho (1960-) Before the Rain 1994; Dust 2001

Mancini, Don Seed of Chucky 2004; Curse of Chucky 2013

Mandel, Robert (1945-) Independence Day 1983; FX: Murder by Illusion 1985; Touch and Go 1986; School Ties 1992; The Substitute 1996

Mandoki, Luis (1954-) Gaby: a True Story 1987; White Palace 1990; Born Yesterday 1993; When a Man Loves a Woman 1994; Message in a Bottle 1998; Angel Eyes 2001; Trapped 2002

Mandt, Neil (1969-) Hijacking Hollywood 1997; Fortune Hunters 1999

Mangold, James (1963-) Heavy 1995; Cop Land 1997; Girl, Interrupted 1999; Kate & Leopold 2002; Identity 2003; Walk the Line 2005; 3:10 to Yuma 2007; Knight and Day 2010; The Wolverine 2013; Wolverine 3 2017

Mankiewicz, Joseph L (1909-1993) Dragonwyck 1946; Somewhere in the Night 1946; The Ghost and Mrs Muir 1947; The Late George Apley 1947; House of Strangers 1949; A Letter to Three Wives 1949; All about Eve 1950; No Way Out 1950; People Will Talk 1951; 5 Fingers 1952; Julius Caesar 1953; The Barefoot Contessa 1954; Guys and Dolls 1955; The Quiet American 1958; Suddenly, Last Summer 1959; Cleopatra 1963; The Honey Pot 1967; King: a Filmed Record... Montgomery to Memphis 1970; There Was a Crooked Man... 1970; Sleuth 1972

Mankiewicz, Tom (1942-2010) Dragnet 1987; Delirious 1991

Mann, Anthony (1906-1967) Dr Broadway 1942; The Great Flamarion 1945; Two o'Clock Courage 1945; The Bamboo Blonde 1946; Desperate 1947; Railroaded! 1947; T-Men 1947; Raw Deal 1948; Border Incident 1949; Reign of Terror 1949; Devil's Doorway 1950; The Furies 1950; Side Street 1950; Winchester '73 1950; The Tall Target 1951; Bend of the River 1952; The Glenn Miller Story

1953; The Naked Spur 1953; Thunder Bay 1953; The Far Country 1954; The Last Frontier 1955; The Man from Laramie 1955; Strategic Air Command 1955; Serenade 1956; Men in War 1957; The Tin Star 1957; God's Little Acre 1958; Man of the West 1958; Cimarron 1960; El Cid 1961; The Fall of the Roman Empire 1964; The Heroes of Telemark 1965

Mann, Daniel (1912-1991) Come Back, Little Sheba 1952; About Mrs Leslie 1954; I'll Cry Tomorrow 1955; The Rose Tattoo 1955; The Teahouse of the August Moon 1956; Hot Spell 1958; The Last Angry Man 1959; Butterfield 8 1960; The Mountain Road 1960; Ada 1961; Five Finger Exercise 1962; Who's Got the Action? 1962; Who's Been Sleeping in My Bed? 1963; Judith 1966; Our Man Flint 1966; For Love of Ivy 1968; A Dream of Kings 1969; Willard 1971; Interval 1973; Lost in the Stars 1974; Matilda 1978; Playing for Time 1980

Mann, Delbert (1920-2007) Marty 1955; The Bachelor Party 1957; Desire under the Elms 1958; Separate Tables 1958; The Dark at the Top of the Stairs 1960; Lover Come Back 1961; The Outsider 1961; That Touch of Mink 1962; Dear Heart 1964; Quick, before It Melts 1965; Fitzwilly 1967; The Pink Jungle 1968; Jane Eyre 1970; Kidnapped 1971; The Man without a Country 1973; Birch Interval 1976; All Quiet on the Western Front 1979; Night Crossing 1981; Against Her Will 1992; Incident in a Small Town 1993

Mann, Michael (1943-) The Jericho Mile 1979; Thief 1981; The Keep 1983; Manhunter 1986; The Last of the Mohicans 1992; Heat 1995; The Insider 1999; Ali 2001; Collateral 2004; Miami Vice 2006; Public Enemies 2009; Blackhat 2015

Mann, Ron (1959-) Comic Book Confidential 1988; Grass 1999; Altman 2014

Mann, Scott The Tournament 2009; Heist 2015

Marcel, Terry aka Marcel, Terence (1942-) There Goes the Bride 1979; Hawk the Slayer 1980; Jane and the Lost City 1987; The Last Seduction 2 1998

March, Alex (1921-1989) Paper Lion 1968; The Big Bounce 1969; Mastermind 1976; The Amazing Captain Nemo 1978

Marcus, Paul Break Up 1998; Eye of the Killer 1999; Heidi 2005

Margheriti, Antonio aka Dawson, Anthony aka Dawson, Anthony M (1930-2002) Vengeance 1968; Blood Money 1974; Flesh for Frankenstein 1974; Take a Hard Ride 1975; Killer Fish 1978; Codename Wildgeese 1984

Marin, Edwin L (1899-1951) The Death Kiss 1933; The Casino Murder Case 1935; Speed 1936; A Christmas Carol 1938; Everybody Sing 1938; Listen, Darling 1938; Fast and Loose 1939; Maisie 1939; Paris Calling 1941; The Invisible Agent 1942; Miss Annie Rooney 1942; Show Business 1944; Tall in the Saddle 1944; Abilene Town 1945; Johnny Angel 1945; Lady Luck 1946; Nocturne 1946; Christmas Eve 1947; Intrigue 1947; Fighting Man of the Plains 1949; The Younger Brothers 1949; The Cariboo Trail 1950; Colt .45 1950; Fort Worth 1951; Sugarfoot 1951

Marker, Chris (1921-2012) La Jetée 1962; Le Joli Mai 1962; Sans Soleil 1982

Marking, Havana Afghan Star 2008; Smash & Grab: the Story of the Pink Panthers 2012

Markle, Fletcher (1921-1991) Jigsaw 1949; The Man with a Cloak 1951; The Incredible Journey 1963

Markle, Peter (1952-) Hot Dog – The Movie 1984; Youngblood 1986; BAT-21 1988; Nightbreaker 1989; Wagons East! 1994; The Last Days of Frankie the Fly 1996; Flight 93 2006; The Tenth Circle 2008; Nora Roberts' High Noon 2009; Nora Roberts' Carnal Innocence 2011

Markowitz, Robert (1935-) The Tuskegee Airmen 1995; Nicholas' Gift 1998; The Great Gatsby 2000; The Big Heist 2001

Marks, Arthur Detroit 9000 1973; Friday Foster 1975

Marlind, Mans aka Marlind & Stein Shelter 2008; Underworld: Awakening 2012

Marquand, Richard (1937-1987) The Legacy 1978; Eye of the Needle 1981; Star Wars Episode VI: Return of the

Jedi 1983; Until September 1984; Jagged Edge 1985; Hearts of Fire 1987

Marsh, James (1963-) The King 2005; Man on Wire 2007; Project Nim 2011; Shadow Dancer 2012; The Theory of Everything 2015; The Mercy 2016

Marshall, Frank (1947-) Arachnophobia 1990; Alive 1992; Congo 1995; Eight Below 2005

Marshall, Garry (1934-) Young Doctors in Love 1982; The Flamingo Kid 1984; Nothing in Common 1986; Overboard 1987; Beaches 1988; Pretty Woman 1990; Frankie & Johnny 1991; Exit to Eden 1994; Dear God 1996; The Other Sister 1999; Runaway Bride 1999; The Princess Diaries 2001; The Princess Diaries 2: Royal Engagement 2004; Raising Helen 2004; Georgia Rule 2007; Valentine's Day 2010; New Year's Eve 2011; Mother's Day 2016

Marshall, George (1891-1975) Pack Up Your Troubles 1932; Their First Mistake 1932; Towed in a Hole 1932; In Old Kentucky 1935; Life Begins at 40 1935; A Message to Garcia 1936; Nancy Steele Is Missing 1937; The Goldwyn Follies 1938; Hold That Co-Ed 1938; Destry Rides Again 1939; You Can't Cheat an Honest Man 1939; The Ghost Breakers 1940; When the Daltons Rode 1940; Pot o' Gold 1941; Texas 1941; The Forest Rangers 1942; Star Spangled Rhythm 1942; Valley of the Sun 1942; Riding High 1943; True to Life 1943; And the Angels Sing 1944; Incendiary Blonde 1945; Murder, He Says 1945; The Blue Dahlia 1946; Monsieur Beaucaire 1946; Variety Girl 1947; My Friend Irma 1949; Fancy Pants 1950; Never a Dull Moment 1950; A Millionaire for Christy 1951; Houdini 1953; Military Policeman 1953; Money from Home 1953; The Savage 1953; Scared Stiff 1953; Destry 1954; Duel in the Jungle 1954; Red Garters 1954; Pillars of the Sky 1956; Guns of Fort Petticoat 1957; The Sad Sack 1957; The Sheepman 1958; The Gazebo 1959; It Started with a Kiss 1959; The Mating Game 1959; Cry for Happy 1961; The Happy Thieves 1962; How the West Was Won 1962; Papa's Delicate Condition 1963; Advance to the Rear 1964; Boy, Did I Get a Wrong Number 1966; Eight on the Lam 1967

Marshall, Neil (1970-) Dog Soldiers 2001; The Descent 2005; Doomsday 2008; Centurion 2009

Marshall, Penny (1942-) Jumpin' Jack Flash 1986; Big 1988; Awakenings 1990; A League of Their Own 1992; Renaissance Man 1994; The Preacher's Wife 1996; Riding in Cars with Boys 2001

Marshall, Rob (1960-) Annie 1999; Chicago 2002; Memoirs of a Geisha 2005; Nine 2009; Pirates of the Caribbean: On Stranger Tides 2011; Into the Woods 2014

Marshall, Scott Keeping Up with the Steins 2006; Blonde Ambition 2007

Marston, Joshua Maria Full of Grace 2003; New York, I Love You 2009

Martel, Lucrecia (1966-) La Ciénaga 2001; The Headless Woman 2008

Martin, Charles (1910-1983) My Dear Secretary 1948; Death of a Scoundrel 1956

Martin, Darnell (1965-) I Like It like That 1994; Their Eyes Were Watching God 2005; Cadillac Records 2008

Martin, Eugenio aka Martin, Gene (1925-) Bad Man's River 1971; Horror Express 1972

Martineau, Jacques (1963-) Drôle de Félix 2000; Ma Vraie Vie à Rouen 2002; Cockles & Muscles 2004; Born in 68: We'll Love Each Other until Death Do Us Part 2008

Martinez, Justin aka Radio Silence V/H/S 2012; Southbound 2015

Martino, Steve Dr Seuss' Horton Hears a Who! 2008; Ice Age 4: Continental Drift 2012; Snoopy and Charlie Brown: the Peanuts Movie 2015

Martinson, Leslie H aka Martinson, Leslie (1915-) The Atomic Kid 1954; Black Gold 1962; PT 109 1963; For Those Who Think Young 1964; Batman 1966; Fathom 1967; Mrs Pollifax - Spy 1970; And Millions Will Die! 1973

Marton, Andrew (1904-1992) King Solomon's Mines 1950; The Devil Makes Three 1952; The Wild North

1952; Green Fire 1954; Men of the Fighting Lady 1954; Prisoner of War 1954; The Longest Day 1962; Crack in the World 1964; The Thin Red Line 1964; Clarence, the Cross-Eyed Lion 1965

Marvin, Mike The Wraith 1986; Wishman 1991

Maselli, Francesco (1930-) Love in the City 1953; Time of Indifference 1964; A Fine Pair 1968

Mason, Herbert (1891-1960) His Lordship 1936; Strange Boarders 1938; A Window in London 1939; Back Room Boy 1942

Massot, Joe Wonderwall 1968; The Song Remains the Same 1976

Masters, Quentin (1946-) Thumb Tripping 1972; The Stud 1978

Masterson, Peter (1934-) The Trip to Bountiful 1985; Blood Red 1988; Full Moon in Blue Water 1988; Convicts 1991; The Only Thrill 1997; Mermaid 2000

Mastorakis, Nico (1941-) Blind Date 1984; Hired to Kill 1990

Mastroianni, Armand (1948-) He Knows You're Alone 1981; Cameron's Closet 1988; Desperate Justice 1993; Victim of Rage 1994; Formula for Death 1995; Fatal Error 1999; First Daughter 1999; First Target 2000; Nowhere to Land 2000; First Shot 2002; Falling in Love with the Girl Next Door 2006; Though None Go with Me 2006; Black Widow 2007; The Gunfighter's Pledge 2008; Our First Christmas 2008

Maté, Rudolph (1898-1964) It Had to Be You 1947; The Dark Past 1948; DOA 1949; Branded 1950; No Sad Songs for Me 1950; Union Station 1950; The Prince Who Was a Thief 1951; When Worlds Collide 1951; Forbidden 1953; The Mississippi Gambler 1953; Second Chance 1953; The Black Shield of Falworth 1954; The Siege at Red River 1954; The Far Horizons 1955; The Violent Men 1955; Miracle in the Rain 1956; The Rawhide Years 1956; Three Violent People 1956; The Deep Six 1958; For the First Time 1959; Seven Seas to Calais 1962; The 300 Spartans 1962

Matthau, Charles (1965-) Mrs Lambert Remembers Love 1991; The Grass Harp 1995

Matthews, Paul The Little Unicorn 1998; Merlin the Return 2000

Maurer, Norman (1926-1986) The Three Stooges Go around the World in a Daze 1963; The Outlaws Is Coming 1965

Maxwell, Garth Jack Be Nimble 1992; When Love Comes 1998

Maxwell, Peter (1932-) Dilemma 1962; Serena 1962; Impact 1963

Maxwell, Ronald F (1947-) Little Darlings 1980; The Night the Lights Went Out in Georgia 1981; Gettysburg 1993; Gods and Generals 2002

May, Bradford (1951-) Darkman II: the Return of Durant 1995; Darkman III: Die Darkman Die 1996; A Kiss at Midnight 2008; The Nanny Express 2008; Flower Girl 2009; Vickery's Wild Ride 2009; After the Fall 2010; Backyard Wedding 2010; Elevator Girl 2010; Love Will Keep Us Together 2010; Working Miracles 2010; Help for the Holidays 2012

May, Elaine (1932-) A New Leaf 1971; The Heartbreak Kid 1972; Ishtar 1987

May, Joe (1880-1954) Asphalt 1928; Confession 1937; The House of the Seven Gables 1940; The Invisible Man Returns 1940; Johnny Doesn't Live Here Anymore 1944

Maybury, John (1958-) Love Is the Devil: Study for a Portrait of Francis Bacon 1998; The Jacket 2005; The Edge of Love 2008

Mayer (1), Michael A Home at the End of the World 2004; Flicka 2006

Mayfield, Les California Man 1992; Miracle on 34th Street 1994; Flubber 1997; Blue Streak 1999; American Outlaws 2001; The Man 2005; Code Name: the Cleaner 2007

Maylam, Tony (1943-) The Riddle of the Sands 1978; The Burning 1981; Split Second 1991

Mayo, Archie (1891-1968) A Handful of Clouds 1930; Illicit 1931; Svengali 1931; Night after Night 1932; Ever in My Heart 1933; The Mayor of Hell 1933; Gambling Lady 1934; Bordertown 1935; The Case of the Lucky Legs 1935; Go into Your Dance 1935; The Petrified Forest 1936; The Black Legion 1937; It's Love I'm After 1937; The Adventures of Marco Polo 1938; They Shall Have

Music 1939; Four Sons 1940; The House across the Bay 1940; Charley's Aunt 1941; Confirm or Deny 1941; The Great American Broadcast 1941; Moontide 1942; Orchestra Wives 1942; Crash Dive 1943; Sweet and Lowdown 1944; Angel on My Shoulder 1946; A Night in Casablanca 1946

Mayron, Melanie (1952-) The Baby-Sitter's Club 1995; Freaky Friday 1995; Slap Her, She's French! 2001

Maysles, Albert (1926-2015) Gimme Shelter 1970; Grey Gardens 1975; Iris 2014

Maysles, David (1931-1987) Gimme Shelter 1970; Grey Gardens 1975

Mazer, Dan I Give It a Year 2013; Dirty Grandpa 2016

Mazin, Craig (1971-) The Specials 2000; Superhero Movie 2008

Mazursky, Paul (1930-2014) Bob & Carol & Ted & Alice 1969; Alex in Wonderland 1970; Blume in Love 1973; Harry and Tonto 1974; Next Stop, Greenwich Village 1976; An Unmarried Woman 1978; Willie and Phil 1980; Tempest 1982; Moscow on the Hudson 1984; Down and Out in Beverly Hills 1986; Moon over Parador 1988; Enemies, a Love Story 1989; Scenes from a Mall 1991; The Pickle 1993; Faithful 1996

McQueen (2), Steve (1969-) Hunger 2008; Shame 2011; 12 Years a Slave 2013

Meadows, Shane (1972-) Smalltime 1996; TwentyFourSeven 1997; A Room for Romeo Brass 1999; Once upon a Time in the Midlands 2002; Dead Man's Shoes 2004; This Is England 2006; Somers Town 2008; Le Donk & Scor-Zay-Zee 2009; Made of Stone 2013

Meckler, Nancy Sister My Sister 1994; Alive and Kicking 1996

Medak, Peter (1937-) A Day in the Death of Joe Egg 1971; The Ruling Class 1972; Ghost in the Noonday Sun 1973; The Odd Job 1978; The Changeling 1980; Zorro, the Gay Blade 1981; The Men's Club 1986; The Krays 1990; Let Him Have It 1991; Romeo Is Bleeding 1992; Pontiac Moon 1994; The Hunchback of Notre Dame 1997; Species II 1998; Sex and Lies in Sin City 2008

Medem, Julio (1958-) Vacas 1991; The Red Squirrel 1993; The Lovers of the Arctic Circle 1998; Sex and Lucia 2001; The Basque Ball: Skin against Stone 2003; 7 Days in Havana 2012; ma ma 2015

Medford, Don (1917-2012) To Trap a Spy 1966; The Hunting Party 1971; The Organization 1971

Megahey, Francis Real Life 1983; Taffin 1988; The Disappearance of Kevin Johnson 1995

Megaton, Olivier Transporter 3 2008; Colombiana 2011; Taken 2 2012; Taken 3 2014

Mehta, Deepa (1949-) Camilla 1993; Fire 1996; Earth 1998; Bollywood/Hollywood 2002; Water 2005; Midnight's Children 2012

Mehta, Ketan (1952-) Mirch Masala 1987; Maya 1992

Meier, Ursula Home 2008; Sister 2012

Meirelles, Fernando (1955-) City of God 2002; The Constant Gardener 2005; Blindness 2008; 360 2011

Melançon, André (1942-) The Dog Who Stopped the War 1984; Bach and Broccoli 1986

Melchior, Ib (1917-2015) The Angry Red Planet 1959; The Time Traveller 1964

Melendez, Bill (1916-2008) A Boy Named Charlie Brown 1969; Snoopy, Come Home 1972; Race for Your Life, Charlie Brown 1977; Bon Voyage, Charlie Brown 1980

Melville, Jean-Pierre (1917-1973) Le Silence de la Mer 1947; Les Enfants Terribles 1949; Bob Le Flambeur 1955; Two Men in Manhattan 1959; Léon Morin, Priest 1961; Le Doulos 1962; L'Aîné des Ferchaux 1963; Le Deuxième Souffle 1966; Le Samouraï 1967; Army of Shadows 1969; The Red Circle 1970; Un Flic 1972

Menaul, Christopher Feast of July 1995; First Night 2010; Summer in February 2012

Mendeluk, George (1948-) The Kidnapping of the President 1980; Her Fatal Flaw 2006; Secrets of an Undercover Wife 2007; Desperate Escape 2009

Mendes, Lothar (1894-1974) The Four Feathers 1929; The Marriage Playground 1929; Paramount on Parade 1930; Ladies' Man 1931; If I

Had a Million 1932; Payment Deferred 1932; Jew Süss 1934; The Man Who Could Work Miracles 1936; Moonlight Sonata 1937; Flight for Freedom 1943

Mendes, Sam (1965-) American Beauty 1999; Road to Perdition 2002; Jarhead 2005; Revolutionary Road 2008; Away We Go 2009; Skyfall 2012; Spectre 2015

Menendez, Ramon Stand and Deliver 1988; Money for Nothing 1993

Menges, Chris (1940-) A World Apart 1987; CrissCross 1992; Second Best 1993; The Lost Son 1998

Menzel, Jiri (1938-) Closely Observed Trains 1966; Capricious Summer 1968; Larks on a String 1969; Cutting It Short 1980; My Sweet Little Village 1986; The Last of the Good Old Days 1989; The Life and Extraordinary Adventures of Private Ivan Chonkin 1994; Ten Minutes Older: the Cello 2002; I Served the King of England 2006

Menzies, William Cameron aka **Menzies, William C** (1886-1957) Chandu the Magician 1932; Things to Come 1936; The Green Cockatoo 1937; The Thief of Bagdad 1940; The Whip Hand 1951; Invaders from Mars 1953; The Maze 1953

Merchant, Ismail (1936-2005) In Custody 1993; The Proprietor 1996; Cotton Mary 1999; The Mystic Masseur 2001

Merhige, E Elias (1964-) Shadow of the Vampire 2000; Suspect Zero 2004

Merrill, Kieth The Great American Cowboy 1973; Windwalker 1980; Harry's War 1981

Meshkini, Marziyeh (1969-) The Day I Became a Woman 2000; Stray Dogs 2004

Mészáros, Marta (1931-) Diary for My Children 1982; Diary for My Loves 1987; Diary for My Father and Mother 1990

Metter, Alan (1933-) Girls Just Want to Have Fun 1985; Back to School 1986; Moving 1988; Cold Dog Soup 1989; Police Academy: Mission to Moscow 1994

Metzstein, Saul (1970-) Late Night Shopping 2001; Guy X 2005

Meyer, Nicholas (1945-) Time after Time 1979; Star Trek II: the Wrath of Khan 1982; Volunteers 1985; The Deceivers 1988; Company Business 1991; Star Trek VI: the Undiscovered Country 1991

Meyer, Russ (1922-2004) Immoral Mr Teas 1959; Eve and the Handyman 1961; Fanny Hill: Memoirs of a Woman of Pleasure 1964; Lorna 1964; Faster, Pussycat! Kill! Kill! 1965; Motor Psycho 1965; Mudhoney 1965; Common-Law Cabin 1967; Good Morning... and Goodbye 1967; Finders Keepers, Lovers Weepers 1968; Vixen! 1968; Cherry, Harry & Raquel 1969; Beyond the Valley of the Dolls 1970; Supervixens 1975; Up 1976; Beneath the Valley of the Ultra Vixens 1979

Meyer, Turi (1964-) Sleepstalker 1995; Candyman: Day of the Dead 1999

Meyers, Nancy (1949-) The Parent Trap 1998; What Women Want 2001; Something's Gotta Give 2003; The Holiday 2006; It's Complicated 2009; The Intern 2015

Michell, Roger (1957-) Persuasion 1995; Titanic Town 1998; Notting Hill 1999; Changing Lanes 2002; The Mother 2003; Enduring Love 2004; Venus 2006; Morning Glory 2010; Hyde Park on Hudson 2012; Le Week-end 2013; My Cousin Rachel 2017

Michôd, David Animal Kingdom 2009; The Rover 2014

Mickle, Jim Stake Land 2010; We Are What We Are 2013; Cold in July 2014

Mihaileanu, Radu (1958-) The Concert 2009; The Source 2011

Mihalka, George (1953-) My Bloody Valentine 1981; Bullet to Beijing 1995

Miike, Takashi (1960-) Audition 1999; The Happiness of the Katakuris 2001; Ichi the Killer 2001; Gozu 2003; Sukiyaki Western Django 2007; YatterMan 2009; 13 Assassins 2010; Hara-Kiri: Death of a Samurai 2011; Yakuza Apocalypse 2015

Mikhalkov, Nikita (1945-) A Slave of Love 1976; An Unfinished Piece for Mechanical Piano 1976; Oblomov 1980; A Private Conversation 1983; Dark Eyes 1987; Urga 1990; Burnt by

the Sun 1995; The Barber of Siberia 1999

Miles, Bernard (1907-1991) Tawny Pipit 1944; Chance of a Lifetime 1950

Miles, Christopher (1939-) The Virgin and the Gypsy 1970; A Time for Loving 1971; The Maids 1974; That Lucky Touch 1975; Priest of Love 1981; The Clandestine Marriage 1999

Milestone, Lewis (1895-1980) The Kid Brother 1927; Two Arabian Knights 1927; The Racket 1928; All Quiet on the Western Front 1930; The Front Page 1931; Rain 1932; Hallelujah, I'm a Bum 1933; The Captain Hates the Sea 1934; Anything Goes 1936; The General Died at Dawn 1936; Of Mice and Men 1939; Lucky Partners 1940; My Life with Caroline 1941; Edge of Darkness 1943; The North Star 1943; The Purple Heart 1944; A Walk in the Sun 1945; The Strange Love of Martha Ivers 1946; Arch of Triumph 1948; No Minor Vices 1948; The Red Pony 1949; Halls of Montezuma 1950; Kangaroo 1952; Les Misérables 1952; They Who Dare 1953; Pork Chop Hill 1959; Ocean's Eleven 1960; Mutiny on the Bounty 1962

Milius, John (1944-) Dillinger 1973; The Wind and the Lion 1975; Big Wednesday 1978; Conan the Barbarian 1982; Red Dawn 1984; Farewell to the King 1988; Flight of the Intruder 1991

Milland, Ray aka **Milland, R** (1905-1986) A Man Alone 1955; Lisbon 1956; The Safecracker 1958; Panic in Year Zero 1962; Hostile Witness 1968

Millar, Gavin (1938-) Dreamchild 1985; Danny, the Champion of the World 1989; Complicity 1999

Millar, Stuart (1929-) When the Legends Die 1972; Rooster Cogburn 1975

Miller, Bennett (1966-) Capote 2005; Moneyball 2011; Foxcatcher 2014

Miller, Chris aka **Miller, Christopher** aka **Miller, Christopher** Shrek the Third 2007; Puss in Boots 2011; 21 Jump Street 2012; The Lego Movie 2014; Han Solo: a Star Wars Story 2018

Miller, Claude (1942-2012) Garde à Vue 1981; An Impudent Girl 1985; La Petite Voleuse 1988; L'Accompagnatrice 1992; Les Enfants de Lumière 1995; La Classe de Neige 1998; Betty Fisher and Other Stories 2001; A Secret 2007; Thérèse Desqueyroux 2012

Miller (1), David (1909-1992) Billy the Kid 1941; Flying Tigers 1942; Love Happy 1949; Our Very Own 1950; Sudden Fear 1952; Beautiful Stranger 1954; Diane 1955; The Opposite Sex 1956; The Story of Esther Costello 1957; Happy Anniversary 1959; Midnight Lace 1960; Back Street 1961; Lonely Are the Brave 1962; Captain Newman, MD 1963; Hammerhead 1968; Hail, Hero! 1969; Executive Action 1973; Bittersweet Love 1976

Miller, Frank (1957-) Sin City 2005; The Spirit 2008; Sin City: a Dame to Kill For 2014

Miller (1), George (1943-) The Man from Snowy River 1982; The Aviator 1985; Les Patterson Saves the World 1987; The NeverEnding Story II: the Next Chapter 1991; Over the Hill 1992; Andre 1994; Daniel Defoe's Robinson Crusoe 1996; Zeus and Roxanne 1997

Miller (2), George (1945-) Mad Max 1979; Mad Max 2 1981; Twilight Zone: the Movie 1983; Mad Max beyond Thunderdome 1985; The Witches of Eastwick 1987; Lorenzo's Oil 1992; Babe: Pig in the City 1998; Happy Feet 2006; Happy Feet Two 2011; Mad Max: Fury Road 2015

Miller, Harvey (1936-1999) Bad Medicine 1985; Getting Away with Murder 1996

Miller (2), Michael Jackson County Jail 1976; National Lampoon's Class Reunion 1982; Silent Rage 1982; Danielle Steel's Palomino 1991; Danielle Steel's Star 1993; Danielle Steel's Once in a Lifetime 1994; Danielle Steel's A Perfect Stranger 1994; Barbara Taylor Bradford's Everything to Gain 1996; Determination of Death 2001

Miller, Randall Class Act 1992; Houseguest 1995; The 6th Man 1997; Marilyn Hotchkiss Ballroom Dancing & Charm School 2005; Bottle Shock 2008

Miller, Rebecca (1962-) Personal Velocity 2001; The Ballad of Jack and Rose 2005; The Private Lives of Pippa Lee 2009; Maggie's Plan 2016

Miller, Robert Ellis (1932-) Any Wednesday 1966; The Heart Is a Lonely Hunter 1968; Sweet November 1968; The Buttercup Chain 1970; The Girl from Petrovka 1974; The Baltimore Bullet 1980; Reuben, Reuben 1983; Hawks 1988; Brenda Starr 1989; Bed & Breakfast 1992

Miller, Sam (1962-) Among Giants 1998; Elephant Juice 1999; No Good Deed 2014

Miller, Troy Jack Frost 1998; Dumb and Dumberer: When Harry Met Lloyd 2003

Mills, Mike Thumbsucker 2005; Beginners 2010

Miner, Steve (1951-) Friday the 13th Part 2 1981; Friday the 13th Part III 1982; House 1986; Soul Man 1986; Warlock 1989; Wild Hearts Can't Be Broken 1991; Forever Young 1992; My Father the Hero 1994; Big Bully 1996; Halloween H20: 20 Years Later 1998; Lake Placid 1999; Texas Rangers 2001; Day of the Dead 2008

Minghella, Anthony (1954-2008) Truly Madly Deeply 1990; Mr Wonderful 1992; The English Patient 1996; The Talented Mr Ripley 1999; Cold Mountain 2003; Breaking and Entering 2006

Minkoff, Rob (1962-) The Lion King 1994; Stuart Little 1999; Stuart Little 2 2002; The Haunted Mansion 2003; The Forbidden Kingdom 2008; Mr Peabody & Sherman 2013

Minnelli, Vincente (1903-1986) Cabin in the Sky 1943; I Dood It 1943; Meet Me in St Louis 1944; Ziegfeld Follies 1944; The Clock 1945; Yolanda and the Thief 1945; Undercurrent 1946; The Pirate 1948; Madame Bovary 1949; Father of the Bride 1950; An American in Paris 1951; Father's Little Dividend 1951; The Bad and the Beautiful 1952; The Band Wagon 1953; The Story of Three Loves 1953; Brigadoon 1954; The Long, Long Trailer 1954; The Cobweb 1955; Kismet 1955; Lust for Life 1956; Tea and Sympathy 1956; Designing Woman 1957; Gigi 1958; The Reluctant Debutante 1958; Some Came Running 1958; Bells Are Ringing 1960; Home from the Hill 1960; The Four Horsemen of the Apocalypse 1962; Two Weeks in Another Town 1962; The Courtship of Eddie's Father 1963; Goodbye Charlie 1964; The Sandpiper 1965; On a Clear Day You Can See Forever 1970; A Matter of Time 1976

Mira, Eugenio Agnosia 2010; Grand Piano 2013

Mirkin, David Romy and Michele's High School Reunion 1997; Heartbreakers 2001

Misiorowski, Bob Shark Attack 1999; Derailed 2002

Misumi, Kenji (1921-1975) Zatoichi 1962; Sword of Vengeance 1972; Shogun Assassin 1980

Mitchell, David Robert aka **Mitchell, David** The Myth of the American Sleepover 2010; It Follows 2014

Mitchell, John Cameron (1963-) Hedwig and the Angry Inch 2001; Shortbus 2006; Rabbit Hole 2010

Mitchell, Mike (1970-) Deuce Bigalow: Male Gigolo 1999; Surviving Christmas 2004; Sky High 2005; Shrek Forever After 2010; Alvin and the Chipmunks: Chipwrecked 2011; Trolls 2016

Mitchell, Oswald (1890-1949) Danny Boy 1941; The Greed of William Hart 1948

Miyazaki, Goro Tales from Earthsea 2006; From Up on Poppy Hill 2011

Miyazaki, Hayao (1941-) The Castle of Cagliostro 1979; Nausicaa of the Valley of the Wind 1984; My Neighbour Totoro 1988; Kiki's Delivery Service 1998; Princess Mononoke 1997; Spirited Away 2001; Laputa: Castle in the Sky 2003; Howl's Moving Castle 2004; Porco Rosso 2005; Ponyo 2008; The Wind Rises 2013

Mizoguchi, Kenji (1898-1956) The Downfall of Osen 1935; Poppy 1935; Osaka Elegy 1936; Sisters of the Gion 1936; Story of the Late Chrysanthemums 1939; The Loyal 47 Ronin 1941; Musashi Miyamoto 1944; The Famous Sword 1945; Five Women around Utamaro 1946; The Victory of Women 1946; The Love of Sumako the Actress 1947; My Love

Has Been Burning 1949; The Lady of Musashino 1951; Miss Oyu 1951; The Life of Oharu 1952; Ugetsu Monogatari 1953; The Crucified Lovers 1954; Sansho the Bailiff 1954; The Princess Yang Kwei Fei 1955; Street of Shame 1955; Tales of the Taira Clan 1955

Mizrahi, Moshe (1931-) Madame Rosa 1977; Every Time We Say Goodbye 1986

Moeller, Philip (?-1958) The Age of Innocence 1934; Break of Hearts 1935

Moguy, Léonie aka **Moguy, Leonide** (1899-1977) Action in Arabia 1944; Whistle Stop 1946

Moland, Hans Petter (1955-) Aberdeen 2000; In Order of Disappearance 2014

Molander, Gustaf aka **Molander, Gustav** (1888-1973) Swedenhielms 1935; Intermezzo 1936; Dollar 1938; A Woman's Face 1938; One Single Night 1939

Molinaro, Edouard (1928-2013) The Seven Deadly Sins 1961; Male Hunt 1964; A Ravishing Idiot 1964; Uncle Benjamin 1969; A Pain in the A...! 1973; La Cage aux Folles 1978; La Cage aux Folles II 1980; Beaumarchais l'Insolent 1996

Moll, Dominik (1962-) Harry, He's Here to Help 2000; Lemming 2005; The Monk 2011

Mollo, Andrew (1930-) It Happened Here 1963; Winstanley 1975

Molloy, Christine Helen 2008; Mister John 2013

Monahan, William London Boulevard 2010; Mojave 2014

Monger, Christopher (1950-) Waiting for the Light 1989; Just like a Woman 1992; The Englishman Who Went up a Hill, but Came down a Mountain 1995; Girl from Rio 2001

Monicelli, Mario (1915-2010) Big Deal on Madonna Street 1958; The Organizer 1963; Casanova '70 1965; Lady Liberty 1971; Viva Italia! 1978; Let's Hope It's a Girl 1985

Monroe, Steven R House of 9 2004; Ice Twisters 2009; I Spit on Your Grave 2010

Montagne, Edward J (1912-2003) The Tattooed Stranger 1950; McHale's Navy 1964

Montesi, Jorge (1950-) Soft Deceit 1994; Freefall: Flight 174 1995

Montgomery, Robert (1904-1981) Lady in the Lake 1947; Eye Witness 1949; Once More, My Darling 1949; The Gallant Hours 1960

Montiel, Dito A Guide to Recognizing Your Saints 2006; Fighting 2009; Boulevard 2014

Monzón, Daniel (1968-) The Kovak Box 2006; Cell 211 2009

Moodysson, Lukas (1969-) Show Me Love 1998; Together 2000; Lilya 4-Ever 2002; A Hole in My Heart 2004; Container 2006; Mammoth 2009; We Are the Best! 2013

Moore, Jason Pitch Perfect 2012; Sisters 2015

Moore (3), John (1970-) Behind Enemy Lines 2001; Flight of the Phoenix 2004; The Omen 2006; Max Payne 2008; A Good Day to Die Hard 2013

Moore (1), Michael aka **Moore, Michael D** (1914-2013) The Fastest Guitar Alive 1966; Paradise, Hawaiian Style 1966; Kill a Dragon 1967; Buckskin 1968

Moore (2), Michael (1954-) Roger & Me 1989; Canadian Bacon 1995; The Big One 1997; Bowling for Columbine 2002; Fahrenheit 9/11 2004; Sicko 2007; Capitalism: a Love Story 2009; Where to Invade Next 2015

Moore, Nick Wild Child 2008; Horrid Henry: the Movie 2011; Pudsey the Dog: the Movie 2014

Moore, Rich Wreck-It Ralph 2012; Zootropolis 2016

Moore, Robert (1927-1984) Murder by Death 1976; The Cheap Detective 1978; Chapter Two 1979

Moore, Simon Under Suspicion 1991; Up on the Roof 1997

Moore, Tom 'Night, Mother 1986; Geppetto 2000

Moore, Tomm The Secret of Kells 2009; Song of the Sea 2014

Moorhouse, Jocelyn (1960-) Proof 1991; How to Make an American Quilt 1995; A Thousand Acres 1997; The Dressmaker 2015

Mora, Philippe (1949-) Mad Dog 1976; The Return of Captain Invincible 1983; A Breed Apart 1984; Howling II: Your Sister Is a Werewolf 1984; Death of a Soldier 1985; Communion 1989

Morahan, Andrew aka **Morahan, Andy** Highlander III: the Sorcerer 1995; Murder in Mind 1996

Morahan, Christopher (1929-) Diamonds for Breakfast 1968; All Neat in Black Stockings 1969; Clockwise 1986; Paper Mask 1990

Moran, Nick (1969-) Telstar: the Joe Meek Story 2008; The Kid 2010

Moreau, David Them 2006; The Eye 2008

Morel, Pierre District 13 2004; Taken 2007; From Paris with Love 2010; The Gunman 2015

Moretti, Nanni (1953-) Dear Diary 1994; Aprile 1998; The Son's Room 2001; The Caiman 2006; We Have a Pope 2011; Mia Madre 2015

Morgan, Glen Willard 2003; Black Christmas 2006

Morgen, Brett The Kid Stays in the Picture 2001; Cobain: Montage of Heck 2015

Morley, Carol Dreams of a Life 2011; The Falling 2014

Morneau, Louis Bats 1999; Made Men 1999; Joy Ride 2: Dead Ahead 2008

Morris (2), David McCullin 2012; Attacking the Devil: Harold Evans and the Last Nazi War Crime 2014

Morris, David Burton (1948-) Patti Rocks 1987; Jersey Girl 1992; And the Beat Goes On: the Sonny and Cher Story 1999; Chasing a Dream 2009; Ice Dreams 2009

Morris, Ernest (1915-1987) Echo of Diana 1963; Shadow of Fear 1963; The Sicilians 1964; The Return of Mr Moto 1965

Morris, Errol (1948-) The Thin Blue Line 1988; The Dark Wind 1991; A Brief History of Time 1992; Mr Death: the Rise and Fall of Fred A Leuchter Jr 1999; The Fog of War: Eleven Lessons from the Life of Robert S McNamara 2003; Standard Operating Procedure 2008; Tabloid 2010; The Unknown Known 2013

Morris, Howard (1919-2005) Who's Minding the Mint? 1967; With Six You Get Eggroll 1968; Don't Drink the Water 1969

Morris, Jacqui McCullin 2012; Attacking the Devil: Harold Evans and the Last Nazi War Crime 2014

Morrison, Paul Solomon and Gaenor 1998; Wondrous Oblivion 2003; Little Ashes 2008

Morrissey, Paul (1939-) Flesh 1968; Trash 1970; Women in Revolt 1971; Heat 1972; Blood for Dracula 1974; Flesh for Frankenstein 1974; The Hound of the Baskervilles 1977

Morse, Hollingsworth Pufnstuf 1970; Daughters of Satan 1972

Morse, Terry aka **Morse, Terrell O** (1906-1984) British Intelligence 1940; Fog Island 1945; Dangerous Money 1946; Unknown World 1951; Young Dillinger 1965

Morton, Rocky DOA 1988; Super Mario Bros 1993

Mosher, Gregory A Life in the Theater 1993; The Prime Gig 2000

Mostow, Jonathan (1961-) Breakdown 1997; U-571 2000; Terminator 3: Rise of the Machines 2003; Surrogates 2009

Mottola, Greg (1964-) The Daytrippers 1998; Superbad 2007; Adventureland 2009; Paul 2010; Clear History 2013; Keeping Up with the Joneses 2016

Moverman, Oren The Messenger 2009; Rampart 2011; Time out of Mind 2014

Mowbray, Malcolm A Private Function 1984; The Boyfriend School 1990; The Revengers' Comedies 1997

Moxey, John Llewellyn aka **Moxey, John** (1925-) The City of the Dead 1960; Foxhole in Cairo 1960; Circus of Fear 1967

Moyle, Allan (1947-) Times Square 1980; Pump Up the Volume 1990; The Gun in Betty Lou's Handbag 1992; Empire Records 1995; XChange 2000; Weirdsville 2006

Muccino, Gabriele (1967-) The Pursuit of Happyness 2006; Seven Pounds 2008; Playing for Keeps 2012; Fathers and Daughters 2015

Mulcahy, Russell (1953-) Razorback 1984; Highlander 1986; Highlander II: the Quickening 1990; Ricochet 1991; Blue Ice 1992; The Real McCoy 1993; The Shadow 1994; Silent Trigger 1996; Talos the Mummy 1997; Resurrection 1999; Swimming Upstream 2003; Resident Evil: Extinction 2007; The Sitter 2007; Prayers for Bobby 2009

Mullan, Peter (1959-) Orphans 1998; The Magdalene Sisters 2002; Neds 2010

Mulligan, Robert (1925-2008) Fear Strikes Out 1957; The Great Impostor 1960; The Rat Race 1960; Come September 1961; The Spiral Road 1962; To Kill a Mockingbird 1962; Love with the Proper Stranger 1963; Baby the Rain Must Fall 1965; Inside Daisy Clover 1965; Up the Down Staircase 1967; The Stalking Moon 1968; The Pursuit of Happiness 1971; Summer of '42 1971; The Other 1972; Bloodbrothers 1978; Same Time, Next Year 1978; Kiss Me Goodbye 1982; Clara's Heart 1988; The Man in the Moon 1991

Münch, Christopher (1962-) The Hours and Times 1992; Color of a Brisk and Leaping Day 1996

Mundhra, Jag (1948-2011) Night Eyes 1990; Improper Conduct 1994; Provoked: a True Story 2006

Mune, Ian (1941-) The End of the Golden Weather 1992; What Becomes of the Broken Hearted? 1999

Mungiu, Cristian 4 Months, 3 Weeks and 2 Days 2007; Tales from the Golden Age 2009; Beyond the Hills 2012

Munk, Andrzej (1921-1961) Eroica 1958; Passenger 1963

Munroe, Kevin TMNT 2007; Ratchet & Clank 2016

Murakami, Jimmy T (1933-2014) Battle beyond the Stars 1980; When the Wind Blows 1986; Christmas Carol: the Movie 2001

Murlowski, John Amityville: a New Generation 1993; Automatic 1994; The Secret Agent Club 1995; Contagion 2001; Next Stop Murder 2010

Murnau, F W aka **Murnau, Friedrich W** (1888-1931) The Haunted Castle 1921; Nosferatu, a Symphony of Horrors 1922; The Last Laugh 1924; Faust 1926; Tartuffe 1926; Sunrise 1927; Tabu 1931

Murphy, Dudley (1897-1968) The Emperor Jones 1933; One Third of a Nation 1939

Murphy, Geoff (1938-) Goodbye Pork Pie 1981; Utu 1983; The Quiet Earth 1985; Young Guns II 1990; Freejack 1992; The Last Outlaw 1993; Under Siege 2 1995; Fortress 2: Re-entry 1999

Murphy, Maeve Silent Grace 2001; Beyond the Fire 2008

Murphy, Nick The Awakening 2011; Blood 2012

Murphy, Pat Anne Devlin 1984; Nora 1999

Murphy, Ryan Running with Scissors 2006; Eat Pray Love 2010; The Normal Heart 2014

Murray, Rupert Unknown White Male 2005; The End of the Line 2009

Murro, Noam Smart People 2007; 300: Rise of an Empire 2013

Musker, John (1953-) Basil the Great Mouse Detective 1986; The Little Mermaid 1989; Aladdin 1992; Hercules 1997; Treasure Planet 2002; The Princess and the Frog 2009

Mustan Baazigar 1993; Aitraaz 2004

Mutrux, Floyd Aloha, Bobby and Rose 1975; American Hot Wax 1977; There Goes My Baby 1994

Myerson, Alan (1940-) Steelyard Blues 1973; Police Academy 5: Assignment Miami Beach 1988; Holiday Affair 1996

Mylod, Mark Ali G indahouse 2002; The Big White 2005; What's Your Number? 2011

N

Na Hong-jin The Chaser 2008; The Yellow Sea 2010

Naess, Petter Elling 2001; Cross of Honour 2012

Nahon, Chris Kiss of the Dragon 2001; Blood: the Last Vampire 2008

Nair, Mira (1957-) Salaam Bombay! 1988; Mississippi Masala 1991; The Perez Family 1995; Kama Sutra: a Tale of Love 1996; Monsoon Wedding 2001; 11'09"01 – September 11 2002; Hysterical Blindness 2002; Vanity Fair 2004; The Namesake 2006; Amelia 2009; New York, I Love You 2009; The Reluctant Fundamentalist 2012

Najafi, Babak Easy Money II 2012; London Has Fallen 2016

Nakache, Olivier Untouchable 2011; Samba 2014

Nakashima, Tetsuya Kamikaze Girls: the End 2004; Memories of Matsuko 2006; Confessions 2010

Nakata, Hideo (1961-) Ring 1997; Ring 2 1998; Chaos 1999; Dark Water 2002; The Ring Two 2004; Chatroom 2010; Death Game 2010

Nalluri, Bharat (1966-) Downtime 1997; Killing Time 1998; Miss Pettigrew Lives for a Day 2007; Spooks: the Greater Good 2015

Naranjo, Gerardo I'm Gonna Explode 2008; Miss Bala 2011

Narizzano, Silvio (1927-2011) Die! Die! My Darling 1964; Georgy Girl 1966; Blue 1968; Loot 1970; Why Shoot the Teacher 1976; The Class of Miss MacMichael 1978

Natali, Vincenzo (1969-) Cube 1997; Cypher 2002; Paris, Je T'Aime 2006; Splice 2009; Haunter 2013

Nava, Gregory (1949-) El Norte 1983; A Time of Destiny 1988; My Family 1994; Selena 1997; Why Do Fools Fall in Love? 1998

Nazarro, Ray (1902-1986) Al Jennings of Oklahoma 1951; Indian Uprising 1951; The Bandits of Corsica 1953; Southwest Passage 1954; The Hired Gun 1957; Apache Territory 1958

Neame, Ronald (1911-2010) Take My Life 1947; Golden Salamander 1949; The Card 1952; The Million Pound Note 1953; The Man Who Never Was 1955; Windom's Way 1957; The Horse's Mouth 1958; Tunes of Glory 1960; Escape from Zahrain 1962; I Could Go On Singing 1963; The Chalk Garden 1964; Gambit 1966; A Man Could Get Killed 1966; Prudence and the Pill 1968; The Prime of Miss Jean Brodie 1969; Scrooge 1970; The Poseidon Adventure 1972; The Odessa File 1974; Meteor 1979; Hopscotch 1980; First Monday in October 1981; Foreign Body 1986

Needham, Hal (1931-2013) Smokey and the Bandit 1977; Hooper 1978; Cactus Jack 1979; Smokey and the Bandit II 1980; The Cannonball Run 1981; Cannonball Run II 1983; Stroker Ace 1983

Negulesco, Jean (1900-1993) The Conspirators 1944; The Mask of Dimitrios 1944; Humoresque 1946; Nobody Lives Forever 1946; Three Strangers 1946; Deep Valley 1947; Johnny Belinda 1948; Road House 1948; Britannia Mews 1949; The Mudlark 1950; Three Came Home 1950; O Henry's Full House 1952; Phone Call from a Stranger 1952; How to Marry a Millionaire 1953; Scandal at Scourie 1953; Titanic 1953; Three Coins in the Fountain 1954; Woman's World 1954; Daddy Long Legs 1955; The Rains of Ranchipur 1955; Boy on a Dolphin 1957; A Certain Smile 1958; The Gift of Love 1958; The Best of Everything 1959; Count Your Blessings 1959; Jessica 1962; The Pleasure Seekers 1964; The Heroes 1968; Hello – Goodbye 1970

Neilan, Marshall aka **Neilan, Marshall A** (1891-1958) Rebecca of Sunnybrook Farm 1917; Stella Maris 1918; Daddy Long Legs 1919; Hell's Angels 1930; The Lemon Drop Kid 1934

Neill, Roy William (1887-1946) The Black Room 1935; The Lone Wolf Returns 1936; Dr Syn 1937; Sherlock Holmes and the Secret Weapon 1942; Frankenstein Meets the Wolf Man 1943; Sherlock Holmes Faces Death 1943; Sherlock Holmes in Washington 1943; The House of Fear 1944; The Pearl of Death 1944; The Scarlet Claw 1944; Sherlock Holmes and the Spider Woman 1944; Pursuit to Algiers 1945; The Woman in Green 1945; Black Angel 1946; Dressed to Kill 1946; Terror by Night 1946

Neilson, James (1909-1979) Night Passage 1957; Bon Voyage! 1962; Moon Pilot 1962; Dr Syn, Alias the Scarecrow 1963; Summer Magic 1963; The Moon-Spinners 1964; The Legend of Young Dick Turpin 1965; The Adventures of Bullwhip Griffin 1967; Where Angels Go... Trouble Follows 1968

Nelson, Gary (1934-) Molly and Lawless John 1972; Santee 1973; Freaky Friday 1976; The Black Hole 1979; Agatha Christie's Murder in Three Acts 1986; Allan Quatermain and the Lost City of Gold 1987; The Return of Ironside 1993

Nelson, Gene (1920-1996) Kissin' Cousins 1964; Your Cheatin' Heart

1964; Harum Scarum 1965; The Cool Ones 1967

Nelson, Jessie Corrina, Corrina 1994; I Am Sam 2001; Christmas with the Coopers 2015

Nelson, Ralph (1916-1987) Requiem for a Heavyweight 1962; Lilies of the Field 1963; Soldier in the Rain 1963; Fate Is the Hunter 1964; Father Goose 1964; Once a Thief 1965; Duel at Diablo 1966; Counterpoint 1967; Charly 1968; tick... tick... tick... 1969; Soldier Blue 1970; Flight of the Doves 1971; The Wrath of God 1972; The Wilby Conspiracy 1975; Embryo 1976; A Hero Ain't Nothin' but a Sandwich 1978

Nelson, Tim Blake (1964-) Eye of God 1997; The Grey Zone 2001; O 2001

Nesher, Avi Timebomb 1991; Doppelganger 1993; Taxman 1998

Neumann, Kurt (1908-1958) Ellery Queen Master Detective 1940; The Unknown Guest 1943; Tarzan and the Amazons 1945; Tarzan and the Leopard Woman 1946; Tarzan and the Huntress 1947; The Kid from Texas 1950; Cattle Drive 1951; The Ring 1952; Son of Ali Baba 1952; Tarzan and the She-Devil 1953; Carnival Story 1954; Mohawk 1956; The Deerslayer 1957; Kronos 1957; The Fly 1958

Neveldine, Mark (1973-) Crank 2006; Gamer 2008; Crank: High Voltage 2009; Ghost Rider: Spirit of Vengeance 2012; The Vatican Tapes 2015

Neville, Morgan Twenty Feet from Stardom 2013; Best of Enemies 2015

Newby, Chris (1957-) Anchoress 1993; Madagascar Skin 1995

Newell, Mike (1942-) The Man in the Iron Mask 1977; The Awakening 1980; Bad Blood 1982; Dance with a Stranger 1984; The Good Father 1986; Amazing Grace and Chuck 1987; Soursweet 1988; Enchanted April 1991; Into the West 1992; An Awfully Big Adventure 1994; Four Weddings and a Funeral 1994; Donnie Brasco 1997; Pushing Tin 1999; Mona Lisa Smile 2003; Harry Potter and the Goblet of Fire 2005; Love in the Time of Cholera 2007; Prince of Persia: the Sands of Time 2010; Great Expectations 2012

Newfield, Sam aka **Scott, Sherman** (1899-1964) Aces and Eights 1936; Knight of the Plains 1939; The Lone Rider in Ghost Town 1941; Sheriff of Sage Valley 1942; The Monster Maker 1944; The Gambler and the Lady 1952

Newland, John (1917-2000) The Spy with My Face 1966; Don't Be Afraid of the Dark 1973

Newley, Anthony (1931-1999) Can Heironymus Merkin Ever Forget Mercy Humppe and Find True Happiness? 1969; Summertree 1971

Newman, Joseph M (1909-2006) 711 Ocean Drive 1950; Love Nest 1951; Pony Soldier 1952; Red Skies of Montana 1952; Kiss of Fire 1955; This Island Earth 1955; Fort Massacre 1958; The Big Circus 1959; The Gunfight at Dodge City 1959; Tarzan, the Ape Man 1959; King of the Roaring 20s – the Story of Arnold Rothstein 1961; A Thunder of Drums 1961

Newman, Kyle Fanboys 2008; Barely Lethal 2015

Newman, Paul (1925-2008) Rachel, Rachel 1968; Sometimes a Great Notion 1971; The Effect of Gamma Rays on Man-in-the-Moon Marigolds 1972; The Shadow Box 1980; Harry and Son 1984; The Glass Menagerie 1987

Newmeyer, Fred C (1888-1967) A Sailor-Made Man 1921; Grandma's Boy 1922; Safety Last 1923; Girl Shy 1924; Hot Water 1924; The Freshman 1925; Fast and Loose 1930

Newton, Joel Jennifer 1953; Main Street to Broadway 1953

Nibbelink, Phil An American Tail: Fievel Goes West 1991; We're Back! A Dinosaur's Story 1993

Niblo, Fred (1874-1948) The Mark of Zorro 1920; The Three Musketeers 1921; Blood and Sand 1922; Ben-Hur: a Tale of the Christ 1925; The Temptress 1926; Camille 1927; The Mysterious Lady 1928

Niccol, Andrew (1964-) Gattaca 1997; SIMØNE 2002; Lord of War 2005; In Time 2011; The Host 2013; Good Kill 2014

Nichetti, Maurizio (1948-) The Icicle Thief 1989; Volere, Volare 1991

Nichols, Dudley (1895-1960) Government Girl 1943; Sister Kenny 1946; Mourning Becomes Electra 1947

Nichols Jr, George (1897-1939) Anne of Green Gables 1934; Finishing School 1934; The Return of Peter Grimm 1935

Nichols, Jeff Shotgun Stories 2007; Take Shelter 2011; Mud 2012; Midnight Special 2015; Loving 2016

Nichols, Mike (1931-2014) Who's Afraid of Virginia Woolf? 1966; The Graduate 1967; Catch-22 1970; Carnal Knowledge 1971; The Day of the Dolphin 1973; The Fortune 1975; Silkwood 1983; Heartburn 1986; Biloxi Blues 1988; Working Girl 1988; Postcards from the Edge 1990; Regarding Henry 1991; Wolf 1994; The Birdcage 1996; Primary Colors 1998; What Planet Are You From? 2000; Wit 2001; Closer 2004; Charlie Wilson's War 2007

Nicholson, Jack (1937-) Drive, He Said 1971; Goin' South 1978; The Two Jakes 1990

Nicloux, Guillaume The Nun 2013; The Kidnapping of Michel Houellebecq 2014; Valley of Love 2015

Nicolaou, Ted TerrorVision 1986; Subspecies 1991; Dragonworld 1994

Nimoy, Leonard (1931-2015) Star Trek III: the Search for Spock 1984; Star Trek IV: the Voyage Home 1986; Three Men and a Baby 1987; The Price of Passion 1988; Funny about Love 1990; Holy Matrimony 1994

Nispel, Marcus (1963-) The Texas Chainsaw Massacre 2003; Frankenstein 2004; Pathfinder 2006; Friday the 13th 2009; Conan the Barbarian 2011; The Asylum 2015

Noé, Gaspar (1963-) Seul contre Tous 1998; Irreversible 2002; Destricted 2006; Enter the Void 2010; 7 Days in Havana 2012; Love 2015

Noer, Michael R 2010; Northwest 2013

Nolan, Christopher (1970-) Following 1998; Memento 2000; Insomnia 2002; Batman Begins 2005; The Prestige 2006; The Dark Knight 2008; Inception 2010; The Dark Knight Rises 2012; Interstellar 2014; Dunkirk 2017

Nolbandov, Sergei (1895-1971) Ships with Wings 1942; Undercover 1943

Noonan, Chris (1952-) Babe 1995; Miss Potter 2006

Norgaard, Mikkel Klown 2010; The Keeper of Lost Causes 2013; The Absent One 2014

Norman, Leslie (1911-1993) The Night My Number Came Up 1955; X the Unknown 1956; The Shiralee 1957; Dunkirk 1958; The Long and the Short and the Tall 1960; Season of Passion 1960; Spare the Rod 1961; Mix Me a Person 1962

Norrington, Stephen (1965-) Death Machine 1994; Blade 1998; The League of Extraordinary Gentlemen 2003

Norris, Aaron (1951-) Braddock: Missing in Action III 1988; Delta Force 2 1990; The Hitman 1991; Top Dog 1995

Norris, Rufus Broken 2012; London Road 2014

Norton, Bill L aka **Norton, B W L** aka **Norton, Bill** (1943-) Cisco Pike 1971; More American Graffiti 1979; Baby: Secret of the Lost Legend 1985; Three for the Road 1987; Deadly Whispers 1995; Thirst 1998; Generation Gap 2008

Nosseck, Max (1902-1972) Overture to Glory 1940; The Brighton Strangler 1945; Dillinger 1945; Black Beauty 1946

Nossiter, Jonathan (1961-) Sunday 1997; Mondovino 2004; Natural Resistance 2014

Noujaim, Jehane Startup.com 2001; The Square 2013

Nourizadeh, Nima Project X 2012; American Ultra 2015

Nowlan, Cherie Thank God He Met Lizzie 1997; Clubland 2008

Noyce, Phillip (1950-) Newsfront 1978; Heatwave 1981; Shadows of the Peacock 1987; Dead Calm 1988; Blind Fury 1990; Patriot Games 1992; Sliver 1993; Clear and Present Danger 1994; The Saint 1997; The Bone Collector 1999; The Quiet American 2002; Rabbit-Proof Fence 2002; Catch a Fire 2006; Salt 2010; The Giver 2014

Nuchtern, Simon Snuff 1976; Savage Dawn 1985

Nugent, Elliott (1899-1980) Life Begins 1932; Enter Madame! 1933; If I Were Free 1933; She Loves Me Not 1934; Splendor 1935; And So They Were Married 1936; The Cat and the Canary 1939; Never Say Die 1939; Nothing but the Truth 1941; The Male Animal 1942; The Crystal Ball 1943; Up in Arms 1944; My Favorite Brunette 1947; Welcome Stranger 1947; My Girl Tisa 1948; The Great Gatsby 1949; Mr Belvedere Goes to College 1949; Just for You 1952

Nunez, Victor (1945-) A Flash of Green 1984; Ruby in Paradise 1993; Ulee's Gold 1997

Nunn, Trevor (1940-) Lady Jane 1985; Twelfth Night 1996

Nussbaum, Joe Sleepover 2004; American Pie Presents the Naked Mile 2006; Sydney White 2007; Prom 2011

Nutley, Colin (1944-) House of Angels 1992; Under the Sun 1998

Nyby, Christian (1913-1993) The Thing from Another World 1951; Operation CIA 1965

Nygard, Roger (1962-) American Yakuza 2: Back to Back 1996; Trekkies 1997

O

Oblowitz, Michael This World, Then the Fireworks 1996; The Breed 2001; The Foreigner 2003; Out for a Kill 2003

Oboler, Arch (1909-1987) Strange Holiday 1942; Bewitched 1945; Five 1951; Bwana Devil 1952; The Bubble 1966

Obrow, Jeffrey The Kindred 1986; Bram Stoker's Legend of the Mummy 1998

O'Callaghan, Matthew Curious George 2006; Open Season 2 2008

Ocelot, Michel Kirikou and the Sorceress 1998; Azur & Asmar: the Princes' Quest 2006; Tales of the Night 2011

O'Connolly, Jim aka **O'Connolly, James** (1926-1987) The Hi-Jackers 1963; Smokescreen 1964; Crooks and Coronets 1969; The Valley of Gwangi 1969; Tower of Evil 1972

O'Connor, Gavin Tumbleweeds 1999; Miracle 2004; Pride and Glory 2007; Warrior 2011; Jane Got a Gun 2015; The Accountant 2016

O'Connor, Pat (1943-) Cal 1984; A Month in the Country 1987; Stars and Bars 1988; The January Man 1989; Fools of Fortune 1990; Circle of Friends 1995; Inventing the Abbotts 1997; Dancing at Lughnasa 1998; Sweet November 2001; Private Peaceful 2012

Odets, Clifford (1906-1963) None but the Lonely Heart 1944; The Story on Page One 1959

O'Donnell, Damien East Is East 1999; Heartlands 2002; Inside I'm Dancing 2004

Oedekerk, Steve (1961-) Ace Ventura: When Nature Calls 1995; Nothing to Lose 1997; Barnyard 2006

O'Fallon, Peter Suicide Kings 1997; A Rumor of Angels 2000

O'Ferrall, George More (1907-1982) Angels One Five 1952; The Holly and the Ivy 1952; The Heart of the Matter 1953; Three Cases of Murder 1953; The Green Scarf 1954; The Woman for Joe 1955; The March Hare 1956

Ogilvie, George (1931-) Mad Max beyond Thunderdome 1985; The Shiralee 1986

O'Hara, Gerry (1925-) The Pleasure Girls 1965; Maroc 7 1966; All the Right Noises 1970; The Bitch 1979; Fanny Hill 1983

O'Haver, Tommy (1967-) Billy's Hollywood Screen Kiss 1998; Get over It 2001; Ella Enchanted 2004

O'Herlihy, Michael (1919-1997) The Fighting Prince of Donegal 1966; The One and Only, Genuine, Original Family Band 1968; Smith! 1969

O'Keefe, Dennis (1908-1968) The Diamond 1954; Angela 1955

Olivier, Laurence (1907-1989) Henry V 1944; Hamlet 1948; Richard III 1955; The Prince and the Showgirl 1957; Three Sisters 1970

Olmi, Ermanno (1931-) Il Posto 1961; The Tree of Wooden Clogs 1978; Long Live the Lady! 1987; The Legend of the Holy Drinker 1988; Tickets 2005

Olsson, Goran Hugo aka **Olsson, Goran** The Black Power Mixtape 1967-1975 2011; Concerning Violence 2014

O'Neil, Robert Vincent *Angel 1984; Avenging Angel 1985*
O'Neill, Kevin *The Secret Policeman's Third Ball 1987; Dinoshark 2010*
Ophüls, Marcel (1927-) *Love at Twenty 1962; Banana Peel 1964; The Sorrow and the Pity 1969; A Sense of Loss 1972; Hotel Terminus: the Life and Times of Klaus Barbie 1987*
Ophüls, Max *aka* **Opuls, Max** (1902-1957) *Liebelei 1932; La Signora di Tutti 1934; Divine 1935; The Exile 1947; Letter from an Unknown Woman 1948; Caught 1949; The Reckless Moment 1949; La Ronde 1950; Le Plaisir 1951; Madame de... 1953; Lola Montès 1955*
Oplev, Niels Arden (1961-) *The Girl with the Dragon Tattoo 2009; Dead Man Down 2013; Flatliners 2017*
Oppenheimer (2), Joshua (1974-) *The Act of Killing 2012; The Look of Silence 2014*
Orme, Stuart (1954-) *The Wolves of Willoughby Chase 1988; The Puppet Masters 1994*
Orr, James (1953-) *Mr Destiny 1990; Man of the House 1994; Christmas in Wonderland 2007*
Ortega, Kenny (1950-) *Hocus Pocus 1993; High School Musical 2006; High School Musical 2 2007; High School Musical 3: Senior Year 2008; Michael Jackson's This Is It 2009*
Oshii, Mamoru (1951-) *Patlabor: the Mobile Police 1989; Ghost in the Shell 1995; Avalon 2000*
Oshima, Nagisa (1932-2013) *Death by Hanging 1968; In the Realm of the Senses 1976; Merry Christmas Mr Lawrence 1982; Max Mon Amour 1986; Gohatto 1999*
Osmond, Louise *Deep Water 2006; Dark Horse 2015; Versus: The Life and Films of Ken Loach 2016*
Ostlund, Ruben *Involuntary 2008; Play 2011; Force Majeure 2014*
O'Sullivan, Shane *Second Generation 1999; Children of the Revolution 2010; Killing Oswald 2013*
O'Sullivan, Thaddeus (1947-) *December Bride 1990; Nothing Personal 1995; Ordinary Decent Criminal 1999; The Heart of Me 2002*
Oswald, Gerd (1919-1989) *The Brass Legend 1956; A Kiss before Dying 1956; Crime of Passion 1957; Valerie 1957; Paris Holiday 1958; Screaming Mimi 1958; Eighty Steps to Jonah 1969; Bunny O'Hare 1971*
Oswald, Richard *aka* **Ornstein, Richard** (1880-1963) *The Living Dead 1932; The Lovable Cheat 1949*
Othenin-Girard, Dominique *After Darkness 1985; Halloween 5: the Revenge of Michael Myers 1989*
Otomo, Katsuhiro (1954-) *Akira 1988; Steamboy 2004*
Ouedraogo, Idrissa (1954-) *Yam Daabo 1986; Yaaba 1989; Tilaï 1990; Samba Traore 1992; Le Cri du Coeur 1994; Kini and Adams 1997; 11'09"01 - September 11 2002*
Ouellette, Jean-Paul *The Unnamable 1988; The Unnamable Returns 1992*
Oury, Gérard (1919-2006) *The Brain 1969; Delusions of Grandeur 1971*
Ové, Horace (1939-) *Pressure 1976; Playing Away 1986*
Owen, Cliff (1919-1993) *A Prize of Arms 1961; The Wrong Arm of the Law 1962; A Man Could Get Killed 1966; That Riviera Touch 1966; The Magnificent Two 1967; The Vengeance of She 1968; Ooh... You Are Awful 1972; Steptoe and Son 1972; No Sex Please - We're British 1973; The Bawdy Adventures of Tom Jones 1976*
Oz, Frank (1944-) *The Dark Crystal 1982; The Muppets Take Manhattan 1984; Little Shop of Horrors 1986; Dirty Rotten Scoundrels 1988; What about Bob? 1991; HouseSitter 1992; The Indian in the Cupboard 1995; In & Out 1997; Bowfinger 1999; The Score 2001; The Stepford Wives 2004; Death at a Funeral 2007*
Ozon, François (1967-) *Sitcom 1997; Criminal Lovers 1999; Water Drops on Burning Rocks 1999; Under the Sand 2000; 8 Women 2001; Swimming Pool 2002; 5x2 2004; Time to Leave 2005; Angel 2006; The Refuge 2009; Potiche 2010; In the House 2012; Jeune & Jolie 2013; The New Girlfriend 2014*
Ozpetek, Ferzan (1959-) *Hamam: the Turkish Bath 1996; Le Fate Ignoranti 2001; Facing Window 2003; Loose Cannons 2010; A Magnificent Haunting 2012*

Ozu, Yasujiro (1903-1963) *Tokyo Chorus 1931; I Was Born, but... 1932; The Only Son 1936; There Was a Father 1942; Record of a Tenement Gentleman 1947; Hen in the Wind 1948; Late Spring 1949; Early Summer 1951; The Flavour of Green Tea over Rice 1952; Tokyo Story 1953; Early Spring 1956; Tokyo Twilight 1957; Equinox Flower 1958; Floating Weeds 1959; Ohayo 1959; Late Autumn 1960; The End of Summer 1961; An Autumn Afternoon 1962*

P

Pabst, G W (1885-1967) *The Joyless Street 1925; Secrets of a Soul 1926; The Love of Jeanne Ney 1927; Crisis 1928; Diary of a Lost Girl 1929; Pandora's Box 1929; Westfront 1918 1930; Kameradschaft 1931; The Threepenny Opera 1931; Don Quixote 1932; Mademoiselle Docteur 1936; Paracelsus 1943*
Pacino, Al (1940-) *Looking for Richard 1996; Wilde Salomé 2011; Salomé 2013*
Padilha, José *Bus 174 2002; The Elite Squad 2007; Elite Squad: the Enemy Within 2010; RoboCop 2014*
Page, Anthony (1935-) *Inadmissible Evidence 1968; Alpha Beta 1973; I Never Promised You a Rose Garden 1977; Absolution 1978; The Lady Vanishes 1979; FDR: the Last Year 1980; Bill 1981; The Patricia Neal Story 1981; Second Serve 1986*
Pagnol, Marcel (1895-1974) *Angèle 1934; César 1936; The Baker's Wife 1938; Topaze 1951; Manon des Sources 1952*
Paine, Chris *Who Killed the Electric Car? 2006; Revenge of the Electric Car 2011*
Pakula, Alan J (1928-1998) *The Sterile Cuckoo 1969; Klute 1971; Love and Pain and the Whole Damn Thing 1973; The Parallax View 1974; All the President's Men 1976; Comes a Horseman 1978; Starting Over 1979; Rollover 1981; Sophie's Choice 1982; Dream Lover 1986; Orphans 1987; See You in the Morning 1989; Presumed Innocent 1990; Consenting Adults 1992; The Pelican Brief 1993; The Devil's Own 1997*
Pal, George (1908-1980) *tom thumb 1958; Atlantis, the Lost Continent 1960; The Time Machine 1960; The Wonderful World of the Brothers Grimm 1962; 7 Faces of Dr Lao 1963*
Palcy, Euzhan (1958-) *Rue Cases Nègres 1983; A Dry White Season 1989*
Palfi, Gyorgy *Hukkle 2002; Taxidermia 2006*
Palmer, Ben *The Inbetweeners Movie 2011; Man Up 2015*
Palmer, Tony (1941-) *200 Motels 1971; Wagner 1983; Testimony 1987; The Children 1990*
Paltenghi, David (1919-1961) *Orders Are Orders 1954; The Love Match 1955; Dick Turpin - Highwayman 1956*
Paltrow, Bruce (1943-2002) *A Little Sex 1981; Duets 2000*
Paltrow, Jake *The Good Night 2005; Bad Land: Road to Fury 2014*
Palud, Xavier *Them 2006; The Eye 2008*
Panahi, Jafar (1960-) *The White Balloon 1995; The Circle 2000; Crimson Gold 2003; Offside 2006*
Panama, Norman (1914-2003) *Callaway Went Thataway 1951; Above and Beyond 1952; Knock on Wood 1954; The Court Jester 1956; That Certain Feeling 1956; The Baited Trap 1959; The Road to Hong Kong 1962; Not with My Wife, You Don't! 1966; How to Commit Marriage 1969; The Maltese Bippy 1969*
Panfilov, Gleb (1934-) *The Theme 1979; Vassa 1983*
Pang, Danny *aka* **Pang Brothers** (1965-) *Bangkok Dangerous 2000; The Eye 2002; The Eye 2 2004; Bangkok Dangerous 2007; The Messengers 2007*
Pang, Oxide *aka* **Pang Brothers** (1965-) *Bangkok Dangerous 2000; The Eye 2002; Ab-normal Beauty 2004; The Eye 2 2004; Bangkok Dangerous 2007; The Messengers 2007*
Panh, Rithy (1964-) *Rice People 1994; S21: the Khmer Rouge Killing Machine 2003; The Sea Wall 2008*
Paquet-Brenner, Gilles *Sarah's Key 2010; Dark Places 2015*

Paradjanov, Sergei (1924-1990) *Shadows of Our Forgotten Ancestors 1964; The Colour of Pomegranates 1969; The Legend of the Suram Fortress 1984; Ashik Kerib 1988*
Parello, Charles *aka* **Parello, Chuck** *Henry: Portrait of a Serial Killer, Part II 1996; Ed Gein 2000; The Hillside Strangler 2004*
Paris, Jerry (1925-1986) *Don't Raise the Bridge, Lower the River 1968; How Sweet It Is! 1968; Viva Max! 1969; The Grasshopper 1970; Evil Roy Slade 1971; Police Academy 2: Their First Assignment 1985; Police Academy 3: Back in Training 1986*
Parisot, Dean (1952-) *Home Fries 1998; Galaxy Quest 1999; Fun with Dick and Jane 2005; Red 2 2013*
Park Chan-wook (1963-) *Sympathy for Mr Vengeance 2002; Oldboy 2003; Sympathy for Lady Vengeance 2005; I'm a Cyborg, but That's OK 2006; Thirst 2009; Stoker 2013*
Park, Nick (1958-) *Chicken Run 2000; Wallace & Gromit in The Curse of the Were-Rabbit 2005; Early Man 2018*
Parker, Alan (1944-) *Bugsy Malone 1976; Midnight Express 1978; Fame 1980; Pink Floyd - The Wall 1982; Shoot the Moon 1982; Birdy 1984; Angel Heart 1987; Mississippi Burning 1988; Come See the Paradise 1990; The Commitments 1991; The Road to Wellville 1994; Evita 1996; Angela's Ashes 1999; The Life of David Gale 2003*
Parker, Alan G *Who Killed Nancy? The True Story... 2009; Status Quo: Hello Quo 2012*
Parker, David (1947-) *Hercules Returns 1993; Diana & Me 1997*
Parker, Ol (1969-) *Imagine Me and You 2005; Now Is Good 2012*
Parker, Oliver (1960-) *Othello 1995; An Ideal Husband 1999; The Importance of Being Earnest 2002; Fade to Black 2006; St Trinian's 2007; Dorian Gray 2009; St Trinian's 2: the Legend of Fritton's Gold 2009; Johnny English Reborn 2011; Dad's Army 2016*
Parker, Trey (1969-) *Cannibal! the Musical 1993; Orgazmo 1997; South Park: Bigger, Longer & Uncut 1999; Team America: World Police 2004*
Parks, Gordon (1912-2006) *The Learning Tree 1969; Shaft 1971; Shaft's Big Score! 1972; The Super Cops 1973; Leadbelly 1976*
Parks Jr, Gordon (1934-1979) *Superfly 1972; Three the Hard Way 1974; Aaron Loves Angela 1975*
Parolini, Gianfranco *aka* **Kramer, Frank** (1930-) *Sartana 1968; Sabata 1969; Adios, Sabata 1970; Return of Sabata 1971; God's Gun 1977*
Parrish, Robert (1916-1995) *Cry Danger 1951; The Mob 1951; Assignment - Paris 1952; Rough Shoot 1952; The San Francisco Story 1952; The Purple Plain 1954; Lucy Gallant 1955; Fire Down Below 1957; Saddle the Wind 1958; The Wonderful Country 1959; In the French Style 1963; Up from the Beach 1965; The Bobo 1967; Casino Royale 1967; Duffy 1968; Journey to the Far Side of the Sun 1969; A Town Called Hell 1971; The Marseille Contract 1974*
Parrott, James (1897-1939) *The Two Tars 1928; Perfect Day 1929; Pardon Us 1931; County Hospital 1932; The Music Box 1932; Twice Two 1933*
Parry, Gordon (1908-1981) *Bond Street 1948; The Gay Adventure 1949; Now Barabbas Was a Robber 1949; Third Time Lucky 1949; Tom Brown's Schooldays 1951; Women of Twilight 1952; Front Page Story 1953; Innocents in Paris 1953; A Yank in Ermine 1955; Sailor Beware! 1956; A Touch of the Sun 1956; Tread Softly Stranger 1958; The Navy Lark 1959*
Parry, Richard *South West Nine 2001; A Night in the Woods 2011*
Pascal, Gabriel (1894-1954) *Major Barbara 1941; Caesar and Cleopatra 1945*
Pasolini, Pier Paolo (1922-1975) *Accattone 1961; Mamma Roma 1962; RoGoPaG 1962; The Gospel According to St Matthew 1964; Hawks and Sparrows 1966; The Witches 1966; Oedipus Rex 1967; Theorem 1968; Pigsty 1969; The Decameron 1970; Medea 1970; The Canterbury Tales 1971; The Arabian*

Nights 1974; Salo, or the 120 Days of Sodom 1975
Pasolini, Uberto *Machan 2008; Still Life 2013*
Pasquin, John (1944-) *The Santa Clause 1994; Jungle 2 Jungle 1997; Joe Somebody 2001; Miss Congeniality 2: Armed & Fabulous 2005*
Pasquini, Dania *aka* **Dania** *StreetDance 2010; StreetDance 2 2012; Walking on Sunshine 2014*
Passer, Ivan (1933-) *Born to Win 1971; Law and Disorder 1974; Crime and Passion 1976; Silver Bears 1977; Cutter's Way 1981; Creator 1985; Haunted Summer 1988*
Pate, Jonas (1970-) *Liar 1997; Shrink 2009*
Pattinson, Michael (1957-) *Ground Zero 1987; Almost 1990; Virtual Nightmare 2000*
Patzak, Peter (1945-) *Midnight Cop 1988; Death of a Schoolboy 1990*
Pawlikowski, Pawel *aka* **Pavlikovsky, Paul** (1957-) *The Stringer 1997; Last Resort 2000; My Summer of Love 2004; The Woman in the Fifth 2011; Ida 2013*
Paxton, Bill (1955-) *Frailty 2001; The Greatest Game Ever Played 2005*
Payne, Alexander (1961-) *Citizen Ruth 1996; Election 1999; About Schmidt 2002; Sideways 2004; Paris, Je T'Aime 2006; The Descendants 2011; Nebraska 2013*
Payne, Dave *aka* **Payne, David** *Addams Family Reunion 1998; Just Can't Get Enough 2001; Reeker 2005*
Pearce, Richard (1943-) *Threshold 1981; Country 1984; No Mercy 1986; The Long Walk Home 1990; Leap of Faith 1992; A Family Thing 1996; Witness Protection 1999; South Pacific 2001; The Blues, a Musical Journey: The Road to Memphis 2003; Plainsong 2004*
Peckinpah, Sam (1925-1984) *The Deadly Companions 1961; Ride the High Country 1962; Major Dundee 1965; The Wild Bunch 1969; The Ballad of Cable Hogue 1970; Straw Dogs 1971; The Getaway 1972; Junior Bonner 1972; Pat Garrett and Billy the Kid 1973; Bring Me the Head of Alfredo Garcia 1974; The Killer Elite 1975; Cross of Iron 1977; Convoy 1978; The Osterman Weekend 1983*
Peerce, Larry (1930-) *One Potato, Two Potato 1964; The Big TNT Show 1966; The Incident 1967; Goodbye, Columbus 1969; Ash Wednesday 1973; The Other Side of the Mountain 1975; Two-Minute Warning 1976; Love Child 1982; Wired 1989; The Court-Martial of Jackie Robinson 1990; Breach of Trust 1999; Man of Miracles 1999*
Peirce, Kimberly (1967-) *Boys Don't Cry 1999; Stop-Loss 2007; Carrie 2013*
Pelissier, Anthony (1912-1988) *The History of Mr Polly 1948; The Rocking Horse Winner 1949; Encore 1951; Night without Stars 1951; Meet Me Tonight 1952; Meet Mr Lucifer 1953; Personal Affair 1953*
Pellerin, Jean *For Hire 1997; Escape under Pressure 2000*
Pellington, Mark (1965-) *Going All the Way 1997; Arlington Road 1998; The Mothman Prophecies 2001; U23D 2007*
Penn, Arthur (1922-2010) *The Left Handed Gun 1958; The Miracle Worker 1962; Mickey One 1965; The Chase 1966; Bonnie and Clyde 1967; Alice's Restaurant 1969; Little Big Man 1970; Visions of Eight 1973; Night Moves 1975; The Missouri Breaks 1976; Target 1985; Dead of Winter 1987; Penn & Teller Get Killed 1989*
Penn, Leo (1921-1998) *A Man Called Adam 1966; Judgment in Berlin 1988*
Penn, Sean (1960-) *The Indian Runner 1991; The Crossing Guard 1995; The Pledge 2000; 11'09"01 - September 11 2002; Into the Wild 2007*
Pennebaker, D A (1925-) *Don't Look Back 1967; Monterey Pop 1968; Ziggy Stardust and the Spiders from Mars 1982; The War Room 1993*
Pennington-Richards, C M (1911-2005) *The Oracle 1952; Inn for Trouble 1960; Dentist on the Job 1961; Double Bunk 1961; Ladies Who Do 1963; A Challenge for Robin Hood 1967*
Pepe, Louis *Lost in La Mancha 2002; Brothers of the Head 2005*

Peploe, Clare *High Season 1987; Rough Magic 1995*
Peploe, Mark *Afraid of the Dark 1991; Victory 1995*
Peralta, Stacy (1957-) *Dogtown and Z-Boys 2001; Riding Giants 2004*
Percival, Brian *A Boy Called Dad 2009; The Book Thief 2014*
Perelman, Vadim *House of Sand and Fog 2003; The Life before Her Eyes 2007*
Périer, Etienne (1931-) *Bridge to the Sun 1961; The Swordsman of Siena 1962; When Eight Bells Toll 1971; Zeppelin 1971*
Perry, Alex Ross *Listen Up Philip 2014; Queen of Earth 2015*
Perry, Frank (1930-1995) *David and Lisa 1962; Ladybug, Ladybug 1963; The Swimmer 1968; Last Summer 1969; Trilogy 1969; Diary of a Mad Housewife 1970; Doc 1971; Play It as It Lays 1972; Rancho Deluxe 1975; Mommie Dearest 1981; Monsignor 1982; Compromising Positions 1985; Hello Again 1987*
Perry, Tyler (1969-) *For Colored Girls 2010; Tyler Perry's Why Did I Get Married Too? 2010*
Peters, Charlie *Passed Away 1992; Music from Another Room 1998*
Petersen, Wolfgang (1941-) *The NeverEnding Story 1984; Enemy Mine 1985; Shattered 1991; In the Line of Fire 1993; Outbreak 1995; Air Force One 1997; Das Boot: the Director's Cut 1997; The Perfect Storm 2000; Troy 2004; Poseidon 2006*
Petit, Christopher (1949-) *Radio On 1979; An Unsuitable Job for a Woman 1981*
Petri, Elio (1929-1982) *The Tenth Victim 1965; Investigation of a Citizen above Suspicion 1970; The Working Class Goes to Heaven 1971*
Petrie, Daniel *aka* **Petrie Sr, Daniel** (1920-2004) *The Bramble Bush 1960; A Raisin in the Sun 1961; The Main Attraction 1962; The Idol 1966; The Spy with a Cold Nose 1966; The Neptune Factor 1973; Buster and Billie 1974; The Betsy 1978; Resurrection 1980; Fort Apache, the Bronx 1981; Six Pack 1982; Bay Boy 1984; The Dollmaker 1984; Square Dance 1987; Cocoon: the Return 1988; Rocket Gibraltar 1988; My Name Is Bill W 1989; Lassie: a New Generation 1994; Kissinger and Nixon 1995; Inherit the Wind 1999*
Petrie Jr, Daniel (1952-) *Toy Soldiers 1991; In the Army Now 1994; Rosemont 2015*
Petrie, Donald (1954-) *Mystic Pizza 1988; Opportunity Knocks 1990; Grumpy Old Men 1993; The Favor 1994; Richie Rich 1994; The Associate 1996; My Favorite Martian 1999; Miss Congeniality 2000; How to Lose a Guy in 10 Days 2003; Welcome to Mooseport 2004; Just My Luck 2006; Driving Aphrodite 2008*
Petzold, Christian (1960-) *Barbara 2012; Phoenix 2014*
Pevney, Joseph (1911-2008) *Undercover Girl 1950; Air Cadet 1951; Iron Man 1951; The Strange Door 1951; Flesh and Fury 1952; Meet Danny Wilson 1952; Back to God's Country 1953; Desert Legion 1953; Playgirl 1954; Three Ring Circus 1954; Six Bridges to Cross 1955; Away All Boats 1956; Istanbul 1957; Man of a Thousand Faces 1957; The Midnight Story 1957; Tammy and the Bachelor 1957; Torpedo Run 1958; Cash McCall 1960; The Crowded Sky 1960*
Peyser, John (1916-2002) *The Murder Men 1961; The Young Warriors 1967*
Peyton, Brad *Cats & Dogs: the Revenge of Kitty Galore 2010; Journey 2 the Mysterious Island 2011; San Andreas 2015*
Philibert, Nicolas *Etre et Avoir 2002; Nénette 2010*
Phillips, Maurice *Riders of the Storm 1986; Over Her Dead Body 1990; Another You 1991*
Phillips, Stan *A Christmas Carol 1997; Madeline: Lost in Paris 1999*
Phillips, Todd (1970-) *Road Trip 2000; Old School 2003; Starsky & Hutch 2004; School for Scoundrels 2006; The Hangover 2009; Due Date 2010; The Hangover: Part II 2011; The Hangover Part III 2013; War Dogs 2016*
Pialat, Maurice (1925-2003) *L'Enfance Nue 1968; The Mouth Agape 1974; Loulou 1980; To Our*

Loves 1984; Police 1985; Sous le Soleil de Satan 1987; Van Gogh 1991
Pichel, Irving (1891-1954) The Most Dangerous Game 1932; She 1935; Hudson's Bay 1940; The Man I Married 1940; Life Begins at 8.30 1942; The Pied Piper 1942; Happy Land 1943; The Moon Is Down 1943; And Now Tomorrow 1944; Colonel Effingham's Raid 1945; A Medal for Benny 1945; Tomorrow Is Forever 1945; The Bride Wore Boots 1946; OSS 1946; Something in the Wind 1947; They Won't Believe Me 1947; The Miracle of the Bells 1948; Mr Peabody and the Mermaid 1948; Destination Moon 1950; The Great Rupert 1950; Quicksand 1950; Santa Fe 1951
Pierce, Charles B (1938-2010) The Legend of Boggy Creek 1972; Winterhawk 1975; Grayeagle 1977; The Norseman 1978; The Evictors 1979
Pierson, Arthur (1901-1975) Dangerous Years 1947; The Fighting O'Flynn 1948; Home Town Story 1951
Pierson, Frank aka **Pierson, Frank R** (1925-2012) The Looking Glass War 1969; A Star Is Born 1976; King of the Gypsies 1978; Truman 1995; Conspiracy 2001
Pilger, John The War on Democracy 2007; Utopia 2013
Pillsbury, Sam Zandalee 1991; Free Willy 3: the Rescue 1997; The King and Queen of Moonlight Bay 2003; Raising Waylon 2004
Pink, Steve (1966-) Accepted 2006; Hot Tub Time Machine 2010; About Last Night 2014; Hot Tub Time Machine 2 2014
Pinkaew, Prachya Ong-Bak 2003; Warrior King 2005; Chocolate 2008
Pintoff, Ernest (1931-2002) Dynamite Chicken 1971; Jaguar Lives! 1979
Pirès, Gérard (1942-) Taxi 1998; Steal 2002
Pirosh, Robert (1910-1989) Go for Broke! 1951; Valley of the Kings 1954; The Girl Rush 1955; Spring Reunion 1957
Pitof Vidocq 2001; Catwoman 2004
Pittman, Bruce (1950-) Captive Heart 1996; Chasing Secrets 1999
Placido, Michele (1946-) Romanzo Criminale 2005; Angels of Evil 2010; The Lookout 2012
Plaza, Paco The Christmas Tale 2005; [Rec] 2007; [Rec]² 2009; [Rec]³ Génesis 2012
Plympton, Bill (1946-) The Tune 1992; I Married a Strange Person 1997
Podeswa, Jeremy (1962-) The Five Senses 1999; Fugitive Pieces 2007
Poe, Amos Alphabet City 1984; Triple Bogey on a Par Five Hole 1991
Poiré, Jean-Marie aka **Gaubert, Jean-Marie** (1945-) Les Visiteurs 1993; Les Visiteurs 2: Les Couloirs du Temps 1998; Just Visiting 2001
Poitier, Sidney (1927-) Buck and the Preacher 1972; A Warm December 1973; Uptown Saturday Night 1974; Let's Do It Again 1975; A Piece of the Action 1977; Stir Crazy 1980; Hanky Panky 1982; Ghost Dad 1990
Polanski, Roman (1933-) Knife in the Water 1962; The Beautiful Swindlers 1964; Repulsion 1965; Cul-de-Sac 1966; The Fearless Vampire Killers 1967; Rosemary's Baby 1968; Macbeth 1971; What? 1973; Chinatown 1974; The Tenant 1976; Tess 1979; Pirates 1986; Frantic 1988; Bitter Moon 1992; Death and the Maiden 1994; The Ninth Gate 1999; The Pianist 2002; Oliver Twist 2005; The Ghost 2010; Carnage 2011; Venus in Fur 2013
Poliakoff, Stephen (1952-) Close My Eyes 1991; Century 1993; Food of Love 1997; Glorious 39 2009
Polish, Michael (1972-) Twin Falls Idaho 1999; Jackpot 2001; Northfork 2002; The Astronaut Farmer 2006
Pollack, Jeff (1959-2013) Above the Rim 1994; Booty Call 1997; Lost & Found 1999
Pollack, Sydney (1934-2008) The Slender Thread 1965; This Property Is Condemned 1966; The Scalphunters 1968; Castle Keep 1969; They Shoot Horses, Don't They? 1969; Jeremiah Johnson 1972; The Way We Were 1973; Three Days of the Condor 1975; The Yakuza 1975; Bobby Deerfield 1977; The Electric Horseman 1979; Absence of Malice 1981; Tootsie 1982; Out of Africa 1985; Havana 1990; The Firm 1993; Sabrina 1995;

Random Hearts 1999; The Interpreter 2005; Sketches of Frank Gehry 2006
Polley, Sarah (1979-) Away from Her 2006; Take This Waltz 2011; Stories We Tell 2012
Pollock, George (1907-1979) Rooney 1958; And the Same to You 1960; Murder She Said 1961; Village of Daughters 1961; Kill or Cure 1962; Murder at the Gallop 1963; Murder Ahoy 1964; Murder Most Foul 1964; Ten Little Indians 1965
Polonsky, Abraham (1910-1999) Force of Evil 1948; Tell Them Willie Boy Is Here 1969; Romance of a Horse Thief 1971
Polson, John (1965-) Siam Sunset 1999; Swimfan 2002; Hide and Seek 2005; Tenderness 2007
Pons, Ventura (1945-) Actresses 1996; Beloved/Friend 1998; Food of Love 2002
Ponsoldt, James Smashed 2012; The End of the Tour 2015
Pontecorvo, Gillo (1919-2006) Kapo 1959; The Battle of Algiers 1965; Burn! 1970
Pooh, D J 3 Strikes 2000; The Wash 2001
Pope, Angela Captives 1994; Hollow Reed 1995
Popogrebsky, Alexei Roads to Koktebel 2003; How I Ended This Summer 2010
Porumboiu, Corneliu 12:08 East of Bucharest 2005; Police, Adjective 2009
Posin, Arie The Chumscrubber 2005; The Face of Love 2013
Post, Ted (1918-2013) The Legend of Tom Dooley 1959; Hang 'Em High 1968; Beneath the Planet of the Apes 1969; The Baby 1973; The Harrad Experiment 1973; Magnum Force 1973; Whiffs 1975; Go Tell the Spartans 1977; Good Guys Wear Black 1977; Cagney & Lacey 1981; Stagecoach 1986
Potter, H C (1904-1977) Beloved Enemy 1936; The Cowboy and the Lady 1938; The Shopworn Angel 1938; Blackmail 1939; The Story of Vernon and Irene Castle 1939; Second Chorus 1940; Hellzapoppin' 1941; Mr Lucky 1943; The Farmer's Daughter 1946; Mr Blandings Builds His Dream House 1948; The Time of Your Life 1948; You Gotta Stay Happy 1948; The Miniver Story 1950; Three for the Show 1955; Top Secret Affair 1957
Potter, Sally (1949-) Gold Diggers 1983; Orlando 1992; The Tango Lesson 1997; The Man Who Cried 2000; Yes 2004; Ginger & Rosa 2012
Potterton, Gerald The Railrodder 1965; Heavy Metal 1981
Poulson, Gerry Under the Doctor 1976; Arthur's Dyke 2001
Powell, Dick (1904-1963) Split Second 1953; The Conqueror 1956; You Can't Run Away from It 1956; The Enemy Below 1957; The Hunters 1958
Powell, Michael (1905-1990) The Phantom Light 1934; Lazybones 1935; The Love Test 1935; The Edge of the World 1937; The Lion Has Wings 1939; The Spy in Black 1939; Contraband 1940; The Thief of Bagdad 1940; 49th Parallel 1941; One of Our Aircraft Is Missing 1942; The Life and Death of Colonel Blimp 1943; A Canterbury Tale 1944; I Know Where I'm Going! 1945; A Matter of Life and Death 1946; Black Narcissus 1947; The Red Shoes 1948; The Small Back Room 1949; The Elusive Pimpernel 1950; Gone to Earth 1950; The Tales of Hoffmann 1951; Oh, Rosalinda!! 1955; The Battle of the River Plate 1956; Ill Met by Moonlight 1956; Honeymoon 1959; Peeping Tom 1960; The Queen's Guards 1960; They're a Weird Mob 1966; Age of Consent 1969; The Boy Who Turned Yellow 1972
Pozdorovkin, Maxim Pussy Riot: a Punk Prayer 2013; The Notorious Mr Bout 2014
Prasad, Udayan (1953-) Brothers in Trouble 1995; My Son the Fanatic 1997; Gabriel & Me 2001
Preece, Michael Logan's War: Bound by Honor 1998; The President's Man 2000
Preminger, Otto (1905-1986) Danger - Love at Work 1937; Margin for Error 1943; In the Meantime, Darling 1944; Laura 1944; Fallen Angel 1945; A Royal Scandal 1945; Centennial Summer 1946; Daisy Kenyon 1947; Forever Amber 1947;

That Lady in Ermine 1948; The Fan 1949; Whirlpool 1949; The 13th Letter 1950; Where the Sidewalk Ends 1950; Angel Face 1953; The Moon Is Blue 1953; Carmen Jones 1954; River of No Return 1954; The Court-Martial of Billy Mitchell 1955; The Man with the Golden Arm 1955; Saint Joan 1957; Bonjour Tristesse 1958; Anatomy of a Murder 1959; Porgy and Bess 1959; Exodus 1960; Advise and Consent 1962; The Cardinal 1963; Bunny Lake Is Missing 1965; In Harm's Way 1965; Hurry Sundown 1967; Skidoo 1968; Tell Me That You Love Me, Junie Moon 1970; Such Good Friends 1971; Rosebud 1975; The Human Factor 1979
Pressburger, Emeric (1902-1988) One of Our Aircraft Is Missing 1942; The Life and Death of Colonel Blimp 1943; A Canterbury Tale 1944; I Know Where I'm Going! 1945; A Matter of Life and Death 1946; Black Narcissus 1947; The Red Shoes 1948; The Small Back Room 1949; The Elusive Pimpernel 1950; Gone to Earth 1950; The Tales of Hoffmann 1951; Oh, Rosalinda!! 1955; The Battle of the River Plate 1956; Ill Met by Moonlight 1956
Pressman, Michael (1950-) The Bad News Bears in Breaking Training 1977; Those Lips, Those Eyes 1980; Doctor Detroit 1983; Teenage Mutant Ninja Turtles II: the Secret of the Ooze 1991; Quicksand: No Escape 1992; To Gillian on Her 37th Birthday 1996; To Gillian on Her 37th Birthday 1996
Preston, Gaylene Mr Wrong 1985; Ruby and Rata 1990
Price, David F (1961-) Children of the Corn II: the Final Sacrifice 1993; Dr Jekyll and Ms Hyde 1995
Prince (1958-2016) Under the Cherry Moon 1986; Sign o' the Times 1987; Graffiti Bridge 1990
Prince-Bythewood, Gina (1969-) Disappearing Acts 2000; Love & Basketball 2000; The Secret Life of Bees 2008; Beyond the Lights 2014
Prince, Harold Something for Everyone 1970; A Little Night Music 1977
Prior, David A (1955-2015) Raw Nerve 1991; Good Cop, Bad Cop 1993
Proctor, Elaine Friends 1993; Kin 2000
Provost, Martin Séraphine 2008; Violette 2013
Proyas, Alex (1965-) The Crow 1994; Dark City 1998; I, Robot 2004; Knowing 2009; Gods of Egypt 2016
Pudovkin, Vsevolod I (1893-1953) Mother 1926; The End of St Petersburg 1927; Storm over Asia 1928
Puenzo, Lucía XXY 2007; Wakolda 2013
Puenzo, Luis (1946-) The Official Story 1985; Old Gringo 1989; The Plague 1992
Puiu, Cristi The Death of Mr Lazarescu 2005; Aurora 2010
Pulcini, Robert (1964-) American Splendor 2003; The Nanny Diaries 2007; Cinema Verite 2011; Girl Most Likely 2012
Purdy, Jon Reflections on a Crime 1994; Dillinger and Capone 1995
Pyun, Albert (1953-) Dangerously Close 1986; Cyborg 1989; Journey to the Center of the Earth 1989; Captain America 1990; Kickboxer 2: the Road Back 1990; Brain Smasher... a Love Story 1993; Nemesis 1993; Adrenalin: Fear the Rush 1995; Omega Doom 1996; Postmortem 1999; Ticker 2001

Q

Quale, Steven Final Destination 5 2011; Into the Storm 2014
Quay, Stephen (1947-) Street of Crocodiles 1986; Institute Benjamenta, or This Dream People Call Human Life 1995
Quay, Timothy (1947-) Street of Crocodiles 1986; Institute Benjamenta, or This Dream People Call Human Life 1995
Quine, Richard (1920-1989) All Ashore 1953; Drive a Crooked Road 1954; Pushover 1954; So This Is Paris 1954; My Sister Eileen 1955; Full of Life 1956; The Solid Gold Cadillac 1956; Operation Mad Ball 1957; Bell, Book and Candle 1958; It Happened to Jane 1959; Strangers When We Meet 1960; The World of Suzie Wong 1960; The Notorious Landlady 1962; Paris When It Sizzles 1964; Sex and

the Single Girl 1964; How to Murder Your Wife 1965; Oh Dad, Poor Dad, Mama's Hung You in the Closet and I'm Feelin' So Sad 1967; The Prisoner of Zenda 1979
Quintano, Gene (1946-) Why Me? 1990; National Lampoon's Loaded Weapon 1 1993; Dollar for the Dead 1998

R

Rademakers, Fons (1920-2007) The Assault 1986; The Rose Garden 1989
Radford, Michael (1946-) Another Time, Another Place 1983; Nineteen Eighty-Four 1984; White Mischief 1987; Il Postino 1994; B Monkey 1996; Dancing at the Blue Iguana 2000; Ten Minutes Older: the Cello 2002; William Shakespeare's The Merchant of Venice 2004; Flawless 2007; Elsa & Fred 2014
Radler, Robert Best of the Best 1989; Best of the Best II 1992
Rafelson, Bob (1933-) Head 1968; Five Easy Pieces 1970; The King of Marvin Gardens 1972; Stay Hungry 1976; The Postman Always Rings Twice 1981; Black Widow 1987; Mountains of the Moon 1989; Man Trouble 1992; Erotic Tales 1994; Blood and Wine 1996; Poodle Springs 1998; No Good Deed 2002
Raffill, Stewart (1945-) The Adventures of the Wilderness Family 1975; Across the Great Divide 1977; High Risk 1981; The Ice Pirates 1984; The Philadelphia Experiment 1984; Mac and Me 1988; Mannequin on the Move 1991; Grizzly Falls 1999; Three - III 2006
Rafkin, Alan (1928-2001) Ski Party 1965; The Ride to Hangman's Tree 1967; The Shakiest Gun in the West 1967; Angel in My Pocket 1968
Raimi, Sam (1959-) The Evil Dead 1981; Crimewave 1985; Evil Dead II 1987; Darkman 1990; Army of Darkness 1993; The Quick and the Dead 1995; A Simple Plan 1998; For Love of the Game 1999; The Gift 2000; Spider-Man 2002; Spider-Man 2 2004; Spider-Man 3 2007; Drag Me to Hell 2009; Oz the Great and Powerful 2013
Rakoff, Alvin (1937-) Passport to Shame 1958; The Treasure of San Teresa 1959; The Comedy Man 1964; Crossplot 1969; Hoffman 1970; Say Hello to Yesterday 1971; City on Fire 1979
Ramati, Alexander The Desperate Ones 1967; The Assisi Underground 1985
Ramirez, Robert C aka **Ramirez, Robert** Joseph: King of Dreams 2000; Clifford's Really Big Movie 2004
Ramis, Harold (1944-2014) Caddyshack 1980; National Lampoon's Vacation 1983; Club Paradise 1986; Groundhog Day 1993; Stuart Saves His Family 1995; Multiplicity 1996; Analyze This 1999; Bedazzled 2000; Analyze That 2002; The Ice Harvest 2005; Year One 2009
Ramsay, Lynne (1969-) Ratcatcher 1999; Morvern Callar 2001; We Need to Talk about Kevin 2011
Randel, Tony (1956-) Hellbound: Hellraiser II 1988; Ticks 1993; Fist of the North Star 1995; One Good Turn 1996
Rappeneau, Jean-Paul (1932-) La Vie de Château 1965; Les Mariés de l'An Deux 1971; Call Him Savage 1975; Cyrano de Bergerac 1990; The Horseman on the Roof 1995; Bon Voyage 2003
Rapper, Irving (1898-1999) One Foot in Heaven 1941; The Gay Sisters 1942; Now, Voyager 1942; The Adventures of Mark Twain 1944; The Corn Is Green 1945; Rhapsody in Blue 1945; Deception 1946; Voice of the Turtle 1947; Anna Lucasta 1949; The Glass Menagerie 1950; Another Man's Poison 1951; Forever Female 1953; Bad for Each Other 1954; The Brave One 1956; Marjorie Morningstar 1958; Pontius Pilate 1961; Born Again 1978
Rash, Steve The Buddy Holly Story 1978; Under the Rainbow 1981; Can't Buy Me Love 1987; Queens Logic 1991; Eddie 1996; Held Up 1999; Good Advice 2001; American Pie Presents Band Camp 2005
Rathnam, Mani (1956-) Bombay 1995; Dil Se... 1998

Ratliff, George Joshua 2007; Salvation Boulevard 2011
Ratner, Brett (1970-) Money Talks 1997; Rush Hour 1998; The Family Man 2000; Rush Hour 2 2001; Red Dragon 2002; After the Sunset 2004; X-Men - the Last Stand 2006; Rush Hour 3 2007; New York, I Love You 2009; Tower Heist 2011; Movie 43 2013; Hercules 2014
Ratoff, Gregory (1897-1960) Lancer Spy 1937; Intermezzo 1939; Rose of Washington Square 1939; Wife, Husband and Friend 1939; Adam Had Four Sons 1941; The Corsican Brothers 1941; The Men in Her Life 1941; Footlight Serenade 1942; Irish Eyes Are Smiling 1944; Madame Pimpernel 1945; Where Do We Go from Here? 1945; Do You Love Me? 1946; Moss Rose 1947; Black Magic 1949; That Dangerous Age 1949; Taxi 1953; Oscar Wilde 1959
Rawlins, John (1902-1997) Arabian Nights 1942; Sherlock Holmes and the Voice of Terror 1942; Sudan 1945; Dick Tracy's Dilemma 1947; Dick Tracy Meets Gruesome 1947
Ray, Billy Shattered Glass 2003; Breach 2006; Secret in Their Eyes 2015
Ray, Fred Olen (1954-) The Alien Dead 1980; Haunting Fear 1990
Ray, Nicholas (1911-1979) They Live by Night 1948; Knock on Any Door 1949; A Woman's Secret 1949; Born to Be Bad 1950; In a Lonely Place 1950; Flying Leathernecks 1951; On Dangerous Ground 1951; The Racket 1951; The Lusty Men 1952; Macao 1952; Johnny Guitar 1954; Rebel without a Cause 1955; Run for Cover 1955; Bigger than Life 1956; Hot Blood 1956; Bitter Victory 1957; The True Story of Jesse James 1957; Party Girl 1958; Wind across the Everglades 1958; The Savage Innocents 1960; King of Kings 1961; 55 Days at Peking 1963; Lightning over Water 1980
Ray, Satyajit (1921-1992) Pather Panchali 1955; Aparajito 1956; The Music Room 1958; The World of Apu 1959; Devi 1960; Teen Kanya 1961; Abhijan 1962; Kangchenjunga 1962; The Big City 1963; Charulata 1964; Nayaak 1966; Days and Nights in the Forest 1969; The Adversary 1970; Company Limited 1971; Distant Thunder 1973; The Middleman 1975; The Chess Players 1977; Sadgati 1981; The Home and the World 1984; An Enemy of the People 1989; Branches of the Tree 1990; The Stranger 1991
Red, Eric (1961-) Cohen and Tate 1988; Body Parts 1991; Bad Moon 1996
Redford, Robert (1936-) Ordinary People 1980; The Milagro Beanfield War 1988; A River Runs through It 1992; Quiz Show 1994; The Horse Whisperer 1998; The Legend of Bagger Vance 2000; Lions for Lambs 2007; The Conspirator 2010; The Company You Keep 2012
Reed, Carol (1906-1976) Midshipman Easy 1935; Bank Holiday 1938; Climbing High 1938; Penny Paradise 1938; The Stars Look Down 1939; The Girl in the News 1940; Night Train to Munich 1940; Kipps 1941; The Young Mr Pitt 1942; The Way Ahead 1944; Odd Man Out 1947; The Fallen Idol 1948; The Third Man 1949; Outcast of the Islands 1951; The Man Between 1953; A Kid for Two Farthings 1955; Trapeze 1956; The Key 1958; Our Man in Havana 1959; The Running Man 1963; The Agony and the Ecstasy 1965; Oliver! 1968; Flap 1970; Follow Me 1971
Reed, Luther (1888-1961) Rio Rita 1929; Hell's Angels 1930
Reed, Peyton (1964-) Bring It On 2000; Down with Love 2003; The Break-Up 2006; Yes Man 2008; Ant-Man 2015
Rees, Clive The Blockhouse 1973; When the Whales Came 1989
Rees, Jerry The Brave Little Toaster 1987; Too Hot to Handle 1991
Reeve, Christopher (1952-2004) In the Gloaming 1997; The Brooke Ellison Story 2004
Reeve, Geoffrey (1932-2010) Puppet on a Chain 1970; Caravan to Vaccares 1974; Shadow Run 1998
Reeves, Matt (1966-) The Pallbearer 1996; Cloverfield 2008; Let Me In 2010; Dawn of the Planet of the Apes 2014; War for the Planet of the Apes 2017

Reeves, Michael (1944-1969) *The She Beast* 1965; *The Sorcerers* 1967; *Witchfinder General* 1968

Refn, Nicolas Winding (1972-) *Pusher* 1996; *Bleeder* 1999; *Fear X* 2002; *Pusher II* 2004; *Pusher 3* 2005; *Bronson* 2008; *Valhalla Rising* 2009; *Drive* 2011; *Only God Forgives* 2012; *The Neon Demon* 2016

Reggio, Godfrey (1940-) *Koyaanisqatsi* 1982; *Powaqqatsi* 1988

Reichardt, Kelly (1964-) *River of Grass* 1994; *Old Joy* 2005; *Wendy and Lucy* 2008; *Meek's Cutoff* 2010; *Night Moves* 2013

Reid, Alastair (1939-) *The Road Builder* 1971; *Something to Hide* 1971; *What Rats Won't Do* 1998

Reiné, Roel *The Delivery* 1998; *Pistol Whipped* 2008

Reiner, Carl (1922-) *Enter Laughing* 1967; *The Comic* 1969; *Where's Poppa?* 1970; *Oh, God!* 1977; *The One and Only* 1978; *The Jerk* 1979; *Dead Men Don't Wear Plaid* 1982; *The Man with Two Brains* 1983; *All of Me* 1984; *Summer Rental* 1985; *Summer School* 1987; *Bert Rigby, You're a Fool* 1989; *Sibling Rivalry* 1990; *Fatal Instinct* 1993; *That Old Feeling* 1997

Reiner, Rob (1945-) *This Is Spinal Tap* 1984; *The Sure Thing* 1985; *Stand by Me* 1986; *The Princess Bride* 1987; *When Harry Met Sally...* 1989; *Misery* 1990; *A Few Good Men* 1992; *North* 1994; *The American President* 1995; *Ghosts of Mississippi* 1996; *The Story of Us* 1999; *Alex & Emma* 2003; *Rumor Has It...* 2005; *The Bucket List* 2008; *And So It Goes* 2014

Reinhardt, Gottfried (1913-1994) *The Story of Three Loves* 1953; *Betrayed* 1954; *Town without Pity* 1961; *Situation Hopeless – but Not Serious* 1965

Reis, Irving (1906-1953) *A Date with the Falcon* 1941; *Footlight Fever* 1941; *The Gay Falcon* 1941; *The Big Street* 1942; *The Falcon Takes Over* 1942; *Crack-Up* 1946; *The Bachelor and the Bobby-Soxer* 1947; *All My Sons* 1948; *Enchantment* 1948; *Dancing in the Dark* 1949; *Roseanna McCoy* 1949; *The Four Poster* 1953

Reisch, Walter (1903-1983) *Men Are Not Gods* 1936; *Song of Scheherazade* 1947

Reisner, Allen (1923-2004) *The Day They Gave Babies Away* 1957; *St Louis Blues* 1958

Reisner, Charles aka Reisner, Charles F (1887-1962) *Steamboat Bill, Jr* 1928; *Hollywood Revue* 1929; *Winter Carnival* 1939; *The Big Store* 1941; *Lost in a Harem* 1944; *Meet the People* 1944

Reisz, Karel (1926-2002) *Saturday Night and Sunday Morning* 1960; *Night Must Fall* 1964; *Morgan – a Suitable Case for Treatment* 1966; *Isadora* 1968; *The Gambler* 1974; *Who'll Stop the Rain?* 1978; *The French Lieutenant's Woman* 1981; *Sweet Dreams* 1985; *Everybody Wins* 1990

Reitherman, Wolfgang (1909-1985) *Sleeping Beauty* 1959; *One Hundred and One Dalmatians* 1960; *The Sword in the Stone* 1963; *The Jungle Book* 1967; *The Aristocats* 1970; *Robin Hood* 1973; *The Many Adventures of Winnie the Pooh* 1977; *The Rescuers* 1977

Reitman, Ivan (1946-) *Cannibal Girls* 1973; *Meatballs* 1979; *Stripes* 1981; *Ghost Busters* 1984; *Legal Eagles* 1986; *Twins* 1988; *Ghostbusters II* 1989; *Kindergarten Cop* 1990; *Dave* 1993; *Junior* 1994; *Fathers' Day* 1997; *Six Days Seven Nights* 1998; *Evolution* 2001; *My Super Ex-Girlfriend* 2006; *No Strings Attached* 2011; *Draft Day* 2014

Reitman, Jason (1977-) *Thank You for Smoking* 2005; *Juno* 2007; *Up in the Air* 2009; *Young Adult* 2011; *Labor Day* 2013; *Men, Women & Children* 2014

Reitz, Edgar (1932-) *Heimat* 1984; *Heimat 2* 1992; *Heimat 3: a Chronicle of Endings and Beginnings* 2004

Relph, Michael (1915-2004) *Saraband for Dead Lovers* 1948; *The Gentle Gunman* 1952; *I Believe in You* 1952; *The Square Ring* 1953; *The Ship That Died of Shame* 1955; *Davy* 1958; *Rockets Galore* 1958; *Desert Mice* 1959

Renaud, Chris *Despicable Me* 2010; *Dr Seuss' The Lorax* 2012; *Despicable Me 2* 2013; *The Secret Life of Pets* 2016

René, Norman (1951-1996) *Longtime Companion* 1990; *Prelude to a Kiss* 1992; *Reckless* 1995

Renfroe, Jeff *Stranger with My Face* 2009; *The Colony* 2013

Renoir, Jean (1894-1979) *Nana* 1926; *La Chienne* 1931; *On Purge Bébé* 1931; *Boudu, Saved from Drowning* 1932; *La Nuit du Carrefour* 1932; *Madame Bovary* 1933; *Le Crime de Monsieur Lange* 1935; *Toni* 1935; *The Lower Depths* 1936; *Une Partie de Campagne* 1936; *La Vie Est à Nous* 1936; *La Grande Illusion* 1937; *La Bête Humaine* 1938; *La Marseillaise* 1938; *La Règle du Jeu* 1939; *Swamp Water* 1941; *This Land Is Mine* 1943; *The Southerner* 1945; *Diary of a Chambermaid* 1946; *The Woman on the Beach* 1947; *The River* 1951; *The Golden Coach* 1953; *French Cancan* 1955; *Elena et les Hommes* 1956; *Lunch on the Grass* 1959; *The Testament of Dr Cordelier* 1959; *The Vanishing Corporal* 1962; *The Little Theatre of Jean Renoir* 1969

Requa, John (1967-) *I Love You Phillip Morris* 2009; *Crazy, Stupid, Love* 2011; *Focus* 2015; *Whiskey Tango Foxtrot* 2016

Resnais, Alain (1922-2014) *Nuit et Brouillard* 1955; *Hiroshima, Mon Amour* 1959; *Last Year at Marienbad* 1961; *Muriel* 1963; *La Guerre Est Finie* 1966; *Far from Vietnam* 1967; *Je T'Aime, Je T'Aime* 1968; *Stavisky* 1974; *Providence* 1977; *Mon Oncle d'Amérique* 1980; *Life Is a Bed of Roses* 1983; *Mélo* 1986; *I Want to Go Home* 1989; *Smoking/No Smoking* 1993; *On Connaît la Chanson* 1997; *Pas sur la Bouche* 2003; *Private Fears in Public Places* 2006; *Wild Grass* 2008; *Life of Riley* 2014

Reygadas, Carlos (1971-) *Japón* 2002; *Silent Light* 2007; *Post Tenebras Lux* 2012

Reynolds, Burt (1936-) *Gator* 1976; *The End* 1978; *Sharky's Machine* 1981; *Stick* 1985; *The Man from Left Field* 1993; *Hard Time* 1998; *The Last Producer* 2000

Reynolds, Kevin (1952-) *Fandango* 1985; *The Beast of War* 1988; *Robin Hood: Prince of Thieves* 1991; *Rapa Nui* 1994; *Waterworld* 1995; *One Eight Seven* 1997; *The Count of Monte Cristo* 2001; *Tristan + Isolde* 2005; *Risen* 2016

Rich, David Lowell (1923-) *Senior Prom* 1958; *Have Rocket, Will Travel* 1959; *Hey Boy! Hey Girl!* 1959; *Madame X* 1966; *The Plainsman* 1966; *Rosie!* 1967; *A Lovely Way to Go* 1968; *Three Guns for Texas* 1968; *Eye of the Cat* 1969; *Airport '79: the Concorde* 1979

Rich, John (1925-2012) *Roustabout* 1964; *Boeing Boeing* 1965; *Easy Come, Easy Go* 1967

Rich, Richard (1951-) *The Fox and the Hound* 1981; *The Black Cauldron* 1985; *The Swan Princess* 1994; *The King and I* 1999

Rich, Roy (1913-1970) *It's Not Cricket* 1948; *My Brother's Keeper* 1948

Richards, Dick (1936-) *The Culpepper Cattle Co* 1972; *Farewell, My Lovely* 1975; *March or Die* 1977; *Death Valley* 1982; *Man, Woman and Child* 1983; *Heat* 1987

Richards, Julian *Darklands* 1996; *The Last Horror Movie* 2003; *Summer Scars* 2007; *Charles Dickens's England* 2009

Richardson, Peter (1952-) *The Supergrass* 1985; *Eat the Rich* 1987; *The Pope Must Die* 1991; *Churchill: the Hollywood Years* 2004; *Stella Street* 2004

Richardson, Tony (1928-1991) *Look Back in Anger* 1959; *The Entertainer* 1960; *Sanctuary* 1961; *A Taste of Honey* 1961; *The Loneliness of the Long Distance Runner* 1962; *Tom Jones* 1963; *The Loved One* 1965; *Mademoiselle* 1966; *The Sailor from Gibraltar* 1967; *The Charge of the Light Brigade* 1968; *Hamlet* 1969; *Laughter in the Dark* 1969; *Ned Kelly* 1970; *A Delicate Balance* 1973; *Dead Cert* 1974; *Joseph Andrews* 1977; *A Death in Canaan* 1978; *The Border* 1981; *The Hotel New Hampshire* 1984; *Women and Men: Stories of Seduction* 1990; *Blue Sky* 1991

Richert, William *The American Success Company* 1979; *Winter Kills* 1979; *A Night in the Life of Jimmy Reardon* 1988

Richet, Jean-François *Assault on Precinct 13* 2005; *Mesrine: Killer Instinct* 2008; *Mesrine: Public*

Enemy No 1 2008; *Blood Father* 2016

Richter, W D (1945-) *The Adventures of Buckaroo Banzai across the 8th Dimension* 1984; *Late for Dinner* 1991

Rickman, Alan (1946-2016) *The Winter Guest* 1996; *A Little Chaos* 2014

Ridley, Philip (1960-) *The Reflecting Skin* 1990; *The Passion of Darkly Noon* 1995; *Heartless* 2009

Riefenstahl, Leni (1902-2003) *The Blue Light* 1932; *Triumph of the Will* 1935; *Olympiad* 1938

Rifkin, Adam (1966-) *The Chase* 1994; *Something about Sex* 1998; *Detroit Rock City* 1999

Riggen, Patricia *Lemonade Mouth* 2011; *The 33* 2014; *Miracles from Heaven* 2016

Riklis, Eran *Cup Final* 1991; *Lemon Tree* 2008; *Zaytoun* 2012

Riley, Stevan *Blue Blood* 2006; *Fire in Babylon* 2010; *Everything or Nothing: the Untold Story of 007* 2012; *Listen to Me Marlon* 2015

Rilla, Wolf (1920-2005) *Marilyn* 1953; *The Black Rider* 1954; *The Blue Peter* 1955; *Stock Car* 1955; *The Scamp* 1957; *Bachelor of Hearts* 1958; *Piccadilly Third Stop* 1960; *Village of the Damned* 1960; *Cairo* 1962; *The World Ten Times Over* 1963

Ripley, Arthur (1895-1961) *The Barber Shop* 1933; *I Met My Love Again* 1938; *The Chase* 1946; *Thunder Road* 1958

Ripoll, María *If Only* 1998; *Tortilla Soup* 2001

Ripstein, Arturo (1943-) *Deep Crimson* 1996; *No One Writes to the Colonel* 1999

Risi, Dino (1916-2008) *Love in the City* 1953; *The Easy Life* 1962; *Le Bambole* 1965; *The Tiger and the Pussycat* 1967; *The Priest's Wife* 1970; *Scent of a Woman* 1974; *Viva Italia!* 1978

Ritchie, Guy (1968-) *Lock, Stock and Two Smoking Barrels* 1998; *Snatch* 2000; *Swept Away* 2002; *Revolver* 2005; *RocknRolla* 2008; *Sherlock Holmes* 2009; *Sherlock Holmes: a Game of Shadows* 2011; *The Man from UNCLE* 2015; *Knights of the Round Table: King Arthur* 2016

Ritchie, Michael (1938-2001) *Downhill Racer* 1969; *The Candidate* 1972; *Prime Cut* 1972; *Smile* 1975; *The Bad News Bears* 1976; *Semi-Tough* 1977; *Divine Madness* 1980; *The Island* 1980; *The Survivors* 1983; *Fletch* 1985; *The Golden Child* 1986; *Wildcats* 1986; *The Couch Trip* 1988; *Fletch Lives* 1989; *Midnight Sting* 1992; *The Positively True Adventures of the Alleged Texas Cheerleader-Murdering Mom* 1993; *Cops and Robbersons* 1994; *The Scout* 1994; *A Simple Wish* 1997

Ritt, Martin (1914-1990) *Edge of the City* 1957; *No Down Payment* 1957; *The Long, Hot Summer* 1958; *The Black Orchid* 1959; *The Sound and the Fury* 1959; *Five Branded Women* 1960; *Paris Blues* 1961; *Hemingway's Adventures of a Young Man* 1962; *Hud* 1963; *The Outrage* 1964; *The Spy Who Came In from the Cold* 1965; *Hombre* 1967; *The Brotherhood* 1968; *The Great White Hope* 1970; *The Molly Maguires* 1970; *Pete 'n' Tillie* 1972; *Sounder* 1972; *The Front* 1976; *Casey's Shadow* 1978; *Norma Rae* 1979; *Back Roads* 1981; *Cross Creek* 1983; *Murphy's Romance* 1985; *Nuts* 1987; *Stanley & Iris* 1989

Rittikrai, Panna (1961-2014) *Born to Fight* 2004; *Ong-Bak: the Beginning* 2008

Rivette, Jacques (1928-2016) *Paris Nous Appartient* 1960; *La Religieuse* 1965; *L'Amour Fou* 1968; *Celine and Julie Go Boating* 1974; *L'Amour par Terre* 1984; *La Belle Noiseuse* 1991; *Jeanne la Pucelle* 1994; *Secret Defense* 1997; *Va Savoir* 2001; *Histoire de Marie et Julien* 2003; *Don't Touch the Axe* 2006

Roach, Hal (1892-1992) *Bogus Bandits* 1933; *One Million BC* 1940

Roach, Jay (1957-) *Austin Powers: International Man of Mystery* 1997; *Austin Powers: the Spy Who Shagged Me* 1999; *Mystery, Alaska* 1999; *Meet the Parents* 2000; *Austin Powers in Goldmember* 2002; *Meet the Fockers* 2004; *Recount* 2008; *Dinner for Schmucks* 2010; *The Campaign* 2012; *Game Change* 2012; *Trumbo* 2015; *All the Way* 2016

Robbe-Grillet, Alain (1922-2008) *Trans-Europ-Express* 1966; *The Blue Villa* 1994

Robbins, Brian (1964-) *Good Burger* 1997; *Varsity Blues* 1999; *Ready to Rumble* 2000; *Hardball* 2001; *The Perfect Score* 2004; *The Shaggy Dog* 2006; *Norbit* 2007; *Meet Dave* 2008

Robbins, Matthew *Corvette Summer* 1978; *Dragonslayer* 1981; *The Legend of Billie Jean* 1985; **batteries not included* 1987; *Bingo* 1991

Robbins, Tim (1958-) *Bob Roberts* 1992; *Dead Man Walking* 1995; *Cradle Will Rock* 1999

Robe, Mike *More than Meets the Eye: the Joan Brock Story* 2003; *While I Was Gone* 2004; *Nora Roberts' Northern Lights* 2009

Robert, Yves (1920-2002) *War of the Buttons* 1962; *The Tall Blond Man with One Black Shoe* 1972; *The Bit Player* 1973; *Pardon Mon Affaire* 1976; *Le Château de Ma Mère* 1990; *La Gloire de Mon Père* 1990

Roberts, Bill *Fantasia* 1940; *Saludos Amigos* 1943; *The Three Caballeros* 1944

Roberts, Johannes *F* 2010; *Storage 24* 2012; *The Other Side of the Door* 2016

Roberts, John *War of the Buttons* 1993; *Paulie* 1998; *Day of the Flowers* 2012

Roberts, Stephen (1917-1999) *If I Had a Million* 1932; *Romance in Manhattan* 1934; *The Man Who Broke the Bank at Monte Carlo* 1935; *Star of Midnight* 1935; *The Ex-Mrs Bradford* 1936

Robertson, John S (1878-1964) *Dr Jekyll and Mr Hyde* 1920; *Tess of the Storm Country* 1922; *Annie Laurie* 1927; *The Single Standard* 1929; *Our Little Girl* 1935

Robins, John *Nearest and Dearest* 1972; *That's Your Funeral* 1972; *Love Thy Neighbour* 1973; *The Best of Benny Hill* 1974; *Man about the House* 1974

Robinson, Bruce (1946-) *Withnail & I* 1986; *How to Get Ahead in Advertising* 1989; *Jennifer Eight* 1992; *The Rum Diary* 2011

Robinson, Julie Anne *The Last Song* 2010; *One for the Money* 2012

Robinson, Phil Alden (1950-) *The Woo Woo Kid* 1987; *Field of Dreams* 1989; *Sneakers* 1992; *Freedom Song* 2000; *The Sum of All Fears* 2002; *The Angriest Man in Brooklyn* 2014

Robson, Mark (1913-1978) *The Ghost Ship* 1943; *The Seventh Victim* 1943; *Isle of the Dead* 1945; *Bedlam* 1946; *Champion* 1949; *Home of the Brave* 1949; *My Foolish Heart* 1949; *Roughshod* 1949; *Edge of Doom* 1950; *Bright Victory* 1951; *I Want You* 1951; *Return to Paradise* 1953; *The Bridges at Toko-Ri* 1954; *Hell below Zero* 1954; *Phffft!* 1954; *A Prize of Gold* 1955; *Trial* 1955; *The Harder They Fall* 1956; *The Little Hut* 1957; *Peyton Place* 1957; *The Inn of the Sixth Happiness* 1958; *From the Terrace* 1960; *The Prize* 1963; *Von Ryan's Express* 1965; *Valley of the Dolls* 1967; *Daddy's Gone A-Hunting* 1969; *Earthquake* 1974; *Avalanche Express* 1979

Rocco, Marc (1965-2009) *Dream a Little Dream* 1989; *Murder in the First* 1994

Rocha, Glauber (1938-1981) *Black God, White Devil* 1964; *Antonio das Mortes* 1969

Rochant, Eric (1961-) *A World without Pity* 1989; *Autobus* 1991

Rocher, Benjamin *The Horde* 2009; *The Sweeney: Paris* 2015

Rock, Chris (1966-) *Head of State* 2003; *Top Five* 2014

Rocksavage, David *Other Voices, Other Rooms* 1995; *Shadows in the Sun* 2008

Rockwell, Alexandre (1956-) *Sons* 1989; *In the Soup* 1992; *Somebody to Love* 1994; *Four Rooms* 1995

Roddam, Franc (1946-) *Quadrophenia* 1979; *The Lords of Discipline* 1983; *The Bride* 1985; *Aria* 1987; *War Party* 1988; *K2* 1991; *Moby Dick* 1998

Rodriguez, Ismael (1917-2004) *The Beast of Hollow Mountain* 1956; *Tizoc* 1956; *Daniel Boone, Trail Blazer* 1957; *The Important Man* 1961

Rodriguez, Robert (1968-) *El Mariachi* 1992; *Roadracers* 1994; *Desperado* 1995; *Four Rooms* 1995; *From Dusk till Dawn* 1995; *The Faculty* 1998; *SPYkids* 2001; *SPYkids 2: the Island of Lost Dreams* 2002;

Once upon a Time in Mexico 2003; *SPYkids 3-D: Game Over* 2003; *The Adventures of Sharkboy and Lavagirl* 2005; *Sin City* 2005; *Planet Terror* 2007; *Shorts* 2009; *Machete* 2010; *SPYkids 4: All the Time in the World* 2011; *Machete Kills* 2013; *Sin City: a Dame to Kill For* 2014

Roeg, Nicolas (1928-) *Performance* 1970; *Walkabout* 1970; *Don't Look Now* 1973; *The Man Who Fell to Earth* 1976; *Bad Timing* 1980; *Eureka* 1982; *Insignificance* 1985; *Castaway* 1986; *Aria* 1987; *Track 29* 1988; *Sweet Bird of Youth* 1989; *The Witches* 1989; *Cold Heaven* 1992; *Two Deaths* 1994; *Puffball* 2006

Roemer, Michael (1928-) *Nothing but a Man* 1964; *The Plot against Harry* 1969

Rogell, Albert S (1901-1988) *Argentine Nights* 1940; *The Black Cat* 1941; *Change of Heart* 1943; *War of the Wildcats* 1943; *Heaven Only Knows* 1947; *The Admiral Was a Lady* 1950

Rogen, Seth (1982-) *This Is the End* 2013; *The Interview* 2014

Rogers, Charles (1890-1960) *Bogus Bandits* 1933; *Babes in Toyland* 1934; *Them Thar Hills!* 1934; *Tit for Tat* 1934; *The Bohemian Girl* 1936

Rogers, James B aka Rogers, J B *American Pie 2* 2001; *Say It Isn't So* 2001

Rogers, Maclean (1899-1962) *Gert and Daisy's Weekend* 1941; *Variety Jubilee* 1942; *Calling Paul Temple* 1948; *Paul Temple's Triumph* 1950; *Something in the City* 1950; *Down among the Z-Men* 1952; *Paul Temple Returns* 1952; *Forces' Sweetheart* 1953; *Assignment Redhead* 1956; *Mark of the Phoenix* 1957; *Not Wanted on Voyage* 1957; *You Pay Your Money* 1957

Rohmer, Eric (1920-2010) *The Sign of Leo* 1959; *The Boulangère de Monceau* 1962; *La Carrière de Suzanne* 1963; *Paris Vu Par...* 1965; *La Collectionneuse* 1967; *My Night with Maud* 1969; *Claire's Knee* 1970; *Love in the Afternoon* 1972; *The Marquise of O* 1976; *Perceval le Gallois* 1978; *The Aviator's Wife* 1980; *Le Beau Mariage* 1982; *Pauline at the Beach* 1983; *Full Moon in Paris* 1984; *Four Adventures of Reinette and Mirabelle* 1986; *The Green Ray* 1986; *My Girlfriend's Boyfriend* 1987; *A Tale of Springtime* 1989; *A Winter's Tale* 1992; *Les Rendez-vous de Paris* 1995; *A Summer's Tale* 1996; *An Autumn Tale* 1998; *The Lady & the Duke* 2001; *Triple Agent* 2003; *The Romance of Astrea and Celadon* 2007

Roley, Sutton *How to Steal the World* 1968; *Chosen Survivors* 1974

Roman, Phil (1930-) *Race for Your Life, Charlie Brown* 1977; *Tom and Jerry: the Movie* 1992

Romanek, Mark (1959-) *Static* 1985; *One Hour Photo* 2001; *Never Let Me Go* 2010

Romero, Eddie (1924-2013) *Black Mama, White Mama* 1972; *Twilight People* 1973; *A Case of Honor* 1988

Romero, George A (1940-) *Night of the Living Dead* 1968; *Season of the Witch* 1972; *The Crazies* 1973; *Dawn of the Dead* 1978; *Martin* 1978; *Knightriders* 1981; *Creepshow* 1982; *Day of the Dead* 1985; *Monkey Shines* 1988; *Two Evil Eyes* 1990; *The Dark Half* 1991; *George A Romero's Land of the Dead* 2005; *Diary of the Dead* 2007; *George A Romero's Survival of the Dead* 2009

Romy, Bruno *Rumba* 2008; *The Fairy* 2011

Ronning, Joachim *Kon-Tiki* 2012; *Pirates of the Caribbean: Dead Men Tell No Tales* 2017

Roodt, Darrell James aka Roodt, Darrell (1963-) *Jobman* 1990; *Sarafina!* 1992; *Father Hood* 1993; *Cry, the Beloved Country* 1995; *Dangerous Ground* 1996

Roome, Alfred (1908-1997) *It's Not Cricket* 1948; *My Brother's Keeper* 1948

Rooney, Bethany *Danielle Steel's Mixed Blessings* 1995; *Danielle Steel's Remembrance* 1996

Rooney, Darrell *The Lion King II: Simba's Pride* 1998; *Lady and the Tramp II: Scamp's Adventure* 2000; *Mulan II* 2004

Roos, Don (1955-) *The Opposite of Sex* 1998; *Bounce* 2000; *Happy Endings* 2005; *Love and Other Impossible Pursuits* 2009

Ropelewski, Tom *Madhouse* 1990; *Look Who's Talking Now!* 1993

Schaffner, Franklin J aka
Schaffner, Franklin (1920-1989)
The Stripper 1963; *The Best Man* 1964; *The War Lord* 1965; *The Double Man* 1967; *Planet of the Apes* 1967; *Patton* 1970; *Nicholas and Alexandra* 1971; *Papillon* 1973; *Islands in the Stream* 1976; *The Boys from Brazil* 1978; *Sphinx* 1980; *Yes, Giorgio* 1982; *Lionheart* 1986; *Welcome Home* 1989

Schatzberg, Jerry (1927-) *Puzzle of a Downfall Child* 1970; *The Panic in Needle Park* 1971; *Scarecrow* 1973; *The Seduction of Joe Tynan* 1979; *Honeysuckle Rose* 1980; *Street Smart* 1987; *Blood Money* 1988; *Reunion* 1989

Scheerer, Robert (1929-) *Adam at 6 AM* 1970; *The World's Greatest Athlete* 1973; *How to Beat the High Cost of Living* 1980

Schell, Maximilian (1930-2014) *First Love* 1970; *The Pedestrian* 1974; *End of the Game* 1976; *Marlene* 1984

Schenkel, Carl (1948-2003) *The Mighty Quinn* 1989; *Knight Moves* 1992; *Tarzan and the Lost City* 1998; *Murder on the Orient Express* 2001

Schepisi, Fred (1939-) *The Devil's Playground* 1976; *The Chant of Jimmie Blacksmith* 1978; *Barbarosa* 1982; *Iceman* 1984; *Plenty* 1985; *Roxanne* 1987; *A Cry in the Dark* 1988; *The Russia House* 1990; *Mr Baseball* 1992; *Six Degrees of Separation* 1993; *IQ* 1994; *Fierce Creatures* 1997; *Last Orders* 2001; *It Runs in the Family* 2002; *The Eye of the Storm* 2011; *Words and Pictures* 2013

Scherfig, Lone (1959-) *Italian for Beginners* 2000; *Wilbur (Wants to Kill Himself)* 2002; *An Education* 2008; *One Day* 2011; *The Riot Club* 2014

Schertzinger, Victor (1880-1941) *Paramount on Parade* 1930; *Friends and Lovers* 1931; *One Night of Love* 1934; *Something to Sing About* 1937; *The Mikado* 1939; *Rhythm on the River* 1940; *Road to Singapore* 1940; *The Birth of the Blues* 1941; *Kiss the Boys Goodbye* 1941; *Road to Zanzibar* 1941; *The Fleet's In* 1942

Schiller, Lawrence (1935-) *The American Dreamer* 1971; *The Executioner's Song* 1982; *The Plot to Kill Hitler* 1990

Schlamme, Thomas (1952-) *Miss Firecracker* 1989; *Crazy from the Heart* 1991; *So I Married an Axe Murderer* 1993; *Kingfish: a Story of Huey P Long* 1995

Schlesinger, John (1926-2003) *A Kind of Loving* 1962; *Billy Liar* 1963; *Darling* 1965; *Far from the Madding Crowd* 1967; *Midnight Cowboy* 1969; *Sunday, Bloody Sunday* 1971; *Visions of Eight* 1973; *The Day of the Locust* 1975; *Marathon Man* 1976; *Yanks* 1979; *Honky Tonk Freeway* 1981; *Separate Tables* 1983; *The Falcon and the Snowman* 1985; *The Believers* 1987; *Madame Sousatzka* 1988; *Pacific Heights* 1990; *The Innocent* 1993; *Eye for an Eye* 1995; *The Next Best Thing* 2000

Schlöndorff, Volker (1939-) *The Lost Honour of Katharina Blum* 1975; *The Tin Drum* 1979; *Circle of Deceit* 1981; *Swann in Love* 1984; *Death of a Salesman* 1985; *The Handmaid's Tale* 1990; *Voyager* 1991; *Palmetto* 1998; *Ten Minutes Older: the Cello* 2002; *Diplomacy* 2014

Schlossberg, Hayden *Harold & Kumar Escape from Guantanamo Bay* 2008; *American Reunion* 2012

Schmid, Hans-Christian *Requiem* 2006; *Storm* 2009

Schmidt, Rob (1965-) *Crime + Punishment in Suburbia* 2000; *Wrong Turn* 2003

Schmitz, Oliver *Mapantsula* 1988; *Paris, Je T'Aime* 2006; *Life, above All* 2010

Schmoeller, David (1947-) *Tourist Trap* 1979; *Puppet Master* 1989

Schnabel, Julian (1951-) *Basquiat* 1996; *Before Night Falls* 2000; *Berlin* 2007; *The Diving-Bell and the Butterfly* 2007; *Miral* 2010

Schneider (1), Paul *Willy/Milly* 1986; *My Boyfriend's Back* 1989; *Cries in the Dark* 2006; *Seventeen and Missing* 2006

Schoedsack, Ernest B (1893-1979) *Grass: a Nation's Battle for Life* 1925; *Chang* 1927; *The Four Feathers* 1929; *The Most Dangerous Game* 1932; *Blind Adventure* 1933; *King Kong* 1933; *Son of Kong* 1933; *Long Lost Father* 1934; *The Last Days of*

Pompeii 1935; *Dr Cyclops* 1940; *Mighty Joe Young* 1949

Schrader, Paul (1946-) *Blue Collar* 1978; *Hardcore* 1979; *American Gigolo* 1980; *Cat People* 1982; *Mishima: a Life in Four Chapters* 1985; *Patty Hearst* 1988; *The Comfort of Strangers* 1991; *Light Sleeper* 1991; *Touch* 1996; *Affliction* 1997; *Forever Mine* 1999; *Auto Focus* 2002; *Dominion: Prequel to the Exorcist* 2005; *The Walker* 2006; *The Canyons* 2013; *Dying of the Light* 2014

Schreier, Jake *Robot & Frank* 2012; *Paper Towns* 2015

Schroeder, Barbet (1941-) *More* 1969; *The Valley* 1972; *Maîtresse* 1976; *Barfly* 1987; *Reversal of Fortune* 1990; *Single White Female* 1992; *Kiss of Death* 1994; *Before and After* 1996; *Desperate Measures* 1998; *Our Lady of the Assassins* 2000; *Murder by Numbers* 2002

Schroeder, Michael (1952-) *Out of the Dark* 1988; *Damned River* 1989; *Cyborg 2: Glass Shadow* 1993; *Cyborg 3: The Recycler* 1994; *The Glass Cage* 1996; *Man in the Chair* 2006

Schulman, Ariel *Catfish* 2010; *Paranormal Activity 3* 2011; *Paranormal Activity 4* 2012; *Nerve* 2016

Schultz, Carl (1939-) *Careful, He Might Hear You* 1983; *Travelling North* 1986; *The Seventh Sign* 1988; *To Walk with Lions* 1999

Schultz, John (1960-) *Drive Me Crazy* 1999; *Like Mike* 2002; *When Zachary Beaver Came to Town* 2003; *The Honeymooners* 2005; *Aliens in the Attic* 2009; *Judy Moody and the Not Bummer Summer* 2011

Schultz, Michael (1938-) *Car Wash* 1976; *Greased Lightning* 1977; *Which Way Is Up?* 1977; *Sgt Pepper's Lonely Hearts Club Band* 1978; *Carbon Copy* 1981; *Disorderlies* 1987; *To Live For* 1999

Schumacher, Joel (1939-) *The Incredible Shrinking Woman* 1981; *DC Cab* 1983; *St Elmo's Fire* 1985; *The Lost Boys* 1987; *Cousins* 1989; *Flatliners* 1990; *Dying Young* 1991; *Falling Down* 1992; *The Client* 1994; *Batman Forever* 1995; *A Time to Kill* 1996; *Batman and Robin* 1997; *8mm* 1999; *Flawless* 1999; *Tigerland* 2000; *Bad Company* 2002; *Phone Booth* 2002; *Veronica Guerin* 2003; *The Phantom of the Opera* 2004; *The Number 23* 2006; *Blood Creek* 2009; *Trespass* 2011

Schünzel, Reinhold (1886-1954) *Viktor und Viktoria* 1933; *The Ice Follies of 1939* 1939

Schuster, Harold aka **Schuster, Harold D** (1902-1986) *Dinner at the Ritz* 1937; *Wings of the Morning* 1937; *My Friend Flicka* 1943; *Marine Raiders* 1944; *So Dear to My Heart* 1949; *Dragoon Wells Massacre* 1957

Schwartz, Stefan *Soft Top, Hard Shoulder* 1992; *Shooting Fish* 1997; *The Abduction Club* 2002; *The Best Man* 2005

Schwarz, Hanns aka **Schwartz, Hans** (1888-1945) *The Wonderful Lie of Nina Petrovna* 1929; *The Return of the Scarlet Pimpernel* 1937

Schwentke, Robert (1968-) *Tattoo* 2002; *Flightplan* 2005; *The Time Traveler's Wife* 2009; *Red* 2010; *R.I.P.D.* 2013; *Insurgent* 2015; *The Divergent Series: Allegiant* 2016

Schwimmer, David (1966-) *Since You've Been Gone* 1998; *Run Fatboy Run* 2007; *Trust* 2010

Sciamma, Céline *Water Lilies* 2007; *Tomboy* 2011; *Girlhood* 2014

Scola, Ettore (1931-2016) *Let's Talk about Women* 1964; *Jealousy, Italian Style* 1970; *We All Loved Each Other So Much* 1974; *Down and Dirty* 1976; *A Special Day* 1977; *Viva Italia!* 1978; *Le Bal* 1983; *La Nuit de Varennes* 1983; *Macaroni* 1985; *The Family* 1987

Scorsese, Martin (1942-) *Who's That Knocking at My Door* 1968; *Boxcar Bertha* 1972; *Mean Streets* 1973; *Alice Doesn't Live Here Anymore* 1974; *Taxi Driver* 1976; *New York, New York* 1977; *The Last Waltz* 1978; *Raging Bull* 1980; *The King of Comedy* 1983; *After Hours* 1985; *The Color of Money* 1986; *The Last Temptation of Christ* 1988; *New York Stories* 1989; *Goodfellas* 1990; *Cape Fear* 1991; *The Age of Innocence* 1993; *Casino* 1995; *Kundun* 1997; *Bringing Out the Dead* 1999; *My Voyage to Italy* 1999;

Gangs of New York 2002; *The Blues, a Musical Journey: Feel like Going Home* 2003; *The Aviator* 2004; *The Departed* 2006; *Shine a Light* 2007; *Shutter Island* 2009; *George Harrison: Living in the Material World* 2011; *Hugo* 2011; *The Wolf of Wall Street* 2013

Scott, George C (1927-1999) *Rage* 1972; *The Savage Is Loose* 1974

Scott, Jake *Plunkett & Macleane* 1999; *Welcome to the Rileys* 2009

Scott (2), Ken *Starbuck* 2011; *Delivery Man* 2013; *Unfinished Business* 2015

Scott, Michael aka **Scott, Michael M** *Deadly Visions* 2004; *Mrs Miracle* 2009; *Call Me Mrs Miracle* 2010; *It's Christmas, Carol!* 2012

Scott, Peter Graham (1923-) *Escape Route* 1952; *Account Rendered* 1957; *The Big Chance* 1957; *Night Creatures* 1962; *The Pot Carriers* 1962; *Bitter Harvest* 1963; *The Cracksman* 1963; *Father Came Too* 1963; *Mister Ten Per Cent* 1967

Scott, Ridley (1937-) *The Duellists* 1977; *Alien* 1979; *Blade Runner* 1982; *Legend* 1985; *Someone to Watch over Me* 1987; *Black Rain* 1989; *Thelma & Louise* 1991; *1492: Conquest of Paradise* 1992; *White Squall* 1996; *GI Jane* 1997; *Gladiator* 2000; *Black Hawk Down* 2001; *Hannibal* 2001; *Matchstick Men* 2003; *Kingdom of Heaven* 2005; *A Good Year* 2006; *American Gangster* 2007; *Body of Lies* 2008; *Robin Hood* 2010; *Prometheus* 2012; *The Counsellor* 2013; *Exodus: Gods and Kings* 2014; *The Martian* 2015

Scott, Tony (1944-2012) *The Hunger* 1983; *Top Gun* 1986; *Beverly Hills Cop II* 1987; *Days of Thunder* 1990; *Revenge* 1990; *The Last Boy Scout* 1991; *True Romance* 1993; *Crimson Tide* 1995; *The Fan* 1996; *Enemy of the State* 1998; *Spy Game* 2001; *Man on Fire* 2004; *Domino* 2005; *Déjà Vu* 2006; *The Taking of Pelham 123* 2009; *Unstoppable* 2010

Searle, Francis (1909-2002) *A Girl in a Million* 1946; *A Case for PC 49* 1950; *Someone at the Door* 1950; *Cloudburst* 1951; *Profile* 1954; *Undercover Girl* 1957; *Dead Man's Evidence* 1962; *Emergency* 1962; *Gaolbreak* 1962; *Night of the Prowler* 1962; *A Hole Lot of Trouble* 1969

Sears, Fred F (1913-1957) *Ambush at Tomahawk Gap* 1953; *The 49th Man* 1953; *Wyoming Renegades* 1955; *Don't Knock the Rock* 1956; *Earth vs the Flying Saucers* 1956; *Rock around the Clock* 1956; *The Werewolf* 1956

Seaton, George (1911-1979) *Billy Rose's Diamond Horseshoe* 1945; *Miracle on 34th Street* 1947; *The Shocking Miss Pilgrim* 1947; *Apartment for Peggy* 1948; *Chicken Every Sunday* 1948; *The Big Lift* 1950; *For Heaven's Sake* 1950; *Anything Can Happen* 1952; *Little Boy Lost* 1953; *The Country Girl* 1954; *Teacher's Pet* 1958; *The Pleasure of His Company* 1961; *The Counterfeit Traitor* 1962; *The Hook* 1962; *36 Hours* 1964; *What's So Bad about Feeling Good?* 1968; *Airport* 1970; *Showdown* 1973

Sedgwick, Edward (1892-1953) *The Cameraman* 1928; *Spite Marriage* 1929; *Doughboys* 1930; *Free and Easy* 1930; *Parlor, Bedroom and Bath* 1931; *The Passionate Plumber* 1932; *Speak Easily* 1932; *What - No Beer?* 1933; *Pick a Star* 1937; *A Southern Yankee* 1948

Segal, Alex (1915-1977) *Ransom!* 1956; *All the Way Home* 1963

Segal, Peter (1962-) *Naked Gun 33⅓: the Final Insult* 1994; *Tommy Boy* 1995; *My Fellow Americans* 1996; *Nutty Professor 2: the Klumps* 2000; *Anger Management* 2003; *50 First Dates* 2004; *The Longest Yard* 2005; *Get Smart* 2008; *Grudge Match* 2013

Seidelman, Arthur Allan aka **Seidelman, Arthur A** *Hercules in New York* 1969; *The Caller* 1987; *Rescue Me* 1991; *The Summer of Ben Tyler* 1996; *Walking across Egypt* 1999; *A Christmas Carol* 2004

Seidelman, Susan (1952-) *Smithereens* 1982; *Desperately Seeking Susan* 1985; *Making Mr Right* 1987; *Cookie* 1989; *She-Devil* 1989; *Erotic Tales* 1994; *A Cooler Climate* 1999

Seidl, Ulrich (1952-) *Dog Days* 2001; *Import Export* 2007

Seiler, Lewis (1891-1963) *Charlie Chan in Paris* 1935; *Dust Be My*

Destiny 1939; *Hell's Kitchen* 1939; *King of the Underworld* 1939; *You Can't Get Away with Murder* 1939; *It All Came True* 1940; *The Big Shot* 1942; *Pittsburgh* 1942; *Guadalcanal Diary* 1943; *Something for the Boys* 1944; *Molly and Me* 1945; *Breakthrough* 1950; *Women's Prison* 1955; *The True Story of Lynn Stuart* 1957

Seiter, William A aka **Seiter, William** (1892-1964) *Sunny* 1930; *If I Had a Million* 1932; *Sons of the Desert* 1933; *The Richest Girl in the World* 1934; *Sing and Like It* 1934; *If You Could Only Cook* 1935; *In Person* 1935; *Roberta* 1935; *Dimples* 1936; *The Moon's Our Home* 1936; *Stowaway* 1936; *Life Begins in College* 1937; *This Is My Affair* 1937; *Room Service* 1938; *Sally, Irene and Mary* 1938; *Thanks for Everything* 1938; *Three Blind Mice* 1938; *The First Rebel* 1939; *Susannah of the Mounties* 1939; *Hired Wife* 1940; *It's a Date* 1940; *Appointment for Love* 1941; *Nice Girl?* 1941; *Broadway* 1942; *You Were Never Lovelier* 1942; *A Lady Takes a Chance* 1943; *Belle of the Yukon* 1944; *The Affairs of Susan* 1945; *It's a Pleasure* 1945; *Little Giant* 1946; *Lover Come Back* 1946; *I'll Be Yours* 1947; *One Touch of Venus* 1948; *Up in Central Park* 1948; *Borderline* 1950; *The Lady Wants Mink* 1953

Seitz, George B (1888-1944) *Danger Lights* 1930; *Buried Loot* 1934; *Woman Wanted* 1935; *The Last of the Mohicans* 1936; *A Family Affair* 1937; *Judge Hardy's Children* 1938; *Love Finds Andy Hardy* 1938; *Out West with the Hardys* 1938; *You're Only Young Once* 1938; *The Hardys Ride High* 1939; *Judge Hardy and Son* 1939; *Andy Hardy Meets Debutante* 1940; *Kit Carson* 1940; *Sky Murder* 1940; *Andy Hardy's Private Secretary* 1941; *Life Begins for Andy Hardy* 1941; *Andy Hardy's Double Life* 1942; *The Courtship of Andy Hardy* 1942; *Andy Hardy's Blonde Trouble* 1944

Sekely, Steve (1899-1979) *Miracle on Main Street* 1940; *Hollow Triumph* 1948; *The Day of the Triffids* 1962

Selander, Lesley (1900-1979) *Cherokee Strip* 1940; *Belle Starr's Daughter* 1948; *Guns of Hate* 1948; *Cavalry Scout* 1951; *Flight to Mars* 1951; *The Raiders* 1952; *Fort Algiers* 1953; *War Paint* 1953; *Arrow in the Dust* 1954; *Tall Man Riding* 1955; *Arizona Bushwhackers* 1968

Selick, Henry *The Nightmare before Christmas* 1993; *James and the Giant Peach* 1996; *Monkeybone* 2000; *Coraline* 2008

Seltzer, Aaron (1974-) *Date Movie* 2006; *Epic Movie* 2007; *Disaster Movie* 2008; *Meet the Spartans* 2008; *Vampires Suck* 2010

Seltzer, David (1940-) *Lucas* 1986; *Punchline* 1988; *Shining Through* 1992

Selwyn, Edgar (1875-1944) *The Sin of Madelon Claudet* 1931; *Skyscraper Souls* 1932

Sembene, Ousmane (1923-2007) *Xala* 1974; *Guelwaar* 1992; *Moolaadé* 2004

Sen, Mrinal (1923-) *And Quiet Rolls the Dawn* 1979; *In Search of Famine* 1980

Sena, Dominic (1949-) *Kalifornia* 1993; *Gone in Sixty Seconds* 2000; *Swordfish* 2001; *Whiteout* 2009; *Season of the Witch* 2010

Serious, Yahoo (1954-) *Young Einstein* 1988; *Reckless Kelly* 1993

Serreau, Coline (1947-) *Pourquoi Pas!* 1977; *3 Men and a Cradle* 1985; *Romuald et Juliette* 1989; *La Crise* 1992

Sewell, Vernon aka **Sewell, Vernon Campbell** (1903-2001) *The Silver Fleet* 1943; *The Ghosts of Berkeley Square* 1947; *The Dark Light* 1951; *Ghost Ship* 1952; *Counterspy* 1953; *Home and Away* 1956; *The Battle of the V1* 1958; *House of Mystery* 1961; *The Man in the Back Seat* 1961; *Strongroom* 1961; *The Wind of Change* 1961; *The Blood Beast Terror* 1967; *Curse of the Crimson Altar* 1968; *Burke & Hare* 1971

Shadyac, Tom (1958-) *Ace Ventura: Pet Detective* 1993; *The Nutty Professor* 1996; *Liar Liar* 1997; *Patch Adams* 1998; *Dragonfly* 2002; *Bruce Almighty* 2003; *Evan Almighty* 2007

Shainberg, Steven *Secretary* 2001; *Fur: an Imaginary Portrait of Diane Arbus* 2006

Shane, Maxwell (1905-1983) *Fear in the Night* 1947; *City across the River* 1949; *The Glass Wall* 1953; *The Naked Street* 1955; *Nightmare* 1956

Shankland, Tom *WAZ* 2006; *The Children* 2008

Shankman, Adam (1964-) *The Wedding Planner* 2001; *A Walk to Remember* 2002; *Bringing Down the House* 2003; *Cheaper by the Dozen 2* 2005; *The Pacifier* 2005; *Hairspray* 2007; *Bedtime Stories* 2008; *Rock of Ages* 2012

Shanley, John Patrick (1950-) *Joe versus the Volcano* 1990; *Doubt* 2008

Shapiro, Alan *The Crush* 1993; *Flipper* 1996

Shapiro, Craig *Our Lips Are Sealed* 2000; *Winning London* 2001; *Dr Dolittle: Tail to the Chief* 2008

Shapiro, Paul (1955-) *Murder at Devil's Glen* 1999; *Deadly Honeymoon* 2009

Sharp, Don (1922-2011) *The Golden Disc* 1958; *Kiss of the Vampire* 1962; *It's All Happening* 1963; *The Devil-Ship Pirates* 1964; *Curse of the Fly* 1965; *The Face of Fu Manchu* 1965; *Rasputin, the Mad Monk* 1965; *The Brides of Fu Manchu* 1966; *Our Man in Marrakesh* 1966; *Jules Verne's Rocket to the Moon* 1967; *The Violent Enemy* 1969; *Psychomania* 1972; *Dark Places* 1973; *Callan* 1974; *Hennessy* 1975; *The Four Feathers* 1978; *The Thirty-Nine Steps* 1978; *Bear Island* 1979

Sharp, Ian (1946-) *Who Dares Wins* 1982; *Mrs Caldicot's Cabbage War* 2000; *Tracker* 2010

Sharpsteen, Ben (1895-1980) *Pinocchio* 1940; *Dumbo* 1941

Shaughnessy, Alfred (1916-2005) *6.5 Special* 1958; *The Impersonator* 1962

Shavelson, Melville (1917-2007) *Seven Little Foys* 1955; *Beau James* 1957; *Houseboat* 1958; *The Five Pennies* 1959; *It Started in Naples* 1960; *On the Double* 1961; *The Pigeon That Took Rome* 1962; *A New Kind of Love* 1963; *Cast a Giant Shadow* 1966; *Yours, Mine and Ours* 1968; *The War between Men and Women* 1972

Shaw, Anthony Pullen aka **Shaw, Anthony** (1952-) *Mrs 'arris Goes to Paris* 1992; *The Unexpected Mrs Pollifax* 1999

Shaw, Larry *Mortal Fear* 1994; *Wes Craven's Don't Look Down* 1998

Shea, Katt aka **Ruben, Katt Shea** (1957-) *Streets* 1990; *Poison Ivy* 1992; *The Rage: Carrie 2* 1999

Shear, Barry (1923-1979) *The Karate Killers* 1967; *Wild in the Streets* 1968; *Across 110th Street* 1972; *The Deadly Trackers* 1973

Sheldon, Sidney (1917-2007) *Dream Wife* 1953; *The Buster Keaton Story* 1957

Shelton, Lynn *Humpday* 2009; *Your Sister's Sister* 2011; *Touchy Feely* 2013; *Say When* 2014

Shelton, Ron (1945-) *Bull Durham* 1988; *Blaze* 1989; *White Men Can't Jump* 1992; *Cobb* 1994; *Tin Cup* 1996; *Play It to the Bone* 2000; *Dark Blue* 2002; *Hollywood Homicide* 2003

Shepard, Richard (1965-) *Cool Blue* 1988; *The Linguini Incident* 1991; *Oxygen* 1999; *The Matador* 2005; *The Hunting Party* 2007; *Dom Hemingway* 2013

Sher, Jack (1913-1988) *The Three Worlds of Gulliver* 1959; *The Wild and the Innocent* 1959

Sheridan, Jim (1949-) *My Left Foot* 1989; *The Field* 1990; *In the Name of the Father* 1993; *The Boxer* 1997; *In America* 2003; *Get Rich or Die Tryin'* 2005; *Brothers* 2009; *Dream House* 2011

Sheridan, Kirsten *Disco Pigs* 2001; *August Rush* 2007

Sherin, Edwin aka **Sherin, Ed** (1930-) *Glory Boy* 1971; *Valdez Is Coming* 1971; *Lena: My 100 Children* 1987

Sherman, Gary aka **Sherman, Gary A** *Death Line* 1972; *Vice Squad* 1982; *Wanted Dead or Alive* 1986; *Poltergeist III* 1988

Sherman, George (1908-1991) *Overland Stage Raiders* 1938; *Red River Range* 1938; *Frontier Horizon* 1939; *The Lady and the Monster* 1944; *The Bandit of Sherwood Forest* 1946; *Relentless* 1948; *Calamity Jane and Sam Bass* 1949; *Red Canyon* 1949; *Comanche Territory* 1950; *The Sleeping City* 1950; *Target Unknown* 1951;

Tomahawk 1951; Against All Flags 1952; The Battle at Apache Pass 1952; The Lone Hand 1953; War Arrow 1953; Dawn at Socorro 1954; Johnny Dark 1954; Chief Crazy Horse 1955; Count Three and Pray 1955; The Treasure of Pancho Villa 1955; Comanche 1956; The Last of the Fast Guns 1958; Son of Robin Hood 1958; Hell Bent for Leather 1960; None but the Brave 1960; The Wizard of Baghdad 1960; The Fiercest Heart 196; Panic Button 1964; Big Jake 1971

Sherman, Lowell (1885-1934) Bachelor Apartment 1931; Broadway through a Keyhole 1933; Morning Glory 1933; She Done Him Wrong 1933; Born to Be Bad 1934

Sherman, Vincent (1906-2006) The Return of Dr X 1939; Saturday's Children 1940; All Through the Night 1942; The Hard Way 1942; Old Acquaintance 1943; In Our Time 1944; Mr Skeffington 1944; Nora Prentiss 1947; The Unfaithful 1947; Adventures of Don Juan 1948; The Hasty Heart 1949; Backfire 1950; The Damned Don't Cry 1950; Harriet Craig 1950; Goodbye, My Fancy 1951; Affair in Trinidad 1952; Lone Star 1952; The Garment Jungle 1957; The Young Philadelphians 1959; Ice Palace 1960; The Second Time Around 1961; Cervantes 1968

Sherwood, John (1959-) The Creature Walks among Us 1956; Raw Edge 1956; The Monolith Monsters 1957

Shimizu, Takashi (1972-) The Grudge: Ju-On 2003; Ju-On: The Grudge 2 2003; The Grudge 2004; Marebito 2004; The Grudge 2 2006

Shindo, Kaneto (1912-2012) The Island 1961; Onibaba 1964

Sholder, Jack (1945-) Alone in the Dark 1982; A Nightmare on Elm Street 2: Freddy's Revenge 1985; The Hidden 1987; Renegades 1989; By Dawn's Early Light 1990; 12:01 1993; Arachnid 2001

Sholem, Lee (1913-2000) Tarzan's Magic Fountain 1949; Tarzan and the Slave Girl 1950; The Redhead from Wyoming 1953; Hell Ship Mutiny 1957

Shonteff, Lindsay (1935-2006) Devil Doll 1964; Licensed to Kill 1965; Sumuru 1967

Shore, Simon Get Real 1998; Things to Do before You're 30 2004

Shortland, Cate Somersault 2004; Lore 2012

Shumlin, Herman (1898-1979) Watch on the Rhine 1943; Confidential Agent 1945

Shyamalan, M Night (1970-) Wide Awake 1998; The Sixth Sense 1999; Unbreakable 2000; Signs 2002; The Village 2004; Lady in the Water 2006; The Happening 2008; The Last Airbender 2010; After Earth 2013; The Visit 2015; Split 2017

Shyer, Charles (1941-) Irreconcilable Differences 1984; Baby Boom 1987; Father of the Bride 1991; I Love Trouble 1994; Father of the Bride Part 2 1995; The Affair of the Necklace 2001; Alfie 2004

Sidney (2), George (1916-2002) Pilot #5 1943; Thousands Cheer 1943; Bathing Beauty 1944; Ziegfeld Follies 1944; Anchors Aweigh 1945; The Harvey Girls 1946; Holiday in Mexico 1946; Cass Timberlane 1947; The Three Musketeers 1948; The Red Danube 1949; Annie Get Your Gun 1950; Key to the City 1950; Show Boat 1951; Scaramouche 1952; Kiss Me Kate 1953; Young Bess 1953; Jupiter's Darling 1955; The Eddy Duchin Story 1956; Jeanne Eagels 1957; Pal Joey 1957; Pepe 1960; Who Was That Lady? 1960; Bye Bye Birdie 1963; A Ticklish Affair 1963; Viva Las Vegas 1964; Half a Sixpence 1967

Siega, Marcos Underclassman 2004; Pretty Persuasion 2005

Siegel, David Suture 1993; The Deep End 2001; Bee Season 2005; What Maisie Knew 2012

Siegel, Don aka **Siegel, Donald** aka **Smithee, Allen** (1912-1991) The Verdict 1946; The Big Steal 1949; Night unto Night 1949; The Duel at Silver Creek 1952; Count the Hours 1953; Private Hell 36 1954; Riot in Cell Block 11 1954; An Annapolis Story 1955; Crime in the Streets 1956; Invasion of the Body Snatchers 1956; Baby Face Nelson 1957; The Gun Runners 1958; The Lineup 1958; Edge of Eternity 1959; Hound Dog Man 1959; Flaming Star 1960; Hell Is

for Heroes 1962; The Killers 1964; Stranger on the Run 1967; Coogan's Bluff 1968; Madigan 1968; Death of a Gunfighter 1969; The Beguiled 1970; Two Mules for Sister Sara 1970; Dirty Harry 1971; Charley Varrick 1973; The Black Windmill 1974; The Shootist 1976; Telefon 1977; Escape from Alcatraz 1979; Rough Cut 1980; Jinxed! 1982

Signorelli, James Easy Money 1983; Elvira, Mistress of the Dark 1988

Silberg, Joel Breakdance 1984; Rappin' 1985; Bad Guys 1986; Lambada 1990

Silberling, Brad (1965-) Casper 1995; City of Angels 1998; Moonlight Mile 2002; Lemony Snicket's A Series of Unfortunate Events 2004; Land of the Lost 2009

Silva, Sebastián (1979-) The Maid 2009; Crystal Fairy and the Magical Cactus 2013; Magic Magic 2013; Nasty Baby 2016

Silver, Joan Micklin (1935-) Hester Street 1975; Between the Lines 1977; Chilly Scenes of Winter 1979; Crossing Delancey 1988; Loverboy 1989; A Private Matter 1992; Stepkids 1992; Invisible Child 1999; Charms for the Easy Life 2001

Silver, Marisa (1960-) Permanent Record 1988; Vital Signs 1990; He Said, She Said 1991

Silver, Scott Johns 1995; The Mod Squad 1999

Silverstein, Elliot (1927-) Cat Ballou 1965; The Happening 1967; A Man Called Horse 1970; The Car 1977

Simmons, Anthony (1924-) Your Money or Your Wife 1960; Four in the Morning 1965; The Optimists of Nine Elms 1973; Black Joy 1977

Simon, S Sylvan (1910-1951) Dancing Co-Ed 1939; Whistling in the Dark 1941; Rio Rita 1942; Song of the Open Road 1944; Abbott and Costello in Hollywood 1945; Son of Lassie 1945; Her Husband's Affairs 1947

Simoneau, Yves (1955-) Perfectly Normal 1990; Mother's Boys 1993; Amelia Earhart: the Final Flight 1994; Free Money 1998; 36 Hours to Die 1999; Bury My Heart at Wounded Knee 2007; America 2009

Simpson, Daniel Spiderhole 2009; The Rendlesham UFO Incident 2014

Sinclair, Andrew (1935-) Under Milk Wood 1971; Blue Blood 1973

Sinclair, Robert B (1905-1970) Dramatic School 1938; That Wonderful Urge 1948

Singer, Alexander (1932-) Psyche '59 1964; Love Has Many Faces 1965; Captain Apache 1971

Singer, Bryan (1966-) Public Access 1993; The Usual Suspects 1995; Apt Pupil 1997; X-Men 2000; X2 2003; Superman Returns 2006; Valkyrie 2008; Jack the Giant Slayer 2013; X-Men: Days of Future Past 2014; X-Men: Apocalypse 2016

Singh, Tarsem aka **Tarsem** (1961-) The Cell 2000; The Fall 2006; Immortals 2011; Mirror Mirror 2012; Self/Less 2015

Singleton, John (1968-) Boyz N the Hood 1991; Poetic Justice 1993; Higher Learning 1995; Rosewood 1997; Shaft 2000; Baby Boy 2001; 2 Fast 2 Furious 2003; Four Brothers 2005; Abduction 2011

Sington, David In the Shadow of the Moon 2006; The Flaw 2011; The Fear of 13 2015

Sinise, Gary (1955-) Miles from Home 1988; Of Mice and Men 1992

Sinyor, Gary (1962-) Leon the Pig Farmer 1992; Solitaire for 2 1994; Stiff Upper Lips 1997; The Bachelor 1999; United We Fall 2014

Siodmak, Robert aka **Siodmark, Robert** (1900-1973) People on Sunday 1929; Pièges 1939; Son of Dracula 1943; Christmas Holiday 1944; Cobra Woman 1944; Phantom Lady 1944; The Suspect 1944; The Strange Affair of Uncle Harry 1945; The Dark Mirror 1946; The Killers 1946; The Spiral Staircase 1946; Time Out of Mind 1947; Cry of the City 1948; Criss Cross 1949; The File on Thelma Jordon 1949; The Great Sinner 1949; The Crimson Pirate 1952; The Rats 1955; The Rough and the Smooth 1959; Custer of the West 1967

Siri, Florent Emilio aka **Siri, Florent** (1965-) Hostage 2004; Intimate Enemies 2007

Sirk, Douglas aka **Sierck, Detlef** (1897-1987) Pillars of Society 1935; Hitler's Madman 1943; Summer Storm 1944; Thieves' Holiday 1946;

Lured 1947; Sleep, My Love 1948; Shockproof 1949; Slightly French 1949; Mystery Submarine 1950; The First Legion 1951; The Lady Pays Off 1951; Thunder on the Hill 1951; Weekend with Father 1951; Has Anybody Seen My Gal? 1952; Meet Me at the Fair 1952; No Room for the Groom 1952; All I Desire 1953; Take Me to Town 1953; Magnificent Obsession 1954; Sign of the Pagan 1954; Taza, Son of Cochise 1954; All That Heaven Allows 1955; Captain Lightfoot 1955; Never Say Goodbye 1955; There's Always Tomorrow 1956; Written on the Wind 1956; Battle Hymn 1957; Interlude 1957; The Tarnished Angels 1957; A Time to Love and a Time to Die 1958; Imitation of Life 1959

Sissako, Abderrahmane Waiting for Happiness 2002; Bamako 2006; Timbuktu 2014

Sitch, Rob (1962-) The Castle 1997; The Dish 2000

Sivan, Santosh The Terrorist 1998; Asoka 2001; Before the Rains 2007

Sivertson, Chris I Know Who Killed Me 2007; All Cheerleaders Die 2013

Six, Tom The Human Centipede (First Sequence) 2009; The Human Centipede II (Full Sequence) 2011; The Human Centipede III (Final Sequence) 2015

Sjöberg, Alf (1903-1980) Torment 1944; Miss Julie 1951

Sjöman, Vilgot (1924-2006) My Sister, My Love 1966; I Am Curious-Yellow 1967

Sjöström, Victor aka **Seastrom, Victor** (1879-1960) The Outlaw and His Wife 1917; Karin Ingmarsdotter 1919; A Dangerous Pledge 1920; The Phantom Carriage 1920; He Who Gets Slapped 1924; The Scarlet Letter 1926; The Divine Woman 1928; The Wind 1928; Under the Red Robe 1937

Skjoldbjaerg, Erik (1964-) Insomnia 1997; Pioneer 2013

Skogland, Kari Liberty Stands Still 2002; Fifty Dead Men Walking 2008

Skolimowski, Jerzy (1938-) The Adventures of Gerard 1970; Deep End 1970; King, Queen, Knave 1972; The Shout 1978; Moonlighting 1982; Success Is the Best Revenge 1984; The Lightship 1985; Torrents of Spring 1989; Essential Killing 2010

Slade, David Hard Candy 2005; 30 Days of Night 2007; Eclipse 2010

Sloane, Paul H aka **Sloane, Paul** (1893-1963) Half Shot at Sunrise 1930; Consolation Marriage 1931

Sluizer, George (1932-2014) The Vanishing 1988; Utz 1992; The Vanishing 1993

Smart, Ralph (1908-2001) Bush Christmas 1947; Quartet 1948; A Boy, a Girl and a Bike 1949; Bitter Springs 1950; Never Take No for an Answer 1951; Curtain Up 1952

Smight, Jack (1926-2003) I'd Rather Be Rich 1964; The Third Day 1965; Harper 1966; Kaleidoscope 1966; The Secret War of Harry Frigg 1967; No Way to Treat a Lady 1968; The Illustrated Man 1969; Rabbit, Run 1970; Banacek: Detour to Nowhere 1972; Double Indemnity 1973; Frankenstein: the True Story 1973; Airport 1975 1974; Battle of Midway 1976; Damnation Alley 1977; Loving Couples 1980; Number One with a Bullet 1986

Smith (3), Brian The Little Mermaid II: Return to the Sea 2000; Tarzan II 2005

Smith, Charles Martin (1953-) Trick or Treat 1986; Fifty/Fifty 1991; Air Bud 1997; Stone of Destiny 2008; Dolphin Tale 2011; Dolphin Tale 2 2014

Smith, Chris The Pool 2007; Collapse 2009

Smith, Christopher (1972-) Creep 2004; Severance 2006; Triangle 2009; Black Death 2010; Get Santa 2014

Smith, John N (1943-) The Masculine Mystique 1984; Sitting in Limbo 1986; Dangerous Minds 1995; A Cool, Dry Place 1998

Smith (2), Kevin (1970-) Clerks 1994; Mallrats 1995; Chasing Amy 1996; Dogma 1999; Jay and Silent Bob Strike Back 2001; Jersey Girl 2003; Clerks II 2006; Zack and Miri Make a Porno 2008; Cop Out 2010; Red State 2011; Yoga Hosers 2016

Smith, Mel (1952-2013) The Tall Guy 1989; Radioland Murders 1994; Bean 1997; High Heels and Low Lifes 2001; Blackball 2003

Smith, Simon J Bee Movie 2007; Penguins of Madagascar 2014

Snyder, Zack (1966-) Dawn of the Dead 2004; 300 2006; Watchmen 2009; Legend of the Guardians: the Owls of Ga'Hoole 2010; Sucker Punch 2011; Man of Steel 2013; Batman v Superman: Dawn of Justice 2016; Justice League 2017

So Yong Kim Treeless Mountain 2008; For Ellen 2012

Soavi, Michele (1957-) Stage Fright - Aquarius 1987; The Church 1988; The Sect 1991; Cemetery Man 1994

Sobel, Mark (1956-) Fall into Darkness 1996; Storm Chasers: Revenge of the Twister 1998

Soderbergh, Steven (1963-) sex, lies, and videotape 1989; Kafka 1991; King of the Hill 1993; The Underneath 1995; Gray's Anatomy 1996; Schizopolis 1996; Out of Sight 1998; The Limey 1999; Erin Brockovich 2000; Traffic 2000; Ocean's Eleven 2001; Full Frontal 2002; Solaris 2002; Eros 2004; Ocean's Twelve 2004; The Good German 2006; Ocean's Thirteen 2007; Che Part One 2008; Che Part Two 2008; The Girlfriend Experience 2009; The Informant! 2009; Contagion 2011; Haywire 2011; Magic Mike 2012; Behind the Candelabra 2013; Side Effects 2013

Softley, Iain (1958-) Backbeat 1993; Hackers 1995; The Wings of the Dove 1997; K-PAX 2001; The Skeleton Key 2005; Inkheart 2007; Trap for Cinderella 2011

Sohn, Peter Ponyo 2008; The Good Dinosaur 2015

Sokurov, Aleksandr (1951-) Whispering Pages 1993; Mother and Son 1997; Moloch 1999; Russian Ark 2002; Father and Son 2003; The Sun 2005; Alexandra 2007; Faust 2011

Solanas, Fernando E (1936-) Tangos, Exilo de Gardel 1985; Sur 1987

Sole, Alfred Alice, Sweet Alice 1977; Pandemonium 1982

Sollett, Peter Raising Victor Vargas 2002; Nick & Norah's Infinite Playlist 2008; Freeheld 2015

Solomon, Courtney (1971-) Dungeons & Dragons 2000; An American Haunting 2005; Getaway 2013

Solondz, Todd (1960-) Fear, Anxiety, and Depression 1989; Welcome to the Dollhouse 1995; Happiness 1998; Storytelling 2001; Palindromes 2004; Life during Wartime 2009; Dark Horse 2011; Wiener-Dog 2016

Solt, Andrew This Is Elvis 1981; Imagine: John Lennon 1988

Sommers, Stephen (1962-) The Adventures of Huck Finn 1993; The Jungle Book 1994; Deep Rising 1998; The Mummy 1999; The Mummy Returns 2001; Van Helsing 2004; GI Joe: the Rise of Cobra 2009; Odd Thomas 2013

Sonnenfeld, Barry (1953-) The Addams Family 1991; Addams Family Values 1993; For Love or Money 1993; Get Shorty 1995; Men in Black 1997; Wild Wild West 1999; Big Trouble 2002; Men in Black 2 2002; RV 2006; Men in Black 3 2012; Nine Lives 2016

Sono, Sion (1961-) Love Exposure 2008; Cold Fish 2010; Guilty of Romance 2011; Himizu 2011; Tokyo Tribe 2014

Sori, Fumihiko aka **Sori** Ping Pong 2002; Vexille 2007

Sorin, Carlos (1944-) Eversmile, New Jersey 1989; Historias Mínimas 2002; Bombón - El Perro 2004

Sorrentino, Paolo (1970-) The Consequences of Love 2004; The Family Friend 2006; Il Divo 2008; This Must Be the Place 2011; The Great Beauty 2013; Youth 2015

Spacey, Kevin (1959-) Albino Alligator 1996; Beyond the Sea 2004

Spasojevic, Srdjan A Serbian Film 2010; The ABCs of Death 2012

Speck, Will Blades of Glory 2007; The Switch 2010

Spector, Col Someone Else 2005; Honeymooner 2010

Spence, Richard Different for Girls 1996; New World Disorder 1999

Spheeris, Penelope (1946-) The Decline of Western Civilization 1980; The Boys Next Door 1985; Dudes 1987; The Decline of Western Civilization Part II: the Metal Years 1988; Wayne's World 1992; The Beverly Hillbillies 1993; The Little Rascals 1994; Black Sheep 1996; The

Decline of Western Civilization Part III 1997; Senseless 1998; Five 2011; The Real St Nick 2012

Spicer, Bryan Mighty Morphin Power Rangers: the Movie 1995; For Richer or Poorer 1997; McHale's Navy 1997

Spielberg, Steven (1946-) Duel 1971; Something Evil 1972; The Sugarland Express 1974; Jaws 1975; Close Encounters of the Third Kind 1977; 1941 1979; Raiders of the Lost Ark 1981; ET the Extra-Terrestrial 1982; Twilight Zone: the Movie 1983; Indiana Jones and the Temple of Doom 1984; The Color Purple 1985; Empire of the Sun 1987; Always 1989; Indiana Jones and the Last Crusade 1989; Hook 1991; Jurassic Park 1993; Schindler's List 1993; Amistad 1997; The Lost World: Jurassic Park 1997; Saving Private Ryan 1998; AI: Artificial Intelligence 2001; Catch Me If You Can 2002; Minority Report 2002; The Terminal 2004; Munich 2005; War of the Worlds 2005; Indiana Jones and the Kingdom of the Crystal Skull 2008; The Adventures of Tintin: the Secret of the Unicorn 2011; War Horse 2011; Lincoln 2012; Bridge of Spies 2015; The BFG 2016

Spierig, Michael aka **Spierig Brothers, The** Undead 2002; Daybreakers 2008; Predestination 2014

Spierig, Peter aka **Spierig Brothers, The** Undead 2002; Daybreakers 2008; Predestination 2014

Spiers, Bob (1945-2008) Spice World: the Movie 1997; That Darn Cat 1997

Spottiswoode, Roger (1943-) Terror Train 1980; The Pursuit of DB Cooper 1981; Under Fire 1983; The Best of Times 1986; Deadly Pursuit 1988; Turner & Hooch 1989; Air America 1990; Stop! or My Mom Will Shoot 1992; And the Band Played On 1993; Tomorrow Never Dies 1997; The 6th Day 2000; Ice Bound 2003

Sprackling, Simon The Funny Man 1994; Breakfast with Jonny Wilkinson 2013

Sprecher, Jill Clockwatchers 1997; Thirteen Conversations about One Thing 2001

Springsteen, R G (1904-1989) Come Next Spring 1956; Showdown 1963; Bullet for a Badman 1964; He Rides Tall 1964; Taggart 1964; Apache Uprising 1965; Johnny Reno 1966; Waco 1966; Tiger by the Tail 1970

Spurlock, Morgan (1970-) Super Size Me 2004; Where in the World Is Osama Bin Laden? 2008; POM Wonderful Presents: The Greatest Movie Ever Sold 2011; One Direction: This Is Us 2013

Stacchi, Anthony Open Season 2006; The Boxtrolls 2014

Stahl, John M (1886-1950) Back Street 1932; Only Yesterday 1933; Imitation of Life 1934; Magnificent Obsession 1935; Parnell 1937; Letter of Introduction 1938; When Tomorrow Comes 1939; Holy Matrimony 1943; The Immortal Sergeant 1943; The Eve of St Mark 1944; The Keys of the Kingdom 1944; Leave Her to Heaven 1945; The Foxes of Harrow 1947; Father Was a Fullback 1949; Oh, You Beautiful Doll 1949

Stallone, Sylvester (1946-) Paradise Alley 1978; Rocky II 1979; Rocky III 1982; Staying Alive 1983; Rocky IV 1985; Rocky Balboa 2006; Rambo 2007; The Expendables 2010

Stamm, Daniel The Last Exorcism 2010; 13 Sins 2013

Standring, Glenn The Truth about Demons 2000; Perfect Creature 2005

Stanley, Richard (1964-) Hardware 1990; Dust Devil 1992

Stanton, Andrew (1965-) Finding Nemo 2003; WALL-E 2008; John Carter 2012; Finding Dory 2016

Starewicz, Ladislaw (1882-1965) Town Rat, Country Rat 1923; The Tale of the Fox 1931

Stark, Graham (1922-2013) Simon, Simon 1970; The Magnificent Seven Deadly Sins 1971

Starrett, Jack (1936-1989) The Strange Vengeance of Rosalie 1972; Cleopatra Jones 1973; Race with the Devil 1975

Stassen, Ben Fly Me to the Moon 2007; A Turtle's Tale: Sammy's Adventures 2010; Sammy's Great Escape 2012; The House of Magic 2013

Steckler, Ray Dennis (1938-2009) *The Incredibly Strange Creatures Who Stopped Living and Became Mixed-up Zombies* 1963; *Rat Pfink a Boo Boo* 1965

Steers, Burr *Igby Goes Down* 2002; *17 Again* 2009; *Death & Life of Charlie St Cloud* 2010; *Pride and Prejudice and Zombies* 2015

Stein, Bjorn aka **Marlind & Stein** *Shelter* 2008; *Underworld: Awakening* 2012

Stein, Darren (1972-) *Jawbreaker* 1999; *GBF* 2013

Stein, Paul L aka **Stein, Paul** (1892-1951) *One Romantic Night* 1930; *Blossom Time* 1934; *Poison Pen* 1939; *The Saint Meets the Tiger* 1943; *Counterblast* 1948

Steinberg, David (1942-) *Paternity* 1981; *Going Berserk* 1983

Steinberg, Michael (1959-) *The Waterdance* 1991; *Bodies, Rest & Motion* 1993; *Wicked* 1998

Steinmann, Danny (1942-2012) *Savage Streets* 1984; *Friday the 13th: a New Beginning* 1985

Stephenson, John (1923-2015) *Animal Farm* 1999; *Five Children and It* 2004; *The Christmas Candle* 2013

Stern, Joshua Michael *Swing Vote* 2008; *jOBS* 2013

Stern, Sandor (1936-) *Passions* 1984; *Pin* 1988; *Amityville: the Evil Escapes* 1989; *Heart of a Child* 1994

Stern, Steven Hilliard aka **Smythe, Allan** (1937-) *The Harrad Summer* 1974; *Running* 1979; *The Devil and Max Devlin* 1981; *Another Woman* 1994

Stettner, Patrick *The Business of Strangers* 2001; *The Night Listener* 2006

Stevens, Art (1915-2007) *The Rescuers* 1977; *The Fox and the Hound* 1981

Stevens, Fisher (1963-) *Just a Kiss* 2002; *Stand Up Guys* 2012

Stevens, George (1904-1975) *Alice Adams* 1935; *Annie Oakley* 1935; *Swing Time* 1936; *A Damsel in Distress* 1937; *Quality Street* 1937; *Vivacious Lady* 1938; *Gunga Din* 1939; *Vigil in the Night* 1940; *Penny Serenade* 1941; *The Talk of the Town* 1942; *Woman of the Year* 1942; *The More the Merrier* 1943; *I Remember Mama* 1948; *A Place in the Sun* 1951; *Something to Live For* 1952; *Shane* 1953; *Giant* 1956; *The Diary of Anne Frank* 1959; *The Greatest Story Ever Told* 1965; *The Only Game in Town* 1970

Stevens (1), Leslie (1924-1998) *Hero's Island* 1962; *Incubus* 1965

Stevens, Robert (1921-1998) *The Big Caper* 1957; *I Thank a Fool* 1962

Stevenson, Robert (1905-1986) *The Man Who Changed His Mind* 1936; *Tudor Rose* 1936; *King Solomon's Mines* 1937; *Owd Bob* 1938; *The Ware Case* 1938; *Young Man's Fancy* 1939; *Return to Yesterday* 1940; *Tom Brown's Schooldays* 1940; *Back Street* 1941; *Joan of Paris* 1942; *Forever and a Day* 1943; *Jane Eyre* 1943; *Dishonored Lady* 1947; *To the Ends of the Earth* 1948; *Walk Softly, Stranger* 1949; *The Woman on Pier 13* 1949; *My Forbidden Past* 1951; *The Las Vegas Story* 1952; *Johnny Tremain* 1957; *Old Yeller* 1957; *Darby O'Gill and the Little People* 1959; *Kidnapped* 1960; *The Absent-Minded Professor* 1961; *In Search of the Castaways* 1961; *Son of Flubber* 1962; *Mary Poppins* 1964; *The Misadventures of Merlin Jones* 1964; *The Monkey's Uncle* 1965; *That Darn Cat!* 1965; *Blackbeard's Ghost* 1967; *The Gnome-Mobile* 1967; *The Love Bug* 1969; *Bedknobs and Broomsticks* 1971; *Herbie Rides Again* 1974; *The Island at the Top of the World* 1974; *One of Our Dinosaurs Is Missing* 1975; *The Shaggy DA* 1976

Stewart, Douglas Day *Thief of Hearts* 1984; *Listen to Me* 1989

Stewart, Scott *Legion* 2010; *Priest* 2010; *Dark Skies* 2013

Stiller, Ben (1965-) *Reality Bites* 1994; *The Cable Guy* 1996; *Zoolander* 2001; *Tropic Thunder* 2008; *The Secret Life of Walter Mitty* 2013; *Zoolander 2* 2016

Stiller, Mauritz (1883-1928) *Gunnar Hede's Saga* 1922; *Gösta Berlings Saga* 1924; *Hotel Imperial* 1927

Stillman, Whit (1952-) *Metropolitan* 1990; *Barcelona* 1994; *The Last Days of Disco* 1998; *Damsels in Distress* 2011; *Love & Friendship* 2016

Stimpson, John *The March Sisters at Christmas* 2012; *Shattered Silence* 2012

Stölzl, Philipp *The North Face* 2008; *The Expatriate* 2012

Stockwell, John (1961-) *crazy/beautiful* 2001; *Blue Crush* 2002; *Into the Blue* 2005; *Paradise Lost* 2006; *Dark Tide* 2012

Stoller, Nicholas (1976-) *Forgetting Sarah Marshall* 2008; *Get Him to the Greek* 2010; *The Five-Year Engagement* 2012; *Bad Neighbours* 2014; *Bad Neighbours 2* 2016; *Storks* 2016

Stoloff, Ben aka **Stoloff, Benjamin** (1895-1960) *Palooka* 1934; *The Affairs of Annabel* 1938; *The Bermuda Mystery* 1944

Stone, Andrew L aka **Stone, Andrew** (1902-1999) *Stormy Weather* 1943; *Sensations* 1944; *The Steel Trap* 1952; *The Night Holds Terror* 1955; *Julie* 1956; *Cry Terror* 1958; *The Decks Ran Red* 1958; *The Last Voyage* 1960; *Ring of Fire* 1961; *The Password Is Courage* 1962; *The Secret of My Success* 1965; *Song of Norway* 1970; *The Great Waltz* 1972

Stone III, Charles *Drumline* 2002; *Mr 3000* 2004

Stone, Oliver (1946-) *Seizure* 1974; *The Hand* 1981; *Platoon* 1986; *Salvador* 1986; *Wall Street* 1987; *Talk Radio* 1988; *Born on the Fourth of July* 1989; *The Doors* 1991; *JFK* 1991; *Heaven and Earth* 1993; *Natural Born Killers* 1994; *Nixon* 1995; *U Turn* 1997; *Any Given Sunday* 1999; *Comandante* 2002; *Alexander* 2004; *World Trade Center* 2006; *W.* 2008; *South of the Border* 2009; *Wall Street: Money Never Sleeps* 2010; *Savages* 2012; *Snowden* 2016

Stone (3), Robert *Guerrilla: the Taking of Patty Hearst* 2004; *Pandora's Promise* 2013

Stone, Simon *The Turning* 2013; *The Daughter* 2016

Stopkewich, Lynne (1964-) *Kissed* 1996; *Suspicious River* 2000

Story, Tim (1974-) *Barbershop* 2002; *Taxi* 2004; *Fantastic Four* 2005; *4: Rise of the Silver Surfer* 2007; *Think like a Man* 2012; *Ride Along* 2014; *Think like a Man Too* 2014; *Ride Along 2* 2016

Strand, Paul (1890-1976) *Manhatta* 1921; *Native Land* 1942

Strause, Colin aka **The Brothers Strause** *AVPR: Aliens vs Predator Requiem* 2007; *Skyline* 2010

Strause, Greg aka **The Brothers Strause** *AVPR: Aliens vs Predator Requiem* 2007; *Skyline* 2010

Strayer, Frank R (1891-1964) *The Vampire Bat* 1933; *Blondie!* 1938

Streisand, Barbra (1942-) *Yentl* 1983; *The Prince of Tides* 1991; *The Mirror Has Two Faces* 1996

Strick, Joseph (1923-2010) *The Balcony* 1963; *Ulysses* 1967; *A Portrait of the Artist as a Young Man* 1977

Strickland, Peter *Katalin Varga* 2008; *Berberian Sound Studio* 2012; *The Duke of Burgundy* 2014

Strock, Herbert L (1918-2005) *Battle Taxi* 1955; *Blood of Dracula* 1957; *I Was a Teenage Frankenstein* 1957; *How to Make a Monster* 1958

Stuart, Mel (1928-2012) *Four Days in November* 1964; *I Love My... Wife* 1970; *Willy Wonka and the Chocolate Factory* 1971; *One Is a Lonely Number* 1972; *Wattstax* 1972; *The White Lions* 1980

Sturges, John (1911-1992) *The Walking Hills* 1949; *The Capture* 1950; *The Magnificent Yankee* 1950; *Mystery Street* 1950; *Right Cross* 1950; *It's a Big Country* 1951; *Kind Lady* 1951; *The People against O'Hara* 1951; *The Girl in White* 1952; *Escape from Fort Bravo* 1953; *Jeopardy* 1953; *Bad Day at Black Rock* 1955; *Underwater!* 1955; *Backlash* 1956; *Gunfight at the OK Corral* 1957; *The Law and Jake Wade* 1958; *The Old Man and the Sea* 1958; *Last Train from Gun Hill* 1959; *Never So Few* 1959; *The Magnificent Seven* 1960; *By Love Possessed* 1961; *A Girl Named Tamiko* 1962; *Sergeants 3* 1962; *The Great Escape* 1963; *The Hallelujah Trail* 1965; *The Satan Bug* 1965; *Hour of the Gun* 1967; *Ice Station Zebra* 1968; *Marooned* 1969; *Joe Kidd* 1972; *The Valdez Horses* 1973; *McQ* 1974; *The Eagle Has Landed* 1976

Sturges, Preston (1898-1959) *Christmas in July* 1940; *The Great McGinty* 1940; *The Lady Eve* 1941; *Sullivan's Travels* 1941; *The Palm Beach Story* 1942; *The Miracle of Morgan's Creek* 1943; *The Great Moment* 1944; *Hail the Conquering*

Hero 1944; *Unfaithfully Yours* 1948; *The Beautiful Blonde from Bashful Bend* 1949; *Mad Wednesday* 1950; *The Diary of Major Thompson* 1955

Sturridge, Charles (1951-) *Runners* 1983; *Aria* 1987; *A Handful of Dust* 1987; *Where Angels Fear to Tread* 1991; *FairyTale: a True Story* 1997; *Lassie* 2005

Styles, Eric *Dreaming of Joseph Lees* 1998; *Relative Values* 2000; *That Good Night* 2017

Sucsy, Michael *Grey Gardens* 2009; *The Vow* 2012

Sugarman, Sara *Mad Cows* 1999; *Very Annie-Mary* 2000; *Confessions of a Teenage Drama Queen* 2004; *Vinyl* 2012

Sugg, Stewart *Fast Food* 1998; *Kiss Kiss (Bang Bang)* 2001

Suleiman, Elia (1960-) *Divine Intervention* 2002; *The Time That Remains: Chronicle of a Present Absentee* 2009; *7 Days in Havana* 2012

Sullivan, Kevin Rodney (1959-) *Soul of the Game* 1996; *How Stella Got Her Groove Back* 1998; *Barbershop 2: Back in Business* 2004; *Guess Who* 2005

Summers, Jeremy (1931-) *The Punch and Judy Man* 1962; *Crooks in Cloisters* 1963; *Ferry Cross the Mersey* 1965; *Five Golden Dragons* 1967; *House of a Thousand Dolls* 1967; *The Vengeance of Fu Manchu* 1967

Summers, Walter (1896-1973) *The Battles of Coronel and Falkland Islands* 1927; *The Return of Bulldog Drummond* 1934; *Music Hath Charms* 1935; *Dark Eyes of London* 1939

Sundvall, Kjell *The Hunters* 1996; *Jagarna 2: False Trail* 2011

Surjik, Stephen *Wayne's World 2* 1993; *I Want Candy* 2006

Sutherland, A Edward aka **Sutherland, Edward** (1895-1974) *It's the Old Army Game* 1926; *The Saturday Night Kid* 1929; *Paramount on Parade* 1930; *Palmy Days* 1931; *International House* 1933; *Murders in the Zoo* 1933; *Mississippi* 1935; *Poppy* 1936; *Every Day's a Holiday* 1937; *The Flying Deuces* 1939; *The Boys from Syracuse* 1940; *The Invisible Woman* 1940; *The Navy Comes Through* 1942; *Dixie* 1943; *Follow the Boys* 1944; *Secret Command* 1944; *Abie's Irish Rose* 1946

Sutherland, Kiefer (1966-) *Last Light* 1993; *Truth or Consequences, NM* 1997

Suzuki, Seijun (1923-) *Gate of Flesh* 1964; *Tokyo Drifter* 1966; *Branded to Kill* 1967

Svankmajer, Jan (1934-) *Alice* 1988; *Faust* 1994; *Conspirators of Pleasure* 1996; *Little Otik* 2000; *Lunacy* 2005; *Surviving Life* 2010

Svatek, Peter *The Call of the Wild* 1996; *Hemoglobin* 1997; *Student Seduction* 2003; *Baby for Sale* 2004; *Widow on the Hill* 2005

Sverak, Jan (1965-) *Elementary School* 1991; *Kolya* 1996; *Dark Blue World* 2001

Swaim, Bob (1943-) *La Balance* 1982; *Half Moon Street* 1986; *Masquerade* 1988

Swanberg, Joe *V/H/S* 2012; *Drinking Buddies* 2013

Swift, David (1919-2001) *Pollyanna* 1960; *The Parent Trap* 1961; *Love Is a Ball* 1963; *Under the Yum Yum Tree* 1963; *Good Neighbor Sam* 1964; *How to Succeed in Business without Really Trying* 1967

Switzer, Michael (1948-) *What Love Sees* 1996; *Miracle on the 17th Green* 1999; *No Higher Love* 1999; *Annie's Point* 2005; *Ordinary Miracles* 2005

Sykes, Peter (1939-) *Demons of the Mind* 1971; *The House in Nightmare Park* 1973; *Steptoe and Son Ride Again* 1973; *To the Devil a Daughter* 1976

Szabó, István (1938-) *Apa* 1966; *Confidence* 1979; *Mephisto* 1981; *Colonel Redl* 1984; *Hanussen* 1988; *Meeting Venus* 1990; *Sweet Emma Dear Böbe* 1992; *Sunshine* 1999; *Taking Sides* 2001; *Ten Minutes Older: the Cello* 2002; *Being Julia* 2004

Szumowska, Malgorzata aka **Szumowska, Malgoska** (1973-) *Elles* 2011; *In the Name of* 2013

Szwarc, Jeannot (1937-) *Extreme Close-Up* 1973; *Bug* 1975; *Jaws 2* 1978; *Somewhere in Time* 1980;

Enigma 1982; *Supergirl* 1984; *Santa Claus* 1985

T

Tacchella, Jean-Charles (1925-) *Cousin, Cousine* 1975; *L'Homme de Ma Vie* 1992

Takacs, Tibor (1954-) *The Gate* 1987; *Gate II* 1992; *Sanctuary* 1997; *NYC: Tornado Terror* 2008

Takahata, Isao (1935-) *Little Norse Prince Valiant* 1968; *Grave of the Fireflies* 1988; *Pom Poko* 1994; *My Neighbours the Yamadas* 1999; *The Tale of the Princess Kaguya* 2013

Takita, Yojiro *When the Last Sword Is Drawn* 2002; *Departures* 2008

Talalay, Rachel *Freddy's Dead: the Final Nightmare* 1991; *Ghost in the Machine* 1993; *Tank Girl* 1995; *Hannah's Law* 2012

Talbert, David E *First Sunday* 2008; *Baggage Claim* 2013

Tamahori, Lee (1950-) *Once Were Warriors* 1994; *Mulholland Falls* 1996; *The Edge* 1997; *Along Came a Spider* 2001; *Die Another Day* 2002; *xXx: the Next Level* 2005; *Next* 2007; *The Devil's Double* 2011

Tancharoen, Kevin *Fame* 2009; *Glee: the 3D Concert Movie* 2011

Tanner, Alain (1929-) *Jonah Who Will Be 25 in the Year 2000* 1976; *Messidor* 1978; *Requiem* 1998

Tanovic, Danis (1969-) *No Man's Land* 2001; *11'09''01 - September 11* 2002; *L'Enfer* 2005; *An Episode in the Life of an Iron Picker* 2013

Taplitz, Daniel *Commandments* 1996; *Breakin' All the Rules* 2004

Tarantino, Quentin (1963-) *Reservoir Dogs* 1991; *Pulp Fiction* 1994; *Four Rooms* 1995; *Jackie Brown* 1997; *Kill Bill Vol 1* 2003; *Kill Bill Vol 2* 2004; *Death Proof* 2007; *Inglourious Basterds* 2009; *Django Unchained* 2012; *The Hateful Eight* 2015

Tarkovsky, Andrei (1932-1986) *Ivan's Childhood* 1962; *Andrei Rublev* 1966; *Solaris* 1972; *Mirror* 1974; *Stalker* 1979; *Nostalgia* 1983; *The Sacrifice* 1986

Tarr, Bela (1955-) *Damnation* 1988; *Werckmeister Harmonies* 2000; *The Man from London* 2007; *The Turin Horse* 2011

Tartakovsky, Genndy *Hotel Transylvania* 2012; *Hotel Transylvania 2* 2015

Tashlin, Frank (1913-1972) *Son of Paleface* 1952; *Marry Me Again* 1953; *Susan Slept Here* 1954; *Artists and Models* 1955; *The Girl Can't Help It* 1956; *Hollywood or Bust* 1956; *Will Success Spoil Rock Hunter?* 1957; *The Geisha Boy* 1958; *Rock-a-Bye Baby* 1958; *Say One for Me* 1959; *Cinderfella* 1960; *Bachelor Flat* 1961; *It'$ Only Money* 1962; *The Man from the Diner's Club* 1963; *Who's Minding the Store?* 1963; *The Disorderly Orderly* 1964; *The Alphabet Murders* 1966; *The Glass Bottom Boat* 1966; *Caprice* 1967; *The Private Navy of Sgt O'Farrell* 1968

Tass, Nadia (1955-) *Malcolm* 1986; *The Big Steal* 1990; *Pure Luck* 1991; *Mr Reliable* 1996; *Fatal Honeymoon* 2012

Tati, Jacques (1908-1982) *Jour de Fête* 1947; *School for Postmen* 1947; *Monsieur Hulot's Holiday* 1953; *Mon Oncle* 1958; *Playtime* 1967; *Traffic* 1970; *Parade* 1974

Taurog, Norman (1899-1981) *Huckleberry Finn* 1931; *Skippy* 1931; *If I Had a Million* 1932; *The Phantom President* 1932; *Mrs Wiggs of the Cabbage Patch* 1934; *We're Not Dressing* 1934; *The Big Broadcast of 1936* 1935; *Rhythm on the Range* 1936; *Strike Me Pink* 1936; *You Can't Have Everything* 1937; *The Adventures of Tom Sawyer* 1938; *Boys Town* 1938; *Mad about Music* 1938; *Broadway Melody of 1940* 1940; *Little Nellie Kelly* 1940; *Young Tom Edison* 1940; *Design for Scandal* 1941; *Men of Boys Town* 1941; *A Yank at Eton* 1942; *Girl Crazy* 1943; *Presenting Lily Mars* 1943; *Ziegfeld Follies* 1944; *The Hoodlum Saint* 1946; *The Beginning or the End* 1947; *Words and Music* 1948; *That Midnight Kiss* 1949; *Mrs O'Malley and Mr Malone* 1950; *Please Believe Me* 1950; *The Toast of New Orleans* 1950; *Rich, Young and Pretty* 1951; *The Stooge* 1951; *Jumping Jacks* 1952; *Room for One More* 1952; *The Caddy* 1953; *Living It Up* 1954; *You're Never Too Young* 1955; *The Birds*

---

and the Bees 1956; *Bundle of Joy* 1956; *Pardners* 1956; *The Fuzzy Pink Nightgown* 1957; *Don't Give Up the Ship* 1959; *GI Blues* 1960; *All Hands on Deck* 1961; *Blue Hawaii* 1961; *Girls! Girls! Girls!* 1962; *It Happened at the World's Fair* 1962; *Palm Springs Weekend* 1963; *Dr Goldfoot and the Bikini Machine* 1965; *Sergeant Deadhead* 1965; *Tickle Me* 1965; *Spinout* 1966; *Double Trouble* 1967; *Live a Little, Love a Little* 1968; *Speedway* 1968

Tavernier, Bertrand (1941-) *The Watchmaker of St Paul* 1973; *Death Watch* 1980; *Coup de Torchon* 1981; *Sunday in the Country* 1984; *'Round Midnight* 1986; *Life and Nothing But* 1989; *These Foolish Things* 1990; *L.627* 1992; *The Undeclared War* 1992; *D'Artagnan's Daughter* 1994; *The Bait* 1995; *Ça Commence Aujourd'hui* 1999; *Laissez-passer* 2001; *In the Electric Mist* 2009; *The Princess of Montpensier* 2010

Taviani, Paolo (1931-) *Padre Padrone* 1977; *The Night of San Lorenzo* 1981; *Kaos* 1984; *Good Morning, Babylon* 1987; *Night Sun* 1990; *Fiorile* 1993; *Caesar Must Die* 2012

Taviani, Vittorio (1929-) *Padre Padrone* 1977; *The Night of San Lorenzo* 1981; *Kaos* 1984; *Good Morning, Babylon* 1987; *Night Sun* 1990; *Fiorile* 1993; *Caesar Must Die* 2012

Taylor-Wood, Sam aka **Taylor-Johnson, Sam** (1967-) *Destricted* 2006; *Nowhere Boy* 2010; *Fifty Shades of Grey* 2015

Taylor, Alan (1965-) *Palookaville* 1995; *The Emperor's New Clothes* 2001; *Thor: the Dark World* 2013; *Terminator: Genisys* 2015

Taylor, Baz (1944-) *Near Mrs* 1990; *Shooting Elizabeth* 1992

Taylor, Brian *Crank* 2006; *Gamer* 2008; *Crank: High Voltage* 2009; *Ghost Rider: Spirit of Vengeance* 2012

Taylor, Don (1920-1998) *Ride the Wild Surf* 1964; *Jack of Diamonds* 1967; *Escape from the Planet of the Apes* 1971; *Tom Sawyer* 1973; *Echoes of a Summer* 1976; *The Great Scout & Cathouse Thursday* 1976; *The Island of Dr Moreau* 1977; *Damien - Omen II* 1978; *The Final Countdown* 1980

Taylor, Jud (1932-2008) *Act of Love* 1980; *Out of the Darkness* 1985; *Foxfire* 1987; *The Old Man and the Sea* 1990

Taylor, Ray (1888-1952) *The Daltons Ride Again* 1945; *The Vigilantes Return* 1947

Taylor (3), Robert (1944-2014) *The Nine Lives of Fritz the Cat* 1974; *Heidi's Song* 1982

Taylor, Sam (1895-1958) *Safety Last* 1923; *Girl Shy* 1924; *Hot Water* 1924; *The Freshman* 1925; *For Heaven's Sake* 1926; *My Best Girl* 1927; *Coquette* 1929; *The Taming of the Shrew* 1929; *The Cat's Paw* 1934; *Nothing but Trouble* 1944; *The Monte Carlo Story* 1957

Taylor, Tate *The Help* 2011; *Get on Up* 2014; *The Girl on the Train* 2016

Taymor, Julie (1953-) *Titus* 1999; *Frida* 2002; *Across the Universe* 2007; *The Tempest* 2010

Teague, Lewis (1938-) *The Lady in Red* 1979; *Alligator* 1980; *Death Vengeance* 1982; *Cujo* 1983; *Cat's Eye* 1984; *The Jewel of the Nile* 1985; *Collision Course* 1987; *Shannon's Deal* 1989; *Navy SEALs* 1990

Téchiné, André (1943-) *The Brontë Sisters* 1979; *Rendez-vous* 1985; *The Scene of the Crime* 1986; *J'Embrasse Pas* 1991; *Ma Saison Préferée* 1993; *Les Roseaux Sauvages* 1994; *Les Voleurs* 1996; *Alice et Martin* 1998; *Far Away* 2001; *Strayed* 2003; *Changing Times* 2004; *The Witnesses* 2006; *The Girl on the Train* 2009

Temple, Julien (1953-) *The Great Rock 'n' Roll Swindle* 1979; *The Secret Policeman's Other Ball* 1982; *Running Out of Luck* 1985; *Absolute Beginners* 1986; *Aria* 1987; *Earth Girls Are Easy* 1988; *Bullet* 1995; *Vigo: Passion for Life* 1997; *The Filth and the Fury* 2000; *Pandaemonium* 2000; *The Future Is Unwritten* 2006; *Glastonbury* 2006; *Oil City Confidential* 2009; *London - Babylon* 2012; *The Ecstasy of Wilko Johnson* 2015

Templeton, George (1906-1980) *The Sundowners* 1950; *A Gift for Heidi* 1958

Tennant, Andy (1955-) *The Amy Fisher Story* 1993; *It Takes Two* 1995; *Fools Rush In* 1997; *Ever After: a Cinderella Story* 1998; *Anna and the King* 1999; *Sweet Home Alabama* 2002; *Hitch* 2005; *Fool's Gold* 2008; *The Bounty Hunter* 2010

Tenney, Kevin S (1955-) *Witchboard* 1987; *Night of the Demons* 1988; *Peacemaker* 1990

Tennyson, Pen aka **Tennyson, Penrose** (1918-1941) *There Ain't No Justice* 1939; *Convoy* 1940; *The Proud Valley* 1940

Teplitzky, Jonathan *Gettin' Square* 2003; *The Railway Man* 2013

Terlesky, John (1961-) *Judgment Day* 1999; *Supreme Sanction* 1999; *Guardian* 2000; *By Appointment Only* 2007

Teshigahara, Hiroshi (1927-2001) *Pitfall* 1962; *Woman of the Dunes* 1963; *The Face of Another* 1966

Tessari, Duccio (1926-1994) *Three Tough Guys* 1974; *Zorro* 1975

Tetzlaff, Ted (1903-1995) *Riff-Raff* 1947; *A Dangerous Profession* 1949; *The Window* 1949; *The White Tower* 1950; *Treasure of Lost Canyon* 1952; *Terror on a Train* 1953; *Son of Sinbad* 1955; *The Young Land* 1959

Tewkesbury, Joan (1936-) *Old Boyfriends* 1979; *Cold Sassy Tree* 1989

Tewksbury, Peter (1924-2003) *Sunday in New York* 1963; *Emil and the Detectives* 1964; *Stay Away, Joe* 1968; *The Trouble with Girls* 1969

Thatcher, Kirk R *It's a Very Merry Muppet Christmas Movie* 2002; *The Muppets' Wizard of Oz* 2005

Thiele, William (1890-1975) *London by Night* 1937; *The Ghost Comes Home* 1940; *Tarzan Triumphs* 1943; *Tarzan's Desert Mystery* 1943

Thomas, Betty (1948-) *Only You* 1992; *The Brady Bunch Movie* 1995; *The Late Shift* 1996; *Private Parts* 1997; *Doctor Dolittle* 1998; *28 Days* 2000; *I Spy* 2002; *John Tucker Must Die* 2006; *Alvin and the Chipmunks: the Squeakquel* 2009

Thomas, Daniela (1959-) *Midnight* 1998; *Paris, Je T'Aime* 2006; *Linha de Passe* 2008

Thomas, Gerald (1920-1993) *Circus Friends* 1956; *Time Lock* 1957; *The Vicious Circle* 1957; *Carry On Sergeant* 1958; *The Duke Wore Jeans* 1958; *Carry On Nurse* 1959; *Carry On Teacher* 1959; *Carry On Constable* 1960; *Carry On Regardless* 1960; *No Kidding* 1960; *Please Turn Over* 1960; *Watch Your Stern* 1960; *Raising the Wind* 1961; *Carry On Cruising* 1962; *The Iron Maiden* 1962; *Twice round the Daffodils* 1962; *Carry On Cabby* 1963; *Carry On Jack* 1963; *Nurse on Wheels* 1963; *Carry On Cleo* 1964; *Carry On Spying* 1964; *The Big Job* 1965; *Carry On Cowboy* 1965; *Carry On - Don't Lose Your Head* 1966; *Carry On Screaming* 1966; *Carry On Follow That Camel* 1967; *Carry On Doctor* 1968; *Carry On Up the Khyber* 1968; *Carry On Again Doctor* 1969; *Carry On Camping* 1969; *Carry On Loving* 1970; *Carry On Up the Jungle* 1970; *Carry On at Your Convenience* 1971; *Carry On Henry* 1971; *Bless This House* 1972; *Carry On Abroad* 1972; *Carry On Matron* 1972; *Carry On Girls* 1973; *Carry On Dick* 1974; *Carry On Behind* 1975; *Carry On England* 1976; *That's Carry On* 1977; *Carry On Emmannuelle* 1978; *The Second Victory* 1986; *Carry On Columbus* 1992

Thomas, Ralph (1915-2001) *Once upon a Dream* 1948; *Traveller's Joy* 1949; *The Clouded Yellow* 1950; *Appointment with Venus* 1951; *Venetian Bird* 1952; *A Day to Remember* 1953; *Doctor in the House* 1954; *Mad about Men* 1954; *Above Us the Waves* 1955; *Doctor at Sea* 1955; *Checkpoint* 1956; *The Iron Petticoat* 1956; *Campbell's Kingdom* 1957; *Doctor at Large* 1957; *A Tale of Two Cities* 1957; *The Wind Cannot Read* 1958; *The Thirty-Nine Steps* 1959; *Upstairs and Downstairs* 1959; *Conspiracy of Hearts* 1960; *Doctor in Love* 1960; *No Love for Johnnie* 1960; *No My Darling Daughter* 1961; *A Pair of Briefs* 1962; *The Wild and the Willing* 1962; *Doctor in Distress* 1963; *Hot Enough for June* 1964; *The High Bright Sun* 1965; *Deadlier than the Male* 1966; *Doctor in Clover* 1966; *Nobody Runs Forever* 1968;

Some Girls Do 1969; *Doctor in Trouble* 1970; *Percy* 1971; *Quest for Love* 1971; *Percy's Progress* 1974; *A Nightingale Sang in Berkeley Square* 1979

Thomas, Ralph L aka **Thomas, R L** *Ticket to Heaven* 1981; *Apprentice to Murder* 1988

Thompson, Barnaby *St Trinian's* 2007; *St Trinian's 2: the Legend of Fritton's Gold* 2009

Thompson, Caroline (1956-) *Black Beauty* 1994; *Buddy* 1997; *Snow White* 2001

Thompson, Danièle (1942-) *La Bûche* 1999; *Orchestra Seats* 2005

Thompson, Ernest (1950-) *1969* 1988; *The West Side Waltz* 1995

Thompson (2), Neil *Clubbed* 2008; *Twenty8k* 2012

Thornton, Billy Bob (1955-) *Sling Blade* 1995; *Daddy and Them* 1999; *All the Pretty Horses* 2000; *Jayne Mansfield's Car* 2012

Thornton, Warwick *Samson & Delilah* 2009; *The Turning* 2013

Thorpe, Jerry (1930-) *The Venetian Affair* 1966; *Day of the Evil Gun* 1968

Thorpe, Richard (1896-1991) *Tarzan Escapes* 1936; *Double Wedding* 1937; *Man-Proof* 1937; *Night Must Fall* 1937; *The Crowd Roars* 1938; *Three Loves Has Nancy* 1938; *The Toy Wife* 1938; *The Adventures of Huckleberry Finn* 1939; *Tarzan Finds a Son!* 1939; *The Earl of Chicago* 1940; *Tarzan's Secret Treasure* 1941; *Apache Trail* 1942; *Joe Smith, American* 1942; *Tarzan's New York Adventure* 1942; *White Cargo* 1942; *Above Suspicion* 1943; *Cry Havoc* 1943; *The Thin Man Goes Home* 1944; *Two Girls and a Sailor* 1944; *Thrill of a Romance* 1945; *Fiesta* 1947; *This Time for Keeps* 1947; *A Date with Judy* 1948; *On an Island with You* 1948; *Challenge to Lassie* 1949; *Malaya* 1949; *The Black Hand* 1950; *Three Little Words* 1950; *The Great Caruso* 1951; *It's a Big Country* 1951; *Vengeance Valley* 1951; *Carbine Williams* 1952; *Ivanhoe* 1952; *The Prisoner of Zenda* 1952; *All the Brothers Were Valiant* 1953; *The Girl Who Had Everything* 1953; *Knights of the Round Table* 1953; *Athena* 1954; *The Student Prince* 1954; *The Prodigal* 1955; *Quentin Durward* 1955; *Jailhouse Rock* 1957; *Ten Thousand Bedrooms* 1957; *The House of the Seven Hawks* 1959; *Killers of Kilimanjaro* 1960; *The Horizontal Lieutenant* 1962; *Follow the Boys* 1963; *Fun in Acapulco* 1963; *The Truth about Spring* 1964; *That Funny Feeling* 1965; *The Last Challenge* 1967

Thraves, Jamie (1969-) *The Low Down* 2000; *The Cry of the Owl* 2009; *Treacle Jr* 2010

Thurber, Rawson Marshall *Dodgeball: a True Underdog Story* 2004; *We're the Millers* 2013; *Central Intelligence* 2016

Thurmeier, Mike aka **Thurmeier, Michael** *Ice Age 3: Dawn of the Dinosaurs* 2009; *Ice Age 4: Continental Drift* 2012; *Ice Age: Collision Course* 2016

Tian Zhuangzhuang (1952-) *Horse Thief* 1986; *The Blue Kite* 1992; *Springtime in a Small Town* 2002

Tiddes, Michael *A Haunted House* 2013; *A Haunted House 2* 2014; *Fifty Shades of Black* 2016

Till, Eric (1929-) *Hot Millions* 1968; *The Walking Stick* 1970; *It Shouldn't Happen to a Vet* 1979; *Improper Channels* 1981; *Oh, What a Night* 1992

Tillman Jr, George *Soul Food* 1997; *Men of Honor* 2000; *Notorious* 2009; *Faster* 2010; *The Longest Ride* 2015

Timoner, Ondi *Dig!* 2004; *We Live in Public* 2009; *Brand: a Second Coming* 2015; *Mapplethorpe* 2016

Tinling, James (1889-1967) *Mr Moto's Gamble* 1938; *Riders of the Purple Sage* 1941

Tirard, Laurent *Molière* 2006; *Up for Love* 2016

Title, Stacy *The Last Supper* 1995; *Let the Devil Wear Black* 1999

Tjahjanto, Timo *The ABCs of Death* 2012; *V/H/S/2* 2013; *Killers* 2014

Tlatli, Moufida *The Silences of the Palace* 1994; *La Saison des Hommes* 2000

To, Johnnie aka **To, Johnny** (1955-) *Fulltime Killer* 2002; *Election* 2005; *Exiled* 2006; *Mad Detective* 2007; *Sparrow* 2008

Toback, James (1943-) *Fingers* 1978; *Love and Money* 1982;

Exposed 1983; *The Pick-Up Artist* 1987; *Two Girls and a Guy* 1997; *Black and White* 1999; *Tyson* 2008; *Seduced and Abandoned* 2013

Tokar, Norman (1920-1979) *Big Red* 1962; *Those Calloways* 1964; *A Tiger Walks* 1964; *Follow Me, Boys!* 1966; *The Ugly Dachshund* 1966; *The Happiest Millionaire* 1967; *The Horse in the Gray Flannel Suit* 1968; *The Boatniks* 1970; *Snowball Express* 1972; *The Apple Dumpling Gang* 1974; *Where the Red Fern Grows* 1974; *No Deposit No Return* 1976; *Candleshoe* 1977; *The Cat from Outer Space* 1978

Toledano, Eric *Untouchable* 2011; *Samba* 2014

Tolkin, Michael (1950-) *The Rapture* 1991; *The New Age* 1994

Tollin, Mike (1956-) *Summer Catch* 2001; *Radio* 2003

Tonderai, Mark *Hush* 2008; *House at the End of the Street* 2012

Tong, Stanley (1960-) *Police Story III: Supercop* 1992; *Jackie Chan's First Strike* 1996; *Rumble in the Bronx* 1996; *Mr Magoo* 1997

Tornatore, Giuseppe (1956-) *Cinema Paradiso* 1988; *Everybody's Fine* 1990; *A Pure Formality* 1994; *The Starmaker* 1994; *The Legend of 1900* 1999; *Malena* 2000; *Baaria* 2009; *Deception* 2013

Tourneur, Jacques (1904-1977) *Nick Carter, Master Detective* 1939; *Phantom Raiders* 1940; *Cat People* 1942; *I Walked with a Zombie* 1943; *The Leopard Man* 1943; *Days of Glory* 1944; *Experiment Perilous* 1944; *Canyon Passage* 1946; *Build My Gallows High* 1947; *Berlin Express* 1948; *Easy Living* 1949; *Circle of Danger* 1950; *The Flame and the Arrow* 1950; *Stars in My Crown* 1950; *Anne of the Indies* 1951; *Way of a Gaucho* 1952; *Appointment in Honduras* 1953; *Stranger on Horseback* 1955; *Wichita* 1955; *Great Day in the Morning* 1956; *Nightfall* 1956; *Night of the Demon* 1957; *The Fearmakers* 1958; *The Giant of Marathon* 1960; *The Comedy of Terrors* 1964; *City under the Sea* 1965

Tourneur, Maurice (1876-1961) *The Pride of the Clan* 1917; *The Last of the Mohicans* 1920; *The Ship of Lost Men* 1929; *Königsmark* 1935; *Volpone* 1941

Towne, Robert (1936-) *Personal Best* 1982; *Tequila Sunrise* 1988; *Without Limits* 1998; *Ask the Dust* 2006

Townsend, Robert (1957-) *Eddie Murphy Raw* 1987; *Hollywood Shuffle* 1987; *The Five Heartbeats* 1991; *The Meteor Man* 1993; *BAPS* 1997

Toye, Wendy (1917-2010) *Three Cases of Murder* 1953; *The Teckman Mystery* 1954; *All for Mary* 1955; *Raising a Riot* 1955; *True as a Turtle* 1956; *We Joined the Navy* 1962

Toynton, Ian *The Maid* 1991; *Bermuda Triangle* 1996

Traill, Phil *All about Steve* 2009; *Chalet Girl* 2010

Tramont, Jean-Claude (1934-1996) *All Night Long* 1981; *As Summers Die* 1986

Tran Anh Hung (1962-) *The Scent of Green Papaya* 1993; *Cyclo* 1995; *At the Height of Summer* 1999; *Norwegian Wood* 2010

Trank, Josh *Chronicle* 2012; *Fantastic Four* 2015

Trapero, Pablo (1971-) *El Bonaerense* 2002; *Born and Bred* 2006; *Lion's Den* 2008; *Carancho* 2010; *7 Days in Havana* 2012; *White Elephant* 2012; *The Clan* 2015

Traucki, Andrew *Black Water* 2007; *The Reef* 2010; *The ABCs of Death* 2012

Travers, Alfred (1906-) *Dual Alibi* 1946; *The Primitives* 1962

Travis, Pete *Vantage Point* 2008; *Dredd* 2012; *City of Tiny Lights* 2016

Traviss, Reg (1970-) *Psychosis* 2006; *Screwed* 2011; *Anti-Social* 2015

Travolta, Joey (1952-) *Too Hard to Die* 1998; *Partners* 2000

Tremaine, Jeff *Jackass: the Movie* 2002; *Jackass number two* 2006; *Jackass 3D* 2010; *jackass presents: Bad Grandpa* 2013

Trenchard-Smith, Brian (1946-) *The Man from Hong Kong* 1975; *Turkey Shoot* 1981; *BMX Bandits* 1983; *Jenny Kissed Me* 1984; *Night of the Demons 2* 1994; *Happy Face Murders* 1999; *Britannic* 2000

Trent, John (?-1983) *Sunday in the Country* 1975; *Find the Lady* 1976;

Middle Age Crazy 1980; *Best Revenge* 1983

Trevorrow, Colin (1976-) *Safety Not Guaranteed* 2012; *Jurassic World* 2015

Trier, Joachim *Reprise* 2006; *Oslo, August 31st* 2011; *Louder than Bombs* 2015

Trikonis, Gus (1937-) *Touched by Love* 1979; *Dance of the Dwarfs* 1983

Troche, Rose (1964-) *Go Fish* 1994; *Bedrooms and Hallways* 1998; *The Safety of Objects* 2001

Troell, Jan (1931-) *The Emigrants* 1971; *The New Land* 1972; *Zandy's Bride* 1974; *Hurricane* 1979; *Hamsun* 1996; *Maria Larsson's Everlasting Moments* 2008

Trousdale, Gary *Beauty and the Beast* 1991; *The Hunchback of Notre Dame* 1996; *Atlantis: the Lost Empire* 2001

Trueba, Fernando (1955-) *Belle Epoque* 1992; *Two Much* 1995; *The Girl of Your Dreams* 1998; *Chico & Rita* 2010; *The Artist and the Model* 2012

Truffaut, François (1932-1984) *The 400 Blows* 1959; *Shoot the Pianist* 1960; *Jules et Jim* 1962; *Love at Twenty* 1962; *La Peau Douce* 1964; *Fahrenheit 451* 1966; *The Bride Wore Black* 1967; *Stolen Kisses* 1968; *Mississippi Mermaid* 1969; *Bed and Board* 1970; *L'Enfant Sauvage* 1970; *Anne and Muriel* 1971; *Une Belle Fille comme Moi* 1973; *Day for Night* 1973; *The Story of Adèle H* 1975; *Small Change* 1976; *The Man Who Loved Women* 1977; *The Green Room* 1978; *Love on the Run* 1979; *The Last Metro* 1980; *The Woman Next Door* 1981; *Confidentially Yours* 1983

Truman, Michael (1910-1974) *Touch and Go* 1955; *Go to Blazes* 1961; *Girl in the Headlines* 1963

Trumbull, Douglas (1942-) *Silent Running* 1971; *Brainstorm* 1983

Tryon, Glenn (1894-1970) *The Law West of Tombstone* 1938; *Beauty for the Asking* 1939

Tsai Ming-liang (1957-) *Rebels of the Neon God* 1992; *Vive L'Amour* 1994; *The River* 1997; *The Hole* 1998; *I Don't Want to Sleep Alone* 2006

Tsui Hark (1951-) *The Butterfly Murders* 1979; *Zu Warriors* 1983; *Peking Opera Blues* 1986; *A Better Tomorrow III* 1989; *Once upon a Time in China* 1991; *Once upon a Time in China II* 1992; *Twin Dragons* 1992; *Double Team* 1997; *Knock Off* 1998; *Time and Tide* 2000; *Seven Swords* 2005; *Detective Dee and the Mystery of the Phantom Flame* 2010; *Flying Swords of Dragon Gate* 2011

Tsukamoto, Shinya (1960-) *Tetsuo: the Iron Man* 1989; *Tetsuo II: Body Hammer* 1991; *Tokyo Fist* 1995; *A Snake of June* 2002; *Vital* 2004

Tucci, Stanley (1960-) *Big Night* 1996; *The Impostors* 1998

Tuchner, Michael (1934-) *Villain* 1971; *Fear Is the Key* 1972; *Mister Quilp* 1975; *The Likely Lads* 1976; *Summer of My German Soldier* 1978; *The Hunchback of Notre Dame* 1982; *Adam* 1983; *Wilt* 1989; *Rainbow Warrior* 1992; *Back to the Secret Garden* 2000; *A Place Called Home* 2004

Tucker, Anand (1963-) *Hilary and Jackie* 1998; *Shopgirl* 2005; *And When Did You Last See Your Father?* 2007; *Leap Year* 2010

Tully, Montgomery (1904-1988) *Boys in Brown* 1949; *The Diamond* 1954; *The Glass Cage* 1955; *The Hypnotist* 1957; *No Road Back* 1957; *The Third Alibi* 1961; *Clash by Night* 1963; *Master Spy* 1964; *Battle beneath the Earth* 1968

Turner (1), Alex *Dead Birds* 2004; *Red Sands* 2009

Turner, Ann (1960-) *Celia* 1988; *Hammers over the Anvil* 1992; *Dallas Doll* 1994; *Irresistible* 2006

Turner, Benjamin *In the Hands of the Gods* 2007; *The Class of '92* 2013

Turner, Gabe *In the Hands of the Gods* 2007; *The Class of '92* 2013; *The Guvnors* 2014

Turteltaub, Jon (1964-) *3 Ninjas* 1992; *Cool Runnings* 1993; *While You Were Sleeping* 1995; *Phenomenon* 1996; *Instinct* 1999; *Disney's The Kid* 2000; *National Treasure* 2004; *National Treasure: Book of Secrets* 2007; *The Sorcerer's Apprentice* 2010; *Last Vegas* 2013

Turturro, John (1957-) *Mac* 1992; *Romance & Cigarettes* 2004; *Fading Gigolo* 2013

Tuttle, Frank (1892-1963) *The Canary Murder Case* 1929; *Her Wedding Night* 1930; *Paramount on Parade* 1930; *It Pays to Advertise* 1931; *The Big Broadcast* 1932; *This Is the Night* 1932; *Roman Scandals* 1933; *Ladies Should Listen* 1934; *The Glass Key* 1935; *Waikiki Wedding* 1937; *Doctor Rhythm* 1938; *Paris Honeymoon* 1939; *This Gun for Hire* 1942; *The Hour before the Dawn* 1944; *Hell on Frisco Bay* 1955; *A Cry in the Night* 1956

Twist, Derek (1905-1979) *The End of the River* 1947; *Green Grow the Rushes* 1951; *Police Dog* 1955

Twohy, David (1956-) *The Arrival* 1996; *Pitch Black* 1999; *Below* 2002; *The Chronicles of Riddick* 2004; *A Perfect Getaway* 2009; *Riddick* 2013

Tykwer, Tom (1965-) *Wintersleepers* 1997; *Run Lola Run* 1998; *The Princess & the Warrior* 2000; *Heaven* 2002; *Paris, Je T'Aime* 2006; *Perfume: the Story of a Murderer* 2006; *The International* 2009; *Cloud Atlas* 2012; *A Hologram for the King* 2016

Tyldum, Morten *Headhunters* 2011; *The Imitation Game* 2014; *Passengers* 2016

Uderzo, Albert (1927-) *Asterix the Gaul* 1967; *Asterix and Cleopatra* 1968; *The 12 Tasks of Asterix* 1975

Ullmann, Liv (1939-) *Sofie* 1992; *Kristin Lavransdatter* 1995; *Private Confessions* 1996; *Faithless* 2000; *Miss Julie* 2014

Ulmer, Edgar G (1900-1972) *People on Sunday* 1929; *The Black Cat* 1934; *Green Fields* 1937; *Bluebeard* 1944; *Detour* 1945; *The Strange Woman* 1946; *Carnegie Hall* 1947; *Ruthless* 1948; *The Man from Planet X* 1951; *The Naked Dawn* 1955; *Daughter of Dr Jekyll* 1957; *Hannibal* 1959; *Beyond the Time Barrier* 1960

Underwood, Ron (1959-) *Tremors* 1989; *City Slickers* 1991; *Heart and Souls* 1993; *Speechless* 1994; *Mighty Joe Young* 1998; *Pluto Nash* 2001; *In the Mix* 2005; *Holiday in Handcuffs* 2007

Unkrich, Lee (1967-) *Toy Story 2* 1999; *Finding Nemo* 2003; *Toy Story 3* 2010

Uno, Michael Toshiyuki *Without Warning: the James Brady Story* 1991; *The Road to Galveston* 1996; *A Face to Kill For* 1999

Urban, Stuart (1959-) *Preaching to the Perverted* 1997; *Revelation* 2001; *Tovarisch, I Am Not Dead* 2007; *may i kill u?* 2012

Ustinov, Peter (1921-2004) *School for Secrets* 1946; *Vice Versa* 1947; *Romanoff and Juliet* 1961; *Billy Budd* 1962; *Lady L* 1965

Uys, Jamie (1921-1996) *The Gods Must Be Crazy* 1980; *The Gods Must Be Crazy II* 1989

V

Vadim, Roger (1928-2000) *And God Created Woman* 1956; *Les Bijoutiers du Clair de Lune* 1957; *Les Liaisons Dangereuses* 1959; *Blood and Roses* 1960; *The Seven Deadly Sins* 1961; *La Ronde* 1964; *The Game Is Over* 1966; *Barbarella* 1967; *Histoires Extraordinaires* 1967; *Pretty Maids All in a Row* 1971; *Don Juan 73, or If Don Juan Were a Woman* 1973; *Night Games* 1979; *The Hot Touch* 1982; *And God Created Woman* 1988

Valdez, Luis (1940-) *Zoot Suit* 1981; *La Bamba* 1987

Valerii, Tonino *A Reason to Live, a Reason to Die* 1972; *My Name Is Nobody* 1973

Vallée, Jean-Marc (1963-) *CRAZY* 2005; *The Young Victoria* 2008; *Café de Flore* 2011; *Dallas Buyers Club* 2013; *Wild* 2014; *Demolition* 2015

Van Dormael, Jaco (1957-) *Toto Le Héros* 1991; *The Eighth Day* 1996; *The Brand New Testament* 2015

Van Dyke, W S aka **Van Dyke II, W S** aka **Van Dyke II, Major W S** (1889-1943) *White Shadows in the South Seas* 1928; *Guilty Hands* 1931; *Trader Horn* 1931; *Tarzan, the Ape Man* 1932; *Penthouse* 1933; *The Prizefighter and the Lady* 1933; *Forsaking All Others* 1934; *Manhattan Melodrama* 1934; *The Thin Man* 1934; *I Live My Life* 1935; *Naughty Marietta* 1935; *After the Thin Man* 1936; *The Devil Is a Sissy*

1936; *His Brother's Wife* 1936; *Love on the Run* 1936; *Rose Marie* 1936; *San Francisco* 1936; *Personal Property* 1937; *Rosalie* 1937; *They Gave Him a Gun* 1937; *Marie Antoinette* 1938; *Sweethearts* 1938; *Andy Hardy Gets Spring Fever* 1939; *Another Thin Man* 1939; *It's a Wonderful World* 1939; *Bitter Sweet* 1940; *I Love You Again* 1940; *I Take This Woman* 1940; *Dr Kildare's Victory* 1941; *The Feminine Touch* 1941; *Rage in Heaven* 1941; *Shadow of the Thin Man* 1941; *I Married an Angel* 1942

Van Horn, Buddy (1929-) *Any Which Way You Can* 1980; *The Dead Pool* 1988; *Pink Cadillac* 1989

Van Peebles, Mario (1958-) *New Jack City* 1991; *Posse* 1993; *Panther* 1995; *Gang in Blue* 1996; *Love Kills* 1998; *Baadasssss!* 2003; *Hard Luck* 2006

Van Peebles, Melvin (1932-) *Watermelon Man* 1970; *Sweet Sweetback's Baad Asssss Song* 1971; *Erotic Tales* 1994; *Gang in Blue* 1996

Van Sant, Gus (1952-) *Drugstore Cowboy* 1989; *My Own Private Idaho* 1991; *Even Cowgirls Get the Blues* 1993; *To Die For* 1995; *Good Will Hunting* 1997; *Psycho* 1998; *Finding Forrester* 2000; *Gerry* 2001; *Elephant* 2003; *Last Days* 2004; *Paris, Je T'Aime* 2006; *Paranoid Park* 2007; *Milk* 2008; *Restless* 2011; *Promised Land* 2012; *The Sea of Trees* 2015

Vane, Norman Thaddeus (1928-2015) *Frightmare* 1981; *Midnight* 1989

Varda, Agnès (1928-) *Cleo from 5 to 7* 1961; *Le Bonheur* 1965; *Les Créatures* 1966; *Far from Vietnam* 1967; *Vagabond* 1985; *Kung-Fu Master* 1987; *Jacquot de Nantes* 1991; *Les Cent et Une Nuits* 1995; *The Gleaners and I* 2000; *The Beaches of Agnès* 2008

Varma, Ram Gopal (1961-) *Company* 2001; *Bhoot* 2003; *Naach* 2004; *Sarkar* 2005; *Sarkar Raj* 2008

Varnel, Marcel (1894-1947) *Chandu the Magician* 1932; *Good Morning, Boys* 1937; *Oh, Mr Porter!* 1937; *Alf's Button Afloat* 1938; *Ask a Policeman* 1938; *Convict 99* 1938; *Hey! Hey! USA* 1938; *Old Bones of the River* 1938; *Band Waggon* 1939; *Where's That Fire?* 1939; *Gasbags* 1940; *Let George Do It* 1940; *The Ghost of St Michael's* 1941; *I Thank You* 1941; *It's Turned Out Nice Again* 1941; *South American George* 1941; *King Arthur Was a Gentleman* 1942; *Much Too Shy* 1942; *Bell-Bottom George* 1943; *I Didn't Do It* 1945; *George in Civvy Street* 1946

Vaughan (1), Tom (1969-) *Starter for 10* 2006; *What Happens in Vegas* 2008; *Extraordinary Measures* 2010; *So Undercover* 2012; *Lessons in Love* 2014

Vaughn, Matthew (1971-) *Layer Cake* 2004; *Stardust* 2007; *Kick-Ass* 2009; *X-Men: First Class* 2011; *Kingsman: The Secret Service* 2015; *Kingsman: The Golden Circle* 2017

Veber, Francis (1937-) *Les Compères* 1983; *Three Fugitives* 1989; *Out on a Limb* 1992; *Le Dîner de Cons* 1998; *The Closet* 2001; *Shut Up!* 2003

Venville, Malcolm *44 Inch Chest* 2009; *Henry's Crime* 2010

Verbinski, Gore (1965-) *Mousehunt* 1997; *The Mexican* 2001; *The Ring* 2002; *Pirates of the Caribbean: the Curse of the Black Pearl* 2003; *The Weather Man* 2005; *Pirates of the Caribbean: Dead Man's Chest* 2006; *Pirates of the Caribbean: at World's End* 2007; *Rango* 2011; *The Lone Ranger* 2013

Verhoeven, Michael (1938-) *The Nasty Girl* 1990; *My Mother's Courage* 1995

Verhoeven, Paul (1938-) *Business Is Business* 1971; *Turkish Delight* 1973; *Keetje Tippel* 1975; *Soldier of Orange* 1977; *Spetters* 1980; *The Fourth Man* 1983; *Flesh + Blood* 1985; *RoboCop* 1987; *Total Recall* 1990; *Basic Instinct* 1992; *Showgirls* 1995; *Starship Troopers* 1997; *Hollow Man* 2000; *Black Book* 2006

Verneuil, Henri (1920-2002) *The Sheep Has Five Legs* 1954; *A Monkey in Winter* 1962; *Any Number Can Win* 1963; *The 25th Hour* 1967; *The Sicilian Clan* 1969; *The Burglars* 1971; *The Serpent* 1972

Vernon, Conrad *Shrek 2* 2004; *Monsters vs Aliens* 2009;

Madagascar 3: Europe's Most Wanted 2012; *Sausage Party* 2016

Vernoux, Marion (1966-) *Love etc* 1997; *Bright Days Ahead* 2013

Verona, Stephen (1940-) *The Lords of Flatbush* 1974; *Pipe Dreams* 1976; *Boardwalk* 1979

VeSota, Bruno (1922-1976) *The Female Jungle* 1955; *The Brain Eaters* 1958

Vicas, Victor (1918-1985) *Count Five and Die* 1957; *The Wayward Bus* 1957

Vidor, Charles (1900-1959) *The Arizonian* 1935; *Blind Alley* 1939; *The Lady in Question* 1940; *My Son, My Son!* 1940; *Ladies in Retirement* 1941; *They Dare Not Love* 1941; *The Tuttles of Tahiti* 1942; *The Desperadoes* 1943; *Cover Girl* 1944; *Together Again* 1944; *Over 21* 1945; *A Song to Remember* 1945; *Gilda* 1946; *The Loves of Carmen* 1948; *It's a Big Country* 1951; *Hans Christian Andersen* 1952; *Thunder in the East* 1953; *Rhapsody* 1954; *Love Me or Leave Me* 1955; *The Swan* 1956; *A Farewell to Arms* 1957; *The Joker Is Wild* 1957; *Song without End* 1960

Vidor, King (1894-1982) *The Big Parade* 1925; *La Bohème* 1926; *The Crowd* 1928; *The Patsy* 1928; *Show People* 1928; *Hallelujah* 1929; *Billy the Kid* 1930; *The Champ* 1931; *Street Scene* 1931; *Bird of Paradise* 1932; *Cynara* 1932; *The Mask of Fu Manchu* 1932; *The Stranger's Return* 1933; *Our Daily Bread* 1934; *So Red the Rose* 1935; *The Wedding Night* 1935; *The Texas Rangers* 1936; *Stella Dallas* 1937; *The Citadel* 1938; *Comrade X* 1940; *Northwest Passage* 1940; *HM Pulham Esq* 1941; *An American Romance* 1944; *Duel in the Sun* 1946; *On Our Merry Way* 1948; *Beyond the Forest* 1949; *The Fountainhead* 1949; *Lightning Strikes Twice* 1951; *Ruby Gentry* 1952; *Man without a Star* 1955; *War and Peace* 1956; *Solomon and Sheba* 1959

Viertel, Berthold (1885-1953) *The Man from Yesterday* 1932; *The Wiser Sex* 1932; *The Passing of the Third Floor Back* 1935; *Rhodes of Africa* 1936

Vigalondo, Nacho *Timecrimes* 2007; *The ABCs of Death* 2012

Vigo, Jean (1905-1934) *A Propos de Nice* 1930; *Zéro de Conduite* 1933; *L'Atalante* 1934

Villella, Chad aka **Radio Silence** *V/H/S* 2012; *Southbound* 2015

Villeneuve, Denis (1967-) *Maelström* 2000; *Incendies* 2010; *Enemy* 2013; *Prisoners* 2013; *Sicario* 2015; *Blade Runner 2* 2017

Vincent, Chuck (1940-1991) *Hollywood Hot Tubs* 1984; *Warrior Queen* 1986

Vinterberg, Thomas (1969-) *Festen* 1998; *It's All about Love* 2002; *Dear Wendy* 2004; *The Hunt* 2012; *Far from the Madding Crowd* 2015; *The Commune* 2016

Virgien, Norton *The Rugrats Movie* 1998; *Rugrats Go Wild* 2003

Visconti, Luchino (1906-1976) *Ossessione* 1942; *La Terra Trema* 1947; *Bellissima* 1951; *Senso* 1954; *White Nights* 1957; *Rocco and His Brothers* 1960; *The Leopard* 1962; *Of a Thousand Delights* 1965; *The Witches* 1966; *The Stranger* 1967; *The Damned* 1969; *Death in Venice* 1971; *Ludwig* 1973; *Conversation Piece* 1974; *L'Innocente* 1976

Viveiros, Craig *Ghosted* 2011; *The Liability* 2012

Vogt-Roberts, Jordan *The Kings of Summer* 2013; *Kong: Skull Island* 2017

von Donnersmarck, Florian Henckel (1973-) *The Lives of Others* 2006; *The Tourist* 2010

von Garnier, Katja (1966-) *Iron Jawed Angels* 2004; *Blood and Chocolate* 2006

von Scherler Mayer, Daisy (1965-) *Madeline* 1998; *Woo* 1998; *The Guru* 2002

von Sternberg, Josef (1894-1969) *The Salvation Hunters* 1925; *The Exquisite Sinner* 1926; *Underworld* 1927; *The Docks of New York* 1928; *The Dragnet* 1928; *The Last Command* 1928; *The Case of Lena Smith* 1929; *Thunderbolt* 1929; *The Blue Angel* 1930; *Morocco* 1930; *An American Tragedy* 1931; *Dishonored* 1931; *Blonde Venus* 1932; *Shanghai Express* 1932; *The Scarlet Empress* 1934; *Crime and Punishment* 1935; *The Devil Is a Woman* 1935; *The King Steps Out* 1936; *Sergeant Madden* 1939; *The Shanghai Gesture* 1941;

Macao 1952; *The Saga of Anatahan* 1953

von Stroheim, Erich (1885-1957) *Blind Husbands* 1919; *Foolish Wives* 1920; *Greed* 1925; *The Merry Widow* 1925; *Queen Kelly* 1928; *The Wedding March* 1928; *Hello Sister!* 1933

von Trier, Lars (1956-) *The Element of Crime* 1984; *Medea* 1988; *Europa* 1991; *The Kingdom* 1994; *Breaking the Waves* 1996; *The Idiots* 1998; *Dancer in the Dark* 2000; *Dogville* 2003; *The Five Obstructions* 2003; *Manderlay* 2005; *The Boss of It All* 2006; *Antichrist* 2009; *Melancholia* 2011; *Nymphomaniac Vol I* 2013; *Nymphomaniac Vol II* 2014

von Trotta, Margarethe (1942-) *The Lost Honour of Katharina Blum* 1975; *Sisters, or the Balance of Happiness* 1979; *The German Sisters* 1981; *Rosa Luxemburg* 1986; *Three Sisters* 1988; *The Promise* 1994; *Hannah Arendt* 2012

Vorhaus, Bernard (1904-2000) *Crime on the Hill* 1933; *The Ghost Camera* 1933; *Dusty Ermine* 1936; *The Last Journey* 1936; *Cotton Queen* 1937; *Meet Mr Christian* 1939; *Three Faces West* 1940; *Lady from Louisiana* 1941

Vromen, Ariel *The Iceman* 2012; *Criminal* 2016

W

Wachowski, Lana aka **Wachowski, Larry** aka **The Wachowski Brothers** (1965-) *Bound* 1996; *The Matrix* 1999; *The Matrix Reloaded* 2002; *The Matrix Revolutions* 2003; *Speed Racer* 2008; *Cloud Atlas* 2012; *Jupiter Ascending* 2014

Wachowski, Lilly aka **Wachowski, Andy** aka **The Wachowski Brothers** (1967-) *Bound* 1996; *The Matrix* 1999; *The Matrix Reloaded* 2002; *The Matrix Revolutions* 2003; *Speed Racer* 2008; *Cloud Atlas* 2012; *Jupiter Ascending* 2014

Wacks, Jonathan *Powwow Highway* 1988; *Mystery Date* 1991; *Motherhood* 1993

Wadleigh, Michael (1941-) *Woodstock* 1970; *Wolfen* 1981

Wadlow, Jeff *Cry_Wolf* 2005; *Never Back Down* 2008; *Kick-Ass 2* 2013

Waggner, George (1894-1984) *Man Made Monster* 1941; *The Wolf Man* 1941; *The Fighting Kentuckian* 1949; *Operation Pacific* 1951

Wai Ka-Fai *Fulltime Killer* 2002; *Mad Detective* 2007

Wain, David *Role Models* 2008; *Wanderlust* 2011; *They Came Together* 2014

Wainwright, Rupert (1962-) *Blank Check* 1994; *Stigmata* 1999; *The Fog* 2005

Waititi, Taika *Eagle vs Shark* 2006; *What We Do in the Shadows* 2014; *Hunt for the Wilderpeople* 2016; *Thor: Ragnarok* 2017

Wajda, Andrzej (1926-) *A Generation* 1954; *Kanal* 1957; *Ashes and Diamonds* 1958; *Love at Twenty* 1962; *Landscape after Battle* 1970; *Man of Marble* 1977; *The Young Ladies of Wilko* 1979; *The Conductor* 1980; *Man of Iron* 1981; *Danton* 1982; *Korczak* 1990; *Miss Nobody* 1997; *Katyn* 2007; *Walesa: Man of Hope* 2013

Walas, Chris (1955-) *The Fly II* 1989; *The Vagrant* 1992

Walker, Giles (1946-) *The Masculine Mystique* 1984; *Ordinary Magic* 1993; *Never Too Late* 1996

Walker, Hal (1896-1972) *Duffy's Tavern* 1945; *Out of This World* 1945; *Road to Utopia* 1945; *The Stork Club* 1945; *At War with the Army* 1950; *My Friend Irma Goes West* 1950; *Sailor Beware* 1951; *That's My Boy* 1951; *Road to Bali* 1952

Walker, Lucy *Waste Land* 2009; *Countdown to Zero* 2010; *The Crash Reel* 2013

Walker, Pete (1935-) *Tiffany Jones* 1973; *Frightmare* 1974; *House of Whipcord* 1974; *House of Mortal Sin* 1975; *Schizo* 1976; *The Comeback* 1977; *House of the Long Shadows* 1983

Walker, Stuart (1887-1941) *The Eagle and the Hawk* 1933; *White Woman* 1933; *The Mystery of Edwin Drood* 1935

Wallace, Randall *The Man in the Iron Mask* 1997; *We Were Soldiers* 2002; *Secretariat* 2010; *Heaven Is for Real* 2014

Wallace, Richard (1894-1951) *The Shopworn Angel* 1928; *Man of the World* 1931; *The Masquerader* 1933; *The Little Minister* 1934; *Wedding Present* 1936; *The Young in Heart* 1938; *The Navy Steps Out* 1941; *A Night to Remember* 1942; *Bombardier* 1943; *The Fallen Sparrow* 1943; *Bride by Mistake* 1944; *It's in the Bag* 1945; *Kiss and Tell* 1945; *Because of Him* 1946; *Framed* 1947; *Sinbad the Sailor* 1947; *Tycoon* 1947; *Let's Live a Little* 1948; *Adventure in Baltimore* 1949; *A Kiss for Corliss* 1949

Wallace, Stephen (1943-) *The Boy Who Had Everything* 1984; *Blood Oath* 1990; *Turtle Beach* 1992

Wallace, Tommy Lee (1949-) *Halloween III: Season of the Witch* 1982; *Aloha Summer* 1988; *Fright Night Part 2* 1988; *Vampires: los Muertos* 2002

Waller, Anthony (1959-) *Mute Witness* 1995; *An American Werewolf in Paris* 1997; *The Guilty* 2000

Walls, Tom (1883-1949) *Rookery Nook* 1930; *A Cuckoo in the Nest* 1933; *Fighting Stock* 1935; *Foreign Affaires* 1935

Walsh, Aisling *Joyriders* 1988; *Song for a Raggy Boy* 2002; *The Daisy Chain* 2008

Walsh, Baillie *Flashbacks of a Fool* 2008; *Springsteen & I* 2013

Walsh, John (1945-) *Ed's Next Move* 1996; *Monarch* 1996; *Toryboy the Movie* 2010

Walsh, Raoul aka **Walsh, R A** (1887-1980) *Regeneration* 1915; *The Thief of Bagdad* 1924; *The Lucky Lady* 1926; *What Price Glory* 1926; *The Red Dance* 1928; *Sadie Thompson* 1928; *The Cock-Eyed World* 1929; *In Old Arizona* 1929; *The Big Trail* 1930; *Me and My Gal* 1932; *The Bowery* 1933; *Going Hollywood* 1933; *Big Brown Eyes* 1936; *Klondike Annie* 1936; *Spendthrift* 1936; *You're in the Army Now* 1936; *Artists and Models* 1937; *Jump for Glory* 1937; *College Swing* 1938; *The Roaring Twenties* 1939; *Dark Command* 1940; *They Drive by Night* 1940; *High Sierra* 1941; *Manpower* 1941; *The Strawberry Blonde* 1941; *They Died with Their Boots On* 1941; *Desperate Journey* 1942; *Gentleman Jim* 1942; *Background to Danger* 1943; *Northern Pursuit* 1943; *Uncertain Glory* 1944; *The Horn Blows at Midnight* 1945; *Objective, Burma!* 1945; *Salty O'Rourke* 1945; *The Man I Love* 1946; *Pursued* 1947; *Fighter Squadron* 1948; *Silver River* 1948; *Colorado Territory* 1949; *White Heat* 1949; *Along the Great Divide* 1951; *Captain Horatio Hornblower RN* 1951; *Distant Drums* 1951; *Blackbeard the Pirate* 1952; *Glory Alley* 1952; *The Lawless Breed* 1952; *Sea Devils* 1952; *The World in His Arms* 1952; *Gun Fury* 1953; *A Lion Is in the Streets* 1953; *Saskatchewan* 1954; *Battle Cry* 1955; *The Tall Men* 1955; *The Revolt of Mamie Stover* 1956; *Band of Angels* 1957; *The Naked and the Dead* 1958; *The Sheriff of Fractured Jaw* 1958; *Esther and the King* 1960; *A Distant Trumpet* 1964

Walters, Charles (1911-1982) *Ziegfeld Follies* 1944; *Good News* 1947; *Easter Parade* 1948; *The Barkleys of Broadway* 1949; *Summer Stock* 1950; *Texas Carnival* 1951; *The Belle of New York* 1952; *Dangerous When Wet* 1953; *Easy to Love* 1953; *Lili* 1953; *Torch Song* 1953; *The Glass Slipper* 1955; *The Tender Trap* 1955; *High Society* 1956; *Don't Go near the Water* 1957; *Ask Any Girl* 1959; *Please Don't Eat the Daisies* 1960; *Two Loves* 1961; *Jumbo* 1962; *The Unsinkable Molly Brown* 1964; *Walk, Don't Run* 1966

Walton, Fred *When a Stranger Calls* 1979; *April Fool's Day* 1986; *The Rosary Murders* 1987

Wan, James (1977-) *Saw* 2004; *Dead Silence* 2007; *Death Sentence* 2007; *Insidious* 2010; *The Conjuring* 2013; *Insidious: Chapter 2* 2013; *Fast & Furious 7* 2014; *The Conjuring 2* 2016; *Aquaman* 2018

Wanamaker, Sam (1919-1993) *The File of the Golden Goose* 1969; *The Executioner* 1970; *Catlow* 1971; *Sinbad and the Eye of the Tiger* 1977

Wang Xiaoshuai (1966-) *Beijing Bicycle* 2001; *Shanghai Dreams* 2005

Wang, Wayne (1949-) *Chan Is Missing* 1982; *Dim Sum: a Little Bit of Heart* 1985; *Slam Dance* 1987; *Eat a*

Bowl of Tea 1989; *Life Is Cheap... but Toilet Paper Is Expensive* 1990; *The Joy Luck Club* 1993; *Blue in the Face* 1995; *Smoke* 1995; *Chinese Box* 1997; *Anywhere but Here* 1999; *The Center of the World* 2001; *Maid in Manhattan* 2002; *Because of Winn-Dixie* 2004; *Last Holiday* 2006; *Snow Flower and the Secret Fan* 2011

Warchus, Matthew *Simpatico* 1999; *Pride* 2014

Ward, David S (1945-) *Cannery Row* 1982; *Major League* 1989; *King Ralph* 1991; *The Program* 1993; *Major League II* 1994; *Down Periscope* 1996

Ward, Vincent (1956-) *Vigil* 1984; *The Navigator - a Medieval Odyssey* 1988; *Map of the Human Heart* 1992; *What Dreams May Come* 1998; *River Queen* 2005

Ware, Clyde (1936-) *No Drums, No Bugles* 1971; *Bad Jim* 1989

Wargnier, Régis (1948-) *Indochine* 1991; *Une Femme Française* 1994; *East-West* 1999

Warhol, Andy (1928-1987) *My Hustler* 1965; *Vinyl* 1965; *The Chelsea Girls* 1966; *Bike Boy* 1967; *Lonesome Cowboys* 1968

Warren, Charles Marquis (1912-1990) *Hellgate* 1952; *Arrowhead* 1953; *Flight to Tangier* 1953; *Seven Angry Men* 1955; *Tension at Table Rock* 1956; *Trooper Hook* 1957; *Cattle Empire* 1958; *Charro!* 1969

Warren, Norman J (1942-) *Satan's Slave* 1976; *Prey* 1977; *Terror* 1979; *Inseminoid* 1981

Washington, Denzel (1954-) *Antwone Fisher* 2002; *The Great Debaters* 2007

Waters (2), John (1946-) *Mondo Trasho* 1970; *Multiple Maniacs* 1970; *Pink Flamingos* 1972; *Female Trouble* 1974; *Desperate Living* 1977; *Polyester* 1981; *Hairspray* 1988; *Cry-Baby* 1989; *Serial Mom* 1994; *Pecker* 1998; *Cecil B Demented* 2000; *A Dirty Shame* 2004

Waters (1), Mark aka **Waters, Mark S** (1964-) *The House of Yes* 1997; *Head over Heels* 2000; *Freaky Friday* 2003; *Mean Girls* 2004; *Just like Heaven* 2005; *The Spiderwick Chronicles* 2008; *Ghosts of Girlfriends Past* 2009; *Mr Popper's Penguins* 2011

Watkins, James *Eden Lake* 2008; *The Woman in Black* 2011; *Bastille Day* 2016

Watkins, Peter (1935-) *The War Game* 1965; *Privilege* 1967; *The Peace Game* 1969; *Punishment Park* 1971

Watt, Harry (1906-1987) *Night Mail* 1936; *Fiddlers Three* 1944; *The Overlanders* 1946; *Eureka Stockade* 1949; *Where No Vultures Fly* 1951; *West of Zanzibar* 1954

Watt, Sarah (1958-2011) *Look Both Ways* 2005; *My Year without Sex* 2009

Watts, Jon *Clown* 2014; *Cop Car* 2015; *Spider-Man: Homecoming* 2017

Waugh, Ric Roman *Felon* 2008; *Snitch* 2013

Waugh, Scott *Act of Valor* 2012; *Need for Speed* 2014

Waxman, Keoni aka **Black, Darby** (1968-) *Sweepers* 1999; *Amber's Story* 2006; *A Dangerous Man* 2009; *The Keeper* 2009; *A Good Man* 2014

Wayans, Keenen Ivory (1958-) *I'm Gonna Git You Sucka* 1988; *A Low Down Dirty Shame* 1994; *Scary Movie* 2000; *Scary Movie 2* 2001; *White Chicks* 2004; *Little Man* 2006

Wayne, John (1907-1979) *The Alamo* 1960; *The Green Berets* 1968

Weaver, David *Fairfield Road* 2010; *Fury* 2012

Webb, Jack (1920-1982) *Dragnet* 1954; *Pete Kelly's Blues* 1955; *-30-* 1959

Webb, Marc (1974-) *(500) Days of Summer* 2009; *The Amazing Spider-Man* 2012; *The Amazing Spider-Man 2* 2014

Webb, Robert D aka **Webb, Robert** (1903-1990) *Beneath the 12-Mile Reef* 1953; *The Glory Brigade* 1953; *White Feather* 1955; *Love Me Tender* 1956; *The Proud Ones* 1956; *Guns of the Timberland* 1960; *A Little of What You Fancy* 1968

Webber, Peter *Girl with a Pearl Earring* 2003; *Hannibal Rising* 2006; *Emperor* 2012

Weber, Bruce (1946-) *Let's Get Lost* 1988; *Chop Suey* 2000; *A Letter to True* 2004

Wedge, Chris Ice Age 2002; Robots 2005; Epic 2013; Monster Trucks 2015

Weeks, Stephen (1948-) I, Monster 1971; Gawain and the Green Knight 1973; Ghost Story 1974; Sword of the Valiant 1984

Weerasethakul, Apichatpong Uncle Boonmee Who Can Recall His Past Lives 2010; Cemetery of Splendour 2015

Weide, Robert B How to Lose Friends & Alienate People 2008; Woody Allen: a Documentary 2012; City Slickers II: the Legend of Curly's Gold 1994; Roseanna's Grave 1996; Sixty Six 2006; Made of Honor 2008

Weill, Claudia (1947-) Girlfriends 1978; It's My Turn 1980

Weir, Peter (1944-) The Cars That Ate Paris 1974; Picnic at Hanging Rock 1975; The Last Wave 1977; The Plumber 1979; Gallipoli 1981; The Year of Living Dangerously 1982; Witness 1985; The Mosquito Coast 1986; Dead Poets Society 1989; Green Card 1990; Fearless 1993; The Truman Show 1998; Master and Commander: the Far Side of the World 2003; The Way Back 2010

Weis, Don (1922-2000) It's a Big Country 1951; The Affairs of Dobie Gillis 1953; I Love Melvin 1953; Remains to Be Seen 1953; The Gene Krupa Story 1959; Critic's Choice 1963; Billie 1965; The Ghost in the Invisible Bikini 1966; The King's Pirate 1967

Weis, Gary Jimi Hendrix 1973; The Rutles - All You Need Is Cash 1978

Weisman, Sam (1947-) D2: the Mighty Ducks 1994; Bye Bye Love 1995; George of the Jungle 1997; The Out-of-Towners 1999; What's the Worst That Could Happen? 2001; Dickie Roberts: Former Child Star 2003

Weitz, Chris (1970-) Down to Earth 2001; About a Boy 2002; The Golden Compass 2007; New Moon 2009; A Better Life 2011

Weitz, Paul (1966-) American Pie 1999; Down to Earth 2001; About a Boy 2002; In Good Company 2004; American Dreamz 2006; Cirque du Freak: the Vampire's Assistant 2009; Little Fockers 2010; Being Flynn 2012; Admission 2013; Grandma 2015

Welles, Orson (1915-1985) Too Much Johnson 1938; Citizen Kane 1941; The Magnificent Ambersons 1942; The Stranger 1945; The Lady from Shanghai 1948; Macbeth 1948; Othello 1952; Confidential Report 1955; Touch of Evil 1958; The Trial 1962; Chimes at Midnight 1966; The Immortal Story 1968; F for Fake 1973

Wellesley, Gordon (1894-1980) Rhythm Serenade 1943; The Silver Fleet 1943

Wellman, William A aka **Wellman, William** (1896-1975) Wings 1927; Beggars of Life 1928; Night Nurse 1931; Other Men's Women 1931; The Public Enemy 1931; The Hatchet Man 1932; Love Is a Racket 1932; The Purchase Price 1932; Central Airport 1933; Heroes for Sale 1933; Looking for Trouble 1934; The Call of the Wild 1935; The Robin Hood of El Dorado 1936; Small Town Girl 1936; Nothing Sacred 1937; A Star Is Born 1937; Men with Wings 1938; Beau Geste 1939; The Light That Failed 1939; The Great Man's Lady 1942; Roxie Hart 1942; Lady of Burlesque 1943; The Ox-Bow Incident 1943; Buffalo Bill 1944; The Story of GI Joe 1945; Magic Town 1947; The Iron Curtain 1948; Yellow Sky 1948; Battleground 1949; The Happy Years 1950; The Next Voice You Hear 1950; Across the Wide Missouri 1951; It's a Big Country 1951; Westward the Women 1951; Island in the Sky 1953; The High and the Mighty 1954; Track of the Cat 1954; Blood Alley 1955; Darby's Rangers 1958

Wells, Audrey (1961-) Guinevere 1999; Under the Tuscan Sun 2003

Wells, John (1936-1998) The Company Men 2010; August: Osage County 2013; Burnt 2015

Wells, Simon (1961-) An American Tail: Fievel Goes West 1991; We're Back! A Dinosaur's Story 1993; Balto 1995; The Prince of Egypt 1998; The Time Machine 2002; Mars Needs Moms 2011

Wenders, Wim (1945-) The Goalkeeper's Fear of the Penalty Kick 1971; Alice in the Cities 1974; Kings of the Road 1976; The American Friend 1977; Lightning

over Water 1980; Hammett 1982; The State of Things 1982; Paris, Texas 1984; Wings of Desire 1987; Notebook on Cities and Clothes 1989; Until the End of the World 1991; Faraway, So Close 1993; Lisbon Story 1994; The End of Violence 1997; Buena Vista Social Club 1998; The Million Dollar Hotel 1999; Ten Minutes Older: the Trumpet 2002; The Blues, a Musical Journey: The Soul of a Man 2003; Don't Come Knocking 2005; Pina 2011; The Salt of the Earth 2014

Wendkos, Paul (1922-2009) The Burglar 1956; Battle of the Coral Sea 1959; Face of a Fugitive 1959; Gidget 1959; Because They're Young 1960; Angel Baby 1961; Johnny Tiger 1966; Attack on the Iron Coast 1968; Guns of the Magnificent Seven 1969; Cannon for Cordoba 1970; Hell Boats 1970; The Mephisto Waltz 1971; Special Delivery 1976

Wenk, Richard Vamp 1986; Just the Ticket 1998

Werker, Alfred (1896-1975) The House of Rothschild 1934; Kidnapped 1938; The Adventures of Sherlock Holmes 1939; The Reluctant Dragon 1941; A-Haunting We Will Go 1942; Repeat Performance 1947; He Walked by Night 1948; Sealed Cargo 1951; Walk East on Beacon 1952; Devil's Canyon 1953; At Gunpoint 1955

Werner, Peter (1947-) No Man's Land 1987; The Image 1990; Call Me Claus 2001; No Ordinary Baby 2001; Vinegar Hill 2005; Mom at Sixteen 2005; Lipstick 2006; The Circuit 2008

Wertmuller, Lina (1928-) The Seduction of Mimi 1972; Seven Beauties 1976; The End of the World (in Our Usual Bed in a Night Full of Rain) 1978; Blood Feud 1979; Camorra 1985; Francesca and Nunziata 2001

West, Jake (1972-) Razor Blade Smile 1998; Evil Aliens 2004; Doghouse 2009; The ABCs of Death 2012

West, Roland (1885-1952) The Monster 1925; Alibi 1929; The Bat Whispers 1930

West, Simon (1961-) Con Air 1997; The General's Daughter 1999; Lara Croft: Tomb Raider 2001; When a Stranger Calls 2006; The Mechanic 2011; The Expendables 2 2012; Stolen 2012; Wild Card 2014

West, Ti (1980-) The Roost 2005; The House of the Devil 2009; The Innkeepers 2011; The ABCs of Death 2012; V/H/S 2012; The Sacrament 2013; In a Valley of Violence 2016

Westmoreland, Wash aka **West, Wash** (1966-) The Fluffer 2001; Echo Park LA 2005; Still Alice 2014; Colette 2018

Weston, Eric Marvin and Tige 1983; The Iron Triangle 1988; To Protect and Serve 1992

Wexler, Tanya Finding North 1997; Hysteria 2011

Whale, James (1896-1957) Journey's End 1930; Frankenstein 1931; Waterloo Bridge 1931; The Impatient Maiden 1932; The Old Dark House 1932; The Invisible Man 1933; The Kiss before the Mirror 1933; By Candlelight 1934; One More River 1934; Bride of Frankenstein 1935; Remember Last Night? 1935; Show Boat 1936; The Great Garrick 1937; Port of Seven Seas 1938; Sinners in Paradise 1938; Wives under Suspicion 1938; Green Hell 1939; The Man in the Iron Mask 1939; They Dare Not Love 1941

Whatham, Claude (1927-2008) That'll Be the Day 1973; All Creatures Great and Small 1974; Swallows and Amazons 1974; Sweet William 1980; Agatha Christie's Murder Is Easy 1982; Buddy's Song 1990

Wheatley, Ben (1972-) Down Terrace 2009; Kill List 2011; The ABCs of Death 2012; Sightseers 2012; A Field in England 2013; High-Rise 2015

Whedon, Joss (1964-) Serenity 2005; Marvel Avengers Assemble 2012; Much Ado about Nothing 2012; Avengers: Age of Ultron 2015

Wheeler, Anne (1946-) Bye Bye Blues 1989; The War between Us 1995

Whelan, Tim (1893-1957) Aunt Sally 1933; The Camels Are Coming 1934; Murder Man 1935; The Perfect Gentleman 1935; The Mill on the Floss 1937; Smash and Grab 1937; The Divorce of Lady X 1938; St

Martin's Lane 1938; Q Planes 1939; The Thief of Bagdad 1940; Seven Days' Leave 1942; Higher and Higher 1943; Step Lively 1944; Badman's Territory 1946; Rage at Dawn 1955; Texas Lady 1955

Whitaker, Forest (1961-) Waiting to Exhale 1995; Hope Floats 1998; First Daughter 2004

White, George (1892-1968) George White's Scandals 1934; George White's 1935 Scandals 1935

White, Susanna Nanny McPhee & the Big Bang 2010; Our Kind of Traitor 2016

White, Sylvain Stomp the Yard 2006; The Losers 2010

Whitecross, Mat The Road to Guantanamo 2006; Sex & Drugs & Rock & Roll 2009; Ashes 2012; Spike Island 2012

Whitesell, John Calendar Girl 1993; See Spot Run 2001; Malibu's Most Wanted 2003; Big Momma's House 2 2006; Deck the Halls 2006; Big Mommas: Like Father, like Son 2011

Whorf, Richard (1906-1966) Blonde Fever 1944; The Sailor Takes a Wife 1945; Till the Clouds Roll By 1946; It Happened in Brooklyn 1947; Love from a Stranger 1947; Champagne for Caesar 1950

Wickes, David Sweeney! 1976; Silver Dream Racer 1980

Wicki, Bernhard (1919-2000) The Bridge 1959; The Longest Day 1962; The Visit 1964; Morituri 1965

Widerberg, Bo (1930-1997) The Pram 1963; Raven's End 1963; Elvira Madigan 1967; Adalen 31 1969; All Things Fair 1995

Wiederhorn, Ken Shock Waves 1975; Eyes of a Stranger 1980; Return of the Living Dead Part II 1988

Wiene, Robert (1881-1938) The Cabinet of Dr Caligari 1919; Hands of Orlac 1924

Wilcox, Fred M aka **Wilcox, Fred** aka **Wilcox, Fred McLeod** (1905-1964) Lassie Come Home 1943; Courage of Lassie 1946; Hills of Home 1948; Three Daring Daughters 1948; The Secret Garden 1949; Tennessee Champ 1954; Forbidden Planet 1956

Wilcox, Herbert (1892-1977) Bitter Sweet 1933; Nell Gwyn 1934; Limelight 1936; London Melody 1937; Victoria the Great 1937; Sixty Glorious Years 1938; Nurse Edith Cavell 1939; Irene 1940; No, No, Nanette 1940; Sunny 1941; They Flew Alone 1941; Forever and a Day 1943; Yellow Canary 1943; I Live in Grosvenor Square 1945; Piccadilly Incident 1946; The Courtneys of Curzon Street 1947; Elizabeth of Ladymead 1948; Spring in Park Lane 1948; Maytime in Mayfair 1949; Odette 1950; The Lady with the Lamp 1951; Derby Day 1952; Trent's Last Case 1952; Trouble in the Glen 1954; King's Rhapsody 1955; Lilacs in the Spring 1955; My Teenage Daughter 1956; The Man Who Wouldn't Talk 1957; The Heart of a Man 1959

Wilde, Cornel (1915-1989) The Devil's Hairpin 1957; Maracaibo 1958; Lancelot and Guinevere 1963; The Naked Prey 1966; Beach Red 1967; No Blade of Grass 1970; Shark's Treasure 1975

Wilde, Ted (1893-1929) The Kid Brother 1927; Speedy 1928

Wilder, Billy (1906-2002) The Major and the Minor 1942; Five Graves to Cairo 1943; Double Indemnity 1944; The Lost Weekend 1945; The Emperor Waltz 1948; A Foreign Affair 1948; Sunset Blvd 1950; Ace in the Hole 1951; Stalag 17 1953; Sabrina 1954; The Seven Year Itch 1955; Love in the Afternoon 1957; The Spirit of St Louis 1957; Witness for the Prosecution 1957; Some Like It Hot 1959; The Apartment 1960; One, Two, Three 1961; Irma la Douce 1963; Kiss Me, Stupid 1964; The Fortune Cookie 1966; The Private Life of Sherlock Holmes 1970; Avanti! 1972; The Front Page 1974; Fedora 1978; Buddy Buddy 1981

Wilder, Gene (1933-) The Adventure of Sherlock Holmes' Smarter Brother 1975; The Woman in Red 1984; Haunted Honeymoon 1986

Williams, Chris Bolt 2008; Big Hero 6 2014

Williams, Paul Andrew London to Brighton 2006; The Cottage 2008; Cherry Tree Lane 2010; Song for Marion 2012

Williams, Tod (1968-) The Adventures of Sebastian Cole 1998;

The Door in the Floor 2004; Paranormal Activity 2 2010; Cell 2016

Willing, Nick Photographing Fairies 1997; Alice in Wonderland 1999

Wills, J Elder Tiger Bay 1934; Song of Freedom 1936; Big Fella 1937

Wilson, Hugh (1943-) Police Academy 1984; Rustler's Rhapsody 1985; Burglar 1987; Guarding Tess 1994; The First Wives Club 1996; Blast from the Past 1998; Dudley Do-Right 1999

Wilson (2), Jim Stacy's Knights 1983; Head above Water 1996

Wilson (1), Richard (1915-1991) Man with the Gun 1955; Raw Wind in Eden 1958; Al Capone 1959; Pay or Die 1960; Invitation to a Gunfighter 1964; Skullduggery 1969; It's All True 1993

Wilson, Sandy (1947-) My American Cousin 1985; American Boyfriends 1989

Wimmer, Kurt Equilibrium 2002; Ultraviolet 2005

Wincer, Simon (1943-) Harlequin 1980; Phar Lap 1983; DARYL 1985; The Lighthorsemen 1987; Quigley Down Under 1990; Harley Davidson and the Marlboro Man 1991; Free Willy 1993; Lightning Jack 1994; Operation Dumbo Drop 1995; The Phantom 1996; Crocodile Dundee in Los Angeles 2001; Monte Walsh 2003; The Cup 2011

Windust, Bretaigne (1906-1960) June Bride 1948; Winter Meeting 1948; Perfect Strangers 1950; Pretty Baby 1950; The Enforcer 1951; Face to Face 1952

Winer, Harry (1947-) SpaceCamp 1986; House Arrest 1996

Wingard, Adam (1982-) You're Next 2011; The ABCs of Death 2012; V/H/S 2012; V/H/S/2 2013; The Guest 2014

Winick, Gary (1961-2011) Sweet Nothing 1995; The Tic Code 1998; Tadpole 2002; 13 Going on 30 2004; Charlotte's Web 2006; Bride Wars 2008; Letters to Juliet 2010

Winkler, Charles Disturbed 1990; Rocky Marciano 1999

Winkler, David Finding Graceland 1999; The Obsession 2006

Winkler, Henry (1945-) Memories of Me 1988; Cop and a Half 1993

Winkler, Irwin (1931-) Guilty by Suspicion 1990; Night and the City 1992; The Net 1995; At First Sight 1998; Life as a House 2001; De-Lovely 2004; Home of the Brave 2006

Winner, Michael (1935-2013) Play It Cool 1962; West 11 1963; The System 1964; You Must Be Joking! 1965; I'll Never Forget What's 'Is Name 1967; The Jokers 1967; Hannibal Brooks 1968; The Games 1970; Chato's Land 1971; Lawman 1971; The Mechanic 1972; The Nightcomers 1972; Scorpio 1973; The Stone Killer 1973; Death Wish 1974; Won Ton Ton, the Dog Who Saved Hollywood 1976; The Sentinel 1977; The Big Sleep 1978; Firepower 1979; Death Wish II 1981; The Wicked Lady 1983; Death Wish 3 1985; Appointment with Death 1988; A Chorus of Disapproval 1988; Bullseye! 1990; Dirty Weekend 1992; Parting Shots 1998

Winsor, Terry Party Party 1983; Essex Boys 1999

Winston, Ron (1932-1973) Ambush Bay 1966; Banning 1967; Don't Just Stand There 1968; The Gamblers 1969

Winston, Stan (1946-2008) Pumpkinhead 1988; Upworld 1992

Winterbottom, Michael (1961-) Butterfly Kiss 1994; Go Now 1995; Jude 1996; Welcome to Sarajevo 1997; I Want You 1998; With or without You 1999; Wonderland 1999; The Claim 2000; 24 Hour Party People 2001; In This World 2002; Code 46 2003; 9 Songs 2004; A Cock and Bull Story 2005; The Road to Guantanamo 2006; A Mighty Heart 2007; Genova 2008; The Killer inside Me 2010; Trishna 2011; Everyday 2012; The Look of Love 2013; The Face of an Angel 2014; The Emperor's New Clothes 2015

Winther, Peter The Librarian: Quest for the Spear 2004; Touch the Top of the World 2006

Wiper, Scott A Better Way to Die 2000; The Condemned 2007

Wirkola, Tommy Dead Snow 2009; Hansel & Gretel: Witch Hunters 2013

Wise, Herbert (1924-2015) The Lovers! 1972; Skokie 1981; Reunion at Fairborough 1985

Wise, Kirk Beauty and the Beast 1991; The Hunchback of Notre Dame 1996; Atlantis: the Lost Empire 2001

Wise, Robert (1914-2005) The Curse of the Cat People 1944; The Silent Bell 1944; The Body Snatcher 1945; Criminal Court 1946; Lady of Deceit 1947; Blood on the Moon 1948; The Set-Up 1949; Three Secrets 1950; Two Flags West 1950; The Day the Earth Stood Still 1951; The House on Telegraph Hill 1951; The Captive City 1952; The Desert Rats 1953; Destination Gobi 1953; So Big 1953; Executive Suite 1954; Helen of Troy 1955; Somebody Up There Likes Me 1956; Tribute to a Bad Man 1956; This Could Be the Night 1957; Until They Sail 1957; I Want to Live! 1958; Run Silent Run Deep 1958; Odds against Tomorrow 1959; West Side Story 1961; Two for the Seesaw 1962; The Haunting 1963; The Sound of Music 1965; The Sand Pebbles 1966; Star! 1968; The Andromeda Strain 1970; Two People 1973; The Hindenburg 1975; Audrey Rose 1977; Star Trek: the Motion Picture 1979; A Storm in Summer 2000

Wiseman, Frederick (1930-) Titicut Follies 1967; High School 1968; La Danse: the Paris Opera Ballet 2009; At Berkeley 2013

Wiseman, Len (1973-) Underworld 2003; Underworld: Evolution 2006; Die Hard 4.0 2007; Total Recall 2012

Wishman, Doris (1925-2002) Nude on the Moon 1961; Deadly Weapons 1974

Witney, William (1915-2002) Bells of San Angelo 1947; Under California Stars 1948; The Far Frontier 1949; Bells of Coronado 1950; North of the Great Divide 1950; Trail of Robin Hood 1950; Twilight in the Sierras 1950; The Outcast 1954; Santa Fe Passage 1955; The Cool and the Crazy 1958; The Secret of the Purple Reef 1960; Master of the World 1961; Apache Rifles 1964; Arizona Raiders 1965; 40 Guns to Apache Pass 1967

Wittman, Peter Play Dead 1981; Ellie 1984

Wolf, Fred The Mouse and His Child 1977; Strange Wilderness 2007; The House Bunny 2008

Wolfe, George C Lackawanna Blues 2005; Nights in Rodanthe 2008

Wolk, Andy Traces of Red 1992; A Stranger's Heart 2007

Wolodarsky, Wallace aka **Wolodarsky, M Wallace** Coldblooded 1995; Sorority Boys 2002

Wong Kar-Wai (1958-) As Tears Go By 1988; Days of Being Wild 1990; Ashes of Time 1994; Chung King Express 1994; Fallen Angels 1995; Happy Together 1997; In the Mood for Love 2000; Eros 2004; 2046 2004; My Blueberry Nights 2007

Wong, James Final Destination 2000; The One 2001; Final Destination 3 2006; Dragonball Evolution 2009

Wong, Kirk aka **Wong, Che-Kirk** (1949-) Crime Story 1993; The Big Hit 1998

Wonke, Anthony Fire in the Night 2013; Ronaldo 2015

Woo, John (1946-) A Better Tomorrow 1986; A Better Tomorrow II 1987; The Killer 1989; Bullet in the Head 1990; Once a Thief 1991; Hard-Boiled 1992; Hard Target 1993; Broken Arrow 1996; Face/Off 1997; Mission: Impossible 2 1999; Windtalkers 2001; Paycheck 2003; Red Cliff 2008

Wood, Duncan (1926-1997) The Bargee 1964; Some Will, Some Won't 1969

Wood Jr, Edward D (1924-1978) Glen or Glenda 1953; Jail Bait 1954; Bride of the Monster 1955; Night of the Ghouls 1959; Plan 9 from Outer Space 1959; Hellborn 1961

Wood, Sam (1883-1949) The Barbarian 1933; Hold Your Man 1933; Stamboul Quest 1934; Let 'Em Have It 1935; A Night at the Opera 1935; Whipsaw 1935; A Day at the Races 1937; Madame X 1937; Navy Blue and Gold 1937; Goodbye, Mr Chips 1939; Raffles 1939; Kitty Foyle 1940; Our Town 1940; The Devil and Miss Jones 1941; Kings Row 1942; The Pride of the Yankees 1942; For Whom the Bell Tolls 1943; Casanova Brown 1944; Guest Wife 1944; Saratoga Trunk 1945; Heartbeat 1946; Ivy 1947; Command Decision 1948; Ambush 1949; The Stratton Story 1949

Wooding, Jeremy Bollywood Queen 2002; Blood Moon 2014
Woodruff, Bille Honey 2003; Beauty Shop 2005; Honey 2 2011
Woods, Arthur B aka **Woods, Arthur** (1904-1944) Music Hath Charms 1935; Busman's Honeymoon 1940
Woods, Rowan (1959-) The Boys 1998; Little Fish 2005; Fragments 2008
Woolcock, Penny The Principles of Lust 2002; Mischief Night 2006; 1 Day 2009
Woolnough, Jeff Universal Soldier 2: Brothers in Arms 1998; Universal Soldier 3: Unfinished Business 1998
Workman, Chuck Superstar: the Life and Times of Andy Warhol 1991; Magician: the Astonishing Life and Work of Orson Welles 2014
Worsley, Wallace (1878-1944) The Ace of Hearts 1921; A Blind Bargain 1922; The Hunchback of Notre Dame 1923
Worth, David Kickboxer 1989; The Prophet's Game 1999; Time Lapse 2001
Wortmann, Sönke (1959-) The Most Desired Man 1994; The Miracle of Bern 2003
Wrede, Casper aka **Wrede, Caspar** (1929-1998) Private Potter 1963; One Day in the Life of Ivan Denisovich 1971; Ransom 1975
Wright, Basil (1907-1987) Song of Ceylon 1934; Night Mail 1936
Wright, Edgar (1974-) A Fistful of Fingers 1995; Shaun of the Dead 2004; Hot Fuzz 2007; Scott Pilgrim vs the World 2010; The World's End 2013
Wright, Geoffrey (1961-) Romper Stomper 1992; Cherry Falls 1999; Macbeth 2006
Wright, Joe (1972-) Pride & Prejudice 2005; Atonement 2007; The Soloist 2008; Hanna 2011; Anna Karenina 2012; Pan 2015
Wright, Jon Tormented 2009; Grabbers 2012; Robot Overlords 2014
Wright, Mack V (1894-1965) Winds of the Wasteland 1936; Hit the Saddle 1937
Wrye, Donald (1934-2015) The Entertainer 1975; Ice Castles 1978; Divorce Wars 1982; Stranger in the Family 1991
Wyatt, Rupert The Escapist 2007; Rise of the Planet of the Apes 2011; The Gambler 2014
Wyler, William aka **Wyler, Lt Col William** (1902-1981) Counsellor-at-Law 1933; Glamour 1934; The Gay Deception 1935; The Good Fairy 1935; Come and Get It 1936; Dodsworth 1936; These Three 1936; Dead End 1937; Jezebel 1938; Raffles 1939; Wuthering Heights 1939; The Letter 1940; The Westerner 1940; The Little Foxes 1941; Mrs Miniver 1942; Memphis Belle 1943; The Best Years of Our Lives 1946; The Heiress 1949; Detective Story 1951; Carrie 1952; Roman Holiday 1953; The Desperate Hours 1955; Friendly Persuasion 1956; The Big Country 1958; Ben-Hur 1959; The Children's Hour 1961; The Collector 1965; How to Steal a Million 1966; Funny Girl 1968; The Liberation of LB Jones 1970
Wynorski, Jim aka **Andrews, Jay** (1950-) Big Bad Mama II 1987; Not of This Earth 1988; The Return of Swamp Thing 1989; Transylvania Twist 1989; The Haunting of Morella 1990; Munchie 1992; 976-EVIL 2 1992; Munchie Strikes Back 1994; Desert Thunder 1998; Stealth Fighter 1999; Militia 2000; Sub Zero 2005; Piranhaconda 2011

Y

Yakin, Boaz (1966-) Fresh 1994; A Price above Rubies 1997; Remember the Titans 2000; Uptown Girls 2003; Safe 2011; Max 2015
Yang, Edward (1947-2007) Taipei Story 1984; A One and a Two 1999
Yarbrough, Jean (1900-1975) Devil Bat 1940; Abbott and Costello in Society 1944; Here Come the Co-Eds 1945; The Naughty Nineties 1945; Under Western Skies 1945; Jack and the Beanstalk 1952; Lost in Alaska 1952
Yates, David (1963-) The Tichborne Claimant 1998; Harry Potter and the Order of the Phoenix 2007; Harry Potter and the Half-Blood Prince 2009; Harry Potter and the Deathly

Hallows: Part 1 2010; Harry Potter and the Deathly Hallows: Part 2 2011; Fantastic Beasts and Where to Find Them 2016; The Legend of Tarzan 2016
Yates (1), Gary aka **Yates, Gary B** Niagara Motel 2005; Taken in Broad Daylight 2009
Yates, Peter (1929-2011) Summer Holiday 1962; One Way Pendulum 1965; Robbery 1967; Bullitt 1968; John and Mary 1969; Murphy's War 1971; The Hot Rock 1972; The Friends of Eddie Coyle 1973; For Pete's Sake 1974; Mother, Jugs & Speed 1976; The Deep 1977; Breaking Away 1979; Eyewitness 1981; The Dresser 1983; Krull 1983; Eleni 1985; The House on Carroll Street 1987; Suspect 1987; An Innocent Man 1989; Year of the Comet 1992; Roommates 1995; The Run of the Country 1995; Curtain Call 1997; Don Quixote 2000
Yauch, Adam aka **Hörnblowér, Nathanial** (1964-2012) Awesome; I F***in' Shot That! 2006; Gunnin' for That #1 Spot 2008
Yeaworth Jr, Irvin S (1926-2004) The Blob 1958; Dinosaurus! 1960
Yee, Derek (1957-) One Nite in Mongkok 2004; Protégé 2007; Shinjuku Incident 2009
Yip, Wilson aka **Yip Wai Shun** aka **Yip Wai-shun** Flash Point 2007; Ip Man 2008
Yonebayashi, Hiromasa Arrietty 2010; When Marnie Was There 2014
Yorkin, Bud (1926-2015) Come Blow Your Horn 1963; Never Too Late 1965; Divorce American Style 1967; Inspector Clouseau 1968; Start the Revolution without Me 1970; The Thief Who Came to Dinner 1973; Twice in a Lifetime 1985; Arthur 2: On the Rocks 1988; Love Hurts 1990
Young, Anthony aka **Young, Tony** (1921-1966) Penny Points to Paradise 1951; Port of Escape 1956
Young, Harold (1897-1970) The Scarlet Pimpernel 1934; The Mummy's Tomb 1942; There's One Born Every Minute 1942; The Frozen Ghost 1944; The Three Caballeros 1944
Young (1), Neil aka **Shakey, Bernard** (1945-) Human Highway 1982; CSNY/Déjà Vu 2008
Young (2), Robert aka **Young, Robert William** (1933-) Vampire Circus 1971; Keep It Up Downstairs 1976; The World Is Full of Married Men 1979; Hostage 1992; Splitting Heirs 1993; Fierce Creatures 1997; Captain Jack 1998
Young, Robert M (1924-) Rich Kids 1979; One-Trick Pony 1980; The Ballad of Gregorio Cortez 1983; Saving Grace 1985; Extremities 1986; Dominick and Eugene 1988; Triumph of the Spirit 1989; Talent for the Game 1991; Caught 1996
Young, Roger (1942-) Lassiter 1984; The Squeeze 1987; Murder in Mississippi 1990; Getting Gotti 1994; A Knight in Camelot 1998; One Special Night 1999
Young, Terence (1915-1994) One Night with You 1948; Woman Hater 1948; They Were Not Divided 1950; Valley of Eagles 1951; The Red Beret 1953; Storm over the Nile 1955; That Lady 1955; Safari 1956; Zarak 1956; No Time to Die 1958; Serious Charge 1959; Too Hot to Handle 1960; Dr No 1962; From Russia with Love 1963; The Amorous Adventures of Moll Flanders 1965; The Dirty Game 1965; Thunderball 1965; The Poppy Is Also a Flower 1966; Triple Cross 1966; The Rover 1967; Wait until Dark 1967; Mayerling 1968; The Christmas Tree 1969; Cold Sweat 1971; Red Sun 1971; The Valachi Papers 1972; Bloodline 1979; Inchon 1981; The Jigsaw Man 1984
Younger, Ben (1973-) Boiler Room 2000; Prime 2005
Youngson, Robert (1917-1974) Days of Thrills and Laughter 1961; MGM's Big Parade of Comedy 1964; Laurel and Hardy's Laughing 20s 1965; 4 Clowns 1970
Yu, Ronny (1950-) The Bride with White Hair 1993; Warriors of Virtue 1996; Bride of Chucky 1998; The 51st State 2001; Freddy vs Jason 2003; Fearless 2006
Yuen Woo-Ping aka **Yuen Wo-Ping** (1945-) Drunken Master 1978; Snake in the Eagle's Shadow 1978; Iron Monkey 1993; Twin Warriors 1993; Crouching Tiger, Hidden Dragon: Sword of Destiny 2016
Yuen, Corey aka **Yuen Kwai** (1951-) No Retreat, No Surrender 1985; The

Legend 1993; The Legend II 1993; The Defender 1994; The Enforcer 1995; And Now You're Dead 1998; So Close 2002; The Transporter 2002; DOA: Dead or Alive 2006
Yuh, Jennifer aka **Yuh Nelson, Jennifer** Kung Fu Panda 2 2011; Kung Fu Panda 3 2016
Yuzna, Brian (1949-) Society 1989; Bride of Re-Animator 1991; Necronomicon 1993; Return of the Living Dead 1993; The Dentist 1996; Progeny 1998; Faust: Love of the Damned 2001

Z

Zaillian, Steven (1953-) Innocent Moves 1993; A Civil Action 1998; All the King's Men 2005
Zamm, Alex Snow 2004; Dr Dolittle: Million Dollar Mutts 2009
Zampi, Mario (1903-1963) Laughter in Paradise 1951; Happy Ever After 1954; The Naked Truth 1957; Too Many Crooks 1958; Bottoms Up 1959
Zanussi, Krzysztof (1939-) Illumination 1972; The Catamount Killing 1974; Camouflage 1977; The Constant Factor 1980; The Contract 1980; Imperative 1982; A Year of the Quiet Sun 1984; The Silent Touch 1992
Zeffirelli, Franco (1923-) The Taming of the Shrew 1967; Romeo and Juliet 1968; Brother Sun, Sister Moon 1972; The Champ 1979; Endless Love 1981; La Traviata 1982; Otello 1986; Young Toscanini 1988; Hamlet 1990; Sparrow 1993; Jane Eyre 1996; Tea with Mussolini 1998; Callas Forever 2002
Zeglio, Primo (1906-1984) Morgan the Pirate 1960; Seven Seas to Calais 1962
Zeman, Karel (1910-1989) Invention of Destruction 1958; Baron Munchhausen 1961
Zemeckis, Robert (1952-) I Wanna Hold Your Hand 1978; Used Cars 1980; Romancing the Stone 1984; Back to the Future 1985; Who Framed Roger Rabbit 1988; Back to the Future Part II 1989; Back to the Future Part III 1990; Death Becomes Her 1992; Forrest Gump 1994; Contact 1997; Cast Away 2000; What Lies Beneath 2000; The Polar Express 2004; Beowulf 2007; A Christmas Carol 2009; Flight 2012; The Walk 2015
Zetterling, Mai (1925-1994) Doctor Glas 1968; Visions of Eight 1973; Scrubbers 1982
Zhang Yimou (1951-) Red Sorghum 1987; Ju Dou 1990; Raise the Red Lantern 1991; The Story of Qiu Ju 1992; To Live 1994; Shanghai Triad 1995; Keep Cool 1997; Not One Less 1999; The Road Home 1999; Happy Times 2001; Hero 2002; House of Flying Daggers 2004; Riding Alone for Thousands of Miles 2005; Curse of the Golden Flower 2006; Zhang Yimou's Blood Simple 2009; The Flowers of War 2012
Zhang Yuan (1963-) Beijing Bastards 1993; Behind the Forbidden City 1996; Little Red Flowers 2006
Zidi, Claude (1934-) Le Cop 1985; Le Cop II 1989; Asterix and Obelix Take On Caesar 1999
Zieff, Howard (1927-2009) Slither 1973; Hearts of the West 1975; House Calls 1978; The Main Event 1979; Private Benjamin 1980; Unfaithfully Yours 1983; The Dream Team 1989; My Girl 1991; My Girl 2 1994
Ziehl, Scott Earth vs the Spider 2001; Road House 2 2006
Ziehm, Howard Flesh Gordon 1974; Flesh Gordon Meets the Cosmic Cheerleaders 1989
Zielinski, Rafal (1957-) Screwballs 1983; Fun 1994
Zimmerman, Vernon Deadhead Miles 1972; The Unholy Rollers 1972; Fade to Black 1980
Zinnemann, Fred (1907-1997) Eyes in the Night 1942; Kid Glove Killer 1942; The Seventh Cross 1944; My Brother Talks to Horses 1946; The Search 1948; Act of Violence 1949; The Men 1950; Teresa 1951; High Noon 1952; The Member of the Wedding 1952; From Here to Eternity 1953; Oklahoma! 1955; A Hatful of Rain 1957; The Nun's Story 1959; The Sundowners 1960; Behold a Pale Horse 1964; A Man for All Seasons 1966; The Day of the Jackal 1973; Julia 1977; Five Days One Summer 1982

Zito, Joseph (1949-) Friday the 13th: the Final Chapter 1984; Missing in Action 1984; Invasion USA 1985; Red Scorpion 1989
Zombie, Rob (1966-) House of 1000 Corpses 2001; The Devil's Rejects 2005; Halloween 2007; Halloween II 2009; The Lords of Salem 2012
Zonca, Erick (1956-) The Dream Life of Angels 1998; Julia 2008
Zondag, Ralph We're Back! A Dinosaur's Story 1993; Dinosaur 2000
Zucker, David (1947-) Airplane! 1980; Top Secret! 1984; Ruthless People 1986; The Naked Gun 1988; The Naked Gun 2½: the Smell of Fear 1991; BASEketball 1998; My Boss's Daughter 2003; Scary Movie 3 2003; Scary Movie 4 2006
Zucker, Jerry (1950-) Airplane! 1980; Top Secret! 1984; Ruthless People 1986; Ghost 1990; First Knight 1995; Rat Race 2001
Zugsmith, Albert (1910-1993) The Private Lives of Adam and Eve 1959; Confessions of an Opium Eater 1962
Zulawski, Andrzej (1940-2016) La Femme Publique 1984; La Fidélité 2000
Zurinaga, Marcos Tango Bar 1988; The Disappearance of Garcia Lorca 1997
Zvyagintsev, Andrey The Return 2003; The Banishment 2007; Elena 2011; Leviathan 2014
Zwart, Harald (1965-) Hamilton 1998; One Night at McCool's 2001; Agent Cody Banks 2003; The Pink Panther 2 2009; The Karate Kid 2010; The Mortal Instruments: City of Bones 2013
Zwerin, Charlotte (1931-2004) Gimme Shelter 1970; Thelonious Monk: Straight No Chaser 1988
Zwick, Edward (1953-) About Last Night... 1986; Glory 1989; Leaving Normal 1992; Legends of the Fall 1994; Courage under Fire 1996; The Siege 1998; The Last Samurai 2003; Blood Diamond 2006; Defiance 2008; Love & Other Drugs 2010; Jack Reacher: Never Go Back 2016
Zwick, Joel (1942-) My Big Fat Greek Wedding 2002; Elvis Has Left the Building 2004; Fat Albert 2004
Zwicky, Karl (1958-) Paws 1997; The Magic Pudding 2000
Zwigoff, Terry (1948-) Crumb 1995; Ghost World 2001; Bad Santa 2003

Actors

A

Aaker, Lee (1943-) Desperate Search 1952; Hondo 1953; Jeopardy 1953

Aaliyah (1979-2001) Romeo Must Die 2000; Queen of the Damned 2002

Aaron, Caroline (1952-) Deconstructing Harry 1997; Tuesdays with Morrie 1999; Beyond the Sea 2004; Revenge of the Middle-Aged Woman 2004

Abatantuono, Diego (1955-) Puerto Escondido 1992; Nirvana 1996; The Best Man 1998; I'm Not Scared 2003

Abbass, Hiam (1960-) Paradise Now 2005; Conversations with My Gardener 2006; The Nativity Story 2006; The Visitor 2007; Lemon Tree 2008; Miral 2010

Abbott, Bruce (1954-) Re-Animator 1985; Bride of Re-Animator 1991

Abbott, Bud (1895-1974) Buck Privates 1941; Hold That Ghost 1941; In the Navy 1941; Keep 'Em Flying 1941; Pardon My Sarong 1942; Ride 'Em Cowboy 1942; Rio Rita 1942; Who Done It? 1942; Hit the Ice 1943; Abbott and Costello in Society 1944; Lost in a Harem 1944; Abbott and Costello in Hollywood 1945; Here Come the Co-Eds 1945; The Naughty Nineties 1945; Little Giant 1946; The Time of Their Lives 1946; Buck Privates Come Home 1947; Abbott and Costello Meet Frankenstein 1948; The Noose Hangs High 1948; Abbott and Costello Meet the Killer, Boris Karloff 1949; Africa Screams 1949; Abbott and Costello in the Foreign Legion 1950; Abbott and Costello Meet the Invisible Man 1951; Abbott and Costello Meet Captain Kidd 1952; Jack and the Beanstalk 1952; Lost in Alaska 1952; Abbott and Costello Go to Mars 1953; Abbott and Costello Meet Dr Jekyll and Mr Hyde 1953; Abbott and Costello Meet the Keystone Cops 1955; Abbott and Costello Meet the Mummy 1955; Dance with Me Henry 1956

Abbott, John (1905-1996) Conquest of the Air 1936; The Falcon in Hollywood 1944; Pursuit to Algiers 1945; The Bandit of Sherwood Forest 1946; Deception 1946; The Web 1947; The Woman in White 1948; Gigi 1958; Gambit 1966; The Jungle Book 1967

Abbott, Philip (1923-1998) The Bachelor Party 1957; The Spiral Road 1962; Sweet Bird of Youth 1962; Those Calloways 1964; Nightmare in Chicago 1968

Abdalla, Khalid The Kite Runner 2007; Green Zone 2010

Abdi, Barkhad Captain Phillips 2013; Eye in the Sky 2015

Abdul-Jabbar, Kareem (1947-) Game of Death 1978; Airplane! 1980; Slam Dunk Ernest 1995

Abe, Hiroshi Chocolate 2008; Still Walking 2008

Abel, Alfred (1879-1937) Dr Mabuse, the Gambler 1922; Metropolis 1926

Abel, Dominique Rumba 2008; The Fairy 2011

Abel, Jake (1987-) Flash of Genius 2008; I Am Number Four 2011; The Host 2013; Percy Jackson: Sea of Monsters 2013; Good Kill 2014; Love & Mercy 2014

Abel, Walter (1898-1987) The Three Musketeers 1935; Fury 1936; Green Light 1937; Men with Wings 1938; Racket Busters 1938; Arise, My Love 1940; Michael Shayne, Private Detective 1940; Miracle on Main Street 1940; Hold Back the Dawn 1941; Skylark 1941; Beyond the Blue Horizon 1942; Holiday Inn 1942; Star Spangled Rhythm 1942; Wake Island 1942; So Proudly We Hail 1943; An American Romance 1944; Mr Skeffington 1944; The Affairs of Susan 1945; Kiss and Tell 1945; The Kid from Brooklyn 1946; 13 Rue Madeleine 1946; Dream Girl 1948; That Lady in Ermine 1948; Island in the Sky 1953; So This Is Love 1953; Night People 1954; The Indian Fighter 1955; Quick, Let's Get Married 1964; Mirage 1965; The Man without a Country 1973

Abelanski, Lionel (1964-) Nationale 7 1999; Ma Femme Est une Actrice 2001; Not Here to Be Loved 2005

Abercrombie, Ian (1934-2012) Army of Darkness 1993; Garfield 2 2006; Star Wars: The Clone Wars 2008

Abineri, John (1928-2000) The McKenzie Break 1970; Death Train 1993

Abkarian, Simon (1962-) When the Cat's Away... 1996; Almost Peaceful 2002; Yes 2004; I Saw Ben Barka Get Killed 2005; Le Serpent 2006; The Army of Crime 2009; The Cut 2014

Able, Whitney All the Boys Love Mandy Lane 2006; Monsters 2010; A Walk among the Tombstones 2014

Aboutboul, Alon One of Us 1989; Body of Lies 2008

Abraham, F Murray (1939-) The Prisoner of Second Avenue 1974; The Sunshine Boys 1975; The Ritz 1976; The Big Fix 1978; Scarface 1983; Amadeus 1984; The Name of the Rose 1986; Beyond the Stars 1988; An Innocent Man 1989; Slipstream 1989; The Bonfire of the Vanities 1990; Mobsters 1991; Stockade 1991; By the Sword 1992; Last Action Hero 1993; National Lampoon's Loaded Weapon 1 1993; Nostradamus 1993; Surviving the Game 1994; Dillinger and Capone 1995; Mighty Aphrodite 1995; Children of the Revolution 1996; Mimic 1997; Star Trek: Insurrection 1998; Muppets from Space 1999; Finding Forrester 2000; Thir13en Ghosts 2001; Goltzius and the Pelican Company 2012; Love, Marilyn 2012; Dead Man Down 2013; Inside Llewyn Davis 2013

Abraham, Jake American Cousins 2003; Tamla Rose 2013

Abraham, John (1972-) Jism 2003; Dhoom 2004; Water 2005

Abrahams, Jon (1977-) Meet the Parents 2000; Scary Movie 2000; They 2002; My Boss's Daughter 2003; House of Wax 2004; Prime 2005

Abrams, Michele Buffy the Vampire Slayer 1992; Cool World 1992

Abreu, Claudia (1971-) Four Days in September 1997; The Man of the Year 2002

Abril, Victoria (1959-) The Moon in the Gutter 1983; After Darkness 1985; Max Mon Amour 1986; Tie Me Up! Tie Me Down! 1990; High Heels 1991; Lovers 1991; Kika 1993; Jimmy Hollywood 1994; Gazon Maudit 1995; 101 Reykjavik 2000

Absolom, Joe (1978-) Long Time Dead 2001; Extreme Ops 2003

Abu Warda, Yussef Cup Final 1991; Yom Yom 1998; Kadosh 1999

Accorsi, Stefano (1971-) Captains of April 2000; Le Fate Ignoranti 2001; Romanzo Criminale 2005; Blame It on Fidel 2006

Acevedo, Kirk Dinner Rush 2000; Invincible 2006

Acker, Sharon (1935-) Lucky Jim 1957; Point Blank 1967; Happy Birthday to Me 1981; Threshold 1981

Ackerman, Leslie (1956-) Law and Disorder 1974; Blame It on the Night 1984

Ackland, Joss (1926-) A Midsummer Night's Dream 1961; Rasputin, the Mad Monk 1965; Crescendo 1970; The House That Dripped Blood 1970; Villain 1971; The Mind Snatchers 1972; England Made Me 1973; Hitler: the Last Ten Days 1973; Penny Gold 1973; The Black Windmill 1974; Great Expectations 1974; The Little Prince 1974; One of Our Dinosaurs Is Missing 1975; Operation Daybreak 1975; Royal Flash 1975; Silver Bears 1977; A Nightingale Sang in Berkeley Square 1979; Saint Jack 1979; The Apple 1980; Rough Cut 1980; Lady Jane 1985; A Zed & Two Noughts 1985; The Sicilian 1987; White Mischief 1987; To Kill a Priest 1988; Lethal Weapon 2 1989; The Bridge 1990; The Hunt for Red October 1990; Spymaker: the Secret Life of Ian Fleming 1990; Bill & Ted's Bogus Journey 1991; The Object of Beauty 1991; The Mighty Ducks 1992; Nowhere to Run 1992; Once upon a Crime 1992; The Princess and the Goblin 1992; Mother's Boys 1993; Mad Dogs and Englishmen 1994; Citizen X 1995; D3: the Mighty Ducks 1996; Surviving Picasso 1996; Amy Foster 1997; Firelight 1997; Milk 1999; Passion of Mind 2000; K-19: the Widowmaker 2002; No Good Deed 2002; I'll Be There 2003; Flawless 2007

Ackland, Oliver 100 Bloody Acres 2012; The Mystery of a Hansom Cab 2012

Ackroyd, David (1940-) Memories of Me 1988; Dark Angel 1989; Love, Cheat & Steal 1994

Acosta, Rodolfo aka **Acosta, Rudolph** aka **Acosta, Rudy** (1920-1974) Appointment in Honduras 1953; Hondo 1953; Drum Beat 1954; A Life in the Balance 1955; Bandido 1956; Flaming Star 1960; Let No Man Write My Epitaph 1960; Return of the Seven 1966

Acovone, Jay (1955-) Cold Steel 1987; Quicksand: No Escape 1992; Lookin' Italian 1994

Acquanetta (1921-2004) Dead Man's Eyes 1944; Tarzan and the Leopard Woman 1946

Acuna, Jason "Wee Man" aka **Wee Man** Jackass: the Movie 2002; jackass number two 2006

Adair, Jean (1873-1953) Arsenic and Old Lace 1944; Something in the Wind 1947

Adair, Robert aka **A'Dair, Robert** (1900-1954) Journey's End 1930; The Ticket of Leave Man 1937; There Is Another Sun 1951

Adam, Marie-Christine Priceless 2006; Paris-Manhattan 2012

Adam, Ronald (1896-1979) Strange Boarders 1938; Obsession 1948; The Lavender Hill Mob 1951; Hindle Wakes 1952; Assignment Redhead 1956; Kill Me Tomorrow 1957; The Golden Disc 1958; Postman's Knock 1961

Adams, Amy (1974-) Drop Dead Gorgeous 1999; Cruel Intentions 2 2000; Catch Me If You Can 2002; Serving Sara 2002; Junebug 2004; The Wedding Date 2004; Charlie Wilson's War 2007; Enchanted 2007; Miss Pettigrew Lives for a Day 2007; Underdog 2007; Doubt 2008; Sunshine Cleaning 2008; Julie & Julia 2009; Night at the Museum 2 2009; The Fighter 2010; Leap Year 2010; The Muppets 2011; On the Road 2011; The Master 2012; Trouble with the Curve 2012; American Hustle 2013; Her 2013; Man of Steel 2013; Big Eyes 2014; Batman v Superman: Dawn of Justice 2016; Nocturnal Animals 2016

Adams, Beverly (1945-) How to Fill a Wild Bikini 1965; Torture Garden 1967

Adams, Brandon aka **Adams, Brandon Quintin** (1979-) Moonwalker 1988; The People under the Stairs 1991; Ghost in the Machine 1993; The Sandlot 1993

Adams, Brooke (1949-) Shock Waves 1975; Days of Heaven 1978; Invasion of the Body Snatchers 1978; Cuba 1979; A Man, a Woman and a Bank 1979; Tell Me a Riddle 1980; The Dead Zone 1983; Almost You 1984; Man on Fire 1987; Bridesmaids 1989; Sometimes They Come Back 1991; Gas, Food, Lodging 1992

Adams, Catlin (1950-) The Jerk 1979; The Jazz Singer 1980; Freaky Friday 1995

Adams, Don (1923-2005) The Nude Bomb 1980; Back to the Beach 1987

Adams, Dorothy (1900-1988) The Devil Commands 1941; Laura 1944; Johnny Concho 1956

Adams, Edie (1927-2008) The Apartment 1960; Lover Come Back 1961; Call Me Bwana 1963; Love with the Proper Stranger 1963; Under the Yum Yum Tree 1963; The Best Man 1964; The Oscar 1966; The Honey Pot 1967; Evil Roy Slade 1971

Adams (2), Jane (1965-) Vital Signs 1990; Light Sleeper 1991; Kansas City 1995; Happiness 1998; Songcatcher 1999; The Anniversary Party 2001; Eternal Sunshine of the Spotless Mind 2003; Stone Cold 2005; Last Holiday 2006; Little Children 2006; Restless 2011

Adams, Jill (1930-2008) The Young Lovers 1954; Value for Money 1955; Brothers in Law 1956; The Green Man 1956; The Scamp 1957

Adams, Joe (1922-) Carmen Jones 1954; Ballad in Blue 1964

Adams, Joey Lauren aka **Adams, Joey** (1971-) SFW 1994; Mallrats 1995; Bio-Dome 1996; Chasing Amy 1996; A Cool, Dry Place 1998; Big Daddy 1999; Beautiful 2000; Jay and Silent Bob Strike Back 2001; The Break-Up 2006; Trucker 2009

Adams, Julie aka **Adams, Julia** (1926-) Bright Victory 1951; Bend of the River 1952; Horizons West 1952; The Lawless Breed 1952; Treasure of Lost Canyon 1952; The Man from the Alamo 1953; The Mississippi Gambler 1953; Creature from the Black Lagoon 1954; The Private War of Major Benson 1955; Six Bridges to Cross 1955; Away All Boats 1956; Slaughter on Tenth Avenue 1957; The Gunfight at Dodge City 1959; Tickle Me 1965; Valley of Mystery 1967; The Last Movie 1971

Adams, Kathryn (1920-) 5th Ave Girl 1939; Argentine Nights 1940

Adams, Kelly Bronson 2008; My Last Five Girlfriends 2009; The Seventh Dimension 2009

Adams (2), Lynne Night Zoo 1987; Airspeed 1997

Adams, Mason (1919-2005) Omen III: the Final Conflict 1980; Adam 1983; Passions 1984; FX: Murder by Illusion 1985; Toy Soldiers 1991; Assault at West Point: the Court Martial of John Whittaker 1994

Adams, Maud (1945-) The Christian Licorice Store 1971; The Man with the Golden Gun 1974; Killer Force 1975; Rollerball 1975; Playing for Time 1980; Tattoo 1980; Target Eagle 1982; Octopussy 1983; Jane and the Lost City 1987

Adams, Neile This Could Be the Night 1957; Steve McQueen: the Man & Le Mans 2015

Adams, Nick (1931-1968) The Last Wagon 1956; No Time for Sergeants 1958; Sing, Boy, Sing 1958; Teacher's Pet 1958; The FBI Story 1959; Pillow Talk 1959; The Hook 1963; Twilight of Honor 1963; Frankenstein Conquers the World 1964; Die, Monster, Die! 1965; Invasion of the Astro-Monster 1965; Young Dillinger 1965

Adams, Polly Kisna - the Warrior Poet 2004; United 93 2006

Adams, Robert (1906-1965) Midshipman Easy 1935; Song of Freedom 1936; Old Bones of the River 1938

Adams, Stanley (1915-1977) Hell on Frisco Bay 1955; Requiem for a Heavyweight 1962; Lilies of the Field 1963; Thunder Alley 1967; The Grasshopper 1970

Adams, Tom (1938-2014) A Prize of Arms 1961; Licensed to Kill 1965; The Fighting Prince of Donegal 1966; Where the Bullets Fly 1966

Adamson, Christopher aka **Adamson, Chris** Dirty Weekend 1992; Razor Blade Smile 1998; Lighthouse 1999

Addams, Dawn (1930-1985) The Hour of 13 1952; Plymouth Adventure 1952; The Moon Is Blue 1953; Khyber Patrol 1954; Return to Treasure Island 1954; Secrets d'Alcove 1954; A King in New York 1957; The Silent Enemy 1958; The Treasure of San Teresa 1959; The Thousand Eyes of Dr Mabuse 1960; The Two Faces of Dr Jekyll 1960; Come Fly with Me 1962; The Black Tulip 1963; Ballad in Blue 1964; Where the Bullets Fly 1966; The Vampire Lovers 1970; The Vault of Horror 1973

Addie, Robert (1960-2003) Excalibur 1981; Another Country 1984; A Knight in Camelot 1998

Addison, Chris (1971-) In the Loop 2009; The Look of Love 2013

Addy, Mark (1963-) The Full Monty 1997; Jack Frost 1998; The Last Yellow 1999; The Flintstones in Viva Rock Vegas 2000; Down to Earth 2001; A Knight's Tale 2001; Heartlands 2002; The Sin Eater 2002; The Time Machine 2002; Barney's Version 2010; It's a Wonderful Afterlife 2010; Robin Hood 2010

Addy, Wesley (1913-1996) Kiss Me Deadly 1955; Ten Seconds to Hell 1959; Hush... Hush, Sweet Charlotte 1964; Network 1976; The Europeans 1979; The Bostonians 1984

Adebimpe, Tunde Jump Tomorrow 2001; Rachel Getting Married 2008; Nasty Baby 2015

Adedayo, Adelayo Sket 2011; Gone Too Far! 2013

Adelstein, Paul Bedazzled 2000; Intolerable Cruelty 2003

Ades, Daniel (1932-1992) The Last Movie 1971; Aguirre, Wrath of God 1972

Adiarte, Patrick (1943-) The King and I 1956; High Time 1960

Adjani, Isabelle (1955-) The Story of Adèle H 1975; The Tenant 1976; The Driver 1978; The Brontë Sisters 1979; Nosferatu, the Vampyre 1979; Quartet 1981; One Deadly Summer 1983; Subway 1985; Ishtar 1987; Camille Claudel 1988; La Reine Margot 1994; Diabolique 1996; Bon Voyage 2003; Monsieur Ibrahim and the Flowers of the Koran 2003; Mammuth 2010

Adkins, Scott (1976-) The Shepherd 2008; The Legend of Hercules 2014

Adkins, Seth (1989-) First Do No Harm 1997; Geppetto 2000; Taming Andrew 2000

Adler, Jay (1896-1978) Cry Danger 1951; The Family Jewels 1965

Adler, Jerry (1929-) The Public Eye 1992; Manhattan Murder Mystery 1993; Getting Away with Murder 1996; Sunday, Sunday 1997; In Her Shoes 2005

Adler, Luther (1903-1984) The Loves of Carmen 1948; Saigon 1948; DOA 1949; House of Strangers 1949; Wake of the Red Witch 1949; Kiss Tomorrow Goodbye 1950; The Desert Fox 1951; M 1951; Hoodlum Empire 1952; Crashout 1955; The Girl in the Red Velvet Swing 1955; Hot Blood 1956; The Last Angry Man 1959; The Three Sisters 1966; The Brotherhood 1968; Absence of Malice 1981

Adler, Matt (1966-) Teen Wolf 1985; Amazon Women on the Moon 1987; North Shore 1987; White Water Summer 1987

Adler, Robert (1906-1987) Green Grass of Wyoming 1948; Yellow Sky 1948

Adolphson, Edvin (1893-1979) Dollar 1938; One Single Night 1939; Paw 1959

Adonis, Frank Eyes of Laura Mars 1978; Ace Ventura: Pet Detective 1993

Adorée, Renée (1898-1933) Day Dreams 1922; The Big Parade 1925; The Black Bird 1926; La Bohème 1926; The Exquisite Sinner 1926

Adorf, Mario (1930-) Station Six-Sahara 1962; Ghosts - Italian Style 1967; The Bird with the Crystal Plumage 1969; The Red Tent 1969; The Short Night of the Glass Dolls 1971; King, Queen, Knave 1972; The Lost Honour of Katharina Blum 1975; The Tin Drum 1979; Lola 1982; The Holcroft Covenant 1985; The Second Victory 1986

Adoti, Razaaq aka **Adoti, Raz** Doom 2005; The Hard Corps 2006; Second in Command 2006

Adrian, Iris (1912-1994) Rumba 1935; Wild Geese Calling 1941; Lady of Burlesque 1943; Bluebeard 1944; The Singing Sheriff 1944; It's a Pleasure 1945; The Stork Club 1945; The Bamboo Blonde 1946; The Paleface 1948

Adrian, Max (1903-1973) Kipps 1941; The Young Mr Pitt 1942; Pool of London 1951; Dr Terror's House of Horrors 1964; The Music Lovers 1970; The Boy Friend 1971; The Devils 1971

Adsit, Scott Appropriate Behaviour 2014; Big Hero 6 2014

Affleck, Ben (1972-) School Ties 1992; Dazed and Confused 1993; Glory Daze 1995; Mallrats 1995; Chasing Amy 1996; Going All the Way 1997; Good Will Hunting 1997; Armageddon 1998; Forces of Nature 1998; Phantoms 1998; Shakespeare in Love 1998; Daddy and Them 1999; Dogma 1999; 200 Cigarettes 1999; Boiler Room 2000; Bounce 2000; Deception 2000; Joseph: King of Dreams 2000; Jay and Silent Bob Strike Back 2001; Pearl Harbor 2001; Changing Lanes 2002; The Sum of All Fears 2002; Daredevil 2003; Gigli 2003; Jersey Girl 2003; Paycheck 2003; Surviving Christmas 2004; Clerks II 2006; Hollywoodland 2006; Smokin' Aces 2006; He's Just Not That into You 2008; Extract 2009; State of Play 2009; The Company Men 2010; The Town 2010; Argo 2012; To the Wonder 2012; Runner Runner 2013; Gone Girl 2014; The Accountant 2016; Batman v Superman: Dawn of Justice 2016; Live by Night 2016; Justice League 2017

Affleck, Casey (1975-) To Die For 1995; Chasing Amy 1996; Race the Sun 1996; Good Will Hunting 1997; Desert Blue 1998; 200 Cigarettes 1999; Committed 2000; Drowning Mona 2000; Gerry 2001; Ocean's Eleven 2001; Soul Survivors 2001; Ocean's Twelve 2004; Lonesome Jim 2005; The Last Kiss 2006; The Assassination of Jesse James by the Coward Robert Ford 2007; Gone Baby Gone 2007; Ocean's Thirteen 2007; The Killer inside Me 2010; Tower Heist 2011; ParaNorman 2012; Ain't Them Bodies Saints 2013; Out of the Furnace 2013; Interstellar 2014; The Finest Hours 2015; Triple 9 2015

Agar, John (1921-2002) Fort Apache 1948; Adventure in Baltimore 1949; Sands of Iwo Jima 1949; She Wore a Yellow Ribbon 1949; The Woman on Pier 13 1949; Breakthrough 1950; Along the Great Divide 1951; The Rocket Man 1954; Revenge of the Creature 1955; Tarantula 1955; The Mole People 1956; Star in the Dust 1956; Daughter of Dr Jekyll 1957; The Brain from Planet Arous 1958; Jet Attack 1958; Johnny Reno 1966; Waco 1966; Miracle Mile 1989

Agashe, Mohan Nishant 1975; Sadgati 1981; Train to Pakistan 1997

Aghdashloo, Shohreh (1952-) House of Sand and Fog 2003; The Exorcism of Emily Rose 2005; The Lake House 2006; The Nativity Story 2006; The Odd Life of Timothy Green 2012; Rosewater 2014; The Last Knights 2015

Agogué, Raphaëlle The Round Up 2010; The Informant 2013

Agron, Dianna Glee: the 3D Concert Movie 2011; I Am Number Four 2011; The Family 2013

Aguilera, Christina Shine a Light 2007; Burlesque 2010; Get Him to the Greek 2010

Agutter, Jenny (1952-) East of Sudan 1964; A Man Could Get Killed 1966; Star! 1968; I Start Counting 1970; The Railway Children 1970; Walkabout 1970; A War of Children 1972; The Eagle Has Landed 1976; Logan's Run 1976; Equus 1977; The Man in the Iron Mask 1977; China 9, Liberty 37 1978; Dominique 1978; The Riddle of the Sands 1978; Mayflower: the Pilgrims' Adventure 1979; Sweet William 1980; An American Werewolf in London 1981; Amy 1981; The Survivor 1981; Dark

Tower 1989; King of the Wind 1989; Child's Play 2 1990 Freddie as FR07 1992; The Parole Officer 2001; Heroes and Villains 2006; Irina Palm 2006; Glorious 39 2009; Outside Bet 2011; Marvel Avengers Assemble 2012; Captain America: the Winter Soldier 2014

Aherne, Brian (1902-1985) Underground 1928 The Constant Nymph 1933; The Song of Songs 1933; What Every Woman Knows 1934; I Live My Life 1935; Beloved Enemy 1936; Sylvia Scarlett 1936; The Great Garrick 1937; Merrily We Live 1938; Juarez 1939; Hired Wife 1940; The Lady in Question 1940; My Son, My Son! 1940; Vigil in the Night 1940; Skylark 1941; Smilin' Through 1941; My Sister Eileen 1942; A Night to Remember 1942; What a Woman! 1943; The Locket 1946; I Confess 1953; Titanic 1953; A Bullet Is Waiting 1954; Prince Valiant 1954; The Swan 1956; The Best of Everything 1959; Susan Slade 1961; Lancelot and Guinevere 1963; Rosie! 1967

Ahlstedt, Börje (1939-) I Am Curious - Yellow 1967; A Lover and His Lass 1975; Fanny and Alexander 1982; Best Intentions 1992; Sunday's Children 1992; Saraband 2003

Ahmed, Lalita (1939-) Wild West 1992; Bhaji on the Beach 1993; Brick Lane 2007

Ahmed, Rizwan aka **Ahmed, Riz** (1982-) The Road to Guantanamo 2006; Shifty 2008; Centurion 2009; Four Lions 2010; Black Gold 2011; Trishna 2011; Ill Manors 2012; The Reluctant Fundamentalist 2012; Closed Circuit 2013; Nightcrawler 2013; City of Tiny Lights 2016; Jason Bourne 2016

Ahn Sung-kee (1952-) Village in the Mist 1983; To the Starry Island 1994; Chihwaseon (Drunk on Women and Poetry) 2002; Duelist 2005

Ahn, Philip (1911-1978) The General Died at Dawn 1936; China 1943; Back to Bataan 1945; Betrayal from the East 1945; China Sky 1945; The Miracle of the Bells 1948; Love Is a Many-Splendored Thing 1955; Confessions of an Opium Eater 1962; Shock Corridor 1963; Jonathan Livingston Seagull 1973

Aidman, Charles (1925-1993) War Hunt 1962; Countdown 1967; Hour of the Gun 1967; Angel, Angel Down We Go 1969; Adam at 6 AM 1970; Kotch 1971; Dirty Little Billy 1972; Zoot Suit 1981

Aiello, Danny (1933-) Fingers 1978; Defiance 1979; Hide in Plain Sight 1980; Fort Apache, the Bronx 1981; Amityville II: the Possession 1982; Once upon a Time in America 1984; The Protector 1985; The Purple Rose of Cairo 1985; The Stuff 1985; Man on Fire 1987; Moonstruck 1987; The Pick-Up Artist 1987; Radio Days 1987; Do the Right Thing 1989; Harlem Nights 1989; The January Man 1989; Jacob's Ladder 1990; Hudson Hawk 1991; Once Around 1991; 29th Street 1991; Mistress 1992; Ruby 1992; The Cemetery Club 1993; Me and the Kid 1993; The Pickle 1993; Leon 1994; Pret-a-Porter 1994; The Road Home 1995; Two Much 1995; City Hall 1996; Mojave Moon 1996; 2 Days in the Valley 1996; Bring Me the Head of Mavis Davis 1997; Dinner Rush 2000

Aiken, Liam (1990-) Henry Fool 1997; Stepmom 1998; Road to Perdition 2002; Good Boy! 2003; Lemony Snicket's A Series of Unfortunate Events 2004; Electrick Children 2012

Aikman, Laura Keith Lemon: the Film 2012; Bula Quo! 2013

Aikman, Luke (1983-) Fever Pitch 1996; Devil's Gate 2002; Freight 2010

Aimée, Anouk aka **Anouk** (1932-) Golden Salamander 1949; The Crimson Curtain 1952; Contraband Spain 1955; Montparnasse 19 1958; La Dolce Vita 1960; Lola 1960; Sodom and Gomorrah 1962; 8½ 1963; Un Homme et une Femme 1966; The Appointment 1968; Justine 1969; Model Shop 1969; Second Chance 1976; The Tragedy of a Ridiculous Man 1981; Success Is the Best Revenge 1984; A Man and a Woman: 20 Years Later 1986; Bethune: the Making of a Hero 1990; Pret-a-Porter 1994; Men, Women: a User's Manual 1996; LA without a Map 1998; Festival in Cannes 2001

Aimos, Raymond aka **Aimos** (1889-1944) La Belle Equipe 1936; The Golem 1936

Ainley, Anthony (1932-2004) Blood on Satan's Claw 1970; The Land That Time Forgot 1974

Ainley, Richard (1910-1967) As You Like It 1936; Stolen Life 1939; Above Suspicion 1943; I Dood It 1943

Aird, Holly (1969-) Intimate Relations 1995; Fever Pitch 1996; Dreaming of Joseph Lees 1999; The Theory of Flight 1998; The Criminal 1999; Scenes of a Sexual Nature 2006

Aird, Jane (1926-1993) Hunted 1952; Dance Little Lady 1954

Airlie, Andrew (1961-) Jack 2004; A Decent Proposal 2006; Apollo 18 2011; 50/50 2011

Aitken, Maria (1945-) A Fish Called Wanda 1988; The Fool 1990; Jinnah 1998

Ajala, David Payback Season 2012; Kill Command 2016

Ajaye, Franklyn (1949-) Car Wash 1976; Convoy 1978; The Jazz Singer 1980; American Yakuza 1994

Akbag, Demet Vizontele 2001; Winter Sleep 2014

Aked, Muriel (1887-1955) Evensong 1934; William at the Circus 1948

Akerman, Chantal (1950-2015) Je, Tu, Il, Elle 1974; Jeanne Dielman, 23 Quai du Commerce, 1080 Bruxelles 1975; No Home Movie 2015

Akerman, Malin (1978-) The Brothers Solomon 2007; The Heartbreak Kid 2007; 27 Dresses 2008; Couples Retreat 2009; Watchmen 2009; Wanderlust 2011; Stolen 2012; The Numbers Station 2013; Misconduct 2016

Akers, Andra (1944-2002) Murder à la Mod 1968; Moment by Moment 1978; Desert Hearts 1985

Akin, Philip (1950-) Iceman 1984; Airborne 1997; P2 2006

Akinnagbe, Gbenga The Savages 2007; The Taking of Pelham 123 2009

Akinnuoye-Agbaje, Adewale aka **Adewale** (1967-) Ace Ventura: When Nature Calls 1995; Legionnaire 1998; The Bourne Identity 2002; Get Rich or Die Tryin' 2005; Faster 2010; Best Laid Plans 2011; The Thing 2011

Akins, Claude (1918-1994) The Burning Hills 1956; The Lonely Man 1957; The Defiant Ones 1958; Yellowstone Kelly 1959; Comanche Station 1960; Black Gold 1962; Merrill's Marauders 1962; A Distant Trumpet 1964; The Killers 1964; Incident at Phantom Hill 1966; Return of the Seven 1966; Waterhole #3 1967; The Great Bank Robbery 1969; Flap 1970; Skyjacked 1972; Battle for the Planet of the Apes 1973; Tentacles 1977; Monster in the Closet 1983; The Curse 1987; Falling from Grace 1992

Alamsyah, Donny Red and White 2009; The Raid 2011

Alard, Nelly Eating 1990; Venice/ Venice 1992

Alaskey, Joe (1952-2016) Casper 1995; Tweety's High Flying Adventure 2000

Alba, Jessica (1981-) Idle Hands 1999; Honey 2003; Fantastic Four 2005; Into the Blue 2005; Sin City 2005; Awake 2007; 4: Rise of the Silver Surfer 2007; Good Luck Chuck 2007; The Eye 2008; The Love Guru 2008; The Killer inside Me 2010; Little Fockers 2010; Machete 2010; Valentine's Day 2010; SPYkids 4: All the Time in the World 2011; Machete Kills 2013; Lessons in Love 2014; Sin City: a Dame to Kill For 2014; Barely Lethal 2015; Mechanic: Resurrection 2016

Albarn, Damon Face 1997; Scott Walker: 30 Century Man 2006; No Distance Left to Run 2009; We Are Many 2014

Alberghetti, Anna Maria (1936-) The Last Command 1955; Ten Thousand Bedrooms 1957; Cinderfella 1960

Alberni, Luis (1887-1962) The Mad Genius 1931; The Big Stampede 1932; Topaze 1933; One Night of Love 1934; The Gay Deception 1935; The Gilded Lily 1935; Roberta 1935; Colleen 1936; Easy Living 1937; The Great Garrick 1937; When You're in Love 1937

Albers, Hans (1892-1960) The Blue Angel 1930; Baron Münchhausen 1943

Albert, Eddie (1906-2005) Four Mothers 1941; Out of the Fog 1941; The Wagons Roll at Night 1941; Bombardier 1943; Rendezvous with Annie 1946; Smash Up - the Story of a Woman 1947; Time Out of Mind 1947; You Gotta Stay Happy 1948; The Fuller Brush Girl 1950; Meet Me after the Show 1951; You're in the Navy Now 1951; Actors and Sin 1952; Carrie 1952; Roman Holiday 1953; The Girl Rush 1955; I'll Cry Tomorrow 1955; Oklahoma! 1955; Attack! 1956; The Teahouse of the August Moon 1956; The Joker Is Wild 1957; The Sun Also Rises 1957; The Gun Runners 1958; Orders to Kill 1958; The Roots of Heaven 1958; Beloved Infidel 1959; The Young Doctors 1961; The Longest Day 1962; Madison Avenue 1962; Who's Got the Action? 1962; Captain Newman, MD 1963; Miracle of the White Stallions 1963; 7 Women 1966; The Heartbreak Kid 1972; McQ 1974; The Mean Machine 1974; The Devil's Rain 1975; Escape to Witch Mountain 1975; Hustle 1975; Las Vegas Roundabout 1975; Whiffs 1975; Birch Interval 1976; Airport '79: the Concorde 1979; Foolin' Around 1980; How to Beat the High Cost of Living 1980; Yes, Giorgio 1982; Dreamscape 1984; Head Office 1986

Albert, Edward (1951-2006) The Fool Killer 1965; Butterflies Are Free 1972; 40 Carats 1973; The Domino Principle 1977; The Purple Taxi 1977; The Greek Tycoon 1978; When Time Ran Out 1980; Butterfly 1982; The House Where Evil Dwells 1982; Ellie 1984; The Rescue 1988; Guarding Tess 1994; The Secret Agent Club 1995

Albert, Shari The Brothers McMullen 1995; No Looking Back 1998

Albertazzi, Giorgio (1923-2016) Last Year at Marienbad 1961; Eva 1962

Alberti, Guido (1909-1996) 8½ 1963; Hands over the City 1963; Ten Days' Wonder 1971; What? 1973

Albertini, Giampiero (1927-1991) Burn! 1970; Return of Sabata 1971; Zorro 1975

Albertson, Frank (1909-1964) Men without Women 1930; A Connecticut Yankee 1931; Air Mail 1932; Ever in My Heart 1933; Alice Adams 1935; Bachelor Mother 1939; When the Daltons Rode 1940; Louisiana Purchase 1941; Man Made Monster 1941; Rosie the Riveter 1944; Nightfall 1956; The Enemy Below 1957

Albertson, Jack (1907-1981) Top Banana 1953; Bring Your Smile Along 1955; The Unguarded Moment 1956; Period of Adjustment 1962; Kissin' Cousins 1964; How to Murder Your Wife 1965; The Flim-Flam Man 1967; The Subject Was Roses 1968; Rabbit, Run 1970; Willy Wonka and the Chocolate Factory 1971; The Poseidon Adventure 1972; The Fox and the Hound 1981; My Body, My Child 1982

Albertson, Mabel (1901-1982) Ransom! 1956; Home before Dark 1958; Don't Give Up the Ship 1959; The Gazebo 1959; Period of Adjustment 1962; On a Clear Day You Can See Forever 1970; What's Up, Doc? 1972

Albinus, Jens (1965-) The Idiots 1998; The Boss of It All 2006

Albright, Hardie (1903-1975) Jewel Robbery 1932; The Purchase Price 1932; So Big 1932; Red Salute 1935; The Jade Mask 1945; Angel on My Shoulder 1946

Albright, Lola (1925-) Champion 1949; Sierra Passage 1950; The Tender Trap 1955; The Monolith Monsters 1957; Kid Galahad 1962; The Love Cage 1964; Lord Love a Duck 1966; How I Spent My Summer Vacation 1967; The Way West 1967; The Helicopter Spies 1968; Where Were You When the Lights Went Out? 1968

Albright, Wally aka **Albright Jr, Wally** (1925-1999) The Trespasser 1929; Zoo in Budapest 1933

Alcázar, Damián (1953-) Men with Guns 1997; El Crimen del Padre Amaro 2002

Alda, Alan (1936-) Gone Are the Days 1963; Paper Lion 1968; The Extraordinary Seaman 1969; The Mephisto Waltz 1971; The Glass House 1972; Kill Me If You Can 1977; California Suite 1978; Same Time, Next Year 1978; The Seduction of Joe Tynan 1979; The Four Seasons 1981; Sweet Liberty 1986; A New Life 1988; Crimes and Misdemeanors 1989; Betsy's Wedding 1990; Whispers in the Dark 1992; And the Band Played On 1993; Manhattan Murder Mystery 1993; White Mile 1994; Canadian Bacon 1995; Everyone Says I Love You 1996; Flirting with Disaster 1996; Mad City 1997; Murder at 1600 1997; The Object of My Affection 1998; What Women Want 2001; The Aviator 2004; Diminished Capacity 2007; Resurrecting the Champ 2007; Flash of Genius 2008; Tower Heist 2011; Wanderlust 2011; Bridge of Spies 2015; The Longest Ride 2015

Alda, Robert (1914-1986) Rhapsody in Blue 1945; The Beast with Five Fingers 1946; Cinderella Jones 1946; Cloak and Dagger 1946; The Man I Love 1946; Nora Prentiss 1947; Tarzan and the Slave Girl 1950; Beautiful but Dangerous 1955; Imitation of Life 1959; The Girl Who Knew Too Much 1969; Bittersweet Love 1976; Perfect Gentlemen 1978

Alda, Rutanya (1945-) The Deer Hunter 1978; Mommie Dearest 1981; Amityville II: the Possession 1982; Racing with the Moon 1984; Apprentice to Murder 1988; Prancer 1989; The Dark Half 1991; Murder without Conviction 2004

Alden, Mary (1883-1946) The Battle of the Sexes 1914; The Birth of a Nation 1915

Alden, Norman (1924-2012) The Sword in the Stone 1963; Man's Favorite Sport? 1964; The Wild Angels 1966; Good Times 1967; Where Does It Hurt? 1971; Kansas City Bomber 1972

Alderson, Brooke Urban Cowboy 1980; Mike's Murder 1984

Alderson, Erville (1882-1957) America 1924; Isn't Life Wonderful 1924; The Thirteenth Guest 1932

Alderton, John (1940-) The System 1964; Duffy 1968; Please Sir! 1971; Zardoz 1973; It Shouldn't Happen to a Vet 1979; Clockwork Mice 1994; Mrs Caldicot's Cabbage War 2000; Calendar Girls 2003

Aldon, Mari (1927-2004) Distant Drums 1951; This Woman Is Dangerous 1952; Mask of Dust 1954; Summertime 1955

Aldredge, Tom (1928-2011) The Troublemaker 1964; The Rain People 1969; *batteries not included 1987; Other People's Money 1991; What about Bob? 1991; The Adventures of Huck Finn 1993; Passion 1996

Aldridge, Kitty Slipstream 1989; Divorcing Jack 1998

Aldridge, Michael (1920-1994) Bullshot 1983; Shanghai Surprise 1986

Aldrin, Buzz In the Shadow of the Moon 2006; Fly Me to the Moon 2007

Aleandro, Norma (1936-) The Official Story 1985; Gaby: a True Story 1987; Cousins 1989; Son of the Bride 2001; Only Human 2004

Ales, John The Nutty Professor 1996; Spy Hard 1996; Nutty Professor 2: the Klumps 2000

Alesi, Fausto Russo In Memory of Myself 2007; Vincere 2009

Alessi, Raquel Ghost Rider 2007; Miss March 2009

Alexander, Ben (1911-1969) High Pressure 1932; Dragnet 1954; Man in the Shadow 1957

Alexander, Denise Crime in the Streets 1956; The Lindbergh Kidnapping Case 1976; Danielle Steel's Zoya 1995

Alexander, Erika (1969-) The Long Walk Home 1990; Love Liza 2001; Déjà Vu 2006; Elsa & Fred 2014

Alexander, Flex Snakes on a Plane 2006; The Hills Have Eyes II 2007

Alexander, Jace (1964-) Matewan 1987; City of Hope 1991; Mistress 1992; Love and a .45 1994

Alexander, Jaimie The Last Stand 2013; London Fields 2015

Alexander, Jane (1939-) The Great White Hope 1970; A Gunfight 1971; The New Centurions 1972; All the President's Men 1976; The Betsy 1978; Kramer vs Kramer 1979; Brubaker 1980; Playing for Time 1980; Night Crossing 1981; Testament 1983; City Heat 1984; Square Dance 1987; The Cider House Rules 1999; The Ring 2002; Sunshine State 2002; Fur: an Imaginary Portrait of Diane Arbus 2006; Feast of Love 2007; Gigantic 2008; The Unborn 2009; Dream House 2011; Mr Morgan's Last Love 2013

Alexander, Jason (1959-) The Burning 1981; The Mosquito Coast 1986; Jacob's Ladder 1990; Pretty Woman 1990; White Palace 1990; Coneheads 1993; Blankman 1994; North 1994; The Paper 1994; For Better or Worse 1995; The Last Supper 1995; Dunston Checks In 1996; The Hunchback of Notre Dame 1996; Love! Valour! Compassion! 1997; Rodgers & Hammerstein's Cinderella 1997; Something about Sex 1998; The Adventures of Rocky & Bullwinkle 1999; Madeline: Lost in Paris 1999; Shallow Hal 2001; A Christmas Carol 2004; The Aristocrats 2005; Hachi: a Dog's Tale 2008

Alexander (1), John (1897-1982) Arsenic and Old Lace 1944; The Horn Blows at Midnight 1945; The Jolson Story 1946; Where There's Life 1947; The Sleeping City 1950; The Marrying Kind 1952

Alexander, Katherine aka **Alexander, Katharine** (1898-1981) The Barretts of Wimpole Street 1934; Death Takes a Holiday 1934; Operator 13 1934; The Painted Veil 1934; After Office Hours 1935; Enchanted April 1935; She Married Her Boss 1935; The Devil Is a Sissy 1936; That Certain Woman 1937; The Great Man Votes 1939; In Name Only 1939; Dance, Girl, Dance 1940; Kiss and Tell 1945

Alexander, Khandi (1957-) Poetic Justice 1993; Tina: What's Love Got to Do with It 1993; Perfect Strangers 2004

Alexander, Olly Enter the Void 2010; God Help the Girl 2012; Great Expectations 2012; Le Week-end 2013

Alexander, Richard (1902-1989) Law and Order 1932; Flash Gordon 1936

Alexander (1), Ross (1907-1937) The Wiser Sex 1932; Flirtation Walk 1934; Captain Blood 1935; A Midsummer Night's Dream 1935; Shipmates Forever 1935; China Clipper 1936

Alexander, Sarah Going Off, Big Time 2000; Perfect Strangers 2004

Alexander, Tad (1922-2012) Rasputin and the Empress 1932; Broadway to Hollywood 1933

Alexander, Terence (1923-2009) The One That Got Away 1957; The Square Peg 1958; The League of Gentlemen 1960; Bitter Harvest 1963; Judith 1966; Only When I Larf 1968; What's Good for the Goose 1969; Waterloo 1970

Alexander, Terry (1947-) Day of the Dead 1985; Conspiracy Theory 1997

Alexandridis, Hélène Thérèse 1986; Lady Chatterley 2006

Alexi-Malle, Adam (1964-) Bowfinger 1999; Hidalgo 2003

Alfonsi, Lidia (1928-) Morgan the Pirate 1960; The Trojan War 1961; Black Sabbath 1963

Alfonso, Yves (1944-) Made in USA 1966; Vladimir et Rosa 1970

Alford, Phillip (1948-) To Kill a Mockingbird 1962; Shenandoah 1965

Alfredson, Hans (1931-) Pippi Longstocking 1968; The Emigrants 1971; The New Land 1972; The Simple-Minded Murderer 1982

Ali, Arsher Four Lions 2010; All in Good Time 2012; Remainder 2015

Ali, Muhammad aka **Clay, Cassius** (1942-2016) Requiem for a Heavyweight 1962; Muhammad Ali, the Greatest 1974; The Greatest 1977; Body and Soul 1981; When We Were Kings 1996; Soul Power 2008

Ali, Tatyana aka **Ali, Tatyana M** (1979-) Eddie Murphy Raw 1987; Fall into Darkness 1996

Alice, Mary (1941-) To Sleep with Anger 1990; Freedom Road: the Vernon Johns Story 1994; Down in the Delta 1997; The Matrix Revolutions 2003

Alidoosti, Taraneh The Beautiful City 2004; Shirin 2008; About Elly 2009

Alis, Jorge Play 2005; Bring Me the Head of the Machine Gun Woman 2013

Alison, Dorothy (1925-1992) The Maggie 1953; Turn the Key Softly 1953; Child's Play 1954; The Long Arm 1956; Reach for the Sky 1956; The Scamp 1957; The Man Upstairs 1958; Life in Emergency Ward 10 1959; Two Living, One Dead 1961; Blind Terror 1971; Dr Jekyll & Sister Hyde 1971; The Amazing Mr Blunden 1972

Allam, Roger (1953-) Wilt 1989; V for Vendetta 2005; Speed Racer 2008; Tamara Drewe 2010; The Iron Lady 2011; The Woman in Black 2011; The Book Thief 2014; Mr Holmes 2014; The Lady in the Van 2015

Allan, Elizabeth (1908-1990) Ace of Aces 1933; Men in White 1934; David Copperfield 1935; Java Head 1935; Mark of the Vampire 1935; A Tale of Two Cities 1935; A Woman Rebels 1936; Camille 1937; Slave Ship 1937; Saloon Bar 1940; The Great Mr Handel 1942; Went the Day Well? 1942; That Dangerous Age 1949; Folly to Be Wise 1952; Front Page Story 1953; The Heart of the Matter 1953; The Brain Machine 1954; Grip of the Strangler 1958

Allan, Marguerite Blossom Time 1934; Doctor's Orders 1934

Allbritton, Louise (1920-1979) Pittsburgh 1942; Who Done It? 1942; Son of Dracula 1943; The Egg and I 1947; Sitting Pretty 1948

Alldredge, Michael (1940-1997) The Incredible Melting Man 1977; About Last Night... 1986; Promise 1986; Robot Jox 1989

Allégret, Catherine (1946-) The Sleeping Car Murders 1965; Last Tango in Paris 1972; Burnt Barns 1973; Paul and Michelle 1974; Chanel Solitaire 1981; Nazi Hunter: the Beate Klarsfeld Story 1984

Allen, Adrianne (1907-1993) Merrily We Go to Hell 1932; The October Man 1947; The Final Test 1953

Allen, Aleisha Are We There Yet? 2005; Are We Done Yet? 2007

Allen, Alfie (1986-) Elizabeth 1998; Powder 2011; SoulBoy 2010; Confine 2012; John Wick 2014; Plastic 2014

Allen, Barbara Jo aka **Vague, Vera** (1905-1974) Kiss the Boys Goodbye 1941; Girl Rush 1944; Rosie the Riveter 1944; Mohawk 1956; Sleeping Beauty 1959

Allen, Chad (1974-) TerrorVision 1986; Murder in New Hampshire 1991

Allen, Chesney (1894-1982) *A Fire Has Been Arranged* 1935; *Alf's Button Afloat* 1938; *Gasbags* 1940; *We'll Smile Again* 1942; *Dreaming* 1944; *Here Comes the Sun* 1945

Allen, Corey (1934-2010) *Rebel without a Cause* 1955; *The Big Caper* 1957; *Party Girl* 1958; *Key Witness* 1960

Allen, Debbie (1950-) *Fame* 1980; *Jo Jo Dancer, Your Life Is Calling* 1986; *Fame* 2009

Allen, Doug *The Firm* 2009; *Screwed* 2011; *The Guvnors* 2014; *We Are Monster* 2014

Allen, Elizabeth (1929-2006) *From the Terrace* 1960; *Donovan's Reef* 1963; *The Carey Treatment* 1972

Allen, Fiona *Gladiatress* 2002; *Fat Slags* 2004

Allen (2), Fred (1894-1956) *Thanks a Million* 1935; *Sally, Irene and Mary* 1938; *It's in the Bag* 1945; *O Henry's Full House* 1952; *We're Not Married* 1952

Allen, Ginger Lynn (1962-) *Buried Alive* 1990; *Leather Jackets* 1991; *Bound & Gagged: a Love Story* 1992

Allen, Gracie (1902-1964) *The Big Broadcast* 1932; *International House* 1933; *Six of a Kind* 1934; *We're Not Dressing* 1934; *The Big Broadcast of 1936* 1935; *The Big Broadcast of 1937* 1936; *A Damsel in Distress* 1937; *College Swing* 1938; *The Gracie Allen Murder Case* 1939; *Honolulu* 1939

Allen, Jack (1907-1995) *The Four Feathers* 1939; *The Sound Barrier* 1952; *Impulse* 1955; *Man from Tangier* 1957; *Life in Danger* 1959; *The Breaking Point* 1961

Allen, Joan (1956-) *Manhunter* 1986; *Peggy Sue Got Married* 1986; *Tucker: the Man and His Dream* 1988; *In Country* 1989; *Without Warning: the James Brady Story* 1991; *Ethan Frome* 1993; *Innocent Moves* 1993; *Josh and SAM* 1993; *Mad Love* 1995; *Nixon* 1995; *The Crucible* 1996; *Face/Off* 1997; *The Ice Storm* 1997; *Pleasantville* 1998; *The Contender* 2000; *When the Sky Falls* 2000; *The Notebook* 2003; *The Bourne Supremacy* 2004; *Yes* 2004; *The Upside of Anger* 2005; *Bonneville* 2006; *The Bourne Ultimatum* 2007; *Death Race* 2008; *Hachi: a dog's Tale* 2008; *Georgia O'Keeffe* 2009; *The Bourne Legacy* 2012; *Room* 2015

Allen, Judith (1911-1996) *This Day and Age* 1933; *Bright Eyes* 1934; *The Old-Fashioned Way* 1934

Allen, Karen (1951-) *The Wanderers* 1979; *Raiders of the Lost Ark* 1981; *Shoot the Moon* 1982; *Split Image* 1982; *Starman* 1984; *Until September* 1984; *Backfire* 1987; *The Glass Menagerie* 1987; *Scrooged* 1988; *Animal Behavior* 1989; *The Turning* 1992; *Ghost in the Machine* 1993; *King of the Hill* 1993; *The Sandlot* 1993; *The Perfect Storm* 2000; *In the Bedroom* 2001; *Indiana Jones and the Kingdom of the Crystal Skull* 2008

Allen, Keith (1953-) *Loose Connections* 1983; *The Supergrass* 1985; *Comrades: a Lanternist's Account of the Tolpuddle Martyrs and What Became of Them* 1986; *Chicago Joe and the Showgirl* 1989; *Kafka* 1991; *Rebecca's Daughters* 1991; *Carry On Columbus* 1992; *Beyond Bedlam* 1993; *Second Best* 1993; *The Young Americans* 1993; *Captives* 1994; *Shallow Grave* 1994; *Blue Juice* 1995; *Loch Ness* 1995; *Rancid Aluminium* 1999; *Ma Femme Est une Actrice* 2001; *Agent Cody Banks 2: Destination London* 2003; *De-Lovely* 2004; *Vinyl* 2012; *Hector* 2015

Allen, Krista *Avalon: beyond the Abyss* 1999; *The Final Destination* 2009

Allen, Lee *Funny Girl* 1968; *Ill Manors* 2012

Allen, Nancy (1950-) *Carrie* 1976; *I Wanna Hold Your Hand* 1978; *Home Movies* 1979; *1941* 1979; *Dressed to Kill* 1980; *Blow Out* 1981; *Strange Invaders* 1983; *The Buddy System* 1984; *Not for Publication* 1984; *The Philadelphia Experiment* 1984; *RoboCop* 1987; *Poltergeist III* 1988; *RoboCop 2* 1990; *RoboCop 3* 1993; *The Man Who Wouldn't Die* 1995; *Dusting Cliff 7* 1996

Allen, Patrick (1927-2006) *Dial M for Murder* 1954; *Confession* 1955; *The Man Who Wouldn't Talk* 1957; *I Was Monty's Double* 1958; *Tread Softly Stranger* 1958; *Never Take Sweets from a Stranger* 1960; *Night Creatures* 1962; *Night of the Big Heat* 1967; *The Body Stealers* 1969; *When Dinosaurs Ruled the Earth* 1969; *Puppet on a Chain* 1970; *The Sea Wolves* 1980; *Agatha Christie's Murder Is Easy* 1982

Allen, Penelope aka **Allen, Penny** *Scarecrow* 1973; *Dog Day Afternoon* 1975

Allen, Rae (1926-) *Damn Yankees* 1958; *Where's Poppa?* 1970

Allen, Rex (1920-1999) *Trail of Robin Hood* 1950; *None but the Brave* 1960; *The Incredible Journey* 1963; *Charlotte's Web* 1973

Allen, Robert (1906-1998) *The Black Room* 1935; *Crime and Punishment* 1935

Allen, Ronald (1930-1991) *A Night to Remember* 1958; *Hell Boats* 1970; *Eat the Rich* 1987

Allen, Rosalind *Children of the Corn II: the Final Sacrifice* 1993; *Ticks* 1993

Allen, Sheila (1932-2011) *Children of the Damned* 1964; *The Alphabet Murders* 1966; *Viva Knievel!* 1977; *Pascali's Island* 1988

Allen, Sian Barbara (1946-) *You'll Like My Mother* 1972; *Billy Two Hats* 1973; *The Lindbergh Kidnapping Case* 1976

Allen, Steve (1921-2000) *The Benny Goodman Story* 1955; *Warning Shot* 1967; *Where Were You When the Lights Went Out?* 1968; *The Comic* 1969

Allen, Tanya (1975-) *Regeneration* 1997; *Silent Hill* 2006

Allen, Tim (1953-) *The Santa Clause* 1994; *Toy Story* 1995; *For Richer or Poorer* 1997; *Jungle 2 Jungle* 1997; *Galaxy Quest* 1999; *Toy Story 2* 1999; *Joe Somebody* 2001; *Big Trouble* 2002; *The Santa Clause 2* 2002; *Christmas with the Kranks* 2004; *The Santa Clause 3: the Escape Clause* 2006; *The Shaggy Dog* 2006; *Zoom* 2006; *Redbelt* 2007; *Wild Hogs* 2007; *Toy Story 3* 2010; *Chimpanzee* 2012; *Toy Story 4* 2017

Allen, Todd (1960-) *Witchboard* 1987; *The Apostle* 1997

Allen, Woody (1935-) *What's New, Pussycat?* 1965; *What's Up, Tiger Lily?* 1966; *Casino Royale* 1967; *Take the Money and Run* 1969; *Bananas* 1971; *Everything You Always Wanted to Know about Sex ... but Were Afraid to Ask* 1972; *Play It Again, Sam* 1972; *Sleeper* 1973; *Love and Death* 1975; *The Front* 1976; *Annie Hall* 1977; *Manhattan* 1979; *Stardust Memories* 1980; *A Midsummer Night's Sex Comedy* 1982; *Zelig* 1983; *Broadway Danny Rose* 1984; *Hannah and Her Sisters* 1986; *King Lear - Fear and Loathing* 1987; *Radio Days* 1987; *Crimes and Misdemeanors* 1989; *New York Stories* 1989; *Scenes from a Mall* 1991; *Shadows and Fog* 1991; *Husbands and Wives* 1992; *Manhattan Murder Mystery* 1993; *Don't Drink the Water* 1994; *Mighty Aphrodite* 1995; *Everyone Says I Love You* 1996; *Deconstructing Harry* 1997; *The Sunshine Boys* 1997; *Wild Man Blues* 1997; *Antz* 1998; *The Impostors* 1998; *Sweet and Lowdown* 1999; *Company Man* 2000; *Picking Up the Pieces* 2000; *Small Time Crooks* 2000; *The Curse of the Jade Scorpion* 2001; *Hollywood Ending* 2002; *Anything Else* 2003; *Scoop* 2006; *Paris-Manhattan* 2012; *To Rome with Love* 2012; *Fading Gigolo* 2013

Allenby, Frank (1898-1953) *The Black Sheep of Whitehall* 1941; *Madame Bovary* 1949; *Soldiers Three* 1951

Allerson, Alexander (1930-) *The McKenzie Break* 1970; *Chinese Roulette* 1976; *I Only Want You to Love Me* 1976; *Despair* 1978

Alley, Kirstie (1951-) *Star Trek II: the Wrath of Khan* 1982; *Champions* 1983; *Blind Date* 1984; *Summer School* 1987; *Deadly Pursuit* 1988; *Look Who's Talking* 1989; *Loverboy* 1989; *Look Who's Talking Too* 1990; *Madhouse* 1990; *Sibling Rivalry* 1990; *Look Who's Talking Now!* 1993; *David's Mother* 1994; *It Takes Two* 1995; *Village of the Damned* 1995; *Deconstructing Harry* 1997; *For Richer or Poorer* 1997; *Drop Dead Gorgeous* 1999; *Profoundly Normal* 2003; *Family Sins* 2004; *While I Was Gone* 2004; *And She Was* 2007

Allgood, Sara (1883-1950) *Blackmail* 1929; *Juno and the Paycock* 1930; *Lazybones* 1935; *It's Love Again* 1936; *Storm in a Teacup* 1937; *How Green Was My Valley* 1941; *That Hamilton Woman* 1941; *Life Begins at 8.30* 1942; *Roxie Hart* 1942; *The War against Mrs Hadley* 1942; *Jane Eyre* 1943; *The Lodger* 1944; *Kitty* 1945; *The Strange Affair of Uncle Harry* 1945; *The Spiral Staircase* 1946; *The Fabulous Dorseys* 1947; *Mother Wore Tights* 1947; *My Wild Irish Rose* 1947; *The Accused* 1949; *Cheaper by the Dozen* 1950

Allister, Claud aka **Allister, Claude** (1888-1970) *Bulldog Drummond* 1929; *Monte Carlo* 1930; *The Return of Bulldog Drummond* 1934; *Those Were the Days* 1934; *Confirm or Deny* 1941

Allman, Jamie Anne *Prairie Fever* 2008; *Any Day Now* 2012

Allnutt, Wendy (1946-) *Oh! What a Lovely War* 1969; *From beyond the Grave* 1973

Allwyn, Astrid (1905-1978) *Love Affair* 1932; *The White Parade* 1934; *Accent on Youth* 1935; *Hands across the Table* 1935; *Dimples* 1936; *Follow the Fleet* 1936; *Love Affair* 1939; *Miracles for Sale* 1939

Allyson, June (1917-2006) *Best Foot Forward* 1943; *Girl Crazy* 1943; *Meet the People* 1944; *Music for Millions* 1944; *Two Girls and a Sailor* 1944; *The Sailor Takes a Wife* 1945; *The Secret Heart* 1946; *Two Sisters from Boston* 1946; *Good News* 1947; *High Barbaree* 1947; *The Three Musketeers* 1948; *Little Women* 1949; *The Stratton Story* 1949; *Right Cross* 1950; *The Girl in White* 1952; *Battle Circus* 1953; *The Glenn Miller Story* 1953; *Remains to Be Seen* 1953; *Executive Suite* 1954; *Woman's World* 1954; *The McConnell Story* 1955; *Strategic Air Command* 1955; *The Opposite Sex* 1956; *You Can't Run Away from It* 1956; *Interlude* 1957; *My Man Godfrey* 1957; *A Stranger in My Arms* 1959; *They Only Kill Their Masters* 1972

Almagor, Gila (1939-) *Sallah* 1964; *Every Time We Say Goodbye* 1986

Alonso, Chelo (1933-) *Goliath and the Barbarians* 1959; *Morgan the Pirate* 1960

Alonso, Daniella *The Hills Have Eyes II* 2007; *Wrong Turn 2: Dead End* 2007; *Paul Blart: Mall Cop 2* 2015

Alonso, Ernesto (1919-2007) *Wuthering Heights* 1953; *The Criminal Life of Archibaldo de la Cruz* 1955

Alonso, Laz (1974-) *Captivity* 2006; *Stomp the Yard* 2006; *This Christmas* 2007; *Fast & Furious* 2009; *Straw Dogs* 2011; *Battle of the Year* 2013

Alonso, Maria Conchita (1957-) *Moscow on the Hudson* 1984; *A Fine Mess* 1986; *Touch and Go* 1986; *Extreme Prejudice* 1987; *The Running Man* 1987; *Colors* 1988; *Vampire's Kiss* 1988; *Predator 2* 1990; *The House of the Spirits* 1993; *Caught* 1996; *High Noon* 2000; *Material Girls* 2006

Alpay, David *Ararat* 2002; *Man of the Year* 2006; *Unstable* 2009

Alt, Carol (1960-) *Ring of Steel* 1994; *Private Parts* 1997

Alterio, Héctor (1929-) *Camila* 1984; *The Official Story* 1985; *I, the Worst of All* 1990; *Son of the Bride* 2001

Altin, Josef *Ruby Blue* 2007; *Vendetta* 2013

Altman, Bruce (1955-) *Regarding Henry* 1991; *My New Gun* 1992; *Rookie of the Year* 1993; *To Gillian on Her 37th Birthday* 1996; *LIE* 2001; *Matchstick Men* 2003; *The American* 2010

Altman, Robert (1925-2006) *Luck, Trust & Ketchup* 1994; *Altman* 2014

Alvarado, Don (1904-1967) *Rio Rita* 1929; *Beau Ideal* 1931; *Lady with a Past* 1932; *Black Beauty* 1933; *The Devil Is a Woman* 1935; *The Big Steal* 1949

Alvarado, Trini (1967-) *Rich Kids* 1979; *Times Square* 1980; *Mrs Soffel* 1984; *Satisfaction* 1988; *Stella* 1990; *American Friends* 1991; *The Babe* 1992; *Little Women* 1994; *The Perez Family* 1995; *The Frighteners* 1996; *Paulie* 1998; *The Last Dance* 2000

Alvarez, Edmundo Rivera *Creature from the Haunted Sea* 1961; *The Possession of Joel Delaney* 1971

Alvin, John (1917-2009) *The Fighting Sullivans* 1944; *Objective, Burma!* 1945; *The Beast with Five Fingers* 1946

Amalric, Mathieu (1965-) *Ma Vie Sexuelle* 1996; *Alice et Martin* 1998; *Late August, Early September* 1998; *Kings & Queen* 2004; *I Saw Ben Barka Get Killed* 2005; *Munich* 2005; *The Singer* 2006; *The Diving-Bell and the Butterfly* 2007; *Heartbeat Detector* 2007; *A Secret* 2007; *A Christmas Tale* 2008; *Mesrine: Public Enemy No 1* 2008; *Quantum of Solace* 2008; *Wild Grass* 2008; *The Extraordinary Adventures of Adèle Blanc-Sec* 2010; *On Tour* 2010; *Cosmopolis* 2012; *Venus in Fur* 2013; *The Forbidden Room* 2015

Amandes, Tom (1956-) *The Long Kiss Goodnight* 1996; *Brokedown Palace* 1999; *Bonneville* 2006

Amann, Betty (1906-1990) *Asphalt* 1928; *Rich and Strange* 1932

Amato, Vincenzo *Respiro* 2002; *Golden Door* 2006

Ambler, Joss (1900-1959) *Come On George* 1939; *Trouble Brewing* 1939; *The Black Sheep of Whitehall* 1941; *Much Too Shy* 1942; *Here Comes the Sun* 1945; *Ghost Ship* 1952; *The Long Arm* 1956

Ambrose, Lauren (1978-) *Can't Hardly Wait* 1998; *Cold Souls* 2008; *Love and Other Impossible Pursuits* 2009; *Where the Wild Things Are* 2009; *Grassroots* 2012

Ameche, Don (1908-1993) *Ladies in Love* 1936; *One in a Million* 1936; *In Old Chicago* 1937; *Love Is News* 1937; *You Can't Have Everything* 1937; *Alexander's Ragtime Band* 1938; *Happy Landing* 1938; *Hollywood Cavalcade* 1939; *Midnight* 1939; *The Story of Alexander Graham Bell* 1939; *Swanee River* 1939; *The Three Musketeers* 1939; *Down Argentine Way* 1940; *Four Sons* 1940; *Lillian Russell* 1940; *Confirm or Deny* 1941; *The Feminine Touch* 1941; *Kiss the Boys Goodbye* 1941; *Moon over Miami* 1941; *That Night in Rio* 1941; *The Magnificent Dope* 1942; *Happy Land* 1943; *Heaven Can Wait* 1943; *Greenwich Village* 1944; *Guest Wife* 1944; *Wing and a Prayer* 1944; *So Goes My Love* 1946; *That's My Man* 1947; *Sleep, My Love* 1948; *Slightly French* 1949; *The Boatniks* 1970; *Suppose They Gave a War and Nobody Came?* 1970; *Trading Places* 1983; *Cocoon* 1985; *Bigfoot and the Hendersons* 1987; *Cocoon: the Return* 1988; *Coming to America* 1988; *Things Change* 1988; *Oscar* 1991; *Folks!* 1992; *Homeward Bound: the Incredible Journey* 1993; *Corrina, Corrina* 1994

Amédée (1923-1985) *Jeux Interdits* 1953; *Gates of Paris* 1957

Ameen, Ami *Kidulthood* 2005; *The Maze Runner* 2014

Amell, Robbie *The Duff* 2015; *Max* 2015

Amell, Stephen *Closing the Ring* 2006; *Teenage Mutant Ninja Turtles - Out of the Shadows* 2016

Amendola, Claudio (1963-) *The Horseman on the Roof* 1995; *Suburra* 2015

America, Paul (1944-1982) *My Hustler* 1965; *Ciao! Manhattan* 1973

Ames, Adrienne (1907-1947) *Sinners in the Sun* 1932; *The Death Kiss* 1933; *George White's Scandals* 1934; *You're Telling Me!* 1934; *Black Sheep* 1935; *Woman Wanted* 1935

Ames, Leon aka **Waycoff, Leon** (1902-1993) *Murders in the Rue Morgue* 1932; *Mysterious Mr Moto* 1938; *Mr Moto in Danger Island* 1939; *Crime Doctor* 1943; *Meet Me in St Louis* 1944; *The Thin Man Goes Home* 1944; *Son of Lassie* 1945; *Yolanda and the Thief* 1945; *The Postman Always Rings Twice* 1946; *Lady in the Lake* 1947; *Merton of the Movies* 1947; *Song of the Thin Man* 1947; *On an Island with You* 1948; *The Velvet Touch* 1948; *Little Women* 1949; *Scene of the Crime* 1949; *The Big Hangover* 1950; *The Happy Years* 1950; *Watch the Birdie* 1950; *Cattle Drive* 1951; *On Moonlight Bay* 1951; *Angel Face* 1953; *By the Light of the Silvery Moon* 1953; *Let's Do It Again* 1953; *From the Terrace* 1960; *The Absent-Minded Professor* 1961; *Son of Flubber* 1962; *The Misadventures of Merlin Jones* 1964; *The Monkey's Uncle* 1965; *Testament* 1983; *Peggy Sue Got Married* 1986

Ames, Ramsay (1919-1998) *Calling Dr Death* 1943; *Ali Baba and the Forty Thieves* 1944; *The Mummy's Ghost* 1944

Ames, Robert (1889-1931) *The Trespasser* 1929; *Holiday* 1930

Amick, Mädchen (1970-) *The Borrower* 1989; *The Boyfriend School* 1990; *Sleepwalkers* 1992; *Twin Peaks: Fire Walk with Me* 1992; *Dream Lover* 1993; *Love, Cheat & Steal* 1994; *The Hunted* 1998; *Hangman* 2000; *Lies and Deception* 2005; *Priest* 2010

Amidou (1942-2013) *Man in the Trunk* 1973; *And Now... Ladies and Gentlemen* 2002

Amis, Suzy (1962-) *The Big Town* 1987; *Plain Clothes* 1988; *Rocket Gibraltar* 1988; *Where the Heart Is* 1990; *The Ballad of Little Jo* 1993; *Blown Away* 1994; *Nadja* 1995; *The Usual Suspects* 1995; *Cadillac Ranch* 1996; *One Good Turn* 1996; *Firestorm* 1998; *Judgment Day* 1999

Amos, John (1941-) *The World's Greatest Athlete* 1973; *Let's Do It Again* 1975; *Touched by Love* 1979; *The Beastmaster* 1982; *Dance of the Dwarfs* 1983; *American Flyers* 1985; *Coming to America* 1988; *Lock Up* 1989; *Die Hard 2: Die Harder* 1990; *Two Evil Eyes* 1990; *Mac* 1992; *Disappearing Acts* 2000; *Dr Dolittle 3* 2006

Amstell, Simon *Black Pond* 2011; *Brand: a Second Coming* 2015

Amsterdam, Morey (1908-1996) *Machine Gun Kelly* 1958; *Beach Party* 1963; *The Horse in the Gray Flannel Suit* 1968

Amstutz, Roland (1942-1997) *Slow Motion* 1980; *Nouvelle Vague* 1990

Amurri, Eva aka **Amurri Martino, Eva** (1985-) *The Banger Sisters* 2002; *The Education of Charlie Banks* 2007; *The Life before Her Eyes* 2007; *That's My Boy* 2012

Anaya, Elena (1975-) *Sex and Lucia* 2001; *Van Helsing* 2004; *Fragile* 2005; *Savage Grace* 2007; *Mesrine: Killer Instinct* 2008; *Hierro* 2009; *Point Blank* 2010; *The Skin I Live In* 2011

Ancona, Ronni (1968-) *Stella Street* 2004; *Penelope* 2006

Anconina, Richard (1953-) *Love Songs* 1984; *Police* 1985

Anders, Glenn (1889-1981) *Laughter* 1930; *The Lady from Shanghai* 1948; *M* 1951; *Tarzan's Peril* 1951

Anders, Luana (1940-1996) *Reform School Girl* 1957; *Pit and the Pendulum* 1961; *Dementia 13* 1963; *That Cold Day in the Park* 1969; *When the Legends Die* 1972; *The Killing Kind* 1973

Anders, Merry (1932-) *The Night Runner* 1957; *Violent Road* 1958; *Beauty and the Beast* 1962; *The Time Traveller* 1964; *Tickle Me* 1965

Andersen, Bridgette (1975-) *Savannah Smiles* 1982; *Fever Pitch* 1985

Andersen, Elga (1939-1994) *A Global Affair* 1964; *Le Mans* 1971

Anderson, Anthony (1970-) *Romeo Must Die* 2000; *Exit Wounds* 2001; *Two Can Play That Game* 2001; *Barbershop* 2002; *Agent Cody Banks 2: Destination London* 2003; *Cradle 2 the Grave* 2003; *Kangaroo Jack* 2003; *Malibu's Most Wanted* 2003; *Scary Movie 3* 2003; *Hoodwinked* 2005; *Hustle & Flow* 2005; *Transformers* 2007; *The Back-Up Plan* 2010; *Barbershop: a Fresh Cut* 2016

Anderson, Barbara (1945-) *Don't Be Afraid of the Dark* 1973; *The Six Million Dollar Man* 1973; *The Return of Ironside* 1993

Anderson, Daphne (1922-2013) *The Beggar's Opera* 1953; *Hobson's Choice* 1953

Anderson, Dion *Roe vs Wade* 1989; *Dying Young* 1991

Anderson, Donna (1925-) *On the Beach* 1959; *Inherit the Wind* 1960

Anderson, Eddie "Rochester" (1905-1977) *What Price Hollywood?* 1932; *Buck Benny Rides Again* 1940; *The Birth of the Blues* 1941; *Cabin in the Sky* 1943; *The Meanest Man in the World* 1943; *Broadway Rhythm* 1944; *Brewster's Millions* 1945; *The Sailor Takes a Wife* 1945

Anderson, Erich *Friday the 13th: the Final Chapter* 1984; *Jack* 2000

Anderson, Erika (1965-) *A Nightmare on Elm Street 5: The Dream Child* 1989; *Zandalee* 1991

Anderson, Esther *Two Gentlemen Sharing* 1969; *A Warm December* 1973

Anderson, Gene (1931-1965) *The Shakedown* 1959; *The Day the Earth Caught Fire* 1961; *The Break* 1962

Anderson, Gillian (1968-) *The Turning* 1992; *Chicago Cab* 1998; *The Mighty* 1998; *Playing by Heart* 1998; *The X-Files* 1998; *The House of Mirth* 2000; *Princess Mononoke* 2001; *A Cock and Bull Story* 2005; *The Mighty Celt* 2005; *The Last King of Scotland* 2006; *Straightheads* 2007; *How to Lose Friends & Alienate People* 2008; *The X-Files: I Want to Believe* 2008; *Boogie Woogie* 2009; *From Up on Poppy Hill* 2011; *Johnny English Reborn* 2011; *Shadow Dancer* 2012; *Sister* 2012; *Mr Morgan's Last Love* 2013; *Robot Overlords* 2014

Anderson, Herbert (1917-1994) *The Male Animal* 1942; *The Benny Goodman Story* 1955; *My Man Godfrey* 1957

Anderson (2), James (1921-1969) *Along the Great Divide* 1951; *Five* 1951; *Ruby Gentry* 1952; *Take the Money and Run* 1969

Anderson, Jean (1908-2001) *The Romantic Age* 1949; *The Kidnappers* 1953; *A Town like Alice* 1956; *Lucky Jim* 1957; *Robbery under Arms* 1957; *SOS Pacific* 1959; *Spare the Rod* 1961; *Waltz of the Toreadors* 1962; *The Three Lives of Thomasina* 1963; *The Road Builder* 1971; *The Lady Vanishes* 1979; *Leon the Pig Farmer* 1992

Anderson (1), Joe (1982-) *Becoming Jane* 2006; *Copying Beethoven* 2006; *Across the Universe* 2007; *Control* 2007; *Amelia* 2009; *Love Happens* 2009; *The Crazies* 2010; *Horns* 2013

Anderson, John (1922-1992) *Ride the High Country* 1962; *The Hallelujah Trail* 1965; *Namu, the Killer Whale* 1966; *Welcome to Hard Times* 1967; *Day of the Evil Gun* 1968; *5 Card Stud* 1968; *The Great Bank Robbery* 1969; *A Man Called Gannon* 1969; *Young Billy Young*

1969; Soldier Blue 1970; Molly and Lawless John 1972; Executive Action 1973; The Dove 1974; Zoot Suit 1981
Anderson, Judith (1897-1992) Rebecca 1940; All through the Night 1942; Kings Row 1942; Edge of Darkness 1943; Stage Door Canteen 1943; Laura 1944; And Then There Were None 1945; Diary of a Chambermaid 1946; Specter of the Rose 1946; The Strange Love of Martha Ivers 1946; Pursued 1947; The Red House 1947; Tycoon 1947; The Furies 1950; Salome 1953; Cat on a Hot Tin Roof 1958; Don't Bother to Knock 1961; A Man Called Horse 1970
Anderson, Kevin (1960-) Orphans 1987; Miles from Home 1988; In Country 1989; Liebestraum 1991; Sleeping with the Enemy 1991; Hoffa 1992; The Night We Never Met 1993; Rising Sun 1993; Eye of God 1997; Firelight 1997; A Thousand Acres 1997; Gregory's Two Girls 1999; Wilde Salomé 2011; Salomé 2013
Anderson, Lindsay (1923-1994) Inadmissible Evidence 1968; Chariots of Fire 1981; Never Apologize 2007
Anderson, Loni (1946-) The Jayne Mansfield Story 1980; Stroker Ace 1983; All Dogs Go to Heaven 1989; Munchie 1992; Munchie Strikes Back 1994; A Night at the Roxbury 1998
Anderson, Mary (1918-2014) Cheers for Miss Bishop 1941; Lifeboat 1944; To Each His Own 1946; The Underworld Story 1950
Anderson, Melissa Sue aka **Anderson, Melissa** (1962-) Happy Birthday to Me 1981; Dead Men Don't Die 1991
Anderson, Melody (1955-) Flash Gordon 1980; The Boy in Blue 1986; Firewalker 1986; Cannonball Fever 1989
Anderson Jr, Michael (1943-) The Sundowners 1960; In Search of the Castaways 1961; Play It Cool 1962; Reach for Glory 1962; Dear Heart 1964; The Glory Guys 1965; Major Dundee 1965; The Sons of Katie Elder 1965; Logan's Run 1976; Sunset Grill 1992
Anderson, Michael J (1953-) Mulholland Drive 2001; Snow White 2001
Anderson, Miles (1953-) Gunbus 1986; Cry Freedom 1987; Fast Food 1998; The King Is Alive 2000
Anderson, Pamela aka **Anderson Lee, Pamela** (1967-) Good Cop, Bad Cop 1993; Snapdragon 1993; Barb Wire 1995; Naked Souls 1995; Borat: Cultural Learnings of America for Make Benefit Glorious Nation of Kazakhstan 2006; Superhero Movie 2008
Anderson (2), Paul The Firm 2009; Passion 2012; Pigg 2012; Electricity 2014; '71 2014
Anderson, Richard (1926-) The Magnificent Yankee 1950; Scaramouche 1952; Escape from Fort Bravo 1953; Give a Girl a Break 1953; I Love Melvin 1953; A Cry in the Night 1956; Forbidden Planet 1956; The Buster Keaton Story 1957; Paths of Glory 1957; The Long, Hot Summer 1958; Compulsion 1959; The Gunfight at Dodge City 1959; Johnny Cool 1963; Seconds 1966; The Ride to Hangman's Tree 1967; The Honkers 1971; The Glass Shield 1995
Anderson (2), Robert (1923-) The Night Runner 1957; Buchanan Rides Alone 1958
Anderson, Rona (1926-2013) Sleeping Car to Trieste 1948; Floodtide 1949; Home to Danger 1951; Scrooge 1951; The Black Rider 1954; The Flaw 1954; Shadow of a Man 1954; Little Red Monkey 1955; Stock Car 1955; The Bay of Saint Michel 1963; Devils of Darkness 1964
Anderson, Ross Paising Waylon 2004; The Silent Storm 2014
Anderson, Stanley (1939-) He Said, She Said 1991; Arlington Road 1998; SIMØNE 2002
Anderson, Sylvia (1927-2016) Thunderbirds Are Go! 1966; Thunderbird 6 1968; Filmed in Supermarionation 2014
Anderson, Warner (1911-1976) Destination Tokyo 1943; Abbott and Costello in Hollywood 1945; Objective, Burma! 1945; My Reputation 1946; High Wall 1947; Destination Moon 1950; Santa Fe 1951; A Lion Is in the Streets 1953; The Star 1953; Drum Beat 1954; The Blackboard Jungle 1955; A Lawless Street 1955; The Violent Men 1955; The Lineup 1958; Rio Conchos 1964
Andersson, Bibi (1935-) Smiles of a Summer Night 1955; The Seventh Seal 1957; So Close to Life 1957; Wild Strawberries 1957; The Magician 1958;

The Devil's Eye 1960; Square of Violence 1961; All These Women 1964; Duel at Diablo 1966; My Sister, My Love 1966; Persona 1966; A Passion 1969; The Touch 1971; Scenes from a Marriage 1973; An Enemy of the People 1977; I Never Promised You a Rose Garden 1977; Airport '79: the Concorde 1979; Quintet 1979; Exposed 1983; Babette's Feast 1987
Andersson, Harriet (1932-) Summer with Monika 1952; Sawdust and Tinsel 1953; Lesson in Love 1954; Dreams 1955; Smiles of a Summer Night 1955; Through a Glass Darkly 1961; All These Women 1964; The Deadly Affair 1966; Cries and Whispers 1972; Dogville 2003
Andersson, Peter The Girl with the Dragon Tattoo 2009; The Girl Who Played with Fire 2009; The Vatican Tapes 2015
Andes, Keith (1920-2005) Blackbeard the Pirate 1952; Clash by Night 1952; Split Second 1953; Away All Boats 1956; Back from Eternity 1956; Pillars of the Sky 1956; The Girl Most Likely 1957; Interlude 1957
Ando, Masanobu (1975-) Kids Return 1996; Battle Royale 2000
Andorai, Peter (1948-) Confidence 1979; Mephisto 1981; Sweet Emma Dear Böbe 1992
Andre, Annette (1939-) This Is My Street 1963; A Funny Thing Happened on the Way to the Forum 1966
André, Marcel (1885-1974) La Belle et la Bête 1946; Les Parents Terribles 1948; Les Mains Sales 1951
Andréani, Jean-Pierre Goto, l'île d'Amour 1968; The Story of O 1975
Andreeff, Starr (1964-) Out of the Dark 1988; Amityville Dollhouse 1996
Andreichenko, Natasha aka **Andreichenko, Natalya** (1956-) Sibiriada 1979; Little Odessa 1994
Andress, Ursula (1936-) Dr No 1962; 4 for Texas 1963; Fun in Acapulco 1963; Nightmare in the Sun 1964; Once before I Die 1965; She 1965; The Tenth Victim 1965; Up to His Ears 1965; What's New, Pussycat? 1965; The Blue Max 1966; Casino Royale 1967; The Southern Star 1969; Perfect Friday 1970; Red Sun 1971; The 5th Musketeer 1979; Clash of the Titans 1981; Cremaster 5 1997
Andreu, Simon (1941-) Bad Man's River 1971; Triumphs of a Man Called Horse 1983; Blood and Sand 1989
Andrews, Anthony (1948-) A War of Children 1972; Take Me High 1973; Operation Daybreak 1975; The Scarlet Pimpernel 1982; Agatha Christie's Sparkling Cyanide 1983; Under the Volcano 1984; The Holcroft Covenant 1985; The Second Victory 1986; The Lighthorsemen 1987; Hanna's War 1988; Lost in Siberia 1991; Haunted 1995; The King's Speech 2010
Andrews, Barry Dracula Has Risen from the Grave 1968; Blood on Satan's Claw 1970
Andrews, Brian Halloween 1978; The Great Santini 1979
Andrews, Carol (1922-1976) The Bullfighters 1945; Blue Skies 1946
Andrews, Dana (1909-1992) Kit Carson 1940; Belle Starr 1941; Swamp Water 1941; Tobacco Road 1941; Berlin Correspondent 1942; Crash Dive 1943; The North Star 1943; The Ox-Bow Incident 1943; Laura 1944; The Purple Heart 1944; Up in Arms 1944; Wing and a Prayer 1944; Fallen Angel 1945; State Fair 1945; A Walk in the Sun 1945; The Best Years of Our Lives 1946; Canyon Passage 1946; Boomerang! 1947; Daisy Kenyon 1947; Night Song 1947; The Iron Curtain 1948; No Minor Vices 1948; Britannia Mews 1949; My Foolish Heart 1949; Edge of Doom 1950; Where the Sidewalk Ends 1950; The Frogmen 1951; I Want You 1951; Sealed Cargo 1951; Assignment - Paris 1952; Duel in the Jungle 1954; Elephant Walk 1954; Smoke Signal 1955; Strange Lady in Town 1955; Beyond a Reasonable Doubt 1956; Comanche 1956; While the City Sleeps 1956; Night of the Demon 1957; Spring Reunion 1957; Zero Hour! 1957; The Fearmakers 1958; The Crowded Sky 1960; Madison Avenue 1962; Crack in the World 1964; Battle of the Bulge 1965; Brainstorm 1965; In Harm's Way 1965; The Loved One 1965; The Satan Bug 1965; The Frozen Dead 1966; Johnny Reno 1966; Airport 1975 1974; Take a Hard Ride 1975; The Last Tycoon 1976; Good Guys Wear Black 1977; Born Again 1978
Andrews (1), David (1952-) Some People 1962; A Face to Go 1993
Andrews (2), David (1952-) Wild Horses 1985; Cherry 2000 1988; Graveyard Shift 1990; Wyatt Earp 1994; Under Pressure 1997; Terminator

3: Rise of the Machines 2003; Dear John 2010
Andrews, Dean The Navigators 2001; My Summer of Love 2004; Love + Hate 2005; Salvage 2009
Andrews, Edward (1914-1985) The Phenix City Story 1955; The Harder They Fall 1956; Tea and Sympathy 1956; Tension at Table Rock 1956; These Wilder Years 1956; The Unguarded Moment 1956; The Tattered Dress 1957; Trooper Hook 1957; Elmer Gantry 1960; The Absent-Minded Professor 1961; The Young Savages 1961; Forty Pounds of Trouble 1962; The Thrill of It All 1963; The Brass Bottle 1964; Kisses for My President 1964; Send Me No Flowers 1964; A Tiger Walks 1964; Youngblood Hawke 1964; Fluffy 1965; The Glass Bottom Boat 1966; The Trouble with Girls 1969; Avanti! 1972
Andrews, Harry (1911-1989) The Red Beret 1953; The Black Knight 1954; The Man Who Loved Redheads 1954; Helen of Troy 1955; Alexander the Great 1956; A Hill in Korea 1956; Moby Dick 1956; Saint Joan 1957; Ice Cold in Alex 1958; Circle of Deception 1960; Barabbas 1961; The Best of Enemies 1961; The Inspector 1962; Reach for Glory 1962; 55 Days at Peking 1963; The Informers 1963; Nothing but the Best 1963; 633 Squadron 1964; The System 1964; The Truth about Spring 1964; The Agony and the Ecstasy 1965; The Hill 1965; Sands of the Kalahari 1965; The Deadly Affair 1966; Modesty Blaise 1966; Danger Route 1967; I'll Never Forget What's 'Is Name 1967; The Jokers 1967; The Long Duel 1967; The Charge of the Light Brigade 1968; The Night They Raided Minsky's 1968; The Sea Gull 1968; Entertaining Mr Sloane 1969; A Nice Girl like Me 1969; Play Dirty 1969; The Southern Star 1969; Country Dance 1970; Too Late the Hero 1970; Wuthering Heights 1970; Burke & Hare 1971; I Want What I Want 1971; Man of La Mancha 1972; The Nightcomers 1972; The Ruling Class 1972; The Mackintosh Man 1973; Man at the Top 1973; Theatre of Blood 1973; The Internecine Project 1974; The Blue Bird 1976; Equus 1977; The Prince and the Pauper 1977; The Big Sleep 1978; Death on the Nile 1978; The Four Feathers 1978; The Medusa Touch 1978; SOS Titanic 1979; Mesmerized 1984
Andrews, Jason Last Exit to Brooklyn 1989; Federal Hill 1994
Andrews, Julie (1935-) The Americanization of Emily 1964; Mary Poppins 1964; The Sound of Music 1965; Hawaii 1966; Torn Curtain 1966; Thoroughly Modern Millie 1967; Star! 1968; Darling Lili 1970; The Tamarind Seed 1974; 10 1979; Little Miss Marker 1980; SOB 1981; Victor/Victoria 1982; The Man Who Loved Women 1983; Duet for One 1986; That's Life 1986; A Touch of Adultery 1991; One Special Night 1999; Relative Values 2000; The Princess Diaries 2001; Eloise at the Plaza 2003; The Princess Diaries 2: Royal Engagement 2004; Shrek 2 2004; Enchanted 2007; Shrek the Third 2007; Tooth Fairy 2009; Despicable Me 2010; Shrek Forever After 2010
Andrews, Laverne (1915-1967) Argentine Nights 1940; Buck Privates 1941; In the Navy 1941
Andrews, Maxene (1916-1995) Argentine Nights 1940; Buck Privates 1941; In the Navy 1941
Andrews, Naveen (1969-) Wild West 1992; The English Patient 1996; Kama Sutra: a Tale of Love 1996; Bombay Boys 1998; Mighty Joe Young 1998; Rollerball 2001; Bride & Prejudice 2004; Provoked: a True Story 2006; The Brave One 2007; Planet Terror 2007; Diana 2013
Andrews, Patty (1918-2013) Argentine Nights 1940; Buck Privates 1941; In the Navy 1941
Andrews, Russell The In-Laws 2003; The Punisher 2004
Andrews, Shawn Dazed and Confused 1993; City of Ghosts 2002
Andrews, Stanley (1891-1969) Shine On, Harvest Moon 1938; Al Jennings of Oklahoma 1951
Andrews, Tod aka **Ames, Michael** (1914-1972) Voodoo Man 1944; From Hell It Came 1957
Anémone (1950-) Death in a French Garden 1985; Le Grand Chemin 1987; Le Petit Prince A Dit 1992
Angarano, Michael (1987-) Dear Wendy 2004; Lords of Dogtown 2005; Sky High 2005; Man in the Chair 2006; The Forbidden Kingdom 2008; Gentlemen Broncos 2009; The Art of Getting By 2011; Red State 2011; The

English Teacher 2013; Wild Card 2014; The Stanford Prison Experiment 2015
Angarola, Richard (1920-2008) Gambit 1966; Three the Hard Way 1974
Angel, Heather (1909-1986) Berkeley Square 1933; Pilgrimage 1933; The Informer 1935; The Mystery of Edwin Drood 1935; The Perfect Gentleman 1935; The Three Musketeers 1935; The Last of the Mohicans 1936; Bulldog Drummond Escapes 1937; Bulldog Drummond in Africa 1938; Bulldog Drummond's Bride 1939; Pride and Prejudice 1940; The Undying Monster 1942; Lifeboat 1944; The Saxon Charm 1948; Peter Pan 1953; The Premature Burial 1962
Angel, Mikel (1917-2005) The Hard Ride 1971; Evil Spirits 1991
Angel, Vanessa (1963-) Kingpin 1996; Kissing a Fool 1998; Made Men 1999; G-Men from Hell 2000; Partners 2000
Angeli, Pier (1932-1971) The Light Touch 1951; Teresa 1951; The Devil Makes Three 1952; Sombrero 1952; The Story of Three Loves 1953; The Silver Chalice 1954; Somebody Up There Likes Me 1956; Merry Andrew 1958; SOS Pacific 1959; The Angry Silence 1960; Sodom and Gomorrah 1962; Battle of the Bulge 1965
Angelis, Michael A Nightingale Sang in Berkeley Square 1979; No Surrender 1985; Fated 2006
Angelou, Maya aka **Angelou, Dr Maya** (1928-2014) Poetic Justice 1993; How to Make an American Quilt 1995; Good Hair 2009
Angelus, Muriel (1909-2004) Hindle Wakes 1931; The Light That Failed 1939; The Great McGinty 1940
Anger, Kenneth (1927-) A Midsummer Night's Dream 1935; Fireworks 1947; Invocation of My Demon Brother 1969; Lucifer Rising 1981
Angers, Avril (1918-2005) The Brass Monkey 1948; The Green Man 1956; Be My Guest 1965; The Family Way 1966; Two a Penny 1968
Anglade, Jean-Hugues (1955-) Subway 1985; Betty Blue 1986; Nikita 1990; Killing Zoe 1993; La Reine Margot 1994; Nelly & Monsieur Arnaud 1995; Maximum Risk 1996; Taking Lives 2004; Villa Amalia 2009
Anglim, Philip (1953-) Testament 1983; Haunted Summer 1988
Angulo, Alex (1953-2014) Acción Mutante 1993; The Day of the Beast 1995; Pan's Labyrinth 2006
Anholt, Christien (1971-) Reunion 1989; One against the Wind 1991; Preaching to the Perverted 1997
Aniston, Jennifer (1969-) Leprechaun 1992; Dream for an Insomniac 1996; She's the One 1996; Picture Perfect 1997; 'Til There Was You 1997; The Object of My Affection 1998; The Iron Giant 1999; Office Space 1999; The Good Girl 2001; Rock Star 2001; Bruce Almighty 2003; Along Came Polly 2004; Derailed 2005; Rumor has It... 2005; The Break-Up 2006; Friends with Money 2006; He's Just Not That into You 2008; Management 2008; Marley & Me 2008; Love Happens 2009; The Bounty Hunter 2010; The Switch 2010; Horrible Bosses 2011; Just Go with It 2011; Wanderlust 2011; Life of Crime 2013; We're the Millers 2013; Horrible Bosses 2 2014; She's Funny That Way 2014; Cake 2015; Unity 2015; Mother's Day 2016; Storks 2016
Anka, Paul (1941-) Girls' Town 1959; The Private Lives of Adam and Eve 1959; The Longest Day 1962; Ordinary Magic 1993
Anker, Conrad The Wildest Dream 2009; Meru 2015
Ankers, Evelyn (1918-1985) Hold That Ghost 1941; The Wolf Man 1941; The Ghost of Frankenstein 1942; Sherlock Holmes and the Voice of Terror 1942; Hers to Hold 1943; Son of Dracula 1943; The Frozen Ghost 1944; The Invisible Man's Revenge 1944; The Pearl of Death 1944; Weird Woman 1944; Black Beauty 1946; Tarzan's Magic Fountain 1949
Ankrum, Morris (1896-1964) Buck Benny Rides Again 1940; Cherokee Strip 1940; Desire Me 1947; Lady in the Lake 1947; Colorado Territory 1949; In a Lonely Place 1950; The Redhead and the Cowboy 1950; Along the Great Divide 1951; Son of Ali Baba 1952; The Moonlighter 1953; Apache 1954; Cattle Queen of Montana 1954; Southwest Passage 1954; Taza, Son of Cochise 1954; Vera Cruz 1954; Earth vs the Flying Saucers 1956; Beginning of the End 1957; Kronos 1957; The Saga of Hemp Brown 1958
Ann-Margret (1941-) Pocketful of Miracles 1961; State Fair 1962; Bye Bye

Birdie 1963; The Pleasure Seekers 1964; Viva Las Vegas 1964; Bus Riley's Back in Town 1965; The Cincinnati Kid 1965; Once a Thief 1965; Stagecoach 1966; The Tiger and the Pussycat 1967; RPM - Revolutions per Minute 1970; Carnal Knowledge 1971; The Outside Man 1973; The Train Robbers 1973; Tommy 1975; The Twist 1976; Joseph Andrews 1977; The Last Remake of Beau Geste 1977; The Cheap Detective 1978; Magic 1978; Cactus Jack 1979; Middle Age Crazy 1980; I Ought to Be in Pictures 1982; The Return of the Soldier 1982; Who Will Love My Children? 1983; Twice in a Lifetime 1985; 52 Pick-Up 1986; A Tiger's Tale 1987; A New Life 1988; Grumpy Old Men 1993; Grumpier Old Men 1996; Any Given Sunday 1999; Happy Face Murders 1999; The Last Producer 2000; A Place Called Home 2004; Taxi 2004; The Santa Clause 3: the Escape Clause 2006
Annabella (1909-1996) Le Million 1931; Caravan 1934; Dinner at the Ritz 1937; Under the Red Robe 1937; Wings of the Morning 1937; The Baroness and the Butler 1938; Hôtel du Nord 1938; Suez 1938; 13 Rue Madeleine 1946
Annis, Francesca (1944-) The Cat Gang 1959; No Kidding 1960; Crooks in Cloisters 1963; Saturday Night Out 1963; Flipper's New Adventure 1964; Murder Most Foul 1964; The Pleasure Girls 1965; The Walking Stick 1970; Macbeth 1971; Penny Gold 1973; Krull 1983; Dune 1984; Under the Cherry Moon 1986; The Debt Collector 1999; Milk 1999; Onegin 1999; The Libertine 2004; Revolver 2005; Shifty 2008
Anozie, Nonso Cass 2008; Brighton Rock 2010; The Grey 2012
Ansara, Michael (1922-2013) Soldiers Three 1951; The Diamond Queen 1953; Serpent of the Nile 1953; Princess of the Nile 1954; Abbott and Costello Meet the Mummy 1955; The Lone Ranger 1956; Last of the Badmen 1957; The Tall Stranger 1957; The Comancheros 1961; Voyage to the Bottom of the Sea 1961; Quick, Let's Get Married 1964; Harum Scarum 1965; How I Spent My Summer Vacation 1967; The Destructors 1968; The Pink Jungle 1968; The Bears and I 1974; Day of the Animals 1977; The Manitou 1978; Assassination 1986; Border Shootout 1990
Anspach, Susan (1939-) Five Easy Pieces 1970; Play It Again, Sam 1972; Blume in Love 1973; The Big Fix 1978; Running 1979; The Devil and Max Devlin 1981; Montenegro 1981
Ant, Adam (1954-) Jubilee 1978; Nomads 1986; Cold Steel 1987; Slam Dance 1987; World Gone Wild 1988; Trust Me 1989; The Blueblack Hussar 2013
Antara, Oka The Raid 2 2013; Killers 2014
Anthony, Lysette (1963-) Krull 1983; Without a Clue 1988; A Ghost in Monte Carlo 1990; Switch 1991; Husbands and Wives 1992; The Hour of the Pig 1993; Look Who's Talking Now! 1993; Dr Jekyll and Ms Hyde 1995; Dracula: Dead and Loving It 1995; Talos the Mummy 1997; The Evil beneath Loch Ness 2001; Strippers vs Werewolves 2012; We Still Kill the Old Way 2014
Anthony, Marc (1969-) Big Night 1996; The Substitute 1996; Bringing Out the Dead 1999; Man on Fire 2004; El Cantante 2006
Anthony, Paul House Party 1990; Cheating Fate 2007
Anthony, Ray (1922-) The Beat Generation 1959; The Big Operator 1959; Girls' Town 1959
Antin, Steve (1956-) The Accused 1988; Without You I'm Nothing 1990
Antonelli, Laura (1941-2015) Dr Goldfoot and the Girl Bombs 1966; Les Mariés de l'An Deux 1971; L'Innocente 1976
Antonio, Lou (1934-) America, America 1963; Cool Hand Luke 1967
Antonov, Aleksander aka **Antonov, Aleksandr** (1898-1962) Strike 1924; The Battleship Potemkin 1925
Antonutti, Omero (1935-) Padre Padrone 1977; The Night of San Lorenzo 1981; El Sur 1983; Kaos 1984; Good Morning, Babylon 1987; El Dorado 1988
Antony, Scott (1950-) Savage Messiah 1972; The Mutations 1973; Dead Cert 1974
Antrim, Harry (1884-1967) Let's Live a Little 1948; Act of Violence 1949; Ma and Pa Kettle 1949; The Bounty Hunter 1954; Teacher's Pet 1958
Anwar, Gabrielle (1969-) Teen Agent 1991; Wild Hearts Can't Be Broken 1991; Scent of a Woman 1992; Body Snatchers 1993; For Love or Money

1993; *The Three Musketeers* 1993; *Innocent Lies* 1995; *Things to Do in Denver When You're Dead* 1995; *The Guilty* 2000; *Without Malice* 2000; *Mary Higgins Clark's Try to Remember* 2004; *The Marsh* 2006; *Nora Roberts' Carnal Innocence* 2011

Anys, Georgette (1909-1993) *Little Boy Lost* 1953; *La Traversée de Paris* 1956; *Bon Voyage!* 1962

Aoki, Devon *DOA: Dead or Alive* 2006; *War* 2007; *Mutant Chronicles* 2008

Aparicio, Rafaela (1906-1996) *Mamá Cumple 100 Años* 1979; *El Sur* 1983

Apatow, Judd (1967-) *Salinger* 2013; *Misery Loves Comedy* 2015

Apfel, Oscar (1878-1938) *The Texan* 1930; *Inspiration* 1931; *The Bowery* 1933

Appel, Anna (1888-1963) *Symphony of Six Million* 1932; *Green Fields* 1937

Appel, Peter *Leon* 1994; *Six Ways to Sunday* 1997; *Tadpole* 2002

Appleby, Shiri (1978-) *Swimfan* 2002; *Undertow* 2004; *Havoc* 2005; *Unstable* 2009

Applegate, Christina (1971-) *Streets* 1990; *Don't Tell Mom the Babysitter's Dead* 1991; *Wild Bill* 1995; *The Big Hit* 1998; *Jane Austen's Mafia* 1998; *Just Visiting* 2001; *Prince Charming* 2001; *The Sweetest Thing* 2002; *Grand Theft Parsons* 2003; *View from the Top* 2003; *Wonderland* 2003; *Anchorman: the Legend of Ron Burgundy* 2004; *Surviving Christmas* 2004; *The Rocker* 2008; *Alvin and the Chipmunks: the Squeakquel* 2009; *Cats & Dogs: the Revenge of Kitty Galore* 2010; *Going the Distance* 2010; *Hall Pass* 2011; *Anchorman 2: the Legend Continues* 2013; *Book of Life* 2014; *Vacation* 2015

Aquino, Amy *Alan & Naomi* 1992; *Danielle Steel's Once in a Lifetime* 1994; *Boys on the Side* 1995

Aragón, Angélica aka **Aragon, Angelica** *A Walk in the Clouds* 1995; *El Crimen del Padre Amaro* 2002; *Bella* 2006

Arahanga, Julian *Once Were Warriors* 1994; *What Becomes of the Broken Hearted?* 1999

Arana, Tomas aka **Arana, Thomas** (1959-) *The Church* 1988; *The Sect* 1991; *The Bodyguard* 1992; *Derailed* 2002; *Frankenfish* 2004

Aranda, Angel (1934-2000) *The Colossus of Rhodes* 1961; *Planet of the Vampires* 1965

Arashi, Kanjuro (1903-1980) *The Profound Desire of the Gods* 1968; *Zatoichi Meets Yojimbo* 1970

Arata (1974-) *After Life* 1998; *Ping Pong* 2002

Arata, Michael *Malpractice* 2001; *Torn Apart* 2004; *The Unexpected Journey* 2004; *Odd Girl Out* 2005

Aratama, Michiyo (1930-2001) *Conflagration* 1958; *The Human Condition* 1958; *The End of Summer* 1961; *Kwaidan* 1964

Arau, Alfonso (1932-) *Scandalous John* 1971; *Romancing the Stone* 1984; *Stones for Ibarra* 1988; *Committed* 2000

Arbuckle, Roscoe "Fatty" (1887-1933) *The Butcher Boy* 1917; *Go West* 1925

Arbus, Allan (1918-2013) *The Christian Licorice Store* 1971; *Coffy* 1973; *The Electric Horseman* 1979; *The Last Married Couple in America* 1980

Arcand, Denys (1941-) *Jesus of Montreal* 1989; *Léolo* 1992

Arcand, Gabriel (1949-) *Agnes of God* 1985; *The Decline of the American Empire* 1986; *The Revolving Doors* 1988

Arcand, Nathaniel *Grey Owl* 1999; *The Unknown* 2005; *Pathfinder* 2006

Archard, Bernard (1916-2008) *The List of Adrian Messenger* 1963; *Play Dirty* 1969; *The Horror of Frankenstein* 1970; *Dad's Army* 1971; *Separate Tables* 1983

Archer, Anne (1947-) *The Honkers* 1971; *Cancel My Reservation* 1972; *The All-American Boy* 1973; *The Blue Knight* 1973; *The Mark of Zorro* 1974; *Good Guys Wear Black* 1977; *Paradise Alley* 1978; *Hero at Large* 1980; *Raise the Titanic* 1980; *Green Ice* 1981; *Too Scared to Scream* 1982; *The Naked Face* 1984; *Fatal Attraction* 1987; *Love at Large* 1990; *Narrow Margin* 1990; *Body of Evidence* 1992; *Patriot Games* 1992; *Short Cuts* 1993; *Clear and Present Danger* 1994; *Luck, Trust & Ketchup* 1993; *Mojave Moon* 1996; *Nico the Unicorn* 1998; *The Art of War* 2000; *Rules of Engagement* 2000; *Whispers: an Elephant's Tale* 2000; *Man of the House* 2005; *End Game* 2006; *Felon* 2008; *Ghosts of Girlfriends Past* 2009

Archer, Beverly (1948-) *Vice Versa* 1988; *The Christmas Wish* 1998

Archer, John (1915-1999) *Curtain Call* 1940; *Sherlock Holmes in Washington* 1943; *The Lost Moment* 1947; *Colorado Territory* 1949; *White Heat* 1949; *Destination Moon* 1950; *High Lonesome* 1950; *Best of the Badmen* 1951; *My Favorite Spy* 1951; *Santa Fe* 1951; *The Big Trees* 1952; *Rock around the Clock* 1956; *Decision at Sundown* 1957; *City of Fear* 1959; *Blue Hawaii* 1961; *Apache Rifles* 1964

Archibald, Stephen (1959-1998) *My Childhood* 1972; *My Ain Folk* 1973; *My Way Home* 1978

Ardant, Fanny (1949-) *Les Chiens* 1978; *The Woman Next Door* 1981; *Confidentially Yours* 1983; *Life Is a Bed of Roses* 1983; *Swann in Love* 1984; *Mélo* 1986; *Le Paltoquet* 1986; *The Family* 1987; *Three Sisters* 1988; *Australia* 1989; *Afraid of the Dark* 1991; *Le Colonel Chabert* 1994; *Beyond the Clouds* 1995; *Ridicule* 1996; *Elizabeth* 1998; *Le Libertin* 2000; *8 Women* 2001; *Callas Forever* 2002; *Nathalie...* 2003; *Il Divo* 2008; *Bright Days Ahead* 2013

Arden, Eve (1908-1990) *Stage Door* 1937; *Having Wonderful Time* 1938; *Letter of Introduction* 1938; *At the Circus* 1939; *Eternally Yours* 1939; *Comrade X* 1940; *No, No, Nanette* 1940; *Manpower* 1941; *That Uncertain Feeling* 1941; *Whistling in the Dark* 1941; *Ziegfeld Girl* 1941; *Bedtime Story* 1942; *Change of Heart* 1943; *Let's Face It* 1943; *Cover Girl* 1944; *The Doughgirls* 1944; *Patrick the Great* 1944; *Earl Carroll Vanities* 1945; *Mildred Pierce* 1945; *The Kid from Brooklyn* 1946; *My Reputation* 1946; *Night and Day* 1946; *Song of Scheherazade* 1947; *The Unfaithful* 1947; *Voice of the Turtle* 1947; *One Touch of Venus* 1948; *My Dream Is Yours* 1949; *Paid in Full* 1950; *Tea for Two* 1950; *Goodbye, My Fancy* 1951; *We're Not Married* 1952; *The Lady Wants Mink* 1953; *Anatomy of a Murder* 1959; *The Dark at the Top of the Stairs* 1960; *The Strongest Man in the World* 1975; *Under the Rainbow* 1981; *Grease 2* 1982; *Pandemonium* 1982

Arden, Robert (1922-2004) *Confidential Report* 1955; *Joe Macbeth* 1955; *Omen III: the Final Conflict* 1980

Arditi, Catherine *Mélo* 1986; *Thérèse Desqueyroux* 2012

Arditi, Pierre (1944-) *Mélo* 1986; *Smoking/No Smoking* 1993; *Men, Women: a User's Manual* 1996; *On Connaît la Chanson* 1997; *Chance or Coincidence* 1999; *Pas sur la Bouche* 2003; *Private Fears in Public Places* 2006

Arévalo, Raúl *Even the Rain* 2010; *I'm So Excited* 2013; *Marshland* 2014

Arena, Maurizio (1933-1979) *Le Bambole* 1965; *The Corrupt Ones* 1966

Arenas, Reynaldo aka **Arenas, Reinaldo** *Hour of the Assassin* 1987; *Sniper* 1992

Arenberg, Lee (1962-) *Cross My Heart* 1987; *Dungeons & Dragons* 2000; *Pirates of the Caribbean: at World's End* 2007

Arend, Geoffrey (1978-) *It Runs in the Family* 2002; *The Ringer* 2005; *(500) Days of Summer* 2009; *Devil* 2010

Arestrup, Niels (1949-) *Je, Tu, Il, Elle* 1974; *Second Chance* 1976; *Meeting Venus* 1990; *The Beat That My Heart Skipped* 2005; *A Prophet* 2009; *The Big Picture* 2010; *Sarah's Key* 2010; *War Horse* 2011; *Our Children* 2012; *You Will Be My Son* 2012; *Diplomacy* 2014; *By the Sea* 2015

Argento, Asia (1975-) *The Church* 1988; *Trauma* 1993; *Il Cielo è Sempre Più Blu* 1995; *B Monkey* 1996; *The Stendhal Syndrome* 1996; *New Rose Hotel* 1998; *The Phantom of the Opera* 1998; *xXx* 2002; *The Keeper* 2003; *Last Days* 2004; *George A Romero's Land of the Dead* 2005; *Marie Antoinette* 2005; *Transylvania* 2006; *The Last Mistress* 2007

Argenziano, Carmen (1943-) *Punishment Park* 1971; *The Accused* 1988; *Stand and Deliver* 1988; *Red Scorpion* 1989; *Unlawful Entry* 1992; *Final Combination* 1993; *The Burning Season* 1994; *Identity* 2003

Argo, Victor aka **Argo, Vic** (1934-2004) *Boxcar Bertha* 1972; *Mean Streets* 1973; *King of New York* 1989; *Bad Lieutenant* 1992; *Dangerous Game* 1993; *Household Saints* 1993; *Next Stop Wonderland* 1998; *Angel Eyes* 2001

Argue, David (1959-) *Gallipoli* 1981; *BMX Bandits* 1983; *Hercules Returns* 1993; *Angel Baby* 1995

Arias, Imanol (1956-) *Labyrinth of Passion* 1982; *Camila* 1984; *The Flower of My Secret* 1995

Arias, Moises *The Kings of Summer* 2013; *The Stanford Prison Experiment* 2015

Arima, Ineko (1932-) *Tokyo Twilight* 1957; *Equinox Flower* 1958; *The Human Condition* 1958

Arizmendi, Yareli *Like Water for Chocolate* 1993; *The Big Green* 1995

Arkin, Adam (1956-) *Full Moon High* 1982; *The Doctor* 1991; *Halloween H20: 20 Years Later* 1998; *Thirst* 1998; *A Slight Case of Murder* 1999; *Hanging Up* 2000; *Hitch* 2005; *A Serious Man* 2009

Arkin, Alan (1934-) *The Russians Are Coming, the Russians Are Coming* 1966; *Wait until Dark* 1967; *Woman Times Seven* 1967; *The Heart Is a Lonely Hunter* 1968; *Inspector Clouseau* 1968; *Catch-22* 1970; *Little Murders* 1971; *Deadhead Miles* 1972; *Freebie and the Bean* 1974; *Hearts of the West* 1975; *Fire Sale* 1977; *The In-Laws* 1979; *The Magician of Lublin* 1979; *The Last Unicorn* 1980; *Simon* 1980; *Improper Channels* 1981; *The Return of Captain Invincible* 1983; *Bad Medicine* 1985; *Big Trouble* 1985; *Joshua Then and Now* 1985; *Escape from Sobibor* 1987; *Coupe de Ville* 1990; *Edward Scissorhands* 1990; *Havana* 1990; *Rocketeer* 1991; *Glengarry Glen Ross* 1992; *Cooperstown* 1993; *Indian Summer* 1993; *North* 1994; *The Jerky Boys* 1995; *Steal Big, Steal Little* 1995; *Mother Night* 1996; *Four Days in September* 1997; *Gattaca* 1997; *Grosse Pointe Blank* 1997; *Slums of Beverly Hills* 1998; *Jakob the Liar* 1999; *Varian's War* 2000; *America's Sweethearts* 2001; *Thirteen Conversations about One Thing* 2001; *Eros* 2004; *Noel* 2004; *Firewall* 2006; *Little Miss Sunshine* 2006; *The Santa Clause 3: the Escape Clause* 2006; *Rendition* 2007; *Get Smart* 2008; *Marley & Me* 2008; *Sunshine Cleaning* 2008; *City Island* 2009; *The Private Lives of Pippa Lee* 2009; *The Change-Up* 2011; *Argo* 2012; *Stand Up Guys* 2012; *Grudge Match* 2013; *The Incredible Burt Wonderstone* 2013; *Million Dollar Arm* 2014; *Christmas with the Coopers* 2015

Arkin, David (1941-1990) *I Love You, Alice B Toklas* 1968; *Up in the Cellar* 1970; *The Long Goodbye* 1973; *Nashville* 1975

Arledge, John (1906-1947) *Daddy Long Legs* 1931; *Flirtation Walk* 1934; *Murder on a Bridle Path* 1936; *You Can't Cheat an Honest Man* 1939

Arlen, Richard (1898-1976) *Wings* 1927; *Beggars of Life* 1928; *The Four Feathers* 1929; *Thunderbolt* 1929; *The Virginian* 1929; *Island of Lost Souls* 1932; *Tiger Shark* 1932; *Alice in Wonderland* 1933; *Let 'Em Have It* 1935; *Artists and Models* 1937; *The Great Barrier* 1937; *The Lady and the Monster* 1944; *When My Baby Smiles at Me* 1948; *Flaming Feather* 1952; *Hurricane Smith* 1952; *The Mountain* 1956; *Warlock* 1959; *Apache Uprising* 1965

Arletty (1898-1992) *Hôtel du Nord* 1938; *Le Jour Se Lève* 1939; *Les Visiteurs du Soir* 1942; *Les Enfants du Paradis* 1945

Arliss, George (1868-1946) *Disraeli* 1929; *The Man Who Played God* 1932; *A Successful Calamity* 1932; *The House of Rothschild* 1934; *Cardinal Richelieu* 1935; *His Lordship* 1936; *Dr Syn* 1937

Armendáriz, Pedro (1912-1963) *Portrait of Maria* 1943; *The Fugitive* 1947; *Fort Apache* 1948; *Three Godfathers* 1948; *Tulsa* 1949; *We Were Strangers* 1949; *El Bruto* 1952; *Diane* 1955; *The Conqueror* 1956; *Manuela* 1957; *The Wonderful Country* 1959; *Francis of Assisi* 1961; *Captain Sinbad* 1963; *From Russia with Love* 1963

Armendáriz Jr, Pedro aka **Armendáriz, Pedro** (1940-2011) *The Magnificent Seven Ride!* 1972; *The Deadly Trackers* 1973; *Don't Be Afraid of the Dark* 1973; *Chosen Survivors* 1974; *Agatha Christie's Murder in Three Acts* 1986; *Old Gringo* 1989; *Highway Patrolman* 1991; *El Crimen del Padre Amaro* 2002; *The Legend of Zorro* 2005; *Casa de Mi Padre* 2011

Armetta, Henry (1888-1945) *The Unholy Garden* 1931; *A Farewell to Arms* 1932; *What - No Beer?* 1933; *The Black Cat* 1934; *Magnificent Obsession* 1935; *Dust Be My Destiny* 1939

Armitage, Richard (1971-) *Frozen* 2004; *The Hobbit: an Unexpected Journey* 2012; *The Hobbit: the Desolation of Smaug* 2013; *The Hobbit: the Battle of the Five Armies* 2014; *Into the Storm* 2014

Armstrong, Alun (1946-) *Get Carter* 1971; *Krull* 1983; *White Hunter, Black Heart* 1990; *American Friends* 1991; *London Kills Me* 1991; *Split Second* 1991; *Blue Ice* 1992; *An Awfully Big Adventure* 1994; *Black Beauty* 1994; *The Saint* 1997; *Onegin* 1999; *With or without You* 1999; *Harrison's Flowers* 2000; *Strictly Sinatra* 2000; *It's All about Love* 2002; *Millions* 2004; *Van Helsing* 2004; *Eragon* 2006; *Golden Years* 2016

Armstrong, Bess (1953-) *The Four Seasons* 1981; *High Road to China* 1983; *Jaws III* 1983; *Nothing in Common* 1986; *Dream Lover* 1993; *The Lies Boys Tell* 1994; *Danielle Steel's Mixed Blessings* 1995; *Forgotten Sins* 1996; *That Darn Cat* 1997; *Pecker* 1998

Armstrong, Bridget *The Amorous Prawn* 1962; *For the Love of Benji* 1977

Armstrong, Curtis (1953-) *Risky Business* 1983; *Revenge of the Nerds* 1984; *Bad Medicine* 1985; *The Clan of the Cave Bear* 1986; *One Crazy Summer* 1986; *Big Bully* 1996; *Southland Tales* 2005; *Akeelah and the Bee* 2006; *Legally Blondes* 2008; *Planes: Fire and Rescue* 2014

Armstrong, Jonas *Twenty8k* 2012; *Edge of Tomorrow* 2014

Armstrong, Kerry (1958-) *The Getting of Wisdom* 1977; *Hunting* 1992; *Lantana* 2001; *Razzle Dazzle: a Journey into Dance* 2006

Armstrong, Lance *You, Me and Dupree* 2006; *The Armstrong Lie* 2013

Armstrong, Louis (1900-1971) *Pennies from Heaven* 1936; *Artists and Models* 1937; *Every Day's a Holiday* 1937; *Going Places* 1938; *Cabin in the Sky* 1943; *Atlantic City* 1944; *Here Comes the Groom* 1951; *Glory Alley* 1952; *High Society* 1956; *The Beat Generation* 1959; *The Five Pennies* 1959; *Jazz on a Summer's Day* 1959; *Paris Blues* 1961; *A Man Called Adam* 1966; *Hello, Dolly!* 1969

Armstrong, R G (1917-2012) *From Hell to Texas* 1958; *No Name on the Bullet* 1959; *Ten Who Dared* 1960; *Ride the High Country* 1962; *He Rides Tall* 1964; *El Dorado* 1967; *Eighty Steps to Jonah* 1969; *The Great White Hope* 1970; *JW Coop* 1971; *The Great Northfield Minnesota Raid* 1972; *My Name Is Nobody* 1973; *Running Wild* 1973; *White Lightning* 1973; *Race with the Devil* 1975; *Stay Hungry* 1976; *The Car* 1977; *Mr Billion* 1977; *The Pack* 1977; *Where the Buffalo Roam* 1980; *The Pursuit of DB Cooper* 1981; *Raggedy Man* 1981; *Hammett* 1982; *Children of the Corn* 1984; *Jocks* 1986; *Warlock: the Armageddon* 1993

Armstrong, Robert (1890-1973) *A Girl in Every Port* 1928; *Big News* 1929; *The Leatherneck* 1929; *Danger Lights* 1930; *The Iron Man* 1931; *The Lost Squadron* 1932; *The Most Dangerous Game* 1932; *The Penguin Pool Murder* 1932; *Blind Adventure* 1933; *King Kong* 1933; *Son of Kong* 1933; *Palooka* 1934; *"G" Men* 1935; *Remember Last Night?* 1935; *The Ex-Mrs Bradford* 1936; *Winter Carnival* 1939; *Dive Bomber* 1941; *Baby Face Morgan* 1942; *My Favorite Spy* 1942; *Action in Arabia* 1944; *Blood on the Sun* 1945; *Criminal Court* 1946; *The Paleface* 1948; *Return of the Bad Men* 1948; *Mighty Joe Young* 1949

Armstrong, Samaire (1980-) *It's a Boy/Girl Thing* 2006; *Just My Luck* 2006; *Stay Alive* 2006; *The Staircase Murders* 2007

Armstrong, Todd (1939-1992) *Jason and the Argonauts* 1963; *King Rat* 1965; *Dead Heat on a Merry-Go-Round* 1966; *A Time for Killing* 1967

Armstrong, William *Riders of the Storm* 1986; *Danny, the Champion of the World* 1989

Arnall, Julia (1931-) *Lost* 1955; *House of Secrets* 1956; *Mark of the Phoenix* 1957

Arnatt, John (1917-1999) *House of Blackmail* 1953; *Only Two Can Play* 1961; *The Third Alibi* 1961; *Shadow of Fear* 1963; *Licensed to Kill* 1965; *Where the Bullets Fly* 1966; *A Challenge for Robin Hood* 1967; *Crucible of Terror* 1971

Arnaud, Yvonne (1892-1958) *A Cuckoo in the Nest* 1933; *Tomorrow We Live* 1942; *The Ghosts of Berkeley Square* 1947; *Mon Oncle* 1958

Arnaz, Desi (1917-1986) *Too Many Girls* 1940; *The Navy Comes Through* 1942; *The Long, Long Trailer* 1954; *Forever, Darling* 1956; *The Escape Artist* 1982

Arnaz Jr, Desi (1953-) *Red Sky at Morning* 1971; *Billy Two Hats* 1973; *Marco* 1973; *A Wedding* 1978; *House of the Long Shadows* 1983

Arndt, Denis (1939-) *Distant Thunder* 1988; *Basic Instinct* 1992; *Amelia Earhart: the Final Flight* 1994

Arne, Peter (1920-1983) *For Those in Peril* 1943; *The Cockleshell Heroes* 1955; *Timeslip* 1955; *The Moonraker* 1957; *Intent to Kill* 1958; *Conspiracy of Hearts* 1960; *Sands of the Desert* 1960; *The Treasure of Monte Cristo* 1960; *The Hellfire Club* 1961; *Girl in the Headlines* 1963; *The Black Torment* 1964; *Battle beneath the Earth* 1968; *The Oblong Box* 1969; *The Return of the Pink Panther* 1974

Arness, James aka **Arness, Jim** (1923-2011) *Sierra* 1950; *Stars in My Crown* 1950; *Wagonmaster* 1950; *Wyoming Mail* 1950; *Cavalry Scout* 1951; *Iron Man* 1951; *The People against O'Hara* 1951; *The Thing from Another World* 1951; *Big Jim McLain* 1952; *Hellgate* 1952; *Horizons West* 1952; *Hondo* 1953; *Island in the Sky* 1953; *The Lone Hand* 1953; *Her Twelve Men* 1954; *Them!* 1954; *Many Rivers to Cross* 1955; *The Sea Chase* 1955; *The First Travelling Saleslady* 1956; *Alias Jesse James* 1959

Arnett, Will (1970-) *RV* 2006; *Wristcutters: a Love Story* 2006; *Blades of Glory* 2007; *The Brothers Solomon* 2007; *Ratatouille* 2007; *Monsters vs Aliens* 2009; *When in Rome* 2009; *Despicable Me* 2010; *Jonah Hex* 2010; *The Lego Movie* 2014; *The Nut Job* 2014; *Teenage Mutant Ninja Turtles* 2014; *Teenage Mutant Ninja Turtles - Out of the Shadows* 2016

Arnezeder, Nora *Paris 36* 2008; *Maniac* 2012

Arnold, Charlotte *Custody of the Heart* 2000; *They Come Back* 2007

Arnold, Edward (1890-1956) *The Barbarian* 1933; *I'm No Angel* 1933; *Jennie Gerhardt* 1933; *Roman Scandals* 1933; *The White Sister* 1933; *Sadie McKee* 1934; *Thirty-Day Princess* 1934; *Cardinal Richelieu* 1935; *Crime and Punishment* 1935; *The Glass Key* 1935; *Remember Last Night?* 1935; *Come and Get It* 1936; *Meet Nero Wolfe* 1936; *Easy Living* 1937; *The Toast of New York* 1937; *The Crowd Roars* 1938; *You Can't Take It with You* 1938; *Idiot's Delight* 1939; *Mr Smith Goes to Washington* 1939; *Slightly Honorable* 1939; *The Earl of Chicago* 1940; *Johnny Apollo* 1940; *Lillian Russell* 1940; *Design for Scandal* 1941; *The Devil and Daniel Webster* 1941; *Johnny Eager* 1941; *Meet John Doe* 1941; *Nothing but the Truth* 1941; *The Penalty* 1941; *Unholy Partners* 1941; *Eyes in the Night* 1942; *The War against Mrs Hadley* 1942; *The Youngest Profession* 1943; *Kismet* 1944; *Mrs Parkington* 1944; *Standing Room Only* 1944; *Week-End at the Waldorf* 1945; *My Brother Talks to Horses* 1946; *Dear Ruth* 1947; *The Hucksters* 1947; *Command Decision* 1948; *Three Daring Daughters* 1948; *Dear Wife* 1949; *Take Me Out to the Ball Game* 1949; *Annie Get Your Gun* 1950; *The Yellow Cab Man* 1950; *Belles on Their Toes* 1952; *City That Never Sleeps* 1953; *Living It Up* 1954; *The Ambassador's Daughter* 1956

Arnold, Henry (1961-) *Heimat 2* 1992; *Heimat 3: a Chronicle of Endings and Beginnings* 2004

Arnold, Marcelle (1917-2010) *The Bride Is Too Beautiful* 1956; *The Seven Deadly Sins* 1961

Arnold, Mark (1957-) *Teen Wolf* 1985; *Threesome* 1994

Arnold, Tom (1959-) *Accidental Hero* 1992; *Undercover Blues* 1993; *True Lies* 1994; *Nine Months* 1995; *The Stupids* 1995; *Big Bully* 1996; *Carpool* 1996; *Touch* 1996; *McHale's Navy* 1997; *Animal Factory* 2000; *Shriek If You Know What I Did Last Friday the 13th* 2000; *Exit Wounds* 2001; *Barely Legal* 2003; *Cradle 2 the Grave* 2003; *Soul Plane* 2004; *Happy Endings* 2005; *Three Wise Guys* 2005; *Pride* 2007; *Good Dick* 2008; *Grassroots* 2012; *Hit & Run* 2012

Arnold, Victor (1936-2012) *Shaft* 1971; *The Seven-Ups* 1973; *The Protector* 1985

Arnoul, Françoise (1931-) *French Cancan* 1955; *The Little Theatre of Jean Renoir* 1969

Arnt, Charles (1908-1990) *Take a Letter, Darling* 1942; *Bride for Sale* 1949

Aronica, Gaetano *Malena* 2000; *Baaria* 2009

Aronson, Judie *Friday the 13th: the Final Chapter* 1984; *American Ninja* 1985; *Weird Science* 1985

Arora, Amrita *Kitne Door... Kitne Paas* 2001; *Awara Paagal Deewana* 2002

Arquette, Alexis (1969-) *Death of a Schoolboy* 1990; *Jumpin' at the Boneyard* 1991; *Jack Be Nimble* 1992; *Of Mice and Men* 1992; *Threesome*

1994; Frank and Jesse 1995; Sometimes They Come Back... Again 1996; Bride of Chucky 1998; Love Kills 1998; The Wedding Singer 1998; Spun 2002

Arquette, David (1971-) Buffy the Vampire Slayer 1992; Fall Time 1994; Roadflower 1994; Roadracers 1994; Johns 1995; Wild Bill 1995; Beautiful Girls 1996; Dream with the Fishes 1996; Scream 1996; The Alarmist 1997; Scream 2 1997; Free Money 1998; Never Been Kissed 1999; Ravenous 1999; The Runner 1999; Scream 3 1999; Ready to Rumble 2000; The Shrink Is In 2000; 3000 Miles to Graceland 2000; Eight Legged Freaks 2001; The Grey Zone 2001; See Spot Run 2001; It's a Very Merry Muppet Christmas Movie 2002; Never Die Alone 2004; The Adventures of Sharkboy and Lavagirl 2005; The Tripper 2006; Hamlet 2 2008; Scre4m 2011

Arquette, Lewis (1935-2001) Nobody's Fool 1986; The Linguini Incident 1991; Waiting for Guffman 1996; The Alarmist 1997; Almost Heroes 1998

Arquette, Patricia (1968-) A Nightmare on Elm Street 3: Dream Warriors 1987; Far North 1988; Prayer of the Rollerboys 1990; The Indian Runner 1991; Wildflower 1991; Ethan Frome 1993; Trouble Bound 1993; True Romance 1993; Ed Wood 1994; Holy Matrimony 1994; Beyond Rangoon 1995; Flirting with Disaster 1996; Infinity 1996; Lost Highway 1996; The Secret Agent 1996; Goodbye Lover 1997; Nightwatch 1997; The Hi-Lo Country 1998; Bringing Out the Dead 1999; Stigmata 1999; Little Nicky 2000; Human Nature 2001; Holes 2003; Fast Food Nation 2006; Boyhood 2014

Arquette, Rosanna (1959-) SOB 1981; The Executioner's Song 1982; Baby It's You 1983; The Parade 1984; After Hours 1985; The Aviator 1985; Desperately Seeking Susan 1985; Silverado 1985; 8 Million Ways to Die 1986; Nobody's Fool 1986; Amazon Women on the Moon 1987; The Big Blue 1988; Promised a Miracle 1988; Black Rainbow 1989; New York Stories 1989; Almost 1990; Sweet Revenge 1990; Flight of the Intruder 1991; The Linguini Incident 1991; Nowhere to Run 1992; Pulp Fiction 1994; Search and Destroy 1995; Crash 1996; Gone Fishin' 1997; Liar 1997; Buffalo '66 1998; Hope Floats 1998; I'm Losing You 1998; Palmer's Pick-Up 1999; Sugar Town 1999; The Whole Nine Yards 2000; Diary of a Sex Addict 2001; Good Advice 2001; Nora Roberts' Northern Lights 2009; Repo Chick 2009; The Divide 2011; Kill Your Friends 2015

Arredondo, Jeri Spirit of the Eagle 1991; Color of a Brisk and Leaping Day 1996

Arreola, Enrique Duck Season 2004; Blue Eyelids 2007

Arrighi, Nike (1946-) The Devil Rides Out 1968; Day for Night 1973

Artaud, Antonin (1896-1948) Napoléon 1927; The Passion of Joan of Arc 1928

Arterton, Gemma (1986-) St Trinian's 2007; Quantum of Solace 2008; RocknRolla 2008; The Disappearance of Alice Creed 2009; St Trinian's 2: the Legend of Fritton's Gold 2009; Clash of the Titans 2010; Prince of Persia: the Sands of Time 2010; Tamara Drewe 2010; A Turtle's Tale: Sammy's Adventures 2010; Byzantium 2012; Song for Marion 2012; Hansel & Gretel: Witch Hunters 2013; Runner Runner 2013; Gemma Bovery 2014; The Voices 2014; The Girl with All the Gifts 2016

Arthur, Beatrice (1922-2009) Lovers and Other Strangers 1970; Mame 1974; For Better or Worse 1995

Arthur, George K (1889-1985) The Salvation Hunters 1925; The Exquisite Sinner 1926

Arthur, Jean (1900-1991) Seven Chances 1925; The Canary Murder Case 1929; The Saturday Night Kid 1929; Danger Lights 1930; Paramount on Parade 1930; The Return of Dr Fu Manchu 1930; If You Could Only Cook 1935; The Whole Town's Talking 1935; The Ex-Mrs Bradford 1936; Mr Deeds Goes to Town 1936; The Plainsman 1936; Easy Living 1937; History Is Made at Night 1937; You Can't Take It with You 1938; Mr Smith Goes to Washington 1939; Only Angels Have Wings 1939; Arizona 1940; Too Many Husbands 1940; The Devil and Miss Jones 1941; The Talk of the Town 1942; A Lady Takes a Chance 1943; The More

the Merrier 1943; A Foreign Affair 1948; Shane 1953

Arthur, Johnny (1883-1951) The Monster 1925; The Desert Song 1929; The Bride Comes Home 1935; Road to Singapore 1940

Arthur, Maureen (1934-) How to Succeed in Business without Really Trying 1967; Thunder Alley 1967; How to Commit Marriage 1969

Arthur (1), Robert (1925-2008) Mother Wore Tights 1947; Nora Prentiss 1947; Green Grass of Wyoming 1948; Yellow Sky 1948; Mother Is a Freshman 1949; Twelve o'Clock High 1949; September Affair 1950; Air Cadet 1951; Belles on Their Toes 1952; Just for You 1952; The Ring 1952

Arun, Ila Well Done Abba 2009; West Is West 2010

Asano, Tadanobu (1973-) Gohatto 1999; Ichi the Killer 2001; Café Lumière 2003; Last Life in the Universe 2003; Zatoichi 2003; Vital 2004; Mongol 2007; Battleship 2012; 47 Ronin 2012; Journey to the Shore 2015

Asbaek, Pilou (1982-) A Hijacking 2012; The Absent One 2014; A War 2015; Ghost in the Shell 2017

Ascaride, Ariane (1954-) Marius et Jeannette 1997; A la Place du Coeur 1998; Drôle de Félix 2000; La Ville Est Tranquille 2000; Ma Vraie Vie à Rouen 2002; A Common Thread 2004; The Snows of Kilimanjaro 2011

Asche, Oscar (1871-1936) Don Quixote 1932; Scrooge 1935

Aselton, Kathryn aka **Aselton, Katie** The Puffy Chair 2005; Easier with Practice 2009; Black Rock 2013

Asensi, Neus (1965-) The Girl of Your Dreams 1998; Arachnid 2001

Ash, Leslie (1960-) Quadrophenia 1979; The Curse of the Pink Panther 1983; Shadey 1985

Ash, William aka **Ash, Will** (1977-) Fanny & Elvis 1999; Mad about Mambo 1999; Until Death 2007; Hush 2008

Ashanti (1980-) Coach Carter 2005; The Muppets' Wizard of Oz 2005; John Tucker Must Die 2006; Resident Evil: Extinction 2007

Ashbourne, Lorraine Distant Voices, Still Lives 1988; Fever Pitch 1996; The Martins 2001; Adult Life Skills 2016

Ashbrook, Dana (1967-) Return of the Living Dead Part II 1988; Waxwork 1988

Ashby, Linden (1960-) Wyatt Earp 1994; Mortal Kombat 1995; Judgment Day 1999; Sub Zero 2005; My Neighbor's Keeper 2007

Ashcroft, Peggy (1907-1991) The Wandering Jew 1933; The 39 Steps 1935; Rhodes of Africa 1936; Quiet Wedding 1940; The Nun's Story 1959; Tell Me Lies 1967; Secret Ceremony 1968; Three into Two Won't Go 1969; Sunday, Bloody Sunday 1971; The Pedestrian 1974; Joseph Andrews 1977; Hullabaloo over Georgie and Bonnie's Pictures 1979; A Passage to India 1984; When the Wind Blows 1986; Madame Sousatzka 1988

Asher, Billy Dead End 2003; Big Nothing 2006

Asher, Jane (1946-) Adventure in the Hopfields 1954; The Greengage Summer 1961; The Prince and the Pauper 1962; Girl in the Headlines 1963; The Masque of the Red Death 1964; Alfie 1966; The Winter's Tale 1966; The Buttercup Chain 1970; Deep End 1970; Henry VIII and His Six Wives 1972; Runners 1983; Dreamchild 1985; Paris by Night 1988; Death at a Funeral 2007

Asherson, Renée aka **Asherson, Renee** aka **Ascherson, Renee** (1915-2014) Henry V 1944; The Way Ahead 1944; The Way to the Stars 1945; Once a Jolly Swagman 1948; The Cure for Love 1949; The Small Back Room 1949; Pool of London 1950; The Magic Box 1951; Malta Story 1953; The Day the Earth Caught Fire 1961; The Smashing Bird I Used to Know 1969; Grey Owl 1999; The Others 2001

Ashfield, Kate (1972-) The War Zone 1999; The Low Down 2000; Late Night Shopping 2001; Pure 2002; Fakers 2004; Shaun of the Dead 2004; The Best Man 2005; The Baker 2007; The Kid 2010; When the Lights Went Out 2010; Still 2014

Ashikawa, Makoto Violent Cop 1989; Boiling Point 1990

Ashkenazi, Lior Walk on Water 2004; Yossi 2012; Big Bad Wolves 2013

Ashley, Edward (1904-2000) Bitter Sweet 1940; Sky Murder 1940; Come Live with Me 1941; The Black Swan 1942; Dick Tracy Meets Gruesome 1947; Tarzan and the Mermaids 1948; Macao 1952

Ashley, Elizabeth (1939-) The Carpetbaggers 1964; Ship of Fools

1965; The Third Day 1965; The Face of Fear 1971; Golden Needles 1974; 92 in the Shade 1975; Rancho Deluxe 1975; The Great Scout & Cathouse Thursday 1976; Coma 1977; Paternity 1981; Split Image 1982; Stagecoach 1986; Vampire's Kiss 1988; Happiness 1998; Just the Ticket 1998

Ashley, John (1934-1997) Dragstrip Girl 1957; Motorcycle Gang 1957; Suicide Battalion 1958; Beach Party 1963; Hud 1963; Bikini Beach 1964; Muscle Beach Party 1964; Beach Blanket Bingo 1965; Sergeant Deadhead 1965; Young Dillinger 1965; Twilight People 1973

Ashmore, Aaron A Christmas Visitor 2002; Brave New Girl 2004

Ashmore, Shawn (1979-) Underclassman 2004; Terry 2005; X-Men - the Last Stand 2006; The Ruins 2008; Frozen 2009; Mariachi Gringo 2012

Ashton-Griffiths, Roger (1957-) Haunted Honeymoon 1986; Seven Minutes 1989; Devil's Gate 2002; Gangs of New York 2002; Grace of Monaco 2014; Mr Turner 2014

Ashton, Frederick (1904-1988) The Tales of Hoffmann 1951; The Tales of Beatrix Potter 1971

Ashton, John (1948-) Beverly Hills Cop 1984; King Kong Lives 1986; Beverly Hills Cop II 1987; Some Kind of Wonderful 1987; Midnight Run 1988; I Want to Go Home 1989; Little Big League 1994; The Shooter 1994; Meet the Deedles 1998; Instinct 1999; Gone Baby Gone 2007

Ashton, Sylvia (1880-1940) Why Change Your Wife? 1920; Greed 1925; The Barker 1928

Askew, Desmond (1972-) Go 1999; The Hills Have Eyes 2006; Paradise Lost 2006

Askew, Luke (1932-2012) The Green Berets 1968; The Culpepper Cattle Co 1972; The Great Northfield Minnesota Raid 1972; The Magnificent Seven Ride! 1972; Posse 1975; Rolling Thunder 1977; Wanda Nevada 1979; The Warrior and the Sorceress 1983; Traveller 1997; Frailty 2001

Askey, Arthur (1900-1982) Band Waggon 1939; Charley's (Big Hearted) Aunt 1940; The Ghost Train 1941; I Thank You 1941; Back Room Boy 1942; King Arthur Was a Gentleman 1942; Bees in Paradise 1943; Miss London Ltd 1943; The Love Match 1955; Make Mine a Million 1959; Rosie Dixon: Night Nurse 1978

Askin, Leon (1907-2005) Desert Legion 1953; South Sea Woman 1953; Knock on Wood 1954; Valley of the Kings 1954; One, Two, Three 1961; Sherlock Holmes and the Deadly Necklace 1962; Do Not Disturb 1965; A Fine Pair 1968; Frightmare 1981

Askwith, Robin (1950-) Bless This House 1972; Tower of Evil 1972; Horror Hospital 1973; Confessions of a Window Cleaner 1974; Confessions of a Pop Performer 1975; Confessions of a Driving Instructor 1976; Confessions from a Holiday Camp 1977; Let's Get Laid 1977; Stand Up Virgin Soldiers 1977; Britannia Hospital 1982

Aslan, Grégoire aka **Aslan, Gregoire** (1908-1982) The Adventurers 1950; Act of Love 1953; Joe Macbeth 1955; Celui Qui Doit Mourir 1957; The Roots of Heaven 1958; Sea Fury 1958; The Three Worlds of Gulliver 1959; The Criminal 1960; Killers of Kilimanjaro 1960; The Rebel 1960; Under Ten Flags 1960; The Devil at Four o'Clock 1961; Invasion Quartet 1961; King of Kings 1961; Village of Daughters 1961; The Happy Thieves 1963; Crooks in Cloisters 1963; Paris When It Sizzles 1964; A Ravishing Idiot 1964; The High Bright Sun 1965; A Man Could Get Killed 1966; Moment to Moment 1966; Our Man in Marrakesh 1966; The 25th Hour 1967; A Flea in Her Ear 1968; Marry Me! Marry Me! 1968; You Can't Win 'Em All 1970; The Golden Voyage of Sinbad 1973; The Girl from Petrovka 1974; The Return of the Pink Panther 1974

Asner, Edward aka **Asner, Ed** (1929-) The Murder Men 1961; The Satan Bug 1965; The Slender Thread 1965; The Venetian Affair 1966; El Dorado 1967; Change of Habit 1969; They Call Me Mister Tibbs! 1970; Skin Game 1971; Fort Apache, the Bronx 1981; Snow White in Happily Ever After 1990; JFK 1991; Gypsy 1993; A Christmas Carol 1997; Hard Rain 1997; Payback 1997; The Bachelor 1999; Above Suspicion 2000; The Animal 2001; Elf 2003; The King and Queen of Moonlight Bay 2003; Out of the Woods 2005; Generation Gap

2008; Gigantic 2008; Up 2009; Too Big to Fail 2011

Aso, Kumiko (1978-) Casshern 2004; Miss Hokusai 2015

Asparagus, Fred (1947-1998) Three Amigos! 1986; Just the Ticket 1998

Asquith, Conrad Hostages 1993; How to Re-Establish a Vodka Empire 2011

Assante, Armand (1949-) Paradise Alley 1978; Prophecy 1979; Little Darlings 1980; Private Benjamin 1980; Love and Money 1982; Unfaithfully Yours 1983; Belizaire the Cajun 1985; The Penitent 1988; Animal Behavior 1989; Q & A 1990; Too Hot to Handle 1991; 1492: Conquest of Paradise 1992; Hoffa 1992; The Mambo Kings 1992; Fatal Instinct 1993; Trial by Jury 1994; Judge Dredd 1995; Striptease 1996; The Odyssey 1997; The Hunley 1999; The Road to El Dorado 2000; After the Storm 2001; Federal Protection 2002; Two for the Money 2005; American Gangster 2007; California Dreamin' 2007; The Line 2008; Assumed Killer 2013; Dead Man Down 2013

Ast, Pat (1941-2001) Heat 1972; The Duchess and the Dirtwater Fox 1976; Reform School Girls 1986

Astaire, Fred (1899-1987) Dancing Lady 1933; Flying down to Rio 1933; The Gay Divorce 1934; Roberta 1935; Top Hat 1935; Follow the Fleet 1936; Swing Time 1936; A Damsel in Distress 1937; Shall We Dance 1937; Carefree 1938; The Story of Vernon and Irene Castle 1939; Broadway Melody of 1940 1940; Second Chorus 1940; You'll Never Get Rich 1941; Holiday Inn 1942; You Were Never Lovelier 1942; The Sky's the Limit 1943; Ziegfeld Follies 1944; Yolanda and the Thief 1945; Blue Skies 1946; Easter Parade 1948; The Barkleys of Broadway 1949; Let's Dance 1950; Three Little Words 1950; Royal Wedding 1951; The Belle of New York 1952; The Band Wagon 1953; Daddy Long Legs 1955; Funny Face 1957; Silk Stockings 1957; On the Beach 1959; The Pleasure of His Company 1961; The Notorious Landlady 1962; Paris When It Sizzles 1964; Finian's Rainbow 1968; Midas Run 1969; The Towering Inferno 1974; The Amazing Dobermans 1976; That's Entertainment, Part II 1976; The Purple Taxi 1977; Ghost Story 1981

Asther, Nils (1897-1981) Laugh, Clown, Laugh 1928; Our Dancing Daughters 1928; The Single Standard 1929; Wild Orchids 1929; The Bitter Tea of General Yen 1932; If I Were Free 1933; By Candlelight 1934; Dr Kildare's Wedding Day 1941; Bluebeard 1944

Asti, Adriana (1933-) Accattone 1961; Before the Revolution 1964; Le Fantôme de la Liberté 1974; The Inheritance 1976

Astin, John (1930-) That Touch of Mink 1962; The Wheeler Dealers 1963; Candy 1968; Viva Max! 1969; Evil Roy Slade 1971; Every Little Crook and Nanny 1972; Get to Know Your Rabbit 1972; Freaky Friday 1976; National Lampoon's European Vacation 1985; Teen Wolf Too 1987; Return of the Killer Tomatoes 1988; Huck and the King of Hearts 1993; The Frighteners 1996

Astin, MacKenzie (1973-) The Garbage Pail Kids Movie 1987; Iron Will 1994; Dream for an Insomniac 1996; The Last Days of Disco 1998; The Long Island Incident 1998; The Mating Habits of the Earthbound Human 1999; Stranger than Fiction 1999

Astin, Sean (1971-) The Goonies 1985; Like Father, like Son 1987; White Water Summer 1987; Staying Together 1989; The War of the Roses 1989; Memphis Belle 1990; Toy Soldiers 1991; California Man 1992; Rudy 1993; Safe Passage 1994; The Low Life 1995; Bulworth 1998; Deterrence 1999; The Last Producer 2000; The Lord of the Rings: The Fellowship of the Ring 2001; The Lord of the Rings: The Two Towers 2002; The Lord of the Rings: The Return of the King 2003; Balto - Wings of Change 2004; Elvis Has Left the Building 2004; 50 First Dates 2004; Marilyn Hotchkiss Ballroom Dancing & Charm School 2005; Click 2006

Astin, Skylar (1987-) Hamlet 2 2008; Pitch Perfect 2012; Pitch Perfect 2 2015

Astor, Gertrude (1887-1977) Stage Struck 1925; The Strong Man 1926; The Cat and the Canary 1927

Astor, Mary (1906-1987) Don Q, Son of Zorro 1925; Don Juan 1926; Two Arabian Knights 1927; Holiday 1930; Other Men's Women 1931; The Lost Squadron 1932; Red Dust 1932; A Successful Calamity 1932; Jennie Gerhardt 1933; The Kennel Murder

Case 1933; The Little Giant 1933; The World Changes 1933; The Case of the Howling Dog 1934; Upper World 1934; Page Miss Glory 1935; And So They Were Married 1936; Dodsworth 1936; The Hurricane 1937; The Prisoner of Zenda 1937; Listen, Darling 1938; Paradise for Three 1938; There's Always a Woman 1938; Midnight 1939; Brigham Young 1940; The Great Lie 1941; The Maltese Falcon 1941; Across the Pacific 1942; The Palm Beach Story 1942; Thousands Cheer 1943; Blonde Fever 1944; Meet Me in St Louis 1944; Claudia and David 1946; Cass Timberlane 1947; Cynthia 1947; Desert Fury 1947; Fiesta 1947; Act of Violence 1949; Any Number Can Play 1949; Little Women 1949; A Kiss before Dying 1956; The Power and the Prize 1956; The Devil's Hairpin 1957; This Happy Feeling 1958; A Stranger in My Arms 1959; Return to Peyton Place 1961; Hush... Hush, Sweet Charlotte 1964; Youngblood Hawke 1964

Ates, Roscoe aka Ates, Rosco (1892-1962) The Champ 1931; Freaks 1932; Alice in Wonderland 1933; What - No Beer? 1933

Atherton, William (1947-) Class of '44 1973; The Sugarland Express 1974; The Day of the Locust 1975; The Hindenburg 1975; Looking for Mr Goodbar 1977; Ghost Busters 1984; Real Genius 1985; No Mercy 1986; Die Hard 1988; Buried Alive 1990; Die Hard 2: Die Harder 1990; Grim Prairie Tales 1990; The Pelican Brief 1993; Broken Trust 1995; Formula for Death 1995; Frank and Jesse 1995; Bio-Dome 1996; Mad City 1997; Race to Space 2001; Aces 'n' Eights 2008

Atika, Aure Le Clan 2004; Fear(s) of the Dark 2007; Mademoiselle Chambon 2009

Atkin, Harvey (1942-) Meatballs 1979; Love and Death on Long Island 1998

Atkine, Féodor aka Atkine, Feodor (1948-) Le Beau Mariage 1982; Pauline at the Beach 1983; Leave All Fair 1985; Lola 1986; Nazi Hunter: the Beate Klarsfeld Story 1986; Sarraouina 1986; El Dorado 1988; High Heels 1991; Three Lives and Only One Death 1996; In the Courtyard 2014

Atkins, Christopher (1961-) The Blue Lagoon 1980; A Night in Heaven 1983; Listen to Me 1989; Die Watching 1993; The Little Unicorn 1998

Atkins, Eileen (1934-) Inadmissible Evidence 1968; I Don't Want to Be Born 1975; Equus 1977; Oliver Twist 1982; The Dresser 1983; Let Him Have It 1991; Wolf 1994; Jack & Sarah 1995; The Avengers 1998; Women Talking Dirty 1999; Gosford Park 2001; Wit 2001; What a Girl Wants 2003; Vanity Fair 2004; Ask the Dust 2006; Scenes of a Sexual Nature 2006; Evening 2007; Last Chance Harvey 2008; Wild Target 2009; Robin Hood 2010; Magic in the Moonlight 2014

Atkins, Essence Dance Flick 2009; A Haunted House 2013; A Haunted House 2 2014

Atkins, Finn Once upon a Time in the Midlands 2002; Eden Lake 2008

Atkins, Tom (1935-) Special Delivery 1976; The Fog 1980; Halloween III: Season of the Witch 1982; Lethal Weapon 1987; Maniac Cop 1988; My Bloody Valentine 2009; Drive Angry 2011

Atkinson, Frank (1893-1963) Ladies' Man 1931; Play Up the Band 1935; The Green Cockatoo 1937

Atkinson, Jayne (1959-) Free Willy 1993; Blank Check 1994; The Village 2004; Twelve and Holding 2005

Atkinson, Kate The Hard Word 2002; Japanese Story 2003

Atkinson, Rowan (1955-) The Tall Guy 1989; The Witches 1989; Hot Shots! Part Deux 1993; Four Weddings and a Funeral 1994; The Lion King 1994; Bean 1997; Maybe Baby 1999; Rat Race 2001; Scooby-Doo 2002; Johnny English 2003; Love Actually 2003; Keeping Mum 2005; Mr Bean's Holiday 2007; Johnny English Reborn 2011

Attal, Henri (1936-2003) Les Biches 1968; Juste avant la Nuit 1971

Attal, Yvan (1965-) A World without Pity 1989; Autobus 1991; Après l'Amour 1992; Portraits Chinois 1996; Love etc 1997; The Criminal 1999; With or without You 1999; Ma Femme Est une Actrice 2001; And Now... Ladies and Gentlemen 2002; Bon Voyage 2003; The Interpreter 2005; Le Serpent 2006; Rush Hour 3 2007; Leaving 2008; Rapt 2009; The Last Diamond 2014

Attaway, Ruth (1910-1987) Porgy and Bess 1959; Being There 1979

Attenborough, Richard (1923-2014) *In Which We Serve* 1942; *Journey Together* 1944; *Dancing with Crime* 1946; *A Matter of Life and Death* 1946; *School for Secrets* 1946; *Brighton Rock* 1947; *The Man Within* 1947; *The Guinea Pig* 1948; *London Belongs to Me* 1948; *Boys in Brown* 1949; *The Lost People* 1949; *Morning Departure* 1950; *Gift Horse* 1951; *The Magic Box* 1951; *Father's Doing Fine* 1952; *Eight o'Clock Walk* 1953; *The Ship That Died of Shame* 1955; *The Baby and the Battleship* 1956; *Brothers in Law* 1956; *Private's Progress* 1956; *The Scamp* 1957; *Danger Within* 1958; *Dunkirk* 1958; *The Man Upstairs* 1958; *Sea of Sand* 1958; *I'm All Right Jack* 1959; *Jet Storm* 1959; *SOS Pacific* 1959; *The Angry Silence* 1960; *The League of Gentlemen* 1960; *All Night Long* 1961; *Only Two Can Play* 1961; *Trial and Error* 1962; *The Great Escape* 1963; *Guns at Batasi* 1964; *Seance on a Wet Afternoon* 1964; *The Third Secret* 1964; *The Flight of the Phoenix* 1965; *The Sand Pebbles* 1966; *Doctor Dolittle* 1967; *The Bliss of Mrs Blossom* 1968; *Only When I Larf* 1968; *The Magic Christian* 1969; *The Last Grenade* 1970; *Loot* 1970; *A Severed Head* 1970; *10 Rillington Place* 1970; *And Then There Were None* 1974; *Brannigan* 1975; *Conduct Unbecoming* 1975; *Rosebud* 1975; *The Chess Players* 1977; *The Human Factor* 1979; *Jurassic Park* 1993; *Miracle on 34th Street* 1994; *Hamlet* 1996; *The Lost World: Jurassic Park* 1997; *Elizabeth* 1998; *Puckoon* 2002; *Cameraman: the Life & Work of Jack Cardiff* 2010

Atterbury, Malcolm (1907-1992) *Crime in the Streets* 1956; *Blood of Dracula* 1957; *How to Make a Monster* 1958; *The Learning Tree* 1969; *Emperor of the North* 1973

Atterton, Edward *The Hunchback of Notre Dame* 1997; *Britannic* 2000; *Relative Values* 2000

Atwater, Barry (1918-1978) *The True Story of Lynn Stuart* 1957; *Pork Chop Hill* 1959

Atwell, Hayley (1982-) *Cassandra's Dream* 2007; *Brideshead Revisited* 2008; *The Duchess* 2008; *Captain America: the First Avenger* 2011; *The Sweeney* 2012; *Jimi: All Is by My Side* 2013; *Testament of Youth* 2014; *Cinderella* 2015

Atwill, Lionel (1885-1946) *Doctor X* 1932; *Murders in the Zoo* 1933; *Mystery of the Wax Museum* 1933; *The Secret of Madame Blanche* 1933; *The Song of Songs* 1933; *The Sphinx* 1933; *The Vampire Bat* 1933; *The Age of Innocence* 1934; *Nana* 1934; *One More River* 1934; *Stamboul Quest* 1934; *Captain Blood* 1935; *The Devil Is a Woman* 1935; *Mark of the Vampire* 1935; *Murder Man* 1935; *Rendezvous* 1935; *Till We Meet Again* 1936; *The Great Garrick* 1937; *Lancer Spy* 1937; *The Last Train from Madrid* 1937; *The Great Waltz* 1938; *Three Comrades* 1938; *The Hound of the Baskervilles* 1939; *Mr Moto Takes a Vacation* 1939; *The Secret of Dr Kildare* 1939; *Son of Frankenstein* 1939; *The Three Musketeers* 1939; *Boom Town* 1940; *Johnny Apollo* 1940; *Man Made Monster* 1941; *The Ghost of Frankenstein* 1942; *The Mad Doctor of Market Street* 1942; *Pardon My Sarong* 1942; *Sherlock Holmes and the Secret Weapon* 1942; *To Be or Not to Be* 1942; *Frankenstein Meets the Wolf Man* 1943; *House of Frankenstein* 1944; *Fog Island* 1945; *House of Dracula* 1945

Atzmon, Anat (1958-) *Lemon Popsicle* 1978; *Every Time We Say Goodbye* 1986; *Double Edge* 1992

Auberjonois, René (1940-) *Lilith* 1964; *Petulia* 1968; *MASH* 1969; *Brewster McCloud* 1970; *McCabe and Mrs Miller* 1971; *Images* 1972; *Pete 'n' Tillie* 1972; *The Big Bus* 1976; *King Kong* 1976; *Eyes of Laura Mars* 1978; *Where the Buffalo Roam* 1980; *3:15* 1986; *Walker* 1987; *Police Academy 5: Assignment Miami Beach* 1988; *The Feud* 1989; *Gore Vidal's Billy the Kid* 1989; *The Little Mermaid* 1989; *The Ballad of Little Jo* 1993; *Cats Don't Dance* 1998; *Geppetto* 2000; *The Cat Returns* 2002

Aubert, K D *Frankenfish* 2004; *Soul Plane* 2004

Aubert, Lenore (1913-1993) *They Got Me Covered* 1943; *Action in Arabia* 1944; *I Wonder Who's Kissing Her Now* 1947; *Abbott and Costello Meet Frankenstein* 1948; *Abbott and Costello Meet the Killer, Boris Karloff* 1949

Aubrey, Anne (1937-) *No Time to Die* 1958; *The Bandit of Zhobe* 1959; *Killers of Kilimanjaro* 1960

Aubrey, James (1947-2010) *Lord of the Flies* 1963; *Terror* 1979; *Riders of the Storm* 1986

Aubrey, Juliet (1969-) *Go Now* 1995; *Food of Love* 1997; *Still Crazy* 1998; *The Lost Lover* 1999; *Iris* 2001; *The Constant Gardener* 2005; *F* 2010; *The Infiltrator* 2016

Aubuchon, Jacques (1924-1991) *Gun Glory* 1957; *Short Cut to Hell* 1957; *Thunder Road* 1958; *Wild and Wonderful* 1964

Auclair, Michel *aka* **Auclair, Michael** (1922-1988) *La Belle et la Bête* 1946; *Funny Face* 1957; *Les Mariés de l'An Deux* 1971; *Story of a Love Story* 1973; *Three Men to Destroy* 1980

Audley, Eleanor (1905-1991) *Cinderella* 1950; *Sleeping Beauty* 1959

Audley, Kentucker *The Sacrament* 2013; *Queen of Earth* 2015

Audley, Maxine (1923-1992) *The Sleeping Tiger* 1954; *A King in New York* 1957; *Hell Is a City* 1959; *Peeping Tom* 1960; *The Trials of Oscar Wilde* 1960; *Petticoat Pirates* 1961; *The Brain* 1962; *A Jolly Bad Fellow* 1964; *The Battle of the Villa Fiorita* 1965; *House of Cards* 1968; *Sinful Davey* 1969

Audran, Stéphane (1932-) *The Sign of Leo* 1959; *Les Bonnes Femmes* 1960; *Bluebeard* 1962; *Paris Vu Par...* 1965; *The Champagne Murders* 1966; *Les Biches* 1968; *La Femme infidèle* 1968; *Le Boucher* 1969; *La Rupture* 1970; *Juste avant la Nuit* 1971; *The Discreet Charm of the Bourgeoisie* 1972; *Les Noces Rouges* 1973; *And Then There Were None* 1974; *Vincent, François, Paul and the Others* 1974; *The Black Bird* 1975; *The Twist* 1976; *Blood Relatives* 1977; *The Devil's Advocate* 1977; *Silver Bears* 1977; *Violette Nozière* 1977; *Eagle's Wing* 1978; *The Big Red One* 1980; *Coup de Torchon* 1981; *Le Choc* 1982; *Bay Boy* 1984; *The Blood of Others* 1984; *Cop au Vin* 1984; *La Cage aux Folles III: "Elles" Se Marient* 1985; *Babette's Feast* 1987; *Sons* 1989; *The Turn of the Screw* 1992; *Maximum Risk* 1996; *Madeline* 1998

Auer, Mischa (1905-1967) *Paramount on Parade* 1930; *Delicious* 1931; *Tarzan the Fearless* 1933; *Bulldog Drummond Strikes Back* 1934; *Stamboul Quest* 1934; *I Dream Too Much* 1935; *My Man Godfrey* 1936; *Winterset* 1936; *One Hundred Men and a Girl* 1937; *Pick a Star* 1937; *Three Smart Girls* 1937; *Vogues of 1938* 1937; *The Rage of Paris* 1938; *Sweethearts* 1938; *You Can't Take It with You* 1938; *Destry Rides Again* 1939; *East Side of Heaven* 1939; *Seven Sinners* 1940; *The Flame of New Orleans* 1941; *Hellzapoppin'* 1941; *Lady in the Dark* 1944; *Up in Mabel's Room* 1944; *And Then There Were None* 1945; *Brewster's Millions* 1945; *A Royal Scandal* 1945; *Sentimental Journey* 1946; *Confidential Report* 1955; *The Monte Carlo Story* 1957; *We Joined the Navy* 1962; *Drop Dead Darling* 1966

Auger, Claudine (1941-) *Le Masque de Fer* 1962; *That Man George* 1965; *Thunderball* 1965; *Triple Cross* 1966; *Bay of Blood* 1971; *Salt on Our Skin* 1992

August, Pernilla *aka* **Wallgren, Pernilla** (1958-) *Fanny and Alexander* 1982; *Best Intentions* 1992; *Jerusalem* 1996; *Private Confessions* 1996; *Star Wars Episode I: the Phantom Menace* 1999; *Star Wars Episode II: Attack of the Clones* 2002; *Call Girl* 2012

Ault, Marie (1870-1951) *The Lodger* 1926; *Hindle Wakes* 1927; *Kitty* 1928

Aumont, Jean-Pierre (1911-2001) *Drôle de Drame* 1937; *Hôtel du Nord* 1938; *The Cross of Lorraine* 1943; *Heartbeat* 1946; *Song of Scheherazade* 1947; *The Gay Adventure* 1949; *Lili* 1953; *Royal Affairs in Versailles* 1953; *Napoléon* 1955; *Hilda Crane* 1956; *The Devil at Four o'Clock* 1961; *Five Miles to Midnight* 1963; *Cauldron of Blood* 1967; *Castle Keep* 1969; *Day for Night* 1973; *The Happy Hooker* 1975; *Mahogany* 1975; *Something Short of Paradise* 1979; *The Blood of Others* 1984; *Becoming Colette* 1991; *Jefferson in Paris* 1995; *The Proprietor* 1996

Aumont, Michel (1936-) *Nada* 1974; *Pourquoi Pas!* 1977; *Les Compères* 1983; *Dangerous Moves* 1984; *Sunday in the Country* 1984; *Le Cop II* 1989; *The King of Paris* 1995; *Angel of Mine* 2008; *Paris-Manhattan* 2012

Aumont, Tina *aka* **Marquand, Tina** (1946-2006) *The Game Is Over* 1966; *Partner* 1968; *Lifespan* 1975; *Casanova* 1976; *Illustrious Corpses* 1976; *A Matter of Time* 1976

Aussey, Germaine (1909-1979) *A Nous la Liberté* 1931; *The Golem* 1936

Austin, Albert (1881-1953) *Behind the Screen* 1916; *The Pawnshop* 1916; *The Cure* 1917; *The Immigrant* 1917; *A Dog's Life* 1918

Austin, Charlotte (1933-) *The Farmer Takes a Wife* 1953; *Desiree* 1954; *Gorilla at Large* 1954; *How to Be Very, Very Popular* 1955; *The Bride and the Beast* 1958

Austin, Jake T *Hotel for Dogs* 2008; *Rio* 2011; *Khumba* 2013

Austin, Jerry (1892-1976) *Saratoga Trunk* 1945; *Adventures of Don Juan* 1948

Austin, Karen (1955-) *Summer Rental* 1985; *Far from Home* 1989

Austin, Pamela *aka* **Austin, Pam** (1942-) *Kissin' Cousins* 1964; *The Perils of Pauline* 1967; *Evil Roy Slade* 1971

Austin, William (1884-1975) *It* 1927; *County Hospital* 1932; *Alice in Wonderland* 1933

Auteuil, Daniel (1950-) *Jean de Florette* 1986; *Manon des Sources* 1986; *Le Paltoquet* 1986; *Romuald et Juliette* 1989; *Un Coeur en Hiver* 1992; *Ma Saison Préférée* 1993; *Une Femme Française* 1994; *La Reine Margot* 1994; *La Séparation* 1994; *The Eighth Day* 1996; *Les Voleurs* 1996; *Le Bossu* 1997; *Lucie Aubrac* 1997; *The Lost Son* 1998; *The Escort* 1999; *The Girl on the Bridge* 1999; *La Veuve de Saint-Pierre* 2000; *The Closet* 2001; *Petites Coupures* 2002; *36 Quai des Orfèvres* 2004; *Hidden* 2005; *Conversations with My Gardener* 2006; *My Best Friend* 2006; *The Well Digger's Daughter* 2010; *The Lookout* 2012; *Marius* 2012; *Before the Winter Chill* 2013; *Fanny* 2013

Autry, Alan *aka* **Brown, Carlos** (1952-) *Southern Comfort* 1981; *World Gone Wild* 1988

Autry, Gene (1907-1998) *Down Mexico Way* 1941; *Riders in the Sky* 1949; *Riders of the Whistling Pines* 1949; *Mule Train* 1950; *Blue Canadian Rockies* 1952; *On Top of Old Smoky* 1953; *Alias Jesse James* 1959

Avalon, Frankie (1940-) *The Alamo* 1960; *Guns of the Timberland* 1960; *Voyage to the Bottom of the Sea* 1961; *Panic in Year Zero* 1962; *Beach Party* 1963; *The Castilian* 1963; *Bikini Beach* 1964; *Muscle Beach Party* 1964; *Beach Blanket Bingo* 1965; *Dr Goldfoot and the Bikini Machine* 1965; *How to Fill a Wild Bikini* 1965; *I'll Take Sweden* 1965; *Sergeant Deadhead* 1965; *Ski Party* 1965; *Fireball 500* 1966; *Sumuru* 1967; *Skidoo* 1968; *The Haunted House of Horror* 1969; *Back to the Beach* 1987

Avari, Erick (1952-) *The Beast of War* 1988; *Home Alone 4* 2002

Avery, James (1948-2013) *Without Warning: Terror in the Towers* 1993; *Death of a Cheerleader* 1994

Avery (2), Margaret (1944-) *Hell Up in Harlem* 1973; *Scott Joplin* 1977; *Which Way Is Up?* 1977; *The Lathe of Heaven* 1979; *The Color Purple* 1985; *Heat Wave* 1990; *The Set Up* 1995; *White Man's Burden* 1995; *Welcome Home Roscoe Jenkins* 2008

Avery, Val (1924-2009) *Edge of the City* 1957; *Hud* 1963; *Faces* 1968; *A Dream of Kings* 1969; *The Anderson Tapes* 1971; *Minnie and Moskowitz* 1971; *Black Caesar* 1973; *Continental Divide* 1981; *Jinxed!* 1982; *Easy Money* 1983; *Assault at West Point: the Court Martial of John Whittaker* 1994

Avile, Keiko (1933-2014) *Stray Dog* 1949; *The Bridges at Toko-Ri* 1954

Avonde, Richard (1914-1981) *Captain Carey, USA* 1950; *The 49th Man* 1953

Awaji, Keiko (1933-2014) *Stray Dog* 1949; *The Bridges at Toko-Ri* 1954

Awashima, Chikage (1924-2012) *Early Summer* 1951; *The Flavour of Green Tea over Rice* 1952; *Early Spring* 1956

Axberg, Eddie (1947-) *The Emigrants* 1971; *The New Land* 1972

Axton, Hoyt (1938-1999) *The Black Stallion* 1979; *Liar's Moon* 1982; *The Black Stallion Returns* 1983; *Heart like a Wheel* 1983; *Gremlins* 1984; *Act of Vengeance* 1986; *Disorganized Crime* 1989; *We're No Angels* 1989; *Buried Alive* 1990

Ayars, Ann (1918-1995) *Dr Kildare's Victory* 1941; *Apache Trail* 1942; *The Youngest Profession* 1943; *The Tales of Hoffmann* 1951

Aycox, Nicki *Dead Birds* 2004; *Joy Ride 2: Dead Ahead* 2008

Aycox, Nicki Lynn *aka* **Aycox, Nicki** (1975-) *Slap Her, She's French!* 2001; *Jeepers Creepers 2* 2003; *Perfect Stranger* 2007

Aykroyd, Dan (1952-) *1941* 1979; *The Blues Brothers* 1980; *Neighbors* 1981; *Doctor Detroit* 1983; *Trading Places* 1983; *Twilight Zone: the Movie* 1983; *Ghost Busters* 1984; *Nothing Lasts Forever* 1984; *Into the Night* 1985; *Spies like Us* 1985; *Dragnet* 1987; *Caddyshack II* 1988; *The Couch Trip* 1988; *The Great Outdoors* 1988; *My Stepmother Is an Alien* 1988; *Driving Miss Daisy* 1989; *Ghostbusters II* 1989; *Loose Cannons* 1990; *My Girl* 1991; *Nothing but Trouble* 1991; *Chaplin* 1992; *Sneakers* 1992; *This Is My Life* 1992; *Coneheads* 1993; *Exit to Eden* 1994; *My Girl 2* 1994; *North* 1994; *Rainbow* 1995; *Tommy Boy* 1995; *Celtic Pride* 1996; *Feeling Minnesota* 1996; *Getting Away with Murder* 1996; *My Fellow Americans* 1996; *Grosse Pointe Blank* 1997; *Antz* 1998; *Blues Brothers 2000* 1998; *Susan's Plan* 1998; *Diamonds* 1999; *The House of Mirth* 2000; *Loser* 2000; *Stardom* 2000; *The Curse of the Jade Scorpion* 2001; *Earth vs the Spider* 2001; *Evolution* 2001; *Pearl Harbor* 2001; *Crossroads* 2002; *Bright Young Things* 2003; *Christmas with the Kranks* 2004; *50 First Dates* 2004; *I Now Pronounce You Chuck & Larry* 2007; *War, Inc* 2008; *Yogi Bear* 2010; *The Campaign* 2012; *Behind the Candelabra* 2013; *Legends of Oz: Dorothy's Return* 2013; *Get on Up* 2014; *Tammy* 2014

Aylesworth, Arthur (1883-1946) *The Plot Thickens* 1936; *Test Pilot* 1938

Aylmer, Felix (1889-1979) *The Ghost Camera* 1933; *The Clairvoyant* 1934; *Doctor's Orders* 1934; *As You Like It* 1936; *Dusty Ermine* 1936; *Seven Sinners* 1936; *Tudor Rose* 1936; *The Mill on the Floss* 1937; *The Vicar of Bray* 1937; *Sixty Glorious Years* 1938; *Charley's (Big Hearted) Aunt* 1940; *The Black Sheep of Whitehall* 1941; *The Ghost of St Michael's* 1941; *I Thank You* 1941; *The Saint's Vacation* 1941; *South American George* 1941; *The Young Mr Pitt* 1942; *The Demi-Paradise* 1943; *Time Flies* 1944; *The Way to the Stars* 1945; *The Wicked Lady* 1945; *The Magic Bow* 1946; *The Years Between* 1946; *The Ghosts of Berkeley Square* 1947; *A Man about the House* 1947; *The Man Within* 1947; *The October Man* 1947; *The Calendar* 1948; *Hamlet* 1948; *Edward, My Son* 1949; *Eye Witness* 1949; *Trio* 1950; *The Lady with the Lamp* 1951; *The Man Who Watched Trains Go By* 1952; *Knights of the Round Table* 1953; *The Master of Ballantrae* 1953; *The Angel Who Pawned Her Harp* 1954; *Anastasia* 1956; *Loser Takes All* 1956; *Saint Joan* 1957; *The Doctor's Dilemma* 1958; *The Mummy* 1959; *The Hands of Orlac* 1960; *Never Take Sweets from a Stranger* 1960; *The Boys* 1961; *The Road to Hong Kong* 1962; *The Running Man* 1963; *The Chalk Garden* 1964; *Hostile Witness* 1968

Aylward, John *Buddy* 1997; *Path to War* 2002

Aynesworth, Alan (1864-1959) *Love, Life and Laughter* 1934; *The Last Days of Dolwyn* 1949

Ayoade, Richard (1977-) *Bunny & the Bull* 2009; *The Watch* 2012

Ayres, Leah (1957-) *The Burning* 1981; *Eddie Macon's Run* 1983; *Bloodsport* 1987

Ayres, Lew *aka* **Ayres, Lewis** (1908-1996) *Big News* 1929; *The Kiss* 1929; *All Quiet on the Western Front* 1930; *A Handful of Clouds* 1930; *The Iron Man* 1931; *The Impatient Maiden* 1932; *State Fair* 1933; *The Last Train from Madrid* 1937; *Holiday* 1938; *Young Dr Kildare* 1938; *Broadway Serenade* 1939; *Calling Dr Kildare* 1939; *The Ice Follies of 1939* 1939; *Remember?* 1939; *The Secret of Dr Kildare* 1939; *Dr Kildare's Strange Case* 1940; *Dr Kildare Goes Home* 1940; *Dr Kildare's Crisis* 1940; *Dr Kildare's Wedding Day* 1941; *Dr Kildare's Victory* 1941; *The People vs Dr Kildare* 1941; *Fingers at the Window* 1942; *The Dark Mirror* 1946; *The Unfaithful* 1947; *Johnny Belinda* 1948; *The Capture* 1950; *Donovan's Brain* 1953; *Advise and Consent* 1962; *The Carpetbaggers* 1964; *The Biscuit Eater* 1972; *The Man* 1972; *Battle for the Planet of the Apes* 1973; *End of the World* 1977; *Damien - Omen II* 1978; *Salem's Lot* 1979

Ayres, Robert (1914-1968) *Cosh Boy* 1952; *River Beat* 1954; *Time Lock* 1957; *First Man into Space* 1958; *A Night to Remember* 1958; *The Sicilians* 1964; *Battle beneath the Earth* 1968

Ayres, Rosalind (1946-) *That'll Be the Day* 1973; *Stardust* 1974; *Beautiful People* 1999

Azabal, Lubna (1973-) *Far Away* 2001; *Almost Peaceful* 2002; *Exiles* 2004;

Paradise Now 2005; *Incendies* 2010; *Free Men* 2011

Azaïs, Kévin *Les Combattants* 2014; *Summertime* 2015

Azaria, Hank (1964-) *Cool Blue* 1988; *Quiz Show* 1994; *The Birdcage* 1996; *Anastasia* 1997; *Godzilla* 1997; *Great Expectations* 1997; *Grosse Pointe Blank* 1997; *Celebrity* 1998; *Homegrown* 1998; *Bartok the Magnificent* 1999; *Cradle Will Rock* 1999; *Mystery, Alaska* 1999; *Mystery Men* 1999; *Tuesdays with Morrie* 1999; *Fail Safe* 2000; *America's Sweethearts* 2001; *Shattered Glass* 2003; *Along Came Polly* 2004; *Dodgeball: a True Underdog Story* 2004; *The Aristocrats* 2005; *Run Fatboy Run* 2007; *The Simpsons Movie* 2007; *Night at the Museum 2* 2009; *Year One* 2009; *Love & Other Drugs* 2010; *Happy Feet Two* 2011; *The Smurfs* 2011; *Lovelace* 2013; *The Smurfs 2* 2013

Azéma, Sabine (1955-) *Life Is a Bed of Roses* 1983; *Sunday in the Country* 1984; *Mélo* 1986; *Life and Nothing But* 1989; *Smoking/No Smoking* 1993; *Le Bonheur Est dans le Pré* 1995; *Mon Homme* 1996; *On Connaît la Chanson* 1997; *La Bûche* 1999; *The Officers' Ward* 2001; *Pas sur la Bouche* 2003; *Private Fears in Public Places* 2006; *Wild Grass* 2008; *The Well Digger's Daughter* 2010; *Life of Riley* 2014

Azito, Tony (1949-1995) *The Pirates of Penzance* 1983; *Bloodhounds of Broadway* 1989; *Necronomicon* 1993

Azmi, Shabana (1948-) *Ankur* 1974; *Nishant* 1975; *The Chess Players* 1977; *Junoon* 1978; *Madame Sousatzka* 1988; *Immaculate Conception* 1991; *City of Joy* 1992; *Son of the Pink Panther* 1993; *Fire* 1996; *Side Streets* 1998; *It's a Wonderful Afterlife* 2010; *The Reluctant Fundamentalist* 2012

Aznavour, Charles (1924-) *Shoot the Pianist* 1960; *Le Testament d'Orphée* 1960; *Candy* 1968; *The Adventurers* 1970; *The Games* 1970; *The Blockhouse* 1973; *And Then There Were None* 1974; *The Twist* 1976; *The Tin Drum* 1979; *Edith et Marcel* 1983; *Il Maestro* 1989; *Ararat* 2002

Azzara, Candy *aka* **Azzara, Candice** (1945-) *House Calls* 1978; *Fatso* 1979; *Divorce Wars* 1982; *Easy Money* 1983

Baal, Karin (1940-) *Hannibal Brooks* 1968; *Berlin Alexanderplatz* 1980; *Lola* 1982

Babatunde, Obba *aka* **Babatundé, Obba** (1951-) *Miami Blues* 1990; *The Importance of Being Earnest* 1992; *Introducing Dorothy Dandridge* 1999; *Life* 1999; *After the Sunset* 2004

Babcock, Barbara (1937-) *The Black Marble* 1980; *The Lords of Discipline* 1983; *That Was Then... This Is Now* 1985; *Happy Together* 1989; *Far and Away* 1992; *Home Alone 4* 2002

Babe, Fabienne (1962-) *Fatherland* 1986; *Les Voleurs* 1996; *I Saw Ben Barka Get Killed* 2005; *You and the Night* 2013

Babluani, Georges *13 (Tzameti)* 2005; *Legacy* 2017

Bacall, Lauren (1924-2014) *To Have and Have Not* 1944; *Confidential Agent* 1945; *The Big Sleep* 1946; *Dark Passage* 1947; *Key Largo* 1948; *Bright Leaf* 1950; *Young Man with a Horn* 1950; *How to Marry a Millionaire* 1953; *Woman's World* 1954; *Blood Alley* 1955; *The Cobweb* 1955; *Written on the Wind* 1956; *Designing Woman* 1957; *The Gift of Love* 1958; *North West Frontier* 1959; *Sex and the Single Girl* 1964; *Harper* 1966; *Murder on the Orient Express* 1974; *The Shootist* 1976; *Perfect Gentlemen* 1978; *HEALTH* 1980; *The Fan* 1981; *Appointment with Death* 1988; *Mr North* 1988; *Tree of Hands* 1988; *Dinner at Eight* 1989; *Misery* 1990; *All I Want for Christmas* 1991; *Pret-a-Porter* 1994; *From the Mixed-Up Files of Mrs Basil E Frankweiler* 1995; *The Mirror Has Two Faces* 1996; *My Fellow Americans* 1996; *Diamonds* 1999; *Madeline: Lost in Paris* 1999; *Dogville* 2003; *Birth* 2004; *Howl's Moving Castle* 2004; *Manderlay* 2005; *These Foolish Things* 2006; *The Walker* 2006; *Cameraman: the Life & Work of Jack Cardiff* 2010

Bacall, Michael *Wait until Spring, Bandini* 1989; *Manic* 2001

Baccaloni, Salvatore *aka* **Baccaloni** (1900-1969) *Full of Life* 1956; *Merry Andrew* 1958; *Rock-a-Bye Baby* 1958; *Fanny* 1961; *The Pigeon That Took Rome* 1962

Baccarin, Morena *Serenity* 2005; *Deadpool* 2016

Bach, Barbara (1947-) *The Short Night of the Glass Dolls* 1971; *The Spy Who Loved Me* 1977; *Force 10 from Navarone* 1978; *The Humanoid* 1979; *Jaguar Lives!* 1979; *Caveman* 1981; *Give My Regards to Broad Street* 1984

Bach, John (1946-) *Battletruck* 1982; *Georgia* 1988; *Blood Oath* 1990

Bachar, Dian (1971-) *Orgazmo* 1997; *BASEketball* 1998

Bacharach, Burt (1928-) *Austin Powers: International Man of Mystery* 1997; *Austin Powers: the Spy Who Shagged Me* 1999

Bachchan, Abhishek (1976-) *Kuch Naa Kaho* 2003; *Dhoom* 2004; *Hum Tum* 2004; *Naach* 2004; *Sarkar* 2005; *Dhoom: 2* 2006; *Guru* 2007; *Sarkar Raj* 2008

Bachchan, Amitabh (1942-) *Sholay* 1975; *Hum* 1991; *Mohabbatein* 2000; *Kabhi Khushi Kabhie Gham...* 2001; *Armaan* 2003; *Black* 2004; *Dev* 2004; *Lakshya* 2004; *Veer-Zaara* 2004; *Paheli* 2005; *Sarkar* 2005; *WAQT: the Race against Time* 2005; *Cheeni Kum* 2007; *Eklavya: the Royal Guard* 2007; *Sarkar Raj* 2008

Bachchan, Jaya aka **Bhaduri, Jaya** (1948-) *The Big City* 1963; *Kabhi Khushi Kabhie Gham...* 2001; *Kal Ho Naa Ho* 2003

Bachleda-Curus, Alicja aka **Bachleda, Alicja** *Summer Storm* 2004; *Trade* 2006; *Ondine* 2009

Backer, Brian (1956-) *The Burning* 1981; *Fast Times at Ridgemont High* 1982; *Moving Violations* 1985

Backus, Georgia (1900-1983) *Apache Drums* 1951; *Cause for Alarm* 1951

Backus, Jim (1913-1989) *A Dangerous Profession* 1949; *The Great Lover* 1949; *Bright Victory* 1951; *Half Angel* 1951; *I'll See You in My Dreams* 1951; *Iron Man* 1951; *M* 1951; *The Man with a Cloak* 1951; *Don't Bother to Knock* 1952; *Angel Face* 1953; *Francis in the Navy* 1955; *Rebel without a Cause* 1955; *The Square Jungle* 1955; *When Magoo Flew* 1955; *The Girl He Left Behind* 1956; *The Great Man* 1956; *Meet Me in Las Vegas* 1956; *You Can't Run Away from It* 1956; *Man of a Thousand Faces* 1957; *Top Secret Affair* 1957; *The High Cost of Loving* 1958; *Macabre* 1958; *Ask Any Girl* 1959; *The Big Operator* 1959; *The Wild and the Innocent* 1959; *Ice Palace* 1960; *The Horizontal Lieutenant* 1962; *My Six Loves* 1962; *The Wonderful World of the Brothers Grimm* 1962; *Johnny Cool* 1963; *Sunday in New York* 1963; *The Wheeler Dealers* 1963; *Advance to the Rear* 1964; *John Goldfarb, Please Come Home* 1964; *Billie* 1965; *Fluffy* 1965; *Where Were You When the Lights Went Out?* 1968; *Hello Down There* 1969; *Myra Breckinridge* 1970; *Crazy Mama* 1975; *Friday Foster* 1975; *Good Guys Wear Black* 1977; *Pete's Dragon* 1977

Baclanova, Olga (1899-1974) *The Docks of New York* 1928; *Freaks* 1932; *Claudia* 1943

Bacon, Irving (1893-1965) *Internes Can't Take Money* 1937; *Blondie!* 1938; *The Howards of Virginia* 1940; *A Guy Named Joe* 1944; *Under Western Skies* 1945; *Cause for Alarm* 1951; *Room for One More* 1952; *The Glenn Miller Story* 1953; *Black Horse Canyon* 1954; *A Star Is Born* 1954; *At Gunpoint* 1955

Bacon, Kevin (1958-) *National Lampoon's Animal House* 1978; *Friday the 13th* 1980; *Hero at Large* 1980; *Diner* 1982; *Footloose* 1984; *Quicksilver* 1986; *End of the Line* 1987; *Planes, Trains and Automobiles* 1987; *Criminal Law* 1988; *She's Having a Baby* 1988; *The Big Picture* 1989; *Tremors* 1989; *Flatliners* 1990; *He Said, She Said* 1991; *JFK* 1991; *Pyrates* 1991; *Queens Logic* 1991; *A Few Good Men* 1992; *The Air Up There* 1993; *Murder in the First* 1994; *The River Wild* 1994; *Apollo 13* 1995; *Balto* 1995; *Sleepers* 1996; *Picture Perfect* 1997; *Telling Lies in America* 1997; *Digging to China* 1998; *Wild Things* 1998; *My Dog Skip* 1999; *Stir of Echoes* 1999; *Hollow Man* 2000; *Novocaine* 2001; *Trapped* 2002; *In the Cut* 2003; *Mystic River* 2003; *The Woodsman* 2004; *Beauty Shop* 2005; *Where the Truth Lies* 2005; *The Air I Breathe* 2007; *Death Sentence* 2007; *Rails & Ties* 2007; *Frost/Nixon* 2008; *Super* 2010; *X-Men: First Class* 2011; *Jayne Mansfield's Car* 2012; *R.I.P.D.* 2013; *Cop Car* 2015; *The Darkness* 2016

Bacon, Lloyd (1890-1955) *The Tramp* 1915; *Behind the Screen* 1916

Bacon, Max (1904-1969) *King Arthur Was a Gentleman* 1942; *Bees in Paradise* 1943; *Miss London Ltd* 1943; *Give Us the Moon* 1944; *Privilege* 1967

Bacri, Jean-Pierre (1951-) *Entre Nous* 1983; *Subway* 1985; *C'est la Vie* 1990;

L'Homme de Ma Vie 1992; *Un Air de Famille* 1996; *On Connaît la Chanson* 1997; *Place Vendôme* 1998; *Le Goût des Autres* 1999; *Look at Me* 2004; *Let's Talk about the Rain* 2008; *Looking for Hortense* 2012; *Under the Rainbow* 2013

Badalucco, Michael (1954-) *Mac* 1992; *Leon* 1994; *Stolen Hearts* 1996; *Love Walked In* 1997; *O Brother, Where Art Thou?* 2000; *The Man Who Wasn't There* 2001

Baddeley, Angela (1904-1976) *The Ghost Train* 1931; *Those Were the Days* 1934

Baddeley, Hermione (1906-1986) *Brighton Rock* 1947; *No Room at the Inn* 1948; *Quartet* 1948; *Dear Mr Prohack* 1949; *Passport to Pimlico* 1949; *The Woman in Question* 1950; *Scrooge* 1951; *There Is Another Sun* 1951; *Tom Brown's Schooldays* 1951; *Cosh Boy* 1952; *The Pickwick Papers* 1952; *Time Gentlemen Please!* 1952; *Counterspy* 1953; *The Belles of St Trinian's* 1954; *Room at the Top* 1958; *Jet Storm* 1959; *Midnight Lace* 1960; *Mary Poppins* 1964; *The Unsinkable Molly Brown* 1964; *Do Not Disturb* 1965; *Marriage on the Rocks* 1965; *The Adventures of Bullwhip Griffin* 1967; *The Happiest Millionaire* 1967; *The Aristocats* 1970; *Up the Front* 1972; *CHOMPS* 1979; *The Secret of NIMH* 1982

Badel, Alan (1923-1982) *Salome* 1953; *Three Cases of Murder* 1953; *Magic Fire* 1956; *Bitter Harvest* 1963; *This Sporting Life* 1963; *Children of the Damned* 1964; *Arabesque* 1966; *Otley* 1968; *Where's Jack?* 1969; *The Adventurers* 1970; *The Day of the Jackal* 1973; *Luther* 1974; *Telefon* 1977; *Agatha* 1978; *The Riddle of the Sands* 1978; *Nijinsky* 1980

Badel, Sarah (1943-) *Not without My Daughter* 1990; *Mrs Dalloway* 1997; *Cotton Mary* 1999

Bader, Diedrich (1966-) *The Beverly Hillbillies* 1993; *Office Space* 1999; *The Country Bears* 2002; *Napoleon Dynamite* 2004; *Surf's Up* 2007; *Meet the Spartans* 2008

Badgley, Penn (1986-) *John Tucker Must Die* 2006; *The Stepfather* 2009; *Easy A* 2010; *Margin Call* 2011; *Cymbeline* 2014

Badham, Mary (1952-) *To Kill a Mockingbird* 1962; *This Property Is Condemned* 1966

Badie, Laurence (1934-) *Jeux Interdits* 1953; *Muriel* 1963

Badland, Annette (1950-) *Jabberwocky* 1977; *Anchoress* 1993; *Captives* 1994; *Angels and Insects* 1995; *Little Voice* 1998; *The Baker* 2007; *Mother's Milk* 2012

Bae Doo-na *Sympathy for Mr Vengeance* 2002; *Take Care of My Cat* 2002; *The Host* 2006

Baek Yun-shik *Save the Green Planet!* 2003; *The Taste of Money* 2012

Baer, Buddy (1915-1986) *Africa Screams* 1949; *The Big Sky* 1952; *Jack and the Beanstalk* 1952; *Dream Wife* 1953; *Fair Wind to Java* 1953; *Slightly Scarlet* 1956

Baer, Edouard aka **Baer, Édouard** *Betty Fisher and Other Stories* 2001; *Molière* 2006; *An Ordinary Execution* 2010

Baer, Harry (1947-) *Gods of the Plague* 1969; *Whity* 1970; *Jail Bait* 1972; *Fox and His Friends* 1975; *The Third Generation* 1979; *La Amiga* 1988

Baer, Max (1909-1959) *The Prizefighter and the Lady* 1933; *Over She Goes* 1937; *The Navy Comes Through* 1942; *Africa Screams* 1949; *Bride for Sale* 1949; *The Harder They Fall* 1956

Baer Jr, Max (1937-) *A Time for Killing* 1967; *Macon County Line* 1973

Baer, Parley (1914-2002) *Comanche Territory* 1950; *Gypsy* 1962; *Bedtime Story* 1964; *Two on a Guillotine* 1964; *The Ugly Dachshund* 1966

Baez, Joan *Festival* 1967; *Woodstock* 1970; *Dynamite Chicken* 1971; *Another Day/Another Time* 2013

Bagby III, Larry aka **Bagby, Larry** (1974-) *Walk the Line* 2005; *Age of the Dragons* 2010

Bagley, Lorri (1973-) *Trick* 1999; *The Stepford Wives* 2004

Bahns, Maxine (1971-) *The Brothers McMullen* 1995; *She's the One* 1996; *Cutaway* 2000

Bai Ling (1970-) *Red Corner* 1997; *Anna and the King* 1999; *The Breed* 2001; *She Hate Me* 2004; *Sky Captain and the World of Tomorrow* 2004; *Edmond* 2005; *Crank: High Voltage* 2009

Bailey, Bill *Terkel in Trouble* 2006; *Burke & Hare* 2010; *Chalet Girl* 2010

Bailey (2), Bill (1964-) *Saving Grace* 2000; *Nanny McPhee & the Big Bang* 2010

Bailey, G W (1945-) *Police Academy* 1984; *Rustler's Rhapsody* 1985; *Warning Sign* 1985; *Short Circuit* 1986; *Burglar* 1987; *Mannequin* 1987; *Police Academy 5: Assignment Miami Beach* 1988; *Police Academy: Mission to Moscow* 1994

Bailey, Jonathan *Five Children and It* 2004; *The Mercy* 2016

Bailey, Laura *The Staircase Murders* 2007; *Space Chimps 2: Zartog Strikes Back* 2009

Bailey, Pearl (1918-1990) *Carmen Jones* 1954; *That Certain Feeling* 1956; *St Louis Blues* 1958; *Porgy and Bess* 1959; *All the Fine Young Cannibals* 1960; *The Landlord* 1970; *The Fox and the Hound* 1981

Bailey, Raymond (1904-1980) *The Incredible Shrinking Man* 1957; *Vertigo* 1958; *The Gallant Hours* 1960

Bailey Jr, Robert *What the #$*! Do We Know!?* 2004; *Coraline* 2008

Bailey, Robin (1919-1999) *Portrait of Clare* 1950; *Catch Us If You Can* 1965; *Blind Terror* 1971; *Jane and the Lost City* 1987

Bain, Barbara (1931-) *Trust Me* 1989; *Gideon* 1999; *Panic* 2000; *American Gun* 2002

Bain, Conrad (1923-2013) *CHOMPS* 1979; *Postcards from the Edge* 1990

Bainter, Fay (1892-1968) *This Side of Heaven* 1934; *Make Way for Tomorrow* 1937; *Quality Street* 1937; *Jezebel* 1938; *The Shining Hour* 1938; *White Banners* 1938; *Daughters Courageous* 1939; *A Bill of Divorcement* 1940; *Maryland* 1940; *Our Town* 1940; *Young Tom Edison* 1940; *Babes on Broadway* 1941; *The War against Mrs Hadley* 1942; *Woman of the Year* 1942; *Cry Havoc* 1943; *The Heavenly Body* 1943; *The Human Comedy* 1943; *Presenting Lily Mars* 1943; *Dark Waters* 1944; *State Fair* 1945; *The Kid from Brooklyn* 1946; *The Virginian* 1946; *Deep Valley* 1947; *The Secret Life of Walter Mitty* 1947; *Give My Regards to Broadway* 1948; *June Bride* 1948; *Close to My Heart* 1951; *The President's Lady* 1953; *The Children's Hour* 1961

Baio, Scott (1961-) *Bugsy Malone* 1976; *Skatetown, USA* 1979; *Foxes* 1980; *Zapped!* 1982; *Danielle Steel's Mixed Blessings* 1995; *Cursed* 2005

Baird, Diora *The Texas Chainsaw Massacre: the Beginning* 2006; *My Best Friend's Girl* 2008

Baird, Harry (1931-2005) *Station Six-Sahara* 1962; *The Oblong Box* 1969

Baird, Jimmy (1945-) *The Return of Dracula* 1958; *The Black Orchid* 1959

Bairstow, Scott (1970-) *White Fang 2: Myth of the White Wolf* 1994; *Wild America* 1997; *Two for Texas* 1998; *To Live For* 1999; *Tuck Everlasting* 2002

Baisho, Mitsuko (1946-) *Vengeance Is Mine* 1979; *Akira Kurosawa's Dreams* 1990; *The Eel* 1997; *Warm Water under a Red Bridge* 2001

Baitz, Jon Robin (1961-) *Last Summer in the Hamptons* 1995; *One Fine Day* 1996

Bajpai, Manoj aka **Bajpayee, Manoj** (1969-) *Bandit Queen* 1994; *Zubeidaa* 2000; *Gangs of Wasseypur* 2012; *Gangs of Wasseypur II* 2012

Bakalyan, Richard aka **Bakalyan, Dick** (1931-2015) *The Delicate Delinquent* 1957; *The Delinquents* 1957; *The Cool and the Crazy* 1958; *The Computer Wore Tennis Shoes* 1969; *Return from Witch Mountain* 1978; *Blame It on the Night* 1984

Bakare, Ariyon *The Secret Laughter of Women* 1998; *Dead Bolt Dead* 1999; *Happy Ever Afters* 2009

Baker, Art (1898-1966) *Abie's Irish Rose* 1946; *The Beginning or the End* 1947; *Homecoming* 1948

Baker, Benny (1907-1994) *Thanks a Million* 1935; *Up in Arms* 1944; *Boy, Did I Get a Wrong Number* 1966

Baker, Blanche (1956-) *French Postcards* 1979; *Nobody's Child* 1986; *The Handmaid's Tale* 1990; *Dead Funny* 1995

Baker, Carroll (1931-) *Easy to Love* 1953; *Baby Doll* 1956; *Giant* 1956; *The Big Country* 1958; *But Not for Me* 1959; *Bridge to the Sun* 1961; *How the West Was Won* 1962; *Station Six-Sahara* 1962; *The Carpetbaggers* 1964; *Cheyenne Autumn* 1964; *Sylvia* 1964; *The Greatest Story Ever Told* 1965; *Harlow* 1965; *Jack of Diamonds* 1967; *Captain Apache* 1971; *Bad* 1976; *The World Is Full of Married Men* 1979; *The Watcher in the Woods* 1982; *Star 80* 1983; *Native Son* 1986; *Ironweed* 1987; *Kindergarten Cop* 1990; *Blonde Fist* 1991; *The Game* 1997

Baker, David Aaron (1963-) *The Tao of Steve* 2000; *Melinda and Melinda* 2004; *Edge of Darkness* 2009

Baker, Diane (1938-) *The Best of Everything* 1959; *The Diary of Anne Frank* 1959; *Journey to the Center of the Earth* 1959; *Tess of the Storm Country* 1960; *The Wizard of Baghdad* 1960; *Hemingway's Adventures of a Young Man* 1962; *The Prize* 1963; *Strait-Jacket* 1963; *Marnie* 1964; *Mirage* 1965; *The Horse in the Gray Flannel Suit* 1968; *Baker's Hawk* 1976; *Imaginary Crimes* 1994; *The Net* 1995; *The Cable Guy* 1996; *Murder at 1600* 1997

Baker, Dylan (1958-) *Planes, Trains and Automobiles* 1987; *The Wizard of Loneliness* 1988; *The Long Walk Home* 1990; *Delirious* 1991; *Love Potion No 9* 1992; *Disclosure* 1994; *True Blue* 1996; *Happiness* 1998; *Oxygen* 1999; *Simply Irresistible* 1999; *Thirteen Days* 2000; *Along Came a Spider* 2001; *Head of State* 2003; *Kinsey* 2004; *Hide and Seek* 2005; *The Matador* 2005; *Diminished Capacity* 2007; *Trick 'r Treat* 2007; *The Benefactor* 2015

Baker, Fay (1917-1987) *Tell It to the Judge* 1949; *The Company She Keeps* 1950; *The House on Telegraph Hill* 1951; *Don't Knock the Rock* 1956

Baker (1), Frank (1892-1980) *The New Adventures of Tarzan* 1935; *Tarzan and the Green Goddess* 1938

Baker, George (1931-2011) *The Intruder* 1953; *The Dam Busters* 1954; *The Ship That Died of Shame* 1955; *The Woman for Joe* 1955; *The Extra Day* 1956; *The Feminine Touch* 1956; *A Hill in Korea* 1956; *The Moonraker* 1957; *No Time for Tears* 1957; *Tread Softly Stranger* 1958; *Lancelot and Guinevere* 1963; *Goodbye, Mr Chips* 1969; *Justine* 1969; *On Her Majesty's Secret Service* 1969; *The Executioner* 1970; *A Warm December* 1973; *The Thirty-Nine Steps* 1978; *For Queen and Country* 1988; *Back to the Secret Garden* 2000

Baker, Henry Judd aka **Baker, Henry** *Seizure* 1974; *Clean and Sober* 1988

Baker, Hylda (1905-1986) *Saturday Night and Sunday Morning* 1960; *Up the Junction* 1967; *Oliver!* 1968; *Nearest and Dearest* 1972

Baker, Joby (1935-) *Gidget* 1959; *The Last Angry Man* 1959; *Key Witness* 1960; *The Wackiest Ship in the Army* 1961; *Girl Happy* 1965; *Blackbeard's Ghost* 1967; *Valley of Mystery* 1967

Baker, Joe (1928-2001) *Where the Bullets Fly* 1966; *Pocahontas* 1995

Baker, Joe Don (1936-) *Guns of the Magnificent Seven* 1969; *Adam at 6 AM* 1970; *Wild Rovers* 1971; *Junior Bonner* 1972; *Charley Varrick* 1973; *The Outfit* 1973; *Golden Needles* 1974; *Framed* 1975; *The Pack* 1977; *Wacko* 1981; *The Natural* 1984; *Fletch* 1985; *The Killing Time* 1987; *Leonard, Part 6* 1987; *The Living Daylights* 1987; *Criminal Law* 1988; *The Children* 1990; *Cape Fear* 1991; *The Distinguished Gentleman* 1992; *Complex of Fear* 1993; *Reality Bites* 1994; *Ring of Steel* 1994; *Congo* 1995; *GoldenEye* 1995; *Panther* 1995; *The Underneath* 1995; *Tomorrow Never Dies* 1997; *The Dukes of Hazzard* 2005; *Strange Wilderness* 2007

Baker, Kathy (1950-) *A Killing Affair* 1985; *Nobody's Child* 1986; *Street Smart* 1987; *Clean and Sober* 1988; *Jacknife* 1988; *Dad* 1989; *Edward Scissorhands* 1990; *The Image* 1990; *Mister Frost* 1990; *Article 99* 1992; *Jennifer Eight* 1992; *Mad Dog and Glory* 1992; *Lush Life* 1993; *To Gillian on Her 37th Birthday* 1996; *Inventing the Abbotts* 1997; *The Cider House Rules* 1999; *Things You Can Tell Just by Looking at Her* 2000; *The Glass House* 2001; *Door to Door* 2002; *Cold Mountain* 2003; *13 Going on 30* 2004; *All the King's Men* 2005; *The Jane Austen Book Club* 2007; *Last Chance Harvey* 2008; *Unstable* 2009; *Machine Gun Preacher* 2011; *Take Shelter* 2011; *Saving Mr Banks* 2013; *Boulevard* 2014; *The Age of Adaline* 2015

Baker (1), Kenny (1912-1985) *The Goldwyn Follies* 1938; *At the Circus* 1939; *The Mikado* 1939; *The Harvey Girls* 1946

Baker (2), Kenny (1934-2016) *Star Wars Episode IV: a New Hope* 1977; *Star Wars Episode V: the Empire Strikes Back* 1980; *Time Bandits* 1981; *Star Wars Episode VI: Return of the Jedi* 1983; *Amadeus* 1984; *UFO* 1993; *Star Wars Episode I: the Phantom Menace* 1999; *Star Wars Episode II: Attack of the Clones* 2002; *Star Wars Episode III: Revenge of the Sith* 2005; *Star Wars Episode VII: the Force Awakens* 2015

Baker, Phil (1896-1963) *The Goldwyn Follies* 1938; *The Gang's All Here* 1943

Baker, Ray aka **Baker, Raymond** (1948-) *Nobody's Child* 1986; *Everybody's All-American* 1988; *Heart Condition* 1990; *Hexed* 1993; *Anywhere but Here* 1999

Baker, Rick aka **Baker, Richard A** (1950-) *King Kong* 1976; *The Kentucky Fried Movie* 1977

Baker, Robert *Seraphim Falls* 2006; *Special (PX) - Specioprin Hydrochloride* 2006

Baker (1), Simon aka **Baker-Denny, Simon** (1969-) *Judas Kiss* 1998; *Ride with the Devil* 1999; *Sunset Strip* 2000; *The Affair of the Necklace* 2001; *The Ring Two* 2004; *George A Romero's Land of the Dead* 2005; *The Devil Wears Prada* 2006; *Something New* 2006; *The Lodger* 2009; *The Killer inside Me* 2010; *I Give It a Year* 2013

Baker (2), Simon (1986-) *Smoke Signals* 1998; *Spooky House* 1999; *Red Planet* 2000

Baker, Stanley (1928-1976) *Captain Horatio Hornblower RN* 1951; *Home to Danger* 1951; *The Cruel Sea* 1952; *Knights of the Round Table* 1953; *The Red Beret* 1953; *Beautiful Stranger* 1954; *The Good Die Young* 1954; *Hell below Zero* 1954; *Helen of Troy* 1955; *Richard III* 1955; *Alexander the Great* 1956; *Checkpoint* 1956; *Child in the House* 1956; *A Hill in Korea* 1956; *Campbell's Kingdom* 1957; *Hell Drivers* 1957; *Sea Fury* 1958; *Violent Playground* 1958; *The Angry Hills* 1959; *Blind Date* 1959; *Hell Is a City* 1959; *Jet Storm* 1959; *Yesterday's Enemy* 1959; *The Criminal* 1960; *The Guns of Navarone* 1961; *A Prize of Arms* 1961; *Eva* 1962; *The Man Who Finally Died* 1962; *Sodom and Gomorrah* 1962; *In the French Style* 1963; *Zulu* 1963; *Sands of the Kalahari* 1965; *Accident* 1967; *Robbery* 1967; *Where's Jack?* 1969; *The Games* 1970; *The Last Grenade* 1970; *Perfect Friday* 1970; *Popsy-Pop* 1970; *Zorro* 1975

Baker, Tom (1934-) *The Canterbury Tales* 1971; *Nicholas and Alexandra* 1971; *Frankenstein: the True Story* 1973; *The Golden Voyage of Sinbad* 1973; *The Mutations* 1973; *The Vault of Horror* 1973; *Dungeons & Dragons* 2000; *The Magic Roundabout* 2005

Bakewell, William (1908-1993) *Gold Diggers of Broadway* 1929; *All Quiet on the Western Front* 1930; *Dance, Fools, Dance* 1931; *Guilty Hands* 1931; *Lucky Devils* 1933; *The Capture* 1950; *Davy Crockett, King of the Wild Frontier* 1955

Bakke, Brenda (1963-) *Gunhed* 1989; *Solar Crisis* 1990; *Hot Shots! Part Deux* 1993; *Twogether* 1994; *Tales from the Crypt: Demon Knight* 1995

Bakri, Muhamad aka **Bacri, Muhamad** aka **Bakri, Mohammad** *Beyond the Walls* 1984; *Cup Final* 1991; *Double Edge* 1992; *Private* 2004

Bakri, Saleh *The Time That Remains: Chronicle of a Present Absentee* 2009; *The Source* 2011; *Salvo* 2013

Baku, Shango *Black Joy* 1977; *Rage* 1999

Bakula, Scott (1954-) *Sibling Rivalry* 1990; *Color of Night* 1994; *Rules of Obsession* 1994; *Lord of Illusions* 1995; *Cats Don't Dance* 1998; *Major League: Back to the Minors* 1998; *American Beauty* 1999; *Above Suspicion* 2000; *Life as a House* 2001; *The Informant!* 2009; *Behind the Candelabra* 2013

Balaban, Bob aka **Balaban, Robert** (1945-) *Catch-22* 1970; *Bank Shot* 1974; *Close Encounters of the Third Kind* 1977; *Girlfriends* 1978; *Altered States* 1980; *Absence of Malice* 1981; *Whose Life Is It Anyway?* 1981; *2010* 1984; *End of the Line* 1987; *Dead-Bang* 1989; *For Love or Money* 1993; *Pie in the Sky* 1995; *The Late Shift* 1996; *Waiting for Guffman* 1996; *Deconstructing Harry* 1997; *Jakob the Liar* 1999; *Swing Vote* 1999; *Three to Tango* 1999; *Best in Show* 2000; *Ghost World* 2001; *Gosford Park* 2001; *The Majestic* 2001; *The Mexican* 2001; *A Mighty Wind* 2003; *Capote* 2005; *Lady in the Water* 2006; *No Reservations* 2007; *Recount* 2008; *Howl* 2010; *A Monster in Paris* 2011; *Hitchcock* 2012; *Trumbo* 2015

Balaban, Liane *Last Chance Harvey* 2008; *The Grand Seduction* 2013

Baladi, Patrick (1971-) *Alpha Male* 2005; *The International* 2009; *Honeymoon for One* 2011; *No Fixed Abode* 2012; *Now Is Good* 2012

Balan, Vidya *Parineeta* 2005; *Eklavya: the Royal Guard* 2007; *Ishqiya* 2010

Balaski, Belinda (1947-) *Cannonball* 1976; *The Food of the Gods* 1976; *The Howling* 1981

Balasko, Josiane (1952-) *Trop Belle pour Toi* 1989; *Gazon Maudit* 1995; *Le Libertin* 2000; *I Saw Ben Barka Get Killed* 2005; *Ruby Blue* 2007; *The Hedgehog* 2009

Baldaque, Leonor *I'm Going Home* 2001; *Belle Toujours* 2006; *The Portuguese Nun* 2009

Baldini, Renato (1921-1995) *The White Warrior* 1959; *Esther and the King* 1960

Baldwin, Adam *My Bodyguard* 1980; *DC Cab* 1983; *Reckless* 1984; *Bad Guys* 1986; *3:15* 1986; *Full Metal Jacket* 1987; *The Chocolate War* 1988; *Cohen and Tate* 1988; *Next of Kin* 1989; *Radio Flyer* 1992; *Bitter Harvest* 1993; *800 Leagues down the Amazon* 1993; *How to Make an American Quilt* 1995; *In the Line of Duty: Smoke Jumpers* 1996; *Independence Day* 1996; *Jackpot* 2001; *Serenity* 2005

Baldwin, Alec (1958-) *Forever Lulu* 1987; *Beetle Juice* 1988; *Married to the Mob* 1988; *She's Having a Baby* 1988; *Talk Radio* 1988; *Working Girl* 1988; *Great Balls of Fire!* 1989; *Alice* 1990; *The Hunt for Red October* 1990; *Miami Blues* 1990; *Too Hot to Handle* 1991; *Glengarry Glen Ross* 1992; *Prelude to a Kiss* 1992; *Malice* 1993; *The Getaway* 1994; *The Shadow* 1994; *Ghosts of Mississippi* 1996; *Heaven's Prisoners* 1996; *The Juror* 1996; *Looking for Richard* 1996; *The Edge* 1997; *Mercury Rising* 1998; *The Confession* 1999; *Outside Providence* 1999; *State and Main* 2000; *Thomas and the Magic Railroad* 2000; *Cats & Dogs* 2001; *Final Fantasy: the Spirits Within* 2001; *Pearl Harbor* 2001; *The Royal Tenenbaums* 2001; *The Cooler* 2002; *Path to War* 2002; *Dr Seuss' The Cat in the Hat* 2003; *Along Came Polly* 2004; *The Aviator* 2004; *The Last Shot* 2004; *The SpongeBob SquarePants Movie* 2004; *Elizabethtown* 2005; *Fun with Dick and Jane* 2005; *The Departed* 2006; *The Good Shepherd* 2006; *Running with Scissors* 2006; *Brooklyn Rules* 2007; *Lymelife* 2008; *Madagascar: Escape 2 Africa* 2008; *My Best Friend's Girl* 2008; *It's Complicated* 2009; *My Sister's Keeper* 2009; *Rise of the Guardians* 2012; *Rock of Ages* 2012; *To Rome with Love* 2012; *Blue Jasmine* 2013; *Seduced and Abandoned* 2013; *Still Alice* 2014; *Concussion* 2015; *Rules Don't Apply* 2016

Baldwin, Daniel (1960-) *Harley Davidson and the Marlboro Man* 1991; *Knight Moves* 1992; *Attack of the 50 Ft Woman* 1993; *Desert Thunder* 1998; *Love Kills* 1998; *Phoenix* 1998; *Vampires* 1998; *Killing Moon* 1999; *In Pursuit* 2000; *King of the Ants* 2003; *Paparazzi* 2004; *Grey Gardens* 2009

Baldwin, Dick (1911-1996) *Life Begins in College* 1937; *Mr Moto's Gamble* 1938

Baldwin, Peter (1931-) *Short Cut to Hell* 1957; *I Married a Monster from Outer Space* 1958; *Teacher's Pet* 1958

Baldwin, Stephen (1966-) *The Beast of War* 1988; *Last Exit to Brooklyn* 1989; *Bitter Harvest* 1993; *Posse* 1993; *8 Seconds* 1994; *Fall Time* 1994; *A Simple Twist of Fate* 1994; *Threesome* 1994; *Under the Hula Moon* 1995; *The Usual Suspects* 1995; *Bio-Dome* 1996; *Fled* 1996; *Mr Murder* 1998; *Scared City* 1998; *Absence of the Good* 1999; *Cutaway* 2000; *The Flintstones in Viva Rock Vegas* 2000; *Mercy* 2000; *XChange* 2001; *Greenmail* 2001; *Earthstorm* 2006

Baldwin, Walter (1887-1977) *Together Again* 1944; *Winter Meeting* 1948

Baldwin, William (1963-) *Flatliners* 1990; *Internal Affairs* 1990; *Backdraft* 1991; *Three of Hearts* 1992; *Sliver* 1993; *Curdled* 1995; *Fair Game* 1995; *A Pyromaniac's Love Story* 1995; *Shattered Image* 1998; *Virus* 1998; *Primary Suspect* 2000; *Relative Values* 2000; *The Squid and the Whale* 2005

Bale, Christian (1974-) *Empire of the Sun* 1987; *Mio in the Land of Faraway* 1987; *Treasure Island* 1990; *Swing Kids* 1993; *Little Women* 1994; *Prince of Jutland* 1994; *Pocahontas* 1995; *The Portrait of a Lady* 1996; *The Secret Agent* 1996; *Metroland* 1997; *All the Little Animals* 1998; *Velvet Goldmine* 1998; *A Midsummer Night's Dream* 1999; *American Psycho* 2000; *Shaft* 2000; *Captain Corelli's Mandolin* 2001; *Reign of Fire* 2001; *Equilibrium* 2002; *Laurel Canyon* 2002; *The Machinist* 2003; *Howl's Moving Castle* 2004; *Batman Begins* 2005; *Harsh Times* 2005; *The New World* 2005; *The Prestige* 2006; *Rescue Dawn* 2006; *I'm Not There.* 2007; *3:10 to Yuma* 2007; *The Dark Knight* 2008; *Public Enemies* 2009; *Terminator: Salvation* 2009; *The Fighter* 2010; *The Dark Knight Rises*

2012; *The Flowers of War* 2012; *American Hustle* 2013; *Out of the Furnace* 2013; *Exodus: Gods and Kings* 2014; *The Big Short* 2015; *Knight of Cups* 2015; *Jungle Book: Origins* 2018

Balenda, Carla (1925-) *Sealed Cargo* 1951; *The Whip Hand* 1951

Balfour, Betty (1903-1978) *Champagne* 1928; *Evergreen* 1934; *Forever England* 1935; *Squibs* 1935; *29 Acacia Avenue* 1945

Balfour, Eric (1977-) *The Texas Chainsaw Massacre* 2003; *Lie with Me* 2005; *Spread* 2008; *Dinoshark* 2010; *Skyline* 2010

Balfour, Michael (1918-1997) *The Small Voice* 1948; *The Quiet Woman* 1950; *Albert, RN* 1953; *Fiend without a Face* 1957; *The Monster of Highgate Ponds* 1961; *The Oblong Box* 1969

Balibar, Jeanne (1968-) *Late August, Early September* 1998; *Comédie de l'Innocence* 2000; *Va Savoir* 2001; *Code 46* 2003; *Clean* 2004; *Don't Touch the Axe* 2008

Balin, Ina (1937-1990) *The Black Orchid* 1959; *From the Terrace* 1960; *The Comancheros* 1961; *The Young Doctors* 1961; *The Patsy* 1964; *Charro!* 1969; *The Projectionist* 1970

Balint, Eszter (1966-) *Stranger than Paradise* 1984; *The Linguini Incident* 1991

Balk, Fairuza (1974-) *Return to Oz* 1985; *Valmont* 1989; *Gas, Food, Lodging* 1992; *Shame* 1992; *Imaginary Crimes* 1994; *Tollbooth* 1994; *Things to Do in Denver When You're Dead* 1995; *The Craft* 1996; *The Island of Dr Moreau* 1996; *American Perfekt* 1997; *The Maker* 1997; *American History X* 1998; *The Waterboy* 1998; *Almost Famous* 2000; *Personal Velocity* 2001; *Don't Come Knocking* 2005; *The Bad Lieutenant - Port of Call: New Orleans* 2009; *Beyond Clueless* 2014

Ball, Angeline (1969-) *The Commitments* 1991; *Brothers in Trouble* 1995; *Trojan Eddie* 1996; *The Gambler* 1997; *The General* 1998; *bl,m* 2003; *The Tiger's Tail* 2006

Ball, Lucille (1911-1989) *The Affairs of Cellini* 1934; *Broadway Bill* 1934; *I Dream Too Much* 1935; *Old Man Rhythm* 1935; *Roberta* 1935; *Follow the Fleet* 1936; *Stage Door* 1937; *The Affairs of Annabel* 1938; *Annabel Takes a Tour* 1938; *Having Wonderful Time* 1938; *Joy of Living* 1938; *Room Service* 1938; *Beauty for the Asking* 1939; *Five Came Back* 1939; *That's Right - You're Wrong* 1939; *Dance, Girl, Dance* 1940; *Too Many Girls* 1940; *Look Who's Laughing* 1941; *The Navy Steps Out* 1941; *The Big Street* 1942; *Seven Days' Leave* 1942; *Valley of the Sun* 1942; *Best Foot Forward* 1943; *DuBarry Was a Lady* 1943; *Meet the People* 1944; *Ziegfeld Follies* 1944; *Without Love* 1945; *The Dark Corner* 1946; *Easy to Wed* 1946; *Lover Come Back* 1946; *Her Husband's Affairs* 1947; *Lured* 1947; *Easy Living* 1949; *Miss Grant Takes Richmond* 1949; *Sorrowful Jones* 1949; *Fancy Pants* 1950; *The Fuller Brush Girl* 1950; *The Long, Long Trailer* 1954; *Forever, Darling* 1956; *The Facts of Life* 1960; *Critic's Choice* 1963; *Yours, Mine and Ours* 1968; *Mame* 1974

Ball, Nicholas (1946-) *Overlord* 1975; *Lifeforce* 1985; *Croupier* 1998; *Sisterhood* 2008

Ball, Suzan (1933-1955) *Untamed Frontier* 1952; *City beneath the Sea* 1953; *East of Sumatra* 1953; *War Arrow* 1953; *Chief Crazy Horse* 1955

Ball, Vincent (1923-) *The Black Rider* 1954; *The Blue Peter* 1955; *Blood of the Vampire* 1958; *Sea of Sand* 1958; *Dentist in the Chair* 1960; *Season of Passion* 1960; *Echo of Diana* 1963; *Breaker Morant* 1979; *Phar Lap* 1983

Ballard, Kaye (1926-) *The Girl Most Likely* 1957; *The Ritz* 1976; *Falling in Love Again* 1980; *Pandemonium* 1982; *Baby Geniuses* 1999; *Fortune Hunters* 1999

Ballesta, Juan José *El Bola* 2000; *Spectre* 2006

Balmer, Jean-François (1946-) *A Strange Affair* 1981; *Golden Eighties* 1986; *Madame Bovary* 1991; *Beaumarchais l'Insolent* 1996; *Rien Ne Va Plus* 1997; *A Comedy of Power* 2006; *Dead Europe* 2012

Balpêtré, Antoine (1898-1963) *Nous Sommes Tous des Assassins* 1952; *Le Rouge et le Noir* 1954; *Lust of the Vampire* 1956

Balsam, Martin aka **Balsam, Marty** (1919-1996) *On the Waterfront* 1954; *Time Limit* 1957; *12 Angry Men* 1957; *Marjorie Morningstar* 1958; *Al Capone* 1959; *Psycho* 1960; *Ada* 1961; *Breakfast at Tiffany's* 1961; *Cape Fear* 1962; *Captive City* 1962; *Who's Been Sleeping in My Bed?* 1963; *The Carpetbaggers*

1964; *Seven Days in May* 1964; *The Bedford Incident* 1965; *Harlow* 1965; *A Thousand Clowns* 1965; *After the Fox* 1966; *Hombre* 1967; *The Good Guys and the Bad Guys* 1969; *Trilogy* 1969; *Catch-22* 1970; *Little Big Man* 1970; *Tora! Tora! Tora!* 1970; *The Anderson Tapes* 1971; *The Man* 1972; *The Six Million Dollar Man* 1973; *The Stone Killer* 1973; *Summer Wishes, Winter Dreams* 1973; *Murder on the Orient Express* 1974; *The Taking of Pelham One Two Three* 1974; *All the President's Men* 1976; *The Lindbergh Kidnapping Case* 1976; *Two-Minute Warning* 1976; *Raid on Entebbe* 1977; *The Sentinel* 1977; *Silver Bears* 1977; *Rainbow* 1978; *Cuba* 1979; *There Goes the Bride* 1979; *The Salamander* 1981; *Death Wish 3* 1985; *St Elmo's Fire* 1985; *The Delta Force* 1986; *Second Serve* 1986; *Private Investigations* 1987; *Two Evil Eyes* 1990; *Cape Fear* 1991; *The Silence of the Hams* 1993

Balsam, Talia (1960-) *The Kindred* 1986; *Private Investigations* 1987; *The Woo Woo Kid* 1987; *Trust Me* 1989; *The Wackness* 2008; *Return* 2011

Balsam, Humbert (1954-2005) *Lancelot du Lac* 1974; *Loulou* 1980

Balson, Allison (1969-) *Legend of the White Horse* 1985; *Best Seller* 1987

Baltz, Kirk *Reservoir Dogs* 1991; *Bulworth* 1998

Baluev, Alexander *The Peacemaker* 1997; *The Banishment* 2007

Bamber, David (1954-) *High Hopes* 1988; *I Capture the Castle* 2002; *Valkyrie* 2008

Bamman, Gerry (1941-) *The Secret of My Success* 1987; *Lorenzo's Oil* 1992; *Superstar* 1999

Bana, Eric (1968-) *Chopper* 2000; *Black Hawk Down* 2001; *Finding Nemo* 2003; *Hulk* 2003; *Troy* 2004; *Munich* 2005; *Lucky You* 2007; *Love the Beast* 2008; *Mary and Max* 2008; *The Other Boleyn Girl* 2008; *The Time Traveler's Wife* 2008; *Funny People* 2009; *Star Trek* 2009; *Hanna* 2011; *Deadfall* 2012; *Closed Circuit* 2013; *Lone Survivor* 2013; *Deliver Us from Evil* 2014; *The Finest Hours* 2015; *Knights of the Round Table: King Arthur* 2016

Bancroft, Anne (1931-2005) *Don't Bother to Knock* 1952; *Tonight We Sing* 1953; *Treasure of the Golden Condor* 1953; *Demetrius and the Gladiators* 1954; *Gorilla at Large* 1954; *The Raid* 1954; *The Last Frontier* 1955; *A Life in the Balance* 1955; *The Naked Street* 1955; *New York Confidential* 1955; *Nightfall* 1956; *Walk the Proud Land* 1956; *The Girl in Black Stockings* 1957; *The Restless Breed* 1957; *The Miracle Worker* 1962; *The Pumpkin Eater* 1964; *The Slender Thread* 1965; *7 Women* 1966; *The Graduate* 1967; *Young Winston* 1972; *The Prisoner of Second Avenue* 1974; *The Hindenburg* 1975; *Lipstick* 1976; *The Turning Point* 1977; *Fatso* 1979; *The Elephant Man* 1980; *To Be or Not to Be* 1983; *Garbo Talks* 1984; *Agnes of God* 1985; *84 Charing Cross Road* 1986; *'Night, Mother* 1986; *Torch Song Trilogy* 1988; *Bert Rigby, You're a Fool* 1989; *Broadway Bound* 1991; *Honeymoon in Vegas* 1992; *Love Potion No 9* 1992; *The Assassin* 1993; *Malice* 1993; *Mr Jones* 1993; *Home for the Holidays* 1995; *How to Make an American Quilt* 1995; *Homecoming* 1996; *Sunchaser* 1996; *Critical Care* 1997; *GI Jane* 1997; *Great Expectations* 1997; *Antz* 1998; *Up at the Villa* 1998; *Keeping the Faith* 2000; *Heartbreakers* 2001

Bancroft, Bradford *Dangerously Close* 1986; *Damned River* 1989

Bancroft, Cameron (1967-) *Love and Human Remains* 1993; *LA without a Map* 1998

Bancroft, George (1882-1956) *The Pony Express* 1925; *Underworld* 1927; *The Docks of New York* 1928; *The Dragnet* 1928; *Thunderbolt* 1929; *Mr Deeds Goes to Town* 1936; *Wedding Present* 1936; *Angels with Dirty Faces* 1938; *Submarine Patrol* 1938; *Each Dawn I Die* 1939; *Green Hell* 1939; *Rulers of the Sea* 1939; *Stagecoach* 1939; *North West Mounted Police* 1940; *When the Daltons Rode* 1940; *Young Tom Edison* 1940; *Texas* 1941; *Syncopation* 1942

Banderas, Antonio (1960-) *Matador* 1986; *The Law of Desire* 1987; *Women on the Verge of a Nervous Breakdown* 1988; *Tie Me Up! Tie Me Down!* 1990; *The Mambo Kings* 1992; *The House of the Spirits* 1993; *Outrage* 1993; *Philadelphia* 1993; *Interview with the Vampire: the Vampire Chronicles* 1994; *Of Love and Shadows* 1994; *Assassins* 1995; *Desperado* 1995; *Four Rooms* 1995; *Miami Rhapsody* 1995; *Two Much* 1995; *Evita* 1996; *The Mask of Zorro*

1998; *The 13th Warrior* 1999; *The Body* 2000; *Play It to the Bone* 2000; *Original Sin* 2001; *SPYkids* 2001; *Ballistic: Ecks vs Sever* 2002; *Femme Fatale* 2002; *Frida* 2002; *SPYkids 2: the Island of Lost Dreams* 2002; *Imagining Argentina* 2003; *Once upon a Time in Mexico* 2003; *SPYkids 3-D: Game Over* 2003; *Shrek 2* 2004; *The Legend of Zorro* 2005; *Take the Lead* 2006; *Shrek the Third* 2007; *My Spy* 2008; *The Other Man* 2008; *Shrek Forever After* 2010; *You Will Meet a Tall Dark Stranger* 2010; *Black Gold* 2011; *Haywire* 2011; *Puss in Boots* 2011; *The Skin I Live In* 2011; *Ruby Sparks* 2012; *I'm So Excited* 2013; *Justin and the Knights of Valour* 2013; *The Expendables 3* 2014; *The 33* 2014; *Knight of Cups* 2015; *The SpongeBob Movie: Sponge out of Water* 2015

Bando, Kotaro (1911-1981) *Five Women around Utamaro* 1946; *Gate of Hell* 1953

Banerjee, Victor aka **Bannerjee, Victor** (1946-) *Hullabaloo over Georgie and Bonnie's Pictures* 1979; *The Home and the World* 1984; *A Passage to India* 1984; *Foreign Body* 1986; *Bitter Moon* 1992; *Bhoot* 2003

Banes, Lisa (1955-) *The Hotel New Hampshire* 1984; *Marie: a True Story* 1985; *Cocktail* 1988; *Legally Blondes* 2008

Bang, Joy (1947-) *Cisco Pike* 1971; *Play It Again, Sam* 1972

Bankhead, Tallulah (1902-1968) *My Sin* 1931; *Tarnished Lady* 1931; *Devil and the Deep* 1932; *Faithless* 1932; *Stage Door Canteen* 1943; *Lifeboat* 1944; *A Royal Scandal* 1945; *Main Street to Broadway* 1953; *Die! Die! My Darling* 1964

Banks, Boyd *George A Romero's Land of the Dead* 2005; *How She Move* 2007

Banks (2), Elizabeth (1974-) *Swept Away* 2002; *Seabiscuit* 2003; *Spider-Man 2* 2004; *The 40 Year Old Virgin* 2005; *Invincible* 2006; *Slither* 2006; *Definitely, Maybe* 2008; *Meet Dave* 2008; *Role Models* 2008; *The Uninvited* 2008; *W.* 2008; *Zack and Miri Make a Porno* 2008; *The Next Three Days* 2010; *The Hunger Games* 2012; *Man on a Ledge* 2012; *People like Us* 2012; *Pitch Perfect* 2012; *What to Expect When You're Expecting* 2012; *The Hunger Games: Mockingjay Part 1* 2014; *The Lego Movie* 2014; *Love & Mercy* 2014; *Magic Mike XXL* 2015; *Pitch Perfect 3* 2017

Banks, Jonathan (1947-) *Beverly Hills Cop* 1984; *Armed and Dangerous* 1986; *Cold Steel* 1987; *Freejack* 1992; *Boiling Point* 1993; *Body Shot* 1994; *Flipper* 1996; *Dollar for the Dead* 1998; *Crocodile Dundee in Los Angeles* 2001

Banks, Lenore *Passion Fish* 1992; *The Unexpected Journey* 2004

Banks, Leslie (1890-1952) *The Most Dangerous Game* 1932; *The Man Who Knew Too Much* 1934; *Sanders of the River* 1935; *Fire over England* 1937; *21 Days* 1937; *Wings of the Morning* 1937; *The Arsenal Stadium Mystery* 1939; *Jamaica Inn* 1939; *Sons of the Sea* 1939; *Busman's Honeymoon* 1940; *Cottage to Let* 1941; *Ships with Wings* 1942; *Went the Day Well?* 1942; *Henry V* 1944; *Eye Witness* 1949; *Madeleine* 1949; *The Small Back Room* 1949

Banks, Tyra (1973-) *Higher Learning* 1995; *Coyote Ugly* 2000; *Life-Size* 2000

Banky, Vilma (1898-1991) *The Eagle* 1925; *The Son of the Sheik* 1926; *The Winning of Barbara Worth* 1926

Bannen, Ian (1928-1999) *The Long Arm* 1956; *Miracle in Soho* 1957; *Behind the Mask* 1958; *Carlton-Browne of the FO* 1958; *A French Mistress* 1960; *Suspect* 1960; *Station Six-Sahara* 1962; *Psyche '59* 1964; *The Flight of the Phoenix* 1965; *The Hill* 1965; *Rotten to the Core* 1965; *Penelope* 1966; *The Sailor from Gibraltar* 1967; *Lock Up Your Daughters!* 1969; *Jane Eyre* 1970; *Too Late the Hero* 1970; *The Deserter* 1971; *Fright* 1971; *Doomwatch* 1972; *The Offence* 1972; *From beyond the Grave* 1973; *The Mackintosh Man* 1973; *The Voyage* 1974; *Bite the Bullet* 1975; *The Driver's Seat* 1975; *Sweeney!* 1976; *Inglorious Bastards* 1978; *Eye of the Needle* 1981; *The Watcher in the Woods* 1982; *Gorky Park* 1983; *Defence of the Realm* 1985; *Lamb* 1985; *Hope and Glory* 1987; *The Big Man* 1990; *Ghost Dad* 1990; *George's Island* 1991; *Damage* 1992; *A Pin for the Butterfly* 1994; *Braveheart* 1995; *Something to Believe In* 1997; *Waking Ned* 1998; *Best* 1999; *To Walk with Lions* 1999; *The Testimony of Taliesin Jones* 2000

Banner, Jill (1946-1982) *Spider Baby* 1964; *The President's Analyst* 1967

Banner, John (1910-1973) *The Blue Angel* 1959; *Hitler* 1962

Bannerjee, Haradhan *The Big City* 1963; *Branches of the Tree* 1990

Bannerjee, Kanu (1905-1985) *Pather Panchali* 1955; *Aparajito* 1956

Bannerjee, Karuna (1919-2001) *Pather Panchali* 1955; *Aparajito* 1956; *Devi* 1960; *Kangchenjunga* 1962

Bannerjee, Satya aka **Bannerji, Satya** *The Middleman* 1975; *And Quiet Rolls the Dawn* 1979

Bannister, Reggie *Phantasm* 1978; *Phantasm II* 1988

Bannon, Jim (1911-1984) *Framed* 1947; *The Man from Colorado* 1948; *Unknown World* 1951

Bansagi, Ildiko (1947-) *Confidence* 1979; *Mephisto* 1981; *Hanussen* 1988; *Diary for My Father and Mother* 1990; *Ten Minutes Older: the Cello* 2002

Baquero, Ivana *The Christmas Tale* 2005; *Pan's Labyrinth* 2006; *The New Daughter* 2009

Baragrey, John (1918-1975) *Shockproof* 1949; *Tall Man Riding* 1955; *Pardners* 1956; *The Colossus of New York* 1958; *Gamera the Invincible* 1965

Barak, Ari *Wishmaster* 1997; *Desert Thunder* 1998

Baranovskaya, Vera (1885-1935) *Mother* 1926; *The End of St Petersburg* 1927

Baranski, Christine (1952-) *Playing for Time* 1980; *Lovesick* 1983; *Nine ½ Weeks* 1985; *Reversal of Fortune* 1990; *Addams Family Values* 1993; *Life with Mikey* 1993; *The Night We Never Met* 1993; *Hostile Hostages* 1994; *Jeffrey* 1995; *The Birdcage* 1996; *Bulworth* 1998; *The Odd Couple II* 1998; *Bowfinger* 1999; *The Grinch* 2000; *Chicago* 2002; *The Guru* 2002; *Eloise at the Plaza* 2003; *Marci X* 2003; *Welcome to Mooseport* 2004; *Bonneville* 2006; *Mamma Mia!* 2008; *The Bounty Hunter* 2010; *Trolls* 2016

Barantini, Philip (1980-) *The Escapist* 2002; *Ned Kelly* 2003

Barash, Olivia (1965-) *Repo Man* 1984; *Patty Hearst* 1988

Barbareschi, Luca (1956-) *Cannibal Holocaust* 1979; *Il Cielo è Sempre Più Blu* 1995

Barbé, Marc (1961-) *Nightshift* 2000; *Regular Lovers* 2005; *Don't Touch the Axe* 2006; *Intimate Enemies* 2007; *Mozart's Sister* 2010

Barbeau, Adrienne (1945-) *Someone's Watching Me!* 1978; *The Fog* 1980; *The Cannonball Run* 1981; *Escape from New York* 1981; *Creepshow* 1982; *Swamp Thing* 1982; *Cannibal Women in the Avocado Jungle of Death* 1989; *Two Evil Eyes* 1990; *Fly Me to the Moon* 2007

Barber, Frances (1958-) *A Zed & Two Noughts* 1985; *Castaway* 1986; *Prick Up Your Ears* 1987; *Sammy and Rosie Get Laid* 1987; *We Think the World of You* 1988; *Secret Friends* 1991; *Young Soul Rebels* 1991; *Soft Top, Hard Shoulder* 1992; *Photographing Fairies* 1997; *Still Crazy* 1998; *The Escort* 1999; *Esther Kahn* 2000; *Shiner* 2000; *The Children's Midsummer Night's Dream* 2001; *Suzie Gold* 2003; *may i kill u?* 2012

Barber, Glynis (1955-) *Terror* 1979; *Yesterday's Hero* 1979; *The Hound of the Baskervilles* 1983; *The Wicked Lady* 1983; *Edge of Sanity* 1989; *Déjà Vu* 1997; *Hammer of the Gods* 2013

Barberini, Urbano (1962-) *Otello* 1986; *Gor* 1987; *Opera* 1987; *Torrents of Spring* 1989

Barbier, Christian (1924-2009) *Trans-Europ-Express* 1966; *Army of Shadows* 1969

Barbier, George (1864-1945) *The Big Pond* 1930; *The Smiling Lieutenant* 1931; *The Big Broadcast* 1932; *No Man of Her Own* 1932; *No One Man* 1932; *One Hour with You* 1932; *The Phantom President* 1932; *Tillie and Gus* 1933; *The Cat's Paw* 1934; *The Merry Widow* 1934; *Life Begins at 40* 1935; *Old Man Rhythm* 1935; *The Milky Way* 1936; *The Princess Comes Across* 1936; *Spendthrift* 1936; *Wife vs Secretary* 1936; *On the Avenue* 1937; *Waikiki Wedding* 1937; *The Adventures of Marco Polo* 1938; *Hold That Co-Ed* 1938; *Little Miss Broadway* 1938; *My Lucky Star* 1938; *Remember?* 1939; *Wife, Husband and Friend* 1939; *Weekend in Havana* 1941; *The Magnificent Dope* 1942; *Song of the Islands* 1942

Barbour, Joyce (1901-1977) *Sabotage* 1936; *Housemaster* 1938; *Saloon Bar* 1940

Barbuscia, Lisa (1971-) *Almost Heroes* 1998; *Highlander: Endgame* 2000; *Rabbit Fever* 2005

Barcis, Artur *No End* 1984; *A Short Film about Love* 1988

Barclay, Emily *In My Father's Den* 2004; *Suburban Mayhem* 2006; *Legend of the Guardians: the Owls of Ga'Hoole* 2010; *Weekender* 2011

Barclay, Joan (1914–2002) *The Falcon Out West* 1944; *The Shanghai Cobra* 1945

Barclay, Stephen aka **Barclay, Steve** (1918–1994) *The Great Flamarion* 1945; *Fool's Gold* 1946

Barcroft, Roy (1902–1969) *My Pal Trigger* 1946; *The Far Frontier* 1949; *North of the Great Divide* 1950; *Six Black Horses* 1962

Bard, Ben (1893–1974) *7th Heaven* 1927; *The Ghost Ship* 1943; *The Seventh Victim* 1943

Bard, Katharine (1916–1983) *The Decks Ran Red* 1958; *Inside Daisy Clover* 1965

Bardem, Carlos (1963–) *Perdita Durango* 1997; *La Zona* 2007; *Che Part Two* 2008; *Cell 211* 2009; *Days of Grace* 2011

Bardem, Javier (1969–) *The Ages of Lulu* 1990; *Jamón, Jamón* 1992; *Golden Balls* 1993; *Mouth to Mouth* 1995; *Live Flesh* 1997; *Perdita Durango* 1997; *Before Night Falls* 2000; *Second Skin* 2000; *The Dancer Upstairs* 2002; *Mondays in the Sun* 2002; *Collateral* 2004; *The Sea Inside* 2004; *Goya's Ghosts* 2006; *Love in the Time of Cholera* 2007; *No Country for Old Men* 2007; *Vicky Cristina Barcelona* 2008; *Biutiful* 2009; *Eat Pray Love* 2010; *Skyfall* 2012; *To the Wonder* 2012; *The Counsellor* 2013; *The Gunman* 2015; *Pirates of the Caribbean: Dead Men Tell No Tales* 2017

Bardem, Pilar (1939–) *Vacas* 1991; *Live Flesh* 1997

Barden, Jessica *Mrs Ratcliffe's Revolution* 2007 *Tamara Drewe* 2010; *Far from the Madding Crowd* 2015

Bardette, Trevor (1902–1977) *The Man from Bitter Ridge* 1955; *Dragoon Wells Massacre* 1957; *The Monolith Monsters* 1957; *Thunder Road* 1958

Bardini, Aleksander (1913–1995) *Landscape after Battle* 1970; *No End* 1984; *The Double Life of Véronique* 1991; *The Silent Touch* 1992

Bardot, Brigitte (1934–) *Act of Love* 1953; *Royal Affairs in Versailles* 1953; *Doctor at Sea* 1955; *Les Grandes Manoeuvres* 1955; *Helen of Troy* 1955; *And God Created Woman* 1956; *The Bride Is Too Beautiful* 1956; *The Light across the Street* 1956; *Les Bijoutiers du Clair de Lune* 1957; *Une Parisienne* 1957; *Le Testament d'Orphée* 1960; *La Vérité* 1960; *A Very Private Affair* 1962; *Le Mépris* 1963; *A Ravishing Idiot* 1964; *Viva Maria!* 1965; *Dear Brigitte* 1966; *Masculine Feminine* 1966; *Histoires Extraordinaires* 1967; *Shalako* 1968; *Don Juan 73, or If Don Juan Were a Woman* 1973

Barea, Ramón (1949–) *La Madre Muerta* 1993; *The Other Side of the Bed* 2002

Bareikis, Arija (1966–) *Deuce Bigalow: Male Gigolo* 1999; *A Painted House* 2003; *Tenderness* 2007

Barhom, Ashraf *The Kingdom* 2007; *Agora* 2009

Bari, Lynn (1913–1989) *Always Goodbye* 1938; *Mr Moto's Gamble* 1938; *Pack Up Your Troubles* 1939; *The Return of the Cisco Kid* 1939; *Kit Carson* 1940; *Blood and Sand* 1941; *Sun Valley Serenade* 1941; *China Girl* 1942; *The Falcon Takes Over* 1942; *The Magnificent Dope* 1942; *Orchestra Wives* 1942; *Hello, Frisco, Hello* 1943; *Sweet and Lowdown* 1944; *Capt Eddie* 1945; *Home Sweet Homicide* 1946; *Margie* 1946; *Nocturne* 1946; *I'd Climb the Highest Mountain* 1951; *Has Anybody Seen My Gal?* 1952; *Francis Joins the WACS* 1954; *Abbott and Costello Meet the Keystone Cops* 1955

Baring, Norah (1907–1985) *Underground* 1928; *A Cottage on Dartmoor* 1929; *Murder* 1930

Barker, Eric (1912–1990) *Brothers in Law* 1956; *Happy Is the Bride* 1957; *Carry On Sergeant* 1958; *Left, Right and Centre* 1959; *Carry On Constable* 1960; *Dentist in the Chair* 1960; *The Pure Hell of St Trinian's* 1960; *Watch Your Stern* 1960; *Dentist on the Job* 1961; *Nearly a Nasty Accident* 1961; *On the Fiddle* 1961; *Raising the Wind* 1961; *On the Beat* 1962; *The Bargee* 1964; *Carry On Spying* 1964

Barker, Jess (1912–2000) *Government Girl* 1943; *Cover Girl* 1944; *The Daltons Ride Again* 1945; *Scarlet Street* 1945; *This Love of Ours* 1945; *The Time of Their Lives* 1946; *Marry Me Again* 1953; *Shack Out on 101* 1955

Barker, Lex (1919–1973) *Return of the Bad Men* 1948; *The Velvet Touch* 1948;

Tarzan's Magic Fountain 1949; *Tarzan and the Slave Girl* 1950; *Tarzan's Peril* 1951; *Tarzan's Savage Fury* 1952; *Tarzan and the She-Devil* 1953; *Thunder over the Plains* 1953; *The Yellow Mountain* 1954; *The Man from Bitter Ridge* 1955; *Away All Boats* 1956; *The Deerslayer* 1957; *The Girl in Black Stockings* 1957; *La Dolce Vita* 1960; *Woman Times Seven* 1967

Barker, Ronnie (1929–2005) *Kill or Cure* 1962; *Father Came Too* 1963; *The Bargee* 1964; *Robin and Marian* 1976; *Porridge* 1979; *My House in Umbria* 2002

Barkin, Ellen (1954–) *Diner* 1982; *Tender Mercies* 1982; *Eddie and the Cruisers* 1983; *Terminal Choice* 1983; *The Adventures of Buckaroo Banzai across the 8th Dimension* 1984; *Harry and Son* 1984; *Desert Bloom* 1985; *Act of Vengeance* 1986; *The Big Easy* 1986; *Down by Law* 1986; *Siesta* 1987; *Blood Money* 1988; *Johnny Handsome* 1989; *Sea of Love* 1989; *Switch* 1991; *Into the West* 1992; *Mac* 1992; *Man Trouble* 1992; *This Boy's Life* 1993; *Bad Company* 1995; *Wild Bill* 1995; *The Fan* 1996; *Trigger Happy* 1996; *Before Women Had Wings* 1997; *Fear and Loathing in Las Vegas* 1998; *Drop Dead Gorgeous* 1999; *Crime + Punishment in Suburbia* 2000; *Mercy* 2000; *Animal Attraction* 2001; *Palindromes* 2004; *She Hate Me* 2004; *Trust the Man* 2006; *Ocean's Thirteen* 2007; *Brooklyn's Finest* 2009; *The Cobbler* 2014

Barklem-Biggs, Theo *Borrowed Time* 2012; *The Man Inside* 2012

Barks, Samantha (1990–) *Les Misérables* 2012; *The Christmas Candle* 2013

Barkworth, Peter (1929–2006) *No My Darling Daughter* 1961; *Two a Penny* 1968; *The Littlest Horse Thieves* 1976; *International Velvet* 1978; *Champions* 1983

Barlow, Patrick (1947–) *Girl from Rio* 2001; *Nanny McPhee* 2005

Barlow, Thelma *Mrs Henderson Presents* 2005; *Is Anybody There?* 2008

Barnard, Aneurin (1987–) *Powder* 2010; *Elfie Hopkins* 2011; *Hunky Dory* 2011; *Trap for Cinderella* 2011; *Citadel* 2012; *The Facility* 2012; *Dunkirk* 2017

Barnard, Ivor (1887–1953) *Sally in Our Alley* 1931; *The Saint's Vacation* 1941; *Great Expectations* 1946; *Esther Waters* 1948; *Beat the Devil* 1953

Barnes, Barry K (1906–1965) *The Return of the Scarlet Pimpernel* 1937; *The Ware Case* 1938; *The Girl in the News* 1940; *Bedelia* 1946; *Dancing with Crime* 1946

Barnes, Ben (1981–) *Bigga than Ben: a Guide to Ripping Off London* 2007; *The Chronicles of Narnia: Prince Caspian* 2008; *Easy Virtue* 2008; *Dorian Gray* 2009; *The Chronicles of Narnia: The Voyage of the Dawn Treader* 2010; *Killing Bono* 2010; *The Words* 2012; *The Big Wedding* 2013; *Seventh Son* 2014

Barnes, Binnie (1903–1998) *The Private Life of Henry VIII* 1933; *The Private Life of Don Juan* 1934; *Rendezvous* 1935; *The Last of the Mohicans* 1936; *Small Town Girl* 1936; *Broadway Melody of 1938* 1937; *Three Smart Girls* 1937; *The Adventures of Marco Polo* 1938; *The Divorce of Lady X* 1938; *Holiday* 1938; *Thanks for Everything* 1938; *Three Blind Mice* 1938; *Frontier Marshal* 1939; *The Three Musketeers* 1939; *Wife, Husband and Friend* 1939; *This Thing Called Love* 1940; *'Til We Meet Again* 1940; *Call Out the Marines* 1941; *Skylark* 1941; *I Married an Angel* 1942; *In Old California* 1942; *The Man from Down Under* 1942; *Barbary Coast Gent* 1944; *The Hour before the Dawn* 1944; *Up in Mabel's Room* 1944; *It's in the Bag* 1945; *The Spanish Main* 1945; *The Time of Their Lives* 1946; *If Winter Comes* 1947; *Decameron Nights* 1953; *Malaga* 1954; *The Trouble with Angels* 1966; *Where Angels Go... Trouble Follows* 1968; *40 Carats* 1973

Barnes, Christopher Daniel aka **Barnes, C D** (1972–) *American Dreamer* 1984; *The Little Mermaid* 1989; *The Brady Bunch Movie* 1995; *A Very Brady Sequel* 1996

Barnes, Joanna (1934–) *Violent Road* 1958; *Tarzan, the Ape Man* 1959; *The Parent Trap* 1961; *Goodbye Charlie* 1964; *Don't Make Waves* 1967; *The War Wagon* 1967

Barnes, Priscilla (1955–) *Erotique* 1994; *The Crossing Guard* 1995; *Alone with a Stranger* 2000

Barnes, Susan *Repo Man* 1984; *Meet the Applegates* 1991; *Where the Money Is* 2000

Barnes, Walter (1918–1998) *Escape to Witch Mountain* 1975; *Every Which Way but Loose* 1978

Barnett, Angus *Copying Beethoven* 2006; *The Wedding Video* 2012

Barnett, Griff (1884–1958) *Apartment for Peggy* 1948; *Holiday Affair* 1949; *Cattle Drive* 1951

Barnett, Samuel *The History Boys* 2006; *Love Tomorrow* 2012

Barnett, Vince (1902–1977) *Flesh* 1932; *Scarface* 1932; *Tiger Shark* 1932; *The Death Kiss* 1933; *The Prizefighter and the Lady* 1933; *The Affairs of Cellini* 1934; *Black Fury* 1935; *The Falcon's Alibi* 1946; *The Killers* 1946; *Mule Train* 1950

Barnev, Ivan aka **Burnev, Ivan** *I Served the King of England* 2006; *The Lesson* 2014

Barney, Matthew (1967–) *Cremaster 4* 1994; *Cremaster 5* 1997; *Cremaster 2* 1999; *Cremaster 3* 2002

Barnwell, Jean Marie *Born to Be Wild* 1995; *From the Mixed-Up Files of Mrs Basil E Frankweiler* 1995

Baron Cohen, Sacha (1971–) *Ali G indahouse* 2002; *Madagascar* 2005; *Borat: Cultural Learnings of America for Make Benefit Glorious Nation of Kazakhstan* 2006; *Talladega Nights: the Ballad of Ricky Bobby* 2006; *Sweeney Todd: the Demon Barber of Fleet Street* 2007; *Madagascar: Escape 2 Africa* 2008; *Brüno* 2009; *Hugo* 2011; *The Dictator* 2012; *Madagascar 3: Europe's Most Wanted* 2012; *Les Misérables* 2012; *Alice through the Looking Glass* 2016; *Grimsby* 2016

Baron, Geraldine *Human Highway* 1982; *The City Girl* 1984

Baron, Joanne *Crazy in Love* 1992; *Pet Shop* 1995

Baron, Lita (1929–) *Jungle Jim* 1948; *Red Sundown* 1956

Baron, Lynda (1942–) *Hands of the Ripper* 1971; *Tiffany Jones* 1973

Baron, Sandy (1937–2001) *Sweet November* 1968; *Targets* 1968; *The Out of Towners* 1970; *Straight Time* 1978; *Birdy* 1984; *Vamp* 1986; *Motorama* 1991

Barondes, Elizabeth (1964–) *Oscar* 1991; *Adrenalin: Fear the Rush* 1995

Barondess, Barbara (1907–2000) *Hold Your Man* 1933; *The Plot Thickens* 1936

Barr, Byron (1917–1966) *Double Indemnity* 1944; *The Affairs of Susan* 1945; *Love Letters* 1945; *Pitfall* 1948

Barr (1), Douglas (1932–) *Hue and Cry* 1947; *Dance Hall* 1950

Barr, Jean-Marc (1960–) *Hope and Glory* 1987; *The Big Blue* 1988; *Europa* 1991; *The Plague* 1992; *Breaking the Waves* 1996; *The Suicide Tunic* 1997; *All for Love* 1999; *Dogville* 2003; *Cockles & Muscles* 2004; *Manderlay* 2005; *Tara Road* 2005

Barr, Patrick (1908–1985) *Midnight at Madame Tussaud's* 1936; *The Return of the Scarlet Pimpernel* 1937; *The Gaunt Stranger* 1938; *Let's Be Famous* 1939; *Escape by Night* 1953; *The Vanquished* 1953; *The Brain Machine* 1954; *The Dam Busters* 1954; *Duel in the Jungle* 1954; *It's Never Too Late* 1956; *Next to No Time* 1958; *Guns in the Heather* 1969; *The Satanic Rites of Dracula* 1973; *House of Whipcord* 1974; *The Godsend* 1980

Barr, Roseanne aka **Arnold, Roseanne** (1952–) *She-Devil* 1989; *Look Who's Talking Too* 1990; *Even Cowgirls Get the Blues* 1993; *Blue in the Face* 1995; *Home on the Range* 2004

Barra, Gianfranco (1940–) *Avanti!* 1972; *Screw Loose* 1999

Barranco, Maria (1961–) *Women on the Verge of a Nervous Breakdown* 1988; *The Ages of Lulu* 1990; *The Red Squirrel* 1993; *Mouth to Mouth* 1995

Barrat, Robert (1889–1970) *Heroes for Sale* 1933; *The Kennel Murder Case* 1933; *Gambling Lady* 1934; *Hi, Nellie!* 1934; *Upper World* 1934; *Bordertown* 1935; *Village Tale* 1935; *The Country Doctor* 1936; *The Last of the Mohicans* 1936; *Mary of Scotland* 1936; *The Trail of the Lonesome Pine* 1936; *The Black Legion* 1937; *God's Country and the Woman* 1937; *The Life of Emile Zola* 1937; *The Texans* 1938; *The Cisco Kid and the Lady* 1939; *The First Rebel* 1939; *The Return of the Cisco Kid* 1939; *The Man from Dakota* 1940; *Northwest Passage* 1940; *Riders of the Purple Sage* 1941; *The Adventures of Mark Twain* 1944; *Road to Utopia* 1945; *Relentless* 1948; *An American Guerrilla in the Philippines* 1950; *The Baron of Arizona* 1950; *Distant Drums* 1951; *Tall Man Riding* 1955

Barratt, Julian *The Principles of Lust* 2002; *Bunny & the Bull* 2009; *Aaaaaaaah!* 2015

Barrault, Jean-Louis (1910–1994) *Beethoven* 1936; *Drôle de Drame* 1937; *Les Enfants du Paradis* 1945; *The Testament of Dr Cordelier* 1959; *La Nuit de Varennes* 1983

Barrault, Marie-Christine (1944–) *My Night with Maud* 1969; *Cousin, Cousine* 1975; *The Medusa Touch* 1978; *Perceval le Gallois* 1978; *Stardust Memories* 1980; *Table for Five* 1983; *Swann in Love* 1984

Barraza, Adriana (1956–) *Babel* 2006; *Drag Me to Hell* 2009; *Mariachi Gringo* 2012; *Cake* 2015

Barrese, Sasha *The Hangover* 2009; *Let Me In* 2010

Barrett, Edith (1907–1977) *Ladies in Retirement* 1941; *Lady for a Night* 1942; *The Ghost Ship* 1943; *I Walked with a Zombie* 1943; *Molly and Me* 1945; *The Lady Gambles* 1949

Barrett, Jacinda (1972–) *The Human Stain* 2003; *Bridget Jones: the Edge of Reason* 2004; *Ladder 49* 2004; *The Last Kiss* 2006; *The Namesake* 2006; *Poseidon* 2006; *School for Scoundrels* 2006

Barrett, Jane (1923–1969) *Eureka Stockade* 1949; *The Sword and the Rose* 1952; *Time Gentlemen Please!* 1952

Barrett, Laurinda *The Wrong Man* 1956; *The Heart Is a Lonely Hunter* 1968

Barrett, Majel aka **Roddenberry, Majel Barrett** (1932–2008) *Star Trek: the Motion Picture* 1979; *Star Trek IV: the Voyage Home* 1986; *Star Trek: Nemesis* 2002

Barrett, Nancy (1941–) *House of Dark Shadows* 1970; *Night of Dark Shadows* 1971; *Belizaire the Cajun* 1985

Barrett, Ray (1927–2009) *The Reptile* 1966; *Thunderbirds Are Go!* 1966; *Don's Party* 1976; *The Chant of Jimmie Blacksmith* 1978; *Where the Green Ants Dream* 1984; *Rebel* 1985; *Waiting* 1990; *Hotel Sorrento* 1994; *Hotel de Love* 1996; *Heaven's Burning* 1997

Barrett (1), Sean (1940–) *Four Sided Triangle* 1953; *Bang! You're Dead* 1954

Barrett, Tim (1928–1990) *Where the Bullets Fly* 1966; *The Deadly Bees* 1967; *A Hole Lot of Trouble* 1969; *White Cargo* 1973

Barrett, Tony (1916–1974) *Dick Tracy Meets Gruesome* 1947; *Guns of Hate* 1948

Barretta, Bill *Muppets from Space* 1999; *It's a Very Merry Muppet Christmas Movie* 2002; *Kermit's Swamp Years* 2002; *The Muppets' Wizard of Oz* 2005

Barrie, Amanda (1939–) *Carry On Cabby* 1963; *Carry On Cleo* 1964; *I've Gotta Horse* 1965

Barrie, Barbara (1931–) *One Potato, Two Potato* 1964; *Summer of My German Soldier* 1978; *Breaking Away* 1979; *End of the Line* 1987; *Real Men* 1987; *Judy Berlin* 1999

Barrie, Chris aka **Barrie, Christopher** (1960–) *Testimony* 1987; *Lara Croft: Tomb Raider* 2001; *Lara Croft, Tomb Raider: the Cradle of Life* 2003

Barrie, John (1917–1980) *Life for Ruth* 1962; *The File of the Golden Goose* 1969

Barrie, Mona (1909–1964) *Charlie Chan in London* 1934; *One Night of Love* 1934; *King of Burlesque* 1936; *Love on the Run* 1936; *I Met Him in Paris* 1937; *Something to Sing About* 1937; *I Take This Woman* 1940; *Never Give a Sucker an Even Break* 1941

Barrie, Wendy (1912–1978) *Wedding Rehearsal* 1932; *The Private Life of Henry VIII* 1933; *Speed* 1936; *Dead End* 1937; *I Am the Law* 1938; *Five Came Back* 1939; *The Hound of the Baskervilles* 1939; *The Saint Strikes Back* 1939; *The Saint Takes Over* 1940; *A Date with the Falcon* 1941; *The Gay Falcon* 1941; *The Saint in Palm Springs* 1941

Barrier, Edgar (1907–1964) *Too Much Johnson* 1938; *They Dare Not Love* 1941; *Phantom of the Opera* 1943; *Cobra Woman* 1944; *Cornered* 1945; *Tarzan and the Leopard Woman* 1946; *Macbeth* 1948; *To the Ends of the Earth* 1948; *The Whip Hand* 1951; *Count the Hours* 1953; *The Golden Blade* 1953; *Princess of the Nile* 1954

Barrier, Maurice (1934–) *Police Story* 1975; *Black and White in Color* 1976; *Life and Nothing But* 1989

Barrile, Anthony *Hamburger Hill* 1987; *Kiss Me, Guido* 1997

Berrit, Desmond *A Midsummer Night's Dream* 1996; *A Christmas Carol* 1999

Berron, Dana (1968–) *National Lampoon's Vacation* 1983; *Death Wish 4: the Crackdown* 1987

Barron, Keith (1936–) *Nothing but the Night* 1972; *The Land That Time Forgot*

1974; *La Passione* 1996; *In Love with Alma Cogan* 2011

Barrowman, John *De-Lovely* 2004; *All Stars* 2013

Barry, Bruce (1934–) *ABBA the Movie* 1977; *Patrick* 1978; *The Good Wife* 1986

Barry, Donald aka **Barry, Don** aka **Barry, Don "Red"** (1912–1980) *The Duke of West Point* 1938; *Days of Jesse James* 1939; *The Purple Heart* 1944; *Bells of Rosarita* 1945; *Seven Men from Now* 1956; *Gun Duel in Durango* 1957; *Frankenstein - 1970* 1958; *Born Reckless* 1959; *Walk on the Wild Side* 1962; *Apache Uprising* 1965; *The Shakiest Gun in the West* 1967

Barry, Gene (1919–2009) *The War of the Worlds* 1953; *Naked Alibi* 1954; *Red Garters* 1954; *The Purple Mask* 1955; *Soldier of Fortune* 1955; *Back from Eternity* 1956; *China Gate* 1957; *The 27th Day* 1957; *Thunder Road* 1958; *Maroc 7* 1966; *Prescription: Murder* 1968; *The Second Coming of Suzanne* 1974; *These Old Broads* 2001; *War of the Worlds* 2005

Barry, Gerald *The Lad* 1935; *The Crimes of Stephen Hawke* 1936

Barry, Jason (1975–) *Noose* 1997; *When the Sky Falls* 2000; *MirrorMask* 2004

Barry, Joan (1903–1989) *Rich and Strange* 1932; *Rome Express* 1932

Barry, Matthew (1962–) *La Luna* 1979; *The Wraith* 1986

Barry, Neill (1965–) *Heat* 1987; *OC and Stiggs* 1987

Barry, Patricia aka **White, Patricia** (1930–) *Cry Wolf* 1947; *Riders of the Whistling Pines* 1949; *The Tattooed Stranger* 1950; *Dear Heart* 1964; *Send Me No Flowers* 1964

Barry, Phyllis (1909–1954) *Cynara* 1932; *What - No Beer?* 1933; *The Moonstone* 1934

Barry, Raymond J aka **Barry, Raymond** (1939–) *Year of the Dragon* 1985; *Three for the Road* 1987; *Cop* 1988; *Born on the Fourth of July* 1989; *K2* 1991; *Rapid Fire* 1992; *The Turning* 1992; *Cool Runnings* 1993; *Hostile Hostages* 1994; *Dead Man Walking* 1995; *Sudden Death* 1995; *The Chamber* 1996; *Flubber* 1997; *New Port South* 2001; *Training Day* 2001; *Little Children* 2006; *Walk Hard: the Dewey Cox Story* 2007

Barry, Roukietou *Yaaba* 1989; *Tilaï* 1990

Barry, Tony (1941–) *Beyond Reasonable Doubt* 1980; *Hard Knocks* 1980; *Goodbye Pork Pie* 1981; *We of the Never Never* 1982; *The Coca-Cola Kid* 1985; *Shame* 1987; *Jack Be Nimble* 1992; *Doing Time for Patsy Cline* 1997; *Mystery Road* 2013

Barrymore, Drew (1975–) *Altered States* 1980; *ET the Extra-Terrestrial* 1982; *Cat's Eye* 1984; *Firestarter* 1984; *Irreconcilable Differences* 1984; *Babes in Toyland* 1986; *Far from Home* 1989; *See You in the Morning* 1989; *Motorama* 1991; *Guncrazy* 1992; *No Place to Hide* 1992; *Poison Ivy* 1992; *The Amy Fisher Story* 1993; *Doppelganger* 1993; *Bad Girls* 1994; *Batman Forever* 1995; *Boys on the Side* 1995; *Mad Love* 1995; *Everyone Says I Love You* 1996; *Scream* 1996; *Best Men* 1997; *Wishful Thinking* 1997; *Ever After: a Cinderella Story* 1998; *Home Fries* 1998; *The Wedding Singer* 1998; *Never Been Kissed* 1999; *Charlie's Angels* 2000; *Titan AE* 2000; *Donnie Darko* 2001; *Freddy Got Fingered* 2001; *Riding in Cars with Boys* 2001; *Confessions of a Dangerous Mind* 2002; *Charlie's Angels: Full Throttle* 2003; *Our House* 2003; *50 First Dates* 2004; *The Perfect Catch* 2005; *Curious George* 2006; *Lucky You* 2007; *Music and Lyrics* 2007; *Beverly Hills Chihuahua* 2008; *He's Just Not That into You* 2008; *Everybody's Fine* 2009; *Grey Gardens* 2009; *Whip It* 2009; *Going the Distance* 2010; *Big Miracle* 2012; *Blended* 2014; *Miss You Already* 2015

Barrymore, Ethel (1879–1959) *Rasputin and the Empress* 1932; *None but the Lonely Heart* 1944; *The Farmer's Daughter* 1946; *The Spiral Staircase* 1946; *Moss Rose* 1947; *Night Song* 1947; *The Paradine Case* 1947; *Moonrise* 1948; *Portrait of Jennie* 1948; *The Great Sinner* 1949; *Pinky* 1949; *The Red Danube* 1949; *That Midnight Kiss* 1949; *It's a Big Country* 1951; *Kind Lady* 1951; *The Secret of Convict Lake* 1951; *Deadline - USA* 1952; *Just for You* 1952; *Main Street to Broadway* 1953; *The Story of Three Loves* 1953; *Young at Heart* 1955; *Johnny Trouble* 1957

Barrymore, John (1882–1942) *Dr Jekyll and Mr Hyde* 1920; *Don Juan* 1926; *When a Man Loves* 1926; *Eternal*

Love 1929; The Show of Shows 1929; Moby Dick 1930; The Mad Genius 1931; Svengali 1931; Arsene Lupin 1932; A Bill of Divorcement 1932; Grand Hotel 1932; Rasputin and the Empress 1932; Counsellor-at-Law 1933; Dinner at Eight 1933; Night Flight 1933; Reunion in Vienna 1933; Topaze 1933; Long Lost Father 1934; Twentieth Century 1934; Romeo and Juliet 1936; Bulldog Drummond Comes Back 1937; Bulldog Drummond's Revenge 1937; Maytime 1937; True Confession 1937; Bulldog Drummond's Peril 1938; Hold That Co-Ed 1938; Marie Antoinette 1938; Spawn of the North 1938; The Great Man Votes 1939; Midnight 1939; The Invisible Woman 1940; Playmates 1941

Barrymore, John Drew aka **Barrymore Jr, John** (1932-2004) High Lonesome 1950; The Sundowners 1950; The Big Night 1951; While the City Sleeps 1956; High School Confidential 1958; Pontius Pilate 1961; The Trojan War 1961; Winchester '73 1967

Barrymore, Lionel (1878-1954) America 1924; The Lucky Lady 1926; The Temptress 1926; Sadie Thompson 1928; West of Zanzibar 1928; Hollywood Revue 1929; Free and Easy 1930; A Free Soul 1931; Guilty Hands 1931; Mata Hari 1931; Arsene Lupin 1932; Grand Hotel 1932; The Man I Killed 1932; Rasputin and the Empress 1932; Dinner at Eight 1933; Night Flight 1933; The Stranger's Return 1933; The Girl from Missouri 1934; This Side of Heaven 1934; Treasure Island 1934; Ah, Wilderness! 1935; David Copperfield 1935; The Little Colonel 1935; Mark of the Vampire 1935; The Return of Peter Grimm 1935; The Devil-Doll 1936; The Gorgeous Hussy 1936; The Road to Glory 1936; Camille 1937; Captains Courageous 1937; A Family Affair 1937; Navy Blue and Gold 1937; Saratoga 1937; Test Pilot 1938; A Yank at Oxford 1938; You Can't Take It with You 1938; Young Dr Kildare 1938; Calling Dr Kildare 1939; The Secret of Dr Kildare 1939; Dr Kildare's Strange Case 1940; Dr Kildare Goes Home 1940; Dr Kildare's Crisis 1940; Dr Kildare's Wedding Day 1941; Dr Kildare's Victory 1941; Lady Be Good 1941; The Penalty 1941; The People vs Dr Kildare 1941; Calling Dr Gillespie 1942; Dr Gillespie's New Assistant 1942; Tennessee Johnson 1942; Dr Gillespie's Criminal Case 1943; Dragon Seed 1944; A Guy Named Joe 1944; Since You Went Away 1944; Three Men in White 1944; The Valley of Decision 1945; Duel in the Sun 1946; It's a Wonderful Life 1946; The Secret Heart 1946; Key Largo 1948; Down to the Sea in Ships 1949; Malaya 1949; Right Cross 1950; Lone Star 1952

Barsi, Judith (1978-1988) Jaws the Revenge 1987; All Dogs Go to Heaven 1989

Bart, Roger (1962-) The Stepford Wives 2004; The Producers 2005; Hostel: Part II 2007; Harold & Kumar Escape from Guantanamo Bay 2008; The Midnight Meat Train 2008; Excision 2012

Bartel (1), Paul (1938-2000) Hollywood Boulevard 1976; Rock 'n' Roll High School 1979; Eating Raoul 1982; Follow That Bird 1985; Killer Party 1986; Out of the Dark 1988; Desire & Hell at Sunset Motel 1991; The Pope Must Die 1991; Shelf Life 1993; The Usual Suspects 1995; Basquiat 1996; Escape from LA 1996; Billy's Hollywood Screen Kiss 1998

Barth, Eddie (1931-2010) Boardwalk 1979; Fame 1980

Bartha, Justin (1978-) Gigli 2003; National Treasure 2004; Failure to Launch 2006; National Treasure: Book of Secrets 2007; The Hangover 2009; The Rebound 2009; Holy Rollers 2010; Dark Horse 2011; The Hangover: Part II 2011; The Hangover Part III 2013

Barthelmess, Richard (1895-1963) Broken Blossoms 1919; Way Down East 1920; Tol'able David 1921; Fury 1923; The Dawn Patrol 1930; The Finger Points 1931; The Last Flight 1931; Cabin in the Cotton 1932; Central Airport 1933; Heroes for Sale 1933; Only Angels Have Wings 1939; The Spoilers 1942

Bartholomew, Freddie (1924-1992) Anna Karenina 1935; David Copperfield 1935; The Devil Is a Sissy 1936; Little Lord Fauntleroy 1936; Lloyd's of London 1936; Captains Courageous 1937; Kidnapped 1938; Listen, Darling 1938; Swiss Family Robinson 1940; Tom Brown's Schooldays 1940; A Yank at Eton 1942

Bartlett, Bennie (1927-1999) The Texas Rangers 1936; The Great Man Votes 1939; Let's Make Music 1940

Bartlett, Bonnie (1929-) Love Letters 1983; Twins 1988; The Lies Boys Tell 1994; Shiloh 1996; Tuesdays with Morrie 1999; Surviving Love 2004

Bartlett, Martine (1925-2006) Kansas City Bomber 1972; Aloha, Bobby and Rose 1975

Bartlett, Robin (1951-) Playing for Time 1980; Deceived 1991; Regarding Henry 1991; Teen Agent 1991; 12:01 1993; Dangerous Minds 1995; Honey, We Shrunk Ourselves 1997

Bartok, Eva (1926-1998) The Crimson Pirate 1952; Venetian Bird 1952; Front Page Story 1953; Spaceways 1953; Break in the Circle 1955; Special Delivery 1955; Ten Thousand Bedrooms 1957; Operation Amsterdam 1958; SOS Pacific 1959; Beyond the Curtain 1960; Blood and Black Lace 1964

Bartok, Jayce subUrbia 1996; Murder at Devil's Glen 1999

Barton, James (1890-1962) The Shepherd of the Hills 1941; Yellow Sky 1948; The Daughter of Rosie O'Grady 1950; Wabash Avenue 1950; Golden Girl 1951; Here Comes the Groom 1951; The Scarf 1951; Quantez 1957; The Misfits 1961

Barton, Margaret (1926-) Brief Encounter 1945; The Romantic Age 1949; The Happy Family 1952

Barton, Mischa (1986-) Lawn Dogs 1997; The Sixth Sense 1999; Octane 2003; Closing the Ring 2006; St Trinian's 2007

Barton, Peter (1956-) Hell Night 1981; Friday the 13th: the Final Chapter 1984

Bartusiak, Skye McCole (1992-2014) Witness Protection 1999; Don't Say a Word 2001; Boogeyman 2005

Barty, Billy (1924-2000) The Undead 1957; Harum Scarum 1965; Pufnstuf 1970; WC Fields and Me 1976; Under the Rainbow 1981; Legend 1985; Rumpelstiltskin 1986; Masters of the Universe 1987; Willow 1988; Life Stinks 1991

Baruchel, Jay (1982-) Million Dollar Baby 2004; Knocked Up 2007; Fanboys 2008; She's out of My League 2008; Tropic Thunder 2008; How to Train Your Dragon 2010; The Sorcerer's Apprentice 2010; Goon 2011; Cosmopolis 2012; The Art of the Steal 2013; This Is the End 2013; How to Train Your Dragon 2 2014

Baryshnikov, Mikhail (1948-) The Turning Point 1977; White Nights 1985; Dancers 1987; Company Business 1991

Basaraba, Gary (1959-) One Magic Christmas 1985; Sweet Dreams 1985; No Mercy 1986; The Dark Wind 1991; Fried Green Tomatoes at the Whistle Stop Cafe 1991; For Their Own Good 1993; Recipe for Murder 2001; The Sports Pages 2001

Basche, David Alan (1968-) War of the Worlds 2005; United 93 2006

Basco, Dante (1975-) Fist of the North Star 1995; Take the Lead 2006; Blood and Bone 2009

Basehart, Richard (1914-1984) Cry Wolf 1947; Repeat Performance 1947; He Walked by Night 1948; Reign of Terror 1949; Roseanna McCoy 1949; Tension 1949; Decision before Dawn 1951; Fixed Bayonets! 1951; Fourteen Hours 1951; The House on Telegraph Hill 1951; The Stranger's Hand 1953; The Good Die Young 1954; La Strada 1954; The Swindle 1955; The Extra Day 1956; The Intimate Stranger 1956; Moby Dick 1956; Time Limit 1957; The Brothers Karamazov 1958; Five Branded Women 1960; None but the Brave 1960; Portrait in Black 1960; Hitler 1962; Four Days in November 1964; The Satan Bug 1965; Chato's Land 1971; City beneath the Sea 1971; Rage 1972; And Millions Will Die! 1973; Mansion of the Doomed 1975; The Island of Dr Moreau 1977; Being There 1979

Basil, Toni (1948-) Easy Rider 1969; Eating 1990

Basinger, Kim (1953-) Hard Country 1981; The Man Who Loved Women 1983; Never Say Never Again 1983; The Natural 1984; Fool for Love 1985; Nine ½ Weeks 1985; No Mercy 1986; Blind Date 1987; Nadine 1987; My Stepmother Is an Alien 1988; Batman 1989; Too Hot to Handle 1991; Cool World 1992; Final Analysis 1992; The Real McCoy 1993; Wayne's World 2 1993; The Getaway 1994; Pret-a-Porter 1994; LA Confidential 1997; Bless the Child 2000; I Dreamed of Africa 2000; 8 Mile 2002; People I Know 2002; Cellular 2004; The Door in the Floor 2004; Elvis Has Left the Building 2004; The Sentinel 2006; The Burning Plain 2008; The Informers 2009; Death & Life of Charlie St Cloud 2010; Grudge Match 2013; Third Person 2013; The

Nice Guys 2016; Fifty Shades Darker 2017

Baskin, Elya (1951-) The Name of the Rose 1986; Streets of Gold 1986

Basler, Antoine Les Rendez-vous de 1995; Dobermann 1997; The Last Diamond 2014

Basler, Marianne (1964-) A Soldier's Tale 1988; Farinelli il Castrato 1994; Va Savoir 2001

Basquette, Lina (1907-1994) The Godless Girl 1928; The Younger Generation 1929

Bass, Alfie (1921-1987) The Hasty Heart 1949; Brandy for the Parson 1951; The Lavender Hill Mob 1951; The Square Ring 1953; Top of the Form 1953; The Angel Who Pawned Her Harp 1954; The Bespoke Overcoat 1955; Jumping for Joy 1955; A Kid for Two Farthings 1955; Behind the Headlines 1956; Child in the House 1956; Hell Drivers 1957; No Road Back 1957; I Was Monty's Double 1958; The Millionairess 1960; The Sandwich Man 1966; The Fearless Vampire Killers 1967; Up the Junction 1967; The Magnificent Seven Deadly Sins 1971; Come Play with Me 1977

Bass, Lance On the Line 2001; Love Wrecked 2005

Bassermann, Albert aka **Bassermann, Albert** (1867-1952) A Dispatch from Reuters 1940; Dr Ehrlich's Magic Bullet 1940; Escape 1940; Foreign Correspondent 1940; Knute Rockne - All American 1940; The Shanghai Gesture 1941; A Woman's Face 1941; The Moon and Sixpence 1942; Once upon a Honeymoon 1942; Reunion in France 1942; Madame Curie 1943; Rhapsody in Blue 1945; The Searching Wind 1946; Escape Me Never 1947; The Red Shoes 1948

Bassett, Angela (1958-) Boyz N the Hood 1991; City of Hope 1991; Malcolm X 1992; Passion Fish 1992; Tina: What's Love Got to Do with It 1993; Strange Days 1995; Vampire in Brooklyn 1995; Waiting to Exhale 1995; Contact 1997; How Stella Got Her Groove Back 1998; Music of the Heart 1999; Boesman & Lena 2000; Supernova 2000; Whispers: an Elephant's Tale 2000; The Score 2001; Sunshine State 2002; Mr 3000 2004; Akeelah and the Bee 2006; Meet the Robinsons 2006; Notorious 2009; This Means War 2012; Olympus Has Fallen 2013; Survivor 2015; London Has Fallen 2016

Bassett, Linda Waiting for the Moon 1987; East Is East 1999; The Martins 2001; Calendar Girls 2003; Separate Lies 2004; Kinky Boots 2005; The Reader 2008; West Is West 2010

Bastedo, Alexandra (1946-2014) The Ghoul 1975; The Lady 1976

Bastoni, Steve The Heartbreak Kid 1993; Macbeth 2006; Suburban Mayhem 2006

Bastos, Othon (1933-) Black God, White Devil 1964; Antonio das Mortes 1969; Central Station 1998

Basu, Bipasha (1979-) Raaz 2001; Jism 2003; Dhoom: 2 2006

Bat-Adam, Michal Madame Rosa 1977; The Ambassador 1984

Bataille, Julie C'est la Vie 1990; Bastards 2013

Bataille, Sylvia (1912-1993) Le Crime de Monsieur Lange 1935; Une Partie de Campagne 1936

Batalov, Alexei (1928-) The Cranes Are Flying 1957; The Lady with the Little Dog 1960; Moscow Distrusts Tears 1979

Batcheff, Pierre (1901-1932) The Chess Player 1927; Un Chien Andalou 1928

Bate, Anthony (1927-2012) A Prize of Arms 1961; Ghost Story 1974

Bateman, Charles Brotherhood of Satan 1970; Interval 1973

Bateman, Jason (1969-) Teen Wolf Too 1987; One Way Out 2002; The Sweetest Thing 2002; Starsky & Hutch 2004; The Break-Up 2006; Smokin' Aces 2006; Juno 2007; The Kingdom 2007; Mr Magorium's Wonder Emporium 2007; Hancock 2008; Couples Retreat 2009; Extract 2009; The Invention of Lying 2009; State of Play 2009; Up in the Air 2009; Paul 2010; The Switch 2010; The Change-Up 2011; Horrible Bosses 2011; Disconnect 2012; Identity Thief 2013; Horrible Bosses 2 2014; The Longest Week 2014; This Is Where I Leave You 2014; The Gift 2015; Central Intelligence 2016; Zootropolis 2016

Bateman, Justine (1966-) Satisfaction 1988; The Night We Never Met 1993; Another Woman 1994; The Hollywood Mom's Mystery 2004; Hybrid 2007

Bates Post, Guy (1875-1968) Fatal Lady 1936; Till We Meet Again 1936

Bates, Alan (1934-2003) The Entertainer 1960; Whistle down the Wind 1961; A Kind of Loving 1962; The Caretaker 1963; Nothing but the Best 1963; The Running Man 1963; Zorba the Greek 1964; Georgy Girl 1966; King of Hearts 1966; Far from the Madding Crowd 1967; Women in Love 1969; Three Sisters 1970; A Day in the Death of Joe Egg 1971; The Go-Between 1971; Butley 1973; Story of a Love Story 1973; In Celebration 1974; Royal Flash 1975; The Shout 1978; An Unmarried Woman 1978; The Rose 1979; Nijinsky 1980; Quartet 1981; Britannia Hospital 1982; The Return of the Soldier 1982; Separate Tables 1983; The Wicked Lady 1983; Duet for One 1986; A Prayer for the Dying 1987; We Think the World of You 1988; Dr M 1989; Hamlet 1990; Mister Frost 1990; Secret Friends 1991; The Grotesque 1995; The Cherry Orchard 1998; Nicholas' Gift 1998; Gosford Park 2001; Evelyn 2002; The Sum of All Fears 2002; The Statement 2003

Bates, Barbara (1925-1969) Strange Holiday 1942; June Bride 1948; The Inspector General 1949; All about Eve 1950; Cheaper by the Dozen 1950; Quicksand 1950; I'd Climb the Highest Mountain 1951; Let's Make It Legal 1951; The Secret of Convict Lake 1951; Belles on Their Toes 1952; All Ashore 1953; The Caddy 1953; Rhapsody 1954; House of Secrets 1956; Town on Trial 1956; Apache Territory 1958

Bates, Florence (1888-1954) Rebecca 1940; Son of Monte Cristo 1940; The Chocolate Soldier 1941; Love Crazy 1941; The Tuttles of Tahiti 1942; Slightly Dangerous 1943; Belle of the Yukon 1944; Kismet 1944; San Antonio 1945; Saratoga Trunk 1945; Claudia and David 1946; Diary of a Chambermaid 1946; Desire Me 1947; The Secret Life of Walter Mitty 1947; My Dear Secretary 1948; Portrait of Jennie 1948; Winter Meeting 1948; The Judge Steps Out 1949; A Letter to Three Wives 1949; On the Town 1949; Lullaby of Broadway 1951; The Second Woman 1951; The San Francisco Story 1952

Bates, Granville (1882-1940) Poppy 1936; The Affairs of Annabel 1938

Bates, Kathy (1948-) Straight Time 1978; Come Back to the Five and Dime, Jimmy Dean, Jimmy Dean 1982; Arthur 2: On the Rocks 1988; Roe vs Wade 1989; Dick Tracy 1990; Men Don't Leave 1990; Misery 1990; White Palace 1990; At Play in the Fields of the Lord 1991; Fried Green Tomatoes at the Whistle Stop Cafe 1991; Shadows and Fog 1991; Prelude to a Kiss 1992; Used People 1992; A Home of Our Own 1993; Hostages 1993; Angus 1995; Dolores Claiborne 1995; The West Side Waltz 1995; Diabolique 1996; The Late Shift 1996; The War at Home 1996; Amy Foster 1997; Titanic 1997; A Civil Action 1998; Primary Colors 1998; The Waterboy 1998; Annie 1999; American Outlaws 2001; Love Liza 2001; Unconditional Love 2001; About Schmidt 2002; Dragonfly 2002; Around the World in 80 Days 2004; Little Black Book 2004; Ambulance Girl 2005; Rumor Has It... 2005; Bonneville 2006; Charlotte's Web 2006; Failure to Launch 2006; Bee Movie 2007; Fred Claus 2007; PS I Love You 2007; The Day the Earth Stood Still 2008; Revolutionary Road 2008; The Blind Side 2009; Chéri 2009; A Little Bit of Heaven 2011; Midnight in Paris 2011; You May Not Kiss the Bride 2011; The Choir 2014; Tammy 2014; The Boss 2015

Bates, Michael (1920-1978) Don't Raise the Bridge, Lower the River 1968; Salt & Pepper 1968; Patton 1970; A Clockwork Orange 1971; No Sex Please - We're British 1973

Bates, Ralph (1940-1991) The Horror of Frankenstein 1970; Lust for a Vampire 1970; Dr Jekyll & Sister Hyde 1971; Fear in the Night 1972; Persecution 1974; I Don't Want to Be Born 1975; King of the Wind 1989

Bateson, Timothy (1926-2009) The Mouse That Roared 1959; There Was a Crooked Man 1960; It's Trad, Dad 1961; The Anniversary 1968; Autobiography of a Princess 1975

Bathurst, Robert (1957-) Heidi 2005; Narcopolis 2014

Batinkoff, Randall (1968-) For Keeps 1987; School Ties 1992; Walking and Talking 1996; Dead Man's Curve 1997; The Peacemaker 1997; The Last Marshal 1999

Battaglia, Matt (1965-) Universal Soldier 2: Brothers in Arms 1998;

Universal Soldier 3: Unfinished Business 1998

Battaglia, Rik aka **Battaglia, Rick** (1930-2015) Hannibal 1959; Esther and the King 1960; Don't Bother to Knock 1961; Sandokan the Great 1963; A Fistful of Dynamite 1971

Battista, Lloyd (1937-) Blind Man 1971; Round Trip to Heaven 1992; In Hell 2003

Battiston, Giuseppe (1968-) Bread and Tulips 2000; Shun Li and the Poet 2011

Battley, David (1935-2003) That's Your Funeral 1972; Krull 1983

Bauchau, Patrick (1938-) La Collectionneuse 1967; The State of Things 1982; Entre Nous 1983; Choose Me 1984; Lola 1986; The Music Teacher 1988; Australia 1989; The Rapture 1991; Lisbon Story 1994; The New Age 1994; Twin Falls Idaho 1999; Secretary 2001; Panic Room 2002; The Five Obstructions 2003

Bauche, Vanessa (1973-) Highway Patrolman 1991; Amores Perros 2000

Bauer, Belinda (1951-) The American Success Company 1979; Winter Kills 1979; The Rosary Murders 1987; RoboCop 2 1990; Poison Ivy 2 1995

Bauer, Chris aka **Bauer, Christopher** (1966-) 8mm 1999; The Hunley 1999; The Notorious Bettie Page 2005

Bauer, Steven aka **Bauer, Steve** (1956-) Scarface 1983; Thief of Hearts 1984; Running Scared 1986; The Beast of War 1988; Gleaming the Cube 1988; A Row of Crows 1991; Raising Cain 1992; Snapdragon 1993; Improper Conduct 1994; Wild Side 1995; The Blackout 1997; Traffic 2000; King of Texas 2002; The Lost City 2005

Baumann, Katherine aka **Baumann, Kathy** (1948-) The Thing with Two Heads 1972; 99 and 44/100% Dead 1974

Baur, Harry (1880-1943) Poil de Carotte 1932; Les Misérables 1934; Crime and Punishment 1935; Moscow Nights 1935; Beethoven 1936; The Golem 1936; Un Carnet de Bal 1937; Volpone 1941

Bautista, Dave (1969-) Guardians of the Galaxy 2014; Heist 2015

Bavier, Frances (1903-1989) The Day the Earth Stood Still 1951; Man in the Attic 1953; A Nice Little Bank That Should Be Robbed 1958

Baxendale, Helen (1970-) Macbeth 1997; Ordinary Decent Criminal 1999; Beyond the Pole 2009

Baxley, Barbara (1923-1990) All Fall Down 1962; Countdown 1967; Nashville 1975; Norma Rae 1979

Baxter, Alan (1908-1976) Big Brown Eyes 1936; Boy Slaves 1938; I Met My Love Again 1938; Each Dawn I Die 1939; Spirit of the People 1940; Shadow of the Thin Man 1941; China Girl 1942; Saboteur 1942; Pilot #5 1943; The Set-Up 1949; The True Story of Jesse James 1957; The Restless Years 1958; Face of a Fugitive 1959; This Property Is Condemned 1966

Baxter, Anne (1923-1985) Charley's Aunt 1941; Swamp Water 1941; The Magnificent Ambersons 1942; The Pied Piper 1942; Crash Dive 1943; Five Graves to Cairo 1943; The North Star 1943; The Eve of St Mark 1944; The Fighting Sullivans 1944; Guest in the House 1944; Sunday Dinner for a Soldier 1944; A Royal Scandal 1945; Angel on My Shoulder 1946; The Razor's Edge 1946; Smoky 1946; Blaze of Noon 1947; Mother Wore Tights 1947; Homecoming 1948; Yellow Sky 1948; You're My Everything 1949; All about Eve 1950; A Ticket to Tomahawk 1950; Follow the Sun: the Ben Hogan Story 1951; O Henry's Full House 1952; The Blue Gardenia 1953; I Confess 1953; Carnival Story 1954; Bedevilled 1955; The Spoilers 1955; The Come On 1956; The Ten Commandments 1956; Three Violent People 1956; Chase a Crooked Shadow 1957; Cimarron 1960; Season of Passion 1960; Mix Me a Person 1962; Walk on the Wild Side 1962; The Busy Body 1967; Stranger on the Run 1967; Dynamite Man from Glory Jail 1971; Jane Austen in Manhattan 1980

Baxter, Jane (1909-1996) The Constant Nymph 1933; Blossom Time 1934; The Clairvoyant 1934; We Live Again 1934; Dusty Ermine 1936; The Ware Case 1938; Ships with Wings 1942

Baxter, Jennifer Perfect Strangers 2004; George A Romero's Land of the Dead 2005

Baxter, Keith (1933-) Chimes at Midnight 1966; Ash Wednesday 1973; Golden Rendezvous 1977

Baxter, Lynsey (1965-) The French Lieutenant's Woman 1981; Real Life 1983

Baxter, Meredith aka **Baxter Birney, Meredith** (1947–) Ben 1972; The Night that Panicked America 1975; All the President's Men 1976; Bittersweet Love 1976; The Rape of Richard Beck 1985; A Woman Scorned 992; Mary Higgins Clark's Let Me Call You Sweetheart 1997; Man of Miracles 1999; Miracle on the 17th Green 1999; Murder on the Orient Express 2001; A Christmas Visitor 2002; Ange in the Family 2004; Bound by a Secret 2008

Baxter, Stanley (1926–) Very Important Person 1961; Crooks Anonymous 1962; The Fast Lady 1963; Father Came Too 1963; Joey Boy 1965

Baxter, Warner (1889-1951) West of Zanzibar 1928; In Old Arizona 1929; Renegades 1930; The Cisco Kid 1931; Daddy Long Legs 1931; 42nd Street 1933; Penthouse 1933; Broadway Bill 1934; Stand Up and Cheer! 1934; King of Burlesque 1936; The Prisoner of Shark Island 1936; The Road to Glory 1936; The Robin Hood of El Dorado 1936; Slave Ship 1937; Vogues of 1938 1937; Wife, Doctor and Nurse 1937; Kidnapped 1938; The Return of the Cisco Kid 1939; Wife, Husband and Friend 1939; Adam Had Four Sons 1941; Crime Doctor 1943; Lady in the Dark 1944

Bay, Frances The Pit and the Pendulum 1991; Single White Female 1992; Happy Gilmore 1996

Baye, Nathalie (1948–) Day for Night 1973; The Mouth Agape 1974; The Man Who Loved Women 1977; The Green Room 1978; Slow Motion 1980; A Strange Affair 1981; La Balance 1982; The Return of Martin Guerre 1982; Right Bank, Left Bank 1984; Detective 1985; C'est la Vie 1990; The Lie 1992; La Machine 1994; Food of Love 1997; Venus Beauty Institute 1998; Une Liaison Pornographique 1999; Catch Me If You Can 2002; Tell No One 2006; Beautiful Lies 2010; Laurence Anyways 2012

Bayldon, Geoffrey (1924–) Sky West and Crooked 1965; Where the Spies Are 1965; Casino Royale 1967; To Sir, with Love 1967; Two a Penny 1968; Tales from the Crypt 1972; The Monster Club 1980; Madame Sousatzka 1988; Asterix Conquers America 1994

Bayliss, Peter (1927-2002) House of Cards 1968; 30 's a Dangerous Age, Cynthia 1968; Vampira 1975

Baylor, Hal (1918-1998) Big Jim McLain 1952; This Is My Love 1954; A Boy and His Dog 1975

Bayly, Lorraine (1944–) Ride a Wild Pony 1976; The Man from Snowy River 1982

Baynaud, Erwan (1983–) La Machine 1994; East-West 1999

Baynton, Matthew 1234 2008; You Instead 2011; Bill 2014; The Falling 2014

Bazeley, Mark The Queen 2006; Flight of Fury 2007

Bazinet, Brenda Dancing in the Dark 1986; No Higher Love 1999

Beach, Adam (1972–) Dance Me Outside 1994; Squanto: the Last Great Warrior 1994; A Boy Called Hate 1995; Smoke Signals 1998; Joe Dirt 2001; Windtalkers 2001; Flags of Our Fathers 2006; Bury My Heart at Wounded Knee 2007

Beach, Michael (1963–) In a Shallow Grave 1988; Late for Dinner 1991; Stockade 1991; One False Move 1992; Bad Company 1995; Waiting to Exhale 1995; A Family Thing 1996; Casualties 1997; Soul Food 1997; Made Men 1999; First Sunday 2008; Relative Stranger 2009

Beacham, Stephanie (1947–) The Ballad of Tam Lin 1970; Dracula AD 1972 1972; The Nightcomers 1972; And Now the Screaming Starts! 1973; House of Mortal Sin 1975; Schizo 1976; Inseminoid 1981; The Wolves of Willoughby Chase 1988; Troop Beverly Hills 1989; Unconditional Love 2001

Beadle, Gary Until Death 2007; Malice in Wonderland 2009

Beahan, Kate The Crocodile Hunter: Collision Course 2002; Flightplan 2005; The Return 2006; The Wicker Man 2006; Southbound 2015

Beal, John (1909-1997) The Little Minister 1934; Break of Hearts 1935; Les Misérables 1935; Danger Patrol 1937; Double Wedding 1937; Madame X 1937; I Am the Law 1938; Port of Seven Seas 1938; The Cat and the Canary 1939; Edge of Darkness 1943; Remains to Be Seen 1953; Ten Who Dared 1960; Amityville II: the Demon 1983

Beale, Simon Russell (1961–) Orlando 1992; Persuasion 1995; The Gathering 2002; Deep Water 2006; The Deep Blue Sea 2011; My Cousin Rachel 2017

Beals, Jennifer (1963–) Flashdance 1983; The Bride 1985; Vampire's Kiss

1988; Dr M 1989; Sons 1989; In the Soup 1992; Dear Diary 1994; Devil in a Blue Dress 1995; Let It Be Me 1995; The Prophecy II 1997; Wishful Thinking 1997; The Last Days of Disco 1998; A House Divided 2000; Militia 2000; Turbulence II: Fear of Flying 2000; Without Malice 2000; After the Storm 2001; Roger Dodger 2002; Runaway Jury 2003; Catch That Kid 2004; The Grudge 2 2006; The Book of Eli 2009; A Fuller Life 2013

Bean, Alan In the Shadow of the Moon 2006; The Last Man on the Moon 2015

Bean, Orson (1928–) How to Be Very, Very Popular 1955; Twinky 1969; Being John Malkovich 1999

Bean, Robert The Wild Ride 1960; Creature from the Haunted Sea 1961

Bean, Sean (1959–) Caravaggio 1986; Stormy Monday 1987; War Requiem 1988; Windprints 1989; The Field 1990; Patriot Games 1992; Shopping 1993; Black Beauty 1994; GoldenEye 1995; When Saturday Comes 1995; Airborne 1997; Anna Karenina 1997; Ronin 1998; Essex Boys 1999; Don't Say a Word 2001; The Lord of the Rings: The Fellowship of the Ring 2001; Equilibrium 2002; Tom & Thomas 2002; National Treasure 2004; Troy 2004; The Dark 2005; Flightplan 2005; The Island 2005; North Country 2005; Outlaw 2006; Silent Hill 2006; Far North 2007; The Hitcher 2007; Black Death 2010; Ca$h! 2010; Percy Jackson & the Lightning Thief 2010; Age of Heroes 2011; Cleanskin 2012; Mirror Mirror 2012; Silent Hill: Revelation 2012; Soldiers of Fortune 2012; Percy Jackson: Sea of Monsters 2013; Jupiter Ascending 2014; The Martian 2015; Pixels 2015

Beard, Matthew When Did You Last See Your Father? 2007; Chatroom 2010; The Imitation Game 2014

Béart, Emmanuelle (1965–) Manon des Sources 1986; La Belle Noiseuse 1991; J'Embrasse Pas 1991; Un Coeur en Hiver 1992; L'Enfer 1993; Une Femme Française 1994; Nelly & Monsieur Arnaud 1995; Mission: Impossible 1996; La Bûche 1999; Elephant Juice 1999; Time Regained 1999; Les Destinées Sentimentales 2000; 8 Women 2001; Histoire de Marie et Julien 2003; Nathalie... 2003; Strayed 2003; L'Enfer 2005; The Witnesses 2006; Vinyan 2008

Beasley, John (1943–) The Apostle 1997; Lost Souls 2000; Walking Tall 2004

Beaton, Norman (1934-1994) Pressure 1976; Black Joy 1977; Real Life 1983; Playing Away 1986

Beatty, May (1880-1945) Mad Love 1935; The Adventures of Sherlock Holmes 1939

Beatty, Ned (1937–) Deliverance 1972; The Life and Times of Judge Roy Bean 1972; The Last American Hero 1973; The Marcus-Nelson Murders 1973; The Thief Who Came to Dinner 1973; White Lightning 1973; The Execution of Private Slovik 1974; Nashville 1975; WW and the Dixie Dancekings 1975; All the President's Men 1976; The Big Bus 1976; Network 1976; Silver Streak 1976; Exorcist II: The Heretic 1977; Gray Lady Down 1978; Superman 1978; The American Success Company 1979; Friendly Fire 1979; 1941 1979; Wise Blood 1979; Hopscotch 1980; Superman II 1980; The Incredible Shrinking Woman 1981; The Toy 1982; Stroker Ace 1983; Restless Natives 1985; The Big Easy 1986; The Fourth Protocol 1987; Switching Channels 1987; The Trouble with Spies 1987; Midnight Crossing 1988; Physical Evidence 1988; The Purple People Eater 1988; The Unholy 1988; Chattahoochee 1989; Time Trackers 1989; Captain America 1990; Going Under 1990; Repossessed 1990; Hear My Song 1991; Prelude to a Kiss 1992; Motherhood 1993; Rudy 1993; Radioland Murders 1994; Just Cause 1995; He Got Game 1998; Cookie's Fortune 1999; Life 1999; Thunderpants 2002; Sweet Land 2005; The Walker 2006; Charlie Wilson's War 2007; In the Electric Mist 2009; The Killer Inside Me 2010; Rampart 2011; Rango 2011

Beatty, Robert (1909-1992) San Demetrio London 1943; Against the Wind 1947; Odd Man Out 1947; Another Shore 1948; Counterblast 1948; Portrait from Life 1948; Calling Bulldog Drummond 1951; Captain Horatio Hornblower RN 1951; The Magic Box 1951; The Gentle Gunman 1952; The Oracle 1952; Albert, RN 1953; Man on a Tightrope 1953; The Net 1953; The Square Ring 1953; The Loves of Three Queens 1954; Out of the Clouds 1954;

Tarzan and the Lost Safari 1956; Something of Value 1957; Time Lock 1957; The Shakedown 1959; The Amorous Prawn 1962; 2001: a Space Odyssey 1968; Where Eagles Dare 1969; The Spaceman and King Arthur 1979

Beatty, Warren (1937–) The Roman Spring of Mrs Stone 1961; Splendor in the Grass 1961; All Fall Down 1962; Lilith 1964; Mickey One 1965; Kaleidoscope 1966; Promise Her Anything 1966; Bonnie and Clyde 1967; The Only Game in Town 1970; Dollars 1971; McCabe and Mrs Miller 1971; The Parallax View 1974; The Fortune 1975; Shampoo 1975; Heaven Can Wait 1978; Reds 1981; Ishtar 1987; Dick Tracy 1990; Bugsy 1991; In Bed with Madonna 1991; Love Affair 1994; Bulworth 1998; Town & Country 2001; Rules Don't Apply 2016

Beaumont, Diana (1909-1964) When London Sleeps 1932; Let George Do It 1940; Home at Seven 1952

Beaumont, Hugh (1909-1982) The Seventh Victim 1943; The Blue Dahlia 1946; Railroaded! 1947; The Mole People 1956

Beaumont, Kathryn (1938–) On an Island with You 1948; Alice in Wonderland 1951; Peter Pan 1953

Beaumont, Lucy (1873-1937) A Free Soul 1931; His Double Life 1933; The Devil-Doll 1936

Beaumont, Susan (1936–) Eyewitness 1956; Innocent Sinners 1957; The Man Who Liked Funerals 1959

Beauvais-Nilon, Garcelle Bad Company 2002; I Know Who Killed Me 2007

Beauvois, Xavier (1967–) Le Vent de la Nuit 1999; Villa Amalia 2009

Beauvy, Nicolas (1958–) Rage 1972; The Toolbox Murders 1978

Beaver, Jim (1950–) Twogether 1994; Next 2007; Crimson Peak 2015

Beavers, Louise (1902-1962) What Price Hollywood? 1932; Imitation of Life 1934; Belle Starr 1941; The Vanishing Virginian 1941; Holiday Inn 1942; Barbary Coast Gent 1944; Lover Come Back 1946; Good Sam 1948; Mr Blandings Builds His Dream House 1948; My Blue Heaven 1950

Becerril, Fernando KM 31: Kilometro 31 2005; Mariachi Gringo 2012

Beck (2), Jennifer (1974–) Tightrope 1984; Troll 1986

Beck, John (1943–) Mrs Pollifax - Spy 1970; Pat Garrett and Billy the Kid 1973; Sleeper 1973; Rollerball 1975; The Big Bus 1976; Audrey Rose 1977; The Other Side of Midnight 1977; A Row of Crows 1991

Beck, Julian (1925-1985) Oedipus Rex 1967; Poltergeist II: the Other Side 1986

Beck, Michael (1949–) Mayflower: the Pilgrims' Adventure 1979; The Warriors 1979; Xanadu 1980; Battletruck 1982; The Golden Seal 1983; Triumphs of a Man Called Horse 1983; Chiller 1985

Beck, Stanley (1936–) John and Mary 1969; Lenny 1974

Beck, Thomas (1909-1995) Charlie Chan in Egypt 1935; Charlie Chan in Paris 1935; Charlie Chan at the Opera 1936; Crack-Up 1936; White Fang 1936; Heidi 1937; Thank You, Mr Moto 1937; Think Fast, Mr Moto 1937

Beckel, Graham (1955–) The Paper Chase 1973; The Road Home 1989; Welcome Home, Roxy Carmichael 1990; Liebestraum 1991; Jennifer Eight 1992; Black Dog 1998; Blue Streak 1999; Northfork 2002

Becker, Gerry (1950–) The Public Eye 1992; Donnie Brasco 1997; The Hunley 1999; Man on the Moon 1999; Mickey Blue Eyes 1999

Becker, Gretchen Firehead 1991; Huck and the King of Hearts 1993

Becker, Kuno (1978–) Imagining Argentina 2003; Goal! 2005; Goal II: Living the Dream 2007

Beckett, James Rotten to the Core 1965; Poor Cow 1967

Beckett, Scotty (1929-1968) Dante's Inferno 1935; Listen, Darling 1938; Days of Jesse James 1939; My Favorite Wife 1940; Circumstantial Evidence 1945; Cynthia 1947; The Happy Years 1950

Beckham, David (1975–) Manchester United: beyond the Promised Land 2000; Goal II: Living the Dream 2007; The Class of '92 2013

Beckinsale, Kate (1973–) One against the Wind 1991; Much Ado about Nothing 1993; Prince of Jutland 1994; Haunted 1995; Shooting Fish 1997; The Last Days of Disco 1998; Brokedown Palace 1999; The Golden Bowl 2000; Pearl Harbor 2001; Serendipity 2001; Laurel Canyon 2002; Underworld 2003; The Aviator 2004; Van Helsing 2004; Click 2006; Underworld: Evolution 2006; Vacancy 2007;

Fragments 2008; Everybody's Fine 2009; Contraband 2012; Total Recall 2012; Underworld: Awakening 2012; The Face of an Angel 2014; Stonehearst Asylum 2014; Absolutely Anything 2015; Love & Friendship 2016

Beckinsale, Richard (1947-1979) The Lovers! 1972; Rentadick 1972; Porridge 1979

Beckley, Tony (1927-1980) The Penthouse 1967; The Lost Continent 1968; The Italian Job 1969; Assault 1970; The Fiend 1971; Diagnosis: Murder 1974; Gold 1974; When a Stranger Calls 1979

Beckman, Henry (1921-2008) The Harness 1971; The Brood 1979

Beckwith, Reginald (1908-1965) Scott of the Antarctic 1948; Mr Drake's Duck 1950; Another Man's Poison 1951; Penny Princess 1952; Genevieve 1953; The Million Pound Note 1953; Dance Little Lady 1954; Lease of Life 1954; Men of Sherwood Forest 1954; The Runaway Bus 1954; Break in the Circle 1955; The Lyons in Paris 1955; They Can't Hang Me 1955; A Yank in Ermine 1955; A Touch of the Sun 1956; Night of the Demon 1957; The Captain's Table 1958; Next to No Time 1958; Up the Creek 1958; Bottoms Up 1959; Desert Mice 1959; The Thirty-Nine Steps 1959; The Night We Got the Bird 1960; There Was a Crooked Man 1960; The Day the Earth Caught Fire 1961; Dentist on the Job 1961; Double Bunk 1961; Night of the Eagle 1961; The Password Is Courage 1962

Becwar, George (1917-1970) Bride of the Monster 1955; War of the Colossal Beast 1958

Bedard, Irene (1967–) Squanto: the Last Great Warrior 1994; Pocahontas 1995; Smoke Signals 1998; Two for Texas 1998

Beddoe, Don (1891-1991) The Amazing Mr Williams 1939; The Man They Could Not Hang 1939; The Face behind the Mask 1941; Sweetheart of the Campus 1941; Texas 1941; Unholy Partners 1941; The Boogie Man Will Get You 1942; The Bachelor and the Bobby-Soxer 1947; Buck Privates Come Home 1947; The Lady Gambles 1949; The Conquest She Keeps 1950; Carson City 1952; Bullwhip 1958; Jack the Giant Killer 1962

Bedelia, Bonnie (1946–) The Gypsy Moths 1969; They Shoot Horses, Don't They? 1969; Lovers and Other Strangers 1970; The Strange Vengeance of Rosalie 1972; The Big Fix 1978; Salem's Lot 1979; Heart like a Wheel 1983; Death of an Angel 1985; The Boy Who Could Fly 1986; Violets Are Blue 1986; Die Hard 1988; The Prince of Pennsylvania 1988; Shadow Makers 1989; Die Hard 2: Die Harder 1990; Presumed Innocent 1990; Needful Things 1993; Speechless 1994; Homecoming 1996; Bad Manners 1997; Gloria 1998; Anywhere but Here 1999; Flowers for Algernon 2000

Bedell, Rodney The Gruesome Twosome 1967; She-Devils on Wheels 1968

Bedford, Barbara (1903-1981) The Last of the Mohicans 1920; Tumbleweeds 1925

Bedford, Brian (1935-2016) Miracle in Soho 1957; Grand Prix 1966; Robin Hood 1973; Nixon 1995

Bedi, Kabir (1945–) The Thief of Bagdad 1978; Ashanti 1979; Octopussy 1983; The Beast of War 1988

Bedoya, Alfonso (1904-1957) The Treasure of the Sierra Madre 1947; Angel in Exile 1948; Border Incident 1949; Streets of Laredo 1949; Ten Wanted Men 1955; The Big Country 1958

Beeby, Bruce (1921-2013) The Man in the Road 1957; Serena 1962

Beecher, Janet (1884-1955) The Mighty Barnum 1934; The Dark Angel 1935; So Red the Rose 1935; Village Tale 1935; Love before Breakfast 1936; Big City 1937; The Story of Vernon and Irene Castle 1939; The Gay Caballero 1940; The Mark of Zorro 1940; The Lady Eve 1941

Beery, Noah aka **Beery Sr, Noah** (1884-1946) The Mark of Zorro 1920; Beau Geste 1926; Beau Sabreur 1928; The Godless Girl 1928; The Four Feathers 1929; Renegades 1930; Riders of the Purple Sage 1931; The Big Stampede 1932; The Kid from Spain 1932; She Done Him Wrong 1933; Caravan 1934; The Trail Beyond 1934; The Avenging Hand 1936; Barbary Coast Gent 1944; Block Busters 1944

Beery Jr, Noah aka **Beery, Noah** (1913-1994) The Trail Beyond 1934; Stormy 1935; Of Mice and Men 1939; Frontier Badmen 1943; Gung Ho! 1943; The Daltons Ride Again 1945; Under

Western Skies 1945; Red River 1948; Two Flags West 1950; The Cimarron Kid 1951; War Arrow 1953; White Feather 1955; The Fastest Gun Alive 1956; Jubal 1956; Decision at Sundown 1957; Escort West 1959; Guns of the Timberland 1960; 7 Faces of Dr Lao 1963; The Spikes Gang 1974

Beery, Wallace (1885-1949) The Last of the Mohicans 1920; Robin Hood 1922; Three Ages 1923; The Sea Hawk 1924; The Lost World 1925; The Pony Express 1925; Beggars of Life 1928; The Big House 1930; Billy the Kid 1930; A Lady's Morals 1930; Min and Bill 1930; The Champ 1931; The Secret Six 1931; Flesh 1932; Grand Hotel 1932; Hell Divers 1932; The Bowery 1933; Dinner at Eight 1933; Tugboat Annie 1933; The Mighty Barnum 1934; Treasure Island 1934; Viva Villa! 1934; Ah, Wilderness! 1935; China Seas 1935; A Message to Garcia 1936; Slave Ship 1937; Bad Man of Brimstone 1938; Port of Seven Seas 1938; Sergeant Madden 1939; The Man from Dakota 1940; Barbary Coast Gent 1944; A Date with Judy 1948

Beesley, Max (1971–) The Match 1999; It Was an Accident 2000; Glitter 2001; Kill Me Later 2001; Anita & Me 2002

Beghe, Jason (1960–) Monkey Shines 1988; Thelma & Louise 1991; Jimmy Hollywood 1994; GI Jane 1997; Taming Andrew 2000; Home Alone 4 2002; One Missed Call 2007; Going Clear 2015

Begley, Ed (1901-1970) Sitting Pretty 1948; Sorry, Wrong Number 1948; The Street with No Name 1948; It Happens Every Spring 1949; Tulsa 1949; Backfire 1950; Dark City 1950; Saddle Tramp 1950; Stars in My Crown 1950; Wyoming Mail 1950; Boots Malone 1951; On Dangerous Ground 1951; Deadline - USA 1952; Lone Star 1952; The Turning Point 1952; Patterns 1956; 12 Angry Men 1957; Odds against Tomorrow 1959; The Green Helmet 1960; Sweet Bird of Youth 1962; The Unsinkable Molly Brown 1964; The Oscar 1966; Billion Dollar Brain 1967; Warning Shot 1967; Firecreek 1968; Hang 'Em High 1968; Wild in the Streets 1968; The Violent Enemy 1969; The Dunwich Horror 1970

Begley Jr, Ed (1949–) Showdown 1973; Blue Collar 1978; The One and Only 1978; The In-Laws 1979; Cat People 1982; Eating Raoul 1982; Get Crazy 1983; Protocol 1984; Transylvania 6-5000 1985; Amazon Women on the Moon 1987; The Accidental Tourist 1988; Scenes from the Class Struggle in Beverly Hills 1989; She-Devil 1989; Meet the Applegates 1991; Dark Horse 1992; Cooperstown 1993; Even Cowgirls Get the Blues 1993; Greedy 1994; The Pagemaster 1994; Renaissance Man 1994; The Late Shift 1996; Project ALF 1996; Addams Family Reunion 1998; I'm Losing You 1998; Diary of a Sex Addict 2001; Get over It 2001; A Mighty Wind 2003; Life on Liberty Street 2004; Who Killed the Electric Car? 2006; Fly Me to the Moon 2007; Recount 2008; Georgia O'Keeffe 2009; Whatever Works 2009

Behan, Paudge Snakes & Ladders 1996; A Secret Affair 1999

Behets, Briony (1951–) Long Weekend 1977; Cassandra 1987

Behr, Dani (1975–) Like It Is 1997; Rancid Aluminium 1999; Goodbye Charlie Bright 2000

Behr, Jason (1973–) Rites of Passage 1999; The Shipping News 2001; The Grudge 2004; Skinwalkers 2006

Behrens, Bernard (1926-2012) The Changeling 1980; Incident in a Small Town 1993; Zero Patience 1993

Behrens, Sam (1950–) Alive 1992; Bermuda Triangle 1996

Beirute, Yerye (1928-1972) Battle Shock 1956; Alien Terror 1969

Bejo, Bérénice OSS 117: Cairo - Nest of Spies 2006; The Artist 2011; Populaire 2012; The Past 2013; The Last Diamond 2014; The Childhood of a Leader 2015

Bekassy, Stephen (1910-1995) A Song to Remember 1945; Arch of Triumph 1948; Black Magic 1949; Hell and High Water 1954

Bekhti, Leïla Sheitan 2006; The Source 2011; Before the Winter Chill 2013

Bel Geddes, Barbara (1922-2005) The Long Night 1947; Blood on the Moon 1948; I Remember Mama 1948; Caught 1949; Panic in the Street 1950; Fourteen Hours 1951; Vertigo 1958; The Five Pennies 1959; Five Branded Women 1960; By Love Possessed 1961; Summertree 1971

Belafonte, Harry (1927–) Bright Road 1953; Carmen Jones 1954; Island in the Sun 1957; Odds against Tomorrow 1959; The World, the Flesh and the

Devil 1959; The Angel Levine 1970; King: a Filmed Record... Montgomery to Memphis 1970; Buck and the Preacher 1972; Uptown Saturday Night 1974; Kansas City 1995; White Man's Burden 1995; Robert Altman's Jazz '34: Remembrances of Kansas City Swing 1996; Swing Vote 1999; Bobby 2006; Sing Your Song 2011

Belafonte, Shari aka Belafonte-Harper, Shari (1954-) Cannonball Fever 1989; Fire, Ice and Dynamite 1990

Belal, Baya Bent Keltoum 2001; Our Children 2012

Belasco, Leon (1902-1988) Everybody Does It 1949; Love Happy 1949

Belcher, Charles (1872-1943) Rosita 1923; The Thief of Bagdad 1924; The Black Pirate 1926

Bélézy, Victoire Marius 2012; Fanny 2013

Belford, Christine (1949-) Banacek: Detour to Nowhere 1972; The Groundstar Conspiracy 1972; Pocket Money 1972; Agatha Christie's Sparkling Cyanide 1983; Christine 1983

Belita (1923-2005) The Man on the Eiffel Tower 1949; Never Let Me Go 1953

Belkhadra, Karim La Haine 1995; The Crimson Rivers 2000; Room to Rent 2000; JCVD 2008

Bell Calloway, Vanessa (1957-) Bebe's Kids 1992; Tina: What's Love Got to Do with It 1993; Love Don't Cost a Thing 2003

Bell, Ann (1940-) A Midsummer Night's Dream 1961; The Witches 1966; The Reckoning 1969; Champions 1983; When Saturday Comes 1995

Bell, Arnold (?-1988) Doss House 1933; The Greed of William Hart 1948; The Master Plan 1954

Bell, Ashley The Last Exorcism 2010; The Last Exorcism Part II 2013

Bell, Drake (1986-) The Neon Bible 1995; Superhero Movie 2008

Bell, Emma Frozen 2009; Final Destination 5 2011

Bell, Geoff (1963-) Green Street 2004; The Business 2005; Botched 2007; Daylight Robbery 2007; Freebird 2007; Route Irish 2010

Bell, James (1891-1973) Holiday Inn 1942; I Walked with a Zombie 1943; The Leopard Man 1943; My Friend Flicka 1943; Thunderhead - Son of Flicka 1945; The Company She Keeps 1950; Red Mountain 1951; About Mrs Leslie 1954; The City Is Dark 1954; A Lawless Street 1955; Texas Lady 1955; -30- 1959

Bell, Jamie (1986-) Billy Elliot 2000; Deathwatch 2002; Nicholas Nickleby 2002; Dear Wendy 2004; Undertow 2004; The Chumscrubber 2005; King Kong 2005; Flags of Our Fathers 2006; Hallam Foe 2006; Defiance 2008; Jumper 2008; The Eagle 2010; The Adventures of Tintin: the Secret of the Unicorn 2011; Jane Eyre 2011; Retreat 2011; Man on a Ledge 2012; Filth 2013; Snowpiercer 2013; Nymphomaniac Vol II 2014; Fantastic Four 2015

Bell, Kristen (1980-) The Cat Returns 2002; The King and Queen of Moonlight Bay 2003; Spartan 2004; Pulse 2006; Fanboys 2008; Forgetting Sarah Marshall 2008; Astro Boy 2009; Couples Retreat 2009; When in Rome 2009; Burlesque 2010; You Again 2010; Scre4m 2011; Big Miracle 2012; Hit & Run 2012; Safety Not Guaranteed 2012; Stuck in Love 2012; Frozen 2013; Veronica Mars 2014; The Boss 2015

Bell, Lake (1979-) Over Her Dead Body 2008; What Happens in Vegas 2008; It's Complicated 2009; Black Rock 2012; In a World... 2013; Million Dollar Arm 2014; No Escape 2014; Man Up 2015

Bell, Marie (1900-1985) Un Carnet de Bal 1937; Hotel Paradiso 1966

Bell, Marshall (1944-) Twins 1988; Total Recall 1990; Leather Jackets 1991; The Vagrant 1992; Virus 1998; Mercy 2000

Bell, Nicholas Father 1990; Hotel Sorrento 1994; Dead Letter Office 1998

Bell, Tobin (1942-) False Identity 1990; The Quick and the Dead 1995; Overnight Delivery 1997; Brown's Requiem 1998; The Road to El Dorado 2000; Saw 2004; Saw II 2005; Saw III 2006; Saw IV 2007; Saw V 2008; Saw VI 2009; Saw: the Final Chapter 2010

Bell, Tom (1933-2006) The Kitchen 1961; Payroll 1961; A Prize of Arms 1961; HMS Defiant 1962; The L-Shaped Room 1962; Ballad in Blue 1964; He Who Rides a Tiger 1965; In Enemy Country 1968; Lock Up Your Daughters! 1969; The Violent Enemy 1969; All the Right Noises 1970; Quest

for Love 1971; Royal Flash 1975; The Innocent 1984; Wish You Were Here 1987; Resurrected 1989; The Krays 1990; Let Him Have It 1991; Prospero's Books 1991; Feast of July 1995; Amy Foster 1997; Preaching to the Perverted 1997; Swing 1998; Lava 2000; Long Time Dead 2001; My Kingdom 2001; Devil's Gate 2002

Bell, Zoë aka Bell, Zoe Death Proof 2007; Hansel & Gretel: Witch Hunters 2013

Bellamy, Bill (1965-) Love Jones 1997; Buying the Cow 2000; The Brothers 2001

Bellamy, Madge (1899-1990) The Iron Horse 1924; White Zombie 1932; Charlie Chan in London 1934

Bellamy, Ned (1957-) Cobb 1994; Tenacious D in The Pick of Destiny 2006; Wind Chill 2007

Bellamy, Ralph (1904-1991) The Secret Six 1931; Air Mail 1932; Forbidden 1932; Ace of Aces 1933; Blind Adventure 1933; Ever in My Heart 1933; Picture Snatcher 1933; Spitfire 1934; This Man Is Mine 1934; Hands across the Table 1935; The Wedding Night 1935; The Man Who Lived Twice 1936; The Awful Truth 1937; Boy Meets Girl 1938; Carefree 1938; Fools for Scandal 1938; Trade Winds 1938; Blind Alley 1939; His Girl Friday 1939; Brother Orchid 1940; Dance, Girl, Dance 1940; Ellery Queen Master Detective 1940; Affectionately Yours 1941; Dive Bomber 1941; Footsteps in the Dark 1941; The Wolf Man 1941; The Ghost of Frankenstein 1942; Lady in a Jam 1942; Men of Texas 1942; Stage Door Canteen 1943; Guest in the House 1944; Lady on a Train 1945; The Court-Martial of Billy Mitchell 1955; Sunrise at Campobello 1960; The Professionals 1966; Rosemary's Baby 1968; Doctors' Wives 1970; Cancel My Reservation 1972; Something Evil 1972; The Boy in the Plastic Bubble 1976; Oh, God! 1977; Trading Places 1983; Amazon Women on the Moon 1987; Disorderlies 1987; Coming to America 1988; The Price of Passion 1988; Pretty Woman 1990

Bellar, Clara Les Rendez-vous de Paris 1995; Dominion: Prequel to the Exorcist 2005

Bellaver, Harry (1905-1993) No Way Out 1950; Perfect Strangers 1950; Something to Live For 1952; Miss Sadie Thompson 1953; Love Me or Leave Me 1955; The Birds and the Bees 1956; Serenade 1956; The Brothers Rico 1957; The Old Man and the Sea 1958; One Potato, Two Potato 1964; Blue Collar 1978; Hero at Large 1980

Belle, Camilla (1986-) Poison Ivy 2 1995; The Ballad of Jack and Rose 2005; The Chumscrubber 2005; When a Stranger Calls 2006; 10,000 BC 2008; Adrift 2009; Push 2009

Belle, David District 13 2004; District 13: Ultimatum 2009; Brick Mansions 2014

Beller, Kathleen (1955-) Something for Joey 1977; The Betsy 1978; Fort Apache, the Bronx 1981; Time Trackers 1989

Belli, Agostina (1949-) Bluebeard 1972; The Seduction of Mimi 1972; Scent of a Woman 1974; Holocaust 2000 1977; The Purple Taxi 1977

Bellingham, Lynda (1948-2014) Sweeney! 1976; Stand Up Virgin Soldiers 1977; Devil's Gate 2002

Bellini, Francesca Bachelor Flat 1961; Who's Minding the Store? 1963

Bellis, Scott Timecop 1994; The Man Who Wouldn't Die 1995

Bellman, Gina (1966-) Secret Friends 1991; Leon the Pig Farmer 1992; Silent Trigger 1996; 7 Days to Live 2000; Married/Unmarried 2001

Bello, Maria (1967-) Payback 1998; Permanent Midnight 1998; Coyote Ugly 2000; Duets 2000; Auto Focus 2002; The Cooler 2002; Secret Window 2004; Silver City 2004; Assault on Precinct 13 2005; The Dark 2005; A History of Violence 2005; Thank You for Smoking 2005; Flicka 2006; World Trade Center 2006; Butterfly on a Wheel 2007; The Jane Austen Book Club 2007; The Mummy: Tomb of the Dragon Emperor 2008; The Private Lives of Pippa Lee 2009; Grown Ups 2010; The Company Men 2010; Grown Ups 2010; Abduction 2011; Grown Ups 2 2013; Prisoners 2013; Lights Out 2016

Bellocchio, Piergiorgio aka Bellocchio, Pier Giorgio Good Morning, Night 2003; Vincere 2009

Bellows, Gil (1967-) Love and a .45 1994; The Shawshank Redemption 1994; Miami Rhapsody 1995; Snow White: a Tale of Terror 1996; The Substance of Fire 1996; Judas Kiss 1998; Beautiful Joe 2000; Blind Horizon 2003; EMR 2004; The

Weather Man 2005; Unthinkable 2010; Fury 2012; House at the End of the Street 2012; The Calling 2014; Extraterrestrial 2014

Bellucci, Monica (1964-) L'Appartement 1996; Dobermann 1997; Malena 2000; Under Suspicion 2000; Asterix & Obelix: Mission Cleopatra 2001; Brotherhood of the Wolf 2001; Irreversible 2002; The Matrix Reloaded 2002; The Matrix Revolutions 2003; Tears of the Sun 2003; The Passion of the Christ 2004; She Hate Me 2004; The Brothers Grimm 2005; Sheitan 2006; Shoot 'Em Up 2007; The Private Lives of Pippa Lee 2009; The Sorcerer's Apprentice 2010; The Whistleblower 2010

Bellwood, Pamela (1951-) Hangar 18 1980; Serial 1980; Agatha Christie's Sparkling Cyanide 1983

Belmadi, Yasmine (1976-) Criminal Lovers 1999; Wild Side 2004

Belmondo, Jean-Paul (1933-) A Bout de Souffle 1959; Classe Tous Risques 1959; Web of Passion 1959; Two Women 1960; Cartouche 1961; Une Femme Est une Femme 1961; Léon Morin, Priest 1961; Le Doulos 1962; A Monkey in Winter 1962; L'Ainé des Ferchaux 1963; Banana Peel 1964; Male Hunt 1964; That Man from Rio 1964; Pierrot le Fou 1965; Up to his Ears 1965; Is Paris Burning? 1966; Casino Royale 1967; The Thief of Paris 1967; The Brain 1969; Mississippi Mermaid 1969; Borsalino 1970; The Burglars 1971; Les Mariés de l'An Deux 1971; Stavisky 1974; The Professional 1981; The Outsider 1983; Hold-Up 1985; Les Misérables 1995

Belmont, Lara The War Zone 1999; Long Time Dead 2001; Someone Else 2005

Belmore, Lionel (1867-1953) Oliver Twist 1922; Three Ages 1923; The Matinee Idol 1928; Monte Carlo 1930; The Rogue Song 1930; Frankenstein 1931; One Heavenly Night 1931; Berkeley Square 1933

Beltran, Robert (1953-) Eating Raoul 1982; Lone Wolf McQuade 1983; Calendar Girl Murders 1984; Night of the Comet 1984; Gaby: a True Story 1987; Slam Dance 1987; Scenes from the Class Struggle In Beverly Hills 1989

Belushi, James aka Belushi, Jim (1954-) Thief 1981; Trading Places 1983; The Man with One Red Shoe 1985; About Last Night... 1986; Jumpin' Jack Flash 1986; Little Shop of Horrors 1986; Salvador 1986; The Principal 1987; Real Men 1987; Red Heat 1988; Homer and Eddie 1989; K-9 1989; Mr Destiny 1990; Taking Care of Business 1990; Curly Sue 1991; Only the Lonely 1991; Diary of a Hitman 1992; Once upon a Crime 1992; Traces of Red 1992; Canadian Bacon 1995; Destiny Turns on the Radio 1995; The Pebble and the Penguin 1995; Separate Lives 1995; Jingle All the Way 1996; Race the Sun 1996; Gang Related 1997; Wag the Dog 1997; Angel's Dance 1999; K-911 1999; Made Men 1999; Return to Me 2000; Joe Somebody 2001; One Way Out 2002; Hoodwinked 2005; The Wild 2006; Underdog 2007; The Ghost 2010; Legends of Oz: Dorothy's Return 2013; The Whole Truth 2016

Belushi, John (1949-1982) Goin' South 1978; National Lampoon's Animal House 1978; The Rutles - All You Need Is Cash 1978; 1941 1979; Old Boyfriends 1979; The Blues Brothers 1980; Continental Divide 1981; Neighbors 1981

Belvaux, Lucas (1961-) Cop au Vin 1984; Madame Bovary 1991; [One] Cavale 2002; [Three] Après la Vie 2002; [Two] Un Couple Epatant 2002

Belzer, Richard (1944-) The Puppet Masters 1994; Get on the Bus 1996

Ben-Victor, Paul Body Parts 1991; Trouble Bound 1993; The Corruptor 1999; The Three Stooges 2000

Benben, Brian (1956-) Dark Angel 1989; Radioland Murders 1994

Benchley, Robert (1889-1945) Dancing Lady 1933; China Seas 1935; Piccadilly Jim 1936; Live, Love and Learn 1937; Foreign Correspondent 1940; Hired Wife 1940; Nice Girl? 1941; The Reluctant Dragon 1941; You'll Never Get Rich 1941; Bedtime Story 1942; I Married a Witch 1942; The Major and the Minor 1942; Take a Letter, Darling 1942; Young and Willing 1942; Flesh and Fantasy 1943; The Sky's the Limit 1943; Practically Yours 1944; It's in the Bag 1945; Kiss and Tell 1945; Road to Utopia 1945; The Stork Club 1945; Week-End at the Waldorf 1945; Blue Skies 1946; The Bride Wore Boots 1946

Bender, Russ (1910-1969) The Amazing Colossal Man 1957; Motorcycle Gang 1957; Suicide

Battalion 1958; War of the Colossal Beast 1958

Bendix, William (1906-1964) The Glass Key 1942; Star Spangled Rhythm 1942; Wake Island 1942; Woman of the Year 1942; China 1943; The Crystal Ball 1943; Guadalcanal Diary 1943; Abroad with Two Yanks 1944; Greenwich Village 1944; The Hairy Ape 1944; Lifeboat 1944; A Bell for Adano 1945; It's in the Bag 1945; The Blue Dahlia 1946; The Dark Corner 1946; Sentimental Journey 1946; Two Years before the Mast 1946; Blaze of Noon 1947; Calcutta 1947; I'll Be Yours 1947; The Web 1947; Where There's Life 1947; The Babe Ruth Story 1948; The Time of Your Life 1948; The Big Steal 1949; A Connecticut Yankee in King Arthur's Court 1949; Streets of Laredo 1949; Detective Story 1951; Submarine Command 1951; Blackbeard the Pirate 1952; A Girl in Every Port 1952; Macao 1952; Dangerous Mission 1954; Crashout 1955; The Deep Six 1958; The Rough and the Smooth 1959; For Love or Money 1963

Benedict, Billy (1917-1999) Ghosts in the Night 1943; Block Busters 1944; Bowery Champs 1944; Come Out Fighting 1945; Docks of New York 1945

Benedict, Brooks (1896-1968) The Freshman 1925; Speedy 1928; What Price Hollywood? 1932

Benedict, Dirk (1945-) Battlestar Galactica 1978; Alaska 1996; Earthstorm 2006; The A-Team 2010

Benedict, Freddie Azur & Asmar: the Princes' Quest 2006; Planet 51 2009

Benedict, Leopold Azur & Asmar: the Princes' Quest 2006; Before the Rains 2007

Benedict, Paul (1938-2008) Taking Off 1971; Deadhead Miles 1972; Jeremiah Johnson 1972; The Goodbye Girl 1977; The Man with Two Brains 1983; Arthur 2: On the Rocks 1988; The Freshman 1990; The Addams Family 1991; Attack of the 50 Ft Woman 1993

Benedict, Richard (1916-1984) OSS 1946; Ace in the Hole 1951; Beginning of the End 1957

Benet, Marianne Shake Hands with the Devil 1959; The Boy Who Stole a Million 1960; A Terrible Beauty 1960

Beneyton, Yves Weekend 1967; The Lacemaker 1977; Rogue Trader 1998

Benfield, John Hidden Agenda 1990; You're Dead 1999

Benge, Wilson (1875-1955) Bulldog Drummond 1929; The Bat Whispers 1930; Charley's Aunt 1930; The Lady Eve 1941

Benham, Joan (1918-1981) King's Rhapsody 1955; Murder Ahoy 1964; Perfect Friday 1970

Bénichou, Maurice (1943-) Drôle de Félix 2000; Time of the Wolf 2003; Hidden 2005

Benicio, Murilo (1972-) Woman on Top 2000; The Man of the Year 2002

Benigni, Roberto (1952-) La Luna 1979; Down by Law 1986; Johnny Stecchino 1991; Night on Earth 1992; Son of the Pink Panther 1993; Life Is Beautiful 1997; Asterix and Obelix Take On Caesar 1999; Pinocchio 2002; Coffee and Cigarettes 2003; To Rome with Love 2012

Bening, Annette (1958-) The Great Outdoors 1988; Valmont 1989; The Grifters 1990; Guilty by Suspicion 1990; Postcards from the Edge 1990; Bugsy 1991; Regarding Henry 1991; Love Affair 1994; The American President 1995; Richard III 1995; Mars Attacks! 1996; In Dreams 1998; The Siege 1998; American Beauty 1999; What Planet Are You From? 2000; Open Range 2003; Being Julia 2004; Running with Scissors 2006; The Women 2008; Mother and Child 2009; The Kids Are All Right 2010; Ginger & Rosa 2012; Girl Most Likely 2012; Ruby Sparks 2012; The Face of Love 2013; Danny Collins 2015

Benjamin, André (1975-) Be Cool 2005; Four Brothers 2005; Revolver 2005; Idlewild 2006; Battle in Seattle 2007; Semi-Pro 2008; Jimi: All Is by My Side 2013

Benjamin, Christopher (1934-) The Plague Dogs 1982; Treasure Island 1998

Benjamin, Paul (1938-) Across 110th Street 1972; The Deadly Trackers 1973; Leadbelly 1976; Escape from Alcatraz 1979; Last Rites 1998; The Station Agent 2003

Benjamin, Richard (1938-) Goodbye, Columbus 1969; Catch-22 1970; Diary of a Mad Housewife 1970; Portnoy's Complaint 1972; The Last of Sheila 1973; Westworld 1973; The Sunshine Boys 1975; House Calls 1978; Love at First Bite 1979; Witches' Brew 1979; First Family 1980; How to Beat the

High Cost of Living 1980; The Last Married Couple in America 1980; Saturday the 14th 1981; Deconstructing Harry 1997; The Pentagon Wars 1998; Marci X 2003

Benn, Tony (1925-2014) Sicko 2007; Taking Liberties 2007; Will & Testament 2014

Bennent, Anne (1963-) Swann in Love 1984; 71 Fragments of a Chronology of Chance 1994; Séraphine 2008

Bennent, David (1966-) The Tin Drum 1979; Legend 1985

Bennent, Heinz (1921-2011) The Lost Honour of Katharina Blum 1975; The Serpent's Egg 1977; The Last Metro 1980; The Death of Mario Ricci 1983; Une Femme Française 1994

Bennes, John Black Rainbow 1989; Stephen King's The Night Flier 1997

Bennett, Alan (1934-) Pleasure at Her Majesty's 1976; Long Shot 1978

Bennett, Andrew Garage 2007; Silence 2012; The Stag 2013

Bennett, Belle (1891-1932) Stella Dallas 1925; The Way of All Flesh 1927; The Iron Mask 1929

Bennett, Brian (1940-) Wonderful Life 1964; Finders Keepers 1966

Bennett, Bruce aka Brix, Herman (1906-2007) The New Adventures of Tarzan 1935; A Million to One 1937; Tarzan and the Green Goddess 1938; Before I Hang 1940; The More the Merrier 1943; Sahara 1943; Mildred Pierce 1945; The Man I Love 1946; A Stolen Life 1946; Dark Passage 1947; Nora Prentiss 1947; The Treasure of the Sierra Madre 1947; Silver River 1948; The Doctor and the Girl 1949; Task Force 1949; The Younger Brothers 1949; Mystery Street 1950; Angels in the Outfield 1951; Sudden Fear 1952; The Big Tip Off 1955; Strategic Air Command 1955; Beyond the River 1956; Three Violent People 1956; Daniel Boone, Trail Blazer 1957; The Alligator People 1959; The Cosmic Man 1959; The Outsider 1961

Bennett, Charles (1899-1995) Tillie's Punctured Romance 1914; America 1924

Bennett, Constance (1904-1965) The Goose Woman 1925; Sally, Irene and Mary 1925; Lady with a Past 1932; Rockabye 1932; What Price Hollywood? 1932; After Tonight 1933; Our Betters 1933; The Affairs of Cellini 1934; After Office Hours 1935; Everything Is Thunder 1936; Ladies in Love 1936; Topper 1937; Merrily We Live 1938; Topper Takes a Trip 1939; Two-Faced Woman 1941; Sin Town 1942; Madame Pimpernel 1945; Centennial Summer 1946; The Unsuspected 1947; As Young as You Feel 1951; Madame X 1966

Bennett, Eliza aka Bennett, Eliza Hope (1992-) The Prince & Me 2004; The Contractor 2007; Inkheart 2007; From Time to Time 2009; F 2010; Confine 2012

Bennett, Enid (1895-1969) Robin Hood 1922; The Sea Hawk 1924; Skippy 1931; Waterloo Bridge 1931; Intermezzo 1939; Meet Dr Christian 1939

Bennett, Haley (1988-) Music and Lyrics 2007; Marley & Me 2008; The Hole 2009; Kaboom 2010; Hardcore Henry 2015; The Magnificent Seven 2016

Bennett, Hywel (1944-) The Family Way 1966; Twisted Nerve 1968; The Virgin Soldiers 1969; The Buttercup Chain 1970; Loot 1970; Endless Night 1971; Percy 1971; Witness in the War Zone 1986; Deadly Advice 1993; Nasty Neighbours 2000; One for the Road 2003

Bennett, Jeff (1962-) Kiki's Delivery Service 1998; Lady and the Tramp II: Scamp's Adventure 2000; Return to Never Land 2002

Bennett, Jill (1931-1990) Hell below Zero 1954; Lust for Life 1956; The Criminal 1960; The Nanny 1965; The Skull 1965; The Charge of the Light Brigade 1968; Inadmissible Evidence 1968; Julius Caesar 1970; I Want What I Want 1971; Mister Quilp 1975; Full Circle 1977; For Your Eyes Only 1981; Britannia Hospital 1982; Lady Jane 1985; Hawks 1988; The Sheltering Sky 1990

Bennett, Jimmy (1996-) Hostage 2004; Winnie the Pooh: Springtime with Roo 2004; The Amityville Horror 2005; Poseidon 2006; Evan Almighty 2007; Shorts 2009

Bennett, Joan (1910-1990) Bulldog Drummond 1929; Disraeli 1929; Moby Dick 1930; Me and My Gal 1932; Little Women 1933; The Man Who Broke the Bank at Monte Carlo 1935; Mississippi 1935; Private Worlds 1935; Big Brown Eyes 1936; Wedding Present 1936; Vogues of 1938 1937; I Met My Love Again 1938; The Texans 1938; Trade

Winds 1938; Green Hell 1939; The Man in the Iron Mask 1939; The House across the Bay 1940; The Man I Married 1940; Son of Monte Cristo 1940; Confirm or Deny 1941; Man Hunt 1941; Wild Geese Calling 1941; Margin for Error 1943; Colonel Effingham's Raid 1945; Nob Hill 1945; Scarlet Street 1945; The Woman in the Window 1945; The Macomber Affair 1947; The Woman on the Beach 1947; Hollow Triumph 1948; Secret beyond the Door 1948; The Reckless Moment 1949; Father of the Bride 1950; For Heaven's Sake 1950; Father's Little Dividend 1951; We're No Angels 1955; There's Always Tomorrow 1956; Desire in the Dust 1960; House of Dark Shadows 1970; Suspiria 1976; Divorce Wars 1982

Bennett, John (1928-2005) The House that Dripped Blood 1970; The House in Nightmare Park 1973; Watership Down 1978

Bennett, Leila (1892-1965) The First Year 1932; Taxi! 1932; Tiger Shark 1932

Bennett, Marcia Prince Charming 2001; Godsend 2003; Widow on the Hill 2005; Mr Magorium's Wonder Emporium 2007

Bennett, Marjorie (1896-1982) Limelight 1952; What Ever Happened to Baby Jane? 1962; Games 1967

Bennett, Nigel (1949-) Soft Deceit 1994; Sanctuary 1997; Cypher 2002

Bennett (1), Richard (1873-1944) Arrowsmith 1931; If I Had a Million 1932; Nana 1934; The Magnificent Ambersons 1942

Benny, Jack (1894-1974) Hollywood Revue 1929; Broadway Melody of 1936 1935; The Big Broadcast of 1937 1936; Artists and Models 1937; Buck Benny Rides Again 1940; Charley's Aunt 1941; George Washington Slept Here 1942; To Be or Not to Be 1942; The Meanest Man in the World 1943; Hollywood Canteen 1944; The Horn Blows at Midnight 1945; It's in the Bag 1945; Without Reservations 1946; Somebody Loves Me 1952; The Man 1972

Benoît, Anne Not Here to Be Loved 2005; On Tour 2010

Benoist, Melissa (1988-) Whiplash 2014; The Longest Ride 2015

Benrath, Martin (1926-2000) Morituri 1965; From the Life of the Marionettes 1980

Benrubi, Abraham (1969-) The Program 1993; Open Range 2003; Without a Paddle 2004

Benson, Deborah September 30, 1955 1977; Just before Dawn 1980

Benson, George (1911-1983) Keep Fit 1937; The Creeping Flesh 1972

Benson, Jodi (1961-) The Little Mermaid 1989; Thumbelina 1994; Joseph: King of Dreams 2000; Lady and the Tramp II: Scamp's Adventure 2000; The Little Mermaid II: Return to the Sea 2000; Balto - Wings of Change 2004

Benson, Lucille (1914-1984) Duel 1971; Tom Sawyer 1973; Huckleberry Finn 1974

Benson, Martin (1918-2010) The Dark Light 1951; West of Zanzibar 1954; The King and I 1955; Man from Tangier 1957; The Strange World of Planet X 1957; Oscar Wilde 1959; The Gentle Trap 1960; Gorgo 1961; Satan Never Sleeps 1962; Goldfinger 1964; The Magnificent Two 1967; Battle beneath the Earth 1963; The Omen 1976

Benson, Perry (1961-) Final Cut 1998; Last Resort 2000; Mum & Dad 2008; Somers Town 2008; Borrowed Time 2012; Vinyl 2012

Benson, Robby (1956-) Jeremy 1973; Lucky Lady 1975; Ode to Billy Joe 1976; Ice Castles 1978; Tribute 1980; The Chosen 1981; National Lampoon's Movie Madness 1981; Harry and Son 1984; Rent-a-Cop 1988; Modern Love 1990; Beauty and the Beast 1991; Beauty and the Beast: the Enchanted Christmas 1997; Belle's Magical World 1997; Dragonheart: a New Beginning 1999

Benson, Roy Sweet and Lowdown 1944; Billy Rose's Diamond Horseshoe 1945

Bentine, Michael (1922-1996) Down among the Z-Men 1952; Forces' Sweetheart 1953; Raising a Riot 1955; We Joined the Navy 1962; The Sandwich Man 1966; Rentadick 1972

Bentivoglio, Fabrizio (1957-) Apartment Zero 1988; Eternity and a Day 1998; The Family Friend 2006; Human Capital 2013

Bentley, Beverly Scent of Mystery 1960; Beyond the Law 1968

Bentley, D ck (1907-1995) Desert Mice 1959; And the Same to You 1960; In the Doghouse 1961; Tamahine 1963; The Adventures of Barry McKenzie

1972; Barry McKenzie Holds His Own 1974

Bentley, John (1916-2009) The Hills of Donegal 1947; Calling Paul Temple 1948; The Happiest Days of Your Life 1950; Paul Temple's Triumph 1950; The Lost Hours 1952; Paul Temple Returns 1952; Tread Softly 1952; Final Appointment 1954; The Flaw 1954; Profile 1954; River Beat 1954; Confession 1955; Istanbul 1957; The Singer Not the Song 1960

Bentley, Wes (1978-) American Beauty 1999; The Claim 2000; Soul Survivors 2001; The Four Feathers 2002; P2 2006; Weirdsville 2006; Ghost Rider 2007; Gone 2012; Pioneer 2013; Interstellar 2014; Welcome to Me 2014; Final Girl 2015; We Are Your Friends 2015; Pete's Dragon 2016

Benton, Jerome Purple Rain 1984; Under the Cherry Moon 1986; Graffiti Bridge 1990

Benton, Mark (1965-) Career Girls 1997; Mr In-Between 2001; Breaking and Entering 2006; Beyond the Pole 2009

Benton, Susanne (1948-) That Cold Day in the Park 1969; A Boy and His Dog 1975

Benussi, Femi (1948-) Hawks and Sparrows 1966; Hatchet for the Honeymoon 1969

Benz, Julie (1972-) Jawbreaker 1999; Shriek If You Know What I Did Last Friday the 13th 2000; The Long Shot 2004; Lackawanna Blues 2005; Circle of Friends 2006; Rambo 2007; Punisher: War Zone 2008; Saw V 2008; Uncorked 2008

Benzali, Daniel (1950-) Messenger of Death 1988; A Day in October 1991; Murder at 1600 1997; All the Little Animals 1998; Screwed 2000; The Grey Zone 2001; Dead Heat 2002

Beranger, George (1893-1973) Broken Blossoms 1919; Road House 1948

Bercot, Emmanuelle La Classe de Neige 1998; Mon Roi 2015

Bercovici, Luca (1957-) Frightmare 1981; Parasite 1982; American Flyers 1985; Clean and Sober 1988; K2 1991; Drop Zone 1994

Beregi (2), Oscar (1918-1976) Anything Can Happen 1952; Desert Legion 1953

Berenger, Tom (1950-) Looking for Mr Goodbar 1977; The Sentinel 1977; In Praise of Older Women 1978; Butch and Sundance: the Early Days 1979; The Dogs of War 1980; The Big Chill 1983; Eddie and the Cruisers 1983; Fear City 1984; Rustler's Rhapsody 1985; Platoon 1986; Someone to Watch over Me 1987; Betrayed 1988; Deadly Pursuit 1988; Last Rites 1988; Born on the Fourth of July 1989; Major League 1989; The Field 1990; Love at Large 1990; At Play in the Fields of the Lord 1991; Shattered 1991; Sniper 1992; Gettysburg 1993; Sliver 1993; Chasers 1994; Major League II 1994; Last of the Dogmen 1995; The Substitute 1996; The Gingerbread Man 1997; A Murder of Crows 1998; Shadow of Doubt 1998; Diplomatic Siege 1999; In the Company of Spies 1999; Cutaway 2000; Turbulence II: Fear of Flying 2000; D-Tox 2001; Training Day 2001; Faster 2010; Inception 2010

Berens, Harold (1903-1995) Dual Alibi 1946; Live Now - Pay Later 1962; Hear My Song 1991

Berenson, Marisa (1946-) Death in Venice 1971; Cabaret 1972; Barry Lyndon 1975; Casanova & Co 1976; Killer Fish 1978; Playing for Time 1980; SOB 1981; Perfume of the Cyclone 1989; White Hunter, Black Heart 1990; I Am Love 2009

Beresford, Harry (1864-1944) Doctor X 1932; High Pressure 1932; The Sign of the Cross 1932; I Cover the Waterfront 1933; Murders in the Zoo 1933; Follow the Fleet 1936; Klondike Annie 1936

Berg, Peter (1964-) Shocker 1989; Crooked Hearts 1991; Late for Dinner 1991; A Midnight Clear 1991; Aspen Extreme 1993; Fire in the Sky 1993; The Last Seduction 1993; FTW 1994; Girl 6 1996; The Great White Hype 1996; Cop Land 1997; Corky Romano 2001; Collateral 2004; Smokin' Aces 2006; Lions for Lambs 2007

Bergé, Francine (1940-) Judex 1963; La Ronde 1964; La Religieuse 1965; Une Histoire Simple 1978

Bergès-Frisbey, Astrid The Sea Wall 2008; The Well Digger's Daughter 2010; Pirates of the Caribbean: on Stranger Tides 2011; I Origins 2014; Knights of the Round Table: King Arthur 2016

Bergen, Candice (1946-) The Group 1966; The Sand Pebbles 1966; The Day the Fish Came Out 1967; Vivre pour

Vivre 1967; The Magus 1968; The Adventurers 1970; Getting Straight 1970; Soldier Blue 1970; Carnal Knowledge 1971; The Hunting Party 1971; TR Baskin 1971; 11 Harrowhouse 1974; Bite the Bullet 1975; The Wind and the Lion 1975; The Domino Principle 1977; The End of the World (in Our Usual Bed in a Night Full of Rain) 1978; Oliver's Story 1978; Starting Over 1979; Rich and Famous 1981; Gandhi 1982; Stick 1985; Miss Congeniality 2000; Sweet Home Alabama 2002; The In-Laws 2003; View from the Top 2003; Bride Wars 2008; The Women 2008; Rules Don't Apply 2016

Bergen, Edgar (1903-1978) The Goldwyn Follies 1938; You Can't Cheat an Honest Man 1939; Look Who's Laughing 1941; Song of the Open Road 1944; I Remember Mama 1948; Don't Make Waves 1967

Bergen, Polly (1930-2014) At War with the Army 1950; The Stooge 1951; That's My Boy 1951; Warpath 1951; Arena 1953; Cry of the Hunted 1953; Escape from Fort Bravo 1953; Cape Fear 1962; The Caretakers 1963; Move Over, Darling 1963; Kisses for My President 1964; Making Mr Right 1987; Cry-Baby 1989; Leave of Absence 1994; Dr Jekyll and Ms Hyde 1995

Bergen, Tushka (1969-) Swing Kids 1993; Barcelona 1994

Berger, Helmut (1944-) The Damned 1969; The Garden of the Finzi-Continis 1971; Ash Wednesday 1973; Ludwig 1973; Conversation Piece 1974; The Romantic Englishwoman 1975; Salon Kitty 1976; Victory at Entebbe 1976; Code Name: Emerald 1985

Berger, Nicole (1935-1967) The Ripening Seed 1953; Shoot the Pianist 1960; The Siege of Sidney Street 1960

Berger, Senta (1941-) The Secret Ways 1961; Sherlock Holmes and the Deadly Necklace 1962; The Victors 1963; The Glory Guys 1965; Major Dundee 1965; Cast a Giant Shadow 1966; Our Man in Marrakesh 1966; The Quiller Memorandum 1966; The Spy with My Face 1966; Diabolically Yours 1967; De Sade 1969; The Swiss Conspiracy 1975

Berger, Toni (1921-2005) The Serpent's Egg 1977; Sugarbaby 1985

Berger, William (1928-1993) Face to Face 1967; Sartana 1968; Sabata 1969; Three Tough Guys 1974; Keoma 1976; Hercules 1983; Hercules II 1984; Dr M 1989

Bergerac, Jacques (1927-2014) Beautiful Stranger 1954; Les Girls 1957; Gigi 1958; Thunder in the Sun 1959

Bergere, Lee (1918-2007) Bob & Carol & Ted & Alice 1969; Time Trackers 1989

Berggren, Thommy (1937-) The Pram 1963; Raven's End 1963; Elvira Madigan 1967; Sunday's Children 1992

Berghof, Herbert (1909-1990) Assignment - Paris 1952; 5 Fingers 1952; Red Planet Mars 1952; Dark Victory 1976; Those Lips, Those Eyes 1980; Times Square 1980; Target 1985

Bergin, Patrick (1954-) Taffin 1988; Mountains of the Moon 1989; Robin Hood 1990; Love Crimes 1991; Sleeping with the Enemy 1991; Highway to Hell 1992; Map of the Human Heart 1992; Patriot Games 1992; Soft Deceit 1994; Lawnmower Man 2: Beyond Cyberspace 1995; The Proposition 1996; The Island on Bird Street 1997; Treasure Island 1998; The Invisible Circus 2000; Merlin the Return 2000; When the Sky Falls 2000; The Evil beneath Loch Ness 2001; Silent Grace 2001; King of Texas 2002; Bloom 2003; Ella Enchanted 2004; The Wee Man 2013

Bergman, Henry (1868-1946) Behind the Screen 1916; The Pawnshop 1916; A Dog's Life 1918; Sunnyside 1919; The Idle Class 1921; The Circus 1928; Modern Times 1936

Bergman, Ingrid (1915-1982) The Count of the Old Town 1935; Swedenhielms 1935; Walpurgis Night 1935; Intermezzo 1936; Dollar 1938; A Woman's Face 1938; Intermezzo 1939; One Single Night 1939; June Night 1940; Adam Had Four Sons 1941; Dr Jekyll and Mr Hyde 1941; Rage in Heaven 1941; Casablanca 1942; For Whom the Bell Tolls 1943; Gaslight 1944; The Bells of St Mary's 1945; Saratoga Trunk 1945; Spellbound 1945; Notorious 1945; Arch of Triumph 1948; Joan of Arc 1948; Under Capricorn 1949; Stromboli 1950; Europa '51 1952; Journey to Italy 1953; Fear 1954; Anastasia 1956; Elena et les Hommes 1956; Indiscreet 1958; The Inn of the Sixth Happiness 1958; Goodbye Again 1961; The Visit 1964; The Yellow Rolls-Royce 1964; Cactus Flower 1969; A

Walk in the Spring Rain 1970; The Hideaways 1973; Murder on the Orient Express 1974; A Matter of Time 1976; Autumn Sonata 1978

Bergman, Mary Kay (1961-1999) The Hunchback of Notre Dame 1996; South Park: Bigger, Longer & Uncut 1999

Bergman, Sandahl (1951-) All That Jazz 1979; Conan the Barbarian 1982; Red Sonja 1985; Hell Comes to Frogtown 1988; Raw Nerve 1991

Bergner, Elisabeth aka Bergner, Elizabeth (1897-1986) Ariane 1931; The Rise of Catherine the Great 1934; Escape Me Never 1935; As You Like It 1936; Stolen Life 1939; Paris Calling 1941; Cry of the Banshee 1970; The Pedestrian 1974

Bergström, Helena (1964-) House of Angels 1992; Still Crazy 1998; Under the Sun 1998

Beristain, Luis (1918-1962) El 1953; The Exterminating Angel 1962

Berkel, Christian (1957-) The Experiment 2000; Downfall 2004; Flame & Citron 2008; Anti-Social 2015

Berkeley, Ballard (1904-1988) The Last Adventurers 1937; The Blue Parrot 1953; Child's Play 1954; Impact 1963

Berkeley, Xander (1955-) The Fabulous Baker Boys 1989; Short Time 1990; Candyman 1992; Roswell 1994; Apollo 13 1995; Barb Wire 1995; Poison Ivy 2 1995; [Safe] 1995; If These Walls Could Talk 1996; Persons Unknown 1996; Air Force One 1997; Gattaca 1997; Universal Soldier - the Return 1999; Shanghai Noon 2000; Quicksand 2003; Taken 2007; Kick-Ass 2009; Repo Chick 2009; Justice 2011

Berkley, Elizabeth (1973-) Showgirls 1995; The First Wives Club 1996; The Real Blonde 1997; Taxman 1998; The Curse of the Jade Scorpion 2001; Roger Dodger 2002; Student Seduction 2003; Black Widow 2007

Berkoff, Steven (1937-) A Clockwork Orange 1971; Barry Lyndon 1975; The Passenger 1975; McVicar 1980; Outland 1981; Octopussy 1983; Beverly Hills Cop 1984; Rambo: First Blood, Part II 1985; Revolution 1985; Absolute Beginners 1986; Under the Cherry Moon 1986; The Krays 1990; Decadence 1993; Fair Game 1995; Flynn 1995; Another 9½ Weeks 1997; Legionnaire 1998; Rancid Aluminium 1999; 9 Dead Gay Guys 2001; Steal 2002 Charlie 2003; Head in the Clouds 2004; The Flying Scotsman 2006; 44 Inch Chest 2009; Just for the Record 2010; The Tourist 2010; Bula...: Big Fat Gypsy Gangster 2011; The Girl with the Dragon Tattoo 2011; Strippers vs Werewolves 2012

Berle, Milton (1908-2002) New Faces of 1937 1937; Sun Valley Serenade 1941; Tall, Dark and Handsome 1941; A Gentleman at Heart 1942; Margin for Error 1943; Always Leave Them Laughing 1949; Let's Make Love 1960; It's a Mad Mad Mad Mad World 1963; Journey back to Oz 1964; The Loved One 1965; The Oscar 1966; The Happening 1967; Who's Minding the Mint? 1967; Where Angels Go... Trouble Follows 1968; Can Heironymus Merkin Ever Forget Mercy Humppe and Find True Happiness? 1969; Evil Roy Slade 1971; Lepke 1975

Berléand, François (1952-) Au Revoir les Enfants 1987; Milou en Mai 1989; Place Vendôme 1998; Romance 1998; The Transporter 2002; A Comedy of Power 2006; Tell No One 2006; La Fille Coupée en Deux 2007; Transporter 3 2008; The Concert 2009

Berley, André (1890-1936) Hara-Kiri 1928; The Passion of Joan of Arc 1928

Berlin, Jeannie (1949-) Bone 1972; The Heartbreak Kid 1972; Margaret 2008

Berliner, Max (1919-) Only Human 2004; To Die in San Hilario 2005

Berling, Charles (1958-) Salt on Our Skin 1992; Ridicule 1996; Love etc 1997; L'Ennui 1998; Those Who Love Me Can Take the Train 1998; The Bridge 1999; Comédie de l'Innocence 2000; Les Destinées Sentimentales 2000; Stardom 2000; Comment J'ai Tué Mon Père 2001; Demonlover 2002; I Saw Ben Barka Get Killed 2005; Summer Hours 2008

Berling, Peter (1934-) Aguirre, Wrath of God 1972; Haunted Summer 1988; Francesco 1989

Berlinger, Warren (1937-) Teenage Rebel 1956; Blue Denim 1959; Because They're Young 1960; All Hands on Deck 1961; The Wackiest Ship in the Army 1961; Billie 1965; Thunder Alley 1967; Lepke 1975; Accidental Hero 1992

Berman, Marc Noir et Blanc 1986; The Last Island 1990; Autobus 1991; The Girl from Paris 2001

Berman, Shelley (1926-) The Best Man 1964; Divorce American Style 1967; Every Home Should Have One 1970; Beware! The Blob 1971

Berman, Susan Smithereens 1982; Making Mr Right 1987

Bernal, Gael García (1978-) Amores Perros 2000; Y Tu Mamá También 2001; El Crimen del Padre Amaro 2002; I'm with Lucy 2002; Dot the i 2003; Bad Education 2004; The Motorcycle Diaries 2004; The King 2005; The Science of Sleep 2005; Babel 2006; Déficit 2007; Blindness 2008; The Limits of Control 2008; Rudo y Cursi 2008; Mammoth 2009; Even the Rain 2010; Letters to Juliet 2010; Casa de Mi Padre 2011; A Little Bit of Heaven 2011; No 2012; Who Is Dayani Cristal? 2013; The Burning 2014; Rosewater 2014

Bernard, Crystal (1961-) Chasing Secrets 1999; A Face to Kill For 1999; Gideon 1999; Single Santa Seeks Mrs Claus 2004; Meet the Santas 2005

Bernard, Ed (1939-) Across 110th Street 1972; Blue Thunder 1983

Bernard, Jason (1938-1996) Going Home 1971; All of Me 1984; No Way Out 1986; While You Were Sleeping 1995; Liar Liar 1997

Bernard, Rukiya Stuck 2007; The Music Teacher 2012

Bernardi, Herschel (1923-1986) Murder by Contract 1958; Irma la Douce 1963; Love with the Proper Stranger 1963; The Front 1976; No Deposit No Return 1976

Bernath, Antonia Kisna - the Warrior Poet 2004; Cuckoo 2009

Berner, Sara (1912-1969) Rear Window 1954; Spring Reunion 1957

Bernhard, Sandra (1955-) Shogun Assassin 1980; Cheech and Chong's Nice Dreams 1981; The King of Comedy 1983; Follow That Bird 1985; Track 29 1988; Without You I'm Nothing 1990; Hudson Hawk 1991; In Bed with Madonna 1991; Dallas Doll 1994; Freaky Friday 1995; Burn Hollywood Burn 1997; Wrongfully Accused 1998; Dinner Rush 2000

Bernhardt, Daniel (1965-) Bloodsport II: The Next Kumite 1996; Precious Cargo 2016

Bernier, Mélanie Delicacy 2011; Populaire 2012

Bernsen, Corbin (1954-) Hello Again 1987; Bert Rigby, You're a Fool 1989; Disorganized Crime 1989; Major League 1989; Shattered 1991; Major League II 1994; Where Are My Children? 1994; Temptress 1995; The Dentist 1996; The Great White Hype 1996; Major League: Back to the Minors 1998; The Misadventures of Margaret 1998; I Saw Mommy Kissing Santa Claus 2001; Atomic Twister 2002; Kiss Kiss Bang Bang 2005; Ordinary Miracles 2005

Bernthal, Jon Snitch 2013; Fury 2014; Sicario 2015

Berrell, George (1849-1933) Straight Shooting 1917; Pollyanna 1920

Berri, Claude (1934-2009) Les Bonnes Femmes 1960; Marry Me! Marry Me! 1968

Berridge, Elizabeth (1962-) The Funhouse 1981; Amadeus 1984; Five Corners 1987; When the Party's Over 1992

Berrington, Elizabeth Secrets & Lies 1995; In Bruges 2008

Berroyer, Jackie (1946-) L'Eau Froide 1994; Rien Ne Va Plus 1997; Calvaire 2004; Le Clan 2004; A Common Thread 2004; Love Is in the Air 2013

Berruti (2), Giulio Goltzius and the Pelican Company 2012; Walking on Sunshine 2014

Berry, Chuck (1926-) Go, Johnny, Go! 1959; Jazz on a Summer's Day 1959; Let the Good Times Roll 1973; Hail! Hail! Rock 'n' Roll! 1987

Berry, Halle (1966-) Jungle Fever 1991; The Last Boy Scout 1991; Boomerang 1992; Father Hood 1993; The Program 1993; The Flintstones 1994; Losing Isaiah 1995; Executive Decision 1996; Race the Sun 1996; The Rich Man's Wife 1996; BAPS 1997; Bulworth 1998; The Wedding 1998; Why Do Fools Fall in Love? 1998; Introducing Dorothy Dandridge 1999; X-Men 2000; Monster's Ball 2001; Swordfish 2001; Die Another Day 2002; Gothika 2003; X2 2003; Catwoman 2004; Robots 2005; Their Eyes Were Watching God 2005; X-Men - the Last Stand 2006; Perfect Stranger 2007; Things We Lost in the Fire 2007; New Year's Eve 2011; Cloud Atlas 2012; Dark Tide 2012; The Call 2013; Movie 43 2013; X-Men: Days of

Harriet Craig 1950; Lorna Doone 1951; The Redhead from Wyoming 1953; Wyoming Renegades 1955; Short Cut to Hell 1957

Bisio, Claudio (1957-) Mediterraneo 1991; Puerto Escondito 1992

Bisley, Steve (1951-) Mad Max 1979; The Chain Reaction 1980; The Big Steal 1990; Over the Hill 1992; Red Hill 2010

Bissell, Whit (1909-1996) Brute Force 1947; He Walked by Night 1948; Anna Lucasta 1949; Wyoming Mail 1950; The Atomic Kid 1954; Creature from the Black Lagoon 1954; Riot in Cell Block 11 1954; Shack Out on 101 1955; I Was a Teenage Frankenstein 1957; I Was a Teenage Werewolf 1957; Johnny Tremain 1957; The Tall Stranger 1957; The Young Strange 1957; No Name on the Bullet 1959; The Time Machine 1960; Hud 1963; Seven Days in May 1964

Bisset, Donald (1911-1995) Murder in the Cathedral 1952; Little Red Monkey 1955

Bisset, Jacqueline aka **Bisset, Jacky** (1944-) Casino Royale 1967; The Sweet Ride 1967; Bullitt 1968; The Detective 1968; Airport 1970; The Grasshopper 1970; The Mephisto Waltz 1971; The Life and Times of Judge Roy Bean 1972; Day for Night 1973; The Thief Who Came to Dinner 1973; Murder on the Orient Express 1974; End of the Game 1976; St Ives 1976; The Deep 1977; The Greek Tycoon 1978; Who Is Killing the Great Chefs of Europe? 1978; When Time Ran Out 1980; Inchon 1981; Rich and Famous 1981; Class 1983; Under the Volcano 1984; Anna Karenina 1985; High Season 1987; Scenes from the Class Struggle In Beverly Hills 1989; Wild Orchid 1990; The Maid 1991; Leave of Absence 1994; La Cérémonie 1995; Dangerous Beauty 1997; Let the Devil Wear Black 1999; Britannic 2000; Dancing at the Harvest Moon 2002; Domino 2005; An Old-Fashioned Thanksgiving 2008; Welcome to New York 2014; Miss You Already 2015

Bisson, Chris (1975-) East Is East 1999; Chicken Tikka Masala 2005

Bisson, Yannick (1969-) Crazy for Christmas 2005; Too Late to Say Goodbye 2009

Bissot, Stéphane Our Children 2012; Alleluia 2014

Biswas, Chhabi (1900-1962) The Music Room 1953; Devi 1960; Kangchenjunga 1962

Biswas, Seema Bandit Queen 1994; Bhoot 2003; Water 2005; Midnight's Children 2012

Bixby, Bill (1934-1993) Irma la Douce 1963; Ride beyond Vengeance 1966; Clambake 1967; Speedway 1968; The Apple Dumpling Gang 1974; The Incredible Hulk 1977; Agatha Christie's Murder Is Easy 1982; The Incredible Hulk Returns 1938; The Trial of the Incredible Hulk 1989; The Death of the Incredible Hulk 1990

Björk aka **Gudmundsdottir, Björk** (1965-) The Juniper Tree 1990; Dancer in the Dark 2000

Björk, Anita (1923-) Miss Julie 1951; Waiting Women 1952; Night People 1954; Square of Violence 1961; Private Confessions 1996

Bjork, Halvar (1928-2000) The New Land 1972; Autumn Sonata 1978

Bjorklund, Irina Lost 2005; The American 2010

Björnstrand, Gunnar (1909-1986) It Rains on Our Love 1946; Waiting Women 1952; Lesson in Love 1954; Dreams 1955; Smiles of a Summer Night 1955; The Seventh Seal 1957; Wild Strawberries 1957; The Magician 1958; The Devil's Eye 1960; Through a Glass Darkly 1961; Winter Light 1962; My Sister, My Love 1966; Persona 1966; Shame 1968; The Rite 1969; Face to Face 1976; Autumn Sonata 1978; Fanny and Alexander 1982

Black, Isobel (1943-) The Magnificent Two 1967; 10 Rillington Place 1970; Twins of Evil 1971

Black, Jack (1969-) The NeverEnding Story III 1994; The Cable Guy 1996; Jesus' Son 1999; High Fidelity 2000; Evil Woman 2001; Orange County 2001; Shallow Hal 2001; Ice Age 2002; Envy 2003; The School of Rock 2003; Shark Tale 2004; King Kong 2005; The Holiday 2006; Nacho Libre 2006; Tenacious D in The Pick of Destiny 2006; Be Kind Rewind 2007; Margot at the Wedding 2007; Kung Fu Panda 2008; Tropic Thunder 2008; Year One 2009; Gulliver's Travels 2010; Mars: Beyond the Lighted Stage 2010; Bernie 2011; The Big Year 2011; Kung Fu Panda 2 2011; The Muppets 2011; Sex Tape

2014; The D Train 2015; Goosebumps 2015; Kung Fu Panda 3 2016

Black, Jennifer Local Hero 1983; Heavenly Pursuits 1986

Black, Karen (1939-2013) You're a Big Boy Now 1966; Easy Rider 1969; Hard Contract 1969; Five Easy Pieces 1970; Born to Win 1971; Cisco Pike 1971; Drive, He Said 1971; A Gunfight 1971; Portnoy's Complaint 1972; The Outfit 1973; Airport 1975 1974; The Great Gatsby 1974; Law and Disorder 1974; Rhinoceros 1974; The Day of the Locust 1975; Nashville 1975; Burnt Offerings 1976; Crime and Passion 1976; Family Plot 1976; Capricorn One 1978; In Praise of Older Women 1978; Killer Fish 1978; Chanel Solitaire 1981; Come Back to the Five and Dime, Jimmy Dean, Jimmy Dean 1982; Can She Bake a Cherry Pie? 1983; Martin's Day 1984; Savage Dawn 1985; Invaders from Mars 1986; It's Alive III: Island of the Alive 1987; The Invisible Kid 1988; Out of the Dark 1988; Homer and Eddie 1989; The Children 1990; Haunting Fear 1990; Evil Spirits 1991; Rubin & Ed 1991; Bound & Gagged: a Love Story 1992; Plan 10 from Outer Space 1995; House of 1000 Corpses 2001

Black, Lewis Grounded 2006; Man of the Year 2006; Inside Out 2015

Black, Lucas (1982-) Sling Blade 1995; Crazy in Alabama 1999; All the Pretty Horses 2000; Friday Night Lights 2004; Jarhead 2005; The Fast and the Furious: Tokyo Drift 2006; Get Low 2009; Legion 2010; 42 2013

Black, Marina Bundy 2002; The Trail to Hope Rose 2004; Wedding Daze 2004

Black, Maurice (1891-1938) Smart Money 1931; I Cover the Waterfront 1933

Blackburn, Richard Eating Raoul 1982; Not for Publication 1984; Under the Piano 1995

Blackley, Jamie (1991-) Vinyl 2012; We Are the Freaks 2013; If I Stay 2014; Irrational Man 2015

Blackman, Honor (1925-) Daughter of Darkness 1948; Quartet 1948; A Boy, a Girl and a Bike 1949; Conspirator 1949; Diamond City 1949; So Long at the Fair 1950; Green Grow the Rushes 1951; The Rainbow Jacket 1954; The Glass Cage 1955; Account Rendered 1957; You Pay Your Money 1957; A Night to Remember 1958; Serena 1962; Jason and the Argonauts 1963; Goldfinger 1964; Life at the Top 1965; The Secret of My Success 1965; Moment to Moment 1966; A Twist of Sand 1967; Shalako 1968; Twinky 1969; The Last Grenade 1970; The Virgin and the Gypsy 1970; Fright 1971; something big 1971; To the Devil a Daughter 1976; The Cat and the Canary 1979; Talos the Mummy 1997; To Walk with Lions 1999; Bridget Jones's Diary 2001; Reuniting the Rubins 2010; Cockneys vs Zombies 2011; I, Anna 2012

Blackman, Joan (1938-) Career 1959; The Great Impostor 1960; Blue Hawaii 1961; Kid Galahad 1962; Twilight of Honor 1963; The Destructors 1968; Macon County Line 1973

Blackmer, Sidney (1895-1973) Deluge 1933; The Count of Monte Cristo 1934; This Man Is Mine 1934; The Little Colonel 1935; Charlie Chan at Monte Carlo 1937; The Last Gangster 1937; Thank You, Mr Moto 1937; This Is My Affair 1937; Wife, Doctor and Nurse 1937; Suez 1938; Trade Winds 1938; Maryland 1940; Cheers for Miss Bishop 1941; Down Mexico Way 1941; Love Crazy 1941; Quiet Please, Murder 1942; War of the Wildcats 1943; The Lady and the Monster 1944; People Will Talk 1951; The San Francisco Story 1952; Johnny Dark 1954; Accused of Murder 1956; Beyond a Reasonable Doubt 1956; High Society 1956; Tammy and the Bachelor 1957; How to Murder Your Wife 1965; Rosemary's Baby 1968

Blackthorne, Paul (1969-) The Truth Game 2000; Lagaan: Once upon a Time in India 2001; Special (PX) - Specioprin Hydrochloride 2006

Blackwood, Vas (1969-) Arthur's Hallowed Ground 1985; Babymother 1998; Lock, Stock and Two Smoking Barrels 1998; Mean Machine 2001; 9 Dead Gay Guys 2001; The Escapist 2002; One Love 2003; Creep 2004; Rollin with the Nines 2005; Daylight Robbery 2007; The Guvnors 2014

Blades, Rubén (1948-) Critical Condition 1987; Fatal Beauty 1987; The Milagro Beanfield War 1988; Disorganized Crime 1989; The Lemon Sisters 1989; Predator 2 1990; The Two Jakes 1990; Crazy from the Heart 1991; The Super 1991; Color of Night 1994; Scorpion Spring 1995; Chinese Box

1997; The Devil's Own 1997; Cradle Will Rock 1999; All the Pretty Horses 2000; Imagining Argentina 2003; The Maldonado Miracle 2003; Once upon a Time in Mexico 2003; Secuestro Express 2004

Blain, Gérard (1930-2000) Le Beau Serge 1958; Les Cousins 1959; Hatari! 1962; The American Friend 1977

Blaine, Vivian (1921-1995) Jitterbugs 1943; Greenwich Village 1944; Something for the Boys 1944; Nob Hill 1945; State Fair 1945; Three Little Girls in Blue 1946; Skirts Ahoy! 1952; Guys and Dolls 1955; The Cracker Factory 1979

Blair, Betsy (1923-2009) The Guilt of Janet Ames 1947; Kind Lady 1951; Marty 1955; Calle Mayor 1956; Il Grido 1957; The Halliday Brand 1957; All Night Long 1961; A Delicate Balance 1973; Descent into Hell 1986; Betrayed 1988

Blair, Isla (1944-) Real Life 1983; Valmont 1989; The Match 1999

Blair, Janet (1921-2007) Broadway 1942; My Sister Eileen 1942; Once upon a Time 1944; Tonight and Every Night 1945; The Fabulous Dorseys 1947; The Black Arrow 1948; Night of the Eagle 1961; Boys' Night Out 1962; The One and Only, Genuine, Original Family Band 1968

Blair, Linda (1959-) The Exorcist 1973; Airport 1975 1974; Victory at Entebbe 1976; Exorcist II: The Heretic 1977; Hell Night 1981; Chained Heat 1983; Savage Streets 1984; Silent Assassins 1988; Witchcraft 1989; Repossessed 1990; Scream 1996

Blair, Lionel (1934-) The Main Attraction 1962; A Hard Day's Night 1964; Run for Your Wife 2013

Blair, Selma (1972-) Brown's Requiem 1998; Cruel Intentions 1999; Down to You 2000; Kill Me Later 2001; Legally Blonde 2001; Storytelling 2001; A Guy Thing 2002; The Sweetest Thing 2002; A Dirty Shame 2004; Hellboy 2004; In Good Company 2004; The Fog 2005; Pretty Persuasion 2005; WAZ 2006; Feast of Love 2007; Hellboy II: the Golden Army 2008; My Spy 2008; Dark Horse 2011

Blake, Amanda (1929-1989) Duchess of Idaho 1950; Stars in My Crown 1950; Scarlet Angel 1952; Lili 1953; A Star Is Born 1954; The Glass Slipper 1955; The Boost 1988

Blake, Catherine The Dark Light 1951; Tale of a Vampire 1992

Blake, Geoffrey (1962-) FernGully: the Last Rainforest 1992; Entertaining Angels: the Dorothy Day Story 1996

Blake, Julia (1936-) Patrick 1978; Lonely Hearts 1981; Man of Flowers 1984; Travelling North 1986; Georgia 1988; Father 1990; Hotel de Love 1996; Innocence 2000; The Boys Are Back 2009

Blake, Larry J aka **Blake, Larry** (1914-1982) The Trap 1947; Earth vs the Flying Saucers 1956; Demon Seed 1977

Blake, Madge (1899-1969) The Prowler 1951; Batman 1966

Blake, Rachael (1971-) Paws 1997; Nowhere to Land 2000; The Three Stooges 2000; Lantana 2001; Summer 2008; Cherry Tree Lane 2010; Sleeping Beauty 2011

Blake, Robert aka **Blake, Bobby** (1933-) China Girl 1942; The Big Noise 1944; The Horn Blows at Midnight 1945; The Black Rose 1950; Pork Chop Hill 1959; Town without Pity 1961; PT 109 1963; This Property Is Condemned 1966; In Cold Blood 1967; Tell Them Willie Boy Is Here 1969; Corky 1972; Electra Glide in Blue 1973; Busting 1974; Coast to Coast 1980; Money Train 1995; Lost Highway 1996

Blakely, Colin (1930-1987) The Informers 1963; The Long Ships 1963; This Sporting Life 1963; A Man for All Seasons 1966; The Spy with a Cold Nose 1966; Charlie Bubbles 1967; The Day the Fish Came Out 1967; Decline and Fall... of a Birdwatcher 1968; The Vengeance of She 1968; Alfred the Great 1969; The Private Life of Sherlock Holmes 1970; Something to Hide 1971; The National Health 1973; Galileo 1974; Murder on the Orient Express 1974; Love among the Ruins 1975; The Pink Panther Strikes Again 1976; Equus 1977; It Shouldn't Happen to a Vet 1979; The Dogs of War 1980; Loophole 1980; Nijinsky 1980; Evil under the Sun 1982

Blakely, Gene (1922-1987) Battle of the Coral Sea 1959; Beach Red 1967

Blakely, Susan (1950-) Savages 1972; The Lords of Flatbush 1974; The Towering Inferno 1974; Capone 1975; Report to the Commissioner 1975; Airport '79: the Concorde 1979; Over

the Top 1987; The Incident 1990; Wildflower 1991; Against Her Will 1992; That Uncertain Feeling 1941; Experiment Perilous 1944

Blakley, Ronee (1946-) Nashville 1975; The Private Files of J Edgar Hoover 1977; The Driver 1978; The Baltimore Bullet 1980; A Nightmare on Elm Street 1984; A Return to Salem's Lot 1987

Blalock, Jolene Slow Burn 2003; I Dream of Murder 2006; Starship Troopers 3: Marauder 2008

Blanc, Dominique (1962-) Milou en Mai 1989; Indochine 1991; La Reine Margot 1994; Total Eclipse 1995; A Soldier's Daughter Never Cries 1998; The Pornographer 2001; [One] Cavale 2002; [Three] Après la Vie 2002; [Two] Un Couple Epatant 2002

Blanc, J B Tristan + Isolde 2005; A Cat in Paris 2010

Blanc, Manuel (1968-) J'Embrasse Pas 1991; The King of Paris 1995; Beaumarchais l'Insolent 1996

Blanc, Mel (1908-1989) A Wild Hare 1940; Neptune's Daughter 1949; Duck Dodgers in the $24\frac{1}{2}$ Century 1953; Birds Anonymous 1957; What's Opera, Doc? 1957; The Phantom Tollbooth 1969; Scalawag 1973; Buck Rogers in the 25th Century 1979; The Bugs Bunny/Road Runner Movie 1979; Looney Looney Looney Bugs Bunny Movie 1981; Bugs Bunny 1001 Rabbit Tales 1982; Daffy Duck's Movie: Fantastic Island 1983; Daffy Duck's Quackbusters 1988; Who Framed Roger Rabbit 1988; Jetsons: the Movie 1990

Blanc, Michel (1952-) Tenue de Soirée 1986; Monsieur Hire 1989; The Favour, the Watch and the Very Big Fish 1991; Merci la Vie 1991; Prospero's Books 1991; Summer Things 2002; The Witnesses 2006; The Girl on the Train 2009

Blancan, Bernard Skin of Man, Heart of Beast 1999; Days of Glory 2006; Leaving 2008

Blancard, René (1897-1965) A Cage of Nightingales 1945; Calle Mayor 1956

Blanchar, Dominique (1927-) Decision before Dawn 1951; L'Avventura 1960

Blanchar, Pierre (1892-1963) The Chess Player 1927; Crime and Punishment 1935; Mademoiselle Docteur 1936; Un Carnet de Bal 1937; La Symphonie Pastorale 1946

Blanchard, Mari (1927-1970) Abbott and Costello Go to Mars 1953; Black Horse Canyon 1954; Destry 1954; Rails into Laramie 1954; Son of Sinbad 1955; Twice Told Tales 1963

Blanchard, Rachel (1976-) Road Trip 2000; Sugar & Spice 2001; Without a Paddle 2004; Where the Truth Lies 2005; Snakes on a Plane 2006; Adoration 2008; Spread 2008

Blanchard, Tammy (1976-) Stealing Harvard 2002; Bella 2006; The Good Shepherd 2006; Deadline 2009; Amish Grace 2010; Rabbit Hole 2010

Blanche, Roland (1943-1999) Les Compères 1983; Trop Belle pour Toi 1989

Blanchett, Cate (1969-) Oscar and Lucinda 1997; Thank God He Met Lizzie 1997; Elizabeth 1998; An Ideal Husband 1999; Pushing Tin 1999; The Talented Mr Ripley 1999; The Gift 2000; The Man Who Cried 2000; Bandits 2001; Charlotte Gray 2001; The Lord of the Rings: The Fellowship of the Ring 2001; The Shipping News 2001; Heaven 2002; The Lord of the Rings: The Two Towers 2002; Coffee and Cigarettes 2003; The Lord of the Rings: The Return of the King 2003; The Missing 2003; Veronica Guerin 2003; The Aviator 2004; The Life Aquatic with Steve Zissou 2004; Little Fish 2005; Babel 2006; The Good German 2006; Notes on a Scandal 2006; Elizabeth: the Golden Age 2007; I'm Not There. 2007; The Curious Case of Benjamin Button 2008; Indiana Jones and the Kingdom of the Crystal Skull 2008; Ponyo 2008; Robin Hood 2010; Hanna 2011; The Hobbit: an Unexpected Journey 2012; Blue Jasmine 2013; The Hobbit: the Desolation of Smaug 2013; The Monuments Men 2013; The Turning 2013; The Hobbit: the Battle of the Five Armies 2014; How to Train Your Dragon 2 2014; Carol 2015; Cinderella 2015; Knight of Cups 2015; Truth 2015; Thor: Ragnarok 2017; Jungle Book: Origins 2018

Blandick, Clara (1880-1962) Romance 1930; Tom Sawyer 1930; Huckleberry Finn 1931; The Bitter Tea of General Yen 1932; Rockabye 1932; Ever in My Heart 1933; The Girl from Missouri 1934; The Adventures of Huckleberry Finn 1939; The Wizard of Oz 1939; Frontier Gal 1945; Pillow of Death 1945

Blankfield, Mark (1950-) Robin Hood: Men in Tights 1993; Dracula: Dead and Loving It 1995

Blanks, Billy (1956-) Bloodfist 1989; Timebomb 1991; Back in Action 1993

Blanton, Kirby Bliss Scar 2007; Project X 2012; The Green Inferno 2013

Blasi, Rosa (1972-) The Grudge 2004; Next Stop Murder 2010

Blatt, Melanie (1975-) Dog Eat Dog 2000; Honest 2000

Blatz, Kelly Prom Night 2008; Skyrunners 2009

Blau, Martin Maria Ginger & Fred 1986; Heimat 2 1992

Blavette, Charles (1902-1967) Toni 1935; Stormy Waters 1941

Blech, Hans Christian (1925-1993) Decision before Dawn 1951; The Visit 1964; Morituri 1965; Les Innocents aux Mains Sales 1975; Knife in the Head 1978; Colonel Redl 1984

Bledel, Alexis (1981-) Tuck Everlasting 2002; The Sisterhood of the Traveling Pants 2005; The Sisterhood of the Traveling Pants 2 2008; Post Grad 2009

Bleek, Memphis Backstage 2000; Fade to Black 2004

Bleibtreu, Monica (1944-2009) The Farewell - Brecht's Last Summer 2000; Tattoo 2002; Four Minutes 2006

Bleibtreu, Moritz (1971-) Run Lola Run 1998; The Experiment 2000; Taking Sides 2001; Chiko 2007; Female Agents 2007; The Baader Meinhof Complex 2008; Angels of Evil 2010; 360 2011

Blessed, Brian (1937-) Till Death Us Do Part 1968; Country Dance 1970; The Trojan Women 1971; Henry VIII and His Six Wives 1972; Man of La Mancha 1972; High Road to China 1983; The Hound of the Baskervilles 1983; Henry V 1989; Prisoner of Honor 1991; Robin Hood: Prince of Thieves 1991; Back in the USSR 1992; Freddie as FRO7 1992; Chasing the Deer 1994; The Bruce 1996; Hamlet 1996; Macbeth 1997; Star Wars Episode I: the Phantom Menace 1999; Tarzan 1999; As You Like It 2006

Blethyn, Brenda (1946-) The Witches 1989; A River Runs through It 1992; Secrets & Lies 1995; Remember Me? 1996; Girls' Night 1997; Little Voice 1998; Music from Another Room 1998; Night Train 1998; Daddy and Them 1999; RKO 281 1999; Saving Grace 2000; Lovely & Amazing 2001; Sonny 2002; The Wild Thornberrys Movie 2003; Beyond the Sea 2004; On a Clear Day 2004; Piccadilly Jim 2004; A Way of Life 2004; Pooh's Heffalump Movie 2005; Pride & Prejudice 2005; Clubland 2006; Atonement 2007; The Calling 2009; Dead Man Running 2009; London River 2009

Bleu, Corbin (1989-) Catch That Kid 2004; High School Musical 2006; High School Musical 2 2007; Jump In! 2007; High School Musical 3: Senior Year 2008

Blick, Newton (1899-1965) The Long Arm 1956; The Gypsy and the Gentleman 1958; Morgan - a Suitable Case for Treatment 1966

Blicker, Jason American Boyfriends 1989; Baby on Board 1993; Superstar 1999; Owning Mahowny 2002

Blier, Bernard (1916-1989) Hôtel du Nord 1938; Le Jour Se Lève 1939; La Nuit Fantastique 1942; Quai des Orfèvres 1947; Secrets d'Alcove 1954; Les Misérables 1957; The Organizer 1963; Male Hunt 1964; Casanova '70 1965; Uncle Benjamin 1969; Catch Me a Spy 1971; The Tall Blond Man with One Black Shoe 1972; Buffet Froid 1979

Bliss, Boti Ann aka **Bliss, Boti** Warlock III: the End of Innocence 1999; Bundy 2002; The Perfect Teacher 2010

Bliss, Caroline (1961-) The Living Daylights 1987; Licence to Kill 1989

Bliss, Ian Siam Sunset 1999; Stealth 2005

Bloch, Bernard Hidden Agenda 1990; The Cow and the President 2000

Blocker, Dan (1928-1972) Come Blow Your Horn 1963; Lady in Cement 1968

Blondell, Joan (1906-1979) Blonde Crazy 1931; God's Gift to Women 1931; Illicit 1931; Night Nurse 1931; Other Men's Women 1931; The Public Enemy 1931; The Crowd Roars 1932; Lawyer Man 1932; Make Me a Star 1932; Three on a Match 1932; Union Depot 1932; Footlight Parade 1933; Gold Diggers of 1933 1933; Havana Widows 1933; Dames 1934; He Was Her Man 1934; Bullets or Ballots 1936; Colleen 1936; Gold Diggers of 1937 1936; Stage Struck 1936; The Perfect Specimen 1937; Stand-In 1937; There's Always a Woman 1938; The Amazing Mr Williams

1939; East Side of Heaven 1939; Topper Returns 1941; Lady for a Night 1942; Cry Havoc 1943; Adventure 1945; A Tree Grows in Brooklyn 1945; Christmas Eve 1947; Nightmare Alley 1947; For Heaven's Sake 1950; The Blue Veil 1951; Desk Set 1957; Lizzie 1957; This Could Be the Night 1957; Will Success Spoil Rock Hunter? 1957; Angel Baby 1961; Advance to the Rear 1964; The Cincinnati Kid 1965; Ride beyond Vengeance 1966; The Spy in the Green Hat 1966; Waterhole #3 1967; Winchester '73 1967; Stay Away, Joe 1968; Support Your Local Gunfighter 1971; Opening Night 1977; The Glove 1978; The Champ 1979

Bloodgood, Moon (1975-) Eight Below 2005; Pathfinder 2006; Terminator: Salvation 2009; Faster 2010; The Sessions 2012

Bloom, Claire (1931-) The Blind Goddess 1948; Limelight 1952; Innocents in Paris 1953; The Man Between 1953; Richard III 1955; Alexander the Great 1956; The Brothers Karamazov 1958; The Buccaneer 1958; Look Back in Anger 1959; The Chapman Report 1962; The Wonderful World of the Brothers Grimm 1962; 80,000 Suspects 1963; The Haunting 1963; The Outrage 1964; The Spy Who Came In from the Cold 1965; Charly 1968; The Illustrated Man 1969; Three into Two Won't Go 1969; A Severed Head 1970; Red Sky at Morning 1971; A Doll's House 1973; Islands in the Stream 1976; Clash of the Titans 1981; Separate Tables 1983; Déjà Vu 1984; Sammy and Rosie Get Laid 1987; Crimes and Misdemeanors 1989; The Princess and the Goblin 1992; Mad Dogs and Englishmen 1994; Mighty Aphrodite 1995; Daylight 1996; Wrestling with Alligators 1998; The Lady in Question 1999; Imagining Argentina 2003; The King's Speech 2010

Bloom, Orlando (1977-) Black Hawk Down 2001; The Lord of the Rings: The Fellowship of the Ring 2001; The Lord of the Rings: The Two Towers 2002; The Calcium Kid 2003; The Lord of the Rings: The Return of the King 2003; Ned Kelly 2003; Pirates of the Caribbean: the Curse of the Black Pearl 2003; Troy 2004; Elizabethtown 2005; Kingdom of Heaven 2005; Pirates of the Caribbean: Dead Man's Chest 2006; Pirates of the Caribbean: at World's End 2007; New York, I Love You 2009; The Three Musketeers 2011; The Hobbit: the Desolation of Smaug 2013; Zulu 2013; The Hobbit: the Battle of the Five Armies 2014

Bloom, Verna (1939-) Medium Cool 1969; The Hired Hand 1971; High Plains Drifter 1973; National Lampoon's Animal House 1978; Playing for Time 1980; Honkytonk Man 1982; After Hours 1985; The Journey of Natty Gann 1985; The Last Temptation of Christ 1988

Blore, Eric (1887-1959) Tarnished Lady 1931; The Gay Divorce 1934; Folies Bergère 1935; The Good Fairy 1935; I Dream Too Much 1935; I Live My Life 1935; Old Man Rhythm 1935; Top Hat 1935; The Ex-Mrs Bradford 1936; Piccadilly Jim 1936; Swing Time 1936; Breakfast for Two 1937; It's Love I'm After 1937; Quality Street 1937; Shall We Dance 1937; Joy of Living 1938; Swiss Miss 1938; The Boys from Syracuse 1940; The Man Who Wouldn't Talk 1940; Music in My Heart 1940; 'Til We Meet Again 1940; Confirm or Deny 1941; The Lady Eve 1941; Road to Zanzibar 1941; The Shanghai Gesture 1941; Sullivan's Travels 1941; The Moon and Sixpence 1942; Passport to Suez 1943; The Sky's the Limit 1943; Abie's Irish Rose 1946; Romance on the High Seas 1948; The Adventures of Ichabod and Mr Toad 1949; Love Happy 1949

Blossom, Roberts (1924-2011) Slaughterhouse-Five 1972; Deranged 1974; Citizens Band 1977; Close Encounters of the Third Kind 1977; Escape from Alcatraz 1979; Resurrection 1980; Reuben, Reuben 1983; Candy Mountain 1987; The Last Temptation of Christ 1988; Always 1989; Home Alone 1990

Blount, Lisa (1957-2010) September 30, 1955 1977; An Officer and a Gentleman 1982; Prince of Darkness 1987; Blind Fury 1990; Femme Fatale 1991; Murder between Friends 1993; Box of Moonlight 1996

Blucas, Marc (1972-) The Mating Habits of the Earthbound Human 1999; I Capture the Castle 2002; They 2002; First Daughter 2004; The Jane Austen Book Club 2007; Deadline 2009

Blue, Ben (1901-1975) Artists and Models 1937; College Swing 1938; Paris

Honeymoon 1939; For Me and My Gal 1942; Broadway Rhythm 1944; Two Sisters from Boston 1946

Blue, Callum (1977-) In Love and War 2001; Devil's Gate 2002; The Princess Diaries 2: Royal Engagement 2004; Red Sands 2009; Colombiana 2011

Blue, Jean (?-1972) The Overlanders 1946; Bitter Springs 1950

Blue, Monte (1890-1963) Orphans of the Storm 1921; The Marriage Circle 1924; Kiss Me Again 1925; So This Is Paris 1926; White Shadows in the South Seas 1928; The Lives of a Bengal Lancer 1935; Hell Town 1937; A Million to One 1937; Silver River 1948; The Younger Brothers 1949; Apache 1954

Blum, Jack Meatballs 1979; Happy Birthday to Me 1981

Blum, Mark (1950-) Desperately Seeking Susan 1985; "Crocodile" Dundee 1986; Blind Date 1987; "Crocodile" Dundee II 1988; The Presidio 1988; Indictment: the McMartin Trial 1995; You Can Thank Me Later 1998

Blum, Steven Jay aka **Lucas, David** aka **Blum, Steve** Perfect Blue 1998; A Cat in Paris 2010

Blundell, Graeme (1945-) Don's Party 1976; The Odd Angry Shot 1979; The Year My Voice Broke 1987; Idiot Box 1996

Blunt, Emily (1983-23/02/1983) My Summer of Love 2004; The Devil Wears Prada 2006; Irresistible 2006; Charlie Wilson's War 2007; The Jane Austen Book Club 2007; Wind Chill 2007; Sunshine Cleaning 2008; The Young Victoria 2008; Wild Target 2009; The Wolfman 2009; The Adjustment Bureau 2010; Gulliver's Travels 2010; Gnomeo & Juliet 2011; Salmon Fishing in the Yemen 2011; Your Sister's Sister 2011; Arthur & Mike 2012; The Five-Year Engagement 2012; Looper 2012; The Wind Rises 2013; Edge of Tomorrow 2014; Into the Woods 2014; Sicario 2015; The Girl on the Train 2016; The Huntsman: Winter's War 2016

Blunt, Erin (1963-) The Bad News Bears in Breaking Training 1977; The Bad News Bears Go to Japan 1978

Bluteau, Lothaire (1957-) Jesus of Montreal 1989; Black Robe 1991; Mrs 'arris Goes to Paris 1992; Orlando 1992; The Silent Touch 1992; The Confessional 1995; I Shot Andy Warhol 1995; Other Voices, Other Rooms 1995; Bent 1996; Dead Heat 2002

Bluthal, John (1929-) The Knack... and How to Get It 1965; Carry On Follow That Camel 1967; The Bliss of Mrs Blossom 1968; Digby, the Biggest Dog in the World 1973

Blyden, Larry (1925-1975) The Bachelor Party 1957; Kiss Them for Me 1957; On a Clear Day You Can See Forever 1970

Blye, Maggie aka **Blye, Margaret** (1942-2016) Waterhole #3 1967; Diamonds for Breakfast 1968; The Italian Job 1969; Every Little Crook and Nanny 1972; Hard Times 1975; The Entity 1981; Liar's Moon 1982

Blyth, Ann (1928-) The Merry Monahans 1944; Mildred Pierce 1945; Brute Force 1947; Killer McCoy 1947; Another Part of the Forest 1948; Mr Peabody and the Mermaid 1948; Once More, My Darling 1949; Red Canyon 1949; Our Very Own 1950; The Great Caruso 1951; Thunder on the Hill 1951; One Minute to Zero 1952; The World in His Arms 1952; All the Brothers Were Valiant 1953; Rose Marie 1954; The Student Prince 1954; The King's Thief 1955; Kismet 1955; The Buster Keaton Story 1957; The Helen Morgan Story 1957

Blythe, Benedick The Little Riders 1996; The Hunchback of Notre Dame 1997

Blythe, John (1921-1993) Bon Voyage 1944; The Frightened Man 1952; Gaolbreak 1962

Blythe, Peter (1934-2004) Frankenstein Created Woman 1966; A Challenge for Robin Hood 1967; Carrington 1995; The Luzhin Defence 2000

Boardman, Eleanor (1898-1991) Sinners in Silk 1924; The Crowd 1928

Boatman, Michael aka **Boatman, Michael Patrick** (1964-) Hamburger Hill 1987; The Glass Shield 1995

Boatman, Ross Hard Men 1996; Bring Me the Head of Mavis Davis 1997

Bobby, Anne (1967-) Nightbreed 1990; Finding North 1997

Bobo, Jonah (1997-) Around the Bend 2004; Zathura: a Space Adventure 2005; The Fox and the Hound 2 2007; Choke 2008; Crazy, Stupid, Love 2011

Bobulova, Barbora In Love and War 2001; Black Souls 2014

Boccardo, Delia (1948-) Inspector Clouseau 1968; Snow Job 1972; Massacre in Rome 1973; Tentacles 1977

Bochner, Hart (1956-) Islands in the Stream 1976; Breaking Away 1979; Terror Train 1980; Rich and Famous 1981; Apartment Zero 1988; Die Hard 1988; Fellow Traveller 1989; Mr Destiny 1990; Batman: Mask of the Phantasm 1993; Complex of Fear 1993; The Innocent 1993; Break Up 1998; Urban Legends: Final Cut 2000; Liberty Stands Still 2002; Baby for Sale 2004

Bochner, Lloyd (1924-2005) The Night Walker 1964; Point Blank 1967; Stranger on the Run 1967; Tony Rome 1967; The Detective 1968; The Horse in the Gray Flannel Suit 1968; Tiger by the Tail 1970; Ulzana's Raid 1972; The Hot Touch 1982; The Lonely Lady 1983; Millennium 1989; The Naked Gun 2½: the Smell of Fear 1991; Bram Stoker's Legend of the Mummy 1998

Bodnia, Kim (1965-) Nightwatch 1994; Pusher 1996; Bleeder 1999; Dragonflies 2001; Love Is All You Need 2012; Rosewater 2014

Bodrov Jr, Sergei (1971-2002) Prisoner of the Mountains 1996; Brother 1997; The Stringer 1997; East-West 1999; War 2002

Boen, Earl (1945-) The Man with Two Brains 1983; The Terminator 1984; Terminator 2: Judgment Day 1991; The Dentist 1996; Terminator 3: Rise of the Machines 2003

Boes, Richard Permanent Vacation 1982; Johnny Suede 1991; Dead Man 1995

Bogaert, Lucienne (1892-1983) Les Dames du Bois de Boulogne 1946; Maigret Sets a Trap 1957

Bogarde, Dirk (1921-1999) Dancing with Crime 1946; Esther Waters 1948; Once a Jolly Swagman 1948; Quartet 1948; The Blue Lamp 1949; Boys in Brown 1949; Dear Mr Prohack 1949; So Long at the Fair 1950; The Woman in Question 1950; Appointment in London 1952; The Gentle Gunman 1952; Hunted 1952; Penny Princess 1952; Desperate Moment 1953; They Who Dare 1953; Doctor in the House 1954; For Better, for Worse 1954; The Sea Shall Not Have Them 1954; The Sleeping Tiger 1954; Doctor at Sea 1955; Simba 1955; Ill Met by Moonlight 1956; The Spanish Gardener 1956; Campbell's Kingdom 1957; Cast a Dark Shadow 1957; Doctor at Large 1957; A Tale of Two Cities 1957; The Doctor's Dilemma 1958; The Wind Cannot Read 1958; Libel 1959; The Angel Wore Red 1960; The Singer Not the Song 1960; Song without End 1960; Victim 1961; HMS Defiant 1962; The Password Is Courage 1962; We Joined the Navy 1962; Doctor in Distress 1963; I Could Go On Singing 1963; The Mind Benders 1963; The Servant 1963; Hot Enough for June 1964; King and Country 1964; Darling 1965; The High Bright Sun 1965; Modesty Blaise 1966; Accident 1967; Our Mother's House 1967; Sebastian 1968; The Damned 1969; Justine 1969; Oh! What a Lovely War 1969; Death in Venice 1971; The Serpent 1972; The Night Porter 1973; Permission to Kill 1975; A Bridge Too Far 1977; Providence 1977; Despair 1978; The Patricia Neal Story 1981; These Foolish Things 1990

Bogart, Humphrey (1899-1957) Up the River 1930; Bad Sister 1931; Body and Soul 1931; Love Affair 1932; Three on a Match 1932; Midnight 1934; Bullets or Ballots 1936; China Clipper 1936; Isle of Fury 1936; The Petrified Forest 1936; The Black Legion 1937; Dead End 1937; The Great O'Malley 1937; Kid Galahad 1937; Marked Woman 1937; San Quentin 1937; Stand-In 1937; Swing Your Lady 1937; The Amazing Dr Clitterhouse 1938; Angels with Dirty Faces 1938; Racket Busters 1938; Dark Victory 1939; Invisible Stripes 1939; King of the Underworld 1939; The Oklahoma Kid 1939; The Return of Dr X 1939; The Roaring Twenties 1939; You Can't Get Away with Murder 1939; Brother Orchid 1940; It All Came True 1940; They Drive by Night 1940; Virginia City 1940; High Sierra 1941; The Maltese Falcon 1941; The Wagons Roll at Night 1941; Across the Pacific 1942; All through the Night 1942; The Big Shot 1942; Casablanca 1942; Action in the North Atlantic 1943; Sahara 1943; Thank Your Lucky Stars 1943; Passage to Marseille 1944; To Have and Have Not 1944; Conflict 1945; The Two Mrs Carrolls 1945; The Big Sleep 1946; Dark Passage 1947; Dead Reckoning 1947; The Treasure of the Sierra Madre 1947; Key Largo 1948; Knock on Any Door 1949; Tokyo Joe 1949; Chain Lightning 1950; In a Lonely

Place 1950; The African Queen 1951; The Enforcer 1951; Sirocco 1951; Deadline - USA 1952; Battle Circus 1953; Beat the Devil 1953; The Love Lottery 1953; The Barefoot Contessa 1954; The Caine Mutiny 1954; Sabrina 1954; The Desperate Hours 1955; The Left Hand of God 1955; We're No Angels 1955; The Harder They Fall 1956

Bogatyrev, Yuri (1947-1989) An Unfinished Piece for Mechanical Piano 1976; Oblomov 1980

Bogdanovich, Peter (1939-) Targets 1968; Saint Jack 1979; Mr Jealousy 1997; Festival in Cannes 2001; Easy Riders, Raging Bulls 2003; Infamous 2006; 'Tis Autumn: the Search for Jackie Paris 2007; Corman's World: Exploits of a Hollywood Rebel 2011; Magician: the Astonishing Life and Work of Orson Welles 2014; Hitchcock Truffaut 2015

Bogosian, Eric (1953-) The Caine Mutiny Court-Martial 1988; Talk Radio 1988; Suffering Bastards 1989; Sex, Drugs, Rock & Roll 1991; Dolores Claiborne 1995; Under Siege 2 1995; Beavis and Butt-head Do America 1996; The Substance of Fire 1996; Deconstructing Harry 1997; Gossip 1999; Ararat 2002; Wonderland 2003; Listen Up Philip 2014

Bohm, Hark (1939-) The American Soldier 1970; Effi Briest 1974; Lili Marleen 1980

Böhm, Karlheinz aka **Boehm, Carl** aka **Boehm, Karl** aka **Bohm, Karl-Heinz** (1928-2014) Peeping Tom 1960; Too Hot to Handle 1960; The Magnificent Rebel 1961; Come Fly with Me 1962; The Wonderful World of the Brothers Grimm 1962; The Venetian Affair 1966; Martha 1973; Fox and His Friends 1975; Mother Küsters Goes to Heaven 1975

Bohm, Marquard (1941-2006) Beware of a Holy Whore 1970; Kings of the Road 1976; Satan's Brew 1976

Bohnen, Roman (1894-1949) Of Mice and Men 1939; They Dare Not Love 1941; The Song of Bernadette 1943; The Hairy Ape 1944; Counter-Attack 1945; The Strange Love of Martha Ivers 1946; Arch of Triumph 1948

Bohrer, Corinne (1959-) Vice Versa 1988; Star Kid 1997

Bohringer, Richard (1942-) Diva 1981; Le Grand Pardon 1981; Death in a French Garden 1985; Subway 1985; Kamikaze 1986; Le Paltoquet 1986; Le Grand Chemin 1987; The Cook, the Thief, His Wife and Her Lover 1989; L'Accompagnatrice 1992; Le Cri du Coeur 1994; Le Parfum d'Yvonne 1994; Crime Spree 2002

Bohringer, Romane (1973-) Kamikaze 1986; L'Accompagnatrice 1992; Les Nuits Fauves 1992; Mina Tannenbaum 1993; Total Eclipse 1995; L'Appartement 1996; Portraits Chinois 1996; Vigo: Passion for Life 1997; The King Is Alive 2000; Renoir 2012

Boht, Jean (1936-) Arthur's Hallowed Ground 1985; To Die For 1994

Boidin, Samuel La Vie de Jésus 1996; Flanders 2005

Bois, Curt (1901-1991) The Great Waltz 1938; Hold Back the Dawn 1941; That Night in Rio 1941; The Tuttles of Tahiti 1942; The Woman in White 1948; Caught 1949; The Lovable Cheat 1949; Wings of Desire 1987

Boisson, Christine (1957-) Emmanuelle 1974; Identification of a Woman 1982; The Truth about Charlie 2002

Boitel, Jeanne (1904-1987) Marie Antoinette 1956; Maigret Sets a Trap 1957

Bok, Erika The Man from London 2007; The Turin Horse 2011

Bolam, James (1938-) The Kitchen 1961; A Kind of Loving 1962; The Loneliness of the Long Distance Runner 1962; Murder Most Foul 1964; Otley 1968; Crucible of Terror 1971; In Celebration 1974; The Likely Lads 1976; The Plague Dogs 1982; Clockwork Mice 1994; The Island on Bird Street 1997; Stella Does Tricks 1997; The End of the Affair 1999; It Was an Accident 2000; To Kill a King 2003

Boland, Eddie (1883-1935) Oliver Twist 1922; The Kid Brother 1927; The Miracle Woman 1931

Boland, Katie (1988-) No Higher Love 1999; Taking a Chance on Love 2009

Boland, Mary (1880-1965) Four Frightened People 1934; Six of a Kind 1934; Ruggles of Red Gap 1935; Danger - Love at Work 1937; The Women 1939; New Moon 1940; Pride and Prejudice 1940; In Our Time 1944; Nothing but Trouble 1944

Bolden, Philip Daniel Are We There Yet? 2005; Are We Done Yet? 2007; Fly Me to the Moon 2007

Boles, John (1895-1969) Fazil 1928; The Last Warning 1928; The Desert Song 1929; Rio Rita 1929; The King of Jazz 1930; Frankenstein 1931; One Heavenly Night 1931; Back Street 1932; Only Yesterday 1933; The Age of Innocence 1934; The White Parade 1934; Curly Top 1935; The Littlest Rebel 1935; Craig's Wife 1936; A Message to Garcia 1936; Stella Dallas 1937; Sinners in Paradise 1938; Thousands Cheer 1943

Bolger, Emma In America 2003; Heidi 2005

Bolger, Franklin aka **Bolger, Franklin H** Common-Law Cabin 1967; Cherry, Harry & Raquel 1969

Bolger, Ray (1904-1987) Rosalie 1937; Sweethearts 1938; The Wizard of Oz 1939; Sunny 1941; Forever and a Day 1943; The Harvey Girls 1946; Look for the Silver Lining 1949; April in Paris 1952; Babes in Toyland 1961; The Entertainer 1975; The Runner Stumbles 1979

Bolger, Sarah (1991-) In America 2003; Stormbreaker 2006; The Spiderwick Chronicles 2008; The Moth Diaries 2010; From Up on Poppy Hill 2011; Emelie 2015

Bolkan, Florinda (1941-) Investigation of a Citizen above Suspicion 1970; The Last Valley 1971; Royal Flash 1975; Some Girls 1988

Boliain, Iciar (1967-) El Sur 1983; Land and Freedom 1995

Bolling, Tiffany (1947-) The Wild Party 1975; Kingdom of the Spiders 1977

Bollman, Ryan (1972-) Children of the Corn II: the Final Sacrifice 1993; The NeverEnding Story III 1994; True Blue 1996

Bologna, Joseph (1936-) Cops and Robbers 1973; The Big Bus 1976; Chapter Two 1979; My Favorite Year 1982; Blame It on Rio 1984; The Woman in Red 1984; Transylvania 6-5000 1985; Coupe de Ville 1990; Alligator II: the Mutation 1991; Jersey Girl 1992; Love Is All There Is 1996; Big Daddy 1999

Bolt, Josh The Be All and End All 2009; Nowhere Boy 2010

Bomer, Matt aka **Bomer, Matthew** (1977-) The Texas Chainsaw Massacre: the Beginning 2006; Magic Mike 2012; The Normal Heart 2014; Magic Mike XXL 2015

Bon Jovi, Jon (1962-) Moonlight and Valentino 1995; The Leading Man 1996; Little City 1997; Homegrown 1998; No Looking Back 1998; Pay It Forward 2000; U-571 2000; Vampires: los Muertos 2002; Cry_Wolf 2005

Bonacelli, Paolo (1939-) Salò, or the 120 Days of Sodom 1975; Illustrious Corpses 1976; Midnight Express 1978; Christ Stopped at Eboli 1979; The Oberwald Mystery 1980; Camorra 1985; Francesco 1989; Johnny Stecchino 1991; The American 2010

Bonaiuto, Anna (1950-) L'Amore Molesto 1995; Il Divo 2008

Bonamy, Olivia (1974-) The Captive 2000; Read My Lips 2001; Them 2006

Bonanova, Fortunio (1893-1969) Citizen Kane 1941; Five Graves to Cairo 1943; Ali Baba and the Forty Thieves 1944; The Red Dragon 1945; Where Do We Go from Here? 1945; Romance on the High Seas 1948; Whirlpool 1949; An Affair to Remember 1957; The Saga of Hemp Brown 1958; Thunder in the Sun 1959

Bonar, Ivan (1924-1988) MacArthur 1977; Same Time, Next Year 1978

Bond, Derek (1919-2006) The Loves of Joanna Godden 1947; Nicholas Nickleby 1947; Uncle Silas 1947; Broken Journey 1948; Scott of the Antarctic 1948; The Weaker Sex 1948; Christopher Columbus 1949; The Quiet Woman 1950; The Hour of 13 1952; Trouble in Store 1953; Stranger from Venus 1954; Wonderful Life 1964; Press for Time 1966; When Eight Bells Toll 1971

Bond, Lillian (1908-1991) Air Mail 1932; The Old Dark House 1932; Blond Cheat 1938

Bond, Raleigh (1935-1989) The Black Marble 1980; Nightmares 1983

Bond (2), Samantha (1961-) Erik the Viking 1989; GoldenEye 1995; Tomorrow Never Dies 1997; What Rats Won't Do 1998; The Bookfair Murders 2000; Die Another Day 2002; Blinded 2004; Strings 2004; Yes 2004; A Bunch of Amateurs 2008

Bond, Sheila The Marrying Kind 1952; The Spirit of St Louis 1957

Bond, Sudie (1928-1984) Tomorrow 1972; Come Back to the Five and Dime, Jimmy Dean, Jimmy Dean 1982

Bond, Ward (1903-1960) The Man Who Lived Twice 1936; Submarine Patrol

1938; *The Cisco Kid and the Lady* 1939; *The Girl from Mexico* 1939; *Buck Benny Rides Again* 1940; *Kit Carson* 1940; *The Long Voyage Home* 1940; *The Maltese Falcon* 1941; *A Man Betrayed* 1941; *Manpower* 1941; *Sergeant York* 1941; *The Shepherd of the Hills* 1941; *The Falcon Takes Over* 1942; *Gentleman Jim* 1942; *Sin Town* 1942; *Ten Gentlemen from West Point* 1942; *Hello, Frisco, Hello* 1943; *The Fighting Sullivans* 1944; *A Guy Named Joe* 1944; *Home in Indiana* 1944; *Tall in the Saddle* 1944; *Dakota* 1945; *They Were Expendable* 1945; *Canyon Passage* 1946; *It's a Wonderful Life* 1946; *My Darling Clementine* 1946; *The Fugitive* 1947; *Unconquered* 1947; *Fort Apache* 1948; *Joan of Arc* 1948; *Three Godfathers* 1948; *The Time of Your Life* 1948; *Kiss Tomorrow Goodbye* 1950; *Only the Valiant* 1950; *Riding High* 1950; *Wagonmaster* 1950; *On Dangerous Ground* 1951; *Operation Pacific* 1951; *Hellgate* 1952; *The Quiet Man* 1952; *Blowing Wild* 1953; *Hondo* 1953; *The Moonlighter* 1953; *Johnny Guitar* 1954; *The Long Gray Line* 1955; *A Man Alone* 1955; *Mister Roberts* 1955; *Dakota Incident* 1956; *Pillars of the Sky* 1956; *The Searchers* 1956; *The Halliday Brand* 1957; *The Wings of Eagles* 1957; *China Doll* 1958; *Rio Bravo* 1958; *Alias Jesse James* 1959

Bondarchuk, Sergei (1920–1994) *Othello* 1955; *Destiny of a Man* 1959; *War and Peace* 1956

Bondi, Beulah (1892–1981) *Arrowsmith* 1931; *Street Scene* 1931; *The Stranger's Return* 1933; *Finishing School* 1934; *The Painted Veil* 1934; *The Good Fairy* 1935; *The Gorgeous Hussy* 1936; *The Invisible Ray* 1936; *The Moon's Our Home* 1936; *The Trail of the Lonesome Pine* 1936; *Make Way for Tomorrow* 1937; *Of Human Hearts* 1938; *The Sisters* 1938; *Vivacious Lady* 1938; *Mr Smith Goes to Washington* 1939; *Our Town* 1940; *Remember the Night* 1940; *One Foot in Heaven* 1941; *Penny Serenade* 1941; *The Shepherd of the Hills* 1941; *Watch on the Rhine* 1943; *And Now Tomorrow* 1944; *I Love a Soldier* 1944; *The Very Thought of You* 1944; *Back to Bataan* 1945; *The Southerner* 1945; *It's a Wonderful Life* 1946; *Sister Kenny* 1946; *The Snake Pit* 1948; *Reign of Terror* 1949; *So Dear to My Heart* 1949; *The Furies* 1950; *Lone Star* 1952; *Latin Lovers* 1953; *Track of the Cat* 1954; *Back from Eternity* 1956; *The Unholy Wife* 1957; *Tammy Tell Me True* 1961; *The Wonderful World of the Brothers Grimm* 1962; *Tammy and the Doctor* 1963

Bonds, De'Aundre (1976–) *Get on the Bus* 1996; *Sunset Park* 1996; *The Wood* 1999

Bonet, Lisa (1967–) *Angel Heart* 1987; *Final Combination* 1993; *Enemy of the State* 1998; *High Fidelity* 2000; *Biker Boyz* 2003

Bonetti, Massimo *The Night of San Lorenzo* 1981; *Night Sun* 1990

Bongard, Pascal *13 (Tzameti)* 2005; *Legacy* 2007

Bonham Carter, Helena (1966–) *Lady Jane* 1985; *A Room with a View* 1985; *Francesco* 1989; *Getting It Right* 1989; *Hamlet* 1990; *Where Angels Fear to Tread* 1991; *Howards End* 1992; *Mary Shelley's Frankenstein* 1994; *Margaret's Museum* 1995; *Mighty Aphrodite* 1995; *Portraits Chinois* 1996; *Twelfth Night* 1996; *Keep the Aspidistra Flying* 1997; *The Revengers' Comedies* 1997; *The Wings of the Dove* 1997; *The Theory of Flight* 1998; *Fight Club* 1999; *Women Talking Dirty* 1999; *Novocaine* 2001; *Planet of the Apes* 2001; *The Heart of Me* 2002; *Live from Baghdad* 2002; *Big Fish* 2003; *Charlie and the Chocolate Factory* 2005; *Conversations with Other Women* 2005; *Tim Burton's Corpse Bride* 2005; *Wallace & Gromit in The Curse of the Were-Rabbit* 2005; *Sixty Six* 2006; *Harry Potter and the Order of the Phoenix* 2007; *Sweeney Todd: the Demon Barber of Fleet Street* 2007; *Harry Potter and the Half-Blood Prince* 2009; *Terminator: Salvation* 2009; *Alice in Wonderland* 2010; *Harry Potter and the Deathly Hallows: Part 1* 2010; *The King's Speech* 2010; *Toast* 2010; *Harry Potter and the Deathly Hallows: Part 2* 2011; *Dark Shadows* 2012; *Great Expectations* 2012; *Les Misérables* 2012; *The Lone Ranger* 2013; *The Young and Prodigious TS Spivet* 2013; *Night Will Fall* 2014; *Cinderella* 2015; *Suffragette* 2015; *Alice through the Looking Glass* 2016

Boniadi, Nazanin *Desert Dancer* 2014; *Ben-Hur* 2015

Bonilla, Jesús (1955–) *The Girl of Your Dreams* 1998; *La Comunidad* 2000

Bonnaffé, Jacques (1958–) *First Name: Carmen* 1983; *Venus Beauty Institute* 1998; *Va Savoir* 2001; *Les Diables* 2002; *Cockles & Muscles* 2004; *Lemming* 2005; *The Page Turner* 2006; *Violette* 2013

Bonnaire, Sandrine (1967–) *To Our Loves* 1984; *Police* 1985; *Vagabond* 1985; *Sous le Soleil de Satan* 1987; *Monsieur Hire* 1989; *Captive of the Desert* 1990; *The Plague* 1992; *Jeanne la Pucelle* 1994; *La Cérémonie* 1995; *Circle of Passion* 1996; *Secret Defense* 1997; *The Colour of Lies* 1999; *East-West* 1999; *Confidences Trop Intimes* 2004; *Angel of Mine* 2008

Bonnell, Lee *Footlight Fever* 1941; *Look Who's Laughing* 1941

Bonner, Priscilla (1898–1996) *The Strong Man* 1926; *Long Pants* 1927

Bonner, Tony (1943–) *Eyewitness* 1970; *You Can't Win 'Em All* 1970; *Creatures the World Forgot* 1971; *The Man from Snowy River* 1982; *The Lighthorsemen* 1987; *Quigley Down Under* 1990

Bonnevie, Maria (1973–) *Jerusalem* 1996; *Insomnia* 1997; *Dragonflies* 2001; *Reconstruction* 2003; *The Banishment* 2007; *A Second Chance* 2014; *The Shamer's Daughter* 2015

Bonneville, Hugh (1963–) *Notting Hill* 1999; *Blow Dry* 2000; *The Emperor's New Clothes* 2001; *Iris* 2001; *Asylum* 2004; *Piccadilly Jim* 2004; *Stage Beauty* 2004; *Underclassman* 2004; *Four Last Songs* 2007; *French Film* 2008; *From Time to Time* 2009; *Glorious 39* 2009; *Third Star* 2010; *The Monuments Men* 2013; *Paddington* 2014

Bonney, John *Paranoiac* 1963; *Saturday Night Out* 1963

Bono (1960–) *U2 Rattle and Hum* 1988; *Leonard Cohen: I'm Your Man* 2005; *The Future Is Unwritten* 2006; *Across the Universe* 2007; *U23D* 2007

Bono, Sonny (1935-1998) *Wild on the Beach* 1965; *Good Times* 1967; *Escape to Athena* 1979; *Airplane II: the Sequel* 1982; *Troll* 1986; *Hairspray* 1988; *First Kid* 1996

Bonsall, Brian (1981–) *Father Hood* 1993; *Blank Check* 1994

Bonvoisin, Bérangère *Hôtel du Paradis* 1986; *Good Morning, Babylon* 1987; *Docteur Petiot* 1990

Booke, Sorrell (1930-1994) *Gone Are the Days* 1963; *Black like Me* 1964; *The Love Cage* 1964; *Up the Down Staircase* 1967; *Bye Bye Braverman* 1968; *Slaughterhouse-Five* 1972; *What's Up, Doc?* 1972; *Bank Shot* 1974; *Freaky Friday* 1976; *Special Delivery* 1976

Boon, Dany *Merry Christmas* 2005; *My Best Friend* 2006; *Micmacs* 2009; *A Perfect Plan* 2012

Boone Junior, Mark (1955–) *Trees Lounge* 1996; *Vampires* 1998; *Buddy Boy* 1999; *Memento* 2000; *2 Fast 2 Furious* 2003; *Dead Birds* 2004; *Frankenfish* 2004; *Lonesome Jim* 2005; *30 Days of Night* 2007; *Frozen River* 2008

Boone, Pat (1934–) *April Love* 1957; *Mardi Gras* 1958; *Journey to the Center of the Earth* 1959; *All Hands on Deck* 1961; *The Main Attraction* 1962; *State Fair* 1962; *The Yellow Canary* 1963; *Goodbye Charlie* 1964; *The Greatest Story Ever Told* 1965; *The Perils of Pauline* 1967; *Roger & Me* 1989

Boone, Richard (1917–1981) *Halls of Montezuma* 1950; *Call Me Mister* 1951; *Kangaroo* 1952; *Red Skies of Montana* 1952; *Way of a Gaucho* 1952; *Beneath the 12-Mile Reef* 1953; *The Robe* 1953; *Dragnet* 1954; *The Raid* 1954; *The Siege at Red River* 1954; *Man without a Star* 1955; *Ten Wanted Men* 1955; *Away All Boats* 1956; *Star in the Dust* 1956; *The Garment Jungle* 1957; *Lizzie* 1957; *The Tall T* 1957; *The Alamo* 1960; *A Thunder of Drums* 1961; *Rio Conchos* 1964; *The War Lord* 1965; *Hombre* 1967; *The Night of the Following Day* 1968; *The Arrangement* 1969; *Madron* 1970; *Big Jake* 1971; *The Shootist* 1976; *God's Gun* 1977; *The Big Sleep* 1978; *Winter Kills* 1979

Boorem, Mika (1987–) *Hearts in Atlantis* 2001; *Blue Crush* 2002; *Dirty Dancing 2* 2003; *Sleepover* 2004

Boorman, Charley (1966–) *The Emerald Forest* 1985; *The Bunker* 2001

Booth, Anthony (1937–) *Pit of Darkness* 1961; *The L-Shaped Room* 1962; *The Hi-Jackers* 1963; *Corruption* 1968; *Till Death Us Do Part* 1968; *Neither the Sea nor the Sand* 1972; *Confessions of a Window Cleaner* 1974; *Confessions of a Pop Performer* 1975;

Confessions of a Driving Instructor 1976; *Confessions from a Holiday Camp* 1977; *Revengers Tragedy* 2002

Booth, Connie (1941–) *And Now for Something Completely Different* 1971; *Monty Python and the Holy Grail* 1975; *The Hound of the Baskervilles* 1983; *Hawks* 1988; *High Spirits* 1988; *American Friends* 1991; *Leon the Pig Farmer* 1992

Booth, Douglas (1992–) *LOL* 2011; *Romeo & Juliet* 2012; *Jupiter Ascending* 2014; *Noah* 2014; *The Riot Club* 2014; *Pride and Prejudice and Zombies* 2015; *Loving Vincent* 2016

Booth, Emma *Clubland* 2006; *Blood Creek* 2009; *The Boys Are Back* 2009

Booth, James (1927–2005) *The Trials of Oscar Wilde* 1960; *In the Doghouse* 1961; *Sparrows Can't Sing* 1962; *Zulu* 1963; *French Dressing* 1964; *The Secret of My Success* 1965; *Robbery* 1967; *The Bliss of Mrs Blossom* 1968; *Fraulein Doktor* 1968; *Adam's Woman* 1970; *Darker than Amber* 1970; *The Man Who Had Power over Women* 1970; *Rentadick* 1972; *Penny Gold* 1973; *That'll Be the Day* 1973; *Zorro, the Gay Blade* 1981; *Avenging Force* 1986; *Bad Guys* 1986; *Keeping Mum* 2005

Booth, Karin (1923-1992) *The Unfinished Dance* 1947; *The Cariboo Trail* 1950; *The Crooked Sky* 1957; *Beloved Infidel* 1959; *Juke Box Rhythm* 1959

Booth, Lindy (1979–) *American Psycho II: All American Girl* 2002; *Wrong Turn* 2003; *Dawn of the Dead* 2004; *Cry_Wolf* 2005

Booth, Shirley (1907–1992) *Come Back, Little Sheba* 1952; *About Mrs Leslie* 1954; *Hot Spell* 1958; *The Matchmaker* 1958

Booth, Zachary *Dark Horse* 2011; *Keep the Lights On* 2012

Boothe, Powers (1948–) *Southern Comfort* 1981; *A Breed Apart* 1984; *Red Dawn* 1984; *The Emerald Forest* 1985; *Extreme Prejudice* 1987; *By Dawn's Early Light* 1990; *Blue Sky* 1991; *Rapid Fire* 1992; *Tombstone* 1993; *Nixon* 1995; *Sudden Death* 1995; *U Turn* 1997; *Men of Honor* 2000; *Frailty* 2001; *Sin City* 2005; *Marvel Avengers Assemble* 2012; *Sin City: a Dame to Kill For* 2014

Boratto, Caterina (1915–2010) *Juliet of the Spirits* 1965; *The Tiger and the Pussycat* 1967; *Salo, or the 120 Days of Sodom* 1975

Borboni, Paola (1900–1995) *Arabella* 1967; *La Cage aux Folles II* 1980; *Yes, Giorgio* 1982

Borchers, Cornell (1925–2014) *The Big Lift* 1950; *The Divided Heart* 1954; *Never Say Goodbye* 1955; *Istanbul* 1957

Borden, Eugene (1897–1971) *So Dark the Night* 1946; *An American in Paris* 1951

Boreanaz, David (1969–) *Valentine* 2001; *I'm with Lucy* 2002; *The Crow: Wicked Prayer* 2005

Borell, Louis (1905–1973) *The Avenging Hand* 1936; *Head over Heels in Love* 1937; *Over the Moon* 1937

Borg, Veda Ann (1915–1973) *San Quentin* 1937; *Miracle on Main Street* 1940; *The Penalty* 1941; *The Unknown Guest* 1943; *The Big Noise* 1944; *The Falcon in Hollywood* 1944; *Fog Island* 1945; *Big Jim McLain* 1952; *You're Never Too Young* 1955; *The Fearmakers* 1958; *Thunder in the Sun* 1959

Borge, Victor (1909–2000) *Higher and Higher* 1943; *The King of Comedy* 1983

Borgeaud, Nelly (1931–2004) *Celà S'Appelle l'Aurore* 1956; *Mississippi Mermaid* 1969; *The Man Who Loved Women* 1977; *Mon Oncle d'Amérique* 1980; *Dandin* 1988; *L'Accompagnatrice* 1992

Borgnine, Ernest (1917–2012) *The Mob* 1951; *From Here to Eternity* 1953; *The Bounty Hunter* 1954; *Demetrius and the Gladiators* 1954; *Johnny Guitar* 1954; *Vera Cruz* 1954; *Bad Day at Black Rock* 1955; *The Last Command* 1955; *Marty* 1955; *Run for Cover* 1955; *The Square Jungle* 1955; *Violent Saturday* 1955; *The Best Things in Life Are Free* 1956; *The Catered Affair* 1956; *Jubal* 1956; *The Badlanders* 1958; *Torpedo Run* 1958; *The Vikings* 1958; *Pay or Die* 1960; *Season of Passion* 1960; *Barabbas* 1961; *Go Naked in the World* 1961; *McHale's Navy* 1964; *The Flight of the Phoenix* 1965; *The Oscar* 1966; *The Dirty Dozen* 1967; *Ice Station Zebra* 1968; *The Legend of Lylah Clare* 1968; *The Split* 1968; *The Wild Bunch* 1969; *The Adventurers* 1970; *A Bullet for Sandoval* 1970; *Suppose They Gave a War and Nobody Came?* 1970; *Bunny O'Hare* 1971; *Hannie Caulder* 1971; *Willard* 1971; *The Poseidon Adventure* 1972; *Emperor of the North* 1973; *The*

Neptune Factor 1973; *Law and Disorder* 1974; *The Devil's Rain* 1975; *Hustle* 1975; *Sunday in the Country* 1975; *The Greatest* 1977; *The Prince and the Pauper* 1977; *Convoy* 1978; *All Quiet on the Western Front* 1979; *The Black Hole* 1979; *When Time Ran Out* 1980; *Deadly Blessing* 1981; *Escape from New York* 1981; *High Risk* 1981; *Young Warriors* 1983; *Codename Wildgeese* 1984; *Gattaca* 1997; *McHale's Navy* 1997; *BASEketball* 1998; *Small Soldiers* 1998; *Blueberry* 2004; *The Trail to Hope Rose* 2004; *A Grandpa for Christmas* 2007; *Strange Wilderness* 2007; *Aces 'n' Eights* 2008; *The Wishing Well* 2009

Borland, Barlowe (1877–1948) *Bluebeard's Eighth Wife* 1938; *The Hound of the Baskervilles* 1939

Boros, Ferike (1880–1951) *Once upon a Honeymoon* 1942; *The Pied Piper* 1942

Borowitz, Katherine *Fellow Traveller* 1989; *Men of Respect* 1990; *Mac* 1992; *The Man Who Wasn't There* 2001

Borrego, Jesse (1962–) *Blood In Blood Out* 1992; *Mi Vida Loca* 1993; *I Like It like That* 1994; *The Maldonado Miracle* 2003

Borstein, Alex *Catwoman* 2004; *The Lookout* 2007

Bory, Jean-Marc (1934–2001) *Les Amants* 1958; *RoGoPaG* 1962

Bosch, Johnny Yong (1976–) *Mighty Morphin Power Rangers: the Movie* 1995; *Turbo: a Power Rangers Adventure* 1997

Bosco, Philip (1930–) *Catholic Boys* 1985; *The Money Pit* 1985; *Walls of Glass* 1985; *Children of a Lesser God* 1986; *Suspect* 1987; *Three Men and a Baby* 1987; *The Dream Team* 1989; *Blue Steel* 1990; *FX 2* 1991; *True Colors* 1991; *Against the Wall* 1994; *Angie* 1994; *Milk Money* 1994; *It Takes Two* 1995; *My Best Friend's Wedding* 1997; *Wonder Boys* 2000; *No Ordinary Baby* 2001; *The Savages* 2007

Bosé, Lucia (1931–) *Chronicle of a Love* 1950; *La Signora senza Camelie* 1953; *Celà S'Appelle l'Aurore* 1956

Bose, Miguel (1956–) *Suspiria* 1976; *High Heels* 1991; *Gazon Maudit* 1995

Bose, Rahul (1968–) *English, August* 1994; *Bombay Boys* 1998; *Split Wide Open* 1999; *Mumbai Matinee* 2003; *Before the Rains* 2007

Boseman, Chadwick *42* 2013; *Get on Up* 2014; *Black Panther* 2018

Bosetti, Giulio (1930–2009) *Imperial Venus* 1963; *Il Divo* 2008

Bosley, Tom (1927–2010) *Love with the Proper Stranger* 1963; *The World of Henry Orient* 1964; *The Secret War of Harry Frigg* 1967; *Yours, Mine and Ours* 1968; *The Night that Panicked America* 1975; *Wicked Stepmother* 1989; *Hidden Places* 2006; *The Back-Up Plan* 2010

Bosson, Barbara (1939–) *Calendar Girl Murders* 1984; *The Last Starfighter* 1984

Bostick, Devon (1991–) *Godsend* 2003; *Knights of the South Bronx* 2005; *Adoration* 2008; *George A Romero's Survival of the Dead* 2009; *Diary of a Wimpy Kid* 2010; *Diary of a Wimpy Kid: Rodrick Rules* 2011; *Diary of a Wimpy Kid 3: Dog Days* 2012

Bostwick, Barry (1945–) *Fantastic Planet* 1973; *The Rocky Horror Picture Show* 1975; *Weekend at Bernie's II* 1992; *800 Leagues down the Amazon* 1993; *Danielle Steel's Once in a Lifetime* 1994; *919 Fifth Avenue* 1995; *The Secret Agent Club* 1995; *Spy Hard* 1996; *Nancy Drew* 2007; *Hannah Montana: the Movie* 2009

Boswall, John (2010–2011) *Three Men and a Little Lady* 1990; *The Statement* 2003

Boswell, Connee (1907–1996) *Syncopation* 1942; *Senior Prom* 1958

Bosworth, Hobart (1867–1943) *The Big Parade* 1925; *Annie Laurie* 1927; *Hangman's House* 1928; *Eternal Love* 1929; *The Show of Shows* 1929; *Abraham Lincoln* 1930; *The Devil's Holiday* 1930; *Mammy* 1930; *Dirigible* 1931; *This Modern Age* 1931

Bosworth, Kate (1983–) *Blue Crush* 2002; *The Rules of Attraction* 2002; *Wonderland* 2003; *Beyond the Sea* 2004; *Win a Date with Tad Hamilton!* 2004; *Bee Season* 2005; *Superman Returns* 2006; *The Girl in the Park* 2007; *21* 2008; *The Warrior's Way* 2010; *Straw Dogs* 2011; *Black Rock* 2012; *Homefront* 2013; *Still Alice* 2014; *Before I Wake* 2015; *Heist* 2015

Boteler, Wade (1888–1943) *Big News* 1929; *Days of Jesse James* 1939

Botet, Javier [Rec]² *Génesis* 2012; *Mama* 2013; *The Other Side of the Door* 2016

Botsford, Sara (1953–) *Murder by Phone* 1982; *Still of the Night* 1982; *The Gunrunner* 1984; *Our Guys: Outrage in Glen Ridge* 1999; *The Fog* 2005; *River* 2015

Botto, María *Only Human* 2004; *Risen* 2016

Bottomley, Christine (1979–) *The Waiting Room* 2007; *Hush* 2008; *The Arbor* 2010; *Strawberry Fields* 2011; *Keeping Rosy* 2014

Bottoms, Joseph (1954–) *The Dove* 1974; *Crime and Passion* 1976; *The Black Hole* 1979; *Cloud Dancer* 1979; *Blind Date* 1984

Bottoms, Sam (1955-2008) *The Last Picture Show* 1971; *Class of '44* 1973; *Zandy's Bride* 1974; *The Outlaw Josey Wales* 1976; *Apocalypse Now* 1979; *Bronco Billy* 1980; *Shopgirl* 2005; *Sherrybaby* 2006

Bottoms, Timothy *aka* Bottoms, Tim (1950–) *Johnny Got His Gun* 1971; *The Last Picture Show* 1971; *Love and Pain and the Whole Damn Thing* 1973; *The Paper Chase* 1973; *The White Dawn* 1974; *Operation Daybreak* 1975; *Rollercoaster* 1977; *Hurricane* 1979; *The High Country* 1981; *Hambone and Hillie* 1984; *The Fantasist* 1986; *Invaders from Mars* 1986; *Mio in the Land of Faraway* 1987; *A Case of Honor* 1988; *Return from the River Kwai* 1988; *Texasville* 1990; *Horses and Champions* 1994; *Elephant* 2003; *The Girl Next Door* 2004; *Ike: Countdown to D-Day* 2004; *Holiday in Handcuffs* 2007; *Bound by a Secret* 2008; *Lone Rider* 2008

Bouajila, Sami (1966–) *The Siege* 1998; *Drôle de Félix* 2000; *Days of Glory* 2006; *The Witnesses* 2006; *London River* 2009; *Beautiful Lies* 2010

Bouchet, Barbara (1943–) *Casino Royale* 1967; *Danger Route* 1967; *Gangs of New York* 2002

Bouchey, Willis (1907–1977) *Red Planet Mars* 1952; *The Big Heat* 1953; *The McConnell Story* 1955; *Last of the Badmen* 1957; *The Night Runner* 1957; *The Sheepman* 1958; *Sergeant Rutledge* 1960

Bouchez, Elodie (1973–) *Les Roseaux Sauvages* 1994; *Clubbed to Death* 1996; *The Dream Life of Angels* 1998; *Lovers* 1999

Bouchitey, Patrick *Nine Months* 1994; *My Afternoons with Margueritte* 2010

Boudet, Jacques *Waiting for the Moon* 1987; *Farinelli il Castrato* 1994; *Marius et Jeannette* 1997; *La Ville Est Tranquille* 2000

Bouise, Jean (1929–1989) *I Am Cuba* 1964; *The Things of Life* 1969; *The Confession* 1970; *Edith et Marcel* 1983; *The Last Battle* 1983; *The Big Blue* 1988

Bouix, Evelyne (1956–) *Les Misérables* 1982; *Edith et Marcel* 1983; *A Man and a Woman: 20 Years Later* 1986

Boujenah, Michel (1952–) *3 Men and a Cradle* 1985; *Les Misérables* 1995

Boulanger, Daniel (1922-2014) *A Bout de Souffle* 1959; *The Bride Wore Black* 1967; *Bed and Board* 1970

Boulanger, Pierre *Monsieur Ibrahim and the Flowers of the Koran* 2003; *God Help the Girl* 2012

Boulter, Robert *Daylight Robbery* 2007; *Donkey Punch* 2007

Boulter, Rosalyn (1917–1997) *Return of a Stranger* 1937; *George in Civvy Street* 1946

Boulton, Matthew (1893-1962) *Sabotage* 1936; *They Met in Bombay* 1941; *The Brighton Strangler* 1945; *The Woman in Green* 1945; *Bulldog Drummond Strikes Back* 1947

Bouquet, Carole (1957–) *That Obscure Object of Desire* 1977; *Buffet Froid* 1979; *For Your Eyes Only* 1981; *Trop Belle pour Toi* 1989; *A Business Affair* 1993; *Lucie Aubrac* 1997; *En Plein Coeur* 1998; *The Bridge* 1999; *Summer Things* 2002; *Red Lights* 2003; *L'Enfer* 2005

Bouquet, Michel (1926–) *Nuit et Brouillard* 1955; *The Bride Wore Black* 1967; *The Road to Corinth* 1967; *La Femme Infidèle* 1968; *Mississippi Mermaid* 1969; *Borsalino* 1970; *La Rupture* 1970; *Juste avant la Nuit* 1971; *Malpertuis* 1971; *The Serpent* 1972; *Two against the Law* 1973; *Les Misérables* 1982; *Cop au Vin* 1984; *Toto Le Héros* 1991; *Tous les Matins du Monde* 1991; *Comment J'ai Tué Mon Père* 2001; *The Last Mitterrand* 2005; *Renoir* 2012

Bourdin, Lise (1925–) *Love in the Afternoon* 1957; *The Last Blitzkrieg* 1958

Bourdon, Didier *La Machine* 1994; *A Good Year* 2006

Bourgeois, John *The Prince & Me* 2004; *Unstable* 2009

Bourgoin, Louise *The Extraordinary Adventures of Adèle Blanc-Sec 2010; The Love Punch 2013; The Nun 2013*
Bourne, J R (1970-) *Thir13en Ghosts 2001; Perfect Romance 2004*
Bourne, Whitney (1914-1988) *Crime without Passion 1934; Flight from Glory 1937; The Mad Miss Manton 1938; Beauty for the Asking 1939*
Bourneuf, Philip (1908-1979) *The Big Night 1951; Beyond a Reasonable Doubt 1956*
Bourvil aka **Bourvil, André** (1917-1970) *La Traversée de Paris 1956; Les Misérables 1957; Le Bossu 1959; The Captain 1960; The Dirty Game 1965; The Brain 1969; The Christmas Tree 1969; Monte Carlo or Bust! 1969; The Red Circle 1970*
Boutefeu, Nathalie *Le Chignon d'Olga 2002; Son Frère 2003; Kings & Queen 2004*
Boutella, Sofia *StreetDance 2 2012; Monsters: Dark Continent 2014; Kingsman: The Secret Service 2015; Tiger Raid 2016; The Mummy 2017*
Boutsikaris, Dennis (1952-) *batteries not included 1987; The Dream Team 1989; The Boy Who Cried Bitch 1991; Boys on the Side 1995; Custody of the Heart 2000; They Crawl 2001*
Bova, Raoul (1971-) *Francesca and Nunziata 2001; Avenging Angelo 2002; Facing Window 2003; Under the Tuscan Sun 2003; AVP: Alien vs Predator 2004*
Bovasso, Julie (1930-1991) *Saturday Night Fever 1977; Willie and Phil 1980; Staying Alive 1983; Wise Guys 1986; Moonstruck 1987*
Bovell, Brian (1959-) *Babylon 1980; Playing Away 1986*
Bow Wow aka **Lil' Bow Wow** (1987-) *Like Mike 2002; Johnson Family Vacation 2004; The Fast and the Furious: Tokyo Drift 2006*
Bow, Clara (1905-1965) *Kiss Me Again 1925; Mantrap 1926; It 1927; Wings 1927; The Saturday Night Kid 1929; The Wild Party 1929; Her Wedding Night 1930; Paramount on Parade 1930*
Bowden, Katrina *Sex Drive 2008; Tucker and Dale vs Evil 2009; Piranha 3DD 2011; Scary Movie V 2013*
Bowdon, Dorris (1914-2005) *Drums along the Mohawk 1939; The Grapes of Wrath 1940; The Moon Is Down 1943*
Bowe, David (1947-) *UHF 1989; Heavyweights 1995*
Bowen, A J *The Signal 2007; The Sacrament 2013*
Bowen, Andrea *After the Fall 2010; GBF 2013*
Bowen, Julie (1970-) *Happy Gilmore 1996; An American Werewolf in Paris 1997; Joe Somebody 2001; Planes: Fire and Rescue 2014*
Bowen, Michael (1957-) *Valley Girl 1983; Echo Park 1985; Less than Zero 1987; Kid 1990; True Crime 1995; Excess Baggage 1997; Jackie Brown 1997; Walking Tall 2004*
Bowens, Malick *Out of Africa 1985; Bophal 1993; Tears of the Sun 2003*
Bower, Antoinette (1932-) *Prom Night 1980; The Evil That Men Do 1984*
Bower, Jamie Campbell (1988-) *Sweeney Todd: the Demon Barber of Fleet Street 2007; Winter in Wartime 2008; London Boulevard 2010; The Mortal Instruments: City of Bones 2013*
Bower, Tom (1938-) *The Ballad of Gregorio Cortez 1983; The Lightship 1985; Distant Thunder 1988; Promised a Miracle 1988; True Believer 1989; Talent for the Game 1991; Raising Cain 1992; The Ballad of Little Jo 1993; Against the Wall 1994; Far from Home: the Adventures of Yellow Dog 1994; White Man's Burden 1995; Buffalo Soldiers 1997; Poodle Springs 1998; High Crimes 2002; Appaloosa 2008; Crazy Heart 2009*
Bowers, John (1893-1936) *The Ace of Hearts 1921; Say It with Songs 1929*
Bowers, Lally (1917-1984) *We Joined the Navy 1962; The Chalk Garden 1964*
Bowie, David (1947-2016) *The Man Who Fell to Earth 1976; Just a Gigolo 1978; Christiane F 1981; Merry Christmas Mr Lawrence 1982; Ziggy Stardust and the Spiders from Mars 1982; The Hunger 1983; Into the Night 1985; Absolute Beginners 1986; Labyrinth 1986; The Last Temptation of Christ 1988; The Linguini Incident 1991; Twin Peaks: Fire Walk with Me 1992; Basquiat 1996; Glastonbury 2006; The Prestige 2006; Scott Walker: 30 Century Man 2006; Bandslam 2009*
Bowker, Judi (1954-) *Brother Sun, Sister Moon 1972; East of Elephant Rock 1976; Clash of the Titans 1981; The Shooting Party 1984; Anna Karenina 1985*

Bowler, Norman (1932-) *Submarine X-1 1967; Renegade 1987*
Bowles, Peter (1936-) *Three Hats for Lisa 1965; Blowup 1966; The Charge of the Light Brigade 1968; Laughter in the Dark 1969; Eyewitness 1970; A Day in the Death of Joe Egg 1971; Endless Night 1971; The Offence 1972; The Legend of Hell House 1973; For the Love of Benji 1977; The Steal 1994; One of the Hollywood Ten 2000; In Love and War 2001; Freebird 2007; Loves Kitchen 2010; In the Blood 2014; Lilting 2014*
Bowman, Jessica (1980-) *Road Kill 2001; Derailed 2002*
Bowman, Lee (1914-1979) *I Met Him in Paris 1937; Internes Can't Take Money 1937; Having Wonderful Time 1938; Dancing Co-Ed 1939; Fast and Furious 1939; Love Affair 1939; Miracles for Sale 1939; Third Finger, Left Hand 1940; Buck Privates 1941; Design for Scandal 1941; Kid Glove Killer 1942; Bataan 1943; Cover Girl 1944; Up in Mabel's Room 1944; Tonight and Every Night 1945; Smash Up - the Story of a Woman 1947; My Dream Is Yours 1949; House by the River 1950; Youngblood Hawke 1964*
Bown, John *Master Spy 1964; Dr Who and the Daleks 1965*
Bown, Paul (1957-) *Morons from Outer Space 1985; Butterfly Kiss 1994*
Boxer, John (1909-1982) *Mr Drake's Duck 1950; The Bridge on the River Kwai 1957*
Boxleitner, Bruce (1950-) *The Baltimore Bullet 1980; Tron 1982; Kuffs 1991; The Babe 1992; Danielle Steel's Zoya 1995; Contagion 2001; Killer Flood 2003; Falling in Love with the Girl Next Door 2006; Aces 'n' Eights 2008; Tron Legacy 2010*
Boyar, Sully (1923-2001) *Dog Day Afternoon 1975; Car Wash 1976; The Jazz Singer 1980; Best Seller 1987; The Lemon Sisters 1989*
Boyce, Alan *Permanent Record 1988; Totally F***ed Up 1993*
Boyd (1), Billy (1968-) *The Lord of the Rings: The Fellowship of the Ring 2001; The Lord of the Rings: The Two Towers 2002; The Lord of the Rings: The Return of the King 2003; Master and Commander: the Far Side of the World 2003; On a Clear Day 2004; Seed of Chucky 2004; The Flying Scotsman 2006; Stone of Destiny 2008; Pimp 2010*
Boyd, Cayden *The Adventures of Sharkboy and Lavagirl 2005; Fireflies in the Garden 2007*
Boyd, Darren (1969-) *High Heels and Low Lifes 2001; Imagine Me and You 2005; Magicians 2007*
Boyd, Guy (1942-) *Ticket to Heaven 1981; Streamers 1983; Body Double 1984; Target 1985; Blue Heat 1990; Black Widow Murders 1993*
Boyd, Jan Gan *A Chorus Line 1985; Assassination 1986*
Boyd, Jenna (1993-) *Dickie Roberts: Former Child Star 2003; The Missing 2003; The Sisterhood of the Traveling Pants 2005*
Boyd, Lynda *Harvey 1996; Final Destination 2 2002*
Boyd, Stephen (1928-1977) *An Alligator Named Daisy 1955; The Man Who Never Was 1955; Les Bijoutiers du Clair de Lune 1957; Seven Thunders 1957; Seven Waves Away 1957; The Bravados 1958; Ben-Hur 1959; The Best of Everything 1959; Woman Obsessed 1959; The Inspector 1962; Jumbo 1962; Imperial Venus 1963; The Fall of the Roman Empire 1964; The Third Secret 1964; The Bible... in the Beginning 1966; Fantastic Voyage 1966; The Oscar 1966; The Poppy Is Also a Flower 1966; Shalako 1968; Slaves 1969; Kill! 1972; The Squeeze 1977*
Boyd (1), William aka **Boyd, Bill** (1898-1972) *The Road to Yesterday 1925; Two Arabian Knights 1927; High Voltage 1929; The Leatherneck 1929; City Streets 1931; The Painted Desert 1931; Lucky Devils 1933; The Devil's Playground 1946; Fool's Gold 1946; The Dead Don't Dream 1948; Silent Conflict 1948*
Boyd, William "Stage" (1889-1935) *The Wiser Sex 1932; Laughing at Life 1933*
Boyega, John (1992-) *Attack the Block 2010; Half of a Yellow Sun 2013; Star Wars Episode VII: the Force Awakens 2015; Star Wars Episode VIII 2017*
Boyer, Charles (1897-1978) *The Man from Yesterday 1932; Red-Headed Woman 1932; Caravan 1934; Break of Hearts 1935; Private Worlds 1935; The Garden of Allah 1936; Mayerling 1936; Conquest 1937; History Is Made at*

Night 1937; Tovarich 1937; Algiers 1938; Love Affair 1939; When Tomorrow Comes 1939; All This, and Heaven Too 1940; Appointment for Love 1941; Back Street 1941; Hold Back the Dawn 1941; Tales of Manhattan 1942; The Constant Nymph 1943; Flesh and Fantasy 1943; Gaslight 1944; Together Again 1944; Confidential Agent 1945; La Bataille du Rail 1946; Cluny Brown 1946; Arch of Triumph 1948; The 13th Letter 1950; The First Legion 1951; The Happy Time 1952; Madame de... 1953; Thunder in the East 1953; The Cobweb 1955; Lucky to Be a Woman 1955; Une Parisienne 1957; The Buccaneer 1958; Fanny 1961; The Four Horsemen of the Apocalypse 1962; Love Is a Ball 1963; How to Steal a Million 1966; Is Paris Burning? 1966; Barefoot in the Park 1967; Casino Royale 1967; The April Fools 1969; The Madwoman of Chaillot 1969; Lost Horizon 1973; Stavisky 1974; A Matter of Time 1976*
Boyer, Myriam (1948-) *Jonah Who Will Be 25 in the Year 2000 1976; Golden Eighties 1986*
Boyle, Lara Flynn (1971-) *Poltergeist III 1988; How I Got Into College 1989; May Wine 1990; The Rookie 1990; Mobsters 1991; Equinox 1992; Red Rock West 1992; Wayne's World 1992; The Temp 1993; Baby's Day Out 1994; The Road to Wellville 1994; Threesome 1994; Afterglow 1997; Happiness 1998; Since You've Been Gone 1998; Susan's Plan 1998; Men in Black 2 2002; Land of the Blind 2006*
Boyle, Liam *Awaydays 2009; Powder 2010; Truth or Dare 2011*
Boyle, Peter (1935-2006) *Joe 1970; Kid Blue 1971; TR Baskin 1971; The Candidate 1972; The Friends of Eddie Coyle 1973; Ghost in the Noonday Sun 1973; Slither 1973; Steelyard Blues 1973; Young Frankenstein 1974; Swashbuckler 1976; Taxi Driver 1976; The Brink's Job 1978; FIST 1978; Beyond the Poseidon Adventure 1979; Hardcore 1979; In God We Trust 1980; Where the Buffalo Roam 1980; Outland 1981; Hammett 1982; Yellowbeard 1983; Johnny Dangerously 1984; Turk 182! 1985; Surrender 1987; Walker 1987; Red Heat 1988; Cannonball Fever 1989; The Dream Team 1989; Kickboxer 2: the Road Back 1990; Men of Respect 1990; Solar Crisis 1990; Killer 1994; The Shadow 1994; Born to Be Wild 1995; While You Were Sleeping 1995; That Darn Cat 1997; Doctor Dolittle 1998; Monster's Ball 2001; The Cat Returns 2002; Scooby-Doo 2: Monsters Unleashed 2004*
Bozonnet, Marcel (1944-) *Right Bank, Left Bank 1984; Jeanne la Pucelle 1994*
Bozzuffi, Marcel (1929-1988) *Tintin and the Mystery of the Golden Fleece 1961; Le Deuxième Souffle 1966; The French Connection 1971; Images 1972; The Valdez Horses 1973; Caravan to Vaccares 1974; The Marseille Contract 1974; Illustrious Corpses 1976; La Cage aux Folles II 1980; Identification of a Woman 1982*
Bracco, Elizabeth *Mystery Train 1989; Jumpin' at the Boneyard 1991; Trees Lounge 1996*
Bracco, Lorraine (1954-) *Someone to Watch over Me 1987; The Dream Team 1989; Sea of Love 1989; Sing 1989; GoodFellas 1990; Switch 1991; Talent for the Game 1991; Medicine Man 1992; Radio Flyer 1992; Traces of Red 1992; Even Cowgirls Get the Blues 1993; Being Human 1994; Getting Gotti 1994; The Basketball Diaries 1995; Custody of the Heart 2000; Ladies' Room 2000; Riding in Cars with Boys 2001; We Are Together 2006*
Bracey, Luke *The Best of Me 2014; The November Man 2014; Point Break 2015*
Bracey, Sidney aka **Bracy, Sidney** (1877-1942) *The Black Bird 1926; The Cameraman 1928; Queen Kelly 1928*
Bracken, Eddie (1920-2002) *Too Many Girls 1940; The Fleet's In 1942; Star Spangled Rhythm 1942; Young and Willing 1942; Happy Go Lucky 1943; The Miracle of Morgan's Creek 1943; Hail the Conquering Hero 1944; Bring On the Girls 1945; Out of This World 1945; Summer Stock 1950; Two Tickets to Broadway 1951; We're Not Married 1952; National Lampoon's Vacation 1983; Arthur Miller's The American Clock 1993; Rookie of the Year 1993*
Bradbury, Kitty (1875-1945) *Our Hospitality 1923; The Pilgrim 1923*
Braddell, Maurice (1900-1990) *Things to Come 1936; Flesh 1968; Women in Revolt 1971*
Bradecki, Tadeusz (1955-) *Camera Buff 1979; The Constant Factor 1980*

Braden, Bernard (1916-1993) *Love in Pawn 1953; Jet Storm 1959; The Day the Earth Caught Fire 1961; Two and Two Make Six 1961*
Bradford, Jesse (1979-) *The Boy Who Cried Bitch 1991; King of the Hill 1993; Far from Home: the Adventures of Yellow Dog 1994; Hackers 1995; William Shakespeare's Romeo + Juliet 1996; A Soldier's Daughter Never Cries 1998; Cherry Falls 1999; Bring It On 2000; Clockstoppers 2002; Swimfan 2002; Happy Endings 2005; Flags of Our Fathers 2006*
Bradford, Marshall (1885-1971) *Hellgate 1952; I Was a Teenage Frankenstein 1957*
Bradford, Richard (1937-) *Goin' South 1978; Hammett 1982; Badge of the Assassin 1985; The Legend of Billie Jean 1985; The Mean Season 1985; The Trip to Bountiful 1985; Resting Place 1986; The Untouchables 1987; Little Nikita 1988; The Milagro Beanfield War 1988; Permanent Record 1988; Sunset 1988; Internal Affairs 1990; Ambition 1991; Cold Heaven 1992; Dr Giggles 1992; Just the Ticket 1998; The Lost City 2005*
Bradin, Jean (1899-1969) *Champagne 1928; Moulin Rouge 1928*
Bradley, Cathleen *About Adam 2000; Silent Grace 2001*
Bradley, Charlotte *About Adam 2000; The Boys & Girl from County Clare 2003*
Bradley (2), David (1942-) *Left Luggage 1997; Tom's Midnight Garden 1998; The King Is Alive 2000; Gabriel & Me 2001; Harry Potter and the Philosopher's Stone 2001; The Daisy Chain 2008; I Know You Know 2008; Harry Brown 2009; Another Year 2010*
Bradley (3), David aka **Bradley, Dai** (1955-) *Kes 1969; Malachi's Cove 1973; Absolution 1978; Hummingbird 2013*
Bradley, Doug (1955-) *Hellraiser 1987; Hellbound: Hellraiser II 1988; Hellraiser III: Hell on Earth 1992; Shepherd on the Rock 1995; Hellraiser: Bloodline 1996; The Cottage 2008*
Bradley, Grace (1913-2010) *The Cat's Paw 1934; Old Man Rhythm 1935; Anything Goes 1936; You're in the Army Now 1936; Wake Up and Live 1937*
Bradley, Leslie (1907-1974) *Play Up the Band 1935; Time Flies 1944; Waterloo Road 1944; Just William's Luck 1947; No Orchids for Miss Blandish 1948; A Case for PC 49 1950; The Crimson Pirate 1952; The Iron Glove 1954; Kiss of Fire 1955; Lady Godiva 1955; Attack of the Crab Monsters 1957; Teenage Caveman 1958; The Sad Horse 1959*
Bradley, Therese *Young Adam 2003; Half Light 2006; Outcast 2010*
Bradna, Olympe (1920-2012) *Souls at Sea 1937; South of Pago Pago 1940*
Bradshaw, Carl *The Harder They Come 1972; The Lunatic 1992; Third World Cop 1999; One Love 2003*
Bradshaw, Cathryn *Bert Rigby, You're a Fool 1989; The Mother 2003*
Bradshaw, Terry (1948-) *The Cannonball Run 1981; Failure to Launch 2006*
Brady, Alice (1892-1972) *Broadway to Hollywood 1933; When Ladies Meet 1933; The Gay Divorce 1934; Gold Diggers of 1935 1935; Let 'Em Have It 1935; Go West, Young Man 1936; My Man Godfrey 1936; In Old Chicago 1937; One Hundred Men and a Girl 1937; Three Smart Girls 1937; Joy of Living 1938; Young Mr Lincoln 1939; Zenobia 1939*
Brady, Moya *Life Is Sweet 1990; Middleton's Changeling 1997*
Brady, Orla (1961-) *Silent Grace 2001; The Price of Desire 2015*
Brady, Pat (1914-1972) *Bells of Coronado 1950; Twilight in the Sierras 1950*
Brady, Scott (1924-1985) *He Walked by Night 1948; The Gal Who Took the West 1949; Port of New York 1949; Undertow 1949; I Was a Shoplifter 1950; Kansas Raiders 1950; Undercover Girl 1950; The Model and the Marriage Broker 1951; Bloodhounds of Broadway 1952; Untamed Frontier 1952; Johnny Guitar 1954; Gentlemen Marry Brunettes 1955; Mohawk 1956; The Restless Breed 1957; John Goldfarb, Please Come Home 1964; Castle of Evil 1966; Arizona Bushwhackers 1968; Dollars 1971; The China Syndrome 1979*
Brady, Wayne (1972-) *Geppetto 2000; Clifford's Really Big Movie 2004; Stuart Little 3: Call of the Wild 2005; The Adventures of Brer Rabbit 2006*
Braeden, Eric (1942-) *Colossus: the Forbin Project 1969; Escape from the Planet of the Apes 1971; The*

Ambulance 1990; Meet the Deedles 1998
Braff, Zach (1975-) *The Broken Hearts Club: a Romantic Comedy 2000; Garden State 2003; Chicken Little 2005; The Last Kiss 2006; Oz the Great and Powerful 2013; Wish I Was Here 2014*
Braga, Alice (1983-) *Lower City 2005; I Am Legend 2007; Redbelt 2007; Blindness 2008; Predators 2010; Repo Men 2010; The Rite 2011; Elysium 2013; The Burning 2014*
Braga, Sonia (1950-) *Gabriela 1983; Kiss of the Spider Woman 1985; The Milagro Beanfield War 1988; Moon over Parador 1988; The Rookie 1990; The Burning Season 1994; Two Deaths 1994; From Dusk till Dawn 3: the Hangman's Daughter 2000; Angel Eyes 2001; Empire 2002*
Braithwaite, Lilian (1870-1946) *Downhill 1927; A Man about the House 1947*
Brake, Richard (1964-) *Death Machine 1994; Doom 2005; Hannibal Rising 2006; Outpost 2007; The Numbers Station 2013; Set Fire to the Stars 2014*
Brambell, Wilfrid aka **Bramble, Wilfred** (1912-1985) *Another Shore 1948; The Boys 1961; Crooks in Cloisters 1963; The Small World of Sammy Lee 1963; A Hard Day's Night 1964; Where the Bullets Fly 1966; Witchfinder General 1968; Some Will, Some Won't 1969; Steptoe and Son 1972; Holiday on the Buses 1973; Steptoe and Son Ride Again 1973; The Terence Davies Trilogy 1984*
Bramly, Virgile *Manderlay 2005; Four Last Songs 2007*
Branagh, Kenneth (1960-) *High Season 1987; A Month in the Country 1987; Henry V 1989; Dead Again 1991; Peter's Friends 1992; Much Ado about Nothing 1993; Swing Kids 1993; Mary Shelley's Frankenstein 1994; Anne Frank Remembered 1995; Othello 1995; Hamlet 1996; Looking for Richard 1996; The Gingerbread Man 1997; Celebrity 1998; The Proposition 1998; The Theory of Flight 1998; Universal Horror 1998; Love's Labour's Lost 1999; Wild Wild West 1999; The Road to El Dorado 2000; Conspiracy 2001; Harry Potter and the Chamber of Secrets 2002; Rabbit-Proof Fence 2002; Five Children and It 2004; Valkyrie 2008; The Boat That Rocked 2009; My Week with Marilyn 2011; Jack Ryan: Shadow Recruit 2013; Dunkirk 2017*
Brancato, Lillo aka **Brancato Jr, Lillo** *A Bronx Tale 1993; Renaissance Man 1994*
Branch, Sarah (1938-2007) *Sands of the Desert 1960; Sword of Sherwood Forest 1960*
Brand, Neville (1920-1992) *DOA 1949; Only the Valiant 1950; The Mob 1951; Kansas City Confidential 1952; Kansas City Confidential 1952; Gun Fury 1953; Stalag 17 1953; Riot in Cell Block 11 1954; The Prodigal 1955; Love Me Tender 1956; Mohawk 1956; The Lonely Man 1957; The Tin Star 1957; Cry Terror 1958; The Adventures of Huckleberry Finn 1960; The Last Sunset 1961; Birdman of Alcatraz 1962; Hero's Island 1962; That Darn Cat! 1965; Three Guns for Texas 1968; Backtrack 1969; Cahill, United States Marshal 1973; The Deadly Trackers 1973; Scalawag 1973; Eaten Alive 1976; The Ninth Configuration 1979; Without Warning 1980*
Brand, Russell (1975-) *St Trinian's 2007; Bedtime Stories 2008; Forgetting Sarah Marshall 2008; Despicable Me 2010; Get Him to the Greek 2010; The Tempest 2010; Arthur 2011; Hop 2011; Rock of Ages 2012; Despicable Me 2 2013; Brand: a Second Coming 2015; The Emperor's New Clothes 2015; Bo66y 2016; Trolls 2016*
Brandauer, Klaus Maria (1944-) *Mephisto 1981; Never Say Never Again 1983; Colonel Redl 1984; The Lightship 1985; Out of Africa 1985; Streets of Gold 1986; Burning Secret 1988; Hanussen 1988; Seven Minutes 1989; The Russia House 1990; Becoming Colette 1991; White Fang 1991; Introducing Dorothy Dandridge 1999; Druids 2001; Tetro 2009*
Brandenburg, Larry (1948-) *The Santa Clause 1994; What the #$*! Do We Know!? 2004*
Brandis, Jonathan (1976-2003) *Stepfather II 1989; The NeverEnding Story II: the Next Chapter 1991; Ladybugs 1992; Fall into Darkness 1996; Outside Providence 1999*
Brando, Jocelyn (1919-2005) *The Big Heat 1953; Ten Wanted Men 1955;*

Nightfall 1956; The Ugly American 1963; Bus Riley's Back in Town 1965
Brando, Luisina Miss Mary 1986; We Don't Want to Talk about It 1993
Brando, Marlon (1924-2004) The Men 1950; A Streetcar Named Desire 1951; Viva Zapata! 1952; Julius Caesar 1953; The Wild One 1953; Desiree 1954; On the Waterfront 1954; Guys and Dolls 1955; The Teahouse of the August Moon 1956; Sayonara 1957; The Young Lions 1958; The Fugitive Kind 1960; One-Eyed Jacks 1961; Mutiny on the Bounty 1962; The Ugly American 1963; Bedtime Story 1964; Morituri 1965; The Appaloosa 1966; The Chase 1966; A Countess from Hong Kong 1967; Reflections in a Golden Eye 1967; Candy 1968; The Night of the Following Day 1968; Burn! 1970; The Godfather 1972; Last Tango in Paris 1972; The Nightcomers 1972; The Missouri Breaks 1976; Superman 1978; Apocalypse Now 1979; The Formula '980; A Dry White Season 1989; The Freshman 1990; Christopher Columbus: the Discovery 1992; Don Juan DeMarco 1995; The Island of Dr Moreau 1996; Free Money 1998; The Score 2001; Superman Returns 2006; Listen to Me Marlon 2015
Brandon, Clark (1958-) My Tutor 1983; Fast Food 1989
Brandon, David All Hands on Deck 1961; State Fair 1962; Stage Fright - Aquarius 1987
Brandon, Henry aka Kleinbach, Henry (1912-1990) Babes in Toyland 1934; Cattle Drive 1951; Tarzan and the She-Devil 1953; War Arrow 1953; Vera Cruz 1954; Bandido 1956; Comanche 1956; The Searchers 1956
Brandon, Michael (1945-) Lovers and Other Strangers 1970; Jennifer on My Mind 1971; FM 1977; A Change of Seasons 1980; Déjà Vu 1997; Contagion 2000
Brandt, Carolyn The Incredibly Strange Creatures Who Stopped Living and Became Mixed-up Zombies 1963; Rat Pfink a Boo Boo 1965
Brandy aka Norwood, Brandy (1979-) Rodgers & Hammerstein's Cinderella 1997; I Still Know What You Did Last Summer 1998; Double Platinum 1999; Osmosis Jones 2001
Branice, Ligia Goto, l'île d'Amour 1968; Blanche 1971
Brannagh, Brigid Acceptance 2009; Next Stop Murder 2010
Brannigan, Paul The Angels' Share 2012; Under the Skin 2013
Brännström, Brasse (1945-) A Lover and His Lass 1975; Happy We 1983
Branson, Richard (1950-) Around the World in 80 Days 2004; Rabbit Fever 2005; Casino Royale 2006; Superman Returns 2006; We Are Many 2014
Brantford, Mickey (1912-1984) The Phantom Light 1934; The Last Journey 1936
Brantley, Betsy (1955-) Five Days One Summer 1982; Another Country 1984; Dark Angel 1989; Havana 1990; Shepherd on the Rock 1995; Schizopolis 1996; Washington Square 1997; Rogue Trader 1998
Braschi, Nicoletta (1960-) Down by Law 1986; Mystery Train 1989; Johnny Stecchino 1991; Life Is Beautiful 1997; Pinocchio 2002
Brasno, George (1911-1982) The Mighty Barnum 1934; Charlie Chan at the Circus 1936
Brass, Steffan (1992-) Dawg 2001; Bundy 2002
Brasselle, Keefe (1923-1981) It's a Big Country 1951; A Place in the Sun 1951; Skirts Ahoy! 1952; The Eddie Cantor Story 1953; Bring Your Smile Along 1955
Brasseur, Claude (1936-) The Vanishing Corporal 1962; Banana Peel 1964; Bande à Part 1964; Une Belle Fille comme Moi 1973; Someone Is Bleeding 1974; Pardon Mon Affaire 1976; Une Histoire Simple 1978; Detective 1985; Descent into Hell 1986; Dandin 1988; The Edge of the Horizon 1993; Orchestra Seats 2005; Les Petites Vacances 2006
Brasseur, Pierre (1903-1972) Caravan 1934; Le Quai des Brumes 1938; Les Enfants du Paradis 1945; Les Portes de la Nuit 1946; Les Mains Sales 1951; Napoléon 1955; Gates of Paris 1957; Eyes without a Face 1959; La Vie de Château 1965; King of Hearts 1966; Goto, l'île d'Amour 1968; Les Mariés de l'An Deux 1971
Brassington, Christian Mrs Ratcliffe's Revolution 2007; Easy Virtue 2008
Bratt, Benjamin (1963-) Chains of Gold 1989; Bright Angel 1990; One Good Cop 1991; Blood In Blood Out 1992; Demolition Man 1993; The River Wild 1994; The Last Producer 2000;

Miss Congeniality 2000; The Next Best Thing 2000; Red Planet 2000; After the Storm 2001; Piñero 2001; Catwoman 2004; The Woodsman 2004; The Great Raid 2005; Thumbsucker 2005; Love in the Time of Cholera 2007; Cloudy with a Chance of Meatballs 2009; Trucker 2009; Cloudy with a Chance of Meatballs 2 2013; Despicable Me 2 2013; Snitch 2013; The Infiltrator 2016; Ride Along 2 2016
Braugher, André aka Braugher, Andre (1962-) Glory 1989; The Court-Martial of Jackie Robinson 1990; The Tuskegee Airmen 1995; Get on the Bus 1996; City of Angels 1998; A Better Way to Die 2000; Duets 2000; Frequency 2000; Standing in the Shadows of Motown 2002; Poseidon 2006; The Mist 2007; Salt 2010; The Baytown Outlaws 2012
Braun, Judith (1930-) Horizons West 1952; Red Ball Express 1952
Braun, Nicholas Poltergeist 2015; The Stanford Prison Experiment 2015; How to Be Single 2016
Brauss, Arthur Dollars 1971; The Goalkeeper's Fear of the Penalty Kick 1971; Knight Moves 1992
Bray, Robert (1917-1983) Return of the Bad Men 1948; Bus Stop 1956; The Traitor 1957
Brazeau, Jay (1953-) We're No Angels 1989; Slam Dunk Ernest 1995; Kissed 1996; Air Bud 1997; Turbulence II: Fear of Flying 2000
Brazzi, Rossano (1916-1994) We the Living 1942; Little Women 1949; The Barefoot Contessa 1954; Three Coins in the Fountain 1954; Angela 1955; Summertime 1955; Loser Takes All 1956; Interlude 1957; Legend of the Lost 1957; The Story of Esther Costello 1957; A Certain Smile 1958; South Pacific 1958; Count Your Blessings 1959; Light in the Piazza 1961; Rome Adventure 1962; The Battle of the Villa Fiorita 1965; The Bobo 1967; Woman Times Seven 1967; The Italian Job 1969; The Adventurers 1970; Mr Kingstreet's War 1970; The Great Waltz 1972; Omen III: the Final Conflict 1980; Fear City 1984
Breakston, George (1920-1973) No Greater Glory 1934; The Return of Peter Grimm 1935
Brealey, Louise Delicious 2013; Containment 2015
Brecher, Egon (1880-1946) The Black Cat 1934; They Dare Not Love 1941; So Dark the Night 1946
Breck, Jonathan Jeepers Creepers 2001; Jeepers Creepers 2 2003
Breck, Kathleen West 11 1963; The Frozen Dead 1966
Breck, Peter (1929-2012) Shock Corridor 1963; The Glory Guys 1965; Benji 1974; Highway 61 1992
Bredice, Leticia Nine Queens 2000; The City of No Limits 2002; Tetro 2009
Bredin, Patricia Left, Right and Centre 1959; The Treasure of Monte Cristo 1960
Breen, Patrick (1960-) For Love or Money 1993; Sweet Nothing 1995; Galaxy Quest 1999; Just a Kiss 2002; Stark Raving Mad 2002; Space Chimps 2008
Breese, Edmund (1871-1936) The Hatchet Man 1932; Madame Butterfly 1932; Duck Soup 1933
Brel, Jacques (1929-1978) Uncle Benjamin 1969; A Pain in the A...! 1973
Bremer, Lucille (1917-1996) Meet Me in St Louis 1944; Yolanda and the Thief 1945; Till the Clouds Roll By 1946; Ruthless 1948
Bremner, Ewen (1971-) Heavenly Pursuits 1986; Conquest of the South Pole 1989; As You Like It 1992; Naked 1993; Trainspotting 1995; The Life of Stuff 1997; The Acid House 1998; Mojo 1998; julien donkey-boy 1999; Snatch 2000; Black Hawk Down 2001; The Reckoning 2001; 16 Years of Alcohol 2003; Welcome to the Jungle 2003; AVP: Alien vs Predator 2004; Match Point 2005; Hallam Foe 2006; Death at a Funeral 2007; Faintheart 2008; Fool's Gold 2008; Perfect Sense 2011; T2: Trainspotting 2 2016
Brendel, El (1890-1964) Wings 1927; Sunny Side Up 1929; The Big Trail 1930; Delicious 1931; The Beautiful Blonde from Bashful Bend 1949
Brendemühl, Alex (1972-) The Hours of the Day 2003; Wakolda 2013
Brendon, Nicholas My Neighbor's Secret 2009; Coherence 2013
Brennan, Brid Anne Devlin 1984; Trojan Eddie 1996; Dancing at Lughnasa 1998; Felicia's Journey 1999
Brennan, Eileen (1932-2013) The Last Picture Show 1971; The Blue Knight 1973; Scarecrow 1973; The Sting 1973;

Daisy Miller 1974; At Long Last Love 1975; Hustle 1975; The Night that Panicked America 1975; Murder by Death 1976; FM 1977; The Cheap Detective 1978; Private Benjamin 1980; Clue 1985; Babes in Toyland 1986; The New Adventures of Pippi Longstocking 1988; Sticky Fingers 1988; Stella 1990; Texasville 1990; White Palace 1990; The Lies Boys Tell 1994; Freaky Friday 1995; Reckless 1995; If These Walls Could Talk 1996; Changing Habits 1997; Jeepers Creepers 2001
Brennan, Michael (1912-1982) Blackout 1950; Morning Departure 1950; They Were Not Divided 1950; It's a Grand Life 1953; Not Wanted on Voyage 1957
Brennan, Walter (1894-1974) The King of Jazz 1930; Law and Order 1932; Barbary Coast 1935; Man on the Flying Trapeze 1935; The Wedding Night 1935; Banjo on My Knee 1936; Come and Get It 1936; Fury 1936; The Adventures of Tom Sawyer 1938; The Buccaneer 1938; The Cowboy and the Lady 1938; Kentucky 1938; The Texans 1938; Stanley and Livingstone 1939; The Story of Vernon and Irene Castle 1939; They Shall Have Music 1939; Maryland 1940; Northwest Passage 1940; The Westerner 1940; Meet John Doe 1941; Nice Girl? 1941; Sergeant York 1941; Swamp Water 1941; The Pride of the Yankees 1942; Stand by for Action 1942; Hangmen Also Die! 1943; The North Star 1943; Slightly Dangerous 1943; Home in Indiana 1944; The Princess and the Pirate 1944; To Have and Have Not 1944; Dakota 1945; Centennial Summer 1946; Driftwood 1946; My Darling Clementine 1946; Nobody Lives Forever 1946; A Stolen Life 1946; Blood on the Moon 1948; Red River 1948; Task Force 1949; A Ticket to Tomahawk 1950; Along the Great Divide 1951; Best of the Badmen 1951; Drums across the River 1954; The Far Country 1954; At Gunpoint 1955; Bad Day at Black Rock 1955; Come Next Spring 1956; The Proud Ones 1956; Tammy and the Bachelor 1957; Rio Bravo 1958; How the West Was Won 1962; Those Calloways 1964; The Oscar 1966; The Gnome-Mobile 1967; Who's Minding the Mint? 1967; The One and Only, Genuine, Original Family Band 1968; Support Your Local Sheriff! 1969
Brenneman, Amy (1964-) Bye Bye Love 1995; Heat 1995; Daylight 1996; Fear 1996; Your Friends & Neighbors 1998; The Suburbans 1999; Things You Can Tell Just by Looking at Her 2000; 88 Minutes 2007; The Jane Austen Book Club 2007; The Face of Love 2013; Words and Pictures 2013
Brenner, Dori (1946-2000) Summer Wishes, Winter Dreams 1973; Next Stop, Greenwich Village 1976; Altered States 1980; Infinity 1996
Brent, Eve aka Brent Ashe, Eve (1929-2011) Tarzan and the Trappers 1958; Tarzan's Fight for Life 1958; Going Berserk 1983; Garfield 2004
Brent, Evelyn (1899-1975) Underworld 1927; Beau Sabreur 1928; The Dragnet 1928; The Last Command 1928; Broadway 1929; High Pressure 1932; The Law West of Tombstone 1938; The Seventh Victim 1943
Brent, George (1899-1979) The Purchase Price 1932; The Rich Are Always with Us 1932; So Big 1932; Baby Face 1933; Female 1933; 42nd Street 1933; The Painted Veil 1934; Stamboul Quest 1934; Front Page Woman 1935; In Person 1935; Special Agent 1935; God's Country and the Woman 1937; Gold Is Where You Find It 1938; Jezebel 1938; Racket Busters 1938; Dark Victory 1939; The Old Maid 1939; The Rains Came 1939; The Fighting 69th 1940; 'Til We Meet Again 1940; The Great Lie 1941; They Dare Not Love 1941; The Gay Sisters 1942; In This Our Life 1942; Experiment Perilous 1944; The Affairs of Susan 1945; Tomorrow Is Forever 1945; Lover Come Back 1946; My Reputation 1946; The Spiral Staircase 1946; Christmas Eve 1947; Out of the Blue 1947; Slave Girl 1947; Bride for Sale 1949; Red Canyon 1949; Born Again 1978
Brent, Romney (1902-1976) Dinner at the Ritz 1937; Head over Heels in Love 1937; Under the Red Robe 1937; Let George Do It 1940; Adventures of Don Juan 1948; Screaming Mimi 1958
Breon, Edmund aka Breon, Edmond (1882-1951) Keep Fit 1937; Crackerjack 1938; Casanova Brown 1944; The Woman in the Window 1945; Dressed to Kill 1946
Breslin, Abigail (1996-) Signs 2002; Keane 2004; Raising Helen 2004; Family Plan 2005; Little Miss Sunshine

2006; No Reservations 2007; Definitely, Maybe 2008; Nim's Island 2008; My Sister's Keeper 2009; Zombieland 2009; Rango 2011; August: Osage County 2013; The Call 2013; Ender's Game 2013; Haunter 2013; Final Girl 2015; Maggie 2015
Breslin, Patricia aka Breslin, Pat (1931-2011) Go, Man, Go! 1953; Andy Hardy Comes Home 1958; Homicidal 1961; I Saw What You Did 1965
Breslin, Spencer (1992-) Disney's The Kid 2000; The Santa Clause 2 2002; Dr Seuss' The Cat in the Hat 2003; Raising Helen 2004; The Santa Clause 3: the Escape Clause 2006; The Shaggy Dog 2006; Zoom 2006; The Happening 2008
Bressart, Felix (1890-1949) Ninotchka 1939; Swanee River 1939; Bitter Sweet 1940; Comrade X 1940; Escape 1940; The Shop around the Corner 1940; Third Finger, Left Hand 1940; Blossoms in the Dust 1941; Crossroads 1942; To Be or Not to Be 1942; Blonde Fever 1944; Greenwich Village 1944; Without Love 1945
Bresslaw, Bernard (1933-1993) Blood of the Vampire 1958; Too Many Crooks 1958; It's All Happening 1963; Carry On Cowboy 1965; Carry On Screaming 1966; Morgan - a Suitable Case for Treatment 1966; Carry On Follow That Camel 1967; Carry On Doctor 1968; Carry On Up the Khyber 1968; Carry On Camping 1969; Moon Zero Two 1969; Carry On Loving 1970; Carry On Up the Jungle 1970; Carry On at Your Convenience 1971; Up Pompeii 1971; Carry On Abroad 1972; Carry On Matron 1972; Carry On Girls 1973; Carry On Dick 1974; Carry On Behind 1975; One of Our Dinosaurs Is Missing 1975; Jabberwocky 1977; Hawk the Slayer 1980; Krull 1983
Brestoff, Richard Car Wash 1976; The Entity 1981; The Man with Two Brains 1983
Brett, Danielle Jill Rips 2000; Rated X 2000
Brett, Jeremy (1935-1995) The Very Edge 1962; The Wild and the Willing 1962; Girl in the Headlines 1963; My Fair Lady 1964; Mad Dogs and Englishmen 1994
Breuls, Laurence Blackrock 1997; Suburban Mayhem 2006
Brewster, Anna (1986-) Anita & Me 2002; Mrs Henderson Presents 2005
Brewster, Diane (1931-1991) Quantrill's Raiders 1958; Torpedo Run 1958; The Young Philadelphians 1959
Brewster, Jordana (1980-) The Faculty 1998; The Invisible Circus 2000; The Fast and the Furious 2001; Annapolis 2005; The Texas Chainsaw Massacre: the Beginning 2006; Fast & Furious 2009; Fast Five 2011; Fast & Furious 6 2013
Brewster, Paget (1969-) The Specials 2000; Grounded 2006; A Perfect Day 2006
Breznahan, Kevin Alive 1992; Winter's Bone 2010
Brialy, Jean-Claude (1933-2007) Le Beau Serge 1958; Les Cousins 1959; Paris Nous Appartient 1960; Cleo from 5 to 7 1961; Une Femme Est une Femme 1961; Male Hunt 1964; La Ronde 1964; King of Hearts 1966; The Bride Wore Black 1967; Claire's Knee 1970; Le Fantôme de la Liberté 1974; Robert et Robert 1978; Edith et Marcel 1983; La Nuit de Varennes 1983; An Impudent Girl 1985; Inspecteur Lavardin 1986; Le Cop II 1989; Une Femme Française 1994; Portraits Chinois 1996
Brian, David (1914-1993) Beyond the Forest 1949; Flamingo Road 1949; Intruder in the Dust 1949; Breakthrough 1950; The Damned Don't Cry 1950; Fort Worth 1951; Million Dollar Mermaid 1952; Springfield Rifle 1952; This Woman Is Dangerous 1952; Ambush at Tomahawk Gap 1953; Dawn at Socorro 1954; The High and the Mighty 1954; Timberjack 1955; Accused of Murder 1956; The First Travelling Saleslady 1956; Castle of Evil 1966; The Rare Breed 1966; The Destructors 1968; The Girl Who Knew Too Much 1969
Brian, Mary (1906-2002) Beau Geste 1926; The Marriage Playground 1929; The Virginian 1929; The Royal Family of Broadway 1930; The Front Page 1931; Blessed Event 1932; Hard to Handle 1933; Charlie Chan in Paris 1935; Man on the Flying Trapeze 1935; The Amazing Quest of Ernest Bliss 1936; Spendthrift 1936
Briant, Shane (1946-) Demons of the Mind 1971; Captain Kronos: Vampire Hunter 1972; Frankenstein and the Monster from Hell 1973; Lady Chatterley's Lover 1981; Agatha

Christie's Murder Is Easy 1982; Constance 1984; Cassandra 1987; Tunnel Vision 1994
Brice, Fanny (1891-1951) Everybody Sing 1938; Ziegfeld Follies 1944
Bridge, Al aka Bridge, Alan (1891-1957) Law and Order 1936; The Falcon's Alibi 1946
Bridgers, Sean The Woman 2011; Room 2015; The Whole Truth 2016
Bridges, Beau (1941-) The Red Pony 1949; Village of the Giants 1965; The Incident 1967; For Love of Ivy 1968; Gaily, Gaily 1969; Adam's Woman 1970; The Landlord 1970; The Christian Licorice Store 1971; Child's Play 1972; The Man without a Country 1973; One Summer Love 1976; The Other Side of the Mountain 1975; Swashbuckler 1976; Two-Minute Warning 1976; Greased Lightning 1977; The Four Feathers 1978; The 5th Musketeer 1979; Norma Rae 1979; The Runner Stumbles 1979; Silver Dream Racer 1980; Honky Tonk Freeway 1981; Night Crossing 1981; Love Child 1982; Witness for the Prosecution 1982; Heart like a Wheel 1983; The Hotel New Hampshire 1984; The Killing Time 1987; The Wild Pair 1987; The Iron Triangle 1988; Seven Hours to Judgment 1988; The Fabulous Baker Boys 1989; Daddy's Dyin'... Who's Got the Will? 1990; Women and Men: Stories of Seduction 1990; Wildflower 1991; Without Warning: the James Brady Story 1991; The Positively True Adventures of the Alleged Texas Cheerleader-Murdering Mom 1993; Kissinger and Nixon 1995; Rocketman 1997; Inherit the Wind 1999; Songs in Ordinary Time 2000; Evel Knievel 2004; The Ballad of Jack and Rose 2005; The Good German 2006; Max Payne 2008; The Descendants 2011; Eden 2012
Bridges, Chris "Ludacris" aka Ludacris (1977-) 2 Fast 2 Furious 2003; Crash 2004; Hustle & Flow 2005; Gamer 2008; Max Payne 2008; RocknRolla 2008; No Strings Attached 2011
Bridges, Jeff (1949-) The Last Picture Show 1971; Bad Company 1972; Fat City 1972; The Last American Hero 1973; The Lolly-Madonna War 1973; Thunderbolt and Lightfoot 1974; Hearts of the West 1975; Rancho Deluxe 1975; King Kong 1976; Stay Hungry 1976; Somebody Killed Her Husband 1978; The American Success Company 1979; Winter Kills 1979; Heaven's Gate 1980; The Last Unicorn 1980; Cutter's Way 1981; Kiss Me Goodbye 1982; Tron 1982; Against All Odds 1984; Starman 1984; Jagged Edge 1985; 8 Million Ways to Die 1986; The Morning After 1986; Nadine 1987; Tucker: the Man and His Dream 1988; Cold Feet 1989; The Fabulous Baker Boys 1989; See You in the Morning 1989; Texasville 1990; The Fisher King 1991; American Heart 1992; Fearless 1993; The Vanishing 1993; Blown Away 1994; Wild Bill 1995; The Mirror Has Two Faces 1996; White Squall 1996; The Big Lebowski 1997; Arlington Road 1998; The Muse 1999; Simpatico 1999; The Contender 2000; K-PAX 2001; Lost in La Mancha 2002; Masked and Anonymous 2003; Seabiscuit 2003; The Door in the Floor 2004; The Moguls 2005; Tideland 2005; Stick It 2006; Surf's Up 2007; How to Lose Friends & Alienate People 2008; Iron Man 2008; Crazy Heart 2009; The Men Who Stare at Goats 2009; Tron Legacy 2010; True Grit 2010; R.I.P.D. 2013; The Giver 2014; Seventh Son 2014; Hell or High Water 2016
Bridges, Lloyd (1913-1998) They Dare Not Love 1941; Passport to Suez 1943; Sahara 1943; The Master Race 1944; Abilene Town 1945; Miss Susie Slagle's 1945; Strange Confession 1945; A Walk in the Sun 1945; Ramrod 1947; Calamity Jane and Sam Bass 1949; Home of the Brave 1949; Red Canyon 1949; Colt .45 1950; The Sound of Fury 1950; The White Tower 1950; High Noon 1952; Last of the Comanches 1952; Plymouth Adventure 1952; Pride of the Blue Grass 1954; Apache Woman 1955; Wichita 1955; The Rainmaker 1956; The Goddess 1958; Attack on the Iron Coast 1968; Running Wild 1973; Bear Island 1979; The 5th Musketeer 1979; Airplane! 1980; Airplane II: the Sequel 1982; The Wild Pair 1987; Tucker: the Man and His Dream 1988; Cousins 1989; Joe versus the Volcano 1990; Hot Shots! 1991; Honey, I Blew Up the Kid 1992; Hot Shots! Part Deux 1993; Blown Away 1994; Jane Austen's Mafia 1998
Bridges, Spencir Daddy Day Camp 2007; The Christmas Gift 2009

Brie, Alison *The Five-Year Engagement* 2012; *Get Hard* 2015; *Sleeping with Other People* 2015; *How to Be Single* 2016

Briers, Richard (1934-2013) *Bottoms Up* 1959; *The Girl on the Boat* 1962; *The Bargee* 1964; *Fathom* 1967; *Rentadick* 1972; *Watership Down* 1978; *A Chorus of Disapproval* 1988; *Henry V* 1989; *Much Ado about Nothing* 1993; *Mary Shelley's Frankenstein* 1994; *In the Bleak Midwinter* 1995; *Hamlet* 1996; *Love's Labour's Lost* 1999; *Unconditional Love* 2001; *Peter Pan* 2003; *As You Like It* 2006; *Cockneys vs Zombies* 2011

Briggs, Johnny (1935-) *Light Up the Sky* 1960; *The Wind of Change* 1961; *The Last Escape* 1970

Briggs, Matt (1883-1962) *The Dancing Masters* 1943; *The Meanest Man in the World* 1943; *The Ox-Bow Incident* 1943

Bright, Cameron (1993-) *Godsend* 2003; *Birth* 2004; *Running Scared* 2005; *Thank You for Smoking* 2005; *Ultraviolet* 2005; *Christmas in Wonderland* 2007

Bright, Richard (1937-2006) *The Panic in Needle Park* 1971; *The Getaway* 1972; *Marathon Man* 1976; *On the Yard* 1978; *Two of a Kind* 1983; *The Ambulance* 1990; *Who's the Man?* 1993; *Sweet Nothing* 1995

Brightwell, Paul *The Innocent Sleep* 1995; *Sliding Doors* 1997

Brill, Patti (1923-1963) *Girl Rush* 1944; *Music in Manhattan* 1944

Brimble, Nick (1944-) *Frankenstein Unbound* 1990; *Robin Hood: Prince of Thieves* 1991; *Loch Ness* 1995; *Gone Fishin'* 1995; *7 Days to Live* 2000; *Out of Reach* 2004

Brimley, Wilford aka **Brimley, A Wilford** (1934-) *The China Syndrome* 1979; *The Electric Horseman* 1979; *Death Valley* 1982; *Tender Mercies* 1982; *The Thing* 1982; *Tough Enough* 1982; *High Road to China* 1983; *10 to Midnight* 1983; *Country* 1984; *Harry and Son* 1984; *The Hotel New Hampshire* 1984; *The Natural* 1984; *The Stone Boy* 1984; *Cocoon* 1985; *Remo - Unarmed and Dangerous* 1985; *Act of Vengeance* 1986; *Cocoon: the Return* 1988; *Gore Vidal's Billy the Kid* 1989; *The Firm* 1993; *Hard Target* 1993; *The Good Old Boys* 1995; *Last of the Dogmen* 1995; *My Fellow Americans* 1996

Brine, Adrian (1936-) *The Girl with Red Hair* 1981; *Vincent and Theo* 1990

Brinegar, Paul (1917-1995) *Cattle Empire* 1958; *How to Make a Monster* 1958

Brinkley, John *The Mobster* 1958; *A Bucket of Blood* 1959

Brinkley, Ritch *Cabin Boy* 1994; *Breakdown* 1997

Brisbane, Syd *Bad Boy Bubby* 1993; *Dead Letter Office* 1998

Briscoe, Brent (1961-) *Another Day in Paradise* 1998; *A Simple Plan* 1998; *Mulholland Drive* 2001

Brissac, Virginia (1894-1979) *Dark Victory* 1939; *The Ghost Breakers* 1940; *The Scarlet Clue* 1945; *About Mrs Leslie* 1954

Brisson, Carl (1893-1958) *The Ring* 1927; *The Manxman* 1929

Britt, May (1936-) *The Hunters* 1958; *The Young Lions* 1958; *The Blue Angel* 1959

Britton, Barbara (1919-1980) *Young and Willing* 1942; *So Proudly We Hail* 1943; *Till We Meet Again* 1944; *Captain Kidd* 1945; *The Virginian* 1946; *I Shot Jesse James* 1949; *Champagne for Caesar* 1950; *Bwana Devil* 1952; *The Raiders* 1952; *Ain't Misbehavin'* 1955; *The Spoilers* 1955

Britton, Connie (1968-) *No Looking Back* 1998; *Friday Night Lights* 2004

Britton, Pamela aka **Britton, Pam** (1923-1974) *Anchors Aweigh* 1945; *DOA* 1949; *Watch the Birdie* 1950

Britton, Tony (1924-) *The Birthday Present* 1957; *Behind the Mask* 1958; *Operation Amsterdam* 1958; *The Heart of a Man* 1959; *The Rough and the Smooth* 1959; *Suspect* 1960; *The Break* 1962; *Dr Syn, Alias the Scarecrow* 1963; *There's a Girl in My Soup* 1970; *Sunday, Bloody Sunday* 1971; *The Day of the Jackal* 1973; *Night Watch* 1973; *The People That Time Forgot* 1977; *Agatha* 1978

Bro, Nicolas (1972-) *The Green Butchers* 2003; *Reconstruction* 2003; *King's Game* 2004; *Allegro* 2005

Broadbent, Jim (1949-) *Brazil* 1985; *Running out of Luck* 1985; *The Good Father* 1986; *Vroom* 1988; *Life Is Sweet* 1990; *Enchanted April* 1991; *The Crying Game* 1992; *Wide Eyed and Legless* 1993; *Widows' Peak* 1993; *Bullets over Broadway* 1994; *Princess Caraboo* 1994; *Richard III* 1995; *Rough Magic* 1995; *The Secret Agent* 1996; *Smilla's Feeling for Snow* 1996; *The Borrowers* 1997; *The Avengers* 1998; *Little Voice* 1998; *Topsy-Turvy* 1999; *Bridget Jones's Diary* 2001; *Iris* 2001; *Moulin Rouge!* 2001; *Gangs of New York* 2002; *Nicholas Nickleby* 2002; *Bright Young Things* 2003; *Tooth* 2003; *Around the World in 80 Days* 2004; *Bridget Jones: the Edge of Reason* 2004; *Vanity Fair* 2004; *The Chronicles of Narnia: The Lion, the Witch and the Wardrobe* 2005; *The Magic Roundabout* 2005; *Robots* 2005; *Valiant* 2005; *Free Jimmy* 2006; *And When Did You Last See Your Father?* 2007; *Hot Fuzz* 2007; *Inkheart* 2007; *Indiana Jones and the Kingdom of the Crystal Skull* 2008; *The Young Victoria* 2008; *The Damned United* 2009; *Harry Potter and the Half-Blood Prince* 2009; *Perrier's Bounty* 2009; *Animals United* 2010; *Another Year* 2010; *Arthur Christmas* 2011; *The Iron Lady* 2011; *Cloud Atlas* 2012; *Closed Circuit* 2013; *Filth* 2013; *Postman Pat: the Movie* 2013; *Le Week-end* 2013; *Big Game* 2014; *Get Santa* 2014; *Paddington* 2014; *Brooklyn* 2015; *The Lady in the Van* 2015; *Bridget Jones's Baby* 2016; *Eddie the Eagle* 2016

Broadhurst, Kent (1940-) *Stars and Bars* 1988; *The Dark Half* 1991

Brocco, Peter (1903-1992) *Appointment with Murder* 1948; *The Balcony* 1963

Brochard, Jean (1893-1972) *Clochemerle* 1948; *Les Diaboliques* 1954

Brochet, Anne (1966-) *Masques* 1987; *Cyrano de Bergerac* 1990; *Tous les Matins du Monde* 1991; *Driftwood* 1996; *Dust* 2001; *Histoire de Marie et Julien* 2003; *Confidences Trop Intimes* 2004; *The Hedgehog* 2009; *The Round Up* 2010

Brochu, Evelyne *Café de Flore* 2011; *Tom at the Farm* 2013

Brock, Phil (1953-) *PoW the Escape* 1986; *The Allnighter* 1987

Brock, Stanley (1931-1991) *Tin Men* 1987; *UHF* 1989

Brocklebank, Daniel *The Hole* 2001; *Release* 2010

Brocksmith, Roy (1945-2001) *Killer Fish* 1978; *Tales of Ordinary Madness* 1981; *Total Recall* 1990; *Kull the Conqueror* 1997

Brockwell, Gladys (1894-1929) *Oliver Twist* 1922; *Long Pants* 1927; *Lights of New York* 1928

Broderick, Beth (1959-) *Hard Evidence* 1994; *Man of the Year* 1995; *Timber Falls* 2007; *Revenge of the Bridesmaids* 2010

Broderick, Helen (1891-1959) *Top Hat* 1935; *The Bride Walks Out* 1936; *Murder on a Bridle Path* 1936; *Swing Time* 1936; *The Rage of Paris* 1938; *Naughty but Nice* 1939; *No, No, Nanette* 1940; *Nice Girl?* 1941; *Because of Him* 1946

Broderick, James (1927-1982) *Girl of the Night* 1960; *Alice's Restaurant* 1969; *The Taking of Pelham One Two Three* 1974; *Dog Day Afternoon* 1975; *The Shadow Box* 1980

Broderick, Matthew (1962-) *Max Dugan Returns* 1983; *WarGames* 1983; *Ladyhawke* 1985; *1918* 1985; *Ferris Bueller's Day Off* 1986; *Project X* 1987; *Biloxi Blues* 1988; *Torch Song Trilogy* 1988; *Family Business* 1989; *Glory* 1989; *The Freshman* 1990; *Out on a Limb* 1992; *A Life in the Theater* 1993; *The Night We Never Met* 1993; *The Lion King* 1994; *Mrs Parker and the Vicious Circle* 1994; *The Road to Wellville* 1994; *The Cable Guy* 1996; *Infinity* 1996; *Addicted to Love* 1997; *Godzilla* 1997; *The Lion King II: Simba's Pride* 1998; *Election* 1999; *Inspector Gadget* 1999; *You Can Count on Me* 1999; *Good Boy!* 2003; *The Last Shot* 2004; *The Stepford Wives* 2004; *The Producers* 2005; *Deck the Halls* 2006; *Bee Movie* 2007; *Diminished Capacity* 2007; *Then She Found Me* 2007; *Margaret* 2008; *The Tale of Despereaux* 2008; *Tower Heist* 2011; *Rules Don't Apply* 2016

Brodie-Sangster, Thomas aka **Sangster, Thomas** aka **Brodie Sangster, Thomas** (1990-) *Nanny McPhee* 2005; *The Last Legion* 2006; *Bright Star* 2009; *Nowhere Boy* 2010; *The Maze Runner* 2014; *Maze Runner: The Scorch Trials* 2015

Brodie, Steve (1919-1992) *A Walk in the Sun* 1945; *Badman's Territory* 1946; *Criminal Court* 1946; *The Falcon's Adventure* 1946; *Build My Gallows High* 1947; *Crossfire* 1947; *Desperate* 1947; *Thunder Mountain* 1947; *Trail Street* 1947; *Bodyguard* 1948; *Guns of Hate* 1948; *Return of the Bad Men* 1948; *Station West* 1948; *The Big Wheel* 1949; *Home of the Brave* 1949; *The Admiral Was a Lady* 1950; *Armored Car Robbery* 1950; *Winchester '73* 1950; *M* 1951; *The Steel Helmet* 1951; *The Sword of Monte Cristo* 1951; *The Beast from 20,000 Fathoms* 1953; *Donovan's Brain* 1953; *Gun Duel in Durango* 1957; *A Girl Named Tamiko* 1962; *The Giant Spider Invasion* 1975; *Delta Pi* 1985

Brodsky, Vlastimil (1920-2002) *All My Good Countrymen* 1968; *Capricious Summer* 1968; *Jacob the Liar* 1974

Brody, Adam (1979-) *Mr & Mrs Smith* 2005; *Thank You for Smoking* 2005; *Jennifer's Body* 2009; *Cop Out* 2010; *Damsels in Distress* 2011; *The Oranges* 2011; *Seeking a Friend for the End of the World* 2011; *Yoga Hosers* 2016

Brody, Adrien (1973-) *The Boy Who Cried Bitch* 1991; *Bullet* 1995; *Solo* 1996; *Six Ways to Sunday* 1997; *Liberty Heights* 1999; *Oxygen* 1999; *Summer of Sam* 1999; *Bread and Roses* 2000; *Harrison's Flowers* 2000; *The Affair of the Necklace* 2001; *Dummy* 2002; *The Pianist* 2002; *The Singing Detective* 2003; *The Village* 2004; *The Jacket* 2005; *King Kong* 2005; *Hollywoodland* 2006; *The Darjeeling Limited* 2007; *The Brothers Bloom* 2008; *Cadillac Records* 2008; *Fantastic Mr Fox* 2009; *Splice* 2009; *Predators* 2010; *Detachment* 2011; *Love, Marilyn* 2012; *Third Person* 2013; *The Grand Budapest Hotel* 2014; *Backtrack* 2015; *Dragon Blade* 2015

Brody, Estelle (1900-1995) *Hindle Wakes* 1927; *Kitty* 1928

Brogi, Giulio *The Spider's Stratagem* 1970; *Voyage to Cythera* 1984

Brolin, James (1940-) *Von Ryan's Express* 1965; *Skyjacked* 1972; *Westworld* 1973; *Gable and Lombard* 1976; *The Car* 1977; *Capricorn One* 1978; *The Amityville Horror* 1979; *Night of the Juggler* 1980; *High Risk* 1981; *Bad Jim* 1989; *Gas, Food, Lodging* 1992; *Paper Hearts* 1993; *Flashpoint* 1997; *Traffic* 2000; *Antwone Fisher* 2002; *Catch Me If You Can* 2002; *A Guy Thing* 2002; *The Master of Disguise* 2002; *Widow on the Hill* 2005; *Wedding Wars* 2006; *The Hunting Party* 2007; *Last Chance Harvey* 2008; *The Goods: Live Hard Sell Hard* 2009; *The 33* 2014

Brolin, Josh (1968-) *The Goonies* 1985; *Thrashin'* 1986; *Roadflower* 1994; *Bed of Roses* 1995; *Flirting with Disaster* 1996; *Gang in Blue* 1996; *Flashpoint* 1997; *Mimic* 1997; *Nightwatch* 1997; *Best Laid Plans* 1999; *The Mod Squad* 1999; *Hollow Man* 2000; *Milwaukee, Minnesota* 2002; *Into the Blue* 2005; *American Gangster* 2007; *In the Valley of Elah* 2007; *No Country for Old Men* 2007; *Planet Terror* 2007; *Milk* 2008; *W.* 2008; *Jonah Hex* 2010; *True Grit* 2010; *Wall Street: Money Never Sleeps* 2010; *You Will Meet a Tall Dark Stranger* 2010; *Gangster Squad* 2012; *Men in Black 3* 2012; *Labor Day* 2013; *Old Boy* 2013; *Inherent Vice* 2014; *Sin City: a Dame to Kill For* 2014; *Everest* 2015; *Sicario* 2015; *Hail, Caesar!* 2016

Brolly, Shane *Underworld* 2003; *Underworld: Evolution* 2006

Bromberg, J Edward (1903-1951) *Stowaway* 1936; *Under Two Flags* 1936; *Charlie Chan on Broadway* 1937; *Fair Warning* 1937; *Seventh Heaven* 1937; *The Baroness and the Butler* 1938; *Four Men and a Prayer* 1938; *Mr Moto Takes a Chance* 1938; *Suez* 1938; *Hollywood Cavalcade* 1939; *Wife, Husband and Friend* 1939; *The Mark of Zorro* 1940; *The Return of Frank James* 1940; *Strange Cargo* 1940; *The Invisible Agent* 1942; *Life Begins at 8.30* 1942; *Tennessee Johnson* 1942; *Lady of Burlesque* 1943; *Son of Dracula* 1943; *Pillow of Death* 1945; *Cloak and Dagger* 1946; *I Shot Jesse James* 1949

Bromfield, John (1922-2005) *Rope of Sand* 1949; *Easy to Love* 1953; *Revenge of the Creature* 1955

Bromiley, Dorothy (1935-) *It's Great to Be Young* 1956; *A Touch of the Sun* 1956

Bron, Eleanor (1940-) *Help!* 1965; *Alfie* 1966; *Bedazzled* 1967; *Two for the Road* 1967; *A Touch of Love* 1969; *Women in Love* 1969; *The National Health* 1973; *Pleasure at Her Majesty's* 1976; *The Hound of the Baskervilles* 1983; *Turtle Diary* 1985; *The Attic: the Hiding of Anne Frank* 1988; *Deadly Advice* 1993; *Black Beauty* 1994; *A Little Princess* 1995; *The House of Mirth* 2000; *Iris* 2001; *The Heart of Me* 2002; *Wimbledon* 2004; *StreetDance* 2010; *Hyde Park on Hudson* 2012

Bronson, Betty (1906-1971) *Ben-Hur: a Tale of the Christ* 1925; *The Singing Fool* 1928; *The Naked Kiss* 1964

Bronson, Charles aka **Buchinski, Charles** aka **Buchinsky, Charles** (1921-2003) *The Mob* 1951; *The People against O'Hara* 1951; *You're in the Navy Now* 1951; *Pat and Mike* 1952; *Red Skies of Montana* 1952; *House of Wax* 1953; *Miss Sadie Thompson* 1953; *Apache* 1954; *The City Is Dark* 1954; *Drum Beat* 1954; *Riding Shotgun* 1954; *Tennessee Champ* 1954; *Big House, USA* 1955; *Jubal* 1956; *Run of the Arrow* 1957; *Gang War* 1958; *Machine Gun Kelly* 1958; *Showdown at Boot Hill* 1958; *Never So Few* 1959; *The Magnificent Seven* 1960; *Master of the World* 1961; *A Thunder of Drums* 1961; *X-15* 1961; *Kid Galahad* 1962; *4 for Texas* 1963; *The Great Escape* 1963; *Battle of the Bulge* 1965; *The Sandpiper* 1965; *This Property Is Condemned* 1966; *The Dirty Dozen* 1967; *Once upon a Time in the West* 1968; *Twinky* 1969; *Rider on the Rain* 1970; *You Can't Win 'Em All* 1970; *Chato's Land* 1971; *Cold Sweat* 1971; *Red Sun* 1971; *Someone behind the Door* 1971; *The Mechanic* 1972; *The Valachi Papers* 1972; *The Stone Killer* 1973; *The Valdez Horses* 1973; *Death Wish* 1974; *Mr Majestyk* 1974; *Breakout* 1975; *Hard Times* 1975; *Breakheart Pass* 1976; *St Ives* 1976; *Raid on Entebbe* 1977; *Telefon* 1977; *The White Buffalo* 1977; *Love and Bullets* 1978; *Borderline* 1980; *Death Hunt* 1981; *Death Wish II* 1981; *10 to Midnight* 1983; *The Evil That Men Do* 1984; *Death Wish 3* 1985; *Act of Vengeance* 1986; *Assassination* 1986; *Murphy's Law* 1986; *Death Wish 4: the Crackdown* 1987; *Messenger of Death* 1988; *Kinjite: Forbidden Subjects* 1989; *The Indian Runner* 1991; *The Sea Wolf* 1993; *Death Wish V: the Face of Death* 1994

Brook-Jones, Elwyn (1911-1962) *Bonnie Prince Charlie* 1948; *The Gilded Cage* 1954; *Passport to Shame* 1958

Brook, Claudio (1929-1995) *The Young One* 1960; *The Exterminating Angel* 1962; *Simon of the Desert* 1965; *Interval* 1973; *Alucarda* 1975; *The Return of a Man Called Horse* 1976; *Cronos* 1992

Brook, Clive (1887-1974) *Underworld* 1927; *The Four Feathers* 1929; *Anybody's Woman* 1930; *Paramount on Parade* 1930; *East Lynne* 1931; *Tarnished Lady* 1931; *The Man from Yesterday* 1932; *Shanghai Express* 1932; *Sherlock Holmes* 1932; *Cavalcade* 1933; *If I Were Free* 1933; *Gallant Lady* 1934; *The Dictator* 1935; *The Ware Case* 1938; *Convoy* 1940; *Freedom Radio* 1940; *Return to Yesterday* 1940; *The List of Adrian Messenger* 1963

Brook, Faith (1922-2012) *Jungle Book* 1942; *The Intimate Stranger* 1956; *Chase a Crooked Shadow* 1957; *The Thirty-Nine Steps* 1959; *To Sir, with Love* 1967; *The Smashing Bird I Used to Know* 1969; *Walk a Crooked Path* 1969; *North Sea Hijack* 1979; *Eye of the Needle* 1981

Brook, Irina (1962-) *The Girl in the Picture* 1985; *Captive* 1986; *The Fool* 1990

Brook, Isabel *Faust: Love of the Damned* 2001; *About a Boy* 2002

Brook, Jayne (1979-) *Clean Slate* 1994; *Ed* 1996; *Last Dance* 1996

Brook, Kelly (1979-) *House of 9* 2004; *Three - III* 2006; *Piranha* 2010; *Keith Lemon: the Film* 2012

Brook, Lesley *Variety Jubilee* 1942; *House of Darkness* 1948

Brook, Lyndon (1926-2004) *The Purple Plain* 1954; *Reach for the Sky* 1956; *The Spanish Gardener* 1956; *The Gypsy and the Gentleman* 1958; *Invasion* 1965; *Who?* 1974

Brooke-Taylor, Tim (1940-) *Twelve plus One* 1969; *Pleasure at Her Majesty's* 1976

Brooke, Hillary (1914-1999) *Sherlock Holmes Faces Death* 1943; *Standing Room Only* 1944; *The Enchanted Cottage* 1945; *Ministry of Fear* 1945; *Road to Utopia* 1945; *The Woman in Green* 1945; *The Strange Woman* 1946; *Africa Screams* 1949; *The Admiral Was a Lady* 1950; *Abbott and Costello Meet Captain Kidd* 1952; *Invaders from Mars* 1953; *Bengazi* 1955; *The Man Who Knew Too Much* 1956

Brooke Jr, Michael *The Magnet* 1950; *The Long Arm* 1956

Brooke, Paul (1944-) *The Lair of the White Worm* 1988; *The Fool* 1990; *Lighthouse* 1999

Brooke, Tom *The Veteran* 2011; *Iona* 2015

Brooke, Tyler (1886-1943) *Fazil* 1928; *Dynamite* 1929; *Monte Carlo* 1930; *Hallelujah, I'm a Bum* 1933

Brooke, Walter (1914-1986) *Conquest of Space* 1955; *The Graduate* 1967; *Sergeant Ryker* 1968; *Zigzag* 1970

Brookes, Jacqueline (1930-2013) *The Gambler* 1974; *Last Embrace* 1979; *Act of Love* 1980; *The Entity* 1981; *Without a Trace* 1983; *The Good Son* 1993

Brooks, Albert (1947-) *Taxi Driver* 1976; *Real Life* 1979; *Private Benjamin* 1980; *Modern Romance* 1981; *Twilight Zone: the Movie* 1983; *Unfaithfully Yours* 1983; *Lost in America* 1985; *Broadcast News* 1987; *Defending Your Life* 1991; *I'll Do Anything* 1994; *The Scout* 1994; *Mother* 1996; *Critical Care* 1997; *Out of Sight* 1998; *The Muse* 1999; *My First Mister* 2001; *Finding Nemo* 2003; *The In-Laws* 2003; *Drive* 2011; *This Is 40* 2012; *A Most Violent Year* 2014; *Finding Dory* 2016; *The Secret Life of Pets* 2016

Brooks, Avery (1948-) *American History X* 1998; *The Big Hit* 1998; *15 Minutes* 2001

Brooks, Carroll *Boy Meets Girl* 1984; *Mauvais Sang* 1986

Brooks, Geraldine (1925-1977) *Cry Wolf* 1947; *Possessed* 1947; *Challenge to Lassie* 1949; *The Reckless Moment* 1949; *The Younger Brothers* 1949; *Johnny Tiger* 1966; *Mr Ricco* 1975

Brooks, Hazel (1924-2002) *Body and Soul* 1947; *Sleep, My Love* 1948

Brooks, Jean (1915-1963) *The Falcon and the Co-Eds* 1943; *The Leopard Man* 1943; *The Seventh Victim* 1943; *The Falcon in Hollywood* 1944

Brooks, Joel (1949-) *Skin Deep* 1989; *Indecent Proposal* 1993

Brooks, Leslie (1922-2011) *You Were Never Lovelier* 1942; *Cover Girl* 1944; *Tonight and Every Night* 1945; *Hollow Triumph* 1948

Brooks, Louise (1906-1985) *It's the Old Army Game* 1926; *Beggars of Life* 1928; *A Girl in Every Port* 1928; *The Canary Murder Case* 1929; *Diary of a Lost Girl* 1929; *Pandora's Box* 1929; *Prix de Beauté* 1930; *God's Gift to Women* 1931; *It Pays to Advertise* 1931; *Overland Stage Raiders* 1938

Brooks, Mel (1926-) *The Twelve Chairs* 1970; *Blazing Saddles* 1974; *Silent Movie* 1976; *High Anxiety* 1977; *History of the World Part 1* 1981; *To Be or Not to Be* 1983; *Spaceballs* 1987; *Look Who's Talking Too* 1990; *Life Stinks* 1991; *Robin Hood: Men in Tights* 1993; *The Little Rascals* 1994; *Dracula: Dead and Loving It* 1995; *Screw Loose* 1999; *Robots* 2005; *Mr Peabody & Sherman* 2013; *Hotel Transylvania 2* 2015

Brooks, Phyllis (1915-1995) *Little Miss Broadway* 1938; *Rebecca of Sunnybrook Farm* 1938; *Charlie Chan in Reno* 1939; *The Shanghai Gesture* 1941; *The Unseen* 1945

Brooks, Rand (1918-2003) *The Devil's Playground* 1946; *Fool's Gold* 1946; *The Dead Don't Dream* 1948; *Silent Conflict* 1948; *Ladies of the Chorus* 1949; *Comanche Station* 1960

Brooks, Randi (1956-) *The Cartier Affair* 1984; *Cop* 1988

Brooks, Randy *Assassination* 1986; *8 Million Ways to Die* 1986; *Colors* 1988; *Reservoir Dogs* 1991

Brooks, Ray (1939-) *Some People* 1962; *The Knack... and How to Get It* 1965; *Daleks - Invasion Earth 2150 AD* 1966; *The Last Grenade* 1970; *Assassin* 1973; *Tiffany Jones* 1973; *House of Whipcord* 1974

Brooks (2), Richard (1962-) *The Hidden* 1987; *Blue Jean Cop* 1988; *84 Charlie Mopic* 1989; *Shocker* 1989; *To Sleep with Anger* 1990; *The Crow: City of Angels* 1996; *The Wedding* 1998

Brooks, Victor (1918-1999) *Cover Girl Killer* 1959; *Life in Danger* 1959; *Give Us Tomorrow* 1978

Brophy, Anthony *The Run of the Country* 1995; *Snow White: a Tale of Terror* 1996; *The Last Bus Home* 1997

Brophy, Edward aka **Brophy, Edward S** (1895-1960) *The Cameraman* 1928; *Doughboys* 1930; *The Champ* 1931; *What - No Beer?* 1933; *Evelyn Prentice* 1934; *Mad Love* 1935; *Great Guy* 1936; *Spendthrift* 1936; *Strike Me Pink* 1936; *The Last Gangster* 1937; *The Amazing Mr Williams* 1939; *Golden Boy* 1939; *Dance, Girl, Dance* 1940; *The Invisible Woman* 1940; *Dumbo* 1941; *The Gay Falcon* 1941; *Broadway* 1942; *Larceny, Inc* 1942; *It Happened Tomorrow* 1944; *The Falcon in San Francisco* 1945; *The Falcon's Adventure* 1946; *The Last Hurrah* 1958

Brophy, Kevin (1953-) *The Long Riders* 1980; *Hell Night* 1981

Brosnan, Pierce (1953-) *The Long Good Friday* 1979; *Nomads* 1985; *The Fourth Protocol* 1987; *The Deceivers* 1988; *Taffin* 1988; *Mister Johnson* 1991; *Victim of Love* 1991; *The Lawnmower Man* 1992; *Live Wire* 1992; *Death Train* 1993; *Mrs Doubtfire* 1993; *Don't Talk to*

Strangers 1994; Love Affair 1994; The Disappearance of Kevin Johnson 1995; GoldenEye 1995; Night Watch 1995; Daniel Defoe's Robinson Crusoe 1996; Mars Attacks! 1996; The Mirror Has Two Faces 1996; Dante's Peak 1997; The Magic Sword: Quest for Camelot 1997; The Nephew 1997; Tomorrow Never Dies 1997; Grey Owl 1999; The Match 1999; The Thomas Crown Affair 1999; The World Is Not Enough 1999; The Tailor of Panama 2000; Die Another Day 2002; Evelyn 2002; Laws of Attraction 2003; After the Sunset 2004; The Matador 2005; Seraphim Falls 2006; The 2006 FIFA World Cup Film: the Grand Finale 2006; Butterfly on a Wheel 2007; Married Life 2007; Mamma Mia! 2008; The Greatest 2009; The Ghost 2010; Percy Jackson & the Lightning Thief 2010; Remember Me 2010; I Don't Know How She Does It 2011; Johnny English Reborn 2011; Salvation Boulevard 2011; Everything or Nothing: the Untold Story of 007 2012; Love Is All You Need 2012; A Long Way Down 2013; The Love Punch 2013; Lessons in Love 2014; No Escape 2014; The November Man 2014; Survivor 2015

Brosset, Claude (1943-) The Outsider 1983; Le Cop 1985

Brothers, Dr Joyce (1928-2013) Oh God! Book II 1980; The Lonely Guy 1984; Age Isn't Everything 1991

Brough, Mary (1863-1934) Rookery Nook 1930; A Cuckoo in the Nest 1933

Brousse, Liliane Maniac 1962; Paranoiac 1963

Brown Findlay, Jessica (1989-) Albatross 2011; A New York Winter's Tale 2014; The Riot Club 2014; Victor Frankenstein 2015

Brown, Barbara (1902-1975) Hollywood Canteen 1944; Born Yesterday 1950; Home Town Story 1951; Jack and the Beanstalk 1952; An Annapolis Story 1955

Brown, Barry (1951-1978) Flesh 1968; Bad Company 1972; Daisy Miller 1974

Brown, Billie (1952-) The Dish 2000; The Man Who Sued God 2001

Brown, Billy Aaron (1981-) Getting There 2002; Jeepers Creepers 2 2003

Brown, Blair (1948-) Altered States 1980; One-Trick Pony 1980; Continental Divide 1981; A Flash of Green 1984; Stealing Home 1988; Strapless 1988; Passed Away 1992; Dogville 2003; The Sentinel 2006

Brown, Bobby (1969-) Panther 1995; A Thin Line between Love and Hate 1996

Brown, Bryan (1947-) The Irishman 1978; Newsfront 1978; Breaker Morant 1979; The Odd Angry Shot 1979; Give My Regards to Broad Street 1984; Kim 1984; FX: Murder by Illusion 1985; Rebel 1985; The Good Wife 1986; The Shiralee 1986; Tai-Pan 1986; Cocktail 1988; Gorillas in the Mist 1988; Blood Oath 1990; FX 2 1991; Blame It on the Bellboy 1992; Dead Heart 1996; Grizzly Falls 1999; Two Hands 1999; Risk 2000; Styx 2000; Dirty Deeds 2002; Along Came Polly 2004; Revenge of the Middle-Aged Woman 2004; Australia 2008; Dean Spanley 2008; Beautiful Kate 2009

Brown, Charles D (1887-1949) Gold Diggers of 1937 1936; The Duke of West Point 1938; The Shopworn Angel 1938; Brother Orchid 1940; The Big Sleep 1946; The Killers 1946; The Senator Was Indiscreet 1947; Smash Up - the Story of a Woman 1947

Brown, Chris This Christmas 2007; Battle of the Year 2013

Brown, Clancy (1959-) The Bride 1985; Highlander 1986; Extreme Prejudice 1987; Deadly Pursuit 1988; Waiting for the Light 1989; Blue Steel 1990; Ambition 1991; Pet Sematary II 1992; Last Light 1993; Pom Poko 1994; The Shawshank Redemption 1994; Flubber 1997; Starship Troopers 1997; The Hurricane 1999; In the Company of Spies 1999; Snow White 2001; Normal 2002; The SpongeBob SquarePants Movie 2004; The Guardian 2006; Pathfinder 2006; The Express 2008; A Nightmare on Elm Street 2010; John Dies at the End 2012; The SpongeBob Movie: Sponge out of Water 2015

Brown, Dwier (1959-) House II: the Second Story 1987; Field of Dreams 1989; The Guardian 1990; The Cutting Edge 1992; Mom and Dad Save the World 1992; Dennis the Menace Strikes Again 1998

Brown, Garrett M aka **Brown, Garrett** Zelig 1983; Uncle Buck 1989

Brown, Georg Stanford (1943-) The Comedians 1967; Bullitt 1968; Colossus: the Forbin Project 1969; Black Jack 1972; The Man 1972; Stir Crazy 1980

Brown, Georgia (1933-1992) Lock Up Your Daughters! 1969; The Raging Moon 1970; Nothing but the Night 1972; Galileo 1974; The Bawdy Adventures of Tom Jones 1976; Victim of Love 1991

Brown (1), James (1920-1992) Corvette K-225 1943; Going My Way 1944; Objective, Burma! 1945; Sands of Iwo Jima 1949; The Younger Brothers 1949; Chain Lightning 1950; The Fireball 1950; Montana 1950; The Pride of St Louis 1952; The Woman They Almost Lynched 1953; A Star Is Born 1954; Targets 1968

Brown (2), James (1933-2006) The Blues Brothers 1980; Rocky IV 1985; When We Were Kings 1996; Blues Brothers 2000 1998; Holy Man 1998; Soul Power 2008

Brown, Janet (1924-2011) Floodtide 1949; For Your Eyes Only 1981

Brown, Jim (1935-) Rio Conchos 1964; Dark of the Sun 1967; The Dirty Dozen 1967; Ice Station Zebra 1968; The Split 1968; Riot 1969; tick... tick... tick... 1969; El Condor 1970; The Grasshopper 1970; Slaughter's Big Rip-Off 1973; Three the Hard Way 1974; Take a Hard Ride 1975; Kid Vengeance 1977; Fingers 1978; Pacific Inferno 1979; The Running Man 1987; Crack House 1989; Original Gangstas 1996; He Got Game 1998; Any Given Sunday 1999; She Hate Me 2004; I Am Ali 2014

Brown (2), Joe (1941-) What a Crazy World 1963; Three Hats for Lisa 1965; Mona Lisa 1986

Brown, Joe E aka **Brown, Joe** (1892-1973) Sunny Side Up 1929; A Midsummer Night's Dream 1935; Pin Up Girl 1944; Show Boat 1951; Some Like It Hot 1959; The Comedy of Terrors 1964

Brown, Johnny Mack aka **Brown, John Mack** (1904-1974) The Divine Woman 1928; Our Dancing Daughters 1928; A Woman of Affairs 1928; Coquette 1929; The Single Standard 1929; The Valiant 1929; Billy the Kid 1930; The Last Flight 1931; The Secret Six 1931; Female 1933; Belle of the Nineties 1934; Hell Town 1937; Apache Uprising 1965

Brown, Jophery (1945-2014) The Bingo Long Travelling All-Stars and Motor Kings 1976; The Squeeze 1987; Sudden Death 1995

Brown, Juanita (1951-1981) Caged Heat 1974; Foxy Brown 1974

Brown, Judith aka **Brown, Judy** Women in Cages 1972; Slaughter's Big Rip-Off 1973

Brown, Julie (1958-) Earth Girls Are Easy 1988; Shakes the Clown 1991; The Opposite Sex and How to Live with Them 1993; Raining Stones 1993

Brown, Kimberly J (1984-) Tumbleweeds 1999; Bringing Down the House 2003

Brown (2), Lew (1925-2014) Crime and Punishment, USA 1959; Grand Theft Auto 1977

Brown, Max Paradise Lost 2006; Love Tomorrow 2012; That Good Night 2017

Brown, Natalie Fairfield Road 2010; Exploding Sun 2013

Brown, Pamela (1917-1975) One of Our Aircraft Is Missing 1942; I Know Where I'm Going! 1945; The Tales of Hoffmann 1951; Personal Affair 1953; Richard III 1955; Lust for Life 1956; The Scapegoat 1959; Cleopatra 1963; Becket 1964; Secret Ceremony 1968; Figures in a Landscape 1970; On a Clear Day You Can See Forever 1970; Wuthering Heights 1970; The Road Builder 1971; Lady Caroline Lamb 1972; Dracula 1974

Brown, Pat Crawford Elvira, Mistress of the Dark 1988; Stuck on You 2003

Brown, Peter (1935-2016) Darby's Rangers 1958; Merrill's Marauders 1962; Ride the Wild Surf 1964; A Tiger Walks 1964; Three Guns for Texas 1968; Backtrack 1969; Foxy Brown 1974

Brown, Phil (1916-2006) Calling Dr Gillespie 1942; The Killers 1946; Without Reservations 1946; Obsession 1948; A King in New York 1957; The Adding Machine 1969; Valdez Is Coming 1971

Brown, Ralph (1957-) The Contractor 2007; Straightheads 2007; Huge 2009; Sus 2009; Dark Tide 2012; I, Anna 2012; Tower Block 2012

Brown (2), Ralph (1960-) Withnail & I 1986; Buster 1988; Impromptu 1991; Alien³ 1992; Wayne's World 2 1993; Up 'n' Under 1997; Mean Machine 2001; The Final Curtain 2002; I'll Be There 2003; Exorcist: the Beginning 2004; Puritan 2004; Dominion: Prequel to the Exorcist 2005

Brown, Reb (1948-) Captain America 1979; Uncommon Valor 1983; Howling II: Your Sister Is a Werewolf 1984; Death of a Soldier 1985; Distant Thunder 1988; Cage 1989

Brown, Rob (1984-) Finding Forrester 2000; Coach Carter 2005; Take the Lead 2006; Live! 2007; Stop-Loss 2007; The Express 2008; Don Jon 2013

Brown, Robert (1918-2003) Time Gentlemen Please! 1952; The Abominable Snowman 1957; The Steel Bayonet 1957; Passport to Shame 1958; Tower of London 1962; One Million Years BC 1966; Octopussy 1983; A View to a Kill 1985; The Living Daylights 1987; Licence to Kill 1989

Brown, Russ (1896-1993) Damn Yankees 1958; South Pacific 1958; It Happened to Jane 1959

Brown, Ruth (1928-2006) Hairspray 1988; Shake, Rattle and Rock 1994

Brown, Sean Dear Frankie 2003; The Flying Scotsman 2006

Brown, Sharon A Chorus Line 1985; For Keeps 1987

Brown, Stanley aka **Taylor, Brad** (1914-2001) The Face behind the Mask 1941; Atlantic City 1944

Brown, Thomas Wilson aka **Brown, Thomas** (1972-) Honey, I Shrunk the Kids 1989; Welcome Home 1989; Welcome Home, Roxy Carmichael 1990; Midnight Sting 1992

Brown, Timothy aka **Brown, Tim** (1937-) Nashville 1975; Pacific Inferno 1979

Brown, Tom (1913-1990) Central Airport 1933; Anne of Green Gables 1934; Judge Priest 1934; This Side of Heaven 1934; Black Sheep 1935; Maytime 1937; Navy Blue and Gold 1937; The Duke of West Point 1938; Merrily We Live 1938; Sergeant Madden 1939; There's One Born Every Minute 1942; Buck Privates Come Home 1947; Fireman Save My Child 1954

Brown, Vanessa (1928-1999) The Foxes of Harrow 1947; The Ghost and Mrs Muir 1947; The Late George Apley 1947; Mother Wore Tights 1947; The Heiress 1949; Tarzan and the Slave Girl 1950; The Bad and the Beautiful 1952; Rosie! 1967

Brown, W Earl The Big White 2005; The Sessions 2012

Brown, Wally (1904-1961) Girl Rush 1944; Step Lively 1944; From This Day Forward 1946; Holiday for Lovers 1959; The Absent-Minded Professor 1961

Brown, Warren Borrowed Time 2012; Captain Webb 2014

Browne, Coral (1913-1991) We're Going to Be Rich 1938; Let George Do It 1940; Piccadilly Incident 1946; The Courtneys of Curzon Street 1947; Beautiful Stranger 1954; Auntie Mame 1958; Go to Blazes 1961; The Roman Spring of Mrs Stone 1961; Dr Crippen 1962; Tamahine 1963; The Night of the Generals 1966; The Killing of Sister George 1968; The Ruling Class 1972; Theatre of Blood 1973; American Dreamer 1984; Dreamchild 1985

Browne, Irene (1891-1965) The Letter 1929; Berkeley Square 1933; Peg o' My Heart 1933; Meet Me at Dawn 1946; Barnacle Bill 1957; Serious Charge 1959

Browne, Leslie (1958-) The Turning Point 1977; Nijinsky 1980; Dancers 1987

Browne, Roscoe Lee (1925-2007) Black like Me 1964; Uptight 1968; Topaz 1969; The Liberation of LB Jones 1970; Cisco Pike 1971; The Cowboys 1972; The World's Greatest Athlete 1974; Logan's Run 1976; Oliver & Company 1988; Babe 1995; Last Summer in the Hamptons 1995; Dear God 1996

Browning, Alistair Merry Christmas Mr Lawrence 1982; Rain 2001

Browning, Emily (1988-) The Man Who Sued God 2001; Lemony Snicket's A Series of Unfortunate Events 2004; The Uninvited 2008; Sleeping Beauty 2011; Sucker Punch 2011; God Help the Girl 2012; Summer in February 2012; Magic Magic 2013; Pompeii 2014; Legend 2015

Browning, Ricou (1930-) Creature from the Black Lagoon 1954; Revenge of the Creature 1955

Broyles, Robert (1933-2011) Eat My Dust! 1976; Norma Rae 1979

Brubaker, Robert (1916-2010) Apache Rifles 1964; 40 Guns to Apache Pass 1966

Bruce, Betty (1920-1974) Gypsy 1962; Island of Love 1963

Bruce, Brenda (1918-1996) While the Sun Shines 1946; When the Bough Breaks 1947; The Final Test 1953; Behind the Mask 1958; Law and Disorder 1958; Peeping Tom 1960;

Nightmare 1963; The Uncle 1964; All Creatures Great and Small 1974; Swallows and Amazons 1974; The Man in the Iron Mask 1977; Steaming 1985; The Tenth Man 1988; December Bride 1990; Splitting Heirs 1993

Bruce, Carol (1919-2007) Keep 'Em Flying 1941; Planes, Trains and Automobiles 1987

Bruce, Cheryl Lynn Music Box 1989; Daughters of the Dust 1991

Bruce, Colin Crusoe 1988; The Dead Can't Lie 1988

Bruce, David (1914-1976) Calling Dr Death 1943; Can't Help Singing 1944; Christmas Holiday 1944; Salome, Where She Danced 1945

Bruce, Nigel (1895-1953) I Was a Spy 1934; The Scarlet Pimpernel 1934; Stand Up and Cheer! 1934; Treasure Island 1934; Becky Sharp 1935; The Man Who Broke the Bank at Monte Carlo 1935; She 1935; The Charge of the Light Brigade 1936; The Trail of the Lonesome Pine 1936; Under Two Flags 1936; The White Angel 1936; The Last of Mrs Cheyney 1937; Thunder in the City 1937; Kidnapped 1938; The Adventures of Sherlock Holmes 1939; The Hound of the Baskervilles 1939; The Rains Came 1939; The Blue Bird 1940; A Dispatch from Reuters 1940; Rebecca 1940; Susan and God 1940; The Chocolate Soldier 1941; Suspicion 1941; Roxie Hart 1942; Sherlock Holmes and the Secret Weapon 1942; Sherlock Holmes and the Voice of Terror 1942; This above All 1942; Lassie Come Home 1943; Sherlock Holmes Faces Death 1943; Sherlock Holmes in Washington 1943; Frenchman's Creek 1944; The House of Fear 1944; The Pearl of Death 1944; The Scarlet Claw 1944; Sherlock Holmes and the Spider Woman 1944; The Corn Is Green 1945; Pursuit to Algiers 1945; Son of Lassie 1945; The Two Mrs Carrolls 1945; The Woman in Green 1945; Dressed to Kill 1946; Terror by Night 1946; The Exile 1947; Julia Misbehaves 1948; Bwana Devil 1952; Limelight 1952; World for Ransom 1953

Bruce, Virginia (1910-1982) Dangerous Corner 1934; The Mighty Barnum 1934; Escapade 1935; Let 'Em Have It 1935; Murder Man 1935; Born to Dance 1936; The Great Ziegfeld 1936; Wife, Doctor and Nurse 1937; Arsene Lupin Returns 1938; Bad Man of Brimstone 1938; There Goes My Heart 1938; Hired Wife 1940; The Invisible Woman 1940; Careful, Soft Shoulder 1942; Pardon My Sarong 1942; Action in Arabia 1944; Brazil 1944; Night Has a Thousand Eyes 1948; Strangers When We Meet 1960

Bruch, Volker The Reader 2008; The Red Baron 2008

Brücher, Christine A la Place du Coeur 1998; La Ville Est Tranquille 2000

Bruckner, Agnes (1985-) Blue Car 2001; Murder by Numbers 2002; Blood and Chocolate 2006; The Woods 2006; The Pact 2011

Bruel, Patrick (1959-) Lost & Found 1999; A Comedy of Power 2006; A Secret 2007; Paris-Manhattan 2012

Brühl, Daniel (1978-) Good Bye Lenin! 2003; Ladies in Lavender 2004; Merry Christmas 2005; 2 Days in Paris 2006; City of War: the Story of John Rabe 2009; Intruders 2011; The Fifth Estate 2013; A Most Wanted Man 2013; Rush 2013; The Face of an Angel 2014; Burnt 2015; Colonia 2015; Woman in Gold 2015

Brumpton, John Long Weekend 2008; The Loved Ones 2009

Brurdin, Bo (1937-) The Great Waldo Pepper 1975; Late for Dinner 1991

Brunetti, Argentina (1907-2005) The Brothers Rico 1957; The Midnight Story 1957

Bruni-Tedeschi, Valéria aka **Bruni Tedeschi, Valeria** (1964-) Mon Homme 1996; Those Who Love Me Can Take the Train 1998; The Colour of Lies 1999; Ten Minutes Older: the Cello 2002; Cockles & Muscles 2004; 5x2 2004; Tickets 2005; Time to Leave 2005; Human Capital 2013

Brunius, Jacques aka **Borel, Jacques** (1906-1967) Une Partie de Campagne 1936; Sea Devils 1952; South of Algiers 1952

Brunning, Nancy When Love Comes 1993; What Becomes of the Broken Hearted? 1999

Bruno, Dylan (1972-) When Trumpets Fade 1998; The Rage: Carrie 2 1999; The Simian Line 2000; Where the Heart Is 2000; The One 2001

Brunot, André (1879-1973) Hôtel du Nord 1938; Pièges 1939; Le Rouge et le Noir 1954

Bruns, Philip aka **Bruns, Phil** (1931-2012) The Out of Towners 1970; Corvette Summer 1978; Return of the Living Dead Part II 1988

Bryan, Arthur Q (1899-1959) A Wild Hare 1940; What's Opera, Doc? 1957

Bryan, Dora (1924-2014) No Room at the Inn 1948; Once upon a Dream 1948; Adam and Evelyne 1949; The Blue Lamp 1949; The Cure for Love 1949; The Interrupted Journey 1949; Now Barabbas Was a Robber 1949; Traveller's Joy 1949; Circle of Danger 1950; No Trace 1950; The Quiet Woman 1950; Something in the City 1950; Gift Horse 1951; Lady Godiva Rides Again 1951; Scarlet Thread 1951; Miss Robin Hood 1952; Time Gentlemen Please! 1952; Women of Twilight 1952; The Intruder 1953; Mad about Men 1954; You Know What Sailors Are 1954; As Long as They're Happy 1955; Child in the House 1956; The Man Who Wouldn't Talk 1957; Carry On Sergeant 1958; Desert Mice 1959; Operation Bullshine 1959; The Night We Got the Bird 1960; A Taste of Honey 1961; The Great St Trinian's Train Robbery 1966; The Sandwich Man 1966; Two a Penny 1968; Hands of the Ripper 1971; Up the Front 1972; Apartment Zero 1988; MirrorMask 2004

Bryan, Jane (1918-2009) The Case of the Black Cat 1936; Confession 1937; Kid Galahad 1937; Marked Woman 1937; The Sisters 1938; A Slight Case of Murder 1938; Each Dawn I Die 1939; Invisible Stripes 1939; The Old Maid 1939; We Are Not Alone 1939

Bryan, Zachery Ty aka **Bryan, Zachery** (1981-) The Rage: Carrie 2 1999; Plainsong 2004; CodeBreakers 2005; The Fast and the Furious: Tokyo Drift 2006

Bryant, Joy (1976-) Antwone Fisher 2002; Baadasssss! 2003; Honey 2003; Get Rich or Die Tryin' 2005; The Skeleton Key 2005; Welcome Home Roscoe Jenkins 2008; About Last Night 2013

Bryant, Lucas More Sex & the Single Mom 2005; The Vow 2012; The Girl King 2015

Bryant, Michael (1928-2002) The Mind Benders 1963; Torture Garden 1967; Goodbye, Mr Chips 1969; Mumsy, Nanny, Sonny & Girly 1970; The Ruling Class 1972; Caravan to Vaccares 1974; The Miracle Maker 1999

Bryant, Nana (1888-1955) The King Steps Out 1936; The Man Who Lived Twice 1936; Meet Nero Wolfe 1936; Pennies from Heaven 1936; The League of Frightened Men 1937; Man-Proof 1937; The Adventures of Tom Sawyer 1938; The Reluctant Dragon 1941; Her Husband's Affairs 1947; Possessed 1947; Ladies of the Chorus 1949; Follow the Sun: the Ben Hogan Story 1951; The Outcast 1954

Bryant, William (1924-2001) The Other Side of the Mountain 1975; Corvette Summer 1978

Bryar, Paul (1910-1985) Easy to Love 1953; Vertigo 1958

Brydon, Rob (1965-) MirrorMask 2004; A Cock and Bull Story 2005; The Unbeatables 2013

Bryggman, Larry (1938-) Die Hard with a Vengeance 1995; Spy Game 2001

Brygmann, Lars (1956-) The Inheritance 2003; King's Game 2004

Bryk, Greg A History of Violence 2005; Weirdsville 2006; Shoot 'Em Up 2007

Bryniarski, Andrew (1969-) Cyborg 3: The Recycler 1994; The Texas Chainsaw Massacre 2003; The Texas Chainsaw Massacre: the Beginning 2006

Brynner, Yul (1915-1985) Port of New York 1949; Anastasia 1956; The King and I 1956; The Ten Commandments 1956; The Brothers Karamazov 1958; The Buccaneer 1958; Solomon and Sheba 1959; The Sound and the Fury 1959; The Magnificent Seven 1960; Surprise Package 1960; Le Testament d'Orphée 1960; Escape from Zahrain 1962; Taras Bulba 1962; Flight from Ashiya 1963; Kings of the Sun 1963; Invitation to a Gunfighter 1964; Morituri 1965; Cast a Giant Shadow 1966; The Poppy Is Also a Flower 1966; Return of the Seven 1966; Triple Cross 1966; The Double Man 1967; The Long Duel 1967; The File of the Golden Goose 1969; The Madwoman of Chaillot 1969; The Magic Christian 1969; Adios, Sabata 1970; Catlow 1971; The Light at the Edge of the World 1971; Romance of a Horse Thief 1971; Fuzz 1972; The Serpent 1972; Westworld 1973; The Ultimate Warrior 1975; Futureworld 1976

Brynolfsson, Reine (1953-) *House of Angels* 1992; *Jerusalem* 1996; *Les Misérables* 1997; *Kitchen Stories* 2003

Buccella, Maria Grazia (1940-) *The Dirty Game* 1965; *Dead Run* 1967

Bucci, Flavio (1947-) *Suspiria* 1976; *Il Divo* 2008

Buccille, Ashley (1986-) *Dusting Cliff 7* 1996; *Phenomenon* 1996

Buccirosso, Carlo *Il Divo* 2008; *The Great Beauty* 2013

Buchan, Andrew *Having You* 2013; *Still Life* 2013

Buchanan, Edgar (1903-1979) *Too Many Husbands* 1940; *Penny Serenade* 1941; *Texas* 1941; *You Belong to Me* 1941; *The Talk of the Town* 1942; *The Desperadoes* 1943; *Bride by Mistake* 1944; *Buffalo Bill* 1944; *Abilene Town* 1945; *The Bandit of Sherwood Forest* 1946; *Framed* 1947; *The Sea of Grass* 1947; *The Black Arrow* 1948; *Coroner Creek* 1948; *The Man from Colorado* 1948; *Red Canyon* 1949; *The Walking Hills* 1949; *The Big Hangover* 1950; *Cheaper by the Dozen* 1950; *Devil's Doorway* 1950; *Cave of Outlaws* 1951; *Rawhide* 1951; *The Big Trees* 1952; *Flaming Feather* 1952; *Shane* 1953; *Beautiful but Dangerous* 1954; *Dawn at Socorro* 1954; *Destry* 1954; *Human Desire* 1954; *Rage at Dawn* 1955; *Wichita* 1955; *Come Next Spring* 1956; *Day of the Bad Man* 1958; *The Sheepman* 1958; *Edge of Eternity* 1959; *Tammy Tell Me True* 1961; *Ride the High Country* 1962; *A Ticklish Affair* 1963; *The Man from Button Willow* 1965; *The Rounders* 1965; *Gunpoint* 1966; *Welcome to Hard Times* 1967; *Angel in My Pocket* 1968; *Benji* 1974

Buchanan, Jack (1891-1957) *Monte Carlo* 1930; *When Knights Were Bold* 1936; *Smash and Grab* 1937; *The Gang's All Here* 1939; *The Band Wagon* 1953; *As Long as They're Happy* 1955; *The Diary of Major Thompson* 1955; *Josephine and Men* 1955

Buchanan, Robert *That Sinking Feeling* 1979; *Gregory's Girl* 1980

Buchholz, Christopher *Eros* 2004; *Free Men* 2011

Buchholz, Horst (1933-2003) *Tiger Bay* 1959; *The Magnificent Seven* 1960; *Fanny* 1961; *One, Two, Three* 1961; *The Empty Canvas* 1963; *Cervantes* 1968; *The Great Waltz* 1972; *The Catamount Killing* 1974; *Raid on Entebbe* 1977; *The Amazing Captain Nemo* 1978; *Avalanche Express* 1979; *From Hell to Victory* 1979; *Sahara* 1983; *Code Name: Emerald* 1985; *Aces: Iron Eagle III* 1992; *Faraway, So Close* 1993; *Life Is Beautiful* 1997; *The Enemy* 2000

Buck, David (1936-1989) *The Mummy's Shroud* 1966; *Deadfall* 1968; *Mosquito Squadron* 1968

Buckler, John (1906-1936) *The Black Room* 1935; *Tarzan Escapes* 1936

Buckley, Betty (1947-) *Carrie* 1976; *Tender Mercies* 1982; *Another Woman* 1988; *Frantic* 1988; *Simply Irresistible* 1999; *Vinegar Hill* 2004; *The Happening* 2008

Buckley, James (1987-) *Everywhere + Nowhere* 2011; *The Inbetweeners Movie* 2011; *Charlie Countryman* 2013; *The Inbetweeners 2* 2014; *The Pyramid* 2014

Buckley, Keith (1941-) *Spring and Port Wine* 1969; *Dr Phibes Rises Again* 1972; *Hanover Street* 1979; *Gunbus* 1986; *Half Moon Street* 1986

Bucur, Dragoş *Boogie* 2007; *Police, Adjective* 2009

Buetel, Jack (1915-1989) *The Outlaw* 1943; *Best of the Badmen* 1951; *The Half-Breed* 1952; *Rose of Cimarron* 1952

Buferd, Marilyn (1925-1990) *Les Belles de Nuit* 1952; *The Unearthly* 1957

Buffalo Bill Jr *aka* **Wilsey, Jay** (1896-1961) *'Neath the Arizona Skies* 1934; *Texas Terror* 1935

Bugallo, Celso *Mondays in the Sun* 2002; *The Sea Inside* 2004; *The Night of the Sunflowers* 2006

Buggy, Niall *Zardoz* 1973; *King David* 1985

Buhr, Gérard (1928-1988) *Bob Le Flambeur* 1955; *Five Days One Summer* 1982

Bujalski, Andrew *Funny Ha Ha* 2002; *Mutual Appreciation* 2005

Bujeau, Christian *Les Visiteurs 2: Les Couloirs du Temps* 1998; *The Cow and the President* 2000

Bujold, Geneviève *aka* **Bujold, Geneviève** (1942-) *La Guerre Est Finie* 1966; *King of Hearts* 1966; *The Thief of Paris* 1967; *Anne of the Thousand Days* 1969; *Act of the Heart* 1970; *The Trojan Women* 1971; *Kamouraska* 1973; *Earthquake* 1974; *Alex and the Gypsy* 1976; *Obsession* 1976; *Swashbuckler* 1976; *Another Man, Another Chance*

1977; *Coma* 1977; *Murder by Decree* 1978; *The Last Flight of Noah's Ark* 1980; *Monsignor* 1982; *Choose Me* 1984; *Tightrope* 1984; *Trouble in Mind* 1985; *Dead Ringers* 1988; *The Moderns* 1988; *A Paper Wedding* 1989; *False Identity* 1990; *Oh, What a Night* 1992; *The Adventures of Pinocchio* 1996; *The House of Yes* 1997; *Last Night* 1998; *You Can Thank Me Later* 1998; *The Bookfair Murders* 2000; *Children of My Heart* 2000

Bull, Peter (1912-1984) *Saraband for Dead Lovers* 1948; *The African Queen* 1951; *Dr Strangelove, or How I Learned to Stop Worrying and Love the Bomb* 1963; *The Old Dark House* 1963; *Licensed to Kill* 1965; *Doctor Dolittle* 1967; *The Tempest* 1979

Bullmore, Amelia (1964-) *Festival* 2005; *The Truth* 2006

Bulloch, Jeremy *aka* **Bullock, Jeremy** *The Cat Gang* 1959; *Summer Holiday* 1962; *Hoffman* 1970; *Can You Keep It Up for a Week?* 1974

Bullock, Sandra (1964-) *Who Shot Patakango?* 1989; *Love Potion No 9* 1992; *When the Party's Over* 1992; *Demolition Man* 1993; *The Thing Called Love* 1993; *The Vanishing* 1993; *Wrestling Ernest Hemingway* 1993; *Speed* 1994; *The Net* 1995; *While You Were Sleeping* 1995; *A Time to Kill* 1996; *Stolen Hearts* 1996; *Speed 2: Cruise Control* 1997; *Forces of Nature* 1998; *Hope Floats* 1998; *Practical Magic* 1998; *The Prince of Egypt* 1998; *Gun Shy* 2000; *Miss Congeniality* 2000; *28 Days* 2000; *Divine Secrets of the Ya-Ya Sisterhood* 2002; *Murder by Numbers* 2002; *Two Weeks Notice* 2002; *Crash* 2004; *Miss Congeniality 2: Armed & Fabulous* 2005; *Infamous* 2006; *The Lake House* 2006; *Premonition* 2007; *All about Steve* 2009; *The Blind Side* 2009; *The Proposal* 2009; *Extremely Loud & Incredibly Close* 2012; *Gravity* 2013; *The Heat* 2013; *Minions* 2015; *Our Brand Is Crisis* 2015

Buloff, Joseph (1899-1985) *Let's Make Music* 1940; *Carnegie Hall* 1947; *The Loves of Carmen* 1948; *A Kiss in the Dark* 1949; *Silk Stockings* 1957

Bumpass, Rodger *The SpongeBob SquarePants Movie* 2004; *The SpongeBob Movie: Sponge out of Water* 2015

Bunce, Alan (1902-1965) *The Last Mile* 1959; *Sunrise at Campobello* 1960; *Homicidal* 1961

Bunce, Stuart *Bring Me the Head of Mavis Davis* 1997; *Regeneration* 1997; *The Lost Lover* 1999

Bunker, Edward *aka* **Bunker, Eddie** (1933-2005) *Reservoir Dogs* 1991; *Animal Factory* 2000

Bunnage, Avis (1923-1990) *The L-Shaped Room* 1962; *The Loneliness of the Long Distance Runner* 1962; *Sparrows Can't Sing* 1962; *What a Crazy World* 1963; *Rotten to the Core* 1965; *The Whisperers* 1967; *No Surrender* 1985; *The Krays* 1990

Bunston, Herbert (1874-1935) *The Last of Mrs Cheyney* 1929; *Dracula* 1931; *The Moonstone* 1934

Bunton, Emma *Spice World: the Movie* 1997; *Absolutely Fabulous: the Movie* 2016

Buono, Cara (1974-) *The Cowboy Way* 1994; *Killer: a Journal of Murder* 1995; *Next Stop Wonderland* 1998; *Hulk* 2003; *Let Me In* 2010

Buono, Victor (1938-1982) *What Ever Happened to Baby Jane?* 1962; *4 for Texas* 1963; *Hush... Hush, Sweet Charlotte* 1964; *Robin and the 7 Hoods* 1964; *Young Dillinger* 1965; *The Silencers* 1966; *Who's Minding the Mint?* 1967; *Beneath the Planet of the Apes* 1969; *The Wrath of God* 1972; *The Man with Bogart's Face* 1980

Bupp, Tommy *aka* **Bupp, Tom** (1925-1983) *It's a Gift* 1934; *Hey! Hey! USA* 1938

Burden, Hugh (1913-1985) *One of Our Aircraft Is Missing* 1942; *The Way Ahead* 1944; *Fame Is the Spur* 1947; *Ghost Ship* 1952; *No Love for Johnnie* 1960; *The Secret Partner* 1961; *Blood from the Mummy's Tomb* 1971; *The Ruling Class* 1972; *The House in Nightmare Park* 1973

Burfield, Kim *Bloomfield* 1969; *Treasure Island* 1972

Burgess, Dorothy (1907-1961) *In Old Arizona* 1929; *Taxi!* 1932; *Hold Your Man* 1933; *Ladies They Talk About* 1933; *Village Tale* 1935

Burgi, Richard (1958-) *Cellular* 2004; *Starship Troopers 2: Hero of the Federation* 2004; *Torn Apart* 2004; *Hostel: Part II* 2007

Buric, Zlatko (1953-) *Pusher* 1996; *Bleeder* 1999; *Pusher 3* 2005; *Pusher* 2012

Buring, MyAnna (1979-) *The Descent* 2005; *City Rats* 2008; *Lesbian Vampire Killers* 2008; *Kill List* 2011; *Way of the Morris* 2011; *Hyena* 2014; *Lost in Karastan* 2014

Burke, Alfred (1918-2011) *Bitter Victory* 1957; *The Angry Silence* 1960; *Children of the Damned* 1964; *The Nanny* 1965; *The Night Caller* 1965; *Guns in the Heather* 1969; *One Day in the Life of Ivan Denisovich* 1971; *Kim* 1984

Burke, Billie (1885-1970) *A Bill of Divorcement* 1932; *Christopher Strong* 1933; *Dinner at Eight* 1933; *Only Yesterday* 1933; *Finishing School* 1934; *Forsaking All Others* 1934; *After Office Hours* 1935; *Becky Sharp* 1935; *Splendor* 1935; *Craig's Wife* 1936; *Piccadilly Jim* 1936; *The Bride Wore Red* 1937; *Navy Blue and Gold* 1937; *Topper* 1937; *Everybody Sing* 1938; *Merrily We Live* 1938; *The Young in Heart* 1938; *Eternally Yours* 1939; *Remember?* 1939; *Topper Takes a Trip* 1939; *The Wizard of Oz* 1939; *Zenobia* 1939; *The Ghost Comes Home* 1940; *Irene* 1940; *The Man Who Came to Dinner* 1941; *Topper Returns* 1941; *They All Kissed the Bride* 1942; *The Cheaters* 1945; *And Baby Makes Three* 1949; *The Barkleys of Broadway* 1949; *Father of the Bride* 1950; *Father's Little Dividend* 1951; *The Young Philadelphians* 1959; *Sergeant Rutledge* 1960

Burke, Billy (1966-) *Jane Austen's Mafia* 1998; *Wes Craven's Don't Look Down* 1998; *Without Limits* 1998; *Komodo* 1999; *Ladder 49* 2004; *Feast of Love* 2007; *Fracture* 2007; *Twilight* 2008; *Untraceable* 2008; *New Moon* 2009; *Eclipse* 2010; *Breaking Dawn Part One* 2011; *Drive Angry* 2011; *Red Riding Hood* 2011; *Breaking Dawn Part Two* 2012; *Lights Out* 2016

Burke, Georgia (1880-1985) *Anna Lucasta* 1958; *The Cool World* 1963

Burke, James (1886-1968) *Great Guy* 1936; *The Dawn Patrol* 1938; *Ellery Queen Master Detective* 1940; *The Saint Takes Over* 1940

Burke, Kathleen (1913-1980) *Island of Lost Souls* 1932; *Murders in the Zoo* 1933; *The Lives of a Bengal Lancer* 1935

Burke, Kathy (1964-) *Scrubbers* 1982; *Eat the Rich* 1987; *Nil by Mouth* 1997; *Dancing at Lughnasa* 1998; *Elizabeth* 1998; *This Year's Love* 1999; *Kevin & Perry Go Large* 2000; *Love, Honour and Obey* 2000; *The Martins* 2001; *Anita & Me* 2002; *Once upon a Time in the Midlands* 2002; *Flushed Away* 2006; *Pan* 2015; *Absolutely Fabulous: the Movie* 2016

Burke, Marie (1894-1980) *Odette* 1950; *Miracle in Soho* 1957

Burke, Marylouise *Series 7: the Contenders* 2001; *Sideways* 2004; *I Love You Phillip Morris* 2009

Burke, Michael Reilly *Bermuda Triangle* 1996; *Bundy* 2002; *The Collector* 2009

Burke, Michelle *aka* **Thomas, Michelle Rene** (1973-) *Coneheads* 1993; *Dazed and Confused* 1993; *Midnight in St Petersburg* 1995

Burke, Patricia (1917-2003) *While I Live* 1947; *Dilemma* 1962; *The Impersonator* 1962

Burke, Paul (1926-2009) *Valley of the Dolls* 1967; *The Thomas Crown Affair* 1968; *Daddy's Gone A-Hunting* 1969

Burke, Robert *aka* **Burke, Robert John** *aka* **Burke, Robert John** (1961-) *The Unbelievable Truth* 1989; *Rambling Rose* 1991; *Dust Devil* 1992; *Simple Men* 1992; *A Far Off Place* 1993; *RoboCop 3* 1993; *Killer: a Journal of Murder* 1995; *Fled* 1996; *If Lucy Fell* 1996; *Stephen King's Thinner* 1996; *Good Night, and Good Luck.* 2005; *Hide and Seek* 2005; *Safe* 2011; *True Story* 2015

Burke, Simon (1961-) *The Devil's Playground* 1976; *The Irishman* 1978; *Passion* 1999

Burke, Tom (1981-) *I Want Candy* 2006; *Donkey Punch* 2007; *Telstar: the Joe Meek Story* 2008; *Third Star* 2010; *Cleanskin* 2012; *The Hooligan Factory* 2014

Burke, Walter (1908-1984) *Jack the Giant Killer* 1962; *The Three Stooges Go around the World in a Daze* 1963; *The Stone Killer* 1973

Burkley, Dennis (1945-) *Mask* 1985; *Murphy's Romance* 1985; *Lambada* 1990; *The Doors* 1991; *Tin Cup* 1996

Burley, Nichola *Love + Hate* 2005; *Donkey Punch* 2007; *Kicks* 2009; *SoulBoy* 2010; *StreetDance* 2010; *Payback Season* 2012; *Twenty8k* 2012; *For Those in Peril* 2013

Burlinson, Tom (1956-) *The Man from Snowy River* 1982; *Phar Lap* 1983; *Flesh + Blood* 1985; *Windrider* 1986; *The Time Guardian* 1987; *Return to Snowy River* 1988

Burmester, Leo (1944-2007) *The Abyss* 1989; *A Perfect World* 1993; *The Neon Bible* 1995; *Old Man* 1997

Burnaby, Davy (1881-1949) *Boys Will Be Boys* 1935; *Song of the Road* 1937

Burnett, Carol (1933-) *Pete 'n' Tillie* 1972; *The Front Page* 1974; *A Wedding* 1978; *Friendly Fire* 1979; *HEALTH* 1980; *The Four Seasons* 1981; *Annie* 1982; *Between Friends* 1983; *Noises Off* 1992; *Seasons of the Heart* 1994; *Dr Seuss' Horton Hears a Who!* 2008; *Post Grad* 2009

Burnette, Olivia (1977-) *Planes, Trains and Automobiles* 1987; *Hard Promises* 1991; *Eye for an Eye* 1995

Burnette, Smiley (1911-1967) *Down Mexico Way* 1941; *On Top of Old Smoky* 1953

Burnham, Edward (1916-2015) *To Sir, with Love* 1967; *The Abominable Dr Phibes* 1971

Burnham, Jeremy *Bachelor of Hearts* 1958; *Law and Disorder* 1958

Burns (2), Bob (1893-1956) *The Big Broadcast of 1937* 1936; *Rhythm on the Range* 1936; *Waikiki Wedding* 1937; *Wells Fargo* 1937; *Belle of the Yukon* 1944

Burns, Carol (1947-2015) *Bad Blood* 1982; *Dusty* 1982

Burns, Catherine *aka* **Burns, Cathy** (1945-) *Last Summer* 1969; *Red Sky at Morning* 1971

Burns, David (1902-1971) *Smash and Grab* 1937; *Hey! Hey! USA* 1938; *The Gang's All Here* 1939; *The Saint in London* 1939; *Knock on Wood* 1954; *It's Always Fair Weather* 1955; *Let's Make Love* 1960; *Who Is Harry Kellerman, and Why Is He Saying Those Terrible Things about Me?* 1971

Burns, Edward (1968-) *The Brothers McMullen* 1995; *She's the One* 1996; *No Looking Back* 1998; *Saving Private Ryan* 1998; *Sidewalks of New York* 2000; *15 Minutes* 2001; *Ash Wednesday* 2002; *Confidence* 2002; *Life or Something like It* 2002; *The Holiday* 2006; *One Missed Call* 2007; *Alex Cross* 2012

Burns, George (1896-1996) *The Big Broadcast* 1932; *International House* 1933; *Six of a Kind* 1934; *We're Not Dressing* 1934; *The Big Broadcast of 1936* 1935; *The Big Broadcast of 1937* 1936; *A Damsel in Distress* 1937; *College Swing* 1938; *Honolulu* 1939; *The Sunshine Boys* 1975; *Oh, God!* 1977; *Sgt Pepper's Lonely Hearts Club Band* 1978; *Going in Style* 1979; *Just You and Me, Kid* 1979; *Oh! God! Book II* 1980; *Oh, God! You Devil* 1984; *18 Again!* 1988; *Radioland Murders* 1994

Burns, Heather (1974-) *Miss Congeniality* 2000; *Two Weeks Notice* 2002; *Bewitched* 2005; *Miss Congeniality 2: Armed & Fabulous* 2005

Burns, Jack (1933-) *The Night They Raided Minsky's* 1968; *Sour Grapes* 1998

Burns, Jere (1954-) *Hit List* 1988; *Greedy* 1994; *My Giant* 1998; *Life-Size* 2000; *Crocodile Dundee in Los Angeles* 2001

Burns, Marilyn (1949-2014) *The Texas Chain Saw Massacre* 1974; *Eaten Alive* 1976; *Texas Chainsaw* 2013

Burns, Marion (1907-1993) *Me and My Gal* 1932; *Born to Be Bad* 1934; *The Dawn Rider* 1935; *Paradise Canyon* 1935

Burns, Mark (1936-2007) *The Adventures of Gerard* 1970; *The Virgin and the Gypsy* 1970; *Death in Venice* 1971; *A Time for Loving* 1971; *The Maids* 1974; *The Bitch* 1979; *Bullseye!* 1990

Burns, Michael (1947-) *40 Guns to Apache Pass* 1966; *Journey to Shiloh* 1967; *Stranger on the Run* 1967; *That Cold Day in the Park* 1969; *Thumb Tripping* 1972; *Santee* 1973

Burns, Paul E (1881-1967) *The Woman on Pier 13* 1949; *Montana* 1950

Burr, Raymond (1917-1993) *Without Reservations* 1946; *Desperate* 1947; *Pitfall* 1948; *Raw Deal* 1948; *Ruthless* 1948; *Sleep, My Love* 1948; *Station West* 1948; *Black Magic* 1949; *Bride of Vengeance* 1949; *Love Happy* 1949; *Red Light* 1949; *Borderline* 1950; *Key to the City* 1950; *His Kind of Woman* 1951; *M* 1951; *A Place in the Sun* 1951; *The Whip Hand* 1951; *Horizons West* 1952; *Mara Maru* 1952; *Meet Danny Wilson* 1952; *The Bandits of Corsica* 1953; *The Blue Gardenia* 1953; *Fort Algiers* 1953; *Serpent of the Nile* 1953; *Tarzan and the She-Devil* 1953; *Casanova's Big Night* 1954; *Gorilla at Large* 1954; *Khyber Patrol* 1954; *Rear Window* 1954; *Count Three and Pray* 1955; *A Man Alone* 1955; *You're Never Too Young* 1955; *The Brass Legend* 1956; *A Cry in the Night* 1956; *Great Day in the Morning* 1956; *Crime of*

Passion 1957; *Desire in the Dust* 1960; *Tomorrow Never Comes* 1977; *Out of the Blue* 1980; *Airplane II: the Sequel* 1982; *The Return of Godzilla* 1984; *Delirious* 1991; *The Return of Ironside* 1993

Burrage, Ron *The Confessional* 1995; *Double Take* 2009

Burrell, Sheila (1922-2011) *Cloudburst* 1951; *Colonel March Investigates* 1953; *Paranoiac* 1963; *The Woodlanders* 1997

Burrell, Ty (1967-) *Dawn of the Dead* 2004; *Friends with Money* 2006; *Fur: an Imaginary Portrait of Diane Arbus* 2006; *The Incredible Hulk* 2008; *Mr Peabody & Sherman* 2013; *Muppets Most Wanted* 2014; *The Skeleton Twins* 2014

Burress, Hedy (1973-) *Foxfire* 1996; *If These Walls Could Talk* 1996

Burroughs, Jackie (1939-2010) *Heavy Metal* 1981; *The Grey Fox* 1982; *The Care Bears Movie* 1985; *Hemoglobin* 1997; *Evidence of Blood* 1998; *Willard* 2003; *Snow* 2004

Burrows, Saffron (1972-) *Welcome II the Terrordome* 1994; *Circle of Friends* 1995; *Hotel de Love* 1996; *Deep Blue Sea* 1999; *The Loss of Sexual Innocence* 1999; *Miss Julie* 1999; *Timecode* 1999; *Wing Commander* 1999; *Gangster No 1* 2000; *Enigma* 2001; *Hotel* 2001; *Tempted* 2001; *Frida* 2002; *Troy* 2004; *Perfect Creature* 2005; *Klimt* 2006; *Dangerous Parking* 2007; *Reign over Me* 2007; *The Bank Job* 2008; *Shrink* 2009

Burstyn, Ellen *aka* **McRae, Ellen** (1932-) *For Those Who Think Young* 1964; *Goodbye Charlie* 1964; *Alex in Wonderland* 1970; *The Last Picture Show* 1971; *The King of Marvin Gardens* 1972; *The Exorcist* 1973; *Alice Doesn't Live Here Anymore* 1974; *Harry and Tonto* 1974; *Providence* 1977; *A Dream of Passion* 1978; *Same Time, Next Year* 1978; *Resurrection* 1980; *Silence of the North* 1981; *The Ambassador* 1984; *Surviving* 1985; *Twice in a Lifetime* 1985; *Act of Vengeance* 1986; *Hanna's War* 1988; *Dying Young* 1991; *Mrs Lambert Remembers Love* 1991; *The Cemetery Club* 1993; *Getting Gotti* 1994; *When a Man Loves a Woman* 1994; *The Baby-Sitter's Club* 1995; *How to Make an American Quilt* 1995; *My Brother's Keeper* 1995; *Roommates* 1995; *The Spitfire Grill* 1996; *Liar* 1997; *Playing by Heart* 1998; *You Can Thank Me Later* 1998; *Walking across Egypt* 1999; *Mermaid* 2000; *Requiem for a Dream* 2000; *The Yards* 2000; *Divine Secrets of the Ya-Ya Sisterhood* 2002; *Red Dragon* 2002; *The Fountain* 2005; *The Wicker Man* 2006; *W.* 2008; *According to Greta* 2009; *Love, Marilyn* 2012; *The Calling* 2014; *When Marnie Was There* 2014; *The Age of Adaline* 2015; *Wiener-Dog* 2016

Burton, Clarence (1882-1933) *The Navigator* 1924; *The Unholy Three* 1930

Burton, Corey (1955-) *The Hunchback of Notre Dame* 1996; *Atlantis: the Lost Empire* 2001; *Cinderella II: Dreams Come True* 2002; *Return to Never Land* 2002

Burton, Frederick (1871-1957) *The Big Trail* 1930; *An American Tragedy* 1931; *One Way Passage* 1932; *The Wet Parade* 1932; *The Man from Dakota* 1940

Burton, Kate (1957-) *Big Trouble in Little China* 1986; *August* 1995; *Swimfan* 2002; *Unfaithful* 2002; *Stay* 2005; *Mariachi Gringo* 2012; *Martyrs* 2015

Burton, LeVar (1957-) *The Hunter* 1980; *Star Trek: Generations* 1994; *Star Trek: First Contact* 1996; *Star Trek: Insurrection* 1998; *Star Trek: Nemesis* 2002; *Taken in Broad Daylight* 2009

Burton, Martin (1904-1976) *Ladies' Man* 1931; *When Ladies Meet* 1933

Burton, Norman *aka* **Burton, Normann** (1923-2003) *Diamonds Are Forever* 1971; *Save the Tiger* 1973; *The Terminal Man* 1974; *The Reincarnation of Peter Proud* 1975; *The Gumball Rally* 1976; *Mausoleum* 1983; *Crimes of Passion* 1984; *Bloodsport* 1987

Burton, Peter (1921-1989) *What the Butler Saw* 1950; *The Wooden Horse* 1950; *Dr No* 1962

Burton, Richard (1925-1984) *The Last Days of Dolwyn* 1949; *Now Barabbas Was a Robber* 1949; *Waterfront* 1950; *Green Grow the Rushes* 1951; *My Cousin Rachel* 1952; *The Desert Rats* 1953; *The Robe* 1953; *Prince of Players* 1955; *The Rains of Ranchipur* 1955; *Alexander the Great* 1956; *Bitter Victory* 1957; *Sea Wife* 1957; *Look Back in Anger* 1959; *The Bramble Bush* 1960; *Ice Palace* 1960; *A Midsummer Night's Dream* 1961; *The Longest Day* 1962; *Cleopatra* 1963; *The VIPs* 1963; *Becket*

1964; Hamlet 1964; The Night of the Iguana 1964; The Sandpiper 1965; The Spy Who Came In from the Cold 1965; What's New, Pussycat? 1965; Who's Afraid of Virginia Woolf? 1966; The Comedians 1967; Doctor Faustus 1967; The Taming of the Shrew 1967; Boom 1968; Candy 1968; Anne of the Thousand Days 1969; Staircase 1969; Where Eagles Dare 1969; Raid on Rommel 1971; Under Milk Wood 1971; Villain 1971; The Assassination of Trotsky 1972; Bluebeard 1972; Massacre in Rome 1973; Brief Encounter 1974; The Voyage 1974; Equus 1977; Exorcist II: The Heretic 1977; Absolution 1978; Breakthrough 1978; The Medusa Touch 1978; The Wild Geese 1978; Lovespell 1979; Circle of Two 1980; Wagner 1983; Nineteen Eighty-Four 1984

Burton, Robert (1895-1964) Above and Beyond 1952; Desperate Search 1952; Cry of the Hunted 1953; The Girl Who Had Everything 1953; A Man Called Peter 1955; The Brass Legend 1956; The Hired Gun 1957; I Was a Teenage Frankenstein 1957; The Gallant Hours 1960

Burton, Tony (1937-2016) Assault on Precinct 13 1976; The Bingo Long Travelling All-Stars and Motor Kings 1976; Rocky II 1979; Inside Moves: the Guys from Max's Bar 1980; Rocky IV 1985; Rocky V 1990; Rocky Balboa 2006

Burton, Wendell (1947-) The Sterile Cuckoo 1969; Fortune and Men's Eyes 1971

Burtwell, Frederick (1900-1948) Dr Syn 1937; The Silver Fleet 1943

Busby, Tom (1936-2003) During One Night 1961; Heavenly Pursuits 1986

Buscemi, Michael Trees Lounge 1996; Interview 2007

Buscemi, Steve (1957-) Parting Glances 1985; Heart 1987; Kiss Daddy Good Night 1987; Call Me 1988; Heart of Midnight 1988; Bloodhounds of Broadway 1989; King of New York 1989; Mystery Train 1989; New York Stories 1989; Slaves of New York 1989; Miller's Crossing 1990; Barton Fink 1991; Billy Bathgate 1991; Reservoir Dogs 1991; Tales from the Darkside: the Movie 1991; Zandalee 1991; CrissCross 1992; In the Soup 1992; The Last Outlaw 1993; Motherhood 1993; Rising Sun 1993; Airheads 1994; Floundering 1994; Pulp Fiction 1994; Somebody to Love 1994; Desperado 1995; Fargo 1995; Kansas City 1995; Living in Oblivion 1995; Things to Do in Denver When You're Dead 1995; Escape from LA 1996; Trees Lounge 1996; The Big Lebowski 1997; Con Air 1997; The Real Blonde 1997; Armageddon 1998; The Impostors 1998; Big Daddy 1999; Animal Factory 2000; 28 Days 2000; Domestic Disturbance 2001; Double Whammy 2001; Final Fantasy: the Spirits Within 2001; Ghost World 2001; The Grey Zone 2001; Monsters, Inc 2001; The Laramie Project 2002; Mr Deeds 2002; SPYkids 2: the Island of Lost Dreams 2002; Coffee and Cigarettes 2003; Home on the Range 2004; Romance & Cigarettes 2004; The Island 2005; Charlotte's Web 2006; Monster House 2006; I Now Pronounce You Chuck & Larry 2007; Interview 2007; Igor 2008; City of War: the Story of John Rabe 2009; G-Force 2009; The Messenger 2009; Youth in Revolt 2009; Blank City 2010; Grown Ups 2010; Hotel Transylvania 2012; The Incredible Burt Wonderstone 2013; Khumba 2013; Monsters University 2013; The Cobbler 2014; Time out of Mind 2014; Hotel Transylvania 2 2015

Busch, Ernst (1900-1980) Kameradschaft 1931; Kühle Wampe 1931

Busch, Mae (1897-1946) Foolish Wives 1920; The Unholy Three 1925; Fazil 1928; Alibi 1929; Their First Mistake 1932; Sons of the Desert 1933; Oliver the Eighth 1934; Them Thar Hills! 1934; Tit for Tat 1934; The Bohemian Girl 1936

Busey, Gary aka Busey, Garey (1944-) The Last American Hero 1973; The Lolly-Madonna War 1973; The Execution of Private Slovik 1974; Thunderbolt and Lightfoot 1974; The Gumball Rally 1976; A Star Is Born 1976; Big Wednesday 1978; The Buddy Holly Story 1978; Straight Time 1978; Carny 1980; Foolin' Around 1980; Barbarosa 1982; DC Cab 1983; Insignificance 1985; Silver Bullet 1985; Eye of the Tiger 1986; Bulletproof 1987; Lethal Weapon 1987; Hider in the House 1989; Predator 2 1990; My Heroes Have Always Been Cowboys 1991; Point Break 1991; Under Siege 1992; Rookie of the Year 1993; Chasers 1994; Drop Zone 1994; Surviving the

Game 1994; Acts of Love 1995; Black Sheep 1996; Lethal Tender 1996; Lost Highway 1996; Diary of a Serial Killer 1997; Fear and Loathing in Las Vegas 1998; Soldier 1998; Too Hard to Die 1998; Universal Soldier 2: Brothers in Arms 1998; Universal Soldier 3: Unfinished Business 1998; Gang Law 1999; Jacob Two Two Meets the Hooded Fang 1999; A Crack in the Floor 2000; G-Men from Hell 2000; Piranha 3DD 2011; Bounty Killer 2013

Busey, Jake (1971-) SFW 1994; Starship Troopers 1997; Home Fries 1998; Held Up 1999; Tomcats 2000; Identity 2003; Christmas with the Kranks 2004; CodeBreakers 2005; Road House 2 2006

Busfield, Timothy (1960-) Revenge of the Nerds 1984; Field of Dreams 1989; Sneakers 1992; Murder between Friends 1993; Striking Distance 1993; Little Big League 1994; Kidnapped 1995; First Kid 1996; Buffalo Soldiers 1997; National Security 2002; Beyond the Blackboard 2011

Bush, Billy Green aka **Bush, Billy "Green"** (1935-) Five Easy Pieces 1970; The Culpepper Cattle Co 1972; Electra Glide in Blue 1973; Alice Doesn't Live Here Anymore 1974; The Jericho Mile 1979; Tom Horn 1980; The River 1984; Critters 1986

Bush, James (1907-1987) The Arizonian 1935; The Return of Peter Grimm 1935; You Can't Cheat an Honest Man 1939

Bush, Sophia John Tucker Must Die 2006; Stay Alive 2006; The Hitcher 2007

Bushell, Anthony (1904-1997) Disraeli 1929; Journey's End 1930; Five Star Final 1931; Crime on the Hill 1933; The Ghoul 1933; The Scarlet Pimpernel 1934; Dusty Ermine 1936; Dark Journey 1937; The Return of the Scarlet Pimpernel 1937; The Arsenal Stadium Mystery 1939; The Miniver Story 1950; The Long Dark Hall 1951; The Red Beret 1953; The Black Knight 1954; The Purple Plain 1954; The Battle of the River Plate 1956; The Black Tent 1956; Bitter Victory 1957; A Night to Remember 1958; The Wind Cannot Read 1958

Bushman, Ralph aka **Bushman Jr, Francis X** (1903-1978) Our Hospitality 1923; Four Sons 1928

Busia, Akosua (1968-) The Color Purple 1985; Native Son 1986

Bussières, Pascale (1968-) When Night Is Falling 1995; The Five Senses 1999; Girls Can't Swim 1999; XChange 2000; Petites Coupures 2002

Bussières, Raymond (1907-1982) Les Portes de la Nuit 1946; Casque d'Or 1952; Gates of Paris 1957; Paris When It Sizzles 1964; The King and the Mockingbird 1980

Busta Rhymes (1972-) The Rugrats Movie 1998; Finding Forrester 2000; Shaft 2000; Narc 2001; Halloween: Resurrection 2002

Butcher, Adam Saint Ralph 2004; Dog Pound 2009

Butel, Mitchell Dark City 1998; The Bank 2001

Butler, Austin Aliens in the Attic 2009; Sharpay's Fabulous Adventure 2011; Yoga Hosers 2016

Butler, David (1894-1979) 7th Heaven 1927; The Corpse 1969

Butler, Gerald Geostorm 2016; London Has Fallen 2016

Butler, Gerard (1969-) Mrs Brown 1997; Fast Food 1998; One More Kiss 1999; Dracula 2001 2000; Shooters 2000; Reign of Fire 2001; Dear Frankie 2003; Lara Croft, Tomb Raider: the Cradle of Life 2003; Timeline 2003; The Phantom of the Opera 2004; 300 2006; Butterfly on a Wheel 2007; PS I Love You 2007; Gamer 2008; Nim's Island 2008; RocknRolla 2008; Law Abiding Citizen 2009; The Ugly Truth 2009; The Bounty Hunter 2010; Coriolanus 2010; How to Train Your Dragon 2010; Machine Gun Preacher 2011; Chasing Mavericks 2012; Playing for Keeps 2012; Movie 43 2013; Olympus Has Fallen 2013; How to Train Your Dragon 2 2014; Gods of Egypt 2016

Butler, Jean (1971-) The Brylcreem Boys 1996; Goldfish Memory 2003

Butler, Jimmy (1921-1945) No Greater Glory 1934; Romance in Manhattan 1934

Butler, Tom (1951-) Scanners II: The New Order 1991; Ernest Rides Again 1993

Butler, William aka **Butler, Bill** Friday the 13th Part VII: the New Blood 1988; Buried Alive 1990; Leatherface: the Texas Chainsaw Massacre III 1990; Night of the Living Dead 1990

Butler, Yancy (1970-) Hard Target 1993; Drop Zone 1994; Let It Be Me 1995; Doomsday Man 1998

Butrick, Merritt (1959-1989) Star Trek II: the Wrath of Khan 1982; Star Trek III: the Search for Spock 1984; Shy People 1987

Butterfield, Asa (1997-) The Boy in the Striped Pyjamas 2008; Nanny McPhee & the Big Bang 2010; Hugo 2011; Ender's Game 2013; X+Y 2014; Miss Peregrine's Home for Peculiar Children 2016

Butterworth, Charles (1896-1946) Illicit 1931; The Mad Genius 1931; Love Me Tonight 1932; Penthouse 1933; Bulldog Drummond Strikes Back 1934; The Cat and the Fiddle 1934; Forsaking All Others 1934; Magnificent Obsession 1935; The Moon's Our Home 1936; Every Day's a Holiday 1937; Swing High, Swing Low 1937; The Boys from Syracuse 1940; Second Chorus 1940; Road Show 1941; This Is the Army 1943; The Bermuda Mystery 1944

Butterworth, Donna The Family Jewels 1965; Paradise, Hawaiian Style 1966

Butterworth, Peter (1919-1979) Mr Drake's Duck 1950; tom thumb 1958; Live Now - Pay Later 1962; Doctor in Distress 1963; Carry On Cowboy 1965; Carry On - Don't Lose Your Head 1966; Carry On Screaming 1966; Carry On Follow That Camel 1967; Carry On Doctor 1968; Carry On Camping 1969; Bless This House 1972; Carry On Abroad 1972; Carry On Girls 1973; Carry On Dick 1974; Carry On Behind 1975; Carry On England 1976; Carry On Emmannuelle 1978

Buttons, Red (1919-2006) Sayonara 1957; The Big Circus 1959; Five Weeks in a Balloon 1962; Gay Purr-ee 1962; Hatari! 1962; The Longest Day 1962; A Ticklish Affair 1963; Your Cheatin' Heart 1964; Harlow 1965; Up from the Beach 1965; Stagecoach 1966; They Shoot Horses, Don't They? 1969; The Poseidon Adventure 1972; Gable and Lombard 1976; Pete's Dragon 1977; Viva Knievel! 1977; CHOMPS 1979; When Time Ran Out 1980; Leave 'Em Laughing 1981; Reunion at Fairborough 1985; 18 Again! 1988; The Ambulance 1990; It Could Happen to You 1994; The Story of Us 1999

Buttram, Pat (1917-1994) Riders in the Sky 1949; Mule Train 1950; Blue Canadian Rockies 1952; Twilight of Honor 1963; Roustabout 1964; Back to the Future Part III 1990

Buy, Margherita (1962-) Il Cielo è Sempre Più Blu 1995; Le Fate Ignoranti 2001; The Caiman 2006; A Magnificent Haunting 2012; Mia Madre 2015

Buzzi, Ruth (1936-) Cactus Jack 1979; Skatetown, USA 1979; Bad Guys 1986

Byers, Christian Opal Dream 2005; December Boys 2007

Byers, Kate Staggered 1993; Career Girls 1997

Bygraves, Max (1922-2012) Tom Brown's Schooldays 1951; Charley Moon 1956; A Cry from the Streets 1957; Bobbikins 1959; Spare the Rod 1961

Byington, Spring (1893-1971) Little Women 1933; Ah, Wilderness! 1935; Way Down East 1935; The Charge of the Light Brigade 1936; Stage Struck 1936; Theodora Goes Wild 1936; A Family Affair 1937; Green Light 1937; The Buccaneer 1938; You Can't Take It with You 1938; The Story of Alexander Graham Bell 1939; The Blue Bird 1940; Lucky Partners 1940; The Devil and Miss Jones 1941; Meet John Doe 1941; The Vanishing Virginian 1941; When Ladies Meet 1941; The Affairs of Martha 1942; Rings on Her Fingers 1942; Roxie Hart 1942; The War against Mrs Hadley 1942; Heaven Can Wait 1943; The Heavenly Body 1943; Presenting Lily Mars 1943; I'll Be Seeing You 1944; The Enchanted Cottage 1945; Salty O'Rourke 1945; Thrill of a Romance 1945; Dragonwyck 1946; My Brother Talks to Horses 1946; Cynthia 1947; It Had to Be You 1947; Living in a Big Way 1947; Singapore 1947; BF's Daughter 1948; The Big Wheel 1949; In the Good Old Summertime 1949; Walk Softly, Stranger 1949; Devil's Doorway 1950; Please Believe Me 1950; Angels in the Outfield 1951; Because You're Mine 1952; No Room for the Groom 1952; The Rocket Man 1954; Please Don't Eat the Daisies 1960

Byner, John (1938-) Stroker Ace 1983; The Black Cauldron 1985; Transylvania 6-5000 1985

Bynes, Amanda (1986-) Big Fat Liar 2002; What a Girl Wants 2003; Love Wrecked 2005; Robots 2005; She's the Man 2006; Hairspray 2007;

Sydney White 2007; Living Proof 2008; Easy A 2010

Byrd, Dan (1985-) A Cinderella Story 2004; The Hills Have Eyes 2006

Byrd, Eugene (1975-) Murder in Mississippi 1990; Whiteboys 1999; 8 Mile 2002; Anacondas: the Hunt for the Blood Orchid 2004; Rails & Ties 2007

Byrd, Ralph (1909-1952) Careful, Soft Shoulder 1942; Jungle Book 1942; Moontide 1942; Dick Tracy's Dilemma 1947; Dick Tracy Meets Gruesome 1947

Byrd, Thomas Jefferson aka **Byrd, Tom** (1960-) Clockers 1995; Get on the Bus 1996; Bamboozled 2000

Byrge, Bill Ernest Goes to Jail 1990; Ernest Scared Stupid 1991

Byrne, Anne The End of the World (in Our Usual Bed in a Night Full of Rain) 1978; Manhattan 1979

Byrne, David (1952-) Stop Making Sense 1984; True Stories 1986; Ride, Rise, Roar 2010

Byrne, Ed Rat 2000; Round Ireland with a Fridge... a True Story 2010

Byrne, Eddie (1911-1982) Lady Godiva Rides Again 1951; The Gentle Gunman 1952; Time Gentlemen Please! 1952; Beautiful Stranger 1954; Children Galore 1954; The Divided Heart 1954; Happy Ever After 1954; Trouble in the Glen 1954; The Man in the Sky 1956; Floods of Fear 1958; Jack the Ripper 1958; The Mummy 1959; The Shakedown 1959; The Break 1962; The Cracksman 1963; Island of Terror 1966

Byrne, Gabriel (1950-) The Outsider 1979; Excalibur 1981; The Keep 1983; Defence of the Realm 1985; Gothic 1986; Lionheart 1986; Hello Again 1987; Julia and Julia 1987; Siesta 1987; A Soldier's Tale 1988; Diamond Skulls 1989; Miller's Crossing 1990; Shipwrecked 1990; Cool World 1992; Into the West 1992; The Assassin 1993; A Dangerous Woman 1993; Little Women 1994; Prince of Jutland 1994; A Simple Twist of Fate 1994; Trial by Jury 1994; Dead Man 1995; Frankie Starlight 1995; The Usual Suspects 1995; The Brylcreem Boys 1996; Last of the High Kings 1996; Smilla's Feeling for Snow 1996; This Is the Sea 1996; Trigger Happy 1996; The End of Violence 1997; The Man in the Iron Mask 1997; Enemy of the State 1998; Polish Wedding 1998; End of Days 1999; Stigmata 1999; Ghost Ship 2002; Spider 2002; Vanity Fair 2004; Assault on Precinct 13 2005; Wah-Wah 2005; Jindabyne 2006; All Things to All Men 2012; I, Anna 2012; The 33 2014; Louder than Bombs 2015

Byrne, Michael (1922-) Butley 1973; Champions 1983; The Plot to Kill Hitler 1990; The Infiltrator 1995; The Island on Bird Street 1997; Battlefield Earth 2000; Gangs of New York 2002

Byrne, Rose (1979-) Dallas Doll 1994; Two Hands 1999; My Mother Frank 2000; City of Ghosts 2002; I Capture the Castle 2002; The Rage in Placid Lake 2002; The Night We Called It a Day 2003; Troy 2004; Wicker Park 2004; Sunshine 2007; 28 Weeks Later 2007; Adam 2009; Knowing 2009; Get Him to the Greek 2010; Insidious 2010; Bridesmaids 2011; X-Men: First Class 2011; I Give It a Year 2013; Insidious: Chapter 2 2013; The Internship 2013; The Turning 2013; Annie 2014; Bad Neighbours 2014; This Is Where I Leave You 2014; The Meddler 2015; Spy 2015; Bad Neighbours 2 2016

Byrnes, Edd aka **Byrnes, Edward** (1933-) Johnny Trouble 1957; Reform School Girl 1957; Darby's Rangers 1958; Yellowstone Kelly 1959; The Secret Invasion 1964; Stardust 1974; Troop Beverly Hills 1989

Byrnes, Jim (1948-) Highlander: Endgame 2000; My Fair Madeline 2002; Highlander: the Source 2007

Byron, Arthur aka **Byron, A S** (1872-1943) The Mummy 1932; Gabriel over the White House 1933; The Mayor of Hell 1933; 20,000 Years in Sing Sing 1933; Fog over Frisco 1934; The House of Rothschild 1934; Marie Galante 1934; The Secret Bride 1934; The Casino Murder Case 1935; The Whole Town's Talking 1935

Byron, Kathleen (1921-2009) A Matter of Life and Death 1946; Black Narcissus 1947; Madness of the Heart 1949; The Small Back Room 1949; Prelude to Fame 1950; The Reluctant Widow 1950; Scarlet Thread 1951; Tom Brown's Schooldays 1951; The Gambler and the Lady 1952; Young Bess 1953; Profile 1954; Night of the Eagle 1961; Twins of Evil 1971; The Abdication 1974; Saving Private Ryan 1998

Byron, Walter (1899-1972) Queen Kelly 1928; The Last Flight 1931; Sinners

in the Sun 1932; Three Wise Girls 1932; British Agent 1934; Folies Bergère 1935

Byun Hee-bong Memories of Murder 2003; The Host 2006

C

Caan, James (1939-) Lady in a Cage 1964; The Glory Guys 1965; Red Line 7000 1965; Countdown 1967; El Dorado 1967; Games 1967; Journey to Shiloh 1967; Submarine X-1 1967; The Rain People 1969; Rabbit, Run 1970; Brian's Song 1971; TR Baskin 1971; The Godfather 1972; Cinderella Liberty 1973; Slither 1973; Freebie and the Bean 1974; The Gambler 1974; Funny Lady 1975; The Killer Elite 1975; Rollerball 1975; Harry and Walter Go to New York 1976; Another Man, Another Chance 1977; A Bridge Too Far 1977; Comes a Horseman 1978; Little Moon & Jud McGraw 1978; Chapter Two 1979; Hide in Plain Sight 1980; Thief 1981; Les Uns et les Autres 1981; Kiss Me Goodbye 1982; Gardens of Stone 1987; Alien Nation 1988; Dick Tracy 1990; Misery 1990; For the Boys 1991; Honeymoon in Vegas 1992; Flesh and Bone 1993; The Program 1993; A Boy Called Hate 1995; Bottle Rocket 1996; Bulletproof 1996; Eraser 1996; North Star 1996; Poodle Springs 1998; Mickey Blue Eyes 1999; This Is My Father 1999; The Way of the Gun 2000; The Yards 2000; City of Ghosts 2002; Dogville 2003; Elf 2003; Cloudy with a Chance of Meatballs 2009; Henry's Crime 2010; Detachment 2011; Small Apartments 2012; That's My Boy 2012; Cloudy with a Chance of Meatballs 2 2013; The Tale of the Princess Kaguya 2013

Caan, Scott (1976-) A Boy Called Hate 1995; Black and White 1999; Varsity Blues 1999; Ready to Rumble 2000; American Outlaws 2001; Novocaine 2001; Ocean's Eleven 2001; Sonny 2002; Ocean's Twelve 2004; Into the Blue 2005; Friends with Money 2006; Lonely Hearts 2006; Brooklyn Rules 2007; Ocean's Thirteen 2007; Meet Dave 2008; Rock the Kasbah 2015

Caba, Emilio Gutiérrez (1942-) The Hunt 1966; La Comunidad 2000

Cabot, Bruce (1904-1972) The Roadhouse Murder 1932; Ann Vickers 1933; King Kong 1933; Lucky Devils 1933; Finishing School 1934; Murder on the Blackboard 1934; Let 'Em Have It 1935; Fury 1936; The Robin Hood of El Dorado 1936; Sinners in Paradise 1938; Smashing the Rackets 1938; Dodge City 1939; Susan and God 1940; The Flame of New Orleans 1941; Sundown 1941; The Desert Song 1944; Fallen Angel 1945; Salty O'Rourke 1945; Smoky 1946; Angel and the Badman 1947; Sorrowful Jones 1949; Fancy Pants 1950; Best of the Badmen 1951; Lost in Alaska 1952; The Quiet American 1958; The Sheriff of Fractured Jaw 1958; Goliath and the Barbarians 1959; The Comancheros 1961; Hatari! 1962; The War Wagon 1967; The Green Berets 1968; Chisum 1970; Big Jake 1971; Diamonds Are Forever 1971

Cabot, Christina The Maldonado Miracle 2003; The Incredible Hulk 2008

Cabot, Sebastian (1918-1977) Kismet 1955; Dragoon Wells Massacre 1957; Johnny Tremain 1957; Omar Khayyam 1957; Terror in a Texas Town 1958; The Angry Hills 1959; The Time Machine 1960; The Sword in the Stone 1963; Twice Told Tales 1963; The Family Jewels 1965; The Jungle Book 1967; The Many Adventures of Winnie the Pooh 1977

Cabot, Susan (1927-1986) Tomahawk 1951; The Battle at Apache Pass 1952; The Duel at Silver Creek 1952; Son of Ali Baba 1952; Gunsmoke 1953; Ride Clear of Diablo 1954; Viking Women and the Sea Serpent 1957; Fort Massacre 1958; Machine Gun Kelly 1958; War of the Satellites 1958; The Wasp Woman 1959

Cadell, Jean (1884-1967) David Copperfield 1935; Love from a Stranger 1936; Whom the Gods Love 1936; Pygmalion 1938; Quiet Wedding 1940; Whisky Galore! 1949; The Late Edwina Black 1951; The Little Hut 1957

Cadell, Selina Not Quite Jerusalem 1985; The Carer 2015

Cadieux, Anne-Marie The Confessional 1995; Four Days 1999

Cady, Frank (1915-2012) Ace in the Hole 1951; Let's Make It Legal 1951; Zandy's Bride 1974

Caesar, Adolph (1933-1986) *A Soldier's Story* 1984; *The Color Purple* 1985; *Club Paradise* 1986

Caesar, Harry (1928-1994) *Emperor of the North* 1973; *The Mean Machine* 1974; *Breakdance 2 - Electric Boogaloo* 1984; *Bird on a Wire* 1990

Caesar, Sid (1922-2014) *The Guilt of Janet Ames* 1947; *It's a Mad Mad Mad Mad World* 1963; *The Busy Body* 1967; *Airport 1975* 1974; *Silent Movie* 1976; *Fire Sale* 1977; *The Cheap Detective* 1978; *The Fiendish Plot of Dr Fu Manchu* 1980; *History of the World Part 1* 1981; *Grease 2* 1982; *Over the Brooklyn Bridge* 1983

Caffrey, Peter *Angel* 1982; *I Went Down* 1997

Caffrey, Sean (1940-) *I Was Happy Here* 1966; *When Dinosaurs Ruled the Earth* 1969

Caffrey, Stephen (1961-) *Longtime Companion* 1990; *Formula for Death* 1995

Cage, Nicolas (1964-) *Rumble Fish* 1983; *Valley Girl* 1983; *Birdy* 1984; *The Cotton Club* 1984; *Racing with the Moon* 1984; *The Boy in Blue* 1986; *Peggy Sue Got Married* 1986; *Moonstruck* 1987; *Raising Arizona* 1987; *Vampire's Kiss* 1988; *Wild at Heart* 1990; *Wings of the Apache* 1990; *Zandalee* 1991; *Honeymoon in Vegas* 1992; *Red Rock West* 1992; *Amos & Andrew* 1993; *Guarding Tess* 1994; *It Could Happen to You* 1994; *Kiss of Death* 1994; *Trapped in Paradise* 1994; *Leaving Las Vegas* 1995; *The Rock* 1996; *Con Air* 1997; *Face/Off* 1997; *City of Angels* 1998; *Snake Eyes* 1998; *Bringing Out the Dead* 1999; *8mm* 1999; *The Family Man* 2000; *Gone in Sixty Seconds* 2000; *Captain Corelli's Mandolin* 2001; *Christmas Carol: the Movie* 2001; *Windtalkers* 2001; *Adaptation.* 2002; *Sonny* 2002; *Matchstick Men* 2003; *National Treasure* 2004; *Lord of War* 2005; *The Weather Man* 2005; *The Ant Bully* 2006; *The Wicker Man* 2006; *World Trade Center* 2006; *Bangkok Dangerous* 2007; *Ghost Rider* 2007; *National Treasure: Book of Secrets* 2007; *Next* 2007; *Astro Boy* 2009; *The Bad Lieutenant - Port of Call: New Orleans* 2009; *G-Force* 2009; *Kick-Ass* 2009; *Knowing* 2009; *Season of the Witch* 2010; *The Sorcerer's Apprentice* 2010; *Drive Angry* 2011; *Justice* 2011; *Trespass* 2011; *Ghost Rider: Spirit of Vengeance* 2012; *Stolen* 2012; *The Croods* 2013; *The Frozen Ground* 2013; *Joe* 2013; *Dying of the Light* 2014; *Left Behind* 2014; *Rage* 2014; *The Runner* 2015; *Snowden* 2016; *The Trust* 2016

Cagney, James (1899-1986) *A Handful of Clouds* 1930; *Blonde Crazy* 1931; *Other Men's Women* 1931; *The Public Enemy* 1931; *Smart Money* 1931; *The Crowd Roars* 1932; *Taxi!* 1932; *Footlight Parade* 1933; *Hard to Handle* 1933; *Lady Killer* 1933; *The Mayor of Hell* 1933; *Picture Snatcher* 1933; *He Was Her Man* 1934; *Here Comes the Navy* 1934; *Jimmy the Gent* 1934; *Ceiling Zero* 1935; *Devil Dogs of the Air* 1935; *Frisco Kid* 1935; *"G" Men* 1935; *The Irish in Us* 1935; *A Midsummer Night's Dream* 1935; *Mutiny on the Bounty* 1935; *Great Guy* 1936; *Something to Sing About* 1937; *Angels with Dirty Faces* 1938; *Boy Meets Girl* 1938; *Each Dawn I Die* 1939; *The Oklahoma Kid* 1939; *The Roaring Twenties* 1939; *City for Conquest* 1940; *The Fighting 69th* 1940; *Torrid Zone* 1940; *The Bride Came COD* 1941; *The Strawberry Blonde* 1941; *Captains of the Clouds* 1942; *Yankee Doodle Dandy* 1942; *Johnny Come Lately* 1943; *Blood on the Sun* 1945; *13 Rue Madeleine* 1946; *The Time of Your Life* 1948; *White Heat* 1949; *Kiss Tomorrow Goodbye* 1950; *The West Point Story* 1950; *Come Fill the Cup* 1951; *What Price Glory?* 1952; *A Lion Is in the Streets* 1953; *Love Me or Leave Me* 1955; *Mister Roberts* 1955; *Run for Cover* 1955; *Seven Little Foys* 1955; *These Wilder Years* 1956; *Tribute to a Bad Man* 1956; *Man of a Thousand Faces* 1957; *Never Steal Anything Small* 1959; *Shake Hands with the Devil* 1959; *The Gallant Hours* 1960; *One, Two, Three* 1961; *Arizona Bushwhackers* 1968; *Ragtime* 1981

Cagney, Jeanne (1908-1984) *Yankee Doodle Dandy* 1942; *The Time of Your Life* 1948; *Quicksand* 1950; *Don't Bother to Knock* 1952; *A Lion Is in the Streets* 1953; *Man of a Thousand Faces* 1957

Cagney, William aka **Cagney, Bill** (1902-1988) *Ace of Aces* 1933; *Palooka* 1934; *Kiss Tomorrow Goodbye* 1950

Cahill, Barry (1921-2012) *Daddy's Gone A-Hunting* 1969; *Coffy* 1973; *Grand Theft Auto* 1977

Cain, Dean (1966-) *The Stone Boy* 1984; *Best Men* 1997; *Futuresport* 1998; *The Broken Hearts Club: a Romantic Comedy* 2000; *Flight of Fancy* 2000; *Militia* 2000; *Firetrap* 2001; *Out of Time* 2003; *Lost* 2005; *The Christmas Gift* 2009; *The Appearing* 2014

Caine, Henry (1888-1962) *The Ghost Train* 1931; *Number Seventeen* 1932

Caine, Howard (1926-1993) *The Man from the Diner's Club* 1963; *Watermelon Man* 1970

Caine, Michael (1933-) *A Hill in Korea* 1956; *Sailor Beware!* 1956; *How to Murder a Rich Uncle* 1957; *The Steel Bayonet* 1957; *Carve Her Name with Pride* 1958; *Danger Within* 1958; *The Key* 1958; *Passport to Shame* 1958; *The Bulldog Breed* 1960; *Foxhole in Cairo* 1960; *The Day the Earth Caught Fire* 1961; *The Wrong Arm of the Law* 1962; *Zulu* 1963; *The Ipcress File* 1965; *Alfie* 1966; *Funeral in Berlin* 1966; *Gambit* 1966; *The Wrong Box* 1966; *Billion Dollar Brain* 1967; *Hurry Sundown* 1967; *Tonite Let's All Make Love in London* 1967; *Woman Times Seven* 1967; *Deadfall* 1968; *The Magus* 1968; *Battle of Britain* 1969; *The Italian Job* 1969; *Play Dirty* 1969; *Simon, Simon* 1970; *Too Late the Hero* 1970; *Get Carter* 1971; *Kidnapped* 1971; *The Last Valley* 1971; *Zee and Co* 1971; *Pulp* 1972; *Sleuth* 1972; *The Black Windmill* 1974; *The Marseille Contract* 1974; *The Man Who Would Be King* 1975; *The Romantic Englishwoman* 1975; *The Wilby Conspiracy* 1975; *The Eagle Has Landed* 1976; *Harry and Walter Go to New York* 1976; *A Bridge Too Far* 1977; *Silver Bears* 1977; *California Suite* 1978; *The Swarm* 1978; *Ashanti* 1979; *Beyond the Poseidon Adventure* 1979; *Dressed to Kill* 1980; *The Island* 1980; *Escape to Victory* 1981; *The Hand* 1981; *Deathtrap* 1982; *Educating Rita* 1983; *The Honorary Consul* 1983; *Blame It on Rio* 1984; *The Jigsaw Man* 1984; *The Holcroft Covenant* 1985; *Water* 1985; *Half Moon Street* 1986; *Hannah and Her Sisters* 1986; *Mona Lisa* 1986; *Sweet Liberty* 1986; *The Whistle Blower* 1986; *The Fourth Protocol* 1987; *Jaws the Revenge* 1987; *Surrender* 1987; *Dirty Rotten Scoundrels* 1988; *Without a Clue* 1988; *Bullseye!* 1990; *Mr Destiny* 1990; *A Shock to the System* 1990; *Blue Ice* 1992; *The Muppet Christmas Carol* 1992; *Noises Off* 1992; *On Deadly Ground* 1994; *Bullet to Beijing* 1995; *Midnight in St Petersburg* 1995; *Blood and Wine* 1996; *Curtain Call* 1997; *Mandela and de Klerk* 1997; *Little Voice* 1998; *Shadow Run* 1998; *The Cider House Rules* 1999; *Get Carter* 2000; *Miss Congeniality* 2000; *Quills* 2000; *Shiner* 2000; *Last Orders* 2001; *Austin Powers in Goldmember* 2002; *The Quiet American* 2002; *The Actors* 2003; *Quicksand* 2003; *Secondhand Lions* 2003; *The Statement* 2003; *Around the Bend* 2004; *Batman Begins* 2005; *Bewitched* 2005; *The Weather Man* 2005; *Children of Men* 2006; *The Prestige* 2006; *Flawless* 2007; *Sleuth* 2007; *The Dark Knight* 2008; *Is Anybody There?* 2008; *Harry Brown* 2009; *Inception* 2010; *Cars 2* 2011; *Gnomeo & Juliet* 2011; *Journey 2 the Mysterious Island* 2011; *The Dark Knight Rises* 2012; *Mr Morgan's Last Love* 2013; *Now You See Me* 2013; *Interstellar* 2014; *Stonehearst Asylum* 2014; *Kingsman: The Secret Service* 2015; *The Last Witch Hunter* 2015; *Youth* 2015; *Now You See Me 2* 2016

Cairney, John (1930-) *Windom's Way* 1957; *A Night to Remember* 1958; *Operation Bullshine* 1959; *The Devil-Ship Pirates* 1964

Cake, Jonathan (1968-) *Honest* 2000; *The One and Only* 2001

Caiamai, Clara (1915-1998) *Ossessione* 1942; *White Nights* 1957; *Deep Red* 1975

Calder, David (1946-) *Defence of the Realm* 1985; *American Friends* 1991; *Mr In-Between* 2001; *Perfume: the Story of a Murderer* 2006

Calderon, Paul aka **Calderone, Paul** (1959-) *King of New York* 1989; *Sea of Love* 1989; *Bad Lieutenant* 1992; *CrissCross* 1992; *The Addiction* 1994; *Sweet Nothing* 1995; *Oxygen* 1999; *Girlfight* 2000; *21 Grams* 2003; *Pistol Whipped* 2008; *Welcome to New York* 2014

Caidicot, Richard (1908-1995) *One Good Turn* 1954; *The Fool* 1990

Caldwell, L Scott *The Switch* 1993; *The Perfect Guy* 2015

Caldwell, Zoe (1933-) *The Purple Rose of Cairo* 1985; *Lilo & Stitch* 2002

Calfa, Don (1940-) *Return of the Living Dead* 1984; *Weekend at Bernie's* 1989; *Chopper Chicks in Zombietown* 1990

Calfan, Nicole (1947-) *The Burglars* 1971; *Permission to Kill* 1975; *Les Chiens* 1978; *Max Mon Amour* 1986

Calhern, Louis (1895-1956) *Blonde Crazy* 1931; *Duck Soup* 1933; *20,000 Years in Sing Sing* 1933; *The Affairs of Cellini* 1934; *The Count of Monte Cristo* 1934; *The Arizonian* 1935; *The Last Days of Pompeii* 1935; *Woman Wanted* 1935; *The Gorgeous Hussy* 1936; *Fast Company* 1938; *Up in Arms* 1944; *Notorious* 1946; *Arch of Triumph* 1948; *The Red Danube* 1949; *The Red Pony* 1949; *Annie Get Your Gun* 1950; *The Asphalt Jungle* 1950; *Devil's Doorway* 1950; *A Life of Her Own* 1950; *The Magnificent Yankee* 1950; *Nancy Goes to Rio* 1950; *The Man with a Cloak* 1951; *The Prisoner of Zenda* 1952; *We're Not Married* 1952; *Julius Caesar* 1953; *Latin Lovers* 1953; *Remains to Be Seen* 1953; *Athena* 1954; *Betrayed* 1954; *Executive Suite* 1954; *Men of the Fighting Lady* 1954; *Rhapsody* 1954; *The Student Prince* 1954; *The Blackboard Jungle* 1955; *The Prodigal* 1955; *Forever, Darling* 1956; *High Society* 1956

Calhoun, Monica (1971-) *Bagdad Café* 1987; *The Players Club* 1998; *The Best Man* 1999

Calhoun, Rory (1922-1999) *The Red House* 1947; *A Ticket to Tomahawk* 1950; *I'd Climb the Highest Mountain* 1951; *Meet Me after the Show* 1951; *Way of a Gaucho* 1952; *With a Song in My Heart* 1952; *How to Marry a Millionaire* 1953; *Powder River* 1953; *A Bullet Is Waiting* 1954; *Dawn at Socorro* 1954; *River of No Return* 1954; *Ain't Misbehavin'* 1955; *The Spoilers* 1955; *The Treasure of Pancho Villa* 1955; *Raw Edge* 1956; *Red Sundown* 1956; *The Big Caper* 1957; *The Hired Gun* 1957; *Apache Territory* 1958; *The Saga of Hemp Brown* 1958; *The Treasure of Monte Cristo* 1961; *The Colossus of Rhodes* 1961; *The Gun Hawk* 1963; *Apache Uprising* 1965; *Motel Hell* 1980; *Angel* 1984; *Avenging Angel* 1985; *Hell Comes to Frogtown* 1988; *Bad Jim* 1989; *Pure Country* 1992

Cali, Joseph (1950-) *Saturday Night Fever* 1977; *The Lonely Lady* 1983

Call, R D (1950-) *Unconquered* 1989; *Young Guns II* 1990; *Other People's Money* 1991; *Jack Reed: Badge of Honor* 1993; *Waterworld* 1995; *Logan's War: Bound by Honor* 1998; *Murder by Numbers* 2002

Callahan, James (1930-2007) *Lady Sings the Blues* 1972; *Outlaw Blues* 1977; *The Burning Bed* 1984

Callan, Michael (1935-) *They Came to Cordura* 1959; *Because They're Young* 1960; *Mysterious Island* 1961; *Bon Voyage!* 1962; *13 West Street* 1962; *Cat Ballou* 1965; *You Must Be Joking!* 1965; *The Magnificent Seven Ride!* 1972; *Lepke* 1975; *The Cat and the Canary* 1979

Callard, Kay (1933-2008) *They Who Dare* 1953; *The Flying Scot* 1957; *The Hypnotist* 1957; *Undercover Girl* 1957

Calleia, Joseph (1897-1975) *After the Thin Man* 1936; *His Brother's Wife* 1936; *Riffraff* 1936; *Algiers* 1938; *Bad Man of Brimstone* 1938; *Golden Boy* 1939; *My Little Chickadee* 1940; *Sundown* 1941; *The Glass Key* 1942; *Jungle Book* 1942; *The Cross of Lorraine* 1943; *The Conspirators* 1944; *Deadline at Dawn* 1946; *Gilda* 1946; *Noose* 1948; *The Noose Hangs High* 1948; *They Passed This Way* 1948; *Branded* 1950; *Captain Carey* 1951; *The Light Touch* 1951; *Valentino* 1951; *The Iron Mistress* 1952; *The Caddy* 1953; *The Treasure of Pancho Villa* 1955; *Underwater!* 1955; *Hot Blood* 1956; *Serenade* 1956; *Wild Is the Wind* 1957; *The Light in the Forest* 1958; *Touch of Evil* 1958; *The Alamo* 1960

Callie, Dayton *Executive Target* 1996; *The Last Days of Frankie the Fly* 1996; *The Other Side of the Door* 2016

Callies, Sarah Wayne (1977-) *Into the Storm* 2014; *The Other Side of the Door* 2016

Callis, James (1971-) *Bridget Jones's Diary* 2001; *Bridget Jones: the Edge of Reason* 2004; *Reuniting the Rubins* 2010

Callow, Simon (1949-) *Amadeus* 1984; *A Room with a View* 1985; *The Good Father* 1986; *Maurice* 1987; *Mr and Mrs Bridge* 1990; *Postcards from the Edge* 1990; *Soft Top, Hard Shoulder* 1992; *Four Weddings and a Funeral* 1994; *Street Fighter* 1994; *Ace Ventura: When Nature Calls* 1995; *Jefferson in Paris* 1995; *James and the Giant Peach* 1996; *The Scarlet Tunic* 1997;

Bedrooms and Hallways 1998; *Shakespeare in Love* 1998; *Christmas Carol: the Movie* 2001; *Merci Docteur Rey* 2002; *Thunderpants* 2002; *Bright Young Things* 2003; *The Phantom of the Opera* 2004; *The Best Man* 2005; *Rag Tale* 2005; *Chemical Wedding* 2008; *Loves Kitchen* 2010; *Acts of Godfrey* 2011; *Golden Years* 2016

Calloway, Cab (1907-1994) *International House* 1933; *Stormy Weather* 1943; *St Louis Blues* 1958; *The Blues Brothers* 1980

Calthrop, Donald (1888-1940) *Blackmail* 1929; *The Ghost Train* 1931; *Rome Express* 1932; *The Clairvoyant* 1934; *The Phantom Light* 1934; *Scrooge* 1935; *Broken Blossoms* 1936; *The Man Who Changed His Mind* 1936

Calvé, Jean-François *Marguerite de la Nuit* 1955; *The Bride Is Too Beautiful* 1956

Calvert, Bill *Six Weeks* 1982; *CHUD II: Bud the Chud* 1989

Calvert, Jennifer *Proteus* 1995; *Infinite Justice* 2006

Calvert, John (1911-2013) *Appointment with Murder* 1948; *Devil's Cargo* 1948; *Search for Danger* 1949

Calvert, Phyllis (1915-2002) *Let George Do It* 1940; *Kipps* 1941; *Uncensored* 1942; *The Young Mr Pitt* 1942; *The Man in Grey* 1943; *Fanny by Gaslight* 1944; *Madonna of the Seven Moons* 1944; *Two Thousand Women* 1944; *They Were Sisters* 1945; *The Magic Bow* 1946; *The Root of All Evil* 1946; *Time Out of Mind* 1947; *Broken Journey* 1948; *Appointment with Danger* 1950; *Mr Denning Drives North* 1951; *Mandy* 1952; *The Net* 1953; *Child in the House* 1956; *It's Never Too Late* 1956; *Indiscreet* 1958; *Oscar Wilde* 1959; *The Battle of the Villa Fiorita* 1965; *Twisted Nerve* 1968; *Oh! What a Lovely War* 1969; *The Walking Stick* 1970

Calvet, Corinne (1925-2001) *Rope of Sand* 1949; *My Friend Irma Goes West* 1950; *When Willie Comes Marching Home* 1950; *On the Riviera* 1951; *Peking Express* 1951; *Sailor Beware* 1951; *What Price Glory?* 1952; *Flight to Tangier* 1953; *Powder River* 1953; *Thunder in the East* 1953; *The Far Country* 1954; *So This Is Paris* 1954; *Hemingway's Adventures of a Young Man* 1962; *Apache Uprising* 1965

Calvin, Henry (1918-1975) *Toby Tyler, or Ten Weeks with a Circus* 1960; *Babes in Toyland* 1961

Calvin, John *Foolin' Around* 1980; *The Magic Bubble* 1992; *Dragonworld* 1994

Cámara, Javier (1967-) *Talk to Her* 2001; *Bad Education* 2004; *I'm So Excited* 2013

Camaso, Claudio aka **Volonté, Claudio** (?-1977) *Vengeance* 1968; *Bay of Blood* 1971

Cambridge, Godfrey (1933-1976) *Gone Are the Days* 1963; *The President's Analyst* 1967; *The Biggest Bundle of Them All* 1968; *Bye Bye Braverman* 1968; *Cotton Comes to Harlem* 1970; *Watermelon Man* 1970; *Beware! The Blob* 1971; *The Biscuit Eater* 1972; *Friday Foster* 1975; *Whiffs* 1975; *Scott Joplin* 1977

Cameron, Dean (1962-) *Summer School* 1987; *Men at Work* 1990; *Sleep with Me* 1994

Cameron, Earl (1917-) *Pool of London* 1950; *Emergency Call* 1952; *The Woman for Joe* 1955; *Sapphire* 1959; *Flame in the Streets* 1961; *Tarzan's Three Challenges* 1963; *Guns at Batasi* 1964; *A Warm December* 1973; *The Interpreter* 2005

Cameron, Hugh (1879-1941) *For the Love of Mike* 1927; *One Heavenly Night* 1931

Cameron, James (1954-) *Tell Me Lies* 1967; *Ray Harryhausen: Special Effects Titan* 2011; *Side by Side* 2012

Cameron, Kirk (1970-) *Like Father, like Son* 1987; *Listen to Me* 1989

Cameron, Rod (1910-1983) *Riding High* 1943; *Frontier Gal* 1945; *Salome, Where She Danced* 1945; *Belle Starr's Daughter* 1948; *The Plunderers* 1948; *Cavalry Scout* 1951; *Southwest Passage* 1954; *Santa Fe Passage* 1955; *Passport to Treason* 1956; *The Gun Hawk* 1963; *Evel Knievel* 1971

Cameron, Trent *The Wood* 1999; *DC Sniper: 23 Days of Fear* 2003

Camilleri, Terry (1949-) *The Cars That Ate Paris* 1974; *Bill & Ted's Excellent Adventure* 1988; *Encounter at Raven's Gate* 1988; *Coffin Rock* 2009

Camp, Bill *Tamara Drewe* 2010; *Compliance* 2012

Camp, Colleen (1953-) *Smile* 1975; *Death Game* 1976; *Game of Death* 1978; *They All Laughed* 1981; *Smokey and the Bandit III* 1983; *Joy of Sex*

1984; DARYL 1985; *Police Academy 2: Their First Assignment* 1985; *Walk like a Man* 1987; *Illegally Yours* 1988; *Track 29* 1988; *Wicked Stepmother* 1989; *The Magic Bubble* 1992; *The Vagrant* 1992; *Sliver* 1993; *Die Hard with a Vengeance* 1995; *Trapped* 2002; *Psych 9* 2010; *Palo Alto* 2013

Camp, Hamilton (1934-2005) *The Perils of Pauline* 1967; *All Night Long* 1981

Campanella, Joseph (1927-) *The St Valentine's Day Massacre* 1967; *Ben* 1972; *Hangar 18* 1980; *My Body, My Child* 1982; *The Glass Cage* 1996

Campbell Moore, Stephen (1979-) *Bright Young Things* 2003; *A Good Woman* 2004; *The History Boys* 2006; *The Bank Job* 2008; *Season of the Witch* 2010; *Man Up* 2015; *The Ones Below* 2015

Campbell-Hughes, Antonia aka **Campbell Hughes, Antonia** *Storage 24* 2012; *Kelly + Victor* 2013; *The Canal* 2014; *Les Cowboys* 2015

Campbell, Adam *Date Movie* 2006; *Epic Movie* 2007

Campbell, Beatrice (1922-1979) *Meet Me at Dawn* 1946; *Silent Dust* 1948; *No Place for Jennifer* 1949; *Now Barabbas Was a Robber* 1949; *Last Holiday* 1950; *The Mudlark* 1950; *Laughter in Paradise* 1951; *Grand National Night* 1953; *The Master of Ballantrae* 1953

Campbell, Bill aka **Campbell, William** aka **Campbell, Billy** (1959-) *Rocketeer* 1991; *Bram Stoker's Dracula* 1992; *The Brylcreem Boys* 1996; *The Second Jungle Book* 1997; *Enough* 2002; *Ghost Town* 2008

Campbell, Brenda *My Neighbor's Keeper* 2007; *Secrets of an Undercover Wife* 2007

Campbell, Bruce (1958-) *The Evil Dead* 1981; *Crimewave* 1985; *Evil Dead II* 1987; *Maniac Cop* 1988; *Maniac Cop 2* 1990; *Lunatics: a Love Story* 1991; *Army of Darkness* 1992; *The Hudsucker Proxy* 1994; *Tornado!* 1996; *From Dusk till Dawn II: Texas Blood Money* 1999; *Bubba Ho-tep* 2002; *Serving Sara* 2002; *Sky High* 2005; *The Ant Bully* 2006; *Touch the Top of the World* 2006; *The Woods* 2006; *My Name Is Bruce* 2008; *Cloudy with a Chance of Meatballs* 2009; *Oz the Great and Powerful* 2013

Campbell, Cheryl (1949-) *Hawk the Slayer* 1980; *McVicar* 1980; *Chariots of Fire* 1981; *Greystoke: the Legend of Tarzan, Lord of the Apes* 1984; *The Shooting Party* 1984

Campbell, Colin (1883-1966) *The Leather Boys* 1963; *Saturday Night Out* 1963; *The High Bright Sun* 1965

Campbell, Eric (1878-1917) *Behind the Screen* 1916; *The Rink* 1916; *The Vagabond* 1916; *The Cure* 1917; *The Immigrant* 1917

Campbell, G Smokey *Bagdad Café* 1987; *Fear of a Black Hat* 1992

Campbell, Glen (1936-) *The Cool Ones* 1967; *True Grit* 1969

Campbell, John *The Fighting Sullivans* 1944; *Sweet and Lowdown* 1944

Campbell, Judy (1916-2004) *Convoy* 1940; *East of Piccadilly* 1941; *Saloon Bar* 1940; *Green for Danger* 1946; *Bonnie Prince Charlie* 1948; *There's a Girl in My Soup* 1970; *Anna Karenina* 1985

Campbell, Julia (1963-) *Opportunity Knocks* 1990; *Diary of a Serial Killer* 1997; *Romy and Michele's High School Reunion* 1997; *Poodle Springs* 1998; *A Slight Case of Murder* 1999

Campbell, Ken (1941-2008) *The Tempest* 1979; *Letter to Brezhnev* 1985; *Hard Men* 1996; *Creep* 2004

Campbell, Louise (1911-1997) *Bulldog Drummond Comes Back* 1937; *Bulldog Drummond's Revenge* 1937; *Bulldog Drummond's Peril* 1938; *Men with Wings* 1938; *The Star Maker* 1939; *Anne of Windy Poplars* 1940

Campbell, Mrs Patrick (1865-1940) *One More River* 1934; *Riptide* 1934; *Crime and Punishment* 1935

Campbell, Naomi (1970-) *Cool as Ice* 1991; *Miami Rhapsody* 1995; *Unzipped* 1995; *Girl 6* 1996; *Burn Hollywood Burn* 1997; *Fat Slags* 2004

Campbell, Nell aka **Little Nell** (1953-) *Lisztomania* 1975; *The Rocky Horror Picture Show* 1975

Campbell, Neve (1973-) *The Canterville Ghost* 1996; *The Craft* 1996; *Scream* 1996; *Scream 2* 1997; *54* 1998; *The Lion King II: Simba's Pride* 1998; *Wild Things* 1998; *Scream 3* 1999; *Three to Tango* 1999; *Drowning Mona* 2000; *Panic* 2000; *Blind Horizon* 2003; *The Company* 2003; *Churchill: the Hollywood Years* 2004; *Closing the Ring* 2006; *Partition* 2006; *Dirty Oil* 2009; *Scre4m* 2011

Campbell, Nicholas (1952-) The Amateur 1981; Terminal Choice 1983; Certain Fury 1985; Rampage 1987; Bordertown Cafe 1991; Naked Lunch 1991; Danielle Steel's No Greater Love 1996; Happy Face Murders 1999

Campbell, Rob The Crucible 1996; Hostile Waters 1996; Boys Don't Cry 1999

Campbell, Scott Michael Radioland Murders 1994; Project ALF 1996; Flight of the Phoenix 2004

Campbell, Tisha (1958-) Little Shop of Horrors 1986; School Daze 1988; House Party 1990

Campbell, William (923-2011) The Breaking Point 1950; Breakthrough 1950; Operation Pacific 1951; Battle Circus 1953; Big Leaguer 1953; Escape from Fort Bravo 1953; Man without a Star 1955; Backlash 1956; Love Me Tender 1956; The Naked and the Dead 1958; The Sheriff of Fractured Jaw 1958; Dementia 13 1963; The Secret Invasion 1964; Pretty Maids All in a Row 1971

Campeau, Frank (1864-1943) 3 Bad Men 1926; Abraham Lincoln 1930

Campion, Cris (1966-) Pirates 1986; Beyond Therapy 1987

Campo, Wally Machine Gun Kelly 1958; Beast from Haunted Cave 1959

Campos, Rafael (1936-1985) Trial 1955; Tonka 1958; Lady in a Cage 1964; Where the Buffalo Roam 1980; The Return of Josey Wales 1986

Campos, Victor Newman's Law 1974; The Master Gunfighter 1975

Canada, Ron Lone Star 1995; The Hunted 2002

Canale, Gianna Maria (1927-2009) The Man from Cairo 1953; Lust of the Vampire 1956; Hercules 1957; The Whole Truth 1958; The Treasure of Monte Cristo 1960

Canals, Maria aka **Canals, María** (1966-) The Master of Disguise 2002; Imagining Argentina 2003

Canary, David (1938-2015) Posse 1975; Shark's Treasure 1975

Candelier, Isabella News from the Good Lord 1996; Strange Gardens 2003; Gemma Bovery 2014

Candido, Candy (1913-1999) Sleeping Beauty 1959; Basil the Great Mouse Detective 1986

Candy, John (1950-1994) Find the Lady 1976; The Silent Partner 1978; Lost and Found 1979; 1941 1979; The Blues Brothers 1980; Heavy Metal 1981; Stripes 1981; Going Berserk 1983; National Lampoon's Vacation 1983; Splash 1984; Brewster's Millions 1985; Follow That Bird 1985; Summer Rental 1985; Volunteers 1985; Armed and Dangerous 1986; Little Shop of Horrors 1986; Planes, Trains and Automobiles 1987; Spaceballs 1987; The Great Outdoors 1988; Hot to Trot 1988; Cannonball Fever 1989; Uncle Buck 1989; Who's Harry Crumb? 1989; Home Alone 1990; The Rescuers Down Under 1990; Career Opportunities 1991; Delirious 1991; JFK 1991; Nothing but Trouble 1991; Only the Lonely 1991; Once upon a Crime 1992; Cool Runnings 1993; Wagons East! 1994; Canadian Bacon 1995

Cane, Charles (1899-1973) Dead Reckoning 1947; The Guilt of Janet Ames 1947; Revenge of the Creature 1955

Canerday, Natalie One False Move 1992; Sling Blade 1995; Shotgun Stories 2007

Canet, Guillaume (1973-) En Plein Coeur 1998; The Beach 2000; La Fidélité 2000; Vidocq 2001; Love Me If You Dare 2003; L'Enfer 2005; Merry Christmas 2005; Tell No One 2006; Rivals 2007; Last Night 2009; Farewell 2010; The Players 2012; The Program 2015

Canfield, Gene The Boy Who Cried Bitch 1991; Love Walked In 1997

Cannavale, Bobby (1970-) The Station Agent 2003; Romance & Cigarettes 2005; Shall We Dance 2004; Happy Endings 2005; Fast Food Nation 2006; The Night Listener 2006; Snakes on a Plane 2006; Diminished Capacity 2007; The Merry Gentleman 2009; Paul Blart: Mall Cop 2009; Win Win 2011; Blue Jasmine 2013; Annie 2014; Ant-Man 2015; Danny Collins 2015

Canning, Sara Taken in Broad Daylight 2009; Hannah's Law 2012

Cannon, Dyan aka **Cannon, Diane** (1937-) The Rise and Fall of Legs Diamond 1960; This Rebel Breed 1960; Bob & Carol & Ted & Alice 1969; Doctors' Wives 1970; The Anderson Tapes 1971; The Burglars 1971; The Love Machine 1971; Such Good Friends 1971; The Last of Sheila 1973; Shamus 1973; Heaven Can Wait 1978; Revenge

of the Pink Panther 1978; Coast to Coast 1980; Honeysuckle Rose 1980; Author! Author! 1982; Deathtrap 1982; Caddyshack II 1988; Christmas in Connecticut 1992; The Pickle 1993; 8 Heads in a Duffel Bag 1997; That Darn Cat 1997; A Kiss at Midnight 2008

Cannon, Esma (1896-1974) The Last Adventurers 1937; Holiday Camp 1947; Sailor Beware! 1956; Carry On Regardless 1960; Raising the Wind 1961; What a Carve Up! 1961; Carry On Cruising 1962; On the Beat 1962; We Joined the Navy 1962; Carry On Cabby 1963

Cannon, J D (1922-2005) An American Dream 1966; Cool Hand Luke 1967; The 1,000 Plane Raid 1969; Scorpio 1973; Death Wish II 1981

Cannon, Nick (1980-) Drumline 2002; Love Don't Cost a Thing 2003; Underclassman 2004; The Adventures of Brer Rabbit 2006; Monster House 2006; Goal II: Living the Dream 2007; Day of the Dead 2008

Cannon, Wanda (1960-) For the Moment 1994; First Shot 2002; They 2002; A Trick of the Mind 2006

Canova, Judy (1916-1983) Artists and Models 1937; The Adventures of Huckleberry Finn 1960

Cantafora, Antonio (1943-) Baron Blood 1972; Gabriela 1983

Canterbury, Chandler After.Life 2009; Knowing 2009

Canti, Aldo aka **Jordan, Nick** (1941-1990) Sabata 1969; Return of Sabata 1971

Cantillo, Jose Pablo Crank 2006; Disturbia 2007

Cantineau, Anne The Last Mitterrand 2005; Don't Touch the Axe 2006

Cantinflas (1911-1993) Around the World in 80 Days 1956; Pepe 1960

Cantó, Toni (1965-) All about My Mother 1999; You're My Hero 2003

Cantona, Eric (1966-) Le Bonheur Est dans le Pré 1995; The Children of the Marshland 1998; Elizabeth 1998; French Film 2008; Looking for Eric 2009; You and the Night 2013

Cantor, Eddie (1892-1964) Whoopee! 1930; Palmy Days 1931; The Kid from Spain 1932; Roman Scandals 1933; Kid Millions 1934; Strike Me Pink 1936; Thank Your Lucky Stars 1943; Show Business 1944

Canutt, Yakima (1895-1986) Riders of Destiny 1933; Blue Steel 1934; The Lucky Texan 1934; The Man from Utah 1934; 'Neath the Arizona Skies 1934; Randy Rides Alone 1934; Sagebrush Trail 1934; The Star Packer 1934; West of the Divide 1934; The Dawn Rider 1935; The Lawless Frontier 1935; Paradise Canyon 1935; Westward Ho 1935

Capaldi, Peter (1958-) Local Hero 1983; Dangerous Liaisons 1988; The Lair of the White Worm 1988; December Bride 1990; Soft Top, Hard Shoulder 1992; Captives 1994; Shooting Fish 1997; What Rats Won't Do 1998; Mrs Caldicot's Cabbage War 2000; Max 2002; House of 9 2004; Wild Country 2005; Magicians 2007; In the Loop 2009; Bulla... Big Fat Gypsy Gangster 2011; The Fifth Estate 2013; Paddington 2014

Capell, Peter (1912-1986) Walk East on Beacon 1952; The Burglar 1956; A Gift for Heidi 1958; For the First Time 1959; One, Two, Three 1961

Caplan, Lizzy (1982-) Mean Girls 2004; Cloverfield 2008; My Best Friend's Girl 2008; Hot Tub Time Machine 2010; 127 Hours 2011; Bachelorette 2012; The Interview 2014; The Night Before 2015; Now You See Me 2 2016

Caplan, Twink Look Who's Talking 1989; Clueless 1995; In Search of a Midnight Kiss 2008

Capodice, John The Hard Way 1991; Honeymoon in Vegas 1992; Ringmaster 1998

Capolicchio, Lino (1943-) The Garden of the Finzi-Continis 1971; The Last Days of Mussolini 1974; Noi Tre 1984; Fiorile 1993

Capote, Truman (1924-1984) Trilogy 1969; Murder by Death 1976

Capotorto, Carl (1959-) American Blue Note 1989; Mac 1992

Capra, Francis (1983-) A Bronx Tale 1993; Free Willy 2: the Adventure Home 1995; Kazaam 1996; A Simple Wish 1997; Veronica Mars 2014

Capri, Ahna aka **Capri, Anna** (1944-2010) Kisses for My President 1964; One of Our Spies Is Missing 1966; Brotherhood of Satan 1970; Payday 1972; Enter the Dragon 1973

Capri, Alaina Common-Law Cabin 1967; Good Morning... and Goodbye 1967

Caprioli, Vittorio (1921-1989) General Della Rovere 1959; The Tragedy of a Ridiculous Man 1981

Capron, Robert Diary of a Wimpy Kid 2010; Diary of a Wimpy Kid: Rodrick Rules 2011; Diary of a Wimpy Kid 3: Dog Days 2012

Capshaw, Jessica (1976-) A Secret Sin 1997; The Love Letter 1999; Valentine 2001; Blind Trust 2007

Capshaw, Kate (1953-) A Little Sex 1981; Best Defense 1984; Dreamscape 1984; Indiana Jones and the Temple of Doom 1984; Windy City 1984; Power 1986; SpaceCamp 1986; The Quick and the Dead 1987; Black Rain 1989; Love at Large 1990; My Heroes Have Always Been Cowboys 1991; Love Affair 1994; How to Make an American Quilt 1995; Just Cause 1995; The Alarmist 1997; A Secret Sin 1997; The Love Letter 1999

Capucine (1928-1990) North to Alaska 1960; Song without End 1960; The Lion 1962; Walk on the Wild Side 1962; The Pink Panther 1963; The 7th Dawn 1964; What's New, Pussycat? 1965; The Honey Pot 1967; Fraulein Doktor 1968; Satyricon 1969; Red Sun 1971; The Con Artists 1976; Arabian Adventure 1979; From Hell to Victory 1979; Jaguar Lives! 1979; Trail of the Pink Panther 1982; The Curse of the Pink Panther 1983

Cara, Irene (1957-) Aaron Loves Angela 1975; Fame 1980; DC Cab 1983; City Heat 1984; Certain Fury 1985; Snow White in Happily Ever After 1990

Carafotes, Paul All the Right Moves 1983; Journey to the Center of the Earth 1989

Caramitru, Ion (1942-) Two Deaths 1994; Amen. 2002

Carano, Gina Haywire 2011; I Am Bruce Lee 2012; Deadpool 2016

Caravaca, Eric (1970-) The Officers' Ward 2001; Son Frère 2003

Carax, Leos (1960-) King Lear - Fear and Loathing 1987; Mister Lonely 2007

Carbone, Antony (1927-) A Bucket of Blood 1959; The Last Woman on Earth 1960; Creature from the Haunted Sea 1961; Pit and the Pendulum 1961

Carbonell, Nestor The Lost City 2005; Imperium 2016

Cardellini, Linda (1975-) Scooby-Doo 2002; Scooby-Doo 2: Monsters Unleashed 2005; Brokeback Mountain 2005; Return 2011; Welcome to Me 2014; Daddy's Home 2015; The Founder 2016

Cardenas, Elsa The Brave One 1956; None but the Brave 1960; Fun in Acapulco 1963; Taggart 1964

Cardinal, Tantoo (1951-) Dances with Wolves 1990; Black Robe 1991; Where the Rivers Flow North 1993; Legends of the Fall 1994; Sioux City 1994; The Education of Little Tree 1997; Smoke Signals 1998

Cardinale, Claudia (1939-) Big Deal on Madonna Street 1958; Upstairs and Downstairs 1959; The Battle of Austerlitz 1960; Rocco and His Brothers 1960; Cartouche 1961; The Leopard 1962; 8½ 1963; The Pink Panther 1963; The Magnificent Showman 1964; Time of Indifference 1964; Of a Thousand Delights 1965; Blindfold 1966; The Professionals 1966; Don't Make Waves 1967; A Fine Pair 1968; The Hell with Heroes 1968; Once upon a Time in the West 1968; The Red Tent 1969; The Adventures of Gerard 1970; Popsy-Pop 1970; Conversation Piece 1974; Escape to Athena 1979; Immortal Bachelor 1980; La Pelle 1981; The Salamander 1981; Fitzcarraldo 1982; A Man in Love 1987; My Best Fiend 1999; And Now... Ladies and Gentlemen 2002; The Artist and the Model 2014; Effie Gray 2014

Cardinali, Julieta Valentín 2002; La Antena 2007

Cardona, Manolo Beverly Hills Chihuahua 2008; Undertow 2009

Cardwell, James (1920-1954) The Fighting Sullivans 1944; Sweet and Lowdown 1944; The Shanghai Cobra 1945; He Walked by Night 1948

Carell, Steve (1962-) Anchorman: the Legend of Ron Burgundy 2004; The 40 Year Old Virgin 2005; Little Miss Sunshine 2006; Over the Hedge 2006; Dan in Real Life 2007; Evan Almighty 2007; Dr Seuss' Horton Hears a Who! 2008; Get Smart 2008; Date Night 2010; Despicable Me 2010; Dinner for Schmucks 2010; Crazy, Stupid, Love 2011; Seeking a Friend for the End of the World 2012; Hope Springs 2012; Anchorman 2: the Legend Continues 2013; Despicable Me 2 2013; The Incredible Burt Wonderstone 2013; The Way Way Back 2013; Alexander and the Terrible, Horrible, No Good, Very Bad Day 2014; Foxcatcher 2014; The Big Short 2015; Freeheld 2015; Café

Society 2016; Battle of the Sexes 2017; Despicable Me 3 2017

Carette, Julien aka **Carette** (1897-1966) La Grande Illusion 1937; La Bête Humaine 1938; La Règle du Jeu 1939

Carew, James (1876-1938) Midnight at Madame Tussaud's 1936; Jericho 1937

Carewe, Arthur Edmund (1884-1937) The Cat and the Canary 1927; Doctor X 1932

Carey, Amie subUrbia 1996; Dog Park 1998

Carey, Drew (1958-) Geppetto 2000; Play It to the Bone 2000; Robots 2005

Carey, Harry aka **Carey Sr, Harry** (1878-1947) The Musketeers of Pig Alley 1912; Straight Shooting 1917; The Trail of '98 1929; Trader Horn 1931; Law and Order 1932; The Last Outlaw 1936; Valiant Is the Word for Carrie 1936; Born Reckless 1937; Danger Patrol 1937; Kid Galahad 1937; Souls at Sea 1937; The Law West of Tombstone 1938; You and Me 1938; Mr Smith Goes to Washington 1939; They Knew What They Wanted 1940; Among the Living 1941; The Shepherd of the Hills 1941; Sundown 1941; The Spoilers 1942; Air Force 1943; Happy Land 1943; The Great Moment 1944; Angel and the Badman 1947; The Sea of Grass 1947; Red River 1948

Carey Jr, Harry aka **Carey, Harry** (1921-2012) Pursued 1947; Red River 1948; Three Godfathers 1948; She Wore a Yellow Ribbon 1949; So Dear to My Heart 1949; Copper Canyon 1950; Rio Grande 1950; Wagonmaster 1950; Warpath 1951; Beneath the 12-Mile Reef 1953; Silver Lode 1954; The Long Gray Line 1955; The Searchers 1956; 7th Cavalry 1956; The River's Edge 1957; Escort West 1959; The Undefeated 1969; Dirty Dingus Magee 1970; Man of the East 1972; Take a Hard Ride 1975; Nickelodeon 1976; The Long Riders 1980; UFOria 1980; Mask 1985; The Whales of August 1987; Cherry 2000 1988; Illegally Yours 1988; Bad Jim 1989; Breaking In 1989; Back to the Future Part III 1990

Carey, Joyce (1898-1993) In Which We Serve 1942; Blithe Spirit 1945; Brief Encounter 1945; The October Man 1947; The Astonished Heart 1949; The Chiltern Hundreds 1949; Cry, the Beloved Country 1951; The Rough and the Smooth 1959; Greyfriars Bobby 1961; A Nice Girl like Me 1969

Carey, Leonard (1887-1977) Laughter 1930; Rebecca 1940

Carey, Macdonald aka **Carey, MacDonald** (1913-1994) Dr Broadway 1942; Shadow of a Doubt 1942; Star Spangled Rhythm 1942; Take a Letter, Darling 1942; Wake Island 1942; Suddenly It's Spring 1947; Dream Girl 1948; Bride of Vengeance 1949; The Great Gatsby 1949; Streets of Laredo 1949; Comanche Territory 1950; Copper Canyon 1950; The Lawless 1950; Mystery Submarine 1950; Cave of Outlaws 1951; Let's Make It Legal 1951; Meet Me after the Show 1951; Count the Hours 1953; Malaga 1954; Blue Denim 1959; The Damned 1961; Tammy and the Doctor 1963; End of the World 1977

Carey, Mariah (1970-) The Bachelor 1999; Glitter 2001; Wisegirls 2001; Precious (Base on Nol by Saf) (Based on the Novel "Push" by Sapphire) 2008

Carey, Michele (1943-) El Dorado 1967; The Sweet Ride 1967; Live a Little, Love a Little 1968; Dirty Dingus Magee 1970; Scandalous John 1971

Carey, Olive (1896-1988) The Searchers 1956; Run of the Arrow 1957

Carey, Philip aka **Carey, Phil** (1925-2009) I Was a Communist for the FBI 1951; Operation Pacific 1951; Springfield Rifle 1952; This Woman Is Dangerous 1952; Calamity Jane 1953; Gun Fury 1953; The Man behind the Gun 1953; Pushover 1954; They Rode West 1954; Count Three and Pray 1955; The Long Gray Line 1955; Wyoming Renegades 1955; Screaming Mimi 1958; Tonka 1958; Black Gold 1962; Dead Ringer 1964; The Time Traveller 1964; Three Guns for Texas 1968; Backtrack 1969; Fighting Mad 1976

Carey, Ron (1935-2007) The Out of Towners 1970; Dynamite Chicken 1971; Silent Movie 1976; High Anxiety 1977; Fatso 1979; History of the World Part I 1981

Carey, Timothy aka **Carey, Timothy Agoglia** (1929-1994) White Witch Doctor 1953; Paths of Glory 1957; A Time for Killing 1967; Waterhole #3 1967; Head 1968; Minnie and

Moskowitz 1971; The Outfit 1973; The Killing of a Chinese Bookie 1976

Carey, Tom Plaza Suite 1971; I Dream of Murder 2006; Touch the Top of the World 2006

Cargill, Patrick (1918-1996) The Hi-Jackers 1963; A Countess from Hong Kong 1967; Inspector Clouseau 1968; Every Home Should Have One 1970; Up Pompeii 1971; Father Dear Father 1972

Carhart, Timothy (1953-) Pink Cadillac 1989; Thelma & Louise 1991; Quicksand: No Escape 1992; Beverly Hills Cop III 1994; Candyman: Farewell to the Flesh 1995; Black Sheep 1996; In the Line of Duty: Smoke Jumpers 1996

Carides, Gia (1964-) Bliss 1985; Daydream Believer 1991; Strictly Ballroom 1992; Bad Company 1995; Austin Powers: the Spy Who Shagged Me 1999; A Secret Affair 1999; My Big Fat Greek Wedding 2002

Caridi, Carmine (1933-) The Gambler 1974; Prince of the City 1981; Life Stinks 1991; Top Dog 1995

Cariou, Len (1939-) A Little Night Music 1977; The Four Seasons 1981; Surviving 1985; Lady in White 1988; The Sea Wolf 1993; The Summer of Ben Tyler 1996; Thirteen Days 2000; About Schmidt 2002; Secret Window 2004; Spotlight 2015

Carle, Richard (1871-1941) The Bride Comes Home 1935; Anything Goes 1936; Spendthrift 1936; Remember? 1939

Carleton, Claire (1913-1966) Witness to Murder 1954; The Buster Keaton Story 1957

Carlin, George (1937-2008) With Six You Get Eggroll 1968; Car Wash 1976; Outrageous Fortune 1987; Bill & Ted's Excellent Adventure 1988; Bill & Ted's Bogus Journey 1991; The Prince of Tides 1991; Dogma 1999; Jay and Silent Bob Strike Back 2001; Jersey Girl 2003; Scary Movie 3 2003; Tarzan II 2005; Cars 2006

Carlin, Lynn (1930-) Faces 1968; tick... tick... tick... 1969; Taking Off 1971; Wild Rovers 1971; Dead of Night 1972; Baxter 1973

Carlini, Paolo (1922-1979) Roman Holiday 1953; It Started in Naples 1960

Carlisi, Olimpia Casanova 1976; The Tragedy of a Ridiculous Man 1981

Carlisle, Kitty (1910-2007) She Loves Me Not 1934; A Night at the Opera 1935

Carlisle, Mary (1916-) Palooka 1934; This Side of Heaven 1934; Doctor Rhythm 1938; Dance, Girl, Dance 1940; Baby Face Morgan 1942

Carlqvist, Margit aka **Carlquist, Margit** (1932-) To Joy 1950; Smiles of a Summer Night 1955

Carlson, Karen (1945-) The Candidate 1972; Matilda 1978; The Octagon 1980; The Man Next Door 1998

Carlson, Les (1933-) Videodrome 1982; The Fly 1986

Carlson, Richard (1912-1977) The Duke of West Point 1938; Dancing Co-Ed 1939; Winter Carnival 1939; The Ghost Breakers 1940; The Howards of Virginia 1940; No, No, Nanette 1940; Too Many Girls 1940; Back Street 1941; Hold That Ghost 1941; The Little Foxes 1941; The Affairs of Martha 1942; White Cargo 1942; The Man from Down Under 1943; Presenting Lily Mars 1943; So Well Remembered 1947; King Solomon's Mines 1950; The Sound of Fury 1950; The Blue Veil 1951; A Millionaire for Christy 1951; Valentino 1951; Retreat, Hell! 1952; All I Desire 1953; It Came from Outer Space 1953; The Maze 1953; Seminole 1953; Creature from the Black Lagoon 1954; Bengazi 1955; The Last Command 1955; The Helen Morgan Story 1957; Kid Rodelo 1966; The Power 1968; The Valley of Gwangi 1969

Carlson, Veronica (1944-) Dracula Has Risen from the Grave 1968; Frankenstein Must Be Destroyed 1969; The Horror of Frankenstein 1970; The Ghoul 1975

Carlyle, Robert (1961-) Silent Scream 1989; Riff-Raff 1991; Priest 1994; Go Now 1995; Trainspotting 1995; Carla's Song 1996; Face 1997; The Full Monty 1997; Angela's Ashes 1999; Plunkett & Macleane 1999; Ravenous 1999; The World Is Not Enough 1999; The Beach 2000; There's Only One Jimmy Grimble 2000; The 51st State 2001; To End All Wars 2001; Black and White 2002; Once upon a Time in the Midlands 2002; Marilyn Hotchkiss Ballroom Dancing & Charm School 2005; The Mighty Celt 2005; Eragon 2006; 28 Weeks Later 2007; I Know You Know 2008; Stone of Destiny 2008; Summer 2008; The Tournament 2009; The Unloved 2009; The Legend of Barney Thomson 2015; T2: Trainspotting 2 2016

Carmack, Chris The Last Ride 2004; Love Wrecked 2005; Deadly Honeymoon 2009; Shark Night 3D 2011

Carman, Michael Hercules Returns 1993; Nim's Island 2008

Carmel, Roger C (1932-1986) Goodbye Charlie 1964; Alvarez Kelly 1966; Gambit 1966; The Venetian Affair 1966; Skullduggery 1969; Myra Breckinridge 1970; Breezy 1973

Carmen, Julie (1960-) Gloria 1980; Night of the Juggler 1980; Blue City 1986; Fright Night Part 2 1988; The Milagro Beanfield War 1988; The Penitent 1988; Gore Vidal's Billy the Kid 1989; Cold Heaven 1992; In the Mouth of Madness 1994

Carmet, Jean (1920-1994) The Vanishing Corporal 1962; The Little Theatre of Jean Renoir 1969; The Tall Blond Man with One Black Shoe 1972; Black and White in Color 1976; Violette Nozière 1977; Buffet Froid 1979; Circle of Deceit 1981; Les Misérables 1982; Merci la Vie 1991; Germinal 1993

Carmi, Vera (1914-1969) Sunday in August 1949; Friends for Life 1955

Carmichael, Hoagy (1899-1981) To Have and Have Not 1944; Johnny Angel 1945; The Best Years of Our Lives 1946; Night Song 1947; Young Man with a Horn 1950; Belles on Their Toes 1952; The Las Vegas Story 1952; Timberjack 1955

Carmichael, Ian (1920-2010) Dear Mr Prohack 1949; Betrayed 1954; The Colditz Story 1954; Simon and Laura 1955; Storm over the Nile 1955; The Big Money 1956; Brothers in Law 1956; Private's Progress 1956; Happy Is the Bride 1957; Lucky Jim 1957; I'm All Right Jack 1959; Left, Right and Centre 1959; Light Up the Sky 1960; School for Scoundrels 1960; Double Bunk 1961; The Amorous Prawn 1962; Heavens Above! 1963; Hide and Seek 1963; Smashing Time 1967; The Magnificent Seven Deadly Sins 1971; From beyond the Grave 1973; The Lady Vanishes 1979; Diamond Skulls 1989

Carminati, Tullio (1894-1971) Gallant Lady 1934; One Night of Love 1934; London Melody 1937; Roman Holiday 1953; A Breath of Scandal 1960; The Swordsman of Siena 1962

Carmine, Michael (1959-1989) *batteries not included 1987; Leviathan 1989

Carnelutti, Francesco The Belly of an Architect 1987; The Sin Eater 2002; Spring 2014

Carnera, Primo (1906-1967) The Prizefighter and the Lady 1933; A Kid for Two Farthings 1955

Carney, Alan (1909-1973) Mr Lucky 1943; Girl Rush 1944; Step Lively 1944; Li'l Abner 1959

Carney, Art (1918-2003) The Yellow Rolls-Royce 1964; Harry and Tonto 1974; WW and the Dixie Dancekings 1975; Won Ton Ton, the Dog Who Saved Hollywood 1976; The Late Show 1977; House Calls 1978; Defiance 1979; Going in Style 1979; Sunburn 1979; Roadie 1980; Better Late than Never 1983; A Doctor's Story 1984; Firestarter 1984; The Naked Face 1984; Last Action Hero 1993

Carney, George (1887-1947) Love on the Dole 1941; In Which We Serve 1942; I Know Where I'm Going! 1945

Carnovsky, Morris (1897-1992) Edge of Darkness 1943; The Master Race 1944; Cornered 1945; Our Vines Have Tender Grapes 1945; Rhapsody in Blue 1945; Dead Reckoning 1947; Dishonored Lady 1947; Gun Crazy 1949; Thieves' Highway 1949; Cyrano de Bergerac 1950; The Second Woman 1951; The Gambler 1974

Carol, Joan Mr Moto's Last Warning 1938; Ghost Ship 1952

Carol, Martine (1922-1967) Les Belles de Nuit 1952; Madame du Barry 1954; Secrets d'Alcove 1954; The Diary of Major Thompson 1955; Lola Montès 1955; Ten Seconds to Hell 1959; The Battle of Austerlitz 1960

Caron, Leslie (1931-) An American in Paris 1951; The Man with a Cloak 1951; Glory Alley 1952; Lili 1953; The Story of Three Loves 1953; Daddy Long Legs 1955; The Glass Slipper 1955; Gaby 1956; The Doctor's Dilemma 1958; Gigi 1958; The Man Who Understood Women 1959; The Battle of Austerlitz 1960; The Subterraneans 1960; Fanny 1961; Guns of Darkness 1962; The L-Shaped Room 1962; Father Goose 1964; Is Paris Burning? 1966; Promise Her Anything 1966; Madron 1970; The Man Who Loved Women 1977; Valentino 1977; Goldengirl 1979; The Contract 1980; Imperative 1982; Dangerous Moves 1984; Courage

Mountain 1989; Damage 1992; Funny Bones 1994; Let It Be Me 1995; Chocolat 2000; Murder on the Orient Express 2001; Le Divorce 2003

Carotenuto, Memmo (1908-1980) Umberto D 1952; Bread, Love & Dreams 1954; Big Deal on Madonna Street 1958

Carpenter, Carleton (1926-) Vengeance Valley 1951; Take the High Ground 1953; Up Periscope 1959

Carpenter, David Crimes of the Heart 1986; Amelia Earhart: the Final Flight 1994

Carpenter, Jack aka **Carpenter, Jack T** Sydney White 2007; I Love You, Beth Cooper 2009

Carpenter, Jennifer (1979-) The Exorcism of Emily Rose 2005; Quarantine 2008; Justice 2011; The Factory 2012; Gone 2012

Carpenter, Ken Spirit of the Eagle 1991; Hellraiser III: Hell on Earth 1992

Carpenter, Paul (1921-1964) Face the Music 1954; Shadow of a Man 1954; The Stranger Came Home 1954; The Young Lovers 1954; Stock Car 1955; Behind the Headlines 1956; Fire Maidens from Outer Space 1956; The Hypnotist 1957; No Road Back 1957; Undercover Girl 1957; Intent to Kill 1958

Carpentieri, Renato (1943-) Puerto Escondido 1992; The Stolen Children 1992

Carr, Alexander (1878-1946) The Death Kiss 1933; Christmas in July 1940

Carr, Darleen (1950-) The Jungle Book 1967; The Beguiled 1970

Carr (1), Jane (1909-1957) Lord Edgware Dies 1934; Those Were the Days 1934; The Lad 1935

Carr, Jimmy (1972-) Alien Autopsy 2006; Confetti 2006; I Want Candy 2006

Carr, Marian The Devil Thumbs a Ride 1947; World for Ransom 1953; Indestructible Man 1956

Carr, Mary (1874-1973) Lights of New York 1928; Kept Husbands 1931; Pack Up Your Troubles 1932

Carr, Paul (1934-2006) Jamboree 1957; Ben 1972; Executive Action 1973

Carradine, David (1936-2009) Taggart 1964; The Violent Ones 1967; The Good Guys and the Bad Guys 1969; Young Billy Young 1969; Boxcar Bertha 1972; Death Race 2000 1975; Bound for Glory 1976; Cannonball 1976; The Serpent's Egg 1977; Deathsport 1978; Gray Lady Down 1978; The Silent Flute 1978; Cloud Dancer 1979; The Long Riders 1980; Americana 1981; Q - the Winged Serpent 1982; Lone Wolf McQuade 1983; The Warrior and the Sorceress 1983; PoW the Escape 1986; Bird on a Wire 1990; Roadside Prophets 1992; Jailbreak 1997; The Outsider 2001; Kill Bill Vol 1 2003; Kill Bill Vol 2 2004; Crank: High Voltage 2009

Carradine, John (1906-1988) The Garden of Allah 1936; Mary of Scotland 1936; The Prisoner of Shark Island 1936; White Fang 1936; Winterset 1936; Captains Courageous 1937; Danger - Love at Work 1937; The Hurricane 1937; The Last Gangster 1937; Nancy Steele Is Missing 1937; Thank You, Mr Moto 1937; This Is My Affair 1937; Alexander's Ragtime Band 1938; Four Men and a Prayer 1938; Kentucky Moonshine 1938; Kidnapped 1938; Mr Moto's Last Warning 1938; Of Human Hearts 1938; Submarine Patrol 1938; Drums along the Mohawk 1939; Five Came Back 1939; Frontier Marshal 1939; The Hound of the Baskervilles 1939; Jesse James 1939; Stagecoach 1939; The Three Musketeers 1939; Brigham Young 1940; Chad Hanna 1940; The Grapes of Wrath 1940; The Return of Frank James 1940; Blood and Sand 1941; Man Hunt 1941; Swamp Water 1941; Western Union 1941; Reunion in France 1942; Son of Fury 1942; Hitler's Madman 1943; The Adventures of Mark Twain 1944; Barbary Coast Gent 1944; Bluebeard 1944; House of Frankenstein 1944; The Invisible Man's Revenge 1944; The Mummy's Ghost 1944; Voodoo Man 1944; Captain Kidd 1945; Fallen Angel 1945; House of Dracula 1945; It's in the Bag 1945; The Private Affairs of Bel Ami 1947; Casanova's Big Night 1954; Johnny Guitar 1954; The Female Jungle 1955; The Kentuckian 1955; Stranger on Horseback 1955; The Black Sleep 1956; The Ten Commandments 1956; Hell Ship Mutiny 1957; The True Story of Jesse James 1957; The Unearthly 1957; Showdown at Boot Hill 1958; The Cosmic Man 1959; The Adventures of Huckleberry Finn 1960; Tarzan the Magnificent 1960; The Man

Who Shot Liberty Valance 1962; Cheyenne Autumn 1964; The Patsy 1964; Billy the Kid vs Dracula 1966; The Hostage 1966; Munster, Go Home! 1966; Blood of Dracula's Castle 1967; The Good Guys and the Bad Guys 1969; The Trouble with Girls 1969; Myra Breckinridge 1970; Boxcar Bertha 1972; Everything You Always Wanted to Know about Sex ... but Were Afraid to Ask 1972; The House of Seven Corpses 1973; Terror in the Wax Museum 1973; The Killer inside Me 1975; Shock Waves 1975; The Last Tycoon 1976; The Shootist 1976; Crash! 1977; Golden Rendezvous 1977; The Sentinel 1977; The White Buffalo 1977; The Monster Club 1980; The Howling 1981; The Secret of NIMH 1982; House of the Long Shadows 1983; Monster in the Closet 1983; The Ice Pirates 1984; Peggy Sue Got Married 1986; Buried Alive 1990

Carradine, Keith (1949-) McCabe and Mrs Miller 1971; Emperor of the North 1973; Thieves like Us 1974; Nashville 1975; Welcome to LA 1976; The Duellists 1977; Pretty Baby 1978; Old Boyfriends 1979; The Long Riders 1980; Southern Comfort 1981; Choose Me 1984; Maria's Lovers 1984; Trouble in Mind 1985; A Winner Never Quits 1986; Backfire 1987; The Moderns 1988; My Father, My Son 1988; Stones for Ibarra 1988; Cold Feet 1989; Street of No Return 1989; The Bachelor 1990; Daddy's Dyin'... Who's Got the Will? 1990; The Ballad of the Sad Café 1991; CrissCross 1992; Andre 1994; The Tie That Binds 1995; Wild Bill 1995; A Thousand Acres 1997; The Outsider 2001; Falcons 2002; Monte Walsh 2003; Balto - Wings of Change 2004; Cowboys & Aliens 2011; Ain't Them Bodies Saints 2013

Carradine, Robert (1954-) Mean Streets 1973; Aloha, Bobby and Rose 1975; Cannonball 1976; Jackson County Jail 1976; Orca... Killer Whale 1977; Coming Home 1978; The Big Red One 1980; The Long Riders 1980; Revenge of the Nerds 1984; Number One with a Bullet 1986; Buy & Cell 1988; All's Fair 1989; Rude Awakening 1989; The Incident 1990; Palmer's Pick-Up 1999; Max Keeble's Big Move 2001; The Lizzie McGuire Movie 2003; Monte Walsh 2003

Carré, Isabelle (1971-) The Children of the Marshland 1998; La Bûche 1999; Les Enfants du Siècle 1999; He Loves Me... He Loves Me Not 2002; Private Fears in Public Places 2006; Anna M. 2007; The Fox and the Child 2007; The Refuge 2009; Romantics Anonymous 2010; Looking for Hortense 2012

Carrel, Dany (1935-) Gates of Paris 1957; The Hands of Orlac 1960

Carrera, Barbara (1951-) The Master Gunfighter 1975; Embryo 1976; The Island of Dr Moreau 1977; When Time Ran Out 1980; Condorman 1981; Lone Wolf McQuade 1983; Never Say Never Again 1983; Wild Geese II 1985; Love at Stake 1987; Loverboy 1989; Wicked Stepmother 1989; Love Is All There Is 1996

Carrere, Tia (1967-) Aloha Summer 1988; Fatal Mission 1990; Harley Davidson and the Marlboro Man 1991; Showdown in Little Tokyo 1991; Wayne's World 1992; Quick 1993; Rising Sun 1993; Wayne's World 2 1993; True Lies 1994; Jury Duty 1995; High School High 1996; Hollow Point 1996; Kull the Conqueror 1997; Top of the World 1997; Scarred City 1998; Merlin the Return 2000; Lilo & Stitch 2002; Torn Apart 2004

Carrey, Jim (1962-) Finders Keepers 1984; Once Bitten 1985; Peggy Sue Got Married 1986; Earth Girls Are Easy 1988; Pink Cadillac 1989; Ace Ventura: Pet Detective 1993; Dumb and Dumber 1994; The Mask 1994; Ace Ventura: When Nature Calls 1995; Batman Forever 1995; The Cable Guy 1996; Liar Liar 1997; The Truman Show 1998; Man on the Moon 1999; The Grinch 2000; Me, Myself & Irene 2000; The Majestic 2001; Bruce Almighty 2003; Eternal Sunshine of the Spotless Mind 2003; Lemony Snicket's A Series of Unfortunate Events 2004; Fun with Dick and Jane 2005; The Number 23 2006; Dr Seuss' Horton Hears a Who! 2008; Yes Man 2008; A Christmas Carol 2009; I Love You Phillip Morris 2009; Mr Popper's Penguins 2011; The Incredible Burt Wonderstone 2013; Kick-Ass 2 2013; Dumb and Dumber To 2014

Carrier, Corey (1980-) After Dark, My Sweet 1990; The Adventures of Pinocchio 1996

Carrière, Mathieu (1950-) Malpertuis 1971; Don Juan 73, or If Don Juan Were

a Woman 1973; India Song 1975; The Aviator's Wife 1980; Bay Boy 1984; Christopher Columbus: the Discovery 1992; Arsène Lupin 2004

Carrillo, Elpidia (1963-) The Border 1981; The Honorary Consul 1983; Salvador 1986; Predator 1987; My Family 1994; Bread and Roses 2000; Seven Pounds 2008

Carrillo, Leo (1880-1961) Four Frightened People 1934; The Gay Bride 1934; Manhattan Melodrama 1934; If You Could Only Cook 1935; In Caliente 1935; History Is Made at Night 1937; Blockade 1938; The Girl of the Golden West 1938; Too Hot to Handle 1938; Lillian Russell 1940; Men of Texas 1942; Sin Town 1942; Frontier Badmen 1943; Phantom of the Opera 1943; Under Western Skies 1945; The Fugitive 1947

Carrol, Regina (1943-1992) The Female Bunch 1969; Dracula vs Frankenstein 1970

Carroll, Beeson Lady Liberty 1971; Werewolf of Washington 1973; Spacehunter: Adventures in the Forbidden Zone 1983; Crimes of the Heart 1986

Carroll, Diahann (1935-) Carmen Jones 1954; Porgy and Bess 1959; Paris Blues 1961; The Split 1968; Claudine 1974; The Five Heartbeats 1991

Carroll, Janet (1940-2012) Risky Business 1983; Memories of Me 1988; Family Business 1989; Talent for the Game 1991; Destiny Turns on the Radio 1995

Carroll, Joan (1932-) Anne of Windy Poplars 1940; Meet Me in St Louis 1944; The Bells of St Mary's 1945

Carroll, John (1906-1979) Go West 1940; Hired Wife 1940; Phantom Raiders 1940; Susan and God 1940; Lady Be Good 1941; Sunny 1941; Flying Tigers 1942; Rio Rita 1942; Change of Heart 1943; The Youngest Profession 1943; Fiesta 1947; Angel in Exile 1948; The Farmer Takes a Wife 1953; Decision at Sundown 1957

Carroll, Leo G (1892-1972) London by Night 1937; Tower of London 1939; Wuthering Heights 1939; Rebecca 1940; The House on 92nd Street 1945; Spellbound 1945; Song of Love 1947; Time Out of Mind 1947; Enchantment 1948; Father of the Bride 1950; The Happy Years 1950; The Desert Fox 1951; The First Legion 1951; Strangers on a Train 1951; The Snows of Kilimanjaro 1952; Treasure of the Golden Condor 1953; Tarantula 1955; We're No Angels 1955; The Swan 1956; North by Northwest 1959; The Parent Trap 1961; That Funny Feeling 1965; One of Our Spies Is Missing 1966; One Spy Too Many 1966; The Spy in the Green Hat 1966; The Spy with My Face 1966; The Helicopter Spies 1968

Carroll, Madeleine (1906-1987) The First Born 1928; Escape 1930; I Was a Spy 1934; The World Moves On 1934; The Dictator 1935; The 39 Steps 1935; The General Died at Dawn 1936; Lloyd's of London 1936; Secret Agent 1936; On the Avenue 1937; The Prisoner of Zenda 1937; Blockade 1938; My Son, My Son! 1940; North West Mounted Police 1940; My Favorite Blonde 1942; The Fan 1949

Carroll, Madeline (1996-) Swing Vote 2008; The Spy Next Door 2009; Machine Gun Preacher 2011; Mr Popper's Penguins 2011

Carroll, Nancy (1904-1965) Abie's Irish Rose 1928; The Shopworn Angel 1928; The Devil's Holiday 1930; Laughter 1930; Paramount on Parade 1930; The Man I Killed 1932; Scarlet Dawn 1932; The Kiss before the Mirror 1933; That Certain Age 1938; There Goes My Heart 1938

Carroll, Pat (1927-) Cinderella 1965; With Six You Get Eggroll 1968; The Little Mermaid 1989; Songcatcher 1999; The Little Mermaid II: Return to the Sea 2000

Carroll, Peter The More Things Change 1985; Sleeping Beauty 2011

Carroll, Rocky The Chase 1994; Crimson Tide 1995; Best Laid Plans 1999

Carruth, Shane Primer 2004; Upstream Color 2013

Carruthers, Ben aka **Carruthers, Benito** (1936-1983) Shadows 1959; A High Wind in Jamaica 1965; Riot 1969

Carson, Charles (1885-1977) Dreyfus 1931; Blossom Time 1934; The Beloved Vagabond 1936; Sixty Glorious Years 1938; We're Going to Be Rich 1938; Cry, the Beloved Country 1951; The Dam Busters 1955; Bobbikins 1959

Carson, Hunter (1976-) Paris, Texas 1984; Invaders from Mars 1986

Carson, Jack (1910-1963) Stage Door 1937; Stand-In 1937; Carefree 1938; The

Saint in New York 1938; Vivacious Lady 1938; I Take This Woman 1940; Lucky Partners 1940; Blues in the Night 1941; The Bride Came COD 1941; Love Crazy 1941; Mr and Mrs Smith 1941; Gentleman Jim 1942; The Hard Way 1942; Larceny, Inc 1942; The Male Animal 1942; Princess O'Rourke 1943; Arsenic and Old Lace 1944; The Doughgirls 1944; Shine On, Harvest Moon 1944; Mildred Pierce 1945; Roughly Speaking 1945; Romance on the High Seas 1948; It's a Great Feeling 1949; My Dream Is Yours 1949; Bright Leaf 1950; Dangerous When Wet 1953; Phffft! 1954; Red Garters 1954; A Star Is Born 1954; Ain't Misbehavin' 1955; Beyond the River 1956; The Tarnished Angels 1957; The Tattered Dress 1957; Cat on a Hot Tin Roof 1958; The Bramble Bush 1960; King of the Roaring 20s - the Story of Arnold Rothstein 1961

Carson, Jeannie aka **Carson, Jean** (1928-) A Date with a Dream 1948; Love in Pawn 1953; An Alligator Named Daisy 1955; As Long as They're Happy 1955; Rockets Galore 1958

Carson, John (1927-) Master Spy 1964; Smokescreen 1964; The Night Caller 1965; The Plague of the Zombies 1965; Captain Kronos: Vampire Hunter 1972; Out of Darkness 1990

Carson, John David (1952-) Pretty Maids All in a Row 1971; The Savage Is Loose 1974; Empire of the Ants 1977

Carson, L M Kit (1947-2014) David Holzman's Diary 1968; Running on Empty 1988

Carson, Lisa Nicole (1969-) Devil in a Blue Dress 1995; Eve's Bayou 1997; Love Jones 1997

Carson, Shawn The Funhouse 1981; Something Wicked This Way Comes 1983

Carsten, Peter (1928-2012) Dark of the Sun 1967; Zeppelin 1971

Carstens, Liezl Renegade Justice 2007; The Keeper 2009

Carstensen, Margit (1940-) The Bitter Tears of Petra von Kant 1972; Martha 1973; Mother Küsters Goes to Heaven 1975; Chinese Roulette 1976; Fear of Fear 1976; Satan's Brew 1976; The Third Generation 1979

Carter Cash, June (1929-2003) The Apostle 1997; My Father and the Man in Black 2012

Carter, Alex (1964-) Time to Say Goodbye? 1997; Guilt by Association 2002; Out of Time 2003

Carter, Ben (1907-1946) Tin Pan Alley 1940; Dark Alibi 1946

Carter, Billy Up on the Roof 1997; Festival 2005

Carter, Finn How I Got Into College 1989; Tremors 1989

Carter, Helena (1923-2000) Intrigue 1947; Something in the Wind 1947; Time Out of Mind 1947; The Fighting O'Flynn 1948; Kiss Tomorrow Goodbye 1950; Double Crossbones 1951; Fort Worth 1951; Bugles in the Afternoon 1952; Invaders from Mars 1953

Carter, Jack (1923-2015) The Horizontal Lieutenant 1962; The Extraordinary Seaman 1969; The Amazing Dobermans 1976; The Happy Hooker Goes to Washington 1977; The Glove 1978; Rainbow 1978; Alligator 1980; Hambone and Hillie 1984; The Opposite Sex and How to Live with Them 1993

Carter, Janis (1913-1994) Framed 1947; And Baby Makes Three 1949; Miss Grant Takes Richmond 1949; Slightly French 1949; The Woman on Pier 13 1949; A Woman of Distinction 1950; My Forbidden Past 1951; Santa Fe 1951; The Half-Breed 1952

Carter, Jim (1951-) A Private Function 1984; Haunted Honeymoon 1986; A Month in the Country 1987; The Rainbow 1988; Soursweet 1988; Blame It on the Bellboy 1992; The Hour of the Pig 1993; Black Beauty 1994; The Grotesque 1995; The Madness of King George 1995; Brassed Off 1996; Keep the Aspidistra Flying 1997; Vigo: Passion for Life 1997; Legionnaire 1998; Shakespeare in Love 1998; The Little Vampire 2000; Heartlands 2002; 16 Years of Alcohol 2003; The Thief Lord 2005; Cassandra's Dream 2007; The Golden Compass 2007; The Oxford Murders 2008; Creation 2009

Carter, Jimmy The Jayhawkers 1959; Countdown to Zero 2010

Carter, Louise (1875-1957) Madame Butterfly 1932; Jennie Gerhardt 1933; You're Telling Me! 1934

Carter, Lynda (1951-) Super Troopers 2001; Sky High 2005

Carter, Nell (1948-2003) Modern Problems 1981; Bebe's Kids 1992; The Grass Harp 1995; The Proprietor 1996

Carter, Reggie (1977-1995) Dr No 1962; The Lunatic 1992
Carter, Sarah aka **Carter, Sarah Sanguin** Final Destination 2 2002; Date with Darkness 2003; DOA: Dead or Alive 2006; Red Mist 2008; Salem Falls 2011
Carter, T K (1956-) Seems like Old Times 1980; Southern Comfort 1981; The Thing 1982; Doctor Detroit 1983; Runaway Train 1985; He's My Girl 1987; Baadasssss! 2003
Carter, Terry (1929-) Foxy Brown 1974; Battlestar Galactica 1978
Carter, Thomas (1953-) Almost Summer 1977; Whose Life Is It Anyway? 1981
Carteris, Gabrielle (1961-) Danielle Steel's Mixed Blessings 1995; Malpractice 2001
Cartlidge, Katrin (1961-2002) Naked 1993; Before the Rain 1994; Breaking the Waves 1996; Career Girls 1997; The Cherry Orchard 1999; Claire Dolan 1998; Hi-Life 1998; The Lost Son 1998; Hotel Splendide 1999; The Weight of Water 2000; From Hell 2001
Carton, Pauline (1884-1974) The Blood of a Poet 1930; Bonne Chance 1935
Cartwright, Nancy (1959-) Yellow Pages 1984; Rugrats Go Wild 2003; The Simpsons Movie 2007
Cartwright, Veronica (1949-) The Children's Hour 1961; The Birds 1963; One Man's Way 1964; Inserts 1975; Goin' South 1978; Invasion of the Body Snatchers 1978; Alien 1979; The Right Stuff 1983; Flight of the Navigator 1986; Wisdom 1986; The Witches of Eastwick 1987; False Identity 1990; Candyman: Farewell to the Flesh 1995; My Brother's Keeper 1995; Money Talks 1997; Scary Movie 2 2001; Just Married 2003; The Invasion 2007
Caruso, Anthony aka **Caruso, Tony** (1916-2003) The Asphalt Jungle 1950; Tarzan and the Slave Girl 1950; Desert Legion 1953; Fort Algiers 1953; The Boy from Oklahoma 1954; Cattle Queen of Montana 1954; Baby Face Nelson 1957; The Big Land 1957; The Badlanders 1958; Fort Massacre 1958; Never Steal Anything Small 1959; The Most Dangerous Man Alive 1961
Caruso, David (1956-) First Blood 1982; An Officer and a Gentleman 1982; Thief of Hearts 1984; Blue City 1986; China Girl 1987; Twins 1988; King of New York 1989; Hudson Hawk 1991; Mad Dog and Glory 1992; Kiss of Death 1994; Jade 1995; Body Count 1997; Deadlocked 2000; Proof of Life 2000; Black Point 2001; Session 9 2001
Carver, Brent (1952-) Millennium 1989; Ararat 2002
Carver, Lynne aka **Carver, Lynn** (1909-1955) The Bride Wore Red 1937; Maytime 1937; A Christmas Carol 1938; Everybody Sing 1938; Young Dr Kildare 1938; The Adventures of Huckleberry Finn 1939; Bitter Sweet 1940; Broadway Melody of 1940 1940
Carver, Mary (1924-2013) Best Seller 1987; [Safe] 1995
Carvey, Dana (1955-) Tough Guys 1986; Moving 1988; Opportunity Knocks 1990; Wayne's World 1992; Wayne's World 2 1993; Clean Slate 1994; The Road to Wellville 1994; Trapped in Paradise 1994; The Master of Disguise 2002
Casadesus, Gisèle Verdict 1974; My Afternoons with Marguerite 2010
Casar, Amira (1971-) Comment J'ai Tué Mon Père 2001; Murder on the Orient Express 2001; Sylvia 2003; Transylvania 2006; Saint Laurent 2014
Casarès, Maria (1922-1996) Les Enfants du Paradis 1945; Les Dames du Bois de Boulogne 1946; Orphée 1950; Le Testament d'Orphée 1960; Someone Else's America 1995
Casella, Max (1967-) Sgt Bilko 1996; Analyze This 1999; The Little Mermaid II: Return to the Sea 2000
Caselli, Chiara (1967-) My Own Private Idaho 1991; Beyond the Clouds 1995; Ripley's Game 2002; BirdWatchers 2008; The Father of My Children 2009
Casey, Bernie (1939-) Guns of the Magnificent Seven 1969; Brian's Song 1971; Boxcar Bertha 1972; Hit Man 1972; Cleopatra Jones 1973; The Man Who Fell to Earth 1976; Sharky's Machine 1981; Never Say Never Again 1983; Spies like Us 1985; Backfire 1987; I'm Gonna Git You Sucka 1988; Rent-a-Cop 1988; Chains of Gold 1989; Another 48 HRS 1990; The Cemetery Club 1993; The Glass Shield 1995; The Simple Life of Noah Dearborn 1999
Cash, Johnny (1932-2003) Door-to-Door Maniac 1961; A Gunfight 1971; Stagecoach 1986; My Father and the Man in Black 2012

Cash, Rosalind (1938-1995) The Omega Man 1971; Hickey and Boggs 1972; The New Centurions 1972; Uptown Saturday Night 1974; The Class of Miss MacMichael 1978
Cashman, Michael (1950-) I've Gotta Horse 1965; Unman, Wittering and Zigo 1971; Zee and Co 1971
Casini, Stefania (1949-) Blood for Dracula 1974; Bad 1976; Suspiria 1976; The Belly of an Architect 1987
Casisa, Francesco Respiro 2002; Golden Door 2006
Caso, Mark Teenage Mutant Ninja Turtles II: the Secret of the Ooze 1991; Teenage Mutant Ninja Turtles III 1992
Caspary, Tina aka **Caspary, Katrina** Can't Buy Me Love 1987; Mac and Me 1988
Cass, Peggy (1924-1999) The Marrying Kind 1952; Auntie Mame 1958
Cassagne, Michel Nightshift 2000; Lemming 2005
Cassavetes, John (1929-1989) Taxi 1953; The Night Holds Terror 1955; Crime in the Streets 1956; Edge of the City 1957; Saddle the Wind 1958; Virgin Island 1958; The Killers 1964; The Dirty Dozen 1967; Rosemary's Baby 1968; Husbands 1970; Capone 1975; Two-Minute Warning 1976; Opening Night 1977; Brass Target 1978; The Fury 1978; Whose Life Is It Anyway? 1981; Tempest 1982; Marvin and Tige 1983
Cassavetes, Katherine (1896-1983) Minnie and Moskowitz 1971; A Woman under the Influence 1974
Cassavetes, Nick (1959-) Black Moon Rising 1985; The Wraith 1986; Mrs Parker and the Vicious Circle 1994; Twogether 1994; Face/Off 1997; The Astronaut's Wife 1999
Cassel, Cécile The Romance of Astrea and Celadon 2007; My Last Five Girlfriends 2009
Cassel, Jean-Pierre (1932-2007) The Vanishing Corporal 1962; The Beautiful Swindlers 1964; Those Magnificent Men in Their Flying Machines 1965; Is Paris Burning? 1966; Army of Shadows 1969; Oh! What a Lovely War 1969; La Rupture 1970; Malpertuis 1971; The Discreet Charm of the Bourgeoisie 1972; Baxter 1973; Murder on the Orient Express 1974; Doctor Françoise Gailland 1975; That Lucky Touch 1975; The Twist 1976; Who Is Killing the Great Chefs of Europe? 1978; From Hell to Victory 1979; Mister Frost 1990; The Favour, the Watch and the Very Big Fish 1991; The Maid 1991; Pétain 1992; La Cérémonie 1995; The Crimson Rivers 2000; The Diving-Bell and the Butterfly 2007; Asterix at the Olympic Games 2008
Cassel, Seymour (1935-) Too Late Blues 1961; Faces 1968; The Revolutionary 1970; Minnie and Moskowitz 1971; Death Game 1976; The Killing of a Chinese Bookie 1976; Scott Joplin 1977; Valentino 1977; Convoy 1978; Eye of the Tiger 1986; Tin Men 1987; Johnny Be Good 1988; Plain Clothes 1988; Track 29 1988; Cold Dog Soup 1989; Sweet Bird of Youth 1989; White Fang 1991; Diary of a Hitman 1992; In the Soup 1992; Boiling Point 1993; Indecent Proposal 1993; Trouble Bound 1993; Chasers 1994; Hand Gun 1994; Tollbooth 1994; Dream for an Insomniac 1996; This World, Then the Fireworks 1996; Motel Blue 1997; Relax... It's Just Sex 1998; Rushmore 1998; Animal Factory 2000; Bartleby 2000; Sonny 2002; Stealing Harvard 2002; The Life Aquatic with Steve Zissou 2004; Lonesome Jim 2005; Staten Island 2009
Cassel, Vincent (1966-) La Haine 1995; L'Appartement 1996; Dobermann 1997; Guest House Paradiso 1999; Joan of Arc 1999; The Crimson Rivers 2000; Birthday Girl 2001; Brotherhood of the Wolf 2001; Read My Lips 2001; The Reckoning 2001; Shrek 2001; Irreversible 2002; Blueberry 2004; Ocean's Twelve 2004; Derailed 2005; Sheitan 2006; Eastern Promises 2007; Mesrine: Killer Instinct 2008; Mesrine: Public Enemy No 1 2008; Adrift 2009; Black Swan 2010; A Dangerous Method 2011; The Monk 2011; Trance 2013; Mon Roi 2015; Partisan 2015; Tale of Tales 2015; Jason Bourne 2016
Cassell, Wally (1915-2015) The Story of GI Joe 1945; Saigon 1948; Sands of Iwo Jima 1949; We Were Strangers 1949; White Heat 1949; Princess of the Nile 1954; The Come On 1956; Until They Sail 1957
Cassetti, Stefano Roberto Succo 2000; Love like Poison 2010
Casseus, Gabriel Get on the Bus 1996; Black Dog 1998; Fallen 1998; Black Hawk Down 2001
Cassidy, Elaine (1980-) Felicia's Journey 1999; Disco Pigs 2001; The

Others 2001; The Truth 2006; And When Did You Last See Your Father? 2007
Cassidy, Jack (1927-1976) Bunny O'Hare 1971; The Eiger Sanction 1975; WC Fields and Me 1976
Cassidy, Joanna (1944-) The Outfit 1973; Bank Shot 1974; The Late Show 1977; The Glove 1978; Night Games 1979; Under Fire 1983; Club Paradise 1986; The Fourth Protocol 1987; 1969 1988; Who Framed Roger Rabbit 1988; The Package 1989; May Wine 1990; Where the Heart Is 1990; Don't Tell Mom the Babysitter's Dead 1991; Barbarians at the Gate 1993; Vampire in Brooklyn 1995; Chain Reaction 1996; Loved 1996; John Carpenter's Ghosts of Mars 2001; The Reading Room 2005; Visions 2014
Cassidy, Katie Black Christmas 2006; Live! 2007; A Nightmare on Elm Street 2010; Monte Carlo 2011
Cassidy, Patrick (1961-) Love at Stake 1987; Longtime Companion 1990
Cassidy, Raffey Molly Moon and the Incredible Book of Hypnotism 2015; Tomorrowland: a World Beyond 2015
Cassidy, Ted (1932-1979) Butch Cassidy and the Sundance Kid 1969; Mackenna's Gold 1969
Cassini, John Catwoman 2004; Cool Money 2005
Casson, Lewis (1875-1969) Escape 1930; Crime on the Hill 1933; Calling the Tune 1936
Casta, Laetitia (1978-) Asterix and Obelix Take On Caesar 1999; Born in 68: We'll Love Each Other until Death Do Us Part 2008; Gainsbourg (Je T'Aime... Moi Non Plus) 2010; Arbitrage 2012
Castaldi, Jean-Pierre (1944-) French Connection II 1975; Le Cop II 1989; A Touch of Adultery 1993
Castañeda, Luis Aceves (1913-1973) Mexican Bus Ride 1951; Wuthering Heights 1953
Castel, Lou (1943-) Fists in the Pocket 1965; A Bullet for the General 1966; Requiescant 1967; Beware of a Holy Whore 1970; Nada 1974; Killer Nun 1978; Treasure Island 1986; Irma Vep 1996
Castellaneta, Dan (1957-) My Giant 1998; Laughter on the 23rd Floor 2000; Recess: School's Out 2001; Hey Arnold! the Movie 2002; Dr Seuss' The Cat in the Hat 2003; The Pursuit of Happyness 2006; The Simpsons Movie 2007
Castellano, Richard (1933-1988) Lovers and Other Strangers 1970; The Godfather 1972; Night of the Juggler 1980
Castellanos, Vincent (1962-) The Crow: City of Angels 1996; Anaconda 1997; The Last Marshal 1999; Primary Suspect 2000
Castellitto, Sergio (1953-) The Big Blue 1988; Three Sisters 1988; The Starmaker 1994; Portraits Chinois 1996; Pronto 1996; Va Savoir 2001; Don't Move 2004; The Chronicles of Narnia: Prince Caspian 2008
Castello, Don (1894-1942) The New Adventures of Tarzan 1935; Tarzan and the Green Goddess 1938
Castelnuovo, Nino (1936-) The Umbrellas of Cherbourg 1964; Les Créatures 1966; A Pain in the A...! 1973
Castile, Christopher (1980-) Beethoven 1992; Beethoven's 2nd 1993
Castillo, Enrique aka **Castillo, Enrique J** Borderline 1980; Blood In Blood Out 1992; The Hi-Lo Country 1998
Castillo, Gloria (1933-1978) Invasion of the Saucer Men 1957; Reform School Girl 1957; Teenage Monster 1958
Castle-Hughes, Keisha (1990-) Whale Rider 2002; The Nativity Story 2006; Red Dog 2011
Castle, Don (1917-1966) Out West with the Hardys 1938; Wake Island 1942; The Big Land 1957
Castle, John (1940-) Blowup 1966; The Lion in Winter 1968; Antony and Cleopatra 1972; Man of La Mancha 1972; Eagle's Wing 1979; Dealers 1989; RoboCop 3 1993; Sparrow 1993
Castle, Keith-Lee Seed of Chucky 2004; Doghouse 2009
Castle, Mary (1931-1998) The Lawless Breed 1952; Gunsmoke 1953
Castle, Peggie (1927-1973) Payment on Demand 1951; The Prince Who Was a Thief 1951; I, the Jury 1953; 99 River Street 1953; Tall Man Riding 1955; Miracle in the Rain 1956; The Oklahoma Woman 1956; Beginning of the End 1957; Seven Hills of Rome 1957
Castle, Roy (1932-1994) Dr Terror's House of Horrors 1964; Dr Who and the Daleks 1965; The Plank 1967; Carry On Up the Khyber 1968; Legend of the Werewolf 1974

Castro, Alfredo Tony Manero 2008; Post Mortem 2010; No 2012; The Club 2015
Catania, Antonio (1952-) Puerto Escondido 1992; Bread and Tulips 2000
Cataño, Diego Duck Season 2004; Año Uña 2007; Lake Tahoe 2008
Cater, John (1932-2009) Loot 1970; Captain Kronos: Vampire Hunter 1972; Rising Damp 1980; Alien Autopsy 2006
Cates, Georgina (1975-) An Awfully Big Adventure 1994; Frankie Starlight 1995; Stiff Upper Lips 1997; Clay Pigeons 1998; jackass presents: Bad Grandpa 2013
Cates, Phoebe (1963-) Fast Times at Ridgemont High 1982; Gremlins 1984; Bright Lights, Big City 1988; Shag 1988; Heart of Dixie 1989; Gremlins 2: the New Batch 1990; Drop Dead Fred 1991; Bodies, Rest & Motion 1993; Princess Caraboo 1994; The Anniversary Party 2001
Catherwood, Emma Large 2000; My Kingdom 2001; Spirit Trap 2004
Cathey, Reg E (1958-) Boycott 2001; The Machinist 2003; Nasty Baby 2016
Catillon, Brigitte (1951-) La Lectrice 1988; Un Coeur en Hiver 1992; Artemisia 1997; Le Goût des Autres 1999; Frankie 2005; Love Is in the Air 2013
Catlett, Mary Jo (1938-) Serial Mom 1994; Bram Stoker's Legend of the Mummy 1998
Catlett, Walter (1889-1960) The Front Page 1931; Rain 1932; Banjo on My Knee 1936; Cain and Mabel 1936; Danger - Love at Work 1937; Every Day's a Holiday 1937; Love Is News 1937; On the Avenue 1937; Bringing Up Baby 1938; Going Places 1938; Zaza 1939; Change of Heart 1943; His Butler's Sister 1943; I'll Be Yours 1947; Are You with It? 1948; The Boy with Green Hair 1948
Caton, Juliette (1975-) The Last Temptation of Christ 1988; Courage Mountain 1989
Caton, Michael (1943-) The Castle 1997; The Animal 2001
Cattrall, Kim (1956-) Tribute 1980; Porky's 1981; Ticket to Heaven 1981; Police Academy 1984; Hold-Up 1985; Turk 182! 1985; Big Trouble in Little China 1986; Mannequin 1987; Masquerade 1988; Midnight Crossing 1988; The Return of the Musketeers 1989; The Bonfire of the Vanities 1990; Split Second 1991; Star Trek VI: the Undiscovered Country 1991; Above Suspicion 1995; Baby Geniuses 1999; 36 Hours to Die 1999; 15 Minutes 2001; Crossroads 2002; Ice Princess 2005; The Tiger's Tail 2006; Sex and the City: the Movie 2008; The Ghost 2010; Sex and the City 2 2010; Meet Monica Velour 2011
Caubère, Philippe (1950-) Le Château de Ma Mère 1990; La Gloire de Mon Père 1990
Cauchy, Daniel (1930-) Bob Le Flambeur 1955; The Gendarme of St Tropez 1964
Cauffiel, Jessica (1976-) Valentine 2001; Ice Dreams 2009
Caulfield, Joan (1922-1991) Miss Susie Slagle's 1945; Blue Skies 1946; Monsieur Beaucaire 1946; Dear Ruth 1947; The Unsuspected 1947; Welcome Stranger 1947; Dear Wife 1949; The Petty Girl 1950; The Rains of Ranchipur 1955; Cattle King 1963; Buckskin 1968
Caulfield, Maxwell (1959-) Grease 2 1982; Electric Dreams 1984; The Parade 1984; The Boys Next Door 1985; Gettysburg 1993; Empire Records 1995; The Real Blonde 1997
Cavadini, Cathy aka **Cavadini, Catherine** An American Tail: Fievel Goes West 1991; The Powerpuff Girls 2002
Cavalli, Valeria Everybody's Fine 1990; Double Team 1997
Cavanagh, Megan A League of Their Own 1992; Robin Hood: Men in Tights 1993; Jimmy Neutron: Boy Genius 2001
Cavanagh, Paul (1888-1964) The Devil to Pay 1930; A Bill of Divorcement 1932; The Kennel Murder Case 1933; The Sin of Nora Moran 1933; Tarzan and His Mate 1934; Goin' to Town 1935; Splendor 1935; I Take This Woman 1940; The Hard Way 1942; The House of Fear 1944; The Scarlet Claw 1944; The Woman in Green 1945; The Verdict 1946; Dishonored Lady 1947; Secret beyond the Door 1948; Rogues of Sherwood Forest 1950; The Strange Door 1951; The All American 1953; The Mississippi Gambler 1953; Khyber Patrol 1954; Francis in the Haunted House 1956
Cavanagh, Tom Snow 2004; Yogi Bear 2010

Cavanah, Robert Pimp 2010; The Fall of the Essex Boys 2012
Cavanaugh, Christine (1963-2014) Babe 1995; The Rugrats Movie 1998; Rugrats in Paris: the Movie 2000
Cavanaugh, Hobart (1886-1950) I Cover the Waterfront 1933; Hi, Nellie! 1934; The Key 1934; A Midsummer Night's Dream 1935; Wings in the Dark 1935; Cain and Mabel 1936; Stage Struck 1936; Wife vs Secretary 1936; The Great O'Malley 1937; Rose of Washington Square 1939; Black Angel 1946; Up in Central Park 1948; A Letter to Three Wives 1949
Cavazos, Lumi (1968-) Like Water for Chocolate 1993; Bottle Rocket 1996; Sugar Town 1999
Cave, Nick (1957-) Ghosts... of the Civil Dead 1988; Johnny Suede 1991; Leonard Cohen: I'm Your Man 2005; 20,000 Days on Earth 2014
Cavell, Marc (1939-2004) Thunder in the East 1953; The Wild Angels 1966
Caven, Ingrid (1943-) Gods of the Plague 1969; The American Soldier 1970; Mother Küsters Goes to Heaven 1975; Fear of Fear 1976; Satan's Brew 1976; In a Year of 13 Moons 1978; 35 Shots of Rum 2008
Cavett, Dick HEALTH 1980; Best of Enemies 2015
Caviezel, Jim aka **Caviezel, James** (1968-) GI Jane 1997; The Thin Red Line 1998; Ride with the Devil 1999; Frequency 2000; Pay It Forward 2000; Angel Eyes 2001; The Count of Monte Cristo 2001; High Crimes 2002; Highwaymen 2003; Bobby Jones: Stroke of Genius 2004; The Final Cut 2004; The Passion of the Christ 2004; Déjà Vu 2006; Unknown 2006; Long Weekend 2008; Outlander 2008; Escape Plan 2013
Cavill, Henry (1983-) I Capture the Castle 2002; Tristan + Isolde 2005; Blood Creek 2009; Whatever Works 2009; Immortals 2011; The Cold Light of Day 2012; Man of Steel 2013; The Man from UNCLE 2015; Batman v Superman: Dawn of Justice 2016; Justice League 2017
Cawdron, Robert (1921-1998) Street of Shadows 1953; Saturday Night and Sunday Morning 1960
Cawthorn, Joseph (1868-1949) The Taming of the Shrew 1929; Love Me Tonight 1932; White Zombie 1932; Glamour 1934; Sweet Adeline 1935; One Rainy Afternoon 1936
Cazale, John (1936-1978) The Conversation 1974; The Godfather Part II 1974; Dog Day Afternoon 1975; The Deer Hunter 1978
Cazalé, Nicolas (1977-) Le Clan 2004; The Grocer's Son 2007
Cazenove, Christopher (1945-2010) Royal Flash 1975; East of Elephant Rock 1976; Eye of the Needle 1981; Heat and Dust 1982; Until September 1984; Mata Hari 1985; The Fantasist 1986; Three Men and a Little Lady 1990; Aces: Iron Eagle III 1992; LaVyrle Spencer's Home Song 1996; The Proprietor 1996; Shadow Run 1998; Contagion 2000; A Knight's Tale 2001
Ceccaldi, Daniel (1927-2003) Bed and Board 1970; Love in the Afternoon 1972
Cecchi, Carlo (1939-) Hamam: the Turkish Bath 1996; The Red Violin 1998
Cecil, Jonathan (1939-2011) Under the Doctor 1976; Thirteen at Dinner 1985; Agatha Christie's Murder in Three Acts 1986; Dead Man's Folly 1986
Cecil, Nora (1878-1951) The Old-Fashioned Way 1934; The Unknown Guest 1943
Cedar, Jon (1931-2011) The Manitou 1978; Death Hunt 1981; Murder in Mind 1996
Cedar, Larry Feds 1988; Midnight Son 2011
Cederlund, Gosta (1888-1980) Torment 1944; It Rains on Our Love 1946
Cedric the Entertainer aka **Cedric "The Entertainer"** aka **Cedric "The Entertainer" Kyles** (1964-) Ride 1998; Barbershop 2002; Serving Sara 2002; Intolerable Cruelty 2003; Barbershop 2: Back in Business 2004; Johnson Family Vacation 2004; Be Cool 2005; The Honeymooners 2005; Madagascar 2005; Man of the House 2005; Charlotte's Web 2006; Code Name: the Cleaner 2007; Talk to Me 2007; Cadillac Records 2008; Madagascar: Escape 2 Africa 2008; Street Kings 2008; Welcome Home Roscoe Jenkins 2008; Grassroots 2012; A Haunted House 2013; Planes 2013; A Haunted House 2 2014; Barbershop: a Fresh Cut 2016
Celano, Guido (1905-1988) Four Steps in the Clouds 1942; Never Take No for an Answer 1951; The Man from Cairo

1953; *The Loves of Three Queens* 1954; *Seven Hills of Rome* 1957

Célarié, Clémentine (1957-) *Betty Blue* 1986; *Le Cri du Coeur* 1994; *The Lawless Heart* 2001

Cele, Henry (1949-) *Out of Darkness* 1990; *Curse III: Blood Sacrifice* 1991

Celi, Adolfo (1922-1986) *That Man from Rio* 1964; *The Agony and the Ecstasy* 1965; *Thunderball* 1965; *The Bobo* 1967; *Danger: Diabolik* 1967; *Grand Slam* 1967; *The Honey Pot* 1967; *Midas Run* 1969; *Fragment of Fear* 1970; *In Search of Gregory* 1970; *Murders in the Rue Morgue* 1971; *Hitler: the Last Ten Days* 1973; *And Then There Were None* 1974; *Le Fantôme de la Liberté* 1974; *The Next Man* 1976; *Monsignor* 1982

Celinska, Stanislawa (1947-) *Landscape after Battle* 1970; *Miss Nobody* 1997

Celio, Teco *Three Colours Red* 1994; *The Truce* 1997

Celli, Teresa (1924-) *Border Incident* 1949; *The Black Hand* 1950; *Right Cross* 1950

Cellier, Antoinette (1913-1981) *Music Hath Charms* 1935; *The Great Barrier* 1937; *Bees in Paradise* 1943; *The End of the River* 1947

Cellier, Caroline (1945-) *Que la Bête Meure* 1969; *A Pain in the A...!* 1973; *Farinelli il Castrato* 1994

Cellier, Frank (1884-1948) *Doss House* 1933; *The Passing of the Third Floor Back* 1935; *The 39 Steps* 1935; *The Man Who Changed His Mind* 1936; *Rhodes of Africa* 1936; *Tudor Rose* 1936; *You're in the Army Now* 1936; *The Black Sheep of Whitehall* 1941; *Love on the Dole* 1941; *Give Us the Moon* 1944; *Quiet Weekend* 1946; *The Blind Goddess* 1948

Cellier, Peter (1940-1994) *Man about the House* 1974; *Man Friday* 1975; *And the Ship Sails On* 1983

Cena, John *12 Rounds* 2008; *Fred: the Movie* 2010

Cepek, Petr (1940-1994) *Cutting It Short* 1980; *My Sweet Little Village* 1986; *Faust* 1994

Cera, Michael (1988-) *Custody of the Heart* 2000; *Juno* 2007; *Superbad* 2007; *Nick & Norah's Infinite Playlist* 2008; *Paper Heart* 2009; *Year One* 2009; *Youth in Revolt* 2009; *Scott Pilgrim vs the World* 2010; *Crystal Fairy and the Magical Cactus* 2013; *Magic Magic* 2013; *Sausage Party* 2016

Cernan, Eugene *In the Shadow of the Moon* 2007; *The Last Man on the Moon* 2015

Cerra, Saturno *Valentina* 1982; *1919* 1983

Cerval, Claude (1921-1975) *Bob Le Flambeur* 1955; *Le Beau Serge* 1958; *Classe Tous Risques* 1959; *Les Cousins* 1959; *Ophélia* 1962

Cervi, Gino (1901-1974) *Four Steps in the Clouds* 1942; *Les Misérables* 1946; *The Little World of Don Camillo* 1951; *La Signora senza Camelie* 1953; *Indiscretion of an American Wife* 1954; *The Naked Maja* 1959; *Becket* 1964

Cervi, Valentina (1974-) *Artemisia* 1997; *Rien sur Robert* 1998; *James Dean* 2001

Cesana, Renzo (1907-1970) *Stromboli* 1950; *For the First Time* 1959

Ceylan, Ebru *Uzak* 2003; *Climates* 2006

Ceylan, Fatma *Uzak* 2003; *Climates* 2006

Chávez, Alan *La Zona* 2007; *We Are What We Are* 2010

Chávez, Hugo *The War on Democracy* 2007; *South of the Border* 2009

Chabat, Alain (1958-) *Six Days, Six Nights* 1994; *Gazon Maudit* 1995; *Le Goût des Autres* 1999; *Asterix & Obelix: Mission Cleopatra* 2005; *The Science of Sleep* 2005; *I Do* 2006; *Night at the Museum 2* 2009; *Mood Indigo* 2013

Chabert, Lacey (1982-) *Lost in Space* 1998; *The Wild Thornberrys Movie* 2003; *The Brooke Ellison Story* 2004; *Mean Girls* 2004; *Be My Baby* 2006; *Black Christmas* 2006; *Ghosts of Girlfriends Past* 2009; *Elevator Girl* 2010; *Imaginary Friend* 2012

Chabrol, Claude (1930-2010) *Les Bonnes Femmes* 1960; *Paris Vu Par...* 1965; *The Road to Corinth* 1967; *Les Biches* 1968

Chabrol, Thomas (1963-) *Rien Ne Va Plus* 1997; *The Flower of Evil* 2002; *A Comedy of Power* 2006

Chadbon, Tom (1946-) *The Beast Must Die* 1974; *Dance with a Stranger* 1984

Chadda, Richa *Gangs of Wasseypur* 2012; *Gangs of Wasseypur II* 2012

Chadov, Alexei (1981-) *War* 2002; *Night Watch* 2004; *9th Company* 2005; *Day Watch* 2006

Chadwick, Cyril (1879-1955) *The Iron Horse* 1924; *The Last of Mrs Cheyney* 1929

Chahine, Youssef (1926-2008) *Cairo Station* 1958; *Alexandria Encore* 1990

Chakiris, George aka **Kerris, George** (1933-) *Meet Me in Las Vegas* 1956; *Two and Two Make Six* 1961; *West Side Story* 1961; *Diamond Head* 1962; *Flight from Ashiya* 1963; *Kings of the Sun* 1963; *633 Squadron* 1964; *The High Bright Sun* 1965; *The Young Girls of Rochefort* 1967; *The Big Cube* 1969

Chakravarty, Lily aka **Chakraborty, Lily** *The Middleman* 1975; *Chokher Bali* 2003

Chalfant, Kathleen *Jumpin' at the Boneyard* 1991; *Georgia O'Keeffe* 2009

Chaliapin Jr, Feodor aka **Chaliapin, Feodor** (1907-1992) *The Name of the Rose* 1986; *The Church* 1988; *Stanley & Iris* 1989; *The King's Whore* 1990; *The Inner Circle* 1991

Chalmers, Thomas (1884-1966) *The Plow That Broke the Plains* 1934; *The River* 1937; *All the Way Home* 1963; *The Outrage* 1964

Chamas, Mohamad *West Beirut* 1998; *Blind Flight* 2003

Chamberlain, Cyril (1909-1974) *Impulse* 1955; *Tiger by the Tail* 1955; *The Great St Trinian's Train Robbery* 1966

Chamberlain, Richard (1935-) *The Secret of the Purple Reef* 1960; *A Thunder of Drums* 1961; *Twilight of Honor* 1963; *Petulia* 1968; *The Madwoman of Chaillot* 1969; *Julius Caesar* 1970; *The Music Lovers* 1970; *Lady Caroline Lamb* 1972; *The Three Musketeers* 1973; *The Count of Monte Cristo* 1974; *The Four Musketeers* 1974; *The Towering Inferno* 1974; *The Slipper and the Rose* 1976; *The Last Wave* 1977; *The Man in the Iron Mask* 1977; *The Swarm* 1978; *Murder by Phone* 1982; *Cook & Peary: the Race to the Pole* 1983; *King Solomon's Mines* 1985; *Allan Quatermain and the Lost City of Gold* 1987; *The Return of the Musketeers* 1989; *I Now Pronounce You Chuck & Larry* 2007

Chamberlin, Howland aka **Chamberlain, Howland** (1911-1984) *The Web* 1947; *Force of Evil* 1948; *The Big Night* 1951; *Kramer vs Kramer* 1979

Chambers, Justin (1970-) *The Musketeer* 2001; *The Wedding Planner* 2001; *Leo* 2002

Chambers, Matthew *Attack Force* 2006; *Lady Godiva* 2007

Chambers (1), Michael aka **Chambers, Michael "Boogaloo Shrimp"** *Breakdance* 1984; *Breakdance 2 - Electric Boogaloo* 1984

Champa, Jo (1969-) *The Family* 1987; *Out for Justice* 1991

Champion, Gower (1919-1980) *Show Boat* 1951; *Lovely to Look At* 1952; *Give a Girl a Break* 1953; *Jupiter's Darling* 1955; *Three for the Show* 1955

Champion, Jean (1914-2001) *The Umbrellas of Cherbourg* 1964; *Day for Night* 1973

Champion, Marge (1921-) *Show Boat* 1951; *Lovely to Look At* 1952; *Give a Girl a Break* 1953; *Jupiter's Darling* 1955; *Three for the Show* 1955; *The Party* 1968; *The Swimmer* 1968

Champion, Michael aka **Champion, Mike** *False Identity* 1990; *Total Recall* 1990

Chan Kwok Kwan *Tsui Hark's Vampire Hunters* 2002; *Kung Fu Hustle* 2004

Chan, Anthony aka **Chan, Anthony "Friend"** *Mr Vampire* 1986; *Twin Dragons* 1992; *Rigor Mortis* 2013

Chan, Dennis *Kickboxer* 1989; *Kickboxer 2: the Road Back* 1990; *Kickboxer III: the Art of War* 1992

Chan, Gemma (1982-) *Exam* 2009; *Submarine* 2010

Chan, Jackie aka **Lung Cheng** (1954-) *Drunken Master* 1978; *Snake in the Eagle's Shadow* 1978; *The Big Brawl* 1980; *The Cannonball Run* 1981; *Cannonball Run II* 1983; *Project A* 1983; *Wheels on Meals* 1984; *Police Story* 1985; *The Protector* 1985; *The Armour of God* 1986; *Police Story 2* 1986; *Project A: Part II* 1987; *Operation Condor: the Armour of God II* 1990; *Police Story III: Supercop* 1992; *Twin Dragons* 1992; *Crime Story* 1993; *Jackie Chan's First Strike* 1996; *Mr Nice Guy* 1996; *Rumble in the Bronx* 1996; *Burn Hollywood Burn* 1997; *Jackie Chan's Who Am I?* 1998; *Rush Hour* 1998; *Shanghai Noon* 2000; *The Accidental Spy* 2001; *Rush Hour 2* 2001; *Shanghai Knights* 2002; *The Tuxedo* 2002; *The Medallion* 2003; *Around the World in 80 Days* 2004; *New Police Story* 2004; *Rush Hour 3* 2007; *The Forbidden Kingdom* 2008; *Kung Fu Panda* 2008; *Shinjuku Incident* 2009; *The Spy Next Door* 2009; *The Karate Kid* 2010; *Little Big Soldier* 2010; *Kung Fu Panda 2* 2011; *Shaolin* 2011; *Chinese Zodiac* 2012; *Dragon Blade* 2015; *Kung Fu Panda 3* 2016

Chan, Jordan (1967-) *Young and Dangerous* 1996; *Kitchen* 1997; *And Now You're Dead* 1998; *Initial D - Drift Racer* 2005

Chan, Philip aka **Chan, Philip Yan Kin** *Bloodsport* 1987; *Double Impact* 1991; *Hard-Boiled* 1992; *Twin Dragons* 1992

Chance, Naomi (1930-2003) *The Gambler and the Lady* 1952; *Blood Orange* 1953

Chancellor, Anna (1964-) *Staggered* 1993; *Four Weddings and a Funeral* 1994; *Heart* 1997; *The Man Who Knew Too Little* 1997; *Crush* 2001; *Agent Cody Banks 2: Destination London* 2003; *The Dreamers* 2003; *What a Girl Wants* 2003; *The Best Man* 2005; *The Hitchhiker's Guide to the Galaxy* 2005; *Breaking and Entering* 2006; *St Trinian's* 2007; *How I Live Now* 2013; *The Carer* 2015

Chandler, Chick (1905-1988) *Melody Cruise* 1933; *Murder on a Honeymoon* 1935; *Mr Moto Takes a Chance* 1938; *Swanee River* 1939; *Baby Face Morgan* 1942; *The Big Shot* 1942; *Johnny Doesn't Live Here Anymore* 1944; *Do You Love Me?* 1946; *Nightmare in the Sun* 1964

Chandler, Helen (1906-1965) *Daybreak* 1931; *Dracula* 1931; *The Last Flight* 1931; *Christopher Strong* 1933; *The Worst Woman in Paris?* 1933; *Long Lost Father* 1934

Chandler, Jeff (1918-1961) *Broken Arrow* 1950; *Two Flags West* 1950; *Bird of Paradise* 1951; *Double Crossbons* 1951; *Iron Man* 1951; *The Battle at Apache Pass* 1952; *Red Ball Express* 1952; *East of Sumatra* 1953; *The Great Sioux Uprising* 1953; *War Arrow* 1953; *Sign of the Pagan* 1954; *The Spoilers* 1955; *Away All Boats* 1956; *Pillars of the Sky* 1956; *Jeanne Eagels* 1957; *Man in the Shadow* 1957; *The Tattered Dress* 1957; *The Lady Takes a Flyer* 1958; *Raw Wind in Eden* 1958; *The Jayhawkers* 1959; *A Stranger in My Arms* 1959; *Ten Seconds to Hell* 1959; *Thunder in the Sun* 1959; *Return to Peyton Place* 1961; *Merrill's Marauders* 1962

Chandler, Joan (1923-1979) *Humoresque* 1946; *Rope* 1948

Chandler, John Davis (1935-2010) *Mad Dog Coll* 1961; *Ride the High Country* 1962; *Once a Thief* 1965; *The Good Guys and the Bad Guys* 1969

Chandler, Kyle (1965-) *Pure Country* 1992; *Angel's Dance* 1999; *King Kong* 2005; *Super 8* 2011; *Zero Dark Thirty* 2012; *Broken City* 2013; *The Wolf of Wall Street* 2013; *Carol* 2015

Chandler, Lane (1899-1972) *The Single Standard* 1929; *Sagebrush Trail* 1934; *Winds of the Wasteland* 1936; *Return to Treasure Island* 1954

Chandler, Simon *The Lord of the Rings* 1978; *Perfume: the Story of a Murderer* 2006

Chandos, John (1917-1987) *Next of Kin* 1942; *The Long Memory* 1952; *The Battle of the River Plate* 1956; *The Green Man* 1956

Chandrasekhar, Jay (1968-) *Super Troopers* 2001; *Broken Lizard's Club Dread* 2004; *Beerfest* 2006

Chaney, Lon (1883-1930) *The Ace of Hearts* 1921; *A Blind Bargain* 1922; *Oliver Twist* 1922; *The Hunchback of Notre Dame* 1923; *He Who Gets Slapped* 1924; *The Monster* 1925; *The Phantom of the Opera* 1925; *The Unholy Three* 1925; *The Black Bird* 1926; *The Road to Mandalay* 1926; *London after Midnight* 1927; *The Unknown* 1927; *Laugh, Clown, Laugh* 1928; *West of Zanzibar* 1928; *The Unholy Three* 1930

Chaney Jr, Lon aka **Chaney, Creighton** aka **Chaney, Lon** (1906-1973) *Bird of Paradise* 1932; *Lucky Devils* 1933; *Frontier Marshal* 1939; *Of Mice and Men* 1939; *Union Pacific* 1939; *One Million BC* 1940; *Billy the Kid* 1941; *Man Made Monster* 1941; *The Wolf Man* 1941; *The Ghost of Frankenstein* 1942; *The Mummy's Tomb* 1942; *Calling Dr Death* 1943; *Frankenstein Meets the Wolf Man* 1943; *Frontier Badmen* 1943; *Son of Dracula* 1943; *Cobra Woman* 1944; *Dead Man's Eyes* 1944; *Follow the Boys* 1944; *The Frozen Ghost* 1944; *House of Frankenstein* 1944; *The Mummy's Curse* 1944; *The Mummy's Ghost* 1944; *Weird Woman* 1944; *The Daltons Ride Again* 1945; *Here Come the Co-Eds* 1945; *House of Dracula* 1945; *Pillow of Death* 1945; *Strange Confession* 1945; *My Favorite Brunette* 1947; *Abbott and Costello Meet Frankenstein* 1948; *Only*

the Valiant 1950; *The Black Castle* 1952; *High Noon* 1952; *Springfield Rifle* 1952; *Thief of Damascus* 1952; *A Lion Is in the Streets* 1953; *Raiders of the Seven Seas* 1953; *The Boy from Oklahoma* 1954; *Casanova's Big Night* 1954; *Big House, USA* 1955; *I Died a Thousand Times* 1955; *The Indian Fighter* 1955; *Not as a Stranger* 1955; *The Black Sleep* 1956; *Indestructible Man* 1956; *Pardners* 1956; *The Cyclops* 1957; *Daniel Boone, Trail Blazer* 1957; *The Defiant Ones* 1958; *The Alligator People* 1959; *Night of the Ghouls* 1959; *The Haunted Palace* 1963; *Spider Baby* 1964; *Apache Uprising* 1965; *Johnny Reno* 1966; *Buckskin* 1968; *The Female Bunch* 1969; *Dracula vs Frankenstein* 1970

Chang Chen (1976-) *Happy Together* 1997; *Crouching Tiger, Hidden Dragon* 2000; *Chinese Odyssey 2002* 2002; *Eros* 2004; *Three Times* 2005; *Red Cliff* 2008; *The Assassin* 2015

Chang, Sylvia (1953-) *Soursweet* 1988; *Eat Drink Man Woman* 1994; *The Red Violin* 1998

Channing, Carol (1921-) *The First Travelling Saleslady* 1956; *Thoroughly Modern Millie* 1967; *Skidoo* 1968; *Snow White in Happily Ever After* 1990

Channing, Stockard (1944-) *The Fortune* 1975; *The Big Bus* 1976; *The Cheap Detective* 1978; *Grease* 1978; *Without a Trace* 1983; *Heartburn* 1986; *The Men's Club* 1986; *A Time of Destiny* 1988; *Staying Together* 1989; *Meet the Applegates* 1991; *Bitter Moon* 1992; *Six Degrees of Separation* 1993; *David's Mother* 1994; *Moll Flanders* 1995; *Smoke* 1995; *To Wong Foo, Thanks for Everything, Julie Newmar* 1995; *Desert Gamble* 1996; *The First Wives Club* 1996; *Up Close & Personal* 1996; *Practical Magic* 1998; *Twilight* 1998; *Isn't She Great* 1999; *Where the Heart Is* 2000; *The Business of Strangers* 2001; *Life or Something like It* 2002; *Anything Else* 2003; *Bright Young Things* 2003; *Le Divorce* 2003; *Jack* 2004; *Must Love Dogs* 2005; *Sparkle* 2006

Chao, Rosalind (1949-) *The Big Brawl* 1980; *An Eye for an Eye* 1981; *The End of Violence* 1997; *What Dreams May Come* 1998; *Freaky Friday* 2003; *Just like Heaven* 2005

Chao, Winston *The Wedding Banquet* 1993; *Eat Drink Man Woman* 1994; *1911* 2011

Chapa, Damian (1963-) *Blood In Blood Out* 1992; *Under Siege* 1992; *Final Combination* 1993; *Street Fighter* 1994; *Sometimes They Come Back... for More* 1998; *Bad Karma* 2001

Chapin, Billy (1943-) *Naked Alibi* 1954; *The Night of the Hunter* 1955; *Tension at Table Rock* 1956

Chapin, Miles (1954-) *French Postcards* 1979; *Buddy Buddy* 1981; *The Funhouse* 1981; *Pandemonium* 1982; *Get Crazy* 1983

Chaplin, Ben (1970-) *The Remains of the Day* 1993; *Feast of July* 1995; *The Truth about Cats and Dogs* 1996; *Washington Square* 1997; *The Thin Red Line* 1998; *Lost Souls* 2000; *Birthday Girl* 2001; *Murder by Numbers* 2002; *Stage Beauty* 2004; *Chromophobia* 2005; *The Water Horse* 2007; *Me and Orson Welles* 2008; *Dorian Gray* 2009; *Twixt* 2011; *War Book* 2014; *Cinderella* 2015

Chaplin, Charles aka **Chaplin, Charlie** (1889-1977) *Tillie's Punctured Romance* 1914; *His New Job* 1915; *The Tramp* 1915; *Work* 1915; *Behind the Screen* 1916; *The Floorwalker* 1916; *The Pawnshop* 1916; *The Rink* 1916; *The Vagabond* 1916; *The Cure* 1917; *The Immigrant* 1917; *A Dog's Life* 1918; *Shoulder Arms* 1918; *A Day's Pleasure* 1919; *Sunnyside* 1919; *The Idle Class* 1921; *The Kid* 1921; *Pay Day* 1922; *The Pilgrim* 1923; *A Woman of Paris* 1923; *The Gold Rush* 1925; *The Circus* 1928; *Show People* 1928; *City Lights* 1931; *Modern Times* 1936; *The Great Dictator* 1940; *Monsieur Verdoux* 1947; *Limelight* 1952; *A King in New York* 1957; *Charlie: the Life and Art of Charles Chaplin* 2003

Chaplin Jr, Charles (1925-1968) *Limelight* 1952; *The Beat Generation* 1959; *The Big Operator* 1959

Chaplin, Christopher (1962-) *Death of a Schoolboy* 1990; *Labyrinth* 1991

Chaplin, Geraldine (1944-) *Limelight* 1952; *Doctor Zhivago* 1965; *Peppermint Frappé* 1967; *Stranger in the House* 1967; *The Hawaiians* 1970; *ZPG: Zero Population Growth* 1971; *The Four Musketeers* 1974; *Cría Cuervos* 1975; *Nashville* 1975; *Buffalo Bill and the Indians, or Sitting Bull's History Lesson* 1976; *Welcome to LA* 1976; *Roseland* 1977; *Remember My Name*

1978; *A Wedding* 1978; *Mamá Cumple 100 Años* 1979; *The Mirror Crack'd* 1980; *Les Uns et les Autres* 1981; *Life Is a Bed of Roses* 1983; *L'Amour par Terre* 1984; *White Mischief* 1987; *The Moderns* 1988; *The Return of the Musketeers* 1989; *The Children* 1990; *Chaplin* 1992; *The Age of Innocence* 1993; *Home for the Holidays* 1995; *Jane Eyre* 1996; *Cousin Bette* 1997; *The Odyssey* 1997; *To Walk with Lions* 1999; *Talk to Her* 2001; *The City of No Limits* 2002; *A Christmas Carol* 2004; *Heidi* 2005; *The Orphanage* 2006; *The Wolfman* 2009; *The Impossible* 2011; *The Monk* 2011; *The Forbidden Room* 2015

Chaplin, Oona (1986-) *Powder Room* 2013; *The Longest Ride* 2015

Chaplin, Syd aka **Chaplin, Sydney** (1885-1965) *A Dog's Life* 1918; *Shoulder Arms* 1918; *A Day's Pleasure* 1919; *Pay Day* 1922; *The Pilgrim* 1923

Chaplin, Sydney (1926-2009) *Limelight* 1952; *Confession* 1955; *Land of the Pharaohs* 1955; *Quantez* 1957; *A Countess from Hong Kong* 1967; *The Adding Machine* 1969

Chapman, Constance (1912-2003) *Say Hello to Yesterday* 1971; *In Celebration* 1974; *Hedda* 1975; *Clockwise* 1986

Chapman, Dean-Charles *Before I Go to Sleep* 2014; *Man Up* 2015

Chapman, Edward (1901-1977) *Juno and the Paycock* 1930; *Murder* 1930; *The Skin Game* 1931; *Blossom Time* 1934; *The Man Who Could Work Miracles* 1936; *Rembrandt* 1936; *Things to Come* 1936; *Poison Pen* 1939; *There Ain't No Justice* 1939; *Convoy* 1940; *The Proud Valley* 1940; *It's Turned Out Nice Again* 1941; *They Flew Alone* 1941; *Ships with Wings* 1942; *It Always Rains on Sunday* 1947; *The October Man* 1947; *The History of Mr Polly* 1948; *Mr Perrin and Mr Traill* 1948; *Madeleine* 1949; *The Spider and the Fly* 1949; *Gone to Earth* 1950; *The Card* 1952; *Folly to Be Wise* 1952; *Mandy* 1952; *A Day to Remember* 1953; *A Yank in Ermine* 1955; *Bhowani Junction* 1956; *X the Unknown* 1956; *Just My Luck* 1957; *The Square Peg* 1958; *Oscar Wilde* 1959; *The Bulldog Breed* 1960; *School for Scoundrels* 1960; *A Stitch in Time* 1963 ; *The Early Bird* 1965

Chapman, Georgina *The Business* 2005; *Awake* 2007

Chapman, Graham (1941-1989) *The Magic Christian* 1969; *Doctor in Trouble* 1970; *And Now for Something Completely Different* 1971; *Monty Python and the Holy Grail* 1975; *Pleasure at Her Majesty's* 1976; *The Odd Job* 1978; *Monty Python's Life of Brian* 1979; *Monty Python Live at the Hollywood Bowl* 1982; *Monty Python's The Meaning of Life* 1983; *Yellowbeard* 1983; *A Liar's Autobiography: the Untrue Story of Monty Python's Graham Chapman* 2012

Chapman, Kevin *Mystic River* 2003; *Sunshine Cleaning* 2008; *Black Dynamite* 2009

Chapman, Lonny (1921-2007) *Baby Doll* 1956; *The Stalking Moon* 1968; *The Reivers* 1969; *Take the Money and Run* 1969; *The Cowboys* 1972; *Where the Red Fern Grows* 1974; *52 Pick-Up* 1986

Chapman, Marguerite (1918-1999) *Counter-Attack* 1945; *Pardon My Past* 1945; *Coroner Creek* 1948; *Relentless* 1948; *Kansas Raiders* 1950; *Flight to Mars* 1951; *Bloodhounds of Broadway* 1952; *The Seven Year Itch* 1955

Chapman, Mark Lindsay *Separate Lives* 1995; *Bram Stoker's Legend of the Mummy* 1998

Chapman, Sean *Party Party* 1983; *Hellraiser* 1987; *For Queen and Country* 1988; *Hellbound: Hellraiser II* 1988; *One of the Hollywood Ten* 2000

Chappell, Lisa *Desperate Remedies* 1993; *Coffin Rock* 2009

Chappelle, Dave (1973-) *Robin Hood: Men in Tights* 1993; *Getting In* 1994; *The Nutty Professor* 1996; *Half-Baked* 1998; *Woo* 1998; *You've Got Mail* 1998; *Blue Streak* 1999; *Screwed* 2000; *Undercover Brother* 2002; *Dave Chappelle's Block Party* 2005

Chappey, Antoine *I'm Going Home* 2001; *5x2* 2004; *Angel of Mine* 2008

Charbonneau, Patricia (1959-) *Desert Hearts* 1985; *Call Me* 1988; *Brain Dead* 1990; *K2* 1991; *One Special Night* 1999

Charendoff, Tara aka **Strong, Tara** (1973-) *The Little Mermaid II: Return to the Sea* 2000; *Rugrats in Paris: the Movie* 2000; *Spirited Away* 2001; *Ice Age* 2002; *The Powerpuff Girls* 2002; *Rugrats Go Wild* 2003

Charisse, Cyd (1922-2008) *Ziegfeld Follies* 1944; *The Harvey Girls* 1946; *Fiesta* 1947; *The Unfinished Dance* 1947; *On an Island with You* 1948; *East Side, West Side* 1949; *The Kissing*

Bandit 1949; Tension 1949; Singin' in the Rain 1952; Sombrero 1952; The Wild North 1952; The Band Wagon 1953; Brigadoon 1954; Deep in My Heart 1954; It's Always Fair Weather 1955; Meet Me in Las Vegas 1956; Silk Stockings 1957; Party Girl 1958; Two Weeks in Another Town 1962; Maroc 7 1966; The Silencers 1966; Warlords of Atlantis 1978

Charles, Craig Asterix Conquers America 1994; Fated 2006

Charles, Josh (1971-) Dead Poets Society 1989; Murder in Mississippi 1990; Don't Tell Mom the Babysitter's Dead 1991; Cooperstown 1993; Threesome 1994; Coldblooded 1995; Pie in the Sky 1995; Crossworlds 1996; Norma Jean & Marilyn 1996; Little City 1997; SWAT 2003; Four Brothers 2005; After.Life 2009

Charles, Nancy Linehan Ed Gein 2000; The Stepfather 2009

Charles, Ray (1930-2004) Ballad in Blue 1964; The Blues Brothers 1980

Charleson, Ian (1949-1990) Jubilee 1978; Chariots of Fire 1981; Greystoke: the Legend of Tarzan, Lord of the Apes 1984; Car Trouble 1985; Opera 1987

Charlesworth, John (1934-1960) Scrooge 1951; Tom Brown's Schooldays 1951; The Blue Peter 1955

Charlita (1921-1997) The Brave Bulls 1951; Bela Lugosi Meets a Brooklyn Gorilla 1952; Ride, Vaquero! 1953; The Naked Dawn 1955

Charmetant, Christian News from the Good Lord 1996; Le Libertin 2000

Charney, Jordan (1937-) Witches' Brew 1979; The Cartier Affair 1984; Do You Remember Love 1985

Charney, Kim (1945-) Suddenly 1954; Quantrill's Raiders 1958; Hey Boy! Hey Girl! 1959

Charo (1941-) Tiger by the Tail 1970; Airport '79: the Concorde 1979; Moon over Parador 1988

Charpin, Fernand (1887-1944) Marius 1931; Fanny 1932; César 1936; Pépé le Moko 1937

Charrier, Jacques (1936-) Les Tricheurs 1958; The Seven Deadly Sins 1961; Les Créatures 1966

Charters, Spencer (1875-1943) Whoopee! 1930; Palmy Days 1931; Jewel Robbery 1932; Spendthrift 1936; Three Faces West 1940

Chartoff, Melanie (1955-) The Rugrats Movie 1998; Rugrats Go Wild 2003

Chase, Alden (1902-1982) The Little Colonel 1935; The Lone Rider in Ghost Town 1941

Chase, Charley (1893-1940) Sons of the Desert 1933; Laurel and Hardy's Laughing 20s 1965; 4 Clowns 1970

Chase, Cheryl Rugrats in Paris: the Movie 2000; Rugrats Go Wild 2003

Chase, Chevy (1943-) Foul Play 1978; Caddyshack 1980; Seems like Old Times 1980; Modern Problems 1981; Under the Rainbow 1981; Deal of the Century 1983; National Lampoon's Vacation 1983; Fletch 1985; Follow That Bird 1985; National Lampoon's European Vacation 1985; Spies like Us 1985; Three Amigos! 1986; Caddyshack II 1988; The Couch Trip 1988; Funny Farm 1988; Fletch Lives 1989; National Lampoon's Christmas Vacation 1989; Nothing but Trouble 1991; Memoirs of an Invisible Man 1992; Cops and Robbersons 1994; Man of the House 1994; Vegas Vacation 1997; Dirty Work 1998; Snow Day 2000; Orange County 2001; Ellie Parker 2005; Zoom 2006; Hot Tub Time Machine 2010; Jack and the Beanstalk 2010; Hot Tub Time Machine 2 2014; Vacation 2015

Chase, Daveigh (1990-) Spirited Away 2001; Lilo & Stitch 2002

Chase, Ilka (1900-1978) The Gay Diplomat 1931; The Animal Kingdom 1932; Now, Voyager 1942; No Time for Love 1943; Miss Tatlock's Millions 1948; Johnny Dark 1954

Chase (1), Stephen aka **Chase, Steven** (1902-1982) Cavalry Scout 1951; My Favorite Spy 1951; When Worlds Collide 1951; The Great Sioux Uprising 1953; The Blob 1958

Chastain, Jessica (1977-) Coriolanus 2010; The Debt 2010; The Tree of Life 2010; The Help 2011; Take Shelter 2011; Texas Killing Fields 2011; Wilde Salomé 2011; Lawless 2012; Madagascar 3: Europe's Most Wanted 2012; Zero Dark Thirty 2012; Mama 2013; Salomé 2013; Seduced and Abandoned 2013; Interstellar 2014; Miss Julie 2014; A Most Violent Year 2014; Crimson Peak 2015; The Martian 2015; The Huntsman: Winter's War 2016

Chatel, Peter (1943-1986) Martha 1973; Fox and His Friends 1975

Chatterjee, Anil aka **Chattopadhyay, Anil** (1929-1996) The Cloud Capped

Star 1960; E Flat 1961; Teen Kanya 1961; Kangchenjunga 1962; The Big City 1963

Chatterjee, Dhritiman aka **Chaterji, Dhritiman** (1946-) The Adversary 1970; In Search of Famine 1980; 36 Chowringhee Lane 1982; An Enemy of the People 1989; The Stranger 1991; Black 2004

Chatterjee, Soumitra (1934-) The World of Apu 1959; Devi 1960; Teen Kanya 1961; Abhijan 1962; Charulata 1964; Days and Nights in the Forest 1969; Distant Thunder 1973; The Home and the World 1984; An Enemy of the People 1989; Branches of the Tree 1990

Chatterton, Ruth (1893-1961) Madame X 1929; Anybody's Woman 1930; Paramount on Parade 1930; Sarah and Son 1930; The Rich Are Always with Us 1932; Female 1933; Dodsworth 1936

Chattopadhyay, Harindranath The Householder 1963; Company Limited 1971

Chatwin, Justin (1982-) War of the Worlds 2005; The Invisible 2007; Dragonball Evolution 2009

Chau, François (1959-) Teenage Mutant Ninja Turtles II: the Secret of the Ooze 1991; Beverly Hills Ninja 1997; 21 and Over 2013

Chaulet, Emmanuelle My Girlfriend's Boyfriend 1987; All the Vermeers in New York 1990

Chaumette, Monique (1927-) La Grande Bouffe 1973; Sunday in the Country 1984; Masques 1987

Chauvin, Lilyan Silent Night, Deadly Night 1984; Going to Pieces: the Rise and Fall of the Slasher Film 2006

Chawla, Juhi Paheli 2005; Salaam E Ishq 2007

Chaykin, Maury (1949-2010) Of Unknown Origin 1983; Def-Con 4 1984; Harry and Son 1984; Act of Vengeance 1986; Stars and Bars 1988; Breaking In 1989; Cold Comfort 1989; Millennium 1989; Dances with Wolves 1990; Mr Destiny 1990; The Adjuster 1991; George's Island 1991; Accidental Hero 1992; Leaving Normal 1992; Camilla 1993; Money for Nothing 1993; Whale Music 1994; CutThroat Island 1995; Devil in a Blue Dress 1995; Unstrung Heroes 1995; Mousehunt 1997; The Sweet Hereafter 1997; Jerry and Tom 1998; Love and Death on Long Island 1998; The Mask of Zorro 1998; Entrapment 1999; Jacob Two Two Meets the Hooded Fang 1999; Mystery, Alaska 1999; The Art of War 2000; Bartleby 2000; Varian's War 2000; What's Cooking? 2000; Crossed Over 2002; Owning Mahowny 2002; Being Julia 2004; Where the Truth Lies 2005; It's a Boy/Girl Thing 2006

Chazel, Marie-Anne (1951-) Les Visiteurs 1993; Les Visiteurs 2: Les Couloirs du Temps 1998; Marius 2012; Fanny 2013

Cheadle, Don (1964-) Hamburger Hill 1987; Colors 1988; Roadside Prophets 1992; Lush Life 1993; Devil in a Blue Dress 1995; Boogie Nights 1997; Rosewood 1997; Volcano 1997; Out of Sight 1998; The Rat Pack 1998; A Lesson before Dying 1999; Mission to Mars 1999; Fail Safe 2000; The Family Man 2000; Traffic 2000; Manic 2001; Ocean's Eleven 2001; Swordfish 2001; The United States of Leland 2002; After the Sunset 2004; The Assassination of Richard Nixon 2004; Crash 2004; Hotel Rwanda 2004; Ocean's Twelve 2004; Ocean's Thirteen 2007; Reign over Me 2007; Talk to Me 2007; Hotel for Dogs 2008; Traitor 2008; Brooklyn's Finest 2009; Iron Man 2 2010; The Guard 2011; Flight 2012; Iron Man Three 2013; Miles Ahead 2015

Checchi, Andrea (1916-1974) La Signora senza Camelie 1953; The Mask of Satan 1960; The Thousand Eyes of Dr Mabuse 1960; Two Women 1960; A Bullet for the General 1966

Cheirel, Micheline (1917-2002) Carnival in Flanders 1935; La Belle Equipe 1936; Cornered 1945; So Dark the Night 1946

Chekhov, Michael (1891-1955) Spellbound 1945; Abie's Irish Rose 1946; Specter of the Rose 1946; Rhapsody 1954

Chen Chao-jung Rebels of the Neon God 1992; Eat Drink Man Woman 1994; Vive L'Amour 1994

Chen Dao Ming (1955-) Hero 2002; Infernal Affairs 3 2003

Chen Kun Balzac and the Little Chinese Seamstress 2002; Flying Swords of Dragon Gate 2011

Chen, Edison (1980-) Infernal Affairs 2002; Infernal Affairs 3 2003; Infernal Affairs 3 2003; Initial D - Drift Racer 2005; The Grudge 2 2006

Chen, Joan (1961-) Tai-Pan 1986; The Last Emperor 1987; The Salute of the Jugger 1989; Where Sleeping Dogs Lie 1991; Turtle Beach 1992; Heaven and Earth 1993; Golden Gate 1994; On Deadly Ground 1994; The Hunted 1995; Wild Side 1995; What's Cooking? 2000; Lust, Caution 2007; 1911 2011

Chen, Kelly (1973-) Tokyo Raiders 2000; Infernal Affairs 2002; Infernal Affairs 3 2003

Chen, Terry Snakes on a Plane 2006; A Dangerous Man 2009

Chen, Tina Alice's Restaurant 1969; The Hawaiians 1970; Three Days of the Condor 1975

Cheng Pei Pei Crouching Tiger, Hidden Dragon 2000; Lilting 2014

Cheng, Adam (1947-) Zu Warriors 1983; The Legend II 1993

Cheng, Ekin (1967-) A Man Called Hero 1999; Tokyo Raiders 2000

Cheng, Kent (1951-) Crime Story 1993; The Defender 1994

Cheng, Sammi Infernal Affairs 2002; Infernal Affairs 3 2003

Chenoweth, Kristin (1968-) Annie 1999; Bewitched 2005; Deck the Halls 2006; The Pink Panther 2006; RV 2006; Tinker Bell 2008; You Again 2010; Hit & Run 2012; The Boy Next Door 2015

Cher (1946-) Wild on the Beach 1965; Good Times 1967; Chastity 1969; Come Back to the Five and Dime, Jimmy Dean, Jimmy Dean 1982; Silkwood 1983; Mask 1985; Moonstruck 1987; Suspect 1987; The Witches of Eastwick 1987; Mermaids 1990; Faithful 1996; If These Walls Could Talk 1996; Tea with Mussolini 1998; Stuck on You 2003; Burlesque 2010; Zookeeper 2011

Chéreau, Patrice (1944-2013) Danton 1982; The Last of the Mohicans 1992; Lucie Aubrac 1997; Time of the Wolf 2003

Cherkassov, Nikolai (1903-1966) Alexander Nevsky 1938; Ivan the Terrible, Part I 1944; Ivan the Terrible, Part II 1946; Don Quixote 1957

Cherrill, Virginia (1908-1996) City Lights 1931; Delicious 1931

Cherry, Helen (1915-2001) Adam and Evelyne 1949; Morning Departure 1950; They Were Not Divided 1950; Young Wives' Tale 1951; His Excellency 1952; Three Cases of Murder 1953; Tomorrow at Ten 1962; Flipper's New Adventure 1964; Hard Contract 1969; 11 Harrowhouse 1974

Cherry, Jake aka **Cherry, Jacob** The Unexpected Journey 2004; Night at the Museum 2006; The Rebound 2009

Cherry, Jonathan Final Destination 2 2002; WolfCop 2014

Chesebro, George (1888-1959) The Lone Rider in Ghost Town 1941; Trail of Robin Hood 1950

Chesnais, Patrick (1947-) Les Enfants du Siècle 1999; Not Here to Be Loved 2005; The Diving-Bell and the Butterfly 2007; You Will Be My Son 2012; Bright Days Ahead 2013

Chester, Colby Executive Action 1973; The Dove 1974; Salvador 1986

Chester, Craig (1965-) Swoon 1992; Kiss Me, Guido 1997; The Misadventures of Margaret 1998

Chester, Vanessa Lee (1984-) A Little Princess 1995; Harriet the Spy 1996

Chestnut, Morris (1969-) Boyz N the Hood 1991; Under Siege 2 1995; GI Jane 1997; The Best Man 1999; The Brothers 2001; Two Can Play That Game 2001; Half Past Dead 2002; Like Mike 2002; Anacondas: the Hunt for the Blood Orchid 2004; Ladder 49 2004; The Cave 2005; The Game Plan 2007; Not Easily Broken 2009; The Best Man Holiday 2013; The Call 2013; Kick-Ass 2 2013

Cheung, Cecilia (1980-) Tokyo Raiders 2000; One Nite in Mongkok 2004

Cheung, Jacky (1960-) As Tears Go By 1988; Bullet in the Head 1990; Once upon a Time in China 1991

Cheung, Leslie aka **Cheung, Leslie Kwok-Wing** (1956-2003) A Better Tomorrow 1986; A Better Tomorrow II 1987; A Chinese Ghost Story 1987; Rouge 1987; Days of Being Wild 1990; Once a Thief 1991; The Bride with White Hair 1993; Farewell My Concubine 1993; Ashes of Time 1994; Temptress Moon 1996; Happy Together 1997

Cheung, Maggie aka **Cheung Man Yuk, Maggie** aka **Cheung Man-Yuk** aka **Cheung Man-Yuk, Maggie** (1964-) Police Story 1985; Police Story 2 1986; Project A: Part II 1987; As Tears Go By 1988; A Better Tomorrow III 1989; Days of Being Wild 1990; The Actress 1992; Police Story III: Supercop 1992; Twin Dragons 1992; Ashes of

Time 1994; Irma Vep 1996; Chinese Box 1997; In the Mood for Love 2000; Hero 2002; Clean 2004; 2046 2004

Cheung, Roy aka **Cheung Yiu-Yeung, Roy** Wild Search 1989; Beast Cops 1998; Exiled 2006

Chevalier, Maurice (1888-1972) The Love Parade 1929; The Big Pond 1930; Paramount on Parade 1930; The Smiling Lieutenant 1931; Love Me Tonight 1932; One Hour with You 1932; The Merry Widow 1934; Folies Bergère 1935; The Beloved Vagabond 1936; Pièges 1939; Man about Town 1947; Love in the Afternoon 1957; Gigi 1958; Count Your Blessings 1959; A Breath of Scandal 1960; Can-Can 1960; Pepe 1960; Fanny 1961; In Search of the Castaways 1961; Jessica 1962; I'd Rather Be Rich 1964; Panic Button 1964; Monkeys, Go Home! 1966

Chew, Laureen Chan Is Missing 1982; Dim Sum: a Little Bit of Heart 1985

Chiaki, Minoru (1917-1999) Rashomon 1950; Seven Samurai 1954; Godzilla Raids Again 1955; Throne of Blood 1957; The Hidden Fortress 1958

Chiang, David The Legend of the 7 Golden Vampires 1974; Once upon a Time in China II 1992

Chiao, Roy (1927-1999) Golden Needles 1974; Indiana Jones and the Temple of Doom 1984; The Protector 1985; Bloodsport 1987

Chiari, Walter (1924-1991) Bellissima 1951; The Little Hut 1957; Bonjour Tristesse 1958; Let's Talk about Women 1964; They're a Weird Mob 1966; The Valachi Papers 1972

Chiaureli, Sofiko (1937-2008) The Colour of Pomegranates 1969; Ashik Kerib 1988

Chiba, Sonny aka **Chiba, Shinichi** (1939-) The Street Fighter 1974; Virus 1980; Aces: Iron Eagle III 1992; Kill Bill Vol 1 2003

Chicot, Etienne (1949-) Le Choc 1982; Ecoute le Temps 2005; The Da Vinci Code 2006

Chikezie, Caroline Babymother 1998; Aeonflux 2005

Chiklis, Michael (1963-) Wired 1989; Taxman 1998; The Three Stooges 2000; Spirited Away 2001; Fantastic Four 2005; 4: Rise of the Silver Surfer 2007; Parker 2013

Chilcott, Barbara The Trap 1966; Lies My Father Told Me 1975

Child, Jeremy (1944-) Privilege 1967; Taffin 1988

Childers, Ambyr The Master 2012; We Are What We Are 2013

Chiles, Linden (1933-2013) Incident at Phantom Hill 1966; Counterpoint 1967; Eye of the Cat 1969

Chiles, Lois (1947-) The Way We Were 1973; The Great Gatsby 1974; Coma 1977; Death on the Nile 1978; Moonraker 1979; Sweet Liberty 1986; Broadcast News 1987; Lush Life 1993; The Babysitter 1995; Curdled 1995; Chilvers, Simon (1939-) The Naked Country 1985; Sky Pirates 1986; Ground Zero 1987

Chin S u-hou Twin Warriors 1993; Fist of Legend 1994; Revenge: a Love Story 2010; Rigor Mortis 2013

Chin, Ashley Cherry Tree Lane 2010; Victim 2011; Snow in Paradise 2014

Ching, William aka **Ching, Bill** (1913-1989) DOA 1949; Never Wave at a WAC 1952; Pat and Mike 1952; Give a Girl a Break 1953; The Moonlighter 1953; Scared Stiff 1953; Tall Man Riding 1955

Chinlund, Nick (1961-) Con Air 1997; Mr Magoo 1997; Tears of the Sun 2003; The Chronicles of Riddick 2004; The Legend of Zorro 2005; Ultraviolet 2005; Avenging Angel 2007

Chistyakov, A (1880-1942) The End of St Petersburg 1927; Storm over Asia 1928

Chitty, Erik (1906-1977) First Men in the Moon 1964; Please Sir! 1971

Chlumsky, Anna (1980-) My Girl 1991; The Mommy Market 1994; My Girl 2 1994; Gold Diggers: the Secret of Bear Mountain 1995; Blood Car 2007; In the Loop 2009; The End of the Tour 2015

Cho Jae-hyeon The Isle 2000; Bad Guy 2001; Moebius 2013

Cho, John (1972-) Better Luck Tomorrow 2001; Earth vs the Spider 2001; Harold & Kumar Get the Munchies 2004; Harold & Kumar Escape from Guantanamo Bay 2008; Star Trek 2009; A Very Harold & Kumar 3D Christmas 2011; Star Trek into Darkness 2013; Star Trek Beyond 2016

Choate, Tim (1954-2004) The Europeans 1979; Jane Austen in Manhattan 1980; Def-Con 4 1984

Choi Min-sik (1962-) The Quiet Family 1998; Shiri 1999; Chihwaseon (Drunk on Women and Poetry) 2002; Oldboy

2003; Sympathy for Lady Vengeance 2005; I Saw the Devil 2010; Lucy 2014

Chokri, Monia Heartbeats 2010; Laurence Anyways 2012

Chomsky, Noam The US vs John Lennon 2006; Manufacturing Dissent: Uncovering Michael Moore 2007; We Are Many 2014; The Divide 2016

Chon, Justin 21 and Over 2012; Revenge of the Green Dragons 2013

Chong, Marcus (1967-) Panther 1995; The Matrix 1999

Chong, Rae Dawn (1961-) Quest for Fire 1981; Choose Me 1984; Fear City 1984; American Flyers 1985; Badge of the Assassin 1985; The Color Purple 1985; Commando 1985; Running Out of Luck 1985; Soul Man 1986; The Principal 1987; The Squeeze 1987; The Borrower 1989; Chaindance 1991; Tales from the Darkside: the Movie 1991; When the Party's Over 1992; Time Runner 1993; Crying Freeman 1995; Hideaway 1995; Jeff, Who Lives at Home 2011

Chong, Tommy aka **Chong, Thomas** (1938-) Cheech & Chong's Up in Smoke 1978; Cheech and Chong's Next Movie 1980; Cheech and Chong's Nice Dreams 1981; Cheech & Chong's Still Smokin' 1983; Yellowbeard 1983; Cheech & Chong's The Corsican Brothers 1984; After Hours 1985; National Lampoon's Senior Trip 1995; Half-Baked 1998

Chopra, Prem (1935-) Bobby 1973; Koi... Mil Gaya 2003

Chopra, Priyanka (1982-) Aitraaz 2004; Mujhse Shaadi Karogi 2004; WAQT: the Race against Time 2005; Salaam E Ishq 2007

Chopra, Uday (1973-) Mohabbatein 2000; Dhoom 2004; Dhoom: 2 2006

Chou, Collin The Matrix Reloaded 2002; Fearless 2006; Flash Point 2007; The Forbidden Kingdom 2008

Chou, Jay Initial D - Drift Racer 2005; Curse of the Golden Flower 2006; The Green Hornet 2011

Chou, Lawrence The Eye 2002; Dream Home 2010

Choudhury, Sarita (1966-) Mississippi Masala 1991; Wild West 1992; Kama Sutra: a Tale of Love 1996; Subway Stories: Tales from the Underground 1997; Just a Kiss 2002; Lady in the Water 2006; The Accidental Husband 2008; Learning to Drive 2014; A Hologram for the King 2016

Choudhury, Supriya The Cloud Capped Star 1960; E Flat 1961

Choureau, Etchika (1923-) The Vanquished 1953; Darby's Rangers 1958

Chow Yun-Fat (1955-) A Better Tomorrow 1986; A Better Tomorrow II 1987; City on Fire 1987; Spiritual Love 1987; A Better Tomorrow III 1989; The Killer 1989; Wild Search 1989; Once a Thief 1991; Full Contact 1992; Hard-Boiled 1992; The Replacement Killers 1998; Anna and the King 1999; The Corruptor 1999; Crouching Tiger, Hidden Dragon 2000; Bulletproof Monk 2002; Curse of the Golden Flower 2006; Pirates of the Caribbean: at World's End 2007; Dragonball Evolution 2009; Confucius 2010

Chow, China (1974-) The Big Hit 1998; Head over Heels 2000; Frankenfish 2004

Chow, Michael Tsui Hark's Vampire Hunters 2002; Kung Phooey! 2003

Chow, Stephen (1962-) Shaolin Soccer 2001; Kung Fu Hustle 2004; CJ7 2008

Chow, Valerie aka **Shane, Rachel** Chung King Express 1994; Bridge of Dragons 1999

Chowdhry, Navin Madame Sousatzka 1988; King of the Wind 1989; The Seventh Coin 1993

Chowdhry, Ranjit Mississippi Masala 1991; Camilla 1993; Fire 1996; Bollywood/Hollywood 2002

Chriqui, Emmanuelle (1977-) Snow Day 2000; On the Line 2001; Wrong Turn 2003; The Crow: Wicked Prayer 2005; In the Mix 2005; Cadillac Records 2008; You Don't Mess with the Zohan 2008; 5 Days of War 2011

Christensen, Carol (1937-2005) The Big Show 1961; The Three Stooges in Orbit 1962

Christensen, Erika (1982-) Traffic 2000; The Banger Sisters 2002; Swimfan 2002; The Perfect Score 2004; Flightplan 2005; The Upside of Anger 2005

Christensen, Hayden (1981-) Life as a House 2001; Star Wars Episode II: Attack of the Clones 2002; Shattered Glass 2003; Star Wars Episode III: Revenge of the Sith 2005; Factory Girl 2006; Awake 2007; Jumper 2008; New York, I Love You 2009; Takers 2010

Christensen, Jesper (1948-) *Sofie* 1992; *Minor Mishaps* 2002; *The Interpreter* 2005; *Maria Larsson's Everlasting Moments* 2008; *Quantum of Solace* 2008

Christian, Claudia (1965-) *The Hidden* 1987; *Clean and Sober* 1988; *Maniac Cop 2* 1990; *Upworld* 1992; *Hexed* 1993; *Atlantis: the Lost Empire* 2001; *Half Past Dead* 2002

Christian, Kurt (1950-) *The Golden Voyage of Sinbad* 1973; *Sinbad and the Eye of the Tiger* 1977

Christian, Linda (1923-2011) *Tarzan and the Mermaids* 1948; *The Happy Time* 1952; *The House of the Seven Hawks* 1959; *The VIPs* 1963; *The Moment of Truth* 1964

Christian, Shawn (1965-) *Tremors 3: Back to Perfection* 2001; *Million Dollar Murder* 2004

Christians, Mady (1900-1951) *Escapade* 1935; *Tender Comrade* 1943; *All My Sons* 1948; *Letter from an Unknown Woman* 1948

Christie, Audrey (1912-1989) *Keeper of the Flame* 1942; *Carousel* 1956; *Splendor in the Grass* 1961; *Frankie & Johnny* 1966; *Mame* 1974

Christie, Julie (1941-) *Crooks Anonymous* 1962; *Billy Liar* 1963; *The Fast Lady* 1963; *Darling* 1965; *Doctor Zhivago* 1965; *Young Cassidy* 1965; *Fahrenheit 451* 1966; *Far from the Madding Crowd* 1967; *Tonite Let's All Make Love in London* 1967; *Petulia* 1968; *In Search of Gregory* 1970; *The Go-Between* 1971; *McCabe and Mrs Miller* 1971; *Don't Look Now* 1973; *Shampoo* 1975; *Demon Seed* 1977; *Heaven Can Wait* 1978; *Heat and Dust* 1982; *The Return of the Soldier* 1982; *Gold Diggers* 1983; *Separate Tables* 1983; *Miss Mary* 1986; *Power* 1986; *Fools of Fortune* 1990; *DragonHeart* 1996; *Hamlet* 1996; *Afterglow* 1997; *The Miracle Maker* 1999; *I'm with Lucy* 2002; *Finding Neverland* 2004; *A Letter to True* 2004; *Troy* 2004; *Away from Her* 2006; *Glorious 39* 2009; *New York, I Love You* 2009; *Red Riding Hood* 2011; *The Company You Keep* 2012

Christie, Linford *Don't Go Breaking My Heart* 1999; *9.79** 2012

Christine, Virginia (1920-1996) *The Mummy's Curse* 1944; *Invasion of the Body Snatchers* 1956; *Nightmare* 1956; *One Man's Way* 1964; *Billy the Kid vs Dracula* 1966

Christmas, Eric (1916-2000) *Harold and Maude* 1972; *An Enemy of the People* 1977; *Attack of the Killer Tomatoes* 1978; *Middle Age Crazy* 1980; *The Philadelphia Experiment* 1984; *Air Bud* 1997; *Mousehunt* 1997

Christophe, Françoise (1923-2012) *Le Testament d'Orphée* 1960; *King of Hearts* 1966; *Borsalino* 1970

Christopher, Dennis (1955-) *September 30, 1955* 1977; *A Wedding* 1978; *Breaking Away* 1979; *Fade to Black* 1980; *Chariots of Fire* 1981; *Circuitry Man* 1990; *Doppelganger* 1993; *Plughead Rewired: Circuitry Man II* 1994; *The Ballad of Lucy Whipple* 2001

Christopher, Jordan (1942-1996) *Return of the Seven* 1966; *Angel, Angel Down We Go* 1969

Christy, Dorothy (1906-1977) *Parlor, Bedroom and Bath* 1931; *Sons of the Desert* 1933

Chrystall, Belle (1910-2003) *Hindle Wakes* 1931; *Friday the Thirteenth* 1933; *Scotland Yard Mystery* 1933; *The Edge of the World* 1937; *Poison Pen* 1939

Chuck D *Burn Hollywood Burn* 1997; *Something from Nothing: the Art of Rap* 2012

Chuillot, Delphine *Pola X* 1999; *Heartbeat Detector* 2007; *Mozart's Sister* 2010; *The Woman in the Fifth* 2011; *Age of Uprising: the Legend of Michael Kohlhaas* 2013

Chung Lam *The Killer* 1989; *Life Is Cheap... but Toilet Paper Is Expensive* 1990

Chung, Cherie aka Chung, Cherry Cho-Hung (1960-) *The Dead and the Deadly* 1983; *Peking Opera Blues* 1986; *Spiritual Love* 1987; *Wild Search* 1989; *Once a Thief* 1991

Chung, David *Missing in Action 2: the Beginning* 1985; *The Ballad of Little Jo* 1993; *Color of a Brisk and Leaping Day* 1996

Chung, Jamie (1983-) *Dragonball Evolution* 2009; *Sorority Row* 2009; *The Hangover: Part II* 2011; *Eden* 2012; *The Man with the Iron Fists* 2012; *Premium Rush* 2012; *Big Hero 6* 2014

Church, Charlotte *I'll Be There* 2003; *Under Milk Wood* 2015

Church, Thomas Haden (1960-) *George of the Jungle* 1997; *Free Money* 1998; *Mr Murder* 1998; *The Specials*

2000; *3000 Miles to Graceland* 2000; *Lone Star State of Mind* 2002; *Sideways* 2004; *Idiocracy* 2006; *Over the Hedge* 2006; *Smart People* 2007; *Spider-Man 3* 2007; *All about Steve* 2009; *Imagine That* 2009; *Easy A* 2010; *Killer Joe* 2011; *We Bought a Zoo* 2011; *John Carter* 2012; *Lucky Them* 2013; *Heaven Is for Real* 2014; *Daddy's Home* 2015; *Max* 2015

Churchill, Berton (1876-1940) *The Big Stampede* 1932; *Cabin in the Cotton* 1932; *I Am a Fugitive from a Chain Gang* 1932; *Dr Bull* 1933; *Heroes for Sale* 1933; *The Little Giant* 1933; *Steamboat round the Bend* 1935; *Daughters Courageous* 1939

Churchill, Diana (1913-1994) *Foreign Affaires* 1935; *Housemaster* 1938; *The History of Mr Polly* 1948; *Scott of the Antarctic* 1948; *The Winter's Tale* 1966

Churchill, Donald (1930-1991) *Victim* 1961; *The Hound of the Baskervilles* 1983

Churchill, Marguerite (1909-2000) *They Had to See Paris* 1929; *The Valiant* 1929; *The Big Trail* 1930; *Born Reckless* 1930; *Quick Millions* 1931; *Riders of the Purple Sage* 1931; *Dracula's Daughter* 1936; *The Walking Dead* 1936

Churchill, Sarah (1914-1982) *Royal Wedding* 1951; *Serious Charge* 1959

Churikova, Inna (1943-) *The Theme* 1979; *Vassa* 1983

Chweneyagae, Presley *Tsotsi* 2005; *More than Just a Game* 2007

Chyra, Andrzej *Katyn* 2007; *Elles* 2011; *In the Name of* 2013

Ciamaca, Julien *Le Château de Ma Mère* 1990; *La Gloire de Mon Père* 1990

Ciannelli, Eduardo aka Cianelli, Eduardo aka Ciannelli, Edward (1887-1969) *Reunion in Vienna* 1933; *Winterset* 1936; *Criminal Lawyer* 1937; *The League of Frightened Men* 1937; *Marked Woman* 1937; *Bulldog Drummond's Bride* 1939; *Gunga Din* 1939; *Foreign Correspondent* 1940; *Kitty Foyle* 1940; *The Mummy's Hand* 1940; *Strange Cargo* 1940; *Dr Broadway* 1942; *Flight for Freedom* 1943; *They Got Me Covered* 1943; *Dillinger* 1945; *The Lost Moment* 1947; *The People against O'Hara* 1951; *The Stranger's Hand* 1953; *The Vanquished* 1953; *Houseboat* 1958; *Monster from Green Hell* 1958; *The Spy in the Green Hat* 1966; *Boot Hill* 1969

Cibrian, Eddie (1973-) *Logan's War: Bound by Honor* 1998; *But I'm a Cheerleader* 1999; *The Cave* 2005; *Nora Roberts' Northern Lights* 2009; *Not Easily Broken* 2009; *Working Miracles* 2010

Ciccolella, Jude *Blue Jean Cop* 1988; *Mad Love* 1995; *A Perfect Day* 2006; *Julia* 2008

Ciepielewska, Anna (1936-2006) *The Devil and the Nun* 1960; *Passenger* 1963

Cigoli, Emilio (1909-1980) *We the Living* 1942; *The Children Are Watching Us* 1943; *Sunday in August* 1949

Cilenti, Enzo (1974-) *Late Night Shopping* 2001; *The Fourth Kind* 2009

Cilento, Diane (1933-2011) *The Angel Who Pawned Her Harp* 1954; *Passage Home* 1955; *The Woman for Joe* 1955; *The Admirable Crichton* 1957; *The Truth about Women* 1958; *Jet Storm* 1959; *The Full Treatment* 1961; *The Naked Edge* 1961; *I Thank a Fool* 1962; *Tom Jones* 1963; *Rattle of a Simple Man* 1964; *The Third Secret* 1964; *The Agony and the Ecstasy* 1965; *Hombre* 1967; *ZPG: Zero Population Growth* 1971; *Hitler: the Last Ten Days* 1973; *The Wicker Man* 1973; *The Boy Who Had Everything* 1984

Cilliers, Jana *A Game for Vultures* 1979; *Quest for Love* 1988

Cimino, Leonardo (1917-2012) *Jeremy* 1973; *Amityville II: the Possession* 1982; *Monsignor* 1982; *Penn & Teller Get Killed* 1989

Cinnante, Kelly *True Love* 1989; *Christmas in Connecticut* 1992

Cintra, Luis Miguel (1949-) *The Divine Comedy* 1992; *Abraham Valley* 1993; *The Convent* 1995; *Un Filme Falado* 2003

Cioffi, Charles (1935-) *Klute* 1971; *Shaft* 1971; *The Thief Who Came to Dinner* 1973; *Time after Time* 1979; *Missing* 1981; *All the Right Moves* 1983; *Remo - Unarmed and Dangerous* 1985

Citran, Roberto (1955-) *Il Cielo è Sempre Più Blu* 1995; *Nora* 1999; *Shun Li and the Poet* 2011

Citti, Christine *The Page Turner* 2006; *The Singer* 2006; *Born in 68: We'll Love Each Other until Death Do Us Part* 2008

Citti, Franco (1935-2016) *Accattone* 1961; *Mamma Roma* 1962; *Requiescant* 1967; *Oedipus Rex* 1967; *The*

Decameron 1970; *The Arabian Nights* 1974

Citti, Marc *The Lie* 1992; *Born in 68: We'll Love Each Other until Death Do Us Part* 2008

CK, Louis (1967-) *Diminished Capacity* 2007; *Welcome Home Roscoe Jenkins* 2008; *American Hustle* 2013; *Blue Jasmine* 2013; *The Secret Life of Pets* 2016

Claflin, Sam (1986-) *Pirates of the Caribbean: on Stranger Tides* 2011; *Snow White and the Huntsman* 2012; *The Quiet Ones* 2013; *Love, Rosie* 2014; *The Riot Club* 2014; *The Hunger Games: Mockingjay Part 2* 2015; *Me before You* 2016; *My Cousin Rachel* 2017

Claire, Cyrielle aka Clair, Cyrielle (1955-) *Sword of the Valiant* 1984; *Code Name: Emerald* 1985; *Triple Agent* 2003

Claire, Imogen *The Lair of the White Worm* 1988; *I Hired a Contract Killer* 1990

Claire, Ina (1892-1985) *The Royal Family of Broadway* 1930; *Ninotchka* 1939; *Claudia* 1943

Clanton, Ralph (1914-2002) *Cyrano de Bergerac* 1950; *They Were Not Divided* 1950; *The 27th Day* 1957

Clapton, Eric (1945-) *The Concert for Bangladesh* 1972; *Jimi Hendrix* 1973; *Tommy* 1975; *Hail! Hail! Rock 'n' Roll!* 1987; *George Harrison: Living in the Material World* 2011

Clare, Diane (1938-2013) *Ice Cold in Alex* 1958; *The Reluctant Debutante* 1958; *The Haunting* 1963; *The Plague of the Zombies* 1965; *The Hand of Night* 1966

Clare, Mary (1894-1970) *The Constant Nymph* 1928; *Hindle Wakes* 1931; *The Constant Nymph* 1933; *The Clairvoyant* 1934; *Lorna Doone* 1934; *The Mill on the Floss* 1937; *Young and Innocent* 1937; *The Challenge* 1938; *The Citadel* 1938; *Climbing High* 1938; *The Lady Vanishes* 1938; *There Ain't No Justice* 1939; *Old Bill and Son* 1940; *The Night Has Eyes* 1942; *My Brother Jonathan* 1947; *The Three Weird Sisters* 1948; *The Black Rose* 1950; *The Beggar's Opera* 1953

Clare, Phyllis (1908-1947) *The Roadhouse Murder* 1932; *Aunt Sally* 1933

Claridge, Jessica *Five Children and It* 2004; *Heidi* 2005

Clariond, Aimé (1894-1960) *Monsieur Vincent* 1947; *Marie Antoinette* 1956

Clark, Anthony (1964-) *Dogfight* 1991; *The Thing Called Love* 1993

Clark, Barney *Oliver Twist* 2005; *Savage Grace* 2007

Clark, Blake (1946-) *Fast Food* 1989; *Shakes the Clown* 1991; *The Waterboy* 1998; *50 First Dates* 2004

Clark, Bobby (1946-) *The Happy Road* 1956; *Gun Duel in Durango* 1957

Clark, Candy (1947-) *Fat City* 1972; *American Graffiti* 1973; *The Man Who Fell to Earth* 1976; *Citizens Band* 1977; *The Big Sleep* 1978; *More American Graffiti* 1979; *Q - the Winged Serpent* 1982; *Amityville III: the Demon* 1983; *Blue Thunder* 1983; *Cat's Eye* 1984; *Hambone and Hillie* 1984; *The Blob* 1988; *Cool as Ice* 1991; *Cherry Falls* 1999

Clark, Cliff (1889-1953) *Miracles for Sale* 1939; *Stranger on the Third Floor* 1940; *The Wagons Roll at Night* 1941; *The Falcon's Brother* 1942; *Kid Glove Killer* 1942; *The Falcon and the Co-Eds* 1943; *The Falcon in Danger* 1943; *The Falcon Out West* 1944; *The Stratton Story* 1949

Clark, Dane (1913-1998) *Action in the North Atlantic* 1943; *Destination Tokyo* 1943; *Hollywood Canteen* 1944; *The Very Thought of You* 1944; *Pride of the Marines* 1945; *A Stolen Life* 1946; *Deep Valley* 1947; *Moonrise* 1948; *Backfire* 1950; *Barricade* 1950; *Highly Dangerous* 1950; *The Gambler and the Lady* 1952; *Go, Man, Go!* 1953; *The Face of Fear* 1971; *Last Rites* 1988

Clark, Dick (1929-2012) *Because They're Young* 1960; *The Young Doctors* 1961; *Bowling for Columbine* 2002

Clark, Ernest (1912-1994) *The Dam Busters* 1954; *The Baby and the Battleship* 1956; *The Safecracker* 1958; *Tomorrow at Ten* 1962; *The Devil-Ship Pirates* 1964; *It!* 1966; *Salt & Pepper* 1968

Clark, Eugene (1955-) *Wilder* 2000; *George A Romero's Land of the Dead* 2005; *Murder at the Presidio* 2005

Clark, Fred (1914-1968) *The Unsuspected* 1947; *Cry of the City* 1948; *Alias Nick Beal* 1949; *Flamingo Road* 1949; *The Jackpot* 1950; *Mrs O'Malley and Mr Malone* 1950; *Sunset Blvd* 1950; *The Lemon Drop Kid* 1951;

Meet Me after the Show 1951; *Dreamboat* 1952; *Here Come the Girls* 1953; *How to Marry a Millionaire* 1953; *Living It Up* 1954; *Abbott and Costello Meet the Keystone Cops* 1955; *Daddy Long Legs* 1955; *How to Be Very, Very Popular* 1955; *Back from Eternity* 1956; *The Birds and the Bees* 1956; *Miracle in the Rain* 1956; *The Solid Gold Cadillac* 1956; *Don't Go near the Water* 1957; *Auntie Mame* 1958; *Mardi Gras* 1958; *It Started with a Kiss* 1959; *The Mating Game* 1959; *Bells Are Ringing* 1960; *Hemingway's Adventures of a Young Man* 1962; *Move Over, Darling* 1963; *The Curse of the Mummy's Tomb* 1964; *John Goldfarb, Please Come Home* 1964; *Dr Goldfoot and the Bikini Machine* 1965; *Sergeant Deadhead* 1965; *The Horse in the Gray Flannel Suit* 1968; *Skidoo* 1968

Clark, Harvey (1885-1938) *Camille* 1927; *Red-Headed Woman* 1932; *Man's Castle* 1933

Clark, Jameson (1907-1984) *The Brave Don't Cry* 1952; *Laxdale Hall* 1953; *The Battle of the Sexes* 1960; *Ring of Bright Water* 1969

Clark, Ken (1927-2009) *Six Bridges to Cross* 1955; *Between Heaven and Hell* 1956; *Attack of the Giant Leeches* 1960

Clark, Marlene *The Beast Must Die* 1974; *Switchblade Sisters* 1975

Clark, Matt (1936-) *The Bridge at Remagen* 1969; *White Lightning* 1973; *The Execution of Private Slovik* 1974; *The Terminal Man* 1974; *Kid Vengeance* 1977; *The Driver* 1978; *Brubaker* 1980; *An Eye for an Eye* 1981; *The Legend of the Lone Ranger* 1981; *Honkytonk Man* 1982; *Love Letters* 1983; *Country* 1984; *Out of the Darkness* 1985; *Return to Oz* 1985; *Class Action* 1991; *Barbarians at the Gate* 1993; *The Haunted Heart* 1995

Clark, Oliver (1939-) *End of the Road* 1970; *Deadhead Miles* 1972; *A Star Is Born* 1976; *Ernest Saves Christmas* 1988

Clark, Petula (1932-) *I Know Where I'm Going!* 1945; *London Town* 1946; *Easy Money* 1947; *Vice Versa* 1947; *Here Come the Huggetts* 1948; *Vote for Huggett* 1948; *Don't Ever Leave Me* 1949; *The Huggetts Abroad* 1949; *The Romantic Age* 1949; *Dance Hall* 1950; *White Corridors* 1951; *The Card* 1952; *Made in Heaven* 1952; *The Runaway Bus* 1954; *That Woman Opposite* 1957; *Finian's Rainbow* 1968; *Goodbye, Mr Chips* 1969

Clark, Roger (1909-1978) *You Belong to Me* 1941; *The Lady Is Willing* 1942; *Detour* 1945; *Angel Baby* 1961

Clark, Spencer Treat (1987-) *Arlington Road* 1998; *Unbreakable* 2000; *Mystic River* 2003; *The Last House on the Left* 2008; *The Last Exorcism Part II* 2013

Clark, Susan (1940-) *Banning* 1967; *Coogan's Bluff* 1968; *Colossus: the Forbin Project* 1969; *Skullduggery* 1969; *Tell Them Willie Boy Is Here* 1969; *Skin Game* 1971; *Valdez Is Coming* 1971; *Showdown* 1973; *The Apple Dumpling Gang* 1974; *Night Moves* 1975; *City on Fire* 1979; *Hill's Angels* 1979; *Porky's* 1981

Clarke-Smith, D A (1888-1959) *Friday the Thirteenth* 1933; *The Ghoul* 1933; *Flying 55* 1939

Clarke, Angela (1969-) *Mrs Mike* 1949; *Captain Carey, USA* 1950; *Beneath the 12-Mile Reef* 1953; *Houdini* 1953; *Seven Little Foys* 1955; *Dancin' thru the Dark* 1989; *Blonde Fist* 1991; *Land and Freedom* 1995

Clarke, Betty Ross aka Clarke, Betsy Ross aka Clark, Betty Ross (1896-1947) *Judge Hardy's Children* 1938; *Love Finds Andy Hardy* 1938

Clarke, Caitlin (1952-2004) *Dragonslayer* 1981; *Penn & Teller Get Killed* 1989; *Blown Away* 1994

Clarke, Emilia (1986-) *Spike Island* 2012; *Dom Hemingway* 2013; *Terminator: Genisys* 2015; *Me before You* 2016

Clarke, Gage aka Clark, Gage (1900-1964) *Nightmare* 1956; *The Return of Dracula* 1958

Clarke, Hope (1943-) *Book of Numbers* 1972; *A Piece of the Action* 1977

Clarke (2), Jason (1969-) *Risk* 2000; *Rabbit-Proof Fence* 2002; *Trust* 2010; *Zero Dark Thirty* 2012; *The Great Gatsby* 2013; *White House Down* 2013; *Child 44* 2014; *Dawn of the Planet of the Apes* 2014; *Terminator: Genisys* 2015

Clarke, Jean *There Was a Crooked Man* 1960; *Goodbye Again* 1961

Clarke (2), John (1948-) *Footrot Flats: the Dog's Tale* 1986; *Blood Oath* 1990; *Death in Brunswick* 1990

Clarke, Justine *Danny Deckchair* 2003; *Look Both Ways* 2005

Clarke, Kathy Keira *The Most Fertile Man in Ireland* 1999; *Bloody Sunday* 2001; *Small Engine Repair* 2006

Clarke, Mae (1910-1992) *Frankenstein* 1931; *The Public Enemy* 1931; *Waterloo Bridge* 1931; *The Impatient Maiden* 1932; *The Penguin Pool Murder* 1932; *Three Wise Girls* 1932; *Penthouse* 1933; *Nana* 1934; *This Side of Heaven* 1934; *Great Guy* 1936; *Flying Tigers* 1942

Clarke, Margi (1954-) *Letter to Brezhnev* 1985; *I Hired a Contract Killer* 1990; *Loser Takes All* 1990; *Blonde Fist* 1991; *Revengers Tragedy* 2002

Clarke, Melinda aka Clarke, Mindy *Return of the Living Dead III* 1993; *Spawn* 1997

Clarke, Noel (1975-) *Kidulthood* 2005; *Adulthood* 2008; *Centurion* 2009; *Doghouse* 2009; *Heartless* 2009; *Huge* 2009; *4.3.2.1* 2010; *Screwed* 2011; *Fast Girls* 2012; *The Knot* 2012; *Storage 24* 2012; *Star Trek into Darkness* 2013; *The Anomaly* 2014; *Brotherhood* 2016

Clarke, Robert (1920-2005) *Hard, Fast and Beautiful* 1951; *The Man from Planet X* 1951; *The Astounding She-Monster* 1958; *Beyond the Time Barrier* 1960

Clarke, Sarah (1972-) *Thirteen* 2003; *Happy Endings* 2005

Clarke, Warren (1947-2014) *A Clockwork Orange* 1971; *Hawk the Slayer* 1980; *Firefox* 1982; *Real Life* 1983; *Lassiter* 1984; *Top Secret!* 1984; *Crusoe* 1988; *ID* 1994; *Blow Dry* 2000; *Greenfingers* 2000; *Arthur's Dyke* 2001

Clarkson, Lana (1962-2003) *Blind Date* 1984; *The Haunting of Morella* 1990

Clarkson, Patricia (1960-) *The Dead Pool* 1988; *Everybody's All-American* 1988; *Rocket Gibraltar* 1988; *Aunt Julia and the Scriptwriter* 1990; *The Old Man and the Sea* 1990; *Jumanji* 1995; *High Art* 1998; *Simply Irresistible* 1999; *The Safety of Objects* 2001; *Wendigo* 2001; *Far from Heaven* 2002; *Pieces of April* 2002; *Welcome to Collinwood* 2002; *All the Real Girls* 2003; *Dogville* 2003; *The Station Agent* 2003; *Miracle* 2004; *All the King's Men* 2005; *Good Night, and Good Luck.* 2005; *The Woods* 2006; *Lars and the Real Girl* 2007; *Married Life* 2007; *No Reservations* 2007; *Elegy* 2008; *Vicky Cristina Barcelona* 2008; *Shutter Island* 2009; *Whatever Works* 2009; *Easy A* 2010; *Friends with Benefits* 2011; *One Day* 2011; *The East* 2013; *Learning to Drive* 2014; *The Maze Runner* 2014

Clary, Robert (1926-) *Thief of Damascus* 1952; *New Faces* 1954

Clash, Kevin (1960-) *Teenage Mutant Ninja Turtles II: the Secret of the Ooze* 1991; *The Adventures of Elmo in Grouchland* 1999; *Being Elmo: a Puppeteer's Journey* 2011

Clausen, Claus (1899-1989) *Westfront 1918* 1930; *The Devil Makes Three* 1952

Clavier, Christian (1952-) *Les Visiteurs* 1993; *Les Visiteurs 2: Les Couloirs du Temps* 1998; *Asterix and Obelix Take On Caesar* 1999; *Asterix & Obelix: Mission Cleopatra* 2001; *Just Visiting* 2001

Clay, Andrew Dice aka Clay, Andrew aka Silverstein, Andrew (1957-) *Wacko* 1981; *Casual Sex?* 1988; *The Adventures of Ford Fairlane* 1990; *Brain Smasher... a Love Story* 1993; *One Night at McCool's* 2001; *Blue Jasmine* 2013

Clay, Juanin (1949-1995) *The Legend of the Lone Ranger* 1981; *The Long Summer of George Adams* 1982; *WarGames* 1983

Clay, Nicholas (1946-2000) *The Road Builder* 1971; *The Darwin Adventure* 1972; *Victor Frankenstein* 1977; *Lovespell* 1979; *Excalibur* 1981; *Lady Chatterley's Lover* 1981; *Evil under the Sun* 1982; *The Hound of the Baskervilles* 1983; *Lionheart* 1986

Clay, Philippe (1927-2007) *French Cancan* 1955; *The Hunchback of Notre Dame* 1956

Clayburgh, Jill (1944-2010) *The Wedding Party* 1966; *The Thief Who Came to Dinner* 1973; *The Terminal Man* 1974; *Gable and Lombard* 1976; *Silver Streak* 1976; *Semi-Tough* 1977; *An Unmarried Woman* 1978; *La Luna* 1979; *Starting Over* 1979; *It's My Turn* 1980; *First Monday in October* 1981; *I'm Dancing as Fast as I Can* 1982; *Miles to Go* 1986; *Shy People* 1987; *Whispers in the Dark* 1992; *Naked in New York* 1994; *The Face on the Milk Carton* 1995; *Going All the Way* 1997; *Running with Scissors* 2006

Clayton, Adam *U2 Rattle and Hum* 1988; *U23D* 2007

Clayton, John (1940-2003) Warm Nights on a Slow Moving Train 1986; High Tide 1987

Clayton, Merry Blame It on the Night 1984; Maid to Order 1987; Twenty Feet from Stardom 2013

Clayworth, June (1912-1993) Criminal Court 1946; Dick Tracy Meets Gruesome 1947; Bodyguard 1948; Sons of the Musketeers 1951; The Marriage-Go-Round 1960

Clément, Suzanne I Killed My Mother 2009; Laurence Anyways 2012; Mommy 2014

Cleere, John War of the Buttons 1993; My Friend Joe 1996

Cleese, John (1939-) The Bliss of Mrs Blossom 1968; Interlude 1968; The Magic Christian 1969; The Rise and Rise of Michael Rimmer 1970; And Now for Something Completely Different 1971; Monty Python and the Holy Grail 1975; Pleasure at Her Majesty's 1976; Monty Python's Life of Brian 1979; The Great Muppet Caper 1981; Time Bandits 1981; Monty Python Live at the Hollywood Bowl 1982; Privates on Parade 1982; Monty Python's The Meaning of Life 1983; Yellowbeard 1983; Silverado 1985; Clockwise 1986; A Fish Called Wanda 1988; The Big Picture 1989; Erik the Viking 1989; An American Tail: Fievel Goes West 1991; Splitting Heirs 1993; The Jungle Book 1994; Mary Shelley's Frankenstein 1994; The Swan Princess 1994; The Wind in the Willows 1996; Fierce Creatures 1997; George of the Jungle 1997; Parting Shots 1998; Isn't She Great 1999; The Out-of-Towners 1999; The World Is Not Enough 1999; The Magic Pudding 2000; Harry Potter and the Philosopher's Stone 2001; Pluto Nash 2001; Rat Race 2001; Die Another Day 2002; Harry Potter and the Chamber of Secrets 2002; Scorched 2002; Charlie's Angels: Full Throttle 2003; Around the World in 80 Days 2004; Shrek 2 2004; Valiant 2005; Charlotte's Web 2006; Shrek the Third 2007; The Day the Earth Stood Still 2008; Igor 2008; The Pink Panther 2 2009; Planet 51 2009; Shrek Forever After 2010; Spud 2010; Winnie the Pooh 2011; A Liar's Autobiography: the Untrue Story of Monty Python's Graham Chapman 2012; Planes 2013; Absolutely Anything 2015; Trolls 2016

Clem, Jimmy Grayeagle 1977; The Evictors 1979

Clemens, Adelaide No One Lives 2012; Silent Hill: Revelation 2012

Clemenson, Christian (1959-) Broadcast News 1987; Bad Influence 1990; Accidental Hero 1992

Clément, Aurore (1945-) Lacombe Lucien 1974; Les Rendez-vous d'Anna 1978; El Sur 1983; Paris, Texas 1984; The Captive 2000; Bon Voyage 2003; The Bridesmaid 2004; A Bigger Splash 2015

Clément, Coralie Diabolo Menthe 1977; The Aviator's Wife 1980

Clement, Jemaine (1974-) Eagle vs Shark 2006; Gentlemen Broncos 2009; Dinner for Schmucks 2010; Rio 2011; Men in Black 3 2012; Rio 2 2014; What We Do in the Shadows 2014; The BFG 2016

Clementi, Margareth Medea 1970; Casanova 1976

Clémenti, Pierre (1942-1999) Belle de Jour 1967; The Milky Way 1968; Partner 1968; Pigsty 1969; The Conformist 1970; Steppenwolf 1974; Quartet 1981; Exposed 1983; Hideous Kinky 1998

Clements, John (1910-1988) South Riding 1938; The Four Feathers 1939; Convoy 1940; Ships with Wings 1942; Tomorrow We Live 1942; Undercover 1943; Train of Events 1949; The Silent Enemy 1958; The Mind Benders 1963; Oh! What a Lovely War 1969

Clements, Stanley aka **Clements, Stanley "Stash"** (1926-1981) Tall, Dark and Handsome 1941; Salty O'Rourke 1945; Destination Murder 1950; Boots Malone 1951; Military Policeman 1953

Clemons, Kiersey Dope 2015; Flatliners 2017

Clennon, David aka **Clennon, Dave** (1943-) Go Tell the Spartans 1977; Being There 1979; Ladies and Gentlemen, the Fabulous Stains 1981; Missing 1981; The Thing 1982; Star 80 1983; Falling in Love 1984; Sweet Dreams 1985; Legal Eagles 1986; He's My Girl 1987; Betrayed 1988; The Couch Trip 1988; Downtown 1990; Light Sleeper 1991; Black Widow Murders 1993

Clerkin, Cavan Miranda 2001; Pierrepoint 2005

Cléry, Corinne (1950-) The Story of O 1975; The Con Artists 1976; The Humanoid 1979; Moonraker 1979

Cleveland, Carol (1943-) And Now for Something Completely Different 1971; Pleasure at Her Majesty's 1976; Monty Python Live at the Hollywood Bowl 1982; A Liar's Autobiography: the Untrue Story of Monty Python's Graham Chapman 2012

Cleveland, George (1886-1957) Blue Steel 1934; The Man from Utah 1934; The Star Packer 1934; The Navy Steps Out 1941; Seven Miles from Alcatraz 1942; Abroad with Two Yanks 1944; The Yellow Rose of Texas 1944; Pillow of Death 1945; Angel on My Shoulder 1946; Courage of Lassie 1946; Little Giant 1946; Wild Beauty 1946; The Plunderers 1948

Clevenot, Philippe (1942-2001) Celine and Julie Go Boating 1974; Roselyne and the Lions 1989; The Hairdresser's Husband 1990

Cliff, Jimmy (1948-) The Harder They Come 1972; Club Paradise 1986; Marley 2012

Cliff, John (1918-2001) Back to God's Country 1953; I Was a Teenage Frankenstein 1957

Clifford, Colleen (1898-1996) Careful, He Might Hear You 1983; Frauds 1992

Clifford, Jefferson (1892-1959) Confession 1955; The Bridal Path 1959

Clift, Montgomery (1920-1966) Red River 1948; The Search 1948; The Heiress 1949; The Big Lift 1950; A Place in the Sun 1951; From Here to Eternity 1953; I Confess 1953; Indiscretion of an American Wife 1954; Raintree County 1957; Lonelyhearts 1958; The Young Lions 1958; Suddenly, Last Summer 1959; Wild River 1960; Judgment at Nuremberg 1961; The Misfits 1961; Freud 1962; The Defector 1966

Climent, Joaquín Goya in Bordeaux 1999; Mondays in the Sun 2002

Cline, Edward aka **Cline, Eddie** aka **Cline, Edward F** (1892-1961) Neighbors 1920; The Scarecrow 1920; Day Dreams 1922

Clinton, Bill The Big One 1997; Shine a Light 2007; Fire in the Blood 2012

Clinton, Roger (1956-) The Revenge of Pumpkinhead - Blood Wings 1994; Bio-Dome 1996

Clitheroe, Jimmy (1916-1973) Rhythm Serenade 1943; Jules Verne's Rocket to the Moon 1967

Clive, Colin (1898-1937) Journey's End 1930; Frankenstein 1931; Christopher Strong 1933; The Key 1934; One More River 1934; Bride of Frankenstein 1935; Clive of India 1935; The Girl from 10th Avenue 1935; Mad Love 1935; The Man Who Broke the Bank at Monte Carlo 1935; History Is Made at Night 1937; The Woman I Love 1937

Clive, E E (1879-1940) Charlie Chan in London 1934; Long Lost Father 1934; Annie Oakley 1935; Cherokee Strip 1940; The Devil's Playground 1946; Fool's Gold 1946; The Dead Don't Dream 1948; Silent Conflict 1948; The Road to Denver 1955; The Mystery of Edwin Drood 1935; Isle of Fury 1936; Libeled Lady 1936; Tarzan Escapes 1936; Trouble for Two 1936; Bulldog Drummond Escapes 1937; Bulldog Drummond Comes Back 1937; Bulldog Drummond's Revenge 1937; Live, Love and Learn 1937; Personal Property 1937; Arsene Lupin Returns 1938; Bulldog Drummond's Peril 1938; Bulldog Drummond in Africa 1938; The Adventures of Sherlock Holmes 1939; Bachelor Mother 1939; Bulldog Drummond's Bride 1939; The Earl of Chicago 1940

Clive, John (1938-2012) Yellow Submarine 1968; Never Too Young to Rock 1975

Clooney, George (1961-) Return to Horror High 1986; Return of the Killer Tomatoes 1988; Red Surf 1990; The Magic Bubble 1992; Without Warning: Terror in the Towers 1993; From Dusk till Dawn 1995; One Fine Day 1996; Batman and Robin 1997; The Peacemaker 1997; Out of Sight 1998; The Thin Red Line 1998; South Park: Bigger, Longer & Uncut 1999; Three Kings 1999; Fail Safe 2000; O Brother, Where Art Thou? 2000; The Perfect Storm 2000; Ocean's Eleven 2001; SPYkids 2001; Confessions of a Dangerous Mind 2002; Solaris 2002; Welcome to Collinwood 2002; Intolerable Cruelty 2003; Ocean's Twelve 2004; Good Night, and Good Luck. 2005; Syriana 2005; The Good German 2006; Leatherheads 2007; Michael Clayton 2007; Ocean's Thirteen 2007; Burn after Reading 2008; Fantastic Mr Fox 2009; The Men Who Stare at Goatsx 2009; Up in the Air 2009; The American 2010; The Descendants 2011; The Ides of March 2011; Radioman 2012; Gravity 2013; The Monuments Men 2013; Tomorrowland: a World Beyond 2015; Hail, Caesar! 2016; Money Monster 2016

Clooney, Rosemary (1928-2002) Here Come the Girls 1953; Deep in My Heart 1954; Red Garters 1954; White Christmas 1954

Close, Glenn (1947-) The World According to Garp 1982; The Big Chill 1983; The Natural 1984; The Stone Boy 1984; Jagged Edge 1985; Maxie 1985; Fatal Attraction 1987; Dangerous Liaisons 1988; Light Years 1988; Stones for Ibarra 1988; Immediate Family 1989; Hamlet 1990; Meeting Venus 1990; Reversal of Fortune 1990; The House of the Spirits 1993; The Paper 1994; Anne Frank Remembered 1995; Mary Reilly 1995; Mars Attacks! 1996; 101 Dalmatians 1996; Air Force One 1997; In & Out 1997; In the Gloaming 1997; Cookie's Fortune 1999; Tarzan 1999; 102 Dalmatians 2000; Things You Can Tell Just by Looking at Her 2000; The Ballad of Lucy Whipple 2001; The Safety of Objects 2001; South Pacific 2001; Le Divorce 2003; The Stepford Wives 2004; Strip Search 2004; The Chumscrubber 2005; Hoodwinked 2005; Tarzan II 2005; Evening 2007; Albert Nobbs 2011; Love, Marilyn 2012; Guardians of the Galaxy 2014; Bastards 2016; The Girl with All the Gifts 2016

Closser Hale, Louise (1872-1933) Platinum Blonde 1931; The Man Who Played God 1932; Shanghai Express 1932; The Barbarian 1933; Today We Live 1933; The White Sister 1933

Clough, John Scott A Cut Above 1989; What Ever Happened to...? 1991

Cloutier, Suzanne (1927-2003) Derby Day 1952; Othello 1952; Doctor in the House 1954

Clouzot, Vera (1921-1960) The Wages of Fear 1953; Les Diaboliques 1954; Les Espions 1957

Clunes, Alec (1912-1970) Saloon Bar 1940; Quentin Durward 1955; Richard III 1955; Tiger in the Smoke 1956; Tomorrow at Ten 1962

Clunes, Martin (1963-) The Russia House 1990; Carry On Columbus 1992; Staggered 1993; The Revengers' Comedies 1997; The Acid House 1998; Shakespeare in Love 1998; Saving Grace 2000; Nativity 3: Dude Where's My Donkey 2014

Clutesi, George (1988-) I Heard the Owl Call My Name 1973; Prophecy 1979

Cluzet, François (1955-) Le Cheval d'Orgeuil 1980; One Deadly Summer 1983; 'Round Midnight 1986; Une Affaire de Femmes 1988; Chocolat 1988; Trop Belle pour Toi 1989; Olivier Olivier 1991; L'Enfer 1993; Les Apprentis 1995; French Kiss 1995; Rien Ne Va Plus 1997; Late August, Early September 1998; Tell No One 2006; Paris 2007; Rivals 2007; Little White Lies 2010; Untouchable 2011

Clyde, Andy (1892-1967) Million Dollar Legs 1932; The Little Minister 1934; Tess of the Storm Country 1932; Land without Music 1936; Treasure Hunt 1952

Clyde, June (1909-1987) Back Street 1932; The Devil's Playground 1946; The Test Pilot...

Coates, Kim (1959-) Cold Front 1989; The Amityville Curse 1990; The Shamrock Conspiracy 1995; Carpool 1996; Lethal Tender 1996; Airborne 1997; Killing Moon 1999; Auggie Rose 2000; Battlefield Earth 2000; XChange 2000; Black Hawk Down 2001; Open Range 2003; Hostage 2004; Unstoppable 2004; Silent Hill 2006; Skinwalkers 2006; The Gunfighter's Pledge 2008; Hero Wanted 2008; Resident Evil: Afterlife 2010; Goon 2011; Cody the Robosapien 2012; A Dark Truth 2012

Coates, Phyllis (1927-) I Was a Teenage Frankenstein 1957; Cattle Empire 1958

Cobain, Kurt (1967-1994) Kurt & Courtney 1997; Hit So Hard 2011

Cobanoglu, Necmettin (1953-) Yol 1982; Journey of Hope 1990

Cobb, Lee J (1911-1976) Golden Boy 1939; This Thing Called Love 1940; Men of Boys Town 1941; Paris Calling 1941; The Moon Is Down 1943; The Song of Bernadette 1943; Anna and the King of Siam 1946; Boomerang! 1947; Captain from Castile 1947; Johnny o'Clock 1947; Call Northside 777 1948; The Dark Past 1948; The Miracle of the Bells 1948; Thieves' Highway 1949; Sirocco 1951; Gorilla at Large 1954; On the Waterfront 1954; The Left Hand of God 1955; The Racers 1955; The Road to Denver 1955; The Man in the Gray Flannel Suit 1956; The Garment Jungle 1957; The Three Faces of Eve 1957; 12 Angry Men 1957; The Brothers Karamazov 1958; Man of the West 1958; Party Girl 1958; The Baited Trap 1959; But Not for Me 1959; Green Mansions 1959; Exodus 1960; The Four Horsemen of the Apocalypse 1962; How the West Was Won 1962; Come Blow Your Horn 1963; Our Man Flint 1966; In like Flint 1967; Coogan's Bluff 1968; They Came to Rob Las Vegas 1968; Mackenna's Gold 1969; The Liberation of LB Jones 1970; Lawman 1971; Double Indemnity 1973; The Exorcist 1973; The Man Who Loved Cat Dancing 1973; That Lucky Touch 1975

Cobb, Randall "Tex" (1950-) Uncommon Valor 1983; The Golden Child 1986; Critical Condition 1987; Buy & Cell 1988; Fletch Lives 1989; Blind Fury 1990; Ernest Goes to Jail 1990; Raw Nerve 1991; Midnight Sting 1992

Cobbs, Bill aka **Cobbs, William** (1935-) The Brother from Another Planet 1984; Dominick and Eugene 1988; The People under the Stairs 1991; The Bodyguard 1992; The Hudsucker Proxy 1994; Ed 1996; Air Bud 1997; Hope Floats 1998; I Still Know What You Did Last Summer 1998; Night at the Museum 2006

Cobo, Eva aka **Cobo de Garcia, Eva** (1967-) Matador 1986; Operation Condor: the Armour of God II 1990

Cobo, Roberto (1930-2002) Los Olvidados 1950; Mexican Bus Ride 1951

Coburn, Charles (1877-1961) Of Human Hearts 1938; Vivacious Lady 1938; Bachelor Mother 1939; Idiot's Delight 1939; In Name Only 1939; Made for Each Other 1939; Stanley and Livingstone 1939; The Story of Alexander Graham Bell 1939; Edison, the Man 1940; Road to Singapore 1940; Three Faces West 1940; The Devil and Miss Jones 1941; HM Pulham Esq 1941; The Lady Eve 1941; George Washington Slept Here 1942; In This Our Life 1942; Kings Row 1942; The Constant Nymph 1943; Forever and a Day 1943; Heaven Can Wait 1943; The More the Merrier 1943; Princess O'Rourke 1943; Knickerbocker Holiday 1944; Together Again 1944; Wilson 1944; Colonel Effingham's Raid 1945; Over 21 1945; Rhapsody in Blue 1945; A Royal Scanda' 1945; The Green Years 1946; Lured 1947; The Paradine Case 1947; BF's Daughter 1948; Green Grass of Wyoming 1948; The Doctor and the Girl 1949; Everybody Does It 1949; The Gal Who Took the West 1949; Impact 1949; Mr Music 1950; Has Anybody Seen My Gal? 1952; Monkey Business 1952; Gentlemen Prefer Blondes 1953; Trouble along the Way 1953; The Rocket Man 1954; How to Be Very, Very Popular 1955; The Power and the Prize 1956; Town on Trial 1956; How to Murder a Rich Uncle 1957; The Remarkable Mr Pennypacker 1959; A Stranger in My Arms 1959; Pepe 1960

Coburn, James (1928-2002) Face of a Fugitive 1959; Ride Lonesome 1959; The Magnificent Seven 1960; The Murder Men 1961; Hell Is for Heroes 1962; Charade 1963; The Great Escape 1963; The Americanization of Emily 1964; A High Wind in Jamaica 1965; The Loved One 1965; Major Dundee 1965; Dead Heat on a Merry-Go-Round 1966; Our Man Flint 1966; What Did You Do in the War, Daddy? 1966; In like Flint 1967; The President's Analyst 1967; Waterhole #3 1967; Candy 1968; Duffy 1968; Hard Contract 1969; Last of the Mobile Hot-Shots 1970; A Fistful of Dynamite 1971; The Honkers 1971; The Carey Treatment 1972; A Reason to Live, a Reason to Die 1972; Harry in Your Pocket 1973; The Last of Sheila 1973; Pat Garrett and Billy the Kid 1973; The Internecine Project 1974; Bite the Bullet 1975; Hard Times 1975; Battle of Midway 1976; The Last Hard Men 1976; Cross of Iron 1977; Firepower 1979; Goldengirl 1979; The Baltimore Bullet 1980; Loving Couples 1980; High Risk 1981; Looker 1981; Martin's Day 1984; Death of a Soldier 1985; Young Guns II 1990; Hudson Hawk 1991; Sister Act 2: Back in the Habit 1993; Maverick 1994; The Disappearance of Kevin Johnson 1995; The Set Up 1995; Eraser 1996; Keys to Tulsa 1996; The Nutty Professor 1996; Skeletons 1996; Affliction 1997; Mr Murder 1998; Payback 1998; The Man from Elysian Fields 2001; Monsters, Inc 2001; American Gun 2002; Snow Dogs 2002

Coca, Imogene (1908-2001) Under the Yum Yum Tree 1963; National Lampoon's Vacation 1983; Nothing Lasts Forever 1984

Cochran, Robert Moscow Nights 1935; Sanders of the River 1935; Scrooge 1935; The Man Who Could Work Miracles 1936

Cochran, Steve (1917-1965) Wonder Man 1945; The Chase 1946; The Kid from Brooklyn 1946; Copacabana 1947; A Song Is Born 1948; White Heat 1949; Dallas 1950; The Damned Don't Cry 1950; Storm Warning 1950; Jim Thorpe - All-American 1951; Back to God's Country 1953; The Desert Song 1953; Carnival Story 1954; Private Hell 36 1954; Come Next Spring 1956; Il Grido 1957; The Mobster 1958; Quantrill's Raiders 1958; The Beat Generation 1959; The Big Operator 1959; The Deadly Companions 1961

Cochrane, Rory (1972-) Dazed and Confused 1993; Love and a .45 1994; Empire Records 1995; The Low Life 1995; Black and White 1998; The Prime Gig 2000; Sunset Strip 2000; Hart's War 2002; Right at Your Door 2006; A Scanner Darkly 2006; Oculus 2013; Black Mass 2015

Cockburn, Arlene The Winter Guest 1996; The Governess 1997

Cocker, Jarvis Leonard Cohen: I'm Your Man 2005; Scott Walker: 30 Century Man 2006; Fantastic Mr Fox 2009; Pulp: a Film about Life, Death and Supermarkets 2014

Cocker, Linzey Salvage 2009; Enemies Closer 2013

Cockrell, Gary Lolita 1961; The War Lover 1962

Coco, James (1930-1987) Ensign Pulver 1964; Generation 1969; End of the Road 1970; Tell Me That You Love Me, Junie Moon 1970; A New Leaf 1971; Such Good Friends 1971; Man of La Mancha 1972; The Wild Party 1975; Murder by Death 1976; Bye Bye Monkey 1978; The Cheap Detective 1978; The Diary of Anne Frank 1980; Only When I Laugh 1981; Hunk 1987

Cocteau, Jean (1889-1963) The Blood of a Poet 1930; Les Parents Terribles 1948; Les Enfants Terribles 1950; Orphée 1950; Le Testament d'Orphée 1960

Coduri, Camille (1966-) Hawks 1988; Nuns on the Run 1990; King Ralph 1991

Cody, Iron Eyes (1907-1999) Sitting Bull 1954; Gun for a Coward 1957; El Condor 1970; Grayeagle 1977; Ernest Goes to Camp 1987

Cody, Lew (1884-1934) What a Widow! 1930; Dishonored 1931; Sporting Blood 1931; Sitting Pretty 1933

Coe, Barry (1934-) The Bravados 1958; But Not for Me 1959; One Foot in Hell 1960; The Wizard of Baghdad 1960; The 300 Spartans 1962; Jaws 2 1978

Coe, George (1929-2015) Kramer vs Kramer 1979; The Amateur 1981; The Entity 1981; A Flash of Green 1984; Remo - Unarmed and Dangerous 1985; Best Seller 1987; Blind Date 1987; My Name Is Bill W 1989; Big Eden 2000; Wrinkles 2011

Coe, Peter (1929-1987) House of Frankenstein 1944; The Mummy's Curse 1944; Hellgate 1952; Road to Bali 1952

Coeur, Paul aka **Jolicoeur, Paul** The High Country 1981; Cool Runnings 1993

Coffey, Denise (1936-) Waltz of the Toreadors 1962; Georgy Girl 1966; Another Time, Another Place 1983

Coffey, Scott (1967-) Satisfaction 1988; Shag 1988; The Temp 1993; Ellie Parker 2005

Coffin, Frederick (1943-2003) Hard to Kill 1989; Crash: the Mystery of Flight 1501 1990; VI Warshawski 1991

Coffin, Pierre Minions 2015; Despicable Me 3 2017

Cohen, Emory (1990-) Afterschool 2008; The Place beyond the Pines 2012

Cohen, Giles The Beat That My Heart Skipped 2005; Mea Culpa 2012

Cohen, J J aka **Cohen, Jeffrey Jay** Fire with Fire 1986; The Principal 1987

Cohen, Jonathan A Perfect Plan 2012; Love Is in the Air 2013

Cohen, Leonard Dynamite Chicken 1971; Leonard Cohen: I'm Your Man 2005

Cohen, Lynn Manhattan Murder Mystery 1993; Vanya on 42nd Street 1994; Hurricane Streets 1997; Then She Found Me 2007

Cohen, Oshri Beaufort 2007; Lebanon 2009

Cohen, Scott (1964-) The Mambo Kings 1992; Kissing Jessica Stein 2001; Love and Other Impossible Pursuits 2009

Colangeli, Giorgio Il Divo 2008; The Wait 2015

Colantoni, Enrico (1963-) Galaxy Quest 1999; Stigmata 1999; James Dean 2001; Criminal 2004

Colasanto, Nicholas (1924-1985) Fat City 1972; Raging Bull 1980

Colbert, Claudette (1903-1996) For the Love of Mike 1927; The Big Pond 1930; Manslaughter 1930; His Woman 1931; Honor among Lovers 1931; The Smiling Lieutenant 1931; The Man from

Yesterday 1932; The Phantom President 1932; The Sign of the Cross 1932; The Wiser Sex 1932; I Cover the Waterfront 1933; Torch Singer 1933; Cleopatra 1934; Four Frightened People 1934; Imitation of Life 1934; It Happened One Night 1934; The Bride Comes Home 1935; The Gilded Lily 1935; Private Worlds 1935; She Married Her Boss 1935; Under Two Flags 1936; I Met Him in Paris 1937; Tovarich 1937; Bluebeard's Eighth Wife 1938; Drums along the Mohawk 1939; It's a Wonderful World 1939; Midnight 1939; Zaza 1939; Arise, My Love 1940; Boom Town 1940; Remember the Day 1941; Skylark 1941; The Palm Beach Story 1942; No Time for Love 1943; So Proudly We Hail 1943; Guest Wife 1944; Practically Yours 1944; Since You Went Away 1944; Tomorrow Is Forever 1945; The Secret Heart 1946; Without Reservations 1946; The Egg and I 1947; Sleep, My Love 1948; Bride for Sale 1949; Three Came Home 1950; Let's Make It Legal 1951; Thunder on the Hill 1951; The Planter's Wife 1952; Royal Affairs in Versailles 1953; Texas Lady 1955; The Love Goddesses 1965

Colbert, Robert aka Colbert, Bob (1931-) Have Rocket, Will Travel 1959; The Lawyer 1969; City beneath the Sea 1971

Colby, Anita (1914-1992) Cover Girl 1944; Brute Force 1947

Cole, Gary (1957-) The Old Man and the Sea 1990; In the Line of Fire 1993; The Switch 1993; The Brady Bunch Movie 1995; A Very Brady Sequel 1996; Gang Related 1997; I'll Be Home for Christmas 1998; A Simple Plan 1998; Office Space 1999; One Hour Photo 2001; I Spy 2002; The Ring Two 2004; Win a Date with Tad Hamilton! 2004; Cry_Wolf 2005; Breach 2006; Talladega Nights: the Ballad of Ricky Bobby 2006; Pineapple Express 2008; The Joneses 2009; Hop 2011; Tammy 2014

Cole, George (1925-2015) Cottage to Let 1941; My Brother's Keeper 1948; Quartet 1948; The Spider and the Fly 1949; Gone to Earth 1950; Lady Godiva Rides Again 1951; Laughter in Paradise 1951; Scrooge 1951; The Happy Family 1952; The Intruder 1953; Our Girl Friday 1953; Will Any Gentleman...? 1953; The Belles of St Trinian's 1954; Happy Ever After 1954; The Constant Husband 1955; A Prize of Gold 1955; Quentin Durward 1955; The Green Man 1956; It's a Wonderful World 1956; Blue Murder at St Trinian's 1957; Too Many Crooks 1958; The Bridal Path 1959; The Pure Hell of St Trinian's 1960; Cleopatra 1963; Dr Syn, Alias the Scarecrow 1963; The Legend of Young Dick Turpin 1965; One Way Pendulum 1965; The Great St Trinian's Train Robbery 1966; The Vampire Lovers 1970; Fright 1971; Take Me High 1973; Gone in 60 Seconds 1974; The Blue Bird 1976; Mary Reilly 1995; The Ghost of Greville Lodge 2000

Cole, Joe In the Blood 2014; Green Room 2015; Pressure 2015

Cole, Lily (1987-) The Imaginarium of Doctor Parnassus 2009; The Moth Diaries 2010; Confession of a Child of the Century 2011; The Messenger 2015

Cole, Nat King (1919-1965) The Blue Gardenia 1953; China Gate 1957; Istanbul 1957; St Louis Blues 1958

Coleby, Robert (1947-) The Plumber 1979; Dynasty: the Making of a Guilty Pleasure 2004; Tracks 2013

Coleman, Bobby Post Grad 2009; The Last Song 2010; Cody the Robosapien 2012

Coleman, Charles (1885-1951) The Rage of Paris 1938; That Certain Age 1938

Coleman, Charlotte (1968-2001) Four Weddings and a Funeral 1994; The Young Poisoner's Handbook 1994; Different for Girls 1996; If Only 1998; Beautiful People 1999

Coleman, Dabney (1932-) The Slender Thread 1965; This Property Is Condemned 1966; The Scalphunters 1968; Downhill Racer 1969; I Love My... Wife 1970; Cinderella Liberty 1973; The Dove 1974; The Other Side of the Mountain 1975; Rolling Thunder 1977; North Dallas Forty 1979; How to Beat the High Cost of Living 1980; Nine to Five 1980; Modern Problems 1981; On Golden Pond 1981; Tootsie 1982; Young Doctors in Love 1982; WarGames 1983; Cloak and Dagger 1984; The Man with One Red Shoe 1985; Dragnet 1987; Hot to Trot 1988; Short Time 1990; Where the Heart Is 1990; Meet the Applegates 1991; Amos & Andrew 1993; The Beverly Hillbillies 1993; Kidnapped 1995; You've Got Mail 1998; Inspector

Gadget 1999; Recess: School's Out 2001; Moonlight Mile 2002

Coleman, Dominic Sex Lives of the Potato Men 2003; Special People 2007

Coleman, Frank J (1889-1948) Behind the Screen 1916; The Cure 1917

Coleman, Gary (1968-2010) Dirty Work 1998; A Carol Christmas 2003; Midgets vs Mascots 2008

Coleman, Holliston (1992-) Supreme Sanction 1999; Bless the Child 2000; Cody the Robosapien 2012

Coleman, Jack (1958-) Bridesmaids 1989; Last Rites 1998; Polar Storm 2009; Rock the House 2011

Coleman, Marilyn Which Way Is Up? 1977; Remember My Name 1978

Coleman, Nancy (1917-2000) Dangerously They Live 1942; Desperate Journey 1942; The Gay Sisters 1942; Kings Row 1942; Edge of Darkness 1943; In Our Time 1944; Devotion 1946; Mourning Becomes Electra 1947

Coleridge, Ethel (1883-1976) Rookery Nook 1930; Penny Paradise 1938

Coles, Michael (1936-2005) Dr Who and the Daleks 1965; A Touch of Love 1969; I Want What I Want 1971; Dracula AD 1972 1972; The Satanic Rites of Dracula 1973

Colgan, Eileen (1933-2014) Quackser Fortune Has a Cousin in the Bronx 1970; The Secret of Roan Inish 1993

Colicos, John (1928-2000) Anne of the Thousand Days 1969; Raid on Rommel 1971; Red Sky at Morning 1971; The Wrath of God 1972; Scorpio 1973; Breaking Point 1976; Drum 1976; Phobia 1980; The Postman Always Rings Twice 1981; Nowhere to Hide 1987

Colin, Grégoire (1975-) Olivier Olivier 1991; Before the Rain 1994; Secret Defense 1997; The Dream Life of Angels 1998; Beau Travail 1999; Sex Is Comedy 2002; Vendredi Soir 2002; The Intruder 2004; 35 Shots of Rum 2008

Colin, Ian (1910-1987) It's Never Too Late to Mend 1937; The Big Chance 1957

Colin, Margaret (1957-) Something Wild 1986; Like Father, like Son 1987; Three Men and a Baby 1987; True Believer 1989; The Butcher's Wife 1991; Amos & Andrew 1993; Independence Day 1996; The Devil's Own 1997; Time to Say Goodbye? 1997; The Adventures of Sebastian Cole 1998; Hit and Run 1999; Blue Car 2001; Unfaithful 2002; First Daughter 2004

Collado, Adrià KM 31: Kilometro 31 2005; To Let 2006

Collard, Kenneth Passion in the Desert 1998; 12 in a Box 2007

Colleano, Bonar (1924-1958) The Way to the Stars 1945; A Matter of Life and Death 1946; Wanted for Murder 1946; While the Sun Shines 1946; Once a Jolly Swagman 1948; One Night with You 1948; Dance Hall 1950; Pool of London 1950; Escape by Night 1953; Is Your Honeymoon Really Necessary? 1953; The Sea Shall Not Have Them 1954; Joe Macbeth 1955; Zarak 1956; Fire Down Below 1957; Interpol 1957; The Man Inside 1958; No Time to Die 1958

Collet, Christopher (1968-) Firstborn 1984; The Deadly Game 1986; Prayer of the Rollerboys 1990

Collette, Toni (1972-) Spotswood 1991; Muriel's Wedding 1994; Cosi 1996; Emma 1996; The Pallbearer 1996; Clockwatchers 1997; Diana & Me 1997; The James Gang 1997; The Boys 1998; Velvet Goldmine 1998; 8½ Women 1999; Hotel Splendide 1999; The Sixth Sense 1999; The Magic Pudding 2000; Shaft 2000; Dinner with Friends 2001; About a Boy 2002; Changing Lanes 2002; Dirty Deeds 2002; The Hours 2002; Japanese Story 2003; Connie and Carla 2004; The Last Shot 2004; In Her Shoes 2005; Like Minds 2006; Little Miss Sunshine 2006; The Night Listener 2006; Evening 2007; Mary and Max 2008; Fright Night 2011; Hitchcock 2012; Mental 2012; Enough Said 2013; A Long Way Down 2013; Lucky Them 2013; The Way Way Back 2013; The Boxtrolls 2014; Glassland 2014; Hector and the Search for Happiness 2014; Krampus 2015; Miss You Already 2015; Imperium 2016; xXx: the Return of Xander Cage 2017

Colley, Don Pedro (1938-) THX 1138 1971; Sugar Hill 1974

Colley, Kenneth aka Colley, Ken (1937-) The Music Lovers 1970; The Triple Echo 1972; Giro City 1982; The Scarlet and the Black 1983; The Whistle Blower 1986; A Summer Story 1987; I Hired a Contract Killer 1990; The Last Island 1990; Prisoner of Honor 1991;

Brassed Off 1996; Shadow Run 1998; Hold Back the Night 1999

Collier, Constance (1878-1955) A Damsel in Distress 1937; Stage Door 1937; Thunder in the City 1937; Zaza 1939; Kitty 1945; The Dark Corner 1946; Monsieur Beaucaire 1946; An Ideal Husband 1947; The Girl from Manhattan 1948; Rope 1948; Whirlpool 1949

Collier, Lois (1919-1999) Cobra Woman 1944; The Naughty Nineties 1945; A Night in Casablanca 1946; Wild Beauty 1946; Slave Girl 1947

Collier, Patience (1910-1987) Countess Dracula 1970; Every Home Should Have One 1970; Perfect Friday 1970

Collier Sr, William (1866-1944) Up the River 1930; Six Cylinder Love 1931; The Bride Comes Home 1935; Invitation to Happiness 1939; Miracle on Main Street 1940

Collier Jr, William aka Collier, William (1902-1987) The Lucky Lady 1926; Rain or Shine 1930; Cimarron 1931; Little Caesar 1931; Street Scene 1931

Collin, John (1928-1987) The Witches 1966; Before Winter Comes 1968; The Last Escape 1970; All Creatures Great and Small 1974; Tess 1979

Collinge, Patricia (1892-1974) The Little Foxes 1941; Shadow of a Doubt 1942; Tender Comrade 1943; Casanova Brown 1944; Teresa 1951; The Nun's Story 1959

Collins Jr, Clifton aka Gonzalez, Clifton Gonzalez aka Gonzáles, Clifton González (1970-) Fortress 1992; One Eight Seven 1997; Light It Up 1999; Price of Glory 2000; Tigerland 2000; Traffic 2000; The Last Castle 2001; I Witness 2003; Capote 2005; Sunshine Cleaning 2008; Crank: High Voltage 2009; Extract 2009; Horsemen 2009; Parker 2013

Collins, Eddie (1884-1940) Drums along the Mohawk 1939; Young Mr Lincoln 1939; The Blue Bird 1940

Collins, Elaine Up 1976; Soft Top, Hard Shoulder 1992

Collins, Gary (1938-2012) Angel in My Pocket 1968; Killer Fish 1978; Hangar 18 1980

Collins, Jackie (1939-2015) Barnacle Bill 1957; Undercover Girl 1957; During One Night 1961

Collins, Joan (1933-) Lady Godiva Rides Again 1951; Cosh Boy 1952; I Believe in You 1952; Decameron Nights 1953; Our Girl Friday 1953; The Square Ring 1953; Turn the Key Softly 1953; The Good Die Young 1954; The Girl in the Red Velvet Swing 1955; Land of the Pharaohs 1955; The Virgin Queen 1955; The Opposite Sex 1956; Island in the Sun 1957; Sea Wife 1957; The Wayward Bus 1957; The Bravados 1958; Esther and the King 1960; Seven Thieves 1960; The Road to Hong Kong 1962; Warning Shot 1967; Can Heironymus Merkin Ever Forget Mercy Humppe and Find True Happiness? 1969; The Executioner 1970; Up in the Cellar 1970; Quest for Love 1971; Fear in the Night 1972; Tales from the Crypt 1972; Dark Places 1973; Alfie Darling 1975; I Don't Want to Be Born 1975; The Bawdy Adventures of Tom Jones 1976; Empire of the Ants 1977; The Big Sleep 1978; The Stud 1978; The Bitch 1979; A Game for Vultures 1979; Sunburn 1979; Nutcracker 1982; The Cartier Affair 1984; Decadence 1993; In the Bleak Midwinter 1995; The Clandestine Marriage 1999; The Flintstones in Viva Rock Vegas 2000; These Old Broads 2001; Saving Santa 2013; Molly Moon and the Incredible Book of Hypnotism 2015

Collins, Judy (1939-) Festival 1967; Junior 1994

Collins, Karl TwentyFourSeven 1997; Life & Lyrics 2006; The Unloved 2009

Collins, Kevin The Garden 1990; Edward II 1991; Wittgenstein 1993; Infinite Justice 2006

Collins, Lewis (1946-2013) Who Dares Wins 1982; Codename Wildgeese 1984; A Ghost in Monte Carlo 1990

Collins, Lily (1989-) The Blind Side 2009; Priest 2010; Abduction 2011; Mirror Mirror 2012; Stuck in Love 2012; The English Teacher 2013; The Mortal Instruments: City of Bones 2013; Love, Rosie 2014; Rules Don't Apply 2016

Collins, Lynn (1979-) William Shakespeare's The Merchant of Venice 2004; Bug 2006; The Lake House 2006; The Number 23 2006; John Carter 2012

Collins, Patricia (1937-) Bear Island 1979; Circle of Two 1980; Speaking Parts 1989

Collins, Paul (1937-) Peter Pan 1953; Mother 1996

Collins, Pauline (1940-) Shirley Valentine 1989; City of Joy 1992; My

Mother's Courage 1995; Mrs Caldicot's Cabbage War 2000; You Will Meet a Tall Dark Stranger 2010; Albert Nobbs 2011; Quartet 2012

Collins, Phil (1951-) Buster 1988; Hook 1991; Frauds 1992; And the Band Played On 1993; Balto 1995; The Jungle Book 2 2003

Collins, Ray (1889-1965) Citizen Kane 1941; The Big Street 1942; The Commandos Strike at Dawn 1942; The Magnificent Ambersons 1942; Crime Doctor 1943; The Human Comedy 1943; Can't Help Singing 1944; The Eve of St Mark 1944; Leave Her to Heaven 1945; Miss Susie Slagle's 1945; Badman's Territory 1946; Crack-Up 1946; The Bachelor and the Bobby-Soxer 1947; A Double Life 1947; The Senator Was Indiscreet 1947; For the Love of Mary 1948; Good Sam 1948; Homecoming 1948; The Man from Colorado 1948; The Fountainhead 1949; Francis 1949; The Heiress 1949; Paid in Full 1950; Summer Stock 1950; The Racket 1951; Vengeance Valley 1951; You're in the Navy Now 1951; Young Man with Ideas 1952; Column South 1953; The Desert Song 1953; Bad for Each Other 1954; Never Say Goodbye 1955; Texas Lady 1955; The Solid Gold Cadillac 1956; Touch of Evil 1958

Collins, Roberta (1944-2008) The Unholy Rollers 1972; Women in Cages 1972; Caged Heat 1974; Death Race 2000 1975; School Spirit 1985

Collins, Russell (1897-1965) Shockproof 1949; Miss Sadie Thompson 1953; The Last Frontier 1955; The Enemy Below 1957

Collins, Stephen (1947-) All the President's Men 1976; Between the Lines 1977; Star Trek: the Motion Picture 1979; Loving Couples 1980; Brewster's Millions 1985; Jumpin' Jack Flash 1986; On Dangerous Ground 1986; Stella 1990; My New Gun 1992; A Woman Scorned 1992; As Time Runs Out 1999; Drive Me Crazy 1999; Blood Diamond 2006

Collison, Frank (1950-) Hope Springs 2002; The Whole Ten Yards 2004

Colloca, Silvia The Detonator 2006; Lesbian Vampire Killers 2008

Collyer, June (1904-1968) Hangman's House 1928; Charley's Aunt 1930

Colman, Olivia (1974-) Confetti 2006; Terkel in Trouble 2006; Hot Fuzz 2007; Le Donk & Scor-Zay-Zee 2009; Arrietty 2010; Tyrannosaur 2010; The Iron Lady 2011; Hyde Park on Hudson 2012; Cuban Fury 2014; Locke 2014; London Road 2014; Pudsey the Dog: the Movie 2014; Thomas & Friends: Tale of the Brave 2014; The Lobster 2015; Thomas & Friends - Sodor's Legend of the Lost Treasure: the Movie 2015

Colman, Ronald (1891-1958) The White Sister 1923; Lady Windermere's Fan 1925; Stella Dallas 1925; Beau Geste 1926; The Winning of Barbara Worth 1926; Bulldog Drummond 1929; Condemned 1929; The Devil to Pay 1930; Raffles 1930; Arrowsmith 1931; The Unholy Garden 1931; Cynara 1932; The Masquerader 1933; Bulldog Drummond Strikes Back 1934; Clive of India 1935; The Man Who Broke the Bank at Monte Carlo 1935; A Tale of Two Cities 1935; Under Two Flags 1936; Lost Horizon 1937; The Prisoner of Zenda 1937; If I Were King 1938; The Light That Failed 1939; Lucky Partners 1940; My Life with Caroline 1941; Random Harvest 1942; The Talk of the Town 1942; Kismet 1944; A Double Life 1947; The Late George Apley 1947; Champagne for Caesar 1950; The Story of Mankind 1957

Colomby, Scott (1952-) Caddyshack 1980; Porky's Revenge 1985

Colon, Alex (1941-1995) Death of an Angel 1985; Invasion USA 1985; Red Scorpion 1989

Colon, Miriam (1936-) Thunder Island 1963; The Appaloosa 1966; Back Roads 1981; Scarface 1983; Lone Star 1995

Colonna, Jerry (1904-1986) Road to Singapore 1940; Atlantic City 1944; Make Mine Music 1946; Alice in Wonderland 1951; Andy Hardy Comes Home 1958

Colosimo, Clara (1922-1994) Alfredo Alfredo 1971; Orchestra Rehearsal 1978; Vampire in Venice 1987

Colosimo, Vince (1966-) Chopper 2000; Lantana 2001; The Hard Word 2002; Opal Dream 2005; Body of Lies 2008

Colpeyn, Louisa aka Colpeyn, Luisa Bande à Part 1964; Marry Me! Marry Me! 1968

Coltrane, Robbie (1950-) Scrubbers 1982; Krull 1983; Loose Connections 1983; Defence of the Realm 1985;

National Lampoon's European Vacation 1985; The Supergrass 1985; Caravaggio 1986; Mona Lisa 1986; Eat the Rich 1987; Bert Rigby, You're a Fool 1989; Danny, the Champion of the World 1989; Henry V 1989; Nuns on the Run 1990; Perfectly Normal 1990; The Pope Must Die 1991; Triple Bogey on a Par Five Hole 1991; Oh, What a Night 1992; The Adventures of Huck Finn 1993; GoldenEye 1995; Buddy 1997; Montana 1997; Message in a Bottle 1998; Alice in Wonderland 1999; The World Is Not Enough 1999; From Hell 2001; Harry Potter and the Philosopher's Stone 2001; Harry Potter and the Chamber of Secrets 2002; Harry Potter and the Prisoner of Azkaban 2004; Ocean's Twelve 2004; Harry Potter and the Goblet of Fire 2005; Provoked: a True Story 2006; Harry Potter and the Order of the Phoenix 2007; The Brothers Bloom 2008; Harry Potter and the Half-Blood Prince 2009; Brave 2012; Great Expectations 2012; Effie Gray 2014

Colvig, Pinto (1892-1967) The Three Little Pigs 1933; Snow White and the Seven Dwarfs 1937

Colvin, Jack (1934-2005) The Incredible Hulk 1977; Child's Play 1988; The Incredible Hulk Returns 1988

Combeau, Muriel Romuald et Juliette 1989; Near Mrs 1990

Combs, Holly Marie (1973-) Sweet Hearts Dance 1988; Dr Giggles 1992; Danielle Steel's A Perfect Stranger 1994; Swearing Allegiance 1997

Combs, Jeffrey aka Combs, Jeffery (1954-) Re-Animator 1985; From Beyond 1986; Bride of Re-Animator 1991; The Pit and the Pendulum 1991; Trancers II: The Return of Jack Deth 1991; Necronomicon 1993; Love and a .45 1994; The Frighteners 1996; Contagion 2001; Faust: Love of the Damned 2001; FearDotCom 2002; Edmond 2005

Combs, Sean aka Combs, Sean "P Diddy" (1969-) Made 2001; Monster's Ball 2001; Fade to Black 2004; Get Him to the Greek 2010; I'm Still Here 2010; Draft Day 2014

Comer, Anjanette (1942-) The Loved One 1965; Quick, before It Melts 1965; The Appaloosa 1966; Banning 1967; In Enemy Country 1968; Rabbit, Run 1970; The Baby 1973; Lepke 1975; Fire Sale 1977; The Long Summer of George Adams 1982

Comer, John (1924-1984) The Family Way 1966; There's a Girl in My Soup 1970; The Lovers! 1972

Comingore, Dorothy (1913-1971) Citizen Kane 1941; The Hairy Ape 1944; The Big Night 1951

Common (1972-) Street Kings 2008; Wanted 2008; Terminator: Salvation 2009; Just Wright 2010; Something from Nothing: the Art of Rap 2012; Selma 2014

Como, Perry (1912-2001) Something for the Boys 1944; Words and Music 1948

Compson, Betty (1897-1974) The Pony Express 1925; The Barker 1928; The Docks of New York 1928; The Great Gabbo 1929; The Gay Diplomat 1931

Compston, Martin (1984-) Sweet Sixteen 2002; Tickets 2005; Wild Country 2005; A Guide to Recognizing Your Saints 2006; Red Road 2006; True North 2006; Red Mist 2008; The Disappearance of Alice Creed 2009; Donkeys 2010; Four 2010; Pimp 2010; SoulBoy 2010; When the Lights Went Out 2010; Ghosted 2011; Piggy 2012; Sister 2012; The Wee Man 2013

Compton, Fay (1894-1978) Waltzes from Vienna 1933; The Mill on the Floss 1937; The Prime Minister 1940; Odd Man Out 1947; Esther Waters 1948; London Belongs to Me 1948; Britannia Mews 1949; Laughter in Paradise 1951; Othello 1952; The Vanquished 1953; Double Cross 1955; The Story of Esther Costello 1957; The Haunting 1963; The Virgin and the Gypsy 1970

Compton, Joyce (1907-1997) The Wild Party 1929; The Awful Truth 1937; Rose of Washington Square 1939; Let's Make Music 1940; Sky Murder 1940; The Villain Still Pursued Her 1940; Bedtime Story 1942; Christmas in Connecticut 1945; Scared to Death 1947

Compton, Juliette (1899-1989) Anybody's Woman 1930; Morocco 1930; Devil and the Deep 1932; No One Man 1932; Westward Passage 1932; The Masquerader 1933; Peg o' My Heart 1933

Compton, O'Neal (1951-) Attack of the 50 Ft Woman 1993; Murder between Friends 1993; Roadracers 1994; Kill Me Later 2001

Conant, Oliver (1955-) Summer of '42 1971; Class of '44 1973

Conaway, Cristi (1965-) Attack of the 50 Ft Woman 1993; Flashpoint 1997

Conaway, Jeff (1950-2011) Grease 1978; The Patriot 1986; Elvira, Mistress of the Dark 1988

Condon, Kerry (1983-) Unleashed 2005; The Last Station 2009; This Must Be the Place 2011; Dom Hemingway 2013; Gold 2014

Condra, Julie (1970-) Crying Freeman 1995; Danielle Steel's Mixed Blessings 1995; Screw Loose 1999

Conklin, Chester (1888-1971) Tillie's Punctured Romance 1914; Greed 1925; The Big Noise 1928; The Virginian 1929; Her Majesty Love 1931; Hallelujah, I'm a Bum 1933; Modern Times 1936; The Beast with a Million Eyes 1955

Conklin, Peggy (1912-2003) The Devil Is a Sissy 1936; Having Wonderful Time 1938

Conley, Brian (1961-) Circus 1999; Arthur's Dyke 2001

Conley, Jack Brown's Requiem 1998; The Unknown 2005; Generation Gap 2008; Harold & Kumar Escape from Guantanamo Bay 2008

Conlin, Jimmy aka **Conlin, James** (1884-1962) Rose Marie 1936; Knock on Any Door 1949; Tulsa 1949; Mad Wednesday 1950

Conn, Didi (1951-) Almost Summer 1977; You Light Up My Life 1977; Grease 2 1982; Thomas and the Magic Railroad 2000

Conn, Shelley Nina's Heavenly Delights 2006; New Town Killers 2009; How Do You Know 2010

Connell, Maureen (1931-) The Abominable Snowman 1957; Lucky Jim 1957; Next to No Time 1958; Danger by My Side 1962

Connelly, Christopher aka **Connelly, Chris** (1941-1988) Corky 1972; They Only Kill Their Masters 1972; The Norseman 1978; Liar's Moon 1982

Connelly, Edward (1859-1928) Camille 1921; Sinners in Silk 1924; The Torrent 1926

Connelly, Erwin (1879-1931) Sherlock Junior 1924; Go West 1925; Seven Chances 1925

Connelly, Jennifer (1970-) Labyrinth 1986; Some Girls 1988; The Hot Spot 1990; Career Opportunities 1991; Rocketeer 1991; The Heart of Justice 1992; Of Love and Shadows 1994; Higher Learning 1995; Mulholland Falls 1996; Inventing the Abbotts 1997; Dark City 1998; Pollock 2000; Requiem for a Dream 2000; Waking the Dead 2000; A Beautiful Mind 2001; House of Sand and Fog 2003; Hulk 2003; Dark Water 2005; Blood Diamond 2006; Little Children 2006; The Day the Earth Stood Still 2008; He's Just Not That into You 2008; Creation 2009; 9 2009; The Dilemma 2011; Salvation Boulevard 2011; Stuck in Love 2012; A New York Winter's Tale 2014; Noah 2014; Shelter 2014; American Pastoral 2016

Connery, Jason (1962-) The Lords of Discipline 1983; The Boy Who Had Everything 1984; Spymaker: the Secret Life of Ian Fleming 1990; Bullet to Beijing 1995; Midnight in St Petersburg 1995; Macbeth 1997; Urban Ghost Story 1998; Shanghai Noon 2000; The Line 2008

Connery, Sean (1930-) Lilacs in the Spring 1955; Hell Drivers 1957; No Road Back 1957; Time Lock 1957; Another Time, Another Place 1958; A Night to Remember 1958; Darby O'Gill and the Little People 1959; Tarzan's Greatest Adventure 1959; The Frightened City 1961; On the Fiddle 1961; Dr No 1962; The Longest Day 1962; From Russia with Love 1963; Goldfinger 1964; Marnie 1964; Woman of Straw 1964; The Hill 1965; Thunderball 1965; A Fine Madness 1966; You Only Live Twice 1967; Shalako 1968; The Red Tent 1969; The Molly Maguires 1970; The Anderson Tapes 1971; Diamonds Are Forever 1971; The Offence 1972; Zardoz 1973; Murder on the Orient Express 1974; The Man Who Would Be King 1975; Ransom 1975; The Wind and the Lion 1975; The Next Man 1976; Robin and Marian 1976; A Bridge Too Far 1977; The First Great Train Robbery 1978; Cuba 1979; Meteor 1979; Outland 1981; Time Bandits 1981; Five Days One Summer 1982; The Man with the Deadly Lens 1982; Never Say Never Again 1983; Sword of the Valiant 1984; Highlander 1986; The Name of the Rose 1986; The Untouchables 1987; Memories of Me 1988; The Presidio 1988; Family Business 1989; Indiana Jones and the Last Crusade 1989; Highlander II: the Quickening 1990; The Hunt for Red

October 1990; The Russia House 1990; Robin Hood: Prince of Thieves 1991; Medicine Man 1992; A Good Man in Africa 1993; Rising Sun 1993; First Knight 1995; Just Cause 1995; DragonHeart 1996; The Rock 1996; The Avengers 1998; Playing by Heart 1998; Entrapment 1999; Finding Forrester 2000; The League of Extraordinary Gentlemen 2003; Sir Billi 2012

Connick Jr, Harry (1967-) Memphis Belle 1990; Little Man Tate 1991; Copycat 1995; Excess Baggage 1997; Hope Floats 1998; The Iron Giant 1999; The Simian Line 2000; South Pacific 2001; Bug 2006; PS I Love You 2007; Living Proof 2008; New in Town 2008; Dolphin Tale 2011; Dolphin Tale 2 2014

Connolly, Andrew Joyriders 1988; Mad Dogs and Englishmen 1994

Connolly, Billy (1942-) Absolution 1978; Bullshot 1983; Water 1985; The Big Man 1990; Indecent Proposal 1993; Pocahontas 1995; Muppet Treasure Island 1996; Middleton's Changeling 1997; Mrs Brown 1997; Paws 1997; The Impostors 1998; Still Crazy 1998; The Boondock Saints 1999; The Debt Collector 1999; Beautiful Joe 2000; An Everlasting Piece 2000; Gabriel & Me 2001; The Man Who Sued God 2001; Prince Charming 2001; White Oleander 2002; The Last Samurai 2003; Timeline 2003; Lemony Snicket's A Series of Unfortunate Events 2004; Overnight 2004; The Aristocrats 2005; Garfield 2 2006; Open Season 2006; Open Season 2 2008; The X-Files: I Want to Believe 2008; Gulliver's Travels 2010; Brave 2012; Quartet 2012; The Hobbit: the Battle of the Five Armies 2014; What We Did on Our Holiday 2014

Connolly, Kevin (1974-) Alan & Naomi 1992; Antwone Fisher 2002; The Notebook 2003; He's Just Not That into You 2008; Secretariat 2010; Entourage 2015

Connolly, Kristen The Cabin in the Woods 2010; The Bay 2012

Connolly, Walter (1887-1940) The Bitter Tea of General Yen 1932; Washington Merry-Go-Round 1932; Lady for a Day 1933; Man's Castle 1933; Broadway Bill 1934; The Captain Hates the Sea 1934; It Happened One Night 1934; Lady by Choice 1934; Twentieth Century 1934; So Red the Rose 1935; The King Steps Out 1936; Libeled Lady 1936; The Good Earth 1937; The League of Frightened Men 1937; Nancy Steele Is Missing 1937; Nothing Sacred 1937; Four's a Crowd 1938; Too Hot to Handle 1938; The Adventures of Huckleberry Finn 1939; 5th Ave Girl 1939

Connor, Edric (1915-1968) Cry, the Beloved Country 1951; West of Zanzibar 1954; Virgin Island 1958; 4 for Texas 1963; Only When I Larf 1968

Connor, Kenneth (1918-1992) Marilyn 1953; The Ladykillers 1955; Carry On Sergeant 1958; Carry On Nurse 1959; Carry On Teacher 1959; Make Mine a Million 1959; Carry On Constable 1960; Carry On Regardless 1960; Dentist in the Chair 1960; His and Hers 1960; Watch Your Stern 1960; Dentist on the Job 1961; Nearly a Nasty Accident 1961; What a Carve Up! 1961; Carry On Cruising 1962; Carry On Cabby 1963; Carry On Cleo 1964; Captain Nemo and the Underwater City 1969; Carry On Up the Jungle 1970; Carry On Henry 1971; Carry On Abroad 1972; Carry On Matron 1972; Carry On Girls 1973; Carry On Dick 1974; Carry On Behind 1975; Carry On England 1976; Carry On Emmannuelle 1978

Connors, Chuck (1921-1992) Pat and Mike 1952; South Sea Woman 1953; Naked Alibi 1954; Good Morning, Miss Dove 1955; The Hired Gun 1957; Old Yeller 1957; The Big Country 1958; The Lady Takes a Flyer 1958; Geronimo 1962; Flipper 1963; Move Over, Darling 1963; Ride beyond Vengeance 1966; Captain Nemo and the Underwater City 1969; The Deserter 1971; Pancho Villa 1971; Support Your Local Gunfighter 1971; Soylent Green 1973; 99 and 44/100% Dead 1974; Tourist Trap 1979; Virus 1980; Airplane II: the Sequel 1982; Target Eagle 1982; Once upon a Texas Train 1988; Salmonberries 1991

Connors, Mike aka **Connors, Touch** aka **Connors, Michael** (1925-) Sudden Fear 1952; The 49th Man 1953; The Day the World Ended 1956; Shake, Rattle and Rock! 1957; Voodoo Woman 1957; Suicide Battalion 1958; Good Neighbor Sam 1964; Panic Button 1964; Where Love Has Gone 1964; Harlow 1965; Situation Hopeless - but Not Serious 1965; Kiss the Girls and Make Them Die 1966; Stagecoach

1966; Avalanche Express 1979; Too Scared to Scream 1982; Gideon 1999

Conrad, Chris Airborne 1993; The Next Karate Kid 1994

Conrad, David (1967-) Snow White: a Tale of Terror 1996; Return to Paradise 1998

Conrad, Jess (1940-) Konga 1960; The Boys 1961; The Punk 1993

Conrad, Michael (1925-1983) They Shoot Horses, Don't They? 1969; Un Flic 1972; The Mean Machine 1974

Conrad, Robert (1935-) Palm Springs Weekend 1963; Young Dillinger 1965; The Lady in Red 1979; The Man with the Deadly Lens 1982; Jingle All the Way 1996

Conrad, William (1920-1994) The Killers 1946; Body and Soul 1947; Sorry, Wrong Number 1948; They Passed This Way 1948; East Side, West Side 1949; Tension 1949; Cry Danger 1951; The Sword of Monte Cristo 1951; Cry of the Hunted 1953; The Naked Jungle 1953; The Conqueror 1956; Johnny Concho 1956; -30- 1959

Conried, Hans (1917-1982) A Lady Takes a Chance 1943; The Senator Was Indiscreet 1947; My Friend Irma 1949; The Affairs of Dobie Gillis 1953; The 5,000 Fingers of Dr T 1953; Peter Pan 1953; Davy Crockett, King of the Wild Frontier 1955; The Birds and the Bees 1956; Bus Stop 1956; The Monster That Challenged the World 1957; Rock-a-Bye Baby 1958; Juke Box Rhythm 1959; My Six Loves 1962; The Patsy 1964

Conroy, Frances (1953-) Rocket Gibraltar 1988; The Neon Bible 1995; Murder in a Small Town 1999; Maid in Manhattan 2002; Catwoman 2004; Broken Flowers 2005; Shopgirl 2005; A Perfect Day 2006; The Wicker Man 2006; The Dark Is Rising 2007; New in Town 2008; Shelter 2008; Love Happens 2009; Stone 2010

Conroy, Frank (1890-1964) Bad Company 1931; Possessed 1931; The White Parade 1934; The Call of the Wild 1935; Charlie Chan in Egypt 1935; All My Sons 1948; Lightning Strikes Twice 1951; The Last Mile 1959; The Bramble Bush 1960

Conroy, Kevin (1955-) Batman: Mask of the Phantasm 1993; Batman of the Future: Return of the Joker 2000; Batman: The Killing Joke 2016

Conroy, Neili The Van 1996; Kisses 2008

Conroy, Ruaidhri (1979-) Into the West 1992; Clockwork Mice 1994; Nothing Personal 1995; The Van 1996

Considine, John (1938-) Buffalo Bill and the Indians, or Sitting Bull's History Lesson 1976; Passions 1984; Trouble in Mind 1985; Hell Camp 1986

Considine, Paddy (1974-) A Room for Romeo Brass 1999; Last Resort 2000; 24 Hour Party People 2001; In America 2003; Dead Man's Shoes 2004; My Summer of Love 2004; Cinderella Man 2005; Stoned 2005; The Bourne Ultimatum 2007; Hot Fuzz 2007; The Cry of the Owl 1999; Le Donk & Scor-Zay-Zee 2009; Blitz 2011; Submarine 2010; Honour 2012; Now Is Good 2012; The World's End 2013; Pride 2014; Macbeth 2015; Miss You Already 2015; The Girl with All the Gifts 2016

Considine, Tim (1940-) The Clown 1952; Her Twelve Men 1954; The Private War of Major Benson 1955; The Shaggy Dog 1959; Sunrise at Campobello 1960

Consigny, Anne (1963-) Not Here to Be Loved 2005; Anna M. 2007; The Diving-Bell and the Butterfly 2007; A Christmas Tale 2008; Wild Grass 2008; City of War: the Story of John Rabe 2009; Rapt 2009

Constance, Nathan (1979-) A Kind of Hush 1998; Dog Eat Dog 2000; London to Brighton 2006; Broken Lines 2008

Constantin, Michel (1924-2003) Le Trou 1959; Cold Sweat 1971; Man in the Trunk 1973

Constantine, Eddie (1917-1993) Passport to Shame 1958; SOS Pacific 1959; The Treasure of San Teresa 1959; Cleo from 5 to 7 1961; The Seven Deadly Sins 1961; Alphaville 1965; Beware of a Holy Whore 1970; It Lives Again 1978; The Long Good Friday 1979; The Third Generation 1979; Europa 1991

Constantine, Michael (1927-) The Hustler 1961; Quick, before It Melts 1965; Skidoo 1968; Don't Drink the Water 1969; The Reivers 1969; The Night that Panicked America 1975; Summer of My German Soldier 1978; Hill's Angels 1979; The Woo Woo Kid 1987; My Life 1993; The Juror 1996; My Big Fat Greek Wedding 2002; My Big Fat Greek Wedding 2 2016

Conte, John (1915-2006) Lost in a Harem 1944; The Man with the Golden Arm 1955

Conte, Richard (1910-1975) Guadalcanal Diary 1943; The Purple Heart 1944; A Bell for Adano 1945; Capt Eddie 1945; A Walk in the Sun 1945; Somewhere in the Night 1946; 13 Rue Madeleine 1946; The Other Love 1947; Call Northside 777 1948; Cry of the City 1948; House of Strangers 1949; Thieves' Highway 1949; Whirlpool 1949; The Sleeping City 1950; The Raiders 1952; The Blue Gardenia 1953; Desert Legion 1953; Mask of Dust 1954; Bengazi 1955; The Big Combo 1955; The Big Tip Off 1955; I'll Cry Tomorrow 1955; Little Red Monkey 1955; New York Confidential 1955; Full of Life 1956; The Brothers Rico 1957; This Angry Age 1957; They Came to Cordura 1959; Ocean's Eleven 1960; Who's Been Sleeping in My Bed? 1963; The Magnificent Showman 1964; Assault on a Queen 1966; Tony Rome 1967; Lady in Cement 1968; The Godfather 1972

Conti, Albert (1887-1967) The Eagle 1925; One Romantic Night 1930; Lady with a Past 1932; Topaze 1933; The Black Cat 1934

Conti, Tom (1941-) Galileo 1974; Slade in Flame 1974; The Duellists 1977; Full Circle 1977; Merry Christmas Mr Lawrence 1982; Reuben, Reuben 1983; American Dreamer 1984; Miracles 1985; Saving Grace 1985; Heavenly Pursuits 1986; Nazi Hunter: the Beate Klarsfeld Story 1986; Beyond Therapy 1987; The Quick and the Dead 1987; Shirley Valentine 1989; Someone Else's America 1995; Something to Believe In 1997; Don't Go Breaking My Heart 1999; The Enemy 2000; Derailed 2005; Rabbit Fever 2005; Dangerous Parking 2007; A Closed Book 2009; StreetDance 2 2012

Contreras, Luis (1950-) Blue City 1986; Straight to Hell 1987

Contreras, Patricio (1947-) Old Gringo 1989; La Frontera 1991; Of Love and Shadows 1994

Converse-Roberts, William 1918 1985; Drive Me Crazy 1999

Convy, Bert (1933-1991) Semi-Tough 1977; Jennifer 1978; Hero at Large 1980

Conway, Denis Boy Eats Girl 2005; Garage 2007

Conway, Gary (1938-) I Was a Teenage Frankenstein 1957; How to Make a Monster 1958; Young Guns of Texas 1962; Once Is Not Enough 1975

Conway, Kevin (1942-) Slaughterhouse-Five 1972; FIST 1978; Paradise Alley 1978; The Lathe of Heaven 1979; One Good Cop 1991; Rambling Rose 1991; Jennifer Eight 1992; Lawnmower Man 2: Beyond Cyberspace 1995; Black Knight 2001; Gods and Generals 2002; Invincible 2006

Conway, Morgan (1903-1981) Looking for Trouble 1934; Brother Orchid 1940; The Saint Takes Over 1940; Dick Tracy 1945; Dick Tracy vs Cueball 1946

Conway, Pat (1931-1981) An Annapolis Story 1955; Geronimo 1962

Conway, Russ (1913-2009) Jennifer 1953; Interval 1973

Conway, Tim (1933-) McHale's Navy 1964; The World's Greatest Athlete 1973; The Apple Dumpling Gang 1974; The Shaggy DA 1976; The Apple Dumpling Gang Rides Again 1979; The Private Eyes 1980; Dear God 1996; Saving Santa 2013

Conway, Tom (1904-1967) Sky Murder 1940; Lady Be Good 1941; Tarzan's Secret Treasure 1941; Cat People 1942; The Falcon's Brother 1942; Rio Rita 1942; The Falcon and the Co-Eds 1943; The Falcon in Danger 1943; The Falcon Strikes Back 1943; I Walked with a Zombie 1943; The Seventh Victim 1943; The Falcon in Hollywood 1944; The Falcon in Mexico 1944; The Falcon Out West 1944; The Falcon in San Francisco 1945; Two o'Clock Courage 1945; Criminal Court 1946; The Falcon's Adventure 1946; The Falcon's Alibi 1946; Whistle Stop 1946; Repeat Performance 1947; One Touch of Venus 1948; Painting the Clouds with Sunshine 1951; Blood Orange 1953; Peter Pan 1953; Tarzan and the She-Devil 1953; Death of a Scoundrel 1956; The She-Creature 1956; Voodoo Woman 1957; The Atomic Submarine 1960

Coogan, Jackie (1914-1984) A Day's Pleasure 1919; The Kid 1921; Oliver Twist 1922; Tom Sawyer 1930; Huckleberry Finn 1931; College Swing 1938; Million Dollar Legs 1939; The Buster Keaton Story 1957; The Joker Is Wild 1957; Lonelyhearts 1958; The Beat

Generation 1959; The Big Operator 1959; The Shakiest Gun in the West 1967; Marlowe 1969; Sherlock Holmes in New York 1976; Dr Heckyl & Mr Hype 1980; The Escape Artist 1982

Coogan, Keith (1970-) Hiding Out 1987; A Night on the Town 1987; Under the Boardwalk 1988; Cheetah 1989; Cousins 1989; Don't Tell Mom the Babysitter's Dead 1991; Toy Soldiers 1991

Coogan, Steve (1965-) The Indian in the Cupboard 1995; The Wind in the Willows 1996; The Revengers' Comedies 1997; The Parole Officer 2001; 24 Hour Party People 2001; Coffee and Cigarettes 2003; Around the World in 80 Days 2004; Ella Enchanted 2004; A Cock and Bull Story 2005; Happy Endings 2005; Marie Antoinette 2006; Night at the Museum 2006; Hamlet 2 2008; Tropic Thunder 2008; In the Loop 2009; Night at the Museum 2 2009; Marmaduke 2010; Percy Jackson & the Lightning Thief 2010; Our Idiot Brother 2011; Ruby Sparks 2012; Alan Partridge: Alpha Papa 2013; Despicable Me 2 2013; The Look of Love 2013; Philomena 2013; What Maisie Knew 2013; Night at the Museum: Secret of the Tomb 2014; Minions 2015

Cook, A J (1978-) The Virgin Suicides 1999; Final Destination 2 2002

Cook, Carole The Gauntlet 1977; Summer Lovers 1982; Grandview, USA 1984; Home on the Range 2004

Cook, Clyde (1891-1984) The Docks of New York 1928; The Taming of the Shrew 1929; The Man from Down Under 1943

Cook, Dane (1972-) Simon Sez 1999; Waiting... 2005; Employee of the Month 2006; Dan in Real Life 2007; Good Luck Chuck 2007; Mr Brooks 2007; My Best Friend's Girl 2008; Planes 2013; Planes: Fire and Rescue 2014

Cook, Donald (1901-1961) The Mad Genius 1931; The Public Enemy 1931; The Man Who Played God 1932; The Penguin Pool Murder 1932; Baby Face 1933; Jennie Gerhardt 1933; The Kiss before the Mirror 1933; The World Changes 1933; Long Lost Father 1934; Viva Villa! 1934; The Casino Murder Case 1935; Confidential 1935; Show Boat 1936; Patrick the Great 1944; Here Come the Co-Eds 1945; Our Very Own 1950

Cook Jr, Elisha aka **Cook, Elisha** (1903-1995) Love Is News 1937; They Won't Forget 1937; My Lucky Star 1938; Stranger on the Third Floor 1940; Hellzapoppin! 1941; I Wake Up Screaming 1941; The Maltese Falcon 1941; A-Haunting We Will Go 1942; A Gentleman at Heart 1942; Dark Waters 1944; Phantom Lady 1944; Up in Arms 1944; Dillinger 1945; The Big Sleep 1946; The Falcon's Alibi 1946; Lady of Deceit 1947; The Long Night 1947; Don't Bother to Knock 1952; Shane 1953; Thunder over the Plains 1953; Drum Beat 1954; The Killing 1956; Baby Face Nelson 1957; Chicago Confidential 1957; The Lonely Man 1957; Plunder Road 1957; House on Haunted Hill 1958; Platinum High School 1960; Black Zoo 1963; The Haunted Palace 1963; The Spy in the Green Hat 1966; The Great Bank Robbery 1969; El Condor 1970; Electra Glide in Blue 1973; The Outfit 1973; The Black Bird 1975; Winterhawk 1975; St Ives 1976; 1941 1979; Carny 1980; Harry's War 1981; Leave 'Em Laughing 1981; National Lampoon's Movie Madness 1981; Hammett 1982

Cook, Mason SPYkids 4: All the Time in the World 2011; Help for the Holidays 2012

Cook, Paul (1956-) The Great Rock 'n' Roll Swindle 1979; Ladies and Gentlemen, the Fabulous Stains 1981

Cook, Peter (1937-1995) The Wrong Box 1966; Bedazzled 1967; The Bed Sitting Room 1969; Monte Carlo or Bust! 1969; The Rise and Rise of Michael Rimmer 1970; The Adventures of Barry McKenzie 1972; Find the Lady 1976; Pleasure at Her Majesty's 1976; The Hound of the Baskervilles 1977; Yellowbeard 1983; Supergirl 1984; Whoops Apocalypse 1986; The Princess Bride 1987; Without a Clue 1988; Getting It Right 1989; Black Beauty 1994

Cook, Rachael Leigh (1979-) The Baby-Sitter's Club 1995; Tom and Huck 1995; Carpool 1996; The Eighteenth Angel 1997; The House of Yes 1997; Strike! 1998; She's All That 1999; Antitrust 2000; Blow Dry 2000; Get Carter 2000; Josie and the Pussycats 2001; Texas Rangers 2001; Scorched 2002; 11:14 2003; Blonde Ambition

2007; Nancy Drew 2007; The Lodger 2009; Stealing Paradise 2011; Left to Die: the Sandra and Tammi Chase Story 2012

Cook, Ron Secrets & Lies 1995; Topsy-Turvy 1999; Lucky Break 2001; On a Clear Day 2004; Thunderbirds 2004

Cook, Tommy (1930-) Tarzan and the Leopard Woman 1946; Cry of the City 1948; An American Guerrilla in the Philippines 1950

Cooke, Baldwin (1888-1953) County Hospital 1932; Twice Two 1933

Cooke, Chris aka **Cooke, Christopher** The Unbelievable Truth 1989; Simple Men 1992; I Married a Strange Person 1997

Cooke, Christian Cemetery Junction 2010; Romeo & Juliet 2012; Electricity 2014; Love, Rosie 2014

Cooke, Olivia The Quiet Ones 2013; Ouija 2014; The Signal 2014; Me and Earl and the Dying Girl 2015

Cookson, Georgina (1918-2011) The Naked Truth 1957; Your Money or Your Wife 1960; Walk a Crooked Path 1969

Cooley, Hallam (1895-1971) The Monster 1925; Sporting Blood 1931

Coolidge, Jennifer (1961-) American Pie 1999; Best in Show 2000; Down to Earth 2001; Legally Blonde 2001; Legally Blonde 2: Red, White & Blonde 2003; A Mighty Wind 2003; A Cinderella Story 2004; Robots 2005; American Dreamz 2006; Click 2006; Date Movie 2006; For Your Consideration 2006; Epic Movie 2007; Igor 2008; The Bad Lieutenant - Port of Call: New Orleans 2009; Gentlemen Broncos 2009; American Reunion 2012; Austenland 2013

Coolio (1963-) Burn Hollywood Burn 1997; Judgment Day 1999; In Pursuit 2000; Shriek If You Know What I Did Last Friday the 13th 2000

Coombes, James Monarch 1996; A Knight in Camelot 1998

Coombs, Pat (1926-2002) Dad's Army 1971; Adolf Hitler - My Part in His Downfall 1972; Ooh... You Are Awful 1972

Cooney, Kevin (1945-) The Trip to Bountiful 1985; Full Moon in Blue Water 1988; Spring Thaw 2007

Cooney, Ray (1932-) Not Now Darling 1972; Not Now, Comrade 1976

Cooper, Alice (1948-) Sgt Pepper's Lonely Hearts Club Band 1978; Sextette 1978; Prince of Darkness 1987; Lemmy 2010; Dark Shadows 2012; SuperMensch: the Legend of Shep Gordon 2013

Cooper, Ben (1930-) The Woman They Almost Lynched 1953; Johnny Guitar 1954; The Outcast 1954; The Rose Tattoo 1955; Gunfight at Comanche Creek 1964; Arizona Raiders 1965

Cooper, Bradley (1975-) My Little Eye 2002; The Last Chance 2003; Failure to Launch 2006; Case 39 2008; The Midnight Meat Train 2008; Yes Man 2008; All about Steve 2009; The Hangover 2009; New York, I Love You 2009; The A-Team 2010; Valentine's Day 2010; The Hangover: Part II 2011; Limitless 2011; Hit & Run 2012; The Place beyond the Pines 2012; Silver Linings Playbook 2012; The Words 2012; American Hustle 2013; The Hangover Part III 2013; Serena 2013; American Sniper 2014; Guardians of the Galaxy 2014; Aloha 2015; Burnt 2015; Joy 2015; 10 Cloverfield Lane 2016; Guardians of the Galaxy Vol 2 2017

Cooper, Camille aka **Cooper, Cami** Like Father, like Son 1987; Shocker 1989; Meet the Applegates 1991; Lawnmower Man 2: Beyond Cyberspace 1995

Cooper, Chris (1951-) Matewan 1987; Guilty by Suspicion 1990; City of Hope 1991; This Boy's Life 1993; Boys 1995; Lone Star 1995; Money Train 1995; Breast Men 1997; Great Expectations 1997; The Horse Whisperer 1998; American Beauty 1999; October Sky 1999; Me, Myself & Irene 2000; The Patriot 2000; Adaptation. 2002; The Bourne Identity 2002; My House in Umbria 2002; Seabiscuit 2003; Silver City 2004; Capote 2005; Jarhead 2005; Syriana 2005; Breach 2006; The Kingdom 2007; Married Life 2007; Where the Wild Things Are 2009; The Company Men 2010; Remember Me 2010; The Tempest 2010; The Town 2010; The Muppets 2011; Mea Maxima Culpa: Silence in the House of God 2012; August: Osage County 2013; The Amazing Spider-Man 2 2014; Demolition 2015; Live by Night 2016

Cooper, Clancy (1906-1975) Distant Drums 1951; A Gift for Heidi 1958

Cooper, Dominic (1978-) The History Boys 2006; Starter for 10 2006; The Escapist 2007; The Duchess 2008; An Education 2008; Mamma Mia! 2008; Tamara Drewe 2010; A Turtle's Tale: Sammy's Adventures 2010; The Devil's Double 2011; My Week with Marilyn 2011; Abraham Lincoln: Vampire Hunter 2012; Summer in February 2012; Dead Man Down 2013; Dracula Untold 2014; Need for Speed 2014; Reasonable Doubt 2014; The Lady in the Van 2015; Miss You Already 2015; Warcraft: the Beginning 2016

Cooper, Garry Quadrophenia 1979; Caravaggio 1986

Cooper, Gary (1901-1961) The Winning of Barbara Worth 1926; It 1927; Wings 1927; Beau Sabreur 1928; Lilac Time 1928; The Shopworn Angel 1928; The Virginian 1929; Morocco 1930; Paramount on Parade 1930; The Texan 1930; City Streets 1931; Fighting Caravans 1931; His Woman 1931; Devil and the Deep 1932; A Farewell to Arms 1932; If I Had a Million 1932; Alice in Wonderland 1933; Design for Living 1933; Today We Live 1933; Now and Forever 1934; Operator 13 1934; The Lives of a Bengal Lancer 1935; Peter Ibbetson 1935; The Wedding Night 1935; Desire 1936; The General Died at Dawn 1936; Mr Deeds Goes to Town 1936; The Plainsman 1936; Souls at Sea 1937; The Adventures of Marco Polo 1938; Bluebeard's Eighth Wife 1938; The Cowboy and the Lady 1938; Beau Geste 1939; The Real Glory 1939; North West Mounted Police 1940; The Westerner 1940; Ball of Fire 1941; Meet John Doe 1941; Sergeant York 1941; The Pride of the Yankees 1942; For Whom the Bell Tolls 1943; Casanova Brown 1944; The Story of Dr Wassell 1944; Along Came Jones 1945; Saratoga Trunk 1945; Cloak and Dagger 1946; Unconquered 1947; Variety Girl 1947; Good Sam 1948; The Fountainhead 1949; It's a Great Feeling 1949; Task Force 1949; Bright Leaf 1950; Dallas 1950; Distant Drums 1951; You're in the Navy Now 1951; High Noon 1952; Springfield Rifle 1952; Blowing Wild 1953; Return to Paradise 1953; Garden of Evil 1954; Vera Cruz 1954; The Court-Martial of Billy Mitchell 1955; Friendly Persuasion 1956; Love in the Afternoon 1957; Man of the West 1958; Ten North Frederick 1958; Alias Jesse James 1959; The Hanging Tree 1959; They Came to Cordura 1959; The Wreck of the Mary Deare 1959; The Naked Edge 1961

Cooper (1), George (1892-1943) The Barker 1928; Lilac Time 1928; The Trail of '98 1929; Renegades 1930; Think Fast, Mr Moto 1937

Cooper (2), George (1920-) Crossfire 1947; Roughshod 1949

Cooper (3), George A (1925-) Violent Playground 1958; Hell Is a City 1959; Nightmare 1963; The Strange Affair 1968; The Rise and Rise of Michael Rimmer 1970

Cooper, Gladys (1888-1971) Kitty Foyle 1940; Rebecca 1940; The Black Cat 1941; The Gay Falcon 1941; That Hamilton Woman 1941; Now, Voyager 1942; This above All 1942; Mr Lucky 1943; The Song of Bernadette 1943; Mrs Parkington 1944; The White Cliffs of Dover 1944; Love Letters 1945; The Valley of Decision 1945; Beware of Pity 1946; The Green Years 1946; The Bishop's Wife 1947; Homecoming 1948; The Pirate 1948; Madame Bovary 1949; The Secret Garden 1949; Sons of the Musketeers 1951; Thunder on the Hill 1951; The Man Who Loved Redheads 1954; Separate Tables 1958; The List of Adrian Messenger 1963; My Fair Lady 1964; The Happiest Millionaire 1967; A Nice Girl like Me 1969

Cooper, Jackie (1922-2011) The Champ 1931; Skippy 1931; The Bowery 1933; Broadway to Hollywood 1933; Treasure Island 1934; The Devil Is a Sissy 1936; That Certain Age 1938; White Banners 1938; The Return of Frank James 1940; Ziegfeld Girl 1941; Men of Texas 1942; The Navy Comes Through 1942; Syncopation 1942; The Love Machine 1971; Chosen Survivors 1974; The Invisible Man 1975; Superman 1978; Superman II 1980; Superman III 1983; Superman IV: the Quest for Peace 1987; Surrender 1987

Cooper, Jeanne (1928-2013) The Man from the Alamo 1953; The Redhead from Wyoming 1953; Plunder Road 1957; The Intruder 1961; Black Zoo 1963; Kansas City Bomber 1972

Cooper, Jeff Born Losers 1967; The Silent Flute 1978

Cooper, Justin (1988-) Liar Liar 1997; Dennis the Menace Strikes Again 1998

Cooper, Maggie An Eye for an Eye 1981; Divorce Wars 1982

Cooper, Maxine (1924-2009) Kiss Me Deadly 1955; Autumn Leaves 1956

Cooper, Melanie The Little Polar Bear: the Mysterious Island 2005; A Turtle's Tale: Sammy's Adventures 2010

Cooper, Melville (1896-1973) The Great Garrick 1937; Tovarich 1937; The Adventures of Robin Hood 1938; The Dawn Patrol 1938; Blind Alley 1939; Rebecca 1940; Too Many Husbands 1940; The Lady Eve 1941; You Belong to Me 1941; Life Begins at 8.30 1942; Change of Heart 1943; Holy Matrimony 1943; The Immortal Sergeant 1943; Heartbeat 1946; 13 Rue Madeleine 1946; Love Happy 1949; Father of the Bride 1950; Let's Dance 1950; The Petty Girl 1950; The Underworld Story 1950; The King's Thief 1955; Bundle of Joy 1956; From the Earth to the Moon 1958

Cooper, Oliver Project X 2012; Runner Runner 2013

Cooper, Terence (1928-1997) Calculated Risk 1963; Sylvia 1984

Cooper, Tommy (1921-1984) And the Same to You 1960; The Plank 1967

Coote, Jonathan Razor Blade Smile 1998; The Last Horror Movie 2003

Coote, Robert (1909-1982) Blond Cheat 1938; Mr Moto's Last Warning 1938; Vigil in the Night 1940; The Commandos Strike at Dawn 1942; A Matter of Life and Death 1946; The Exile 1947; The Ghost and Mrs Muir 1947; Berlin Express 1948; The Elusive Pimpernel 1950; Soldiers Three 1951; Othello 1952; Scaramouche 1952; The Horse's Mouth 1958; Merry Andrew 1958; The League of Gentlemen 1960; A Man Could Get Killed 1966; The Cool Ones 1967; Prudence and the Pill 1968; Theatre of Blood 1973

Cope, Jason Bunny Chow: Know Thyself 2006; District 9 2009

Cope, Kenneth (1934-) Naked Fury 1959; The Damned 1961; Tomorrow at Ten 1962; Night of the Big Heat 1967; Carry On Matron 1972; Rentadick 1972; George and Mildred 1980; Captives 1994

Copeland, James aka **Copeland, Jimmy** (1923-2002) Innocents in Paris 1953; The Maggie 1953; Mask of Dust 1954

Copeland, Joan (1922-) Drums across the River 1954; So This Is Paris 1954; The Man from Bitter Ridge 1955; Man without a Star 1955; Tarantula 1955; A Day of Fury 1956; Raw Edge 1956; The Black Scorpion 1957

Copeland, Miles Bring On the Night 1985; Eat the Rich 1987

Copley, Peter (1915-2008) Golden Salamander 1949; The Sword and the Rose 1952; Victim 1961; King and Country 1964; The Knack... and How to Get It 1965

Copley, Sharlto (1973-) District 9 2009; The A-Team 2010; Elysium 2013; Old Boy 2013; Maleficent 2014; Chappie 2015; Hardcore Henry 2015

Copley, Teri (1961-) Transylvania Twist 1989; Brain Donors 1992

Copperfield, David Terror Train 1980; The Incredible Burt Wonderstone 2013

Coppola, Chris Beowulf 2007; Shadow 2009

Coppola, Francis Ford (1939-) Apocalypse Now 1979; Easy Riders, Raging Bulls 2003

Coppola, Sofia (1971-) Peggy Sue Got Married 1986; The Godfather Part III 1990; Star Wars Episode I: the Phantom Menace 1999

Corban, Teodor aka **Corban, Teo** 12:08 East of Bucharest 2005; Tales from the Golden Age 2009

Corbet, Brady (1988-) Thirteen 2003; Mysterious Skin 2004; Thunderbirds 2004; Funny Games US 2008; Martha Marcy May Marlene 2011; Simon Killer 2012; Clouds of Sils Maria 2014; Escobar: Paradise Lost 2014

Corbett, Glenn (1930-1993) The Crimson Kimono 1959; All the Young Men 1960; The Mountain Road 1960; Homicidal 1961; The Pirates of Blood River 1961; Shenandoah 1965; Guns in the Heather 1969; Chisum 1970; Dead Pigeon on Beethoven Street 1972

Corbett, Harry H (1925-1982) Floods of Fear 1958; Cover Girl Killer 1959; The Shakedown 1959; Ladies Who Do 1963; Sammy Going South 1963; What a Crazy World 1963; The Bargee 1964; Rattle of a Simple Man 1964; Joey Boy 1965; Carry On Screaming 1966; The Sandwich Man 1966; Crooks and Coronets 1969; The Magnificent Seven Deadly Sins 1971; Steptoe and Son 1972; Steptoe and Son Ride Again 1973; Percy's Progress 1974; Adventures of a Private Eye 1977; Jabberwocky 1977; Silver Dream Racer 1980

Corbett, John (1961-) Volcano 1997; Prancer Returns 2001; Serendipity 2001; My Big Fat Greek Wedding 2002; Elvis Has Left the Building 2004; Raise Your Voice 2004; Raising Helen 2004; Hunt for Justice 2005; The Messengers 2007; The Burning Plain 2008; November Christmas 2010; Ramona and Beezus 2010; The Boy Next Door 2015; My Big Fat Greek Wedding 2 2016

Corbett, Leonora (1907-1960) The Constant Nymph 1933; Under Your Hat 1940

Corbett, Ronnie (1930-2016) Top of the Form 1953; Rockets Galore 1958; Casino Royale 1967; Some Will, Some Won't 1969; The Rise and Rise of Michael Rimmer 1970; No Sex Please - We're British 1973; Fierce Creatures 1997; Burke & Hare 2010

Corbin, Barry (1940-) Stir Crazy 1980; Urban Cowboy 1980; Honkytonk Man 1982; Six Pack 1982; WarGames 1983; My Science Project 1985; Nothing in Common 1986; Who's Harry Crumb? 1989; Ghost Dad 1990; The Hot Spot 1990; Short Time 1990; Career Opportunities 1991; Curdled 1995; Formula for Death 1995; Solo 1996; Held Up 1999; Monte Walsh 2003; Hidden Places 2006; No Country for Old Men 2007

Corby, Ellen (1913-1999) I Remember Mama 1948; Caged 1950; Harriet Craig 1950; On Moonlight Bay 1951; Shane 1953; The Bowery Boys Meet the Monsters 1954; Illegal 1955; Macabre 1958; Vertigo 1958

Corcoran, Donna (1942-) Angels in the Outfield 1951; Don't Bother to Knock 1952; Million Dollar Mermaid 1952; Young Man with Ideas 1952; Dangerous When Wet 1953; Scandal at Scourie 1953

Corcoran, Kevin (1949-2015) Old Yeller 1957; The Shaggy Dog 1959; Swiss Family Robinson 1960; Toby Tyler, or Ten Weeks with a Circus 1960; Babes in Toyland 1961; A Tiger Walks 1964

Corcoran, Noreen (1943-2016) I Love Melvin 1953; Tanganyika 1954

Cord, Alex (1931-) Stagecoach 1966; The Brotherhood 1968; The Last Grenade 1970; Chosen Survivors 1974; Grayeagle 1977

Corday, Mara (1932-) Drums across the River 1954; So This Is Paris 1954; The Man from Bitter Ridge 1955; Man without a Star 1955; Tarantula 1955; A Day of Fury 1956; Raw Edge 1956; The Black Scorpion 1957

Corday, Rita aka **Croset, Paula** aka **Corday, Paula** (1920-1992) The Falcon and the Co-Eds 1943; The Falcon Strikes Back 1943; The Falcon in Hollywood 1944; The Body Snatcher 1945; The Falcon in San Francisco 1945; Dick Tracy vs Cueball 1946; The Falcon's Alibi 1946; The Exile 1947; The Sword of Monte Cristo 1951; Because You're Mine 1952; The Black Castle 1952

Corddry, Nathan aka **Corddry, Nate** The Nanny Diaries 2007; The Ugly Truth 2009; Yogi Bear 2010

Corddry, Rob (1971-) The Heartbreak Kid 2007; Harold & Kumar Escape from Guantanamo Bay 2008; What Happens in Vegas 2008; Hot Tub Time Machine 2010; Warm Bodies 2012; Escape from Planet Earth 2013; In a World... 2013; Hot Tub Time Machine 2 2014; Sex Tape 2014

Corden, James (1978-) All or Nothing 2002; Heroes and Villains 2006; The History Boys 2006; Starter for 10 2006; Lesbian Vampire Killers 2008; Telstar: the Joe Meek Story 2008; Animals United 2010; Begin Again 2013; One Chance 2013; Into the Woods 2014; Kill Your Friends 2015

Cordero, Joaquin (1926-2013) A Woman without Love 1951; The River and Death 1954

Cording, John One Day in the Life of Ivan Denisovich 1971; Ransom 1975

Corduner, Allan (1950-) Topsy-Turvy 1999; Kiss Kiss (Bang Bang) 2001; Food of Love 2002; Moonlight Mile 2002; De-Lovely 2004; The White Countess 2005; Defiance 2008; A Thousand Kisses Deep 2011; Florence Foster Jenkins 2016

Cordy, Annie (1928-) Rider on the Rain 1970; La Rupture 1970

Cordy, Raymond (1898-1956) A Nous la Liberté 1931; La Belle Equipe 1936; Les Belles de Nuit 1952

Corey, Isabelle (1939-2011) Bob Le Flambeur 1955; It Happened in Rome 1956

Corey, Jeff (1914-2002) My Friend Flicka 1943; Kidnapped 1948; City across the River 1949; Home of the Brave 1949; Roughshod 1949; The Next Voice You Hear 1950; Only the Valiant 1951; The Outriders 1950; The Prince Who Was a Thief 1951; Red Mountain 1951; The Balcony 1963; Lady in a Cage 1964; Mickey One 1965; Once a Thief 1965; Seconds 1966; In Cold Blood 1967; The Boston Strangler 1968; Butch Cassidy and the Sundance Kid 1969; True Grit 1969; Getting Straight 1970; Little Big Man 1970; They Call Me Mister Tibbs! 1970; Catlow 1971; Shoot Out 1971; Something Evil 1972; Butch and Sundance: the Early Days 1979; Bird on a Wire 1990; Surviving the Game 1994

Corey, Wendell (1914-1968) Desert Fury 1947; I Walk Alone 1947; The Search 1948; Sorry, Wrong Number 1948; The Accused 1949; Any Number Can Play 1949; The File on Thelma Jordon 1949; Holiday Affair 1949; The Furies 1950; Harriet Craig 1950; No Sad Songs for Me 1950; Rich, Young and Pretty 1951; Carbine Williams 1952; The Wild North 1952; Jamaica Run 1953; Rear Window 1954; The Big Knife 1955; The Bold and the Brave 1956; The Killer Is Loose 1956; The Rack 1956; The Rainmaker 1956; Loving You 1957; The Light in the Forest 1958; Alias Jesse James 1959; Waco 1966; Buckskin 1968

Corley, Annie (1952-) The Bridges of Madison County 1995; Box of Moonlight 1996; Free Willy 3: the Rescue 1997; Here on Earth 2000; Monster 2003

Corley, Pat (1930-2006) The Black Marble 1980; Night Shift 1982; Against All Odds 1984; Calendar Girl Murders 1984

Corman, Maddie (1969-) The Adventures of Ford Fairlane 1990; My New Gun 1992; Mickey Blue Eyes 1999

Corman, Roger (1926-) War of the Satellites 1958; Cannonball 1976; The State of Things 1982; Scream 3 1999; Searchers 2.0 2007; Dinoshark 2010; Corman's World: Exploits of a Hollywood Rebel 2011

Cormie, Lee Darkness Falls 2003; December Boys 2007

Cornell, Ellie (1963-) Halloween 4: the Return of Michael Myers 1988; Halloween 5: the Revenge of Michael Myers 1989

Cornilliac, Clovis (1968-) A Very Long Engagement 2004; Le Serpent 2006; Asterix at the Olympic Games 2008; Paris 36 2008

Cornish, Abbie (1982-) The Monkey's Mask 2000; Somersault 2004; Candy 2005; A Good Year 2006; Elizabeth: the Golden Age 2007; Stop-Loss 2007; Bright Star 2009; Limitless 2011; Sucker Punch 2011; W.E. 2011; Seven Psychopaths 2012; RoboCop 2014; Solace 2015; Geostorm 2016

Cornthwaite, Robert (1917-2006) The Thing from Another World 1951; The War of the Worlds 1953; The Spirit of St Louis 1957; Ten Seconds to Hell 1959; Waterhole #3 1967

Cornwell, Judy (1942-) The Wild Racers 1968; Country Dance 1970; Every Home Should Have One 1970; Wuthering Heights 1970; Who Slew Auntie Roo? 1971; Santa Claus 1985; Persuasion 1995

Cornwell, Phil (1957-) Stella Street 2004; Alan Partridge: Alpha Papa 2013

Corr, Andrea (1974-) Evita 1996; The Magic Sword: Quest for Camelot 1997; The Boys & Girl from County Clare 2005

Corr, Ryan The Water Diviner 2014; Holding the Man 2015

Corradi, Nelly (1914-1968) La Signora di Tutti 1934; The Barber of Seville 1946

Corraface, Georges aka **Corraface, George** (1952-) Not without My Daughter 1991; Impromptu 1991; Christopher Columbus: the Discovery 1992; Escape from LA 1996

Corri, Adrienne (1930-2016) The Romantic Age 1949; The River 1951; The Kidnappers 1953; Lease of Life 1954; Behind the Headlines 1956; The Feminine Touch 1956; The Big Chance 1957; The Rough and the Smooth 1959; The Hellfire Club 1961; Corridors of Blood 1962; A Study in Terror 1965; The Viking Queen 1967; Moon Zero Two 1969; A Clockwork Orange 1971; Vampire Circus 1971; Madhouse 1974; Rosebud 1975

Corri, Nick Gotcha! 1985; Slaves of New York 1989; Candyman: Day of the Dead 1999

Corrieri, Sergio (1939-2008) I Am Cuba 1964; Memories of Underdevelopment 1968

Corrigan, Kevin (1969-) Zebrahead 1992; Walking and Talking 1996; Henry Fool 1997; Kicked in the Head 1997; Slums of Beverly Hills 1998; Lonesome Jim 2005; The Next Three Days 2010; Results 2015

Corrigan, Lloyd (1900-1969) The Ghost Breakers 1940; The Lady in Question 1940; The Great Man's Lady 1942; Hitler's Children 1943; Tarzan's

Desert Mystery 1943; Rosie the Riveter 1944; The Chase 1946; And Baby Makes Three 1949; Dancing in the Dark 1949; Cyrano de Bergerac 1950; My Friend Irma Goes West 1950; Sierra Passage 1950; When Willie Comes Marching Home 1950; Son of Paleface 1952; Marry Me Again 1953; The Bowery Boys Meet the Monsters 1954

Corrigan, Ray "Crash" (1902-1976) Hit the Saddle 1937; Overland Stage Raiders 1938; Red River Range 1938; Frontier Horizon 1939; It! The Terror from beyond Space 958

Corseaut, Aneta aka **Corsaut, Aneta** (1933-1995) The Blob 1958; The Toolbox Murders 1978

Corsini, Silvana Accattone 1961; Mamma Roma 1962

Cort, Bud (1950-) Brewster McCloud 1970; Gas-s-s-s, or It Became Necessary to Destroy the World in Order to Save It 1970; The Strawberry Statement 1970; Harold and Maude 1972; Why Shoot the Teacher 1976; She Dances Alone 1981; Love Letters 1983; Electric Dreams 1984; Maria's Lovers 1984; Love at Stake 1987; The Chocolate War 1988; Out of the Dark 1988; Brain Dead 1990; Going Under 1990; Theodore Rex 1995; But I'm a Cheerleader 1999; Dogma 1999; The Million Dollar Hotel 1999; Pollock 2000; South of Heaven, West of Hell 2000; The Life Aquatic with Steve Zissou 2004

Cortese, Joe (1949-) Death Collector 1976; Monsignor 1982; Ruby 1992; To Protect and Serve 1992; Against the Ropes 2003

Cortese, Valentina aka **Cortesa, Valentina** (1924-) Les Misérables 1946; Black Magic 1949; The Glass Mountain 1949; Malaya 1949; Thieves' Highway 1949; The House on Telegraph Hill 1951; The Secret People 1951; The Barefoot Contessa 1954; Le Amiche 1955; Magic Fire 1956; Barabbas 1961; Square of Violence 1961; The Visit 1964; The Legend of Lylah Clare 1968; First Love 1970; The Assassination of Trotsky 1972; Brother Sun, Sister Moon 1972; Day for Night 1973; The Adventures of Baron Munchausen 1988

Cortez, Julia The Adventures of Priscilla, Queen of the Desert 1994; Mighty Morphin Power Rangers: the Movie 1995

Cortez, Ricardo 1899-1977) The Pony Express 1925; The Torrent 1926; The Private Life of Helen of Troy 1927; The Younger Generation 1929; Bad Company 1931; Dangerous Female 1931; Illicit 1931; Flesh 1932; No One Man 1932; Symphony of Six Million 1932; Torch Singer 1933; Mandalay 1934; Wonder Bar 1934; Frisco Kid 1935; Special Agent 1935; The Case of the Black Cat 1936; The Walking Dead 1936; Mr Moto's Last Warning 1938; Charlie Chan in Reno 1939; The Locket 1946

Corti, Jesse Revenge 1990; Beauty and the Beast 1991

Cosby, Bill (1937-) Hickey and Boggs 1972; Uptown Saturday Night 1974; Let's Do It Again 1975; Mother, Jugs & Speed 1976; A Piece of the Action 1977; California Suite 1978; The Devil and Max Devlin 1981; Leonard, Part 6 1987; Ghost Dad 1990; The Meteor Man 1993; Jack 1996; Fat Albert 2004

Cosgrove, Daniel (1970-) They Crawl 2001; Van Wilder: Party Liaison 2002

Cosgrove, Douglas (1895-1944) Lucky Killer 1933; Winds of the Wasteland 1936

Cosgrove, Miranda (1993-) The School of Rock 2003; Despicable Me 2010; Despicable Me 2 2013; Despicable Me 3 2017

Cosmo, James (1948-) Stormy Monday 1987; Braveheart 1995; Trainspotting 1996; Emma 1996; Sunset Heights 1996; Urban Ghost Story 1998; The Match 1999; One More Kiss 1999; Honest 2000; All the Queen's Men 2001; To End All Wars 2001; Man Dancin' 2003; One Last Chance 2003; Greyfriars Bobby 2005; The Lives of the Saints 2005; Half Light 2006; The Dark Is Rising 2007; Donkeys 2010; No Saints for Sinners 2010; Outcast 2010; Citadel 2012; The Christmas Candle 2013; Hammer of the Gods 2013; Breakdown 2015; The Legend of Barney Thomson 2015; Whisky Galore 2016

Cossart, Ernest (1876-1951) The Scoundrel 1935; Desire 1936; The Great Ziegfeld 1936; Angel 1937; Lancer Spy 1937; The Light That Failed 1939; Never Say Die 1939; A Bill of Divorcement 1940; Kitty Foyle 1940; Knickerbocker Holiday 1944; Love from a Stranger 1947

Cossins, James (1933-1997) The Anniversary 1968; The Rise and Rise of Michael Rimmer 1970; Wuthering Heights 1970; Fear in the Night 1972

Costa-Gavras (1933-) Madame Rosa 1977; The Stupids 1995; Henri-Georges Clouzot's Inferno 2009

Costa, Mary (1930-) Marry Me Again 1953; The Big Caper 1957; Sleeping Beauty 1959; The Great Waltz 1972

Costanzo, Paulo (1978-) Road Trip 2000; 40 Days and 40 Nights 2002; Scorched 2002

Costanzo, Robert (1942-) The Lightship 1985; Man's Best Friend 1993; For Better or Worse 1995; In the Mix 2005

Costello, Anthony (1938-1983) Blue 1968; Night Moves 1975

Costello, Dolores aka **Barrymore, Dolores Costello** (1905-1979) When a Man Loves 1926; Little Lord Fauntleroy 1936; The Magnificent Ambersons 1942

Costello (1), Don (1901-1945) A-Haunting We Will Go 1942; Crime Doctor 1943; A Lady Takes a Chance 1943; The Whistler 1944

Costello, Elvis (1954-) Americathon 1979; No Surrender 1985; Straight to Hell 1987; Austin Powers: the Spy Who Shagged Me 1999

Costello, Helene (1903-1957) Don Juan 1926; Lights of New York 1928

Costello, Lou (1906-1959) Buck Privates 1941; Hold That Ghost 1941; In the Navy 1941; Keep 'Em Flying 1941; Pardon My Sarong 1942; Ride 'Em Cowboy 1942; Rio Rita 1942; Who Done It? 1942; Hit the Ice 1943; Abbott and Costello in Society 1944; Lost in a Harem 1944; Abbott and Costello in Hollywood 1945; Here Come the Co-Eds 1945; The Naughty Nineties 1945; Little Giant 1946; The Time of Their Lives 1946; Buck Privates Come Home 1947; Abbott and Costello Meet Frankenstein 1948; The Noose Hangs High 1948; Abbott and Costello Meet the Killer, Boris Karloff 1949; Africa Screams 1949; Abbott and Costello in the Foreign Legion 1950; Abbott and Costello Meet the Invisible Man 1951; Abbott and Costello Meet Captain Kidd 1952; Jack and the Beanstalk 1952; Lost in Alaska 1952; Abbott and Costello Go to Mars 1953; Abbott and Costello Meet Dr Jekyll and Mr Hyde 1953; Abbott and Costello Meet the Keystone Cops 1955; Abbott and Costello Meet the Mummy 1955; Dance with Me Henry 1956

Costello, Ward (1919-2009) The Gallant Hours 1960; MacArthur 1977; Return from Witch Mountain 1978

Coster-Waldau, Nikolaj aka **Waldau, Nikolaj** aka **Coster Waldau, Nikolaj** (1970-) Nightwatch 1994; Bent 1996; Enigma 2001; Wimbledon 2004; The Baker 2007; Blackthorn 2011; Headhunters 2011; Mama 2013; A Thousand Times Good Night 2013; The Other Woman 2014; A Second Chance 2014; Gods of Egypt 2016

Coster, Nicolas aka **Coster, Nicholas** (1934-) My Blood Runs Cold 1965; MacArthur 1977; The Big Fix 1978; Slow Dancing in the Big City 1978; The Electric Horseman 1979; Just You and Me, Kid 1979; Reds 1981; By Dawn's Early Light 1990

Coster, Ritchie The Tuxedo 2002; The Sentinel 2006

Costigan, George (1947-) Rita, Sue and Bob Too 1986; Shirley Valentine 1989; The Hawk 1992; Girls' Night 1997; Garage 2007

Costner, Kevin (1955-) Sizzle Beach, USA 1974; Chasing Dreams 1982; Night Shift 1982; Stacy's Knights 1983; Testament 1983; The Gunrunner 1984; American Flyers 1985; Fandango 1985; Silverado 1985; No Way Out 1986; The Untouchables 1987; Bull Durham 1988; Field of Dreams 1989; Dances with Wolves 1990; Revenge 1990; In Bed with Madonna 1991; JFK 1991; Robin Hood: Prince of Thieves 1991; The Bodyguard 1992; A Perfect World 1993; The War 1994; Wyatt Earp 1994; Waterworld 1995; Tin Cup 1996; The Postman 1997; Message in a Bottle 1998; For Love of the Game 1999; Play It to the Bone 2000; Thirteen Days 2000; 3000 Miles to Graceland 2000; Dragonfly 2002; Open Range 2003; Rumor Has It... 2005; The Upside of Anger 2005; The Guardian 2006; Mr Brooks 2007; Swing Vote 2008; The New Daughter 2009; The Company Men 2010; Jack Ryan: Shadow Recruit 2013; Man of Steel 2013; The Man Who Saved the World 2013; Draft Day 2014; Hollywood Banker 2014; 3 Days to Kill 2014; McFarland, USA 2015; Criminal 2016

Cothran Jr, John Jimmy Hollywood 1994; Black Snake Moan 2006

Cotillard, Marion (1975-) Taxi 1998; Taxi 2 2000; Big Fish 2003; Love Me If You Dare 2003; Innocence 2004; A Very Long Engagement 2004; A Good Year 2006; La Vie en Rose 2007; Nine 2009; Public Enemies 2009; Inception 2010; Little White Lies 2010; Contagion 2011; Midnight in Paris 2011; The Dark Knight Rises 2012; Rust and Bone 2012; Blood Ties 2013; The Immigrant 2013; Dior and I 2014; Two Days, One Night 2014; Macbeth 2015; Assassin's Creed 2016

Cotrona, D J Dear John 2010; GI Joe: Retaliation 2013

Cotten, Joseph (1905-1994) Too Much Johnson 1938; Citizen Kane 1941; Lydia 1941; Journey into Fear 1942; The Magnificent Ambersons 1942; Shadow of a Doubt 1942; Hers to Hold 1943; Gaslight 1944; I'll Be Seeing You 1944; Since You Went Away 1944; Love Letters 1945; Duel in the Sun 1946; The Farmer's Daughter 1946; Portrait of Jennie 1948; Beyond the Forest 1949; The Third Man 1949; Under Capricorn 1949; Walk Softly, Stranger 1949; September Affair 1950; Two Flags West 1950; Half Angel 1951; The Man with a Cloak 1951; Peking Express 1951; The Steel Trap 1952; Untamed Frontier 1952; Niagara 1953; Special Delivery 1955; Beyond the River 1956; The Killer Is Loose 1956; The Halliday Brand 1957; From the Earth to the Moon 1958; Touch of Evil 1958; The Angel Wore Red 1960; The Last Sunset 1961; Hush... Hush, Sweet Charlotte 1964; The Oscar 1966; Jack of Diamonds 1967; Petulia 1968; White Comanche 1968; Latitude Zero 1969; The Grasshopper 1970; Tora! Tora! 1970; The Abominable Dr Phibes 1971; City beneath the Sea 1971; Baron Blood 1972; A Delicate Balance 1973; F for Fake 1973; Soylent Green 1973; The Lindbergh Kidnapping Case 1976; Airport '77 1977; Twilight's Last Gleaming 1977; Heaven's Gate 1980; The Survivor 1981

Cottençon, Fanny (1957-) Golden Eighties 1986; Conversations with My Gardener 2006; Bright Days Ahead 2013

Cotterill, Chrissie (1955-) Scrubbers 1982; Nil by Mouth 1997; Underground 1998; Weak at Denise 2000

Cotterill, Ralph (1932-) The Chain Reaction 1980; The Survivor 1981; Burke and Wills 1985; Lorca and the Outlaws 1985; Bad Boy Bubby 1993

Cottet, Mia (1968-) Romy and Michele's High School Reunion 1997; The Tuxedo 2002

Cotton, Ben Cheating Fate 2007; Scar 2007

Cotton, Oliver (1944-) Oliver Twist 1982; Eleni 1985; Hiding Out 1987; Christopher Columbus: the Discovery 1992; The Innocent Sleep 1995; The Dancer Upstairs 2002

Cottrell, Mickey Paper Hearts 1993; Apt Pupil 1997

Coughlan, Marisa (1973-) Gossip 1999; Teaching Mrs Tingle 1999; Freddy Got Fingered 2001; Super Troopers 2001

Coulouris, George (1903-1989) The Lady in Question 1940; Citizen Kane 1941; Watch on the Rhine 1943; Between Two Worlds 1944; The Master Race 1944; Mr Skeffington 1944; None but the Lonely Heart 1944; Confidential Agent 1945; Hotel Berlin 1945; Lady on a Train 1945; A Song to Remember 1945; California 1946; Nobody Lives Forever 1946; The Verdict 1946; Where There's Life 1947; Sleep, My Love 1948; A Southern Yankee 1948; Appointment with Venus 1951; Outcast of the Islands 1951; Venetian Bird 1952; A Day to Remember 1953; The Heart of the Matter 1953; Duel in the Jungle 1954; Mask of Dust 1954; The Runaway Bus 1954; The Teckman Mystery 1954; The Big Money 1956; Tarzan and the Lost Safari 1956; Kill Me Tomorrow 1957; The Woman Eater 1957; Law and Disorder 1958; Son of Robin Hood 1958; The Boy Who Stole a Million 1960; Surprise Package 1960; Fury at Smugglers Bay 1961; The Crooked Road 1964; The Skull 1965; Arabesque 1966; Land Raiders 1969; Blood from the Mummy's Tomb 1971; The Final Programme 1973; Papillon 1973; Shout at the Devil 1976; The Long Good Friday 1979

Coulson, Bernie The Accused 1988; Eddie and the Cruisers II: Eddie Lives! 1989

Couper, Barbara (1903-1992) The Last Days of Dolwyn 1949; Paul Temple's Triumph 1950

Coupland, Diana (1930-2006) Spring and Port Wine 1969; The Twelve Chairs 1970; The Best Pair of Legs in the

Business 1972; Bless This House 1972; Operation Daybreak 1975

Courau, Clotilde (1969-) Map of the Human Heart 1992; The Pickle 1993; The Bait 1995; Deterrence 1999; Milk 1999; Almost Peaceful 2002; La Vie en Rose 2007

Courcel, Nicole (1930-) The Case of Dr Laurent 1957; Sundays and Cybèle 1962

Courcet, Richard Clubbed to Death 1996; Beau Travail 1999

Court, Hazel (1926-2008) Dreaming 1944; Carnival 1946; Gaiety George 1946; Meet Me at Dawn 1946; Holiday Camp 1947; Bond Street 1948; Ghost Ship 1952; Counterspy 1953; Behind the Headlines 1956; The Curse of Frankenstein 1957; The Man Who Could Cheat Death 1959; The Shakedown 1959; Doctor Blood's Coffin 1960; The Premature Burial 1962; The Raven 1963; The Masque of the Red Death 1964

Courtenay, Tom (1937-) The Loneliness of the Long Distance Runner 1962; Billy Liar 1963; Private Potter 1963; King and Country 1964; Doctor Zhivago 1965; King Rat 1965; Operation Crossbow 1965; The Night of the Generals 1966; The Day the Fish Came Out 1967; Otley 1968; Catch Me a Spy 1971; One Day in the Life of Ivan Denisovich 1971; I Heard the Owl Call My Name 1973; The Dresser 1983; Happy New Year 1987; Leonard, Part 6 1987; The Last Butterfly 1990; Let Him Have It 1991; The Boy from Mercury 1996; Whatever Happened to Harold Smith? 1999; Last Orders 2001; Nicholas Nickleby 2002; The Golden Compass 2007; Gambit 2012; Quartet 2012; Night Train to Lisbon 2013; The First Film 2015; 45 Years 2015; Dad's Army 2016

Courtland, Jerome (1926-2012) Together Again 1944; Kiss and Tell 1945; The Man from Colorado 1948; Battleground 1949; Tokyo Joe 1949; A Woman of Distinction 1950; Santa Fe 1951; Tonka 1958

Courtneidge, Cicely (1893-1980) The Ghost Train 1931; Aunt Sally 1933; The Perfect Gentleman 1935; Under Your Hat 1940; The L-Shaped Room 1962; Not Now Darling 1972

Courtney, Alex (1940-) Enter the Ninja 1981; Murder between Friends 1993

Courtney, Chuck aka **Courtney, Charles** (1930-2000) Teenage Monster 1958; Billy the Kid vs Dracula 1966

Courtney, Inez (1908-1975) Break of Hearts 1935; Beauty for the Asking 1939; The Shop around the Corner 1940

Courtney, Jai (1986-) Felony 2013; A Good Day to Die Hard 2013; I, Frankenstein 2013; Unbroken 2014; The Water Diviner 2014; Terminator: Genisys 2015; Suicide Squad 2016

Cousins, Christopher (1960-) Earth vs the Spider 2001; The Long Shot 2004; Legally Blondes 2008; William & Kate 2011

Covert, Allen aka **Covert, Alan** (1964-) Bulletproof 1996; Happy Gilmore 1996; The Wedding Singer 1998; Big Daddy 1999; Little Nicky 2000; 50 First Dates 2004; Strange Wilderness 2007

Cowan, Elliot Hammer of the Gods 2013; Narcopolis 2014

Cowan, Jerome (1897-1972) Beloved Enemy 1936; New Faces of 1937 1937; Shall We Dance 1937; Vogues of 1938 1937; There's Always a Woman 1938; East Side of Heaven 1939; The Gracie Allen Murder Case 1939; The Saint Strikes Back 1939; Castle on the Hudson 1940; Torrid Zone 1940; Victory 1940; Affectionately Yours 1941; The Great Lie 1941; Kiss the Boys Goodbye 1941; The Maltese Falcon 1941; A Gentleman at Heart 1942; Moontide 1942; Guest in the House 1944; Fog Island 1945; Deadline at Dawn 1946; My Reputation 1946; Cry Wolf 1947; Dangerous Years 1947; Miracle on 34th Street 1947; Riff-Raff 1947; The Unfaithful 1947; So This Is New York 1948; Always Leave Them Laughing 1949; Dallas 1950; The Fuller Brush Girl 1950; Young Man with a Horn 1950; Have Rocket, Will Travel 1959; All in a Night's Work 1960; Black Zoo 1963; The Gnome-Mobile 1967

Coward, Noël (1899-1973) Hearts of the World 1918; The Scoundrel 1935; In Which We Serve 1942; The Astonished Heart 1949; Around the World in 80 Days 1956; Our Man in Havana 1959; Surprise Package 1960; Paris When It Sizzles 1964; Bunny Lake Is Missing 1965; Boom 1968; The Italian Job 1969

Cowl, Jane (1884-1950) Once More, My Darling 1949; No Man of Her Own 1950; Payment on Demand 1951

Cowling, Bruce (1919-1986) Battleground 1949; The Stratton Story 1949; A Lady without Passport 1950; Cause for Alarm 1951; The Battle at Apache Pass 1952

Cowper, Nicola (1967-) Dreamchild 1985; Lionheart 1986; Journey to the Center of the Earth 1989

Cox, Alan (1970-) Young Sherlock Holmes 1985; Death of a Schoolboy 1990; Mrs Dalloway 1997

Cox, Alex (1954-) Dead Beat 1994; The Winner 1996; Perdita Durango 1997; Searchers 2.0 2007; The Oxford Murders 2008

Cox (1), Brian (1946-) In Celebration 1974; Manhunter 1986; Hidden Agenda 1990; Iron Will 1994; Prince of Jutland 1994; Rob Roy 1995; Chain Reaction 1996; The Glimmer Man 1996; The Long Kiss Goodnight 1996; The Boxer 1997; Kiss the Girls 1997; Desperate Measures 1998; Poodle Springs 1998; Rushmore 1998; Complicity 1999; The Corruptor 1999; For Love of the Game 1999; Mad about Mambo 1999; The Minus Man 1999; Saltwater 1999; A Shot at Glory 2000; Strictly Sinatra 2000; The Affair of the Necklace 2001; LIE 2001; The Reckoning 2001; Super Troopers 2001; Adaptation. 2002; The Bourne Identity 2002; The Ring 2002; The Rookie 2002; 25th Hour 2002; X2 2003; The Bourne Supremacy 2004; Troy 2004; Match Point 2005; Red Eye 2005; The Ringer 2005; The Flying Scotsman 2006; Running with Scissors 2006; Battle for Terra 2007; The Escapist 2007; Trick 'r Treat 2007; The Water Horse 2007; Zodiac 2007; Fantastic Mr Fox 2009; Coriolanus 2010; Ironclad 2010; Rise of the Planet of the Apes 2011; The Veteran 2011; Believe 2012; Blood 2012; The Campaign 2012; The Anomaly 2014; The Carer 2015; Forsaken 2015

Cox, Charlie (1982-) Dot the i 2003; William Shakespeare's The Merchant of Venice 2004; Casanova 2005; Stardust 2007; Stone of Destiny 2008; Glorious 39 2009; Hello Carter 2013; The Theory of Everything 2015

Cox, Courteney aka **Cox Arquette, Courteney** (1964-) Masters of the Universe 1987; Cocoon: the Return 1988; Ace Ventura: Pet Detective 1993; The Opposite Sex and How to Live with Them 1993; Commandments 1996; Scream 1996; Scream 2 1997; The Runner 1999; Scream 3 1999; The Shrink Is In 2000; 3000 Miles to Graceland 2000; Get Well Soon 2001; Barnyard 2006; The Tripper 2006; Zoom 2006; Bedtime Stories 2008; Scre4m 2011

Cox, Jennifer Elise (1973-) The Brady Bunch Movie 1995; Sometimes They Come Back... Again 1996; A Very Brady Sequel 1996

Cox, Julie (1973-) 20,000 Leagues under the Sea 1997; The War Bride 2001; King of Texas 2002; Second in Command 2006; The Oxford Murders 2008

Cox, Paul (1940-2016) Golden Braid 1991; Careful 1992

Cox, Ronny (1938-) Deliverance 1972; The Mind Snatchers 1972; Bound for Glory 1976; Gray Lady Down 1978; Harper Valley PTA 1978; The Onion Field 1979; Taps 1981; Beverly Hills Cop 1984; Vision Quest 1985; Beverly Hills Cop II 1987; RoboCop 1987; Captain America 1990; Loose Cannons 1990; Total Recall 1990; Scissors 1991; Murder at 1600 1997; Forces of Nature 1998; Angel in the Family 2004; Imagine That 2009; Beyond the Reach 2014

Cox, Tony (1958-) Bad Santa 2003; Date Movie 2006; The Warrior's Way 2010

Cox, Veanne Miss Firecracker 1989; Rodgers & Hammerstein's Cinderella 1997

Cox, Wally (1924-1973) State Fair 1962; Spencer's Mountain 1963; Fate Is the Hunter 1964; The Yellow Rolls-Royce 1964; The Bedford Incident 1965; Morituri 1965; The Boatniks 1970; The Barefoot Executive 1971

Coy, Johnny (1920-1973) Bring On the Girls 1945; Top Banana 1953

Coy, Jonathan (1953-) The Wolves of Willoughby Chase 1988; Conspiracy 2001

Coy, Walter (1909-1974) Barricade 1950; The Lusty Men 1952; Cult of the Cobra 1955

Coyle, Brendan The Last Bus Home 1997; I Could Read the Sky 1999; Conspiracy 2001

Coyle, Richard (1972-) The Libertine 2004; Prince of Persia: the Sands of

Time 2010; 5 Days of War 2011; W.E. 2011; Grabbers 2012; Pusher 2012

Coyote, Peter (1942-) Southern Comfort 1981; ET the Extra-Terrestrial 1982; Cross Creek 1983; Strangers Kiss 1983; Heartbreakers 1984; Jagged Edge 1985; The Legend of Billie Jean 1985; A Man in Love 1987; Outrageous Fortune 1987; Season of Dreams 1987; Heart of Midnight 1988; Unconquered 1989; Crooked Hearts 1991; Bitter Moon 1992; Kika 1993; That Eye, the Sky 1994; Moonlight and Valentino 1995; Unforgettable 1996; Sphere 1998; Two for Texas 1998; Execution of Justice 1999; Random Hearts 1999; Erin Brockovich 2000; Midwives 2001; Femme Fatale 2002; Northfork 2002; A Walk to Remember 2002; Bon Voyage 2003; Kursk: a Submarine in Troubled Waters 2004; Enron: the Smartest Guys in the Room 2005; Behind Enemy Lines II: Axis of Evil 2006; Dr Dolittle: Tail to the Chief 2008

Cozart, Cylk (1957-) White Men Can't Jump 1992; Conspiracy Theory 1997; Three to Tango 1999; 16 Blocks 2006

Crabbe, Larry "Buster" aka **Crabbe, Buster** aka **Crabbe, Larry** (1908-1983) Island of Lost Souls 1932; Tarzan the Fearless 1933; You're Telling Me! 1934; Flash Gordon 1936; Million Dollar Legs 1939; Sheriff of Sage Valley 1942; Arizona Raiders 1965; The Alien Dead 1980

Crabtree, Michael Tender Mercies 1982; Whore 1991

Craig, Alec (1878-1945) Vivacious Lady 1938; Sherlock Holmes and the Spider Woman 1944

Craig, Carolyn (1934-1970) Gunsight Ridge 1957; Apache Territory 1958; House on Haunted Hill 1958

Craig, Catherine (1915-2004) Here Come the Waves 1944; Appointment with Murder 1948

Craig, Daniel (1968-) The Power of One 1991; Love Is the Devil: Study for a Portrait of Francis Bacon 1998; Hotel Splendide 1999; The Trench 1999; I Dreamed of Africa 2000; Some Voices 2000; Lara Croft: Tomb Raider 2001; Road to Perdition 2002; Ten Minutes Older: the Cello 2002; The Mother 2003; Sylvia 2003; Enduring Love 2004; Layer Cake 2004; The Jacket 2005; Munich 2005; Casino Royale 2006; Infamous 2006; Renaissance 2006; The Golden Compass 2007; The Invasion 2007; Defiance 2008; Flashbacks of a Fool 2008; Quantum of Solace 2008; The Adventures of Tintin: the Secret of the Unicorn 2011; Cowboys & Aliens 2011; Dream House 2011; The Girl with the Dragon Tattoo 2011; One Life 2011; Everything or Nothing: the Untold Story of 007 2012; Skyfall 2012; Spectre 2015; Star Wars Episode VII: the Force Awakens 2015

Craig, Davina The Ghost Camera 1933; Dusty Ermine 1936; Sweeney Todd, the Demon Barber of Fleet Street 1936

Craig, Diane (1949-) Double Deal 1981; Travelling North 1986

Craig, Helen (1912-1986) The Snake Pit 1948; They Live by Night 1948

Craig, James (1912-1985) Kitty Foyle 1940; The Devil and Daniel Webster 1941; Seven Miles from Alcatraz 1942; Valley of the Sun 1942; The Heavenly Body 1943; The Human Comedy 1943; Lost Angel 1943; Kismet 1944; Marriage Is a Private Affair 1944; Our Vines Have Tender Grapes 1945; A Lady without Passport 1950; Side Street 1950; The Strip 1951; Hurricane Smith 1952; The Cyclops 1957; Shoot-Out at Medicine Bend 1957; Arizona Bushwhackers 1968

Craig, Michael (1928-) The Black Tent 1956; Eyewitness 1956; House of Secrets 1956; Yield to the Night 1956; Campbell's Kingdom 1957; High Tide at Noon 1957; Nor the Moon by Night 1958; Sea of Sand 1958; The Silent Enemy 1958; Life in Emergency Ward 10 1959; Sapphire 1959; Upstairs and Downstairs 1959; The Angry Silence 1960; Cone of Silence 1960; Doctor in Love 1960; Mysterious Island 1961; No My Darling Daughter 1961; A Pair of Briefs 1961; Payroll 1961; Captive City 1962; The Iron Maiden 1962; Life for Ruth 1962; Life at the Top 1965; Of a Thousand Delights 1965; Modesty Blaise 1966; Star! 1968; The Royal Hunt of the Sun 1969; Twinky 1969; Country Dance 1970; A Town Called Hell 1971; The Vault of Horror 1973; Ride a Wild Pony 1976; The Irishman 1978; Turkey Shoot 1981

Craig, Nell (1891-1965) Dr Kildare's Victory 1941; Dr Gillespie's New Assistant 1942; Dr Gillespie's Criminal Case 1943

Craig, Wendy (1934-) The Mind Benders 1963; The Servant 1963; The Nanny 1965; Just like a Woman 1966; I'll Never Forget What's 'Is Name 1967

Craig, Yvonne (1937-2015) The Gene Krupa Story 1959; The Young Land 1959; High Time 1960; By Love Possessed 1961; Kissin' Cousins 1964; Ski Party 1965; One of Our Spies Is Missing 1966; One Spy Too Many 1966

Craigie, Ingrid The Dead 1987; Da 1988

Crain, Jeanne (1925-2003) Home in Indiana 1944; In the Meantime, Darling 1944; Winged Victory 1944; Leave Her to Heaven 1945; State Fair 1945; Centennial Summer 1946; Margie 1946; Apartment for Peggy 1948; You Were Meant for Me 1948; The Fan 1949; A Letter to Three Wives 1949; Pinky 1949; Cheaper by the Dozen 1950; The Model and the Marriage Broker 1951; People Will Talk 1951; Belles on Their Toes 1952; O Henry's Full House 1952; Duel in the Jungle 1954; Gentlemen Marry Brunettes 1955; Man without a Star 1955; The Fastest Gun Alive 1956; The Joker Is Wild 1957; The Tattered Dress 1957; Guns of the Timberland 1960; Nefertite, Queen of the Nile 1961; Pontius Pilate 1961; Madison Avenue 1962; Skyjacked 1972

Cramer, Marc (1918-1988) Isle of the Dead 1945; Those Endearing Young Charms 1945

Cramer, Richard aka **Cramer, Rychard** (1889-1960) Pack Up Your Troubles 1932; Scram! 1932; Knight of the Plains 1939; Saps at Sea 1940

Crampton, Barbara (1962-) Re-Animator 1985; From Beyond 1986; Robot Wars 1993; Space Truckers 1996

Crane, Norma (1928-1973) Tea and Sympathy 1956; All in a Night's Work 1960; The Sweet Ride 1967; They Call Me Mister Tibbs! 1970; Fiddler on the Roof 1971

Crane, Richard (1918-1969) Happy Land 1943; None Shall Escape 1944; The Alligator People 1959

Cranham, Kenneth (1944-) Brother Sun, Sister Moon 1972; Joseph Andrews 1977; Dead Man's Folly 1986; Chocolat 1988; Hellbound: Hellraiser II 1988; Stealing Heaven 1988; Prospero's Books 1991; Under Suspicion 1991; Tale of a Vampire 1992; The Last Yellow 1999; The Most Fertile Man in Ireland 1999; Women Talking Dirty 1999; Gangster No 1 2000; Two Men Went to War 2002; Blackball 2003; Man Dancin' 2003; Layer Cake 2004; Trauma 2004; Flying Blind 2012; Closed Circuit 2013

Cranitch, Lorcan (1969-) Food of Love 1997; Dancing at Lughnasa 1998; Night Train 1998; Titanic Town 1998

Cranston, Bryan (1956-) Erotique 1994; Detachment 2011; Drive 2011; Larry Crowne 2011; The Lincoln Lawyer 2011; Argo 2012; Total Recall 2012; Cold Comes the Night 2013; Godzilla 2014; Trumbo 2015; All the Way 2016; The Infiltrator 2016; Kung Fu Panda 3 2016; Why Him? 2016

Crauchet, Paul (1920-2012) The Swimming Pool 1968; Army of Shadows 1969; Un Flic 1972; Burnt Barns 1973; La Gloire de Mon Père 1990; The King's Whore 1990

Cravat, Nick (1912-1994) The Flame and the Arrow 1950; The Crimson Pirate 1952; Run Silent Run Deep 1958; The Island of Dr Moreau 1977

Craven, Eddie (1909-1991) The Gilded Lily 1935; The Invisible Menace 1938

Craven, Frank (1875-1945) He Was Her Man 1934; Barbary Coast 1935; Small Town Girl 1936; You're Only Young Once 1938; Miracles for Sale 1939; City for Conquest 1940; Our Town 1940; Pittsburgh 1942; Son of Dracula 1943; Jack London 1944

Craven, Gemma (1950-) The Slipper and the Rose 1976; Wagner 1983; Double X: the Name of the Game 1991; The Mystery of Edwin Drood 1993; The Last Bus Home 1997

Craven, Matt (1956-) Happy Birthday to Me 1981; Jacob's Ladder 1990; K2 1991; Indian Summer 1993; Killer 1994; Crimson Tide 1995; Kingfish: a Story of Huey P Long 1995; Never Too Late 1996; Masterminds 1997; Varian's War 2000; The Life of David Gale 2003; The Statement 2003; Timeline 2003; The Clearing 2004; Assault on Precinct 13 2005

Craven, Wes (1939-2015) Wes Craven's New Nightmare 1994; Scream 1996; Going to Pieces: the Rise and Fall of the Slasher Film 2006

Crawford, Andrew (1917-1994) The Brothers 1947; Boys in Brown 1949; Diamond City 1949; Trottie True 1949; Morning Departure 1950

Crawford, Anne (1920-1956) Millions like Us 1943; Two Thousand Women 1944; They Were Sisters 1945; Bedelia 1946; Caravan 1946; The Master of Bankdam 1947; The Blind Goddess 1948; Daughter of Darkness 1948; Trio 1950; Thunder on the Hill 1951; Knights of the Round Table 1953; Mad about Men 1954

Crawford, Broderick (1911-1986) Woman Chases Man 1937; Beau Geste 1939; Eternally Yours 1939; The Real Glory 1939; Slightly Honorable 1939; Seven Sinners 1940; When the Daltons Rode 1940; The Black Cat 1941; Broadway 1942; Larceny, Inc 1942; Men of Texas 1942; Sin Town 1942; Black Angel 1946; Slave Girl 1947; The Time of Your Life 1948; All the King's Men 1949; Anna Lucasta 1949; A Kiss in the Dark 1949; Night unto Night 1949; Born Yesterday 1950; Convicted 1950; The Mob 1951; Last of the Comanches 1952; Lone Star 1952; Stop, You're Killing Me 1952; Down Three Dark Streets 1954; Human Desire 1954; Night People 1954; Big House, USA 1955; New York Confidential 1955; Not as a Stranger 1955; The Swindle 1955; Between Heaven and Hell 1956; The Fastest Gun Alive 1956; The Decks Ran Red 1958; Square of Violence 1961; Convicts Four 1962; The Castilian 1963; Up from the Beach 1965; Kid Rodelo 1966; The Oscar 1966; Terror in the Wax Museum 1973; The Private Files of J Edgar Hoover 1977; A Little Romance 1979; Harlequin 1980; Liar's Moon 1982

Crawford, Cindy (1966-) Fair Game 1995; Unzipped 1995; The Simian Line 2000

Crawford, Clayne (1978-) Swimfan 2002; A Walk to Remember 2002; A Love Song for Bobby Long 2004; The Baytown Outlaws 2012

Crawford, Joan (1908-1977) Sally, Irene and Mary 1925; Tramp, Tramp, Tramp 1926; The Unknown 1927; Our Dancing Daughters 1928; Hollywood Revue 1929; Our Modern Maidens 1929; Dance, Fools, Dance 1931; Laughing Sinners 1931; Possessed 1931; This Modern Age 1931; Grand Hotel 1932; Rain 1932; Dancing Lady 1933; Today We Live 1933; Chained 1934; Forsaking All Others 1934; Sadie McKee 1934; I Live My Life 1935; The Gorgeous Hussy 1936; Love on the Run 1936; The Bride Wore Red 1937; The Last of Mrs Cheyney 1937; Mannequin 1937; The Shining Hour 1938; The Ice Follies of 1939 1939; The Women 1939; Strange Cargo 1940; Susan and God 1940; When Ladies Meet 1941; A Woman's Face 1941; Reunion in France 1942; They All Kissed the Bride 1942; Above Suspicion 1943; Hollywood Canteen 1944; Mildred Pierce 1945; Humoresque 1946; Daisy Kenyon 1947; Possessed 1947; Flamingo Road 1949; It's a Great Feeling 1949; The Damned Don't Cry 1950; Harriet Craig 1950; Goodbye, My Fancy 1951; Sudden Fear 1952; This Woman Is Dangerous 1952; Torch Song 1953; Johnny Guitar 1954; Queen Bee 1955; Autumn Leaves 1956; The Story of Esther Costello 1957; The Best of Everything 1959; What Ever Happened to Baby Jane? 1962; The Caretakers 1963; Strait-Jacket 1963; I Saw What You Did 1965; Berserk 1967; The Karate Killers 1967; Trog 1970

Crawford, John (1926-2010) Floods of Fear 1958; Orders to Kill 1958; Hell Is a City 1959; Solomon and Sheba 1959; Piccadilly Third Stop 1960; The Impersonator 1962; Night Moves 1975; The Enforcer 1976; Outlaw Blues 1977

Crawford, Johnny (1946-) Village of the Giants 1965; El Dorado 1967

Crawford, Michael (1942-) A French Mistress 1960; The War Lover 1962; Two Left Feet 1963; The Knack... and How to Get It 1965; A Funny Thing Happened on the Way to the Forum 1966; How I Won the War 1967; The Jokers 1967; Hello, Dolly! 1969; The Games 1970; Hello - Goodbye 1970; Alice's Adventures in Wonderland 1972; Condorman 1981; Once upon a Forest 1992

Crawford, Rachael (1969-) When Night Is Falling 1995; Captive Heart 1996; The Man 2005

Crayne, Dani (1934-) Ain't Misbehavin' 1955; The Unguarded Moment 1956; Shoot-Out at Medicine Bend 1957

Craze, Michael (1942-1998) Two Left Feet 1963; Neither the Sea nor the Sand 1972; Satan's Slave 1976; Terror 1979

Créton, Lola Bluebeard 2009; Goodbye First Love 2011; Something in the Air 2012; Bastards 2013

Creed-Miles, Charlie (1972-) The Punk 1993; Nil by Mouth 1997; Essex Boys 1999; The Last Yellow 1999; Harry Brown 2009; Wild Bill 2011

Cregar, Laird (1916-1944) Hudson's Bay 1940; Blood and Sand 1941; Charley's Aunt 1941; I Wake Up Screaming 1941; The Black Swan 1942; Joan of Paris 1942; Rings on Her Fingers 1942; Ten Gentlemen from West Point 1942; Heaven Can Wait 1943; Hello, Frisco, Hello 1943; Holy Matrimony 1943; The Lodger 1944; Hangover Square 1945

Crehan, Joseph (1883-1966) Front Page Woman 1935; Special Agent 1935; Girls Can Play 1937; Meeting at Midnight 1944; Dick Tracy 1945; Dangerous Money 1946; Roadblock 1951

Cremer, Bruno (1929-2010) The Stranger 1967; The Flesh of the Orchid 1974; Une Histoire Simple 1978; Tenue de Soirée 1986; Under the Sand 2000

Cremieux, Henri (1896-1980) Orphée 1950; Le Testament d'Orphée 1960

Crenna, Richard (1926-2003) It Grows on Trees 1952; The Pride of St Louis 1952; John Goldfarb, Please Come Home 1964; The Sand Pebbles 1966; Wait until Dark 1967; Star! 1968; Marooned 1969; Midas Run 1969; Doctors' Wives 1970; Catlow 1971; The Deserter 1971; Red Sky at Morning 1971; Un Flic 1972; Double Indemnity 1973; Breakheart Pass 1976; Mayflower: the Pilgrims' Adventure 1979; Body Heat 1981; First Blood 1982; Table for Five 1983; The Flamingo Kid 1984; Passions 1984; Rambo: First Blood, Part II 1985; The Rape of Richard Beck 1985; Summer Rental 1985; Rambo III 1988; Leviathan 1989; Hot Shots! Part Deux 1993; Jade 1995; A Pyromaniac's Love Story 1995; Sabrina 1995; 20,000 Leagues under the Sea 1997; Wrongfully Accused 1998

Crew, Amanda (1986-) Sex Drive 2008; The Haunting in Connecticut 2009; Death & Life of Charlie St Cloud 2010; What If 2013; The Age of Adaline 2015

Crews, Laura Hope (1879-1942) Blind Adventure 1933; Ever in My Heart 1933; The Silver Cord 1933; The Age of Innocence 1934; Escapade 1935; Angel 1937; Camille 1937; Doctor Rhythm 1938; Gone with the Wind 1939; The Star Maker 1939; One Foot in Heaven 1941

Crews, Terry aka **Crews, Terry Alan** (1968-) The 6th Day 2000; Serving Sara 2002; Baadasssss! 2003; White Chicks 2004; Harsh Times 2005; Idiocracy 2006; Balls of Fury 2007; Norbit 2007; Street Kings 2008; Cloudy with a Chance of Meatballs 2 2013; Blended 2014

Crewson, Wendy (1956-) The Doctor 1991; Folks! 1992; The Good Son 1993; Corrina, Corrina 1994; The Santa Clause 1994; To Gillian on Her 37th Birthday 1996; Air Force One 1997; The Eighteenth Angel 1997; Gang Related 1997; Bicentennial Man 1999; Mercy 2000; The Santa Clause 2 2002; The Clearing 2004; Jack 2004; Eight Below 2005; Hunt for Justice 2005; Niagara Motel 2005; Away from Her 2006; The Covenant 2006; The Santa Clause 3: the Escape Clause 2006

Cribbins, Bernard (1928-) Make Mine a Million 1959; Tommy the Toreador 1959; Two Way Stretch 1960; The World of Suzie Wong 1960; The Best of Enemies 1961; The Girl on the Boat 1962; The Wrong Arm of the Law 1962; Carry On Jack 1963; Crooks in Cloisters 1963; The Mouse on the Moon 1963; Carry On Spying 1964; She 1965; You Must Be Joking! 1965; Daleks - Invasion Earth 2150 AD 1966; The Sandwich Man 1966; Casino Royale 1967; Don't Raise the Bridge, Lower the River 1968; The Railway Children 1970; Frenzy 1972; The Water Babies 1978; Carry On Columbus 1992; Blackball 2003

Crichlow, Lenora (1985-) Wilderness 2006; Fast Girls 2012; Electricity 2014

Crider, Missy aka **Crider, Melissa** (1974-) Desperate Justice 1993; A Boy Called Hate 1995; The Sex Monster 1998; Firefly 2001; Gigli 2003; Out of the Woods 2005

Crisham, Walter (1906-1985) No Orchids for Miss Blandish 1948; The Beachcomber 1954

Crisp, Donald (1880-1974) The Battle of the Sexes 1914; The Escape 1914; Broken Blossoms 1919; Don Q, Son of Zorro 1925; The Black Pirate 1926; Svengali 1931; Red Dust 1932; The Key 1934; The Little Minister 1934; What Every Woman Knows 1934; Mutiny on the Bounty 1935; The Charge of the Light Brigade 1936; Mary of Scotland 1936; The White Angel 1936; A Woman Rebels 1936; Confession 1937; The Life of Emile Zola 1937; Parnell 1937; That Certain Woman 1937; The Amazing Dr Clitterhouse 1938; The Dawn Patrol 1938; Jezebel 1938; Daughters Courageous 1939; Juarez 1939; The Oklahoma Kid 1939; The Old Maid 1939; The Private Lives of Elizabeth and Essex 1939; Wuthering Heights 1939; Brother Orchid 1940; City for Conquest 1940; Dr Ehrlich's Magic Bullet 1940; Knute Rockne - All American 1940; The Sea Hawk 1940; Dr Jekyll and Mr Hyde 1941; How Green Was My Valley 1941; The Battle of Midway 1942; The Gay Sisters 1942; Lassie Come Home 1943; The Adventures of Mark Twain 1944; National Velvet 1944; The Uninvited 1944; Son of Lassie 1945; The Valley of Decision 1945; Hills of Home 1948; Whispering Smith 1948; Challenge to Lassie 1949; Bright Leaf 1950; Home Town Story 1951; Prince Valiant 1954; The Long Gray Line 1955; The Man from Laramie 1955; The Last Hurrah 1958; Saddle the Wind 1958; Pollyanna 1960; Greyfriars Bobby 1961; Spencer's Mountain 1963

Crisp, Quentin (1908-1999) The Bride 1985; Orlando 1992; Naked in New York 1994; The Celluloid Closet 1995

Criss, Anthony "Treach" Jason's Lyric 1994; Today You Die 2005

Criss, Darren Glee: the 3D Concert Movie 2011; Girl Most Likely 2012; The Tale of the Princess Kaguya 2013

Cristal, Linda (1934-) Comanche 1956; The Last of the Fast Guns 1958; The Perfect Furlough 1958; The Alamo 1960; Two Rode Together 1961; Mr Majestyk 1974

Cristal, Perla (1937-) The Awful Dr Orlof 1962; White Comanche 1968

Cristofer, Michael (1945-) The Entertainer 1975; An Enemy of the People 1977; The Little Drummer Girl 1984

Crivello, Anthony Spellbinder 1988; Dillinger and Capone 1995

Crocker, Barry (1935-) The Adventures of Barry McKenzie 1972; Barry McKenzie Holds His Own 1974; Razzle Dazzle: a Journey into Dance 2006

Cromwell, James (1940-) The Man with Two Brains 1983; Explorers 1985; The Babe 1992; Babe 1995; Eraser 1996; The People vs Larry Flynt 1996; Star Trek: First Contact 1996; The Education of Little Tree 1997; LA Confidential 1997; Babe: Pig in the City 1998; Deep Impact 1998; Species II 1998; The Bachelor 1999; The General's Daughter 1999; The Green Mile 1999; RKO 281 1999; A Slight Case of Murder 1999; Snow Falling on Cedars 1999; Fail Safe 2000; Space Cowboys 2000; The Magnificent Ambersons 2001; Spirit: Stallion of the Cimarron 2002; The Sum of All Fears 2002; Blackball 2003; I, Robot 2004; The Longest Yard 2005; Wal-Mart: the High Cost of Low Price 2005; Becoming Jane 2006; The Queen 2006; Spider-Man 3 2007; W. 2008; Surrogates 2009; Secretariat 2010; The Artist 2011; Soldiers of Fortune 2012; Big Hero 6 2014

Cromwell, John (1888-1979) Top Secret Affair 1957; 3 Women 1977

Cromwell, Richard (1910-1960) Emma 1932; The Strange Love of Molly Louvain 1932; This Day and Age 1933; Life Begins at 40 1935; The Lives of a Bengal Lancer 1935; Poppy 1936; Jezebel 1938; The Villain Still Pursued Her 1940; Baby Face Morgan 1942

Cronauer, Gail Positive ID 1986; The Newton Boys 1998

Cronenberg, David (1943-) The Fly 1986; Nightbreed 1990; The Stupids 1995; To Die For 1995; Extreme Measures 1996; Last Night 1998; Jason X 2001

Cronin, Jeanette The Boys 1998; The Three Stooges 2000

Cronkite, Walter (1916-2009) We're Back! A Dinosaur's Story 1993; The US vs John Lennon 2006

Cronyn, Hume (1911-2003) Shadow of a Doubt 1942; The Cross of Lorraine 1943; Lifeboat 1944; The Seventh Cross 1944; The Sailor Takes a Wife 1945; The Green Years 1946; The Postman Always Rings Twice 1946; The Beginning or the End 1947; Brute Force 1947; People Will Talk 1951; Sunrise at Campobello 1960; Cleopatra 1963; Hamlet 1964; The Arrangement 1969; Gaily, Gaily 1969; There Was a Crooked Man... 1970; The Parallax View 1974; Honky Tonk Freeway 1981; Rollover 1981; The World According to Garp 1982; Impulse 1984; Brewster's Millions 1985; Cocoon 1985; *batteries not included 1987; Foxfire 1987; Cocoon: the Return 1988; Day One 1989; Broadway Bound 1991; Camilla

1993; The Pelican Brief 1993; Marvin's Room 1996; 12 Angry Men 1997

Crook, Mackenzie (1971-) Sex Lives of the Potato Men 2003; Churchill: the Hollywood Years 2004; William Shakespeare's The Merchant of Venice 2004; Pirates of the Caribbean: at World's End 2007; Three and Out 2008; Solomon Kane 2009; Ironclad 2010; The Adventures of Tintin: the Secret of the Unicorn 2011; In Secret 2013; One Chance 2013

Cropper, Linda Blackrock 1997; Passion 1999

Crosbie, Annette (1934-) Sky West and Crooked 1965; Follow Me 1971; The Slipper and the Rose 1976; Hawk the Slayer 1980; The Pope Must Die 1991; Leon the Pig Farmer 1992; Solitaire for 2 1994; Shooting Fish 1997; The Debt Collector 1999; Calendar Girls 2003

Crosby, Bing (1904-1977) The King of Jazz 1930; The Big Broadcast 1932; Going Hollywood 1933; She Loves Me Not 1934; We're Not Dressing 1934; The Big Broadcast of 1936 1935; Mississippi 1935; Anything Goes 1936; Pennies from Heaven 1936; Rhythm on the Range 1936; Waikiki Wedding 1937; Doctor Rhythm 1938; East Side of Heaven 1939; Paris Honeymoon 1939; The Star Maker 1939; Rhythm on the River 1940; Road to Singapore 1940; The Birth of the Blues 1941; Road to Zanzibar 1941; Holiday Inn 1942; My Favorite Blonde 1942; Road to Morocco 1942; Star Spangled Rhythm 1942; Dixie 1943; Going My Way 1944; Here Come the Waves 1944; The Princess and the Pirate 1944; The Bells of St Mary's 1945; Duffy's Tavern 1945; Out of This World 1945; Road to Utopia 1945; Blue Skies 1946; My Favorite Brunette 1947; Road to Rio 1947; Variety Girl 1947; Welcome Stranger 1947; The Emperor Waltz 1948; The Adventures of Ichabod and Mr Toad 1949; A Connecticut Yankee in King Arthur's Court 1949; Mr Music 1950; Riding High 1950; Here Comes the Groom 1951; The Greatest Show on Earth 1952; Just for You 1952; Road to Bali 1952; Little Boy Lost 1953; Scared Stiff 1953; The Country Girl 1954; White Christmas 1954; Anything Goes 1956; High Society 1956; Alias Jesse James 1959; Say One for Me 1959; High Time 1960; Let's Make Love 1960; Pepe 1960; The Road to Hong Kong 1962; Robin and the 7 Hoods 1964; Stagecoach 1966

Crosby, Bob (1913-1993) Let's Make Music 1940; The Singing Sheriff 1944; Two Tickets to Broadway 1951; Senior Prom 1958; The Five Pennies 1959

Crosby, Cathy Lee (1944-) The Dark 1979; The Real Howard Spitz 1998

Crosby, Denise (1957-) Miracle Mile 1989; Pet Sematary 1989; Max 1994; Jackie Brown 1997; Trekkies 1997

Crosby, Gary (1933-1995) Mardi Gras 1958; Holiday for Lovers 1959; Battle at Bloody Beach 1961 Girl Happy 1965

Crosby, Mary (1959-) The Ice Pirates 1984; Tapeheads 1988; Eating 1990

Crosby, Norm (1927-) Amore! 1993; Adam Sandler's Eight Crazy Nights 2003

Crosman, Henrietta (1861-1944) The Royal Family of Broadway 1930; Pilgrimage 1933; The Dark Angel 1935; The Moon's Our Home 1936; Personal Property 1937

Cross, Ben (1947-) Chariots of Fire 1981; The Assisi Underground 1985; Paperhouse 1988; The Unholy 1988; Live Wire 1992; The Ascent 1994; First Knight 1995; Temptress 1995; Turbulence 1997; 20,000 Leagues under the Sea 1997; The Order 2001; Exorcist: the Beginning 2004; Behind Enemy Lines II: Axis of Evil 2006; Species: the Awakening 2007; Star Trek 2009; William & Kate 2011

Cross (2), David (1964-) Eternal Sunshine of the Spotless Mind 2003; Curious George 2006; School for Scoundrels 2006; She's the Man 2006; Alvin and the Chipmunks 2007; I'm Not There. 2007; Kung Fu Panda 2008; Alvin and the Chipmunks: the Squeakquel 2009; Year One 2009; Megamind 2010; Alvin and the Chipmunks: Chipwrecked 2011; Kung Fu Panda 2 2011; Kill Your Darlings 2013

Cross, Harley (1978-) The Believers 1987; Cohen and Tate 1988; Stanley & Iris 1989; The Boy Who Cried Bitch 1991; Perdita Durango 1997; Shriek If You Know What I Did Last Friday the 13th 2000

Cross, Hugh (1925-1989) Just William's Luck 1947; William at the Circus 1948; Seven Days to Noon 1950

Cross, Joseph (1986-) Desperate Measures 1998; Jack Frost 1998; Wide Awake 1998; Running with Scissors 2006; Untraceable 2008

Cross, Kendall Flight 93 2006; White Noise: the Light 2006

Crothers, Scatman aka Crothers, Benjamin "Scatman" aka Crothers, Sherman "Scatman" (1910-1986) Meet Me at the Fair 1952; East of Sumatra 1953; The Sins of Rachel Cade 1960; Three on a Couch 1966; The Aristocats 1970; The King of Marvin Gardens 1972; Detroit 9000 1973; Black Belt Jones 1974; Friday Foster 1975; One Flew over the Cuckoo's Nest 1975; Silver Streak 1976; Stay Hungry 1976; The Cheap Detective 1978; Bronco Billy 1980; The Shining 1980; Zapped! 1982; Two of a Kind 1983; The Journey of Natty Gann 1985

Crouse, Lindsay (1948-) Between the Lines 1977; Slap Shot 1977; The Verdict 1982; Iceman 1984; Places in the Heart 1984; House of Games 1987; Communion 1989; Desperate Hours 1990; Being Human 1994; Out of Darkness 1994; Bye Bye Love 1995; The Indian in the Cupboard 1995; The Arrival 1996; If These Walls Could Talk 1996; The Juror 1996; Prefontaine 1997; Progeny 1998; The Insider 1999; Impostor 2001; Mr Brooks 2007

Crow, Ashley (1960-) The Good Son 1993; Little Big League 1994

Crowden, Graham (1922-2010) Leo the Last 1970; The Rise and Rise of Michael Rimmer 1970; The Road Builder 1971; Something to Hide 1971; Up the Chastity Belt 1971; The Ruling Class 1972; The Final Programme 1973; The Abdication 1974; The Little Prince 1974; Hardcore 1977; Britannia Hospital 1982; The Missionary 1982; The Company of Wolves 1984; Code Name: Emerald 1985; Possession 2002

Crowe, Eileen (1899-1978) The Plough and the Stars 1936; Hungry Hill 1946; The Rising of the Moon 1957

Crowe, Russell (1964-) Blood Oath 1990; Proof 1991; Spotswood 1991; Hammers over the Anvil 1992; Romper Stomper 1992; The Silver Brumby 1992; For the Moment 1994; The Quick and the Dead 1995; Rough Magic 1995; The Sum of Us 1995; Virtuosity 1995; Breaking Up 1996; No Way Back 1996; Heaven's Burning 1997; LA Confidential 1997; The Insider 1999; Mystery, Alaska 1999; Gladiator 2000; Proof of Life 2000; A Beautiful Mind 2001; Master and Commander: the Far Side of the World 2003; Cinderella Man 2005; A Good Year 2006; American Gangster 2007; Tenderness 2007; 3:10 to Yuma 2007; Body of Lies 2008; State of Play 2009; The Next Three Days 2010; Robin Hood 2010; The Man with the Iron Fists 2012; Les Misérables 2012; Broken City 2013; Man of Steel 2013; A New York Winter's Tale 2014; Noah 2014; The Water Diviner 2014; Fathers and Daughters 2015; The Nice Guys 2016; The Mummy 2017

Crowell, Josephine (1849-1932) Home, Sweet Home 1914; Intolerance 1916; Hearts of the World 1918; Hot Water 1924; Mantrap 1926

Crowley, Kathleen (1931-) The Female Jungle 1955; Showdown 1963; The Lawyer 1969

Crowley, Matt (1904-1983) The Mob 1951; April Love 1957

Crowley, Pat aka Crowley, Patricia (1929-) Forever Female 1953; Money from Home 1953; Red Garters 1954; The Square Jungle 1955; Hollywood or Bust 1956; There's Always Tomorrow 1956; Walk the Proud Land 1956; Key Witness 1960; The Wheeler Dealers 1963; To Trap a Spy 1966; The Biscuit Eater 1972

Croze, Marie-Josée (1970-) Maelström 2000; Ararat 2002; The Barbarian Invasions 2003; Tell No One 2006; The Diving-Bell and the Butterfly 2007

Crudup, Billy (1968-) Sleepers 1996; Inventing the Abbotts 1997; Noose 1997; The Hi-Lo Country 1998; Without Limits 1998; Jesus' Son 1999; Almost Famous 2000; Waking the Dead 2000; Charlotte Gray 2001; Princess Mononoke 2001; Big Fish 2003; Stage Beauty 2004; The Good Shepherd 2006; Mission: Impossible III 2006; Trust the Man 2006; Pretty Bird 2008; Public Enemies 2009; Watchmen 2009; Eat Pray Love 2010; Too Big to Fail 2011; Blood Ties 2013; The Longest Week 2014; The Stanford Prison Experiment 2015

Cruickshank, Andrew (1907-1988) Eye Witness 1956; There Was a Crooked Man 1960; El Cid 1961; Greyfriars Bobby 1961; We Joined the Navy 1962; Murder Most Foul 1964

Cruise, Tom (1962-) Endless Love 1981; Taps 1981; All the Right Moves 1983; Losin' It 1983; The Outsiders 1983; Risky Business 1983; Legend 1985; The Color of Money 1986; Top Gun 1986; Cocktail 1988; Rain Man 1988; Born on the Fourth of July 1989; Days of Thunder 1990; Far and Away 1992; A Few Good Men 1992; The Firm 1993; Interview with the Vampire: the Vampire Chronicles 1994; Jerry Maguire 1996; Mission: Impossible 1996; Eyes Wide Shut 1999; Magnolia 1999; Mission: Impossible 2 1999; Vanilla Sky 2001; Minority Report 2002; The Last Samurai 2003; Collateral 2004; War of the Worlds 2005; Mission: Impossible III 2006; Lions for Lambs 2007; Tropic Thunder 2008; Valkyrie 2008; Knight and Day 2010; Mission: Impossible - Ghost Protocol 2011; Jack Reacher 2012; Rock of Ages 2012; Oblivion 2013; Edge of Tomorrow 2014; Mission: Impossible - Rogue Nation 2016; Mena 2017; The Mummy 2017

Crumb, Robert Comic Book Confidential 1988; Crumb 1995

Crutchley, Jeremy The Mangler 1994; Out on a Limb 2005; Ask the Dust 2006

Crutchley, Rosalie (1920-1997) Take My Life 1947; Prelude to Fame 1950; The Sword and the Rose 1952; Miracle in Soho 1957; Seven Thunders 1957; A Tale of Two Cities 1957; Beyond This Place 1959; The Nun's Story 1959; No Love for Johnnie 1960; Greyfriars Bobby 1961; Girl in the Headlines 1963; The Haunting 1963; Wuthering Heights 1970; Blood from the Mummy's Tomb 1971; Creatures the World Forgot 1971; Who Slew Auntie Roo? 1971; And Now the Screaming Starts! 1973; The House in Nightmare Park 1973; Mahler 1974; The Fool 1990; Four Weddings and a Funeral 1994

Cruttenden, Abigail (1969-) P'Tang, Yang, Kipperbang 1982; Hideous Kinky 1998

Cruttwell, Greg Naked 1993; 2 Days in the Valley 1996; George of the Jungle 1997

Cruz, Ernesto Gómez (1933-) El Norte 1983; El Crimen del Padre Amaro 2002

Cruz, Lito (1941-) Sur 1987; La Amiga 1988

Cruz, Penélope (1974-) Belle Epoque 1992; Jamón, Jamón 1992; Live Flesh 1997; Open Your Eyes 1997; The Girl of Your Dreams 1998; The Hi-Lo Country 1998; If Only 1998; Talk of Angels 1998; All about My Mother 1999; All the Pretty Horses 2000; Waking Up in Reno 2000; Woman on Top 2000; Blow 2001; Captain Corelli's Mandolin 2001; Vanilla Sky 2001; Gothika 2003; Masked and Anonymous 2003; Don't Move 2004; Head in the Clouds 2004; Noel 2004; Chromophobia 2005; The Good Night 2005; Sahara 2005; Volver 2006; Elegy 2008; Vicky Cristina Barcelona 2008; Broken Embraces 2009; G-Force 2009; Nine 2009; Pirates of the Caribbean: on Stranger Tides 2011; To Rome with Love 2012; The Counsellor 2013; I'm So Excited 2013; ma ma 2015; Grimsby 2016; Zoolander 2 2016

Cruz, Raymond The Substitute 1996; From Dusk till Dawn II: Texas Blood Money 1999

Cruz, Wilson (1973-) All over Me 1996; Supernova 2000; Party Monster 2003

Cryer, Barry (1935-) A Little of What You Fancy 1968; Bloodbath at the House of Death 1983

Cryer, Jon (1965-) Pretty in Pink 1986; Dudes 1987; Hiding Out 1987; OC and Stiggs 1987; Superman IV: the Quest for Peace 1987; Penn & Teller Get Killed 1989; Hot Shots! 1991; Holy Man 1998; Shorts 2009

Crystal, Billy (1947-) Animalympics 1979; This Is Spinal Tap 1984; Running Scared 1986; The Princess Bride 1987; Throw Momma from the Train 1987; Memories of Me 1988; When Harry Met Sally... 1989; City Slickers 1991; Mr Saturday Night 1992; City Slickers II: the Legend of Curly's Gold 1994; Forget Paris 1995; Deconstructing Harry 1997; Fathers' Day 1997; My Giant 1998; The Adventures of Rocky & Bullwinkle 1999; Analyze This 1999; America's Sweethearts 2001; Monsters, Inc 2001; Analyze That 2002; Howl's Moving Castle 2004; Tooth Fairy 2009; Parental Guidance 2012; Small Apartments 2012; Monsters University 2013

Csokas, Marton (1966-) The Monkey's Mask 2000; Rain 2001; xXx 2002; Kangaroo Jack 2003; Asylum 2004; The Bourne Supremacy 2004; Aeonflux 2005; The Great Raid 2005; Kingdom of Heaven 2005; The Debt 2010; The Tree 2010; Abraham Lincoln: Vampire Hunter 2012; Dead Europe 2012; The Equalizer 2014; Loving 2016

Cucciolla, Riccardo (1932-1999) Grand Slam 1967; Un Flic 1972; Borsalino and Co 1974

Cucinotta, Maria Grazia (1969-) Il Postino 1994; The Day of the Beast 1995; Picking Up the Pieces 2000; The Rite 2011

Cudlitz, Michael Thirst 1998; Running Scared 2005

Cugat, Xavier (1900-1990) Holiday in Mexico 1946; A Date with Judy 1948; Neptune's Daughter 1949

Cuka, Frances (1936-) Henry VIII and His Six Wives 1972; The Attic: the Hiding of Anne Frank 1988; Oliver Twist 2005

Cukic, Dejan Just Another Love Story 2007; Easy Money 2010

Culkin, Kieran (1982-) Father of the Bride 1991; Nowhere to Run 1992; It Runs in the Family 1994; Father of the Bride Part 2 1995; The Mighty 1998; She's All That 1999; The Dangerous Lives of Altar Boys 2001; Igby Goes Down 2002; Lymelife 2008; Margaret 2008; Scott Pilgrim vs the World 2010; Wiener-Dog 2016

Culkin, Macaulay (1980-) Rocket Gibraltar 1988; Uncle Buck 1989; Home Alone 1990; Jacob's Ladder 1990; My Girl 1991; Only the Lonely 1991; Home Alone 2: Lost in New York 1992; George Balanchine's The Nutcracker 1993; The Good Son 1993; Getting Even with Dad 1994; The Pagemaster 1994; Richie Rich 1994; Party Monster 2003

Culkin, Michael Chicken 2015; Mortdecai 2015

Culkin, Rory (1989-) You Can Count on Me 1999; Igby Goes Down 2002; It Runs in the Family 2002; Signs 2002; Down in the Valley 2004; Mean Creek 2004; The Chumscrubber 2005; The Night Listener 2006; Lymelife 2008; Scre4m 2011; Electrick Children 2012

Cullen, Brett (1956-) By the Sword 1992; Leaving Normal 1992; Complex of Fear 1993; Prehysteria! 1993; Something to Talk About 1995; Life on Liberty Street 2004; Suburban Madness 2004; The Life before Her Eyes 2007; The Burning Plain 2008; Skateland 2010; The Guilt Trip 2013; The Shallows 2016

Cullen, Max (1940-) Sunday Too Far Away 1974; My Brilliant Career 1979; Hard Knocks 1980; Rough Diamonds 1994

Cullen, Peter Heidi's Song 1982; Winnie the Pooh's Most Grand Adventure 1997; The Tigger Movie 2000; Piglet's Big Movie 2003; Pooh's Heffalump Movie 2005

Cullen, Tom Weekend 2011; Desert Dancer 2014; Black Mountain Poets 2015

Culley, Frederick (1879-1942) Conquest of the Air 1936; The Four Feathers 1939; Uncensored 1942

Cullum, John (1930-) All the Way Home 1963; Held Up 1999; The Night Listener 2006

Cullum, John David aka Cullum, J D (1966-) Willy/Milly 1986; Ambition 1991

Culp, Robert (1930-2010) PT 109 1963; Sunday in New York 1963; Rhino! 1964; Bob & Carol & Ted & Alice 1969; Hannie Caulder 1971; Hickey and Boggs 1972; The Castaway Cowboy 1974; Inside Out 1975; Breaking Point 1976; The Great Scout & Cathouse Thursday 1976; Goldengirl 1979; National Lampoon's Movie Madness 1981; Calendar Girl Murders 1984; Turk 182! 1985; Big Bad Mama II 1987; The Pelican Brief 1993; Most Wanted 1997

Culp, Steven (1955-) Jason Goes to Hell: the Final Friday 1993; Thirteen Days 2000; The Emperor's Club 2002; Firehouse Dog 2006

Culver, Roland (1900-1984) French without Tears 1939; The Day Will Dawn 1942; The First of the Few 1942; Secret Mission 1942; Unpublished Story 1942; The Life and Death of Colonel Blimp 1943; English without Tears 1944; Give Us the Moon 1944; Dead of Night 1945; Perfect Strangers 1945; To Each His Own 1946; Wanted for Murder 1946; Down to Earth 1947; Singapore 1947; The Emperor Waltz 1948; Isn't It Romantic 1948; The Great Lover 1949; Trio 1950; Encore 1951; Hotel Sahara 1951; The Late Edwina Black 1951; Folly to Be Wise 1952; The Hour of 13 1952; Rough Shoot 1952; Betrayed 1954; The Man Who Loved Redheads 1954; The Teckman Mystery 1954; An Alligator Named Daisy 1955; The Ship That Died of Shame 1955; Touch and Go 1955; Safari 1956; The Hypnotist 1957; The Vicious Circle 1957; Next to No Time 1958; Rockets Galore 1958; A Pair of Briefs 1961; Term of Trial 1962; A Man Could Get Killed 1966; In Search of Gregory 1970; The Legend of Hell House 1973; The Mackintosh Man 1973

Cumberbatch, Benedict (1976-) Amazing Grace 2006; Starter for 10 2006; Atonement 2007; Creation 2009; Four Lions 2010; Third Star 2010; The Whistleblower 2010; Wreckers 2010; Tinker Tailor Soldier Spy 2011; War Horse 2011; The Hobbit: an Unexpected Journey 2012; August: Osage County 2013; The Fifth Estate 2013; The Hobbit: the Desolation of Smaug 2013; Star Trek into Darkness 2013; 12 Years a Slave 2013; The Hobbit: the Battle of the Five Armies 2014; The Imitation Game 2014; Penguins of Madagascar 2014; Black Mass 2015; Doctor Strange 2016; How the Grinch Stole Christmas 2017; Jungle Book: Origins 2018

Cumming, Alan (1965-) Black Beauty 1994; Circle of Friends 1995; Emma 1996; Buddy 1997; Romy and Michele's High School Reunion 1997; Spice World: the Movie 1997; Annie 1999; Eyes Wide Shut 1999; Plunkett & Macleane 1999; Titus 1999; Company Man 2000; The Flintstones in Viva Rock Vegas 2000; Get Carter 2000; The Anniversary Party 2001; Josie and the Pussycats 2001; SPYkids 2001; Nicholas Nickleby 2002; X2 2003; Son of the Mask 2004; Sweet Land 2005; Boogie Woogie 2009; Burlesque 2010; Jackboots on Whitehall 2010; The Smurfs 2011; Any Day Now 2012; Sir Billi 2012; Strange Magic 2015

Cumming, Dorothy (1899-1983) The King of Kings 1927; The Divine Woman 1928; Kitty 1928; Our Dancing Daughters 1928; The Wind 1928

Cummings, Constance (1910-2005) The Criminal Code 1930; American Madness 1932; Movie Crazy 1932; Night after Night 1932; Washington Merry-Go-Round 1932; Broadway through a Keyhole 1933; The Mind Reader 1933; Glamour 1934; Looking for Trouble 1934; This Man Is Mine 1934; Remember Last Night? 1935; Seven Sinners 1936; Busman's Honeymoon 1940; The Foreman Went to France 1941; Blithe Spirit 1945; John and Julie 1955; The Intimate Stranger 1956; Battle of the Sexes 1960; Sammy Going South 1963; Dead Man's Folly 1986

Cummings, Jim (1953-) The Lion King 1994; Balto 1995; A Goofy Movie 1995; Winnie the Pooh's Most Grand Adventure 1997; The Road to El Dorado 2000; The Tigger Movie 2000; The Jungle Book 2 2003; Piglet's Big Movie 2003; Winnie the Pooh: Springtime with Roo 2004; Pooh's Heffalump Movie 2005; The Princess and the Frog 2009; Winnie the Pooh 2011

Cummings, Robert aka Cummings, Bob (1910-1990) So Red the Rose 1935; The Last Train from Madrid 1937; Souls at Sea 1937; Wells Fargo 1937; The Texans 1938; Three Smart Girls Grow Up 1939; The Devil and Miss Jones 1941; It Started with Eve 1941; Moon over Miami 1941; Kings Row 1942; Saboteur 1942; Flesh and Fantasy 1943; Princess O'Rourke 1943; The Bride Wore Boots 1946; The Chase 1946; Heaven Only Knows 1947; The Lost Moment 1947; Let's Live a Little 1948; Sleep, My Love 1948; The Accused 1949; Reign of Terror 1949; Tell It to the Judge 1949; For Heaven's Sake 1950; Paid in Full 1950; The Petty Girl 1950; Marry Me Again 1953; Dial M for Murder 1954; Lucky Me 1954; How to Be Very, Very Popular 1955; My Geisha 1962; Beach Party 1963; The Carpetbaggers 1964; What a Way to Go! 1964; Promise Her Anything 1966; Stagecoach 1966; Five Golden Dragons 1967

Cummins, Martin (1969-) Liberty Stands Still 2002; Murder at the Presidio 2005; I Dream of Murder 2006

Cummins, Peggy (1925-) English without Tears 1944; The Late George Apley 1947; Moss Rose 1947; Green Grass of Wyoming 1948; Gun Crazy 1949; That Dangerous Age 1949; The Love Lottery 1953; Meet Mr Lucifer 1953; To Dorothy, a Son 1954; The March Hare 1956; Carry On Admiral 1957; Hell Drivers 1957; Night of the Demon 1957; The Captain's Table 1958; Dentist in the Chair 1960; Your Money or Your Wife 1960; In the Doghouse 1961

Cummins, Peter (1931-) Sunday Too Far Away 1974; Double Deal 1981; Kangaroo 1986

Cung Le Pandorum 2009; The Man with the Iron Fists 2012

Daddario, Matthew Breathe In 2013; Cabin Fever 2016

Daddo, Cameron A Kiss at Midnight 2008; Oliver's Ghost 2010

Dade, Frances (1910-1968) Grumpy 1930; Raffles 1930; Dracula 1931

Dafoe, Willem (1955-) The Loveless 1981; Streets of Fire 1984; To Live and Die in LA 1985; Platoon 1986; The Last Temptation of Christ 1988; Mississippi Burning 1988; Saigon 1988; Born on the Fourth of July 1939; Cry-Baby 1989; Triumph of the Spirit 1989; Wild at Heart 1990; Flight of the Intruder 1991; Light Sleeper 1991; Body of Evidence 1992; White Sands 1992; Faraway, So Close 1993; Clear and Present Danger 1994; Tom & Viv 1994; Victory 1995; Basquiat 1996; The English Patient 1996; Speed 2: Cruise Control 1997; Lulu on the Bridge 1998; New Rose Hotel 1998; The Boondock Saints 1999; eXistenZ 1999; American Psycho 2000; Animal Factory 2000; Shadow of the Vampire 2000; The Reckoning 2001; Auto Focus 2002; Spider-Man 2002; Finding Nemo 2003; Once upon a Time in Mexico 2003; The Clearing 2004; The Life Aquatic with Steve Zissou 2004; Overnight 2004; Manderlay 2005; xXx: the Next Level 2005; American Dreamz 2006; Inside Man 2006; Tales from Earthsea 2006; The Walker 2006; Fireflies in the Garden 2007; Mr Bean's Holiday 2007; Daybreakers 2008; Antichrist 2009; Cirque du Freak: the Vampire's Assistant 2009; Fantastic Mr Fox 2009; My Son, My Son, What Have Ye Done 2009; Farewell 2010; Miral 2010; The Hunter 2011; Joan Carter 2012; A Most Wanted Man 2013; Odd Thomas 2013; Out of the Furnace 2013; The Fault in Our Stars 2014; Nymphomaniac Vol II 2014; Pasolini 2014

Daggett, Jensen Friday the 13th Part VIII: Jason Takes Manhattan 1989; Project ALF 1996

Dagover, Lil (1897-1980) The Cabinet of Dr Caligari 1919; The Spiders 1919; Destiny 1921; Tartuffe 1926; Congress Dances 1931; The Pedestrian 1974

Dahl, Arlene (1924-) My Wild Irish Rose 1947; A Southern Yankee 1948; Ambush 1949; Reign of Terror 1949; Scene of the Crime 1949; The Outriders 1950; Three Little Words 1950; Watch the Birdie 1950; Desert Legion 1953; The Diamond Queen 1953; Here Come the Girls 1953; Jamaica Run 1953; Woman's World 1954; Fortune Is a Woman 1956; Slightly Scarlet 1956; Journey to the Center of the Earth 1959; Kisses for My President 1964; Land Raiders 1969

Dahlbeck, Eva (1920-2008) Waiting Women 1952; Lesson in Love 1954; Dreams 1955; Smiles of a Summer Night 1955; So Close to Life 1957; The Counterfeit Traitor 1962; All These Women 1964; Les Créatures 1966

Daike, Yuko Kikujiro 1999; Zatoichi 2003

Dailey, Dan aka Dailey Jr, Dan (1914-1978) Lady Be Good 1941; Mother Wore Tights 1947; Chicken Every Sunday 1948; Give My Regards to Broadway 1948; When My Baby Smiles at Me 1948; You Were Meant for Me 1948; You're My Everything 1949; My Blue Heaven 1950; A Ticket to Tomahawk 1950; When Willie Comes Marching Home 1950; Call Me Mister 1951; I Can Get It for You Wholesale 1951; Meet Me at the Fair 1952; The Pride of St Louis 1952; What Price Glory? 1952; The Girl Next Door 1953; Taxi 1953; There's No Business like Show Business 1954; It's Always Fair Weather 1955; The Best Things in Life Are Free 1956; Meet Me in Las Vegas 1956; Oh, Men! Oh, Women! 1957; The Wayward Bus 1957; The Wings of Eagles 1957; Pepe 1960; Hemingway's Adventures of a Young Man 1962; The Private Files of J Edgar Hoover 1977

Daily, Elizabeth aka Daily, E G (1962-) Wacko 1981; The Escape Artist 1982; One Dark Night 1982; Valley Girl 1983; Fandango 1985; Pee-wee's Big Adventure 1985; Dogfight 1991; Driving Me Crazy 1991; Babe: Pig in the City 1998; The Rugrats Movie 1998; Rugrats in Paris: the Movie 2000; The Powerpuff Girls 2002; Rugrats Go Wild 2003

Dainton, Patricia (1930-) The Dancing Years 1949; Paul Temple Returns 1952; Tread Softly 1952; No Road Back 1957; The Passionate Stranger 1957; The Third Alibi 1961

Dalban, Max (1903-1960) Boudu, Saved from Drowning 1932; Toni 1935

Dalbert, Suzanne (1927-1970) The Accused 1949; Target Unknown 1951; The 49th Man 1953

D'Albie, Julian (1892-1978) The Gay Adventure 1949; The Lady with the Lamp 1951

Dale, Esther (1885-1961) Crime without Passion 1934; Curly Top 1935; Private Worlds 1935; The Wedding Night 1935; The Awful Truth 1937; Condemned Women 1938; Blackmail 1939; Unfinished Business 1941; Dangerously They Live 1942; Margie 1946; Smoky 1946; The Unfinished Dance 1947; Holiday Affair 1949; Ma and Pa Kettle 1949

Dale, James Badge (1978-) Shame 2011; The Grey 2012; The Lone Ranger 2013; World War Z 2013; The Walk 2015; 13 Hours: the Secret Soldiers of Benghazi 2016

Dale, Jennifer (1955-) Ticket to Heaven 1981; Of Unknown Origin 1983; The Adjuster 1991; Whale Music 1994

Dale, Jim (1935-) Raising the Wind 1961; Carry On Cabby 1963; Carry On Cleo 1964; Carry On Spying 1964; The Big Job 1965; Carry On Cowboy 1965; Carry On - Don't Lose Your Head 1966; Carry On Screaming 1966; The Winter's Tale 1966; Carry On Follow That Camel 1967; The Plank 1967; Carry On Doctor 1968; Carry On Again Doctor 1969; Lock Up Your Daughters! 1969; Adolf Hitler - My Part in His Downfall 1972; Digby, the Biggest Dog in the World 1973; The National Health 1973; Joseph Andrews 1977; Pete's Dragon 1977; Hot Lead and Cold Feet 1978; The Spaceman and King Arthur 1979; Carry On Columbus 1992; Arthur Miller's The American Clock 1993; The Hunchback of Notre Dame 1997

Dale, Virginia (1917-1994) Buck Benny Rides Again 1940; Kiss the Boys Goodbye 1941; Holiday Inn 1942

Daley, Cass (1915-1975) The Fleet's In 1942; Riding High 1943; Out of This World 1945

Dalio, Marcel aka Dalio (1900-1983) Les Affaires Publiques 1934; La Grande Illusion 1937; La Règle du Jeu 1939; The Shanghai Gesture 1941; The Desert Song 1944; Snowbound 1948; On the Riviera 1951; Rich, Young and Pretty 1951; Black Jack 1952; Flight to Tangier 1953; Lucky Me 1954; Sabrina 1954; The Perfect Furlough 1958; Classe Tous Risques 1959; The Man Who Understood Women 1959; Can-Can 1960; Cartouche 1961; The List of Adrian Messenger 1963; How to Steal a Million 1966; The 25th Hour 1967; How Sweet It Is! 1968; La Bête 1975

Dalkowska, Ewa (1947-) A Year of the Quiet Sun 1984; Korczak 1990

Dall, Evelyn (1918-2010) King Arthur Was a Gentleman 1942; Miss London Ltd 1943; Time Flies 1944

Dall, John (1918-1971) The Corn Is Green 1945; Something in the Wind 1947; Another Part of the Forest 1948; Rope 1948; Gun Crazy 1949; Atlantis, the Lost Continent 1960

Dalle, Béatrice (1964-) Betty Blue 1986; Night on Earth 1992; Six Days, Six Nights 1994; Clubbed to Death 1996; The Blackout 1997; Trouble Every Day 2000; Time of the Wolf 2003; Clean 2004; The Intruder 2004

Dallesandro, Joe (1948-) Flesh 1968; Lonesome Cowboys 1968; Trash 1970; Heat 1972; Black Moon 1974; Blood for Dracula 1974; Flesh for Frankenstein 1974; Killer Nun 1978; Critical Condition 1987; Sunset 1988; Cry-Baby 1989; Guncrazy 1992; Wild Orchid 2: Two Shades of Blue 1992; Beefcake 1998; LA without a Map 1998; The Limey 1999

Dallimore, Maurice (1912-1973) The Three Stooges Go around the World in a Daze 1963; The Collector 1965

D'Aloja, Francesca Apartment Zero 1988; Hamam: the Turkish Bath 1996

Dalton, Abby (1935-) Rock All Night 1957; Viking Women and the Sea Serpent 1957; Stakeout on Dope Street 1958; The Plainsman 1966

Dalton, Audrey (1934-) My Cousin Rachel 1952; Titanic 1953; Casanova's Big Night 1954; Drum Beat 1954; Confession 1955; The Prodigal 1955; The Monster That Challenged the World 1957; This Other Eden 1959; Mr Sardonicus 1961

Dalton, Darren (1965-) Red Dawn 1984; Brotherhood of Justice 1986

Dalton, Timothy (1944-) The Lion in Winter 1968; Cromwell 1970; Wuthering Heights 1970; Mary, Queen of Scots 1971; Permission to Kill 1975; Agatha 1978; Sextette 1978; Flash Gordon 1980; Chanel Solitaire 1981; The Doctor and the Devils 1985; The Living Daylights 1987; Hawks 1988; Brenda Starr 1989; Licence to Kill 1989; The King's Whore 1990; Rocketeer 1991; Naked in New York 1994; The Beautician and the Beast 1997; Made

Men 1999; Bitter Suite 2000; Possessed 2000; American Outlaws 2001; Looney Tunes: Back in Action 2004; Tales from Earthsea 2006; Hot Fuzz 2007; The Tourist 2010; Toy Story 3 2010; Everything or Nothing: the Untold Story of 007 2012; Tinkerbell and the Secret of the Wings 2012

Daltrey, Roger (1944-) Lisztomania 1975; Tommy 1975; The Kids Are Alright 1978; The Legacy 1978; McVicar 1980; Mack the Knife 1989; Buddy's Song 1990; Teen Agent 1991; Lightning Jack 1994; Like It Is 1997; Best 1999; Dark Prince - the Legend of Dracula 2000; Lambert & Stamp 2014; The Ecstasy of Wilko Johnson 2015

Daly, Andrew Semi-Pro 2008; Yogi Bear 2010

Daly, Eileen Razor Blade Smile 1998; Sacred Flesh 2000; Cradle of Fear 2001; Messages 2007

Daly, James (1918-1978) The Young Stranger 1957; I Aim at the Stars 1960; Planet of the Apes 1967; The Big Bounce 1969

Daly, Mark (1887-1957) Doss House 1933; Command Performance 1937; Good Morning, Boys 1937

Daly, Timothy aka Daly, Tim (1956-) Diner 1982; Made in Heaven 1987; Spellbinder 1988; Year of the Comet 1992; Denise Calls Up 1995; Dr Jekyll and Ms Hyde 1995; The Associate 1996; The Object of My Affection 1998; Execution of Justice 1999; A House Divided 2000; The Outsider 2001; Against the Ropes 2003; Basic 2003

Daly, Tyne (1946-) John and Mary 1969; The Entertainer 1975; The Enforcer 1976; Telefon 1977; Cagney & Lacey 1981; Zoot Suit 1981; The Aviator 1985; Movers and Shakers 1985; Absence of the Good 1999; Execution of Justice 1999; The Simian Line 2000

Damas, Bertila Fires Within 1991; Nothing but Trouble 1991

d'Amboise, Jacques (1934-) Seven Brides for Seven Brothers 1954; The Best Things in Life Are Free 1956; Off Beat 1986

Damici, Nick In the Cut 2003; Stake Land 2010

Damiens, François JCVD 2008; Heartbreaker 2010; Delicacy 2011; La Famille Bélier 2014; The Brand New Testament 2015; Les Cowboys 2015

Damita, Lili (1901-1994) The Cock-Eyed World 1929; Fighting Caravans 1931; Friends and Lovers 1931; This Is the Night 1932; Frisco Kid 1935

Damon, Cathryn (1930-1987) How to Beat the High Cost of Living 1980; Who Will Love My Children? 1983

Damon, Gabriel (1976-) The Land before Time 1988; RoboCop 2 1990; Iron Maze 1991

Damon, Mark (1933-) Between Heaven and Hell 1956; The Fall of the House of Usher 1960; This Rebel Breed 1960; Beauty and the Beast 1962; Black Sabbath 1963; Requiescant 1967; Anzio 1968

Damon, Matt (1970-) School Ties 1992; Geronimo: an American Legend 1993; Glory Daze 1995; The Good Old Boys 1995; Chasing Amy 1996; Courage under Fire 1996; Good Will Hunting 1997; John Grisham's The Rainmaker 1997; Rounders 1998; Saving Private Ryan 1998; Dogma 1999; The Talented Mr Ripley 1999; All the Pretty Horses 2000; The Legend of Bagger Vance 2000; Titan AE 2000; Gerry 2001; Jay and Silent Bob Strike Back 2001; Ocean's Eleven 2001; The Bourne Identity 2002; Spirit: Stallion of the Cimarron 2002; Jersey Girl 2003; Stuck on You 2003; The Bourne Supremacy 2004; EuroTrip 2004; Ocean's Twelve 2004; The Brothers Grimm 2005; Syriana 2005; The Departed 2006; The Good Shepherd 2006; The Bourne Ultimatum 2007; Ocean's Thirteen 2007; Che Part Two 2008; Margaret 2008; Ponyo 2008; The Informant! 2009; Invictus 2009; The Adjustment Bureau 2010; Green Zone 2010; Hereafter 2010; Inside Job 2010; True Grit 2010; Contagion 2011; Happy Feet Two 2011; We Bought a Zoo 2011; Promised Land 2012; Radioman 2012; Behind the Candelabra 2013; Elysium 2013; The Man Who Saved the World 2013; The Monuments Men 2013; The Zero Theorem 2013; Interstellar 2014; The Martian 2015; Jason Bourne 2016

Damone, Vic (1928-) Rich, Young and Pretty 1951; Athena 1954; Deep in My Heart 1954; Hit the Deck 1955; Kismet 1955; Hell to Eternity 1960

Damus, Mike (1979-) Lost in Yonkers 1993; A Pig's Tale 1994

Dan, Reiko (1935-2003) When a Woman Ascends the Stairs 1960; Sanjuro 1962

Dana, Leora (1923-1983) 3:10 to Yuma 1957; Change of Habit 1969; Wild Rovers 1971; Amityville III: the Demon 1983

Danare, Malcolm (1962-) The Curse 1987; Popcorn 1991

Dance, Charles (1946-) For Your Eyes Only 1981; Plenty 1985; The Golden Child 1986; Good Morning, Babylon 1987; White Mischief 1987; Pascali's Island 1986; Alien³ 1992; Century 1993; Last Action Hero 1993; China Moon 1994; Michael Collins 1996; Space Truckers 1996; Hilary and Jackie 1998; What Rats Won't Do 1998; Don't Go Breaking My Heart 1999; Dark Blue World 2001; Gosford Park 2001; Ali G indahouse 2002; Black and White 2002; Swimming Pool 2002; Scoop 2006; Starter for 10 2006; The Contractor 2007; Ironclad 2010; Your Highness 2010; St George's Day 2012; Underworld: Awakening 2012; Dracula Untold 2014; The Imitation Game 2014; Despite the Falling Snow 2016; Me before You 2016

Dancy, Hugh (1975-) Black Hawk Down 2001; Ella Enchanted 2004; King Arthur 2004; Shooting Dogs 2005; Basic Instinct 2: Risk Addiction 2006; Blood and Chocolate 2006; Evening 2007; The Jane Austen Book Club 2007; Savage Grace 2007; Adam 2009; Confessions of a Shopaholic 2009; The Wildest Dream 2009; Hysteria 2011; Martha Marcy May Marlene 2011; Our Idiot Brother 2011; Legends of Oz: Dorothy's Return 2013

D'Andrea, Tom (1909-1998) Humoresque 1946; Dark Passage 1947; Fighter Squadron 1948; Silver River 1948; Tension 1949; The Next Voice You Hear 1950

Dandridge, Dorothy (1923-1965) Lady from Louisiana 1941; Sun Valley Serenade 1941; Sundown 1941; Ride 'Em Cowboy 1942; Change of Heart 1943; Atlantic City 1944; Tarzan's Peril 1951; Bright Road 1953; Remains to Be Seen 1953; Carmen Jones 1954; Island in the Sun 1957; The Decks Ran Red 1958; Porgy and Bess 1959; Moment of Danger 1960; The Murder Men 1961

Dane, Eric Adrift 2006; Wedding Wars 2006; Marley & Me 2008

Dane, Karl (1886-1934) The Big Parade 1925; La Bohème 1926; The Scarlet Letter 1926; The Son of the Sheik 1925; The Trail of '98 1929; The Big House 1930; Billy the Kid 1930

Dane, Lawrence (1937-) Find the Lady 1976; Bear Island 1979; Running 1979; Head On 1980; Scanners 1980; Happy Birthday to Me 1981; Of Unknown Origin 1983; Mr and Mrs Loving 1993; Darkman II: the Return of Durant 1995; National Lampoon's Senior Trip 1995; Bride of Chucky 1998; Family Gathering 2010

Dane, Patricia aka Dane, Pat (1918-1995) Johnny Eager 1941; Life Begins for Andy Hardy 1941; Rio Rita 1942; I Dood It 1943; Are You with It? 1948

Daneman, Paul (1925-2001) Time without Pity 1957; Zulu 1963; Oh! What a Lovely War 1969

Danes, Claire (1979-) Little Women 1994; Home for the Holidays 1995; How to Make an American Quilt 1995; To Gillian on Her 37th Birthday 1996; William Shakespeare's Romeo + Juliet 1996; I Love You, I Love You Not 1997; John Grisham's The Rainmaker 1997; Les Misérables 1997; U Turn 1997; Polish Wedding 1998; Brokedown Palace 1999; The Mod Squad 1999; Princess Mononoke 2001; The Hours 2002; Igby Goes Down 2002; It's All about Love 2002; Terminator 3: Rise of the Machines 2003; Stage Beauty 2004; The Family Stone 2005; Shopgirl 2005; Evening 2007; The Flock 2007; Stardust 2007; Me and Orson Welles 2008; Temple Grandin 2010

Danese, Shera (1950-) Risky Business 1983; The Magic Bubble 1992

Danet, Jean (1924-2001) Diary of a Country Priest 1950; The Hunchback of Notre Dame 1956

D'Angelo, Angelo BMX Bandits 1983; The Big Steal 1990

D'Angelo, Beverly (1953-) First Love 1977; The Sentinel 1977; Every Which Way but Loose 1978; Hair 1979; Coal Miner's Daughter 1980; Honky Tonk Freeway 1981; Paternity 1981; National Lampoon's Vacation 1983; Finders Keepers 1984; Big Trouble 1985; National Lampoon's European Vacation 1985; Aria 1987; Maid to Order 1987; The Woo Woo Kid 1987; High Spirits 1988; Trading Hearts 1988;

Cold Front 1989; National Lampoon's Christmas Vacation 1989; Daddy's Dyin'... Who's Got the Will? 1990; The Miracle 1990; The Pope Must Die 1991; Man Trouble 1992; The Switch 1993; Lightning Jack 1994; Eye for an Eye 1996; Desert Gamble 1996; Vegas Vacation 1997; American History X 1998; Lansky 1999; Sugar Town 1999; Battle for Terra 2007; The House Bunny 2008; Bounty Killer 2013; Vacation 2015

D'Angelo, Mirella (1956-) Tenebrae 1982; Hercules 1983; Apartment Zero 1988; Hard Men 1996

Dangerfield, Rodney (1921-2004) The Projectionist 1970; Caddyshack 1980; Easy Money 1983; Back to School 1986; Ladybugs 1992; Natural Born Killers 1994; Casper: a Spirited Beginning 1997; Little Nicky 2000

Dangler, Anita (1922-2000) Law and Disorder 1974; Slow Dancing in the Big City 1978; Hero at Large 1980

Dani (1944-) Day for Night 1973; Love on the Run 1979; Orchestra Seats 2005

Daniel, Brittany (1976-) Joe Dirt 2001; Broken Lizard's Club Dread 2004; White Chicks 2004; Skyline 2010

Daniel, Jennifer Kiss of the Vampire 1962; The Reptile 1966

Danieli, Isa Camorra 1985; Macaroni 1985

Daniell, Henry (1894-1963) Camille 1937; Madame X 1937; Holiday 1938; We Are Not Alone 1939; The Great Dictator 1940; The Philadelphia Story 1940; The Sea Hawk 1940; Sherlock Holmes and the Voice of Terror 1942; Jane Eyre 1943; Sherlock Holmes in Washington 1943; The Suspect 1944; The Body Snatcher 1945; The Woman in Green 1945; The Bandit of Sherwood Forest 1946; The Exile 1947; Song of Love 1947; Lust for Life 1956; Les Girls 1957; Mister Cory 1957; Witness for the Prosecution 1957; From the Earth to the Moon 1958; The Comancheros 1961; Madison Avenue 1962

Danielle, Suzanne (1957-) Carry On Emmannuelle 1978; Long Shot 1978; The Boys in Blue 1983

Daniels, Alex Cyborg 1989; Star Kid 1997

Daniels, Anthony (1946-) Star Wars Episode IV: a New Hope 1977; The Lord of the Rings 1978; Star Wars Episode V: the Empire Strikes Back 1980; Star Wars Episode VI: Return of the Jedi 1983; I Bought a Vampire Motorcycle 1989; Star Wars Episode I: the Phantom Menace 1999; Star Wars Episode II: Attack of the Clones 2002; Star Wars Episode III: Revenge of the Sith 2005; Star Wars: The Clone Wars 2008; The Lego Movie 2014; Star Wars Episode VII: the Force Awakens 2015

Daniels, Bebe (1901-1971) Male and Female 1919; Why Change Your Wife? 1920; Rio Rita 1929; Dangerous Female 1931; Counsellor-at-Law 1933; 42nd Street 1933; Life with the Lyons 1953; The Lyons in Paris 1955

Daniels, Ben (1964-) Beautiful Thing 1995; I Want You 1998; Madeline 1998; Passion in the Desert 1998; Fanny & Elvis 1999; Britannic 2000; Conspiracy 2001; Married/Unmarried 2001; Doom 2005; Locke 2014; Luna 2014

Daniels, Erin House of 1000 Corpses 2001; One Hour Photo 2001

Daniels Jr, Henry H (1919-1973) Meet Me in St Louis 1944; Bewitched 1945

Daniels, Jeff (1955-) Terms of Endearment 1983; Marie: a True Story 1985; The Purple Rose of Cairo 1985; Heartburn 1986; Something Wild 1986; The House on Carroll Street 1987; The Caine Mutiny Court-Martial 1988; Checking Out 1988; Sweet Hearts Dance 1988; Arachnophobia 1990; Love Hurts 1990; Welcome Home, Roxy Carmichael 1990; The Butcher's Wife 1991; Gettysburg 1993; Dumb and Dumber 1994; Speed 1994; Fly Away Home 1996; 101 Dalmatians 1996; 2 Days in the Valley 1996; Trial and Error 1997; Pleasantville 1998; My Favorite Martian 1999; Blood Work 2002; Gods and Generals 2002; The Hours 2002; I Witness 2003; Because of Winn-Dixie 2004; Imaginary Heroes 2004; Good Night, and Good Luck. 2005; The Squid and the Whale 2005; Infamous 2006; RV 2006; The Lookout 2007; Space Chimps 2008; State of Play 2009; Howl 2010; Looper 2012; Dumb and Dumber To 2014; The Martian 2015; Steve Jobs 2015; The Divergent Series: Allegiant 2016

Daniels, Mark (1916-1990) The Vanishing Virginian 1941; Candyman 1992

Daniels, Phil (1958-) The Class of Miss MacMichael 1978; Quadrophenia 1979; Scum 1979; Breaking Glass 1980;

Number One 1984; *The Bride* 1985; *Bad Behaviour* 1992; *Still Crazy* 1998; *Chicken Run* 2000; *Goodbye Charlie Bright* 2000; *Nasty Neighbours* 2000; *Free Jimmy* 2006; *Freebird* 2007; *Vinyl* 2012

Daniels (2), William (1927–) *Ladybug, Ladybug* 1963; *A Thousand Clowns* 1965; *The Graduate* 1967; *Two for the Road* 1967; *Marlowe* 1969; *The Parallax View* 1974; *Black Sunday* 1976; *Oh, God!* 1977; *The One and Only* 1978; *Sunburn* 1979; *The Blue Lagoon* 1980; *All Night Long* 1981; *Blind Date* 1987; *Her Alibi* 1989

Danielsen Lie, Anders *Reprise* 2006; *Oslo, August 31st* 2011

Daniely, Lisa (1930–2014) *Hindle Wakes* 1952; *Tiger by the Tail* 1955; *The Man in the Road* 1957

Danker, Eli *The Little Drummer Girl* 1984; *Impulse* 1990; *Upworld* 1992

Danner, Blythe (1944–) *Hearts of the West* 1975; *Futureworld* 1976; *The Great Santini* 1979; *Man, Woman and Child* 1983; *Guilty Conscience* 1985; *Brighton Beach Memoirs* 1986; *Another Woman* 1988; *Alice* 1990; *Mr and Mrs Bridge* 1990; *The Prince of Tides* 1991; *Husbands and Wives* 1992; *Leave of Absence* 1994; *Homage* 1995; *Napoleon* 1995; *To Wong Foo, Thanks for Everything, Julie Newmar* 1995; *The Myth of Fingerprints* 1996; *Mad City* 1997; *Forces of Nature* 1998; *No Looking Back* 1998; *The Proposition* 1998; *The Love Letter* 1999; *The Invisible Circus* 2000; *Meet the Parents* 2000; *Sylvia* 2003; *Howl's Moving Castle* 2004; *Meet the Fockers* 2004; *The Last Kiss* 2006; *Detachment* 2011; *What's Your Number?* 2011; *The Lucky One* 2012; *I'll See You in My Dreams* 2015

Danning, Sybil (1952–) *Death in the Sun* 1975; *God's Gun* 1977; *Battle beyond the Stars* 1980; *The Salamander* 1981; *Chained Heat* 1983; *Hercules* 1983; *Howling II: Your Sister Is a Werewolf* 1984; *Reform School Girls* 1986; *Warrior Queen* 1986; *Amazon Women on the Moon* 1987

Dano, Paul aka **Dano, Paul Franklin** (1984–) *L.I.E.* 2001; *The Emperor's Club* 2002; *The Girl Next Door* 2004; *Taking Lives* 2004; *The Ballad of Jack and Rose* 2005; *The King* 2005; *Fast Food Nation* 2006; *Little Miss Sunshine* 2006; *There Will Be Blood* 2007; *Gigantic* 2008; *Where the Wild Things Are* 2009; *Knight and Day* 2010; *Meek's Cutoff* 2010; *Being Flynn* 2012; *For Ellen* 2012; *Looper* 2012; *Ruby Sparks* 2012; *Prisoners* 2013; *12 Years a Slave* 2013; *Love & Mercy* 2014; *Youth* 2015; *Swiss Army Man* 2016

Dano, Royal (1922–1994) *Undercover Girl* 1950; *The Red Badge of Courage* 1951; *The Trouble with Harry* 1954; *Tension at Table Rock* 1956; *Crime of Passion* 1957; *Man in the Shadow* 1957; *Trooper Hook* 1957; *Man of the West* 1958; *Saddle the Wind* 1958; *Never Steal Anything Small* 1959; *Gunpoint* 1966; *Backtrack* 1969; *Cahill, United States Marshal* 1973; *Electra Glide in Blue* 1973; *Big Bad Mama* 1974; *The Wild Party* 1975; *Something Wicked This Way Comes* 1983; *Teachers* 1984; *House II: the Second Story* 1987; *Killer Klowns from Outer Space* 1988; *Once upon a Texas Train* 1988

Danova, Cesare (1926–1992) *Crossed Swords* 1954; *The Man Who Understood Women* 1959; *Tarzan, the Ape Man* 1959; *Tender Is the Night* 1961; *Cleopatra* 1963; *Viva Las Vegas* 1964; *Boy, Did I Get a Wrong Number* 1966; *Chamber of Horrors* 1966; *Che!* 1969; *Mean Streets* 1973; *Tentacles* 1977

Danson, Ted (1947–) *The Onion Field* 1979; *Once upon a Spy* 1980; *Body Heat* 1981; *Creepshow* 1982; *Little Treasure* 1985; *A Fine Mess* 1986; *Just between Friends* 1986; *Three Men and a Baby* 1987; *Cousins* 1989; *Dad* 1989; *Three Men and a Little Lady* 1990; *Made in America* 1993; *Getting Even with Dad* 1994; *Pontiac Moon* 1994; *Loch Ness* 1995; *Homegrown* 1998; *Jerry and Tom* 1998; *Saving Private Ryan* 1998; *Mumford* 1999; *Surviving Love* 2004; *Knights of the South Bronx* 2005; *The Moguls* 2005; *Mad Money* 2008; *Big Miracle* 2012

Dante, Joe (1946–) *Cannonball* 1976; *Sleepwalkers* 1992

Dante, Michael (1931–) *Westbound* 1959; *Seven Thieves* 1960; *Apache Rifles* 1964; *The Naked Kiss* 1964; *Arizona Raiders* 1965; *Willard* 1971; *Winterhawk* 1975; *Cage* 1989

Dantine, Helmut (1917–1982) *Edge of Darkness* 1943; *Northern Pursuit* 1943; *Passage to Marseille* 1944; *Hotel Berlin* 1945; *Stranger from Venus* 1954; *War*

and Peace 1956; *Tempest* 1959; *Bring Me the Head of Alfredo Garcia* 1974

Danton, Ray (1931–1992) *Chief Crazy Horse* 1955; *I'll Cry Tomorrow* 1955; *The Spoilers* 1955; *The Night Runner* 1957; *Too Much, Too Soon* 1958; *The Beat Generation* 1959; *The Big Operator* 1959; *Yellowstone Kelly* 1959; *Ice Palace* 1960; *The Rise and Fall of Legs Diamond* 1960; *A Majority of One* 1961

Danza, Tony (1951–) *Going Ape!* 1981; *Angels in the Outfield* 1994; *Deadly Whispers* 1995; *illtown* 1996; *12 Angry Men* 1997; *Don Jon* 2013

Danziger, Maia *The Magician of Lublin* 1979; *Dr Heckyl & Mr Hype* 1980

Dapkunaite, Ingeborga (1963–) *Burnt by the Sun* 1995; *War* 2002; *Kiss of Life* 2003

D'Arbanville, Patti aka **D'Arbanville-Quinn, Patti** (1951–) *Flesh* 1968; *Big Wednesday* 1978; *The Main Event* 1979; *Time after Time* 1979; *Modern Problems* 1981; *The Boys Next Door* 1985; *Real Genius* 1985; *Call Me* 1988; *Fresh Horses* 1988; *Wired* 1989; *The Fan* 1996; *Personal Velocity* 2001

Darbo, Patrika (1952–) *Daddy's Dyin'... Who's Got the Will?* 1990; *Leaving Normal* 1992; *The Vagrant* 1992

Darby, Kim (1947–) *Generation* 1969; *True Grit* 1969; *The Strawberry Statement* 1970; *The Grissom Gang* 1971; *Don't Be Afraid of the Dark* 1973; *The One and Only* 1978; *Better Off Dead* 1985; *Teen Wolf Too* 1987; *Halloween 6: the Curse of Michael Myers* 1995

Darby, Rhys *Yes Man* 2008; *The Boat That Rocked* 2009; *What We Do in the Shadows* 2014

Darc, Mireille (1938–) *Weekend* 1967; *Monte Carlo or Bust!* 1969; *The Tall Blond Man with One Black Shoe* 1972; *Man in the Trunk* 1973; *Someone Is Bleeding* 1974

Darcel, Denise (1925–2012) *Tarzan and the Slave Girl* 1950; *Westward the Women* 1951; *Young Man with Ideas* 1952; *Dangerous When Wet* 1953; *Vera Cruz* 1954

Darcey, Janine (1917–1993) *French without Tears* 1939; *Rififi* 1955

Darcy-Smith, Kieran *The Cave* 2005; *The Reef* 2010

D'Arcy, Alex aka **D'Arcy, Alexandre** aka **D'Arcy, Alexander** (1908–1996) *A Nous la Liberté* 1931; *The Awful Truth* 1937; *Topper Takes a Trip* 1939; *How to Marry a Millionaire* 1953; *Man on a Tightrope* 1953; *Fanny Hill: Memoirs of a Woman of Pleasure* 1964; *Blood of Dracula's Castle* 1967; *Dead Pigeon on Beethoven Street* 1972

D'Arcy, James (1975–) *The Trench* 1999; *Revelation* 2001; *Dot the i* 2003; *Master and Commander: the Far Side of the World* 2003; *Exorcist: the Beginning* 2004; *An American Haunting* 2005; *Age of Heroes* 2011; *Screwed* 2011; *W.E.* 2011; *Hitchcock* 2012; *Let's Be Cops* 2014; *Survivor* 2015

D'Arcy, Roy (1894–1969) *The Merry Widow* 1925; *La Bohème* 1926; *The Temptress* 1926; *The Last Warning* 1928

Darden, Severn (1929–1995) *The President's Analyst* 1967; *Model Shop* 1969; *The Hired Hand* 1971; *Conquest of the Planet of the Apes* 1972; *Battle for the Planet of the Apes* 1973; *Jackson County Jail* 1976; *Wanda Nevada* 1979; *In God We Trust* 1980; *Saturday the 14th* 1981; *The Telephone* 1988

Dare, John *Girl on Approval* 1962; *The Impersonator* 1962

Darien, Frank (1876–1955) *Bad Girl* 1931; *The Outlaw* 1943

Darin, Bobby (1936–1973) *Pepe* 1960; *Come September* 1961; *Too Late Blues* 1961; *Hell Is for Heroes* 1962; *If a Man Answers* 1962; *Pressure Point* 1962; *State Fair* 1962; *Captain Newman, MD* 1963; *That Funny Feeling* 1965; *Gunfight in Abilene* 1967; *Stranger in the House* 1967; *Happy Mother's Day... Love, George* 1973

Darin, Ricardo aka **Darín, Ricardo** (1957–) *Nine Queens* 2000; *Son of the Bride* 2001; *El Aura* 2005; *XXY* 2007; *The Secret in Their Eyes* 2009; *Carancho* 2010; *White Elephant* 2012

Dark, Christopher aka **Dark, Chris** (1920–1971) *Suddenly* 1954; *World without End* 1955; *Baby Face Nelson* 1957; *The Halliday Brand* 1957

Darling, Candy (1946–1974) *Flesh* 1968; *Women in Revolt* 1971

Darmon, Gérard (1948–) *Diva* 1981; *Les Princes* 1982; *Betty Blue* 1986; *The Tit and the Moon* 1994; *The Good Thief* 2002

Darnell, Linda (1921–1965) *Brigham Young* 1940; *Chad Hanna* 1940; *The*

Mark of Zorro 1940; *Star Dust* 1940; *Blood and Sand* 1941; *The Song of Bernadette* 1943; *Buffalo Bill* 1944; *It Happened Tomorrow* 1944; *Summer Storm* 1944; *Sweet and Lowdown* 1944; *Fallen Angel* 1945; *Hangover Square* 1945; *Anna and the King of Siam* 1946; *Centennial Summer* 1946; *My Darling Clementine* 1946; *Forever Amber* 1947; *Unfaithfully Yours* 1948; *Everybody Does It* 1949; *A Letter to Three Wives* 1949; *Slattery's Hurricane* 1949; *No Way Out* 1950; *The 13th Letter* 1950; *Two Flags West* 1950; *The Lady Pays Off* 1951; *Blackbeard the Pirate* 1952; *Island of Desire* 1952; *Second Chance* 1953; *This Is My Love* 1954; *Dakota Incident* 1956; *Zero Hour!* 1957

Darren, James (1936–) *The Brothers Rico* 1957; *Operation Mad Ball* 1957; *Gunman's Walk* 1958; *The Gene Krupa Story* 1959; *Gidget* 1959; *All the Young Men* 1960; *Because They're Young* 1960; *Let No Man Write My Epitaph* 1960; *The Guns of Navarone* 1961; *Diamond Head* 1962; *For Those Who Think Young* 1964

Darrieux, Danielle (1917–) *Club de Femmes* 1936; *Mayerling* 1936; *The Rage of Paris* 1938; *La Ronde* 1950; *Le Plaisir* 1951; *Rich, Young and Pretty* 1951; *5 Fingers* 1952; *Madame de...* 1953; *Le Rouge et le Noir* 1954; *Napoléon* 1955; *Alexander the Great* 1956; *The Greengage Summer* 1961; *Bluebeard* 1962; *The Young Girls of Rochefort* 1967; *The Scene of the Crime* 1986; *8 Women* 2001

Darro, Frankie (1917–1976) *The Mad Genius* 1931; *The Mayor of Hell* 1933; *No Greater Glory* 1934

Darroussin, Jean-Pierre (1953–) *L'Eau Froide* 1994; *Un Air de Famille* 1996; *A la Place du Coeur* 1998; *La Bûche* 1999; *La Ville Est Tranquille* 2000; *Red Lights* 2003; *A Very Long Engagement* 2004; *Conversations with My Gardener* 2006; *22 Bullets* 2010; *The Well Digger's Daughter* 2010; *Le Havre* 2011; *The Snows of Kilimanjaro* 2011; *Marius* 2012; *Fanny* 2013

Darrow, Barbara (1931–) *The Mountain* 1956; *Queen of Outer Space* 1958

Darrow, Henry (1933–) *The Invisible Man* 1975; *Losin' It* 1983; *Blue Heat* 1990; *A Girl like Me* 2006

Darrow, John (1907–1980) *The Racket* 1928; *Hell's Angels* 1930

Darrow, Tony *GoodFellas* 1990; *Small Time Crooks* 2000

Darvas, Lili (1906–1974) *Meet Me in Las Vegas* 1956; *Love* 1971

Darvi, Bella (1928–1971) *Hell and High Water* 1954; *The Racers* 1955

Darwell, Jane (1879–1967) *Tom Sawyer* 1930; *Bright Eyes* 1934; *Change of Heart* 1934; *The White Parade* 1934; *Curly Top* 1935; *Life Begins at 40* 1935; *Captain January* 1936; *The Country Doctor* 1936; *Craig's Wife* 1936; *Poor Little Rich Girl* 1936; *White Fang* 1936; *Love Is News* 1937; *Slave Ship* 1937; *Wife, Doctor and Nurse* 1937; *Little Miss Broadway* 1938; *Jesse James* 1939; *Brigham Young* 1940; *Chad Hanna* 1940; *The Grapes of Wrath* 1940; *Miracle on Main Street* 1940; *The Devil and Daniel Webster* 1941; *All through the Night* 1942; *The Battle of Midway* 1942; *The Ox-Bow Incident* 1943; *Tender Comrade* 1943; *Music in Manhattan* 1944; *I Live in Grosvenor Square* 1945; *Three Godfathers* 1948; *Red Canyon* 1949; *Caged* 1950; *The Daughter of Rosie O'Grady* 1950; *Wagonmaster* 1950; *The Lemon Drop Kid* 1951; *Affair with a Stranger* 1953; *The Bigamist* 1953; *Mary Poppins* 1964

Dary, René (1905–1974) *Honour among Thieves* 1954; *Goto, l'île d'Amour* 1968

Das, Nandita (1969–) *Fire* 1996; *Earth* 1998; *Provoked: a True Story* 2006; *Before the Rains* 2007

Dash, Stacey (1966–) *Moving* 1988; *Mo' Money* 1992; *Renaissance Man* 1994; *Clueless* 1995

Dassin, Jules aka **Vita, Perlo** (1911–2008) *Rififi* 1955; *Never on Sunday* 1960

Dasté, Jean (1904–1994) *Boudu, Saved from Drowning* 1932; *Zéro de Conduite* 1933; *L'Atalante* 1934; *La Vie Est à Nous* 1936; *La Grande Illusion* 1937; *La Guerre Est Finie* 1966; *The Green Room* 1978

Dauder, Jordi *Spectre* 2006; *The Monk* 2011

Dauphin, Claude (1903–1978) *English without Tears* 1944; *Le Plaisir* 1951; *April in Paris* 1952; *Casque d'Or* 1952; *Innocents in Paris* 1953; *Little Boy Lost* 1953; *The Quiet American* 1958; *The Full Treatment* 1961; *Tiara Tahiti* 1962; *Lady L* 1965; *Barbarella* 1967; *Two for*

the Road 1967; *Hard Contract* 1969; *The Madwoman of Chaillot* 1969; *Rosebud* 1975; *Madame Rosa* 1977; *Les Misérables* 1978

Davalos, Alexa (1982–) *The Chronicles of Riddick* 2004; *Surrender Dorothy* 2006; *Feast of Love* 2007; *Defiance* 2008; *Clash of the Titans* 2010

Davalos, Elyssa *The Apple Dumpling Gang Rides Again* 1979; *Herbie Goes Bananas* 1980

Davalos, Richard (1930–2016) *East of Eden* 1955; *The Sea Chase* 1955; *The Cabinet of Caligari* 1962

Davenport, Harry (1866–1949) *My Sin* 1931; *The Cowboy and the Lady* 1938; *The Hunchback of Notre Dame* 1939; *Made for Each Other* 1939; *All This, and Heaven Too* 1940; *Lucky Partners* 1940; *Too Many Husbands* 1940; *The Bride Came COD* 1941; *One Foot in Heaven* 1941; *That Uncertain Feeling* 1941; *Ten Gentlemen from West Point* 1942; *The Amazing Mrs Holliday* 1943; *Government Girl* 1943; *Princess O'Rourke* 1943; *Jack London* 1944; *Kismet* 1944; *Meet Me in St Louis* 1944; *The Thin Man Goes Home* 1944; *Pardon My Past* 1945; *This Love of Ours* 1945; *Claudia and David* 1946; *Courage of Lassie* 1946; *Lady Luck* 1946; *The Bachelor and the Bobby-Soxer* 1947; *For the Love of Mary* 1948; *That Lady in Ermine* 1948; *Three Daring Daughters* 1948; *Down to the Sea in Ships* 1949; *The Forsyte Saga* 1949; *Tell It to the Judge* 1949

Davenport, Jack (1973–) *Talos the Mummy* 1997; *The Wisdom of Crocodiles* 1998; *The Talented Mr Ripley* 1999; *The Bunker* 2001; *Pirates of the Caribbean: the Curse of the Black Pearl* 2003; *The Libertine* 2004; *The Wedding Date* 2004; *Pirates of the Caribbean: Dead Man's Chest* 2006; *Pirates of the Caribbean: at World's End* 2007; *Mother's Milk* 2012; *Kingsman: The Secret Service* 2015; *A United Kingdom* 2016

Davenport, Madison *The Sitter* 2007; *Love Will Keep Us Together* 2010; *The Possession* 2012; *Sisters* 2015

Davenport, Nigel (1928–2013) *Lunch Hour* 1962; *Ladies Who Do* 1963; *The Third Secret* 1964; *Sands of the Kalahari* 1965; *A Man for All Seasons* 1966; *Sebastian* 1968; *Play Dirty* 1969; *The Royal Hunt of the Sun* 1969; *Sinful Davey* 1969; *The Virgin Soldiers* 1969; *The Mind of Mr Soames* 1970; *No Blade of Grass* 1970; *The Last Valley* 1971; *Mary, Queen of Scots* 1971; *Villain* 1971; *Living Free* 1972; *Phase IV* 1973; *Dracula* 1974; *The Island of Dr Moreau* 1977; *Stand Up Virgin Soldiers* 1977; *Zulu Dawn* 1979; *Chariots of Fire* 1981; *Nighthawks* 1981; *A Christmas Carol* 1984; *Greystoke: the Legend of Tarzan, Lord of the Apes* 1984; *Caravaggio* 1986; *Without a Clue* 1988

Davey-Fitzpatrick, Seamus *The Omen* 2006; *Before Midnight* 2013

Davey, Belinda *Death of a Soldier* 1985; *Proof* 1991

Davi, Robert (1951–) *The Goonies* 1985; *Raw Deal* 1986; *Action Jackson* 1988; *Licence to Kill* 1989; *Maniac Cop 2* 1990; *Peacemaker* 1990; *Christopher Columbus: the Discovery* 1992; *Wild Orchid 2: Two Shades of Blue* 1992; *Quick* 1993; *Son of the Pink Panther* 1993; *Cops and Robbersons* 1994; *Showgirls* 1995; *The Hot Chick* 2002; *In the Mix* 2005; *Everything or Nothing: the Untold Story of 007* 2012

Davich, Jacob *The Adventures of Sharkboy and Lavagirl* 2005; *Mr Woodcock* 2007

David, Alki *Flight of Fury* 2007; *The Bank Job* 2008

David, Angel *The Crow* 1994; *Two Girls and a Guy* 1997

David, Clifford *The Last Mile* 1959; *The Party's Over* 1965; *Resurrection* 1980

David, Eleanor (1956–) *Pink Floyd – The Wall* 1982; *The Scarlet Pimpernel* 1982; *Comfort and Joy* 1984; *Sylvia* 1984; *84 Charing Cross Road* 1986; *The Wolves of Willoughby Chase* 1988; *London Kills Me* 1991

David, Joanna (1947–) *Anna Karenina* 1985; *Secret Friends* 1991; *Cotton Mary* 1999

David, Keith (1954–) *The Thing* 1982; *Platoon* 1986; *Bird* 1988; *Saigon* 1988; *They Live* 1988; *Always* 1989; *Marked for Death* 1990; *Men at Work* 1990; *Article 99* 1992; *Final Analysis* 1992; *The Last Outlaw* 1993; *The Puppet Masters* 1994; *Clockers* 1995; *Dead Presidents* 1995; *Johns* 1995; *Executive Target* 1996; *Flipping* 1996; *Don King: Only in America* 1997; *Volcano* 1997; *Armageddon* 1998; *Pitch Black* 1999; *Requiem for a Dream* 2000; *Where the Heart Is* 2000; *Final Fantasy: the*

Spirits Within 2001; *Novocaine* 2001; *Agent Cody Banks* 2003; *Head of State* 2003; *Hollywood Homicide* 2003; *The Chronicles of Riddick* 2004; *Mr & Mrs Smith* 2005; *The Transporter 2* 2005; *Behind Enemy Lines II: Axis of Evil* 2006; *Coraline* 2008; *First Sunday* 2008; *All about Steve* 2009; *The Princess and the Frog* 2009; *The Nice Guys* 2016

David, Larry (1947–) *Whatever Works* 2009; *The Three Stooges* 2012; *Clear History* 2013

David, Mario (1930–1996) *Les Bonnes Femmes* 1960; *L'Enfer* 1993

David, Michael *Let's Make Love* 1960; *The Fiercest Heart* 1961

David, Thayer (1927–1978) *A Time to Love and a Time to Die* 1958; *Journey to the Center of the Earth* 1959; *The Story of Ruth* 1960; *House of Dark Shadows* 1970; *Night of Dark Shadows* 1971; *Savages* 1972; *Save the Tiger* 1973; *The Duchess and the Dirtwater Fox* 1976; *Rocky* 1976

Davidovich, Lolita (1961–) *Blaze* 1989; *The Inner Circle* 1991; *The Object of Beauty* 1991; *Leap of Faith* 1992; *Raising Cain* 1992; *Boiling Point* 1993; *Younger and Younger* 1993; *Cobb* 1994; *Intersection* 1994; *For Better or Worse* 1995; *Indictment: the McMartin Trial* 1995; *Jungle 2 Jungle* 1997; *Gods and Monsters* 1998; *Four Days* 1999; *Mystery, Alaska* 1999; *Play It to the Bone* 2000; *Dark Blue* 2002; *Hollywood Homicide* 2003; *Cinema Verite* 2011

Davidson, Holly *Food of Love* 1997; *Final Cut* 1998

Davidson, Jack *Shock Waves* 1975; *Baby It's You* 1983

Davidson, Jaye (1968–) *The Crying Game* 1992; *Stargate* 1994

Davidson, John (1886–1968) *The Happiest Millionaire* 1967; *The One and Only, Genuine, Original Family Band* 1968; *Airport '79: the Concorde* 1979; *The Squeeze* 1987

Davidson, Tommy (1965–) *Ace Ventura: When Nature Calls* 1995; *Booty Call* 1997; *Woo* 1998; *Bamboozled* 2000; *Santa Who?* 2000; *Black Dynamite* 2009

Davidtz, Embeth (1965–) *Army of Darkness* 1993; *Schindler's List* 1993; *Murder in the First* 1994; *Feast of July* 1995; *Matilda* 1996; *The Gingerbread Man* 1997; *Fallen* 1998; *Last Rites* 1998; *Simon Magus* 1998; *Bicentennial Man* 1999; *Mansfield Park* 1999; *Bridget Jones's Diary* 2001; *The Hole* 2001; *Thir13en Ghosts* 2001; *The Emperor's Club* 2002; *Junebug* 2004; *Fracture* 2007; *Fragments* 2008; *The Girl with the Dragon Tattoo* 2011; *The Amazing Spider-Man 2* 2014

Davies, Alan *Dog Eat Dog* 2000; *Angus, Thongs and Perfect Snogging* 2008

Davies, Betty Ann (1910–1955) *Play Up the Band* 1935; *It Always Rains on Sunday* 1947; *The History of Mr Polly* 1948; *The Passionate Friends* 1948; *Outcast of the Islands* 1951; *Cosh Boy* 1952; *Meet Me Tonight* 1952; *Grand National Night* 1953; *The Belles of St Trinian's* 1954

Davies, Brian *Convoy* 1978; *American Gigolo* 1980; *Masquerade* 1988

Davies, Jeremy (1969–) *Nell* 1994; *Spanking the Monkey* 1994; *Going All the Way* 1997; *A Secret Sin* 1997; *Saving Private Ryan* 1998; *Up at the Villa* 1998; *The Million Dollar Hotel* 1999; *Ravenous* 1999; *Secretary* 2001; *Solaris* 2002; *Dogville* 2003; *Rescue Dawn* 2006; *It's Kind of a Funny Story* 2010

Davies, John Howard (1939–2011) *Oliver Twist* 1948; *The Rocking Horse Winner* 1949; *Tom Brown's Schooldays* 1951

Davies, Marion (1897–1961) *The Patsy* 1928; *Show People* 1928; *Hollywood Revue* 1929; *The Bachelor Father* 1931; *Blondie of the Follies* 1932; *Polly of the Circus* 1932; *Going Hollywood* 1933; *Peg o' My Heart* 1933; *Operator 13* 1934; *Page Miss Glory* 1935; *Cain and Mabel* 1936

Davies, Morgana *The Tree* 2010; *The Hunter* 2011

Davies (2), Richard (1926–2015) *Please Sir!* 1971; *Blue Blood* 1973

Davies, Rudi *The Lonely Passion of Judith Hearne* 1987; *Resurrected* 1989; *Frankie Starlight* 1995

Davies, Rupert (1916–1976) *The Traitor* 1957; *The Criminal* 1960; *The Uncle* 1965; *The Spy Who Came In from the Cold* 1965; *Five Golden Dragons* 1967; *Submarine X-1* 1967; *Curse of the Crimson Altar* 1968; *Dracula Has Risen from the Grave* 1968; *Witchfinder General* 1968; *The*

Night Visitor 1970; Zeppelin 1971; Frightmare 1974

Davies, Stephen Inserts 1975; Dillinger and Capone 1995

Davies, Windsor (1930–) Adolf Hitler – My Part in His Downfall 1972; Carry On Behind 1975; Carry On England 1976; Confessions of a Driving Instructor 1976; Not Now, Comrade 1976; Old Scores 1991

Davion, Alexander aka **Davion, Alex** (1929–) Paranoiac 1963; The Plague of the Zombies 1965; Valley of the Dolls 1967; Incense for the Damned 1970

Davis, Altovise (1943–2009) Pipe Dreams 1976; Kingdom of the Spiders 1977

Davis, Bette (1908–1989) Bad Sister 1931; Waterloo Bridge 1931; Cabin in the Cotton 1932; Hell's House 1932; The Man Who Played God 1932; The Rich Are Always with Us 1932; So Big 1932; Three on a Match 1932; Ex-Lady 1933; 20,000 Years in Sing Sing 1933; Fashions of 1934 1934; Fog over Frisco 1934; Jimmy the Gent 1934; Of Human Bondage 1934; Bordertown 1935; Dangerous 1935; Front Page Woman 1935; The Girl from 10th Avenue 1935; Special Agent 1935; The Petrified Forest 1936; Satan Met a Lady 1936; It's Love I'm After 1937; Kid Galahad 1937; Marked Woman 1937; That Certain Woman 1937; Jezebel 1938; The Sisters 1938; Dark Victory 1939; Juarez 1939; The Old Maid 1939; The Private Lives of Elizabeth and Essex 1939; All This, and Heaven Too 1940; The Letter 1940; The Bride Came COD 1941; The Great Lie 1941; The Little Foxes 1941; The Man Who Came to Dinner 1941; In This Our Life 1942; Now, Voyager 1942; Old Acquaintance 1943; Watch on the Rhine 1943; Hollywood Canteen 1944; Mr Skeffington 1944; The Corn Is Green 1945; Deception 1946; A Stolen Life 1946; June Bride 1948; Winter Meeting 1948; Beyond the Forest 1949; All about Eve 1950; Another Man's Poison 1951; Payment on Demand 1951; Phone Call from a Stranger 1952; The Star 1953; The Virgin Queen 1955; The Catered Affair 1956; Storm Center 1956; The Scapegoat 1959; Pocketful of Miracles 1961; What Ever Happened to Baby Jane? 1962; The Empty Canvas 1963; Dead Ringer 1964; Hush... Hush, Sweet Charlotte 1964; Where Love Has Gone 1964; The Love Goddesses 1965; The Nanny 1965; The Anniversary 1968; Connecting Rooms 1969; Bunny O'Hare 1971; Madame Sin 1972; Burnt Offerings 1976; The Disappearance of Aimee 1976; Death on the Nile 1978; Return from Witch Mountain 1978; A Piano for Mrs Cimino 1982; The Watcher in the Woods 1982; Agatha Christie's Murder with Mirrors 1985; As Summers Die 1986; The Whales of August 1987; Wicked Stepmother 1989

Davis, Brad (1949–1991) Midnight Express 1978; Chariots of Fire 1981; Querelle 1982; Cold Steel 1987; Heart 1987; The Caine Mutiny Court-Martial 1988; Rosalie Goes Shopping 1989; The Plot to Kill Hitler 1990

Davis (1), Charles (1925–1990) The Man from Planet X 1951; The Desert Rats 1953

Davis, Clifton (1945–) Lost in the Stars 1974; Scott Joplin 1977

Davis, Dana Raise Your Voice 2004; Prom Night 2008; Relative Stranger 2009

Davis, Daniel (1945–) K-9 1989; Havana 1990; The Prestige 2006

Davis, DeRay The Fog 2005; Code Name: the Cleaner 2007; License to Wed 2007; Imagine That 2009

Davis, Duane Midnight Sting 1992; Rocky Marciano 1999

Davis, Essie (1970–) The Custodian 1993; Dad and Dave: on Our Selection 1995; Blackrock 1997; Code 46 2003; Girl with a Pearl Earring 2003; Isolation 2005; The Babadook 2013

Davis, Gail (1925–1997) The Far Frontier 1949; Blue Canadian Rockies 1952; On Top of Old Smoky 1953; Alias Jesse James 1959; Race for Your Life, Charlie Brown 1977

Davis, Geena (1956–) Tootsie 1982; Fletch 1985; Transylvania 6-5000 1985; The Fly 1986; The Accidental Tourist 1988; Beetle Juice 1988; Earth Girls Are Easy 1988; Quick Change 1990; Thelma & Louise 1991; Accidental Hero 1992; A League of Their Own 1992; Angie 1994; Speechless 1994; CutThroat Island 1995; The Long Kiss Goodnight 1996; Stuart Little 1999; Stuart Little 2 2002; Stuart Little 3: Call of the Wild 2005; When Marnie Was There 2014

Davis, Gene aka **Davis, Eugene M** Night Games 1979; 10 to Midnight 1983; Fear X 2002; Hidden Places 2006

Davis, George (1889–1965) The Circus 1928; The Kiss 1929; I Met Him in Paris 1937

Davis, Harry (1907–1993) America, America 1963; One of Our Spies Is Missing 1966; Rollercoaster 1977

Davis, Hope (1964–) Guy 1996; Mr Wrong 1996; The Myth of Fingerprints 1996; Arlington Road 1998; The Daytrippers 1998; The Impostors 1998; Next Stop Wonderland 1998; Mumford 1999; Hearts in Atlantis 2001; About Schmidt 2002; American Splendor 2003; The Secret Lives of Dentists 2003; Duma 2005; The Matador 2005; Proof 2005; The Weather Man 2005; The Hoax 2006; Infamous 2006; Charlie Bartlett 2007; The Nines 2007; Genova 2008; Synecdoche, New York 2008; The Lodger 2009; Disconnect 2012

Davis (1), Jim aka **Davis, James** (1909–1981) Winter Meeting 1948; The Cariboo Trail 1950; Cavalry Scout 1951; The Big Sky 1952; Rose of Cimarron 1952; The Outcast 1954; Timberjack 1955; The Restless Breed 1957; Monster from Green Hell 1958; Alias Jesse James 1959; Dracula vs Frankenstein 1970; Monte Walsh 1970; Bad Company 1972; Comes a Horseman 1978; The Day Time Ended 1980

Davis, Joan (1907–1961) Life Begins in College 1937; On the Avenue 1937; Thin Ice 1937; Hold That Co-Ed 1938; Just around the Corner 1938; My Lucky Star 1938; Sally, Irene and Mary 1938; Hold That Ghost 1941; Sun Valley Serenade 1941; Show Business 1944

Davis, Johnnie aka **Davis, Johnnie "Scat"** (1910–1983) Hollywood Hotel 1937; Knickerbocker Holiday 1944

Davis, Judy (1955–) My Brilliant Career 1979; Heatwave 1982; Who Dares Wins 1982; A Passage to India 1984; Kangaroo 1986; High Tide 1987; Georgia 1988; Barton Fink 1991; Impromptu 1991; Naked Lunch 1991; One against the Wind 1991; Where Angels Fear to Tread 1991; Husbands and Wives 1992; On My Own 1992; Hostile Hostages 1994; The New Age 1994; Absolute Power 1996; Blood and Wine 1996; Children of the Revolution 1996; Deconstructing Harry 1997; Celebrity 1998; A Cooler Climate 1999; The Man Who Sued God 2001; Swimming Upstream 2003; Marie Antoinette 2005; The Eye of the Storm 2011; To Rome with Love 2012; The Young and Prodigious TS Spivet 2013; The Dressmaker 2015

Davis, Julia (1966–) Wilbur (Wants to Kill Himself) 2002; Sex Lives of the Potato Men 2003; Cemetery Junction 2010; Four Lions 2010

Davis, Kristin (1965–) Take Me Home: the John Denver Story 2000; The Adventures of Sharkboy and Lavagirl 2005; Deck the Halls 2006; The Shaggy Dog 2006; Sex and the City: the Movie 2008; Couples Retreat 2009; Sex and the City 2 2010; Journey 2 the Mysterious Island 2011

Davis, Lucy (1973–) Sex Lives of the Potato Men 2003; Shaun of the Dead 2004; Rag Tale 2005; Garfield 2 2006

Davis, Mac (1942–) North Dallas Forty 1979; The Sting II 1983; Jackpot 2001

Davis, Mackenzie Breathe In 2013; That Awkward Moment 2013

Davis, Matthew aka **Davis, Matt** (1978–) Tigerland 2000; Urban Legends: Final Cut 2000; Legally Blonde 2001; Below 2002; Blue Crush 2002; Lone Star State of Mind 2002

Davis, Mildred (1900–1969) A Sailor-Made Man 1921; Grandma's Boy 1922; Safety Last 1923

Davis, Miles (1926–1991) Listen Up: the Lives of Quincy Jones 1990; Dingo 1991

Davis, Nancy (1921–2016) The Doctor and the Girl 1949; East Side, West Side 1949; The Next Voice You Hear 1950; It's a Big Country 1951; Donovan's Brain 1953

Davis, Nathan aka **Davis, Nate** Code of Silence 1985; Flowers in the Attic 1987; Dunston Checks In 1996; Holes 2003

Davis, Ossie (1917–2005) The Cardinal 1963; Gone Are the Days 1963; The Hill 1965; A Man Called Adam 1966; The Scalphunters 1968; Sam Whiskey 1969; Slaves 1969; Harry and Son 1984; Avenging Angel 1985; School Daze 1988; Do the Right Thing 1989; Joe versus the Volcano 1990; Jungle Fever 1991; Gladiator 1992; Grumpy Old Men 1993; I'm Not Rappaport 1996; Miss Evers' Boys 1997; 12 Angry Men 1997; Doctor Dolittle 1998; Chasing Secrets 1999; Dinosaur 2000; Bubba Ho-tep

2002; Baadasssss! 2003; She Hate Me 2004

Davis Jr, Owen (1907–1949) They Had to See Paris 1929; Murder on a Bridle Path 1936; The Plot Thickens 1936

Davis, Philip aka **Davis, Phil** (1953–) Quadrophenia 1979; The Bounty 1984; Comrades: a Lanternist's Account of the Tolpuddle Martyrs and What Became of Them 1986; High Hopes 1988; Blue Ice 1992; Face 1997; Photographing Fairies 1997; Still Crazy 1998; Vera Drake 2004; Notes on a Scandal 2006; Cassandra's Dream 2007; Dead Man Running 2009; Another Year 2010; Brighton Rock 2010; Just for the Record 2010; Outside Bet 2011; Borrowed Time 2012; Fast Girls 2012; Having You 2013; Golden Years 2016

Davis, Roger (1939–) House of Dark Shadows 1970; Ruby 1977

Davis, Sammi (1964–) Mona Lisa 1986; Hope and Glory 1987; A Prayer for the Dying 1987; Consuming Passions 1988; The Lair of the White Worm 1988; The Rainbow 1988

Davis Jr, Sammy (1925–1990) Anna Lucasta 1958; Porgy and Bess 1959; Ocean's Eleven 1960; Pepe 1960; Convicts Four 1962; Sergeants 3 1962; Johnny Cool 1963; Nightmare in the Sun 1964; Robin and the 7 Hoods 1964; A Man Called Adam 1966; Salt & Pepper 1968; Sweet Charity 1968; One More Time 1970; Little Moon & Jud McGraw 1978; The Cannonball Run 1981; Heidi's Song 1982; Cannonball Run II 1983; Moon over Parador 1988; Tap 1989

Davis, Sonny Carl aka **Davis, Sonny** Roadie 1980; Thelma & Louise 1991

Davis, Stringer (1896–1973) Murder at the Gallop 1963; Murder Ahoy 1964; Murder Most Foul 1964

Davis, Taryn Danielle Steel's Zoya 1995; Snow White: a Tale of Terror 1996

Davis, Viola (1965–) The Pentagon Wars 1998; The Shrink Is In 2001; Antwone Fisher 2002; Far from Heaven 2002; Solaris 2002; Get Rich or Die Tryin' 2005; Stone Cold 2005; Doubt 2008; Nights in Rodanthe 2008; Law Abiding Citizen 2009; Eat Pray Love 2010; It's Kind of a Funny Story 2010; Trust 2010; The Help 2011; Extremely Loud & Incredibly Close 2012; Won't Back Down 2012; Beautiful Creatures 2013; Ender's Game 2013; Prisoners 2013; Get on Up 2014; Blackhat 2015

Davis, Viveka (1969–) Shoot the Moon 1982; To Live For 1999

Davis, Warwick (1970–) Willow 1988; Leprechaun 1992; Prince Valiant 1997; The New Adventures of Pinocchio 1999; Snow White 2001; The Chronicles of Narnia: Prince Caspian 2008; Get Santa 2014; Star Wars Episode VII: the Force Awakens 2015

Davis, William B (1938–) Heart of a Child 1994; The X-Files 1998; The Proposal 2000; Mary Higgins Clark's The Cradle Will Fall 2004; Her Fatal Flaw 2006

Davison, Bruce (1946–) Last Summer 1969; The Strawberry Statement 1970; Willard 1971; The Jerusalem File 1972; Ulzana's Raid 1972; The Affair 1973; Mame 1974; Mother, Jugs & Speed 1976; Brass Target 1978; Summer of My German Soldier 1978; The Lathe of Heaven 1979; High Risk 1981; Crimes of Passion 1984; Spies like Us 1985; Longtime Companion 1990; Desperate Justice 1993; Short Cuts 1993; Six Degrees of Separation 1993; Far from Home: the Adventures of Yellow Dog 1994; The Baby-Sitter's Club 1995; The Cure 1995; Homage 1995; The Crucible 1996; Grace of My Heart 1996; Apt Pupil 1997; At First Sight 1998; Paulie 1998; The King Is Alive 2000; X-Men 2000; crazy/beautiful 2001; Summer Catch 2001; Dahmer 2002; High Crimes 2002; Runaway Jury 2003; X2 2003; Breach 2006; Camp Hell 2010; The Lords of Salem 2012; Words and Pictures 2013

Davison, Davey (1942–) Angel, Angel Down We Go 1969; No Drums, No Bugles 1971

Davison, Peter (1951–) Black Beauty 1994; Parting Shots 1998

Davitian, Ken Borat: Cultural Learnings of America for Make Benefit Glorious Nation of Kazakhstan 2006; Meet the Spartans 2008

Davoli, Andrew Knockaround Guys 2001; Welcome to Collinwood 2002

Davoli, Ninetto (1948–) Hawks and Sparrows 1966; Oedipus Rex 1967; The Decameron 1970; The Arabian Nights 1974

Davy, Jean (1911–2001) Le Masque de Fer 1962; Eloge de l'Amour 2001

Dawber, Pam (1951–) Wild Horses 1985; Stay Tuned 1992; I'll Remember April 1999

Dawson, Anthony (1916–1992) The Queen of Spades 1948; The Wooden Horse 1950; The Long Dark Hall 1951; Valley of Eagles 1951; Dial M for Murder 1954; Grip of the Strangler 1958; Libel 1959; Tiger Bay 1959; The Curse of the Werewolf 1961; Dr No 1962; Seven Seas to Calais 1962; Pirates 1986

Dawson, Hal K (1896–1987) Dr Socrates 1935; Billy Rose's Diamond Horseshoe 1945; Cattle Empire 1958

Dawson, Kamala aka **Lopez, Kamala** aka **Lopez-Dawson, Kamala** Born in East LA 1987; The Burning Season 1994; Erotique 1994; Lightning Jack 1994

Dawson, Richard (1932–2012) Munster, Go Home! 1966; The Running Man 1987

Dawson, Rosario (1979–) kids 1995; He Got Game 1998; Light It Up 1999; Down to You 2000; Sidewalks of New York 2000; Josie and the Pussycats 2001; Pluto Nash 2001; Ash Wednesday 2002; Men in Black 2 2002; 25th Hour 2002; Shattered Glass 2003; Welcome to the Jungle 2003; Alexander 2004; Rent 2005; Sin City 2005; Clerks II 2006; Death Proof 2007; Eagle Eye 2008; Seven Pounds 2008; Percy Jackson & the Lightning Thief 2010; Unstoppable 2010; 10 Years 2011; Zookeeper 2011; Fire with Fire 2012; Trance 2013; The Captive 2014; Sin City: a Dame to Kill For 2014; Tinker Bell and the Legend of the NeverBeast 2014; Top Five 2014; Ratchet & Clank 2016

Dax, Micheline Paris Vu Par... 1965; Tintin and the Lake of Sharks 1972

Day George, Lynda aka **Day, Lynda** (1944–) The Gentle Rain 1966; Day of the Animals 1977; The Amazing Captain Nemo 1978; Pieces 1982; Young Warriors 1983

Day-Lewis, Daniel (1957–) The Bounty 1984; My Beautiful Laundrette 1985; A Room with a View 1985; Stars and Bars 1988; The Unbearable Lightness of Being 1988; Eversmile, New Jersey 1989; My Left Foot 1989; The Last of the Mohicans 1992; The Age of Innocence 1993; In the Name of the Father 1993; The Crucible 1996; The Boxer 1997; Gangs of New York 2002; The Ballad of Jack and Rose 2005; There Will Be Blood 2007; Nine 2009; Lincoln 2012

Day, Charlie Going the Distance 2010; Horrible Bosses 2011; Pacific Rim 2013; Horrible Bosses 2 2014

Day, Dennis (1912–1988) Buck Benny Rides Again 1940; Music in Manhattan 1944; Golden Girl 1951; The Girl Next Door 1953

Day, Doris (1924–) Romance on the High Seas 1948; It's a Great Feeling 1949; My Dream Is Yours 1949; Storm Warning 1950; Tea for Two 1950; The West Point Story 1950; Young Man with a Horn 1950; I'll See You in My Dreams 1951; Lullaby of Broadway 1951; On Moonlight Bay 1951; April in Paris 1952; By the Light of the Silvery Moon 1953; Calamity Jane 1953; Lucky Me 1954; Love Me or Leave Me 1955; Young at Heart 1955; Julie 1956; The Man Who Knew Too Much 1956; The Pajama Game 1957; Teacher's Pet 1958; The Tunnel of Love 1958; It Happened to Jane 1959; Pillow Talk 1959; Midnight Lace 1960; Please Don't Eat the Daisies 1960; Lover Come Back 1961; Jumbo 1962; That Touch of Mink 1962; Move Over, Darling 1963; The Thrill of It All 1963; Send Me No Flowers 1964; Do Not Disturb 1965; The Glass Bottom Boat 1966; Caprice 1967; The Ballad of Josie 1968; Where Were You When the Lights Went Out? 1968; With Six You Get Eggroll 1968

Day, Frances (1907–1984) The Girl in the Taxi 1937; Fiddlers Three 1944; Tread Softly 1952

Day, Josette (1914–1978) Club de Femmes 1936; La Belle et la Bête 1946; Les Parents Terribles 1948

Day, Laraine (1917–2007) Calling Dr Kildare 1939; The Secret of Dr Kildare 1939; Sergeant Madden 1939; Tarzan Finds a Son! 1939; Dr Kildare's Strange Case 1940; Dr Kildare Goes Home 1940; Dr Kildare's Crisis 1940; Foreign Correspondent 1940; I Take This Woman 1940; My Son, My Son! 1940; Dr Kildare's Wedding Day 1941; The People vs Dr Kildare 1941; Unholy Partners 1941; Fingers at the Window 1942; Mr Lucky 1943; Bride by Mistake 1944; The Story of Dr Wassell 1944; Keep Your Powder Dry 1945; Those Endearing Young Charms 1945; The Locket 1946; Tycoon 1947; My Dear Secretary 1948; The Woman on Pier 13

1949; The High and the Mighty 1954; The Third Voice 1960

Day, Marceline (1907–2000) London after Midnight 1927; The Cameraman 1928; The Wild Party 1929

Day, Matt (1971–) Muriel's Wedding 1994; Love and Other Catastrophes 1996; Doing Time for Patsy Cline 1997; My Year without Sex 2009

Day, Morris (1957–) Purple Rain 1984; The Adventures of Ford Fairlane 1990; Graffiti Bridge 1990

Day, Rosie The Seasoning House 2012; Sixteen 2013; Howl 2015

Day, Vera (1939–) It's a Great Day 1955; A Kid for Two Farthings 1955; Quatermass II 1957; The Woman Eater 1957; Grip of the Strangler 1958; Too Many Crooks 1958; Up the Creek 1958; And the Same to You 1960; Saturday Night Out 1963

Dayan, Assi aka **Dayan, Assaf** (1945–2014) A Walk with Love and Death 1969; The Sellout 1975; Beyond the Walls 1984; Time of Favor 2000

Dayton, Dan (1923–1999) At War with the Army 1950; The Turning Point 1952

De Acutis, William (1957–1991) Nine ½ Weeks 1985; Chattahoochee 1989

de Almeida, Joaquim (1957–) The Honorary Consul 1983; Good Morning, Babylon 1987; Clear and Present Danger 1994; Only You 1994; Desperado 1995; Dollar for the Dead 1998; Captains of April 2000; Behind Enemy Lines 2001; The Burning Plain 2008; Che Part Two 2008; Cody the Robosapien 2012; Our Brand Is Crisis 2015

de Armas, Ana (1988–) Knock Knock 2015; Exposed 2016; War Dogs 2016

De Baer, Jean A Flash of Green 1984; 84 Charing Cross Road 1986

de Bankole, Isaach aka **de Bankolé, Isaach** aka **De Bankolé, Isaach** (1957–) Chocolat 1988; Night on Earth 1992; Ghost Dog: the Way of the Samurai 1999; Coffee and Cigarettes 2003; Manderlay 2005; The Limits of Control 2008; White Material 2009; Calvary 2013

de Banzie, Brenda (1915–1981) Hobson's Choice 1953; The Purple Plain 1954; As Long as They're Happy 1955; Doctor at Sea 1955; A Kid for Two Farthings 1955; House of Secrets 1956; The Man Who Knew Too Much 1956; Passport to Shame 1958; Too Many Crooks 1958; The Thirty-Nine Steps 1959; The Entertainer 1960; Flame in the Streets 1961; The Mark 1961; A Pair of Briefs 1961; The Pink Panther 1963; Pretty Polly 1967

de Blas, Manuel (1941–) A Bullet for Sandoval 1970; Callas Forever 2002

de Boer, Nicole (1970–) Cube 1997; Rated X 2000; NYC: Tornado Terror 2008

de Bray, Yvonne (1889–1954) Eternal Love 1943; Les Parents Terribles 1948; Olivia 1950

de Brulier, Nigel (1877–1948) The Three Musketeers 1921; Salome 1922; The Hunchback of Notre Dame 1923; Moby Dick 1930; The Three Musketeers 1935

De Burgh, Celia (1958–) The Getting of Wisdom 1977; Phar Lap 1983

De Cadenet, Amanda (1972–) The Rachel Papers 1989; Four Rooms 1995

De Caestecker, Iain In Fear 2012; Shell 2012; Not Another Happy Ending 2013; Lost River 2014

De Capitani, Grace (1959–) Le Cop 1985; Le Cop II 1989

De Carlo, Yvonne (1922–2007) True to Life 1943; Practically Yours 1944; Frontier Gal 1945; Salome, Where She Danced 1945; Brute Force 1947; Slave Girl 1947; Song of Scheherazade 1947; Casbah 1948; Calamity Jane and Sam Bass 1949; Criss Cross 1949; The Gal Who Took the West 1949; Hotel Sahara 1951; Tomahawk 1951; Hurricane Smith 1952; The San Francisco Story 1952; Scarlet Angel 1952; Sea Devils 1952; Sombrero 1952; The Captain's Paradise 1953; Fort Algiers 1953; Happy Ever After 1954; Death of a Scoundrel 1956; Magic Fire 1956; Raw Edge 1956; The Ten Commandments 1956; Band of Angels 1957; The Sword and the Cross 1958; McLintock! 1963; A Global Affair 1964; Munster, Go Home! 1966; Arizona Bushwhackers 1968; The Power 1968; The Delta Factor 1970; The Mark of Zorro 1974; Play Dead 1981; Liar's Moon 1982; American Gothic 1987

de Casalis, Jeanne (1897–1966) Nell Gwyn 1934; Sailors Three 1940; Cottage to Let 1941; Woman Hater 1948

de Caunes, Emma (1976–) Ma Mère 2004; The Science of Sleep 2005; Mr Bean's Holiday 2007

De Cordoba, Pedro (1881-1950) *Devil's Island 1940; The Ghost Breakers 1940; Tarzan Triumphs 1943; Comanche Territory 1950*

de Cordova, Arturo (1908-1973) *For Whom the Bell Tolls 1943; Frenchman's Creek 1944; Incendiary Blonde 1945; A Medal for Benny 1945; El 1953*

De Corsia, Ted (1903-1973) *The Lady from Shanghai 1948; The Naked City 1948; It Happens Every Spring 1949; Three Secrets 1950; The Enforcer 1951; Ride, Vaquero! 1953; The City Is Dark 1954; 20,000 Leagues under the Sea 1954; The Big Combo 1955; The Conqueror 1956; The Killing 1956; Showdown at Abilene 1956; Slightly Scarlet 1956; Baby Face Nelson 1957*

de Fougerolles, Hélène (1973-) *Va Savoir 2001; Innocence 2004*

de France, Cécile (1976-) *Pot Luck 2002; Switchblade Romance 2003; Around the World in 80 Days 2004; Orchestra Seats 2005; Russian Dolls 2005; The Singer 2006; A Secret 2007; Mesrine: Killer Instinct 2008; Hereafter 2010; The Kid with a Bike 2011; Chinese Puzzle 2013; En Equilibre 2015; Summertime 2015*

De Franciscis, Valeria aka **De Franciscis Bendoni, Valeria** *The Ferragosto Dinner 2008; The Salt of Life 2011*

De Funès, Louis (1914-1983) *The Sheep Has Five Legs 1954; La Traversée de Paris 1956; The Gendarme of St Tropez 1964; Delusions of Grandeur 1971*

De Gouw, Jessica *The Mystery of a Hansom Cab 2012; These Final Hours 2013*

De Grasse, Sam (1875-1953) *Blind Husbands 1919; Robin Hood 1922; The Black Pirate 1926; When a Man Loves 1926*

de Guillebon, Xavier *The Page Turner 2006; Le Week-end 2013*

de Havilland, Olivia aka **de Haviland, Olivia** (1916-) *Captain Blood 1935; The Irish in Us 1935; A Midsummer Night's Dream 1935; Anthony Adverse 1936; The Charge of the Light Brigade 1936; The Great Garrick 1937; It's Love I'm After 1937; The Adventures of Robin Hood 1938; Four's a Crowd 1938; Gold Is Where You Find It 1938; Hard to Get 1938; Dodge City 1939; Gone with the Wind 1939; The Private Lives of Elizabeth and Essex 1939; Raffles 1939; Santa Fe Trail 1940; Hold Back the Dawn 1941; The Strawberry Blonde 1941; They Died with Their Boots On 1941; In This Our Life 1942; The Male Animal 1942; Government Girl 1943; Princess O'Rourke 1943; The Dark Mirror 1946; Devotion 1946; To Each His Own 1946; The Well Groomed Bride 1946; The Snake Pit 1948; The Heiress 1949; My Cousin Rachel 1952; Not as a Stranger 1955; That Lady 1955; The Ambassador's Daughter 1956; The Proud Rebel 1958; Libel 1959; Light in the Piazza 1961; Hush... Hush, Sweet Charlotte 1964; Lady in a Cage 1964; The Adventurers 1970; Pope Joan 1972; Airport '77 1977; The Swarm 1978; The 5th Musketeer 1979; Agatha Christie's Murder Is Easy 1982*

De Keyser, David *Leo the Last 1970; Leon the Pig Farmer 1992; The Designated Mourner 1997; Sunshine 1999*

De Kova, Frank (1910-1981) *Shack Out on 101 1955; Teenage Caveman 1958; Atlantis, the Lost Continent 1960; The Mechanic 1972*

de la Brosse, Simon (1965-1998) *Pauline at the Beach 1983; La Petite Voleuse 1988; Loser Takes All 1990*

de la Huerta, Paz *A Walk to Remember 2002; Choke 2008; My Scientology Movie 2019*

De La Paz, Danny (1957-) *Barbarosa 1982; 3:15 1986; The Wild Pair 1987; American Me 1992*

De La Pena, George (1955-) *Nijinsky 1980; Kuffs 1991; Brain Donors 1992*

de la Reguera, Ana *Nacho Libre 2006; Cop Out 2010*

de la Tour, Frances (1945-) *Our Miss Fred 1972; Wombling Free 1977; Rising Damp 1980; Agatha Christie's Murder with Mirrors 1985; Loser Takes All 1990; The Cherry Orchard 1998; Harry Potter and the Goblet of Fire 2005; The History Boys 2006; The Book of Eli 2009; The Nutcracker in 3D 2009; Private Peaceful 2012; Mr Holmes 2014; The Lady in the Van 2015*

De Lacy, Philippe (1917-1995) *The Student Prince in Old Heidelberg 1927; Sarah and Son 1930*

de Lancie, John (1948-) *The Hand That Rocks the Cradle 1992; Fearless 1993; Woman on Top 2000; Pathology 2007*

de Lencquesaing, Louis-Do *The Father of My Children 2009; Elles 2011; Paris-Manhattan 2012*

de Lint, Derek aka **de Lint, Derek** (1950-) *Soldier of Orange 1977; The Assault 1986; Mascara 1987; Stealing Heaven 1988; The Unbearable Lightness of Being 1988; Black Book 2006; When a Stranger Calls 2006*

de Marney, Derrick (1906-1978) *Land without Music 1936; Things to Come 1936; Young and Innocent 1937; Flying 55 1939; Dangerous Moonlight 1941; Uncle Silas 1947; Sleeping Car to Trieste 1948*

de Marney, Terence (1909-1971) *Dual Alibi 1946; The Hand of Night 1966*

de Medeiros, Maria (1965-) *Henry & June 1990; The Divine Comedy 1992; L'Homme de Ma Vie 1992; Golden Balls 1993; Pulp Fiction 1994; News from the Good Lord 1996; Captains of April 2000; My Life without Me 2002; The Saddest Music in the World 2003; Pasolini 2014*

de Medina, Nieve *Mondays in the Sun 2002; Blame 2006*

de Mendoza, Alberto aka **Mendoza, Albert** (1923-2011) *That Man George 1965; A Bullet for Sandoval 1970; Delusions of Grandeur 1971; Horror Express 1972; Open Season 1974; What Changed Charley Farthing? 1974*

De Metz, Danielle *Return of the Fly 1959; Raid on Rommel 1971*

De Monaghan, Laurence *Claire's Knee 1970; Story of a Love Story 1973*

de Montalembert, Thibault *Love etc 1997; Lovers 1999; The Pornographer 2001; In My Skin 2002*

De Mornay, Rebecca (1959-) *Risky Business 1983; Testament 1983; Runaway Train 1985; The Slugger's Wife 1985; The Trip to Bountiful 1985; Beauty and the Beast 1987; And God Created Woman 1988; Feds 1988; Dealers 1989; By Dawn's Early Light 1990; Backdraft 1991; The Hand That Rocks the Cradle 1992; Guilty as Sin 1993; The Three Musketeers 1993; The Con 1998; Raise Your Voice 2004; Lords of Dogtown 2005; Mother's Day 2010*

De Niro, Robert aka **DeNero, Robert** (1943-) *Trois Chambres à Manhattan 1965; The Wedding Party 1966; Greetings 1968; Sam's Song 1969; Bloody Mama 1970; Hi, Mom! 1970; Born to Win 1971; The Gang That Couldn't Shoot Straight 1971; Jennifer on My Mind 1971; Bang the Drum Slowly 1973; Mean Streets 1973; The Godfather Part II 1974; The Last Tycoon 1976; 1900 1976; Taxi Driver 1976; New York, New York 1977; The Deer Hunter 1978; Raging Bull 1980; The King of Comedy 1983; Falling in Love 1984; Once upon a Time in America 1984; Brazil 1985; The Mission 1986; Angel Heart 1987; Dear America: Letters Home from Vietnam 1987; The Untouchables 1987; Jacknife 1988; Midnight Run 1988; Stanley & Iris 1989; We're No Angels 1989; Awakenings 1990; GoodFellas 1990; Guilty by Suspicion 1991; Backdraft 1991; Cape Fear 1991; Mad Dog and Glory 1992; Mistress 1992; Night and the City 1992; A Bronx Tale 1993; This Boy's Life 1993; Mary Shelley's Frankenstein 1994; Casino 1995; Heat 1995; The Fan 1996; Marvin's Room 1996; Sleepers 1996; Cop Land 1997; Great Expectations 1997; Jackie Brown 1997; Wag the Dog 1997; Ronin 1998; The Adventures of Rocky & Bullwinkle 1999; Analyze This 1999; Flawless 1999; Meet the Parents 2000; Men of Honor 2000; 15 Minutes 2001; The Score 2001; Analyze That 2002; City by the Sea 2002; Showtime 2002; Godsend 2003; Meet the Fockers 2004; Shark Tale 2004; Hide and Seek 2005; Arthur and the Invisibles 2006; The Good Shepherd 2006; Stardust 2007; What Just Happened? 2007; Righteous Kill 2008; Everybody's Fine 2009; Little Fockers 2010; Machete 2010; Stone 2010; Corman's World: Exploits of a Hollywood Rebel 2011; Killer Elite 2011; Limitless 2011; New Year's Eve 2011; Being Flynn 2012; Red Lights 2012; Silver Linings Playbook 2012; American Hustle 2013; The Big Wedding 2013; The Family 2013; Grudge Match 2013; Killing Season 2013; Last Vegas 2013; The Man Who Saved the World 2013; Heist 2015; The Intern 2015; Joy 2015; Dirty Grandpa 2016*

de Oliveira, Vinicius *Central Station 1998; Linha de Passe 2008*

de Palma, Rossy (1965-) *Women on the Verge of a Nervous Breakdown 1988; Kika 1993; The Flower of My Secret 1995; Broken Embraces 2009; Julieta 2016*

de Ravin, Emilie (1981-) *Brick 2005; The Hills Have Eyes 2006; Nora Roberts' High Noon 2009; Public Enemies 2009; Remember Me 2010*

De Rienzo, Libero *A Ma Soeur! 2001; My House in Umbria 2002*

De Rita, Joe (1909-1993) *Have Rocket, Will Travel 1959; The Three Stooges in Orbit 1962; The Three Stooges Meet Hercules 1962; The Three Stooges Go around the World in a Daze 1963; The Outlaws Is Coming 1965*

de Rossi, Portia (1973-) *Sirens 1994; I Witness 2003; The Night We Called It a Day 2003; Cursed 2005*

De Sade, Ana *The Return of a Man Called Horse 1976; Triumphs of a Man Called Horse 1983*

De Salvo, Anne (1949-) *My Favorite Year 1982; Compromising Positions 1985; Perfect 1985; Burglar 1987; Taking Care of Business 1990*

De Santis, Eliana *The Monk 1972; Les Noces Rouges 1973*

De Santis, Joe aka **De Santis, Joseph** (1909-1989) *The Man with a Cloak 1951; Deadline - USA 1952; Full of Life 1956; Tension at Table Rock 1956; Jeanne Eagels 1957; The Unholy Wife 1957; Al Capone 1959; The Professionals 1966; Blue 1968*

De Sapio, Francesca *Blood Red 1988; Torrents of Spring 1989*

De Sica, Vittorio (1902-1974) *Bread, Love & Dreams 1953; Madame de... 1953; Gold of Naples 1954; Secrets d'Alcove 1954; The Miller's Wife 1955; Too Bad She's Bad 1955; It Happened in Rome 1955; A Farewell to Arms 1957; The Monte Carlo Story 1957; General Della Rovere 1959; The Angel Wore Red 1960; It Started in Naples 1960; The Millionairess 1960; The Amorous Adventures of Moll Flanders 1965; The Biggest Bundle of Them All 1968; The Shoes of the Fisherman 1968; Twelve plus One 1969; Snow Job 1972; Blood for Dracula 1974; Blood for Dracula 1974; We All Loved Each Other So Much 1974*

De Soto, Rosana (1950-) *La Bamba 1987; Stand and Deliver 1988; Family Business 1989*

De Sousa, Melissa *Ride 1998; The Best Man 1999; The Triumph 2006*

De Souza, Edward (1933-) *Kiss of the Vampire 1962; The Phantom of the Opera 1962; The Return of the Soldier 1982*

De Souza, Sebastian *Plastic 2014; Kids in Love 2016*

De Turckheim, Charlotte (1955-) *Right Bank, Left Bank 1984; Mon Père Ce Héros 1991*

de Van, Marina (1971-) *Sitcom 1997; In My Skin 2002*

De Villalonga, José-Luis aka **Vilallonga** (1920-2007) *Breakfast at Tiffany's 1961; Cleo from 5 to 7 1961; Any Number Can Win 1963; Darling 1965*

de Villiers, Gys *Mandela: Long Walk to Freedom 2013; Vehicle 19 2013*

De Voogdt, Titus *Ben X 2007; Cub 2014*

de Vries, Dolf (1937-) *Turkish Delight 1973; The Fourth Man 1983*

de Wilde, Brandon (1942-1972) *The Member of the Wedding 1952; Shane 1953; Night Passage 1957; Blue Denim 1959; All Fall Down 1962; Hud 1963; Those Calloways 1964; In Harm's Way 1965; The Deserter 1971; Black Jack 1972*

de Wit, Jacqueline (1912-1998) *Meeting at Midnight 1944; Little Giant 1946; Wild Beauty 1946; All That Heaven Allows 1955; Tea and Sympathy 1956; Twice Told Tales 1963*

De Wolfe, Billy (1907-1974) *Dixie 1943; Miss Susie Slagle's 1945; Blue Skies 1946; Dear Ruth 1947; Isn't It Romantic 1948; Dear Wife 1949; Tea for Two 1950; Lullaby of Broadway 1951; Call Me Madam 1953; Billie 1965*

De Wolff, Francis (1913-1984) *Scrooge 1951; The Kidnappers 1953; The Diamond 1954; Geordie 1955; King's Rhapsody 1955; The Hound of the Baskervilles 1959; The Man Who Could Cheat Death 1959; The Two Faces of Dr Jekyll 1960; The World Ten Times Over 1963; Devil Doll 1964; Licensed to Kill 1965*

de Woolfson, Luke (1976-) *Large 2000; Late Night Shopping 2001; Stoned 2005; Reverb 2006*

De Young, Cliff (1945-) *The Night That Panicked America 1975; The Lindbergh Kidnapping Case 1976; The Hunger 1983; Independence Day 1983; Protocol 1984; Reckless 1984; FX: Murder by Illusion 1985; Secret Admirer 1985; Flight of the Navigator 1986; Fear 1988; Pulse 1988; Rude Awakening*

1989; *Flashback 1990; Dr Giggles 1992; The Craft 1996*

Déa, Marie (1919-1992) *Pièges 1939; Les Visiteurs du Soir 1942; Orphée 1950*

Deacon, Adam (1983-) *Kidulthood 2005; Sugarhouse 2007; Adulthood 2008; Bonded by Blood 2010; Everywhere + Nowhere 2011; Outside Bet 2011; Payback Season 2012*

Deacon, Brian (1949-) *The Triple Echo 1972; Separate Tables 1983; A Zed & Two Noughts 1985*

Deacon, Kim (1959-) *The Getting of Wisdom 1977; Rebel 1985*

Deacon, Richard (1921-1984) *Abbott and Costello Meet the Mummy 1955; Blackbeard's Ghost 1967; The Gnome-Mobile 1967*

Deakin, Julia *Dancin' thru the Dark 1989; Down Terrace 2009*

Deakins, Lucy (1971-) *The Boy Who Could Fly 1986; Cheetah 1989; There Goes My Baby 1994; A Mother's Gift 1995*

Dean, Allison *Coming to America 1988; Ruby in Paradise 1993*

Dean, Bill (1921-2000) *Family Life 1971; Night Watch 1973*

Dean, Billy (1962-) *Blue Valley Songbird 1999; A Face to Kill For 1999*

Dean, Calvin *Tormented 2009; Howl 2015*

Dean, Felicity *Steaming 1985; The Whistle Blower 1986*

Dean, Isabel (1918-1997) *The Passionate Friends 1948; The Story of Gilbert and Sullivan 1953; Out of the Clouds 1954; Virgin Island 1958; Light in the Piazza 1961; Ransom 1975; Rough Cut 1980; Five Days One Summer 1982*

Dean (1), James (1931-1955) *Sailor Beware 1951; Has Anybody Seen My Gal? 1952; East of Eden 1955; Rebel without a Cause 1955; Giant 1956*

Dean, Julia (1878-1952) *The Curse of the Cat People 1944; Nightmare Alley 1947*

Dean, Laura (1963-) *Fame 1980; Almost You 1984*

Dean, Loren (1969-) *Billy Bathgate 1991; 1492: Conquest of Paradise 1992; The Passion of Darkly Noon 1995; Mrs Winterbourne 1996; The End of Violence 1997; Gattaca 1997; Rosewood 1997; Mumford 1999; Space Cowboys 2000; The War Bride 2001*

Dean, Margia (1921-) *The Quatermass Xperiment 1955; The Secret of the Purple Reef 1960; The Big Show 1961*

Deane, Lezlie *976-EVIL 1988; Freddy's Dead: the Final Nightmare 1991; To Protect and Serve 1992*

Dearing, Edgar (1893-1974) *Free and Easy 1930; They Gave Him a Gun 1937*

Dearman, Glyn (1939-1997) *The Small Voice 1948; Scrooge 1951; Four Sided Triangle 1953*

Deayton, Angus (1956-) *Elizabeth 1998; Fat Slags 2004; Swinging with the Finkels 2010*

Debbouze, Jamel (1975-) *Asterix & Obelix: Mission Cleopatra 2001; Angel-A 2005; Days of Glory 2006; Let's Talk about the Rain 2008*

DeBell, Kristine (1954-) *Meatballs 1979; The Big Brawl 1980*

DeBello, James (1980-) *Detroit Rock City 1999; Crime + Punishment in Suburbia 2000; Cabin Fever 2002*

DeBenning, Burr (1936-2003) *Beach Red 1967; Sweet November 1968; City beneath the Sea 1971; The Face of Fear 1971; The Incredible Melting Man 1977; The Amazing Captain Nemo 1978*

Debicki, Elizabeth (1990-) *Macbeth 2015; The Man from UNCLE 2015*

Debnam-Carey, Alycia *Into the Storm 2014; Friend Request 2016*

DeBonis, Marcia *Commandments 1996; Twelve and Holding 2005*

Debourcourt, Jean (1894-1958) *Beethoven 1936; Mayerling 1936; Devil in the Flesh 1947; Monsieur Vincent 1947; The Eagle Has Two Heads 1948; Madame de... 1953; The Witches of Salem 1957*

DeCamp, Rosemary (1910-2001) *Hold Back the Dawn 1941; Jungle Book 1942; Yankee Doodle Dandy 1942; This Is the Army 1943; The Merry Monahans 1944; Practically Yours 1944; Blood on the Sun 1945; Pride of the Marines 1945; Rhapsody in Blue 1945; From This Day Forward 1946; Nora Prentiss 1947; Look for the Silver Lining 1949; Night unto Night 1949; On Moonlight Bay 1951; Treasure of Lost Canyon 1952; By the Light of the Silvery Moon 1953; Main Street to Broadway 1953; So This Is Love 1953; 13 Ghosts 1959; Saturday the 14th 1981*

Dechent, Antonio *Intacto 2001; Carmen 2003; You're My Hero 2003; The Baby's Room 2006*

Decker, Brooklyn (1987-) *Just Go with It 2011; Battleship 2012; Results 2015*

Decker, Diana (1926-) *Fiddlers Three 1944; When You Come Home 1947; Is Your Honeymoon Really Necessary? 1953; Knave of Hearts 1954; A Yank in Ermine 1955; Lolita 1961; Devils of Darkness 1964*

Deckers, Eugene (1917-1977) *Highly Dangerous 1950; Hotel Sahara 1951; Foreign Intrigue 1956; Seven Thunders 1957; North West Frontier 1959*

Decleir, Jan (1946-) *Daens 1992; Antonia's Line 1995; Character 1997; Running Free 1999*

Decomble, Guy (1910-1964) *Jour de Fête 1947; Bob Le Flambeur 1955; Les Cousins 1959; The 400 Blows 1959*

Dee, Frances (1907-2004) *An American Tragedy 1931; If I Had a Million 1932; Love Is a Racket 1932; Little Women 1933; The Silver Cord 1933; Finishing School 1934; Of Human Bondage 1934; Becky Sharp 1935; The Gay Deception 1935; Souls at Sea 1937; Wells Fargo 1937; If I Were King 1938; A Man Betrayed 1941; So Ends Our Night 1941; Happy Land 1943; I Walked with a Zombie 1943; Patrick the Great 1944; The Private Affairs of Bel Ami 1947; They Passed This Way 1948; Payment on Demand 1951*

Dee, Jack (1962-) *The Steal 1994; Londinium 1999*

Dee, Ruby (1924-2014) *The Tall Target 1951; Go, Man, Go! 1953; Edge of the City 1957; St Louis Blues 1958; Take a Giant Step 1959; A Raisin in the Sun 1961; The Balcony 1963; Gone Are the Days 1963; The Incident 1967; Uptight 1968; King: a Filmed Record... Montgomery to Memphis 1970; Buck and the Preacher 1972; Cat People 1982; Do the Right Thing 1989; The Court-Martial of Jackie Robinson 1990; Jungle Fever 1991; Cop and a Half 1993; Mr and Mrs Loving 1993; Captive Heart 1996; A Simple Wish 1997; Baby Geniuses 1999; A Storm in Summer 2000; Their Eyes Were Watching God 2005; American Gangster 2007; America 2009*

Dee, Sandra (1942-2005) *Until They Sail 1957; The Reluctant Debutante 1958; The Restless Years 1958; Gidget 1959; Imitation of Life 1959; A Stranger in My Arms 1959; A Summer Place 1959; The Wild and the Innocent 1959; Portrait in Black 1960; Come September 1961; Romanoff and Juliet 1961; Tammy Tell Me True 1961; If a Man Answers 1962; Take Her, She's Mine 1963; Tammy and the Doctor 1963; I'd Rather Be Rich 1964; That Funny Feeling 1965; A Man Could Get Killed 1966; Rosie! 1967; The Dunwich Horror 1970*

Deezen, Eddie (1957-) *Midnight Madness 1980; Delta Pi 1985; The Polar Express 2004*

DeFore, Don (1917-1993) *The Affairs of Susan 1945; The Stork Club 1945; Without Reservations 1946; It Happened on Fifth Avenue 1947; Romance on the High Seas 1948; My Friend Irma 1949; Dark City 1950; A Girl in Every Port 1952; No Room for the Groom 1952; She's Working Her Way through College 1952; Battle Hymn 1957; A Time to Love and a Time to Die 1958; The Facts of Life 1960*

DeGeneres, Ellen (1958-) *Coneheads 1993; Mr Wrong 1996; Goodbye Lover 1997; Edtv 1999; The Love Letter 1999; If These Walls Could Talk 2 2000; Finding Nemo 2003; Finding Dory 2016*

Degermark, Pia (1949-) *Elvira Madigan 1967; The Looking Glass War 1969*

DeHaan, Dane (1986-) *Chronicle 2012; The Place beyond the Pines 2012; Devil's Knot 2013; Kill Your Darlings 2013; Metallica: Through the Never 2013; The Amazing Spider-Man 2 2014; Life after Beth 2014; Life 2015; Valérian and the City of a Thousand Planets 2017*

DeHaven, Gloria aka **De Haven, Gloria** (1924-) *Best Foot Forward 1943; Broadway Rhythm 1944; Step Lively 1944; The Thin Man Goes Home 1944; Two Girls and a Sailor 1944; Summer Holiday 1948; The Doctor and the Girl 1949; Scene of the Crime 1949; Summer Stock 1950; Three Little Words 1950; The Yellow Cab Man 1950; Two Tickets to Broadway 1951; So This Is Paris 1954; The Girl Rush 1955*

Dehner, John (1915-1992) *Ten Tall Men 1951; Fort Algiers 1953; Powder River 1953; Apache 1954; The Bowery Boys Meet the Monsters 1954; The King's Thief 1955; The Man from Bitter Ridge 1955; The Girl in Black Stockings 1957; The Iron Sheriff 1957; Trooper Hook 1957; Apache Territory 1958; The*

Left Handed Gun 1958; Man of the West 1958; Cast a Long Shadow 1959; Critic's Choice 1963; Winchester '73 1967; The Helicopter Spies 1968; Dirty Dingus Magee 1970; Tiger by the Tail 1970; The Killer inside Me 1975; Creator 1985; Jagged Edge 1985

Dekker, Albert (1904-1968) Beau Geste 1939; Paris Honeymoon 1939; Dr Cyclops 1940; Seven Sinners 1940; Strange Cargo 1940; Among the Living 1941; Honky Tonk 1941; The Forest Rangers 1942; In Old California 1942; Once upon a Honeymoon 1942; Wake Island 1942; War of the Wildcats 1943; Experiment Perilous 1944; Incendiary Blonde 1945; Salome, Where She Danced 1945; California 1946; The Killers 1946; Two Years before the Mast 1946; Cass Timberlane 1947; Gentleman's Agreement 1947; Slave Girl 1947; Fury at Furnace Creek 1948; Lulu Belle 1948; Bride of Vengeance 1949; Search for Danger 1949; Tarzan's Magic Fountain 1949; Destination Murder 1950; The Kid from Texas 1950; Wait 'til the Sun Shines, Nellie 1952; East of Eden 1955; Illegal 1955; Kiss Me Deadly 1955; Suddenly, Last Summer 1959; These Thousand Hills 1959; The Wonderful Country 1959; Gamera the Invincible 1965

Dekker, Thomas (1987-) My Sister's Keeper 2009; Kaboom 2010; A Nightmare on Elm Street 2010

Deklin, Mark The Wish List 2010; Tarzan 2013

del Castillo, Kate Trade 2006; Julia 2008; Book of Life 2014; No Good Deed 2014

del Lago, Alicia Tizoc 1956; El Norte 1983

Del Pozo, Angel (1934-) Pancho Villa 1971; Treasure Island 1972

Del Prete, Duilio (1938-1998) The Assassination of Trotsky 1972; Daisy Miller 1974; At Long Last Love 1975

Del Rio, Dolores (1905-1983) What Price Glory 1926; The Red Dance 1928; The Trail of '98 1929; Bird of Paradise 1932; Flying down to Rio 1933; Madame Du Barry 1934; Wonder Bar 1934; In Caliente 1935; Accused 1936; Lancer Spy 1937; The Man from Dakota 1940; Journey into Fear 1942; Portrait of Maria 1943; The Fugitive 1947; Flaming Star 1960; Cheyenne Autumn 1964; More than a Miracle 1967; The Children of Sanchez 1978

Del Sol, Laura (1961-) Carmen 1983; The Hit 1984; El Amor Brujo 1986; Killing Dad 1989

Del Toro, Benicio (1967-) Big Top Pee-wee 1988; Licence to Kill 1989; Christopher Columbus: the Discovery 1992; Fearless 1993; Golden Balls 1993; Money for Nothing 1993; China Moon 1994; Swimming with Sharks 1994; The Usual Suspects 1995; Basquiat 1996; The Fan 1996; The Funeral 1996; Excess Baggage 1997; Fear and Loathing in Las Vegas 1998; The Pledge 2000; Snatch 2000; Traffic 2000; The Way of the Gun 2000; The Hunted 2002; 21 Grams 2003; Sin City 2005; Things We Lost in the Fire 2007; Che Part One 2008; Che Part Two 2008; The Wolfman 2009; Escobar: Paradise Lost 2014; Inherent Vice 2014; Sicario 2015; Guardians of the Galaxy Vol 2 2017

Delahaye, Michel (1929-) Alphaville 1965; Shiver of the Vampires 1970; Une Belle Fille comme Moi 1973

Delair, Suzy (1916-) Quai des Orfèvres 1947; Utopia 1950; Gervaise 1956; Rocco and His Brothers 1960

Delamare, Lise (1913-2006) La Marseillaise 1938; Monsieur Vincent 1947; Les Grandes Manoeuvres 1955; Lola Montès 1955

Delamere, Matthew Under the Skin 1997; 8½ Women 1999

Delamere, Victorien Le Château de Ma Mère 1990; La Gloire de Mon Père 1990

Delaney, Cathleen The Dead 1987; The Miracle 1990

Delaney, Joan The President's Analyst 1967; Don't Drink the Water 1969; Bunny O'Hare 1971

Delaney, Kim (1961-) That Was Then... This Is Now 1985; Body Parts 1991; Darkman II: the Return of Durant 1995; Temptress 1995; Finding a Family 2011

Delaney, Maureen (1888-1961) Another Shore 1948; Jacqueline 1956; The Scamp 1957; Tread Softly Stranger 1958

Delaney, Padraic The Wind That Shakes the Barley 2006; Perrier's Bounty 2009; Blackthorn 2011

Delano, Michael (1940-) Catlow 1971; Not of This Earth 1988

Delany, Dana (1956-) The Adventures of Mowgli 1967; Almost You 1984; Masquerade 1988; Patty Hearst 1988;

Light Sleeper 1991; HouseSitter 1992; Batman: Mask of the Phantasm 1993; The Enemy Within 1994; Exit to Eden 1994; Fly Away Home 1996; Wide Awake 1998; Baby for Sale 2004; Camp Hell 2010

Delevanti, Cyril (1887-1975) The Night of the Iguana 1964; The Killing of Sister George 1968

Delevingne, Cara (1992-) The Face of an Angel 2014; London Fields 2015; Paper Towns 2015; Kids in Love 2016; Suicide Squad 2016; Valérian and the City of a Thousand Planets 2017

Delfino, Majandra Shriek If You Know What I Did Last Friday the 13th 2000; Life as We Know It 2010

Delgado, Roger (1918-1973) The Road to Hong Kong 1962; Hot Enough for June 1964; The Mummy's Shroud 1966

D'Elia, Jorge The Lost Embrace 2003; El Aura 2005

Dell, Gabriel (1919-1988) Dead End 1937; Angels with Dirty Faces 1938; Angels Wash Their Faces 1939; Hell's Kitchen 1939; Block Busters 1944; Bowery Champs 1944; Come Out Fighting 1945; Who Is Harry Kellerman, and Why Is He Saying Those Terrible Things about Me? 1971; Framed 1975; The Escape Artist 1982

Dell, Myrna (1924-2011) The Falcon's Adventure 1946; Nocturne 1946; Guns of Hate 1948; The Gal Who Took the West 1949; The Judge Steps Out 1949; Roughshod 1949; Search for Danger 1949; Destination Murder 1950

Delle Piane, Carlo (1936-) What? 1973; Noi Tre 1984; Tickets 2005

Delmont, Edouard aka Delmont (1883-1955) Angèle 1934; The Sheep Has Five Legs 1954

Delon, Alain (1935-) Plein Soleil 1960; Rocco and His Brothers 1960; The Eclipse 1962; The Leopard 1962; Any Number Can Win 1963; The Black Tulip 1963; The Love Cage 1964; The Yellow Rolls-Royce 1964; Once a Thief 1965; Is Paris Burning? 1966; Texas across the River 1966; Diabolically Yours 1967; Histoires Extraordinaires 1967; Le Samouraï 1967; The Adventurers 1968; The Girl on a Motorcycle 1968; The Swimming Pool 1968; The Sicilian Clan 1969; Borsalino 1970; The Red Circle 1970; Red Sun 1971; The Widow Couderc 1971; The Assassination of Trotsky 1972; Un Flic 1972; Burnt Barns 1973; Scorpio 1973; Shock Treatment 1973; Two against the Law 1973; Borsalino and Co 1974; Someone Is Bleeding 1974; Police Story 1975; Zorro 1975; Mr Klein 1976; Airport '79: the Concorde 1979; Three Men to Destroy 1980; Le Choc 1982; Swann in Love 1984; Nouvelle Vague 1990; Asterix at the Olympic Games 2008

Delon, Nathalie (1938-) Le Samouraï 1967; When Eight Bells Toll 1971; Bluebeard 1972; The Monk 1972; The Romantic Englishwoman 1975

DeLorenzo, Michael (1959-) Somebody to Love 1994; Phantoms 1998

Delorme, Danièle (1926-2015) Les Misérables 1957; Cleo from 5 to 7 1961; Pardon Mon Affaire 1976

Delpy, Albert The Hairdresser's Husband 1990; Before Sunset 2004; 2 Days in Paris 2006; 2 Days in New York 2011

Delpy, Julie (1969-) Detective 1985; Mauvais Sang 1986; Europa Europa 1991; Voyager 1991; Killing Zoe 1993; Three Colours White 1993; The Three Musketeers 1993; Younger and Younger 1993; Before Sunrise 1995; An American Werewolf in Paris 1997; LA without a Map 1998; But I'm a Cheerleader 1999; Waking Life 2001; Villa des Roses 2002; Before Sunset 2004; Broken Flowers 2005; The Hoax 2006; 2 Days in Paris 2006; The Air I Breathe 2007; 2 Days in New York 2011; Before Midnight 2013; Wiener-Dog 2016

Deltgen, René (1909-1979) Special Delivery 1955; The Tiger of Eschnapur 1959

Delubac, Jacqueline (1910-1997) Bonne Chance 1935; The Story of a Cheat 1936

DeLuise, Dom (1933-2009) The Glass Bottom Boat 1966; The Busy Body 1967; What's So Bad about Feeling Good? 1968; The Twelve Chairs 1970; Evil Roy Slade 1971; Who Is Harry Kellerman, and Why Is He Saying Those Terrible Things about Me? 1971; Every Little Crook and Nanny 1972; The Adventure of Sherlock Holmes' Smarter Brother 1975; Silent Movie 1976; The Cheap Detective 1978; The End 1978; Sextette 1978; Fatso 1979; The Last Married Couple in America 1980; Smokey and the Bandit II 1980; The Cannonball Run 1981; History of

the World Part I 1981; The Best Little Whorehouse in Texas 1982; The Secret of NIMH 1982; Cannonball Run II 1983; Johnny Dangerously 1984; An American Tail 1986; Haunted Honeymoon 1986; Spaceballs 1987; Oliver & Company 1988; All Dogs Go to Heaven 1989; Loose Cannons 1990; Snow White in Happily Ever After 1990; An American Tail: Fievel Goes West 1991; Munchie 1992; Robin Hood: Men in Tights 1993; The Silence of the Hams 1993; Don't Drink the Water 1994; Munchie Strikes Back 1994; Stanley's Magic Garden 1994; The Secret of NIMH II: Timmy to the Rescue 1998; Baby Geniuses 1999; Lion of Oz 2000

DeLuise, Michael (1970-) California Man 1992; Wayne's World 1992; The Man without a Face 1993

Demange, Paul School for Postmen 1947; Clochemerle 1948

Demarest, William (1892-1983) The Jazz Singer 1927; Hands across the Table 1935; Murder Man 1935; Wedding Present 1936; Easy Living 1937; Rosalie 1937; Christmas in July 1940; The Great McGinty 1940; The Devil and Miss Jones 1941; The Lady Eve 1941; Sullivan's Travels 1941; All through the Night 1942; Life Begins at 8.30 1942; Pardon My Sarong 1942; The Miracle of Morgan's Creek 1943; Stage Door Canteen 1943; True to Life 1943; The Great Moment 1944; Hail the Conquering Hero 1944; Once upon a Time 1944; Along Came Jones 1945; Pardon My Past 1945; Salty O'Rourke 1945; The Jolson Story 1946; Night Has a Thousand Eyes 1948; On Our Merry Way 1948; Whispering Smith 1948; Jolson Sings Again 1949; Sorrowful Jones 1949; Never a Dull Moment 1950; Riding High 1950; When Willie Comes Marching Home 1950; The First Legion 1951; The Strip 1951; What Price Glory? 1952; Dangerous When Wet 1953; Escape from Fort Bravo 1953; Here Come the Girls 1953; The Lady Wants Mink 1953; The Yellow Mountain 1954; The Far Horizons 1955; Hell on Frisco Bay 1955; Jupiter's Darling 1955; Lucy Gallant 1955; The Private War of Major Benson 1955; Sincerely Yours 1955; The Mountain 1956; The Rawhide Years 1956; Pepe 1960; Son of Flubber 1962; Viva Las Vegas 1964; That Darn Cat! 1965; Don't Be Afraid of the Dark 1973

Demazis, Orane (1904-1991) Marius 1931; Fanny 1932; Angèle 1934; César 1936

Demetral, Chris (1976-) Sometimes They Come Back 1991; Blank Check 1994

Demick, Irina (1936-2004) The Visit 1964; Up from the Beach 1965; Prudence and the Pill 1968; The Sicilian Clan 1969

DeMille, Cecil B (1881-1959) Free and Easy 1930; Star Spangled Rhythm 1942; Son of Paleface 1952; The Buster Keaton Story 1957

DeMille, Katherine (1911-1995) Belle of the Nineties 1934; The Black Room 1935; The Crusades 1935; Banjo on My Knee 1936; Charlie Chan at the Olympics 1937; Black Gold 1947; Unconquered 1947

Demongeot, Mylène aka Nicole, **Mylene** (1936-) It's a Wonderful World 1956; The Witches of Salem 1957; Bonjour Tristesse 1958; Upstairs and Downstairs 1959; The Giant of Marathon 1960; The Singer Not the Song 1960; Under Ten Flags 1960; Romulus and the Sabines 1961; Doctor in Distress 1963; The Private Navy of Sgt O'Farrell 1968; Twelve plus One 1969

Demoustier, Anaïs (1987-) Time of the Wolf 2003; Give Me Your Hand 2008; Elles 2011; Thérèse Desqueyroux 2012; The New Girlfriend 2014

Dempsey, Jack (1895-1983) The Prizefighter and the Lady 1933; Military Policeman 1952; Requiem for a Heavyweight 1962

Dempsey, Patrick (1966-) Catholic Boys 1985; Can't Buy Me Love 1987; The Woo Woo Kid 1987; In a Shallow Grave 1988; Some Girls 1988; Happy Together 1989; Loverboy 1989; Coupe de Ville 1990; Mobsters 1991; Run 1991; For Better and for Worse 1993; With Honors 1994; Outbreak 1995; Something about Sex 1998; Scream 3 1999; The Emperor's Club 2002; Sweet Home Alabama 2002; Iron Jawed Angels 2004; Freedom Writers 2006; Enchanted 2007; Made of Honor 2008; Transformers: Dark of the Moon 2011; Bridget Jones's Baby 2016

Dempster, Carol (1901-1991) Dream Street 1921; America 1924; Isn't Life Wonderful 1924; Sally of the Sawdust 1925

Dempster, Hugh (1900-1987) Anna Karenina 1947; Paul Temple's Triumph 1950

DeMunn, Jeffrey (1947-) Windy City 1984; Warning Sign 1985; The Hitcher 1986; Betrayed 1988; The Blob 1988; Blaze 1989; By Dawn's Early Light 1990; Crash: the Mystery of Flight 1501 1990; Eyes of an Angel 1991; Barbarians at the Gate 1993; Citizen X 1995; Killer: a Journal of Murder 1995; Rocketman 1997; Turbulence 1997; The Majestic 2001; The Mist 2007; Shelter 2008

Demy, Mathieu (1972-) Kung-Fu Master 1987; Les Cent et Une Nuits 1995; Ecoute le Temps 2005; The Girl on the Train 2009; Tomboy 2011

Denberg, Susan (1944-) An American Dream 1956; Frankenstein Created Woman 1966

Dench, Judi (1934-) The Third Secret 1964; Four in the Morning 1965; He Who Rides a Tiger 1965; A Study in Terror 1965; A Midsummer Night's Dream 1959; Dead Cert 1974; Luther 1974; The Angelic Conversation 1985; A Room with a View 1985; Wetherby 1985; 84 Charing Cross Road 1986; A Handful of Dust 1987; Henry V 1989; GoldenEye 1995; Jack & Sarah 1995; Hamlet 1996; Mrs Brown 1997; Tomorrow Never Dies 1997; Shakespeare in Love 1998; Tea with Mussolini 1998; The World Is Not Enough 1999; Chocolat 2000; Into the Arms of Strangers: Stories of the Kindertransport 2000; Iris 2001; The Shipping News 2001; Die Another Day 2002; The Importance of Being Earnest 2002; The Chronicles of Riddick 2004; Home on the Range 2004; Ladies in Lavender 2004; Mrs Henderson Presents 2005; Pride & Prejudice 2005; Casino Royale 2006; Notes on a Scandal 2006; Quantum of Solace 2008; Nine 2009; The Best Exotic Marigold Hotel 2011; J Edgar 2011; Jane Eyre 2011; My Week with Marilyn 2011; Everything or Nothing: the Untold Story of 007 2012; Skyfall 2012; Philomena 2013; Run for Your Wife 2013; The Second Best Exotic Marigold Hotel 2015

Dencik, David Call Girl 2012; A Royal Affair 2012; The Absent One 2014; Men & Chicken 2015; Regression 2015

Denden Cold Fish 2010; Like Someone in Love 2012

Deneuve, Catherine (1943-) The Beautiful Swindlers 1964; Male Hunt 1964; The Umbrellas of Cherbourg 1964; Repulsion 1965; La Vie de Château 1965; Les Créatures 1966; Belle de Jour 1967; The Young Girls of Rochefort 1967; La Chamade 1968; Mayerling 1968; The April Fools 1969; Mississippi Mermaid 1969; The Magic Donkey 1970; Tristana 1970; Un Flic 1972; The Lady with Red Boots 1972; Call Him Savage 1975; Hustle 1975; Second Chance 1976; March or Die 1977; Ecoute Voir... 1978; An Adventure for Two 1979; Je Vous Aime 1980; The Last Metro 1980; Choice of Arms 1981; Le Choc 1982; The Hunger 1983; Fort Saganne 1984; Love Songs 1984; Let's Hope It's a Girl 1985; The Scene of the Crime 1986; Indochine 1991; Ma Saison Préférée 1993; The Convent 1995; Les Voleurs 1996; Généalogies d'un Crime 1997; Place Vendôme 1998; East-West 1999; Pola X 1999; Time Regained 1999; Le Vent de la Nuit 1999; Dancer in the Dark 2000; 8 Women 2001; I'm Going Home 2001; The Musketeer 2001; Un Filme Falado 2003; Changing Times 2004; Kings & Queen 2004; Persepolis 2007; A Christmas Tale 2008; I Want to See 2008; The Girl on the Train 2009; The Big Picture 2010; Potiche 2010; Beloved 2011; In the Courtyard 2014; The Brand New Testament 2015

Deng Chao Assembly 2007; Detective Dee and the Mystery of the Phantom Flame 2010; Mermaid 2016

Denham, Maurice (1909-2002) Daybreak 1946; Captain Boycott 1947; Take My Life 1947; Blanche Fury 1948; The Blind Goddess 1948; It's Not Cricket 1948; Oliver Twist 1948; Once upon a Dream 1948; A Boy, a Girl and a Bike 1949; Landfall 1949; Madness of the Heart 1949; The Spider and the Fly 1949; Traveller's Joy 1949; Eight o'Clock Walk 1953; The Net 1953; Terror on a Train 1953; Animal Farm 1954; Carrington VC 1954; The Purple Plain 1954; Doctor at Sea 1955; Simon and Laura 1955; Checkpoint 1956; 23 Paces to Baker Street 1956; Barnacle Bill 1957; Night of the Demon 1957; The Captain's Table 1958; Sink the Bismarck! 1960; Two Way Stretch 1960; Invasion Quartet 1961; HMS Defiant 1962; The Very Edge 1962; Paranoiac 1963; Hysteria 1964; The 7th

Dawn 1964; The Legend of Young Dick Turpin 1965; The Nanny 1965; The Night Caller 1965; The Alphabet Murders 1966; Danger Route 1967; The Long Duel 1967; Torture Garden 1967; Attack on the Iron Coast 1968; The Best House in London 1968; Midas Run 1969; Some Girls Do 1969; Countess Dracula 1970; The Virgin and the Gypsy 1970; Sunday, Bloody Sunday 1971; Luther 1974; Shout at the Devil 1976; The Chain 1984; 84 Charing Cross Road 1986

Denham, Tony The Shouting Men 2009; Vendetta 2013

Denicourt, Marianne (1966-) La Belle Noiseuse 1991; Ma Vie Sexuelle 1996; The Lost Son 1998; Me without You 2001; Hippocrates 2014

Denis, Jacques (1943-) The Watchmaker of St Paul 1973; Jonah Who Will Be 25 in the Year 2000 1976; Chocolat 1988

Denisof, Alexis (1966-) Innocent Lies 1995; Much Ado about Nothing 2012

Denison, Anthony John (1950-) Little Vegas 1990; The Amy Fisher Story 1993; Full Eclipse 1993; The Harvest 1993; Getting Gotti 1994

Denison, Michael (1915-1998) Hungry Hill 1946; My Brother Jonathan 1947; The Blind Goddess 1948; The Glass Mountain 1949; Landfall 1949; The Franchise Affair 1950; Angels One Five 1952; The Importance of Being Earnest 1952; Contraband Spain 1955; The Truth about Women 1958; Faces in the Dark 1960; Shadowlands 1993

Denman, David Smart People 2007; Shutter 2008; 13 Hours: the Secret Soldiers of Benghazi 2016

Denman, Tony (1979-) Fargo 1995; Sorority Boys 2002; Barely Legal 2003

Dennehy, Brian (1939-) Semi-Tough 1977; A Death in Canaan 1978; Foul Play 1978; Butch and Sundance: the Early Days 1979; The Jericho Mile 1979; 10 1979; Little Miss Marker 1980; Skokie 1981; First Blood 1982; Split Image 1982; Gorky Park 1983; Never Cry Wolf 1983; The River Rat 1984; Cocoon 1985; FX: Murder by Illusion 1985; Silverado 1985; Legal Eagles 1986; The Belly of an Architect 1987; Best Seller 1987; Miles from Home 1988; Return to Snowy River 1988; Day One 1989; Seven Minutes 1989; Blue Heat 1990; Evidence of Love 1990; Presumed Innocent 1990; FX 2 1991; Gladiator 1992; Jack Reed: Badge of Honor 1993; Leave of Absence 1994; The Stars Fell on Henrietta 1995; Tommy Boy 1995; William Shakespeare's Romeo + Juliet 1996; A Father's Betrayal 1997; Fail Safe 2000; Summer Catch 2001; Stolen Summer 2002; She Hate Me 2004; Assault on Precinct 13 2005; Ratatouille 2007; Righteous Kill 2008; The Next Three Days 2010; The Big Year 2011; Meet Monica Velour 2011; Knight of Cups 2015

Dennehy, Ned Reign of Fire 2001; Tyrannosaur 2010; Storage 24 2012; Downhill 2014

Dennen, Barry (1938-) Jesus Christ Superstar 1973; Brannigan 1975; The Dark Crystal 1982

Denner, Charles (1926-1995) Bluebeard 1962; The Bride Wore Black 1967; Z 1968; Une Belle Fille comme Moi 1973; And Now My Love 1974; Mado 1976; Second Chance 1976; The Man Who Loved Women 1977; Robert et Robert 1978; Golden Eighties 1986

Denning, Richard (1914-1998) Adam Had Four Sons 1941; Beyond the Blue Horizon 1942; The Glass Key 1942; Quiet Please, Murder 1942; Black Beauty 1946; No Man of Her Own 1950; Weekend with Father 1951; Scarlet Angel 1952; The 49th Man 1953; The Glass Web 1953; Creature from the Black Lagoon 1954; Creature with the Atom Brain 1955; Assignment Redhead 1956; The Day the World Ended 1956; The Oklahoma Woman 1956; An Affair to Remember 1957; The Black Scorpion 1957; The Lady Takes a Flyer 1958; Twice Told Tales 1963

Dennings, Kat (1986-) Big Momma's House 2 2006; Charlie Bartlett 2007; The House Bunny 2008; Nick & Norah's Infinite Playlist 2008; Defendor 2009; Shorts 2009

Dennis, Les (1954-) Intimate Relations 1995; Large 2000

Dennis, Nick (1904-1980) Sirocco 1951; A Streetcar Named Desire 1951; Ten Tall Men 1951; Anything Can Happen 1952; The Glory Brigade 1953; Kiss Me Deadly 1955; Too Late Blues 1961; Gunpoint 1966

Dennis, Sandy (1937-1992) Splendor in the Grass 1961; The Three Sisters 1966; Who's Afraid of Virginia Woolf? 1966; The Fox 1967; Up the Down

Staircase 1967; Sweet November 1968; That Cold Day in the Park 1969; A Touch of Love 1969; The Out of Towners 1970; Something Evil 1972; Mr Sycamore 1974; Nasty Habits 1976; Perfect Gentlemen 1978; The Four Seasons 1981; Come Back to the Five and Dime, Jimmy Dean, Jimmy Dean 1982; Another Woman 1988; 976-EVIL 1988; Parents 1988; The Indian Runner 1991

Denny, Reginald (1891-1967) A Lady's Morals 1930; Madam Satan 1930; Parlor, Bedroom and Bath 1931; Private Lives 1931; The Barbarian 1933; Only Yesterday 1933; The Lost Patrol 1934; Of Human Bondage 1934; One More River 1934; The Richest Girl in the World 1934; The World Moves On 1934; Anna Karenina 1935; Remember Last Night? 1935; Bulldog Drummond Escapes 1937; Bulldog Drummond Comes Back 1937; Bulldog Drummond's Revenge 1937; Bulldog Drummond's Peril 1938; Bulldog Drummond in Africa 1938; Bulldog Drummond's Bride 1939; Rebecca 1940; Seven Sinners 1940; Appointment for Love 1941; Captains of the Clouds 1942; Sherlock Holmes and the Voice of Terror 1942; Christmas Eve 1947; Escape Me Never 1947; The Macomber Affair 1947; My Favorite Brunette 1947; The Secret Life of Walter Mitty 1947; Abbott and Costello Meet Dr Jekyll and Mr Hyde 1953; World for Ransom 1953; Cat Ballou 1965

Denny, Susan (1934-) The Pursuers 1961; The Sicilians 1964

Denton, Christa The Burning Bed 1984; The Gate 1987

Denton, Crahan (1914-1966) The Young One 1960; Birdman of Alcatraz 1962; Hud 1963; Bus Riley's Back in Town 1965

Denton, Will Palindromes 2004; Camp Hell 2010

Denver, Bob (1935-2005) For Those Who Think Young 1964; The Sweet Ride 1967; Who's Minding the Mint? 1967

Denver, John (1943-1997) Oh, God! 1977; Foxfire 1987

Denzongpa, Danny (1948-) Hum 1991; Seven Years in Tibet 1997; Asoka 2001

Deol, Abhay Manorama Six Feet Under 2007; Oye Lucky! Lucky Oye! 2008

Depardieu, Elisabeth (1941-) Jean de Florette 1986; Manon des Sources 1986

Depardieu, Gérard aka Depardieu, Gerard (1948-) Les Valseuses 1974; Vincent, François, Paul and the Others 1974; Maîtresse 1976; 1900 1976; Get Out Your Handkerchiefs 1977; Bye Bye Monkey 1978; Les Chiens 1978; Buffet Froid 1979; Je Vous Aime 1980; The Last Metro 1980; Loulou 1980; Mon Oncle d'Amérique 1980; Choice of Arms 1981; The Woman Next Door 1981; Danton 1982; The Return of Martin Guerre 1982; Les Compères 1983; The Moon in the Gutter 1983; Fort Saganne 1984; Right Bank, Left Bank 1984; Police 1985; Jean de Florette 1986; Tenue de Soirée 1986; Sous le Soleil de Satan 1987; Camille Claudel 1988; I Want to Go Home 1989; Trop Belle pour Toi 1989; Cyrano de Bergerac 1990; Green Card 1990; Merci la Vie 1991; Mon Père Ce Héros 1991; Tous les Matins du Monde 1991; 1492: Conquest of Paradise 1992; Germinal 1993; Hélas pour Moi 1993; Le Colonel Chabert 1994; La Machine 1994; My Father the Hero 1994; A Pure Formality 1994; The Horseman on the Roof 1995; Bogus 1996; Hamlet 1996; The Secret Agent 1996; Unhook the Stars 1996; The Man in the Iron Mask 1997; Asterix and Obelix Take On Caesar 1999; The Bridge 1999; 102 Dalmatians 2000; Vatel 2000; Asterix & Obelix: Mission Cleopatra 2001; The Closet 2001; Vidocq 2001; City of Ghosts 2002; Crime Spree 2002; Bon Voyage 2003; Nathalie... 2003; Shut Up! 2003; Changing Times 2004; Nouvelle-France 2004; 36 Quai des Orfèvres 2004; Last Holiday 2006; The Singer 2006; La Vie en Rose 2007; Asterix at the Olympic Games 2008; Babylon AD 2008; Mesrine: Killer Instinct 2008; Mammuth 2010; My Afternoons with Margueritte 2010; Potiche 2010; Life of Pi 2012; Welcome to New York 2014; Valley of Love 2015

Depardieu, Guillaume (1971-2008) Tous les Matins du Monde 1991; Wild Target 1993; Les Apprentis 1995; Pola X 1999; Don't Touch the Axe 2006; Fear(s) of the Dark 2007

Depardieu, Julie (1973-) Les Destinées Sentimentales 2000; Blame

It on Fidel 2006; The Witnesses 2006; Female Agents 2007; A Secret 2007

Depp, Johnny (1963-) A Nightmare on Elm Street 1984; Private Resort 1985; Platoon 1986; Cry-Baby 1989; Edward Scissorhands 1990; Arizona Dream 1991; Benny & Joon 1993; What's Eating Gilbert Grape 1993; Ed Wood 1994; Dead Man 1995; Don Juan DeMarco 1995; Nick of Time 1995; Donnie Brasco 1997; Fear and Loathing in Las Vegas 1998; LA without a Map 1998; The Astronaut's Wife 1999; The Ninth Gate 1999; Sleepy Hollow 1999; Before Night Falls 2000; Chocolat 2000; The Man Who Cried 2000; Blow 2001; From Hell 2001; Once upon a Time in Mexico 2003; Pirates of the Caribbean: the Curse of the Black Pearl 2003; Finding Neverland 2004; The Libertine 2004; Secret Window 2004; Charlie and the Chocolate Factory 2005; Tim Burton's Corpse Bride 2005; The Future Is Unwritten 2006; Pirates of the Caribbean: Dead Man's Chest 2006; Pirates of the Caribbean: at World's End 2007; Sweeney Todd: the Demon Barber of Fleet Street 2007; Gonzo: the Life and Work of Dr Hunter S Thompson 2008; The Imaginarium of Doctor Parnassus 2009; Public Enemies 2009; When You're Strange 2009; Alice in Wonderland 2010; The Tourist 2010; Pirates of the Caribbean: on Stranger Tides 2011; Rango 2011; The Rum Diary 2011; Dark Shadows 2012; For No Good Reason 2012; Radioman 2012; 21 Jump Street 2012; The Lone Ranger 2013; Lucky Them 2013; Into the Woods 2014; Transcendence 2014; Black Mass 2015; London Fields 2015; Mortdecai 2015; Alice through the Looking Glass 2016; Yoga Hosers 2016; Pirates of the Caribbean: Dead Men Tell No Tales 2017

Derr, Richard (1918-1992) A Gentleman at Heart 1942; The Secret Heart 1946; When Worlds Collide 1951; Something to Live For 1952

Derricks, Cleavant (1953-) Moscow on the Hudson 1984; The Slugger's Wife 1985; Off Beat 1986

Derryberry, Debi Whispers: an Elephant's Tale 2000; Jimmy Neutron: Boy Genius 2001

Derzsi, Janos Werckmeister Harmonies 2000; The Man from London 2007; The Turin Horse 2011

Des Barres, Michael (1948-) Ghoulies 1985; Pink Cadillac 1989; Sugar Town 1999; Diary of a Sex Addict 2001; Catch That Kid 2004

Desailly, Jean (1920-2008) La Symphonie Pastorale 1946; Les Grandes Manoeuvres 1955; Maigret Sets a Trap 1957; Le Doulos 1962; La Peau Douce 1964

DeSando, Anthony Federal Hill 1994; Kiss Me, Guido 1997

DeSantis, Stanley (1953-2005) Broken Trust 1995; The Truth about Cats and Dogs 1996; Clockwatchers 1997

Descamps, Patrick [Three] Après la Vie 2002; Private Property 2006

Descas, Alex (1958-) Le Cri du Coeur 1994; Trouble Every Day 2000; Coffee and Cigarettes 2003; The Intruder 2004; 35 Shots of Rum 2008; Rapt 2009; Bastards 2013

Deschamps, Hubert (1923-1998) Zazie dans le Métro 1960; Le Feu Follet 1963; The Mouth Agape 1974

Deschanel, Zooey (1980-) Mumford 1999; Almost Famous 2000; The Good Girl 2001; Manic 2001; The New Guy 2002; All the Real Girls 2003; Elf 2003; The Hitchhiker's Guide to the Galaxy 2005; Bridge to Terabithia 2006; Failure to Launch 2006; The Assassination of Jesse James by the Coward Robert Ford 2007; Surf's Up 2007; Gigantic 2008; The Happening 2008; Yes Man 2008; (500) Days of Summer 2009; Your Highness 2010; Our Idiot Brother 2011; Rock the Kasbah 2015; Trolls 2016

Descher, Sandy (1948-) It Grows on Trees 1952; A Gift for Heidi 1958

Desiderio, Robert (1951-) Oh, God! You Devil 1984; A Cut Above 1989

Desmond, Florence (1905-1993) Sally in Our Alley 1931; No Limit 1935; Accused 1936; Keep Your Seats, Please 1936; Three Came Home 1950; Charley Moon 1956

Desmond, Johnny (1920-1985) China Doll 1958; The Bubble 1966

Desmonde, Jerry (1908-1967) London Town 1946; Cardboard Cavalier 1949; Trouble in Store 1953; The Angel Who Pawned Her Harp 1954; Man of the Moment 1955; Up in the World 1956; Follow a Star 1959; A Stitch in Time 1963 ; The Early Bird 1965

Desni, Tamara (1913-2008) Jack Ahoy! 1934; Fire over England 1937; The Squeaker 1937; The Hills of Donegal 1947

Desny, Ivan aka Desny, Yvan (1928-2002) Madeleine 1949; La Signora senza Camelie 1953; Lola Montès 1955; Anastasia 1956; Song without End 1960; The Magnificent Rebel 1961; Sherlock Holmes and the Deadly Necklace 1962; Paper Tiger 1974; The Marriage of Maria Braun 1978; Lola 1982; J'Embrasse Pas 1991

Desselle, Natalie BAPS 1997; Rodgers & Hammerstein's Cinderella 1997

Detmer, Amanda (1971-) Boys and Girls 2000; Final Destination 2000; Evil Woman 2001; Big Fat Liar 2002; You, Me and Dupree 2006

Detmers, Maruschka (1962-) First Name: Carmen 1983; Hanna's War 1988; The Mambo Kings 1992; Love in the Strangest Way 1994; The Shooter 1994

Deutch, Zoey Dirty Grandpa 2016; Everybody Wants Some!! 2016; Why Him? 2016

Deutsch, Ernst (1890-1969) The Golem 1920; The Third Man 1949

Dev, Rahul Asoka 2001; Awara Paagal Deewana 2002

Devane, William (1939-) Glory Boy 1971; Lady Liberty 1971; McCabe and

Mrs Miller 1971; The Pursuit of Happiness 1971; Fear on Trial 1975; Report to the Commissioner 1975; Family Plot 1976; Marathon Man 1976; The Bad News Bears in Breaking Training 1977; Rolling Thunder 1977; The Dark 1979; Yanks 1979; Honky Tonk Freeway 1981; Testament 1983; Formula for Death 1995; Freefall: Flight 174 1995; Night Watch 1995; Forgotten Sins 1996; Payback 1998; Hollow Man 2000; Space Cowboys 2000; Race to Space 2001; A Christmas Visitor 2002; Monte Walsh 2003

Devereaux, Ed (1925-2003) Watch Your Stern 1960; The Password Is Courage 1962; Live It Up 1963; They're a Weird Mob 1966; Pressure 1976

Devgan, Ajay (1967-) Hum Dil De Chuke Sanam 1999; Company 2001; Bhoot 2003

Devillers, Renée (1903-2001) J'Accuse 1938; Thérèse Desqueyroux 1962

Devine, Adam aka DeVine, Adam (1983-) The Intern 2015; Pitch Perfect 2 2015; Mike and Dave Need Wedding Dates 2016

Devine, Andy (1905-1977) The Impatient Maiden 1932; The Man from Yesterday 1932; Three Wise Girls 1932; Dr Bull 1933; Upper World 1934; The Farmer Takes a Wife 1935; In Old Chicago 1937; A Star Is Born 1937; Doctor Rhythm 1938; Men with Wings 1938; Never Say Die 1939; Stagecoach 1939; Little Old New York 1940; Torrid Zone 1940; When the Daltons Rode 1940; The Flame of New Orleans 1941; Sin Town 1942; Corvette K-225 1943; Frontier Badmen 1943; Ali Baba and the Forty Thieves 1944; Frontier Gal 1945; Sudan 1945; Canyon Passage 1946; Bells of San Angelo 1947; Slave Girl 1947; The Vigilantes Return 1947; Under California Stars 1948; The Far Frontier 1949; Never a Dull Moment 1950; The Red Badge of Courage 1951; Pete Kelly's Blues 1955; The Adventures of Huckleberry Finn 1960; Two Rode Together 1961; The Man Who Shot Liberty Valance 1962; The Ballad of Josie 1968; Myra Breckinridge 1970; Robin Hood 1973; The Mouse and His Child 1977

Devine, George (1910-1966) The Beggar's Opera 1953; Tom Jones 1963

Devine, Loretta (1949-) Sticky Fingers 1988; Waiting to Exhale 1995; The Preacher's Wife 1996; Down in the Delta 1997; Love Kills 1998; Urban Legend 1998; Introducing Dorothy Dandridge 1999; Freedom Song 2000; Urban Legends: Final Cut 2000; I Am Sam 2001; This Christmas 2007; First Sunday 2008; My Son, My Son, What Have Ye Done 2009; Death at a Funeral 2010; For Colored Girls 2010

DeVito, Danny (1944-) Lady Liberty 1971; Scalawag 1973; One Flew over the Cuckoo's Nest 1975; Goin' South 1978; Going Ape! 1981; Terms of Endearment 1983; Johnny Dangerously 1984; Romancing the Stone 1984; The Jewel of the Nile 1985; Head Office 1986; Ruthless People 1986; Wise Guys 1986; Throw Momma from the Train 1987; Tin Men 1987; Twins 1988; The War of the Roses 1989; Other People's Money 1991; Batman Returns 1992; Hoffa 1992; Jack the Bear 1993; Look Who's Talking Now! 1993; Junior 1994; Renaissance Man 1994; Get Shorty 1995; Mars Attacks! 1996; Matilda 1996; Hercules 1997; John Grisham's The Rainmaker 1997; LA Confidential 1997; Space Jam 1997; Living Out Loud 1998; The Big Kahuna 1999; Man on the Moon 1999; The Virgin Suicides 1999; Drowning Mona 2000; Screwed 2000; Heist 2001; What's the Worst That Could Happen? 2001; Death to Smoochy 2002; Anything Else 2003; Be Cool 2005; The Good Night 2005; Marilyn Hotchkiss Ballroom Dancing & Charm School 2005; Deck the Halls 2006; Solitary Man 2009; When in Rome 2009; Dr Seuss' The Lorax 2012; Salinger 2013; Wiener-Dog 2016

Devlin, Alan (1948-2011) Angel 1982; The Lonely Passion of Judith Hearne 1987; The Playboys 1992; High Boot Benny 1993; Song for a Raggy Boy 2002; bl,m 2003

Devlin, J G (1907-1991) No Surrender 1985; The Miracle 1990

Devlin, William (1911-1987) Blood of the Vampire 1958; The Shuttered Room 1967

Devon, Laura (1940-2007) Goodbye Charlie 1964; Red Line 7000 1965; Chamber of Horrors 1966

Devon, Richard (1926-2010) Viking Women and the Sea Serpent 1957; War of the Satellites 1958

Devos, Emmanuelle (1964-) Ma Vie Sexuelle 1996; Esther Kahn 2000; Read My Lips 2001; Petites Coupures

2002; Kings & Queen 2004; The Beat That My Heart Skipped 2005; A Christmas Tale 2008; Wild Grass 2008; Coco avant Chanel 2009; Violette 2013

Devry, Elaine (1935-) Diary of a Madman 1963; A Guide for the Married Man 1967; The Cheyenne Social Club 1970

Dewaele, David Hadewijch 2009; Hors Satan 2011

Dewaere, Patrick (1947-1982) Les Valseuses 1974; Get Out Your Handkerchiefs 1977

Dewan, Jenna Step Up 2006; Take the Lead 2006; Set Up 2011

Dewhurst, Colleen (1924-1991) The Nun's Story 1959; A Fine Madness 1966; The Last Run 1971; The Cowboys 1972; McQ 1974; Annie Hall 1977; Ice Castles 1978; When a Stranger Calls 1979; Tribute 1980; The Dead Zone 1983; The Boy Who Could Fly 1986; Dying Young 1991; Bed & Breakfast 1992

DeWitt, Rosemarie (1971-) Afterschool 2008; Rachel Getting Married 2008; The Company Men 2010; Your Sister's Sister 2011; Promised Land 2012; Touchy Feely 2013; Kill the Messenger 2014; Men, Women & Children 2014; Poltergeist 2015

Dexter, Alan (1918-1983) Forbidden 1953; Time Limit 1957; Paint Your Wagon 1969

Dexter, Anthony (1913-2001) Valentino 1951; Captain Kidd and the Slave Girl 1954; Fire Maidens from Outer Space 1956; He Laughed Last 1956

Dexter, Brad (1917-2002) The Las Vegas Story 1952; Macao 1952; 99 River Street 1953; House of Bamboo 1955; Between Heaven and Hell 1956; Beyond the River 1956; The Oklahoman 1957; Run Silent Run Deep 1958; Last Train from Gun Hill 1959; The Magnificent Seven 1960; X-15 1961; Taras Bulba 1962; Johnny Cool 1963; Kings of the Sun 1963; Invitation to a Gunfighter 1964; Bus Riley's Back in Town 1965; None but the Brave 1965; Von Ryan's Express 1965; Blindfold 1966; Vigilante Force 1975

Dexter, William (1974-) The Knack... and How to Get It 1965; The Hand of Night 1966

Dey, Dipankar The Middleman 1975; In Search of Famine 1980; An Enemy of the People 1989; Branches of the Tree 1990; The Stranger 1991

Dey, Susan (1952-) Skyjacked 1972; First Love 1977; Looker 1981; Echo Park 1985; Sad Inheritance 1993

Deyn, Agyness Pusher 2012; Electricity 2014; Sunset Song 2015; The White King 2016

Dharkar, Ayesha aka Dharker, Ayesha (1977-) City of Joy 1992; The Terrorist 1998; Split Wide Open 1999; The Mystic Masseur 2001; Mad, Sad & Bad 2009

Dharmendra (1935-) Bandini 1963; Sholay 1975; Dharam Veer 1977

Dhavernas, Caroline Niagara Motel 2005; Breach 2006; Passchendaele 2007; The Cry of the Owl 2009

Di Gregorio, Gianni The Ferragosto Dinner 2008; The Salt of Life 2011

Di Stefano, Andrea The Phantom of the Opera 1998; Before Night Falls 2000; Angela 2002

Diamantidou, Despo (1916-2004) Love and Death 1975; A Dream of Passion 1978

Diamantopoulos, Chris The Three Stooges 2012; The Art of the Steal 2013

Diamond, Neil (1941-) The Jazz Singer 1980; Evil Woman 2001

Diamond, Reed aka Diamond, Reed Edward (1964-) Memphis Belle 1990; 919 Fifth Avenue 1995; A Father's Betrayal 1997; High Noon 2000

Diamond, Selma (1920-1985) Bang the Drum Slowly 1973; All of Me 1984

Diarra, Hélène Moolaadé 2004; Bamako 2006

Diaz, Cameron (1972-) The Mask 1994; The Last Supper 1995; Feeling Minnesota 1996; Head above Water 1996; Keys to Tulsa 1996; She's the One 1996; A Life Less Ordinary 1997; My Best Friend's Wedding 1997; Fear and Loathing in Las Vegas 1998; There's Something about Mary 1998; Very Bad Things 1998; Any Given Sunday 1999; Being John Malkovich 1999; Charlie's Angels 2000; The Invisible Circus 2000; Things You Can Tell Just by Looking at Her 2000; Shrek 2001; Slackers 2001; Vanilla Sky 2001; Gangs of New York 2002; The Sweetest Thing 2002; Charlie's Angels: Full Throttle 2003; Shrek 2 2004; In Her Shoes 2005; The Holiday 2006; Shrek the Third 2007; The Box 2008;

What Happens in Vegas 2008; *My Sister's Keeper* 2009; *Knight and Day* 2010; *Shrek Forever After* 2010; *Bad Teacher* 2011; *The Green Hornet* 2011; *Gambit* 2012; *What to Expect When You're Expecting* 2012; *The Counsellor* 2013; *Annie* 2014; *The Other Woman* 2014; *Sex Tape* 2014

Diaz, Guillermo (1975-) *Stonewall* 1995; *High School High* 1996; *I'm Not Rappaport* 1996; *Half-Baked* 1998; *Cop Out* 2010

Diaz, Melonie *Raising Victor Vargas* 2002; *A Guide to Recognizing Your Saints* 2006; *Be Kind Rewind* 2007; *Fruitvale Station* 2013

Diaz, Vic (1932-) *Operation CIA* 1965; *Bloodfist* 1989

Diberti, Luigi (1939-) *The Seduction of Mimi* 1972; *The Oberwald Mystery* 1980; *The Stendhal Syndrome* 1996

DiCaprio, Leonardo (1974-) *Poison Ivy* 1992; *This Boy's Life* 1993; *What's Eating Gilbert Grape* 1993; *The Basketball Diaries* 1995; *The Quick and the Dead* 1995; *Total Eclipse* 1995; *Marvin's Room* 1996; *William Shakespeare's Romeo + Juliet* 1996; *The Man in the Iron Mask* 1997; *Titanic* 1997; *Celebrity* 1998; *The Beach* 2000; *Catch Me If You Can* 2002; *Gangs of New York* 2002; *The Aviator* 2004; *Blood Diamond* 2006; *The Departed* 2006; *The 11th Hour* 2007; *Body of Lies* 2008; *Revolutionary Road* 2008; *Shutter Island* 2009; *Inception* 2010; *J Edgar* 2011; *Django Unchained* 2012; *The Great Gatsby* 2013; *The Wolf of Wall Street* 2013; *The Revenant* 2015

DiCenzo, George (1940-2010) *Going Home* 1971; *The Frisco Kid* 1979; *Starflight One* 1983; *About Last Night...* 1986; *Walk like a Man* 1987; *18 Again!* 1988; *Sing* 1989; *Tempted* 2001

DiCicco, Bobby (1955-) *I Wanna Hold Your Hand* 1978; *The Big Red One* 1980; *Night Shift* 1982; *The Philadelphia Experiment* 1984; *Tiger Warsaw* 1988

Dick, Andy (1965-) *...And God Spoke* 1993; *In the Army Now* 1994; *Best Men* 1997; *The Lion King II: Simba's Pride* 1998; *Inspector Gadget* 1999; *Hoodwinked* 2005; *Employee of the Month* 2006; *Happily N'Ever After* 2006; *The Reef* 2006; *Blonde Ambition* 2007

Dick, Bryan *Brothers of the Head* 2005; *Blood and Chocolate* 2006; *Day of the Flowers* 2012

Dick, Douglas (1920-) *The Searching Wind* 1946; *Casbah* 1948; *Saigon* 1948; *The Accused* 1949; *Home of the Brave* 1949; *The Red Badge of Courage* 1951; *Something to Live For* 1952; *The Oklahoman* 1957

Dick, William *The Company* 2003; *The Merry Gentleman* 2009

Dickens, Kim (1965-) *Great Expectations* 1997; *Truth or Consequences, NM* 1997; *Zero Effect* 1997; *Mercury Rising* 1998; *Hollow Man* 2000; *House of Sand and Fog* 2003; *At Any Price* 2012; *Gone Girl* 2014

Dickerson, George (1933-2015) *Blue Velvet* 1986; *Death Wish 4: the Crackdown* 1987; *After Dark, My Sweet* 1990; *Death Warrant* 1990

Dickey, Dale *Winter's Bone* 2010; *Regression* 2015; *Hell or High Water* 2016

Dickey, Lucinda *Breakdance* 1984; *Breakdance 2 - Electric Boogaloo* 1984

Dickie, Kate (1971-) *Red Road* 2006; *Somers Town* 2008; *Donkeys* 2010; *Outcast* 2010; *For Those in Peril* 2013; *The Silent Storm* 2014; *Couple in a Hole* 2015; *The Witch* 2015

Dickinson, Angie (1931-) *Lucky Me* 1954; *Man with the Gun* 1955; *Tension at Table Rock* 1956; *China Gate* 1957; *Shoot-Out at Medicine Bend* 1957; *Cry Terror* 1958; *I Married a Woman* 1958; *Rio Bravo* 1958; *The Bramble Bush* 1960; *Ocean's Eleven* 1960; *The Sins of Rachel Cade* 1960; *Jessica* 1962; *Rome Adventure* 1962; *Captain Newman, MD* 1963; *The Killers* 1964; *Art of Love* 1965; *Cast a Giant Shadow* 1966; *The Chase* 1966; *The Poppy Is Also a Flower* 1966; *The Last Challenge* 1967; *Point Blank* 1967; *Sam Whiskey* 1969; *Young Billy Young* 1969; *Pretty Maids All in a Row* 1971; *The Outside Man* 1973; *Big Bad Mama* 1974; *Dressed to Kill* 1980; *Charlie Chan and the Curse of the Dragon Queen* 1981; *Death Hunt* 1981; *Big Bad Mama II* 1987; *Once upon a Texas Train* 1988; *Even Cowgirls Get the Blues* 1993; *The Maddening* 1995; *Sabrina* 1995; *Danielle Steel's Remembrance* 1996; *Duets* 2000; *Pay It Forward* 2000; *Elvis Has Left the Building* 2004; *A View from Here* 2009

Dickson, Gloria (1916-1945) *They Won't Forget* 1937; *Racket Busters*

1938; *They Made Me a Criminal* 1939; *This Thing Called Love* 1940; *Lady of Burlesque* 1943

Dickson, Neil *Biggles* 1986; *Lionheart* 1986; *King of the Wind* 1989

Diddley, Bo (1928-2008) *Trading Places* 1983; *Eddie and the Cruisers II: Eddie Lives!* 1989

Diefenthal, Frédéric (1968-) *Taxi* 1998; *Taxi 2* 2000

Diego, Gabino (1966-) *Ay, Carmela!* 1990; *Belle Epoque* 1992; *Two Much* 1995

Diego, Juan (1942-) *Los Santos Inocentes* 1984; *Jamón, Jamón* 1992

Diehl, August (1976-) *Tattoo* 2002; *Mouth to Mouth* 2005; *The Counterfeiters* 2007; *Salt* 2010; *Confession of a Child of the Century* 2011; *Night Train to Lisbon* 2013

Diehl, John (1956-) *Angel* 1984; *Kickboxer 2: the Road Back* 1990; *Madhouse* 1990; *Motorama* 1991; *A Row of Crows* 1991; *Whore* 1991; *Mo' Money* 1992; *Stargate* 1994; *Three Wishes* 1995; *Casualties* 1997; *Anywhere but Here* 1999; *Jurassic Park III* 2001; *Down in the Valley* 2004

Dier, Brett *Seventeen and Missing* 2006; *The Asylum* 2015

Dierkes, John (1905-1975) *Macbeth* 1948; *The Red Badge of Courage* 1951; *The Moonlighter* 1953; *The Naked Jungle* 1953; *Shane* 1953; *Daughter of Dr Jekyll* 1957; *The Hanging Tree* 1959

Dierkop, Charles (1936-) *The Face of Fear* 1971; *Messenger of Death* 1988

Diesel, Vin (1967-) *Saving Private Ryan* 1998; *The Iron Giant* 1999; *Pitch Black* 1999; *Boiler Room* 2000; *The Fast and the Furious* 2001; *Knockaround Guys* 2001; *xXx* 2002; *A Man Apart* 2003; *The Chronicles of Riddick* 2004; *The Pacifier* 2005; *Find Me Guilty* 2006; *Babylon AD* 2008; *Fast & Furious* 2009; *Fast Five* 2011; *Fast & Furious 6* 2013; *Riddick* 2013; *Fast & Furious 7* 2014; *Guardians of the Galaxy* 2014; *The Last Witch Hunter* 2015; *Guardians of the Galaxy Vol 2* 2017; *xXx: the Return of Xander Cage* 2017

Diessl, Gustav (1899-1948) *Crisis* 1928; *Westfront 1918* 1930; *The Testament of Dr Mabuse* 1933

Dieterle, William aka **Dieterle, Wilhelm** (1893-1972) *Waxworks* 1924; *Faust* 1926

Dietrich, Marlene (1901-1992) *The Joyless Street* 1925; *The Ship of Lost Men* 1929; *Three Loves* 1929; *The Blue Angel* 1930; *Morocco* 1930; *Dishonored* 1931; *Blonde Venus* 1932; *Shanghai Express* 1932; *The Song of Songs* 1933; *The Scarlet Empress* 1934; *The Devil Is a Woman* 1935; *Desire* 1936; *The Garden of Allah* 1936; *Angel* 1937; *Knight without Armour* 1937; *Destry Rides Again* 1939; *Seven Sinners* 1940; *The Flame of New Orleans* 1941; *Manpower* 1941; *The Lady Is Willing* 1942; *Pittsburgh* 1942; *The Spoilers* 1942; *Follow the Boys* 1944; *Kismet* 1944; *Martin Roumagnac* 1946; *Golden Earrings* 1947; *A Foreign Affair* 1948; *Jigsaw* 1949; *Stage Fright* 1949; *No Highway* 1951; *Rancho Notorious* 1952; *Around the World in 80 Days* 1956; *The Monte Carlo Story* 1957; *Witness for the Prosecution* 1957; *Touch of Evil* 1958; *Judgment at Nuremberg* 1961; *The Black Fox* 1962; *Paris When It Sizzles* 1964; *The Love Goddesses* 1965; *Just a Gigolo* 1978; *Marlene* 1984

Diffring, Anton (1918-1989) *Albert, RN* 1953; *Double Cross* 1955; *I Am a Camera* 1955; *The Black Tent* 1956; *House of Secrets* 1956; *The Crooked Sky* 1957; *Mark of the Phoenix* 1957; *The Traitor* 1957; *The Man Who Could Cheat Death* 1959; *Circus of Horrors* 1960; *The Heroes of Telemark* 1965; *The Blue Max* 1966; *Fahrenheit 451* 1966; *Counterpoint* 1967; *The Double Man* 1967; *Where Eagles Dare* 1969; *Zeppelin* 1971; *Dead Pigeon on Beethoven Street* 1972; *The Beast Must Die* 1974; *Shatter* 1974; *Operation Daybreak* 1975; *The Swiss Conspiracy* 1975

Digard, Uschi aka **Lillimor, Astrid** (1948-) *Cherry, Harry & Raquel* 1969; *Supervixens* 1975; *Beneath the Valley of the Ultra Vixens* 1979

Digges, Dudley (1879-1947) *Condemned* 1929; *Dangerous Female* 1931; *The First Year* 1932; *The Hatchet Man* 1932; *Tess of the Storm Country* 1932; *The Emperor Jones* 1933; *The Mayor of Hell* 1933; *What Every Woman Knows* 1934; *China Seas* 1935; *Mutiny on the Bounty* 1935; *The General Died at Dawn* 1936; *Valiant Is the Word for Carrie* 1936; *Love Is News* 1937; *The Light That Failed* 1939; *Raffles* 1939; *The Searching Wind* 1946

Diggs, Taye (1971-) *How Stella Got Her Groove Back* 1998; *The Best Man* 1999; *House on Haunted Hill* 1999; *The Wood* 1999; *The Way of the Gun* 2000; *Brown Sugar* 2002; *Chicago* 2002; *Equilibrium* 2002; *Just a Kiss* 2002; *Basic* 2003; *Malibu's Most Wanted* 2003; *Slow Burn* 2003; *Rent* 2005; *Baggage Claim* 2013; *The Best Man Holiday* 2013

Dignam, Arthur (1939-) *The Devil's Playground* 1976; *We of the Never Never* 1982; *The Wild Duck* 1983

Dignam, Basil (1905-1979) *Seven Seas to Calais* 1962; *80,000 Suspects* 1963

Dignam, Mark (1909-1989) *The Siege of the Saxons* 1963; *Hamlet* 1969; *Dead Cert* 1974

Dignard, Holly Elissa aka **Dignard, Holly** *Kill Switch* 2008; *Polar Storm* 2009

Dillahunt, Garret (1964-) *No Country for Old Men* 2007; *The Last House on the Left* 2008; *Oliver Sherman* 2010; *Winter's Bone* 2010; *Any Day Now* 2012

Dillane, Richard *The Dinosaur Project* 2012; *Mindscape* 2013

Dillane, Stephen (1957-) *Hamlet* 1990; *Stolen Hearts* 1996; *Déjà Vu* 1997; *Firelight* 1997; *Welcome to Sarajevo* 1997; *The Darkest Light* 1999; *Ordinary Decent Criminal* 1999; *The Parole Officer* 2001; *Spy Game* 2001; *The Gathering* 2002; *The Hours* 2002; *The Truth about Charlie* 2002; *King Arthur* 2004; *Goal!* 2005; *The Greatest Game Ever Played* 2005; *Klimt* 2006; *Fugitive Pieces* 2007; *Goal II: Living the Dream* 2007; *Savage Grace* 2007; *Red Mist* 2008; *44 Inch Chest* 2009; *Storm* 2009; *Perfect Sense* 2011; *Papadopoulos & Sons* 2012; *Twenty8k* 2012; *Zero Dark Thirty* 2012

Dillard, Victoria (1969-) *Ricochet* 1991; *Deep Cover* 1992; *The Best Man* 1999

Dillaway, Donald aka **Dillaway, Don** (1903-1982) *Min and Bill* 1930; *Body and Soul* 1931; *Platinum Blonde* 1931; *The Animal Kingdom* 1932; *Pack Up Your Troubles* 1932; *The Little Giant* 1933; *The Magnificent Ambersons* 1942

Diller, Phyllis (1917-2012) *Boy, Did I Get a Wrong Number* 1966; *Mad Monster Party* 1966; *Eight on the Lam* 1967; *The Private Navy of Sgt O'Farrell* 1968; *The Adding Machine* 1969; *Snow White in Happily Ever After* 1990; *The Silence of the Hams* 1993; *A Bug's Life* 1998; *Who Killed the Electric Car?* 2006

Dillman, Bradford aka **Dillman, Brad** (1930-) *A Certain Smile* 1958; *In Love and War* 1958; *Compulsion* 1959; *Circle of Deception* 1960; *Crack in the Mirror* 1960; *Francis of Assisi* 1961; *Sanctuary* 1961; *The Plainsman* 1966; *The Helicopter Spies* 1968; *Jigsaw* 1968; *Sergeant Ryker* 1968; *The Bridge at Remagen* 1969; *Brother John* 1970; *Suppose They Gave a War and Nobody Came?* 1970; *Escape from the Planet of the Apes* 1971; *The Mephisto Waltz* 1971; *The Way We Were* 1973; *Chosen Survivors* 1974; *Gold* 1974; *99 and 44/100% Dead* 1974; *Bug* 1975; *The Enforcer* 1976; *Mastermind* 1976; *The Amsterdam Kill* 1978; *Love and Bullets* 1978; *Piranha* 1978; *Sudden Impact* 1983; *The Heart of Justice* 1992

Dillon, Edward aka **Dillon, Eddie** (1879-1933) *The Broadway Melody* 1929; *The Iron Man* 1931

Dillon, Kevin (1965-) *Catholic Boys* 1985; *Platoon* 1986; *The Blob* 1988; *Remote Control* 1988; *The Rescue* 1988; *War Party* 1988; *Immediate Family* 1989; *The Doors* 1991; *A Midnight Clear* 1991; *No Escape* 1994; *True Crime* 1995; *Poseidon* 2006; *Hotel for Dogs* 2009; *Entourage* 2015

Dillon, Matt (1964-) *Over the Edge* 1979; *Little Darlings* 1980; *My Bodyguard* 1980; *Liar's Moon* 1982; *Tex* 1982; *The Outsiders* 1983; *Rumble Fish* 1983; *The Flamingo Kid* 1984; *Rebel* 1985; *Target* 1985; *Native Son* 1986; *The Big Town* 1987; *Kansas* 1988; *Bloodhounds of Broadway* 1989; *Drugstore Cowboy* 1989; *A Kiss before Dying* 1991; *Mr Wonderful* 1992; *Singles* 1992; *The Saint of Fort Washington* 1993; *Golden Gate* 1994; *Frankie Starlight* 1995; *To Die For* 1995; *Albino Alligator* 1996; *Beautiful Girls* 1996; *Grace of My Heart* 1996; *In & Out* 1997; *There's Something about Mary* 1998; *Wild Things* 1998; *One Night at McCool's* 2001; *City of Ghosts* 2002; *Crash* 2004; *Factotum (A Man Who Fully Loaded)* 2005; *The Future Is Unwritten* 2006; *Once in a Lifetime: the Extraordinary Story of the New York Cosmos* 2006; *You, Me and Dupree* 2006; *Armored* 2009; *Old*

Dogs 2009; *Takers* 2010; *Girl Most Likely* 2012; *The Art of the Steal* 2013

Dillon, Melinda (1939-) *The April Fools* 1969; *Bound for Glory* 1976; *Close Encounters of the Third Kind* 1977; *FIST* 1978; *The Shadow Box* 1980; *Absence of Malice* 1981; *A Christmas Story* 1983; *Songwriter* 1984; *Bigfoot and the Hendersons* 1987; *Nightbreaker* 1989; *Staying Together* 1989; *Captain America* 1990; *The Prince of Tides* 1991; *Sioux City* 1994; *To Wong Foo, Thanks for Everything, Julie Newmar* 1995; *Magnolia* 1999; *A Painted House* 2003; *Reign over Me* 2007

Dillon, Paul *Kiss Daddy Good Night* 1987; *Blink* 1994; *CutThroat Island* 1995; *Chicago Cab* 1998

DiMaggio, John *Pirates of Silicon Valley* 1999; *Asterix and the Vikings* 2006

Dimitriades, Alex (1973-) *The Heartbreak Kid* 1993; *Head On* 1997; *La Spagnola* 2001; *Ghost Ship* 2002

Dinehart, Alan (1889-1944) *Lawyer Man* 1932; *Washington Merry-Go-Round* 1932; *Bureau of Missing Persons* 1933; *The Sin of Nora Moran* 1933; *Supernatural* 1933; *Baby, Take a Bow* 1934; *Jimmy the Gent* 1934; *Dante's Inferno* 1935; *Born to Dance* 1936; *Human Cargo* 1936; *Step Lively, Jeeves* 1937; *This Is My Affair* 1937; *Fast and Loose* 1939; *Second Fiddle* 1939; *Sweet Rosie O'Grady* 1943; *What a Woman!* 1943; *The Whistler* 1944

Dingle, Charles (1887-1956) *The Little Foxes* 1941; *Unholy Partners* 1941; *Somewhere I'll Find You* 1942; *The Talk of the Town* 1942; *Lady of Burlesque* 1943; *Guest Wife* 1944; *Home in Indiana* 1944; *Together Again* 1944; *A Medal for Benny* 1945; *The Beast with Five Fingers* 1946; *Cinderella Jones* 1946; *Sister Kenny* 1946; *My Favorite Brunette* 1947; *Never Wave at a WAC* 1952

Dingo, Ernie (1956-) *"Crocodile" Dundee II* 1988; *Until the End of the World* 1991; *Dead Heart* 1996

Dingwall, Shaun *Villa des Roses* 2002; *Someone Else* 2005; *Outlanders* 2006; *Summer in February* 2012

Dinicol, Joe *Weirdsville* 2006; *Diary of the Dead* 2007; *Passchendaele* 2007

Dinklage, Peter (1969-) *The Station Agent* 2003; *Lassie* 2005; *Find Me Guilty* 2006; *Penelope* 2006; *Death at a Funeral* 2007; *Underdog* 2007; *The Chronicles of Narnia: Prince Caspian* 2008; *Death at a Funeral* 2010; *The Angriest Man in Brooklyn* 2014; *The Boss* 2015; *Pixels* 2015; *The Angry Birds Movie* 2016

Dinsdale, Reece (1959-) *A Private Function* 1984; *ID* 1994; *Hamlet* 1996

Dio, Ronnie James *Tenacious D in The Pick of Destiny* 2006; *Iron Maiden: Flight 666* 2009

Dione, Rose (1875-1936) *Salome* 1922; *Freaks* 1932

Dionisi, Stefano (1966-) *Farinelli il Castrato* 1994; *The Truce* 1997; *Shooting the Moon* 1998; *Les Enfants du Siècle* 1999; *The Loss of Sexual Innocence* 1999

Dionisotti, Paola *Vigo: Passion for Life* 1997; *The Tichborne Claimant* 1998

Diop, Mati *35 Shots of Rum* 2008; *Simon Killer* 2012

Director, Kim *Book of Shadows: Blair Witch 2* 2000; *Split* 2017

Dishy, Bob aka **Dishy, Robert** (1934-) *Lovers and Other Strangers* 1970; *The Big Bus* 1976; *First Family* 1980; *Author! Author!* 1982; *Brighton Beach Memoirs* 1986; *Critical Condition* 1987; *Used People* 1992; *Don Juan DeMarco* 1995; *Judy Berlin* 1999

Diskin, Ben *Top Cat: the Movie* 2011; *Top Cat Begins* 2016

Disney, Walt (1901-1966) *Steamboat Willie* 1928; *The Reluctant Dragon* 1941

Ditson, Harry *The Sender* 1982; *Back in the USSR* 1992

Divine (1945-1988) *Mondo Trasho* 1970; *Multiple Maniacs* 1970; *Pink Flamingos* 1972; *Female Trouble* 1974; *Polyester* 1981; *Lust in the Dust* 1984; *Trouble in Mind* 1985; *Hairspray* 1988; *Out of the Dark* 1988; *I Am Divine* 2013

Divoff, Andrew (1955-) *Another 48 HRS* 1990; *Graveyard Shift* 1990; *Toy Soldiers* 1991; *Back in the USSR* 1992; *Running Cool* 1993; *A Low Down Dirty Shame* 1994; *Adrenalin: Fear the Rush* 1995; *Wishmaster* 1997; *Captured* 1998; *Stealth Fighter* 1999; *Faust: Love of the Damned* 2001

Dix, Richard (1894-1949) *The Ten Commandments* 1923; *Cimarron* 1931; *The Lost Squadron* 1932; *Ace of Aces* 1933; *The Arizonian* 1935; *Cherokee Strip* 1940; *The Ghost Ship* 1943; *The Whistler* 1944

Dix, William (1956-) *The Nanny* 1965; *Doctor Dolittle* 1967

Dixit, Madhuri (1967-) *Saajan* 1991; *Hum Tumhare Hain Sanam* 2000; *Devdas* 2002

Dixon, Donna (1957-) *Doctor Detroit* 1983; *Spies like Us* 1985; *The Couch Trip* 1988; *Cannonball Fever* 1989

Dixon, Ivan (1931-2008) *The Murder Men* 1961; *A Raisin in the Sun* 1961; *Nothing but a Man* 1964; *A Patch of Blue* 1965; *Suppose They Gave a War and Nobody Came?* 1970

Dixon, James *It's Alive* 1974; *It Lives Again* 1978; *Q - the Winged Serpent* 1982; *The Stuff* 1985; *It's Alive III: Island of the Alive* 1987

Dixon, Jean (1896-1981) *The Kiss before the Mirror* 1933; *She Married Her Boss* 1935; *My Man Godfrey* 1936; *Swing High, Swing Low* 1937; *You Only Live Once* 1937; *Holiday* 1938; *Joy of Living* 1938

Dixon, Jill *Just My Luck* 1957; *A Night to Remember* 1958

Dixon, Lee (1914-1953) *Gold Diggers of 1937* 1936; *Angel and the Badman* 1947

Dixon, MacIntyre (1931-) *Starting Over* 1979; *Funny Farm* 1988

Dixon, Reg (1914-1983) *Love in Pawn* 1953; *No Smoking* 1954

Djalili, Omid (1965-) *The Mummy* 1999; *The Calcium Kid* 2003; *Sky Captain and the World of Tomorrow* 2004; *Casanova* 2005; *Alien Autopsy* 2006; *Grow Your Own* 2007; *The Love Guru* 2008; *The Infidel* 2010; *Mr Nice* 2010; *Bulla... Big Fat Gypsy Gangster* 2011; *Shaun the Sheep Movie* 2015

Djaoro, Youssouf *Daratt* 2006; *A Screaming Man* 2010

Djola, Badja (1948-2005) *The Lightship* 1985; *The Serpent and the Rainbow* 1987; *An Innocent Man* 1989; *A Rage in Harlem* 1991; *Who's the Man?* 1993; *Heaven's Prisoners* 1996; *Deterrence* 1999

Dmochowski, Mariusz (1930-1992) *The Scar* 1976; *Camouflage* 1977

Dobie, Alan (1932-) *Alfred the Great* 1969; *The Chairman* 1969

Dobkin, Lawrence (1919-2002) *The Gene Krupa Story* 1959; *The Cabinet of Caligari* 1962; *Geronimo* 1962

Dobrev, Nina (1989-) *Chloe* 2009; *The Perks of Being a Wallflower* 2012; *Let's Be Cops* 2014; *Flatliners* 2017; *xXx: the Return of Xander Cage* 2017

Dobrowolska, Gosia (1958-) *A Woman's Tale* 1991; *Careful* 1992; *Erotic Tales* 1994

Dobson, Anita (1949-) *Beyond Bedlam* 1993; *Darkness Falls* 1998; *Charlie* 2003; *London Road* 2014

Dobson, James (1920-1987) *The Tall Stranger* 1957; *Jet Attack* 1958; *Impulse* 1975

Dobson, Peter (1964-) *Last Exit to Brooklyn* 1989; *Sing* 1989; *Too Hot to Handle* 1991; *The Frighteners* 1996; *Norma Jean & Marilyn* 1996; *A Stranger's Heart* 2007; *The Nanny Express* 2008

Dobson, Tamara (1947-2006) *Cleopatra Jones* 1973; *Cleopatra Jones and the Casino of Gold* 1975; *Chained Heat* 1983

Dobtcheff, Vernon (1934-) *India Song* 1975; *Condorman* 1981; *Berlin Jerusalem* 1989; *Venice/Venice* 1992; *M Butterfly* 1993; *Déjà Vu* 1997; *All for Love* 1999; *The Order* 2001; *Before Sunset* 2004; *Priceless* 2006

Dockery, Michelle (1981-) *Non-Stop* 2014; *Self/Less* 2015

Dr Dre (1965-) *Who's the Man?* 1993; *Set It Off* 1996; *Ride* 1998; *Training Day* 2001; *The Wash* 2001; *Something from Nothing: the Art of Rap* 2012; *Unity* 2015

Dodd, Claire (1908-1973) *Lawyer Man* 1932; *Ex-Lady* 1933; *Hard to Handle* 1933; *Gambling Lady* 1934; *The Glass Key* 1935; *Roberta* 1935; *The Case of the Velvet Claws* 1936; *Fast Company* 1938; *Three Loves Has Nancy* 1938; *Slightly Honorable* 1939; *In the Navy* 1941; *The Mad Doctor of Market Street* 1942

Dodds, Megan *Ever After: a Cinderella Story* 1998; *The Contract* 2006

Dodsworth, John (1910-1964) *Here Comes the Sun* 1945; *The Maze* 1953

Doe, John (1954-) *Slam Dance* 1987; *Great Balls of Fire!* 1989; *Without You I'm Nothing* 1990; *Pure Country* 1992; *Roadside Prophets* 1992; *Georgia* 1995; *Sugar Town* 1999

Doherty, James *Inbred* 2011; *Verity's Summer* 2012

Doherty, Shannen (1971-) *Night Shift* 1982; *The Secret of NIMH* 1982; *Girls Just Want to Have Fun* 1985; *Heathers* 1989; *Mallrats* 1995; *Jay and Silent Bob Strike Back* 2001; *The Battle of Mary Kay* 2002

Dolan, Michael (1965-) Hamburger Hill 1987; Biloxi Blues 1988; The Turning 1992

Dolan, Monica (1969-) A Midsummer Night's Dream 1996; The Arbor 2010; Sightseers 2012; The Falling 2014

Dolan, Xavier (1989-) I Killed My Mother 2009; Heartbeats 2010; Tom at the Farm 2013

Doleman, Guy (1923-1996) The Ipcress File 1965; Thunderball 1965; Funeral in Berlin 1966; The Idol 1966; Billion Dollar Brain 1967; The Deadly Bees 1967; A Twist of Sand 1967

Dolenz, Ami (1969-) Rescue Me 1991; Ticks 1993; The Revenge of Pumpkinhead - Blood Wings 1994

Dolenz, George (1908-1963) Enter Arsene Lupin 1944; My Cousin Rachel 1952; Scared Stiff 1953; Sign of the Pagan 1954; A Bullet for Joey 1955; The Purple Mask 1955; The Sad Sack 1957

Dolera, Leticia Imagining Argentina 2003; Man Push Cart 2005; [Rec]³ Génesis 2012

Doll, Birgit (1958-) The Second Victory 1986; The Seventh Continent 1989

Doll, Dora (1922-2015) Honour among Thieves 1954; Calle Mayor 1956; Black and White in Color 1976; L'Enfer 1993

Domasin, Larry (1955-) Fun in Acapulco 1963; Island of the Blue Dolphins 1964

Dombasle, Arielle (1955-) Le Beau Mariage 1982; Pauline at the Beach 1983; The Blue Villa 1994; Three Lives and Only One Death 1996; L'Ennui 1998; Le Libertin 2000

Domeier, Richard Evil Dead II 1987; The Unnamable Returns 1992

Domergue, Faith (1924-1999) Where Danger Lives 1950; The Duel at Silver Creek 1952; The Great Sioux Uprising 1953; This Is My Love 1954; Cult of the Cobra 1955; It Came from beneath the Sea 1955; Santa Fe Passage 1955; This Island Earth 1955; Timeslip 1955; Escort West 1959; Voyage to the Prehistoric Planet 1965; The Gamblers 1969; The House of Seven Corpses 1973

Dominczyk, Dagmara (1976-) The Count of Monte Cristo 2001; Rock Star 2001; They 2002; The Immigrant 2013

Domingo, Placido (1941-) La Traviata 1982; Carmen 1984; Otello 1986

Dominguez D, Berta Where Is Parsifal? 1983; The Rainbow Thief 1990

Dominguez, Columba (1929-) The River and Death 1954; The Important Man 1961

Dominguez, Wade (1966-1999) City of Industry 1996; Shadow of Doubt 1998; Taxman 1998

Dominici, Arturo (1918-1992) Hercules 1957; Goliath and the Barbarians 1959; The Mask of Satan 1960; The Trojan War 1961; Investigation of a Citizen above Suspicion 1970

Dommartin, Solveig (1961-2007) Wings of Desire 1987; Until the End of the World 1991; Faraway, So Close 1993

Donahue, Elinor (1937-) Love Is Better than Ever 1951; Girls' Town 1959

Donahue, Heather (1974-) The Blair Witch Project 1998; Boys and Girls 2000

Donahue, Troy (1936-2001) The Tarnished Angels 1957; Wild Heritage 1958; A Summer Place 1959; The Crowded Sky 1960; Susan Slade 1961; Rome Adventure 1962; Palm Springs Weekend 1963; A Distant Trumpet 1964; My Blood Runs Cold 1965; Jules Verne's Rocket to the Moon 1967; Seizure 1974; Grandview, USA 1984; Cry-Baby 1990

Donald, James (1917-1993) The Way Ahead 1944; Broken Journey 1948; The Small Voice 1948; Edward, My Son 1949; Trottie True 1949; Cage of Gold 1950; Brandy for the Parson 1951; Gift Horse 1951; White Corridors 1951; The Pickwick Papers 1952; The Net 1953; Beau Brummell 1954; Lust for Life 1956; The Bridge on the River Kwai 1957; The Vikings 1958; The Great Escape 1963; King Rat 1965; The Jokers 1967; Quatermass and the Pit 1967; The Royal Hunt of the Sun 1969

Donaldson, Ted (1933-) Mr Winkle Goes to War 1944; Once upon a Time 1944; A Tree Grows in Brooklyn 1945

Donat, Peter (1928-) The China Syndrome 1979; Ladies and Gentlemen, the Fabulous Stains 1981; Bay Boy 1984; Skin Deep 1989; The War of the Roses 1989; The Babe 1992; The Game 1997; Red Corner 1997; The Deep End 2001

Donat, Robert (1905-1958) The Private Life of Henry VIII 1933; The Count of Monte Cristo 1934; The Ghost Goes West 1935; The 39 Steps 1935; Knight without Armour 1937; The Citadel 1938; Goodbye, Mr Chips 1939; The Young Mr Pitt 1942; The Adventures of Tartu 1943; Perfect Strangers 1945; Captain Boycott 1947; The Winslow Boy 1948; The Cure for Love 1949; The Magic Box 1951; Lease of Life 1954; The Inn of the Sixth Happiness 1958

Donath, Ludwig (1900-1967) The Jolson Story 1946; To the Ends of the Earth 1948; Jolson Sings Again 1949; Mystery Submarine 1950; Torn Curtain 1966

Donato, Marc A Map of the World 1999; The Final 2010

Donde, Manuel (1906-1976) The Treasure of the Sierra Madre 1947; Mexican Bus Ride 1951; El 1953

Donlan, James (1888-1938) Big News 1929; Belle of the Nineties 1934

Donlan, Yolande (1920-2014) Traveller's Joy 1949; Mr Drake's Duck 1950; Penny Princess 1952; They Can't Hang Me 1955; Tarzan and the Lost Safari 1956; Expresso Bongo 1959; Jigsaw 1962; 80,000 Suspects 1963

Donlevy, Brian aka McGinty (1899-1972) Barbary Coast 1935; Crack-Up 1936; Human Cargo 1936; Strike Me Pink 1936; Born Reckless 1937; This Is My Affair 1937; We're Going to Be Rich 1938; Beau Geste 1939; Destry Rides Again 1939; The First Rebel 1939; Jesse James 1939; Union Pacific 1939; Brigham Young 1940; The Great McGinty 1940; When the Daltons Rode 1940; Billy the Kid 1941; The Birth of the Blues 1941; I Wanted Wings 1941; The Glass Key 1942; The Great Man's Lady 1942; Stand by for Action 1942; Wake Island 1942; Hangmen Also Die! 1943; The Miracle of Morgan's Creek 1943; An American Romance 1944; Canyon Passage 1946; Two Years before the Mast 1946; The Virginian 1946; The Beginning or the End 1947; Heaven Only Knows 1947; Killer McCoy 1947; Kiss of Death 1947; Song of Scheherazade 1947; Command Decision 1948; A Southern Yankee 1948; Impact 1949; Kansas Raiders 1950; Hoodlum Empire 1952; The Woman They Almost Lynched 1953; The Big Combo 1955; The Quatermass Xperiment 1955; A Cry in the Night 1956; Quatermass II 1957; Cowboy 1958; Juke Box Rhythm 1959; Never So Few 1959; The Errand Boy 1961; Curse of the Fly 1965; Gamera the Invincible 1965; How to Fill a Wild Bikini 1965; Waco 1966; Five Golden Dragons 1967; Arizona Bushwhackers 1968

Donlin, Mike (1878-1933) Beggars of Life 1928; The Iron Man 1931

Donnadieu, Bernard-Pierre (1949-2010) The Return of Martin Guerre 1982; Max Mon Amour 1986; The Vanishing 1988; Shadow of the Wolf 1992; Druids 2001; Paris 36 2008

Donnell, Jeff (1921-1988) The Boogie Man Will Get You 1942; A Night to Remember 1942; Over 21 1945; Easy Living 1949; Roughshod 1949; Walk Softly, Stranger 1949; The Fuller Brush Girl 1950; In a Lonely Place 1950; Because You're Mine 1952; Thief of Damascus 1952; The Blue Gardenia 1953; So This Is Love 1953; Guns of Fort Petticoat 1957; Sweet Smell of Success 1957; The Iron Maiden 1962

Donnelly, Donal aka Donnelly, Donald (1931-2010) The Knack... and How to Get It 1965; The Mind of Mr Soames 1970; Waterloo 1970; The Dead 1987; Squanto: the Last Great Warrior 1994

Donnelly, Ruth (1896-1982) Blessed Event 1932; Bureau of Missing Persons 1933; Ever in My Heart 1933; Female 1933; Hard to Handle 1933; Mandalay 1934; Hands across the Table 1935; Red Salute 1935; Fatal Lady 1936; The Affairs of Annabel 1938; Annabel Takes a Tour 1938; A Slight Case of Murder 1938; The Amazing Mr Williams 1939; My Little Chickadee 1940; You Belong to Me 1941; The Bells of St Mary's 1945; Cinderella Jones 1946; Where the Sidewalk Ends 1950; I'd Climb the Highest Mountain 1951; A Lawless Street 1955; Autumn Leaves 1956

Donner, Robert (1931-2006) Vanishing Point 1971; The Man Who Loved Cat Dancing 1973; Under the Rainbow 1981; Allan Quatermain and the Lost City of Gold 1987

D'Onofrio, Vincent aka D'Onofrio, Vincent (1959-) Full Metal Jacket 1987; A Night on the Town 1987; Mystic Pizza 1988; The Salute of the Jugger 1989; Naked Tango 1990; Crooked Hearts 1991; Dying Young 1991; Fires Within 1991; Mr Wonderful 1992; The Player 1992; Salt on Our Skin 1992; Household Saints 1993; Being Human 1994; Ed Wood 1994; Imaginary Crimes 1994; Strange Days 1995; Stuart Saves His Family 1995; Feeling Minnesota 1996; Good Luck 1996; Guy 1996; The Whole Wide World 1996; The Winner 1996; Men in Black 1997; Claire Dolan 1998; The Newton Boys 1998; The Velocity of Gary 1998; The Thirteenth Floor 1999; The Cell 2000; The Dangerous Lives of Altar Boys 2001; Impostor 2001; The Salton Sea 2002; Overnight 2004; Thumbsucker 2005; The Break-Up 2006; Brooklyn's Finest 2009; Staten Island 2009; Kill the Irishman 2011; Chained 2012; Fire with Fire 2012; Sinister 2012; The Judge 2014; Broken Horses 2015; Jurassic World 2015; Run All Night 2015; The Magnificent Seven 2016

Donohoe, Amanda (?-) Castaway 1986; Foreign Body 1986; The Lair of the White Worm 1988; The Rainbow 1988; Diamond Skulls 1989; Paper Mask 1990; Shame 1992; The Madness of King George 1995; Liar Liar 1997; I'm Losing You 1998; A Knight in Camelot 1998; The Real Howard Spitz 1998; Wild about Harry 2000; Starship Troopers 3: Marauder 2008; The Calling 2009

Donovan (1946-) Festival 1967; Message to Love 1995

Donovan, Daisy Millions 2004; Death at a Funeral 2007; Wild Child 2008

Donovan, Jason (1968-) Blood Oath 1990; Rough Diamonds 1994; Sorted 2000

Donovan, Jeffrey (1968-) Book of Shadows: Blair Witch 2 2000; Changeling 2008; J Edgar 2011; Sicario 2015

Donovan, King (1918-1987) The Enforcer 1951; Easy to Love 1953; Private Hell 36 1954; Invasion of the Body Snatchers 1956; The Defiant Ones 1958

Donovan, Martin The Great Gatsby 2000; The Sentinel 2006; Wind Chill 2007; Unthinkable 2010

Donovan (2), Martin (1957-) Trust 1990; Simple Men 1992; Quick 1993; Amateur 1994; Hollow Reed 1995; Nadja 1995; The Portrait of a Lady 1996; The Book of Life 1998; Heaven 1998; Living Out Loud 1998; The Opposite of Sex 1998; When Trumpets Fade 1998; Onegin 1999; Custody of the Heart 2000; Insomnia 2002; The United States of Leland 2002; Agent Cody Banks 2003; The Haunting in Connecticut 2009

Donovan, Tate (1963-) SpaceCamp 1986; Clean and Sober 1988; Dead-Bang 1989; Memphis Belle 1990; Equinox 1992; Little Noises 1992; Love Potion No 9 1992; Ethan Frome 1993; Holy Matrimony 1994; Hercules 1997; G-Men from Hell 2000; Get Well Soon 2001; Nancy Drew 2007; Shooter 2007; Argo 2012

Donovan, Terence (1939-) Breaker Morant 1979; Emma's War 1985

Doody, Alison (1966-) Taffin 1988; Indiana Jones and the Last Crusade 1989; We Still Kill the Old Way 2014

Doohan, James (1920-2005) Pretty Maids All in a Row 1971; Star Trek: the Motion Picture 1979; Star Trek II: the Wrath of Khan 1982; Star Trek III: the Search for Spock 1984; Star Trek IV: the Voyage Home 1986; Star Trek V: the Final Frontier 1989; Star Trek VI: the Undiscovered Country 1991; Star Trek: Generations 1994; The Duke 1999

Doolan, Jack Cemetery Junction 2010; may i kill u? 2012; It's a Lot 2013

Dooley, Paul (1928-) A Wedding 1978; Breaking Away 1979; A Perfect Couple 1979; Rich Kids 1979; HEALTH 1980; Popeye 1980; Paternity 1981; Kiss Me Goodbye 1982; Monster in the Closet 1983; Big Trouble 1985; OC and Stiggs 1987; Last Rites 1988; Flashback 1990; Shakes the Clown 1991; Cooperstown 1993; The Underneath 1995; Loved 1996; Telling Lies in America 1997; Guinevere 1999; Runaway Bride 1999; Insomnia 2002; Horsemen 2009

Dooley, Shaun Salvage 2009; Junkhearts 2011; The Woman in Black 2011; Blood Moon 2014

Doonan, Patric (1925-1958) The Blue Lamp 1949; Blackout 1950; Seagulls over Sorrento 1954

Dopud, Mike Snowman's Pass 2004; White Noise 2004

DoQui, Robert (1934-2008) Coffy 1973; Nashville 1975; RoboCop 1987; RoboCop 2 1990

Dor, Christiane (1892-1939) Poil de Carotte 1932; Madame Bovary 1933

Dor, Karin (1936-) The Face of Fu Manchu 1965; You Only Live Twice 1967; Topaz 1969

Doran, Ann (1911-2000) Blondie! 1938; Blind Alley 1939; Penny Serenade 1941; Here Come the Waves 1944; I Love a Soldier 1944; Pride of the Marines 1945; Roughly Speaking 1945; The Strange Love of Martha Ivers 1946; Fear in the Night 1947; Magic Town 1947; Pitfall 1948; No Sad Songs for Me 1950; Love Is Better than Ever 1951; Tomahawk 1951; So This Is Love 1953; Rebel without a Cause 1955; It! The Terror from beyond Space 1958; Violent Road 1958; Voice in the Mirror 1958; The Brass Bottle 1964; All Night Long 1981

Doran, Johnny (1962-) The Hideaways 1973; Treasure of Matecumbe 1976

Doran, Mary (1907-1995) The Criminal Code 1930; The Divorcee 1930

Doran, Matt Macbeth 2006; Battle of the Damned 2013

Doran, Richard The Harrad Summer 1974; Hollywood Boulevard 1976

Dorat, Charles (1906-1997) La Belle Equipe 1936; The Golem 1936

Doré, Edna (1921-2014) High Hopes 1988; Nil by Mouth 1997; Weak at Denise 2000

Doret, Thomas The Kid with a Bike 2011; Renoir 2012

Dorff, Stephen (1973-) The Gate 1987; The Power of One 1991; Rescue Me 1991; Backbeat 1993; Judgment Night 1993; SFW 1994; I Shot Andy Warhol 1995; Innocent Lies 1995; Reckless 1995; Blood and Wine 1996; City of Industry 1996; Space Truckers 1996; Blade 1998; Earthly Possessions 1999; Cecil B Demented 2000; FearDotCom 2002; Steal 2002; Cold Creek Manor 2003; World Trade Center 2006; Botched 2007; Felon 2008; Public Enemies 2009; Somewhere 2010; Immortals 2011; The Iceman 2012; The Motel Life 2012; Zaytoun 2012

Dorfman, David (1993-) Invisible Child 1999; Panic 2000; The Ring 2002; The Texas Chainsaw Massacre 2003; The Ring Two 2004; Drillbit Taylor 2007

Doria, Diogo (1953-) The Divine Comedy 1992; Journey to the Beginning of the World 1997; Eccentricities of a Blonde-Haired Girl 2009

Doria, Malena (?-1999) Little Treasure 1985; Highway Patrolman 1991

Dorléac, Françoise (1942-1967) Male Hunt 1964; La Peau Douce 1964; That Man from Rio 1964; Where the Spies Are 1965; Cul-de-Sac 1966; Billion Dollar Brain 1967; The Young Girls of Rochefort 1967

Dorman, Michael Suburban Mayhem 2006; Daybreakers 2008; Triangle 2009

Dormer, Natalie W.E. 2011; A Long Way from Home 2013; The Riot Club 2014; The Forest 2016

Dormer, Richard (1969-) Middletown 2006; Five Minutes of Heaven 2009; Good Vibrations 2012; '71 2014; Shooting for Socrates 2014

Dorn, Dolores (1935-) The Bounty Hunter 1954; Underworld USA 1961; 13 West Street 1962; Truck Stop Women 1974; Tell Me a Riddle 1980

Dorn, Michael (1952-) Star Trek: Generations 1994; Star Trek: First Contact 1996; Star Trek: Insurrection 1998; The Prophet's Game 1999; Shadow Hours 2000; Star Trek: Nemesis 2002

Dorn, Philip (1901-1975) Escape 1940; Tarzan's Secret Treasure 1941; Calling Dr Gillespie 1942; Random Harvest 1942; Reunion in France 1942; Blonde Fever 1944; Passage to Marseille 1944; I Remember Mama 1948; The Fighting Kentuckian 1949; Sealed Cargo 1951

Dornan, Jamie (1982-) Shadows in the Sun 2008; Fifty Shades of Grey 2015; Fifty Shades Darker 2017

Dorne, Sandra (1925-1992) Hindle Wakes 1952; Marilyn 1953; Police Dog 1955; Devil Doll 1964

Dorning, Robert (1913-1989) Die! Die! My Darling 1964; Ups and Downs of a Handyman 1975

Dors, Diana (1931-1984) Dancing with Crime 1946; The Calendar 1948; Here Come the Huggetts 1948; It's Not Cricket 1948; Oliver Twist 1948; Vote for Huggett 1948; A Boy, a Girl and a Bike 1949; Diamond City 1949; Dance Hall 1950; Lady Godiva Rides Again 1951; My Wife's Lodger 1952; Is Your Honeymoon Really Necessary? 1953; It's a Grand Life 1953; The Weak and the Wicked 1953; An Alligator Named Daisy 1955; As Long as They're Happy 1955; A Kid for Two Farthings 1955; Value for Money 1955; Yield to the Night 1956; The Unholy Wife 1957; I Married a Woman 1958; Passport to Shame 1958; Tread Softly Stranger 1958; Scent of Mystery 1960; King of the Roaring 20s - the Story of Arnold Rothstein 1961; On the Double 1961; West 11 1963; The Sandwich Man 1966; Berserk 1967; Danger Route 1967; Hammerhead 1968; Deep End 1970; There's a Girl in My Soup 1970; Hannie Caulder 1971; The Amazing Mr Blunden 1972; Nothing but the Night 1972; Craze 1973; From beyond the Grave 1973; Steptoe and Son Ride Again 1973; The Amorous Milkman 1974; Adventures of a Taxi Driver 1975; Keep It Up Downstairs 1976; Adventures of a Private Eye 1977; Steaming 1985

D'Orsay, Fifi (1904-1983) They Had to See Paris 1929; Going Hollywood 1933

Dorsey, Joe (1925-) Brainstorm 1983; The Philadelphia Experiment 1984

Dorsey, Tommy (1905-1956) Presenting Lily Mars 1943; The Fabulous Dorseys 1947

Dorval, Anne I Killed My Mother 2009; Heartbeats 2010; Mommy 2014

Dorziat, Gabrielle (1880-1979) Mayerling 1936; The End of the Day 1939; Monsieur Vincent 1947; Les Parents Terribles 1948; Act of Love 1953; Little Boy Lost 1953; Gigot 1962; A Monkey in Winter 1962

Dossett, John Longtime Companion 1990; That Night 1992

Dotrice, Karen (1955-) The Three Lives of Thomasina 1963; Mary Poppins 1964; The Gnome-Mobile 1967; The Thirty-Nine Steps 1978

Dotrice, Michele (1947-) The Witches 1966; And Soon the Darkness 1970; Blood on Satan's Claw 1970; Not Now, Comrade 1976

Dotrice, Roy (1923-) A Twist of Sand 1967; Lock Up Your Daughters! 1969; The Buttercup Chain 1970; Toomorrow 1970; Tales from the Crypt 1972; Amadeus 1984; Cheech & Chong's The Corsican Brothers 1984; The Cutting Edge 1992; Swimming with Sharks 1994; The Scarlet Letter 1995

Doty, David Full Moon in Blue Water 1988; Vacancy 2007

Doubleday, Kaitlin Waiting... 2005; The March Sisters at Christmas 2012

Doubleday, Portia Youth in Revolt 2009; Big Mommas: Like Father, like Son 2011; Carrie 2013

Doucet, Catherine aka Doucet, Catharine (1875-1958) Little Man, What Now? 1934; Poppy 1936; These Three 1936; When You're in Love 1937; There's One Born Every Minute 1942

Doucette, John (1921-1994) Cavalry Scout 1951; Gang War 1958; The Fastest Guitar Alive 1966; One Little Indian 1973; Fighting Mad 1976

Doug, Doug E (1970-) Hangin' with the Homeboys 1991; Cool Runnings 1993; Operation Dumbo Drop 1995; That Darn Cat 1997; Eight Legged Freaks 2001

Doughty, Kenny Crush 2001; The Aryan Couple 2004; City Rats 2008; In the Blood 2014

Douglas, Angela (1940-) Some People 1962; It's All Happening 1963; The Comedy Man 1964; Carry On Cowboy 1965; Carry On Follow That Camel 1967; Digby, the Biggest Dog in the World 1973

Douglas, Craig It's Trad, Dad 1961; The Painted Smile 1961

Douglas, Diana (1923-2015) The Indian Fighter 1955; It Runs in the Family 2002

Douglas, Don aka Douglas, Donald (1905-1945) The Great Gabbo 1929; Smashing the Rackets 1938; I Love You Again 1940; The Falcon Out West 1944; Show Business 1944; Tall in the Saddle 1944

Douglas, Donna (1933-2015) Career 1959; Frankie & Johnny 1966

Douglas, Illeana (1965-) Cape Fear 1991; Alive 1992; Search and Destroy 1995; To Die For 1995; Grace of My Heart 1996; Picture Perfect 1997; Message in a Bottle 1998; Happy, Texas 1999; Lansky 1999; Stir of Echoes 1999; The Next Best Thing 2000; Ghost World 2001; Dummy 2002; The New Guy 2002; Factory Girl 2006; Expired 2007

Douglas, Jack (1927-2008) Carry On Abroad 1972; Carry On Girls 1973; Carry On Dick 1974; Carry On Behind 1975; Carry On England 1976; Carry On Emmannuelle 1978; The Boys in Blue 1983

Douglas, James GI Blues 1960; A Thunder of Drums 1961

Douglas, Kirk (1916-) The Strange Love of Martha Ivers 1946; Build My Gallows High 1947; I Walk Alone 1947; Mourning Becomes Electra 1947; My Dear Secretary 1948; Champion 1949; A Letter to Three Wives 1949; The Glass Menagerie 1950; Young Man with a Horn 1950; Ace in the Hole 1951; Along the Great Divide 1951; Detective Story 1951; The Bad and the Beautiful 1952; The Big Sky 1952; The Big Trees 1952; Act of Love 1953; The Juggler 1953; The Story of Three Loves 1953; 20,000 Leagues under the Sea 1954; Ulysses 1954; The Indian Fighter 1955;

Man without a Star 1955; The Racers 1955; Lust for Life 1956; Gunfight at the OK Corral 1957; Paths of Glory 1957; Top Secret Affair 1957; The Vikings 1958; Last Train from Gun Hill 1959; Spartacus 1960; Strangers When We Meet 1960; The Last Sunset 1961; Town without Pity 1961; The Hook 1962; Lonely Are the Brave 1962; Two Weeks in Another Town 1962; For Love or Money 1963; The List of Adrian Messenger 1963; Seven Days in May 1964; The Heroes of Telemark 1965; In Harm's Way 1965; Cast a Giant Shadow 1966; Is Paris Burning? 1966; The War Wagon 1967; The Way West 1967; The Brotherhood 1968; A Lovely Way to Go 1968; The Arrangement 1969; There Was a Crooked Man... 1970; Catch Me a Spy 1971; A Gunfight 1971; The Light at the Edge of the World 1971; Scalawag 1973; Once Is Not Enough 1975; Posse 1975; Victory at Entebbe 1976; Holocaust 2000 1977; The Fury 1978; Cactus Jack 1979; Home Movies 1979; The Final Countdown 1980; Saturn 3 1980; The Man from Snowy River 1982; Eddie Macon's Run 1983; Tough Guys 1986; Inherit the Wind 1988; Oscar 1991; Greedy 1994; The Lies Boys Tell 1994; Diamonds 1999; It Runs in the Family 2002; Cameraman: the Life & Work of Jack Cardiff 2010

Douglas, Melvyn (1901-1981) As You Desire Me 1932; The Old Dark House 1932; The Wiser Sex 1932; Counsellor-at-Law 1933; The Vampire Bat 1933; Dangerous Corner 1934; Annie Oakley 1935; She Married Her Boss 1935; And So They Were Married 1936; The Gorgeous Hussy 1936; The Lone Wolf Returns 1936; Theodora Goes Wild 1936; Angel 1937; Captains Courageous 1937; I Met Him in Paris 1937; I'll Take Romance 1937; Arsene Lupin Returns 1938; Fast Company 1938; The Shining Hour 1938; That Certain Age 1938; There's Always a Woman 1938; The Toy Wife 1938; The Amazing Mr Williams 1939; Ninotchka 1939; Tell No Tales 1939; Third Finger, Left Hand 1940; This Thing Called Love 1940; Too Many Husbands 1940; That Uncertain Feeling 1941; Two-Faced Woman 1941; A Woman's Face 1941; They All Kissed the Bride 1942; The Guilt of Janet Ames 1947; The Sea of Grass 1947; Mr Blandings Builds His Dream House 1948; The Great Sinner 1949; A Woman's Secret 1949; My Forbidden Past 1951; Billy Budd 1962; Hud 1963; Advance to the Rear 1964; The Americanization of Emily 1964; Rapture 1965; I Never Sang for My Father 1970; The Candidate 1972; One Is a Lonely Number 1972; The Tenant 1976; Twilight's Last Gleaming 1977; Being There 1979; The Seduction of Joe Tynan 1979; The Changeling 1980; Tell Me a Riddle 1980; Ghost Story 1981; The Hot Touch 1982

Douglas, Michael Summertree 1971; SuperMensch: the Legend of Shep Gordon 2013

Douglas (1), Michael (1944-) Hail, Hero! 1969; Adam at 6 AM 1970; Napoleon and Samantha 1972; Coma 1977; The China Syndrome 1979; Running 1979; It's My Turn 1980; The Star Chamber 1983; Romancing the Stone 1984; A Chorus Line 1985; The Jewel of the Nile 1985; Fatal Attraction 1987; Wall Street 1987; Black Rain 1989; The War of the Roses 1989; Basic Instinct 1992; Falling Down 1992; Shining Through 1992; Disclosure 1994; The American President 1995; The Ghost and the Darkness 1996; The Game 1997; One Day in September 1999; Traffic 2000; Wonder Boys 2000; Don't Say a Word 2001; One Night at McCool's 2001; It Runs in the Family 2002; The In-Laws 2003; The Sentinel 2006; You, Me and Dupree 2006; Beyond a Reasonable Doubt 2009; Ghosts of Girlfriends Past 2009; Solitary Man 2009; Wall Street: Money Never Sleeps 2010; Haywire 2011; Behind the Candelabra 2013; Last Vegas 2013; And So It Goes 2014; Beyond the Reach 2014; Ant-Man 2015

Douglas, Paul (1907-1959) Everybody Does It 1949; It Happens Every Spring 1949; A Letter to Three Wives 1949; The Big Lift 1950; Panic in the Streets 1950; Angels in the Outfield 1951; Fourteen Hours 1951; Clash by Night 1952; Never Wave at a WAC 1952; We're Not Married 1952; Forever Female 1953; The Maggie 1953; Executive Suite 1954; Green Fire 1954; Joe Macbeth 1955; The Solid Gold Cadillac 1956; Beau James 1957; This Could Be the Night 1957; The Mating Game 1959

Douglas, Robert (1909-1999) Death Drives Through 1935; London Melody 1937; Over the Moon 1937; The Challenge 1938; The Lion Has Wings 1939; The End of the River 1947; Adventures of Don Juan 1948; The Fountainhead 1949; Barricade 1950; The Flame and the Arrow 1950; Kim 1950; Mystery Submarine 1950; Sons of the Musketeers 1951; Target Unknown 1951; Thunder on the Hill 1951; Ivanhoe 1952; The Desert Rats 1953; Fair Wind to Java 1953; Flight to Tangier 1953; King Richard and the Crusaders 1954; Saskatchewan 1954; Good Morning, Miss Dove 1955; Tarzan, the Ape Man 1959; Secret Ceremony 1968

Douglas, Sarah (1952-) The People That Time Forgot 1977; Superman II 1980; Conan the Destroyer 1984; The Return of Swamp Thing 1989; Strippers vs Werewolves 2012

Douglas, Shirley (1934-) Dead Ringers 1988; Barney's Great Adventure 1998; A House Divided 2000

Douglas, Suzzanne (1957-) Tap 1989; Jason's Lyric 1994; How Stella Got Her Groove Back 1998

Douglass, Robyn (1953-) Breaking Away 1979; Partners 1982; Romantic Comedy 1983; The Lonely Guy 1984

Dourdan, Gary (1966-) Alien: Resurrection 1997; Scarred City 1998; Muhammad Ali: King of the World 2000; Impostor 2001; Perfect Stranger 2007

Dourif, Brad (1950-) One Flew over the Cuckoo's Nest 1975; Eyes of Laura Mars 1978; Wise Blood 1979; Heaven's Gate 1980; Ragtime 1981; Dune 1984; Blue Velvet 1986; Fatal Beauty 1987; Child's Play 1988; Mississippi Burning 1988; Child's Play 2 1990; The Exorcist III 1990; Grim Prairie Tales 1990; Hidden Agenda 1990; Graveyard Shift 1990; Body Parts 1991; Chaindance 1991; Child's Play 3 1991; Jungle Fever 1991; London Kills Me 1991; Scream of Stone 1991; Amos & Andrew 1993; Trauma 1993; Color of Night 1994; Death Machine 1994; Murder in the First 1994; Nightwatch 1997; Bride of Chucky 1998; Brown's Requiem 1998; Progeny 1998; Senseless 1998; Urban Legend 1998; The Ghost 2000; The Prophecy 3: the Ascent 2000; Shadow Hours 2000; Seed of Chucky 2004; The Wild Blue Yonder 2005; Halloween 2007; Halloween II 2009; My Son, My Son, What Have Ye Done 2009; Curse of Chucky 2013; Rosemont 2015

Dourif, Fiona After the Fall 2010; Curse of Chucky 2013

Doutey, Mélanie (1978-) The Flower of Evil 2002; The Connection 2014

Dove, Billie (1900-1997) The Black Pirate 1926; Blondie of the Follies 1932

Dow, Ellen Albertini (1913-2015) The Wedding Singer 1998; Annie's Point 2005

Dow, Peggy (1928-) Undertow 1949; Harvey 1950; The Sleeping City 1950; Bright Victory 1951; I Want You 1951

Dowd, Ann (1956-) Bushwhacked 1995; Kingfish: a Story of Huey P Long 1995; All over Me 1996; Shiloh 1996; Apt Pupil 1997; Garden State 2003; Lucy 2003; Compliance 2012; The Drop 2014; Our Brand Is Crisis 2015

Dowie, Freda Distant Voices, Still Lives 1988; Butterfly Kiss 1994

Dowling, Constance (1920-1969) Knickerbocker Holiday 1944; Up in Arms 1944; Black Angel 1946; The Well Groomed Bride 1946

Dowling, Doris (1923-2004) The Lost Weekend 1945; The Blue Dahlia 1946; Bitter Rice 1949

Dowling, Joan (1928-1954) No Room at the Inn 1948; Train of Events 1949; Murder without Crime 1950; Pool of London 1950; Women of Twilight 1952

Dowling, Kathryn Diner 1982; Stranger in the Family 1991

Dowling, Rachael aka **Dowling, Rachel** The Dead 1987; Bogwoman 1997; The Tichborne Claimant 1998

Down, Lesley-Anne (1954-) Assault 1970; Countess Dracula 1970; Pope Joan 1972; From beyond the Grave 1973; Scalawag 1973; Brannigan 1975; The Pink Panther Strikes Again 1976; A Little Night Music 1977; The Betsy 1978; The First Great Train Robbery 1978; Hanover Street 1979; Rough Cut 1980; Sphinx 1980; Agatha Christie's Murder Is Easy 1982; The Hunchback of Notre Dame 1982; Nomads 1985; Indiscreet 1988; Death Wish V: the Face of Death 1994; Munchie Strikes Back 1994; The Secret Agent Club 1996

Downey, Brian George's Island 1991; Hobo with a Shotgun 2011

Downey Sr, Robert (1936-) Is There Sex after Death? 1971; To Live and Die in LA 1985; Johnny Be Good 1988

Downey Jr, Robert (1965-) Baby It's You 1983; Weird Science 1985; Back to School 1986; Less than Zero 1987; The Pick-Up Artist 1987; Johnny Be Good 1988; 1969 1988; Chances Are 1989; True Believer 1989; Air America 1990; Too Much Sun 1990; Soapdish 1991; Chaplin 1992; Heart and Souls 1993; The Last Party 1993; Short Cuts 1993; Natural Born Killers 1994; Only You 1994; Home for the Holidays 1995; Restoration 1995; Richard III 1995; Danger Zone 1996; The Gingerbread Man 1997; One Night Stand 1997; Two Girls and a Guy 1997; In Dreams 1998; US Marshals 1998; Black and White 1999; Bowfinger 1999; Wonder Boys 2000; Gothika 2003; The Singing Detective 2003; Eros 2004; Good Night, and Good Luck. 2005; Kiss Kiss Bang Bang 2005; Fur: an Imaginary Portrait of Diane Arbus 2006; A Guide to Recognizing Your Saints 2006; A Scanner Darkly 2006; The Shaggy Dog 2006; Charlie Bartlett 2007; Zodiac 2007; The Incredible Hulk 2008; Iron Man 2008; The Soloist 2008; Tropic Thunder 2008; Sherlock Holmes 2009; Due Date 2010; Iron Man 2 2010; Sherlock Holmes: a Game of Shadows 2011; Marvel Avengers Assemble 2012; Iron Man Three 2013; Chef 2014; The Judge 2014; Avengers: Age of Ultron 2015; Captain America: Civil War 2016; Spider-Man: Homecoming 2017

Downing, Vernon (1913-1973) Clive of India 1935; Sherlock Holmes and the Spider Woman 1944

Downs, Cathy (1924-1976) The Dark Corner 1946; My Darling Clementine 1946; The Noose Hangs High 1948; The Sundowners 1950; The Big Tip Off 1955; The Oklahoma Woman 1956; The She-Creature 1956; The Amazing Colossal Man 1957

Downs, Johnny (1913-1994) Pigskin Parade 1936; Adam Had Four Sons 1941

Dowse, Denise (1958-) Bio-Dome 1996; Coach Carter 2005

Doyen, Jacqueline Entre Nous 1983; The Frog Prince 1984

Doyle Kennedy, Maria aka **Doyle, Maria** (1964-) The Commitments 1991; The General 1998; Gregory's Two Girls 1999; I Could Read the Sky 1999; Miss Julie 1999; A Thousand Times Good Night 2013; Sing Street 2015

Doyle-Murray, Brian (1945-) Modern Problems 1981; JFK 1991; Wayne's World 1992; Groundhog Day 1993; Cabin Boy 1994; Jury Duty 1995; My Brother's Keeper 1995; Dennis the Menace Strikes Again 1998; Legalese 1998; Snow Dogs 2002; Daddy Day Camp 2007

Doyle, David (1929-1997) Paper Lion 1968; The April Fools 1969; Loving 1970; The Comeback 1977

Doyle, Shawn Frequency 2000; Don't Say a Word 2001

Doyle, Tony (1941-2000) Loophole 1980; Who Dares Wins 1982; Eat the Peach 1986; Secret Friends 1991

Drache, Heinz (1923-2002) Coast of Skeletons 1964; The Brides of Fu Manchu 1966; Circus of Fear 1967

Drago, Billy (1949-) Windwalker 1980; The Untouchables 1987; Delta Force 2 1990; Guncrazy 1992; Cyborg 2: Glass Shadow 1993; Mysterious Skin 2004; The Hills Have Eyes 2006

Drake, Betsy (1923-2015) Every Girl Should Be Married 1948; Dancing in the Dark 1949; Pretty Baby 1950; The Second Woman 1951; Room for One More 1952; Will Success Spoil Rock Hunter? 1957; Intent to Kill 1958; Next to No Time 1958; Clarence, the Cross-Eyed Lion 1965

Drake, Charles (1914-1994) Air Force 1943; Conflict 1945; A Night in Casablanca 1946; Tarzan's Magic Fountain 1949; Comanche Territory 1950; Harvey 1950; I Was a Shoplifter 1950; Winchester '73 1950; Air Cadet 1951; Red Ball Express 1952; Treasure of Lost Canyon 1952; The Glenn Miller Story 1953; Gunsmoke 1953; It Came from Outer Space 1953; The Lone Hand 1953; War Arrow 1953; All That Heaven Allows 1955; To Hell and Back 1955; Walk the Proud Land 1956; Jeanne Eagels 1957; Until They Sail 1957; No Name on the Bullet 1959; Back Street 1961; Tammy Tell Me True 1961; Showdown 1963; Dear Heart 1964; Valley of the Dolls 1967; The Counterfeit Killer 1968; Hail, Hero! 1969

Drake, Charlie (1925-2006) Sands of the Desert 1960; Petticoat Pirates 1961; The Cracksman 1963; Mister Ten Per Cent 1967

Drake, Dona (1914-1989) Louisiana Purchase 1941; Road to Morocco 1942; Without Reservations 1946; Another Part of the Forest 1948; So This Is New York 1948; Beyond the Forest 1949; Valentino 1951; Kansas City Confidential 1952; The Bandits of Corsica 1953; Princess of the Nile 1954

Drake, Fabia (1904-1990) Not Wanted on Voyage 1957; Operation Bullshine 1959; Valmont 1989

Drake, Frances (1908-2000) Bolero 1934; Forsaking All Others 1934; Ladies Should Listen 1934; Mad Love 1935; Les Misérables 1935; The Invisible Ray 1936; There's Always a Woman 1938; It's a Wonderful World 1939; I Take This Woman 1940; The Affairs of Martha 1942

Drake, Gabrielle (1944-) Connecting Rooms 1969; There's a Girl in My Soup 1970

Drake, Larry (1950-2016) Darkman 1990; Murder in New Hampshire 1991; Dr Giggles 1992; Darkman II: the Return of Durant 1995; The Journey of August King 1995; Bean 1997; Overnight Delivery 1997; Desert Heat 1999

Drake, Tom (1918-1982) Meet Me in St Louis 1944; Two Girls and a Sailor 1944; Courage of Lassie 1946; The Green Years 1946; The Beginning or the End 1947; Cass Timberlane 1947; I'll Be Yours 1947; Hills of Home 1948; Words and Music 1948; Mr Belvedere Goes to College 1949; Scene of the Crime 1949; The Great Rupert 1950; The Cyclops 1957; Warlock 1959; The Bramble Bush 1960; Johnny Reno 1966

Draper, Paul (1909-1996) Colleen 1936; The Time of Your Life 1948

Draper, Polly (1955-) Gold Diggers: the Secret of Bear Mountain 1995; LaVyrle Spencer's Home Song 1996; The Tic Code 1998; Obvious Child 2014; Demolition 2015

Dratch, Rachel Down with Love 2003; Driving Aphrodite 2008

Draxl, Tom Swimming Upstream 2003; A Few Best Men 2011

Dray, Albert La Balance 1982; Crime Spree 2002

Drayton, Alfred (1881-1949) Friday the Thirteenth 1933; Jack Ahoy! 1934; The Dictator 1935; First a Girl 1935; Look Up and Laugh 1935; The Halfway House 1943; Don't Take It to Heart 1944; Nicholas Nickleby 1947

Drescher, Fran (1957-) American Hot Wax 1977; Doctor Detroit 1983; Cadillac Man 1990; Without Warning: Terror in the Towers 1993; Jack 1996; The Beautician and the Beast 1997; Picking Up the Pieces 2000; The Reef 2006

Dresdel, Sonia (1909-1976) While I Live 1947; The Fallen Idol 1948; The Clouded Yellow 1950; The Break 1962

Dresser, Louise (1878-1965) Ruggles of Red Gap 1923; The Eagle 1925; The Goose Woman 1925; Mammy 1930; Dr Bull 1933; State Fair 1933; The Scarlet Empress 1934; The World Moves On 1934

Dressler, Lieux (1930-) Truck Stop Women 1974; Kingdom of the Spiders 1977

Dressler, Marie (1869-1934) Tillie's Punctured Romance 1914; The Divine Lady 1928; The Patsy 1928; Hollywood Revue 1929; Anna Christie 1930; Min and Bill 1930; One Romantic Night 1930; Emma 1932; Dinner at Eight 1933; Tugboat Annie 1933

Drew, Ben aka **Drew, Ben "Plan B"** Adulthood 2008; Harry Brown 2009; The Sweeney 2012

Drew, Ellen (1915-2003) If I Were King 1938; French without Tears 1939; The Gracie Allen Murder Case 1939; Buck Benny Rides Again 1940; Christmas in July 1940; My Favorite Spy 1942; The Impostor 1944; China Sky 1945; Isle of the Dead 1945; Johnny o'Clock 1947; The Man from Colorado 1948; The Baron of Arizona 1950; Stars in My Crown 1950; Man in the Saddle 1951

Drew, Roland (1900-1988) The Bermuda Mystery 1944; Two o'Clock Courage 1945

Drexel, Ruth (1930-2009) Jail Bait 1972; The Marquise of O 1976

Dreyfus, James (1964-) Boyfriends 1996; Notting Hill 1999; Fat Slags 2004

Dreyfus, Jean-Claude (1946-) Delicatessen 1990; Pétain 1992; The City of Lost Children 1995; The Lady & the Duke 2001; Two Brothers 2004; A Very Long Engagement 2004

Dreyfuss, Richard (1947-) Hello Down There 1969; American Graffiti 1973; Dillinger 1973; The Apprenticeship of Duddy Kravitz 1974; The Second Coming of Suzanne 1974; Inserts 1975; Jaws 1975; Victory at Entebbe 1976; Close Encounters of the Third Kind 1977; The Goodbye Girl 1977; The Big Fix 1978; Whose Life Is It Anyway? 1981; The Buddy System 1984; Down and Out in Beverly Hills 1986; Stand by Me 1986; Nuts 1987; Stakeout 1987; Tin Men 1987; Moon over Parador 1988;

Always 1989; Postcards from the Edge 1990; Rosencrantz and Guildenstern Are Dead 1990; Once Around 1991; Prisoner of Honor 1991; What about Bob? 1991; Another Stakeout 1993; Lost in Yonkers 1993; Silent Fall 1994; The American President 1995; Mr Holland's Opus 1995; The Call of the Wild 1996; James and the Giant Peach 1996; Trigger Happy 1996; Night Falls on Manhattan 1997; Krippendorf's Tribe 1998; Lansky 1999; Fail Safe 2000; The Old Man Who Read Love Stories 2000; Silver City 2004; Poseidon 2006; Driving Aphrodite 2008; W. 2008; Piranha 2010; Red 2010; Paranoia 2013

Drier, Moosie (1964-) The War between Men and Women 1972; American Hot Wax 1977; Rainbow 1978

Dring, Micaiah One for the Road 2003; Crying with Laughter 2009

Drinkwater, Carol (1948-) The Shout 1978; Father 1990

Driscoll, Bobby (1937-1968) The Fighting Sullivans 1944; From This Day Forward 1946; So Goes My Love 1946; Song of the South 1946; So Dear to My Heart 1949; The Window 1949; Treasure Island 1950; The Happy Time 1952; Peter Pan 1953

Driscoll, Patricia (1927-) Charley Moon 1956; The Wackiest Ship in the Army 1961

Drivas, Robert (1938-1986) Cool Hand Luke 1967; The Illustrated Man 1969

Driver, Adam (1983-) Frances Ha 2012; Tracks 2013; What If 2013; This Is Where I Leave You 2014; While We're Young 2014

Driver, Betty (1920-2011) Boots! Boots! 1934; Penny Paradise 1938; Let's Be Famous 1939

Driver, Edgar (1887-1964) Doss House 1933; Song of the Road 1937

Driver, Minnie (1970-) Circle of Friends 1995; Big Night 1996; Sleepers 1996; Good Will Hunting 1997; The Governess 1997; Grosse Pointe Blank 1997; Hard Rain 1997; An Ideal Husband 1999; South Park: Bigger, Longer & Uncut 1999; Tarzan 1999; Beautiful 2000; Return to Me 2000; High Heels and Low Lifes 2001; Princess Mononoke 2001; Hope Springs 2002; Owning Mahowny 2002; Ella Enchanted 2004; The Phantom of the Opera 2004; Motherhood 2009; Barney's Version 2010; Conviction 2010; Hunky Dory 2011; I Give It a Year 2013; Beyond the Lights 2014

Drouot, Jean-Claude Le Bonheur 1965; Laughter in the Dark 1969; The Light at the Edge of the World 1971

Dru, Joanne (1922-1996) Abie's Irish Rose 1946; Red River 1948; All the King's Men 1949; She Wore a Yellow Ribbon 1949; 711 Ocean Drive 1950; Wagonmaster 1950; Mr Belvedere Rings the Bell 1951; Vengeance Valley 1951; The Pride of St Louis 1952; Forbidden 1953; Thunder Bay 1953; The Siege at Red River 1954; Southwest Passage 1954; Three Ring Circus 1954; The Dark Avenger 1955; Hell on Frisco Bay 1955; Sincerely Yours 1955; The Light in the Forest 1958; The Wild and the Innocent 1959; Sylvia 1964

Drukarova, Dinara (1976-) Don't Move, Die and Rise Again 1989; Of Freaks and Men 1998

Drummond, Alice Awakenings 1990; Pieces of April 2002; Doubt 2008

Drury, James (1934-) Ten Who Dared 1960; Toby Tyler, or Ten Weeks with a Circus 1960; Ride the High Country 1962; The Young Warriors 1967; Backtrack 1969; The Virginian 2000

Drynan, Jeanie Muriel's Wedding 1994; Paperback Hero 1999; Soft Fruit 1999

du Maurier, Gerald (1873-1934) Escape 1930; Scotland Yard Mystery 1933; I Was a Spy 1934; Jew Süss 1934; The Rise of Catherine the Great 1934

Duane, Michael (1914-1963) Dr Gillespie's Criminal Case 1943; The Prince of Thieves 1948

Dubbins, Don (1928-1991) These Wilder Years 1956; Tribute to a Bad Man 1956; From the Earth to the Moon 1958; The Illustrated Man 1969; Banacek: Detour to Nowhere 1972

Dube, Desmond The Long Run 2000; Hotel Rwanda 2004

Duberg, Axel (1927-2001) The Devil's Eye 1960; The Virgin Spring 1960

Dubey, Satyadev (1936-2011) Nishant 1975; Maya 1992

Dubin, Ellen Lies and Deception 2005; Abducted 2007

Dubois, Marie (1937-2014) Shoot the Pianist 1960; Une Femme Est une Femme 1961; Jules et Jim 1962; La Ronde 1964; The Thief of Paris 1967; Vincent, François, Paul and the Others

1974; L'Innocente 1976; Mon Oncle d'Amérique 1980; Descent into Hell 1986

Dubost, Paulette (1910-2011) La Règle du Jeu 1939; Lola Montès 1955; Le Bossu 1959; Viva Maria! 1965; The Last Metro 1980

Dubov, Paul (1918-1979) China Gate 1957; Voodoo Woman 1957; Verboten! 1959; The Atomic Submarine 1960; Underworld USA 1961

Duchaussoy, Michel (1938-2012) La Femme Infidèle 1968; Que la Bête Meure 1969; Shock Treatment 1973; Nada 1974; Fort Saganne 1984; Milou en Mai 1989; Road to Ruin 1992; La Veuve de Saint-Pierre 2000; Amen. 2002; The Bridesmaid 2004; Confidences Trop Intimes 2004

Duchesne, Roger (1906-1996) The Golem 1936; Bob Le Flambeur 1955

Duchovny, David (1960-) Bad Influence 1990; Don't Tell Mom the Babysitter's Dead 1991; The Rapture 1991; Beethoven 1992; Chaplin 1992; Ruby 1992; Venice/Venice 1992; Kalifornia 1993; Playing God 1997; The X-Files 1998; Return to Me 2000; Evolution 2001; Zoolander 2001; Full Frontal 2002; Connie and Carla 2004; Trust the Man 2006; Things We Lost in the Fire 2007; The X-Files: I Want to Believe 2008; The Joneses 2009

Duclos, Philippe The Bait 1995; Ma Mère 2004

Ducommun, Rick (1952-2015) The 'Burbs 1989; Ghost in the Machine 1993; Groundhog Day 1993

Dudgeon, Neil (1961-) Different for Girls 1996; It Was an Accident 2000; Son of Rambow 2007; The Arbor 2010

Dudikoff, Michael (1954-) American Ninja 1985; Avenging Force 1986; River of Death 1989; Rescue Me 1991; In Her Defense 1998; The Silencer 1999

Dudley Ward, Penelope (1919-1982) Escape Me Never 1935; Moscow Nights 1935; Convoy 1940; The Demi-Paradise 1943

Dudley, Doris (1917-1985) A Woman Rebels 1936; The Moon and Sixpence 1942

Dudley, Olivia aka **Taylor Dudley, Olivia** Chernobyl Diaries 2012; The Vatican Tapes 2015

Duel, Pete (1940-1971) The Hell with Heroes 1968; Generation 1969; Cannon for Cordoba 1970

Duell, William (1923-2011) Deadhead Miles 1972; Grace Quigley 1984

Dueñas, Lola (1971-) The Sea Inside 2004; Volver 2006; The Women on the 6th Floor 2010; Alleluia 2014

Duering, Carl (1923-) Arabesque 1966; Duffy 1968; A Clockwork Orange 1971

Duff, Amanda (1914-2006) Just around the Corner 1938; Mr Moto in Danger Island 1939; The Devil Commands 1941

Duff, Anne-Marie (1970-) The Magdalene Sisters 2002; Garage 2007; The Waiting Room 2007; French Film 2008; Is Anybody There? 2008; The Last Station 2009; Nowhere Boy 2010; Before I Go to Sleep 2014; Molly Moon and the Incredible Book of Hypnotism 2015; Suffragette 2015

Duff, Haylie (1985-) Napoleon Dynamite 2004; Material Girls 2006; A Nanny's Secret 2008

Duff, Hilary (1987-) Casper Meets Wendy 1998; Agent Cody Banks 2003; Cheaper by the Dozen 2003; The Lizzie McGuire Movie 2003; A Cinderella Story 2004; Raise Your Voice 2004; Cheaper by the Dozen 2 2005; The Perfect Man 2005; Material Girls 2006; War, Inc 2008; According to Greta 2009

Duff, Howard (1913-1990) All My Sons 1948; The Naked City 1948; Calamity Jane and Sam Bass 1949; Red Canyon 1949; Jennifer 1953; Spaceways 1953; Private Hell 36 1954; Tanganyika 1954; The Yellow Mountain 1954; Women's Prison 1955; While the City Sleeps 1956; Boys' Night Out 1962; Kramer vs Kramer 1979; Monster in the Closet 1983; No Way Out 1986; Too Much Sun 1990

Duff, Julia (1951-) Wacko 1981; Intolerable Cruelty 2003; Be My Baby 2006; Together Again for the First Time 2008

Duffy, Karen (1962-) Blank Check 1994; Dumb and Dumber 1994; Memory Run 1995

Duffy, Patrick (1949-) Desolation Canyon 2006; Falling in Love with the Girl Next Door 2006; Working Miracles 2010

Dufilho, Jacques (1914-2005) War of the Buttons 1962; Black and White in Color 1976; Le Cheval d'Orgueil 1980; Pétain 1992

Dugan, Dennis (1946-) The Spaceman and King Arthur 1979; The Howling

1981; Can't Buy Me Love 1987; The New Adventures of Pippi Longstocking 1988; Happy Gilmore 1996

Dugan (1), Tom (1889-1955) Lights of New York 1928; Pennies from Heaven 1936; Wife vs Secretary 1936; The Lone Wolf Spy Hunt 1939; To Be or Not to Be 1942; Take Me Out to the Ball Game 1949; Painting the Clouds with Sunshine 1951

Dugay, Yvette aka **Duguay, Yvette** (1932-1986) The Cimarron Kid 1951; The People against O'Hara 1951; Francis Covers the Big Town 1953; Cattle Queen of Montana 1954

Duggan, Andrew (1923-1988) Decision at Sundown 1957; Westbound 1959; The Chapman Report 1962; Merrill's Marauders 1962; Palm Springs Weekend 1963; The Glory Guys 1965; In like Flint 1967; The Secret War of Harry Frigg 1967; Skin Game 1971; Bone 1972; The Bears and I 1974; It's Alive 1974; It Lives Again 1978; A Return to Salem's Lot 1987

Duggan, Tom (1915-1969) Frankenstein - 1970 1958; Born Reckless 1959

Duhamel, Josh (1972-) Win a Date with Tad Hamilton! 2004; Paradise Lost 2006; Transformers 2007; Transformers: Revenge of the Fallen 2009; When in Rome 2009; Life as We Know It 2010; Ramona and Beezus 2010; Transformers: Dark of the Moon 2011; Fire with Fire 2012; Safe Haven 2013; Misconduct 2016

Dujardin, Jean (1972-) OSS 117: Cairo - Nest of Spies 2006; Ca$h 2008; OSS 117: Lost in Rio 2009; Little White Lies 2010; The Artist 2011; The Players 2012; The Monuments Men 2013; The Wolf of Wall Street 2013; The Connection 2014; Up for Love 2016

Dukakis, Olympia (1931-) John and Mary 1969; The Idolmaker 1980; National Lampoon's Movie Madness 1981; Walls of Glass 1985; Moonstruck 1987; Working Girl 1988; Dad 1989; Look Who's Talking 1989; Steel Magnolias 1989; Look Who's Talking Too 1990; Over the Hill 1992; The Cemetery Club 1993; Look Who's Talking Now! 1993; I Love Trouble 1994; The Haunted Heart 1995; Jeffrey 1995; Mighty Aphrodite 1995; Mr Holland's Opus 1995; Jerusalem 1996; Never Too Late 1996; Picture Perfect 1997; Jane Austen's Mafia 1998; The Librarian: Quest for the Spear 2004; Away from Her 2006

Duke, Bill (1943-) Car Wash 1976; American Gigolo 1980; Commando 1985; No Man's Land 1987; Predator 1987; Action Jackson 1988; Street of No Return 1989; Bird on a Wire 1990; Menace II Society 1993; Payback 1998; Exit Wounds 2001; National Security 2002; Get Rich or Die Tryin' 2005; Henry's Crime 2010; A Fuller Life 2013

Duke, Clark (1985-) Sex Drive 2008; Kick-Ass 2009; Hot Tub Time Machine 2010; The Croods 2013; Hot Tub Time Machine 2 2014

Duke, Patty aka **Duke Astin, Patty** (1946-2016) Happy Anniversary 1959; The Miracle Worker 1962; Billie 1965; Valley of the Dolls 1967; You'll Like My Mother 1972; The Swarm 1978; Willy/ Milly 1986; Amityville: the Evil Escapes 1989; Prelude to a Kiss 1992; Murder without Conviction 2004; Falling in Love with the Girl Next Door 2006

Dukes, David (1945-2000) The Wild Party 1975; A Little Romance 1979; Only When I Laugh 1981; Without a Trace 1983; The Men's Club 1986; Rawhead Rex 1986; See You in the Morning 1989; Me and the Kid 1993; Norma Jean & Marilyn 1996; Gods and Monsters 1998; Supreme Sanction 1999

Dullaghan (1), John Sweet Sweetback's Baad Asssss Song 1971; The Thing with Two Heads 1972

Dullea, Keir (1936-) The Hoodlum Priest 1961; David and Lisa 1962; Mail Order Bride 1963; The Thin Red Line 1964; Bunny Lake Is Missing 1965; Madame X 1966; The Fox 1967; 2001: a Space Odyssey 1968; De Sade 1969; Pope Joan 1972; Black Christmas 1974; Paul and Michelle 1974; Full Circle 1977; Brainwaves 1982; Blind Date 1984; 2010 1984; Oh, What a Night 1992; The Audrey Hepburn Story 2000; The Good Shepherd 2006; The Accidental Husband 2008; Infinitely Polar Bear 2014

Dullin, Charles (1885-1949) The Chess Player 1927; Mademoiselle Docteur 1936; Quai des Orfèvres 1947

Dumas, Roger (1932-2016) The Bride Is Too Beautiful 1956; La Femme Publique 1984; Masques 1987; The First Day of the Rest of Your Life 2007

Dumas, Sandrine (1957-) Beyond Therapy 1987; The Legend of the Holy Drinker 1988

Dumbrille, Douglass aka **Dumbrille, Douglas** (1890-1974) His Woman 1931; Blondie of the Follies 1932; Broadway Bill 1934; Fog over Frisco 1934; Hi, Nellie! 1934; The Secret Bride 1934; Stambool Quest 1934; Cardinal Richelieu 1935; Crime and Punishment 1935; The Lives of a Bengal Lancer 1935; Naughty Marietta 1935; Peter Ibbetson 1935; The Lone Wolf Returns 1936; Mr Deeds Goes to Town 1936; The Princess Comes Across 1936; The Emperor's Candlesticks 1937; The Firefly 1937; The Buccaneer 1938; Fast Company 1938; Kentucky 1938; Charlie Chan at Treasure Island 1939; Mr Moto in Danger Island 1939; Tell No Tales 1939; The Three Musketeers 1939; Michael Shayne, Private Detective 1940; South of Pago Pago 1940; Ten Gentlemen from West Point 1942; DuBarry Was a Lady 1943; The Frozen Ghost 1944; Lost in a Harem 1944; Uncertain Glory 1944; A Medal for Benny 1945; Pardon My Past 1945; Road to Utopia 1945; Christmas Eve 1947; Dishonored Lady 1947; Riders of the Whistling Pines 1949; Tell It to the Judge 1949; Abbott and Costello in the Foreign Legion 1950; A Millionaire for Christy 1951; Son of Paleface 1952; World for Ransom 1953; Shake, Rattle and Rock! 1957

Dumke, Ralph (1899-1964) All the King's Men 1949; The Breaking Point 1950; The Fireball 1950; Where Danger Lives 1950; Invasion of the Body Snatchers 1956; The Solid Gold Cadillac 1956

Dumont, José (1950-) Hour of the Star 1985; Behind the Sun 2001

Dumont, Margaret (1889-1965) The Cocoanuts 1929; Animal Crackers 1930; Duck Soup 1933; A Night at the Opera 1935; A Day at the Races 1937; Dramatic School 1938; At the Circus 1939; The Big Store 1941; Never Give a Sucker an Even Break 1941; The Dancing Masters 1943; Billy Rose's Diamond Horseshoe 1945; The Horn Blows at Midnight 1945; Little Giant 1946; Stop, You're Killing Me 1952; Shake, Rattle and Rock! 1957

Dumont, Ulises (1937-2008) Sur 1987; Wind with the Gone 1998; To Die in San Hilario 2005

Dun, Dennis Big Trouble in Little China 1986; The Last Emperor 1987; Prince of Darkness 1987

Duna, Steffi (1910-1992) Anthony Adverse 1936; Phantom Raiders 1940

Dunagan, Deanna The Naked Face 1984; The Visit 2015

Dunaway, Faye (1941-) Bonnie and Clyde 1967; The Happening 1967; Hurry Sundown 1967; A Place for Lovers 1968; The Thomas Crown Affair 1968; The Arrangement 1969; The Extraordinary Seaman 1969; Little Big Man 1970; Puzzle of a Downfall Child 1970; The Deadly Trap 1971; Doc 1971; Oklahoma Crude 1973; The Three Musketeers 1973; Chinatown 1974; The Four Musketeers 1974; The Towering Inferno 1974; Three Days of the Condor 1975; The Disappearance of Aimee 1976; Network 1976; Voyage of the Damned 1976; Eyes of Laura Mars 1978; The Champ 1979; Mommie Dearest 1981; The Wicked Lady 1983; Supergirl 1984; Thirteen at Dinner 1985; Barfly 1987; Burning Secret 1988; Midnight Crossing 1988; Cold Sassy Tree 1989; Wait until Spring, Bandini 1989; The Handmaid's Tale 1990; Arizona Dream 1991; Scorchers 1991; Double Edge 1992; The Temp 1993; Don Juan DeMarco 1995; Albino Alligator 1996; The Chamber 1996; Dunston Checks In 1996; Gia 1998; Joan of Arc 1999; The Thomas Crown Affair 1999; The Yards 2000; The Rules of Attraction 2002; Blind Horizon 2003; Nora Roberts' Midnight Bayou 2009

Dunbar, Adrian (1958-) Dealers 1989; Hear My Song 1991; The Crying Game 1992; Widows' Peak 1993; Innocent Lies 1995; The Near Room 1995; The General 1998; Shooters 2000; The Wedding Tackle 2000; Wild about Harry 2000; Triggermen 2002; Good Vibrations 2012; Mother's Milk 2012

Dunbar, Dixie (1919-1991) One in a Million 1936; Pigskin Parade 1936

Duncan, Andrew Loving 1970; Slap Shot 1977; An Unmarried Woman 1978; A Little Romance 1979; The Gig 1985

Duncan, Archie (1914-1979) Counterspy 1953; Rob Roy, the Highland Rogue 1953; Trouble in the Glen 1954; Tess of the Storm Country 1960; Lancelot and Guinevere 1963

Duncan, Carmen (1942-) Harlequin 1980; Turkey Shoot 1981

Duncan, Kenne (1903-1972) My Pal Trigger 1946; On Top of Old Smoky 1953; The Astounding She-Monster 1958; Night of the Ghouls 1959; Hellborn 1961

Duncan, Lindsay (1950-) Loose Connections 1983; Prick Up Your Ears 1987; The Reflecting Skin 1990; Body Parts 1991; City Hall 1996; A Midsummer Night's Dream 1996; An Ideal Husband 1999; Mansfield Park 1999; Star Wars Episode I: the Phantom Menace 1999; AfterLife 2003; Under the Tuscan Sun 2003; Starter for 10 2006; Last Passenger 2013; Le Week-end 2013; Birdman or (The Unexpected Virtue of Ignorance) 2014

Duncan, Michael Clarke (1957-2012) The Green Mile 1999; The Whole Nine Yards 2000; Planet of the Apes 2001; See Spot Run 2001; The Scorpion King 2002; Daredevil 2003; Racing Stripes 2004; The Island 2005; School for Scoundrels 2006; Talladega Nights: the Ballad of Ricky Bobby 2006; The Last Mimzy 2007; Welcome Home Roscoe Jenkins 2008; Cats & Dogs: the Revenge of Kitty Galore 2010

Duncan, Michelle Driving Lessons 2006; The Broken 2008; Iona 2015

Duncan, Pamela (1931-2005) Attack of the Crab Monsters 1957; The Undead 1957

Duncan, Sandy (1946-) The Million Dollar Duck 1971; The Cat from Outer Space 1978; The Fox and the Hound 1981; My Boyfriend's Back 1989

Dundas, Jennie The Hotel New Hampshire 1984; Mrs Soffel 1984

Dunford, Christine Reversal of Fortune 1990; Ulee's Gold 1997

Dunham, Joanna (1936-2014) The Breaking Point 1961; Dangerous Afternoon 1961; The House That Dripped Blood 1970

Dunn-Hill, John Bullet to Beijing 1995; Wilder 2000

Dunn, Clive (1920-2012) She'll Have to Go 1961; Just like a Woman 1966; The Bliss of Mrs Blossom 1968; The Magic Christian 1969; Dad's Army 1971

Dunn, Emma (1875-1966) Manslaughter 1930; The Texan 1930; Bad Sister 1931; This Modern Age 1931; Hell's House 1932; The Wet Parade 1932; George White's 1935 Scandals 1935; The Cowboy and the Lady 1938; Young Dr Kildare 1938; The Llano Kid 1939; Dr Kildare's Strange Case 1940; Dr Kildare's Crisis 1940; Ladies in Retirement 1941; The Penalty 1941; Life with Father 1947

Dunn, James (1905-1967) Bad Girl 1931; Hello Sister! 1933; Baby, Take a Bow 1934; Bright Eyes 1934; Change of Heart 1934; George White's 1935 Scandals 1935; Government Girl 1943; A Tree Grows in Brooklyn 1945; Killer McCoy 1947; The Bramble Bush 1960; Hemingway's Adventures of a Young Man 1962

Dunn, Josephine (1906-1983) The Singing Fool 1928; Our Modern Maidens 1929

Dunn, Kevin (1956-) Blue Steel 1990; The Bonfire of the Vanities 1990; Hot Shots! 1991; Only the Lonely 1991; Chaplin 1992; 1492: Conquest of Paradise 1992; Dave 1993; Little Big League 1994; Chain Reaction 1996; Godzilla 1997; Picture Perfect 1997; The 6th Man 1997; Almost Heroes 1998; Snake Eyes 1998; Stir of Echoes 1999; Gridiron Gang 2006; Vicky Cristina Barcelona 2008; Transformers: Revenge of the Fallen 2009; Unstoppable 2010

Dunn, Liam (1916-1976) What's Up, Doc? 1972; Blazing Saddles 1974

Dunn, Michael (1934-1973) You're a Big Boy Now 1966; Boom 1968; No Way to Treat a Lady 1968; The Mutations 1973; Werewolf of Washington 1973; The Abdication 1974

Dunn, Nora (1952-) Miami Blues 1990; The Last Supper 1995; Three Kings 1999; Max Keeble's Big Move 2001; Laws of Attraction 2003; Southland Tales 2005

Dunn, Roger No Higher Love 1999; Owning Mahowny 2002

Dunn, Ryan (1977-2011) Jackass: the Movie 2002; jackass number two 2006; Jackass 3D 2010

Dunne, Griffin (1955-) Chilly Scenes of Winter 1979; An American Werewolf in London 1981; Almost You 1984; Johnny Dangerously 1984; After Hours 1985; Who's That Girl 1987; The Big Blue 1988; My Girl 1991; Stepkids 1992; Straight Talk 1992; The Pickle 1993; I Like It like That 1994; Search and Destroy 1995; 40 Days and 40 Nights 2002; Last Night 2009

Dunne, Irene (1898-1990) Bachelor Apartment 1931; Cimarron 1931; Consolation Marriage 1931; Back Street 1932; Symphony of Six Million 1932; Ann Vickers 1933; If I Were Free 1933; The Secret of Madame Blanche 1933; The Silver Cord 1933; The Age of Innocence 1934; This Man Is Mine 1934; Magnificent Obsession 1935; Roberta 1935; Sweet Adeline 1935; Show Boat 1936; Theodora Goes Wild 1936; The Awful Truth 1937; High, Wide and Handsome 1937; Joy of Living 1938; Invitation to Happiness 1939; Love Affair 1939; When Tomorrow Comes 1939; My Favorite Wife 1940; Penny Serenade 1941; Unfinished Business 1941; Lady in a Jam 1942; A Guy Named Joe 1944; Together Again 1944; The White Cliffs of Dover 1944; Over 21 1945; Anna and the King of Siam 1946; Life with Father 1947; I Remember Mama 1948; The Mudlark 1950; Never a Dull Moment 1950; It Grows on Trees 1952

Dunne, Robin (1976-) Cruel Intentions 2 2000; American Psycho II: All American Girl 2002

Dunne, Steve aka **Dunne, Stephen** (1918-1977) The Dark Past 1948; Above and Beyond 1952; Home before Dark 1958; I Married a Woman 1958

Dunning, Ruth (1911-1983) It's a Great Day 1955; And Women Shall Weep 1960; Dangerous Afternoon 1961; Hoffman 1970; The House in Nightmare Park 1973

Dunnock, Mildred (1901-1991) The Corn Is Green 1945; Death of a Salesman 1951; I Want You 1951; The Girl in White 1952; The Jazz Singer 1952; Bad for Each Other 1954; The Trouble with Harry 1954; Baby Doll 1956; Love Me Tender 1956; The Nun's Story 1959; The Story on Page One 1959; Butterfield 8 1960; Sweet Bird of Youth 1962; Behold a Pale Horse 1964; 7 Women 1966; Whatever Happened to Aunt Alice? 1969; One Summer Love 1975; The Pick-Up Artist 1987

Dunsmore, Rosemary (1952-) Dancing in the Dark 1986; Miles to Go 1986; The Boys 1991; Profoundly Normal 2003; They Come Back 2007

Dunst, Kirsten (1982-) Interview with the Vampire: the Vampire Chronicles 1994; Little Women 1994; Jumanji 1995; Mother Night 1996; Anastasia 1997; Wag the Dog 1997; Kiki's Delivery Service 1998; Small Soldiers 1998; Strike! 1998; The Devil's Arithmetic 1999; Dick 1999; Drop Dead Gorgeous 1999; The Virgin Suicides 1999; Bring It On 2000; The Cat's Meow 2001; crazy/ beautiful 2001; Get over It 2001; Levity 2002; Spider-Man 2002; Eternal Sunshine of the Spotless Mind 2003; Mona Lisa Smile 2003; Spider-Man 2 2004; Wimbledon 2004; Elizabethtown 2005; Marie Antoinette 2005; Spider-Man 3 2007; How to Lose Friends & Alienate People 2008; All Good Things 2010; Melancholia 2011; On the Road 2011; Bachelorette 2012; The Two Faces of January 2013; Midnight Special 2015

Duperey, Anny (1947-) Two or Three Things I Know about Her 1966; Stavisky 1974; No Problem! 1975; Pardon Mon Affaire 1976; Bobby Deerfield 1977; Le Grand Pardon 1981; Les Compères 1983

Duplass, Mark (1976-) The Puffy Chair 2005; Humpday 2009; Your Sister's Sister 2011; Safety Not Guaranteed 2012

DuPois, Starletta Hollywood Shuffle 1987; Convicts 1991; The Road to Galveston 1996

Dupontel, Albert (1964-) A Self-Made Hero 1995; Irreversible 2002; Orchestra Seats 2005; Intimate Enemies 2007; Paris 2007; En Equilibre 2015

Duprez, June (1918-1984) The Four Feathers 1939; The Lion Has Wings 1939; The Spy in Black 1939; The Thief of Bagdad 1940; None but the Lonely Heart 1944; And Then There Were None 1945; The Brighton Strangler 1945; Calcutta 1947

Dupuis, Paul (1913-1976) Johnny Frenchman 1945; Against the Wind 1947; Sleeping Car to Trieste 1948; Madness of the Heart 1949; The Romantic Age 1949; The Reluctant Widow 1950

Dupuis, Roy (1963-) Being at Home with Claude 1992; Screamers 1995; Hemoglobin 1997; Mesrine: Killer Instinct 2008; The Forbidden Room 2015

Durand, Kevin (1974-) Walking Tall 2004; Wild Hogs 2007; I Am Number Four 2011; Real Steel 2011; Cosmopolis 2012; A Dark Truth 2012; Resident Evil: Retribution 2012; Devil's Knot 2013;

Eckhart, Aaron (1968-) *In the Company of Men* 1997; *Thursday* 1998; *Your Friends & Neighbors* 1998; *Any Given Sunday* 1999; *Molly* 1999; *Erin Brockovich* 2000; *Nurse Betty* 2000; *The Pledge* 2000; *The Core* 2002; *Possession* 2002; *Paycheck* 2003; *Suspect Zero* 2004; *Conversations with Other Women* 2005; *Thank You for Smoking* 2005; *The Black Dahlia* 2006; *No Reservations* 2007; *The Dark Knight* 2008; *Love Happens* 2009; *Rabbit Hole* 2010; *Battle Los Angeles* 2011; *The Rum Diary* 2011; *The Expatriate* 2012; *I, Frankenstein* 2013; *Olympus Has Fallen* 2013; *London Has Fallen* 2016; *Sully* 2016

Eckholdt, Steven (1961-) *Santa Who?* 2000; *Our First Christmas* 2008

Ecoffey, Jean-Philippe (1959-) *Henry & June* 1990; *Mina Tannenbaum* 1993; *L'Appartement* 1996; *Ma Vie en Rose* 1997

Eddington, Paul (1927-1995) *The Devil Rides Out* 1968; *Baxter* 1973

Eddison, Robert (1908-1991) *The Angel Who Pawned Her Harp* 1954; *The Boy Who Turned Yellow* 1972; *American Friends* 1991

Eddy, Duane (1938-) *Because They're Young* 1960; *A Thunder of Drums* 1961

Eddy, Helen Jerome (1897-1990) *Rebecca of Sunnybrook Farm* 1917; *Pollyanna* 1920; *Skippy* 1931; *Madame Butterfly* 1932; *Klondike Annie* 1936

Eddy, Nelson (1901-1967) *Broadway to Hollywood* 1933; *Dancing Lady* 1933; *Naughty Marietta* 1935; *Rose Marie* 1936; *Maytime* 1937; *Rosalie* 1937; *The Girl of the Golden West* 1938; *Sweethearts* 1938; *Bitter Sweet* 1940; *New Moon* 1940; *The Chocolate Soldier* 1941; *I Married an Angel* 1942; *Phantom of the Opera* 1943; *Knickerbocker Holiday* 1944; *Make Mine Music* 1946

Edelman, Gregg (1958-) *Green Card* 1990; *Passion* 1996; *Little Children* 2006

Edelman, Herb aka **Edelman, Herbert** (1930-1996) *Barefoot in the Park* 1967; *I Love You, Alice B Toklas* 1968; *The Odd Couple* 1968; *The War between Men and Women* 1972; *The Way We Were* 1973; *Hearts of the West* 1975; *The Yakuza* 1975

Edelstein, Eric *The Hills Have Eyes II* 2007; *Good Dick* 2008

Edelstein, Lisa (1967-) *Keeping the Faith* 2000; *Date with Darkness* 2003

Eden, Barbara (1934-) *Flaming Star* 1960; *All Hands on Deck* 1961; *Voyage to the Bottom of the Sea* 1961; *Five Weeks in a Balloon* 1962; *The Wonderful World of the Brothers Grimm* 1962; *7 Faces of Dr Lao* 1963; *The Yellow Canary* 1963; *The Brass Bottle* 1964; *Quick, Let's Get Married* 1964; *Ride the Wild Surf* 1964; *The Amazing Dobermans* 1976; *Harper Valley PTA* 1978; *Always and Forever* 2008

Eden, Harry (1990-) *Pure* 2002; *Oliver Twist* 2005; *Flashbacks of a Fool* 2008

Eden, Mark (1928-) *Seance on a Wet Afternoon* 1964; *The Pleasure Girls* 1965; *Attack on the Iron Coast* 1968; *Curse of the Crimson Altar* 1968; *A Little of What You Fancy* 1968

Edeson, Robert (1868-1931) *The Prisoner of Zenda* 1922; *The King of Kings* 1927

Edgerly, Chris *Top Cat: the Movie* 2011; *Top Cat Begins* 2016

Edgerton, Joel (1974-) *The Hard Word* 2002; *Ned Kelly* 2003; *The Night We Called It a Day* 2003; *Kinky Boots* 2005; *The Square* 2008; *Animal Kingdom* 2009; *The Thing* 2011; *Warrior* 2011; *The Odd Life of Timothy Green* 2012; *Wish You Were Here* 2012; *Zero Dark Thirty* 2012; *Felony* 2013; *The Great Gatsby* 2013; *Exodus: Gods and Kings* 2014; *Black Mass* 2015; *The Gift* 2015; *Jane Got a Gun* 2015; *Life* 2015; *Midnight Special* 2015; *Loving* 2016; *Bright* 2017

Edmond, J Trevor (1969-) *Return of the Living Dead III* 1993; *The Revenge of Pumpkinhead - Blood Wings* 1994

Edmond, Valerie *One More Kiss* 1999; *Saving Grace* 2000

Edmondson, Adrian (1957-) *The Supergrass* 1985; *Eat the Rich* 1987; *Guest House Paradiso* 1999; *Terkel in Trouble* 2006; *Bob* 2012

Edney, Beatie (1962-) *Highlander* 1986; *Mister Johnson* 1991; *In the Name of the Father* 1993; *Highlander: Endgame* 2000

Edson, Richard (1954-) *Stranger than Paradise* 1984; *Platoon* 1986; *Do the Right Thing* 1989; *Eyes of an Angel* 1991; *Joey Breaker* 1993; *Super Mario Bros* 1993; *Love, Cheat & Steal* 1994; *Jury Duty* 1995; *The Winner* 1996;

Frankenfish 2004; *Momma's Man* 2008; *Black Dynamite* 2009

Edwall, Allan (1924-1997) *Winter Light* 1962; *The Emigrants* 1971; *The New Land* 1972; *Fanny and Alexander* 1982; *The Sacrifice* 1986

Edwards, Alan (1892-1954) *The White Sister* 1933; *If You Could Only Cook* 1935; *The Gentle Trap* 1960

Edwards, Anthony (1962-) *Fast Times at Ridgemont High* 1982; *Heart like a Wheel* 1983; *Revenge of the Nerds* 1984; *Gotcha!* 1985; *The Sure Thing* 1985; *Top Gun* 1986; *Hawks* 1988; *Mr North* 1988; *How I Got Into College* 1989; *Miracle Mile* 1989; *Downtown* 1990; *Pet Sematary II* 1992; *Charlie's Ghost Story* 1994; *The Client* 1994; *Playing by Heart* 1998; *Don't Go Breaking My Heart* 1999; *Northfork* 2002; *The Forgotten* 2004; *Thunderbirds* 2004; *Zodiac* 2007; *Motherhood* 2009

Edwards, Bill aka **Edwards, Billy** (1918-1999) *Hail the Conquering Hero* 1944; *The Virginian* 1946; *First Man into Space* 1958; *The Primitives* 1962; *The War Lover* 1962

Edwards, Bruce (1914-2002) *The Fallen Sparrow* 1943; *Betrayal from the East* 1945

Edwards, Cliff (1895-1971) *Doughboys* 1930; *Dance, Fools, Dance* 1931; *Laughing Sinners* 1931; *Parlor, Bedroom and Bath* 1931; *The Sin of Madelon Claudet* 1931; *Hell Divers* 1932; *George White's Scandals* 1934; *George White's Scandals* 1935; *Red Salute* 1935; *Saratoga* 1937; *They Gave Him a Gun* 1937; *His Girl Friday* 1939; *Maisie* 1939; *Pinocchio* 1940; *Dumbo* 1941; *Seven Miles from Alcatraz* 1942; *The Falcon Strikes Back* 1943

Edwards, Daryl *The Brother from Another Planet* 1984; *Blue Jean Cop* 1988

Edwards, Glynn (1931-) *The Hi-Jackers* 1963; *Zulu* 1963; *Smokescreen* 1964; *The Blood Beast Terror* 1967; *Burke & Hare* 1971; *Rising Damp* 1980

Edwards, Henry (1882-1952) *East of Piccadilly* 1940; *Take My Life* 1947; *The Brass Monkey* 1948; *Oliver Twist* 1948

Edwards, Hilton (1903-1982) *Othello* 1952; *Cat and Mouse* 1958; *The Quare Fellow* 1962; *Half a Sixpence* 1967

Edwards, James (1918-1970) *Home of the Brave* 1949; *Bright Victory* 1951; *The Steel Helmet* 1951; *The Member of the Wedding* 1952; *Battle Hymn* 1957; *Anna Lucasta* 1958; *Tarzan's Fight for Life* 1958; *Pork Chop Hill* 1959

Edwards, Jennifer (1959-) *SOB* 1981; *A Fine Mess* 1986; *That's Life* 1986; *Sunset* 1988; *All's Fair* 1989; *Son of the Pink Panther* 1993

Edwards, Jimmy (1920-1988) *Treasure Hunt* 1952; *Innocents in Paris* 1953; *Three Men in a Boat* 1956; *Bottoms Up* 1959; *Nearly a Nasty Accident* 1961; *The Plank* 1967; *The Bed Sitting Room* 1969

Edwards, Luke (1980-) *Guilty by Suspicion* 1990; *Mother's Boys* 1993; *Little Big League* 1994

Edwards, Mark (1942-) *Blood from the Mummy's Tomb* 1971; *Tower of Evil* 1972

Edwards, Maudie (1906-1991) *Only Two Can Play* 1961; *Band of Thieves* 1962

Edwards, Meredith (1917-1999) *A Run for Your Money* 1949; *The Magnet* 1950; *There Is Another Sun* 1951; *Where No Vultures Fly* 1951; *The Gambler and the Lady* 1952; *The Conquest of Everest* 1953; *A Day to Remember* 1953; *Devil on Horseback* 1954; *Final Appointment* 1954; *Mask of Dust* 1954; *Circus Friends* 1956; *Dunkirk* 1958; *This Is My Street* 1963; *Gulliver's Travels* 1977

Edwards, Penny (1928-1998) *North of the Great Divide* 1950; *Trail of Robin Hood* 1950; *Pony Soldier* 1952; *Powder River* 1953

Edwards, Snitz (1862-1937) *The Thief of Bagdad* 1924; *The Phantom of the Opera* 1925; *Seven Chances* 1925; *Battling Butler* 1926; *College* 1927

Edwards, Stacy (1965-) *Dinner at Eight* 1989; *In the Company of Men* 1997; *Black and White* 1999; *Four Dogs Playing Poker* 1999; *Driven* 2001; *Prancer Returns* 2001

Edwards, Vince aka **Edwards, Vincent** (1928-1996) *Sailor Beware* 1951; *The Night Holds Terror* 1955; *The Killing* 1956; *Serenade* 1956; *The Hired Gun* 1957; *Murder by Contract* 1958; *City of Fear* 1959; *The Victors* 1963; *Hammerhead* 1968; *Deal of the Century* 1983; *Return to Horror High* 1986

Efron, Inés *Glue* 2006; *XXY* 2007; *The Headless Woman* 2008

Efron, Marshall (1938-) *Dynamite Chicken* 1971; *Is There Sex after Death?* 1971

Efron, Zac (1987-) *The Unexpected Journey* 2004; *High School Musical* 2006; *Hairspray* 2007; *High School Musical 2* 2007; *High School Musical 3: Senior Year* 2008; *Me and Orson Welles* 2008; *17 Again* 2009; *Death & Life of Charlie St Cloud* 2010; *Liberal Arts* 2011; *New Year's Eve* 2011; *At Any Price* 2012; *Dr Seuss' The Lorax* 2012; *The Lucky One* 2012; *The Paperboy* 2012; *Parkland* 2013; *That Awkward Moment* 2013; *Bad Neighbours* 2014; *We Are Your Friends* 2015; *Bad Neighbours 2* 2016; *Dirty Grandpa* 2016; *Mike and Dave Need Wedding Dates* 2016; *Baywatch* 2017

Egan, Christopher *Alpha Male* 2005; *Resident Evil: Extinction* 2007; *Letters to Juliet* 2010

Egan, Eddie (1930-1995) *Out of the Darkness* 1985; *Cold Steel* 1987

Egan, Peter (1946-) *The Hireling* 1973; *Callan* 1974; *Hennessy* 1975; *The Wedding Date* 2004

Egan, Richard (1921-1987) *Kansas Raiders* 1950; *Undercover Girl* 1950; *The Devil Makes Three* 1952; *One Minute to Zero* 1952; *The Glory Brigade* 1953; *Split Second* 1953; *Khyber Patrol* 1954; *Underwater!* 1955; *Untamed* 1955; *Violent Saturday* 1955; *Love Me Tender* 1956; *The Revolt of Mamie Stover* 1956; *Tension at Table Rock* 1956; *Slaughter on Tenth Avenue* 1957; *The Hunters* 1958; *Voice in the Mirror* 1958; *A Summer Place* 1959; *These Thousand Hills* 1959; *Esther and the King* 1960; *Pollyanna* 1960; *The 300 Spartans* 1962; *Valley of Mystery* 1967; *The Destructors* 1968; *The Big Cube* 1969; *The Amsterdam Kill* 1978

Egan, Susan (1970-) *Hercules* 1997; *Spirited Away* 2001; *Porco Rosso* 2005

Ege, Julie (1943-2008) *Every Home Should Have One* 1970; *Creatures the World Forgot* 1971; *The Magnificent Seven Deadly Sins* 1971; *Up Pompeii* 1971; *Go for a Take* 1972; *Not Now Darling* 1972; *Rentadick* 1972; *Craze* 1973; *The Mutations* 1973; *The Amorous Milkman* 1974; *The Legend of the 7 Golden Vampires* 1974; *Percy's Progress* 1974

Egerton, Tamsin (1988-) *Keeping Mum* 2005; *Huge* 2009; *Chalet Girl* 2010; *4.3.2.1* 2010; *Grand Piano* 2013; *The Look of Love* 2013; *Love, Rosie* 2014; *Queen and Country* 2014

Egerton, Taron (1989-) *Testament of Youth* 2014; *Kingsman: The Secret Service* 2015; *Eddie the Eagle* 2016; *Sing* 2016; *Kingsman: The Golden Circle* 2017

Eggar, Samantha (1939-) *Dr Crippen* 1962; *The Wild and the Willing* 1962; *Doctor in Distress* 1963; *Psyche '59* 1964; *The Collector* 1965; *Return from the Ashes* 1965; *Walk, Don't Run* 1966; *Doctor Dolittle* 1967; *The Molly Maguires* 1970; *The Walking Stick* 1970; *The Light at the Edge of the World* 1971; *Double Indemnity* 1973; *Why Shoot the Teacher* 1977; *The Uncanny* 1977; *The Brood* 1979; *The Exterminator* 1980; *The Hot Touch* 1982; *A Ghost in Monte Carlo* 1990; *Dark Horse* 1992; *Barbara Taylor Bradford's Everything to Gain* 1996; *Hercules* 1997; *The Astronaut's Wife* 1999

Egger, Josef (1889-1966) *A Fistful of Dollars* 1964; *For a Few Dollars More* 1965

Eggert, Nicole (1972-) *Kinjite: Forbidden Subjects* 1989; *The Haunting of Morella* 1990; *Siberia* 1998; *Snowman's Pass* 2004

Eggerth, Marta (1912-2013) *For Me and My Gal* 1942; *Presenting Lily Mars* 1943

Egglesfield, Colin *Nora Roberts' Carnal Innocence* 2011; *Something Borrowed* 2011

Egi, Stan *Come See the Paradise* 1990; *Rising Sun* 1993; *Golden Gate* 1994

Egoyan, Atom (1960-) *Calendar* 1993; *This Film Is Not Yet Rated* 2006

Ehara, Tatsuyoshi *Red Beard* 1965; *Rebellion* 1967

Ehle, Jennifer (1969-) *Backbeat* 1993; *Wilde* 1997; *Bedrooms and Hallways* 1998; *Sunshine* 1999; *This Year's Love* 1999; *Possession* 2002; *Alpha Male* 2005; *Before the Rains* 2007; *Pride and Glory* 2007; *The Greatest* 2009; *The King's Speech* 2010; *Contagion* 2011; *Zero Dark Thirty* 2012; *A Little Chaos* 2014; *Fifty Shades of Grey* 2015; *The Fundamentals of Caring* 2015; *Spooks: the Greater Good* 2015

Ehrenreich, Alden *Tetro* 2009; *Beautiful Creatures* 2013; *Rules Don't Apply* 2016

Eichhorn, Lisa (1952-) *The Europeans* 1979; *Yanks* 1979; *Cutter's Way* 1981; *Agatha Christie's Murder in Three Acts* 1986; *Hell Camp* 1986; *Grim Prairie Tales* 1990; *Moon 44* 1990; *King of the Hill* 1993; *The Vanishing* 1993; *First Kid* 1996; *About Time* 2013

Eidem, Erik *Conversations with Other Women* 2005; *Ordinary Miracles* 2005

Eigeman, Chris aka **Eigeman, Christopher** (1965-) *Metropolitan* 1990; *Barcelona* 1994; *Mr Jealousy* 1997; *The Last Days of Disco* 1998; *Maid in Manhattan* 2002

Eigenberg, David *Garfield* 2004; *Sex and the City: the Movie* 2008; *Sex and the City 2* 2010; *Cody the Robosapien* 2012

Eikenberry, Jill (1947-) *Between the Lines* 1977; *Hide in Plain Sight* 1980; *Arthur* 1981; *The Deadly Game* 1986; *My Boyfriend's Back* 1989; *Taken Away* 1996; *Something Borrowed* 2011; *Young Adult* 2011

Eilbacher, Lisa (1957-) *An Officer and a Gentleman* 1982; *10 to Midnight* 1983; *Beverly Hills Cop* 1984; *Leviathan* 1989; *Live Wire* 1992; *919 Fifth Avenue* 1995

Eilers, Sally (1908-1978) *Doughboys* 1930; *Bad Girl* 1931; *Parlor, Bedroom and Bath* 1931; *Central Airport* 1933; *State Fair* 1933; *Remember Last Night?* 1935; *Strike Me Pink* 1936; *Danger Patrol* 1937; *Condemned Women* 1938; *Coroner Creek* 1948

Eisenberg, Aron (1969-) *Amityville: the Evil Escapes* 1989; *House III: The Horror Show* 1989

Eisenberg, Hallie Kate (1992-) *Nicholas' Gift* 1998; *Paulie* 1998; *Beautiful* 2000

Eisenberg, Jesse (1983-) *The Emperor's Club* 2002; *Roger Dodger* 2002; *Cursed* 2005; *The Squid and the Whale* 2005; *The Education of Charlie Banks* 2007; *The Hunting Party* 2007; *Adventureland* 2009; *Solitary Man* 2009; *Zombieland* 2009; *Camp Hell* 2010; *Holy Rollers* 2010; *The Social Network* 2010; *Rio* 2011; *30 Minutes or Less* 2011; *To Rome with Love* 2012; *The Double* 2013; *Night Moves* 2013; *Now You See Me* 2013; *Rio 2* 2014; *American Ultra* 2015; *The End of the Tour* 2015; *Louder than Bombs* 2015; *Batman v Superman: Dawn of Justice* 2016; *Café Society* 2016; *Now You See Me 2* 2016

Eisenberg, Ned *The Burning* 1981; *Moving Violations* 1985; *Last Man Standing* 1996

Eisenmann, Ike (1962-) *Escape to Witch Mountain* 1975; *Return from Witch Mountain* 1978

Eisley, Anthony aka **Eisley, Fred** (1925-2003) *The Wasp Woman* 1959; *The Naked Kiss* 1964; *The Navy vs the Night Monsters* 1966; *Dracula vs Frankenstein* 1970

Eita *Memories of Matsuko* 2006; *Hara-Kiri: Death of a Samurai* 2011

Ejiofor, Chiwetel (1977-) *GMT Greenwich Mean Time* 1998; *It Was an Accident* 2000; *Dirty Pretty Things* 2002; *Slow Burn* 2003; *Melinda and Melinda* 2004; *Red Dust* 2004; *She Hate Me* 2004; *Four Brothers* 2005; *Kinky Boots* 2005; *Serenity* 2005; *Children of Men* 2006; *Inside Man* 2006; *American Gangster* 2007; *Redbelt* 2007; *Talk to Me* 2007; *2012* 2009; *Salt* 2010; *Half of a Yellow Sun* 2013; *Phil Spector* 2013; *12 Years a Slave* 2013; *Secret in Their Eyes* 2015; *Triple 9* 2015; *Doctor Strange* 2016

Ejogo, Carmen (1975-) *I Want You* 1998; *Love's Labour's Lost* 1999; *Boycott* 2001; *What's the Worst That Could Happen?* 2001; *Lackawanna Blues* 2005; *The Brave One* 2007; *Sparkle* 2012; *Selma* 2014; *Born to Be Blue* 2015

Ek, Anders (1916-1979) *Sawdust and Tinsel* 1953; *The Rite* 1969

Ekberg, Anita (1931-2015) *Abbott and Costello Go to Mars* 1953; *Artists and Models* 1955; *Blood Alley* 1955; *Back from Eternity* 1956; *Hollywood or Bust* 1956; *War and Peace* 1956; *Zarak* 1956; *Interpol* 1957; *Valerie* 1957; *The Man Inside* 1958; *Paris Holiday* 1958; *Screaming Mimi* 1958; *La Dolce Vita* 1960; *The Mongols* 1961; *Call Me Bwana* 1963; *4 for Texas* 1963; *The Alphabet Murders* 1966; *Woman Times Seven* 1967; *Killer Nun* 1978; *Intervista* 1987

Ekborg, Lars (1926-1969) *Summer with Monika* 1952; *The Magician* 1958

Ekerot, Bengt (1920-1971) *The Seventh Seal* 1957; *The Magician* 1958

Ekland, Britt aka **Ekman, Brita** (1942-) *The Happy Thieves* 1962; *After the Fox* 1966; *The Bobo* 1967; *The Double Man* 1967; *The Night They Raided Minsky's* 1968; *Endless Night* 1971; *Get Carter* 1971; *Percy* 1971; *A Time for Loving* 1971; *Asylum* 1972;

Baxter 1973; *The Wicker Man* 1973; *The Man with the Golden Gun* 1974; *Royal Flash* 1975; *Casanova & Co* 1976; *High Velocity* 1977; *Slavers* 1977; *The Monster Club* 1980; *Fraternity Vacation* 1985; *Scandal* 1988; *The Children* 1990

Eklund, Bengt (1925-1998) *Night Is My Future* 1948; *Port of Call* 1948; *Three Strange Loves* 1949

Eklund, Michael *The Divide* 2011; *The Call* 2013

Ekman (1), Gösta (1890-1938) *Faust* 1926; *Swedenhielms* 1935; *Intermezzo* 1936

Ekman, Hasse (1915-2004) *Intermezzo* 1936; *The Devil's Wanton* 1949; *Three Strange Loves* 1949

Ekman, John (1880-1949) *The Outlaw and His Wife* 1917; *To Joy* 1950

Elam, Jack (1916-2003) *An American Guerrilla in the Philippines* 1950; *High Lonesome* 1950; *The Sundowners* 1950; *Bird of Paradise* 1951; *Rawhide* 1951; *High Noon* 1952; *Kansas City Confidential* 1952; *Rancho Notorious* 1952; *The Ring* 1952; *Appointment in Honduras* 1953; *Count the Hours* 1953; *The Moonlighter* 1953; *Ride, Vaquero!* 1953; *Cattle Queen of Montana* 1954; *The Far Country* 1954; *Princess of the Nile* 1954; *Ride Clear of Diablo* 1954; *Artists and Models* 1955; *Kismet* 1955; *The Man from Laramie* 1955; *Thunder over Arizona* 1956; *Dragoon Wells Massacre* 1957; *The Gun Runners* 1958; *Edge of Eternity* 1959; *The Rare Breed* 1966; *The Last Challenge* 1967; *The Way West* 1967; *Support Your Local Sheriff!* 1969; *Dirty Dingus Magee* 1970; *Rio Lobo* 1970; *Hannie Caulder* 1971; *Support Your Local Gunfighter* 1971; *Pat Garrett and Billy the Kid* 1973; *Grayeagle* 1977; *Hot Lead and Cold Feet* 1978; *The Norseman* 1978; *The Apple Dumpling Gang Rides Again* 1979; *Cactus Jack* 1979; *The Cannonball Run* 1981; *Jinxed!* 1982; *Once upon a Texas Train* 1988; *Suburban Commando* 1991

Elba, Idris (1972-) *One Love* 2003; *Sometimes in April* 2005; *The Reaping* 2006; *This Christmas* 2007; *RocknRolla* 2008; *Obsessed* 2009; *Legacy: Black Ops* 2010; *The Losers* 2010; *Takers* 2010; *Thor* 2011; *Ghost Rider: Spirit of Vengeance* 2012; *Prometheus* 2012; *Mandela: Long Walk to Freedom* 2013; *Pacific Rim* 2013; *Thor: the Dark World* 2013; *No Good Deed* 2014; *Second Coming* 2014; *Beasts of No Nation* 2015; *The Gunman* 2015; *Bastille Day* 2016; *Finding Dory* 2016; *The Jungle Book* 2016; *Star Trek Beyond* 2016; *Zootropolis* 2016; *The Dark Tower* 2017; *Thor: Ragnarok* 2017

Elcar, Dana (1927-2005) *The Fool Killer* 1965; *The Learning Tree* 1969; *Adam at 6 AM* 1970; *Soldier Blue* 1970; *Zigzag* 1970; *The Great Northfield Minnesota Raid* 1972; *WC Fields and Me* 1976; *The Nude Bomb* 1980; *Buddy Buddy* 1981; *Condorman* 1981; *All of Me* 1984; *2010* 1984; *Agatha Christie's Murder in Three Acts* 1986

Eldard, Ron (1965-) *True Love* 1989; *The Last Supper* 1995; *Sex and the Other Man* 1995; *Sleepers* 1996; *When Trumpets Fade* 1998; *The Runner* 1999; *Black Hawk Down* 2001; *Ghost Ship* 2002; *Just a Kiss* 2002; *House of Sand and Fog* 2003; *Freedomland* 2006; *The Tenth Circle* 2008; *Super 8* 2011

Elder, Ann *One of Our Spies Is Missing* 1966; *Don't Make Waves* 1967

Eldon, Kevin *High Heels and Low Lifes* 2001; *Hot Fuzz* 2007

Eldredge, John (1917-1960) *Flirtation Walk* 1934; *Dangerous* 1935; *The Girl from 10th Avenue* 1935; *The Woman in Red* 1935; *His Brother's Wife* 1936; *Charlie Chan at the Olympics* 1937; *Blind Alley* 1939; *King of the Underworld* 1939

Eldridge, Florence (1901-1988) *The Divorcee* 1930; *Mary of Scotland* 1936; *Another Part of the Forest* 1948; *Christopher Columbus* 1949; *Inherit the Wind* 1960

Electra, Carmen (1972-) *The Mating Habits of the Earthbound Human* 1999; *Scary Movie* 2000; *My Boss's Daughter* 2003; *Starsky & Hutch* 2004; *Cheaper by the Dozen 2* 2005; *I Want Candy* 2006; *Scary Movie 4* 2006; *Christmas in Wonderland* 2007; *Disaster Movie* 2008; *Meet the Spartans* 2008

Elejalde, Karra (1960-) *Vacas* 1991; *La Madre Muerta* 1993; *Timecrimes* 2007; *Even the Rain* 2010

Eleniak, Erika (1969-) *ET the Extra-Terrestrial* 1982; *Under Siege* 1992; *The Beverly Hillbillies* 1993; *Chasers* 1994; *A Pyromaniac's Love Story* 1995; *Stealth Fighter* 1999

Elerick, John *Dark Victory* 1976; *Embryo* 1976

Eles, Sandor (1936-2002) *Evil of Frankenstein* 1964; *And Soon the Darkness* 1970; *Countess Dracula* 1970
Elfman, Danny (1949-) *The Nightmare before Christmas* 1993; *Tim Burton's Corpse Bride* 2005
Elfman, Jenna (1971-) *Krippendorf's Tribe* 1998; *Edtv* 1999; *Keeping the Faith* 2000; *Town & Country* 2001; *Clifford's Really Big Movie* 2004; *Looney Tunes: Back in Action* 2004; *Friends with Benefits* 2011
Elg, Taina (1931-) *Diane* 1955; *Gaby* 1956; *Les Girls* 1957; *The Thirty-Nine Steps* 1959; *Hercules in New York* 1969
Elgar, Avril (1932-) *Ladies Who Do* 1963; *Betrayal* 1982
Elgort, Ansel (1994-) *Divergent* 2014; *The Fault in Our Stars* 2014; *Men, Women & Children* 2014; *Insurgent* 2015
Elias, Alix *John and Mary* 1969; *A Night in Heaven* 1983; *True Stories* 1986; *Munchies* 1987
Elias, Hector (1941-) *The Master Gunfighter* 1975; *Lsin' It* 1983; *Buddy Boy* 1999; *Envy* 2003; *Me and You and Everyone We Know* 2005
Elic, Josip *The Producers* 1968; *Dirty Little Billy* 1972
Elise, Christine (1955-) *Child's Play 2* 1990; *Body Snatchers* 1993; *Boiling Point* 1993; *Nowhere to Land* 2000
Elise, Kimberly (1971-) *Set It Off* 1996; *Beloved* 1998; *John Q* 2001; *The Manchurian Candidate* 2004; *Pride* 2007; *Gifted Hands: the Ben Carson Story* 2009; *Dope* 2015
Elizabeth, Shannon (1973-) *American Pie* 1999; *Scary Movie* 2000; *Tomcats* 2000; *American Pie 2* 2001; *Jay and Silent Bob Strike Back* 2001; *Thir13en Ghosts* 2001; *Johnson Family Vacation* 2004; *Confessions of an American Bride* 2005; *Night of the Demons* 2010
Elizondo, Hector (1936-) *Born to Win* 1971; *Valdez Is Coming* 1971; *Deadhead Miles* 1972; *Pocket Money* 1972; *The Taking of Pelham One Two Three* 1974; *Report to the Commissioner* 1975; *Cuba* 1979; *American Gigolo* 1980; *The Fan* 1981; *Young Doctors in Love* 1982; *The Flamingo Kid* 1984; *Out of the Darkness* 1985; *Private Resort* 1985; *Nothing in Common* 1986; *Chains of Gold* 1989; *Leviathan* 1989; *Pretty Woman* 1990; *Taking Care of Business* 1990; *Final Approach* 1991; *Frankie & Johnny* 1991; *Being Human* 1994; *Beverly Hills Cop III* 1994; *Exit to Eden* 1994; *Getting Even with Dad* 1994; *Perfect Alibi* 1994; *Dear God* 1996; *Turbulence* 1997; *Runaway Bride* 1999; *The Princess Diaries* 2001; *Tortilla Soup* 2001; *The Princess Diaries 2: Royal Engagement* 2004; *Raising Helen* 2004; *Love in the Time of Cholera* 2007; *Mother's Day* 2016
Ellefsen, Per Christian *Elling* 2001; *Rare Exports from the Land of the Original Santa Claus* 2010
Ellerbe, Harry (1905-1992) *Murder on a Honeymoon* 1935; *So Red the Rose* 1935; *The Fall of the House of Usher* 1960
Elliot, Biff (1923-2012) *I, the Jury* 1953; *Good Morning, Miss Dove* 1955; *The Dark* 1979
Elliot, Laura *aka* **Elliott, Laura** (1926-2006) *Strangers on a Train* 1951; *Denver & Rio Grande* 1952; *Jamaica Run* 1953
Elliot, Mike (1946-2014) *Eden Valley* 1994; *Billy Elliot* 2000
Elliott (2), Alison (1970-) *Indictment: the McMartin Trial* 1995; *The Underneath* 1995; *The Spitfire Grill* 1996; *The Wings of the Dove* 1997; *The Eternal* 1998; *Birth* 2004
Elliott, Bill *aka* **Elliott, Gordon** *aka* **Elliott, Wild Bill** (1903-1965) *The Case of the Black Cat* 1936; *The Case of the Velvet Claws* 1936; *Bells of Rosarita* 1945
Elliott, Bob (1923-) *Author! Author!* 1982; *Quick Change* 1990
Elliott, Brennan (1975-) *The Silencer* 1999; *Flight 93* 2006; *The Nanny Express* 2008; *Curse of Chucky* 2013
Elliott, Chris (1960-) *Gremlins* 1990; *CB4* 1993; *Groundhog Day* 1993; *Cabin Boy* 1994; *Kingpin* 1996; *There's Something about Mary* 1998; *Snow Day* 2000; *The Rewrite* 2014
Elliott, David James (1960-) *Holiday Affair* 1996; *The Shrink Is In* 2001; *Love Will Keep Us Together* 2010; *Exploding Sun* 2013
Elliott, Denholm (1922-1992) *Dear Mr Prohack* 1949; *The Cruel Sea* 1952; *The Holly and the Ivy* 1952; *The Sound Barrier* 1952; *The Heart of the Matter* 1953; *They Who Dare* 1953; *Lease of Life* 1954; *The Man Who Loved Redheads* 1954; *The Night My Number Came Up* 1955; *Scent of Mystery* 1960; *Station Six-Sahara* 1962; *Nothing but*

the Best 1963; *The High Bright Sun* 1965; *King Rat* 1965; *You Must Be Joking!* 1965; *Alfie* 1966; *Maroc 7* 1966; *The Spy with a Cold Nose* 1966; *Here We Go round the Mulberry Bush* 1967; *The Night They Raided Minsky's* 1968; *The Sea Gull* 1968; *The House That Dripped Blood* 1970; *The Rise and Rise of Michael Rimmer* 1970; *Too Late the Hero* 1970; *Percy* 1971; *Quest for Love* 1971; *Madame Sin* 1972; *A Doll's House* 1973; *The Vault of Horror* 1973; *The Apprenticeship of Duddy Kravitz* 1974; *Percy's Progress* 1974; *Robin and Marian* 1976; *To the Devil a Daughter* 1976; *The Hound of the Baskervilles* 1977; *The Boys from Brazil* 1978; *Sweeney 2* 1978; *Cuba* 1979; *A Game for Vultures* 1979; *Saint Jack* 1979; *Zulu Dawn* 1979; *Bad Timing* 1980; *Rising Damp* 1980; *Raiders of the Lost Ark* 1981; *Brimstone and Treacle* 1982; *The Missionary* 1982; *The Hound of the Baskervilles* 1983; *Trading Places* 1983; *The Wicked Lady* 1983; *A Private Function* 1984; *The Razor's Edge* 1984; *Defence of the Realm* 1985; *A Room with a View* 1985; *Mrs Delafield Wants to Marry* 1986; *Maurice* 1987; *September* 1987; *Return from the River Kwai* 1988; *Stealing Heaven* 1988; *Indiana Jones and the Last Crusade* 1989; *Killing Dad* 1989; *One against the Wind* 1991; *Scorchers* 1991; *Toy Soldiers* 1991; *Noises Off* 1992
Elliott, Robert (1879-1951) *Lights of New York* 1928; *The Divorcee* 1930; *A Handful of Clouds* 1930; *Dangerous Female* 1931; *The Finger Points* 1931; *Trade Winds* 1938; *The Saint Strikes Back* 1939; *The Devil's Playground* 1946
Elliott, Sam (1944-) *The Adventures of Mowgli* 1967; *Frogs* 1972; *Molly and Lawless John* 1972; *The Blue Knight* 1973; *The Legacy* 1978; *Mask* 1985; *Fatal Beauty* 1987; *The Quick and the Dead* 1987; *Blue Jean Cop* 1988; *Prancer* 1989; *Road House* 1989; *Sibling Rivalry* 1990; *Rush* 1991; *Gettysburg* 1993; *Tombstone* 1993; *The Hi-Lo Country* 1998; *The Contender* 2000; *Fail Safe* 2000; *We Were Soldiers* 2002; *Hulk* 2003; *Thank You for Smoking* 2005; *Barnyard* 2006; *Ghost Rider* 2007; *The Golden Compass* 2007; *Did You Hear about the Morgans?* 2009; *Up in the Air* 2009; *Marmaduke* 2010; *November Christmas* 2010; *The Company You Keep* 2012; *Draft Day* 2014; *Grandma* 2015; *I'll See You in My Dreams* 2015
Elliott, Shawn *Hurricane Streets* 1997; *Thirteen Conversations about One Thing* 2001
Elliott (1), Stephen *aka* **Elliot, Stephen** (1918-2005) *The Hospital* 1971; *Arthur* 1981; *Cutter's Way* 1981; *My Body, My Child* 1982; *Assassination* 1986; *Walk like a Man* 1987; *Arthur 2: On the Rocks* 1988; *Taking Care of Business* 1990
Elliott, William (1934-1983) *Where Does It Hurt?* 1971; *Coffy* 1973
Ellis, Aunjanue (1969-) *Men of Honor* 2000; *Lovely & Amazing* 2001; *Undercover Brother* 2002; *Ray* 2004; *Freedomland* 2006; *Racing for Time* 2008; *Gifted Hands: the Ben Carson Story* 2009; *The Resident* 2010
Ellis, Chris (1956-) *Bean* 1997; *Armageddon* 1998; *The Watcher* 2000
Ellis, Diane (1909-1930) *High Voltage* 1929; *Laughter* 1930
Ellis, Edward (1870-1952) *I Am a Fugitive from a Chain Gang* 1932; *After Tonight* 1933; *The Return of Peter Grimm* 1935; *Village Tale* 1935; *Fury* 1936; *The Texas Rangers* 1936; *Little Miss Broadway* 1938; *A Man Betrayed* 1941
Ellis, James (1931-2014) *No Surrender* 1985; *Priest* 1994; *Resurrection Man* 1997
Ellis, Patricia (1916-1970) *Three on a Match* 1932; *Picture Snatcher* 1933; *The World Changes* 1933; *The Case of the Lucky Legs* 1935; *Step Lively, Jeeves* 1937; *Blockheads* 1938
Ellis, Robert (1933-1973) *Broadway* 1929; *The McConnell Story* 1955; *Space Master X 7* 1958
Ellison, James (1910-1993) *The Plainsman* 1936; *Vivacious Lady* 1938; *5th Ave Girl* 1939; *Zenobia* 1939; *Anne of Windy Poplars* 1940; *Charley's Aunt* 1941; *Careful, Soft Shoulder* 1942; *The Undying Monster* 1942; *The Gang's All Here* 1943; *I Walked with a Zombie* 1943; *Johnny Doesn't Live Here Anymore* 1944
Ellison, Jennifer (1983-) *The Phantom of the Opera* 2004; *The Cottage* 2008
Elmaleh, Gad (1971-) *Salut Cousin!* 1996; *Priceless* 2006; *The Round Up* 2010; *Mood Indigo* 2013

Elmosnino, Eric *The Father of My Children* 2009; *Gainsbourg (Je T'Aime... Moi Non Plus)* 2010; *La Famille Bélier* 2014
Elphick, Michael (1946-2002) *Hamlet* 1969; *Where's Jack?* 1969; *The Buttercup Chain* 1970; *Blind Terror* 1971; *The First Great Train Robbery* 1978; *The Odd Job* 1978; *The Elephant Man* 1980; *Gorky Park* 1983; *The Element of Crime* 1984; *Arthur's Hallowed Ground* 1985; *Withnail & I* 1986; *I Bought a Vampire Motorcycle* 1989; *Buddy's Song* 1990; *Let Him Have It* 1991
Elsayed, Fady *My Brother the Devil* 2012; *Sixteen* 2013
Elsom, Isobel (1893-1981) *Ladies in Retirement* 1941; *You Were Never Lovelier* 1942; *The Two Mrs Carrolls* 1945; *The Unseen* 1945; *Two Sisters from Boston* 1946; *Escape Me Never* 1947; *Love from a Stranger* 1947; *Love Is a Many-Splendored Thing* 1955; *Rock-a-Bye Baby* 1958; *The Second Time Around* 1961; *My Fair Lady* 1964
Elwes, Cary (1962-) *Another Country* 1984; *Oxford Blues* 1984; *Lady Jane* 1985; *The Princess Bride* 1987; *Glory* 1989; *Days of Thunder* 1990; *Hot Shots!* 1991; *Leather Jackets* 1991; *Bram Stoker's Dracula* 1992; *The Crush* 1993; *Robin Hood: Men in Tights* 1993; *The Jungle Book* 1994; *Whisper of the Heart* 1995; *Twister* 1996; *Kiss the Girls* 1997; *Liar Liar* 1997; *The Magic Sword: Quest for Camelot* 1997; *The Pentagon Wars* 1998; *Cradle Will Rock* 1999; *Shadow of the Vampire* 2000; *The Cat's Meow* 2001; *The Cat Returns* 2002; *Ella Enchanted* 2004; *The Riverman* 2004; *Saw* 2004; *Porco Rosso* 2005; *Georgia Rule* 2007; *A Christmas Carol* 2009; *Psych 9* 2010; *Saw: the Final Chapter* 2010; *No Strings Attached* 2011
Ely, Ron (1938-) *The Remarkable Mr Pennypacker* 1959; *Once before I Die* 1965; *Doc Savage: the Man of Bronze* 1975; *Slavers* 1977
Embry, Ethan *aka* **Randall, Ethan** (1978-) *All I Want for Christmas* 1991; *Driving Me Crazy* 1991; *A Far Off Place* 1993; *Empire Records* 1995; *That Thing You Do!* 1996; *Vegas Vacation* 1997; *Can't Hardly Wait* 1998; *Dancer, Texas Pop 81* 1998; *Sweet Home Alabama* 2002; *They* 2002; *Timeline* 2003; *Life on Liberty Street* 2004; *Vacancy* 2007; *Eagle Eye* 2008; *Imaginary Friend* 2012; *Cheap Thrills* 2013
Emerson, Faye (1917-1983) *The Hard Way* 1942; *Between Two Worlds* 1944; *The Desert Song* 1944; *The Mask of Dimitrios* 1944; *Uncertain Glory* 1944; *The Very Thought of You* 1944; *Hotel Berlin* 1945; *Nobody Lives Forever* 1946
Emerson, Hope (1897-1960) *Cry of the City* 1948; *Adam's Rib* 1949; *Dancing in the Dark* 1949; *Caged* 1950; *Double Crossbones* 1951; *Westward the Women* 1951; *The Lady Wants Mink* 1953; *Untamed* 1955; *Guns of Fort Petticoat* 1957
Emerton, Roy (1892-1944) *Lorna Doone* 1934; *Everything Is Thunder* 1936; *Big Fella* 1937; *Dr Syn* 1937; *The Last Adventurers* 1937
Emery, Dick (1917-1983) *The Case of the Mukkinese Battle Horn* 1955; *Light Up the Sky* 1960; *The Fast Lady* 1963; *The Big Job* 1965; *Yellow Submarine* 1968; *Loot* 1970; *Ooh... You Are Awful* 1972; *Find the Lady* 1976
Emery, Gilbert (1875-1945) *A Lady's Morals* 1930; *Sarah and Son* 1930; *Ladies' Man* 1931; *Now and Forever* 1934; *Goin' to Town* 1935; *Magnificent Obsession* 1935; *The Brighton Strangler* 1945
Emery, John (1905-1964) *Eyes in the Night* 1942; *The Silent Bell* 1944; *Blood on the Sun* 1945; *The Spanish Main* 1945; *Spellbound* 1945; *The Woman in White* 1948; *Frenchie* 1950; *Double Crossbones* 1951; *The Mad Magician* 1954; *A Lawless Street* 1955; *Forever, Darling* 1956; *The Girl Can't Help It* 1956; *Kronos* 1957; *Ten North Frederick* 1958
Emery, Katherine (1906-1980) *Eyes in the Night* 1942; *Isle of the Dead* 1945; *Untamed Frontier* 1952; *The Maze* 1953
Emery, Tania (1976-) *The Truth Game* 2000; *Club le Monde* 2001; *Brothers of the Head* 2005
Emhardt, Robert (1914-1994) *3:10 to Yuma* 1957; *The Badlanders* 1958; *The Intruder* 1961; *Underworld USA* 1961; *Change of Habit* 1969; *Alex and the Gypsy* 1976
Emil, Michael (1937-) *Tracks* 1977; *Sitting Ducks* 1979; *Can She Bake a Cherry Pie?* 1983; *Insignificance* 1985; *Someone to Love* 1987

Emile, Taungaroa *Once Were Warriors* 1994; *Flight of the Albatross* 1995
Emilfork, Daniel (1924-2006) *Lady L* 1965; *Kill!* 1972; *The City of Lost Children* 1995
Eminem (1972-) *How to Make Money Selling Drugs* 2012; *Something from Nothing: the Art of Rap* 2012
Emmanuel, Takis (1933-) *Zorba the Greek* 1964; *The Magus* 1968; *The Golden Voyage of Sinbad* 1973; *Caddie* 1976
Emmerich, Noah (1966-) *Beautiful Girls* 1996; *The Truman Show* 1998; *Frequency* 2000; *Love & Sex* 2000; *Windtalkers* 2001; *Beyond Borders* 2003; *Miracle* 2004; *Little Children* 2006; *Pride and Glory* 2007; *Fair Game* 2010; *Super 8* 2011; *Jane Got a Gun* 2015
Empson, Tameka *Beautiful Thing* 1995; *Food of Love* 1997; *Babymother* 1998
Endre, Lena (1955-) *Best Intentions* 1992; *Kristin Lavransdatter* 1995; *Jerusalem* 1996; *Faithless* 2000; *The Girl with the Dragon Tattoo* 2009; *The Girl Who Played with Fire* 2009; *The Girl Who Kicked the Hornet's Nest* 2009
Enfield, Harry (1961-) *Kevin & Perry Go Large* 2000; *Tooth* 2003; *Churchill: the Hollywood Years* 2004; *Stella Street* 2004; *Acts of Godfrey* 2011; *The Bad Education Movie* 2015; *Swallows and Amazons* 2016
Engel, Georgia *aka* **Engel, Georgia B** (1948-) *Taking Off* 1971; *The Outside Man* 1973; *The Care Bears Movie* 1985; *The Sweetest Thing* 2002
Engel, Roy (1913-1980) *The Man from Planet X* 1951; *The Naked Dawn* 1955
Engel, Susan (1935-) *King Lear* 1970; *Butley* 1973
England, Audie (1971-) *Delta of Venus* 1995; *One Good Turn* 1996; *Free Enterprise* 1998
England, Sue (1928-) *This Love of Ours* 1945; *Kidnapped* 1948
Englert, Alice *Ginger & Rosa* 2012; *In Fear* 2012; *Beautiful Creatures* 2013
English, Arthur (1919-1995) *The Hi-Jackers* 1963; *For the Love of Ada* 1972; *Malachi's Cove* 1973; *Are You Being Served?* 1977; *The Boys in Blue* 1983
English, Marla (1935-2012) *The She-Creature* 1956; *Voodoo Woman* 1957
Englund, Robert (1947-) *Buster and Billie* 1974; *Eaten Alive* 1976; *St Ives* 1976; *Stay Hungry* 1976; *Starflight One* 1983; *A Nightmare on Elm Street* 1984; *A Nightmare on Elm Street 2: Freddy's Revenge* 1985; *A Nightmare on Elm Street 3: Dream Warriors* 1987; *A Nightmare on Elm Street 4: The Dream Master* 1988; *A Nightmare on Elm Street 5: The Dream Child* 1989; *The Phantom of the Opera* 1989; *The Adventures of Ford Fairlane* 1990; *Freddy's Dead: the Final Nightmare* 1991; *The Mangler* 1994; *Mortal Fear* 1994; *Wes Craven's New Nightmare* 1994; *Wishmaster* 1997; *Meet the Deedles* 1998; *Urban Legend* 1998; *Python* 2000; *Freddy vs Jason* 2003; *Hatchet* 2006; *Zombie Strippers!* 2007; *Strippers vs Werewolves* 2012
Eno, Brian *Scott Walker: 30 Century Man* 2006; *Ride, Rise, Roar* 2010; *The British Guide to Showing Off* 2011
Enos, John *aka* **Enos III, John** (1962-) *Bullet* 1995; *Dead Sexy* 2001
Enos, Lisa *ivansxtc.* 1999; *Snuff-Movie* 2005; *Boxing Day* 2012
Enos, Mireille *Devil's Knot* 2013; *World War Z* 2013; *The Captive* 2014; *If I Stay* 2014
Enriquez, Rene (1933-1990) *The Evil That Men Do* 1984; *Bulletproof* 1987
Ensign, Michael (1944-) *Buddy Buddy* 1981; *House* 1986; *Inherit the Wind* 1988; *Life Stinks* 1991; *Born Yesterday* 1993; *Children of the Corn III: Urban Harvest* 1995
Epps, Mike (1970-) *Next Friday* 1999; *The Fighting Temptations* 2003; *Resident Evil: Apocalypse* 2004; *The Honeymooners* 2005; *Something New* 2006; *Resident Evil: Extinction* 2007; *Talk to Me* 2007; *Open Season 2* 2008; *Welcome Home Roscoe Jenkins* 2008; *Sparkle* 2012; *Fifty Shades of Black* 2016
Epps, Omar (1973-) *Juice* 1991; *The Program* 1993; *Major League II* 1994; *Higher Learning* 1995; *Scream 2* 1997; *Breakfast of Champions* 1999; *In Too Deep* 1999; *The Mod Squad* 1999; *Love & Basketball* 2000; *Against the Ropes* 2003; *Alfie* 2004

Ercy, Elizabeth *Phaedra* 1962; *The Sorcerers* 1967
Erdman, Richard (1925-) *The Admiral Was a Lady* 1950; *The Men* 1950; *Cry Danger* 1951; *The Stooge* 1951; *The San Francisco Story* 1952; *The Blue Gardenia* 1953; *Stalag 17* 1953; *Bengazi* 1955; *Francis in the Navy* 1955; *Namu, the Killer Whale* 1966; *Heidi's Song* 1982
Erdogan, Yilmaz (1967-) *Vizontele* 2001; *Once upon a Time in Anatolia* 2011; *The Water Diviner* 2014
Ergun, Halil (1946-) *Yol* 1982; *Hamam: the Turkish Bath* 1996
Erickson, Ethan (1973-) *Two-Bits and Pepper* 1995; *The In Crowd* 2000
Erickson, Leif (1911-1986) *Conquest* 1937; *Waikiki Wedding* 1937; *One Third of a Nation* 1939; *HM Pulham Esq* 1941; *Nothing but the Truth* 1941; *Arabian Nights* 1942; *Pardon My Sarong* 1942; *Joan of Arc* 1948; *The Snake Pit* 1948; *Sorry, Wrong Number* 1948; *Dallas* 1950; *Stella* 1950; *Three Secrets* 1950; *The Cimarron Kid* 1951; *Sailor Beware* 1951; *Abbott and Costello Meet Captain Kidd* 1952; *Never Wave at a WAC* 1952; *Fort Algiers* 1953; *Invaders from Mars* 1953; *On the Waterfront* 1954; *The Fastest Gun Alive* 1956; *Star in the Dust* 1956; *Tea and Sympathy* 1956; *Istanbul* 1957; *Kiss Them for Me* 1957; *Strait-Jacket* 1963; *Roustabout* 1964; *I Saw What You Did* 1965; *Mirage* 1965; *Winterhawk* 1975
Ericson, John (1926-) *Teresa* 1951; *Green Fire* 1954; *Rhapsody* 1954; *The Student Prince* 1954; *Bad Day at Black Rock* 1955; *Forty Guns* 1957; *Day of the Bad Man* 1958; *Under Ten Flags* 1960; *7 Faces of Dr Lao* 1963; *The Destructors* 1968; *Bedknobs and Broomsticks* 1971; *Crash!* 1977
Ermey, R Lee *aka* **Ermey, Lee** *aka* **Ermey, Ronald Lee** *aka* **Lee Ermey** (1944-) *The Boys in Company C* 1978; *Purple Hearts* 1984; *Full Metal Jacket* 1987; *Mississippi Burning* 1988; *Fletch Lives* 1989; *Kid* 1990; *Toy Soldiers* 1991; *Body Snatchers* 1993; *Hexed* 1993; *Sommersby* 1993; *Murder in the First* 1994; *On Deadly Ground* 1994; *Dead Man Walking* 1995; *Se7en* 1995; *Soul of the Game* 1996; *Dead Men Can't Dance* 1997; *Prefontaine* 1997; *Switchback* 1997; *Evil Woman* 2001; *Taking Sides* 2001; *The Texas Chainsaw Massacre* 2003; *Willard* 2003; *Man of the House* 2005; *The Reef* 2006; *The Texas Chainsaw Massacre: the Beginning* 2006
Errol, Leon (1881-1951) *Her Majesty Love* 1931; *One Heavenly Night* 1931; *Alice in Wonderland* 1933; *We're Not Dressing* 1934; *Dancing Co-Ed* 1939; *The Girl from Mexico* 1939; *Mexican Spitfire* 1940; *Never Give a Sucker an Even Break* 1941; *Higher and Higher* 1943; *The Invisible Man's Revenge* 1944; *Under Western Skies* 1945; *The Noose Hangs High* 1948
Ershadi, Homayoun *The Kite Runner* 2007; *Agora* 2009
Erskine, Marilyn (1926-) *Westward the Women* 1951; *Above and Beyond* 1952; *The Girl in White* 1952; *The Eddie Cantor Story* 1953
Erwin, Bill (1914-2010) *Somewhere in Time* 1980; *The Land before Time* 1988; *Silent Assassins* 1988; *Desert Heat* 1999
Erwin, Stuart (1903-1967) *The Big Broadcast* 1932; *Make Me a Star* 1932; *Going Hollywood* 1933; *Hold Your Man* 1933; *International House* 1933; *The Stranger's Return* 1933; *Chained* 1934; *Palooka* 1934; *Viva Villa!* 1934; *After Office Hours* 1935; *Ceiling Zero* 1935; *Pigskin Parade* 1936; *Checkers* 1937; *I'll Take Romance* 1937; *Slim* 1937; *Three Blind Mice* 1938; *Hollywood Cavalcade* 1939; *When the Daltons Rode* 1940; *The Bride Came COD* 1941; *Heaven Only Knows* 1947; *None but the Brave* 1960; *The Misadventures of Merlin Jones* 1964
Escarpeta, Arlen *Brotherhood* 2010; *Final Destination 5* 2011
Esformes, Nate *Black Belt Jones* 1974; *Gore Vidal's Billy the Kid* 1989
Eshley, Norman (1945-) *The Immortal Story* 1968; *Blind Terror* 1971; *House of Mortal Sin* 1975; *George and Mildred* 1980
Esmond, Annie (1873-1945) *Thunder in the City* 1937; *Gert and Daisy's Weekend* 1941
Esmond, Carl (1902-2004) *Blossom Time* 1934; *Evensong* 1934; *The Dawn Patrol* 1938; *The Navy Comes Through* 1942; *Margin for Error* 1943; *Experiment Perilous* 1944; *The Master Race* 1944; *The Story of Dr Wassell* 1944; *Ministry of Fear* 1945; *This Love of Ours* 1945; *Without Love* 1945; *Lover Come Back* 1946; *Smash Up -*

the Story of a Woman 1947; Mystery Submarine 1950; The World in His Arms 1952; Thunder in the Sun 1959

Esmond, Jill (1908-1990) The Skin Game 1931; The Pied Piper 1942; Casanova Brown 1944; The Bandit of Sherwood Forest 1946; Bedelia 1946; A Man Called Peter 1955

Esposito, Giancarlo (1958-) School Daze 1988; Do the Right Thing 1989; King of New York 1989; Mo' Better Blues 1990; Harley Davidson and the Marlboro Man 1991; Bob Roberts 1992; Night on Earth 1992; Fresh 1994; Reckless 1995; Smoke 1995; The Usual Suspects 1995; Nothing to Lose 1997; Thirst 1998; Twilight 1998; Monkeybone 2000; Piñero 2001; Blind Horizon 2003; Derailed 2005; Last Holiday 2006; Sherrybaby 2006; Rabbit Hole 2010; Maze Runner: The Scorch Trials 2015

Esposito, Gianni (1930-1974) French Cancan 1955; Celà S'Appelle l'Aurore 1956; Les Misérables 1957; Paris Nous Appartient 1960

Esposito, Jennifer (1973-) Summer of Sam 1999; Dracula 2001 2000; The Proposal 2000; Don't Say a Word 2001; The Master of Disguise 2002; Breakin' All the Rules 2004; Taxi 2004; The Wish List 2010

Essell, Eileen Our House 2003; Finding Neverland 2004

Essex, David (1947-) That'll Be the Day 1973; Stardust 1974; Silver Dream Racer 1980; Shogun Warrior 1991; The Guvnors 2014

Essman, Susie The Man 2005; Bolt 2008

Estefan, Gloria (1957-) Music of the Heart 1999; For Love or Country: the Arturo Sandoval Story 2000

Estes, Will (1978-) The Road Home 1995; New Port South 2001; Dangerous Attraction 2012

Estevez, Emilio (1962-) Tex 1982; Nightmares 1983; The Outsiders 1983; Repo Man 1984; The Breakfast Club 1985; St Elmo's Fire 1985; That Was Then... This Is Now 1985; Maximum Overdrive 1986; Wisdom 1986; Stakeout 1987; Young Guns 1988; Nightbreaker 1989; Men at Work 1990; Young Guns II 1990; Freejack 1992; The Mighty Ducks 1992; Another Stakeout 1993; Judgment Night 1993; National Lampoon's Loaded Weapon 1 1993; D2: the Mighty Ducks 1994; D3: the Mighty Ducks 1996; The War at Home 1996; Dollar for the Dead 1998; Rated X 2000; Arthur and the Invisibles 2006; Bobby 2006; The Way 2010

Estevez, Renée (1967-) Running Wild 1992; Paper Hearts 1993; Storm 1999

Estrada, Erik (1949-) The New Centurions 1972; Where Is Parsifal? 1983; Hour of the Assassin 1987; A Show of Force 1990

Eszterhas, Joe (1944-) Burn Hollywood Burn 1997; The First Film 2015

Etel, Alex Millions 2004; The Water Horse 2007; From Time to Time 2009

Etienne, Pauline The Nun 2013; Eden 2014

Eure, Wesley (1955-) The Toolbox Murders 1978; CHOMPS 1979

Evans, Alice (1974-) 102 Dalmatians 2000; The Abduction Club 2002; Blackball 2003; The Christmas Card 2006; Dangerous Parking 2007

Evans, Art (1942-) Leadbelly 1976; A Soldier's Story 1984; Jo Jo Dancer, Your Life Is Calling 1986; Native Son 1986; Ruthless People 1986; White of the Eye 1986; School Daze 1988; The Mighty Quinn 1989; Die Hard 2: Die Harder 1990; Downtown 1990; Trespass 1992; Metro 1997

Evans, Barry (1943-1997) Here We Go round the Mulberry Bush 1967; Adventures of a Taxi Driver 1975; Under the Doctor 1976

Evans, Charles Black Beauty 1946; The Dark Mirror 1946; It Had to Be You 1947

Evans, Chris (1981-) Not Another Teen Movie 2001; Cellular 2004; The Perfect Score 2004; Fantastic Four 2005; Battle for Terra 2007; 4: Rise of the Silver Surfer 2007; The Nanny Diaries 2007; Sunshine 2007; TMNT 2007; Street Kings 2008; Push 2009; The Losers 2010; Scott Pilgrim vs the World 2010; Captain America: the First Avenger 2011; What's Your Number? 2011; The Iceman 2012; Marvel Avengers Assemble 2012; Snowpiercer 2013; Captain America: the Winter Soldier 2014; Playing It Cool 2014; Avengers: Age of Ultron 2015; Captain America: Civil War 2016

Evans, Clifford (1912-1985) Calling the Tune 1936; The Foreman Went to France 1941; Love on the Dole 1941; The Saint Meets the Tiger 1943; The Silver

Darlings 1947; While I Live 1947; Escape Route 1947; Valley of Song 1953; The Gilded Cage 1954; Passport to Treason 1956; Violent Playground 1958; The Curse of the Werewolf 1961; Kiss of the Vampire 1962; The Long Ships 1963

Evans, Dale (1912-2001) War of the Wildcats 1943; The Yellow Rose of Texas 1944; Bells of Rosarita 1945; My Pal Trigger 1946; Bells of San Angelo 1947; Bells of Coronado 1950; Twilight in the Sierras 1950

Evans, Daniel (1974-) A Midsummer Night's Dream 1996; Otherworld 2003

Evans, Edith aka Evans, Dame Edith (1888-1976) The Queen of Spades 1948; The Last Days of Dolwyn 1949; The Importance of Being Earnest 1952; Look Back in Anger 1959; The Nun's Story 1959; Tom Jones 1963; The Chalk Garden 1964; Young Cassidy 1965; Fitzwilly 1967; The Whisperers 1967; Prudence and the Pill 1968; Crooks and Coronets 1969; The Madwoman of Chaillot 1969; Scrooge 1970; Craze 1973; A Doll's House 1973; The Slipper and the Rose 1976

Evans, Edward (1914-2001) Valley of Song 1953; It's a Great Day 1955

Evans, Estelle (1906-1985) To Kill a Mockingbird 1962; The Learning Tree 1969

Evans, Evans (1936-) All Fall Down 1962; Bonnie and Clyde 1967; Story of a Love Story 1973

Evans, Gene (1922-1998) Fixed Bayonets! 1951; Force of Arms 1951; The Steel Helmet 1951; Mutiny 1952; Park Row 1952; Donovan's Brain 1953; The Golden Blade 1953; Cattle Queen of Montana 1954; Hell and High Water 1954; Crashout 1955; Wyoming Renegades 1955; The Helen Morgan Story 1957; The Sad Sack 1957; The Hangman 1959; Operation Petticoat 1959; Shock Corridor 1963; Apache Uprising 1965; Waco 1966; The War Wagon 1967; The Intruders 1970

Evans, John (1934-) I've Heard the Mermaids Singing 1987; Lena: My 100 Children 1987

Evans, Josh (1971-) Born on the Fourth of July 1989; The Doors 1991

Evans, Lee (1965-) Funny Bones 1994; The Fifth Element 1997; Mousehunt 1997; There's Something about Mary 1998; The Ladies Man 2000; The Martins 2001; Freeze Frame 2003; The Medallion 2003; The Magic Roundabout 2005

Evans, Linda (1942-) Those Calloways 1964; Beach Blanket Bingo 1965; Avalanche Express 1979; Tom Horn 1980

Evans, Luke (1979-) Blitz 2010; Tamara Drewe 2010; Immortals 2011; The Three Musketeers 2011; Ashes 2012; No One Lives 2012; The Raven 2012; Fast & Furious 6 2013; The Hobbit: the Desolation of Smaug 2013; Dracula Untold 2014; The Hobbit: the Battle of the Five Armies 2014; High-Rise 2015; The Girl on the Train 2016; Beauty and the Beast 2017

Evans, Madge (1909-1981) Guilty Hands 1931; Sporting Blood 1931; Broadway to Hollywood 1933; Dinner at Eight 1933; Hallelujah, I'm a Bum 1933; The Mayor of Hell 1933; Stand Up and Cheer! 1934; What Every Woman Knows 1934; David Copperfield 1935; Pennies from Heaven 1936; Piccadilly Jim 1936; Sinners in Paradise 1938

Evans, Maurice (1901-1989) Wedding Rehearsal 1932; Kind Lady 1951; Androcles and the Lion 1952; The Story of Gilbert and Sullivan 1953; The War Lord 1965; One of Our Spies Is Missing 1966; Jack of Diamonds 1967; Planet of the Apes 1967; Rosemary's Baby 1968; Beneath the Planet of the Apes 1969; The Body Stealers 1969; Terror in the Wax Museum 1973

Evans (1), Michael (1920-2007) Blackout 1950; The 1,000 Plane Raid 1969

Evans, Monica The Odd Couple 1968; Robin Hood 1973

Evans, Peggy (1925-) The Blue Lamp 1949; Calling Bulldog Drummond 1951

Evans, Rex (1903-1969) The Brighton Strangler 1945; Merry Andrew 1958

Evans, Richard (1935-) Too Soon to Love 1960; Dirty Little Billy 1972; Islands in the Stream 1976

Evans, Robert (1930-) Man of a Thousand Faces 1957; The Sun Also Rises 1957; The Best of Everything 1959; Burn Hollywood Burn 1997; The Kid Stays in the Picture 2001

Evans (2), Rupert (1976-) Hellboy 2004; Agora 2009; Elfie Hopkins 2011; The Canal 2014; The Boy 2016

Evans, Shaun (1980-) The Boys & Girl from County Clare 2003; Being Julia 2004; Cashback 2005; Gone 2006; Sparkle 2006; Dread 2009; Wreckers 2010; War Book 2014

Evans, Troy (1948-) Kuffs 1991; Under Siege 1992; Ace Ventura: Pet Detective 1993; It Runs in the Family 1994

Evanson, Edith (1900-1980) The Jade Mask 1945; Rope 1948; The Magnificent Yankee 1950

Eve (1978-) Barbershop 2002; Barbershop 2: Back in Business 2004; The Woodsman 2004; Flashbacks of a Fool 2008; Barbershop: a Fresh Cut 2016

Eve, Alice (1982-) Big Nothing 2006; Starter for 10 2006; Crossing Over 2008; She's out of My League 2008; The Decoy Bride 2011; ATM 2012; Men in Black 3 2012; The Raven 2012; Cold Comes the Night 2013; Decoding Annie Parker 2013; Criminal 2016; Misconduct 2016

Eve, Trevor (1951-) Dracula 1979; Aspen Extreme 1993; Possession 2002

Evelyn, Judith (1913-1967) The 13th Letter 1950; Rear Window 1954; Hilda Crane 1956; The Brothers Karamazov 1958; The Tingler 1959

Everest, Barbara (1890-1968) When London Sleeps 1932; The Lad 1935; Old Mother Riley 1937; Gaslight 1944; The Uninvited 1944; Wanted for Murder 1946; Madeleine 1949; The Safecracker 1958; The Man Who Finally Died 1962; Nurse on Wheels 1963

Everett, Chad (1936-2012) Rome Adventure 1962; Get Yourself a College Girl 1964; Johnny Tiger 1966; The Singing Nun 1966; The Last Challenge 1967; Airplane II: the Sequel 1982; Fever Pitch 1985; Psycho 1998; Mulholland Drive 2001

Everett, Rupert (1959-) Real Life 1983; Another Country 1984; Dance with a Stranger 1984; Duet for One 1986; Chronicle of a Death Foretold 1987; Hearts of Fire 1987; The Comfort of Strangers 1991; Cemetery Man 1994; Pret-a-Porter 1994; The Madness of King George 1995; B Monkey 1996; Dunston Checks In 1996; My Best Friend's Wedding 1997; Shakespeare in Love 1998; An Ideal Husband 1999; Inspector Gadget 1999; A Midsummer Night's Dream 1999; Paragraph 175 1999; The Next Best Thing 2000; Unconditional Love 2001; The Importance of Being Earnest 2002; To Kill a King 2003; The Wild Thornberrys Movie 2003; Separate Lies 2004; Shrek 2 2004; Stage Beauty 2004; The Chronicles of Narnia: The Lion, the Witch and the Wardrobe 2005; St Trinian's 2007; Shrek the Third 2007; Stardust 2007; St Trinian's 2: the Legend of Fritton's Gold 2009; Wild Target 2009; A Royal Night Out 2015

Everett, Tom Leatherface: the Texas Chainsaw Massacre III 1990; xXx 2002

Everhard, Nancy (1959-) DeepStar Six 1989; The Trial of the Incredible Hulk 1989

Everhart, Angie (1969-) Executive Target 1996; Another 9½ Weeks 1997; The Hollywood Mom's Mystery 2004; Mary Higgins Clark's The Cradle Will Fall 2004

Evermore, J D 99 Homes 2014; Maggie 2015

Evers, Jason (1922-2005) The Brain That Wouldn't Die 1959; The Illustrated Man 1969; Escape from the Planet of the Apes 1971; Basket Case 2 1990

Evets, Steve (1959-) Summer 2008; A Boy Called Dad 2009; Looking for Eric 2009; Brighton Rock 2010; Wuthering Heights 2011; The Facility 2012

Evigan, Briana (1986-) Step Up 2 the Streets 2008; Sorority Row 2009; Mother's Day 2010; Step Up: All In 2014

Evigan, Greg (1953-) DeepStar Six 1989; Murder among Friends 2001; Straight from the Heart 2003; After the Fall 2010

Evison, Pat (1924-2010) Tim 1979; Emma's War 1985

Ewart, John (1928-1994) Newsfront 1978; Bush Christmas 1983

Ewell, Dwight Stonewall 1995; Chasing Amy 1996

Ewell, Tom (1909-1994) Adam's Rib 1949; An American Guerrilla in the Philippines 1950; A Life of Her Own 1950; Mr Music 1950; Lost in Alaska 1952; The Seven Year Itch 1955; The Girl Can't Help It 1956; A Nice Little Bank That Should Be Robbed 1958; Tender Is the Night 1961; State Fair 1962; Suppose They Gave a War and Nobody Came? 1970; They Only Kill Their Masters 1972; Easy Money 1983

Ewing, Barbara Dracula Has Risen from the Grave 1968; Eye of the Needle 1981; When the Whales Came 1989

Ewing, Diana Eighty Steps to Jonah 1969; Play It as It Lays 1972; The Way We Were 1973

Eyer, Richard (1945-) The Desperate Hours 1955; Sincerely Yours 1955; Come Next Spring 1956; Friendly Persuasion 1956; The 7th Voyage of Sinbad 1958

Eyre, Peter (1942-) Hedda 1975; Dragonslayer 1981; Princess Caraboo 1994

Eythe, William (1918-1957) The Ox-Bow Incident 1943; The Song of Bernadette 1943; The Eve of St Mark 1944; Wing and a Prayer 1944; Colonel Effingham's Raid 1945; The House on 92nd Street 1945; A Royal Scandal 1945; Centennial Summer 1946; Meet Me at Dawn 1946

Eziashi, Maynard Mister Johnson 1991; Twenty-One 1991; Bopha! 1993; Ace Ventura: When Nature Calls 1995

F

Fabares, Shelley (1944-) Never Say Goodbye 1955; Ride the Wild Surf 1964; Girl Happy 1965; Spinout 1966; Clambake 1967; Brian's Song 1971; Hot Pursuit 1987

Fabbri, Jacques (1925-1997) Le Défroqué 1953; Diva 1981

Fabian aka **Forte, Fabian** (1942-) Hound Dog Man 1959; High Time 1960; North to Alaska 1960; Five Weeks in a Balloon 1962; The Longest Day 1962; Mr Hobbs Takes a Vacation 1962; Ride the Wild Surf 1964; Ten Little Indians 1965; Dear Brigitte 1966; Dr Goldfoot and the Girl Bombs 1966; Fireball 500 1966; Thunder Alley 1967; The Wild Racers 1968; Get Crazy 1983

Fabian, Françoise (1932-) The Thief of Paris 1967; My Night with Maud 1969; The Bit Player 1969; Reunion 1989; La Bûche 1999; 5x2 2004; Rapt 2009; Me, Myself and Mum 2013

Fabian, Patrick Snow 2004; The Last Exorcism 2010

Fabray, Nanette (1920-) The Band Wagon 1953; Harper Valley PTA 1978; Amy 1981

Fabre, Saturnin (1884-1961) La Nuit Fantastique 1942; Les Portes de la Nuit 1946

Fabregas, Manolo (1920-1996) Captain Scarlett 1953; The Candy Man 1969; Two Mules for Sister Sara 1970

Fabrizi, Aldo (1905-1990) Rome, Open City 1945; Francis, God's Jester 1950; The Angel Wore Red 1960

Fabrizi, Franco (1926-1995) I Vitelloni 1953; Le Amiche 1955; The Swindle 1955; The Birds, the Bees, and the Italians 1965; Ginger & Fred 1986

Fabrizi, Mario (1925-1963) The Running, Jumping and Standing Still Film 1959; The Punch and Judy Man 1962

Facinelli, Peter (1973-) Touch Me 1997; Can't Hardly Wait 1998; Dancer, Texas Pop 81 1998; Telling You 1998; The Big Kahuna 1999; Honest 2000; Supernova 2000; Tempted 2001; The Scorpion King 2002; Hollow Man II 2006; Touch the Top of the World 2006; Twilight 2008; New Moon 2009; Eclipse 2010

Fackeldey, Gisela (1975-) The Bitter Tears of Petra von Kant 1972; Martha 1973

Fagerbakke, Bill (1957-) Lady and the Tramp II: Scamp's Adventure 2000; Balto - Wings of Change 2004; The SpongeBob SquarePants Movie 2004; The SpongeBob Movie: Sponge out of Water 2015

Faget, Huguette (1922-) The Last Stage 1947; Le Beau Mariage 1982

Fahey, Jeff (1954-) Psycho III 1986; Backfire 1987; Blue Heat 1990; Impulse 1990; White Hunter, Black Heart 1990; Body Parts 1991; Iron Maze 1991; The Lawnmower Man 1992; Quick 1993; Wyatt Earp 1994; Darkman III: Die Darkman Die 1996; Lethal Tender 1996; Operation Delta Force 1996; Too Hard to Die 1998; Messages 2007; Planet Terror 2007; Tornado Warning 2012

Fahey, Myrna (1933-1973) Face of a Fugitive 1959; The Fall of the House of Usher 1960

Fairbank, Christopher Anazapta 2001; The Bunker 2001

Fairbanks, Douglas (1883-1939) The Mark of Zorro 1920; The Three Musketeers 1921; Robin Hood 1922; The Thief of Bagdad 1924; Don Q, Son of Zorro 1925; The Black Pirate 1926; The Gaucho 1927; Show People 1928; The Iron Mask 1929; The Taming of the

Shrew 1929; The Private Life of Don Juan 1934; The Great Chase 1961

Fairbanks Jr, Douglas (1909-2000) Stella Dallas 1925; The Barker 1928; A Woman of Affairs 1928; Our Modern Maidens 1929; The Show of Shows 1929; The Dawn Patrol 1930; Party Girl 1930; Little Caesar 1931; Love Is a Racket 1932; Scarlet Dawn 1932; Union Depot 1932; Morning Glory 1933; The Rise of Catherine the Great 1934; Accused 1936; Jump for Glory 1937; The Prisoner of Zenda 1937; Having Wonderful Time 1938; Joy of Living 1938; The Rage of Paris 1938; The Young in Heart 1938; Green Hell 1939; Gunga Din 1939; Rulers of the Sea 1939; Angels over Broadway 1940; The Corsican Brothers 1941; The Exile 1947; Sinbad the Sailor 1947; The Fighting O'Flynn 1948; That Lady in Ermine 1948; Mr Drake's Duck 1950; State Secret 1950; Ghost Story 1981

Fairbanks, Craig (1951-) For Queen and Country 1988; Beyond Bedlam 1993; Cliffhanger 1993; Proteus 1995; Darklands 1996; Killing Time 1998; Weak at Denise 2000; Rise of the Footsoldier 2006; White Noise: the Light 2006; The Shouting Men 2009; 31 North 62 East 2009; Freight 2010; Just for the Record 2010; St George's Day 2012; Bula Quo! 2013; Breakdown 2015

Fairchild, Max Death of a Soldier 1985; The Salute of the Jugger 1989

Fairchild, Morgan (1950-) Midnight Cop 1988; Gospa 1995; Holy Man 1998

Faire, Virginia Brown (1904-1980) The Temptress 1926; West of the Divide 1934

Fairley, Michelle Philomena 2013; Ironclad 2 2014

Fairman, Michael (1934-) Forces of Nature 1998; Thirteen Days 2000; Dead Silence 2007

Faison, Donald aka **Faison, Donald Adeosun** (1974-) Clueless 1995; Remember the Titans 2000; Big Fat Liar 2002; Uptown Girls 2003; Something New 2006; Skyline 2010

Faison, Frankie aka **Faison, Frankie R** (1949-) Sommersby 1993; The Rich Man's Wife 1996; Julian Po 1997; The Thomas Crown Affair 1999; Hannibal 2001; Thirteen Conversations about One Thing 2001; Gods and Generals 2002; Red Dragon 2002; Showtime 2002; Highwaymen 2003; In Good Company 2004; White Chicks 2004; Adam 2009

Faison, Sandy aka **Faison, Sandra** The Sterile Cuckoo 1969; All the Right Moves 1983

Faith, Adam (1940-2003) Beat Girl 1960; Never Let Go 1960; What a Whopper! 1961; Mix Me a Person 1962; Stardust 1974; Yesterday's Hero 1979; Foxes 1980; McVicar 1980

Faithfull, Marianne (1946-) I'll Never Forget What's 'Is Name 1967; The Girl on a Motorcycle 1968; Hamlet 1969; Ghost Story 1974; Lucifer Rising 1981; The Turn of the Screw 1992; Shopping 1993; Intimacy 2000; A Letter to True 2004; Marie Antoinette 2005; Irina Palm 2006

Fajardo, Eduardo (1918-) Tizoc 1956; A Professional Gun 1968

Falco, Edie (1963-) The Unbelievable Truth 1989; Trust 1990; Laws of Gravity 1992; The Addiction 1994; Hurricane Streets 1997; The Sunshine Boys 1997; Judy Berlin 1999; Sunshine State 2002; Freedomland 2006

Falk, Lisanne Heathers 1989; Shattered Image 1998

Falk, Peter (1927-2011) Wind across the Everglades 1958; The Secret of the Purple Reef 1960; Pocketful of Miracles 1961; Pressure Point 1962; The Balcony 1963; Robin and the 7 Hoods 1964; The Great Race 1965; Penelope 1966; Luv 1967; Anzio 1968; Prescription: Murder 1968; Castle Keep 1969; Husbands 1970; Ransom for a Dead Man 1971; A Woman under the Influence 1974; Murder by Death 1976; The Brink's Job 1978; The Cheap Detective 1978; The In-Laws 1979; The California Dolls 1981; The Great Muppet Caper 1981; Big Trouble 1985; Happy New Year 1987; The Princess Bride 1987; Wings of Desire 1987; Vibes 1988; Cookie 1989; Aunt Julia and the Scriptwriter 1990; Faraway, So Close 1993; Roommates 1995; Pronto 1996; The Sunshine Boys 1997; A Storm in Summer 2000; Corky Romano 2001; Made 2001; Undisputed 2002; Shark Tale 2004; Next 2007

Falk, Rossella (1926-2013) 8½ 1963; Modesty Blaise 1966; The Legend of Lylah Clare 1968

Fallon, Jimmy (1974-) Anything Else 2003; Taxi 2004; The Perfect Catch 2005; Arthur and the Invisibles 2006; Factory Girl 2006; Whip It 2009

Fallon, Siobhan aka **Hogan, Siobhan**
Fallon aka **Fallon Hogan, Siobhan** (1972-) Only You 1994; Fools Rush In 1997; The Negotiator 1998; Daddy Day Care 2003; Funny Games US 2008; New in Town 2008; Fred: the Movie 2010; We Need to Talk about Kevin 2011

Fann, Al (1925-) Parasite 1982; Frankie & Johnny 1991; Stop! or My Mom Will Shoot 1992

Fanning, Dakota (1994-) My Neighbour Totoro 1988; I Am Sam 2001; Trapped 2002; Dr Seuss' The Cat in the Hat 2003; Uptown Girls 2003; Man on Fire 2004; Dreamer 2005; Hide and Seek 2005; War of the Worlds 2005; Charlotte's Web 2006; Coraline 2008; Fragments 2008; The Secret Life of Bees 2008; Push 2009; Eclipse 2010; The Runaways 2010; Breaking Dawn Part Two 2012; The Motel Life 2012; Now Is Good 2012; Night Moves 2013; Effie Gray 2014; The Benefactor 2015; American Pastoral 2016

Fanning, Elle (1998-) My Neighbour Totoro 1988; Because of Winn-Dixie 2004; The Door in the Floor 2004; Babel 2006; The Nines 2007; The Curious Case of Benjamin Button 2008; The Nutcracker in 3D 2010; Somewhere 2010; Super 8 2011; Twixt 2011; We Bought a Zoo 2011; Ginger & Rosa 2012; Bad Land: Road to Fury 2014; The Boxtrolls 2014; Maleficent 2014; Trumbo 2015; Live by Night 2016; The Neon Demon 2016

Fanning, Neil (1967-) Scooby-Doo 2002; Scooby-Doo 2: Monsters Unleashed 2004

Fantastichini, Ennio Loose Cannons 2010; The Arrival of Wang 2011

Fantoni, Sergio (1930-) Esther and the King 1960; The Giant of Marathon 1960; Do Not Disturb 1965; Von Ryan's Express 1965; What Did You Do in the War, Daddy? 1966; Diabolically Yours 1967; The Belly of an Architect 1987

Faracy, Stephanie (1949-) The Great Outdoors 1988; Bridesmaids 1989

Farahani, Golshifteh (1983-) Body of Lies 2008; Shirin 2008; About Elly 2009; The Patience Stone 2012; Rosewater 2014

Farebrother, Violet (1888-1969) Easy Virtue 1927; The Woman for Joe 1955; Fortune Is a Woman 1956

Farentino, Debrah (1961-) Sherlock Holmes Returns 1993; Son of the Pink Panther 1993

Farentino, James (1938-2012) The War Lord 1965; Banning 1967; The Ride to Hangman's Tree 1967; Rosie! 1967; The Final Countdown 1980; Her Alibi 1989; Bulletproof 1996

Fares, Fares (1973-) Easy Money II 2012; The Keeper of Lost Causes 2013; The Absent One 2014; The Commune 2016

Farès, Nadia Love in the Strangest Way 1994; The Crimson Rivers 2000

Fargas, Antonio (1946-) Cisco Pike 1971; Across 110th Street 1972; Cleopatra Jones 1973; Foxy Brown 1974; Car Wash 1976; Next Stop, Greenwich Village 1976; Pretty Baby 1978; Crimewave 1985; Blue Jean Cop 1988; I'm Gonna Git You Sucka 1988; The Borrower 1989; Whore 1991

Farías, Roberto Los Debutantes 2003; The Club 2015

Farina, Dennis (1944-2013) Thief 1981; The Killing Floor 1984; Manhunter 1986; Midnight Run 1988; Men of Respect 1990; Romeo Is Bleeding 1992; Another Stakeout 1993; Striking Distance 1993; Little Big League 1994; Get Shorty 1995; Eddie 1996; That Old Feeling 1997; Out of Sight 1998; The Mod Squad 1999; Deception 2000; Sidewalks of New York 2000; Snatch 2000; Big Trouble 2002; Stealing Harvard 2002; Paparazzi 2004; You Kill Me 2007; Bottle Shock 2008; What Happens in Vegas 2008

Farinacci, Daniela Lantana 2001; Look Both Ways 2005

Faris, Anna (1976-) Scary Movie 2000; Scary Movie 2 2001; The Hot Chick 2002; Lost in Translation 2003; Scary Movie 3 2003; Brokeback Mountain 2005; Just Friends 2005; Waiting... 2005; My Super Ex-Girlfriend 2006; Scary Movie 4 2006; Frequently Asked Questions about Time Travel 2008; The House Bunny 2008; Alvin and the Chipmunks: the Squeakquel 2009; Cloudy with a Chance of Meatballs 2009; Observe and Report 2009; Yogi Bear 2010; Take Me Home Tonight 2011; What's Your Number? 2011; The Dictator 2012; Cloudy with a Chance of Meatballs 2 2013; I Give It a Year 2013; Movie 43 2013

Faris, Sean Sleepover 2004; Never Back Down 2008

Farley, Chris (1964-1997) Coneheads 1993; Airheads 1994; Tommy Boy 1995; Black Sheep 1996; Beverly Hills Ninja 1997; Almost Heroes 1998; Dirty Work 1998

Farley, James aka **Farley, Jim** (1882-1947) The General 1927; Westward Ho 1935

Farley, John Black Sheep 1996; Beverly Hills Ninja 1997; The Straight Story 1999

Farley, Kevin aka **Farley, Kevin P** (1965-) Black Sheep 1996; Beverly Hills Ninja 1997; The Straight Story 1999

Farley, Morgan (1898-1988) The Devil's Holiday 1930; Barricade 1950; The Wild North 1952

Farmer, Bill A Goofy Movie 1995; Casper: a Spirited Beginning 1997

Farmer, Frances (1913-1970) Come and Get It 1936; Rhythm on the Range 1936; The Toast of New York 1937; South of Pago Pago 1940; Among the Living 1941; Son of Fury 1942

Farmer, Gary (1953-) Powwow Highway 1988; The Dark Wind 1991; Dead Man 1995; Smoke Signals 1998; The Score 2001

Farmer, Mimsy (1945-) Spencer's Mountain 1963; The Wild Racers 1968; More 1969; Two against the Law 1973; The Black Cat 1981; The Death of Mario Ricci 1983; Codename Wildgeese 1984

Farmer, Suzan (1943-) Die, Monster, Die! 1965; Dracula - Prince of Darkness 1965; Rasputin, the Mad Monk 1965

Farmer, Virginia (1898-1988) Born to Be Bad 1950; Cyrano de Bergerac 1950; The Men 1950; Darling, How Could You! 1951

Farmiga, Taissa The Bling Ring 2013; Mindscape 2013; In a Valley of Violence 2016

Farmiga, Vera (1973-) Return to Paradise 1998; Autumn in New York 2000; The Opportunists 2000; Dummy 2002; Running Scared 2005; Breaking and Entering 2006; The Departed 2006; Joshua 2007; The Boy in the Striped Pyjamas 2008; Orphan 2009; Up in the Air 2009; Henry's Crime 2010; Source Code 2011; Safe House 2012; The Conjuring 2013; Closer to the Moon 2014; The Judge 2014; The Conjuring 2 2016

Farnaby, Simon Bunny & the Bull 2009; Bill 2014

Farnsworth, Richard (1920-2000) Comes a Horseman 1978; Resurrection 1980; Tom Horn 1980; The Legend of the Lone Ranger 1981; The Grey Fox 1982; Independence Day 1983; The Natural 1984; Rhinestone 1984; Into the Night 1985; Sylvester 1985; Wild Horses 1985; Misery 1990; The Two Jakes 1990; Highway to Hell 1992; The Getaway 1994; The Straight Story 1999

Farnum, William (1876-1953) A Connecticut Yankee 1931; The Painted Desert 1931; Supernatural 1933; The Count of Monte Cristo 1934; Shine On, Harvest Moon 1938; Trail of Robin Hood 1950; Lone Star 1952

Farr, Derek (1912-1986) Freedom Radio 1940; Quiet Wedding 1940; Quiet Weekend 1946; The Shop at Sly Corner 1946; Wanted for Murder 1946; Bond Street 1948; Noose 1948; Silent Dust 1948; Murder without Crime 1950; Young Wives' Tale 1951; Eight o'Clock Walk 1953; Front Page Story 1953; Bang! You're Dead 1954; The Dam Busters 1954; Value for Money 1955; Town on Trial 1956; Doctor at Large 1957; The Man in the Road 1957; The Vicious Circle 1957

Farr, Felicia (1932-) The First Texan 1956; Jubal 1956; The Last Wagon 1956; 3:10 to Yuma 1957; Hell Bent for Leather 1960; Kiss Me, Stupid 1964; The Venetian Affair 1966; Kotch 1971; Charley Varrick 1973; That's Life 1986

Farr, Jamie (1934-) Who's Minding the Mint? 1967; The Cannonball Run 1981; Cannonball Run II 1983; Curse II: The Bite 1989; A Grandpa for Christmas 2007

Farrar, David (1908-1995) Danny Boy 1941; Went the Day Well? 1942; For Those in Peril 1943; Black Narcissus 1947; Frieda 1947; Mr Perrin and Mr Traill 1948; Diamond City 1949; The Small Back Room 1949; Cage of Gold 1950; Gone to Earth 1950; The Late Edwina Black 1951; Night without Stars 1951; The Black Shield of Falworth 1954; Duel in the Jungle 1954; Escape to Burma 1955; Lilacs in the Spring 1955; Lost 1955; Pearl of the South Pacific 1955; The Sea Chase 1955; The Woman and the Hunter 1957; I Accuse! 1958; Son of Robin Hood 1958; Solomon and Sheba 1959; Beat Girl 1960; The 300 Spartans 1962

Farrell (1), Charles (1906-1988) Boys Will Be Boys 1935; Bell-Bottom George 1943; Final Appointment 1954

Farrell (2), Colin aka **Farrell, Colin J** (1976-) The War Zone 1999; Tigerland 2000; American Outlaws 2001; Hart's War 2002; Minority Report 2002; Phone Booth 2002; The Recruit 2002; Daredevil 2003; interMission 2003; SWAT 2003; Veronica Guerin 2003; Alexander 2004; A Home at the End of the World 2004; The New World 2005; Ask the Dust 2006; Miami Vice 2006; Cassandra's Dream 2007; Pride and Glory 2007; In Bruges 2008; Crazy Heart 2009; The Imaginarium of Doctor Parnassus 2009; Ondine 2009; London Boulevard 2010; The Way Back 2010; Fright Night 2011; Horrible Bosses 2011; Seven Psychopaths 2012; Total Recall 2012; Dead Man Down 2013; Epic 2013; Saving Mr Banks 2013; Miss Julie 2014; A New York Winter's Tale 2014; The Lobster 2015; Solace 2015; Fantastic Beasts and Where to Find Them 2016

Farrell, Glenda (1904-1971) Little Caesar 1931; I Am a Fugitive from a Chain Gang 1932; Life Begins 1932; Bureau of Missing Persons 1933; Havana Widows 1933; Lady for a Day 1933; Man's Castle 1933; Mystery of the Wax Museum 1933; Hi, Nellie! 1934; The Secret Bride 1934; Go into Your Dance 1935; Gold Diggers of 1935 1935; In Caliente 1935; Gold Diggers of 1937 1936; Smart Blonde 1936; Breakfast for Two 1937; Hollywood Hotel 1937; Johnny Eager 1941; The Talk of the Town 1942; Lulu Belle 1948; Secret of the Incas 1954; Susan Slept Here 1954; The Girl in the Red Velvet Swing 1955; The Disorderly Orderly 1964; Kissin' Cousins 1964; Tiger by the Tail 1970

Farrell, Nicholas (1955-) Chariots of Fire 1981; Playing Away 1986; In the Bleak Midwinter 1995; Othello 1995; Hamlet 1996; Twelfth Night 1996; Legionnaire 1998; Beautiful People 1999; Arthur's Dyke 2001; Bloody Sunday 2001; Driving Lessons 2006

Farrell, Sharon (1946-) The Spy with My Face 1966; A Lovely Way to Go 1968; Marlowe 1969; The Reivers 1969; It's Alive 1974; Out of the Blue 1980; The Stunt Man 1980

Farrell, Terry (1963-) Back to School 1986; Hellraiser III: Hell on Earth 1992; Danielle Steel's Star 1993

Farrell, Timothy (1923-1989) Glen or Glenda 1953; Jail Bait 1954

Farrell, Tommy (1921-2004) At War with the Army 1950; Meet Danny Wilson 1952

Farrow, Mia (1945-) Guns at Batasi 1964; Rosemary's Baby 1968; Secret Ceremony 1968; John and Mary 1969; Blind Terror 1971; Follow Me 1971; The Great Gatsby 1974; Full Circle 1977; Avalanche 1978; Death on the Nile 1978; A Wedding 1978; Hurricane 1979; The Last Unicorn 1980; A Midsummer Night's Sex Comedy 1982; Zelig 1983; Broadway Danny Rose 1984; Supergirl 1984; The Purple Rose of Cairo 1985; Hannah and Her Sisters 1986; Radio Days 1987; September 1987; Another Woman 1988; Crimes and Misdemeanors 1989; New York Stories 1989; Alice 1990; Shadows and Fog 1991; Husbands and Wives 1992; Widows' Peak 1993; Miami Rhapsody 1995; Reckless 1995; Private Parts 1997; Forget Me Never 1999; Arthur and the Invisibles 2006; The Omen 2006; Be Kind Rewind 2007; Roman Polanski: Wanted and Desired 2008; Dark Horse 2011

Farrow, Tisa (1951-) And Hope to Die 1972; Fingers 1978; Zombie Flesh Eaters 1979

Fassbender, Michael (1977-) Angel 2006; 300 2006; Eden Lake 2008; Hunger 2008; Blood Creek 2009; Centurion 2009; Fish Tank 2009; Inglourious Basterds 2009; Jonah Hex 2010; A Dangerous Method 2011; Haywire 2011; Jane Eyre 2011; Shame 2011; X-Men: First Class 2011; Prometheus 2012; The Counsellor 2013; Frank 2013; 12 Years a Slave 2013; X-Men: Days of Future Past 2014; Macbeth 2015; Slow West 2015; Steve Jobs 2015; Assassin's Creed 2016; X-Men: Apocalypse 2016

Fassbinder, Rainer Werner (1945-1982) Gods of the Plague 1969; Love Is Colder than Death 1969; The American Soldier 1970; Beware of a Holy Whore 1970; Whity 1970; Fear Eats the Soul 1973; Fox and His Friends 1975

Fatone, Joey (1977-) On the Line 2001; My Big Fat Greek Wedding 2002

Faulds, Andrew (1923-2000) The One That Got Away 1957; Blood of the Vampire 1958

Faulkner, James (1948-) The Great Waltz 1972; The Abdication 1974; Death in the Sun 1975; Real Life 1983; The Maid 1991; Vigo: Passion for Life 1997; All the Little Animals 1998; Agent Cody Banks 2: Destination London 2003; The Bank Job 2008; Franklyn 2008

Faulkner, Keith The Man in the Back Seat 1961; Strongroom 1961

Faulkner, Lisa (1973-) The Lover 1992; A Feast at Midnight 1994; Honeymooner 2010

Favino, Pierfrancesco (1969-) The Keys to the House 2004; Romanzo Criminale 2005; Angels & Demons 2009; Rush 2013; Suburra 2015

Favreau, Jon (1966-) Rudy 1993; PCU 1994; Just Your Luck 1996; Persons Unknown 1996; Swingers 1996; Very Bad Things 1998; Rocky Marciano 1999; Love & Sex 2000; The Replacements 2000; Made 2001; Daredevil 2003; Something's Gotta Give 2003; Wimbledon 2004; The Break-Up 2006; Open Season 2006; Four Christmases 2008; I Love You, Man 2009; Couples Retreat 2009; G-Force 2009; Iron Man 2 2010; Zookeeper 2011; Identity Thief 2013; Iron Man Three 2013; The Wolf of Wall Street 2013; Chef 2014; Misery Loves Comedy 2015

Fawcett, Alan aka **Fawcett, Allan** Afterglow 1997; Ladies' Room 2000; Hidden Agenda 2001

Fawcett, Farrah aka **Fawcett-Majors, Farrah** (1947-2009) Myra Breckinridge 1970; Logan's Run 1976; Somebody Killed Her Husband 1978; Sunburn 1979; Saturn 3 1980; The Cannonball Run 1981; The Burning Bed 1984; Extremities 1986; Nazi Hunter: the Beate Klarsfeld Story 1986; See You in the Morning 1989; Man of the House 1994; The Apostle 1997; Dr T & the Women 2000

Fawcett, George (1860-1939) Flesh and the Devil 1926; The Son of the Sheik 1926; Love 1927; The Private Life of Helen of Troy 1927; The Wedding March 1928; Ladies of Leisure 1930

Fay, Frank (1897-1961) The Show of Shows 1929; God's Gift to Women 1931; Nothing Sacred 1937; They Knew What They Wanted 1940; Love Nest 1951

Fay, Megan The Country Bears 2002; Working Miracles 2010

Faye, Alice (1915-1998) George White's Scandals 1934; George White's 1935 Scandals 1935; King of Burlesque 1936; Poor Little Rich Girl 1936; Sing, Baby, Sing 1936; Stowaway 1936; In Old Chicago 1937; On the Avenue 1937; Wake Up and Live 1937; You Can't Have Everything 1937; Alexander's Ragtime Band 1938; Sally, Irene and Mary 1938; Hollywood Cavalcade 1939; Rose of Washington Square 1939; Lillian Russell 1940; Little Old New York 1940; Tin Pan Alley 1940; The Great American Broadcast 1941; That Night in Rio 1941; Weekend in Havana 1941; The Gang's All Here 1943; Hello, Frisco, Hello 1943; Fallen Angel 1945; State Fair 1962; The Magic of Lassie 1978

Faye, Herbie (1899-1980) Top Banana 1953; Requiem for a Heavyweight 1962

Faye, Janina Don't Talk to Strange Men 1962; The Beauty Jungle 1964; The Dance of Death 1969

Faye, Julia (1893-1966) The Ten Commandments 1923; Dynamite 1929; Samson and Delilah 1949

Faylen, Frank (1905-1985) It's a Wonderful Life 1946; Road to Rio 1947; Suddenly It's Spring 1947; Welcome Stranger 1947; Blood on the Moon 1948; Whispering Smith 1948; Convicted 1950; Copper Canyon 1950; Detective Story 1951; Hangman's Knot 1952; The Lusty Men 1952; The Sniper 1952; 99 River Street 1953; Riot in Cell Block 11 1954; The McConnell Story 1955; 7th Cavalry 1956; Gunfight at the OK Corral 1957; Fluffy 1965; The Monkey's Uncle 1965

Faysse, Dominique Your Beating Heart 1991; L'Eau Froide 1994

Fazenda, Louise (1895-1962) The Desert Song 1929; Rain or Shine 1930; Alice in Wonderland 1933; Colleen 1936; Swing Your Lady 1937

Fearn, Sheila (1940-) The Likely Lads 1976; George and Mildred 1980

Featherstone, Katie Paranormal Activity 2007; Paranormal Activity 2 2010; Paranormal Activity 3 2011; Paranormal Activity 4 2012

Featherstone, Angela (1965-) Zero Effect 1997; The Wedding Singer 1998; 200 Cigarettes 1999; The Guilty 2000; Soul Survivors 2001; Federal Protection 2002; One Way Out 2002

Feder, Frédérique Acción Mutante 1993; Three Colours Red 1994

Feeney, Caroleen Denise Calls Up 1995; Cadillac Ranch 1996; Bad Manners 1997

Fehling, Alexander Storm 2009; Labyrinth of Lies 2014

Fehmiu, Bekim (1936-2010) I Even Met Happy Gypsies 1967; The Adventurers 1970; The Deserter 1971; Permission to Kill 1975; Black Sunday 1976; Salon Kitty 1976

Fehr, Brendan (1977-) The Forsaken 2001; Biker Boyz 2003

Fehr, Darcy The Saddest Music in the World 2003; My Winnipeg 2007

Fehr, Oded (1970-) Deuce Bigalow: Male Gigolo 1999; The Mummy 1999; The Mummy Returns 2001; Resident Evil: Apocalypse 2004; Dreamer 2005; Resident Evil: Extinction 2007

Feig, Paul (1962-) Zombie High 1987; Heavyweights 1995

Feild, J J (1978-) Blood: the Last Vampire 2008; Telstar: the Joe Meek Story 2008; Centurion 2009; Third Star 2010; Austenland 2013

Feinberg, Ron (1932-2005) Brian's Song 1971; A Boy and His Dog 1975

Feld, Fritz (1900-1993) The Affairs of Annabel 1938; Bringing Up Baby 1938; Heidi's Song 1982

Felder, Clarence The Killing Floor 1984; Ruthless People 1986; The Hidden 1987

Feldman, Andrea (1948-1972) Trash 1970; Heat 1972

Feldman, Ben (1980-) The Perfect Man 2005; As Above, So Below 2014

Feldman, Corey (1971-) Friday the 13th: the Final Chapter 1984; The Goonies 1985; Stand by Me 1986; The Lost Boys 1987; License to Drive 1988; The 'Burbs 1989; Dream a Little Dream 1989; Round Trip to Heaven 1992; Fortune Hunters 1999

Feldman, Marty (1933-1982) The Bed Sitting Room 1969; Every Home Should Have One 1970; Young Frankenstein 1974; The Adventure of Sherlock Holmes' Smarter Brother 1975; Silent Movie 1976; The Last Remake of Beau Geste 1977; In God We Trust 1980; Yellowbeard 1983

Feldon, Barbara (1941-) Fitzwilly 1967; Smile 1975; No Deposit No Return 1976

Feldshuh, Tovah (1952-) The Idolmaker 1980; Brewster's Millions 1985; A Day in October 1991; A Walk on the Moon 1999; Kissing Jessica Stein 2001; Just My Luck 2006

Felix, Maria (1914-2002) French Cancan 1955; Tizoc 1956; La Fièvre Monte à el Pao 1959

Fell, Norman (1924-1998) Pork Chop Hill 1959; The Killers 1964; Fitzwilly 1967; Bullitt 1968; Sergeant Ryker 1968; The Boatniks 1970; The Stone Killer 1973; Cleopatra Jones and the Casino of Gold 1975; The End 1978; Paternity 1981; For the Boys 1991

Fellaq, Mohamed aka **Fellaq** Intimate Enemies 2007; Monsieur Lazhar 2011

Fellini, Federico (1920-1993) L'Amore 1948; Alex in Wonderland 1970; Fellini's Roma 1972; We All Loved Each Other So Much 1974; Intervista 1987

Fellner, Rosie Magicians 2007; Do Elephants Pray? 2009; The Face of an Angel 2014

Fellowes, Julian (1949-) The Scarlet Pimpernel 1982; Baby: Secret of the Lost Legend 1985; Fellow Traveller 1989; Damage 1992; Shadowlands 1993; A Christmas Star 2015

Fellowes, Rockliffe (1883-1950) Regeneration 1915; Monkey Business 1931

Fellows, Edith (1923-2011) She Married Her Boss 1935; And So They Were Married 1936; Pennies from Heaven 1936; Music in My Heart 1940

Fellows, Graham aka **John Shuttleworth** Southern Softies 2009; Southern Softies 2009

Felmy, Hansjörg aka **Felmy, Hansjoerg** (1931-2007) Station Six-Sahara 1962; Torn Curtain 1966

Felton, Felix (1911-1972) Night Was Our Friend 1951; It's That, Dad 1961

Felton, Tom (1987-) Anna and the King 1999; Harry Potter and the Philosopher's Stone 2001; The Disappeared 2008; Harry Potter and the Half-Blood Prince 2009; Rise of the Planet of the Apes 2011; Belle 2013; In Secret 2013; Risen 2016; A United Kingdom 2017

Felton, Verna (1890-1966) Dumbo 1941; Cinderella 1950; The Gunfighter 1950; Alice in Wonderland 1951; Don't Bother to Knock 1952; Lady and the

Tramp 1955; The Oklahoman 1957; Sleeping Beauty 1959; Guns of the Timberland 1960; The Jungle Book 1967

Fenemore, Hilda (1919-2004) Adventure in the Hopfields 1954; The Tommy Steele Story 1957; The Wind of Change 1961

Feng Yuanzheng Sacrificed Youth 1985; Ten Minutes Older: the Trumpet 2002

Fenn, Sherilyn (1965-) Thrashin' 1986; The Wraith 1986; Zombie High 1987; Two Moon Junction 1988; Backstreet Dreams 1990; Desire & Hell at Sunset Motel 1991; Diary of a Hitman 1992; Of Mice and Men 1992; Ruby 1992; Three of Hearts 1992; Boxing Helena 1993; Fatal Instinct 1993; Darkness Falls 1998

Fennelly, Parker (1891-1988) The Trouble with Harry 1954; Angel in My Pocket 1968

Fenton, Frank (1906-1957) Buffalo Bill 1944; The Clay Pigeon 1949

Fenton, Lance Night of the Demons 1988; Heathers 1989

Fenton, Leslie (1902-1978) The Dragnet 1928; The Public Enemy 1931; The Hatchet Man 1932; The Strange Love of Molly Louvain 1932; Lady Killer 1933; Marie Galante 1934; Star of Midnight 1935; Boys Town 1938

Fenton, Sarah-Jane The Bachelor 1990; A Good Man in Africa 1993

Fenwick, Perry (1962-) Party Party 1983; ID 1994

Feore, Colm (1958-) Beautiful Dreamers 1990; Bethune: the Making of a Hero 1990; Thirty Two Short Films about Glenn Gould 1993; Truman 1995; Night Falls on Manhattan 1997; City of Angels 1998; The Red Violin 1998; Forget Me Never 1999; Titus 1999; The Virginian 2000; Pearl Harbor 2001; Chicago 2002; National Security 2002; The Sum of All Fears 2002; Highwaymen 2003; Paycheck 2003; The Chronicles of Riddick 2004; Lies My Mother Told Me 2004; The Exorcism of Emily Rose 2005; Bury My Heart at Wounded Knee 2007; Changeling 2008; Jack Ryan: Shadow Recruit 2013

Ferch, Heino (1963-) Lucie Aubrac 1997; Wintersleepers 1997; Run Lola Run 1998; Extreme Ops 2003; Downfall 2004

Ferdin, Pamelyn (1959-) A Boy Named Charlie Brown 1969; The Beguiled 1970; The Mephisto Waltz 1971; The Toolbox Murders 1978

Ferdinando, Peter Tony 2009; Hyena 2014; Tommy's Honour 2016

Ferguson, Craig (1962-) The Big Tease 1999; Born Romantic 2000; Saving Grace 2000; I'll Be There 2003; Niagara Motel 2005; How to Train Your Dragon 2010; Winnie the Pooh 2011; Brave 2012; How to Train Your Dragon 2 2014

Ferguson, Frank (1899-1978) Abbott and Costello Meet Frankenstein 1948; Caught 1949; Gun Duel in Durango 1957; Andy Hardy Comes Home 1958

Ferguson, Jessie Lawrence (1941-) Darkman 1990; To Protect and Serve 1992

Ferguson, Matthew (1973-) On My Own 1992; Love and Human Remains 1993

Ferguson, Rebecca (1983-) Hercules 2014; Mission: Impossible - Rogue Nation 2015; Despite the Falling Snow 2016; Florence Foster Jenkins 2016; The Girl on the Train 2016

Ferguson, Stacy aka **Fergie** Planet Terror 2007; Marmaduke 2010

Ferjac, Anouk (1932-) Vivre pour Vivre 1967; Je T'Aime, Je T'Aime 1968; Que la Bête Meure 1969; Diabolo Menthe 1977

Ferland, Jodelle (1994-) Mermaid 2000; Tideland 2005; Silent Hill 2006; Case 39 2008

Ferlito, Vanessa Man of the House 2005; Death Proof 2007; Julie & Julia 2009

Fernandel (1903-1971) On Purge Bébé 1931; Angèle 1934; Un Carnet de Bal 1937; The Little World of Don Camillo 1951; Topaze 1951; The Sheep Has Five Legs 1954; Paris Holiday 1958

Fernández, Ana (1963-) Solas 1998; The City of No Limits 2002; To Die in San Hilario 2005

Fernández, Eduard Che Part Two 2008; Biutiful 2009

Fernandez, Emilio (1904-1986) The Reward 1965; The Appaloosa 1966; Return of the Seven 1966; The Wild Bunch 1969; Bring Me the Head of Alfredo Garcia 1974

Fernandez, Jaime (1937-2005) The Adventures of Robinson Crusoe 1952; The River and Death 1954; A Bullet for the General 1966

Fernandez, Jesus Simon of the Desert 1965; Tristana 1970

Fernandez, Juan aka **Fernández, Juan** (1956-) "Crocodile" Dundee II 1988; Kinjite: Forbidden Subjects 1989; Extralarge: Moving Target 1990; A Show of Force 1990; Solas 1998; A Man Apart 2003; You're My Hero 2003; The Collector 2009

Fernandez, Shiloh (1985-) Skateland 2010; Red Riding Hood 2011; The East 2013; Evil Dead 2013; White Bird in a Blizzard 2014; Return to Sender 2015; We Are Your Friends 2015

Ferns, Alex (1969-) Man Dancin' 2003; Merry Christmas 2005

Fernside, John The Overlanders 1946; Bush Christmas 1947; Eureka Stockade 1949

Ferraday, Lisa (1921-2004) The Belle of New York 1952; Death of a Scoundrel 1956

Ferrara, Abel aka **Laine, Jimmy** (1952-) The Driller Killer 1979; Ms 45 1981

Ferrara, Jerry Brooklyn Rules 2007; Think like a Man 2012

Ferratti, Rebecca (1964-) Gor 1987; Cyborg 3: The Recycler 1994

Ferreira, Sky The Green Inferno 2013; The Trust 2016

Ferrell, Conchata (1943-) For Keeps 1987; Mystic Pizza 1988; Chains of Gold 1989; True Romance 1993; Stranger Inside 2001; Mr Deeds 2002; Krampus 2015

Ferrell, Tyra (1962-) Lady Beware 1987; Boyz N the Hood 1991; Equinox 1992; White Men Can't Jump 1992; Poetic Justice 1993; The Perfect Score 2004

Ferrell, Will (1967-) A Night at the Roxbury 1998; Austin Powers: the Spy Who Shagged me 1999; Dick 1999; The Suburbans 1999; Superstar 1999; Drowning Mona 2000; The Ladies Man 2000; Jay and Silent Bob Strike Back 2001; Zoolander 2001; Elf 2003; Old School 2003; Anchorman: the Legend of Ron Burgundy 2004; Melinda and Melinda 2004; Bewitched 2005; Kicking & Screaming 2005; The Producers 2005; Curious George 2006; Stranger than Fiction 2006; Talladega Nights: the Ballad of Ricky Bobby 2006; Blades of Glory 2007; Semi-Pro 2008; Step Brothers 2008; The Goods: Live Hard Sell Hard 2009; Land of the Lost 2009; Everything Must Go 2010; Megamind 2010; The Other Guys 2010; Casa de Mi Padre 2011; The Campaign 2012; Anchorman 2: the Legend Continues 2013; The Internship 2013; The Lego Movie 2014; Daddy's Home 2015; A Deadly Adoption 2015; Get Hard 2015; Zoolander 2 2016

Ferréol, Andréa (1947-) La Grande Bouffe 1973; Despair 1978; The Last Metro 1980; Three Brothers 1980; A Zed & Two Noughts 1985; Francesco 1989; Il Maestro 1989; Street of No Return 1989; Wings of Fame 1990; The Edge of the Horizon 1993

Ferrer, José (1909-1992) Joan of Arc 1948; Whirlpool 1949; Crisis 1950; Cyrano de Bergerac 1950; Anything Can Happen 1952; Moulin Rouge 1952; Miss Sadie Thompson 1953; The Caine Mutiny 1954; Deep in My Heart 1954; The Cockleshell Heroes 1955; The Great Man 1956; The High Cost of Loving 1958; I Accuse! 1958; Lawrence of Arabia 1962; The Greatest Story Ever Told 1965; Ship of Fools 1965; Enter Laughing 1967; Cervantes 1968; The Marcus-Nelson Murders 1973; The Big Bus 1976; Crash! 1977; The Private Files of J Edgar Hoover 1977; The Sentinel 1977; Who Has Seen the Wind 1977; Zoltan... Hound of Dracula 1977; The Amazing Captain Nemo 1978; Fedora 1978; The Swarm 1978; The 5th Musketeer 1979; The Big Brawl 1980; Gideon's Trumpet 1980; A Midsummer Night's Sex Comedy 1982; To Be or Not to Be 1983; Dune 1984; The Evil That Men Do 1984; Hired to Kill 1990

Ferrer, Leilani aka **Ferrer, Leilani Sarelle** (1966-) Barbarians at the Gate 1993; The Harvest 1993

Ferrer, Mel (1917-2008) Born to Be Bad 1950; The Brave Bulls 1951; Rancho Notorious 1952; Scaramouche 1952; Knights of the Round Table 1953; Lili 1953; Saadia 1953; Oh, Rosalinda!! 1955; Elena et les Hommes 1956; War and Peace 1956; The Sun Also Rises 1957; The World, the Flesh and the Devil 1959; Blood and Roses 1960; The Hands of Orlac 1960; The Longest Day 1962; The Fall of the Roman Empire 1964; Paris When It Sizzles 1964; Sex and the Single Girl 1964; A Time for Loving 1971; Brannigan 1975; Eaten Alive 1976; The Amazing Captain Nemo 1978; The Norseman 1978; Lili Marleen 1980; The Visitor 1980

Ferrer, Miguel (1955-) RoboCop 1987; DeepStar Six 1989; Shannon's Deal 1989; The Guardian 1990; Another Stakeout 1993; The Assassin 1993; The Harvest 1993; Hot Shots! Part Deux 1993; It's All True 1993; Blank Check 1994; Project ALF 1996; The Disappearance of Garcia Lorca 1997; Stephen King's The Night Flier 1997; Mulan 1998; Traffic 2000; The Manchurian Candidate 2004; The Man 2005; Wrong Turn at Tahoe 2009

Ferrera, America (1984-) Real Women Have Curves 2002; Plainsong 2004; The Sisterhood of the Traveling Pants 2005; The Sisterhood of the Traveling Pants 2 2008; Tinker Bell 2008; How to Train Your Dragon 2010; Our Family Wedding 2010; End of Watch 2012

Ferreri, Marco (1928-1997) Casanova '70 1965; Pigsty 1969

Ferrero, Martin (1947-) I Ought to Be in Pictures 1982; Stop! or My Mom Will Shoot 1992; Jurassic Park 1993; The Tailor of Panama 2000

Ferres, Veronica Ladies' Room 2000; Klimt 2006

Ferret, Eve Foreign Body 1986; Haunted Honeymoon 1986

Ferri, Claudia The Assignment 1997; Mambo Italiano 2003

Ferrier, Julie Heartbreaker 2010; On Tour 2010

Ferrier, Noel (1920-1997) Turkey Shoot 1981; The Year of Living Dangerously 1982

Ferrigno, Lou (1951-) Pumping Iron 1976; The Incredible Hulk 1977; Hercules 1983; Hercules II 1984; The Incredible Hulk Returns 1988; All's Fair 1989; Cage 1989; The Trial of the Incredible Hulk 1989; The Death of the Incredible Hulk 1990; ...And God Spoke 1993; Hulk 2003

Ferris, Barbara (1942-) A Place to Go 1963; Children of the Damned 1964; The System 1964; Catch Us If You Can 1965; Interlude 1968; A Nice Girl like Me 1969; The Krays 1990

Ferris, Pam (1948-) Matilda 1996; Death to Smoochy 2002; Gladiatress 2002; Children of Men 2006; Telstar: the Joe Meek Story 2008; Malice in Wonderland 2009; Nativity! 2009; Nativity 2: Danger in the Manger! 2012; The Raven 2012; Saving Santa 2013

Ferro, Turi (1921-2001) The Seduction of Mimi 1972; Blood Feud 1979

Ferzetti, Gabriele (1925-2015) Le Amiche 1955; L'Avventura 1960; Jessica 1962; Imperial Venus 1963; Trois Chambres à Manhattan 1965; Once upon a Time in the West 1968; On Her Majesty's Secret Service 1969; The Confession 1970; Hitler: the Last Ten Days 1973; The Night Porter 1973; End of the Game 1976; A Matter of Time 1976; Julia and Julia 1987; I Am Love 2009

Fessenden, Larry (1963-) River of Grass 1994; Wendy and Lucy 2008

Fetchit, Stepin aka **Fetchit, Step'n** aka **Fetchit, Stepin'** (1902-1985) Judge Priest 1934; Stand Up and Cheer! 1934; Steamboat round the Bend 1935; Dimples 1936; Love Is News 1937; Zenobia 1939; Bend of the River 1952; The Sun Shines Bright 1953

Fetty, Darrell The Wind and the Lion 1975; Big Wednesday 1978; Blood Beach 1981

Feuer, Debra Moment by Moment 1978; To Live and Die in LA 1985

Feuerstein, Mark (1971-) The Muse 1999; Woman on Top 2000; What Women Want 2001; In Her Shoes 2005; Defiance 2008

Feuillère, Edwige (1907-1998) The Eagle Has Two Heads 1948; Woman Hater 1948; Olivia 1950; The Ripening Seed 1953; The Flesh of the Orchid 1974

Feulner, Miles A Home of Our Own 1993; Little Big League 1994

Fey, Tina (1970-) Mean Girls 2004; Man of the Year 2006; Baby Mama 2008; Ponyo 2008; The Invention of Lying 2009; Date Night 2010; Megamind 2010; Admission 2013; Muppets Most Wanted 2014; This Is Where I Leave You 2014; Sisters 2015; Whiskey Tango Foxtrot 2016

Ffrangcon-Davies, Gwen (1891-1992) The Witches 1966; The Devil Rides Out 1968; Leo the Last 1970

Fiander, Lewis (1938-2016) Dr Jekyll & Sister Hyde 1971; Dr Phibes Rises Again 1972; The Abdication 1974; The Doctor and the Devils 1985; Georgia 1988

Fichtner, William (1956-) The Underneath 1995; Albino Alligator 1996; Contact 1997; Drowning Mona 2000; Passion of Mind 2000; The Perfect Storm 2000; Black Hawk Down 2001; Equilibrium 2002; Crash 2004; The Longest Yard 2005; The Moguls 2005; Ultraviolet 2005; Blades of Glory 2007; Drive Angry 2011; The Homesman 2014; Teenage Mutant Ninja Turtles 2014

Fiedler, John (1925-2005) 12 Angry Men 1957; A Raisin in the Sun 1961; Fitzwilly 1967; The Odd Couple 1968; Winnie the Pooh's Most Grand Adventure 1997; The Tigger Movie 2000; Piglet's Big Movie 2003; Winnie the Pooh: Springtime with Roo 2004; Pooh's Heffalump Movie 2005

Field, Alexander (1892-1971) When London Sleeps 1932; Limelight 1936; Dark Eyes of London 1939; Naked Fury 1959

Field, Ben (1878-1939) When London Sleeps 1932; The Clairvoyant 1934

Field, Betty (1913-1973) Of Mice and Men 1939; Victory 1940; Blues in the Night 1941; The Shepherd of the Hills 1941; Kings Row 1942; Flesh and Fantasy 1943; The Great Moment 1944; The Southerner 1945; The Great Gatsby 1949; Picnic 1955; Bus Stop 1956; Butterfield 8 1960; Birdman of Alcatraz 1962; 7 Women 1966; Coogan's Bluff 1968

Field, Chelsea (1957-) Prison 1987; Skin Deep 1989; The Dark Half 1991; Harley Davidson and the Marlboro Man 1991; The Last Boy Scout 1991; Dust Devil 1992; Complex of Fear 1993; Snapdragon 1993; Andre 1994; Rules of Obsession 1994; Indictment: the McMartin Trial 1995; Flipper 1996; Wicked 1998

Field, David aka **Field, Dave** Ghosts... of the Civil Dead 1988; Dad and Dave: on Our Selection 1995; To Have & to Hold 1996; Two Hands 1999; Chopper 2000; Gettin' Square 2003; The Night We Called It a Day 2003; Feed 2005; Battle of the Damned 2013; The Rover 2014

Field, Mary (1896-1968) The Crystal Ball 1943; A Lady Takes a Chance 1943; The Affairs of Susan 1945; Ride a Crooked Trail 1958; Seven Ways from Sundown 1960

Field, Sally (1946-) The Way West 1967; Stay Hungry 1976; Smokey and the Bandit 1977; The End 1978; Hooper 1978; Beyond the Poseidon Adventure 1979; Norma Rae 1979; Smokey and the Bandit II 1980; Absence of Malice 1981; Back Roads 1981; Kiss Me Goodbye 1982; Places in the Heart 1984; Murphy's Romance 1985; Surrender 1987; Punchline 1988; Steel Magnolias 1989; Not without My Daughter 1990; Soapdish 1991; Homeward Bound: the Incredible Journey 1993; Mrs Doubtfire 1993; Forrest Gump 1994; Eye for an Eye 1995; Homeward Bound II: Lost in San Francisco 1996; A Cooler Climate 1999; Where the Heart Is 2000; Say It Isn't So 2001; Legally Blonde 2: Red, White & Blonde 2003; The Amazing Spider-Man 2012; Lincoln 2012; The Amazing Spider-Man 2 2014

Field, Shirley Anne aka **Field, Shirley Ann** (1936-) It's Never Too Late 1956; Horrors of the Black Museum 1959; Beat Girl 1960; The Entertainer 1960; Man in the Moon 1960; Peeping Tom 1960; Saturday Night and Sunday Morning 1960; The Damned 1961; Lunch Hour 1962; The War Lover 1962; Kings of the Sun 1963; Alfie 1966; Doctor in Clover 1966; My Beautiful Laundrette 1985; Shag 1988; Getting It Right 1989; The Rachel Papers 1989; Hear My Song 1991; UFO 1993; A Monkey's Tale 1999

Field, Sid (1904-1950) London Town 1946; Cardboard Cavalier 1949

Field, Todd (1964-) A Cut Above 1989; Ruby in Paradise 1993; Sleep with Me 1994; Frank and Jesse 1995; Walking and Talking 1996; Eyes Wide Shut 1999; Stranger than Fiction 1999; New Port South 2001

Field, Virginia (1917-1992) Lloyd's of London 1936; Thank You, Jeeves 1936; Charlie Chan at Monte Carlo 1937; Lancer Spy 1937; London by Night 1937; Think Fast, Mr Moto 1937; Mr Moto's Last Warning 1938; The Cisco Kid and the Lady 1939; Mr Moto Takes a Vacation 1939; Dance, Girl, Dance 1940; Hudson's Bay 1940; Waterloo Bridge 1940; The Crystal Ball 1943; Christmas Eve 1947; The Imperfect Lady 1947; Repeat Performance 1947; Dream Girl 1948; The Lady Pays Off 1951; Weekend with Father 1951; The Earth Dies Screaming 1964

Fielding, Dorothy Kiss Me Goodbye 1982; Fright Night 1985

Fielding, Edward (1875-1945) The Major and the Minor 1942; What a Woman! 1943; Dead Man's Eyes 1944

Fielding, Emma (1971-) The Scarlet Tunic 1997; Pandaemonium 2000; The Great Ghost Rescue 2011

Fielding, Fenella (1930-) Follow a Star 1959; Foxhole in Cairo 1960; In the Doghouse 1961; The Old Dark House 1963; Carry On Screaming 1966; Doctor in Clover 1966; Drop Dead Darling 1966; Lock Up Your Daughters! 1969; Dougal and the Blue Cat 1970; Guest House Paradiso 1999

Fielding, Marjorie (1892-1956) Quiet Wedding 1940; The Demi-Paradise 1943; Yellow Canary 1943; Quiet Weekend 1946; Easy Money 1947; Spring in Park Lane 1948; The Chiltern Hundreds 1949; Conspirator 1949; The Franchise Affair 1950; Portrait of Clare 1950; The Lavender Hill Mob 1951; Mandy 1952

Fielding, Noel Bunny & the Bull 2009; Horrid Henry: the Movie 2011; Aaaaaaaah! 2015; Set the Thames on Fire 2015

Fielding, Tom Model Shop 1969; A Walk in the Spring Rain 1970

Fields, Gracie (1898-1979) Looking on the Bright Side 1931; Sally in Our Alley 1931; Love, Life and Laughter 1934; Sing as We Go 1934; Look Up and Laugh 1935; The Show Goes On 1937; We're Going to Be Rich 1938; Shipyard Sally 1939; Holy Matrimony 1943; Stage Door Canteen 1943; Madame Pimpernel 1945; Molly and Me 1945

Fields, Stanley (1884-1941) City Streets 1931; Little Caesar 1931; Riders of the Purple Sage 1931; All over Town 1937; Way Out West 1937; Pack Up Your Troubles 1939; New Moon 1940

Fields, Tony (1958-1995) Trick or Treat 1986; Backstreet Dreams 1990

Fields, W C (1879-1946) Sally of the Sawdust 1925; It's the Old Army Game 1926; Her Majesty Love 1931; The Dentist 1932; If I Had a Million 1932; Million Dollar Legs 1932; Alice in Wonderland 1933; The Barber Shop 1933; International House 1933; Tillie and Gus 1933; It's a Gift 1934; Mrs Wiggs of the Cabbage Patch 1934; The Old-Fashioned Way 1934; Six of a Kind 1934; You're Telling Me! 1934; David Copperfield 1935; Man on the Flying Trapeze 1935; Mississippi 1935; Poppy 1936; The Big Broadcast of 1938 1937; You Can't Cheat an Honest Man 1939; The Bank Dick 1940; My Little Chickadee 1940; Never Give a Sucker an Even Break 1941; Follow the Boys 1944; Sensations 1944; Song of the Open Road 1944

Fiennes, Joseph (1970-) Stealing Beauty 1995; Martha - Meet Frank, Daniel and Laurence 1997; Elizabeth 1998; Shakespeare in Love 1998; Forever Mine 1999; Rancid Aluminium 1999; Dust 2001; Enemy at the Gates 2001; Killing Me Softly 2001; Leo 2002; Sinbad: Legend of the Seven Seas 2003; William Shakespeare's The Merchant of Venice 2004; The Great Raid 2005; Running with Scissors 2006; The Escapist 2007; Goodbye Bafana 2007; The Red Baron 2008; Hercules 2014; Strangerland 2015; Risen 2016

Fiennes, Ralph (1962-) Wuthering Heights 1992; The Baby of Macon 1993; Schindler's List 1993; Quiz Show 1994; Strange Days 1995; The English Patient 1996; Oscar and Lucinda 1997; The Avengers 1998; The Prince of Egypt 1998; The End of the Affair 1999; The Miracle Maker 1999; Onegin 1999; Sunshine 1999; Maid in Manhattan 2002; Red Dragon 2002; Spider 2002; Chromophobia 2005; The Chumscrubber 2005; The Constant Gardener 2005; Harry Potter and the Goblet of Fire 2005; Wallace & Gromit in The Curse of the Were-Rabbit 2005; The White Countess 2005; Bernard and Doris 2006; Land of the Blind 2006; Harry Potter and the Order of the Phoenix 2007; The Duchess 2008; The Hurt Locker 2008; In Bruges 2008; The Reader 2008; The Wildest Dream 2009; Cemetery Junction 2010; Clash of the Titans 2010; Harry Potter and the Deathly Hallows: Part 1 2010; Nanny McPhee & the Big Bang 2010; Harry Potter and the Deathly Hallows: Part 2 2011; Great Expectations 2012; Skyfall 2012; Wrath of the Titans 2012; The Invisible Woman 2014; The Grand Budapest Hotel 2014; A Bigger Splash 2015; Spectre 2015; Hail, Caesar! 2016; Kubo and the Two Strings 2016

Fiermonte, Enzo (1908-1993) Romeo and Juliet 1954; Angela 1955; A Black Veil for Lisa 1969

Fierstein, Harvey (1954-) The Times of Harvey Milk 1983; Torch Song Trilogy 1988; The Harvest 1993; Mrs Doubtfire 1993; Bullets over Broadway

1994; The Celluloid Closet 1995; Dr Jekyll and Ms Hyde 1995; Independence Day 1996; Kull the Conqueror 1997; Mulan 1998; Safe Men 1998; Death to Smoochy 2002; Our House 2003; Mulan II 2004

Figura, Katarzyna (1962-) Near Mrs 1990; Yuma 2012

Fillières, Hélène Vendredi Soir 2002; Lady Chatterley 2006

Fillion, Nathan (1971-) Serenity 2005; Slither 2006; White Noise: the Light 2006; Waitress 2007; Trucker 2009; Super 2010; Much Ado about Nothing 2012

Fillmore, Clyde (1875-1946) The More the Merrier 1943; Laura 1944

Fimple, Dennis (1940-2002) Truck Stop Women 1974; The Evictors 1979

Finch, Jon (1941-2012) The Vampire Lovers 1970; Macbeth 1971; Frenzy 1972; Lady Caroline Lamb 1972; The Final Programme 1973; Diagnosis: Murder 1974; Death on the Nile 1978; Breaking Glass 1980; Giro City 1982; Darklands 1996; Anazapta 2001; Kingdom of Heaven 2005

Finch, Peter (1916-1977) Train of Events 1949; The Miniver Story 1950; The Story of Robin Hood and His Merrie Men 1952; The Heart of the Matter 1953; The Story of Gilbert and Sullivan 1953; Elephant Walk 1954; Father Brown 1954; The Dark Avenger 1955; Josephine and Men 1955; Passage Home 1955; Simon and Laura 1955; The Battle of the River Plate 1956; A Town like Alice 1956; Robbery under Arms 1957; The Shiralee 1957; Windom's Way 1957; Operation Amsterdam 1958; The Nun's Story 1959; Kidnapped 1950; No Love for Johnnie 1960; The Sins of Rachel Cade 1960; The Trials of Oscar Wilde 1960; I Thank a Fool 1962; Girl with Green Eyes 1963; The Pumpkin Eater 1964; The Flight of the Phoenix 1965; Judith 1966; 10:30 PM Summer 1966; Far from the Madding Crowd 1967; The Legend of Lylah Clare 1968; The Red Tent 1969; Something to Hide 1971; Sunday, Bloody Sunday 1971; Bequest to the Nation 1972; England Made Me 1973; Lost Horizon 1973; The Abdication 1974; Network 1976; Raid on Entebbe 1977

Fincher, David (1962-) Full Frontal 2002; Side by Side 2012; Hitchcock Truffaut 2015

Findlay, Deborah Truly Madly Deeply 1990; The Ones Below 2015

Fine, Larry (1902-1975) Meet the Baron 1933; Hollywood Party 1934; Time Out for Rhythm 1941; Have Rocket, Will Travel 1959; The Three Stooges in Orbit 1962; The Three Stooges Meet Hercules 1962; The Three Stooges Go around the World in a Daze 1963; The Outlaws Is Coming 1965

Fine, Travis (1968-) Child's Play 3 1991; Vanished without a Trace 1993

Fink, Isabella Love Letters 1999; Children of My Heart 2000

Fink, John Ransom for a Dead Man 1971; The Carey Treatment 1972

Finlay, Frank (1926-2016) The Informers 1963; Private Potter 1963; The Wild Affair 1963; The Comedy Man 1964; Othello 1965; A Study in Terror 1965; The Deadly Bees 1967; I'll Never Forget What's 'Is Name 1967; The Jokers 1967; Robbery 1967; Inspector Clouseau 1968; Twisted Nerve 1968; Assault 1970; Cromwell 1970; The Molly Maguires 1970; Gumshoe 1971; Neither the Sea nor the Sand 1972; Sitting Target 1972; Shaft in Africa 1973; The Three Musketeers 1973; The Four Musketeers 1974; Murder by Decree 1978; The Thief of Baghdad 1978; The Wild Geese 1978; Enigma 1982; The Return of the Soldier 1982; The Ploughman's Lunch 1983; A Christmas Carol 1984; Nineteen Nineteen 1984; Lifeforce 1985; King of the Wind 1989; The Return of the Musketeers 1989; Sparrow 1993; Gospa 1995; Stiff Upper Lips 1997; Dreaming of Joseph Lees 1998; The Martins 2001; The Pianist 2002; The Statement 2003; The Waiting Room 2007

Finlayson, James (1887-1953) Big Business 1929; Men o' War 1929; The Dawn Patrol 1930; Pardon Us 1931; Pack Up Your Troubles 1932; Bogus Bandits 1933; Bonnie Scotland 1935; Thicker than Water 1935; The Bohemian Girl 1936; All over Town 1937; Way Out West 1937; Blockheads 1938; A Chump at Oxford 1940; Saps at Sea 1940; Laurel and Hardy's Laughing 20s 1965

Finley, Cameron (1987-) Leave It to Beaver 1997; Hope Floats 1998; Bitter Suite 2000

Finley, William (1940-2012) Murder à la Mod 1968; Dionysus in '69 1970; Sisters 1973; Phantom of the Paradise 1974; Eaten Alive 1976; Silent Rage 1982

Finn, John aka Finn, John Joseph (1952-) Glory 1989; Quicksand: No Escape 1992; Blown Away 1994; Turbulence 1997; Deadlocked 2000; Analyze That 2002; The Hunted 2002

Finneran, Siobhan Rita, Sue and Bob Too 1986; The Selfish Giant 2013

Finney, Albert (1936-) The Entertainer 1960; Saturday Night and Sunday Morning 1960; Tom Jones 1963; The Victors 1963; Night Must Fall 1964; Charlie Bubbles 1967; Two for the Road 1967; The Picasso Summer 1969; Scrooge 1970; Gumshoe 1971; Alpha Beta 1973; Murder on the Orient Express 1974; The Duellists 1977; Loophole 1980; Looker 1981; Wolfen 1981; Annie 1982; Shoot the Moon 1982; The Dresser 1983; Under the Volcano 1984; Orphans 1987; The Image 1990; Miller's Crossing 1990; The Playboys 1992; The Browning Version 1994; A Man of No Importance 1994; The Run of the Country 1995; Washington Square 1997; Breakfast of Champions 1999; Simpatico 1999; Erin Brockovich 2000; Traffic 2000; Big Fish 2003; Tim Burton's Corpse Bride 2005; Amazing Grace 2006; A Good Year 2006; Before the Devil Knows You're Dead 2007; The Bourne Ultimatum 2007; The Bourne Legacy 2012; Skyfall 2012

Finocchiaro, Angela (1955-) Volere, Volare 1991; Don't Move 2004; My Brother Is an Only Child 2006

Finsches, Erich Dog Days 2001; Import Export 2007

Fiore, Elena The Seduction of Mimi 1972; Seven Beauties 1976

Fiorentino, Linda (1960-) After Hours 1985; Gotcha! 1985; Vision Quest 1985; The Moderns 1988; Queens Logic 1991; Shout 1991; The Last Seduction 1993; Charlie's Ghost Story 1994; Fixing the Shadow 1994; Jade 1995; Larger than Life 1996; Unforgettable 1996; Body Count 1997; Kicked in the Head 1997; Men in Black 1997; Dogma 1999; Ordinary Decent Criminal 1999; What Planet Are You From? 2000; Where the Money Is 2000; Liberty Stands Still 2002

Firbank, Ann Behind the Mask 1958; The Servant 1963; Accident 1967; A Severed Head 1970

Firestone, Eddie (1920-2007) The Brass Legend 1956; The Great Locomotive Chase 1956; The Law and Jake Wade 1958; Two for the Seesaw 1962; Duel 1971; Play It as It Lays 1972; The Stone Killer 1973

Firth, Anne aka Firth, Annie (1918-1967) The First of the Few 1942; The Goose Steps Out 1942; Bell-Bottom George 1943; Scott of the Antarctic 1948

Firth, Colin (1960-) Another Country 1984; Nineteen Nineteen 1984; A Month in the Country 1987; The Secret Garden 1987; Apartment Zero 1988; Valmont 1989; Wings of Fame 1990; Femme Fatale 1991; Hostages 1993; The Hour of the Pig 1993; Circle of Friends 1995; The English Patient 1996; Fever Pitch 1996; A Thousand Acres 1997; The Secret Laughter of Women 1998; Shakespeare in Love 1998; Londinium 1999; My Life So Far 1999; Relative Values 2000; Bridget Jones's Diary 2001; Conspiracy 2001; Hope Springs 2002; The Importance of Being Earnest 2002; Girl with a Pearl Earring 2003; Love Actually 2003; What a Girl Wants 2003; Bridget Jones: the Edge of Reason 2004; Trauma 2004; Nanny McPhee 2005; Where the Truth Lies 2005; The Last Legion 2006; And When Did You Last See Your Father? 2007; St Trinian's 2007; Then She Found Me 2007; The Accidental Husband 2008; Easy Virtue 2008; Genova 2008; Mamma Mia! 2008; A Christmas Carol 2009; Dorian Gray 2009; St Trinian's 2: the Legend of Fritton's Gold 2009; A Single Man 2009; The King's Speech 2010; Tinker Tailor Soldier Spy 2011; Arthur & Mike 2012; Gambit 2012; Devil's Knot 2013; The Railway Man 2013; Before I Go to Sleep 2014; Magic in the Moonlight 2014; Genius 2015; Kingsman: The Secret Service 2015; Bridget Jones's Baby 2016; The Mercy 2016

Firth, Julian Scum 1979; Oxford Blues 1984

Firth, Peter (1953-) Aces High 1976; Equus 1977; Joseph Andrews 1977; Tess 1979; Letter to Brezhnev 1985; Lifeforce 1985; Tree of Hands 1988; The Hunt for Red October 1990; The Incident 1990; Prisoner of Honor 1991;

Shadowlands 1993; An Awfully Big Adventure 1994; Mighty Joe Young 1998; Chill Factor 1999; The Greatest Game Ever Played 2005; Spooks: the Greater Good 2015; Risen 2016

Fischer, Jenna (1974-) Blades of Glory 2007; Walk Hard: the Dewey Cox Story 2007; Solitary Man 2009; Hall Pass 2011

Fischer, Kai (1934-) The Hellfire Club 1961; The Goalkeeper's Fear of the Penalty Kick 1971

Fischer, Kate (1973-) Sirens 1994; Blood Surf 2000

Fish aka **Dick, Derek** (1958-) Chasing the Deer 1994; The Jacket 2005; Electric Man 2012

Fish, Nancy (1938-) Birdy 1984; The Exorcist III 1990; Death Becomes Her 1992; Ghost in the Machine 1993; Reflections on a Crime 1994

Fishburne, Laurence aka Fishburne, Larry (1961-) Apocalypse Now 1979; Rumble Fish 1983; The Cotton Club 1984; Quicksilver 1986; A Nightmare on Elm Street 3: Dream Warriors 1987; Red Heat 1988; School Daze 1988; King of New York 1989; Boyz N the Hood 1991; Class Action 1991; Stockade 1991; Deep Cover 1992; Innocent Moves 1993; Tina: What's Love Got to Do with It 1993; Bad Company 1995; Higher Learning 1995; Just Cause 1995; Othello 1995; The Tuskegee Airmen 1995; Fled 1996; Event Horizon 1997; Hoodlum 1997; Miss Evers' Boys 1997; The Matrix 1999; Osmosis Jones 2001; The Matrix Reloaded 2002; Biker Boyz 2003; The Matrix Revolutions 2003; Mystic River 2003; Assault on Precinct 13 2005; Akeelah and the Bee 2006; Bobby 2006; Mission: Impossible III 2006; 4: Rise of the Silver Surfer 2007; TMNT 2007; 21 2008; Armored 2009; Predators 2010; Contagion 2011; The Colony 2013; Khumba 2013; Ride Along 2014; The Signal 2014; Batman v Superman: Dawn of Justice 2016; Passengers 2016

Fisher, Carrie (1956-) Shampoo 1975; Star Wars Episode IV: a New Hope 1977; The Blues Brothers 1980; Star Wars Episode V: the Empire Strikes Back 1980; Under the Rainbow 1981; Star Wars Episode VI: Return of the Jedi 1983; Garbo Talks 1984; The Man with One Red Shoe 1985; Hannah and Her Sisters 1986; Amazon Women on the Moon 1987; The Time Guardian 1987; Appointment with Death 1988; The 'Burbs 1989; Loverboy 1989; When Harry Met Sally... 1989; Sibling Rivalry 1990; Sweet Revenge 1990; Drop Dead Fred 1991; Soapdish 1991; This Is My Life 1992; Scream 3 1999; Heartbreakers 2001; Jay and Silent Bob Strike Back 2001; Wonderland 2003; Fanboys 2008; White Lightnin' 2008; The Women 2008; Sorority Row 2009; It's Christmas, Carol! 2012; Star Wars Episode VII: the Force Awakens 2015

Fisher, Cindy Liar's Moon 1982; The Stone Boy 1984

Fisher, Eddie (1928-2010) Bundle of Joy 1956; Butterfield 8 1960; Nothing Lasts Forever 1984

Fisher, Elsie Despicable Me 2010; Despicable Me 2 2013

Fisher, Frances (1952-) Can She Bake a Cherry Pie? 1983; Heart 1987; Patty Hearst 1988; Cold Sassy Tree 1989; Pink Cadillac 1989; Welcome Home, Roxy Carmichael 1990; Unforgiven 1992; Attack of the 50 Ft Woman 1993; Babyfever 1994; The Stars Fell on Henrietta 1995; Female Perversions 1996; Titanic 1997; Wild America 1997; The Big Tease 1999; The Audrey Hepburn Story 2000; Blue Car 2001; House of Sand and Fog 2003; Laws of Attraction 2003; Wal-Mart: the High Cost of Low Price 2005; In the Valley of Elah 2007; Backyard Wedding 2010; The Roommate 2011; Any Day Now 2012; The Host 2013

Fisher, Gregor (1953-) Another Time, Another Place 1983; Nineteen Eighty-Four 1984; The Girl in the Picture 1985; To Kill a Priest 1988; Lassie 2005; Wild Target 2009; Whisky Galore! 2016

Fisher, Isla (1976-) Scooby-Doo 2002; Wedding Crashers 2005; Wedding Daze 2006; Hot Rod 2007; The Lookout 2007; Definitely, Maybe 2008; Dr Seuss' Horton Hears a Who! 2008; Confessions of a Shopaholic 2009; Burke & Hare 2010; Rango 2011; Bachelorette 2012; Rise of the Guardians 2012; The Great Gatsby 2013; Life of Crime 2013; Now You See Me 2013; Visions 2015; Grimsby 2016; Keeping Up with the Joneses 2016; Nocturnal Animals 2016

Fisher, Jaishon Lakeview Terrace 2008; Christmas in Canaan 2009

Fisher, Joely (1967-) Thirst 1998; When the Bough Breaks 2: Perfect Prey 1998; Inspector Gadget 1999

Fisher, Noel Teenage Mutant Ninja Turtles 2014; Teenage Mutant Ninja Turtles - Out of the Shadows 2016

Fisher, Tom aka Fisher, Thomas (1968-) The Nine Lives of Tomas Katz 1999; The Truth Game 1999; Shanghai Knights 2002; The Illusionist 2005; Treacle Jr 2010

Fisk, Schuyler (1982-) The Baby-Sitter's Club 1995; My Friend Joe 1996; Snow Day 2000; Orange County 2001; Restless 2011

Fiske, Robert (1899-1944) Old Louisiana 1938; Along the Rio Grande 1941

Fitzgerald, Barry (1888-1961) The Plough and the Stars 1936; Bringing Up Baby 1938; The Dawn Patrol 1938; The Saint Strikes Back 1939; The Long Voyage Home 1940; How Green Was My Valley 1941; The Sea Wolf 1941; Tarzan's Secret Treasure 1941; The Amazing Mrs Holliday 1943; Corvette K-225 1943; Going My Way 1944; None but the Lonely Heart 1944; And Then There Were None 1945; The Stork Club 1945; California 1946; Two Years before the Mast 1946; Welcome Stranger 1947; Miss Tatlock's Millions 1948; The Naked City 1948; Union Station 1950; The Quiet Man 1952; Happy Ever After 1954; The Catered Affair 1956; Rooney 1958

Fitzgerald, Ciaran (1983-) Into the West 1992; The Canterville Ghost 1996; The Boxer 1997

Fitzgerald, Ella (1917-1996) Ride 'Em Cowboy 1942; Pete Kelly's Blues 1955; St Louis Blues 1958; Let No Man Write My Epitaph 1960; Listen Up: the Lives of Quincy Jones 1990

Fitzgerald, Geraldine (1914-2005) The Lad 1935; The Mill on the Floss 1937; Dark Victory 1939; Wuthering Heights 1939; 'Til We Meet Again 1940; The Gay Sisters 1942; Watch on the Rhine 1943; Wilson 1944; The Strange Affair of Uncle Harry 1945; Nobody Lives Forever 1946; OSS 1946; Three Strangers 1946; The Late Edwina Black 1951; Ten North Frederick 1958; The Fiercest Heart 1961; The Pawnbroker 1965; The Last American Hero 1973; Harry and Tonto 1974; Echoes of a Summer 1976; Bye Bye Monkey 1978; Lovespell 1979; Arthur 1981; Easy Money 1983; Do You Remember Love 1985; Poltergeist II: the Other Side 1986; Arthur 2: On the Rocks 1988

Fitzgerald, Glenn A Price above Rubies 1997; The Sixth Sense 1999; The Believer 2001; Series 7: the Contenders 2001

Fitz-Gerald, Lewis (1958-) We of the Never Never 1982; The Boy Who Had Everything 1984; The More Things Change 1985; The Shiralee 1986; Warm Nights on a Slow Moving Train 1986; Dead Heart 1996; Pitch Black 1999

Fitzgerald, Nuala The Brood 1979; Circle of Two 1980

FitzGerald, Tara (1968-) Hear My Song 1991; A Man of No Importance 1994; Sirens 1994; The Englishman Who Went up a Hill, but Came down a Mountain 1995; Brassed Off 1996; New World Disorder 1999; Rancid Aluminium 1999; Dark Blue World 2001; I Capture the Castle 2002; Five Children and It 2004; Legend 2015

Fitzgerald, Walter (1896-1976) San Demetrio London 1943; Great Day 1944; Blanche Fury 1948; The Fallen Idol 1948; Edward, My Son 1949; Treasure Island 1950; Our Girl Friday 1953; Personal Affair 1953; Lease of Life 1954; The Man in the Sky 1956; The Birthday Present 1957; Something of Value 1957; The Camp on Blood Island 1958; Darby O'Gill and the Little People 1959; HMS Defiant 1962

Fitzpatrick, Colleen aka Fitzpatrick, Colleen Ann (1970-) Hairspray 1988; Dracula 2001 2000

Fitzpatrick, Emma The Collection 2011; Bloodsucking Bosses 2015

Fitzpatrick, Leo (1978-) kids 1995; Personal Velocity 2001; Cold Comes the Night 2013

Fitzpatrick, Neil (1934-2005) Ground Zero 1987; A Cry in the Dark 1988

Fitzpatrick, Richard Jill Rips 2000; George A Romero's Survival of the Dead 2009

Fitzroy, Emily (1860-1954) Love 1927; The Case of Lena Smith 1929; Don Quixote 1932

Fiuzat, Allen Benji 1974; For the Love of Benji 1977

Fix, Paul (1901-1983) Zoo in Budapest 1933; The Desert Trail 1935; The Plot Thickens 1936; Dr Cyclops 1940; Down Mexico Way 1941; The Unknown Guest 1943; Tall in the Saddle 1944; Angel in

Exile 1948; The Plunderers 1948; Wake of the Red Witch 1949; Warpath 1951; Blood Alley 1955; The Bad Seed 1956; Santiago 1956; Toward the Unknown 1956; The Devil's Hairpin 1957; Mail Order Bride 1963; Baby the Rain Must Fall 1965; Day of the Evil Gun 1968; Zabriskie Point 1970; Grayeagle 1977; Wanda Nevada 1979

Flaherty, Danny King Jack 2015; Goat 2016

Flaherty, Joe (1941-) Going Berserk 1983; Follow That Bird 1985; One Crazy Summer 1986; Cannonball Fever 1989; A Pig's Tale 1994

Flaherty, Lanny The Ballad of the Sad Café 1991; Sommersby 1993

Flamand, Didier (1947-) India Song 1975; Merci Docteur Rey 2002; Factotum (A Man Who Preforms Many Jobs) 2005

Flanagan, Bud (1896-1968) A Fire Has Been Arranged 1935; Alf's Button Afloat 1938; Gasbags 1940; We'll Smile Again 1942; Dreaming 1944; Here Comes the Sun 1945; The Wild Affair 1963

Flanagan, Fionnula aka Flanagan, Fionnuala (1941-) Sinful Davey 1969; A Winner Never Quits 1986; Money for Nothing 1993; 919 Fifth Avenue 1995; Some Mother's Son 1996; Waking Ned 1998; A Secret Affair 1999; With or without You 1999; The Others 2001; Divine Secrets of the Ya-Ya Sisterhood 2002; Tears of the Sun 2003; Four Brothers 2005; Transamerica 2005; The Guard 2011; Life's a Breeze 2013; Song of the Sea 2014

Flanagan, John (1947-) Sweeney 2 1978; Arthur's Hallowed Ground 1985

Flanagan, Tommy aka Flanagan, Tommy J (1965-) Ratcatcher 1999; Strictly Sinatra 2000; AVP: Alien vs Predator 2004; Trauma 2004; When a Stranger Calls 2006; Hero Wanted 2008

Flanders, Ed (1934-1995) MacArthur 1977; The Ninth Configuration 1979; Salem's Lot 1979; The Pursuit of DB Cooper 1981; The Exorcist III 1990; Bye Bye Love 1995

Flanery, Sean Patrick (1965-) The Grass Harp 1995; Powder 1995; Just Your Luck 1996; Best Men 1997; Suicide Kings 1997; Body Shots 1999; The Boondock Saints 1999; Simply Irresistible 1999; Run the Wild Fields 2000; D-Tox 2001; Saw: the Final Chapter 2010; Broken Horses 2015

Flanigan, Joe The Other Sister 1999; Six Bullets 2012

Flatman, Barry Cruel Intentions 2 2000; Saw II 2006

Flavin, James (1906-1976) Corvette K-225 1943; Abroad with Two Yanks 1944; Laura 1944; Uncertain Glory 1944; Angel on My Shoulder 1946; Desert Fury 1947; The Fabulous Dorseys 1947; Destination Murder 1950; Francis in the Haunted House 1956; In Cold Blood 1967

Flawless StreetDance 2010; StreetDance 2 2012

Flea (1962-) Dudes 1987; The Blue Iguana 1988; The Wild Thornberrys Movie 2003

Fleet, James (1954-) Blue Black Permanent 1992; Four Weddings and a Funeral 1994; Sense and Sensibility 1995; Remember Me? 1996; Milk 1999; Kevin & Perry Go Large 2000; Charlotte Gray 2001; Two Men Went to War 2002; Blackball 2003

Fleetwood, Susan (1944-1995) Clash of the Titans 1981; Heat and Dust 1982; Young Sherlock Holmes 1985; The Sacrifice 1986; Dream Demon 1988; The Krays 1990; Persuasion 1995

Fleischer, Charles (1950-) Who Framed Roger Rabbit 1988; Back to the Future Part II 1989; We're Back! A Dinosaur's Story 1993; Gridlock'd 1996; G-Men from Hell 2000; The Polar Express 2004; Zodiac 2007

Fleiss, Noah (1984-) Josh and SAM 1993; Under Pressure 1997; Brick 2005; Hard Luck 2006

Fleming, Eric (1925-1966) Conquest of Space 1955; Queen of Outer Space 1958; The Glass Bottom Boat 1966

Fleming, Ian (1908-1964) They Met in the Dark 1943; I Didn't Do It 1945; George in Civvy Street 1946

Fleming, Rhonda (1923-) Abilene Town 1945; Spellbound 1945; The Spiral Staircase 1946; Build My Gallows High 1947; A Connecticut Yankee in King Arthur's Court 1949; The Great Lover 1949; The Redhead and the Cowboy 1950; Cry Danger 1951; Inferno 1953; Pony Express 1953; Serpent of the Nile 1953; The Killer Is Loose 1956; Slightly Scarlet 1956; While the City Sleeps 1956; The Buster Keaton Story 1957; Gun Glory 1957; Gunfight at the OK Corral 1957; Bullwhip 1958; Home before Dark 1958; Alias Jesse James 1959; The Big Circus 1959; The Crowded Sky 1960; Backtrack 1969; The Nude Bomb 1980

Flemming, Peter First Target 2000; Mermaid 2000

Flemyng, Jason (1966-) The Jungle Book 1994; Hollow Reed 1995; Alive and Kicking 1996; The James Gang 1997; The Life of Stuff 1997; Deep Rising 1998; Lock, Stock and Two Smoking Barrels 1998; The Red Violin 1998; The Body 2000; Snatch 2000; Anazapta 2001; The Bunker 2001; From Hell 2001; Mean Machine 2001; Rock Star 2001; Below 2002; The League of Extraordinary Gentlemen 2003; Seed of Chucky 2004; Rollin with the Nines 2005; The Transporter 2 2005; Stardust 2007; The Curious Case of Benjamin Button 2008; Mirrors 2008; Shifty 2008; City of Life 2009; Kick-Ass 2009; Solomon Kane 2009; Clash of the Titans 2010; Ironclad 2010; Hanna 2011; Great Expectations 2012; Welcome to the Punch 2012; I Give It a Year 2013; Gemma Bovery 2014; Stonehearst Asylum 2014

Flemyng, Robert (1912-1995) Head over Heels in Love 1937; The Guinea Pig 1948; The Blue Lamp 1949; Conspirator 1949; The Man Who Never Was 1955; Funny Face 1957; Windom's Way 1957; Blind Date 1959; A Touch of Larceny 1959; The Blood Beast Terror 1967; The Body Stealers 1969; The Darwin Adventure 1972

Fletcher, Bramwell (1904-1988) Raffles 1930; Svengali 1931; The Mummy 1932; The Scarlet Pimpernel 1934; The Undying Monster 1942; White Cargo 1942; The Immortal Sergeant 1943

Fletcher, Brendan (1981-) The Five Senses 1999; Freddy vs Jason 2003; The Final Cut 2004; Tideland 2005; The Revenant 2015

Fletcher, Dexter (1966-) Revolution 1985; Gothic 1986; Lionheart 1986; The Raggedy Rawney 1987; The Rachel Papers 1989; Lock, Stock and Two Smoking Barrels 1998; Below 2002; Stander 2003; Doom 2005; Kick-Ass 2009; St George's Day 2012

Fletcher, Jay Born to Win 1971; California Split 1974

Fletcher, Louise (1934-) Thieves like Us 1974; One Flew over the Cuckoo's Nest 1975; Exorcist II: The Heretic 1977; The Cheap Detective 1978; The Lady in Red 1979; The Magician of Lublin 1979; The Lucky Star 1980; Brainstorm 1983; Strange Invaders 1983; Firestarter 1984; Invaders from Mars 1986; Nobody's Fool 1986; Flowers in the Attic 1987; Two Moon Junction 1988; Blue Steel 1990; Shadowzone 1990; Tollbooth 1994; Virtuosity 1995; Desert Gamble 1996; High School High 1996; Breast Men 1997; Love Kills 1998; Cruel Intentions 1999; The Devil's Arithmetic 1999; A Map of the World 1999; Big Eden 2000; Cassadaga 2011

Flicker, Theodore J aka Flicker, Ted (1930-2014) The Troublemaker 1964; The Legend of the Lone Ranger 1981

Flint, Helen (1898-1967) The Black Legion 1937; Step Lively, Jeeves 1937

Flint, Sam (1882-1980) Winds of the Wasteland 1936; Abbott and Costello Meet the Keystone Cops 1955; The Big Tip Off 1955

Flippen, Jay C (1898-1971) They Live by Night 1948; Oh, You Beautiful Doll 1949; A Woman's Secret 1949; Two Flags West 1950; Winchester '73 1950; Flying Leathernecks 1951; The Lemon Drop Kid 1951; The People against O'Hara 1951; The Las Vegas Story 1952; Devil's Canyon 1953; East of Sumatra 1953; Thunder Bay 1953; The Wild One 1953; Carnival Story 1954; The Far Country 1954; Kismet 1955; Man without a Star 1955; Oklahoma! 1955; Six Bridges to Cross 1955; Strategic Air Command 1955; The Killing 1956; 7th Cavalry 1956; The Deerslayer 1957; The Halliday Brand 1957; The Midnight Story 1957; The Restless Breed 1957; Run of the Arrow 1957; From Hell to Texas 1958; Wild River 1960

Flitter, Josh The Greatest Game Ever Played 2005; License to Wed 2007; Nancy Drew 2007

Floberg, Bjørn (1947-) Insomnia 1997; Kitchen Stories 2003; O'Horten 2007

Flockhart, Calista (1964-) Getting In 1994; The Birdcage 1996; Telling Lies in America 1997; A Midsummer Night's Dream 1999; Things You Can Tell Just by Looking at Her 2000; The Last Shot 2004; Fragile 2005

Flon, Suzanne (1918-2005) Moulin Rouge 1952; A Monkey in Winter 1962; The Trial 1962; The Train 1964; The Silent One 1973; Mr Klein 1976; One Deadly Summer 1983; The Children of

the Marshland 1998; The Flower of Evil 2002; Strange Gardens 2003; The Bridesmaid 2004

Florance, Sheila (1916-1991) Cactus 1986; A Woman's Tale 1991

Florelle aka Florelle, Odette (1901-1974) Les Misérables 1934; Le Crime de Monsieur Lange 1935

Flower, George "Buck" (1937-2004) Across the Great Divide 1977; They Live 1988

Floyd, James Everywhere + Nowhere 2011; My Brother the Devil 2012

Fluegel, Darlanne (1956-) Battle beyond the Stars 1980; To Live and Die in LA 1985; Running Scared 1986; Tough Guys 1986; Bulletproof 1987; Lock Up 1989; Scanner Cop 1994; Darkman III: Die Darkman Die 1996

Flueger, Patrick Brothers 2009; Mother's Day 2010

Fluellen, Joel (1907-1990) Monster from Green Hell 1958; The Learning Tree 1969; The Great White Hope 1970

Flynn, Barbara You're Dead 1999; Miss Potter 2006

Flynn, Colleen (1962-) Late for Dinner 1991; The Temp 1993

Flynn, Errol (1909-1959) Captain Blood 1935; The Charge of the Light Brigade 1936; Another Dawn 1937; Green Light 1937; The Perfect Specimen 1937; The Prince and the Pauper 1937; The Adventures of Robin Hood 1938; The Dawn Patrol 1938; Four's a Crowd 1938; The Sisters 1938; Dodge City 1939; The Private Lives of Elizabeth and Essex 1939; Santa Fe Trail 1940; The Sea Hawk 1940; Virginia City 1940; Dive Bomber 1941; Footsteps in the Dark 1941; They Died with Their Boots On 1941; Desperate Journey 1942; Gentleman Jim 1942; Edge of Darkness 1943; Northern Pursuit 1943; Uncertain Glory 1944; Objective, Burma! 1945; San Antonio 1945; Never Say Goodbye 1946; Cry Wolf 1947; Escape Me Never 1947; Adventures of Don Juan 1948; Silver River 1948; The Forsyte Saga 1949; It's a Great Feeling 1949; Kim 1950; Montana 1950; Rocky Mountain 1950; Adventures of Captain Fabian 1951; Against All Flags 1952; Mara Maru 1952; The Master of Ballantrae 1953; Crossed Swords 1954; The Dark Avenger 1955; King's Rhapsody 1955; Lilacs in the Spring 1955; Istanbul 1957; The Sun Also Rises 1957; The Roots of Heaven 1958; Too Much, Too Soon 1958

Flynn, Jerome (1963-) A Summer Story 1987; Edward II 1991; Best 1999

Flynn, Joe (1925-1974) McHale's Navy 1964; Divorce American Style 1967; The Computer Wore Tennis Shoes 1969; The Love Bug 1969; The Barefoot Executive 1971; The Million Dollar Duck 1971; The Strongest Man in the World 1975; The Rescuers 1977

Flynn, Miriam (1952-) National Lampoon's Class Reunion 1982; For Keeps 1987; 18 Again! 1988; National Lampoon's Christmas Vacation 1989; Babe 1995

Flynn, Steven Without Warning: the James Brady Story 1991; Ulee's Gold 1997

Foà, Arnoldo (1916-2014) Angela 1955; The Angel Wore Red 1960; The Captain 1960; The Trial 1962

Focas, Spiros (1937-) Shaft in Africa 1973; The Jewel of the Nile 1985; Rambo III 1988

Foch, Nina (1924-2008) The Return of the Vampire 1943; Cry of the Werewolf 1944; My Name Is Julia Ross 1945; A Song to Remember 1945; The Guilt of Janet Ames 1947; Johnny o'Clock 1947; The Dark Past 1948; The Undercover Man 1949; An American in Paris 1951; Scaramouche 1952; Sombrero 1952; Young Man with Ideas 1952; Executive Suite 1954; Illegal 1955; You're Never Too Young 1955; The Ten Commandments 1956; Cash McCall 1960; Spartacus 1960; Prescription: Murder 1968; Such Good Friends 1971; Mahogany 1975; Jennifer 1978; Hush 1998; Shadow of Doubt 1998

Fogerty, Adam Greenfingers 2000; Bait 2015

Fogler, Dan (1976-) Balls of Fury 2007; Good Luck Chuck 2007; Dr Seuss' Horton Hears a Who! 2008; Fanboys 2008; Love Happens 2009; Taking Woodstock 2009; Mars Needs Moms 2011; Take Me Home Tonight 2011; Fantastic Beasts and Where to Find Them 2016

Folch, Aida Mondays in the Sun 2002; The Artist and the Model 2012

Foley, Dave (1963-) Kids in the Hall: Brain Candy 1996; Blast from the Past 1998; A Bug's Life 1998; Dick 1999;

Monkeybone 2000; Stark Raving Mad 2002; Monsters University 2013

Foley, Jeremy (1983-) Casper: a Spirited Beginning 1997; Dante's Peak 1997; Casper Meets Wendy 1998

Foley, Scott (1973-) Scream 3 1999; Below 2002

Folland, Alison (1978-) To Die For 1995; All over Me 1996; Boys Don't Cry 1999; Milwaukee, Minnesota 2002

Follows, Megan (1968-) Silver Bullet 1985; Season of Dreams 1987; Inherit the Wind 1988; The Nutcracker Prince 1990; Under the Piano 1995; Plainsong 2004

Fonda, Bridget (1964-) Aria 1987; Light Years 1988; Scandal 1988; Shag 1988; Strapless 1988; Frankenstein Unbound 1990; The Godfather Part III 1990; Doc Hollywood 1991; Drop Dead Fred 1991; Iron Maze 1991; Leather Jackets 1991; Single White Female 1992; Singles 1992; Army of Darkness 1993; The Assassin 1993; Bodies, Rest & Motion 1993; Camilla 1993; Little Buddha 1993; It Could Happen to You 1994; The Road to Wellville 1994; Balto 1995; Rough Magic 1995; City Hall 1996; Grace of My Heart 1996; Touch 1996; In the Gloaming 1997; Jackie Brown 1997; Mr Jealousy 1997; Break Up 1998; A Simple Plan 1998; Finding Graceland 1999; Lake Placid 1999; Monkeybone 2000; South of Heaven, West of Hell 2000; Kiss of the Dragon 2001; No Ordinary Baby 2001

Fonda, Henry (1905-1982) The Farmer Takes a Wife 1935; I Dream Too Much 1935; Way Down East 1935; The Moon's Our Home 1936; Spendthrift 1936; The Trail of the Lonesome Pine 1936; Slim 1937; That Certain Woman 1937; Wings of the Morning 1937; You Only Live Once 1937; Blockade 1938; I Met My Love Again 1938; Jezebel 1938; The Mad Miss Manton 1938; Spawn of the North 1938; Drums along the Mohawk 1939; Jesse James 1939; The Story of Alexander Graham Bell 1939; Young Mr Lincoln 1939; Chad Hanna 1940; The Grapes of Wrath 1940; Lillian Russell 1940; The Return of Frank James 1940; The Lady Eve 1941; Wild Geese Calling 1941; You Belong to Me 1941; The Battle of Midway 1942; The Big Street 1942; The Magnificent Dope 1942; The Male Animal 1942; Rings on Her Fingers 1942; Tales of Manhattan 1942; The Immortal Sergeant 1943; The Ox-Bow Incident 1943; My Darling Clementine 1946; Daisy Kenyon 1947; The Fugitive 1947; The Long Night 1947; Fort Apache 1948; On Our Merry Way 1948; Jigsaw 1949; Mister Roberts 1955; War and Peace 1956; The Wrong Man 1956; The Tin Star 1957; 12 Angry Men 1957; Stage Struck 1958; The Man Who Understood Women 1959; Warlock 1959; Advise and Consent 1962; How the West Was Won 1962; The Longest Day 1962; Spencer's Mountain 1963; The Best Man 1964; Fail-Safe 1964; Sex and the Single Girl 1964; Battle of the Bulge 1965; In Harm's Way 1965; The Rounders 1965; A Big Hand for a Little Lady 1966; Stranger on the Run 1967; Welcome to Hard Times 1967; The Boston Strangler 1968; Firecreek 1968; Madigan 1968; Once upon a Time in the West 1968; Yours, Mine and Ours 1968; The Cheyenne Social Club 1970; There Was a Crooked Man... 1970; Too Late the Hero 1970; Sometimes a Great Notion 1971; The Serpent 1972; Ash Wednesday 1973; My Name Is Nobody 1973; The Last Days of Mussolini 1974; Battle of Midway 1976; Rollercoaster 1977; Tentacles 1977; Fedora 1978; City on Fire 1979; Meteor 1979; Wanda Nevada 1979; Gideon's Trumpet 1980; On Golden Pond 1981

Fonda, Jane (1937-) The Chapman Report 1962; Period of Adjustment 1962; Walk on the Wild Side 1962; Sunday in New York 1963; The Love Cage 1964; La Ronde 1964; Cat Ballou 1965; Any Wednesday 1966; The Chase 1966; The Game Is Over 1966; Barbarella 1967; Barefoot in the Park 1967; Histoires Extraordinaires 1967; Hurry Sundown 1967; They Shoot Horses, Don't They? 1969; Klute 1971; FTA 1972; Tout Va Bien 1972; A Doll's House 1973; Steelyard Blues 1973; The Blue Bird 1976; Fun with Dick and Jane 1977; Julia 1977; California Suite 1978; Comes a Horseman 1978; Coming Home 1978; The China Syndrome 1979; The Electric Horseman 1979; Nine to Five 1980; On Golden Pond 1981; Rollover 1981; The Dollmaker 1984; Agnes of God 1985; The Morning After 1986; Leonard, Part 6 1987; Old Gringo 1989; Stanley & Iris 1989; Monster-in-Law 2005; Georgia Rule 2007; Peace, Love & Misunderstanding 2011; The

Butler 2013; Better Living through Chemistry 2014; This Is Where I Leave You 2014; Youth 2015

Fonda, Peter (1940-) Tammy and the Doctor 1963; The Victors 1963; Lilith 1964; The Wild Angels 1966; Histoires Extraordinaires 1967; The Trip 1967; Easy Rider 1969; The Hired Hand 1971; The Last Movie 1971; Two People 1973; Open Season 1974; Killer Force 1975; 92 in the Shade 1975; Race with the Devil 1975; Fighting Mad 1976; Futureworld 1976; Outlaw Blues 1977; Wanda Nevada 1979; The Cannonball Run 1981; Split Image 1982; Dance of the Dwarfs 1983; Certain Fury 1985; The Rose Garden 1989; Fatal Mission 1990; Love and a .45 1994; Nadja 1995; Escape from LA 1996; Ulee's Gold 1997; The Limey 1999; South of Heaven, West of Hell 2000; Thomas and the Magic Railroad 2000; The Laramie Project 2002; The Maldonado Miracle 2003; Ghost Rider 2007; 3:10 to Yuma 2007; Wild Hogs 2007; Corman's World: Exploits of a Hollywood Rebel 2011; The Runner 2015

Fondacaro, Phil (1958-) Troll 1986; The Garbage Pail Kids Movie 1987

Fong, Alex (1963-) One Nite in Mongkok 2004; Kung Fu Killer 2014

Fong, Benson (1916-1987) Charlie Chan in the Chinese Cat 1944; Charlie Chan in the Secret Service 1944; The Red Dragon 1945; The Scarlet Clue 1945; The Shanghai Cobra 1945; Dark Alibi 1946; Deception 1946; Peking Express 1951; His Majesty O'Keefe 1953; Flower Drum Song 1961; Girls! Girls! Girls! 1962; Our Man Flint 1966; The Love Bug 1969; Oliver's Story 1978

Fonseca, Lyndsy (1987-) Ordinary Miracles 2005; Kick-Ass 2009; Hot Tub Time Machine 2010; John Carpenter's The Ward 2010

Fontaine, Frank (1920-1978) Stella 1950; The Model and the Marriage Broker 1951

Fontaine, Joan (1917-2013) A Damsel in Distress 1937; A Million to One 1937; Quality Street 1937; Blond Cheat 1938; The Duke of West Point 1938; Maid's Night Out 1938; Gunga Din 1939; The Women 1939; Rebecca 1940; Suspicion 1941; This above All 1942; The Constant Nymph 1943; Jane Eyre 1943; Frenchman's Creek 1944; The Affairs of Susan 1945; From This Day Forward 1946; Ivy 1947; Blood on My Hands 1948; The Emperor Waltz 1948; Letter from an Unknown Woman 1948; You Gotta Stay Happy 1948; Born to Be Bad 1950; September Affair 1950; Darling, How Could You! 1951; Ivanhoe 1952; Something to Live For 1952; The Bigamist 1953; Decameron Nights 1953; Flight to Tangier 1953; Casanova's Big Night 1954; Beyond a Reasonable Doubt 1956; Serenade 1956; Island in the Sun 1957; Until They Sail 1957; A Certain Smile 1958; South Pacific 1958; Tender Is the Night 1961; Voyage to the Bottom of the Sea 1961; The Witches 1966

Fontenoy, Catherine (1879-1966) Poil de Carotte 1932; Divine 1935

Foran, Dick aka **Foran, Richard** (1910-1979) Dangerous 1935; Shipmates Forever 1935; The Petrified Forest 1936; The Black Legion 1937; The Perfect Specimen 1937; Boy Meets Girl 1938; Four Daughters 1938; Daughters Courageous 1939; The House of the Seven Gables 1940; The Mummy's Hand 1940; My Little Chickadee 1940; Keep 'Em Flying 1941; Unfinished Business 1941; The Mummy's Tomb 1942; Ride 'Em Cowboy 1942; Guest Wife 1944; Al Jennings of Oklahoma 1951; Chicago Confidential 1957; The Fearmakers 1958; Violent Road 1958; The Atomic Submarine 1960; Taggart 1964

Foray, June (1919-) Daffy Duck's Movie: Fantastic Island 1983; Duck Tales: the Movie - Treasure of the Lost Lamp 1990; Thumbelina 1994; The Adventures of Rocky & Bullwinkle 1999; Tweety's High Flying Adventure 2000

Forbes, Bryan (1926-2013) Appointment in London 1952; Sea Devils 1952; The World in His Arms 1952; The Colditz Story 1954; An Inspector Calls 1954; Passage Home 1955; The Baby and the Battleship 1956; Satellite in the Sky 1956; Quatermass II 1957; The Key 1958; The League of Gentlemen 1960; The Guns of Navarone 1961; Restless Natives 1985

Forbes, Mary (1883-1974) Sunny Side Up 1929; The Devil to Pay 1930; Blonde Bombshell 1933; We Live Again 1934; Tender Comrade 1943

Forbes, Meriel (1913-2000) Come On George 1939; The Bells Go Down 1943; Home at Seven 1952

Forbes, Michelle (1967-) Kalifornia 1993; Roadflower 1994; Swimming with Sharks 1994; Escape from LA 1996

Forbes, Ralph (1902-1951) Beau Geste 1926; The Trail of '98 1929; Her Wedding Night 1930; The Bachelor Father 1931; Beau Ideal 1931; Smilin' Through 1932; The Barretts of Wimpole Street 1934; Riptide 1934; Piccadilly Jim 1936; The Last of Mrs Cheyney 1937; Annabel Takes a Tour 1938; Kidnapped 1938; Frenchman's Creek 1944

Forbes, Scott (1920-1997) Rocky Mountain 1950; Operation Pacific 1951; The Mind of Mr Soames 1970

Ford Davies, Oliver Titanic Town 1998; Star Wars Episode I: the Phantom Menace 1999; Johnny English 2003; The Mother 2003

Ford, Alan (1938-) The Squeeze 1977; Snatch 2000; Exorcist: the Beginning 2004; Cockneys vs Zombies 2011; The 100-Year-Old Man Who Climbed out of the Window and Disappeared 2013

Ford, Constance (1923-1993) The Last Hunt 1956; The Iron Sheriff 1957; A Summer Place 1959; All Fall Down 1962; The Cabinet of Caligari 1962; Rome Adventure 1962; 99 and 44/100% Dead 1974

Ford, Dorothy (1923-2010) On Our Merry Way 1948; Jack and the Beanstalk 1952

Ford, Faith (1964-) Sometimes They Come Back... for More 1998; The Pacifier 2005; A Kiss at Midnight 2008

Ford, Francis (1881-1953) Charlie Chan at the Circus 1936; South of Pago Pago 1940; The Ox-Bow Incident 1943; The Plunderers 1948; The Far Frontier 1949; The Sun Shines Bright 1953

Ford, Fritz (1927-2006) The Bridge at Remagen 1969; Challenge to Be Free 1972

Ford, Glenn (1916-2006) The Lady in Question 1940; So Ends Our Night 1941; Texas 1941; The Desperadoes 1943; Gilda 1946; A Stolen Life 1946; Framed 1947; The Loves of Carmen 1948; The Man from Colorado 1948; The Return of October 1948; The Doctor and the Girl 1949; The Undercover Man 1949; Convicted 1950; The Redhead and the Cowboy 1950; The White Tower 1950; Follow the Sun: the Ben Hogan Story 1951; The Secret of Convict Lake 1951; Affair in Trinidad 1952; Young Man with Ideas 1952; Appointment in Honduras 1953; The Big Heat 1953; The Man from the Alamo 1953; Terror on a Train 1953; Human Desire 1954; The Americano 1955; The Blackboard Jungle 1955; Interrupted Melody 1955; Trial 1955; The Violent Men 1955; The Fastest Gun Alive 1956; Jubal 1956; Ransom! 1956; The Teahouse of the August Moon 1956; Don't Go near the Water 1957; 3:10 to Yuma 1957; Cowboy 1958; The Sheepman 1958; Torpedo Run 1958; The Gazebo 1959; It Started with a Kiss 1959; Cimarron 1960; Cry for Happy 1961; Pocketful of Miracles 1961; The Four Horsemen of the Apocalypse 1962; The Courtship of Eddie's Father 1963; Love Is a Ball 1963; Advance to the Rear 1964; Dear Heart 1964; Fate Is the Hunter 1964; The Rounders 1965; Is Paris Burning? 1966; Rage 1966; The Last Challenge 1967; A Time for Killing 1967; Day of the Evil Gun 1968; Smith! 1969; Santee 1973; Battle of Midway 1976; Superman 1978; Virus 1980; The Visitor 1980; Happy Birthday to Me 1981; Border Shootout 1990; Raw Nerve 1991

Ford, Harrison (1942-) Dead Heat on a Merry-Go-Round 1966; Journey to Shiloh 1967; A Time for Killing 1967; Getting Straight 1970; The Intruders 1970; American Graffiti 1973; The Conversation 1974; Star Wars Episode IV: a New Hope 1977; Force 10 from Navarone 1978; Apocalypse Now 1979; The Frisco Kid 1979; Hanover Street 1979; More American Graffiti 1979; Star Wars Episode V: the Empire Strikes Back 1980; Raiders of the Lost Ark 1981; Blade Runner 1982; Star Wars Episode VI: Return of the Jedi 1983; Indiana Jones and the Temple of Doom 1984; Witness 1985; The Mosquito Coast 1986; Frantic 1988; Working Girl 1988; Indiana Jones and the Last Crusade 1989; Presumed Innocent 1990; Regarding Henry 1991; Patriot Games 1992; The Fugitive 1993; Clear and Present Danger 1994; Jimmy Hollywood 1994; Sabrina 1995; Air Force One 1997; The Devil's Own 1997; Six Days Seven Nights 1998; Random Hearts 1999; What Lies Beneath 2000; K-19: the Widowmaker 2002; Hollywood Homicide 2003; Firewall

2006; Crossing Over 2008; Indiana Jones and the Kingdom of the Crystal Skull 2008; Brüno 2009; Extraordinary Measures 2010; Morning Glory 2010; Cowboys & Aliens 2011; Anchorman 2: the Legend Continues 2013; Ender's Game 2013; 42 2013; Paranoia 2013; The Expendables 3 2014; The Age of Adaline 2015; Star Wars Episode VII: the Force Awakens 2015; Blade Runner 2 2017

Ford, John aka Ford, Jack (1894-1973) The Birth of a Nation 1915; His Lordship 1936; The Tales of Hoffmann 1951

Ford, Julia A Room for Romeo Brass 1999; Vinyl 2012; Radiator 2014

Ford, Luke The Mummy: Tomb of the Dragon Emperor 2008; Red Dog 2011; Charlie's Country 2013

Ford, Maria (1966-) The Haunting of Morella 1990; Ring of Fire 1991; The Unnamable Returns 1992

Ford, Paul (1901-1976) Perfect Strangers 1950; The Teahouse of the August Moon 1956; The Matchmaker 1958; The Music Man 1962; Who's Got the Action? 1962; Never Too Late 1965; A Big Hand for a Little Lady 1966; The Russians Are Coming, the Russians Are Coming 1966; The Comedians 1967

Ford, Ross (1923-1988) Challenge to Lassie 1949; Force of Arms 1951; Blue Canadian Rockies 1952; Reform School Girl 1957

Ford, Ruth (1911-2009) Too Much Johnson 1938; Circumstantial Evidence 1945; Act One 1963; Play It as It Lays 1972; Too Scared to Scream 1982

Ford, Wallace aka Ford, Wally (1898-1966) Possessed 1931; The Beast of the City 1932; Freaks 1932; The Wet Parade 1932; Employees' Entrance 1933; The Lost Patrol 1934; The Informer 1935; The Whole Town's Talking 1935; You're in the Army Now 1936; Jericho 1937; The Mummy's Hand 1940; Blues in the Night 1941; A Man Betrayed 1941; All through the Night 1942; The Mummy's Tomb 1942; Seven Days' Leave 1942; Shadow of a Doubt 1942; Secret Command 1944; Blood on the Sun 1945; Black Angel 1946; Crack-Up 1945; Dead Reckoning 1947; Magic Town 1947; T-Men 1947; Belle Starr's Daughter 1948; Coroner Creek 1948; The Set-Up 1949; The Breaking Point 1950; Harvey 1950; He Ran All the Way 1951; Painting the Clouds with Sunshine 1951; Warpath 1951; Flesh and Fury 1952; Beautiful but Dangerous 1954; The Boy from Oklahoma 1954; Destry 1954; Three Ring Circus 1954; A Lawless Street 1955; Lucy Gallant 1955; The Man from Laramie 1955; The Spoilers 1955; Wichita 1955; The First Texan 1956; Johnny Concho 1956; The Rainmaker 1956; Thunder over Arizona 1956; The Matchmaker 1958; Warlock 1959; Tess of the Storm Country 1960; A Patch of Blue 1965

Foree, Ken (1941-) Dawn of the Dead 1978; From Beyond 1986; Leatherface: the Texas Chainsaw Massacre III 1990; Without You I'm Nothing 1990; The Dentist 1996; The Lords of Salem 2012

Foreman, Amanda Silver 1993; All I Want for Christmas 2007

Foreman, Deborah (1962-) Valley Girl 1983; April Fool's Day 1986; My Chauffeur 1986; 3:15 1986; Waxwork 1988; The Experts 1989; Lobster Man from Mars 1989; Lunatics: a Love Story 1991

Foreman, George Muhammad Ali, the Greatest 1974; When We Were Kings 1996; Play It to the Bone 2000; I Am Ali 2014

Foreman, Jamie (1958-) Gangster No 1 2000; Goodbye Charlie Bright 2000; Saving Grace 2000; I'll Sleep When I'm Dead 2003; The Football Factory 2004; Layer Cake 2004; Oliver Twist 2005; Botched 2007; Screwed 2011

Forest, Michael (1929-) Beast from Haunted Cave 1959; Atlas 1960; Deathwatch 1966

Forke, Farrah (1967-) Complex of Fear 1993; Hitman's Run 1999

Forlani, Claire (1971-) Mallrats 1995; Basquiat 1996; The Last Time I Committed Suicide 1996; Basil 1998; Meet Joe Black 1998; Antitrust 2000; Boys and Girls 2000; Triggermen 2002; The Medallion 2003; Bobby Jones: Stroke of Genius 2004; Green Street 2004; Hallam Foe 2006; Loves Kitchen 2010; Precious Cargo 2016

Forman, Milos (1932-) Heartburn 1986; Keeping the Faith 2000; Beloved 2011

Formby, Beryl (?- 960) Boots! Boots! 1934; Off the Dole 1935

Formby, George (1904-1961) Boots! Boots! 1934; No Limit 1935; Off the

Dole 1935; Keep Your Seats, Please 1936; Keep Fit 1937; I See Ice 1938; It's in the Air 1938; Come On George 1939; Trouble Brewing 1939; Let George Do It 1940; Spare a Copper 1940; It's Turned Out Nice Again 1941; South American George 1941; Much Too Shy 1942; Bell-Bottom George 1943; I Didn't Do It 1945; George in Civvy Street 1946

Forner, Lola (1960-) Wheels on Meals 1984; The Armour of God 1986

Foronjy, Richard (1937-) Prince of the City 1981; The Morning After 1986; Midnight Run 1988

Forqué, Verónica (1955-) What Have I Done to Deserve This? 1984; Kika 1993

Forquet, Philippe (1940-) In the French Style 1963; Take Her, She's Mine 1963

Forrest, Christine Martin 1978; Knightriders 1981; Monkey Shines 1988

Forrest, Frederic (1936-) When the Legends Die 1972; The Conversation 1974; Permission to Kill 1975; The Missouri Breaks 1976; It Lives Again 1978; Apocalypse Now 1979; The Rose 1979; Hammett 1982; One from the Heart 1982; Who Will Love My Children? 1983; The Parade 1984; The Stone Boy 1984; Season of Dreams 1987; The Dead Can't Lie 1988; Tucker: the Man and His Dream 1988; Cat Chaser 1989; Music Box 1989; The Two Jakes 1990; Falling Down 1992; Trauma 1993; Against the Wall 1994; Lassie: a New Generation 1994; Before the Night 1995; Point Blank 1997; Whatever 1998; Militia 2000; Shadow Hours 2000; Path to War 2002

Forrest, Sally (1928-2015) Mystery Street 1950; Hard, Fast and Beautiful 1951; The Strange Door 1951; The Strip 1951; Vengeance Valley 1951; Son of Sinbad 1955; While the City Sleeps 1956

Forrest, Steve (1925-2013) Dream Wife 1953; So Big 1953; Take the High Ground 1953; Prisoner of War 1954; Rogue Cop 1954; Bedevilled 1955; The Living Idol 1955; It Happened to Jane 1959; Five Branded Women 1960; Flaming Star 1960; Heller in Pink Tights 1960; The Second Time Around 1961; The Yellow Canary 1963; Captain America 1979; North Dallas Forty 1979; Mommie Dearest 1981; Spies like Us 1985; Amazon Women on the Moon 1987; Killer: a Journal of Murder 1995

Forster, Robert (1941-) Reflections in a Golden Eye 1967; The Stalking Moon 1968; Justine 1969; Medium Cool 1969; Pieces of Dreams 1970; Journey through Rosebud 1972; The Black Hole 1979; Alligator 1980; The Delta Force 1986; Peacemaker 1990; 29th Street 1991; American Yakuza 1994; American Perfekt 1997; Jackie Brown 1997; Psycho 1998; Rear Window 1998; Me, Myself & Irene 2000; Supernova 2000; Human Nature 2001; Mulholland Drive 2001; Murder in Greenwich 2002; Grand Theft Parsons 2003; Firewall 2006; Ghosts of Girlfriends Past 2009; The Descendants 2011; Survivor 2015

Forster, Rudolf (1884-1968) Ariane 1931; The Threepenny Opera 1931

Forsyth, Bruce (1928-) Star! 1968; Can Hieronymus Merkin Ever Forget Mercy Humppe and Find True Happiness? 1969; Bedknobs and Broomsticks 1971; The Magnificent Seven Deadly Sins 1971; House! 2000

Forsyth, Rosemary (1944-) Shenandoah 1965; The War Lord 1965; Texas across the River 1966; Whatever Happened to Aunt Alice? 1969; How Do I Love Thee? 1970; City beneath the Sea 1971; Gray Lady Down 1978; Disclosure 1994

Forsythe, Drew (1950-) Annie's Coming Out 1984; Burke and Wills 1985

Forsythe, Henderson (1917-2006) Dead of Night 1972; End of the Line 1987

Forsythe, John (1918-2010) The Captive City 1952; Escape from Fort Bravo 1953; The Glass Web 1953; The Trouble with Harry 1954; The Ambassador's Daughter 1956; Madame X 1966; In Cold Blood 1967; Topaz 1969; ...And Justice for All 1979; Scrooged 1988; Charlie's Angels 2000; Charlie's Angels: Full Throttle 2003

Forsythe, William aka Forsythe, Bill (1955-) Once upon a Time in America 1984; The Lightship 1985; Savage Dawn 1985; Extreme Prejudice 1987; Raising Arizona 1987; Weeds 1987; Patty Hearst 1988; Dead-Bang 1989; Sons 1989; Torrents of Spring 1989; Dick Tracy 1990; Out for Justice 1991; Stone Cold 1991; The Waterdance 1991; American Me 1992; The Gun in Betty Lou's Handbag 1992; Palookaville 1995; Things to Do in Denver When You're Dead 1995; Virtuosity 1995; The Rock 1996; The Substitute 1996; Dollar for

the Dead 1998; Firestorm 1998; Deuce Bigalow: Male Gigolo 1999; Four Days 1999; G-Men from Hell 2000; Luck of the Draw 2000; City by the Sea 2002; The Devil's Rejects 2005; Freedomland 2006; 88 Minutes 2007

Forte, Will (1970-) Beerfest 2006; The Brothers Solomon 2007; MacGruber 2010; Cloudy with a Chance of Meatballs 2 2013; Life of Crime 2013; Nebraska 2013; Run and Jump 2013; She's Funny That Way 2014; Keanu 2016

Fortier, Robert (1926-2005) Incubus 1965; 3 Women 1977

Fortineau, Thierry (1953-2006) Your Beating Heart 1991; L'Homme de Ma Vie 1992

Fortune, John (1939-2013) Pleasure at Her Majesty's 1976; Bloodbath at the House of Death 1983; Calendar Girls 2003

Fosse, Bob aka Fosse, Robert (1927-1987) The Affairs of Dobie Gillis 1953; Give a Girl a Break 1953; Kiss Me Kate 1953; My Sister Eileen 1955; Damn Yankees 1958; The Little Prince 1974

Fossey, Brigitte (1946-) Jeux Interdits 1953; The Happy Road 1956; Les Valseuses 1974; The Man Who Loved Women 1977; Quintet 1979; Enigma 1982; Imperative 1982; The Last Butterfly 1990

Foster, Barry (1931-2002) Sea Fury 1958; Sea of Sand 1958; Surprise Package 1960; King and Country 1964; The Family Way 1966; Robbery 1967; Inspector Clouseau 1968; Twisted Nerve 1968; The Guru 1969; Ryan's Daughter 1970; Frenzy 1972; Sweeney! 1976; Heat and Dust 1982; The Whistle Blower 1986; King of the Wind 1989

Foster, Ben (1980-) Liberty Heights 1999; Get over It 2001; 11:14 2003; Hostage 2004; The Punisher 2004; Alpha Dog 2006; 30 Days of Night 2007; 3:10 to Yuma 2007; The Messenger 2009; Pandorum 2009; The Mechanic 2011; Rampart 2011; 360 2011; Contraband 2012; Ain't Them Bodies Saints 2013; Kill Your Darlings 2013; Lone Survivor 2013; The Finest Hours 2015; The Program 2015; Hell or High Water 2016; Inferno 2016; Warcraft: the Beginning 2016

Foster, Dianne (1928-) The Quiet Woman 1950; Isn't Life Wonderful! 1952; The Last Hours 1952; Bad for Each Other 1954; Drive a Crooked Road 1954; The Kentuckian 1955; The Violent Men 1955; The Brothers Rico 1957; Night Passage 1957; The Deep Six 1958; Gideon's Day 1958; The Last Hurrah 1958; King of the Roaring 20s - the Story of Arnold Rothstein 1961

Foster, Dudley (1925-1973) Moon Zero Two 1969; Where's Jack? 1969; Dulcima 1971

Foster, Gloria (1936-2001) The Cool World 1963; Nothing but a Man 1964; The Angel Levine 1970; Leonard, Part 6 1987; The Matrix 1999; The Matrix Reloaded 2002

Foster, Jodie (1962-) Kansas City Bomber 1972; Napoleon and Samantha 1972; One Little Indian 1973; Tom Sawyer 1973; Alice Doesn't Live Here Anymore 1974; Bugsy Malone 1976; Echoes of a Summer 1976; Freaky Friday 1976; The Little Girl Who Lives Down the Lane 1976; Taxi Driver 1976; Candleshoe 1977; Carny 1980; Foxes 1980; The Blood of Others 1984; The Hotel New Hampshire 1984; Mesmerized 1984; Five Corners 1987; Siesta 1987; The Accused 1988; Stealing Home 1988; Catchfire 1989; Little Man Tate 1991; Shadows and Fog 1991; The Silence of the Lambs 1991; Sommersby 1993; Maverick 1994; Nell 1994; Contact 1997; Anna and the King 1999; The Dangerous Lives of Altar Boys 2001; Panic Room 2002; A Very Long Engagement 2004; Flightplan 2005; Inside Man 2006; The Brave One 2007; Nim's Island 2008; Motherhood 2009; The Beaver 2010; Carnage 2011; Elysium 2013

Foster (1), Jon (1984-) Murder in Greenwich 2002; The Door in the Floor 2004; Stay Alive 2006; Tenderness 2007; The Informers 2009; Brotherhood 2010

Foster, Julia (1942-) The Loneliness of the Long Distance Runner 1962; The Small World of Sammy Lee 1963; Two Left Feet 1963; The Bargee 1964; The System 1964; One Way Pendulum 1965; Alfie 1966; Half a Sixpence 1967; Simon, Simon 1970; Percy 1971; The Great McGonagall 1974

Foster, Meg (1948-) Adam at 6 AM 1970; Thumb Tripping 1972; Carny 1980; Ticket to Heaven 1981; The Osterman Weekend 1983; The Emerald Forest 1985; Masters of the Universe 1987; They Live 1988; Leviathan 1989;

Relentless 1989; Stepfather II 1989; Blind Fury 1990; Best of the Best II 1992; The Lords of Salem 2012

Foster, Norman (1900-1976) It Pays to Advertise 1931; Skyscraper Souls 1932; Pilgrimage 1933; State Fair 1933; Fatal Lady 1936; How Much Does Your Building Weigh, Mr Foster? 2009

Foster, Phil (1914-1985) Conquest of Space 1955; Bang the Drum Slowly 1973

Foster, Phoebe (1896-1975) Tarnished Lady 1931; Our Betters 1933; Anna Karenina 1935

Foster, Preston aka Foster, Preston S (1900-1970) Doctor X 1932; I Am a Fugitive from a Chain Gang 1932; Two Seconds 1932; Ladies They Talk About 1933; Annie Oakley 1935; The Arizonian 1935; The Informer 1935; The Last Days of Pompeii 1935; Love before Breakfast 1936; The Plough and the Stars 1936; Submarine Patrol 1938; North West Mounted Police 1940; Unfinished Business 1941; Guadalcanal Diary 1943; My Friend Flicka 1943; The Bermuda Mystery 1944; Thunderhead - Son of Flicka 1945; The Valley of Decision 1945; The Harvey Girls 1946; Ramrod 1947; I Shot Jesse James 1949; The Big Night 1951; Tomahawk 1951; Kansas City Confidential 1952; I, the Jury 1953; Law and Order 1953; The Time Traveller 1964

Foster, Sara (1981-) The Big Bounce 2004; Psych 9 2010

Fouldes, Angela The Small Voice 1948; The Secret People 1951

Foulger, Byron (1899-1968) Arizona 1940; Circumstantial Evidence 1945; The River's Edge 1957

Foulk, Robert (1908-1989) The 49th Man 1953; Last of the Badmen 1957

Foundas, George (1924-) Stella 1955; Never on Sunday 1960; Zorba the Greek 1964

Fourçade, Christian Little Boy Lost 1953; The Captain 1960

Fowlds, Derek aka Fowldes, Derek (1937-) We Joined the Navy 1962; East of Sudan 1964; Frankenstein Created Woman 1966; Hotel Paradiso 1966; The Smashing Bird I Used to Know 1969; Tower of Evil 1972; Over the Hill 1992

Fowler, Harry (1926-2012) Went the Day Well? 1942; Painted Boats 1945; Hue and Cry 1947; I Believe in You 1952; Conflict of Wings 1953; A Day to Remember 1953; The Blue Peter 1955; Stock Car 1955; Behind the Headlines 1956; Fire Maidens from Outer Space 1956; Booby Trap 1957; Clash by Night 1963

Fowley, Douglas (1911-1998) Big Brown Eyes 1936; Charlie Chan on Broadway 1937; On the Avenue 1937; Mr Moto's Gamble 1938; Charlie Chan at Treasure Island 1939; Jitterbugs 1943; Desperate 1947; Scared to Death 1947; Mighty Joe Young 1949; Search for Danger 1949; Armored Car Robbery 1950; Mrs O'Malley and Mr Malone 1950; Tarzan's Peril 1951; Singin' in the Rain 1952; The Naked Jungle 1953; Bandido 1956; A Gift for Heidi 1958

Fox, Bernard (1927-) One of Our Spies Is Missing 1966; The Hound of the Baskervilles 1972; The Private Eyes 1980

Fox, Colin (1938-) Food of the Gods II 1989; Beautiful Dreamers 1990; Scanners III: the Takeover 1992; Prince Charming 2001

Fox, David Ordinary Magic 1993; When Night Is Falling 1995; Dangerous Offender: the Marlene Moore Story 1996; The Saddest Music in the World 2003

Fox, Edward (1937-) The Mind Benders 1963; The Frozen Dead 1966; I'll Never Forget What's 'Is Name 1967; The Jokers 1967; The Naked Runner 1967; Skullduggery 1969; The Go-Between 1971; The Day of the Jackal 1973; A Doll's House 1973; Galileo 1974; A Bridge Too Far 1977; The Duellists 1977; Soldier of Orange 1977; The Squeeze 1977; The Big Sleep 1978; Force 10 from Navarone 1978; The Cat and the Canary 1979; The Mirror Crack'd 1980; Gandhi 1982; The Dresser 1983; Never Say Never Again 1983; The Bounty 1984; The Shooting Party 1984; Wild Geese II 1985; Return from the River Kwai 1988; Robin Hood 1990; A Feast at Midnight 1994; A Month by the Lake 1994; Forbidden Territory: Stanley's Search for Livingstone 1997; Prince Valiant 1997; All the Queen's Men 2001; The Importance of Being Earnest 2002; Nicholas Nickleby 2002; Stage Beauty 2004; Lassie 2005

Fox, Emilia (1974-) The Pianist 2002; Things to Do before You're 30 2004; Cashback 2005; Keeping Mum 2005; Free Jimmy 2006; Dorian Gray 2009;

Vanishing of the Bees 2009; A Thousand Kisses Deep 2011; Suspension of Disbelief 2012; The Carer 2015

Fox, Freddie (1989-) Pride 2014; The Riot Club 2014; Victor Frankenstein 2015

Fox, Huckleberry (1975-) Terms of Endearment 1983; American Dreamer 1984; A Winner Never Quits 1986

Fox, James aka Fox, William (1939-) The Magnet 1950; The Lavender Hill Mob 1951; The Servant 1963; Tamahine 1963; King Rat 1965; Those Magnificent Men in Their Flying Machines 1965; The Chase 1966; Arabella 1967; Thoroughly Modern Millie 1967; Duffy 1968; Isadora 1968; Performance 1970; Runners 1983; Greystoke: the Legend of Tarzan, Lord of the Apes 1984; A Passage to India 1984; Absolute Beginners 1986; Comrades: a Lanternist's Account of the Tolpuddle Martyrs and What Became of Them 1986; The Whistle Blower 1986; High Season 1987; Farewell to the King 1988; The Mighty Quinn 1989; The Russia House 1990; Afraid of the Dark 1991; As You Like It 1992; Hostage 1992; Patriot Games 1992; The Remains of the Day 1993; Circle of Passion 1996; Anna Karenina 1997; Jinnah 1998; Shadow Run 1998; Up at the Villa 1998; Mickey Blue Eyes 1999; The Golden Bowl 2000; Sexy Beast 2000; The Mystic Masseur 2001; The Prince & Me 2004; Charlie and the Chocolate Factory 2005; Mister Lonely 2007; Sherlock Holmes 2009; The Kid 2010; W.E. 2011; The Double 2013; A Long Way from Home 2013

Fox, Kerry (1966-) An Angel at My Table 1990; The Last Days of Chez Nous 1992; Rainbow Warrior 1992; Friends 1993; Country Life 1994; Shallow Grave 1994; The Hanging Garden 1997; Welcome to Sarajevo 1997; The Wisdom of Crocodiles 1998; The Darkest Light 1999; Fanny & Elvis 1999; To Walk with Lions 1999; Intimacy 2000; The Point Men 2000; Black and White 2002; The Gathering 2002; Rag Tale 2005; The Ferryman 2007; Bright Star 2009; Storm 2009; Intruders 2011; Trap for Cinderella 2011; Mental 2012; War Book 2014; Holding the Man 2015

Fox, Laurence (1978-) The Hole 2001; Deathwatch 2002; W.E. 2011

Fox, Matthew (1966-) My Boyfriend's Back 1993; Behind the Mask 1999; Speed Racer 2008; Vantage Point 2008; Alex Cross 2012; Emperor 2012; World War Z 2013; Bone Tomahawk 2015

Fox, Megan (1986-) Confessions of a Teenage Drama Queen 2004; Transformers 2007; How to Lose Friends & Alienate People 2008; Jennifer's Body 2009; Transformers: Revenge of the Fallen 2009; Jonah Hex 2010; Friends with Kids 2011; The Dictator 2012; This Is 40 2012; Teenage Mutant Ninja Turtles 2014; Teenage Mutant Ninja Turtles - Out of the Shadows 2016

Fox, Michael (1921-1996) Top Secret Affair 1957; War of the Satellites 1958

Fox, Michael J (1961-) Midnight Madness 1980; Class of 1984 1982; Back to the Future 1985; Teen Wolf 1985; Dear America: Letters Home from Vietnam 1987; The Secret of My Success 1987; Bright Lights, Big City 1988; Back to the Future Part II 1989; Casualties of War 1989; Back to the Future Part III 1990; Doc Hollywood 1991; The Hard Way 1991; For Love or Money 1993; Homeward Bound: the Incredible Journey 1993; Life with Mikey 1993; Where the Rivers Flow North 1993; Don't Drink the Water 1994; Greedy 1994; The American President 1995; Blue in the Face 1995; Coldblooded 1995; The Frighteners 1996; Homeward Bound II: Lost in San Francisco 1996; Mars Attacks! 1996; Stuart Little 1999; Atlantis: the Lost Empire 2001; Stuart Little 2 2002; Stuart Little 3: Call of the Wild 2005; Mr Calzaghe 2015

Fox, Ronnie Clubbed 2008; Harrigan 2013

Fox, Sidney (1910-1942) Bad Sister 1931; Six Cylinder Love 1931; Don Quixote 1932; Murders in the Rue Morgue 1932; Midnight 1934

Fox, Virginia (1902-1982) Neighbors 1920; The Paleface 1921

Fox, Vivica A (1964-) Independence Day 1996; Set It Off 1996; Booty Call 1997; Soul Food 1997; Why Do Fools Fall in Love? 1998; Idle Hands 1999; Two Can Play That Game 2001; Boat Trip 2002; Kill Bill Vol 1 2003; Ella Enchanted 2004; The Hard Corps 2006; Farewell Mr Kringle 2010;

Sharknado 2: the Second One 2014; Independence Day: Resurgence 2016
Foxe, Earle (1891-1973) Four Sons 1928; Hangman's House 1928; Dance, Fools, Dance 1931
Foxworth, Robert (1941-) The Astral Factor 1976; Treasure of Matecumbe 1976; Airport '77 1977; Damien - Omen II 1978; Prophecy 1979; Act of Love 1980; The Black Marble 1980; Beyond the Stars 1988
Foxworthy, Jeff Racing Stripes 2004; The Fox and the Hound 2 2007
Foxx, Jamie (1967-) The Truth about Cats and Dogs 1996; Booty Call 1997; The Players Club 1998; Any Given Sunday 1999; Held Up 1999; Ali 2001; Breakin' All the Rules 2004; Collateral 2004; Ray 2004; Jarhead 2005; Stealth 2005; Dreamgirls 2006; Miami Vice 2006; The Kingdom 2007; The Soloist 2008; Law Abiding Citizen 2009; Due Date 2010; Horrible Bosses 2011; Rio 2011; Django Unchained 2012; White House Down 2013; The Amazing Spider-Man 2 2014; Annie 2014; Horrible Bosses 2 2014; Rio 2 2014
Foxx, Redd (1922-1991) Cotton Comes to Harlem 1970; Harlem Nights 1989
Foy, Claire (1984-) Season of the Witch 2010; Wreckers 2010; Rosewater 2014
Foy Jr, Eddie (1905-1983) Dixie 1943; And the Angels Sing 1944; The Farmer Takes a Wife 1953; Lucky Me 1954; Seven Little Foys 1955; The Pajama Game 1957; Bells Are Ringing 1960; 30 Is a Dangerous Age, Cynthia 1968
Foy, Mackenzie Breaking Dawn Part Two 2012; The Conjuring 2013; Interstellar 2014
Foyt, Victoria Babyfever 1994; Last Summer in the Hamptons 1995; Déjà Vu 1997
Frain, James (1969-) Loch Ness 1995; Nothing Personal 1995; Daniel Defoe's Robinson Crusoe 1996; Rasputin 1996; Vigo: Passion for Life 1997; Hilary and Jackie 1998; What Rats Won't Do 1998; Sunshine 1999; Deception 2000; Where the Heart Is 2000; The Count of Monte Cristo 2001; Path to War 2002; Into the Blue 2005; The Front Line 2006; Tron Legacy 2010; Water for Elephants 2011
Frakes, Jonathan (1952-) Star Trek: Generations 1994; Star Trek: First Contact 1996; Star Trek: Insurrection 1998; Star Trek: Nemesis 2002
Frame, Grazina What a Crazy World 1963; Every Day's a Holiday 1964
François, Déborah (1987-) L'Enfant 2005; The Page Turner 2006; Female Agents 2007; The First Day of the Rest of Your Life 2007; Unmade Beds 2009; The Monk 2011; Populaire 2012
France, C V (1868-1949) The Skin Game 1931; Lord Edgware Dies 1934; Scrooge 1935; Victoria the Great 1937; If I Were King 1938; Strange Boarders 1938; The Ware Case 1938; A Yank at Oxford 1938; Cheer Boys Cheer 1939; Went the Day Well? 1942
Francella, Guillermo Rudo y Cursi 2008; The Clan 2015
Francen, Victor (1888-1977) J'Accuse 1938; The End of the Day 1939; Hold Back the Dawn 1941; Ten Gentlemen from West Point 1942; The Tuttles of Tahiti 1942; The Conspirators 1944; The Desert Song 1944; In Our Time 1944; Passage to Marseille 1944; Confidential Agent 1945; San Antonio 1945; The Beast with Five Fingers 1946; Night and Day 1946; Adventures of Captain Fabian 1951; Hell and High Water 1954; Bedevilled 1955; Fanny 1961
Francey, Micheline (1919-1969) The Raven 1943; A Cage of Nightingales 1945
Franchi, Franco (1928-1992) Dr Goldfoot and the Girl Bombs 1966; Kaos 1984
Francine, Francis Flaming Creatures 1963; Lonesome Cowboys 1968
Franciosa, Anthony aka **Franciosa, Tony** (1928-2006) A Face in the Crowd 1957; A Hatful of Rain 1957; This Could Be the Night 1957; Wild Is the Wind 1957; The Long, Hot Summer 1958; Career 1959; The Naked Maja 1959; The Story on Page One 1959; Go Naked in the World 1961; Period of Adjustment 1962; The Pleasure Seekers 1964; Rio Conchos 1964; Assault on a Queen 1966; A Man Could Get Killed 1966; Fathom 1967; The Sweet Ride 1967; In Enemy Country 1968; A Man Called Gannon 1969; Across 110th Street 1972; Ghost in the Noonday Sun 1973; The Drowning Pool 1975; Firepower 1979; The World Is Full of Married Men 1979; Death Wish II 1981; Tenebrae 1982; Backstreet Dreams 1990; City Hall 1996

Francis, Alec B aka **Francis, Alec** (1867-1934) Camille 1927; Feet First 1930
Francis, Anne (1930-2011) Dreamboat 1952; A Lion Is in the Streets 1953; The Rocket Man 1954; Rogue Cop 1954; Susan Slept Here 1954; Bad Day at Black Rock 1955; The Blackboard Jungle 1955; Forbidden Planet 1956; Don't Go near the Water 1957; The Hired Gun 1957; The Crowded Sky 1960; Girl of the Night 1960; Brainstorm 1965; The Satan Bug 1965; Funny Girl 1968; The Intruders 1970; Pancho Villa 1971; Born Again 1978; Little Vegas 1990
Francis, Arlene (1908-2001) Too Much Johnson 1938; All My Sons 1948; One, Two, Three 1961; The Thrill of It All 1963
Francis, Connie (1938-) Where the Boys Are 1960; Follow the Boys 1963
Francis, Derek (1923-1984) The Hi-Jackers 1963; The Tomb of Ligeia 1964; Press for Time 1966; What's Good for the Goose 1969
Francis, Dick (1920-2010) Dreaming 1944; Here Comes the Sun 1945
Francis, Jan (1951-) Dracula 1979; Champions 1983
Francis, Kay (1899-1968) The Marriage Playground 1929; Raffles 1930; The Virtuous Sin 1930; Guilty Hands 1931; Ladies' Man 1931; Cynara 1932; Jewel Robbery 1932; One Way Passage 1932; Trouble in Paradise 1932; British Agent 1934; Mandalay 1934; Wonder Bar 1934; I Found Stella Parish 1935; The White Angel 1936; Another Dawn 1937; Confession 1937; In Name Only 1939; King of the Underworld 1939; It's a Date 1940; When the Daltons Rode 1940; Charley's Aunt 1941; The Feminine Touch 1941; Always in My Heart 1942
Francis, Noel (1906-1959) Bachelor Apartment 1931; Blonde Crazy 1931; Smart Money 1931; I Am a Fugitive from a Chain Gang 1932
Francis, Raymond (1911-1987) Carrington VC 1954; Double Cross 1955
Francis, Robert (1930-1955) The Caine Mutiny 1954; They Rode West 1954; The Long Gray Line 1955
Franciscus, James (1934-1991) The Outsider 1961; Miracle of the White Stallions 1963; Youngblood Hawke 1964; Beneath the Planet of the Apes 1969; Marooned 1969; The Valley of Gwangi 1969; Hell Boats 1970; Cat o'Nine Tails 1971; Jonathan Livingston Seagull 1973; The Amazing Dobermans 1976; Good Guys Wear Black 1977; The Greek Tycoon 1978; Killer Fish 1979; City on Fire 1979; When Time Ran Out 1980; Butterfly 1982
Francks, Don (1932-2016) Finian's Rainbow 1968; My Bloody Valentine 1981; Terminal Choice 1983; Lie with Me 2005
Franco, Dave (1985-) Death & Life of Charlie St Cloud 2010; 21 Jump Street 2012; Bad Neighbours 2014; Unfinished Business 2015; Bad Neighbours 2 2016; Nerve 2016; Now You See Me 2 2016
Franco, James (1978-) James Dean 2001; City by the Sea 2002; Sonny 2002; Spider-Man 2002; The Company 2003; Spider-Man 2 2004; Annapolis 2005; The Great Raid 2005; Tristan + Isolde 2005; Flyboys 2006; In the Valley of Elah 2007; Spider-Man 3 2007; Milk 2008; Nights in Rodanthe 2008; Pineapple Express 2008; Date Night 2010; Eat Pray Love 2010; Howl 2010; Your Highness 2010; 127 Hours 2011; Rise of the Planet of the Apes 2011; Cherry 2012; The Iceman 2012; Spring Breakers 2012; As I Lay Dying 2013; A Fuller Life 2013; Homefront 2013; Lovelace 2013; Oz the Great and Powerful 2013; Palo Alto 2013; Third Person 2013; This Is the End 2013; Good People 2014; The Interview 2014; True Story 2015; Goat 2016; Sausage Party 2016; Why Him? 2016
François, Emilie Sense and Sensibility 1995; Paws 1997
François, Jacques (1920-2003) South of Algiers 1952; To Paris with Love 1954; Les Grandes Manoeuvres 1955; North Star 1996
Frank, Horst (1929-1999) Dead Run 1967; Django, Prepare a Coffin 1968; Death in the Sun 1975
Frank, Jason David (1973-) Mighty Morphin Power Rangers: the Movie 1995; Turbo: a Power Rangers Adventure 1997
Frankau, Ronald (1894-1951) Dual Alibi 1946; The Ghosts of Berkeley Square 1947
Frankel, Mark (1962-1996) Leon the Pig Farmer 1992; Solitaire for 2 1994; Roseanna's Grave 1996

Franken, Al (1951-) Stuart Saves His Family 1995; Manufacturing Dissent: Uncovering Michael Moore 2007
Franken, Steve (1932-2012) Which Way to the Front? 1970; Avalanche 1978
Frankeur, Paul (1905-1975) Jour de Fête 1947; Nous Sommes Tous des Assassins 1952; Honour among Thieves 1954; A Monkey in Winter 1962; The Milky Way 1969; The Discreet Charm of the Bourgeoisie 1972
Frankfather, William (1944-1998) Alamo Bay 1985; Cool World 1992
Frankham, David aka **Frankham, Dave** (1926-) Return of the Fly 1959; One Hundred and One Dalmatians 1960; Master of the World 1961
Franklin, Aretha (1942-) The Blues Brothers 1980; Blues Brothers 2000 1998
Franklin, Diane Amityville II: the Possession 1982; Better Off Dead 1985; TerrorVision 1986
Franklin, Marcus Carl aka **Franklin, Marcus** Lackawanna Blues 2005; Be Kind Rewind 2007; I'm Not There. 2007; The Art of Getting By 2011
Franklin, Pamela (1949-) The Innocents 1961; The Lion 1962; Flipper's New Adventure 1964; The Third Secret 1964; A Tiger Walks 1964; The Nanny 1965; Our Mother's House 1967; The Night of the Following Day 1968; The Prime of Miss Jean Brodie 1969; Sinful Davey 1969; And Soon the Darkness 1970; Ace Eli and Rodger of the Skies 1973; The Legend of Hell House 1973; The Food of the Gods 1976
Franklyn, Leo (1897-1975) The Night We Dropped a Clanger 1959; And the Same to You 1960; The Night We Got the Bird 1960
Franklyn, William (1926-2006) Quatermass II 1957; That Woman Opposite 1957; Pit of Darkness 1961; The Intelligence Men 1965; Cul-de-Sac 1966; Ooh... You Are Awful 1972; The Satanic Rites of Dracula 1973; Nutcracker 1982
Franks, Chloe (1959-) Who Slew Auntie Roo? 1971; A Little Night Music 1977
Franky G The Italian Job 2003; Wonderland 2003; Saw II 2005
Franz, Arthur (1920-2006) Abbott and Costello Meet the Invisible Man 1951; Flight to Mars 1951; The Member of the Wedding 1952; The Sniper 1952; The Eddie Cantor Story 1953; Invaders from Mars 1953; Bad for Each Other 1954; Battle Taxi 1955; Beyond a Reasonable Doubt 1956; The Devil's Hairpin 1957; The Unholy Wife 1957; Woman Obsessed 1959; The Atomic Submarine 1960; The Human Factor 1975; That Championship Season 1982
Franz, Dennis (1944-) Dressed to Kill 1980; Blow Out 1981; Psycho II 1983; Body Double 1984; A Fine Mess 1986; The Package 1989; Die Hard 2: Die Harder 1990; American Buffalo 1995; City of Angels 1998
Franz, Eduard (1902-1983) Hollow Triumph 1948; Outpost in Morocco 1949; Wake of the Red Witch 1949; Whirlpool 1949; The Magnificent Yankee 1950; The Jazz Singer 1952; Dream Wife 1953; Latin Lovers 1953; Broken Lance 1954; Sign of the Pagan 1954; Lady Godiva 1955; White Feather 1955; The Burning Hills 1956; A Certain Smile 1958; The Last of the Fast Guns 1958; Beauty and the Beast 1962
Franz, Elizabeth (1941-) Jacknife 1988; Christmas with the Kranks 2004
Franzese, Daniel Mean Girls 2004; I Spit on Your Grave 2010
Frappat, Francis Noir et Blanc 1986; Requiem 1998
Fraser, Bill (1908-1987) The Captain's Paradise 1953; Orders Are Orders 1954; The Man Who Liked Funerals 1959; I've Gotta Horse 1965; Joey Boy 1965; Masquerade 1965; The Best House in London 1968; Captain Nemo and the Underwater City 1969; Up Pompeii 1971; Up the Chastity Belt 1971; That's Your Funeral 1972; Up the Front 1972; The Amorous Milkman 1974
Fraser, Brendan (1968-) California Man 1992; School Ties 1992; Younger and Younger 1993; Airheads 1994; The Scout 1994; With Honors 1994; The Passion of Darkly Noon 1995; Mrs Winterbourne 1996; George of the Jungle 1997; Blast from the Past 1998; Gods and Monsters 1998; Dudley Do-Right 1999; The Mummy 1999; Bedazzled 2000; Monkeybone 2000; The Mummy Returns 2001; The Quiet American 2002; Crash 2004; Looney Tunes: Back in Action 2004; The Air I Breathe 2007; Inkheart 2007; Journey to the Center of the Earth 2008; The Mummy: Tomb of the Dragon Emperor 2008; GI Joe: the Rise of Cobra 2009;

Extraordinary Measures 2010; Furry Vengeance 2010; Escape from Planet Earth 2013; The Nut Job 2014
Fraser, Brent The Chocolate War 1988; Wild Orchid 2: Two Shades of Blue 1992
Fraser, David Teenage Mutant Ninja Turtles III 1992; Airborne 1993
Fraser, Duncan Watchers 1988; The Reflecting Skin 1990; Needful Things 1993; Alaska 1996; Unforgettable 1996
Fraser, Elisabeth (1920-2005) One Foot in Heaven 1941; So Big 1953; Young at Heart 1955; The Tunnel of Love 1958; Ask Any Girl 1959; Two for the Seesaw 1962; A Patch of Blue 1965
Fraser, Helen (1942-) Billy Liar 1963; The Uncle 1964; Something to Hide 1971
Fraser, Hugh The Draughtsman's Contract 1982; 101 Dalmatians 1996
Fraser, John (1931-) Valley of Song 1953; The Dam Busters 1954; Touch and Go 1955; The Good Companions 1956; The Wind Cannot Read 1958; The Trials of Oscar Wilde 1960; Tunes of Glory 1960; El Cid 1961; Fury at Smugglers Bay 1961; Waltz of the Toreadors 1962; Tamahine 1963; Repulsion 1965; A Study in Terror 1965; Doctor in Clover 1966; Isadora 1968; Schizo 1976
Fraser, Laura (1976-) Small Faces 1995; Cousin Bette 1997; Left Luggage 1997; Divorcing Jack 1998; The Match 1999; Titus 1999; Virtual Sexuality 1999; Whatever Happened to Harold Smith? 1999; Kevin & Perry Go Large 2000; A Knight's Tale 2001; Devil's Gate 2002; 16 Years of Alcohol 2003; The Flying Scotsman 2006; Land of the Blind 2006; Nina's Heavenly Delights 2006; The Boys Are Back 2009; Cuckoo 2009; Castles in the Sky 2014
Fraser, Liz (1933-) Desert Mice 1959; I'm All Right Jack 1959; The Night We Dropped a Clanger 1959; Carry On Regardless 1960; Doctor in Love 1960; The Night We Got the Bird 1960; The Rebel 1960; Two Way Stretch 1960; Double Bunk 1961; The Painted Smile 1961; A Pair of Briefs 1961; Raising the Wind 1961; The Amorous Prawn 1962; Carry On Cruising 1962; Live Now - Pay Later 1962; Carry On Cabby 1963; The Americanization of Emily 1964; Every Day's a Holiday 1965; Up the Junction 1967; Dad's Army 1971; Adventures of a Taxi Driver 1975; Carry On Behind 1975; Confessions of a Driving Instructor 1976; Under the Doctor 1976; Adventures of a Private Eye 1977; Rosie Dixon: Night Nurse 1978; Chicago Joe and the Showgirl 1989
Fraser, Richard (1913-1971) A Yank in the RAF 1941; The Picture of Dorian Gray 1945; Bedlam 1946
Fraser, Ronald (1930-1997) The Long and the Short and the Tall 1960; The Best of Enemies 1961; The Pot Carriers 1962; The Punch and Judy Man 1962; Crooks in Cloisters 1963; Girl in the Headlines 1963; Private Potter 1963; The Beauty Jungle 1964; The Flight of the Phoenix 1965; Fathom 1967; The Whisperers 1967; The Killing of Sister George 1968; Sebastian 1968; Sinful Davey 1969; The Rise and Rise of Michael Rimmer 1970; Too Late the Hero 1970; The Magnificent Seven Deadly Sins 1971; Ooh... You Are Awful 1972; Rentadick 1972; Paper Tiger 1974; Swallows and Amazons 1974; Come Play with Me 1977; Hardcore 1977; Let Him Have It 1991; The Mystery of Edwin Drood 1993
Fraser, Sally It Conquered the World 1956; Roadracers 1958; War of the Colossal Beast 1958
Fraser, Shelagh (1922-2000) The History of Mr Polly 1948; Raising a Riot 1955
Frawley, James (1937-) Ladybug, Ladybug 1963; The Troublemaker 1964
Frawley, John (1936-1999) The Devil's Playground 1976; Dallas Doll 1994
Frawley, William (1887-1966) Bolero 1934; The Lemon Drop Kid 1934; Desire 1936; The General Died at Dawn 1936; The Princess Comes Across 1936; Strike Me Pink 1936; Something to Sing About 1937; Mad about Music 1938; The Adventures of Huckleberry Finn 1939; Rose of Washington Square 1939; Rhythm on the River 1940; The Bride Came COD 1941; Footsteps in the Dark 1941; Gentleman Jim 1942; Roxie Hart 1942; The Fighting Seabees 1944; Flame of the Barbary Coast 1945; I Wonder Who's Kissing Her Now 1947; Miracle on 34th Street 1947; Mother Wore Tights 1947; The Babe Ruth Story 1948; The Girl from Manhattan 1948; Abbott and Costello Meet the Invisible Man 1951; The Lemon Drop Kid 1951; Rhubarb 1951; Rancho Notorious 1952

Frazee, Jane (1918-1985) Buck Privates 1941; Hellzapoppin' 1941; Rosie the Riveter 1944; Under California Stars 1948
Frazer, Dan (1921-2011) Lilies of the Field 1963; Cleopatra Jones 1973; The Super Cops 1973
Frazer, Robert (1891-1944) White Zombie 1932; The Trail Beyond 1934
Frazer, Rupert (1891-1944) The Shooting Party 1984; Third Star 2010
Frazier, Ron (1939-2003) Rollover 1981; The Road Home 1989; Shadow Makers 1989
Frazier, Sheila (1948-) Superfly 1972; The Super Cops 1973; Three the Hard Way 1974
Frears, Stephen (1941-) Long Shot 1978; Chéri 2009
Frechette, Peter (1956-) Grease 2 1982; The Unholy 1988
Frecheville, James Animal Kingdom 2009; Adore 2013
Fred, Gunnel (1955-) Ake and His World 1984; Saraband 2003
Frederici, Blanche (1878-1933) Sadie Thompson 1928; The Trespasser 1929; Billy the Kid 1930; Night Nurse 1931; A Farewell to Arms 1932; If I Had a Million 1932; The Barbarian 1933; Secrets 1933; It Happened One Night 1934
Frederick, Lynne (1954-1994) No Blade of Grass 1970; Nicholas and Alexandra 1971; Vampire Circus 1971; The Amazing Mr Blunden 1972; Henry VIII and His Six Wives 1972; Phase IV 1973; Schizo 1976; Voyage of the Damned 1976; The Prisoner of Zenda 1979
Frederick, Pauline (1883-1938) This Modern Age 1931; Thank You, Mr Moto 1937
Frederick, Vicki (1954-) The California Dolls 1981; A Chorus Line 1985; Scissors 1991
Freed, Alan (1922-1965) Don't Knock the Rock 1956; Rock around the Clock 1956; Go, Johnny, Go! 1959
Freed, Bert (1919-1994) The Company She Keeps 1950; Where the Sidewalk Ends 1950; Detective Story 1951; Red Mountain 1951; Men of the Fighting Lady 1954; The Gazebo 1959; Evel Knievel 1971
Freeman Jr, Al (1934-2012) Dutchman 1966; The Lost Man 1969; Seven Hours to Judgment 1988; Malcolm X 1992; Down in the Delta 1997
Freeman, Alan (1927-2006) Dr Terror's House of Horrors 1964; Sebastian 1968
Freeman, Howard (1899-1967) Hitler's Madman 1943; Margin for Error 1943; Slightly Dangerous 1943; Once upon a Time 1944; Abilene Town 1945; The Blue Dahlia 1946; The Long Night 1947; The Girl from Manhattan 1948; Letter from an Unknown Woman 1948; Perfect Strangers 1950; Double Dynamite 1951; Million Dollar Mermaid 1952
Freeman, J E (1946-2014) Miller's Crossing 1990; Dream with the Fishes 1996; Mystery Woman 2003
Freeman, Joan (1941-) Panic in Year Zero 1962; Tower of London 1962; The Three Stooges Go around the World in a Daze 1963; Roustabout 1964; The Rounders 1965; The Fastest Guitar Alive 1966
Freeman, K Todd The End of Violence 1997; Grosse Pointe Blank 1997
Freeman, Kathleen (1919-2001) Love Is Better than Ever 1951; The Fly 1958; The Ladies' Man 1961; Madison Avenue 1962; The Nutty Professor 1963; The Disorderly Orderly 1964; The Rounders 1965; Three on a Couch 1966; The Blues Brothers 1980; Reckless Kelly 1993; Naked Gun 33⅓: the Final Insult 1994; ...At First Sight 1995; Shrek 2001
Freeman, Martin (1971-) Ali G indahouse 2002; The Good Night 2005; The Hitchhiker's Guide to the Galaxy 2005; Breaking and Entering 2006; Confetti 2006; The All Together 2007; Nativity! 2009; Wild Target 2009; Swinging with the Finkels 2010; The Hobbit: an Unexpected Journey 2012; The Pirates! in an Adventure with Scientists! 2012; The Hobbit: the Desolation of Smaug 2013; Saving Santa 2013; Svengali 2013; The World's End 2013; The Hobbit: the Battle of the Five Armies 2014; Whiskey Tango Foxtrot 2016
Freeman, Mona (1926-2014) Till We Meet Again 1944; Together Again 1944; Black Beauty 1946; Dear Ruth 1947; Mother Wore Tights 1947; Isn't It Romantic 1948; Dear Wife 1949; The Heiress 1949; Streets of Laredo 1949; Branded 1950; Copper Canyon 1950; I Was a Shoplifter 1950; Darling, How Could You! 1951; Flesh and Fury 1952; Jumping Jacks 1952; Angel Face 1953;

Battle Cry 1955; The Road to Denver 1955; Dragoon Wells Massacre 1957

Freeman, Morgan (1937-) Who Says I Can't Ride a Rainbow? 1971; Brubaker 1980; Eyewitness 1981; Harry and Son 1984; Teachers 1984; Marie: a True Story 1985; That Was Then... This Is Now 1985; Resting Place 1986; Street Smart 1987; Blood Money 1988; Clean and Sober 1988; Driving Miss Daisy 1989; Glory 1989; Johnny Handsome 1989; Lean on Me 1989; The Bonfire of the Vanities 1990; The Power of One 1991; Robin Hood: Prince of Thieves 1991; Unforgiven 1992; The Shawshank Redemption 1994; Moll Flanders 1995; Outbreak 1995; Se7en 1995; Chain Reaction 1996; The Long Way Home 1996; Amistad 1997; Hard Rain 1997; Kiss the Girls 1997; Deep Impact 1998; Nurse Betty 2000; Under Suspicion 2000; Along Came a Spider 2001; High Crimes 2002; Levity 2002; The Sum of All Fears 2002; Bruce Almighty 2003; Dreamcatcher 2003; The Big Bounce 2004; Million Dollar Baby 2004; Batman Begins 2005; Edison 2005; March of the Penguins 2005; An Unfinished Life 2005; Unleashed 2005; War of the Worlds 2005; The Contract 2006; Lucky Number Slevin 2006; Evan Almighty 2007; Feast of Love 2007; Gone Baby Gone 2007; The Bucket List 2008; The Dark Knight 2008; Wanted 2008; The Heist 2009; Invictus 2009; Red 2010; Dolphin Tale 2011; The Dark Knight Rises 2012; The Life of Riley 2012; Last Vegas 2013; Now You See Me 2013; Oblivion 2013; Olympus Has Fallen 2013; Dolphin Tale 2 2014; The Lego Movie 2014; Lucy 2014; Ruth & Alex 2014; Transcendence 2014; The Last Knights 2015; Momentum 2015; Ted 2 2015; Ben-Hur 2016; London Has Fallen 2016; Now You See Me 2 2016

Freeman, Paul (1943-) The Dogs of War 1980; Raiders of the Lost Ark 1981; An Unsuitable Job for a Woman 1981; The Sender 1982; Shanghai Surprise 1986; A World Apart 1987; Without a Clue 1988; The Last Island 1990; May Wine 1990; Aces: Iron Eagle III 1992; Just like a Woman 1992; Mighty Morphin Power Rangers: the Movie 1995; Double Team 1997; The Devil's Arithmetic 1999; A Fantastic Fear of Everything 2012

Frees, Paul (1920-1986) Riot in Cell Block 11 1954; Suddenly 1954; Francis in the Haunted House 1956; Space Master X 7 1958; Gay Purr-ee 1962

Frégis, Lucien (1904-1979) Monsieur Hulot's Holiday 1953; Mon Oncle 1958

Freindlikh, Alisa (1934-) Agony 1975; Stalker 1979

Freiss, Stéphane (1960-) Vagabond 1985; The King's Whore 1990; Betty Fisher and Other Stories 2001; Crime Spree 2002; Monsieur N 2003; 5x2 2004

Frémont, Thierry Merci la Vie 1991; Femme Fatale 2002

French, Andrew Exorcist: the Beginning 2004; Dominion: Prequel to the Exorcist 2005

French, Bruce Pipe Dreams 1976; Black Eagle 1988

French, Dawn (1957-) The Supergrass 1985; Eat the Rich 1987; The Adventures of Pinocchio 1996; Maybe Baby 1999; Milk 1999; The Chronicles of Narnia: The Lion, the Witch and the Wardrobe 2005; Coraline 2008; Animals United 2010

French, Harold (1897-1997) When London Sleeps 1932; A Fire Has Been Arranged 1935

French, Leslie (1904-1999) Orders to Kill 1958; The Singer Not the Song 1960; The Leopard 1962; More than a Miracle 1967

French, Valerie (1931-1990) Jubal 1956; Decision at Sundown 1957; The Garment Jungle 1957; The 27th Day 1957; Shalako 1968

French, Victor (1934-1989) Charro! 1969; Rio Lobo 1970; Chato's Land 1971; Wild Rovers 1971; The Other 1972

Fresnay, Pierre (1897-1975) Marius 1931; Fanny 1932; The Man Who Knew Too Much 1934; Königsmark 1935; César 1936; Mademoiselle Docteur 1936; La Grande Illusion 1937; The Raven 1943; Monsieur Vincent 1947; Le Défroqué 1953

Fresson, Bernard (1931-2002) Hiroshima, Mon Amour 1959; Je T'Aime, Je T'Aime 1968; French Connection II 1975; The Tenant 1976; Right Bank, Left Bank 1984; Street of No Return 1989; Place Vendôme 1998

Frewer, Matt (1958-) Cannonball Fever 1989; Far from Home 1989; Honey, I Shrunk the Kids 1989; Short Time 1990; The Positively True Adventures of the Alleged Texas

Cheerleader-Murdering Mom 1993; Kissinger and Nixon 1995; Lawnmower Man 2: Beyond Cyberspace 1995; National Lampoon's Senior Trip 1995; Breast Men 1997; A Home at the End of the World 2004; Watchmen 2009; Battle of the Bulbs 2010

Frey, Barbara Love at Twenty 1962; Requiescant 1967

Frey, Leonard (1938-1988) The Magic Christian 1969; The Boys in the Band 1970; Fiddler on the Roof 1971; Tattoo 1980; Where the Buffalo Roam 1980

Frey, Nathaniel (1913-1970) Kiss Them for Me 1957; Damn Yankees 1958; What's So Bad about Feeling Good? 1968

Frey, Sami (1937-) La Vérité 1960; Cleo from 5 to 7 1961; Thérèse Desqueyroux 1962; Bande à Part 1964; Les Mariés de l'An Deux 1971; César and Rosalie 1972; Pourquoi Pas! 1977; Ecoute Voir... 1978; The Little Drummer Girl 1984; Black Widow 1987; D'Artagnan's Daughter 1994; Traps 1994

Fricker, Brenda (1944-) My Left Foot 1989; The Field 1990; Utz 1992; Deadly Advice 1993; So I Married an Axe Murderer 1993; Angels in the Outfield 1994; A Man of No Importance 1994; Moll Flanders 1995; Swann 1996; A Time to Kill 1996; Masterminds 1997; Resurrection Man 1997; The War Bride 2001; Veronica Guerin 2003; Inside I'm Dancing 2004; Trauma 2004; Tara Road 2005; Closing the Ring 2006; A Long Way from Home 2013

Frid, Jonathan (1924-2012) House of Dark Shadows 1970; Seizure 1974

Fridh, Gertrud (1921-1984) A Ship to India 1947; The Magician 1958; The Devil's Eye 1960

Friedel, Christian The White Ribbon 2009; Amour Fou 2014; 13 Minutes 2015

Friedlander, Judah American Splendor 2003; The Wrestler 2008

Friedman, Peter (1949-) The Seventh Sign 1988; Single White Female 1992; Blink 1994; [Safe] 1995; The Savages 2007

Friedman, Shraga (1923-1970) Sallah 1964; Bloomfield 1969

Friedrich, Georg Import Export 2007; The North Face 2008; Breathing 2011; Faust 2011

Friedrich, John Almost Summer 1977; The Wanderers 1979

Friel, Anna (1976-) The Land Girls 1997; The Stringer 1997; Rogue Trader 1998; All for Love 1999; Mad Cows 1999; A Midsummer Night's Dream 1999; An Everlasting Piece 2000; Sunset Strip 2000; Me without You 2001; The War Bride 2001; Timeline 2003; Perfect Strangers 2004; Goal! 2005; Niagara Motel 2005; Goal II: Living the Dream 2007; Bathory 2008; Land of the Lost 2009; London Boulevard 2010; Limitless 2011; Having You 2013; The Look of Love 2013

Friels, Colin (1952-) Kangaroo 1986; Malcolm 1986; Warm Nights on a Slow Moving Train 1986; Ground Zero 1987; High Tide 1987; Darkman 1990; Class Action 1991; Dingo 1991; A Good Man in Africa 1993; Angel Baby 1995; Back of Beyond 1995; Cosi 1996; Mr Reliable 1996; Dark City 1998; The Man Who Sued God 2001; Black and White 2002; The Mystery of Natalie Wood 2004; The Book of Revelation 2006

Friend, Philip (1915-1987) The Bells Go Down 1943; Great Day 1944; Enchantment 1948; Thunder on the Hill 1951; Background 1953; Desperate Moment 1953; The Diamond 1954; Dick Turpin - Highwayman 1956; Son of Robin Hood 1958

Friend, Rupert (1981-) Mrs Palfrey at The Claremont 2005; Outlaw 2006; The Boy in the Striped Pyjamas 2008; The Young Victoria 2008; Chéri 2009; The Kid 2010; 5 Days of War 2011; Starred Up 2013; Hitman: Agent 47 2015

Frinton, Freddie (1911-1968) Forces' Sweetheart 1953; What a Whopper! 1961

Frisch, Arno Benny's Video 1992; Funny Games 1997

Friske, Zhanna Night Watch 2004; Day Watch 2006

Frith, Rebecca Me Myself I 1999; Strange Planet 1999

Fritsch, Willy (1901-1973) Spies 1928; The Woman in the Moon 1929; Congress Dances 1931

Frizzell, Lou (1920-1979) The Stalking Moon 1968; Duel 1971; Hickey and Boggs 1972; The Other 1972

Fröbe, Gert aka **Froebe, Gert** aka **Frobe, Gert** (1913-1988) Celui Qui Doit Mourir 1957; The Thousand Eyes of Dr Mabuse 1960; Banana Peel 1964; Goldfinger 1964; A High Wind in

Jamaica 1965; Those Magnificent Men in Their Flying Machines 1965; Triple Cross 1966; Jules Verne's Rocket to the Moon 1967; Chitty Chitty Bang Bang 1968; Monte Carlo or Bust! 1969; Dollars 1971; Ludwig 1973; And Then There Were None 1974; The Serpent's Egg 1977

Froboess, Cornelia aka **Froboess, Conny** (1943-) The Vanishing Corporal 1962; Veronika Voss 1982

Froggatt, Joanne In Our Name 2010; Filth 2013; Still Life 2013

Fröhlich, Gustav (1902-1987) Metropolis 1926; Asphalt 1928

Froler, Samuel (1957-) Best Intentions 1992; Private Confessions 1996

Fröling, Ewa (1952-) Fanny and Alexander 1982; The Ox 1991

Frost, Alex Elephant 2003; Drillbit Taylor 2007

Frost, Lindsay (1962-) Dead Heat 1988; Danielle Steel's Palomino 1991; In the Line of Duty: Smoke Jumpers 1996; Death in the Shadows: the Sam Sheppard Story 1998; The Ring 2002

Frost, Nick (1972-) Shaun of the Dead 2004; Kinky Boots 2005; Hot Fuzz 2007; Wild Child 2008; The Boat That Rocked 2009; Attack the Block 2011; Paul 2010; The Adventures of Tintin: the Secret of the Unicorn 2011; Snow White and the Huntsman 2012; The World's End 2013; Cuban Fury 2014; Unfinished Business 2015; The Huntsman: Winter's War 2016

Frost, Sadie (1968-) Diamond Skulls 1989; Bram Stoker's Dracula 1992; Shopping 1993; Splitting Heirs 1993; Magic Hunter 1994; A Pyromaniac's Love Story 1995; Captain Jack 1998; Final Cut 1998; Rancid Aluminium 1999; Love, Honour and Obey 2000; Set the Thames on Fire 2015

Frot, Catherine (1956-) Un Air de Famille 1996; Le Dîner de Cons 1998; La Nouvelle Eve 1998; [One] Cavale 2002; [Three] Après la Vie 2002; [Two] Un Couple Epatant 2002; The Page Turner 2006; Angel of Mine 2008; Marguerite 2015

Fry, Stephen (1957-) The Good Father 1986; Peter's Friends 1992; IQ 1994; The Steal 1994; The Wind in the Willows 1996; Wilde 1997; A Civil Action 1998; The Tichborne Claimant 1998; Londinium 1999; Whatever Happened to Harold Smith? 1999; Relative Values 2000; Gosford Park 2001; Thunderpants 2002; Bright Young Things 2003; Le Divorce 2003; The Life and Death of Peter Sellers 2003; Tooth 2003; MirrorMask 2004; A Cock and Bull Story 2005; The Hitchhiker's Guide to the Galaxy 2005; V for Vendetta 2005; St Trinian's 2007; Alice in Wonderland 2010; Animals United 2010; Sherlock Holmes: a Game of Shadows 2011; The Hobbit: the Desolation of Smaug 2013; The Man Who Knew Infinity 2015; Alice through the Looking Glass 2016; The Killing$ of Tony Blair 2016; Love & Friendship 2016

Frye, Dwight (1899-1943) Dracula 1931; Frankenstein 1931; The Vampire Bat 1933

Frye, Soleil Moon (1976-) The Revenge of Pumpkinhead - Blood Wings 1994; Motel Blue 1997

Fuchs, Jason Spooky House 1999; Holy Rollers 2010

Fuchs, Leo (1911-1994) The Frisco Kid 1979; Avalon 1990

Fudge, Alan (1944-) Two People 1973; Bug 1975; Chapter Two 1979; My Demon Lover 1987

Fugard, Athol (1932-) Meetings with Remarkable Men 1979; The Killing Fields 1984

Fugit, Patrick (1982-) Almost Famous 2000; Spun 2002; White Oleander 2002; Dead Birds 2004; The Moguls 2005; Wristcutters: a Love Story 2006; Cirque du Freak: the Vampire's Assistant 2009; Horsemen 2009; Cinema Verite 2011; We Bought a Zoo 2011; Thanks for Sharing 2012; Queen of Earth 2015

Fuhrman, Isabelle Orphan 2009; Sammy's Great Escape 2012; Cell 2016

Fuji, Takako (1972-) The Grudge: Ju-On 2003; Ju-On: The Grudge 2 2003

Fujiki, Yu (1931-2005) King Kong vs Godzilla 1962; Godzilla vs Mothra 1964; War of the Gargantuas 1970

Fujita, Susumu (1912-1991) Sanshiro Sugata 1943; No Regrets for Our Youth 1946; Escapade in Japan 1957; The Hidden Fortress 1958; Yojimbo 1961

Fujiwara, Kamatari (1905-1985) Seven Samurai 1954; The Hidden Fortress 1958; Mickey One 1965

Fujiwara, Tatsuya (1982-) Battle Royale 2000; Battle Royale 2: Requiem 2003; Death Game 2010

Fujiwara, Toshizo A Scene at the Sea 1991; Mr Baseball 1992

Fukada, Kyoko Ring 2 1998; Dolls 2002; Kamikaze Girls: the End 2004; YatterMan 2009

Fukatsu, Eri Villain 2010; Journey to the Shore 2015

Fukikoshi, Mitsuru The Twilight Samurai 2002; Cold Fish 2010; Himizu 2011

Fulford, Christopher aka **Fulford, Chris** (1955-) Resurrected 1989; Bedrooms and Hallways 1998; One of the Hollywood Ten 2000; D-Tox 2001; The Aryan Couple 2004; Millions 2004; Pierrepoint 2005; Tower Block 2012; Queen of the Desert 2015

Fuller, Amanda Red White & Blue 2010; Cheap Thrills 2013

Fuller, Dale (1885-1948) The Wedding March 1923; Twentieth Century 1934

Fuller, Dolores (1923-2011) Glen or Glenda 1953; Jail Bait 1954

Fuller, Kurt (1952-) Elvira, Mistress of the Dark 1988; Miracle Mile 1989; Bingo 1991; Eve of Destruction 1991; Calendar Girl 1993; Reflections on a Crime 1994; Diamonds 1999; Auto Focus 2002; Anger Management 2003; The Pursuit of Happyness 2006

Fuller, Lance (1928-2001) Cattle Queen of Montana 1954; Apache Woman 1955; Pearl of the South Pacific 1955; This Island Earth 1955; The She-Creature 1956; Slightly Scarlet 1956; Voodoo Woman 1957; The Bride and the Beast 1958

Fuller, Penny (1940-) A Piano for Mrs Cimino 1982; Miss Rose White 1992

Fuller, Robert (1934-) The Brain from Planet Arous 1958; Incident at Phantom Hill 1966; Return of the Seven 1966; Whatever Happened to Aunt Alice? 1969; The Hard Ride 1971; Mustang Country 1976

Fuller, Samuel aka **Fuller, Sam** (1911-1997) Pierrot le Fou 1965; The Last Movie 1971; The American Friend 1977; 1941 1979; The State of Things 1982; A Return to Salem's Lot 1987; Sons 1989; Somebody to Love 1994

Fullerton, Fiona (1956-) Run Wild, Run Free 1969; Nicholas and Alexandra 1971; Alice's Adventures in Wonderland 1972; A View to a Kill 1985; A Ghost in Monte Carlo 1990

Fulton, Rad (1934-) Hell Bent for Leather 1960; The Last Sunset 1961; No My Darling Daughter 1961

Fulton, Rikki (1924-2004) Gorky Park 1983; Local Hero 1983; Comfort and Joy 1984; The Girl in the Picture 1985

Funicello, Annette aka **Annette** (1942-2013) The Shaggy Dog 1959; Babes in Toyland 1961; Beach Party 1963; Bikini Beach 1964; The Misadventures of Merlin Jones 1964; Muscle Beach Party 1964; Beach Blanket Bingo 1965; Dr Goldfoot and the Bikini Machine 1965; How to Fill a Wild Bikini 1965; The Monkey's Uncle 1965; Ski Party 1965; Fireball 500 1966; Thunder Alley 1967; Head 1968; Back to the Beach 1987

Funk, Terry (1944-) Paradise Alley 1978; Over the Top 1987

Furlong, Edward (1977-) Terminator 2: Judgment Day 1991; American Heart 1992; Pet Sematary II 1992; A Home of Our Own 1993; Brainscan 1994; Little Odessa 1994; The Grass Harp 1995; Before and After 1996; American History X 1998; Pecker 1998; Detroit Rock City 1999; Animal Factory 2000; The Crow: Wicked Prayer 2005; Night of the Demons 2010; The Green Hornet 2011

Furlong, John (1933-2008) Mudhoney 1965; Common-Law Cabin 1967; The Man Next Door 1998

Fürmann, Benno (1972-) Anatomy 2000; The Princess & the Warrior 2000; My House in Umbria 2003; The Sin Eater 2002; Sword of Xanten 2004; Merry Christmas 2005; Mutant Chronicles 2008; The North Face 2008; Speed Racer 2008; In Darkness 2011

Furneaux, Yvonne (1928-) The Master of Ballantrae 1953; Le Amiche 1955; The Dark Avenger 1955; Lisbon 1956; The Mummy 1959; La Dolce Vita 1960; Repulsion 1965; The Champagne Murders 1966

Furness, Betty (1916-1994) Dangerous Corner 1934; Magnificent Obsession 1935; Swing Time 1936; Fair Warning 1937

Furness, Deborra-Lee (1960-) Jenny Kissed Me 1984; Shame 1987; Blue Heat 1990; Waiting 1990; Voyager 1991; Angel Baby 1995; Jindabyne 2006

Furst, Joseph (1916-2005) The High Bright Sun 1965; The Brides of Fu Manchu 1966; Diamonds Are Forever 1971

Furst, Stephen (1955-) National Lampoon's Animal House 1978; Midnight Madness 1980; National Lampoon's Class Reunion 1982; Silent Rage 1982; The Dream Team 1989; Shake, Rattle and Rock 1994; American Yakuza 2: Back to Back 1996; The Little Mermaid II: Return to the Sea 2000; Path of Destruction 2005

Furtado, Ruy (1919-1991) Recollections of the Yellow House 1989; The Divine Comedy 1992

Furth, George (1932-2008) Butch Cassidy and the Sundance Kid 1969; The Man with Two Brains 1983

Fury, Billy (1941-1983) Play It Cool 1962; I've Gotta Horse 1965; That'll Be the Day 1973

Futterman, Dan (1967-) Stepkids 1992; The Birdcage 1996; Shooting Fish 1997; Enough 2002; A Mighty Heart 2007; Righteous Kill 2008

Fyfe, Jim A Kiss before Dying 1991; Kill the Man 1999

Fyffe, Will (1885-1947) Cotton Queen 1937; Owd Bob 1938; Rulers of the Sea 1939; For Freedom 1940; The Prime Minister 1940; The Brothers 1947

G

G, Q On the Line 2001; Drumline 2002

Gaal, Franciska (1904-1972) The Buccaneer 1938; Paris Honeymoon 1939

Gabel, Elyes Everywhere + Nowhere 2011; A Most Violent Year 2014; Spooks: the Greater Good 2015

Gabel, Martin (1912-1986) M 1951; Deadline - USA 1952; The James Dean Story 1957; Goodbye Charlie 1964; Marnie 1964; Divorce American Style 1967; Lady in Cement 1968

Gabel, Scilla (1938-) Tarzan's Greatest Adventure 1959; The White Warrior 1959; Romulus and the Sabines 1961; Village of Daughters 1961; Modesty Blaise 1966

Gabin, Jean (1904-1976) La Belle Equipe 1936; The Lower Depths 1936; La Grande Illusion 1937; Pépé le Moko 1937; La Bête Humaine 1938; Le Quai des Brumes 1938; Le Jour Se Lève 1939; Stormy Waters 1941; Moontide 1942; The Impostor 1944; Martin Roumagnac 1946; Le Plaisir 1951; Honour among Thieves 1954; French Cancan 1955; Napoléon 1955; La Traversée de Paris 1956; The Case of Dr Laurent 1957; Maigret Sets a Trap 1957; Les Misérables 1957; A Monkey in Winter 1962; Any Number Can Win 1963; The Sicilian Clan 1969; Two against the Law 1973; Verdict 1974

Gable, Christopher (1940-1998) The Music Lovers 1970; The Boy Friend 1971; The Slipper and the Rose 1976; The Rainbow 1988

Gable, Clark (1901-1960) Dance, Fools, Dance 1931; The Finger Points 1931; A Free Soul 1931; Laughing Sinners 1931; The Painted Desert 1931; Possessed 1931; The Secret Six 1931; Sporting Blood 1931; Susan Lenox: Her Fall and Rise 1931; Hell Divers 1932; No Man of Her Own 1932; Polly of the Circus 1932; Red Dust 1932; Strange Interlude 1932; Dancing Lady 1933; Hold Your Man 1933; Night Flight 1933; The White Sister 1933; Chained 1934; Forsaking All Others 1934; It Happened One Night 1934; Manhattan Melodrama 1934; Men in White 1934; After Office Hours 1935; The Call of the Wild 1935; China Seas 1935; Mutiny on the Bounty 1935; Cain and Mabel 1936; Love on the Run 1936; San Francisco 1936; Wife vs Secretary 1936; Parnell 1937; Saratoga 1937; Test Pilot 1938; Too Hot to Handle 1938; Gone with the Wind 1939; Idiot's Delight 1939; Boom Town 1940; Comrade X 1940; Strange Cargo 1940; Honky Tonk 1941; They Met in Bombay 1941; Somewhere I'll Find You 1942; Adventure 1945; The Hucksters 1947; Command Decision 1948; Homecoming 1948; Any Number Can Play 1949; Key to the City 1950; To Please a Lady 1950; Across the Wide Missouri 1951; Callaway Went Thataway 1951; Lone Star 1952; Mogambo 1953; Never Let Me Go 1953; Betrayed 1954; Soldier of Fortune 1955; The Tall Men 1955; Band of Angels 1957; Run Silent Run Deep 1958; Teacher's Pet 1958; But Not for Me 1959; It Started in Naples 1960; The Misfits 1961

Gabor, Eva (1919-1995) Captain Kidd and the Slave Girl 1954; The Last Time I Saw Paris 1954; The Mad Magician 1954; Artists and Models 1955; My Man Godfrey 1957; Gigi 1958; The Truth about Women 1958; It Started with a Kiss 1959; A New Kind of Love 1963; Youngblood Hawke 1964; The

Aristocats 1970; The Rescuers 1977; The Rescuers Down Under 1990

Gabor, Miklos (1919-1998) Somewhere in Europe 1947; Apa 1966

Gabor, Zsa Zsa (1917-) Lovely to Look At 1952; Moulin Rouge 1952; We're Not Married 1952; Lili 1953; Three Ring Circus 1954; Death of a Scoundrel 1956; The Man Who Wouldn't Talk 1957; Queen of Outer Space 1958; Touch of Evil 1958; For the First Time 1959; Pepe 1960; The Road to Hong Kong 1962; Drop Dead Darling 1966; Jack of Diamonds 1967; Up the Front 1972; Snow White in Happily Ever After 1990; The Beverly Hillbillies 1993

Gabriel, John (1931-) The Hunters 1958; The Cat Gang 1959

Gabriel, Ron Getting Gotti 1994; A Sister's Secret 2009

Gabriello, André aka **Gabriello** (1896-1975) The Lower Depths 1936; Une Partie de Campagne 1936

Gad, Josh (1981-) The Rocker 2008; 21 2008; Love & Other Drugs 2010; Thanks for Sharing 2012; Frozen 2013; jOBS 2013; Pixels 2015; The Wedding Ringer 2015; The Angry Birds Movie 2016; Beauty and the Beast 2017

Gadd, Renee aka **Gadd, Renée** (1908-2003) The Man in the Mirror 1936; Brief Ecstasy 1937

Gade, Ariel Dark Water 2005; AVPR: Aliens vs Predator Requiem 2007

Gadebois, Grégory Angel and Tony 2010; An Ordinary Execution 2010

Gaden, John (1941-) Children of the Revolution 1996; Thank God He Met Lizzie 1997; The Eye of the Storm 2011

Gades, Antonio (1936-2004) Blood Wedding 1981; Carmen 1983; El Amor Brujo 1986

Gadon, Sarah (1987-) The Moth Diaries 2010; A Dangerous Method 2011; Antiviral 2012; Cosmopolis 2012; Belle 2013; Enemy 2013; Dracula Untold 2014; The Girl King 2015; A Royal Night Out 2015

Gadot, Gal (1985-) Fast & Furious 2009; Batman v Superman: Dawn of Justice 2016; Criminal 2016; Keeping Up with the Joneses 2016; Justice League 2017; Wonder Woman 2017

Gaffney, Liam (1911-1994) Curtain Up 1952; Street of Shadows 1953

Gaga, Lady (1986-) Muppets Most Wanted 2014; Sin City: a Dame to Kill For 2014

Gage, Erford (1912-1945) The Falcon Strikes Back 1943; The Seventh Victim 1943; The Curse of the Cat People 1944

Gage, Kevin Point Blank 1997; Paparazzi 2004

Gage, Patricia Rabid 1976; Perfectly Normal 1990; Dangerous Offender: the Marlene Moore Story 1996

Gago, Jenny (1953-) Old Gringo 1989; My Family 1994

Gaier, Dana Despicable Me 2010; Despicable Me 2 2013; Despicable Me 3 2017

Gail, Jane (1890-1963) Traffic in Souls 1913; 20,000 Leagues under the Sea 1916

Gail, Max (1943-) DC Cab 1983; Heartbreakers 1984; Judgment in Berlin 1988; The Switch 1993; Mortal Fear 1994; Pontiac Moon 1994; Sodbusters 1994; Good Luck 1996; Always and Forever 2008

Gaines, Boyd (1953-) Fame 1980; The Sure Thing 1985; Heartbreak Ridge 1986; Call Me 1988; I'm Not Rappaport 1996; The Confession 1999; Funny Games US 2008

Gaines, Lynn Quest for Love 1988; Jobman 1990

Gaines, Richard (1904-1975) The More the Merrier 1943; The Enchanted Cottage 1945; Do You Love Me? 1946; So Goes My Love 1946; Dangerous Years 1947; Flight to Mars 1951; Marry Me Again 1953; Love Me or Leave Me 1955

Gainey, M C (1948-) Leap of Faith 1992; Citizen Ruth 1996; Breakdown 1997; Happy, Texas 1999; The Country Bears 2002; The Last Chance 2003; Wonderland 2003; Broken Lizard's Club Dread 2004; Sideways 2004; Are We There Yet? 2005; The Dukes of Hazzard 2005; Wild Hogs 2007; Tangled 2010; Stolen 2012

Gains, Courtney (1965-) Children of the Corn 1984; Can't Buy Me Love 1987; The 'Burbs 1989

Gainsbourg, Charlotte (1971-) Love Songs 1984; An Impudent Girl 1985; Kung-Fu Master 1987; La Petite Voleuse 1988; Night Sun 1990; Autobus 1991; Merci la Vie 1991; The Cement Garden 1992; Jane Eyre 1996; Love etc 1997; La Bûche 1999; Ma Femme Est une Actrice 2001; 21 Grams 2003; Lemming 2005; The Science of Sleep 2005; Golden Door 2006; I Do 2006; I'm Not There. 2007; Antichrist

2009; The Tree 2010; Confession of a Child of the Century 2011; Melancholia 2011; Nymphomaniac Vol I 2013; Misunderstood 2014; Nymphomaniac Vol II 2014; Samba 2014; Independence Day: Resurgence 2016

Gainsbourg, Serge (1928-1991) The Looters 1966; Romance of a Horse Thief 1971; Je Vous Aime 1980

Gaitan, Paulina aka **Gaitán, Paulina** Trade 2006; We Are What We Are 2010

Gajos, Janusz (1939-) The Contract 1980; Interrogation 1982; Three Colours White 1993

Galabru, Michel (1924-) The Gendarme of St Tropez 1964; La Cage aux Folles 1978; La Cage aux Folles II 1980; Choice of Arms 1981; Double Dare 1981; One Deadly Summer 1983; La Cage aux Folles III: "Elles" Se Marient 1985; Subway 1985; Kamikaze 1986; Soigne Ta Droite 1986; Asterix and Obelix Take On Caesar 1999; Love like Poison 2010

Galbraith, Alastair Conquest of the South Pole 1989; The Debt Collector 1999; Intimacy 2000

Gale, David (1936-1991) Gold Diggers 1983; Re-Animator 1985; Bride of Re-Animator 1991; The Guyver 1991; The Hollywood Mom's Mystery 2004

Galecki, Johnny (1975-) National Lampoon's Christmas Vacation 1989; Bean 1997; Suicide Kings 1997; The Opposite of Sex 1998; Bounce 2000; Hancock 2008

Galeya, Abhin The Blue Tower 2008; Cleanskin 2012

Galiena, Anna (1954-) The Hairdresser's Husband 1990; Jamón, Jamón 1992; Being Human 1994; The Leading Man 1996; Three Lives and Only One Death 1996; Fade to Black 2006

Galifianakis, Zach (1969-) Below 2002; What Happens in Vegas 2008; G-Force 2009; The Hangover 2009; Youth in Revolt 2009; Dinner for Schmucks 2010; Due Date 2010; It's Kind of a Funny Story 2010; The Hangover: Part II 2011; The Muppets 2011; Puss in Boots 2011; The Campaign 2012; The Hangover Part III 2013; Birdman or (The Unexpected Virtue of Ignorance) 2014; Masterminds 2015; Keeping Up with the Joneses 2016

Galik, Denise Melvin and Howard 1980; Monster 1980; Eye of the Tiger 1986

Galindo, Nacho (1973-) Thunder over Arizona 1956; Born Reckless 1959

Galipeau, Annie Map of the Human Heart 1992; Grey Owl 1999

Gallacher, Frank (1943-) Dallas Doll 1994; Dark City 1998

Gallagher, Bronagh (1972-) The Commitments 1991; Mary Reilly 1995; The Most Fertile Man in Ireland 1999; Wild about Harry 2000; Tristan + Isolde 2005; Botched 2007; Faintheart 2008; Malice in Wonderland 2009

Gallagher, David (1985-) Look Who's Talking Now! 1993; Whisper of the Heart 1995; Bermuda Triangle 1996; Phenomenon 1996

Gallagher Jr, John Pieces of April 2002; Whatever Works 2009; Short Term 12 2013; 10 Cloverfield Lane 2016

Gallagher, Megan (1960-) The Ambulance 1990; Contagion 2001

Gallagher, Peter (1955-) The Idolmaker 1980; Summer Lovers 1982; Dreamchild 1985; The Caine Mutiny Court-Martial 1988; High Spirits 1988; sex, lies, and videotape 1989; Late for Dinner 1991; The Player 1992; Malice 1993; Mother's Boys 1993; Short Cuts 1993; While Mile 1994; The Underneath 1995; While You Were Sleeping 1995; Last Dance 1996; To Gillian on Her 37th Birthday 1996; The Man Who Knew Too Little 1997; American Beauty 1999; House on Haunted Hill 1999; Center Stage 2000; The Last Debate 2000; The Adventures of Tom Thumb and Thumbelina 2002; Mr Deeds 2002; Adam 2009; Conviction 2010

Gallagher, Richard "Skeets" aka **Gallagher, Skeets** (1891-1955) Her Wedding Night 1930; It Pays to Advertise 1931; Possessed 1931; Bird of Paradise 1932; Merrily We Go to Hell 1932; Riptide 1934

Gallagher, Sean La Passione 1996; Elephant Juice 1999

Galland, Jean (1887-1967) The House of the Spaniard 1936; Le Plaisir 1951; Madame de... 1953

Gallaudet, John (1903-1983) Pennies from Heaven 1936; Girls Can Play 1937; Holiday Inn 1942; Julie 1956; The Decks Ran Red 1958; In Cold Blood 1967

Gallian, Ketti (1912-1972) Marie Galante 1934; Shall We Dance 1937

Gallienne, Guillaume aka **Gallienne de la Comédie-Française, Guillaume** Me,

Myself and Mum 2013; YSL: Yves Saint Laurent 2014

Galligan, Zach (1963-) Gremlins 1984; Nothing Lasts Forever 1984; Surviving 1985; Waxwork 1988; Gremlins 2: the New Batch 1990; Round Trip to Heaven 1992; Cyborg 3: The Recycler 1994

Gallner, Kyle (1986-) The Haunting in Connecticut 2009; A Nightmare on Elm Street 2010; Red State 2011; American Sniper 2014; Dear White People 2014

Gallo, Vincent (1961-) Arizona Dream 1991; The House of the Spirits 1993; Palookaville 1995; The Funeral 1996; Truth or Consequences, NM 1997; Buffalo '66 1998; LA without a Map 1998; Confessions of a Trickbaby 1999; Hide and Seek 2000; Trouble Every Day 2000; Get Well Soon 2001; The Brown Bunny 2003; Tetro 2009; Essential Killing 2010

Galloway, Don (1937-2009) The Rare Breed 1966; Gunfight in Abilene 1967; The Ride to Hangman's Tree 1967; Rough Night in Jericho 1967; The Big Chill 1983; Two Moon Junction 1988; The Return of Ironside 1993

Galvani, Graziella Kapo 1959; Pierrot le Fou 1965

Gam, Rita (1927-2016) Saadia 1953; Night People 1954; Sign of the Pagan 1954; Magic Fire 1956; Mohawk 1956; Hannibal 1959; King of Kings 1961; Klute 1971; Shoot Out 1971; Midnight 1989

Gamble, Mason (1986-) Dennis 1993; Bad Moon 1996; Arlington Road 1998; Rushmore 1998

Gamble, Nathan Marley & Me 2008; The Hole 2009; Dolphin Tale 2011; Dolphin Tale 2 2014

Gamble, Warburton (1893-1945) By Candlelight 1934; Spare a Copper 1940

Gamblin, Jacques (1957-) The Children of the Marshland 1998; The Colour of Lies 1999; Laissez-passer 2001; L'Enfer 2005; The First Day of the Rest of Your Life 2007; Hippocrates 2014

Gambon, Michael (1940-) Nothing but the Night 1972; The Beast Must Die 1974; Turtle Diary 1985; Paris by Night 1988; The Cook, the Thief, His Wife and Her Lover 1989; Missing Link 1989; The Rachel Papers 1989; Mobsters 1991; Toys 1992; The Browning Version 1994; Clean Slate 1994; A Man of No Importance 1994; Squanto: the Last Great Warrior 1994; Two Deaths 1994; Bullet to Beijing 1995; The Innocent Sleep 1995; Mary Reilly 1995; Midnight in St Petersburg 1995; Nothing Personal 1995; The Gambler 1997; The Wings of the Dove 1997; Dancing at Lughnasa 1998; The Insider 1999; The Last September 1999; A Monkey's Tale 1999; Plunkett & Macleane 1999; Sleepy Hollow 1999; Charlotte Gray 2001; Christmas Carol: the Movie 2001; Gosford Park 2001; High Heels and Low Lifes 2001; Ali G indahouse 2002; Path to War 2002; The Actors 2003; Deep Blue 2003; Open Range 2003; Sylvia 2003; Being Julia 2004; Harry Potter and the Prisoner of Azkaban 2004; Layer Cake 2004; The Life Aquatic with Steve Zissou 2004; Sky Captain and the World of Tomorrow 2004; The Good Night 2005; Harry Potter and the Goblet of Fire 2005; Amazing Grace 2006; The Good Shepherd 2006; The Omen 2006; The Baker 2007; Harry Potter and the Order of the Phoenix 2007; Brideshead Revisited 2008; The Book of Eli 2009; Fantastic Mr Fox 2009; Harry Potter and the Half-Blood Prince 2009; The King's Speech 2010; Harry Potter and the Deathly Hallows: Part 2 2011; Quartet 2012; Paddington 2014; Unity 2015; Dad's Army 2016

Gamelon, Laurent Shut Up! 2003; Confidences Trop Intimes 2004

Gammell, Robin (1936-) Lipstick 1976; Full Circle 1977; Circle of Two 1980; Murder by Phone 1982; Project X 1987; Bone Daddy 1998; Last Night 1998

Gammon, James (1940-2010) The 1,000 Plane Raid 1969; The Ballad of Gregorio Cortez 1983; Made in Heaven 1987; The Milagro Beanfield War 1988; Major League 1989; Roe vs Wade 1989; Coupe de Ville 1990; Revenge 1990; CrissCross 1992; Leaving Normal 1992; The Adventures of Huck Finn 1993; Cabin Boy 1994; Major League II 1994; Truman 1995; Traveller 1997; The Iron Giant 1999; The Country Bears 2002; Life or Something like It 2002; Cold Mountain 2003; Monte Walsh 2003; Don't Come Knocking 2005; What I Did for Love 2006

Gampu, Ken (1929-2003) The Naked Prey 1966; King Solomon's Mines 1985

Ganatra, Nitin Shifty 2008; Mad, Sad & Bad 2009

Ganatra, Nitin Chandra aka **Ganatra, Nitin** (1967-) Guru in Seven 1997; Second Generation 1999; Bride & Prejudice 2004

Gandolfini, James (1961-2013) Money for Nothing 1993; True Romance 1993; Angie 1994; Italian Movie 1994; Terminal Velocity 1994; Crimson Tide 1995; Get Shorty 1995; The Juror 1996; Night Falls on Manhattan 1997; Perdita Durango 1997; She's So Lovely 1997; 12 Angry Men 1997; A Civil Action 1998; Fallen 1998; 8mm 1999; The Last Castle 2001; The Man Who Wasn't There 2001; The Mexican 2001; Romance & Cigarettes 2004; Surviving Christmas 2004; All the King's Men 2005; Lonely Hearts 2006; In the Loop 2009; The Taking of Pelham 123 2009; Welcome to the Rileys 2009; Where the Wild Things Are 2009; Cinema Verite 2011; Killing Them Softly 2012; Zero Dark Thirty 2012; Enough Said 2013; The Incredible Burt Wonderstone 2013; The Drop 2014

Ganios, Tony (1959-) The Wanderers 1979; Continental Divide 1981; Porky's 1981; Porky's Revenge 1985

Ganoung, Richard Parting Glances 1985; Billy's Hollywood Screen Kiss 1998

Gant, Richard (1940-) Rocky V 1990; Stone Cold 1991; Divorcing Jack 1998; Nutty Professor 2: the Klumps 2000; Daddy Day Camp 2007

Gantzler, Peter Italian for Beginners 2000; The Boss of It All 2006

Ganz, Bruno (1941-) The Marquise of O 1976; The American Friend 1977; The Boys from Brazil 1978; Knife in the Head 1978; Nosferatu, the Vampyre 1979; Circle of Deceit 1981; Wings of Desire 1987; Strapless 1988; The Last Days of Chez Nous 1992; Faraway, So Close 1993; Eternity and a Day 1998; Bread and Tulips 2000; Downfall 2004; The Manchurian Candidate 2004; Youth without Youth 2007; The Baader Meinhof Complex 2008; The Reader 2008; Unknown 2011; Age of Uprising: the Legend of Michael Kohlhaas 2013; Night Train to Lisbon 2013; In Order of Disappearance 2014; Remember 2015

Gao Yuanyuan (1979-) Beijing Bicycle 2001; Shanghai Dreams 2005; City of Life and Death 2009

Garai, Romola (1982-) I Capture the Castle 2002; Dirty Dancing 2 2003; Inside I'm Dancing 2004; Vanity Fair 2004; Amazing Grace 2006; Angel 2006; As You Like It 2006; Renaissance 2006; Atonement 2007; The Other Man 2008; Glorious 39 2009; Junkhearts 2011; One Day 2011; Having You 2013; The Last Days on Mars 2013; Suffragette 2015

Garas, Kaz (1940-) The Last Safari 1967; Ben 1972

Garber, Matthew (1956-1977) Mary Poppins 1964; The Gnome-Mobile 1967

Garber, Victor (1949-) Godspell 1973; Light Sleeper 1991; Sleepless in Seattle 1993; Exotica 1994; Mary Higgins Clark's Let Me Call You Sweetheart 1997; Rodgers & Hammerstein's Cinderella 1997; Annie 1999; Invisible Child 1999; Laughter on the 23rd Floor 2000; Call Me Claus 2001; Legally Blonde 2001; Tuck Everlasting 2002; Milk 2008; You Again 2010; Argo 2012; Big Game 2014; Self/Less 2015

Garbo, Greta (1905-1990) The Joyless Street 1925; Flesh and the Devil 1926; The Temptress 1926; The Torrent 1926; Love 1927; The Divine Woman 1928; The Mysterious Lady 1928; A Woman of Affairs 1928; The Kiss 1929; The Single Standard 1929; Wild Orchids 1929; Anna Christie 1930; Romance 1930; Inspiration 1931; Mata Hari 1931; Susan Lenox: Her Fall and Rise 1931; As You Desire Me 1932; Grand Hotel 1932; Queen Christina 1933; The Painted Veil 1934; Anna Karenina 1935; Camille 1937; Conquest 1937; Ninotchka 1939; Two-Faced Woman 1941; The Love Goddesses 1965

Garcés, Paula (1974-) Clockstoppers 2002; Marci X 2003; Harold & Kumar Get the Munchies 2004; Man of the House 2005; A Very Harold & Kumar 3D Christmas 2011

Garcia, Adam (1973-) Bootmen 2000; Coyote Ugly 2000; Riding in Cars with Boys 2001; Confessions of a Teenage Drama Queen 2004; Nativity 3: Dude Where's My Donkey 2014

Garcia, Allan (1887-1938) The Circus 1928; City Lights 1931

Garcia, Andres House of Evil 1968; Tintorera 1977

Garcia, Andy (1956-) A Night in Heaven 1983; The Mean Season 1985; 8 Million Ways to Die 1986; The Untouchables 1987; Blood Money 1988; Stand and Deliver 1988; Black Rain

1989; The Godfather Part III 1990; Internal Affairs 1990; A Show of Force 1990; Dead Again 1991; Accidental Hero 1992; Jennifer Eight 1992; When a Man Loves a Woman 1994; Steal Big, Steal Little 1995; Things to Do in Denver When You're Dead 1995; The Disappearance of Garcia Lorca 1997; Hoodlum 1997; Night Falls on Manhattan 1997; Desperate Measures 1998; Just the Ticket 1998; Swing Vote 1999; For Love or Country: the Arturo Sandoval Story 2000; The Man from Elysian Fields 2001; Ocean's Eleven 2001; Confidence 2002; Twisted 2003; Ocean's Twelve 2004; The Lost City 2005; Smokin' Aces 2006; The Air I Breathe 2007; Ocean's Thirteen 2007; Beverly Hills Chihuahua 2008; The Line 2008; City Island 2009; The Pink Panther 2 2009; A Dark Truth 2012; Let's Be Cops 2014

Garcia, Jesse aka **García, Jesse** Echo Park LA 2005; Good Dick 2008

Garcia, Joanna Man of Miracles 1999; Revenge of the Bridesmaids 2010

Garcia, Juan (1905-1980) Blowing Wild 1953; The Tall Men 1955

Garcia, Luis Alberto The Last Supper 1976; Guantanamera 1995

Garcia, Nicole (1946-) Mon Oncle d'Amérique 1980; Les Uns et les Autres 1981; Order of Death 1983; Death in a French Garden 1985; Betty Fisher and Other Stories 2001; Histoire de Marie et Julien 2003; Fear(s) of the Dark 2007

Garcia, Stella (1942-2006) The Last Movie 1971; Joe Kidd 1972

Garcia, Stenio (1933-) At Play in the Fields of the Lord 1991; Me, You, Them 2000

Garcin, Ginette (1928-2010) Cousin, Cousine 1975; L'Homme de Ma Vie 1992

Garcin, Henri (1929-) La Vie de Château 1965; Someone behind the Door 1971; Kill! 1972; Verdict 1974; The Woman Next Door 1981; Les Cent et Une Nuits 1995; The Eighth Day 1996

Garde, Betty (1905-1989) Call Northside 777 1948; Cry of the City 1948; Caged 1950; The Prince Who Was a Thief 1951

Gardenia, Vincent (1920-1992) Mad Dog Coll 1961; Where's Poppa? 1970; Little Murders 1971; Bang the Drum Slowly 1973; Lucky Luciano 1973; Death Wish 1974; The Front Page 1974; Fire Sale 1977; Greased Lightning 1977; Heaven Can Wait 1978; Firepower 1979; Home Movies 1979; The Last Flight of Noah's Ark 1980; Death Wish II 1981; Movers and Shakers 1985; Little Shop of Horrors 1986; Moonstruck 1987; Skin Deep 1989; The Super 1991

Gardiner, Reginald (1903-1980) A Damsel in Distress 1937; The Flying Deuces 1939; The Doctor Takes a Wife 1940; The Great Dictator 1940; The Man Who Came to Dinner 1941; My Life with Caroline 1941; Sundown 1941; A Yank in the RAF 1941; Captains of the Clouds 1942; Claudia 1943; The Immortal Sergeant 1943; Sweet Rosie O'Grady 1943; Christmas in Connecticut 1945; The Dolly Sisters 1945; The Horn Blows at Midnight 1945; Molly and Me 1945; Cluny Brown 1946; Do You Love Me? 1946; I Wonder Who's Kissing Her Now 1947; Fury at Furnace Creek 1948; That Lady in Ermine 1948; That Wonderful Urge 1948; Halls of Montezuma 1950; Wabash Avenue 1950; Androcles and the Lion 1952; Black Widow 1954; Ain't Misbehavin' 1955; The Birds and the Bees 1956; Rock-a-Bye Baby 1958; Back Street 1961; Do Not Disturb 1965

Gardner, Ava (1922-1990) Calling Dr Gillespie 1942; Joe Smith, American 1942; Kid Glove Killer 1942; Reunion in France 1942; Ghosts in the Night 1943; Hitler's Madman 1943; Pilot #5 1943; Three Men in White 1944; Two Girls and a Sailor 1944; The Killers 1946; Whistle Stop 1946; The Hucksters 1947; Singapore 1947; One Touch of Venus 1948; The Bribe 1949; East Side, West Side 1949; The Great Sinner 1949; Pandora and the Flying Dutchman 1950; My Forbidden Past 1951; Show Boat 1951; Lone Star 1952; The Snows of Kilimanjaro 1952; The Band Wagon 1953; Knights of the Round Table 1953; Mogambo 1953; Ride, Vaquero! 1953; The Barefoot Contessa 1954; Bhowani Junction 1956; The Little Hut 1957; The Sun Also Rises 1957; The Naked Maja 1959; On the Beach 1959; The Angel Wore Red 1960; 55 Days at Peking 1963; The Night of the Iguana 1964; Seven Days in May 1964; The Bible... in the Beginning 1966; Mayerling 1968; The Ballad of Tam Lin 1970; The Life and Times of Judge Roy Bean 1972; Earthquake 1974; Permission to Kill

1975; The Blue Bird 1976; The Cassandra Crossing 1976; The Sentinel 1977; City on Fire 1979; The Kidnapping of the President 1980; Priest of Love 1981; Regina 1982

Gardner, Joan (1914-1999) Wedding Rehearsal 1932; The Private Life of Don Juan 1934; The Scarlet Pimpernel 1934; The Man Who Could Work Miracles 1936; Dark Journey 1937; The Challenge 1938

Gardner, Virginia Project Almanac 2014; Goat 2016

Garfield, Allen aka **Garfield, Alan** aka **Goorwitz, Allen** (1939-) Greetings 1968; Hi, Mom! 1970 The Owl and the Pussycat 1970; The Organization 1971; The Candidate 1972; Get to Know Your Rabbit 1972; The Marcus-Nelson Murders 1973; Slither 1973; Busting 1974; The Conversation 1974; The Front Page 1974; Nashville 1975; Gable and Lombard 1976; Mother, Jugs & Speed 1976; The Brink's Job 1978; One-Trick Pony 1980; The Stunt Man 1980; Continental Divide 1981; Leave 'Em Laughing 1981; One from the Heart 1982; The State of Things 1982; The Black Stallion Returns 1983; Get Crazy 1983; The Cotton Club 1984; Irreconcilable Differences 1984; Teachers 1984; Desert Bloom 1985; Beverly Hills Cop II 1987; Never Cry Devil 1989; Cyborg 2: Glass Shadow 1993; Wild Side 1995; Crime of the Century 1996; Diabolique 1996; Absence of the Good 1999; The Majestic 2001

Garfield, Andrew (1983-) Lions for Lambs 2007; The Imaginarium of Doctor Parnassus 2009; Never Let Me Go 2010; The Social Network 2010; The Amazing Spider-Man 2012; The Amazing Spider-Man 2 2014; 99 Homes 2014

Garfield, John (1913-1952) Daughters Courageous 1939; Dust Be My Destiny 1939; Four Wives 1939; Juarez 1939; They Made Me a Criminal 1939; Castle on the Hudson 1940; East of the River 1940; Saturday's Children 1940; Out of the Fog 1941; The Sea Wolf 1941; Dangerously They Live 1942; Tortilla Flat 1942; Air Force 1943; Destination Tokyo 1943; The Fallen Sparrow 1943; Thank Your Lucky Stars 1943; Between Two Worlds 1944; Hollywood Canteen 1944; Pride of the Marines 1945; Humoresque 1946; Nobody Lives Forever 1946; The Postman Always Rings Twice 1946; Body and Soul 1947; Daisy Kenyon 1947; Gentleman's Agreement 1947; Force of Evil 1948; Jigsaw 1949; We Were Strangers 1949; The Breaking Point 1950; He Ran All the Way 1951

Garfunkel, Art aka **Garfunkel, Arthur** (1941-) Catch-22 1970; Carnal Knowledge 1971; Bad Timing 1980; Boxing Helena 1993; The Rebound 2009

Gargan, Edward aka **Gargan, Ed** (1902-1964) Danger Patrol 1937; The Falcon Takes Over 1942; The Falcon and the Co-Eds 1943; The Falcon in Danger 1943; The Falcon Out West 1944

Gargan, William (1905-1979) The Animal Kingdom 1932; Rain 1932; Lucky Devils 1933; British Agent 1934; Four Frightened People 1934; Black Fury 1935; The Milky Way 1936; You Only Live Once 1937; The Crowd Roars 1938; Star Dust 1940; They Knew What They Wanted 1940; Cheers for Miss Bishop 1941; I Wake Up Screaming 1941; Keep 'Em Flying 1941; Miss Annie Rooney 1942; The Canterville Ghost 1944; The Bells of St Mary's 1945; Till the End of Time 1946; The Rawhide Years 1956

Garity, Troy (1973-) Bandits 2001; Barbershop 2002; Milwaukee, Minnesota 2004; Barbershop 2: Back in Business 2004; Sunshine 2007

Garko, Gabriel (1974-) Le Fate Ignoranti 2001; Callas Forever 2002; Misunderstood 2014

Garko, Gianni aka **Garko, John** (1935-) Kapo 1959; The Mongols 1961; Pontius Pilate 1961; Santana 1968

Garland, Beverly aka **Campbell, Beverly** (1926-2008) DOA 1949; It Conquered the World 1956; Not of This Earth 1956; Chicago Confidential 1957; The Joker Is Wild 1957; The Saga of Hemp Brown 1958; The Alligator People 1959; Twice Told Tales 1963; Pretty Poison 1968; Where the Red Fern Grows 1974; It's My Turn 1980

Garland, Judy (1922-1969) Every Sunday 1936; Pigskin Parade 1936; Broadway Melody of 1938 1937; Thoroughbreds Don't Cry 1937; Everybody Sing 1938; Listen, Darling 1938; Love Finds Andy Hardy 1938; Babes in Arms 1939; The Wizard of Oz

1939; Andy Hardy Meets Debutante 1940; Little Nellie Kelly 1940; Strike Up the Band 1940; Babes on Broadway 1941; Life Begins for Andy Hardy 1941; Ziegfeld Girl 1941; For Me and My Gal 1942; Girl Crazy 1943; Presenting Lily Mars 1943; Meet Me in St Louis 1944; Ziegfeld Follies 1946; The Clock 1945; The Harvey Girls 1946; Till the Clouds Roll By 1946; Easter Parade 1948; The Pirate 1948; Words and Music 1948; In the Good Old Summertime 1949; Summer Stock 1950; A Star Is Born 1954; Pepe 1960; Judgment at Nuremberg 1961; A Child Is Waiting 1962; Gay Purr-ee 1962; I Could Go On Singing 1963

Garland, Richard (1927-1969) Rage at Dawn 1955; Attack of the Crab Monsters 1957; The Undead 1957; Panic in Year Zero 1962

Garlin, Jeff (1962-) Daddy Day Care 2003; Strange Wilderness 2007; The Rocker 2008; WALL-E 2008; The Bounty Hunter 2010; ParaNorman 2012

Garlington, Lee (1953-) Cobra 1986; Psycho III 1986; Cold Sassy Tree 1989; Evidence of Love 1990; My Life 1993; Reflections on a Crime 1994; The Babysitter 1995

Garner, Alice (1969-) Love and Other Catastrophes 1996; Strange Planet 1999; Jindabyne 2006

Garner, James (1928-2014) The Girl He Left Behind 1956; Toward the Unknown 1956; Sayonara 1957; Shoot-Out at Medicine Bend 1957; Darby's Rangers 1958; Alias Jesse James 1959; Up Periscope 1959; Cash McCall 1960; The Children's Hour 1961; Boys' Night Out 1962; The Great Escape 1963; Move Over, Darling 1963; The Thrill of It All 1963; The Wheeler Dealers 1963; The Americanization of Emily 1964; 36 Hours 1964; Art of Love 1965; Duel at Diablo 1966; Grand Prix 1966; A Man Could Get Killed 1966; Hour of the Gun 1967; How Sweet It Is! 1968; The Pink Jungle 1968; Marlowe 1969; Support Your Local Sheriff! 1969; Skin Game 1971; Support Your Local Gunfighter 1971; They Only Kill Their Masters 1972; One Little Indian 1973; The Castaway Cowboy 1974; The Rockford Files 1974; HEALTH 1980; The Fan 1981; The Long Summer of George Adams 1982; Victor/Victoria 1982; Murphy's Romance 1985; Promise 1986; Sunset 1988; My Name Is Bill W 1989; The Distinguished Gentleman 1992; Barbarians at the Gate 1993; Fire in the Sky 1993; Breathing Lessons 1994; Maverick 1994; My Fellow Americans 1996; Legalese 1998; Twilight 1998; One Special Night 1999; The Last Debate 2000; Space Cowboys 2000; Atlantis: the Lost Empire 2001; Divine Secrets of the Ya-Ya Sisterhood 2002; The Notebook 2003; Battle for Terra 2007

Garner, Jennifer (1972-) Mr Magoo 1997; Washington Square 1997; Dude, Where's My Car? 2000; Catch Me If You Can 2002; Daredevil 2003; 13 Going on 30 2004; Elektra 2005; Catch and Release 2006; Juno 2007; The Kingdom 2007; Ghosts of Girlfriends Past 2009; The Invention of Lying 2009; Valentine's Day 2010; Arthur 2011; The Odd Life of Timothy Green 2012; Dallas Buyers Club 2013; Alexander and the Terrible, Horrible, No Good, Very Bad Day 2014; Draft Day 2014; Men, Women & Children 2014; Danny Collins 2015; Miracles from Heaven 2016; Nine Lives 2016

Garner, Julia Electrick Children 2012; The Last Exorcism Part II 2013; We Are What We Are 2013; Grandma 2015

Garner, Kelli (1984-) Bully 2001; Thumbsucker 2005; Lars and the Real Girl 2007; Horns 2013; The Secret Life of Marilyn Monroe 2015

Garner, Peggy Ann (1931-1984) Jane Eyre 1943; Nob Hill 1945; A Tree Grows in Brooklyn 1945; Home Sweet Homicide 1946; Bob, Son of Battle 1947; Daisy Kenyon 1947; The Lovable Cheat 1949; Teresa 1951; Black Widow 1954

Garnett, Gale (1942-) Mad Monster Party 1966; Tribute 1980

Garnett, Tony (1936-) The Boys 1961; Versus: The Life and Films of Ken Loach 2016

Garofalo, Janeane (1964-) Reality Bites 1994; Bye Bye Love 1995; Coldblooded 1995; The Cable Guy 1996; Larger than Life 1996; Touch 1996; The Truth about Cats and Dogs 1996; Cop Land 1997; The Matchmaker 1997; Romy and Michele's High School Reunion 1997; Clay Pigeons 1998; Dog Park 1998; Kiki's Delivery Service 1998; Permanent Midnight 1998; Dogma 1999; The Minus Man 1999; Mystery Men 1999; 200 Cigarettes 1999; Titan

AE 2000; The Search for John Gissing 2001; Big Trouble 2002; The Laramie Project 2002; Wonderland 2003; Stay 2005; The Wild 2006; Manufacturing Dissent: Uncovering Michael Moore 2007; Ratatouille 2007; Misery Loves Comedy 2015

Garr, Teri aka **Garr, Terry** (1947-) The Cool Ones 1967; Head 1968; The Young Frankenstein 1974; Won Ton Ton, the Dog Who Saved Hollywood 1976; Close Encounters of the Third Kind 1977; Oh, God! 1977; The Black Stallion 1979; Witches' Brew 1979; Honky Tonk Freeway 1981; The Escape Artist 1982; One from the Heart 1982; Tootsie 1982; The Black Stallion Returns 1983; Mr Mom 1983; The Sting II 1983; Firstborn 1984; After Hours 1985; Miracles 1985; Full Moon in Blue Water 1988; Waiting for the Light 1989; Short Time 1990; Stranger in the Family 1991; Mom and Dad Save the World 1992; Dumb and Dumber 1994; Perfect Alibi 1994; Pret-a-Porter 1994; Michael 1996; Changing Habits 1997; A Simple Wish 1997; Casper Meets Wendy 1998; Dick 1999; Kill the Man 1999; Ghost World 2001; Expired 2007

Garralaga, Martin (1894-1981) A Message to Garcia 1936; They Passed This Way 1948; The Ring 1952

Garrani, Ivo (1924-2015) Hercules 1957; General Della Rovere 1959; The Giant of Marathon 1960; The Mask of Satan 1960; Morgan the Pirate 1960; The Rover 1967

Garrel, Louis (1983-) The Dreamers 2003; Ma Mère 2004; Regular Lovers 2005; Inside Paris 2006; Love Songs 2007; Beloved 2011; Jealousy 2013; Saint Laurent 2014; Mon Roi 2015

Garrel, Maurice (1923-2011) Nada 1974; Son Frère 2003; Kings & Queen 2004

Garrett, Beau Paradise Lost 2006; Tron Legacy 2010

Garrett, Betty (1919-2011) Words and Music 1948; Neptune's Daughter 1949; On the Town 1949; Take Me Out to the Ball Game 1949; My Sister Eileen 1955; The Long Way Home 1998

Garrett, Brad (1960-) Casper 1995; Tarzan II 2005; Asterix and the Vikings 2006; Music and Lyrics 2007; Ratatouille 2007; Planes 2013

Garrett, Leif (1961-) God's Gun 1977; Kid Vengeance 1977; The Outsiders 1983

Garrett, Patsy (1921-) Benji 1974; For the Love of Benji 1977

Garrick, John (1902-1966) Song o' My Heart 1930; Bad Company 1931; Chu Chin Chow 1934; D'Ye Ken John Peel? 1934

Garrick, Rian Battle of the Coral Sea 1959; Edge of Eternity 1959

Garrison, Sean (1937-) Violent Road 1958; Bridge to the Sun 1961; Moment to Moment 1966

Garrone, Riccardo (1926-2016) Pontius Pilate 1961; Eva 1962; The Swordsman of Siena 1962

Garson, Greer (1904-1996) Goodbye, Mr Chips 1939; Remember? 1939; Pride and Prejudice 1940; Blossoms in the Dust 1941; When Ladies Meet 1941; Mrs Miniver 1942; Random Harvest 1942; Madame Curie 1943; Mrs Parkington 1944; Adventure 1945; The Valley of Decision 1945; Desire Me 1947; Julia Misbehaves 1948; The Forsyte Saga 1949; The Miniver Story 1950; The Law and the Lady 1951; Julius Caesar 1953; Scandal at Scourie 1953; Her Twelve Men 1954; Strange Lady in Town 1955; Pepe 1960; Sunrise at Campobello 1960; The Singing Nun 1966; The Happiest Millionaire 1967

Garson, Willie (1964-) Untamed Heart 1993; Fortress 2: Re-entry 1999; Little Manhattan 2005; The Perfect Catch 2005; Sex and the City: the Movie 2008

Garth, Jennie (1972-) Danielle Steel's Star 1993; Flashpoint 1997; The Last Chance 2003

Gartin, Christopher (1968-) Johns 1995; Tremors II: Aftershocks 1995

Garwood, John Hell's Angels on Wheels 1967; The Stunt Man 1980

Gary, Lorraine (1937-) The Marcus-Nelson Murders 1973; Jaws 1975; I Never Promised You a Rose Garden 1977; Jaws 2 1978; Just You and Me, Kid 1979; 1941 1979; Jaws the Revenge 1987

Gascoine, Jill (1937-) Confessions of a Pop Performer 1975; King of the Wind 1989

Gassman, Alessandro (1965-) Golden Balls 1993; A Month by the Lake 1994; Hamam: the Turkish Bath 1996; The Transporter 2 2005; Calm Chaos 2008

Gassman, Vittorio (1922-2000) Bitter Rice 1949; Sombrero 1952; Cry of the

Hunted 1953; The Glass Wall 1953; Rhapsody 1954; Beautiful but Dangerous 1955; War and Peace 1956; Big Deal on Madonna Street 1958; Barabbas 1961; The Easy Life 1962; Let's Talk about Women 1964; The Dirty Game 1965; Ghosts - Italian Style 1967; The Tiger and the Pussycat 1967; Woman Times Seven 1967; Twelve plus One 1969; Scent of a Woman 1974; We All Loved Each Other So Much 1974; Viva Italia! 1978; A Wedding 1978; Quintet 1979; Immortal Bachelor 1980; The Nude Bomb 1980; Sharky's Machine 1981; Tempest 1982; Life Is a Bed of Roses 1983; The Family 1987; Sleepers 1996

Gastaldi, Johanna The Miracle of Bern 2003; Sophie Scholl: the Final Days 2005

Gasteyer, Ana (1967-) Dick 1999; Woman on Top 2000; Mean Girls 2004

Gastoni, Lisa (1935-) The Baby and the Battleship 1956; Three Men in a Boat 1956; Man from Tangier 1957; Intent to Kill 1958; The Breaking Point 1961; Eva 1962; RoGoPaG 1962; The Last Days of Mussolini 1974

Gates, Larry (1915-1996) Above and Beyond 1952; Glory Alley 1952; Has Anybody Seen My Gal? 1952; Francis Covers the Big Town 1953; Take Me to Town 1953; Invasion of the Body Snatchers 1956; The Brothers Rico 1957; Jeanne Eagels 1957; Cat on a Hot Tin Roof 1958; One Foot in Hell 1960; Ada 1961; The Hoodlum Priest 1961; Underworld USA 1961; The Young Savages 1961; Toys in the Attic 1963; The Sand Pebbles 1966; FDR: the Last Year 1980

Gates, Nancy (1926-) The Master Race 1944; Nevada 1944; Sons of the Musketeers 1951; The Member of the Wedding 1952; Suddenly 1954; Stranger on Horseback 1955; World without End 1955; The Brass Legend 1956; Death of a Scoundrel 1956; Some Came Running 1958; The Gunfight at Dodge City 1959; Comanche Station 1960

Gateson, Marjorie (1891-1977) Goin' to Town 1935; Big Brown Eyes 1936; Vogues of 1938 1937; The Sky's the Limit 1943

Gatiss, Mark (1966-) Sex Lives of the Potato Men 2003; The League of Gentlemen's Apocalypse 2005; Starter for 10 2006; Dad's Army 2016; Denial 2016; Our Kind of Traitor 2016

Gatliff, Frank (1927-1990) The Ipcress File 1965; Déjà Vu 1984

Gaubert, Danièle (1943-1987) Flight from Ashiya 1963; Snow Job 1972

Gauge, Alexander (1914-1960) Murder in the Cathedral 1952; The Pickwick Papers 1952; Counterspy 1953; House of Blackmail 1953

Gauthier, Vincent The Green Ray 1986; Nazi Hunter: the Beate Klarsfeld Story 1986

Gautier, Dick (1937-) Black Jack 1972; Fun with Dick and Jane 1977

Gautier, Jean-Yves The Promise 1994; Three Lives and Only One Death 1996; Journey to the Beginning of the World 1997

Gava, Cassandra High Road to China 1983; The Amityville Curse 1990

Gaven, Jean (1922-2014) Rider on the Rain 1970; And Hope to Die 1972; The Story of O 1975

Gavin, Erica (1949-) Vixen! 1968; Beyond the Valley of the Dolls 1970; Caged Heat 1974

Gavin, John (1928-) Quantez 1957; A Time to Love and a Time to Die 1958; Imitation of Life 1959; A Breath of Scandal 1960; Midnight Lace 1960; Psycho 1960; Spartacus 1960; Back Street 1961; Romanoff and Juliet 1961; Tammy Tell Me True 1961; Thoroughly Modern Millie 1967; The Madwoman of Chaillot 1969

Gavron, Rafi Breaking and Entering 2006; Nick & Norah's Infinite Playlist 2008

Gawthorne, Peter (1884-1962) The Camels Are Coming 1934; No Limit 1935; The Amazing Quest of Ernest Bliss 1936; Good Morning, Boys 1937; The Last Adventurers 1937; The Ticket of Leave Man 1937; Alf's Button Afloat 1938; Ask a Policeman 1938; Convict 99 1938; Band Waggon 1939; Flying 55 1939; Where's That Fire? 1939; I Thank You 1941; Pimpernel Smith 1941; Paul Temple Returns 1952

Gaxton, William (1890-1963) It's the Old Army Game 1926; Best Foot Forward 1943; Billy Rose's Diamond Horseshoe 1945

Gaye, Gregory (1900-1993) Renegades 1930; Charlie Chan at the Opera 1936; Dodsworth 1936; Ninotchka 1939; Black Magic 1949;

Creature with the Atom Brain 1955; The Eddy Duchin Story 1956

Gaye, Lisa (1935-) Drums across the River 1954; Rock around the Clock 1956; Shake, Rattle and Rock! 1957; Ten Thousand Bedrooms 1957; Castle of Evil 1966; The Violent Ones 1967

Gaye, Nona (1974-) The Matrix Reloaded 2002; The Polar Express 2004; xXx: the Next Level 2005; Blood and Bone 2009

Gayet, Julie (1972-) Les Cent et Une Nuits 1995; Almost Peaceful 2002; My Best Friend 2006; Paper Souls 2013

Gayheart, Rebecca (1972-) Urban Legend 1998; Jawbreaker 1999; From Dusk till Dawn 3: the Hangman's Daughter 2000; Shadow Hours 2000

Gayle, Jackie (1926-2002) Tin Men 1987; Plain Clothes 1988; Bert Rigby, You're a Fool 1989

Gaylor, Anna (1932-) Seven Thunders 1957; Nor the Moon by Night 1958

Gaynes, George (1917-2016) Dead Men Don't Wear Plaid 1982; Tootsie 1982; Micki & Maude 1984; Police Academy 1984; Police Academy 4: Citizens on Patrol 1987; Police Academy 5: Assignment Miami Beach 1988; Police Academy: Mission to Moscow 1994; Vanya on 42nd Street 1994

Gaynor, Janet (1906-1984) 7th Heaven 1927; Sunrise 1927; Street Angel 1928; Sunny Side Up 1929; Daddy Long Legs 1931; Delicious 1931; The First Year 1932; Tess of the Storm Country 1932; State Fair 1933; Change of Heart 1934; The Farmer Takes a Wife 1935; Ladies in Love 1936; Small Town Girl 1936; A Star Is Born 1937; Three Loves Has Nancy 1938; The Young in Heart 1938

Gaynor, Mitzi (1930-) My Blue Heaven 1950; Golden Girl 1951; Bloodhounds of Broadway 1952; The I Don't Care Girl 1952; We're Not Married 1952; There's No Business like Show Business 1954; Anything Goes 1956; The Birds and the Bees 1956; Les Girls 1957; The Joker Is Wild 1957; South Pacific 1958; Happy Anniversary 1959; Surprise Package 1960; For Love or Money 1963

Gayson, Eunice (1931-) Dance Hall 1950; Dance Little Lady 1954; Out of the Clouds 1954; Zarak 1956; Carry On Admiral 1957; The Revenge of Frankenstein 1958; Dr No 1962; From Russia with Love 1963

Gazelle, Wendy Hot Pursuit 1987; Sammy and Rosie Get Laid 1987; The In Crowd 1988; Triumph of the Spirit 1989; The Net 1995

Gazzara, Ben (1930-2012) Anatomy of a Murder 1959; The Young Doctors 1961; Captive City 1962; Convicts Four 1962; The Bridge at Remagen 1969; Husbands 1970; King: a Filmed Record... Montgomery to Memphis 1970; The Neptune Factor 1973; Capone 1975; The Killing of a Chinese Bookie 1976; Voyage of the Damned 1976; High Velocity 1977; Opening Night 1977; Bloodline 1979; Saint Jack 1979; Inchon 1981; Tales of Ordinary Madness 1981; They All Laughed 1981; An Early Frost 1985; Road House 1989; Shadow Conspiracy 1996; The Spanish Prisoner 1997; Buffalo '66 1998; Happiness 1998; The Thomas Crown Affair 1999; Hysterical Blindness 2002; Dogville 2003

Gazzo, Michael V aka **Gazzo, Michael** (1923-1995) The Godfather Part II 1974; Black Sunday 1976; Fingers 1978; Alligator 1980; Back Roads 1981; Body and Soul 1981; Fear City 1984; Cookie 1989

Ge You (1957-) Farewell My Concubine 1993; To Live 1994; Keep Cool 1997; Big Shot's Funeral 2001; The Banquet 2006

Gear, Luella (1897-1980) Carefree 1938; Phffft! 1954

Gearon, Valerie (1937-2003) Invasion 1965; Anne of the Thousand Days 1969

Geary, Anthony (1947-) Disorderlies 1987; Crack House 1989; UHF 1989; Scorchers 1991

Geary, Karl (1972-) Nadja 1995; The Eternal 1998; Hamlet 2000

Gebert, Gordon (1941-) Holiday Affair 1949; The House on Telegraph Hill 1951; The Narrow Margin 1952

Gedeck, Martina (1961-) The Lives of Others 2006; The Baader Meinhof Complex 2008; Agnosia 2010; The Wall 2012; Night Train to Lisbon 2013; The Nun 2013

Gedmintas, Ruta The Athlete 2009; You Instead 2011

Gedrick, Jason (1965-) The Heavenly Kid 1985; Iron Eagle 1985; Season of Dreams 1987; Promised Land 1988; Backdraft 1991; Summer Catch 2001; Date with Darkness 2003; Hidden Places 2006; The Wishing Tree 2012

Gee, Robbie (1970-) *Mean Machine 2001; Underworld 2003; Out of Reach 2004; Rollin with the Nines 2005; Hush 2008; Shank 2010*

Geer, Ellen (1941-) *Kotch 1971; Harold and Maude 1972; Over the Edge 1979; Our House 2006*

Geer, Will (1902-1978) *Anna Lucasta 1949; Intruder in the Dust 1949; Broken Arrow 1950; Comanche Territory 1950; The Kid from Texas 1950; To Please a Lady 1950; Winchester '73 1950; Bright Victory 1951; Double Crossbones 1951; The Tall Target 1951; Salt of the Earth 1954; Seconds 1966; In Cold Blood 1967; Bandolero! 1968; The Reivers 1969; Brother John 1970; Pieces of Dreams 1970; Jeremiah Johnson 1972; Napoleon and Samantha 1972; Executive Action 1973*

Geeson, Judy (1948-) *Berserk 1967; Here We Go round the Mulberry Bush 1967; To Sir, with Love 1967; Hammerhead 1968; Prudence and the Pill 1968; Three into Two Won't Go 1969; Two Gentlemen Sharing 1969; The Executioner 1970; Goodbye Gemini 1970; 10 Rillington Place 1970; Doomwatch 1972; Fear in the Night 1972; Diagnosis: Murder 1974; Percy's Progress 1974; Adventures of a Taxi Driver 1975; Brannigan 1975; Carry On England 1976; The Eagle Has Landed 1976; Dominique 1978; Inseminoid 1981; The Duke 1999; The Lords of Salem 2012*

Geeson, Sally (1950-) *What's Good for the Goose 1969; Bless This House 1972*

Gégauff, Paul (1922-1983) *Weekend 1967; Une Partie de Plaisir 1974*

Gehman, Martha *The Legend of Billie Jean 1985; A Kiss before Dying 1991; Threesome 1994*

Geldof, Bob (1954-) *Pink Floyd - The Wall 1982; Number One 1984; Diana & Me 1997; New York Doll 2005; Sketches of Frank Gehry 2006*

Gélin, Daniel (1921-2002) *La Ronde 1950; Les Mains Sales 1951; Le Plaisir 1951; Napoléon 1955; The Man Who Knew Too Much 1956; Le Souffle au Coeur 1971; Dandin 1988*

Gellar, Sarah Michelle (1977-) *I Know What You Did Last Summer 1997; Scream 2 1997; Small Soldiers 1998; Cruel Intentions 1999; Simply Irresistible 1999; Scooby-Doo 2002; The Grudge 2004; Scooby-Doo 2: Monsters Unleashed 2004; Southland Tales 2005; The Grudge 2 2006; Happily N'Ever After 2006; The Return 2006; The Air I Breathe 2007; TMNT 2007*

Gellman, Yani *Children of My Heart 2000; The Lizzie McGuire Movie 2003*

Gemmell, Ruth *Fever Pitch 1996; Good 2008; F 2010*

Genaro, Tony *Tremors 1990; Phenomenon 1996; Tremors 3: Back to Perfection 2001*

Gendron, François-Eric (1954-) *My Girlfriend's Boyfriend 1987; Sweet Revenge 1990*

Genest, Emile (1921-2003) *Big Red 1962; The Incredible Journey 1963*

Géniat, Marcelle (1879-1959) *Crime and Punishment 1935; La Belle Equipe 1936; Le Défroqué 1953*

Génin, René (1890-1967) *Le Jour Se Lève 1939; A Cage of Nightingales 1945*

Genn, Leo (1905-1978) *Henry V 1944; Green for Danger 1946; Mourning Becomes Electra 1947; The Snake Pit 1948; The Velvet Touch 1948; No Place for Jennifer 1949; The Miniver Story 1950; The Wooden Horse 1950; Quo Vadis 1951; Plymouth Adventure 1952; Personal Affair 1953; The Red Beret 1953; The Green Scarf 1954; Moby Dick 1956; The Steel Bayonet 1957; I Accuse! 1958; No Time to Die 1958; Too Hot to Handle 1960; Ten Little Indians 1965; Circus of Fear 1967; The Bloody Judge 1969; The Silent One 1973*

Gentile, Troy *Bad News Bears 2005; Drillbit Taylor 2007*

Gentle, Lili *Will Success Spoil Rock Hunter? 1957; Sing, Boy, Sing 1958; Mr Hobbs Takes a Vacation 1962*

Gentry, Minnie (1915-1993) *Black Caesar 1973; Def by Temptation 1990*

Gentry, Race (1934-) *Black Horse Canyon 1954; The Bold and the Brave 1956*

Geoffrey, Paul *Excalibur 1981; Zina 1985*

Geoffreys, Stephen (1964-) *Fraternity Vacation 1985; Fright Night 1985; 976-EVIL 1988; Moon 44 1990*

George, Chief Dan (1899-1981) *Smith! 1969; Little Big Man 1970; Dan Candy's Law 1973; The Bears and I 1974; Harry and Tonto 1974; The Outlaw Josey Wales 1976*

George, Christopher (1929-1983) *The Gentle Rain 1966; The 1,000 Plane Raid 1969; Chisum 1970; The Delta Factor 1970; Tiger by the Tail 1970; The Train Robbers 1973; Dixie Dynamite 1976; Grizzly 1976; Day of the Animals 1977; The Exterminator 1980; Enter the Ninja 1981; Pieces 1982*

George, Florence (1917-1998) *College Swing 1938; Tell No Tales 1939*

George, Gladys (1900-1954) *Valiant Is the Word for Carrie 1936; Madame X 1937; They Gave Him a Gun 1937; Marie Antoinette 1938; The Roaring Twenties 1939; The House across the Bay 1940; The Way of All Flesh 1940; The Maltese Falcon 1941; The Hard Way 1942; The Crystal Ball 1943; Christmas Holiday 1944; Flamingo Road 1949; Bright Leaf 1950; Undercover Girl 1950; He Ran All the Way 1951; Lullaby of Broadway 1951*

George, Heinrich (1893-1945) *Berlin Alexanderplatz 1931; Pillars of Society 1935*

George, Jan *Gods of the Plague 1969; The American Soldier 1970*

George, Maude (1888-1963) *Foolish Wives 1920; The Wedding March 1928*

George, Melissa (1976-) *Dark City 1998; The Limey 1999; New Port South 2001; Sugar & Spice 2001; The Amityville Horror 2005; Derailed 2005; Paradise Lost 2006; WAZ 2006; 30 Days of Night 2007; Triangle 2009; Swinging with the Finkels 2010; A Lonely Place to Die 2011; Felony 2013*

George, Muriel (1883-1965) *Limelight 1936; Song of the Road 1937; Went the Day Well? 1942; Last Holiday 1950*

George, Susan (1950-) *The Sorcerers 1967; The Strange Affair 1968; All Neat in Black Stockings 1969; The Looking Glass War 1969; Spring and Port Wine 1969; Twinky 1969; Eyewitness 1970; Fright 1971; Straw Dogs 1971; Mandingo 1975; Out of Season 1975; Tintorera 1977; Tomorrow Never Comes 1977; Enter the Ninja 1981; Venom 1981; The House Where Evil Dwells 1982; The Jigsaw Man 1984*

Georges-Picot, Olga (1944-1997) *Je T'Aime, Je T'Aime 1968; The Man Who Haunted Himself 1970; Persecution 1974; Love and Death 1975*

Georgeson, Tom (1937-) *No Surrender 1985; A Fish Called Wanda 1988; Downtime 1997; The Land Girls 1997; Man Dancin' 2003*

Geraghty, Brian (1975-) *Jarhead 2005; When a Stranger Calls 2006; I Know Who Killed Me 2007; The Hurt Locker 2008; Easier with Practice 2009; ATM 2012*

Geraghty, Carmelita (1901-1966) *The Pleasure Garden 1925; My Best Girl 1927*

Geraghty, Marita *Sleeping with the Enemy 1991; This Is My Life 1992; Groundhog Day 1993*

Gérald, Jim (1889-1958) *An Italian Straw Hat 1927; Adventures of Captain Fabian 1951; The Crimson Curtain 1952*

Geray, Steven *aka Geray, Steve* (1904-1973) *The Moon and Sixpence 1942; Cornered 1945; Gilda 1946; So Dark the Night 1946; The Unfaithful 1947; The Dark Past 1948; Once More, My Darling 1949; A Lady without Passport 1950; The Big Sky 1952; The Golden Blade 1953*

Gere, Richard (1949-) *Report to the Commissioner 1975; Looking for Mr Goodbar 1977; Bloodbrothers 1978; Days of Heaven 1978; Yanks 1979; American Gigolo 1980; An Officer and a Gentleman 1982; Breathless 1983; The Honorary Consul 1983; The Cotton Club 1984; King David 1985; No Mercy 1986; Power 1986; Miles from Home 1988; Internal Affairs 1990; Pretty Woman 1990; Final Analysis 1992; And the Band Played On 1993; Mr Jones 1993; Sommersby 1993; Intersection 1994; First Knight 1995; Primal Fear 1996; The Jackal 1997; Red Corner 1997; Runaway Bride 1999; Autumn in New York 2000; Dr T & the Women 2000; The Mothman Prophecies 2001; Chicago 2002; Unfaithful 2002; Shall We Dance 2004; Bee Season 2005; The Hoax 2006; The Flock 2007; The Hunting Party 2007; I'm Not There. 2007; Hachi: a Dog's Tale 2008; Nights in Rodanthe 2008; Amelia 2009; Brooklyn's Finest 2009; The Double 2011; Arbitrage 2012; Movie 43 2013; Time out of Mind 2014; The Benefactor 2015; The Second Best Exotic Marigold Hotel 2015*

Geret, Georges *aka Géret, Georges* (1924-1996) *The Diary of a Chambermaid 1964; Dead Run 1967; The Stranger 1967; They Came to Rob Las Vegas 1968; Z 1968*

Gerety, Peter *Mrs Winterbourne 1996; My Dog Tulip 2009*

Gerini, Claudia (1971-) *Francesca and Nunziata 2001; Don't Move 2004; The Passion of the Christ 2004*

Germaine, Mary (1933-) *Cloudburst 1951; Father's Doing Fine 1952; House of Blackmail 1953*

German, Lauren *A Walk to Remember 2002; Surrender Dorothy 2006; Hostel: Part II 2007; The Divide 2011*

Germann, Greg (1962-) *Jesus' Son 1999; The Last Producer 2000; Down to Earth 2001; Joe Somebody 2001; Family Plan 2005; Friends with Money 2006; All I Want for Christmas 2007; Quarantine 2008; Here Comes the Boom 2012*

Germano, Elio *Respiro 2002; My Brother Is an Only Child 2006; A Magnificent Haunting 2012; Suburra 2015*

Germon, Nane (1909-2001) *La Belle et la Bête 1946; Les Biches 1968*

Gerrard, Joanne *The Snapper 1993; The Boy from Mercury 1996*

Gerroll, Daniel (1951-) *84 Charing Cross Road 1986; Happy New Year 1987; Big Business 1988; Drop Dead Fred 1991; A Far Off Place 1993; Still Alice 2014*

Gerry, Alex (1904-1993) *The Jazz Singer 1952; The Eddie Cantor Story 1953; The Come On 1956; The Bellboy 1960*

Gershon, Gina (1962-) *3:15 1986; Cocktail 1988; Red Heat 1988; Suffering Bastards 1989; Out for Justice 1991; Miss Rose White 1992; Joey Breaker 1993; Showgirls 1995; Bound 1996; This World, Then the Fireworks 1996; Touch 1996; Face/Off 1997; Black and White 1998; I'm Losing You 1998; Legalese 1998; Lulu on the Bridge 1998; Palmetto 1998; Guinevere 1999; The Insider 1999; Driven 2001; Demonlover 2002; PS I Love You 2007; Killer Joe 2011*

Gerson, Betty Lou (1914-1999) *The Fly 1958; One Hundred and One Dalmatians 1960*

Gerstle, Frank (1915-1970) *Top Secret Affair 1957; The Wasp Woman 1959*

Gert, Valeska (1892-1978) *The Joyless Street 1925; The Threepenny Opera 1931*

Gertz, Jami (1965-) *Alphabet City 1984; Crossroads 1986; Quicksilver 1986; Less than Zero 1987; The Lost Boys 1987; Listen to Me 1989; Renegades 1989; The Boyfriend School 1990; Sibling Rivalry 1990; Jersey Girl 1992; Twister 1996; Keeping Up with the Steins 2006; Lost Holiday: the Jim and Suzanne Shemwell Story 2007*

Gervais, Ricky (1961-) *Dog Eat Dog 2000; Valiant 2005; For Your Consideration 2006; Night at the Museum 2006; Stardust 2007; Ghost Town 2008; The Invention of Lying 2009; Night at the Museum 2 2009; Cemetery Junction 2010; SPYkids 4: All the Time in the World 2011; Escape from Planet Earth 2013; Muppets Most Wanted 2014; Night at the Museum: Secret of the Tomb 2014; Life on the Road 2016*

Gerwig, Greta (1983-) *Greenberg 2009; The House of the Devil 2009; Arthur 2011; Damsels in Distress 2011; No Strings Attached 2011; Frances Ha 2012; Lola Versus 2012; Mistress America 2015; Maggie's Plan 2016; Wiener-Dog 2016*

Getty, Balthazar *aka Getty, Paul Balthazar* (1975-) *Lord of the Flies 1990; Young Guns II 1990; My Heroes Have Always Been Cowboys 1991; The Pope Must Die 1991; Dead Beat 1994; Lost Highway 1996; Four Dogs Playing Poker 1999; Shadow Hours 2000; The Center of the World 2001; Ladder 49 2004; The Tripper 2006*

Getty, Estelle (1923-2008) *Mask 1985; Mannequin 1987; Stop! or My Mom Will Shoot 1992; Fortune Hunters 1999*

Getz, John (1947-) *Tattoo 1980; Blood Simple 1983; Thief of Hearts 1984; The Fly 1986; The Fly II 1989; Men at Work 1990; Curly Sue 1991; Don't Tell Mom the Babysitter's Dead 1991; Rules of Obsession 1994; The Perfect Guy 2015*

Gheorghiu, Luminita *4 Months, 3 Weeks and 2 Days 2007; Child's Pose 2013*

Ghir, Kulvinder *Brothers in Trouble 1995; Up There 2011; Jadoo 2013*

Ghosh, Robi (1931-1997) *Abhijan 1962; Days and Nights in the Forest 1969*

Ghostley, Alice (1926-2007) *New Faces 1954; The Flim-Flam Man 1967; With Six You Get Eggroll 1968; Viva Max! 1969; Ace Eli and Rodger of the Skies 1973; Gator 1976; Not for Publication 1984; Palmer's Pick-Up 1999; Whispers: an Elephant's Tale 2000*

Giallelis, Stathis (1939-) *America, America 1963; Blue 1968; The Children of Sanchez 1978*

Giamatti, Paul (1967-) *Private Parts 1997; The Negotiator 1998; Safe Men 1998; Man on the Moon 1999; Big Momma's House 2000; Duets 2000; Planet of the Apes 2001; Storytelling 2001; Big Fat Liar 2002; Confidence 2002; Thunderpants 2002; American Splendor 2003; Paycheck 2003; Sideways 2004; Cinderella Man 2005; The Illusionist 2005; The Ant Bully 2006; Asterix and the Vikings 2006; Lady in the Water 2006; Fred Claus 2007; The Nanny Diaries 2007; Shoot 'Em Up 2007; Cold Souls 2008; Pretty Bird 2008; Duplicity 2009; The Last Station 2009; Barney's Version 2010; Ironclad 2010; The Hangover: Part II 2011; The Ides of March 2011; Too Big to Fail 2011; Win Win 2011; Cosmopolis 2012; John Dies at the End 2012; Love, Marilyn 2012; Rock of Ages 2012; Romeo & Juliet 2012; The Congress 2013; Parkland 2013; Saving Mr Banks 2013; Turbo 2013; 12 Years a Slave 2013; The Amazing Spider-Man 2 2014; Love & Mercy 2014; Madame Bovary 2014; San Andreas 2015; Straight Outta Compton 2015; Morgan 2016; Ratchet & Clank 2016*

Giannini, Adriano (1971-) *Swept Away 2002; Sinbad: Legend of the Seven Seas 2003; The Consequences of Love 2004*

Giannini, Giancarlo (1942-) *Anzio 1968; Jealousy, Italian Style 1970; The Seduction of Mimi 1972; L'Innocente 1976; Seven Beauties 1976; The End of the World (in Our Usual Bed in a Night Full of Rain) 1978; Blood Feud 1979; Immortal Bachelor 1980; Lili Marleen 1980; American Dreamer 1984; Fever Pitch 1985; Saving Grace 1985; Blood Red 1988; New York Stories 1989; Once upon a Crime 1992; A Walk in the Clouds 1995; The Disappearance of Garcia Lorca 1997; Mimic 1997; Francesca and Nunziata 2001; Hannibal 2001; Darkness 2002; My House in Umbria 2002; Man on Fire 2004; Casino Royale 2006; Quantum of Solace 2008*

Giatti, Ian (1977-) *The Great Outdoors 1988; The Rescue 1988*

Gibb, Cynthia (1963-) *Salvador 1986; Youngblood 1986; Malone 1987; Jack's Back 1988; Short Circuit 2 1988; Death Warrant 1990; Gypsy 1993; Holiday Affair 1996; Accused at 17 2009*

Gibb, Donald *Bloodsport 1987; Bloodsport II: The Next Kumite 1996*

Gibney, Rebecca (1965-) *Clubland 2006; Mental 2012*

Gibson, Henry (1935-2009) *Evil Roy Slade 1971; Charlotte's Web 1973; The Long Goodbye 1973; Nashville 1975; The Last Remake of Beau Geste 1977; A Perfect Couple 1979; The Blues Brothers 1980; HEALTH 1980; The Incredible Shrinking Woman 1981; Monster in the Closet 1983; Switching Channels 1987; The 'Burbs 1989; Tom and Jerry: the Movie 1992; Color of a Brisk and Leaping Day 1996; Magnolia 1999*

Gibson, Hoot (1892-1962) *Straight Shooting 1917; The Last Outlaw 1936; The Horse Soldiers 1959*

Gibson, Mel (1956-) *Mad Max 1979; Tim 1979; Attack Force Z 1981; Gallipoli 1981; Mad Max 2 1981; The Year of Living Dangerously 1982; The Bounty 1984; Mrs Soffel 1984; The River 1984; Mad Max beyond Thunderdome 1985; Lethal Weapon 1987; Tequila Sunrise 1988; Lethal Weapon 2 1989; Air America 1990; Bird on a Wire 1990; Hamlet 1990; Forever Young 1992; Lethal Weapon 3 1992; The Man without a Face 1993; Maverick 1994; Braveheart 1995; Casper 1995; Pocahontas 1995; Ransom 1996; Conspiracy Theory 1997; FairyTale: a True Story 1997; Lethal Weapon 4 1998; Payback 1998; The Million Dollar Hotel 1999; Chicken Run 2000; The Patriot 2000; What Women Want 2001; Signs 2002; We Were Soldiers 2002; The Singing Detective 2003; Paparazzi 2004; Who Killed the Electric Car? 2006; Edge of Darkness 2009; The Beaver 2010; How I Spent My Summer Vacation 2012; Machete Kills 2013; The Expendables 3 2014; Blood Father 2016*

Gibson, Thomas (1962-) *Far and Away 1992; Love and Human Remains 1993; Barcelona 1994; Stardom 2000; Raising Waylon 2004*

Gibson, Tyrese *aka Tyrese* (1978-) *Baby Boy 2001; 2 Fast 2 Furious 2003; Flight of the Phoenix 2004; Annapolis 2005; Four Brothers 2005; Waist Deep 2006; Transformers 2007; Death Race 2008; Transformers: Revenge of the Fallen 2009; Legion 2010; Fast Five 2011; Transformers: Dark of the Moon 2011; Fast & Furious 6 2013; Fast & Furious 7 2014*

Gibson, Virginia (1928-2013) *Stop, You're Killing Me 1952; Athena 1954*

Gibson, Wynne (1899-1987) *City Streets 1931; Man of the World 1931; If I Had a Million 1932; Night after Night 1932; The Captain Hates the Sea 1934; Miracle on Main Street 1940*

Gidley, Pamela (1966-) *Thrashin' 1986; The Blue Iguana 1988; Cherry 2000 1988; Permanent Record 1988; Disturbed 1990; Liebestraum 1991; Highway to Hell 1992; Paper Hearts 1993; SFW 1994; Jane Austen's Mafia 1998; The Little Vampire 2000*

Giehse, Thérèse (1898-1975) *Black Moon 1974; Lacombe Lucien 1974*

Gielgud, John (1904-2000) *The Good Companions 1933; Secret Agent 1936; The Prime Minister 1940; Julius Caesar 1953; Romeo and Juliet 1954; Richard III 1955; Around the World in 80 Days 1956; The Barretts of Wimpole Street 1956; Saint Joan 1957; To Die in Madrid 1963; Becket 1964; The Loved One 1965; Chimes at Midnight 1966; The Charge of the Light Brigade 1968; Sebastian 1968; The Shoes of the Fisherman 1968; Oh! What a Lovely War 1969; Julius Caesar 1970; Eagle in a Cage 1971; Frankenstein: the True Story 1973; Lost Horizon 1973; 11 Harrowhouse 1974; Galileo 1974; Gold 1974; Murder on the Orient Express 1974; Aces High 1976; Joseph Andrews 1977; A Portrait of the Artist as a Young Man 1977; Providence 1977; Les Misérables 1978; Murder by Decree 1978; Caligula 1979; The Human Factor 1979; The Conductor 1980; The Elephant Man 1980; The Formula 1980; Sphinx 1980; Arthur 1981; Chariots of Fire 1981; Lion of the Desert 1981; Priest of Love 1981; Gandhi 1982; The Hunchback of Notre Dame 1982; Invitation to the Wedding 1983; Scandalous 1983; The Scarlet and the Black 1983; Wagner 1983; The Wicked Lady 1983; The Shooting Party 1984; Leave All Fair 1985; Plenty 1985; The Whistle Blower 1986; Appointment with Death 1988; Arthur 2: On the Rocks 1988; A Man for All Seasons 1988; Getting It Right 1989; Loser Takes All 1990; The Power of One 1991; Prospero's Books 1991; Shining Through 1992; Haunted 1995; DragonHeart 1996; Hamlet 1996; The Portrait of a Lady 1996; Shine 1996; The Magic Sword: Quest for Camelot 1997; Elizabeth 1998; The Tichborne Claimant 1998*

Gierasch, Stefan (1926-) *Jeremiah Johnson 1972; What's Up, Doc? 1972; High Plains Drifter 1973; Blood Beach 1981; Perfect 1985; Shannon's Deal 1989; Jack the Bear 1993*

Gierszal, Jakub *Yuma 2012; The Fold 2013*

Gifford, Alan (1905-1989) *The Flying Scot 1957; The Look 1957; Screaming Mimi 1958; Phase IV 1973*

Gifford, Frances (1920-1994) *The Reluctant Dragon 1941; Beyond the Blue Horizon 1942; Cry Havoc 1943; Tarzan Triumphs 1943; Marriage Is a Private Affair 1944; Thrill of a Romance 1945; Riding High 1950*

Gifford, Frank (1930-2015) *Up Periscope 1959; Viva Knievel! 1977*

Gifford, Gloria *DC Cab 1983; Vice Versa 1988*

Gift, Roland (1963-) *Sammy and Rosie Get Laid 1987; Scandal 1988*

Gigandet, Cam (1982-) *Never Back Down 2008; The Unborn 2008; Pandorum 2009; Burlesque 2010; Easy A 2010; Priest 2010; The Roommate 2011; Trespass 2011*

Giggs, Ryan *Manchester United: beyond the Promised Land 2000; The Class of '92 2013*

Giglio, Sandro (1900-1979) *Assignment - Paris 1952; The War of the Worlds 1953*

Gil, Ariadna (1969-) *Belle Epoque 1992; Second Skin 2000; Pan's Labyrinth 2006*

Gil, Vincent (1939-) *Encounter at Raven's Gate 1988; Ghosts... of the Civil Dead 1988; Body Melt 1993*

Gilbert, Andrew S *Paperback Hero 1998; Look Both Ways 2005*

Gilbert, Billy (1894-1971) *County Hospital 1932; The Music Box 1932; Pack Up Your Troubles 1932; Their First Mistake 1932; Towed in a Hole 1932; Them Thar Hills! 1934; The Bride Walks Out 1936; Poor Little Rich Girl 1936; One Hundred Men and a Girl 1937; Rosalie 1937; Snow White and the Seven Dwarfs 1937; Blockheads 1938; Happy Landing 1938; Maid's Night Out 1938; My Lucky Star 1938; His Girl*

Friday 1939; The Great Dictator 1940; Lucky Partners 1940 No, No, Nanette 1940; Seven Sinners 1940; The Villain Still Pursued Her 1940; Weekend in Havana 1941; Song of the Islands 1942; Stage Door Canteen 1943; Anchors Aweigh 1945; Bride of Vengeance 1949

Gilbert, Helen (1915-1995) Andy Hardy Gets Spring Fever 1939; The Secret of Dr Kildare 1939; Beyond the Blue Horizon 1942; The Falcon Takes Over 1942

Gilbert, Joanne Red Garters 1954; The Great Man 1956; The High Cost of Loving 1958

Gilbert, Jody (1916-1979) House by the River 1950; Willard 1971

Gilbert (1), John (1895-1936) He Who Gets Slapped 1924; The Big Parade 1925; The Merry Widow 1925; La Bohème 1926; Flesh and the Devil 1926; Love 1927; Show People 1928; A Woman of Affairs 1928; Hollywood Revue 1929; Queen Christina 1933; The Captain Hates the Sea 1934

Gilbert, Lou (1909-1978) The Great White Hope 1970; Jennifer on My Mind 1971

Gilbert, Marcus Biggles 1986; A Ghost in Monte Carlo 1990; Army of Darkness 1993

Gilbert, Melissa (1964-) The Diary of Anne Frank 1980; Sylvester 1985; Danielle Steel's Zoya 1995; Thicker than Water 2005; Spring Thaw 2007; The Christmas Pageant 2011

Gilbert, Paul (1918-1976) So This Is Paris 1954; You Can't Run Away from It 1956

Gilbert, Philip (1931-2004) Bachelor of Hearts 1958; The Frozen Dead 1966

Gilbert, Sara (1975-) Poison Ivy 1992; Dead Beat 1994; Desert Blue 1998; Light It Up 1999; Riding in Cars with Boys 2001

Gilchrist, Connie (1901-1985) A Woman's Face 1941; Apache Trail 1942; Act of Violence 1949; A Letter to Three Wives 1949; A Ticket to Tomahawk 1950; Flesh and Fury 1952; The Half-Breed 1952; Houdini 1953; It Should Happen to You 1954; Long John Silver 1954; Say One for Me 1959; The Misadventures of Merlin Jones 1964; Two on a Guillotine 1964; Tickle Me 1965

Gilchrist, Keir (1992-) It's Kind of a Funny Story 2010; It Follows 2014

Gilder, Sean The Fall 2006; The Selfish Giant 2013

Giles, Selina The Truth Game 2000; Until Death 2007

Gilford, Jack (1907-1990) A Funny Thing Happened on the Way to the Forum 1966; Enter Laughing 1967; The Incident 1967; Catch-22 1970; They Might Be Giants 1971; Save the Tiger 1973; Caveman 1981; Cocoon 1985; Cocoon: the Return 1988

Gilford, Zach Post Grad 2009; Devil's Due 2014; The Purge: Anarchy 2014

Gilgun, Joe aka Gilgun, Joseph This Is England 2006; Pride 2014

Gill, Basil (1877-1955) The Wandering Jew 1933; Knight without Armour 1937

Gill, Dan Paranormal Activity: the Ghost Dimension 2015; The Wedding Ringer 2015

Gill, Tom (1916-1971) Something in the City 1950; Behind the Headlines 1956; Up the Creek 1958

Gillain, Marie (1975-) Mon Père Ce Héros 1991; The Bait 1995; Le Bossu 1997; Laissez-passer 2001; L'Enfer 2005; Female Agents 2007; Coco avant Chanel 2009

Gillan, Karen (1937-) Outcast 2010; Not Another Happy Ending 2013; Oculus 2013; Guardians of the Galaxy 2014; The Big Short 2015; In a Valley of Violence 2016; Guardians of the Galaxy Vol 2 2017

Gillen, Aidan (1968-) Circle of Friends 1995; Some Mother's Son 1996; Mojo 1998; Buddy Boy 1999; The Low Down 2000; My Kingdom 2001; The Final Curtain 2002; Shanghai Knights 2002; 12 Rounds 2008; Blitz 2010; Treacle Jr 2010; Wake Wood 2010; Shadow Dancer 2012; Calvary 2013; Mister John 2013; Still 2014; Maze Runner: The Scorch Trials 2015; Sing Street 2015; You're Ugly Too 2015

Gillespie, Dana The People That Time Forgot 1977; Bad Timing 1980; Scrubbers 1982

Gillett, Aden The Winslow Boy 1999; Shadow of the Vampire 2000

Gillette, Anita (1936-) Boys on the Side 1995; Larger than Life 1996

Gilliam, Seth Assault at West Point: the Court Martial of John Whittaker 1994; Jefferson in Paris 1995; Courage under Fire 1996

Gilliam, Terry (1940-) And Now for Something Completely Different 1971; Monty Python and the Holy Grail 1975;

Pleasure at Her Majesty's 1976; Monty Python's Life of Brian 1979; Monty Python Live at the Hollywood Bowl 1982; Monty Python's The Meaning of Life 1983; Not the Messiah: He's a Very Naughty Boy 2009; Ray Harryhausen: Special Effects Titan 2011; For No Good Reason 2012; A Liar's Autobiography: the Untrue Story of Monty Python's Graham Chapman 2012; Absolutely Anything 2015

Gilliard Jr, Larry aka Gilliard Jr, Lawrence (1971-) Straight out of Brooklyn 1991; Next Stop Wonderland 1998; The Waterboy 1998; Simply Irresistible 1999; Cecil B Demented 2000; The Machinist 2003

Gillie, Jean (1915-1949) The Girl in the Taxi 1937; The Gentle Sex 1943; The Saint Meets the Tiger 1943; Tawny Pipit 1944

Gillies, Coco Jack Maya the Bee 2014; Oddball and the Penguins 2015

Gillies, Daniel Bride & Prejudice 2004; Captivity 2006

Gilliland, Richard (1950-) Bug 1975; Evidence of Love 1990; The Lies Boys Tell 1994; Star Kid 1997

Gillin, Hugh (1925-2004) Psycho II 1983; Psycho III 1986

Gilling, Rebecca (1953-) The Naked Country 1985; Heaven Tonight 1990

Gillingwater, Claude aka Gillingwater Sr, Claude (1870-1939) Little Lord Fauntleroy 1921; Daddy Long Legs 1931; Tess of the Storm Country 1932; The Prisoner of Shark Island 1936; Just around the Corner 1938

Gillis, Ann aka Gillis, Anne (1927-) The Adventures of Tom Sawyer 1938; Nice Girl? 1941; Abbott and Costello in Society 1944; The Cheaters 1945

Gillmer, Caroline Hotel Sorrento 1994; Paws 1997; The Monkey's Mask 2000

Gillmore, Margalo (1897-1986) The Happy Years 1950; Perfect Strangers 1950; Cause for Alarm 1951; Gaby 1956

Gilman, Sam (1915-1985) Macon County Line 1973; Every Which Way but Loose 1978

Gilmore, Alexie World's Greatest Dad 2009; Willow Creek 2013

Gilmore, Craig The Living End 1992; Totally F***ed Up 1993

Gilmore, Lowell (1906-1960) Days of Glory 1944; Johnny Angel 1945; The Picture of Dorian Gray 1945; Calcutta 1947; The Black Arrow 1948; Dream Girl 1948; King Solomon's Mines 1950; Rogues of Sherwood Forest 1950; Roadblock 1951; Lone Star 1952; Comanche 1956

Gilmore, Peter (1898-1968) I've Gotta Horse 1965; The Abominable Dr Phibes 1971; Warlords of Atlantis 1978

Gilmore, Virginia (1919-1986) Swamp Water 1941; Tall, Dark and Handsome 1941; Western Union 1941; Berlin Correspondent 1942; Orchestra Wives 1942; Walk East on Beacon 1952

Gilmour, Ian (1955-) The Odd Angry Shot 1979; The Boy Who Had Everything 1984

Gilpin, Jack (1951-) Something Wild 1986; Funny Farm 1988; Reversal of Fortune 1990

Gilpin, Peri (1961-) Laughter on the 23rd Floor 2000; Final Fantasy: the Spirits Within 2001

Gimenez Cacho, Daniel aka Giménez-Cacho, Daniel aka Giménez Cacho, Daniel (1961-) Deep Crimson 1996; Bad Education 2004; La Zona 2007; I'm Gonna Explode 2008; Blancanieves 2011; Come Out and Play 2012; How I Spent My Summer Vacation 2012

Ging, Jack (1931-) Tess of the Storm Country 1960; High Plains Drifter 1973; Where the Red Fern Grows 1974

Gingold, Hermione (1897-1987) Cosh Boy 1952; The Pickwick Papers 1952; Our Girl Friday 1953; Around the World in 80 Days 1956; Bell, Book and Candle 1958; Gigi 1958; The Naked Edge 1961; Gay Purr-ee 1962; The Music Man 1962; I'd Rather Be Rich 1964; Munster, Go Home! 1966; Promise Her Anything 1966; Jules Verne's Rocket to the Moon 1967; A Little Night Music 1977

Ginsberg, Allen (1926-1997) Pull My Daisy 1959; Magic Trip: Ken Kesey's Search for a Kool Place 2011

Ginty, Robert (1948-2009) Coming Home 1978; The Exterminator 1980; The Alchemist 1981; Loverboy 1989; Madhouse 1990; Harley Davidson and the Marlboro Man 1991

Giordani, Rocky After Dark, My Sweet 1990; Cop and a Half 1993

Giordano, Domiziana (1960-) Nostalgia 1983; Zina 1985; Nouvelle Vague 1990; Interview with the Vampire: the Vampire Chronicles 1994

Giorgelli, Gabriella (1942-) The Organizer 1963; The Beautiful Swindlers 1964

Giorgetti, Florence (1944-) La Grande Bouffe 1973; The Lacemaker 1977

Girard, Philippe Wild Target 1993; Les Apprentis 1995

Girard, Rémy (1950-) The Decline of the American Empire 1986; Jesus of Montreal 1989; The Barbarian Invasions 2003; Incendies 2010

Girardon, Michèle (1938-1975) The Sign of Leo 1959; The Seven Deadly Sins 1961; The Boulangère de Monceau 1962; Hatari! 1962

Girardot, Annie (1931-2011) Maigret Sets a Trap 1957; Rocco and His Brothers 1960; The Organizer 1963; The Dirty Game 1965; Trois Chambres à Manhattan 1965; The Witches 1966; Vivre pour Vivre 1967; Shock Treatment 1973; Doctor Françoise Gailland 1975; Les Misérables 1995; The Piano Teacher 2001; Hidden 2005

Girardot, Etienne (1856-1939) Twentieth Century 1934; Breakfast for Two 1937; Port of Seven Seas 1938; Fast and Loose 1939; The Story of Vernon and Irene Castle 1939

Girardot, Hippolyte (1955-) First Name: Carmen 1983; Manon des Sources 1986; A World without Pity 1989; Hors la Vie 1991; Après l'Amour 1992; Le Parfum d'Yvonne 1994; Jump Tomorrow 2001; House of 9 2004; Kings & Queen 2004; Lady Chatterley 2006; The Flight of the Red Balloon 2007; Calm Chaos 2008; Life of Riley 2014

Giraud, Roland (1942-) 3 Men and a Cradle 1985; Mister Frost 1990

Giraudeau, Bernard (1947-2010) Le Grand Pardon 1981; Après l'Amour 1992; Ridicule 1996; Water Drops on Burning Rocks 1999

Girling, Cindy The Kidnapping of the President 1980; Heart of a Child 1994

Girotti, Massimo (1918-2003) Ossessione 1942; Chronicle of a Love 1950; Senso 1954; Marguerite de la Nuit 1955; It Happened in Rome 1956; Duel of the Titans 1961; Imperial Venus 1963; Theorem 1968; The Red Tent 1969; Medea 1970; Baron Blood 1972; L'Innocente 1976; Facing Window 2003

Gish, Annabeth (1971-) Desert Bloom 1985; Hiding Out 1987; Mystic Pizza 1988; Shag 1988; Coupe de Ville 1990; The Last Supper 1995; Beautiful Girls 1996; What Love Sees 1996; Steel 1997; Double Jeopardy 1999; No Higher Love 1999; SLC Punk! 1999; Buying the Cow 2000; Race to Space 2001; Life on Liberty Street 2004; Texas Killing Fields 2011; Before I Wake 2015

Gish, Dorothy (1898-1968) Home, Sweet Home 1914; Hearts of the World 1918; Orphans of the Storm 1921; Fury 1923; Centennial Summer 1946; The Cardinal 1963

Gish, Lillian (1893-1993) The Musketeers of Pig Alley 1912; The Battle of Elderbush 1914; The Battle of the Sexes 1914; Home, Sweet Home 1914; The Birth of a Nation 1915; Intolerance 1916; Hearts of the World 1918; Broken Blossoms 1919; Way Down East 1920; Orphans of the Storm 1921; The White Sister 1923; La Bohème 1926; The Scarlet Letter 1926; Annie Laurie 1927; The Wind 1928; One Romantic Night 1930; His Double Life 1933; The Commandos Strike at Dawn 1942; Miss Susie Slagle's 1945; Duel in the Sun 1946; Portrait of Jennie 1948; The Cobweb 1955; The Night of the Hunter 1955; Orders to Kill 1958; The Unforgiven 1960; The Great Chase 1961; The Love Goddesses 1965; Follow Me, Boys! 1966; The Comedians 1967; Warning Shot 1967; Twin Detectives 1976; A Wedding 1978; Hambone and Hillie 1984; Sweet Liberty 1986; The Whales of August 1987

Gish, Sheila (1942-2005) A Day in the Death of Joe Egg 1971; Highlander 1986; Mansfield Park 1999; Highlander: Endgame 2000

Gist, Robert (1924-1998) The Band Wagon 1953; D-Day the Sixth of June 1956

Giuffre, Aldo (1924-2010) The Best of Enemies 1961; Ghosts - Italian Style 1967

Giuffrè, Carlo (1928-) Madame 1961; Pinocchio 2002

Giuntoli, Neil Child's Play 1988; The Borrower 1989; Henry: Portrait of a Serial Killer, Part II 1996; Palmer's Pick-Up 1999

Giustini, Carlo (1923-) The Passionate Stranger 1957; The Savage Innocents 1960

Givens, Robin (1964-) A Rage in Harlem 1991; Boomerang 1992; Blankman 1994; Foreign Student 1994; Head of State 2003

Givney, Kathryn (1897-1978) My Friend Irma 1949; Lightning Strikes

Twice 1951; Operation Pacific 1951; Three Coins in the Fountain 1954

Givot, George (1903-1984) Step Lively, Jeeves 1937; DuBarry Was a Lady 1943; The Falcon and the Co-Eds 1943; Riff-Raff 1947; April in Paris 1952; Three Sailors and a Girl 1953; China Gate 1957

Gladwin, Joe (1906-1987) Night Must Fall 1964; Nearest and Dearest 1972

Glascott, Fiona Goldfish Memory 2003; Apartment 143 2011

Glaser, Paul Michael aka Glaser, Michael (1943-) Fiddler on the Roof 1971; Butterflies Are Free 1972; Phobia 1980; Something's Gotta Give 2003

Glass, Ned (1906-1984) Jennifer 1953; West Side Story 1961; Kid Galahad 1962; Charade 1963; The All-American Boy 1973

Glasser, Isabel Forever Young 1992; Pure Country 1992; Tactical Assault 1998

Glasser, Phillip (1955-) An American Tail 1986; An American Tail: Fievel Goes West 1991; Stanley's Magic Garden 1994

Glau, Summer Serenity 2005; Deadly Honeymoon 2009; Help for the Holidays 2012

Glaubrecht, Frank The Bridge 1959; Codename Wildgeese 1984

Glaudini, Robert aka Glaudini, Bob The Alchemist 1981; Parasite 1982

Gleason, Jackie (1916-1987) All through the Night 1941; Larceny, Inc 1942; Orchestra Wives 1942; Springtime in the Rockies 1942; The Hustler 1961; Gigt 1962; Requiem for a Heavyweight 1962; Papa's Delicate Condition 1963; Soldier in the Rain 1963; Skidoo 1968; Don't Drink the Water 1969; How to Commit Marriage 1969; How Do I Love Thee? 1970; Mr Billion 1977; Smokey and the Bandit 1977; Smokey and the Bandit II 1980; The Toy 1982; Smokey and the Bandit III 1983; The Sting II 1983; Nothing in Common 1986

Gleason, James (1886-1959) A Free Soul 1931; Blondie of the Follies 1932; The Penguin Pool Murder 1932; Murder on the Blackboard 1934; Murder on a Honeymoon 1935; The Ex-Mrs Bradford 1936; Murder on a Bridle Path 1936; The Plot Thickens 1936; Affectionately Yours 1941; A Date with the Falcon 1941; Here Comes Mr Jordan 1941; Meet John Doe 1941; The Falcon Takes Over 1942; Footlight Serenade 1942; My Gal Sal 1942; Crash Dive 1943; Arsenic and Old Lace 1944; A Guy Named Joe 1944; Once upon a Time 1944; The Clock 1945; A Tree Grows in Brooklyn 1945; Home Sweet Homicide 1946; The Hoodlum Saint 1946; Lady Luck 1946; The Well Groomed Bride 1946; The Bishop's Wife 1947; Down to Earth 1947; Tycoon 1947; The Return of October 1948; When My Baby Smiles at Me 1948; Miss Grant Takes Richmond 1949; The Jackpot 1950; Key to the City 1950; Riding High 1950; Come Fill the Yellow Cab Man 1950; I'll See You in My Dreams 1951; Forever Female 1953; Suddenly 1954; The Girl Rush 1955; The Night of the Hunter 1955; Star in the Dust 1956; Loving You 1957; Man in the Shadow 1957; Spring Reunion 1957; The Last Hurrah 1958; Rock-a-Bye Baby 1958

Gleason, Joanna (1950-) Crimes and Misdemeanors 1989; The Boys 1991; FX 2 1991; American Perfekt 1997; Wedding Daze 2006; The Skeleton Twins 2014

Gleason, Paul (1939-2006) Doc Savage: the Man of Bronze 1975; He Knows You're Alone 1981; The Pursuit of DB Cooper 1981; Trading Places 1983; The Breakfast Club 1985; Forever Lulu 1987; Die Hard 1988; Johnny Be Good 1988; Wishman 1991; Running Cool 1993; Money Talks 1997

Gleckler, Robert (1887-1939) The Glass Key 1935; Whipsaw 1935

Gleeson, Brendan (1955-) The Snapper 1993; Braveheart 1995; Trojan Eddie 1996; I Went Down 1997; Turbulence 1997; The General 1998; Lake Placid 1999; Saltwater 1999; Harrison's Flowers 2000; The Tailor of Panama 2000; Wild about Harry 2000; AI: Artificial Intelligence 2001; Dark Blue 2002; Gangs of New York 2002; 28 Days Later... 2002; Cold Mountain 2003; In My Country 2004; Troy 2004; The Village 2004; Breakfast on Pluto 2005; Kingdom of Heaven 2005; The Tiger's Tail 2006; Beowulf 2007; In Bruges 2008; Perrier's Bounty 2009; The Secret of Kells 2009; Green Zone 2010; Harry Potter and the Deathly Hallows: Part 1 2010; Albert Nobbs 2011; The Cup 2011; The Guard 2011; The Company You Keep 2012; The Pirates! in an Adventure with Scientists! 2012;

The Raven 2012; Safe House 2012; Calvary 2013; The Grand Seduction 2013; The Smurfs 2 2013; Edge of Tomorrow 2014; Song of the Sea 2014; Stonehearst Asylum 2014; In the Heart of the Sea 2015; Suffragette 2015; Assassin's Creed 2016

Gleeson, Brian aka Gleeson, Briain The Tiger's Tail 2006; Life's a Breeze 2013; The Stag 2013; Tiger Raid 2016

Gleeson, Domhnall (1983-) True Grit 2010; Dredd 2012; Shadow Dancer 2012; About Time 2013; Frank 2013; Ex Machina 2014; Unbroken 2014; Brooklyn 2015; The Revenant 2015; Star Wars Episode VII: the Force Awakens 2015; Goodbye Christopher Robin 2017; Mena 2017

Gleeson, Paul Komodo 1999; Virtual Nightmare 2000

Glen, Georgie Mrs Brown 1997; Calendar Girls 2003

Glen, Iain (1961-) Gorillas in the Mist 1988; Paris by Night 1988; Mountains of the Moon 1989; Silent Scream 1989; Fools of Fortune 1990; Rosencrantz and Guildenstern Are Dead 1990; The Young Americans 1993; Beautiful Creatures 2000; Gabriel & Me 2001; Lara Croft: Tomb Raider 2001; Darkness 2002; Song for a Raggy Boy 2002; Kingdom of Heaven 2005; Tara Road 2005; The Last Legion 2006; Small Engine Repair 2006; Mrs Ratcliffe's Revolution 2007; Resident Evil: Extinction 2007; Harry Brown 2009; Eye in the Sky 2015; My Cousin Rachel 2017; Resident Evil: the Final Chapter 2017

Glendenning, Candace Nicholas and Alexandra 1971; Satan's Slave 1976

Glenister, Philip ID 1994; Calendar Girls 2003; Tu£sday 2007; Bel Ami 2010

Glenn, Roy aka Glenn Sr, Roy E (1914-1971) Carmen Jones 1954; Guess Who's Coming to Dinner 1967

Glenn, Scott (1942-) Fighting Mad 1976; Apocalypse Now 1979; Cattle Annie and Little Britches 1980; Urban Cowboy 1980; The Challenge 1982; Personal Best 1982; The Keep 1983; The Right Stuff 1983; The River 1984; Silverado 1985; Wild Geese II 1985; As Summers Die 1986; Man on Fire 1987; Saigon 1988; Miss Firecracker 1989; The Hunt for Red October 1990; Backdraft 1991; My Heroes Have Always Been Cowboys 1991; The Silence of the Lambs 1991; Night of the Running Man 1994; Tall Tale 1994; Reckless 1995; Absolute Power 1996; Carla's Song 1996; Courage under Fire 1996; Desert Gamble 1996; Firestorm 1998; The Last Marshal 1999; Vertical Limit 2000; Buffalo Soldiers 2001; The Shipping News 2001; Training Day 2001; A Painted House 2003; CodeBreakers 2005; Freedom Writers 2006; The Bourne Ultimatum 2007; Nights in Rodanthe 2008; W. 2008; Secretariat 2010; The Bourne Legacy 2012; The Paperboy 2012

Glenville, Peter (1913-1996) Uncensored 1942; Madonna of the Seven Moons 1944

Gless, Sharon (1943-) Las Vegas Roundabout 1975; The Star Chamber 1983

Glick, Stacey Brighton Beach Memoirs 1986; Three o'Clock High 1987

Glover, Brian (1934-1997) Kes 1969; Sweeney! 1976; Trial by Combat 1976; An American Werewolf in London 1981; The Company of Wolves 1984; To Kill a Priest 1988; Kafka 1991; Alien³ 1992; Leon the Pig Farmer 1992; 1942: a Love Story 1994; Prince of Jutland 1994; Bob's Weekend 1996; Snow White: a Tale of Terror 1996; Stiff Upper Lips 1997

Glover, Bruce (1932-) Diamonds Are Forever 1971; One Little Indian 1973; Big Bad Mama II 1987; Hider in the House 1989; Chaindance 1991; Warlock: the Armageddon 1993

Glover, Crispin aka Glover, Crispin Hellion (1964-) My Tutor 1983; Friday the 13th: the Final Chapter 1984; Teachers 1984; Back to the Future 1985; River's Edge 1987; Where the Heart Is 1990; Wild at Heart 1990; Rubin & Ed 1991; Little Noises 1992; Even Cowgirls Get the Blues 1993; What's Eating Gilbert Grape 1993; Chasers 1994; Dead Man 1995; The People vs Larry Flynt 1996; Bartleby 2000; Charlie's Angels 2000; Like Mike 2002; Charlie's Angels: Full Throttle 2003; Willard 2003; Beowulf 2007; Epic Movie 2007; 9 2009; Alice in Wonderland 2010; Hot Tub Time Machine 2010

Glover, Danny (1947-) Iceman 1984; Places in the Heart 1984; The Color Purple 1985; Silverado 1985; Witness 1985; Lethal Weapon 1987; BAT-21

1988; Lethal Weapon 2 1989; Predator 2 1990; To Sleep with Anger 1990; Flight of the Intruder 1991; Grand Canyon 1991; Pure Luck 1991; A Rage in Harlem 1991; Lethal Weapon 3 1992; Bopha! 1993; The Saint of Fort Washington 1993; Angels in the Outfield 1994; Operation Dumbo Drop 1995; Buffalo Soldiers 1997; Gone Fishin' 1997; John Grisham's The Rainmaker 1997; Switchback 1997; Antz 1998; Beloved 1998; Lethal Weapon 4 1998; The Prince of Egypt 1998; Boesman & Lena 2000; Freedom Song 2000; The Royal Tenenbaums 2001; Saw 2004; Manderlay 2005; The Adventures of Brer Rabbit 2006; Bamako 2006; Barnyard 2006; Dreamgirls 2006; The Shaggy Dog 2006; Battle for Terra 2007; Be Kind Rewind 2007; Honeydripper 2007; Shooter 2007; Blindness 2008; 2012 2009; Age of the Dragons 2010; Alpha and Omega 2010; Death at a Funeral 2010; Beyond the Lights 2014; Rage 2014; We Are Many 2014

Glover, Edmund (1911-1978) The Ghost Ship 1943; Marine Raiders 1944
Glover, Joan The Neon Bible 1995; Lolita 1997
Glover, John (1944-) Somebody Killed Her Husband 1978; The American Success Company 1979; Last Embrace 1979; A Little Sex 1981; The Evil That Men Do 1984; A Flash of Green 1984; An Early Frost 1985; A Killing Affair 1985; White Nights 1985; 52 Pick-Up 1986; Willy/Milly 1986; The Chocolate War 1988; Masquerade 1988; Rocket Gibraltar 1988; Scrooged 1988; Gremlins 2: the New Batch 1990; What Ever Happened to...? 1991; Motherhood 1993; Automatic 1994; In the Mouth of Madness 1994; Night of the Running Man 1994; Love! Valour! Compassion! 1997; Payback 1998
Glover, Julian (1935-) Girl with Green Eyes 1963; I Was Happy Here 1966; Theatre of Death 1966; Quatermass and the Pit 1967; The Magus 1968; The Adding Machine 1969; Alfred the Great 1969; The Last Grenade 1970; The Rise and Rise of Michael Rimmer 1970; Dead Cert 1974; Luther 1974; For Your Eyes Only 1981; Heat and Dust 1982; Kim 1984; Hearts of Fire 1987; The Secret Garden 1987; Indiana Jones and the Last Crusade 1989; Treasure Island 1990; King Ralph 1991; The Infiltrator 1995; Vatel 2000; Two Men Went to War 2002; Strings 2004; Big Nothing 2006; Mirrors 2008
Glover, Richard Sightseers 2012; A Field in England 2013
Glover, Savion (1973-) Tap 1989; Bamboozled 2000
Glynn, Carlin (1940-) Continental Divide 1981; The Trip to Bountiful 1985; Blood Red 1988; Convicts 1991; Judy Berlin 1999
Glynne, Mary (1898-1954) The Good Companions 1933; Scrooge 1935
Gobbi, Tito (1913-1984) The Barber of Seville 1946; Rigoletto 1946; Pagliacci 1948; The Glass Mountain 1949
Gobel, George (1919-1991) The Birds and the Bees 1956; I Married a Woman 1958; Ellie 1984
Godard, Jean-Luc (1930-) A Bout de Souffle 1959; The Sign of Leo 1959; Le Petit Soldat 1960; Cleo from 5 to 7 1961; RoGoPaG 1962; Vivre Sa Vie 1962; Bande à Part 1964; The Defector 1966; Two or Three Things I Know about Her 1966; Vladimir et Rosa 1970; Number Two 1975; First Name: Carmen 1983; Soigne Ta Droite 1986; King Lear - Fear and Loathing 1987; Notre Musique 2004
Goddard, Paulette (1910-1990) Pack Up Your Troubles 1932; Modern Times 1936; Dramatic School 1938; The Young in Heart 1938; The Cat and the Canary 1939; The Women 1939; The Ghost Breakers 1940; The Great Dictator 1940; North West Mounted Police 1940; Second Chorus 1940; Hold Back the Dawn 1941; Nothing but the Truth 1941; Pot o' Gold 1941; The Forest Rangers 1942; Reap the Wild Wind 1942; Star Spangled Rhythm 1942; The Crystal Ball 1943; So Proudly We Hail 1943; I Love a Soldier 1944; Standing Room Only 1944; Duffy's Tavern 1945; Kitty 1945; Diary of a Chambermaid 1946; An Ideal Husband 1947; Suddenly It's Spring 1947; Unconquered 1947; Variety Girl 1947; On Our Merry Way 1948; Anna Lucasta 1949; Bride of Vengeance 1949; Vice Squad 1953; The Stranger Came Home 1954; Time of Indifference 1964
Godfrey, Derek (1924-1983) Guns of Darkness 1962; The Vengeance of She 1968; A Midsummer Night's Dream 1969; Hands of the Ripper 1971

Godfrey, Patrick Heat and Dust 1982; Ever After: a Cinderella Story 1998; For No Good Reason 2012
Godfrey, Peter (1899-1970) Good Morning, Boys 1937; Dr Jekyll and Mr Hyde 1941
Godino, Javier The Secret in Their Eyes 2009; Everybody Has a Plan 2012
Godley, Adam The Golden Compass 2007; Son of Rambow 2007; The X-Files: I Want to Believe 2008
Godrèche, Judith aka **Godreche, Judith** (1972-) The Man in the Iron Mask 1997; Pot Luck 2002; Quicksand 2003; Potiche 2010; The Overnight 2015
Godridge, Constance First a Girl 1935; Return of a Stranger 1937
Godsell, Vanda (1919-1990) The Brain Machine 1954; Bitter Harvest 1963; Clash by Night 1963; This Sporting Life 1963; The Earth Dies Screaming 1964
Godunov, Alexander (1949-1995) The Money Pit 1985; Witness 1985; Die Hard 1988
Goelz, Dave (1946-) The Muppet Movie 1979; The Great Muppet Caper 1981; The Muppets Take Manhattan 1984; The Muppet Christmas Carol 1992; Muppet Treasure Island 1996; Muppets from Space 1999; It's a Very Merry Muppet Christmas Movie 2002; Kermit's Swamp Years 2002; The Muppets' Wizard of Oz 2005; The Muppets 2011; Muppets Most Wanted 2014
Goenaga, Bárbara Timecrimes 2007; Agnosia 2010
Goethals, Angela (1977-) Heartbreak Hotel 1988; Triple Bogey on a Par Five Hole 1991; VI Warshawski 1991
Goetz, Peter Michael (1941-) Best Defense 1984; Beer 1985; Jumpin' Jack Flash 1986; My Little Girl 1986; Promise 1986; Dad 1989; Infinity 1996
Goetzke, Bernhard (1884-1964) Destiny 1921; Dr Mabuse, the Gambler 1922
Goggins, Walton The Apostle 1997; Shanghai Noon 2000; Predators 2010; Mojave 2014; The Hateful Eight 2015
Goic, Alejandro The Maid 2009; The Club 2015
Going, Joanna (1963-) Wyatt Earp 1994; Inventing the Abbotts 1997; Little City 1997; Heaven 1998; Phantoms 1998; Chasing a Dream 1998; The Tree of Life 2010
Golan, Gila (1940-) Our Man Flint 1966; Three on a Couch 1966; The Valley of Gwangi 1969
Gold, Brandy (1977-) Wildcats 1986; Amityville: the Evil Escapes 1989
Gold, Jimmy (1886-1967) Alf's Button Afloat 1938; Gasbags 1940
Goldberg, Adam (1970-) Dazed and Confused 1993; The Prophecy 1994; Saving Private Ryan 1998; Sunset Strip 2000; A Beautiful Mind 2001; The Salton Sea 2002; How to Lose a Guy in 10 Days 2003; Frankenstein 2004; Déjà Vu 2006; Stay Alive 2006; 2 Days in Paris 2002; A Monster in Paris 2011
Goldberg, Bill (1966-) Ready to Rumble 2000; Looney Tunes: Back in Action 2004
Goldberg, Iddo Suzie Gold 2003; Unmade Beds 2009; Last Passenger 2013
Goldberg, Whoopi (1949-) The Color Purple 1985; Jumpin' Jack Flash 1986; Burglar 1987; Fatal Beauty 1987; Clara's Heart 1988; The Telephone 1988; Homer and Eddie 1989; Ghost 1990; The Long Walk Home 1990; Soapdish 1991; The Player 1992; Sarafina! 1992; Sister Act 1992; Made in America 1993; Sister Act 2: Back in the Habit 1993; Corrina, Corrina 1994; The Lion King 1994; The Little Rascals 1994; Naked in New York 1994; The Pagemaster 1994; Star Trek: Generations 1994; Boys on the Side 1995; The Celluloid Closet 1995; Moonlight and Valentino 1995; Theodore Rex 1995; The Associate 1996; Bogus 1996; Eddie 1996; Ghosts of Mississippi 1996; Burn Hollywood Burn 1997; A Christmas Carol 1997; In & Out 1997; In the Gloaming 1997; Rodgers & Hammerstein's Cinderella 1997; How Stella Got Her Groove Back 1998; A Knight in Camelot 1998; Rudolph the Red-Nosed Reindeer 1998; The Rugrats Movie 1998; The Adventures of Rocky & Bullwinkle 1999; Alice in Wonderland 1999; The Deep End of the Ocean 1999; Girl, Interrupted 1999; Monkeybone 2000; Call Me Claus 2001; Rat Race 2001; It's a Very Merry Muppet Christmas Movie 2002; My Fair Madame 2002; Star Trek: Nemesis 2002; Racing Stripes 2004; The Aristocrats 2005; For Colored Girls 2010; Being Elmo: a Puppeteer's Journey 2011; A Little Bit

of Heaven 2011; Misery Loves Comedy 2015
Goldblatt, Harold (?-1982) The Reluctant Saint 1962; The Mind Benders 1963; The Running Man 1963; The Scarlet Blade 1963; The Reptile 1966
Goldblum, Jeff (1952-) Death Wish 1974; Nashville 1975; St Ives 1976; Special Delivery 1976; Between the Lines 1977; The Sentinel 1977; Invasion of the Body Snatchers 1978; Remember My Name 1978; Thank God It's Friday 1978; Threshold 1981; The Big Chill 1983; The Adventures of Buckaroo Banzai across the 8th Dimension 1984; Into the Night 1985; Silverado 1985; Transylvania 6-5000 1985; The Fly 1986; Beyond Therapy 1987; Earth Girls Are Easy 1988; Vibes 1988; The Tall Guy 1989; Mister Frost 1990; The Favour, the Watch and the Very Big Fish 1991; Deep Cover 1992; Shooting Elizabeth 1992; Jurassic Park 1993; Lush Life 1993; Hideaway 1995; Nine Months 1995; Powder 1995; The Great White Hype 1996; Independence Day 1996; Trigger Happy 1996; The Lost World: Jurassic Park 1997; Holy Man 1998; The Prince of Egypt 1998; Auggie Rose 2000; One of the Hollywood Ten 2000; Cats & Dogs 2001; Igby Goes Down 2002; The Life Aquatic with Steve Zissou 2004; Man of the Year 2006; Morning Glory 2010; The Switch 2010; Le Week-end 2013; Independence Day: Resurgence 2016
Golden, Annie (1951-) Hair 1979; Forever Lulu 1987; The Pebble and the Penguin 1995
Golden, Geoffrey This Other Eden 1959; December Bride 1990
Goldie, Wyndham (1897-1957) Under the Red Robe 1937; Old Bones of the River 1938; The Girl in the News 1940; The Strange World of Planet X 1957
Goldin, Ricky Paull (1968-) The Blob 1988; Lambada 1990
Goldman, Danny The World's Greatest Athlete 1973; Where the Buffalo Roam 1980
Goldner, Charles (1900-1955) The Rocking Horse Winner 1949; Third Time Lucky 1949; The Secret People 1951; South of Algiers 1952; The Captain's Paradise 1953; Duel in the Jungle 1954
Goldoni, Lelia (1937-) Shadows 1959; Hysteria 1964; Theatre of Death 1966; Alice Doesn't Live Here Anymore 1974; The Disappearance of Aimee 1976; Bloodbrothers 1978
Goldstein, Brett SuperBob 2015; Adult Life Skills 2016
Goldstein, Jenette (1960-) Aliens 1986; Near Dark 1987
Goldthwait, Bobcat aka **Goldthwait, Bob** (1962-) Police Academy 2: Their First Assignment 1985; One Crazy Summer 1986; Police Academy 3: Back in Training 1986; Burglar 1987; Police Academy 4: Citizens on Patrol 1987; Hot to Trot 1988; Scrooged 1988; Shakes the Clown 1991; American Yakuza 2: Back to Back 1996; G-Men from Hell 2000; Lion of Oz 2000
Goldwyn, Tony (1960-) Ghost 1990; Kuffs 1991; Traces of Red 1992; The Pelican Brief 1993; Reckless 1995; Truman 1995; The Boys Next Door 1996; The Substance of Fire 1996; Kiss the Girls 1997; Tarzan 1999; Bounce 2000; The 6th Day 2000; An American Rhapsody 2001; The Last Samurai 2003; The Last House on the Left 2008; The Mechanic 2011; Divergent 2014
Golightly, Gage The Long Shot 2004; The Asylum 2015; Cabin Fever 2016
Golino, Valeria (1966-) Big Top Pee-wee 1988; Rain Man 1988; Three Sisters 1988; Torrents of Spring 1989; The King's Whore 1990; Hot Shots! 1991; The Indian Runner 1991; Year of the Gun 1991; Puerto Escondido 1992; Hot Shots! Part Deux 1993; Clean Slate 1994; Immortal Beloved 1994; Leaving Las Vegas 1995; Shooting the Moon 1998; Side Streets 1998; Things You Can Tell Just by Looking at Her 2000; Frida 2002; Respiro 2002; 36 Quai des Orfèvres 2004; Calm Chaos 2008; Ca$h 2008; Human Capital 2013
Golonka, Arlene (1939-) The Busy Body 1967; Hang 'Em High 1968; The In-Laws 1979; The Last Married Couple in America 1980; My Tutor 1983; Skeletons 1996
Gombell, Minna (1892-1973) Bad Girl 1931; The First Year 1932; Hello Sister! 1933; The Lemon Drop Kid 1934; The Merry Widow 1934; The Thin Man 1934; Banjo on My Knee 1936; Blockheads 1938; Johnny Doesn't Live Here Anymore 1944
Gomez, Carlos (1962-) Fools Rush In 1997; In Hell 2003

Gomez, Carmelo Vacas 1991; The Red Squirrel 1993; Secrets of the Heart 1997
Gómez, Fernando Fernán (1921-2007) The Spirit of the Beehive 1973; Mamá Cumple 100 Años 1979; Belle Epoque 1992; Butterfly's Tongue 1999; The City of No Limits 2002
Gomez, Ian (1964-) My Big Fat Greek Wedding 2002; Connie and Carla 2004; Underclassman 2004
Gómez, José Luis (1940-) Goya's Ghosts 2006; Broken Embraces 2009
Gomez, Selena (1992-) Ramona and Beezus 2010; Monte Carlo 2011; Hotel Transylvania 2012; Spring Breakers 2012; Getaway 2013; The Fundamentals of Caring 2015; Hotel Transylvania 2 2015; Bad Neighbours 2 2016
Gomez, Thomas (1905-1971) Sherlock Holmes and the Voice of Terror 1942; Who Done It? 1942; White Savage 1943; Abbott and Costello in Society 1944; Dead Man's Eyes 1944; Patrick the Great 1944; Phantom Lady 1944; The Daltons Ride Again 1945; Johnny o'Clock 1947; Singapore 1947; Angel in Exile 1948; Casbah 1948; Force of Evil 1948; Key Largo 1948; Come to the Stable 1949; Sorrowful Jones 1949; That Midnight Kiss 1949; The Woman on Pier 13 1949; The Furies 1950; Kim 1950; Anne of the Indies 1951; Macao 1952; The Merry Widow 1952; Pony Soldier 1952; The Conqueror 1956; Trapeze 1956; But Not for Me 1959; Stay Away, Joe 1968
Gong Li (1965-) Red Sorghum 1987; Ju Dou 1990; Raise the Red Lantern 1991; The Story of Qiu Ju 1992; Farewell My Concubine 1993; To Live 1994; Shanghai Triad 1995; Temptress Moon 1996; Chinese Box 1997; The Emperor and the Assassin 1999; Eros 2004; 2046 2004; Memoirs of a Geisha 2005; Curse of the Golden Flower 2006; Hannibal Rising 2006; Miami Vice 2006
Gonzales, George (1967-) The Bad News Bears in Breaking Training 1977; The Bad News Bears Go to Japan 1978
Gonzalez, Nicholas (1976-) Anacondas: the Hunt for the Blood Orchid 2004; Behind Enemy Lines II: Axis of Evil 2006; Left to Die: the Sandra and Tammi Chase Story 2012
Gonzalez, Rick (1979-) The Rookie 2002; Coach Carter 2005; Pulse 2006; Apartment 143 2011
Good, Meagan (1981-) Eve's Bayou 1997; Stomp the Yard 2006; Waist Deep 2006; The Love Guru 2008; Saw V 2008; The Unborn 2008; Think like a Man 2012; Anchorman 2: the Legend Continues 2013
Goodall, Caroline (1959-) Hook 1991; The Silver Brumby 1992; Cliffhanger 1993; Schindler's List 1993; Disclosure 1994; Hotel Sorrento 1994; White Squall 1996; Casualties 1997; The Princess Diaries 2001; Chasing Liberty 2004; The Thief Lord 2005; The Cold Light of Day 2012; Mental 2012; The Dressmaker 2015
Goodall, Louise Carla's Song 1996; My Name Is Joe 1998; Aberdeen 2000; Neds 2010
Goode, Matthew (1976-) Chasing Liberty 2004; Imagine Me and You 2005; Match Point 2005; Copying Beethoven 2006; The Lookout 2007; Brideshead Revisited 2008; A Single Man 2009; Watchmen 2009; Cemetery Junction 2010; Leap Year 2010; Stoker 2013; The Imitation Game 2014; Pressure 2015; Self/Less 2015
Goodfellow, Joan Buster and Billie 1974; A Flash of Green 1984
Gooding Jr, Cuba (1968-) Boyz N the Hood 1991; Gladiator 1992; Judgment Night 1993; Lightning Jack 1994; Losing Isaiah 1995; Outbreak 1995; The Tuskegee Airmen 1995; Jerry Maguire 1996; As Good as It Gets 1997; A Murder of Crows 1998; What Dreams May Come 1998; Chill Factor 1999; Instinct 1999; Men of Honor 2000; Pearl Harbor 2001; Rat Race 2001; Boat Trip 2002; Snow Dogs 2002; The Fighting Temptations 2003; Radio 2003; Home on the Range 2004; End Game 2006; American Gangster 2007; Daddy Day Camp 2007; Norbit 2007; Hero Wanted 2008; Linewatch 2008; Gifted Hands: the Ben Carson Story 2009; Wrong Turn at Tahoe 2009; Red Tails 2012; Machete Kills 2013; Selma 2014
Goodliffe, Michael (1914-1976) The Wooden Horse 1950; Sea Devils 1952; Front Page Story 1953; The End of the Affair 1954; The Battle of the River Plate 1956; The One That Got Away 1957; Up the Creek 1958; The Thirty-Nine Steps 1959; Conspiracy of Hearts 1960; Peeping Tom 1960; The Day the Earth Caught Fire 1961; Jigsaw 1962;

80,000 Suspects 1963; The Gorgon 1964; The 7th Dawn 1964; 633 Squadron 1964; Henry VIII and His Six Wives 1972; To the Devil a Daughter 1976
Goodman-Hill, Tom Fat Slags 2004; Down Dog 2014
Goodman, Benny (1909-1986) The Big Broadcast of 1937 1936; Hollywood Hotel 1937; Sweet and Lowdown 1944; A Song Is Born 1948
Goodman, Dody (1914-2008) Bedtime Story 1964; Max Dugan Returns 1983; Splash 1984; Private Resort 1985; Cool as Ice 1991
Goodman, Henry (1950-) The Saint 1997; The Final Curtain 2002; Green Street 2004; Out on a Limb 2005; Taking Woodstock 2009
Goodman, John (1952-) Eddie Macon's Run 1983; Maria's Lovers 1984; Sweet Dreams 1985; The Big Easy 1986; True Stories 1986; Burglar 1987; Raising Arizona 1987; Everybody's All-American 1988; Punchline 1988; Always 1989; Sea of Love 1989; Arachnophobia 1990; Stella 1990; Barton Fink 1991; King Ralph 1991; The Babe 1992; Born Yesterday 1993; Matinee 1993; We're Back! A Dinosaur's Story 1993; The Flintstones 1994; Kingfish: a Story of Huey P Long 1995; Pie in the Sky 1995; Mother Night 1996; The Big Lebowski 1997; The Borrowers 1997; Blues Brothers 2000 1998; Fallen 1998; Rudolph the Red-Nosed Reindeer 1998; Bringing Out the Dead 1999; The Jack Bull 1999; The Runner 1999; Coyote Ugly 2000; The Emperor's New Groove 2000; O Brother, Where Art Thou? 2000; What Planet Are You From? 2000; Monsters, Inc 2001; My First Mister 2001; One Night at McCool's 2001; Storytelling 2001; Dirty Deeds 2002; The Jungle Book 2 2003; Masked and Anonymous 2003; Beyond the Sea 2004; Clifford's Really Big Movie 2004; Kronk's New Groove 2005; Marilyn Hotchkiss Ballroom Dancing & Charm School 2005; Bee Movie 2007; Death Sentence 2007; Evan Almighty 2007; Gigantic 2008; Speed Racer 2008; Confessions of a Shopaholic 2009; In the Electric Mist 2009; The Princess and the Frog 2009; You Don't Know Jack 2010; Red State 2011; Argo 2012; Extremely Loud & Incredibly Close 2012; Flight 2012; ParaNorman 2012; Trouble with the Curve 2012; Inside Llewyn Davis 2013; The Internship 2013; Monsters University 2013; The Monuments Men 2013; The Gambler 2014; Christmas with the Coopers 2015; Ratchet & Clank 2016; 10 Cloverfield Lane 2016; The Coldest City 2017; Kong: Skull Island 2017; Valérian and the City of a Thousand Planets 2017
Goodrich, Deborah April Fool's Day 1986; Remote Control 1988
Goodwin, Alexander (1987-) Box of Moonlight 1996; Mimic 1997
Goodwin, Angela (1925-2016) Julia and Julia 1987; The Consequences of Love 2004
Goodwin, Bill (1910-1958) Riding High 1943; Bathing Beauty 1944; The Stork Club 1945; The Jolson Story 1946; To Each His Own 1946; Heaven Only Knows 1947; So This Is New York 1948; It's a Great Feeling 1949; Jolson Sings Again 1949; The Atomic Kid 1954; Lucky Me 1954; Bundle of Joy 1956
Goodwin, Ginnifer (1978-) Mona Lisa Smile 2003; Win a Date with Tad Hamilton! 2004; Walk the Line 2005; He's Just Not That into You 2008; A Single Man 2009; Ramona and Beezus 2010; Something Borrowed 2011; Killing Kennedy 2013; Tinker Bell and the Legend of the NeverBeast 2014; Zootropolis 2016
Goodwin (1), Harold (1902-1987) College 1927; The Cameraman 1928; Flight 1929; Dirigible 1931
Goodwin (2), Harold (1917-2004) Angels One Five 1952; Barnacle Bill 1957; Sea Wife 1957; The Hi-Jackers 1963
Goodwin, Laurel (1942-) Girls! Girls! Girls! 1962; Papa's Delicate Condition 1963
Goodwin, Raven (1992-) Lovely & Amazing 2001; The Station Agent 2003
Goorjian, Michael (1971-) David's Mother 1994; Hard Rain 1997; SLC Punk! 1999
Gopal, Ram (1917-2003) The Planter's Wife 1952; The Purple Plain 1954; The Blue Peter 1955
Gorbachev, Mikhail Faraway, So Close 1993; The 11th Hour 2007; Countdown to Zero 2010
Gorcey, Bernard (1886-1955) Abie's Irish Rose 1928; No Minor Vices 1948;

The Bowery Boys Meet the Monsters 1954

Gorcey, David (1921-1984) Sergeant Madden 1939; Pride of the Bowery 1941; Spooks Run Wild 1941

Gorcey, Leo (1915-1969) Dead End 1937; Mannequin 1937; Angels with Dirty Faces 1938; Angels Wash Their Faces 1939; Hell's Kitchen 1939; They Made Me a Criminal 1939; Boys of the City 1940; Pride of the Bowery 1941; Spooks Run Wild 1941; Ghosts in the Night 1943; Block Busters 1944; Bowery Champs 1944; Come Out Fighting 1945; Docks of New York 1945; So This Is New York 1948; The Bowery Boys Meet the Monsters 1954

Gordon-Levitt, Joseph (1981-) Angels in the Outfield 1994; Holy Matrimony 1994; Roadflower 1994; The Juror 1996; Halloween H20: 20 Years Later 1998; 10 Things I Hate about You 1999; Manic 2001; Treasure Planet 2002; Mysterious Skin 2004; Brick 2005; Havoc 2005; The Lookout 2007; Stop-Loss 2007; (500) Days of Summer 2009; GI Joe: the Rise of Cobra 2009; Inception 2010; 50/50 2011; The Dark Knight Rises 2012; Lincoln 2012; Looper 2012; Premium Rush 2012; Don Jon 2013; The Wind Rises 2013; Sin City: a Dame to Kill For 2014; The Night Before 2015; The Walk 2015; Snowden 2016

Gordon-Sinclair, John aka **Sinclair, Gordon John** (1962-) That Sinking Feeling 1979; Gregory's Girl 1980; The Girl in the Picture 1985; Erik the Viking 1989; The Brylcreem Boys 1996; Gregory's Two Girls 1999; World War Z 2013

Gordon, C Henry (1883-1940) Renegades 1930; Mata Hari 1931; Rasputin and the Empress 1932; Scarface 1932; Gabriel over the White House 1933; Penthouse 1933; Stamboul Quest 1934; The Charge of the Light Brigade 1936; Charlie Chan at the Olympics 1937; Conquest 1937; Stand-In 1937; The Return of the Cisco Kid 1939

Gordon, Claire And Women Shall Weep 1960; Beat Girl 1960; Konga 1960

Gordon, Colin (1911-1972) Traveller's Joy 1949; Green Grow the Rushes 1951; Folly to Be Wise 1952; Little Red Monkey 1955; The Extra Day 1956; Up in the World 1956; The One That Got Away 1957; Virgin Island 1958; Bobbikins 1959; House of Mystery 1961; In the Doghouse 1961; Night of the Eagle 1961; Strongroom 1961; Three on a Spree 1961; Don't Raise the Bridge, Lower the River 1968

Gordon, Don (1926-) Bullitt 1968; The Gamblers 1969; Cannon for Cordoba 1970; WUSA 1970; The Last Movie 1971; ZPG: Zero Population Growth 1971; Papillon 1973; Omen III: the Final Conflict 1980; The Borrower 1989; Skin Deep 1989

Gordon, Dorothy The Silver Fleet 1943; House of Whipcord 1974

Gordon, Eve (1954-) Avalon 1990; The Boys 1991; Paradise 1991; Leaving Normal 1992; Honey, We Shrunk Ourselves 1997; 'Il Be Home for Christmas 1998

Gordon, Fiona Rumba 2008; The Fairy 2011

Gordon, Gale (1906-1995) Francis Covers the Big Town 1953; Don't Give Up the Ship 1959; All in a Night's Work 1960; All Hands on Deck 1961; Sergeant Deadhead 1965; Speedway 1968

Gordon, Gavin (1901-1983) Romance 1930; American Madness 1932; The Bitter Tea of General Yen 1932; Black Beauty 1933; Hard to Handle 1933; Mystery of the Wax Museum 1933; The Scarlet Empress 1934; Bordertown 1935; Bride of Frankenstein 1935; The Bat 1959

Gordon, Hannah (1941-) Spring and Port Wine 1969; Alfie Darling 1975; Watership Down 1978; The Elephant Man 1980

Gordon, Harold (1919-1959) The Jazz Singer 1952; Viva Zapata! 1952; East of Eden 1955

Gordon, Hilary (1977-) The Mosquito Coast 1986; The Great Outdoors 1988

Gordon, Huntley (1887-1956) The Marriage Playground 1929; Anybody's Woman 1930

Gordon, Jack Truth or Dare 2011; Life Just Is 2012; Northern Soul 2012

Gordon, Keith (1961-) Home Movies 1979; Dressed to Kill 1980; Christine 1983; The Legend of Billie Jean 1985; Static 1985; Back to School 1986

Gordon, Leo (1922-2000) Gun Fury 1953; Hondo 1953; Riot in Cell Block 11 1954; The Yellow Mountain 1954; Seven Angry Men 1955; Great Day in the Morning 1956; 7th Cavalry 1956; Baby Face Nelson 1957; The Restless

Breed 1957; Apache Territory 1958; Quantrill's Raiders 1958; Ride a Crooked Trail 1958; Escort West 1959; The Jayhawkers 1959; Tarzan Goes to India 1962; The Haunted Palace 1963; Kings of the Sun 1963; Beau Geste 1966; Tobruk 1966; My Name Is Nobody 1973; Savage Dawn 1985

Gordon, Luanne Stickmen 2000; Mee-Shee: the Water Giant 2005

Gordon, Lucy (1980-2009) Russian Dolls 2005; Gainsbourg (Je T'Aime... Moi Non Plus) 2010

Gordon, Mary (1882-1963) The Irish in Us 1935; The Great O'Malley 1937; Pot o' Gold 1941; Little Giant 1946

Gordon, Matt Terry 2005; Earthstorm 2006

Gordon, Nora (1894-1970) Night Was Our Friend 1951; Police Dog 1955; Woman in a Dressing Gown 1957

Gordon, Rebecca (1977-) The Mosquito Coast 1986; The Great Outdoors 1988

Gordon, Ruth (1896-1985) Dr Ehrlich's Magic Bullet 1940; Spirit of the People 1940; Two-Faced Woman 1941; Action in the North Atlantic 1943; Edge of Darkness 1943; Inside Daisy Clover 1965; Lord Love a Duck 1966; Rosemary's Baby 1968; Whatever Happened to Aunt Alice? 1969; Where's Poppa? 1970; Harold and Maude 1972; The Big Bus 1976; Every Which Way but Loose 1978; Perfect Gentlemen 1978; Boardwalk 1979; Any Which Way You Can 1980; My Bodyguard 1980; Delta Pi 1985; Maxie 1985; The Trouble with Spies 1987

Gordon, Zachary Diary of a Wimpy Kid 2010; Diary of a Wimpy Kid: Rodrick Rules 2011; Diary of a Wimpy Kid 3: Dog Days 2012

Gorham, Mel (1959-) Blue in the Face 1995; Curdled 1995; Wishful Thinking 1997; The Center of the World 2001

Goring, Marius (1912-1998) Flying 55 1939; The Spy in Black 1939; Pastor Hall 1940; A Matter of Life and Death 1946; Night Boat to Dublin 1946; Take My Life 1947; Mr Perrin and Mr Traill 1948; The Red Shoes 1948; Circle of Danger 1950; Highly Dangerous 1950; Odette 1950; Pandora and the Flying Dutchman 1950; The Man Who Watched Trains Go By 1952; Rough Shoot 1952; The Barefoot Contessa 1954; Break in the Circle 1955; Quentin Durward 1955; Ill Met by Moonlight 1956; The Moonraker 1957; I Was Monty's Double 1958; Son of Robin Hood 1958; The Treasure of San Teresa 1959; Beyond the Curtain 1960; The Inspector 1962; The Crooked Road 1964; Up from the Beach 1965; The 25th Hour 1967; The Girl on a Motorcycle 1968; First Love 1970; Zeppelin 1971

Gorman, Bud (1921-2010) Bowery Champs 1944; Docks of New York 1945

Gorman, Burn The Oxford Murders 2008; Up There 2011; Jimi: All Is by My Side 2013; Imperium 2016

Gorman, Cliff (1936-2002) The Boys in the Band 1970; Cops and Robbers 1973; Rosebud 1975; An Unmarried Woman 1978; All That Jazz 1979; Night of the Juggler 1980; Angel 1984; Night and the City 1992; Ghost Dog: the Way of the Samurai 1999

Gorman, Robert Hy aka **Gorman, Robert** (1980-) The Accidental Tourist 1988; Sometimes They Come Back 1991; Leprechaun 1992; Mr Nanny 1992

Gorshin, Frank (1933-2005) Dragstrip Girl 1957; Invasion of the Saucer Men 1957; Bells Are Ringing 1960; Ring of Fire 1961; Batman 1966; Skidoo 1968; Midnight 1989; Twelve Monkeys 1995; Beethoven's 3rd 2000; Luck of the Draw 2000

Gortner, Marjoe (1944-) The Marcus-Nelson Murders 1973; Earthquake 1974; The Food of the Gods 1976; Mausoleum 1983

Gosling, Ryan (1980-) The Believer 2001; Murder by Numbers 2002; The United States of Leland 2002; The Notebook 2003; Stay 2005; Half Nelson 2006; Fracture 2007; Lars and the Real Girl 2007; All Good Things 2010; Blue Valentine 2010; Crazy, Stupid, Love 2011; Drive 2011; The Ides of March 2011; Gangster Squad 2012; Only God Forgives 2012; The Place beyond the Pines 2012; Seduced and Abandoned 2013; The Big Short 2015; La La Land 2016; The Nice Guys 2016; Blade Runner 2 2017

Goss, Luke (1968-) Blade II 2002; Charlie 2003; The Man 2005; Mercenary for Justice 2006

Gosselaar, Mark-Paul (1974-) Dead Man on Campus 1998; Atomic Twister 2002; 12 Dates of Christmas 2011; Precious Cargo 2016

Gossett Jr, Louis aka **Gossett, Louis** aka **Gossett, Lou** (1936-) A Raisin in the Sun 1961; The Landlord 1970; Skin Game 1971; Travels with My Aunt 1972; The White Dawn 1974; The Choirboys 1977; The Deep 1977; An Officer and a Gentleman 1982; Jaws III 1983; Finders Keepers 1984; Enemy Mine 1985; Iron Eagle 1985; Firewalker 1986; The Principal 1987; Iron Eagle II 1988; The Punisher 1989; Toy Soldiers 1991; Aces: Iron Eagle III 1992; Midnight Sting 1992; A Good Man in Africa 1993; Blue Chips 1994; Iron Eagle IV 1995; Captive Heart 1996; Bram Stoker's Legend of the Mummy 1998; Strange Justice 1999

Gostukhin, Vladimir (1946-) The Ascent 1976; Urga 1990

Gotell, Walter (1924-1997) The African Queen 1951; The Bandit of Zhobe 1959; The Treasure of San Teresa 1959; The Damned 1961; The Road to Hong Kong 1962; From Russia with Love 1963; The Spy Who Loved Me 1977; The Stud 1978; Octopussy 1983; A View to a Kill 1985

Gothard, Michael (1939-1992) Up the Junction 1967; The Devils 1971; Who Slew Auntie Roo? 1971; The Valley 1972; Warlords of Atlantis 1978; For Your Eyes Only 1981; Lifeforce 1985

Gottfried, Gilbert (1955-) The Adventures of Ford Fairlane 1990; Problem Child 1990; Problem Child 2 1991; Aladdin 1992; Aladdin and the King of Thieves 1996

Gottschalk, Ferdinand (1869-1944) The Sign of the Cross 1932; Female 1933; The Man Who Broke the Bank at Monte Carlo 1935

Gough, Lloyd (1907-1984) All My Sons 1948; A Southern Yankee 1948; That Wonderful Urge 1948; Tension 1949; Storm Warning 1950; Sunset Blvd 1950; The Scarf 1951; Glory Boy 1971

Gough, Michael (1916-2011) Anna Karenina 1947; Blanche Fury 1948; Saraband for Dead Lovers 1948; No Resting Place 1950; The Man in the White Suit 1951; Night Was Our Friend 1951; The Sword and the Rose 1952; Rob Roy, the Highland Rogue 1953; Richard III 1955; Ill Met by Moonlight 1956; House in the Woods 1957; Dracula 1958; Horrors of the Black Museum 1959; Konga 1960; Mr Topaze 1961; What a Carve Up! 1961; The Phantom of the Opera 1962; Black Zoo 1963; Tamahine 1963; The Skull 1965; Berserk 1967; They Came from beyond Space 1967; Curse of the Crimson Altar 1968; The Corpse 1969; Women in Love 1969; Trog 1970; The Go-Between 1971; Henry VIII and His Six Wives 1972; Savage Messiah 1972; Horror Hospital 1973; The Legend of Hell House 1973; Galileo 1974; Satan's Slave 1976; The Boys from Brazil 1978; The Dresser 1983; Oxford Blues 1984; Top Secret! 1984; Out of Africa 1985; Caravaggio 1986; The Serpent and the Rainbow 1987; Strapless 1988; Batman 1989; The Garden 1990; Let Him Have It 1991; Batman Returns 1992; The Hour of the Pig 1993; Wittgenstein 1993; Batman Forever 1995; Batman and Robin 1997; All for Love 1999; Tim Burton's Corpse Bride 2005

Gouix, Guillaume Attila Marcel 2013; The Connection 2014

Gould, Elliott (1938-) Quick, Let's Get Married 1964; The Night They Raided Minsky's 1968; Bob & Carol & Ted & Alice 1969; MASH 1969; Getting Straight 1970; I Love My... Wife 1970; Little Murders 1971; The Touch 1971; The Long Goodbye 1973; Busting 1974; California Split 1974; Who? 1974; Whiffs 1975; Harry and Walter Go to New York 1976; A Bridge Too Far 1977; Capricorn One 1978; Matilda 1978; The Silent Partner 1978; Escape to Athena 1979; The Lady Vanishes 1979; Falling in Love Again 1980; The Last Flight of Noah's Ark 1980; The Devil and Max Devlin 1981; Over the Brooklyn Bridge 1983; The Naked Face 1984; The Telephone 1988; The Big Picture 1989; The Lemon Sisters 1989; Never Cry Devil 1989; Bugsy 1991; Dead Men Don't Die 1991; Amore! 1993; A Boy Called Hate 1995; The Glass Shield 1995; Let It Be Me 1995; City of Industry 1996; American History X 1998; The Big Hit 1998; Picking Up the Pieces 2000; Ocean's Eleven 2001; The Cat Returns 2002; Puckoon 2002; Ocean's Twelve 2004; Uncorked 2008

Gould, Harold (1923-2010) The Lawyer 1969; Mrs Pollifax - Spy 1970; Ransom for a Dead Man 1971; Where Does It Hurt? 1971; The Sting 1973; Love and Death 1975; The Strongest Man in the World 1975; The Big Bus 1976; Silent Movie 1976; The One and Only 1978; Seems like Old Times 1980; Mrs Delafield Wants to Marry 1986; Romero

1989; Brown's Requiem 1998; My Giant 1998; The Master of Disguise 2002; Freaky Friday 2003

Gould, Jason (1966-) Say Anything... 1989; The Prince of Tides 1991

Goulem, Alain aka **Goulem, Al** 36 Hours to Die 1999; Agent of Influence 2002; Reverse Angle 2008

Goulet, Robert (1933-2007) Gay Purr-ee 1962; Honeymoon Hotel 1964; I'd Rather Be Rich 1964; Atlantic City, USA 1980; Beetle Juice 1988; The Naked Gun 2½: the Smell of Fear 1991; Mr Wrong 1996; G-Men from Hell 2000; Recess: School's Out 2001

Goullet, Arthur (1894-1978) Hey! Hey! USA 1938; Caravan 1946

Gourmet, Olivier (1963-) La Promesse 1996; Nationale 7 1999; Rosetta 1999; Read My Lips 2001; The Son 2002; Time of the Wolf 2003; L'Enfant 2005; Home 2008; The Silence of Lorna 2008; The Lookout 2012; Grand Central 2013; Violette 2013

Govinda (1958-) Partner 2007; Salaam E Ishq 2007

Gowland, Gibson aka **Gibson-Gowland, T H** (1877-1951) Blind Husbands 1919; Greed 1925; The Phantom of the Opera 1925; The Secret of the Loch 1934; Cotton Queen 1937

Goyo, Dakota My Neighbor's Secret 2009; Real Steel 2011; Dark Skies 2013

Goz, Harry (1932-2003) Bill 1981; Mommie Dearest 1981

Gozlino, Paolo Vengeance 1968; Django the Bastard 1970

Gozzi, Patricia Sundays and Cybèle 1962; Rapture 1965

Grabeel, Lucas High School Musical 2006; High School Musical 2 2007; High School Musical 3: Senior Year 2008; Milk 2008

Grable, Betty (1916-1973) Melody Cruise 1933; The Gay Divorce 1934; Old Man Rhythm 1935; Follow the Fleet 1936; Pigskin Parade 1936; College Swing 1938; Million Dollar Legs 1939; Down Argentine Way 1940; Tin Pan Alley 1940; I Wake Up Screaming 1941; Moon over Miami 1941; A Yank in the RAF 1941; Footlight Serenade 1942; Song of the Islands 1942; Springtime in the Rockies 1942; Coney Island 1943; Sweet Rosie O'Grady 1943; Pin Up Girl 1944; Billy Rose's Diamond Horseshoe 1945; The Dolly Sisters 1945; Mother Wore Tights 1947; The Shocking Miss Pilgrim 1947; That Lady in Ermine 1948; When My Baby Smiles at Me 1948; The Beautiful Blonde from Bashful Bend 1949; My Blue Heaven 1950; Wabash Avenue 1950; Call Me Mister 1951; Meet Me after the Show 1951; The Farmer Takes a Wife 1953; How to Marry a Millionaire 1953; How to Be Very, Very Popular 1955; Three for the Show 1955

Grabol, Sofie (1968-) The Wolf at the Door 1986; The Silent Touch 1992; Nightwatch 1994; Mifune 1999; The Hour of the Lynx 2013

Grabowski, Norman (1933-2012) The Monkey's Uncle 1965; Blackbeard's Ghost 1967

Grace, April (1962-) Finding Forrester 2000; The Assassination of Richard Nixon 2004

Grace, Maggie (1983-) Murder in Greenwich 2002; The Fog 2005; The Jane Austen Book Club 2007; Taken 2007; Malice in Wonderland 2009; Faster 2010; Knight and Day 2010; Lockout 2012; Taken 2 2012; Decoding Annie Parker 2013; Taken 3 2014; We'll Never Have Paris 2014; The Choice 2016

Grace, Nickolas (1949-) Heat and Dust 1982; Dream Demon 1988; Salome's Last Dance 1988; The Man in the Brown Suit 1989; Tom & Viv 1994; Two Deaths 1994; Shooting Fish 1997; Puckoon 2002

Grace, Topher (1978-) In Good Company 2004; Win a Date with Tad Hamilton! 2004; Spider-Man 3 2007; Predators 2010; The Double 2011; Take Me Home Tonight 2011; Too Big to Fail 2011; The Calling 2014; Playing It Cool 2014; American Ultra 2015; Truth 2015

Gracen, Elizabeth (1960-) The Death of the Incredible Hulk 1990; Marked for Death 1990; Coherence 2013

Gracia, Sancho (1936-2012) La Comunidad 2000; El Crimen del Padre Amaro 2002; The Baby's Room 2006

Grad, Geneviève (1944-) Sandokan the Great 1963; The Gendarme of St Tropez 1964

Grad, Tzahi Eyes Wide Open 2009; Big Bad Wolves 2013

Graetz, Paul (1889-1937) Blossom Time 1934; Bulldog Jack 1934; Jew Süss 1934; Isle of Fury 1936

Graf, David (1950-2001) The Long Summer of George Adams 1982; Police

Academy 1984; Police Academy 2: Their First Assignment 1985; Police Academy 3: Back in Training 1986; Love at Stake 1987; Police Academy 4: Citizens on Patrol 1987; Police Academy 5: Assignment Miami Beach 1988; Police Academy 6: City under Siege 1989; Police Academy: Mission to Moscow 1994

Graff, Todd (1959-) Not Quite Jerusalem 1985; Five Corners 1987; Dominick and Eugene 1988; The Abyss 1989; An Innocent Man 1989; Opportunity Knocks 1990

Graff, Wilton (1903-1969) Bulldog Drummond Strikes Back 1947; The Dark Past 1948; Miss Sadie Thompson 1953

Graham, Currie Unlocking the Mask 1999; The Accidental Witness 2006; By Appointment Only 2007

Graham, David Thunderbirds Are Go! 1966; Thunderbird 6 1968; Filmed in Supermarionation 2014

Graham, Gerrit aka **Chud, Bud T** (1949-) Greetings 1968; Hi, Mom! 1970; Phantom of the Paradise 1974; Cannonball 1976; Special Delivery 1976; Demon Seed 1977; Home Movies 1979; Used Cars 1980; National Lampoon's Class Reunion 1982; TerrorVision 1986; It's Alive III: Island of the Alive 1987; CHUD II: Bud the Chud 1989; Perfume of the Cyclone 1989; Child's Play 2 1990

Graham, Heather (1970-) License to Drive 1988; Drugstore Cowboy 1989; Guilty as Charged 1991; Shout 1991; Midnight Sting 1992; The Ballad of Little Jo 1993; Even Cowgirls Get the Blues 1993; Six Degrees of Separation 1993; Entertaining Angels: the Dorothy Day Story 1996; Swingers 1996; Boogie Nights 1997; Nowhere 1997; Two Girls and a Guy 1997; Lost in Space 1998; Austin Powers: the Spy Who Shagged Me 1999; Bowfinger 1999; Committed 2000; Sidewalks of New York 2000; From Hell 2001; Killing Me Softly 2001; Say It Isn't So 2001; The Guru 2002; Hope Springs 2002; Bobby 2006; Boogie Woogie 2009; The Hangover 2009; 5 Days of War 2011; Judy Moody and the Not Bummer Summer 2011; At Any Price 2012; Cherry 2012; The Hangover Part III 2013; Horns 2013; Norm of the North 2016

Graham, Julie (1965-) The Near Room 1995; Preaching to the Perverted 1997; Bedrooms and Hallways 1998; With or without You 1999; Some Voices 2000; Tower Block 2012

Graham, Katerina Our First Christmas 2008; 17 Again 2009; Honey 2 2011

Graham, Lauren (1967-) Nightwatch 1997; One True Thing 1998; Bad Santa 2003; The Moguls 2005; The Pacifier 2005; Because I Said So 2007; Evan Almighty 2007; Flash of Genius 2008; It's Kind of a Funny Story 2010

Graham, Morland (1891-1949) Old Bill and Son 1940; The Ghost Train 1941; Gaiety George 1946; The Upturned Glass 1947; Bonnie Prince Charlie 1948; Esther Waters 1948

Graham (2), Richard Return from the River Kwai 1988; ID 1994; Arthur's Dyke 2001

Graham, Stephen (1973-) Downtime 1997; Gangs of New York 2002; American Cousins 2003; This Is England 2006; Awaydays 2009; The Damned United 2009; Doghouse 2009; Season of the Witch 2010; Best Laid Plans 2011; Pirates of the Caribbean: on Stranger Tides 2011; Texas Killing Fields 2011; Blood 2012; Get Santa 2014; Hyena 2014; Orthodox 2015; A Patch of Fog 2015

Graham, Stuart (1967-) Song for a Raggy Boy 2002; Small Engine Repair 2006; Hunger 2008; Parked 2010; In the Blood 2014

Graham, William Just William's Luck 1947; William at the Circus 1948

Grahame, Gloria (1923-1981) Blonde Fever 1944; Without Love 1945; It's a Wonderful Life 1946; Crossfire 1947; It Happened in Brooklyn 1947; Merton of the Movies 1947; Roughshod 1949; A Woman's Secret 1949; In a Lonely Place 1950; The Bad and the Beautiful 1952; The Greatest Show on Earth 1952; Macao 1952; Sudden Fear 1952; The Big Heat 1953; The Glass Wall 1953; Man on a Tightrope 1953; Prisoners of the Casbah 1953; The Good Die Young 1954; Human Desire 1954; Naked Alibi 1954; The Cobweb 1955; The Man Who Never Was 1955; Not as a Stranger 1955; Oklahoma! 1955; Odds against Tomorrow 1959; Ride beyond Vengeance 1966; Mama's Dirty Girls 1974; Mansion of the Doomed 1975; Chilly Scenes of Winter

1979; A Nightingale Sang in Berkeley Square 1979; Melvin and Howard 1980
Grahame, Margot (1911-1982) Rookery Nook 1930; The Arizonian 1935; The Informer 1935; The Three Musketeers 1935; Criminal Lawyer 1937; The Buccaneer 1938; Broken Journey 1948; Black Magic 1949; The Romantic Age 1949; The Crimson Pirate 1952; Venetian Bird 1952; The Beggar's Opera 1953; Orders Are Orders 1954
Grainger, Gawn (1940-) Mastermind 1976; August 1995; Love and Death on Long Island 1998
Grainger, Holliday (1988-) Awaydays 2009; The Scouting Book for Boys 2009; Bel Ami 2010; Great Expectations 2012; The Riot Club 2014; The Finest Hours 2015; My Cousin Rachel 2017
Grammer, Kelsey (1954-) Down Periscope 1996; Anastasia 1997; The Pentagon Wars 1998; The Real Howard Spitz 1998; Animal Farm 1999; Bartok the Magnificent 1999; Toy Story 2 1999; 15 Minutes 2001; The Sports Pages 2001; A Christmas Carol 2004; Teacher's Pet 2004; X-Men - the Last Stand 2006; The Simpsons Movie 2007; Swing Vote 2008; Fame 2009; I Don't Know How She Does It 2011; Legends of Oz: Dorothy's Return 2013; Breaking the Bank 2014; Transformers: Age of Extinction 2014; Best of Enemies 2015; Storks 2016
Gran, Albert (1862-1932) 7th Heaven 1927; Four Sons 1928; Employees' Entrance 1938
Granach, Alexander (1893-1945) Nosferatu, a Symphony of Horrors 1922; Kameradschaft 1931; Ninotchka 1939; Joan of Paris 1942; Hangmen Also Die! 1943
Granados, Rosario (1925-1997) The Great Madcap 1949; A Woman without Love 1951
Grand'Henry, Philippe Les Convoyeurs Attendent 1999; Calvaire 2004
Granger, Farley (1925-2011) The North Star 1943; The Purple Heart 1944; Enchantment 1948; Rope 1948; They Live by Night 1948; Roseanna McCoy 1949; Edge of Doom 1950; Our Very Own 1950; Side Street 1950; I Want You 1951; Strangers on a Train 1951; Hans Christian Andersen 1952; O Henry's Full House 1952; The Story of Three Loves 1953; Senso 1954; The Girl in the Red Velvet Swing 1955; The Naked Street 1955; They Call Me Trinity 1970; The Serpent 1972
Granger, Michael (1923-1981) Tarzan and the She-Devil 1953; Creature with the Atom Brain 1955; Murder by Contract 1958
Granger, Stewart (1913-1993) Convoy 1940; Secret Mission 1942; The Lamp Still Burns 1943; The Man in Grey 1943; Fanny by Gaslight 1944; Love Story 1944; Madonna of the Seven Moons 1944; Waterloo Road 1944; Caesar and Cleopatra 1945; Caravan 1946; The Magic Bow 1946; Captain Boycott 1947; Blanche Fury 1948; Saraband for Dead Lovers 1948; Woman Hater 1948; Adam and Evelyne 1949; King Solomon's Mines 1950; The Light Touch 1951; Soldiers Three 1951; The Prisoner of Zenda 1952; Scaramouche 1952; The Wild North 1952; All the Brothers Were Valiant 1953; Salome 1953; Young Bess 1953; Beau Brummell 1954; Green Fire 1954; Footsteps in the Fog 1955; Moonfleet 1955; Bhowani Junction 1956; The Last Hunt 1956; Gun Glory 1957; The Little Hut 1957; Harry Black and the Tiger 1958; The Whole Truth 1958; North to Alaska 1960; The Secret Partner 1961; Sodom and Gomorrah 1962; The Swordsman of Siena 1962; The Crooked Road 1964; The Secret Invasion 1964; The Last Safari 1967; The Trygon Factor 1967; The Hound of the Baskervilles 1972; The Wild Geese 1978
Granstedt, Greta (1907-1987) Crime without Passion 1934; The Eddie Cantor Story 1953; The Return of Dracula 1958
Grant, Beth (1949-) Love Field 1992; City Slickers II: the Legend of Curly's Gold 1994; To Wong Foo, Thanks for Everything, Julie Newmar 1995; Dance with Me 1998; The Rookie 2002; Matchstick Men 2003; Factory Girl 2006; All about Steve 2009
Grant, Bob (1932-2003) On the Buses 1971; Mutiny on the Buses 1972; Holiday on the Buses 1973
Grant, Cary (1904-1986) Blonde Venus 1932; Devil and the Deep 1932; Madame Butterfly 1932; Merrily We Go to Hell 1932; Sinners in the Sun 1932; This Is the Night 1932; Alice in Wonderland 1933; The Eagle and the Hawk 1933; Enter Madame! 1933; I'm

No Angel 1933; She Done Him Wrong 1933; Born to Be Bad 1934; Kiss and Make-Up 1934; Ladies Should Listen 1934; Thirty-Day Princess 1934; The Last Outpost 1935; Wings in the Dark 1935; The Amazing Quest of Ernest Bliss 1936; Big Brown Eyes 1936; Suzy 1936; Sylvia Scarlett 1936; Wedding Present 1936; The Awful Truth 1937; The Toast of New York 1937; Topper 1937; When You're in Love 1937; Bringing Up Baby 1938; Holiday 1938; Gunga Din 1939; His Girl Friday 1939; In Name Only 1939; Only Angels Have Wings 1939; Topper Takes a Trip 1939; The Howards of Virginia 1940; My Favorite Wife 1940; The Philadelphia Story 1940; Penny Serenade 1941; Suspicion 1941; Once upon a Honeymoon 1942; The Talk of the Town 1942; Destination Tokyo 1943; Mr Lucky 1943; Arsenic and Old Lace 1944; None but the Lonely Heart 1944; Once upon a Time 1944; Night and Day 1946; Notorious 1946; Without Reservations 1946; The Bachelor and the Bobby-Soxer 1947; The Bishop's Wife 1947; Every Girl Should Be Married 1948; Mr Blandings Builds His Dream House 1948; I Was a Male War Bride 1949; Crisis 1950; People Will Talk 1951; Monkey Business 1952; Room for One More 1952; Dream Wife 1953; To Catch a Thief 1955; An Affair to Remember 1957; Kiss Them for Me 1957; The Pride and the Passion 1957; Houseboat 1958; Indiscreet 1958; North by Northwest 1959; Operation Petticoat 1959; The Grass Is Greener 1960; That Touch of Mink 1962; Charade 1963; Father Goose 1964; Walk, Don't Run 1966; Elvis: That's the Way It Is 1970
Grant, Cy (1919-2010) Sea Wife 1957; Shaft in Africa 1973; At the Earth's Core 1976
Grant, David Marshall aka **Grant, David** (1955-) French Postcards 1979; American Flyers 1985; The Big Town 1987; BAT-21 1988; Air America 1990; Three Wishes 1995; The Stepford Wives 2004
Grant, Faye (1957-) The January Man 1989; Traces of Red 1992; Drive Me Crazy 1999
Grant, Hugh (1960-) Maurice 1987; White Mischief 1987; The Dawning 1988; The Lair of the White Worm 1988; The Big Man 1990; Impromptu 1991; Bitter Moon 1992; Night Train to Venice 1993; The Remains of the Day 1993; An Awfully Big Adventure 1994; Four Weddings and a Funeral 1994; Sirens 1994; The Englishman Who Went up a Hill, but Came down a Mountain 1995; Nine Months 1995; Restoration 1995; Sense and Sensibility 1995; Extreme Measures 1996; Mickey Blue Eyes 1999; Notting Hill 1999; Small Time Crooks 2000; Bridget Jones's Diary 2001; About a Boy 2002; Two Weeks Notice 2002; Love Actually 2003; Bridget Jones: the Edge of Reason 2004; American Dreamz 2006; Music and Lyrics 2007; Did You Hear about the Morgans? 2009; Cloud Atlas 2012; The Pirates! in an Adventure with Scientists! 2012; The Rewrite 2014; The Man from UNCLE 2015; Florence Foster Jenkins 2016
Grant, Kathryn (1933-) The Phenix City Story 1955; The Brothers Rico 1957; Guns of Fort Petticoat 1957; Mister Cory 1957; Operation Mad Ball 1957; Gunman's Walk 1958; The 7th Voyage of Sinbad 1958; Anatomy of a Murder 1959; The Big Circus 1959
Grant, Kirby (1914-1985) Red River Range 1938; Abbott and Costello in Society 1944
Grant, Lawrence (1870-1952) Bulldog Drummond 1929; The Unholy Garden 1931; The Mask of Fu Manchu 1932; Shanghai Express 1932; Speak Easily 1932; By Candlelight 1934; Under the Red Robe 1937
Grant, Lee (1927-) Detective Story 1951; The Balcony 1963; In the Heat of the Night 1967; Valley of the Dolls 1967; Buona Sera, Mrs Campbell 1968; The Big Bounce 1969; Marooned 1969; The Landlord 1970; Plaza Suite 1971; Ransom for a Dead Man 1971; Portnoy's Complaint 1972; The Internecine Project 1974; Shampoo 1975; Voyage of the Damned 1976; Airport '77 1977; Damien - Omen II 1978; The Swarm 1978; Little Miss Marker 1980; Charlie Chan and the Curse of the Dragon Queen 1981; Teachers 1984; The Big Town 1987; Defending Your Life 1991; It's My Party 1996; The Substance of Fire 1996; Mulholland Drive 2001
Grant, Olivia Wah-Wah 2005; Breakdown 2015
Grant, Richard E (1957-) Withnail & I 1986; How to Get Ahead in Advertising

1989; Killing Dad 1989; Mountains of the Moon 1989; Warlock 1989; Henry & June 1990; Hudson Hawk 1991; LA Story 1991; Bram Stoker's Dracula 1992; The Player 1992; The Age of Innocence 1993; Pret-a-Porter 1994; Jack & Sarah 1995; The Portrait of a Lady 1996; Twelfth Night 1996; Food of Love 1997; Keep the Aspidistra Flying 1997; The Serpent's Kiss 1997; Spice World: the Movie 1997; All for Love 1999; A Christmas Carol 1999; The Match 1999; The Miracle Maker 1999; The Little Vampire 2000; Strictly Sinatra 2000; Gosford Park 2001; Monsieur N 2003; Tooth 2003; The Story of an African Farm 2004; Tim Burton's Corpse Bride 2005; Penelope 2006; Cuckoo 2009; First Night 2010; Jackboots on Whitehall 2010; Horrid Henry: the Movie 2011; The Iron Lady 2011; Dom Hemingway 2013; Khumba 2013; Queen and Country 2014; Wolverine 3 2017
Grant, Rodney A (1959-) Dances with Wolves 1990; Geronimo: an American Legend 1993; Wagons East! 1994; The Jack Bull 1999
Grant, Salim (1977-) Ghost Dad 1990; The Hitman 1991
Grant, Stacy One Special Night 1999; A Trick of the Mind 2006
Grantham, Leslie (1947-) Shadow Run 1998; Lava 2000; The Wedding Tackle 2000; Charlie 2003
Granval, Charles (1882-1943) Boudu, Saved from Drowning 1932; La Nuit Fantastique 1942
Granville, Bonita (1923-1988) These Three 1936; Hard to Get 1938; Merrily We Live 1938; Nancy Drew - Detective 1938; White Banners 1938; Angels Wash Their Faces 1939; The Mortal Storm 1940; Third Finger, Left Hand 1940; The People vs Dr Kildare 1941; The Glass Key 1942; Now, Voyager 1942; Seven Miles from Alcatraz 1942; Syncopation 1942; Hitler's Children 1943; Andy Hardy's Blonde Trouble 1944; Song of the Open Road 1944; Love Laughs at Andy Hardy 1946; The Lone Ranger 1956
Grapewin, Charley aka **Grapewin, Charles** (1869-1956) Hell's House 1932; The Kiss before the Mirror 1933; Pilgrimage 1933; Torch Singer 1933; Anne of Green Gables 1934; Ah, Wilderness! 1935; Alice Adams 1935; Libeled Lady 1936; The Petrified Forest 1936; Big City 1937; Captains Courageous 1937; A Family Affair 1937; The Good Earth 1937; Of Human Hearts 1938; The Shopworn Angel 1938; Dust Be My Destiny 1939; The Wizard of Oz 1939; Ellery Queen Master Detective 1940; The Grapes of Wrath 1940; Johnny Apollo 1940; Rhythm on the River 1940; They Died with Their Boots On 1941; Tobacco Road 1941; Atlantic City 1944; Follow the Boys 1944
Graves (1), Peter (1911-1994) King Arthur Was a Gentleman 1942; Bees in Paradise 1943; Miss London Ltd 1943; Give Us the Moon 1944; I'll Be Your Sweetheart 1945; Gaiety George 1946; Spring in Park Lane 1948; Maytime in Mayfair 1949; Derby Day 1952; Lilacs in the Spring 1955; The Admirable Crichton 1957; The Adventurers 1970
Graves (2), Peter (1926-2010) Red Planet Mars 1952; Beneath the 12-Mile Reef 1953; East of Sumatra 1953; Stalag 17 1953; War Paint 1953; The Raid 1954; The Court-Martial of Billy Mitchell 1955; The Naked Street 1955; The Night of the Hunter 1955; Wichita 1955; It Conquered the World 1956; Beginning of the End 1957; A Stranger in My Arms 1959; Texas across the River 1966; Valley of Mystery 1967; The Ballad of Josie 1968; Sergeant Ryker 1968; Airplane! 1980; Airplane II: the Sequel 1982; Savannah Smiles 1982; Number One with a Bullet 1986; These Old Broads 2001
Graves, Ralph (1900-1977) Dream Street 1921; Flight 1929; Ladies of Leisure 1930; Dirigible 1931
Graves, Rupert (1963-) A Room with a View 1985; A Handful of Dust 1987; Maurice 1987; The Children 1990; Where Angels Fear to Tread 1991; Damage 1992; The Innocent Sleep 1995; Intimate Relations 1995; The Madness of King George 1995; Different for Girls 1996; Mrs Dalloway 1997; The Revengers' Comedies 1997; Dreaming of Joseph Lees 1998; Room to Rent 2000; Extreme Ops 2003; Rag Tale 2005; V for Vendetta 2005; Death at a Funeral 2007; The Waiting Room 2007; Fast Girls 2012
Gravet, Fernand aka **Graavey, Fernand** aka **Gravey, Fernand** (1904-1970) Bitter Sweet 1933; Fools

for Scandal 1938; The Great Waltz 1938; La Nuit Fantastique 1942; La Ronde 1950; How to Steal a Million 1966
Gravina, Carla (1941-) Big Deal on Madonna Street 1958; Alfredo Alfredo 1971; The Bit Player 1973; And Now My Love 1974
Gray, Billy (1938-) The Day the Earth Stood Still 1951; On Moonlight Bay 1951; All I Desire 1953; By the Light of the Silvery Moon 1953; The Girl Next Door 1953; Some Like It Hot 1959; Two for the Seesaw 1962; The Navy vs the Night Monsters 1966
Gray, Bruce Between Friends 1983; Dragnet 1987
Gray, Carole (1940-) The Young Ones 1961; Devils of Darkness 1964; Curse of the Fly 1965; The Brides of Fu Manchu 1966; Island of Terror 1966
Gray, Charles (1928-2000) Tommy the Toreador 1959; Man in the Moon 1960; Masquerade 1965; The Night of the Generals 1966; The Secret War of Harry Frigg 1967; The Devil Rides Out 1968; Mosquito Squadron 1968; The File of the Golden Goose 1969; The Executioner 1970; Diamonds Are Forever 1971; The Beast Must Die 1974; The Rocky Horror Picture Show 1975; Seven Nights in Japan 1976; The Legacy 1978; The Jigsaw Man 1984; The Tichborne Claimant 1998
Gray, Coleen (1922-2015) Kiss of Death 1947; Nightmare Alley 1947; Fury at Furnace Creek 1948; Red River 1948; Riding High 1950; The Sleeping City 1950; Apache Drums 1951; Kansas City Confidential 1952; Arrow in the Dust 1954; The Twinkle in God's Eye 1955; Death of a Scoundrel 1956; The Killing 1956; Star in the Dust 1956; The Leech Woman 1960; The Phantom Planet 1961; Town Tamer 1965
Gray, David Barry Mr Wonderful 1992; Cops and Robbersons 1994; Lawn Dogs 1997
Gray, Dolores (1924-2002) It's Always Fair Weather 1955; Kismet 1955; The Opposite Sex 1956; Designing Woman 1957
Gray, Donald (1914-1978) The Four Feathers 1939; We'll Meet Again 1942; Island of Desire 1952; Timeslip 1955
Gray, Dulcie (1915-2011) A Place of One's Own 1944; They Were Sisters 1945; Wanted for Murder 1946; The Years Between 1946; A Man about the House 1947; Mine Own Executioner 1947; My Brother Jonathan 1947; The Glass Mountain 1949; The Franchise Affair 1950; Angels One Five 1952; A Man Could Get Killed 1966
Gray, Erin (1950-) Buck Rogers in the 25th Century 1979; Six Pack 1982; Jason Goes to Hell: the Final Friday 1993
Gray, Eve (1900-1983) Moulin Rouge 1928; The Vicar of Bray 1937
Gray, Gary (1936-2006) Rachel and the Stranger 1948; The Next Voice You Hear 1950
Gray, Lawrence (1898-1970) Stage Struck 1925; The Patsy 1928; Sunny 1930; Man of the World 1931
Gray, Lorna aka **Booth, Adrian** (1918-) Red River Range 1938; The Man They Could Not Hang 1939; The Plunderers 1948
Gray, Macy Idlewild 2006; The Paperboy 2012
Gray, Nadia (1923-1994) The Spider and the Fly 1949; Night without Stars 1951; Valley of Eagles 1951; Crossed Swords 1954; Une Parisienne 1957; The Captain's Table 1958; La Dolce Vita 1960; Mr Topaze 1961; Maniac 1962; The Crooked Road 1964; The Naked Runner 1967; Two for the Road 1967
Gray, Robert (1940-) Elvis - the Movie 1979; UFOria 1980
Gray, Sally (1916-2006) Calling the Tune 1936; Over She Goes 1937; The Saint in London 1939; A Window in London 1939; Dangerous Moonlight 1941; The Saint's Vacation 1941; Green for Danger 1946; The Mark of Cain 1947; They Made Me a Fugitive 1947; Obsession 1948; Silent Dust 1948; Escape Route 1952; The Keeper 1976
Gray, Spalding (1941-2004) The Killing Fields 1984; True Stories 1986; Swimming to Cambodia 1987; Beaches 1988; Clara's Heart 1988; The Image 1990; Straight Talk 1992; King of the Hill 1993; The Paper 1994; Bad Company 1995; Beyond Rangoon 1995; Diabolique 1996; Gray's Anatomy 1996; Bliss 1997; Kate & Leopold 2002
Gray, Vernon A Day to Remember 1953; To Paris with Love 1954
Gray, Vivean Picnic at Hanging Rock 1975; The Last Wave 1977
Gray, Willoughby (1916-1993) Stranger from Venus 1954; Absolution 1978
Grayden, Sprague Paranormal Activity 2 2010; Paranormal Activity 3 2011

Graye, Devon Scar 2007; 13 Sins 2013
Graynor, Ari (1983-) Nick & Norah's Infinite Playlist 2008; Holy Rollers 2010; The Sitter 2011; Celeste & Jesse Forever 2012; For a Good Time, Call... 2012
Grayson, Diane (1948-) The Prime of Miss Jean Brodie 1969; Blind Terror 1971
Grayson, Jerry Bullet 1995; Striptease 1996
Grayson, Kathryn (1922-2010) Andy Hardy's Private Secretary 1941; The Vanishing Virginian 1941; Rio Rita 1942; Thousands Cheer 1943; Ziegfeld Follies 1944; Anchors Aweigh 1945; Two Sisters from Boston 1946; It Happened in Brooklyn 1947; The Kissing Bandit 1949; That Midnight Kiss 1949; The Toast of New Orleans 1950; Show Boat 1951; Lovely to Look At 1952; The Desert Song 1953; Kiss Me Kate 1953; So This Is Love 1953; The Vagabond King 1956
Graziosi, Franco A Fistful of Dynamite 1971; We Have a Pope 2011
Greco, José (1918-2000) Sombrero 1952; Ship of Fools 1965
Greco, Juliette aka **Gréco, Juliette** (1927-) Orphée 1950; Elena et les Hommes 1956; The Sun Also Rises 1957; Bonjour Tristesse 1958; The Roots of Heaven 1958; Crack in the Mirror 1960
Greczyn, Alice Shrooms 2006; Sex Drive 2008
Green, Adolph (1915-2002) Simon 1980; Lily in Love 1985; I Want to Go Home 1989
Green, Brian Austin (1973-) Kid 1990; The Wild Girl 2010
Green, Danny (1903-1973) Someone at the Door 1950; The Ladykillers 1955; Assignment Redhead 1956; The 7th Voyage of Sinbad 1958; The Old Dark House 1963
Green, Dorothy (1920-2008) Face of a Fugitive 1959; The Six Million Dollar Man 1973
Green, Eva (1980-) The Dreamers 2003; Arsène Lupin 2004; Kingdom of Heaven 2005; Casino Royale 2006; The Golden Compass 2007; Franklyn 2008; Cracks 2009; Clone 2010; Perfect Sense 2011; Dark Shadows 2012; 300: Rise of an Empire 2013; The Salvation 2014; Sin City: a Dame to Kill For 2014; White Bird in a Blizzard 2014; Miss Peregrine's Home for Peculiar Children 2016
Green, Garard (1924-2004) Profile 1954; Emergency 1962
Green, Gilbert (1914-1984) Dark Intruder 1965; Executive Action 1973
Green, Harry (1892-1958) This Day and Age 1933; The Cisco Kid and the Lady 1939; A King in New York 1957; Next to No Time 1958
Green (3), Johnny The Face on the Milk Carton 1995; Eight Days a Week 1996
Green, Kerri (1967-) The Goonies 1985; Summer Rental 1985; Lucas 1986; Three for the Road 1987
Green, Marika Pickpocket 1959; Emmanuelle 1974
Green, Martyn (1899-1975) The Mikado 1939; The Story of Gilbert and Sullivan 1953; A Lovely Way to Go 1968
Green, Mitzi (1920-1969) Paramount on Parade 1930; Tom Sawyer 1930; Huckleberry Finn 1931; Skippy 1931; Bloodhounds of Broadway 1952; Lost in Alaska 1952
Green, Nigel (1924-1972) Sword of Sherwood Forest 1960; Pit of Darkness 1961; The Man Who Finally Died 1962; Saturday Night Out 1963; Zulu 1963; The Masque of the Red Death 1964; The Face of Fu Manchu 1965; The Ipcress File 1965; The Skull 1965; Deadlier than the Male 1966; Khartoum 1966; Tobruk 1966; The Pink Jungle 1968; Play Dirty 1969; The Wrecking Crew 1969; Countess Dracula 1970; The Ruling Class 1972; Gawain and the Green Knight 1973
Green, Scott Last Days 2004; Paranoid Park 2007
Green, Seth (1974-) The Hotel New Hampshire 1984; Willy/Milly 1986; Can't Buy Me Love 1987; Radio Days 1987; Big Business 1988; My Stepmother Is an Alien 1988; Airborne 1993; Ticks 1993; Austin Powers: International Man of Mystery 1997; Austin Powers: the Spy Who Shagged Me 1999; Idle Hands 1999; Knockaround Guys 2001; Austin Powers in Goldmember 2002; The Italian Job 2003; Party Monster 2003; Scooby-Doo 2: Monsters Unleashed 2004; Without a Paddle 2004; The Best Man 2005; Sex Drive 2008; Old Dogs 2009; Mars Needs Moms 2011
Green, Teddy The Young Ones 1961; Summer Holiday 1962

Green (1), Tom *Freddy Got Fingered* 2001; *Stealing Harvard* 2002

Greenberg, Bryan (1978-) *The Perfect Score* 2004; *Prime* 2005; *Bride Wars* 2008

Greene, Ashley (1987-) *Twilight* 2008; *New Moon* 2009; *Eclipse* 2010; *Skateland* 2010; *LOL* 2011

Greene, David (1921-2003) *The Small Voice* 1948; *The Wooden Horse* 1950; *The Dark Light* 1951

Greene, Ellen (1951-) *Next Stop, Greenwich Village* 1976; *Little Shop of Horrors* 1986; *Talk Radio* 1988; *Dinner at Eight* 1989; *Pump Up the Volume* 1990; *Stepping Out* 1991; *Leon* 1994; *Naked Gun 33⅓: the Final Insult* 1994; *Wagons East!* 1994; *Killer: a Journal of Murder* 1995; *One Fine Day* 1996; *Fielder's Choice* 2005

Greene (2), Graham (1952-) *Dances with Wolves* 1990; *Clearcut* 1992; *Thunderheart* 1992; *Benefit of the Doubt* 1993; *Camilla* 1993; *Cooperstown* 1993; *Huck and the King of Hearts* 1993; *Maverick* 1994; *Die Hard with a Vengeance* 1995; *The Education of Little Tree* 1997; *Shattered Image* 1998; *The Green Mile* 1999; *Transamerica* 2005

Greene, Leon *A Challenge for Robin Hood* 1967; *The Devil Rides Out* 1968

Greene, Lorne (1915-1987) *The Silver Chalice* 1954; *Tight Spot* 1955; *Autumn Leaves* 1956; *The Buccaneer* 1958; *The Gift of Love* 1958; *The Last of the Fast Guns* 1958; *The Baited Trap* 1959; *The Harness* 1971; *Earthquake* 1974; *Battlestar Galactica* 1978; *Heidi's Song* 1982

Greene, Michael (1934-) *Americana* 1981; *Lost in America* 1985; *To Live and Die in LA* 1985; *Moon over Parador* 1988; *Eve of Destruction* 1991; *Rubin & Ed* 1991

Greene, Michele (1962-) *Heart of a Child* 1994; *Determination of Death* 2001; *Killer Flood* 2003

Greene, Peter (1965-) *Laws of Gravity* 1992; *Judgment Night* 1993; *The Mask* 1994; *Pulp Fiction* 1994; *The Rich Man's Wife* 1996; *Blue Streak* 1999; *Shadow Hours* 2000; *End Game* 2006

Greene, Richard (1918-1985) *Four Men and a Prayer* 1938; *Kentucky* 1938; *My Lucky Star* 1938; *Submarine Patrol* 1938; *The Hound of the Baskervilles* 1939; *The Little Princess* 1939; *Stanley and Livingstone* 1939; *Little Old New York* 1940; *Unpublished Story* 1942; *Yellow Canary* 1943; *Don't Take It to Heart* 1944; *Gaiety George* 1946; *Forever Amber* 1947; *The Fighting O'Flynn* 1948; *The Fan* 1949; *Now Barabbas Was a Robber* 1949; *That Dangerous Age* 1949; *Lorna Doone* 1951; *The Black Castle* 1952; *The Bandits of Corsica* 1953; *Captain Scarlett* 1953; *Contraband Spain* 1955; *Beyond the Curtain* 1960; *Sword of Sherwood Forest* 1960; *The Blood of Fu Manchu* 1968; *The Castle of Fu Manchu* 1968; *Tales from the Crypt* 1972

Greenleaf, Raymond (1892-1963) *Harriet Craig* 1950; *Storm Warning* 1950; *Al Jennings of Oklahoma* 1951; *A Millionaire for Christy* 1951; *Angel Face* 1953; *The Bandits of Corsica* 1953; *Three Sailors and a Girl* 1953

Greenlees, Billy aka **Greenlees, William** *That Sinking Feeling* 1979; *Gregory's Girl* 1980

Greenstreet, Sydney (1879-1954) *The Maltese Falcon* 1941; *They Died with Their Boots On* 1941; *Across the Pacific* 1942; *Casablanca* 1942; *Background to Danger* 1943; *Between Two Worlds* 1944; *The Conspirators* 1944; *Hollywood Canteen* 1944; *The Mask of Dimitrios* 1944; *Passage to Marseille* 1944; *Christmas in Connecticut* 1945; *Conflict* 1945; *Devotion* 1946; *Three Strangers* 1946; *The Verdict* 1946; *The Hucksters* 1947; *Ruthless* 1948; *The Velvet Touch* 1948; *The Woman in White* 1948; *Flamingo Road* 1949; *It's a Great Feeling* 1949; *Malaya* 1949

Greenwood, Bruce (1956-) *Wild Orchid* 1990; *Passenger 57* 1992; *Exotica* 1994; *Heart of a Child* 1994; *Treacherous Beauties* 1994; *Danielle Steel's Mixed Blessings* 1995; *The Sweet Hereafter* 1997; *Disturbing Behavior* 1998; *The Lost Son* 1998; *Double Jeopardy* 1999; *Here on Earth* 2000; *Hide and Seek* 2000; *Rules of Engagement* 2000; *Thirteen Days* 2000; *The Magnificent Ambersons* 2001; *Ararat* 2002; *Below* 2002; *The Core* 2002; *Swept Away* 2002; *Hollywood Homicide* 2003; *Being Julia* 2004; *I, Robot* 2004; *Racing Stripes* 2004; *The Riverman* 2004; *Capote* 2005; *Eight Below* 2005; *Mee-Shee: the Water Giant* 2005; *Déjà Vu* 2006; *Firehouse Dog* 2006; *I'm Not There.*

2007; *National Treasure: Book of Secrets* 2007; *Star Trek* 2009; *Barney's Version* 2010; *Dinner for Schmucks* 2010; *Meek's Cutoff* 2010; *Flight* 2012; *Devil's Knot* 2013; *Star Trek into Darkness* 2013; *Endless Love* 2014; *Good Kill* 2014

Greenwood, Charlotte (1890-1978) *Palmy Days* 1931; *Parlor, Bedroom and Bath* 1931; *Down Argentine Way* 1940; *Star Dust* 1940; *Young People* 1940; *Moon over Miami* 1941; *Tall, Dark and Handsome* 1941; *Springtime in the Rockies* 1942; *The Gang's All Here* 1943; *Home in Indiana* 1944; *Up in Mabel's Room* 1944; *Driftwood* 1946; *Oh, You Beautiful Doll* 1949; *Dangerous When Wet* 1953

Greenwood, Joan (1921-1987) *The Gentle Sex* 1943; *A Girl in a Million* 1946; *The Man Within* 1947; *The October Man* 1947; *Saraband for Dead Lovers* 1948; *The Bad Lord Byron* 1949; *Kind Hearts and Coronets* 1949; *Whisky Galore!* 1949; *The Man in the White Suit* 1951; *Young Wives' Tale* 1951; *The Importance of Being Earnest* 1952; *Father Brown* 1954; *Knave of Hearts* 1954; *Moonfleet* 1955; *Stage Struck* 1958; *Mysterious Island* 1961; *The Amorous Prawn* 1962; *The Moon-Spinners* 1964; *The Hound of the Baskervilles* 1977; *The Uncanny* 1977; *The Water Babies* 1978; *Little Dorrit* 1987

Greer, Dabbs (1917-2007) *Affair with a Stranger* 1953; *Riot in Cell Block 11* 1954; *It! The Terror from beyond Space* 1958; *The Cheyenne Social Club* 1970

Greer, Germaine *Jimi Hendrix* 1973; *Rabbit Fever* 2005

Greer, Jane aka **Greer, Bettejane** (1924-2001) *Dick Tracy* 1945; *Two o'Clock Courage* 1945; *The Bamboo Blonde* 1946; *The Falcon's Alibi* 1946; *Build My Gallows High* 1947; *Sinbad the Sailor* 1947; *They Won't Believe Me* 1947; *Station West* 1948; *The Big Steal* 1949; *The Company She Keeps* 1950; *You're in the Navy Now* 1951; *The Clown* 1952; *Desperate Search* 1952; *Run for the Sun* 1956; *Man of a Thousand Faces* 1957; *Where Love Has Gone* 1964; *Billie* 1965; *The Outfit* 1973; *Against All Odds* 1984; *Immediate Family* 1989

Greer, Judy aka **Greer, Judy Evans** (1971-) *Jawbreaker* 1999; *The Specials* 2000; *The Wedding Planner* 2001; *What Women Want* 2001; *Adaptation.* 2002; *The Cat Returns* 2002; *13 Going on 30* 2004; *The Village* 2004; *Cursed* 2005; *Elizabethtown* 2005; *27 Dresses* 2008; *Love Happens* 2009; *Henry's Crime* 2010; *Love & Other Drugs* 2010; *Marmaduke* 2010; *The Descendants* 2011; *Jeff, Who Lives at Home* 2011; *Playing for Keeps* 2012; *Carrie* 2013; *Men, Women & Children* 2014; *Addicted to Fresno* 2015; *Ant-Man* 2015; *Grandma* 2015; *War for the Planet of the Apes* 2017

Gregg, Bradley *Class of 1999* 1990; *Madhouse* 1990; *Fire in the Sky* 1993

Gregg, Christina *Cover Girl Killer* 1959; *Don't Talk to Strange Men* 1962

Gregg, Clark (1964-) *The Adventures of Sebastian Cole* 1998; *State and Main* 2000; *Lovely & Amazing* 2001; *The Human Stain* 2003; *In Good Company* 2004; *When a Stranger Calls* 2006; *Choke* 2008; *(500) Days of Summer* 2009; *Labor Day* 2013; *The To Do List* 2013

Gregg, Everley (1903-1959) *The Private Life of Henry VIII* 1933; *The Ghost Goes West* 1935; *Pygmalion* 1938; *Brief Encounter* 1945

Gregg, Hubert (1914-2004) *29 Acacia Avenue* 1945; *The Root of All Evil* 1946; *The Story of Robin Hood and His Merrie Men* 1952; *The Maggie* 1953; *Final Appointment* 1954; *Doctor at Sea* 1955; *Simon and Laura* 1955

Gregg, John (1940-) *Heatwave* 1981; *To End All Wars* 2001

Gregg, Virginia (1916-1986) *Dragnet* 1954; *Love Is a Many-Splendored Thing* 1955; *Crime in the Streets* 1956; *The Hanging Tree* 1959; *Spencer's Mountain* 1963; *Two on a Guillotine* 1964; *A Walk in the Spring Rain* 1970

Greggio, Ezio (1954-) *The Silence of the Hams* 1993; *Screw Loose* 1999

Greggory, Pascal (1954-) *The Brontë Sisters* 1979; *Pauline at the Beach* 1983; *Lucie Aubrac* 1997; *Those Who Love Me Can Take the Train* 1998; *Joan of Arc* 1999; *Time Regained* 1999; *La Fidélité* 2000; *Arsène Lupin* 2004; *Gabrielle* 2005; *The Page Turner* 2006; *La Vie en Rose* 2007

Gregory, Andre aka **Gregory, André** (1934-) *My Dinner with Andre* 1981; *Protocol* 1984; *Street Smart* 1987; *The Last Temptation of Christ* 1988; *Some Girls* 1988; *The Linguini Incident* 1991;

Vanya on 42nd Street 1994; *Last Summer in the Hamptons* 1995

Gregory, Celia (1949-2008) *Agatha* 1978; *The Inside Man* 1984; *The Baby of Macon* 1993

Gregory, David *Gaolbreak* 1962; *The Hi-Jackers* 1963

Gregory, James (1911-2002) *Nightfall* 1956; *The Big Caper* 1957; *Gun Glory* 1957; *The Young Stranger* 1957; *Al Capone* 1959; *Hey Boy! Hey Girl!* 1959; *The Manchurian Candidate* 1962; *Two Weeks in Another Town* 1962; *PT 109* 1963; *Twilight of Honor* 1963; *A Distant Trumpet* 1964; *Quick, before It Melts* 1965; *The Silencers* 1966; *Clambake* 1967; *Beneath the Planet of the Apes* 1969; *The Million Dollar Duck* 1971; *Shoot Out* 1971

Gregory, Leo (1978-) *Octane* 2003; *Suzie Gold* 2003; *Green Street* 2004; *Perfect Creature* 2005; *Stoned* 2005; *Reverb* 2006; *Daylight Robbery* 2007; *Cass* 2008; *Wild Bill* 2011; *All Things to All Men* 2012; *Payback Season* 2012

Gregory, Thea (1929-) *Profile* 1954; *Satellite in the Sky* 1956

Gregson Wagner, Natasha aka **Wagner, Natasha** (1970-) *Dead Beat* 1994; *Lost Highway* 1996; *Two Girls and a Guy* 1997; *Another Day in Paradise* 1998; *Stranger than Fiction* 1999; *High Fidelity* 2000; *Play It to the Bone* 2000; *Vampires: los Muertos* 2002; *Wonderland* 2003; *Angel in the Family* 2004; *The Accidental Witness* 2006

Gregson, John (1919-1975) *The Lavender Hill Mob* 1951; *Angels One Five* 1952; *The Brave Don't Cry* 1952; *The Holly and the Ivy* 1952; *The Titfield Thunderbolt* 1952; *Venetian Bird* 1952; *Conflict of Wings* 1953; *Genevieve* 1953; *Three Cases of Murder* 1953; *The Weak and the Wicked* 1953; *To Dorothy, a Son* 1954; *Above Us the Waves* 1955; *Value for Money* 1955; *The Battle of the River Plate* 1956; *Jacqueline* 1956; *True as a Turtle* 1956; *Miracle in Soho* 1957; *The Captain's Table* 1958; *Rooney* 1958; *Sea of Sand* 1958; *SOS Pacific* 1959; *Faces in the Dark* 1960; *The Treasure of Monte Cristo* 1960; *The Frightened City* 1961; *Live Now - Pay Later* 1962; *Tomorrow at Ten* 1962; *Fright* 1971

Greig, Robert (1880-1958) *Love Me Tonight* 1932; *The Devil-Doll* 1936; *Rose Marie* 1936; *The Lady Eve* 1941; *Sullivan's Travels* 1941

Greig, Tamsin *Tamara Drewe* 2010; *Breaking the Bank* 2014; *The Second Best Exotic Marigold Hotel* 2015

Greist, Kim (1958-) *CHUD* 1984; *Brazil* 1985; *Manhunter* 1986; *Throw Momma from the Train* 1987; *Punchline* 1988; *Why Me?* 1990; *Homeward Bound: the Incredible Journey* 1993; *Roswell* 1994; *Houseguest* 1995; *Homeward Bound II: Lost in San Francisco* 1996

Grenfell, Joyce (1910-1979) *The Demi-Paradise* 1943; *The Lamp Still Burns* 1943; *While the Sun Shines* 1946; *A Run for Your Money* 1949; *Stage Fright* 1949; *The Happiest Days of Your Life* 1950; *Laughter in Paradise* 1951; *The Pickwick Papers* 1952; *Genevieve* 1953; *The Million Pound Note* 1953; *The Belles of St Trinian's* 1954; *Forbidden Cargo* 1954; *The Good Companions* 1956; *Blue Murder at St Trinian's* 1957; *Happy Is the Bride* 1957; *The Pure Hell of St Trinian's* 1960; *The Old Dark House* 1963; *The Americanization of Emily* 1964; *The Yellow Rolls-Royce* 1964

Grenier, Adrian (1976-) *The Adventures of Sebastian Cole* 1998; *Drive Me Crazy* 1999; *Cecil B Demented* 2000; *The Devil Wears Prada* 2006; *Entourage* 2015

Grenier, Zach (1954-) *Liebestraum* 1991; *Gang in Blue* 1996; *Maximum Risk* 1996; *Rescue Dawn* 2006; *Zodiac* 2007

Gress, Googy *Maxie* 1985; *Promised Land* 1988; *Vibes* 1988

Gretsch, Joel (1963-) *The Legend of Bagger Vance* 2000; *The Emperor's Club* 2002

Grévill, Laurent (1961-) *Jack & Sarah* 1995; *Look at Me* 2004; *I've Loved You So Long* 2008

Grey, Anne (1907-1987) *Number Seventeen* 1932; *The Wandering Jew* 1933; *Bonnie Scotland* 1935

Grey, Denise (1896-1996) *Devil in the Flesh* 1947; *Carve Her Name with Pride* 1958

Grey, Jennifer (1960-) *Reckless* 1984; *Red Dawn* 1984; *American Flyers* 1985; *Ferris Bueller's Day Off* 1986; *Dirty Dancing* 1987; *Light Years* 1988; *Bloodhounds of Broadway* 1989; *Murder in Mississippi* 1990; *Wind* 1992; *The West Side Waltz* 1995

Grey, Joel (1932-) *Cabaret* 1972; *Buffalo Bill and the Indians, or Sitting Bull's History Lesson* 1976; *Remo - Unarmed and Dangerous* 1985; *Kafka* 1991; *The Music of Chance* 1993; *A Christmas Carol* 1999; *Dancer in the Dark* 2000; *Choke* 2008

Grey, Nan (1918-1993) *Dracula's Daughter* 1936; *Three Smart Girls* 1937; *Three Smart Girls Grow Up* 1939; *Tower of London* 1939; *The House of the Seven Gables* 1940; *The Invisible Man Returns* 1940

Grey, Shirley (1910-1981) *Back Street* 1932; *The Little Giant* 1933

Grey, Virginia (1917-2004) *Another Thin Man* 1939; *Broadway Serenade* 1939; *The Big Store* 1941; *Whistling in the Dark* 1941; *Tarzan's New York Adventure* 1942; *Sweet Rosie O'Grady* 1943; *Flame of the Barbary Coast* 1945; *Jungle Jim* 1948; *So This Is New York* 1948; *The Bullfighter and the Lady* 1951; *All That Heaven Allows* 1955; *The Rose Tattoo* 1955; *Accused of Murder* 1956; *Crime of Passion* 1957; *Jeanne Eagels* 1957; *The Restless Years* 1958; *No Name on the Bullet* 1959; *Portrait in Black* 1960; *Bachelor in Paradise* 1961; *Back Street* 1961; *Tammy Tell Me True* 1961; *Black Zoo* 1963; *The Naked Kiss* 1964; *Love Has Many Faces* 1965

Grey, Zena (1988-) *Snow Day* 2000; *Max Keeble's Big Move* 2001; *The Shaggy Dog* 2006; *My Soul to Take* 2010

Greyeyes, Michael (1967-) *Dance Me Outside* 1994; *The New World* 2005; *Passchendaele* 2007

Grieco, Richard (1965-) *Mobsters* 1991; *Teen Agent* 1991; *A Night at the Roxbury* 1998

Griem, Helmut (1932-2004) *The Damned* 1969; *The McKenzie Break* 1970; *Cabaret* 1972; *Ludwig* 1973; *Breakthrough* 1978; *Les Rendez-vous d'Anna* 1978; *The Second Victory* 1986; *The Plot to Kill Hitler* 1990

Grier, David Alan (1955-) *Streamers* 1983; *A Soldier's Story* 1984; *Beer* 1985; *Amazon Women on the Moon* 1987; *Boomerang* 1992; *Blankman* 1994; *In the Army Now* 1994; *Jumanji* 1995; *McHale's Navy* 1997; *Top of the World* 1997; *Return to Me* 2000; *3 Strikes* 2000; *King of Texas* 2002; *Baadasssss!* 2003; *The Woodsman* 2004; *The Muppets' Wizard of Oz* 2005

Grier, Pam (1949-) *The Big Bird Cage* 1972; *Black Mama, White Mama* 1972; *Hit Man* 1972; *Women in Cages* 1972; *Coffy* 1973; *Twilight People* 1973; *Foxy Brown* 1974; *Friday Foster* 1975; *Drum* 1976; *Greased Lightning* 1977; *Fort Apache, the Bronx* 1981; *Tough Enough* 1982; *Something Wicked This Way Comes* 1983; *Badge of the Assassin* 1985; *The Allnighter* 1987; *Nico* 1988; *The Package* 1989; *Class of 1999* 1990; *Escape from LA* 1996; *Original Gangstas* 1996; *Jackie Brown* 1997; *Holy Smoke* 1999; *In Too Deep* 1999; *Jawbreaker* 1999; *Snow Day* 2000; *Wilder* 2000; *Bones* 2001; *John Carpenter's Ghosts of Mars* 2001; *Pluto Nash* 2001; *Ladies of the House* 2008; *Just Wright* 2010; *Larry Crowne* 2011; *The Man with the Iron Fists* 2012

Grier, Rosey aka **Grier, Roosevelt** (1932-) *Skyjacked* 1972; *The Thing with Two Heads* 1972; *The Pure Hell of St Trinian's* 1960; *The Old Dark House* 1963; *The Americanization of Emily* 1964

Gries, Jonathan aka **Gries, Jon** (1957-) *TerrorVision* 1986; *Fright Night Part 2* 1988; *Kill Me Again* 1989; *Get Shorty* 1995; *Casualties* 1997; *Jackpot* 2001; *Northfork* 2002; *Welcome to the Jungle* 2003; *Napoleon Dynamite* 2004; *The Astronaut Farmer* 2006

Grieve, Helen *The Overlanders* 1946; *Bush Christmas* 1947

Grifasi, Joe (1944-) *On the Yard* 1978; *Something Short of Paradise* 1979; *Hide in Plain Sight* 1980; *Still of the Night* 1982; *FX: Murder by Illusion* 1985; *The Feud* 1989; *Benny & Joon* 1993; *Heavy* 1995; *One Fine Day* 1996; *Sunday* 1997

Griffeth, Simone (1955-) *Death Race 2000* 1975; *Hot Target* 1985; *The Patriot* 1986

Griffies, Ethel (1878-1975) *Waterloo Bridge* 1931; *We Live Again* 1934; *Stranger on the Third Floor* 1940; *Billy Liar* 1963; *The Birds* 1963

Griffin, David (1943-) *The Blood Beast Terror* 1967; *Trog* 1970

Griffin, Eddie (1968-) *The Meteor Man* 1993; *Deuce Bigalow: Male Gigolo* 1999; *John Q* 2001; *Undercover Brother* 2002; *Deuce Bigalow: European Gigolo* 2005; *Date Movie* 2006; *Norbit* 2007; *Redemption: Justice* 2007

Griffin, Josephine (1928-2005) *The Man Who Never Was* 1955; *The Extra Day* 1956; *The Spanish Gardener* 1956

Griffin, Kathy *Lion of Oz* 2000; *Joan Rivers: a Piece of Work* 2010

Griffin, Merv (1925-2007) *So This Is Love* 1953; *The Boy from Oklahoma* 1954; *Hello Down There* 1969; *The Lonely Guy* 1984

Griffin, Robert aka **Griffin, Robert E** (1902-1960) *Barricade* 1950; *Gunsight Ridge* 1957; *Monster from Green Hell* 1958

Griffis, Rhoda *Love Field* 1992; *Odd Girl Out* 2005

Griffith, Andy (1926-2012) *A Face in the Crowd* 1957; *No Time for Sergeants* 1958; *The Second Time Around* 1967; *Angel in My Pocket* 1968; *Hearts of the West* 1975; *Rustler's Rhapsody* 1985; *Spy Hard* 1996; *Daddy and Them* 1999; *Waitress* 2007

Griffith, Anthony *Panther* 1995; *Dead Man's Curve* 1997

Griffith, Gattlin *The New Daughter* 2009; *Labor Day* 2013

Griffith, Gordon (1907-1958) *Tarzan of the Apes* 1918; *Little Annie Rooney* 1925

Griffith, Hugh (1912-1980) *Kind Hearts and Coronets* 1949; *The Last Days of Dolwyn* 1949; *A Run for Your Money* 1949; *Gone to Earth* 1950; *The Titfield Thunderbolt* 1952; *The Beggar's Opera* 1953; *The Sleeping Tiger* 1954; *Passage Home* 1955; *The Good Companions* 1956; *Lucky Jim* 1957; *Ben-Hur* 1959; *The Story on Page One* 1959; *The Day They Robbed the Bank of England* 1960; *Exodus* 1960; *The Counterfeit Traitor* 1962; *The Inspector* 1962; *Mutiny on the Bounty* 1962; *Term of Trial* 1962; *Hide and Seek* 1963; *Tom Jones* 1963; *The Bargee* 1964; *The Amorous Adventures of Moll Flanders* 1965; *How to Steal a Million* 1966; *Oh Dad, Poor Dad, Mama's Hung You in the Closet and I'm Feelin' So Sad* 1967; *On My Way to the Crusades, I Met a Girl Who...* 1967; *The Sailor from Gibraltar* 1967; *Oliver!* 1968; *Cry of the Banshee* 1970; *Start the Revolution without Me* 1970; *The Abominable Dr Phibes* 1971; *Who Slew Auntie Roo?* 1971; *Dr Phibes Rises Again* 1972; *Craze* 1973; *The Final Programme* 1973; *Take Me High* 1973; *What?* 1973; *Legend of the Werewolf* 1974; *Luther* 1974; *Casanova & Co* 1976

Griffith, James (1919-1993) *Apache Drums* 1951; *Red Skies of Montana* 1952; *Tribute to a Bad Man* 1956; *Bullwhip* 1958; *Lorna* 1964

Griffith, Kenneth (1921-2006) *The Shop at Sly Corner* 1946; *Blue Scar* 1947; *Waterfront* 1950; *The Prisoner* 1955; *Circus of Horrors* 1960; *A French Mistress* 1960; *Only Two Can Play* 1961; *The Painted Smile* 1961; *Payroll* 1961; *Rotten to the Core* 1965; *The Bobo* 1967; *The Whisperers* 1967; *Great Catherine* 1968; *The Gamblers* 1969; *The House in Nightmare Park* 1973; *Callan* 1974; *Who Dares Wins* 1982; *The Englishman Who Went up a Hill, but Came down a Mountain* 1995

Griffith, Kristin *Interiors* 1978; *The Europeans* 1979; *The Long Way Home* 1998

Griffith, Melanie (1957-) *The Harrad Experiment* 1973; *The Drowning Pool* 1975; *Night Moves* 1975; *Smile* 1975; *Roar* 1981; *Body Double* 1984; *Fear City* 1984; *Something Wild* 1986; *Stormy Monday* 1987; *Cherry 2000* 1988; *The Milagro Beanfield War* 1988; *Working Girl* 1988; *The Bonfire of the Vanities* 1990; *Pacific Heights* 1990; *Women and Men: Stories of Seduction* 1990; *Paradise* 1991; *Shining Through* 1992; *A Stranger among Us* 1992; *Born Yesterday* 1993; *Milk Money* 1994; *Nobody's Fool* 1994; *Now and Then* 1995; *Two Much* 1995; *Mulholland Falls* 1996; *Lolita* 1997; *Another Day in Paradise* 1998; *Celebrity* 1998; *Shadow of Doubt* 1998; *Crazy in Alabama* 1999; *RKO 281* 1999; *Cecil B Demented* 2000; *Stuart Little 2* 2002; *The Night We Called It a Day* 2003; *Dino Time* 2012

Griffith, Raymond (1894-1937) *Hands Up!* 1926; *All Quiet on the Western Front* 1930

Griffith, Thomas Ian (1962-) *The Karate Kid III* 1989; *Excessive Force* 1993; *Hollow Point* 1996; *Kull the Conqueror* 1997; *Vampires* 1998; *The Unexpected Mrs Pollifax* 1999; *Black Point* 2001

Griffith, Tracy (1965-) *Fast Food* 1989; *The First Power* 1990; *The Finest Hour* 1991

Griffiths, Jane (1929-1975) *The Million Pound Note* 1953; *The Green Scarf* 1954; *Shadow of a Man* 1954; *The Traitor* 1957; *Tread Softly Stranger* 1958; *The Third Alibi* 1961; *Dead Man's Evidence* 1962; *The Impersonator* 1962

Griffiths, Lucy (1919-1982) *Children Galore* 1954; *The Third Alibi* 1961
Griffiths, Rachel (1968-) *Muriel's Wedding* 1994; *Children of the Revolution* 1996; *Cosi* 1996; *Jude* 1996; *To Have & to Hold* 1996; *My Best Friend's Wedding* 1997; *My Son the Fanatic* 1997; *Among Giants* 1998; *Divorcing Jack* 1998; *Hilary and Jackie* 1998; *Me Myself I* 1999; *Blow Dry* 2000; *Very Annie-Mary* 2000; *Blow* 2001; *The Adventures of Tom Thumb and Thumbelina* 2002; *The Hard Word* 2002; *The Rookie* 2002; *Plainsong* 2004; *Step Up* 2006; *Beautiful Kate* 2009
Griffiths, Richard (1947-2013) *Chariots of Fire* 1981; *Gorky Park* 1983; *Greystoke: the Legend of Tarzan, Lord of the Apes* 1984; *A Private Function* 1984; *Shanghai Surprise* 1986; *Withnail & I* 1986; *King Ralph* 1991; *The Naked Gun 2½: the Smell of Fear* 1991; *Blame It on the Bellboy* 1992; *Funny Bones* 1994; *Guarding Tess* 1994; *Sleepy Hollow* 1999; *Harry Potter and the Philosopher's Stone* 2001; *Harry Potter and the Chamber of Secrets* 2002; *Stage Beauty* 2004; *The History Boys* 2006; *Venus* 2006; *Harry Potter and the Order of the Phoenix* 2007; *Bedtime Stories* 2008; *Private Peaceful* 2012
Grillo, Frank (1963-) *Pride and Glory* 2007; *My Soul to Take* 2010; *Disconnect* 2012; *The Grey* 2012; *Homefront* 2013; *The Purge: Anarchy* 2014
Grimaudo, Nicole *Baarìa* 2009; *Loose Cannons* 2010
Grimes, Frank *The Outsider* 1979; *Britannia Hospital* 1982; *The Whales of August* 1987
Grimes, Gary (1955-) *Summer of '42* 1971; *The Culpepper Cattle Co* 1972; *Cahill, United States Marshal* 1973; *Class of '44* 1973; *The Spikes Gang* 1974
Grimes, Luke *American Sniper* 2014; *Freeheld* 2015
Grimes, Tammy (1934-) *Play It as It Lays* 1972; *Somebody Killed Her Husband* 1978; *The Runner Stumbles* 1979; *Can't Stop the Music* 1980; *The Last Unicorn* 1980; *High Art* 1998
Grimm, Oliver (1948-) *The Magnificent Rebel* 1961; *Reach for Glory* 1962
Grinberg, Anouk (1963-) *Merci la Vie* 1991; *A Self-Made Hero* 1995; *Mon Homme* 1996
Grinko, Nikolai (1920-1989) *Andrei Rublev* 1966; *Stalker* 1979
Grint, Rupert (1988-) *Harry Potter and the Philosopher's Stone* 2001; *Harry Potter and the Chamber of Secrets* 2002; *Thunderpants* 2002; *Harry Potter and the Prisoner of Azkaban* 2004; *Harry Potter and the Goblet of Fire* 2005; *Driving Lessons* 2006; *Harry Potter and the Order of the Phoenix* 2007; *Cherrybomb* 2008; *Harry Potter and the Half-Blood Prince* 2009; *Wild Target* 2009; *Harry Potter and the Deathly Hallows: Part 1* 2010; *Harry Potter and the Deathly Hallows: Part 2* 2011; *Cross of Honour* 2012; *Postman Pat: the Movie* 2013; *The Unbeatables* 2013
Grives, Steven (1951-) *Inseminoid* 1981; *Jenny Kissed Me* 1984; *Scooby-Doo* 2002
Grizzard, George (1928-2007) *Advise and Consent* 1962; *Warning Shot* 1967; *Comes a Horseman* 1978; *Seems like Old Times* 1980; *The Man with the Deadly Lens* 1982; *Bachelor Party* 1984; *Caroline?* 1990; *Small Time Crooks* 2000
Grochowska, Agnieszka *In Darkness* 2011; *Walesa: Man of Hope* 2013
Grodin, Charles (1935-) *Catch-22* 1970; *The Heartbreak Kid* 1972; *11 Harrowhouse* 1974; *King Kong* 1976; *Heaven Can Wait* 1978; *Sunburn* 1979; *It's My Turn* 1980; *Seems like Old Times* 1980; *The Great Muppet Caper* 1981; *The Incredible Shrinking Woman* 1981; *The Lonely Guy* 1984; *The Woman in Red* 1984; *Movers and Shakers* 1985; *Ishtar* 1987; *The Couch Trip* 1988; *Midnight Run* 1988; *Taking Care of Business* 1990; *Beethoven* 1992; *Beethoven's 2nd* 1993; *Dave* 1993; *Heart and Souls* 1993; *So I Married an Axe Murderer* 1993; *It Runs in the Family* 1994; *While We're Young* 2014
Grody, Kathryn (1946-) *Parents* 1988; *The Lemon Sisters* 1989
Groener, Harry (1951-) *Buddy Boy* 1999; *The Day the World Ended* 2001; *About Schmidt* 2002
Groff, Jonathan *Taking Woodstock* 2009; *Frozen* 2013

Grogan, Clare aka **Grogan, C P** (1962-) *Gregory's Girl* 1980; *Comfort and Joy* 1984; *The Wee Man* 2013
Groh, David (1939-2008) *A Hero Ain't Nothin' but a Sandwich* 1978; *Hot Shot* 1986; *Blowback* 1999
Grondin, Marc-André *CRAZY* 2005; *The First Day of the Rest of Your Life* 2007; *Che Part Two* 2008
Groome, Georgia (1992-) *London to Brighton* 2006; *Angus, Thongs and Perfect Snogging* 2008; *The Disappeared* 2008; *The Great Ghost Rescue* 2011; *Papadopoulos & Sons* 2012
Gross, Arye (1960-) *Soul Man* 1986; *House II: the Second Story* 1987; *The Couch Trip* 1988; *The Experts* 1989; *Coupe de Ville* 1990; *For the Boys* 1991; *A Midnight Clear* 1991; *Hexed* 1993; *The Opposite Sex and How to Live with Them* 1993; *Mother Night* 1996; *Big Eden* 2000; *Three Wise Guys* 2005; *Grey Gardens* 2009
Gross, Mary (1953-) *Casual Sex?* 1988; *The Couch Trip* 1988; *Feds* 1988; *Troop Beverly Hills* 1989
Gross, Michael (1947-) *FDR: the Last Year* 1980; *Cook & Peary: the Race to the Pole* 1983; *Big Business* 1988; *Tremors* 1989; *Cool as Ice* 1991; *Alan & Naomi* 1992; *Tremors II: Aftershocks* 1995; *Sometimes They Come Back... Again* 1996; *Tremors 3: Back to Perfection* 2001; *Rosemont* 2015
Gross, Paul (1959-) *Cold Comfort* 1989; *Aspen Extreme* 1993; *Whale Music* 1994; *20,000 Leagues under the Sea* 1997; *Passchendaele* 2007
Grossmith, Lawrence (1877-1944) *Sing as We Go* 1934; *Tiger Bay* 1934; *The Girl in the Taxi* 1937
Grove, Richard *Army of Darkness* 1993; *Scanner Cop* 1994
Grover, Deborah *The Gate* 1987; *A Sister's Secret* 2009
Grover, Ricky *Tony* 2009; *Bulla... Big Fat Gypsy Gangster* 2011
Groves, Fred (1880-1955) *Sally in Our Alley* 1931; *The Great Barrier* 1937; *The Challenge* 1938; *An Ideal Husband* 1947
Groyne, Pili *Two Days, One Night* 2014; *The Brand New Testament* 2015
Grubb, Robert (1950-) *My Brilliant Career* 1979; *Gallipoli* 1981
Grubbs, Gary (1949-) *The Burning Bed* 1984; *Foxfire* 1987; *JFK* 1991; *Gone Fishin'* 1997; *The Astronaut's Wife* 1999; *For One Night* 2006
Gruffudd, Ioan (1974-) *Wilde* 1997; *Solomon and Gaenor* 1998; *Another Life* 2000; *102 Dalmatians* 2000; *Shooters* 2000; *Very Annie-Mary* 2000; *Black Hawk Down* 2001; *The Gathering* 2002; *Otherworld* 2003; *King Arthur* 2004; *Fantastic Four* 2005; *Amazing Grace* 2006; *Fireflies in the Garden* 2007; *4: Rise of the Silver Surfer* 2007; *The Secret of Moonacre* 2008; *W.* 2008; *The Kid* 2010; *Sanctum* 2010; *San Andreas* 2015
Grunberg, Greg *Hollow Man* 2000; *Big Ass Spider* 2013
Gründgens, Gustaf (1899-1963) *M* 1931; *Liebelei* 1932
Gruner, Mark (1958-) *Fantastic Planet* 1973; *Jaws 2* 1978
Gruner, Olivier (1960-) *Nemesis* 1993; *Automatic* 1994
Guard, Christopher (1953-) *A Little Night Music* 1977; *The Lord of the Rings* 1978; *Dead Man's Folly* 1986
Guard, Dominic (1956-) *The Go-Between* 1971; *Bequest to the Nation* 1972; *Picnic at Hanging Rock* 1975; *Absolution* 1978; *The Lord of the Rings* 1978; *An Unsuitable Job for a Woman* 1981
Guardino, Harry (1925-1995) *Houseboat* 1958; *The Five Pennies* 1959; *Pork Chop Hill* 1959; *Five Branded Women* 1960; *King of Kings* 1961; *Hell Is for Heroes* 1962; *The Pigeon That Took Rome* 1962; *Rhino!* 1964; *The Adventures of Bullwhip Griffin* 1967; *Valley of Mystery* 1967; *The Hell with Heroes* 1968; *Jigsaw* 1968; *Madigan* 1968; *Lovers and Other Strangers* 1970; *Dirty Harry* 1971; *Red Sky at Morning* 1971; *They Only Kill Their Masters* 1972; *Capone* 1975; *Whiffs* 1975; *The Enforcer* 1976; *St Ives* 1976; *Rollercoaster* 1977; *Matilda* 1978; *Any Which Way You Can* 1980
Guastaferro, Vincent (1950-) *Eyes of an Angel* 1991; *Homicide* 1991; *Sweet and Lowdown* 1999
Guazzini, Coca *Play* 2005; *Gloria* 2013
Gubler, Matthew Gray *Alvin and the Chipmunks* 2007; *Alvin and the Chipmunks: the Squeakquel* 2009; *(500) Days of Summer* 2009; *Alvin and the Chipmunks: Chipwrecked* 2011; *Alvin and the Chipmunks: the Road Chip* 2015

Guerra, Castulo *Stick* 1985; *Terminator 2: Judgment Day* 1991
Guerra, Saverio *The Winner* 1996; *Summer of Sam* 1999; *Lucky You* 2007
Guerrasio, John *Jane Austen in Manhattan* 1980; *Boo, Zino and the Snurks* 2004
Guerrero, Evelyn (1949-) *Cheech and Chong's Next Movie* 1980; *Cheech and Chong's Nice Dreams* 1981
Guers, Paul (1927-) *Bay of the Angels* 1963; *Le Parfum d'Yvonne* 1994
Guesmi, Samir *L'Afrance* 2001; *The Woman in the Fifth* 2011
Guest, Christopher (1948-) *Girlfriends* 1978; *The Long Riders* 1980; *Heartbeeps* 1981; *A Piano for Mrs Cimino* 1982; *This Is Spinal Tap* 1984; *Little Shop of Horrors* 1986; *Beyond Therapy* 1987; *The Princess Bride* 1987; *Sticky Fingers* 1988; *Waiting for Guffman* 1996; *Best in Show* 2000; *A Mighty Wind* 2003; *Mrs Henderson Presents* 2005; *For Your Consideration* 2006; *The Invention of Lying* 2009; *Night at the Museum 2* 2009; *Misery Loves Comedy* 2015
Guest, Lance (1960-) *Halloween II* 1981; *I Ought to Be in Pictures* 1982; *The Last Starfighter* 1984; *Jaws the Revenge* 1987; *The Wizard of Loneliness* 1988
Guest, Nicholas (1951-) *The Long Riders* 1980; *Appointment with Death* 1988; *Adrenalin: Fear the Rush* 1995
Gugino, Carla (1971-) *This Boy's Life* 1993; *The War at Home* 1996; *Judas Kiss* 1998; *Snake Eyes* 1998; *The Center of the World* 2001; *The One* 2001; *She Creature* 2001; *SPYkids* 2001; *SPYkids 2: the Island of Lost Dreams* 2002; *The Singing Detective* 2003; *SPYkids 3-D: Game Over* 2003; *Sin City* 2005; *Night at the Museum* 2006; *American Gangster* 2007; *The Lookout* 2007; *Righteous Kill* 2008; *Race to Witch Mountain* 2009; *Watchmen* 2009; *Faster* 2010; *Mr Popper's Penguins* 2011; *Sucker Punch* 2011; *San Andreas* 2015
Guidall, George *Golden Gate* 1994; *The Impostors* 1998
Guilbert, Jean-Claude aka **Guilbert, J C** *Au Hasard, Balthazar* 1966; *Mouchette* 1966
Guild, Nancy (1925-1999) *Somewhere in the Night* 1946; *Give My Regards to Broadway* 1948; *Black Magic* 1949; *Abbott and Costello Meet the Invisible Man* 1951; *Francis Covers the Big Town* 1953
Guilfoyle (1), Paul (1902-1961) *Winterset* 1936; *Behind the Headlines* 1937; *Flight from Glory* 1937; *The Woman I Love* 1937; *The Saint in New York* 1938; *Remember the Night* 1940; *The Saint Takes Over* 1940; *The Saint in Palm Springs* 1941; *The Woman on Pier 13* 1949; *Apache* 1954; *Chief Crazy Horse* 1955
Guilfoyle (2), Paul (1955-) *Billy Galvin* 1986; *Howard, a New Breed of Hero* 1986; *Dealers* 1989; *Cadillac Man* 1990; *True Colors* 1991; *Final Analysis* 1992; *Mother's Boys* 1993; *Amelia Earhart: the Final Flight* 1994; *Little Odessa* 1994; *Celtic Pride* 1996; *Extreme Measures* 1996; *Striptease* 1996; *Air Force One* 1997; *LA Confidential* 1997; *Primary Colors* 1998; *Session 9* 2001; *Live from Baghdad* 2002
Guillaume, Robert (1932-) *Seems like Old Times* 1980; *Wanted Dead or Alive* 1986; *Lean on Me* 1989; *Death Warrant* 1990; *The Meteor Man* 1993; *The Lion King* 1994; *The Lion King II: Simba's Pride* 1998; *The Adventures of Tom Thumb and Thumbelina* 2002; *Big Fish* 2003
Guillemin, Sophie (1977-) *L'Ennui* 1998; *Harry, He's Here to Help* 2000; *He Loves Me... He Loves Me Not* 2002; *My Afternoons with Margueritte* 2010
Guillen-Cuervo, Fernando aka **Guillen, Fernando** aka **Guillén, Fernando** (1963-) *Women on the Verge of a Nervous Breakdown* 1988; *The Ages of Lulu* 1990; *Acción Mutante* 1993; *A Business Affair* 1993; *Mouth to Mouth* 1995
Guillon, Stéphane *Comment J'ai Tué Mon Père* 2001; *Paper Souls* 2013
Guillory, Sienna (1975-) *Sorted* 2000; *Kiss Kiss (Bang Bang)* 2001; *Late Night Shopping* 2001; *The Principles of Lust* 2002; *The Time Machine* 2002; *Resident Evil: Apocalypse* 2004; *Rabbit Fever* 2005; *Eragon* 2006; *Resident Evil: Retribution* 2012; *The Goob* 2014
Guinan, Francis *Shining Through* 1992; *Guinevere* 1999
Guinee, Tim (1962-) *Tai-Pan* 1986; *American Blue Note* 1989; *Once Around* 1991; *Vampires* 1998; *Impostor* 2001; *Personal Velocity* 2001; *Ladder*

49 2004; *Vinegar Hill* 2004; *Sweet Land* 2005; *99 Homes* 2014
Guinness, Alec (1914-2000) *Evensong* 1934; *Great Expectations* 1946; *Oliver Twist* 1948; *Kind Hearts and Coronets* 1949; *A Run for Your Money* 1949; *Last Holiday* 1950; *The Mudlark* 1950; *The Lavender Hill Mob* 1951; *The Man in the White Suit* 1951; *The Card* 1952; *The Captain's Paradise* 1953; *Malta Story* 1953; *Father Brown* 1954; *To Paris with Love* 1954; *The Ladykillers* 1955; *The Prisoner* 1955; *The Swan* 1956; *Barnacle Bill* 1957; *The Bridge on the River Kwai* 1957; *The Horse's Mouth* 1958; *Our Man in Havana* 1959; *The Scapegoat* 1959; *Tunes of Glory* 1960; *A Majority of One* 1961; *HMS Defiant* 1962; *Lawrence of Arabia* 1962; *The Fall of the Roman Empire* 1964; *Doctor Zhivago* 1965; *Situation Hopeless – but Not Serious* 1965; *Hotel Paradiso* 1966; *The Quiller Memorandum* 1966; *The Comedians* 1967; *Cromwell* 1970; *Scrooge* 1970; *Brother Sun, Sister Moon* 1972; *Hitler: the Last Ten Days* 1973; *Murder by Death* 1976; *Star Wars Episode IV: a New Hope* 1977; *Raise the Titanic* 1980; *Star Wars Episode V: the Empire Strikes Back* 1980; *Lovesick* 1983; *Star Wars Episode VI: Return of the Jedi* 1983; *A Passage to India* 1984; *A Handful of Dust* 1987; *Little Dorrit* 1987; *Kafka* 1991; *Mute Witness* 1995
Guiomar, Julien (1928-2010) *King of Hearts* 1966; *The Thief of Paris* 1967; *Mado* 1976; *Double Dare* 1981; *Le Cop* 1985; *Léolo* 1992
Guiry, Tom aka **Guiry, Thomas** (1981-) *The Sandlot* 1993; *Strike!* 1998; *Wrestling with Alligators* 1998; *Ride with the Devil* 1999; *Songs in Ordinary Time* 2000; *Tigerland* 2000; *Mystic River* 2003; *Strip Search* 2004
Guisol, Henri (1904-1994) *Le Crime de Monsieur Lange* 1935; *Drôle de Drame* 1937; *Lola Montès* 1955
Guitry, Sacha (1885-1957) *Bonne Chance* 1935; *The Story of a Cheat* 1936; *Royal Affairs in Versailles* 1953; *Napoléon* 1955
Guizar, Tito (1908-1999) *The Llano Kid* 1939; *Brazil* 1944
Gulager, Clu (1928-) *The Killers* 1964; *Winning* 1969; *The Last Picture Show* 1971; *The Glass House* 1972; *Molly and Lawless John* 1972; *McQ* 1974; *A Force of One* 1979; *Touched by Love* 1979; *The Initiation* 1984; *Return of the Living Dead* 1984; *A Nightmare on Elm Street 2: Freddy's Revenge* 1985; *The Hidden* 1987; *I'm Gonna Git You Sucka* 1988; *Tapeheads* 1988
Gulpilil, David aka **Gulpilil** (1954-) *Walkabout* 1970; *Mad Dog* 1976; *The Last Wave* 1977; *"Crocodile" Dundee* 1986; *Rabbit-Proof Fence* 2002; *The Proposition* 2004; *Charlie's Country* 2013
Gummer, Grace *The Homesman* 2014; *Learning to Drive* 2014
Gummer, Mamie *Evening* 2007; *John Carpenter's The Ward* 2010; *The End of the Tour* 2015; *Ricki and the Flash* 2015
Gummersall, Devon (1978-) *Lured Innocence* 1999; *Earth vs the Spider* 2001; *Reeker* 2005
Gunn, Janet (1961-) *Night of the Running Man* 1994; *The Quest* 1996
Gunn, Judy (1915-1991) *The Love Test* 1935; *The Last Journey* 1936
Gunn, Moses (1929-1993) *Eagle in a Cage* 1971; *Shaft* 1971; *Wild Rovers* 1971; *The Hot Rock* 1972; *Shaft's Big Score!* 1972; *Aaron Loves Angela* 1975; *Rollerball* 1975; *Remember My Name* 1978; *The Ninth Configuration* 1979; *Ragtime* 1981; *The Killing Floor* 1984; *The NeverEnding Story* 1984; *Certain Fury* 1985; *Heartbreak Ridge* 1986; *Leonard, Part 6* 1987
Gunn, Peter *Resurrected* 1989; *Blue Juice* 1995; *Brassed Off* 1996; *A Bunch of Amateurs* 2008; *Hannah Montana: the Movie* 2009
Gunton, Bob (1945-) *Rollover* 1981; *Static* 1985; *Matewan* 1987; *Unconquered* 1989; *Demolition Man* 1993; *Roswell* 1994; *The Shawshank Redemption* 1994; *Ace Ventura: When Nature Calls* 1995; *Kingfish: a Story of Huey P Long* 1995; *Broken Arrow* 1996; *The Glimmer Man* 1996; *Buffalo Soldiers* 1997; *Changing Habits* 1997; *Patch Adams* 1998; *Bats* 1999; *When Billie Beat Bobby* 2001; *Boat Trip* 2002; *Dead Silence* 2007; *The Lazarus Project* 2008
Gupta, Arjun *Motherhood* 2009; *The Diabolical* 2015
Gupta, Neena *In Custody* 1993; *Cotton Mary* 1999
Gur, Alizia *The Hand of Night* 1966; *Kill a Dragon* 1967; *Tarzan and the Jungle Boy* 1968

Gurie, Sigrid (1911-1969) *The Adventures of Marco Polo* 1938; *Algiers* 1938; *Three Faces West* 1940
Gurney, Sharon *The Corpse* 1969; *Death Line* 1972
Gurry, Eric *Bad Boys* 1983; *Willy/Milly* 1986
Gusman, Martina *Born and Bred* 2006; *Lion's Den* 2008; *Carancho* 2010; *White Elephant* 2012
Guthrie, Arlo (1947-) *Alice's Restaurant* 1969; *Roadside Prophets* 1992
Guthrie, Kevin *Sunshine on Leith* 2013; *Sunset Song* 2015
Guthrie, Tyrone (1900-1971) *St Martin's Lane* 1938; *Vessel of Wrath* 1938
Gutiérrez, Javier *The Baby's Room* 2006; *Marshland* 2014
Gutierrez, Zaide Silvia *El Norte* 1983; *Highway Patrolman* 1991
Guttenberg, Steve (1958-) *The Chicken Chronicles* 1977; *Something for Joey* 1977; *The Boys from Brazil* 1978; *Players* 1979; *Can't Stop the Music* 1980; *Diner* 1982; *Police Academy* 1984; *Bad Medicine* 1985; *Cocoon* 1985; *Police Academy 2: Their First Assignment* 1985; *Police Academy 3: Back in Training* 1986; *Short Circuit* 1986; *Amazon Women on the Moon* 1987; *The Bedroom Window* 1987; *Police Academy 4: Citizens on Patrol* 1987; *Surrender* 1987; *Three Men and a Baby* 1987; *Cocoon: the Return* 1988; *High Spirits* 1988; *The Boyfriend School* 1990; *Three Men and a Little Lady* 1990; *The Big Green* 1995; *Home for the Holidays* 1995; *It Takes Two* 1995; *Airborne* 1997; *Casper: a Spirited Beginning* 1997; *Zeus and Roxanne* 1997; *Home Team* 1998; *Single Santa Seeks Mrs Claus* 2004; *Meet the Santas* 2005
Gutteridge, Lucy (1956-) *Top Secret!* 1984; *The Secret Garden* 1987; *The Trouble with Spies* 1987
Gutteridge, Melanie *GMT Greenwich Mean Time* 1998; *Large* 2000; *Long Time Dead* 2001
Guy, Jasmine (1964-) *Harlem Nights* 1989; *Cats Don't Dance* 1998; *Guinevere* 1999
Guyler, Deryck (1914-1999) *A Hard Day's Night* 1964; *The Big Job* 1965; *Please Sir!* 1971
Guzman, Luis aka **Guzmán, Luis** (1956-) *Q & A* 1990; *The Hard Way* 1991; *Jumpin' at the Boneyard* 1991; *Carlito's Way* 1993; *Pronto* 1996; *The Substitute* 1996; *The Bone Collector* 1999; *The Limey* 1999; *Magnolia* 1999; *Traffic* 2000; *The Count of Monte Cristo* 2001; *Double Whammy* 2001; *Pluto Nash* 2001; *Confidence* 2002; *Punch-Drunk Love* 2002; *The Salton Sea* 2002; *Welcome to Collinwood* 2002; *Anger Management* 2003; *Dumb and Dumberer: When Harry Met Lloyd* 2003; *Dreamer* 2005; *Waiting...* 2005; *Fast Food Nation* 2006; *Hard Luck* 2006; *School for Scoundrels* 2006; *Cleaner* 2007; *War* 2007; *Fighting* 2009; *The Taking of Pelham 123* 2009; *Arthur* 2011; *Journey 2 the Mysterious Island* 2011; *The Last Stand* 2013; *Turbo* 2013; *Keanu* 2016
Guzman, Ryan *Step Up: All In* 2014; *The Boy Next Door* 2015; *Jem and the Holograms* 2015
Gwaltney, Jack (1960-) *Casualties of War* 1989; *Vital Signs* 1990
Gwenn, Edmund (1875-1959) *Hindle Wakes* 1931; *The Skin Game* 1931; *Friday the Thirteenth* 1933; *The Good Companions* 1933; *Waltzes from Vienna* 1933; *I Was a Spy* 1934; *Java Head* 1935; *Anthony Adverse* 1936; *Sylvia Scarlett* 1936; *The Walking Dead* 1936; *Parnell* 1937; *Penny Paradise* 1938; *South Riding* 1938; *A Yank at Oxford* 1938; *Cheer Boys Cheer* 1939; *The Doctor Takes a Wife* 1940; *The Earl of Chicago* 1940; *Foreign Correspondent* 1940; *Pride and Prejudice* 1940; *Charley's Aunt* 1941; *Cheers for Miss Bishop* 1941; *The Devil and Miss Jones* 1941; *Random Harvest* 1942; *A Yank at Eton* 1942; *Forever and a Day* 1943; *Lassie Come Home* 1943; *The Meanest Man in the World* 1943; *Between Two Worlds* 1944; *The Keys of the Kingdom* 1944; *Bewitched* 1945; *Of Human Bondage* 1946; *Undercurrent* 1946; *Bob, Son of Battle* 1947; *Green Dolphin Street* 1947; *Life with Father* 1947; *Miracle on 34th Street* 1947; *Apartment for Peggy* 1948; *Hills of Home* 1948; *Challenge to Lassie* 1949; *For Heaven's Sake* 1950; *Mister 880* 1950; *Pretty Baby* 1950; *A Woman of Distinction* 1950; *Peking Express* 1951; *Les Misérables* 1952; *The Bigamist* 1953; *The Student Prince* 1954; *Them!* 1954; *The Trouble with Harry* 1954

Gwillim, Jack (1909-2001) *The Battle of the River Plate* 1956; *The One That Got Away* 1957; *North West Frontier* 1959; *Circus of Horrors* 1960; *Sword of Sherwood Forest* 1960; *A Midsummer Night's Dream* 1961; *Jason and the Argonauts* 1963; *The Curse of the Mummy's Tomb* 1964; *Clash of the Titans* 1981

Gwilym, Mike aka **Gwilym, Michael** (1949-) *On the Black Hill* 1987; *The Plot to Kill Hitler* 1990

Gwynn, Michael (1916-1976) *The Revenge of Frankenstein* 1958; *Village of the Damned* 1960; *Jason and the Argonauts* 1963; *The Scars of Dracula* 1970

Gwynne, Anne (1918-2003) *The Black Cat* 1941; *Broadway* 1942; *Men of Texas* 1942; *Ride 'Em Cowboy* 1942; *Sin Town* 1942; *Frontier Badmen* 1943; *House of Frankenstein* 1944; *Weird Woman* 1944; *Dick Tracy Meets Gruesome* 1947; *Teenage Monster* 1958

Gwynne, Fred (1926-1993) *On the Waterfront* 1954; *Munster, Go Home!* 1966; *La Luna* 1979 *Simon* 1980; *So Fine* 1981; *The Cotton Club* 1984; *Water* 1985; *The Boy Who Could Fly* 1986; *Off Beat* 1986; *Fatal Attraction* 1987; *Ironweed* 1987; *The Land before Time* 1988; *Disorganized Crime* 1989; *Pet Sematary* 1989; *My Cousin Vinny* 1992

Gwynne, Haydn (1960-) *Remember Me?* 1996; *Hunky Dory* 2011

Gwynne, Michael C (1942-) *Payday* 1972; *Harry in Your Pocket* 1973; *The Terminal Man* 1974; *Special Delivery* 1976; *Butch and Sundance: the Early Days* 1979; *Blue Heat* 1990

Gyasi, David *Shooting Dogs* 2005; *Interstellar* 2014

Gyllenhaal, Jake aka **Gyllenhaal, Jacob** (1980-) *A Dangerous Woman* 1993; *October Sky* 1999; *Bubble Boy* 2001; *Donnie Darko* 2001; *The Good Girl* 2001; *Lovely & Amazing* 2001; *Moonlight Mile* 2002; *The Day after Tomorrow* 2004; *Brokeback Mountain* 2005; *Jarhead* 2005; *Proof* 2005; *Rendition* 2007; *Zodiac* 2007; *Brothers* 2009; *Love & Other Drugs* 2010; *Prince of Persia: the Sands of Time* 2010; *Source Code* 2011; *End of Watch* 2012; *Accidental Love* 2013; *Enemy* 2013; *Nightcrawler* 2013; *Prisoners* 2013; *Demolition* 2015; *Everest* 2015; *Southpaw* 2015; *Nocturnal Animals* 2016

Gyllenhaal, Maggie (1977-) *A Dangerous Woman* 1993; *Cecil B Demented* 2000; *Donnie Darko* 2001; *Secretary* 2001; *Adaptation.* 2002; *Confessions of a Dangerous Mind* 2002; *40 Days and 40 Nights* 2002; *Casa de los Babys* 2003; *Mona Lisa Smile* 2003; *Criminal* 2004; *Strip Search* 2004; *Happy Endings* 2005; *Monster House* 2006; *Sherrybaby* 2006; *Stranger than Fiction* 2006; *Trust the Man* 2006; *World Trade Center* 2006; *The Dark Knight* 2008; *Away We Go* 2009; *Crazy Heart* 2009; *Nanny McPhee & the Big Bang* 2010; *Hysteria* 2011; *Won't Back Down* 2012; *Frank* 2013; *White House Down* 2013

Gyngell, Kim (1952-) *Heaven Tonight* 1990; *Love and Other Catastrophes* 1996

Gynt, Greta (1916-2000) *Sexton Blake and the Hooded Terror* 1938; *The Arsenal Stadium Mystery* 1939; *Dark Eyes of London* 1939; *Crooks' Tour* 1940; *The Common Touch* 1941; *It's That Man Again* 1942; *Tomorrow We Live* 1942; *London Town* 1946; *Dear Murderer* 1947; *Easy Money* 1947; *Take My Life* 1947; *The Calendar* 1948; *Mr Perrin and Mr Traill* 1948; *Soldiers Three* 1951; *Forbidden Cargo* 1954; *The Blue Peter* 1955

H

Ha Ji-won *Phone* 2002; *Duelist* 2005

Ha Jung-woo *The Chaser* 2008; *The Yellow Sea* 2010

Haas, Dolly (1910-1994) *Broken Blossoms* 1936; *I Confess* 1953

Haas, Hugo (1901-1968) *Days of Glory* 1944; *Summer Storm* 1944; *Dakota* 1945; *Holiday in Mexico* 1946; *Casbah* 1948; *For the Love of Mary* 1948; *My Girl Tisa* 1948; *The Fighting Kentuckian* 1949; *King Solomon's Mines* 1950; *Lizzie* 1957

Haas, Lukas (1976-) *Testament* 1983; *Witness* 1985; *Lady in White* 1988; *The Wizard of Loneliness* 1988; *Music Box* 1989; *See You in the Morning* 1989; *Convicts* 1991; *Rambling Rose* 1991; *Alan & Naomi* 1992; *Leap of Faith* 1992; *Boys* 1995; *Johns* 1995; *Everyone Says I Love You* 1996; *David and Lisa* 1998; *Breakfast of Champions* 1999; *Running Free* 1999; *Long Time Dead* 2001; *Last Days* 2004; *Brick* 2005; *Material Girls* 2006; *The Tripper* 2006; *Inception* 2010; *Red Riding Hood* 2011; *Contraband* 2012; *jOBS* 2013; *The Revenant* 2015

Habich, Matthias (1940-) *Imperative* 1982; *Nowhere in Africa* 2001; *Downfall* 2004

Hack, Olivia (1983-) *The Brady Bunch Movie* 1995; *A Very Brady Sequel* 1996

Hack, Shelley (1952-) *The Stepfather* 1986; *Troll* 1986; *Bridesmaids* 1989; *Freefall: Flight 174* 1995

Hackett, Buddy (1924-2003) *Fireman Save My Child* 1954; *God's Little Acre* 1958; *All Hands on Deck* 1961; *The Music Man* 1962; *It's a Mad Mad Mad Mad World* 1963; *The Love Bug* 1969; *The Little Mermaid* 1989; *Paulie* 1998; *The Little Mermaid II: Return to the Sea* 2000

Hackett, Joan (1934-1983) *The Group* 1966; *Will Penny* 1967; *Support Your Local Sheriff!* 1969; *The Last of Sheila* 1973; *The Terminal Man* 1974; *Treasure of Matecumbe* 1976; *One-Trick Pony* 1980; *Only When I Laugh* 1981; *The Long Summer of George Adams* 1982

Hackl, Karlheinz aka **Hackl, Karl-Heinz** aka **Hackl, Karl Heinz** (1949-2014) *The Assisi Underground* 1985; *The Wall* 2012

Hackman, Gene (1930-) *Mad Dog Coll* 1961; *Lilith* 1964; *Hawaii* 1966; *Banning* 1967; *Bonnie and Clyde* 1967; *The Split* 1968; *Downhill Racer* 1969; *The Gypsy Moths* 1969; *Marooned* 1969; *Riot* 1969; *Doctors' Wives* 1970; *I Never Sang for My Father* 1970; *Cisco Pike* 1971; *The French Connection* 1971; *The Hunting Party* 1971; *The Poseidon Adventure* 1972; *Prime Cut* 1972; *Scarecrow* 1973; *The Conversation* 1974; *Young Frankenstein* 1974; *Zandy's Bride* 1974; *Bite the Bullet* 1975; *French Connection II* 1975; *Lucky Lady* 1975; *Night Moves* 1975; *A Bridge Too Far* 1977; *The Domino Principle* 1977; *March or Die* 1977; *Superman* 1978; *Superman II* 1980; *All Night Long* 1981; *Reds* 1981; *Eureka* 1982; *Uncommon Valor* 1983; *Under Fire* 1983; *Target* 1985; *Twice in a Lifetime* 1985; *Hoosiers* 1986; *No Way Out* 1986; *Power* 1986; *Superman IV: the Quest for Peace* 1987; *Another Woman* 1988; *BAT-21* 1988; *Full Moon in Blue Water* 1988; *Mississippi Burning* 1988; *The Package* 1989; *Loose Cannons* 1990; *Narrow Margin* 1990; *Postcards from the Edge* 1990; *Class Action* 1991; *Company Business* 1991; *Unforgiven* 1992; *The Firm* 1993; *Geronimo: an American Legend* 1993; *Wyatt Earp* 1994; *Crimson Tide* 1995; *Get Shorty* 1995; *The Quick and the Dead* 1995; *Absolute Power* 1996; *The Birdcage* 1996; *The Chamber* 1996; *Extreme Measures* 1996; *Antz* 1998; *Enemy of the State* 1998; *Twilight* 1998; *The Replacements* 2000; *Under Suspicion* 2000; *Behind Enemy Lines* 2001; *Heartbreakers* 2001; *Heist* 2001; *The Mexican* 2001; *The Royal Tenenbaums* 2001; *Runaway Jury* 2003; *Welcome to Mooseport* 2004

Haddock, Laura *The Inbetweeners Movie* 2011; *Storage 24* 2012; *SuperBob* 2015

Haddon, Dayle (1949-) *The World's Greatest Athlete* 1973; *North Dallas Forty* 1979; *Love Songs* 1984; *Cyborg* 1989

Haddon, Peter *The Silent Passenger* 1935; *The House of the Spaniard* 1936; *Over the Moon* 1937

Haden, Sara (1897-1981) *Anne of Green Gables* 1934; *Mad Love* 1935; *Magnificent Obsession* 1935; *Captain January* 1936; *Poor Little Rich Girl* 1936; *Out West with the Hardys* 1938; *Andy Hardy Gets Spring Fever* 1939; *Judge Hardy and Son* 1939; *Andy Hardy Meets Debutante* 1940; *The Shop around the Corner* 1940; *Life Begins for Andy Hardy* 1941; *Andy Hardy's Double Life* 1942; *The Courtship of Andy Hardy* 1942; *Andy Hardy's Blonde Trouble* 1944; *Love Laughs at Andy Hardy* 1946; *The Great Rupert* 1950; *Andy Hardy Comes Home* 1958

Hader, Bill (1978-) *Hot Rod* 2007; *Superbad* 2007; *Forgetting Sarah Marshall* 2008; *Pineapple Express* 2008; *Adventureland* 2009; *Cloudy with a Chance of Meatballs* 2009; *Paul* 2010; *Men in Black 3* 2012; *Clear History* 2013; *Cloudy with a Chance of Meatballs 2* 2013; *The To Do List* 2013; *The Skeleton Twins* 2014; *They Came Together* 2014; *Inside Out* 2015; *Trainwreck* 2015; *The Angry Birds Movie* 2016; *Maggie's Plan* 2016; *Sausage Party* 2016

Hadley, Reed (1911-1974) *Circumstantial Evidence* 1945; *The Dark Corner* 1946; *I Shot Jesse James* 1949; *The Baron of Arizona* 1950; *Dallas* 1950; *The Half-Breed* 1952; *Big House, USA* 1955

Haenel, Adèle (1989-) *Les Diables* 2002; *Water Lilies* 2007; *Les Combattants* 2014

Haft, Linal *Soft Fruit* 1999; *Tu£sday* 2007

Hagan, Molly (1962-) *Some Kind of Wonderful* 1987; *The Dentist* 1996; *Ringmaster* 1998; *Election* 1999

Hageman, Richard (1882-1966) *The Toast of New Orleans* 1950; *The Great Caruso* 1951; *Rhapsody* 1954

Hagen, Jean (1923-1977) *Adam's Rib* 1949; *Ambush* 1949; *The Asphalt Jungle* 1950; *A Life of Her Own* 1950; *Side Street* 1950; *Carbine Williams* 1952; *Singin' in the Rain* 1952; *Arena* 1953; *Latin Lovers* 1953; *The Big Knife* 1955; *Spring Reunion* 1957; *The Shaggy Dog* 1959; *Sunrise at Campobello* 1960; *Panic in Year Zero* 1962; *Dead Ringer* 1964

Hagen, Pal Sverre Valheim aka **Hagen, Pal Sverre** *Kon-Tiki* 2012; *In Order of Disappearance* 2014; *The Last King* 2016

Hagen, Ross (1938-2011) *Speedway* 1968; *Avenging Angel* 1985

Hagen, Uta (1919-2004) *The Other* 1972; *The Boys from Brazil* 1978; *Reversal of Fortune* 1990

Hager, Kristen *AVPR: Aliens vs Predator Requiem* 2007; *Sorority Wars* 2009

Hagerthy, Ron *I Was a Communist for the FBI* 1951; *The Hostage* 1966

Hagerty, Julie aka **Haggerty, Julie** (1955-) *Airplane!* 1980; *Airplane II: the Sequel* 1982; *A Midsummer Night's Sex Comedy* 1982; *Bad Medicine* 1985; *Lost in America* 1985; *Aria* 1987; *Beyond Therapy* 1987; *What about Bob?* 1991; *Noises Off* 1992; *U Turn* 1997; *The Story of Us* 1999; *Freddy Got Fingered* 2001; *Storytelling* 2001; *A Guy Thing* 2002; *Just Friends* 2005; *She's the Man* 2006; *Confessions of a Shopaholic* 2009

Hagerty, Michael G aka **Hagerty, Michael** (1953-) *Overboard* 1987; *Speed 2: Cruise Control* 1997; *Best Laid Plans* 1999; *Inspector Gadget* 1999

Haggerty, Don (1914-1988) *Armored Car Robbery* 1950; *The Sundowners* 1950; *Cause for Alarm* 1951; *Cry Vengeance* 1954; *Cattle Empire* 1958

Hagiwara, Masato (1971-) *Chaos* 1999; *Café Lumière* 2003

Hagman, Larry (1931-2012) *Ensign Pulver* 1964; *Fail-Safe* 1964; *The Group* 1966; *Up in the Cellar* 1970; *Beware! The Blob* 1971; *Harry and Tonto* 1974; *Stardust* 1974; *The Big Bus* 1976; *Mother, Jugs & Speed* 1976; *Superman* 1978; *S.O.B.* 1981; *Primary Colors* 1998

Hagney, Frank (1884-1973) *The General* 1927; *The Lone Rider in Ghost Town* 1941

Hahn, Jess (1922-1998) *The Sign of Leo* 1959; *Cartouche* 1961; *The Trial* 1962; *Topkapi* 1964; *The Night of the Following Day* 1968

Hahn, Kathryn (1974-) *Anchorman: the Legend of Ron Burgundy* 2004; *Win a Date with Tad Hamilton!* 2004; *A Lot like Love* 2005; *The Last Mimzy* 2007; *Revolutionary Road* 2008; *Step Brothers* 2008; *The Goods: Live Hard Sell Hard* 2009; *How Do You Know* 2010; *Wanderlust* 2011; *Afternoon Delight* 2013; *She's Funny That Way* 2014; *The D Train* 2015; *Tomorrowland: a World Beyond* 2015; *The Visit* 2015

Haid, Charles (1943-) *Oliver's Story* 1978; *Who'll Stop the Rain?* 1978; *Altered States* 1980; *Divorce Wars* 1982; *Cop* 1988; *The Rescue* 1988; *Nightbreed* 1990; *Storyville* 1992; *Cooperstown* 1993; *For Their Own Good* 1993; *Broken Trust* 1995; *Home on the Range* 2004

Haiduk, Stacy (1968-) *Danielle Steel's A Perfect Stranger* 1994; *Desert Thunder* 1998

Haig, Sid (1939-) *Spider Baby* 1964; *THX 1138* 1971; *The Big Bird Cage* 1972; *Black Mama, White Mama* 1972; *Coffy* 1973; *Lambada! The Forbidden Dance* 1990; *House of 1000 Corpses* 2001; *The Devil's Rejects* 2005

Haigh, Kenneth (1929-) *My Teenage Daughter* 1956; *Cleopatra* 1963; *A Hard Day's Night* 1964; *The Deadly Affair* 1966; *A Lovely Way to Go* 1968; *Eagle in a Cage* 1971; *Man at the Top* 1973; *Robin and Marian* 1976; *The Bitch* 1979; *Wild Geese II* 1985

Haim, Corey (1971-2010) *Firstborn* 1984; *Murphy's Romance* 1985; *Silver Bullet* 1985; *Lucas* 1986; *The Lost Boys* 1987; *License to Drive* 1988; *Watchers* 1988; *Dream a Little Dream* 1989; *Oh, What a Night* 1992; *Never Too Late* 1996; *Without Malice* 2000

Haines, Donald (1941-) *No Greater Glory* 1934; *Pride of the Bowery* 1941; *Spooks Run Wild* 1941

Haines, Larry (1918-2008) *The Odd Couple* 1968; *The Seven-Ups* 1973

Haines, Patricia (?-1976) *The Night Caller* 1965; *Walk a Crooked Path* 1969

Haines, William (1900-1973) *Little Annie Rooney* 1925; *Sally, Irene and Mary* 1925; *Show People* 1928

Haji (1946-2013) *Faster, Pussycat! Kill! Kill!* 1965; *Motor Psycho* 1965; *Good Morning... and Goodbye* 1967

Hale, Alan (1892-1950) *The Four Horsemen of the Apocalypse* 1921; *Robin Hood* 1922; *The Covered Wagon* 1923; *The Leatherneck* 1929; *The Sin of Madelon Claudet* 1931; *Susan Lenox: Her Fall and Rise* 1931; *Union Depot* 1932; *It Happened One Night* 1934; *Little Man, What Now?* 1934; *The Little Minister* 1934; *The Lost Patrol* 1934; *Of Human Bondage* 1934; *The Good Fairy* 1935; *The Last Days of Pompeii* 1935; *A Message to Garcia* 1936; *Our Relations* 1936; *God's Country and the Woman* 1937; *Jump for Glory* 1937; *The Prince and the Pauper* 1937; *Stella Dallas* 1937; *The Adventures of Marco Polo* 1938; *The Adventures of Robin Hood* 1938; *Algiers* 1938; *Four Men and a Prayer* 1938; *Listen, Darling* 1938; *Dodge City* 1939; *Dust Be My Destiny* 1939; *Green Hell* 1939; *The Man in the Iron Mask* 1939; *The Private Lives of Elizabeth and Essex* 1939; *The Fighting 69th* 1940; *Santa Fe Trail* 1940; *The Sea Hawk* 1940; *They Drive by Night* 1940; *Virginia City* 1940; *Footsteps in the Dark* 1941; *Manpower* 1941; *The Strawberry Blonde* 1941; *Captains of the Clouds* 1942; *Desperate Journey* 1942; *Gentleman Jim* 1942; *Action in the North Atlantic* 1943; *Destination Tokyo* 1943; *This Is the Army* 1943; *The Adventures of Mark Twain* 1944; *Hotel Berlin* 1945; *Roughly Speaking* 1945; *The Man I Love* 1946; *Night and Day* 1946; *My Wild Irish Rose* 1947; *Pursued* 1947; *Adventures of Don Juan* 1948; *My Girl Tisa* 1948; *Always Leave Them Laughing* 1949; *The Inspector General* 1949; *South of St Louis* 1949; *The Younger Brothers* 1949; *Colt .45* 1950; *Rogues of Sherwood Forest* 1950; *Stars in My Crown* 1950

Hale Jr, Alan aka **Hale, Alan** (1921-1990) *Sweetheart of the Campus* 1941; *Riders in the Sky* 1949; *Sierra Passage* 1950; *The West Point Story* 1950; *Home Town Story* 1951; *Sons of the Musketeers* 1951; *The Big Trees* 1952; *Wait 'til the Sun Shines, Nellie* 1952; *Captain Kidd and the Slave Girl* 1954; *Destry* 1954; *The Iron Glove* 1954; *A Man Alone* 1955; *Many Rivers to Cross* 1955; *Young at Heart* 1955; *The Killer Is Loose* 1956; *Battle Hymn* 1957; *The True Story of Jesse James* 1957; *Up Periscope* 1959; *The Iron Maiden* 1962; *Bullet for a Badman* 1964; *Hang 'Em High* 1968; *Tiger by the Tail* 1970; *The Giant Spider Invasion* 1975; *The 5th Musketeer* 1979; *Hambone and Hillie* 1984

Hale, Barbara (1922-) *Higher and Higher* 1943; *The Falcon in Hollywood* 1944; *The Falcon Out West* 1944; *Lady Luck* 1946; *The Boy with Green Hair* 1948; *And Baby Makes Three* 1949; *The Clay Pigeon* 1949; *Jolson Sings Again* 1949; *The Window* 1949; *The Jackpot* 1950; *Lorna Doone* 1951; *Last of the Comanches* 1953; *A Lion Is in the Streets* 1953; *The Lone Hand* 1953; *Seminole* 1953; *The Far Horizons* 1955; *7th Cavalry* 1956; *The Oklahoman* 1957; *Buckskin* 1968; *The Giant Spider Invasion* 1975; *Big Wednesday* 1978

Hale, Binnie (1899-1984) *The Phantom Light* 1934; *Love from a Stranger* 1936; *Take a Chance* 1937

Hale, Creighton (1882-1965) *The Marriage Circle* 1924; *Annie Laurie* 1927; *The Cat and the Canary* 1927; *The Masquerader* 1933

Hale, Diana *My Friend Flicka* 1943; *Thunderhead - Son of Flicka* 1945

Hale, Elvi (1931-) *True as a Turtle* 1956; *Happy Is the Bride* 1957; *The Navy Lark* 1959

Hale, Georgia (1903-1985) *The Gold Rush* 1925; *The Salvation Hunters* 1925

Hale, Georgina (1943-) *The Devils* 1971; *Eagle in a Cage* 1971; *Butley* 1973; *Mahler* 1974; *The World Is Full of Married Men* 1979; *McVicar* 1980; *Castaway* 1986; *Beyond Bedlam* 1993; *Preaching to the Perverted* 1997

Hale, Jean *Taggart* 1964; *In like Flint* 1967; *The St Valentine's Day Massacre* 1967

Hale, Jennifer *Cinderella II: Dreams Come True* 2002; *The Powerpuff Girls* 2002

Hale, Jonathan (1891-1966) *Charlie Chan at the Olympics* 1937; *Madame X* 1937; *Blondie* 1938; *The Saint in New York* 1938; *The Amazing Mr Williams* 1939; *In Name Only* 1939; *The Saint Strikes Back* 1939; *The Saint Takes Over* 1940; *The Saint's Double Trouble* 1940; *The Saint in Palm Springs* 1941; *Joe Smith, American* 1942; *Miss Annie Rooney* 1942; *Dead Man's Eyes* 1944; *Hollywood Canteen* 1944; *Her Husband's Affairs* 1947; *The Vigilantes Return* 1947; *Silver River* 1948; *Strangers on a Train* 1951

Hale, Lucy (1989-) *Sorority Wars* 2009; *Tinkerbell and the Secret of the Wings* 2012

Hale, Richard (1893-1981) *Knickerbocker Holiday* 1944; *None Shall Escape* 1944; *Abilene Town* 1945; *The Other Love* 1947; *The Man with a Cloak* 1951; *The Miracle of Our Lady of Fatima* 1952; *The Diamond Queen* 1953; *Julius Caesar* 1953

Hale, Sonnie (1902-1959) *Friday the Thirteenth* 1933; *Evergreen* 1934; *First a Girl* 1935; *It's Love Again* 1936; *The Gaunt Stranger* 1938; *Let's Be Famous* 1939; *Fiddlers Three* 1944; *London Town* 1946

Haley, Bill (1925-1981) *Don't Knock the Rock* 1956; *Rock around the Clock* 1956

Haley, Brian (1963-) *Into the Sun* 1992; *Baby's Day Out* 1994; *Gran Torino* 2008

Haley, Jack (1897-1979) *Sitting Pretty* 1933; *Pigskin Parade* 1936; *Poor Little Rich Girl* 1936; *Danger - Love at Work* 1937; *Pick a Star* 1937; *Wake Up and Live* 1937; *Alexander's Ragtime Band* 1938; *Hold That Co-Ed* 1938; *Rebecca of Sunnybrook Farm* 1938; *Thanks for Everything* 1938; *The Wizard of Oz* 1939; *Moon over Miami* 1941; *Beyond the Blue Horizon* 1942; *Higher and Higher* 1943

Haley, Jackie Earle (1961-) *The Bad News Bears* 1976; *The Bad News Bears in Breaking Training* 1977; *Damnation Alley* 1977; *The Bad News Bears Go to Japan* 1978; *Breaking Away* 1979; *Losin' It* 1983; *Little Children* 2006; *Fragments* 2008; *Shutter Island* 2009; *Watchmen* 2009; *A Nightmare on Elm Street* 2010; *The Dark Tower* 2017

Hall-Davis, Lillian (1897-1933) *The Ring* 1927; *The Farmer's Wife* 1928

Hall, Albert aka **Hall, Albert P** (1937-) *Leadbelly* 1976; *Apocalypse Now* 1979; *Betrayed* 1988; *Malcolm X* 1992; *Rookie of the Year* 1993; *Devil in a Blue Dress* 1995; *Get on the Bus* 1996; *Beloved* 1998

Hall, Anthony Michael (1968-) *National Lampoon's Vacation* 1983; *Sixteen Candles* 1984; *The Breakfast Club* 1985; *Weird Science* 1985; *Johnny Be Good* 1988; *Edward Scissorhands* 1990; *Into the Sun* 1992; *Upworld* 1992; *Six Degrees of Separation* 1993; *Pirates of Silicon Valley* 1999; *Freddy Got Fingered* 2001; *61** 2001; *The Dark Knight* 2008; *Results* 2015

Hall, Arsenio (1956-) *Coming to America* 1988; *Harlem Nights* 1989; *Blankman* 1994; *Black Dynamite* 2009

Hall, Berta (1906-1990) *Port of Call* 1948; *My Sister, My Love* 1966

Hall, Bug (1985-) *The Little Rascals* 1994; *The Stupids* 1995; *Honey, We Shrunk Ourselves* 1997; *The King and Queen of Moonlight Bay* 2003

Hall, Charlie (1899-1959) *The Music Box* 1932; *Twice Two* 1933; *Them Thar Hills!* 1934; *Tit for Tat* 1934; *Thicker than Water* 1935; *Saps at Sea* 1940

Hall, Craig *Eagle vs Shark* 2006; *The Ferryman* 2007; *The Devil's Rock* 2011

Hall, Grayson (1927-1985) *Satan in High Heels* 1962; *The Night of the Iguana* 1964; *Adam et 6 AM* 1970; *End of the Road* 1970; *House of Dark Shadows* 1970; *Night of Dark Shadows* 1971

Hall, Hanna (1987-) *Homecoming* 1996; *The Virgin Suicides* 1999

Hall, Harriet *Foxfire* 1987; *Relentless* 1989

Hall, Huntz (1920-1999) *Dead End* 1937; *Angels with Dirty Faces* 1938; *Angels Wash Their Faces* 1939; *Hell's Kitchen* 1939; *The Return of Dr X* 1939; *They Made Me a Criminal* 1939; *Spooks Run Wild* 1941; *Ghosts in the Night* 1943; *Block Busters* 1944; *Bowery Champs* 1944; *Come Out Fighting* 1945; *Docks of New York* 1945; *A Walk in the Sun* 1945; *The Bowery Boys Meet the Monsters* 1954; *Herbie Rides Again* 1974; *Valentino* 1977

Hall, Irma P aka **Hall, Irma** (1937-) *A Family Thing* 1996; *Buddy* 1997; *Midnight in the Garden of Good and Evil* 1997; *Steel* 1997; *Patch Adams* 1998; *A Lesson before Dying* 1999; *Collateral* 2004; *The Ladykillers* 2004; *My Son, My Son, What Have Ye Done* 2009

Hall, James (1900-1940) *Hotel Imperial* 1927; *Four Sons* 1928; *The Canary Murder Case* 1929; *The Case of Lena Smith* 1929; *The Saturday Night Kid* 1929; *Hell's Angels* 1930

Hall, Jane *The Craic* 1999; *Razzle Dazzle: a Journey into Dance* 2006

Hall, Jerry (1956-) *Running Out of Luck* 1985; *Batman* 1989; *Diana & Me* 1997; *Merci Docteur Rey* 2002; *Tooth* 2003

Hall, Jon aka **Locher, Charles** (1913-1979) *Charlie Chan in Shanghai* 1935; *The Hurricane* 1937; *Kit Carson* 1940; *South of Pago Pago* 1940; *Arabian Nights* 1942; *The Invisible Agent* 1942; *The Tuttles of Tahiti* 1942; *White Savage* 1943; *Ali Baba and the Forty Thieves* 1944; *Cobra Woman* 1944; *The Invisible Man's Revenge* 1944; *Lady in the Dark* 1944; *Sudan* 1945; *The Vigilantes Return* 1947; *The Prince of Thieves* 1948; *Hell Ship Mutiny* 1957

Hall, Juanita (1901-1968) *South Pacific* 1958; *Flower Drum Song* 1961

Hall, Kevin Peter (1955-1991) *One Dark Night* 1982; *Monster in the Closet* 1983; *Bigfoot and the Hendersons* 1987; *Predator* 1987; *Predator 2* 1990

Hall, Michael C *Paycheck* 2003; *Gamer* 2008; *Kill Your Darlings* 2013; *Cold in July* 2014

Hall, Philip Baker (1931-) *Secret Honor* 1984; *Three o'Clock High* 1987; *How I Got Into College* 1989; *Live Wire* 1992; *Kiss of Death* 1994; *Hard Eight* 1996; *Psycho* 1998; *Rush Hour* 1998; *Cradle Will Rock* 1999; *The Insider* 1999; *Let the Devil Wear Black* 1999; *Magnolia* 1999; *The Talented Mr Ripley* 1999; *The Contender* 2000; *Lost Souls* 2000; *Rules of Engagement* 2000; *Path to War* 2002; *The Sum of All Fears* 2002; *Bruce Almighty* 2003; *Dogville* 2003; *In Good Company* 2004; *The Amityville Horror* 2005; *The Matador* 2005; *You Kill Me* 2007; *Zodiac* 2007; *Fired Up!* 2009; *The Lodger* 2009; *All Good Things* 2010; *50/50* 2011; *Mr Popper's Penguins* 2011; *People like Us* 2012; *Clear History* 2013

Hall, Porter (1888-1953) *The Thin Man* 1934; *The General Died at Dawn* 1936; *The Petrified Forest* 1936; *The Plainsman* 1936; *Satan Met a Lady* 1936; *Bulldog Drummond Escapes* 1937; *Make Way for Tomorrow* 1937; *True Confession* 1937; *Wells Fargo* 1937; *Bulldog Drummond's Peril* 1938; *Men with Wings* 1938; *His Girl Friday* 1939; *Arizona* 1940; *Dark Command* 1940; *Sullivan's Travels* 1941; *The Desperadoes* 1943; *The Miracle of Morgan's Creek* 1943; *Double Indemnity* 1944; *Going My Way* 1944; *The Great Moment* 1944; *Standing Room Only* 1944; *Kiss and Tell* 1945; *Murder, He Says* 1945; *Miracle on 34th Street* 1947; *Singapore* 1947; *That Wonderful Urge* 1948; *The Beautiful Blonde from Bashful Bend* 1949; *Intruder in the Dust* 1949; *Ace in the Hole* 1951; *Pony Express* 1953; *Vice Squad* 1953; *Return to Treasure Island* 1954

Hall, Rebecca (1982-) *The Prestige* 2006; *Starter for 10* 2006; *Frost/Nixon* 2008; *Vicky Cristina Barcelona* 2008; *Dorian Gray* 2009; *Everything Must Go* 2010; *Please Give* 2010; *The Town* 2010; *The Awakening* 2011; *Lay the Favorite* 2012; *Closed Circuit* 2013; *Iron Man Three* 2013; *A Promise* 2013; *Transcendence* 2014; *The Gift* 2015; *The BFG* 2016

Hall, Regina (1971-) *Disappearing Acts* 2000; *Scary Movie* 2000; *Scary Movie 2* 2001; *Malibu's Most Wanted* 2003; *The Honeymooners* 2005; *Scary Movie 4* 2006; *First Sunday* 2008; *Law Abiding Citizen* 2009; *Death at a Funeral* 2010; *Think like a Man* 2012; *About Last Night* 2013; *The Best Man Holiday* 2013; *Barbershop: a Fresh Cut* 2016

Hall, Ruth (1910-2003) *Monkey Business* 1931; *The Kid from Spain* 1932; *Ride Him, Cowboy* 1932

Hall, Scott H (1924-1995) *Blood Feast* 1963; *Color Me Blood Red* 1965

Hall, Thurston (1883-1958) *The Black Room* 1935; *The Lone Wolf Returns* 1936; *The Man Who Lived Twice* 1936; *Theodora Goes Wild* 1936; *The Affairs of Annabel* 1938; *The Amazing Dr Clitterhouse* 1938; *Dancing Co-Ed* 1939; *The Star Maker* 1939; *The Blue Bird* 1940; *The Great Man's Lady* 1942; *I Dood It* 1943; *Without Reservations* 1946; *Black Gold* 1947; *It Had to Be You* 1947; *The Secret Life of Walter Mitty* 1947; *The Unfinished Dance* 1947; *Up in Central Park* 1948

Hall, Winter (1872-1947) *A Romance of the Redwoods* 1917; *Kitty* 1928

Hall, Zooey (1946-) *Fortune and Men's Eyes* 1971; *I Dismember Mama* 1972

Hallahan, Charles (1943-1997) *Going in Style* 1979; *The Thing* 1982; *Twilight Zone: the Movie* 1983; *Vision Quest* 1985; *Warlock: the Armageddon* 1993; *The Rich Man's Wife* 1996; *Dante's Peak* 1997

Hallam, John (1941-2006) *A Walk with Love and Death* 1969; *Murphy's War* 1971; *The Offence* 1972; *Dragonslayer* 1981; *When the Whales Came* 1989

Hallaren, Jane *Hero at Large* 1980; *Body Heat* 1981; *Modern Romance* 1981; *A Night in the Life of Jimmy Reardon* 1988

Hallett, Neil (1925-2005) *The Brain Machine* 1954; *Can You Keep It Up for a Week?* 1974

Halliday, Bryant (1928-1996) *Devil Doll* 1964; *Tower of Evil* 1972

Halliday, John (1880-1947) *Consolation Marriage* 1931; *Bird of Paradise* 1932; *The Impatient Maiden* 1932; *Finishing School* 1934; *The Dark Angel* 1935; *Peter Ibbetson* 1935; *Desire* 1936; *Fatal Lady* 1936; *Arsene Lupin Returns* 1938; *Blockade* 1938; *That Certain Age* 1938; *Intermezzo* 1939; *The Philadelphia Story* 1940; *Lydia* 1941

Hallier, Lori *My Bloody Valentine* 1981; *A Woman Scorned* 1992; *Incident in a Small Town* 1993

Halloran, John *Blood on the Sun* 1945; *The Deerslayer* 1957

Hallyday, Johnny (1943-) *Detective* 1985; *The Iron Triangle* 1988; *Crime Spree* 2002; *L'Homme du train* 2002

Halop, Billy (1920-1976) *Dead End* 1937; *Angels with Dirty Faces* 1938; *Angels Wash Their Faces* 1939; *Dust Be My Destiny* 1939; *Hell's Kitchen* 1939; *They Made Me a Criminal* 1939; *You Can't Get Away with Murder* 1939; *Tom Brown's Schooldays* 1940; *Dangerous Years* 1947

Halpin, Luke (1948-) *Flipper* 1963; *Flipper's New Adventure* 1964; *Shock Waves* 1975; *Flipper* 1996

Halprin, Daria *Zabriskie Point* 1970; *The Jerusalem File* 1972

Halsey, Brett (1933-) *The Cry Baby Killer* 1958; *The Best of Everything* 1959; *Return of the Fly* 1959; *The Atomic Submarine* 1960; *Desire in the Dust* 1960; *Return to Peyton Place* 1961; *Twice Told Tales* 1963

Halton, Charles (1876-1959) *Woman Chases Man* 1937; *Bluebeard's Eighth Wife* 1938; *Dr Cyclops* 1940; *Stranger on the Third Floor* 1940; *Mr and Mrs Smith* 1941; *Across the Pacific* 1942; *Because of Him* 1946; *Three Little Girls in Blue* 1946

Hama, Mie (1943-) *King Kong vs Godzilla* 1962; *The Beautiful Swindlers* 1964; *What's Up, Tiger Lily?* 1966; *You Only Live Twice* 1967

Hamdouchi, Aymen *Up There* 2011; *My Brother the Devil* 2012; *Snow in Paradise* 2014; *We Are Monster* 2014

Hamel, Veronica (1945-) *Cannonball* 1976; *Beyond the Poseidon Adventure* 1979; *A New Life* 1988; *Taking Care of Business* 1990; *Determination of Death* 2001

Hamer, Gerald (1886-1972) *Blond Cheat* 1938; *The Scarlet Claw* 1944

Hamill, John *The Beast in the Cellar* 1970; *No Blade of Grass* 1970; *Trog* 1970

Hamill, Mark (1951-) *Star Wars Episode IV: a New Hope* 1977; *Corvette Summer* 1978; *The Big Red One* 1980; *Star Wars Episode V: the Empire Strikes Back* 1980; *The Night the Lights Went Out in Georgia* 1981; *Britannia Hospital* 1982; *Star Wars Episode VI: Return of the Jedi* 1983; *Slipstream* 1989; *The Guyver* 1991; *Time Runner* 1993; *Village of the Damned* 1995; *Hamilton* 1998; *Walking across Egypt* 1999; *Batman of the Future: Return of the Joker* 2000; *Joseph: King of Dreams* 2000; *Jay and Silent Bob Strike Back* 2001; *Laputa: Castle in the Sky* 2003; *Battle for Terra* 2007; *Kingsman: The Secret Service* 2015; *Star Wars Episode VII: the Force Awakens* 2015; *Batman: The Killing Joke* 2016; *Star Wars Episode VIII* 2017

Hamilton, Bernie (1928-2008) *The Young One* 1960; *Captain Sindbad* 1963; *One Potato, Two Potato* 1964; *The Organization* 1971; *Hammer* 1972

Hamilton, Gay *A Challenge for Robin Hood* 1967; *Barry Lyndon* 1975

Hamilton, George (1939-) *The Well* 1951; *Crime and Punishment, USA* 1959; *All the Fine Young Cannibals* 1960; *Home from the Hill* 1960; *Where the Boys Are* 1960; *Angel Baby* 1961; *By Love Possessed* 1961; *Light in the Piazza* 1961; *A Thunder of Drums* 1961; *Two Weeks in Another Town* 1962; *Act*

One 1963; *The Victors* 1963; *Your Cheatin' Heart* 1964; *That Man George* 1965; *Viva Maria!* 1965; *Jack of Diamonds* 1967; *A Time for Killing* 1967; *The Power* 1968; *Evel Knievel* 1971; *The Man Who Loved Cat Dancing* 1973; *Once Is Not Enough* 1975; *The Happy Hooker Goes to Washington* 1977; *Sextette* 1978; *From Hell to Victory* 1979; *Love at First Bite* 1979; *Zorro, the Gay Blade* 1981; *The Godfather Part III* 1990; *Doc Hollywood* 1991; *Once upon a Crime* 1992; *Amore!* 1993; *8 Heads in a Duffel Bag* 1997; *Casper Meets Wendy* 1998; *The Little Unicorn* 1998; *Hollywood Ending* 2002; *The Hollywood Mom's Mystery* 2004

Hamilton, Hale (1883-1942) *The Champ* 1931; *Strangers May Kiss* 1931; *Susan Lenox: Her Fall and Rise* 1931; *Black Beauty* 1933; *Employees' Entrance* 1933; *After Office Hours* 1935

Hamilton, Josh (1968-) *Alive* 1992; *With Honors* 1994; *The House of Yes* 1997; *Dark Skies* 2013

Hamilton, Kipp (1934-1981) *Good Morning, Miss Dove* 1955; *War of the Gargantuas* 1970

Hamilton, Linda (1956-) *Children of the Corn* 1984; *The Terminator* 1984; *Black Moon Rising* 1985; *King Kong Lives* 1986; *Mr Destiny* 1990; *Terminator 2: Judgment Day* 1991; *Silent Fall* 1994; *Separate Lives* 1995; *Shadow Conspiracy* 1996; *Dante's Peak* 1997; *Holy Water* 2009

Hamilton, Lisa Gay aka **Hamilton, Lisagay** (1964-) *Jackie Brown* 1997; *Beloved* 1998; *Swing Vote* 1999; *True Crime* 1999; *A House Divided* 2000; *The Truth about Charlie* 2002; *Honeydripper* 2007; *Deception* 2008; *The Soloist* 2009; *Beastly* 2010

Hamilton, Margaret (1902-1985) *Way Down East* 1935; *The Moon's Our Home* 1936; *I'll Take Romance* 1937; *You Only Live Once* 1937; *A Slight Case of Murder* 1938; *The Wizard of Oz* 1939; *The Invisible Woman* 1940; *My Little Chickadee* 1940; *The Villain Still Pursued Her* 1940; *The Affairs of Martha* 1942; *Driftwood* 1946; *The Red Pony* 1949; *Mad Wednesday* 1950; *Wabash Avenue* 1950; *People Will Talk* 1951; *13 Ghosts* 1959; *Rosie!* 1967; *The Anderson Tapes* 1971

Hamilton, Melinda Page *Sleeping Dogs Lie.* 2006; *God Bless America* 2011

Hamilton, Murray (1923-1986) *The Girl He Left Behind* 1956; *Toward the Unknown* 1956; *The Spirit of St Louis* 1957; *Houseboat* 1958; *No Time for Sergeants* 1958; *Too Much, Too Soon* 1958; *The FBI Story* 1959; *The Hustler* 1961; *An American Dream* 1966; *The Graduate* 1967; *The Boston Strangler* 1968; *The Brotherhood* 1968; *No Way to Treat a Lady* 1968; *The Harness* 1971; *The Way We Were* 1973; *The Drowning Pool* 1975; *Jaws* 1975; *Casey's Shadow* 1978; *Jaws 2* 1978; *1941* 1979; *Brubaker* 1980

Hamilton, Neil (1899-1984) *America* 1924; *Isn't Life Wonderful* 1924; *Beau Geste* 1926; *The Patriot* 1928; *The Dawn Patrol* 1930; *The Return of Dr Fu Manchu* 1930; *Laughing Sinners* 1931; *The Sin of Madelon Claudet* 1931; *Strangers May Kiss* 1931; *This Modern Age* 1931; *The Animal Kingdom* 1932; *Payment Deferred* 1932; *Tarzan, the Ape Man* 1932; *The Wet Parade* 1932; *What Price Hollywood?* 1932; *Tarzan and His Mate* 1934; *The Saint Strikes Back* 1939; *Betrayed* 1944; *Batman* 1966

Hamilton, Richard (1920-2004) *Ladybug, Ladybug* 1963; *Greetings* 1968; *In Country* 1989; *On Deadly Ground* 1994

Hamilton, Suzanna (1960-) *Brimstone and Treacle* 1982; *Nineteen Eighty-Four* 1984; *Out of Africa* 1985; *Wetherby* 1985; *Tale of a Vampire* 1992

Hamilton, Victoria *Before You Go* 2002; *French Film* 2008; *Toast* 2010

Hamlett, Dilys (1928-2002) *Assault* 1970; *Diagnosis: Murder* 1974; *What Changed Charley Farthing?* 1974

Hamlin, Harry (1951-) *Clash of the Titans* 1981; *Making Love* 1982; *Dinner at Eight* 1989; *The Hunted* 1998; *Strange Wilderness* 2007; *Family Gathering* 2010; *Dangerous Attraction* 2012

Hamm, Jon (1971-) *The Day the Earth Stood Still* 2008; *Howl* 2010; *Shrek Forever After* 2010; *The Town* 2010; *Bridesmaids* 2011; *Friends with Kids* 2011; *Clear History* 2013; *The Congress* 2013; *Million Dollar Arm* 2014; *Minions* 2015; *Keeping Up with the Joneses* 2016

Hammer, Armie (1986-) *The Social Network* 2010; *J Edgar* 2011; *Mirror*

Mirror 2012; *The Lone Ranger* 2013; *The Man from UNCLE* 2015

Hammond, Darrell (1960-) *The King and I* 1999; *New York Minute* 2004

Hammond, Earl (1921-2002) *Satan in High Heels* 1962; *Light Years* 1988

Hammond, Kay (1909-1980) *The Trespasser* 1929; *Abraham Lincoln* 1930; *Blithe Spirit* 1945

Hammond, Nicholas (1950-) *The Sound of Music* 1965; *20,000 Leagues under the Sea* 1997; *The Rage in Placid Lake* 2002

Hammond, Peter (1923-2011) *Holiday Camp* 1947; *Vote for Huggett* 1948; *The Adventurers* 1950; *The Reluctant Widow* 1950; *Confession* 1955; *X the Unknown* 1956

Hammond, Virginia (1893-1972) *Anybody's Woman* 1930; *No One Man* 1932

Hamnett, Olivia (1927-2001) *The Last Wave* 1977; *The Earthling* 1980

Hampden, Walter (1879-1955) *The Hunchback of Notre Dame* 1939; *All This, and Heaven Too* 1940; *They Died with Their Boots On* 1941; *5 Fingers* 1952; *Treasure of the Golden Condor* 1953; *Sabrina* 1954; *The Silver Chalice* 1954; *The Prodigal* 1955; *Strange Lady in Town* 1955; *The Vagabond King* 1956

Hampshire, Emily (1981-) *The Life before This* 1999; *Snow Cake* 2005

Hampshire, Susan (1938-) *During One Night* 1961; *The Three Lives of Thomasina* 1963; *Night Must Fall* 1964; *Wonderful Life* 1964; *The Fighting Prince of Donegal* 1966; *The Trygon Factor* 1967; *Monte Carlo or Bust!* 1969; *The Violent Enemy* 1969; *Malpertuis* 1971; *A Time for Loving* 1971; *Living Free* 1972; *Neither the Sea nor the Sand* 1972

Hampton, James aka **Hampton, Jim** (1936-) *The Mean Machine* 1974; *WW and the Dixie Dancekings* 1975; *The China Syndrome* 1979; *Condorman* 1981; *Teen Wolf* 1985; *Teen Wolf Too* 1987; *Sling Blade* 1995

Hampton, Paul (1945-) *Senior Prom* 1958; *Lady Sings the Blues* 1972; *Hit!* 1973; *Shivers* 1975

Han Suk-kyu (1964-) *Shiri* 1999; *Tell Me Something* 1999

Han, Maggie (1959-) *The Last Emperor* 1987; *Open Season* 1995

Hanauer, Terri *Communion* 1989; *The Rapture* 1991

Hanayagi, Shotaro (1894-1965) *Story of the Late Chrysanthemums* 1939; *The Famous Sword* 1945

Hancock, Herbie (1940-) *'Round Midnight* 1986; *Indecent Proposal* 1993

Hancock, John (1942-1992) *The Black Marble* 1980; *Collision Course* 1987; *The Bonfire of the Vanities* 1990; *Why Me?* 1990

Hancock, Lou *Evil Dead II* 1987; *Miracle Mile* 1989

Hancock, Sheila (1933-) *Light Up the Sky* 1960; *The Girl on the Boat* 1962; *Twice round the Daffodils* 1962; *Carry On Cleo* 1964; *The Moon-Spinners* 1964; *Night Must Fall* 1964; *The Anniversary* 1968; *Take a Girl like You* 1970; *The Wildcats of St Trinian's* 1980; *Buster* 1988; *Hawks* 1988; *Three Men and a Little Lady* 1990; *A Business Affair* 1993; *Love and Death on Long Island* 1998; *Hold Back the Night* 1999; *Yes* 2004; *The Boy in the Striped Pyjamas* 2008; *Delicious* 2013

Hancock, Tony (1924-1968) *Orders Are Orders* 1954; *The Rebel* 1960; *The Punch and Judy Man* 1962; *Those Magnificent Men in Their Flying Machines* 1965; *The Wrong Box* 1966

Handl, Irene (1901-1987) *Strange Boarders* 1938; *The Girl in the News* 1940; *Uncensored* 1942; *Rhythm Serenade* 1943; *Give Us the Moon* 1944; *Brief Encounter* 1945; *The Hills of Donegal* 1947; *Adam and Evelyne* 1949; *Cardboard Cavalier* 1949; *The Perfect Woman* 1949; *Stage Fright* 1949; *Mad about Men* 1954; *A Kid for Two Farthings* 1955; *Brothers in Law* 1956; *It's Never Too Late* 1956; *Who Done It?* 1956; *Desert Mice* 1959; *I'm All Right Jack* 1959; *Doctor in Love* 1960; *A French Mistress* 1960; *Make Mine Mink* 1960; *The Night We Got the Bird* 1960; *No Kidding* 1960; *The Pure Hell of St Trinian's* 1960; *The Rebel* 1960; *School for Scoundrels* 1960; *Two Way Stretch* 1960; *Double Bunk* 1961; *Heavens Above!* 1963; *Morgan - a Suitable Case for Treatment* 1966; *Smashing Time* 1967; *Wonderwall* 1968; *The Italian Job* 1969; *Doctor in Trouble* 1970; *On a Clear Day You Can See Forever* 1970; *The Private Life of Sherlock Holmes* 1970; *For the Love of Ada* 1972; *Confessions of a Driving Instructor* 1976; *Adventures of a Private Eye* 1977; *Come Play with Me* 1977; *The*

Hound of the Baskervilles 1977; *The Last Remake of Beau Geste* 1977; *Stand Up Virgin Soldiers* 1977

Handler, Chelsea *Fun Size* 2012; *This Means War* 2012

Handler, Evan *The Three Stooges* 2000; *Sex and the City: the Movie* 2008; *Sex and the City 2* 2010

Handley, Taylor *The Texas Chainsaw Massacre: the Beginning* 2006; *Chasing Mavericks* 2012

Handley, Tommy (1894-1949) *Elstree Calling* 1930; *It's That Man Again* 1942; *Time Flies* 1944

Hands, Marina *The Barbarian Invasions* 2003; *Lady Chatterley* 2006; *An Ordinary Execution* 2010

Handy, James *Burglar* 1987; *Bird* 1988; *K-9* 1989; *Rocketeer* 1991; *K-911* 1999; *Ash Wednesday* 2002

Haney-Jardine, Perla *Genova* 2008; *Untraceable* 2008

Haney, Anne (1934-2001) *Liar Liar* 1997; *Psycho* 1998

Haney, Carol (1924-1964) *Invitation to the Dance* 1956; *The Pajama Game* 1957

Hanft, Helen (1937-) *Stardust Memories* 1980; *License to Drive* 1988

Hanin, Roger (1925-2015) *A Bout de Souffle* 1959; *Rocco and His Brothers* 1960; *They Came to Rob Las Vegas* 1968; *Le Grand Pardon* 1981

Hankin, Larry (1945-) *Escape from Alcatraz* 1979; *Ratboy* 1986; *Out on a Limb* 1992; *Billy Madison* 1995

Hanks, Colin (1977-) *Get over It* 2001; *Orange County* 2001; *11:14* 2003; *King Kong* 2005; *The House Bunny* 2008; *My Spy* 2008; *Untraceable* 2008; *The Guilt Trip* 2012; *Parkland* 2013; *Elvis & Nixon* 2016

Hanks, Tom (1956-) *He Knows You're Alone* 1981; *Bachelor Party* 1984; *Splash* 1984; *The Man with One Red Shoe* 1985; *The Money Pit* 1985; *Volunteers* 1985; *Every Time We Say Goodbye* 1986; *Nothing in Common* 1986; *Dragnet* 1987; *Big* 1988; *Punchline* 1988; *The 'Burbs* 1989; *Turner & Hooch* 1989; *The Bonfire of the Vanities* 1990; *Joe versus the Volcano* 1990; *A League of Their Own* 1992; *Radio Flyer* 1992; *Philadelphia* 1993; *Sleepless in Seattle* 1993; *Forrest Gump* 1994; *Apollo 13* 1995; *Toy Story* 1995; *That Thing You Do!* 1996; *Saving Private Ryan* 1998; *You've Got Mail* 1998; *The Green Mile* 1999; *Toy Story 2* 1999; *Cast Away* 2000; *Catch Me If You Can* 2002; *Road to Perdition* 2002; *Elvis Has Left the Building* 2004; *The Ladykillers* 2004; *The Polar Express* 2004; *The Terminal* 2004; *The Da Vinci Code* 2006; *Charlie Wilson's War* 2007; *Angels & Demons* 2009; *Toy Story 3* 2010; *Larry Crowne* 2011; *Cloud Atlas* 2012; *Extremely Loud & Incredibly Close* 2012; *Radioman* 2012; *Captain Phillips* 2013; *Saving Mr Banks* 2013; *Bridge of Spies* 2015; *Ithaca* 2015; *A Hologram for the King* 2016; *Inferno* 2016; *Sully* 2016; *Toy Story 4* 2017

Hanley, Jimmy (1918-1970) *Boys Will Be Boys* 1935; *Forever England* 1935; *Cotton Queen* 1937; *Housemaster* 1938; *There Ain't No Justice* 1939; *Gaslight* 1940; *The Way Ahead* 1944; *29 Acacia Avenue* 1945; *Holiday Camp* 1947; *The Master of Bankdam* 1947; *Here Come the Huggetts* 1948; *The Blue Lamp* 1949; *Boys in Brown* 1949; *Don't Ever Leave Me* 1949; *The Huggetts Abroad* 1949; *Room to Let* 1949; *The Black Rider* 1954; *Satellite in the Sky* 1956

Hanley, Katie *Godspell* 1973; *Xanadu* 1980

Hann-Byrd, Adam (1982-) *Little Man Tate* 1991; *The Ice Storm* 1997; *Halloween H20: 20 Years Later* 1998

Hannah, Daryl (1960-) *Hard Country* 1981; *Blade Runner* 1982; *Summer Lovers* 1982; *The Pope of Greenwich Village* 1984; *Reckless* 1984; *Splash* 1984; *The Clan of the Cave Bear* 1986; *Legal Eagles* 1986; *Roxanne* 1987; *Wall Street* 1987; *High Spirits* 1988; *Steel Magnolias* 1989; *Crazy People* 1990; *At Play in the Fields of the Lord* 1991; *Memoirs of an Invisible Man* 1992; *Attack of the 50 Ft Woman* 1993; *Grumpy Old Men* 1993; *The Little Rascals* 1994; *The Tie That Binds* 1995; *Two Much* 1995; *Grumpier Old Men* 1996; *The Last Days of Frankie the Fly* 1996; *The Gingerbread Man* 1997; *The Real Blonde* 1997; *Addams Family Reunion* 1998; *Hi-Life* 1998; *Rear Window* 1998; *Diplomatic Siege* 1999; *My Favorite Martian* 1999; *Dancing at the Blue Iguana* 2000; *First Target* 2000; *Hide and Seek* 2000; *Jackpot* 2001; *Northfork* 2002; *A Walk to Remember* 2002; *Casa de los Babys* 2003; *Kill Bill Vol 1* 2003; *Kill Bill Vol 2*

2004; Silver City 2004; A Closed Book 2009

Hannah, John (1962-) Four Weddings and a Funeral 1994; The Innocent Sleep 1995; Madagascar Skin 1995; The James Gang 1997; Resurrection Man 1997; Sliding Doors 1997; Circus 1999; The Hurricane 1999; The Mummy 1999; Pandaemonium 2000; The Mummy Returns 2001; Before You Go 2002; I'm with Lucy 2002; The Last Legion 2006; The Mummy: Tomb of the Dragon Emperor 2008; The Wee Man 2013; Shooting to Socrates 2014

Hannigan, Alyson (1974-) My Stepmother Is an Alien 1988; Dead Man on Campus 1998; American Pie 1999; Boys and Girls 2000; American Pie 2 2001; American Pie: the Wedding 2003; Date Movie 2006; American Reunion 2012

Hanover, Donna (1950-) The People vs Larry Flynt 1996; Series 7: the Contenders 2001

Hanray, Lawrence aka **Hanray, Laurence** (1874-1947) The Man Who Could Work Miracles 1936; It's Never Too Late to Mend 1937; Moonlight Sonata 1937; My Learned Friend 1943; Mine Own Executioner 1947

Hansard, Glen The Commitments 1991; Once 2006

Hansen, Gale (1969-) Dead Poets Society 1989; The Finest Hour 1991

Hansen, Myrna (1934-) Cult of the Cobra 1955; Man without a Star 1955

Hansen, William (1911-1975) The Member of the Wedding 1952; Fail-Safe 1964; Save the Tiger 1973; The Terminal Man 1974

Hanson, Lars (1836-1965) Gösta Berlings Saga 1924; Flesh and the Devil 1926; The Scarlet Letter 1926; The Divine Woman 1928; The Wind 1928; Walpurgis Night 1935

Hanson, Peter aka **Hansen, Peter** (1922-) Branded 1950; Darling, How Could You! 1951; When Worlds Collide 1951; The Savage 1953; A Bullet for Joey 1955

Hanson, Rosamund This Is England 2006; Benny & Jolene 2014

Hanzlik, Jaromir (1948-) Cutting It Short 1980; The Last of the Good Old Days 1989

Hara, Setsuko (1920-2015) No Regrets for Our Youth 1946; Late Spring 1949; Early Summer 1951; The Idiot 1951; Tokyo Story 1953; Tokyo Twilight 1957; Late Autumn 1960; The End of Summer 1961

Harada, Mieko (1958-) Ran 1985; Akira Kurosawa's Dreams 1990

Harareet, Haya (1931-) Ben-Hur 1959; The Secret Partner 1961

Harbord, Carl (1908-1958) Dressed to Kill 1946; The Macomber Affair 1947

Harbour, David The Green Hornet 2011; W.E. 2011; The Equalizer 2014

Harcourt, James (1873-1951) The Old Curiosity Shop 1935; The Avenging Hand 1936; Return of a Stranger 1937; Night Train to Munich 1940; Obsession 1948

Hardcastle, Diana A Good Woman 2004; If Only 2004; The Boy 2016

Harden, Jacques (1925-1992) Gervaise 1956; The Long Absence 1961

Harden, Marcia Gay (1959-) Miller's Crossing 1990; Late for Dinner 1991; Crush 1992; Used People 1992; Safe Passage 1994; The Spitfire Grill 1996; Spy Hard 1996; Curtain Call 1997; Flubber 1997; Desperate Measures 1998; Meet Joe Black 1998; Pollock 2000; Space Cowboys 2000; King of Texas 2002; Casa de los Babys 2003; Mona Lisa Smile 2003; Mystic River 2003; Welcome to Mooseport 2004; Bad News Bears 2005; American Dreamz 2006; The Hoax 2006; Into the Wild 2007; The Invisible 2007; The Mist 2007; Rails & Ties 2007; Sex and Lies in Sin City 2008; The Courageous Heart of Irena Sendler 2009; The Heist 2009; Whip It 2009; A Cat in Paris 2010; Detachment 2011; If I Were You 2012; Parkland 2013; Elsa & Fred 2014; Magic in the Moonlight 2014; Fifty Shades of Grey 2015; Grandma 2015

Hardie, Kate (1969-) Runners 1983; Mona Lisa 1986; Tree of Hands 1988; Melancholia 1989; The Krays 1990; Jack & Sarah 1995; Heart 1997; Croupier 1998

Hardie, Russell (1904-1973) Broadway to Hollywood 1933; Operator 13 1934; In Old Kentucky 1935; Camille 1937

Hardin, Jerry (1929-) Chilly Scenes of Winter 1979; Wolf Lake 1979; Missing 1981; Honkytonk Man 1982; Warning Sign 1985; Wanted Dead or Alive 1986; Blaze 1989; The Hot Spot 1990; Where Are My Children? 1994; Bermuda Triangle 1996

Hardin, Melora (1967-) Soul Man 1986; Lambada 1990; Reckless Kelly

1993; The Hot Chick 2002; Dynasty: the Making of a Guilty Pleasure 2004; 27 Dresses 2008

Hardin, Ty (1930-) Merrill's Marauders 1962; PT 109 1963; Palm Springs Weekend 1963; Battle of the Bulge 1965; Berserk 1967; Custer of the West 1967; Bad Jim 1989

Harding, Ann (1901-1981) Condemned 1929; Holiday 1930; East Lynne 1931; The Animal Kingdom 1932; Westward Passage 1932; When Ladies Meet 1933; Gallant Lady 1934; Enchanted April 1935; Peter Ibbetson 1935; Love from a Stranger 1936; Eyes in the Night 1942; Mission to Moscow 1943; Those Endearing Young Charms 1945; Christmas Eve 1947; The Magnificent Yankee 1950; The Man in the Gray Flannel Suit 1956

Harding, Gilbert (1907-1960) The Gentle Gunman 1952; The Oracle 1952

Harding, John Crime and Punishment, USA 1959; This Property Is Condemned 1966

Harding, Kay (1924-1984) The Mummy's Curse 1944; The Scarlet Claw 1944

Harding, Lyn (1867-1952) The Constant Nymph 1933; An Old Spanish Custom 1935; The Man Who Changed His Mind 1936; Fire over England 1937; Goodbye, Mr Chips 1939

Hardison, Kadeem (1965-) Def by Temptation 1990; White Men Can't Jump 1992; Gunmen 1994; Renaissance Man 1994; Panther 1995; Vampire in Brooklyn 1995; The 6th Man 1997; Made of Honor 2008

Hardwick, Omari Linewatch 2008; Kick-Ass 2010; For Colored Girls 2010

Hardwicke, Cedric aka **Hardwicke, Sir Cedric** (1893-1964) Dreyfus 1931; Rome Express 1932; The Ghoul 1933; Jew Süss 1934; Nell Gwyn 1934; Becky Sharp 1935; Les Misérables 1935; Things to Come 1936; Tudor Rose 1936; Green Light 1937; King Solomon's Mines 1937; The Hunchback of Notre Dame 1939; Stanley and Livingstone 1939; The Howards of Virginia 1940; The Invisible Man Returns 1940; Tom Brown's Schooldays 1940; Victory 1940; Sundown 1941; Suspicion 1941; The Commandos Strike at Dawn 1942; The Ghost of Frankenstein 1942; The Invisible Agent 1942; Valley of the Sun 1942; The Cross of Lorraine 1943; Forever and a Day 1943; The Moon Is Down 1943; The Keys of the Kingdom 1944; The Lodger 1944; Wilson 1944; Wing and a Prayer 1944; Beware of Pity 1946; Sentimental Journey 1946; The Imperfect Lady 1947; Ivy 1947; Lured 1947; Nicholas Nickleby 1947; Tycoon 1947; I Remember Mama 1948; Rope 1948; The Winslow Boy 1948; A Connecticut Yankee in King Arthur's Court 1949; Now Barabbas Was a Robber 1949; The White Tower 1950; The Desert Fox 1951; Mr Imperium 1951; Botany Bay 1952; Salome 1953; The War of the Worlds 1953; Diane 1955; Helen of Troy 1955; Richard III 1955; Gaby 1956; The Power and the Prize 1956; The Ten Commandments 1956; The Vagabond King 1956; Baby Face Nelson 1957; Five Weeks in a Balloon 1962; The Pumpkin Eater 1964

Hardwicke, Edward aka **Hardwick, Edward** (1932-2011) The Odd Job 1978; Baby: Secret of the Lost Legend 1985; Shadowlands 1993; The Scarlet Letter 1995; Photographing Fairies 1997; Oliver Twist 2005

Hardy, Jonathan (1940-2012) The Devil's Playground 1976; Lonely Hearts 1981

Hardy, Oliver (1892-1957) Three Ages 1923; The Wizard of Oz 1925; The Two Tars 1928; Big Business 1929; Hollywood Revue 1929; Men o' War 1929; Perfect Day 1929; The Rogue Song 1930; Pardon Us 1931; County Hospital 1932; The Music Box 1932; Pack Up Your Troubles 1932; Scram! 1932; Their First Mistake 1932; Towed in a Hole 1932; Bogus Bandits 1933; Sons of the Desert 1933; Twice Two 1933; Babes in Toyland 1934; Hollywood Party 1934; Oliver the Eighth 1934; Them Thar Hills! 1934; Tit for Tat 1934; Bonnie Scotland 1935; Thicker than Water 1935; The Bohemian Girl 1936; Our Relations 1936; Pick a Star 1937; Way Out West 1937; Blockheads 1938; Swiss Miss 1938; The Flying Deuces 1939; Zenobia 1939; A Chump at Oxford 1940; Saps at Sea 1940; Great Guns 1941; A-Haunting We Will Go 1942; The Dancing Masters 1943; Jitterbugs 1943; The Big Noise 1944; Nothing but Trouble 1944; The Bullfighters 1945; The Fighting Kentuckian 1949; Utopia 1950; Laurel and Hardy's Laughing 20s 1965; 4 Clowns 1970

Hardy, Robert (1925-) Berserk 1967; Demons of the Mind 1971; Psychomania 1972; Dark Places 1973; Gawain and the Green Knight 1973; The Silent One 1973; The Shooting Party 1984; Paris by Night 1988; A Feast at Midnight 1994; Mary Shelley's Frankenstein 1994; Sense and Sensibility 1995; The Tichborne Claimant 1998; The Gathering 2002; Lassie 2005

Hardy, Sam (1883-1935) The Big Noise 1928; Big News 1929; The Miracle Woman 1931; Ann Vickers 1933; Aunt Sally 1933; King Kong 1933; The Gay Bride 1934; Break of Hearts 1935

Hardy, Sophie (1944-) Three Hats for Lisa 1965; The Trygon Factor 1967

Hardy, Tom (1977-) The Reckoning 2001; Star Trek: Nemesis 2002; Dot the i 2003; EMR 2004; Layer Cake 2004; Bronson 2008; Inception 2010; From the Ashes 2011; Tinker Tailor Soldier Spy 2011; Warrior 2011; The Dark Knight Rises 2012; Lawless 2012; This Means War 2012; Child 44 2014; The Drop 2014; Locke 2014; London Road 2014; Legend 2015; Mad Max: Fury Road 2015; The Revenant 2015; Dunkirk 2017

Hare, Doris (1905-2000) A Place to Go 1963; On the Buses 1971; Mutiny on the Buses 1972; Holiday on the Buses 1973; Confessions of a Pop Performer 1975; Confessions of a Driving Instructor 1976; Confessions from a Holiday Camp 1977; Nuns on the Run 1990

Hare, Lumsden (1875-1964) Svengali 1931; His Double Life 1933; The Little Minister 1934; The World Moves On 1934; Folies Bergère 1935; She 1935; Northwest Passage 1940; Forever and a Day 1943; The Fighting O'Flynn 1948

Hare, Robertson aka **Hare, J Robertson** (1891-1979) Rookery Nook 1930; A Cuckoo in the Nest 1933; Friday the Thirteenth 1933; Car of Dreams 1935; Fighting Stock 1935; Foreign Affaires 1935; Our Girl Friday 1953; The Night We Got the Bird 1960; Crooks Anonymous 1962

Hare, Will (1916-1997) The Electric Horseman 1979; Enter the Ninja 1981; Grim Prairie Tales 1990

Harelik, Mark (1951-) Upworld 1992; Election 1999

Harens, Dean (1920-1996) Christmas Holiday 1944; The Suspect 1944; Crack-Up 1946

Härenstam, Magnus (1941-2015) Father to Be 1979; Happy We 1983

Harewood, David (1965-) The Hawk 1992; Separate Lies 2004; Strings 2004; Blood Diamond 2006; The Hot Potato 2011; The Man Inside 2012; 9.79* 2012; SuperBob 2015; Grimsby 2016

Harewood, Dorian (1950-) Gray Lady Down 1978; Looker 1981; Against All Odds 1984; The Falcon and the Snowman 1985; Full Metal Jacket 1987; Pacific Heights 1990; Sudden Death 1995; 12 Angry Men 1997; Levity 2002; Gothika 2003

Harfouch, Corinna (1954-) The Promise 1994; Downfall 2004

Hargreaves, Amy Brainscan 1994; Blue Ruin 2013

Hargreaves, John (1945-1996) Don's Party 1976; Long Weekend 1977; The Odd Angry Shot 1979; Beyond Reasonable Doubt 1980; Careful, He Might Hear You 1983; My First Wife 1984; Malcolm 1986; Sky Pirates 1986; Cry Freedom 1987; Sweet Revenge 1990; Country Life 1994; Hotel Sorrento 1994

Harington, Kit (1986-) Silent Hill: Revelation 2012; Pompeii 2014; Seventh Son 2014; Testament of Youth 2014; Spooks: the Greater Good 2015

Harker, Gordon (1885-1967) Champagne 1928; The Farmer's Wife 1928; Escape 1930; Rome Express 1932; Friday the Thirteenth 1933; The Phantom Light 1934; Boys Will Be Boys 1935; The Lad 1935; Squibs 1935; Saloon Bar 1940; 29 Acacia Avenue 1945; Derby Day 1952; Bang! You're Dead 1954; Out of the Clouds 1954; A Touch of the Sun 1956; Left, Right and Centre 1959

Harker, Susannah (1965-) Surviving Picasso 1996; Intimacy 2000; Offending Angels 2000; The Calling 2009

Harker, Wiley Crimewave 1985; Guilty Conscience 1985

Harkins, John (1932-1999) The Cracker Factory 1979; Absence of Malice 1981; Six Weeks 1982; Amityville III: the Demon 1984; Birdy 1984; Inherit the Wind 1988

Harlan, Otis (1865-1940) Broadway 1929; Ride Him, Cowboy 1932; Snow White and the Seven Dwarfs 1937; Laurel and Hardy's Laughing 20s 1965; 4 Clowns 1970

Harlow, Jean (1911-1937) The Love Parade 1929; The Saturday Night Kid

1929; Hel's Angels 1930; City Lights 1931; The Iron Man 1931; Platinum Blonde 1931; The Public Enemy 1931; The Secret Six 1931; The Beast of the City 1932; Red Dust 1932; Red-Headed Woman 1932; Three Wise Girls 1932; Blonde Bombshell 1933; Dinner at Eight 1933; Hold Your Man 1933; The Girl from Missouri 1934; China Seas 1935; Reckless 1935; Libeled Lady 1936; Riffraff 1936; Suzy 1936; Wife vs Secretary 1936; Personal Property 1937; Saratoga 1937; The Love Goddesses 1965

Harlow, Shalom (1973-) Head over Heels 2000; How to Lose a Guy in 10 Days 2003

Harmon, Angie (1972-) Batman of the Future: Return of the Joker 2000; Good Advice 2001; Agent Cody Banks 2003; Fun with Dick and Jane 2005; End Game 2006; Living Proof 2008

Harmon, Mark (1951-) Comes a Horseman 1978; Beyond the Poseidon Adventure 1979; Summer School 1987; The Presidio 1988; Stealing Home 1988; Sweet Bird of Youth 1989; Cold Heaven 1992; Wyatt Earp 1994; The Last Supper 1995; Magic in the Water 1995; Casualties 1997; Fear and Loathing in Las Vegas 1998; I'll Remember April 1999; Freaky Friday 2003; Chasing Liberty 2004

Harmon, Pat (1886-1958) Hot Water 1924; The Freshman 1925

Harnett, Ricci The Object of Beauty 1991; Rise of the Footsoldier 2006

Harnick, Aaron (1970-) Happy Together 1989; Judy Berlin 1999

Harnois, Elisabeth (1979-) One Magic Christmas 1985; Pretty Persuasion 2005; Mars Needs Moms 2011

Harnos, Christine aka **Harnos, Christina** The Rescue 1988; Cold Dog Soup 1989

Harolde, Ralf (1899-1974) Check and Double Check 1930; Smart Money 1931; Deluge 1933; I'm No Angel 1933; Picture Snatcher 1933; He Was Her Man 1934

Harper, Frank (1959-) A Room for Romeo Brass 1999; Shiner 2000; The Football Factory 2004; StreetDance 2010; Screwed 2011; St George's Day 2012

Harper, Gerald (1929-) The Admirable Crichton 1957; The Lady Vanishes 1979

Harper, Hill (1966-) Get on the Bus 1996; The Nephew 1997; Hav Plenty 1998; He Got Game 1998; The Skulls 2000; The Breed 2006

Harper, Jessica (1949-) Phantom of the Paradise 1974; Inserts 1975; Suspiria 1976; The Evictors 1979; Stardust Memories 1980; Pennies from Heaven 1981; My Favorite Year 1982; The Blue Iguana 1988

Harper, Tess (1950-) Tender Mercies 1982; Amityville III: the Demon 1983; Crimes of the Heart 1986; Ishtar 1987; Criminal Law 1988; Far North 1988; Her Alibi 1989; Unconquered 1989; Daddy's Dyin'... Who's Got the Will? 1990; The Man in the Moon 1991; My Heroes Have Always Been Cowboys 1991; My New Gun 1992; The Turning 1992; The Road to Galveston 1996; The In Crowd 2000; Angel in the Family 2004; No Country for Old Men 2007

Harper, Valerie (1940-) Freebie and the Bean 1974; Chapter Two 1979; The Last Married Couple in America 1980; The Shadow Box 1980; Blame It on Rio 1984; Death of a Cheerleader 1994; Dancing at the Harvest Moon 2002

Harrelson, Brett The People vs Larry Flynt 1996; From Dusk till Dawn II: Texas Blood Money 1999

Harrelson, Woody (1962-) Wildcats 1986; Cool Blue 1988; Doc Hollywood 1991; White Men Can't Jump 1992; Indecent Proposal 1993; The Cowboy Way 1994; Natural Born Killers 1994; Money Train 1995; Kingpin 1996; The People vs Larry Flynt 1996; Sunchaser 1996; Wag the Dog 1997; Welcome to Sarajevo 1997; The Hi-Lo Country 1998; Palmetto 1998; The Thin Red Line 1998; Edtv 1999; Grass 1999; Play It to the Bone 2000; Scorched 2002; Anger Management 2003; After the Sunset 2004; She Hate Me 2004; The Big White 2005; North Country 2005; Free Jimmy 2006; A Prairie Home Companion 2006; A Scanner Darkly 2006; The Walker 2006; Battle in Seattle 2007; No Country for Old Men 2007; Management 2008; Semi-Pro 2008; Seven Pounds 2008; Transsiberian 2008; Defendor 2009; The Messenger 2009; Zombieland 2009; Bunraku 2010; Friends with Benefits 2011; Rampart 2011; Game Change 2012; How to Make Money Selling Drugs 2012; The Hunger Games 2012; Seven Psychopaths 2012; Free Birds 2013; The Hunger Games: Catching Fire 2013; Now You See Me

2013; Out of the Furnace 2013; The Hunger Games: Mockingjay Part 1 2014; The Hunger Games: Mockingjay Part 2 2015; Triple 9 2015; Now You See Me 2 2016; War for the Planet of the Apes 2017

Harrigan, William (1894-1966) Born Reckless 1930; The Invisible Man 1933; "G" Men 1935; Whipsaw 1935; Back Door to Heaven 1939; Desert Fury 1947; Flying Leathernecks 1951

Harring, Laura aka **Herring, Laura** aka **Herring, Laura Elena** (1964-) Lambada! The Forbidden Dance 1990; Mulholland Drive 2001; Derailed 2002; Willard 2003; The Punisher 2004; The King 2005; My Neighbor's Keeper 2007; Nancy Drew 2007

Harrington, Desmond (1976-) The Hole 2001; My First Mister 2001; Ghost Ship 2002; Wrong Turn 2003

Harrington, Jay Lipstick 2006; A Monster in Paris 2011

Harrington, Kate (1903-1978) Rachel, Rachel 1968; Child's Play 1972

Harrington, Kevin The Dish 2000; Red Hill 2010

Harrington, Laura (1958-) The City Girl 1984; Maximum Overdrive 1986; What's Eating Gilbert Grape 1993

Harrington, Pat (1929-2016) Stage Struck 1958; Easy Come, Easy Go 1967; The President's Analyst 1967; The Affair 1973

Harrington, Richard Leaving Lenin 1993; House of America 1996; The All Together 2007

Harris, Barbara (1935-) A Thousand Clowns 1965; Oh Dad, Poor Dad, Mama's Hung You in the Closet and I'm Feelin' So Sad 1967; Plaza Suite 1971; Who Is Harry Kellerman, and Why Is He Saying Those Terrible Things about Me? 1971; The War between Men and Women 1972; Family Plot 1976; Freaky Friday 1976; Movie Movie 1978; Hill's Angels 1979; The Seduction of Joe Tynan 1979; Peggy Sue Got Married 1986; Dirty Rotten Scoundrels 1988

Harris, Barbara Eve (1959-) 36 Hours to Die 1999; The Midnight Meat Train 2008

Harris, Brad (1933-) The Mutations 1973; Hercules 1983

Harris, Danielle (1977-) Halloween 4: the Return of Michael Myers 1988; Halloween 5: the Revenge of Michael Myers 1989; Marked for Death 1990; The Last Boy Scout 1991; American Yakuza 2: Back to Back 1996; The Wild Thornberrys Movie 2003; Halloween 2007; Halloween II 2009; Stake Land 2010

Harris, Danneel Harold & Kumar Escape from Guantanamo Bay 2008; Fired Up! 2009; A Very Harold & Kumar 3D Christmas 2011

Harris, David (1959-) The Warriors 1979; Purple Hearts 1984; A Soldier's Story 1984; Badge of the Assassin 1985

Harris, Ed (1950-) Borderline 1980; Knightriders 1981; Creepshow 1982; The Right Stuff 1983; Under Fire 1983; A Flash of Green 1984; Places in the Heart 1984; Swing Shift 1984; Alamo Bay 1985; Code Name: Emerald 1985; Sweet Dreams 1985; Walker 1987; Jacknife 1988; To Kill a Priest 1988; The Abyss 1989; State of Grace 1990; Paris Trout 1991; Glengarry Glen Ross 1992; The Firm 1993; Needful Things 1993; China Moon 1994; Milk Money 1994; Apollo 13 1995; Eye for an Eye 1995; Just Cause 1995; Nixon 1995; Absolute Power 1996; The Rock 1996; Stepmom 1998; The Truman Show 1998; Pollock 2000; The Prime Gig 2000; Waking the Dead 2000; A Beautiful Mind 2001; Buffalo Soldiers 2001; Enemy at the Gates 2001; The Hours 2002; The Human Stain 2003; Radio 2003; A History of Violence 2005; Copying Beethoven 2006; Cleaner 2007; Gone Baby Gone 2007; National Treasure: Book of Secrets 2007; Appaloosa 2008; The Way Back 2010; Salvation Boulevard 2011; Game Change 2012; Man on a Ledge 2012; The Face of Love 2013; Gravity 2013; Pain & Gain 2013; Snowpiercer 2013; Cymbeline 2014; Frontera 2014; Planes: Fire and Rescue 2014; Run All Night 2015

Harris, Estelle (1932-) Addams Family Reunion 1998; Good Advice 2001; Tarzan II 2005

Harris (2), George (1949-) Camilla 1993; Layer Cake 2004; The Interpreter 2005

Harris, Jamie (1963-) The Big Heist 2001; The Kreutzer Sonata 2008

Harris, Jared (1961-) The Public Eye 1992; Tall Tale 1994; Blue in the Face 1995; I Shot Andy Warhol 1995; Nadja 1995; B Monkey 1996; Chinese Box 1997; Sunday 1997; The Eternal 1998;

Happiness 1998; Lost in Space 1998; Two of Us 2000; Dummy 2002; Igby Goes Down 2002; Mr Deeds 2002; Sylvia 2003; Resident Evil: Apocalypse 2004; The Notorious Bettie Page 2005; Extraordinary Measures 2010; John Carpenter's The Ward 2010; Sherlock Holmes: a Game of Shadows 2011; The Mortal Instruments: City of Bones 2013; The Quiet Ones 2013; Pompeii 2014; The Man from UNCLE 2015; Poltergeist 2015

Harris, Jason Top Cat: the Movie 2011; Top Cat Begins 2016

Harris, Jet (1939-2011) The Young Ones 1961; Summer Holiday 1962

Harris, Johnny (1973-) London to Brighton 2006; Daylight Robbery 2007; Huge 2009; The Last Days on Mars 2013; Monsters: Dark Continent 2014

Harris, Jonathan (1914-2002) Botany Bay 1952; A Bug's Life 1998

Harris (2), Julie (1925-2013) The Member of the Wedding 1952; East of Eden 1955; I Am a Camera 1955; The Truth about Women 1958; Requiem for a Heavyweight 1962; The Haunting 1963; Harper 1966; You're a Big Boy Now 1966; Reflections in a Golden Eye 1967; The Split 1968; Voyage of the Damned 1976; Gorillas in the Mist 1988; The Dark Half 1991; HouseSitter 1992; Vanished without a Trace 1993; Acts of Love 1995; Bad Manners 1997; The First of May 1999

Harris, Julius aka **Harris, Julius W** (1923-2004) Nothing but a Man 1964; Shaft's Big Score! 1972; Superfly 1972; Trouble Man 1972; Black Caesar 1973; Hell Up in Harlem 1973; Live and Let Die 1973; Islands in the Stream 1976; Victory at Entebbe 1976; Prayer of the Rollerboys 1990

Harris, Lara (1962-) No Man's Land 1987; Blood Red 1988; The Fourth War 1990

Harris, Laura (1976-) The Faculty 1998; Severance 2006

Harris, Mel (1957-) Wanted Dead or Alive 1986; Cameron's Closet 1988; K-9 1989; Suture 1993; The Pagemaster 1994; Firetrap 2001; Out of the Woods 2005

Harris, Moira The Fantasist 1986; Breakdown 1997; Chicago Cab 1998

Harris, Naomie (1976-) 28 Days Later... 2002; After the Sunset 2004; Trauma 2004; A Cock and Bull Story 2005; Miami Vice 2006; Pirates of the Caribbean: Dead Man's Chest 2006; Street Kings 2008; Morris: a Life with Bells On 2009; My Last Five Girlfriends 2009; Ninja Assassin 2009; Sex & Drugs & Rock & Roll 2009; The First Grader 2010; Skyfall 2012; Mandela: Long Walk to Freedom 2013; Southpaw 2015; Spectre 2015; Collateral Beauty 2016; Our Kind of Traitor 2016; Jungle Book: Origins 2018

Harris, Neil Patrick (1973-) Clara's Heart 1988; The Purple People Eater 1988; Cold Sassy Tree 1989; Stranger in the Family 1991; Starship Troopers 1997; The Christmas Wish 1998; The Proposition 1998; The Next Best Thing 2000; Undercover Brother 2002; Harold & Kumar Get the Munchies 2004; Harold & Kumar Escape from Guantanamo Bay 2008; Cloudy with a Chance of Meatballs 2009; Beastly 2010; Cats & Dogs: the Revenge of Kitty Galore 2010; The Smurfs 2011; Cloudy with a Chance of Meatballs 2 2013; The Smurfs 2 2013; Gone Girl 2014; A Million Ways to Die in the West 2014

Harris, Paul (1917-1985) All Night Long 1961; Truck Turner 1974

Harris, Phil (1904-1995) Melody Cruise 1933; Buck Benny Rides Again 1940; Wabash Avenue 1950; The High and the Mighty 1954; Anything Goes 1956; The Wheeler Dealers 1963; The Patsy 1964; The Cool Ones 1967; The Jungle Book 1967; The Aristocats 1970; Robin Hood 1973

Harris, Rachael aka **Harris, Rachel** Showtime 2002; Diary of a Wimpy Kid 2010; Diary of a Wimpy Kid: Rodrick Rules 2011; Diary of a Wimpy Kid 3: Dog Days 2012

Harris, Richard (1932-2002) Alive and Kicking 1958; The Wreck of the Mary Deare 1959; The Long and the Short and the Tall 1960; A Terrible Beauty 1960; The Guns of Navarone 1961; Mutiny on the Bounty 1962; This Sporting Life 1963; Red Desert 1964; The Heroes of Telemark 1965; Major Dundee 1965; The Bible... in the Beginning 1966; Hawaii 1966; Camelot 1967; Caprice 1967; Bloomfield 1969; Cromwell 1970; A Man Called Horse 1970; The Molly Maguires 1970; Man in the Wilderness 1971; The Deadly Trackers 1973; Juggernaut 1974; 99

and 44/100% Dead 1974; The Cassandra Crossing 1976; Echoes of a Summer 1976; The Return of a Man Called Horse 1976; Robin and Marian 1976; Golden Rendezvous 1977; Gulliver's Travels 1977; Orca... Killer Whale 1977; The Wild Geese 1978; A Game for Vultures 1979; Tarzan, the Ape Man 1981; Triumphs of a Man Called Horse 1981; Martin's Day 1984; King of the Wind 1989; Mack the Knife 1989; The Field 1990; Patriot Games 1992; Unforgiven 1992; Wrestling Ernest Hemingway 1993; Cry, the Beloved Country 1995; Smilla's Feeling for Snow 1996; This Is the Sea 1996; Trojan Eddie 1996; The Hunchback of Notre Dame 1997; The Barber of Siberia 1999; Grizzly Falls 1999; To Walk with Lions 1999; Gladiator 2000; The Count of Monte Cristo 2001; Harry Potter and the Philosopher's Stone 2001; My Kingdom 2001; Harry Potter and the Chamber of Secrets 2002

Harris, Robert (1900-1995) Undercover 1943; That Lady 1955; The Big Caper 1957; Decline and Fall... of a Birdwatcher 1968; Ransom 1975

Harris, Rosemary (1930-) Beau Brummell 1954; The Shiralee 1957; A Flea in Her Ear 1968; The Boys from Brazil 1978; The Ploughman's Lunch 1983; The Bridge 1990; Tom & Viv 1994; The Little Riders 1996; My Life So Far 1999; Sunshine 1999; Blow Dry 2000; Spider-Man 2002; Spider-Man 2 2004; Before the Devil Knows You're Dead 2007; Spider-Man 3 2007; Is Anybody There? 2008

Harris, Rossie aka **Harris, Ross** (1969-) Another Man, Another Chance 1977; Testament 1983

Harris, Sean (1966-) 24 Hour Party People 2001; Tom & Thomas 2002; Asylum 2004; Creep 2004; Frozen 2004; Trauma 2004; Brothers of the Head 2005; Isolation 2005; Outlaw 2006; A Lonely Place to Die 2011; Serena 2013; The Goob 2014; '71 2014; Macbeth 2015; Mission: Impossible - Rogue Nation 2015

Harris, Stacy (1918-1973) Appointment with Danger 1950; The Great Sioux Uprising 1953; Dragnet 1954; Comanche 1956; The Hunters 1958

Harris, Steve (1965-) The Mod Squad 1999; The Skulls 2000; Quarantine 2008; 12 Rounds 2008

Harris, Tip aka **Harris, Tip "TI"** aka **TI** (1980-) Takers 2010; Identity Thief 2013; Get Hard 2015

Harris, Wood Remember the Titans 2000; Not Easily Broken 2009; Dredd 2012

Harris, Zelda Crooklyn 1994; The Baby-Sitter's Club 1995

Harrison, Blake (1985-) Reuniting the Rubins 2010; The Inbetweeners Movie 2011; The Inbetweeners 2 2014; Keeping Rosy 2014; Dad's Army 2016

Harrison, Cathryn (1960-) Images 1972; Black Moon 1974; The Dresser 1983; Duet for One 1986

Harrison, George (1943-2001) A Hard Day's Night 1964; Help! 1965; The Concert for Bangladesh 1972; The Rutles - All You Need Is Cash 1978; Shanghai Surprise 1986; George Harrison: Living in the Material World 2011

Harrison, Gregory (1950-) Razorback 1984; North Shore 1987; Mortal Fear 1994; First Daughter 1999; First Target 2000

Harrison, Jenna My Brother Tom 2001; Heroes and Villains 2006

Harrison, Kathleen (1892-1995) The Ghoul 1933; Night Must Fall 1937; Bank Holiday 1938; The Ghost Train 1941; I Thank You 1941; Much Too Shy 1942; The Shop at Sly Corner 1946; Wanted for Murder 1946; Holiday Camp 1947; Bond Street 1948; Here Come the Huggetts 1948; Vote for Huggett 1948; The Winslow Boy 1948; The Gay Adventure 1949; The Huggetts Abroad 1949; Now Barabbas Was a Robber 1949; Trio 1950; Waterfront 1950; Scrooge 1951; The Happy Family 1952; The Pickwick Papers 1952; Turn the Key Softly 1953; All for Mary 1955; Lilacs in the Spring 1955; The Big Money 1956; Home and Away 1956; It's a Wonderful World 1956; Cast a Dark Shadow 1957; A Cry from the Streets 1957; Seven Thunders 1957; Alive and Kicking 1958; On the Fiddle 1961; The Fast Lady 1963; West 11 1963; Lock Up Your Daughters! 1969

Harrison, Linda (1945-) A Guide for the Married Man 1967; Planet of the Apes 1967; Beneath the Planet of the Apes 1969

Harrison, Noel (1934-2013) The Best of Enemies 1961; Where the Spies Are 1965; Take a Girl like You 1970

Harrison, Rex (1908-1990) Men Are Not Gods 1936; Over the Moon 1937; Storm in a Teacup 1937; The Citadel 1938; St Martin's Lane 1938; Night Train to Munich 1940; Major Barbara 1941; Blithe Spirit 1945; I Live in Grosvenor Square 1945; The Rake's Progress 1945; Anna and the King of Siam 1946; The Foxes of Harrow 1947; The Ghost and Mrs Muir 1947; Unfaithfully Yours 1948; The Long Dark Hall 1951; The Four Poster 1953; King Richard and the Crusaders 1954; The Constant Husband 1955; The Reluctant Debutante 1958; Midnight Lace 1960; The Happy Thieves 1962; Cleopatra 1963; My Fair Lady 1964; The Yellow Rolls-Royce 1964; The Agony and the Ecstasy 1965; Doctor Dolittle 1967; The Honey Pot 1967; A Flea in Her Ear 1968; Staircase 1969; The Prince and the Pauper 1977; Ashanti 1979; The 5th Musketeer 1979

Harrison, Richard (1935-) Master of the World 1961; Vengeance 1968

Harrison, Susan (1938-) Sweet Smell of Success 1957; Key Witness 1960

Harrold, Kathryn (1950-) Nightwing 1979; The Hunter 1980; Modern Romance 1981; The Pursuit of DB Cooper 1981; The Sender 1982; Yes, Giorgio 1982; Heartbreakers 1984; Into the Night 1985; Raw Deal 1986

Harron, Robert (1893-1920) The Battle of Elderbush 1914; The Battle of the Sexes 1914; The Escape 1914; Intolerance 1916; Hearts of the World 1918

Harrow, Lisa (1943-) All Creatures Great and Small 1974; It Shouldn't Happen to a Vet 1979; Omen III: the Final Conflict 1980; The Last Days of Chez Nous 1992; That Eye, the Sky 1994; Sunday 1997

Harry, Deborah aka **Harry, Debbie** (1945-) Union City 1980; Downtown 81 1981; Videodrome 1982; Forever Lulu 1987; Hairspray 1988; Satisfaction 1988; Tales from the Darkside: the Movie 1991; Dead Beat 1994; Heavy 1995; Six Ways to Sunday 1997; The Fluffer 2001; My Life without Me 2002; Spun 2002; Elegy 2008; Blank City 2010; Mapplethorpe: Look at the Pictures 2016

Hart, Diane (1926-2002) Happy Go Lovely 1951; Father's Doing Fine 1952; Dick Turpin - Highwayman 1956

Hart, Dolores (1938-) Loving You 1957; Wild Is the Wind 1957; King Creole 1958; Lonelyhearts 1958; Where the Boys Are 1960; Francis of Assisi 1961; Come Fly with Me 1962; The Inspector 1962

Hart, Dorothy (1922-2004) The Countess of Monte Cristo 1948; The Naked City 1948; Calamity Jane and Sam Bass 1949; Undertow 1949; I Was a Communist for the FBI 1951; Tarzan's Savage Fury 1952

Hart, Ian (1964-) The Hours and Times 1992; Backbeat 1993; Clockwork Mice 1994; The Englishman Who Went up a Hill, but Came down a Mountain 1995; Hollow Reed 1995; Land and Freedom 1995; Nothing Personal 1995; B Monkey 1996; Daniel Defoe's Robinson Crusoe 1996; Michael Collins 1996; The Butcher Boy 1997; Noose 1997; Enemy of the State 1998; Mojo 1998; Best 1999; The End of the Affair 1999; This Year's Love 1999; Wonderland 1999; Aberdeen 2000; Born Romantic 2000; The Closer You Get 2000; Strictly Sinatra 2000; Harry Potter and the Philosopher's Stone 2001; Killing Me Softly 2001; Blind Flight 2003; Finding Neverland 2004; Strings 2004; A Boy Called Dad 2009; Morris: a Life with Bells On 2009

Hart, John (1917-2009) The Man Who Loved Redheads 1954; The Legend of the Lone Ranger 1981

Hart, Kevin (1979-) Soul Plane 2004; Fool's Gold 2008; Superhero Movie 2008; Not Easily Broken 2009; Think like a Man 2012; About Last Night 2013; Grudge Match 2013; Ride Along 2014; Think like a Man Too 2014; Top Five 2014; Get Hard 2015; The Wedding Ringer 2015; Central Intelligence 2016; Ride Along 2 2016; The Secret Life of Pets 2016

Hart, Linda Stella 1990; Tin Cup 1996

Hart, Melissa Joan (1976-) Can't Hardly Wait 1998; Drive Me Crazy 1999; Recess: School's Out 2001; Holiday in Handcuffs 2007; My Fake Fiancé 2009

Hart, Miranda (1972-) 12 in a Box 2007; Spy 2015

Hart, Richard (1915-1951) Desire Me 1947; Green Dolphin Street 1947; BF's Daughter 1948; Reign of Terror 1949

Hart, Roxanne (1952-) Oh, God! You Devil 1984; Highlander 1986; Pulse 1988; Once Around 1991; Wilde Salomé 2011; Salomé 2013

Hart, Susan (1941-) City under the Sea 1965; Dr Goldfoot and the Bikini Machine 1965

Hart, Teddy (1897-1971) After the Thin Man 1936; A Girl in Every Port 1952; Mickey One 1965

Hartley, Jo (1972-) This Is England 2006; Crying with Laughter 2009; SoulBoy 2010; Inbred 2011; Up There 2011; Ill Manors 2012; Eddie the Eagle 2016; Life on the Road 2016

Hartley, John (1912-2000) Million Dollar Legs 1939; The Way of All Flesh 1940

Hartley, Mariette (1940-) Ride the High Country 1962; Marnie 1964; Marooned 1969; Barquero 1970; The Return of Count Yorga 1971; The Magnificent Seven Ride! 1972; Improper Channels 1981; 1969 1988; Freefall: Flight 174 1995; Meet the Santas 2005

Hartley, Ted (1935-) Walk, Don't Run 1966; Barefoot in the Park 1967; High Plains Drifter 1973

Hartman, David (1935-) The Ballad of Josie 1968; The Island at the Top of the World 1974

Hartman, Elizabeth (1943-1987) A Patch of Blue 1965; The Group 1966; You're a Big Boy Now 1966; The Beguiled 1970; Full Moon High 1982; The Secret of NIMH 1982

Hartman, Lisa aka Hartman Black, Lisa (1956-) Deadly Blessing 1981; Back to You and Me 2005

Hartman, Paul (1904-1973) Sunny 1941; Soldier in the Rain 1963

Hartman, Phil (1948-1998) Blind Date 1987; The Brave Little Toaster 1987; CB4 1993; Coneheads 1993; So I Married an Axe Murderer 1993; Greedy 1994; Houseguest 1995; Jingle All the Way 1996; Sgt Bilko 1996; Kiki's Delivery Service 1998; Small Soldiers 1998

Hartmann, Paul (1889-1977) Anna Boleyn 1920; The Haunted Castle 1921

Hartnell, William aka **Hartnell, Billy** (1908-1975) Midnight at Madame Tussaud's 1936; The Bells Go Down 1943; The Way Ahead 1944; Brighton Rock 1947; The Lost People 1949; Now Barabbas Was a Robber 1949; Will Any Gentleman...? 1953; Double Cross 1955; Footsteps in the Fog 1955; Josephine and Men 1955; Private's Progress 1956; Yangtse Incident 1956; Hell Drivers 1957; The Hypnotist 1957; Carry On Sergeant 1958; The Mouse That Roared 1959; The Night We Dropped a Clanger 1959; And the Same to You 1960; Piccadilly Third Stop 1960; Tomorrow at Ten 1962; This Sporting Life 1963; The World Ten Times Over 1963

Hartnett, Josh (1978-) The Faculty 1998; Halloween H20: 20 Years Later 1998; The Virgin Suicides 1999; Blow Dry 2000; Here on Earth 2000; Black Hawk Down 2001; O 2001; Pearl Harbor 2001; Town & Country 2001; 40 Days and 40 Nights 2002; Hollywood Homicide 2003; Wicker Park 2004; Sin City 2005; The Black Dahlia 2006; Lucky Number Slevin 2006; Resurrecting the Champ 2007; 30 Days of Night 2007; Bunraku 2010

Harvey, Don (1960-) The Beast of War 1988; Casualties of War 1989; American Heart 1992; The Glass Shield 1995; Tank Girl 1995

Harvey, Forrester (1884-1945) Guilty Hands 1931; Red Dust 1932; Tarzan, the Ape Man 1932; The Eagle and the Hawk 1933; Tarzan and His Mate 1934; Thoroughbreds Don't Cry 1937

Harvey, John (1911-1982) Pin Up Girl 1944; X the Unknown 1956; The Deadly Bees 1967

Harvey, Laurence aka **Harvey, Lawrence** (1928-1973) House of Darkness 1948; Landfall 1949; Cairo Road 1950; Scarlet Thread 1951; There Is Another Sun 1951; I Believe in You 1952; Women of Twilight 1952; Innocents in Paris 1953; The Good Die Young 1954; King Richard and the Crusaders 1954; Romeo and Juliet 1954; I Am a Camera 1955; Storm over the Nile 1955; Three Men in a Boat 1956; Room at the Top 1958; The Silent Enemy 1958; The Truth about Women 1958; Expresso Bongo 1959; The Alamo 1960; Butterfield 8 1960; The Long and the Short and the Tall 1960; Summer and Smoke 1961; Two Loves 1961; A Girl Named Tamiko 1962; The Manchurian Candidate 1962; Walk on the Wild Side 1962; The Wonderful World of the Brothers Grimm 1962; The Ceremony 1963; The Running Man 1963; Of Human Bondage 1964; The Outrage 1964; Darling 1965; Life at the Top 1965; The Spy with a Cold Nose 1966; The Winter's Tale 1966; The Magic Christian 1969; WUSA 1970;

Night Watch 1973; Welcome to Arrow Beach 1974

Harvey, Laurence R The Human Centipede II (Full Sequence) 2011; The Human Centipede III (Final Sequence) 2015

Harvey, Morris (1877-1944) Sing as We Go 1934; The Love Test 1935; Squibs 1935

Harvey, Paul (1882-1955) Born to Be Bad 1934; The Walking Dead 1936; Meet Dr Christian 1939; Never Say Die 1939; Arizona 1940; Side Street 1950; April in Paris 1952; Dreamboat 1952; Calamity Jane 1953; Three for the Show 1955

Harvey, Steve (1956-) The Fighting Temptations 2003; Love Don't Cost a Thing 2003; Johnson Family Vacation 2004; Think like a Man 2012

Harvey, Terence Gunbus 1986; The Phantom of the Opera 1989

Harvey, Verna The Nightcomers 1972; Assassin 1973

Hasegawa, Kazuo (1908-1984) Gate of Hell 1953; The Crucified Lovers 1954; An Actor's Revenge 1963

Haskell, David (1948-2000) Godspell 1973; Body Double 1984

Haskell, Peter (1934-2010) The Cracker Factory 1979; Child's Play 3 1991

Hassall, Imogen (1942-1980) The Long Duel 1967; El Condor 1970; Incense for the Damned 1970; Mumsy, Nanny, Sonny & Girly 1970; White Cargo 1973

Hassan, Tamer (1968-) The Calcium Kid 2003; The Football Factory 2004; The Business 2005; The Ferryman 2007; Cass 2008; City Rats 2008; Dead Man Running 2009; Bonded by Blood 2010; The Last Seven 2010; Breakdown 2015

Hasse, O E (1903-1978) The Big Lift 1950; Decision before Dawn 1951; I Confess 1953; Betrayed 1954; Above Us the Waves 1955; Les Espions 1957; Trois Chambres à Manhattan 1965; State of Siege 1972

Hassel, Danny A Nightmare on Elm Street 4: The Dream Master 1988; A Nightmare on Elm Street 5: The Dream Child 1989

Hasselhoff, David (1952-) The Cartier Affair 1984; Witchcraft 1989; The Big Tease 1999; The SpongeBob SquarePants Movie 2004; Click 2006; Hop 2011; Piranha 3DD 2011; The Christmas Consultant 2012; Keith Lemon: the Film 2012; Baywatch 2017

Hassett, Marilyn (1947-) The Other Side of the Mountain 1975; Two-Minute Warning 1976; Messenger of Death 1988

Hassing, Anne Louise The Idiots 1998; Goltzius and the Pelican Company 2012; The Hunt 2012

Hasso, Signe (1910-2002) The Seventh Cross 1944; The Story of Dr Wassell 1944; The House on 92nd Street 1945; Johnny Angel 1945; Thieves' Holiday 1946; A Double Life 1947; Where There's Life 1947; To the Ends of the Earth 1948; Crisis 1950; A Reflection of Fear 1973; The Black Bird 1975; Sherlock Holmes in New York 1976

Hatami, Leila The Deserted Station 2002; Nader and Simin, a Separation 2011

Hatch, Richard aka **Hatch, Richard L** (1945-) Battlestar Galactica 1978; Charlie Chan and the Curse of the Dragon Queen 1981; The Ghost 2000

Hatcher, Mary Variety Girl 1947; Isn't It Romantic 1948; The Big Wheel 1949

Hatcher, Teri (1964-) The Big Picture 1989; Tango & Cash 1989; Soapdish 1991; Straight Talk 1992; Brain Smasher... a Love Story 1993; Heaven's Prisoners 1996; 2 Days in the Valley 1996; Tomorrow Never Dies 1997; Since You've Been Gone 1998; SPYkids 2001; Resurrecting the Champ 2007; Coraline 2008; Planes 2013

Hatfield, Hurd (1917-1998) Dragon Seed 1944; The Picture of Dorian Gray 1945; Diary of a Chambermaid 1946; The Beginning or the End 1947; The Unsuspected 1947; Destination Murder 1950; Tarzan and the Slave Girl 1950; The Left Handed Gun 1958; El Cid 1961; King of Kings 1961; Mickey One 1965; The Boston Strangler 1968; King David 1985; Crimes of the Heart 1986; Her Alibi 1989

Hathaway, Anne (1982-) The Princess Diaries 2001; The Cat Returns 2002; Nicholas Nickleby 2002; Ella Enchanted 2004; The Princess Diaries 2: Royal Engagement 2004; Brokeback Mountain 2005; Havoc 2005; Hoodwinked 2005; Becoming Jane 2006; The Devil Wears Prada 2006; Bride Wars 2008; Get Smart 2008; Rachel Getting Married 2008; Alice in

Wonderland 2010; Love & Other Drugs 2010; Valentine's Day 2010; One Day 2011; Rio 2011; The Dark Knight Rises 2012; Les Misérables 2012; Interstellar 2014; Rio 2 2014; The Intern 2015; Alice through the Looking Glass 2016

Hathaway, Noah (1971-) Battlestar Galactica 1978; The NeverEnding Story 1984; Troll 1986

Hatosy, Shawn (1975-) The Faculty 1998; Anywhere but Here 1999; The Joyriders 1999; Outside Providence 1999; Witness Protection 1999; Down to You 2000; The Cooler 2002; A Guy Thing 2002; 11:14 2003; Alpha Dog 2006; Factory Girl 2006; The Bad Lieutenant - Port of Call: New Orleans 2009

Hattab, Yoram (1966-) Kadosh 1999; Kippur 2000

Hatton, Raymond (1887-1971) A Romance of the Redwoods 1917; Male and Female 1919; The Ace of Hearts 1921; The Hunchback of Notre Dame 1923; Law and Order 1932; Polly of the Circus 1932; Lady Killer 1933; The Texans 1938; Frontier Horizon 1939; Black Gold 1947; Invasion of the Saucer Men 1957; Motorcycle Gang 1957

Haudepin, Didier (1951-) L'Innocente 1976; Ecoute Voir... 1978

Haudepin, Sabine (1955-) Jules et Jim 1962; The Last Metro 1980

Hauer, Rutger (1944-) Turkish Delight 1973; Keetje Tippel 1975; The Wilby Conspiracy 1975; Soldier of Orange 1977; Spetters 1980; Chanel Solitaire 1981; Nighthawks 1981; Blade Runner 1982; Eureka 1982; The Osterman Weekend 1983; A Breed Apart 1984; Flesh + Blood 1985; Ladyhawke 1985; The Hitcher 1986; Wanted Dead or Alive 1986; Escape from Sobibor 1987; The Legend of the Holy Drinker 1988; Bloodhounds of Broadway 1989; The Salute of the Jugger 1989; Blind Fury 1990; Split Second 1991; Buffy the Vampire Slayer 1992; Nostradamus 1993; Amelia Earhart: the Final Flight 1994; Surviving the Game 1994; The Call of the Wild 1996; Crossworlds 1996; Hostile Waters 1996; Omega Doom 1996; Hemoglobin 1997; Bone Daddy 1998; Simon Magus 1998; Tactical Assault 1998; New World Disorder 1999; Wilder 2000; Confessions of a Dangerous Mind 2002; Batman Begins 2005; Sin City 2005; Hobo with a Shotgun 2011; The Rite 2011

Haun, Lindsey (1984-) Brave New Girl 2004; Broken Bridges 2006; Shrooms 2006

Haupt, Ullrich aka **Haupt, Ulrich** (1887-1931) Morocco 1930; The Unholy Garden 1931

Hauser, Cole (1975-) School Ties 1992; Higher Learning 1995; All over Me 1996; The Hi-Lo Country 1998; Pitch Black 1999; Hart's War 2002; White Oleander 2002; Tears of the Sun 2003; 2 Fast 2 Furious 2003; Paparazzi 2004; The Cave 2005; The Break-Up 2006; A Good Day to Die Hard 2013

Hauser, Fay Marvin and Tige 1983; Jo Jo Dancer, Your Life Is Calling 1986; Candyman: Farewell to the Flesh 1995

Hauser, Wings (1948-) Vice Squad 1982; Mutant 1984; Tough Guys Don't Dance 1987; Avenging Angel 2007; Rubber 2010

Havens, Richie (1941-2013) Catch My Soul 1973; Greased Lightning 1977; Hearts of Fire 1987

Haver, June (1926-2005) Home in Indiana 1944; Irish Eyes Are Smiling 1944; The Dolly Sisters 1945; Where Do We Go from Here? 1945; Three Little Girls in Blue 1946; I Wonder Who's Kissing Her Now 1947; Look for the Silver Lining 1949; Oh, You Beautiful Doll 1949; The Daughter of Rosie O'Grady 1950; Love Nest 1951; The Girl Next Door 1953

Haver, Phyllis (1899-1960) What Price Glory 1926; The Way of All Flesh 1927

Havers, Nigel (1949-) Chariots of Fire 1981; A Passage to India 1984; Burke and Wills 1985; The Whistle Blower 1986; Empire of the Sun 1987; Farewell to the King 1988; The Burning Season 1994; The Life and Death of Peter Sellers 2003

Havill, Andrew The Heart of Me 2002; Sylvia 2003

Havoc, June (1912-2010) Hello, Frisco, Hello 1943; No Time for Love 1943; Brewster's Millions 1945; Gentleman's Agreement 1947; Intrigue 1947; The Iron Curtain 1948; When My Baby Smiles at Me 1948; Follow the Sun: the Ben Hogan Story 1951; Can't Stop the Music 1980; A Return to Salem's Lot 1987

Hawdon, Robin (1939-) When Dinosaurs Ruled the Earth 1969; Burke & Hare 1971

Hawes, Keeley (1977-) Complicity 1999; The Last September 1999; A Cock and Bull Story 2005; Death at a Funeral 2007; The Bank Job 2008; Flashbacks of a Fool 2008

Hawk, Kali Get Him to the Greek 2010; Fifty Shades of Black 2016

Hawke, Ethan (1970-) Explorers 1985; Dad 1989; Dead Poets Society 1989; A Midnight Clear 1991; Mystery Date 1991; White Fang 1991; Alive 1992; Waterland 1992; Floundering 1994; Reality Bites 1994; White Fang 2: Myth of the White Wolf 1994; Before Sunrise 1995; Search and Destroy 1995; Gattaca 1997; Great Expectations 1997; The Newton Boys 1998; Snow Falling on Cedars 1999; Hamlet 2000; Tape 2001; Training Day 2001; Waking Life 2001; Before Sunset 2004; Taking Lives 2004; Assault on Precinct 13 2005; Lord of War 2005; Fast Food Nation 2006; Before the Devil Knows You're Dead 2007; Daybreakers 2008; Brooklyn's Finest 2009; New York, I Love You 2009; Staten Island 2009; The Woman in the Fifth 2011; Mea Maxima Culpa: Silence in the House of God 2012; Sinister 2012; Before Midnight 2013; Getaway 2013; The Purge 2013; Boyhood 2014; Cymbeline 2014; Good Kill 2014; Predestination 2014; Born to Be Blue 2015; Regression 2015; In a Valley of Violence 2016; Maggie's Plan 2016; The Magnificent Seven 2016; Valérian and the City of a Thousand Planets 2017

Hawkes, John (1959-) Roadracers 1994; Hardball 2001; Identity 2003; Me and You and Everyone We Know 2005; American Gangster 2007; Winter's Bone 2010; Martha Marcy May Marlene 2011; The Sessions 2012; Life of Crime 2013

Hawking, Stephen (1942-) The 11th Hour 2007; Hawking 2013

Hawkins, Jack aka **Hawkins, 2nd Lt Jack** (1910-1973) Next of Kin 1942; Bonnie Prince Charlie 1948; The Fallen Idol 1948; The Small Back Room 1949; The Adventurers 1950; The Black Rose 1950; The Elusive Pimpernel 1950; State Secret 1950; No Highway 1951; Angels One Five 1952; The Cruel Sea 1952; Home at Seven 1952; Mandy 1952; The Planter's Wife 1952; Front Page Story 1953; The Intruder 1953; Malta Story 1953; The Seekers 1954; Land of the Pharaohs 1955; The Prisoner 1955; Touch and Go 1955; Fortune Is a Woman 1956; The Long Arm 1956; The Man in the Sky 1956; The Bridge on the River Kwai 1957; Gideon's Day 1958; Ben-Hur 1959; The League of Gentlemen 1960; Two Loves 1961; Five Finger Exercise 1962; Lawrence of Arabia 1962; Zulu 1963; Guns at Batasi 1964; The Third Secret 1964; Lord Jim 1965; Masquerade 1965; Judith 1966; Great Catherine 1968; Shalako 1968; Monte Carlo or Bust! 1969; Oh! What a Lovely War 1969; Twinky 1969; The Adventures of Gerard 1970; Jane Eyre 1970; Waterloo 1970; Kidnapped 1971; When Eight Bells Toll 1971; Sin 1972; Theatre of Blood 1973

Hawkins, Sally (1976-) Vera Drake 2004; Cassandra's Dream 2007; Happy-Go-Lucky 2007; Happy Ever Afters 2009; Made in Dagenham 2010; Never Let Me Go 2010; Submarine 2010; Jane Eyre 2011; Blue Jasmine 2013; Godzilla 2014; Paddington 2014; X+Y 2014

Hawkins, Screamin' Jay (1929-2000) Mystery Train 1989; Perdita Durango 1997

Hawley, Andrew The Innocent 1984; A Night in the Woods 2011

Hawley, Richard Paper Marriage 1991; Captives 1994

Hawn, Goldie aka **Hawn, Goldie Jeanne** (1945-) The One and Only, Genuine, Original Family Band 1968; Cactus Flower 1969; There's a Girl in My Soup 1970; Dollars 1971; Butterflies Are Free 1972; The Girl from Petrovka 1974; The Sugarland Express 1974; Shampoo 1975; The Duchess and the Dirtwater Fox 1976; Foul Play 1978; Private Benjamin 1980; Seems like Old Times 1980; Best Friends 1982; Protocol 1984; Swing Shift 1984; Wildcats 1986; Overboard 1987; Bird on a Wire 1990; Deceived 1991; CrissCross 1992; Death Becomes Her 1992; HouseSitter 1992; Everyone Says I Love You 1996; The First Wives Club 1996; The Out-of-Towners 1999; Town & Country 2001; The Banger Sisters 2002

Haworth, Jill (1945-2011) The Mysteries of Paris 1962; In Harm's Way 1965; It! 1966; The Haunted House of Horror 1969; Tower of Evil 1972; The Mutations 1973

Hawthorne, Nigel (1929-2001) Sweeney 2 1978; The Hunchback of Notre Dame 1982; The Plague Dogs 1982; The Chain 1984; The Black Cauldron 1985; Turtle Diary 1985; King of the Wind 1989; Freddie as FRO7 1992; Demolition Man 1993; The Madness of King George 1995; Richard III 1995; Murder in Mind 1996; Twelfth Night 1996; Amistad 1997; Forbidden Territory: Stanley's Search for Livingstone 1997; Madeline 1998; The Object of My Affection 1998; The Clandestine Marriage 1999; A Reasonable Man 1999; Tarzan 1999; The Winslow Boy 1999; Call Me Claus 2001

Hawtrey, Charles (1914-1988) Where's That Fire? 1939; The Ghost of St Michael's 1941; The Goose Steps Out 1942; A Canterbury Tale 1944; Room to Let 1949; Brandy for the Parson 1951; Timeslip 1955; The March Hare 1956; Who Done It? 1956; Carry On Sergeant 1958; Carry On Nurse 1959; Carry On Teacher 1959; Carry On Constable 1960; Carry On Regardless 1960; Inn for Trouble 1960; Please Turn Over 1960; Dentist on the Job 1961; What a Whopper! 1961; Carry On Cabby 1963; Carry On Jack 1963; Carry On Cleo 1964; Carry On Spying 1964; Carry On Cowboy 1965; Carry On - Don't Lose Your Head 1966; Carry On Screaming 1966; Carry On Follow That Camel 1967; Carry On Doctor 1968; Carry On Up the Khyber 1968; Carry On Again Doctor 1969; Carry On Camping 1969; Carry On Loving 1970; Carry On Up the Jungle 1970; Carry On at Your Convenience 1971; Carry On Henry 1971; Carry On Abroad 1972; Carry On Matron 1972

Hay, Will (1888-1949) Those Were the Days 1934; Boys Will Be Boys 1935; Where There's a Will 1936; Windbag the Sailor 1936; Good Morning, Boys 1937; Oh, Mr Porter! 1937; Ask a Policeman 1938; Convict 99 1938; Hey! Hey! USA 1938; Old Bones of the River 1938; Where's That Fire? 1939; The Black Sheep of Whitehall 1941; The Ghost of St Michael's 1941; The Big Blockade 1942; The Goose Steps Out 1942; My Learned Friend 1943

Hayakawa, Sessue (1889-1973) The Cheat 1915; Tokyo Joe 1949; Three Came Home 1950; House of Bamboo 1955; The Bridge on the River Kwai 1957; The Geisha Boy 1958; Green Mansions 1959; Hell to Eternity 1960; Swiss Family Robinson 1960

Hayashibara, Megumi Cowboy Bebop: the Movie 2001; Paprika 2006

Hayden, Harry (1884-1955) The Meanest Man in the World 1943; The Unknown Guest 1943; Two Sisters from Boston 1946; Double Dynamite 1951

Hayden, Linda (1953-) Taste the Blood of Dracula 1969; Blood on Satan's Claw 1970; Something to Hide 1971; Confessions of a Window Cleaner 1974; Madhouse 1974; Exposé 1975; Vampira 1975; Confessions from a Holiday Camp 1977; Let's Get Laid 1977

Hayden, Nora Plunder Road 1957; The Angry Red Planet 1959

Hayden, Sterling (1916-1986) Blaze of Noon 1947; The Asphalt Jungle 1950; Denver & Rio Grande 1952; Flaming Feather 1952; Hellgate 1952; So Big 1953; The Star 1953; Take Me to Town 1953; Arrow in the Dust 1954; The City Is Dark 1954; Johnny Guitar 1954; Naked Alibi 1954; Prince Valiant 1954; Suddenly 1954; Battle Taxi 1955; The Last Command 1955; Timberjack 1955; The Come On 1956; The Killing 1956; Crime of Passion 1957; The Iron Sheriff 1957; Valerie 1957; Zero Hour! 1957; Terror in a Texas Town 1958; Dr Strangelove, or How I Learned to Stop Worrying and Love the Bomb 1963; Hard Contract 1969; Sweet Hunters 1969; Loving 1970; The Godfather 1972; The Final Programme 1973; The Long Goodbye 1973; 1900 1976; King of the Gypsies 1978; The Outsider 1979; Winter Kills 1979; Nine to Five 1980; Venom 1981

Haydn, Richard aka **Rancyd, Richard** (1905-1985) No Time for Love 1943; Adventure 1945; Forever Amber 1947; The Foxes of Harrow 1947; The Late George Apley 1947; Singapore 1947; The Emperor Waltz 1948; Miss Tatlock's Millions 1948; Sitting Pretty 1948; Alice in Wonderland 1951; The Merry Widow 1952; Money from Home 1953; Never Let Me Go 1953; Her Twelve Men 1954; Jupiter's Darling 1955; The Lost World 1960; Please Don't Eat the Daisies 1960; Five Weeks in a Balloon 1962; Mutiny on the Bounty 1962; Clarence, the Cross-Eyed

Lion 1965; The Sound of Music 1965; The Adventures of Bullwhip Griffin 1967; Young Frankenstein 1974

Haydon, Julie (1910-1994) The Age of Innocence 1934; The Scoundrel 1935; A Family Affair 1937

Haye, Helen (1874-1957) The Skin Game 1931; The Dictator 1935; The 39 Steps 1935; Cotton Queen 1937; Wings of the Morning 1937; The Spy in Black 1939; Kipps 1941; A Place of One's Own 1944; Third Time Lucky 1949; Hobson's Choice 1953; Lilacs in the Spring 1955; My Teenage Daughter 1956; The Gypsy and the Gentleman 1958

Hayek, Salma aka **Hayek Pinault, Salma** (1966-) Roadracers 1994; Desperado 1995; Fair Game 1995; Four Rooms 1995; From Dusk till Dawn 1995; Breaking Up 1996; Fled 1996; Fools Rush In 1997; The Hunchback of Notre Dame 1997; The Faculty 1998; 54 1998; The Velocity of Gary 1998; Dogma 1999; No One Writes to the Colonel 1999; Timecode 1999; Wild Wild West 1999; Hotel 2001; Frida 2002; Once upon a Time in Mexico 2003; After the Sunset 2004; Ask the Dust 2006; Lonely Hearts 2006; Across the Universe 2007; Cirque du Freak: the Vampire's Assistant 2009; Grown Ups 2010; Puss in Boots 2011; Here Comes the Boom 2012; The Pirates! in an Adventure with Scientists! 2012; Savages 2012; Grown Ups 2 2013; Everly 2014; Lessons in Love 2014; Tale of Tales 2015; Sausage Party 2016

Hayes, Allison (1930-1977) Sign of the Pagan 1954; Count Three and Pray 1955; Mohawk 1956; The Undead 1957; The Unearthly 1957; Attack of the 50 Foot Woman 1958

Hayes, Anthony (1977-) The Boys 1998; Bootmen 2000; Look Both Ways 2005; Suburban Mayhem 2006; The Square 2008

Hayes, Bernadene (1903-1987) Great Guy 1936; The Emperor's Candlesticks 1937; Dick Tracy's Dilemma 1947

Hayes, George "Gabby" aka **Hayes, George** (1885-1969) Riders of Destiny 1933; Blue Steel 1934; The Lucky Texan 1934; The Man from Utah 1934; 'Neath the Arizona Skies 1934; Randy Rides Alone 1934; The Star Packer 1934; West of the Divide 1934; The Lawless Frontier 1935; Texas Terror 1935; Land without Music 1936; The Arizona Kid 1939; Come On George 1939; Days of Jesse James 1939; Dark Command 1940; War of the Wildcats 1943; Tall in the Saddle 1944; Bells of Rosarita 1945; Badman's Territory 1946; My Pal Trigger 1946; Trail Street 1947; Return of the Bad Men 1948; The Cariboo Trail 1950

Hayes, Grace (1895-1989) Babes in Arms 1939; Always Leave Them Laughing 1949

Hayes, Helen (1900-1993) Arrowsmith 1931; The Sin of Madelon Claudet 1931; A Farewell to Arms 1932; Night Flight 1933; The White Sister 1933; What Every Woman Knows 1934; Vanessa, Her Love Story 1935; Stage Door Canteen 1943; My Son John 1952; Anastasia 1956; Airport 1970; Herbie Rides Again 1974; One of Our Dinosaurs Is Missing 1975; Victory at Entebbe 1976; Candleshoe 1977; Agatha Christie's Murder Is Easy 1982; Agatha Christie's A Caribbean Mystery 1983; Agatha Christie's Murder with Mirrors 1985

Hayes, Isaac (1942-2008) Three Tough Guys 1974; Truck Turner 1974; Escape from New York 1981; I'm Gonna Git You Sucka 1988; Guilty as Charged 1991; Posse 1993; Robin Hood: Men in Tights 1993; It Could Happen to You 1994; Flipper 1996; illtown 1996; Six Ways to Sunday 1997; South Park: Bigger, Longer & Uncut 1999; Dr Dolittle 2 2001; Hustle & Flow 2005; Kill Switch 2008; Soul Men 2008

Hayes, Linda (1922-1995) The Girl from Mexico 1939; Mexican Spitfire 1940; The Saint in Palm Springs 1941

Hayes, Margaret aka **Hayes, Maggie** (1916-1977) The Blackboard Jungle 1955; Violent Saturday 1955; Beyond the River 1956; Omar Khayyam 1957; The Beat Generation 1959; Girls' Town 1959; 13 West Street 1962

Hayes, Melvyn (1934-) Adventure in the Hopfields 1954; No Trees in the Street 1959; Bottoms Up 1959; The Young Ones 1961; Summer Holiday 1962; Crooks in Cloisters 1963; Wonderful Life 1964; Carry On England 1976

Hayes, Patricia (1909-1996) Went the Day Well? 1942; The Sicilians 1964; Can Heironymus Merkin Ever Forget Mercy Humppe and Find True Happiness? 1969; Goodbye, Mr Chips 1969; The Best of Benny Hill 1974; The

NeverEnding Story 1984; Little Dorrit 1987; A Fish Called Wanda 1988; War Requiem 1988; Willow 1988; The Fool 1990; The Last Island 1990

Hayes, Peter Lind (1915-1998) Playmates 1941; Seven Days' Leave 1942; The Senator Was Indiscreet 1947; The 5,000 Fingers of Dr T 1953

Hayes, Sean aka **Hayes, Sean P** (1970-) Billy's Hollywood Screen Kiss 1998; Cats & Dogs 2001; Martin and Lewis 2002; Pieces of April 2002; Dr Seuss' The Cat in the Hat 2003; Win a Date with Tad Hamilton! 2004; The Bucket List 2008; Igor 2008; Soul Men 2008; Cats & Dogs: the Revenge of Kitty Galore 2010; The Three Stooges 2012

Haygarth, Tony aka **Haygarth, Anthony** (1945-) Unman, Wittering and Zigo 1971; Dracula 1979; A Private Function 1984; The Dressmaker 1988; Tree of Hands 1988; London Kills Me 1991; The Infiltrator 1995; Amy Foster 1997; The Woodlanders 1997; Fakers 2004

Hayman, Cyd (1944-) Percy 1971; The Godsend 1980

Hayman, David (1950-) Eye of the Needle 1981; Heavenly Pursuits 1986; Sid and Nancy 1986; Hope and Glory 1987; Venus Peter 1989; The Near Room 1995; Regeneration 1997; Ordinary Decent Criminal 1999; Gladiatress 2002; The Last Great Wilderness 2002; Rag Tale 2005; Where the Truth Lies 2005; Castles in the Sky 2014

Hayman, Bob aka **Stanton, Robert** (1923-1989) Mr Winkle Goes to War 1944; Abbott and Costello in Hollywood 1945

Haymes, Dick (1918-1980) Dramatic School 1938; Irish Eyes Are Smiling 1944; Billy Rose's Diamond Horseshoe 1945; State Fair 1945; Do You Love Me? 1946; The Shocking Miss Pilgrim 1947; One Touch of Venus 1948; Up in Central Park 1948; All Ashore 1953

Haynes, Linda (1947-) Latitude Zero 1969; The Drowning Pool 1975; Rolling Thunder 1977

Haynes, Lloyd (1934-1986) Good Guys Wear Black 1977; The Greatest 1977

Haynes, Roberta (1929-) Gun Fury 1953; Return to Paradise 1953; Hell Ship Mutiny 1957

Haynie, Jim (1940-) Country 1984; Pretty in Pink 1986; Jack's Back 1988; Dark Angel 1989; Staying Together 1989; Too Much Sun 1990; Sleepwalkers 1992; The Bridges of Madison County 1995

Hays, Kathryn (1933-) Ladybug, Ladybug 1963; Ride beyond Vengeance 1966; Counterpoint 1967

Hays, Robert (1947-) Airplane! 1980; Airplane II: the Sequel 1982; Scandalous 1983; Cat's Eye 1984; Fifty/Fifty 1991; Good Cop, Bad Cop 1993; Homeward Bound: the Incredible Journey 1993; Homeward Bound II: Lost in San Francisco 1996

Haysbert, Dennis (1955-) Love Field 1992; Mr Baseball 1992; Suture 1993; Major League II 1994; Waiting to Exhale 1995; Absolute Power 1996; Major League: Back to the Minors 1998; The Minus Man 1999; Random Hearts 1999; The Thirteenth Floor 1999; Love & Basketball 2000; What's Cooking? 2000; Far from Heaven 2002; Sinbad: Legend of the Seven Seas 2003; Jarhead 2005; Breach 2006; Goodbye Bafana 2007; Dear White People 2014; Sin City: a Dame to Kill For 2014

Hayter, James (1907-1983) Big Fella 1937; Sailors Three 1940; The End of the River 1947; Once a Jolly Swagman 1948; The Blue Lagoon 1949; Trio 1950; Tom Brown's Schooldays 1951; The Crimson Pirate 1952; The Pickwick Papers 1952; The Story of Robin Hood and His Merrie Men 1952; A Day to Remember 1953; Four Sided Triangle 1953; Will Any Gentleman...? 1953; Beau Brummell 1954; Land of the Pharaohs 1955; The Big Money 1956; It's a Wonderful World 1956; Seven Waves Away 1957; Gideon's Day 1958; The Thirty-Nine Steps 1959; A Challenge for Robin Hood 1967

Hayward, Louis (1909-1985) The Love Test 1935; Anthony Adverse 1936; Trouble for Two 1936; The Woman I Love 1937; Condemned Women 1938; The Duke of West Point 1938; The Rage of Paris 1938; The Saint in New York 1938; Dance, Girl, Dance 1940; My Son, My Son! 1940; Son of Monte Cristo 1940; Ladies in Retirement 1941; And Then There Were None 1945; The Strange Woman 1946; Repeat Performance 1947; The Black Arrow 1948; Ruthless 1948; House by the River 1950

Hayward, Susan (1918-1975) Hollywood Hotel 1937; The Amazing Dr Clitterhouse 1938; The Sisters 1938; Beau Geste 1939; Adam Had Four Sons 1941; Among the Living 1941; The Forest Rangers 1942; I Married a Witch 1942; Reap the Wild Wind 1942; Star Spangled Rhythm 1942; Young and Willing 1942; Change of Heart 1943; And Now Tomorrow 1944; The Fighting Seabees 1944; The Hairy Ape 1944; Jack London 1944; Canyon Passage 1946; Deadline at Dawn 1946; The Lost Moment 1947; Smash Up – the Story of a Woman 1947; They Won't Believe Me 1947; The Saxon Charm 1948; House of Strangers 1949; My Foolish Heart 1949; Tulsa 1949; David and Bathsheba 1951; I Can Get It for You Wholesale 1951; I'd Climb the Highest Mountain 1951; Rawhide 1951; The Lusty Men 1952; The Snows of Kilimanjaro 1952; With a Song in My Heart 1952; The President's Lady 1953; White Witch Doctor 1953; Demetrius and the Gladiators 1954; Garden of Evil 1954; I'll Cry Tomorrow 1955; Soldier of Fortune 1955; Untamed 1955; The Conqueror 1956; Top Secret Affair 1957; I Want to Live! 1958; Thunder in the Sun 1959; Woman Obsessed 1959; The Marriage-Go-Round 1960; Ada 1961; Back Street 1961; I Thank a Fool 1962; Where Love Has Gone 1964; The Honey Pot 1967; Valley of the Dolls 1967

Haywood, Chris (1949-) Breaker Morant 1979; Attack Force Z 1981; Heatwave 1981; The Man from Snowy River 1982; Man of Flowers 1984; Razorback 1984; The Coca-Cola Kid 1985; A Street to Die 1985; Dogs in Space 1986; Malcolm 1986; The Navigator – a Medieval Odyssey 1988; Quigley Down Under 1990; Golden Braid 1991; A Woman's Tale 1991; Blackrock 1997; The Boys Are Back 2009; Sleeping Beauty 2011

Haywood, Roy Bronco Bullfrog 1970; Looks and Smiles 1981

Hayworth, Rita aka **Cansino, Rita** (1918-1987) Charlie Chan in Egypt 1935; Dante's Inferno 1935; Human Cargo 1936; Meet Nero Wolfe 1936; Girls Can Play 1937; Hit the Saddle 1937; Old Louisiana 1938; There's Always a Woman 1938; The Lone Wolf Spy Hunt 1939; Only Angels Have Wings 1939; Angels over Broadway 1940; The Lady in Question 1940; Music in My Heart 1940; Susan and God 1940; Affectionately Yours 1941; Blood and Sand 1941; The Strawberry Blonde 1941; You'll Never Get Rich 1941; My Gal Sal 1942; Tales of Manhattan 1942; You Were Never Lovelier 1942; Cover Girl 1944; Tonight and Every Night 1945; Gilda 1946; Down to Earth 1947; The Lady from Shanghai 1948; The Loves of Carmen 1948; Affair in Trinidad 1952; Miss Sadie Thompson 1953; Salome 1953; Fire Down Below 1957; Pal Joey 1957; Separate Tables 1958; The Story on Page One 1959; They Came to Cordura 1959; The Happy Thieves 1962; The Magnificent Showman 1964; The Love Goddesses 1965; The Poppy Is Also a Flower 1966; The Rover 1967; The Wrath of God 1972

Haze, Jonathan (1929-) Not of This Earth 1956; Stakeout on Dope Street 1958; The Little Shop of Horrors 1960

Hazen, Maya Shrooms 2006; Shutter 2008

Hazlehurst, Noni (1954-) The Shiralee 1986; Waiting 1990; Candy 2005; Little Fish 2005

He Caifei Raise the Red Lantern 1991; Temptress Moon 1996

Head, Anthony (1954-) Lady Chatterley's Lover 1981; Fat Slags 2004; Imagine Me and You 2005; Sparkle 2006; The Great Ghost Rescue 2011; The Iron Lady 2011; Ghost Rider: Spirit of Vengeance 2012; The Unbeatables 2013; Despite the Falling Snow 2016

Head, Edith (1897-1981) Lucy Gallant 1955; The Pleasure of His Company 1961; The Oscar 1966

Head, Jae The Blind Side 2009; Cody the Robosapien 2012

Head, Murray (1946-) Sunday, Bloody Sunday 1971; Gawain and the Green Knight 1973

Headey, Lena (1973-) Waterland 1992; Century 1993; The Jungle Book 1994; The Grotesque 1995; Face 1997; Mrs Dalloway 1997; If Only 1998; Gossip 1999; Onegin 1999; Aberdeen 2000; Anazapta 2001; The Parole Officer 2001; Possession 2002; Ripley's Game 2002; The Actors 2003; The Brothers Grimm 2005; The Cave 2005; Imagine Me and You 2005; 300 2006; The Contractor 2007; St Trinian's 2007; The Broken 2008; The Red Baron

2008; Dredd 2012; The Mortal Instruments: City of Bones 2013; The Purge 2013; 300: Rise of an Empire 2013; Pride and Prejudice and Zombies 2015

Headly, Glenne (1955-) Eleni 1985; Making Mr Right 1987; Nadine 1987; Dirty Rotten Scoundrels 1988; Paperhouse 1988; Dick Tracy 1990; Mortal Thoughts 1991; And the Band Played On 1993; Ordinary Magic 1993; Getting Even with Dad 1994; Mr Holland's Opus 1995; Pronto 1996; Sgt Bilko 1996; 2 Days in the Valley 1996; Babe: Pig in the City 1998; Breakfast of Champions 1999; Timecode 1999; Bartleby 2000; What's the Worst That Could Happen? 2001; Around the Bend 2004; Confessions of a Teenage Drama Queen 2004; The Moguls 2005; The Joneses 2009; Don Jon 2013

Heald, Anthony (1944-) Orphans 1987; Outrageous Fortune 1987; The Silence of the Lambs 1991; Bushwhacked 1995; Deep Rising 1998; 8mm 1999; Red Dragon 2002; Accepted 2006

Healey, Myron (1922-2005) Count Three and Prey 1955; Rage at Dawn 1955; The Unearthly 1957; The Incredible Melting Man 1977

Healy, Darren Disco Pigs 2001; Dead Bodies 2003

Healy, David (1932-1995) The Sign of Four 1983; The Unbelievable Truth 1989

Healy, Dorian For Queen and Country 1988; Young Soul Rebels 1991

Healy, Mary (1918-2015) Second Fiddle 1939; Star Dust 1940; The 5,000 Fingers of Dr T 1953

Healy, Pat Undertow 2004; The Innkeepers 2011; Compliance 2012; Cheap Thrills 2013

Healy, Ted (1896-1937) Blonde Bombshell 1933; Dancing Lady 1933; Meet the Baron 1933; Hollywood Party 1934; Operator 13 1934; The Casino Murder Case 1935; Mad Love 1935; Reckless 1935; San Francisco 1936; Sing, Baby, Sing 1936; Speed 1936; Hollywood Hotel 1937

Healy, Tim (1952-) Shadow Run 1998; Purely Belter 2000; Faintheart 2008

Heard, Amber (1986-) All the Boys Love Mandy Lane 2006; Never Back Down 2008; Pineapple Express 2008; The Informers 2009; The Joneses 2009; The Stepfather 2009; Zombieland 2009; John Carpenter's The Ward 2010; Drive Angry 2011; The Rum Diary 2011; Machete Kills 2013; Paranoia 2013; 3 Days to Kill 2014; The Danish Girl 2015; London Fields 2015; Magic Mike XXL 2015

Heard, John (1946-) Between the Lines 1977; First Love 1977; On the Yard 1978; Chilly Scenes of Winter 1979; Heart Beat 1979; Cutter's Way 1981; Cat People 1982; Too Scared to Scream 1982; Best Revenge 1983; CHUD 1984; After Hours 1985; Catholic Boys 1985; The Trip to Bountiful 1985; Beaches 1988; Betrayed 1988; Big 1988; The Milagro Beanfield War 1988; The Seventh Sign 1988; The Telephone 1988; The Package 1989; Awakenings 1990; Home Alone 1990; Deceived 1991; Rambling Rose 1991; Gladiator 1992; Home Alone 2: Lost in New York 1992; Radio Flyer 1992; Waterland 1992; The Pelican Brief 1993; Before and After 1996; My Fellow Americans 1996; One Eight Seven 1997; Desert Blue 1998; Snake Eyes 1998; Animal Factory 2000; Pollock 2000; The Big Heist 2001; White Chicks 2004; Edison 2005; Sweet Land 2005; The Guardian 2006; The Great Debaters 2007; Sharknado 2013

Hearn, Ann The Dollmaker 1984; The Accused 1988; My Father the Hero 1994; The War at Home 1996

Hearn, George (1934-) A Piano for Mrs Cimino 1982; See You in the Morning 1989; The Vanishing 1993; The Devil's Own 1997; Barney's Great Adventure 1998

Hearne, Richard (1908-1979) Miss London Ltd 1943; Something in the City 1950; Miss Robin Hood 1952; The Time of His Life 1955

Hearst, Patricia (1954-) Cry-Baby 1989; Serial Mom 1994; Bio-Dome 1996; Pecker 1998; A Dirty Shame 2004

Heath, Gordon (1918-1991) Animal Farm 1954; Sapphire 1959; Asterix vs Caesar 1985

Heathcote, Bella (1987-) The Rewrite 2014; The Neon Demon 2016

Heather, Jean (1921-1995) Double Indemnity 1944; Going My Way 1944; Murder, He Says 1945

Heatherley, Clifford (1888-1937) Champagne 1928; Bitter Sweet 1933

Heatherton, Joey (1944-) Twilight of Honor 1963; Where Love Has Gone 1964; My Blood Runs Cold 1965; Bluebeard 1972; The Happy Hooker Goes to Washington 1977

Heche, Anne (1969-) The Adventures of Huck Finn 1993; Against the Wall 1994; Milk Money 1994; Kingfish: a Story of Huey P Long 1995; Pie in the Sky 1995; Wild Side 1995; If These Walls Could Talk 1996; The Juror 1996; Walking and Talking 1996; Donnie Brasco 1997; I Know What You Did Last Summer 1997; Subway Stories: Tales from the Underground 1997; Volcano 1997; Wag the Dog 1997; Psycho 1998; Return to Paradise 1998; Six Days Seven Nights 1998; Auggie Rose 2000; John Q 2001; Birth 2004; Spread 2008; Cedar Rapids 2011; Rampart 2011; Arthur & Mike 2012; Wild Card 2014

Hecht, Ben (1894-1964) The Scoundrel 1935; Specter of the Rose 1946

Hecht, Gina (1953-) Night Shift 1982; A Stranger's Heart 2007

Hecht, Jessica (1965-) The Forgotten 2004; Sideways 2004

Hecht, Paul (1941-) The Reincarnation of Peter Proud 1975; My Dog Tulip 2009

Heckart, Eileen (1919-2001) The Bad Seed 1956; Bus Stop 1956; Miracle in the Rain 1956; Somebody Up There Likes Me 1956; Hot Spell 1958; Heller in Pink Tights 1960; My Six Loves 1962; Up the Down Staircase 1967; No Way to Treat a Lady 1968; Butterflies Are Free 1972; Zandy's Bride 1974; Burnt Offerings 1976; FDR: the Last Year 1980; Heartbreak Ridge 1986; Breathing Lessons 1994

Hedaya, Dan (1940-) Night of the Juggler 1980; Blood Simple 1983; The Hunger 1983; Reckless 1984; Tightrope 1984; Commando 1985; Running Scared 1986; Wise Guys 1986; Aunt Julia and the Scriptwriter 1990; Joe versus the Volcano 1990; The Addams Family 1991; Mr Wonderful 1992; Benny & Joon 1993; Rookie of the Year 1993; Clueless 1995; To Die For 1995; The Usual Suspects 1995; Daylight 1996; The First Wives Club 1996; Freeway 1996; Marvin's Room 1996; Alien: Resurrection 1997; A Life Less Ordinary 1997; A Civil Action 1998; A Night at the Roxbury 1998; Dick 1999; The Hurricane 1999; Shaft 2000; Mulholland Drive 2001; Swimfan 2002; American Cousins 2003

Heder, Jon (1977-) Napoleon Dynamite 2004; Just like Heaven 2005; The Benchwarmers 2006; Monster House 2006; School for Scoundrels 2006; Blades of Glory 2007; Surf's Up 2007; When in Rome 2009; For Ellen 2012

Hedison, David aka **Hedison, Al** (1927-) The Enemy Below 1957; The Fly 1958; Son of Robin Hood 1958; The Lost World 1960; Live and Let Die 1973; North Sea Hijack 1979; The Naked Face 1984

Hedley, Jack (1930-) Left, Right and Centre 1959; Make Mine Mink 1960; The Very Edge 1962; In the French Style 1963; The Scarlet Blade 1963; Of Human Bondage 1964; How I Won the War 1967; The Anniversary 1968; Brief Encounter 1974

Hedlund, Garrett (1984-) Friday Night Lights 2004; Four Brothers 2005; Eragon 2006; Death Sentence 2007; Georgia Rule 2007; Country Strong 2010; Tron Legacy 2010; On the Road 2011; Inside Llewyn Davis 2013; Mojave 2014; Unbroken 2014; Pan 2015

Hedren, Tippi aka **Hedren, "Tippi"** (1930-) The Petty Girl 1950; The Birds 1963; Marnie 1964; A Countess from Hong Kong 1967; Mr Kingstreet's War 1970; Tiger by the Tail 1970; The Harrad Experiment 1973; Roar 1981; Pacific Heights 1990; Treacherous Beauties 1994; Citizen Ruth 1996; Break Up 1998; I Woke Up Early the Day I Died 1998; Nora Roberts' Tribute 2009; Jayne Mansfield's Car 2012

Heffernan, John (1934-) Puzzle of a Downfall Child 1970; The Sting 1973

Heffernan, Kevin (1968-) Broken Lizard's Club Dread 2004; Sky High 2005; Beerfest 2006; Strange Wilderness 2007

Heffner, Kyle T Flashdance 1983; Runaway Train 1985

Heflin, Marta (1945-2013) A Star Is Born 1976; A Perfect Couple 1979; Come Back to the Five and Dime, Jimmy Dean, Jimmy Dean 1982

Heflin, Nora Fantastic Planet 1973; Chilly Scenes of Winter 1979

Heflin, Van (1910-1971) A Woman Rebels 1936; Flight from Glory 1937; Back Door to Heaven 1939; Santa Fe

Trail 1940; The Feminine Touch 1941; HM Pulham Esq 1941; Johnny Eager 1941; Kid Glove Killer 1942; Tennessee Johnson 1942; Presenting Lily Mars 1943; The Strange Love of Martha Ivers 1946; Till the Clouds Roll By 1946; Green Dolphin Street 1947; Possessed 1947; BF's Daughter 1948; The Three Musketeers 1948; Act of Violence 1949; East Side, West Side 1949; Madame Bovary 1949; The Prowler 1951; Tomahawk 1951; Weekend with Father 1951; My Son John 1952; South of Algiers 1952; Shane 1953; Black Widow 1954; The Raid 1954; Tanganyika 1954; Woman's World 1954; Battle Cry 1955; Count Three and Pray 1955; Patterns 1956; 3:10 to Yuma 1957; Gunman's Walk 1958; Tempest 1959; They Came to Cordura 1959; Five Branded Women 1960; Under Ten Flags 1960; Once a Thief 1965; Stagecoach 1966; The Big Bounce 1969; Airport 1970

Hefner, Hugh Inside Deep Throat 2005; The House Bunny 2008

Heggie, O P (1879-1936) The Letter 1929; One Romantic Night 1930; East Lynne 1931; Smilin' Through 1932; Zoo in Budapest 1933; Anne of Green Gables 1934; The Count of Monte Cristo 1934; Midnight 1934

Hehir, Peter (1949-) A Street to Die 1985; Kangaroo 1986

Heigl, Katherine (1978-) That Night 1992; My Father the Hero 1994; Under Siege 2 1995; Prince Valiant 1997; Bride of Chucky 1998; Valentine 2001; The Ringer 2005; Knocked Up 2007; 27 Dresses 2008; The Ugly Truth 2009; Killers 2010; Life as We Know It 2010; New Year's Eve 2011; One for the Money 2012; The Big Wedding 2013; The Nut Job 2014

Heinemann, Laurie Save the Tiger 1973; The Lady in Red 1979

Heinz, Gerard (1904-1972) Caravan 1946; The Lost People 1949; That Dangerous Age 1949; Traveller's Joy 1949; Desperate Moment 1953

Heiskanen, Maria Lights in the Dusk 2006; Maria Larsson's Everlasting Moments 2008

Helberg, Simon We'll Never Have Paris 2014; Florence Foster Jenkins 2016

Held, Ingrid Gunbus 1986; The Last Butterfly 1990; Après l'Amour 1992

Helgenberger, Marg (1958-) After Midnight 1989; The Cowboy Way 1994; Where Are My Children? 1994; Bad Boys 1995; Species 1995; Fire Down Below 1997; Species II 1998; Happy Face Murders 1999; Erin Brockovich 2000; In Good Company 2004; Mr Brooks 2007

Hélia, Jenny Toni 1935; La Bête Humaine 1938

Hell, Erik (1911-1973) Port of Call 1948; A Passion 1969; The Rite 1969

Hellman, Jaclyn aka **Hellman, Jacqueline** Flight to Fury 1966; Two-Lane Blacktop 1971

Helm, Anne (1938-) Follow That Dream 1962; The Iron Maiden 1962; The Magic Sword 1962

Helm, Brigitte (1906-1996) Metropolis 1926; The Love of Jeanne Ney 1927; Crisis 1928; The Wonderful Lie of Nina Petrovna 1929

Helm, Fay (1913-2003) Blondie! 1938; Calling Dr Death 1943; Phantom Lady 1944; The Falcon in San Francisco 1945

Helm, Levon (1943-2012) Coal Miner's Daughter 1980; Best Revenge 1983; The Dollmaker 1984; Smooth Talk 1985; End of the Line 1987; Staying Together 1989; Feeling Minnesota 1996; The Right Stuff 1983; Shady 1985; Overboard 1987; Lady in White 1988; Amore! 1993; A Grandpa for Christmas 2007

Helmore, Tom (1904-1995) Trouble along the Way 1953; Lucy Gallant 1955; Designing Woman 1957; Vertigo 1958; Count Your Blessings 1959; The Time Machine 1960; Flipper's New Adventure 1964

Helms, Ed (1974-) Meet Dave 2008; The Goods: Live Hard Sell Hard 2009; The Hangover 2009; Cedar Rapids 2011; The Hangover: Part II 2011; Jeff, Who Lives at Home 2011; Dr Seuss' The Lorax 2012; The Hangover Part III 2013; We're the Millers 2013; They Came Together 2014; Vacation 2015; Bastards 2016

Helpmann, Robert (1909-1986) Caravan 1946; The Red Shoes 1948; The Tales of Hoffmann 1951; The Big Money 1956; The Iron Petticoat 1956; The Quiller Memorandum 1966; Alice's Adventures in Wonderland 1972; Don Quixote 1973; Patrick 1978

Helstad, Benjamin King of Devil's Island 2010; The Last King 2016

Hemblen, David Family Viewing 1987; Short Circuit 2 1988; Speaking Parts

1989; The Adjuster 1991; Brainscan 1994; Exotica 1994; Hollow Point 1996; Rollerball 2001

Hembrow, Mark (1955-) High Tide 1987; Return to Snowy River 1988; The Last Island 1990

Hemingway, Margaux (1955-1996) Lipstick 1976; Killer Fish 1978; Over the Brooklyn Bridge 1983

Hemingway, Mariel (1961-) Lipstick 1976; Manhattan 1979; Personal Best 1982; Star 80 1983; Creator 1985; The Mean Season 1985; Superman IV: the Quest for Peace 1987; Sunset 1988; Delirious 1991; Falling from Grace 1992; Bad Moon 1996; Deconstructing Harry 1997; The Sex Monster 1998; First Daughter 1999; Londinium 1999; First Shot 2002

Hemingway, Toby (1983-) The Covenant 2006; Feast of Love 2007

Hemmings, David (1941-2003) The Painted Smile 1961; The Wind of Change 1961; Some People 1962; Live It Up 1963; Two Left Feet 1963; The System 1964; Be My Guest 1965; Blowup 1966; Eye of the Devil 1966; Barbarella 1967; Camelot 1967; The Best House in London 1968; The Charge of the Light Brigade 1968; Only When I Larf 1968; Alfred the Great 1969; Fragment of Fear 1970; The Walking Stick 1970; The Love Machine 1971; Unman, Wittering and Zigo 1971; Juggernaut 1974; Deep Red 1975; Mister Quilp 1975; Islands in the Stream 1976; Blood Relatives 1977; The Disappearance 1977; The Prince and the Pauper 1977; The Squeeze 1977; Just a Gigolo 1978; Murder by Decree 1978; Power Play 1978; Thirst 1979; Beyond Reasonable Doubt 1980; Harlequin 1980; Man, Woman and Child 1983; The Rainbow 1988; Last Orders 2001; Mean Machine 2001; Spy Game 2001; Gangs of New York 2002; The League of Extraordinary Gentlemen 2003; The Night We Called It a Day 2003

Hempel, Anouska (1941-) The Scars of Dracula 1970; Tiffany Jones 1973

Hempstead-Wright, Isaac The Awakening 2011; The Boxtrolls 2014

Hemsley, Estelle (1887-1968) Take a Giant Step 1959; America, America 1963; Baby the Rain Must Fall 1965

Hemsley, Sherman (1938-2012) Love at First Bite 1979; Mr Nanny 1992; Screwed 2000

Hemsworth, Chris (1983-) The Cabin in the Woods 2010; Ca$h! 2010; Thor 2011; Marvel Avengers Assemble 2012; Red Dawn 2012; Snow White and the Huntsman 2012; Rush 2013; Thor: the Dark World 2013; Avengers: Age of Ultron 2015; Blackhat 2015; In the Heart of the Sea 2015; Vacation 2015; Ghostbusters 2016; The Huntsman: Winter's War 2016; Thor: Ragnarok 2017

Hemsworth, Liam (1990-) Triangle 2009; The Last Song 2010; The Expendables 2 2012; The Hunger Games 2012; The Hunger Games: Catching Fire 2013; Paranoia 2013; The Hunger Games: Mockingjay Part 1 2014; The Dressmaker 2015; The Hunger Games: Mockingjay Part 2 2015; Independence Day: Resurgence 2016

Hendel, Paolo (1952-) The Night of San Lorenzo 1981; Three Sisters 1988

Henderson, Bill (1925-) Trouble Man 1972; Inside Moves: the Guys from Max's Bar 1980; Continental Divide 1981; Murphy's Law 1986; Wisdom 1986

Henderson, Dell (1883-1956) The Crowd 1928; The Patsy 1928; Show People 1928

Henderson, Don (1931-1997) Callan 1974; The Ghoul 1975; The Island 1980; As You Like It 1992; The Baby of Macon 1993; No Escape 1994

Henderson, Florence (1934-) Song of Norway 1970; Shakes the Clown 1991; Ladies of the House 2008

Henderson, Marcia (1929-1987) All I Desire 1953; Back to God's Country 1953; The Glass Web 1953; Thunder Bay 1953; Naked Alibi 1954

Henderson, Martin (1974-) The Ring 2002; Torque 2003; Bride & Prejudice 2004; Little Fish 2005; Flyboys 2006; Battle in Seattle 2007; Miracles from Heaven 2016

Henderson, Shirley (1965-) Salt on Our Skin 1992; Topsy-Turvy 1999; Wonderland 1999; The Claim 2000; Bridget Jones's Diary 2001; 24 Hour Party People 2001; Harry Potter and the Chamber of Secrets 2002; Once upon a Time in the Midlands 2002; Villa des Roses 2002; Wilbur (Wants to Kill Himself) 2002; AfterLife 2003; American Cousins 2003; interMission 2003; Bridget Jones: the Edge of Reason 2004; Frozen 2004; Yes 2004; A Cock and Bull Story 2005; Marie

Antoinette 2005; Miss Pettigrew Lives for a Day 2007; Wild Child 2008; Life during Wartime 2009; Meek's Cutoff 2010; The Nutcracker in 3D 2010; Everyday 2012; Filth 2013; In Secret 2013; Set Fire to the Stars 2014; Tale of Tales 2015

Hendler, Daniel (1976-) The Lost Embrace 2003; Whisky 2004

Hendricks, Christina (1975-) Life as We Know It 2010; Detachment 2011; Drive 2011; From Up on Poppy Hill 2011; Ginger & Rosa 2012; God's Pocket 2014; Lost River 2014; TinkerBell and the Pirate Fairy 2014; Dark Places 2015; The Neon Demon 2016

Hendrickson, Benjamin (1950-2006) Manhunter 1986; Spanking the Monkey 1994

Hendrix, Elaine (1971-) Romy and Michele's High School Reunion 1997; The Parent Trap 1998; Superstar 1999; What the #$*! Do We Know!? 2004

Hendrix, Jimi (1942-1970) Woodstock 1970; Dynamite Chicken 1971; Jimi Hendrix 1973; Message to Love 1995

Hendrix, Wanda (1928-1981) Confidential Agent 1945; Welcome Stranger 1947; Miss Tatlock's Millions 1948; Prince of Foxes 1949; The Admiral Was a Lady 1950; Captain Carey, USA 1950; Saddle Tramp 1950; Sierra 1950; South of Algiers 1952

Hendry, Gloria (1945-) Black Caesar 1973; Hell Up in Harlem 1973; Live and Let Die 1973; Slaughter's Big Rip-Off 1973; Black Belt Jones 1974; The Revenge of Pumpkinhead - Blood Wings 1994

Hendry, Ian (1931-1984) Live Now - Pay Later 1962; Girl in the Headlines 1963; This Is My Street 1963; The Beauty Jungle 1964; Children of the Damned 1964; The Hill 1965; Repulsion 1965; The Sandwich Man 1966; Journey to the Far Side of the Sun 1969; The Southern Star 1969; The McKenzie Break 1970; Get Carter 1971; Captain Kronos - Vampire Hunter 1972; The Jerusalem File 1972; Tales from the Crypt 1972; Assassin 1973; Theatre of Blood 1973; The Internecine Project 1974; The Passenger 1975; The Bitch 1979; McVicar 1980

Henfrey, Janet She'll Be Wearing Pink Pyjamas 1984; The Nine Lives of Tomas Katz 1999

Henie, Sonja (1912-1969) One in a Million 1936; Thin Ice 1937; Happy Landing 1938; My Lucky Star 1938; Second Fiddle 1939; Sun Valley Serenade 1941; Wintertime 1943; It's a Pleasure 1945; The Countess of Monte Cristo 1948

Henke, Brad aka Henke, Brad William The Assassination of Richard Nixon 2004; Split 2017

Henke, Brad William Me and You and Everyone We Know 2005; Sherrybaby 2006; Choke 2008

Henley, Barry "Shabaka" aka Henley, Barry Shabaka Collateral 2004; The Terminal 2004; Miami Vice 2006

Henley, Georgia The Chronicles of Narnia: The Lion, the Witch and the Wardrobe 2005; The Chronicles of Narnia: Prince Caspian 2008; The Chronicles of Narnia: The Voyage of the Dawn Treader 2010

Henner, Marilu (1952-) Between the Lines 1977; Bloodbrothers 1978; Hammett 1982; The Man Who Loved Women 1983; Johnny Dangerously 1984; Perfect 1985; Rustler's Rhapsody 1985; Chains of Gold 1989; LA Story 1991; Noises Off! 1992

Hennessy, Jill (1969-) RoboCop 3 1993; Most Wanted 1997; A Smile like Yours 1997; Komodo 1999; Molly 1999; Exit Wounds 2001; Lymelife 2008

Henney, Del Straw Dogs 1971; Brannigan 1975

Hennicke, Andre aka Hennicke, André aka Hennicke, Andre M Antibodies 2005; In Memory of Myself 2007; Youth without Youth 2007; A Dangerous Method 2011

Hennie, Aksel Headhunters 2011; Pioneer 2013; Hercules 2014; The Last Knights 2015

Henning, Eva (1920-) The Devil's Wanton 1949; Three Strange Loves 1949

Henning, Uno (1895-1970) The Love of Jeanne Ney 1927; A Cottage on Dartmoor 1929; Three Loves 1929

Henreid, Paul (1908-1992) Goodbye, Mr Chips 1939; Night Train to Munich 1940; Casablanca 1942; Joan of Paris 1942; Now, Voyager 1942; Between Two Worlds 1944; The Conspirators 1944; In Our Time 1944; The Spanish Main 1945; Deception 1946; Devotion 1946; Of Human Bondage 1946; Song of Love 1947; Hollow Triumph 1948; Rope of Sand 1949; Mantrap 1952; Stolen Face 1952; Thief of Damascus

1952; Deep in My Heart 1954; Battle Shock 1956; Ten Thousand Bedrooms 1957; Holiday for Lovers 1959; Never So Few 1959; The Four Horsemen of the Apocalypse 1962; Operation Crossbow 1965; The Madwoman of Chaillot 1969; Exorcist II: The Heretic 1977

Henriksen, Lance (1940-) Mansion of the Doomed 1975; Damien - Omen II 1978; The Visitor 1980; Piranha II: the Spawning 1981; The Right Stuff 1983; The Terminator 1984; Jagged Edge 1985; Savage Dawn 1985; Aliens 1986; On Dangerous Ground 1986; Near Dark 1987; Hit List 1988; Pumpkinhead 1988; House III: The Horror Show 1989; Johnny Handsome 1989; The Pit and the Pendulum 1991; Stone Cold 1991; Alien³ 1992; Jennifer Eight 1992; Excessive Force 1993; Hard Target 1993; Man's Best Friend 1993; Bad Company 1994; Color of Night 1994; No Escape 1994; Dead Man 1995; Powder 1995; The Quick and the Dead 1995; Dusting Cliff 7 1996; The Day Lincoln Was Shot 1998; Scream 3 1999; Tarzan 1999; The Last Chance 2003; AVP: Alien vs Predator 2004; Evel Knievel 2004; Madhouse 2004; Tarzan II 2005; Appaloosa 2008; Ladies of the House 2008; Pistol Whipped 2008; Prairie Fever 2008

Henrikson, Anders (1896-1965) A Woman's Face 1938; The Devil's Wanton 1949

Henriksson, Krister (1946-) Faithless 2000; Reconstruction 2003

Henritze, Bette Other People's Money 1991; Judy Berlin 1999

Henry, Buck (1930-) The Troublemaker 1964; Catch-22 1970; Is There Sex after Death? 1971; Taking Off 1971; The Man Who Fell to Earth 1976; Heaven Can Wait 1978; Old Boyfriends 1979; First Family 1980; Gloria 1980; Eating Raoul 1982; Aria 1987; Rude Awakening 1989; Defending Your Life 1991; The Linguini Incident 1991; Even Cowgirls Get the Blues 1993; Grumpy Old Men 1993; Curtain Call 1997; I'm Losing You 1998; Breakfast of Champions 1999; Town & Country 2001

Henry, Charlotte (1913-1980) Alice in Wonderland 1933; Babes in Toyland 1934; Charlie Chan at the Opera 1936

Henry, Gloria (1923-) Bulldog Drummond Strikes Back 1947; Miss Grant Takes Richmond 1949; Riders in the Sky 1949; Al Jennings of Oklahoma 1951; Rancho Notorious 1952; Gang War 1958

Henry, Gregg (1952-) Just before Dawn 1980; Body Double 1984; The Patriot 1986; Raising Cain 1992; Payback 1998; Ballistic: Ecks vs Sever 2002; Femme Fatale 2002; Slither 2006

Henry, Guy Bright Young Things 2003; EMR 2004

Henry, Hank (1906-1981) Pal Joey 1957; Pepe 1960; Robin and the 7 Hoods 1964; The Only Game in Town 1970

Henry, Judith Germinal 1993; Les Apprentis 1995

Henry, Justin (1971-) Kramer vs Kramer 1979; Martin's Day 1984; Sixteen Candles 1984; Sweet Hearts Dance 1988; Lost 2005

Henry, Lenny (1958-) True Identity 1991; MirrorMask 2004

Henry, Linda Beautiful Thing 1995; The Business 2005

Henry, Louise (1911-2011) Reckless 1935; Remember Last Night? 1935; The Gaunt Stranger 1938

Henry, Martha (1938-) Dancing in the Dark 1986; Clean 2004

Henry, Mike (1939-) Tarzan and the Valley of Gold 1966; Tarzan and the Great River 1967; Tarzan and the Jungle Boy 1968; Smokey and the Bandit 1977; Smokey and the Bandit III 1983

Henry, Thomas Browne aka Henry, Tom Browne aka Henry, Thomas B (1907-1980) Earth vs the Flying Saucers 1956; Blood of Dracula 1957; 20 Million Miles to Earth 1957; The Brain from Planet Arous 1958; Showdown at Boot Hill 1958; Space Master X 7 1958

Henry, Tim Eye of the Cat 1969; Lies My Mother Told Me 2004

Henry, Victor (1943-1985) The Sorcerers 1967; All Neat in Black Stockings 1969

Henry, William (1918-1982) Tarzan Escapes 1936; Madame X 1937; Four Men and a Prayer 1938; The Way of All Flesh 1940; The Adventures of Mark Twain 1944; Secret of the Incas 1954

Henshall, Daniel Snowtown 2011; The Babadook 2013; These Final Hours 2013

Henshall, Douglas (1967-) Angels and Insects 1995; Kull the Conqueror 1997; Fast Food 1998; If Only 1998; Orphans 1998; This Year's Love 1999; The Lawless Heart 2001; It's All about Love 2002; French Film 2008; Iona 2015

Henshaw, John Looking for Eric 2009; In Our Name 2010; The Angels' Share 2012

Hensley, John Teeth 2007; Shutter 2008

Hensley, Pamela (1950-) Rollerball 1975; Buck Rogers in the 25th Century 1979

Henson, Brian (1963-) Return to Oz 1985; Labyrinth 1986

Henson, Elden (1977-) The Mighty 1998; Idle Hands 1999; Manic 2001; The Butterfly Effect 2003; Dumb and Dumberer: When Harry Met Lloyd 2003; Déjà Vu 2006

Henson, Gladys (1897-1982) The Captive Heart 1946; The Blue Lamp 1949; The Cure for Love 1949; Train of Events 1949; Dance Hall 1950; The Magnet 1950; Lady Godiva Rides Again 1951; Derby Day 1952; The Leather Boys 1963

Henson, Jim (1936-1990) The Muppet Movie 1979; The Great Muppet Caper 1981; The Muppets Take Manhattan 1984; Follow That Bird 1985

Henson, Nicky (1945-) Witchfinder General 1968; Crooks and Coronets 1969; There's a Girl in My Soup 1970; Psychomania 1972; Penny Gold 1973; Vampira 1975; The Bawdy Adventures of Tom Jones 1976; Me without You 2001; Blitz 2010; Truth or Dare 2011; Narcopolis 2014; We Still Kill the Old Way 2014

Henson, Taraji P (1970-) Baby Boy 2001; Hustle & Flow 2005; Talk to Me 2007; Not Easily Broken 2009; Date Night 2010; The Karate Kid 2010; No Good Deed 2014

Henstridge, Natasha (1974-) Adrenalin: Fear the Rush 1995; Species 1995; Maximum Risk 1996; Dog Park 1998; Species II 1998; A Better Way to Die 2000; Bounce 2000; It Had to Be You 2000; The Whole Nine Yards 2000; John Carpenter's Ghosts of Mars 2001; Steal 2002; The Whole Ten Yards 2004; Widow on the Hill 2005; Deception 2008; The Devil's Teardrop 2010; Family Gathering 2010

Hepburn, Audrey (1929-1993) Laughter in Paradise 1951; The Lavender Hill Mob 1951; The Secret People 1951; Young Wives' Tale 1951; Roman Holiday 1953; Sabrina 1954; War and Peace 1956; Funny Face 1957; Love in the Afternoon 1957; Green Mansions 1959; The Nun's Story 1959; The Unforgiven 1960; Breakfast at Tiffany's 1961; The Children's Hour 1961; Charade 1963; My Fair Lady 1964; Paris When It Sizzles 1964; The Love Goddesses 1965; How to Steal a Million 1966; Two for the Road 1967; Wait until Dark 1967; Robin and Marian 1976; Bloodline 1979; They All Laughed 1981; Always 1989

Hepburn, Katharine (1907-2003) A Bill of Divorcement 1932; Christopher Strong 1933; Little Women 1933; Morning Glory 1933; The Little Minister 1934; Spitfire 1934; Alice Adams 1935; Break of Hearts 1935; Mary of Scotland 1936; Sylvia Scarlett 1936; A Woman Rebels 1936; Quality Street 1937; Stage Door 1937; Bringing Up Baby 1938; Holiday 1938; The Philadelphia Story 1940; Keeper of the Flame 1942; Woman of the Year 1942; Stage Door Canteen 1943; Dragon Seed 1944; Without Love 1945; Undercurrent 1946; The Sea of Grass 1947; Song of Love 1947; State of the Union 1948; Adam's Rib 1949; The African Queen 1951; Pat and Mike 1952; Summertime 1955; The Iron Petticoat 1956; The Rainmaker 1956; Desk Set 1957; Suddenly, Last Summer 1959; Long Day's Journey into Night 1962; Guess Who's Coming to Dinner 1967; The Lion in Winter 1968; The Madwoman of Chaillot 1969; The Trojan Women 1971; A Delicate Balance 1973; Love among the Ruins 1975; Rooster Cogburn 1975; The Great Balloon Adventure 1978; On Golden Pond 1981; Grace Quigley 1984; Mrs Delafield Wants to Marry 1986; Love Affair 1994

Hepton, Bernard (1925-) Henry VIII and His Six Wives 1970; The Plague Dogs 1982; Shadey 1985; Stealing Heaven 1988

Herbert, Charles (1948-) The Colossus of New York 1958; The Fly 1958; 13 Ghosts 1959

Herbert, Holmes (1882-1956) When a Man Loves 1926; The Kiss 1929; Madame X 1929; Say It with Songs 1929; Dr Jekyll and Mr Hyde 1931; Accent on Youth 1935; Mark of the

Vampire 1935; British Intelligence 1940; Calling Dr Death 1943; The House of Fear 1944; Bulldog Drummond Strikes Back 1947; Johnny Belinda 1948; Anne of the Indies 1951

Herbert, Hugh (1887-1952) Danger Lights 1930; Friends and Lovers 1931; Faithless 1932; Bureau of Missing Persons 1933; Dames 1934; Fashions of 1934 1934; Fog over Frisco 1934; Sweet Adeline 1935; Colleen 1936; One Rainy Afternoon 1936; Hollywood Hotel 1937; The Perfect Specimen 1937; Four's a Crowd 1938; The Great Waltz 1938; Eternally Yours 1939; The Villain Still Pursued Her 1940; The Black Cat 1941; Hellzapoppin' 1941; There's One Born Every Minute 1942; Kismet 1944; Music for Millions 1944; The Beautiful Blonde from Bashful Bend 1949

Herbert, Leon Double X: the Name of the Game 1991; Emotional Backgammon 2003

Herbert, Percy (1920-1992) The Cockleshell Heroes 1955; Barnacle Bill 1957; Sea of Sand 1958; Serious Charge 1959; Mutiny on the Bounty 1962; Carry On Jack 1963; The Cracksman 1963; Joey Boy 1965; One Million Years BC 1966; Tobruk 1966; Too Late the Hero 1970; Captain Apache 1971; The Fiend 1971; Man in the Wilderness 1971; Doomwatch 1972

Herd, Richard (1932-) Wolf Lake 1979; Trancers 1985; Gleaming the Cube 1988

Heredia, Dolores (1966-) Rudo y Cursi 2008; A Better Life 2011; Days of Grace 2011; How I Spent My Summer Vacation 2012

Heredia, Wilson Jermaine (1971-) Flawless 1999; Rent 2005

Herfurth, Karoline Perfume: the Story of a Murderer 2006; We Are the Night 2010; Passion 2012

Hériat, Philippe (1898-1971) L'Inhumaine 1923; Divine 1935

Herlie, Eileen (1918-2008) Hamlet 1948; Isn't Life Wonderful! 1952; The Story of Gilbert and Sullivan 1953; For Better, for Worse 1954; Hamlet 1964; The Sea Gull 1968

Herlihy, David Veronica Guerin 2003; The Price of Desire 2015

Herlin, Jacques (1927-2014) Torrents of Spring 1989; Of Gods and Men 2010

Herman, David (1968-) Office Space 1999; Dude, Where's My Car? 2000; Idiocracy 2006

Hermann, Irm aka Herrmann, Irm (1942-) The Merchant of Four Seasons 1971; The Bitter Tears of Petra von Kant 1972; Fear Eats the Soul 1973; Mother Küsters Goes to Heaven 1975; Fear of Fear 1976; Ten Minutes Older: the Cello 2002; Anonyma: a Woman in Berlin 2008

Hernandez, Jay (1978-) crazy/beautiful 2001; The Rookie 2002; Torque 2003; Friday Night Lights 2004; Hostel 2005; World Trade Center 2006; Live! 2007; Lakeview Terrace 2008; Quarantine 2008; Takers 2010; LOL 2011; Max 2015

Hernandez, Juano (1901-1970) Intruder in the Dust 1949; The Breaking Point 1950; Young Man with a Horn 1950; Kiss Me Deadly 1955; Trial 1955; Ransom! 1956; Something of Value 1957; Sergeant Rutledge 1960; The Sins of Rachel Cade 1960; Two Loves 1961; Hemingway's Adventures of a Young Man 1962; The Extraordinary Seaman 1969; The Reivers 1969; They Call Me Mister Tibbs! 1970

Herrand, Marcel (1897-1953) Les Visiteurs du Soir 1942; Les Enfants du Paradis 1945; Martin Roumagnac 1946; Fanfan la Tulipe 1951

Herrier, Mark Porky's 1981; Porky's Revenge 1985

Herriman, Damon The Big Steal 1990; 100 Bloody Acres 2012

Herrmann, Edward (1943-2014) The Day of the Dolphin 1973; The Paper Chase 1973; The Great Waldo Pepper 1975; Brass Target 1978; Hill's Angels 1979; Harry's War 1981; A Little Sex 1981; Reds 1981; Death Valley 1982; Mrs Soffel 1984; Compromising Positions 1985; The Man with One Red Shoe 1985; The Lost Boys 1987; Overboard 1987; Big Business 1988; Born Yesterday 1993; My Boyfriend's Back 1993; Don't Drink the Water 1994; Foreign Student 1994; Richie Rich 1994; The Face on the Milk Carton 1995; Soul of the Game 1996; What Love Sees 1996; Frank Lloyd Wright 1997; Walking across Egypt 1999; The Cat's Meow 2001; James Dean 2001; The Emperor's Club 2002; Intolerable Cruelty 2003; Wedding Daze 2006; The Christmas Pageant 2011

Hersent, Philippe (1912-1982) The Sword and the Cross 1958; The Giant of Marathon 1960

Hershey, Barbara aka Seagull, Barbara (1948-) With Six You Get Eggroll 1968; Last Summer 1969; The Liberation of LB Jones 1970; The Pursuit of Happiness 1971; Boxcar Bertha 1972; Diamonds 1975; The Last Hard Men 1976; Trial by Combat 1976; The Stunt Man 1980; Americana 1981; The Entity 1981; The Right Stuff 1983; The Natural 1984; Hannah and Her Sisters 1986; Hoosiers 1986; Shy People 1987; Tin Men 1987; A World Apart 1987; Beaches 1988; The Last Temptation of Christ 1988; Aunt Julia and the Scriptwriter 1990; Evidence of Love 1990; Defenseless 1991; Paris Trout 1991; Falling Down 1992; The Public Eye 1992; A Dangerous Woman 1993; Splitting Heirs 1993; Swing Kids 1993; Last of the Dogmen 1995; The Pallbearer 1996; The Portrait of a Lady 1996; A Soldier's Daughter Never Cries 1998; Breakfast of Champions 1999; Passion 1999; Lantana 2001; 11:14 2003; Black Swan 2010; Insidious 2010; Left to Die: the Sandra and Tammi Chase Story 2012; Insidious: Chapter 2 2013

Hersholt, Jean (1886-1956) Tess of the Storm Country 1922; Sinners in Silk 1924; Don Q, Son of Zorro 1925; Greed 1925; Stella Dallas 1925; The Student Prince in Old Heidelberg 1927; Abie's Irish Rose 1928; The Younger Generation 1929; Daybreak 1931; Private Lives 1931; The Sin of Madelon Claudet 1931; Susan Lenox: Her Fall and Rise 1931; The Beast of the City 1932; Emma 1932; Flesh 1932; Grand Hotel 1932; The Mask of Fu Manchu 1932; Skyscraper Souls 1932; Dinner at Eight 1933; The Cat and the Fiddle 1934; Men in White 1934; The Painted Veil 1934; Break of Hearts 1935; Mark of the Vampire 1935; The Country Doctor 1936; His Brother's Wife 1936; One in a Million 1936; Heidi 1937; Seventh Heaven 1937; Alexander's Ragtime Band 1938; Happy Landing 1938; Meet Dr Christian 1939; Mr Moto in Danger Island 1939; Stage Door Canteen 1943; Run for Cover 1955

Herter, Gerard The White Warrior 1959; Adios, Sabata 1970

Herthum, Louis The Last Exorcism 2010; The Last Exorcism Part II 2013

Hervey, Irene (1910-1998) The Stranger's Return 1933; Charlie Chan in Shanghai 1935; The League of Frightened Men 1937; East Side of Heaven 1939; The Boys from Syracuse 1940; Mr Peabody and the Mermaid 1948; A Cry in the Night 1956; Cactus Flower 1969

Herzi, Hafsia Couscous 2007; House of Tolerance 2011; The Source 2011

Herzog, Werner (1942-) Man of Flowers 1984; Little Dieter Needs to Fly 1997; julien donkey-boy 1999; My Best Friend 1999; Encounters at the End of the World 2007; Mister Lonely 2007; Cave of Forgotten Dreams 2010; Into the Abyss: a Tale of Death, a Tale of Life 2011; Jack Reacher 2012; Life Itself 2014

Heslov, Grant (1963-) Congo 1995; Black Sheep 1996; Dante's Peak 1997; The Scorpion King 2002

Hesme, Annelise Priceless 2006; Sparks and Embers 2014

Hesme, Clotilde (1979-) Regular Lovers 2005; The Grocer's Son 2007; Love Songs 2007; Angel and Tony 2010; Mysteries of Lisbon 2010

Hess, David aka Hess, David A (1942-2011) Last House on the Left 1972; Avalanche Express 1979; Swamp Thing 1982

Hesseman, Howard (1940-) Steelyard Blues 1973; The Sunshine Boys 1975; Jackson County Jail 1976; Honky Tonk Freeway 1981; Doctor Detroit 1983; Police Academy 2: Their First Assignment 1985; Flight of the Navigator 1986; My Chauffeur 1986; Heat 1987; Murder in New Hampshire 1991; Rubin & Ed 1991; Munchie Strikes Back 1994; Gridlock'd 1996; About Schmidt 2002; Crazy for Christmas 2005; The Rocker 2008; All about Steve 2009; Halloween II 2009

Heston, Charlton (1923-2008) Dark City 1950; The Greatest Show on Earth 1952; Ruby Gentry 1952; Arrowhead 1953; The Naked Jungle 1953; Pony Express 1953; The President's Lady 1953; The Savage 1953; Bad for Each Other 1954; Secret of the Incas 1954; The Far Horizons 1955; Lucy Gallant 1955; The Private War of Major Benson 1955; The Ten Commandments 1956; Three Violent People 1956; The Big Country 1958; The Buccaneer 1958; Touch of Evil 1958; Ben-Hur 1959; The Wreck of the Mary Deare 1959; El Cid

1961; *Diamond Head* 1962; *The Pigeon That Took Rome* 1962; *55 Days at Peking* 1963; *The Agony and the Ecstasy* 1965; *The Greatest Story Ever Told* 1965; *Major Dundee* 1965; *The War Lord* 1965; *Khartoum* 1966; *The Adventures of Mowgli* 1967; *Counterpoint* 1967; *Planet of the Apes* 1967; *Will Penny* 1967; *Beneath the Planet of the Apes* 1969; *Number One* 1969; *The Hawaiians* 1970; *Julius Caesar* 1970; *King: a Filmed Record... Montgomery to Memphis* 1970; *The Omega Man* 1971; *Antony and Cleopatra* 1972; *Call of the Wild* 1972; *Skyjacked* 1972; *Soylent Green* 1973; *The Three Musketeers* 1973; *Airport 1975* 1974; *Earthquake* 1974; *The Four Musketeers* 1974; *Battle of Midway* 1976; *The Last Hard Men* 1976; *Two-Minute Warning* 1976; *The Prince and the Pauper* 1977; *Gray Lady Down* 1978; *The Awakening* 1980; *A Man for All Seasons* 1988; *Almost an Angel* 1990; *Solar Crisis* 1990; *Treasure Island* 1990; *Tombstone* 1993; *In the Mouth of Madness* 1994; *True Lies* 1994; *Alaska* 1996; *Hamlet* 1996; *Hercules* 1997; *Armageddon* 1998; *Any Given Sunday* 1999; *Gideon* 1999; *Cats & Dogs* 2001; *The Order* 2001; *Town & Country* 2001; *Bowling for Columbine* 2002

Hetherington, Jason (1965-) *Complicity* 1999; *Aberdeen* 2000; *Perfect Romance* 2004

Hewer, John (1922-2008) *Colonel March Investigates* 1953; *Mister Ten Per Cent* 1967

Hewett, Christopher (1922-2001) *The Producers* 1968; *Ratboy* 1986

Hewitt, Alan (1915-1986) *Days of Wine and Roses* 1962; *That Touch of Mink* 1962; *The Misadventures of Merlin Jones* 1964; *How to Murder Your Wife* 1965; *The Computer Wore Tennis Shoes* 1969; *The Barefoot Executive* 1971

Hewitt, Henry (1885-1968) *Sailors Three* 1940; *The Black Sheep of Whitehall* 1941

Hewitt, Jennifer Love aka **Hewitt, Love** (1979-) *Munchie* 1992; *Sister Act 2: Back in the Habit* 1993; *House Arrest* 1996; *I Know What You Did Last Summer* 1997; *Can't Hardly Wait* 1998; *I Still Know What You Did Last Summer* 1998; *Telling You* 1998; *The Suburbans* 1999; *The Audrey Hepburn Story* 2000; *Heartbreakers* 2001; *The Adventures of Tom Thumb and Thumbelina* 2002; *The Tuxedo* 2002; *A Christmas Carol* 2004; *Garfield* 2004; *If Only* 2004; *The Truth about Love* 2004; *Garfield 2* 2006

Hewitt, Martin (1958-) *Endless Love* 1981; *Killer Party* 1986; *Two Moon Junction* 1988

Hewitt, Sean *The Sender* 1982; *Swann* 1996

Hewlett, David (1968-) *Pin* 1988; *Where the Heart Is* 1990; *Desire & Hell at Sunset Motel* 1991; *Scanners II: The New Order* 1991; *Cube* 1997; *Cypher* 2002; *Splice* 2009

Heyburn, Weldon (1910-1951) *Speed* 1936; *Charlie Chan in The Chinese Cat* 1944

Heydt, Louis Jean (1905-1960) *The Great McGinty* 1940; *Let's Make Music* 1940; *The Great Moment* 1944; *The Big Sleep* 1946; *Roadblock* 1951; *The Boy from Oklahoma* 1954

Heyerdahl, Christopher *Silent Trigger* 1996; *The Peacekeeper* 1997

Heyes, Herbert (1889-1958) *Union Station* 1950; *Bedtime for Bonzo* 1951; *A Place in the Sun* 1951; *Carbine Williams* 1952; *Park Row* 1952; *Something to Live For* 1952; *Seven Little Foys* 1955

Heyman, Barton (1937-1996) *Valdez Is Coming* 1971; *Static* 1985; *Billy Galvin* 1986; *Against Her Will* 1992

Heywood, Anne (1932-) *Dangerous Exile* 1957; *Floods of Fear* 1958; *Violent Playground* 1958; *The Heart of a Man* 1959; *Upstairs and Downstairs* 1959; *A Terrible Beauty* 1960; *Petticoat Pirates* 1961; *The Brain* 1962; *The Very Edge* 1962; *The Fox* 1967; *The Chairman* 1969; *Midas Run* 1969; *I Want What I Want* 1971

Heywood, Pat (1927-) *Romeo and Juliet* 1968; *Mumsy, Nanny, Sonny & Girly* 1970; *10 Rillington Place* 1970; *Wish You Were Here* 1987; *Young Toscanini* 1988

Hiatt, Philippa *The Bells Go Down* 1943; *The Halfway House* 1943; *George in Civvy Street* 1946

Hibbert, Geoffrey (1922-1969) *The Common Touch* 1941; *Love on the Dole* 1941; *In Which We Serve* 1942; *Gaolbreak* 1962

Hibler, Winston (1910-1976) *The Living Desert* 1953; *Jungle Cat* 1959; *King of the Grizzlies* 1969

Hickey, John Benjamin (1963-) *Only You* 1994; *Eddie* 1996; *Finding North* 1997; *Love! Valour! Compassion!* 1997; *The Bone Collector* 1999; *The Anniversary Party* 2001; *Flags of Our Fathers* 2006; *Transformers: Revenge of the Fallen* 2009

Hickey, Tom (1944-) *Fools of Fortune* 1990; *Raining Stones* 1993; *Possession* 2002; *Inside I'm Dancing* 2004; *Garage* 2007

Hickey, William (1927-1997) *A Hatful of Rain* 1957; *The Producers* 1968; *92 in the Shade* 1975; *Wise Blood* 1979; *Prizzi's Honor* 1985; *Walls of Glass* 1985; *The Name of the Rose* 1986; *One Crazy Summer* 1986; *Da* 1988; *Pink Cadillac* 1989; *Puppet Master* 1989; *Sea of Love* 1989; *Sons* 1989; *My Blue Heaven* 1990; *Tales from the Darkside: the Movie* 1991; *The Nightmare before Christmas* 1993; *The Jerky Boys* 1995; *The Maddening* 1995; *Love Is All There Is* 1996; *Mousehunt* 1997

Hickman, Bill (1921-1986) *The French Connection* 1971; *The Seven-Ups* 1973

Hickman, Darryl (1931-) *Men of Boys Town* 1941; *Joe Smith, American* 1942; *Kiss and Tell* 1945; *Salty O'Rourke* 1945; *A Kiss for Corliss* 1949; *The Happy Years* 1950; *Lightning Strikes Twice* 1951; *Destination Gobi* 1953; *Southwest Passage* 1954; *Tea and Sympathy* 1956; *The Iron Sheriff* 1957; *The Tingler* 1959

Hickman, Dwayne (1934-) *Cat Ballou* 1965; *Dr Goldfoot and the Bikini Machine* 1965; *How to Fill a Wild Bikini* 1965; *Ski Party* 1965

Hicks, Catherine (1951-) *Death Valley* 1982; *Better Late than Never* 1983; *Garbo Talks* 1984; *The Razor's Edge* 1984; *Fever Pitch* 1985; *Peggy Sue Got Married* 1986; *Star Trek IV: the Voyage Home* 1986; *Like Father, like Son* 1987; *Child's Play* 1988; *Dillinger and Capone* 1995; *Eight Days a Week* 1996; *Stranger with My Face* 2009

Hicks, Danny aka **Hicks, Dan** *Evil Dead II* 1987; *Darkman* 1990

Hicks, Kevin *Dance Me Outside* 1994; *Time to Say Goodbye?* 1997

Hicks, Russell (1895-1957) *Charlie Chan in Shanghai* 1935; *The Woman in Red* 1935; *Follow the Fleet* 1936; *The Big Broadcast of 1938* 1937; *Kentucky* 1938; *Swanee River* 1939; *The Bank Dick* 1940; *Flame of the Barbary Coast* 1945; *The Bandit of Sherwood Forest* 1946; *The Black Arrow* 1948

Hicks, Seymour (1871-1949) *The Secret of the Loch* 1934; *Scrooge* 1935; *Young Man's Fancy* 1939; *Busman's Honeymoon* 1940; *Pastor Hall* 1940

Hicks, Taral (1975-) *A Bronx Tale* 1993; *Belly* 1998

Hickson, Joan (1906-1998) *Love from a Stranger* 1936; *Don't Take It to Heart* 1944; *The Guinea Pig* 1948; *Seven Days to Noon* 1950; *The Card* 1952; *Hindle Wakes* 1952; *Deadly Nightshade* 1953; *Mad about Men* 1954; *Jumping for Joy* 1955; *Child in the House* 1956; *The Extra Day* 1956; *Port of Escape* 1956; *Sea Wife* 1957; *Law and Disorder* 1958; *Upstairs and Downstairs* 1959; *Carry On Regardless* 1960; *No Kidding* 1960; *Please Turn Over* 1960; *Murder She Said* 1961; *I Thank a Fool* 1962; *Nurse on Wheels* 1963; *Carry On Loving* 1970; *A Day in the Death of Joe Egg* 1971; *Carry On Girls* 1973; *Confessions of a Window Cleaner* 1974; *The Wicked Lady* 1983; *Clockwise* 1986; *King of the Wind* 1989; *Century* 1993

Hiddleston, Tom (1981-) *Unrelated* 2007; *Archipelago* 2010; *The Deep Blue Sea* 2011; *Midnight in Paris* 2011; *Thor* 2011; *War Horse* 2011; *Marvel Avengers Assemble* 2012; *Exhibition* 2013; *Only Lovers Left Alive* 2013; *Thor: the Dark World* 2013; *Muppets Most Wanted* 2014; *TinkerBell and the Pirate Fairy* 2014; *Crimson Peak* 2015; *High-Rise* 2015; *I Saw the Light* 2015; *Unity* 2015; *Kong: Skull Island* 2017; *Thor: Ragnarok* 2017

Hiegel, Catherine *Gazon Maudit* 1995; *Violette* 2013

Higareda, Martha *Mariachi Gringo* 2012; *McFarland, USA* 2015

Higashiyama, Chieko (1890-1980) *Early Summer* 1951; *Tokyo Story* 1953

Higelin, Izïa *Samba* 2014; *Summertime* 2015

Higgins, Anthony aka **Corlan, Anthony** (1947-) *Taste the Blood of Dracula* 1969; *A Walk with Love and Death* 1969; *Something for Everyone* 1970; *Quartet* 1981; *Raiders of the Lost Ark* 1981; *The Draughtsman's Contract* 1982; *She'll Be Wearing Pink Pyjamas* 1984; *The Bride* 1985; *Young Sherlock Holmes* 1985; *Max Mon Amour* 1986;

The Bridge 1990; *One against the Wind* 1991; *For Love or Money* 1993; *Nostradamus* 1993; *Sherlock Holmes Returns* 1993; *Alive and Kicking* 1996; *Chromophobia* 2005

Higgins, Clare (1955-) *Nineteen Nineteen* 1984; *Hellraiser* 1987; *Hellbound: Hellraiser II* 1988; *Bad Behaviour* 1992; *Small Faces* 1995; *The Golden Compass* 2007; *Toast* 2010; *A Fantastic Fear of Everything* 2012

Higgins, John Michael (1962-) *The Late Shift* 1996; *Best in Show* 2000; *A Mighty Wind* 2003; *Evan Almighty* 2007; *Fred Claus* 2007; *Yes Man* 2008; *Fired Up!* 2009; *Bad Teacher* 2011; *We Bought a Zoo* 2011; *Planes: Fire and Rescue* 2014

Higgins, Jonathan *No Good Deed* 2002; *Crimes of Passion* 2005; *The Devil's Teardrop* 2010; *Stealing Paradise* 2011

Higgins, Michael (1920-2008) *The Arrangement* 1969; *Wanda* 1971; *The Conversation* 1974; *An Enemy of the People* 1977; *The Black Stallion* 1979; *A Midsummer Night's Sex Comedy* 1982; *Angel Heart* 1987

Higgins, Paul *Complicity* 1999; *Red Road* 2006; *Couple in a Hole* 2015

Highmore, Freddie (1992-) *Finding Neverland* 2004; *Five Children and It* 2004; *Two Brothers* 2004; *Charlie and the Chocolate Factory* 2005; *Arthur and the Invisibles* 2006; *A Good Year* 2006; *August Rush* 2007; *The Spiderwick Chronicles* 2008; *Astro Boy* 2009; *Toast* 2010; *The Art of Getting By* 2011; *Justin and the Knights of Valour* 2013

Hiken, Gerald (1927-) *The Goddess* 1958; *The Three Sisters* 1966

Hilary, Jennifer (1942-) *The Heroes of Telemark* 1965; *The Idol* 1966; *Five Days One Summer* 1982

Hill, Amy (1953-) *Dim Sum: a Little Bit of Heart* 1985; *Dr Seuss' The Cat in the Hat* 2003; *50 First Dates* 2004

Hill, Arthur (1922-2006) *Scarlet Thread* 1951; *The Deep Blue Sea* 1955; *The Ugly American* 1963; *Harper* 1966; *Moment to Moment* 1966; *Petulia* 1968; *The Chairman* 1969; *The Andromeda Strain* 1970; *Rabbit, Run* 1970; *The Pursuit of Happiness* 1971; *The Killer Elite* 1975; *Futureworld* 1976; *The Champ* 1979; *A Little Romance* 1979; *The Amateur* 1981; *Making Love* 1982; *Something Wicked This Way Comes* 1983; *One Magic Christmas* 1985

Hill, Benny (1924-1992) *Who Done It?* 1956; *Light Up the Sky* 1960; *Those Magnificent Men in Their Flying Machines* 1965; *Chitty Chitty Bang Bang* 1968; *The Italian Job* 1969; *The Best of Benny Hill* 1974

Hill, Bernard (1944-) *The Bounty* 1984; *The Chain* 1984; *No Surrender* 1985; *Restless Natives* 1985; *Bellman & True* 1987; *Drowning by Numbers* 1988; *Mountains of the Moon* 1989; *Shirley Valentine* 1989; *Double X: the Name of the Game* 1991; *Madagascar Skin* 1995; *Shepherd on the Rock* 1995; *The Ghost and the Darkness* 1996; *The Wind in the Willows* 1996; *Titanic* 1997; *The Criminal* 1999; *The Loss of Sexual Innocence* 1999; *A Midsummer Night's Dream* 1999; *True Crime* 1999; *Going Off, Big Time* 2000; *The Lord of the Rings: The Two Towers* 2002; *The Scorpion King* 2002; *The Boys & Girl from County Clare* 2003; *Gothika* 2003; *The Lord of the Rings: The Return of the King* 2003; *Wimbledon* 2004; *The League of Gentlemen's Apocalypse* 2005; *Joy Division* 2006; *Franklyn* 2008; *The Kid* 2010; *Golden Years* 2016

Hill, Conleth *Shooting for Socrates* 2014; *A Patch of Fog* 2015

Hill, Craig (1927-) *Detective Story* 1951; *Fixed Bayonets!* 1951; *The I Don't Care Girl* 1952; *What Price Glory?* 1952; *The Siege at Red River* 1954

Hill, Dana (1964-1996) *Shoot the Moon* 1982; *Cross Creek* 1983; *National Lampoon's European Vacation* 1985; *Tom and Jerry: the Movie* 1992

Hill, Dave *Slade in Flame* 1974; *The Draughtsman's Contract* 1982; *The Raggedy Rawney* 1987

Hill, Dulé *Holes* 2003; *Edmond* 2005

Hill, Jonah (1983-) *Accepted* 2006; *Knocked Up* 2007; *Strange Wilderness* 2007; *Superbad* 2007; *Forgetting Sarah Marshall* 2008; *Funny People* 2009; *The Invention of Lying* 2009; *Cyrus* 2010; *Get Him to the Greek* 2010; *How to Train Your Dragon* 2010; *Megamind* 2010; *Moneyball* 2011; *The Sitter* 2011; *21 Jump Street* 2012; *The Watch* 2012; *This Is the End* 2013; *The Wolf of Wall Street* 2013; *How to Train Your Dragon 2* 2014; *22 Jump Street* 2014; *True Story* 2015; *Hail, Caesar!*

2016; *Sausage Party* 2016; *War Dogs* 2016

Hill, Lauryn (1975-) *Sister Act 2: Back in the Habit* 1993; *Dave Chappelle's Block Party* 2005; *Concerning Violence* 2014

Hill, Marianna aka **Hill, Mariana** (1941-) *Red Line 7000* 1965; *Paradise, Hawaiian Style* 1966; *Medium Cool* 1969; *El Condor* 1970; *Thumb Tripping* 1972; *The Baby* 1973; *High Plains Drifter* 1973; *Blood Beach* 1981

Hill, Matt *Teenage Mutant Ninja Turtles III* 1992; *A Monkey's Tale* 1999

Hill, Melanie (1963-) *The Hawk* 1992; *When Saturday Comes* 1995; *Brassed Off* 1996

Hill, Robin *Down Terrace* 2009; *The Borderlands* 2013

Hill, Steven (1922-) *The Goddess* 1958; *A Child Is Waiting* 1962; *The Slender Thread* 1965; *It's My Turn* 1980; *Rich and Famous* 1981; *Garbo Talks* 1984; *Heartburn* 1986; *Legal Eagles* 1986; *The Boost* 1988; *White Palace* 1990; *Billy Bathgate* 1991

Hill, Terence aka **Girotti, Mario** (1939-) *The Sword and the Cross* 1958; *Hannibal* 1959; *The Leopard* 1962; *Seven Seas to Calais* 1962; *God Forgives... I Don't!* 1967; *Ace High* 1968; *Django, Prepare a Coffin* 1968; *Boot Hill* 1969; *They Call Me Trinity* 1970; *Man of the East* 1972; *My Name Is Nobody* 1973; *March or Die* 1977; *Mr Billion* 1977; *Renegade* 1987

Hill, Thelma (1906-1938) *The Two Tars* 1928; *The Miracle Woman* 1931

Hillaire, Marcel (1908-1988) *Sabrina* 1954; *Take the Money and Run* 1969

Hiller, Wendy (1912-2003) *Pygmalion* 1938; *Major Barbara* 1941; *I Know Where I'm Going!* 1945; *Outcast of the Islands* 1951; *Sailor of the King* 1953; *How to Murder a Rich Uncle* 1957; *Something of Value* 1957; *Separate Tables* 1958; *Sons and Lovers* 1960; *Toys in the Attic* 1963; *A Man for All Seasons* 1966; *Murder on the Orient Express* 1974; *The Cat and the Canary* 1979; *The Elephant Man* 1980; *Making Love* 1982; *Witness for the Prosecution* 1982; *The Lonely Passion of Judith Hearne* 1987

Hillerman, John (1932-) *Paper Moon* 1973; *Chinatown* 1974; *At Long Last Love* 1975; *Lucky Lady* 1975; *Kill Me If You Can* 1977; *Sunburn* 1979

Hillie, Verna (1914-1997) *The Star Packer* 1934; *The Trail Beyond* 1934

Hillier, James *Long Time Dead* 2001; *Fathers of Girls* 2010

Hills, Gillian (1946-) *Beat Girl* 1960; *Blowup* 1966; *Demons of the Mind* 1971

Hilton, George (1934-) *The Battle of El Alamein* 1968; *A Bullet for Sandoval* 1970

Hilton, Paris (1981-) *House of Wax* 2004; *The Hottie & the Nottie* 2008

Hilton, Paul *Strange Holiday* 1942; *Wuthering Heights* 2011

Hilton, Tyler (1983-) *Walk the Line* 2005; *Charlie Bartlett* 2007

Hinde, Madeline *I Used to Know* 1969; *Incense for the Damned* 1970; *The Fiend* 1971; *The Last Valley* 1971

Hindle, Art (1948-) *Black Christmas* 1974; *Invasion of the Body Snatchers* 1978; *The Brood* 1979; *The Octagon* 1980; *Blind Trust* 2007

Hindman, Earl (1942-2003) *The Parallax View* 1974; *The Taking of Pelham One Two Three* 1974; *Greased Lightning* 1977

Hinds, Aisha *Assault on Precinct 13* 2005; *Mr Brooks* 2007

Hinds, Ciaran aka **Hinds, Ciarán** (1953-) *December Bride* 1990; *Hostages* 1993; *Circle of Friends* 1995; *Persuasion* 1995; *Some Mother's Son* 1996; *The Life of Stuff* 1997; *Oscar and Lucinda* 1997; *The Lost Son* 1998; *Titanic Town* 1998; *The Lost Lover* 1999; *The Weight of Water* 2000; *The Sum of All Fears* 2002; *Calendar Girls* 2003; *Lara Croft, Tomb Raider: the Cradle of Life* 2003; *The Statement* 2003; *Veronica Guerin* 2003; *The Phantom of the Opera* 2004; *Munich* 2005; *Amazing Grace* 2006; *Hallam Foe* 2006; *Miami Vice* 2006; *The Nativity Story* 2006; *The Tiger's Tail* 2006; *Margot at the Wedding* 2007; *Miss Pettigrew Lives for a Day* 2007; *There Will Be Blood* 2007; *In Bruges* 2008; *Life during Wartime* 2009; *Race to Witch Mountain* 2009; *The Debt* 2010; *The Rite* 2011; *The Woman in Black* 2011; *Ghost Rider: Spirit of Vengeance* 2012; *John Carter* 2012; *Closed Circuit* 2013; *The Sea* 2013; *Hitman: Agent 47* 2015

Hinds, Samuel S aka **Hinds, Samuel** aka **Hinds, Sam** (1875-1948) *Deluge* 1933; *Gabriel over the White House* 1933; *Private Worlds* 1935; *The Raven*

1935; *Rendezvous* 1935; *She* 1935; *His Brother's Wife* 1936; *Rhythm on the Range* 1936; *Navy Blue and Gold* 1937; *Stage Door* 1937; *Test Pilot* 1938; *Wives under Suspicion* 1938; *You Can't Take It with You* 1938; *Young Dr Kildare* 1938; *Calling Dr Kildare* 1939; *The Secret of Dr Kildare* 1939; *The Boys from Syracuse* 1940; *Dr Kildare's Strange Case* 1940; *Dr Kildare Goes Home* 1940; *It's a Date* 1940; *Seven Sinners* 1940; *Back Street* 1941; *Blossoms in the Dust* 1941; *Dr Kildare's Wedding Day* 1941; *Man Made Monster* 1941; *The Shepherd of the Hills* 1941; *Kid Glove Killer* 1942; *Lady in a Jam* 1942; *Ride 'Em Cowboy* 1942; *Hers to Hold* 1943; *Son of Dracula* 1943; *Cobra Woman* 1944; *The Singing Sheriff* 1944; *The Strange Affair of Uncle Harry* 1945; *The Boy with Green Hair* 1948; *The Bribe* 1949

Hines, Cheryl (1965-) *Herbie: Fully Loaded* 2005; *Keeping Up with the Steins* 2006; *RV* 2006; *Waitress* 2007; *Space Chimps* 2008; *Space Chimps 2: Zartog Strikes Back* 2009; *The Ugly Truth* 2009; *The Benefactor* 2015

Hines, Damon *Lethal Weapon* 1987; *Lethal Weapon 3* 1992

Hines, Gregory (1946-2003) *History of the World Part 1* 1981; *Wolfen* 1981; *Deal of the Century* 1983; *The Cotton Club* 1984; *White Nights* 1985; *Running Scared* 1986; *Saigon* 1988; *Tap* 1989; *Eve of Destruction* 1991; *A Rage in Harlem* 1991; *Renaissance Man* 1994; *Waiting to Exhale* 1995; *Good Luck* 1996; *The Preacher's Wife* 1996; *Trigger Happy* 1996; *Subway Stories: Tales from the Underground* 1997; *The Tic Code* 1998; *Things You Can Tell Just by Looking at Her* 2000

Hingle, Pat (1924-2009) *No Down Payment* 1957; *Splendor in the Grass* 1961; *All the Way Home* 1963; *The Ugly American* 1963; *Nevada Smith* 1966; *Hang 'Em High* 1968; *Jigsaw* 1968; *Bloody Mama* 1970; *WUSA* 1970; *The Carey Treatment* 1972; *One Little Indian* 1973; *Running Wild* 1973; *The Super Cops* 1973; *The Gauntlet* 1977; *Elvis - the Movie* 1979; *Norma Rae* 1979; *Going Berserk* 1983; *Sudden Impact* 1983; *Brewster's Millions* 1985; *The Falcon and the Snowman* 1985; *The Rape of Richard Beck* 1985; *Maximum Overdrive* 1986; *Baby Boom* 1987; *The Land before Time* 1988; *Batman* 1989; *The Grifters* 1990; *Lightning Jack* 1994; *Batman Forever* 1995; *Truman* 1995; *The Member of the Wedding* 1997; *A Thousand Acres* 1997

Hinkle, Marin *Fielder's Choice* 2005; *Rails & Ties* 2007

Hinkley, Tommy (1958-) *Back to the Beach* 1987; *The Little Vampire* 2000

Hinnant, Skip (1940-) *Fritz the Cat* 1972; *The Nine Lives of Fritz the Cat* 1974

Hinshaw, Ashley (1988-) *Cherry* 2012; *Chronicle* 2012; *The Pyramid* 2014

Hintermann, Carlo (1923-1988) *A Breath of Scandal* 1960; *A Black Veil for Lisa* 1969

Hira, Mikijiro (1933-) *The Face of Another* 1966; *The Empty Table* 1985; *13 Assassins* 2010

Hirata, Akihiko (1927-1984) *Godzilla* 1954; *The H-Man* 1954; *Terror of Mechagodzilla* 1975

Hird, Thora (1911-2003) *The Big Blockade* 1942; *Next of Kin* 1942; *Went the Day Well?* 1942; *Once a Jolly Swagman* 1948; *Portrait from Life* 1948; *The Weaker Sex* 1948; *A Boy, a Girl and a Bike* 1949; *Boys in Brown* 1949; *Conspirator* 1949; *The Cure for Love* 1949; *Fools Rush In* 1949; *Madness of the Heart* 1949; *Maytime in Mayfair* 1949; *The Magnet* 1950; *Emergency Call* 1952; *The Frightened Man* 1952; *The Long Memory* 1952; *The Lost Hours* 1952; *Time Gentlemen Please!* 1952; *A Day to Remember* 1953; *Personal Affair* 1953; *Turn the Key Softly* 1953; *One Good Turn* 1954; *Lost* 1955; *The Love Match* 1955; *The Quatermass Xperiment* 1955; *Simon and Laura* 1955; *The Good Companions* 1956; *Home and Away* 1956; *Sailor Beware!* 1956; *Further up the Creek* 1958; *The Entertainer* 1960; *A Kind of Loving* 1962; *Term of Trial* 1962; *Rattle of a Simple Man* 1964; *Some Will, Some Won't* 1969; *The Nightcomers* 1972; *Consuming Passions* 1988; *Wide Eyed and Legless* 1993; *Julie and the Cadillacs* 1998

Hirosue, Ryoko *Departures* 2008; *Goemon* 2009

Hirsch, Emile (1985-) *The Dangerous Lives of Altar Boys* 2001; *The Emperor's Club* 2002; *The Girl Next Door* 2004; *Imaginary Heroes* 2004;

Lords of Dogtown 2005; Alpha Dog 2006; The Air I Breathe 2007; Into the Wild 2007; Milk 2008; Speed Racer 2008; Taking Woodstock 2009; The Darkest Hour 2011; Killer Joe 2011; The Motel Life 2012; Prince Avalanche 2012; Lone Survivor 2013; Just Jim 2015

Hirsch, Judd (1935-) King of the Gypsies 1978; Ordinary People 1980; Without a Trace 1983; Teachers 1984; Running on Empty 1988; Independence Day 1996; Rocky Marciano 1999; A Beautiful Mind 2001; This Must Be the Place 2011; Independence Day: Resurgence 2016

Hirsch, Robert (1925-) The Hunchback of Notre Dame 1956; Shock Treatment 1973

Hirschmüller, Hans Love Is Colder than Love 1969; The Merchant of Four Seasons 1971

Hirt, Christianne (1968-) For the Moment 1994; Tokyo Cowboy 1994; Firestorm 1998

Hirt, Eléonore A Very Private Affair 1962; Seven Nights in Japan 1976; Get Out Your Handkerchiefs 1977; La Nuit de Varennes 1983

Hitchcock, Alfred (1899-1980) Night Will Fall 2014; Hitchcock Truffaut 2015

Hitchcock, Patricia (1928-) Stage Fright 1949; Strangers on a Train 1951

Hitchens, Christopher (1949-2011) Manufacturing Dissent: Uncovering Michael Moore 2007; Best of Enemies 2015

Hivju, Kristofer Force Majeure 2014; In Order of Disappearance 2014; The Last King 2016

Hjejle, Iben (1971-) Mifune 1999; High Fidelity 2000; The Emperor's New Clothes 2001; The Boss of It All 2006; Chéri 2009

Hjelm, Keve (1922-2004) Raven's End 1963; Best Intentions 1992

Hoath, Florence (1984-) A Pin for the Butterfly 1994; Innocent Lies 1995; FairyTale: a True Story 1997; The Governess 1997; Tom's Midnight Garden 1998; Back to the Secret Garden 2000

Hobart, Rose (1906-2000) Dr Jekyll and Mr Hyde 1931; A Gentleman at Heart 1942; The Brighton Strangler 1945; Conflict 1945; Claudia and David 1946; The Farmer's Daughter 1946

Hobbes, Halliwell (1877-1962) Charley's Aunt 1930; Grumpy 1930; Dr Jekyll and Mr Hyde 1931; The Masquerader 1933; British Agent 1934; The Key 1934; Cardinal Richelieu 1935; Charlie Chan in Shanghai 1935; The Earl of Chicago 1940; Sherlock Holmes Faces Death 1943

Hobbs, Chelsea More Sex & the Single Mom 2005; The Unknown 2005

Hobbs, Jack (1893-1968) No Limit 1935; It's in the Air 1938

Hobbs, Peter (1918-2011) The Lady in Red 1979; The Man with Two Brains 1983

Hobbs, Rebecca Siam Sunset 1999; Lucy 2003

Hobel, Mara (1971-) The Hand 1981; Mommie Dearest 1981

Hobson, Valerie (1917-1998) Bride of Frankenstein 1935; The Mystery of Edwin Drood 1935; Jump for Glory 1937; The Drum 1938; Q Planes 1939; The Spy in Black 1939; Contraband 1940; Unpublished Story 1942; The Adventures of Tartu 1943; Great Expectations 1946; The Years Between 1946; Blanche Fury 1948; The Small Voice 1948; The Interrupted Journey 1949; Kind Hearts and Coronets 1949; The Rocking Horse Winner 1949; Train of Events 1949; The Card 1952; Meet Me Tonight 1952; Voice of Merrill 1952; Background 1953; Knave of Hearts 1954

Hoch, Danny (1970-) Whiteboys 1999; We Own the Night 2007

Hockney, David Tonite Let's All Make Love in London 1967; A Bigger Splash 1974; Hockney 2014

Hodder, Kane (1951-) Friday the 13th Part VII: the New Blood 1988; Friday the 13th Part VIII: Jason Takes Manhattan 1989; Jason Goes to Hell: the Final Friday 1993; Wishmaster 1997; Jason X 2001; Hatchet 2006; Frozen 2009

Hodge, Douglas (1960-) Salome's Last Dance 1988; Dealers 1989; Diamond Skulls 1989; Buddy's Song 1990; The Descent: Part 2 2009; Diana 2013

Hodge, Edwin All the Boys Love Mandy Lane 2006; The Purge 2013; As Above, So Below 2014

Hodge, Kate Leatherface: the Texas Chainsaw Massacre III 1990; Rapid Fire 1992

Hodge, Patricia (1946-) Betrayal 1982; Sunset 1988; Spymaker: the Secret Life of Ian Fleming 1990; The

Leading Man 1996; Before You Go 2002

Hodges, Eddie (1947-) The Adventures of Huckleberry Finn 1960; Summer Magic 1963; The Happiest Millionaire 1967

Hodges, Horace (1865-1951) Escape 1930; London Melody 1937; The Show Goes On 1937

Hodges, Tom aka **Hodges, Thomas E** (1965-) Lucas 1986; Excessive Force 1993; Vanished without a Trace 1993; Heavyweights 1995

Hodgins, Earle aka **Hodgins, Earl** (1893-1964) Paradise Canyon 1935; Aces and Eights 1936; Silent Conflict 1948

Hodgson, Leyland aka **Hodgson, Leyland** (1899-1949) Enter Arsene Lupin 1944; Bedlam 1946

Hodgson, Michael The One and Only 2001; brilliantlove 2010

Hodiak, John (1914-1955) Lifeboat 1944; Marriage Is a Private Affair 1944; Sunday Dinner for a Soldier 1944; A Bell for Adano 1945; The Harvey Girls 1946; Somewhere in the Night 1946; Desert Fury 1947; Love from a Stranger 1947; Command Decision 1948; Homecoming 1948; Ambush 1949; Battleground 1949; The Bribe 1949; Malaya 1949; A Lady without Passport 1950; The Miniver Story 1950; Across the Wide Missouri 1951; The People against O'Hara 1951; Ambush at Tomahawk Gap 1953; Trial 1955

Hoechlin, Tyler Road to Perdition 2002; Everybody Wants Some!! 2016

Hoeks, Sylvia aka **Hoecks, Sylvia** Frankie 2005; Deception 2013

Hoenig, Heinz (1951-) Judgment in Berlin 1988; Antibodies 2005

Hoey, Dennis (1893-1960) The Good Companions 1933; Chu Chin Chow 1934; Sherlock Holmes and the Secret Weapon 1942; Sherlock Holmes Faces Death 1943; The House of Fear 1944; The Pearl of Death 1944; Sherlock Holmes and the Spider Woman 1944; Kitty 1945; A Thousand and One Nights 1945; Anna and the King of Siam 1946; Terror by Night 1946; Golden Earrings 1947; Where There's Life 1947

Hoey, Iris (1885-1979) Those Were the Days 1934; Just William 1939

Hofer, Johanna (1896-1988) The Lost One 1951; I Only Want You to Love Me 1976

Hoff, Halvard Leaves from Satan's Book 1919; The President 1919

Hoffman, Basil (1941-) My Favorite Year 1982; Communion 1989; Lambada 1990

Hoffman, David (1904-1961) Flesh and Fantasy 1943; The Beast with Five Fingers 1946; Desire Me 1947; Top Cat Begins 2016

Hoffman, Dustin (1937-) The Graduate 1967; Madigan's Millions 1967; John and Mary 1969; Midnight Cowboy 1969; Little Big Man 1970; Alfredo Alfredo 1971; Straw Dogs 1971; Who Is Harry Kellerman, and Why Is He Saying Those Terrible Things about Me? 1971; Papillon 1973; Lenny 1974; All the President's Men 1976; Marathon Man 1976; Agatha 1978; Straight Time 1978; Kramer vs Kramer 1979; Tootsie 1982; Death of a Salesman 1985; Ishtar 1987; Rain Man 1988; Common Threads: Stories from the Quilt 1989; Family Business 1989; Dick Tracy 1990; Billy Bathgate 1991; Hook 1991; Accidental Hero 1992; American Buffalo 1995; Outbreak 1995; Sleepers 1996; Mad City 1997; Wag the Dog 1997; Sphere 1998; Joan of Arc 1999; Confidence 2002; Moonlight Mile 2002; Runaway Jury 2003; Finding Neverland 2004; I ♥ Huckabees 2004; Meet the Fockers 2004; Racing Stripes 2004; The Lost City 2005; Perfume: the Story of a Murderer 2006; Stranger than Fiction 2006; Mr Magorium's Wonder Emporium 2007; Kung Fu Panda 2008; Last Chance Harvey 2008; The Tale of Despereaux 2008; Barney's Version 2010; Little Fockers 2010; Kung Fu Panda 2 2011; Chef 2014; The Choir 2014; The Cobbler 2014; The Program 2015; Kung Fu Panda 3 2016

Hoffman, Elizabeth Fear No Evil 1980; Dante's Peak 1997

Hoffman, Jane (1911-2004) Ladybug, Ladybug 1963; Up the Sandbox 1972; Static 1985

Hoffman, Linda The Dentist 1996; Captured 1998

Hoffman, Philip Seymour aka **Hoffman, Philip S** (1967-2014) Triple Bogey on a Par Five Hole 1991; Leap of Faith 1992; My New Gun 1992; Scent of a Woman 1992; Joey Breaker 1993; When a Man Loves a Woman 1994; Hard Eight 1996; Twister 1996; The Big Lebowski 1997; Montana 1997;

Happiness 1998; Next Stop Wonderland 1998; Patch Adams 1998; Flawless 1999; Magnolia 1999; The Talented Mr Ripley 1999; State and Main 2000; Love Liza 2001; Owning Mahowny 2002; Punch-Drunk Love 2002; Red Dragon 2002; 25th Hour 2002; Cold Mountain 2003; Along Came Polly 2004; Capote 2005; Mission: Impossible III 2006; Before the Devil Knows You're Dead 2007; Charlie Wilson's War 2007; The Savages 2007; Doubt 2008; Mary and Max 2008; Synecdoche, New York 2008; The Boat That Rocked 2009; The Invention of Lying 2009; Jack Goes Boating 2010; The Ides of March 2011; Moneyball 2011; A Late Quartet 2012; The Master 2012; The Hunger Games: Catching Fire 2013; A Most Wanted Man 2013; Salinger 2013; Child 44 2014; God's Pocket 2014; The Hunger Games: Mockingjay Part 1 2014; The Hunger Games: Mockingjay Part 2 2015

Hoffman, Robert She's the Man 2006; Shrooms 2006; Step Up 2 the Streets 2008; Aliens in the Attic 2009

Hoffman, Thom (1957-) The Fourth Man 1983; Orlando 1992; Black Book 2006

Hoffmann, Gaby aka **Hoffman, Gaby** (1982-) Field of Dreams 1989; Uncle Buck 1989; This Is My Life 1992; The Man without a Face 1993; Freaky Friday 1995; Now and Then 1995; Everyone Says I Love You 1996; Volcano 1997; Strike! 1998; Black and White 1999; Crystal Fairy and the Magical Cactus 2013; Obvious Child 2014; Wild 2014

Hoffmann, Robert (1939-) Grand Slam 1967; A Black Veil for Lisa 1969

Hofheimer, Charlie Boys 1995; Fathers' Day 1997

Hofschneider, Marco (1969-) Europa Europa 1991; Foreign Student 1994; The Island of Dr Moreau 1996

Hofstätter, Maria Dog Days 2001; Import Export 2007

Hogan, Bosco Zardoz 1973; A Portrait of the Artist as a Young Man 1977; Anne Devlin 1984

Hogan, Gabriel (1973-) Head in the Clouds 2004; Accidental Friendship 2008; The Devil's Teardrop 2010

Hogan, Hulk aka **Hogan, Terry "Hulk"** (1953-) Rocky III 1982; Suburban Commando 1991; Mr Nanny 1992; The Secret Agent Club 1995

Hogan, Jonathan (1951-) Dreams of Gold: the Mel Fisher Story 1986; The House on Carroll Street 1987

Hogan (3), Michael (1949-) The Peanut Butter Solution 1985; Clearcut 1992; Stay Tuned 1992

Hogan, Pat (1920-1966) Davy Crockett, King of the Wild Frontier 1955; The Last Frontier 1955

Hogan, Paul (1939-) "Crocodile" Dundee 1986; "Crocodile" Dundee II 1988; Almost an Angel 1990; Lightning Jack 1994; Flipper 1996; Crocodile Dundee in Los Angeles 2001; Charlie & Boots 2009

Hogan, Susan (1951-) The Brood 1979; Title Shot 1979; Phobia 1980; Narrow Margin 1990; Bordertown Cafe 1991; White Fang 1991

Hogg, Edward White Lightnin' 2008; Bunny & the Bull 2009; Ollie Kepler's Expanding Purple World 2010; The Comedian 2012

Hogg, Ian (1937-) Tell Me Lies 1967; Dead Cert 1974; Hennessy 1975; The Legacy 1978; Lady Jane 1985; A Pin for the Butterfly 1994

Hohl, Arthur (1889-1964) Baby Face 1933; Man's Castle 1933; Cleopatra 1934; Jimmy the Gent 1934; Lady by Choice 1934; Romance in Manhattan 1934; Village Tale 1935; The Whole Town's Talking 1935; The Adventures of Sherlock Holmes 1939; Blackmail 1939; The Scarlet Claw 1944; Sherlock Holmes and the Spider Woman 1944; The Vigilantes Return 1947

Holbrook, Boyd The Skeleton Twins 2014; Wolverine 3 2017

Holbrook, Hal (1925-) The Group 1966; Wild in the Streets 1968; The Great White Hope 1970; They Only Kill Their Masters 1972; Jonathan Livingston Seagull 1973; Magnum Force 1973; The Girl from Petrovka 1974; All the President's Men 1976; Battle of Midway 1976; Julia 1977; Capricorn One 1978; The Fog 1980; The Kidnapping of the President 1980; Creepshow 1982; The Star Chamber 1983; Wall Street 1987; The Unholy 1988; Day One 1989; Fletch Lives 1989; Evidence of Love 1990; The Firm 1993; Acts of Love 1995; Operation Delta Force 1996; Eye of God 1997; Cats Don't Dance 1998; Hush 1998; The Bachelor 1999; Men of Honor 2000; Waking the Dead 2000; The Majestic

2001; Into the Wild 2007; Water for Elephants 2011; Lincoln 2012; Promised Land 2012; Planes: Fire and Rescue 2014; Go with Me 2015

Holcombe, Harry (1906-1987) Kisses for My President 1964; The Fortune Cookie 1966; Foxy Brown 1974

Holden, Alexandra (1977-) Dancer, Texas Pop 81 1998; Sugar & Spice 2001; American Gun 2002; The Hot Chick 2002; Dead End 2003; Special (PX) - Specioprin Hydrochloride 2006; A Trick of the Mind 2006; Lovely Molly 2012

Holden, Fay (1895-1973) Bulldog Drummond Escapes 1937; Judge Hardy's Children 1938; Love Finds Andy Hardy 1938; Out West with the Hardys 1938; Sweethearts 1938; You're Only Young Once 1938; Andy Hardy Gets Spring Fever 1939; The Hardys Ride High 1939; Judge Hardy and Son 1939; Sergeant Madden 1939; Andy Hardy Meets Debutante 1940; Andy Hardy's Private Secretary 1941; Blossoms in the Dust 1941; Dr Kildare's Wedding Day 1941; HM Pulham Esq 1941; Life Begins for Andy Hardy 1941; Andy Hardy's Double Life 1942; The Courtship of Andy Hardy 1942; Andy Hardy's Blonde Trouble 1944; Love Laughs at Andy Hardy 1946; Whispering Smith 1948; Samson and Delilah 1949; The Big Hangover 1950; Andy Hardy Comes Home 1958

Holden, Frankie (1952-) High Tide 1987; Hammers over the Anvil 1992; Clubland 2006

Holden, Gloria (1908-1991) Dracula's Daughter 1936; The Life of Emile Zola 1937; This Thing Called Love 1940; Miss Annie Rooney 1942; Strange Holiday 1942; Dream Wife 1953; The Eddy Duchin Story 1956

Holden, Jan (1931-2005) Assignment Redhead 1956; The Primitives 1962

Holden, Jennifer Jailhouse Rock 1957; Gang War 1958

Holden, Laurie (1972-) The Majestic 2001; Silent Hill 2006; The Mist 2007; Dumb and Dumber To 2014

Holden (1), William (1872-1932) The Trespasser 1929; Holiday 1930; What a Widow! 1930; Dance, Fools, Dance 1931

Holden (2), William (1918-1981) Golden Boy 1939; Invisible Stripes 1939; Arizona 1940; Our Town 1940; I Wanted Wings 1941; Texas 1941; The Fleet's In 1942; Young and Willing 1942; Blaze of Noon 1947; Dear Ruth 1947; Variety Girl 1947; Apartment for Peggy 1948; The Dark Past 1948; The Man from Colorado 1948; Rachel and the Stranger 1948; Dear Wife 1949; Miss Grant Takes Richmond 1949; Streets of Laredo 1949; Born Yesterday 1950; Sunset Blvd 1950; Union Station 1950; Boots Malone 1951; Force of Arms 1951; Submarine Command 1951; The Turning Point 1952; Escape from Fort Bravo 1953; Forever Female 1953; The Moon Is Blue 1953; Stalag 17 1953; The Bridges at Toko-Ri 1954; The Country Girl 1954; Executive Suite 1954; Sabrina 1954; Samurai 1954; Love Is a Many-Splendored Thing 1955; Picnic 1955; Toward the Unknown 1956; The Bridge on the River Kwai 1957; The Key 1958; The Horse Soldiers 1959; The World of Suzie Wong 1960; The Counterfeit Traitor 1962; The Lion 1962; Satan Never Sleeps 1962; Paris When It Sizzles 1964; The 7th Dawn 1964; Alvarez Kelly 1966; Casino Royale 1967; The Christmas Tree 1969; The Wild Bunch 1969; Wild Rovers 1971; The Blue Knight 1973; Breezy 1973; Open Season 1974; The Towering Inferno 1974; Network 1976; Damien - Omen II 1978; Fedora 1978; Ashanti 1979; Escape to Athena 1979; The Earthling 1980; When Time Ran Out 1980; SOB 1981

Holder, Geoffrey (1930-2014) Live and Let Die 1973; The Man without a Country 1973; Swashbuckler 1976; Annie 1982; Boomerang 1992; Chance or Coincidence 1999

Holder, Ram John Half Moon Street 1986; Song for Marion 2012

Holder, Roy (1946-) Whistle down the Wind 1961; Loot 1970; Psychomania 1972

Holding, Thomas (1880-1929) The Three Musketeers 1921; Ruggles of Red Gap 1923

Holgado, Ticky (1944-2004) Delicatessen 1990; Gazon Maudit 1995; And Now... Ladies and Gentlemen 2002; A Very Long Engagement 2004

Holiday, Hope (1938-) The Apartment 1960; The Rounders 1965

Holland, Anthony (1928-1988) Lucky Lady 1975; The Lonely Lady 1983

Holland, John (1908-1993) Ladies' Man 1931; The Girl in Black Stockings 1957

Holland (2), Tom (1996-) Arrietty 2010; The Impossible 2011; How I Live Now 2013; Locke 2014; Spider-Man: Homecoming 2017

Holland, Willa Genova 2008; Straw Dogs 2011

Hollander, Tom (1967-) Some Mother's Son 1996; Martha - Meet Frank, Daniel and Laurence 1997; Bedrooms and Hallways 1998; The Clandestine Marriage 1999; Maybe Baby 1999; Enigma 2001; The Lawless Heart 2001; Possession 2002; The Libertine 2004; Paparazzi 2004; Pride & Prejudice 2005; A Good Year 2006; Land of the Blind 2006; Elizabeth: the Golden Age 2007; The Soloist 2008; In the Loop 2009; Hanna 2011; About Time 2013; The Invisible Woman 2013; The Riot Club 2014

Holles, Antony (1901-1950) Limelight 1936; Smash and Grab 1937; The Dark Road 1948

Holliday, Judy (1921-1965) Too Much Johnson 1938; Winged Victory 1944; Adam's Rib 1949; Born Yesterday 1950; The Marrying Kind 1952; It Should Happen to You 1954; Phffft! 1954; Full of Life 1956; The Solid Gold Cadillac 1956; Bells Are Ringing 1960

Holliday, Polly (1937-) The One and Only 1978; Gremlins 1984; Mrs Doubtfire 1993

Holliman, Earl (1928-) The Bridges at Toko-Ri 1954; Broken Lance 1954; Tennessee Champ 1954; I Died a Thousand Times 1955; The Burning Hills 1956; Forbidden Planet 1956; The Rainmaker 1956; Don't Go near the Water 1957; Gunfight at the OK Corral 1957; Trooper Hook 1957; Hot Spell 1958; The Baited Trap 1959; Last Train from Gun Hill 1959; The Sons of Katie Elder 1965; Anzio 1968; The Power 1968; The Biscuit Eater 1972; Sharky's Machine 1981

Hollis, Kelli The Principles of Lust 2002; Mischief Night 2006

Hollis, Tommy (1954-2001) Malcolm X 1992; Freedom Road: the Vernon Johns Story 1994

Holloman, Laurel (1971-) The Incredibly True Adventures of Two Girls in Love 1995; The Myth of Fingerprints 1996; Tumbleweeds 1999

Holloway, Ann Two a Penny 1968; Father Dear Father 1972

Holloway, Josh Mission: Impossible - Ghost Protocol 2011; Battle of the Year 2013

Holloway, Stanley (1890-1982) D'Ye Ken John Peel? 1934; Sing as We Go 1934; Play Up the Band 1935; Squibs 1935; Cotton Queen 1937; The Vicar of Bray 1937; Champagne Charlie 1944; This Happy Breed 1944; The Way Ahead 1944; Brief Encounter 1945; The Way to the Stars 1945; Carnival 1946; Meet Me at Dawn 1946; Wanted for Murder 1946; Nicholas Nickleby 1947; Another Shore 1948; Hamlet 1948; Noose 1948; One Night with You 1948; Snowbound 1948; Passport to Pimlico 1949; The Perfect Woman 1949; Lady Godiva Rides Again 1951; The Lavender Hill Mob 1951; The Magic Box 1951; The Happy Family 1952; Meet Me Tonight 1952; The Titfield Thunderbolt 1952; The Beggar's Opera 1953; A Day to Remember 1953; Meet Mr Lucifer 1953; An Alligator Named Daisy 1955; Jumping for Joy 1955; Alive and Kicking 1958; No Trees in the Street 1958; No Love for Johnnie 1960; On the Fiddle 1961; My Fair Lady 1964; In Harm's Way 1965; Ten Little Indians 1965; The Sandwich Man 1966; The Private Life of Sherlock Holmes 1970; Flight of the Doves 1971; Up the Front 1972

Holloway, Sterling (1905-1992) Faithless 1932; When Ladies Meet 1933; The Merry Widow 1934; Life Begins at 40 1935; Remember the Night 1940; Cheers for Miss Bishop 1941; Dumbo 1941; A Walk in the Sun 1945; Make Mine Music 1946; The Beautiful Blonde from Bashful Bend 1949; Alice in Wonderland 1951; Shake, Rattle and Rock! 1957; The Jungle Book 1967; Live a Little, Love a Little 1968; The Aristocats 1970; The Many Adventures of Winnie the Pooh 1977

Holly, Ellen (1931-) Take a Giant Step 1959; Cops and Robbers 1973; School Daze 1988

Holly, Lauren (1963-) The Adventures of Ford Fairlane 1990; Dragon: the Bruce Lee Story 1993; Dumb and Dumber 1994; Sabrina 1995; Beautiful Girls 1996; Down Periscope 1996; A Smile like Yours 1997; Turbulence 1997; No Looking Back 1998; The Last Producer 2000; Spirited Away 2001; What Women Want 2001; King of Texas 2002; The Chumscrubber 2005; Before You Say "I Do" 2009; Too Late to Say Goodbye 2009; Call Me Mrs Miracle 2010; The Town Christmas Forgot 2010

Holm, Astrid (1893-1961) The Phantom Carriage 1920; Master of the House 1925

Holm, Celeste (1917-2012) Three Little Girls in Blue 1946; Gentleman's Agreement 1947; Chicken Every Sunday 1947; Road House 1948; The Snake Pit 1948; Come to the Stable 1949; Everybody Does It 1949; A Letter to Three Wives 1949; All about Eve 1950; Champagne for Caesar 1950; The Tender Trap 1955; High Society 1956; Bachelor Flat 1961; Cinderella 1965; Tom Sawyer 1973; Bittersweet Love 1976; The Private Files of J Edgar Hoover 1977; Three Men and a Baby 1987

Holm, Claus (1918-1996) The Indian Tomb 1959; The Tiger of Eschnapur 1959

Holm, Ian (1931-) The Bofors Gun 1968; A Midsummer Night's Dream 1969; Oh! What a Lovely War 1969; A Severed Head 1970; Mary, Queen of Scots 1971; Young Winston 1972; The Homecoming 1973; Juggernaut 1974; Robin and Marian 1976; Shout at the Devil 1976; The Man in the Iron Mask 1977; March or Die 1977; Les Misérables 1978; The Thief of Baghdad 1978; Alien 1979; All Quiet on the Western Front 1979; SOS Titanic 1979; Chariots of Fire 1981; Time Bandits 1981; The Return of the Soldier 1982; Dance with a Stranger 1984; Greystoke: the Legend of Tarzan, Lord of the Apes 1984; Brazil 1985; Dreamchild 1985; Wetherby 1985; Another Woman 1988; Henry V 1989; Hamlet 1990; Kafka 1991; Naked Lunch 1991; Blue Ice 1992; The Hour of the Pig 1993; Mary Shelley's Frankenstein 1994; Loch Ness 1995; The Madness of King George 1995; Big Night 1996; The Fifth Element 1997; Night Falls on Manhattan 1997; The Sweet Hereafter 1997; Simon Magus 1998; Animal Farm 1999; eXistenZ 1999; The Match 1999; The Miracle Maker 1999; Beautiful Joe 2000; Bless the Child 2000; Esther Kahn 2000; The Emperor's New Clothes 2001; From Hell 2001; The Lord of the Rings: The Fellowship of the Ring 2001; Garden State 2003; The Aviator 2004; The Day after Tomorrow 2004; Chromophobia 2005; Lord of War 2005; Renaissance 2006; Ratatouille 2007; The Hobbit: an Unexpected Journey 2012

Holm, Sonia (1922-1974) Miranda 1947; Broken Journey 1948; The Calendar 1948; The Bad Lord Byron 1949

Holman, Clare Afraid of the Dark 1991; Let Him Have It 1991; Tom & Viv 1994

Holman, Vincent (1886-1962) Love Story 1944; The Sound Barrier 1952

Holmes, Adrian Cries in the Dark 2006; White Noise: the Light 2006

Holmes, Ashton A History of Violence 2005; Smart People 2007; Wind Chill 2007

Holmes, Katie (1978-) The Ice Storm 1997; Disturbing Behavior 1998; Go 1999; Teaching Mrs Tingle 1999; The Gift 2000; Wonder Boys 2000; Phone Booth 2002; Pieces of April 2002; The Singing Detective 2003; First Daughter 2004; Batman Begins 2005; Thank You for Smoking 2005; Mad Money 2008; Don't Be Afraid of the Dark 2010; Jack and Jill 2011; The Giver 2014; Woman in Gold 2015

Holmes, Phillips (1907-1942) The Criminal Code 1930; The Devil's Holiday 1930; Grumpy 1930; An American Tragedy 1931; The Man I Killed 1932; Penthouse 1933; The Secret of Madame Blanche 1933; Caravan 1934; Nana 1934; Housemaster 1938

Holmes, Stuart (1887-1971) The Prisoner of Zenda 1922; When a Man Loves 1926; Belle of the Nineties 1934

Holmes, Taylor (1872-1959) Boomerang! 1947; Kiss of Death 1947; Nightmare Alley 1947; The Plunderers 1948; Act of Violence 1949; Rhubarb 1951; Beware, My Lovely 1952; Gentlemen Prefer Blondes 1953; The Outcast 1954; Sleeping Beauty 1959

Holmes, Tina Keane 2004; Half Nelson 2006

Holt, Charlene (1928-1996) Man's Favorite Sport? 1964; Red Line 7000 1965; El Dorado 1967

Holt, Jack (1888-1951) Flight 1929; Dirigible 1931; The Littlest Rebel 1935; San Francisco 1936; Cat People 1942; They Were Expendable 1945; The Chase 1946; My Pal Trigger 1946; Task Force 1949; Trail of Robin Hood 1950; Across the Wide Missouri 1951

Holt, Jany (1911-2005) Beethoven 1936; The Golem 1936; The Lower Depths 1936; Les Anges du Péché 1943

Holt, Patrick (1912-1993) The Mark of Cain 1947; When the Bough Breaks 1947; Portrait from Life 1948; A Boy, a Girl and a Bike 1949; Boys in Brown 1949; Men of Sherwood Forest 1954; The Stranger Came Home 1954; The Dark Avenger 1955; The Girl in the Picture 1956; I Was Monty's Double 1958; Night of the Prowler 1962; Serena 1962; No Blade of Grass 1970; Psychomania 1972

Holt, Sandrine (1972-) Black Robe 1991; Rapa Nui 1994; Resident Evil: Apocalypse 2004; Chinese Puzzle 2013

Holt, Tim (1918-1973) Stella Dallas 1937; Gold Is Where You Find It 1938; The Law West of Tombstone 1938; 5th Ave Girl 1939; Stagecoach 1939; Swiss Family Robinson 1940; Along the Rio Grande 1941; Back Street 1941; The Magnificent Ambersons 1942; Hitler's Children 1943; My Darling Clementine 1946; Thunder Mountain 1947; The Treasure of the Sierra Madre 1947; Guns of Hate 1948; His Kind of Woman 1951; The Monster That Challenged the World 1957

Holt, Ula The New Adventures of Tarzan 1935; Tarzan and the Green Goddess 1938

Holton, Mark Pee-wee's Big Adventure 1985; Teen Wolf Too 1987; Leprechaun 1992

Holub, Miroslav aka Holub, Miloslav (1915-1999) Invention of Destruction 1958; The Ear 1969

Homar, Lluís (1957-) Bad Education 2004; To Die in San Hilario 2005; Fermat's Room 2007; Broken Embraces 2009; Julia's Eyes 2010

Homeier, Skip (1930-) The Gunfighter 1950; Halls of Montezuma 1950; Fixed Bayonets! 1951; Sealed Cargo 1951; Has Anybody Seen My Gal? 1952; Cry Vengeance 1954; At Gunpoint 1955; The Road to Denver 1955; Ten Wanted Men 1955; The Burning Hills 1956; Thunder over Arizona 1956; No Road Back 1957; The Tall T 1957; Day of the Bad Man 1958; Comanche Station 1960; Showdown 1963; Bullet for a Badman 1964

Homolka, Oscar aka Homolka, Oskar (1898-1978) Everything Is Thunder 1936; Rhodes of Africa 1936; Sabotage 1936; Comrade X 1940; The Invisible Woman 1940; Seven Sinners 1940; Ball of Fire 1941; Rage in Heaven 1941; Mission to Moscow 1943; The Shop at Sly Corner 1946; I Remember Mama 1948; Anna Lucasta 1949; The White Tower 1950; Prisoner of War 1954; The Seven Year Itch 1955; War and Peace 1956; A Farewell to Arms 1957; The Key 1958; Tempest 1959; Mr Sardonicus 1961; Boys' Night Out 1962; The Wonderful World of the Brothers Grimm 1962; The Long Ships 1963; Funeral in Berlin 1966; Billion Dollar Brain 1967; The Happening 1967; The Madwoman of Chaillot 1969; The Executioner 1970; Song of Norway 1970; The Tamarind Seed 1974

Hong, James (1929-) Yes, Giorgio 1982; Missing in Action 1984; Big Trouble in Little China 1986; The Golden Child 1986; Black Widow 1987; Vice Versa 1988; Tango & Cash 1989; Shadowzone 1990; Wayne's World 2 1993; Bloodsport II: The Next Kumite 1996; The Art of War 2000; Balls of Fury 2007; Safe 2011

Hood, Don (1941-2003) Marie: a True Story 1985; Inherit the Wind 1988

Hood, Ed My Hustler 1965; The Chelsea Girls 1966; Bike Boy 1967

Hood, Noel (1910-1979) The Curse of Frankenstein 1957; How to Murder a Rich Uncle 1957; The Inn of the Sixth Happiness 1958

Hooks, Brian Runaway Car 1997; 3 Strikes 2000; Soul Plane 2004

Hooks, Kevin (1958-) Sounder 1972; Aaron Loves Angela 1975; A Hero Ain't Nothin' but a Sandwich 1978

Hooks, Robert (1937-) Hurry Sundown 1967; Last of the Mobile Hot-Shots 1970; Trouble Man 1972; Aaron Loves Angela 1975; Fast-Walking 1982; Passenger 57 1992; Fled 1996

Hooper, Ewan (1935-) Dracula Has Risen from the Grave 1968; Kinky Boots 2005

Hoosier, Trula Sidewalk Stories 1989; Daughters of the Dust 1991

Hooten, Peter Orca... Killer Whale 1977; Inglorious Bastards 1978

Hootkins, William (1948-2005) Zina 1985; Biggles 1986; American Gothic 1987; Hardware 1990; Hear My Song 1991; The Pope Must Die 1991; Dust Devil 1992; Death Machine 1994; This World, Then the Fireworks 1996; The Magnificent Ambersons 2001

Hope, Barclay (1958-) The Boy Next Door 2008; The Christmas Consultant 2012

Hope, Bob (1903-2003) The Big Broadcast of 1938 1937; College Swing 1938; The Cat and the Canary 1939; Never Say Die 1939; Some Like It Hot 1939; The Ghost Breakers 1940; Road to Singapore 1940; Louisiana Purchase 1941; Nothing but the Truth 1941; Road to Zanzibar 1941; My Favorite Blonde 1942; Road to Morocco 1942; Star Spangled Rhythm 1942; Let's Face It 1943; They Got Me Covered 1943; The Princess and the Pirate 1944; Road to Utopia 1945; Monsieur Beaucaire 1946; My Favorite Brunette 1947; Road to Rio 1947; Variety Girl 1947; Where There's Life 1947; The Paleface 1948; The Great Lover 1949; Sorrowful Jones 1949; Fancy Pants 1950; The Lemon Drop Kid 1951; My Favorite Spy 1951; The Greatest Show on Earth 1952; Road to Bali 1952; Son of Paleface 1952; Here Come the Girls 1953; Military Policeman 1953; Scared Stiff 1953; Casanova's Big Night 1954; Seven Little Foys 1955; The Iron Petticoat 1956; That Certain Feeling 1956; Beau James 1957; Paris Holiday 1958; Alias Jesse James 1959; The Five Pennies 1959; The Facts of Life 1960; Bachelor in Paradise 1961; The Road to Hong Kong 1962; Call Me Bwana 1963; Critic's Choice 1963; A Global Affair 1964; I'll Take Sweden 1965; Boy, Did I Get a Wrong Number 1966; The Oscar 1966; Eight on the Lam 1967; The Private Navy of Sgt O'Farrell 1968; How to Commit Marriage 1969; Cancel My Reservation 1972; Spies like Us 1985

Hope, Leslie (1965-) Kansas 1988; Talk Radio 1988; Men at Work 1990; Doppelganger 1993; Fun 1994; Never Back Down 2008

Hope, Nicholas (1959-) Bad Boy Bubby 1993; The Darkest Light 1999

Hope, Richard Bellman & True 1987; My Brother Tom 2001

Hope, Vida (1918-1963) They Made Me a Fugitive 1947; Vice Versa 1947; Green Grow the Rushes 1951; The Man in the White Suit 1951; Women of Twilight 1952; Marilyn 1953

Hope, William Aliens 1986; Hellbound: Hellraiser II 1988; The Detonator 2006; Sherlock Holmes 2009

Hopkins, Anthony (1937-) The Lion in Winter 1968; Hamlet 1969; The Looking Glass War 1969; When Eight Bells Toll 1971; Young Winston 1972; A Doll's House 1973; All Creatures Great and Small 1974; The Girl from Petrovka 1974; Juggernaut 1974; Dark Victory 1976; The Lindbergh Kidnapping Case 1976; Victory at Entebbe 1976; Audrey Rose 1977; A Bridge Too Far 1977; International Velvet 1978; Magic 1978; Mayflower: the Pilgrims' Adventure 1979; A Change of Seasons 1980; The Elephant Man 1980; The Hunchback of Notre Dame 1982; The Bounty 1984; Guilty Conscience 1985; 84 Charing Cross Road 1986; The Good Father 1986; A Chorus of Disapproval 1988; The Dawning 1988; The Tenth Man 1988; Desperate Hours 1990; The Silence of the Lambs 1991; Spotswood 1991; Bram Stoker's Dracula 1992; Chaplin 1992; Freejack 1992; Howards End 1992; The Innocent 1993; The Remains of the Day 1993; Shadowlands 1993; The Trial 1993; Legends of the Fall 1994; The Road to Wellville 1994; August 1995; Nixon 1995; Surviving Picasso 1996; Amistad 1997; The Edge 1997; The Mask of Zorro 1998; Meet Joe Black 1998; Instinct 1999; Mission: Impossible 2 1999; Titus 1999; The Grinch 2000; Hannibal 2001; Hearts in Atlantis 2001; Bad Company 2002; Red Dragon 2002; The Human Stain 2003; Alexander 2004; All the King's Men 2005; Proof 2005; The World's Fastest Indian 2005; Bobby 2006; Beowulf 2007; Fracture 2007; The Wolfman 2009; You Will Meet a Tall Dark Stranger 2010; The Rite 2011; Thor 2011; 360 2011; Hitchcock 2012; Red 2 2013; Thor: the Dark World 2013; Noah 2014; Go with Me 2015; Kidnapping Freddy Heineken 2015; Solace 2015; Misconduct 2016; Thor: Ragnarok 2017

Hopkins, Bo (1942-) The Culpepper Cattle Co 1972; American Graffiti 1973; The Man Who Loved Cat Dancing 1973; White Lightning 1973; The Killer Elite 1975; Posse 1975; Tentacles 1977; Midnight Express 1978; More American Graffiti 1979; Mutant 1984; The Ballad of Little Jo 1993; U Turn 1997; The Newton Boys 1998; From Dusk till Dawn II: Texas Blood Money 1999; A Crack in the Floor 2000; South of Heaven, West of Hell 2000

Hopkins, Harold (1944-2011) Age of Consent 1969; Don's Party 1976; The Club 1980; Gallipoli 1981

Hopkins, Jermaine (1973-) Lean on Me 1989; Juice 1991

Hopkins, Joan (1915-2002) We Dive at Dawn 1943; The Weaker Sex 1948

Hopkins, Josh (1970-) Pirates of Silicon Valley 1999; Love & Sex 2000; Surrender Dorothy 2006

Hopkins, Miriam (1902-1972) Fast and Loose 1930; Dr Jekyll and Mr Hyde 1931; The Smiling Lieutenant 1931; Trouble in Paradise 1932; Design for Living 1933; The Stranger's Return 1933; The Richest Girl in the World 1934; She Loves Me Not 1934; Barbary Coast 1935; Becky Sharp 1935; Splendor 1935; Men Are Not Gods 1936; These Three 1936; Woman Chases Man 1937; The Woman I Love 1937; The Old Maid 1939; Virginia City 1940; Old Acquaintance 1943; The Heiress 1949; The Mating Season 1951; Carrie 1952; The Children's Hour 1961; Fanny Hill: Memoirs of a Woman of Pleasure 1964; The Chase 1966

Hopkins, Nikita The Tigger Movie 2000; Piglet's Big Movie 2003; Pooh's Heffalump Movie 2005

Hoppe, Rolf (1930-) Mephisto 1981; Palmetto 1998

Hopper, Dennis (1936-2010) I Died a Thousand Times 1955; Rebel without a Cause 1955; Giant 1956; Gunfight at the OK Corral 1957; From Hell to Texas 1958; The Young Land 1959; Key Witness 1960; The Sons of Katie Elder 1965; Planet of Blood 1966; Cool Hand Luke 1967; The Glory Stompers 1967; The Trip 1967; Hang 'Em High 1968; Easy Rider 1969; True Grit 1969; The American Dreamer 1971; Kid Blue 1971; The Last Movie 1971; Mad Dog 1976; The American Friend 1977; Tracks 1977; Apocalypse Now 1979; Out of the Blue 1980; Human Highway 1982; The Osterman Weekend 1983; Rumble Fish 1983; The Inside Man 1984; My Science Project 1985; Running Out of Luck 1985; Blue Velvet 1986; Hoosiers 1986; Riders of the Storm 1986; The Texas Chainsaw Massacre Part 2 1986; Black Widow 1987; OC and Stiggs 1987; The Pick-Up Artist 1987; River's Edge 1987; Straight to Hell 1987; Blood Red 1988; Catchfire 1989; Chattahoochee 1989; Flashback 1990; Hearts of Darkness: a Film-Maker's Apocalypse 1991; The Indian Runner 1991; Paris Trout 1991; The Heart of Justice 1992; Red Rock West 1992; Boiling Point 1993; Super Mario Bros 1993; True Romance 1993; Speed 1994; Acts of Love 1995; Search and Destroy 1995; Waterworld 1995; Basquiat 1996; The Last Days of Frankie the Fly 1996; Space Truckers 1996; The Blackout 1997; Top of the World 1997; Meet the Deedles 1998; Edtv 1999; Jesus' Son 1999; Lured Innocence 1999; The Prophet's Game 1999; Luck of the Draw 2000; Knockaround Guys 2001; Ticker 2001; Leo 2002; Easy Riders, Raging Bulls 2003; The Keeper 2003; The Night We Called It a Day 2003; House of 9 2004; The Last Ride 2004; The Crow: Wicked Prayer 2005; George A Romero's Land of the Dead 2005; Inside Deep Throat 2005; Sketches of Frank Gehry 2006; Elegy 2008; Not Quite Hollywood 2008; Swing Vote 2008; Alpha and Omega 2010

Hopper, Hal (1912-1970) Lorna 1964; Mudhoney 1965

Hopper, Hedda (1890-1966) Sinners in Silk 1924; Wings 1927; The Last of Mrs Cheyney 1929; Holiday 1930; As You Desire Me 1932; Skyscraper Souls 1932; Speak Easily 1932; Pilgrimage 1933; Alice Adams 1935; Dracula's Daughter 1936; Nothing Sacred 1937; Topper 1937; Vogues of 1938 1937; Maid's Night Out 1938; Midnight 1939; The Women 1939; The Oscar 1966

Hopper, Victoria (1909-2007) The Constant Nymph 1933; Lorna Doone 1934; Whom the Gods Love 1936; The Mill on the Floss 1937

Hopper, William (1915-1970) Track of the Cat 1954; Conquest of Space 1955; Rebel without a Cause 1955; The Bad Seed 1956; The Deadly Mantis 1957; 20 Million Miles to Earth 1957

Hopton, Russell (1900-1945) Arrowsmith 1931; The Miracle Woman 1931; Air Mail 1932; Law and Order 1932; Lady Killer 1933; The Little Giant 1933; He Was Her Man 1934; Star of Midnight 1935; Wings in the Dark 1935

Horan, Xavier The Dark Horse 2014; The Dead Lands 2014

Hordern, Michael (1911-1995) School for Secrets 1946; The Astonished Heart 1949; Highly Dangerous 1950; Trio 1950; Scrooge 1951; Tom Brown's Schooldays 1951; The Card 1952; The Hour of 13 1952; Grand National Night 1953; Personal Affair 1953; The Beachcomber 1954; You Know What Sailors Are 1954; The Dark Avenger 1955; The Man Who Never Was 1955; The Night My Number Came Up 1955; Storm over the Nile 1955; Alexander the Great 1956; The Baby and the Battleship 1956; The Spanish Gardener 1956; Windom's Way 1957; I Was Monty's Double 1958; Man in the Moon 1960; Moment of Danger 1960; Sink the Bismarck! 1960; El Cid 1961; Dr Syn, Alias the Scarecrow 1963; The Yellow Rolls-Royce 1964; A Funny Thing Happened on the Way to the Forum 1966; Khartoum 1966; How I Won the War 1967; I'll Never Forget What's 'Is Name 1967; The Jokers 1967; The Taming of the Shrew 1967; Anne of the Thousand Days 1969; The Bed Sitting Room 1969; Some Will, Some Won't 1969; Where Eagles Dare 1969; Demons of the Mind 1971; The Possession of Joel Delaney 1971; Up Pompeii 1971; Alice's Adventures in Wonderland 1972; England Made Me 1973; The Mackintosh Man 1973; Theatre of Blood 1973; Lucky Lady 1975; Mister Quilp 1975; Royal Flash 1975; The Slipper and the Rose 1976; Joseph Andrews 1977; The Medusa Touch 1978; Watership Down 1978; The Wildcats of St Trinian's 1980; The Missionary 1982; Oliver Twist 1982; Yellowbeard 1983; Lady Jane 1985; Comrades: a Lanternist's Account of the Tolpuddle Martyrs and What Became of Them 1986; Labyrinth 1986; The Secret Garden 1987; The Trouble with Spies 1987; Danny, the Champion of the World 1989; Diamond Skulls 1989; Freddie as FRO7 1992

Horgan, Sharon Run and Jump 2013; Man Up 2015

Horler, Sacha Soft Fruit 1999; My Year without Sex 2009

Horn, Camilla (1903-1996) Faust 1926; Eternal Love 1929

Horn, Cody End of Watch 2012; Magic Mike 2012

Horne, David (1898-1970) Crimes at the Dark House 1939; The First of the Few 1942; Don't Take It to Heart 1944; The Man from Morocco 1944; The Seventh Veil 1945; The Wicked Lady 1945; Once upon a Dream 1948; The Sheriff of Fractured Jaw 1958

Horne, Geoffrey (1933-) The Bridge on the River Kwai 1957; Bonjour Tristesse 1958; Tempest 1959

Horne, Lena (1917-2010) Cabin in the Sky 1943; Stormy Weather 1943; Broadway Rhythm 1944; Ziegfeld Follies 1944; Duchess of Idaho 1950; Death of a Gunfighter 1969; The Wiz 1978

Horne, Mathew (1978-) Lesbian Vampire Killers 2008; Horrid Henry: the Movie 2011; Breaking the Bank 2014; The Bad Education Movie 2015

Horne, Victoria (1920-2003) Pillow of Death 1945; Harvey 1950

Horneff, Wil (1979-) Ghost in the Machine 1993; Born to Be Wild 1995; The Roost 2005

Horner, Penelope Half a Sixpence 1967; The Man Who Had Power over Women 1970; Dracula 1974

Horney, Brigitte (1911-1988) The House of the Spaniard 1936; Baron Münchhausen 1943; The Trygon Factor 1967

Horovitch, David (1945-) An Unsuitable Job for a Woman 1981; Solomon and Gaenor 1998; Max 2002

Horovitz, Adam (1966-) The Road Home 1989; Roadside Prophets 1992; The Punk Singer 2013; While We're Young 2014

Horrocks, Jane (1964-) The Dressmaker 1988; The Wolves of Willoughby Chase 1988; Getting It Right 1989; The Witches 1989; Life Is Sweet 1990; Memphis Belle 1990; Deadly Advice 1993; Second Best 1993; Bring Me the Head of Mavis Davis 1997; Little Voice 1998; Born Romantic 2000; Chicken Run 2000; Lion of Oz 2000; Christmas Carol: the Movie 2001; Tim Burton's Corpse Bride 2005; Tinker Bell 2008; Sunshine on Leith 2013; Absolutely Fabulous: the Movie 2016

Horsfall, Bernard (1930-2013) On Her Majesty's Secret Service 1969; Gold 1974

Horsford, Anna Maria (1948-) Times Square 1980; Bill 1981; The Fan 1981; Friday 1995; Dear God 1996; Nutty Professor 2: the Klumps 2000

Horsley, John (1920-2014) Deadly Nightshade 1953; Circus Friends 1956; Night of the Prowler 1962; Serena 1962

Horsley, Lee (1955-) Danielle Steel's Palomino 1991; LaVyrle Spencer's Home Song 1996

Horton, Edward Everett aka **Horton, Edward** (1886-1970) Ruggles of Red Gap 1923; La Bohème 1926; Holiday 1930; The Front Page 1931; Six Cylinder Love 1931; Trouble in Paradise 1932; Alice in Wonderland 1933; Design for Living 1933; The Gay Divorce 1934; Kiss and Make-Up 1934; Ladies Should Listen 1934; The Merry Widow 1934; Sing and Like It 1934; The Devil Is a Woman 1935; In Caliente 1935; Top Hat 1935; The Man in the Mirror 1936; The Singing Kid 1936; Angel 1937; Danger - Love at Work 1937; The Great Garrick 1937; Lost Horizon 1937; The Perfect Specimen 1937; Shall We Dance 1937; Bluebeard's Eighth Wife 1938; College Swing 1938; Holiday 1938; The Gang's All Here 1939; Paris Honeymoon 1939; That's Right - You're Wrong 1939; Here Comes Mr Jordan 1941; Sunny 1941; Ziegfeld Girl 1941; I Married an Angel 1942; The Magnificent Dope 1942; Springtime in the Rockies 1942; The Gang's All Here 1943; Thank Your Lucky Stars 1943; Arsenic and Old Lace 1944; Brazil 1944; Summer Storm 1944; Lady on a Train 1945; Cinderella Jones 1946; Down to Earth 1947; Her Husband's Affairs 1947; Pocketful of Miracles 1961; Sex and the Single Girl 1964; The Perils of Pauline 1967
Horton, Helen (1923-2009) Phase IV 1973; Alien 1979
Horton, Louisa (1924-2008) All My Sons 1948; Walk East on Beacon 1952
Horton, Michael My Father, My Son 1988; Snow White in Happily Ever After 1990
Horton, Peter (1953-) Children of the Corn 1984; 2 Days in the Valley 1996; While I Was Gone 2004
Horton, Robert (1924-) When Knights Were Bold 1936; Pony Soldier 1952; Arena 1953; Bright Road 1953; Men of the Fighting Lady 1954
Hoshi, Shizuko Come See the Paradise 1990; M Butterfly 1993
Hoshi, Yuriko (1943-) Godzilla vs Mothra 1964; Gnidrah, the Three-Headed Monster 1965
Hoskins, Bob (1942-2014) Up the Front 1972; The National Health 1973; Inserts 1975; The Long Good Friday 1979; Zulu Dawn 1979; Pink Floyd - The Wall 1982; The Honorary Consul 1983; The Cotton Club 1984; Lassiter 1984; Brazil 1985; Mona Lisa 1986; Sweet Liberty 1986; The Lonely Passion of Judith Hearne 1987; A Prayer for the Dying 1987; The Raggedy Rawney 1987; Who Framed Roger Rabbit 1988; Heart Condition 1990; Mermaids 1990; The Favour, the Watch and the Very Big Fish 1991; Hook 1991; The Inner Circle 1991; Shattered 1991; Passed Away 1992; Super Mario Bros 1993; Balto 1995; Nixon 1995; Rainbow 1995; Michael 1996; The Secret Agent 1996; Cousin Bette 1997; TwentyFourSeven 1997; Captain Jack 1998; Parting Shots 1998; Felicia's Journey 1999; A Room for Romeo Brass 1999; Don Quixote 2000; Live Virgin 2000; Enemy at the Gates 2001; Last Orders 2001; Maid in Manhattan 2002; Beyond the Sea 2004; Son of the Mask 2004; Vanity Fair 2004; Mrs Henderson Presents 2005; Stay 2005; Unleashed 2005; Garfield 2 2006; Hollywoodland 2006; Outlaw 2006; Sparkle 2006; Ruby Blue 2007; Doomsday 2008; A Christmas Carol 2009; Made in Dagenham 2010; Outside Bet 2011; Will 2011
Hoss, Nina (1975-) Anonyma: a Woman in Berlin 2008; We Are the Night 2010; Barbara 2012; A Most Wanted Man 2013; Phoenix 2014
Hossein, Robert (1927-) Madame 1961; The Dirty Game 1965; The Battle of El Alamein 1968; The Burglars 1971; Don Juan 73, or If Don Juan Were a Woman 1973; Le Grand Pardon 1981; The Professional 1981; Les Uns et les Autres 1981; Wax Mask 1997
Hosseini, Shahab About Elly 2009; Nader and Simin, a Separation 2011
Hotchkis, Joan (1927-) Breezy 1973; Ode to Billy Joe 1976; Old Boyfriends 1979
Hotton, Donald (1941-2008) One Dark Night 1982; Brainstorm 1983
Houde, Serge Hidden Agenda 2001; 50/50 2011
Hough, Julianne Footloose 2011; Rock of Ages 2012; Safe Haven 2013
Houghton, Katharine (1945-) Guess Who's Coming to Dinner 1967; Ethan Frome 1993
Hoult, Nicholas (1989-) About a Boy 2002; Wah-Wah 2005; A Single Man 2009; X-Men: First Class 2011; Warm Bodies 2012; Jack the Giant Slayer 2013; Bad Land: Road to Fury 2014; X-Men: Days of Future Past 2014; Dark Places 2015; Kill Your Friends 2015;

Mad Max: Fury Road 2015; X-Men: Apocalypse 2016
Hounsou, Djimon (1964-) Amistad 1997; Gladiator 2000; The Four Feathers 2002; Biker Boyz 2003; In America 2003; Lara Croft, Tomb Raider: the Cradle of Life 2003; Blueberry 2004; Beauty Shop 2005; Constantine 2005; The Island 2005; Blood Diamond 2006; Eragon 2006; Never Back Down 2008; Push 2009; The Tempest 2010; Special Forces 2011; Baggage Claim 2013; The Vatican Tapes 2015; Knights of the Round Table: King Arthur 2016
House, Billy (1890-1961) Bedlam 1946; The Egg and I 1947; Trail Street 1947; Rogues of Sherwood Forest 1950; Where Danger Lives 1950
House, Rachel Eagle vs Shark 2006; Hunt for the Wilderpeople 2016
Houseman, John (1902-1988) The Paper Chase 1973; Rollerball 1975; Three Days of the Condor 1975; St Ives 1976; The Cheap Detective 1978; Old Boyfriends 1979; The Fog 1980; Gideon's Trumpet 1980; My Bodyguard 1980; Ghost Story 1981; Murder by Phone 1982; Another Woman 1988; Bright Lights, Big City 1988
Houser, Jerry (1952-) Summer of '42 1971; Bad Company 1972; Class of '44 1973; Slap Shot 1977; Magic 1978; Another You 1991
Housman, Arthur (1888-1942) The Singing Fool 1928; Scram! 1932
Houston, Donald (1923-1991) The Blue Lagoon 1949; A Run for Your Money 1949; Dance Hall 1950; The Red Beret 1953; Doctor in the House 1954; The Flaw 1954; Double Cross 1955; The Girl in the Picture 1956; Yangtse Incident 1956; Danger Within 1958; The Man Upstairs 1958; Room at the Top 1958; The Mark 1961; Maniac 1962; The Prince and the Pauper 1962; The 300 Spartans 1962; Twice round the Daffodils 1962; Carry On Jack 1963; Doctor in Distress 1963; 633 Squadron 1964; A Study in Terror 1965; The Viking Queen 1967; Where Eagles Dare 1969; Sunstruck 1972
Houston, Glyn (1926-) The Cruel Sea 1952; Turn the Key Softly 1953; River Beat 1954; The Sleeping Tiger 1954; The Wind of Change 1961; Emergency 1962; A Stitch in Time 1963 ; Old Scores 1991; The Mystery of Edwin Drood 1993
Houston, Marques aka **Houston, Marques B** (1981-) Fat Albert 2004; You Got Served 2004
Houston, Renee (1902-1980) Old Bill and Son 1940; Two Thousand Women 1944; Lady Godiva Rides Again 1951; The Big Money 1956; A Town like Alice 1956; Time without Pity 1957; The Horse's Mouth 1958; The Flesh and the Fiends 1959; And the Same to You 1960; No My Darling Daughter 1961; Three on a Spree 1961; Repulsion 1965; Cul-de-Sac 1966; Legend of the Werewolf 1974
Houston, Whitney (1963-2012) The Bodyguard 1992; Waiting to Exhale 1995; The Preacher's Wife 1996; Rodgers & Hammerstein's Cinderella 1997; Sparkle 2012
Hoven, Adrian (1922-1981) Foxhole in Cairo 1960; I Aim at the Stars 1960; Fox and His Friends 1975; Inside Out 1975; Fear of Fear 1976
Howard, Alan (1937-2015) Oxford Blues 1984; Strapless 1988; The Cook, the Thief, His Wife and Her Lover 1989; The Secret Rapture 1993
Howard, Andrew (1969-) Rancid Aluminium 1999; Shooters 2000; Mr In-Between 2001; Revolver 2005; I Spit on Your Grave 2010; Limitless 2011
Howard, Arliss (1955-) The Lightship 1985; Full Metal Jacket 1987; Plain Clothes 1988; Tequila Sunrise 1988; Men Don't Leave 1990; CrissCross 1992; Ruby 1992; Wilder Napalm 1993; Erotic Tales 1994; The Infiltrator 1995; Johns 1995; To Wong Foo, Thanks for Everything, Julie Newmar 1995; Beyond the Call 1996; The Man Who Captured Eichmann 1996; The Lost World: Jurassic Park 1997; Old Man 1997; A Map of the World 1999; Birth 2004; Awake 2007; The Time Traveler's Wife 2008
Howard, Arthur (1910-1995) Bottoms Up 1959; Paradisio 1962; The Love Cage 1964; Steptoe and Son 1972
Howard, Bryce Dallas (1981-) The Village 2004; Manderlay 2005; As You Like It 2006; Lady in the Water 2006; Spider-Man 3 2007; Terminator: Salvation 2009; Eclipse 2010; Hereafter 2010; 50/50 2011; The Help 2011; Jurassic World 2015; Gold 2016; Pete's Dragon 2016; Jurassic World 2 2018

Howard, Clint (1959-) The Jungle Book 1967; Eat My Dust! 1976; The Many Adventures of Winnie the Pooh 1977; Rock 'n' Roll High School 1979; Night Shift 1982; The Wraith 1986; Disturbed 1990; Dillinger and Capone 1995; Edtv 1999; The Grinch 2000
Howard, Curly (1903-1952) Hollywood Party 1934; Time Out for Rhythm 1941
Howard, Esther (1892-1965) Detour 1945; Dick Tracy vs Cueball 1946; The Falcon's Alibi 1946; Lady of Deceit 1947
Howard, Jean (1910-2000) Claudia 1943; The Bermuda Mystery 1944
Howard, Jeremy Black Widow 2007; Sydney White 2007; Teenage Mutant Ninja Turtles - Out of the Shadows 2016
Howard (1), John (1913-1995) Valiant Is the Word for Carrie 1936; Bulldog Drummond Comes Back 1937; Bulldog Drummond's Revenge 1937; Lost Horizon 1937; Bulldog Drummond's Peril 1938; Bulldog Drummond in Africa 1938; Bulldog Drummond's Bride 1939; Green Hell 1939; The Invisible Woman 1940; The Man from Dakota 1940; The Philadelphia Story 1940; The Undying Monster 1942; Love from a Stranger 1947; The Fighting Kentuckian 1949
Howard (2), John (1952-) The Club 1980; Bush Christmas 1983; Young Einstein 1988
Howard, Joyce (1922-2010) Freedom Radio 1940; The Common Touch 1941; Love on the Dole 1941; Back Room Boy 1942; The Night Has Eyes 1942; The Gentle Sex 1943; They Met in the Dark 1943
Howard, Kathleen (1879-1956) Death Takes a Holiday 1934; It's a Gift 1934; You're Telling Me! 1934; Man on the Flying Trapeze 1935; Young People 1940; Blossoms in the Dust 1941; The Navy Steps Out 1941; Sweetheart of the Campus 1941; Take a Letter, Darling 1942; Laura 1944
Howard, Ken (1944-2016) Tell Me That You Love Me, Junie Moon 1970; Such Good Friends 1971; The Strange Vengeance of Rosalie 1972; The Man in the Brown Suit 1989; Murder in New Hampshire 1991; Oscar 1991; The Net 1995; At First Sight 1998; Tactical Assault 1998; In Her Shoes 2005; Spring Thaw 2007
Howard, Kevyn Major Alien Nation 1988; War Party 1988
Howard, Kyle (1978-) House Arrest 1996; Skeletons 1996; Baby Geniuses 1999
Howard, Leslie (1893-1943) A Free Soul 1931; The Animal Kingdom 1932; Smilin' Through 1932; Berkeley Square 1933; Secrets 1933; British Agent 1934; Of Human Bondage 1934; The Scarlet Pimpernel 1934; The Petrified Forest 1936; Romeo and Juliet 1936; It's Love I'm After 1937; Stand-In 1937; Pygmalion 1938; Gone with the Wind 1939; Intermezzo 1939; 49th Parallel 1941; Pimpernel Smith 1941; The First of the Few 1942
Howard, Mary (1913-2009) All over Town 1937; Spirit of the People 1940; Billy the Kid 1941; Riders of the Purple Sage 1941; Swamp Water 1941
Howard, Michael (1916-1988) I See a Dark Stranger 1946; Out of the Clouds 1954; The Baby and the Battleship 1956
Howard, Moe (1897-1975) Meet the Baron 1933; Hollywood Party 1934; Time Out for Rhythm 1941; Have Rocket, Will Travel 1959; The Three Stooges in Orbit 1962; The Three Stooges Meet Hercules 1962; The Three Stooges Go around the World in a Daze 1963; The Outlaws Is Coming 1965
Howard, Norah (1901-1968) Love, Life and Laughter 1934; Car of Dreams 1935; The Last Adventurers 1937; Two Loves 1961
Howard, Rance (1928-) Where the Lilies Bloom 1974; Eat My Dust! 1976; A Crack in the Floor 2000; Toolbox Murders 2003
Howard, Ron aka **Howard, Ronnie** aka **Howard, Ronny** (1954-) Door-to-Door Maniac 1961; The Music Man 1962; The Courtship of Eddie's Father 1963; Village of the Giants 1965; American Graffiti 1973; Happy Mother's Day... Love, George 1973; The Spikes Gang 1974; Eat My Dust! 1976; The Shootist 1976; Grand Theft Auto 1977; More American Graffiti 1979; Act of Love 1980; Corman's World: Exploits of a Hollywood Rebel 2011
Howard, Ronald (1918-1996) While the Sun Shines 1946; My Brother Jonathan 1947; Bond Street 1948; The Queen of Spades 1948; Now Barabbas Was a Robber 1949; Portrait of Clare 1950; The Browning Version 1951; Night Was Our Friend 1951; House in the Woods

1957; Gideon's Day 1958; No Trees in the Street 1958; The Monster of Highgate Ponds 1961; Live Now - Pay Later 1962; The Bay of Saint Michel 1963; Nurse on Wheels 1963; The Siege of the Saxons 1963; The Curse of the Mummy's Tomb 1964; The Hunting Party 1971
Howard, Shemp (1895-1955) The Bank Dick 1940; Arabian Nights 1942
Howard, Terrence aka **Howard, Terrence Dashon** (1969-) Mr Holland's Opus 1995; Sunset Park 1996; Best Laid Plans 1999; The Best Man 1999; Big Momma's House 2000; Muhammad Ali: King of the World 2000; Angel Eyes 2001; Boycott 2001; Hart's War 2002; Crash 2004; Ray 2004; Four Brothers 2005; Get Rich or Die Tryin' 2005; Hustle & Flow 2005; Their Eyes Were Watching God 2005; Idlewild 2006; August Rush 2007; Awake 2007; The Brave One 2007; The Hunting Party 2007; Pride 2007; Iron Man 2008; Fighting 2009; The Company You Keep 2012; Red Tails 2012; The Best Man Holiday 2013; Dead Man Down 2013; Prisoners 2013; Sabotage 2013; St Vincent 2014
Howard, Traylor (1966-) Dirty Work 1998; Son of the Mask 2004
Howard, Trevor (1913-1988) Brief Encounter 1945; The Way to the Stars 1945; Green for Danger 1946; I See a Dark Stranger 1946; So Well Remembered 1947; They Made Me a Fugitive 1947; The Passionate Friends 1948; Golden Salamander 1949; The Third Man 1949; The Clouded Yellow 1950; Odette 1950; Gift Horse 1951; Outcast of the Islands 1951; The Heart of the Matter 1953; The Stranger's Hand 1953; The Cockleshell Heroes 1955; Around the World in 80 Days 1956; Run for the Sun 1956; Interpol 1957; Manuela 1957; The Key 1958; The Roots of Heaven 1958; Moment of Danger 1960; Sons and Lovers 1960; The Lion 1962; Mutiny on the Bounty 1962; Father Goose 1964; Morituri 1965; Operation Crossbow 1965; Von Ryan's Express 1965; The Liquidator 1966; The Poppy Is Also a Flower 1966; Triple Cross 1966; The Long Duel 1967; Pretty Polly 1967; The Charge of the Light Brigade 1968; Battle of Britain 1969; Twinky 1969; The Night Visitor 1970; Ryan's Daughter 1970; Catch Me a Spy 1971; Kidnapped 1971; Mary, Queen of Scots 1971; The Offence 1972; Pope Joan 1972; Craze 1973; A Doll's House 1973; Ludwig 1973; The Count of Monte Cristo 1974; 11 Harrowhouse 1974; Persecution 1974; Who? 1974; Conduct Unbecoming 1975; Death in the Sun 1975; Hennessy 1975; Aces High 1976; The Bawdy Adventures of Tom Jones 1976; The Last Remake of Beau Geste 1977; Slavers 1977; Stevie 1978; Superman 1978; Hurricane 1979; Meteor 1979; The Sea Wolves 1980; Windwalker 1980; Gandhi 1982; The Missionary 1982; Sword of the Valiant 1984; Dust 1985; Foreign Body 1986; White Mischief 1987; The Dawning 1988; The Unholy 1988
Howard, Vanessa (1948-2010) The Blood Beast Terror 1967; Here We Go round the Mulberry Bush 1967; Mumsy, Nanny, Sonny & Girly 1970; The Rise and Rise of Michael Rimmer 1970
Howarth, Kevin Razor Blade Smile 1998; The Last Horror Movie 2003; Summer Scars 2007; The Seasoning House 2012
Howe, Brian Catch Me If You Can 2002; The Pursuit of Happyness 2006; Gran Torino 2008
Howell, C Thomas aka **Howell, Tom** (1966-) ET the Extra-Terrestrial 1982; The Outsiders 1983; Grandview, USA 1984; Red Dawn 1984; Secret Admirer 1985; The Hitcher 1986; Soul Man 1986; A Tiger's Tale 1987; Young Toscanini 1988; The Return of the Musketeers 1989; Kid 1990; That Night 1992; To Protect and Serve 1992; Gettysburg 1993; Mad Dogs and Englishmen 1994; Fortune Hunters 1999; Gang Law 1999; Hitman's Run 1999; Red Team 1999; Gods and Generals 2002; The Hillside Strangler 2004; Ordinary Miracles 2005; The Gunfighter's Pledge 2008; The Amazing Spider-Man 2012
Howell, Hoke (1930-1997) Grand Theft Auto 1977; The Alarmist 1997
Howell, Kenneth (1913-1966) The Eagle and the Hawk 1933; Pride of the Bowery 1941
Howells, Ursula (1922-2005) The Oracle 1952; The Gilded Cage 1954; They Can't Hang Me 1955; Account Rendered 1957; The Sicilians 1964; Mumsy, Nanny, Sonny & Girly 1970
Howerd, Frankie (1917-1992) The Runaway Bus 1954; Jumping for Joy

1955; The Ladykillers 1955; A Touch of the Sun 1956; Further up the Creek 1958; The Great St Trinian's Train Robbery 1966; Carry On Doctor 1968; Carry On Up the Jungle 1970; Up Pompeii 1971; Up the Chastity Belt 1971; Up the Front 1972; The House in Nightmare Park 1973; Sgt Pepper's Lonely Hearts Club Band 1978
Howes, Hans aka **Howes, Hans R** Fire and Ice 1983; Terminal Velocity 1994
Howes, Reed (1900-1964) The Singing Fool 1928; The Dawn Rider 1935; Paradise Canyon 1935; A Million to One 1937; The Lone Rider in Ghost Town 1941
Howes, Sally Ann (1930-) The Halfway House 1943; Dead of Night 1945; Pink String and Sealing Wax 1945; Anna Karenina 1947; Nicholas Nickleby 1947; The History of Mr Polly 1948; Fools Rush In 1949; The Admirable Crichton 1957; Chitty Chitty Bang Bang 1968; The Hound of the Baskervilles 1972
Howey, Steve Bride Wars 2008; Something Borrowed 2011
Howland, Jobyna (1880-1936) Rockabye 1932; Topaze 1933
Howlett, Noel (1901-1984) Serious Charge 1959; Murder at the Gallop 1963; Please Sir! 1971
Howlin, Olin (1886-1959) Belle Starr 1941; The Blob 1958
Howman, Karl (1952-) Babylon 1980; Party Party 1983; The Truth about Love 2004
Howze, Leonard Earl Barbershop 2: Back in Business 2004; The Ringer 2005
Hoyos, Cristina Blood Wedding 1981; Carmen 1983; El Amor Brujo 1986
Hoyos, Rodolfo aka **Hoyos Jr, Rodolfo** (1896-1980) The Americano 1955; The Brave One 1956
Hoyt, Arthur (1874-1953) Camille 1921; The Lost World 1925; Shanghai Madness 1933; It Happened One Night 1934; The Great McGinty 1940; Sullivan's Travels 1941
Hoyt, John (1905-1991) OSS 1946; Brute Force 1947; My Favorite Brunette 1947; The Unfaithful 1947; To the Ends of the Earth 1948; Winter Meeting 1948; The Bribe 1949; Everybody Does It 1949; The Lady Gambles 1949; The Company She Keeps 1950; The Lawless 1950; When Worlds Collide 1951; The Blackboard Jungle 1955; The Purple Mask 1955; The Come On 1956; The Conqueror 1956; Death of a Scoundrel 1956; Forever, Darling 1956; Mohawk 1956; Merrill's Marauders 1962; The Man with the X-Ray Eyes 1963; The Time Traveller 1964; Operation CIA 1965; Duel at Diablo 1966; Winchester '73 1967; Flesh Gordon 1974
Hrusinsky, Rudolf (1921-1994) Baron Munchhausen 1961; Capricious Summer 1968; The Cremator 1968; Cutting It Short 1980; My Sweet Little Village 1986; The Last of the Good Old Days 1989; Elementary School 1991
Hu Jun Behind the Forbidden City 1996; Red Cliff 2008
Hu, Kelly (1968-) The Scorpion King 2002; Cradle 2 the Grave 2003; The Librarian: Quest for the Spear 2004; Underclassman 2004; The Tournament 2009
Huang Lei Life on a String 1991; CJ7 2008
Huard, Patrick Starbuck 2011; Mommy 2014
Hubbard, John aka **Allan, Anthony** (1914-1988) Dramatic School 1938; Maisie 1939; One Million BC 1940; Road Show 1941; You'll Never Get Rich 1941; The Mummy's Tomb 1942; Up in Mabel's Room 1944; The Bullfighter and the Lady 1951; Escort West 1959; Gunfight at Comanche Creek 1964
Hubbert, Cork (1952-2003) Caveman 1981; Under the Rainbow 1981; Not for Publication 1984; Legend 1985; The Ballad of the Sad Café 1991
Huber, Harold (1904-1959) He Was Her Man 1934; Klondike Annie 1936; Charlie Chan at Monte Carlo 1937; Charlie Chan on Broadway 1937; Going Places 1938; Mysterious Mr Moto 1938; Kit Carson 1940; Charlie Chan in Rio 1941; Down Mexico Way 1941; Crime Doctor 1943
Hubley, Season (1951-) Catch My Soul 1973; The Lolly-Madonna War 1973; Elvis - the Movie 1979; Hardcore 1979; Vice Squad 1982; Agatha Christie's A Caribbean Mystery 1983
Hubley, Whip (1957-) Russkies 1987; Desire & Hell at Sunset Motel 1991; Lake Consequence 1992
Hubschmid, Paul (1917-2001) The Indian Tomb 1959; The Tiger of Eschnapur 1959; Funeral in Berlin 1966;

Track of the Cat 1954; Battle Cry 1955; The Sea Chase 1955; The Burning Hills 1956; The Girl He Left Behind 1956; Damn Yankees 1958; Gunman's Walk 1958; That Kind of Woman 1959; They Came to Cordura 1959; The Pleasure of His Company 1961; Ride the Wild Surf 1964; City under the Sea 1965; The Loved One 1965; The Life and Times of Judge Roy Bean 1972; Polyester 1981; Pandemonium 1982; Lust in the Dust 1984; Cameron's Closet 1988; Out of the Dark 1988; Dark Horse 1992; I Am Divine 2013

Hunter, Thomas The Hills Run Red 1966; Anzio 1968

Huntington-Whiteley, Rosie (1987–) Transformers: Dark of the Moon 2011; Mad Max: Fury Road 2015

Huntington, Sam (1982–) Jungle 2 Jungle 1997; Detroit Rock City 1999; Sleepover 2004; Superman Returns 2006; Fanboys 2008

Huntley, Raymond (1904–1990) Freedom Radio 1940; The Ghost of St Michael's 1941; The Ghost Train 1941; Pimpernel Smith 1941; The Way Ahead 1944; I See a Dark Stranger 1946; School for Secrets 1946; Broken Journey 1948; Mr Perrin and Mr Traill 1948; The Long Dark Hall 1951; Mr Denning Drives North 1951; Laxdale Hall 1953; Orders Are Orders 1954; The Constant Husband 1955; Brothers in Law 1956; The Green Man 1956; Carlton-Browne of the FO 1958; Room at the Top 1958; Bottoms Up 1959; The Mummy 1959; A French Mistress 1960; Sands of the Desert 1960; Suspect 1960; On the Beat 1962; The Black Torment 1964; Hostile Witness 1968; The Adding Machine 1969; That's Your Funeral 1972

Huppert, Isabelle (1955–) César and Rosalie 1972; Les Valseuses 1974; Doctor Françoise Gailland 1975; The Lacemaker 1977; Violette Nozière 1977; The Brontë Sisters 1979; Heaven's Gate 1980; Loulou 1980; Slow Motion 1980; Coup de Torchon 1981; Passion 1982; Entre Nous 1983; Storia di Piera 1983; Cactus 1986; The Bedroom Window 1987; Une Affaire de Femmes 1988; Madame Bovary 1991; Après l'Amour 1992; The Flood 1993; Amateur 1994; La Séparation 1994; La Cérémonie 1995; Rien Ne Va Plus 1997; Comédie de l'Innocence 2000; Les Destinées Sentimentales 2000; Merci pour le Chocolat 2000; 8 Women 2001; The Piano Teacher 2001; Time of the Wolf 2003; I ♥ Huckabees 2004; Ma Mère 2004; Gabrielle 2005; A Comedy of Power 2006; Private Property 2006; Home 2008; The Sea Wall 2008; Villa Amalia 2009; White Material 2009; Amour 2012; Dead Man Down 2013; The Nun 2013; Louder than Bombs 2015; Valley of Love 2015; Things to Come 2016

Hurd-Wood, Rachel (1990–) Peter Pan 2003; An American Haunting 2005; Perfume: the Story of a Murderer 2006; Dorian Gray 2009; Solomon Kane 2009; Tomorrow, When the War Began 2010

Hurlbut, Gladys (1898–1988) The Long, Long Trailer 1954; A Man Called Peter 1955

Hurley, Elizabeth (1965–) Aria 1987; Passenger 57 1992; Beyond Bedlam 1993; Mad Dogs and Englishmen 1994; The Shamrock Conspiracy 1995; Dangerous Ground 1996; Austin Powers: International Man of Mystery 1997; Permanent Midnight 1998; Austin Powers: The Spy Who Shagged Me 1999; Edtv 1999; My Favorite Martian 1999; Bedazzled 2000; The Weight of Water 2000; Dawg 2001; Double Whammy 2001; Serving Sara 2002

Hursey, Sherry (1940–) Friendly Fire 1979; Mrs Lambert Remembers Love 1991; Bring It On 2000

Hurst, Brandon (1866–1947) Dr Jekyll and Mr Hyde 1920; The Hunchback of Notre Dame 1923; The Thief of Bagdad 1924; Annie Laurie 1927; Love 1927; Murders in the Rue Morgue 1932

Hurst, Paul (1888–1953) Bad Company 1931; The Secret Six 1931; The Sphinx 1933; Topper Takes a Trip 1939; The Westerner 1940; Girl Rush 1944

Hurst, Ryan (1976–) Remember the Titans 2000; Lone Star State of Mind 2002; The Ladykillers 2004

Hurst, Veronica (1931–) Laughter in Paradise 1951; Angels One Five 1952; The Maze 1953; Will Any Gentleman...? 1953; Bang! You're Dead 1954; The Gilded Cage 1954; Dead Man's Evidence 1962; Licensed to Kill 1965

Hurt, John (1940–) The Wild and the Willing 1962; This Is My Street 1963; A Man for All Seasons 1966; Before Winter Comes 1968; Sinful Davey 1969; In Search of Gregory 1970; 10 Rillington

Place 1970; The Ghoul 1975; East of Elephant Rock 1976; The Disappearance 1977; The Lord of the Rings 1978; Midnight Express 1978; The Shout 1978; Watership Down 1978; Alien 1979; The Elephant Man 1980; Heaven's Gate 1980; Night Crossing 1981; Partners 1982; The Plague Dogs 1982; Champions 1983; The Osterman Weekend 1983; The Hit 1984; Nineteen Eighty-Four 1984; Success Is the Best Revenge 1984; After Darkness 1985; The Black Cauldron 1985; Rocinante 1986; Aria 1987; From the Hip 1987; Spaceballs 1987; Vincent: the Life and Death of Vincent Van Gogh 1987; White Mischief 1987; Scandal 1988; Windprints 1989; The Field 1990; Frankenstein Unbound 1990; King Ralph 1991; Lapse of Memory 1992; Even Cowgirls Get the Blues 1993; Second Best 1993; Dead Man 1995; Rob Roy 1995; Wild Bill 1995; Contact 1997; All the Little Animals 1998; Love and Death on Long Island 1998; Night Train 1998; A Monkey's Tale 1999; You're Dead 1999; Lost Souls 2000; The Tigger Movie 2000; Captain Corelli's Mandolin 2001; Harry Potter and the Philosopher's Stone 2001; Miranda 2001; Owning Mahowny 2002; Hellboy 2004; The Proposition 2004; Shooting Dogs 2005; The Skeleton Key 2005; V for Vendetta 2005; Valiant 2005; Perfume: the Story of a Murderer 2006; Hellboy II: the Golden Army 2008; Indiana Jones and the Kingdom of the Crystal Skull 2008; The Limits of Control 2008; Outlander 2008; The Oxford Murders 2008; Recount 2008; 44 Inch Chest 2009; New York, I Love You 2009; Brighton Rock 2010; Harry Potter and the Deathly Hallows: Part 1 2010; A Turtle's Tale: Sammy's Adventures 2010; Harry Potter and the Deathly Hallows: Part 2 2011; Immortals 2011; In Love with Alma Cogan 2011; Melancholia 2011; Tinker Tailor Soldier Spy 2011; Jayne Mansfield's Car 2012; More than Honey 2012; Benjamin Britten: Peace and Conflict 2013; Only Lovers Left Alive 2013; Snowpiercer 2013; Thomas & Friends – Sodor's Legend of the Lost Treasure: the Movie 2015; That Good Night 2017

Hurt, Mary Beth (1948–) Interiors 1978; Chilly Scenes of Winter 1979; A Change of Seasons 1980; The World According to Garp 1982; Compromising Positions 1985; DARYL 1985; Parents 1988; Slaves of New York 1989; Defenseless 1991; Light Sleeper 1991; The Age of Innocence 1993; My Boyfriend's Back 1993; Six Degrees of Separation 1993; Affliction 1997; Bringing Out the Dead 1999; No Ordinary Baby 2001; The Exorcism of Emily Rose 2005; Untraceable 2008

Hurt, William (1950–) Altered States 1980; Body Heat 1981; Eyewitness 1981; The Big Chill 1983; Gorky Park 1983; Kiss of the Spider Woman 1985; Children of a Lesser God 1986; Broadcast News 1987; The Accidental Tourist 1988; A Time of Destiny 1988; Alice 1990; I Love You to Death 1990; The Doctor 1991; Until the End of the World 1991; Mr Wonderful 1992; The Plague 1992; Second Best 1993; Trial by Jury 1994; Smoke 1995; Jane Eyre 1996; Loved 1996; Michael 1996; Dark City 1998; Lost in Space 1998; One True Thing 1998; The Proposition 1998; The Miracle Maker 1999; Sunshine 1999; Contagion 2000; The Simian Line 2000; Varian's War 2000; AI: Artificial Intelligence 2001; Changing Lanes 2002; Tuck Everlasting 2002; The Village 2004; A History of Violence 2005; Hunt for Justice 2005; The King 2005; Syriana 2005; The Good Shepherd 2006; Into the Wild 2007; Mr Brooks 2007; The Incredible Hulk 2008; Vantage Point 2008; Robin Hood 2010; Too Big to Fail 2011; The Host 2013; A New York Winter's Tale 2014; Race 2016

Huss, Toby Down Periscope 1996; Bedazzled 2000

Hussain, Adil Ishqiya 2010; Life of Pi 2012

Hussain (1), Nasir Parineeta 1953; Devdas 1955; Naya Daur 1957

Hussenot, Olivier (1913–1978) Fanfan la Tulipe 1951; Maigret Sets a Trap 1957

Hussey, Olivia (1951–) The Battle of the Villa Fiorita 1965; Romeo and Juliet 1968; All the Right Noises 1970; Lost Horizon 1973; Black Christmas 1974; Death on the Nile 1978; The Cat and the Canary 1979; The Man with Bogart's Face 1980; Virus 1980; Turkey Shoot 1981; Psycho IV: the Beginning 1990

Hussey, Ruth (1911–2005) Man-Proof 1937; Another Thin Man 1939; Blackmail 1939; Fast and Furious 1939;

Maisie 1939; Flight Command 1940; Northwest Passage 1940; The Philadelphia Story 1940; Susan and God 1940; HM Pulham Esq 1941; Tennessee Johnson 1942; Tender Comrade 1943; Marine Raiders 1944; The Uninvited 1944; The Great Gatsby 1949; Mr Music 1950; That's My Boy 1951; Stars and Stripes Forever 1952; The Lady Wants Mink 1953; The Facts of Life 1960

Huster, Francis (1947–) Second Chance 1976; Another Man, Another Chance 1977; Edith et Marcel 1983; La Femme Publique 1984; Le Dîner de Cons 1998

Huston, Anjelica (1951–) Hamlet 1969; Sinful Davey 1969; A Walk with Love and Death 1969; The Last Tycoon 1976; Swashbuckler 1976; The Postman Always Rings Twice 1981; The Ice Pirates 1984; This Is Spinal Tap 1984; Prizzi's Honor 1985; The Dead 1987; Gardens of Stone 1987; A Handful of Dust 1987; Mr North 1988; Crimes and Misdemeanors 1989; Enemies, a Love Story 1989; The Witches 1989; The Grifters 1990; The Addams Family 1991; Addams Family Values 1993; And the Band Played On 1993; Manhattan Murder Mystery 1993; The Crossing Guard 1995; The Perez Family 1995; Buffalo '66 1998; Ever After: a Cinderella Story 1998; Phoenix 1998; Agnes Browne 1999; The Golden Bowl 2000; The Man from Elysian Fields 2001; The Royal Tenenbaums 2001; Blood Work 2002; Daddy Day Care 2003; Iron Jawed Angels 2004; The Life Aquatic with Steve Zissou 2004; Material Girls 2006; Seraphim Falls 2006; These Foolish Things 2006; The Darjeeling Limited 2007; Choke 2008; The Kreutzer Sonata 2008; Tinker Bell 2008; When in Rome 2009; A Cat in Paris 2010; The Big Year 2011; 50/50 2011; Horrid Henry: the Movie 2011; Tinkerbell and the Secret of the Wings 2012; Tinker Bell and the Legend of the NeverBeast 2014

Huston, Danny (1962–) Anna Karenina 1997; ivansxtc. 1999; Hotel 2001; 21 Grams 2003; The Aviator 2004; Birth 2004; The Proposition 2004; Silver City 2004; Alpha Male 2006; The Constant Gardener 2005; Children of Men 2006; Fade to Black 2006; The Number 23 2006; 30 Days of Night 2007; How to Lose Friends & Alienate People 2008; The Kreutzer Sonata 2008; Boogie Woogie 2009; Edge of Darkness 2009; X-Men Origins: Wolverine 2009; Clash of the Titans 2010; The Conspirator 2010; Robin Hood 2010; The Warrior's Way 2010; A Monster in Paris 2011; Boxing Day 2012; Stolen 2012; Wrath of the Titans 2012; The Congress 2013; Big Eyes 2014; Frankenstein 2015; Pressure 2015

Huston, Jack (1982–) Factory Girl 2006; Shrooms 2006; Outlander 2008; Boogie Woogie 2009; The Hot Potato 2011; Kill Your Darlings 2013; Night Train to Lisbon 2013; The Longest Ride 2015; Pride and Prejudice and Zombies 2015; Ben-Hur 2016

Huston, John (1906–1987) The Treasure of the Sierra Madre 1947; The Cardinal 1963; The List of Adrian Messenger 1963; The Bible... in the Beginning 1966; Casino Royale 1967; Candy 1968; De Sade 1969; Myra Breckinridge 1970; The Deserter 1971; Man in the Wilderness 1971; The Life and Times of Judge Roy Bean 1972; Battle for the Planet of the Apes 1973; Chinatown 1974; Breakout 1975; The Wind and the Lion 1975; Sherlock Holmes in New York 1976; Tentacles 1977; Winter Kills 1979; Wise Blood 1979; Head on 1980; The Visitor 1980; Cannery Row 1982; The Black Cauldron 1985; Mr Corbett's Ghost 1986

Huston, Virginia (1925–1981) Nocturne 1946; Build My Gallows High 1947; Flamingo Road 1949; Flight to Mars 1951; Tarzan's Peril 1951

Huston, Walter (1884–1950) The Virginian 1929; Abraham Lincoln 1930; The Criminal Code 1930; The Virtuous Sin 1930; American Madness 1932; The Beast of the City 1932; Law and Order 1932; Rain 1932; The Wet Parade 1932; Ann Vickers 1933; Gabriel over the White House 1933; The Prizefighter and the Lady 1933; Dodsworth 1936; Rhodes of Africa 1936; Of Human Hearts 1938; The Light That Failed 1939; The Devil and Daniel Webster 1941; The Shanghai Gesture 1941; Swamp Water 1941; Always in My Heart 1942; In This Our Life 1942; Yankee Doodle Dandy 1942; The Battle of Russia 1943; Edge of Darkness 1943; Mission to Moscow 1943; The North Star 1943; The Outlaw 1943; Prelude to War 1943; Dragon Seed 1944; And

Then There Were None 1945; Dragonwyck 1946; Duel in the Sun 1946; The Treasure of the Sierra Madre 1947; Summer Holiday 1948; The Great Sinner 1949; The Furies 1950

Hutchence, Michael (1960–1997) Dogs in Space 1986; Frankenstein Unbound 1990

Hutcherson, Josh (1992–) Howl's Moving Castle 2004; Kicking & Screaming 2005; Little Manhattan 2005; Zathura: a Space Adventure 2005; Bridge to Terabithia 2006; Firehouse Dog 2006; RV 2006; Fragments 2008; Journey to the Center of the Earth 2008; Cirque du Freak: the Vampire's Assistant 2009; The Kids Are All Right 2010; Journey 2 the Mysterious Island 2011; The Hunger Games 2012; Red Dawn 2012; 7 Days in Havana 2012; Epic 2013; Escobar: Paradise Lost 2014; The Hunger Games: Catching Fire 2013; The Hunger Games: Mockingjay Part 1 2014; The Hunger Games: Mockingjay Part 2 2015

Hutcheson, David (1905–1976) The Love Test 1935; The Life and Death of Colonel Blimp 1943; Vice Versa 1947; Woman Hater 1948

Hutchings, Geoffrey (1939–2010) Clockwise 1986; Wish You Were Here 1987; It's All about Love 2002; She, a Chinese 2009

Hutchins, Will (1932–) No Time for Sergeants 1958; Merrill's Marauders 1962; Clambake 1967; The Shooting 1967

Hutchinson, Josephine (1903–1998) The Story of Louis Pasteur 1936; Son of Frankenstein 1939; My Son, My Son! 1940; Tom Brown's Schooldays 1940; Somewhere in the Night 1946; Adventure in Baltimore 1949; Love Is Better than Ever 1951; Ruby Gentry 1952; Miracle in the Rain 1956; Gun for a Coward 1957; Sing, Boy, Sing 1958; Walk like a Dragon 1960; Baby the Rain Must Fall 1965

Hutchison, Doug (1960–) The Chocolate War 1988; The Green Mile 1999; No Good Deed 2002; The Salton Sea 2002; Punisher: War Zone 2008

Hutchison, Fiona (1960–) Biggles 1986; American Gothic 1987

Hutchison, Ken Straw Dogs 1971; The Wrath of God 1972; Sweeney 2 1978; Ladyhawke 1985; Blonde Fist 1991

Huth, Harold (1892–1967) A Honeymoon Adventure 1931; Rome Express 1932; The Ghoul 1933; The Camels Are Coming 1934

Hutton, Betty (1921–2007) The Fleet's In 1942; Star Spangled Rhythm 1942; Happy Go Lucky 1943; Let's Face It 1943; The Miracle of Morgan's Creek 1943; And the Angels Sing 1944; Here Come the Waves 1944; Duffy's Tavern 1945; Incendiary Blonde 1945; The Stork Club 1945; Dream Girl 1948; Annie Get Your Gun 1950; Let's Dance 1950; Sailor Beware 1951; The Greatest Show on Earth 1952; Somebody Loves Me 1952; Spring Reunion 1957

Hutton, Jim (1934–1979) The Subterraneans 1960; Where the Boys Are 1960; Bachelor in Paradise 1961; The Horizontal Lieutenant 1962; Period of Adjustment 1962; The Hallelujah Trail 1965; Major Dundee 1965; Never Too Late 1965; Walk, Don't Run 1966; Who's Minding the Mint? 1967; The Green Berets 1968; Don't Be Afraid of the Dark 1973

Hutton, Lauren (1943–) Paper Lion 1968; Pieces of Dreams 1970; The Gambler 1974; Gator 1976; Welcome to LA 1976; Viva Knievel! 1977; Someone's Watching Me! 1978; American Gigolo 1980; Paternity 1981; Zorro, the Gay Blade 1981; Starflight One 1983; Lassiter 1984; Once Bitten 1985; Malone 1987; Guilty as Charged 1991; My Father the Hero 1994; The Joneses 2009

Hutton, Marion (1919–1987) Orchestra Wives 1942; Abbott and Costello in Society 1944; Love Happy 1949

Hutton, Robert (1920–1994) Destination Tokyo 1943; Hollywood Canteen 1944; Roughly Speaking 1945; Time Out of Mind 1947; and Baby Makes Three 1949; The Man on the Eiffel Tower 1949; The Younger Brothers 1949; The Racket 1951; The Steel Helmet 1951; Man from Tangier 1957; The Colossus of New York 1958; Showdown at Boot Hill 1958; Cinderfella 1960; The Sicilians 1964; They Came from beyond Space 1967; Torture Garden 1967

1990; The Dark Half 1991; Mr and Mrs Loving 1993; The Temp 1993; French Kiss 1995; Beautiful Girls 1996; City of Industry 1996; The Substance of Fire 1996; Playing God 1997; Aldrich Ames: Traitor Within 1998; Deterrence 1999; The General's Daughter 1999; Sunshine State 2002; Kinsey 2004; Secret Window 2004; The Good Shepherd 2006; The Kovak Box 2006; Last Holiday 2006; The Last Mimzy 2007; Lymelife 2008; The Ghost 2010

Huxtable, Judy The Psychopath 1966; Scream and Scream Again 1969

Hwang Jang Lee aka **Huang Cheng Li** Drunken Master 1978; Snake in the Eagle's Shadow 1978

Hyams, Leila (1905–1977) Spite Marriage 1929; The Big House 1930; The Big Broadcast 1932; Freaks 1932; Island of Lost Souls 1932; Red-Headed Woman 1932; Ruggles of Red Gap 1935

Hyde-White, Alex (1958–) Biggles 1986; The Phantom of the Opera 1989; Time Trackers 1989; Pretty Woman 1990

Hyde White, Wilfrid aka **Hyde-White, Wilfrid** (1903–1991) Elephant Boy 1937; Poison Pen 1939; It's Turned Out Nice Again 1941; The Demi-Paradise 1943; While the Sun Shines 1946; The Winslow Boy 1948; Adam and Evelyne 1949; Britannia Mews 1949; Conspirator 1949; Golden Salamander 1949; The Man on the Eiffel Tower 1949; The Third Man 1949; Highly Dangerous 1950; Last Holiday 1950; Mr Drake's Duck 1950; Trio 1950; The Browning Version 1951; Mr Denning Drives North 1951; The Million Pound Note 1953; The Story of Gilbert and Sullivan 1953; Betrayed 1954; Duel in the Jungle 1954; The Rainbow Jacket 1954; To Dorothy, a Son 1954; John and Julie 1955; Quentin Durward 1955; The March Hare 1956; My Teenage Daughter 1956; Tarzan and the Lost Safari 1956; That Woman Opposite 1957; The Vicious Circle 1957; Up the Creek 1958; Carry On Nurse 1959; Libel 1959; Life in Emergency Ward 10 1959; North West Frontier 1959; His and Hers 1960; Let's Make Love 1960; Two Way Stretch 1960; Ada 1961; In Search of the Castaways 1961; On the Double 1961; On the Fiddle 1961; Crooks Anonymous 1962; John Goldfarb, Please Come Home 1964; My Fair Lady 1964; Ten Little Indians 1965; You Must Be Joking! 1965; Chamber of Horrors 1966; The Liquidator 1966; Our Man in Marrakesh 1966; The Sandwich Man 1966; Sumuru 1967; Gaily, Gaily 1969; The Magic Christian 1969; Skullduggery 1969; Fragment of Fear 1970; The Cat and the Canary 1979; A Touch of the Sun 1979; In God We Trust 1980; Oh God! Book II 1980; Tarzan, the Ape Man 1981; The Toy 1982; Fanny Hill 1983

Hyde, Jonathan (1947–) Deadly Advice 1993; Being Human 1994; Richie Rich 1994; Jumanji 1995; Anaconda 1997; The Mummy 1999; The Contract 2006; Land of the Blind 2006

Hyer, Martha (1924–2014) Thunder Mountain 1947; The Clay Pigeon 1949; Roughshod 1949; Abbott and Costello Go to Mars 1953; So Big 1953; Cry Vengeance 1954; Down Three Dark Streets 1954; Lucky Me 1954; Sabrina 1954; Francis in the Navy 1955; Kiss of Fire 1955; Wyoming Renegades 1955; Red Sundown 1956; Showdown at Abilene 1956; Battle Hymn 1957; The Delicate Delinquent 1957; Mister Cory 1957; My Man Godfrey 1957; Houseboat 1958; Paris Holiday 1958; Some Came Running 1958; The Best of Everything 1959; The Big Fisherman 1959; Desire in the Dust 1960; Ice Palace 1960; A Girl Named Tamiko 1962; The Man from the Diner's Club 1963; Bikini Beach 1964; The Carpetbaggers 1964; First Men in the Moon 1964; The Sons of Katie Elder 1965; The Happening 1967; House of a Thousand Dolls 1967; Crossplot 1969

Hyland, Diana (1936–1977) One Man's Way 1964; Jigsaw 1968; The Boy in the Plastic Bubble 1976

Hylands, Scott (1943–) Daddy's Gone A-Hunting 1969; Fools 1970; Bittersweet Love 1976; The Boys in Company C 1978; Freefall: Flight 174 1995; The Accidental Witness 2006

Hylton, Jane (1926–1979) Daybreak 1946; It Always Rains on Sunday 1947; Here Come the Huggetts 1948; My Brother's Keeper 1948; Dance Hall 1950; The Quiet Woman 1950; It Started in Paradise 1952; The Weak and the Wicked 1953; You Pay Your Money 1957; Circus of Horrors 1960; House of Mystery 1961

Hylton, Richard (1920–1962) Halls of Montezuma 1950; Fixed Bayonets! 1951; The Pride of St Louis 1952

Hymer, Warren (1906-1948) *Born Reckless* 1930; *Men without Women* 1930; *Up the River* 1930; *One Way Passage* 1932; *20,000 Years in Sing Sing* 1933; *She Loves Me Not* 1934; *Confidential* 1935; *Mr Deeds Goes to Town* 1936; *Rhythm on the Range* 1936; *You Only Live Once* 1937; *Bluebeard's Eighth Wife* 1938; *You and Me* 1938; *Destry Rides Again* 1939; *Mr Moto in Danger Island* 1939; *The Birth of the Blues* 1941; *Baby Face Morgan* 1942
Hynde, Chrissie *Rugrats Go Wild* 2003; *New York Doll* 2005
Hynes, Tyler *Home Team* 1998; *Mom at Sixteen* 2005
Hyson, Dorothy (1914-1996) *The Ghoul* 1933; *Sing as We Go* 1934; *Spare a Copper* 1940
Hytten, Olaf (1888-1955) *Kitty* 1928; *Blond Cheat* 1938; *Bells of San Angelo* 1947

I

Ibarra, Mirta aka **Ibarra, Mirtha** *Strawberry and Chocolate* 1993; *Guantanamera* 1995; *7 Days in Havana* 2012
Ice Cube (1969-) *Boyz N the Hood* 1991; *Trespass* 1992; *CB4* 1993; *Friday* 1995; *The Glass Shield* 1995; *Higher Learning* 1995; *Dangerous Ground* 1996; *Anaconda* 1997; *I Got the Hook Up* 1998; *The Players Club* 1998; *Next Friday* 1999; *Three Kings* 1999; *John Carpenter's Ghosts of Mars* 2001; *Barbershop* 2002; *Torque* 2003; *Barbershop 2: Back in Business* 2004; *Are We There Yet?* 2005; *xXx: the Next Level* 2005; *Are We Done Yet?* 2007; *First Sunday* 2008; *Rampart* 2011; *Something from Nothing: the Art of Rap* 2012; *21 Jump Street* 2012; *Book of Life* 2014; *Ride Along* 2014; *22 Jump Street* 2014; *Barbershop: a Fresh Cut* 2016; *Ride Along 2* 2016
Ice-T aka **Ice T** (1958-) *New Jack City* 1991; *Ricochet* 1991; *Trespass* 1992; *CB4* 1993; *Who's the Man?* 1993; *Surviving the Game* 1994; *Johnny Mnemonic* 1995; *Tank Girl* 1995; *Jacob Two Two Meets the Hooded Fang* 1999; *Judgment Day* 1999; *Stealth Fighter* 1999; *Guardian* 2000; *Luck of the Draw* 2000; *Hood Rat* 2001; *Good Hair* 2009; *Something from Nothing: the Art of Rap* 2012
Ichikawa, Raizo (1931-1969) *Tales of the Taira Clan* 1955; *Conflagration* 1958
Ichikawa, Yui (1986-) *The Grudge: Ju-On* 2003; *Ju-On: The Grudge 2* 2003
Idle, Eric (1943-) *And Now for Something Completely Different* 1971; *Monty Python and the Holy Grail* 1975; *The Rutles - All You Need Is Cash* 1978; *Monty Python's Life of Brian* 1979; *Monty Python Live at the Hollywood Bowl* 1982; *Monty Python's The Meaning of Life* 1983; *Yellowbeard* 1983; *National Lampoon's European Vacation* 1985; *Transformers - the Movie* 1986; *The Adventures of Baron Munchausen* 1988; *Nuns on the Run* 1990; *Too Much Sun* 1990; *Mom and Dad Save the World* 1992; *Splitting Heirs* 1993; *Casper* 1995; *The Wind in the Willows* 1996; *Burn Hollywood Burn* 1997; *The Magic Sword: Quest for Camelot* 1997; *Rudolph the Red-Nosed Reindeer* 1998; *The Secret of NIMH II: Timmy to the Rescue* 1998; *Dudley Do-Right* 1999; *South Park: Bigger, Longer & Uncut* 1999; *102 Dalmatians* 2000; *Ella Enchanted* 2004; *Not the Messiah: He's a Very Naughty Boy* 2009; *Shrek Forever After* 2010; *Absolutely Anything* 2015
Ifans, Rhys (1968-) *Heart* 1997; *Twin Town* 1997; *Dancing at Lughnasa* 1998; *Janice Beard 45 WPM* 1999; *Notting Hill* 1999; *Rancid Aluminium* 1999; *You're Dead* 1999; *Kevin & Perry Go Large* 2000; *Little Nicky* 2000; *Love, Honour and Obey* 2000; *The Replacements* 2000; *Christmas Carol: the Movie* 2001; *The 51st State* 2001; *Hotel* 2001; *Human Nature* 2001; *The Shipping News* 2001; *Once upon a Time in the Midlands* 2002; *Danny Deckchair* 2003; *Enduring Love* 2004; *Vanity Fair* 2004; *Chromophobia* 2005; *Hannibal Rising* 2006; *Elizabeth: the Golden Age* 2007; *The Boat That Rocked* 2009; *Greenberg* 2009; *Exit through the Gift Shop* 2010; *Mr Nice* 2010; *Nanny McPhee & the Big Bang* 2010; *Anonymous* 2011; *The Amazing Spider-Man* 2012; *The Five-Year Engagement* 2012; *Serena* 2013; *Madame Bovary* 2014; *She's Funny That Way* 2014; *Under Milk Wood* 2015

Igawa, Hisashi (1936-) *Pitfall* 1962; *Dodes'ka-Den* 1970; *Ran* 1985; *Boiling Point* 1990; *Rhapsody in August* 1990; *No, Not Yet* 1993
Iglesias, Eugene aka **Iglesias, Gene** (1926-) *The Brave Bulls* 1951; *The Duel at Silver Creek* 1952; *Taza, Son of Cochise* 1954; *The Naked Dawn* 1955; *Underwater!* 1955
Ihnat, Steve (1934-1972) *Countdown* 1967; *Hour of the Gun* 1967; *Zigzag* 1970
Iida, Choko (1897-1972) *Tokyo Chorus* 1931; *The Only Son* 1936; *Record of a Tenement Gentleman* 1947
Ilkley, William *Paper Marriage* 1991; *The Jealous God* 2005
Illig, Rolf (1925-2005) *Alpine Fire* 1985; *Salt on Our Skin* 1992
Illing, Peter (1899-1966) *Eureka Stockade* 1949; *Outcast of the Islands* 1951; *Mask of Dust* 1954; *The Battle of the River Plate* 1956; *Bhowani Junction* 1956; *Passport to Treason* 1956; *Miracle in Soho* 1957; *The Angry Hills* 1959; *Sands of the Desert* 1960; *Echo of Diana* 1963; *Devils of Darkness* 1964
Ilyin, Vladimir (1947-) *Lost in Siberia* 1991; *The Life and Extraordinary Adventures of Private Ivan Chonkin* 1994; *The Stringer* 1997
Iman (1955-) *The Human Factor* 1979; *No Way Out* 1986; *Surrender* 1987; *House Party 2* 1991; *The Linguini Incident* 1991; *Star Trek VI: The Undiscovered Country* 1991; *Exit to Eden* 1994
Imhof, Roger (1875-1958) *The Farmer Takes a Wife* 1935; *Riffraff* 1936
Imperioli, Michael (1966-) *Household Saints* 1993; *Hand Gun* 1994; *Postcards from America* 1994; *Sweet Nothing* 1995; *Girl 6* 1996; *Last Man Standing* 1996; *Shark Tale* 2004; *The Lovely Bones* 2009; *Old Boy* 2013
Imrie, Celia (1952-) *Blue Black Permanent* 1992; *In the Bleak Midwinter* 1995; *The Borrowers* 1997; *Hilary and Jackie* 1998; *Star Wars Episode I: the Phantom Menace* 1999; *Bridget Jones's Diary* 2001; *Revelation* 2001; *Heartlands* 2002; *Thunderpants* 2002; *Calendar Girls* 2003; *Imagine Me and You* 2005; *Nanny McPhee* 2005; *Wah-Wah* 2005; *St Trinian's* 2007; *St Trinian's 2: the Legend of Fritton's Gold* 2009; *Acts of Godfrey* 2011; *The Best Exotic Marigold Hotel* 2011; *The Love Punch* 2013; *Nativity 3: Dude Where's My Donkey* 2014; *What We Did on Our Holiday* 2014; *Molly Moon and the Incredible Book of Hypnotism* 2015; *The Second Best Exotic Marigold Hotel* 2015; *Absolutely Fabulous: the Movie* 2016; *Bridget Jones's Baby* 2016
Inaba, Yoshio (1921-1998) *Seven Samurai* 1954; *Harakiri* 1962
Ince, Ralph (1881-1937) *Little Caesar* 1931; *Law and Order* 1932
Inclan, Miguel (1900-1956) *Fort Apache* 1948; *Indian Uprising* 1951
Inescort, Frieda (1900-1976) *If You Could Only Cook* 1935; *Another Dawn* 1937; *The Great O'Malley* 1937; *Beauty for the Asking* 1939; *Tarzan Finds a Son!* 1939; *Pride and Prejudice* 1940; *Sunny* 1941; *You'll Never Get Rich* 1941; *Mission to Moscow* 1943; *The Return of the Vampire* 1943; *The Judge Steps Out* 1949; *The Eddy Duchin Story* 1956; *Senior Prom* 1958; *The Alligator People* 1959
Ineson, Ralph *Shooting Fish* 1997; *Cass* 2008; *The Witch* 2015
Ingham, Barrie (1932-2015) *Dr Who and the Daleks* 1965; *A Challenge for Robin Hood* 1967; *Basil the Great Mouse Detective* 1986
Ingleby, Lee *Master and Commander: the Far Side of the World* 2003; *Doghouse* 2009
Ingram (2), Rex (1895-1969) *The Adventures of Huckleberry Finn* 1939; *The Thief of Bagdad* 1940; *Cabin in the Sky* 1943; *Sahara* 1943; *Dark Waters* 1944; *A Thousand and One Nights* 1945; *Moonrise* 1948; *Anna Lucasta* 1958; *Escort West* 1959; *Your Cheatin' Heart* 1964
Ingrassia, Ciccio (1923-2003) *Dr Goldfoot and the Girl Bombs* 1966; *Amarcord* 1973; *Kaos* 1984
Inkijinoff, Valery aka **Inkishinov, Valeri** (1895-1973) *Storm over Asia* 1928; *The Indian Tomb* 1959; *The Tiger of Eschnapur* 1959; *Up to His Ears* 1965
Innes, George (1938-) *Gumshoe* 1971; *Master and Commander: the Far Side of the World* 2003; *Things to Do before You're 30* 2004
Innes, Neil (1944-) *The Rutles - All You Need Is Cash* 1978; *Monty Python Live at the Hollywood Bowl* 1982
Interlenghi, Franco (1931-2015) *Shoeshine* 1946; *Sunday in August* 1949; *The Little World of Don Camillo*

1951; *The Vanquished* 1953; *I Vitelloni* 1953
Irani, Boman *Being Cyrus* 2005; *Well Done Abba* 2009
Irby, Michael *Piñero* 2001; *Law Abiding Citizen* 2009
Ireland, Anthony (1902-1957) *Jump for Glory* 1937; *The Gambler and the Lady* 1952
Ireland, Celia *Dad and Dave: on Our Selection* 1995; *My Mother Frank* 2000
Ireland, Jill (1936-1990) *The Big Money* 1956; *Three Men in a Boat* 1956; *Hell Drivers* 1957; *Robbery under Arms* 1957; *Twice round the Daffodils* 1962; *Rider on the Rain* 1970; *Cold Sweat* 1971; *Someone behind the Door* 1971; *The Mechanic* 1972; *The Valachi Papers* 1972; *The Valdez Horses* 1973; *Breakout* 1975; *Hard Times* 1975; *Breakheart Pass* 1976; *Love and Bullets* 1978; *Death Wish II* 1981; *Assassination* 1986
Ireland, John (1914-1992) *A Walk in the Sun* 1945; *My Darling Clementine* 1946; *Railroaded!* 1947; *Raw Deal* 1948; *Red River* 1948; *A Southern Yankee* 1948; *All the King's Men* 1949; *Anna Lucasta* 1949; *I Shot Jesse James* 1949; *Roughshod* 1949; *The Walking Hills* 1949; *Red Mountain* 1951; *The Scarf* 1951; *Vengeance Valley* 1951; *Hurricane Smith* 1952; *The 49th Man* 1953; *The Good Die Young* 1954; *Southwest Passage* 1954; *The Glass Cage* 1955; *Queen Bee* 1955; *Gunfight at the OK Corral* 1957; *Party Girl* 1958; *Faces in the Dark* 1960; *Wild in the Country* 1961; *The Ceremony* 1963; *55 Days at Peking* 1963; *The Fall of the Roman Empire* 1964; *I Saw What You Did* 1965; *Arizona Bushwhackers* 1968; *The Adventurers* 1970; *The House of Seven Corpses* 1973; *Welcome to Arrow Beach* 1974; *Farewell, My Lovely* 1975; *The Swiss Conspiracy* 1975; *Maniac* 1977; *Tomorrow Never Comes* 1977; *Martin's Day* 1984; *Thunder Run* 1986
Ireland, Kathy (1963-) *Journey to the Center of the Earth* 1989; *Mom and Dad Save the World* 1992; *Amore!* 1993; *National Lampoon's Loaded Weapon 1* 1993
Ireland, Kenny (1945-2014) *The Big Man* 1990; *Blinded* 2004
Irons, Jeremy (1948-) *The French Lieutenant's Woman* 1981; *Betrayal* 1982; *Moonlighting* 1982; *The Wild Duck* 1983; *Swann in Love* 1984; *The Mission* 1986; *A Chorus of Disapproval* 1988; *Dead Ringers* 1988; *Australia* 1989; *Danny, the Champion of the World* 1989; *Reversal of Fortune* 1990; *Kafka* 1991; *Damage* 1992; *Waterland* 1992; *The House of the Spirits* 1993; *M Butterfly* 1993; *The Lion King* 1994; *Die Hard with a Vengeance* 1995; *Stealing Beauty* 1995; *Chinese Box* 1997; *Lolita* 1997; *The Man in the Iron Mask* 1997; *Dungeons & Dragons* 2000; *The Fourth Angel* 2001; *And Now... Ladies and Gentlemen* 2002; *Callas Forever* 2002; *The Time Machine* 2002; *Being Julia* 2004; *William Shakespeare's The Merchant of Venice* 2004; *Casanova* 2005; *Kingdom of Heaven* 2005; *Eragon* 2006; *Inland Empire* 2006; *Appaloosa* 2008; *Georgia O'Keeffe* 2009; *The Pink Panther 2* 2009; *Margin Call* 2011; *Trashed* 2012; *The Words* 2012; *Beautiful Creatures* 2013; *Night Train to Lisbon* 2013; *High-Rise* 2015; *The Man Who Knew Infinity* 2015; *Assassin's Creed* 2016; *Batman v Superman: Dawn of Justice* 2016; *Race* 2016
Irons, Max (1985-) *Red Riding Hood* 2011; *The Host* 2013; *The Riot Club* 2014; *Woman in Gold* 2015
Ironside, Michael (1950-) *Scanners* 1980; *Spacehunter: Adventures in the Forbidden Zone* 1983; *Top Gun* 1986; *Extreme Prejudice* 1987; *Nowhere to Hide* 1987; *Watchers* 1988; *Highlander II: the Quickening* 1990; *Total Recall* 1990; *Chaindance* 1991; *Guncrazy* 1992; *A Passion for Murder* 1992; *The Vagrant* 1992; *Father Hood* 1993; *The Next Karate Kid* 1994; *The Glass Shield* 1995; *Starship Troopers* 1997; *Chicago Cab* 1998; *Desert Blue* 1998; *Crime + Punishment in Suburbia* 2000; *The Machinist* 2003; *Guy X* 2005; *Reeker* 2005; *Surveillance* 2007; *Extraterrestrial* 2014; *Turbo Kid* 2014
Irvine, Jeremy (1990-) *War Horse* 2011; *Great Expectations* 2012; *Now Is Good* 2012; *The Railway Man* 2013; *Beyond the Reach* 2014; *The Woman in Black: Angel of Death* 2014; *The Bad Education Movie* 2015; *Stonewall* 2015
Irvine, Robin (1901-1933) *Downhill* 1927; *Easy Virtue* 1927; *The Ship of Lost Men* 1929
Irving, Amy (1953-) *Carrie* 1976; *The Fury* 1978; *Honeysuckle Rose* 1980;

Yentl 1983; *Micki & Maude* 1984; *Rumpelstiltskin* 1986; *Crossing Delancey* 1988; *Who Framed Roger Rabbit* 1988; *A Show of Force* 1990; *An American Tail: Fievel Goes West* 1991; *Benefit of the Doubt* 1993; *Acts of Love* 1995; *I'm Not Rappaport* 1996; *Deconstructing Harry* 1997; *The Confession* 1999; *The Rage: Carrie 2* 1999; *Traffic* 2000; *Thirteen Conversations about One Thing* 2001; *Tuck Everlasting* 2002; *Hide and Seek* 2005; *Adam* 2009
Irving, George (1874-1961) *Bringing Up Baby* 1938; *Maid's Night Out* 1938
Irving, Margaret (1898-1988) *Charlie Chan at the Opera* 1936; *Abbott and Costello in Society* 1944
Irwin, Bill aka **Irwin, William** (1950-) *My Blue Heaven* 1990; *Scenes from a Mall* 1991; *Stepping Out* 1991; *Subway Stories: Tales from the Underground* 1997; *The Grinch* 2000; *Rachel Getting Married* 2008
Irwin, Charles (1887-1969) *Bob, Son of Battle* 1947; *The Iron Glove* 1954
Irwin, Steve (1962-2006) *The Crocodile Hunter: Collision Course* 2002; *Happy Feet* 2006
Irwin, Tom (1956-) *Deceived* 1991; *Mr Jones* 1993; *Holiday Affair* 1996; *No Higher Love* 1999; *Snow White* 2001
Isaac, Oscar (1979-) *The Nativity Story* 2006; *The Life before Her Eyes* 2007; *Body of Lies* 2008; *Agora* 2009; *Robin Hood* 2010; *Drive* 2011; *Sucker Punch* 2011; *W.E.* 2011; *Won't Back Down* 2012; *Another Day/Another Time* 2013; *In Secret* 2013; *Inside Llewyn Davis* 2013; *The Two Faces of January* 2013; *Ex Machina* 2014; *Mojave* 2014; *A Most Violent Year* 2014; *Star Wars Episode VII: the Force Awakens* 2015; *X-Men: Apocalypse* 2016; *Star Wars Episode VIII* 2017
Isaacs, Jason (1963-) *Solitaire for 2* 1994; *DragonHeart* 1996; *Event Horizon* 1997; *Armageddon* 1998; *Divorcing Jack* 1998; *Soldier* 1998; *All for Love* 1999; *The End of the Affair* 1999; *The Patriot* 2000; *Black Hawk Down* 2001; *Sweet November* 2001; *Harry Potter and the Chamber of Secrets* 2002; *The Tuxedo* 2002; *Peter Pan* 2003; *Nouvelle-France* 2004; *Friends with Money* 2006; *Good* 2008; *Green Zone* 2010; *Harry Potter and the Deathly Hallows: Part 1* 2010; *Skeletons* 2010; *Abduction* 2011; *Cars 2* 2011; *The Great Ghost Rescue* 2011
Isaak, Chris (1956-) *The Silence of the Lambs* 1991; *Twin Peaks: Fire Walk with Me* 1992; *Little Buddha* 1993; *Grace of My Heart* 1996; *That Thing You Do!* 1996; *A Dirty Shame* 2004
Isabelle, Katharine aka **Isobel, Katherine** (1982-) *Knight Moves* 1992; *Ginger Snaps* 2000; *Freddy vs Jason* 2003; *American Mary* 2012
Iscan, Elit *Times and Winds* 2006; *Mustang* 2015
Iseya, Yusuke (1976-) *Casshern* 2004; *Memories of Matsuko* 2006; *Sukiyaki Western Django* 2007; *Blindness* 2008; *13 Assassins* 2010
Ishibashi, Renji (1941-) *The Sea Is Watching* 2002; *Gozu* 2003
Ishibashi, Ryo (1956-) *American Yakuza* 1994; *Blue Tiger* 1994; *American Yakuza 2: Back to Back* 1996; *Kids Return* 1996; *Audition* 1999; *Mitsuko Delivers* 2011
Ishihama, Akira (1935-) *The Human Condition* 1958; *Harakiri* 1962
Israel, Neal (1945-) *It's Alive III: Island of the Alive* 1987; *Look Who's Talking Too* 1990
Issyanov, Ravil aka **Isyanov, Ravil** *Back in the USSR* 1992; *Arachnid* 2001
Ito, Emi (1941-) *Mothra* 1962; *Godzilla vs Mothra* 1964
Ito, Robert (1931-) *The Adventures of Buckaroo Banzai across the 8th Dimension* 1984; *The War between Us* 1995
Ito, Yumi (1941-) *Mothra* 1962; *Godzilla vs Mothra* 1964
Ito, Yunosuke (1919-1980) *The Burmese Harp* 1956; *The Ballad of Narayama* 1958
Iturbi, José (1895-1980) *Thousands Cheer* 1943; *Music for Millions* 1944; *Anchors Aweigh* 1945; *Holiday in Mexico* 1946; *Three Daring Daughters* 1948; *That Midnight Kiss* 1949
Itzin, Gregory (1948-) *The Fabulous Baker Boys* 1989; *Born to Be Wild* 1995; *Original Sin* 2001; *I Know Who Killed Me* 2007
Iures, Marcel (1951-) *Mission: Impossible* 1996; *The Peacemaker* 1997; *Amen.* 2002; *Hart's War* 2002; *Layer Cake* 2004; *The Cave* 2005; *Goal!* 2005; *Youth without Youth* 2007
Ivan, Rosalind (1884-1959) *The Suspect* 1944; *The Corn Is Green* 1945; *Pillow of Death* 1945; *Pursuit to Algiers*

1945; *Scarlet Street* 1945; *The Verdict* 1946; *Elephant Walk* 1954
Ivanek, Zeljko (1957-) *The Sender* 1982; *Mass Appeal* 1984; *My Brother's Keeper* 1995; *Donnie Brasco* 1997; *A Civil Action* 1998; *The Rat Pack* 1998; *In Bruges* 2008
Ivanir, Mark *Holy Rollers* 2010; *A Late Quartet* 2012
Ivanov, Vlad *4 Months, 3 Weeks and 2 Days* 2007; *Police, Adjective* 2009; *Tales from the Golden Age* 2009
Ivernel, Daniel (1920-1999) *Madame du Barry* 1954; *Ulysses* 1954; *Sundays and Cybèle* 1962; *The Diary of a Chambermaid* 1964; *That Man George* 1965; *Borsalino and Co* 1974
Ivers, Robert (1934-2003) *The Delicate Delinquent* 1957; *Short Cut to Hell* 1957; *I Married a Monster from Outer Space* 1958; *GI Blues* 1960
Ives, Burl (1909-1995) *Smoky* 1946; *Green Grass of Wyoming* 1948; *Station West* 1948; *So Dear to My Heart* 1949; *Sierra* 1950; *East of Eden* 1955; *The Power and the Prize* 1956; *The Big Country* 1958; *Cat on a Hot Tin Roof* 1958; *Desire under the Elms* 1958; *Wind across the Everglades* 1958; *Day of the Outlaw* 1959; *Our Man in Havana* 1959; *Let No Man Write My Epitaph* 1960; *The Spiral Road* 1962; *Summer Magic* 1963; *The Brass Bottle* 1964; *Ensign Pulver* 1964; *Jules Verne's Rocket to the Moon* 1967; *Baker's Hawk* 1976; *Just You and Me, Kid* 1979; *White Dog* 1981; *Two Moon Junction* 1988
Ivey, Dana (1942-) *Explorers* 1985; *Dirty Rotten Scoundrels* 1988; *The Addams Family* 1991; *The Adventures of Huck Finn* 1993; *Guilty as Sin* 1993; *Simon Birch* 1998; *Walking across Egypt* 1999; *Disney's The Kid* 2000; *Two Weeks Notice* 2002; *Legally Blonde 2: Red, White & Blonde* 2003; *Ghost Town* 2008
Ivey, Judith (1951-) *Harry and Son* 1984; *The Lonely Guy* 1984; *The Woman in Red* 1984; *Compromising Positions* 1985; *Brighton Beach Memoirs* 1986; *Hello Again* 1987; *In Country* 1989; *Everybody Wins* 1990; *Love Hurts* 1990; *The Devil's Advocate* 1997; *Washington Square* 1997
Ivgi, Moshe (1953-) *Cup Final* 1991; *Yom Yom* 1998
Ivgy, Dana *Cupcakes* 2013; *Next to Her* 2014
Ivo, Tommy (1936-) *Treasure of Lost Canyon* 1952; *Dragstrip Girl* 1957
Iwashita, Shima (1941-) *An Autumn Afternoon* 1962; *Harakiri* 1962; *Twin Sisters of Kyoto* 1963; *The Empty Table* 1985
Izzard, Eddie (1962-) *The Secret Agent* 1996; *The Avengers* 1998; *Velvet Goldmine* 1998; *Circus* 1999; *The Criminal* 1999; *Shadow of the Vampire* 2000; *All the Queen's Men* 2001; *The Cat's Meow* 2001; *Revengers Tragedy* 2002; *Blueberry* 2004; *Five Children and It* 2004; *Ocean's Twelve* 2004; *Romance & Cigarettes* 2004; *The Aristocrats* 2005; *My Super Ex-Girlfriend* 2006; *The Wild* 2006; *Across the Universe* 2007; *The Chronicles of Narnia: Prince Caspian* 2008; *Igor* 2008; *Valkyrie* 2008; *Castles in the Sky* 2014; *The Choir* 2014; *Absolutely Anything* 2015; *Whisky Galore!* 2016
Izzo, Lorenza *The Green Inferno* 2013; *Knock Knock* 2015

J

Ja Rule aka **Atkins, Jeffrey "Ja Rule"** (1976-) *Half Past Dead* 2002; *Assault on Precinct 13* 2005
Jaa, Tony (1976-) *Ong-Bak* 2003; *Warrior King* 2005; *Ong-Bak: the Beginning* 2008; *xXx: the Return of Xander Cage* 2017
Jackman, Hugh (1968-) *Paperback Hero* 1998; *X-Men* 2000; *Animal Attraction* 2001; *Swordfish* 2001; *Kate & Leopold* 2002; *X2* 2003; *Van Helsing* 2004; *The Fountain* 2005; *Flushed Away* 2006; *Happy Feet* 2006; *The Prestige* 2006; *Scoop* 2006; *X-Men - the Last Stand* 2006; *Australia* 2008; *Deception* 2008; *X-Men Origins: Wolverine* 2009; *Real Steel* 2011; *Snow Flower and the Secret Fan* 2011; *X-Men: First Class* 2011; *Les Misérables* 2012; *Rise of the Guardians* 2012; *Movie 43* 2013; *Prisoners* 2013; *The Wolverine* 2013; *X-Men: Days of Future Past* 2014; *Chappie* 2015; *Pan* 2015; *Eddie the Eagle* 2016; *The Greatest Showman on Earth* 2017; *Wolverine 3* 2017
Jackson-Cohen, Oliver *Faster* 2010; *The Raven* 2012
Jackson, Anne (1925-2016) *Dirty Dingus Magee* 1970; *Zigzag* 1970; *Nasty Habits* 1976; *The Shining* 1980;

Leave 'Em Laughing 1981; Sam's Son 1984; Folks! 1992

Jackson, Barry (1938-2013) The Bofors Gun 1968; Alfred the Great 1969

Jackson, Brad April Love 1957; Viking Women and the Sea Serpent 1957

Jackson, Brandon T (1984-) Tropic Thunder 2008; Percy Jackson & the Lightning Thief 2010; Big Mommas: Like Father, like Son 2011; Percy Jackson: Sea of Monsters 2013

Jackson, Curtis "50 Cent" aka **Jackson, Curtis** aka **50 Cent** (1975-) Get Rich or Die Tryin' 2005; Home of the Brave 2006; Righteous Kill 2008; Dead Man Running 2009; Morning Glory 2010; Set Up 2011; Fire with Fire 2012; Escape Plan 2013; The Frozen Ground 2013; Southpaw 2015

Jackson, Freda (1909-1990) Beware of Pity 1946; No Room at the Inn 1948; Women of Twilight 1952; The Brides of Dracula 1960; The Shadow of the Cat 1961; West 11 1963; Die, Monster, Die! 1965; The Valley of Gwangi 1969

Jackson, Glenda (1936-) Marat/Sade 1966; Tell Me Lies 1967; Women in Love 1969; The Music Lovers 1970; Mary, Queen of Scots 1971; Sunday, Bloody Sunday 1971; Bequest to the Nation 1972; The Triple Echo 1972; A Touch of Class 1973; The Maids 1974; Hedda 1975; The Romantic Englishwoman 1975; Nasty Habits 1976; The Class of Miss MacMichael 1978; House Calls 1978; Stevie 1978; Lost and Found 1979; HEALTH 1980; Hopscotch 1980; The Patricia Neal Story 1981; Giro City 1982; The Return of the Soldier 1982; Turtle Diary 1985; Beyond Therapy 1987; Business as Usual 1987; The Rainbow 1988; Salome's Last Dance 1988; King of the Wind 1989

Jackson, Gordon (1923-1990) The Foreman Went to France 1941; Millions like Us 1943; San Demetrio London 1943; Pink String and Sealing Wax 1945; The Captive Heart 1946; Against the Wind 1947; Eureka Stockade 1949; Floodtide 1949; Whisky Galore! 1949; Bitter Springs 1950; Happy Go Lovely 1950; The Love Lottery 1953; Meet Mr Lucifer 1953; Passage Home 1955; The Quatermass Xperiment 1955; The Baby and the Battleship 1956; Sailor Beware! 1956; Hell Drivers 1957; Seven Waves Away 1957; Rockets Galore 1958; Blind Date 1959; The Bridal Path 1959; The Navy Lark 1959; Yesterday's Enemy 1959; Cone of Silence 1960; Tunes of Glory 1960; Greyfriars Bobby 1961; Mutiny on the Bounty 1962; The Great Escape 1963; The Long Ships 1963; The Ipcress File 1965; The Fighting Prince of Donegal 1966; Danger Route 1967; Hamlet 1969; The Prime of Miss Jean Brodie 1969; Run Wild, Run Free 1969; Scrooge 1970; Kidnapped 1971; Madame Sin 1972; Golden Rendezvous 1977; The Medusa Touch 1978; The Shooting Party 1984; The Whistle Blower 1986

Jackson, Harry (1923-1973) The Night Runner 1957; The True Story of Lynn Stuart 1957

Jackson, Janet (1966-) Poetic Justice 1993; Nutty Professor 2: the Klumps 2000; For Colored Girls 2010; Tyler Perry's Why Did I Get Married Too? 2010

Jackson, Jay (1919-2005) Days of Thrills and Laughter 1961; Laurel and Hardy's Laughing 20s 1965

Jackson, John M aka **Jackson, John** (1950-) Cold Sassy Tree 1989; Career Opportunities 1991; Eve of Destruction 1991; Black Widow Murders 1993; The Glimmer Man 1996

Jackson, Jonathan (1982-) The Deep End of the Ocean 1999; Insomnia 2002; Tuck Everlasting 2002; Dirty Dancing 2 2003

Jackson, Joshua (1978-) The Mighty Ducks 1992; Andre 1994; Magic in the Water 1995; D3: the Mighty Ducks 1996; Apt Pupil 1997; Urban Legend 1998; Cruel Intentions 1999; Gossip 1999; The Skulls 2000; The Safety of Objects 2001; Lone Star State of Mind 2002; Racing Stripes 2004; Cursed 2005; Shutter 2008; Lay the Favorite 2012

Jackson, Kate (1948-) Night of Dark Shadows 1971; Making Love 1982; Loverboy 1989; Hard Evidence 1994

Jackson, Mahalia (1911-1972) St Louis Blues 1958; Jazz on a Summer's Day 1959

Jackson, Mary (1910-2005) Targets 1968; A Family Thing 1996

Jackson (3), Michael (1958-2009) The Wiz 1978; Moonwalker 1988; Michael Jackson's This Is It 2009

Jackson, Peter (1961-) Bad Taste 1987; Braindead 1992; Ray Harryhausen: Special Effects Titan 2011

Jackson, Philip (1948-) High Hopes 1988; Bad Behaviour 1992; Brassed Off 1996; Little Voice 1998; Mike Bassett: England Manager 2001; I Want Candy 2006; Grow Your Own 2007; Believe 2012; Deception 2008

Jackson, Ray (1931-1989) The Final Test 1953; Dunkirk 1958

Jackson, Roger L Scream 3 1999; The Powerpuff Girls 2002

Jackson, Rose aka **Jackson, Rosemarie** Hangin' with the Homeboys 1991; Dead Presidents 1995

Jackson, Samuel L aka **Jackson, Sam** (1948-) Eddie Murphy Raw 1987; School Daze 1988; Do the Right Thing 1989; Betsy's Wedding 1990; Def by Temptation 1990; The Exorcist III 1990; A Shock to the System 1990; Johnny Suede 1991; Juice 1991; Jumpin' at the Boneyard 1991; Jungle Fever 1991; Patriot Games 1992; White Sands 1992; Amos & Andrew 1993; Jurassic Park 1993; Menace II Society 1993; National Lampoon's Loaded Weapon 1 1993; True Romance 1993; Against the Wall 1994; Assault at West Point: the Court Martial of John Whittaker 1994; Fresh 1994; Kiss of Death 1994; Pulp Fiction 1994; Die Hard with a Vengeance 1995; Fluke 1995; Losing Isaiah 1995; The Great White Hype 1996; Hard Eight 1996; The Long Kiss Goodnight 1996; A Time to Kill 1996; Eve's Bayou 1997; Jackie Brown 1997; One Eight Seven 1997; The Negotiator 1998; Out of Sight 1998; The Red Violin 1998; Sphere 1998; Deep Blue Sea 1999; Star Wars Episode I: the Phantom Menace 1999; Rules of Engagement 2000; Shaft 2000; Unbreakable 2000; The 51st State 2001; Changing Lanes 2002; No Good Deed 2002; Star Wars Episode II: Attack of the Clones 2002; xXx 2002; Basic 2003; SWAT 2003; Twisted 2003; In My Country 2004; The Incredibles 2004; Kill Bill Vol 2 2004; Coach Carter 2005; The Man 2005; Star Wars Episode III: Revenge of the Sith 2005; xXx: the Next Level 2005; Black Snake Moan 2006; Freedomland 2006; Home of the Brave 2006; Snakes on a Plane 2006; Cleaner 2007; 1408 2007; Resurrecting the Champ 2007; Jumper 2008; Lakeview Terrace 2008; Soul Men 2008; The Spirit 2008; Star Wars: The Clone Wars 2008; Astro Boy 2009; In the Land of the Free... 2009; Inglourious Basterds 2009; Mother and Child 2009; Iron Man 2 2010; The Other Guys 2010; The Sunset Limited 2010; Unthinkable 2010; Thor 2011; Django Unchained 2012; Fury 2012; Marvel Avengers Assemble 2012; Old Boy 2013; Turbo 2013; Big Game 2014; Captain America: the Winter Soldier 2014; Reasonable Doubt 2014; RoboCop 2014; Avengers: Age of Ultron 2015; Barely Lethal 2015; The Hateful Eight 2015; Kingsman: The Secret Service 2015; Cell 2016; The Legend of Tarzan 2016; Miss Peregrine's Home for Peculiar Children 2016; Kong: Skull Island 2017; xXx: the Return of Xander Cage 2017

Jackson, Sherry (1942-) The Miracle of Our Lady of Fatima 1952; Trouble along the Way 1953; Come Next Spring 1956; Wild on the Beach 1965

Jackson, Stoney (1960-) By the Sword 1992; Trespass 1992

Jackson, Thomas E aka **Jackson, Thomas** (1886-1967) Broadway 1929; Little Caesar 1931; The Woman in the Window 1945

Jackson, Victoria (1959-) Casual Sex? 1988; Family Business 1989; UHF 1989

Jacob, Catherine (1959-) Tatie Danielle 1990; Merci la Vie 1991; Mon Père Ce Héros 1991; Nine Months 1994

Jacob, Irène (1966-) The Double Life of Véronique 1991; The Secret Garden 1993; Three Colours Red 1994; All Men Are Mortal 1995; Beyond the Clouds 1995; Othello 1995; Victory 1995; Incognito 1997; US Marshals 1998; History Is Made at Night 1999; Londinium 1999; My Life So Far 1999; Nouvelle-France 2004; Dying of the Light 2014

Jacobi, Derek (1938-) Othello 1965; Three Sisters 1970; Blue Blood 1973; The Day of the Jackal 1973; The Odessa File 1974; The Medusa Touch 1978; The Human Factor 1979; Enigma 1982; The Hunchback of Notre Dame 1982; The Secret of NIMH 1982; Little Dorrit 1987; The Tenth Man 1988; Henry V 1989; The Fool 1990; Dead Again 1991; Hamlet 1996; Looking for Richard 1996; Basil 1998; Love Is the Devil: Study for a Portrait of Francis Bacon 1998; Up at the Villa 1999; The Body 2000; Gladiator 2000; The Children's

Midsummer Night's Dream 2001; Gosford Park 2001; Revelation 2001; Revengers Tragedy 2002; Two Men Went to War 2002; Cloud Cuckoo Land 2004; Strings 2004; Nanny McPhee 2005; Underworld: Evolution 2006; The Golden Compass 2007; A Bunch of Amateurs 2008; Charles Dickens's England 2009; Morris: a Life with Bells On 2009; Ironclad 2010; The King's Speech 2010; Grace of Monaco 2014

Jacobi, Ernst Hamsun 1996; The White Ribbon 2009

Jacobi, Lou (1913-2009) The Diary of Anne Frank 1959; Irma la Douce 1963; Everything You Always Wanted to Know about Sex ... but Were Afraid to Ask 1972; Roseland 1977; The Magician of Lublin 1979; The Lucky Star 1980; My Favorite Year 1982; Avalon 1990; IQ 1994

Jacobs, Gillian Seeking a Friend for the End of the World 2011; Visions 2014

Jacobs, Lawrence-Hilton aka **Hilton-Jaques, Lawrence** aka **Hilton-Jacobs, Lawrence** (1953-) Claudine 1974; Indecent Behavior 1993

Jacobs, Martin Over the Hill 1992; Turtle Beach 1992

Jacobs, Paula She'll Be Wearing Pink Pyjamas 1984; The Remains of the Day 1993

Jacobs, Steve aka **Jacobs, Steven** (1967-) Shadows of the Peacock 1987; Father 1990; To Have & to Hold 1996

Jacobson, Dean Lobster Man from Mars 1989; Child's Play 3 1991

Jacobson, Eric It's a Very Merry Muppet Christmas Movie 2002; The Muppets' Wizard of Oz 2005; The Muppets 2011; Muppets Most Wanted 2014

Jacobson, Shane Kenny 2006; Charlie & Boots 2009; The Mystery of a Hansom Cab 2012; Oddball and the Penguins 2015

Jacobsson, Ulla (1929-1982) Smiles of a Summer Night 1955; Zulu 1963; The Heroes of Telemark 1965; Fox and His Friends 1975

Jacoby, Bobby (1973-) Tremors 1989; Meet the Applegates 1991; Night of the Demons 2 1994

Jacoby, Scott (1956-) Baxter 1973; The Little Girl Who Lives down the Lane 1976; The Diary of Anne Frank 1980

Jacott, Carlos Mr Jealousy 1997; Being John Malkovich 1999; Fun with Dick and Jane 2005

Jacques, Hattie (1924-1980) Trottie True 1949; Chance of a Lifetime 1950; Scrooge 1951; The Pickwick Papers 1952; Our Girl Friday 1953; Carry On Sergeant 1958; The Square Peg 1958; Carry On Nurse 1959; Carry On Teacher 1959; Follow a Star 1959; The Navy Lark 1959; Carry On Constable 1960; Carry On Regardless 1960; Make Mine Mink 1960; School for Scoundrels 1960; Watch Your Stern 1960; In the Doghouse 1961; She'll Have to Go 1961; Carry On Cabby 1963; The Bobo 1967; The Plank 1967; Carry On Doctor 1968; Carry On Again Doctor 1969; Carry On Camping 1969; Crooks and Coronets 1969; The Magic Christian 1969; Monte Carlo or Bust! 1969; Carry On Loving 1970; Carry On at Your Convenience 1971; Carry On Abroad 1972; Carry On Matron 1972; Carry On Dick 1974

Jacques, Jennie Cherry Tree Lane 2010; Demons Never Die 2011

Jacques, Sylvain Those Who Love Me Can Take the Train 1998; Son Frère 2003

Jacques, Yves (1956-) The Decline of the American Empire 1986; Jesus of Montreal 1989; The Barbarian Invasions 2003; A Secret 2007

Jade, Claude (1948-2006) Stolen Kisses 1968; Topaz 1969; Uncle Benjamin 1969; Bed and Board 1970; Love on the Run 1979

Jaeckel, Richard (1926-1997) Guadalcanal Diary 1943; Wing and a Prayer 1944; Come Back, Little Sheba 1952; My Son John 1952; Big Leaguer 1953; Attack! 1956; 3:10 to Yuma 1957; Cowboy 1958; The Gun Runners 1958; The Lineup 1958; The Naked and the Dead 1958; The Gallant Hours 1960; Platinum High School 1960; Town without Pity 1961; Nightmare in the Sun 1964; Once before I Die 1965; The Dirty Dozen 1967; Latitude Zero 1969; Chisum 1970; Sometimes a Great Notion 1971; Ulzana's Raid 1972; The Outfit 1973; Pat Garrett and Billy the Kid 1973; Chosen Survivors 1974; The Drowning Pool 1975; Grizzly 1976; Day of the Animals 1977; The Dark 1979; Pacific Inferno 1979; Herbie Goes Bananas 1980; The California Dolls 1981; Starman 1984; Black Moon Rising 1985; Delta Force 2 1990

Jaeger, Sam The Riverman 2004; Catch and Release 2007

Jaenada, Oscar The Losers 2010; The Shallows 2016

Jaenicke, Hannes (1960-) The Hunted 1998; Mary Higgins Clark's Pretend You Don't See Her 2002

Jaffe, Carl (1902-1974) I Didn't Do It 1945; State Secret 1950; Desperate Moment 1953; Child's Play 1954; The Traitor 1957; First Man into Space 1958; Subway in the Sky 1958

Jaffe, Sam (1891-1984) The Scarlet Empress 1934; We Live Again 1934; Lost Horizon 1937; Gunga Din 1939; Stage Door Canteen 1943; 13 Rue Madeleine 1946; The Accused 1949; Rope of Sand 1949; The Asphalt Jungle 1950; The Day the Earth Stood Still 1951; I Can Get It for You Wholesale 1951; Les Espions 1957; The Barbarian and the Geisha 1958; Ben-Hur 1959; The Great Bank Robbery 1969; The Dunwich Horror 1970; Bedknobs and Broomsticks 1971; Battle beyond the Stars 1980; Gideon's Trumpet 1980

Jaffer, Melissa (1936-) Caddie 1976; Ride a Wild Pony 1976

Jaffrey, Madhur (1933-) Shakespeare Wallah 1965; The Guru 1969; Autobiography of a Princess 1975; Heat and Dust 1982; The Assam Garden 1985; The Perfect Murder 1988; Vanya on 42nd Street 1994; ABCD 1999; Cotton Mary 1999; Partition 2006; Jadoo 2013

Jaffrey, Saeed (1929-2015) The Horsemen 1971; The Man Who Would Be King 1975; The Wilby Conspiracy 1975; The Chess Players 1977; Hullabaloo over Georgie and Bonnie's Pictures 1979; Sphinx 1980; A Passage to India 1984; The Razor's Edge 1984; My Beautiful Laundrette 1985; The Deceivers 1988; After Midnight 1990; Henna 1990; Masala 1991; Guru in Seven 1997; The Journey 1997; Second Generation 1999; Mr In-Between 2001; Chicken Tikka Masala 2005

Jagger, Bianca (1945-) The Rutles - All You Need Is Cash 1978; The American Success Company 1979; The Cannonball Run 1981

Jagger, Dean (1903-1991) Wings in the Dark 1935; Having Wonderful Time 1938; Brigham Young 1940; The Men in Her Life 1941; Western Union 1941; Valley of the Sun 1942; Betrayed 1944; I Live in Grosvenor Square 1945; Driftwood 1946; Sister Kenny 1946; Pursued 1947; Twelve o'Clock High 1949; Sierra 1950; Rawhide 1951; Warpath 1951; Denver & Rio Grande 1952; It Grows on Trees 1952; My Son John 1952; The Robe 1953; Private Hell 36 1954; White Christmas 1954; Bad Day at Black Rock 1955; The Great Man 1956; Red Sundown 1956; X the Unknown 1956; Forty Guns 1957; King Creole 1958; The Proud Rebel 1958; The Nun's Story 1959; Cash McCall 1960; Elmer Gantry 1960; Jumbo 1962; Day of the Evil Gun 1968; Firecreek 1968; Smith! 1969; Tiger by the Tail 1970; Vanishing Point 1971; The Glass House 1972; I Heard the Owl Call My Name 1973; End of the World 1977; Game of Death 1978; Alligator 1980; Gideon's Trumpet 1980

Jagger, Mick (1943-) Tonite Let's All Make Love in London 1967; Gimme Shelter 1970; Ned Kelly 1970; Performance 1970; The Concert for Bangladesh 1972; Jimi Hendrix 1973; Running Out of Luck 1985; Freejack 1992; Bent 1996; The Man from Elysian Fields 2001; Manufacturing Dissent: Uncovering Michael Moore 2007; Shine a Light 2007; Twenty Feet from Stardom 2013

Jaglom, Henry (1941-) Drive, He Said 1971; The Last Movie 1971; Sitting Ducks 1979; Always 1985; Someone to Love 1987; Venice/Venice 1992; Last Summer in the Hamptons 1995

Jakub, Lisa (1978-) Rambling Rose 1991; Matinee 1993; Mrs Doubtfire 1993; A Pig's Tale 1994; Bermuda Triangle 1996; The Beautician and the Beast 1997

Jalal, Farida The Chess Players 1977; Dilwale Dulhania Le Jayenge 1995

James, Anthony The Last Days of Dolwyn 1949; Return from Witch Mountain 1978; Wacko 1981; Nightmares 1983; World Gone Wild 1988; The Naked Gun 2½: the Smell of Fear 1991

James, Brion (1945-1999) Blue Sunshine 1977; Southern Comfort 1981; Blade Runner 1982; The Ballad of Gregorio Cortez 1983; A Breed Apart 1984; Crimewave 1985; Enemy Mine 1985; Armed and Dangerous 1986; Cherry 2000 1988; DOA 1988; House III: The Horror Show 1989; Red Scorpion 1989; Tango & Cash 1989;

Another 48 HRS 1990; Over Her Dead Body 1990; Wishman 1991; The Player 1992; Brain Smasher... a Love Story 1993; Striking Distance 1993; Time Runner 1993; Bad Company 1994; Cabin Boy 1994; FTW 1994; The Fifth Element 1997; Brown's Requiem 1998

James, Clifton (1921-) David and Lisa 1962; Black like Me 1964; Cool Hand Luke 1967; The Reivers 1969; The Biscuit Eater 1972; The New Centurions 1972; The Last Detail 1973; Live and Let Die 1973; Werewolf of Washington 1973; Bank Shot 1974; Buster and Billie 1974; The Man with the Golden Gun 1974; Rancho Deluxe 1975; Silver Streak 1976; The Bad News Bears in Breaking Training 1977; Eight Men Out 1988; Lone Star 1995

James, Dalton (1971-) California Man 1992; My Father the Hero 1994

James, Gennie (1977-) Places in the Heart 1984; The Secret Garden 1987

James, Geraldine (1950-) Sweet William 1980; The Wolves of Willoughby Chase 1988; The Tall Guy 1989; The Bridge 1990; Teen Agent 1991; Moll Flanders 1995; The Man Who Knew Too Little 1997; The Luzhin Defence 2000; The Testimony of Taliesin Jones 2000; Tom & Thomas 2002; Calendar Girls 2003; Sherlock Holmes 2009; Made in Dagenham 2010; Arthur 2011; Sherlock Holmes: a Game of Shadows 2011; Diana 2013; Robot Overlords 2014; 45 Years 2015

James, Godfrey The Land That Time Forgot 1974; At the Earth's Core 1976

James, Harry (1916-1983) Springtime in the Rockies 1942; Do You Love Me? 1946

James, Jesse (1989-) Message in a Bottle 1998; A Dog of Flanders 1999; Slap Her, She's French! 2001; The Amityville Horror 2005

James, Kevin (1965-) Hitch 2005; Barnyard 2006; Monster House 2006; I Now Pronounce You Chuck & Larry 2007; Paul Blart: Mall Cop 2009; Grown Ups 2010; The Dilemma 2011; Zookeeper 2011; Here Comes the Boom 2012; Hotel Transylvania 2012; Grown Ups 2 2013; Hotel Transylvania 2 2015; Paul Blart: Mall Cop 2 2015; Pixels 2015

James, Lennie (1965-) Among Giants 1998; Elephant Juice 1999; Lucky Break 2001; 24 Hour Party People 2001; Outlaw 2006; The Next Three Days 2010; Colombiana 2011; Lockout 2012; Get on Up 2014

James, Liam Christmas Comes Home to Canaan 2011; The Way Way Back 2013

James, Lily (1989-) Fast Girls 2012; Cinderella 2015; Pride and Prejudice and Zombies 2015

James, Oliver (1980-) What a Girl Wants 2003; Raise Your Voice 2004

James, Oscar Pressure 1976; Black Joy 1977

James, Pell The King 2005; Surveillance 2007

James, Raji East Is East 1999; Nina's Heavenly Delights 2006

James, Sidney (1913-1976) No Orchids for Miss Blandish 1948; Last Holiday 1950; Lady Godiva Rides Again 1951; The Lavender Hill Mob 1951; Emergency Call 1952; Father's Doing Fine 1952; I Believe in You 1952; Miss Robin Hood 1952; Time Gentleman Please! 1952; The Titfield Thunderbolt 1952; Venetian Bird 1952; The Yellow Balloon 1952; Escape by Night 1953; Is Your Honeymoon Really Necessary? 1953; The Square Ring 1953; The Weak and the Wicked 1953; Will Any Gentleman...? 1953; Father Brown 1954; For Better, for Worse 1954; Orders Are Orders 1954; The Rainbow Jacket 1954; Seagulls over Sorrento 1954; The Deep Blue Sea 1955; The Glass Cage 1955; It's a Great Day 1955; Joe Macbeth 1955; John and Julie 1955; A Kid for Two Farthings 1955; Dry Rot 1956; The Extra Day 1956; The Iron Petticoat 1956; Trapeze 1956; Campbell's Kingdom 1957; Hell Drivers 1957; A King in New York 1957; Quatermass II 1957; The Shiralee 1957; The Smallest Show on Earth 1957; The Story of Esther Costello 1957; I Was Monty's Double 1958; The Man Inside 1958; The Silent Enemy 1958; Too Many Crooks 1958; Desert Mice 1959; Make Mine a Million 1959; Tommy the Toreador 1959; Upstairs and Downstairs 1959; And the Same to You 1960; Carry On Constable 1960; Carry On Regardless 1960; The Green Helmet 1960; The Pure Hell of St Trinian's 1960; Watch Your Stern 1960; Double Bunk 1961; Raising the Wind 1961; What a Carve Up! 1961; What a Whopper! 1961; Carry On Cruising 1962; We Joined the Navy 1962; Carry On Cabby 1963; Carry On Cleo 1964; The Big Job

1965; Carry On Cowboy 1965; Three Hats for Lisa 1965; Carry On – Don't Lose Your Head 1966; Where the Bullets Fly 1966; Carry On Doctor 1968; Carry On Up the Khyber 1968; Carry On Again Doctor 1969; Carry On Camping 1969; Carry On Loving 1970; Carry On Up the Jungle 1970; Carry On at Your Convenience 1971; Carry On Henry 1971; Bless This House 1972; Carry On Abroad 1972; Carry On Matron 1972; Carry On Girls 1973; Carry On Dick 1974

James (1), Steve (1955-1993) The Exterminator 1980; The Brother from Another Planet 1984; American Ninja 1985; To Live and Die in LA 1985; Avenging Force 1986; PoW the Escape 1986; Hero and the Terror 1988; I'm Gonna Git You Sucka 1988; Johnny Be Good 1988; Weekend at Bernie's II 1992

James, Theo (1984-) Underworld: Awakening 2012; Divergent 2014; The Benefactor 2015; Insurgent 2015; London Fields 2015; The Divergent Series: Allegiant 2016

James, Walter (1882-1946) Little Annie Rooney 1925; Battling Butler 1926; The Kid Brother 1927

Jameson, Joyce (1932-1987) Tales of Terror 1962; The Balcony 1963; The Comedy of Terrors 1964

Jameson, Pauline (1920-2007) Two Living, One Dead 1961; Crooks Anonymous 1962; I Could Go On Singing 1963

Jampanoï, Mylène Martyrs 2008; Gainsbourg (Je T'Aime... Moi Non Plus) 2010

Janda, Krystyna (1955-) Man of Marble 1977; The Conductor 1980; Man of Iron 1981; Interrogation 1982; Elles 2011

Jane, Thomas aka **Jane, Tom** (1969-) The Crow: City of Angels 1996; The Last Time I Committed Suicide 1996; Thursday 1998; The Velocity of Gary 1998; Deep Blue Sea 1999; Molly 1999; Under Suspicion 2000; Original Sin 2001; 61* 2001; The Sweetest Thing 2002; Dreamcatcher 2003; Stander 2003; The Punisher 2004; The Tripper 2006; The Mist 2007; Mutant Chronicles 2008; LOL 2011; Before I Wake 2015; Broken Horses 2015

Jang Dong-gun aka **Jang Dong-Keon** (1972-) Nowhere to Hide 1999; Brotherhood 2004; The Warrior's Way 2010

Janis, Conrad (1928-) Margie 1946; The Happy Hooker 1975; The Duchess and the Dirtwater Fox 1976; The Buddy Holly Story 1978; Oh God! Book II 1980

Janney, Allison (1959-) Dead Funny 1995; First Do No Harm 1997; David and Lisa 1998; The Object of My Affection 1998; Six Days Seven Nights 1998; American Beauty 1999; Drop Dead Gorgeous 1999; The Hours 2002; Finding Nemo 2003; Piccadilly Jim 2004; The Chumscrubber 2005; Over the Hedge 2006; Juno 2007; Margaret 2008; Away We Go 2009; Life during Wartime 2009; The Help 2011; Liberal Arts 2011; The Oranges 2011; Mr Peabody & Sherman 2013; Touchy Feely 2013; The Way Way Back 2013; The Rewrite 2014; Tammy 2014; Minions 2015; Spy 2015; Miss Peregrine's Home for Peculiar Children 2016

Janney, Leon (1917-1980) A Handful of Clouds 1930; The Last Mile 1959; Charly 1968

Janney, William (1908-1992) The Dawn Patrol 1930; A Successful Calamity 1932; Bonnie Scotland 1935

Jannings, Emil (1884-1950) Anna Boleyn 1920; The Last Laugh 1924; Waxworks 1924; Vaudeville 1925; Faust 1926; Tartuffe 1926; The Way of All Flesh 1927; The Last Command 1928; The Patriot 1928; The Blue Angel 1930

Jansen, Tom (1945-) Suite 16 1994; The Gambler 1997

Janson, Horst (1935-) The McKenzie Break 1970; Murphy's War 1971; Captain Kronos: Vampire Hunter 1972

Janssen, David (1930-1980) Chief Crazy Horse 1955; Cult of the Cobra 1955; Francis in the Navy 1955; Never Say Goodbye 1955; The Square Jungle 1955; Francis in the Haunted House 1956; The Girl He Left Behind 1956; Showdown at Abilene 1956; Hell to Eternity 1960; King of the Roaring 20s - the Story of Arnold Rothstein 1961; Ring of Fire 1961; My Six Loves 1962; Warning Shot 1967; The Green Berets 1968; The Shoes of the Fisherman 1968; Marooned 1969; Once Is Not Enough 1975; The Swiss Conspiracy 1975; Two-Minute Warning 1976; Golden Rendezvous 1977; SOS Titanic 1979; Inchon 1981

Janssen, Eilene aka **Janssen, Eileen** (1937-) On Our Merry Way 1948; About Mrs Leslie 1954

Janssen, Famke (1964-) GoldenEye 1995; Lord of Illusions 1995; City of Industry 1996; The Gingerbread Man 1997; Noose 1997; The Adventures of Sebastian Cole 1998; Celebrity 1998; Deep Rising 1998; The Faculty 1998; Rounders 1998; Circus 1999; House on Haunted Hill 1999; Love & Sex 2000; X-Men 2000; Don't Say a Word 2001; Made 2001; I Spy 2002; X2 2003; Hide and Seek 2005; X-Men - the Last Stand 2006; Taken 2007; The Wackness 2008; Taken 2 2012; Hansel & Gretel: Witch Hunters 2013; The Wolverine 2013; Taken 3 2014

Jaoui, Agnès (1964-) Un Air de Famille 1996; On Connaît la Chanson 1997; Le Goût des Autres 1999; Look at Me 2004; Let's Talk about the Rain 2008; Under the Rainbow 2013

Jaray, Hans (1906-1990) The Love of Jeanne Ney 1927; Lydia 1941; Carnegie Hall 1947

Jaregard, Ernst-Hugo (1928-1998) Europa 1991; The Kingdom 1994

Jarman Jr, Claude (1934-) The Yearling 1946; High Barbaree 1947; Intruder in the Dust 1949; Roughshod 1949; The Outriders 1950; Rio Grande 1950; Hangman's Knot 1952; Fair Wind to Java 1953

Jarman, Derek (1942-1994) Blue 1993; The British Guide to Showing Off 2011

Jarmusch, Jim (1953-) Leningrad Cowboys Go America 1989; In the Soup 1992; Blue in the Face 1995; Sling Blade 1995; Blank City 2010

Jarratt, John (1952-) The Odd Angry Shot 1979; We of the Never Never 1982; The Naked Country 1985; Dead Heart 1996; Wolf Creek 2005; Rogue 2007; 100 Bloody Acres 2012

Järrel, Stig (1910-1998) Torment 1944; The Devil's Eye 1960

Jarvet, Juri (1919-1995) King Lear 1970; Solaris 1972

Jarvis, Graham (1930-2003) RPM – Revolutions per Minute 1970; Middle Age Crazy 1980; Parents 1988; Misery 1990; The Sports Pages 2001

Jason, David (1940-) White Cargo 1973; Wombling Free 1977; The Odd Job 1978

Jason, Harvey (1940-) Oklahoma Crude 1973; The Gumball Rally 1976

Jason, Peter (1950-) Alien Nation 1988; They Live 1988; A View from Here 2009

Jason, Rick (1926-2000) Sombrero 1952; This Is My Love 1954; The Wayward Bus 1957

Jason, Sybil (1927-2011) I Found Stella Parish 1935; The Singing Kid 1936; The Great O'Malley 1937; The Little Princess 1939

Jasper, Star True Love 1989; Hand Gun 1994

Jay-Z (1969-) Backstage 2000; Fade to Black 2004

Jay, Ernest (1893-1957) Broken Blossoms 1936; School for Secrets 1946

Jay, Ricky (1948-) Things Change 1988; The Spanish Prisoner 1997; Tomorrow Never Dies 1997; Last Days 2004

Jay, Tony (1933-2006) Tom and Jerry: the Movie 1992; The Jungle Book 2 2003

Jayne, Jennifer (1931-2006) It's a Grand Life 1953; The Trollenberg Terror 1958; Band of Thieves 1962; On the Beat 1962; Clash by Night 1963; Hysteria 1964; They Came from beyond Space 1967

Jayston, Michael (1935-) A Midsummer Night's Dream 1969; Follow Me 1971; Nicholas and Alexandra 1971; Alice's Adventures in Wonderland 1972; Bequest to the Nation 1972; Craze 1973; The Homecoming 1973; The Internecine Project 1974; Dominique 1978; 20,000 Leagues under the Sea 1997

Jean-Baptiste, Marianne (1967-) Secrets & Lies 1995; Mr Jealousy 1997; A Murder of Crows 1998; New Year's Day 1999; The 24 Hour Woman 1999; The Cell 2000; 28 Days 2000; Spy Game 2001; City of Ember 2008; Secrets in the Walls 2010; Takers 2010; 360 2011

Jean, Gloria (1927-) Never Give a Sucker an Even Break 1941; Copacabana 1947

Jean, Wyclef Dave Chappelle's Block Party 2005; Ghosts of Cité Soleil 2005

Jeanmaire, Zizi aka **Jeanmaire** (1924-) Hans Christian Andersen 1952; Anything Goes 1956

Jeans, Isabel (1891-1985) Downhill 1927; Easy Virtue 1927; Tovarich 1937; Fools for Scandal 1938; Suspicion 1941; Great Day 1944; It Happened in Rome

1956; Gigi 1958; A Breath of Scandal 1960; Heavens Above! 1963

Jeans, Ursula (1906-1973) Cavalcade 1933; Friday the Thirteenth 1933; The Man in the Mirror 1936; Dark Journey 1937; Over the Moon 1937; Storm in a Teacup 1937; Gaiety George 1946; The Weaker Sex 1948; The Dam Busters 1954; The Night My Number Came Up 1955; North West Frontier 1959; The Green Helmet 1960; The Queen's Guards 1960; The Battle of the Villa Fiorita 1965

Jeavons, Colin (1929-) Bartleby 1971; Diagnosis: Murder 1974; The Island 1980; Secret Friends 1991

Jeayes, Allan (1885-1963) The Ghost Train 1931; The Impassive Footman 1932; The Camels Are Coming 1934; Königsmark 1935; The House of the Spaniard 1936; Rembrandt 1936; Elephant Boy 1937; The Green Cockatoo 1937; The Squeaker 1937; The Four Feathers 1939; The Stars Look Down 1939; Convoy 1940; Pimpernel Smith 1941; Blanche Fury 1948

Jeevan (1915-1987) Tarana 1951; Ek Hi Rasta 1956; Naya Daur 1957

Jefferies, Marc John (1990-) The Haunted Mansion 2003; Get Rich or Die Tryin' 2005

Jefford, Barbara (1930-) A Midsummer Night's Dream 1961; Ulysses 1967; The Shoes of the Fisherman 1968; A Midsummer Night's Dream 1969; Lust for a Vampire 1970; And the Ship Sails On 1983; When the Whales Came 1989; Where Angels Fear to Tread 1991; The Ninth Gate 1999; Philomena 2013

Jeffrey, Peter (1929-1999) if... 1968; Anne of the Thousand Days 1969; Ring of Bright Water 1969; The Abominable Dr Phibes 1971; The Horsemen 1971; The Odessa File 1974; The Return of the Pink Panther 1974; Britannia Hospital 1982; The Adventures of Baron Munchausen 1988

Jeffreys, Anne (1923-) Nevada 1944; Dick Tracy 1945; Dillinger 1945; Those Endearing Young Charms 1945; Dick Tracy vs Cueball 1946; Riff-Raff 1947; Trail Street 1947; Return of the Bad Men 1948

Jeffreys, Ellis (1872-1943) Limelight 1936; Return of a Stranger 1937

Jeffries, Fran (1939-) Sex and the Single Girl 1964; Harum Scarum 1965

Jeffries, Lionel (1926-2010) The Black Rider 1954; The Colditz Story 1954; No Smoking 1954; All for Mary 1955; Jumping for Joy 1955; The Quatermass Xperiment 1955; The Baby and the Battleship 1956; The Man in the Sky 1956; Blue Murder at St Trinian's 1957; Doctor at Large 1957; The Vicious Circle 1957; Behind the Mask 1958; Further up the Creek 1958; Law and Disorder 1958; Orders to Kill 1958; The Revenge of Frankenstein 1958; Bobbikins 1959; The Nun's Story 1959; Please Turn Over 1960; Tarzan the Magnificent 1960; The Trials of Oscar Wilde 1960; Two Way Stretch 1960; Fanny 1961; Kill or Cure 1962; The Notorious Landlady 1962; Operation Snatch 1962; The Wrong Arm of the Law 1962; Call Me Bwana 1963; The Long Ships 1963; The Scarlet Blade 1963; First Men in the Moon 1964; Murder Ahoy 1964; The Truth about Spring 1964; The Secret of My Success 1965; You Must Be Joking! 1965; Drop Dead Darling 1966; The Spy with a Cold Nose 1966; Camelot 1967; Jules Verne's Rocket to the Moon 1967; Oh Dad, Poor Dad, Mama's Hung You in the Closet and I'm Feelin' So Sad 1967; Chitty Chitty Bang Bang 1968; Twinky 1969; Eyewitness 1970; Who Slew Auntie Roo? 1971; What Changed Charley Farthing? 1974; Royal Flash 1975; Wombling Free 1977; The Prisoner of Zenda 1979; Better Late than Never 1983; A Chorus of Disapproval 1988; Danny, the Champion of the World 1989

Jehanne, Edith The Chess Player 1927; The Love of Jeanne Ney 1927

Jemison, Anna Heatwave 1981; Smash Palace 1981

Jemison, Eddie Schizopolis 1996; Ocean's Twelve 2004; Waitress 2007

Jenkins, Allen (1900-1974) Blessed Event 1932; I Am a Fugitive from a Chain Gang 1932; Lawyer Man 1932; Bureau of Missing Persons 1933; Hard to Handle 1933; Havana Widows 1933; The Mayor of Hell 1933; The Mind Reader 1933; The Case of the Howling Dog 1934; Jimmy the Gent 1934; The Case of the Lucky Legs 1935; The Irish in Us 1935; Cain and Mabel 1936; The Singing Kid 1936; Dead End 1937; Marked Woman 1937; The Perfect Specimen 1937; Swing Your Lady 1937;

The Amazing Dr Clitterhouse 1938; Fools for Scandal 1938; Going Places 1938; Hard to Get 1938; Racket Busters 1938; A Slight Case of Murder 1938; Destry Rides Again 1939; Five Came Back 1939; Naughty but Nice 1939; Brother Orchid 1940; Tin Pan Alley 1940; A Date with the Falcon 1941; Dive Bomber 1941; Footsteps in the Dark 1941; The Gay Falcon 1941; Time Out for Rhythm 1941; Eyes in the Night 1942; The Falcon Takes Over 1942; They All Kissed the Bride 1942; Lady on a Train 1945; Wonder Man 1945; The Senator Was Indiscreet 1947; The Big Wheel 1949; Robin and the 7 Hoods 1964; The Spy in the Green Hat 1966

Jenkins, Jackie "Butch" aka **Jenkins, "Butch"** (1937-2001) National Velvet 1944; Our Vines Have Tender Grapes 1945; My Brother Talks to Horses 1946; Summer Holiday 1948

Jenkins, Ken (1940-) Matewan 1987; Air America 1990; Thirst 1998

Jenkins, Megs (1917-1998) Millions like Us 1943; Green for Danger 1946; The History of Mr Polly 1948; Saraband for Dead Lovers 1948; A Boy, a Girl and a Bike 1949; The Secret People 1951; Personal Affair 1953; Trouble in Store 1953; Tiger Bay 1959; The Green Helmet 1960; The Innocents 1961; Life for Ruth 1962; Murder Most Foul 1964; The Smashing Bird I Used to Know 1969

Jenkins, Rebecca (1959-) Bye Bye Blues 1989; Bob Roberts 1992; Clearcut 1992

Jenkins, Richard (1947-) The Witches of Eastwick 1987; Little Nikita 1988; Blaze 1989; Sea of Love 1989; Trapped in Paradise 1994; Wolf 1994; The Indian in the Cupboard 1995; Eddie 1996; Flirting with Disaster 1996; Eye of God 1997; The Man Who Wasn't There 2001; Say It Isn't So 2001; Changing Lanes 2002; The Core 2002; Stealing Harvard 2002; Intolerable Cruelty 2003; Shall We Dance 2004; Fun with Dick and Jane 2005; North Country 2005; Rumor Has It... 2005; The Visitor 2007; The Broken 2008; Step Brothers 2008; The Cabin in the Woods 2010; Dear John 2010; Eat Pray Love 2010; Let Me In 2010; Friends with Benefits 2011; Hall Pass 2011; Liberal Arts 2011; The Rum Diary 2011; Jack Reacher 2012; Killing Them Softly 2012; White House Down 2013; God's Pocket 2014; Bone Tomahawk 2015

Jenks, Frank (1902-1962) Back Street 1941; The Flame of New Orleans 1941; Seven Miles from Alcatraz 1942; Rosie the Riveter 1944; Christmas in Connecticut 1945

Jenney, Lucinda (1954-) Wired 1989; Thelma & Louise 1991; American Heart 1992; Matinee 1993; Stephen King's Thinner 1996; GI Jane 1997; The Mothman Prophecies 2001

Jennings, Alex (1957-) A Midsummer Night's Dream 1996; The Wings of the Dove 1997; The Hunley 1999; The Four Feathers 2002; The Queen 2006; The Disappeared 2008; Trap for Cinderella 2011; Castles in the Sky 2014; The Lady in the Van 2015

Jennings, Brent (1951-) Witness 1985; The Serpent and the Rainbow 1987; A Lesson before Dying 1999

Jennings, Claudia (1949-1979) The Unholy Rollers 1972; Truck Stop Women 1974; Deathsport 1978

Jennings, DeWitt (1879-1937) The Valiant 1929; The Criminal Code 1930; Min and Bill 1930; Little Man, What Now? 1934

Jenns, Elizabeth The Fortunate Fool 1933; A Star Is Born 1937

Jens, Salome (1935-) Angel Baby 1961; The Fool Killer 1965; Seconds 1966; Savages 1972; Harry's War 1981

Jensen, Ashley (1969-) Taking Liberties 2007; Nativity! 2009; Arthur Christmas 2011; Gnomeo & Juliet 2011; Hysteria 2011; The Pirates! in an Adventure with Scientists! 2012; All Stars 2013; The Legend of Barney Thomson 2015; The Lobster 2015

Jensen, David Tornado Warning 2012; The Last Exorcism Part II 2013

Jensen (2), David (1952-) Schizopolis 1996; A Love Song for Bobby Long 2004

Jensen, Maren (1957-) Battlestar Galactica 1978; Beyond the Reef 1981; Deadly Blessing 1981

Jensen, Todd Cyborg Cop 1993; Operation Delta Force 1996; Operation Delta Force II: Mayday 1998

Jenson, Roy (1927-2007) Cry for Me Billy 1972; Journey through Rosebud 1972; Chinatown 1974; The Wind and the Lion 1975; Breakheart Pass 1976; The Duchess and the Dirtwater Fox 1976

Jenson, Sasha Dazed and Confused 1993; Bad Company 1994

Jentsch, Julia (1978-) Sophie Scholl: the Final Days 2005; I Served the King of England 2006; Hannah Arendt 2012

Jeong, Ken (1969-) All about Steve 2009; Furry Vengeance 2010; Vampires Suck 2010; The Hangover: Part II 2011; The Hangover Part III 2013; Norm of the North 2016

Jeremy, Ron Orgazmo 1997; Midgets vs Mascots 2008

Jergens, Adele (1917-2002) A Thousand and One Nights 1945; Down to Earth 1947; The Dark Past 1948; The Prince of Thieves 1948; Ladies of the Chorus 1949; Slightly French 1949; Armored Car Robbery 1950; The Sound of Fury 1950; Abbott and Costello Meet the Invisible Man 1951; Sugarfoot 1951; Somebody Loves Me 1952; Fireman Save My Child 1954; The Day the World Ended 1956

Jergens, Diane (1937-) High School Confidential 1958; Sing, Boy, Sing 1958; The FBI Story 1959

Jerins, Sterling And So It Goes 2014; No Escape 2014

Jerrold, Mary (1877-1955) Friday the Thirteenth 1933; Doctor's Orders 1934; Mr Perrin and Mr Traill 1948; The Queen of Spades 1948; Woman Hater 1948; Top of the Form 1953

Jessel, George (1898-1981) Juke Box Rhythm 1959; Can Heironymus Merkin Ever Forget Mercy Humppe and Find True Happiness? 1969

Jessel, Patricia (1920-1968) The Man Upstairs 1958; The City of the Dead 1960; A Funny Thing Happened on the Way to the Forum 1966

Jesson, Paul All or Nothing 2002; Mr Turner 2014

Jeter, Michael (1952-2003) The Fisher King 1991; Sister Act 2: Back in the Habit 1993; Drop Zone 1994; Waterworld 1995; The Boys Next Door 1996; Mrs Santa Claus 1996; Air Bud 1997; Thursday 1998; The Green Mile 1999; Jakob the Liar 1999; Jurassic Park III 2001; Welcome to Collinwood 2002; Open Range 2003; The Polar Express 2004

Jewel, Jimmy (1909-1995) Rhythm Serenade 1943; Nearest and Dearest 1972; Arthur's Hallowed Ground 1985; Rocinante 1986; The Krays 1990

Jewell, Isabel (1909-1972) Counsellor-at-Law 1933; Design for Living 1933; Evelyn Prentice 1934; Ceiling Zero 1935; Big Brown Eyes 1936; Go West, Young Man 1936; The Man Who Lived Twice 1936; Valiant Is the Word for Carrie 1936; Lost Horizon 1937; Marked Woman 1937; The Falcon and the Co-Eds 1943; The Leopard Man 1943; The Seventh Victim 1943; The Merry Monahans 1944; Badman's Territory 1946; Lady of Deceit 1947; Belle Starr's Daughter 1948; Ciao! Manhattan 1973

Jhangiani, Preeti (1980-) Mohabbatein 2000; Awara Paagal Deewana 2002

Jhutti, Ronny Immaculate Conception 1991; Wild West 1992; Nina's Heavenly Delights 2006

Jiang Wen (1963-) Red Sorghum 1987; Keep Cool 1997; Devils on the Doorstep 2000; The Missing Gun 2002

Jillette, Penn aka **Penn** (1955-) My Chauffeur 1986; Penn & Teller Get Killed 1989; Fantasia 2000 1999; Tim's Vermeer 2013

Jimenez, Juan Antonio Blood Wedding 1981; Carmen 1983; El Amor Brujo 1986

Jobert, Marlène (1943-) Masculine Feminine 1966; Rider on the Rain 1970; Catch Me a Spy 1971; Les Mariés de l'An Deux 1971; Ten Days' Wonder 1971

Jodorowsky, Adan Santa Sangre 1989; 2 Days in Paris 2006

Jodorowsky, Alexandro (1929-) El Topo 1971; The Holy Mountain 1973; Midnight Movies: from the Margins to the Mainstream 2005; The Dance of Reality 2013

Jodorowsky, Brontis El Topo 1971; The Dance of Reality 2013

Johann, Zita (1904-1993) The Struggle 1931; The Mummy 1932; Tiger Shark 1932; The Sin of Nora Moran 1933

Johansen, David (1950-) Candy Mountain 1987; Scrooged 1988; Desire & Hell at Sunset Motel 1991; Tales from the Darkside: the Movie 1991; Freejack 1992

Johansson, Paul (1964-) Soapdish 1991; A Trick of the Mind 2006

Johansson, Scarlett (1984-) The Horse Whisperer 1998; My Brother the Pig 1999; An American Rhapsody 2001; Eight Legged Freaks 2001; Ghost World 2001; The Man Who Wasn't There 2001; Girl with a Pearl Earring 2003; Lost in Translation 2003; A Good

Woman 2004; In Good Company 2004; A Love Song for Bobby Long 2004; The Perfect Score 2004; The SpongeBob SquarePants Movie 2004; The Island 2005; Match Point 2005; The Black Dahlia 2006; The Prestige 2006; Scoop 2006; The Nanny Diaries 2007; He's Just Not That into You 2008; The Other Boleyn Girl 2008; The Spirit 2008; Vicky Cristina Barcelona 2008; Iron Man 2 2010; We Bought a Zoo 2011; Hitchcock 2012; Marvel Avengers Assemble 2012; Don Jon 2013; Her 2013; Under the Skin 2013; Captain America: the Winter Soldier 2014; Chef 2014; Lucy 2014; Avengers: Age of Ultron 2015; Captain America: Civil War 2016; Hail, Caesar! 2016; The Jungle Book 2016; Sing 2016; Ghost in the Shell 2017

Johar, I S (1920-1984) Harry Black and the Tiger 1958; North West Frontier 1959; Death on the Nile 1978

John, Elton (1947-) Born to Boogie 1972; Tommy 1975; The Road to El Dorado 2000

John, Errol (1924-1988) The Sins of Rachel Cade 1960; PT 109 1963; Guns at Batasi 1964; Assault on a Queen 1966

John, Georg (1879-1934) The Spiders 1919; Dr Mabuse, the Gambler 1922

John, Gottfried (1942-2014) Mother Küsters Goes to Heaven 1975; In a Year of 13 Moons 1978; The Marriage of Maria Braun 1978; Berlin Alexanderplatz 1980; Wings of Fame 1990; Institute Benjamenta, or This Dream People Call Human Life 1995; Asterix and Obelix Take On Caesar 1999

John, Karl (1905-1977) The Lost One 1951; The Devil's General 1955

John, Rosamund (1913-1998) The First of the Few 1942; The Gentle Sex 1943; The Lamp Still Burns 1943; Tawny Pipit 1944; The Way to the Stars 1945; Green for Danger 1946; Fame Is the Spur 1947; The Upturned Glass 1947; When the Bough Breaks 1947; No Place for Jennifer 1949

Johnes, Alexandra Zelly and Me 1988; The NeverEnding Story II: the Next Chapter 1991

Johns, Glynis (1923-) South Riding 1938; 49th Parallel 1941; The Adventures of Tartu 1943; The Halfway House 1943; Perfect Strangers 1945; Frieda 1947; An Ideal Husband 1947; Miranda 1947; Dear Mr Prohack 1949; Third Time Lucky 1949; State Secret 1950; Appointment with Venus 1951; Encore 1951; The Magic Box 1951; No Highway 1951; The Card 1952; The Sword and the Rose 1952; Personal Affair 1953; Rob Roy, the Highland Rogue 1953; The Weak and the Wicked 1953; The Beachcomber 1954; Mad about Men 1954; The Seekers 1954; Josephine and Men 1955; The Court Jester 1956; Loser Takes All 1956; The Day They Gave Babies Away 1957; Another Time, Another Place 1958; Shake Hands with the Devil 1959; The Sundowners 1960; The Cabinet of Caligari 1962; The Chapman Report 1962; Papa's Delicate Condition 1963; Mary Poppins 1964; Dear Brigitte 1965; Don't Just Stand There 1968; Lock Up Your Daughters! 1969; Under Milk Wood 1971; The Vault of Horror 1973; Zelly and Me 1988; Hostile Hostages 1994; While You Were Sleeping 1995; Superstar 1999

Johns, Harriette (1921-1990) An Ideal Husband 1947; Edward, My Son 1949

Johns, Mervyn (1899-1992) Saloon Bar 1940; Next of Kin 1942; Went the Day Well? 1942; The Bells Go Down 1943; The Halfway House 1943; My Learned Friend 1943; San Demetrio London 1943; Dead of Night 1945; Pink String and Sealing Wax 1945; The Captive Heart 1946; Captain Boycott 1947; Easy Money 1947; Counterblast 1948; Diamond City 1949; Edward, My Son 1949; Scrooge 1951; The Oracle 1952; The Master of Ballantrae 1953; Valley of Song 1953; Romeo and Juliet 1954; The Blue Peter 1955; 1984 1955; The Intimate Stranger 1956; The Vicious Circle 1957; Never Let Go 1960; The Day of the Triffids 1962; 80,000 Suspects 1963; The Old Dark House 1963; The Heroes of Telemark 1965

Johns, Stratford (1925-2002) The Great St Trinian's Train Robbery 1966; The Plank 1967; The Fiendish Plot of Dr Fu Manchu 1980; George and Mildred 1980; Dance with a Stranger 1984; Car Trouble 1985; Wild Geese II 1985; The Lair of the White Worm 1988; Salome's Last Dance 1988; Splitting Heirs 1993

Johnson, Aaron aka Taylor-Johnson, Aaron (1990-) Shanghai Knights 2002; Tom & Thomas 2002; The Thief Lord 2005; Angus, Thongs and Perfect Snogging 2008; The Greatest 2009; Kick-Ass 2009; Chatroom 2010; Nowhere Boy 2010; Albert Nobbs 2011; Anna Karenina 2012; Savages 2012; Kick-Ass 2 2013; Godzilla 2014; Nocturnal Animals 2016

Johnson, Adrienne-Joi aka Johnson, A J (1963-) House Party 1990; Baby Boy 2001

Johnson, Alexz Final Destination 3 2006; Stranger with My Face 2009

Johnson, Amy Jo (1970-) Mighty Morphin Power Rangers: the Movie 1995; Hard Ground 2003

Johnson, Anne-Marie (1960-) Hollywood Shuffle 1987; Robot Jox 1989; True Identity 1991; Uncorked 2008

Johnson, Anthony aka Johnson, A J BAPS 1997; I Got the Hook Up 1998; The Players Club 1998

Johnson, Arch (1924-1997) Gun Glory 1957; GI Blues 1960; The Cheyenne Social Club 1970; Napoleon and Samantha 1972

Johnson, Arte (1929-) Love at First Bite 1979; Evil Spirits 1991; Munchie 1992

Johnson, Ashley (1983-) AWOL 1990; Dancer, Texas Pop 81 1998; Recess: School's Out 2001; What Women Want 2001; Fast Food Nation 2006; Spread 2008

Johnson (1), Ben (1918-1996) Mighty Joe Young 1949; She Wore a Yellow Ribbon 1949; Rio Grande 1950; Wagonmaster 1950; Shane 1953; Ten Who Dared 1960; One-Eyed Jacks 1961; Will Penny 1967; Hang 'Em High 1968; The Undefeated 1969; The Wild Bunch 1969; Chisum 1970; Kid Blue 1971; The Last Picture Show 1971; something big 1971; Corky 1972; The Getaway 1972; Junior Bonner 1972; Dillinger 1973; The Train Robbers 1973; The Sugarland Express 1974; Bite the Bullet 1975; Hustle 1975; Breakheart Pass 1976; Grayeagle 1977; The Greatest 1977; The Swarm 1978; The Hunter 1980; Terror Train 1980; Tex 1982; Champions 1983; Red Dawn 1984; Wild Horses 1985; Cherry 2000 1988; My Heroes Have Always Been Cowboys 1991; Radio Flyer 1992; Angels in the Outfield 1994; The Evening Star 1996

Johnson (1), Bill (1916-1957) It's a Pleasure 1945; Keep Your Powder Dry 1945

Johnson, Brad (1959-) Always 1989; Flight of the Intruder 1991; Victim of Rage 1994

Johnson, Bryce Sleeping Dogs Lie. 2006; Willow Creek 2013

Johnson, Celia (1908-1982) In Which We Serve 1942; This Happy Breed 1944; Brief Encounter 1945; The Astonished Heart 1949; The Holly and the Ivy 1952; I Believe in You 1952; The Captain's Paradise 1953; A Kid for Two Farthings 1955; The Good Companions 1956; The Prime of Miss Jean Brodie 1969; Les Misérables 1978

Johnson, Chic (1891-1962) All over Town 1937; Hellzapoppin' 1941

Johnson, Chubby (1903-1974) Treasure of Lost Canyon 1952; Back to God's Country 1953; Calamity Jane 1953; Law and Order 1953; Cattle Queen of Montana 1954; The River's Edge 1957

Johnson, Corey (1966-) Out for a Kill 2003; The Contract 2006; The All Together 2007; Pimp 2010; Blood Moon 2014

Johnson, Dakota (1989-) For Ellen 2012; Cymbeline 2014; A Bigger Splash 2015; Fifty Shades of Grey 2015; How to Be Single 2016; Fifty Shades Darker 2017

Johnson, Don (1949-) Good Morning... and Goodbye 1967; The Harrad Experiment 1973; A Boy and His Dog 1975; Return to Macon County 1975; Sweet Hearts Dance 1988; Dead-Bang 1989; The Hot Spot 1990; Harley Davidson and the Marlboro Man 1991; Paradise 1991; Born Yesterday 1993; Guilty as Sin 1993; Tin Cup 1996; Goodbye Lover 1997; Machete 2010; Django Unchained 2012; Cold in July 2014

Johnson, Dwayne aka The Rock aka Johnson, Dwayne "The Rock" (1972-) The Mummy Returns 2001; The Scorpion King 2002; Welcome to the Jungle 2003; Walking Tall 2004; Be Cool 2005; Doom 2005; Southland Tales 2005; Gridiron Gang 2006; The Game Plan 2007; Get Smart 2008; Planet 51 2009; Race to Witch Mountain 2009; Tooth Fairy 2009; Faster 2010; The Other Guys 2010; You Again 2010; Fast Five 2011; Journey 2 the Mysterious Island 2011; Fast & Furious 6 2013; GI Joe: Retaliation 2013; Pain & Gain 2013; Snitch 2013; Fast & Furious 7 2014; Hercules 2014;

San Andreas 2015; Central Intelligence 2016; Baywatch 2017

Johnson, Dyke Ride Lonesome 1959; Comanche Station 1960

Johnson (3), Eric (1979-) Honeymoon with Mom 2006; A Nanny's Secret 2008; Call Me Mrs Miracle 2010

Johnson, Fred (1899-1971) Native Land 1942; Break in the Circle 1955; Doctor Blood's Coffin 1960

Johnson, Georgann (1926-) Short Cut to Hell 1957; The Hideaways 1973; Murphy's Romance 1985

Johnson, Greg Rainbow Warrior 1992; The Insatiable Moon 2010

Johnson, Jake aka Johnson, Jake M (1978-) Paper Heart 2009; No Strings Attached 2011; Safety Not Guaranteed 2012; Drinking Buddies 2013; Let's Be Cops 2014

Johnson (2), Karl (1948-) Jubilee 1978; The Tempest 1979; Close My Eyes 1991; Wittgenstein 1993; Love Is the Devil: Study for a Portrait of Francis Bacon 1998; Pure 2002; Hot Fuzz 2007; I Know You Know 2008

Johnson, Katie (1878-1957) The Last Adventurers 1937; The Ladykillers 1955; How to Murder a Rich Uncle 1957

Johnson, Kay (1904-1975) Dynamite 1929; Billy the Kid 1930; Madam Satan 1930; American Madness 1932; Of Human Bondage 1934; This Man Is Mine 1934; Village Tale 1935; White Banners 1938; The Real Glory 1939

Johnson, Kurt R (1952-1986) Jane Austen in Manhattan 1980; The Fan 1981

Johnson, Lamont (1922-2010) The Brothers Rico 1957; Shogun Assassin 1980; Live Virgin 2000

Johnson, Laura (1957-) Chiller 1985; Paper Hearts 1993; Trauma 1993; Judge & Jury 1995; And the Beat Goes On: the Sonny and Cher Story 1999

Johnson, Lynn-Holly (1958-) Ice Castles 1978; For Your Eyes Only 1981; The Watcher in the Woods 1982

Johnson, Melodie (1943-) The Ride to Hangman's Tree 1967; Coogan's Bluff 1968

Johnson, Michelle (1965-) Blame It on Rio 1984; Waxwork 1988; Dr Giggles 1992; Far and Away 1992; A Woman Scorned 1992; Body Shot 1994; The Glimmer Man 1996

Johnson, Noble (1881-1978) The Navigator 1924; Hands Up! 1926; The Four Feathers 1929; The Most Dangerous Game 1932; Murders in the Rue Morgue 1932; King Kong 1933; She 1935; The Ghost Breakers 1940

Johnson, Penny Automatic 1994; The Road to Galveston 1996

Johnson, Rafer (1935-) The Fiercest Heart 1961; Wild in the Country 1961; Tarzan and the Jungle Boy 1968; The Last Grenade 1970

Johnson, Reggie Platoon 1986; Seven Hours to Judgment 1988

Johnson, Richard (1927-2015) Never So Few 1959; Cairo 1962; 80,000 Suspects 1963; The Haunting 1963; The Pumpkin Eater 1964; The Amorous Adventures of Moll Flanders 1965; Operation Crossbow 1965; Deadlier than the Male 1966; Khartoum 1966; Danger Route 1967; Oedipus the King 1967; The Rover 1967; A Twist of Sand 1967; Some Girls Do 1969; Julius Caesar 1970; Sin 1972; Hennessy 1975; Aces High 1976; The Four Feathers 1978; A Nightingale Sang in Berkeley Square 1979; Zombie Flesh Eaters 1979; The Monster Club 1980; Turtle Diary 1985; A Man for All Seasons 1988; Spymaker: the Secret Life of Ian Fleming 1990; Treasure Island 1990; Milk 1999; The Boy in the Striped Pyjamas 2008; Radiator 2014

Johnson, Rita (1913-1965) London by Night 1937; Man-Proof 1937; Letter of Introduction 1938; Smashing the Rackets 1938; Broadway Serenade 1939; Nick Carter, Master Detective 1939; Edison, the Man 1940; Appointment for Love 1941; Here Comes Mr Jordan 1941; The Major and the Minor 1942; My Friend Flicka 1943; The Affairs of Susan 1945; The Naughty Nineties 1945; Pardon My Past 1945; They Won't Believe Me 1947; The Big Clock 1948; Sleep, My Love 1948

Johnson, Robin (1964-) Times Square 1980; DOA 1988

Johnson, Russell (1924-2014) It Came from Outer Space 1953; Law and Order 1953; Seminole 1953; Tumbleweed 1953; Ride Clear of Diablo 1954; This Island Earth 1955; Attack of the Crab Monsters 1957; The Saga of Hemp Brown 1958

Johnson, Scarlett Alice aka Johnson, Scarlett Adulthood 2008; Pimp 2010

Johnson, Sunny (1953-1984) Dr Heckyl & Mr Hype 1980; Flashdance 1983

Johnson, Tor (1903-1971) Bride of the Monster 1955; The Black Sleep 1956; The Unearthly 1957; Night of the Ghouls 1959

Johnson, Van (1916-2008) Too Many Girls 1940; Dr Gillespie's New Assistant 1942; Somewhere I'll Find You 1942; The War against Mrs Hadley 1942; Dr Gillespie's Criminal Case 1943; The Human Comedy 1943; Pilot #5 1943; A Guy Named Joe 1944; Thirty Seconds over Tokyo 1944; Three Men in White 1944; Two Girls and a Sailor 1944; The White Cliffs of Dover 1944; Thrill of a Romance 1945; Week-End at the Waldorf 1945; Easy to Wed 1946; High Barbaree 1947; Command Decision 1948; State of the Union 1948; Battleground 1949; In the Good Old Summertime 1949; Scene of the Crime 1949; The Big Hangover 1950; Duchess of Idaho 1950; Go for Broke! 1951; It's a Big Country 1951; Plymouth Adventure 1952; Easy to Love 1953; Remains to Be Seen 1953; Brigadoon 1954; The Caine Mutiny 1954; The End of the Affair 1954; The Last Time I Saw Paris 1954; Men of the Fighting Lady 1954; The Siege at Red River 1954; Beyond the River 1956; Miracle in the Rain 1956; 23 Paces to Baker Street 1956; The Last Blitzkrieg 1958; Subway in the Sky 1958; Beyond This Place 1959; Divorce American Style 1967; Where Angels Go... Trouble Follows 1968; Yours, Mine and Ours 1968; The Kidnapping of the President 1980; The Purple Rose of Cairo 1985

Johnson, Wil Babymother 1998; South West Nine 2001; Emotional Backgammon 2003

Johnson, Wilko Oil City Confidential 2009; The Ecstasy of Wilko Johnson 2015

Johnston, Amy The Buddy Holly Story 1978; Jennifer 1978

Johnston, J J Things Change 1988; K-911 1999

Johnston, Jamie More than Meets the Eye: the Joan Brock Story 2003; The Tenth Circle 2008

Johnston, John Dennis (1945-) A Breed Apart 1984; Communion 1989; Pink Cadillac 1989

Johnston, Kristen aka Johnson, Kristen (1967-) Austin Powers: the Spy Who Shagged Me 1999; The Flintstones in Viva Rock Vegas 2000; Music and Lyrics 2007; Bride Wars 2008

Johnston, Margaret (1917-2002) A Man about the House 1947; Portrait of Clare 1950; The Magic Box 1951; Knave of Hearts 1954; Touch and Go 1955; Night of the Eagle 1961; Girl in the Headlines 1963; The Psychopath 1966; Sebastian 1968

Johnston, Oliver (1888-1966) A King in New York 1957; A Touch of Larceny 1959; Dr Crippen 1962; The Tomb of Ligeia 1964; It! 1966; A Countess from Hong Kong 1967

Johnston, Sue (1943-) Brassed Off 1996; Face 1997; New Year's Day 1999; Imagine Me and You 2005; Golden Years 2016

Jokovic, Mirjana (1967-) Eversmile, New Jersey 1989; Underground 1995; Side Streets 1998

Jolie, Angelina aka Jolie Pitt, Angelina (1975-) Cyborg 2: Glass Shadow 1993; Hackers 1995; Foxfire 1996; Love Is All There Is 1996; Mojave Moon 1996; Playing God 1997; Gia 1998; Playing by Heart 1998; The Bone Collector 1999; Girl, Interrupted 1999; Pushing Tin 1999; Gone in Sixty Seconds 2000; Lara Croft: Tomb Raider 2001; Original Sin 2001; Life or Something like It 2002; Beyond Borders 2003; Lara Croft, Tomb Raider: the Cradle of Life 2003; Alexander 2004; Shark Tale 2004; Sky Captain and the World of Tomorrow 2004; Taking Lives 2004; Mr & Mrs Smith 2005; The Good Shepherd 2006; Beowulf 2007; A Mighty Heart 2007; Changeling 2008; Kung Fu Panda 2008; Wanted 2008; Salt 2010; The Tourist 2010; Kung Fu Panda 2 2011; Maleficent 2014; By the Sea 2015; Kung Fu Panda 3 2016

Jolson, Al (1886-1950) The Jazz Singer 1927; The Singing Fool 1928; Say It with Songs 1929; Mammy 1930; Hallelujah, I'm a Bum 1933; Wonder Bar 1934; Go into Your Dance 1935; The Singing Kid 1936; Rose of Washington Square 1939; Swanee River 1939

Jonas, Joe Camp Rock 2008; Hannah Montana & Miley Cyrus: Best of Both Worlds Concert 2008; Jonas Brothers: the 3D Concert Experience 2009

Jonas, Kevin Camp Rock 2008; Hannah Montana & Miley Cyrus: Best of Both Worlds Concert 2008; Jonas Brothers: the 3D Concert Experience 2009

Jonas, Nick Camp Rock 2008; Hannah Montana & Miley Cyrus: Best of Both Worlds Concert 2008; Jonas Brothers: the 3D Concert Experience 2009; Goat 2016

Joner, Kristoffer King of Devil's Island 2010; Babycall 2011

Jones-Davies, Sue Radio On 1979; Elenya 1992; Solomon and Gaenor 1998

Jones-Moreland, Betsy (1930-2006) The Last Woman on Earth 1960; Creature from the Haunted Sea 1961

Jones, Allan (1907-1992) A Night at the Opera 1935; Show Boat 1936; A Day at the Races 1937; The Firefly 1937; Everybody Sing 1938; The Boys from Syracuse 1940

Jones, Angus T See Shoot Run 2001; The Rookie 2002; Bringing Down the House 2003

Jones, Barry (1893-1981) Dancing with Crime 1946; Madeleine 1949; The Clouded Yellow 1950; Seven Days to Noon 1950; Appointment with Venus 1951; White Corridors 1951; Plymouth Adventure 1952; Return to Paradise 1953; Brigadoon 1954; Demetrius and the Gladiators 1954; The Glass Slipper 1955; Alexander the Great 1956; Saint Joan 1957; The Safecracker 1958; The Thirty-Nine Steps 1959

Jones, Bruce (1953-) Raining Stones 1993; Bob's Weekend 1996; The Full Monty 1997

Jones, Caleb Landry (1989-) The Last Exorcism 2010; Antiviral 2012; Tom at the Farm 2013; God's Pocket 2014; Queen and Country 2014; Stonewall 2015; Mena 2017

Jones, Carolyn (1930-1983) House of Wax 1953; The Tender Trap 1955; Invasion of the Body Snatchers 1956; Baby Face Nelson 1957; The Bachelor Party 1957; Johnny Trouble 1957; King Creole 1958; Marjorie Morningstar 1958; Career 1959; Last Train from Gun Hill 1959; Ice Palace 1960; How the West Was Won 1962; A Ticklish Affair 1963; The Dance of Death 1969; Eaten Alive 1976

Jones, Cherry (1956-) Julian Po 1997; Cradle Will Rock 1999; The Lady in Question 1999; Murder in a Small Town 1999; Erin Brockovich 2000; Signs 2002; The Village 2004; Amelia 2009; The Beaver 2010; I Saw the Light 2015

Jones, Christopher (1941-2014) Wild in the Streets 1968; The Looking Glass War 1969; Ryan's Daughter 1970

Jones, Claude Earl Impulse 1984; Bride of Re-Animator 1991

Jones, Clifton (1942-) Only When I Larf 1968; Sheena 1984

Jones, Dean (1931-2015) Tea and Sympathy 1956; These Wilder Years 1956; Jailhouse Rock 1957; Until They Sail 1957; Torpedo Run 1958; Never So Few 1959; Under the Yum Yum Tree 1963; Two on a Guillotine 1964; That Darn Cat! 1965; Any Wednesday 1966; Monkeys, Go Home! 1966; The Ugly Dachshund 1966; Blackbeard's Ghost 1967; The Horse in the Gray Flannel Suit 1968; The Love Bug 1969; The Million Dollar Duck 1971; Snowball Express 1972; The Shaggy DA 1976; Herbie Goes to Monte Carlo 1977; Born Again 1978; Other People's Money 1991; Beethoven 1992; That Darn Cat 1997

Jones, Dickie aka Jones, Dick (1927-2014) Pinocchio 1940; Rocky Mountain 1950; Fort Worth 1951; The Cool and the Crazy 1958

Jones, Doug (1960-) Hellboy 2004; Pan's Labyrinth 2006; 4: Rise of the Silver Surfer 2007; Hellboy II: the Golden Army 2008; Gainsbourg (Je T'Aime... Moi Non Plus) 2010

Jones, Eddie (1937-) Year of the Dragon 1985; Apprentice to Murder 1988; Return to Me 2000; Seabiscuit 2003

Jones, Emrys (1915-1972) One of Our Aircraft Is Missing 1942; Blue Scar 1947; The Small Back Room 1949; Deadly Nightshade 1953; Three Cases of Murder 1953; Serena 1962

Jones, Evan 8 Mile 2002; Glory Road 2006

Jones, Felicity (1983-) Brideshead Revisited 2008; Chéri 2009; Cemetery Junction 2010; Chalet Girl 2010; SoulBoy 2010; The Tempest 2010; Albatross 2011; Hysteria 2011; Like Crazy 2011; Breathe In 2013; The Invisible Woman 2013; The Theory of Everything 2015; True Story 2015; Inferno 2016; A Monster Calls 2016; Rogue One: a Star Wars Story 2016

Jones, Freddie (1927–) Marat/Sade 1966; The Bliss of Mrs Blossom 1968; Otley 1968; Frankenstein Must Be Destroyed 1969; Assault 1970; Doctor in Trouble 1970; Goodbye Gemini 1970; Antony and Cleopatra 1972; Sitting Target 1972; The Satanic Rites of Dracula 1973; All Creatures Great and Small 1974; Never Too Young to Rock 1975; Zulu Dawn 1979; The Elephant Man 1980; Agatha Christie's Murder Is Easy 1982; Firefox 1982; And the Ship Sails On 1983; Krull 1983; Dune 1984; Firestarter 1984; The Black Cauldron 1985; Young Sherlock Holmes 1985; Consuming Passions 1988; The Last Butterfly 1990; The NeverEnding Story III 1994; House! 2000; Ladies in Lavender 2004; By Our Selves 2015

Jones, Gemma (1942–) The Devils 1971; On the Black Hill 1987; Paperhouse 1988; Feast of July 1995; Sense and Sensibility 1995; Wilde 1997; Captain Jack 1998; The Theory of Flight 1998; The Winslow Boy 1999; Bridget Jones's Diary 2001; Bridget Jones: the Edge of Reason 2004; Fragile 2005; The Contractor 2007; Good 2008; Forget Me Not 2009; You Will Meet a Tall Dark Stranger 2010; Radiator 2014; Bridget Jones's Baby 2016

Jones, Gillian Shame 1987; The Tree 2010; The Rover 2014

Jones, Gordon (1911–1963) Red Salute 1935; Strike Me Pink 1936; Among the Living 1941; The Feminine Touch 1941; Flying Tigers 1942; The Secret Life of Walter Mitty 1947; Tokyo Joe 1949; North of the Great Divide 1950; Trail of Robin Hood 1950; Smoke Signal 1955

Jones, Grace (1952–) Gordon's War 1973; Conan the Destroyer 1984; A View to a Kill 1985; Vamp 1986; Siesta 1987; Straight to Hell 1987; Boomerang 1992; Palmer's Pick-Up 1999

Jones, Griffith (1910–2007) The Rise of Catherine the Great 1934; Escape Me Never 1935; First a Girl 1935; The Mill on the Floss 1937; Return of a Stranger 1937; A Yank at Oxford 1938; The Four Just Men 1939; Young Man's Fancy 1939; Uncensored 1942; The Rake's Progress 1945; The Wicked Lady 1945; Miranda 1947; They Made Me a Fugitive 1947; Once upon a Dream 1948; Account Rendered 1957; Not Wanted on Voyage 1957

Jones, Hannah Blackmail 1929; Piccadilly 1929

Jones, Helen Bliss 1985; Waiting 1990

Jones, Henry (1912–1999) The Bad Seed 1956; The Girl Can't Help It 1956; The Girl He Left Behind 1956; 3:10 to Yuma 1957; Will Success Spoil Rock Hunter? 1957; Vertigo 1958; The Bramble Bush 1960; Cash McCall 1960; Angel Baby 1961; Never Too Late 1965; Angel in My Pocket 1968; Butch Cassidy and the Sundance Kid 1969; Support Your Local Sheriff! 1969; Skin Game 1971; Support Your Local Gunfighter 1971; Napoleon and Samantha 1972; The Outfit 1973; Tom Sawyer 1973; Nine to Five 1980; Deathtrap 1982; Arachnophobia 1990; The Grifters 1990; Over Her Dead Body 1990; Breathing Lessons 1994

Jones (2), Jack (1938–) Juke Box Rhythm 1959; The Comeback 1977; Airplane II: the Sequel 1982

Jones, James Earl (1931–) Dr Strangelove, or How I Learned to Stop Worrying and Love the Bomb 1963; The Comedians 1967; End of the Road 1970; The Great White Hope 1970; King: a Filmed Record... Montgomery to Memphis 1970; The Man 1972; Claudine 1974; The Bingo Long Travelling All-Stars and Motor Kings 1976; Swashbuckler 1976; Exorcist II: The Heretic 1977; The Greatest 1977; The Last Remake of Beau Geste 1977; A Piece of the Action 1977; Star Wars Episode IV: a New Hope 1977; Star Wars Episode V: the Empire Strikes Back 1980; Conan the Barbarian 1982; Star Wars Episode VI: Return of the Jedi 1983; My Little Girl 1986; Soul Man 1986; Allan Quatermain and the Lost City of Gold 1987; Gardens of Stone 1987; Matewan 1987; Coming to America 1988; Best of the Best 1989; Field of Dreams 1989; Three Fugitives 1989; The Ambulance 1990; By Dawn's Early Light 1990; Grim Prairie Tales 1990; Heat Wave 1990; The Hunt for Red October 1990; Convicts 1991; Scorchers 1991; Patriot Games 1992; Sneakers 1992; Excessive Force 1993; The Meteor Man 1993; The Sandlot 1993; Sommersby 1993; Clean Slate 1994; Freedom Road: the Vernon Johns Story 1994; The Lion King 1994; Cry, the Beloved Country 1995; Jefferson in Paris 1995; A Family Thing 1996; Good Luck 1996; Looking for

Richard 1996; Casper: a Spirited Beginning 1997; Gang Related 1997; The Lion King II: Simba's Pride 1998; Fantasia 2000 1999; The Reading Room 2005; Star Wars Episode III: Revenge of the Sith 2005; Welcome Home Roscoe Jenkins 2008; Jack and the Beanstalk 2010; The Angriest Man in Brooklyn 2014

Jones, January (1978–) American Pie: the Wedding 2003; Dirty Dancing 2 2003; The Three Burials of Melquiades Estrada 2005; The Boat That Rocked 2009; Justice 2011; Unknown 2011; X-Men: First Class 2011; Good Kill 2014

Jones, Jeffrey (1947–) Easy Money 1983; Amadeus 1984; Transylvania 6-5000 1985; Ferris Bueller's Day Off 1986; Howard, a New Breed of Hero 1986; Beetle Juice 1988; Without a Clue 1988; Valmont 1989; Who's Harry Crumb? 1989; Over Her Dead Body 1990; Mom and Dad Save the World 1992; Out on a Limb 1992; Stay Tuned 1992; Ed Wood 1994; The Crucible 1996; The Devil's Advocate 1997; Ravenous 1999; Sleepy Hollow 1999; Stuart Little 1999; Dr Dolittle 2 2001; Heartbreakers 2001

Jones, Jennifer aka Isley, Phyllis (1919–2009) Frontier Horizon 1939; The Song of Bernadette 1943; Since You Went Away 1944; Love Letters 1945; Cluny Brown 1946; Duel in the Sun 1946; Portrait of Jennie 1948; Madame Bovary 1949; We Were Strangers 1949; Gone to Earth 1950; Carrie 1952; Ruby Gentry 1952; Beat the Devil 1953; Indiscretion of an American Wife 1954; Good Morning, Miss Dove 1955; Love Is a Many-Splendored Thing 1955; The Barretts of Wimpole Street 1956; The Man in the Gray Flannel Suit 1956; A Farewell to Arms 1957; Tender Is the Night 1961; The Idol 1966; Angel, Angel Down We Go 1969; The Towering Inferno 1974

Jones, L Q aka McQueen, Justus E (1927–) An Annapolis Story 1955; Battle Cry 1955; Santiago 1956; Toward the Unknown 1956; Men in War 1957; Buchanan Rides Alone 1958; Torpedo Run 1958; Battle of the Coral Sea 1959; Ten Who Dared 1960; Hell Is for Heroes 1962; Ride the High Country 1962; Showdown 1963; Apache Rifles 1964; Stay Away, Joe 1968; Backtrack 1969; The Ballad of Cable Hogue 1970; Brotherhood of Satan 1970; The Hunting Party 1971; White Line Fever 1975; Winterhawk 1975; Mother, Jugs & Speed 1976; Lone Wolf McQuade 1983; Bulletproof 1987; River of Death 1989; Lightning Jack 1994; The Edge 1997; The Mask of Zorro 1998; The Jack Bull 1999

Jones, Mark Lewis Paper Mask 1990; Solomon and Gaenor 1998; Master and Commander: the Far Side of the World 2003; Queen of the Desert 2015

Jones, Mick New York Doll 2005; The Future Is Unwritten 2006; Lemmy 2010

Jones (1), Morgan Apache Woman 1955; Not of This Earth 1956

Jones, Nathan B aka Jones, Nathan (1969–) Warrior King 2005; Fearless 2006

Jones, Nicholas (1946–) The Blockhouse 1973; Daisy Miller 1974; Flawless 2007

Jones, Norah (1979–) My Blueberry Nights 2007; Ted 2012

Jones, Orlando (1968–) Liberty Heights 1999; Magnolia 1999; Bedazzled 2000; The Replacements 2000; Evolution 2001; Say It Isn't So 2001; Drumline 2002; The Time Machine 2002; Biker Boyz 2003; Primeval 2007; Beyond a Reasonable Doubt 2009; Enemies Closer 2013

Jones, Paul (1942–) Privilege 1967; Demons of the Mind 1971

Jones, Peter (1920–2000) The Blue Lagoon 1949; Miss Robin Hood 1952; The Yellow Balloon 1952; A Day to Remember 1953; Private's Progress 1956; Never Let Go 1960; School for Scoundrels 1960; Nearly a Nasty Accident 1961; Just like a Woman 1966; The Sandwich Man 1966; Carry On England 1976; Milk 1999

Jones, Quincy (1933–) Listen Up: the Lives of Quincy Jones 1990; A Great Day in Harlem 1994; Fantasia 2000 1999

Jones, Rashida (1976–) I Love You, Man 2008; The Social Network 2010; The Big Year 2011; The Muppets 2011; Celeste & Jesse Forever 2012; Cuban Fury 2014

Jones, Renee Friday the 13th Part VI: Jason Lives 1986; Talkin' Dirty after Dark 1991

Jones, Richard T (1972–) Renaissance Man 1994; The Trigger Effect 1996; Event Horizon 1997; The Wood 1999

Auggie Rose 2000; Moonlight Mile 2002; Phone Booth 2002; Twisted 2003

Jones, Sam aka Jones, Sam J (1954–) 10 1979; Flash Gordon 1980; My Chauffeur 1986; Jane and the Lost City 1987; Silent Assassins 1988; American Strays 1996

Jones, Samantha Wait until Dark 1967; Get to Know Your Rabbit 1972

Jones, Shirley (1934–) Oklahoma! 1955; Carousel 1956; April Love 1957; Bobbikins 1959; Never Steal Anything Small 1959; Elmer Gantry 1960; Pepe 1960; Two Rode Together 1961; The Music Man 1962; The Courtship of Eddie's Father 1963; A Ticklish Affair 1963; Bedtime Story 1964; Fluffy 1965; The Secret of My Success 1965; The Cheyenne Social Club 1970; Beyond the Poseidon Adventure 1979; Gideon 1999; Hidden Places 2006; Nora Roberts' Carnal Innocence 2011

Jones, Simon (1950–) Green Card 1990; American Friends 1991; Miracle on 34th Street 1994

Jones, Steve (1955–) The Great Rock 'n' Roll Swindle 1979; Ladies and Gentlemen, the Fabulous Stains 1981

Jones, Tamala (1974–) Booty Call 1997; The Brothers 2001; On the Line 2001; Two Can Play That Game 2001; Head of State 2003; Daddy Day Camp 2007

Jones, Terry (1942–) And Now for Something Completely Different 1971; Monty Python and the Holy Grail 1975; Pleasure at Her Majesty's 1976; Monty Python's Life of Brian 1979; Monty Python Live at the Hollywood Bowl 1982; Monty Python's The Meaning of Life 1983; Erik the Viking 1989; The Wind in the Willows 1996; Help, I'm a Fish! 2000; Not the Messiah: He's a Very Naughty Boy 2009; A Liar's Autobiography: the Untrue Story of Monty Python's Graham Chapman 2012; Absolutely Anything 2015

Jones, Toby (1967–) In Love and War 2001; Infamous 2006; The Painted Veil 2006; The Mist 2007; St Trinian's 2007; City of Ember 2008; Frost/Nixon 2008; W. 2008; Creation 2009; St Trinian's 2: the Legend of Fritton's Gold 2009; Sex & Drugs & Rock & Roll 2009; Your Highness 2010; The Adventures of Tintin: the Secret of the Unicorn 2011; Captain America: the First Avenger 2011; The Rite 2011; Tinker Tailor Soldier Spy 2011; Berberian Sound Studio 2012; Red Lights 2012; Snow White and the Huntsman 2012; Leave to Remain 2013; Serena 2013; Captain America: the Winter Soldier 2014; By Our Selves 2015; The Man Who Knew Infinity 2015; Tale of Tales 2015; Dad's Army 2016; The Coldest City 2017

Jones, Tom (1940–) Mars Attacks! 1996; Agnes Browne 1999

Jones, Tommy Lee aka Jones, Tom Lee (1946–) Love Story 1970; Jackson County Jail 1976; Rolling Thunder 1977; The Betsy 1978; Eyes of Laura Mars 1978; Coal Miner's Daughter 1980; Back Roads 1981; The Executioner's Song 1982; Savage Islands 1983; The River Rat 1984; Black Moon Rising 1985; The Big Town 1987; Stormy Monday 1987; The Dead Can't Lie 1988; The Package 1989; Wings of the Apache 1990; Blue Sky 1991; JFK 1991; Under Siege 1992; The Fugitive 1993; Heaven and Earth 1993; House of Cards 1993; Blown Away 1994; The Client 1994; Cobb 1994; Natural Born Killers 1994; Batman Forever 1995; The Good Old Boys 1995; Men in Black 1997; Volcano 1997; Small Soldiers 1998; US Marshals 1998; Double Jeopardy 1999; Rules of Engagement 2000; Space Cowboys 2000; The Hunted 2002; Men in Black 2 2002; The Missing 2003; Man of the House 2005; The Three Burials of Melquiades Estrada 2005; A Prairie Home Companion 2006; In the Valley of Elah 2007; No Country for Old Men 2007; In the Electric Mist 2009; The Company Men 2010; The Sunset Limited 2010; Captain America: the First Avenger 2011; Emperor 2012; Hope Springs 2012; Lincoln 2012; Men in Black 3 2012; The Family 2013; The Homesman 2014; Criminal 2016; Jason Bourne 2016; Mechanic: Resurrection 2016

Jones, Vinnie (1965–) Lock, Stock and Two Smoking Barrels 1998; Snatch 2000; Mean Machine 2001; Swordfish 2001; Tooth 2003; The Big Bounce 2004; EuroTrip 2004; She's the Man 2006; The Condemned 2007; Rush Hour 3 2007; The Midnight Meat Train 2008; The Heavy 2009; Age of the Dragons 2010; Kill the Irishman 2011; You May Not Kiss the Bride 2011; Escape Plan 2013

Jonet, Jaclyn Searchers 2.0 2007; Repo Chick 2009

Jonz, Jo D Deadlocked 2000; Midnight Son 2011

Jonze, Spike (1969–) Three Kings 1999; jackass presents: Bad Grandpa 2013

Jordan, Bobby aka Jordan, Bobbie (1923–1965) Dead End 1937; Angels with Dirty Faces 1938; Angels Wash Their Faces 1939; Dust Be My Destiny 1939; Hell's Kitchen 1939; They Made Me a Criminal 1939; Boys of the City 1940; Young Tom Edison 1940; Pride of the Bowery 1941; Spooks Run Wild 1941; Ghosts in the Night 1943; Bowery Champs 1944

Jordan, Dorothy (1906–1988) Min and Bill 1930; Cabin in the Cotton 1932; Hell Divers 1932; The Lost Squadron 1932; The Roadhouse Murder 1932; The Wet Parade 1932

Jordan, Jeremy Joyful Noise 2012; The Last 5 Years 2014

Jordan, Joanne Moore Faces 1968; The Dunwich Horror 1970; I Dismember Mama 1972

Jordan, Lydia The Secret Lives of Dentists 2003; Pistol Whipped 2008

Jordan, Michael (1963–) Space Jam 1997; Hardball 2001

Jordan, Michael B (1987–) Chronicle 2012; Red Tails 2012; Fruitvale Station 2013; That Awkward Moment 2013; Creed 2015; Fantastic Four 2015

Jordan, Patrick (1923–) Dilemma 1962; The Last Escape 1970

Jordan, Richard (1938–1993) Valdez Is Coming 1971; The Friends of Eddie Coyle 1973; Kamouraska 1973; Rooster Cogburn 1975; The Yakuza 1975; Logan's Run 1976; Interiors 1978; Les Misérables 1978; A Nightingale Sang in Berkeley Square 1979; Old Boyfriends 1979; Raise the Titanic 1980; Dune 1984; A Flash of Green 1984; The Mean Season 1985; The Men's Club 1986; The Secret of My Success 1987; Romero 1989; The Hunt for Red October 1990; Shout 1991; Timebomb 1991; Gettysburg 1993

Jordan, William A Man Called Horse 1970; The Buddy Holly Story 1978; Kingpin 1996

Jorge, Seu The Life Aquatic with Steve Zissou 2004; The Escapist 2007

Jorgensen, Bodil (1961–) The Idiots 1998; The Green Butchers 2003

Jory, Victor (1902–1982) Renegades 1930; He Was Her Man 1934; Madame Du Barry 1934; A Midsummer Night's Dream 1935; Meet Nero Wolfe 1936; The Adventures of Tom Sawyer 1938; Susannah of the Mounties 1939; Cherokee Strip 1940; Charlie Chan in Rio 1941; The Unknown Guest 1943; The Loves of Carmen 1948; Fighting Man of the Plains 1949; South of St Louis 1949; A Woman's Secret 1949; The Capture 1950; The Cariboo Trail 1950; Cave of Outlaws 1951; Flaming Feather 1952; Son of Ali Baba 1952; The Man from the Alamo 1953; Valley of the Kings 1954; Death of a Scoundrel 1956; The Fugitive Kind 1960; The Miracle Worker 1962; Jigsaw 1968; Flap 1970; Papillon 1973

Joseph, Allen (1919–2012) Eraserhead 1976; Marathon Man 1976

Joseph, Paterson (1964–) The Beach 2000; Greenfingers 2000; The Long Run 2000; The Other Man 2008

Josephson, Erland (1923–2012) So Close to Life 1957; The Magician 1958; The Hour of the Wolf 1967; A Passion 1969; Cries and Whispers 1972; Scenes from a Marriage 1973; Face to Face 1976; Autumn Sonata 1978; Montenegro 1981; Fanny and Alexander 1982; Nostalgia 1983; After the Rehearsal 1984; Saving Grace 1985; The Sacrifice 1986; Hanussen 1988; The Unbearable Lightness of Being 1988; The Ox 1991; Prospero's Books 1991; Sofie 1992; Kristin Lavransdatter 1995; Ulysses' Gaze 1995; Faithless 2000; Saraband 2003

Joshi, Sharman Rang De Basanti 2006; Life in a... METRO 2007

Joshua, Larry The Burning 1981; A Midnight Clear 1991; Sugar Hill 1993

Joslin, Samuel The Impossible 2011; Paddington 2014

Joslyn, Allyn (1901–1981) They Won't Forget 1937; The Shining Hour 1938; Fast and Furious 1939; The Great McGinty 1940; No Time for Comedy 1940; This Thing Called Love 1940; The Affairs of Martha 1942; Bedtime Story 1942; My Sister Eileen 1942; Heaven Can Wait 1943; The Immortal Sergeant 1943; Bride by Mistake 1944; The Impostor 1944; Sweet and Lowdown 1944; Colonel Effingham's Raid 1945; The Horn Blows at Midnight 1945; The Shocking Miss Pilgrim 1947; Moonrise 1948; Harriet Craig 1950; The Jazz

Singer 1952; I Love Melvin 1953; The Fastest Gun Alive 1956; Nightmare in the Sun 1964

Jostyn, Jennifer Telling You 1998; House of 1000 Corpses 2001

Jourdan, Louis (1921–2015) The Paradine Case 1947; Letter from an Unknown Woman 1948; No Minor Vices 1948; Madame Bovary 1949; Anne of the Indies 1951; Bird of Paradise 1951; The Happy Time 1952; Decameron Nights 1953; Three Coins in the Fountain 1954; The Bride Is Too Beautiful 1956; Julie 1956; The Swan 1956; Dangerous Exile 1957; Gigi 1958; The Best of Everything 1959; Can-Can 1960; The VIPs 1963; Cervantes 1968; A Flea in Her Ear 1968; The Count of Monte Cristo 1974; The Man in the Iron Mask 1977; Silver Bears 1977; Double Deal 1981; Swamp Thing 1982; Octopussy 1983; The Return of Swamp Thing 1989; Year of the Comet 1992

Jouvet, Louis (1887–1951) Carnival in Flanders 1935; The Lower Depths 1936; Mademoiselle Docteur 1936; Un Carnet de Bal 1937; Drôle de Drame 1937; Hôtel du Nord 1938; La Marseillaise 1938; The End of the Day 1939; Volpone 1941; Quai des Orfèvres 1947

Jover, Arly Blade 1998; Vampires: los Muertos 2002; Little Ashes 2008

Jovovich, Milla (1975–) Kuffs 1991; Return to the Blue Lagoon 1991; Chaplin 1992; Dazed and Confused 1993; The Fifth Element 1997; He Got Game 1998; Joan of Arc 1999; The Million Dollar Hotel 1999; The Claim 2000; Zoolander 2001; Dummy 2002; No Good Deed 2002; Resident Evil 2002; Resident Evil: Apocalypse 2004; Ultraviolet 2005; Resident Evil: Extinction 2007; The Fourth Kind 2009; A Perfect Getaway 2009; Resident Evil: Afterlife 2010; Stone 2010; The Three Musketeers 2011; Resident Evil: Retribution 2012; Cymbeline 2014; Survivor 2015; Resident Evil: the Final Chapter 2017

Joy, Leatrice (1893–1985) The Ace of Hearts 1921; The Ten Commandments 1923; First Love 1939; Love Nest 1951

Joy, Mark Black Rainbow 1989; Pecker 1998

Joy, Nicholas (1894–1964) The Iron Curtain 1948; And Baby Makes Three 1949; Native Son 1951; Affair with a Stranger 1953

Joy, Robert (1951–) Atlantic City, USA 1980; Ragtime 1981; Amityville III: the Demon 1983; Terminal Choice 1985; Desperately Seeking Susan 1985; Millennium 1989; The Dark Half 1991; Harriet the Spy 1996; George A Romero's Land of the Dead 2005; The Hills Have Eyes 2006; It's a Boy/Girl Thing 2006

Joyce, Alice (1890–1955) Stella Dallas 1925; Beau Geste 1926

Joyce, Brenda (1917–2009) The Rains Came 1939; Little Old New York 1940; Maryland 1940; Pillow of Death 1945; Strange Confession 1945; Tarzan and the Amazons 1945; Little Giant 1946; Tarzan and the Leopard Woman 1946; Tarzan and the Huntress 1947; Tarzan and the Mermaids 1948; Tarzan's Magic Fountain 1949

Joyce, Elaine (1945–) Motel Hell 1980; Trick or Treat 1988

Joyce, Paddy (1923–2000) The Girl in the Picture 1956; The Cat Gag 1959

Joyce, Patricia The Visitors 1972; The Catamount Killing 1974

Joyce, Yootha (1927–1980) Die! Die! My Darling 1964; Stranger in the House 1967; Burke & Hare 1971; The Road Builder 1971; Nearest and Dearest 1972; Man about the House 1974; George and Mildred 1980

Joyner, Michelle Grim Prairie Tales 1990; Traces of Red 1992

Judd, Ashley (1968–) Kuffs 1991; Ruby in Paradise 1993; Heat 1995; Normal Life 1995; The Passion of Darkly Noon 1995; Smoke 1995; Norma Jean & Marilyn 1996; Kiss the Girls 1997; A Secret Sin 1997; Simon Birch 1998; Double Jeopardy 1999; Eye of the Beholder 1999; Where the Heart Is 2000; Animal Attraction 2001; Divine Secrets of the Ya-Ya Sisterhood 2002; Frida 2002; High Crimes 2002; Twisted 2003; De-Lovely 2004; Bug 2006; Crossing Over 2008; Tooth Fairy 2009; Dolphin Tale 2011; Divergent 2014; Dolphin Tale 2 2014

Judd, Edward (1932–2009) The Day the Earth Caught Fire 1961; The Long Ships 1963; The World Ten Times Over 1963; First Men in the Moon 1964; Invasion 1965; Strange Bedfellows 1965; Island of Terror 1966; The Vengeance of She 1968; Living Free 1972; Assassin 1973; The Vault of Horror 1973; The Boys in Blue 1983;

The Hound of the Baskervilles 1983; *The Kitchen Toto* 1987

Judels, Charles (1882-1969) *Sweetheart of the Campus* 1941; *Baby Face Morgan* 1942

Judge, Arline (1912-1974) *Looking for Trouble* 1934; *George White's 1935 Scandals* 1935; *King of Burlesque* 1936; *One in a Million* 1935; *Pigskin Parade* 1936; *Valiant Is the Word for Carrie* 1936; *The Lady Is Willing* 1942; *Mad Wednesday* 1950

Judge, Mike (1962-) *Beavis and Butthead Do America* 1996; *SPYkids 2: the Island of Lost Dreams* 2002; *SPYkids 3-D: Game Over* 2003

Juerging, Arno (1947-) *Blood for Dracula* 1974; *Flesh for Frankenstein* 1974

Julia, Raul (1940-1994) *The Organization* 1971; *The Panic in Needle Park* 1971; *The Gumball Rally* 1976; *Eyes of Laura Mars* 1978; *The Escape Artist* 1982; *One from the Heart* 1982; *Tempest* 1982; *Compromising Positions* 1985; *Kiss of the Spider Woman* 1985; *The Morning After* 1986; *Moon over Parador* 1988; *The Penitent* 1988; *Tango Bar* 1988; *Tequila Sunrise* 1988; *Trading Hearts* 1988; *Mack the Knife* 1989; *Romero* 1989; *Frankenstein Unbound* 1990; *Havana* 1990; *Presumed Innocent* 1990; *The Rookie* 1990; *The Addams Family* 1991; *The Plague* 1992; *Addams Family Values* 1993; *The Burning Season* 1994; *Street Fighter* 1994

Julian, Janet (1959-) *On Dangerous Ground* 1986; *King of New York* 1989

July, Miranda *Me and You and Everyone We Know* 2005; *The Future* 2011

Jumbo, Cush *Remainder* 2015; *City of Tiny Lights* 2016

Jun, Gianna aka **Gianna** *Blood: the Last Vampire* 2008; *Snow Flower and the Secret Fan* 2011

Junco, Tito (1915-1983) *A Woman without Love* 1951; *Death in the Garden* 1956

Junco, Victor (1917-1988) *Bandido* 1956; *La Fièvre Monte à el Pao* 1959

Jung Woo-sung aka **Jung Woo-Sung** *The Good the Bad the Weird* 2008; *Reign of Assassins* 2010

Jungmann, Eric (1981-) *Winning London* 2001; *Monster Man* 2003

Junkin, John (1930-2006) *A Hard Day's Night* 1964; *Simon, Simon* 1970; *Rosie Dixon: Night Nurse* 1978

Jurado, Katy (1927-2002) *The Bullfighter and the Lady* 1951; *El Bruto* 1952; *High Noon* 1952; *Arrowhead* 1953; *Broken Lance* 1954; *Trial* 1955; *Trapeze* 1956; *The Badlanders* 1958; *Barabbas* 1961; *One-Eyed Jacks* 1961; *Stay Away, Joe* 1968; *Pat Garrett and Billy the Kid* 1973; *The Children of Sanchez* 1978; *Under the Volcano* 1984

Jurasik, Peter (1950-) *Born Again* 1978; *Tron* 1982; *Crash: the Mystery of Flight 1501* 1990

Jurgens, Curt aka **Jürgens, Curd** (1912-1982) *The Devil's General* 1955; *The Rats* 1955; *And God Created Woman* 1956; *Bitter Victory* 1957; *The Enemy Below* 1957; *Les Espions* 1957; *Ferry to Hong Kong* 1958; *The Inn of the Sixth Happiness* 1958; *Me and the Colonel* 1958; *This Happy Feeling* 1958; *The Blue Angel* 1959; *I Aim at the Stars* 1960; *Hide and Seek* 1963; *Miracle of the White Stallions* 1963; *Psyche '59* 1964; *Lord Jim* 1965; *The Karate Killers* 1967; *The Heroes* 1968; *The Assassination Bureau* 1969; *Battle of Britain* 1969; *Hello - Goodbye* 1970; *The Mephisto Waltz* 1971; *Kill!* 1972; *Soft Beds, Hard Battles* 1973; *The Vault of Horror* 1973; *The Twist* 1976; *The Spy Who Loved Me* 1977; *Breakthrough* 1978; *Just a Gigolo* 1978; *Goldengirl* 1979

Justice, Katherine (1942-) *The Way West* 1967; *5 Card Stud* 1968; *Prescription: Murder* 1968

Justin, John (1917-2002) *The Thief of Bagdad* 1940; *The Gentle Sex* 1943; *The Sound Barrier* 1952; *King of the Khyber Rifles* 1953; *The Man Who Loved Redheads* 1954; *Seagulls over Sorrento* 1954; *The Teckman Mystery* 1954; *Untamed* 1955; *Safari* 1956

K

Kaa, Wi Kuki (1938-2006) *Utu* 1983; *Ngati* 1987

Kaaren, Suzanne (1912-2004) *A Million to One* 1937; *Devil Bat* 1940

Kaas, Nikolaj Lie (1973-) *The Idiots* 1998; *Open Hearts* 2002; *The Green Butchers* 2003; *Reconstruction* 2003; *Brothers* 2004; *Just Another Love Story* 2007; *Angels & Demons* 2009;

The Keeper of Lost Causes 2013; *The Absent One* 2014; *A Second Chance* 2014; *Men & Chicken* 2015

Kaci, Nadia *Ça Commence Aujourd'hui* 1999; *Nationale 7* 1999

Kaczmarek, Jane (1955-) *Falling in Love* 1984; *The Heavenly Kid* 1985; *DOA* 1988; *Vice Versa* 1988; *All's Fair* 1989

Kadochnikov, Pavel (1915-1988) *Ivan the Terrible, Part I* 1944; *Ivan the Terrible, Part II* 1946

Kady, Charlotte *These Foolish Things* 1990; *L.627* 1992; *D'Artagnan's Daughter* 1994; *Laissez-passer* 2001

Kae-Kazim, Hakeem *The Front Line* 2006; *The Fourth Kind* 2009

Kagan, Elaine *By the Sword* 1992; *Babyfever* 1994

Kagan, Marilyn (1951-) *Foxes* 1980; *The Initiation* 1984

Kagawa, Kyoko (1931-) *The Crucified Lovers* 1954; *Sansho the Bailiff* 1954; *The Lower Depths* 1956; *Mothra* 1962; *High and Low* 1963; *No, Not Yet* 1963

Kagawa, Teruyuki (1965-) *Devils on the Doorstep* 2000; *Tokyo Sonata* 2008

Kagurazaka, Megumi *Cold Fish* 2010; *Guilty of Romance* 2011; *Himizu* 2011

Kahan, Steve aka **Kahan, Stephen** (1930-) *Inside Moves: the Guys from Max's Bar* 1980; *Lethal Weapon* 1987; *Lethal Weapon 2* 1989; *Lethal Weapon 3* 1992; *Warlock: the Armageddon* 1993; *Assassins* 1995; *Conspiracy Theory* 1997; *Lethal Weapon 4* 1998

Kahn, Madeline (1942-1999) *What's Up, Doc?* 1972; *The Hideaways* 1973; *Paper Moon* 1973; *Blazing Saddles* 1974; *Young Frankenstein* 1974; *The Adventure of Sherlock Holmes' Smarter Brother* 1975; *At Long Last Love* 1975; *Won Ton Ton, the Dog Who Saved Hollywood* 1976; *High Anxiety* 1977; *The Cheap Detective* 1978; *First Family* 1980; *Simon* 1980; *History of the World Part I* 1981; *City Heat* 1984; *Clue* 1985; *An American Tail* 1986; *Betsy's Wedding* 1990; *Mixed Nuts* 1994; *A Bug's Life* 1998; *Judy Berlin* 1999

Kaidanovsky, Alexander (1946-1995) *Stalker* 1979; *Magic Hunter* 1994

Kain, Khalil (1965-) *Juice* 1991; *Renaissance Man* 1994; *Execution of Justice* 1999; *Bones* 2001

Kaiser, Oldrich *Dark Blue World* 2001; *I Served the King of England* 2006

Kajol (1975-) *Baazigar* 1993; *Dilwale Dulhania Le Jayenge* 1995; *Kabhi Khushi Kabhie Gham...* 2001; *My Name Is Khan* 2010

Kalem, Toni *The Wanderers* 1979; *Silent Rage* 1982; *Billy Galvin* 1986

Kalember, Patricia (1957-) *Stepkids* 1992; *A Far Off Place* 1993; *Signs* 2002; *Straight from the Heart* 2003

Kaler, Berwick *Go Now* 1995; *Jude* 1996

Kalfon, Jean-Pierre (1938-) *Weekend* 1967; *L'Amour Fou* 1968; *The Valley* 1972; *The Lady Cop* 1979; *Condorman* 1981; *A Strange Affair* 1981; *Confidentially Yours* 1983; *L'Amour par Terre* 1984; *Le Cri du Hibou* 1987; *Heartbeat Detector* 2007

Kallianiotes, Helena *Kansas City Bomber* 1972; *Stay Hungry* 1976; *Eureka* 1982

Kalyagin, Aleksandr (1942-) *A Slave of Love* 1976; *An Unfinished Piece for Mechanical Piano* 1976

Kamekona, Danny (1935-1996) *The Karate Kid Part II* 1986; *Robot Jox* 1989

Kamerling, Antonie (1966-) *Suite 16* 1994; *Dominion: Prequel to the Exorcist* 2005

Kaminska, Ida (1899-1980) *The Shop on the High Street* 1965; *The Angel Levine* 1970

Kammer, Salome (1959-) *Heimat 2* 1992; *Heimat 3: a Chronicle of Endings and Beginnings* 2004

Kampers, Fritz (1891-1950) *Westfront 1918* 1930; *Kameradschaft* 1931

Kanakaredes, Melina (1967-) *15 Minutes* 2001; *Snitch* 2013

Kanaly, Steve (1946-) *Dillinger* 1973; *The Sugarland Express* 1974; *The Wind and the Lion* 1975

Kanaoka, Nobu (1959-) *Tetsuo: the Iron Man* 1989; *Tetsuo II: Body Hammer* 1991

Kane, Carol (1952-) *Carnal Knowledge* 1971; *Desperate Characters* 1971; *The Last Detail* 1973; *Dog Day Afternoon* 1975; *Hester Street* 1975; *Annie Hall* 1977; *Valentino* 1977; *When a Stranger Calls* 1979; *Norman Loves Rose* 1982; *Pandemonium* 1982; *Over the Brooklyn Bridge* 1983; *Transylvania 6-5000* 1985; *Jumpin' Jack Flash* 1986; *Ishtar* 1987; *License to Drive* 1988; *Scrooged* 1988; *Sticky Fingers* 1988; *The Lemon Sisters* 1989; *Flashback* 1990; *My Blue*

Heaven 1990; *In the Soup* 1992; *Addams Family Values* 1993; *Baby on Board* 1993; *Even Cowgirls Get the Blues* 1993; *Freaky Friday* 1995; *Napoleon* 1995; *Theodore Rex* 1995; *American Strays* 1996; *Big Bully* 1996; *The Pallbearer* 1996; *Sunset Park* 1996; *Trees Lounge* 1996; *Gone Fishin'* 1997; *Jawbreaker* 1999; *The Shrink Is In* 2000; *My First Mister* 2001; *Confessions of a Teenage Drama Queen* 2004; *The Pacifier* 2005

Kane, Christian (1974-) *Life or Something like It* 2002; *Just Married* 2003; *Secondhand Lions* 2003; *Taxi* 2004

Kane, Eddie (1889-1969) *The Mummy* 1932; *All over Town* 1937

Kane, Jackson D *Showdown* 1973; *The Man Who Fell to Earth* 1976

Kane, Marjorie aka **Kane, Margie "Babe"** aka **Kane, "Babe"** (1909-1992) *The Great Gabbo* 1929; *The Dentist* 1932

Kane, Michael *Lonely Are the Brave* 1962; *The Bedford Incident* 1965

Kane, Tom *The Powerpuff Girls* 2002; *The Wild Thornberrys Movie* 2003; *Star Wars: The Clone Wars* 2008

Kaneko, Nobuo (1923-1995) *Ikiru* 1952; *The Yakuza Papers* 1973; *The Return of Godzilla* 1984

Kaneshiro, Takeshi (1973-) *Chung King Express* 1994; *Fallen Angels* 1995; *House of Flying Daggers* 2004; *Red Cliff* 2008; *The Warlords* 2008; *Dragon* 2011

Kani, John (1943-) *Sarafina!* 1992; *The Ghost and the Darkness* 1996; *Kini and Adams* 1997; *The Tichborne Claimant* 1998; *Coriolanus* 2010

Kanner, Alexis (1942-2003) *Connecting Rooms* 1969; *Crossplot* 1969; *Goodbye Gemini* 1970; *Kings and Desperate Men* 1981

Kanter, Marin *Ladies and Gentlemen, the Fabulous Stains* 1981; *The Loveless* 1981

Kants, Ivar (1949-) *The Plumber* 1979; *Jenny Kissed Me* 1984; *The Naked Country* 1985

Kao Jai *Daughter of the Nile* 1987; *A City of Sadness* 1989

Kapadia, Dimple (1957-) *Bobby* 1973; *Being Cyrus* 2005

Kapelos, John (1956-) *The Breakfast Club* 1985; *Roxanne* 1987; *The Boost* 1988; *All's Fair* 1989; *The Deep End of the Ocean* 1999; *The Sports Pages* 2001; *Identity Theft: the Michelle Brown Story* 2004

Kaplan, Marvin (1924-) *Angels in the Outfield* 1951; *I Can Get It for You Wholesale* 1951

Kapoor, Anil (1959-) *1942: a Love Story* 1994; *Taal* 1999; *Armaan* 2003; *Salaam E Ishq* 2007; *Slumdog Millionaire* 2008; *Mission: Impossible - Ghost Protocol* 2011

Kapoor, Kareena (1980-) *Asoka* 2001; *Kabhi Khushi Kabhie Gham...* 2001; *Yaadein* 2001; *Aitraaz* 2004; *Dev* 2004; *Hulchul* 2004; *Kambakkht Ishq* 2009

Kapoor, Karishma (1974-) *Zubeidaa* 2000; *Shakti - the Power* 2002

Kapoor, Pincho *Bombay Talkie* 1970; *Siddhartha* 1972

Kapoor, Prithviraj aka **Prithviraj** (1906-1972) *Awara* 1951; *Mughal-e-Azam* 1960

Kapoor, Raj (1924-1988) *Andaz* 1949; *Barsaat* 1949; *Awara* 1951; *Shree 420* 1955; *Chori Chori* 1956; *Anari* 1959; *Sangam* 1964

Kapoor, Rajat *Kisna - the Warrior Poet* 2004; *Midnight's Children* 2012

Kapoor, Rishi (1952-) *Bobby* 1973; *Henna* 1990; *Hum Tum* 2004

Kapoor, Shashi aka **Shashiraj** (1938-) *Awara* 1951; *The Householder* 1963; *Shakespeare Wallah* 1965; *Waqt* 1965; *Pretty Polly* 1967; *Bombay Talkie* 1970; *Siddhartha* 1972; *Junoon* 1978; *Heat and Dust* 1982; *Sammy and Rosie Get Laid* 1987; *The Deceivers* 1988; *In Custody* 1993; *Jinnah* 1998; *Side Streets* 1998

Kaprisky, Valérie (1963-) *Breathless* 1983; *La Femme Publique* 1984

Karaman, Bushra *Wedding in Galilee* 1987; *Canticle of the Stones* 1990

Karan, Amara *The Darjeeling Limited* 2007; *All in Good Time* 2012; *A Fantastic Fear of Everything* 2012; *Jadoo* 2013

Karanovic, Mirjana (1957-) *When Father Was Away on Business* 1985; *Underground* 1995; *Esma's Secret* 2006

Karen, Anna (1936-2009) *On the Buses* 1971; *Mutiny on the Buses* 1972; *Holiday on the Buses* 1973

Karen, James (1923-) *Hercules in New York* 1970; *FDR: the Last Year* 1980; *Frances* 1982; *Return of the Living Dead* 1984; *Invaders from Mars*

1986; *Return of the Living Dead Part II* 1988; *Apt Pupil* 1997; *To Live For* 1999; *The Pursuit of Happyness* 2006

Karewicz, Emil (1923-) *The Shadow* 1956; *Kanal* 1957

Karin, Rita (1919-1993) *Sophie's Choice* 1982; *Enemies, a Love Story* 1989

Karina, Anna (1940-) *Le Petit Soldat* 1960; *Cleo from 5 to 7* 1961; *Une Femme Est une Femme* 1961; *She'll Have to Go* 1961; *Le Joli Mai* 1962; *Vivre Sa Vie* 1962; *Bande à Part* 1964; *La Ronde* 1964; *Alphaville* 1965; *Pierrot le Fou* 1965; *La Religieuse* 1965; *Made in USA* 1966; *The Stranger* 1967; *Before Winter Comes* 1968; *The Magus* 1968; *Justine* 1969; *Laughter in the Dark* 1969; *Chinese Roulette* 1976; *Regina* 1982; *Treasure Island* 1986

Karkanis, Athena *The Art of War II: Betrayal* 2008; *George A Romero's Survival of the Dead* 2009

Karlatos, Olga (1947-) *Zombie Flesh Eaters* 1979; *Purple Rain* 1984

Karlen, John (1933-) *Daughters of Darkness* 1970; *House of Dark Shadows* 1970; *Night of Dark Shadows* 1971; *Pennies from Heaven* 1981; *Impulse* 1984; *Racing with the Moon* 1984; *Native Son* 1986; *The Dark Wind* 1991; *Surf Ninjas* 1993; *Without Warning: Terror in the Towers* 1993

Karlin, Miriam (1925-2011) *The Deep Blue Sea* 1955; *The Entertainer* 1960; *The Millionairess* 1960; *Ladies Who Do* 1963; *The Small World of Sammy Lee* 1963; *The Bargee* 1964; *Just like a Woman* 1966; *A Clockwork Orange* 1971; *Mahler* 1974; *Utz* 1992; *The Man Who Cried* 2000; *Suzie Gold* 2003; *Flashbacks of a Fool* 2008

Karloff, Boris aka **?** aka **Karloff** (1887-1969) *The Last of the Mohicans* 1920; *Two Arabian Knights* 1927; *The Criminal Code* 1930; *Five Star Final* 1931; *Frankenstein* 1931; *The Mad Genius* 1931; *Smart Money* 1931; *The Mask of Fu Manchu* 1932; *The Mummy* 1932; *The Old Dark House* 1932; *Scarface* 1932; *The Ghoul* 1933; *The Black Cat* 1934; *The House of Rothschild* 1934; *The Lost Patrol* 1934; *The Black Room* 1935; *Bride of Frankenstein* 1935; *The Raven* 1935; *Charlie Chan at the Opera* 1936; *The Invisible Ray* 1936; *The Man Who Changed His Mind* 1936; *The Walking Dead* 1936; *The Invisible Menace* 1938; *The Man They Could Not Hang* 1939; *Son of Frankenstein* 1939; *Tower of London* 1939; *The Ape* 1940; *Before I Hang* 1940; *British Intelligence* 1940; *Devil's Island* 1940; *You'll Find Out* 1940; *The Devil Commands* 1941; *The Boogie Man Will Get You* 1942; *House of Frankenstein* 1944; *The Body Snatcher* 1945; *Isle of the Dead* 1945; *Bedlam* 1946; *Dick Tracy Meets Gruesome* 1947; *Lured* 1947; *The Secret Life of Walter Mitty* 1947; *Unconquered* 1947; *Abbott and Costello Meet the Killer, Boris Karloff* 1949; *The Strange Door* 1951; *The Black Castle* 1952; *Abbott and Costello Meet Dr Jekyll and Mr Hyde* 1953; *Colonel March Investigates* 1953; *Frankenstein - 1970* 1958; *Grip of the Strangler* 1958; *Corridors of Blood* 1962; *Black Sabbath* 1963; *The Raven* 1963; *The Terror* 1963; *Bikini Beach* 1964; *The Comedy of Terrors* 1964; *Die, Monster, Die!* 1965; *The Ghost in the Invisible Bikini* 1966; *Mad Monster Party* 1966; *The Venetian Affair* 1966; *Cauldron of Blood* 1967; *The Sorcerers* 1967; *Curse of the Crimson Altar* 1968; *House of Evil* 1968; *Targets* 1968; *Alien Terror* 1969

Karlsen, John *Le Bambole* 1965; *The She Beast* 1965; *Screw Loose* 1999

Karlweis, Oscar (1894-1956) *Anything Can Happen* 1952; *5 Fingers* 1952; *Meet Me in Las Vegas* 1956

Karns, Roscoe (1893-1970) *The Shopworn Angel* 1928; *Dirigible* 1931; *Today We Live* 1933; *It Happened One Night* 1934; *Twentieth Century* 1934; *Front Page Woman* 1935; *Wings in the Dark* 1935; *Cain and Mabel* 1936; *You and Me* 1938; *Dancing Co-Ed* 1939; *Saturday's Children* 1940; *They Drive by Night* 1940; *That's My Man* 1947; *Devil's Cargo* 1948; *Man's Favorite Sport?* 1964

Karpluk, Erin aka **Karpuk, Erin** *Surviving Love* 2004; *Mrs Miracle* 2009

Karr, Sarah Rose (1984-) *Beethoven* 1992; *Beethoven's 2nd* 1993

Karras, Alex (1935-2012) *Blazing Saddles* 1974; *FM* 1977; *Victor/Victoria* 1982; *Against All Odds* 1984

Kartheiser, Vincent (1979-) *Alaska* 1996; *Masterminds* 1997; *Another Day in Paradise* 1998; *Strike!* 1998; *Crime +*

Punishment in Suburbia 2000; *In Time* 2011

Karvan, Claudia (1973-) *High Tide* 1987; *The Big Steal* 1990; *The Heartbreak Kid* 1993; *Flynn* 1995; *Paperback Hero* 1998; *Passion* 1999; *Strange Planet* 1999; *Risk* 2000; *Aquamarine* 2006; *Daybreakers* 2008; *Long Weekend* 2008

Karyo, Tchéky (1953-) *The Outsider* 1983; *Full Moon in Paris* 1984; *The Bear* 1988; *Australia* 1989; *Nikita* 1990; *1492: Conquest of Paradise* 1992; *Nostradamus* 1993; *Bad Boys* 1995; *Crying Freeman* 1995; *GoldenEye* 1995; *Operation Dumbo Drop* 1995; *To Have & to Hold* 1996; *Addicted to Love* 1997; *Dobermann* 1997; *Joan of Arc* 1999; *My Life So Far* 1999; *Wing Commander* 1999; *The Patriot* 2000; *Le Roi Danse* 2000; *Saving Grace* 2000; *Kiss of the Dragon* 2001; *The Core* 2002; *The Good Thief* 2002; *Blueberry* 2004; *Taking Lives* 2004; *A Very Long Engagement* 2004; *The Way* 2010; *Special Forces* 2011; *Belle and Sebastian - the Adventure Continues* 2015

Kasch, Max *Right at Your Door* 2006; *Shrooms* 2006

Kasdorf, Lenore (1948-) *Missing in Action* 1984; *Kid* 1990

Kase, Ryo *Letters from Iwo Jima* 2006; *Like Someone in Love* 2012; *Our Little Sister* 2015

Kash, Linda (1961-) *Ernest Rides Again* 1993; *The Bookfair Murders* 2000; *Are We Done Yet?* 2007

Kashfi, Anna (1934-2015) *The Mountain* 1956; *Battle Hymn* 1957; *Cowboy* 1958

Kasket, Harold (1926-2002) *The 7th Voyage of Sinbad* 1958; *The Boy Who Stole a Million* 1960; *Sands of the Desert* 1960

Kassovitz, Mathieu (1967-) *See How They Fall* 1993; *A Self-Made Hero* 1995; *Mon Homme* 1996; *News from the Good Lord* 1996; *Amélie* 2001; *Birthday Girl* 2001; *Amen.* 2002; *Munich* 2005; *Louise-Michel* 2008; *Rebellion* 2011; *The Lookout* 2012

Kastner, Daphna (1961-) *Eating* 1990; *Venice/Venice* 1992

Kasznar, Kurt (1913-1979) *The Light Touch* 1951; *Anything Can Happen* 1952; *Glory Alley* 1952; *All the Brothers Were Valiant* 1953; *Give a Girl a Break* 1953; *Kiss Me Kate* 1953; *Lili* 1953; *Ride, Vaquero!* 1953; *The Last Time I Saw Paris* 1954; *Valley of the Kings* 1954; *My Sister Eileen* 1955; *Anything Goes* 1956; *A Farewell to Arms* 1957; *Legend of the Lost* 1957; *For the First Time* 1959; *The King's Pirate* 1967; *The Perils of Pauline* 1967

Katarina, Anna *The Salute of the Jugger* 1989; *Omega Doom* 1996; *The Game* 1997

Katch, Kurt (1896-1958) *Berlin Correspondent* 1942; *Ali Baba and the Forty Thieves* 1944; *Abbott and Costello Meet the Mummy* 1955

Kateb, Reda *A Prophet* 2009; *Hippocrates* 2014

Kates, Kimberley (1971-) *Shadow of Doubt* 1998; *Blue Valley Songbird* 1999

Kath, Katherine (1928-) *Moulin Rouge* 1952; *A Touch of the Sun* 1956; *The Man Who Wouldn't Talk* 1957; *Seven Thunders* 1957; *Subway in the Sky* 1958; *Gigot* 1962; *The High Bright Sun* 1965

Kato, Daisuke *Seven Samurai* 1954; *When a Woman Ascends the Stairs* 1960

Kato, Masaya (1963-) *Brother* 2000; *Shinjuku Incident* 2009

Katsaros, Andonia *Age of Consent* 1969; *Time after Time* 1979

Katsu, Shintaro (1931-1997) *Zatoichi* 1962; *Zatoichi Meets Yojimbo* 1970

Katsulas, Andreas (1946-2006) *Someone to Watch over Me* 1987; *Communion* 1989; *Next of Kin* 1989; *The Death of the Incredible Hulk* 1990; *True Identity* 1991; *Blame It on the Bellboy* 1992

Katt, Nicky (1970-) *The Babysitter* 1995; *subUrbia* 1996; *One True Thing* 1998; *Phantoms* 1998; *The Limey* 1999; *Boiler Room* 2000; *The Way of the Gun* 2000; *Full Frontal* 2002; *Insomnia* 2002; *Secondhand Lions* 2003; *The Brave One* 2007

Katt, William (1955-) *Carrie* 1976; *First Love* 1977; *Big Wednesday* 1978; *Butch and Sundance: the Early Days* 1979; *Baby: Secret of the Lost Legend* 1985; *House* 1986; *Double X: the Name of the Game* 1991; *Tollbooth* 1994; *Determination of Death* 1997

Kattan, Chris (1970-) *A Night at the Roxbury* 1998; *House on Haunted Hill* 1999; *Monkeybone* 2001; *Corky Romano* 2001; *Undercover Brother* 2002; *Christmas in Wonderland* 2007

Katz, Jonathan Daddy Day Care 2003; Are We Done Yet? 2007
Katz, Omri (1976-) Hocus Pocus 1993; Matinee 1993
Kaufman, Adam Between 2005; Lying to Be Perfect 2010
Kaufman, Andy (1949-1984) In God We Trust 1980; Heartbeeps 1981
Kaufman, Lloyd (1945-) Terror Firmer 1999; Big Ass Spider 2013
Kaufman, Maurice (1927-1997) Die! Die! My Darling 1964; The Abominable Dr Phibes 1971
Kaufmann, Christine (1944-) The Last Days of Pompeii 1960; Constantine and the Cross 1961; Town without Pity 1961; The Swordsman of Siena 1962; Taras Bulba 1962; Wild and Wonderful 1964; Murders in the Rue Morgue 1971; Bagdad Café 1987
Kaufmann, Günther (1947-2012) Gods of the Plague 1969; Whity 1970; The Third Generation 1979; Querelle 1982
Kaufmann, Maurice (1927-1997) The Girl in the Picture 1956; Gorgo 1961; House of Mystery 1961; Bloomfield 1969
Kava, Caroline (1949-) Year of the Dragon 1985; Nobody's Child 1986; Little Nikita 1988; Born on the Fourth of July 1989
Kavanagh, John The Country Girls 1983; Cal 1984; The Fantasist 1986; Bellman & True 1987; Joyriders 1988; Fools of Fortune 1990; Widows' Peak 1993
Kavli, Karin (1906-1990) Walpurgis Night 1935; A Woman's Face 1938
Kavner, Julie (1950-) National Lampoon's Movie Madness 1981; Hannah and Her Sisters 1986; Radio Days 1987; Surrender 1987; New York Stories 1989; Awakenings 1990; Shadows and Fog 1991; This Is My Life 1992; Don't Drink the Water 1994; I'll Do Anything 1994; Forget Paris 1995; Deconstructing Harry 1997; Judy Berlin 1999; Click 2006; The Simpsons Movie 2007
Kawahara, Takashi Eat the Peach 1986; Road to Ruin 1992
Kawarazaki, Chojuro (1903-1981) Humanity and Paper Balloons 1937; The Loyal 47 Ronin 1941; Musashi Miyamoto 1944
Kay, Beatrice (1907-1986) Billy Rose's Diamond Horseshoe 1945; Underworld USA 1961
Kay, Bernard (1928-2014) Doctor Zhivago 1965; The Shuttered Room 1967; They Came from beyond Space 1967; Interlude 1968; Trog 1970
Kay, Billy (1984-) Bitter Suite 2000; LIE 2001
Kay, Charles (1930-) Bachelor of Hearts 1958; Amadeus 1984
Kay, Dominic Scott Single Santa Seeks Mrs Claus 2004; Meet the Santas 2005; Charlotte's Web 2006
Kay, Robbie Fugitive Pieces 2007; Made in Dagenham 2010
Kayama, Yuzo (1937-) Sanjuro 1962; Red Beard 1965
Kaye, Celia (1941-) Island of the Blue Dolphins 1964; The Final Comedown 1972
Kaye, Clarissa aka Kaye-Mason, Clarissa (1931-1994) Age of Consent 1969; The Good Wife 1986
Kaye, Danny (1913-1987) Up in Arms 1944; Wonder Man 1945; The Kid from Brooklyn 1946; The Secret Life of Walter Mitty 1947; A Song Is Born 1948; The Inspector General 1949; It's a Great Feeling 1949; On the Riviera 1951; Hans Christian Andersen 1952; Knock on Wood 1954; White Christmas 1954; The Court Jester 1956; Me and the Colonel 1958; Merry Andrew 1958; The Five Pennies 1959; On the Double 1961; The Man from the Diner's Club 1963; The Madwoman of Chaillot 1969; Skokie 1981
Kaye, David Mermaid 2000; Ratchet & Clank 2016
Kaye, Davy (1916-1998) The Wrong Arm of the Law 1962; Crooks in Cloisters 1963; The World Ten Times Over 1963
Kaye, Lila (1929-) An American Werewolf in London 1981; Nuns on the Run 1990; Mrs 'arris Goes to Paris 1992; Dragonworld 1994
Kaye, Norman (1927-2007) Lonely Hearts 1981; Man of Flowers 1984; Where the Green Ants Dream 1984; Cactus 1986; Warm Nights on a Slow Moving Train 1986; Golden Braid 1991; A Woman's Tale 1991; Turtle Beach 1992; Bad Boy Bubby 1993
Kaye, Paul (1965-) Blackball 2003; It's All Gone Pete Tong 2004; WAZ 2006; Cass 2008; Malice in Wonderland 2009; The Infidel 2010; 8 minutes idle 2012; Pusher 2012; Blackwood 2013
Kaye, Stubby (1918-1997) Guys and Dolls 1955; You Can't Run Away from It

1956; Li'l Abner 1959; Forty Pounds of Trouble 1962; The Way West 1967; Sweet Charity 1968; Can Hieronymus Merkin Ever Forget Mercy Humppe and Find True Happiness? 1969; Who Framed Roger Rabbit 1988
Kazan, Elia (1909-2003) City for Conquest 1940; Blues in the Night 1941
Kazan, Lainie (1942-) Lady in Cement 1968; Romance of a Horse Thief 1971; My Favorite Year 1982; One from the Heart 1982; Lust in the Dust 1984; The Journey of Natty Gann 1985; The Delta Force 1986; Bigfoot and the Hendersons 1987; Beaches 1988; Out of the Dark 1988; 29th Street 1991; The Associate 1996; Love Is All There Is 1996; The Big Hit 1998; My Big Fat Greek Wedding 2002; Gigli 2003; Returning Lily 2003; You Don't Mess with the Zohan 2008; My Big Fat Greek Wedding 2 2016
Kazan, Zoe (1983-) Revolutionary Road 2008; Meek's Cutoff 2010; Ruby Sparks 2012; What If 2013
Keach, James (1948-) FM 1977; Hurricane 1979; The Long Riders 1980; Love Letters 1983; National Lampoon's Vacation 1983; The Razor's Edge 1984; Moving Violations 1985; Wildcats 1986; The Experts 1989
Keach, Stacy (1941-) The Heart Is a Lonely Hunter 1968; Brewster McCloud 1970; End of the Road 1970; Doc 1971; Fat City 1972; The Life and Times of Judge Roy Bean 1972; The New Centurions 1972; Luther 1974; Conduct Unbecoming 1975; James Dean - the First American Teenager 1975; The Killer inside Me 1975; The Squeeze 1977; Cheech & Chong's Up in Smoke 1978; Gray Lady Down 1978; The Ninth Configuration 1979; The Long Riders 1980; Cheech and Chong's Nice Dreams 1981; Road Games 1981; Butterfly 1982; That Championship Season 1982; Class of 1999 1990; False Identity 1990; Sunset Grill 1992; Batman: Mask of the Phantasm 1993; Good Cop, Bad Cop 1993; Escape from LA 1996; American History X 1998; Militia 2000; Desolation Canyon 2006; Honeydripper 2007; Lone Rider 2008; The Bourne Legacy 2012; Nebraska 2013; Planes 2013; If I Stay 2014; Cell 2016
Kean, Marie (1922-1994) Rooney 1958; Girl with Green Eyes 1963; I Was Happy Here 1966; Ryan's Daughter 1970; Barry Lyndon 1975; The Lonely Passion of Judith Hearne 1987
Keane, Edward (1884-1959) The Singing Kid 1936; Devil's Island 1940
Keane, James (1952-) Cannery Row 1982; Crazy Heart 2009
Keane, Kerrie Second Serve 1986; Distant Thunder 1988
Keane, Robert Emmett aka Keane, Robert E (1883-1981) The Saint Takes Over 1940; The Red Dragon 1945; Fool's Gold 1946; Fear in the Night 1947
Kearney, Gerard War of the Buttons 1993; The Wind That Shakes the Barley 2006
Kearns, Billy aka Kearns, Bill (1923-1992) Plein Soleil 1960; Playtime 1967; Asterix vs Caesar 1985; Asterix in Britain 1986
Kearns, Gerard Looking for Eric 2009; Honeymooner 2010; The Rise 2012
Keating, Charles (1941-2014) The Thomas Crown Affair 1999; Deuce Bigalow: European Gigolo 2005
Keating, Larry (1896-1963) Three Secrets 1950; Follow the Sun: the Ben Hogan Story 1951; The Light Touch 1951; The Mating Season 1951; When Worlds Collide 1951; Above and Beyond 1952; Carson City 1952; Inferno 1953; The Buster Keaton Story 1957; The Wayward Bus 1957; Who Was That Lady? 1960
Keating, Ronan Goddess 2013; Postman Pat: the Movie 2013
Keaton, Buster (1895-1966) The Butcher Boy 1917; Neighbors 1920; One Week 1920; The Saphead 1920; The Scarecrow 1920; The Paleface 1921; Day Dreams 1922; Our Hospitality 1923; Three Ages 1923; The Navigator 1924; Sherlock Junior 1924; Go West 1925; Seven Chances 1925; Battling Butler 1926; College 1927; The General 1927; The Cameraman 1928; Steamboat Bill, Jr 1928; Hollywood Revue 1929; Spite Marriage 1929; Doughboys 1930; Free and Easy 1930; Parlor, Bedroom and Bath 1931; The Passionate Plumber 1932; Speak Easily 1932; What - No Beer? 1933; An Old Spanish Custom 1935; The Villain Still Pursued Her 1940; Forever and a Day 1943; In the Good Old Summertime 1949; The Lovable Cheat 1949; You're My Everything 1949; Limelight 1952; Around the World in 80 Days 1956;

The Adventures of Huckleberry Finn 1960; The Great Chase 1961; Beach Blanket Bingo 1965; Film 1965; How to Fill a Wild Bikini 1965; The Railrodder 1965; Sergeant Deadhead 1965; A Funny Thing Happened on the Way to the Forum 1966; 4 Clowns 1970; The Golden Age of Buster Keaton 1975
Keaton, Diane (1946-) Lovers and Other Strangers 1970; The Godfather 1972; Play It Again, Sam 1972; Sleeper 1973; The Godfather Part II 1974; Love and Death 1975; Harry and Walter Go to New York 1976; Annie Hall 1977; Looking for Mr Goodbar 1977; Interiors 1978; Manhattan 1979; Reds 1981; Shoot the Moon 1982; The Little Drummer Girl 1984; Mrs Soffel 1984; Crimes of the Heart 1986; Baby Boom 1987; Radio Days 1987; The Price of Passion 1988; The Lemon Sisters 1989; The Godfather Part III 1990; Father of the Bride 1991; Look Who's Talking Now! 1993; Manhattan Murder Mystery 1993; Amelia Earhart: the Final Flight 1994; Father of the Bride Part 2 1995; The First Wives Club 1996; Marvin's Room 1996; The Only Thrill 1997; The Other Sister 1999; Hanging Up 2000; Town & Country 2001; Crossed Over 2002; Something's Gotta Give 2003; The Family Stone 2005; Surrender Dorothy 2006; Because I Said So 2007; Mad Money 2008; Morning Glory 2010; The Big Wedding 2013; And So It Goes 2014; Ruth & Alex 2014; Christmas with the Coopers 2015; Finding Dory 2016
Keaton, Joe aka Keaton, Joseph (1867-1946) Neighbors 1920; The Scarecrow 1920; Day Dreams 1922; Our Hospitality 1923; Sherlock Junior 1924; Go West 1925
Keaton, Michael (1951-) Night Shift 1982; Mr Mom 1983; Johnny Dangerously 1984; Gung Ho 1986; Touch and Go 1986; The Squeeze 1987; Beetle Juice 1988; Clean and Sober 1988; Batman 1989; The Dream Team 1989; Pacific Heights 1990; One Good Cop 1991; Batman Returns 1992; Much Ado about Nothing 1993; My Life 1993; The Paper 1994; Speechless 1994; Multiplicity 1996; Jackie Brown 1997; Desperate Measures 1998; Jack Frost 1998; Out of Sight 1998; A Shot at Glory 2000; Live from Baghdad 2002; Quicksand 2003; First Daughter 2004; White Noise 2004; Herbie: Fully Loaded 2005; Porco Rosso 2005; Cars 2006; The Merry Gentleman 2009; Post Grad 2009; The Other Guys 2010; Toy Story 3 2010; Cars 2 2011; Clear History 2013; Birdman or (The Unexpected Virtue of Ignorance) 2014; RoboCop 2014; Minions 2015; Spotlight 2015; The Founder 2016; Spider-Man: Homecoming 2017
Keats, Ele (1973-) The Haunted Heart 1995; Eros 2004
Keats, Steven (1945-1994) The Friends of Eddie Coyle 1973; Death Wish 1974; The Gambler 1974; Hester Street 1975; Black Sunday 1976; The American Success Company 1979; The Executioner's Song 1982; Silent Rage 1982; Badge of the Assassin 1985; Turk 182! 1985
Keays-Byrne, Hugh (1947-) The Man from Hong Kong 1975; Mad Max 1979; The Chain Reaction 1980; Lorca and the Outlaws 1985; Kangaroo 1986; Les Patterson Saves the World 1987; The Salute of the Jugger 1989; Sleeping Beauty 2011; Mad Max: Fury Road 2015
Kebbel, Arielle (1985-) American Pie Presents Band Camp 2005; Reeker 2005; Aquamarine 2006; The Grudge 2 2006; John Tucker Must Die 2006; Red Mist 2008; The Uninvited 2008
Kebbell, Toby (1982-) Dead Man's Shoes 2004; Wilderness 2006; Control 2007; Prince of Persia: the Sands of Time 2010; The Veteran 2011; War Horse 2011; The East 2013; Dawn of the Planet of the Apes 2014; Fantastic Four 2015; Ben-Hur 2016; Gold 2016; A Monster Calls 2016; Warcraft: the Beginning 2016
Kechiouche, Salim (1979-) Criminal Lovers 1999; Le Clan 2004; Blue Is the Warmest Colour 2013
Kedrova, Lila (1918-2000) Calle Mayor 1956; Montparnasse 19 1958; Zorba the Greek 1964; A High Wind in Jamaica 1965; Torn Curtain 1966; A Time for Loving 1971; Soft Beds, Hard Battles 1973; The Tenant 1976; Tell Me a Riddle 1980; Sword of the Valiant 1984
Keefer, Don (1916-) Riot in Cell Block 11 1954; Ace Eli and Rodger of the Skies 1973
Keegan, Andrew (1979-) 10 Things I Hate about You 1999; The Broken Hearts Club: a Romantic Comedy 2000; O 2001

Keehne, Virginya Ticks 1993; The Dentist 1996
Keel, Howard aka Keel, Harold (1917-2004) The Small Voice 1948; Annie Get Your Gun 1950; Across the Wide Missouri 1951; Callaway Went Thataway 1951; Show Boat 1951; Texas Carnival 1951; Desperate Search 1952; Lovely to Look at 1952; Calamity Jane 1953; Kiss Me Kate 1953; Ride, Vaquero! 1953; Deep in My Heart 1954; Rose Marie 1954; Seven Brides for Seven Brothers 1954; Jupiter's Darling 1955; Kismet 1955; Floods of Fear 1958; The Big Fisherman 1959; The Day of the Triffids 1962; The Man from Button Willow 1965; Waco 1966; The War Wagon 1967; Arizona Bushwhackers 1968
Keelan, Claire Hush 2008; Mister John 2013
Keeler, Ruby (1909-1993) Footlight Parade 1933; 42nd Street 1933; Gold Diggers of 1933 1933; Dames 1934; Flirtation Walk 1934; Go into Your Dance 1935; Shipmates Forever 1935; Colleen 1936; Sweetheart of the Campus 1941
Keen, Diane (1946-) Here We Go round the Mulberry Bush 1967; Sweeney! 1976; Silver Dream Racer 1980; Thirteen at Dinner 1985
Keen, Geoffrey (1916-2005) Chance of a Lifetime 1950; Cry, the Beloved Country 1951; Green Grow the Rushes 1951; Hunted 1952; The Long Memory 1952; Genevieve 1953; The Maggie 1953; Rob Roy, the Highland Rogue 1953; Turn the Key Softly 1953; Carrington VC 1954; The Divided Heart 1954; Face the Music 1954; The Glass Cage 1955; Passage Home 1955; Storm over the Nile 1955; House of Secrets 1956; The Long Arm 1956; Sailor Beware! 1956; Yield to the Night 1956; The Birthday Present 1957; Nowhere to Go 1958; Horrors of the Black Museum 1959; The Scapegoat 1959; The Angry Silence 1960; Sink the Bismarck! 1960; Spare the Rod 1961; Live Now - Pay Later 1962; The Spiral Road 1962; Dr Syn, Alias the Scarecrow 1963; The Mind Benders 1963; Born Free 1966; Berserk 1967; Taste the Blood of Dracula 1969; Doomwatch 1972; Living Free 1972; The Spy Who Loved Me 1977; Octopussy 1983
Keen, Malcolm (1888-1970) The Lodger 1926; The Manxman 1929; The Great Mr Handel 1942; Operation Amsterdam 1958; Two and Two Make Six 1961; Life for Ruth 1962
Keen, Noah Battle for the Planet of the Apes 1973; Gable and Lombard 1976
Keen, Pat (1933-2013) A Kind of Loving 1962; Clockwise 1986; Without a Clue 1988
Keena, Monica (1979-) Snow White: a Tale of Terror 1996; First Daughter 1999; Crime + Punishment in Suburbia 2000; The Simian Line 2000; Freddy vs Jason 2003; Man of the House 2005; Night of the Demons 2010
Keenan, Will Tromeo & Juliet 1996; Terror Firmer 1999
Keene, Tom aka Powers, Richard (1896-1963) Our Daily Bread 1934; Old Louisiana 1938; Thunder Mountain 1947; Return of the Bad Men 1948; Trail of Robin Hood 1950; Plan 9 from Outer Space 1959
Keener, Catherine (1959-) Johnny Suede 1991; Living in Oblivion 1995; Box of Moonlight 1996; If These Walls Could Talk 1996; Walking and Talking 1996; The Real Blonde 1997; Your Friends & Neighbors 1998; Being John Malkovich 1999; 8mm 1999; Simpatico 1999; Lovely & Amazing 2001; Death to Smoochy 2002; Full Frontal 2002; SiMONE 2002; The Ballad of Jack and Rose 2005; Capote 2005; The 40 Year Old Virgin 2005; The Interpreter 2005; Friends with Money 2006; Into the Wild 2007; What Just Happened? 2007; Genova 2008; Hamlet 2 2008; The Soloist 2008; Synecdoche, New York 2008; Where the Wild Things Are 2009; Cyrus 2010; Percy Jackson & the Lightning Thief 2010; Please Give 2010; Trust 2010; The Oranges 2011; Peace, Love & Misunderstanding 2011; A Late Quartet 2012; Accidental Love 2013; Captain Phillips 2013; The Croods 2013; Enough Said 2013

Untouchables 1987; Young Guns II 1990
Keillor, Garrison The Big One 1997; A Prairie Home Companion 2006
Keim, Betty Lou (1938-2010) Teenage Rebel 1956; These Wilder Years 1956; The Wayward Bus 1957
Keim, Claire (1975-) The Girl 1999; Le Roi Danse 2000
Keir, Andrew (1926-1997) The Brave Don't Cry 1952; The Pirates of Blood River 1961; Cleopatra 1963; The Devil-Ship Pirates 1964; Dracula - Prince of Darkness 1965; Daleks - Invasion Earth 2150 AD 1966; The Fighting Prince of Donegal 1966; The Long Duel 1967; Quatermass and the Pit 1967; The Viking Queen 1967; Attack on the Iron Coast 1968; The Royal Hunt of the Sun 1969; Adam's Woman 1970; The Last Grenade 1970; The Night Visitor 1970; Blood from the Mummy's Tomb 1971; Zeppelin 1971; Absolution 1978; Lion of the Desert 1981; Dragonworld 1994; Rob Roy 1995
Keitel, Harvey (1939-) Who's That Knocking at My Door 1968; Mean Streets 1973; Alice Doesn't Live Here Anymore 1974; Buffalo Bill and the Indians, or Sitting Bull's History Lesson 1976; Mother, Jugs & Speed 1976; Taxi Driver 1976; Welcome to LA 1976; The Duellists 1977; Blue Collar 1978; Eagle's Wing 1978; Fingers 1978; Bad Timing 1980; Death Watch 1980; Saturn 3 1980; The Border 1981; Exposed 1983; La Nuit de Varennes 1983; Order of Death 1983; Falling in Love 1984; Camorra 1985; The Men's Club 1986; Off Beat 1986; Wise Guys 1986; The Pick-Up Artist 1987; The Last Temptation of Christ 1988; The January Man 1989; Two Evil Eyes 1990; The Two Jakes 1990; Bugsy 1991; Mortal Thoughts 1991; Reservoir Dogs 1991; Thelma & Louise 1991; Bad Lieutenant 1992; Sister Act 1992; The Assassin 1993; Dangerous Game 1993; The Piano 1993; Rising Sun 1993; The Young Americans 1993; Imaginary Crimes 1994; Monkey Trouble 1994; Pulp Fiction 1994; Somebody to Love 1994; Blue in the Face 1995; Clockers 1995; From Dusk till Dawn 1995; Smoke 1995; Ulysses' Gaze 1995; City of Industry 1996; Head above Water 1996; Cop Land 1997; FairyTale: a True Story 1997; Lulu on the Bridge 1998; Finding Graceland 1999; Holy Smoke 1999; Three Seasons 1999; Fail Safe 2000; Little Nicky 2000; U-571 2000; The Grey Zone 2001; Taking Sides 2001; Crime Spree 2002; Red Dragon 2002; National Treasure 2004; Be Cool 2005; Arthur and the Invisibles 2006; National Treasure: Book of Secrets 2007; Wrong Turn at Tahoe 2009; Little Fockers 2010; Fatal Honeymoon 2012; Moonrise Kingdom 2012; The Congress 2013; Youth 2015
Keith-Johnston, Colin (1896-1980) Berkeley Square 1933; Blood on My Hands 1948
Keith, Brian (1921-1997) Arrowhead 1953; Tight Spot 1955; The Violent Men 1955; Nightfall 1956; Storm Center 1956; Chicago Confidential 1957; Run of the Arrow 1957; Violent Road 1958; The Young Philadelphians 1959; Ten Who Dared 1960; The Deadly Companions 1961; The Parent Trap 1961; Moon Pilot 1962; The Pleasure Seekers 1964; Those Calloways 1964; A Tiger Walks 1964; The Hallelujah Trail 1965; Nevada Smith 1966; The Rare Breed 1966; The Russians Are Coming, the Russians Are Coming 1966; Reflections in a Golden Eye 1967; With Six You Get Eggroll 1968; Gaily, Gaily 1969; The McKenzie Break 1970; Suppose They Gave a War and Nobody Came? 1970; Scandalous John 1971; something big 1971; The Wind and the Lion 1975; The Yakuza 1975; Nickelodeon 1976; Hooper 1978; Meteor 1979; Charlie Chan and the Curse of the Dragon Queen 1981; Sharky's Machine 1981; Welcome Home 1989
Keith, David (1954-) The Rose 1979; Brubaker 1980; Back Roads 1981; An Officer and a Gentleman 1982; Independence Day 1983; The Lords of Discipline 1983; Firestarter 1984; White of the Eye 1986; Heartbreak Hotel 1988; The Two Jakes 1990; Running Wild 1992; Good Cop, Bad Cop 1993; Gold Diggers: the Secret of Bear Mountain 1995; Judge & Jury 1995; Poodle Springs 1998; When the Bough Breaks 2: Perfect Prey 1998; Men of Honor 2000; U-571 2000; Behind Enemy Lines 2001; The Stickup 2001; Daredevil 2003; Raise Your Voice 2004; Path of Destruction 2005; Meet Monica Velour 2011

Keith, Ian (1899-1960) *The Divine Lady* 1928; *The Big Trail* 1930; *The Sign of the Cross* 1932; *Queen Christina* 1933; *Cleopatra* 1934; *Dangerous Corner* 1934; *The Crusades* 1935; *The Three Musketeers* 1935; *The Buccaneer* 1938; *Charlie Chan in The Chinese Cat* 1944; *Under Western Skies* 1945; *Dick Tracy vs Cueball* 1946; *Dick Tracy's Dilemma* 1947; *Nightmare Alley* 1947; *The Black Shield of Falworth* 1954; *It Came from beneath the Sea* 1955
Keith, Penelope (1940-) *Every Home Should Have One* 1970; *Rentadick* 1972; *Ghost Story* 1974; *The Hound of the Baskervilles* 1977; *Priest of Love* 1981
Keith (1), Robert (1898-1966) *Boomerang!* 1947; *My Foolish Heart* 1949; *Branded* 1950; *Edge of Doom* 1950; *Fourteen Hours* 1951; *I Want You* 1951; *Somebody Loves Me* 1952; *Battle Circus* 1953; *Devil's Canyon* 1953; *The Wild One* 1953; *Drum Beat* 1954; *Guys and Dolls* 1955; *Love Me or Leave Me* 1955; *Underwater!* 1955; *Young at Heart* 1955; *Between Heaven and Hell* 1956; *Ransom!* 1956; *Written on the Wind* 1956; *Men in War* 1957; *My Man Godfrey* 1957; *The Lineup* 1958; *Tempest* 1959
Keith, Rosalind (1912-2000) *The Glass Key* 1935; *Theodora Goes Wild* 1936
Keith, Sheila (1920-2004) *Frightmare* 1974; *House of Whipcord* 1974; *House of Mortal Sin* 1975; *The Comeback* 1977
Keleghan, Peter *Screwballs* 1983; *Niagara Motel* 2005
Kell, Joseph *Bone Daddy* 1998; *Lies and Deception* 2005; *If I Were You* 2012
Kellaway, Cecil aka **Kelloway, Cecil** (1891-1973) *Blond Cheat* 1938; *Maid's Night Out* 1938; *Intermezzo* 1939; *Brother Orchid* 1940; *The House of the Seven Gables* 1940; *The Invisible Man Returns* 1940; *Mexican Spitfire* 1940; *The Mummy's Hand* 1940; *Phantom Raiders* 1940; *Appointment for Love* 1941; *I Married a Witch* 1942; *Take a Letter, Darling* 1942; *The Crystal Ball* 1943; *And Now Tomorrow* 1944; *Frenchman's Creek* 1944; *Practically Yours* 1944; *Kitty* 1945; *Love Letters* 1945; *Easy to Wed* 1946; *Monsieur Beaucaire* 1946; *The Postman Always Rings Twice* 1946; *Unconquered* 1947; *Portrait of Jennie* 1948; *Down to the Sea in Ships* 1949; *Harvey* 1950; *Kim* 1950; *Francis Goes to the Races* 1951; *Half Angel* 1951; *The Beast from 20,000 Fathoms* 1953; *Thunder in the East* 1953; *Interrupted Melody* 1955; *Johnny Trouble* 1957; *The Proud Rebel* 1958; *The Private Lives of Adam and Eve* 1959; *The Shaggy Dog* 1959; *Tammy Tell Me True* 1961; *The Cardinal* 1963; *Hush... Hush, Sweet Charlotte* 1964; *The Adventures of Bullwhip Griffin* 1967; *Fitzwilly* 1967; *Guess Who's Coming to Dinner* 1967; *Getting Straight* 1970
Kelleghan, Tina *The Snapper* 1993; *Puffball* 2006
Keller, Hiram (1944-1997) *Satyricon* 1969; *Lifespan* 1975
Keller, Marthe (1945-) *And Now My Love* 1974; *Black Sunday* 1976; *Marathon Man* 1976; *Bobby Deerfield* 1977; *Fedora* 1978; *The Formula* 1980; *The Amateur* 1981; *Rouge Baiser* 1985; *Dark Eyes* 1987; *Lapse of Memory* 1992; *Hereafter* 2010
Kellerman, Barbara (1949-) *Satan's Slave* 1976; *The Quatermass Conclusion* 1979; *The Monster Club* 1980; *The Sea Wolves* 1980
Kellerman, Sally (1938-) *Reform School Girl* 1957; *The Boston Strangler* 1968; *The April Fools* 1969; *MASH* 1969; *Brewster McCloud* 1970; *Lost Horizon* 1973; *A Reflection of Fear* 1973; *Slither* 1973; *The Big Bus* 1976; *Welcome to LA* 1976; *The Mouse and His Child* 1977; *A Little Romance* 1979; *Foxes* 1980; *Head On* 1980; *Loving Couples* 1980; *Serial* 1980; *Moving Violations* 1985; *Back to School* 1986; *That's Life* 1986; *Someone to Love* 1987; *Three for the Road* 1987; *All's Fair* 1989; *Snow White in Happily Ever After* 1990; *Doppelganger* 1993; *Younger and Younger* 1993; *Pret-a-Porter* 1994; *Live Virgin* 2000; *The Wishing Well* 2009
Kelley, Alice *Against All Flags* 1952; *Francis Goes to West Point* 1952
Kelley, Barry (1908-1991) *Knock on Any Door* 1949; *Ma and Pa Kettle* 1949; *The Undercover Man* 1949; *The Asphalt Jungle* 1950; *The Black Hand* 1950; *The Capture* 1950; *Right Cross* 1950; *711 Ocean Drive* 1950; *Wabash Avenue* 1950; *Francis Goes to the Races* 1951; *The Well* 1951; *Carrie* 1952; *Law and Order* 1953; *South Sea Woman* 1953; *The Tall Stranger* 1957;

Buchanan Rides Alone 1958; *The Extraordinary Seaman* 1969
Kelley, DeForest (1920-1999) *Fear in the Night* 1947; *Variety Girl* 1947; *Malaya* 1949; *Illegal* 1955; *Tension at Table Rock* 1956; *Gunfight at the OK Corral* 1957; *The Law and Jake Wade* 1958; *Warlock* 1959; *Gunfight at Comanche Creek* 1964; *Where Love Has Gone* 1964; *Apache Uprising* 1965; *Waco* 1966; *Star Trek: the Motion Picture* 1979; *Star Trek II: the Wrath of Khan* 1982; *Star Trek III: the Search for Spock* 1984; *Star Trek IV: The Voyage Home* 1986; *Star Trek V: the Final Frontier* 1989; *Star Trek VI: The Undiscovered Country* 1991
Kelley, Elijah *Hairspray* 2007; *Strange Magic* 2015
Kelley, James T (1854-1933) *The Rink* 1916; *The Cure* 1917
Kelley, Ryan *Mean Creek* 2004; *Prayers for Bobby* 2009; *Shattered Silence* 2012
Kelley (1), Sheila (1961-) *Some Girls* 1988; *Breaking In* 1989; *The Fulfillment of Mary Gray* 1989; *Pure Luck* 1991; *Singles* 1992; *House of Obsession* 1994; *Matchstick Men* 2003; *The Guest* 2014
Kellin, Mike (1922-1983) *At War with the Army* 1950; *Hurricane Smith* 1952; *Hell Is for Heroes* 1962; *Invitation to a Gunfighter* 1964; *The Boston Strangler* 1968; *Riot* 1969; *Freebie and the Bean* 1974; *On the Yard* 1978; *Just before Dawn* 1980; *So Fine* 1981
Kellino, Pamela aka **Mason, Pamela** (1916-1996) *The Upturned Glass* 1947; *Door-to-Door Maniac* 1961; *The Navy vs the Night Monsters* 1966
Kellogg, Bruce (1910-1967) *Barbary Coast Gent* 1944; *Unknown World* 1951
Kellogg, John (1916-2000) *Johnny o'Clock* 1947; *Twelve o'Clock High* 1949; *The Greatest Show on Earth* 1952; *Go Naked in the World* 1961; *Violets Are Blue* 1986; *Orphans* 1987
Kelly, Barbara (?-2007) *Love in Pawn* 1953; *Jet Storm* 1959
Kelly, Brett (1993-) *Bad Santa* 2003; *Grounded* 2006
Kelly, Carol *Daniel Boone, Trail Blazer* 1957; *Terror in a Texas Town* 1958
Kelly, Claire (1934-1998) *The Badlanders* 1958; *Party Girl* 1958; *Ask Any Girl* 1959; *A Guide for the Married Man* 1967
Kelly, Clare (?-2001) *Georgy Girl* 1966; *All Neat in Black Stockings* 1969; *And Soon the Darkness* 1970
Kelly (2), Craig (1970-) *Beyond Bedlam* 1993; *The Young Americans* 1993; *When Saturday Comes* 1995
Kelly, David (1929-2012) *Pirates* 1986; *Joyriders* 1988; *Into the West* 1992; *The Run of the Country* 1995; *Waking Ned* 1998; *Greenfingers* 2000; *Mean Machine* 2001; *Charlie and the Chocolate Factory* 2005; *The Kovak Box* 2006
Kelly, David Patrick (1952-) *Dreamscape* 1984; *Commando* 1985; *Penn & Teller Get Killed* 1989; *The Adventures of Ford Fairlane* 1990; *Crooklyn* 1994; *The Crow* 1994; *Heavy* 1995; *Last Man Standing* 1996; *K-PAX* 2001; *Flags of Our Fathers* 2006
Kelly, Dean Lennox *The Low Down* 2000; *Deathwatch* 2002; *Frequently Asked Questions about Time Travel* 2008
Kelly, Frank (1938-2016) *Rat* 2000; *Evelyn* 2002
Kelly, Gene (1912-1996) *For Me and My Gal* 1942; *The Cross of Lorraine* 1943; *DuBarry Was a Lady* 1943; *Pilot #5* 1943; *Thousands Cheer* 1943; *Christmas Holiday* 1944; *Cover Girl* 1944; *Ziegfeld Follies* 1944; *Anchors Aweigh* 1945; *Living in a Big Way* 1947; *The Pirate* 1948; *The Three Musketeers* 1948; *Words and Music* 1948; *On the Town* 1949; *Take Me Out to the Ball Game* 1949; *The Black Hand* 1950; *Summer Stock* 1950; *An American in Paris* 1951; *It's a Big Country* 1951; *Love Is Better than Ever* 1951; *The Devil Makes Three* 1952; *Singin' in the Rain* 1952; *Brigadoon* 1954; *Deep in My Heart* 1954; *Seagulls over Sorrento* 1954; *It's Always Fair Weather* 1955; *The Happy Road* 1956; *Invitation to the Dance* 1956; *Les Girls* 1957; *Marjorie Morningstar* 1958; *Inherit the Wind* 1960; *Let's Make Love* 1960; *What a Way to Go!* 1964; *The Young Girls of Rochefort* 1967; *40 Carats* 1973; *That's Entertainment, Part II* 1976; *Viva Knievel!* 1977; *Xanadu* 1980
Kelly, Grace aka **Princess Grace of Monaco** (1929-1982) *Fourteen Hours* 1951; *High Noon* 1952; *Mogambo* 1953; *The Bridges at Toko-Ri* 1954; *The Country Girl* 1954; *Dial M for Murder* 1954; *Green Fire* 1954; *Rear Window* 1954; *To Catch a Thief* 1955; *High Society* 1956; *The Swan* 1956; *The

Poppy Is Also a Flower* 1966; *The Children of Theatre Street* 1977
Kelly, Jack (1927-1992) *No Room for the Groom* 1952; *Gunsmoke* 1953; *Law and Order* 1953; *The Redhead from Wyoming* 1953; *Drive a Crooked Road* 1954; *Cult of the Cobra* 1955; *The Night Holds Terror* 1955; *To Hell and Back* 1955; *Forbidden Planet* 1956; *Young Billy Young* 1969
Kelly, Jean Louisa (1972-) *Uncle Buck* 1989; *The Day Lincoln Was Shot* 1998; *The Christmas Gift* 2009
Kelly, Jim (1946-2013) *Enter the Dragon* 1973; *Black Belt Jones* 1974; *Golden Needles* 1974; *Three the Hard Way* 1974; *Take a Hard Ride* 1975
Kelly (3), John *Tarzan and the Valley of Gold* 1966; *Two Mules for Sister Sara* 1970; *Buck and the Preacher* 1972
Kelly, Judy (1913-1991) *Crime on the Hill* 1933; *Over She Goes* 1937; *Tomorrow We Live* 1942; *Dead of Night* 1945; *Dancing with Crime* 1946
Kelly, Laura Michelle *Sweeney Todd: the Demon Barber of Fleet Street* 2007; *Goddess* 2013
Kelly, Michael *Defendor* 2009; *Did You Hear about the Morgans?* 2009
Kelly (2), Michael (1969-) *Dawn of the Dead* 2004; *Tenderness* 2007; *Changeling* 2008; *Fair Game* 2010; *Chronicle* 2012; *Secret in Their Eyes* 2015
Kelly, Moira (1968-) *The Boy Who Cried Bitch* 1991; *Chaplin* 1992; *The Cutting Edge* 1992; *Twin Peaks: Fire Walk with Me* 1992; *The Lion King* 1994; *Little Odessa* 1994; *With Honors* 1994; *The Tie That Binds* 1995; *Entertaining Angels: the Dorothy Day Story* 1996; *Unhook the Stars* 1996; *Changing Habits* 1997; *Dangerous Beauty* 1997; *Love Walked In* 1997; *Hi-Life* 1998; *The Lion King II: Simba's Pride* 1998; *The Safety of Objects* 2001
Kelly, Nancy (1921-1995) *Submarine Patrol* 1938; *Frontier Marshal* 1939; *Jesse James* 1939; *Stanley and Livingstone* 1939; *To the Shores of Tripoli* 1942; *Tarzan's Desert Mystery* 1943; *Show Business* 1944; *Betrayal from the East* 1945; *The Bad Seed* 1956
Kelly, Patsy (1910-1981) *Going Hollywood* 1933; *The Girl from Missouri* 1934; *Go into Your Dance* 1935; *Thanks a Million* 1935; *Pigskin Parade* 1936; *Sing, Baby, Sing* 1936; *Pick a Star* 1937; *Wake Up and Live* 1937; *The Cowboy and the Lady* 1938; *Merrily We Live* 1938; *There Goes My Heart* 1938; *Playmates* 1941; *Road Show* 1941; *Topper Returns* 1941; *In Old California* 1942; *The Crowded Sky* 1960; *Please Don't Eat the Daisies* 1960; *The Naked Kiss* 1964; *Freaky Friday* 1976; *Hill's Angels* 1979
Kelly (1), Paul (1899-1956) *Broadway through a Keyhole* 1933; *Star of Midnight* 1935; *Invisible Stripes* 1939; *Flight Command* 1940; *The Howards of Virginia* 1940; *Call Out the Marines* 1941; *Flying Tigers* 1942; *Tarzan's New York Adventure* 1942; *Dead Man's Eyes* 1944; *Crossfire* 1947; *Fear in the Night* 1947; *The File on Thelma Jordon* 1949; *Frenchie* 1950; *Gunsmoke* 1953; *Split Second* 1953; *The High and the Mighty* 1954; *Johnny Dark* 1954; *The Square Jungle* 1955; *Storm Center* 1956
Kelly, Paula (1943-) *Sweet Charity* 1968; *The Andromeda Strain* 1970; *Trouble Man* 1972; *Three Tough Guys* 1974
Kelly, Roz (1943-) *The Owl and the Pussycat* 1970; *Full Moon High* 1982
Kelly, Sam (1943-2014) *Blue Ice* 1992; *All or Nothing* 2002; *Common People* 2013
Kelly, Sean *The Man Inside* 1958; *The Green Helmet* 1960
Kelly, Tommy (1925-2016) *The Adventures of Tom Sawyer* 1938; *They Shall Have Music* 1939
Kelsall, Moultrie (1901-1980) *The Dark Avenger* 1955; *Violent Playground* 1958; *The Battle of the Sexes* 1960; *The Birthday Party* 1968
Kelton, Pert (1907-1968) *The Bowery* 1933; *Sing and Like It* 1934; *Annie Oakley* 1935; *The Music Man* 1962; *The Comic* 1969
Keltz, Jonathan *Acceptance* 2009; *21 and Over* 2012
Kemble-Cooper, Violet aka **Kemble Cooper, Violet** (1886-1961) *Vanessa, Her Love Story* 1935; *The Invisible Ray* 1936
Kemmerling, Warren aka **Kemmerling, Warren J** (1928-2005) *The Lawyer* 1969; *Brother John* 1970; *Hit!* 1973; *Eat My Dust!* 1976; *Family Plot* 1976; *Close Encounters of the Third Kind* 1977; *The Dark* 1979

Kemp-Welch, Joan (1906-1999) *Busman's Honeymoon* 1940; *They Flew Alone* 1941
Kemp, Elizabeth *He Knows You're Alone* 1981; *Eating* 1990
Kemp, Gary (1960-) *The Krays* 1990; *Paper Marriage* 1991; *The Bodyguard* 1992; *Killing Zoe* 1993; *Magic Hunter* 1994; *Dog Eat Dog* 2000; *Soul Boys of the Western World* 2014
Kemp, Jeremy (1934-) *Operation Crossbow* 1965; *The Blue Max* 1966; *A Twist of Sand* 1967; *The Strange Affair* 1968; *Darling Lili* 1970; *Eyewitness* 1970; *The Games* 1970; *The Belstone Fox* 1973; *The Blockhouse* 1973; *East of Elephant Rock* 1976; *The Return of the Soldier* 1982; *Top Secret!* 1984; *Prisoner of Honor* 1991; *Angels and Insects* 1995
Kemp, Lindsay *Savage Messiah* 1972; *The Wicker Man* 1973
Kemp, Martin (1961-) *The Krays* 1990; *Daydream Believer* 1991; *Aspen Extreme* 1993; *Murder between Friends* 1993; *Embrace of the Vampire* 1994; *Monk Dawson* 1997; *Sugar Town* 1999; *Soul Boys of the Western World* 2014
Kemp, Will (1977-) *Van Helsing* 2004; *Step Up 2 the Streets* 2008
Kemper, Charles (1900-1950) *The Southerner* 1945; *Belle Starr's Daughter* 1948; *Yellow Sky* 1948; *Adventure in Baltimore* 1949; *A Ticket to Tomahawk* 1950; *Wagonmaster* 1950; *Where Danger Lives* 1950; *On Dangerous Ground* 1951
Kemper, Ellie *Bridesmaids* 2011; *Say When* 2014; *Sex Tape* 2014; *They Came Together* 2014; *The Secret Life of Pets* 2016
Kempson, Rachel (1910-2003) *The Captive Heart* 1946; *The Third Secret* 1964; *Georgy Girl* 1966; *The Charge of the Light Brigade* 1968; *A Touch of Love* 1969; *Two Gentlemen Sharing* 1969; *The Virgin Soldiers* 1969; *Out of Africa* 1985
Kendal, Felicity (1946-) *Shakespeare Wallah* 1965; *Valentino* 1977; *We're Back! A Dinosaur's Story* 1993; *Parting Shots* 1998
Kendal, Geoffrey (1910-1998) *Shakespeare Wallah* 1965; *36 Chowringhee Lane* 1982
Kendal, Jennifer (1934-1984) *Bombay Talkie* 1970; *Junoon* 1978; *Heat and Dust* 1982; *36 Chowringhee Lane* 1982
Kendall, Cy aka **Kendall, Cyrus W** (1898-1953) *The Saint Takes Over* 1940; *Tarzan's New York Adventure* 1942; *Charlie Chan in The Chinese Cat* 1944; *Laura* 1944
Kendall, Henry (1897-1962) *Rich and Strange* 1932; *The Ghost Camera* 1933; *The Amazing Quest of Ernest Bliss* 1936; *Take a Chance* 1937; *29 Acacia Avenue* 1945; *Voice of Merrill* 1952; *An Alligator Named Daisy* 1955
Kendall, Kay (1926-1959) *London Town* 1946; *Dance Hall* 1950; *Lady Godiva Rides Again* 1951; *Curtain Up* 1952; *It Started in Paradise* 1952; *Genevieve* 1953; *Meet Mr Lucifer* 1953; *The Square Ring* 1953; *Street of Shadows* 1953; *Doctor in the House* 1954; *The Constant Husband* 1955; *Quentin Durward* 1955; *Simon and Laura* 1955; *Les Girls* 1957; *The Reluctant Debutante* 1958
Kendall, Suzy (1944-) *The Sandwich Man* 1966; *Circus of Fear* 1967; *The Penthouse* 1967; *To Sir, with Love* 1967; *Up the Junction* 1967; *Fraulein Doktor* 1968; *30 Is a Dangerous Age, Cynthia* 1968; *The Bird with the Crystal Plumage* 1969; *The Gamblers* 1969; *Assault* 1970; *Darker than Amber* 1970; *Fear Is the Key* 1972; *Craze* 1973; *Adventures of a Private Eye* 1977
Kendrick, Anna (1985-) *Camp* 2003; *Rocket Science* 2007; *Up in the Air* 2009; *Scott Pilgrim vs the World* 2010; *Breaking Dawn Part One* 2011; *50/50* 2011; *End of Watch* 2012; *ParaNorman* 2012; *Pitch Perfect* 2012; *Drinking Buddies* 2013; *Into the Woods* 2014; *The Last 5 Years* 2014; *Life after Beth* 2014; *The Voices* 2014; *Cake* 2015; *Pitch Perfect 2* 2015; *The Accountant* 2016; *Mike and Dave Need Wedding Dates* 2016; *Trolls* 2016; *Pitch Perfect 3* 2017
Kenin, Alexa (1962-1985) *Honkytonk Man* 1982; *A Piano for Mrs Cimino* 1982; *Animal Behavior* 1989
Kennard, Malcolm *Diana & Me* 1997; *The Mystery of Natalie Wood* 2004
Kenney, Arthur (1914-1990) *City for Conquest* 1940; *High Sierra* 1941; *They Died with Their Boots On* 1941; *Desperate Journey* 1942; *Air Force* 1943; *Devotion* 1946; *Boomerang!* 1947; *Champion* 1949; *The Walking Hills* 1949; *The Window* 1949; *The Glass Menagerie* 1950; *Bright Victory* 1951; *Red Mountain* 1951; *Bend of the River*

1952; *The Girl in White* 1952; *The Lusty Men* 1952; *Rancho Notorious* 1952; *Crashout* 1955; *The Desperate Hours* 1955; *Impulse* 1955; *The Man from Laramie* 1955; *The Naked Dawn* 1955; *Trial* 1955; *The Rawhide Years* 1956; *Peyton Place* 1957; *Some Came Running* 1958; *A Summer Place* 1959; *Elmer Gantry* 1960; *Barabbas* 1961; *Murder She Said* 1961; *Hemingway's Adventures of a Young Man* 1962; *Lawrence of Arabia* 1962; *Cheyenne Autumn* 1964; *Fantastic Voyage* 1966; *Nevada Smith* 1966; *Anzio* 1968; *Day of the Evil Gun* 1968; *Hail, Hero!* 1969; *Shark!* 1969; *Glory Boy* 1971; *The Living Dead at the Manchester Morgue* 1974; *The Sentinel* 1977; *The Humanoid* 1979
Kennedy, David *Reign of Fire* 2001; *Attack Force* 2006
Kennedy, Deborah *Tim* 1979; *The Sum of Us* 1995; *Idiot Box* 1996; *Swimming Upstream* 2003
Kennedy, Douglas (1915-1973) *Fighting Man of the Plains* 1949; *South of St Louis* 1949; *The Cariboo Trail* 1950; *Montana* 1950; *Cry Vengeance* 1954; *Sitting Bull* 1954; *Wyoming Renegades* 1955; *Last of the Badmen* 1957
Kennedy, Edgar (1890-1948) *The Two Tars* 1928; *Perfect Day* 1929; *Murder on the Blackboard* 1934; *Woman Wanted* 1935; *The Robin Hood of El Dorado* 1936; *Double Wedding* 1937; *True Confession* 1937; *Hey! Hey! USA* 1938; *The Falcon Strikes Back* 1943; *Hitler's Madman* 1943; *It Happened Tomorrow* 1944; *Unfaithfully Yours* 1948; *My Dream Is Yours* 1949; *Mad Wednesday* 1950; *Laurel and Hardy's Laughing 20s* 1965
Kennedy, George (1925-2016) *Lonely Are the Brave* 1962; *Charade* 1963; *The Man from the Diner's Club* 1963; *Strait-Jacket* 1963; *Hush... Hush, Sweet Charlotte* 1964; *Island of the Blue Dolphins* 1964; *In Harm's Way* 1965; *Mirage* 1965; *Shenandoah* 1965; *The Sons of Katie Elder* 1965; *Cool Hand Luke* 1967; *The Dirty Dozen* 1967; *Hurry Sundown* 1967; *The Ballad of Josie* 1968; *Bandolero!* 1968; *The Boston Strangler* 1968; *The Pink Jungle* 1968; *Gaily, Gaily* 1969; *The Good Guys and the Bad Guys* 1969; *Guns of the Magnificent Seven* 1969; *tick... tick... tick...* 1969; *Airport* 1970; *Dirty Dingus Magee* 1970; *Zigzag* 1970; *Dynamite Man from Glory Jail* 1971; *Cahill, United States Marshal* 1973; *Lost Horizon* 1973; *Airport 1975* 1974; *Earthquake* 1974; *Thunderbolt and Lightfoot* 1974; *The Eiger Sanction* 1975; *The Human Factor* 1975; *Airport '77* 1977; *Brass Target* 1978; *Death on the Nile* 1978; *Airport '79* 1979; *The Concorde* 1979; *Just before Dawn* 1980; *Virus* 1980; *Modern Romance* 1981; *Wacko* 1981; *Bolero* 1984; *Savage Dawn* 1985; *The Delta Force* 1986; *Creepshow 2* 1987; *The Naked Gun* 1988; *Brain Dead* 1990; *Hired to Kill* 1990; *The Naked Gun 2½: the Smell of Fear* 1991; *Naked Gun 33⅓: the Final Insult* 1994; *Cats Don't Dance* 1998; *Dennis the Menace Strikes Again* 1998; *Small Soldiers* 1998
Kennedy, Gerard (1932-) *Newsfront* 1978; *Body Melt* 1993
Kennedy, Gordon *Just like a Woman* 1992; *With or without You* 1999; *The Borderlands* 2013
Kennedy, Graham (1934-2005) *The Odd Angry Shot* 1979; *The Club* 1980; *The Return of Captain Invincible* 1983; *The Killing Fields* 1984; *Travelling North* 1986
Kennedy, Jamie (1970-) *Scream* 1996; *Clockwatchers* 1997; *Scream 2* 1997; *Bowfinger* 1999; *Three Kings* 1999; *The Specials* 2000; *Max Keeble's Big Move* 2001; *Malibu's Most Wanted* 2003; *Son of the Mask* 2004
Kennedy, Leon Isaac (1949-) *Penitentiary* 1979; *Body and Soul* 1981; *Too Scared to Scream* 1982; *Lone Wolf McQuade* 1983
Kennedy, Madge (1891-1987) *The Marrying Kind* 1952; *The Catered Affair* 1956; *Lust for Life* 1956; *A Nice Little Bank That Should Be Robbed* 1958
Kennedy, Merle (1967-) *Nemesis* 1993; *Night of the Demons 2* 1994
Kennedy, Merna (1908-1944) *The Circus* 1928; *Broadway* 1929; *Lady with a Past* 1932
Kennedy, Mimi (1949-) *Pump Up the Volume* 1990; *Buddy* 1997; *Man in the Chair* 2006; *The Christmas Gift* 2009
Kennedy, Neil *Sebastiane* 1976; *Jubilee* 1978
Kennedy, Patricia (1917-2012) *The Getting of Wisdom* 1977; *My Brilliant Career* 1979; *Country Life* 1994
Kennedy, Tom (1885-1965) *Mantrap* 1926; *Big News* 1929; *Monkey Business*

Flatbush 1974; Mandingo 1975; The Wild Party 1975; Bad 1976; Lipstick 1976; The Choirboys 1977; The Cracker Factory 1979; Class of 1984 1982; Switch 1991

King, Regina (1971-) Poetic Justice 1993; Friday 1995; Jerry Maguire 1996; A Thin Line between Love and Hate 1996; Enemy of the State 1998; How Stella Got Her Groove Back 1998; Mighty Joe Young 1998; Down to Earth 2001; Daddy Day Care 2003; Legally Blonde 2: Red, White & Blonde 2003; A Cinderella Story 2004; Ray 2004; Miss Congeniality 2: Armed & Fabulous 2005; The Ant Bully 2006; This Christmas 2007; Year of the Dog 2007; Living Proof 2008; Our Family Wedding 2010

King, Rowena Darklands 1996; A Perfect Day 2006; The Bucket List 2008

King, Stephen (1947-) Knightriders 1981; Creepshow 1982; Sleepwalkers 1992

King, Tony Gordon's War 1973; Hell Up in Harlem 1973; Report to the Commissioner 1975

King, Wright (1923-) The Young Guns 1956; Journey through Rosebud 1972

King, Zalman (1942-2012) The Intruders 1970; Blue Sunshine 1977; Tell Me a Riddle 1980

Kingsford, Walter (1881-1958) The Mystery of Edwin Drood 1935; The Invisible Ray 1936; Trouble for Two 1936; I'll Take Romance 1937; Carefree 1938; Young Dr Kildare 1938; Calling Dr Kildare 1939; The Man in the Iron Mask 1939; Miracles for Sale 1939; The Devil and Miss Jones 1941; Dr Kildare's Wedding Day 1941; Dr Kildare's Victory 1941; Unholy Partners 1941; Fingers at the Window 1942; My Favorite Blonde 1942; Dr Gillespie's Criminal Case 1943; Flight for Freedom 1943; The Velvet Touch 1948; Slattery's Hurricane 1949

Kingsley, Ben aka **Kingsley, Sir Ben** (1943-) Fear Is the Key 1972; Betrayal 1982; Gandhi 1982; Turtle Diary 1985; Maurice 1987; Testimony 1987; Pascali's Island 1988; Without a Clue 1988; Slipstream 1989; The Children 1990; The 5th Monkey 1990; Bugsy 1991; Freddie as FRO7 1992; Sneakers 1992; Dave 1993; Innocent Moves 1993; Schindler's List 1993; Death and the Maiden 1994; Species 1995; Twelfth Night 1996; The Assignment 1997; Photographing Fairies 1997; Parting Shots 1998; Alice in Wonderland 1999; The Confession 1999; Spooky House 1999; Rules of Engagement 2000; Sexy Beast 2000; What Planet Are You From? 2000; A.I. Artificial Intelligence 2001; Tuck Everlasting 2002; House of Sand and Fog 2003; Suspect Zero 2004; Thunderbirds 2004; Oliver Twist 2005; The Last Legion 2006; Lucky Number Slevin 2006; I Have Never Forgotten You: the Life and Legacy of Simon Wiesenthal 2007; You Kill Me 2007; Elegy 2008; Fifty Dead Men Walking 2008; The Love Guru 2008; Transsiberian 2008; The Wackness 2008; War, Inc 2008; Shutter Island 2009; Prince of Persia: the Sands of Time 2010; Hugo 2011; The Dictator 2012; Ender's Game 2013; Iron Man Three 2013; The Boxtrolls 2014; Exodus: Gods and Kings 2014; Learning to Drive 2014; Night at the Museum: Secret of the Tomb 2014; Robot Overlords 2014; Stonehearst Asylum 2014; Life 2015; Self/Less 2015; Unity 2015; The Walk 2015; The Jungle Book 2016

Kingston, Alex (1963-) The Cook, the Thief, His Wife and Her Lover 1989; Carrington 1995; The Infiltrator 1995; Croupier 1998; Essex Boys 1999; Sweet Land 2005; Like Crazy 2011

Kinkade, Amelia (1959-) Night of the Demons 1988; Night of the Demons 2 1994; Demon House 1997

Kinlan, Laurence (1983-) Saltwater 1999; Ned Kelly 2003; Small Engine Repair 2006

Kinnaman, Joel (1979-) Easy Money 2010; The Darkest Hour 2011; Easy Money II 2012; Lola Versus 2012; Easy Money III: Life Deluxe 2013; Child 44 2014; RoboCop 2014; Run All Night 2015; Suicide Squad 2016

Kinnear, Greg (1963-) Blankman 1994; Sabrina 1995; Dear God 1996; As Good as It Gets 1997; A Smile like Yours 1997; You've Got Mail 1998; Mystery Men 1999; The Gift 2000; Loser 2000; Nurse Betty 2000; What Planet Are You From? 2000; Animal Attraction 2001; Dinner with Friends 2001; Auto Focus 2002; We Were Soldiers 2002; Godsend 2003; Stuck on You 2003; Bad News Bears 2005; The Matador 2006; Robots 2005; Fast Food Nation 2006; Invincible 2006; Little Miss Sunshine 2006; Unknown 2006; Feast of Love 2007; Baby Mama 2008; Flash of Genius 2008; Ghost Town 2008; Green Zone 2010; The Last Song 2010; I Don't Know How She Does It 2011; Salvation Boulevard 2011; Stuck in Love 2012; The English Teacher 2013; Heaven Is for Real 2014

Kinnear, Rory Broken 2012; Cuban Fury 2014; The Imitation Game 2014; Man Up 2015

Kinnear, Roy (1934-1988) Sparrows Can't Sing 1962; Tiara Tahiti 1962; A Place to Go 1963; The Small World of Sammy Lee 1963; French Dressing 1964; Help! 1965; The Hill 1965; The Deadly Affair 1966; How I Won the War 1967; The Bed Sitting Room 1969; Lock Up Your Daughters! 1969; Taste the Blood of Dracula 1969; On a Clear Day You Can See Forever 1970; Scrooge 1970; Willy Wonka and the Chocolate Factory 1971; Alice's Adventures in Wonderland 1972; Madame Sin 1972; That's Your Funeral 1972; The Three Musketeers 1973; The Amorous Milkman 1974; Barry McKenzie Holds His Own 1974; The Adventure of Sherlock Holmes' Smarter Brother 1975; One of Our Dinosaurs Is Missing 1975; Royal Flash 1975; Not Now, Comrade 1976; Herbie Goes to Monte Carlo 1977; The Hound of the Baskervilles 1977; The Last Remake of Beau Geste 1977; Watership Down 1978; Hawk the Slayer 1980; Hammett 1982; The Boys in Blue 1983; Pirates 1986; A Man for All Seasons 1988; The Return of the Musketeers 1989; The Princess and the Goblin 1992

Kinnell, Murray (1889-1954) The Purchase Price 1932; Zoo in Budapest 1933; Anne of Green Gables 1934; Think Fast, Mr World 1934

Kinney, Taylor The Other Woman 2014; The Forest 2016

Kinney, Terry (1954-) No Mercy 1986; Talent for the Game 1991; Body Snatchers 1993; The Firm 1993; Devil in a Blue Dress 1995; The Good Old Boys 1995; Fly Away Home 1996; Wes Craven's Don't Look Down 1998; Oxygen 1999; The House of Mirth 2000; Save the Last Dance 2000; Midwives 2001

Kinsey, Lance (1960-) Police Academy 6: City under Siege 1989; Dollar for the Dead 1998

Kinskey, Leonid (1903-1998) Duck Soup 1933; The Great Waltz 1938; Ball of Fire 1941; That Night in Rio 1941; Weekend in Havana 1941; Lady for a Night 1942; Can't Help Singing 1944; The Fighting Seabees 1944

Kinski, Klaus aka **Kinsky, Klaus** (1926-1991) A Time to Love and a Time to Die 1958; Doctor Zhivago 1965; For a Few Dollars More 1965; The Pleasure Girls 1965; A Bullet for the General 1966; Our Man in Marrakesh 1966; Circus of Fear 1967; Five Golden Dragons 1967; Grand Slam 1967; The Great Silence 1967; Sumuru 1967; Sartana 1968; Count Dracula 1970; Aguirre, Wrath of God 1972; Lifespan 1975; Woyzeck 1978; Nosferatu, the Vampyre 1979; Buddy Buddy 1981; Venom 1981; Android 1982; Fitzcarraldo 1982; Love and Money 1982; Codename Wildgeese 1984; The Little Drummer Girl 1984; Vampire in Venice 1987; Cobra Verde 1988; My Best Fiend 1999

Kinski, Nastassja aka **Kinski, Nastassia** (1959-) To the Devil a Daughter 1976; Tess 1979; Cat People 1982; One from the Heart 1982; Exposed 1983; The Moon in the Gutter 1983; Unfaithfully Yours 1983; The Hotel New Hampshire 1984; Maria's Lovers 1984; Paris, Texas 1984; Revolution 1985; Torrents of Spring 1989; Night Sun 1990; Faraway, So Close 1993; Terminal Velocity 1994; Father's Day 1997; One Night Stand 1997; Savior 1997; The Lost Son 1998; Playing by Heart 1998; Susan's Plan 1998; Your Friends & Neighbors 1998; Bitter Suite 2000; The Claim 2000; A Storm in Summer 2000; An American Rhapsody 2001; The Day the World Ended 2001; Diary of a Sex Addict 2001; Town & Country 2001

Kinski, Nikolai Tortilla Soup 2001; Klimt 2006; YSL: Yves Saint Laurent 2014

Kirby, Bruno aka **Kirby Jr, Bruno** aka **Kirby Jr, B** (1949-2006) Cinderella Liberty 1973; The Harrad Experiment 1973; Almost Summer 1977; Between the Lines 1977; Borderline 1980; Where the Buffalo Roam 1980; Modern Romance 1981; Birdy 1984; This Is Spinal Tap 1984; Good Morning, Vietnam 1987; Tin Men 1987; The In Crowd 1988; Bert Rigby, You're a Fool 1989; We're No Angels 1989; When Harry Met Sally... 1989; The Freshman 1990; City Slickers 1991; Golden Gate 1994; The Basketball Diaries 1995; Donnie Brasco 1997; History Is Made at Night 1999

Kirby, Christopher aka **Kirby, Chris** Salute 2008; Iron Sky 2012; Predestination 2014

Kirby, Luke Mambo Italiano 2003; Take This Waltz 2011; Fury 2012

Kirby, Michael (1925-2002) The Countess of Monte Cristo 1948; The Silent Partner 1978; Swoon 1992

Kirby, Simone Jimmy's Hall 2014; Notes on Blindness 2016

Kirby, Vanessa The Rise 2012; Queen and Country 2014; Kill Command 2016

Kirienko, Zinaida (1933-) And Quiet Flows the Don 1957; Destiny of a Man 1959

Kirilmis, Nazan aka **Kesal, Nazan** Uzak 2003; Climates 2006

Kirk, Justin (1969-) Love! Valour! Compassion! 1997; Ask the Dust 2006; Mr Morgan's Last Love 2013

Kirk, Phyllis (1926-2006) Mrs O'Malley and Mr Malone 1950; Our Very Own 1950; The Iron Mistress 1952; House of Wax 1953; Thunder over the Plains 1953; The City Is Dark 1954; River Beat 1954; Back from Eternity 1956; Johnny Concho 1956; The Sad Sack 1957; That Woman Opposite 1957

Kirk, Robert aka **Kirk, Robert C** The Killing of John Lennon 2006; Everyday 2012

Kirk, Tommy (1941-) Old Yeller 1957; The Shaggy Dog 1959; Swiss Family Robinson 1960; The Absent-Minded Professor 1961; Babes in Toyland 1961; Bon Voyage! 1962; Son of Flubber 1962; The Misadventures of Merlin Jones 1964; The Monkey's Uncle 1965; Village of the Giants 1965; The Ghost in the Invisible Bikini 1966

Kirke, Lola (1990-) Reaching for the Moon 2013; Mistress America 2015

Kirkland, Alexander (1901-?) Tarnished Lady 1931; Strange Interlude 1932; Black Beauty 1933

Kirkland, Muriel (1903-1971) Hold Your Man 1933; Little Man, What Now? 1934; Nana 1934; The White Parade 1934

Kirkland, Sally (1944-) Blue 1968; Going Home 1971; A Star Is Born 1976; Human Highway 1982; Anna 1987; Best of the Best 1989; Cold Feet 1989; Bullseye! 1990; Heat Wave 1990; Revenge 1990; Two Evil Eyes 1990; Eye of the Stranger 1993; Paper Hearts 1993; Gunmen 1994; Edtv 1999

Kirkwood, Jack (1894-1964) Fancy Pants 1950; Never a Dull Moment 1950

Kirkwood, Pat (1921-2008) Band Waggon 1939; Come On George 1939

Kirshner, Mia (1976-) Love and Human Remains 1993; Exotica 1994; The Crow: City of Angels 1996; Anna Karenina 1997; Mad City 1997; Not Another Teen Movie 2001; The Black Dahlia 2006; They Come Back 2007; The Barrens 2012

Kirwan, Dervla (1971-) December Bride 1990; With or without You 1999; Dangerous Parking 2007; Ondine 2009; Luna 2014

Kirwan, Kitty The Vicar of Bray 1937; Odd Man Out 1947

Kiser, Terry (1939-) Rachel, Rachel 1968; Rich Kids 1979; Six Pack 1982; Friday the 13th Part VII: the New Blood 1988; Weekend at Bernie's 1989; Mannequin on the Move 1991; Into the Sun 1992; Weekend at Bernie's II 1992; Pet Shop 1995; Tornado Warning 2012

Kishi, Keiko (1932-) The Thick-Walled Room 1953; Early Spring 1956; Kwaidan 1964; The Yakuza 1975; Mastermind 1976; The Makioka Sisters 1983

Kishimoto, Kayoko (1960-) Hana-Bi 1997; Kikujiro 1999

Kitabayashi, Tanie (1911-2010) The Burmese Harp 1956; The Key 1959; The Burmese Harp 1985

Kitaen, Tawny (1961-) Bachelor Party 1984; Witchboard 1987

Kitamura, Kazuki Freezer 2000; Killers 2014

Kitamura, Kazuo (1927-2007) The Profound Desire of the Gods 1968; Black Rain 1988; Warm Water under a Red Bridge 2001

Kitano, Takeshi aka **Takeshi** aka **Takeshi, "Beat"** (1947-) Merry Christmas Mr Lawrence 1982; Violent Cop 1989; Sonatine 1993; Johnny Mnemonic 1995; Hana-Bi 1997; Gohatto 1999; Kikujiro 1999; Battle Royale 2000; Brother 2000; Battle Royale 2: Requiem 2003; Zatoichi 2003; Ghost in the Shell 2017

Kitchen, Michael (1948-) Out of Africa 1985; Fools of Fortune 1990; The Russia House 1990; Enchanted April 1991; Hostage 1992; Mrs Dalloway 1997; New Year's Day 1999

Kitsch, Taylor (1981-) The Covenant 2006; X-Men Origins: Wolverine 2009; Battleship 2012; John Carter 2012; Savages 2012; The Grand Seduction 2013; Lone Survivor 2013; The Normal Heart 2014

Kitt, Eartha (1927-2008) Casbah 1948; New Faces 1954; Anna Lucasta 1958; St Louis Blues 1958; Up the Chastity Belt 1971; Friday Foster 1975; Dragonard 1987; Erik the Viking 1989; Ernest Scared Stupid 1991; Boomerang 1992; Unzipped 1995; Harriet the Spy 1996; The Emperor's New Groove 2000; Holes 2003; Kronk's New Groove 2005

Kittelsen, Agnes Happy, Happy 2010; Kon-Tiki 2012

Kittles, Tory Frankenfish 2004; Get Rich or Die Tryin' 2005; Next 2007

Kitzmiller, John (1913-1965) Dolina Mira 1956; Dr No 1962

Kjellin, Alf aka **Kent, Christopher** (1920-1988) Torment 1944; Madame Bovary 1949; Summer Interlude 1950; The Juggler 1953; Two Living, One Dead 1961; Assault on a Queen 1966; Ice Station Zebra 1968

Kjellman, Björn (1963-) Best Intentions 1992; All Things Fair 1995

Klaussner, Burghart (1949-) Good Bye Lenin! 2003; Requiem 2006; The Silence 2010; Diplomacy 2014; 13 Minutes 2015

Klauzner, Uri Ran Kadosh 1999; Kippur 2000

Klebba, Martin Snow White 2001; Oz the Great and Powerful 2013

Klein-Rogge, Rudolf (1888-1955) Destiny 1921; Dr Mabuse, the Gambler 1922; Metropolis 1926; Spies 1928; The Testament of Dr Mabuse 1932

Klein, Chris (1979-) American Pie 1999; Election 1999; Here on Earth 2000; American Pie 2 2001; Rollerball 2001; Say It Isn't So 2001; The United States of Leland 2002; We Were Soldiers 2002; Just Friends 2005; American Dreamz 2006; American Reunion 2012

Klein, Kacey Mottet Home 2008; Sister 2012

Klein, Nita Muriel 1963; Total Eclipse 1995

Klein, Robert (1942-) The Thirteenth Guest 1932; The Landlord 1970; The Owl and the Pussycat 1970; The Pursuit of Happiness 1971; Hooper 1978; The Last Unicorn 1980; Mixed Nuts 1994; Jeffrey 1995; The Safety of Objects 2001; Two Weeks Notice 2002; How to Lose a Guy in 10 Days 2003; Reign over Me 2007

Klemperer, Werner (1920-2000) Kiss Them for Me 1957; Dark Intruder 1965; Ship of Fools 1965

Kline, Kevin (1947-) Sophie's Choice 1982; The Big Chill 1983; The Pirates of Penzance 1983; Silverado 1985; Violets Are Blue 1986; Cry Freedom 1987; A Fish Called Wanda 1988; The January Man 1989; I Love You to Death 1990; Grand Canyon 1991; Soapdish 1991; Chaplin 1992; Consenting Adults 1992; Dave 1993; George Balanchine's The Nutcracker 1993; Princess Caraboo 1994; French Kiss 1995; The Hunchback of Notre Dame 1996; Looking for Richard 1996; Fierce Creatures 1997; The Ice Storm 1997; In & Out 1997; A Midsummer Night's Dream 1999; Wild Wild West 1999; The Road to El Dorado 2000; The Anniversary Party 2001; Life as a House 2001; Orange County 2001; The Emperor's Club 2002; De-Lovely 2004; As You Like It 2006; The Pink Panther 2006; A Prairie Home Companion 2006; Trade 2006; Definitely, Maybe 2008; The Tale of Despereaux 2008; The Conspirator 2010; No Strings Attached 2011; Last Vegas 2013; My Old Lady 2014; Ricki and the Flash 2015; Beauty and the Beast 2017

Kling, Heidi (1967-) The Mighty Ducks 1992; Out on a Limb 1992; D3: the Mighty Ducks 1996

Klugman, Jack (1922-2012) 12 Angry Men 1957; Cry Terror 1958; Days of Wine and Roses 1962; Act One 1963; I Could Go On Singing 1963; The Yellow Canary 1963; The Detective 1968; The Split 1968; Goodbye, Columbus 1969; Who Says I Can't Ride a Rainbow? 1971; Two-Minute Warning 1976

Knaggs, Skelton (1911-1955) The Ghost Ship 1943; Terror by Night 1946; Dick Tracy Meets Gruesome 1947

Knapp, Beau The Signal 2014; The Gift 2015

Knapp, Evalyn (1908-1981) Smart Money 1931; High Pressure 1932; A Successful Calamity 1932; Confidential 1935

Knaup, Herbert (1956-) Run Lola Run 1998; In Darkness 2011

Knepper, Robert aka **Knepper, Rob** (1959-) DOA 1988; Renegades 1989; Gas, Food, Lodging 1992; When the Bough Breaks 1993; The Stinger 1997; Absence of the Good 1999; Love & Sex 2000; Hitman 2007; Transporter 3 2008; Jack Reacher: Never Go Back 2016

Knight, David (1928-) Out of the Clouds 1954; The Young Lovers 1954; Lost 1955; Eyewitness 1956; Across the Bridge 1957; The Battle of the V1 1958; Nightmare 1963; Who Shot Patakango? 1989

Knight, Don (1933-1997) The Hell with Heroes 1968; The Hawaiians 1970; something big 1971; Swamp Thing 1982

Knight, Esmond (1906-1987) Waltzes from Vienna 1933; The Vicar of Bray 1937; The Arsenal Stadium Mystery 1939; Contraband 1940; The Halfway House 1943; The Silver Fleet 1943; Henry V 1944; Black Narcissus 1947; The End of the River 1947; Uncle Silas 1947; The Red Shoes 1948; Gone to Earth 1950; The River 1951; The Battle of the V1 1958; Peeping Tom 1960; The Winter's Tale 1966; The Boy Who Turned Yellow 1972; Robin and Marian 1976; The Element of Crime 1984

Knight, Fuzzy (1901-1976) The Cowboy and the Lady 1938; Spawn of the North 1938; My Little Chickadee 1940; The Singing Sheriff 1944; Frontier Gal 1945

Knight, Gladys (1944-) Pipe Dreams 1976; Hollywood Homicide 2003

Knight, Jack (1938-) The Long Goodbye 1973; Touch the Top of the World 2006

Knight, Shirley (1937-) The Dark at the Top of the Stairs 1960; Sweet Bird of Youth 1962; Flight from Ashiya 1963; Dutchman 1966; The Group 1966; The Counterfeit Killer 1968; Petulia 1968; The Rain People 1969; Juggernaut 1974; Beyond the Poseidon Adventure 1979; Endless Love 1981; The Sender 1982; Desperate Justice 1993; Indictment: the McMartin Trial 1995; Stuart Saves His Family 1995; Diabolique 1996; If These Walls Could Talk 1996; As Good as It Gets 1997; The Wedding 1998; Angel Eyes 2001; Divine Secrets of the Ya-Ya Sisterhood 2002; Paul Blart: Mall Cop 2009

Knight, Ted (1923-1986) Nightmare in Chicago 1968; Caddyshack 1980

Knight, Trenton (1982-) Charlie's Ghost Story 1994; Munchie Strikes Back 1994

Knight, Wayne (1955-) Dead Again 1991; Jurassic Park 1993; To Die For 1995; Space Jam 1997; Punisher: War Zone 2008

Knight, Wyatt (1955-) Porky's 1981; Porky's Revenge 1985

Knightley, Keira (1985-) Bend It like Beckham 2001; The Hole 2001; Love Actually 2003; Pirates of the Caribbean: the Curse of the Black Pearl 2003; King Arthur 2004; Domino 2005; The Jacket 2005; Pride & Prejudice 2005; Pirates of the Caribbean: Dead Man's Chest 2006; Atonement 2007; Pirates of the Caribbean: at World's End 2007; Silk 2007; The Duchess 2008; The Edge of Love 2008; Last Night 2009; London Boulevard 2010; Never Let Me Go 2010; A Dangerous Method 2011; Seeking a Friend for the End of the World 2011; Anna Karenina 2012; Begin Again 2013; Jack Ryan: Shadow Recruit 2013; The Imitation Game 2014; Say When 2014; Everest 2015; Collateral Beauty 2016; Colette 2018

Knoller, Ohad Beaufort 2007; Yossi 2012

Knott, Andrew (1979-) The Secret Garden 1993; Black Beauty 1994; In Our Name 2010; Ollie Kepler's Expanding Purple World 2010

Knotts, Don (1924-2006) No Time for Sergeants 1958; Move Over, Darling 1963; The Shakiest Gun in the West 1967; The Apple Dumpling Gang 1974; No Deposit No Return 1976; Herbie Goes to Monte Carlo 1977; Hot Lead and Cold Feet 1978; The Apple Dumpling Gang Rides Again 1979; The Private Eyes 1980; Pleasantville 1998; Chicken Little 2005

Knowland, Marilyn (1927-) Les Misérables 1935; The Way of All Flesh 1940

Knowles, Beyoncé (1981-) Austin Powers in Goldmember 2002; The Fighting Temptations 2003; Fade to Black 2004; Dreamgirls 2006; The Pink Panther 2006; Cadillac Records 2008; Obsessed 2009; Epic 2013

Knowles, Patric (1911-1995) The Charge of the Light Brigade 1936; It's Love I'm After 1937; The Adventures of

Robin Hood 1938; Four's a Crowd 1938; Another Thin Man 1939; Beauty for the Asking 1939; Anne of Windy Poplars 1940; A Bill of Divorcement 1940; The Wolf Man 1941; Lady in a Jam 1942; Sin Town 1942; Who Done It? 1942; Frankenstein Meets the Wolf Man 1943; Hit the Ice 1943; Kitty 1945; The Bride Wore Boots 1946; Monsieur Beaucaire 1946; OSS 1946; Of Human Bondage 1946; Ivy 1947; Dream Girl 1948; Isn't It Romantic 1948; The Big Steal 1949; Three Came Home 1950; Mutiny 1952; Tarzan's Savage Fury 1952; Jamaica Run 1953; World for Ransom 1953; Khyber Patrol 1954; Band of Angels 1957; Auntie Mame 1958
Knox, Alexander (1907-1995) The Gaunt Stranger 1938; Cheer Boys Cheer 1939; The Sea Wolf 1941; This above All 1942; None Shall Escape 1944; Wilson 1944; Over 21 1945; Sister Kenny 1946; The Judge Steps Out 1949; Tokyo Joe 1949; I'd Climb the Highest Mountain 1951; Man in the Saddle 1951; Europa '51 1952; The Divided Heart 1954; The Sleeping Tiger 1954; The Night My Number Came Up 1955; Reach for the Sky 1956; Chase a Crooked Shadow 1957; High Tide at Noon 1957; Davy 1958; Intent to Kill 1958; Operation Amsterdam 1958; Passionate Summer 1958; The Vikings 1958; Oscar Wilde 1959; The Wreck of the Mary Deare 1959; Crack in the Mirror 1960; The Damned 1961; The Longest Day 1962; Crack in the World 1964; Woman of Straw 1964; Khartoum 1966; The Psychopath 1966; Accident 1967; The 25th Hour 1967; Fraulein Doktor 1968; Shalako 1968; Skullduggery 1969; Puppet on a Chain 1970; Holocaust 2000 1977
Knox, Elyse (1917-2012) Footlight Fever 1941; The Mummy's Tomb 1942; Hit the Ice 1943; Black Gold 1947
Knox, Mickey (1921-2013) Knock on Any Door 1949; White Heat 1949; Beyond the Law 1968; Cemetery Man 1994
Knox, Teddy (1894-1974) Alf's Button Afloat 1938; Gasbags 1940
Knoxville, Johnny (1971-) Big Trouble 2002; Jackass: the Movie 2002; Men in Black 2 2002; Grand Theft Parsons 2003; A Dirty Shame 2004; Walking Tall 2004; The Dukes of Hazzard 2005; Lords of Dogtown 2005; The Ringer 2005; jackass number two 2006; Jackass 3D 2010; Fun Size 2012; Small Apartments 2012; jackass presents: Bad Grandpa 2013; The Last Stand 2013; Elvis & Nixon 2016
Knudsen, Erik Saw II 2005; Client Seduction 2014
Knudsen, Peggy (1923-1980) The Big Sleep 1946; Humoresque 1946; A Stolen Life 1946; The Unfaithful 1947; Good Morning, Miss Dove 1955; Beyond the River 1956; Hilda Crane 1956; Istanbul 1957
Knudsen, Sidse Babett After the Wedding 2006; The Duke of Burgundy 2014; A Hologram for the King 2016
Knudson, Barbara (1927-2014) Meet Danny Wilson 1952; The Cry Baby Killer 1958
Kober, Jeff (1953-) Alien Nation 1988; The First Power 1990; Automatic 1994; Tank Girl 1995; Logan's War: Bound by Honor 1998; Aces 'n' Eights 2008
Kobiela, Bogumil (1932-1969) Ashes and Diamonds 1958; Eroica 1958
Koch, Marianne (1931-) The Devil's General 1955; Death Drums along the River 1963; A Fistful of Dollars 1964
Koch, Peter aka **Koch, Pete** Sunset Grill 1992; Body Shot 1994
Koch, Sebastian (1962-) Black Book 2006; The Lives of Others 2006; Albatross 2011; Suspension of Disbelief 2012; A Good Day to Die Hard 2013; Bridge of Spies 2015
Köchl, Franz The Goalkeeper's Fear of the Penalty Kick 1971; Alice in the Cities 1974
Kodet, Jiri (1937-2005) Mandragora 1997; Divided We Fall 2000
Kodjoe, Boris Brown Sugar 2002; Surrogates 2009; Baggage Claim 2013
Koechner, David (1962-) A Guy Thing 2002; My Boss's Daughter 2003; Anchorman: the Legend of Ron Burgundy 2004; The Dukes of Hazzard 2005; Thank You for Smoking 2005; Yours, Mine & Ours 2005; The Goods: Live Hard Sell Hard 2009; Final Destination 5 2011; Anchorman 2: the Legend Continues 2013; Cheap Thrills 2013; A Haunted House 2013; Krampus 2015
Koehler, Frederick aka **Koehler, Fred** (1975-) Mr Mom 1983; The Positively True Adventures of the Alleged Texas Cheerleader-Murdering Mom 1993
Koenig, Walter (1936-) Star Trek: the Motion Picture 1979; Star Trek II: the

Wrath of Khan 1982; Star Trek III: the Search for Spock 1984; Star Trek IV: the Voyage Home 1986; Star Trek V: the Final Frontier 1989; Star Trek VI: the Undiscovered Country 1991; Star Trek: Generations 1994
Kogure, Michiyo (1918-1990) Drunken Angel 1948; The Flavour of Green Tea over Rice 1952; Street of Shame 1955; Tales of the Taira Clan 1955
Kohler, Fred (1889-1938) The Iron Horse 1924; Riders of the Purple Sage 1925; Underworld 1927; The Way of All Flesh 1927; The Dragnet 1928; The Case of Lena Smith 1929; The Leatherneck 1929; Say It with Songs 1929; Fighting Caravans 1931; Other Men's Women 1931; Deluge 1933; Goin' to Town 1935
Köhler, Juliane (1965-) Aimée and Jaguar 1999; Nowhere in Africa 2001; Downfall 2004
Kohner, Susan (1936-) To Hell and Back 1955; The Last Wagon 1956; Trooper Hook 1957; The Big Fisherman 1959; The Gene Krupa Story 1959; Imitation of Life 1959; All the Fine Young Cannibals 1961; By Love Possessed 1961; Freud 1962
Koirala, Manisha (1970-) 1942: a Love Story 1994; Bombay 1995; Dil Se... 1998; Company 2001
Koizumi, Hiroshi (1926-2015) Godzilla Raids Again 1955; Mothra 1962; Godzilla vs Mothra 1964; Ghidrah, the Three-Headed Monster 1965
Kojo, Nikola (1969-) Pretty Village Pretty Flame 1996; Life Is a Miracle 2004
Kolb, Clarence (1875-1964) The Toast of New York 1937; The Law West of Tombstone 1938; The Amazing Mr Williams 1939; His Girl Friday 1939; Honolulu 1939; No Time for Comedy 1940; Nothing but the Truth 1941; True to Life 1943; Standing Room Only 1944; Adam's Rib 1949
Kolk, Scott (1905-1993) All Quiet on the Western Front 1930; My Sin 1931
Kolker, Henry (1870-1947) The Valiant 1929; Jewel Robbery 1932; Baby Face 1933; Meet the Baron 1933; The Power and the Glory 1933; The Black Room 1935; Mad Love 1935; Great Guy 1936; The Cowboy and the Lady 1938; Holiday 1938; The Invisible Menace 1938; Too Hot to Handle 1938
Kolldehoff, Reinhard aka **Kolldehoff, Reinhardt** aka **Kolldehoff, Rene** (1914-1995) Borsalino and Co 1974; Shout at the Devil 1976
Koman, Jacek The Hunter 2011; Son of a Gun 2013
Komorowska, Liliana Scanners III: the Takeover 1992; The Assignment 1997; The Art of War 2000
Komorowska, Maja (1937-) The Young Ladies of Wilko 1979; The Contract 1980; A Year of the Quiet Sun 1984
Koné, Djénéba Bamako 2006; A Screaming Man 2010
Konstam, Phyllis (1907-1976) Murder 1930; The Skin Game 1931
Koo, Louis Election 2005; Flash Point 2007; Protégé 2007
Koock, Guich (1944-) Seven 1979; American Ninja 1985; Square Dance 1987
Kopache, Thomas Liebestraum 1991; Stigmata 1999
Kopecky, Milos (1922-1996) Baron Munchhausen 1961; Labyrinth 1991
Kopins, Karen Creator 1985; Once Bitten 1985
Korff, Arnold (1870-1944) The Haunted Castle 1921; Diary of a Lost Girl 1929; Doughboys 1930; The Royal Family of Broadway 1930
Korine, Harmony (1974-) Last Days 2004; Manglehorn 2014
Korkes, Jon Little Murders 1971; The Day of the Dolphin 1973
Korman, Harvey (1927-2008) Lord Love a Duck 1966; Don't Just Stand There 1968; The April Fools 1969; Blazing Saddles 1974; Huckleberry Finn 1974; High Anxiety 1977; Americathon 1979; Herbie Goes Bananas 1980; History of the World Part I 1981; Trail of the Pink Panther 1982; The Curse of the Pink Panther 1983; Munchies 1987; Dracula: Dead and Loving It 1995; The Secret of NIMH II: Timmy to the Rescue 1998; The Flintstones in Viva Rock Vegas 2000
Korsmo, Charlie (1978-) Dick Tracy 1990; Men Don't Leave 1990; The Doctor 1991; Hook 1991; What about Bob? 1991; Can't Hardly Wait 1998
Kortner, Fritz (1892-1970) Hands of Orlac 1924; Pandora's Box 1929; The Ship of Lost Men 1929; Three Loves 1929; Chu Chin Chow 1934; Evensong 1934
Korvin, Charles (1907-1998) Enter Arsene Lupin 1944; This Love of Ours

1945; Berlin Express 1948; Tarzan's Savage Fury 1952; The Man Who Had Power over Women 1970
Korzun, Dina (1971-) Last Resort 2000; Cold Souls 2008
Koscina, Sylva (1933-1994) Hercules 1957; Jessica 1962; Le Masque de Fer 1962; The Swordsman of Siena 1962; Hot Enough for June 1964; Let's Talk about Women 1964; Juliet of the Spirits 1965; Deadlier than the Male 1966; The Secret War of Harry Frigg 1967; A Lovely Way to Go 1968; Lisa and the Devil 1974
Kosleck, Martin (1907-1994) Berlin Correspondent 1942; The Frozen Ghost 1944; The Mummy's Curse 1944; Pursuit to Algiers 1945; Hitler 1962; The Flesh Eaters 1964
Koslo, Paul (1944-) The Omega Man 1971; Vanishing Point 1971; Joe Kidd 1972; Mr Majestyk 1974; Tomorrow Never Comes 1977; A Night in the Life of Jimmy Reardon 1988; Robot Jox 1989; Judge & Jury 1995
Kossoff, David (1919-2005) The Young Lovers 1954; The Bespoke Overcoat 1955; A Kid for Two Farthings 1955; 1984 1955; The Woman for Joe 1955; House of Secrets 1956; The Iron Petticoat 1956; Who Done It? 1956; Count Five and Die 1957; Innocent Sinners 1957; Indiscreet 1958; The House of the Seven Hawks 1959; Jet Storm 1959; The Mouse That Roared 1959; Conspiracy of Hearts 1960; Inn for Trouble 1960; The Two Faces of Dr Jekyll 1960; The Mouse on the Moon 1963; Ring of Spies 1963
Kosugi, Kane Shogun Warrior 1991; DOA: Dead or Alive 2006
Kosugi, Sho (1948-) Enter the Ninja 1981; Aloha Summer 1988; Black Eagle 1988; Blind Fury 1990; Shogun Warrior 1991; Ninja Assassin 2009
Kotamanidou, Eva (1936-) The Travelling Players 1975; Trilogy: the Weeping Meadow 2004
Koteas, Elias (1961-) One Magic Christmas 1985; Some Kind of Wonderful 1987; Blood Red 1988; Full Moon in Blue Water 1988; Tucker: the Man and His Dream 1988; Almost an Angel 1990; Desperate Hours 1990; Look Who's Talking Too 1990; Teenage Mutant Ninja Turtles 1990; The Adjuster 1991; Teenage Mutant Ninja Turtles III 1992; Camilla 1993; Cyborg 2: Glass Shadow 1993; Exotica 1994; The Prophecy 1994; Crash 1996; Gattaca 1997; Fallen 1998; Living Out Loud 1998; The Thin Red Line 1998; Harrison's Flowers 2000; Lost Souls 2000; Collateral Damage 2001; Novocaine 2001; Ararat 2002; The Greatest Game Ever Played 2005; Skinwalkers 2006; The Girl in the Park 2007; Shooter 2007; The Curious Case of Benjamin Button 2008; Two Lovers 2008; Defendor 2009; The Fourth Kind 2009; The Haunting in Connecticut 2009; Let Me In 2010; Dream House 2011; A Very Harold & Kumar 3D Christmas 2011; Devil's Knot 2013; The Last Days on Mars 2013
Kotto, Yaphet (1937-) Nothing but a Man 1964; 5 Card Stud 1968; The Thomas Crown Affair 1968; The Liberation of LB Jones 1970; Across 110th Street 1972; Bone 1972; Live and Let Die 1973; Truck Turner 1974; Friday Foster 1975; Report to the Commissioner 1975; Shark's Treasure 1975; Drum 1976; Raid on Entebbe 1977; Blue Collar 1978; Alien 1979; Brubaker 1980; Death Vengeance 1982; The Star Chamber 1983; Badge of the Assassin 1985; Warning Sign 1985; Eye of the Tiger 1986; The Running Man 1987; Midnight Run 1988; Freddy's Dead: The Final Nightmare 1991; Intent to Kill 1992; The Puppet Masters 1994; Bitter Hearts 1996
Kouyate, Sotigui aka **Kouyaté, Sotigui** (1936-2010) Dirty Pretty Things 2002; London River 2009
Kovack, Nancy (1935-) Diary of a Madman 1963; Jason and the Argonauts 1963; The Outlaws Is Coming 1965; Frankie & Johnny 1966; Tarzan and the Valley of Gold 1966; Marooned 1969
Kovacs, Ernie (1919-1962) Operation Mad Ball 1957; Bell, Book and Candle 1958; It Happened to Jane 1959; Our Man in Havana 1959; North to Alaska 1960; Pepe 1960; Strangers When We Meet 1960

Kovic, Ron (1946-) The US vs John Lennon 2006; We Are Many 2014
Kowalski, Wladyslaw (1936-) The Double Life of Véronique 1991; Avalon 2000
Koyuki (1976-) The Last Samurai 2003; Blood: the Last Vampire 2008
Kozak, Harley Jane aka **Kozak, Harley** (1957-) Parenthood 1989; Arachnophobia 1990; All I Want for Christmas 1991; The Amy Fisher Story 1993; The Favor 1994; Magic in the Water 1995
Kozlowski, Linda (1958-) "Crocodile" Dundee 1986; "Crocodile" Dundee II 1988; Almost an Angel 1990; Village of the Damned 1995; Crocodile Dundee in Los Angeles 2001
Kozlowski, Piotr Korczak 1990; Europa Europa 1991
Krabbé, Jeroen (1944-) Soldier of Orange 1977; Spetters 1980; The Fourth Man 1983; Turtle Diary 1985; No Mercy 1986; The Living Daylights 1987; A World Apart 1987; Crossing Delancey 1988; Scandal 1988; Melancholia 1989; The Punisher 1989; Robin Hood 1990; Kafka 1991; The Prince of Tides 1991; King of the Hill 1993; Farinelli il Castrato 1994; Immortal Beloved 1994; The Disappearance of Garcia Lorca 1997; Left Luggage 1997; The Odyssey 1997; An Ideal Husband 1999; Ocean's Twelve 2004; Deuce Bigalow: European Gigolo 2005; Snuff-Movie 2005; Transporter 3 2008
Kraft, Scott For the Moment 1994; The Stupids 1995
Krakowski, Jane (1968-) Stepping Out 1991; Mrs Winterbourne 1996; Dance with Me 1998; The Flintstones in Viva Rock Vegas 2000; Marci X 2003; When Zachary Beaver Came to Town 2003; Alfie 2004; A Christmas Carol 2004; Mom at Sixteen 2005; Pretty Persuasion 2005; Open Season 2006; Surf's Up 2007; Open Season 2 2008
Kramer, Chris Circle of Friends 2006; Her Fatal Flaw 2006
Kramer, Eric Allan aka **Kramer, Eric** The Incredible Hulk Returns 1988; Robin Hood: Men in Tights 1993
Kramer, Jeffrey aka **Kramer, Jeffrey C** (1952-) Jaws 1975; Hollywood Boulevard 1976; Jaws 2 1978; Halloween II 1981; Santa Claus 1985; Hero and the Terror 1988
Kranz, Fran The Cabin in the Woods 2010; Much Ado about Nothing 2012; Bloodsucking Bosses 2015
Krasinski, John (1979-) Leatherheads 2007; License to Wed 2007; Away We Go 2009; It's Complicated 2009; Something Borrowed 2011; Big Miracle 2012; Promised Land 2012; The Wind Rises 2013; 13 Hours: the Secret Soldiers of Benghazi 2016
Krause, Brian (1972-) Return to the Blue Lagoon 1991; Sleepwalkers 1992; Naked Souls 1995; 919 Fifth Avenue 1995; Next Stop Murder 2010
Krause, Peter (1965-) We Don't Live Here Anymore 2003; Steep 2007; Beastly 2010
Krauss, Werner (1884-1959) The Cabinet of Dr Caligari 1919; Waxworks 1924; The Joyless Street 1925; Nana 1926; Secrets of a Soul 1926; Tartuffe 1926; Paracelsus 1943
Kravitz, Zoë aka **Kravitz, Zoe** aka **Kravitz, Zoë Isabella** (1988-) The Greatest 2009; It's Kind of a Funny Story 2010; After Earth 2013; Good Kill 2014; Mad Max: Fury Road 2015; The Divergent Series: Allegiant 2016
Kretschmann, Thomas (1962-) The Stendhal Syndrome 1996; Prince Valiant 1997; Blade II 2002; The Pianist 2002; Downfall 2004; Frankenstein 2004; Head in the Clouds 2004; Resident Evil: Apocalypse 2004; King Kong 2005; Next 2007; Transsiberian 2008; Valkyrie 2008; Wanted 2008; The Young Victoria 2008; Stalingrad 2013; Hitman: Agent 47 2015
Kreuger, Kurt (1916-2006) The Silent Bell 1944; Madame Pimpernel 1945; The Dark Corner 1946; Unfaithfully Yours 1948; Fear 1954; The Enemy Below 1957
Kreuk, Kristin (1982-) Snow White 2001; EuroTrip 2004; Partition 2006
Kreuzer, Lisa (1945-) Kings of the Road 1976; The American Friend 1977; Radio On 1979; Berlin Jerusalem 1989
Krige, Alice (1955-) Chariots of Fire 1981; Ghost Story 1981; King David 1985; Second Serve 1986; Barfly 1987; Haunted Summer 1988; See You in the Morning 1989; Sleepwalkers 1992; Jack Reed: Badge of Honor 1993; Institute Benjamenta, or This Dream People Call Human Life 1995; Star Trek: First Contact 1996; A Father's Betrayal 1997; In the Company of Spies 1999; The Little Vampire 2000; Dynasty: the Making of a Guilty Pleasure 2004; The

Mystery of Natalie Wood 2004; The Contract 2006; Lonely Hearts 2006; Silent Hill 2006; Skin 2008; Solomon Kane 2009; Will 2011
Krisch, Johannes Revanche 2008; Labyrinth of Lies 2014
Kristel, Sylvia (1952-2012) Emmanuelle 1974; Emmanuelle 2 1975; Airport '79: the Concorde 1979; The 5th Musketeer 1979; The Nude Bomb 1980; Lady Chatterley's Lover 1981; Mata Hari 1985; Dracula's Widow 1988
Kristofferson, Kris (1936-) Cisco Pike 1971; The Last Movie 1971; Blume in Love 1973; Pat Garrett and Billy the Kid 1973; Alice Doesn't Live Here Anymore 1974; Bring Me the Head of Alfredo Garcia 1974; Vigilante Force 1975; The Sailor Who Fell from Grace with the Sea 1976; A Star Is Born 1976; Semi-Tough 1977; Convoy 1978; Heaven's Gate 1980; Rollover 1981; Songwriter 1984; Trouble in Mind 1985; Stagecoach 1986; Big Top Pee-wee 1988; Millennium 1989; Perfume of the Cyclone 1989; Welcome Home 1989; Christmas in Connecticut 1992; No Place to Hide 1992; Paper Hearts 1993; Sodbusters 1994; Lone Star 1995; The Road Home 1995; Fire Down Below 1997; Girls' Night 1997; Blade 1998; Dance with Me 1998; Payback 1998; A Soldier's Daughter Never Cries 1998; Two for Texas 1998; The Joyriders 1999; Limbo 1999; D-Tox 2001; Blade II 2002; Blade: Trinity 2004; Dreamer 2005; The Jacket 2005; Fast Food Nation 2006; Dolphin Tale 2011; Deadfall 2012; The Motel Life 2012; Dolphin Tale 2 2014
Kroeger, Berry (1912-1991) Cry of the City 1948; The Dark Past 1948; The Iron Curtain 1948; Act of Violence 1949; Black Magic 1949; Down to the Sea in Ships 1949; Gun Crazy 1949; The Sword of Monte Cristo 1951; Blood Alley 1955; Atlantis, the Lost Continent 1960; Seven Thieves 1960; Demon Seed 1977
Król, Joachim (1957-) The Most Desired Man 1994; The Princess & the Warrior 2000
Kross, David (1990-) The Reader 2008; Cross of Honour 2012; Age of Uprising: the Legend of Michael Kohlhaas 2013
Kruger, Alma (1871-1960) Craig's Wife 1936; These Three 1936; One Hundred Men and a Girl 1937; Vogues of 1938 1937; The Toy Wife 1938; Calling Dr Kildare 1939; Dr Kildare's Strange Case 1940; Dr Kildare's Victory 1941; The People vs Dr Kildare 1941; Dr Gillespie 1942; Dr Gillespie's New Assistant 1942; Saboteur 1942; Dr Gillespie's Criminal Case 1943; Three Men in White 1944; Do You Love Me? 1946
Kruger, Diane (1976-) National Treasure 2004; Troy 2004; Wicker Park 2004; Frankie 2005; Merry Christmas 2005; Copying Beethoven 2006; Goodbye Bafana 2007; The Hunting Party 2007; National Treasure: Book of Secrets 2007; Anything for Her 2008; Inglourious Basterds 2009; Special Forces 2011; Unknown 2011; A Perfect Plan 2012; The Host 2013; Me, Myself and Mum 2013; Disorder 2015; Fathers and Daughters 2015; The Infiltrator 2016
Kruger, Hardy (1928-) The One That Got Away 1957; Bachelor of Hearts 1958; Blind Date 1959; Hatari! 1962; Sundays and Cybèle 1962; The Flight of the Phoenix 1966; The Defector 1966; The Red Tent 1969; The Secret of Santa Vittoria 1969; Paper Tiger 1974; Barry Lyndon 1975; A Bridge Too Far 1977; The Wild Geese 1978; The Inside Man 1984
Kruger, Otto (1885-1974) Ever in My Heart 1933; The Prizefighter and the Lady 1933; Chained 1934; Gallant Lady 1934; Men in White 1934; Treasure Island 1934; Vanessa, Her Love Story 1935; Dracula's Daughter 1936; They Won't Forget 1937; Housemaster 1938; I Am the Law 1938; Another Thin Man 1939; The Gang's All Here 1939; A Dispatch from Reuters 1940; Dr Ehrlich's Magic Bullet 1940; The Man I Married 1940; The Men in Her Life 1941; Saboteur 1942; Hitler's Children 1943; Stage Door Canteen 1943; Tarzan's Desert Mystery 1943; Cover Girl 1944; Farewell My Lovely 1944; Earl Carroll Vanities 1945; Wonder Man 1945; Duel in the Sun 1946; Lulu Belle 1948; 711 Ocean Drive 1950; Valentino 1951; High Noon 1952; Black Widow 1954; Magnificent Obsession 1954; The Colossus of New York 1958; The Young Philadelphians 1959; Cash McCall 1960
Krumholtz, David (1978-) Life with Mikey 1993; The Santa Clause 1994; Slums of Beverly Hills 1998; 10 Things I

Hate about You 1999; Sidewalks of New York 2000; The Santa Clause 2 2002; Scorched 2002; Harold & Kumar Get the Munchies 2004; Live! 2007

Krupa, Olek (1955-) Black Rainbow 1989; Mac 1992; Home Alone 3 1997; Blue Streak 1999; Behind Enemy Lines 2001

Kruschen, Jack (1922-2002) Cry Terror 1958; The Decks Ran Red 1958; The Angry Red Planet 1959; The Apartment 1960; The Last Voyage 1960; Cape Fear 1952; Follow That Dream 1962; McLintock! 1963; The Unsinkable Molly Brown 1964; Caprice 1967; The Million Dollar Duck 1971; Freebie and the Bean 1974

Kubo, Akira (1926-) Invasion of the Astro-Monster 1965; Son of Godzilla 1967; Destroy All Monsters 1968

Kudoh, Youki (1971-) Mystery Train 1989; Picture Bride 1994; Heaven's Burning 1997; Snow Falling on Cedars 1999; Memoirs of a Geisha 2005

Kudrow, Lisa (1963-) Mother 1996; Clockwatchers 1997; Romy and Michele's High School Reunion 1997; The Opposite of Sex 1998; Analyze This 1999; Hanging Up 2000; Dr Dolittle 2 2001; Analyze That 2002; Marci X 2003; Wonderland 2003; Happy Endings 2005; PS I Love You 2007; Hotel for Dogs 2008; Bandslam 2009; Love and Other Impossible Pursuits 2009; Easy A 2010; Bad Neighbours 2014

Kuga, Yoshiko (1931-) The Idiot 1951; Tales of the Taira Clan 1955; Ohayo 1959

Kulig, Joanna Elles 2011; The Woman in the Fifth 2011

Kulky, Henry (1911-1965) The 5,000 Fingers of Dr T 1953; Abbott and Costello Meet the Keystone Cops 1955

Kulle, Jarl (1927-1997) Waiting Women 1952; The Devil's Eye 1960; All These Women 1964; Dear John 1964; My Sister, My Love 1966; Fanny and Alexander 1982; Babette's Feast 1987

Kuluva, Will (1917-1990) Odds against Tomorrow 1959; Go Naked in the World 1961; The Spiral Road 1962; To Trap a Spy 1966

Kumar, Akshay (1967-) Awara Paagal Deewana 2002; Aitraaz 2004; Mujhse Shaadi Karogi 2004; WAQT: the Race against Time 2005; Kambakkht Ishq 2009

Kumar, Ashok (1911-2001) Mahal 1949; Parineeta 1953; Ek Hi Rasta 1956; Kanoon 1960; Bandini 1963

Kumar, Dilip (1922-) Shaheed 1948; Andaz 1949; Babul 1950; Tarana 1951; Devdas 1955; Naya Daur 1957; Madhumati 1958; Yahudi 1958; Mughal-e-Azam 1960

Kumar, Raaj (1926-1996) Mother India 1957; Waqt 1965

Kumar, Rajendra (1929-1999) Mother India 1957; Kanoon 1960; Sangam 1964

Kumar, Sanjeev (1937-1985) Sholay 1975; The Chess Players 1977

Kumari, Meena (1932-1972) Parineeta 1953; Ek Hi Rasta 1956; Yahudi 1958

Kunene, Vusi Cry, the Beloved Country 1995; Jerusalema 1997; A Reasonable Man 1999; The First Grader 2010

Kunimura, Jun (1955-) Chaos 1999; Vital 2004

Kunis, Mila (1983-) American Psycho II: All American Girl 2002; Forgetting Sarah Marshal 2008; Max Payne 2008; The Book of Eli 2009; Extract 2009; Black Swan 2010; Date Night 2010; Friends with Benefits 2011; Ted 2012; Blood Ties 2013; Oz the Great and Powerful 2013; Third Person 2013; The Angriest Man in Brooklyn 2014; Jupiter Ascending 2014

Kunstmann, Doris (1944-) Hitler: the Last Ten Days 1973; Funny Games 1997

Kuosmanen, Sakari Drifting Clouds 1996; Juha 1999; The Man without a Past 2002

Kupchenko, Irina (1948-) A Private Conversation 1983; Lonely Woman Seeks Lifetime Companion 1987

Küppenheim, Aline Machuca 2004; Play 2005

Kurata, Yasuaki Fist of Legend 1994; So Close 2002

Kurosawa, Asuka A Snake of June 2002; Memories of Matsuko 2006; Cold Fish 2010

Kurts, Alwyn (1915-2000) And Millions Will Die! 1973; Tim 1979; The Earthling 1980; Spotswood 1991

Kurtz, Marcia Jean Born to Win 1971; The Panic in Needle Park 1971

Kurtz, Swoosie (1944-) First Love 1977; Oliver's Story 1978; The World According to Garp 1982; Agatha Christie's A Caribbean Mystery 1983; Against All Odds 1984; Guilty Conscience 1985; True Stories 1986; Wildcats 1986; Bright Lights, Big City

1988; Dangerous Liaisons 1988; Vice Versa 1988; Stanley & Iris 1989; The Image 1990; A Shock to the System 1990; The Positively True Adventures of the Alleged Texas Cheerleader-Murdering Mom 1993; Reality Bites 1994; Citizen Ruth 1996; Harvey 1996; Liar Liar 1997; Bubble Boy 2001; Get over It 2001; The Rules of Attraction 2002; Our House 2003

Kurylenko, Olga (1979-) Hitman 2007; Quantum of Solace 2008; Centurion 2009; The Expatriate 2012; Seven Psychopaths 2012; To the Wonder 2012; Oblivion 2013; The November Man 2014; The Water Diviner 2014; Momentum 2015

Kusatsu, Clyde (1948-) The Choirboys 1977; Shanghai Surprise 1986; Made in America 1993; Top Dog 1995

Kussman, Dylan Dead Poets Society 1989; Wild Hearts Can't Be Broken 1991; Wolverine 3 2017

Kusturica, Emir (1954-) La Veuve de Saint-Pierre 2000; The Good Thief 2002; Farewell 2010; 7 Days in Havana 2012

Kutcher, Ashton (1978-) Down to You 2000; Dude, Where's My Car? 2000; Texas Rangers 2001; The Butterfly Effect 2003; Just Married 2003; My Boss's Daughter 2003; Guess Who 2005; A Lot like Love 2005; Bobby 2006; The Guardian 2006; Open Season 2006; Spread 2008; What Happens in Vegas 2008; Killers 2010; Valentine's Day 2010; New Year's Eve 2011; No Strings Attached 2011; jOBS 2013

Kuter, Kay E (1925-2003) Watermelon Man 1970; The Last Starfighter 1984; Zombie High 1987

Kuznetsova, Maria Russian Ark 2002; The Italian 2005

Kuzyk, Mimi (1952-) Miles to Go 1986; The Kiss 1988; Cannonball Fever 1989; The Final Cut 2004

Kwan, Nancy (1939-) The World of Suzie Wong 1960; Flower Drum Song 1961; The Main Attraction 1962; Tamahine 1963; The Wild Affair 1963; Fate Is the Hunter 1964; Honeymoon Hotel 1964; The Corrupt Ones 1966; Drop Dead Darling 1966; Lt Robin Crusoe, USN 1966; The Girl Who Knew Too Much 1969; The Wrecking Crew 1969; Cold Dog Soup 1989; Dragon: the Bruce Lee Story 1993

Kwan, Rosamund aka Kwan, Rosamund Chi-Lam (1962-) The Armour of God 1986; Once upon a Time in China 1991; Once upon a Time in China II 1992; Big Shot's Funeral 2001

Kwanten, Ryan (1976-) Flicka 2006; Dead Silence 2007; Legend of the Guardians: the Owls of Ga'Hoole 2010; Red Hill 2010; Mystery Road 2013; Kidnapping Freddy Heineken 2015

Kwouk, Burt aka Kwouk, Bert (1930-2016) The Inn of the Sixth Happiness 1958; Satan Never Sleeps 1962; A Shot in the Dark 1964; Curse of the Fly 1965; The Return of the Pink Panther 1974; The Pink Panther Strikes Again 1976; Revenge of the Pink Panther 1978; Trail of the Pink Panther 1982; The Curse of the Pink Panther 1983; Plenty 1985; Empire of the Sun 1987; I Bought a Vampire Motorcycle 1989; Leon the Pig Farmer 1992; Shooting Elizabeth 1992; Son of the Pink Panther 1993; Bullet to Beijing 1995; Kiss of the Dragon 2001

Kydd, Sam (1917-1982) Trent's Last Case 1952; Devil on Horseback 1954; Final Appointment 1954; Circus Friends 1956; The Treasure of Monte Cristo 1960; Island of Terror 1966; Steptoe and Son Ride Again 1973; Yesterday's Hero 1979

Kyle, Jackson Aria 1987; A Handful of Dust 1987

Kyo, Machiko (1924-) Rashomon 1950; Gate of Hell 1953; Ugetsu Monogatari 1953; The Princess Yang Kwei Fei 1955; Street of Shame 1955; The Teahouse of the August Moon 1956; Floating Weeds 1959; The Key 1959; The Face of Another 1966

Kyser, Kay (1897-1985) That's Right - You're Wrong 1939; You'll Find Out 1940; Playmates 1941; My Favorite Spy 1942

L

L L Cool J aka Smith, James Todd aka James Todd Smith aka LL Cool J (1968-) The Hard Way 1991; Toys 1992; Touch 1996; Halloween H20: 20 Years Later 1998; Woo 1998; Any Given Sunday 1999; Deep Blue Sea 1999; In Too Deep 1999; Rollerball 2001; Mindhunters 2003; Slow Burn 2003;

SWAT 2003; Edison 2005; Last Holiday 2006

La Haye, David Anzapta 2001; Head in the Clouds 2004; Nouvelle-France 2004

La Plante, Laura (1904-1996) The Cat and the Canary 1927; The Last Warning 1928; The King of Jazz 1930; God's Gift to Women 1931; Spring Reunion 1957

La Rocque, Rod (1896-1969) The Ten Commandments 1923; Our Modern Maidens 1929; One Romantic Night 1930; Till We Meet Again 1936

La Roy, Rita (1907-1993) Blonde Venus 1932; Sinners in the Sun 1932

La Rue, Eva aka LaRue Callahan, Eva Cries in the Dark 2006; Help for the Holidays 2012

La Salle, Eriq (1962-) Rappin' 1985; Coming to America 1988; Jacob's Ladder 1990; DROP Squad 1994; One Hour Photo 2001; Relative Stranger 2009; Wolverine 3 2017

La Verne, Lucille (1869-1945) Pilgrimage 1933; The Mighty Barnum 1934; Snow White and the Seven Dwarfs 1937

Laage, Barbara (1925-1988) Act of Love 1953; The Happy Road 1956; Bed and Board 1970

Labaki, Nadine Caramel 2007; Where Do We Go Now? 2011; Mea Culpa 2012

Labarthe, André S aka Labarthe, André (1931-) Vivre Sa Vie 1962; L'Amour Fou 1968

LaBelle, Patti (1944-) A Soldier's Story 1984; Sing 1989; Lipstick 2006

LaBeouf, Shia (1986-) Charlie's Angels: Full Throttle 2003; Holes 2003; Constantine 2005; The Greatest Game Ever Played 2005; A Guide to Recognizing Your Saints 2006; Disturbia 2007; Surf's Up 2007; Transformers 2007; Eagle Eye 2008; Indiana Jones and the Kingdom of the Crystal Skull 2008; New York, I Love You 2009; Transformers: Revenge of the Fallen 2009; Wall Street: Money Never Sleeps 2010; Transformers: Dark of the Moon 2011; The Company You Keep 2012; Lawless 2012; Charlie Countryman 2013; Fury 2014; Nymphomaniac Vol I 2013; Nymphomaniac Vol II 2014; American Honey 2016

Labine, Tyler Flyboys 2006; Tucker and Dale vs Evil 2009; The Boss 2015

Labiosa, David The Entity 1981; Mega Piranha 2010

Laborteaux, Matthew (1966-) A Woman under the Influence 1974; Deadly Friend 1986

Labourdette, Elina (1919-2014) Les Dames du Bois de Boulogne 1946; To Paris with Love 1954; Lola 1960

Labourier, Dominique Celine and Julie Go Boating 1974; Jonah Who Will Be 25 in the Year 2000 1976

Labovic, Slavko Pusher 1996; Pusher 3 2005

Labuda, Marian (1944-) My Sweet Little Village 1986; The Last of the Good Old Days 1989; Meeting Venus 1990

Labus, Jiri Conspirators of Pleasure 1996; I Served the King of England 2006

Lacey, Catherine (1904-1979) Poison Pen 1939; Pink String and Sealing Wax 1945; Carnival 1946; The October Man 1947; Whisky Galore! 1949; Innocent Sinners 1957; Crack in the Mirror 1960; The Servant 1963; The Sorcerers 1967; The Private Life of Sherlock Holmes 1970

Lacey, Ronald (1935-1991) The Boys 1961; Take a Girl like You 1970; Crucible of Terror 1971; Gawain and the Green Knight 1973; Raiders of the Lost Ark 1981; Firefox 1982; The Hound of the Baskervilles 1983; Sword of the Valiant 1984; Red Sonja 1985; Gunbus 1986

Lacher, Taylor (1942-2005) Mr Majestyk 1974; Baker's Hawk 1976; Spirit of the Eagle 1991

Lack, Simon (1915-1980) Sons of the Sea 1939; The Proud Valley 1940; The Silver Darlings 1947

Lack, Stephen (1946-) Head On 1980; Scanners 1980; Dead Ringers 1988; All the Vermeers in New York 1990

LaCroix, Lisa aka Lacroix, Lisa Dance Me Outside 1994; Les Convoyeurs Attendent 1999

LaCroix, Peter The Hunted 1998; The Silencer 1999

Lacy, Jake Obvious Child 2014; Carol 2015

Ladd, Alan (1913-1964) Island of Lost Souls 1932; Pigskin Parade 1936; Hell Town 1937; The Goldwyn Follies 1938; Rulers of the Sea 1939; The Howards of Virginia 1940; The Black Cat 1941; The Glass Key 1942; Joan of Paris 1942; Star Spangled Rhythm 1942; This Gun for Hire 1942; China 1943; And Now Tomorrow 1944; Duffy's Tavern 1945; Salty O'Rourke 1945; The Blue

Dahlia 1946; OSS 1946; Two Years before the Mast 1946; Calcutta 1947; My Favorite Brunette 1947; Variety Girl 1947; Saigon 1948; Whispering Smith 1948; The Great Gatsby 1949; Appointment with Danger 1950; Branded 1950; Captain Carey, USA 1950; Red Mountain 1951; Botany Bay 1953; The Red Beret 1953; Desert Legion 1953; Shane 1953; Thunder in the East 1953; The Black Knight 1954; Drum Beat 1954; Hell below Zero 1954; Saskatchewan 1954; Hell on Frisco Bay 1955; The McConnell Story 1955; A Cry in the Night 1956; Santiago 1956; The Big Land 1957; Boy on a Dolphin 1957; The Badlanders 1958; The Deep Six 1958; The Proud Rebel 1958; All the Young Men 1960; Guns of the Timberland 1960; One Foot in Hell 1960; 13 West Street 1962; The Carpetbaggers 1964

Ladd, Alana (1943-) Guns of the Timberland 1960; Young Guns of Texas 1962

Ladd, Cheryl (1951-) Purple Hearts 1984; The Fulfillment of Mary Gray 1989; Millennium 1989; Crash: the Mystery of Flight 1501 1990; Poison Ivy 1992; A Dog of Flanders 1999; Though None Go with Me 2006

Ladd, David (1947-) The Big Land 1957; The Proud Rebel 1958; The Sad Horse 1959; Death Line 1972; Jonathan Livingston Seagull 1973

Ladd, Diane (1939-) Rebel Rousers 1967; The Reivers 1969; White Lightning 1973; Alice Doesn't Live Here Anymore 1974; Chinatown 1974; Embryo 1976; All Night Long 1981; Something Wicked This Way Comes 1983; Black Widow 1987; Plain Clothes 1988; National Lampoon's Christmas Vacation 1989; Wild at Heart 1990; A Kiss before Dying 1991; Rambling Rose 1991; The Cemetery Club 1993; Father Hood 1993; The Haunted Heart 1995; Citizen Ruth 1996; Primary Colors 1998; Daddy and Them 1999; Redemption of the Ghost 2000; 28 Days 2000; The World's Fastest Indian 2005; Inland Empire 2006

Ladd, Jordan (1975-) Embrace of the Vampire 1994; Cabin Fever 2002; Broken Lizard's Club Dread 2004; Madhouse 2004; Death Proof 2007; The Wishing Well 2009

Laffan, Patricia (1919-) Quo Vadis 1951; Escape Route 1952; Rough Shoot 1952; 23 Paces to Baker Street 1956

LaFleur, Art aka La Fleur, Art (1943-) Trancers 1985; Air America 1990; Death Warrant 1990; Oscar 1991; Jack the Bear 1993; Man of the House 1994; First Kid 1996

Lafont, Bernadette (1938-2013) Le Beau Serge 1958; Web of Passion 1959; Les Bonnes Femmes 1960; Male Hunt 1964; Catch Me a Spy 1971; Une Belle Fille comme Moi 1973; La Maman et la Putain 1973; An Impudent Girl 1985; Inspecteur Lavardin 1986; Masques 1987; Waiting for the Moon 1987; Dingo 1991; Généalogies d'un Crime 1997; Rien sur Robert 1998; I Do 2006; Les Petites Vacances 2006; Attila Marcel 2013

Lafont, Jean-Philippe Carmen 1984; Babette's Feast 1987

Laforêt, Marie (1939-) Plein Soleil 1960; Male Hunt 1964; Jack of Diamonds 1967; Tangos, Exilo de Gardel 1985

Lagarde, Stéphanie Two Brothers 2004; Beautiful Lies 2010

Lagerwall, Sture (1908-1964) Walpurgis Night 1935; The Devil's Eye 1960

Lagrange, Valérie (1942-) Morgan the Pirate 1960; La Ronde 1964; Up to His Ears 1965; Un Homme et une Femme 1966; Weekend 1967; The Valley 1972

Laguna, Sylvie Delicatessen 1990; Road to Ruin 1992

Lahr, Bert (1895-1967) Just around the Corner 1938; The Wizard of Oz 1939; Zaza 1939; Ship Ahoy 1942; Meet the People 1944; Always Leave Them Laughing 1949; Rose Marie 1954

Lahti, Christine (1950-) ...And Justice for All 1979; Ladies and Gentlemen, the Fabulous Stains 1981; Whose Life Is It Anyway? 1981; The Executioner's Song 1982; Swing Shift 1984; Just between Friends 1986; Housekeeping 1987; Season of Dreams 1987; Running on Empty 1988; A Cut Above 1989; Funny about Love 1990; Crazy from the Heart 1991; The Doctor 1991; Leaving Normal 1992; Hideaway 1995; Pie in the Sky 1995; Subway Stories: Tales from the Underground 1997; Revenge of the Middle-Aged Woman 2004; Obsessed 2009

Lai, Leon (1966-) Fallen Angels 1995; Infernal Affairs 3 2003; Seven Swords 2005

Lail, Leah (1966-) Heavyweights 1995; Something about Sex 1998

Laine, Cleo (1927-) The Roman Spring of Mrs Stone 1961; The Third Alibi 1961

Laine, Frankie (1913-2007) Bring Your Smile Along 1955; He Laughed Last 1956

Laing, Stuart (1969-) The Truth Game 2000; Cradle of Fear 2001; South West Nine 2001; The Great Ecstasy of Robert Carmichael 2005

Laird, Jenny (1917-2001) Just William 1939; Painted Boats 1945; Black Narcissus 1947; Village of the Damned 1960

Lake, Arthur (1905-1987) Indiscreet 1931; Topper 1937; Blondie! 1938

Lake, Florence (1904-1980) The Rogue Song 1930; Romance 1930

Lake, Ricki (1968-) Hairspray 1988; Cry-Baby 1989; Last Exit to Brooklyn 1989; Serial Mom 1994; Mrs Winterbourne 1996; I Am Divine 2013

Lake, Veronica (1919-1973) Hold Back the Dawn 1941; I Wanted Wings 1941; Sullivan's Travels 1941; The Glass Key 1942; I Married a Witch 1942; Star Spangled Rhythm 1942; This Gun for Hire 1942; So Proudly We Hail 1943; The Hour before the Dawn 1944; Bring On the Girls 1945; Duffy's Tavern 1945; Miss Susie Slagle's 1945; Out of This World 1945; The Blue Dahlia 1946; Ramrod 1947; Isn't It Romantic 1948; Saigon 1948; Slattery's Hurricane 1949; Flesh Feast 1970

Lally, Mick (1945-2010) The Fantasist 1986; Fools of Fortune 1990; The Secret of Roan Inish 1993; Circle of Friends 1995; The Secret of Kells 2009

Lam Ching Ying (1952-1997) The Prodigal Son 1983; Mr Vampire 1986

Lam Ka Tung Election 2005; Mad Detective 2007; Ip Man 2008; Sparrow 2008

Lam Suet Tsui Hark's Vampire Hunters 2002; Election 2005; Exiled 2006

LaMarche, Maurice Pom Poko 1994; Balto - Wings of Change 2004; Team America: World Police 2004

Lamarr, Hedy aka Kiesler, Hedy (1914-2000) Ecstasy 1933; Algiers 1938; Lady of the Tropics 1939; Boom Town 1940; Comrade X 1940; I Take This Woman 1940; Come Live with Me 1941; HM Pulham Esq 1941; Ziegfeld Girl 1941; Crossroads 1942; Tortilla Flat 1942; White Cargo 1942; The Heavenly Body 1943; The Conspirators 1944; Experiment Perilous 1944; The Strange Woman 1946; Dishonored Lady 1947; Let's Live a Little 1948; Samson and Delilah 1949; Copper Canyon 1950; A Lady without Passport 1950; My Favorite Spy 1951; The Loves of Three Queens 1954; The Story of Mankind 1957; The Female Animal 1958

LaMarr, Phil Kill the Man 1999; The Adventures of Brer Rabbit 2006; Real Steel 2011

Lamas, Fernando (1915-1982) The Law and the Lady 1951; Rich, Young and Pretty 1951; The Merry Widow 1952; Dangerous When Wet 1953; The Diamond Queen 1953; The Girl Who Had Everything 1953; Rose Marie 1954; The Girl Rush 1955; The Lost World 1960; Kill a Dragon 1967; Valley of Mystery 1967; The Violent Ones 1967; Backtrack 1969; The Cheap Detective 1978

Lamb, Gil (1906-1995) The Fleet's In 1942; Riding High 1943; Practically Yours 1944

Lamb, Larry Shadey 1985; Buster 1988; Essex Boys 1999; Fakers 2004

Lambert, Anne Louise aka Lambert, Anne (1956-) Picnic at Hanging Rock 1975; The Draughtsman's Contract 1982

Lambert, Christopher aka Lambert, Christophe (1957-) Greystoke: the Legend of Tarzan, Lord of the Apes 1984; Love Songs 1984; Subway 1985; Highlander 1986; The Sicilian 1987; To Kill a Priest 1988; Highlander II: the Quickening 1990; Why Me? 1990; Fortress 1992; Knight Moves 1992; Gunmen 1994; Roadflower 1994; Adrenalin: Fear the Rush 1995; Highlander III: the Sorcerer 1995; The Hunted 1995; Mortal Kombat 1995; Nirvana 1996; North Star 1996; Fortress 2: Re-entry 1999; Gideon 1999; Resurrection 1999; Highlander: Endgame 2000; The Point Men 2000; Druids 2001; White Material 2009; Ghost Rider: Spirit of Vengeance 2012

Lambert, Jack (1920-2002) A Honeymoon Adventure 1931; Abilene Town 1945; Dick Tracy's Dilemma 1947; The Unsuspected 1947; Belle Starr's Daughter 1948; Eureka Stockade 1949;

Floodtide 1949; North of the Great Divide 1950; The Lost Hours 1952; Scared Stiff 1953; At Gunpoint 1955; Run for Cover 1955; Storm over the Nile 1955; Machine Gun Kelly 1958; The Bridal Path 1959; Winchester '73 1967; Neither the Sea nor the Sand 1972

Lambert, Paul (1922–1997) The Big Mouth 1967; Play It as It Lays 1972; Mama's Dirty Girls 1974

Lamont, Duncan (1918–1978) The Golden Coach 1953; The Teckman Mystery 1954; Passage Home 1955; The Devil-Ship Pirates 1964; Evil of Frankenstein 1964; Arabesque 1966; The Witches 1966; Quatermass and the Pit 1967; The Creeping Flesh 1972

Lamont, Molly (1910–2000) The Awful Truth 1937; The Suspect 1944; So Goes My Love 1946; Scared to Death 1947

Lamont, Nicholas aka **Lamont, Nick** The Long Day Closes 1992; Going Off, Big Time 2000

Lamorisse, Pascal (1950–) White Mane 1952; The Red Balloon 1956

LaMotta, John American Ninja 1985; Lookin' Italian 1994

Lamour, Dorothy (1914–1996) The Big Broadcast of 1938 1937; High, Wide and Handsome 1937; The Hurricane 1937; The Last Train from Madrid 1937; Swing High, Swing Low 1937; Spawn of the North 1938; Chad Hanna 1940; Johnny Apollo 1940; Road to Singapore 1940; Typhoon 1940; Road to Zanzibar 1941; Beyond the Blue Horizon 1942; The Fleet's In 1942; Road to Morocco 1942; Star Spangled Rhythm 1942; Dixie 1943; Riding High 1943; They Got Me Covered 1943; And the Angels Sing 1944; Duffy's Tavern 1945; A Medal for Benny 1945; Road to Utopia 1945; My Favorite Brunette 1947; Road to Rio 1947; Variety Girl 1947; The Girl from Manhattan 1948; Lulu Belle 1948; On Our Merry Way 1948; Slightly French 1949; Here Comes the Groom 1951; The Greatest Show on Earth 1952; Road to Bali 1952; The Road to Hong Kong 1962; Donovan's Reef 1963; Creepshow 2 1987

Lampe, Jutta Sisters, or the Balance of Happiness 1979; The German Sisters 1981

Lampert, Zohra (1937–) Pay or Die 1960; Hey, Let's Twist! 1961; Splendor in the Grass 1961; Bye Bye Braverman 1968; Opening Night 1977; Alphabet City 1984; American Blue Note 1989; Stanley & Iris 1989

Lampkin, Charles (1913–1989) Five 1951; Hammer 1972

Lampreave, Chus (1930–) Dark Habits 1983; What Have I Done to Deserve This? 1984; Matador 1986; The Flower of My Secret 1995; Volver 2006; The Artist and the Model 2012

Lamprecht, Günter aka **Lamprecht, Günther** (1930–) Berlin Alexanderplatz 1980; Rouge Baiser 1985

Lancashire, Sarah And When Did You Last See Your Father? 2007; The First Film 2015; Dad's Army 2016

Lancaster, Burt (1913–1994) The Killers 1946; Brute Force 1947; Desert Fury 1947; I Walk Alone 1947; All My Sons 1948; Blood on My Hands 1948; Sorry, Wrong Number 1948; Criss Cross 1949; Rope of Sand 1949; The Flame and the Arrow 1950; Mister 880 1950; Jim Thorpe – All-American 1951; Ten Tall Men 1951; Vengeance Valley 1951; Come Back, Little Sheba 1952; The Crimson Pirate 1952; From Here to Eternity 1953; His Majesty O'Keefe 1953; South Sea Woman 1953; Apache 1954; Vera Cruz 1954; The Kentuckian 1955; The Rose Tattoo 1955; The Rainmaker 1956; Trapeze 1956; Gunfight at the OK Corral 1957; Sweet Smell of Success 1957; Run Silent Run Deep 1958; Separate Tables 1958; Elmer Gantry 1960; The Unforgiven 1960; Judgment at Nuremberg 1961; The Young Savages 1961; Birdman of Alcatraz 1962; A Child Is Waiting 1962; The Leopard 1962; The List of Adrian Messenger 1963; Seven Days in May 1964; The Train 1964; The Hallelujah Trail 1965; The Professionals 1966; The Scalphunters 1968; The Swimmer 1968; Castle Keep 1969; The Gypsy Moths 1969; Airport 1970; King: a Filmed Record... Montgomery to Memphis 1970; Lawman 1971; Valdez Is Coming 1971; Ulzana's Raid 1972; Executive Action 1973; Scorpio 1973; Conversation Piece 1974; Moses 1975; Buffalo Bill and the Indians, or Sitting Bull's History Lesson 1976; The Cassandra Crossing 1976; 1900 1976; Victory at Entebbe 1976; Go Tell the Spartans 1977; Twilight's Last Gleaming 1977; Zulu Dawn 1979; Atlantic City, USA 1980; Cattle Annie and Little Britches

1980; La Pelle 1981; Local Hero 1983; The Osterman Weekend 1983; Little Treasure 1985; Tough Guys 1986; Rocket Gibraltar 1988; Field of Dreams 1989

Lancaster, Stuart (1920–2000) Faster, Pussycat! Kill! Kill! 1965; Mudhoney 1965; Good Morning... and Goodbye 1967

Lance, James Late Night Shopping 2001; City Rats 2008; Northern Soul 2012

Lanchester, Elsa (1902–1986) The Private Life of Henry VIII 1933; Bride of Frankenstein 1935; David Copperfield 1935; The Ghost Goes West 1935; Naughty Marietta 1935; Rembrandt 1936; Vessel of Wrath 1938; Ladies in Retirement 1941; Son of Fury 1942; Tales of Manhattan 1942; Lassie Come Home 1943; The Razor's Edge 1946; The Spiral Staircase 1946; The Bishop's Wife 1947; The Big Clock 1948; Come to the Stable 1949; The Inspector General 1949; The Secret Garden 1949; Frenchie 1950; Mystery Street 1950; The Petty Girl 1950; Androcles and the Lion 1952; Dreamboat 1952; Les Misérables 1952; Three Ring Circus 1954; The Glass Slipper 1955; Witness for the Prosecution 1957; Bell, Book and Candle 1958; Honeymoon Hotel 1964; Mary Poppins 1964; That Darn Cat! 1965; Blackbeard's Ghost 1967; Easy Come, Easy Go 1967; Willard 1971; Terror in the Wax Museum 1973; Murder by Death 1976

Landau, David (1878–1935) Street Scene 1931; Horse Feathers 1932; I Am a Fugitive from a Chain Gang 1932; Lawyer Man 1932; Polly of the Circus 1932; The Purchase Price 1932; Taxi! 1932; Gabriel over the White House 1933; She Done Him Wrong 1933; Judge Priest 1934

Landau, Juliet (1965–) Theodore Rex 1995; Toolbox Murders 2003

Landau, Martin (1928–) The Gazebo 1959; North by Northwest 1959; Pork Chop Hill 1959; Stagecoach to Dancer's Rock 1962; Cleopatra 1963; The Greatest Story Ever Told 1965; The Hallelujah Trail 1965; Nevada Smith 1966; They Call Me Mister Tibbs! 1970; A Town Called Hell 1971; Meteor 1979; Without Warning 1980; Alone in the Dark 1982; Treasure Island 1986; Tucker: the Man and His Dream 1988; Crimes and Misdemeanors 1989; By Dawn's Early Light 1990; Firehead 1991; Mistress 1992; No Place to Hide 1992; Eye of the Stranger 1993; Sliver 1993; 12:01 1993; Ed Wood 1994; Intersection 1994; The Adventures of Pinocchio 1996; City Hall 1996; BAPS 1997; Rounders 1998; The X-Files 1998; Edtv 1999; The Joyriders 1999; The New Adventures of Pinocchio 1999; Ready to Rumble 2000; Shiner 2000; The Majestic 2001; Hollywood Homicide 2003; The Aryan Couple 2004; City of Ember 2008; 9 2009; Frankenweenie 2012; Remember 2015

Landeau, Alexia 2 Days in Paris 2006; 2 Days in New York 2011

Landen, Dinsdale (1932–2003) Operation Snatch 1962; We Joined the Navy 1962; Mosquito Squadron 1968; Every Home Should Have One 1970; Digby, the Biggest Dog in the World 1973; International Velvet 1978; Morons from Outer Space 1985; The Steal 1994

Landes, Michael (1972–) When the Party's Over 1992; Danielle Steel's No Greater Love 1996; Dream for an Insomniac 1996; Final Destination 2 2002; A Carol Christmas 2003

Landfield, Timothy Cheetah 1989; Without Warning: the James Brady Story 1991

Landgard, Janet The Swimmer 1968; Land Raiders 1969

Landgré, Inga (1927–) Crisis 1945; Dreams 1955

Landham, Sonny (1941–) Firewalker 1986; Predator 1987; Lock Up 1989; Best of the Best II 1992

Landi, Elissa (1904–1948) Underground 1928; Body and Soul 1931; The Sign of the Cross 1932; Enter Madame! 1933; The Masquerader 1933; By Candlelight 1934; The Count of Monte Cristo 1934; Königsmark 1935; After the Thin Man 1936

Landi, Marla (1937–) Across the Bridge 1957; Dublin Nightmare 1958; First Man into Space 1958; The Hound of the Baskervilles 1959; The Pirates of Blood River 1961

Landis, Carole (1919–1948) Hollywood Hotel 1937; One Million BC 1940; I Wake Up Screaming 1941; Moon over Miami 1941; Road Show 1941; Topper Returns 1941; A Gentleman at Heart 1942; My Gal 1942; Orchestra Wives 1942; Wintertime 1943; Secret Command 1944; Thieves' Holiday 1946; Out of the

Blue 1947; The Brass Monkey 1948; Noose 1948

Landis, Forrest (1994–) Cheaper by the Dozen 2003; Cheaper by the Dozen 2 2005

Landis, Jessie Royce (1904–1972) Mr Belvedere Goes to College 1949; My Foolish Heart 1949; To Catch a Thief 1955; The Girl He Left Behind 1956; The Swan 1956; My Man Godfrey 1957; I Married a Woman 1958; North by Northwest 1959; Goodbye Again 1961; Bon Voyage! 1962; Boys' Night Out 1962; Critic's Choice 1963

Landis, John (1950–) Schlock 1971; 1941 1979; Into the Night 1985; Sleepwalkers 1992; Venice/Venice 1992; Diamonds 1999

Landis, Monte aka **Landis, Monty** Targets 1968; Pee-wee's Big Adventure 1985

Lando, Joe (1961–) No Code of Conduct 1998; Killer Flood 2003

Landon, Laurene (1958–) The California Dolls 1981; It's Alive III: Island of the Alive 1987; Maniac Cop 1988; Maniac Cop 2 1990

Landon, Michael (1936–1991) I Was a Teenage Werewolf 1957; Maracaibo 1958; The Legend of Tom Dooley 1959; Sam's Son 1984

Landone, Avice (1910–1976) True as a Turtle 1956; Gaolbreak 1962; The Leather Boys 1963; This Is My Street 1963; The Adventures of Barry McKenzie 1972

Landry, Gérard (1914–1999) La Bête Humaine 1938; Night without Stars 1951; Trapeze 1956

Lane, Abbe (1932–) Ride Clear of Diablo 1954; The Americano 1955; Maracaibo 1958

Lane, Allan aka **Lane, Allan "Rocky"** (1904–1973) Charlie Chan at the Olympics 1937; The Law West of Tombstone 1938; Maid's Night Out 1938; Bells of Rosarita 1945; Trail of Robin Hood 1950; The Saga of Hemp Brown 1958

Lane (1), Charles (1869–1945) Dr Jekyll and Mr Hyde 1920; The White Sister 1923; The Winning of Barbara Worth 1926; Sadie Thompson 1928; The Canary Murder Case 1929

Lane (2), Charles aka **Levison, Charles** (1905–2007) Blonde Crazy 1931; Twentieth Century 1934; The Affairs of Dobie Gillis 1953; The Juggler 1953; Teacher's Pet 1958; But Not for Me 1959; Good Neighbor Sam 1964; Billie 1965; The Ugly Dachshund 1966; What's So Bad about Feeling Good? 1968

Lane (3), Charles (1953–) Sidewalk Stories 1989; True Identity 1991; Posse 1993

Lane, Diane (1965–) A Little Romance 1979; Touched by Love 1979; Cattle Annie and Little Britches 1980; Ladies and Gentlemen, the Fabulous Stains 1981; National Lampoon's Movie Madness 1981; Six Pack 1982; The Outsiders 1983; Rumble Fish 1983; The Cotton Club 1984; Streets of Fire 1984; The Big Town 1987; Lady Beware 1987; Vital Signs 1990; Chaplin 1992; Knight Moves 1992; My New Gun 1992; Indian Summer 1993; Judge Dredd 1995; Wild Bill 1995; Jack 1996; Trigger Happy 1996; Murder at 1600 1997; The Only Thrill 1997; My Dog Skip 1999; A Walk on the Moon 1999; The Perfect Storm 2000; The Virginian 2000; The Glass House 2001; Hardball 2001; Unfaithful 2002; Under the Tuscan Sun 2003; Must Love Dogs 2005; Hollywoodland 2006; Jumper 2008; Nights in Rodanthe 2008; Untraceable 2008; Secretariat 2010; Cinema Verite 2011; Man of Steel 2013; Inside Out 2015; Trumbo 2015; Batman v Superman: Dawn of Justice 2016

Lane, Jocelyn aka **Lane, Jackie** (1937–) Goodbye Again 1961; Two and Two Make Six 1961; Operation Snatch 1962; Tickle Me 1965; Incident at Phantom Hill 1966; Land Raiders 1969

Lane, Lenita (1901–1995) The Mad Magician 1954; The Bat 1959

Lane, Lola (1909–1981) Murder on a Honeymoon 1935; Hollywood Hotel 1937; Marked Woman 1937; Four Daughters 1938; Daughters Courageous 1939; Four Wives 1939; Four Mothers 1941; Deadline at Dawn 1946

Lane, Mara (1930–) Decameron Nights 1953; Angela 1955

Lane, Nathan (1956–) Frankie & Johnny 1991; He Said, She Said 1991; Life with Mikey 1993; The Lion King 1994; Jeffrey 1995; The Birdcage 1996; The Boys Next Door 1996; Mousehunt 1997; At First Sight 1998; Isn't She Great 1999; Love's Labour's Lost 1999; Stuart Little 1999; Laughter on the 23rd Floor 2000; Titan AE 2000; Trixie

2000; Nicholas Nickleby 2002; Stuart Little 2 2002; Teacher's Pet 2004; Win a Date with Tad Hamilton! 2004; The Producers 2005; Stuart Little 3: Call of the Wild 2005; Swing Vote 2008; The Nutcracker in 3D 2010; Mirror Mirror 2012; The English Teacher 2013

Lane, Priscilla (1915–1995) Four Daughters 1938; Daughters Courageous 1939; Dust Be My Destiny 1939; Four Wives 1939; The Roaring Twenties 1939; Blues in the Night 1941; Four Mothers 1941; Million Dollar Baby 1941; Saboteur 1942; The Meanest Man in the World 1943; Arsenic and Old Lace 1944; Bodyguard 1948

Lane, Richard (1899–1982) Flight from Glory 1937; Mr Moto in Danger Island 1939; The Biscuit Eater 1940; Hellzapoppin' 1941; Meet Boston Blackie 1941; Riders of the Purple Sage 1941; Arabian Nights 1942; Dr Broadway 1942; Corvette K-225 1943; The Bermuda Mystery 1944; Brazil 1944; Mr Winkle Goes to War 1944; The Bullfighters 1945; Two o'Clock Courage 1945; Take Me Out to the Ball Game 1949

Lane, Rosemary (1914–1974) Hollywood Hotel 1937; Four Daughters 1938; Daughters Courageous 1939; Four Wives 1939; The Oklahoma Kid 1939; The Return of Dr X 1939; The Boys from Syracuse 1940; Four Mothers 1941; Time Out for Rhythm 1941

Lane, Rusty (1899–1986) Bigger than Life 1956; Johnny Tremain 1957

Laneuville, Eric (1952–) The Omega Man 1971; Black Belt Jones 1974; A Force of One 1979

Lang, Harold (1923–1971) Cairo Road 1950; Cloudburst 1951; Adventure in the Hopfields 1954; Dance Little Lady 1954; It's a Wonderful World 1956

Lang, June (1917–2005) Bonnie Scotland 1935; Captain January 1936; The Country Doctor 1936; The Road to Glory 1936; Nancy Steele Is Missing 1937; Wee Willie Winkie 1937; Footlight Serenade 1942

lang, k d (1961–) Salmonberries 1991; Eye of the Beholder 1999

Lang, Perry (1959–) Alligator 1980; Body and Soul 1981; Sahara 1983; Jocks 1986; Little Vegas 1990; Jennifer Eight 1992

Lang, Robert (1934–2004) Othello 1965; The Dance of Death 1969; Night Watch 1973; Hawks 1988; Mrs Palfrey at The Claremont 2005

Lang, Stephen (1952–) Death of a Salesman 1985; Twice in a Lifetime 1985; Manhunter 1986; Project X 1987; Last Exit to Brooklyn 1989; Another You 1991; The Hard Way 1991; Gettysburg 1993; Guilty as Sin 1993; Murder between Friends 1993; Tall Tale 1994; The Amazing Panda Adventure 1995; Gang in Blue 1996; Shadow Conspiracy 1996; Fire Down Below 1997; Niagara Niagara 1997; The Proposal 2000; Trixie 2000; Gods and Generals 2002; The I Inside 2003; Avatar 2009; The Men Who Stare at Goatsx 2009; Conan the Barbarian 2011; The Nut Job 2014; The Asylum 2015; Avatar 2 2018

Langan, Glenn aka **Langan, Glen** (1917–1991) Something for the Boys 1944; A Bell for Adano 1945; Hangover Square 1945; Dragonwyck 1946; Margie 1946; Sentimental Journey 1946; Forever Amber 1947; Fury at Furnace Creek 1948; The Snake Pit 1948; The Amazing Colossal Man 1957

Langdon, Harry (1884–1944) The Strong Man 1926; Tramp, Tramp, Tramp 1926; Long Pants 1927; Hallelujah, I'm a Bum 1933; Zenobia 1939; Block Busters 1944

Langdon, Libby Federal Hill 1994; A Shot at Glory 2000

Langdon, Sue Ane aka **Langdon, Sue Ann** aka **Langdon, Sue Anne** (1936–) Roustabout 1964; The Rounders 1965; Frankie & Johnny 1966; A Guide for the Married Man 1967; The Cheyenne Social Club 1970; The Evictors 1979; Without Warning 1980

Lange, Allison The Hillside Strangler 2004; Next Stop Murder 2010

Lange, Artie (1967–) Dirty Work 1998; The Bachelor 1999; Lost & Found 1999

Lange, Hope (1933–2003) Bus Stop 1956; Peyton Place 1957; The True Story of Jesse James 1957; In Love and War 1958; The Young Lions 1958; The Best of Everything 1959; Pocketful of Miracles 1961; Wild in the Country 1961; Love Is a Ball 1963; Jigsaw 1968; Death Wish 1974; A Nightmare on Elm Street 2: Freddy's Revenge 1985; Blue Velvet 1986; Aunt Julia and the Scriptwriter 1990

Lange, Jessica (1949–) King Kong 1976; All That Jazz 1979; How to Beat the High Cost of Living 1980; The Postman Always Rings Twice 1981; Frances 1982; Tootsie 1982; Country 1984; Sweet Dreams 1985; Crimes of the Heart 1986; Everybody's All-American 1988; Far North 1988; Music Box 1989; Men Don't Leave 1990; Blue Sky 1991; Cape Fear 1991; Night and the City 1992; Losing Isaiah 1995; Rob Roy 1995; Cousin Bette 1997; A Thousand Acres 1997; Hush 1998; Titus 1999; Normal 2002; Big Fish 2003; Masked and Anonymous 2003; Broken Flowers 2005; Don't Come Knocking 2005; Bonneville 2006; Grey Gardens 2009; The Vow 2012; In Secret 2013; The Gambler 2014

Langella, Frank (1940–) Diary of a Mad Housewife 1970; The Twelve Chairs 1970; The Deadly Trap 1971; The Wrath of God 1972; The Mark of Zorro 1974; Dracula 1979; Sphinx 1980; Those Lips, Those Eyes 1980; The Men's Club 1986; Masters of the Universe 1987; And God Created Woman 1988; True Identity 1991; Dave 1993; Brainscan 1994; Junior 1994; Bad Company 1995; CutThroat Island 1995; Eddie 1996; Lolita 1997; I'm Losing You 1998; Small Soldiers 1998; The Ninth Gate 1999; Stardom 2000; Sweet November 2001; Good Night, and Good Luck. 2005; Superman Returns 2006; The Box 2008; Frost/Nixon 2008; All Good Things 2010; Wall Street: Money Never Sleeps 2010; Unknown 2011; Robot & Frank 2012; Draft Day 2014; Grace of Monaco 2014; All the Way 2016

Langenkamp, Heather (1964–) A Nightmare on Elm Street 1984; Passions 1984; A Nightmare on Elm Street 3: Dream Warriors 1987; Shocker 1989; Wes Craven's New Nightmare 1994

Langer, A J (1974–) The People under the Stairs 1991; Escape from LA 1996; Meet the Deedles 1998

Langford, Frances (1914–2005) Born to Dance 1936; Too Many Girls 1940; Girl Rush 1944; The Bamboo Blonde 1946

Langlet, Amanda Pauline at the Beach 1983; A Summer's Tale 1996; Triple Agent 2003

Langlois, Lisa (1959–) Blood Relatives 1977; Phobia 1980; Class of 1984 1982; Joy of Sex 1984; The Slugger's Wife 1985

Langrick, Margaret (1971–) My American Cousin 1985; Bigfoot and the Hendersons 1987; American Boyfriends 1989; Cold Comfort 1989; Death of a Cheerleader 1994

Langrishe, Caroline (1958–) Eagle's Wing 1978; Hawks 1988; Rogue Trader 1998; Kisna – the Warrior Poet 2004

Langton, Brooke (1970–) The Replacements 2000; Primeval 2007

Langton, Paul (1913–1980) They Were Expendable 1945; Till the Clouds Roll By 1946; Big Leaguer 1953; Chicago Confidential 1957; The Incredible Shrinking Man 1957; The Cosmic Man 1959

Lanners, Bouli Les Convoyeurs Attendent 1999; Louise-Michel 2008; Mammuth 2010

Lanning, Frank (1872–1945) The Kid Brother 1927; The Unknown 1927

Lanoux, Victor (1936–) Two against the Law 1973; Cousin, Cousine 1975; Pardon Mon Affaire 1976; Un Moment d'Egarement 1977; Les Chiens 1978; The Scene of the Crime 1986

Lansbury, Angela (1925–) Gaslight 1944; National Velvet 1944; The Picture of Dorian Gray 1945; The Harvey Girls 1946; The Hoodlum Saint 1946; If Winter Comes 1947; The Private Affairs of Bel Ami 1947; State of the Union 1948; The Three Musketeers 1948; The Red Danube 1949; Samson and Delilah 1949; Kind Lady 1951; Mutiny 1952; Remains to Be Seen 1953; A Lawless Street 1955; The Purple Mask 1955; The Court Jester 1956; The Reluctant Debutante 1958; A Breath of Scandal 1960; The Dark at the Top of the Stairs 1960; Season of Passion 1960; Blue Hawaii 1961; All Fall Down 1962; The Manchurian Candidate 1962; Dear Heart 1964; The World of Henry Orient 1964; The Amorous Adventures of Moll Flanders 1965; The Greatest Story Ever Told 1965; Harlow 1965; Something for Everyone 1970; Bedknobs and Broomsticks 1971; Death on the Nile 1978; The Lady Vanishes 1979; The Last Unicorn 1980; The Mirror Crack'd 1980; The Pirates of Penzance 1983; The Company of Wolves 1984; Beauty and the Beast 1991; Mrs 'arris Goes to Paris 1992; Mrs Santa Claus 1996; Anastasia 1997; Beauty and the Beast: the Enchanted Christmas 1997;

Fantasia 2000 1999; The Unexpected Mrs Pollifax 1999; Nanny McPhee 2005; Mr Popper's Penguins 2011
Lansing, Joi (1928-1972) The Brave One 1956; The Atomic Submarine 1960
Lansing, Robert (1929-1994) Under the Yum Yum Tree 1963; Namu, the Killer Whale 1966; The Grissom Gang 1971; Black Jack 1972; Bittersweet Love 1976; Empire of the Ants 1977
Lanter, Matt Disaster Movie 2008; Star Wars: The Clone Wars 2008; Vampires Suck 2010
Lanvin, Gérard (1949-) Choice of Arms 1981; Double Dare 1981; A Strange Affair 1981; Mon Homme 1996; En Plein Coeur 1998; Le Goût des Autres 1999; Mesrine: Public Enemy No 1 2008; Point Blank 2010
Lanza, Mario (1921-1959) That Midnight Kiss 1949; The Toast of New Orleans 1950; The Great Caruso 1951; Because You're Mine 1952; The Student Prince 1954; Serenade 1956; Seven Hills of Rome 1957; For the First Time 1959
LaPaglia, Anthony (1959-) Slaves of New York 1989; Betsy's Wedding 1990; He Said, She Said 1991; One Good Cop 1991; 29th Street 1991; Innocent Blood 1992; Whispers in the Dark 1992; The Custodian 1993; So I Married an Axe Murderer 1993; The Client 1994; Killer 1994; Mixed Nuts 1994; Empire Records 1995; Commandments 1996; Trees Lounge 1996; Phoenix 1998; Lansky 1999; Sweet and Lowdown 1999; Autumn in New York 2000; Company Man 2000; The House of Mirth 2000; The Bank 2001; Lantana 2001; Dead Heat 2002; The Guys 2002; I'm with Lucy 2002; The Salton Sea 2002; Happy Feet 2006; Legend of the Guardians: the Owls of Ga'Hoole 2010; Mental 2012; Holding the Man 2015
Lapaine, Daniel Polish Wedding 1998; Brokedown Palace 1999; Elephant Juice 1999; The Abduction 2009
Laplace, Victor (1943-) Funny Dirty Little War 1983; La Amiga 1988
Lapotaire, Jane (1944-) Crescendo 1970; Antony and Cleopatra 1972; The Asphyx 1973; Eureka 1982; Lady Jane 1985; Surviving Picasso 1996; There's Only One Jimmy Grimble 2000
Lara, Alexandra Maria (1978-) Downfall 2004; Control 2007; Youth without Youth 2007; The Reader 2008; City of Life 2009; Farewell 2010; Rush 2013
Larbi, Doghmi (1930-1992) The Man Who Would Be King 1975; The Black Stallion 1979
Larch, John (1922-2005) Seven Men from Now 1956; The Careless Years 1957; Man in the Shadow 1957; Quantez 1957; The Saga of Hemp Brown 1958; Miracle of the White Stallions 1963; Hail, Hero! 1969; The Wrecking Crew 1969; Dirty Harry 1971; Play Misty for Me 1971; Santee 1973
Lardi, Ursina The White Ribbon 2009; Lore 2012
Laresca, Vincent (1974-) Juice 1991; Forever Mine 1999; Empire 2002
Larive, Léon aka **Larive** (1886-1961) Zéro de Conduite 1933; La Marseillaise 1938
Larkin, Chris Angels and Insects 1995; Master and Commander: the Far Side of the World 2003
Larkin, John (1912-1965) Those Calloways 1964; The Satan Bug 1965
Larkin, Linda (1970-) Aladdin 1992; Aladdin and the King of Thieves 1996
Laroche, Gérald Nightshift 2000; Love Crime 2010
LaRoche, Mary (1920-1999) The Lineup 1958; Gidget 1959
Laroque, Michèle (1960-) Ma Vie en Rose 1997; The Closet 2001
Larquey, Pierre (1884-1962) Madame Bovary 1933; The Raven 1943; Topaze 1951; Les Diaboliques 1954
Larroquette, John (1947-) Green Ice 1981; Stripes 1981; Choose Me 1984; Summer Rental 1985; Blind Date 1987; Madhouse 1990; Richie Rich 1994; Wedding Daze 2004
Larsen, Keith (1924-2006) War Paint 1953; Arrow in the Dust 1954; Chief Crazy Horse 1955; Wichita 1955; Last of the Badmen 1957
Larsen, Thomas Bo (1963-) Festen 1998; The Hunt 2012; A Second Chance 2014
Larson, Brie (1989-) Sleepover 2004; Hoot 2006; Greenberg 2009; 21 Jump Street 2012; Don Jon 2013; Short Term 12 2013; The Gambler 2014; Room 2015; Trainwreck 2015; Kong: Skull Island 2017
Larson, Darrell (1951-) Kotch 1971; UFOria 1980; Brainstorm 1983; Mike's Murder 1984; Twice in a Lifetime 1985; Eye for an Eye 1995

Larter, Ali (1976-) House on Haunted Hill 1999; Final Destination 2000; American Outlaws 2001; Legally Blonde 2001; Final Destination 2 2002; A Lot like Love 2005; Marigold 2007; Resident Evil: Extinction 2007; Obsessed 2009; Resident Evil: Afterlife 2010; The Diabolical 2015; Resident Evil: the Final Chapter 2017
LaRue, Jack aka **La Rue, Jack** (1902-1984) A Farewell to Arms 1932; The Kennel Murder Case 1933; The Gang's All Here 1939; Cornered 1945; Road to Utopia 1945; My Favorite Brunette 1947; No Orchids for Miss Blandish 1948; For Heaven's Sake 1950; Robin and the 7 Hoods 1964; The Spy in the Green Hat 1966
Lasalle, Martin aka **Lassalle, Martin** aka **Lasalle, Martino** Pickpocket 1959; Alamo Bay 1985
Lascher, David (1972-) Victim of Rage 1994; White Squall 1996
Laser, Dieter (1942-) The Lost Honour of Katharina Blum 1975; The Human Centipede (First Sequence) 2009; The Human Centipede III (Final Sequence) 2015
Laskin, Larissa Recipe for Murder 2001; More Sex & the Single Mom 2005
Lasowski, Elisa The Comedian 2012; Hyena 2014; Keeping Rosy 2014
Lassander, Dagmar (1943-) Hatchet for the Honeymoon 1969; The Black Cat 1981
Lasser, Louise (1939-) What's Up, Tiger Lily? 1966; Bananas 1971; Such Good Friends 1971; Everything You Always Wanted to Know about Sex ... but Were Afraid to Ask 1972; Slither 1973; In God We Trust 1980; Crimewave 1985; Surrender 1987; Rude Awakening 1989; Sing 1989; Frankenhooker 1990; Happiness 1998; Requiem for a Dream 2000
Lassez, Sarah The Blackout 1997; In Pursuit 2000
Lassgard, Rolf (1955-) The Hunters 1996; Under the Sun 1998; After the Wedding 2006; Storm 2009; Jagarna 2: False Trail 2011
Lassick, Sydney aka **Lassick, Sidney** (1922-2003) One Flew over the Cuckoo's Nest 1975; Alligator 1980; Ratboy 1986; Cool as Ice 1991; Shakes the Clown 1991; Deep Cover 1992
Latell, Lyle (1905-1967) Dick Tracy 1945; Dick Tracy vs Cueball 1946; Dick Tracy's Dilemma 1947; Dick Tracy Meets Gruesome 1947
Latham, Louise (1922-) Marnie 1964; Adam at 6 AM 1970; The Harness 1971; White Lightning 1973; The Sugarland Express 1974; Mass Appeal 1984; Crazy from the Heart 1991; Paradise 1991; Love Field 1992
Lathan, Sanaa (1971-) The Best Man 1999; Disappearing Acts 2000; Love & Basketball 2000; Brown Sugar 2002; Out of Time 2003; AVP: Alien vs Predator 2004; Something New 2006; The Perfect Guy 2015
Lathouris, Nico Death in Brunswick 1990; The Heartbreak Kid 1993
Latimer, Hugh (1913-2006) Someone at the Door 1950; Ghost Ship 1952; Counterspy 1953; The Strange World of Planet X 1957; The Gentle Trap 1960
Latimer, Louise (1913-1971) Murder on a Bridle Path 1936; The Plot Thickens 1936; California Straight Ahead 1937
Latimore, Frank (1925-1998) In the Meantime, Darling 1944; The Dolly Sisters 1945; 13 Rue Madeleine 1946; Three Little Girls in Blue 1946; Black Magic 1949; Plein Soleil 1960; The Sergeant 1968; Patton 1970
Lattanzi, Matt (1959-) Rich and Famous 1981; My Tutor 1983
Lau Ching Wan (1964-) Black Mask 1996; Full Alert 1997; Mad Detective 2007
Lau Siu-Ming Eat a Bowl of Tea 1989; Kitchen 1997
Lau, Andy (1961-) As Tears Go By 1988; Fulltime Killer 2002; Infernal Affairs 2002; Infernal Affairs 3 2003; House of Flying Daggers 2004; Protégé 2006; The Warlords 2008; Detective Dee and the Mystery of the Phantom Flame 2010; Shaolin 2011; A Simple Life 2011
Lau, Carina (1964-) Days of Being Wild 1990; The Actress 1992; Flowers of Shanghai 1998; Infernal Affairs II 2003; 2046 2004; Detective Dee and the Mystery of the Phantom Flame 2010
Lau, Frederick The Wave 2008; Victoria 2015
Lauchlan, Agnes (1905-1993) Oh, Mr Porter! 1937; The Spy in Black 1939
Laudenbach, Philippe Confidentially Yours 1983; Four Adventures of Reinette and Mirabelle 1986; Of Gods and Men 2010

Laughlin, John (1956-) Crimes of Passion 1984; Footloose 1984; Midnight Crossing 1988; Improper Conduct 1994; American Yakuza 2: Back to Back 1996
Laughlin, Tom (1931-2013) These Wilder Years 1956; The Delinquents 1957; Senior Prom 1958; Gidget 1959; Born Losers 1967; The Master Gunfighter 1975
Laughton, Charles (1899-1962) Piccadilly 1929; Devil and the Deep 1932; If I Had a Million 1932; Island of Lost Souls 1932; The Old Dark House 1932; Payment Deferred 1932; The Sign of the Cross 1932; The Private Life of Henry VIII 1933; White Woman 1933; The Barretts of Wimpole Street 1934; Les Misérables 1935; Mutiny on the Bounty 1935; Ruggles of Red Gap 1935; Rembrandt 1936; St Martin's Lane 1938; Vessel of Wrath 1938; The Hunchback of Notre Dame 1939; Jamaica Inn 1939; They Knew What They Wanted 1940; It Started with Eve 1941; Stand by for Action 1942; Tales of Manhattan 1942; The Tuttles of Tahiti 1942; Forever and a Day 1943; The Man from Down Under 1943; This Land Is Mine 1943; The Canterville Ghost 1944; The Suspect 1944; Captain Kidd 1945; Because of Him 1946; The Paradine Case 1947; Arch of Triumph 1948; The Big Clock 1948; The Girl from Manhattan 1948; The Bribe 1949; The Man on the Eiffel Tower 1949; The Blue Veil 1951; The Strange Door 1951; Abbott and Costello Meet Captain Kidd 1952; O Henry's Full House 1952; Hobson's Choice 1953; Salome 1953; Young Bess 1953; Witness for the Prosecution 1957; Spartacus 1960; Under Ten Flags 1960; Advise and Consent 1962
Launer, S John (1919-2006) Creature with the Atom Brain 1955; The Werewolf 1956; Marnie 1964
Lauper, Cyndi (1953-) Vibes 1988; Life with Mikey 1993; The Opportunists 2000
Laurance, Matthew (1950-) Eddie and the Cruisers 1983; Eddie and the Cruisers II: Eddie Lives! 1989
Laurance, Mitchell (1950-) Stepfather II 1989; The Hand That Rocks the Cradle 1992
Laure, Carole (1951-) Get Out Your Handkerchiefs 1977; Maria Chapdelaine 1982; Heartbreakers 1984
Laurel, Stan aka **Laurel, Stanley** (1890-1965) The Two Tars 1928; Big Business 1929; Hollywood Revue 1929; Men o' War 1929; Perfect Day 1929; The Rogue Song 1930; Pardon Us 1931; County Hospital 1932; The Music Box 1932; Pack Up Your Troubles 1932; Scram! 1932; Their First Mistake 1932; Towed in a Hole 1932; Bogus Bandits 1933; Sons of the Desert 1933; Twice Two 1933; Babes in Toyland 1934; Hollywood Party 1934; Oliver the Eighth 1934; Them Thar Hills! 1934; Tit for Tat 1934; Bonnie Scotland 1935; Thicker than Water 1935; The Bohemian Girl 1936; Our Relations 1936; Pick a Star 1937; Way Out West 1937; Blockheads 1938; Swiss Miss 1938; The Flying Deuces 1939; A Chump at Oxford 1940; Saps at Sea 1940; Great Guns 1941; A-Haunting We Will Go 1942; The Dancing Masters 1943; Jitterbugs 1943; The Big Noise 1944; Nothing but Trouble 1944; The Bullfighters 1945; Utopia 1950; Laurel and Hardy's Laughing 20s 1965; 4 Clowns 1970
Lauren, Rod (1940-) Black Zoo 1963; The Gun Hawk 1963; Once before I Die 1965
Lauren, Tammy (1968-) The Last Flight of Noah's Ark 1980; Wishmaster 1997
Lauren, Veronica (1980-) Homeward Bound: the Incredible Journey 1993; Homeward Bound II: Lost in San Francisco 1996
Laurence, Ashley aka **Lauren, Ashley** (1971-) Hellraiser 1987; Hellbound: Hellraiser II 1988; A Murder of Crows 1998; Warlock III: the End of Innocence 1999
Laurence (1), Michael Piccadilly Incident 1946; Elizabeth of Ladymead 1948; Return to Glennascaul 1951; Othello 1952
Laurenson, James (1940-) Assault 1970; The Monster Club 1980; Pink Floyd - The Wall 1982; Heartbreakers 1984; Dead Bolt Dead 1999; AfterLife 2003
Laurent, Mélanie (1983-) The Bridge 1999; Paris 2007; The Concert 2009; Inglourious Basterds 2009; Beginners 2010; The Round Up 2009; Enemy 2013; Night Train to Lisbon 2013; By the Sea 2015

Lauria, Dan (1947-) Stakeout 1987; Hangman 2000; Contagion 2001
Laurie, Hugh (1959-) Strapless 1988; Peter's Friends 1992; A Pin for the Butterfly 1994; Sense and Sensibility 1995; 101 Dalmatians 1996; The Borrowers 1997; Cousin Bette 1997; The Man in the Iron Mask 1997; Maybe Baby 1999; Stuart Little 1999; Girl from Rio 2001; Stuart Little 2 2002; Flight of the Phoenix 2004; Stuart Little 3: Call of the Wild 2005; Valiant 2005; Street Kings 2008; Monsters vs Aliens 2009; Arthur Christmas 2011; Hop 2011; The Oranges 2011; Tomorrowland: a World Beyond 2015
Laurie, John (1897-1980) Juno and the Paycock 1930; The 39 Steps 1935; As You Like It 1936; The Edge of the World 1937; Jericho 1937; Convoy 1940; The Ghost of St Michael's 1941; The Lamp Still Burns 1943; The Way Ahead 1944; I Know Where I'm Going! 1945; School for Secrets 1946; The Brothers 1947; Jassy 1947; Mine Own Executioner 1947; Bonnie Prince Charlie 1948; Floodtide 1949; Happy Go Lovely 1950; No Trace 1950; Pandora and the Flying Dutchman 1950; Treasure Island 1950; Laughter in Paradise 1951; Island of Desire 1952; Tread Softly 1952; Campbell's Kingdom 1957; Kidnapped 1960; The Siege of the Saxons 1963; The Reptile 1966; Dad's Army 1971
Laurie, Piper (1932-) Francis Goes to the Races 1951; The Prince Who Was a Thief 1951; Has Anybody Seen My Gal? 1952; No Room for the Groom 1952; Son of Ali Baba 1952; The Golden Blade 1953; The Mississippi Gambler 1953; Dangerous Mission 1954; Dawn at Socorro 1954; Johnny Dark 1954; Ain't Misbehavin' 1955; Smoke Signal 1955; Until They Sail 1957; The Hustler 1961; Carrie 1976; Ruby 1977; Rainbow 1978; Tim 1979; Return to Oz 1985; Children of a Lesser God 1986; Promise 1986; Appointment with Death 1988; Tiger Warsaw 1988; Dream a Little Dream 1989; Other People's Money 1991; Sad Inheritance 1993; Trauma 1993; Wrestling Ernest Hemingway 1993; The Crossing Guard 1995; The Grass Harp 1995; The Road to Galveston 1996; The Faculty 1998; Inherit the Wind 1999; Palmer's Pick-Up 1999; Possessed 2000; Midwives 2001
Lauter, Ed (1938-2013) Executive Action 1973; The Last American Hero 1973; The Mean Machine 1974; Breakheart Pass 1976; Family Plot 1976; King Kong 1976; The Chicken Chronicles 1977; Magic 1978; The Jericho Mile 1979; The Amateur 1981; Eureka 1982; Cujo 1983; Finders Keepers 1984; Lassiter 1984; Death Wish 3 1985; 3:15 1986; Youngblood 1986; Gleaming the Cube 1988; Rocketeer 1991; School Ties 1992; Trial by Jury 1994; Wagons East! 1994; Dollar for the Dead 1998; Seabiscuit 2003; Starship Troopers 2: Hero of the Federation 2004; Seraphim Falls 2006
Lauter, Harry (1914-1990) Return to Treasure Island 1954; The Werewolf 1956; The Cry Baby Killer 1958; Ambush Bay 1966
Lautner, Taylor (1992-) The Adventures of Sharkboy and Lavagirl 2005; Twilight 2008; New Moon 2009; Eclipse 2010; Valentine's Day 2010; Abduction 2011; Breaking Dawn Part One 2011; Breaking Dawn Part Two 2012; Grown Ups 2 2013
Lavanant, Dominique (1944-) Love Songs 1984; Rendez-vous 1985; 3 Men and a Cradle 1985; Kamikaze 1986
Lavant, Denis (1961-) Boy Meets Girl 1984; Mauvais Sang 1986; Les Amants du Pont-Neuf 1990; Beau Travail 1999; Married/Unmarried 2001; Mister Lonely 2007; Holy Motors 2012
Lavender, Ian (1946-) Dad's Army 1971; Adventures of a Taxi Driver 1975; Adventures of a Private Eye 1977; 31 North 62 East 2009; Dad's Army 2016
Laverick, June (1931-) It Happened in Rome 1956; The Duke Wore Jeans 1958; The Gypsy and the Gentleman 1958; Son of Robin Hood 1958; The Flesh and the Fiends 1959; Follow a Star 1959
Lavi, Daliah (1940-) Lord Jim 1965; Ten Little Indians 1965; The Silencers 1966; The Spy with a Cold Nose 1966; Nobody Runs Forever 1968; Some Girls Do 1969; Catlow 1971
Lavia, Gabriele (1942-) Deep Red 1975; The Legend of 1900 1999
Lavigne, Avril (1984-) Fast Food Nation 2006; The Flock 2007
Lavin, Linda (1937-) Lena: My 100 Children 1987; I Want to Go Home 1989; The Back-Up Plan 2010
Lavoine, Marc L'Enfer 1993; The Good Thief 2002

LaVorgna, Adam (1981-) The Beautician and the Beast 1997; I'll Be Home for Christmas 1998
Lavronenko, Konstantin The Return 2003; The Banishment 2007
Law, John Phillip (1937-2008) Barbarella 1967; Danger: Diabolik 1967; Death Rides a Horse 1967; Hurry Sundown 1967; The Sergeant 1968; Skidoo 1968; The Hawaiians 1970; The Love Machine 1971; The Golden Voyage of Sinbad 1973; Open Season 1974; The Cassandra Crossing 1976; Attack Force Z 1981; Tarzan, the Ape Man 1981; A Case of Honor 1988
Law, Jude (1972-) Shopping 1993; Bent 1996; Gattaca 1997; I Love You, I Love You Not 1997; Midnight in the Garden of Good and Evil 1997; Wilde 1997; Final Cut 1998; Music from Another Room 1998; The Wisdom of Crocodiles 1998; eXistenZ 1999; The Talented Mr Ripley 1999; Love, Honour and Obey 2000; AI: Artificial Intelligence 2001; Enemy at the Gates 2001; Road to Perdition 2002; Cold Mountain 2003; Alfie 2004; The Aviator 2004; Closer 2004; I ♥ Huckabees 2004; Lemony Snicket's A Series of Unfortunate Events 2004; Sky Captain and the World of Tomorrow 2004; All the King's Men 2005; Breaking and Entering 2006; The Holiday 2006; My Blueberry Nights 2007; Sleuth 2007; The Imaginarium of Doctor Parnassus 2009; Sherlock Holmes 2009; Repo Men 2010; Contagion 2011; Hugo 2011; Sherlock Holmes: a Game of Shadows 2011; 360 2011; Anna Karenina 2012; Radioman 2012; Rise of the Guardians 2012; Dom Hemingway 2013; Side Effects 2013; Black Sea 2014; Genius 2015; Spy 2015; Knights of the Round Table: King Arthur 2016
Law, Phyllida (1932-) Tree of Hands 1988; Peter's Friends 1992; Much Ado about Nothing 1993; Before the Rain 1994; Emma 1996; The Winter Guest 1996; Anna Karenina 1997; The Lost Lover 1999; Mad Cows 1999; Milk 1999; The Time Machine 2002; Two Men Went to War 2002; I'll Be There 2003; Tooth 2003; Blinded 2004; Mee-Shee: the Water Giant 2005; Copying Beethoven 2006; Miss Potter 2006; The Waiting Room 2007; Arrietty 2010
Lawford, Betty (1910-1960) Love before Breakfast 1936; Criminal Lawyer 1937; The Devil Thumbs a Ride 1947
Lawford, Christopher aka **Lawford, Chris** (1955-) Blankman 1994; Kiss Me, Guido 1997; The World's Fastest Indian 2005
Lawford, Peter (1923-1984) A Yank at Eton 1942; Pilot #5 1943; The Sky's the Limit 1943; The Canterville Ghost 1944; The White Cliffs of Dover 1944; The Picture of Dorian Gray 1945; Son of Lassie 1945; Cluny Brown 1946; My Brother Talks to Horses 1946; Two Sisters from Boston 1946; Good News 1947; It Happened in Brooklyn 1947; Easter Parade 1948; Julia Misbehaves 1948; On an Island with You 1948; Little Women 1949; The Red Danube 1949; Please Believe Me 1950; Royal Wedding 1951; The Hour of 13 1952; Kangaroo 1952; It Should Happen to You 1954; Never So Few 1959; Exodus 1960; Ocean's Eleven 1960; Pepe 1960; Advise and Consent 1962; The Longest Day 1962; Sergeants 3 1962; Dead Ringer 1964; Sylvia 1964; Harlow 1965; A Man Called Adam 1966; The Oscar 1966; Dead Run 1967; How I Spent My Summer Vacation 1967; Buona Sera, Mrs Campbell 1968; Salt & Pepper 1968; Skidoo 1968; The April Fools 1969; One More Time 1970; They Only Kill Their Masters 1972; Rosebud 1975; Body and Soul 1981; Where Is Parsifal? 1983
Lawless, Lucy (1968-) EuroTrip 2004; Boogeyman 2005; Bedtime Stories 2008
Lawley, Yvonne (1914-1999) Death in Brunswick 1990; Ruby and Rata 1990
Lawlor, Sean Reefer and the Model 1988; The Disappearance of Finbar 1996; Mega Shark vs Giant Octopus 2008
Lawrance, Jody aka **Lawrence, Jody** (1930-1986) Ten Tall Men 1951; All Ashore 1953; Hot Spell 1958; Stagecoach to Dancer's Rock 1962
Lawrence, Andre (1939-) The Pleasure Seekers 1964; And Hope to Die 1972
Lawrence, Barbara (1930-2013) Margie 1946; Give My Regards to Broadway 1948; The Street with No Name 1948; Unfaithfully Yours 1948; You Were Meant for Me 1948; A Letter to Three Wives 1949; Mother Is a Freshman 1949; Thieves' Highway 1949; Two Tickets to Broadway 1951;

Arena 1953; Her Twelve Men 1954; Oklahoma! 1955; Kronos 1957; Man in the Shadow 1957

Lawrence, Bruno (1941-1995) Race for the Yankee Zephyr 1981; Smash Palace 1981; Battletruck 1982; Utu 1983; The Quiet Earth 1985; Spotswood 1991; Jack Be Nimble 1992

Lawrence, Delphi (1926-2002) Blood Orange 1953; Double Cross 1955; The Feminine Touch 1956; Just My Luck 1957; Son of Robin Hood 1958; Too Many Crooks 1958; The Man Who Could Cheat Death 1959; The Last Challenge 1967

Lawrence, Doug aka Mr Lawrence The SpongeBob SquarePants Movie 2004; The SpongeBob Movie: Sponge out of Water 2015

Lawrence, Elizabeth (1922-2000) We're No Angels 1989; Sleeping with the Enemy 1991

Lawrence, Gertrude (1898-1952) Men Are Not Gods 1936; Rembrandt 1936; Stage Door Canteen 1943; The Glass Menagerie 1950

Lawrence (2), Jennifer (1990-) The Burning Plain 2008; The Beaver 2010; Winter's Bone 2010; Like Crazy 2011; X-Men: First Class 2011; House at the End of the Street 2012; The Hunger Games 2012; Silver Linings Playbook 2012; American Hustle 2013; The Hunger Games: Catching Fire 2013; Serena 2013; Dior and I 2014; The Hunger Games: Mockingjay Part 1 2014; X-Men: Days of Future Past 2014; The Hunger Games: Mockingjay Part 2 2015; Joy 2015; Passengers 2016; X-Men: Apocalypse 2016

Lawrence, Joey aka Lawrence, Joseph (1976-) Summer Rental 1985; Oliver & Company 1988; Pulse 1988; Chains of Gold 1989; Urban Legends: Final Cut 2000; Together Again for the First Time 2008; My Fake Fiancé 2009

Lawrence, Josie (1959-) Riders of the Storm 1986; Enchanted April 1991; Round Ireland with a Fridge... a True Story 2010; Bonobo 2013

Lawrence (1), Marc (1910-2005) Blind Alley 1939; Sergeant Madden 1939; Johnny Apollo 1940; Hold That Ghost 1941; Hit the Ice 1943; Dillinger 1945; Key Largo 1948; Calamity Jane and Sam Bass 1949; Jigsaw 1949; The Asphalt Jungle 1950; The Black Hand 1950; Johnny Tiger 1966; The Man with the Golden Gun 1974; Marathon Man 1976; Ruby 1992; From Dusk till Dawn 1995

Lawrence, Martin (1965-) House Party 1990; House Party 2 1991; Talkin' Dirty after Dark 1991; Boomerang 1992; Bad Boys 1995; A Thin Line between Love and Hate 1996; Nothing to Lose 1997; Blue Streak 1999; Life 1999; Big Momma's House 2000; Black Knight 2001; What's the Worst That Could Happen? 2001; National Security 2002; Bad Boys II 2003; Rebound 2005; Big Momma's House 2 2006; Open Season 2006; Wild Hogs 2007; College Road Trip 2008; Welcome Home Roscoe Jenkins 2008; Death at a Funeral 2010; Big Mommas: Like Father, like Son 2011

Lawrence, Matthew) Pulse 1988; Tales from the Darkside: the Movie 1991; Mrs Doubtfire 1993; Kiki's Delivery Service 1998; The Hot Chick 2002

Lawrence, Rosina (1912-1997) Pick a Star 1937; Way Out West 1937

Lawrence, Sharon (1963-) The Face on the Milk Carton 1995; The Only Thrill 1997; Gossip 1999; Atomic Twister 2002

Lawrence, Sheldon The Crooked Sky 1957; Mark of the Phoenix 1957; The Pursuers 1961

Lawrence, Stephanie (1949-2000) Buster 1988; The Phantom of the Opera 1989

Lawrence, Steve (1935-) The Lonely Guy 1984; The Yards 2000

Laws, Sam (1924-1990) Hit Man 1972; Truck Turner 1974; White Line Fever 1975

Lawson, Bianca (1979-) Save the Last Dance 2000; Bones 2001; Breakin' All the Rules 2004

Lawson, Denis (1947-) Providence 1977; Local Hero 1983; The Chain 1984; Perfect Sense 2011; The Machine 2013; The Wee Man 2013

Lawson, Leigh (1945-) Brother Sun, Sister Moon 1972; Ghost Story 1974; Percy's Progress 1974; Love among the Ruins 1975; The Devil's Advocate 1977; Tess 1979; Agatha Christie's Murder Is Easy 1982; Sword of the Valiant 1984; Madame Sousatzka 1988; Back to the Secret Garden 2000

Lawson, Linda (1936-) Apache Rifles 1964; Sometimes a Great Notion 1971

Lawson, Mary (1911-1941) D'Ye Ken John Peel? 1934; A Fire Has Been Arranged 1935; Cotton Queen 1937

Lawson, Priscilla (1914-1958) Flash Gordon 1936; The Girl of the Golden West 1938

Lawson, Richard (1947-) Sugar Hill 1974; The Jericho Mile 1979; The Main Event 1979; Stick 1985; How Stella Got Her Groove Back 1998

Lawson, Sarah (1928-) You Know What Sailors Are 1954; The Blue Peter 1955; It's Never Too Late 1956; The World Ten Times Over 1963; Night of the Big Heat 1967; The Devil Rides Out 1968

Lawson, Shannon The War between Us 1995; Forever Mine 1999

Lawson, Wilfrid (1900-1966) The Gaunt Stranger 1938; Pygmalion 1938; The First Rebel 1939; Stolen Life 1939; The Long Voyage Home 1940; Pastor Hall 1940; Danny Boy 1941; Jeannie 1941; The Great Mr Handel 1942; The Night Has Eyes 1942; Fanny by Gaslight 1944; The Prisoner 1955; Hell Drivers 1957; Postman's Knock 1961; The Wrong Box 1966; The Viking Queen 1967

Lawther, Alex Benjamin Britten: Peace and Conflict 2013; Departure 2015

Lawton, Frank (1904-1969) Birds of Prey 1930; The Skin Game 1931; Friday the Thirteenth 1933; One More River 1934; David Copperfield 1935; The Devil-Doll 1936; The Invisible Ray 1936; The Mill on the Floss 1937; The Four Just Men 1939; Went the Day Well? 1942; The Winslow Boy 1948; Rough Shoot 1952; Double Cross 1955

Laydu, Claude (1927-2011) Diary of a Country Priest 1950; Nous Sommes Tous des Assassins 1952

Laye, Dilys (1934-2009) Please Turn Over 1960; Carry On Cruising 1962; Carry On Spying 1964

Laye, Evelyn (1900-1996) One Heavenly Night 1931; Evensong 1934; Theatre of Death 1966; Say Hello to Yesterday 1971

Layton, George (1943-) Confessions of a Driving Instructor 1976; Stand Up Virgin Soldiers 1977

Lazar, Veronica aka Lazare, Veronica (1938-2014) La Luna 1979; Identification of a Woman 1982; Berlin Jerusalem 1989; Me and You 2012

Lazard, Justin (1967-) Species II 1998; Universal Soldier - the Return 1999

Lazenby, George (1939-) On Her Majesty's Secret Service 1969; The Man from Hong Kong 1975; The Kentucky Fried Movie 1977; Saint Jack 1979; Gettysburg 1993; Four Dogs Playing Poker 1999; Not Quite Hollywood 2008; Everything or Nothing: the Untold Story of 007 2012

Le Beau, Bettine (1936-) Village of Daughters 1961; The Best of Benny Hill 1974

Le Besco, Isild Girls Can't Swim 1999; Roberto Succo 2000; The New Girlfriend 2014

Le Bihan, Samuel aka LeBihan, Samuel (1965-) Three Colours Red 1994; Venus Beauty Institute 1998; Brotherhood of the Wolf 2001; He Loves Me... He Loves Me Not 2002; Frontier(s) 2007; Mesrine: Public Enemy No 1 2008

Le Bon, Charlotte Mood Indigo 2013; YSL: Yves Saint Laurent 2014; The Walk 2015; Bastille Day 2016

Le Coq, Bernard (1950-) Burnt Barns 1973; Van Gogh 1991; The Flower of Evil 2002; The Bridesmaid 2004; Hidden 2005

Le Mat, Paul (1952-) American Graffiti 1973; Aloha, Bobby and Rose 1975; Citizens Band 1977; More American Graffiti 1979; Melvin and Howard 1980; Death Valley 1982; Strange Invaders 1983; The Burning Bed 1984; Private Investigations 1987; Puppet Master 1989; Wishman 1991; The Long Shot 2004

Le Mesurier, John (1912-1983) The Blue Parrot 1953; Police Dog 1955; Brothers in Law 1956; Happy Is the Bride 1957; The Moonraker 1957; Blood of the Vampire 1958; Carlton-Browne of the FO 1958; I Was Monty's Double 1958; Jack the Ripper 1958; Law and Disorder 1958; Too Many Crooks 1958; Follow a Star 1959; The Hound of the Baskervilles 1959; I'm All Right Jack 1959; The Bulldog Breed 1960; The Day They Robbed the Bank of England 1960; Never Let Go 1960; The Night We Got the Bird 1960; The Rebel 1960; School for Scoundrels 1960; Don't Bother to Knock 1961; Invasion Quartet 1961; Only Two Can Play 1961; Village of Daughters 1962; Jigsaw 1962; The Main Attraction 1962; The Punch and Judy Man 1962; Waltz of the Toreadors

1962; We Joined the Navy 1962; The Wrong Arm of the Law 1962; The Mouse on the Moon 1963; The Pink Panther 1963; Hot Enough for June 1964; The Moon-Spinners 1964; City under the Sea 1965; The Early Bird 1965; Masquerade 1965; Where the Spies Are 1965; Eye of the Devil 1966; Finders Keepers 1966; Our Man in Marrakesh 1966; The Sandwich Man 1966; Mister Ten Per Cent 1967; The 25th Hour 1967; Salt & Pepper 1968; The Italian Job 1969; Midas Run 1969; Doctor in Trouble 1970; On a Clear Day You Can See Forever 1970; Dad's Army 1971; Barry McKenzie Holds His Own 1974; Brief Encounter 1974; Confessions of a Window Cleaner 1974; The Adventure of Sherlock Holmes' Smarter Brother 1975; Jabberwocky 1977; Stand Up Virgin Soldiers 1977; Rosie Dixon: Night Nurse 1978; The Spaceman and King Arthur 1979; The Fiendish Plot of Dr Fu Manchu 1980

Le Ny, Anne Untouchable 2011; Attila Marcel 2013

Le Poulain, Jean (1924-1988) Le Bossu 1959; The Sign of Leo 1959

Le Saché, Bernadette aka Simone Lemorne Le Cheval d'Orgueil 1980; The Vanishing 1988

Le Vaillant, Nigel (1958-) Seven Minutes 1989; Tom's Midnight Garden 1998

Lea, Ron The Gunrunner 1984; Criminal Law 1988; Clearcut 1992; Victor 2008; Goodnight for Justice 2011

Leach, Rosemary (1925-) That'll Be the Day 1973; Brief Encounter 1974; A Room with a View 1985; Turtle Diary 1985; The Children 1990; The Hawk 1992; The Mystery of Edwin Drood 1993; may i kill u? 2012

Leachman, Cloris (1926-) Kiss Me Deadly 1955; The Rack 1956; Butch Cassidy and the Sundance Kid 1969; WUSA 1970; The Last Picture Show 1971; Charley and the Angel 1973; Dillinger 1973; Happy Mother's Day... Love, George 1973; Daisy Miller 1974; Young Frankenstein 1974; Crazy Mama 1975; High Anxiety 1977; The Mouse and His Child 1977; Hill's Angels 1979; SOS Titanic 1979; Foolin' Around 1980; Herbie Goes Bananas 1980; History of the World Part 1 1981; Walk like a Man 1987; Prancer 1989; Love Hurts 1990; Texasville 1990; The Beverly Hillbillies 1993; Stanley's Magic Garden 1994; Beavis and Butt-head Do America 1996; Never Too Late 1996; The Iron Giant 1999; Music of the Heart 1999; Alex & Emma 2003; Laputa: Castle in the Sky 2003; Spanglish 2004; Sky High 2005; Beerfest 2006; Scary Movie 4 2006; Ponyo 2008; Gambit 2012; The Croods 2013

Leak, Jennifer Yours, Mine and Ours 1968; Eye of the Cat 1969

Leal, Sharon (1972-) Dreamgirls 2006; This Christmas 2007; Linewatch 2008; Soul Men 2008; Tyler Perry's Why Did I Get Married Too? 2010

Learned, Michael (1939-) Touched by Love 1979; The Parade 1984; Power 1986; Murder in New Hampshire 1991; Dragon: the Bruce Lee Story 1993

Leary, Denis (1957-) Demolition Man 1993; Judgment Night 1993; The Sandlot 1993; Who's the Man? 1993; Gunmen 1994; Hostile Hostages 1994; The Neon Bible 1995; Operation Dumbo Drop 1995; Stolen Hearts 1996; Love Walked In 1997; The Matchmaker 1997; Noose 1997; The Real Blonde 1997; Subway Stories: Tales from the Underground 1997; Suicide Kings 1997; Wag the Dog 1997; A Bug's Life 1998; Small Soldiers 1998; Wide Awake 1998; Jesus' Son 1999; The Thomas Crown Affair 1999; True Crime 1999; Company Man 2000; Dawg 2001; Double Whammy 2001; Ice Age 2002; The Secret Lives of Dentists 2003; Ice Age: the Meltdown 2006; Recount 2008; Ice Age 3: Dawn of the Dinosaurs 2009; Ice Age 4: Continental Drift 2012; Draft Day 2014; Ice Age: Collision Course 2016

Lease, Rex (1901-1966) The Younger Generation 1929; Aces and Eights 1936; Law and Order 1936

Léaud, Jean-Pierre (1944-) The 400 Blows 1959; Le Testament d'Orphée 1960; Love at Twenty 1962; Pierrot le Fou 1965; Made in USA 1966; Masculine Feminine 1966; La Chinoise 1967; Weekend 1967; Le Gai Savoir 1968; Stolen Kisses 1968; Pigsty 1969; Bed and Board 1970; Anne and Muriel 1971; Last Tango in Paris 1972; Day for Night 1973; La Maman et la Putain 1973; Love on the Run 1979; Detective 1985; Grandeur et Décadence d'un Petit Commerce de Cinéma 1986; Treasure Island 1986; I Hired a

Contract Killer 1990; Irma Vep 1996; Mon Homme 1996; The Pornographer 2001; I Saw Ben Barka Get Killed 2005; Le Havre 2011

Leaver, Philip (1904-1981) Dr Morelle - the Case of the Missing Heiress 1949; Spaceways 1953

Lebeau, Madeleine (1923-2016) Casablanca 1942; Cage of Gold 1950; Une Parisienne 1957

Lebedeff, Ivan (1899-1953) Bachelor Apartment 1931; The Gay Diplomat 1931; Blonde Bombshell 1933; Goin' to Town 1935; Love on the Run 1936; Angel 1937; History Is Made at Night 1937

LeBlanc, Matt (1967-) Lookin' Italian 1994; Ed 1996; Lost in Space 1998; Charlie's Angels 2000; All the Queen's Men 2001; Charlie's Angels: Full Throttle 2003

LeBrock, Kelly (1960-) The Woman in Red 1984; Weird Science 1985; Hard to Kill 1989; Wrongfully Accused 1998

Lebrun, Françoise La Maman et la Putain 1973; The Nun 2013; The Kidnapping of Michel Houellebecq 2014

Lechtenbrink, Volker The Bridge 1959; When Santa Fell to Earth 2011

Leclerc, Ginette (1912-1992) The Baker's Wife 1938; The Raven 1943; Goto, l'Ile d'Amour 1968; Popsy-Pop 1970

Ledebur, Friedrich (1900-1986) Moby Dick 1956; The 27th Day 1957; The Christmas Tree 1969

Lederer, Francis aka Lederer, Franz (1899-2000) Pandora's Box 1929; The Wonderful Lie of Nina Petrovna 1929; Romance in Manhattan 1934; The Gay Deception 1935; One Rainy Afternoon 1936; Confessions of a Nazi Spy 1939; Midnight 1939; The Man I Married 1940; Diary of a Chambermaid 1946; A Woman of Distinction 1950; The Ambassador's Daughter 1956; Lisbon 1956; Maracaibo 1958; The Return of Dracula 1958

Ledford, Brandy First Target 2000; Mary Higgins Clark's We'll Meet Again 2002

Ledger, Heath (1979-2008) Blackrock 1997; 10 Things I Hate about You 1999; Two Hands 1999; The Patriot 2000; A Knight's Tale 2001; Monster's Ball 2001; The Four Feathers 2002; The Sin Eater 2002; Ned Kelly 2003; Brokeback Mountain 2005; Candy 2005; Casanova 2005; Lords of Dogtown 2005; I'm Not There. 2007; The Dark Knight 2008; The Imaginarium of Doctor Parnassus 2009

Ledoux, Fernand (1897-1993) La Bête Humaine 1938; Volpone 1941; Les Visiteurs du Soir 1942; Les Misérables 1957; The Magic Donkey 1970

Ledoyen, Virginie (1976-) L'Eau Froide 1994; La Cérémonie 1995; En Plein Coeur 1998; Late August, Early September 1998; The Beach 2000; 8 Women 2001; Bon Voyage 2003; The Army of Crime 2009

Lee Byung-hun A Bittersweet Life 2005; The Good the Bad the Weird 2008; I Saw the Devil 2010; Terminator: Genisys 2015

Lee Eun-joo (1979-2005) Take Care of My Cat 2002; Brotherhood 2004

Lee Kang-sheng (1968-) Rebels of the Neon God 1992; Vive L'Amour 1994; I Don't Want to Sleep Alone 2006

Lee Mi-yeon Whispering Corridors 1998; Typhoon 2005

Lee Seon-gyun aka Lee Sunkyun R-Point 2004; Nobody's Daughter Haewon 2013

Lee Waise A Better Tomorrow 1986; Bullet in the Head 1990; The Actress 1992

Lee, Anna (1913-2004) The Camels Are Coming 1934; First a Girl 1935; The Passing of the Third Floor Back 1935; The Man Who Changed His Mind 1936; You're in the Army Now 1936; King Solomon's Mines 1937; The Four Just Men 1939; Young Man's Fancy 1939; Return to Yesterday 1940; Seven Sinners 1940; How Green Was My Valley 1941; My Life with Caroline 1941; The Commandos Strike at Dawn 1942; Flying Tigers 1942; Hangmen Also Die! 1943; Summer Storm 1944; Bedlam 1946; The Ghost and Mrs Muir 1947; Gideon's Day 1958; The Crimson Kimono 1959; The Horse Soldiers 1959; What Ever Happened to Baby Jane? 1962; 7 Women 1966; In like Flint 1967

Lee, Belinda (1935-1961) No Smoking 1954; The Runaway Bus 1954; Footsteps in the Fog 1955; Man of the Moment 1955; The Big Money 1956; Eyewitness 1956; The Feminine Touch 1956; Who Done It? 1956; Dangerous Exile 1957; Miracle in Soho 1957; Nor

the Moon by Night 1958; Constantine and the Cross 1961

Lee, Bernard (1908-1981) Rhodes of Africa 1936; Let George Do It 1940; Spare a Copper 1940; Elizabeth of Ladymead 1948; The Fallen Idol 1948; The Blue Lamp 1949; The Third Man 1949; The Adventurers 1950; Cage of Gold 1950; Last Holiday 1950; Odette 1950; Appointment with Venus 1951; Gift Horse 1951; The Yellow Balloon 1952; Beat the Devil 1953; Sailor of the King 1953; Father Brown 1954; The Purple Plain 1954; Seagulls over Sorrento 1954; The Ship That Died of Shame 1955; The Battle of the River Plate 1956; The Spanish Gardener 1956; Across the Bridge 1957; Danger Within 1958; Dunkirk 1958; The Key 1958; The Man Upstairs 1958; Nowhere to Go 1958; Beyond This Place 1959; The Angry Silence 1960; Cone of Silence 1960; Kidnapped 1960; Fury at Smugglers Bay 1961; The Secret Partner 1961; Whistle down the Wind 1961; The Brain 1962; Dr No 1962; The L-Shaped Room 1962; From Russia with Love 1963; A Place to Go 1963; Ring of Spies 1963; Saturday Night Out 1963; Two Left Feet 1963; Goldfinger 1964; The Legend of Young Dick Turpin 1965; Thunderball 1965; You Only Live Twice 1967; Crossplot 1969; On Her Majesty's Secret Service 1969; The Raging Moon 1970; Diamonds Are Forever 1971; Dulcima 1971; Frankenstein and the Monster from Hell 1973; Live and Let Die 1973; The Man with the Golden Gun 1974; The Spy Who Loved Me 1977; Moonraker 1979

Lee, Brandon (1965-1993) Showdown in Little Tokyo 1991; Rapid Fire 1992; The Crow 1994

Lee, Bruce (1940-1973) Marlowe 1969; The Big Boss 1971; Fist of Fury 1972; Enter the Dragon 1973; The Way of the Dragon 1973; Game of Death 1978

Lee, Canada (1907-1952) Lifeboat 1944; Body and Soul 1947; Cry, the Beloved Country 1951

Lee, Carl (1926-1986) The Cool World 1963; Superfly 1972; Gordon's War 1973

Lee, Christopher (1922-2015) Captain Horatio Hornblower RN 1951; Valley of Eagles 1951; The Crimson Pirate 1952; Paul Temple Returns 1952; Storm over the Nile 1955; That Lady 1955; Fortune Is a Woman 1957; Bitter Victory 1957; The Curse of Frankenstein 1957; A Tale of Two Cities 1957; The Traitor 1957; The Battle of the V1 1958; Dracula 1958; The Hound of the Baskervilles 1959; The Man Who Could Cheat Death 1959; The Mummy 1959; The Treasure of San Teresa 1959; Beat Girl 1960; The City of the Dead 1960; The Hands of Orlac 1960; Too Hot to Handle 1960; The Two Faces of Dr Jekyll 1960; The Pirates of Blood River 1961; Taste of Fear 1961; Corridors of Blood 1962; The Longest Day 1962; Sherlock Holmes and the Deadly Necklace 1962; The Devil-Ship Pirates 1964; Dr Terror's House of Horrors 1964; The Gorgon 1964; Dracula - Prince of Darkness 1965; The Face of Fu Manchu 1965; Rasputin, the Mad Monk 1965; She 1965; The Skull 1965; The Brides of Fu Manchu 1966; Theatre of Death 1966; Circus of Fear 1967; Five Golden Dragons 1967; Night of the Big Heat 1967; The Vengeance of Fu Manchu 1967; The Blood of Fu Manchu 1968; The Castle of Fu Manchu 1968; Curse of the Crimson Altar 1968; The Devil Rides Out 1968; Dracula Has Risen from the Grave 1968; The Bloody Judge 1969; The Magic Christian 1969; The Oblong Box 1969; Scream and Scream Again 1969; Taste the Blood of Dracula 1969; Count Dracula 1970; The House That Dripped Blood 1970; One More Time 1970; The Private Life of Sherlock Holmes 1970; The Scars of Dracula 1970; Hannie Caulder 1971; I, Monster 1971; The Creeping Flesh 1972; Death Line 1972; Dracula AD 1972 1972; Horror Express 1972; Nothing but the Night 1972; Dark Places 1973; The Satanic Rites of Dracula 1973; The Three Musketeers 1973; The Wicker Man 1973; Diagnosis: Murder 1974; The Four Musketeers 1974; The Man with the Golden Gun 1974; Death in the Sun 1975; Killer Force 1975; The Keeper 1976; To the Devil a Daughter 1976; Airport '77 1977; End of the World 1977; The Passage 1978; Return from Witch Mountain 1978; The Silent Flute 1978; Arabian Adventure 1979; Bear Island 1979; Jaguar Lives! 1979; 1941 1979; The Last Unicorn 1982; Once upon a Spy 1980; Serial 1980; An Eye for an Eye 1981; The Salamander 1981; House of the Long Shadows 1983; The

Return of Captain Invincible 1983; Howling II: Your Sister Is a Werewolf 1984; The Girl 1986; Jocks 1986; Mio in the Land of Faraway 1987; The Return of the Musketeers 1989; Gremlins 2: the New Batch 1990; The Rainbow Thief 1990; Treasure Island 1990; Curse III: Blood Sacrifice 1991; Shogun Warrior 1991; Death Train 1993; A Feast at Midnight 1994; The Funny Man 1994; Police Academy: Mission to Moscow 1994; The Stupids 1995; Talos the Mummy 1997; Jinnah 1998; The Lord of the Rings: The Fellowship of the Ring 2001; The Lord of the Rings: The Two Towers 2002; Star Wars Episode II: Attack of the Clones 2002; Charlie and the Chocolate Factory 2005; Greyfriars Bobby 2005; Star Wars Episode III: Revenge of the Sith 2005; Tim Burton's Corpse Bride 2005; Sweeney Todd: the Demon Barber of Fleet Street 2007; Not Quite Hollywood 2008; Star Wars: The Clone Wars 2008; Boogie Woogie 2009; Glorious 39 2009; The Heavy 2009; Alice in Wonderland 2010; Burke & Hare 2010; The Resident 2010; Season of the Witch 2010; Hugo 2011; Dark Shadows 2012; The Hobbit: an Unexpected Journey 2012; The Hobbit: the Battle of the Five Armies 2014

Lee, Cinqué (1968-) Mystery Train 1989; Coffee and Cigarettes 2003

Lee, Danny aka **Lee Sau Yin** City on Fire 1987; The Killer 1989

Lee, Davey (1924-2008) The Singing Fool 1928; Say It with Songs 1929

Lee, Gwen (1904-1961) Laugh, Clown, Laugh 1928; Free and Easy 1930

Lee, Gypsy Rose aka **Hovick, Louise** (1914-1970) You Can't Have Everything 1937; My Lucky Star 1938; Sally, Irene and Mary 1938; Stage Door Canteen 1943; Belle of the Yukon 1944; Screaming Mimi 1958; Wind across the Everglades 1958; The Stripper 1963; The Trouble with Angels 1966

Lee, Jason (1970-) Mallrats 1995; Chasing Amy 1996; Enemy of the State 1998; Kissing a Fool 1998; Dogma 1999; Mumford 1999; Almost Famous 2000; Heartbreakers 2001; Vanilla Sky 2001; A Guy Thing 2002; Stealing Harvard 2002; Dreamcatcher 2003; Jersey Girl 2003; The Incredibles 2004; The Ballad of Jack and Rose 2005; Monster House 2006; Alvin and the Chipmunks 2007; Underdog 2007; Alvin and the Chipmunks: the Squeakquel 2009; Cop Out 2010; Alvin and the Chipmunks: Chipwrecked 2011; Alvin and the Chipmunks: the Road Chip 2015

Lee, Jason Scott (1966-) Map of the Human Heart 1992; Dragon: the Bruce Lee Story 1993; The Jungle Book 1994; Rapa Nui 1994; Murder in Mind 1996; Talos the Mummy 1997; Soldier 1998; Lilo & Stitch 2002; Crouching Tiger, Hidden Dragon: Sword of Destiny 2016

Lee, Jesse (1984-) Matinee 1993; The Brady Bunch Movie 1995; From the Mixed-Up Files of Mrs Basil E Frankweiler 1995; A Very Brady Sequel 1996

Lee, Joie (1962-) She's Gotta Have It 1986; Mo' Better Blues 1990; Coffee and Cigarettes 2003

Lee, Jon Seeing Double 2003; Telstar: the Joe Meek Story 2008

Lee, Kaiulani Zelly and Me 1988; Hush 1998

Lee, Lila (1901-1973) Male and Female 1919; Terror Island 1920; Blood and Sand 1922; Fight 1929; The Unholy Three 1930; Stand Up and Cheer! 1934; The Ex-Mrs Bradford 1936

Lee, Margaret (1943-) Kiss the Girls and Make Them Die 1966; Circus of Fear 1967; Five Golden Dragons 1967; Ghosts - Italian Style 1967; The Bloody Judge 1969

Lee (1), Mark (1958-) Gallipoli 1981; Emma's War 1985

Lee, Michele (1942-) How to Succeed in Business without Really Trying 1967; The Comic 1969; The Love Bug 1969; Dark Victory 1976; Broadway Bound 1991

Lee, Oliver Awaydays 2009; Powder 2010

Lee, Peggy (1920-2002) Stage Door Canteen 1943; The Jazz Singer 1952; Lady and the Tramp 1955; Pete Kelly's Blues 1955

Lee, Robbie Big Bad Mama 1974; Switchblade Sisters 1975

Lee, Robinne (1974-) Hav Plenty 1998; National Security 2002

Lee, Ruta (1936-) Gaby 1956; Sergeants 3 1962; The Gun Hawk 1963; Bullet for a Badman 1964

Lee, Sam aka **Lee Chan-Sam, Sam** (1975-) Made in Hong Kong 1997; Beast Cops 1998; Ping Pong 2002

Lee, Shannon (1969-) And Now You're Dead 1998; I Am Bruce Lee 2012

Lee, Sheryl (1967-) Jersey Girl 1992; Twin Peaks: Fire Walk with Me 1992; Backbeat 1993; Fall Time 1994; Homage 1995; Mother Night 1996; This World, Then the Fireworks 1996; Bliss 1997; Vampires 1998; Angel's Dance 1999; Texas Killing Fields 2011

Lee, Sophie (1968-) The Castle 1997; Holy Smoke 1999; Bootmen 2000

Lee, Spike (1957-) She's Gotta Have It 1986; School Daze 1988; Do the Right Thing 1989; Mo' Better Blues 1990; Jungle Fever 1991; Malcolm X 1992; Crooklyn 1994; Girl 6 1996; When We Were Kings 1996; Summer of Sam 1999

Lee, Stan (1922-) Comic Book Confidential 1988; The Ambulance 1990; Mallrats 1995; Daredevil 2003; Hulk 2003; Fantastic Four 2005; 4: Rise of the Silver Surfer 2007; Iron Man 2008; Thor 2011; Marvel Avengers Assemble 2012; Yoga Hosers 2016

Lee, Stephen (1951-) Purple Hearts 1984; Dolls 1987; RoboCop 2 1990; Prehysteria! 1993

Lee, Will Yun (1975-) Die Another Day 2002; Torque 2003; Elektra 2005; Red Dawn 2012

Leech, Allen (1981-) In Fear 2012; The Imitation Game 2014

Leech, Richard (1922-2004) Dublin Nightmare 1958; Ice Cold in Alex 1958

Leeds, Andrea (1914-1984) Come and Get It 1936; Stage Door 1937; The Goldwyn Follies 1938; Letter of Introduction 1938; The Real Glory 1939; Swanee River 1939; They Shall Have Music 1939

Leeds, Peter (1917-1996) The Lady Gambles 1949; Tight Spot 1955; The Facts of Life 1960

Leeds, Thelma (1912-2006) New Faces of 1937 1937; The Toast of New York 1937

Leerhsen, Erica (1977-) Book of Shadows: Blair Witch 2 2000; Anything Else 2003; The Texas Chainsaw Massacre 2003; Wrong Turn 2: Dead End 2007

Leeves, Jane (1963-) Miracle on 34th Street 1994; James and the Giant Peach 1996; Don't Go Breaking My Heart 1999; Music of the Heart 1999; The Adventures of Tom Thumb and Thumbelina 2002

Lefebvre, Jean (1919-2004) Gigot 1962; The Gendarme of St Tropez 1964; Man in the Trunk 1973; No Problem! 1975

Lefebvre (2), Philippe OSS 117: Cairo - Nest of Spies 2006; Tell No One 2006

LeFevre, Adam (1950-) Return of the Secaucus Seven 1980; Only You 1994; No Ordinary Baby 2001; Tadpole 2002

Lefevre, Rachelle New Moon 2009; Barney's Version 2010

Lefèvre, René (1898-1991) Le Million 1931; Le Crime de Monsieur Lange 1935; Le Doulos 1962

Legeno, Dave (1963-2014) Bonded by Blood 2000; Sword of Vengeance 2015

Leggatt, Alison (1904-1990) This Happy Breed 1944; Waterloo Road 1944; Encore 1951; Touch and Go 1955; Never Take Sweets from a Stranger 1960; The Day of the Triffids 1962; Nothing but the Best 1963; One Way Pendulum 1965; Far from the Madding Crowd 1967

Legge, Michael (1978-) Angela's Ashes 1999; Whatever Happened to Harold Smith? 1999; The Stag 2013

LeGros, James aka **Le Gros, James** (1962-) Phantasm II 1988; Drugstore Cowboy 1989; Leather Jackets 1991; Point Break 1991; Guncrazy 1992; My New Gun 1992; Singles 1992; Bad Girls 1994; Floundering 1994; Boys 1995; Destiny Turns on the Radio 1995; Living in Oblivion 1995; The Low Life 1995; [Safe] 1995; The Myth of Fingerprints 1996; Pronto 1996; Wishful Thinking 1997; Thursday 1998; Lovely & Amazing 2001; Catch That Kid 2004; Trust the Man 2006

Leguizamo, John (1964-) Casualties of War 1989; Hangin' with the Homeboys 1991; Whispers in the Dark 1992; Carlito's Way 1993; Super Mario Bros 1993; A Pyromaniac's Love Story 1995; To Wong Foo, Thanks for Everything, Julie Newmar 1995; Executive Decision 1996; The Fan 1996; William Shakespeare's Romeo + Juliet 1996; Body Count 1997; Spawn 1997; Summer of Sam 1999; Titan AE 2000; Collateral Damage 2001; Moulin Rouge! 2001; What's the Worst That Could Happen? 2001; Empire 2002; Ice Age 2002; Spun 2002; Assault on Precinct 13 2005; George A Romero's Land of the Dead 2005; The Honeymooners 2005; Ice Age: the Meltdown 2006;

Gamer 2008; The Happening 2008; Righteous Kill 2008; Ice Age 3: Dawn of the Dinosaurs 2009; The Lincoln Lawyer 2011; Ice Age 4: Continental Drift 2012; One for the Money 2012; Kick-Ass 2 2013; Walking with Dinosaurs: the 3D Movie 2013; Chef 2014; Cymbeline 2014; Experimenter: the Stanley Milgram Story 2014; Ride Along 2014; American Ultra 2015; Sisters 2015; Ice Age: Collision Course 2016; The Infiltrator 2016

Lehman, Kristin (1972-) Hemoglobin 1997; Dog Park 1998

Lehmann, Beatrix (1903-1979) The Key 1958; Psyche '59 1964; Staircase 1969; The Cat and the Canary 1979

Lehmann, Carla (1917-1990) Sailors Three 1940; Cottage to Let 1941; Secret Mission 1942; Candlelight in Algeria 1943; 29 Acacia Avenue 1945

Lehne, Fredric aka **Lehne, Frederic** aka **Lehne, Fredrick** (1959-) Ordinary People 1980; Amityville: the Evil Escapes 1989; Dream Lover 1993; Man's Best Friend 1993; Payback 1997

Lehne, John (1925-2007) Who? 1974; Bound for Glory 1976; The Disappearance of Aimee 1976; American Hot Wax 1977; Carny 1980; Ladies and Gentlemen, the Fabulous Stains 1981

Lei, Lydia Hammett 1982; Doctor Detroit 1983

Leiber, Fritz (1882-1949) The Story of Louis Pasteur 1936; Pack Up Your Troubles 1939; All This, and Heaven Too 1940; The Web 1947

Leibman, Ron (1937-) Where's Poppa? 1970; The Hot Rock 1972; Slaughterhouse-Five 1972; The Super Cops 1973; Won Ton Ton, the Dog Who Saved Hollywood 1976; Norma Rae 1979; Zorro, the Gay Blade 1981; Phar Lap 1983; Romantic Comedy 1983; Rhinestone 1984; Seven Hours to Judgment 1988; Just the Ticket 1998; Personal Velocity 2001; Auto Focus 2002; Dummy 2002; Garden State 2003

Leigh-Hunt, Barbara (1935-) A Midsummer Night's Dream 1961; Bequest to the Nation 1972; Frenzy 1972; Henry VIII and His Six Wives 1972; Paper Mask 1990; Keep the Aspidistra Flying 1997; The Martins 2001

Leigh-Hunt, Ronald (1916-2005) Where the Bullets Fly 1966; Le Mans 1971

Leigh, Barbara (1946-) Junior Bonner 1972; Seven 1979

Leigh, Janet (1927-2004) If Winter Comes 1947; Hills of Home 1948; Words and Music 1948; Act of Violence 1949; The Doctor and the Girl 1949; The Forsyte Saga 1949; Holiday Affair 1949; Little Women 1949; The Red Danube 1949; Angels in the Outfield 1951; It's a Big Country 1951; Two Tickets to Broadway 1951; Scaramouche 1952; Houdini 1953; The Naked Spur 1953; The Black Shield of Falworth 1954; Living It Up 1954; Prince Valiant 1954; Rogue Cop 1954; My Sister Eileen 1955; Pete Kelly's Blues 1955; Safari 1956; The Perfect Furlough 1958; Touch of Evil 1958; The Vikings 1958; Pepe 1960; Psycho 1960; Who Was That Lady? 1960; The Manchurian Candidate 1962; Bye Bye Birdie 1963; An American Dream 1966; Harper 1966; Kid Rodelo 1966; The Spy in the Green Hat 1966; Three on a Couch 1966; Grand Slam 1967; Hello Down There 1969; One Is a Lonely Number 1972; Boardwalk 1979; The Fog 1980; Halloween H20: 20 Years Later 1998

Leigh, Jennifer Jason (1962-) Eyes of a Stranger 1980; Fast Times at Ridgemont High 1982; Easy Money 1983; Grandview, USA 1984; Flesh + Blood 1985; The Hitcher 1986; The Men's Club 1986; Heart of Midnight 1988; The Big Picture 1989; Last Exit to Brooklyn 1989; Buried Alive 1990; Miami Blues 1990; Backdraft 1991; Crooked Hearts 1991; Rush 1991; Single White Female 1992; Short Cuts 1993; The Hudsucker Proxy 1994; Luck, Trust & Ketchup 1994; Mrs Parker and the Vicious Circle 1994; Dolores Claiborne 1995; Georgia 1995; Kansas City 1995; A Thousand Acres 1997; Washington Square 1997; eXistenZ 1999; The King Is Alive 2000; The Anniversary Party 2001; Crossed Over 2002; Hey Arnold! the Movie 2002; Road to Perdition 2002; In the Cut 2003; The Machinist 2003; Palindromes 2004; The Jacket 2005; Rag Tale 2005; Margot at the Wedding 2007; Synecdoche, New York 2008; Greenberg 2009; Kill Your Darlings 2013; Welcome to Me 2014; Anomalisa 2015; The Hateful Eight 2015; Morgan 2016

Leigh, Nelson (1905-1985) Thief of Damascus 1952; World without End 1955

Leigh, Spencer Caravaggio 1986; The Garden 1990

Leigh, Suzanna (1945-) Boeing Boeing 1965; Deadlier than the Male 1966; Paradise, Hawaiian Style 1966; The Deadly Bees 1967; The Lost Continent 1968; Lust for a Vampire 1970; The Fiend 1971

Leigh, Vivien (1913-1967) Look Up and Laugh 1935; Dark Journey 1937; Fire over England 1937; Storm in a Teacup 1937; 21 Days 1937; St Martin's Lane 1938; A Yank at Oxford 1938; Gone with the Wind 1939; Waterloo Bridge 1940; That Hamilton Woman 1941; Caesar and Cleopatra 1945; Anna Karenina 1947; A Streetcar Named Desire 1951; The Deep Blue Sea 1955; The Roman Spring of Mrs Stone 1961; Ship of Fools 1965

Leighton, Laura (1968-) Mary Higgins Clark's We'll Meet Again 2002; A View from Here 2000

Leighton, Margaret (1922-1976) Bonnie Prince Charlie 1948; The Winslow Boy 1948; The Astonished Heart 1949; Under Capricorn 1949; The Elusive Pimpernel 1950; Calling Bulldog Drummond 1951; The Holly and the Ivy 1952; Home at Seven 1952; Carrington VC 1954; The Good Die Young 1954; The Teckman Mystery 1954; The Constant Husband 1955; The Passionate Stranger 1957; The Sound and the Fury 1959; Waltz of the Toreadors 1962; The Best Man 1964; 7 Women 1966; The Madwoman of Chaillot 1969; The Go-Between 1971; Zee and Co 1971; Bequest to the Nation 1972; Lady Caroline Lamb 1972; From beyond the Grave 1973; Galileo 1974; Great Expectations 1974; Trial by Combat 1976

Leister, Frederick (1885-1970) Next of Kin 1942; We'll Meet Again 1942; The Captive Heart 1946; Green Grow the Rushes 1951; Footsteps in the Fog 1955; The Time of His Life 1955

Leitch, Donovan (1968-) And God Created Woman 1988; The Blob 1988; The In Crowd 1988; Cutting Class 1989; Glory 1989; Love Kills 1998

Leith, Virginia (1932-) Fear and Desire 1953; Black Widow 1954; Violent Saturday 1955; White Feather 1955; A Kiss before Dying 1956; Toward the Unknown 1956; The Brain That Wouldn't Die 1959

Leland, David (1947-) Nothing but Trouble 1944; Gawain and the Green Knight 1973

Lellouche, Gilles (1972-) Love Me If You Dare 2003; Mesrine: Killer Instinct 2008; The Extraordinary Adventures of Adèle Blanc-Sec 2010; Little White Lies 2010; Point Blank 2010; Mea Culpa 2012; The Players 2012; Thérèse Desqueyroux 2012; The Informant 2013; The Connection 2014

Lemaire, Philippe (1927-2004) Cartouche 1961; Arsène Lupin 2004

Lembeck, Harvey (1923-1982) Stalag 17 1953; The Command 1954; Beach Party 1963; Love with the Proper Stranger 1963; Bikini Beach 1964; The Unsinkable Molly Brown 1964; Beach Blanket Bingo 1965; How to Fill a Wild Bikini 1965; Sergeant Deadhead 1965; Fireball 500 1966; The Ghost in the Invisible Bikini 1966; Hello Down There 1969

Lemche, Kris (1978-) Ginger Snaps 2000; My Little Eye 2002; Final Destination 3 2006

Lemercier, Valérie (1964-) Les Visiteurs 1993; Vendredi Soir 2002; Orchestra Seats 2005

Lemke, Anthony Reverse Angle 2008; Family Gathering 2010; Exploding Sun 2013

Lemkow, Tutte (1918-1991) The Captain's Paradise 1953; The Boy Who Stole a Million 1960

Lemme, Steve (1973-) Super Troopers 2001; Broken Lizard's Club Dread 2004; Beerfest 2006

Lemmon, Chris (1954-) Just before Dawn 1980; Yellow Pages 1984; That's Life 1986; Lena's Holiday 1990; Firehead 1991

Lemmon, Jack (1925-2001) It Should Happen to You 1954; Phffft! 1954; Mister Roberts 1955; My Sister Eileen 1955; Three for the Show 1955; You Can't Run Away from It 1956; Fire Down Below 1957; Operation Mad Ball 1957; Bell, Book and Candle 1958; Cowboy 1958; It Happened to Jane 1959; Some Like It Hot 1959; The Apartment 1960; Pepe 1960; The Wackiest Ship in the Army 1961; Days of Wine and Roses 1962; The Notorious Landlady 1962; Irma La Douce 1963; Under the Yum Yum Tree 1963; Good

Neighbor Sam 1964; The Great Race 1965; How to Murder Your Wife 1965; The Fortune Cookie 1966; Luv 1967; The Odd Couple 1968; The April Fools 1969; The Out of Towners 1970; Avanti! 1972; The War between Men and Women 1972; Save the Tiger 1973; The Front Page 1974; The Prisoner of Second Avenue 1974; The Entertainer 1975; Alex and the Gypsy 1976; Airport '77 1977; The China Syndrome 1979; Tribute 1980; Buddy Buddy 1981; Missing 1981; Mass Appeal 1984; Macaroni 1985; That's Life 1986; Dad 1989; JFK 1991; Glengarry Glen Ross 1992; Grumpy Old Men 1993; A Life in the Theater 1993; Short Cuts 1993; Luck, Trust & Ketchup 1994; The Grass Harp 1995; Getting Away with Murder 1996; Grumpier Old Men 1996; Hamlet 1996; My Fellow Americans 1996; 12 Angry Men 1997; The Long Way Home 1998; The Odd Couple II 1998; Inherit the Wind 1999; Tuesdays with Morrie 1999

Lemmons, Kasi (1961-) Vampire's Kiss 1988; The Court-Martial of Jackie Robinson 1990; The Silence of the Lambs 1991; Candyman 1992; Fear of a Black Hat 1992; Hard Target 1993

Lemmy (1945-2015) Eat the Rich 1987; Tromeo & Juliet 1996; Lemmy 2010

Lemon, Geneviève Sweetie 1989; The Piano 1993; Soft Fruit 1999

Lenard, Mark (1928-1996) Star Trek III: the Search for Spock 1984; Star Trek IV: the Voyage Home 1986; Star Trek VI: the Undiscovered Country 1991

Lenart, Istvan The Man from London 2007; Clone 2010

Lengies, Vanessa The Perfect Man 2005; Stick It 2006

Lennix, Harry aka **Lennix, Harry J** (1965-) The Five Heartbeats 1991; Bob Roberts 1992; Mo' Money 1992; Get on the Bus 1996; Titus 1999; Love & Basketball 2000; The Human Stain 2003; Barbershop 2: Back in Business 2004; Ray 2004; Suspect Zero 2004; Lennon, John (1940-1980) A Hard Day's Night 1964; Help! 1965; How I Won the War 1967; Dynamite Chicken 1971; Imagine: John Lennon 1988; The US vs John Lennon 2006

Lennon, Julian (1963-) Hail! Hail! Rock 'n' Roll! 1987; Leaving Las Vegas 1995

Lennon, Sean Moonwalker 1988; A Monster in Paris 2011

Lennon (3), Thomas Reno 911!: Miami 2007; 17 Again 2009; Monster Trucks 2015

Lennox, Annie Revolution 1985; Edward II 1991

Lennox, Kai Beginners 2010; Apartment 143 2011

Leno, Jay (1950-) American Hot Wax 1977; Silver Bears 1977; Americathon 1979; Collision Course 1987; We're Back! A Dinosaur's Story 1993; In & Out 1997; Ice Age: the Meltdown 2006; Igor 2008; Love the Beast 2008

Lenska, Rula (1947-) Alfie Darling 1975; Paradise Grove 2003; Fakers 2004; Gypo 2005; Bait 2015

Lenya, Lotte (1898-1981) The Threepenny Opera 1931; The Roman Spring of Mrs Stone 1961; From Russia with Love 1963; The Appointment 1968; Semi-Tough 1977

Lenz, Kay (1953-) Breezy 1973; White Line Fever 1975; The Great Scout & Cathouse Thursday 1976; The Passage 1978; Fast-Walking 1982; House 1986; Death Wish 4: the Crackdown 1987; Fear 1988; Physical Evidence 1988; Falling from Grace 1992

Lenz, Rick (1939-) Cactus Flower 1969; Scandalous John 1971; Where Does It Hurt? 1971

Leo, Melissa (1960-) Always 1985; A Time of Destiny 1988; Immaculate Conception 1991; Last Summer in the Hamptons 1995; 21 Grams 2003; Hide and Seek 2005; The Three Burials of Melquiades Estrada 2005; Frozen River 2008; According to Greta 2009; Everybody's Fine 2009; Welcome to the Rileys 2009; Conviction 2010; The Fighter 2010; Red State 2011; Flight 2012; Oblivion 2013; Olympus Has Fallen 2013; The Angriest Man in Brooklyn 2014; The Equalizer 2014; The Big Short 2015; All the Way 2016; Snowden 2016

Leon aka **Robinson, Leon** (1962-) The Five Heartbeats 1991; Cliffhanger 1993; Cool Runnings 1993; Above the Rim 1994; Runaway Car 1997; Side Streets 1998; Bats 1999; Buffalo Soldiers 2001

Leon, David (1954-) Boy Eats Girl 2005; The Lives of the Saints 2005; These Foolish Things 2006

Leon, Joseph (1918-2001) Sweet Smell of Success 1957; Act One 1963

Leon, Loles (1950-) Tie Me Up! Tie Me Down! 1990; The Girl of Your Dreams 1998

Leon, Valerie (1945-) *Blood from the Mummy's Tomb* 1971; *Ups and Downs of a Handyman* 1975

Leonard, Joshua (1975-) *The Blair Witch Project* 1998; *Cubbyhouse* 2001; *Scorched* 2002; *Madhouse* 2004; *Humpday* 2009; *The Motel Life* 2012; *If I Stay* 2014

Leonard, Lu (1932-2004) *Circuitry Man* 1990; *Shadowzone* 1990; *Without You I'm Nothing* 1990

Leonard, Queenie (1905-2002) *Moonlight Sonata* 1937; *The Lodger* 1944; *Molly and Me* 1945; *The Narrow Margin* 1952

Leonard, Robert Sean (1969-) *Dead Poets Society* 1989; *Mr and Mrs Bridge* 1990; *The Age of Innocence* 1993; *Much Ado about Nothing* 1993; *Swing Kids* 1993; *Safe Passage* 1994; *Killer: a Journal of Murder* 1995; *The Boys Next Door* 1996; *In the Gloaming* 1997; *The Last Days of Disco* 1998; *Tape* 2001; *The I Inside* 2003; *A Painted House* 2003

Leonard, Sheldon (1907-1997) *Tall, Dark and Handsome* 1941; *Weekend in Havana* 1941; *Tortilla Flat* 1942; *Hit the Ice* 1943; *Passport to Suez* 1943; *The Falcon in Hollywood* 1944; *To Have and Have Not* 1944; *Frontier Gal* 1945; *Abbott and Costello Meet the Invisible Man* 1951; *The Diamond Queen* 1953; *Guys and Dolls* 1955; *The Brink's Job* 1978

Leonardi, Marco (1971-) *Cinema Paradiso* 1988; *Like Water for Chocolate* 1993; *The Stendhal Syndrome* 1996; *The Five Senses* 1999; *From Dusk till Dawn 3: the Hangman's Daughter* 2000; *Black Souls* 2014

Leong, Al (1952-) *Bill & Ted's Excellent Adventure* 1988; *Cage* 1989

Leoni, Téa (1966-) *Bad Boys* 1995; *Flirting with Disaster* 1996; *Deep Impact* 1998; *The Family Man* 2000; *Jurassic Park III* 2001; *Hollywood Ending* 2002; *People I Know* 2002; *Spanglish* 2004; *Fun with Dick and Jane* 2005; *You Kill Me* 2007; *Ghost Town* 2008; *Tower Heist* 2011

Leonidas, Dimitri *Tormented* 2009; *Rosewater* 2014

Leonidas, Stephanie (1984-) *MirrorMask* 2004; *Yes* 2004; *Luna* 2014

Leontovich, Eugenie (1894-1993) *Four Sons* 1940; *The Men in Her Life* 1941; *Anything Can Happen* 1952; *The World in His Arms* 1952; *The Rains of Ranchipur* 1955; *Homicidal* 1961

Leopardi, Chauncey (1981-) *Huck and the King of Hearts* 1993; *The Sandlot* 1993; *The Big Green* 1995; *Houseguest* 1995

Léotard, Philippe (1940-2001) *Anne and Muriel* 1971; *Une Belle Fille comme Moi* 1973; *Kamouraska* 1973; *The Mouth Agape* 1974; *La Balance* 1982; *Le Choc* 1982; *Tangos, Exilo de Gardel* 1985; *Le Paltoquet* 1986; *Sur* 1987; *Death of a Schoolboy* 1990; *Les Misérables* 1995

Lepage, Robert (1957-) *Jesus of Montreal* 1989; *Stardom* 2000

Leprince-Ringuet, Grégoire *Strayed* 2003; *Love Songs* 2007; *The Army of Crime* 2009; *The Princess of Montpensier* 2010

Lerman, Logan (1992-) *A Painted House* 2003; *Hoot* 2006; *The Number 23* 2006; *Gamer* 2008; *Percy Jackson & the Lightning Thief* 2010; *The Three Musketeers* 2011; *The Perks of Being a Wallflower* 2012; *Stuck in Love* 2012; *Percy Jackson: Sea of Monsters* 2013; *Fury* 2014; *Noah* 2014

Lerner, Ken *Relentless* 1989; *Unlawful Entry* 1992

Lerner, Michael (1941-) *Alex in Wonderland* 1970; *The Candidate* 1972; *Newman's Law* 1974; *Dark Victory* 1976; *The Other Side of Midnight* 1977; *Outlaw Blues* 1977; *The Baltimore Bullet* 1980; *Borderline* 1980; *Coast to Coast* 1980; *The Postman Always Rings Twice* 1981; *Threshold* 1981; *National Lampoon's Class Reunion* 1982; *Strange Invaders* 1983; *Movers and Shakers* 1985; *Anguish* 1986; *Vibes* 1988; *Harlem Nights* 1989; *Maniac Cop 2* 1990; *Barton Fink* 1991; *Amos & Andrew* 1993; *Blank Check* 1994; *The Road to Wellville* 1994; *A Pyromaniac's Love Story* 1995; *No Way Back* 1996; *The Beautician and the Beast* 1997; *For Richer or Poorer* 1997; *Godzilla* 1997; *Talos the Mummy* 1997; *Safe Men* 1998; *My Favorite Martian* 1999; *The Calcium Kid* 2003; *Elf* 2003; *Life during Wartime* 2009

Lerner, Sam *Monster House* 2006; *Project Almanac* 2014

Leroux, Adelaïde *Flanders* 2005; *Home* 2008

Leroy-Beaulieu, Philippine (1963-) *3 Men and a Cradle* 1985; *Nine Months* 1994; *Two Brothers* 2004

LeRoy, Baby (1932-) *Tillie and Gus* 1933; *It's a Gift* 1934; *The Lemon Drop Kid* 1934; *The Old-Fashioned Way* 1934

LeRoy, Gloria *Welcome to Arrow Beach* 1974; *Barfly* 1987; *Cool Blue* 1988

Leroy, Philippe (1930-) *Le Trou* 1959; *The Married Woman* 1964; *The Night Porter* 1973

Lesaffre, Roland (1927-2009) *Thérèse Raquin* 1953; *Les Tricheurs* 1958; *Trois Chambres à Manhattan* 1965

Lesley, Carole (1935-1974) *Woman in a Dressing Gown* 1957; *Operation Bullshine* 1959; *Doctor in Love* 1960; *Three on a Spree* 1961; *What a Whopper!* 1961; *The Pot Carriers* 1962

Leslie, Bethel (1929-1999) *Captain Newman, MD* 1963; *The Molly Maguires* 1970; *Old Boyfriends* 1979

Leslie, Ewen *Sleeping Beauty* 2011; *Dead Europe* 2012; *The Daughter* 2016

Leslie, Joan (1925-2015) *High Sierra* 1941; *Sergeant York* 1941; *The Wagons Roll at Night* 1941; *The Hard Way* 1942; *The Male Animal* 1942; *Yankee Doodle Dandy* 1942; *The Sky's the Limit* 1943; *Thank Your Lucky Stars* 1943; *This Is the Army* 1943; *Hollywood Canteen* 1944; *Rhapsody in Blue* 1945; *Where Do We Go from Here?* 1945; *Cinderella Jones* 1946; *Repeat Performance* 1947; *Born to Be Bad* 1950; *Man in the Saddle* 1951; *Hellgate* 1952; *The Woman They Almost Lynched* 1953; *The Revolt of Mamie Stover* 1956

Leslie, Nan (1926-2000) *The Devil Thumbs a Ride* 1947; *The Woman on the Beach* 1947; *Guns of Hate* 1948

Leslie, Rose *Honeymoon* 2014; *The Last Witch Hunter* 2015; *Morgan* 2016

Leslie, William (1925-2005) *Bring Your Smile Along* 1955; *The Long Gray Line* 1955; *The Lineup* 1958; *Up Periscope* 1959

Lespert, Jalil (1976-) *Human Resources* 1999; *Pas sur la Bouche* 2003; *The Last Mitterrand* 2005

Lesser, Anton (1952-) *The Assam Garden* 1985; *Esther Kahn* 2000; *Charlotte Gray* 2001; *Otherworld* 2003; *River Queen* 2005; *Miss Potter* 2006; *Closer to the Moon* 2014

Lessey, George (1879-1947) *Sky Murder* 1940; *Strike Up the Band* 1940; *Blossoms in the Dust* 1941

Lester, Adrian (1970-) *Up on the Roof* 1997; *Primary Colors* 1998; *Love's Labour's Lost* 1999; *Maybe Baby* 1999; *Born Romantic* 2000; *Dust* 2001; *The Final Curtain* 2002; *The Day after Tomorrow* 2004; *As You Like It* 2006; *Scenes of a Natural Nature* 2006; *Case 39* 2008; *Doomsday* 2008

Lester, Bruce (1912-2008) *Boy Meets Girl* 1938; *British Intelligence* 1940; *The Letter* 1940; *My Son, My Son!* 1940; *Pride and Prejudice* 1940; *Golden Earrings* 1947

Lester, Buddy (1917-2002) *Sergeants 3* 1962; *Three on a Couch* 1966; *The Big Mouth* 1967; *The Party* 1968

Lester (2), Mark (1958-) *Our Mother's House* 1967; *Oliver!* 1968; *Run Wild, Run Free* 1969; *Eyewitness* 1970; *Black Beauty* 1971; *Melody* 1971; *Who Slew Auntie Roo?* 1971; *Scalawag* 1973; *The Prince and the Pauper* 1977

Lester, Ron (1970-2016) *Good Burger* 1997; *Varsity Blues* 1999

Lester, Vicki *The Mad Miss Manton* 1938; *Tom, Dick and Harry* 1941

Letch, David *Sylvia* 1984; *Mr Wrong* 1985

Leto, Jared (1971-) *Last of the High Kings* 1996; *Prefontaine* 1997; *Switchback* 1997; *Basil* 1998; *Urban Legend* 1998; *Black and White* 1999; *Fight Club* 1999; *Girl, Interrupted* 1999; *American Psycho* 2000; *Requiem for a Dream* 2000; *Sunset Strip* 2000; *Panic Room* 2002; *Alexander* 2004; *Lord of War* 2005; *Lonely Hearts* 2006; *Dallas Buyers Club* 2013; *Suicide Squad* 2016

Letondal, Henri (1901-1955) *On the Riviera* 1951; *Monkey Business* 1952

Letscher, Matt (1970-) *The Mask of Zorro* 1998; *When Billie Beat Bobby* 2001; *Amish Grace* 2010

Lett, Dan *Under the Piano* 1995; *The Secret Laughter of Women* 1998

Lettieri, Al aka **Lettieri, Alfredo** (1928-1975) *The Bobo* 1967; *The Getaway* 1972; *Pulp* 1972; *The Deadly Trackers* 1973; *Mr Majestyk* 1974

Lettinger, Rudolf (1865-1937) *The Cabinet of Dr Caligari* 1919; *The Spiders* 1919

Leung Siu-lung *Kung Fu Hustle* 2004; *Gallants* 2010

Leung, Andrew *Lilting* 2014; *Containment* 2015

Leung, Anson *Ab-normal Beauty* 2004; *One Nite in Mongkok* 2004

Leung (1), Tony aka **Leung, Tony Kar-Fai** aka **Leung, Tony** aka **Leung Kar-Fai, Tony** aka **Leung Ka-fai, Tony** aka **Leung Ka Fai, Tony** (1958-) *A Better Tomorrow III* 1989; *The Actress* 1992; *The Lover* 1992; *Ashes of Time* 1994; *Double Vision* 2002; *Election* 2005; *Detective Dee and the Mystery of the Phantom Flame* 2010

Leung (2), Tony aka **Leung, Tony Chiu-Wai** aka **Leung Chiu-Wai, Tony** (1962-) *A City of Sadness* 1989; *Bullet in the Head* 1990; *Days of Being Wild* 1990; *Hard-Boiled* 1992; *Ashes of Time* 1994; *Chung King Express* 1994; *Cyclo* 1995; *Happy Together* 1997; *Flowers of Shanghai* 1998; *In the Mood for Love* 2000; *Tokyo Raiders* 2000; *Chinese Odyssey 2002* 2002; *Hero* 2002; *Infernal Affairs* 2002; *Infernal Affairs 3* 2003; *2046* 2004; *Lust, Caution* 2007; *Red Cliff* 2008

Levant, Oscar (1906-1972) *Rhythm on the River* 1940; *Kiss the Boys Goodbye* 1941; *Humoresque* 1946; *Romance on the High Seas* 1948; *You Were Meant for Me* 1948; *The Barkleys of Broadway* 1949; *An American in Paris* 1951; *The I Don't Care Girl* 1952; *O Henry's Full House* 1952; *The Band Wagon* 1953

Levels, Calvin (1954-) *A Night on the Town* 1987; *Johnny Suede* 1991

Levene, Sam (1905-1980) *The Mad Miss Manton* 1938; *Golden Boy* 1939; *Shadow of the Thin Man* 1941; *The Big Street* 1942; *Action in the North Atlantic* 1943; *I Dood It* 1943; *The Killers* 1946; *Boomerang!* 1947; *Brute Force* 1947; *Crossfire* 1947; *Killer McCoy* 1947; *The Babe Ruth Story* 1948; *Three Sailors and a Girl* 1953; *Designing Woman* 1957; *Sweet Smell of Success* 1957; *Act One* 1963; *A Dream of Kings* 1969; *...And Justice for All* 1979; *Last Embrace* 1979

Lever, Johnny (1950-) *Baazigar* 1993; *Koi... Mil Gaya* 2003

Levesque, Joanna "JoJo" (1990-) *Aquamarine* 2006; *RV* 2006

Levi, Zachary (1980-) *Big Momma's House 2* 2006; *Alvin and the Chipmunks: the Squeakquel* 2009; *Tangled* 2010

Levieva, Margarita *The Invisible* 2007; *Spread* 2008; *For Ellen* 2012; *The Diary of a Teenage Girl* 2015

Levine, Anna aka **Thomson, Anna** (1957-) *Unforgiven* 1992; *Hand Gun* 1994; *Angus* 1995; *Other Voices, Other Rooms* 1995; *Water Drops on Burning Rocks* 1999

Levine, Jerry (1957-) *Teen Wolf* 1985; *Casual Sex?* 1988

Levine, Samm *Pulse* 2006; *Inglourious Basterds* 2009

Levine, Ted (1958-) *Betrayed* 1988; *The Fulfillment of Mary Gray* 1989; *The Silence of the Lambs* 1991; *Nowhere to Run* 1992; *Death Train* 1993; *The Last Outlaw* 1993; *The Mangler* 1994; *Bullet* 1995; *Georgia* 1995; *Flubber* 1997; *Mad City* 1997; *Switchback* 1997; *You Can Thank Me Later* 1998; *Wild Wild West* 1999; *Evolution* 2001; *The Truth about Charlie* 2002; *Wonderland* 2003; *The Manchurian Candidate* 2004; *The Hills Have Eyes* 2006; *American Gangster* 2007; *Big Game* 2014

Levy, Ariel *Aftershock* 2012; *The Green Inferno* 2013

Levy, Eugene (1946-) *Cannibal Girls* 1973; *Running* 1979; *Going Berserk* 1983; *Splash* 1984; *Armed and Dangerous* 1986; *Club Paradise* 1986; *Stay Tuned* 1992; *Multiplicity* 1996; *Waiting for Guffman* 1996; *Almost Heroes* 1998; *American Pie* 1999; *Best in Show* 2000; *American Pie 2* 2001; *Down to Earth* 2001; *Serendipity* 2001; *American Pie: the Wedding* 2003; *Bringing Down the House* 2003; *Dumb and Dumberer: When Harry Met Lloyd* 2003; *A Mighty Wind* 2003; *New York Minute* 2004; *American Pie Presents Band Camp* 2005; *Cheaper by the Dozen 2* 2005; *The Man* 2005; *American Pie Presents the Naked Mile* 2006; *Curious George* 2006; *For Your Consideration* 2006; *Over the Hedge* 2006; *Taking Woodstock* 2009; *Goon* 2011; *American Reunion* 2012; *Finding Dory* 2016

Levy, Jane *Fun Size* 2012; *Evil Dead* 2013; *Monster Trucks* 2016

Levy, Ori *Before Winter Comes* 1968; *The Chairman* 1969; *Moon Zero Two* 1969; *The Sellout* 1975

Lewgoy, José (1920-2003) *Fitzcarraldo* 1982; *Blame It on Rio* 1984; *Kiss of the Spider Woman* 1985; *Cobra Verde* 1988

Lewis, Al (1923-2006) *Munster, Go Home!* 1966; *They Shoot Horses, Don't They?* 1969

Lewis, Carl *Atomic Twister* 2002; *9.79** 2012

Lewis, Charlotte (1967-) *The Golden Child* 1986; *Pirates* 1986; *Storyville* 1992; *Excessive Force* 1993; *Embrace of the Vampire* 1994; *The Glass Cage* 1996

Lewis, Damian (1971-) *Daniel Defoe's Robinson Crusoe* 1996; *Dreamcatcher* 2003; *Keane* 2004; *Chromophobia* 2005; *An Unfinished Life* 2005; *Stormbreaker* 2006; *The Baker* 2007; *The Escapist* 2007; *Your Highness* 2010; *Will* 2011; *Romeo & Juliet* 2012; *The Sweeney* 2012; *The Silent Storm* 2014; *Queen of the Desert* 2015; *Our Kind of Traitor* 2016

Lewis (1), David (1916-2000) *That Certain Feeling* 1956; *The Apartment* 1960; *Generation* 1969

Lewis, Diana (1919-1997) *Bitter Sweet* 1940; *Go West* 1940; *The People vs Dr Kildare* 1941; *Cry Havoc* 1943

Lewis, Fiona (1946-) *Otley* 1968; *Where's Jack?* 1969; *Villain* 1971; *Blue Blood* 1973; *Dracula* 1974; *Lisztomania* 1975; *Drum* 1976; *The Fury* 1978; *Wanda Nevada* 1979; *Strange Invaders* 1983; *Innerspace* 1987

Lewis, Forrest (1899-1977) *Take Me to Town* 1953; *Man's Favorite Sport?* 1964

Lewis, Gary (1946-) *Carla's Song* 1996; *My Name Is Joe* 1998; *Orphans* 1998; *Postmortem* 1999; *Billy Elliot* 2000; *The Escapist* 2002; *Gangs of New York* 2002; *Pure* 2002; *The Rocket Post* 2003; *Yes* 2004; *Merry Christmas* 2005; *True North* 2006; *Blessed* 2007; *Three and Out* 2008; *Valhalla Rising* 2009; *Catch Me Daddy* 2014

Lewis, Geoffrey (1935-2015) *The Culpepper Cattle Co* 1972; *Dillinger* 1973; *Macon County Line* 1973; *Thunderbolt and Lightfoot* 1974; *The Great Waldo Pepper* 1975; *Lucky Lady* 1975; *Smile* 1975; *The Wind and the Lion* 1975; *The Return of a Man Called Horse* 1976; *Every Which Way but Loose* 1978; *Salem's Lot* 1979; *Any Which Way You Can* 1980; *Bronco Billy* 1980; *10 to Midnight* 1983; *Lust in the Dust* 1984; *Night of the Comet* 1984; *Pink Cadillac* 1989; *Tango & Cash* 1989; *Disturbed* 1990; *Double Impact* 1991; *Wishman* 1991; *The Lawnmower Man* 1992; *The Man without a Face* 1993; *Only the Strong* 1993; *Maverick* 1994; *White Fang 2: Myth of the White Wolf* 1994; *American Perfekt* 1997; *A Painted House* 2003; *Down in the Valley* 2004; *Plainsong* 2004; *Wild Hearts* 2006

Lewis, Harry (1920-) *Key Largo* 1948; *Gun Crazy* 1949

Lewis, Huey (1950-) *Shadow of Doubt* 1998; *Duets* 2000

Lewis, Jason *Mr Brooks* 2007; *Sex and the City: the Movie* 2008; *Nora Roberts' Tribute* 2009; *Sex and the City 2* 2010

Lewis, Jenifer (1957-) *Tina: What's Love Got to Do with It* 1993; *Corrina, Corrina* 1994; *Girl 6* 1996; *The Preacher's Wife* 1996; *Partners* 2000; *Not Easily Broken* 2009; *The Princess and the Frog* 2009

Lewis, Jenny (1976-) *Trading Hearts* 1988; *Shannon's Deal* 1989; *Foxfire* 1996

Lewis, Jerry (1926-) *My Friend Irma* 1949; *At War with the Army* 1950; *My Friend Irma Goes West* 1950; *Sailor Beware* 1951; *The Stooge* 1951; *That's My Boy* 1951; *Jumping Jacks* 1952; *The Caddy* 1953; *Money from Home* 1953; *Scared Stiff* 1953; *Living It Up* 1954; *Three Ring Circus* 1954; *Artists and Models* 1955; *You're Never Too Young* 1955; *Hollywood or Bust* 1956; *Pardners* 1956; *The Delicate Delinquent* 1957; *The Sad Sack* 1957; *The Geisha Boy* 1958; *Rock-a-Bye Baby* 1958; *Don't Give Up the Ship* 1959; *Li'l Abner* 1959; *The Bellboy* 1960; *Cinderfella* 1960; *The Errand Boy* 1961; *The Ladies' Man* 1961; *It'S Only Money* 1962; *The Nutty Professor* 1963; *Who's Minding the Store?* 1963; *The Disorderly Orderly* 1964; *The Patsy* 1964; *Boeing Boeing* 1965; *The Family Jewels* 1965; *Three on a Couch* 1966; *The Big Mouth* 1967; *Don't Raise the Bridge, Lower the River* 1968; *Which Way to the Front?* 1970; *The King of Comedy* 1983; *Cookie* 1989; *Arizona Dream* 1991; *Mr Saturday Night* 1992; *Funny Bones* 1994; *The Trust* 2016

Lewis, Jerry Lee (1935-) *High School Confidential* 1958; *Hail! Hail! Rock 'n' Roll!* 1987

Lewis, Johnny (1983-2012) *AVPR: Aliens vs Predator Requiem* 2007; *One Missed Call* 2007; *Lovely Molly* 2012

Lewis, Juliette (1973-) *National Lampoon's Christmas Vacation* 1989; *Cape Fear* 1991; *Crooked Hearts* 1991; *Husbands and Wives* 1992; *Romeo Is Bleeding* 1992; *That Night* 1992; *Kalifornia* 1993; *What's Eating Gilbert Grape* 1993; *Mixed Nuts* 1994; *Natural Born Killers* 1994; *The Basketball Diaries* 1995; *From Dusk till Dawn* 1995; *Strange Days* 1995; *The Evening Star* 1996; *The Other Sister* 1999; *Room to Rent* 2000; *The Way of the Gun* 2000; *Enough* 2002; *Hysterical Blindness* 2002; *Cold Creek Manor* 2003; *Old School* 2003; *Blueberry* 2004; *Starsky & Hutch* 2004; *Catch and Release* 2007; *Whip It* 2009; *Conviction* 2010; *Due Date* 2010; *The Switch* 2010; *August: Osage County* 2013; *Hellion* 2014; *Jem and the Holograms* 2015

Lewis, Matthew *Harry Potter and the Goblet of Fire* 2005; *The Rise* 2012

Lewis, Mitchell (1880-1956) *Salome* 1922; *Beau Sabreur* 1928; *The Docks of New York* 1928; *Ann Vickers* 1933

Lewis, Ralph (1872-1937) *The Escape* 1914; *The Birth of a Nation* 1915; *Dillinger* 1945

Lewis, Richard (1947-) *Once upon a Crime* 1992; *Robin Hood: Men in Tights* 1993; *Wagons East!* 1994; *Leaving Las Vegas* 1995

Lewis, Robert Q (1921-1991) *An Affair to Remember* 1957; *Ski Party* 1965

Lewis, Ronald (1928-1982) *The Square Ring* 1953; *The Prisoner* 1955; *Storm over the Nile* 1955; *A Hill in Korea* 1956; *Sailor Beware!* 1956; *Robbery under Arms* 1957; *Bachelor of Hearts* 1958; *The Wind Cannot Read* 1958; *Conspiracy of Hearts* 1960; *The Full Treatment* 1961; *Mr Sardonicus* 1961; *Taste of Fear* 1961; *Billy Budd* 1962; *Jigsaw* 1962; *Twice round the Daffodils* 1962; *Nurse on Wheels* 1963; *The Siege of the Saxons* 1963; *Paul and Michelle* 1974

Lewis, Stephen (1936-2015) *Staircase* 1969; *On the Buses* 1971; *Mutiny on the Buses* 1972; *Holiday on the Buses* 1973

Lewis, Tommy aka **Lewis, Tom E** (1957-) *The Chant of Jimmie Blacksmith* 1978; *We of the Never Never* 1982; *The Naked Country* 1985; *Red Hill* 2010

Lewis, Vera (1873-1956) *Stella Dallas* 1925; *The Iron Mask* 1929; *Man on the Flying Trapeze* 1935

Lewis, Vicki (1960-) *Mousehunt* 1997; *The Ugly Truth* 2009

Lexy, Edward (1897-1970) *The Mark of Cain* 1947; *Blanche Fury* 1948; *Night Was Our Friend* 1951

Leysen, Johan (1950-) *The Girl with Red Hair* 1981; *Je Vous Salue, Marie* 1984; *The Music Teacher* 1988; *True Blue* 1996; *The Gambler* 1997; *Le Roi Danse* 2000; *Tattoo* 2002; *The American* 2010; *Jeune & Jolie* 2013

Leyton, John (1939-) *The Great Escape* 1963; *Every Day's a Holiday* 1964; *Guns at Batasi* 1964; *Von Ryan's Express* 1965; *The Idol* 1966; *Schizo* 1976

Leza, Conchita *Valentina* 1982; *1919* 1983

Lhermitte, Thierry (1957-) *Until September* 1984; *Le Cop* 1985; *Le Cop II* 1989; *Love in the Strangest Way* 1994; *An American Werewolf in Paris* 1997; *Le Dîner de Cons* 1998; *The Closet* 2001; *And Now... Ladies and Gentlemen* 2002; *Le Divorce* 2003; *Strange Gardens* 2003

Li Baotian *Ju Dou* 1990; *Shanghai Triad* 1995; *Keep Cool* 1997

Li Jai-Xing *The Legend* 1993; *The Legend II* 1993

Li Kangsheng *The River* 1997; *The Hole* 1998

Li Tianlu (?-1998) *Dust in the Wind* 1987; *A City of Sadness* 1989; *The Puppetmaster* 1993

Li Wei (1919-2005) *Spring in a Small Town* 1948; *Ju Dou* 1990

Li Xuejian *Shanghai Triad* 1995; *The Emperor and the Assassin* 1999; *Happy Times* 2001

Li, Bingbing aka **Lee Bingbing** *The Forbidden Kingdom* 2008; *1911* 2011; *Snow Flower and the Secret Fan* 2011

Li, Jet (1963-) *Once upon a Time in China* 1991; *Once upon a Time in China II* 1992; *The Legend* 1993; *The Legend II* 1993; *Twin Warriors* 1993; *The Defender* 1994; *Fist of Legend* 1994; *The Enforcer* 1995; *Black Mask* 1996; *Lethal Weapon 4* 1998; *Romeo Must Die* 2000; *Kiss of the Dragon* 2001; *The One* 2001; *Hero* 2002; *Cradle 2 the Grave* 2003; *Unleashed* 2005; *Fearless* 2006; *War* 2007; *The Forbidden Kingdom* 2008; *The Mummy: Tomb of the Dragon Emperor* 2008; *The Warlords* 2008; *The Expendables* 2010; *Flying Swords of Dragon Gate* 2011; *The Expendables 2* 2012

Liao Fan *Assembly* 2007; *Chinese Zodiac* 2012; *Black Coal, Thin Ice* 2014

Liao, James aka L ao, James Hiroyuki *Hard Luck* 2006; *Management* 2008

Libaire, Dorothy *Baby, Take a Bow* 1934; *Murder on a Honeymoon* 1935

Libéreau, Johan *The Witnesses* 2006; *Grand Central* 2013

Liberace (1919-1987) *Sincerely Yours* 1955; *The Loved One* 1965

Liberato, Liana (1995-) *Trust* 2010; *Trespass* 2011; *The Expatriate* 2012; *The Best of Me* 2014

Libertini, Richard (1933-2016) *Don't Drink the Water* 1969; *The In-Laws* 1979; *Popeye* 1980; *Sharky's Machine* 1981; *Unfaithfully Yours* 1983; *All of Me* 1984; *Big Trouble* 1985; *Animal Behavior* 1989; *Fletch Lives* 1989; *The Lemon Sisters* 1989; *Duck Tales: the Movie - Treasure of the Lost Lamp* 1990; *Nell* 1994; *Telling You* 1998; *A Grandpa for Christmas* 2007

Liberty, Richard 1932-2000) *The Crazies* 1973; *Day of the Dead* 1985

Libman, Andrea (1984-) *Andre* 1994; *Madeline: Lost in Paris* 1999

Libolt, Alain *Army of Shadows* 1969; *An Autumn Tale* 1998; *The Lady & the Duke* 2001

Lichtenstein, Mitchell (1956-) *Streamers* 1983; *The Wedding Banquet* 1993

Liden, Anki *Father to Be* 1979; *My Life as a Dog* 1985

Liebmann, Gerhard *Lourdes* 2009; *Breathing* 2011; *Blood Glacier* 2013

Lien, Jennifer (1974-) *American History X* 1998; *SLC Punk!* 1999

Lieven, Albert (1906-1971) *For Freedom* 1940; *Jeannie* 1941; *Yellow Canary* 1943; *The Seventh Veil* 1945; *Beware of Pity* 1946; *Frieda* 1947; *Sleeping Car to Trieste* 1948; *The Dark Light* 1951; *Hotel Sahara* 1951; *Desperate Moment* 1953; *The Devil's General* 1955; *Subway in the Sky* 1958; *Conspiracy of Hearts* 1960; *Foxhole in Cairo* 1960

Lifford, Tina *Grand Canyon* 1991; *Paris Trout* 1991; *Mandela and de Klerk* 1997; *Blood Work* 2002

Light, Judith (1949-) *My Boyfriend's Back* 1989; *Joseph: King of Dreams* 2000

Lightner, Winnie (1899-1971) *Gold Diggers of Broadway* 1929; *Dancing Lady* 1933

Lightning, Cody *Smoke Signals* 1998; *Manic* 2001

Lightstone, Marilyn (1941-) *Lies My Father Told Me* 1975; *In Praise of Older Women* 1978; *Heavy Metal* 1981

Lillard, Matthew (1970-) *Serial Mom* 1994; *Hackers* 1995; *Mad Love* 1995; *Scream* 1996; *Dead Man's Curve* 1997; *Senseless* 1998; *Telling You* 1998; *Without Limits* 1998; *Love's Labour's Lost* 1999; *SLC Punk!* 1999; *She's All That* 1999; *Wing Commander* 1999; *Summer Catch* 2001; *Thir13en Ghosts* 2001; *Scooby-Doo* 2002; *The Perfect Score* 2004; *Scooby-Doo 2: Monsters Unleashed* 2004; *Wicker Park* 2004; *Without a Paddle* 2004; *The Descendants* 2011; *Trouble with the Curve* 2012

Lillie, Beatrice (1894-1989) *Doctor Rhythm* 1938; *Thoroughly Modern Millie* 1967

Lilly, Evangeline (1979-) *The Hurt Locker* 2008; *Real Steel* 2011; *The Hobbit: the Desolation of Smaug* 2013; *The Hobbit: the Battle of the Five Armies* 2014; *Ant-Man* 2015

Lim Kay Siu *Night Watch* 1995; *Anna and the King* 1999

Lim Kay Tong *Shanghai Surprise* 1986; *Saigon* 1988; *Fifty/Fifty* 1991; *Dragon: the Bruce Lee Story* 1993

Lin Xiuling *A Summer at Grandpa's* 1984; *Taipei Story* 1984

Lin, Brigitte aka **Lin Ching Hsia** aka **Lin Ching Hsia, Brigitte** aka **Lin, Qingxia** (1954-) *Zu Warriors* 1983; *Police Story* 1985; *Peking Opera Blues* 1986; *Peking Opera Blues* 1986; *The Bride with White Hair* 1993; *Ashes of Time* 1994; *Chung King Express* 1994

Lin, Kelly *Fulltime Killer* 2002; *Mad Detective* 2007; *Sparrow* 2008

Linaker, Kay (1913-2008) *Crack-Up* 1936; *Charlie Chan at Monte Carlo* 1937

Lincoln, Abbey (1930-2010) *Nothing but a Man* 1964; *For Love of Ivy* 1968

Lincoln, Andrew (1973-) *Boston Kickout* 1995; *Gangster No 1* 2000; *Offending Angels* 2000; *Enduring Love* 2004; *Scenes of a Sexual Nature* 2006; *These Foolish Things* 2006

Lind, Emily Alyn *November Christmas* 2010; *Lights Out* 2016

Lind, Gillian (1904-1983) *The Oracle* 1952; *Don't Talk to Strange Men* 1962

Lind, Traci aka **Lin, Traci** (1966-) *Fright Night Part 2* 1988; *Class of 1999* 1990; *The Handmaid's Tale* 1990; *Voyager* 1991; *My Boyfriend's Back*

1993; *The Road to Wellville* 1994; *The End of Violence* 1997

Lindberg, Chad (1976-) *The Velocity of Gary* 1998; *October Sky* 1999; *The Fast and the Furious* 2001; *The Rookie* 2002

Lindberg, Sven (1918-2006) *Dreams* 1955; *Face to Face* 1976

Lindblom, Gunnel (1935-) *The Virgin Spring* 1960; *Winter Light* 1962; *The Silence* 1963; *Rapture* 1965; *Hunger* 1966

Linden, Eric (1909-1994) *The Crowd Roars* 1932; *Life Begins* 1932; *The Roadhouse Murder* 1932; *The Silver Cord* 1933; *Ah, Wilderness!* 1935; *Let 'Em Have It* 1935; *A Family Affair* 1937

Linden, Hal (1931-) *Starflight One* 1983; *A New Life* 1988

Linden, Jennie (1939-) *Nightmare* 1963; *Dr Who and the Daleks* 1965; *Women in Love* 1969; *A Severed Head* 1970; *Hedda* 1975; *Vampira* 1975

Linden, Marta (1903-1990) *A Yank at Eton* 1942; *The Youngest Production* 1943; *Keep Your Powder Dry* 1945

Linder, Cec (1921-1992) *Subway in the Sky* 1958; *Goldfinger* 1964; *A Touch of Class* 1973; *Sunday in the Country* 1975

Lindfors, Viveca (1920-1995) *Adventures of Don Juan* 1948; *Night unto Night* 1949; *Backfire* 1950; *No Sad Songs for Me* 1950; *The Raiders* 1952; *Moonfleet* 1955; *Run for Cover* 1955; *The Halliday Brand* 1957; *I Accuse!* 1958; *Tempest* 1959; *The Story of Ruth* 1960; *The Damned* 1961; *King of Kings* 1961; *Sylvia* 1964; *Brainstorm* 1965; *Cauldron of Blood* 1967; *Puzzle of a Downfall Child* 1970; *The Way We Were* 1973; *Welcome to LA* 1976; *The Hand* 1981; *A Doctor's Story* 1984; *Passions* 1984; *Yellow Pages* 1984; *The Sure Thing* 1985; *The Linguini Incident* 1991; *Zandalee* 1991; *Stargate* 1994; *Last Summer in the Hamptons* 1995

Lindhardt, Thure *Brotherhood* 2008; *Keep the Lights On* 2012; *Kill Command* 2016

Lindinger, Natacha *Double Team* 1997; *Coco Chanel & Igor Stravinsky* 2009

Lindley, Audra (1918-1997) *Taking Off* 1971; *The Heartbreak Kid* 1972; *Best Friends* 1982; *Cannery Row* 1982; *Desert Hearts* 1985; *Spellbinder* 1988; *Bridesmaids* 1989; *Troop Beverly Hills* 1989

Lindo, Delroy (1952-) *Mountains of the Moon* 1989; *The Salute of the Jugger* 1989; *Bright Angel* 1990; *The Hard Way* 1991; *Blood In Blood Out* 1992; *Malcolm X* 1992; *Mr Jones* 1993; *Crooklyn* 1994; *Clockers* 1995; *Get Shorty* 1995; *Broken Arrow* 1996; *Feeling Minnesota* 1996; *Ransom* 1996; *Soul of the Game* 1996; *The Winner* 1996; *A Life Less Ordinary* 1997; *The Cider House Rules* 1999; *Strange Justice* 1999; *Gone in Sixty Seconds* 2000; *Romeo Must Die* 2000; *Heist* 2001; *The Last Castle* 2001; *The One* 2001; *The Core* 2002; *Profoundly Normal* 2003; *Wondrous Oblivion* 2003; *Sahara* 2005; *This Christmas* 2007; *Up* 2009; *Point Break* 2015

Lindo, Olga (1899-1968) *The Last Journey* 1936; *Return to Yesterday* 1940; *Time Flies* 1944; *Obsession* 1948; *Train of Events* 1949; *An Inspector Calls* 1954; *Raising a Riot* 1955; *Yield to the Night* 1956; *Make Mine a Million* 1959; *Sapphire* 1959

Lindon, Vincent (1959-) *A Man in Love* 1987; *La Crise* 1992; *Vendredi Soir* 2002; *Anything for Her* 2008; *Mademoiselle Chambon* 2009; *Welcome* 2009; *Mea Culpa* 2012; *Bastards* 2013; *The Measure of a Man* 2015

Lindsay, Margaret (1910-1981) *Baby Face* 1933; *Lady Killer* 1933; *The World Changes* 1933; *Fog over Frisco* 1934; *Bordertown* 1935; *Dangerous* 1935; *Devil Dogs of the Air* 1935; *Frisco Kid* 1935; *"G" Men* 1935; *Isle of Fury* 1936; *Green Light* 1937; *Slim* 1937; *Gold Is Where You Find It* 1938; *Jezebel* 1938; *Hell's Kitchen* 1939; *British Intelligence* 1940; *Ellery Queen Master Detective* 1940; *The House of the Seven Gables* 1940; *The Spoilers* 1942; *Crime Doctor* 1943; *Scarlet Street* 1945; *The Vigilantes Return* 1947; *BF's Daughter* 1948; *The Restless Years* 1958; *Tammy and the Doctor* 1963

Lindsay, Nigel *Rogue Trader* 1998; *First Night* 2010; *Four Lions* 2010; *Breakfast with Jonny Wilkinson* 2013

Lindsay, Robert (1949-) *That'll Be the Day* 1973; *Adventures of a Taxi Driver* 1975; *Bert Rigby, You're a Fool* 1989; *Loser Takes All* 1990; *Remember Me?* 1996; *Fierce Creatures* 1997; *Divorcing Jack* 1998; *Wimbledon* 2004; *Grace of Monaco* 2014

Lindström, Jörgen (1951-) *The Silence* 1963; *Persona* 1966

Lineback, Richard (1952-) *Speed* 1994; *The Jackal* 1997; *Varsity Blues* 1999

Linehan, Rosaleen (1937-) *A Portrait of the Artist as a Young Man* 1977; *About Adam* 2000

Linklater, Hamish (1976-) *Groove* 2000; *Fantastic Four* 2005; *The Future* 2011; *Lola Versus* 2012; *Magic in the Moonlight* 2014

Linklater, Richard (1961-) *Slacker* 1989; *Beavis and Butt-head Do America* 1996

Linley, Cody *When Zachary Beaver Came to Town* 2003; *Hoot* 2006

Linn-Baker, Mark (1954-) *My Favorite Year* 1982; *Noises Off* 1992; *Laughter on the 23rd Floor* 2000; *Adam* 2009; *How Do You Know* 2010

Linn, Rex (1956-) *Cliffhanger* 1993; *CutThroat Island* 1995; *Tin Cup* 1996; *Breakdown* 1997; *Blast from the Past* 1998; *Rush Hour* 1998

Linnane, Joe (1910-1981) *The Woman in Question* 1950; *Hunted* 1952; *The Angel Who Pawned Her Harp* 1954

Linney, Laura (1964-) *Lorenzo's Oil* 1992; *A Simple Twist of Fate* 1994; *Congo* 1995; *Absolute Power* 1996; *Primal Fear* 1996; *The Truman Show* 1998; *Love Letters* 1999; *You Can Count on Me* 1999; *The House of Mirth* 2000; *The Mothman Prophecies* 2001; *The Laramie Project* 2002; *The Life of David Gale* 2003; *Love Actually* 2003; *Mystic River* 2003; *Kinsey* 2004; *The Exorcism of Emily Rose* 2005; *The Squid and the Whale* 2005; *Breach* 2006; *Driving Lessons* 2006; *Jindabyne* 2006; *Man of the Year* 2006; *The Nanny Diaries* 2007; *The Savages* 2007; *The Other Man* 2008; *Hyde Park on Hudson* 2012; *The Fifth Estate* 2013; *Mr Holmes* 2014; *Genius* 2015; *Nocturnal Animals* 2016; *Sully* 2016; *Teenage Mutant Ninja Turtles - Out of the Shadows* 2016

Linow, Ivan (1888-1940) *The Red Dance* 1928; *The Unholy Three* 1930; *Scarlet Dawn* 1932

Linville, Joanne (1928-) *Gable and Lombard* 1976; *James Dean* 2001

Linz, Alex D (1989-) *One Fine Day* 1996; *Home Alone 3* 1997; *My Brother the Pig* 1999; *Bounce* 2000; *Titan AE* 2000; *Max Keeble's Big Move* 2001; *Race to Space* 2001

Lio (1962-) *Golden Eighties* 1986; *Après l'Amour* 1992; *La Madre Muerta* 1993; *Love like Poison* 2010

Lion, Leon M (1879-1947) *Number Seventeen* 1932; *The Amazing Quest of Ernest Bliss* 1936; *Crackerjack* 1938

Liotard, Thérèse *Death Watch* 1980; *Full Moon in Paris* 1984; *Le Château de Ma Mère* 1990; *La Gloire de Mon Père* 1990

Liotta, Ray (1954-) *The Lonely Lady* 1983; *Something Wild* 1986; *Dominick and Eugene* 1988; *Field of Dreams* 1989; *GoodFellas* 1990; *Article 99* 1992; *Unlawful Entry* 1992; *Corrina, Corrina* 1994; *No Escape* 1994; *Operation Dumbo Drop* 1995; *Unforgettable* 1996; *Cop Land* 1997; *Turbulence* 1997; *Phoenix* 1998; *The Rat Pack* 1998; *Forever Mine* 1999; *Muppets from Space* 1999; *A Rumor of Angels* 2000; *Blow* 2001; *Hannibal* 2001; *Heartbreakers* 2001; *John Q* 2001; *Narc* 2001; *Identity* 2003; *Slow Burn* 2003; *The Last Shot* 2004; *Revolver* 2005; *Smokin' Aces* 2006; *Battle in Seattle* 2007; *Bee Movie* 2007; *Wild Hogs* 2007; *Crossing Over* 2008; *Hero Wanted* 2008; *The Line* 2008; *Observe and Report* 2009; *Youth in Revolt* 2009; *Death & Life of Charlie St Cloud* 2010; *The Iceman* 2012; *Killing Them Softly* 2012; *Better Living through Chemistry* 2014; *Kill the Messenger* 2014; *Sin City: a Dame to Kill For* 2014; *Go with Me* 2015

Lipinski, Eugene (1956-) *Moonlighting* 1982; *Riders of the Storm* 1986; *Perfectly Normal* 1990; *Aldrich Ames: Traitor Within* 1998; *The Recruit* 2002

Lipman, Maureen (1946-) *Up the Junction* 1967; *The Smashing Bird I Used to Know* 1969; *Gumshoe* 1971; *The Wildcats of St Trinian's* 1980; *Educating Rita* 1983; *National Lampoon's European Vacation* 1985; *Water* 1985; *Carry On Columbus* 1992; *Captain Jack* 1998; *Solomon and Gaenor* 1998; *The Pianist* 2002

Lipnicki, Jonathan (1990-) *Jerry Maguire* 1996; *Stuart Little* 1999; *The Little Vampire* 2000; *Like Mike* 2002; *Stuart Little 2* 2002; *When Zachary Beaver Came to Town* 2003; *Stuart Little 3: Call of the Wild* 2005

Lipper, David *Swearing Allegiance* 1997; *Federal Protection* 2002

Lipscomb, Dennis (1942-2014) *Union City* 1980; *WarGames* 1983; *A Soldier's Story* 1984; *Crossroads* 1986; *Amazing Grace and Chuck* 1987

Lipton, Peggy (1947-) *Blue* 1968; *The Purple People Eater* 1988; *Kinjite: Forbidden Subjects* 1989; *Jackpot* 2001

Lisi, Virna (1937-2014) *Duel of the Titans* 1961; *Eva* 1962; *The Black Tulip* 1963; *Le Bambole* 1965; *The Birds, the Bees, and the Italians* 1965; *Casanova '70* 1965; *How to Murder Your Wife* 1965; *Assault on a Queen* 1966; *Not with My Wife, You Don't!* 1966; *Arabella* 1967; *The Girl and the General* 1967; *The 25th Hour* 1967; *The Christmas Tree* 1969; *The Secret of Santa Vittoria* 1969; *Bluebeard* 1972; *The Serpent* 1972; *La Reine Margot* 1994

List, Peyton aka **List, Peyton Roi** *The Greatest Game Ever Played* 2005; *Secrets in the Walls* 2010; *Diary of a Wimpy Kid: Rodrick Rules* 2011; *Diary of a Wimpy Kid 3: Dog Days* 2012

Lister, Francis (1899-1951) *Cardinal Richelieu* 1935; *Clive of India* 1935; *The Return of the Scarlet Pimpernel* 1937; *Home to Danger* 1951

Lister, Moira (1923-2007) *Love Story* 1944; *Another Shore* 1948; *A Run for Your Money* 1949; *Pool of London* 1950; *White Corridors* 1951; *Grand National Night* 1953; *Trouble in Store* 1953; *The Deep Blue Sea* 1955; *John and Julie* 1955; *Seven Waves Away* 1957; *The Double Man* 1967; *Stranger in the House* 1967; *Not Now Darling* 1972

Lister Jr, Tom "Tiny" aka **Lister Jr, "Tiny"** aka **Lister, Tiny** aka **Lister Jr, Tiny "Zeus"** aka **Lister, Tiny "Zeus"** aka **Lister Jr, Tommy "Tiny"** (1958-) *Talkin' Dirty after Dark* 1991; *Trespass* 1992; *Posse* 1993; *Friday* 1995; *The Set Up* 1995; *Jackie Brown* 1997; *I Got the Hook Up* 1998; *Circus* 1999; *Judgment Day* 1999; *Supreme Sanction* 1999; *Little Nicky* 2000; *The Wash* 2001

Litefoot *The Indian in the Cupboard* 1995; *Kull the Conqueror* 1997

Litel, John (1892-1972) *Gold Is Where You Find It* 1938; *Nancy Drew - Detective* 1938; *A Slight Case of Murder* 1938; *Dodge City* 1939; *The Return of Dr X* 1939; *You Can't Get Away with Murder* 1939; *It All Came True* 1940; *Virginia City* 1940; *They Died with Their Boots On* 1941; *Crime Doctor* 1943; *Heaven Only Knows* 1947; *Pitfall* 1948; *Outpost in Morocco* 1949; *The Sundowners* 1950; *Flight to Mars* 1951; *Sitting Bull* 1954; *Comanche* 1956; *The Hired Gun* 1957

Lithgow, John (1945-) *Obsession* 1976; *The Big Fix* 1978; *Rich Kids* 1979; *Blow Out* 1981; *I'm Dancing as Fast as I Can* 1982; *The World According to Garp* 1982; *Terms of Endearment* 1983; *The Adventures of Buckaroo Banzai across the 8th Dimension* 1984; *Footloose* 1984; *Mesmerized* 1984; *2010* 1984; *Santa Claus* 1985; *The Deadly Game* 1986; *Resting Place* 1986; *Bigfoot and the Hendersons* 1987; *Distant Thunder* 1988; *Memphis Belle* 1990; *At Play in the Fields of the Lord* 1991; *The Boys* 1991; *Ricochet* 1991; *Raising Cain* 1992; *Cliffhanger* 1993; *A Good Man in Africa* 1993; *The Pelican Brief* 1993; *Love, Cheat & Steal* 1994; *My Brother's Keeper* 1995; *The Tuskegee Airmen* 1995; *Hollow Point* 1996; *A Civil Action* 1998; *Homegrown* 1998; *Don Quixote* 2000; *Orange County* 2001; *Shrek* 2001; *The Life and Death of Peter Sellers* 2003; *Kinsey* 2004; *Dreamgirls* 2006; *Confessions of a Shopaholic* 2009; *Leap Year* 2010; *Rise of the Planet of the Apes* 2011; *The Campaign* 2012; *This Is 40* 2012; *The Homesman* 2014; *Interstellar* 2014; *Love Is Strange* 2014; *Best of Enemies* 2015; *The Accountant* 2016

Little Richard (1932-) *Don't Knock the Rock* 1956; *Let the Good Times Roll* 1973; *Down and Out in Beverly Hills* 1986; *Hail! Hail! Rock 'n' Roll!* 1987; *The Purple People Eater* 1988; *The Pickle* 1993; *Why Do Fools Fall in Love?* 1998; *Mystery, Alaska* 1999

Little Sky, Eddie aka **Little, Eddie** (1926-1997) *Ride a Crooked Trail* 1958; *Journey through Rosebud* 1972

Little, Cleavon (1939-1992) *What's So Bad about Feeling Good?* 1968; *Cotton Comes to Harlem* 1970; *Vanishing Point* 1971; *Blazing Saddles* 1974; *FM* 1977; *Greased Lightning* 1977; *High Risk* 1981; *The Salamander* 1981; *The Gig* 1985; *Once Bitten* 1985

Little, Natasha (1970-) *The Clandestine Marriage* 1999; *The Criminal* 1999; *Another Life* 2000; *Greenfingers* 2000

Little, Ralf (1980-) *Frozen* 2004; *The Waiting Room* 2007; *Telstar: the Joe Meek Story* 2008; *Powder* 2010; *The Unbeatables* 2013; *Nativity 3: Dude Where's My Donkey* 2014

Littlefield, Lucien (1895-1960) *The Sheik* 1921; *Tumbleweeds* 1925; *My Best Girl* 1927; *Tom Sawyer* 1930; *It Pays to Advertise* 1931; *The Bitter Tea of General Yen* 1932; *Shopworn* 1932; *Kiss and Make-Up* 1934; *I Dream Too Much* 1935; *Man on the Flying Trapeze* 1935; *Ruggles of Red Gap* 1935; *Rose Marie* 1936

Littler, Susan (1949-1982) *The Lovers!* 1972; *Rough Cut* 1980

Littman, Julian *Evita* 1996; *Mad about Mambo* 1999

Liu Peiqi *The Story of Qiu Ju* 1992; *Together with You* 2002

Liu Ye *Balzac and the Little Chinese Seamstress* 2002; *Curse of the Golden Flower* 2006; *City of Life and Death* 2009

Liu, Gordon aka **Liu Chia-hui** aka **Chia Hui Liu** *The 36th Chamber of Shaolin* 1978; *Clan of the White Lotus* 1980; *Kill Bill Vol 2* 2004

Liu, Harrison *Bethune: the Making of a Hero* 1990; *Black Robe* 1991

Liu, Lucy (1968-) *Guy* 1996; *The Mating Habits of the Earthbound Human* 1999; *Charlie's Angels* 2000; *Play It to the Bone* 2000; *Shanghai Noon* 2000; *Hotel* 2001; *Ballistic: Ecks vs Sever* 2002; *Chicago* 2002; *Cypher* 2002; *Charlie's Angels: Full Throttle* 2003; *Kill Bill Vol 1* 2003; *Mulan II* 2004; *Domino* 2005; *Lucky Number Slevin* 2006; *Code Name: the Cleaner* 2007; *Kung Fu Panda* 2008; *Tinker Bell* 2008; *Detachment* 2011; *Kung Fu Panda 2* 2011; *The Man with the Iron Fists* 2012; *Tinkerbell and the Secret of the Wings* 2012; *The Tale of the Princess Kaguya* 2013; *Tinker Bell and the Legend of the NeverBeast* 2014; *TinkerBell and the Pirate Fairy* 2014; *Kung Fu Panda 3* 2016

Lively, Blake (1987-) *The Sisterhood of the Traveling Pants* 2005; *Accepted* 2006; *The Sisterhood of the Traveling Pants 2* 2008; *The Private Lives of Pippa Lee* 2009; *The Town* 2010; *Green Lantern* 2011; *Savages* 2012; *The Age of Adaline* 2015; *Café Society* 2016; *The Shallows* 2016

Lively, Eric *The Breed* 2006; *Live!* 2007

Lively, Robyn (1966-1976) *Wildcats* 1986; *The Karate Kid III* 1989; *Crazy from the Heart* 1991; *Santa Who?* 2000

Livesay, Jack (1901-1961) *The Wandering Jew* 1933; *It's Never Too Late to Mend* 1937; *Old Bones of the River* 1938; *Penny Paradise* 1938; *Paul Temple's Triumph* 1950

Livesey, Roger (1906-1976) *Lorna Doone* 1934; *Midshipman Easy* 1935; *Rembrandt* 1936; *The Drum* 1938; *The Girl in the News* 1940; *The Life and Death of Colonel Blimp* 1943; *I Know Where I'm Going!* 1945; *A Matter of Life and Death* 1946; *Vice Versa* 1947; *That Dangerous Age* 1949; *Green Grow the Rushes* 1951; *The Master of Ballantrae* 1953; *The Intimate Stranger* 1956; *The Entertainer* 1960; *The League of Gentlemen* 1960; *No My Darling Daughter* 1961; *Of Human Bondage* 1964; *Oedipus the King* 1967; *Hamlet* 1969

Livesey, Sam (1873-1936) *Dreyfus* 1931; *Calling the Tune* 1936

Livingston, John (1970-) *Mr Wrong* 1996; *The Stickup* 2001

Livingston, Margaret (1895-1984) *Sunrise* 1927; *The Last Warning* 1928; *What a Widow!* 1930; *Smart Money* 1931

Livingston, Robert (1904-1988) *Buried Loot* 1934; *Speed* 1936; *Hit the Saddle* 1937; *Brazil* 1944; *Bells of Rosarita* 1945; *The Cheaters* 1945; *Riders in the Sky* 1949; *Mule Train* 1950

Livingston, Ron (1967-) *The Low Life* 1995; *Swingers* 1996; *Body Shots* 1999; *Office Space* 1999; *A Rumor of Angels* 2000; *The Cooler* 2002; *King of the Ants* 2003; *Little Black Book* 2004; *Pretty Persuasion* 2005; *The Time Traveler's Wife* 2008; *Dinner for Schmucks* 2010; *Going the Distance* 2010; *Game Change* 2012; *The Conjuring* 2013; *Drinking Buddies* 2013; *The End of the Tour* 2015; *The 5th Wave* 2016

Lizaran, Anna aka **Lizaran, Ana** *High Heels* 1991; *Actresses* 1996

Llewellyn, Robert (1956-) *Christmas Carol: the Movie* 2001; *MirrorMask* 2004

Llewellyn, Suzette *Playing Away* 1986; *Sammy and Rosie Get Laid* 1987; *Welcome II the Terrordome* 1994

Llewelyn, Desmond (1914-1999) *From Russia with Love* 1963; *Goldfinger* 1964; *Thunderball* 1965; *You Only Live Twice* 1967; *On Her Majesty's Secret Service* 1969; *Diamonds Are Forever*

1971; *The Man with the Golden Gun* 1974; *The Spy Who Loved Me* 1977; *Moonraker* 1979; *For Your Eyes Only* 1981; *Octopussy* 1983; *A View to a Kill* 1985; *The Living Daylights* 1987; *Licence to Kill* 1989; *GoldenEye* 1995; *Tomorrow Never Dies* 1997; *The World Is Not Enough* 1999

Lloyd Pack, Charles (1902-1983) *River Beat* 1954; *Quatermass II* 1957; *The Revenge of Frankenstein* 1958; *Cover Girl Killer* 1959; *The Three Worlds of Gulliver* 1959; *The Siege of the Saxons* 1963; *The Reptile* 1966

Lloyd Pack, Roger (1944-2014) *Nineteen Eighty-Four* 1984; *Wilt* 1989; *American Friends* 1991; *UFO* 1993; *The Young Poisoner's Handbook* 1994; *Harry Potter and the Goblet of Fire* 2005; *Made in Dagenham* 2010; *In Love with Alma Cogan* 2011

Lloyd-Hughes, Henry *Unrelated* 2007; *Weekender* 2011

Lloyd, Christopher aka **Lloyd, Chris** (1938-) *One Flew over the Cuckoo's Nest* 1975; *Goin' South* 1978; *Butch and Sundance: the Early Days* 1979; *The Lady in Red* 1979; *The Onion Field* 1979; *The Legend of the Lone Ranger* 1981; *National Lampoon's Movie Madness* 1981; *The Postman Always Rings Twice* 1981; *Mr Mom* 1983; *To Be or Not to Be* 1983; *The Adventures of Buckaroo Banzai across the 8th Dimension* 1984; *Star Trek III: the Search for Spock* 1984; *Back to the Future* 1985; *Clue* 1985; *Legend of the White Horse* 1985; *Miracles* 1985; *Walk like a Man* 1987; *Track 29* 1988; *Who Framed Roger Rabbit* 1988; *Back to the Future Part II* 1989; *The Dream Team* 1989; *Back to the Future Part III* 1990; *Duck Tales: the Movie - Treasure of the Lost Lamp* 1990; *Why Me?* 1990; *The Addams Family* 1991; *Suburban Commando* 1991; *Rent-a-Kid* 1992; *Addams Family Values* 1993; *Dennis* 1993; *Angels in the Outfield* 1994; *The Pagemaster* 1994; *Radioland Murders* 1994; *Things to Do in Denver When You're Dead* 1995; *Cadillac Ranch* 1996; *Anastasia* 1997; *Changing Habits* 1997; *The Real Blonde* 1997; *Baby Geniuses* 1999; *My Favorite Martian* 1999; *Wit* 2001; *Hey Arnold! the Movie* 2002; *A Perfect Day* 2006; *Fly Me to the Moon* 2007; *Jack and the Beanstalk* 2010; *Piranha* 2010; *Piranha 3DD* 2011

Lloyd, Doris (1896-1968) *The Black Bird* 1926; *Charley's Aunt* 1930; *Sarah and Son* 1930; *Waterloo Bridge* 1931; *Back Street* 1932; *Tarzan, the Ape Man* 1932; *Secrets* 1933; *Glamour* 1934; *The Letter* 1940; *Molly and Me* 1945; *My Name Is Julia Ross* 1945; *Kind Lady* 1951; *The Time Machine* 1960

Lloyd, Emily (1970-) *Wish You Were Here* 1987; *Chicago Joe and the Showgirl* 1989; *Cookie* 1989; *In Country* 1989; *Scorchers* 1991; *A River Runs through It* 1992; *Under the Hula Moon* 1995; *When Saturday Comes* 1995; *Welcome to Sarajevo* 1997

Lloyd, Eric (1986-) *The Santa Clause* 1994; *Seasons of the Heart* 1994; *Dunston Checks In* 1996; *The Santa Clause 2* 2006; *The Santa Clause 3: the Escape Clause* 2006

Lloyd, George aka **Lloyd, George H** (1897-1967) *Singapore* 1947; *Under California Stars* 1948

Lloyd, Harold (1893-1971) *A Sailor-Made Man* 1921; *Grandma's Boy* 1922; *Safety Last* 1923; *Girl Shy* 1924; *Hot Water* 1924; *The Freshman* 1925; *For Heaven's Sake* 1926; *The Kid Brother* 1927; *Speedy* 1928; *Feet First* 1930; *Movie Crazy* 1932; *The Cat's Paw* 1934; *The Milky Way* 1936; *Mad Wednesday* 1950

Lloyd Jr, Harold (1931-1971) *A Yank in Ermine* 1955; *Girls' Town* 1959; *Platinum High School* 1960

Lloyd, Harry *The Iron Lady* 2011; *Closer to the Moon* 2014

Lloyd, Hugh (1923-2008) *The Punch and Judy Man* 1962; *White Cargo* 1973; *August* 1995

Lloyd, Jake (1989-) *Jingle All the Way* 1996; *Unhook the Stars* 1996; *Star Wars Episode I: the Phantom Menace* 1999

Lloyd, Jeremy (1930-2014) *We Joined the Navy* 1962; *Death Drums along the River* 1963; *The Liquidator* 1966; *Smashing Time* 1967

Lloyd, Jimmy (1918-1988) *The Story of GI Joe* 1945; *Riders of the Whistling Pines* 1949

Lloyd, John Bedford *Tough Guys Don't Dance* 1987; *The Abyss* 1989; *Waiting for the Light* 1989

Lloyd, Kathleen (1949-) *The Missouri Breaks* 1976; *The Car* 1977; *It Lives Again* 1978; *The Jayne Mansfield Story* 1980

Lloyd, Norman (1914-) *Saboteur* 1942; *The Southerner* 1945; *The Unseen* 1945; *A Walk in the Sun* 1945; *No Minor Vices* 1948; *Calamity Jane and Sam Bass* 1949; *Reign of Terror* 1949; *Scene of the Crime* 1949; *He Ran All the Way* 1951; *Limelight* 1952; *Audrey Rose* 1977; *FM* 1977; *Amityville: the Evil Escapes* 1989; *Dead Poets Society* 1989; *Shogun Warrior* 1991; *In Her Shoes* 2005

Lloyd, Rollo (1883-1938) *Today We Live* 1933; *Anthony Adverse* 1936

Lloyd, Sue (1939-2011) *Hysteria* 1964; *The Ipcress File* 1965; *Attack on the Iron Coast* 1968; *Corruption* 1968; *Where's Jack?* 1969; *Go for a Take* 1972; *That's Your Funeral* 1972; *Penny Gold* 1973; *Ups and Downs of a Handyman* 1975; *Revenge of the Pink Panther* 1978; *The Stud* 1978; *The Bitch* 1979; *UFO* 1993; *Bullet to Beijing* 1995

Lloyd, Suzanne *Seven Ways from Sundown* 1960; *The Return of Mr Moto* 1965; *The Champagne Murders* 1966; *That Riviera Touch* 1966

Lo Cascio, Luigi (1967-) *Good Morning, Night* 2003; *Human Capital* 2013

Lo Hoi-pang *Sparrow* 2008; *Rigor Mortis* 2013

Lo Lieh (1939-2002) *King Boxer* 1972; *Blood Money* 1974; *The 36th Chamber of Shaolin* 1978

Lo Verso, Enrico (1964-) *The Stolen Children* 1992; *Farinelli il Castrato* 1994; *Il Cielo è Sempre Più Blu* 1994

Lo, Candy *Time and Tide* 2000; *The Eye* 2002

Loach, Ken (1936-) *We Are Many* 2014; *Versus: The Life and Films of Ken Loach* 2016

LoBianco, Tony (1935-) *The Honeymoon Killers* 1969; *The French Connection* 1971; *The Seven-Ups* 1973; *Bloodbrothers* 1978; *FIST* 1978; *City Heat* 1984; *City of Hope* 1991; *Boiling Point* 1993; *The Ascent* 1994; *The Juror* 1996; *Mary Higgins Clark's Let Me Call You Sweetheart* 1997; *Rocky Marciano* 1999

Lobre, Jane *A Gentle Creature* 1969; *The Green Room* 1978

Loc, Tone (1966-) *Bebe's Kids* 1992; *Ace Ventura: Pet Detective* 1993; *Whispers: an Elephant's Tale* 2000; *They Crawl* 2001

Locane, Amy (1971-) *Cry-Baby* 1989; *The Road Home* 1989; *Blue Sky* 1991; *School Ties* 1992; *Airheads* 1994; *Acts of Love* 1995; *Going All the Way* 1997; *Bram Stoker's Legend of the Mummy* 1998; *Bad Karma* 2001; *Secretary* 2001; *Mystery Woman* 2003

Lochary, David (1944-1977) *Mondo Trasho* 1970; *Multiple Maniacs* 1970; *Pink Flamingos* 1972; *Female Trouble* 1974

Locke, Harry (1913-1987) *A Yank in Ermine* 1955; *Light Up the Sky* 1960; *The Man in the Back Seat* 1961; *The Creeping Flesh* 1972

Locke, Katherine (1910-1995) *The Sound of Fury* 1950; *Flesh and Fury* 1952

Locke, Philip (1928-2004) *The Girl on the Boat* 1962; *Tom & Viv* 1994

Locke, Sondra (1944-) *The Heart Is a Lonely Hunter* 1968; *Willard* 1971; *A Reflection of Fear* 1973; *The Second Coming of Suzanne* 1974; *Death Game* 1976; *The Outlaw Josey Wales* 1976; *The Gauntlet* 1977; *Every Which Way but Loose* 1978; *Any Which Way You Can* 1980; *Bronco Billy* 1980; *Sudden Impact* 1983; *Ratboy* 1986; *The Prophet's Game* 1999

Locke, Spencer *Monster House* 2006; *Resident Evil: Extinction* 2007; *Tarzan* 2013

Lockhart, Anne (1953-) *Young Warriors* 1983; *Hambone and Hillie* 1984; *Dark Tower* 1989

Lockhart, Calvin (1934-2007) *Cotton Comes to Harlem* 1970; *Leo the Last* 1970; *The Beast Must Die* 1974; *Let's Do It Again* 1975; *The Baltimore Bullet* 1980; *Coming to America* 1988

Lockhart, Gene (1891-1957) *Star of Midnight* 1935; *The Devil Is a Sissy* 1936; *Wedding Present* 1936; *Something to Sing About* 1937; *Algiers* 1938; *Blondie!* 1938; *A Christmas Carol* 1938; *Sinners in Paradise* 1938; *Blackmail* 1939; *His Girl Friday* 1939; *The Story of Alexander Graham Bell* 1939; *Tell No Tales* 1939; *A Dispatch from Reuters* 1940; *Dr Kildare Goes Home* 1940; *Edison, the Man* 1940; *South of Pago Pago* 1940; *Spirit of the People* 1940; *Billy the Kid* 1941; *The Devil and Daniel Webster* 1941; *Meet John Doe* 1941; *One Foot in Heaven* 1941; *The Sea Wolf* 1941; *They Died with Their Boots On* 1941; *The Gay Sisters* 1942; *Forever and a Day* 1943; *Hangmen Also Die!* 1943; *Mission to Moscow* 1943; *Northern Pursuit* 1943; *Action in Arabia* 1944; *The Desert Song* 1944; *Going My Way* 1944; *The House on 92nd Street* 1945; *Leave Her to Heaven* 1945; *The Strange Woman* 1946; *Thieves' Holiday* 1946; *Cynthia* 1947; *The Foxes of Harrow* 1947; *Her Husband's Affairs* 1947; *Miracle on 34th Street* 1947; *The Shocking Miss Pilgrim* 1947; *Apartment for Peggy* 1948; *Joan of Arc* 1948; *That Wonderful Urge* 1948; *Down to the Sea in Ships* 1949; *The Inspector General* 1949; *Madame Bovary* 1949; *Red Light* 1949; *I'd Climb the Highest Mountain* 1951; *Rhubarb* 1951; *Androcles and the Lion* 1952; *Face to Face* 1952; *A Girl in Every Port* 1952; *Hoodlum Empire* 1952; *Francis Covers the Big Town* 1953; *The Lady Wants Mink* 1953; *World for Ransom* 1953; *Carousel* 1956; *The Man in the Gray Flannel Suit* 1956; *Jeanne Eagels* 1957

Lockhart, June (1925-) *Adam Had Four Sons* 1941; *Meet Me in St Louis* 1944; *Son of Lassie* 1945; *Easy to Wed* 1946; *T-Men* 1947; *Time Limit* 1957; *Lassie's Great Adventure* 1963; *Holiday in Handcuffs* 2007

Lockhart, Kathleen (1894-1978) *Blondie!* 1938; *A Christmas Carol* 1938; *Love Crazy* 1941; *Bewitched* 1945; *I'd Climb the Highest Mountain* 1951

Locklear, Heather (1962-) *Firestarter* 1984; *The Return of Swamp Thing* 1989; *Wayne's World 2* 1993; *Money Talks* 1997; *Uptown Girls* 2003; *Looney Tunes: Back in Action* 2004; *The Perfect Man* 2005; *Scary Movie V* 2013

Locklin, Loryn *Taking Care of Business* 1990; *Fortress* 1992

Lockwood, Gary (1937-) *Wild in the Country* 1961; *It Happened at the World's Fair* 1962; *The Magic Sword* 1962; *Firecreek* 1968; *They Came to Rob Las Vegas* 1968; *2001: a Space Odyssey* 1968; *Model Shop* 1969; *RPM - Revolutions per Minute* 1970; *The Wild Pair* 1987

Lockwood, Julia (1941-) *My Teenage Daughter* 1956; *No Kidding* 1960; *Please Turn over* 1960

Lockwood, Margaret (1916-1990) *Lorna Doone* 1934; *Midshipman Easy* 1935; *The Beloved Vagabond* 1936; *Dr Syn* 1937; *Bank Holiday* 1938; *The Lady Vanishes* 1938; *Owd Bob* 1938; *Rulers of the Sea* 1939; *The Stars Look Down* 1939; *Susannah of the Mounties* 1939; *The Girl in the News* 1940; *Night Train to Munich* 1940; *Quiet Wedding* 1940; *The Man in Grey* 1943; *Give Us the Moon* 1944; *Love Story* 1944; *A Place of One's Own* 1945; *I'll Be Your Sweetheart* 1945; *The Wicked Lady* 1945; *Bedelia* 1946; *Hungry Hill* 1946; *Jassy* 1947; *Cardboard Cavalier* 1949; *Madness of the Heart* 1949; *Highly Dangerous* 1950; *Trent's Last Case* 1952; *Trouble in the Glen* 1954; *Cast a Dark Shadow* 1957; *The Slipper and the Rose* 1976

Loden, Barbara (1932-1980) *Splendor in the Grass* 1961; *Wanda* 1971

Loder, John (1898-1988) *The First Born* 1928; *Wedding Rehearsal* 1932; *Lorna Doone* 1934; *Love, Life and Laughter* 1934; *Sing as We Go* 1934; *Java Head* 1935; *The Silent Passenger* 1935; *The Man Who Changed His Mind* 1936; *Sabotage* 1936; *Whom the Gods Love* 1936; *Dr Syn* 1937; *King Solomon's Mines* 1937; *Owd Bob* 1938; *Tin Pan Alley* 1940; *Confirm or Deny* 1941; *How Green Was My Valley* 1941; *Gentleman Jim* 1942; *Now, Voyager* 1942; *Old Acquaintance* 1943; *Abroad with Two Yanks* 1944; *The Hairy Ape* 1944; *Passage to Marseille* 1944; *The Brighton Strangler* 1945; *Dishonored Lady* 1947; *The Story of Esther Costello* 1957; *The Woman and the Hunter* 1957

Lodge, David (1921-2003) *The Cockleshell Heroes* 1955; *The Running, Jumping and Standing Still Film* 1959; *The Bulldog Breed* 1960; *Two Way Stretch* 1960; *Watch Your Stern* 1960; *The Hellfire Club* 1961; *On the Beat* 1962; *Trial and Error* 1962; *The Long Ships* 1963; *Saturday Night Out* 1963; *Two Left Feet* 1963; *Catch Us If You Can* 1965; *Corruption* 1968; *Scream and Scream Again* 1969; *What's Good for the Goose* 1969; *Hoffman* 1970; *Incense for the Damned* 1970; *The Fiend* 1971; *Go for a Take* 1972; *The Return of the Pink Panther* 1974; *Edge of Sanity* 1989

Lodge, Jean *Dr Morelle - the Case of the Missing Heiress* 1949; *Brandy for the Parson* 1951; *Final Appointment* 1954

Lodge, John aka **Lodge, John Davis** (1903-1985) *Little Women* 1933; *Murders in the Zoo* 1933; *The Scarlet Empress* 1934; *Königsmark* 1935; *The Little Colonel* 1935; *Bank Holiday* 1938

Loff, Jeanette (1906-1942) *The King of Jazz* 1930; *Party Girl* 1930

Löfgren, Marianne (1910-1957) *June Night* 1940; *Crisis* 1945

Loft, Arthur (1897-1947) *I Am the Law* 1938; *Days of Jesse James* 1939; *My Friend Flicka* 1943; *Charlie Chan in the Secret Service* 1944; *Along Came Jones* 1945; *Scarlet Street* 1945; *The Shanghai Cobra* 1945; *The Woman in the Window* 1945

Loftus, Cecilia (1876-1943) *East Lynne* 1931; *It's a Date* 1940; *Lucky Partners* 1940

Logan, Jacqueline (1901-1983) *A Blind Bargain* 1922; *The King of Kings* 1927

Logan, Jimmy (1928-2001) *Floodtide* 1949; *The Wild Affair* 1963; *Carry On Abroad* 1972

Logan, Phyllis (1956-) *Another Time, Another Place* 1983; *The Chain* 1984; *Nineteen Eighty-Four* 1984; *The Doctor and the Devils* 1985; *The Kitchen Toto* 1987; *Freddie as FR07* 1992; *Soft Top, Hard Shoulder* 1992; *Secrets & Lies* 1995

Logan, Robert aka **Logan, Robert F** (1941-) *The Adventures of the Wilderness Family* 1975; *Across the Great Divide* 1977; *A Night in Heaven* 1983

Loggia, Robert (1930-2015) *Somebody Up There Likes Me* 1956; *The Garment Jungle* 1957; *Cattle King* 1963; *The Greatest Story Ever Told* 1965; *Che!* 1969; *First Love* 1977; *Revenge of the Pink Panther* 1978; *The Ninth Configuration* 1979; *SOB* 1981; *An Officer and a Gentleman* 1982; *Trail of the Pink Panther* 1982; *The Curse of the Pink Panther* 1983; *Psycho II* 1983; *Scarface* 1983; *Jagged Edge* 1985; *Prizzi's Honor* 1985; *Armed and Dangerous* 1986; *That's Life* 1986; *The Believers* 1987; *Gaby: a True Story* 1987; *Hot Pursuit* 1987; *Over the Top* 1987; *Big* 1988; *Oliver & Company* 1988; *Relentless* 1989; *Triumph of the Spirit* 1989; *Opportunity Knocks* 1990; *Too Hot to Handle* 1991; *Gladiator* 1992; *Innocent Blood* 1992; *Bad Girls* 1994; *I Love Trouble* 1994; *White Mile* 1994; *Coldblooded* 1995; *Independence Day* 1996; *Lost Highway* 1996; *Smilla's Feeling for Snow* 1996; *Hard Time* 1998; *Holy Man* 1998; *The Proposition* 1998; *Wide Awake* 1998; *Live Virgin* 2000; *Return to Me* 2000; *Shrink* 2009

Logue, Donal (1966-) *Blade* 1998; *The Big Tease* 1999; *Deception* 2000; *The Opportunists* 2000; *The Tao of Steve* 2000; *Confidence* 2002; *Just like Heaven* 2005; *The Reef* 2006; *Ghost Rider* 2007; *Max Payne* 2008; *Death & Life of Charlie St Cloud* 2010; *Oliver Sherman* 2010

Lohan, Lindsay (1986-) *The Parent Trap* 1998; *Life-Size* 2000; *Freaky Friday* 2003; *Confessions of a Teenage Drama Queen* 2004; *Mean Girls* 2004; *Herbie: Fully Loaded* 2005; *Bobby* 2006; *Just My Luck* 2006; *A Prairie Home Companion* 2006; *Georgia Rule* 2007; *I Know Who Killed Me* 2007; *Machete* 2010; *Liz & Dick* 2012; *Love, Marilyn* 2012; *The Canyons* 2013

Lohman, Alison (1979-) *Fortune Hunters* 1999; *White Oleander* 2002; *Big Fish* 2003; *Matchstick Men* 2003; *The Big White* 2005; *Where the Truth Lies* 2005; *Flicka* 2006; *Beowulf* 2007; *Things We Lost in the Fire* 2007; *Gamer* 2008; *Drag Me to Hell* 2009

Lohr, Marie (1890-1975) *Fighting Stock* 1935; *Foreign Affaires* 1935; *Pygmalion* 1938; *South Riding* 1938; *Went the Day Well?* 1942; *Anna Karenina* 1947; *The Winslow Boy* 1948; *A Town like Alice* 1956; *Seven Waves Away* 1957; *Great Catherine* 1968

Loiret Caille, Florence aka **Loiret-Caille, Florence** *Trouble Every Day* 2000; *Le Chignon d'Olga* 2002; *Vendredi Soir* 2002; *The Intruder* 2004; *Let's Talk about the Rain* 2008

Loken, Kristanna (1979-) *Terminator 3: Rise of the Machines* 2003; *Sword of Xanten* 2004; *Bounty Killer* 2013

Lollobrigida, Gina (1927-) *Pagliacci* 1948; *Fanfan la Tulipe* 1951; *Les Belles de Nuit* 1952; *Beat the Devil* 1953; *Bread, Love & Dreams* 1953; *Crossed Swords* 1954; *Beautiful but Dangerous* 1955; *The Hunchback of Notre Dame* 1956; *Trapeze* 1956; *Never So Few* 1959; *Solomon and Sheba* 1959; *Come September* 1961; *Go Naked in the World* 1961; *Imperial Venus* 1963; *Woman of Straw* 1964; *Le Bambole* 1965; *Strange Bedfellows* 1965; *Hotel Paradiso* 1966; *Buona Sera, Mrs Campbell* 1968; *Cervantes* 1968; *The Private Navy of Sgt O'Farrell* 1968; *Bad Man's River* 1971; *King, Queen, Knave* 1972

Lom, Herbert (1917-2012) *Secret Mission* 1942; *Tomorrow We Live* 1942; *Hotel Reserve* 1944; *The Seventh Veil* 1945; *Dual Alibi* 1946; *Night Boat to Dublin* 1946; *The Brass Monkey* 1948; *Portrait from Life* 1948; *Snowbound* 1948; *Golden Salamander* 1949; *The Black Rose* 1950; *Cage of Gold* 1950; *Night and the City* 1950; *State Secret* 1950; *Mr Denning Drives North* 1951; *The Man Who Watched Trains Go By* 1952; *Rough Shoot* 1952; *The Love Lottery* 1953; *The Net* 1953; *Beautiful Stranger* 1954; *Star of India* 1954; *The Ladykillers* 1955; *War and Peace* 1956; *Chase a Crooked Shadow* 1957; *Fire Down Below* 1957; *Hell Drivers* 1957; *I Accuse!* 1958; *Intent to Kill* 1958; *No Trees in the Street* 1958; *Passport to Shame* 1958; *The Roots of Heaven* 1958; *The Big Fisherman* 1959; *North West Frontier* 1959; *I Aim at the Stars* 1960; *El Cid* 1961; *The Frightened City* 1961; *Mr Topaze* 1961; *Mysterious Island* 1961; *The Phantom of the Opera* 1962; *Tiara Tahiti* 1962; *A Shot in the Dark* 1964; *Return from the Ashes* 1965; *Gambit* 1966; *Our Man in Marrakesh* 1966; *The Karate Killers* 1967; *Journey to the Far Side of the Sun* 1969; *Mister Jerico* 1969; *Count Dracula* 1970; *Mark of the Devil* 1970; *Murders in the Rue Morgue* 1971; *Asylum* 1972; *And Now the Screaming Starts!* 1973; *Dark Places* 1973; *And Then There Were None* 1974; *The Return of the Pink Panther* 1974; *The Pink Panther Strikes Again* 1976; *Revenge of the Pink Panther* 1978; *The Lady Vanishes* 1979; *Hopscotch* 1980; *The Man with Bogart's Face* 1980; *Trail of the Pink Panther* 1982; *The Curse of the Pink Panther* 1983; *The Dead Zone* 1983; *King Solomon's Mines* 1985; *Whoops Apocalypse* 1986; *River of Death* 1989; *The Pope Must Die* 1991; *The Sect* 1991; *Son of the Pink Panther* 1993

Lomas, Herbert (1887-1961) *When London Sleeps* 1932; *Java Head* 1935; *Knight without Armour* 1937; *Ask a Policeman* 1938

Lombard, Carole aka **Lombard, Carol** (1908-1942) *Big News* 1929; *High Voltage* 1929; *Fast and Loose* 1930; *It Pays to Advertise* 1931; *Ladies' Man* 1931; *Man of the World* 1931; *No Man of Her Own* 1932; *No One Man* 1932; *Sinners in the Sun* 1932; *The Eagle and the Hawk* 1933; *Supernatural* 1933; *White Woman* 1933; *Bolero* 1934; *The Gay Bride* 1934; *Lady by Choice* 1934; *Now and Forever* 1934; *Twentieth Century* 1934; *We're Not Dressing* 1934; *Hands across the Table* 1935; *Love before Breakfast* 1936; *My Man Godfrey* 1936; *The Princess Comes Across* 1936; *Nothing Sacred* 1937; *Swing High, Swing Low* 1937; *True Confession* 1937; *Fools for Scandal* 1938; *In Name Only* 1939; *Made for Each Other* 1939; *They Knew What They Wanted* 1940; *Vigil in the Night* 1940; *Mr and Mrs Smith* 1941; *To Be or Not to Be* 1942

Lombard, Karina (1964-) *Wide Sargasso Sea* 1992; *Legends of the Fall* 1994; *Last Man Standing* 1996; *Kull the Conqueror* 1997

Lombard, Louise (1970-) *Talos the Mummy* 1997; *My Kingdom* 2001; *Hidalgo* 2003

Lombard, Michael (1934-) *Fatso* 1979; *'Crocodile' Dundee* 1986; *Blood Money* 1988; *Pet Sematary* 1989

Lombardi, Paolo *A Month by the Lake* 1994; *A Pure Formality* 1994

Lommel, Ulli (1944-) *Fanny Hill: Memoirs of a Woman of Pleasure* 1964; *Love Is Colder than Death* 1969; *The American Soldier* 1970; *Whity* 1970; *Effi Briest* 1974; *Chinese Roulette* 1976; *Satan's Brew* 1976

Lomnicki, Tadeusz (1927-1992) *A Generation* 1954; *Man of Marble* 1977; *The Contract* 1980; *Blind Chance* 1987

Loncar, Beba (1943-) *The Long Ships* 1963; *The Birds, the Bees, and the Italians* 1965; *Some Girls Do* 1969

Londez, Guilaine *Night and Day* 1991; *Skin of Man, Heart of Beast* 1999

London, Alexandra *Van Gogh* 1991; *Les Destinées Sentimentales* 2000

London, Daniel *Patch Adams* 1998; *Four Dogs Playing Poker* 1999; *Old Joy* 2005; *Concussion* 2013

London, Jason (1972-) *The Man in the Moon* 1991; *Dazed and Confused* 1993; *Fall Time* 1994; *Safe Passage* 1994; *To Wong Foo, Thanks for Everything, Julie Newmar* 1995; *If These Walls Could Talk* 1996; *The Rage: Carrie 2* 1999; *Identity Theft: the Michelle Brown Story* 2004; *Out of the Woods* 2005; *The Wishing Well* 2009

London, Jeremy (1972-) The Babysitter 1995; Mallrats 1995; What I Did for Love 2006

London, Julie (1926-2000) The Red House 1947; Task Force 1949; The Great Man 1956; Man of the West 1958; Saddle the Wind 1958; Voice in the Mirror 1958; The Wonderful Country 1959; The Third Voice 1960

London, Lauren This Christmas 2007; I Love You, Beth Cooper 2009

Lone, John (1952-) Iceman 1984; Year of the Dragon 1985; The Last Emperor 1987; Shadows of the Peacock 1987; The Moderns 1988; M Butterfly 1993; The Shadow 1994; The Hunted 1995; Rush Hour 2 2001; War 2007

Long, Audrey (1922-2014) Tall in the Saddle 1944; Desperate 1947; Lady of Deceit 1947; The Petty Girl 1950; Cavalry Scout 1951; Indian Uprising 1951

Long, Howie (1960-) Broken Arrow 1996; Dollar for the Dead 1998; Firestorm 1998; 3000 Miles to Graceland 2000

Long, Jodi Patty Hearst 1988; Soursweet 1988

Long, Joseph Queen of Hearts 1989; The Unexpected Mrs Pollifax 1999

Long, Justin (1978-) Jeepers Creepers 2001; Crossroads 2002; Dodgeball: a True Underdog Story 2004; Herbie: Fully Loaded 2005; Waiting... 2005; Accepted 2006; Alvin and the Chipmunks 2007; Battle for Terra 2007; Die Hard 4.0 2007; Strange Wilderness 2007; Walk Hard: the Dewey Cox Story 2007; Just Not That into You 2008; After.Life 2009; Alvin and the Chipmunks: the Squeakquel 2009; Drag Me to Hell 2009; Planet 51 2009; Youth in Revolt 2009; Alpha and Omega 2010; The Conspirator 2010; Going the Distance 2010; Alvin and the Chipmunks: Chipwrecked 2011; 10 Years 2011; For a Good Time, Call... 2012; Walking with Dinosaurs: the 3D Movie 2013; Comet 2014; Alvin and the Chipmunks: the Road Chip 2015; Yoga Hosers 2016

Long, Mark Stormy Monday 1987; Ten Minutes Older: the Cello 2002

Long, Matt Ghost Rider 2007; Sydney White 2007

Long, Nia (1970-) Buried Alive 1990; Boyz N the Hood 1991; Made in America 1993; Friday 1995; Love Jones 1997; Soul Food 1997; The Secret Laughter of Women 1998; The Best Man 1999; Held Up 1999; In Too Deep 1999; Stigmata 1999; Big Momma's House 2000; Boiler Room 2000; Baadasssss! 2003; Alfie 2004; Are We There Yet? 2005; Big Momma's House 2 2006; Are We Done Yet? 2007; Premonition 2007; Good Hair 2009

Long, Richard aka **Long, Dick** (1927-1974) Tomorrow Is Forever 1945; The Dark Mirror 1946; The Stranger 1946; The Egg and I 1947; Criss Cross 1949; Ma and Pa Kettle 1949; Kansas Raiders 1950; Air Cadet 1951; The All American 1953; All I Desire 1953; Playgirl 1954; Cult of the Cobra 1955; He Laughed Last 1956; House on Haunted Hill 1958

Long, Shelley (1949-) The Cracker Factory 1979; Caveman 1981; Night Shift 1982; Losin' It 1983; Irreconcilable Differences 1984; The Money Pit 1985; Hello Again 1987; Outrageous Fortune 1987; Troop Beverly Hills 1989; The Boyfriend School 1990; The Brady Bunch Movie 1995; Freaky Friday 1995; A Very Brady Sequel 1996; Dr T & the Women 2000; Falling in Love with the Girl Next Door 2006; Honeymoon with Mom 2006

Long, Tom Strange Planet 1999; The Dish 2000; The Book of Revelation 2006

Long, Walter (1879-1952) The Birth of a Nation 1915; A Romance of the Redwoods 1917; The Sheik 1921; Blood and Sand 1922; Moby Dick 1930; Other Men's Women 1931; Pardon Us 1931

Longden, John (1900-1971) Blackmail 1929; Juno and the Paycock 1930; The Skin Game 1931; Young and Innocent 1937; Quatermass II 1957

Longdon, Terence (1922-2011) Carry On Nurse 1959; Carry On Regardless 1960; Clash by Night 1963; The Return of Mr Moto 1965

Longley, Victoria (1962-) The More Things Change 1985; Celia 1988; Turtle Beach 1992; Dallas Doll 1994

Longo, Tony (1961-2015) Bloodhounds of Broadway 1989; Prehysteria! 1993

Longoria, Eva aka **Longoria Parker, Eva** (1975-) Harsh Times 2005; The Sentinel 2006; Over Her Dead Body 2008; The Baytown Outlaws 2012; A Dark Truth 2012; Frontera 2014; Visions 2014

Longstreth, Emily Private Resort 1985; The Big Picture 1989

Lonsdale, Michel aka **Lonsdale, Michael** (1931-) The Trial 1962; The Bride Wore Black 1967; Stolen Kisses 1968; Le Souffle au Coeur 1971; The Day of the Jackal 1973; Caravan to Vaccares 1974; Le Fantôme de la Liberté 1974; Galileo 1974; Stavisky 1974; India Song 1975; The Romantic Englishwoman 1975; Mr Klein 1976; The Passage 1978; Moonraker 1979; Enigma 1982; The Holcroft Covenant 1985; The Name of the Rose 1986; The Remains of the Day 1993; Jefferson in Paris 1995; Ronin 1998; 5x2 2004; Munich 2005; Goya's Ghosts 2006; Heartbeat Detector 2007; The Last Mistress 2007; Agora 2009; Of Gods and Men 2010; Free Men 2011

Loo, Richard (1903-1983) The Bitter Tea of General Yen 1932; Back to Bataan 1945; Betrayal from the East 1945; China Sky 1945; The Clay Pigeon 1949; The Steel Helmet 1951; Love Is a Many-Splendored Thing 1955; Confessions of an Opium Eater 1962; The Man with the Golden Gun 1974

Loomis, Rod The Beastmaster 1982; Bill & Ted's Excellent Adventure 1988; Jack's Back 1988

Loos, Theodor aka **Loos, Theodore** (1883-1954) The Nibelungen 1924; Metropolis 1926; Ariane 1931; M 1931

Lopert, Tanya Navajo Joe 1966; Tales of Ordinary Madness 1981

Lopez de Ayala, Pilar aka **López de Ayala, Pilar** In the City of Sylvia 2007; Intruders 2011

Lopez Moctezuma, Carlos (1909-1980) The Proud Ones 1953; Viva Maria! 1965

Lopez, George (1961-) Real Women Have Curves 2002; The Adventures of Sharkboy and Lavagirl 2005; Balls of Fury 2007; Beverly Hills Chihuahua 2008; Swing Vote 2008

Lopez, Gerry Conan the Barbarian 1982; North Shore 1987

Lopez, Jennifer (1970-) Money Train 1995; Blood and Wine 1996; Jack 1996; Anaconda 1997; Selena 1997; U Turn 1997; Antz 1998; Out of Sight 1998; The Cell 2000; Angel Eyes 2001; The Wedding Planner 2001; Enough 2002; Maid in Manhattan 2002; Gigli 2003; Jersey Girl 2003; Shall We Dance 2004; Monster-in-Law 2005; An Unfinished Life 2005; El Cantante 2006; The Back-Up Plan 2010; Ice Age 4: Continental Drift 2012; What to Expect When You're Expecting 2012; Parker 2013; Home 2014; The Boy Next Door 2015

Lopez, Mario (1973-) A Crack in the Floor 2000; Holiday in Handcuffs 2007

Lopez, Perry (1929-2008) Hell on Frisco Bay 1955; I Died a Thousand Times 1955; The Lone Ranger 1956; Violent Road 1958; Taras Bulba 1962; Chinatown 1974; Death Wish 4: the Crackdown 1987; Kinjite: Forbidden Subjects 1989

Lopez, Sergi aka **López, Sergi** (1965-) Western 1997; La Nouvelle Eve 1998; Une Liaison Pornographique 1999; Lisboa 1999; Harry, He's Here to Help 2000; Dirty Pretty Things 2002; Pan's Labyrinth 2006; Leaving 2008

Lopez, Trini (1937-) Marriage on the Rocks 1965; The Dirty Dozen 1967

Lorain, Sophie (1957-) In Her Defense 1998; Mambo Italiano 2003

Lord, Jack (1920-1998) The Court-Martial of Billy Mitchell 1955; The Vagabond King 1956; The True Story of Lynn Stuart 1957; God's Little Acre 1958; Man of the West 1958; The Hangman 1959; Walk like a Dragon 1960; Dr No 1962; The Ride to Hangman's Tree 1967; The Counterfeit Killer 1968

Lord, Marion aka **Lord, Marian** (1883-1942) Broadway 1929; One Heavenly Night 1931

Lord, Marjorie (1922-) Johnny Come Lately 1943; Sherlock Holmes in Washington 1943; Boy, Did I Get a Wrong Number 1966

Lord, Stephen Reverb 2006; The Truth 2006; Until Death 2007; The Shepherd 2008; The Violators 2015

Lords, Traci (1968-) Not of This Earth 1988; Cry-Baby 1989; Fast Food 1989; Raw Nerve 1991; Intent to Kill 1992; Plughead Rewired: Circuitry Man II 1994; Serial Mom 1994; Blade 1998; Zack and Miri Make a Porno 2008; Excision 2012

Loren, Sophia (1934-) Quo Vadis 1951; Gold of Naples 1954; Lucky to Be a Woman 1955; The Miller's Wife 1955; Too Bad She's Bad 1955; Boy on a Dolphin 1957; Legend of the Lost 1957; The Pride and the Passion 1957; Desire under the Elms 1958; Houseboat 1958; The Key 1958; The Black Orchid 1959;

That Kind of Woman 1959; A Breath of Scandal 1960; Heller in Pink Tights 1960; It Started in Naples 1960; The Millionairess 1960; Two Women 1960; El Cid 1961; Madame 1961; Five Miles to Midnight 1963; Yesterday, Today and Tomorrow 1963; The Fall of the Roman Empire 1964; Marriage - Italian Style 1964; Lady L 1965; The Love Goddesses 1965; Operation Crossbow 1965; Arabesque 1966; Judith 1966; A Countess from Hong Kong 1967; Ghosts - Italian Style 1967; More than a Miracle 1967; Sunflower 1969; The Priest's Wife 1970; Lady Liberty 1971; Man of La Mancha 1972; Brief Encounter 1974; Verdict 1974; The Voyage 1974; The Cassandra Crossing 1976; A Special Day 1977; Brass Target 1978; Blood Feud 1979; Firepower 1979; Pret-a-Porter 1994; Grumpier Old Men 1996; Francesca and Nunziata 2001; Nine 2009

Lorenzon, Livio (1923-1971) Goliath and the Barbarians 1959; Pontius Pilate 1961

Lorimer, Glennis (1913-1968) Alf's Button Afloat 1938; Ask a Policeman 1938

Loring, Natasha The Dinosaur Project 2012; Zulu 2013

Loring, Teala (1922-2007) Bluebeard 1944; Dark Alibi 1946

Lorinz, James Frankenhooker 1990; The Jerky Boys 1995

Lorit, Jean-Pierre Jeanne la Pucelle 1994; Three Colours Red 1994; Alice et Martin 1998

Lorne, Marion (1888-1968) Strangers on a Train 1951; The Girl Rush 1955

Lorre, Peter (1904-1964) M 1931; The Man Who Knew Too Much 1934; Crime and Punishment 1935; Mad Love 1935; Crack-Up 1936; Secret Agent 1936; Lancer Spy 1937; Nancy Steele Is Missing 1937; Thank You, Mr Moto 1937; Think Fast, Mr Moto 1937; Mr Moto Takes a Chance 1938; Mr Moto's Gamble 1938; Mr Moto's Last Warning 1938; Mysterious Mr Moto 1938; Mr Moto in Danger Island 1939; Mr Moto Takes a Vacation 1939; Strange Cargo 1940; Stranger on the Third Floor 1940; You'll Find Out 1940; The Face behind the Mask 1941; The Maltese Falcon 1941; They Met in Bombay 1941; All through the Night 1942; The Boogie Man Will Get You 1942; Casablanca 1942; The Invisible Agent 1942; Background to Danger 1943; The Constant Nymph 1943; The Cross of Lorraine 1943; Arsenic and Old Lace 1944; The Conspirators 1944; Hollywood Canteen 1944; The Mask of Dimitrios 1944; Passage to Marseille 1944; Confidential Agent 1945; Hotel Berlin 1945; The Beast with Five Fingers 1946; Black Angel 1946; The Chase 1946; Three Strangers 1946; The Verdict 1946; My Favorite Brunette 1947; Casbah 1948; Rope of Sand 1949; Quicksand 1950; The Lost One 1951; Beat the Devil 1953; 20,000 Leagues under the Sea 1954; Around the World in 80 Days 1956; The Buster Keaton Story 1957; Hell Ship Mutiny 1957; The Sad Sack 1957; Silk Stockings 1957; The Big Circus 1959; Scent of Mystery 1960; Voyage to the Bottom of the Sea 1961; Five Weeks in a Balloon 1962; Tales of Terror 1962; The Raven 1963; The Comedy of Terrors 1964; Muscle Beach Party 1964; The Patsy 1964

Lorring, Joan (1926-2014) The Corn Is Green 1945; Three Strangers 1946; The Verdict 1946; The Lost Moment 1947; The Other Love 1947; Good Sam 1948; The Big Night 1951

Lorys, Diana (1940-) The Awful Dr Orlof 1962; Bad Man's River 1971

Losch, Tilly (1904-1975) The Garden of Allah 1936; The Good Earth 1937

Lothar, Susanne (1960-2012) Funny Games 1997; The Piano Teacher 2001

Lotis, Dennis (1928-) The City of the Dead 1960; She'll Have to Go 1961

Lottimer, Eb Streets 1990; The Finest Hour 1991

Lotz, Caity The Pact 2011; Battle of the Year 2013; The Machine 2013

Louanne (1970-) Oh God! Book II 1980; A Night in the Life of Jimmy Reardon 1988

Loughlin, Lori (1965-) Amityville III: the Demon 1983; Secret Admirer 1985; Brotherhood of Justice 1986; Back to the Beach 1987; The Night Before 1988; Old Dogs 2009; A Soldier's Love Story 2010

Louie, "Ducky" Back to Bataan 1945; China Sky 1945; Black Gold 1947

Louie, John (1970-) Oh God! Book II 1980; Gremlins 1984

Louis-Dreyfus, Julia (1961-) Troll 1986; North 1994; Deconstructing Harry 1997; Fathers' Day 1997; A Bug's Life 1998; Animal Farm 1999; Geppetto 2000; Enough Said 2013; Planes 2013

Louis, Joe (1914-1981) This Is the Army 1943; The Square Jungle 1955

Louis, Justin (1967-) The Marsh 2006; Saw IV 2007; Grey Gardens 2009

Louis, Willard (1886-1926) Robin Hood 1922; Kiss Me Again 1925; Don Juan 1926

Louise, Anita (1915-1970) Our Betters 1933; Judge Priest 1934; Madame Du Barry 1934; A Midsummer Night's Dream 1935; Anthony Adverse 1936; The Story of Louis Pasteur 1936; Green Light 1937; That Certain Woman 1937; Tovarich 1937; Going Places 1938; Marie Antoinette 1938; The Sisters 1938; The Little Princess 1939; The Villain Still Pursued Her 1940; Casanova Brown 1944; Love Letters 1945; The Bandit of Sherwood Forest 1946; Retreat, Hell! 1952

Louise, Tina (1934-) God's Little Acre 1958; The Baited Trap 1959; Day of the Outlaw 1959; The Hangman 1959; For Those Who Think Young 1964; The Good Guys and the Bad Guys 1969; The Wrecking Crew 1969; The Stepford Wives 1975

Louiso, Todd (1970-) Jerry Maguire 1996; 8 Heads in a Duffel Bag 1997; High Fidelity 2000; The Switch 2010

Louvigny, Jacques (1880-1951) On Purge Bébé 1931; La Symphonie Pastorale 1946

Louwyck, Sam Bullhead 2011; The Wonders 2014

Lovato, Demi Camp Rock 2008; Jonas Brothers: the 3D Concert Experience 2009

Love, Alan That Sinking Feeling 1979; The Apple 1980

Love, Bessie (1898-1986) The Lost World 1925; The Matinee Idol 1928; The Broadway Melody 1929; Hollywood Revue 1929; Next to No Time 1958; Nowhere to Go 1958; Isadora 1968; Catlow 1971; Lady Chatterley's Lover 1981; Reds 1981

Love, Courtney (1964-) Sid and Nancy 1986; Straight to Hell 1987; Basquiat 1996; Feeling Minnesota 1996; The People vs Larry Flynt 1996; Kurt & Courtney 1997; Man on the Moon 1999; 200 Cigarettes 1999; Trapped 2002; Hit So Hard 2011; Cobain: Montage of Heck 2015

Love, Darlene (1938-) Lethal Weapon 1987; Lethal Weapon 2 1989; Lethal Weapon 3 1992; Lethal Weapon 4 1998; Twenty Feet from Stardom 2013

Love, Faizon (1968-) Bebe's Kids 1992; 3 Strikes 2000; Wonderland 2003; Idlewild 2006; Just My Luck 2006; Couples Retreat 2009

Love, Gary The Krays 1990; Russian Dolls 2005

Love, Montagu aka **Love, Montague** (1877-1943) Hands Up! 1926; The Son of the Sheik 1926; The Last Warning 1928; The Wind 1928; Bulldog Drummond 1929; His Double Life 1933; The Man Who Broke the Bank at Monte Carlo 1935; A Million 1936; One in a Million 1936; Sing, Baby, Sing 1936; A Damsel in Distress 1937; London by Night 1937; Gunga Din 1939; Rulers of the Sea 1939; We Are Not Alone 1939; Dr Ehrlich's Magic Bullet 1940; The Mark of Zorro 1940; Son of Monte Cristo 1940; The Devil and Miss Jones 1941; Sherlock Holmes and the Voice of Terror 1942; Forever and a Day 1943

Love, Patti Terror 1979; Steaming 1985

Lovejoy, Frank (1914-1982) Home of the Brave 1949; Breakthrough 1950; In a Lonely Place 1950; The Sound of Fury 1950; Three Secrets 1950; Force of Arms 1951; Goodbye, My Fancy 1951; I Was a Communist for the FBI 1951; I'll See You in My Dreams 1951; Retreat, Hell! 1952; The Charge at Feather River 1953; The Hitch-Hiker 1953; House of Wax 1953; Men of the Fighting Lady 1954; The Americano 1955; Shack Out on 101 1955; Strategic Air Command 1955; Julie 1956

Lovelace, Linda (1949-2002) Deep Throat 1972; Inside Deep Throat 2005

Lovell, Raymond (1900-1953) Contraband 1940; The Common Touch 1941; Uncensored 1942; The Young Mr Pitt 1942; Candlelight in Algeria 1943; The Man in Grey 1943; Hotel Reserve 1944; Caesar and Cleopatra 1945; Night Boat to Dublin 1946; The End of the River 1947; The Blind Goddess 1948; The Calendar 1948; My Brother's Keeper 1948; The Three Weird Sisters 1948; The Bad Lord Byron 1949; Fools Rush In 1949; Madness of the Heart 1949; The Romantic Age 1949; The Mudlark 1950; Time Gentlemen Please! 1952

Lovelock, Raymond (1950-) Fiddler on the Roof 1971; The Living Dead at the Manchester Morgue 1974

Lovett, Dorothy (1915-1998) Meet Dr Christian 1939; Call Out the Marines 1941; Look Who's Laughing 1941

Lovett, Lyle (1957-) Pret-a-Porter 1994; Breast Men 1997; Fear and Loathing in Las Vegas 1998; The Opposite of Sex 1998; The New Guy 2002

Lovibond, Ophelia (1986-) Shadows in the Sun 2008; 4.3.2.1 2010; Mr Popper's Penguins 2011; 8 minutes idle 2012; Man Up 2015; Tommy's Honour 2016

Lovitz, Jon (1957-) The Brave Little Toaster 1987; Big 1988; My Stepmother Is an Alien 1988; Mr Destiny 1990; An American Tail: Fievel Goes West 1991; Mom and Dad Save the World 1992; Coneheads 1993; National Lampoon's Loaded Weapon 1 1993; City Slickers II: the Legend of Curly's Gold 1994; North 1994; Trapped in Paradise 1994; The Great White Hype 1996; High School High 1996; Happiness 1998; Lost & Found 1999; Small Time Crooks 2000; Good Advice 2001; Rat Race 2001; Adam Sandler's Eight Crazy Nights 2002; Dickie Roberts: Former Child Star 2003; The Stepford Wives 2004; The Producers 2005; The Benchwarmers 2006; Bula Quo! 2013

Lovsky, Celia (1897-1979) Captain Carey, USA 1950; Man of a Thousand Faces 1957; The Mobster 1958; The Gene Krupa Story 1959; 36 Hours 1964

Lowe, Alex Peter's Friends 1992; Haunted 1995

Lowe, Alice Sightseers 2012; Black Mountain Poets 2015; Adult Life Skills 2016

Lowe, Andrea The Unloved 2009; Route Irish 2010; When the Lights Went Out 2010

Lowe, Arthur (1915-1982) Final Appointment 1954; This Sporting Life 1963; if.... 1968; The Bed Sitting Room 1969; A Hole Lot of Trouble 1969; The Rise and Rise of Michael Rimmer 1970; Dad's Army 1971; Adolf Hitler - My Part in His Downfall 1972; The Ruling Class 1972; No Sex Please - We're British 1973; O Lucky Man! 1973; Theatre of Blood 1973; Man about the House 1974; The Bawdy Adventures of Tom Jones 1976; The Lady Vanishes 1979

Lowe, Barry (1931-2011) Cash on Demand 1961; Sands of the Kalahari 1965

Lowe, Chad (1968-) Apprentice to Murder 1988; Highway to Hell 1992; Take Me Home: the John Denver Story 2000; Unfaithful 2002; Fielder's Choice 2005

Lowe, Edmund (1890-1971) What Price Glory 1926; The Cock-Eyed World 1929; In Old Arizona 1929; Born Reckless 1930; The Cisco Kid 1931; Chandu the Magician 1932; Dinner at Eight 1933; Black Sheep 1935; Seven Sinners 1936; Every Day's a Holiday 1937; The Squeaker 1937; I Love You Again 1940; Call Out the Marines 1941; Dillinger 1945; Good Sam 1948; The Wings of Eagles 1957; Heller in Pink Tights 1960

Lowe, Rob (1964-) Class 1983; The Outsiders 1983; The Hotel New Hampshire 1984; Oxford Blues 1984; St Elmo's Fire 1985; About Last Night... 1986; Youngblood 1986; Square Dance 1987; Illegally Yours 1988; Masquerade 1988; Bad Influence 1990; The Finest Hour 1991; Wayne's World 1992; Frank and Jesse 1995; Tommy Boy 1995; Contact 1997; For Hire 1997; Austin Powers: the Spy Who Shagged Me 1999; Escape under Pressure 2000; The Specials 2000; View from the Top 2003; Perfect Strangers 2004; Thank You for Smoking 2005; A Perfect Day 2006; The Invention of Lying 2009; Too Late to Say Goodbye 2009; Behind the Candelabra 2013; Killing Kennedy 2013; Sex Tape 2014; Monster Trucks 2015

Lowe, Simon Large 2000; No Fixed Abode 2012

Lowell, Carey (1961-) Dangerously Close 1986; Licence to Kill 1989; The Guardian 1990; Road to Ruin 1992; Fierce Creatures 1997; More than Meets the Eye: the Joan Brock Story 2003

Lowell, Helen (1866-1937) Isn't Life Wonderful 1924; Devil Dogs of the Air 1935; Strike Me Pink 1936

Lowenadler, Holger (1904-1977) A Ship to India 1947; Lacombe Lucien 1974

Lowensohn, Elina aka **Löwensohn, Elina** (1967-) Simple Men 1992; Amateur 1994; Nadja 1995; I'm Not Rappaport 1996; Six Ways to Sunday

1997; *The Wisdom of Crocodiles* 1998; *Lourdes* 2009

Lowery, Andrew (1970-) *School Ties* 1992; *My Boyfriend's Back* 1993; *Color of Night* 1994

Lowery, Robert (1913-1971) *Four Sons* 1940; *The Mummy's Ghost* 1944; *The Rise and Fall of Legs Diamond* 1960

Löwitsch, Klaus aka **Lowitsch, Klaus** aka **Loewitsch, Klaus** (1936-2002) *The Odessa File* 1974; *Cross of Iron* 1977; *Breakthrough* 1978; *Despair* 1978; *The Marriage of Maria Braun* 1978; *Gotcha!* 1985; *Extreme Ops* 2003

Lowry, Lynn (1947-) *The Crazies* 1973; *Shivers* 1975; *Fighting Mad* 1976

Lowry, Morton (1908-1987) *The Dawn Patrol* 1938; *A Yank in the RAF* 1941; *Pursuit to Algiers* 1945; *The Verdict* 1946

Lowther, T J (1986-) *A Home of Our Own* 1993; *A Perfect World* 1993

Loy, Myrna (1905-1993) *Don Juan* 1926; *The Exquisite Sinner* 1926; *So This Is Paris* 1926; *The Jazz Singer* 1927; *The Desert Song* 1929; *The Show of Shows* 1929; *The Devil to Pay* 1930; *Renegades* 1930; *Arrowsmith* 1931; *Body and Soul* 1931; *A Connecticut Yankee* 1931; *Consolation Marriage* 1931; *The Animal Kingdom* 1932; *Emma* 1932; *Love Me Tonight* 1932; *The Mask of Fu Manchu* 1932; *The Wet Parade* 1932; *The Barbarian* 1933; *Night Flight* 1933; *Penthouse* 1933; *The Prizefighter and the Lady* 1933; *Topaze* 1933; *When Ladies Meet* 1933; *Broadway Bill* 1934; *Evelyn Prentice* 1934; *Manhattan Melodrama* 1934; *Men in White* 1934; *Stamboul Quest* 1934; *The Thin Man* 1934; *Whipsaw* 1935; *Wings in the Dark* 1935; *After the Thin Man* 1936; *The Great Ziegfeld* 1936; *Libeled Lady* 1936; *Wife vs Secretary* 1936; *Double Wedding* 1937; *Man-Proof* 1937; *Parnell* 1937; *Test Pilot* 1938; *Too Hot to Handle* 1938; *Another Thin Man* 1939; *The Rains Came* 1939; *I Love You Again* 1940; *Third Finger, Left Hand* 1940; *Love Crazy* 1941; *Shadow of the Thin Man* 1941; *The Thin Man Goes Home* 1944; *The Best Years of Our Lives* 1946; *So Goes My Love* 1946; *The Bachelor and the Bobby-Soxer* 1947; *The Senator Was Indiscreet* 1947; *Song of the Thin Man* 1947; *Mr Blandings Builds His Dream House* 1948; *The Red Pony* 1949; *That Dangerous Age* 1949; *Cheaper by the Dozen* 1950; *Belles on Their Toes* 1952; *The Ambassador's Daughter* 1956; *Lonelyhearts* 1958; *From the Terrace* 1960; *Midnight Lace* 1960; *The April Fools* 1969; *Airport 1975* 1974; *The End* 1978; *Just Tell Me What You Want* 1980

Lozano, Manuel *Butterfly's Tongue* 1999; *You're My Hero* 2013

Lozano, Margarita (1931-) *Viridiana* 1961; *A Fistful of Dollars* 1964; *The Night of San Lorenzo* 1981; *Kaos* 1984; *Manon des Sources* 1986; *Night Sun* 1990

Lu, Lisa (1931-) *The Mountain Road* 1960; *Demon Seed* 1977; *The Joy Luck Club* 1993

Lualdi, Antonella (1931-) *Le Rouge et le Noir* 1954; *Web of Passion* 1959; *The Mongols* 1961; *Let's Talk about Women* 1964; *Vincent, François, Paul and the Others* 1974

Lucas, Isabel *Daybreakers* 2008; *Transformers: Revenge of the Fallen* 2009; *Immortals* 2011

Lucas, Jessica (1985-) *The Covenant* 2006; *Cloverfield* 2008; *Drag Me to Hell* 2009; *Big Mommas: Like Father, like Son* 2011; *Evil Dead* 2013; *That Awkward Moment* 2013

Lucas, Josh (1971-) *True Blue* 1996; *The Weight of Water* 2000; *A Beautiful Mind* 2001; *The Deep End* 2001; *Session 9* 2001; *Sweet Home Alabama* 2002; *Hulk* 2003; *Wonderland* 2003; *Around the Bend* 2004; *Undertow* 2004; *Stealth* 2005; *An Unfinished Life* 2005; *Glory Road* 2006; *Poseidon* 2006; *Life as We Know It* 2010; *J Edgar* 2011; *The Lincoln Lawyer* 2011; *Red Dog* 2011; *Stolen* 2012; *The Choir* 2014

Lucas, Laurent (1965-) *La Nouvelle Eve* 1998; *Rien sur Robert* 1998; *Pola X* 1999; *Harry, He's Here to Help* 2000; *In My Skin* 2002; *Calvaire* 2004; *Lemming* 2005; *Alleluia* 2013

Lucas, Matt (1974-) *Astro Boy* 2009; *Alice in Wonderland* 2010; *The Infidel* 2010; *Arthur Christmas* 2011; *Bridesmaids* 2011; *Gnomeo & Juliet* 2011; *Small Apartments* 2012; *The Harry Hill Movie* 2013; *In Secret* 2013; *The Look of Love* 2013; *Alice through the Looking Glass* 2016

Lucas, Wilfred (1871-1940) *Dishonored* 1931; *Pardon Us* 1931; *Criminal Lawyer* 1937

Lucas, William (1925-2016) *X the Unknown* 1956; *Crack in the Mirror* 1960; *Sons and Lovers* 1960; *Payroll* 1961; *The Shadow of the Cat* 1961; *The Break* 1962; *Calculated Risk* 1963; *Night of the Big Heat* 1967; *Man at the Top* 1973

Luce, Angela (1938-) *The Decameron* 1970; *L'Amore Molesto* 1995

Luce, Claire (1903-1989) *Up the River* 1930; *Lazybones* 1935; *Over She Goes* 1937

Lucero, Enrique (1920-1989) *Macario* 1960; *Tarzan and the Valley of Gold* 1966; *Shark!* 1969; *Two Mules for Sister Sara* 1970; *The Return of a Man Called Horse* 1976; *Green Ice* 1981

Luchini, Fabrice (1951-) *Immoral Tales* 1974; *Perceval le Gallois* 1978; *Full Moon in Paris* 1984; *Hôtel du Paradis* 1986; *Le Colonel Chabert* 1994; *Beaumarchais l'Insolent* 1996; *Men, Women: a User's Manual* 1996; *Le Bossu* 1997; *Rien sur Robert* 1998; *Confidences Trop Intimes* 2004; *Molière* 2006; *Paris* 2007; *Potiche* 2010; *The Women on the 6th Floor* 2010; *In the House* 2012; *Cycling with Molière* 2013; *Gemma Bovery* 2014

Luckham, Cyril (1907-1989) *Stranger from Venus* 1954; *The Naked Runner* 1967; *Providence* 1977

Luckinbill, Laurence (1934-) *The Boys in the Band* 1970; *Such Good Friends* 1971; *Not for Publication* 1984; *Cocktail* 1988; *Messenger of Death* 1988; *Star Trek V: the Final Frontier* 1989

Lucking, William aka **Lucking, Bill** (1941-) *The Magnificent Seven Ride!* 1972; *Oklahoma Crude* 1973; *Doc Savage: the Man of Bronze* 1975; *Birch Interval* 1976; *The Return of a Man Called Horse* 1976; *The A-Team* 1983; *Rescue Me* 1991; *The River Wild* 1994; *Welcome to the Jungle* 2003

Luddy, Barbara (1908-1979) *Lady and the Tramp* 1955; *Sleeping Beauty* 1959

Ludlow, Patrick (1903-1996) *Evergreen* 1934; *Gangway* 1937; *Old Mother Riley* 1937

Ludwig, Alexander *The Dark Is Rising* 2007; *Race to Witch Mountain* 2009; *Final Girl* 2015; *Go with Me* 2015

Ludwig, Pamela *Over the Edge* 1979; *Death of an Angel* 1985

Lugagne, Françoise (1914-1991) *The Witches of Salem* 1957; *The Diary of a Chambermaid* 1964

Lugosi, Bela (1882-1956) *Renegades* 1930; *Dracula* 1931; *Chandu the Magician* 1932; *Island of Lost Souls* 1932; *Murders in the Rue Morgue* 1932; *White Zombie* 1932; *The Death Kiss* 1933; *International House* 1933; *The Black Cat* 1934; *Mark of the Vampire* 1935; *The Raven* 1935; *The Invisible Ray* 1936; *Dark Eyes of London* 1939; *Ninotchka* 1939; *Son of Frankenstein* 1939; *Devil Bat* 1940; *The Saint's Double Trouble* 1940; *You'll Find Out* 1940; *The Black Cat* 1941; *Invisible Ghost* 1941; *Spooks Run Wild* 1941; *The Wolf Man* 1941; *The Ghost of Frankenstein* 1942; *Frankenstein Meets the Wolf Man* 1943; *Ghosts in the Night* 1943; *The Return of the Vampire* 1943; *Voodoo Man* 1944; *The Body Snatcher* 1945; *Scared to Death* 1947; *Abbott and Costello Meet Frankenstein* 1948; *Bela Lugosi Meets a Brooklyn Gorilla* 1952; *Glen or Glenda* 1953; *Bride of the Monster* 1955; *The Black Sleep* 1956; *Plan 9 from Outer Space* 1959

Luguet, André (1892-1979) *The Mad Genius* 1931; *Jewel Robbery* 1932; *The Man Who Played God* 1932; *Madame du Barry* 1954; *Une Parisienne* 1957; *A Ravishing Idiot* 1964

Lukas, Florian *Good Bye Lenin!* 2003; *The North Face* 2008; *Cross of Honour* 2012

Lukas, Paul (1891-1971) *The Shopworn Angel* 1928; *Anybody's Woman* 1930; *The Devil's Holiday* 1930; *Grumpy* 1930; *City Streets* 1931; *No One Man* 1932; *Rockabye* 1932; *The Kiss before the Mirror* 1933; *Little Women* 1933; *By Candlelight* 1934; *Glamour* 1934; *The Casino Murder Case* 1935; *I Found Stella Parish* 1935; *The Three Musketeers* 1935; *Dodsworth* 1936; *Ladies in Love* 1936; *Brief Ecstasy* 1937; *Dinner at the Ritz* 1937; *The Lady Vanishes* 1938; *Confessions of a Nazi Spy* 1939; *A Window in London* 1939; *The Ghost Breakers* 1940; *Strange Cargo* 1940; *They Dare Not Love* 1941; *Watch on the Rhine* 1943; *Experiment Perilous* 1944; *Uncertain Glory* 1944; *Deadline at Dawn* 1946; *Berlin Express* 1948; *Kim* 1950; *20,000 Leagues under the Sea* 1954; *The Roots of Heaven* 1958; *Scent of Mystery* 1960; *Tender Is the Night* 1961; *Fun in Acapulco* 1963; *Lord Jim* 1965

Luke, Benny *La Cage aux Folles* 1978; *La Cage aux Folles II* 1980; *La Cage aux Folles III: "Elles" Se Marient* 1985

Luke, Derek (1974-) *Antwone Fisher* 2002; *Pieces of April* 2002; *Biker Boyz* 2003; *Friday Night Lights* 2004; *Spartan* 2004; *Catch a Fire* 2006; *Glory Road* 2006; *Lions for Lambs* 2007; *Notorious* 2009; *Sparkle* 2012; *Baggage Claim* 2013; *Self/Less* 2015

Luke, Jorge *Ulzana's Raid* 1972; *The Return of a Man Called Horse* 1976; *Eagle's Wing* 1978

Luke, Keye (1904-1991) *Charlie Chan in Paris* 1935; *Charlie Chan in Shanghai* 1935; *Charlie Chan at the Circus* 1936; *Charlie Chan at the Opera* 1936; *Charlie Chan at Monte Carlo* 1937; *Charlie Chan at the Olympics* 1937; *Charlie Chan on Broadway* 1937; *The Good Earth* 1937; *Mr Moto's Gamble* 1938; *Dr Gillespie's New Assistant* 1942; *Dr Gillespie's Criminal Case* 1943; *Andy Hardy's Blonde Trouble* 1944; *Three Men in White* 1944; *Sleep, My Love* 1948; *Yangtse Incident* 1956; *The Amsterdam Kill* 1978; *Just You and Me, Kid* 1979; *Gremlins* 1984; *Dead Heat* 1988

Lukschy, Wolfgang (1905-1983) *Sherlock Holmes and the Deadly Necklace* 1962; *A Fistful of Dollars* 1964; *Inside Out* 1975

Lulu (1948-) *To Sir, with Love* 1967; *Whatever Happened to Harold Smith?* 1999; *Scott Walker: 30 Century Man* 2006; *Absolutely Fabulous: the Movie* 2016

Lumbly, Carl (1952-) *The Bedroom Window* 1987; *Everybody's All-American* 1988; *Judgment in Berlin* 1988; *Pacific Heights* 1990; *To Sleep with Anger* 1990; *South Central* 1992; *Out of Darkness* 1994; *Buffalo Soldiers* 1997; *The Wedding* 1998

Lumet, Baruch (1898-1992) *The Killer Shrews* 1959; *The Pawnbroker* 1965

Lumley, Joanna (1946-) *The Ballad of Tam Lin* 1970; *Don't Just Lie There, Say Something!* 1973; *The Satanic Rites of Dracula* 1973; *Trail of the Pink Panther* 1982; *The Curse of the Pink Panther* 1983; *Shirley Valentine* 1989; *A Ghost in Monte Carlo* 1990; *Innocent Lies* 1995; *James and the Giant Peach* 1996; *Prince Valiant* 1997; *Parting Shots* 1998; *Mad Cows* 1999; *Maybe Baby* 1999; *Whispers: an Elephant's Tale* 2000; *The Cat's Meow* 2001; *Ella Enchanted* 2004; *The Magic Roundabout* 2005; *Tim Burton's Corpse Bride* 2005; *Boogie Woogie* 2009; *Animals United* 2010; *The Wolf of Wall Street* 2013; *Absolutely Anything* 2015; *Absolutely Fabulous: the Movie* 2016

Luna, Barbara (1939-) *The Devil at Four o'Clock* 1961; *Mail Order Bride* 1963; *Che!* 1969

Luna, Diego (1979-) *Y Tu Mamá También* 2001; *Vampires: los Muertos* 2002; *Dirty Dancing 2* 2003; *Open Range* 2003; *Criminal* 2004; *The Terminal* 2004; *Fade to Black* 2006; *Mister Lonely* 2007; *Milk* 2008; *Rudo y Cursi* 2008; *Casa de Mi Padre* 2011; *Elysium* 2013; *Book of Life* 2014; *Blood Father* 2016; *Rogue One: a Star Wars Story* 2016; *Flatliners* 2017

Lund, Art (1915-1990) *The Molly Maguires* 1970; *Black Caesar* 1973; *The Last American Hero* 1973

Lund, John (1913-1992) *To Each His Own* 1946; *A Foreign Affair* 1948; *Miss Tatlock's Millions* 1948; *Night Has a Thousand Eyes* 1948; *Bride of Vengeance* 1949; *My Friend Irma* 1949; *Duchess of Idaho* 1950; *My Friend Irma Goes West* 1950; *No Man of Her Own* 1950; *Darling, How Could You!* 1951; *The Mating Season* 1951; *The Battle at Apache Pass* 1952; *Latin Lovers* 1953; *The Woman They Almost Lynched* 1953; *Chief Crazy Horse* 1955; *White Feather* 1955; *Dakota Incident* 1956; *High Society* 1956; *The Wackiest Ship in the World* 1961; *If a Man Answers* 1962

Lundgren, Dolph (1957-) *Rocky IV* 1985; *Masters of the Universe* 1987; *Dark Angel* 1989; *The Punisher* 1989; *Red Scorpion* 1989; *Showdown in Little Tokyo* 1991; *Universal Soldier* 1992; *The Shooter* 1994; *Johnny Mnemonic* 1995; *Silent Trigger* 1996; *The Peacekeeper* 1997; *Bridge of Dragons* 1999; *Storm Catcher* 1999; *Sweepers* 1999; *Agent Red* 2000; *Jill Rips* 2000; *Hidden Agenda* 2001; *Fat Slags* 2004; *Universal Soldier: Regeneration* 2009; *The Expendables* 2010; *The Expendables 2* 2012; *Battle of the Damned* 2013

Lundigan, William (1914-1975) *Wives under Suspicion* 1938; *Three Smart Girls Grow Up* 1939; *East of the River* 1940; *Andy Hardy's Double Life* 1942;

Apache Trail* 1942; *The Courtship of Andy Hardy* 1942; *Dishonored Lady* 1947; *The Fabulous Dorseys* 1947; *Pinky* 1949; *The House on Telegraph Hill* 1951; *I'd Climb the Highest Mountain* 1951; *Love Nest* 1951; *Inferno* 1953; *Serpent of the Nile* 1953

Lundy, Jessica (1966-) *Vampire's Kiss* 1988; *Madhouse* 1990; *The Stupids* 1995; *Rocketman* 1997

Lung Sihung (1930-2002) *Pushing Hands* 1991; *The Wedding Banquet* 1993; *Eat Drink Man Woman* 1994

Lunge, Romilly (1904-1994) *Königsmark* 1935; *His Lordship* 1936

Lunghi, Cherie (1953-) *Excalibur* 1981; *Oliver Twist* 1982; *The Sign of Four* 1983; *King David* 1985; *The Mission* 1986; *To Kill a Priest* 1988; *Jack & Sarah* 1995; *The Canterville Ghost* 1996; *Burn Hollywood Burn* 1997; *Back to the Secret Garden* 2000; *Loves Kitchen* 2010

Lupi, Roldano (1908-1989) *Crossed Swords* 1954; *The Mongols* 1961

Lupien, Tabitha (1990-) *Rent-a-Kid* 1992; *Look Who's Talking Now!* 1993

Lupino, Ida (1914-1995) *The Ghost Camera* 1933; *Peter Ibbetson* 1935; *Anything Goes* 1936; *One Rainy Afternoon* 1936; *Artists and Models* 1937; *The Adventures of Sherlock Holmes* 1939; *The Light That Failed* 1939; *The Lone Wolf Spy Hunt* 1939; *They Drive by Night* 1940; *High Sierra* 1941; *Ladies in Retirement* 1941; *Out of the Fog* 1941; *The Sea Wolf* 1941; *The Hard Way* 1942; *Life Begins at 8.30* 1942; *Moontide* 1942; *Forever and a Day* 1943; *In Our Time* 1944; *Devotion* 1946; *The Man I Love* 1946; *Deep Valley* 1947; *Escape Me Never* 1947; *Road House* 1948; *On Dangerous Ground* 1951; *Beware, My Lovely* 1952; *The Bigamist* 1953; *Jennifer* 1953; *Private Hell 36* 1954; *The Big Knife* 1955; *Women's Prison* 1955; *While the City Sleeps* 1956; *Backtrack* 1969; *Deadhead Miles* 1972; *Junior Bonner* 1972; *The Devil's Rain* 1975; *The Food of the Gods* 1976

Lupino, Stanley (1893-1942) *Honeymoon for Three* 1935; *Over She Goes* 1937

Lupo, Alberto (1924-1984) *The Giant of Marathon* 1960; *The Agony and the Ecstasy* 1965

LuPone, Patti (1949-) *Death Vengeance* 1982; *Witness* 1985; *Wise Guys* 1986; *Driving Miss Daisy* 1989; *The 24 Hour Woman* 1999; *State and Main* 2000; *Heist* 2001; *City by the Sea* 2002

Luppi, Federico (1934-) *Funny Dirty Little War* 1983; *La Amiga* 1988; *Cronos* 1992; *Men with Guns* 1997; *Lisboa* 1999; *The Devil's Backbone* 2001; *Machuca* 2004; *Fermat's Room* 2007

Lupton, John (1926-1993) *Man with the Gun* 1955; *The Great Locomotive Chase* 1956

Lurie, John (1952-) *Permanent Vacation* 1982; *Stranger than Paradise* 1984; *Down by Law* 1986

Luttazzi, Lelio (1923-2010) *L'Avventura* 1960; *Snow Job* 1972

Lutter, Alfred aka **Lutter, Alfred W** (1962-) *Alice Doesn't Live Here Anymore* 1974; *The Bad News Bears* 1976

Lutz, Adele *Beyond Rangoon* 1995; *Dead Funny* 1995

Lutz, Kellan (1985-) *Stick It* 2006; *A Nightmare on Elm Street* 2010; *Immortals* 2011; *Tarzan* 2013; *Experimenter: the Stanley Milgram Story* 2014; *The Legend of Hercules* 2014

Lvovsky, Noémie *Ma Femme Est une Actrice* 2001; *House of Tolerance* 2011; *Summertime* 2015

Lyadova, Elena *Elena* 2011; *Leviathan* 2014

Lydon, Gary *Nothing Personal* 1995; *Small Engine Repair* 2006

Lydon, James aka **Lydon, Jimmy** (1923-) *Back Door to Heaven* 1939; *Tom Brown's Schooldays* 1940; *Cynthia* 1947; *Life with Father* 1947; *September Affair* 1950; *When Willie Comes Marching Home* 1950

Lydon, John aka **Rotten, Johnny** (1956-) *The Great Rock 'n' Roll Swindle* 1979; *Order of Death* 1983

Lye, Reg (1912-1988) *Smiley Gets a Gun* 1959; *The Amorous Prawn* 1962; *Sunday Too Far Away* 1974; *Tarka the Otter* 1978

Lynas, Jeffrey aka **Lynas, Jeff** *Lies My Father Told Me* 1975; *Something for Joey* 1977

Lynch, Alfred (1933-2003) *On the Fiddle* 1961; *Two and Two Make Six* 1961; *The Password Is Courage* 1962; *West 11* 1963; *The Hill* 1965; *The Taming*

of the Shrew* 1967; *The Blockhouse* 1973; *Loophole* 1980

Lynch, David (1946-) *Zelly and Me* 1988; *Midnight Movies: from the Margins to the Mainstream* 2005; *Side by Side* 2012; *Brand: a Second Coming* 2015

Lynch, Evanna *Harry Potter and the Half-Blood Prince* 2009; *Harry Potter and the Deathly Hallows: Part 2* 2011

Lynch, Jane (1960-) *Best in Show* 2000; *A Mighty Wind* 2003; *Sleepover* 2004; *The 40 Year Old Virgin* 2005; *Talladega Nights: the Ballad of Ricky Bobby* 2006; *Role Models* 2008; *Julie & Julia* 2009; *Post Grad* 2009; *Paul* 2010; *Shrek Forever After* 2010; *Dino Time* 2012; *The Three Stooges* 2012; *Wreck-It Ralph* 2012; *Afternoon Delight* 2013

Lynch, Joe (1925-2001) *Loot* 1970; *Never Too Young to Rock* 1975; *Eat the Peach* 1986; *Thumbelina* 1994

Lynch, John (1961-) *Cal* 1984; *Hardware* 1990; *In the Name of the Father* 1993; *The Secret Garden* 1993; *The Secret of Roan Inish* 1993; *Angel Baby* 1995; *Moll Flanders* 1995; *Nothing Personal* 1995; *Some Mother's Son* 1996; *This Is the Sea* 1996; *Sliding Doors* 1997; *Best* 1999; *Puckoon* 2002; *Alien Hunter* 2003; *Isolation* 2005; *Lassie* 2005; *Holy Water* 2009; *Black Death* 2010; *Ghosted* 2011; *The Hot Potato* 2011; *Private Peaceful* 2012

Lynch, John Carroll (1963-) *Dead Men Can't Dance* 1997; *Bubble Boy* 2001; *Gothika* 2003; *Catch That Kid* 2004; *Things We Lost in the Fire* 2007; *Love Happens* 2009; *Hot Pursuit* 2015; *Miracles from Heaven* 2016

Lynch, Kate (1959-) *Meatballs* 1979; *Def-Con 4* 1984

Lynch, Kelly (1959-) *Cocktail* 1988; *Drugstore Cowboy* 1989; *Road House* 1989; *Desperate Hours* 1990; *Curly Sue* 1991; *Three of Hearts* 1992; *For Better and for Worse* 1993; *Imaginary Crimes* 1994; *Virtuosity* 1995; *White Man's Burden* 1995; *Heaven's Prisoners* 1996; *Persons Unknown* 1996; *Mr Magoo* 1997; *Homegrown* 1998; *Charlie's Angels* 2000; *Joe Somebody* 2001; *Homeless to Harvard: the Liz Murray Story* 2003; *The Jacket* 2005; *Rock the Kasbah* 2015

Lynch, Ken (1910-1990) *I Married a Monster from Outer Space* 1958; *The Legend of Tom Dooley* 1959; *Seven Ways from Sundown* 1960; *Apache Rifles* 1964

Lynch, Richard (1940-2012) *Scarecrow* 1973; *The Seven-Ups* 1973; *Open Season* 1974; *The Happy Hooker* 1975; *Deathsport* 1978; *Invasion USA* 1985; *Savage Dawn* 1985; *Little Nikita* 1988; *Lambada!* 1990; *The Forbidden Dance* 1990; *Alligator II: the Mutation* 1991; *Necronomicon* 1993; *Cyborg 3: The Recycler* 1994; *Scanner Cop* 1994; *Darklands* 1996; *The Proposition* 1996

Lynch, Sean *Sympathy for the Devil* 1968; *At the Earth's Core* 1976

Lynch, Susan (1971-) *The Secret of Roan Inish* 1993; *Downtime* 1997; *Waking Ned* 1998; *Nora* 1999; *Beautiful Creatures* 2000; *Casa de los Babys* 2003; *16 Years of Alcohol* 2003; *Enduring Love* 2004; *Someone Else* 2005; *City Rats* 2008; *Holy Water* 2009; *The Scouting Book for Boys* 2009; *The Unloved* 2009; *Away* 2016

Lynde, Paul (1926-1982) *New Faces* 1954; *Son of Flubber* 1962; *Bye Bye Birdie* 1963; *Under the Yum Yum Tree* 1963; *For Those Who Think Young* 1964; *Send Me No Flowers* 1964; *Beach Blanket Bingo* 1965; *The Glass Bottom Boat* 1966; *How Sweet It Is!* 1968; *Charlotte's Web* 1973; *Cactus Jack* 1979

Lyndhurst, Nicholas (1961-) *Bullshot* 1983; *Lassie* 2005

Lyndon, Simon *Blackrock* 1997; *Chopper* 2000

Lynley, Carol (1942-) *The Light in the Forest* 1958; *Blue Denim* 1959; *Holiday for Lovers* 1959; *Hound Dog Man* 1959; *The Last Sunset* 1961; *Return to Peyton Place* 1961; *The Cardinal* 1963; *The Stripper* 1963; *Under the Yum Yum Tree* 1963; *The Pleasure Seekers* 1964; *Bunny Lake Is Missing* 1965; *Danger Route* 1967; *The Shuttered Room* 1967; *The Helicopter Spies* 1968; *The Maltese Bippy* 1969; *Beware! The Blob* 1971; *The Poseidon Adventure* 1972; *The Cat and the Canary* 1979; *Dark Tower* 1989

Lynn, Ann (1934-) *Strongroom* 1961; *The Wind of Change* 1961; *The Black Torment* 1964; *The System* 1964; *The Uncle* 1964; *Four in the Morning* 1965; *The Party's Over* 1965

Lynn, Betty (1926-) *June Bride* 1948; *Father Was a Fullback* 1949; *Mother Is a Freshman* 1949; *Cheaper by the Dozen* 1950; *Payment on Demand* 1951;

Meet Me in Las Vegas 1956; *Gun for a Coward* 1957

Lynn, Diana *aka Loehr, Dolly* (1926-1971) *They Shall Have Music* 1939; *The Major and the Minor* 1942; *The Miracle of Morgan's Creek* 1943; *And the Angels Sing* 1944; *Out of This World* 1945; *The Bride Wore Boots* 1946; *Every Girl Should Be Married* 1948; *Ruthless* 1948; *My Friend Irma* 1949; *My Friend Irma Goes West* 1950; *Paid in Full* 1950; *Rogues of Sherwood Forest* 1950; *Bedtime for Bonzo* 1951; *The People against O'Hara* 1951; *Meet Me at the Fair* 1952; *Track of the Cat* 1954; *An Annapolis Story* 1955; *The Kentuckian* 1955; *You're Never Too Young* 1955

Lynn, George (1906-1967) *The Werewolf* 1956; *I Was a Teenage Frankenstein* 1957

Lynn, Jeffrey (1909-1995) *Daughters Courageous* 1939; *The Roaring Twenties* 1939; *A'l This, and Heaven Too* 1940; *The Fighting 69th* 1940; *It All Came True* 1940; *Four Mothers* 1941; *Million Dollar Baby* 1941; *For the Love of Mary* 1948; *A Letter to Three Wives* 1949; *Home Town Story* 1951; *Butterfield 8* 1960; *Tony Rome* 1967

Lynn, Ralph (1832-1964) *Rookery Nook* 1930; *A Cuckoo in the Nest* 1933; *Fighting Stock* 1935; *Foreign Affaires* 1935

Lynn, Vera (1917-) *We'll Meet Again* 1942; *Rhythm Serenade* 1943

Lynn, William Harvey 1950; *Mr Belvedere Rings the Bell* 1951

Lynne, Sharon *aka Lynn, Sharon* (1901-1963) *Sunny Side Up* 1929; *Up the River* 1930; *The Big Broadcast* 1932; *Enter Madame!* 1933; *Go into Your Dance* 1935; *Way Out West* 1937

Lynskey, Melanie (1977-) *Heavenly Creatures* 1994; *Ever After: a Cinderella Story* 1998; *But I'm a Cheerleader* 1999; *Shattered Glass* 2003; *Away We Go* 2009; *The Informant!* 2009; *Up in the Air* 2009; *Seeking a Friend for the End of the World* 2011; *Win Win* 2011; *The Perks of Being a Wallflower* 2012; *We'll Never Have Paris* 2014

Lyon, Barbara (1931-1995) *Life with the Lyons* 1953; *The Lyons in Paris* 1955

Lyon, Ben (1901-1979) *For the Love of Mike* 1927; *Hell's Angels* 1930; *Her Majesty Love* 1931; *Indiscreet* 1931; *Night Nurse* 1931; *Lady with a Past* 1932; *I Cover the Waterfront* 1933; *Life with the Lyons* 1953; *The Lyons in Paris* 1955

Lyon, Richard (1934-) *The Unseen* 1945; *Anna and the King of Siam* 1946; *The Boy with Green Hair* 1948; *The Great Lover* 1949; *Life with the Lyons* 1953; *The Lyons in Paris* 1955

Lyon, Sue (1946-) *Lolita* 1961; *The Night of the Iguana* 1964; *7 Women* 1966; *The Flim-Flam Man* 1967; *Evel Knievel* 1971; *The Astral Factor* 1976; *Crash!* 1977; *End of the World* 1977

Lyonne, Natasha (1979-) *Dennis* 1993; *Everyone Says I Love You* 1996; *Krippendorf's Tribe* 1998; *Slums of Beverly Hills* 1998; *American Pie* 1999; *But I'm a Cheerleader* 1999; *Confessions of a Trickbaby* 1999; *American Pie 2* 2001; *The Grey Zone* 2001; *Kate & Leopold* 2002; *Party Monster* 2003; *Blade: Trinity* 2004; *Madhouse* 2004; *Addicted to Fresno* 2015; *Sleeping with Other People* 2015; *Yoga Hosers* 2016

Lyons, Phyllis (1960-) *The Bridges of Madison County* 1995; *Thirst* 1998

Lyons, Robert F (1940-) *Pendulum* 1969; *Getting Straight* 1970; *Shoot Out* 1971; *10 to Midnight* 1983; *Avenging Angel* 1985; *Murphy's Law* 1986; *Annie's Point* 2005

Lyons, Tom Burn! 1970; *Factotum (A Man Who Preforms Many Jobs)* 2005

Lys, Lya (1908-1986) *L'Age d'Or* 1930; *Confessions of a Nazi Spy* 1939; *The Return of Dr X* 1939

M

Ma Jingwu *Raise the Red Lantern* 1991; *The Day the Sun Turned Cold* 1994; *The Banquet* 2006

Ma Tzi (1962-) *Rapid Fire* 1992; *Golden Gate* 1994; *The Quiet American* 2002; *The Ladykillers* 2004; *Akeelah and the Bee* 2006

Maaskri, Moussa *Vidocq* 2001; *Two Brothers* 2004; *District 13: Ultimatum* 2009

Maberly, Kate *The Secret Garden* 1993; *Like Minds* 2006

Mabius, Eric (1971-) *The Journey of August King* 1995; *Lawn Dogs* 1997; *The Minus Man* 1999; *Splendor* 1999;

Dancing at the Harvest Moon 2002; *Resident Evil* 2002; *Reeker* 2005

Mably, Luke (1976-) *The Prince & Me* 2004; *Spirit Trap* 2004; *Exam* 2009

Mac, Bernie (1957-2008) *Above the Rim* 1994; *Get on the Bus* 1996; *The Players Club* 1998; *Life* 1999; *Ocean's Eleven* 2001; *What's the Worst That Could Happen?* 2001; *Bad Santa* 2003; *Charlie's Angels: Full Throttle* 2003; *Head of State* 2003; *Mr 3000* 2004; *Ocean's Twelve* 2004; *Guess Who* 2005; *Ocean's Thirteen* 2007; *Pride* 2007; *Madagascar: Escape 2 Africa* 2008; *Soul Men* 2008; *Old Dogs* 2009

McAdams, Rachel (1976-) *Guilt by Association* 2002; *The Hot Chick* 2002; *The Notebook* 2003; *Mean Girls* 2004; *The Family Stone* 2005; *Red Eye* 2005; *Wedding Crashers* 2005; *Married Life* 2007; *The Time Traveler's Wife* 2008; *Sherlock Holmes* 2009; *State of Play* 2009; *Morning Glory* 2010; *Midnight in Paris* 2011; *Sherlock Holmes: a Game of Shadows* 2011; *Passion* 2012; *To the Wonder* 2012; *The Vow* 2012; *About Time* 2013; *A Most Wanted Man* 2013; *Aloha* 2015; *Southpaw* 2015; *Spotlight* 2015; *Doctor Strange* 2016

McAleer, Des *Anne Devlin* 1984; *Butterfly Kiss* 1994

McAnally, Ray (1926-1989) *Sea of Sand* 1958; *The Naked Edge* 1961; *Billy Budd* 1962; *He Who Rides a Tiger* 1965; *The Looking Glass War* 1969; *Quest for Love* 1971; *Fear Is the Key* 1972; *Angel* 1982; *Cal* 1984; *No Surrender* 1985; *The Mission* 1986; *The Fourth Protocol* 1987; *The Sicilian* 1987; *White Mischief* 1987; *High Spirits* 1988; *Taffin* 1988; *My Left Foot* 1989; *Venus Peter* 1989; *We're No Angels* 1989

MacAninch, Cal (1982-) *The Woodlanders* 1997; *Best* 1999; *The Point Men* 2000

McArdle, Aidan *Ella Enchanted* 2004; *The Duchess* 2008; *The Borderlands* 2013

McArthur, Alex (1957-) *Rampage* 1987; *Perfect Alibi* 1994; *Conspiracy Theory* 1997; *Kiss the Girls* 1997

MacArthur, James (1937-2010) *The Young Stranger* 1957; *The Light in the Forest* 1958; *Kidnapped* 1960; *Swiss Family Robinson* 1960; *Spencer's Mountain* 1963; *The Truth about Spring* 1964; *The Bedford Incident* 1965; *Ride beyond Vengeance* 1966; *Hang 'Em High* 1968; *Storm Chasers: Revenge of the Twister* 1998

McAuley, Alphonso *Fat Albert* 2004; *Glory Road* 2006

Macauley, Tom *The Chiltern Hundreds* 1949; *The Planter's Wife* 1952

McAuliffe, Callan *I Am Number Four* 2011; *The Great Gatsby* 2013; *Robot Overlords* 2014

McAvoy, James (1979-) *Bollywood Queen* 2002; *Bright Young Things* 2003; *Inside I'm Dancing* 2004; *Strings* 2004; *Wimbledon* 2004; *The Chronicles of Narnia: The Lion, the Witch and the Wardrobe* 2005; *Becoming Jane* 2006; *The Last King of Scotland* 2006; *Penelope* 2006; *Starter for 10* 2006; *Atonement* 2007; *Wanted* 2008; *The Last Station* 2009; *The Conspirator* 2010; *Arthur Christmas* 2011; *Gnomeo & Juliet* 2011; *X-Men: First Class* 2011; *Welcome to the Punch* 2012; *Filth* 2013; *Trance* 2013; *Muppets Most Wanted* 2014; *X-Men: Days of Future Past* 2014; *Victor Frankenstein* 2015; *X-Men: Apocalypse* 2016; *The Coldest City* 2017; *Split* 2017

McAvoy, May (1899-1984) *Ben-Hur: a Tale of the Christ* 1925; *Lady Windermere's Fan* 1925; *The Jazz Singer* 1927

McBain, Diane (1941-) *Ice Palace* 1960; *Black Gold* 1962; *Mary, Mary* 1963; *A Distant Trumpet* 1964; *Spinout* 1966; *Thunder Alley* 1967; *The Delta Factor* 1970

McBrayer, Jack *Wreck-It Ralph* 2012; *Cooties* 2014

McBride, Chi (1961-) *Mercury Rising* 1998; *Disney's The Kid* 2000; *Gone in Sixty Seconds* 2000; *Narc* 2001; *Undercover Brother* 2002; *I, Robot* 2004; *The Terminal* 2004; *Waiting...* 2005; *The Brothers Solomon* 2007

McBride (2), Danny *aka McBride, Danny R* (1976-) *All the Real Girls* 2003; *The Foot Fist Way* 2006; *Drillbit Taylor* 2007; *The Heartbreak Kid* 2007; *Hot Rod* 2007; *Pineapple Express* 2008; *Tropic Thunder* 2008; *Land of the Lost* 2009; *Up in the Air* 2009; *Due Date* 2010; *Your Highness* 2010; *30 Minutes or Less* 2011; *As I Lay Dying* 2013; *This Is the End* 2013; *The Angry Birds Movie* 2016

MacBride, Donald (1889-1957) *Annabel Takes a Tour* 1938; *The Amazing Mr Williams* 1939; *The Girl*

from Mexico 1939; *The Great Man Votes* 1939; *Curtain Call* 1940; *Michael Shayne, Private Detective* 1940; *My Favorite Wife* 1940; *Northwest Passage* 1940; *Footlight Fever* 1941; *Out of This World* 1945; *The Killers* 1946; *Good News* 1947; *Meet Danny Wilson* 1952

McBurney, Simon (1957-) *The Reckoning* 2001; *Friends with Money* 2006; *The Last King of Scotland* 2006; *Body of Lies* 2008; *The Duchess* 2008; *Magic in the Moonlight* 2014; *The Conjuring 2* 2016

McCabe, Richard *Notting Hill* 1999; *The Constant Gardener* 2005; *The Duchess* 2008

McCabe, Ruth *My Left Foot* 1989; *The Field* 1990; *The Snapper* 1993; *Talk of Angels* 1998; *The Closer You Get* 2000; *Wake Wood* 2010

McCafferty, Alan *Pasty Faces* 2000; *Night People* 2005

McCaffrey, James (1960-) *The Truth about Cats and Dogs* 1996; *American Splendor* 2003; *Compliance* 2012

McCain, Frances Lee (1944-) *Tex* 1982; *Gremlins* 1984; *The Rape of Richard Beck* 1985; *Patch Adams* 1998

McCall, Mitzi *You're Never Too Young* 1955; *World's Greatest Dad* 2009

McCallany, Holt (1964-) *Alien³* 1992; *Below* 2002; *Bound by a Secret* 2008; *The Losers* 2010

McCallister, Lon (1923-2005) *Stage Door Canteen* 1943; *Home in Indiana* 1944; *Winged Victory* 1944; *Bob, Son of Battle* 1947; *The Red House* 1947

McCallum (1), David (1933-) *Hell Drivers* 1957; *Robbery under Arms* 1957; *A Night to Remember* 1958; *Violent Playground* 1958; *The Long and the Short and the Tall* 1960; *Billy Budd* 1962; *The Great Escape* 1963; *The Greatest Story Ever Told* 1965; *One of Our Spies Is Missing* 1966; *One Spy Too Many* 1966; *The Spy in the Green Hat* 1966; *The Spy with My Face* 1966; *To Trap a Spy* 1966; *The Karate Killers* 1967; *The Helicopter Spies* 1968; *How to Steal the World* 1968; *Mosquito Squadron* 1968; *Frankenstein: the True Story* 1973; *The Invisible Man* 1975; *Dogs* 1976; *The Watcher in the Woods* 1982; *Terminal Choice* 1983; *The Haunting of Morella* 1990; *Hear My Song* 1991; *Dirty Weekend* 1992

McCallum, John (1918-2010) *The Root of All Evil* 1946; *Bush Christmas* 1947; *It Always Rains on Sunday* 1947; *The Loves of Joanna Godden* 1947; *Miranda* 1947; *The Calendar* 1948; *A Boy, a Girl and a Bike* 1949; *Traveller's Joy* 1949; *The Woman in Question* 1950; *Lady Godiva Rides Again* 1951; *Valley of Eagles* 1951; *Derby Day* 1952; *The Long Memory* 1952; *Trent's Last Case* 1952; *Devil on Horseback* 1954; *Trouble in the Glen* 1954; *Port of Escape* 1956; *Smiley* 1956

McCallum, Neil (1929-1976) *Dr Terror's House of Horrors* 1964; *The Lost Continent* 1968

McCambridge, Mercedes (1916-2004) *All the King's Men* 1949; *Lightning Strikes Twice* 1951; *The Scarf* 1951; *Johnny Guitar* 1954; *Giant* 1956; *A Farewell to Arms* 1957; *Touch of Evil* 1958; *Suddenly, Last Summer* 1959; *Cimarron* 1960; *Angel Baby* 1961; *The Exorcist* 1973; *Airport '79: the Concorde* 1979

McCamus, Tom (1955-) *The Sweet Hereafter* 1997; *Possible Worlds* 2000; *Room* 2015

McCann, Chuck (1934-) *The Heart Is a Lonely Hunter* 1968; *The Projectionist* 1970; *CHOMPS* 1979; *Cameron's Closet* 1988; *Duck Tales: the Movie - Treasure of the Lost Lamp* 1990; *Storyville* 1992

McCann, Donal (1943-1999) *Cal* 1984; *The Dead* 1987; *December Bride* 1990; *The Miracle* 1990; *Stealing Beauty* 1995; *The Nephew* 1997

McCann, Martin *'71* 2014; *X+Y* 2014; *The Survivalist* 2015

McCann, Sean (1935-) *Bordertown Cafe* 1991; *Run* 1991; *The Air Up There* 1993; *Swann* 1996; *Evidence of Blood* 1998; *A House Divided* 2000; *Possible Worlds* 2000; *Miracle* 2004; *Ambulance Girl* 2005

McCardie, Brian (1965-) *Rob Roy* 1995; *Speed 2: Cruise Control* 1997; *In the Blood* 2014

McCarren, Fred (1951-2006) *Xanadu* 1980; *National Lampoon's Class Reunion* 1982

McCarron, Conor *Neds* 2010; *Catch Me Daddy* 2014

McCarthy, Andrew (1963-) *Class* 1983; *Catholic Boys* 1985; *St Elmo's Fire* 1985; *Pretty in Pink* 1986; *Less than Zero* 1987; *Mannequin* 1987; *Waiting for the Moon* 1987; *Fresh Horses* 1988; *Kansas* 1988; *Weekend at Bernie's* 1989; *Year of the Gun* 1991; *Only You* 1992; *Weekend at Bernie's II*

1992; Getting In 1994; *Mrs Parker and the Vicious Circle* 1994; *Night of the Running Man* 1994; *Dead Funny* 1995; *I Woke Up Early the Day I Died* 1998; *I'm Losing You* 1998; *New World Disorder* 1999; *A Storm in Summer* 2000; *Straight from the Heart* 2003; *The Hollywood Mom's Mystery* 2004; *The Spiderwick Chronicles* 2008; *The National Tree* 2009; *Camp Hell* 2010

McCarthy, Jenny (1972-) *BASEketball* 1998; *Diamonds* 1999; *Scream 3* 1999; *John Tucker Must Die* 2006

McCarthy, Kevin (1914-2010) *Death of a Salesman* 1951; *Drive a Crooked Road* 1954; *An Annapolis Story* 1955; *Stranger on Horseback* 1955; *Invasion of the Body Snatchers* 1956; *Nightmare* 1956; *The Misfits* 1961; *The Best Man* 1964; *Mirage* 1965; *A Big Hand for a Little Lady* 1966; *The Three Sisters* 1966; *Ace High* 1968; *The Hell with Heroes* 1968; *Kansas City Bomber* 1972; *Dan Candy's Law* 1973; *Buffalo Bill and the Indians, or Sitting Bull's History Lesson* 1976; *Invasion of the Body Snatchers* 1978; *Piranha* 1978; *Hero at Large* 1980; *The Howling* 1981; *My Tutor* 1983; *Innerspace* 1987; *Dark Tower* 1989; *UHF* 1989; *Final Approach* 1991; *The Distinguished Gentleman* 1992; *Addams Family Reunion* 1998

McCarthy, Melissa (1970-) *The Nines* 2007; *Bridesmaids* 2011; *This Is 40* 2012; *The Heat* 2013; *Identity Thief* 2013; *St Vincent* 2014; *Tammy* 2014; *The Boss* 2015; *Spy* 2015; *Ghostbusters* 2016

McCarthy, Neil (1933-1985) *Sands of the Desert* 1960; *Zulu* 1963; *Steptoe and Son Ride Again* 1973

McCarthy, Nobu *aka McCarthy, Nobu Atsumi* (1934-2002) *The Geisha Boy* 1958; *Walk like a Dragon* 1960; *Two Loves* 1961; *The Karate Kid Part II* 1986; *Pacific Heights* 1990

McCarthy, Sheila (1956-) *I've Heard the Mermaids Singing* 1987; *Beautiful Dreamers* 1990; *George's Island* 1991; *Paradise* 1991; *Stepping Out* 1991; *A Private Matter* 1992; *Being Julia* 2004; *Confessions of a Teenage Drama Queen* 2004

McCarthy, Thomas *aka McCarthy, Tom* (1969-) *Year of the Dog* 2007; *Duplicity* 2009; *2012* 2009; *Jack Goes Boating* 2010

McCartney, Jesse *Alvin and the Chipmunks* 2007; *Alvin and the Chipmunks: the Squeakquel* 2009; *Alvin and the Chipmunks: Chipwrecked* 2011; *Chernobyl Diaries* 2012; *Alvin and the Chipmunks: the Road Chip* 2015

McCartney, Linda *Give My Regards to Broad Street* 1984; *Get Back* 1991

McCartney, Paul (1942-) *A Hard Day's Night* 1964; *Help!* 1965; *Breaking Glass* 1980; *Give My Regards to Broad Street* 1984; *Eat the Rich* 1987; *Get Back* 1991; *George Harrison: Living in the Material World* 2011; *God Bless Ozzy Osbourne* 2011

McCarty, Mary (1923-1980) *The French Line* 1954; *Somebody Killed Her Husband* 1978

McCary, Rod *No Drums, No Bugles* 1971; *Night of the Demons 2* 1994

Macchio, Ralph (1961-) *The Outsiders* 1983; *The Karate Kid* 1984; *Teachers* 1984; *Crossroads* 1986; *The Karate Kid Part II* 1986; *Distant Thunder* 1988; *The Karate Kid III* 1989; *Too Much Sun* 1990; *My Cousin Vinny* 1992; *Naked in New York* 1994; *The Secret of NIMH II: Timmy to the Rescue* 1998

McClanahan, Rue (1934-2010) *They Might Be Giants* 1971; *Rainbow* 1978; *The Man in the Brown Suit* 1989; *Modern Love* 1990; *Dear God* 1996; *This World, Then the Fireworks* 1996; *Back to You and Me* 2005; *Generation Gap* 2008

McClintock, Eddie *Confessions of an American Bride* 2005; *Three Wise Guys* 2005

McClory, Belinda (1968-) *Hotel de Love* 1996; *Cubbyhouse* 2001

McClory, Sean (1924-2003) *The Daughter of Rosie O'Grady* 1950; *Anne of the Indies* 1951; *Lorna Doone* 1951; *The King's Thief* 1955; *The Gnome-Mobile* 1967; *My Chauffeur* 1986

McCloskey, Leigh (1955-) *Inferno* 1980; *Fraternity Vacation* 1985; *Cameron's Closet* 1988

McClure, Doug (1934-1995) *Because They're Young* 1960; *Shenandoah* 1965; *Beau Geste* 1966; *The King's Pirate* 1967; *Backtrack* 1969; *The Land That Time Forgot* 1974; *What Changed Charley Farthing?* 1974; *At the Earth's Core* 1976; *The People That Time Forgot* 1977; *Warlords of Atlantis* 1978; *Monster* 1980; *The House Where Evil Dwells* 1982; *52 Pick-Up* 1986; *Tapeheads* 1988

McClure, Greg (1918-) *Lulu Belle* 1948; *Breakthrough* 1950

McClure, Marc (1957-) *I Wanna Hold Your Hand* 1978; *Pandemonium* 1982; *Back to the Future* 1985; *Superman IV: the Quest for Peace* 1987; *After Midnight* 1989; *Grim Prairie Tales* 1990; *The Vagrant* 1992; *Storm* 1999; *Imaginary Friend* 2012

McClure, Molly *Daddy's Dyin'... Who's Got the Will?* 1990; *Pure Country* 1992

McClure, Vicky *A Room for Romeo Brass* 1999; *This Is England* 2006; *Hummingbird* 2013; *Svengali* 2013

McClurg, Edie (1950-) *Ferris Bueller's Day Off* 1986; *Elvira, Mistress of the Dark* 1988; *The Little Mermaid* 1989; *A River Runs through It* 1992; *Airborne* 1993; *Flubber* 1997; *Kiki's Delivery Service* 1998; *The Master of Disguise* 2002; *Dickie Roberts: Former Child Star* 2003

McCole, Stephen *The Acid House* 1998; *Orphans* 1998; *Postmortem* 1999; *Crying with Laughter* 2009; *The Wee Man* 2013

McComb, Heather (1977-) *New York Stories* 1989; *Stay Tuned* 1992; *The Joyriders* 1999

McConaughey, Matthew (1969-) *Dazed and Confused* 1993; *Angels in the Outfield* 1994; *Texas Chainsaw Massacre: the Next Generation* 1994; *Boys on the Side* 1995; *Glory Daze* 1995; *Lone Star* 1995; *Scorpion Spring* 1995; *Larger than Life* 1996; *A Time to Kill* 1996; *Amistad* 1997; *Contact* 1997; *The Newton Boys* 1998; *Edtv* 1999; *U-571* 2000; *Frailty* 2001; *Reign of Fire* 2001; *Thirteen Conversations about One Thing* 2001; *The Wedding Planner* 2001; *How to Lose a Guy in 10 Days* 2003; *Sahara* 2005; *Two for the Money* 2005; *Failure to Launch* 2006; *Fool's Gold* 2008; *Tropic Thunder* 2008; *Ghosts of Girlfriends Past* 2009; *Bernie* 2011; *Killer Joe* 2011; *The Lincoln Lawyer* 2011; *Magic Mike* 2012; *Mud* 2012; *The Paperboy* 2012; *Dallas Buyers Club* 2013; *The Wolf of Wall Street* 2013; *Interstellar* 2014; *The Sea of Trees* 2015; *Gold* 2016; *Kubo and the Two Strings* 2016; *Sing* 2016; *The Dark Tower* 2017

McConnell, John (1958-) *Malpractice* 2001; *The Reaping* 2006; *The Mechanic* 2011

McConnohie, Michael *Fist of the North Star* 1986; *The Little Polar Bear* 2001

MacCorkindale, Simon (1952-2010) *Death on the Nile* 1978; *The Riddle of the Sands* 1978; *The Quatermass Conclusion* 1979; *Jaws III* 1983; *Danielle Steel's No Greater Love* 1996; *A Closed Book* 2009

McCormack, Catherine (1972-) *Loaded* 1994; *Braveheart* 1995; *North Star* 1996; *Dangerous Beauty* 1997; *The Land Girls* 1997; *Dancing at Lughnasa* 1998; *This Year's Love* 1999; *Born Romantic* 2000; *A Rumor of Angels* 2000; *Shadow of the Vampire* 2000; *The Tailor of Panama* 2000; *The Weight of Water* 2000; *Spy Game* 2001; *Strings* 2004; *Renaissance* 2006; *28 Weeks Later* 2007; *The Fold* 2013

McCormack, Eric (1973-) *The Man Who Wouldn't Die* 1995; *Free Enterprise* 1998; *Holy Man* 1998; *The Audrey Hepburn Story* 2000

McCormack, Mary (1969-) *The Alarmist* 1997; *Private Parts* 1997; *The Big Tease* 1999; *Mystery, Alaska* 1999; *The Broken Hearts Club: a Romantic Comedy* 2000; *Gun Shy* 2000; *High Heels and Low Lifes* 2001; *K-PAX* 2001; *Full Frontal* 2002; *Dickie Roberts: Former Child Star* 2003; *Right at Your Door* 2006; *1408* 2007; *Escape from Polygamy* 2013

McCormack, Patty (1945-) *The Bad Seed* 1956; *The Day They Gave Babies Away* 1957; *The Adventures of Huckleberry Finn* 1960; *Saturday the 14th Strikes Back* 1988; *Elevator Girl* 2010

McCormick, F J (1891-1947) *The Plough and the Stars* 1936; *Hungry Hill* 1946; *Odd Man Out* 1947

McCormick, Gilmer (1947-) *Godspell* 1973; *Silent Night, Deadly Night* 1984

McCormick, Maureen (1956-) *The Idolmaker* 1980; *Fortune Hunters* 1999

McCormick, Myron (1908-1962) *One Third of a Nation* 1939; *China Girl* 1942; *Jigsaw* 1949; *Jolson Sings Again* 1949; *Not as a Stranger* 1955; *Three for the Show* 1955; *No Time for Sergeants* 1958; *The Man Who Understood Women* 1959; *The Hustler* 1961

McCormick, Pat (1934-2005) *Smokey and the Bandit* 1977; *Smokey and the Bandit III* 1983; *Broadway Bound* 1991

McCourt, Emer *London Kills Me* 1991; *Riff-Raff* 1991; *Boston Kickout* 1995

McCourt, Malachy Q - the Winged Serpent 1982; Ash Wednesday 2002; The Guru 2002

McCowen, Alec (1925-) The Cruel Sea 1952; The Deep Blue Sea 1955; The Good Companions 1956; The Long Arm 1956; Town on Trial 1956; The One That Got Away 1957; Time without Pity 1957; The Silent Enemy 1958; A Midsummer Night's Dream 1961; The Witches 1966; The Hawaiians 1970; Frenzy 1972; Travels with My Aunt 1972; Stevie 1978; Hanover Street 1979; Never Say Never Again 1983; The Assam Garden 1985; Cry Freedom 1987; Personal Services 1987; Henry V 1989; The Age of Innocence 1993; Gangs of New York 2002

McCoy, Larry Bulletproof 1996; Boss'n Up 2005

McCoy, Matt (1958-) Police Academy 5: Assignment Miami Beach 1988; DeepStar Six 1989; Police Academy 6: City under Siege 1989; The Hand That Rocks the Cradle 1992; Rent-a-Kid 1992; Snapdragon 1993; Little Bigfoot 1995; Memory Run 1995; LA Confidential 1997; National Security 2002

McCoy, Sylvester The Hobbit: an Unexpected Journey 2012; The Christmas Candle 2013

McCrackin, Daisy A Crack in the Floor 2000; Halloween: Resurrection 2002

McCrary, Darius Don King: Only in America 1997; Vampires: los Muertos 2002

McCrea, Jody (1934-2009) The First Texan 1956; Young Guns of Texas 1962; Beach Party 1963; Muscle Beach Party 1964; Beach Blanket Bingo 1965; The Glory Stompers 1967

McCrea, Joel (1905-1990) Dynamite 1929; Kept Husbands 1931; Bird of Paradise 1932; The Lost Squadron 1932; The Most Dangerous Game 1932; Rockabye 1932; The Silver Cord 1933; Gambling Lady 1934; The Richest Girl in the World 1934; Barbary Coast 1935; Our Little Girl 1935; Private Worlds 1935; Splendor 1935; Woman Wanted 1935; Banjo on My Knee 1936; Come and Get It 1936; These Three 1936; Dead End 1937; Internes Can't Take Money 1937; Wells Fargo 1937; Woman Chases Man 1937; Three Blind Mice 1938; They Shall Have Music 1939; Union Pacific 1939; Foreign Correspondent 1940; Primrose Path 1940; Sullivan's Travels 1941; The Great Man's Lady 1942; The Palm Beach Story 1942; The More the Merrier 1943; Buffalo Bill 1944; The Great Moment 1944; The Unseen 1945; The Virginian 1946; Ramrod 1947; They Passed This Way 1948; Colorado Territory 1949; South of St Louis 1949; Frenchie 1950; The Outriders 1950; Saddle Tramp 1950; Cattle Drive 1951; Rough Shoot 1952; The San Francisco Story 1952; The Lone Hand 1953; Black Horse Canyon 1954; Stranger on Horseback 1955; Wichita 1955; The First Texan 1956; Gunsight Ridge 1957; The Oklahoman 1957; The Tall Stranger 1957; Trooper Hook 1957; Cattle Empire 1958; Fort Massacre 1958; The Gunfight at Dodge City 1959; Ride the High Country 1962; The Great American Cowboy 1973; Mustang Country 1976

McCrory, Helen (1968-) Dad Savage 1997; The James Gang 1997; Hotel Splendide 1999; The Count of Monte Cristo 2001; Enduring Love 2004; The Queen 2006; Flashbacks of a Fool 2008; Hugo 2011; Flying Blind 2012; Skyfall 2012; Bill 2014; A Little Chaos 2014; The Woman in Black: Angel of Death 2014; Loving Vincent 2016

McCulloch, Bruce (1961-) Kids in the Hall: Brain Candy 1996; Dog Park 1998; Dick 1999

McCulloch, Ian (1939-) The Ghoul 1975; Zombie Flesh Eaters 1979; Zombie Holocaust 1979

McCullough, Julie (1965-) Big Bad Mama II 1987; Round Trip to Heaven 1992

McCullough, Rohan Strapless 1988; War Requiem 1988

McCullough, Suli (1968-) Terminal Velocity 1994; Don't Be a Menace to South Central while Drinking Your Juice in the Hood 1996

McCurley, Mathew North 1994; The Secret Agent Club 1995

McCutcheon, Bill (1924-2002) Family Business 1989; Aunt Julia and the Scriptwriter 1990; Mr Destiny 1990

McCutcheon, Martine (1976-) Kiss Kiss (Bang Bang) 2001; Love Actually 2003

McDaniel, Hattie aka McDaniels, Hattie (1895-1952) Blonde Venus 1932; Hello Sister! 1933; Judge Priest 1934; Alice Adams 1935; The Little Colonel 1935; The Bride Walks Out 1936; Nothing Sacred 1937; True Confession 1937; The Mad Miss Manton 1938; The Shining Hour 1938; The Shopworn Angel 1938; Vivacious Lady 1938; Gone with the Wind 1939; Zenobia 1939; Maryland 1940; Affectionately Yours 1941; The Great Lie 1941; They Died with Their Boots On 1941; George Washington Slept Here 1942; In This Our Life 1942; The Male Animal 1942; Johnny Come Lately 1943; Since You Went Away 1944; Margie 1946; Never Say Goodbye 1946; Song of the South 1946

McDaniel, James (1958-) The Road to Galveston 1996; Sunshine State 2002

McDermott, Charlie Frozen River 2008; Safe Harbor 2009

McDermott, Dean (1966-) A Christmas Visitor 2002; Open Range 2003; Always and Forever 2008

McDermott, Dylan (1961-) Hamburger Hill 1987; The Blue Iguana 1988; Steel Magnolias 1989; Hardware 1990; Where Sleeping Dogs Lie 1991; Jersey Girl 1992; In the Line of Fire 1993; The Cowboy Way 1994; Miracle on 34th Street 1994; Destiny Turns on the Radio 1995; Home for the Holidays 1995; 'Til There Was You 1997; Three to Tango 1999; Texas Rangers 2001; Party Monster 2003; Wonderland 2003; Edison 2005; The Messengers 2007; The Campaign 2012; The Perks of Being a Wallflower 2012; Olympus Has Fallen 2013; Survivor 2015

McDermott, Hugh (1908-1972) Where's That Fire? 1939; Pimpernel Smith 1941; The Seventh Veil 1945; No Orchids for Miss Blandish 1948; The Huggetts Abroad 1949; Trent's Last Case 1952; Malaga 1954; The Man Who Wouldn't Talk 1957; You Pay Your Money 1957; The Adding Machine 1969; Guns in the Heather 1969

MacDermott, John My Hustler 1965; Vinyl 1965

McDermott, Keith Tourist Trap 1979; Without a Trace 1983

MacDermott, Marc (1881-1929) He Who Gets Slapped 1924; The Sea Hawk 1924; The Lucky Lady 1926; The Temptress 1926

McDevitt, Ruth (1895-1976) The Birds 1963; Love Is a Ball 1963; The Shakiest Gun in the West 1967

McDiarmid, Ian (1947-) Dragonslayer 1981; Star Wars Episode VI: Return of the Jedi 1983; Dirty Rotten Scoundrels 1988; Restoration 1995; Star Wars Episode I: the Phantom Menace 1999; Star Wars Episode II: Attack of the Clones 2002; Star Wars Episode III: Revenge of the Sith 2005

MacDonald, Aimi Take a Girl like You 1970; Keep It Up Downstairs 1976

MacDonald, Audra (1970-) Annie 1999; The Last Debate 2000; Wit 2001

MacDonald, Christopher (1955-) Grease 2 1982; Breakdance 1984; The Boys Next Door 1985; Chances are 1989; Driving Me Crazy 1991; Thelma & Louise 1991; Wild Orchid 2: Two Shades of Blue 1992; Benefit of the Doubt 1993; Fatal Instinct 1993; Monkey Trouble 1994; Roadflower 1994; Terminal Velocity 1994; Fair Game 1995; Happy Gilmore 1996; The Rich Man's Wife 1996; Unforgettable 1996; The Eighteenth Angel 1997; Flubber 1997; Lawn Dogs 1997; Leave It to Beaver 1997; A Smile like Yours 1997; Dirty Work 1998; The Iron Giant 1999; SLC Punk! 1999; Requiem for a Dream 2000; The Skulls 2000; Rumor Has It... 2005; Awake 2007; Superhero Movie 2008; The Collection 2011; Exposed 2016

MacDonald, Donald The Kentuckian 1955; The Brass Legend 1956; Constance 1984

MacDonald, Edmund (1908-1951) The Gay Caballero 1940; Grand Guns 1941; Detour 1945

MacDonald, Francis (1891-1968) Battling Butler 1926; The Dragnet 1928; A Girl in Every Port 1928; Morocco 1930

McDonald, Gary Struck by Lightning 1990; The Shepherd 2008

McDonald, Grace (1918-1999) Gung Ho! 1943; Follow the Boys 1944

MacDonald, Ian (1914-1978) Ramrod 1947; Colt .45 1950; Comanche Territory 1950; Montana 1950; This Woman Is Dangerous 1952; Blowing Wild 1953; Apache 1954

MacDonald, J Farrell (1875-1952) 3 Bad Men 1926; Sunrise 1927; Abie's Irish Rose 1928; In Old Arizona 1929; Dangerous Female 1931; Other Men's Women 1931; The Painted Desert 1931; Sporting Blood 1931; Me and My Gal 1932; The Thirteenth Guest 1932; Peg o' My Heart 1933; Star of Midnight 1935; Stormy 1935; Riffraff 1936; Slim 1937; White Banners 1938; Susannah of the Mounties 1939

MacDonald, Jeanette (1901-1965) The Love Parade 1929; Monte Carlo 1930; Love Me Tonight 1932; One Hour with You 1932; The Cat and the Fiddle 1934; The Merry Widow 1934; Naughty Marietta 1935; Rose Marie 1936; San Francisco 1936; The Firefly 1937; Maytime 1937; The Girl of the Golden West 1938; Sweethearts 1938; Broadway Serenade 1939; Bitter Sweet 1940; New Moon 1940; Smilin' Through 1941; I Married an Angel 1942; Follow the Boys 1944; Three Daring Daughters 1948

MacDonald, Kelly (1976-) Trainspotting 1995; Cousin Bette 1997; Stella Does Tricks 1997; The Loss of Sexual Innocence 1999; My Life So Far 1999; Splendor 1999; House! 2000; Some Voices 2000; Strictly Sinatra 2000; Gosford Park 2001; interMission 2003; Finding Neverland 2004; Nanny McPhee 2005; No Country for Old Men 2007; Choke 2008; In the Electric Mist 2009; The Merry Gentleman 2009; The Decoy Bride 2011; Anna Karenina 2012; Brave 2012; Swallows and Amazons 2016

McDonald, Kevin (1961-) Kids in the Hall: Brain Candy 1996; Lilo & Stitch 2002

McDonald, Marie (1923-1965) Guest in the House 1944; It's a Pleasure 1945; Living in a Big Way 1947; Tell It to the Judge 1949; The Geisha Boy 1958

MacDonald, Norm (1963-) Billy Madison 1995; Dirty Work 1998; Screwed 2000

McDonald, Peter (1972-) I Went Down 1997; Captain Jack 1998; Felicia's Journey 1999; Nora 1999; Saltwater 1999; The Opportunists 2000; Some Voices 2000; When Brendan Met Trudy 2000; The Damned United 2009; Wreckers 2010; The Stag 2013

MacDonald, Ray (1920-1959) Babes on Broadway 1941; Life Begins for Andy Hardy 1941; Good News 1947; All Ashore 1953

McDonald, Ryan (1984-) The Ballad of Jack and Rose 2005; Terry 2005

Macdonald, Shauna (1981-) Late Night Shopping 2001; The Rocket Post 2003

Macdonald, Shauna (1981-) The Descent 2005; The Descent: Part 2 2009; Howl 2015

MacDonald, William Wes Craven's Don't Look Down 1998; Hollow Man II 2006; White Noise: the Light 2006

McDonnell, Mary (1952-) Tiger Warsaw 1988; Dances with Wolves 1990; Grand Canyon 1991; Passion Fish 1992; Sneakers 1992; Arthur Miller's The American Clock 1993; Blue Chips 1994; Independence Day 1996; Evidence of Blood 1998; Behind the Mask 1999; Mumford 1999; Donnie Darko 2001; Scre4m 2011

McDonough, Neal (1966-) Timeline 2003; Walking Tall 2004; The Guardian 2006; The Hitcher 2007; I Know Who Killed Me 2007; Traitor 2008; Paul Blart: Mall Cop 2 2015

McDormand, Frances (1957-) Blood Simple 1983; Raising Arizona 1987; Mississippi Burning 1988; Chattahoochee 1989; Darkman 1990; Hidden Agenda 1990; The Butcher's Wife 1991; Crazy in Love 1992; Passed Away 1992; Short Cuts 1993; Beyond Rangoon 1995; Fargo 1995; The Good Old Boys 1995; Lone Star 1995; Palookaville 1995; Primal Fear 1996; Madeline 1998; Talk of Angels 1998; Almost Famous 2000; Wonder Boys 2000; The Man Who Wasn't There 2001; City by the Sea 2002; Laurel Canyon 2002; Something's Gotta Give 2003; Aeonflux 2005; North Country 2005; Friends with Money 2006; Miss Pettigrew Lives for a Day 2007; Burn after Reading 2008; This Must Be the Place 2011; Transformers: Dark of the Moon 2011; Moonrise Kingdom 2012; Promised Land 2012; The Good Dinosaur 2015

McDowall, Betty (1933-1993) Time Lock 1957; Jack the Ripper 1958; Spare the Rod 1961; Echo of Diana 1963; Ballad in Blue 1964; First Men in the Moon 1964

McDowall, Roddy (1928-1998) Just William 1939; Confirm or Deny 1941; How Green Was My Valley 1941; Man Hunt 1941; The Pied Piper 1942; Son of Fury 1942; Lassie Come Home 1943; My Friend Flicka 1943; The Keys of the Kingdom 1944; The White Cliffs of Dover 1944; Molly and Me 1945; Thunderhead - Son of Flicka 1945; Holiday in Mexico 1946; Kidnapped 1948; Macbeth 1948; Midnight Lace 1960; The Subterraneans 1960; The Longest Day 1962; Cleopatra 1963; The Greatest Story Ever Told 1965; Inside Daisy Clover 1965; That Darn Cat! 1965; The Third Day 1965; The Defector 1966; It! 1966; Lord Love a Duck 1966; The Adventures of Bullwhip Griffin 1967; The Cool Ones 1967; Planet of the Apes 1967; 5 Card Stud 1968; Angel, Angel Down We Go 1969; Beneath the Planet of the Apes 1969; Hello Down There 1969; Midas Run 1969; Bedknobs and Broomsticks 1971; Escape from the Planet of the Apes 1971; Pretty Maids All in a Row 1971; Conquest of the Planet of the Apes 1972; The Life and Times of Judge Roy Bean 1972; The Poseidon Adventure 1972; Battle for the Planet of the Apes 1973; The Legend of Hell House 1973; Funny Lady 1975; Embryo 1976; The Cat from Outer Space 1978; The Silent Flute 1978; The Thief of Baghdad 1978; Charlie Chan and the Curse of the Dragon Queen 1981; Class of 1984 1982; Evil under the Sun 1982; Fright Night 1985; Dead of Winter 1987; Overboard 1987; Fright Night Part 2 1988; Cutting Class 1989; Going Under 1990; Last Summer in the Hamptons 1995; It's My Party 1996; The Second Jungle Book 1997; Something to Believe In 1997; A Bug's Life 1998

MacDowell, Andie (1958-) Greystoke: the Legend of Tarzan, Lord of the Apes 1984; St Elmo's Fire 1985; sex, lies, and videotape 1989; Green Card 1990; Hudson Hawk 1991; The Object of Beauty 1991; Ruby Cairo 1992; Groundhog Day 1993; Short Cuts 1993; Bad Girls 1994; Four Weddings and a Funeral 1994; Luck, Trust & Ketchup 1994; Unstrung Heroes 1995; Michael 1996; Multiplicity 1996; The End of Violence 1997; Just the Ticket 1998; Muppets from Space 1999; The Muse 1999; Harrison's Flowers 2000; Crush 2001; Dinner with Friends 2001; Town & Country 2001; Beauty Shop 2005; Tara Road 2008; Barnyard 2006; Footloose 2011; Monte Carlo 2011; Magic Mike XXL 2015

McDowell, Claire (1877-1966) The Mark of Zorro 1920; Ben-Hur: a Tale of the Christ 1925; The Big Parade 1925; An American Tragedy 1931

McDowell, Malcolm (1943-) Poor Cow 1967; if... 1968; Figures in a Landscape 1970; The Raging Moon 1970; A Clockwork Orange 1971; O Lucky Man! 1973; Royal Flash 1975; Aces High 1976; Voyage of the Damned 1976; The Passage 1978; Caligula 1979; Time after Time 1979; Britannia Hospital 1982; Cat People 1982; The Compleat Beatles 1982; Blue Thunder 1983; Cross Creek 1983; Get Crazy 1983; The Caller 1987; Buy & Cell 1988; Sunset 1988; Il Maestro 1989; Class of 1999 1990; Disturbed 1990; Moon 44 1990; Out of Darkness 1990; Snow White in Happily Ever After 1990; Assassin of the Tsar 1991; Bopha! 1993; Night Train to Venice 1993; Cyborg 3: The Recycler 1994; Milk Money 1994; Seasons of the Heart 1994; Star Trek: Generations 1994; Fist of the North Star 1995; The Man Who Wouldn't Die 1995; Tank Girl 1995; The Little Riders 1996; Mr Magoo 1997; My Life So Far 1999; Gangster No 1 2000; Just Visiting 2001; I Spy 2002; The Company 2003; I'll Sleep When I'm Dead 2003; Bobby Jones: Stroke of Genius 2004; Rag Tale 2005; Halloween 2007; Never Apologize 2007; Bolt 2008; Doomsday 2008; Halloween II 2009; Easy A 2010; The Artist 2011; Antiviral 2012; Excision 2012; Silent Hill: Revelation 2012; Vamps 2012; Lessons in Love 2014

McEachin, James (1930-) Play Misty for Me 1971; Buck and the Preacher 1972; Fuzz 1972; The Groundstar Conspiracy 1972

Macedo, Rita (1928-1993) The Criminal Life of Archibaldo de la Cruz 1955; Nazarín 1958

McElduff, Ellen Maximum Overdrive 1986; Working Girls 1986

McElhatton, Michael I Went Down 1997; The Actors 2003; interMission 2003; Moon Man 2012; The Hallow 2015

McElhone, Jack Dear Frankie 2003; Young Adam 2003

McElhone, Natascha (1969-) Surviving Picasso 1996; The Devil's Own 1997; Mrs Dalloway 1997; Ronin 1998; The Truman Show 1998; What Rats Won't Do 1998; Love's Labour's Lost 1999; Contagion 2000; Killing Me Softly 2001; City of Ghosts 2002; FearDotCom 2002; Laurel Canyon 2002; Solaris 2002; Ladies in Lavender 2004; Guy X 2005; Big Nothing 2006; Blessed 2007; The Secret of Moonacre 2008; The Kid 2010; Believe 2012; Romeo & Juliet 2012; The Sea 2013

McEnery, John (1945-) Romeo and Juliet 1968; Bartleby 1971; Nicholas and Alexandra 1971; The Land That Time Forgot 1974; Hamlet 1990; Black Beauty 1994; When Saturday Comes 1995

McEnery, Peter (1940-) Beat Girl 1960; Victim 1961; The Moon-Spinners 1964; The Fighting Prince of Donegal 1966; The Game Is Over 1966; Entertaining Mr Sloane 1969; The Adventures of Gerard 1970; The Cat and the Canary 1979

McEnnan, Jaime And God Created Woman 1988; Munchie 1992

McEnroe, Annie The Hand 1981; Battletruck 1982; The Survivors 1983; Howling II: Your Sister Is a Werewolf 1984; True Stories 1986

McEnroe, John Wimbledon 2004; Venus and Serena 2012

McEntire, Reba (1955-) Tremors 1989; The Man from Left Field 1993; One Night at McCool's 2001; Charlotte's Web 2006; The Fox and the Hound 2 2007

McEvoy, Barry Gloria 1998; An Everlasting Piece 2000

McEwan, Geraldine (1932-2015) No Kidding 1960; The Dance of Death 1969; The Bawdy Adventures of Tom Jones 1976; The Littlest Horse Thieves 1976; Foreign Body 1986; Robin Hood: Prince of Thieves 1991; The Love Letter 1999; Love's Labour's Lost 1999; Contagion 2000; Food of Love 2002; The Magdalene Sisters 2002; Pure 2002; Vanity Fair 2004; Arrietty 2010

McFadden, Davenia Stranger Inside 2001; Hachi: a Dog's Tale 2008

McFadden, Gates (1949-) Star Trek: Generations 1994; Star Trek: First Contact 1996; Star Trek: Insurrection 1998; Star Trek: Nemesis 2002

McFadden, Joseph (1975-) Small Faces 1995; Dad Savage 1997

MacFadyen, Angus (1964-) Braveheart 1995; The Brylcreem Boys 1996; Warriors of Virtue 1996; The Rat Pack 1998; Cradle Will Rock 1999; Titus 1999; Styx 2000; Divine Secrets of the Ya-Ya Sisterhood 2002; Saw III 2006; Saw IV 2007

Macfadyen, Matthew (1974-) In My Father's Den 2004; Pride & Prejudice 2005; Middletown 2006; Death at a Funeral 2007; Frost/Nixon 2008; Incendiary 2008; Robin Hood 2010; The Three Musketeers 2011; Anna Karenina 2012; Lost in Karastan 2014

McFarlane, Colin Chunky Monkey 2001; Fragile 2005

MacFarlane, Seth (1973-) Tooth Fairy 2009; Ted 2012; A Million Ways to Die in the West 2014; Ted 2 2015; Sing 2016

McFerran, Douglas Sliding Doors 1997; Antitrust 2000; Charlie 2003

McGann, Joe (1958-) The Brylcreem Boys 1996; Food of Love 1997

McGann, Mark (1961-) Business as Usual 1987; Let Him Have It 1991

McGann, Paul (1959-) Withnail & I 1986; Empire of the Sun 1987; The Rainbow 1988; Tree of Hands 1988; Dealers 1989; Paper Mask 1990; Afraid of the Dark 1991; Alien³ 1992; The Three Musketeers 1993; Downtime 1997; FairyTale: a True Story 1997; My Kingdom 2001; Queen of the Damned 2002; Otherworld 2003; Gypo 2005; Lesbian Vampire Killers 2008

McGavin, Darren (1922-2006) The Court-Martial of Billy Mitchell 1955; The Man with the Golden Arm 1955; Summertime 1955; Beau James 1957; The Delicate Delinquent 1957; Bullet for a Badman 1964; Mrs Pollifax - Spy 1970; Something Evil 1972; The Six Million Dollar Man 1973; No Deposit No Return 1976; Airport '77 1977; Hot Lead and Cold Feet 1978; Hangar 18 1980; A Christmas Story 1983; Turk 182! 1985; From the Hip 1987; Dead Heat 1988; Inherit the Wind 1988; By Dawn's Early Light 1990; Captain America 1990; Arthur Miller's The American Clock 1993; Danielle Steel's A Perfect Stranger 1994; Billy Madison 1995

McGaw, Patrick (1967-) The Basketball Diaries 1995; Scorpion Spring 1995; Dream with the Fishes 1996

McGee, Henry (1929-2006) The Best of Benny Hill 1974; Adventures of a Taxi Driver 1975; Asterix Conquers America 1994

McGee, Jack Across the Tracks 1990; Star Kid 1997; Bread and Roses 2000; The Fighter 2010

McGee, Vonetta (1945-2010) The Great Silence 1969; Blacula 1972; Hammer 1972; Detroit 9000 1973; Shaft in Africa 1973; The Eiger Sanction 1975; To Sleep with Anger 1990

McGhee, Johnny Ray White Line Fever 1975; Project: X 1987

McGill, Bruce (1950-) Citizens Band 1977; The Hand 1981; Tough Enough 1982; The Ballad of Gregorio Cortez 1983; Into the Night 1985; Waiting for the Moon 1987; Little Vegas 1990; The Last Boy Scout 1991; My Cousin Vinny 1992; Black Widow Murders 1993; Timecop 1994; Black Sheep 1996; Lawn Dogs 1997; Rosewood 1997; Everything That Rises 1998; A Dog of Flanders 1999; The Legend of Bagger Vance 2000; The Ballad of Lucy Whipple 2001; Shallow Hal 2001; 61* 2001; Live from Baghdad 2002; Path to War 2002; The Sum of All Fears 2002; Legally Blonde 2: Red, White & Blonde 2003; Matchstick Men 2003; Runaway Jury 2003; Slow Burn 2003; Collateral 2004; Cinderella Man 2005; Elizabethtown 2005; The Lookout 2007; Recount 2008; Law Abiding Citizen 2009; Obsessed 2009; Fair Game 2010; Ride Along 2014

McGill, Everett (1945-) Union City 1980; Quest for Fire 1981; Silver Bullet 1985; Heartbreak Ridge 1986; Licence to Kill 1989; The People under the Stairs 1991; Under Siege 2 1995; The Straight Story 1999

MacGill, Moyna (1895-1975) The Strange Affair of Uncle Harry 1945; Black Beauty 1946

McGillis, Kelly (1957-) Reuben, Reuben 1983; Witness 1985; Top Gun 1986; The House on Carroll Street 1987; Made in Heaven 1987; The Accused 1988; Cat Chaser 1989; The Babe 1992; At First Sight 1998; Storm Chasers: Revenge of the Twister 1998; When the Bough Breaks 2: Perfect Prey 1998; The Monkey's Mask 2000; Stake Land 2010; The Innkeepers 2011; We Are What We Are 2013

McGillivray, David (1947-) House of Whipcord 1974; Satan's Slave 1976

McGinley, John C (1959-) Platoon 1986; Blood Money 1988; Talk Radio 1988; Shadow Makers 1989; Suffering Bastards 1989; Highlander II: the Quickening 1990; A Midnight Clear 1991; Point Break 1991; Article 99 1992; Little Noises 1992; Hear No Evil 1993; The Last Outlaw 1993; On Deadly Ground 1994; Surviving the Game 1994; Wagons East! 1994; Born to Be Wild 1995; Se7en 1995; Mother 1996; The Rock 1996; Set It Off 1996; Nothing to Lose 1997; The Pentagon Wars 1998; The Jack Bull 1999; Office Space 1999; Three to Tango 1999; Dean Koontz's Sole Survivor 2000; The Animal 2001; Stealing Harvard 2002; Identity 2003; Are We Done Yet? 2007; 42 2013

McGinley, Sean (1956-) The Disappearance of Finbar 1996; Trojan Eddie 1996; Bogwoman 1997; Resurrection Man 1997; The General 1998; Simon Magus 1998; The Closer You Get 2000; Dead Bodies 2003; Freeze Frame 2003; On a Clear Day 2004; The Mighty Celt 2005; Shrooms 2006; The Tiger's Tail 2006

McGinley, Ted (1958-) Revenge of the Nerds 1984; Physical Evidence 1988; Major League: Back to the Minors 1998

McGinn, Walter (1936-1977) The Parallax View 1974; The Night that Panicked America 1975; Three Days of the Condor 1975; Bobby Deerfield 1977

MacGinnis, Niall (1913 1978) The Edge of the World 1937; The Last Adventurers 1937; East of Piccadilly 1940; 49th Parallel 1941; The Day Will Dawn 1942; Undercover 1943; We Dive at Dawn 1943; Tawny Pipit 1944; Anna Karenina 1947; Captain Boycott 1947; Diamond City 1949; Chance of a Lifetime 1950; Conflict of Wings 1953; Betrayed 1954; Hell below Zero 1954; Helen of Troy 1955; Special Delivery 1955; Lust for Life 1956; Night of the Demon 1957; Behind the Mask 1958; Tarzan's Greatest Adventure 1959; This Other Eden 1959; Foxhole in Cairo 1960; Kidnapped 1960; Never Take Sweets from a Stranger 1960; Sword of Sherwood Forest 1960; A Terrible Beauty 1960; The Man Who Finally Died 1962; The Playboy of the Western World 1962; The Prince and the Pauper 1962; Jason and the Argonauts 1963; The Truth about Spring 1964; The War Lord 1965; The Viking Queen 1967

McGinnis, Scott Wacko 1981; Gunbus 1986; 3:15 1986

McGiver, John (1912-1975) Love in the Afternoon 1957; I Married a Woman 1958; The Gazebo 1959; Breakfast at Tiffany's 1961; The Manchurian Candidate 1962; Mr Hobbs Takes a Vacation 1962; My Six Loves 1962; Period of Adjustment 1962; Take Her, She's Mine 1963; Who's Minding the Store? 1963; Man's Favorite Sport?

1964; Marriage on the Rocks 1965; The Glass Bottom Boat 1966; Fitzwilly 1967; Midnight Cowboy 1969

McGlone, Mike (1972-) The Brothers McMullen 1995; She's the One 1996; The Bone Collector 1999; Dinner Rush 2000; Hardball 2001

McGlynn Sr, Frank (1866-1951) Riders of the Purple Sage 1931; The Littlest Rebel 1935; The Plainsman 1936

McGoohan, Patrick (1928-2009) Passage Home 1955; Zarak 1956; Hell Drivers 1957; High Tide at Noon 1957; The Gypsy and the Gentleman 1958; Nor the Moon by Night 1958; All Night Long 1961; Two Living, One Dead 1961; Life for Ruth 1962; The Quare Fellow 1962; Dr Syn, Alias the Scarecrow 1963; The Three Lives of Thomasina 1963; Ice Station Zebra 1968; Mary, Queen of Scots 1971; Silver Streak 1976; The Man in the Iron Mask 1977; Brass Target 1978; Escape from Alcatraz 1979; Scanners 1980; Kings and Desperate Men 1981; Baby: Secret of the Lost Legend 1985; Braveheart 1995; Treasure Planet 2002

McGovern, Elizabeth (1961-) Ordinary People 1980; Ragtime 1981; Lovesick 1983; Once upon a Time in America 1984; Racing with the Moon 1984; Native Son 1986; The Bedroom Window 1987; She's Having a Baby 1988; Johnny Handsome 1989; Aunt Julia and the Scriptwriter 1990; The Handmaid's Tale 1990; A Shock to the System 1990; Women and Men: Stories of Seduction 1990; King of the Hill 1993; The Favor 1994; Broken Trust 1995; The Summer of Ben Tyler 1996; The Wings of the Dove 1997; If Only 1998; The Misadventures of Margaret 1998; The House of Mirth 2000; Buffalo Soldiers 2001; The Truth 2006

McGowan, Rose (1973-) California Man 1992; Doom Generation 1995; Scream 1996; Going All the Way 1997; Phantoms 1998; Jawbreaker 1999; Ready to Rumble 2000; Death Proof 2007; Planet Terror 2007; Fifty Dead Men Walking 2008; Conan the Barbarian 2011

McGowan, Tom (1958-) Mrs Parker and the Vicious Circle 1994; Heavyweights 1995; Twelve and Holding 2005

MacGowran, Jack (1918-1973) No Resting Place 1950; Sailor Beware! 1956; Manuela 1957; The Rising of the Moon 1957; Rooney 1958; Cul-de-Sac 1966; The Fearless Vampire Killers 1967; How I Won the War 1967; Wonderwall 1968; Age of Consent 1969; King Lear 1970; Start the Revolution without Me 1970; The Exorcist 1973

McGrath, Doug Twilight Zone: the Movie 1983; Pale Rider 1985

McGrath, Frank (1903-1967) Riders of the Purple Sage 1941; The Shakiest Gun in the West 1967

MacGrath, Leueen (1914-1992) The Saint's Vacation 1941; Edward, My Son 1949

McGrath, Matt (1969-) Boys Don't Cry 1999; The Broken Hearts Club: a Romantic Comedy 2000

McGrath, Michael Boyfriends 1996; The Secret of Kells 2009

McGrath, Pat Somewhere on Leave 1942; Confession 1955

MacGraw, Ali (1938-) A Lovely Way to Go 1968; Goodbye, Columbus 1969; Love Story 1970; The Getaway 1972; Convoy 1978; Players 1979; Just Tell Me What You Want 1980

McGraw, Charles (1914-1980) The Killers 1946; T-Men 1947; Reign of Terror 1949; Armored Car Robbery 1950; Side Street 1950; Double Crossbones 1951; His Kind of Woman 1951; Roadblock 1951; The Narrow Margin 1952; One Minute to Zero 1952; Thunder over the Plains 1953; War Paint 1953; The Bridges at Toko-Ri 1954; Toward the Unknown 1956; Slaughter on Tenth Avenue 1957; The Defiant Ones 1958; Saddle the Wind 1958; The Wonderful Country 1959; The Horizontal Lieutenant 1962; The Birds 1963; In Cold Blood 1967; Pendulum 1969; Tell Them Willie Boy Is Here 1969; Johnny Got His Gun 1971; A Boy and His Dog 1975; The Killer inside Me 1975

McGraw, Melinda Nutty Professor 2: the Klumps 2000; Skateland 2010

McGraw, Tim Friday Night Lights 2004; Flicka 2006; The Blind Side 2009; Country Strong 2010

McGreevey, Michael (1948-) The Way West 1967; Snowball Express 1972

McGregor-Stewart, Kate [Safe] 1995; The Maker 1997

McGregor, Angela Punch aka **Punch, Angela** (1953-) The Chant of Jimmie

Blacksmith 1978; Newsfront 1978; The Island 1980; Double Deal 1981; The Survivor 1981; We of the Never Never 1982; Annie's Coming Out 1984; The Delinquents 1989

McGregor, Charles (?-1996) Superfly 1972; Three the Hard Way 1974

McGregor, Ewan (1971-) Being Human 1994; Shallow Grave 1994; Blue Juice 1995; The Pillow Book 1995; Trainspotting 1995; Brassed Off 1996; Emma 1996; A Life Less Ordinary 1997; Nightwatch 1997; The Serpent's Kiss 1997; Little Voice 1998; Rogue Trader 1998; Velvet Goldmine 1998; Eye of the Beholder 1999; Nora 1999; Star Wars Episode I: the Phantom Menace 1999; Black Hawk Down 2001; Moulin Rouge! 2001; Star Wars Episode II: Attack of the Clones 2002; Big Fish 2003; Down with Love 2003; Young Adam 2003; The Island 2005; Robots 2005; Star Wars Episode III: Revenge of the Sith 2005; Stay 2005; Valiant 2005; Miss Potter 2006; Scenes of a Sexual Nature 2006; Stormbreaker 2006; Cassandra's Dream 2007; Deception 2008; Incendiary 2008; Amelia 2009; Angels & Demons 2009; I Love You Phillip Morris 2009; The Men Who Stare at Goatsx 2009; Beginners 2010; The Ghost 2010; Jackboots on Whitehall 2010; Haywire 2011; The Impossible 2011; Perfect Sense 2011; Salmon Fishing in the Yemen 2011; August: Osage County 2013; Jack the Giant Slayer 2013; Son of a Gun 2013; Jane Got a Gun 2015; Miles Ahead 2015; Mortdecai 2015; American Pastoral 2016; Our Kind of Traitor 2016; T2: Trainspotting 2 2016; Beauty and the Beast 2017

McGuire, Biff (1926-) The Phenix City Story 1955; Station Six-Sahara 1962; The Heart Is a Lonely Hunter 1968; The Thomas Crown Affair 1968; Serpico 1973; Werewolf of Washington 1973

McGuire, Don (1919-1999) Armored Car Robbery 1950; Double Dynamite 1951

McGuire, Dorothy (1918-2001) Claudia 1943; The Enchanted Cottage 1945; A Tree Grows in Brooklyn 1945; Claudia and David 1946; The Spiral Staircase 1946; Till the End of Time 1946; Gentleman's Agreement 1947; Mister 880 1950; Callaway Went Thataway 1951; I Want You 1951; Three Coins in the Fountain 1954; Trial 1955; Friendly Persuasion 1956; Old Yeller 1957; The Remarkable Mr Pennypacker 1959; A Summer Place 1959; This Earth Is Mine 1959; The Dark at the Top of the Stairs 1960; Swiss Family Robinson 1960; Susan Slade 1961; Summer Magic 1963; The Greatest Story Ever Told 1965; Flight of the Doves 1971; Caroline? 1990

McGuire, John (1910-1980) Steamboat round the Bend 1935; Stranger on the Third Floor 1940; Invisible Ghost 1941; Bells of San Angelo 1947

McGuire, Kathryn (1903-1978) The Navigator 1924; Sherlock Junior 1924

McGuire, Marcy (1926-) Seven Days' Leave 1942; Higher and Higher 1943

McGuire, Michael (1934-) Hard Times 1975; Report to the Commissioner 1975; Bird 1988

McGuire, Tucker (1913-1988) Shipyard Sally 1939; The Night Has Eyes 1942

McHale, Joel (1971-) Open Season 2 2008; The Informant! 2009; SPYkids 4: All the Time in the World 2011; What's Your Number? 2011; Ted 2012

McHattie, Stephen (1947-) The Ultimate Warrior 1975; Tomorrow Never Comes 1977; Gray Lady Down 1978; Death Valley 1982; Best Revenge 1983; Belizaire the Cajun 1985; Call Me 1988; Sticky Fingers 1988; Bloodhounds of Broadway 1989; Beverly Hills Cop III 1994; Theodore Rex 1995; My Friend Joe 1996; Secretary 2001; The Fountain 2005; A History of Violence 2005; Stone Cold 2005; The Covenant 2006; Shoot 'Em Up 2007; Pontypool 2008; Haunter 2013; Wolves 2013; Born to Be Blue 2015

Machiavelli, Nicoletta (1944-2015) The Hills Run Red 1966; Navajo Joe 1966; Someone Is Bleeding 1974

Machowski, Ignacy (1919-2001) The Shadow 1956; Eroica 1958

Macht, Gabriel (1972-) The Audrey Hepburn Story 2000; American Outlaws 2001; Behind Enemy Lines 2001; Bad Company 2002; The Recruit 2003; A Love Song for Bobby Long 2004; Because I Said So 2007; The Spirit 2008; Love & Other Drugs 2010

Macht, Stephen (1942-) The Choirboys 1977; Nightwing 1979; Agatha Christie's A Caribbean Mystery 1983; The Monster Squad 1987; My

Boyfriend's Back 1989; Graveyard Shift 1990

McHugh, Frank (1898-1981) Bad Company 1931; The Crowd Roars 1932; High Pressure 1932; One Way Passage 1932; The Strange Love of Molly Louvain 1932; Union Depot 1932; Ex-Lady 1933; Mystery of the Wax Museum 1933; Fashions of 1934 1934; Here Comes the Navy 1934; Devil Dogs of the Air 1935; The Irish in Us 1935; A Midsummer Night's Dream 1935; Page Miss Glory 1935; Bullets or Ballots 1936; Stage Struck 1936; Swing Your Lady 1937; Boy Meets Girl 1938; Daughters Courageous 1939; Dodge City 1939; Dust Be My Destiny 1939; The Roaring Twenties 1939; The Fighting 69th 1940; I Love You Again 1940; 'Til We Meet Again 1940; Virginia City 1940; Back Street 1941; Manpower 1941; All through the Night 1942; Her Cardboard Lover 1942; Going My Way 1944; Marine Raiders 1944; A Medal for Benny 1945; State Fair 1945; Carnegie Hall 1947; The Velvet Touch 1948; Mighty Joe Young 1949; Miss Grant Takes Richmond 1949; Paid in Full 1950; My Son John 1952; A Lion Is in the Streets 1953; Career 1959; Say One for Me 1959; Easy Come, Easy Go 1967

McHugh, Matt (1894-1971) Street Scene 1931; Taxi! 1932

McIlhinney, Ian This Is the Sea 1996; A Patch of Fog 2015

McIlwraith, David Outrageous! 1977; On My Own 1992; Hollow Man II 2006

McInnerny, Tim (1956-) Wetherby 1985; Erik the Viking 1989; 101 Dalmatians 1996; Rogue Trader 1998; Notting Hill 1999; 102 Dalmatians 2000; The Emperor's New Clothes 2001; Severance 2006; Black Death 2010; Spooks: the Greater Good 2015; Eddie the Eagle 2016

MacInnes, Angus (1947-) Force 10 from Navarone 1978; Flight of Fury 2007

McInnes, William (1963-) The Heartbreak Kid 1993; Dirty Deeds 2002; Look Both Ways 2005; Irresistible 2006

McIntire, John aka **McIntyre, John** (1907-1991) The Street with No Name 1948; Down to the Sea in Ships 1949; Francis 1949; Red Canyon 1949; Scene of the Crime 1949; The Asphalt Jungle 1950; No Sad Songs for Me 1950; Saddle Tramp 1950; Winchester '73 1950; That's My Boy 1951; Westward the Women 1951; You're in the Navy Now 1951; Glory Alley 1952; Horizons West 1952; The Lawless Breed 1952; The World in His Arms 1952; A Lion Is in the Streets 1953; The Mississippi Gambler 1953; The President's Lady 1953; War Arrow 1953; Apache 1954; The Far Country 1954; The Yellow Mountain 1954; The Kentuckian 1955; The Phenix City Story 1955; The Spoilers 1955; Stranger on Horseback 1955; Backlash 1956; The Tin Star 1957; The Light in the Forest 1958; Sing, Boy, Sing 1958; The Gunfight at Dodge City 1959; Elmer Gantry 1960; Flaming Star 1960; Psycho 1960; Seven Ways from Sundown 1960; Who Was That Lady? 1960; Summer and Smoke 1961; Two Rode Together 1961; Rough Night in Jericho 1967; Challenge to Be Free 1972; Herbie Rides Again 1974; Rooster Cogburn 1975; Honkytonk Man 1982; Cloak and Dagger 1984; Turner & Hooch 1989

McIntire, Tim (1944-1986) The Sterile Cuckoo 1969; Aloha, Bobby and Rose 1975; The Gumball Rally 1976; American Hot Wax 1977; The Choirboys 1977; Brubaker 1980; Fast-Walking 1982

McIntosh, Burr (1862-1942) Way Down East 1920; The Last Warning 1928; Lilac Time 1928

Macintosh, Keegan (1984-) Don't Talk to Strangers 1994; The Road Home 1995

McIntosh, Neve (1972-) One Last Chance 2003; The Be All and End All 2009; Salvage 2009

McIntosh, Pollyanna The Woman 2011; Let Us Prey 2014

McIntyre, Marvin J The Running Man 1987; Wilder Napalm 1993; Born to Be Wild 1995

MacIsaac, Martha Superbad 2007; The Last House on the Left 2008

Mack, Allison (1982-) Desperate Justice 1993; Honey, We Shrunk Ourselves 1997

Mack, Charles Emmett (1900-1927) Dream Street 1921; America 1924

Mack, Helen (1913-1986) Blind Adventure 1933; Melody Cruise 1933; Son of Kong 1933; Kiss and Make-Up 1934; The Lemon Drop Kid 1934; The Return of Peter Grimm 1935; She 1935;

The Milky Way 1936; The Last Train from Madrid 1937

Mack, James aka **Mack, James T** (1871-1948) Anna Christie 1930; Bonnie Scotland 1935

Mackaill, Dorothy (1903-1990) Love Affair 1932; No Man of Her Own 1932

Mackay, Barry (1906-1985) Evergreen 1934; Forever England 1935; Gangway 1937; The Great Barrier 1937; A Christmas Carol 1938; Sailing Along 1938

McKay, Christian Me and Orson Welles 2008; Mr Nice 2010; Rush 2013; Chicklit 2016

McKay, David The Girl in the Picture 1985; My Name Is Joe 1998

Mackay, Fulton (1922-1987) The Brave Don't Cry 1952; Laxdale Hall 1953; Gumshoe 1971; Nothing but the Night 1972; Porridge 1979; Britannia Hospital 1982; Local Hero 1983; Defence of the Realm 1985; Water 1985

MacKay, George (1992-) The Thief Lord 2005; The Boys Are Back 2009; Private Peaceful 2012; Breakfast with Jonny Wilkinson 2013; For Those in Peril 2013; How I Live Now 2013; Sunshine on Leith 2013; Bypass 2014; Captain Fantastic 2015

MacKay, John The Rejuvenator 1988; Trust 1990; Niagara Niagara 1997

Mackay, Mathew The Peanut Butter Solution 1985; Lapse of Memory 1992

McKay, Scott (1922-1987) Guest in the House 1944; Thirty Seconds over Tokyo 1944

McKay, Wanda (1916-1996) The Monster Maker 1944; Voodoo Man 1944

McKean, Michael (1947-) Used Cars 1980; Young Doctors in Love 1982; This Is Spinal Tap 1984; Clue 1985; DARYL 1985; Planes, Trains and Automobiles 1987; Earth Girls Are Easy 1988; Short Circuit 2 1988; The Big Picture 1989; Hider in the House 1989; Flashback 1990; True Identity 1991; Man Trouble 1992; Memoirs of an Invisible Man 1992; Coneheads 1993; Airheads 1994; Radioland Murders 1994; The Brady Bunch Movie 1995; Jack 1996; Casper: a Spirited Beginning 1997; Nothing to Lose 1997; The Sunshine Boys 1997; That Darn Cat 1997; Kill the Man 1999; Teaching Mrs Tingle 1999; True Crime 1999; Best in Show 2000; Slap Her, She's French! 2001; The Guru 2002; A Mighty Wind 2003; For Your Consideration 2006; Joshua 2007; Surf's Up 2007; Whatever Works 2009

McKechnie, James (1911-1964) The Life and Death of Colonel Blimp 1943; The Years Between 1946

McKee, Gina (1964-) The Lair of the White Worm 1988; The Life of Stuff 1997; Croupier 1998; Joan of Arc 1999; The Loss of Sexual Innocence 1999; Notting Hill 1999; Women Talking Dirty 1999; Wonderland 1999; There's Only One Jimmy Grimble 2000; The Reckoning 2001; Divine Secrets of the Ya-Ya Sisterhood 2002; MirrorMask 2004; Greyfriars Bobby 2005; Scenes of a Sexual Nature 2006; And When Did You Last See Your Father? 2007; Atonement 2007; In the Loop 2009; Hector 2015

McKee, John (1916-2002) That Touch of Mink 1962; Monte Walsh 1970

McKee, Lafe (1872-1959) Riders of Destiny 1933; The Man from Utah 1934; The Desert Trail 1935

McKee, Lonette (1954-) Which Way Is Up? 1977; The Cotton Club 1984; Brewster's Millions 1985; 'Round Midnight 1986; Jungle Fever 1991; Malcolm X 1992; He Got Game 1998; Honey 2003; Honey 2 2011

McKee, Roxanne Vendetta 2013; Ironclad 2 2014

McKellar, Don (1963-) Highway 61 1992; Exotica 1994; When Night Is Falling 1995; Last Night 1998; eXistenZ 1999; waydowntown 2000; Clean 2004

McKellen, Ian (1939-) Alfred the Great 1969; A Touch of Love 1969; Priest of Love 1981; The Scarlet Pimpernel 1982; The Keep 1983; Plenty 1985; Zina 1985; Scandal 1988; And the Band Played On 1993; The Ballad of Little Jo 1993; Last Action Hero 1993; Six Degrees of Separation 1993; I'll Do Anything 1994; The Shadow 1994; To Die For 1994; Jack & Sarah 1995; Restoration 1995; Richard III 1995; Bent 1996; A Bit of Scarlet 1996; Rasputin 1996; Amy Foster 1997; Apt Pupil 1997; Gods and Monsters 1998; X-Men 2000; The Lord of the Rings: The Fellowship of the Ring 2001; The Lord of the Rings: The Two Towers 2002; Emile 2003; The Lord of the Rings: The Return of the King 2003; X2 2003; Asylum 2004; The Magic Roundabout 2005; The Da

Vinci Code 2006; Flushed Away 2006; X-Men - the Last Stand 2006; The Hobbit: an Unexpected Journey 2012; The Hobbit: the Desolation of Smaug 2013; The Hobbit: the Battle of the Five Armies 2014; Mr Holmes 2014; X-Men: Days of Future Past 2014; Beauty and the Beast 2017

Macken, Eoin Suspension of Disbelief 2012; The Forest 2016

McKenna, Alan aka **Mckenna, Alan** Second in Command 2006; Pressure 2015

McKenna, Bernard My Childhood 1972; My Ain Folk 1973

MacKenna, Kenneth (1899-1962) Men without Women 1930; The Virtuous Sin 1930; 13 West Street 1962

McKenna, Siobhan (1923-1986) Daughter of Darkness 1948; The Lost People 1949; The Adventurers 1950; King of Kings 1961; The Playboy of the Western World 1962; Of Human Bondage 1964; Doctor Zhivago 1965

McKenna, T P (1929-2011) The Siege of Sidney Street 1960; Girl with Green Eyes 1963; Ulysses 1967; The Beast in the Cellar 1970; Perfect Friday 1970; Straw Dogs 1971; Villain 1971; All Creatures Great and Small 1974; A Portrait of the Artist as a Young Man 1977; The Outsider 1979; The Doctor and the Devils 1985; Pascali's Island 1988; Red Scorpion 1989; Valmont 1989; Monarch 1996

McKenna, Virginia (1931-) The Cruel Sea 1952; Father's Doing Fine 1952; The Oracle 1952; The Ship That Died of Shame 1955; Simba 1955; The Barretts of Wimpole Street 1956; A Town like Alice 1956; The Smallest Show on Earth 1957; Carve Her Name with Pride 1958; Passionate Summer 1958; The Wreck of the Mary Deare 1959; Two Living, One Dead 1961; Born Free 1966; An Elephant Called Slowly 1969; Ring of Bright Water 1969; Waterloo 1970; Swallows and Amazons 1974; The Disappearance 1977; Holocaust 2000 1977; Sliding Doors 1997; Golden Years 2016

Mackenzie (2), Alastair The Last Great Wilderness 2002; Snuff-Movie 2005; The Edge of Love 2008; New Town Killers 2009

Mackenzie, Alex (1885-1965) The Maggie 1953; The Bridal Path 1959; The Battle of the Sexes 1960; Greyfriars Bobby 1961

McKenzie, Fay (1918-) Down Mexico Way 1941; The Singing Sheriff 1944

McKenzie, Jacqueline (1967-) Romper Stomper 1992; Traps 1994; Angel Baby 1995; Mr Reliable 1996; Deep Blue Sea 1999; Kiss Kiss (Bang Bang) 2001; Opal Dream 2005

MacKenzie, Joyce (1929-) Broken Arrow 1950; Destination Murder 1950; The Racket 1951; Wait 'til the Sun Shines, Nellie 1952; Tarzan and the She-Devil 1953; The French Line 1954; Rails into Laramie 1954

McKenzie, Julia (1941-) The Wildcats of St Trinian's 1980; Those Glory, Glory Days 1983; Shirley Valentine 1989; Bright Young Things 2003; These Foolish Things 2006

Mackenzie, Mary (1922-1966) Stolen Face 1952; The Master Plan 1954; Yield to the Night 1956

McKenzie, Tim Gallipoli 1981; The Lighthorsemen 1987

McKeon, Doug (1966-) Night Crossing 1981; On Golden Pond 1981

McKeon, Nancy (1966-) A Mother's Gift 1995; Wild Hearts 2006

McKern, Leo (1920-2002) Murder in the Cathedral 1952; All for Mary 1955; X the Unknown 1956; Time without Pity 1957; Beyond This Place 1959; The Mouse That Roared 1959; The Running, Jumping and Standing Still Film 1959; Yesterday's Enemy 1959; The Day the Earth Caught Fire 1961; Mr Topaze 1961; The Inspector 1962; Doctor in Distress 1963; Hot Enough for June 1964; A Jolly Bad Fellow 1964; King and Country 1964; The Amorous Adventures of Moll Flanders 1965; Help! 1965; A Man for All Seasons 1966; Decline and Fall... of a Birdwatcher 1968; The Shoes of the Fisherman 1968; Ryan's Daughter 1970; Massacre in Rome 1973; The Adventure of Sherlock Holmes' Smarter Brother 1975; The Omen 1976; Candleshoe 1977; The Blue Lagoon 1980; The French Lieutenant's Woman 1981; The Chain 1984; Agatha Christie's Murder with Mirrors 1985; Ladyhawke 1985; Travelling North 1986; Dad and Dave: on Our Selection 1995

Mackey, Brendan 9 Dead Gay Guys 2001; Touching the Void 2003; Fated 2006

Mackichan, Doon With or without You 1999; Gladiatress 2002

McKidd, Kevin (1973-) Small Faces 1995; Trainspotting 1995; Dad Savage 1997; The Acid House 1998; Bedrooms and Hallways 1998; Topsy-Turvy 1999; Dog Soldiers 2001; AfterLife 2003; One Last Chance 2003; The Rocket Post 2003; 16 Years of Alcohol 2003; De-Lovely 2004; Kingdom of Heaven 2005; Hannibal Rising 2006; The Last Legion 2006; Made of Honor 2008; Bunraku 2010; Percy Jackson & the Lightning Thief 2010; The Great Ghost Rescue 2011; Brave 2012; Comes a Bright Day 2012

Mackie, Anthony (1978-) Million Dollar Baby 2004; She Hate Me 2004; The Man 2005; Freedomland 2006; Half Nelson 2006; The Hurt Locker 2008; Notorious 2009; The Adjustment Bureau 2010; Real Steel 2011; Abraham Lincoln: Vampire Hunter 2012; Man on a Ledge 2012; The Fifth Estate 2013; Pain & Gain 2013; Runner Runner 2013; Captain America: the Winter Soldier 2014; Playing It Cool 2014; Shelter 2014; Ant-Man 2015; The Night Before 2015; Our Brand Is Crisis 2015; Triple 9 2015; All the Way 2016

McKim, Robert (1886-1927) The Mark of Zorro 1920; The Strong Man 1926

McKinnel, Norman (1870-1932) Hindle Wakes 1927; Hindle Wakes 1931

McKinney, Bill (1931-2011) She Freak 1967; Deliverance 1972; Junior Bonner 1972; Cleopatra Jones 1973; Cannonball 1976; The Outlaw Josey Wales 1976; The Shootist 1976; The Gauntlet 1977; Bronco Billy 1980; Tex 1982; Heart like a Wheel 1983; Kinjite: Forbidden Subjects 1989; City Slickers II: the Legend of Curly's Gold 1994; Undertow 2004

McKinney, Mark (1959-) Kids in the Hall: Brain Candy 1996; Jacob Two Two Meets the Hooded Fang 1999; The Out-of-Towners 1999; Superstar 1999; The Saddest Music in the World 2003

McKinney, Nina Mae (1913-1967) Hallelujah 1929; Sanders of the River 1935

McKinnon, Ray (1961-) Paris Trout 1991; The Gun in Betty Lou's Handbag 1992; Needful Things 1993; The Net 1995; Goodbye Lover 1997; Old Man 1997; The Missing 2003; The Blind Side 2009; Take Shelter 2011

Mackintosh, Kenneth (1919-2005) Othello 1965; Three Sisters 1970

Mackintosh, Louise (1864-1933) The Phantom President 1932; The Little Giant 1933

Mackintosh, Steven (1967-) London Kills Me 1991; Blue Juice 1995; The Grotesque 1995; Different for Girls 1996; House of America 1996; Twelfth Night 1996; The Land Girls 1997; Lock, Stock and Two Smoking Barrels 1998; The Criminal 1999; The Mother 2003; The Aryan Couple 2004; The Jacket 2005; Small Engine Repair 2006; Underworld: Evolution 2006; The Escapist 2007; Sugarhouse 2007; The Daisy Chain 2008; Good 2008; The Scouting Book for Boys 2009; Underworld: Rise of the Lycans 2009; Elfie Hopkins 2011; The Great Ghost Rescue 2011; The Sweeney 2012; Robot Overlords 2014

McKuen, Rod (1933-2015) Rock, Pretty Baby 1956; Wild Heritage 1958

MacLachlan, Janet (1933-2010) Uptight 1968; tick... tick... tick... 1969; The Man 1972; Dark Victory 1976; The Boy Who Could Fly 1986

MacLachlan, Kyle (1959-) Dune 1984; Blue Velvet 1986; The Hidden 1987; The Boyfriend School 1990; The Doors 1991; Twin Peaks: Fire Walk with Me 1992; The Trial 1993; Against the Wall 1994; The Flintstones 1994; Roswell 1994; Showgirls 1995; The Trigger Effect 1996; Trigger Happy 1996; One Night Stand 1997; Timecode 1999; Hamlet 2000; XChange 2000; Me without You 2001; Miranda 2001; Northfork 2002; The Librarian: Quest for the Spear 2004; Free Jimmy 2006; Peace, Love & Misunderstanding 2011; Breathe In 2013; Inside Out 2015

McLaglen, Victor (1886-1959) The Unholy Three 1925; Beau Geste 1926; What Price Glory 1926; A Girl in Every Port 1928; Hangman's House 1928; The Cock-Eyed World 1929; Dishonored 1931; Laughing at Life 1933; The Captain Hates the Sea 1934; The Lost Patrol 1934; The Informer 1935; Klondike Annie 1936; Under Two Flags 1936; Nancy Steele Is Missing 1937; This Is My Affair 1937; Wee Willie Winkie 1937; We're Going to Be Rich 1938; Gunga Din 1939; South of Pago Pago 1940; Call Out the Marines 1941; China Girl 1942; The Princess and the Pirate 1944; Whistle Stop 1946; The Foxes of Harrow 1947; Fort Apache

1948; She Wore a Yellow Ribbon 1949; Rio Grande 1950; The Quiet Man 1952; Fair Wind to Java 1953; Prince Valiant 1954; Trouble in the Glen 1954; Bengazi 1955; Lady Godiva 1955; Many Rivers to Cross 1955; Sea Fury 1958

MacLaine, Shirley (1934-) The Trouble with Harry 1954; Artists and Models 1955; Around the World in 80 Days 1956; Hot Spell 1958; The Matchmaker 1958; The Sheepman 1958; Some Came Running 1958; Ask Any Girl 1959; Career 1959; All in a Night's Work 1960; The Apartment 1960; Can-Can 1960; The Children's Hour 1961; Two Loves 1961; My Geisha 1962; Two for the Seesaw 1962; Irma la Douce 1963; John Goldfarb, Please Come Home 1964; What a Way to Go! 1964; The Yellow Rolls-Royce 1964; Gambit 1966; Woman Times Seven 1967; The Bliss of Mrs Blossom 1968; Sweet Charity 1968; Two Mules for Sister Sara 1970; Desperate Characters 1971; The Possession of Joel Delaney 1971; The Turning Point 1977; Being There 1979; A Change of Seasons 1980; Loving Couples 1980; Cannonball Run II 1983; Terms of Endearment 1983; Madame Sousatzka 1988; Steel Magnolias 1989; Waiting for the Light 1989; Postcards from the Edge 1990; Used People 1992; Wrestling Ernest Hemingway 1993; Guarding Tess 1994; The Celluloid Closet 1995; The West Side Waltz 1995; The Evening Star 1996; Mrs Winterbourne 1996; A Smile like Yours 1997; These Old Broads 2001; The Battle of Mary Kay 2002; Bewitched 2005; In Her Shoes 2005; Rumor Has It... 2005; Closing the Ring 2006; Bernie 2011; The Secret Life of Walter Mitty 2013; Elsa & Fred 2014

MacLane, Barton (1900-1969) Tillie and Gus 1933; Black Fury 1935; The Case of the Lucky Legs 1935; Ceiling Zero 1935; Dr Socrates 1935; Frisco Kid 1935; "G" Men 1935; Go into Your Dance 1935; Bullets or Ballots 1936; Smart Blonde 1936; The Walking Dead 1936; Born Reckless 1937; God's Country and the Woman 1937; The Prince and the Pauper 1937; San Quentin 1937; You Only Live Once 1937; Gold Is Where You Find It 1938; You and Me 1938; Come Live with Me 1941; Dr Jekyll and Mr Hyde 1941; High Sierra 1941; The Maltese Falcon 1941; Manpower 1941; Western Union 1941; Wild Geese Calling 1941; All through the Night 1942; The Big Street 1942; Bombardier 1943; Cry of the Werewolf 1944; Marine Raiders 1944; The Mummy's Ghost 1944; Secret Command 1944; The Spanish Main 1945; Tarzan and the Amazons 1945; Tarzan and the Huntress 1947; The Treasure of the Sierra Madre 1947; Angel in Exile 1948; Relentless 1948; Silver River 1948; Red Light 1949; Let's Dance 1950; Best of the Badmen 1951; Bugles in the Afternoon 1952; The Half-Breed 1952; Rails into Laramie 1954; Backlash 1956; Three Violent People 1956; The Geisha Boy 1958; The Pounders 1965; Arizona Bushwhackers 1968

McLaren, Brandon Jay Scar 2007; Tucker and Dale vs Evil 2009

McLaren, Hollis Sunday in the Country 1975; Outrageous! 1977; Lost and Found 1979; Atlantic City, USA 1980; Mom at Sixteen 2005

MacLaren, Ian (1875-1952) Journey's End 1930; Body and Soul 1931; Cleopatra 1934

McLaughlin, Dylan Kicking & Screaming 2005; You've Got a Friend 2007

McLaughlin, Gibb (1884-1960) The Farmer's Wife 1928; Congress Dances 1931; Bulldog Jack 1934; The Old Curiosity Shop 1935; Broken Blossoms 1936; Where There's a Will 1936; The Lavender Hill Mob 1951; The Man Who Watched Trains Go By 1952; The Brain Machine 1954

McLean, David (1922-1995) X-15 1961; Kingdom of the Spiders 1977; Deathsport 1978

McLean, Ian The Arsenal Stadium Mystery 1939; Dreaming 1944

McLeavy, Robin The Loved Ones 2009; Backtrack 2015

McLellan, Zoe (1974-) Dungeons & Dragons 2000; Deadly Honeymoon 2009

McLendon-Covey, Wendi Reno 911!: Miami 2007; Blended 2014

McLeod, Catherine (1921-1997) That's My Man 1947; The Outcast 1954

Macleod, Gavin (1930-) War Hunt 1962; Deathwatch 1966; The Party 1968; A Man Called Gannon 1969; The 1,000 Plane Raid 1969

McLeod, Gordon (1890-1961) The Saint in London 1939; Crook's' Tour 1940;

The Saint's Vacation 1941; We'll Smile Again 1942; The Saint Meets the Tiger 1943; A Case for PC 49 1950

MacLeod, John-Paul The Testimony of Taliesin Jones 2000; Calendar Girls 2003

McLerie, Allyn Ann aka **McLerie, Allyn** (1926-) Calamity Jane 1953; The Desert Song 1953; Jeremiah Johnson 1972; Cinderella Liberty 1973; The Way We Were 1973

MacLiam, Eanna My Left Foot 1989; The Snapper 1993; The General 1998; Angela's Ashes 1999

McLiam, John (1918-1994) Showdown 1973; The Dove 1974; The Food of the Gods 1976; The Missouri Breaks 1976; Walk like a Man 1987

MacLiammoir, Michael (1899-1978) Othello 1952; What's the Matter with Helen? 1971

McLynn, Pauline (1962-) My Friend Joe 1996; Angela's Ashes 1999; The Most Fertile Man in Ireland 1999; An Everlasting Piece 2000; When Brendan Met Trudy 2000; Gypo 2005; Heidi 2005; The Calling 2009

MacMahon, Aline (1899-1991) Life Begins 1932; One Way Passage 1932; Gold Diggers of 1933 1933; Heroes for Sale 1933; The World Changes 1933; Ah, Wilderness! 1935; I Live My Life 1935; When You're in Love 1937; Back Door to Heaven 1939; Out of the Fog 1941; The Lady Is Willing 1942; Dragon Seed 1944; Guest in the House 1944; The Search 1948; The Flame and the Arrow 1950; The Eddie Cantor Story 1953; The Man from Laramie 1955; Diamond Head 1962; All the Way Home 1963; I Could Go On Singing 1963

McMahon, Ed (1923-2009) Slaughter's Big Rip-Off 1973; Fun with Dick and Jane 1977; Butterfly 1982; Full Moon High 1982

McMahon, Horace (1906-1971) Detective Story 1951; Abbott and Costello Go to Mars 1953; Susan Slept Here 1954; Beau James 1957; The Delicate Delinquent 1957; Never Steal Anything Small 1959; The Detective 1968

McMahon, Julian (1968-) Fantastic Four 2005; 4: Rise of the Silver Surfer 2007; Premonition 2007; Fire with Fire 2012

McMartin, John (1929-2016) Sweet Charity 1968; What's So Bad about Feeling Good? 1968; Blow Out 1981; Pennies from Heaven 1981; Dream Lover 1986; Legal Eagles 1986; Native Son 1986; Who's That Girl 1987; Day One 1989

McMenamin, Ciaran (1975-) Titanic Town 1998; To End All Wars 2001; Bollywood Queen 2002; Shooting for Socrates 2014

McMillan, Kenneth (1932-1989) Bloodbrothers 1978; Oliver's Story 1978; Chilly Scenes of Winter 1979; Salem's Lot 1979; Borderline 1980; Carny 1980; Hide in Plain Sight 1980; Little Miss Marker 1980; Eyewitness 1981; Heartbeeps 1981; Ragtime 1981; Whose Life Is It Anyway? 1981; Partners 1982; Cat's Eye 1984; Dune 1984; The Pope of Greenwich Village 1984; Reckless 1984; Runaway Train 1985; Armed and Dangerous 1986; Malone 1987; Three Fugitives 1989

McMillan, Roddy (1923-1979) The Bridal Path 1959; Ring of Bright Water 1969

McMullan, Jim aka **McMullan, James** (1938-) Downhill Racer 1969; Extreme Close-Up 1971

MacMurray, Fred (1908-1991) Alice Adams 1935; The Bride Comes Home 1935; The Gilded Lily 1935; Hands across the Table 1935; The Princess Comes Across 1936; The Texas Rangers 1936; The Trail of the Lonesome Pine 1936; Swing High, Swing Low 1937; True Confession 1937; Men with Wings 1938; Invitation to Happiness 1939; Little Old New York 1940; Remember the Night 1940; Too Many Husbands 1940; Dive Bomber 1941; The Forest Rangers 1942; The Lady Is Willing 1942; Star Spangled Rhythm 1942; Take a Letter, Darling 1942; Above Suspicion 1943; Flight for Freedom 1943; No Time for Love 1943; And the Angels Sing 1944; Double Indemnity 1944; Practically Yours 1944; Standing Room Only 1944; Capt Eddie 1945; Murder, He Says 1945; Pardon My Past 1945; Where Do We Go from Here? 1945; Smoky 1946; The Egg and I 1947; Singapore 1947; Suddenly It's Spring 1947; The Miracle of the Bells 1948; On Our Merry Way 1948; Father Was a Fullback 1949; Borderline 1950; Never a Dull Moment 1950; Callaway Went Thataway 1951; A Millionaire for Christy 1951; Fair Wind to Java 1953; The Moonlighter 1953; The Caine

Mutiny 1954; Pushover 1954; Woman's World 1954; At Gunpoint 1955; The Far Horizons 1955; The Rains of Ranchipur 1955; There's Always Tomorrow 1956; Gun for a Coward 1957; Quantez 1957; Day of the Bad Man 1958; Face of a Fugitive 1959; The Shaggy Dog 1959; The Apartment 1960; The Absent-Minded Professor 1961; Bon Voyage! 1962; Son of Flubber 1962; Kisses for My President 1964; Follow Me, Boys! 1966; The Happiest Millionaire 1967; Charley and the Angel 1973; The Swarm 1978

McMurray, Sam (1941-) Union City 1980; LA Story 1991; Stone Cold 1991; Getting Even with Dad 1994; Drop Dead Gorgeous 1999; Lone Star State of Mind 2002

McMurtrey, Joan The Betty Ford Story 1987; Welcome Home, Roxy Carmichael 1990

MacNab, Calum The Firm 2009; Outside Bet 2011

McNair, Barbara (1934-2007) Change of Habit 1969; They Call Me Mister Tibbs! 1970; The Organization 1971

McNairy, Scoot (1977-) In Search of a Midnight Kiss 2008; Monsters 2010; A Night in the Woods 2011; Argo 2012; Killing Them Softly 2012; Promised Land 2012; Frank 2013; Touchy Feely 2013; Black Sea 2014; Non-Stop 2014; The Rover 2014

McNally, Kevin aka **McNally, Kevin R** (1956-) Enigma 1982; Not Quite Jerusalem 1985; Cry Freedom 1987; Entrapment 1999; When the Sky Falls 2000; High Heels and Low Lifes 2001; Johnny English 2003; Pirates of the Caribbean: the Curse of the Black Pearl 2003; De-Lovely 2004; Pirates of the Caribbean: Dead Man's Chest 2006; TuEsday 2007; Pirates of the Caribbean: on Stranger Tides 2011; The Raven 2012

McNally, Stephen aka **McNally, Horace** aka **McNally, Horace** (1913-1994) Dr Gillespie's New Assistant 1942; Eyes in the Night 1942; For Me and My Gal 1942; Keeper of the Flame 1942; The Man from Down Under 1943; Magnificent Doll 1946; Johnny Belinda 1948; City across the River 1949; Criss Cross 1949; The Lady Gambles 1949; No Way Out 1950; Winchester '73 1950; Wyoming Mail 1950; Air Cadet 1951; Apache Drums 1951; Iron Man 1951; The Lady Pays Off 1951; The Black Castle 1952; Diplomatic Courier 1952; The Duel at Silver Creek 1952; Devil's Canyon 1953; Split Second 1953; A Bullet Is Waiting 1954; The Man from Bitter Ridge 1955; Violent Saturday 1955; Tribute to a Bad Man 1956; Hell Bent for Leather 1960

McNamara, Brian (1960-) The Flamingo Kid 1984; Short Circuit 1986; Arachnophobia 1990; Mystery Date 1991; When the Party's Over 1992

McNamara, J Patrick Obsession 1976; Close Encounters of the Third Kind 1977

McNamara, John (1925-1968) From Hell It Came 1957; The Return of Dracula 1958

McNamara, Maggie (1928-1978) The Moon Is Blue 1953; Three Coins in the Fountain 1954; Prince of Players 1955

McNamara, Pat The Last Time I Committed Suicide 1996; The Daytrippers 1998; Ash Wednesday 2002

McNamara, Robert S (1916-2009) The Fog of War: Eleven Lessons from the Life of Robert S McNamara 2003; Countdown to Zero 2010

McNamara, William (1965-) Stealing Home 1988; Texasville 1990; Wildflower 1991; Chasers 1994; Surviving the Game 1994; Copycat 1995; The Brylcreem Boys 1996; Something to Believe In 1997; Ringmaster 1998; Time Lapse 2001

MacNaughtan, Alan (1920-2002) Frankenstein Created Woman 1966; Family Life 1971

McNaughton, Gus (1881-1969) Keep Your Seats, Please 1936; Keep Fit 1937; Storm in a Teacup 1937; The Divorce of Lady X 1938; St Martin's Lane 1938; We're Going to Be Rich 1938; Trouble Brewing 1939; Old Bill and Son 1940; Jeannie 1941

McNaughton, Jack (1905-1990) Cardboard Cavalier 1949; Trent's Last Case 1952; The Purple Plain 1954

McNear, Howard (1905-1969) Bachelor Flat 1961; Blue Hawaii 1961; The Errand Boy 1961

Macnee, Patrick (1922-2015) Scrooge 1951; The Battle of the River Plate 1956; Les Girls 1957; Mister Jerico 1969; Incense for the Damned 1970; Sherlock Holmes in New York 1976; The Sea Wolves 1980; The Howling 1981; The Hot Touch 1982; Young Doctors in

Love 1982; This Is Spinal Tap 1984; Shadey 1985; A View to a Kill 1985; Waxwork 1988; The Avengers 1998
McNeice, Ian (1950-) The Lonely Passion of Judith Hearne 1987; The Raggedy Rawney 1987; The Russia House 1990; Year of the Comet 1992; No Escape 1994; Ace Ventura: When Nature Calls 1995; The Englishman Who Went up a Hill, but Came down a Mountain 1995; The Beautician and the Beast 1997; A Life Less Ordinary 1997; A Christmas Carol 1999; The Nine Lives of Tomas Katz 1999; Anazapta 2001; Conspiracy 2001; The Fourth Angel 2001; The Final Curtain 2002; Blackball 2003; Freeze Frame 2003; I'll Be There 2003; White Noise 2004; Day of the Dead 2008
McNeil, Claudia (1917-1993) A Raisin in the Sun 1961; Black Girl 1972
MacNeill, Meredith Confetti 2006; Frequently Asked Questions about Time Travel 2008
MacNeill, Peter aka **MacNeil, Peter** Whispers 1990; Crash 1996; The Hanging Garden 1997; A History of Violence 2005; Victor 2008
MacNeille, Tress (1951-) Pom Poko 1994; Kiki's Delivery Service 1998; Rugrats in Paris: the Movie 2000; Cinderella II: Dreams Come True 2002; Hey Arnold! the Movie 2002
McNichol, Kristy (1962-) Summer of My German Soldier 1978; Little Darlings 1980; The Night the Lights Went Out in Georgia 1981; Only When I Laugh 1981; White Dog 1981; Dream Lover 1986; Two Moon Junction 1988
MacNicol, Peter (1954-) Dragonslayer 1981; Sophie's Choice 1982; Heat 1987; American Blue Note 1989; Ghostbusters II 1989; By Dawn's Early Light 1990; Hard Promises 1991; HouseSitter 1992; Addams Family Values 1993; Roswell 1994; Dracula: Dead and Loving It 1995; Bean 1997; The Secret of NIMH II: Timmy to the Rescue 1998; Baby Geniuses 1999; Recess: School's Out 2001; Breakin' All the Rules 2004; Stuart Little 3: Call of the Wild 2005; Game Change 2012
McNulty, Kevin (1955-) Family Sins 2004; Fantastic Four 2005; The Uninvited 2008
McNulty, Matthew Little Ashes 2008; Toast 2010; The Knot 2012
Macowan, Norman (1877-1961) The Dark Light 1951; The City of the Dead 1960
McPhee, Katharine The House Bunny 2008; Shark Night 3D 2011; You May Not Kiss the Bride 2011
Macpherson, Elle (1964-) Sirens 1994; If Lucy Fell 1996; Jane Eyre 1996; The Mirror Has Two Faces 1996; The Edge 1997
McQuarrie, Stuart (1963-) The Life of Stuff 1997; Young Adam 2003; Hush 2008
McQueen, Butterfly (1911-1995) Gone with the Wind 1939; Affectionately Yours 1941; Mildred Pierce 1945; Duel in the Sun 1946
McQueen (1), Steve aka **McQueen, Steven** (1930-1980) Somebody Up There Likes Me 1956; The Blob 1958; Never So Few 1959; The Magnificent Seven 1960; Hell Is for Heroes 1962; The War Lover 1962; The Great Escape 1963; Love with the Proper Stranger 1963; Soldier in the Rain 1963; Baby the Rain Must Fall 1965; The Cincinnati Kid 1965; Nevada Smith 1966; The Sand Pebbles 1966; Bullitt 1968; The Thomas Crown Affair 1968; The Reivers 1969; Le Mans 1971; On Any Sunday 1971; The Getaway 1972; Junior Bonner 1972; Papillon 1973; The Towering Inferno 1974; An Enemy of the People 1977; The Hunter 1980; Tom Horn 1980; Steve McQueen: the Man & Le Mans 2015
Macrae, Duncan (1905-1967) The Brothers 1947; The Woman in Question 1950; The Kidnappers 1953; Rockets Galore 1958; The Best of Enemies 1961; Greyfriars Bobby 1961; A Jolly Bad Fellow 1964; 30 Is a Dangerous Age, Cynthia 1963
McRae, Frank (1952-) Paradise Alley 1978; Used Cars 1980; Cannery Row 1982; 48 HRS 1982; *batteries not included 1987; Farewell to the King 1988; Licence to Kill 1989; Lock Up 1989; Last Action Hero 1993; National Lampoon's Loaded Weapon 1 1993; Lightning Jack 1994
MacRae, Gordon (1921-1986) Look for the Silver Lining 1949; Backfire 1950; The Daughter of Rosie O'Grady 1950; Tea for Two 1950; The West Point Story 1950; On Moonlight Bay 1951; By the Light of the Silvery Moon 1953; The Desert Song 1953; Three Sailors and a Girl 1953; Oklahoma! 1955; The Best

Things in Life Are Free 1956; Carousel 1956
McRae, Hilton The French Lieutenant's Woman 1981; The Secret Rapture 1993
McRaney, Gerald (1948-) The NeverEnding Story 1984; Take Me Home: the John Denver Story 2000; Ike: Countdown to D-Day 2004; Get Low 2009; The Best of Me 2014; Focus 2015
Macready, George (1908-1973) The Conspirators 1944; Follow the Boys 1944; Counter-Attack 1945; My Name Is Julia Ross 1945; A Song to Remember 1945; The Bandit of Sherwood Forest 1946; Gilda 1946; Down to Earth 1947; The Big Clock 1948; The Black Arrow 1948; Coroner Creek 1948; Alias Nick Beal 1949; Knock on Any Door 1949; A Lady without Passport 1950; Rogues of Sherwood Forest 1950; The Desert Fox 1951; Detective Story 1951; Tarzan's Peril 1951; The Golden Blade 1953; Julius Caesar 1953; Treasure of the Golden Condor 1953; Vera Cruz 1954; A Kiss before Dying 1956; Thunder over Arizona 1956; Paths of Glory 1957; The Alligator People 1959; Taras Bulba 1962; Dead Ringer 1964; Seven Days in May 1964; Where Love Has Gone 1964
McRobbie, Peter (1943-) The Neon Bible 1995; The Visit 2015
McShane, Ian (1942-) The Wild and the Willing 1962; The Pleasure Girls 1965; Sky West and Crooked 1965; Battle of Britain 1969; The Ballad of Tam Lin 1970; Villain 1971; Sitting Target 1972; The Last of Sheila 1973; Ransom 1975; The 5th Musketeer 1979; Yesterday's Hero 1979; Too Scared to Scream 1982; Exposed 1983; Torchlight 1984; Sexy Beast 2000; Bollywood Queen 2002; Agent Cody Banks 2003; Scoop 2006; The Dark Is Rising 2007; Hot Rod 2007; Shrek the Third 2007; Case 39 2008; Coraline 2008; Death Race 2008; Kung Fu Panda 2008; 44 Inch Chest 2009; Shrek Forever After 2010; Pirates of the Caribbean: on Stranger Tides 2011; Snow White and the Huntsman 2012; How We Used to Live 2013; Jack the Giant Slayer 2013; Hercules 2014; John Wick 2014; Grimsby 2016
McShane, Micheal aka **McShane, Michael** aka **McShane, Mike** (1957-) Robin Hood: Prince of Thieves 1991; Richie Rich 1994; Tom and Huck 1995; A Bug's Life 1998
McSorley, Gerard (1950-) The Boxer 1997; Felicia's Journey 1999; Bloody Sunday 2001; Dead Bodies 2003; Veronica Guerin 2003; Inside I'm Dancing 2004; The Front Line 2006; Middletown 2006
McTavish, Graham (1961-) Macbeth 1997; Rambo 2007; Sisterhood 2008; The Wicker Tree 2010
McTeer, Janet (1962-) Hawks 1988; Wuthering Heights 1992; Carrington 1995; Velvet Goldmine 1998; Songcatcher 1999; Tumbleweeds 1999; The King Is Alive 2000; Waking the Dead 2000; Tideland 2005; Albert Nobbs 2011; Island 2011; The Woman in Black 2011; Hannah Arendt 2012; Me before You 2016
McVey, Patrick aka **McVey, Pat** (1910-1973) The Big Caper 1957; The Visitors 1972; Bang the Drum Slowly 1973
McVey, Paul (1898-1973) Force of Evil 1948; Bwana Devil 1952
McVey, Tyler (1912-2003) The Come On 1956; Attack of the Giant Leeches 1960; Lt Robin Crusoe, USN 1966
MacVittie, Bruce Stonewall 1995; Where the Money Is 2000
McWade, Margaret (1872-1956) The Lost World 1925; Theodora Goes Wild 1936
McWade, Robert (1872-1938) Feet First 1930; Kept Husbands 1931; The First Year 1932; The Lemon Drop Kid 1934; Anything Goes 1936; Next Time We Love 1936; California Straight Ahead 1937
McWhirter, Jillian After Midnight 1989; Progeny 1998
McWilliams, Caroline (1945-2010) White Water Summer 1987; Mermaids 1990
Macy, Bill (1922-) The Late Show 1977; The Jerk 1979; Serial 1980; My Favorite Year 1982; Bad Medicine 1985; Movers and Shakers 1985; Analyze This 1999; Surviving Christmas 2004
Macy, William H aka **Macy, Bill** (1950-) Homicide 1991; The Heart of Justice 1992; Benny & Joon 1993; Being Human 1994; Murder in the First 1994; Oleanna 1994; Above Suspicion 1995; Fargo 1995; Mr Holland's Opus 1995; Down Periscope 1996; Ghosts of Mississippi 1996; Air Force One 1997;

Boogie Nights 1997; Wag the Dog 1997; A Civil Action 1998; The Con 1998; Jerry and Tom 1998; Pleasantville 1998; Psycho 1998; Happy, Texas 1999; Magnolia 1999; Mystery Men 1999; A Slight Case of Murder 1999; Panic 2000; State and Main 2000; Focus 2001; Jurassic Park III 2001; The Cooler 2002; Door to Door 2002; It's a Very Merry Muppet Christmas Movie 2002; Welcome to Collinwood 2002; Easy Riders, Raging Bulls 2003; Seabiscuit 2003; Cellular 2004; Spartan 2004; Edmond 2005; Sahara 2005; Thank You for Smoking 2005; Bobby 2006; Inland Empire 2006; He Was a Quiet Man 2007; Wild Hogs 2007; The Heist 2009; Shorts 2009; Marmaduke 2010; The Lincoln Lawyer 2011; The Sessions 2012; Cake 2015; Room 2015; Blood Father 2016
Madden, Ciaran (1945-) Gawain and the Green Knight 1973; The Beast Must Die 1974
Madden, Dave (1931-2014) Charlotte's Web 1973; Eat My Dust! 1976
Madden, Peter (1905-1976) The Loneliness of the Long Distance Runner 1962; The Road to Hong Kong 1962; He Who Rides a Tiger 1965
Madden, Richard (1986-) A Promise 2013; Cinderella 2015; Bastille Day 2016
Maddern, Victor (1926-1993) Sailor of the King 1953; Street of Shadows 1953; Terror on a Train 1953; Carrington VC 1954; The Cockleshell Heroes 1955; Child in the House 1956; The Man in the Sky 1956; Barnacle Bill 1957; Seven Waves Away 1957; Blood of the Vampire 1958; Cat and Mouse 1958; I Was Monty's Double 1958; The Safecracker 1958; Light Up the Sky 1960; Petticoat Pirates 1961; HMS Defiant 1962; Rotten to the Core 1965; A Hole Lot of Trouble 1969; Steptoe and Son 1972
Madhubala (1933-1969) Mahal 1949; Tarana 1951; Mr and Mrs '55 1955; Mughal-e-Azam 1960
Madigan, Amy (1950-) Love Child 1982; Love Letters 1983; Places in the Heart 1984; Streets of Fire 1984; Alamo Bay 1985; Twice in a Lifetime 1985; Nowhere to Hide 1987; The Prince of Pennsylvania 1988; Field of Dreams 1989; Roe vs Wade 1989; Uncle Buck 1989; The Dark Half 1991; Female Perversions 1996; Loved 1996; Pollock 2000; Frontera 2014
Madison, Bailee (1999-) Bridge to Terabithia 2006; Brothers 2009; Don't Be Afraid of the Dark 2010; Parental Guidance 2012
Madison, Guy (1922-1996) Till the End of Time 1946; The Charge at Feather River 1953; The Command 1954; The Last Frontier 1955; The Beast of Hollow Mountain 1956; Hilda Crane 1956; Bullwhip 1958
Madison, Mae (1914-2004) The Big Stampede 1932; So Big 1932
Madison, Noel (1897-1975) A Handful of Clouds 1930; Me and My Gal 1932; Gangway 1937; Climbing High 1938; Crackerjack 1938; Sailing Along 1938
Madoc, Philip (1934-2012) Dr Jekyll & Sister Hyde 1971; Zina 1985; Otherworld 2003
Madonna (1958-) Desperately Seeking Susan 1985; Shanghai Surprise 1986; Who's That Girl 1987; Bloodhounds of Broadway 1989; Dick Tracy 1990; In Bed with Madonna 1991; Shadows and Fog 1991; Body of Evidence 1992; A League of Their Own 1992; Dangerous Game 1993; Blue in the Face 1995; Four Rooms 1995; Evita 1996; Girl 6 1996; The Next Best Thing 2000; Die Another Day 2002; Swept Away 2002; Arthur and the Invisibles 2006
Madrell, Red Kidulthood 2005; It's a Lot 2014
Madsen, Michael (1958-) The Killing Time 1987; Blood Red 1988; Kill Me Again 1989; The Doors 1991; Reservoir Dogs 1991; Thelma & Louise 1991; Straight Talk 1992; Final Combination 1993; Free Willy 1993; Money for Nothing 1993; Trouble Bound 1993; Fixing the Shadow 1994; The Getaway 1994; Wyatt Earp 1994; Free Willy 2: the Adventure Home 1995; Species 1995; Executive Target 1996; The Last Days of Frankie the Fly 1996; Mulholland Falls 1996; The Winner 1996; Diary of a Serial Killer 1997; Donnie Brasco 1997; The Maker 1997; Species II 1998; Too Hard to Die 1998; Supreme Sanction 1999; The Ghost 2000; High Noon 2000; Luck of the Draw 2000; Die Another Day 2002; Kill Bill Vol 1 2003; My Boss's Daughter 2003; Blueberry 2004; Frankenstein 2004; Kill Bill Vol 2 2004; Sin City 2005; Scary Movie 4 2006; Piranhaconda 2012; The Hateful Eight 2015

Madsen, Virginia (1961-) Dune 1984; Electric Dreams 1984; Creator 1985; Fire with Fire 1986; Slam Dance 1987; Zombie High 1987; The Dead Can't Lie 1988; Hot to Trot 1988; Mr North 1988; Heart of Dixie 1989; Highlander II: the Quickening 1990; The Hot Spot 1990; Becoming Colette 1991; Victim of Love 1991; Candyman 1992; Blue Tiger 1994; The Prophecy 1994; Just Your Luck 1996; John Grisham's The Rainmaker 1997; The Haunting 1999; American Gun 2002; Returning Lily 2003; Brave New Girl 2004; Sideways 2004; Stuart Little 3: Call of the Wild 2005; The Astronaut Farmer 2006; Firewall 2006; The Number 23 2006; A Prairie Home Companion 2006; Diminished Capacity 2007; The Haunting in Connecticut 2009; Red Riding Hood 2011; Joy 2015
Maestro, Mia (1978-) For Love or Country: the Arturo Sandoval Story 2000; Frida 2002; The Motorcycle Diaries 2004; Secuestro Express 2004; Poseidon 2006; First Night 2010
Maffia, Roma (1958-) Disclosure 1994; Nick of Time 1995
Magee, Francis London River 2009; Jimmy's Hall 2014
Magee, Patrick (1922-1982) The Criminal 1960; Dementia 13 1963; The Masque of the Red Death 1964; Seance on a Wet Afternoon 1964; The Skull 1965; Marat/Sade 1966; The Birthday Party 1968; Hard Contract 1969; Cromwell 1970; King Lear 1970; You Can't Win 'Em All 1970; A Clockwork Orange 1971; Demons of the Mind 1971; The Fiend 1971; The Trojan Women 1971; Asylum 1972; Tales from the Crypt 1972; And Now the Screaming Starts! 1973; The Final Programme 1973; Luther 1974; Barry Lyndon 1975; Telefon 1977; The Brontë Sisters 1979; Rough Cut 1980; The Black Cat 1981; Chariots of Fire 1981
Magimel, Benoît (1974-) Life Is a Long Quiet River 1988; Les Voleurs 1996; Les Enfants du Siècle 1999; Le Roi Danse 2000; The Piano Teacher 2001; The Flower of Evil 2002; Strange Gardens 2003; The Bridesmaid 2004; La Fille Coupée en Deux 2007; Intimate Enemies 2007; Little White Lies 2010; Special Forces 2011
Maglietta, Licia (1954-) L'Amore Molesto 1995; Bread and Tulips 2000
Magnan, Philippe (1948-) Le Parfum d'Yvonne 1994; La Veuve de Saint-Pierre 2000; Arsène Lupin 2004
Magnani, Anna (1907-1973) Rome, Open City 1945; L'Amore 1948; Bellissima 1951; The Golden Coach 1953; The Rose Tattoo 1955; Wild Is the Wind 1957; The Fugitive Kind 1960; Mamma Roma 1962; The Secret of Santa Vittoria 1969; Fellini's Roma 1972
Magnuson, Ann (1956-) Making Mr Right 1987; Checking Out 1988; A Night in the Life of Jimmy Reardon 1988; Tequila Sunrise 1988; Before and After 1996; Small Soldiers 1998; Love & Sex 2000; Glitter 2001; Panic Room 2002
Magowan, Kate (1975-) It's All Gone Pete Tong 2004; TuEsday 2007; Elfie Hopkins 2011; A Lonely Place to Die 2011; Screwed 2011; The Fall of the Essex Boys 2012
Magre, Judith (1926-) Les Amants 1958; Nathalie... 2003
Magree, Frank Danny Deckchair 2003; The Subjects 2015
Maguelon, Pierre Garde à Vue 1981; Cyrano de Bergerac 1990; Alice et Martin 1998
Maguire, Kathleen (1925-1989) Edge of the City 1957; Flipper 1963; Bill 1981
Maguire, Mary (1917-1974) Confession 1937; Mysterious Mr Moto 1938
Maguire, Sean Prince Charming 2001; Meet the Spartans 2008
Maguire, Tobey (1975-) This Boy's Life 1993; The Ice Storm 1997; Fear and Loathing in Las Vegas 1998; Pleasantville 1998; The Cider House Rules 1999; Ride with the Devil 1999; Wonder Boys 2000; Cats & Dogs 2001; Spider-Man 2002; Seabiscuit 2003; Spider-Man 2 2004; The Good German 2006; Spider-Man 3 2007; Brothers 2009; The Great Gatsby 2013; Labor Day 2013
Mahaffey, Valerie (1953-) National Lampoon's Senior Trip 1995; Jungle 2 Jungle 1997; No Ordinary Baby 2001; If I Were You 2012
Maharis, George (1928-) Sylvia 1964; Quick, before It Melts 1965; The Satan Bug 1965; The Happening 1967; Land Raiders 1969; Doppelganger 1993
Maher, Bill (1956-) House II: the Second Story 1987; Cannibal Women in the Avocado Jungle of Death 1989; Tomcats 2000; Religulous 2008
Maher, Joseph (1934-1998) Under the Rainbow 1981; The Evil That Men Do

1984; Funny Farm 1988; My Stepmother Is an Alien 1988; IQ 1994; Killer 1994; Surviving Picasso 1996
Maher, Sean Serenity 2005; Much Ado about Nothing 2012
Mahler, Bruce (1950-) Police Academy 2: Their First Assignment 1985; Police Academy 6: City under Siege 1989
Mahoney, Jock (1919-1989) A Day of Fury 1956; Showdown at Abilene 1956; Battle Hymn 1957; The Last of the Fast Guns 1958; A Time to Love and a Time to Die 1958; Tarzan the Magnificent 1960; Tarzan Goes to India 1962; Tarzan's Three Challenges 1963; The Glory Stompers 1967
Mahoney, John (1940-) The Deadly Game 1986; Moonstruck 1987; Suspect 1987; Tin Men 1987; Betrayed 1988; Eight Men Out 1988; Frantic 1988; Dinner at Eight 1989; Say Anything... 1989; The Image 1990; Love Hurts 1990; The Russia House 1990; Barton Fink 1991; Article 99 1992; In the Line of Fire 1993; Striking Distance 1993; The Hudsucker Proxy 1994; The American President 1995; Primal Fear 1996; She's the One 1996; Antz 1998; The Iron Giant 1999; The Broken Hearts Club: a Romantic Comedy 2000; Atlantis: the Lost Empire 2001; Kronk's New Groove 2005; Dan in Real Life 2007
Mahoney, Louis Praise Marx and Pass the Ammunition 1968; Shooting Dogs 2005
Maiden, Rita The Married Woman 1964; Playtime 1967
Maïga, Aïssa Bamako 2006; Mood Indigo 2013
Mailer, Norman (1923-2007) Beyond the Law 1968; Ragtime 1981; King Lear - Fear and Loathing 1987; When We Were Kings 1996; Cremaster 2 1999
Mailer, Stephen (1966-) Reversal of Fortune 1990; Getting In 1994
Mailes, Charles Hill aka **Mailes, Charles H** (1870-1937) The Battle of Elderbush 1914; The Mark of Zorro 1920
Mailhouse, Robert (1962-) A Secret Affair 1999; Thicker than Water 2005; All I Want for Christmas 2007; The Christmas Pageant 2011
Maille, Claudette Like Water for Chocolate 1993; KM 31: Kilometro 31 2005
Mailman, Deborah (1973-) Rabbit-Proof Fence 2002; The Book of Revelation 2006; Mental 2012; The Sapphires 2012; Paper Planes 2014
Main, Laurie (1929-) The Master Plan 1954; Time after Time 1979
Main, Marjorie (1890-1975) Dead End 1937; Stella Dallas 1937; Too Hot to Handle 1938; The Women 1939; I Take This Woman 1940; Honky Tonk 1941; The Shepherd of the Hills 1941; A Woman's Face 1941; The Affairs of Martha 1942; Tennessee Johnson 1942; Heaven Can Wait 1943; Johnny Come Lately 1943; Meet Me in St Louis 1944; Murder, He Says 1945; The Harvey Girls 1946; The Egg and I 1947; Ma and Pa Kettle 1949; Mrs O'Malley and Mr Malone 1950; Summer Stock 1950; The Law and the Lady 1951; Mr Imperium 1951; The Belle of New York 1952; The Long, Long Trailer 1954; Rose Marie 1954; Friendly Persuasion 1956
Mairesse, Valérie (1955-) [Three] Après la Vie 2002; [Two] Un Couple Epatant 2002
Maistre, François (1925-2016) Paris Nous Appartient 1960; Les Innocents aux Mains Sales 1975
Maitland, Gary Tickets 2005; The Angels' Share 2012
Maitland, Lorna Lorna 1964; Mudhoney 1965
Maitland, Marne (1920-1991) Bhowani Junction 1956; The Wind Cannot Read 1958; Sands of the Desert 1960; The Return of Mr Moto 1965; The Reptile 1966; The Bobo 1967
Majorino, Tina (1985-) Andre 1994; Corrina, Corrina 1994; When a Man Loves a Woman 1994; Waterworld 1995; Before Women Had Wings 1997; Alice in Wonderland 1999; Napoleon Dynamite 2004; Veronica Mars 2014
Majors, Lee (1939-) Will Penny 1967; The Liberation of LB Jones 1970; The Six Million Dollar Man 1973; Killer Fish 1978; The Norseman 1978; Agency 1981; Starflight One 1983; Primary Suspect 2000; Big Fat Liar 2002; The Trail to Hope Rose 2004; The Brothers Solomon 2007
Majumdar, Sreela And Quiet Rolls the Dawn 1979; In Search of Famine 1980
Makatsch, Heike (1971-) Aimée and Jaguar 1999; Late Night Shopping 2001; Mrs Ratcliffe's Revolution 2007
Makeba, Miriam Sarafina! 1992; Soul Power 2008

Makeham, Eliot (1882-1956) *Rome Express* 1932; *Friday the Thirteenth* 1933; *Dark Journey* 1937; *Head over Heels in Love* 1937; *Bell-Bottom George* 1943; *Daybreak* 1946; *Green Grow the Rushes* 1951; *Scarlet Thread* 1951; *The Yellow Balloon* 1952

Makepeace, Chris (1964-) *My Bodyguard* 1980; *Vamp* 1986; *Aloha Summer* 1988; *Memory Run* 1995

Makhmalbaf, Mohsen (1957-) *Close-Up* 1989; *A Moment of Innocence* 1996

Makkena, Wendy (1958-) *Sister Act* 1992; *Sister Act 2: Back in the Habit* 1993; *Air Bud* 1997; *Finding North* 1997

Mako (1933-2006) *The Sand Pebbles* 1966; *The Ugly Dachshund* 1966; *The Private Navy of Sgt O'Farrell* 1968; *The Great Bank Robbery* 1969; *The Hawaiians* 1970; *The Island at the Top of the World* 1974; *The Killer Elite* 1975; *The Big Brawl* 1980; *An Eye for an Eye* 1981; *Under the Rainbow* 1981; *Conan the Barbarian* 1982; *Conan the Destroyer* 1984; *PoW the Escape* 1986; *Silent Assassins* 1988; *Tucker: the Man and His Dream* 1988; *Fatal Mission* 1990; *Pacific Heights* 1990; *Rising Sun* 1993; *RoboCop 3* 1993; *Crying Freeman* 1995; *Highlander III: the Sorcerer* 1995; *Seven Years in Tibet* 1997; *Bulletproof Monk* 2002; *TMNT* 2007

Makoare, Lawrence *What Becomes of the Broken Hearted?* 1999; *The Dead Lands* 2014

Makovetsky, Sergei (1958-) *Rothschild's Violin* 1996; *Of Freaks and Men* 1998

Maksimovic, Dragan (1949-2001) *Meetings with Remarkable Men* 1979; *Pretty Village Pretty Flame* 1996

Malahide, Patrick (1945-) *Comfort and Joy* 1984; *A Month in the Country* 1987; *December Bride* 1990; *A Man of No Importance* 1994; *Two Deaths* 1994; *CutThroat Island* 1995; *The Long Kiss Goodnight* 1996; *The Beautician and the Beast* 1997; *Captain Jack* 1998; *Heaven* 1999; *Fortress 2: Re-entry* 1999; *Ordinary Decent Criminal* 1999; *Quills* 2000; *The Abduction Club* 2002; *The Final Curtain* 2002; *The Rocket Post* 2003; *Sahara* 2005; *Like Minds* 2006; *Brideshead Revisited* 2008

Malambri, Rick *After the Fall* 2010; *Step Up 3* 2010

Malavoy, Christophe (1952-) *La Balance* 1982; *Death in a French Garden* 1985; *Le Cri du Hibou* 1987; *Madame Bovary* 1991

Malco, Romany (1968-) *The 40 Year Old Virgin* 2005; *Blades of Glory* 2007; *Baby Mama* 2008; *The Love Guru* 2008; *A Little Bit of Heaven* 2011; *Think like a Man Too* 2014

Malcolm, Christopher (1946-2014) *Figures in a Landscape* 1970; *Labyrinth* 1986

Malden, Karl (1912-2009) *They Knew What They Wanted* 1940; *Kiss of Death* 1947; *The Gunfighter* 1950; *Halls of Montezuma* 1950; *Where the Sidewalk Ends* 1950; *A Streetcar Named Desire* 1951; *Diplomatic Courier* 1952; *Ruby Gentry* 1952; *I Confess* 1953; *Take the High Ground* 1953; *On the Waterfront* 1954; *Baby Doll* 1956; *Bombers B-52* 1957; *Fear Strikes Out* 1957; *The Hanging Tree* 1959; *Pollyanna* 1960; *One-Eyed Jacks* 1961; *All Fall Down* 1962; *Birdman of Alcatraz* 1962; *Come Fly with Me* 1962; *Gypsy* 1962; *How the West Was Won* 1962; *Cheyenne Autumn* 1964; *Dead Ringer* 1964; *The Cincinnati Kid* 1965; *Nevada Smith* 1966; *The Adventures of Bullwhip Griffin* 1967; *Billion Dollar Brain* 1967; *Blue* 1968; *Hot Millions* 1968; *Patton* 1970; *Cat o'Nine Tails* 1971; *Wild Rovers* 1971; *Beyond the Poseidon Adventure* 1979; *Meteor* 1979; *The Sting II* 1983; *Billy Galvin* 1986; *Nuts* 1987; *My Father, My Son* 1988; *Vanished without a Trace* 1993

Malek, Rami *The Master* 2012; *Ain't Them Bodies Saints* 2013; *Night at the Museum: Secret of the Tomb* 2014

Malet, Arthur (1927-2013) *Lt Robin Crusoe, USN* 1966; *Halloween* 1978; *The Secret of NIMH* 1982; *The Black Cauldron* 1985; *Toys* 1992; *A Little Princess* 1995

Malet, Laurent (1955-) *Blood Relatives* 1977; *Roads to the South* 1978; *Querelle* 1982

Maley, Peggy (1926-) *The Wild One* 1953; *Human Desire* 1954

Mali, Antara *Company* 2001; *Naach* 2004

Malick, Wendie (1950-) *The Emperor's New Groove* 2000; *Racing Stripes* 2004

Malik, Art aka **Malik, Athar** (1952-) *Arabian Adventure* 1979; *A Passage to India* 1984; *The Living Daylights* 1987; *City of Joy* 1992; *Hostage* 1992; *Turtle Beach* 1992; *Year of the Comet* 1992;

Clockwork Mice 1994; *True Lies* 1994; *Booty Call* 1997; *Side Streets* 1998; *Fakers* 2004; *Nina's Heavenly Delights* 2006; *Dean Spanley* 2008; *Franklyn* 2008; *The Wolfman* 2009; *Ghosted* 2011

Malikyan, Kevork *The Man Who Haunted Himself* 1970; *Flight of the Phoenix* 1984; *Renaissance* 2006

Malin, Eddie (1894-1977) *A Hard Day's Night* 1964; *Nearest and Dearest* 1972

Malina, Joshua aka **Malina, Josh** (1966-) *Kill the Man* 1999; *View from the Top* 2003

Malina, Judith (1926-2015) *Enemies, a Love Story* 1989; *The Addams Family* 1991; *Household Saints* 1993

Malinger, Ross (1984-) *Sleepless in Seattle* 1993; *Little Bigfoot* 1995; *Sudden Death* 1995

Malkovich, John (1953-) *The Killing Fields* 1984; *Places in the Heart* 1984; *Death of a Salesman* 1985; *Eleni* 1985; *Empire of the Sun* 1987; *The Glass Menagerie* 1987; *Making Mr Right* 1987; *Dangerous Liaisons* 1988; *Miles from Home* 1988; *The Sheltering Sky* 1990; *The Object of Beauty* 1991; *Queens Logic* 1991; *Shadows and Fog* 1991; *Jennifer Eight* 1992; *Of Mice and Men* 1992; *In the Line of Fire* 1993; *Beyond the Clouds* 1995; *The Convent* 1995; *Mary Reilly* 1995; *Mulholland Falls* 1996; *The Portrait of a Lady* 1996; *Con Air* 1997; *The Man in the Iron Mask* 1997; *Rounders* 1998; *Being John Malkovich* 1999; *Joan of Arc* 1999; *RKO 281* 1999; *Time Regained* 1999; *Ladies' Room* 2000; *Shadow of the Vampire* 2000; *Hotel* 2001; *I'm Going Home* 2001; *Knockaround Guys* 2001; *Ripley's Game* 2002; *Un Filme Falado* 2003; *Johnny English* 2003; *The Libertine* 2004; *The Hitchhiker's Guide to the Galaxy* 2005; *Eragon* 2006; *Klimt* 2006; *Beowulf* 2007; *Burn after Reading* 2008; *Changeling* 2008; *Disgrace* 2008; *Mutant Chronicles* 2008; *Jonah Hex* 2010; *Red* 2010; *Secretariat* 2010; *Transformers: Dark of the Moon* 2011; *Warm Bodies* 2012; *Red 2* 2013; *Penguins of Madagascar* 2014

Mallalieu, Aubrey (1873-1948) *Music Hath Charms* 1935; *The Face at the Window* 1939; *Gert and Daisy's Weekend* 1941; *My Learned Friend* 1943

Malle, Louis (1932-1995) *Phantom India* 1968; *God's Country* 1985

Malleson, Miles (1888-1969) *Nell Gwyn* 1934; *The Thief of Bagdad* 1940; *While the Sun Shines* 1946; *Golden Salamander* 1949; *Kind Hearts and Coronets* 1949; *The Perfect Woman* 1949; *Stage Fright* 1949; *The Man in the White Suit* 1951; *Folly to Be Wise* 1952; *Treasure Hunt* 1952; *Trent's Last Case* 1952; *The Captain's Paradise* 1953; *Brothers in Law* 1956; *Dracula* 1958; *The Hound of the Baskervilles* 1959; *And the Same to You* 1960; *The Brides of Dracula* 1960; *Kidnapped* 1960; *Double Bunk* 1961; *Fury at Smugglers Bay* 1961; *Go to Blazes* 1961; *The Hellfire Club* 1961; *Postman's Knock* 1961; *A Jolly Bad Fellow* 1964; *Murder Ahoy* 1964

Malling, Soren *A Hijacking* 2012; *The Hour of the Lynx* 2013; *Men & Chicken* 2015; *The Shamer's Daughter* 2015; *A War* 2015

Mallinson, Rory (1903-1976) *Deep Valley* 1947; *Cavalry Scout* 1951

Malloy, Matt *Boys* 1995; *In the Company of Men* 1997; *Wedding Daze* 2006

Malm, Mona (1935-) *Fanny and Alexander* 1982; *Best Intentions* 1992

Malmsjö, Jan (1932-) *Scenes from a Marriage* 1973; *Fanny and Alexander* 1982

Malmsten, Birger (1920-1991) *It Rains on Our Love* 1946; *A Ship to India* 1947; *Night Is My Future* 1948; *The Devil's Wanton* 1949; *Three Strange Loves* 1949; *Summer Interlude* 1950; *Waiting Women* 1952

Malo, Gina (1909-1963) *Where There's a Will* 1936; *Over She Goes* 1937

Malone, Bonz *Slam* 1998; *Whiteboys* 1999

Malone, Dorothy (1925-) *The Big Sleep* 1946; *Night and Day* 1946; *Colorado Territory* 1949; *South of St Louis* 1949; *Convicted* 1950; *Mrs O'Malley and Mr Malone* 1950; *Law and Order* 1953; *Scared Stiff* 1953; *Private Hell 36* 1954; *Pushover* 1954; *Artists and Models* 1955; *At Gunpoint* 1955; *Sincerely Yours* 1955; *Tall Man Riding* 1955; *Young at Heart* 1955; *Pillars of the Sky* 1956; *Tension at Table Rock* 1956; *Written on the Wind* 1956; *Man of a Thousand Faces* 1957; *Quantez* 1957; *The Tarnished Angels* 1957; *Too Much, Too Soon* 1958; *Warlock* 1959; *The Last Voyage* 1960; *The Last Sunset* 1961;

Beach Party 1963; *Fate Is the Hunter* 1964; *Golden Rendezvous* 1977; *Winter Kills* 1979; *The Day Time Ended* 1980

Malone, Jena (1984-) *Stepmom* 1998; *For Love of the Game* 1999; *The Ballad of Lucy Whipple* 2001; *The Dangerous Lives of Altar Boys* 2001; *Donnie Darko* 2001; *The United States of Leland* 2002; *The Ballad of Jack and Rose* 2005; *Pride & Prejudice* 2005; *Container* 2006; *Four Last Songs* 2007; *Into the Wild* 2007; *The Ruins* 2008; *The Messenger* 2009; *Sucker Punch* 2011; *For Ellen* 2012; *Teenage* 2013; *Time out of Mind* 2014; *The Neon Demon* 2016

Malone, Mark *Dead of Winter* 1987; *Straight out of Brooklyn* 1991

Maloney, Michael (1957-) *Henry V* 1989; *Hamlet* 1990; *Truly Madly Deeply* 1990; *In the Bleak Midwinter* 1995; *Othello* 1995; *Hamlet* 1996; *Kisna - the Warrior Poet* 2004; *Notes on a Scandal* 2006; *Luna* 2014

Maloney, Peter *The Thing* 1982; *Washington Square* 1997

Maltby, H F (1880-1963) *Where There's a Will* 1936; *Under Your Hat* 1940

Mamet, Zosia *Mapplethorpe* 2016; *Wiener-Dog* 2016

Mammone, Robert *Heaven's Burning* 1997; *The Condemned* 2007

Man, Alex (1957-) *Rouge* 1987; *As Tears Go By* 1988

Manahan, Anna (1924-2009) *A Business Affair* 1993; *A Man of No Importance* 1994

Manahan, Sheila (1924-1988) *Another Shore* 1948; *Seven Days to Noon* 1950; *Only Two Can Play* 1961

Mancini, Al (1932-2007) *Miller's Crossing* 1990; *It Runs in the Family* 1994

Mancini, Ray aka **Mancini, Ray "Boom Boom"** (1961-) *Timebomb* 1991; *Aces: Iron Eagle III* 1992

Mancuso, Nick (1948-) *Nightwing* 1979; *Ticket to Heaven* 1981; *Maria Chapdelaine* 1982; *Blame It on the Night* 1984; *Heartbreakers* 1984; *Love Songs* 1984; *Death of an Angel* 1985; *Lena's Holiday* 1990; *Rapid Fire* 1992; *Under Siege 2* 1995; *Mary Higgins Clark's Let Me Call You Sweetheart* 1997; *Captured* 1998; *Today You Die* 2005

Mandan, Robert (1932-) *The Best Little Whorehouse in Texas* 1982; *Zapped!* 1982

Mandel, Howie (1955-) *A Fine Mess* 1986; *Walk like a Man* 1987; *Gremlins 2: the New Batch* 1990; *Shake, Rattle and Rock* 1994

Mander, Miles (1888-1946) *The Pleasure Garden* 1925; *The First Born* 1928; *Murder* 1930; *Don Quixote* 1932; *Bitter Sweet* 1933; *Death Drives Through* 1935; *Kidnapped* 1938; *The Man in the Iron Mask* 1939; *The Three Musketeers* 1939; *Primrose Path* 1940; *Apache Trail* 1942; *Fingers at the Window* 1942; *Five Graves to Cairo* 1943; *The Return of the Vampire* 1943; *Enter Arsene Lupin* 1944; *Farewell My Lovely* 1944; *The Pearl of Death* 1944; *The Brighton Strangler* 1945

Mandvi, Aasif *ABCD* 1999; *The Mystic Masseur* 2001; *The Internship* 2013; *Weirdsville* 2006; *Experimenter: the Stanley Milgram Story* 2014

Mandylor, Costas (1965-) *Triumph of the Spirit* 1989; *Mobsters* 1991; *Delta of Venus* 1995; *Fist of the North Star* 1995; *Stealth Fighter* 1999; *Sub Zero* 2005; *Saw IV* 2007; *Saw V* 2008; *Saw VI* 2009; *Saw: the Final Chapter* 2010

Mandylor, Louis (1966-) *The Heartbreak Kid* 1993; *The Set Up* 1995; *My Big Fat Greek Wedding* 2002

Mane, Tyler *X-Men* 2000; *Halloween* 2007; *Halloween II* 2009

Manesh, Marshall *Kazaam* 1996; *A Girl Walks Home Alone at Night* 2014

Manetti, Larry (1947-) *Back to You and Me* 2005; *Cool Money* 2005

Manfredi, Nino (1921-2004) *Le Bambole* 1965; *We All Loved Each Other So Much* 1974; *Down and Dirty* 1976

Mangan, Stephen (1968-) *Festival* 2005; *Someone Else* 2005; *Confetti* 2006; *Beyond the Pole* 2009; *Postman Pat: the Movie* 2013

Manganiello, Joe *Magic Mike* 2012; *Sabotage* 2013; *Magic Mike XXL* 2015

Mangano, Silvana (1930-1989) *Bitter Rice* 1949; *Gold of Naples* 1954; *Ulysses* 1954; *This Angry Age* 1957; *Tempest* 1959; *Five Branded Women* 1960; *Barabbas* 1961; *The Witches* 1966; *Oedipus Rex* 1967; *Theorem* 1968; *Death in Venice* 1971; *Ludwig* 1973; *Conversation Piece* 1974; *Dune* 1984; *Dark Eyes* 1987

Mango, Alec (1911-1989) *They Who Dare* 1953; *Mask of Dust* 1954; *Interpol* 1957; *The Strange World of Planet X*

1957; The 7th Voyage of Sinbad 1958; *Gothic* 1986

Mangold, Erni (1927-) *I Only Want You to Love Me* 1976; *Before Sunrise* 1995

Manheim, Camryn (1961-) *Scary Movie 3* 2003; *Twisted* 2003; *Dark Water* 2005; *An Unfinished Life* 2005; *Pregnancy Pact* 2010

Mankuma, Blu (1948-) *Stockade* 1991; *Whale Music* 1994; *Bliss* 1997; *Bone Daddy* 1998

Mann, Alakina *The Others* 2001; *Girl with a Pearl Earring* 2003

Mann, Byron (1967-) *Crying Freeman* 1995; *Red Corner* 1997; *The Corruptor* 1999; *Belly of the Beast* 2003

Mann, Claude (1940-) *Bay of the Angels* 1963; *Army of Shadows* 1969; *India Song* 1975

Mann, Gabriel (1972-) *High Art* 1998; *Cherry Falls* 1999; *Live Virgin* 2000; *Josie and the Pussycats* 2001; *The Life of David Gale* 2003; *The Bourne Supremacy* 2004; *Dominion: Prequel to the Exorcist* 2005; *Don't Come Knocking* 2005; *A Lot like Love* 2005; *Psych 9* 2010

Mann, Leonard (1947-) *The Humanoid* 1979; *Order of Death* 1983

Mann, Leslie (1972-) *The Cable Guy* 1996; *George of the Jungle* 1997; *Big Daddy* 1999; *Stealing Harvard* 2002; *The 40 Year Old Virgin* 2005; *Drillbit Taylor* 2007; *Knocked Up* 2007; *Funny People* 2009; *I Love You Phillip Morris* 2009; *17 Again* 2009; *Shorts* 2009; *The Change-Up* 2011; *Rio* 2011; *ParaNorman* 2012; *This Is 40* 2012; *The Bling Ring* 2013; *The Other Woman* 2014; *Vacation* 2015; *How to Be Single* 2016

Mann, Terrence aka **Mann, Terrence V** (1951-) *A Chorus Line* 1985; *Critters* 1986; *Big Top Pee-wee* 1988; *Mrs Santa Claus* 1996

Mann (2), Thomas (1991-) *Fun Size* 2012; *Project X* 2012; *Me and Earl and the Dying Girl* 2015; *The Stanford Prison Experiment* 2015

Mann, Wesley (1959-) *My Stepmother Is an Alien* 1988; *Race to Space* 2001

Manners, David (1901-1998) *Journey's End* 1930; *Dracula* 1931; *The Last Flight* 1931; *The Miracle Woman* 1931; *A Bill of Divorcement* 1932; *Lady with a Past* 1932; *The Mummy* 1932; *The Death Kiss* 1933; *Roman Scandals* 1933; *Torch Singer* 1933; *The Black Cat* 1934; *The Moonstone* 1934; *The Mystery of Edwin Drood* 1935; *A Woman Rebels* 1936

Mannhardt, Renate (1923-) *The Lost One* 1951; *Fear* 1954

Mannheim, Lucie (1899-1976) *The 39 Steps* 1935; *Yellow Canary* 1943; *Hotel Reserve* 1944; *Tawny Pipit* 1944; *Beyond the Curtain* 1960

Manni, Ettore (1927-1979) *Le Amiche* 1955; *Mademoiselle* 1966; *City of Women* 1980

Manninen, Sarah *Martin and Lewis* 2002; *Touch the Top of the World* 2006

Manning, Irene (1912-2004) *The Big Shot* 1942; *Yankee Doodle Dandy* 1942; *The Desert Song* 1944; *Shine On, Harvest Moon* 1944

Manning, Taryn (1978-) *Crossroads* 2002; *Hustle & Flow* 2005; *A Lot like Love* 2005; *The Breed* 2006; *Weirdsville* 2006; *Experimenter: the Stanley Milgram Story* 2014

Mannion, Tom *That Sinking Feeling* 1979; *Beautiful Creatures* 2000

Manoff, Dinah (1958-) *Ordinary People* 1980; *I Ought to Be in Pictures* 1982; *Child's Play* 1988; *Staying Together* 1989; *A Carol Christmas* 2003

Manojlovic, Miki aka **Manojlovic, Pedrag** (1950-) *When Father Was Away on Business* 1985; *Tito and Me* 1992; *Someone Else's America* 1995; *Underground* 1995; *Artemisia* 1997; *Criminal Lovers* 1999; *L'Enfer* 2005; *Irina Palm* 2006; *Largo Winch* 2008

Manookian, Roland *Goodbye Charlie Bright* 2000; *The Football Factory* 2004; *The Business* 2005; *Rise of the Footsoldier* 2006

Mansard, Claude (1922-1967) *A Bout de Souffle* 1959; *Shoot the Pianist* 1960

Mansfield, Jayne (1933-1967) *The Female Jungle* 1955; *Hell on Frisco Bay* 1955; *Illegal* 1955; *The Burglar* 1956; *The Girl Can't Help It* 1956; *Kiss Them for Me* 1957; *The Wayward Bus* 1957; *Will Success Spoil Rock Hunter?* 1957; *The Sheriff of Fractured Jaw* 1958; *The Challenge* 1960; *Too Hot to Handle* 1960; *Panic Button* 1964; *Single Room Furnished* 1968

Manson, Alan (1918-2002) *Whiffs* 1975; *Leadbelly* 1976

Manson, Amy *Harrigan* 2013; *Not Another Happy Ending* 2013

Manson, Marilyn (1969-) *Bowling for Columbine* 2002; *Party Monster* 2003

Mantee, Paul (1931-2013) *Robinson Crusoe on Mars* 1964; *Breakout* 1975; *Wolf Lake* 1979

Mantegna, Joe (1947-) *Compromising Positions* 1985; *The Money Pit* 1985; *Off Beat* 1986; *Critical Condition* 1987; *House of Games* 1987; *Suspect* 1987; *Weeds* 1987; *Things Change* 1988; *Wait until Spring, Bandini* 1989; *Alice* 1990; *The Godfather Part III* 1990; *Bugsy* 1991; *Homicide* 1991; *Queens Logic* 1991; *Body of Evidence* 1992; *Innocent Moves* 1993; *Airheads* 1994; *Baby's Day Out* 1994; *Above Suspicion* 1995; *The Bomber Boys* 1995; *Eye for an Eye* 1995; *For Better or Worse* 1995; *Forget Paris* 1995; *Albino Alligator* 1996; *Persons Unknown* 1996; *Stephen King's Thinner* 1996; *Up Close & Personal* 1996; *Airspeed* 1997; *For Hire* 1997; *Celebrity* 1998; *Hoods* 1998; *Jerry and Tom* 1998; *The Rat Pack* 1998; *Liberty Heights* 1999; *The Runner* 1999; *Edmond* 2005; *Redbelt* 2007; *The Simpsons Movie* 2007

Mantel, Henriette *The Brady Bunch Movie* 1995; *A Very Brady Sequel* 1996

Mantell, Joe (1920-2010) *Marty* 1955; *Storm Center* 1956; *Beau James* 1957; *The Sad Sack* 1957; *The Murder Men* 1961

Mantzoukas, Jason *Search Party* 2014; *They Came Together* 2014; *Sleeping with Other People* 2015

Manuel, Robert (1916-1995) *Rififi* 1955; *The Black Tulip* 1963

Manukov, Grigori aka **Manoukov, Grigori** *East-West* 1999; *The Triple Agent* 2003; *Coco Chanel & Igor Stravinsky* 2009

Manver, Kiti (1953-) *Women on the Verge of a Nervous Breakdown* 1988; *Take My Eyes* 2003

Manville, Lesley (1956-) *Dance with a Stranger* 1984; *High Season* 1987; *High Hopes* 1988; *Secrets & Lies* 1995; *Milk* 1999; *Topsy-Turvy* 1999; *All or Nothing* 2002; *The Great Ecstasy of Robert Carmichael* 2005; *Sparkle* 2006; *Another Year* 2010; *Clone* 2010; *Ashes* 2012; *Spike Island* 2012; *The Christmas Candle* 2013; *Maleficent* 2014; *Mr Turner* 2014

Manz, Linda (1961-) *Days of Heaven* 1978; *The Wanderers* 1979; *Out of the Blue* 1980

Manza, Ralph (1921-2000) *Gang War* 1958; *Too Soon to Love* 1960; *Lookin' Italian* 1994

Maples, Marla (1963-) *Happiness* 1998; *Black and White* 1999

Mapother, William (1965-) *In the Bedroom* 2001; *The Grudge* 2004; *Another Earth* 2011; *Escape from Polygamy* 2013; *I Origins* 2014

Mara, Adele (1923-2010) *You Were Never Lovelier* 1942; *Reveille with Beverly* 1943; *Atlantic City* 1944; *Bells of Rosarita* 1945; *Angel in Exile* 1948; *Sands of Iwo Jima* 1949; *Wake of the Red Witch* 1949

Mara, Kate (1983-) *Brokeback Mountain* 2005; *Zoom* 2006; *Shooter* 2007; *Stone of Destiny* 2008; *Transsiberian* 2008; *Ironclad* 2010; *127 Hours* 2011; *Deadfall* 2012; *Transcendence* 2014; *Captive* 2015; *Fantastic Four* 2015; *The Martian* 2015; *Morgan* 2016

Mara, Mary (1960-) *The Hard Way* 1991; *Love Potion No 9* 1992; *Mr Saturday Night* 1992; *Bound* 1996; *Stranger Inside* 2001

Mara, Rooney (1985-) *A Nightmare on Elm Street* 2010; *The Social Network* 2010; *The Girl with the Dragon Tattoo* 2011; *Ain't Them Bodies Saints* 2013; *Her* 2013; *Side Effects* 2013; *Trash* 2014; *Carol* 2015; *Pan* 2015; *Kubo and the Two Strings* 2016

Marachuk, Steve *Piranha II: the Spawning* 1981; *Hot Target* 1985

Marais, Jean (1913-1998) *Drôle de Drame* 1937; *Eternal Love* 1943; *La Belle et la Bête* 1946; *The Eagle Has Two Heads* 1948; *Les Parents Terribles* 1948; *Orphée* 1950; *Royal Affairs in Versailles* 1953; *Napoléon* 1955; *Elena et les Hommes* 1956; *White Nights* 1957; *Le Bossu* 1959; *The Battle of Austerlitz* 1960; *The Captain* 1960; *Le Testament d'Orphée* 1960; *Pontius Pilate* 1961; *Romulus and the Sabines* 1961; *Le Masque de Fer* 1962; *The Mysteries of Paris* 1962; *The Magic Donkey* 1970; *Stealing Beauty* 1995

Maranne, André *Darling Lili* 1970; *The Return of the Pink Panther* 1974; *The Pink Panther Strikes Again* 1976; *Revenge of the Pink Panther* 1978; *Plenty* 1985

Marceau, Sophie (1966-) *Fort Saganne* 1984; *Police* 1985; *Descent into Hell* 1986; *D'Artagnan's Daughter* 1994; *Beyond the Clouds* 1995; *Braveheart* 1995; *Anna Karenina* 1997; *Firelight* 1997; *Lost & Found* 1999; *A*

Midsummer Night's Dream 1999; The World Is Not Enough 1999; La Fidélité 2000; Alex & Emma 2003; Female Agents 2007

March, Elspeth (1911-1999) The Playboy of the Western World 1962; Psyche '59 1964

March, Eve (1910-1974) The Curse of the Cat People 1944; Adam's Rib 1949

March, Fredric (1897-1975) The Marriage Playground 1929; The Wild Party 1929; Laughter 1930; Manslaughter 1930; Paramount on Parade 1930; The Royal Family of Broadway 1930; Sarah and Son 1930; Dr Jekyll and Mr Hyde 1931; Honor among Lovers 1931; My Sin 1931; Merrily We Go to Hell 1932; The Sign of the Cross 1932; Smilin' Through 1932; Design for Living 1933; The Eagle and the Hawk 1933; The Affairs of Cellini 1934; The Barretts of Wimpole Street 1934; Death Takes a Holiday 1934; We Live Again 1934; Anna Karenina 1935; The Dark Angel 1935; Les Misérables 1935; Anthony Adverse 1936; Mary of Scotland 1936; The Road to Glory 1936; Nothing Sacred 1937; A Star Is Born 1937; The Buccaneer 1938; There Goes My Heart 1938; Trade Winds 1938; Susan and God 1940; Victory 1940; One Foot in Heaven 1941; So Ends Our Night 1941; Bedtime Story 1942; I Married a Witch 1942; The Adventures of Mark Twain 1944; The Best Years of Our Lives 1946; Another Part of the Forest 1948; Christopher Columbus 1949; Death of a Salesman 1951; It's a Big Country 1951; Man on a Tightrope 1953; The Bridges at Toko-Ri 1954; Executive Suite 1954; The Desperate Hours 1955; Alexander the Great 1956; The Man in the Gray Flannel Suit 1956; Inherit the Wind 1960; The Young Doctors 1961; Seven Days in May 1964; Hombre 1967; tick... tick... tick... 1969

March, Jane (1973-) The Lover 1992; Color of Night 1994; Circle of Passion 1996; Tarzan and the Lost City 1998; Dark Prince - the Legend of Dracula 2000; My Last Five Girlfriends 2009

Marchal, Georges (1920-1997) Celà S'Appelle l'Aurore 1956; Death in the Garden 1956; The Colossus of Rhodes 1961; The Milky Way 1968

Marchand, Corinne (1937-) Cleo from 5 to 7 1961; Borsalino 1970; Rider on the Rain 1970; Le Parfum d'Yvonne 1994

Marchand, Guy (1937-) Une Belle Fille comme Moi 1973; Cousin, Cousine 1975; Loulou 1980; Coup de Torchon 1981; Garde à Vue 1981; Entre Nous 1983; Hold-Up 1985; Le Cop II 1989; May Wine 1990; Inside Paris 2006

Marchand, Nancy (1928-2000) The Bachelor Party 1957; The Hospital 1971; Agatha Christie's Sparkling Cyanide 1983; The Bostonians 1984; The Naked Gun 1988; Brain Donors 1992; Sabrina 1995

Marcil, Vanessa The Rock 1996; The Nanny Express 2008

Marcon, André (1948-) Jeanne la Pucelle 1994; Requiem 1998; Les Destinées Sentimentales 2000; The Pornographe 2001; Rapt 2009; Me, Myself and Mum 2013; Marguerite 2015; Things to Come 2016

Marcovicci, Andrea (1948-) The Front 1976; The Hand 1981; Kings and Desperate Men 1981; Spacehunter: Adventures in the Forbidden Zone 1983; The Stuff 1985; Someone to Love 1987

Marcus, James A (1867-1937) Regeneration 1915; Little Lord Fauntleroy 1921; The Iron Horse 1924; The Eagle 1925; The Texan 1930

Marcus, Richard Enemy Mine 1985; Deadly Friend 1986; Tremors 1989

Marcus, Stephen (1962-) Lock, Stock and Two Smoking Barrels 1998; Londinium 1999; The Greatest Game Ever Played 2005

Marcuse, Theo (1920-1967) Harum Scarum 1965; The Picasso Summer 1969

Marescotti, Ivano (1946-) Johnny Stecchino 1991; Il Cielo è Sempre Più Blu 1995

Margaritis, Gilles (1912-1965) Les Affaires Publiques 1934; L'Atalante 1934

Margera, Bam (1979-) Jackass: the Movie 2002; jackass number two 2006; Jackass 3D 2010

Margetson, Arthur (1887-1951) Music Hath Charms 1935; Broken Blossoms 1936; Smash and Grab 1937; Sherlock Holmes Faces Death 1943

Margo (1917-1985) Crime without Passion 1934; Rumba 1935; The Robin Hood of El Dorado 1936; Winterset 1936; Lost Horizon 1937; Miracle on Main Street 1940; The Leopard Man 1943; Viva Zapata! 1952; I'll Cry

Tomorrow 1955; Who's Got the Action? 1962

Margo, George (1915-2002) Who Done It? 1956; Mark of the Phoenix 1957

Margolin, Janet (1943-1993) David and Lisa 1962; Bus Riley's Back in Town 1965; Morituri 1965; Nevada Smith 1966; Enter Laughing 1967; Buona Sera, Mrs Campbell 1968; Take the Money and Run 1969; Annie Hall 1977; Last Embrace 1979; Distant Thunder 1988

Margolin, Stuart (1940-) The Gamblers 1969; The Intruders 1970; Kelly's Heroes 1970; Death Wish 1974; Futureworld 1976; Days of Heaven 1978; S.O.B. 1981; Class 1983; A Fine Mess 1986; Iron Eagle II 1988; Bye Bye Blues 1989; Arbitrage 2012

Margolis, Mark (1939-) Delta Force 2 1990; Pi 1997; The Fountain 2005

Margolyes, Miriam (1941-) Stand Up Virgin Soldiers 1977; The Apple 1980; The Awakening 1980; Electric Dreams 1984; The Good Father 1986; Little Dorrit 1987; I Love You to Death 1990; The Butcher's Wife 1991; As You Like It 1992; The Age of Innocence 1993; Motherhood 1993; Immortal Beloved 1994; Babe 1995; Different for Girls 1996; James and the Giant Peach 1996; William Shakespeare's Romeo + Juliet 1996; Babe: Pig in the City 1998; Dreaming of Joseph Lees 1998; Mulan 1998; End of Days 1999; House! 2000; Cats & Dogs 2001; Harry Potter and the Chamber of Secrets 2002; The Life and Death of Peter Sellers 2003; Being Julia 2004; Ladies in Lavender 2004; Happy Feet 2006; A Closed Book 2009; Sir Billi 2012; The Wedding Video 2012; The Guilt Trip 2013; Maya the Bee 2014

Margotta, Michael (1946-) Drive, He Said 1971; Can She Bake a Cherry Pie? 1983

Margulies, David (1937-2016) Dressed to Kill 1980; Times Square 1980; Nine ½ Weeks 1985; Out on a Limb 1992

Margulies, Julianna (1966-) A Price above Rubies 1997; Traveller 1997; The Newton Boys 1998; Dinosaur 2000; What's Cooking? 2000; The Man from Elysian Fields 2001; Evelyn 2002; Ghost Ship 2002; Snakes on a Plane 2006; City Island 2009; Stand Up Guys 2012

Maricle, Leona (1905-1988) Woman Chases Man 1937; Beauty for the Asking 1939

Marie, Constance (1969-) Selena 1997; The Last Marshal 1999; Tortilla Soup 2001; Class 2010

Marielle, Jean-Pierre (1932-) Banana Peel 1964; Man in the Trunk 1973; Un Moment d'Egarement 1977; Coup de Torchon 1981; Hold-Up 1985; Tenue de Soirée 1986; Tous les Matins du Monde 1991; Le Parfum d'Yvonne 1994; Micmacs 2009

Marienthal, Eli (1986-) Slums of Beverly Hills 1998; The Iron Giant 1999; The Country Bears 2002; Confessions of a Teenage Drama Queen 2004

Marietto (1951-) It Started in Naples 1960; The Pigeon That Took Rome 1962

Marihugh, Tammy The Last Voyage 1960; Back Street 1961

Marin, Jacques (1919-2001) Jeux Interdits 1953; Gigot 1962; Tiara Tahiti 1962; Charade 1963; How to Steal a Million 1966; Darling Lili 1970; The Island at the Top of the World 1974; Herbie Goes to Monte Carlo 1977

Marin, Richard "Cheech" aka **Marin, Cheech** (1946-) Cheech & Chong's Up in Smoke 1978; Cheech and Chong's Next Movie 1980; Cheech and Chong's Nice Dreams 1981; Cheech & Chong's Still Smokin' 1983; Yellowbeard 1983; Cheech & Chong's The Corsican Brothers 1984; After Hours 1985; Echo Park 1985; Born in East LA 1987; Fatal Beauty 1987; Oliver & Company 1988; Rude Awakening 1989; Charlie's Ghost Story 1994; The Lion King 1994; Desperado 1995; From Dusk till Dawn 1995; The Great White Hype 1996; Tin Cup 1996; Paulie 1998; Picking Up the Pieces 2000; SPYkids 2001; SPYkids 2: the Island of Lost Dreams 2002; Once upon a Time in Mexico 2003; SPYkids 3-D: Game Over 2003; Christmas with the Kranks 2004; Underclassman 2004; Cars 2006; Tales from Earthsea 2006; Beverly Hills Chihuahua 2008; The Miracle of Dommatina 2009; Machete 2010

Marin, Rikki Cheech and Chong's Next Movie 1980; Cheech & Chong's The Corsican Brothers 1984

Marinca, Anamaria Boogie 2007; 4 Months, 3 Weeks and 2 Days 2007; Five Minutes of Heaven 2009; Storm 2009

Marinne, Morgan The Son 2002; The Silence of Lorna 2008

Mario Freedom Writers 2006; Step Up 2006

Marion-Crawford, Howard aka **Marion-Crawford, H** (1914-1969) Forever England 1935; Freedom Radio 1940; The Hasty Heart 1949; Mr Drake's Duck 1950; The Man in the White Suit 1951; The Birthday Present 1957; Nowhere to Go 1958; Virgin Island 1958; Life in Danger 1959; The Face of Fu Manchu 1965; The Brides of Fu Manchu 1966; The Vengeance of Fu Manchu 1967; The Blood of Fu Manchu 1968; The Castle of Fu Manchu 1968

Marion, George F (1860-1945) Anna Christie 1930; The Big House 1930

Maris, Mona (1903-1991) Kiss and Make-Up 1934; A Date with the Falcon 1941; Berlin Correspondent 1942; The Falcon in Mexico 1944

Mark, Michael (1886-1975) Frankenstein 1931; Search for Danger 1949; The Wasp Woman 1959

Marken, Jane aka **Marken, Jeanne** (1895-1976) Beethoven 1936; Une Partie de Campagne 1936; Hôtel du Nord 1938; Eternal Love 1943; And God Created Woman 1956

Markey, Enid (1896-1981) Civilization 1916; Tarzan of the Apes 1918

Markham, David (1913-1983) Blood from the Mummy's Tomb 1971; ZPG: Zero Population Growth 1971; Tess 1979

Markham, Kika Anne and Muriel 1971; Outland 1981; The Innocent 1984; Wonderland 1999; Killing Me Softly 2001

Markham, Monte (1935-) Guns of the Magnificent Seven 1969; One Is a Lonely Number 1972; Ginger in the Morning 1973; Hot Pursuit 1987; ...At First Sight 1995

Markinson, Brian Forgotten Sins 1996; Sweet and Lowdown 1999; Take Me Home: the John Denver Story 2000; The Curse of the Jade Scorpion 2001; The Sports Pages 2001

Markland, Ted (1933-2011) The Hired Hand 1971; Wanda Nevada 1979; Fatal Mission 1990

Marks, Alfred (1921-1996) Penny Points to Paradise 1951; Desert Mice 1959; There Was a Crooked Man 1960; The Frightened City 1961; She'll Have to Go 1961; Scream and Scream Again 1969; Our Miss Fred 1972; Fanny Hill 1983

Marks, Howard (2945-2016) Human Traffic 1999; Dirty Sanchez: the Movie 2006

Marlé, Arnold (1887-1970) Portrait from Life 1948; Break in the Circle 1955; Little Red Monkey 1955

Marley, Bob (1945-1981) Time Will Tell 1992; Marley 2012

Marley, Cedella Joey Breaker 1993; Marley 2012

Marley, John (1907-1984) Cat Ballou 1965; Faces 1968; Love Story 1970; Dead of Night 1972; The Godfather 1972; Framed 1975; WC Fields and Me 1976; The Car 1977; The Greatest 1977; Kid Vengeance 1977; Hooper 1978; It Lives Again 1978; Tribute 1980; The Amateur 1981; Threshold 1981

Marlier, Carla Zazie dans le Métro 1960; Any Number Can Win 1963

Marling, Brit (1982-) Another Earth 2011; Sound of My Voice 2011; Arbitrage 2012; The East 2013; I Origins 2014; The Keeping Room 2014

Marlow, Lucy (1932-) A Star Is Born 1954; Bring Your Smile Along 1955; My Sister Eileen 1955; He Laughed Last 1956

Marlowe, Hugh (1911-1982) Marriage Is a Private Affair 1944; Come to the Stable 1949; Twelve o'Clock High 1949; All about Eve 1950; Night and the City 1950; The Day the Earth Stood Still 1951; Mr Belvedere Rings the Bell 1951; Rawhide 1951; Bugles in the Afternoon 1952; Monkey Business 1952; Wait 'til the Sun Shines, Nellie 1952; Way of a Gaucho 1952; Garden of Evil 1954; Illegal 1955; World without End 1955; Earth vs the Flying Saucers 1956; Birdman of Alcatraz 1962; Seven Days in May 1964; Castle of Evil 1966

Marlowe, Jo Ann (1935-1991) Mildred Pierce 1945; Thieves' Holiday 1946

Marlowe, Linda Impact 1963; The World Ten Times Over 1963

Marlowe, Scott (1932-2001) Gaby 1956; The Young Guns 1956; The Cool and the Crazy 1958

Marlowe, William (1932-2003) The Uncle 1964; Robbery 1967; Where's Jack? 1969

Marly, Florence (1919-1978) Tokyo Joe 1949; Planet of Blood 1966

Marmaï, Pio The First Day of the Rest of Your Life 2007; In Your Hands 2010; Delicacy 2011; In the Courtyard 2014

Marmont, Percy (1883-1977) Mantrap 1926; Rich and Strange 1932; Secret Agent 1936; Young and Innocent 1937; Four Sided Triangle 1953; Knave of Hearts 1954; Lisbon 1956

Marner, Richard (1922-2004) The Password Is Courage 1962; Where the Spies Are 1965; Tiffany Jones 1973

Maross, Joe (1923-2009) Elmer Gantry 1960; Zigzag 1970

Marotte, Carl (1959-) Defending Our Kids: the Julie Posey Story 2003; Abducted 2007

Marquand, Christian (1927-2000) And God Created Woman 1956; Behold a Pale Horse 1964; The Corrupt Ones 1966; The Road to Corinth 1967; Ciao! Manhattan 1973; The Other Side of Midnight 1977; Je Vous Aime 1980; Choice of Arms 1981

Marquand, Serge (1930-2004) The Last Train 1972; The Big Red One 1980

Marques, Maria Elena (1926-2008) Across the Wide Missouri 1951; Ambush at Tomahawk Gap 1953

Marquet, Mary (1895-1979) Bluebeard 1962; La Vie de Château 1965

Marquette, Christopher aka **Marquette, Chris** (1984-) Just Friends 2005; Broken Horses 2015

Marquette, Christopher George aka **Marquette, Chris** (1984-) The Tic Code 1998; Freddy vs Jason 2003; The Girl Next Door 2004; The Invisible 2007; Fanboys 2008; Life during Wartime 2009

Marquez, William Deal of the Century 1983; The Lost City 2005

Marr, Eddie aka **Marr, Edward** (1900-1987) The Steel Trap 1952; The Night Holds Terror 1955

Marriott, Moore (1885-1949) Windbag the Sailor 1936; Oh, Mr Porter! 1937; Ask a Policeman 1938; Convict 99 1938; Old Bones of the River 1938; Owd Bob 1938; Band Waggon 1939; Cheer Boys Cheer 1939; Where's That Fire? 1939; Charley's (Big Hearted) Aunt 1940; Gasbags 1940; I Thank You 1941; Back Room Boy 1942; Time Flies 1944; I'll Be Your Sweetheart 1945; Green for Danger 1946; The Hills of Donegal 1947; The History of Mr Polly 1948

Marriott, Steve aka **Marriott, Stephen** (1947-1991) Live It Up 1963; Be My Guest 1965

Marriott, Sylvia (1917-1995) Return of a Stranger 1937; Crimes at the Dark House 1939; Anne and Muriel 1971; The Story of Adèle H 1975

Mars, Kenneth (1936-2011) The Producers 1968; The April Fools 1969; Viva Max! 1969; Desperate Characters 1971; What's Up, Doc? 1972; Young Frankenstein 1974; Night Moves 1975; The Apple Dumpling Gang Rides Again 1979; Full Moon High 1982; Beer 1985; For Keeps 1987; Illegally Yours 1988; The Little Mermaid 1989; Thumbelina 1994; Rough Magic 1995; Citizen Ruth 1996; The Little Mermaid II: Return to the Sea 2000

Marsalis, Branford (1960-) Bring On the Night 1985; Throw Momma from the Train 1987; School Daze 1988; Eve's Bayou 1997

Marsan, Eddie aka **Marsan, Edward** (1968-) The Emperor's New Clothes 2001; The Rocket Post 2004; 21 Grams 2003; Vera Drake 2004; The Illusionist 2005; Pierrepoint 2005; Sixty Six 2006; Grow Your Own 2007; Happy-Go-Lucky 2007; Faintheart 2008; Hancock 2008; Me and Orson Welles 2008; The Disappearance of Alice Creed 2009; Heartless 2009; Sherlock Holmes 2009; London Boulevard 2010; Junkhearts 2011; Sherlock Holmes: a Game of Shadows 2011; I, Anna 2012; Still Life 2013; The World's End 2013; God's Pocket 2014; X+Y 2014; The Coldest City 2017

Marsden, Betty (1919-1998) The Young Lovers 1954; The Leather Boys 1963; The Wild Affair 1963; Eyewitness 1970; The Dresser 1983

Marsden, James (1973-) Taken Away 1996; Disturbing Behavior 1998; Gossip 1999; X-Men 2000; Sugar & Spice 2001; The Notebook 2003; X2 2003; Superman Returns 2006; X-Men - the Last Stand 2006; Enchanted 2007; Hairspray 2007; The Box 2008; Sex Drive 2008; 27 Dresses 2008; Cats & Dogs: the Revenge of Kitty Galore 2010; Death at a Funeral 2010; Hop 2011; Straw Dogs 2011; Bachelorette 2012; Robot & Frank 2012; Small Apartments 2012; Accidental Love 2013; Anchorman 2: the Legend Continues 2013; 2 Guns 2013; The Best of Me 2014; The D Train 2015; Unfinished Business 2015

Marsden, Jason (1975-) A Goofy Movie 1995; The Lion King II: Simba's Pride 1998; Spirited Away 2001; Garfield Gets Real 2007

Marsden, Matthew (1972-) Anacondas: the Hunt for the Blood Orchid 2004; DOA: Dead or Alive 2006; Rambo 2007; Resident Evil: Extinction 2007; Bounty Killer 2013

Marsden, Roy (1941-) Toomorrow 1970; The Squeeze 1977

Marsh, Carol (1926-2010) Brighton Rock 1947; The Romantic Age 1949; Scrooge 1951; Dracula 1958

Marsh, Garry (1902-1981) Dreyfus 1931; Number Seventeen 1932; Scrooge 1935; The Man in the Mirror 1936; When Knights Were Bold 1936; The Vicar of Bray 1937; Bank Holiday 1938; Convict 99 1938; I See Ice 1938; It's in the Air 1938; Trouble Brewing 1939; Let George Do It 1940; Pink String and Sealing Wax 1945; Dancing with Crime 1946; The Shop at Sly Corner 1946; Just William's Luck 1947; William at the Circus 1948; Someone at the Door 1950; Something in the City 1950; The Lost Hours 1952; Man of the Moment 1955; Who Done It? 1956

Marsh, Jamie Montenegro 1981; Brainscan 1994; Best Laid Plans 1999; Beethoven's 3rd 2000

Marsh, Jean (1934-) Frenzy 1972; The Eagle Has Landed 1976; The Changeling 1980; Return to Oz 1985; Willow 1988; Danny, the Champion of the World 1989; Monarch 1996

Marsh, Joan (1913-2000) You're Telling Me! 1934; Charlie Chan on Broadway 1937

Marsh, Linda Hamlet 1964; Freebie and the Bean 1974

Marsh, Mae (1895-1968) The Battle of Elderbush 1914; The Escape 1914; The Birth of a Nation 1915; Intolerance 1916; Three Godfathers 1948; Impact 1949

Marsh, Marian (1913-2006) Five Star Final 1931; The Mad Genius 1931; Svengali 1931; The Black Room 1935; Crime and Punishment 1935; The Man Who Lived Twice 1936

Marsh, Matthew (1954-) Diamond Skulls 1989; Miranda 2002; Bad Company 2002; Quicksand 2003; An American Haunting 2005

Marsh, Reginald (1926-2001) Shadow of Fear 1963; The Sicilians 1964

Marsh, Sally Ann The Princess and the Goblin 1992; A Monkey's Tale 1999

Marsh, William Proteus 1995; Dead Babies 2000

Marshal, Alan (1909-1961) After the Thin Man 1936; Conquest 1937; Night Must Fall 1937; Parnell 1937; Dramatic School 1938; I Met My Love Again 1938; The Adventures of Sherlock Holmes 1939; The Hunchback of Notre Dame 1939; The Howards of Virginia 1940; Irene 1940; Lydia 1941; Tom, Dick and Harry 1941; Bride by Mistake 1944; The White Cliffs of Dover 1944; House on Haunted Hill 1958; Day of the Outlaw 1959

Marshal, Lyndsey Festival 2005; 1234 2008; Hereafter 2010

Marshall-Green, Logan (1976-) Devil 2010; Prometheus 2012; As I Lay Dying 2013; Cold Comes the Night 2013; Madame Bovary 2014

Marshall, Brenda (1915-1992) East of the River 1940; The Sea Hawk 1940; Footsteps in the Dark 1941; Captains of the Clouds 1942; Background to Danger 1943; The Constant Nymph 1943; Whispering Smith 1948

Marshall, Bryan (1938-) I Start Counting 1970; The Spy Who Loved Me 1977; The Long Good Friday 1979; BMX Bandits 1983; Bliss 1985; Hot Target 1985; Return to Snowy River 1988; The Punisher 1989

Marshall, Chan aka **Power, Cat** My Blueberry Nights 2007; Janis: Little Girl Blue 2015

Marshall, Connie (1938-) Sunday Dinner for a Soldier 1944; Home Sweet Homicide 1946; Mother Wore Tights 1947; Mr Blandings Builds His Dream House 1948

Marshall, David Anthony Across the Tracks 1990; Another 48 HRS 1990; Roadside Prophets 1992

Marshall, Dodie Spinout 1966; Easy Come, Easy Go 1967

Marshall, Don (1936-) The Thing with Two Heads 1972; Terminal Island 1973

Marshall, E G (1910-1998) Broken Lance 1954; The Caine Mutiny 1954; Pushover 1954; The Left Hand of God 1955; The Mountain 1956; The Bachelor Party 1957; 12 Angry Men 1957; The Buccaneer 1958; Compulsion 1959; Cash McCall 1960; Town without Pity 1961; The Chase 1966; The Poppy Is Also a Flower 1966; The Bridge at Remagen 1969; Tora! Tora! Tora! 1970; The Pursuit of Happiness 1971; Interiors 1978; Superman II 1980; Creepshow 1982; My Chauffeur 1986; National Lampoon's Christmas Vacation 1989; Two Evil Eyes 1990; Consenting Adults

1992; Nixon 1995; Absolute Power 1996; Miss Evers' Boys 1997

Marshall, Garry (1934-) Never Been Kissed 1999; Chicken Little 2005; Keeping Up with the Steins 2006; Race to Witch Mountain 2009

Marshall, Herbert (1890-1966) The Letter 1929; Murder 1930; Blonde Venus 1932; Trouble in Paradise 1932; Four Frightened People 1934; I Was a Spy 1934; The Painted Veil 1934; Riptide 1934; Accent on Youth 1935; The Dark Angel 1935; The Good Fairy 1935; If You Could Only Cook 1935; Till We Meet Again 1936; A Woman Rebels 1936; Angel 1937; Breakfast for Two 1937; Always Goodbye 1938; Mad about Music 1938; Zaza 1939; A Bill of Divorcement 1940; Foreign Correspondent 1940; The Letter 1940; The Little Foxes 1941; When Ladies Meet 1941; The Moon and Sixpence 1942; Flight for Freedom 1943; Andy Hardy's Blonde Trouble 1944; The Enchanted Cottage 1945; The Unseen 1945; Crack-Up 1946; Duel in the Sun 1946; The Razor's Edge 1946; High Wall 1947; Ivy 1947; The Secret Garden 1949; The Underworld Story 1950; Anne of the Indies 1951; Black Jack 1952; Angel Face 1953; The Black Shield of Falworth 1954; The Virgin Queen 1955; The Fly 1958; Stage Struck 1958; Midnight Lace 1960; The Caretakers 1963; The List of Adrian Messenger 1963; The Third Day 1965

Marshall, James (1967-) Stockade 1991; A Few Good Men 1992; Gladiator 1992; Doomsday Man 1998; Luck of the Draw 2000

Marshall, Ken (1950-) La Pelle 1981; Krull 1983; Feds 1988

Marshall, Kris (1974-) The Most Fertile Man in Ireland 1999; The Four Feathers 2002; William Shakespeare's The Merchant of Venice 2004; Death at a Funeral 2007; Easy Virtue 2008; A Few Best Men 2011; Sparks and Embers 2014

Marshall, Marion (1929-) I Was a Male War Bride 1949; Stella 1950; Sailor Beware 1951; The Stooge 1951; That's My Boy 1951

Marshall, Paula (1964-) Hellraiser III: Hell on Earth 1992; Warlock: the Armageddon 1993; The New Age 1994; That Old Feeling 1997; Thursday 1998

Marshall, Penny (1942-) Evil Roy Slade 1971; Movers and Shakers 1985; The Hard Way 1991

Marshall, Trudy (1922-2004) The Dancing Masters 1943; The Fighting Sullivans 1944; Circumstantial Evidence 1945

Marshall, Tully (1864-1943) A Romance of the Redwoods 1917; The Fall of Babylon 1919; The Covered Wagon 1923; The Hunchback of Notre Dame 1923; He Who Gets Slapped 1924; The Merry Widow 1925; The Cat and the Canary 1927; Thunderbolt 1929; The Trail of '98 1929; The Big Trail 1930; Mammy 1930; Tom Sawyer 1930; Fighting Caravans 1931; The Unholy Garden 1931; Arsene Lupin 1932; The Beast of the City 1932; The Hatchet Man 1932; Red Dust 1932; Murder on the Blackboard 1934; California Straight Ahead 1937; Ball of Fire 1941; This Gun for Hire 1942

Marshall (2), William (1924-2003) Something of Value 1957; To Trap a Spy 1966; The Hell with Heroes 1968; Zigzag 1970; Blacula 1972

Marshall, Zena (1926-2009) The Lost People 1949; Deadly Nightshade 1953; Dr No 1962

Marsillach, Cristina (1963-) 1919 1983; Every Time We Say Goodbye 1986; Opera 1987

Marson, Ania Puppet on a Chain 1970; Nicholas and Alexandra 1971; The Abdication 1974

Marsters, James Cool Money 2005; PS I Love You 2007; Dragonball Evolution 2009

Marstini, Rosita (1887-1948) Blood and Sand 1922; The Big Parade 1925

Marston, Nathaniel (1975-) The Craft 1996; Love Is All There Is 1996

Martel, K C The Amityville Horror 1979; ET the Extra-Terrestrial 1982; White Water Summer 1987

Martell, Chris The Gruesome Twosome 1967; Flesh Feast 1970

Martelli, Norma The Night of San Lorenzo 1981; Everybody's Fine 1990

Marthouret, François (1943-) Marquis 1989; Sitcom 1997; The Lady & the Duke 2001

Martin, Andra (1935-) The Lady Takes a Flyer 1958; Up Periscope 1959

Martin, Andrea (1947-) Cannibal Girls 1973; Black Christmas 1974; Too Much Sun 1990; Bogus 1996; Wag the Dog 1997; Bartok the Magnificent 1999; Hedwig and the Angry Inch 2001; Jimmy Neutron: Boy Genius 2001; Prince Charming 2001; My Big Fat Greek Wedding 2002; New York Minute 2004; Black Christmas 2006

Martin, Chris-Pin (1893-1953) The Cisco Kid and the Lady 1939; Stagecoach 1939; The Gay Caballero 1940

Martin (2), Christopher (1963-) House Party 1990; House Party 2 1991; Class Act 1992

Martin, Damon Pee-wee's Big Adventure 1985; Kid 1990

Martin, Daniel A Fistful of Dollars 1964; Rebellion 2011

Martin, Dean (1917-1995) My Friend Irma 1949; At War with the Army 1950; My Friend Irma Goes West 1950; Sailor Beware 1951; The Stooge 1951; That's My Boy 1951; Jumping Jacks 1952; The Caddy 1953; Money from Home 1953; Scared Stiff 1953; Living It Up 1954; Three Ring Circus 1954; Artists and Models 1955; You're Never Too Young 1955; Hollywood or Bust 1956; Pardners 1956; Ten Thousand Bedrooms 1957; Rio Bravo 1958; Some Came Running 1958; The Young Lions 1958; Career 1959; All in a Night's Work 1960; Bells Are Ringing 1960; Ocean's Eleven 1960; Pepe 1960; Who Was That Lady? 1960; Ada 1961; The Road to Hong Kong 1962; Sergeants 3 1962; Who's Got the Action? 1962; Come Blow Your Horn 1963; 4 for Texas 1963; Toys in the Attic 1963; Who's Been Sleeping in My Bed? 1963; Kiss Me, Stupid 1964; Robin and the 7 Hoods 1964; What a Way to Go! 1964; Marriage on the Rocks 1965; The Sons of Katie Elder 1965; The Silencers 1966; Texas across the River 1966; Rough Night in Jericho 1967; Bandolero! 1968; 5 Card Stud 1968; The Wrecking Crew 1969; Airport 1970; something big 1971; Showdown 1973; Mr Ricco 1975; The Cannonball Run 1981; Cannonball Run II 1983

Martin, Dean Paul (1951-1987) Players 1979; Heart like a Wheel 1983; Backfire 1987

Martin, Demetri Taking Woodstock 2009; In a World... 2013

Martin, Dewey (1923-) Kansas Raiders 1950; The Thing from Another World 1951; The Big Sky 1952; Men of the Fighting Lady 1954; Prisoner of War 1954; Tennessee Champ 1954; The Desperate Hours 1955; Land of the Pharaohs 1955; Ten Thousand Bedrooms 1957; Flight to Fury 1966

Martin, Dick (1922-2008) The Maltese Bippy 1969; Carbon Copy 1981; Bartleby 2000

Martin, Duane Above the Rim 1994; Woo 1998

Martin, D'Urville (1939-1984) Watermelon Man 1970; The Final Comedown 1972; Black Caesar 1973; Hell Up in Harlem 1973

Martin, Edie (1880-1964) The Demi-Paradise 1943; The Lavender Hill Mob 1951; The Ladykillers 1955; Bright Star 2009

Martin, Eugene Terror in a Texas Town 1958; This Rebel Breed 1960; Tower of London 1962

Martin (1), George CHUD 1984; Falling in Love 1984; The Associate 1996

Martin (2), George (1926-2016) Give My Regards to Broad Street 1984; George Harrison: Living in the Material World 2011

Martin, Helen (1909-2000) A Hero Ain't Nothin' but a Sandwich 1978; Hollywood Shuffle 1987; Don't Be a Menace to South Central while Drinking Your Juice in the Hood 1996

Martin, Jared (1943-) Murder à la Mod 1968; The Second Coming of Suzanne 1974; The Lonely Lady 1983

Martin, Jean (1922-2009) Jamboree 1957; The Battle of Algiers 1965; My Name Is Nobody 1973; The King and the Mockingbird 1980; Lucie Aubrac 1997

Martin, Jesse L A Christmas Carol 2004; Rent 2005

Martin, José Manuel (1924-) A Bullet for the General 1966; A Bullet for Sandoval 1970

Martin, Kellie (1975-) Matinee 1993; Death of a Cheerleader 1994; The Face on the Milk Carton 1995; A Goofy Movie 1995; Mystery Woman 2003

Martin, Lewis (1894-1969) Ace in the Hole 1951; The War of the Worlds 1953; Witness to Murder 1954; Diary of a Madman 1963

Martin, Marion (1908-1985) Sinners in Paradise 1938; Sergeant Madden 1939; The Big Street 1942; They Got Me Covered 1943

Martin, Mary (1913-1990) Rhythm on the River 1940; The Birth of the Blues 1941; Kiss the Boys Goodbye 1941; Star Spangled Rhythm 1942; Happy Go Lucky 1943; True to Life 1943

Martin, Millicent (1934-) Libel 1959; Invasion Quartet 1961; The Girl on the Boat 1962; Nothing but the Best 1963; Alfie 1966; Stop the World, I Want to Get Off 1966; Mrs Palfrey at The Claremont 2005

Martin, Nan (1927-2010) Toys in the Attic 1963; For Love of Ivy 1968; Goodbye, Columbus 1969; The Other Side of the Mountain 1975; Jackson County Jail 1976; Loving Couples 1980; Animal Behavior 1989; Big Eden 2000; Thicker than Water 2005

Martin, Pamela Sue (1953-) The Poseidon Adventure 1972; Buster and Billie 1974; The Lady in Red 1979; Torchlight 1984

Martin (1), Richard (1919-1994) Tender Comrade 1943; Marine Raiders 1944; Nevada 1944; The Bamboo Blonde 1946; Thunder Mountain 1947; Guns of Hate 1948

Martin, Rosemary (1936-1998) Tess 1979; The Dressmaker 1988; The Object of Beauty 1991

Martin, Ross (1920-1981) Conquest of Space 1955; The Colossus of New York 1958; Geronimo 1962

Martin, Sandy (1950-) Extremities 1986; Barfly 1987

Martin, Stacy Nymphomaniac Vol I 2013; Nymphomaniac Vol II 2014; The Childhood of a Leader 2015

Martin, Steve (1945-) Sgt Pepper's Lonely Hearts Club Band 1978; The Jerk 1979; Pennies from Heaven 1981; Dead Men Don't Wear Plaid 1982; The Man with Two Brains 1983; All of Me 1984; The Lonely Guy 1984; Movers and Shakers 1985; Little Shop of Horrors 1986; Three Amigos! 1986; Planes, Trains and Automobiles 1987; Roxanne 1987; Dirty Rotten Scoundrels 1988; Parenthood 1989; My Blue Heaven 1990; Father of the Bride 1991; Grand Canyon 1991; LA Story 1991; HouseSitter 1992; Leap of Faith 1992; And the Band Played On 1993; Mixed Nuts 1994; A Simple Twist of Fate 1994; Father of the Bride Part 2 1995; Sgt Bilko 1996; The Spanish Prisoner 1997; The Prince of Egypt 1998; Bowfinger 1999; Fantasia 2000 1999; The Out-of-Towners 1999; Novocaine 2001; Bringing Down the House 2003; Cheaper by the Dozen 2003; Looney Tunes: Back in Action 2004; Cheaper by the Dozen 2 2005; Shopgirl 2005; The Pink Panther 2006; Baby Mama 2008; It's Complicated 2009; The Pink Panther 2 2009; The Big Year 2011; Home 2014

Martin, Strother (1919-1980) The Deadly Companions 1961; Showdown 1963; Invitation to a Gunfighter 1964; Cool Hand Luke 1967; Butch Cassidy and the Sundance Kid 1969; The Ballad of Cable Hogue 1970; Brotherhood of Satan 1970; Dynamite Man from Glory Jail 1971; Hannie Caulder 1971; Pocket Money 1972; Hard Times 1975; Rooster Cogburn 1975; The Great Scout & Cathouse Thursday 1976; Slap Shot 1977; Cheech & Chong's Up in Smoke 1978; The End 1978; Love and Bullets 1978; Cactus Jack 1979; The Champ 1979; Nightwing 1979

Martin, Todd (1927-) The Thomas Crown Affair 1968; Alex and the Gypsy 1976

Martin (1), Tony aka **Martin, Anthony** (1913-2012) Banjo on My Knee 1936; Pigskin Parade 1936; Life Begins in College 1937; You Can't Have Everything 1937; Kentucky Moonshine 1938; Sally, Irene and Mary 1938; Music in My Heart 1940; The Big Store 1941; Ziegfeld Girl 1941; Casbah 1948; Two Tickets to Broadway 1951; Easy to Love 1953; Here Come the Girls 1953; Deep in My Heart 1954; Hit the Deck 1955

Martindale, Margo (1951-) Lorenzo's Oil 1992; Critical Care 1997; Eye of God 1997; First Do No Harm 1997; It's All about Love 2002; Wedding Daze 2006; Rocket Science 2007; Walk Hard: the Dewey Cox Story 2007; Management 2008; Hannah Montana: the Movie 2009

Martindel, Edward (1873-1955) Lady Windermere's Fan 1925; The Singing Fool 1928; The Desert Song 1929; Check and Double Check 1930

Martinelli, Elsa (1932-) The Indian Fighter 1955; Manuela 1957; Blood and Roses 1960; The Captain 1960; Hatari! 1962; The Pigeon That Took Rome 1962; The Trial 1962; The VIPs 1963; The Tenth Victim 1965; Maroc 7 1966; Madigan's Millions 1967

Martinelli, Jean (1910-1983) Le Rouge et le Noir 1954; To Catch a Thief 1955

Martines, Alessandra (1963-) Les Misérables 1995; Men, Women: a User's Manual 1996; Chance or Coincidence 1999; And Now... Ladies and Gentlemen 2002

Martinez, A (1948-) The Honorary Consul 1983; Powwow Highway 1988; Before the Night 1995; Last Rites 1998; Desolation Canyon 2006; Little Girl Lost: the Delimar Vera Story 2008; Curse of Chucky 2013

Martinez, Alma Barbarosa 1982; Under Fire 1983

Martinez, Fele (1976-) Tesis 1996; Open Your Eyes 1997; The Lovers of the Arctic Circle 1998; Captains of April 2000; Darkness 2002; Bad Education 2004

Martinez, Joaquin (1930-2012) Jeremiah Johnson 1972; Ulzana's Raid 1972; Revenge 1990

Martinez, Natalie Death Race 2008; Self/Less 2015

Martinez, Olivier (1966-) IP5 1992; The Horseman on the Roof 1995; Mon Homme 1996; Before Night Falls 2000; Unfaithful 2002; SWAT 2003; Taking Lives 2004; Blood and Chocolate 2006; Dark Tide 2012

Martínez, Petra Bad Education 2004; Sleep Tight 2011

Martinez, Vanessa (1979-) Limbo 1999; Casa de los Babys 2003

Martini, Max Mary Higgins Clark's Try to Remember 2004; Redbelt 2007

Martini, Nino (1904-1976) Paramount on Parade 1930; One Night with You 1948

Martins, Orlando (1899-1985) The End of the River 1947; West of Zanzibar 1954; Safari 1956

Martyn, Peter (1928-1955) Child's Play 1954; Mad about Men 1954; No Smoking 1954

Marull, Laia (1973-) Lisboa 1999; Take My Eyes 2003

Marvin, Hank (1941-) The Young Ones 1961; Summer Holiday 1962; Wonderful Life 1964; Finders Keepers 1966

Marvin, Lee (1924-1987) You're in the Navy Now 1951; The Duel at Silver Creek 1952; Hangman's Knot 1952; We're Not Married 1952; The Big Heat 1953; The Glory Brigade 1953; Gun Fury 1953; Seminole 1953; The Wild One 1953; The Caine Mutiny 1954; Gorilla at Large 1954; The Raid 1954; Bad Day at Black Rock 1955; I Died a Thousand Times 1955; A Life in the Balance 1955; Not as a Stranger 1955; Pete Kelly's Blues 1955; Shack Out on 101 1955; Violent Saturday 1955; Attack! 1956; Pillars of the Sky 1956; The Rack 1956; Seven Men from Now 1956; Raintree County 1957; The Comancheros 1961; The Man Who Shot Liberty Valance 1962; Donovan's Reef 1963; The Killers 1964; Cat Ballou 1965; Ship of Fools 1965; The Professionals 1966; The Dirty Dozen 1967; Point Blank 1967; Tonite Let's All Make Love in London 1967; Hell in the Pacific 1968; Sergeant Ryker 1968; Paint Your Wagon 1969; Monte Walsh 1970; Pocket Money 1972; Prime Cut 1972; Emperor of the North 1973; The Spikes Gang 1974; The Great Scout & Cathouse Thursday 1976; Shout at the Devil 1976; Avalanche Express 1979; The Big Red One 1980; Death Hunt 1981; Gorky Park 1983; The Delta Force 1986

Marwa, Emil East Is East 1999; Doghouse 2009; West Is West 2010

Marx, Brett (1964-) The Bad News Bears Go to Japan 1978; The Lucky Star 1980; Thrashin' 1986

Marx, Chico (1886-1961) The Cocoanuts 1929; Animal Crackers 1930; Monkey Business 1931; Horse Feathers 1932; Duck Soup 1933; A Night at the Opera 1935; A Day at the Races 1937; Room Service 1938; At the Circus 1939; Go West 1940; The Big Store 1941; A Night in Casablanca 1946; Love Happy 1949; The Story of Mankind 1957

Marx, Groucho (1890-1977) The Cocoanuts 1929; Animal Crackers 1930; Monkey Business 1931; Horse Feathers 1932; Duck Soup 1933; A Night at the Opera 1935; A Day at the Races 1937; Room Service 1938; At the Circus 1939; Go West 1940; The Big Store 1941; A Night in Casablanca 1946; Copacabana 1947; Love Happy 1949; Double Dynamite 1951; A Girl in Every Port 1952; The Story of Mankind 1957; Will Success Spoil Rock Hunter? 1957; Skidoo 1968

Marx, Harpo (1888-1964) The Cocoanuts 1929; Animal Crackers 1930; Monkey Business 1931; Horse Feathers 1932; Duck Soup 1933; A Night at the Opera 1935; A Day at the Races 1937; Room Service 1938; At the Circus 1939; Go West 1940; The Big Store 1941; Stage Door Canteen 1943; A Night in Casablanca 1946; Love Happy 1949; The Story of Mankind 1957

Marx, Zeppo (1901-1979) The Cocoanuts 1929; Animal Crackers 1930; Monkey Business 1931; Horse Feathers 1932; Duck Soup 1933

Mascolo, Joseph (1935-) Shaft's Big Score! 1972; Happy Mother's Day... Love, George 1973; Jaws 2 1978; Heat 1987; The Trial of the Incredible Hulk 1989

Mase, Marino (1939-) Les Carabiniers 1963; Fists in the Pocket 1965

Mashkov, Vladimir (1963-) The Thief 1997; Mission: Impossible - Ghost Protocol 2011

Masina, Giulietta (1921-1994) The White Sheik 1951; Europa '51 1952; La Strada 1954; The Swindle 1955; Nights of Cabiria 1957; Juliet of the Spirits 1965; The Madwoman of Chaillot 1969; Ginger & Fred 1986

Mask, Ace (1948-) Not of This Earth 1988; The Return of Swamp Thing 1989; Transylvania Twist 1989

Maskell, Neil (1976-) The Football Factory 2004; Bonded by Blood 2010; Kill List 2011; Wild Bill 2011; Piggy 2012; Hyena 2014

Maskell, Virginia (1936-1968) The Man Upstairs 1958; Virgin Island 1958; Jet Storm 1959; Doctor in Love 1960; Suspect 1960; Only Two Can Play 1961; The Wild and the Willing 1962; Interlude 1968

Maslany, Tatiana Dawn Anna 2005; An Old-Fashioned Thanksgiving 2008; Woman in Gold 2015

Maslow, Walter The Cosmic Man 1959; Atlas 1960

Mason, Brewster (1922-1987) Private Potter 1963; The Quatermass Conclusion 1979

Mason, Connie (1937-) Blood Feast 1963; Two Thousand Maniacs! 1964

Mason, Elliot (1897-1949) The Ghost of St Michael's 1941; It's Turned Out Nice Again 1941

Mason, Hilary (1917-2006) Don't Look Now 1973; I Don't Want to Be Born 1975; Dolls 1987; Robot 2xx 1989

Mason, James (1909-1984) Fire over England 1937; The Mill on the Floss 1937; The Return of the Scarlet Pimpernel 1937; Hatter's Castle 1941; The Night Has Eyes 1942; Secret Mission 1942; Thunder Rock 1942; The Bells Go Down 1943; Candlelight in Algeria 1943; The Man in Grey 1943; They Met in the Dark 1943; Fanny by Gaslight 1944; Hotel Reserve 1944; A Place of One's Own 1944; The Seventh Veil 1945; They Were Sisters 1945; The Wicked Lady 1945; Odd Man Out 1947; The Upturned Glass 1947; Caught 1949; East Side, West Side 1949; Madame Bovary 1949; The Reckless Moment 1949; Pandora and the Flying Dutchman 1950; The Desert Fox 1951; Botany Bay 1952; Face to Face 1952; 5 Fingers 1952; The Prisoner of Zenda 1952; The Desert Rats 1953; Julius Caesar 1953; The Man Between 1953; The Story of Three Loves 1953; Prince Valiant 1954; A Star Is Born 1954; 20,000 Leagues under the Sea 1954; Bigger than Life 1956; Forever, Darling 1956; Island in the Sun 1957; Cry Terror 1958; The Decks Ran Red 1958; Journey to the Center of the Earth 1959; North by Northwest 1959; A Touch of Larceny 1959; The Marriage-Go-Round 1960; The Trials of Oscar Wilde 1960; Lolita 1961; Escape from Zahrain 1962; Hero's Island 1962; Tiara Tahiti 1962; The Fall of the Roman Empire 1964; The Pumpkin Eater 1964; Lord Jim 1965; The Blue Max 1966; The Deadly Affair 1966; Georgy Girl 1966; Stranger in the House 1967; Duffy 1968; Mayerling 1968; The Sea Gull 1968; Age of Consent 1969; Spring and Port Wine 1969; Bad Man's River 1971; Cold Sweat 1971; Child's Play 1972; Kill! 1972; Frankenstein: the True Story 1973; The Last of Sheila 1973; The Mackintosh Man 1973; 11 Harrowhouse 1974; Great Expectations 1974; The Marseille Contract 1974; Autobiography of a Princess 1975; Inside Out 1975; Mandingo 1975; The Masters 1975; Voyage of the Damned 1976; Cross of Iron 1977; The Boys from Brazil 1978; Heaven Can Wait 1978; Murder by Decree 1978; The Passage 1978; The Water Babies 1978; Bloodline 1979; North Sea Hijack 1979; Salem's Lot 1979; Evil under the Sun 1982; The Verdict 1982; Yellowbeard 1983; The Shooting Party 1984; The Assisi Underground 1985

Mason, LeRoy (1903-1947) Texas Terror 1935; Riders of the Purple Sage 1941; My Pal Trigger 1946

Mason, Marsha (1942-) Blume in Love 1973; Cinderella Liberty 1973; Audrey Rose 1977; The Goodbye Girl 1977; The Cheap Detective 1978; Chapter Two 1979; Only When I Laugh 1981; Max Dugan Returns 1983; Surviving 1985; Heartbreak Ridge 1986; Dinner at Eight

1989; The Image 1990; Stella 1990; Drop Dead Fred 1991; I Love Trouble 1994; Broken Trust 1995; Nick of Time 1995; 2 Days in the Valley 1996; The Long Shot 2004

Mason, Reginald (1875-1962) Shanghai Madness 1933; Topaze 1933

Mason, Tom (1949-) Men Don't Leave 1990; The Puppet Masters 1994

Massari, Lea (1933-) L'Avventura 1960; The Colossus of Rhodes 1961; Captive City 1962; The Four Days of Naples 1962; The Things of Life 1969; Le Souffle au Coeur 1971; And Hope to Die 1972; The Silent One 1973; Story of a Love Story 1973; Les Rendez-vous d'Anna 1978; Christ Stopped at Eboli 1979

Massee, Michael Guy 1996; Lost Highway 1996; Playing God 1997

Massen, Osa (1914-2006) A Woman's Face 1941; You'll Never Get Rich 1941; Background to Danger 1943; Cry of the Werewolf 1944; Jack London 1944; The Master Race 1944; Deadline at Dawn 1946; Night unto Night 1949

Massey, Anna (1937-2011) Gideon's Day 1958; Peeping Tom 1960; Bunny Lake Is Missing 1965; De Sade 1969; Frenzy 1972; A Doll's House 1973; The Vault of Horror 1973; Sweet William 1980; Five Days One Summer 1982; Another Country 1984; The Chain 1984; The Little Drummer Girl 1984; Anna Karenina 1985; Foreign Body 1986; Killing Dad 1989; The Tall Guy 1989; Impromptu 1991; The Grotesque 1995; Haunted 1995; Driftwood 1996; The Slab Boys 1997; Captain Jack 1998; Mad Cows 1999; Room to Rent 2000; The Importance of Being Earnest 2002; Possession 2002; The Machinist 2003; Mrs Palfrey at The Claremont 2005; The Gigolos 2006; The Oxford Murders 2008

Massey, Daniel (1933-1998) In Which We Serve 1942; Operation Bullshine 1959; Upstairs and Downstairs 1959; The Entertainer 1960; The Queen's Guards 1960; Go to Blazes 1961; The Jokers 1967; Star! 1968; Fragment of Fear 1971; Mary, Queen of Scots 1971; The Vault of Horror 1973; The Devil's Advocate 1977; Warlords of Atlantis 1978; The Cat and the Canary 1979; Bad Timing 1980; Escape to Victory 1981; Scandal 1988

Massey, Edith (1918-1984) Pink Flamingos 1972; Female Trouble 1974; Desperate Living 1977; Polyester 1981

Massey, Ilona (1910-1974) Rosalie 1937; The Invisible Agent 1942; Frankenstein Meets the Wolf Man 1943; Holiday in Mexico 1946; The Plunderers 1948; Love Happy 1949

Massey, Raymond (1896-1983) The Old Dark House 1932; The Scarlet Pimpernel 1934; Things to Come 1936; Fire over England 1937; The Hurricane 1937; The Prisoner of Zenda 1937; Under the Red Robe 1937; The Drum 1938; Santa Fe Trail 1940; Spirit of the People 1940; 49th Parallel 1941; Dangerously They Live 1942; Desperate Journey 1942; Reap the Wild Wind 1942; Action in the North Atlantic 1943; Arsenic and Old Lace 1944; Hotel Berlin 1945; The Woman in the Window 1945; A Matter of Life and Death 1946; Mourning Becomes Electra 1947; Possessed 1947; The Fountainhead 1949; Roseanna McCoy 1949; Barricade 1950; Chain Lightning 1950; Dallas 1950; Come Fill the Cup 1951; David and Bathsheba 1951; Sugarfoot 1951; Carson City 1952; The Desert Song 1953; Battle Cry 1955; East of Eden 1955; Prince of Players 1955; Seven Angry Men 1955; Omar Khayyam 1957; The Naked and the Dead 1958; The Queen's Guards 1960; The Fiercest Heart 1961; How the West Was Won 1962; Mackenna's Gold 1969

Massey, Walter (1928-2014) Blood Relatives 1977; The Boy in Blue 1986

Massie, Paul (1932-2011) Orders to Kill 1958; Libel 1959; Sapphire 1959; The Rebel 1960; The Two Faces of Dr Jekyll 1960; Raising the Wind 1961; The Pot Carriers 1962

Massine, Léonide (1896-1979) The Red Shoes 1948; The Tales of Hoffmann 1951; Honeymoon 1959

Massoglia, Chris Cirque du Freak: the Vampire's Assistant 2009; The Hole 2009

Master P (1969-) I Got the Hook Up 1998; Gang Law 1999; Hollywood Homicide 2003

Masters, Ben (1947-) The Shadow Box 1980; Dream Lover 1986; Making Mr Right 1987

Masterson, Chris (1980-) Dragonheart: a New Beginning 1999; Scary Movie 2 2001

Masterson, Fay (1974-) The Power of One 1991; The Man without a Face

1993; Cops and Robbersons 1994; Forbidden Territory: Stanley's Search for Livingstone 1997; Sorted 2000; Amish Grace 2010

Masterson, Mary Stuart (1966-) At Close Range 1985; Catholic Boys 1985; My Little Girl 1986; Gardens of Stone 1987; Some Kind of Wonderful 1987; Mr North 1988; Chances Are 1989; Immediate Family 1989; Funny about Love 1990; Fried Green Tomatoes at the Whistle Stop Cafe 1991; Benny & Joon 1993; Bad Girls 1994; Radioland Murders 1994; Bed of Roses 1995; Heaven's Prisoners 1996; Digging to China 1998; Leo 2002

Masterson, Peter (1934-) Ambush Bay 1966; Tomorrow 1972; The Stepford Wives 1975

Masterson, Ronnie (1926-2014) The Dawning 1988; Angela's Ashes 1999

Mastrantonio, Mary Elizabeth (1958-) Scarface 1983; The Color of Money 1986; Slam Dance 1987; The Abyss 1989; The January Man 1989; Fools of Fortune 1990; Class Action 1991; Robin Hood: Prince of Thieves 1991; Consenting Adults 1992; White Sands 1992; Three Wishes 1995; Two Bits 1995; Limbo 1999; My Life So Far 1999; Witness Protection 1999; The Perfect Storm 2000; The Brooke Ellison Story 2004

Mastroianni, Chiara (1972-) Ma Saison Préférée 1993; All Men Are Mortal 1995; Ma Vie Sexuelle 1996; Three Lives and Only One Death 1996; Nowhere 1997; Time Regained 1999; Hotel 2001; Love Songs 2007; Persepolis 2007; A Christmas Tale 2008; Beloved 2011; Bastards 2013

Mastroianni, Marcello (1924-1996) Sunday in August 1949; Lucky to Be a Woman 1955; The Miller's Wife 1955; Too Bad She's Bad 1955; White Nights 1957; Big Deal on Madonna Street 1958; La Dolce Vita 1960; Divorce - Italian Style 1961; La Notte 1961; A Very Private Affair 1962; 8½ 1963; The Organizer 1963; Yesterday, Today and Tomorrow 1963; Marriage - Italian Style 1964; Casanova '70 1965; The Tenth Victim 1965; The Poppy Is Also a Flower 1966; Ghosts - Italian Style 1967; The Stranger 1967; Diamonds for Breakfast 1968; A Place for Lovers 1968; Sunflower 1969; Jealousy, Italian Style 1970; Leo the Last 1970; The Priest's Wife 1970; Fellini's Roma 1972; The Bit Player 1973; La Grande Bouffe 1973; Massacre in Rome 1973; What? 1973; A Special Day 1977; Bye Bye Monkey 1978; Blood Feud 1979; City of Women 1980; La Pelle 1981; Gabriela 1983; La Nuit de Varennes 1983; Storia di Piera 1983; Macaroni 1985; The Bee Keeper 1986; Ginger & Fred 1986; Dark Eyes 1987; Intervista 1987; Everybody's Fine 1990; A Touch of Adultery 1991; Used People 1992; We Don't Want to Talk about It 1993; Pret-a-Porter 1994; Beyond the Clouds 1995; Les Cent et Une Nuits 1995; Three Lives and Only One Death 1996; Journey to the Beginning of the World 1997

Masur, Richard (1948-) Semi-Tough 1977; Who'll Stop the Rain? 1978; Hanover Street 1979; Heaven's Gate 1980; The Thing 1982; Adam 1983; Risky Business 1983; The Burning Bed 1984; The Mean Season 1985; My Science Project 1985; Wild Horses 1985; Heartburn 1986; The Believers 1987; Walker 1987; Deadly Pursuit 1988; License to Drive 1988; Rent-a-Cop 1988; Far from Home 1989; Flashback 1990; My Girl 1991; California Man 1992; The Man without a Face 1993; Six Degrees of Separation 1993; My Girl 2 1994; The Face on the Milk Carton 1995; Forget Paris 1995; My Brother's Keeper 1995; Multiplicity 1996; Play It to the Bone 2000; 61* 2001; Palindromes 2004

Matania, Clelia (1918-1981) The Monte Carlo Story 1957; Seven Hills of Rome 1957; Don't Look Now 1973

Matarazzo, Heather (1982-) Welcome to the Dollhouse 1995; Our Guys: Outrage in Glen Ridge 1999; The Princess Diaries 2001; Sorority Boys 2002; The Princess Diaries 2: Royal Engagement 2004; Hostel: Part II 2007

Matchett, Kari Plague City: Sars in Toronto 2005; The National Tree 2009; The Tree of Life 2010

Mate, Gabor Ten Minutes Older: the Cello 2002; Taxidermia 2006

Mateos, Julian (1938-1996) Return of the Seven 1966; 10:30 PM Summer 1966; Catlow 1971

Mather, Aubrey (1885-1958) The Man in the Mirror 1936; When Knights Were Bold 1936; Careful, Soft Shoulder 1942; The Undying Monster 1942; The House

of Fear 1944; The Lodger 1944; The Hucksters 1947; South of Algiers 1952

Matheron, Marie Le Grand Chemin 1987; Western 1997; Presque Rien 2000

Mathers, Jerry (1948-) The Trouble with Harry 1954; That Certain Feeling 1956

Matheson, Hans (1975-) Les Misérables 1997; Stella Does Tricks 1997; Mojo 1998; Half Light 2006; Bathory 2008; The Christmas Candle 2013

Matheson, Murray (1912-1985) Botany Bay 1952; Hurricane Smith 1952; Love Is a Many-Splendored Thing 1955; How to Succeed in Business without Really Trying 1967; Banacek: Detour to Nowhere 1972

Matheson, Tim (1947-) How to Commit Marriage 1969; Magnum Force 1973; Almost Summer 1977; National Lampoon's Animal House 1978; The Apple Dumpling Gang Rides Again 1979; 1941 1979; A Little Sex 1981; To Be or Not to Be 1983; Impulse 1984; Fletch 1985; Cannonball Fever 1989; Buried Alive 1990; Solar Crisis 1990; Drop Dead Fred 1991; Sometimes They Come Back 1991; Quicksand: No Escape 1992; Black Sheep 1996; The Story of Us 1999; Van Wilder: Party Liaison 2002; The King and Queen of Moonlight Bay 2003

Mathews, Carole (1920-) The Great Gatsby 1949; Meet Me at the Fair 1952; Assignment Redhead 1956; Showdown at Boot Hill 1958; Tender Is the Night 1961

Mathews, Dorothy (1912-1977) A Girl in Every Port 1928; A Handful of Clouds 1930

Mathews, George (1911-1984) Up in Arms 1944; Last of the Comanches 1952; City beneath the Sea 1953; The Man with the Golden Arm 1955; Heller in Pink Tights 1960

Mathews, Al Rough Cut 1980; Aliens 1986; Riders of the Storm 1986

Mathews, Christopher The Scars of Dracula 1970; Blind Terror 1971

Mathews, Dakin (1940-) The Fabulous Baker Boys 1989; Formula for Death 1995; True Grit 2010

Mathews, Francis (1927-2014) Bhowani Junction 1956; The Revenge of Frankenstein 1958; The Pursuers 1961; Dracula - Prince of Darkness 1965; Rasputin, the Mad Monk 1965; Just like a Woman 1966; Crossplot 1969

Mathews, Jessie (1907-1981) Friday the Thirteenth 1933; The Good Companions 1933; Waltzes from Vienna 1933; Evergreen 1934; First a Girl 1935; It's Love Again 1936; Gangway 1937; Head over Heels in Love 1937; Climbing High 1938; Sailing Along 1938; Forever and a Day 1943; tom thumb 1958

Mathews, Lester (1900-1975) The Raven 1935; Crack-Up 1936; Thank You, Jeeves 1936; Rulers of the Sea 1939; The Biscuit Eater 1940; The Pied Piper 1942; Two o'Clock Courage 1945; Rogues of Sherwood Forest 1950; Lorna Doone 1951

Mathews, Liesel (1984-) A Little Princess 1995; Air Force One 1997

Mattick, Patricia aka **Mattick, Pattye** (1951-2003) The Beguiled 1970; Ransom for a Dead Man 1971

Mattox, Matt (1921-2013) Seven Brides for Seven Brothers 1954; Pepe 1960

Mattson, Robin (1956-) Namu, the Killer Whale 1966; Return to Macon County 1975; Captain America 1979; Wolf Lake 1979

Mature, Victor (1915-1999) No, No, Nanette 1940; One Million BC 1940; I Wake Up Screaming 1941; The Shanghai Gesture 1941; Footlight Serenade 1942; My Gal Sal 1942; Seven Days' Leave 1942; Song of the Islands 1942; My Darling Clementine 1946; Kiss of Death 1947; Moss Rose 1947; Cry of the City 1948; Fury at Furnace Creek 1948; Easy Living 1949; Samson and Delilah 1949; Stella 1950; Wabash Avenue 1950; Androcles and the Lion 1952; The Las Vegas Story 1952; Million Dollar Mermaid 1952; Affair with a Stranger 1953; The Glory Brigade 1953; The Robe 1953; Betrayed 1954; Dangerous Mission 1954; Demetrius and the Gladiators 1954; The Egyptian 1954; Chief Crazy Horse 1955; The Last Frontier 1955; Violent Saturday 1955; Safari 1956; Zarak 1956; Interpol 1957; China Doll 1958; No Time to Die 1958; The Bandit of Zhobe 1959; The Big Circus 1959; Escort West 1959; Hannibal 1959; After the Fox 1966; Head 1968; Every Little Crook and Nanny 1972; Firepower 1979

Matuszak, John (1950-1989) Caveman 1981; The Ice Pirates 1984; The Goonies 1985

Mauban, Maria (1924-) Cage of Gold 1950; Cairo Road 1950; Journey to Italy 1953

Mauch, Billy (1924-2006) Anthony Adverse 1936; The Prince and the Pauper 1937

Maude-Roxby, Roddy (1930-) The Aristocats 1970; Shadowlands 1993

Maudsley, Tony The Nine Lives of Tomas Katz 1999; The Scouting Book for Boys 2009

Maughan, Monica (1938-) Annie's Coming Out 1984; Cactus 1986; Golden Braid 1991

Maur-Thorp, Sarah Edge of Sanity 1989; River of Death 1989

Maura, Carmen (1945-) Pepi, Luci, Bom... 1980; Dark Habits 1983; What Have I Done to Deserve This? 1984; Matador 1986; The Law of Desire 1987; Women on the Verge of a Nervous Breakdown 1988; Ay, Carmela! 1990; How to Be a Woman and Not Die in the Attempt 1991; Le Bonheur Est dans le Pré 1995; Alice et Martin 1998; Lisboa 1999; La Comunidad 2000; Valentín 2002; Volver 2006; Tetro 2009; The Women on the 6th Floor 2010

Maurey, Nicole (1925-) Diary of a Country Priest 1950; Little Boy Lost 1953; Secret of the Incas 1954; The Constant Husband 1955; The Bold and the Brave 1956; Me and the Colonel 1958; The House of the Seven Hawks 1959; The Jayhawkers 1959; The Scapegoat 1959; High Time 1960; His and Hers 1960; Don't Bother to Knock 1961; The Day of the Triffids 1962; The Very Edge 1962

Maurier, Claire (1929-) The 400 Blows 1959; La Cage aux Folles 1978; Un Air de Famille 1996; My Afternoons with Margueritte 2010

Maurus, Gerda (1903-1968) Spies 1928; The Woman in the Moon 1929

Maury, Jean-Louis Ophélia 1962; Madame Bovary 1991

Mawle, Joseph (1974-) Heartless 2009; The Awakening 2011; Shell 2012; Half of a Yellow Sun 2013; The Hallow 2015; Kill Your Friends 2015

Maximova, Antonina (1916-1986) Othello 1955; Ballad of a Soldier 1959

Maxwell Martin, Anna Becoming Jane 2006; Philomena 2013

Maxwell, Edwin (1886-1948) The Taming of the Shrew 1929; Inspiration 1931; Tiger Shark 1932; Mystery of the Wax Museum 1933; The Blue Bird 1940; The Great Moment 1944

Maxwell, Frank (1916-2004) Lonelyhearts 1958; Ada 1961; The Intruder 1961; The Haunted Palace 1963; Mr Majestyk 1974

Maxwell, James (1929-1995) Girl on Approval 1962; Private Potter 1963; One Day in the Life of Ivan Denisovich 1971

Maxwell, John (1918-1982) The Prowler 1951; The Bigamist 1953

Maxwell, Lois (1927-2007) The Dark Past 1948; Mantrap 1952; Women of Twilight 1952; Passport to Treason 1956; Satellite in the Sky 1956; Kill Me Tomorrow 1957; Time without Pity 1957; Come Fly with Me 1962; Dr No 1962; From Russia with Love 1963; The Haunting 1963; Goldfinger 1964; Thunderball 1965; You Only Live Twice 1967; On Her Majesty's Secret Service 1969; The Adventurers 1970; Diamonds Are Forever 1971; Endless Night 1971; Live and Let Die 1973; The Man with the Golden Gun 1974; The Spy Who Loved Me 1977; Moonraker 1979; For Your Eyes Only 1981; Octopussy 1983; A View to a Kill 1985

Maxwell, Marilyn (1921-1972) Stand by for Action 1942; Lost in a Harem 1944; Three Men in White 1944; High Barbaree 1947; Summer Holiday 1948; Champion 1949; Key to the City 1950; The Lemon Drop Kid 1951; East of Sumatra 1953; Military Policeman 1953; New York Confidential 1955; Rock-a-Bye Baby 1958; Critic's Choice 1963; Arizona Bushwhackers 1968

Maxwell, Paul (1921-1991) Shadow of Fear 1963; It! 1966; Madame Sin 1972; Baxter 1973

Maxwell, Roberta (1944-) Rich Kids 1979; Popeye 1980; Psycho III 1986; Last Night 1998

May, Anthony (1946-) No Blade of Grass 1970; The Triple Echo 1972

May, Elaine (1932-) Enter Laughing 1967; Luv 1967; A New Leaf 1971; California Suite 1978; Small Time Crooks 2000

May, Jack (1922-1997) Trog 1970; The Man Who Would Be King 1975

May, Jodhi (1975-) A World Apart 1987; The Last of the Mohicans 1992; Sister My Sister 1994; The Scarlet Letter 1995; The Gambler 1997; The Woodlanders 1997; The House of Mirth 2000; The Escapist 2002; Blinded 2004; On a Clear Day 2004; The Best Man 2005; Defiance 2008; Flashbacks of a Fool 2008; I, Anna 2012

May, Mathilda (1965-) *Lifeforce* 1985; *Le Cri du Hibou* 1987; *Naked Tango* 1990; *Becoming Colette* 1991; *Scream of Stone* 1991; *The Tit and the Moon* 1994; *The Jackal* 1997

Mayall, Rik (1958-2014) *An American Werewolf in London* 1981; *Whoops Apocalypse* 1986; *Eat the Rich* 1987; *Drop Dead Fred* 1991; *Carry On Columbus* 1992; *Little Noises* 1992; *The Princess and the Goblin* 1992; *Remember Me?* 1996; *Bring Me the Head of Mavis Davis* 1997; *Guest House Paradiso* 1999; *A Monkey's Tale* 1999; *Merlin the Return* 2000; *Churchill: the Hollywood Years* 2004; *Valiant* 2005; *Just for the Record* 2010

Mayance, Mélusine *Sarah's Key* 2010; *Age of Uprising: the Legend of Michael Kohlhaas* 2013

Mayehoff, Eddie (1911-1992) *The Stooge* 1951; *That's My Boy* 1951; *Military Policeman* 1953; *Artists and Models* 1955; *How to Murder Your Wife* 1965; *Luv* 1967

Mayhew, Peter (1944-) *Star Wars Episode IV: a New Hope* 1977; *Star Wars Episode V: the Empire Strikes Back* 1980; *Star Wars Episode VI: Return of the Jedi* 1983; *Star Wars Episode III: Revenge of the Sith* 2005; *Star Wars Episode VII: the Force Awakens* 2015

Maynard, Bill (1928-) *Till Death Us Do Part* 1968; *A Hole Lot of Trouble* 1969; *Carry On Loving* 1970; *Carry On at Your Convenience* 1971; *Carry On Henry* 1971; *Adolf Hitler - My Part in His Downfall* 1972; *Bless This House* 1972; *Carry On Matron* 1972; *Steptoe and Son Ride Again* 1973; *Confessions of a Window Cleaner* 1974; *Confessions of a Pop Performer* 1975; *Confessions of a Driving Instructor* 1976; *Robin and Marian* 1976; *Confessions from a Holiday Camp* 1977; *It Shouldn't Happen to a Vet* 1979

Maynard, Terence *Revolver* 2005; *All Things to All Men* 2012

Mayne, Ferdy aka Mayne, Ferdinand (1916-1998) *The Blue Parrot* 1953; *Marilyn* 1953; *Beautiful Stranger* 1954; *Gentlemen Marry Brunettes* 1955; *The Big Chance* 1957; *The Fearless Vampire Killers* 1967; *The Vampire Lovers* 1970; *The Walking Stick* 1970; *Eagle in a Cage* 1971; *When Eight Bells Toll* 1971; *Frightmare* 1981; *The Black Stallion Returns* 1983; *Pirates* 1986; *Knight Moves* 1992; *Benefit of the Doubt* 1993

Maynial, Juliette (1936-) *Les Cousins* 1959; *Eyes without a Face* 1959; *The Trojan War* 1961; *Bluebeard* 1962; *Ophélia* 1962

Mayo, Alfredo (1911-1985) *The Hunt* 1966; *Peppermint Frappé* 1967

Mayo, Virginia (1920-2005) *Jack London* 1944; *The Princess and the Pirate* 1944; *Wonder Man* 1945; *The Best Years of Our Lives* 1946; *The Kid from Brooklyn* 1946; *Out of the Blue* 1947; *The Secret Life of Walter Mitty* 1947; *A Song Is Born* 1948; *Always Leave Them Laughing* 1949; *Colorado Territory* 1949; *Red Light* 1949; *White Heat* 1949; *Backfire* 1950; *The Flame and the Arrow* 1950; *The West Point Story* 1950; *Along the Great Divide* 1951; *Captain Horatio Hornblower RN* 1951; *Painting the Clouds with Sunshine* 1951; *The Iron Mistress* 1952; *She's Working Her Way through College* 1952; *Devil's Canyon* 1953; *South Sea Woman* 1953; *King Richard and the Crusaders* 1954; *The Silver Chalice* 1954; *Pearl of the South Pacific* 1955; *Great Day in the Morning* 1956; *The Proud Ones* 1956; *The Big Land* 1957; *The Story of Mankind* 1957; *The Tall Stranger* 1957; *Westbound* 1959; *Castle of Evil* 1966; *Evil Spirits* 1991; *The Man Next Door* 1998

Mayron, Gale *Heart of Midnight* 1988; *The Feud* 1989

Mayron, Melanie (1952-) *Harry and Tonto* 1974; *Gable and Lombard* 1976; *You Light Up My Life* 1977; *Girlfriends* 1978; *Heartbeeps* 1981; *Missing* 1981; *Checking Out* 1988; *Sticky Fingers* 1988; *My Blue Heaven* 1990

Mays, Daniel (1978-) *Vera Drake* 2004; *Middletown* 2006; *The Bank Job* 2008; *Shifty* 2008; *The Firm* 2009; *Made in Dagenham* 2010; *Byzantium* 2012; *Welcome to the Punch* 2013; *Dad's Army* 2016

Mays, Jayma (1979-) *Red Eye* 2005; *Epic Movie* 2007; *Paul Blart: Mall Cop* 2009; *The Smurfs* 2011; *The Smurfs 2* 2013; *Mena* 2017

Maza, Bob (1939-2000) *The Fringe Dwellers* 1985; *Ground Zero* 1987; *Reckless Kelly* 1993; *Back of Beyond* 1995

Maza, Jason (1987-) *Special People* 2007; *Fish Tank* 2009; *Demons Never Die* 2011; *Victim* 2011; *The Knot* 2012;

The Man Inside 2012; *The Hooligan Factory* 2014

Mazar, Debi (1964-) *Little Man Tate* 1991; *Beethoven's 2nd* 1993; *Money for Nothing* 1993; *So I Married an Axe Murderer* 1993; *Batman Forever* 1995; *Empire Records* 1995; *Girl 6* 1996; *Space Truckers* 1996; *Nowhere* 1997; *She's So Lovely* 1997; *David and Lisa* 1998; *Hush* 1998; *The Insider* 1999; *The Tuxedo* 2002

Mazur, Monet (1976-) *Just Married* 2003; *Torque* 2003; *Monster-in-Law* 2005; *Stoned* 2005; *Live!* 2007; *Dead Man Running* 2009

Mazurki, Mike (1907-1990) *The Shanghai Gesture* 1941; *Farewell My Lovely* 1944; *Abbott and Costello in Hollywood* 1945; *Dick Tracy* 1945; *Nightmare Alley* 1947; *Sinbad the Sailor* 1947; *The Noose Hangs High* 1948; *Relentless* 1948; *Neptune's Daughter* 1949; *Dark City* 1950; *Night and the City* 1950; *Ten Tall Men* 1951; *Blood Alley* 1955; *Kismet* 1955; *Hell Ship Mutiny* 1957; *Pocketful of Miracles* 1961; *Donovan's Reef* 1963; *7 Women* 1966; *Challenge to Be Free* 1972

Mazurowna, Ernestine *Jean de Florette* 1986; *Manon des Sources* 1986

Mazursky, Paul (1930-2014) *Fear and Desire* 1953; *Deathwatch* 1966; *Alex in Wonderland* 1970; *Blume in Love* 1973; *A Star Is Born* 1976; *A Man, a Woman and a Bank* 1979; *Punchline* 1988; *Scenes from the Class Struggle in Beverly Hills* 1989; *Scenes from a Mall* 1991; *Love Affair* 1994; *Miami Rhapsody* 1995; *Faithful* 1996; *Touch* 1996; *2 Days in the Valley* 1996; *Antz* 1998; *Why Do Fools Fall in Love?* 1998; *Big Shot's Funeral* 2001

Mazzello, Joseph (1983-) *Jersey Girl* 1992; *Radio Flyer* 1992; *Jurassic Park* 1993; *Shadowlands* 1993; *The River Wild* 1994; *The Cure* 1995; *Three Wishes* 1995; *Star Kid* 1997; *Simon Birch* 1998; *The Social Network* 2010

Mbatha-Raw, Gugu *Belle* 2013; *Odd Thomas* 2013; *Beyond the Lights* 2014; *Concussion* 2015; *The Whole Truth* 2016

Ménochet, Denis *Special Forces* 2011; *In the House* 2012; *Grand Central* 2013

Meacham, Anne (1925-2006) *Lilith* 1964; *Seizure* 1974

Mead, Courtland (1987-) *Lake Consequence* 1992; *Dragonworld* 1994; *Recess: School's Out* 2001

Mead, Taylor (1924-2013) *Lonesome Cowboys* 1968; *Coffee and Cigarettes* 2003

Meade, Julia (1928-2016) *Pillow Talk* 1959; *Tammy Tell Me True* 1961

Meadows, Audrey (1922-1996) *That Touch of Mink* 1962; *Take Her, She's Mine* 1963; *Rosie!* 1967

Meadows, Jayne (1919-2015) *Lady in the Lake* 1947; *Enchantment* 1948; *David and Bathsheba* 1951

Meadows, Shane (1972-) *Smalltime* 1996; *A Room for Romeo Brass* 1999; *Once upon a Time in the Midlands* 2002; *Le Donk & Scor-Zay-Zee* 2009

Meadows, Tim (1961-) *The Ladies Man* 2000; *Mean Girls* 2004; *The Benchwarmers* 2006; *Walk Hard: the Dewey Cox Story* 2007

Meaney, Colm (1953-) *Far and Away* 1992; *Under Siege* 1992; *The Snapper* 1993; *War of the Buttons* 1993; *The Road to Wellville* 1994; *The Englishman Who Went up a Hill, but Came down a Mountain* 1995; *Last of the High Kings* 1996; *The Van* 1996; *Con Air* 1997; *Noose* 1997; *Claire Dolan* 1998; *Four Days* 1999; *Mystery, Alaska* 1999; *This Is My Father* 1999; *King of Texas* 2002; *The Boys & Girl from County Clare* 2003; *interMission* 2003; *Blueberry* 2004; *Layer Cake* 2004; *Three and Out* 2008; *The Damned United* 2009; *Law Abiding Citizen* 2009; *Bel Ami* 2010; *Get Him to the Greek* 2010; *Parked* 2010; *The Hot Potato* 2011; *Soldiers of Fortune* 2012; *Alan Partridge: Alpha Papa* 2013; *A Belfast Story* 2013; *Free Birds* 2013; *One Chance* 2013; *Norm of the North* 2016

Means, Russell (1939-2012) *The Last of the Mohicans* 1992; *Thomas and the Magic Railroad* 2000; *Pathfinder* 2006

Meara, Anne (1929-2015) *The Out of Towners* 1970; *Nasty Habits* 1976; *My Little Girl* 1986; *The Daytrippers* 1998; *Judy Berlin* 1999; *Get Well Soon* 2001; *Zoolander* 2001; *Like Mike* 2002; *Planes: Fire and Rescue* 2014

Meat Loaf aka Aday, Meat Loaf (1947-) *The Rocky Horror Picture Show* 1975; *Americathon* 1979; *Roadie* 1980; *Motorama* 1991; *Leap of Faith* 1992; *Black Dog* 1998; *Everything That Rises* 1998; *The Mighty* 1998; *Crazy in Alabama* 1999; *Fight Club* 1999; *The Ballad of Lucy Whipple* 2001; *The 51st*

State 2001; *Focus* 2001; *Tenacious D in The Pick of Destiny* 2006

Mechlowicz, Scott (1981-) *EuroTrip* 2004; *Mean Creek* 2004; *Gone* 2006; *Eden* 2012

Mechoso, Julio Oscar *Virus* 1998; *The Legend of Zorro* 2005

Medford, Kay (1914-1980) *Jamboree* 1957; *Girl of the Night* 1960; *The Rat Race* 1960; *Ensign Pulver* 1964; *The Busy Body* 1967; *Angel in My Pocket* 1968; *Funny Girl* 1968

Medina, Patricia (1919-2012) *Don't Take It to Heart* 1944; *The Foxes of Harrow* 1947; *Moss Rose* 1947; *The Fighting O'Flynn* 1948; *Francis* 1949; *Abbott and Costello in the Foreign Legion* 1950; *The Jackpot* 1950; *Valentino* 1951; *Botany Bay* 1952; *Desperate Search* 1952; *The Black Knight* 1954; *Confidential Report* 1955; *The Beast of Hollow Mountain* 1956; *The Battle of the V1* 1958; *The Killing of Sister George* 1968; *Latitude Zero* 1969

Medvedev, Vadim (1929-1988) *Hamlet* 1964; *Vassa* 1983

Medwin, Michael (1923-) *The Courtneys of Curzon Street* 1947; *Another Shore* 1948; *Trottie True* 1949; *Someone at the Door* 1950; *Miss Robin Hood* 1952; *The Oracle* 1952; *The Intruder* 1953; *Spaceways* 1953; *Bang! You're Dead* 1954; *The Teckman Mystery* 1954; *Above Us the Waves* 1955; *Doctor at Sea* 1955; *Charley Moon* 1956; *Checkpoint* 1956; *A Hill in Korea* 1956; *Doctor at Large* 1957; *The Steel Bayonet* 1957; *The Duke Wore Jeans* 1958; *The Heart of a Man* 1959; *Crooks Anonymous* 1962; *It's All Happening* 1963; *Night Must Fall* 1964; *Rattle of a Simple Man* 1964; *I've Gotta Horse* 1965; *The Sandwich Man* 1966; *A Countess from Hong Kong* 1967; *Scrooge* 1970; *The Jigsaw Man* 1984; *Hôtel du Paradis* 1986

Mee, Michelle *The Butterfly Murders* 1979; *Ab-normal Beauty* 2004

Meehan, Tony (1942-) *The Young Ones* 1961; *Summer Holiday* 1962

Meek, Donald (1880-1946) *Mrs Wiggs of the Cabbage Patch* 1934; *Accent on Youth* 1935; *The Bride Comes Home* 1935; *The Gilded Lily* 1935; *Mark of the Vampire* 1935; *The Return of Peter Grimm* 1935; *Top Hat* 1935; *Village Tale* 1935; *The Whole Town's Talking* 1935; *And So They Were Married* 1936; *One Rainy Afternoon* 1936; *Pennies from Heaven* 1936; *Artists and Models* 1937; *Behind the Headlines* 1937; *Breakfast for Two* 1937; *The Toast of New York* 1937; *The Adventures of Tom Sawyer* 1938; *Hold That Co-Ed* 1938; *Nick Carter, Master Detective* 1939; *Stagecoach* 1939; *The Ghost Comes Home* 1940; *The Man from Dakota* 1940; *My Little Chickadee* 1940; *Phantom Raiders* 1940; *The Return of Frank James* 1940; *Sky Murder* 1940; *Star Dust* 1940; *Babes on Broadway* 1941; *Come Live with Me* 1941; *Design for Scandal* 1941; *The Feminine Touch* 1941; *A Woman's Face* 1941; *Keeper of the Flame* 1942; *Tortilla Flat* 1942; *DuBarry Was a Lady* 1943; *They Got Me Covered* 1943; *Bathing Beauty* 1944; *State Fair* 1945; *Because of Him* 1946; *Magic Town* 1947

Meek, Jeffrey aka Meek, Jeff (1959-) *Perfume of the Cyclone* 1989; *Heart Condition* 1990

Meeker, George (1904-1984) *Four Sons* 1928; *Back Street* 1932; *The First Year* 1932; *Tess of the Storm Country* 1932; *Only Yesterday* 1933; *The Richest Girl in the World* 1934; *Murder on a Honeymoon* 1935; *Remember Last Night?* 1935; *History Is Made at Night* 1937; *Twilight in the Sierras* 1950

Meeker, Ralph (1920-1988) *Teresa* 1951; *Glory Alley* 1952; *Somebody Loves Me* 1952; *Jeopardy* 1953; *The Naked Spur* 1953; *Big House, USA* 1955; *Kiss Me Deadly* 1955; *Battle Shock* 1956; *The Fuzzy Pink Nightgown* 1957; *Paths of Glory* 1957; *Run of the Arrow* 1957; *Ada* 1961; *The Dirty Dozen* 1967; *The St Valentine's Day Massacre* 1967; *The Detective* 1968; *The Anderson Tapes* 1971; *The Mind Snatchers* 1972; *The Food of the Gods* 1976; *Winter Kills* 1979

Meester, Leighton (1986-) *Country Strong* 2010; *Date Night* 2010; *Monte Carlo* 2011; *The Oranges* 2011; *The Roommate* 2011; *That's My Boy* 2012

Meeten, Tom *Weekender* 2011; *Aaaaaaaah!* 2015

Megowan, Don (1922-1981) *The Creature Walks among Us* 1956; *The Werewolf* 1956; *Tarzan and the Valley of Gold* 1966

Meier, Armin (1943-1978) *Mother Küsters Goes to Heaven* 1975; *Fear of Fear* 1976

Meier, Shane (1977-) *Andre* 1994; *Taken Away* 1996

Meighan, Thomas (1879-1936) *Male and Female* 1919; *Why Change Your Wife?* 1920; *The Racket* 1928

Meillon, John (1934-1989) *The Long and the Short and the Tall* 1960; *Cairo* 1962; *Walkabout* 1970; *Sunstruck* 1972; *The Cars That Ate Paris* 1974; *Heatwave* 1981; *The Wild Duck* 1983; *"Crocodile" Dundee* 1986; *"Crocodile" Dundee II* 1988

Meintjes, Tertius *Jobman* 1990; *Friends* 1993

Meisner, Günter (1928-1994) *Inside Out* 1975; *Roselyne and the Lions* 1989

Mejias, Isabelle *Bay Boy* 1984; *Scanners II: The New Order* 1991

Melamed, Fred *Suspect* 1987; *A Serious Man* 2009; *In a World...* 2013

Melato, Mariangela (1941-2013) *The Working Class Goes to Heaven* 1971; *The Seduction of Mimi* 1972; *Moses* 1975; *So Fine* 1981

Melchior, Lauritz (1890-1973) *Thrill of a Romance* 1945; *Two Sisters from Boston* 1946; *This Time for Keeps* 1947

Meldrum, Wendel (1958-) *Beautiful Dreamers* 1990; *Sodbusters* 1994

Melendez, Bill (1916-2008) *Snoopy, Come Home* 1972; *Snoopy and Charlie Brown: the Peanuts Movie* 2015

Melford, Jack (1899-1972) *Honeymoon for Three* 1935; *Jump for Glory* 1937

Melford, Jill (1934-) *A Stitch in Time* 1963 ; *The Vengeance of She* 1968

Melia, Joe (1935-2012) *Too Many Crooks* 1958; *Four in the Morning* 1965; *Modesty Blaise* 1966; *Oh! What a Lovely War* 1969; *The Wildcats of St Trinian's* 1980; *The Sign of Four* 1983

Melki, Gilbert (1958-) *[One] Cavale* 2002; *[Three] Après la Vie* 2002; *[Two] Un Couple Epatant* 2002; *Monsieur Ibrahim and the Flowers of the Koran* 2003; *Changing Times* 2004; *Cockles & Muscles* 2004; *Confidences Trop Intimes* 2004; *Angel-A* 2005; *Anna M.* 2007; *Largo Winch* 2008

Mell, Marisa (1939-1992) *French Dressing* 1964; *Casanova '70* 1965; *Masquerade* 1965; *Danger: Diabolik* 1967; *Mahogany* 1975; *Casanova & Co* 1976

Mellencamp, John (1951-) *Falling from Grace* 1992; *Lone Star State of Mind* 2002

Mellish Jr, Fuller (1895-1930) *Applause* 1929; *Sarah and Son* 1930

Melly, Andrée (1932-) *Nowhere to Go* 1958; *Beyond the Curtain* 1960

Meloni, Christopher aka Meloni, Chris (1961-) *Bound* 1996; *Runaway Bride* 1999; *Murder in Greenwich* 2002; *Harold & Kumar Get the Munchies* 2004; *Carriers* 2008; *Nights in Rodanthe* 2008; *42* 2013; *They Came Together* 2014; *White Bird in a Blizzard* 2014; *The Diary of a Teenage Girl* 2015

Melton, Frank (1907-1951) *Stand Up and Cheer!* 1934; *Second Chorus* 1940; *Pot o' Gold* 1941

Melton, Sid (1917-2011) *The Steel Helmet* 1951; *Lady Sings the Blues* 1972

Melville, Jean-Pierre (1917-1973) *A Bout de Souffle* 1959; *Two Men in Manhattan* 1959

Melville, Sam (1936-1989) *The Thomas Crown Affair* 1968; *Big Wednesday* 1978

Melvin, Murray (1932-) *A Taste of Honey* 1961; *HMS Defiant* 1962; *Kaleidoscope* 1966; *A Day in the Death of Joe Egg* 1971; *The Devils* 1971; *Gawain and the Green Knight* 1973; *Ghost Story* 1974; *The Emperor's New Clothes* 2001

Memmoli, George (1938-1985) *Phantom of the Paradise* 1974; *New York, New York* 1977; *Blue Collar* 1978

Mencia, Carlos *The Heartbreak Kid* 2007; *Our Family Wedding* 2010

Mendelsohn, Ben (1969-) *The Year My Voice Broke* 1987; *The Big Steal* 1990; *Spotswood* 1991; *Cosi* 1996; *Idiot Box* 1996; *Black and White* 2002; *Animal Kingdom* 2009; *Beautiful Kate* 2009; *Knowing* 2009; *Trespass* 2011; *Killing Them Softly* 2012; *The Place beyond the Pines* 2012; *Starred Up* 2013; *Black Sea* 2014; *Exodus: Gods and Kings* 2014; *Lost River* 2014; *Mississippi Grind* 2015; *Slow West* 2015; *Rogue One: a Star Wars Story* 2016

Mendenhall, David (1971-) *Over the Top* 1987; *Streets* 1990

Mendes, Eva (1974-) *My Brother the Pig* 1999; *Once upon a Time in Mexico* 2003; *Out of Time* 2003; *Stuck on You* 2003; *2 Fast 2 Furious* 2003; *Hitch* 2005; *Trust the Man* 2006; *Cleaner* 2007; *Ghost Rider* 2007; *Live!* 2007; *We Own the Night* 2007; *The Spirit* 2008; *The Women* 2008; *The Bad Lieutenant - Port of Call: New Orleans*

2009; *Last Night* 2009; *The Other Guys* 2010; *Holy Motors* 2012; *The Place beyond the Pines* 2012; *Radioman* 2012; *Lost River* 2014

Mendillo, Stephen *City of Hope* 1991; *Ethan Frome* 1993; *Lone Star* 1995

Mendonca, Maria Luisa (1970-) *The Three Marias* 2002; *Carandiru* 2003

Mendoza, Natalie *South Pacific* 2001; *The Descent* 2005; *The Descent: Part 2* 2009

Mendoza, Victor Manuel aka Mendoza, Victor (1913-1995) *The Proud Ones* 1953; *Garden of Evil* 1954; *Cowboy* 1958; *The Wonderful Country* 1959

Menez, Bernard (1944-) *Day for Night* 1973; *Day for Night* 1973; *No Problem!* 1975

Menjou, Adolphe (1890-1963) *The Sheik* 1921; *The Three Musketeers* 1921; *A Woman of Paris* 1923; *The Marriage Circle* 1924; *Sinners in Silk* 1924; *Morocco* 1930; *Friends and Lovers* 1931; *The Front Page* 1931; *A Farewell to Arms* 1932; *Forbidden* 1932; *Morning Glory* 1933; *The Worst Woman in Paris?* 1933; *Little Miss Marker* 1934; *The Mighty Barnum* 1934; *Gold Diggers of 1935* 1935; *The Milky Way* 1936; *One in a Million* 1936; *Sing, Baby, Sing* 1936; *Café Metropole* 1937; *One Hundred Men and a Girl* 1937; *Stage Door* 1937; *A Star Is Born* 1937; *The Goldwyn Follies* 1938; *Letter of Introduction* 1938; *Thanks for Everything* 1938; *Golden Boy* 1939; *That's Right - You're Wrong* 1939; *A Bill of Divorcement* 1940; *Road Show* 1941; *Roxie Hart* 1942; *Syncopation* 1942; *You Were Never Lovelier* 1942; *Sweet Rosie O'Grady* 1943; *Step Lively* 1944; *Heartbeat* 1946; *The Hucksters* 1947; *I'll Be Yours* 1947; *State of the Union* 1948; *Dancing in the Dark* 1949; *My Dream Is Yours* 1949; *To Please a Lady* 1950; *Across the Wide Missouri* 1951; *The Tall Target* 1951; *The Sniper* 1952; *Man on a Tightrope* 1953; *Timberjack* 1955; *The Ambassador's Daughter* 1956; *Bundle of Joy* 1956; *The Fuzzy Pink Nightgown* 1957; *Paths of Glory* 1957; *I Married a Woman* 1958; *Pollyanna* 1960

Menon, Kay Kay *Sarkar* 2005; *Life in a... METRO* 2007

Menshikov, Oleg (1960-) *Burnt by the Sun* 1995; *Prisoner of the Mountains* 1996; *The Barber of Siberia* 1999; *East-West* 1999

Menshov, Vladimir (1939-) *Night Watch* 2004; *Day Watch* 2006

Mensik, Vladimir (1924-1988) *A Blonde in Love* 1965; *All My Good Countrymen* 1968

Menzel, Idina (1971-) *Rent* 2005; *Ask the Dust* 2006; *Enchanted* 2007; *Frozen* 2013

Menzel, Jiri (1938-) *Capricious Summer* 1968; *The Cremator* 1968; *Elementary School* 1991

Menzer, Ernest *Bande à Part* 1964; *Made in USA* 1966

Menzies, Heather (1949-) *The Sound of Music* 1965; *Hawaii* 1966; *Piranha* 1978; *Captain America* 1979

Menzies, Robert (1955-) *Cactus* 1986; *Golden Braid* 1991; *Innocence* 2000

Menzies, Tobias *The Low Down* 2000; *Forget Me Not* 2009

Merad, Kad *Paris 36* 2008; *22 Bullets* 2010; *The Well Digger's Daughter* 2010

Merande, Doro (1892-1975) *Mr Belvedere Rings the Bell* 1951; *The Gazebo* 1959

Mercado, Hector (1949-) *Nomads* 1985; *Delta Force 2* 1990

Mercer, Beryl (1882-1939) *All Quiet on the Western Front* 1930; *East Lynne* 1931; *Inspiration* 1931; *The Miracle Woman* 1931; *The Public Enemy* 1931; *Smilin' Through* 1932; *Berkeley Square* 1933; *Cavalcade* 1933; *Supernatural* 1933; *Change of Heart* 1934; *The Little Minister* 1934; *The Richest Girl in the World* 1934; *The Hound of the Baskervilles* 1939

Mercer, Frances (1915-2000) *Annabel Takes a Tour* 1938; *The Mad Miss Manton* 1938; *Smashing the Rackets* 1938; *Vivacious Lady* 1938; *Beauty for the Asking* 1939; *Piccadilly Incident* 1946

Mercer, Mae (1932-2008) *The Beguiled* 1970; *Dirty Harry* 1971

Mercer, Marian (1935-) *The Cracker Factory* 1979; *Out on a Limb* 1992

Merchant, Stephen (1974-) *Tooth Fairy* 2009; *Burke & Hare* 2010; *Gnomeo & Juliet* 2011; *Hall Pass* 2011; *I Give It a Year* 2013; *Brand: a Second Coming* 2015; *Misery Loves Comedy* 2015; *Wolverine 3* 2017

Merchant, Vivien (1929-1983) *Alfie* 1966; *Accident* 1967; *Alfred the Great* 1969; *Under Milk Wood* 1971; *Frenzy* 1972; *The Offence* 1972; *A War of*

Children 1972; The Homecoming 1973; The Maids 1974; The Man in the Iron Mask 1977

Mercier, Michèle ('939-) Shoot the Pianist 1960; Fury at Smugglers Bay 1961; Goodbye Again 1961; L'Aîné des Ferchaux 1963; Black Sabbath 1963; A Global Affair 1964; Casanova '70 1965; You Can't Win 'Em All 1970; Call of the Wild 1972

Mercouri, Melina (1920-1994) Stella 1955; The Gypsy and the Gentleman 1958; Never on Sunday 1960; Phaedra 1962; The Victors 1963; Topkapi 1964; A Man Could Get Killed 1966; 10:30 PM Summer 1966; Gaily, Gaily 1969; Once Is Not Enough 1975; Nasty Habits 1976; A Dream of Passion 1978

Mercure, Jean (1909-1998) Le Rouge et le Noir 1954; The Battle of Austerlitz 1960

Mercure, Monique (1930-) My Uncle Antoine 1971; Naked Lunch 1991

Mercurio, Gus (1928-) The Blue Lagoon 1980; Harlequin 1980; Turkey Shoot 1981; The Man from Snowy River 1982; "Crocodile" Dundee II 1988; Doing Time for Patsy Cline 1997

Mercurio, Micole (1938-2016) Mask 1985; Gleaming the Cube 1988; Roe vs Wade 1989; Wrestling Ernest Hemingway 1993; While You Were Sleeping 1995

Mercurio, Paul ('963-) Strictly Ballroom 1992; Exit to Eden 1994; Back of Beyond 1995

Meredith, Burgess (1908-1997) The Scoundrel 1935; Winterset 1936; Idiot's Delight 1939; Of Mice and Men 1939; Castle on the Hudson 1940; Second Chorus 1940; That Uncertain Feeling 1941; Tom, Dick and Harry 1941; The Story of GI Joe 1945; Diary of a Chambermaid 1946; Magnificent Doll 1946; Mine Own Executioner 1947; On Our Merry Way '948; The Gay Adventure 1949; The Man on the Eiffel Tower 1949; Advise and Consent 1962; The Cardinal 1963; Batman 1966; A Big Hand for a Little Lady 1966; Madame X 1966; Hurry Sundown 1967; Torture Garden 1967; Skidoo 1968; Stay Away, Joe 1968; Hard Contract 1969; The Reivers 1969; There Was a Crooked Man... 1970; Such Good Friends 1971; The Man 1972; Golden Needles 1974; The Day of the Locust 1975; The Hindenburg 1975; 92 in the Shade 1975; Burnt Offerings 1976; Rocky 1976; Golden Rendezvous 1977; The Sentinel 1977; The Amazing Captain Nemo 1978; Foul Play 1978; Magic 1978; Rocky II 1979; When Time Ran Out 1980; Clash of the Titans 1981; Rocky III 1982; Twilight Zone: the Movie 1983; Santa Claus 1985; Mr Corbett's Ghost 1986; King Lear - Fear and Loathing 1987; Full Moon in Blue Water 1988; Rocky V 1990; State of Grace 1990; Grumpy Old Men 1993; Grumpier Old Men 1996

Meredith, Judi aka **Meredith, Judy** aka **Meredith, Judith** (1936-) Wild Heritage 1958; Jack the Giant Killer 1962; The Night Walker 1964; Dark Intruder 1965; Planet of Blood 1966

Meredith, Lee (1947-) The Producers 1968; The Sunshine Boys 1975

Meredith, Madge (1921-) Child of Divorce 1946; The Falcon's Adventure 1946; Trail Street 1947

Merhar, Stanislas (1971-) The Captive 2000; Almost Peaceful 2002; Merci Docteur Rey 2002; Legacy 2007

Méril, Macha (1940-) Who's Been Sleeping in My Bed? 1963; The Married Woman 1964; The Defector 1966; Belle de Jour 1967; Deep Red 1975; Chinese Roulette 1976; Robert et Robert 1978; Vagabond 1985

Meritz, Michèle Le Beau Serge 1958; Les Cousins 1959

Merivale, John (1917-1990) The List of Adrian Messenger 1963; Arabesque 1966

Merivale, Philip (1886-1946) Mr and Mrs Smith 1941; Lady for a Night 1942; This above All 1942; Lost Angel 1943; The Hour before the Dawn 1944; Nothing but Trouble 1944; Sister Kenny 1946; The Stranger 1946

Meriwether, Lee (1935-) Batman 1966; Namu, the Killer Whale 1966; Angel in My Pocket 1968; The Undefeated '969

Merkel, Una (1903-1986) Abraham Lincoln 1930; Daddy Long Legs 1931; Dangerous Female 1931; Private Lives 1931; Six Cylinder Love 1931; The Impatient Maiden 1932; Red-Headed Woman 1932; Blonde Bombshell 1933; 42nd Street 1933; Reunion in Vienna 1933; The Secret of Madame Blanche 1933; Bulldog Drummond Strikes Back 1934; The Cat's Paw 1934; Evelyn Prentice 1934; The Merry Widow 1934; This Side of Heaven 1934; Broadway

Melody of 1936 1935; Born to Dance 1936; Riffraff 1936; Speed 1936; Checkers 1937; Saratoga 1937; True Confession 1937; Destry Rides Again 1939; Some Like It Hot 1939; The Bank Dick 1940; Road to Zanzibar 1941; The Mad Doctor of Market Street 1942; My Blue Heaven 1950; Golden Girl 1951; A Millionaire for Christy 1951; Rich, Young and Pretty 1951; The Merry Widow 1952; With a Song in My Heart 1952; I Love Melvin 1953; The Kentuckian 1955; Bundle of Joy 1956; The Girl Most Likely 1957; The Mating Game 1959; The Parent Trap 1961; Summer and Smoke 1961; Summer Magic 1963

Merkerson, S Epatha aka **Merkinson, Epatha** (1952-) She's Gotta Have It 1986; Terminator 2: Judgment Day 1991; A Place for Annie 1994; Radio 2003; Lackawanna Blues 2005; Black Snake Moan 2006; Mother and Child 2009

Merli, Adalberto Maria (1938-) The Lady with Red Boots 1974; The Card Player 2004

Merlin, Jan (1925-) Hell Bent for Leather 1960; Gunfight at Comanche Creek 1964; Take the Money and Run 1969

Merlin, Joanna (1931-) Love Child 1982; Baby It's You 1983; Mystic Pizza 1988; Class Action 1991

Merlini, Marisa (1923-2008) Bread, Love & Dreams 1953; Jealousy, Italian Style 1970

Merman, Ethel (1908-1984) Kid Millions 1934; We're Not Dressing 1934; The Big Broadcast of 1936 1935; Anything Goes 1936; Strike Me Pink 1936; Alexander's Ragtime Band 1938; Happy Landing 1938; Stage Door Canteen 1943; Call Me Madam 1953; There's No Business like Show Business 1954; It's a Mad Mad Mad Mad World 1963; Journey back to Oz 1964; Art of Love 1965

Merr, Juliano (1957-) Yom Yom 1998; Kippur 2000

Merrall, Mary (1890-1976) Love on the Dole 1941; Dead of Night 1945; Pink String and Sealing Wax 1945; Nicholas Nickleby 1947; They Made Me a Fugitive 1947; The Three Weird Sisters 1948; The Late Edwina Black 1951; It's Great to Be Young 1956

Merrick, Doris The Big Noise 1944; Child of Divorce 1946

Merrill, Dina (1925-) Desk Set 1957; A Nice Little Bank That Should Be Robbed 1958; Don't Give Up the Ship 1959; Operation Petticoat 1959; Butterfield 8 1960; The Sundowners 1960; The Young Savages 1961; The Courtship of Eddie's Father 1963; I'll Take Sweden 1965; Running Wild 1973; Caddyshack II 1988; True Colors 1991; Suture 1993; Open Season 1995; The Magnificent Ambersons 2001

Merrill, Gary (1915-1990) Slattery's Hurricane 1949; Twelve o'Clock High 1949; All about Eve 1950; Where the Sidewalk Ends 1950; Another Man's Poison 1951; Decision before Dawn 1951; The Frogmen 1951; The Girl in White 1952; Phone Call from a Stranger 1952; Witness to Murder 1954; The Wonderful Country 1959; The Great Impostor 1960; Mysterious Island 1961; The Pleasure of His Company 1961; A Girl Named Tamiko 1962; Cast a Giant Shadow 1966; Ride beyond Vengeance 1966; Clambake 1967; The Last Challenge 1967; The Power 1968; Huckleberry Finn 1974

Merriman, Ryan (1983-) Everything That Rises 1998; The Deep End of the Ocean 1999; The Ring Two 2004; Final Destination 3 2006; Elevator Girl 2010

Merrison, Clive (1945-) The Sign of Four 1983; Rebecca's Daughters 1991; Heavenly Creatures 1994; The History Boys 2006

Merritt (1), George (1890-1977) Dreyfus 1931; The Ghost Camera 1933; Dr Syn 1937; Q Planes 1939; Spare a Copper 1940; I, Monster 1971

Merritt, Theresa (1922-1998) The Goodbye Girl 1977; The Wiz 1978; The Great Santini 1979; The Serpent and the Rainbow 1987

Merrow, Jane (1941-) The System 1964; Night of the Big Heat 1967; The Lion in Winter 1968; Adam's Woman 1970; Hands of the Ripper 1971; Diagnosis: Murder 1974; The Patricia Neal Story 1981

Mervyn, William (1912-1976) Murder Ahoy 1964; The Railway Children 1970; The Ruling Class 1972; Up the Front 1972

Mescudi, Scott Two Night Stand 2013; Need for Speed 2014

Mesquida, Roxane (1981-) A Ma Soeur! 2001; Sex Is Comedy 2002; Sheitan 2006; The Last Mistress 2007; Kaboom 2010; Rubber 2010

Messemer, Hannes (1924-1991) General Della Rovere 1959; The Defector 1966

Messick, Don (1926-1997) Charlotte's Web 1973; Jetsons: the Movie 1990

Messina, Chris (1974-) Vicky Cristina Barcelona 2008; Greenberg 2009; Julie & Julia 2009; Devil 2010; Celeste & Jesse Forever 2012; Manglehorn 2014

Messing, Debra (1968-) A Walk in the Clouds 1995; McHale's Navy 1997; The Mothman Prophecies 2001; Hollywood Ending 2002; Along Came Polly 2004; Garfield 2004; The Wedding Date 2004; Open Season 2006; Lucky You 2007; The Women 2008

Messner, Johnny (1970-) Anacondas: the Hunt for the Blood Orchid 2004; The Whole Ten Yards 2004; Running Scared 2005; Wrong Turn at Tahoe 2009; A Soldier's Love Story 2010

Mestral, Armand (1917-2000) Gervaise 1956; Morgan the Pirate 1960; That Riviera Touch 1966; Uncle Benjamin 1969

Metcalf, Laurie (1955-) Desperately Seeking Susan 1985; Candy Mountain 1987; Making Mr Right 1987; Miles from Home 1988; Stars and Bars 1988; Uncle Buck 1989; Internal Affairs 1990; Pacific Heights 1990; JFK 1991; Mistress 1992; A Dangerous Woman 1993; Blink 1994; Leaving Las Vegas 1995; Dear God 1996; Scream 2 1997; Chicago Cab 1998; The Long Island Incident 1998; Runaway Bride 1999; Toy Story 2 1999; Treasure Planet 2002; Meet the Robinsons 2006

Metcalf, Mark (1946-) The Heavenly Kid 1985; One Crazy Summer 1986; Hijacking Hollywood 1997; Drive Me Crazy 1999

Metcalfe, Jesse John Tucker Must Die 2006; Beyond a Reasonable Doubt 2009; Fairfield Road 2010

Metchik, Asher (1986-) The Mommy Market 1994; Freaky Friday 1995

Method Man (1971-) Belly 1998; Backstage 2000; Garden State 2003; Soul Plane 2004; Meet the Spartans 2008; The Cobbler 2014; Keanu 2016

Methot, Mayo (1904-1951) The Mind Reader 1933; Marked Woman 1937

Methven, Eleanor The Boxer 1997; Disco Pigs 2001

Metrano, Art (1936-) The All-American Boy 1973; Seven 1979; Going Ape! 1981; Breathless 1983; Police Academy 2: Their First Assignment 1985; Police Academy 3: Back in Training 1986

Metwally, Omar Rendition 2007; Miral 2010

Metzler, Jim (1955-) Tex 1982; Do You Remember Love 1985; Hot to Trot 1988; 976-EVIL 1988; Old Gringo 1989; Circuitry Man 1990; Crash: the Mystery of Flight 1501 1990; One False Move 1992; Plughead Rewired: Circuitry Man II 1994; Children of the Corn III: Urban Harvest 1995; Cadillac Ranch 1996

Meurisse, Paul (1912-1979) Les Diaboliques 1954; Lunch on the Grass 1959; La Vérité 1960; Le Deuxième Souffle 1966; Army of Shadows 1969

Meury, Anne-Laure The Aviator's Wife 1980; My Girlfriend's Boyfriend 1987

Mewes, Jason (1974-) Clerks 1994; Mallrats 1995; Chasing Amy 1996; Dogma 1999; Jay and Silent Bob Strike Back 2001; Clerks II 2006; The Tripper 2006; Midgets vs Mascots 2008; Zack and Miri Make a Porno 2008

Meyer, Breckin (1974-) Freddy's Dead: the Final Nightmare 1991; The Craft 1993; Prefontaine 1997; Dancer, Texas Pop 81 1998; 54 1998; Road Trip 2000; Kate & Leopold 2002; Garfield 2004; Herbie: Fully Loaded 2005; Rebound 2005; Garfield 2 2006; Ghosts of Girlfriends Past 2009; The Heist 2009

Meyer, David (1947-) The Tempest 1979; Octopussy 1983

Meyer, Dina (1968-) Johnny Mnemonic 1995; DragonHeart 1996; Starship Troopers 1997; Poodle Springs 1998; Bats 1999; Stranger than Fiction 1999; Time Lapse 2001; Federal Protection 2002; Saw 2004; Crimes of Passion 2005; Saw III 2006; The Boy Next Door 2008

Meyer, Emile aka **Meyer, Emil** (1910-1987) The Big Night 1951; Shane 1953; Riot in Cell Block 11 1954; Silver Lode 1954; The Blackboard Jungle 1955; Man with the Gun 1955; Stranger on Horseback 1955; The Tall Men 1955; White Feather 1955; Baby Face Nelson 1957; The Lineup 1958; The Blue Knight 1973

Meyer, Russ (1922-2004) Cherry, Harry & Raquel 1969; Amazon Women on the Moon 1987

Meyers, Ari (1969-) Driving Me Crazy 1991; Dark Horse 1992; LaVyrle Spencer's Home Song 1996

Meylan, Gérard Marius et Jeannette 1997; A la Place du Coeur 1998; La Ville Est Tranquille 2000; The Snows of Kilimanjaro 2011

Meyrink, Michelle (1962-) Valley Girl 1983; Joy of Sex 1984; Revenge of the Nerds 1984; Real Genius 1985; Permanent Record 1988

Mézières, Myriam (1947-) Jonah Who Will Be 25 in the Year 2000 1976; Mouth to Mouth 1995

Mezzogiorno, Giovanna (1974-) Facing Window 2003; Love in the Time of Cholera 2007; Vincere 2009

Mezzogiorno, Vittorio (1941-1994) Three Brothers 1980; The Moon in the Gutter 1983; Scream of Stone 1991

Miano, Robert (1942-) Storm Catcher 1999; The Stickup 2001

Miao Tien (1925-2005) The River 1997; The Hole 1998

Miao, Cora Dim Sum: a Little Bit of Heart 1985; Eat a Bowl of Tea 1989; Life Is Cheap... but Toilet Paper Is Expensive 1990

Miao, Nora The Big Boss 1971; Fist of Fury 1972; The Way of the Dragon 1973

Michael, Gertrude (1911-1964) Ann Vickers 1933; I'm No Angel 1933; Bolero 1934; Cleopatra 1934; Murder on the Blackboard 1934; The Last Outpost 1935; Till We Meet Again 1936

Michael, Ralph (1907-1994) For Those in Peril 1943; San Demetrio London 1943; Dead of Night 1945; Johnny Frenchman 1945; The Astonished Heart 1949; The Hasty Heart 1949; The Sound Barrier 1952; Private Potter 1963; Murder Most Foul 1964; House of Cards 1968

Michaels, Dolores (1933-2001) April Love 1957; Time Limit 1957; The Wayward Bus 1957; Warlock 1959; One Foot in Hell 1960; Battle at Bloody Beach 1961

Michalka, Alyson aka **Michalka, Aly** (1989-) Bandslam 2009; The Roommate 2011

Michalka, Amanda aka **Michalka, A J** Secretariat 2010; Salem Falls 2011; Super 8 2011

Michel, Marc Le Trou 1959; Lola 1960; The Umbrellas of Cherbourg 1964

Michele, Michael (1966-) New Jack City 1991; The 6th Man 1997; Dark Blue 2002; How to Lose a Guy in 10 Days 2003; Relative Stranger 2009

Michell, Keith (1926-2015) True as a Turtle 1956; Dangerous Exile 1957; The Gypsy and the Gentleman 1958; All Night Long 1961; The Hellfire Club 1961; Seven Seas to Calais 1962; House of Cards 1968; Prudence and the Pill 1968; Henry VIII and His Six Wives 1972; The Deceivers 1988

Michie, John Monk Dawson 1997; To Walk with Lions 1999

Middlemass, Frank (1919-2006) The Island 1980; Mrs Caldicot's Cabbage War 2000

Middleton, Charles aka **Middleton, Charles B** (1879-1949) The Miracle Woman 1931; Duck Soup 1933; Mrs Wiggs of the Cabbage Patch 1934; Flash Gordon 1936; Blackmail 1939; The Flying Deuces 1939; The Oklahoma Kid 1939

Middleton, Guy (1906-1973) Keep Fit 1937; French without Tears 1939; For Freedom 1940; Night Boat to Dublin 1946; A Man about the House 1947; Once upon a Dream 1948; One Night with You 1948; Snowbound 1948; No Place for Jennifer 1949; The Happiest Days of Your Life 1950; Laughter in Paradise 1951; Young Wives' Tale 1951; Albert, RN 1953; Conflict of Wings 1953; Malaga 1954; Break in the Circle 1955; Gentlemen Marry Brunettes 1955; A Yank in Ermine 1955; Passionate Summer 1958

Middleton, Noelle (1926-) Carrington VC 1954; Happy Ever After 1954; John and Julie 1955; A Yank in Ermine 1955; The Vicious Circle 1957

Middleton, Ray (1907-1984) Lady from Louisiana 1941; Lady for a Night 1942; The Road to Denver 1955

Middleton, Robert (1911-1977) The Big Combo 1955; Trial 1955; The Court Jester 1956; Friendly Persuasion 1956; Love Me Tender 1956; The Proud Ones 1956; Red Sundown 1956; The Lonely Man 1957; The Tarnished Angels 1957; Day of the Bad Man 1958; The Law and Jake Wade 1958; Career 1959; Don't Give Up the Ship 1959; The Great Impostor 1960; Hell Bent for Leather 1960; Cattle King 1963; A Big Hand for a Little Lady 1966; The Cheyenne Social Club 1970; Which Way to the Front? 1970; The Mark of Zorro 1974

Middleton, Tuppence (1987-) Tormented 2009; Skeletons 2010; Trap

for Cinderella 2011; Cleanskin 2012; The Love Punch 2013; Jupiter Ascending 2014; Spooks: the Greater Good 2015

Midkiff, Dale (1959-) Pet Sematary 1989; Love Potion No 9 1992; Torn Apart 2004; Back to You and Me 2005

Midler, Bette (1945-) The Rose 1979; Jinxed! 1982; Down and Out in Beverly Hills 1986; Ruthless People 1986; Outrageous Fortune 1987; Beaches 1988; Big Business 1988; Oliver & Company 1988; Stella 1990; For the Boys 1991; Scenes from a Mall 1991; Gypsy 1993; Hocus Pocus 1993; The First Wives Club 1996; That Old Feeling 1997; Fantasia 2000 1999; Isn't She Great 1999; Drowning Mona 2000; What Women Want 2001; The Stepford Wives 2004; Then She Found Me 2007; The Women 2008; Cats & Dogs: the Revenge of Kitty Galore 2010; Parental Guidance 2012; Twenty Feet from Stardom 2013

Midwinter, Danny Fast Food 1998; Freight 2010

Mifune, Toshiro (1920-1997) Drunken Angel 1948; Stray Dog 1949; Rashomon 1950; Scandal 1950; The Idiot 1951; The Life of Oharu 1952; Samurai 1954; Seven Samurai 1954; I Live in Fear 1955; The Lower Depths 1956; Throne of Blood 1957; The Hidden Fortress 1958; The Bad Sleep Well 1960; The Important Man 1961; Yojimbo 1961; Sanjuro 1962; High and Low 1963; Red Beard 1965; Grand Prix 1966; Rebellion 1967; Hell in the Pacific 1968; Zatoichi Meets Yojimbo 1970; Red Sun 1971; Paper Tiger 1974; Battle of Midway 1976; 1941 1979; Winter Kills 1979; The Challenge 1982; Shogun Warrior 1991; Shadow of the Wolf 1992; Picture Bride 1994

Migenes-Johnson, Julia (1949-) Carmen 1984; Mack the Knife 1989

Migicovsky, Allan Shivers 1975; A Man, a Woman and a Bank 1979

Mihashi, Tatsuya (1923-2004) The Burmese Harp 1956; High and Low 1963; None but the Brave 1965; What's Up, Tiger Lily? 1966; Tora! Tora! Tora! 1970; Dolls 2002

Mihok, Dash (1974-) William Shakespeare's Romeo + Juliet 1996; Telling You 1998; Whiteboys 1999; Dark Blue 2002; The Day after Tomorrow 2004; Kiss Kiss Bang Bang 2005; Firehouse Dog 2006; I Am Legend 2007; Punisher: War Zone 2008

Mikell, George Beyond the Curtain 1960; The Primitives 1962

Mikhalkov, Nikita (1945-) Sibiriada 1979; Burnt by the Sun 1995

Mikhelson, André Desperate Moment 1953; The Intimate Stranger 1956

Mikkelsen, Lars (1964-) King's Game 2004; What Richard Did 2012

Mikkelsen, Mads (1965-) Bleeder 1999; Open Hearts 2002; Wilbur (Wants to Kill Himself) 2002; The Green Butchers 2003; King Arthur 2004; Pusher II 2004; After the Wedding 2006; Casino Royale 2006; Flame & Citron 2008; Coco Chanel & Igor Stravinsky 2009; The Door 2009; Valhalla Rising 2009; Clash of the Titans 2010; The Three Musketeers 2011; The Hunt 2012; A Royal Affair 2012; Age of Uprising: the Legend of Michael Kohlhaas 2013; Charlie Countryman 2013; The Salvation 2014; Men & Chicken 2015; Doctor Strange 2016; Rogue One: a Star Wars Story 2016

Miko, Izabella (1981-) Coyote Ugly 2000; The Forsaken 2001; Age of Heroes 2011; Step Up: All In 2014

Mikuni, Rentaro (1923-2013) Samurai 1954; The Burmese Harp 1956; Harakiri 1962; Kwaidan 1964; Kwaidan 1964; The Profound Desire of the Gods 1968; Vengeance Is Mine 1979

Milan, Lita The Left Handed Gun 1958; The Mobster 1958

Milano, Alyssa (1972-) Commando 1985; Double Dragon 1994; Embrace of the Vampire 1994; Glory Daze 1995; Poison Ivy 2 1995; Fear 1996; Buying the Cow 2000; Lady and the Tramp II: Scamp's Adventure 2000; Dickie Roberts: Former Child Star 2003; Pathology 2007

Milburn, Oliver (1973-) Loaded 1994; Me without You 2001; Wuthering Heights 2011

Miles, Ben V for Vendetta 2005; Ninja Assassin 2009

Miles, Bernard (1907-1991) The Love Test 1935; Midnight at Madame Tussaud's 1936; The Big Blockade 1942; Thunder Rock 1942; In Which We Serve 1942; One of Our Aircraft Is Missing 1942; Tawny Pipit 1944; Carnival 1946; Great Expectations 1946; Fame Is the Spur 1947; Nicholas Nickleby 1947; The Guinea Pig 1948; Chance of a Lifetime

1950; Never Let Me Go 1953; The Man Who Knew Too Much 1956; Moby Dick 1956; Tiger in the Smoke 1956; Zarak 1956; Saint Joan 1957; The Smallest Show on Earth 1957; tom thumb 1958; Sapphire 1959; Heavens Above! 1963; Run Wild, Run Free 1969

Miles, Joanna (1940-) Bug 1975; The Ultimate Warrior 1975; Rosencrantz and Guildenstern Are Dead 1990; The Heart of Justice 1992; Barbara Taylor Bradford's Everything to Gain 1996

Miles, Peter (1938-2002) Heaven Only Knows 1947; The Red Pony 1949; Monarch 1996

Miles, Sarah (1941-) Term of Trial 1962; The Ceremony 1963; The Servant 1963; Those Magnificent Men in Their Flying Machines 1965; Blowup 1966; I Was Happy Here 1966; Ryan's Daughter 1970; Lady Caroline Lamb 1972; The Hireling 1973; The Man Who Loved Cat Dancing 1974; Great Expectations 1974; The Sailor Who Fell from Grace with the Sea 1976; The Big Sleep 1978; Priest of Love 1981; Venom 1981; Steaming 1985; Hope and Glory 1987; White Mischief 1987; A Ghost in Monte Carlo 1990; The Silent Touch 1992

Miles, Sylvia (1932-) Midnight Cowboy 1969; Heat 1972; Farewell, My Lovely 1975; 92 in the Shade 1975; The Great Scout & Cathouse Thursday 1976; Evil under the Sun 1982; Critical Condition 1987; Wall Street 1987; Crossing Delancey 1988; She-Devil 1989

Miles, Vera (1929-) The Charge at Feather River 1953; Pride of the Blue Grass 1954; Wichita 1955; Autumn Leaves 1956; The Searchers 1956; 23 Paces to Baker Street 1956; The Wrong Man 1956; Beau James 1957; Beyond This Place 1959; The FBI Story 1959; A Touch of Larceny 1959; Five Branded Women 1960; Psycho 1960; Back Street 1961; The Man Who Shot Liberty Valance 1962; Those Calloways 1964; A Tiger Walks 1964; Follow Me, Boys! 1966; One of Our Spies Is Missing 1966; Sergeant Ryker 1968; Molly and Lawless John 1972; One Little Indian 1973; The Castaway Cowboy 1974; Brainwaves 1982; Psycho II 1983; The Initiation 1984; Separate Lives 1995

Milford, Penelope (1948-) Coming Home 1978; The Golden Seal 1983; The Burning Bed 1984; Heathers 1989; Henry: Portrait of a Serial Killer, Part II 1996

Milian, Christina (1981-) Love Don't Cost a Thing 2003; Man of the House 2005; Pulse 2006

Milian, Tomas (1937-) Time of Indifference 1964; Face to Face 1967; A Fine Pair 1968; Beatrice Cenci 1969; The Last Movie 1971; La Luna 1979; Winter Kills 1979; Identification of a Woman 1982; Cat Chaser 1989; Havana 1990; Revenge 1990; Fools Rush In 1997; The Lost City 2005

Milicevic, Ivana (1978-) Head over Heels 2000; Frankenstein 2004; Just like Heaven 2005

Military, Frank Dead-Bang 1989; Everybody Wins 1990

Milius, John (1944-) Deadhead Miles 1972; Milius 2013

Miljan, John (1892-1960) Free and Easy 1930; The Unholy Three 1930; Inspiration 1931; The Iron Man 1931; Susan Lenox: Her Fall and Rise 1931; Arsene Lupin 1932; The Beast of the City 1932; Emma 1932; Flesh 1932; The Kid from Spain 1932; The Rich Are Always with Us 1932; Blind Adventure 1933; The Mad Game 1933; What - No Beer? 1933; Belle of the Nineties 1934; The Plainsman 1936; Fast and Furious 1939; The Merry Monahans 1944; Mrs Mike 1949

Millais, Hugh (1929-2009) Images 1972; The Dogs of War 1980

Milland, Ray aka Milland, Raymond (1905-1986) Piccadilly 1929; The Bachelor Father 1931; Blonde Crazy 1931; Payment Deferred 1932; Polly of the Circus 1932; Bolero 1934; Charlie Chan in London 1934; We're Not Dressing 1934; The Gilded Lily 1935; The Glass Key 1935; The Big Broadcast of 1937 1936; Next Time We Love 1936; Bulldog Drummond Escapes 1937; Easy Living 1937; Three Smart Girls 1937; Men with Wings 1938; Beau Geste 1939; French without Tears 1939; Arise, My Love 1940; The Doctor Takes a Wife 1940; Irene 1940; I Wanted Wings 1941; Skylark 1941; The Major and the Minor 1942; Reap the Wild Wind 1942; Star Spangled Rhythm 1942; The Crystal Ball 1943; Forever and a Day 1943; Lady in the Dark 1944; Till We Meet Again 1944; The Uninvited 1944; Kitty 1945; The Lost Weekend 1945; Ministry of Fear 1945; California 1946; The Well Groomed Bride 1946; Golden Earrings

1947; The Imperfect Lady 1947; Variety Girl 1947; The Big Clock 1948; Miss Tatlock's Millions 1948; Alias Nick Beal 1949; It Happens Every Spring 1949; Circle of Danger 1950; Copper Canyon 1950; A Life of Her Own 1950; A Woman of Distinction 1950; Close to My Heart 1951; Rhubarb 1951; Bugles in the Afternoon 1952; Something to Live For 1952; Jamaica Run 1953; Let's Do It Again 1953; Dial M for Murder 1954; The Girl in the Red Velvet Swing 1955; A Man Alone 1955; Lisbon 1956; The River's Edge 1957; The Safecracker 1958; Panic in Year Zero 1962; The Premature Burial 1962; The Man with the X-Ray Eyes 1963; Quick, Let's Get Married 1964; Hostile Witness 1968; Love Story 1970; Frogs 1972; The Thing with Two Heads 1972; The House in Nightmare Park 1973; Terror in the Wax Museum 1973; Gold 1974; Escape to Witch Mountain 1975; The Swiss Conspiracy 1975; Aces High 1976; The Last Tycoon 1976; Slavers 1977; The Uncanny 1977; Oliver's Story 1978; A Game for Vultures 1979; Starflight One 1983

Millar, Marjie (1930-1970) Money from Home 1953; About Mrs Leslie 1954

Millard, Helene (1905-1974) The Divorcee 1930; Break of Hearts 1935; The Biscuit Eater 1940

Millay, Diana Tarzan and the Great River 1967; Night of Dark Shadows 1971

Mille, Patrick Mon Père Ce Héros 1991; Love Crime 2010; En Equilibre 2015

Miller, Allison Blood: the Last Vampire 2008; 17 Again 2009; Devil's Due 2014

Miller, Andrew Last of the Dogmen 1995; Cube 1997

Miller, Ann (1923-2004) New Faces of 1937 1937; Stage Door 1937; Room Service 1938; You Can't Take It with You 1938; Too Many Girls 1940; Time Out for Rhythm 1941; Reveille with Beverly 1943; Easter Parade 1948; The Kissing Bandit 1949; On the Town 1949; Watch the Birdie 1950; Texas Carnival 1951; Two Tickets to Broadway 1951; Lovely to Look At 1952; Kiss Me Kate 1953; Deep in My Heart 1954; Hit the Deck 1955; The Opposite Sex 1956; Mulholland Drive 2001

Miller, Barry (1958-) Saturday Night Fever 1977; The Chosen 1981; The Journey of Natty Gann 1985; Peggy Sue Got Married 1986; The Pickle 1993; Flawless 1999

Miller, Ben (1966-) The Parole Officer 2001; Johnny English 2003; The Prince & Me 2004; Razzle Dazzle: a Journey into Dance 2006; 4.3.2.1 2010; Johnny English Reborn 2011; What We Did on Our Holiday 2014

Miller, Carl (1893-1979) The Kid 1921; A Woman of Paris 1923

Miller, Colleen (1932-) Playgirl 1954; The Purple Mask 1955; The Rawhide Years 1956; Man in the Shadow 1957; The Night Runner 1957; Gunfight at Comanche Creek 1964

Miller, Dean (1924-2004) Because You're Mine 1952; Skirts Ahoy! 1952

Miller, Dennis (1953-) Heatwave 1981; Madhouse 1990; Disclosure 1994; The Net 1995; Murder at 1600 1997; Joe Dirt 2001

Miller, Denny (1934-) Tarzan, the Ape Man 1959; The Party 1968; Buck and the Preacher 1972

Miller, Dick aka Miller, Richard (1928-) Not of This Earth 1956; Rock All Night 1957; War of the Satellites 1958; A Bucket of Blood 1959; The Terror 1963; The Trip 1967; Hollywood Boulevard 1976; Mr Billion 1977; Piranha 1978; Rock 'n' Roll High School 1979; Heartbeeps 1981; The Howling 1981; Get Crazy 1983; Gremlins 1984; The Terminator 1984; Explorers 1985; Gremlins 2: the New Batch 1990; Batman: Mask of the Phantasm 1993; Shake, Rattle and Rock 1994; Tales from the Crypt: Demon Knight 1995

Miller, Eve (1923-1973) April in Paris 1952; The Big Trees 1952

Miller, Ezra (1992-) Afterschool 2008; We Need to Talk about Kevin 2011; The Perks of Being a Wallflower 2012; Madame Bovary 2014; The Stanford Prison Experiment 2015

Miller, Glenn (1904-1944) Sun Valley Serenade 1941; Orchestra Wives 1942

Miller, Jason (1939-2001) The Exorcist 1973; The Devil's Advocate 1977; The Ninth Configuration 1979; Monsignor 1982; The Exorcist III 1990

Miller, Joan (1910-1988) Yield to the Night 1956; No Trees in the Street 1958

Miller, Jonny Lee (1972-) Hackers 1995; Trainspotting 1995; Afterglow 1997; Regeneration 1997; Complicity 1999; Mansfield Park 1999; Plunkett & Macleane 1999; Dracula 2001 2000; Love, Honour and Obey 2000; The

Escapist 2002; Mindhunters 2003; Melinda and Melinda 2004; Aeonflux 2005; The Flying Scotsman 2006; Byzantium 2012; Dark Shadows 2012; T2: Trainspotting 2 2016

Miller, Joshua John aka Miller, Joshua (1974-) Near Dark 1987; River's Edge 1987

Miller, Kristine (1929-) Desert Fury 1947; I Walk Alone 1947; High Lonesome 1950; Thunder over Arizona 1956

Miller, Larry (1953-) Suburban Commando 1991; Dream Lover 1993; Undercover Blues 1993; Corrina, Corrina 1994; The Favor 1994; The Nutty Professor 1996; The Big Tease 1999; Carnival of Souls 1999; Nutty Professor 2: the Klumps 2000; Max Keeble's Big Move 2001; What's the Worst That Could Happen? 2001; Kiss Kiss Bang Bang 2005; Keeping Up with the Steins 2006; Alpha and Omega 2010

Miller, Linda (1942-) One Summer Love 1975; Alice, Sweet Alice 1977; An Unmarried Woman 1978

Miller (1), Mandy (1944-) Mandy 1952; Background 1953; Adventure in the Hopfields 1954; Dance Little Lady 1954; Raising a Riot 1955; Child in the House 1956

Miller, Marilyn (1898-1936) Sunny 1930; Her Majesty Love 1931

Miller, Mark Ginger in the Morning 1973; Savannah Smiles 1982

Miller, Martin (1899-1969) Hotel Reserve 1944; Night Boat to Dublin 1946; Mark of the Phoenix 1957; Libel 1959; The Phantom of the Opera 1962

Miller, Marvin (1913-1985) Johnny Angel 1946; Deadline at Dawn 1946; Dead Reckoning 1947; Intrigue 1947; Peking Express 1951; Red Planet Mars 1952; Forbidden 1953; Forbidden Planet 1956; Senior Prom 1958; Fantastic Planet 1973

Miller, Omar Benson aka Miller, Omar (1978-) 8 Mile 2002; Shall We Dance 2004; American Pie Presents Band Camp 2005; Get Rich or Die Tryin' 2005; Things We Lost in the Fire 2007; The Express 2008

Miller, Patsy Ruth (1904-1995) The Hunchback of Notre Dame 1923; So This Is Paris 1926

Miller, Penelope Ann (1964-) A Night on the Town 1987; Big Top Pee-wee 1988; Biloxi Blues 1988; Dead-Bang 1989; Awakenings 1990; Downtown 1990; The Freshman 1990; Kindergarten Cop 1990; Other People's Money 1991; Chaplin 1992; The Gun in Betty Lou's Handbag 1992; Year of the Comet 1992; Carlito's Way 1993; The Shadow 1994; The Relic 1996; Little City 1997; Break Up 1998; Killing Moon 1999; Rocky Marciano 1999; Along Came a Spider 2001; Blonde Ambition 2007; The Messengers 2007; The Artist 2011; Cody the Robosapien 2012

Miller, Rebecca (1962-) Seven Minutes 1989; Regarding Henry 1991; Consenting Adults 1992; Wind 1992

Miller, Sherry Rent-a-Kid 1992; It's a Boy/Girl Thing 2006

Miller, Sienna (1981-) Alfie 2004; Layer Cake 2004; Casanova 2005; Factory Girl 2006; Interview 2007; Stardust 2007; The Edge of Love 2008; GI Joe: the Rise of Cobra 2009; American Sniper 2014; Foxcatcher 2014; Burnt 2015; High-Rise 2015; Mississippi Grind 2015; Unfinished Business 2015; Live by Night 2016; The Lost City of Z 2016

Miller, T J Cloverfield 2008; Big Hero 6 2014; Search Party 2014; Deadpool 2016

Miller, Walter aka Miller, W Chrystie (1892-1940) The Musketeers of Pig Alley 1912; The Battle of Elderbush 1914; Stormy 1935

Miller, Wentworth The Human Stain 2003; Resident Evil: Afterlife 2010

Milli, Robert (1933-) The Curse of the Living Corpse 1964; Hamlet 1964

Millican, James (1910-1955) The Man from Colorado 1948; Mister 880 1950; Cavalry Scout 1951; I Was a Communist for the FBI 1951; Warpath 1951; Bugles in the Afternoon 1952; Carson City 1952; Diplomatic Courier 1952; Springfield Rifle 1952; Riding Shotgun 1954; The Big Tip Off 1955; Red Sundown 1956

Milligan, Dustin The Messengers 2007; Shark Night 3D 2011

Milligan, Spike (1918-2002) Penny Points to Paradise 1951; Down among the Z-Men 1952; The Case of the Mukkinese Battle Horn 1955; The Running, Jumping and Standing Still Film 1959; Suspect 1960; Watch Your Stern 1960; Invasion Quartet 1961;

Postman's Knock 1961; What a Whopper! 1961; The Bed Sitting Room 1969; The Magic Christian 1969; The Magnificent Seven Deadly Sins 1971; Adolf Hitler - My Part in His Downfall 1972; The Adventures of Barry McKenzie 1972; Alice's Adventures in Wonderland 1972; Rentadick 1972; Digby, the Biggest Dog in the World 1973; Ghost in the Noonday Sun 1973; The Three Musketeers 1973; The Great McGonagall 1974; Man about the House 1974; The Hound of the Baskervilles 1977; The Last Remake of Beau Geste 1977; Yellowbeard 1983

Milliken, Angie Rough Diamonds 1994; Dead Heart 1996; Paperback Hero 1998

Millot, Charles (1921-2003) Trans-Europ-Express 1966; French Connection II 1975

Mills, Donna (1942-) The Incident 1967; Play Misty for Me 1971; Ladies of the House 2008

Mills, Frank Witness for the Prosecution 1982; Mrs Caldicot's Cabbage War 2000

Mills, Freddie (1919-1965) Emergency Call 1952; Kill Me Tomorrow 1957; Saturday Night Out 1963

Mills, Hayley (1946-) Tiger Bay 1959; Pollyanna 1960; In Search of the Castaways 1961; The Parent Trap 1961; Whistle down the Wind 1961; Summer Magic 1963; The Chalk Garden 1964; The Moon-Spinners 1964; The Truth about Spring 1964; Sky West and Crooked 1965; That Darn Cat! 1965; The Family Way 1966; The Trouble with Angels 1966; Pretty Polly 1967; Twisted Nerve 1968; Take a Girl like You 1970; Endless Night 1971; What Changed Charley Farthing? 1974; Appointment with Death 1988; After Midnight 1990; Stanley's Magic Garden 1994

Mills, John aka Mills, Sir John (1908-2005) The Ghost Camera 1933; Doctor's Orders 1934; Those Were the Days 1934; Car of Dreams 1935; Forever England 1935; Tudor Rose 1936; You're in the Army Now 1936; The Green Cockatoo 1937; Goodbye, Mr Chips 1939; Old Bill and Son 1940; The Black Sheep of Whitehall 1941; Cottage to Let 1941; The Big Blockade 1942; In Which We Serve 1942; We Dive at Dawn 1943; This Happy Breed 1944; Waterloo Road 1944; The Way to the Stars 1945; Great Expectations 1946; The October Man 1947; So Well Remembered 1947; The History of Mr Polly 1948; Scott of the Antarctic 1948; The Rocking Horse Winner 1949; Morning Departure 1950; Mr Denning Drives North 1951; The Gentle Gunman 1952; The Long Memory 1952; Hobson's Choice 1953; The Colditz Story 1954; The End of the Affair 1954; Above Us the Waves 1955; Around the World in 80 Days 1956; The Baby and the Battleship 1956; It's Great to Be Young 1956; Town on Trial 1956; War and Peace 1956; The Vicious Circle 1957; Dunkirk 1958; I Was Monty's Double 1958; Ice Cold in Alex 1958; Tiger Bay 1959; Season of Passion 1960; The Singer Not the Song 1960; Swiss Family Robinson 1960; Tunes of Glory 1960; Flame in the Streets 1961; Tiara Tahiti 1962; The Chalk Garden 1964; The Truth about Spring 1964; King Rat 1965; Operation Crossbow 1965; The Family Way 1966; The Wrong Box 1966; A Black Veil for Lisa 1969; Oh! What a Lovely War 1969; Run Wild, Run Free 1969; Adam's Woman 1970; Ryan's Daughter 1970; Dulcima 1971; Lady Caroline Lamb 1972; Young Winston 1972; Oklahoma Crude 1973; The Human Factor 1975; Trial by Combat 1976; The Devil's Advocate 1977; The Big Sleep 1978; The Thirty-Nine Steps 1978; The Quatermass Conclusion 1979; Zulu Dawn 1979; Gandhi 1982; Sahara 1983; Agatha Christie's Murder with Mirrors 1985; When the Wind Blows 1986; Who's That Girl 1987; Deadly Advice 1993; Bright Young Things 2003

Mills, Juliet (1941-) The October Man 1947; So Well Remembered 1947; No My Darling Daughter 1961; Twice round the Daffodils 1962; Carry On Jack 1963; Nurse on Wheels 1963; The Rare Breed 1966; Avanti! 1972; Jonathan Livingston Seagull 1973; The Cracker Factory 1979; The Other Sister 1999

Mills, Mort (1919-1993) Davy Crockett and the River Pirates 1956; Ride a Crooked Trail 1958; The Outlaws Is Coming 1965

Milner, Bill Son of Rambow 2007; Is Anybody There? 2008; Sex & Drugs & Rock & Roll 2009; Locke 2014

Milner, Martin aka Milner, Marty (1931-2015) Life with Father 1947; Operation Pacific 1951; Springfield Rifle

1952; Destination Gobi 1953; Francis in the Navy 1955; Sweet Smell of Success 1957; Marjorie Morningstar 1958; Too Much, Too Soon 1958; Compulsion 1959; The Private Lives of Adam and Eve 1959; 13 Ghosts 1959; Valley of the Dolls 1967; Three Guns for Texas 1968

Milo, Jean-Roger (1957-) Sarraouina 1986; L.627 1992; Germinal 1993; Lucie Aubrac 1997; Bent Keltoum 2001

Milo, Sandra (1933-) Classe Tous Risques 1959; General Della Rovere 1959; 8½ 1963; Juliet of the Spirits 1965

Milton, Billy (1905-1989) Aunt Sally 1933; Music Hath Charms 1935

Milton, Ernest (1890-1974) It's Love Again 1936; The Foreman Went to France 1941

Mimieux, Yvette (1942-) Platinum High School 1960; The Time Machine 1960; Where the Boys Are 1960; Light in the Piazza 1961; Diamond Head 1962; The Wonderful World of the Brothers Grimm 1962; Toys in the Attic 1963; The Reward 1965; Monkeys, Go Home! 1966; Dark of the Sun 1967; The Picasso Summer 1969; The Delta Factor 1970; Skyjacked 1972; The Neptune Factor 1973; Jackson County Jail 1976; The Black Hole 1979

Minazzoli, Christiane (1931-) The Story of O 1975; L'Enfer 1993

Minchenberg, Richard Wisdom 1986; One Good Turn 1996

Minciotti, Esther (1888-1962) Shockproof 1949; Marty 1955; Full of Life 1956; The Wrong Man 1956

Mineo, Sal (1939-1976) The Private War of Major Benson 1955; Rebel without a Cause 1955; Six Bridges to Cross 1955; Crime in the Streets 1956; Giant 1956; Rock, Pretty Baby 1956; Somebody Up There Likes Me 1956; Tonka 1958; The Gene Krupa Story 1959; Exodus 1960; Escape from Zahrain 1962; The Longest Day 1962; Cheyenne Autumn 1964; The Greatest Story Ever Told 1965; Stranger on the Run 1967; Eighty Steps to Jonah 1969; Escape from the Planet of the Apes 1971

Miner, Jan (1917-2004) Lenny 1974; Willie and Phil 1980; Mermaids 1990

Ming-Na aka Wen Ming-Na (1963-) The Joy Luck Club 1993; Street Fighter 1994; One Night Stand 1997; Mulan 1998; Final Fantasy: the Spirits Within 2001; Mulan II 2004; Push 2009

Minghella, Max (1985-) Bee Season 2005; How to Lose Friends & Alienate People 2008; Agora 2009; The Social Network 2010; The Darkest Hour 2011; The Ides of March 2011; 10 Years 2011; The Internship 2013

Minguez, Elvira The Reckoning 2001; The Dancer Upstairs 2002

Minnelli, Liza (1946-) In the Good Old Summertime 1949; Journey back to Oz 1964; Charlie Bubbles 1967; The Sterile Cuckoo 1969; Tell Me That You Love Me, Junie Moon 1970; Cabaret 1972; Lucky Lady 1975; A Matter of Time 1976; New York, New York 1977; Arthur 1981; The King of Comedy 1983; Arthur 2: On the Rocks 1988; Rent-a-Cop 1988; Stepping Out 1991; The West Side Waltz 1995

Minnette, Dylan Let Me In 2010; Alexander and the Terrible, Horrible, No Good, Very Bad Day 2014; Goosebumps 2015

Minogue, Kylie (1968-) The Delinquents 1989; Street Fighter 1994; Bio-Dome 1996; Diana & Me 1997; Cut 2000; Moulin Rouge! 2001; The Magic Roundabout 2005; Holy Motors 2012; 20,000 Days on Earth 2014

Minotis, Alexis (1898-1990) Land of the Pharaohs 1955; Boy on a Dolphin 1957

Minter, Kelly Jo aka Minter, Kelly Miracle Mile 1989; A Nightmare on Elm Street 5: The Dream Child 1989

Minter, Kristin Cool as Ice 1991; There Goes My Baby 1994

Mintz-Plasse, Christopher (1989-) Superbad 2007; Role Models 2008; Kick-Ass 2009; Year One 2009; How to Train Your Dragon 2010; Fright Night 2011; ParaNorman 2012; Kick-Ass 2 2013; Bad Neighbours 2014; Trolls 2016

Mioni, Fabrizio (1930-) Hercules 1957; The Blue Angel 1959; Get Yourself a College Girl 1964; Girl Happy 1965; The Spy with My Face 1966

Miou-Miou (1950-) Burnt Barns 1973; Les Valseuses 1974; No Problem! 1975; Jonah Who Will Be 25 in the Year 2000 1976; Roads to the South 1978; The Lady Cop 1979; Double Dare 1981; Entre Nous 1983; Tenue de Soirée 1986; La Lectrice 1988; The Revolving Doors 1988; Milou en Mai 1989; Germinal 1993; The Eighth Day 1996; The Science of Sleep 2005; The Concert 2009; Populaire 2012

Mira, Brigitte (1910-2005) Fear Eats the Soul 1973; The Enigma of Kaspar Hauser 1974; Mother Küsters Goes to Heaven 1975; Chinese Roulette 1976; Fear of Fear 1976; Berlin Alexanderplatz 1980

Miracle, Irene (1954-) Midnight Express 1978; Inferno 1980; Puppet Master 1989

Mirallegro, Nico Spike Island 2012; Shooting for Socrates 2014

Miranda, Aurora 1915-2005) Brazil 1944; Phantom Lady 1944

Miranda, Carmen (1909-1955) Down Argentine Way 1940; That Night in Rio 1941; Weekend in Havana 1941; Springtime in the Rockies 1942; The Gang's All Here 1943; Greenwich Village 1944; Something for the Boys 1944; Copacabana 1947; A Date with Judy 1948; Nancy Goes to Rio 1950; Scared Stiff 1953

Miranda, Isa (1905-1982) La Signora di Tutti 1934; Summertime 1955; The Empty Canvas 1963; The Night Porter 1973

Miranda, Robert Sons 1989; Sister Act 1992; Judge & Jury 1995; Blue Streak 1999

Miranda, Soledad (1943-1970) Count Dracula 1970; Vampyros Lesbos 1970

Mirel, Nicole Léon Morin, Priest 1961; The Seven Deadly Sins 1961

Miroslava (1925-1955) The Brave Bulls 1951; The Criminal Life of Archibaldo de la Cruz 1955; Stranger on Horseback 1955

Mirren, Helen (1945-) Age of Consent 1969; A Midsummer Night's Dream 1969; Savage Messiah 1972; O Lucky Man! 1973; Caligula 1979; The Long Good Friday 1979; SOS Titanic 1979; The Fiendish Plot of Dr Fu Manchu 1980; Excalibur 1981; Cal 1984; 2010 1984; White Nights 1985; Heavenly Pursuits 1986; The Mosquito Coast 1986; Pascali's Island 1988; The Cook, the Thief, His Wife and Her Lover 1989; When the Whales Came 1989; Bethune: the Making of a Hero 1990; The Comfort of Strangers 1991; Where Angels Fear to Tread 1991; The Hawk 1992; Prince of Jutland 1994; The Madness of King George 1995; Some Mother's Son 1996; Critical Care 1997; The Prince of Egypt 1998; Teaching Mrs Tingle 1999; Greenfingers 2000; The Pledge 2000; Gosford Park 2001; Last Orders 2001; Door to Door 2002; Calendar Girls 2003; The Clearing 2004; Raising Helen 2004; The Hitchhiker's Guide to the Galaxy 2005; The Queen 2006; Inkheart 2007; National Treasure: Book of Secrets 2007; The Last Station 2009; State of Play 2009; Brighton Rock 2010; The Debt 2010; Legend of the Guardians: the Owls of Ga'Hoole 2010; Red 2010; The Tempest 2010; Arthur 2011; Hitchcock 2012; Radioman 2012; Monsters University 2013; Phil Spector 2013; Red 2 2013; The Hundred-Foot Journey 2014; Eye in the Sky 2015; Trumbo 2015; Unity 2015; Woman in Gold 2015; Collateral Beauty 2016

Mirza, Jeff Infinite Justice 2006; Bigga than Ben: a Guide to Ripping Off London 2007

Mison, Tom Salmon Fishing in the Yemen 2011; Jadoo 2013

Mistal, Karen Return of the Killer Tomatoes 1988; Cannibal Women in the Avocado Jungle of Death 1989

Mr T (1952-) Rocky III 1982; The A-Team 1983; DC Cab 1983; Freaked 1993; Not Another Teen Movie 2001; Cloudy with a Chance of Meatballs 2009

Mistral, Jorge (1920-1972) Wuthering Heights 1939; Boy on a Dolphin 1957; The Sword and the Cross 1958

Mistry, Jimi (1973-) East Is East 1999; Born Romantic 2000; My Kingdom 2001; The Guru 2002; Ella Enchanted 2004; Things to Do before You're 30 2004; The Truth about Love 2004; Partition 2006; Exam 2009; Basement 2010; West Is West 2010

Mitchell, Mary Panic in Year Zero 1962; Dementia 13 1963; Spider Baby 1964

Mitchell-Smith, Ilan (1969-) The Wild Life 1984; Weird Science 1985; The Chocolate War 1988; Journey to the Center of the Earth 1989

Mitchell, Ann Lady Chatterley's Lover 1981; Paper Marriage 1991

Mitchell, Brian Stokes (1958-) Double Platinum 1999; Call Me Claus 2001

Mitchell, Cameron (1918-1994) High Barbaree 1947; Command Decision 1948; Homecoming 1948; Death of a Salesman 1951; Flight to Mars 1951; Les Misérables 1952; Pony Soldier 1952; How to Marry a Millionaire 1953; Man on a Tightrope 1953; Powder River

1953; Desiree 1954; Garden of Evil 1954; Gorilla at Large 1954; Hell and High Water 1954; House of Bamboo 1955; Love Me or Leave Me 1955; Strange Lady in Town 1955; The Tall Men 1955; Carousel 1956; Tension at Table Rock 1956; The Day They Gave Babies Away 1957; Escapade in Japan 1957; No Down Payment 1957; Blood and Black Lace 1964; Hombre 1967; Rebel Rousers 1967; Buck and the Preacher 1972; Viva Knievel! 1977; The Toolbox Murders 1978; Without Warning 1980

Mitchell, Charlotte (1926-2012) Curtain Up 1952; Blood on Satan's Claw 1970; The French Lieutenant's Woman 1981

Mitchell, Chuck (1927-1992) Porky's 1981; Porky's Revenge 1985

Mitchell, Daryl aka **Mitchell, Daryl "Chill"** Sgt Bilko 1996; A Thin Line between Love and Hate 1996; Galaxy Quest 1999; The Country Bears 2002

Mitchell, Donna Less than Zero 1987; Psycho IV: the Beginning 1990; Two Bits 1995

Mitchell, Eddy (1942-) Coup de Torchon 1981; Le Bonheur Est dans le Pré 1995

Mitchell, Elizabeth (1970-) Gia 1998; Molly 1999; Frequency 2000; The Santa Clause 2 2002; The Santa Clause 3: the Escape Clause 2006

Mitchell, Frank (1905-1991) Stand Up and Cheer! 1934; The Singing Kid 1936

Mitchell, George (1905-1972) The Wild and the Innocent 1959; The Andromeda Strain 1970

Mitchell (1), Gordon (1923-2003) The Good Die First 1967; Reflections in a Golden Eye 1967

Mitchell, Grant (1874-1957) No Man of Her Own 1932; A Successful Calamity 1932; Central Airport 1933; Our Betters 1933; 20,000 Years in Sing Sing 1933; The Case of the Howling Dog 1934; The Secret Bride 1934; Gold Diggers of 1935 1935; In Person 1935; A Midsummer Night's Dream 1935; The Ex-Mrs Bradford 1936; Next Time We Love 1936; Hell's Kitchen 1939; The Great Lie 1941; One Foot in Heaven 1941; Skylark 1941; Dixie 1943; Arsenic and Old Lace 1944; Guest Wife 1944; Laura 1944; Bring On the Girls 1945; Conflict 1945

Mitchell, Heather Proof 1991; Rogue 2007

Mitchell, James (1920-2010) Border Incident 1949; Colorado Territory 1949; Devil's Doorway 1950; Stars in My Crown 1950; The Toast of New Orleans 1950; The Band Wagon 1953; The Prodigal 1955

Mitchell, Joanne Before Dawn 2012; Bait 2015

Mitchell, Julien (1884-1954) The Last Journey 1936; It's in the Air 1938; Vigil in the Night 1940; The Goose Steps Out 1942; Rhythm Serenade 1943; Hotel Reserve 1944; Chance of a Lifetime 1950

Mitchell, Justine Goldfish Memory 2003; The Honeymooners 2003

Mitchell, Kel (1978-) Good Burger 1997; Mystery Men 1999; Clifford's Really Big Movie 2004

Mitchell, Kirsty (1974-) Greyfriars Bobby 2005; TuEsday 2007

Mitchell, Millard (1900-1953) A Double Life 1947; A Foreign Affair 1948; Everybody Does It 1949; Thieves' Highway 1949; Twelve o'Clock High 1949; Convicted 1950; The Gunfighter 1950; Mister 880 1950; Winchester '73 1950; You're in the Navy Now 1951; Singin' in the Rain 1952; Here Come the Girls 1953; The Naked Spur 1953

Mitchell, Norman (1918-2001) Dick Turpin - Highwayman 1956; Nearest and Dearest 1972; Frankenstein and the Monster from Hell 1973

Mitchell, Radha (1973-) Love and Other Catastrophes 1996; High Art 1998; Pitch Black 1999; Dead Heat 2002; Phone Booth 2002; Finding Neverland 2004; Man on Fire 2004; Melinda and Melinda 2004; Silent Hill 2006; Feast of Love 2007; Rogue 2007; Surrogates 2009; The Crazies 2010; Silent Hill: Revelation 2012; The Frozen Ground 2013; The Darkness 2016

Mitchell, Sasha (1967-) Kickboxer 2: the Road Back 1990; Kickboxer III: the Art of War 1992

Mitchell, Thomas (1892-1962) Theodora Goes Wild 1936; The Hurricane 1937; Lost Horizon 1937; Make Way for Tomorrow 1937; When You're in Love 1937; Trade Winds 1938; Gone with the Wind 1939; The Hunchback of Notre Dame 1939; Mr Smith Goes to Washington 1939; Only Angels Have Wings 1939; Stagecoach 1939; Angels over Broadway 1940; The

Long Voyage Home 1940; Our Town 1940; Swiss Family Robinson 1940; Out of the Fog 1941; The Black Swan 1942; Joan of Paris 1942; Moontide 1942; Song of the Islands 1942; This above All 1942; Bataan 1943; The Immortal Sergeant 1943; The Outlaw 1943; Buffalo Bill 1944; Dark Waters 1944; The Fighting Sullivans 1944; The Keys of the Kingdom 1944; Wilson 1944; Adventure 1945; Capt Eddie 1945; The Dark Mirror 1946; It's a Wonderful Life 1946; High Barbaree 1947; Silver River 1948; Alias Nick Beal 1949; The Big Wheel 1949; High Noon 1952; Destry 1954; Secret of the Incas 1954; While the City Sleeps 1956; By Love Possessed 1961; Pocketful of Miracles 1961

Mitchell, Warren (1926-2015) Barnacle Bill 1957; Manuela 1957; The Trollenberg Terror 1958; Tommy the Toreador 1959; The Boy Who Stole a Million 1960; Surprise Package 1960; Don't Bother to Knock 1961; Postman's Knock 1961; The Main Attraction 1962; Calculated Risk 1963; The Small World of Sammy Lee 1963; Carry On Cleo 1964; The Sicilians 1964; The Night Caller 1965; Drop Dead Darling 1966; The Sandwich Man 1966; The Jokers 1967; The Best House in London 1968; Diamonds for Breakfast 1968; Till Death Us Do Part 1968; The Assassination Bureau 1969; Moon Zero Two 1969; What Changed Charley Farthing? 1974; Jabberwocky 1977; Stand Up Virgin Soldiers 1977; Meetings with Remarkable Men 1979; Norman Loves Rose 1982; The Plague Dogs 1982; The Chain 1984; Foreign Body 1986

Mitchell, Yvonne (1925-1979) The Queen of Spades 1948; Turn the Key Softly 1953; The Divided Heart 1954; Yield to the Night 1956; Woman in a Dressing Gown 1957; Passionate Summer 1958; Sapphire 1959; Tiger Bay 1959; Conspiracy of Hearts 1960; The Trials of Oscar Wilde 1960; The Main Attraction 1962; The Corpse 1969; Demons of the Mind 1971; The Great Waltz 1972

Mitchum, Bentley (1967-) The Man in the Moon 1991; Ruby in Paradise 1993; Shark Attack 1999; A Crack in the Floor 2000

Mitchum, Christopher aka **Mitchum, Chris** (1943-) Rio Lobo 1970; Big Jake 1971; The Day Time Ended 1980

Mitchum, James aka **Mitchum, Jim** (1941-) Thunder Road 1958; The Beat Generation 1959; Young Guns of Texas 1962; Ambush Bay 1966; The Heroes 1968; Maniac 1977; Fatal Mission 1990

Mitchum, John (1919-2001) Hitler 1962; Dirty Harry 1971; The Enforcer 1976

Mitchum, Robert aka **Mitchum, Bob** (1917-1997) Corvette K-225 1943; The Dancing Masters 1943; Gung Ho! 1943; Betrayed 1944; Girl Rush 1944; Johnny Doesn't Live Here Anymore 1944; Mr Winkle Goes to War 1944; Nevada 1944; Thirty Seconds over Tokyo 1944; The Story of GI Joe 1945; The Locket 1946; Till the End of Time 1946; Undercurrent 1946; Build My Gallows High 1947; Crossfire 1947; Desire Me 1947; Pursued 1947; Blood on the Moon 1948; Rachel and the Stranger 1948; The Big Steal 1949; Holiday Affair 1949; The Red Pony 1949; Where Danger Lives 1950; His Kind of Woman 1951; My Forbidden Past 1951; The Racket 1951; The Lusty Men 1952; Macao 1952; One Minute to Zero 1952; Angel Face 1953; Second Chance 1953; White Witch Doctor 1953; Beautiful but Dangerous 1954; River of No Return 1954; Track of the Cat 1954; Man with the Gun 1955; The Night of the Hunter 1955; Not as a Stranger 1955; Bandido 1956; Foreign Intrigue 1956; The Enemy Below 1957; Fire Down Below 1957; Heaven Knows, Mr Allison 1957; The Hunters 1958; Thunder Road 1958; The Angry Hills 1959; The Wonderful Country 1959; The Grass Is Greener 1960; Home from the Hill 1960; The Sundowners 1960; A Terrible Beauty 1960; Cape Fear 1962; The Longest Day 1962; Two for the Seesaw 1962; The List of Adrian Messenger 1963; What a Way to Go! 1964; El Dorado 1967; The Way West 1967; Anzio 1968; 5 Card Stud 1968; Secret Ceremony 1968; The Good Guys and the Bad Guys 1969; Young Billy Young 1969; Ryan's Daughter 1970; Going Home 1971; The Wrath of God 1972; The Friends of Eddie Coyle 1973; Farewell, My Lovely 1975; The Yakuza 1975; Battle of Midway 1976; The Last Tycoon 1976; The Amsterdam Kill 1978; The Big Sleep 1978; Breakthrough 1978;

Matilda 1978; Agency 1981; That Championship Season 1982; The Ambassador 1984; Maria's Lovers 1984; Reunion at Fairborough 1985; Mr North 1988; Scrooged 1988; Cape Fear 1991; Tombstone 1993; Dead Man 1995

Mitevska, Labina (1975-) Before the Rain 1994; I Want You 1998

Mito, Mitsuko (1919-1981) There Was a Father 1942; My Love Has Been Burning 1949; Ugetsu Monogatari 1953

Mitra, Rhona (1976-) Get Carter 2000; Ali G indahouse 2002; Highwaymen 2003; The Life of David Gale 2003; The Number 23 2006; Skinwalkers 2006; Shooter 2007; Doomsday 2008; Underworld: Rise of the Lycans 2009; Reuniting the Rubins 2010

Mitsuishi, Ken (1961-) The Pillow Book 1995; Chaos 1999; Eureka 2000

Mitsushima, Hikari Love Exposure 2008; Hara-Kiri: Death of a Samurai 2011

Mittal, Madhur Slumdog Millionaire 2008; Million Dollar Arm 2014

Miura, Mitsuko The Loyal 47 Ronin 1941; The Victory of Women 1946

Mixon, Katy Take Shelter 2011; Hell or High Water 2016

Miyaguchi, Seiji (1913-1985) Seven Samurai 1954; The Ballad of Narayama 1958; Twin Sisters of Kyoto 1963

Miyake, Kuniko (1916-1992) Poppy 1935; Hen in the Wind 1948; My Love Has Been Burning 1949; Early Summer 1951; The Flavour of Green Tea over Rice 1952; Tokyo Story 1953; Early Spring 1956; Escapade in Japan 1957; Ohayo 1959; An Autumn Afternoon 1962

Miyamoto, Nobuko (1945-) Death Japanese Style 1984; Tampopo 1986; A Taxing Woman 1987

Miyasako, Hiroyuki Casshern 2004; Kamikaze Girls: the End 2004

Miyazaki, Aoi Eureka 2000; Wolf Children 2012

Miyazawa, Rie (1973-) The Twilight Samurai 2002; Tony Takitani 2004

Miyori, Kim (1951-) The Big Picture 1989; The Punisher 1989; Body Shot 1994; Metro 1997

Miyoshi, Eiko (1894-1963) No Regrets for Our Youth 1946; I Live in Fear 1955

Mizrahi, Isaac For Love or Money 1993; Unzipped 1995

Mizuno, Kumi (1937-) Frankenstein Conquers the World 1964; Invasion of the Astro-Monster 1965; Ebirah, Horror of the Deep 1966; War of the Gargantuas 1970

Mnene, Charles The Great Ecstasy of Robert Carmichael 2005; New Town Killers 2009

Mnich, Geneviève Sunday in the Country 1984; Anna M. 2007; Séraphine 2008

Mo'Nique Two Can Play That Game 2001; Precious (Base on Nol by Saf) (Based on the Novel "Push" by Sapphire) 2008; Welcome Home Roscoe Jenkins 2008

Mobley, Mary Ann (1937-2014) Get Yourself a College Girl 1964; Girl Happy 1965; Harum Scarum 1965; Three on a Couch 1966; The King's Pirate 1967

Mobley, Roger (1949-) Jack the Giant Killer 1962; Emil and the Detectives 1964

Mocky, Jean-Pierre (1929-) The Vanquished 1953; Grandeur et Décadence d'un Petit Commerce de Cinéma 1986

Modine, Matthew (1959-) Baby It's You 1983; Streamers 1983; Birdy 1984; The Hotel New Hampshire 1984; Mrs Soffel 1984; Vision Quest 1985; Full Metal Jacket 1987; Orphans 1987; Married to the Mob 1988; A Cut Above 1989; Memphis Belle 1990; Pacific Heights 1990; Equinox 1992; Wind 1992; And the Band Played On 1993; Short Cuts 1993; The Browning Version 1994; Bye Bye Love 1995; CutThroat Island 1995; Fluke 1995; The Blackout 1997; The Maker 1997; The Real Blonde 1997; Any Given Sunday 1999; Flowers for Algernon 2000; Le Divorce 2003; The Transporter 2 2005; Sex and Lies in Sin City 2008; A Cat in Paris 2010; Too Big to Fail 2011; Wrinkles 2011; The Dark Knight Rises 2012; jOBS 2013

Modot, Gaston (1887-1970) The Ship of Lost Men 1929; L'Age d'Or 1930; Sous les Toits de Paris 1930; La Grande Illusion 1937; La Règle du Jeu 1939; Casque d'Or 1952

Moeller, Ralph (1959-) Best of the Best II 1992; Universal Soldier 1992

Moffat, Donald (1930-) Rachel, Rachel 1968; The Great Northfield Minnesota Raid 1972; Showdown 1973; The Terminal Man 1974; Popeye 1980; The White Lions 1980; The Thing 1982; Monster in the Closet 1983; The Right Stuff 1983; Who Will Love My Children?

1983; Alamo Bay 1985; The Best of Times 1986; Far North 1988; The Unbearable Lightness of Being 1988; Music Box 1989; Class Action 1991; Regarding Henry 1991; HouseSitter 1992; Clear and Present Danger 1994; Love, Cheat & Steal 1994; Trapped in Paradise 1994

Moffett, Graham (1919-1965) Where There's a Will 1936; Windbag the Sailor 1936; Dr Syn 1937; Good Morning, Boys 1937; Oh, Mr Porter! 1937; Ask a Policeman 1938; Convict 99 1938; Old Bones of the River 1938; Owd Bob 1938; Cheer Boys Cheer 1939; Where's That Fire? 1939; Charley's (Big Hearted) Aunt 1940; I Thank You 1941; Back Room Boy 1942; Time Flies 1944

Moffett, D W (1954-) An Early Frost 1985; Sad Inheritance 1993; Rough Magic 1995; Stealing Beauty 1995; When the Bough Breaks 2: Perfect Prey 1998; Molly 1999; Kill Me Later 2001; Thirteen 2003; Twisted 2003

Moffett, Gregory Let's Dance 1950; Robot Monster 1953

Moffett, Michelle Hired to Kill 1990; Indecent Behavior 1993

Moffett, Sharyn (1936-) The Body Snatcher 1945; The Falcon in San Francisco 1945; Child of Divorce 1946; The Locket 1946; Mr Blandings Builds His Dream House 1948; The Judge Steps Out 1949

Mohner, Carl (1921-2005) Rififi 1955; Celui Qui Doit Mourir 1957; Behind the Mask 1958; The Camp on Blood Island 1958; Passionate Summer 1958; The Challenge 1960; Sink the Bismarck! 1960; The Kitchen 1961; Callan 1974

Mohr, Gerald (1914-1968) Gilda 1946; Undercover Girl 1950; Sirocco 1951; The Duel at Silver Creek 1952; The Ring 1952; The Sniper 1952; The Eddie Cantor Story 1953; Raiders of the Seven Seas 1953; The Angry Red Planet 1959; This Rebel Breed 1960

Mohr, Jay (1970-) For Better or Worse 1995; Jerry Maguire 1996; Picture Perfect 1997; Suicide Kings 1997; Jane Austen's Mafia 1998; Paulie 1998; Cherry Falls 1999; 200 Cigarettes 1999; Pay It Forward 2000; Pluto Nash 2001; SIMØNE 2002; Are We There Yet? 2005; Street Kings 2008; Hereafter 2010

Möhring, Wotan Wilke Antibodies 2005; The Silence 2010

Mohyeddin, Zia (1933-) Sammy Going South 1963; Khartoum 1966; The Sailor from Gibraltar 1967; They Came from beyond Space 1967; Bombay Talkie 1970; The Assam Garden 1985 (sic) (The Assam Garden 1985); Out of the Fog (see above)

Moir, Richard (1950-) The Odd Angry Shot 1979; Heatwave 1981

Mok, Karen (1970-) Fallen Angels 1995; Black Mask 1996; Kitchen 1997; So Close 2002; Man of Tai Chi 2013

Mokae, Zakes (1935-2009) Agatha Christie's A Caribbean Mystery 1983; Cry Freedom 1987; The Serpent and the Rainbow 1987; Dad 1989; A Dry White Season 1989; Body Parts 1991; A Rage in Harlem 1991; Dust Devil 1992; Vampire in Brooklyn 1995

Mol, Gretchen (1972-) The Funeral 1996; Girl 6 1996; The Last Time I Committed Suicide 1996; Subway Stories: Tales from the Underground 1997; Music from Another Room 1998; Rounders 1998; Finding Graceland 1999; Forever Mine 1999; Sweet and Lowdown 1999; The Thirteenth Floor 1999; Attraction 2000; Get Carter 2000; The Magnificent Ambersons 2001; The Shape of Things 2003; The Notorious Bettie Page 2005; 3:10 to Yuma 2007; The Memory Keeper's Daughter 2008; Say When 2014; True Story 2015

Molina, Alfred (1953-) Raiders of the Lost Ark 1981; Number One 1984; Eleni 1985; Ladyhawke 1985; Letter to Brezhnev 1985; Prick Up Your Ears 1987; Not without My Daughter 1990; American Friends 1991; Enchanted April 1991; The Trial 1993; Maverick 1994; The Steal 1994; White Fang 2: Myth of the White Wolf 1994; Hideaway 1995; The Perez Family 1995; Scorpion Spring 1995; Species 1995; Before and After 1996; Mojave Moon 1996; Anna Karenina 1997; The Man Who Knew Too Little 1997; The Impostors 1998; Dudley Do-Right 1999; Magnolia 1999; Chocolat 2000; Murder on the Orient Express 2001; Texas Rangers 2001; Frida 2002; My Life without Me 2002; Coffee and Cigarettes 2003; Identity 2003; Spider-Man 2 2004; Steamboy 2004; As You Like It 2006; The Da Vinci Code 2006; The Hoax 2006; Silk 2007; An Education 2008; The Lodger 2009; The Pink Panther 2 2009; Prince of Persia: the Sands of Time 2010; The Sorcerer's Apprentice 2010; The Tempest 2010; Abduction 2011;

Rango 2011; Justin and the Knights of Valour 2013; Monsters University 2013; Love Is Strange 2014; The Normal Heart 2014; We'll Never Have Paris 2014; Whiskey Tango Foxtrot 2016

Molina, Angela (1955-) That Obscure Object of Desire 1977; Camorra 1985; Lola 1986; Streets of Gold 1986; 1492: Conquest of Paradise 1992; Live Flesh 1997; Wind with the Gone 1998; One of the Hollywood Ten 2000; Baaria 2009; Broken Embraces 2009

Molina, Miguel (1963-) 1919 1983; The Law of Desire 1987

Moll, Giorgia aka Moll, Georgia (1938-) The Quiet American 1958; The White Warrior 1959; Island of Love 1963; Le Mépris 1963

Moll, Richard (1943-) House 1986; Wicked Stepmother 1989; The Secret Agent Club 1995; The Glass Cage 1996

Mollà, Jordi aka Molla, Jordi (1968-) Jamón, Jamón 1992; Dollar for the Dead 1998; Second Skin 2000; Blow 2001; Bad Boys II 2003; The Alamo 2004; Elizabeth: the Golden Age 2007; Riddick 2013

Moller, Roland R 2010; A Hijacking 2012

Mollet, Clotilde The Page Turner 2006; Untouchable 2011

Mollison, Henry (1905-1985) The Lone Wolf Returns 1936; The Loves of Joanna Godden 1947; What the Butler Saw 1950; The Man in the White Suit 1951

Molloy, Dearbhla Taffin 1988; The Run of the Country 1995; This Is the Sea 1996

Molnar, Tibor (1921-1982) The Round-Up 1966; The Red and the White 1967

Momoa, Jason (1979-) Returning Lily 2003; Conan the Barbarian 2011; Bullet to the Head 2012; Wolves 2013; Aquaman 2018

Momoi, Kaori (1952-) Memoirs of a Geisha 2005; The Sun 2005

Momsen, Taylor The Grinch 2000; Paranoid Park 2007; Underdog 2007

Monaghan, Dominic (1976-) The Lord of the Rings: The Fellowship of the Ring 2001; The Lord of the Rings: The Two Towers 2002; The Lord of the Rings: The Return of the King 2003; X-Men Origins: Wolverine 2009; Molly Moon and the Incredible Book of Hypnotism 2015

Monaghan, Michelle (1976-) It Runs in the Family 2002; Kiss Kiss Bang Bang 2005; Mr & Mrs Smith 2005; North Country 2005; Mission: Impossible III 2006; Gone Baby Gone 2007; The Heartbreak Kid 2007; Eagle Eye 2008; Made of Honor 2008; Trucker 2009; Due Date 2010; Somewhere 2010; Machine Gun Preacher 2011; Mission: Impossible - Ghost Protocol 2011; Source Code 2011; The Best of Me 2014; Better Living through Chemistry 2014; Playing It Cool 2014; Pixels 2015

Monahan, Dan Porky's 1981; Porky's Revenge 1985; Stephen King's The Night Flier 1997

Mondesir, Merwin Plague City: Sars in Toronto 2005; Grave Encounters 2010

Mondy, Pierre (1925-) The Battle of Austerlitz 1960; The Mysteries of Paris 1962; The Sleeping Car Murders 1965

Monette, Richard (1944-2008) Dancing in the Dark 1986; I've Heard the Mermaids Singing 1987

Monfort, Sylvia (1925-1991) The Eagle Has Two Heads 1948; The Case of Dr Laurent 1957

Mong, William V (1875-1940) The Strong Man 1926; What Price Glory 1926; Treasure Island 1934

Monk, Debra (1949-) Center Stage 2000; Milwaukee, Minnesota 2002; Eloise at the Plaza 2003; Palindromes 2004

Monk, Thelonious (1917-1982) Jazz on a Summer's Day 1959; Thelonious Monk: Straight No Chaser 1988

Monkhouse, Bob (1928-2003) The Secret People 1951; Carry On Sergeant 1958; Dentist in the Chair 1960; Dentist on the Job 1961; She'll Have to Go 1961; Thunderbirds Are Go! 1966; The Bliss of Mrs Blossom 1968; Simon, Simon 1970

Monlaur, Yvonne The Brides of Dracula 1960; Circus of Horrors 1960; Inn for Trouble 1960

Monod, Jacques (1918-1985) A Ravishing Idiot 1964; The Game Is Over 1966

Monoson, Lawrence (1965-) Gaby: a True Story 1987; Starship Troopers 2: Hero of the Federation 2004

Monroe, Maika The Guest 2014; It Follows 2014

Monroe, Marilyn (1926-1962) Dangerous Years 1947; Ladies of the Chorus 1949; Love Happy 1949; All about Eve 1950; The Asphalt Jungle 1950; The Fireball 1950; Right Cross 1950; A Ticket to Tomahawk 1950; As Young as You Feel 1951; Home Town Story 1951; Let's Make It Legal 1951; Love Nest 1951; Clash by Night 1952; Don't Bother to Knock 1952; Monkey Business 1952; O Henry's Full House 1952; We're Not Married 1952; Gentlemen Prefer Blondes 1953; How to Marry a Millionaire 1953; Niagara 1953; River of No Return 1954; There's No Business like Show Business 1954; The Seven Year Itch 1955; Bus Stop 1956; The Prince and the Showgirl 1957; Some Like It Hot 1959; Let's Make Love 1960; The Misfits 1961; The Love Goddesses 1965; Cameraman: the Life & Work of Jack Cardiff 2010

Montagu, Felicity I Want Candy 2006; Alan Partridge: Alpha Papa 2013

Montague, Lee (1927-) The Secret Partner 1961; Operation Snatch 1962; How I Won the War 1967; Nobody Runs Forever 1968; Eagle in a Cage 1971; The Best Pair of Legs in the Business 1972; Brother Sun, Sister Moon 1972; Mahler 1974; The Legacy 1978; Silver Dream Racer 1980; Kim 1984; Madame Sousatzka 1988

Montalà, Irene (1976-) Beloved/Friend 1998; Russian Dolls 2005

Montalban, Carlos (1903-1991) The Harder They Fall 1956; Pepe 1960; Bananas 1971

Montalban, Ricardo (1920-2009) Fiesta 1947; On an Island with You 1948; Battleground 1949; Border Incident 1949; The Kissing Bandit 1949; Neptune's Daughter 1949; Mystery Street 1950; Right Cross 1950; Across the Wide Missouri 1951; Sombrero 1952; Latin Lovers 1953; A Life in the Balance 1955; Sayonara 1957; Let No Man Write My Epitaph 1960; Gordon the Black Pirate 1961; Hemingway's Adventures of a Young Man 1962; The Reluctant Saint 1962; Love Is a Ball 1963; Cheyenne Autumn 1964; Madame X 1966; The Singing Nun 1966; Blue 1968; Sweet Charity 1968; The Deserter 1971; The Face of Fear 1971; Conquest of the Planet of the Apes 1972; The Train Robbers 1973; The Mark of Zorro 1974; Star Trek II: The Wrath of Khan 1982; The Naked Gun 1988; SPYkids 2: the Island of Lost Dreams 2002; SPYkids 3-D: Game Over 2003

Montand, Yves (1921-1991) Les Portes de la Nuit 1946; The Wages of Fear 1953; Marguerite de la Nuit 1955; Napoléon 1955; The Witches of Salem 1957; Let's Make Love 1960; Goodbye Again 1961; Sanctuary 1961; Le Joli Mai 1962; My Geisha 1962; The Sleeping Car Murders 1965; Grand Prix 1966; La Guerre Est Finie 1966; Is Paris Burning? 1966; Vivre pour Vivre 1967; Z 1968; The Confession 1970; On a Clear Day You Can See Forever 1970; The Red Circle 1970; Delusions of Grandeur 1971; César and Rosalie 1972; State of Siege 1972; Tout Va Bien 1972; Vincent, François, Paul and the Others 1974; Call Him Savage 1975; Roads to the South 1978; Choice of Arms 1981; Jean de Florette 1986; Manon des Sources 1986; IP5 1992

Monteith, Cory (1982-2013) Hybrid 2007; Monte Carlo 2011

Montell, Lisa (1933-) Escape to Burma 1955; Ten Thousand Bedrooms 1957

Montenegro, Conchita (1912-2007) The Cisco Kid 1931; Laughing at Life 1933; Caravan 1934

Montenegro, Fernanda (1929-) Hour of the Star 1985; Central Station 1998; Love in the Time of Cholera 2007

Montero, Germaine (1909-2000) Knave of Hearts 1954; Le Masque de Fer 1962; Any Number Can Win 1963; Robert et Robert 1978

Monteros, Rosenda (1935-) Battle Shock 1956; The Magnificent Seven 1960; Tiara Tahiti 1962; She 1965; Cauldron of Blood 1967

Montés, Elisa (1936-) Return of the Seven 1966; Texas Adios 1966; Captain Apache 1971

Montevecchi, Liliane (1932-) The Living Idol 1955; Moonfleet 1955; Meet Me in Las Vegas 1956; King Creole 1958

Montez, Maria (1918-1951) That Night in Rio 1941; Arabian Nights 1942; White Savage 1943; Ali Baba and the Forty Thieves 1944; Cobra Woman 1944; Follow the Boys 1944; Sudan 1945; The Exile 1947

Montgomery, Belinda J aka

Montgomery, Belinda (1950-) The Other Side of the Mountain 1975; Breaking Point 1976

Montgomery, Douglass aka Douglass, Kent (1907-1966) Waterloo Bridge 1931; Little Women 1933; Little Man, What Now? 1934; The Mystery of Edwin Drood 1935; Everything Is Thunder 1936; The Cat and the Canary 1939; The Way to the Stars 1945

Montgomery, Elizabeth (1933-1995) The Court-Martial of Billy Mitchell 1955; Johnny Cool 1963; Who's Been Sleeping in My Bed? 1963; How to Fill a Wild Bikini 1965; Dark Victory 1976; Black Widow Murders 1993

Montgomery, Flora (1974-) When Brendan Met Trudy 2000; Goldfish Memory 2003; Rabbit Fever 2005

Montgomery, George (1916-2000) The Cisco Kid and the Lady 1939; Young People 1940; Riders of the Purple Sage 1941; China Girl 1942; Orchestra Wives 1942; Roxie Hart 1942; Ten Gentlemen from West Point 1942; Coney Island 1943; Three Little Girls in Blue 1946; Belle Starr's Daughter 1948; The Girl from Manhattan 1948; Lulu Belle 1948; Indian Uprising 1951; The Sword of Monte Cristo 1951; Gun Duel in Durango 1957; Last of the Badmen 1957; Battle of the Bulge 1965

Montgomery, Lee aka Montgomery, Lee H aka Montgomery, Lee Harcourt (1961-) The Harness 1971; The Million Dollar Duck 1971; Ben 1972; Pete 'n' Tillie 1972; The Savage Is Loose 1974; Baker's Hawk 1976; Burnt Offerings 1976; Mutant 1984; Girls Just Want to Have Fun 1985

Montgomery, Poppy (1975-) Dead Man on Campus 1998; The Other Sister 1999; Million Dollar Murder 2004; Raising Waylon 2004; Between 2005; Lying to Be Perfect 2010; Magic beyond Words: the JK Rowling Story 2011

Montgomery, Robert (1904-1981) The Big House 1930; The Divorcee 1930; Free and Easy 1930; Inspiration 1931; Private Lives 1931; Strangers May Kiss 1931; Blondie of the Follies 1932; Faithless 1932; Night Flight 1933; When Ladies Meet 1933; Forsaking All Others 1934; Riptide 1934; Vanessa, Her Love Story 1935; Piccadilly Jim 1936; Trouble for Two 1936; The Last of Mrs Cheyney 1937; Live, Love and Learn 1937; Night Must Fall 1937; Three Loves Has Nancy 1938; Fast and Loose 1939; Busman's Honeymoon 1940; The Earl of Chicago 1940; Here Comes Mr Jordan 1941; Mr and Mrs Smith 1941; Rage in Heaven 1941; Unfinished Business 1941; They Were Expendable 1945; Lady in the Lake 1947; June Bride 1948; The Saxon Charm 1948; Eye Witness 1949; Once More, My Darling 1949

Montiel, Sarita (1928-) Vera Cruz 1954; Serenade 1956; Run of the Arrow 1957

Montoute, Edouard La Haine 1995; Femme Fatale 2002

Moody, Jim (1932-) Personal Best 1982; Bad Boys 1983; Who's the Man? 1993

Moody, Lynne (1946-) White Dog 1981; Last Light 1993

Moody, Ralph (1887-1971) Road to Bali 1952; The Legend of Tom Dooley 1959

Moody, Ron (1924-2015) A Pair of Briefs 1962; Ladies Who Do 1963; The Mouse on the Moon 1963; Every Day's a Holiday 1964; Murder Most Foul 1964; The Sandwich Man 1966; Oliver! 1968; The Twelve Chairs 1970; Flight of the Doves 1971; Dogpound Shuffle 1974; Legend of the Werewolf 1974; Dominique 1978; The Spaceman and King Arthur 1979; Where Is Parsifal? 1983; A Ghost in Monte Carlo 1990; Revelation 2001; Paradise Grove 2003

Moog, Heinz (1908-1989) Senso 1954; The Secret Ways 1961

Moon, Keith (1947-1978) 200 Motels 1971; That'll Be the Day 1973; Stardust 1974; Tommy 1975; The Kids Are Alright 1978; Sextette 1978

Moon, Sheri aka Moon Zombie, Sheri (1970-) House of 1000 Corpses 2001; The Devil's Rejects 2005; Halloween 2007; Halloween II 2009

Mooney, Paul Dance with a Stranger 1984; Bamboozled 2000

Moore, Alvy (1921-1997) The Glory Brigade 1953; Riot in Cell Block 11 1954; Susan Slept Here 1954; An Annapolis Story 1955; Brotherhood of Satan 1970; A Boy and His Dog 1975

Moore, Bobby (1941-1993) Escape to Victory 1981; Bo66y 2016

Moore, Clayton (1908-1999) The Far Frontier 1949; Riders of the Whistling Pines 1949; The Lone Ranger 1956

Moore, Colleen (1899-1988) Lilac Time 1928; The Power and the Glory 1933

Moore, Constance (1919-2005) Wives under Suspicion 1938; You Can't Cheat an Honest Man 1939; Argentine Nights 1940; I Wanted Wings 1941; Take a Letter, Darling 1942; Atlantic City 1944; Show Business 1944; Earl Carroll Vanities 1945

Moore (1), Deborah aka Barrymore, Deborah aka Moore, Deborah Maria (1963-) Lionheart 1986; Bullseye! 1990; Into the Sun 1992

Moore, Del (1916-1970) Stagecoach to Dancer's Rock 1962; The Nutty Professor 1963; The Disorderly Orderly 1964; The Big Mouth 1967

Moore, Demi (1962-) Parasite 1982; Young Doctors in Love 1982; Blame It on Rio 1984; St Elmo's Fire 1985; About Last Night... 1986; One Crazy Summer 1986; Wisdom 1986; The Seventh Sign 1988; We're No Angels 1989; Ghost 1990; The Butcher's Wife 1991; Mortal Thoughts 1991; Nothing but Trouble 1991; A Few Good Men 1992; Indecent Proposal 1993; Disclosure 1994; Now and Then 1995; The Scarlet Letter 1995; Beavis and Butt-head Do America 1996; The Hunchback of Notre Dame 1996; If These Walls Could Talk 1996; The Juror 1996; Striptease 1996; Deconstructing Harry 1997; GI Jane 1997; Passion of Mind 2000; Charlie's Angels: Full Throttle 2003; Bobby 2006; Half Light 2006; Flawless 2007; Mr Brooks 2007; The Joneses 2009; Bunraku 2010; LOL 2011; Margin Call 2011; Forsaken 2015

Moore, Dennie (1907-1978) Sylvia Scarlett 1936; Saturday's Children 1940

Moore, Dennis aka Meadows, Denny (1908-1964) The Dawn Rider 1935; The Mummy's Curse 1944

Moore, Dickie (1925-2015) Blonde Venus 1932; So Big 1932; Union Depot 1932; Gabriel over the White House 1933; Man's Castle 1933; Gallant Lady 1934; Upper World 1934; Peter Ibbetson 1935; So Red the Rose 1935; Miss Annie Rooney 1942; Sweet and Lowdown 1944

Moore, Dudley (1935-2002) The Wrong Box 1966; Bedazzled 1967; 30 Is a Dangerous Age, Cynthia 1968; The Bed Sitting Room 1969; Monte Carlo or Bust! 1969; Alice's Adventures in Wonderland 1972; Pleasure at Her Majesty's 1976; The Hound of the Baskervilles 1977; Foul Play 1978; 10 1979; Arthur 1981; Six Weeks 1982; Lovesick 1983; Romantic Comedy 1983; Unfaithfully Yours 1983; Best Defense 1984; Micki & Maude 1984; Santa Claus 1985; The Adventures of Milo and Otis 1986; Like Father, like Son 1987; Arthur 2: On the Rocks 1988; Crazy People 1990; Blame It on the Bellboy 1992; The Pickle 1993; The Disappearance of Kevin Johnson 1995

Moore, Duke aka Moore, James "Duke" (1913-1976) Plan 9 from Outer Space 1959; Hellborn 1961

Moore, Eileen (1932-) Mr Denning Drives North 1951; The Happy Family 1952; An Inspector Calls 1954; Men of Sherwood Forest 1954

Moore, Frank Rabid 1976; Food of the Gods II 1989

Moore, Gar (1920-1985) Abbott and Costello Meet the Killer, Boris Karloff 1949; The Underworld Story 1950

Moore, Grace aka Moore, Miss Grace (1898-1947) A Lady's Morals 1930; One Night of Love 1934; The King Steps Out 1936; I'll Take Romance 1937; When You're in Love 1937

Moore, Joanna (1934-1997) Ride a Crooked Trail 1958; Touch of Evil 1958; The Last Angry Man 1959; Follow That Dream 1962; Son of Flubber 1962; Walk on the Wild Side 1962; Countdown 1967

Moore, Joel David Hatchet 2006; The Hottie & the Nottie 2008; Beyond a Reasonable Doubt 2009; Grassroots 2012

Moore, Juanita (1914-2014) The Girl Can't Help It 1956; Imitation of Life 1959; Walk on the Wild Side 1962; The Singing Nun 1966; Paternity 1981

Moore, Julianne (1961-) Tales from the Darkside: the Movie 1991; Body of Evidence 1992; The Gun in Betty Lou's Handbag 1992; The Hand That Rocks the Cradle 1992; Benny & Joon 1993; The Fugitive 1993; Short Cuts 1993; Vanya on 42nd Street 1994; Assassins 1995; Nine Months 1995; Roommates 1995; [Safe] 1995; The Myth of Fingerprints 1996; Surviving Picasso 1996; The Big Lebowski 1997; Boogie Nights 1997; The Lost World: Jurassic Park 1997; Chicago Cab 1998; Psycho 1998; Cookie's Fortune 1999; The End of the Affair 1999; An Ideal Husband 1999; Magnolia 1999; A Map of the World 1999; Evolution 2001; Hannibal 2001; The Shipping News 2001; Far from Heaven 2002; The Hours 2002; Laws of Attraction 2003; The Forgotten 2004; Children of Men 2006; Freedomland 2006; Trust the Man 2006; I'm Not There. 2007; Next 2007; Savage Grace 2007; Blindness 2008; Shelter 2008; Chloe 2009; The Private Lives of Pippa Lee 2009; A Single Man 2009; The Kids Are All Right 2010; Crazy, Stupid, Love 2011; Being Flynn 2012; Game Change 2012; Carrie 2013; Don Jon 2013; The English Teacher 2013; What Maisie Knew 2013; The Hunger Games: Mockingjay Part 1 2014; Maps to the Stars 2014; Non-Stop 2014; Seventh Son 2014; Still Alice 2014; Freeheld 2015; The Hunger Games: Mockingjay Part 2 2015; Maggie's Plan 2016; Kingsman: The Golden Circle 2017

Moore, Kaycee Killer of Sheep 1977; Daughters of the Dust 1991

Moore, Kieron (1924-2007) Anna Karenina 1947; A Man about the House 1947; Mine Own Executioner 1947; David and Bathsheba 1951; Ten Tall Men 1951; Mantrap 1952; Conflict of Wings 1953; The Green Scarf 1954; The Blue Peter 1955; Satellite in the Sky 1956; The Steel Bayonet 1957; The Key 1958; Darby O'Gill and the Little People 1959; The Day They Robbed the Bank of England 1960; Doctor Blood's Coffin 1960; The League of Gentlemen 1960; The Siege of Sidney Street 1960; The Day of the Triffids 1962; I Thank a Fool 1962; The Main Attraction 1962; Girl in the Headlines 1963; Hide and Seek 1963; Crack in the World 1964; Son of a Gunfighter 1964; Arabesque 1966

Moore, Mandy (1984-) The Princess Diaries 2001; A Walk to Remember 2002; Chasing Liberty 2004; Racing Stripes 2004; Romance & Cigarettes 2004; Southland Tales 2005; American Dreamz 2006; Because I Said So 2007; License to Wed 2007; Swinging with the Finkels 2010; Tangled 2010

Moore, Mary Tyler (1936-) X-15 1961; Thoroughly Modern Millie 1967; Don't Just Stand There 1968; What's So Bad about Feeling Good? 1968; Change of Habit 1969; Ordinary People 1980; Six Weeks 1982; Just between Friends 1986; Flirting with Disaster 1996; Keys to Tulsa 1996; Payback 1997

Moore, Matt (1888-1960) Traffic in Souls 1913; 20,000 Leagues under the Sea 1916; The Pride of the Clan 1917; The Unholy Three 1925; Coquette 1929; Consolation Marriage 1931; Deluge 1933

Moore, Melba (1945-) Lost in the Stars 1974; All Dogs Go to Heaven 1989; Def by Temptation 1990; The Fighting Temptations 2003

Moore (2), Michael (1954-) Roger & Me 1989; The Big One 1997; Edtv 1999; Bowling for Columbine 2002; Manufacturing Dissent: Uncovering Michael Moore 2007; Sicko 2007; Capitalism: a Love Story 2009; Where to Invade Next 2015

Moore, Owen (1886-1939) The Battle of the Sexes 1914; The Escape 1914; The Black Bird 1926; The Road to Mandalay 1926; High Voltage 1929; What a Widow! 1930; As You Desire Me 1932; She Done Him Wrong 1933; A Star Is Born 1937

Moore, Pauline (1914-2001) Charlie Chan at the Olympics 1937; Heidi 1937; Love Is News 1937; Three Blind Mice 1938; Charlie Chan at Treasure Island 1939; Charlie Chan in Reno 1939; Days of Jesse James 1939; The Three Musketeers 1939; Young Mr Lincoln 1939

Moore, Roger (1927-) Piccadilly Incident 1946; The Last Time I Saw Paris 1954; Diane 1955; Interrupted Melody 1955; The King's Thief 1955; The Sins of Rachel Cade 1961; Romulus and the Sabines 1961; Crossplot 1969; The Man Who Haunted Himself 1970; Live and Let Die 1973; Gold 1974; The Man with the Golden Gun 1974; That Lucky Touch 1975; Sherlock Holmes in New York 1976; Shout at the Devil 1976; The Spy Who Loved Me 1977; The Wild Geese 1978; Escape to Athena 1979; Moonraker 1979; North Sea Hijack 1979; The Sea Wolves 1980; The Cannonball Run 1981; For Your Eyes Only 1981; The Curse of the Pink Panther 1983; Octopussy 1983; The Naked Face 1984; A View to a Kill 1985; Bullseye! 1990; Fire, Ice and Dynamite 1990; Bed & Breakfast 1992; The Man Who Wouldn't Die 1995; The Quest 1996; The Enemy 2000; Boat Trip 2002; Cats & Dogs: the Revenge of Kitty Galore 2010; Everything or Nothing: the Untold Story of 007 2012; The Carer 2015

Moore, Sheila (1938-) Bye Bye Blues 1989; The Reflecting Skin 1990

Moore, Stephen (1937-) A Midsummer Night's Dream 1961; Clockwise 1986

Moore, Terry (1929-) The Return of October 1948; Mighty Joe Young 1949; The Great Rupert 1950; Come Back, Little Sheba 1952; Beneath the 12-Mile Reef 1953; King of the Khyber Rifles 1953; Man on a Tightrope 1953; Daddy

Long Legs 1955; Shack Out on 101 1955; Between Heaven and Hell 1956; Cast a Long Shadow 1959; Platinum High School 1960; Waco 1966

Moore, Victor (1876-1962) Gold Diggers of 1937 1936; Swing Time 1936; Make Way for Tomorrow 1937; Louisiana Purchase 1941; Star Spangled Rhythm 1942; Riding High 1943; True to Life 1943; It Happened on Fifth Avenue 1947; On Our Merry Way 1948; A Kiss in the Dark 1949; We're Not Married 1952; The Seven Year Itch 1955

Moorehead, Agnes (1906-1974) Citizen Kane 1941; The Big Street 1942; Journey into Fear 1942; The Magnificent Ambersons 1942; Government Girl 1943; Jane Eyre 1943; The Youngest Profession 1943; Dragon Seed 1944; Mrs Parkington 1944; The Seventh Cross 1944; Since You Went Away 1944; Keep Your Powder Dry 1945; Our Vines Have Tender Grapes 1945; Dark Passage 1947; The Lost Moment 1947; Johnny Belinda 1948; Station West 1948; Summer Holiday 1948; The Woman in White 1948; The Great Sinner 1949; The Stratton Story 1949; Caged 1950; Adventures of Captain Fabian 1951; The Blue Veil 1951; Fourteen Hours 1951; Show Boat 1951; Black Jack 1952; Main Street to Broadway 1953; Scandal at Scourie 1953; The Story of Three Loves 1953; Magnificent Obsession 1954; All That Heaven Allows 1955; The Left Hand of God 1955; Untamed 1955; The Conqueror 1956; Meet Me in Las Vegas 1956; The Opposite Sex 1956; Pardners 1956; The Revolt of Mamie Stover 1956; The Swan 1956; Jeanne Eagels 1957; Raintree County 1957; The Story of Mankind 1957; The True Story of Jesse James 1957; The Bat 1959; Tempest 1959; Pollyanna 1960; How the West Was Won 1962; Jessica 1962; Who's Minding the Store? 1963; Hush... Hush, Sweet Charlotte 1964; The Singing Nun 1966; What's the Matter with Helen? 1971; Charlotte's Web 1973

Moorhead, Natalie (1901-1992) Manslaughter 1930; Illicit 1931; Three Wise Girls 1932; The Mind Reader 1933; Lady of the Tropics 1939

Mooy, Genevieve Thank God He Met Lizzie 1997; The Dish 2000

Moraghan, Mark Thomas & Friends: Tale of the Brave 2014; Thomas & Friends - Sodor's Legend of the Lost Treasure: the Movie 2015

Morahan, Hattie Summer in February 2012; Mr Holmes 2014

Morales, Esai (1962-) Bad Boys 1983; La Bamba 1987; The Principal 1987; Naked Tango 1990; The Burning Season 1994; In the Army Now 1994; My Family 1994; Rapa Nui 1994; Scorpion Spring 1995; The Disappearance of Garcia Lorca 1997; Doomsday Man 1998; The Adventures of Tom Thumb and Thumbelina 2002; Fast Food Nation 2006; The Line 2008

Morales, Jacobo (1934-) Bananas 1971; Up the Sandbox 1972

Moran, Dolores (1924-1982) Old Acquaintance 1943; To Have and Have Not 1944; The Horn Blows at Midnight 1945; The Man I Love 1946; Christmas Eve 1947; Count the Hours 1953; Silver Lode 1954

Moran, Dylan (1971-) The Actors 2003; Shaun of the Dead 2004; A Cock and Bull Story 2005; Run Fatboy Run 2007; The Decoy Bride 2011; Good Vibrations 2012; Calvary 2013

Moran, Erin (1961-) Eighty Steps to Jonah 1969; Watermelon Man 1970

Moran, Jackie (1923-1990) And So They Were Married 1936; The Adventures of Tom Sawyer 1938; Mad about Music 1938; Song of the Open Road 1944

Moran, Kate Goltzius and the Pelican Company 2012; You and the Night 2013

Moran, Lois (1909-1990) Stella Dallas 1925; The Road to Mandalay 1926; Mammy 1930; Alice in the Cities 1974

Morán, Mercedes (1955-) La Ciénaga 2001; The Motorcycle Diaries 2004

Moran, Nick (1969-) Buddy's Song 1990; Lock, Stock and Two Smoking Barrels 1998 Another Life 2000; The Proposal 2000; The Musketeer 2001; Puritan 2004; Down Dog 2014

Moran, Peggy (1918-2002) Argentine Nights 1940; The Mummy's Hand 1940; There's One Born Every Minute 1942

Moran, Polly (1884-1952) The Divine Woman 1928; Guilty Hands 1931; The Passionate Plumber 1932; Red River Range 1938; Adam's Rib 1949

Moranis, Rick (1953-) Ghost Busters 1984; Streets of Fire 1984; The Wild Life 1984; Brewster's Millions 1985; Club Paradise 1986; Head Office 1986; Little Shop of Horrors 1986; Spaceballs 1987; Ghostbusters II 1989; Honey, I Shrunk the Kids 1989; Parenthood 1989; My Blue Heaven 1990; Honey, I Blew Up the Kid 1992; Splitting Heirs 1993; The Flintstones 1994; Little Giants 1994; Big Bully 1996; Honey, We Shrunk Ourselves 1997; Brother Bear 2003

Morante, Laura (1956-) The Tragedy of a Ridiculous Man 1981; Man on Fire 1987; The Son's Room 2001; The Dancer Upstairs 2002; Orchestra Seats 2005; Molière 2006; Private Fears in Public Places 2006

Morassi, Kestie Dirty Deeds 2002; Wolf Creek 2005

More, Kenneth (1914-1982) Look Up and Laugh 1935; Scott of the Antarctic 1948; Now Barabbas Was a Robber 1949; Chance of a Lifetime 1950; The Clouded Yellow 1950; The Franchise Affair 1950; Appointment with Venus 1951; Brandy for the Parson 1951; The Yellow Balloon 1952; Genevieve 1953; Never Let Me Go 1953; Our Girl Friday 1953; Doctor in the House 1954; The Deep Blue Sea 1955; Raising a Riot 1955; Reach for the Sky 1956; The Admirable Crichton 1957; Next to No Time 1958; A Night to Remember 1958; The Sheriff of Fractured Jaw 1958; North West Frontier 1959; The Thirty-Nine Steps 1959; Man in the Moon 1960; Sink the Bismarck! 1960; The Greengage Summer 1961; The Longest Day 1962; Some People 1962; We Joined the Navy 1962; The Comedy Man 1964; Dark of the Sun 1967; Fraulein Doktor 1968; Battle of Britain 1969; Oh! What a Lovely War 1969; Scrooge 1970; The Slipper and the Rose 1976; The Spaceman and King Arthur 1979

Moreau, Jeanne (1928-) Honour among Thieves 1954; La Reine Margot 1954; Secrets d'Alcove 1954; Lift to the Scaffold 1957; Les Amants 1958; Les Liaisons Dangereuses 1959; Five Branded Women 1960; Une Femme Est une Femme 1961; La Notte 1961; Eva 1962; Jules et Jim 1962; The Trial 1962; Bay of the Angels 1963; Le Feu Follet 1963; The Victors 1963; Banana Peel 1964; The Diary of a Chambermaid 1964; The Train 1964; The Yellow Rolls-Royce 1964; Viva Maria! 1965; Chimes at Midnight 1966; Mademoiselle 1966; The Bride Wore Black 1967; The Sailor from Gibraltar 1967; Great Catherine 1968; The Immortal Story 1968; The Little Theatre of Jean Renoir 1969; Alex in Wonderland 1970; Monte Walsh 1970; Les Valseuses 1974; The Last Tycoon 1976; Mr Klein 1976; Querelle 1982; Le Paltoquet 1986; Hotel Terminus: the Life and Times of Klaus Barbie 1987; Nikita 1990; The Old Lady Who Walked in the Sea 1991; Until the End of the World 1991; Map of the Human Heart 1992; Beyond the Clouds 1995; The Proprietor 1996; I Love You, I Love You Not 1997; Time to Leave 2005

Moreau, Marguerite Queen of the Damned 2002; Easier with Practice 2009

Moreau, Yolande (1953-) Vagabond 1985; Amélie 2001; The Last Mistress 2007; Louise-Michel 2008; Séraphine 2008; Mammuth 2010; The Brand New Testament 2015; The Childhood of a Leader 2015

Morecambe, Eric (1926-1984) The Intelligence Men 1965; That Riviera Touch 1966; The Magnificent Two 1967; Simon, Simon 1970

Moreira, Ana The Portuguese Nun 2009; Tabu 2012

Morel, François (1959-) Le Bonheur Est dans le Pré 1995; [Three] Après la Vie 2002; [Two] Un Couple Epatant 2002

Morel, Jacques (1922-2008) Topaze 1951; Marie Antoinette 1956

Moreland, Mantan (1902-1973) Footlight Serenade 1942; Charlie Chan in the Chinese Cat 1944; Charlie Chan in the Secret Service 1944; Meeting at Midnight 1944; The Jade Mask 1945; The Scarlet Clue 1945; The Shanghai Cobra 1945; Dark Alibi 1946; The Trap 1947; Spider Baby 1964; Watermelon Man 1970

Morell, André aka **Morell, Andre** (1909-1978) Madeleine 1949; Stage Fright 1949; The Clouded Yellow 1950; Seven Days to Noon 1950; Stolen Face 1952; His Majesty O'Keefe 1953; The Black Knight 1954; The Man Who Never Was 1955; They Can't Hang Me 1955; The Black Tent 1956; The Bridge on the River Kwai 1957; The Camp on Blood Island 1958; Paris Holiday 1958; The Hound of the Baskervilles 1959; Cone of Silence 1960; Cash on Demand 1961; The Shadow of the Cat 1961; The Plague of the Zombies 1965; The Mummy's Shroud 1966

Morelli, Rina (1908-1976) Senso 1954; The Leopard 1963; L'Innocente 1976

Moreno, Antonio (1887-1967) Mare Nostrum 1926; The Temptress 1926; It 1927; The Bohemian Girl 1936; Valley of the Sun 1942; Captain from Castile 1947; Dallas 1950; Creature from the Black Lagoon 1954

Moreno, Catalina Sandino (1981-) Maria Full of Grace 2003; Fast Food Nation 2006; Love in the Time of Cholera 2007; Magic Magic 2013

Moreno, Rita (1931-) The Ring 1952; Singin' in the Rain 1952; Garden of Evil 1954; Untamed 1955; The King and I 1956; The Vagabond King 1956; The Deerslayer 1957; This Rebel Breed 1960; Summer and Smoke 1961; West Side Story 1961; The Night of the Following Day 1968; Marlowe 1969; Carnal Knowledge 1971; The Ritz 1976; The Four Seasons 1981; Age Isn't Everything 1991; Italian Movie 1994; Angus 1995; Slums of Beverly Hills 1998; Piñero 2001; Casa de los Babys 2003

Moreno, Rosita (1907-1993) Her Wedding Night 1930; The Scoundrel 1935

Moretti, Michèle Les Roseaux Sauvages 1994; Look at Me 2004; In the Courtyard 2014

Moretti, Nanni (1953-) Dear Diary 1994; Aprile 1998; The Son's Room 2001; Calm Chaos 2008; Mia Madre 2015

Moretz, Chloë Grace aka **Moretz, Chloë** aka **Moretz, Chloe Grace** (1997-) The Amityville Horror 2005; Big Momma's House 2 2006; The Eye 2008; (500) Days of Summer 2009; Kick-Ass 2009; Diary of a Wimpy Kid 2010; Jack and the Beanstalk 2010; Let Me In 2010; Hugo 2011; Texas Killing Fields 2011; Dark Shadows 2012; Carrie 2013; Kick-Ass 2 2013; The Tale of the Princess Kaguya 2013; Clouds of Sils Maria 2014; The Equalizer 2014; If I Stay 2014; Say When 2014; Dark Places 2015; Bad Neighbours 2 2016; The 5th Wave 2016

Morfitt, Darren Dog Soldiers 2001; Doomsday 2008; Harrigan 2013; K-Shop 2015

Morfogen, George (1933-) The Thief Who Came to Dinner 1973; Those Lips, Those Eyes 1980

Morgan, Cindy (1954-) Caddyshack 1980; Tron 1982

Morgan, Colin Parked 2010; Island 2011

Morgan, Debbi (1956-) Eve's Bayou 1997; The Hurricane 1999; Love & Basketball 2000; Coach Carter 2005

Morgan, Dennis (1910-1994) The Return of Dr X 1939; Kitty Foyle 1940; Affectionately Yours 1941; Captains of the Clouds 1942; The Hard Way 1942; In This Our Life 1942; Thank Your Lucky Stars 1943; The Desert Song 1944; Shine On, Harvest Moon 1944; The Very Thought of You 1944; Christmas in Connecticut 1945; My Wild Irish Rose 1947; It's a Great Feeling 1949; Perfect Strangers 1950; Pretty Baby 1950; Painting the Clouds with Sunshine 1951; This Woman Is Dangerous 1952; Pearl of the South Pacific 1955

Morgan, Frank (1890-1949) Fast and Loose 1930; Laughter 1930; The Half Naked Truth 1932; Blonde Bombshell 1933; Broadway to Hollywood 1933; Hallelujah, I'm a Bum 1933; The Kiss before the Mirror 1933; Reunion in Vienna 1933; When Ladies Meet 1933; The Affairs of Cellini 1934; The Cat and the Fiddle 1934; Enchanted April 1935; Escapade 1935; The Good Fairy 1935; I Live My Life 1935; Naughty Marietta 1935; The Perfect Gentleman 1935; Dimples 1936; The Great Ziegfeld 1936; Piccadilly Jim 1936; Trouble for Two 1936; The Emperor's Candlesticks 1937; The Last of Mrs Cheyney 1937; Rosalie 1937; Saratoga 1937; The Crowd Roars 1938; Paradise for Three 1938; Port of Seven Seas 1938; Sweethearts 1938; Broadway Serenade 1939; The Wizard of Oz 1939; Boom Town 1940; Broadway Melody of 1940 1940; The Ghost Comes Home 1940; The Mortal Storm 1940; The Shop around the Corner 1940; Honky Tonk 1941; The Vanishing Virginian 1941; Tortilla Flat 1942; White Cargo 1942; The Human Comedy 1943; Casanova Brown 1944; The White Cliffs of Dover 1944; Yolanda and the Thief 1945; Courage of Lassie 1946; Lady Luck 1946; Green Dolphin Street 1947; Summer Holiday 1948; The Three Musketeers 1948; Any Number Can Play 1949; The Great Sinner 1949; The Stratton Story 1949; Key to the City 1950

Morgan, Gary Logan's Run 1976; Matilda 1978

Morgan, Gene (1893-1940) Blonde Venus 1932; If You Could Only Cook 1935

Morgan, Harry aka **Morgan, Henry** (1915-2011) To the Shores of Tripoli 1942; Happy Land 1943; The Ox-Bow Incident 1943; The Eve of St Mark 1944; A Bell for Adano 1945; From This Day Forward 1946; Moonrise 1948; The Saxon Charm 1948; Yellow Sky 1948; Down to the Sea in Ships 1949; Holiday Affair 1949; Appointment with Danger 1950; Dark City 1950; The Well 1951; High Noon 1952; Arena 1953; The Glenn Miller Story 1954; Torch Song 1953; The Far Country 1954; The Teahouse of the August Moon 1956; Inherit the Wind 1960; The Mountain Road 1960; Frankie & Johnny 1966; What Did You Do in the War, Daddy? 1966; The Flim-Flam Man 1967; Support Your Local Sheriff! 1969; Viva Max! 1969; The Barefoot Executive 1971; Scandalous John 1971; Support Your Local Gunfighter 1971; Snowball Express 1972; Charley and the Angel 1973; The Apple Dumpling Gang 1974; The Shootist 1976; The Cat from Outer Space 1978; The Apple Dumpling Gang Rides Again 1979; Dragnet 1987; The Incident 1990; Against Her Will 1992; Incident in a Small Town 1993

Morgan (I), Helen (1900-1941) Applause 1929; Marie Galante 1934; Go into Your Dance 1935; Show Boat 1936

Morgan, Horace aka **Morgan, Horace "Cupid"** aka **Morgan, H A** Three Ages 1923; Beggars of Life 1928

Morgan, Jeffrey Dean (1966-) Live! 2007; PS I Love You 2007; The Accidental Husband 2008; Taking Woodstock 2009; Watchmen 2009; The Losers 2010; The Resident 2010; Peace, Love & Misunderstanding 2011; Texas Killing Fields 2011; The Possession 2012; Red Dawn 2012; The Salvation 2014; Heist 2015; The Secret Life of Marilyn Monroe 2015; Solace 2015

Morgan, Michèle (1920-) Le Quai des Brumes 1938; Stormy Waters 1941; Joan of Paris 1942; Higher and Higher 1943; Passage to Marseille 1944; The Chase 1946; La Symphonie Pastorale 1946; The Fallen Idol 1948; The Seven Deadly Sins 1952; The Proud Ones 1953; Les Grandes Manoeuvres 1955; Marguerite de la Nuit 1955; Napoléon 1955; Marie Antoinette 1956; Bluebeard 1962; Everybody's Fine 1990

Morgan, Nancy (1949-) Grand Theft Auto 1977; Americathon 1979

Morgan, Ralph (1882-1956) Rasputin and the Empress 1932; Strange Interlude 1932; The Kennel Murder Case 1933; The Mad Game 1933; The Power and the Glory 1933; Shanghai Madness 1933; Stand Up and Cheer! 1934; Magnificent Obsession 1935; Star of Midnight 1935; Crack-Up 1936; Human Cargo 1936; Speed 1936; Mannequin 1937; Wells Fargo 1937; Wives under Suspicion 1938; Fast and Loose 1939; The Lone Wolf Spy Hunt 1939; Hitler's Madman 1943; The Impostor 1944; Jack London 1944; The Monster Maker 1944; Weird Woman 1944; Sleep, My Love 1948

Morgan, Robbi What's the Matter with Helen? 1971; Friday the 13th 1980

Morgan, Robert The Craic 1999; Opal Dream 2005; Suburban Mayhem 2006

Morgan, Russ (1904-1969) The Great Man 1956; Mister Cory 1957

Morgan, Terence (1921-2005) Hamlet 1948; Captain Horatio Hornblower RN 1951; Encore 1951; It Started in Paradise 1952; Mandy 1952; Turn the Key Softly 1953; Dance Little Lady 1954; Forbidden Cargo 1954; They Can't Hang Me 1955; It's a Wonderful World 1956; The March Hare 1956; The Scamp 1957; Tread Softly Stranger 1958; The Shakedown 1959; Piccadilly Third Stop 1960; The Curse of the Mummy's Tomb 1964; The Penthouse 1967

Morgan, Tracy (1968-) Are We There Yet? 2005; Little Man 2006; First Sunday 2008; Superhero Movie 2008; G-Force 2009; Cop Out 2010; Death at a Funeral 2010; Accidental Love 2013

Morgan, Trevor (1986-) Barney's Great Adventure 1998; I'll Remember April 1999; The Sixth Sense 1999; A Rumor of Angels 2000; The Glass House 2001; Jurassic Park III 2001; Mean Creek 2004; My Spy 2008; Brotherhood 2010

Morgan, Wendy Yanks 1979; 84 Charing Cross Road 1986

Morgenstern, Maia (1962-) Ulysses' Gaze 1995; The Passion of the Christ 2004

Mori, Masayuki (1911-1973) Rashomon 1950; The Idiot 1951; The Lady of Musashino 1951; Ugetsu Monogatari 1953; The Princess Yang Kwei Fei 1955; The Bad Sleep Well 1960; When a Woman Ascends the Stairs 1960; Alone on the Pacific 1963

Mori, Paola (1930-1986) Crossed Swords 1954; Confidential Report 1955

Moriarty, Cathy aka **Moriarty-Gentile, Cathy** (1960-) Raging Bull 1980; Neighbors 1981; White of the Eye 1986; Kindergarten Cop 1990; Soapdish 1991; The Gun in Betty Lou's Handbag 1992; The Mambo Kings 1992; Another Stakeout 1993; Matinee 1993; Me and the Kid 1993; Pontiac Moon 1994; Casper 1995; Dream with the Fishes 1996; Cop Land 1997; Casper Meets Wendy 1998; Digging to China 1998; Gloria 1998; But I'm a Cheerleader 1999; Crazy in Alabama 1999; Red Team 1999; Analyze That 2002

Moriarty, Michael (1941-) Glory Boy 1971; The Last Detail 1973; Report to the Commissioner 1975; Who'll Stop the Rain? 1978; Q - the Winged Serpent 1982; Pale Rider 1985; The Stuff 1985; Troll 1986; It's Alive III: Island of the Alive 1987; A Return to Salem's Lot 1987; Dark Tower 1989; Full Fathom Five 1990; Courage under Fire 1996; Crime of the Century 1996; Shiloh 1996; The Art of Murder 1999; Children of My Heart 2000; Along Came a Spider 2001; James Dean 2001

Moriarty, P H (1939-) Jaws 1983; Number One 1984; Lock, Stock and Two Smoking Barrels 1998

Morice, Tara (1964-) Strictly Ballroom 1992; Hotel Sorrento 1994; Razzle Dazzle: a Journey into Dance 2006; Oranges and Sunshine 2010

Morier-Genoud, Philippe Au Revoir les Enfants 1987; Cyrano de Bergerac 1990; Laissez-passer 2001

Morison, Patricia (1915-) Beyond the Blue Horizon 1942; Calling Dr Death 1943; The Fallen Sparrow 1943; Hitler's Madman 1943; Without Love 1945; Dressed to Kill 1946; Song of the Thin Man 1947; Tarzan and the Huntress 1947; The Prince of Thieves 1948; Song without End 1960

Morissette, Alanis (1974-) Dogma 1999; Jay and Silent Bob Strike Back 2001; The Price of Desire 2015

Morita, Pat aka **Morita, Noriyuki "Pat"** (1932-2005) Evil Roy Slade 1971; Full Moon High 1982; The Karate Kid 1984; Babes in Toyland 1986; The Karate Kid Part II 1986; Collision Course 1987; The Karate Kid III 1989; Lena's Holiday 1990; Honeymoon in Vegas 1992; Even Cowgirls Get the Blues 1993; The Next Karate Kid 1994; Bloodsport II: The Next Kumite 1996; Mulan 1998; I'll Remember April 1999; The Center of the World 2001; Mulan II 2004

Moritzen, Henning (1928-2012) Cries and Whispers 1972; Festen 1998; Allegro 2005

Morley, Karen (1905-2003) Mata Hari 1931; Arsene Lupin 1932; Flesh 1932; The Mask of Fu Manchu 1932; Scarface 1932; Gabriel over the White House 1933; Our Daily Bread 1934; Black Fury 1935; The Littlest Rebel 1935; Beloved Enemy 1936; The Last Train from Madrid 1937; Kentucky 1938; Pride and Prejudice 1940; Framed 1947; M 1951

Morley, Robert (1908-1992) Marie Antoinette 1938; The Foreman Went to France 1941; Major Barbara 1941; The Big Blockade 1942; The Young Mr Pitt 1942; I Live in Grosvenor Square 1945; The Ghosts of Berkeley Square 1947; The Small Back Room 1949; The African Queen 1951; Outcast of the Islands 1951; Curtain Up 1952; Beat the Devil 1953; The Final Test 1953; The Story of Gilbert and Sullivan 1953; Beau Brummell 1954; The Good Die Young 1954; The Rainbow Jacket 1954; Quentin Durward 1955; Around the World in 80 Days 1956; Loser Takes All 1956; The Doctor's Dilemma 1958; Law and Disorder 1958; The Sheriff of Fractured Jaw 1958; Libel 1959; Oscar Wilde 1959; The Battle of the Sexes 1960; The Boys 1961; Go to Blazes 1961; The Young Ones 1961; The Road to Hong Kong 1962; Ladies Who Do 1963; Murder at the Gallop 1963; The Old Dark House 1963; Take Her, She's Mine 1963; Hot Enough for June 1964; Of Human Bondage 1964; Topkapi 1964; The Dot and the Line 1965; Life at the Top 1965; A Study in Terror 1965; Those Magnificent Men in Their Flying Machines 1965; The Alphabet Murders 1966; Finders Keepers 1966; Hotel Paradiso 1966; The Trygon Factor 1967; Woman Times Seven 1967; Hot Millions 1968; Sinful Davey 1969; Some Girls Do 1969; Twinky 1969; Cromwell

1970; Doctor in Trouble 1970; Song of Norway 1970; When Eight Bells Toll 1971; Theatre of Blood 1973; Great Expectations 1974; The Blue Bird 1976; Who Is Killing the Great Chefs of Europe? 1978; The Human Factor 1979; Loophole 1980; The Great Muppet Caper 1981; High Road to China 1983; The Trouble with Spies 1987

Mornar, Lea Joy Division 2006; The Truth 2006

Morón, Mañuel El Bola 2000; Cell 211 2009

Morris, Anita (1943-1994) Maria's Lovers 1984; Blue City 1986; Ruthless People 1986; Aria 1987; 18 Again! 1988; Me and the Kid 1993

Morris, Aubrey (1926-2015) Blood from the Mummy's Tomb 1971; A Clockwork Orange 1971; Oxford Blues 1984; The Rachel Papers 1989; Bram Stoker's Legend of the Mummy 1998

Morris, Barboura (1932-1975) A Bucket of Blood 1959; The Wasp Woman 1959; Atlas 1960; The Trip 1967

Morris, Beth (1949-) Crucible of Terror 1971; Old Scores 1991

Morris, Chester (1901-1970) Alibi 1929; The Bat Whispers 1930; The Big House 1930; The Divorcee 1930; Red-Headed Woman 1932; Sinners in the Sun 1932; The Gay Bride 1934; Flight from Glory 1937; Smashing the Rackets 1938; Blind Alley 1939; Five Came Back 1939; Meet Boston Blackie 1941; Secret Command 1944; The She-Creature 1956; The Great White Hope 1970

Morris, Garrett (1944-) The Stuff 1985; Jackpot 2001

Morris, Haviland (1959-) Sixteen Candles 1984; Who's That Girl 1987; Home Alone 3 1997

Morris, Howard (1919-2005) Forty Pounds of Trouble 1962; Fluffy 1965; High Anxiety 1977; Life Stinks 1991

Morris, Jeff (1936-2004) Goin' South 1978; The Border 1981

Morris, Judy (1947-) The Plumber 1979; Phar Lap 1983; The More Things Change 1985

Morris, Julian Cry_Wolf 2005; Donkey Punch 2007; Kelly + Victor 2013

Morris, Kathryn (1969-) Sleepstalker 1995; Mindhunters 2003; Resurrecting the Champ 2007

Morris, Lana (1930-1998) The Weaker Sex 1948; The Chiltern Hundreds 1949; Trottie True 1949; Morning Departure 1950; The Woman in Question 1950; Trouble in Store 1953; Man of the Moment 1955; Home and Away 1956; I Start Counting 1970

Morris, Libby Tiara Tahiti 1962; The Adding Machine 1969

Morris, Mary (1915-1988) Victoria the Great 1937; The Thief of Bagdad 1940; Pimpernel Smith 1941; Undercover 1943; The Man from Morocco 1944; Train of Events 1949

Morris, Phyllis (1893-1982) The Adventures of Tartu 1943; The Silver Darlings 1947; Three Came Home 1950

Morris, Wayne (1914-1959) Kid Galahad 1937; The Return of Dr X 1939; I Wanted Wings 1941; Deep Valley 1947; Voice of the Turtle 1947; The Time of Your Life 1948; A Kiss in the Dark 1949; Task Force 1949; The Younger Brothers 1949; Sierra Passage 1950; The Master Plan 1954; Riding Shotgun 1954; The Crooked Sky 1957; Paths of Glory 1957; Plunder Road 1957

Morrison, Jennifer aka **Morrison, Jenny** (1979-) Intersection 1994; Stir of Echoes 1999; Urban Legends: Final Cut 2000; Surviving Christmas 2004; Warrior 2011

Morrison, Kenny (1974-) The Quick and the Dead 1987; The NeverEnding Story II: the Next Chapter 1991

Morrison, "Sunshine Sammy" aka **Morrison, Sunshine** aka **Morrison, Sammy** (1912-1989) Boys of the City 1940; Pride of the Bowery 1941; Spooks Run Wild 1941; Ghosts in the Night 1943

Morrison, Temuera (1961-) Once Were Warriors 1994; Barb Wire 1995; The Island of Dr Moreau 1996; Speed 2: Cruise Control 1997; Six Days Seven Nights 1998; What Becomes of the Broken Hearted? 1999; From Dusk till Dawn 3: the Hangman's Daughter 2000; Star Wars Episode II: Attack of the Clones 2002; Blueberry 2004; River Queen 2005; Tracker 2010; Green Lantern 2011

Morrissey, Betty (1908-1944) A Woman of Paris 1923; The Gold Rush 1925

Morrissey, David (1964-) Drowning by Numbers 1988; Robin Hood 1990; Waterland 1992; Hilary and Jackie 1998; Fanny & Elvis 1999; Born Romantic 2000; Some Voices 2000; Captain Corelli's Mandolin 2001; Derailed 2005; Stoned 2005; Basic

Instinct 2: Risk Addiction 2006; The Reaping 2006; The Water Horse 2007; Is Anybody There? 2008; The Other Boleyn Girl 2008; Centurion 2009; Blitz 2010; Nowhere Boy 2010; Welcome to the Punch 2012; The Ones Below 2015; Ronaldo 2015

Morrissey, Neil (1962-) I Bought a Vampire Motorcycle 1989; Up 'n' Under 1997; Triggermen 2002; Clubbed 2008; Run for Your Wife 2013

Morrow, Jeff (1913-1993) The Siege at Red River 1954; Sign of the Pagan 1954; Tanganyika 1954; Captain Lightfoot 1955; This Island Earth 1955; The Creature Walks among Us 1956; The First Texan 1956; Pardners 1956; Kronos 1957; The Story of Ruth 1960

Morrow, Jo (1940-) Juke Box Rhythm 1959; The Legend of Tom Dooley 1959; Our Man in Havana 1959; 13 Ghosts 1959; The Three Worlds of Gulliver 1959; Sunday in New York 1963; He Rides Tall 1964

Morrow, Max (1991-) Jacob Two Two Meets the Hooded Fang 1999; Santa Who? 2000

Morrow, Rob (1962-) Private Resort 1985; Quiz Show 1994; Last Dance 1996; Mother 1996; The Day Lincoln Was Shot 1998; The Emperor's Club 2002; The Guru 2002; The Bucket List 2008

Morrow, Susan (1931-1985) The Savage 1953; Macabre 1958

Morrow, Vic (1932-1982) Tribute to a Bad Man 1956; Men in War 1957; God's Little Acre 1958; King Creole 1958; The Glass House 1972; The Night that Panicked America 1975; The Bad News Bears 1976; Treasure of Matecumbe 1976; The Evictors 1979; Monster 1980; Twilight Zone: the Movie 1983

Morse, Barry (1918-2008) Daughter of Darkness 1948; No Trace 1950; Kings of the Sun 1963; Puzzle of a Downfall Child 1970; Asylum 1972; Power Play 1978; The Changeling 1980; Murder by Phone 1982; Reunion at Fairborough 1985

Morse, David (1953-) Inside Moves: the Guys from Max's Bar 1980; The Indian Runner 1991; The Good Son 1993; The Getaway 1994; The Crossing Guard 1995; Twelve Monkeys 1995; Extreme Measures 1996; The Long Kiss Goodnight 1996; The Rock 1996; Contact 1997; The Negotiator 1998; Crazy in Alabama 1999; The Green Mile 1999; Dancer in the Dark 2000; Proof of Life 2000; Diary of a City Priest 2001; Hearts in Atlantis 2001; Double Vision 2002; Down in the Valley 2004; The Dreamer 2005; 16 Blocks 2006; Disturbia 2007; The Hurt Locker 2008; Mother and Child 2009; Drive Angry 2011; The Odd Life of Timothy Green 2012; World War Z 2013

Morse, Helen (1947-) Picnic at Hanging Rock 1975; Caddie 1976; Agatha 1978; The Eye of the Storm 2011

Morse, Laila Nil by Mouth 1997; Bulla... Big Fat Gypsy Gangster 2011

Morse, Natalie Anchoress 1993; My Mother's Courage 1995

Morse, Robert (1931-) The Matchmaker 1958; Honeymoon Hotel 1964; The Loved One 1965; Quick, before It Melts 1965; A Guide for the Married Man 1967; How to Succeed in Business without Really Trying 1967; Oh Dad, Poor Dad, Mama's Hung You in the Closet and I'm Feelin' So Sad 1967; Where Were You When the Lights Went Out? 1968; The Boatniks 1970; Calendar Girl Murders 1984; Hunk 1987

Morshower, Glenn 84 Charlie Mopic 1989; Runaway Car 1997; After Earth 2013

Mortensen, Viggo (1958-) Witness 1985; Prison 1987; Leatherface: the Texas Chainsaw Massacre III 1990; The Reflecting Skin 1990; The Indian Runner 1991; Ruby Cairo 1992; Boiling Point 1993; Carlito's Way 1993; The Young Americans 1993; American Yakuza 1994; The Prophecy 1994; Crimson Tide 1995; The Passion of Darkly Noon 1995; Albino Alligator 1996; Daylight 1996; The Portrait of a Lady 1996; GI Jane 1997; Psycho 1998; A Walk on the Moon 1999; 28 Days 2000; The Lord of the Rings: The Fellowship of the Ring 2001; The Lord of the Rings: The Two Towers 2002; Hidalgo 2003; The Lord of the Rings: The Return of the King 2003; A History of Violence 2005; Eastern Promises 2007; Appaloosa 2008; Good 2008; The Road 2009; A Dangerous Method 2011; On the Road 2011; Everybody Has a Plan 2012; The Two Faces of January 2013; Jauja 2014; Captain Fantastic 2015

Mortimer, Bob (1959-) Once upon a Time in the Midlands 2002; Churchill: the Hollywood Years 2004

Mortimer, Caroline (1942-) A Place for Lovers 1968; The Hireling 1973

Mortimer, Emily (1971-) The Ghost and the Darkness 1996; Last of the High Kings 1996; Love's Labour's Lost 1999; Disney's The Kid 2000; The 51st State 2001; Lovely & Amazing 2001; Bright Young Things 2003; Dear Frankie 2003; Young Adam 2003; Howl's Moving Castle 2004; Match Point 2005; The Pink Panther 2006; Lars and the Real Girl 2007; Redbelt 2007; Transsiberian 2008; City Island 2009; Harry Brown 2009; The Pink Panther 2 2009; Shutter Island 2009; Cars 2 2011; Hugo 2011; Our Idiot Brother 2011

Morton, Alexander London to Brighton 2006; Valhalla Rising 2009

Morton, Alicia (1987-) Annie 1999; Odd Girl Out 2005

Morton, Amy Rookie of the Year 1993; Up in the Air 2009

Morton, Clive (1904-1975) Kind Hearts and Coronets 1949; A Run for Your Money 1949; The Lavender Hill Mob 1951; Carrington VC 1954; Orders Are Orders 1954; Lucky Jim 1957; The Moonraker 1957; Seven Waves Away 1957; The Duke Wore Jeans 1958; Stranger in the House 1967

Morton, James C (1884-1942) Tit for Tat 1934; Wild Geese Calling 1941

Morton, Joe (1947-) The Brother from Another Planet 1984; Trouble in Mind 1985; Crossroads 1986; The Price of Passion 1988; Zelly and Me 1988; Tap 1989; City of Hope 1991; Terminator 2: Judgment Day 1991; Forever Young 1992; Of Mice and Men 1992; Speed 1994; Lone Star 1995; Executive Decision 1996; Miss Evers' Boys 1997; Blues Brothers 2000 1998; The Astronaut's Wife 1999; Bounce 2000; What Lies Beneath 2000; Dragonfly 2002; Paycheck 2003; Stealth 2005; The Night Listener 2006

Morton, Samantha (1977-) This Is the Sea 1996; Under the Skin 1997; Dreaming of Joseph Lees 1998; Jesus' Son 1999; The Last Yellow 1999; Sweet and Lowdown 1999; Pandaemonium 2000; Morvern Callar 2002; Minority Report 2002; Code 46 2003; In America 2003; Enduring Love 2004; The Libertine 2004; Lassie 2005; River Queen 2005; Free Jimmy 2006; Control 2007; Elizabeth: the Golden Age 2007; Expired 2007; Mister Lonely 2007; The Daisy Chain 2008; Synecdoche, New York 2008; The Messenger 2009; John Carter 2012; Decoding Annie Parker 2013; Miss Julie 2014

Morton, Tom aka **Morton, Tommy** Wait 'til the Sun Shines, Nellie 1952; Main Street to Broadway 1953

Mos Def aka **Bey, Yasiin** (1973-) Monster's Ball 2001; Brown Sugar 2002; The Italian Job 2003; The Woodsman 2004; Dave Chappelle's Block Party 2005; The Hitchhiker's Guide to the Galaxy 2005; Lackawanna Blues 2005; 16 Blocks 2006; Be Kind Rewind 2007; Cadillac Records 2008; In Prison My Whole Life 2008; Begin Again 2013; Life of Crime 2013

Moschin, Gastone (1929-) The Birds, the Bees, and the Italians 1965; The Conformist 1970

Moscovich, Maurice aka **Moscovitch, Maurice** (1871-1940) Winterset 1936; Lancer Spy 1937; Make Way for Tomorrow 1937; Suez 1938; In Name Only 1939; Love Affair 1939; Susannah of the Mounties 1939

Moscow, David (1974-) Big 1988; Honey 2003; Just Married 2003

Moseley, Bill aka **Mosley, Bill** (1953-) The Texas Chainsaw Massacre Part 2 1986; Night of the Living Dead 1990; White Fang 1991; House of 1000 Corpses 2001; The Devil's Rejects 2005; Texas Chainsaw 2013

Moseley, William (1987-) The Chronicles of Narnia: The Lion, the Witch and the Wardrobe 2005; The Chronicles of Narnia: Prince Caspian 2008; Friend Request 2016

Moses, Mark (1958-) Dead Men Don't Die 1991; Race to Space 2001; Big Momma's House 2 2006; Ice Twisters 2009

Moses, William R (1959-) Mystic Pizza 1988; Fun 1994; Wicked 1998; Alone with a Stranger 2000; The Perfect Marriage 2006; The Sitter 2007

Moshesh, Nthati Kini and Adams 1997; The Long Run 2000

Mosley, Roger E (1944-) Leadbelly 1976; Stay Hungry 1976; Semi-Tough 1977; The Jericho Mile 1979; Heart Condition 1990; Unlawful Entry 1992; A Thin Line between Love and Hate 1996

Moss-Bachrach, Ebon Stealth 2005; The Lake House 2006; Come Out and Play 2012

Moss, Arnold (1910-1989) The Loves of Carmen 1948; Border Incident 1949; Reign of Terror 1949; Kim 1950; My Favorite Spy 1951; Viva Zapata! 1952; The 27th Day 1957; The Fool Killer 1965; Gambit 1966

Moss, Carrie-Anne (1967-) Lethal Tender 1996; The Matrix 1999; Chocolat 2000; Memento 2000; Red Planet 2000; The Matrix Reloaded 2002; The Matrix Revolutions 2003; Suspect Zero 2004; The Chumscrubber 2005; Snow Cake 2005; Disturbia 2007; Fireflies in the Garden 2007; Unthinkable 2010; Silent Hill: Revelation 2012; Pompeii 2014; Frankenstein 2015

Moss, Elisabeth (1983-) Once upon a Forest 1992; Separate Lives 1995; Earthly Possessions 1999; The Joyriders 1999; Did You Hear about the Morgans? 2009; Get Him to the Greek 2010; Listen Up Philip 2014; High-Rise 2015; Queen of Earth 2015; Truth 2015

Moss, Jesse Ginger Snaps 2000; Final Destination 3 2006; Tucker and Dale vs Evil 2009; Extraterrestrial 2014

Moss, Nick Going Off, Big Time 2000; Kicks 2009

Moss, Tegan Seventeen and Missing 2006; NYC: Tornado Terror 2008; Dr Dolittle: Million Dollar Mutts 2009

Mossé, Mireille The City of Lost Children 1995; Swimming Pool 2002

Mostel, Josh (1946-) Going Home 1971; Sophie's Choice 1982; Star 80 1983; Almost You 1984; Windy City 1984; The Money Pit 1985; Radio Days 1987; Animal Behavior 1989; Naked Tango 1990; The Chase 1994; Billy Madison 1995; The Maddening 1995; Great Expectations 1997; Rounders 1998; Big Daddy 1999

Mostel, Zero (1915-1977) DuBarry Was a Lady 1943; Panic in the Streets 1950; The Enforcer 1951; Mr Belvedere Rings the Bell 1951; The Model and the Marriage Broker 1951; Sirocco 1951; A Funny Thing Happened on the Way to the Forum 1966; Great Catherine 1968; The Producers 1968; The Great Bank Robbery 1969; The Angel Levine 1970; The Hot Rock 1972; Marco 1973; Rhinoceros 1974; The Front 1976; Mastermind 1976; Watership Down 1978

Motlal (1910-1965) Devdas 1955; Anari 1959

Mouchet, Catherine (1959-) Thérèse 1986; Extension du Domaine de la Lutte 1999; The Pornographer 2001; The Monk 2011

Mouglalis, Anna (1978-) Merci pour le Chocolat 2000; Romanzo Criminale 2005; Coco Chanel & Igor Stravinsky 2009; Gainsbourg (Je T'Aime... Moi Non Plus) 2010; Jealousy 2013

Moulder-Brown, John (1953-) Deep End 1970; First Love 1970; Vampire Circus 1971; King, Queen, Knave 1972; Rumpelstiltskin 1986

Mouloudji, Marcel aka **Mouloudji** (1922-1994) Nous Sommes Tous des Assassins 1952; Secrets d'Alcove 1954

Mount, Anson (1973-) Urban Legends: Final Cut 2000; City by the Sea 2002; Crossroads 2002; All the Boys Love Mandy Lane 2006; The Two Mr Kissels 2008; Safe 2011; Visions 2014

Mount, Peggy (1916-2001) Dry Rot 1956; Sailor Beware! 1956; The Naked Truth 1957; Inn for Trouble 1960; Ladies Who Do 1963; One Way Pendulum 1965; Hotel Paradiso 1966; Oliver! 1968; The Princess and the Goblin 1992

Moura, Wagner (1976-) The Three Marias 2002; Lower City 2005; The Elite Squad 2007; Elite Squad: the Enemy Within 2010; Elysium 2013; Trash 2014

Mouton, Benjamin And God Created Woman 1988; Whore 1991; The Whole Wide World 1996; All the Real Girls 2003

Mowbray, Alan (1896-1969) God's Gift to Women 1931; Guilty Hands 1931; The Man from Yesterday 1932; Sherlock Holmes 1932; Berkeley Square 1933; Our Betters 1933; Peg o' My Heart 1933; Roman Scandals 1933; Charlie Chan in London 1934; The Girl from Missouri 1934; Long Lost Father 1934; One More River 1934; The Gay Deception 1935; In Person 1935; Desire 1936; My Man Godfrey 1936; On the Avenue 1937; Stand-In 1937; Topper 1937; Vogues of 1938 1937; Merrily We Live 1938; There Goes My Heart 1938; The Llano Kid 1939; Never Say Die 1939; Topper Takes a Trip 1939; The Boys from Syracuse 1940; Curtain Call 1940; Music in My Heart 1940; The

Villain Still Pursued Her 1940; Footlight Fever 1941; I Wake Up Screaming 1941; That Hamilton Woman 1941; That Uncertain Feeling 1941; Holy Matrimony 1943; Slightly Dangerous 1943; Earl Carroll Vanities 1945; Where Do We Go from Here? 1945; Terror by Night 1946; Lured 1947; Merton of the Movies 1947; Every Girl Should Be Married 1948; The Prince of Thieves 1948; The Lovable Cheat 1949; The Jackpot 1950; Wagonmaster 1950; Androcles and the Lion 1952; Blackbeard the Pirate 1952; The King and I 1956; The Man Who Knew Too Much 1956

Mower, Patrick (1940-) The Devil Rides Out 1968; The Smashing Bird I Used to Know 1969; Cry of the Banshee 1970; Incense for the Damned 1970; Black Beauty 1971; Catch Me a Spy 1971; Carry On England 1976; The Devil's Advocate 1977

Mowry, Tia aka **Mowry-Hardrict, Tia** Double Wedding 2010; The Mistle-Tones 2012

Moy, Colin In My Father's Den 2004; Emperor 2012

Moya, Antoinette Pétain 1992; Son Frère 2003

Moyer, Stephen (1969-) Prince Valiant 1997; Priest 2010; The Double 2011; The Barrens 2012; Devil's Knot 2013

Moynahan, Bridget (1972-) Serendipity 2001; The Recruit 2002; The Sum of All Fears 2002; I, Robot 2004; Lord of War 2005; Unknown 2006; Ramona and Beezus 2010; Battle Los Angeles 2011; John Wick 2014

Mozgovoy, Leonid Moloch 1999; Russian Ark 2002

Mrozowska, Zofia (1922-1983) The Constant Factor 1980; The Contract 1980

Mrsic, Dragomir Easy Money 2010; Easy Money II 2012

Mueller-Stahl, Armin (1930-) Jacob the Liar 1974; Lola 1982; Colonel Redl 1984; Forget Mozart 1985; Midnight Cop 1988; Music Box 1989; Avalon 1990; Kafka 1991; The Power of One 1991; Night on Earth 1992; Utz 1992; The House of the Spirits 1993; Holy Matrimony 1994; A Pyromaniac's Love Story 1995; Theodore Rex 1995; Shine 1996; The Game 1997; The Peacemaker 1997; 12 Angry Men 1997; The X-Files 1998; Jakob the Liar 1999; Mission to Mars 1999; The Thirteenth Floor 1999; The Long Run 2000; The Story of an African Farm 2004; Eastern Promises 2007; Angels & Demons 2009; The International 2009

Mueller, Cookie (1949-1989) Multiple Maniacs 1970; Pink Flamingos 1972; Female Trouble 1974; Desperate Living 1977; Polyester 1981

Mueller, Elisabeth (1926-) The Power and the Prize 1956; The Angry Hills 1959

Mueller, Maureen In a Shallow Grave 1988; Over Her Dead Body 1990

Muellerleile, Marianne Curse II: The Bite 1989; The Hottie & the Nottie 2008

Mühe, Ulrich (1953-2007) Benny's Video 1992; Funny Games 1997; Amen. 2002; The Lives of Others 2006

Muhich, Donald F (1931-2012) Bob & Carol & Ted & Alice 1969; Blume in Love 1973; Down and Out in Beverly Hills 1986

Mui, Anita (1963-2003) Rouge 1987; A Better Tomorrow III 1989; The Enforcer 1995; Rumble in the Bronx 1995

Muir, Gavin (1900-1972) Mary of Scotland 1936; Fair Warning 1937; Sherlock Holmes in Washington 1943; The Merry Monahans 1944; Calcutta 1947; Abbott and Costello Meet the Invisible Man 1951

Muir, Jean (1911-1996) The World Changes 1933; A Midsummer Night's Dream 1935; White Fang 1936

Muirhead, Oliver The Duke 1999; Like Crazy 2011

Mukherjee, Arun Kangchenjunga 1962; And Quiet Rolls the Dawn 1979

Mukherjee, Madhabi (1943-) The Golden Thread 1962; The Big City 1963; Charulata 1964

Mukherji, Rani aka **Mukerji, Rani** aka **Mukherjee, Rani** (1978-) Saathiya 2002; Black 2004; Hum Tum 2004; Veer-Zaara 2004; Paheli 2005

Mulay, Suhasini Lagaan: Once upon a Time in India 2001; Kuch Naa Kaho 2003

Muldaur, Diana (1938-) The Lawyer 1969; Number One 1969; The Other 1972; Chosen Survivors 1974; McQ 1974

Muldoon, Patrick (1968-) Wicked 1998; Red Team 1999; Bad Karma 2001

Mulgrew, Kate (1955-) Lovespell 1979; Remo - Unarmed and Dangerous 1985; Throw Momma from the Train 1987; The Bomber Boys 1995; Star Trek: Nemesis 2002

Mulhare, Edward (1923-1997) Signpost to Murder 1964; Von Ryan's Express 1965; Eye of the Devil 1966; Our Man Flint 1966; Caprice 1967

Mulhern, Matt (1960-) Extreme Prejudice 1987; Biloxi Blues 1988; Sunchaser 1996

Mulkey, Chris (1948-) Patti Rocks 1987; Heartbreak Hotel 1988; Roe vs Wade 1989; Bound & Gagged: a Love Story 1992; Gas, Food, Lodging 1992; Ghost in the Machine 1993; The Switch 1993; Radio 2003; Whiplash 2014

Mull, Martin (1943-) FM 1977; Serial 1980; Mr Mom 1983; Clue 1985; Cutting Class 1989; Desert Gamble 1996; Jingle All the Way 1996; Oliver's Ghost 2010

Mullally, Megan (1958-) Stealing Harvard 2002; Rebound 2005; Bee Movie 2007; Smashed 2012; The Kings of Summer 2013; Why Him? 2016

Mullan, Peter (1959-) Trainspotting 1995; Bogwoman 1997; My Name Is Joe 1998; Miss Julie 1999; Ordinary Decent Criminal 1999; The Claim 2000; Session 9 2001; Kiss of Life 2003; Young Adam 2003; Blinded 2004; Criminal 2004; On a Clear Day 2004; Children of Men 2006; The Last Legion 2006; True North 2006; Stone of Destiny 2008; Neds 2010; Tyrannosaur 2010; War Horse 2011; The Liability 2012; The Man Inside 2012; Welcome to the Punch 2012; Sunshine on Leith 2013; Hector 2015; Sunset Song 2015; Tommy's Honour 2016

Mullaney, Jack (1932-1982) The Young Stranger 1957; All the Fine Young Cannibals 1960; Dr Goldfoot and the Bikini Machine 1965; Tickle Me 1965; Spinout 1966

Mullard, Arthur (1912-1995) It's Trad, Dad 1961; Band of Thieves 1962; Smashing Time 1967; Crooks and Coronets 1969; Holiday on the Buses 1973; Adventures of a Plumber's Mate 1978

Mullen, Barbara (1914-1979) Jeannie 1941; Thunder Rock 1942; A Place of One's Own 1944; The Gentle Gunman 1952; Innocent Sinners 1957; The Very Edge 1962

Mullen, Conor Saltwater 1999; Silent Grace 2001; The Honeymooners 2003

Mullen, Marie The Disappearance of Finbar 1996; When Brendan Met Trudy 2000

Muller, Paul (1923-) Journey to Italy 1953; Checkpoint 1956; Lust of the Vampire 1956; Count Dracula 1970; Vampyros Lesbos 1970; Treasure Island 1972

Mulligan, Carey (1985-) Pride & Prejudice 2005; And When Did You Last See Your Father? 2007; An Education 2008; Brothers 2009; The Greatest 2009; Never Let Me Go 2010; Wall Street: Money Never Sleeps 2010; Drive 2011; Shame 2011; Another Day/ Another Time 2013; The Great Gatsby 2013; Inside Llewyn Davis 2013; Far from the Madding Crowd 2015; Suffragette 2015

Mulligan, Richard (1932-2000) One Potato, Two Potato 1964; The Group 1966; Little Big Man 1970; The Hideaways 1973; S0B 1981; Trail of the Pink Panther 1982; Micki & Maude 1984; Teachers 1984; The Heavenly Kid 1985; Babes in Toyland 1986; A Fine Mess 1986; Oliver & Company 1988

Mullinar, Rod (1942-) Patrick 1978; Thirst 1979; Dead Calm 1988

Mullins, Aimee Cremaster 3 2002; Bad Land: Road to Fury 2014

Mulock, Al (1925-1970) Tarzan's Greatest Adventure 1959; Battle beneath the Earth 1968

Mulroney, Dermot (1963-) Young Guns 1988; Staying Together 1989; Unconquered 1989; Bright Angel 1990; Career Opportunities 1991; The Heart of Justice 1992; The Assassin 1993; The Last Outlaw 1993; The Thing Called Love 1993; Angels in the Outfield 1994; Bad Girls 1994; There Goes My Baby 1994; Copycat 1995; How to Make an American Quilt 1995; Kansas City 1995; Living in Oblivion 1995; The Trigger Effect 1996; Goodbye Lover 1997; My Best Friend's Wedding 1997; Trixie 2000; Where the Money Is 2000; Lovely & Amazing 2001; The Safety of Objects 2001; About Schmidt 2002; Undertow 2004; The Wedding Date 2004; The Family Stone 2005; Must Love Dogs 2005; Georgia Rule 2007; Zodiac 2007; Flash of Genius 2008; The Memory Keeper's Daughter 2008; J Edgar 2011; Big Miracle 2012; The Grey 2012; jOBS 2013; Stoker 2013;

Insidious: Chapter 3 2015; Dirty Grandpa 2016

Mulroney, Kieran (1965-) Career Opportunities 1991; The Spitfire Grill 1996

Mumba, Samantha (1983-) The Time Machine 2002; Boy Eats Girl 2005

Mumy, Bill aka Mumy, Billy (1954-) Palm Springs Weekend 1963; A Ticklish Affair 1963; Dear Brigitte 1966; Papillon 1973

Mumy, Liliana (1995-) The Santa Clause 2 2002; Cheaper by the Dozen 2003; Cheaper by the Dozen 2 2005; The Santa Clause 3: the Escape Clause 2006

Mundin, Herbert (1898-1939) Chandu the Magician 1932; Cavalcade 1933; Shanghai Madness 1933; Mutiny on the Bounty 1935; The Perfect Gentleman 1935; A Message to Garcia 1936; Tarzan Escapes 1936; Under Two Flags 1936; Angel 1937; Another Dawn 1937

Mune, Ian (1941-) The Piano 1993; Ike: Countdown to D-Day 2004; The Insatiable Moon 2010

Muni, Paul (1895-1967) The Valiant 1929; I Am a Fugitive from a Chain Gang 1932; Scarface 1932; The World Changes 1933; Hi, Nellie! 1934; Black Fury 1935; Bordertown 1935; Dr Socrates 1935; The Story of Louis Pasteur 1936; The Good Earth 1937; The Life of Emile Zola 1937; The Woman I Love 1937; Juarez 1939; We Are Not Alone 1939; Hudson's Bay 1940; The Commandos Strike at Dawn 1942; Stage Door Canteen 1943; Counter-Attack 1945; A Song to Remember 1945; Angel on My Shoulder 1946; The Last Angry Man 1959

Muniz, Frankie (1985-) My Dog Skip 1999; Big Fat Liar 2002; Agent Cody Banks 2003; Agent Cody Banks 2: Destination London 2003; Racing Stripes 2004; Stay Alive 2006

Munn, Olivia (1980-) I Don't Know How She Does It 2011; Magic Mike 2012; Deliver Us from Evil 2014; Mortdecai 2015

Munro, Caroline (1950-) Captain Kronos: Vampire Hunter 1972; Dracula AD 1972 1972; The Golden Voyage of Sinbad 1973; I Don't Want to Be Born 1975; At the Earth's Core 1976; The Spy Who Loved Me 1977; To Die For 1994

Munro, Janet (1934-1972) The Trollenberg Terror 1958; Darby O'Gill and the Little People 1959; Tommy the Toreador 1959; Swiss Family Robinson 1960; The Day the Earth Caught Fire 1961; Life for Ruth 1962; Bitter Harvest 1963; Hide and Seek 1963; A Jolly Bad Fellow 1964; Sebastian 1968

Munro, Lochlyn (1966-) Dead Man on Campus 1998; Scary Movie 2000; Kill Me Later 2001; A Guy Thing 2002; The Keeper 2003; White Chicks 2004; Little Man 2006; Daddy Day Camp 2007; The Art of War II: Betrayal 2008

Munro, Neil Dancing in the Dark 1986; Gate II 1992

Munroe, Kathleen Accidental Friendship 2008; George A Romero's Survival of the Dead 2009; The Wild Girl 2010

Munshin, Jules (1915-1970) Easter Parade 1948; On the Town 1949; Take Me Out to the Ball Game 1949; That Midnight Kiss 1949; Silk Stockings 1957; Mastermind 1976

Munson, Ona (1903-1955) Five Star Final 1931; Gone with the Wind 1939; Lady from Louisiana 1941; The Shanghai Gesture 1941; Wild Geese Calling 1941; The Cheaters 1945; Dakota 1945

Murat, Jean (1888-1968) Carnival in Flanders 1935; Eternal Love 1943; On the Riviera 1951

Murata, Takehiro (1960-) Godzilla vs Mothra 1992; When the Last Sword Is Drawn 2003

Murcell, George (1925-1998) The Pursuers 1961; Pascali's Island 1988; Year of the Gun 1991

Murdoch, Richard (1907-1990) Band Waggon 1939; Charley's (Big Hearted) Aunt 1940; The Ghost Train 1941; I Thank You 1941; The Gay Adventure 1949

Murdock, George (1939-2012) Certain Fury 1985; Man in the Chair 2006

Murdock, Jack (1922-2001) Big Top Pee-wee 1988; Rain Man 1988

Murgia, Tiberio (1929-2010) Big Deal on Madonna Street 1958; That Man George 1965

Murnik, Peter (1965-) Body Parts 1991; Golden Gate 1994

Murphy, Aaron Rain 2001; The World's Fastest Indian 2005

Murphy, Audie (1924-1971) Kansas Raiders 1950; The Kid from Texas 1950; Sierra 1950; The Cimarron Kid

1951; The Red Badge of Courage 1951; The Duel at Silver Creek 1952; Column South 1953; Gunsmoke 1953; Tumbleweed 1953; Destry 1954; Drums across the River 1954; Ride Clear of Diablo 1954; To Hell and Back 1955; Walk the Proud Land 1956; Guns of Fort Petticoat 1957; Night Passage 1957; The Gun Runners 1958; The Quiet American 1958; Ride a Crooked Trail 1958; Cast a Long Shadow 1959; No Name on the Bullet 1959; The Wild and the Innocent 1959; Hell Bent for Leather 1960; Seven Ways from Sundown 1960; The Unforgiven 1960; Battle at Bloody Beach 1961; Six Black Horses 1962; Showdown 1963; Apache Rifles 1964; Bullet for a Badman 1964; Gunfight at Comanche Creek 1964; Arizona Raiders 1965; 40 Guns to Apache Pass 1966; Gunpoint 1966

Murphy, Ben (1942-) Yours, Mine and Ours 1968; The 1,000 Plane Raid 1969

Murphy, Bill The Story of GI Joe 1945; A Foreign Affair 1948

Murphy, Brian (1933-) Sparrows Can't Sing 1962; The Ragman's Daughter 1972; Man about the House 1974; George and Mildred 1980

Murphy, Brittany (1977-2009) Clueless 1995; The Prophecy II 1997; David and Lisa 1998; Cherry Falls 1999; The Devil's Arithmetic 1999; Drop Dead Gorgeous 1999; Girl, Interrupted 1999; Sidewalks of New York 2000; Trixie 2000; Don't Say a Word 2001; Riding in Cars with Boys 2001; Summer Catch 2001; 8 Mile 2002; Spun 2002; Just Married 2003; Uptown Girls 2003; Little Black Book 2004; Sin City 2005; Happy Feet 2006; Deadline 2009; Nora Roberts' Tribute 2009

Murphy, Cillian (1976-) Disco Pigs 2001; 28 Days Later... 2002; Girl with a Pearl Earring 2003; interMission 2003; Batman Begins 2005; Breakfast on Pluto 2005; Red Eye 2005; The Wind That Shakes the Barley 2006; Sunshine 2007; The Edge of Love 2008; Waveriders 2008; Perrier's Bounty 2009; Inception 2010; In Time 2011; Retreat 2011; Broken 2012; Red Lights 2012; Transcendence 2014; In the Heart of the Sea 2015; Dunkirk 2017

Murphy, Donna (1958-) Jade 1995; Passion 1996; The Day Lincoln Was Shot 1998; Star Trek: Insurrection 1998; The Astronaut's Wife 1999; Center Stage 2000; The Last Debate 2000; Spider-Man 2 2004; The Fountain 2005; The Nanny Diaries 2007; Tangled 2010

Murphy, Eddie (1961-) 48 HRS 1982; Trading Places 1983; Best Defense 1984; Beverly Hills Cop 1984; The Golden Child 1986; Beverly Hills Cop II 1987; Eddie Murphy Raw 1987; Coming to America 1988; Harlem Nights 1989; Another 48 HRS 1990; Boomerang 1992; The Distinguished Gentleman 1992; Beverly Hills Cop III 1994; Vampire in Brooklyn 1995; The Nutty Professor 1996; Metro 1997; Doctor Dolittle 1998; Holy Man 1998; Mulan 1998; Bowfinger 1999; Life 1999; Nutty Professor 2: the Klumps 2000; Dr Dolittle 2 2001; Pluto Nash 2001; Shrek 2001; I Spy 2002; Showtime 2002; Daddy Day Care 2003; The Haunted Mansion 2003; Shrek 2 2004; Dreamgirls 2006; Norbit 2007; Shrek the Third 2007; Meet Dave 2008; Imagine That 2009; Shrek Forever After 2010; Tower Heist 2011

Murphy, George (1902-1992) Kid Millions 1934; Broadway Melody of 1938 1937; London by Night 1937; Hold That Co-Ed 1938; Letter of Introduction 1938; Little Miss Broadway 1938; Broadway Melody of 1940 1940; Little Nellie Kelly 1940; The Navy Steps Out 1941; Tom, Dick and Harry 1941; For Me and My Gal 1942; The Navy Comes Through 1942; Bataan 1943; This Is the Army 1943; Broadway Rhythm 1944; Show Business 1944; Step Lively 1944; Cynthia 1947; Battleground 1949; Border Incident 1949; Walk East on Beacon 1952

Murphy, Gerard (1956-) The Brink's Job 1978; Waterworld 1995

Murphy, Johnny (1943-2016) The Commitments 1991; Into the West 1992

Murphy (1), Mary (1931-2011) Main Street to Broadway 1953; The Wild One 1953; The Mad Magician 1954; Sitting Bull 1954; The Desperate Hours 1955; A Man Alone 1955; The Intimate Stranger 1956; Crime and Punishment, USA 1959; Junior Bonner 1972

Murphy, Maurice (1913-1978) Faithless 1932; Pilgrimage 1933; Curly Top 1935; Tovarich 1937

Murphy (1), Michael (1938-) Countdown 1967; Brewster McCloud 1970; Count Yorga, Vampire 1970;

What's Up, Doc? 1972; Phase IV 1973; The Thief Who Came to Dinner 1973; The Autobiography of Miss Jane Pittman 1974; The Front 1976; The Class of Miss MacMichael 1978; An Unmarried Woman 1978; Hot Money 1979; Manhattan 1979; The Year of Living Dangerously 1982; Cloak and Dagger 1984; Mesmerized 1984; Salvador 1986; Shocker 1989; Batman Returns 1992; Clean Slate 1994; Kansas City 1995; Silver City 2004; Away from Her 2006; According to Greta 2009

Murphy, Reilly Body Snatchers 1993; Dangerous Game 1993

Murphy, Rosemary (1925-2014) To Kill a Mockingbird 1962; Any Wednesday 1966; Ben 1972; You'll Like My Mother 1972; Ace Eli and Rodger of the Skies 1973; Julia 1977; The Hand 1981; For the Boys 1991; Dust 2001

Murphy, Tom The General 1998; Adam & Paul 2004

Murray Hill, Peter (1908-1957) The Ghost Train 1941; Bell-Bottom George 1943; Rhythm Serenade 1943; Madonna of the Seven Moons 1944; They Were Sisters 1945

Murray, Barbara (1929-2014) Boys in Brown 1949; Passport to Pimlico 1949; Another Man's Poison 1951; The Frightened Man 1952; Meet Mr Lucifer 1953; Campbell's Kingdom 1957; A Cry from the Streets 1957; Operation Bullshine 1959; The Punch and Judy Man 1962; Doctor in Distress 1963; Some Will, Some Won't 1969; Up Pompeii 1971

Murray, Bill (1950-) Meatballs 1979; Caddyshack 1980; Where the Buffalo Roam 1980; Stripes 1981; Tootsie 1982; Ghost Busters 1984; Nothing Lasts Forever 1984; The Razor's Edge 1984; Little Shop of Horrors 1986; Scrooged 1988; Ghostbusters II 1989; Quick Change 1990; What about Bob? 1991; Mad Dog and Glory 1992; Groundhog Day 1993; Ed Wood 1994; Kingpin 1996; Larger than Life 1996; The Man Who Knew Too Little 1997; Space Jam 1997; Rushmore 1998; Wild Things 1998; Cradle Will Rock 1999; Charlie's Angels 2000; Hamlet 2000; Osmosis Jones 2001; The Royal Tenenbaums 2001; Coffee and Cigarettes 2003; Lost in Translation 2003; Garfield 2004; The Life Aquatic with Steve Zissou 2004; Broken Flowers 2005; The Lost City 2005; Garfield 2 2006; The Darjeeling Limited 2007; City of Ember 2008; Get Smart 2008; The Limits of Control 2008; Fantastic Mr Fox 2009; Get Low 2009; Zombieland 2009; Hyde Park on Hudson 2012; Moonrise Kingdom 2012; The Monuments Men 2013; The Grand Budapest Hotel 2014; St Vincent 2014; Aloha 2015; Rock the Kasbah 2015; The Jungle Book 2016

Murray, Billy (1941-) Poor Cow 1967; McVicar 1980; Essex Boys 1999; Rollin with the Nines 2005; Freight 2010; Strippers vs Werewolves 2012

Murray, Brian Treasure Planet 2002; My Dog Tulip 2009

Murray, Chad Michael (1981-) Freaky Friday 2003; A Cinderella Story 2004; House of Wax 2004; Fruitvale Station 2013; Left Behind 2014

Murray, Chic (1919-1985) Ups and Downs of a Handyman 1975; Gregory's Girl 1980

Murray, Don (1929-) Bus Stop 1956; The Bachelor Party 1957; A Hatful of Rain 1957; From Hell to Texas 1958; Shake Hands with the Devil 1959; These Thousand Hills 1959; One Foot in Hell 1960; The Hoodlum Priest 1961; Advise and Consent 1962; One Man's Way 1964; Baby the Rain Must Fall 1965; Kid Rodelo 1966; The Plainsman 1966; The Viking Queen 1967; The Intruders 1970; Conquest of the Planet of the Apes 1972; Rainbow 1978; Endless Love 1981; Peggy Sue Got Married 1986; Made in Heaven 1987; Ghosts Can't Do It 1990

Murray, Hannah Chatroom 2010; Clone 2010; God Help the Girl 2012

Murray (1), James (1901-1936) The Crowd 1928; Central Airport 1933

Murray, Jan (1917-2006) The Busy Body 1967; Tarzan and the Great River 1967; Thunder Alley 1967; Which Way to the Front? 1970

Murray, Joel One Crazy Summer 1986; God Bless America 2011; Monsters University 2013; Bloodsucking Bosses 2015

Murray, Ken (1903-1988) The Man Who Shot Liberty Valance 1962; Son of Flubber 1962

Murray, Mae (1889-1965) The Merry Widow 1925; Bachelor Apartment 1931

Murray, Mary The Magdalene Sisters 2002; Adam & Paul 2004

Murray, Stephen (1912-1983) The Prime Minister 1940; The Master of

Bankam 1947; My Brother Jonathan 1947; London Belongs to Me 1948; Silent Dust 1948; Now Barabbas Was a Robber 1949; The Magnet 1950; Four Sided Triangle 1953; The End of the Affair 1954; A Tale of Two Cities 1957; Master Spy 1964

Murton, Lionel (1915-2006) The Pickwick Papers 1952; The Battle of the River Plate 1956; Surprise Package 1960; The Truth about Spring 1964; The Revolutionary 1970

Murua, Lautaro (1926-1995) Triumphs of a Man Called Horse 1983; I, the Worst of All 1990; The Plague 1992

Musante, Tony (1936-2013) The Incident 1967; A Professional Gun 1968; The Bird with the Crystal Plumage 1969; The Grissom Gang 1971; The Last Run 1971; The Pope of Greenwich Village 1984; We Own the Night 2007

Muse, Clarence (1889-1979) Dirigible 1931; Huckleberry Finn 1931; Washington Merry-Go-Round 1932; White Zombie 1932; The Mind Reader 1933; Broadway Bill 1934; Invisible Ghost 1941; Riding High 1950; Apache Drums 1951; The Black Stallion 1979

Mutambirwa, Garikayi aka Mutambirwa, Garikayi "G K" Clockstoppers 2002; Jeepers Creepers 2 2003

Muti, Ornella (1955-) Viva Italia! 1978; Flash Gordon 1980; Tales of Ordinary Madness 1981; Love and Money 1982; Swann in Love 1984; Chronicle of a Death Foretold 1987; Wait until Spring, Bandini 1989; Oscar 1991; Once upon a Crime 1992; [One] Cavale 2002; [Three] Après la Vie 2002; [Two] Un Couple Epatant 2002

Muzquiz, Carlos (1906-1960) Captain Scarlett 1953; The Black Scorpion 1957

Myers, Cynthia (1950-) Beyond the Valley of the Dolls 1970; Molly and Lawless John 1972

Myers, Mike (1963-) Wayne's World 1992; So I Married an Axe Murderer 1993; Wayne's World 2 1993; Austin Powers: International Man of Mystery 1997; 54 1998; Austin Powers: the Spy Who Shagged Me 1999; Mystery, Alaska 1999; Shrek 2001; Austin Powers in Goldmember 2002; Dr Seuss' The Cat in the Hat 2003; View from the Top 2003; Shrek 2 2004; Shrek the Third 2007; The Love Guru 2008; Inglourious Basterds 2009; Shrek Forever After 2010

Myers, Peter Bachelor of Hearts 1958; The Reluctant Debutante 1958; Hello - Goodbye 1970

Myles, Sophia (1980-) The Abduction Club 2002; Underworld 2003; Thunderbirds 2004; Tristan + Isolde 2005; Hallam Foe 2006; Outlander 2008; Blackwood 2013; Transformers: Age of Extinction 2014

Mynster, Karen-Lise (1952-) Sofie 1992; Minor Mishaps 2002

N

Nable, Matt Riddick 2013; Son of a Gun 2013

Nabors, Jim (1930-) The Best Little Whorehouse in Texas 1982; Stroker Ace 1983

Naceri, Samy (1961-) Taxi 1998; Taxi 2 2000; Days of Glory 2006

Nachtergaele, Matheus (1969-) Four Days in September 1997; City of God 2002

Nadeau, Claire Nelly & Monsieur Arnaud 1995; Les Petites Vacances 2006

Nader, George (1921-2002) Robot Monster 1953; Carnival Story 1954; Lady Godiva 1955; Six Bridges to Cross 1955; Away All Boats 1956; The Unguarded Moment 1956; The Female Animal 1958; Nowhere to Go 1958; House of a Thousand Dolls 1967; Sumuru 1967

Nader, Ralph Manufacturing Dissent: Uncovering Michael Moore 2007; POM Wonderful Presents: The Greatest Movie Ever Sold 2011

Nadira (1932-2006) Shree 420 1955; Bombay Talkie 1970

Nag, Anant (1948-) Ankur 1974; Nishant 1975

Nagase, Masatoshi (1966-) Mystery Train 1989; Autumn Moon 1992; Cold Fever 1994; The Sea Is Watching 2002

Nagel, Anne (1912-1966) The Case of the Stuttering Bishop 1937; Argentine Nights 1940; Man Made Monster 1941; Never Give a Sucker an Even Break 1941

Nagel, Conrad (1897-1970) Sinners in Silk 1924; The Exquisite Sinner 1926; London after Midnight 1927; The Mysterious Lady 1928; Dynamite 1929; Hollywood Revue 1929; The Kiss 1929; The Divorcee 1930; One Romantic

Night 1930; Bad Sister 1931; East Lynne 1931; Hell Divers 1932; Ann Vickers 1933; Dangerous Corner 1934; Wedding Present 1936; One Million BC 1940; All That Heaven Allows 1955; The Man Who Understood Women 1959; A Stranger in My Arms 1959

Nagra, Parminder Bend It like Beckham 2001; Horrid Henry: the Movie 2011; Twenty8k 2012

Nagy, Bill (1900-1973) The Brain Machine 1954; Shadow of a Man 1954; Across the Bridge 1957; First Man into Space 1958; The Boy Who Stole a Million 1960; Never Take Sweets from a Stranger 1960; Surprise Package 1960; Danger by My Side 1962; Night of the Prowler 1962

Nagy, Zsolt Kontroll 2003; Freight 2010

Nahon, Alex aka **Nahon, Alexandre** 2 Days in Paris 2006; 2 Days in New York 2011

Nahon, Philippe (1938-) Seul contre Tous 1998; Irreversible 2002; Switchblade Romance 2003; Calvaire 2004

Naidu, Ajay (1972-) Touch and Go 1986; subUrbia 1996; Office Space 1999

Naidu, Leela (1940-2009) The Householder 1963; Electric Moon 1992

Nail, Jimmy (1954-) Morons from Outer Space 1985; Crusoe 1988; Dream Demon 1988; Danny, the Champion of the World 1989; Evita 1996; Still Crazy 1998

Nail, Joanne Switchblade Sisters 1975; The Visitor 1980; Full Moon High 1982

Naish, J Carrol aka **Naish, J Carroll** (1900-1973) The Hatchet Man 1932; The Kid from Spain 1932; Tiger Shark 1932; Two Seconds 1932; The Mad Game 1933; British Agent 1934; Upper World 1934; Black Fury 1935; Confidential 1935; The Lives of a Bengal Lancer 1935; The Robin Hood of El Dorado 1936; Bulldog Drummond Comes Back 1937; Bulldog Drummond in Africa 1938; Beau Geste 1939; Down Argentine Way 1940; Typhoon 1940; The Birth of the Blues 1941; Blood and Sand 1941; The Corsican Brothers 1941; That Night in Rio 1941; Dr Broadway 1942; A Gentleman at Heart 1942; The Pied Piper 1942; Calling Dr Death 1943; Gung Ho! 1943; Sahara 1943; Enter Arsene Lupin 1944; House of Frankenstein 1944; The Monster Maker 1944; The Whistler 1944; A Medal for Benny 1945; The Southerner 1945; Strange Confession 1945; The Beast with Five Fingers 1946; Humoresque 1946; The Fugitive 1947; Joan of Arc 1948; The Kissing Bandit 1949; That Midnight Kiss 1949; Annie Get Your Gun 1950; The Black Hand 1950; Please Believe Me 1950; Rio Grande 1950; The Toast of New Orleans 1950; Across the Wide Missouri 1951; Clash by Night 1952; Denver & Rio Grande 1952; Beneath the 12-Mile Reef 1953; Saskatchewan 1954; Sitting Bull 1954; The Last Command 1955; New York Confidential 1955; Rage at Dawn 1955; Violent Saturday 1955; Dracula vs Frankenstein 1970

Naismith, Laurence (1908-1992) Train of Events 1949; Mogambo 1953; The Black Knight 1954; Carrington VC 1954; The Man Who Never Was 1955; The Extra Day 1956; Tiger in the Smoke 1956; Boy on a Dolphin 1957; Robbery under Arms 1957; Seven Waves Away 1957; Solomon and Sheba 1959; The Angry Silence 1960; Sink the Bismarck! 1960; Village of the Damned 1960; The World of Suzie Wong 1960; Greyfriars Bobby 1961; The Prince and the Pauper 1962; We Joined the Navy 1962; Jason and the Argonauts 1963; The Three Lives of Thomasina 1963; Sky West and Crooked 1965; Camelot 1967; The Long Duel 1967; Eye of the Cat 1969; The Valley of Gwangi 1969; Scrooge 1970; Quest for Love 1971; The Amazing Mr Blunden 1972

Najimy, Kathy (1957-) Soapdish 1991; Sister Act 1992; Hocus Pocus 1993; Sister Act 2: Back in the Habit 1993; Cats Don't Dance 1998; Hope Floats 1998; Rat Race 2001; WALL-E 2008

Nakadai, Tatsuya (1932-) Conflagration 1958; The Human Condition 1958; The Key 1959; Harakiri 1962; Sanjuro 1962; High and Low 1963; Kwaidan 1964; The Face of Another 1966; Portrait of Hell 1969; The Wolves 1971; Kagemusha 1980; The Empty Table 1985; Ran 1985

Nakai, Kiichi (1961-) The Burmese Harp 1985; The Empty Table 1985; When the Last Sword Is Drawn 2003; Riding Alone for Thousands of Miles 2005

Nakamura, Ganjiro (1902-1983) The Lower Depths 1956; Conflagration 1958; Floating Weeds 1959; The Key 1959; The End of Summer 1961; An Actor's Revenge 1963

Nakamura, Kanemon (1901-1982) Humanity and Paper Balloons 1937; The Loyal 47 Ronin 1941; Musashi Miyamoto 1944

Nakamura, Shidou aka **Nakamura, Shido** Ping Pong 2002; Fearless 2006; Letters from Iwo Jima 2006

Nakamura, Toru (1965-) Blue Tiger 1994; Tokyo Raiders 2000

Nakatani, Miki (1976-) Ring 1997; Ring 2 1998; Chaos 1999; When the Last Sword Is Drawn 2003; Memories of Matsuko 2006

Nalder, Reggie (1911-1991) The Man Who Knew Too Much 1956; Mark of the Devil 1970; Zoltan... Hound of Dracula 1977; Salem's Lot 1979

Naldi, Nita (1897-1961) Dr Jekyll and Mr Hyde 1920; Blood and Sand 1922; The Pleasure Garden 1925

Nance, Jack aka **Nance, John** (1943-1996) Eraserhead 1976; Ghoulies 1985; Blue Velvet 1986; Barfly 1987; Motorama 1991; The Secret Agent Club 1995; Lost Highway 1996

Nanty, Isabelle (1962-) Tatie Danielle 1990; Pas sur la Bouche 2003

Naor, Igal Rendition 2007; The Infidel 2010; Dead Europe 2012

Napier, Alan (1903-1988) The Four Just Men 1939; We Are Not Alone 1939; The Invisible Man Returns 1940; Cat People 1942; Lost Angel 1943; The Silent Bell 1944; The Uninvited 1944; Ministry of Fear 1945; Macbeth 1948; Tarzan's Magic Fountain 1949; Across the Wide Missouri 1951; Double Crossbones 1951; Big Jim McLain 1952; Julius Caesar 1953; The Mole People 1956; Until They Sail 1957; The Premature Burial 1962; The Sword in the Stone 1963; Marnie 1964; 36 Hours 1964; Batman 1966

Napier, Charles (1936-2011) Cherry, Harry & Raquel 1969; Beyond the Valley of the Dolls 1970; Supervixens 1975; Citizens Band 1977; Last Embrace 1979; Rambo: First Blood, Part II 1985; Hit List 1988; Ernest Goes to Jail 1990; Miami Blues 1990; Good Cop, Bad Cop 1993; Philadelphia 1993; Jury Duty 1995; Jailbreak 1997; Steel 1997; The Big Tease 1999

Napier, Marshall Bad Blood 1982; Georgia 1988; The Navigator - a Medieval Odyssey 1988; The Big Steal 1990; The Water Horse 2007

Napier, Neil Stealing Paradise 2011; The Expatriate 2012

Napier, Russell (1910-1974) The Brain Machine 1954; The Stranger Came Home 1954; The Blue Peter 1955; Little Red Monkey 1955

Nardini, Daniela (1968-) Elephant Juice 1999; Festival 2005

Nares, Owen (1888-1943) The Impassive Footman 1932; The Show Goes On 1937

Nargis (1929-1981) Andaz 1949; Barsaat 1949; Babul 1950; Awara 1951; Shree 420 1955; Chori Chori 1956; Mother India 1957

Nascarella, Arthur aka **Nascarella, Arthur J** After the Storm 2001; Wisegirls 2001; The Cooler 2002

Nash, Johnny (1940-) Take a Giant Step 1959; Key Witness 1960

Nash, Mary (1885-1976) Easy Living 1937; Heidi 1937; Wells Fargo 1937; The Little Princess 1939; The Philadelphia Story 1940; Cobra Woman 1944; In the Meantime, Darling 1944; The Lady and the Monster 1944; Yolanda and the Thief 1945; Till the Clouds Roll By 1946

Nat, Marie-José (1940-) La Vérité 1960; The Seven Deadly Sins 1961

Nath, Alok (1956-) Pardes 1997; Taal 1999; Hum Tumhare Hain Sanam 2000

Nathan, Vivian (1921-2015) The Outsider 1961; The Young Savages 1961; Klute 1971

Nathenson, Zoe Those Glory, Glory Days 1983; Mona Lisa 1986; The Raggedy Rawney 1987

Natividad, Kitten aka **Natividad, Francesca "Kitten"** (1948-) Beneath the Valley of the Ultra Vixens 1979; My Tutor 1983

Natsukawa, Daijiro The Downfall of Osen 1935; Poppy 1935

Natsukawa, Yui (1968-) When the Last Sword Is Drawn 2003; Zatoichi 2003; Still Walking 2008; I Wish 2011

Natwick, Mildred (1905-1994) The Long Voyage Home 1940; The Enchanted Cottage 1945; Yolanda and the Thief 1945; The Late George Apley 1947; Three Godfathers 1948; The Kissing Bandit 1949; She Wore a Yellow Ribbon 1949; Cheaper by the Dozen 1950; Against All Flags 1952; The Trouble with Harry 1954; The Court

Jester 1956; Teenage Rebel 1956; Tammy and the Bachelor 1957; Barefoot in the Park 1967; The Maltese Bippy 1969; Trilogy 1969; Daisy Miller 1974; At Long Last Love 1975; Kiss Me Goodbye 1982; Dangerous Liaisons 1988

Naughton, Charlie (1887-1976) Alf's Button Afloat 1938; Gasbags 1940

Naughton, David (1951-) Midnight Madness 1980; An American Werewolf in London 1981; Hot Dog - The Movie 1984; Not for Publication 1984; The Boy in Blue 1986; Amityville: a New Generation 1993

Naughton, James (1945-) My Body, My Child 1982; Cat's Eye 1984; The Glass Menagerie 1987; The Price of Passion 1988; Danielle Steel's Mixed Blessings 1995; First Kid 1996; Oxygen 1999; Factory Girl 2006

Navarre, Elodie (1979-) Love etc 1997; He Loves Me... He Loves Me Not 2002; Love Me If You Dare 2003; Conversations with My Gardener 2006

Nayar, Nisha K aka **Nayar, Nisha** Bhaji on the Beach 1993; The Darkest Light 1999

Naylor, Zoe (1977-) The Book of Revelation 2006; The Reef 2010

Naymark, Lola A Common Thread 2004; The Army of Crime 2009

Nazimova, Alla aka **Nazimova** (1879-1945) Camille 1921; Salome 1922; Escape 1940; Blood and Sand 1941

Nazzari, Amedeo (1907-1979) Nights of Cabiria 1957; The Naked Maja 1959; The Best of Enemies 1961; Nefertite, Queen of the Nile 1961; The Sicilian Clan 1969; The Valachi Papers 1972

Ne-Yo Stomp the Yard 2006; Battle Los Angeles 2011; Red Tails 2012

Nélisse, Sophie Monsieur Lazhar 2011; The Book Thief 2014

Neagle, Anna (1904-1986) Bitter Sweet 1933; Nell Gwyn 1934; Limelight 1936; London Melody 1937; Victoria the Great 1937; Sixty Glorious Years 1938; Nurse Edith Cavell 1939; Irene 1940; No, No, Nanette 1940; Sunny 1941; They Flew Alone 1941; Forever and a Day 1943; Yellow Canary 1943; I Live in Grosvenor Square 1945; Piccadilly Incident 1946; The Courtneys of Curzon Street 1947; Elizabeth of Ladymead 1948; Spring in Park Lane 1948; Maytime in Mayfair 1949; Odette 1950; The Lady with the Lamp 1951; Derby Day 1952; King's Rhapsody 1955; Lilacs in the Spring 1955; My Teenage Daughter 1956; The Man Who Wouldn't Talk 1957; No Time for Tears 1957

Neal, Billie (1955-1999) Down by Law 1986; Mortal Thoughts 1991; Sweet Nothing 1995

Neal, Dylan The President's Man 2000; My Family's Secret 2010

Neal, Elise (1970-) Rosewood 1997; Scream 2 1997; Hustle & Flow 2005

Neal, Luke Wilderness 2006; The Borderlands 2013

Neal, Patricia (1926-2010) The Fountainhead 1949; The Hasty Heart 1949; It's a Great Feeling 1949; The Breaking Point 1950; Bright Leaf 1950; Three Secrets 1950; The Day the Earth Stood Still 1951; Operation Pacific 1951; Weekend with Father 1951; Diplomatic Courier 1952; Stranger from Venus 1954; A Face in the Crowd 1957; Breakfast at Tiffany's 1961; Hud 1963; Psyche '59 1964; In Harm's Way 1965; The Subject Was Roses 1968; The Road Builder 1971; Baxter 1973; Happy Mother's Day... Love, George 1973; The Passage 1978; All Quiet on the Western Front 1979; Ghost Story 1981; Caroline? 1990; Cookie's Fortune 1999

Neal, Tom (1914-1972) Andy Hardy Meets Debutante 1940; Detour 1945

Nealon, Kevin (1953-) All I Want for Christmas 1991; Adam Sandler's Eight Crazy Nights 2003; Daddy Day Care 2003; Good Boy! 2003; Blended 2014

Neame (2), Christopher (1947-) Dracula AD 1972 1972; DOA 1988

Near, Holly Angel, Angel Down We Go 1969; FTA 1972; Dogfight 1991

Neckar, Vaclav (1943-) Closely Observed Trains 1966; Larks on a String 1969

Nedeljakova, Barbara Hostel 2005; Pimp 2010

Nedell, Bernard (1898-1972) Lazybones 1935; Some Like It Hot 1939

Nedjari, Al Frantz Fanon: Black Skin White Mask 1996; Strong Language 1998

Needham, Tracey (1967-) Lush Life 1993; Angel in the Family 2004; Murder 101 2006

Needles, Nique (1964-) The Boy Who Had Everything 1984; Dogs in Space 1986

Neeson, Liam (1952-) Excalibur 1981; Krull 1983; The Bounty 1984; The Innocent 1984; Lamb 1985; The Mission

1986; A Prayer for the Dying 1987; Suspect 1987; The Dead Pool 1988; High Spirits 1988; The Price of Passion 1988; Satisfaction 1988; Next of Kin 1989; The Big Man 1990; Darkman 1990; Under Suspicion 1991; Husbands and Wives 1992; Leap of Faith 1992; Ruby Cairo 1992; Shining Through 1992; Ethan Frome 1993; Schindler's List 1993; Nell 1994; Rob Roy 1995; Before and After 1996; Michael Collins 1996; Les Misérables 1997; The Haunting 1999; Star Wars Episode I: the Phantom Menace 1999; The Endurance: Shackleton's Legendary Antarctic Expedition 2000; Gun Shy 2000; Gangs of New York 2002; K-19: the Widowmaker 2002; Love Actually 2003; Kinsey 2004; Batman Begins 2005; Breakfast on Pluto 2005; The Chronicles of Narnia: The Lion, the Witch and the Wardrobe 2005; Kingdom of Heaven 2005; Seraphim Falls 2006; Taken 2007; The Chronicles of Narnia: Prince Caspian 2008; The Other Man 2008; Ponyo 2008; After.Life 2009; Chloe 2009; Five Minutes of Heaven 2009; The Wildest Dream 2009; The A-Team 2010; The Chronicles of Narnia: The Voyage of the Dawn Treader 2010; Clash of the Titans 2010; The Next Three Days 2010; Unknown 2011; Battleship 2012; The Grey 2012; Taken 2 2012; Wrath of the Titans 2012; Khumba 2013; Third Person 2013; The Lego Movie 2014; A Million Ways to Die in the West 2014; Non-Stop 2014; The Nut Job 2014; Road 2014; Taken 3 2014; A Walk among the Tombstones 2014; A Christmas Star 2015; Entourage 2015; Run All Night 2015; Ted 2 2015; A Monster Calls 2016

Neff, Hildegarde aka **Knef, Hildegarde** (1925-2002) Decision before Dawn 1951; Diplomatic Courier 1952; The Snows of Kilimanjaro 1952; The Man Between 1953; Subway in the Sky 1958; The Lost Continent 1968; Fedora 1978; Witchcraft 1989

Negga, Ruth Breakfast on Pluto 2005; Fury 2012; Iona 2015; Loving 2016

Negin, Louis The Saddest Music in the World 2003; My Winnipeg 2007

Negishi, Toshie Akira Kurosawa's Dreams 1990; Rhapsody in August 1990

Négret, François Mister Frost 1990; Night and Day 1991

Negri, Pola (1899-1987) Hotel Imperial 1927; The Moon-Spinners 1964

Negron, Taylor (1957-2015) Easy Money 1983; The Last Boy Scout 1991; Nothing but Trouble 1991; Call Me Claus 2001; The Fluffer 2001

Neil, Christopher Adventures of a Private Eye 1977; Adventures of a Plumber's Mate 1978

Neil, Hildegard (1939-) The Man Who Haunted Himself 1970; Antony and Cleopatra 1972; England Made Me 1973; A Touch of Class 1973; The Legacy 1978; Macbeth 1997

Neill, James (1860-1931) The Cheat 1915; The Ten Commandments 1923; The King of Kings 1927

Neill, Sam (1947-) My Brilliant Career 1979; Omen III: the Final Conflict 1980; Attack Force Z 1981; Enigma 1982; The Country Girls 1983; The Blood of Others 1984; Plenty 1985; The Good Wife 1986; A Cry in the Dark 1988; Dead Calm 1988; Death in Brunswick 1990; The Hunt for Red October 1990; One against the Wind 1991; Until the End of the World 1991; Hostage 1992; Memoirs of an Invisible Man 1992; Rainbow Warrior 1992; Jurassic Park 1993; The Piano 1993; Country Life 1994; In the Mouth of Madness 1994; The Jungle Book 1994; Sirens 1994; Restoration 1995; Victory 1995; Children of the Revolution 1996; Snow White: a Tale of Terror 1996; Event Horizon 1997; The Revengers' Comedies 1997; The Horse Whisperer 1998; Bicentennial Man 1999; The Dish 2000; The Magic Pudding 2000; My Mother Frank 2000; Jurassic Park III 2001; Dirty Deeds 2002; Wimbledon 2004; Yes 2004; Little Fish 2005; Angel 2006; Irresistible 2006; Daybreakers 2008; Dean Spanley 2008; Skin 2008; The Hunter 2011; The Vow 2012; Escape Plan 2013; A Long Way Down 2013; Backtrack 2015; The Daughter 2016; Hunt for the Wilderpeople 2016; Tommy's Honour 2016

Neise, George N aka **Neise, George** (1916-1996) The Tall Stranger 1957; The Three Stooges in Orbit 1962

Nelkin, Stacey Going Ape! 1981; Halloween III: Season of the Witch 1982

Nelligan, Kate (1951-) The Count of Monte Cristo 1974; The Romantic Englishwoman 1975; Dracula 1979; Eye

of the Needle 1981; Without a Trace 1983; Eleni 1985; Frankie & Johnny 1991; The Prince of Tides 1991; Fatal Instinct 1993; Wolf 1994; How to Make an American Quilt 1995; Margaret's Museum 1995; Captive Heart 1996; Up Close & Personal 1996; US Marshals 1998; The Cider House Rules 1999; Swing Vote 1999; Premonition 2007

Nelson, Barry (1917-2007) Shadow of the Thin Man 1941; The Affairs of Martha 1942; A Guy Named Joe 1944; The First Travelling Saleslady 1956; Mary, Mary 1963; Pete 'n' Tillie 1972; The Shining 1980

Nelson, Bob Brain Donors 1992; This Is My Life 1992

Nelson, Charlie aka **Nelson, Charles** Wild Target 1993; Le Bossu 1997; L'Homme du Train 2002

Nelson, Craig T (1945-) Stir Crazy 1980; Poltergeist 1982; All the Right Moves 1983; Man, Woman and Child 1983; The Osterman Weekend 1983; Silkwood 1983; The Killing Fields 1984; Poltergeist II: the Other Side 1986; Action Jackson 1988; Troop Beverly Hills 1989; Turner & Hooch 1989; The Switch 1993; The Lies Boys Tell 1994; Ghosts of Mississippi 1996; I'm Not Rappaport 1996; The Devil's Advocate 1997; Wag the Dog 1997; The Skulls 2000; The Incredibles 2004; The Family Stone 2005; Blades of Glory 2007; The Proposal 2009; The Company Men 2010; Soul Surfer 2011; Get Hard 2015

Nelson (1), David (1936-2011) The Big Circus 1959; The Remarkable Mr Pennypacker 1959; -30- 1959; The Big Show 1961

Nelson, Ed aka **Nelson, Edwin** (1928-2014) The Brain Eaters 1958; A Bucket of Blood 1959; For the Love of Benji 1977; Jackie Chan's Who Am I? 1998

Nelson, Gene (1920-1996) I Wonder Who's Kissing Her Now 1947; The Daughter of Rosie O'Grady 1950; Tea for Two 1950; The West Point Story 1950; Lullaby of Broadway 1951; Painting the Clouds with Sunshine 1951; She's Working Her Way through College 1952; Three Sailors and a Girl 1953; The City Is Dark 1954; So This Is Paris 1954; Oklahoma! 1955; Timeslip 1955; Thunder Island 1963

Nelson, Gwen (1901-1990) Don't Talk to Strange Men 1962; A Kind of Loving 1962; Say Hello to Yesterday 1971

Nelson, Harriet aka **Hilliard, Harriet** (1909-1994) Follow the Fleet 1936; New Faces of 1937 1937; Sweetheart of the Campus 1941; The Falcon Strikes Back 1943

Nelson, Jerry (1934-) The Muppet Movie 1979; The Muppet Christmas Carol 1992; Muppets from Space 1999

Nelson, John Allen (1959-) Hunk 1987; Killer Klowns from Outer Space 1988

Nelson, Judd (1959-28/11/1959) The Breakfast Club 1985; Fandango 1985; St Elmo's Fire 1985; Blue City 1986; Transformers - the Movie 1986; From the Hip 1987; Relentless 1989; New Jack City 1991; Airheads 1994; Steel 1997; Light It Up 1999; Three Wise Guys 2005

Nelson, Lori (1933-) Bend of the River 1952; Francis Goes to West Point 1952; The All American 1953; All I Desire 1953; Tumbleweed 1953; Destry 1954; I Died a Thousand Times 1955; Revenge of the Creature 1955; Sincerely Yours 1955; Underwater! 1955; The Day the World Ended 1956; Mohawk 1956; Pardners 1956

Nelson, Mimi (1922-1999) Port of Call 1948; Three Strange Loves 1949

Nelson, Novella (1939-) Orphans 1987; Dear Wendy 2004

Nelson, Ricky (1940-1985) The Story of Three Loves 1953; Rio Bravo 1958; The Wackiest Ship in the Army 1961

Nelson, Ruth (1905-1992) The Eve of St Mark 1944; Wilson 1944; A Tree Grows in Brooklyn 1945; Humoresque 1946; Mother Wore Tights 1947; The Sea of Grass 1947; Arch of Triumph 1948; 3 Women 1977; Awakenings 1990

Nelson, Sean Fresh 1994; American Buffalo 1995; The Wood 1999

Nelson, Tim Blake (1964-) O Brother, Where Art Thou? 2000; The Good Girl 2001; Minority Report 2002; Holes 2003; Wonderland 2003; The Last Shot 2004; Meet the Fockers 2004; Scooby-Doo 2: Monsters Unleashed 2004; The Big White 2005; The Moguls 2005; Syriana 2005; The Astronaut Farmer 2006; Hoot 2006; The Incredible Hulk 2008; Detachment 2011; As I Lay Dying 2013; Kill the Messenger 2014

Nelson, Tracy (1963-) Down and Out in Beverly Hills 1986; A Grandpa for Christmas 2007

Nelson, Willie (1933-) A Poem Is a Naked Person 1974; The Electric Horseman 1979; Honeysuckle Rose 1980; Thief 1981; Barbarosa 1982; Songwriter 1984; Stagecoach 1986; Once upon a Texas Train 1988; Gone Fishin' 1997; Wag the Dog 1997; Half-Baked 1998; The Big Bounce 2004; The Dukes of Hazzard 2005

Nemec, Corin aka Nemec, Corin "Corky" (1971-) Solar Crisis 1990; Drop Zone 1994; Operation Dumbo Drop 1995; The War at Home 1996; Shadow Hours 2000

Neri, Francesca (1964-) The Ages of Lulu 1990; Outrage 1993; Live Flesh 1997; Collateral Damage 2001; Hannibal 2001

Nero, Franco (1941-) The Bible... in the Beginning 1966; Django 1966; Texas Adios 1966; Camelot 1967; A Professional Gun 1968; Tristana 1970; The Virgin and the Gypsy 1970; The Monk 1972; The Last Days of Mussolini 1974; The Masters 1975; Keoma 1976; Force 10 from Navarone 1978; The Man with Bogart's Face 1980; Enter the Ninja 1981; The Salamander 1981; Querelle 1982; The Girl 1986; Die Hard 2: Die Harder 1990; The Innocent Sleep 1995; Talk of Angels 1998; Bathory 2008; Letters to Juliet 2010

Nervo, Jimmy (1890-1975) Alf's Button Afloat 1938; Gasbags 1940

Nesbitt, Cathleen (1888-1982) The Passing of the Third Floor Back 1935; The Lamp Still Burns 1943; Fanny by Gaslight 1944; So Long at the Fair 1950; Desiree 1954; Three Coins in the Fountain 1954; An Affair to Remember 1957; Separate Tables 1958; The Parent Trap 1961; The Trygon Factor 1967; Staircase 1969; French Connection II 1975; Family Plot 1976; Full Circle 1977

Nesbitt, Derren (1935-) Life in Danger 1959; The Man in the Back Seat 1961; Strongroom 1961; The Informers 1963; The Naked Runner 1967; Burke & Hare 1971; Not Now Darling 1972; Ooh... You Are Awful 1972; Give Us Tomorrow 1978; Bullseye! 1990; Double X: the Name of the Game 1991

Nesbitt, James (1965-) Hear My Song 1991; Go Now 1995; Resurrection Man 1997; Welcome to Sarajevo 1997; Waking Ned 1998; The Most Fertile Man in Ireland 1999; Women Talking Dirty 1999; Wild about Harry 2000; Bloody Sunday 2001; Lucky Break 2001; Millions 2004; Match Point 2005; Blessed 2007; Cherrybomb 2009; Five Minutes of Heaven 2009; Outcast 2010; The Way 2010; The Hobbit: an Unexpected Journey 2012; Gold 2014

Nettleton, John (1929-) And Soon the Darkness 1970; Black Beauty 1971; Burning Secret 1988

Nettleton, Lois (1929-2008) Come Fly with Me 1962; Period of Adjustment 1962; Mail Order Bride 1963; Valley of Mystery 1967; The Good Guys and the Bad Guys 1969; Dirty Dingus Magee 1970; The Honkers 1971; Echoes of a Summer 1976; Deadly Blessing 1981; The Best Little Whorehouse in Texas 1982; Butterfly 1982; The Christmas Card 2006

Neuberger, Alex Running Scared 2005; Underdog 2007

Neuvic, Thierry Code Unknown 2000; Hereafter 2010; Love like Poison 2010; Belle and Sebastian - the Adventure Continues 2015

Neuwirth, Bebe (1958-) Say Anything... 1989; Green Card 1990; Bugsy 1991; Malice 1993; Jumanji 1995; The Adventures of Pinocchio 1996; The Associate 1996; Celebrity 1998; Liberty Heights 1999; The Adventures of Tom Thumb and Thumbelina 2002; Tadpole 2002; Le Divorce 2003; How to Lose a Guy in 10 Days 2003; The Big Bounce 2004; Fame 2009

Neuwirth, Chantal Nationale 7 1999; Gabrielle 2005

Neve, Suzanne Mosquito Squadron 1968; Scrooge 1970

Nevern, Nick The Fall of the Essex Boys 2012; The Hooligan Factory 2014; Spring 2014

Neville, John (1925-2011) Oscar Wilde 1959; Mr Topaze 1961; Billy Budd 1962; A Study in Terror 1965; The Adventures of Gerard 1970; The Adventures of Baron Munchausen 1988; The Road to Wellville 1994; Swann 1996; Regeneration 1997; Time to Say Goodbye? 1997; The X-Files 1998; The Duke 1999; Spider 2002; Separate Lies 2004

Nevin, Robyn (1942-) The Irishman 1978; Careful, He Might Hear You 1983

Newark, Derek (1933-1998) City under the Sea 1965; The Blue Max 1966; Dad's Army 1971; The Offence 1972; Bellman & True 1987

Newbern, George (1964-) Switching Channels 1987; Father of the Bride 1991; Doppelganger 1993; Father of the Bride Part 2 1995; Theodore Rex 1995; The Evening Star 1996; The Simple Life of Noah Dearborn 1999

Newell, Patrick (1932-1988) Go for a Take 1972; Man about the House 1974

Newhart, Bob (1929-) Hell Is for Heroes 1962; Hot Millions 1968; Catch-22 1970; On a Clear Day You Can See Forever 1970; The Rescuers 1977; First Family 1980; Little Miss Marker 1980; The Rescuers Down Under 1990; Rudolph the Red-Nosed Reindeer 1998; The Sports Pages 2001; Elf 2003; Legally Blonde 2: Red, White & Blonde 2003; The Librarian: Quest for the Spear 2004

Newlands, Anthony (1926-1995) Hysteria 1964; Kaleidoscope 1966; Circus of Fear 1967; Scream and Scream Again 1969

Newley, Anthony (1931-1999) Vice Versa 1947; Oliver Twist 1948; A Boy, a Girl and a Bike 1949; Don't Ever Leave Me 1949; Top of the Form 1953; Above Us the Waves 1955; The Blue Peter 1955; The Cockleshell Heroes 1955; The Good Companions 1956; Fire Down Below 1957; How to Murder a Rich Uncle 1957; The Man Inside 1958; No Time to Die 1958; The Bandit of Zhobe 1959; The Heart of a Man 1959; Killers of Kilimanjaro 1960; The Small World of Sammy Lee 1963; Doctor Dolittle 1967; Sweet November 1968; Can Heironymus Merkin Ever Forget Mercy Humppe and Find True Happiness? 1969; Mister Quilp 1975; The Garbage Pail Kids Movie 1987

Newman, Alec (1974-) GMT Greenwich Mean Time 1998; Long Time Dead 2001; The Principles of Lust 2002

Newman, Barry (1938-) The Lawyer 1969; Vanishing Point 1971; Fear Is the Key 1972; City on Fire 1979; Amy 1981; Bowfinger 1999; The Limey 1999; G-Men from Hell 2000; Good Advice 2001; What the #$*! Do We Know!? 2004

Newman, Jaime Ray Wedding Daze 2004; Tarzan 2013

Newman, Laraine (1952-) American Hot Wax 1977; Perfect 1985; Invaders from Mars 1986; Problem Child 2 1991; Coneheads 1993

Newman, Nanette (1934-) Faces in the Dark 1960; House of Mystery 1961; The Painted Smile 1961; Pit of Darkness 1961; Twice round the Daffodils 1962; The Wrong Arm of the Law 1962; Of Human Bondage 1964; Seance on a Wet Afternoon 1964; The Wrong Box 1966; The Whisperers 1967; Deadfall 1968; Captain Nemo and the Underwater City 1969; The Madwoman of Chaillot 1969; The Raging Moon 1970; Man at the Top 1973; The Stepford Wives 1975; International Velvet 1978; Restless Natives 1985; The Mystery of Edwin Drood 1993

Newman, Paul (1925-2008) The Silver Chalice 1954; The Rack 1956; Somebody Up There Likes Me 1956; The Helen Morgan Story 1957; Until They Sail 1957; Cat on a Hot Tin Roof 1958; The Left Handed Gun 1958; The Long, Hot Summer 1958; The Young Philadelphians 1959; Exodus 1960; From the Terrace 1960; The Hustler 1961; Paris Blues 1961; Hemingway's Adventures of a Young Man 1962; Sweet Bird of Youth 1962; Hud 1963; A New Kind of Love 1963; The Prize 1963; The Outrage 1964; What a Way to Go! 1964; Lady L 1965; Harper 1966; Torn Curtain 1966; Cool Hand Luke 1967; Hombre 1967; The Secret War of Harry Frigg 1967; Butch Cassidy and the Sundance Kid 1969; Winning 1969; King: a Filmed Record... Montgomery to Memphis 1970; WUSA 1970; Sometimes a Great Notion 1971; The Life and Times of Judge Roy Bean 1972; Pocket Money 1972; The Mackintosh Man 1973; The Sting 1973; The Towering Inferno 1974; The Drowning Pool 1975; Buffalo Bill and the Indians, or Sitting Bull's History Lesson 1976; Slap Shot 1977; Quintet 1979; When Time Ran Out 1980; Absence of Malice 1981; Fort Apache, the Bronx 1981; The Verdict 1982; Harry and Son 1984; The Color of Money 1986; Blaze 1989; Shadow Makers 1989; Mr and Mrs Bridge 1990; The Hudsucker Proxy 1994; Nobody's Fool 1994; Message in a Bottle 1998; Twilight 1998; Where the Money Is 2000; Road to Perdition 2002; Cars 2006; The Meerkats 2007

Newman, Phyllis (1935-) Bye Bye Braverman 1968; The Beautician and the Beast 1997

Newmar, Julie (1935-) Li'l Abner 1959; The Marriage-Go-Round 1960; For Love or Money 1963; Mackenna's Gold 1969; The Maltese Bippy 1969; Ghosts Can't Do It 1990

Newton-John, Olivia (1948-) Toomorrow 1970; Grease 1978; Xanadu 1980; Two of a Kind 1983; It's My Party 1996; A Few Best Men 2011

Newton (2), John aka Newton, John Haymes Alive 1992; The Christmas Card 2006

Newton, Robert (1905-1956) The Green Cockatoo 1937; The Squeaker 1937; 21 Days 1937; Vessel of Wrath 1938; Jamaica Inn 1939; Poison Pen 1939; Busman's Honeymoon 1940; Gaslight 1940; Hatter's Castle 1941; Major Barbara 1941; They Flew Alone 1941; Henry V 1944; This Happy Breed 1944; Night Boat to Dublin 1946; Odd Man Out 1947; Blood on My Hands 1948; Obsession 1948; Oliver Twist 1948; Snowbound 1948; Treasure Island 1950; Waterfront 1950; Soldiers Three 1951; Tom Brown's Schooldays 1951; Androcles and the Lion 1952; Blackbeard the Pirate 1952; Les Misérables 1952; The Desert Rats 1953; The Beachcomber 1954; The High and the Mighty 1954; Long John Silver 1954; Around the World in 80 Days 1956

Newton, Thandie (1972-) Flirting 1989; The Young Americans 1993; Loaded 1994; Jefferson in Paris 1995; The Journey of August King 1995; Gridlock'd 1996; The Leading Man 1996; Beloved 1998; Besieged 1998; Mission: Impossible 2 1999; It Was an Accident 2000; The Truth about Charlie 2002; The Chronicles of Riddick 2004; Crash 2004; The Pursuit of Happyness 2006; Norbit 2007; Run Fatboy Run 2007; RocknRolla 2008; W. 2008; Huge 2009; 2012 2009; For Colored Girls 2010; Retreat 2011; Half of a Yellow Sun 2013

Newton, Theodore (1904-1963) Ace of Aces 1933; The Sphinx 1933; Upper World 1934; The Come On 1956

Newton, Wayne (1942-) Eighty Steps to Jonah 1969; Licence to Kill 1989; The Adventures of Ford Fairlane 1990; Best of the Best II 1992; Vegas Vacation 1997

Ney, Marie (1895-1981) The Wandering Jew 1933; Scrooge 1935; Brief Ecstasy 1937; Night Was Our Friend 1951; Simba 1955

Ney, Richard (1915-2004) Mrs Miniver 1942; The War against Mrs Hadley 1942; Ivy 1947; The Late George Apley 1947; The Lovable Cheat 1949; The Premature Burial 1962

Neyland, Anne Jailhouse Rock 1957; Motorcycle Gang 1957

Ng, Francis aka Ng Chun-yu (1961-) The Bride with White Hair 1993; Full Alert 1997; Infernal Affairs II 2003; Exiled 2006

Ng, Irene (1974-) Night Watch 1995; Hard Men 1996; Rogue Trader 1998

Ngoombujarra, David (1967-2011) Black and White 2002; Kangaroo Jack 2003

Ngor, Haing S aka Ngor, Dr Haing S (1940-1996) The Killing Fields 1984; The Iron Triangle 1988; Ambition 1991; Heaven and Earth 1993; My Life 1993

Ngqobe, Zenzo Tsotsi 2005; The Forgotten Kingdom 2013

Nguyen Nhu Quynh Cyclo 1995; At the Height of Summer 1999

Nguyen, Dustin (1962-) Doom Generation 1995; Little Fish 2005

Ni Dahong Curse of the Golden Flower 2006; Zhang Yimou's Blood Simple 2009

Niblo, Fred (1874-1948) Free and Easy 1930; Ellery Queen Master Detective 1940

Nicastro, Michelle (1960-) Bad Guys 1986; The Swan Princess 1994

Nichetti, Maurizio (1948-) The Icicle Thief 1989; Volere, Volare 1991

Nicholas, Denise aka Nicholas-Hill, Denise (1944-) Blacula 1972; Let's Do It Again 1975; Mr Ricco 1975; A Piece of the Action 1977; Marvin and Tige 1983; Ghost Dad 1990

Nicholas, Paul (1945-) Blind Terror 1971; Stardust 1974; Lisztomania 1975; Tommy 1975; Sgt Pepper's Lonely Hearts Club Band 1978; The World Is Full of Married Men 1979; Yesterday's Hero 1979; The Jazz Singer 1980; Nutcracker 1982; Invitation to the Wedding 1983

Nicholas, Thomas Ian (1980-) Rookie of the Year 1993; Judge & Jury 1995; American Pie 1999; American Pie 2 2001; The Rules of Attraction 2002; American Pie: the Wedding 2003

Nicholls, Allan Buffalo Bill and the Indians, or Sitting Bull's History Lesson 1976; Threshold 1981

Nicholls, Anthony (1902-1977) The Dancing Years 1949; The Hasty Heart 1949; No Place for Jennifer 1949; The Franchise Affair 1950; The Weak and the Wicked 1953; Dunkirk 1958; Night of the Eagle 1961; Victim 1961; Othello 1965; Mister Ten Per Cent 1967; A Walk with Love and Death 1969

Nicholls, Paul (1979-) The Clandestine Marriage 1999; The Trench 1999; Goodbye Charlie Bright 2000; If Only 2004; Daylight Robbery 2007; Faintheart 2008; Life Just Is 2012; A Long Way from Home 2013

Nicholls, Phoebe aka Nicholls, Sarah (1958-) Our Mother's House 1967; Women in Love 1969; The Missionary 1982; Party Party 1983; Persuasion 1995; FairyTale: a True Story 1997

Nicholls, Austin (1980-) The Day after Tomorrow 2004; Wimbledon 2004; Glory Road 2006; Prayers for Bobby 2009

Nichols, Barbara (1929-1976) Miracle in the Rain 1956; The Pajama Game 1957; Pal Joey 1957; Sweet Smell of Success 1957; The Naked and the Dead 1958; That Kind of Woman 1959; Woman Obsessed 1959; Where the Boys Are 1960; Who Was That Lady? 1960; Dear Heart 1964

Nichols, Dandy (1907-1986) The Fallen Idol 1948; Dance Hall 1950; The Happy Family 1952; The Deep Blue Sea 1955; Don't Talk to Strange Men 1962; Ladies Who Do 1963; The Birthday Party 1968; Till Death Us Do Part 1968; O Lucky Man! 1973; Confessions of a Window Cleaner 1974; Britannia Hospital 1982

Nichols, George (1864-1927) The Eagle 1925; The Wedding March 1928

Nichols, Marisol Vegas Vacation 1997; Felon 2008

Nichols, Nichelle (1933-) Truck Turner 1974; Star Trek: the Motion Picture 1979; Star Trek II: the Wrath of Khan 1982; Star Trek III: the Search for Spock 1984; Star Trek IV: the Voyage Home 1986; Star Trek V: the Final Frontier 1989; Star Trek VI: the Undiscovered Country 1991; Snow Dogs 2002; Are We There Yet? 2005

Nichols, Rachel (1980-) Dumb and Dumberer: When Harry Met Lloyd 2003; The Amityville Horror 2005; P2 2006; The Woods 2006; The Sisterhood of the Traveling Pants 2 2008; GI Joe: the Rise of Cobra 2009; Conan the Barbarian 2011; Alex Cross 2012; Rage 2014

Nichols, Robert (1924-2013) Jennifer 1953; The Out of Towners 1970

Nichols, Stephen (1951-) Witchboard 1987; The Glass Cage 1996

Nichols, Taylor Metropolitan 1990; Barcelona 1994; Norma Jean & Marilyn 1996

Nicholson, Jack (1937-) The Cry Baby Killer 1958; The Little Shop of Horrors 1960; Too Soon to Love 1960; The Wild Ride 1960; The Raven 1963; The Terror 1963; Back Door to Hell 1964; Ensign Pulver 1964; Flight to Fury 1966; Hell's Angels on Wheels 1967; Rebel Rousers 1967; The St Valentine's Day Massacre 1967; The Shooting 1967; Easy Rider 1969; Five Easy Pieces 1970; On a Clear Day You Can See Forever 1970; Carnal Knowledge 1971; A Safe Place 1971; The King of Marvin Gardens 1972; The Last Detail 1973; Chinatown 1974; The Fortune 1975; One Flew over the Cuckoo's Nest 1975; The Passenger 1975; Tommy 1975; The Last Tycoon 1976; The Missouri Breaks 1976; Goin' South 1978; The Shining 1980; The Border 1981; The Postman Always Rings Twice 1981; Reds 1981; Terms of Endearment 1983; Prizzi's Honor 1985; Heartburn 1986; Broadcast News 1987; Ironweed 1987; The Witches of Eastwick 1987; Batman 1989; The Two Jakes 1990; A Few Good Men 1992; Hoffa 1992; Man Trouble 1992; Wolf 1994; The Crossing Guard 1995; Blood and Wine 1996; The Evening Star 1996; Mars Attacks! 1996; As Good as It Gets 1997; The Pledge 2000; About Schmidt 2002; Anger Management 2003; Something's Gotta Give 2003; The Departed 2006; The Bucket List 2008; How Do You Know 2010; Corman's World: Exploits of a Hollywood Rebel 2011

Nicholson, Julianne (1971-) The Love Letter 1999; I'm with Lucy 2002; Kinsey 2004; Little Black Book 2004; Staten Island 2009; Keep the Lights On 2012

Nicholson, Nora (1892-1973) The Blue Lagoon 1949; Tread Softly 1952; Upstairs and Downstairs 1959;

Dangerous Afternoon 1961; Devil Doll 1964

Nickson-Soul, Julia aka Nickson, Julia (1959-) Rambo: First Blood, Part II 1985; China Cry 1990; K2 1991; Amityville: a New Generation 1993; Double Dragon 1994

Nicol, Alex (1916-2001) The Sleeping City 1950; Air Cadet 1951; Target Unknown 1951; Tomahawk 1951; Meet Danny Wilson 1952; Red Ball Express 1952; Law and Order 1953; The Lone Hand 1953; The Redhead from Wyoming 1953; About Mrs Leslie 1954; Dawn at Socorro 1954; Face the Music 1954; The Gilded Cage 1955; The Man from Laramie 1955; Sincerely Yours 1955; Strategic Air Command 1955; Great Day in the Morning 1956; Under Ten Flags 1960; Bloody Mama 1970

Nicoll, Jackson Fun Size 2012; jackass presents: Bad Grandpa 2013

Nicolodi, Daria (1950-) Deep Red 1975; Inferno 1980; Macaroni 1985; Opera 1987

Nielsen, Brigitte (1963-) Red Sonja 1985; Rocky IV 1985; Cobra 1986; Beverly Hills Cop II 1987; 976-EVIL 2 1992

Nielsen, Connie (1964-) The Devil's Advocate 1997; Soldier 1998; Mission to Mars 1999; Gladiator 2000; One Hour Photo 2001; Demonlover 2002; The Hunted 2002; Basic 2003; Brothers 2004; The Great Raid 2005; The Ice Harvest 2005; Battle in Seattle 2007; Perfect Sense 2011; 3 Days to Kill 2014; The Runner 2015; Wonder Woman 2017

Nielsen, Leslie (1926-2010) Forbidden Planet 1956; The Opposite Sex 1956; Ransom! 1956; The Vagabond King 1956; Tammy and the Bachelor 1957; The Sheepman 1958; Dark Intruder 1965; Harlow 1965; Beau Geste 1966; The Plainsman 1966; Counterpoint 1967; Gunfight in Abilene 1967; Rosie! 1967; How to Steal the World 1968; How to Commit Marriage 1969; The Poseidon Adventure 1972; And Millions Will Die! 1973; Day of the Animals 1977; Viva Knievel! 1977; The Amsterdam Kill 1978; City on Fire 1979; Airplane! 1980; Prom Night 1980; Creepshow 1982; The Man with the Deadly Lens 1982; The Patriot 1986; Soul Man 1986; The Naked Gun 1988; Repossessed 1990; All I Want for Christmas 1991; The Naked Gun 2½: the Smell of Fear 1991; Rent-a-Kid 1992; Surf Ninjas 1993; Naked Gun 33⅓: the Final Insult 1994; Dracula: Dead and Loving It 1995; Harvey 1996; Spy Hard 1996; Family Plan 1997; Mr Magoo 1997; Wrongfully Accused 1998; Santa Who? 2000; Scary Movie 3 2003; Scary Movie 4 2006; Superhero Movie 2008

Nielsen, William Johnk Juels aka Nielsen, William Johnk In a Better World 2010; A Royal Affair 2012

Niemczyk, Leon (1923-2006) Eroica 1958; Knife in the Water 1962

Nieto, José aka Nieto, Pepe (1903-1982) Contraband Spain 1955; Les Bijoutiers du Clair de Lune 1957; The Pride and the Passion 1957; Solomon and Sheba 1959; Kid Rodelo 1966

Nigh, Jane (1925-1993) Give My Regards to Broadway 1948; Fighting Man of the Plains 1949

Nighy, Bill (1949-) The Little Drummer Girl 1984; Thirteen at Dinner 1985; The Phantom of the Opera 1989; Alive and Kicking 1996; FairyTale: a True Story 1997; Still Crazy 1998; Guest House Paradiso 1999; Blow Dry 2000; The Lawless Heart 2001; Lucky Break 2001; I Capture the Castle 2002; Love Actually 2003; Underworld 2003; Enduring Love 2004; Shaun of the Dead 2004; The Constant Gardener 2005; The Hitchhiker's Guide to the Galaxy 2005; The Magic Roundabout 2005; Flushed Away 2006; Notes on a Scandal 2006; Pirates of the Caribbean: Dead Man's Chest 2006; Stormbreaker 2006; Underworld: Evolution 2006; Hot Fuzz 2007; Pirates of the Caribbean: at World's End 2007; Valkyrie 2008; Astro Boy 2009; The Boat That Rocked 2009; G-Force 2009; Glorious 39 2009; Underworld: Rise of the Lycans 2009; Wild Target 2009; Chalet Girl 2010; The Chronicles of Narnia: The Voyage of the Dawn Treader 2010; Arthur Christmas 2011; The Best Exotic Marigold Hotel 2011; Rango 2011; Total Recall 2012; Wrath of the Titans 2012; About Time 2013; I, Frankenstein 2013; Jack the Giant Slayer 2013; Pride 2014; The Second Best Exotic Marigold Hotel 2015; Dad's Army 2016; Norm of the North 2016

Nihill, Julie (1957-) *Careful, He Might Hear You* 1983; *Rebel* 1985; *Kangaroo* 1986

Nikaido, Fumi *Himizu* 2011; *Au Revoir l'Été* 2013

Nikaido, Miho *Tokyo Decadence* 1992; *The Book of Life* 1998; *Side Streets* 1998

Nikkari, Esko (1938-2006) *Crime and Punishment* 1983; *Hamlet Goes Business* 1987; *The Match Factory Girl* 1990

Niklas, Jan *Colonel Redl* 1984; *Dr M* 1989; *The Rose Garden* 1989

Nilsson, Maj-Britt (1924-2006) *Summer Interlude* 1950; *To Joy* 1950; *Waiting Women* 1952

Nimmo, Derek (1930-1999) *It's Trad, Dad* 1961; *The Amorous Prawn* 1962; *Tamahine* 1963; *The Bargee* 1964; *Murder Ahoy* 1964; *The Liquidator* 1966; *Casino Royale* 1967; *Mister Ten Per Cent* 1967; *One of Our Dinosaurs Is Missing* 1975

Nimoy, Leonard (1931-2015) *Them!* 1954; *The Brain Eaters* 1958; *The Balcony* 1963; *Deathwatch* 1966; *Catlow* 1971; *Invasion of the Body Snatchers* 1978; *Star Trek: the Motion Picture* 1979; *Star Trek II: the Wrath of Khan* 1982; *Star Trek IV: the Voyage Home* 1986; *Transformers - the Movie* 1986; *Star Trek V: the Final Frontier* 1989; *Star Trek VI: the Undiscovered Country* 1991; *The Halloween Tree* 1993; *The Pagemaster* 1994; *Atlantis: the Lost Empire* 2001; *Land of the Lost* 2009; *Star Trek* 2009; *Star Trek into Darkness* 2013

Nimri, Najwa (1972-) *Open Your Eyes* 1997; *The Lovers of the Arctic Circle* 1998; *Sex and Lucia* 2001

Ninchi, Carlo (1897-1974) *La Beauté du Diable* 1949; *Two Women* 1960

Niney, Pierre aka Niney de la Comédie-Française, Pierre *Romantics Anonymous* 2010; *YSL: Yves Saint Laurent* 2014

Ning Jing *Red Firecracker, Green Firecracker* 1993; *The Missing Gun* 2002

Ninidze, Merab (1965-) *Repentance* 1984; *Nowhere in Africa* 2001

Nishii, Yukito *Confessions* 2010; *Wolf Children* 2012

Nishijima, Hidetoshi (1971-) *Dolls* 2002; *Tony Takitani* 2004

Nissen, Aud Egede (1893-1974) *Anna Boleyn* 1920; *Dr Mabuse, the Gambler* 1922

Nissen, Greta (1906-1988) *The Lucky Lady* 1926; *Fazil* 1928; *Melody Cruise* 1933

Niven, Barbara (1953-) *Alone with a Stranger* 2000; *Back to You and Me* 2005

Niven, David (1909-1983) *Mutiny on the Bounty* 1935; *Splendor* 1935; *Beloved Enemy* 1936; *The Charge of the Light Brigade* 1936; *Dodsworth* 1936; *Rose Marie* 1936; *Thank You, Jeeves* 1936; *Dinner at the Ritz* 1937; *The Prisoner of Zenda* 1937; *Bluebeard's Eighth Wife* 1938; *The Dawn Patrol* 1938; *Four Men and a Prayer* 1938; *Three Blind Mice* 1938; *Bachelor Mother* 1939; *Eternally Yours* 1939; *Raffles* 1939; *The Real Glory* 1939; *Wuthering Heights* 1939; *The First of the Few* 1942; *The Way Ahead* 1944; *Magnificent Doll* 1946; *A Matter of Life and Death* 1946; *The Bishop's Wife* 1947; *The Other Love* 1947; *Bonnie Prince Charlie* 1948; *Enchantment* 1948; *A Kiss for Corliss* 1949; *A Kiss in the Dark* 1949; *The Elusive Pimpernel* 1950; *Happy Go Lovely* 1950; *The Toast of New Orleans* 1950; *Appointment with Venus* 1951; *Soldiers Three* 1951; *The Love Lottery* 1953; *The Moon Is Blue* 1953; *Carrington VC* 1954; *Happy Ever After* 1954; *The King's Thief* 1955; *Around the World in 80 Days* 1956; *The Birds and the Bees* 1956; *The Little Hut* 1957; *My Man Godfrey* 1957; *Oh, Men! Oh, Women!* 1957; *Bonjour Tristesse* 1958; *Separate Tables* 1958; *Ask Any Girl* 1959; *Happy Anniversary* 1959; *Please Don't Eat the Daisies* 1960; *The Best of Enemies* 1961; *The Guns of Navarone* 1961; *Captive City* 1962; *Guns of Darkness* 1962; *The Road to Hong Kong* 1962; *55 Days at Peking* 1963; *The Pink Panther* 1963; *Bedtime Story* 1964; *Lady L* 1965; *Where the Spies Are* 1965; *Eye of the Devil* 1966; *Casino Royale* 1967; *Before Winter Comes* 1968; *Prudence and the Pill* 1968; *The Brain* 1969; *The Extraordinary Seaman* 1969; *King, Queen, Knave* 1972; *Paper Tiger* 1974; *Vampira* 1975; *Murder by Death* 1976; *No Deposit No Return* 1976; *Candleshoe* 1977; *Death on the Nile* 1978; *Escape to Athena* 1979; *A Nightingale Sang in Berkeley Square* 1979; *Rough Cut* 1980; *The Sea Wolves* 1980; *Trail of the Pink Panther* 1982; *Better Late than Never* 1983; *The Curse of the Pink Panther* 1983

Nivola, Alessandro (1972-) *Face/Off* 1997; *I Want You* 1998; *Best Laid Plans* 1999; *Love's Labour's Lost* 1999; *Mansfield Park* 1999; *Jurassic Park III* 2001; *Laurel Canyon* 2002; *The Clearing* 2004; *Junebug* 2004; *Goal!* 2005; *The Girl in the Park* 2007; *Goal II: Living the Dream* 2007; *The Eye* 2008; *Coco avant Chanel* 2009; *Howl* 2010; *Ginger & Rosa* 2012; *Devil's Knot* 2013; *A Most Violent Year* 2014; *Selma* 2014

Nixon, Cynthia (1966-) *Tattoo* 1980; *The Deadly Game* 1986; *Baby's Day Out* 1994; *Igby Goes Down* 2002; *Little Manhattan* 2005; *Lymelife* 2008; *Sex and the City: the Movie* 2008; *Sex and the City 2* 2010; *Rampart* 2011; *Ruth & Alex* 2014

Nixon, Kimberley (1985-) *Cherrybomb* 2008; *Easy Virtue* 2008; *Black Death* 2010; *Resistance* 2011

Nixon, Marian aka Nixon, Marion (1904-1983) *Hands Up!* 1926; *Say It with Songs* 1929; *Dr Bull* 1933; *Pilgrimage* 1933

Nkosi, Kenneth *Tsotsi* 2005; *District 9* 2009

Nobile, Roberto *Everybody's Fine* 1990; *We Have a Pope* 2011

Noble, James (1922-2016) *Who?* 1974; *One Summer Love* 1975; *Summer of My German Soldier* 1978

Noble, John (1948-) *Virtual Nightmare* 2000; *The Lord of the Rings: The Return of the King* 2003; *Risen* 2010

Noël-Noël *A Cage of Nightingales* 1945; *The Seven Deadly Sins* 1952; *The Diary of Major Thompson* 1955; *Jessica* 1962

Noel, Chris (1941-) *Get Yourself a College Girl* 1964; *The Glory Stompers* 1967

Noël, Hubert aka Noel, Hubert (1924-1987) *Le Bossu* 1959; *Devils of Darkness* 1964

Noël, Magali (1932-2015) *Rififi* 1955; *Elena et les Hommes* 1956; *La Dolce Vita* 1960; *Amarcord* 1973; *Les Rendez-vous d'Anna* 1978; *The Death of Mario Ricci* 1983; *La Fidélité* 2000

Nono, Clare *Fire and Ice* 1983; *Nightmares* 1983

Nonyela, Valentine *Young Soul Rebels* 1991; *Welcome II the Terrordome* 1994

Noonan, Tom (1951-) *Gloria* 1980; *Wolfen* 1981; *Eddie Macon's Run* 1983; *Manhunter* 1986; *Collision Course* 1987; *The Monster Squad* 1987; *RoboCop 2* 1990; *Last Action Hero* 1993; *Phoenix* 1998; *Knockaround Guys* 2001; *The Roost* 2005; *Seraphim Falls* 2006; *The House of the Devil* 2009; *Anomalisa* 2015

Noonan, Tommy (1921-1968) *Gentlemen Prefer Blondes* 1953; *A Star Is Born* 1954; *How to Be Very, Very Popular* 1955; *Violent Saturday* 1955; *The Ambassador's Daughter* 1956; *The Best Things in Life Are Free* 1956; *Bundle of Joy* 1956; *The Girl Most Likely* 1957

Noone, Nora-Jane (1984-) *The Magdalene Sisters* 2002; *The Descent* 2005

Norby, Ghita (1935-) *Best Intentions* 1992; *Sofie* 1992; *The Kingdom* 1994; *Hamsun* 1996; *The Inheritance* 2003; *O'Horten* 2007; *Maria Larsson's Everlasting Moments* 2008; *Jauja* 2014

Norden, Christine (1924-1988) *An Ideal Husband* 1947; *Mine Own Executioner* 1947; *The Interrupted Journey* 1949; *A Case for PC 49* 1950

Nordling, Jeffrey (1962-) *Ruby* 1992; *The Shamrock Conspiracy* 1995; *D3: the Mighty Ducks* 1996; *Danielle Steel's Remembrance* 1996; *Turbulence II: Fear of Flying* 2000; *Flight 93* 2006

Noriega, Eduardo *Blackthorn* 2011; *The Last Stand* 2013

Noriega (1), Eduardo (1918-2007) *Captain Scarlett* 1953; *The Far Horizons* 1955; *The Living Idol* 1955; *The Beast of Hollow Mountain* 1956; *Tarzan and the Valley of Gold* 1966

Noriega (2), Eduardo (1973-) *Tesis* 1996; *Open Your Eyes* 1997; *The Devil's Backbone* 2001; *Transsiberian* 2008; *Agnosia* 2010

Norman, Lucille (1921-1998) *Painting the Clouds with Sunshine* 1951; *Carson City* 1952

Norman, Maidie (1913-1998) *The Well* 1951; *Bright Road* 1953; *What Ever Happened to Baby Jane?* 1962

Norman, Zack *Sitting Ducks* 1979; *Romancing the Stone* 1984; *Cadillac Man* 1990; *Babyfever* 1994

Noro, Line (1900-1985) *Pépé le Moko* 1937; *J'Accuse* 1938; *La Symphonie Pastorale* 1946

Norris, Chuck (1940-) *The Wrecking Crew* 1969; *The Way of the Dragon* 1973; *Good Guys Wear Black* 1977; *Game of Death* 1978; *A Force of One* 1979; *The Octagon* 1980; *An Eye for an Eye* 1981; *Silent Rage* 1982; *Lone Wolf McQuade* 1983; *Missing in Action* 1984; *Code of Silence* 1985; *Invasion USA* 1985; *Missing in Action 2: the Beginning* 1985; *The Delta Force* 1986; *Firewalker* 1986; *Braddock: Missing in Action III* 1988; *Hero and the Terror* 1988; *Delta Force 2* 1990; *The Hitman* 1991; *Top Dog* 1995; *Logan's War: Bound by Honor* 1998; *The President's Man* 2000; *The Expendables 2* 2012

Norris, Daran *The Little Polar Bear* 2001; *Team America: World Police* 2004

Norris, Dean (1963-) *Hard to Kill* 1989; *The Lawnmower Man* 1992; *The Last Seduction* 1993; *Forgotten Sins* 1996; *Linewatch* 2008; *Secret in Their Eyes* 2015

Norris, Edward (1911-2002) *They Won't Forget* 1937; *Boys Town* 1938; *Frontier Marshal* 1939; *The Singing Sheriff* 1944

Norstrom, Tomas *The Hunters* 1996; *Kitchen Stories* 2003

North, Alan (1920-2000) *Billy Galvin* 1986; *Highlander* 1986; *Blood Money* 1988; *Lean on me* 1989; *See No Evil, Hear No Evil* 1989; *Crazy People* 1990; *The Jerky Boys* 1995

North, Sheree (1933-2005) *Living It Up* 1954; *How to Be Very, Very Popular* 1955; *The Best Things in Life Are Free* 1956; *No Down Payment* 1957; *In Love and War* 1958; *Mardi Gras* 1958; *Madigan* 1968; *The Gypsy Moths* 1969; *The Trouble with Girls* 1969; *Lawman* 1971; *The Organization* 1971; *Charley Varrick* 1973; *The Outfit* 1973; *Breakout* 1975; *The Shootist* 1976; *Telefon* 1977; *Cold Dog Soup* 1989

North, Ted aka North, Michael (1916-) *Chad Hanna* 1940; *Charlie Chan in Rio* 1941; *Syncopation* 1942; *The Devil Thumbs a Ride* 1947; *The Unsuspected* 1947

North, Virginia (1946-2004) *The Long Duel* 1967; *The Abominable Dr Phibes* 1971

Northam, Jeremy (1961-) *Soft Top, Hard Shoulder* 1992; *Wuthering Heights* 1992; *Carrington* 1995; *The Net* 1995; *Emma* 1996; *Amistad* 1997; *Mimic* 1997; *Gloria* 1998; *The Misadventures of Margaret* 1998; *Happy, Texas* 1999; *An Ideal Husband* 1999; *The Winslow Boy* 1999; *The Golden Bowl* 2000; *Enigma* 2001; *Gosford Park* 2001; *Cypher* 2002; *Martin and Lewis* 2002; *Possession* 2002; *The Singing Detective* 2003; *The Statement* 2003; *Bobby Jones: Stroke of Genius* 2004; *A Cock and Bull Story* 2005; *Guy X* 2005; *The Invasion* 2007; *Dean Spanley* 2008; *Creation* 2009; *Glorious 39* 2009; *Eye in the Sky* 2015; *The Man Who Knew Infinity* 2015; *Our Kind of Traitor* 2016

Northup, Harry (1940-) *Over the Edge* 1979; *Kansas* 1988

Norton, Alex (1950-) *Gregory's Girl* 1980; *Comfort and Joy* 1984; *Comrades: a Lanternist's Account of the Tolpuddle Martyrs and What Became of Them* 1986; *Robin Hood* 1990; *Orphans* 1998; *Beautiful Creatures* 2000; *Sir Billi* 2012; *The Unbeatables* 2013

Norton, Barry (1905-1956) *Dishonored* 1931; *Lady for a Day* 1933

Norton, DeeDee *Confessions of a Serial Killer* 1987; *Dakota* 1988

Norton, Edgar (1868-1953) *The Love Parade* 1929; *One Romantic Night* 1930; *Dr Jekyll and Mr Hyde* 1931

Norton, Edward (1969-) *Everyone Says I Love You* 1996; *The People vs Larry Flynt* 1996; *Primal Fear* 1996; *American History X* 1998; *Rounders* 1998; *Fight Club* 1999; *Keeping the Faith* 2000; *The Score* 2001; *Death to Smoochy* 2002; *Frida* 2002; *Red Dragon* 2002; *25th Hour* 2002; *The Italian Job* 2003; *Down in the Valley* 2004; *The Illusionist* 2005; *Kingdom of Heaven* 2005; *The Painted Veil* 2006; *Pride and Glory* 2007; *Bustin' Down the Door* 2008; *The Incredible Hulk* 2008; *The Invention of Lying* 2009; *Stone* 2010; *The Bourne Legacy* 2012; *Moonrise Kingdom* 2012; *Salinger* 2013; *Birdman or (The Unexpected Virtue of Ignorance)* 2014; *The Grand Budapest Hotel* 2014; *Collateral Beauty* 2016; *Sausage Party* 2016

Norton, Jack (1889-1958) *The Big Noise* 1944; *The Scarlet Clue* 1945

Norton, James *Bonobo* 2013; *Mr Turner* 2014; *Flatliners* 2017

Norton, Jim (1938-) *Straw Dogs* 1971; *Adolf Hitler - My Part in His Downfall* 1972; *Hidden Agenda* 1990; *Memoirs of an Invisible Man* 1992; *Sunset Heights* 1996; *Driving Lessons* 2006; *Water for Elephants* 2011; *Jimmy's Hall* 2014; *The Boy* 2016

Norton, Ken (1945-2013) *Mandingo* 1975; *Drum* 1976

Norton, Richard (1950-) *China O'Brien* 1988; *Mr Nice Guy* 1996; *Road House 2* 2006

Noseworthy, Jack (1969-) *A Place for Annie* 1994; *Barb Wire* 1995; *Mojave Moon* 1996; *Breakdown* 1997; *Idle Hands* 1999; *Murder at Devil's Glen* 1999; *Cecil B Demented* 2000; *Aces 'n' Eights* 2008; *Killing Kennedy* 2013; *The Secret Life of Marilyn Monroe* 2015

Noth, Christopher aka Noth, Chris (1956-) *Where Are My Children?* 1994; *Double Whammy* 2001; *The Glass House* 2001; *The Perfect Man* 2005; *Sex and the City: the Movie* 2008; *Sex and the City 2* 2010; *Elsa & Fred* 2014

Nouri, Michael (1945-) *Flashdance* 1983; *The Hidden* 1987; *Little Vegas* 1990; *A Passion for Murder* 1992; *American Yakuza* 1994; *Finding Forrester* 2000; *Lovely & Amazing* 2001; *Last Holiday* 2006; *The Proposal* 2009

Novak, B J *Inglourious Basterds* 2009; *Saving Mr Banks* 2013

Novak, Kayvan (1978-) *Four Lions* 2010; *Cuban Fury* 2014

Novak, Kim (1933-) *Pfffft!* 1954; *Pushover* 1954; *The Man with the Golden Arm* 1955; *Picnic* 1955; *Son of Sinbad* 1955; *The Eddy Duchin Story* 1956; *Jeanne Eagels* 1957; *Pal Joey* 1957; *Bell, Book and Candle* 1958; *Vertigo* 1958; *Pepe* 1960; *Strangers When We Meet* 1960; *Boys' Night Out* 1962; *The Notorious Landlady* 1962; *Kiss Me, Stupid* 1964; *Of Human Bondage* 1964; *The Amorous Adventures of Moll Flanders* 1965; *The Legend of Lylah Clare* 1968; *The Great Bank Robbery* 1969; *The White Buffalo* 1977; *Just a Gigolo* 1978; *The Mirror Crack'd* 1980; *The Children* 1990; *Liebestraum* 1991

Novakovic, Bojana *Edge of Darkness* 2009; *Devil* 2010; *A Funny Kind of Love* 2014; *The Hallow* 2015

Novarro, Ramon aka Samaniegos, Ramon (1899-1968) *The Prisoner of Zenda* 1922; *Scaramouche* 1923; *The Arab* 1924; *Ben-Hur: a Tale of the Christ* 1925; *The Student Prince in Old Heidelberg* 1927; *Daybreak* 1931; *Mata Hari* 1931; *The Barbarian* 1933; *The Cat and the Fiddle* 1934; *The Big Steal* 1949; *We Were Strangers* 1949; *Crisis* 1950; *The Outriders* 1950; *Heller in Pink Tights* 1960

Novello, Don (1943-) *Head Office* 1986; *Before the Night* 1995; *Atlantis: the Lost Empire* 2001

Novello, Ivor (1893-1951) *The Lodger* 1926; *Downhill* 1927; *The Constant Nymph* 1928

Novello, Jay (1904-1982) *Blood on My Hands* 1948; *The Miracle of Our Lady of Fatima* 1952; *The Diamond Queen* 1953; *The City Is Dark* 1954; *Bengazi* 1955; *Son of Sinbad* 1955; *Lisbon* 1956; *The Pride and the Passion* 1957; *The Perfect Furlough* 1958; *This Rebel Breed* 1960; *Harum Scarum* 1965

Novembre, Tom *An American Werewolf in Paris* 1997; *An Ordinary Execution* 2010

Novo, Nancho (1958-) *The Red Squirrel* 1993; *The Lovers of the Arctic Circle* 1998

Novotna, Jarmila (1908-1994) *The Search* 1948; *The Great Caruso* 1951

Novotny, Tuva *Stoned* 2005; *A War* 2015

Novy, Pavel (1948-) *Conspirators of Pleasure* 1996; *Little Otik* 2000; *Lunacy* 2005

Nowak, Jerzy (1923-2013) *Camera Buff* 1979; *Three Colours White* 1993

Nowicki, Jan (1939-) *Diary for My Children* 1982; *Diary for My Loves* 1987; *Diary for My Father and Mother* 1990

Noy, Zachi (1953-) *Lemon Popsicle* 1978; *Enter the Ninja* 1981

Nozick, Bruce *And the Beat Goes On: the Sonny and Cher Story* 1999; *Liz & Dick* 2012

Nsengiyumva, Roger aka Nsengiyumva, Roger Jean *Africa United* 2010; *Sixteen* 2013

Ntshona, Winston *The Wild Geese* 1978; *A Dry White Season* 1989; *The Air Up There* 1993; *Tarzan and the Lost City* 1998

Nucci, Danny (1968-) *Rescue Me* 1991; *Homage* 1995; *Eraser* 1996; *That Old Feeling* 1997; *American Cousins* 2003

Nugent, Edward aka Nugent, Eddie (1904-1995) *Our Dancing Daughters* 1928; *Our Modern Maidens* 1929; *Night Nurse* 1931; *This Day and Age* 1933; *She Loves Me Not* 1934

Nugent, Elliott (1899-1980) Romance 1930; The Unholy Three 1930; The Last Flight 1931

Nunez Jr, Miguel A aka **Nunez, Miguel A** (1964-) Shadowzone 1990; Why Do Fools Fall in Love? 1998; Life 1999; Scooby-Doo 2002

Nunn, Bill (1953-) School Daze 1988; Do the Right Thing 1989; Def by Temptation 1990; New Jack City 1991; Regarding Henry 1991; Sister Act 1992; The Last Seduction 1993; Mr and Mrs Loving 1993; Canadian Bacon 1995; Candyman: Farewell to the Flesh 1995; Things to Do in Denver When You're Dead 1995; True Crime 1995; Extreme Measures 1996; Kiss the Girls 1997; He Got Game 1998; The Legend of 1900 1999; Firehouse Dog 2006

Nunn, Larry (1925-1974) Strike Up the Band 1940; Men of Boys Town 1941

Nureyev, Rudolf (1938-1993) Romeo and Juliet 1966; Don Quixote 1973; Valentino 1977; Exposed 1983

Nussbaum, Danny TwentyFourSeven 1997; One More Kiss 1999; Chunky Monkey 2001; Club le Monde 2001; Things to Do before You're 30 2004

Nussbaum, Mike (1923-) House of Games 1987; Things Change 1988; Desperate Hours 1990; The Con 1998

Nutan (1936-1991) Anari 1959; Bandini 1963

Nuttall, Jeff (1933-2004) Robin Hood 1990; The Baby of Macon 1993; Captives 1994; Anazapta 2001

Nutter, Tarah Chilly Scenes of Winter 1979; Without Warning 1980

Nuyen, France (1939-) In Love and War 1958; South Pacific 1958; Diamond Head 1962; A Girl Named Tamiko 1962; Satan Never Sleeps 1962; China Cry 1990; The Joy Luck Club 1993

N!xau (1944-2003) The Gods Must Be Crazy 1980; The Gods Must Be Crazy II 1989

Nye, Carrie (1936-2006) The Seduction of Joe Tynan 1979; Too Scared to Scream 1982

Nye, Louis (1913-2005) The Facts of Life 1960; The Stripper 1963; Who's Been Sleeping in My Bed? 1963; Harper Valley PTA 1978; Full Moon High 1982

Nyman, Andy Dead Babies 2000; Severance 2006; Death at a Funeral 2007; Black Death 2010

Nyman, Lena (1944-2011) I Am Curious - Yellow 1967; Autumn Sonata 1978

Nyong'o, Lupita (1983-) Non-Stop 2014; Star Wars Episode VII: the Force Awakens 2015

Nyqvist, Michael (1960-) Together 2000; The Girl with the Dragon Tattoo 2009; The Girl Who Played with Fire 2009; The Girl Who Kicked the Hornet's Nest 2009; Abduction 2011; Mission: Impossible - Ghost Protocol 2011; John Wick 2014; Colonia 2015; The Girl King 2015

O

O, Henry Dragonheart: a New Beginning 2000; Romeo Must Die 2000

Oakes, Lee Dragon Heart 1996; Large 2000; Club le Monde 2001

Oakie, Jack (1903-1978) Paramount on Parade 1930; If I Had a Million 1932; Million Dollar Legs 1932; The Eagle and the Hawk 1933; Sitting Pretty 1933; Looking for Trouble 1934; The Big Broadcast of 1936 1935; The Call of the Wild 1935; Colleen 1936; King of Burlesque 1936; The Texas Rangers 1936; The Toast of New York 1937; The Affairs of Annabel 1938; Annabel Takes a Tour 1938; Thanks for Everything 1938; The Great Dictator 1940; Tin Pan Alley 1940; Young People 1940; The Great American Broadcast 1941; Song of the Islands 1942; Hello, Frisco, Hello 1943; Wintertime 1943; It Happened Tomorrow 1944; The Merry Monahans 1944; Sweet and Lowdown 1944; When My Baby Smiles at Me 1948; Thieves' Highway 1949; Tomahawk 1951; The Wonderful Country 1959; The Rat Race 1960; Lover Come Back 1961

Oakland, Simon (1922-1983) I Want to Live! 1958; Psycho 1960; The Rise and Fall of Legs Diamond 1960; West Side Story 1961; Tony Rome 1967; Bullitt 1968; On a Clear Day You Can See Forever 1970; Chato's Land 1971; The Hunting Party 1971; Scandalous John 1971; Emperor of the North 1973; Happy Mother's Day... Love, George 1973

Oakman, Wheeler (1890-1949) Lights of New York 1928; Aces and Eights 1936

Oates, Cicely (1888-1934) The Wandering Jew 1933; The Man Who Knew Too Much 1934

Oates, Warren (1928-1982) Yellowstone Kelly 1959; The Rise and Fall of Legs Diamond 1960; Hero's Island 1962; Ride the High Country 1962; Mail Order Bride 1963; Return of the Seven 1966; In the Heat of the Night 1967; The Shooting 1967; Welcome to Hard Times 1967; The Split 1968; Crooks and Coronets 1969; Smith! 1969; The Wild Bunch 1969; Barquero 1970; There Was a Crooked Man... 1970; The Hired Hand 1971; Kid Blue 1971; Two-Lane Blacktop 1971; Badlands 1973; Dillinger 1973; The Thief Who Came to Dinner 1973; Tom Sawyer 1973; Bring Me the Head of Alfredo Garcia 1974; The White Dawn 1974; 92 in the Shade 1975; Race with the Devil 1975; Dixie Dynamite 1976; Drum 1976; The Brink's Job 1978; China 9, Liberty 37 1978; 1941 1979; The Border 1981; Stripes 1981; Tough Enough 1982; Blue Thunder 1983

Obata, Toshishiro Showdown in Little Tokyo 1991; Teenage Mutant Ninja Turtles II: the Secret of the Ooze 1991

Ober, Philip (1902-1982) The Magnificent Yankee 1950; Never a Dull Moment 1950; The Clown 1952; Come Back, Little Sheba 1952; From Here to Eternity 1953; The High Cost of Loving 1958; Ten North Frederick 1958; Torpedo Run 1958; Beloved Infidel 1959; North by Northwest 1959; The Facts of Life 1960; Go Naked in the World 1961

Oberoi, Vivek (1976-) Company 2001; Saathiya 2002; Kisna - the Warrior Poet 2004

Oberon, Merle (1911-1979) Wedding Rehearsal 1932; The Private Life of Henry VIII 1933; The Private Life of Don Juan 1934; The Scarlet Pimpernel 1934; The Dark Angel 1935; Folies Bergère 1935; Beloved Enemy 1936; These Three 1936; Over the Moon 1937; The Cowboy and the Lady 1938; The Divorce of Lady X 1938; The Lion Has Wings 1939; Wuthering Heights 1939; 'Til We Meet Again 1940; Affectionately Yours 1941; Lydia 1941; That Uncertain Feeling 1941; Forever and a Day 1943; Stage Door Canteen 1943; Dark Waters 1944; The Lodger 1944; A Song to Remember 1945; This Love of Ours 1945; Night Song 1947; Berlin Express 1948; Deep in My Heart 1954; Desiree 1954; The Oscar 1966; Interval 1973

Obradors, Jacqueline (1967-) Six Days Seven Nights 1998; Atlantis: the Lost Empire 2001; Tortilla Soup 2001; A Man Apart 2003; Unstoppable 2004

O'Brady, Frédéric aka **O'Brady** aka **O'Brady, Frederick** (1903-?) La Vie Est à Nous 1936; Foreign Intrigue 1956

O'Brian, Hugh (1925-) Cave of Outlaws 1951; Vengeance Valley 1951; The Lawless Breed 1952; Meet Me at the Fair 1952; The Raiders 1952; Red Ball Express 1952; Son of Ali Baba 1952; Back to God's Country 1953; The Man from the Alamo 1953; Seminole 1953; Broken Lance 1954; Drums across the River 1954; Fireman Save My Child 1954; Saskatchewan 1954; There's No Business like Show Business 1954; The Twinkle in God's Eye 1955; The Brass Legend 1956; Alias Jesse James 1959; Come Fly with Me 1962; Love Has Many Faces 1965; Ten Little Indians 1965; Ambush Bay 1966; Killer Force 1975; The Shootist 1976; Game of Death 1978

O'Brien-Moore, Erin (1902-1979) Dangerous Corner 1934; Our Little Girl 1935; The Black Legion 1937; Green Light 1937; The Life of Emile Zola 1937; Destination Moon 1950

O'Brien, Austin (1981-) Last Action Hero 1993; Prehysteria! 1993; My Girl 2 1994; Lawnmower Man 2: Beyond Cyberspace 1995

O'Brien, Clay (1961-) Cahill, United States Marshal 1973; One Little Indian 1973

O'Brien, Dave aka **O'Brien, David** (1912-1969) The Little Colonel 1935; Reefer Madness 1936; Boys of the City 1940; Devil Bat 1940; Tennessee Champ 1954

O'Brien (1), Dylan (1991-) The Maze Runner 2014; Maze Runner: The Scorch Trials 2015

O'Brien, Edmond (1915-1985) The Hunchback of Notre Dame 1939; The Navy Steps Out 1941; The Amazing Mrs Holliday 1943; Winged Victory 1944; The Killers 1946; A Double Life 1947; The Web 1947; Another Part of the Forest 1948; Fighter Squadron 1948; For the Love of Mary 1948; DOA 1949; White Heat 1949; The Admiral Was a Lady 1950; Backfire 1950; The Redhead and the Cowboy 1950; 711 Ocean Drive 1950; Warpath 1951; Denver & Rio Grande 1952; The

Turning Point 1952; The Bigamist 1953; The Hitch-Hiker 1953; Julius Caesar 1953; The Barefoot Contessa 1954; 1984 1955; Pete Kelly's Blues 1955; A Cry in the Night 1956; D-Day the Sixth of June 1956; The Girl Can't Help It 1956; The Rack 1956; The Big Land 1957; Sing, Boy, Sing 1958; Up Periscope 1959; The Great Impostor 1960; The Last Voyage 1960; The Third Voice 1960; Birdman of Alcatraz 1962; The Longest Day 1962; The Man Who Shot Liberty Valance 1962; Moon Pilot 1962; Rio Conchos 1964; Seven Days in May 1964; Sylvia 1964; Fantastic Voyage 1966; The Wild Bunch 1969; The Intruders 1970; 99 and 44/100% Dead 1974

O'Brien, George (1899-1985) The Iron Horse 1924; 3 Bad Men 1926; Sunrise 1927; Riders of the Purple Sage 1931; My Wild Irish Rose 1947; Fort Apache 1948

O'Brien, Joan (1936-) Operation Petticoat 1959; The Alamo 1960; It Happened at the World's Fair 1962; It'$ Only Money 1962; Six Black Horses 1962; We Joined the Navy 1962; Get Yourself a College Girl 1964

O'Brien, Kieran (1973-) Bellman & True 1987; Virtual Sexuality 1999; 9 Songs 2004

O'Brien, Margaret (1937-) Dr Gillespie's Criminal Case 1943; Jane Eyre 1943; Lost Angel 1943; The Canterville Ghost 1944; Meet Me in St Louis 1944; Music for Millions 1944; Our Vines Have Tender Grapes 1945; The Unfinished Dance 1947; Little Women 1949; The Secret Garden 1949; Heller in Pink Tights 1960; Amy 1981

O'Brien, Mariah (1971-) Halloween 6: the Curse of Michael Myers 1995; Diamonds 1999

O'Brien, Maureen (1943-) She'll Be Wearing Pink Pyjamas 1984; The Land Girls 1997

O'Brien, Niall The Outsider 1979; Half Moon Street 1986; Rawhead Rex 1986; Broken Harvest 1994; The Legend of 1900 1999

O'Brien, Pat (1899-1983) Consolation Marriage 1931; The Front Page 1931; Honor among Lovers 1931; Air Mail 1932; American Madness 1932; Hell's House 1932; Blonde Bombshell 1933; Bureau of Missing Persons 1933; Flirtation Walk 1934; Gambling Lady 1934; Here Comes the Navy 1934; Ceiling Zero 1935; Devil Dogs of the Air 1935; In Caliente 1935; The Irish in Us 1935; Page Miss Glory 1935; China Clipper 1936; The Great O'Malley 1937; San Quentin 1937; Slim 1937; Angels with Dirty Faces 1938; Boy Meets Girl 1938; Slightly Honorable 1939; Castle on the Hudson 1940; The Fighting 69th 1940; Knute Rockne - All American 1940; 'Til We Meet Again 1940; Torrid Zone 1940; Broadway 1942; The Navy Comes Through 1942; Bombardier 1943; His Butler's Sister 1943; Marine Raiders 1944; Secret Command 1944; Crack-Up 1946; Riff-Raff 1947; The Boy with Green Hair 1948; A Dangerous Profession 1949; The Fireball 1950; The People against O'Hara 1951; Kill Me Tomorrow 1957; The Last Hurrah 1958; Some Like It Hot 1959; Ragtime 1981

O'Brien (2), Peter (1960-) Hotel de Love 1996; The Return 2006

O'Brien, Richard (1942-) The Andromeda Strain 1970; Pieces of Dreams 1970; The Rocky Horror Picture Show 1975; The Pack 1977; Jubilee 1978; Flash Gordon 1980; Revolution 1985; The Wolves of Willoughby Chase 1988; Dark City 1998; Dungeons & Dragons 2000; Midnight Movies: from the Margins to the Mainstream 2005; The British Guide to Showing Off 2011

O'Brien, Tom (1890-1947) The Big Parade 1925; Moby Dick 1930; The Accused 1988; Physical Evidence 1988; DC Sniper: 23 Days of Fear 2003

O'Brien, Trever (1984-) Lawnmower Man 2: Beyond Cyberspace 1995; Homecoming 1996

O'Brien, Virginia (1919-2001) Lady Be Good 1941; Ship Ahoy 1942; Meet the People 1944; Ziegfeld Follies 1944; The Harvey Girls 1946; Merton of the Movies 1947

O'Bryan, Patrick 976-EVIL 1988; Relentless 1989; 976-EVIL 2 1992

O'Byrne, Brian F (1967-) The Last Bus Home 1997; An Everlasting Piece 2000; Bandits 2001; Disco Pigs 2001; interMission 2003; Bug 2006; Before the Devil Knows You're Dead 2007; No Reservations 2007; Brooklyn's Finest 2009; The International 2009

O'Callaghan, Richard (1940-) The Bofors Gun 1968; Butley 1973

O'Carroll, Brendan The Van 1996; Mrs Brown's Boys D'Movie 2014

O'Casey, Ronan (1922-2012) Tiger by the Tail 1955; Inn for Trouble 1960

Occhini, Ilaria (1936-) Two against the Law 1973; Loose Cannons 2010

Occhipinti, Andrea (1957-) Bolero 1984; The Family 1987

Ochsenknecht, Uwe (1956-) Forget Mozart 1985; Fire, Ice and Dynamite 1990

O'Connell, Arthur (1908-1981) Bus Stop 1956; The Proud Ones 1956; The Solid Gold Cadillac 1956; April Love 1957; The Monte Carlo Story 1957; Operation Mad Ball 1957; Man of the West 1958; Voice in the Mirror 1958; Anatomy of a Murder 1959; Gidget 1959; Hound Dog Man 1959; Operation Petticoat 1959; Cimarron 1960; The Great Impostor 1960; Pocketful of Miracles 1961; A Thunder of Drums 1961; Follow That Dream 1962; 7 Faces of Dr Lao 1963; Kissin' Cousins 1964; Nightmare in the Sun 1964; Your Cheatin' Heart 1964; The Great Race 1965; The Monkey's Uncle 1965; The Third Day 1965; Fantastic Voyage 1966; Ride beyond Vengeance 1966; The Silencers 1966; There Was a Crooked Man... 1970; The Last Valley 1971; Ben 1972; Huckleberry Finn 1974

O'Connell, Deirdre Straight Talk 1992; Fearless 1993; Imaginary Heroes 2004; You Don't Know Jack 2010

O'Connell, Hugh (1898-1943) The Smiling Lieutenant 1931; Broadway through a Keyhole 1933; That Certain Woman 1937

O'Connell (2), Jack (1990-) Eden Lake 2008; Harry Brown 2009; Weekender 2011; The Liability 2012; Private Peaceful 2012; Tower Block 2012; Starred Up 2013; 300: Rise of an Empire 2013; '71 2014; Unbroken 2014; Money Monster 2016

O'Connell, Jerry (1974-) Stand by Me 1986; Calendar Girl 1993; Jerry Maguire 1996; Joe's Apartment 1996; Scream 2 1997; Body Shots 1999; Mission to Mars 1999; Buying the Cow 2000; Tomcats 2000; Kangaroo Jack 2003; Fat Slags 2004; Yours, Mine & Ours 2005; Nora Roberts' Midnight Bayou 2009; Obsessed 2009; Piranha 2010

O'Connell, Patrick (1934-) The McKenzie Break 1970; The Ragman's Daughter 1972

O'Connell, William Paint Your Wagon 1969; Big Bad Mama 1974

O'Connor, Carroll (1924-2001) By Love Possessed 1961; Lonely Are the Brave 1962; Hawaii 1966; Not with My Wife, You Don't! 1966; What Did You Do in the War, Daddy? 1966; Point Blank 1967; Warning Shot 1967; Waterhole #3 1967; For Love of Ivy 1968; Death of a Gunfighter 1969; Marlowe 1969; Doctors' Wives 1970; Kelly's Heroes 1970; Law and Disorder 1974; Gideon 1999; 36 Hours to Die 1999; Return to Me 2000

O'Connor, Derrick Sweeney 2 1978; Bloody Kids 1979; Dealers 1989; Lethal Weapon 2 1989; Deep Rising 1998

O'Connor, Donald (1925-2003) Men with Wings 1938; Million Dollar Legs 1939; Follow the Boys 1944; The Merry Monahans 1944; Patrick the Great 1944; Something in the Wind 1947; Are You with It? 1948; Francis 1949; Double Crossbones 1951; Francis Goes to the Races 1951; Francis Goes to West Point 1952; Singin' in the Rain 1952; Call Me Madam 1953; Francis Covers the Big Town 1953; I Love Melvin 1953; Francis Joins the WACS 1954; There's No Business like Show Business 1954; Francis in the Navy 1955; Anything Goes 1956; The Buster Keaton Story 1957; Cry for Happy 1961; That Funny Feeling 1965; Pandemonium 1982; Toys 1992

O'Connor, Frances (1969-) Love and Other Catastrophes 1996; Thank God He Met Lizzie 1997; Mansfield Park 1999; About Adam 2000; Bedazzled 2000; AI: Artificial Intelligence 2001; The Importance of Being Earnest 2002; Timeline 2003; Iron Jawed Angels 2004; Piccadilly Jim 2004; The Hunter 2011; Jayne Mansfield's Car 2012; The Conjuring 2 2016

O'Connor, Glynnis (1956-) Jeremy 1973; The Boy in the Plastic Bubble 1976; Ode to Billy Joe 1976; Kid Vengeance 1977; Those Lips, Those Eyes 1980; The White Lions 1980; Night Crossing 1981; Johnny Dangerously 1984

O'Connor, Hazel (1955-) Breaking Glass 1980; Car Trouble 1985

O'Connor, Kevin J (1964-) Peggy Sue Got Married 1986; Candy Mountain 1987; The Moderns 1988; FX 2 1991; Accidental Hero 1992; Equinox 1992; Color of Night 1994; No Escape 1994; Canadian Bacon 1995; Lord of Illusions

1995; Chicago Cab 1998; Deep Rising 1998; Gods and Monsters 1998; The Mummy 1999; Van Helsing 2004; Seraphim Falls 2006; There Will Be Blood 2007

O'Connor, Raymond (1955-) Life Stinks 1991; Mr Nanny 1992

O'Connor, Robert Emmett (1885-1962) The Public Enemy 1931; Blonde Venus 1932

O'Connor, Sinead (1966-) Wuthering Heights 1992; The Butcher Boy 1997

O'Connor, Tim (1927-) Black Jack 1972; The Groundstar Conspiracy 1972; Buck Rogers in the 25th Century 1979; The Naked Gun 2½: the Smell of Fear 1991

O'Connor, Una (1880-1959) Cavalcade 1933; The Invisible Man 1933; The Barretts of Wimpole Street 1934; Chained 1934; Bride of Frankenstein 1935; David Copperfield 1935; The Perfect Gentleman 1935; Lloyd's of London 1936; Rose Marie 1936; Personal Property 1937; The Adventures of Robin Hood 1938; We Are Not Alone 1939; It All Came True 1940; Lillian Russell 1940; The Sea Hawk 1940; The Strawberry Blonde 1941; Always in My Heart 1942; My Favorite Spy 1942; Holy Matrimony 1943; Christmas in Connecticut 1945; Child of Divorce 1946; Witness for the Prosecution 1957

O'Conor, Hugh (1975-) Lamb 1985; Da 1988; My Left Foot 1989; The Three Musketeers 1993; The Young Poisoner's Handbook 1994; The Boy from Mercury 1996; Hotel Splendide 1999; bl_m 2003; Botched 2007; Reuniting the Rubins 2010; The Stag 2013

O'Conor, Joseph (1916-2001) Gorgo 1961; Oliver! 1968; Doomwatch 1972; Penny Gold 1973; The Black Windmill 1974

Odaka, Megumi (1972-) Godzilla vs King Ghidorah 1991; Godzilla vs Mothra 1992

O'Dea, Denis (1905-1978) The Plough and the Stars 1936; The Mark of Cain 1947; The Fallen Idol 1948; Under Capricorn 1949; Treasure Island 1950; The Long Dark Hall 1951; Never Take No for an Answer 1951; Sea Devils 1952; Niagara 1953; The Rising of the Moon 1957; The Story of Esther Costello 1957; Esther and the King 1960

O'Dea, Jimmy (1899-1965) Penny Paradise 1938; Cheer Boys Cheer 1939; Let's Be Famous 1939; The Rising of the Moon 1957; Darby O'Gill and the Little People 1959

Odetta (1930-2008) Sanctuary 1961; The Autobiography of Miss Jane Pittman 1974

O'Donnell, Cathy (1925-1970) The Best Years of Our Lives 1946; They Live by Night 1948; The Miniver Story 1950; Side Street 1950; Detective Story 1951; Eight o'Clock Walk 1953; The Loves of Three Queens 1954; The Man from Laramie 1955; The Deerslayer 1957; Ben-Hur 1959

O'Donnell, Chris (1970-) Men Don't Leave 1990; Blue Sky 1991; Scent of a Woman 1992; School Ties 1992; The Three Musketeers 1993; Batman Forever 1995; Circle of Friends 1995; Mad Love 1995; The Chamber 1996; Batman and Robin 1997; The Bachelor 1999; Cookie's Fortune 1999; Vertical Limit 2000; Kinsey 2004; Max Payne 2008; Cats & Dogs: the Revenge of Kitty Galore 2010

O'Donnell, Rosie (1962-) A League of Their Own 1992; Another Stakeout 1993; Sleepless in Seattle 1993; Exit to Eden 1994; The Flintstones 1994; Now and Then 1995; Beautiful Girls 1996; Harriet the Spy 1996; Wide Awake 1998; America 2009

O'Donnell, Steve aka **O'Donnell, Steven** (1963-) The Pope Must Die 1991; The Cottage 2008; The Hooligan Factory 2014

O'Donoghue, Colin The Rite 2011; Storage 24 2012

O'Dowd, Chris (1979-) Festival 2005; Frequently Asked Questions about Time Travel 2008; The Boat That Rocked 2009; Gulliver's Travels 2010; Bridesmaids 2011; Friends with Kids 2011; The Sapphires 2012; This Is 40 2012; Calvary 2013; Epic 2013; Cuban Fury 2014; St Vincent 2014; The Program 2015; Loving Vincent 2016

O'Driscoll, Martha (1922-1998) The Lady Eve 1941; Young and Willing 1942; The Fallen Sparrow 1943; The Daltons Ride Again 1945; Here Come the Co-Eds 1945; House of Dracula 1945; Under Western Skies 1945; Criminal Court 1946; Carnegie Hall 1947

Oestermann, Grégoire Look at Me 2004; I Do 2006

O'Farrell, Bernadette (1924-1999) *The Happiest Days of Your Life* 1950; *Lady Godiva Rides Again* 1951
O'Farrell, Peter *Hawk the Slayer* 1980; *Legend* 1985
Offerman, Nick (1970-) *Casa de Mi Padre* 2011; *Smashed* 2012; *The Kings of Summer* 2013; *Danny Collins* 2015; *Me and Earl and the Dying Girl* 2015; *The Founder* 2016
O'Flynn, Damian (1907-1982) *The Gay Falcon* 1941; *Crack-Up* 1946; *Riders of the Whistling Pines* 1949; *The Half-Breed* 1952; *Daniel Boone, Trail Blazer* 1957; *Gunfight at Comanche Creek* 1964
O'Flynn, Kate *Happy-Go-Lucky* 2007; *Up There* 2011
Oftebro, Jakob *Kon-Tiki* 2012; *In Order of Disappearance* 2014; *The Last King* 2016
Ogata, Issey (1952-) *A One and a Two* 1999; *Tony Takitani* 2004; *The Sun* 2005
Ogata, Ken (1937-2008) *Vengeance Is Mine* 1979; *Virus* 1980; *The Ballad of Narayama* 1983; *Mishima: a Life in Four Chapters* 1985; *The Pillow Book* 1995
Ogier, Bulle (1939-) *L'Amour Fou* 1968; *The Discreet Charm of the Bourgeoisie* 1972; *The Valley* 1972; *Celine and Julie Go Boating* 1974; *Maîtresse* 1976; *The Third Generation* 1979; *Candy Mountain* 1987; *See How They Fall* 1993; *Irma Vep* 1996; *Shattered Image* 1998; *Venus Beauty Institute* 1998; *The Colour of Lies* 1999; *Merci Docteur Rey* 2002; *Belle Toujours* 2006
Ogilvy, Ian (1943-) *The She Beast* 1965; *The Day the Fish Came Out* 1967; *The Sorcerers* 1967; *Stranger in the House* 1967; *The Heroes* 1968; *Witchfinder General* 1968; *And Now the Screaming Starts!* 1973; *From beyond the Grave* 1973; *No Sex Please - We're British* 1973; *Anna Karenina* 1985; *Death Becomes Her* 1992; *The Disappearance of Kevin Johnson* 1995; *We Still Kill the Old Way* 2014
Ogle, Charles (1865-1940) *Rebecca of Sunnybrook Farm* 1917; *A Romance of the Redwoods* 1917; *The Covered Wagon* 1923; *Ruggles of Red Gap* 1923
O'Grady, Gail (1963-) *Celtic Pride* 1996; *That Old Feeling* 1997; *Deuce Bigalow: Male Gigolo* 1999; *Walking across Egypt* 1999; *More Sex & the Single Mom* 2005; *All I Want for Christmas* 2007; *The Sitter* 2007; *Shadow on the Mesa* 2013
Oh Dal-su (1968-) *Oldboy* 2003; *Sympathy for Lady Vengeance* 2005
Oh, Sandra (1971-) *Last Night* 1998; *Dancing at the Blue Iguana* 2000; *Waking the Dead* 2000; *Under the Tuscan Sun* 2003; *Mulan II* 2004; *Sideways* 2004; *Hard Candy* 2005; *The Night Listener* 2006; *Blindness* 2008; *Defendor* 2009; *Rabbit Hole* 2010
Oh, Soon-Teck *aka* **Oh, Soon Taik** *aka* **Oh, Soon-Tek** (1943-) *The Man with the Golden Gun* 1974; *Missing in Action 2: the Beginning* 1985; *Death Wish 4: the Crackdown* 1987; *Soursweet* 1988; *A Home of Our Own* 1993; *Beverly Hills Ninja* 1997
O'Halloran, Brian *Clerks* 1994; *Clerks II* 2006
O'Halloran, Jack (1943-) *Farewell, My Lovely* 1975; *March or Die* 1977; *The Baltimore Bullet* 1980; *Superman II* 1980; *Dragnet* 1987; *Hero and the Terror* 1988
O'Hanlon, Ardal (1965-) *The Butcher Boy* 1997; *Greyfriars Bobby* 2005
O'Hanlon, George (1912-1989) *Park Row* 1952; *Kronos* 1957; *Jetsons: the Movie* 1990
O'Hara, Catherine (1954-) *Heartburn* 1986; *Beetle Juice* 1988; *Betsy's Wedding* 1990; *Home Alone* 1990; *Little Vegas* 1990; *Home Alone 2: Lost in New York* 1992; *The Nightmare before Christmas* 1993; *The Paper* 1994; *A Simple Twist of Fate* 1994; *Tall Tale* 1994; *Wyatt Earp* 1994; *Last of the High Kings* 1996; *Waiting for Guffman* 1996; *Pippi Longstocking* 1997; *Home Fries* 1998; *Bartok the Magnificent* 1999; *The Life before This* 1999; *Best in Show* 2000; *Orange County* 2001; *A Mighty Wind* 2003; *Surviving Christmas* 2004; *For Your Consideration* 2006; *Monster House* 2006; *Penelope* 2006; *Away We Go* 2009; *Where the Wild Things Are* 2009; *Killers* 2010; *Temple Grandin* 2010; *Frankenweenie* 2012; *When Marnie Was There* 2014

O'Hara, David *aka* **O'Hara, David Patrick** (1965-) *Link* 1986; *The Bridge* 1990; *Braveheart* 1995; *The Near Room* 1995; *Some Mother's Son* 1996; *The Devil's Own* 1997; *The Matchmaker* 1997; *Janice Beard 45 WPM* 1999;

Stander 2003; *Hotel Rwanda* 2004; *Tristan + Isolde* 2005; *Doomsday* 2008; *Wanted* 2008; *Jack Said* 2009; *The Kid* 2010; *Best Laid Plans* 2011
O'Hara, Jenny (1942-) *Career Opportunities* 1991; *Angie* 1994
O'Hara, Maureen (1920-2015) *The Hunchback of Notre Dame* 1939; *Jamaica Inn* 1939; *A Bill of Divorcement* 1940; *Dance, Girl, Dance* 1940; *How Green Was My Valley* 1941; *The Black Swan* 1942; *Ten Gentlemen from West Point* 1942; *To the Shores of Tripoli* 1942; *The Fallen Sparrow* 1943; *The Immortal Sergeant* 1943; *This Land Is Mine* 1943; *Buffalo Bill* 1944; *The Spanish Main* 1945; *Do You Love Me?* 1946; *Sentimental Journey* 1946; *The Foxes of Harrow* 1947; *Miracle on 34th Street* 1947; *Sinbad the Sailor* 1947; *Sitting Pretty* 1948; *Britannia Mews* 1949; *Father Was a Fullback* 1949; *A Woman's Secret* 1949; *Comanche Territory* 1950; *Rio Grande* 1950; *Sons of the Musketeers* 1951; *Against All Flags* 1952; *Kangaroo* 1952; *The Quiet Man* 1952; *The Redhead from Wyoming* 1953; *War Arrow* 1953; *Malaga* 1954; *Lady Godiva* 1955; *The Long Gray Line* 1955; *Lisbon* 1956; *The Wings of Eagles* 1957; *Our Man in Havana* 1959; *The Deadly Companions* 1961; *The Parent Trap* 1961; *Mr Hobbs Takes a Vacation* 1962; *McLintock!* 1963; *Spencer's Mountain* 1963; *The Battle of the Villa Fiorita* 1965; *The Rare Breed* 1966; *How Do I Love Thee?* 1970; *Big Jake* 1971; *Only the Lonely* 1991; *The Last Dance* 2000
O'Hara, Paige (1961-) *Beauty and the Beast* 1991; *Beauty and the Beast: the Enchanted Christmas* 1997; *Belle's Magical World* 1997
O'Hare, Denis (1962-) *Michael Clayton* 2007; *The Proposal* 2009; *The Eagle* 2010; *Dallas Buyers Club* 2013; *The Pyramid* 2014
O'Herlihy, Dan *aka* **O'Herlihy, Daniel** (1919-2005) *Kidnapped* 1948; *Macbeth* 1948; *Soldiers Three* 1951; *Sons of the Musketeers* 1951; *Actors and Sin* 1952; *The Adventures of Robinson Crusoe* 1952; *The Black Shield of Falworth* 1954; *The Purple Mask* 1955; *The Virgin Queen* 1955; *That Woman Opposite* 1957; *Home before Dark* 1958; *Imitation of Life* 1959; *The Young Land* 1959; *One Foot in Hell* 1960; *A Terrible Beauty* 1960; *King of the Roaring 20s - the Story of Arnold Rothstein* 1961; *The Cabinet of Caligari* 1962; *Fail-Safe* 1964; *The Big Cube* 1969; *Waterloo* 1970; *The Carey Treatment* 1972; *The Tamarind Seed* 1974; *MacArthur* 1977; *Halloween III: Season of the Witch* 1982; *The Last Starfighter* 1984; *The Dead* 1987; *RoboCop* 1987; *RoboCop 2* 1990; *Love, Cheat & Steal* 1994
O'Herlihy, Gavan (1954-) *Death Wish 3* 1985; *The Shooter* 1994; *The Descent: Part 2* 2009
Ohmart, Carol (1927-) *House on Haunted Hill* 1958; *Born Reckless* 1959; *Spider Baby* 1964
Ojeda, Manuel *Eagle's Wing* 1978; *Romancing the Stone* 1984
Okada, Eiji (1920-1995) *Hiroshima, Mon Amour* 1959; *The Ugly American* 1963; *Woman of the Dunes* 1963
Okada, Mariko (1933-) *Late Autumn* 1960; *An Autumn Afternoon* 1962
Okada, Masaki *Confessions* 2010; *Villain* 2010
O'Kane, Deirdre *interMission* 2003; *Boy Eats Girl* 2005
O'Keefe, Dennis (1908-1968) *Bad Man of Brimstone* 1938; *That's Right - You're Wrong* 1939; *Arise, My Love* 1940; *You'll Find Out* 1940; *Topper Returns* 1941; *Hangmen Also Die!* 1943; *The Leopard Man* 1943; *Abroad with Two Yanks* 1944; *The Fighting Seabees* 1944; *Sensations* 1944; *The Story of Dr Wassell* 1944; *Up in Mabel's Room* 1944; *The Affairs of Susan* 1945; *Brewster's Millions* 1945; *Earl Carroll Vanities* 1945; *Dishonored Lady* 1947; *T-Men* 1947; *Raw Deal* 1948; *The Company She Keeps* 1950; *Follow the Sun: the Ben Hogan Story* 1951; *The Lady Wants Mink* 1953; *The Diamond* 1954; *Angela* 1955; *Dragoon Wells Massacre* 1957; *All Hands on Deck* 1961
O'Keefe, Jodi Lyn (1978-) *Halloween H20: 20 Years Later* 1998; *She's All That* 1999; *Whatever It Takes* 2000; *Three Wise Guys* 2005; *Class* 2010
O'Keefe, Michael (1955-) *The Great Santini* 1979; *Caddyshack* 1980; *Split Image* 1982; *Savage Islands* 1983; *Finders Keepers* 1984; *The Slugger's Wife* 1985; *Ironweed* 1987; *Nina Takes a Lover* 1993; *Three Wishes* 1995; *The Pledge* 2000; *Prancer Returns* 2001; *Defending Our Kids: the Julie Posey Story* 2003; *Michael Clayton* 2007;

Frozen River 2008; *Apartment 143* 2011
O'Keeffe, Miles (1954-) *Tarzan, the Ape Man* 1981; *Sword of the Valiant* 1984; *Waxwork* 1988; *The Unknown* 2005
O'Kelly, Don *aka* **Kelly, Don** (1924-1966) *Bombers B-52* 1957; *The Hostage* 1966
O'Kelly, Donal *The Van* 1996; *The Last Bus Home* 1997
Okhlopkov, Nikolai P *aka* **Okhlopkov, N P** (1900-1967) *Lenin in October* 1937; *Alexander Nevsky* 1938
Okina, Megumi *The Grudge: Ju-On* 2003; *Shutter* 2008
Okiyama, Hideko (1945-2011) *The Profound Desire of the Gods* 1968; *Dodes'ka-Den* 1970
Okochi, Denjiro (1898-1962) *Sanshiro Sugata* 1943; *No Regrets for Our Youth* 1946
Okonedo, Sophie (1969-) *Young Soul Rebels* 1991; *Ace Ventura: When Nature Calls* 1995; *Go Now* 1995; *This Year's Love* 1999; *Peaches* 2000; *Dirty Pretty Things* 2002; *Hotel Rwanda* 2004; *Aeonflux* 2005; *Scenes of a Sexual Nature* 2006; *Stormbreaker* 2006; *The Secret Life of Bees* 2008; *Skin* 2008; *After Earth* 2013; *War Book* 2014
Okumoto, Yuji (1960-) *The Karate Kid Part II* 1986; *Aloha Summer* 1988; *True Believer* 1989; *Blue Tiger* 1994; *I'll Remember April* 1999
Okura, Chiyoko *Poppy* 1935; *Osaka Elegy* 1936
Olaf, Pierre (1928-1995) *Wild and Wonderful* 1964; *Art of Love* 1965; *Camelot* 1967; *The Gamblers* 1969; *The Little Theatre of Jean Renoir* 1969
Olafsson, Olafur Darri *The Deep* 2012; *The White King* 2016
Oland, Warner (1880-1938) *Don Q, Son of Zorro* 1925; *Riders of the Purple Sage* 1925; *Don Juan* 1926; *When a Man Loves* 1926; *The Jazz Singer* 1927; *The Return of Dr Fu Manchu* 1930; *Dishonored* 1931; *Shanghai Express* 1932; *Bulldog Drummond Strikes Back* 1934; *Charlie Chan in London* 1934; *Mandalay* 1934; *The Painted Veil* 1934; *Charlie Chan in Egypt* 1935; *Charlie Chan in Paris* 1935; *Charlie Chan in Shanghai* 1935; *Charlie Chan at the Circus* 1936; *Charlie Chan at the Opera* 1936; *Charlie Chan at Monte Carlo* 1937; *Charlie Chan at the Olympics* 1937; *Charlie Chan on Broadway* 1937
Olandt, Ken (1958-) *April Fool's Day* 1986; *Leprechaun* 1992
Olbrychski, Daniel (1945-) *Landscape after Battle* 1970; *The Young Ladies of Wilko* 1979; *Les Uns et les Autres* 1981; *Dangerous Moves* 1984; *Rosa Luxemburg* 1986; *The Barber of Siberia* 1999; *Salt* 2010
Oldfield, Finnegan *Bang Gang (A Modern Love Story)* 2015; *Les Cowboys* 2015
Oldham, Will *Matewan* 1987; *Old Joy* 2005
Oldman, Gary (1958-) *Sid and Nancy* 1986; *Prick Up Your Ears* 1987; *Criminal Law* 1988; *Track 29* 1988; *We Think the World of You* 1988; *Chattahoochee* 1989; *Rosencrantz and Guildenstern Are Dead* 1990; *State of Grace* 1990; *JFK* 1991; *Bram Stoker's Dracula* 1992; *Romeo Is Bleeding* 1992; *True Romance* 1993; *Immortal Beloved* 1994; *Leon* 1994; *Murder in the First* 1994; *The Scarlet Letter* 1995; *Basquiat* 1996; *Air Force One* 1997; *The Fifth Element* 1997; *The Magic Sword: Quest for Camelot* 1997; *Lost in Space* 1998; *The Contender* 2000; *Hannibal* 2001; *Harry Potter and the Prisoner of Azkaban* 2004; *Batman Begins* 2005; *Harry Potter and the Order of the Phoenix* 2007; *The Dark Knight* 2008; *The Unborn* 2008; *The Book of Eli* 2009; *A Christmas Carol* 2009; *Planet 51* 2009; *One Night in Turin* 2010; *Kung Fu Panda 2* 2011; *Red Riding Hood* 2011; *Tinker Tailor Soldier Spy* 2011; *The Dark Knight Rises* 2012; *Lawless* 2012; *Paranoia* 2013; *Child 44* 2014; *Dawn of the Planet of the Apes* 2014; *RoboCop* 2014; *Criminal* 2016
O'Leary, Jack *Inside Moves: the Guys from Max's Bar* 1980; *Death Valley* 1982
O'Leary, Matt (1987-) *Domestic Disturbance* 2001; *Frailty* 2001; *Brick* 2005; *Havoc* 2005; *Mother's Day* 2010; *Eden* 2012
O'Leary, William (1957-) *Bull Durham* 1988; *Hot Shots!* 1991; *Candyman: Farewell to the Flesh* 1995; *Project ALF* 1996
Oleynik, Larisa (1981-) *The Baby-Sitter's Club* 1995; *10 Things I Hate about You* 1999; *Together Again for the First Time* 2008
Olin, Lena (1955-) *After the Rehearsal* 1984; *The Unbearable Lightness of*

Being 1988; *Enemies, a Love Story* 1989; *Havana* 1990; *Romeo Is Bleeding* 1992; *Mr Jones* 1993; *Night Falls on Manhattan* 1997; *Hamilton* 1998; *Polish Wedding* 1998; *The Ninth Gate* 1999; *Chocolat* 2000; *Darkness* 2002; *Queen of the Damned* 2002; *The United States of Leland* 2002; *Hollywood Homicide* 2003; *Casanova* 2005; *Awake* 2007; *The Reader* 2008; *Remember Me* 2010; *Night Train to Lisbon* 2013
Olin, Stig (1920-2008) *Crisis* 1945; *The Devil's Wanton* 1949; *To Joy* 1950
Oliver, Anthony (1923-1995) *Lost* 1955; *They Can't Hang Me* 1955; *Danger by My Side* 1962
Oliver, Barret (1973-) *The NeverEnding Story* 1984; *Cocoon* 1985; *DARYL* 1985; *The Secret Garden* 1987
Oliver, Charles (1907-1983) *The Avenging Hand* 1936; *Midnight at Madame Tussaud's* 1936; *The Green Cockatoo* 1937; *Ask a Policeman* 1938; *Sexton Blake and the Hooded Terror* 1938; *Crooks' Tour* 1940; *Under Your Hat* 1940
Oliver, Christian *The Good German* 2006; *Nora Roberts' Tribute* 2009
Oliver, Edna May (1883-1942) *The Saturday Night Kid* 1929; *Half Shot at Sunrise* 1930; *The Penguin Pool Murder* 1932; *Alice in Wonderland* 1933; *Ann Vickers* 1933; *Little Women* 1933; *Meet the Baron* 1933; *Only Yesterday* 1933; *Murder on the Blackboard* 1934; *David Copperfield* 1935; *Murder on a Honeymoon* 1935; *A Tale of Two Cities* 1935; *Romeo and Juliet* 1936; *Parnell* 1937; *Rosalie* 1937; *Little Miss Broadway* 1938; *Paradise for Three* 1938; *Drums along the Mohawk* 1939; *Nurse Edith Cavell* 1939; *Second Fiddle* 1939; *The Story of Vernon and Irene Castle* 1939; *Pride and Prejudice* 1940; *Lydia* 1941
Oliver, Gordon (1911-1995) *Blondie!* 1938; *Sweetheart of the Campus* 1941; *The Spiral Staircase* 1946; *Station West* 1948; *My Forbidden Past* 1951; *The Las Vegas Story* 1952
Oliver, Guy (1878-1932) *The Covered Wagon* 1923; *The Docks of New York* 1928
Oliver, Michael (1982-) *Problem Child* 1990; *Problem Child 2* 1991; *Dillinger and Capone* 1995
Oliver, Susan (1932-1990) *The Gene Krupa Story* 1959; *The Disorderly Orderly* 1964; *Your Cheatin' Heart* 1964; *A Man Called Gannon* 1969; *Ginger in the Morning* 1973
Oliver, Vic (1898-1964) *Give Us the Moon* 1944; *I'll Be Your Sweetheart* 1945
Olivier, Laurence (1907-1989) *Friends and Lovers* 1931; *Westward Passage* 1932; *Moscow Nights* 1935; *As You Like It* 1936; *Conquest of the Air* 1936; *Fire over England* 1937; *21 Days* 1937; *The Divorce of Lady X* 1938; *Q Planes* 1939; *Wuthering Heights* 1939; *Pride and Prejudice* 1940; *Rebecca* 1940; *49th Parallel* 1941; *That Hamilton Woman* 1941; *The Demi-Paradise* 1943; *Henry V* 1944; *This Happy Breed* 1944; *Hamlet* 1948; *The Magic Box* 1951; *Carrie* 1952; *The Beggar's Opera* 1953; *Richard III* 1955; *The Prince and the Showgirl* 1957; *The Entertainer* 1960; *Spartacus* 1960; *Term of Trial* 1962; *Bunny Lake Is Missing* 1965; *Othello* 1965; *Khartoum* 1966; *Romeo and Juliet* 1968; *The Shoes of the Fisherman* 1968; *Battle of Britain* 1969; *The Dance of Death* 1969; *Oh! What a Lovely War* 1969; *Three Sisters* 1970; *Lady Caroline Lamb* 1972; *Sleuth* 1972; *Love among the Ruins* 1975; *Marathon Man* 1976; *A Bridge Too Far* 1977; *The Betsy* 1978; *The Boys from Brazil* 1978; *Dracula* 1979; *A Little Romance* 1979; *The Jazz Singer* 1980; *Clash of the Titans* 1981; *Inchon* 1981; *Wagner* 1983; *The Bounty* 1984; *The Jigsaw Man* 1984; *Wild Geese II* 1985; *War Requiem* 1988
Olivier, Paul (1877-1948) *A Nous la Liberté* 1931; *Le Million* 1931
Olkewicz, Walter (1948-) *The Executioner's Song* 1982; *Pronto* 1996
Olmos, Edward James *aka* **Olmos, Eddie** (1947-) *Aloha, Bobby and Rose* 1975; *Virus* 1980; *Wolfen* 1981; *Zoot Suit* 1981; *Blade Runner* 1982; *The Ballad of Gregorio Cortez* 1983; *Saving Grace* 1985; *Stand and Deliver* 1988; *Triumph of the Spirit* 1989; *Talent for the Game* 1991; *American Me* 1992; *The Burning Season* 1994; *My Family* 1994; *Caught* 1996; *The Disappearance of Garcia Lorca* 1997; *Selena* 1997; *12 Angry Men* 1997; *Gossip* 1999; *The Road to El Dorado* 2000; *The Green Hornet* 2011; *2 Guns* 2013

Being 1988; Continued:

O'Loughlin, Alex *Feed* 2005; *The Back-Up Plan* 2010
O'Loughlin, Gerald S *aka* **O'Loughlin, Gerald** (1921-2015) *A Hatful of Rain* 1957; *Ensign Pulver* 1964; *In Cold Blood* 1967; *Riot* 1969; *Desperate Characters* 1971; *The Organization* 1971; *The Valachi Papers* 1972; *Something for Joey* 1977; *Frances* 1982
Olsen, Ashley (1986-) *It Takes Two* 1995; *Our Lips Are Sealed* 2000; *Winning London* 2001; *Getting There* 2002; *New York Minute* 2004
Olsen, Christopher *aka* **Olsen, Chris** (1947-) *Bigger than Life* 1956; *The Tarnished Angels* 1957
Olsen, Elizabeth (1989-) *Liberal Arts* 2011; *Martha Marcy May Marlene* 2011; *Peace, Love & Misunderstanding* 2011; *Silent House* 2011; *Red Lights* 2012; *In Secret* 2013; *Kill Your Darlings* 2013; *Old Boy* 2013; *Godzilla* 2014; *I Saw the Light* 2015
Olsen, Eric Christian (1976-) *Not Another Teen Movie* 2001; *The Hot Chick* 2002; *Dumb and Dumberer: When Harry Met Lloyd* 2003; *Cellular* 2004; *And She Was* 2007; *License to Wed* 2007; *Sunshine Cleaning* 2008; *Fired Up!* 2009; *The Back-Up Plan* 2010; *The Thing* 2011
Olsen, Gary (1957-2000) *Party Party* 1983; *The Cook, the Thief, his Wife and Her Lover* 1989; *Up 'n' Under* 1997
Olsen, Mary-Kate (1986-) *It Takes Two* 1995; *Our Lips Are Sealed* 2000; *Winning London* 2001; *Getting There* 2002; *New York Minute* 2004; *The Wackness* 2008; *Beastly* 2010
Olsen, Moroni (1889-1954) *Annie Oakley* 1935; *The Three Musketeers* 1935; *Snow White and the Seven Dwarfs* 1937; *Kentucky* 1938; *Rose of Washington Square* 1939; *East of the River* 1940; *One Foot in Heaven* 1941; *Dangerously They Live* 1942; *Ali Baba and the Forty Thieves* 1944; *Buffalo Bill* 1944; *Cobra Woman* 1944; *Mildred Pierce* 1945; *High Wall* 1947; *The Long Night* 1947; *Possessed* 1947; *Father of the Bride* 1950; *Father's Little Dividend* 1951; *Submarine Command* 1951; *The Long, Long Trailer* 1954
Olsen, Ole (1892-1963) *All over Town* 1937; *Hellzapoppin'* 1941
Olson, James (1930-) *The Three Sisters* 1966; *Rachel, Rachel* 1968; *Moon Zero Two* 1969; *The Andromeda Strain* 1970; *Crescendo* 1970; *Wild Rovers* 1971; *The Groundstar Conspiracy* 1972; *Amityville II: the Possession* 1982; *The Parade* 1984; *Commando* 1985
Olson, Nancy (1928-) *Mr Music* 1950; *Sunset Blvd* 1950; *Union Station* 1950; *Force of Arms* 1951; *Submarine Command* 1951; *Big Jim McLain* 1952; *So Big* 1953; *The Boy from Oklahoma* 1954; *Battle Cry* 1955; *Pollyanna* 1960; *The Absent-Minded Professor* 1961; *Son of Flubber* 1963; *Smith!* 1969; *Snowball Express* 1972; *Making Love* 1982
Olyphant, Timothy (1968-) *Go* 1999; *Auggie Rose* 2000; *The Broken Hearts Club: a Romantic Comedy* 2000; *Rock Star* 2001; *The Safety of Objects* 2001; *Dreamcatcher* 2003; *A Man Apart* 2003; *The Girl Next Door* 2004; *Catch and Release* 2007; *Die Hard 4.0* 2007; *Hitman* 2007; *Stop-Loss* 2007; *A Perfect Getaway* 2009; *The Crazies* 2010; *I Am Number Four* 2011; *Mother's Day* 2016; *Snowden* 2016
O'Malley, Daragh (1954-) *Withnail & I* 1986; *Puckoon* 2002
O'Malley, J Pat (1904-1985) *Alice in Wonderland* 1951; *One Hundred and One Dalmatians* 1960; *Apache Rifles* 1964; *The Jungle Book* 1967
O'Malley, Mike *aka* **O'Malley, Michael** (1969-) *28 Days* 2000; *The Perfect Man* 2005; *Meet Dave* 2008; *So Undercover* 2012; *R.I.P.D.* 2013
O'Malley, Rex (1901-1976) *Camille* 1937; *Midnight* 1939; *Taxi* 1953
O'Mara, Jason *Resident Evil: Extinction* 2007; *One for the Money* 2012
O'Mara, Kate (1939-2014) *Corruption* 1968; *The Horror of Frankenstein* 1970; *The Vampire Lovers* 1970
Omen, Judd *Howling II: Your Sister Is a Werewolf* 1984; *Pee-wee's Big Adventure* 1985
O'Moore, Patrick *aka* **O'Moore, Pat** (1909-1983) *Evensong* 1934; *Smilin' Through* 1941; *Conflict* 1945; *The Two Mrs Carrolls* 1945; *Bulldog Drummond Strikes Back* 1947; *Khyber Patrol* 1954
On, Andy *New Police Story* 2004; *Mad Detective* 2007
Ondine (1937-1989) *Vinyl* 1965; *The Chelsea Girls* 1966; *Dynamite Chicken* 1971
Ondra, Anny (1903-1987) *Blackmail* 1929; *The Manxman* 1929

O'Neal, Frederick (1905-1992) Anna Lucasta 1958; Take a Giant Step 1959

O'Neal, Griffin (1964-) The Escape Artist 1982; April Fool's Day 1986; The Wraith 1986

O'Neal (1), Patrick (1927-1994) The Mad Magician 1954; In Harm's Way 1965; King Rat 1965; Alvarez Kelly 1966; Chamber of Horrors 1966; A Fine Madness 1966; Where Were You When the Lights Went Out? 1968; Castle Keep 1969; El Condor 1970; Corky 1972; The Way We Were 1973; The Stepford Wives 1975; Twin Detectives 1976; The Stuff 1985; Like Father, like Son 1987; Alice 1990; Q & A 1990; For the Boys 1991; Under Siege 1992

O'Neal, Ron (1937-2004) The Organization 1971; Superfly 1972; The Master Gunfighter 1975; A Force of One 1979; When a Stranger Calls 1979; The Final Countdown 1980; Hero and the Terror 1988; Original Gangstas 1996

O'Neal, Ryan (194 -) The Big Bounce 1969; The Games 1970; Love Story 1970; Wild Rovers 1971; What's Up, Doc? 1972; Paper Moon 1973; The Thief Who Came to Dinner 1973; Barry Lyndon 1975; Nickelodeon 1976; A Bridge Too Far 1977; The Driver 1978; Oliver's Story 1978; The Main Event 1979; Green Ice 1981; So Fine 1981; Partners 1982; Irreconcilable Differences 1984; Fever Pitch 1985; Tough Guys Don't Dance 1987; Chances Are 1989; Faithful 1996; Burn Hollywood Burn 1997; Zero Effect 1997; People I Know 2002; Malibu's Most Wanted 2003

O'Neal, Shaquille (1972-) CB4 1993; Blue Chips 1994; Kazaam 1996; Steel 1997; Scary Movie 4 2006

O'Neal, Tatum (1953-) Paper Moon 1973; The Bad News Bears 1976; Nickelodeon 1976; International Velvet 1978; Circle of Two 1980; Little Darlings 1980; Certain Fury 1985; Little Noises 1992; Basquiat 1996; The Runaways 2010

O'Neil, Barbara (1910-1980) Stella Dallas 1937; I Am the Law 1938; The Toy Wife 1938; Gone with the Wind 1939; Tower of London 1939; When Tomorrow Comes 1939; All This, and Heaven Too 1940; Secret beyond the Door 1948; Whirlpool 1949; Angel Face 1953

O'Neil, Nance (1874-1965) Ladies of Leisure 1930; The Rogue Song 1930; Cimarron 1931

O'Neil, Nancy (1911-1995) Jack Ahoy! 1934; The Secret of the Loch 1934

O'Neil, Paddie aka O'Neil, Paddy (1926-2010) Penny Points to Paradise 1951; The Early Bird 1965

O'Neil, Sally (1908-1968) Sally, Irene and Mary 1925; Battling Butler 1926

O'Neill, Chris (1946-1997) Backbeat 1993; Beyond the Fire 2008

O'Neill, Con Dancin' thru the Dark 1989; The Last Seduction 2 1998; Telstar: the Joe Meek Story 2008

O'Neill, Dick (1928-1998) Gamera the Invincible 1965; The Taking of Pelham One Two Three 1974; House Calls 1978; The Jerk 1979; Wolfen 1981; Chiller 1985

O'Neill, Ed (1946-) A Winner Never Quits 1986; Disorganized Crime 1989; K-9 1989; Sibling Rivalry 1990; Driving Me Crazy 1991; Blue Chips 1994; Little Giants 1994; Prefontaine 1997; The Bone Collector 1999; Spartan 2004; Finding Dory 2016

O'Neill, Henry (1891-1961) Lady Killer 1933; Fashions of 1934 1934; Flirtation Walk 1934; The Key 1934; Madame Du Barry 1934; The Secret Bride 1934; Black Fury 1935; Special Agent 1935; The Story of Louis Pasteur 1936; The Walking Dead 1936; The White Angel 1936; The Great O'Malley 1937; Green Light 1937; Wells Fargo 1937; Jezebel 1938; Racket Busters 1938; White Banners 1938; Angels Wash Their Faces 1939; Confessions of a Nazi Spy 1939; Castle on the Hudson 1940; Billy the Kid 1941; Men of Boys Town 1941; Whistling in the Dark 1941; White Cargo 1942; The Heavenly Body 1943; Nothing but Trouble 1944; Two Girls and a Sailor 1944; Anchors Aweigh 1945; The Virginian 1946; The Return of October 1948; Holiday Affair 1949; The Reckless Moment 1949; No Man of Her Own 1950; The Second Woman 1951; Scarlet Angel 1952

O'Neill, Jennifer (1948-) Rio Lobo 1970; Such Good Friends 1971; Summer of '42 1971; The Carey Treatment 1972; The Masters 1975; The Reincarnation of Peter Proud 1975; Whiffs 1975; L'Innocente 1976; Cloud Dancer 1979; A Force of One 1979; Scanners 1980

O'Neill, Kel XX/XY 2001; Easier with Practice 2009

O'Neill, Maggie (1967-) Seven Minutes 1989; Under Suspicion 1991; All Men Are Mortal 1995

O'Neill, Seamus Le Donk & Scor-Zay-Zee 2009; Inbred 2011

Ongg, Judy Zu Warriors 1983; The Pillow Book 1995

Ono, Yoko aka Ono Lennon, Yoko The US vs John Lennon 2006; George Harrison: Living in the Material World 2011

Onorati, Peter (1954-) Wings of the Apache 1990; The Art of Murder 1999

Ontiveros, Lupe (1942-2012) Born in East LA 1987; As Good as It Gets 1997; Chuck & Buck 2000; Real Women Have Curves 2002; A Girl like Me 2006

Ontkean, Michael (1950-) Slap Shot 1977; Willie and Phil 1980; Making Love 1982; The Blood of Others 1984; The Allnighter 1987; Maid to Order 1987; Clara's Heart 1988; Bye Bye Blues 1989; Cold Front 1989; Swann 1996; Nico the Unicorn 1998

Opatoshu, David (1918-1996) The Best of Enemies 1961; Guns of Darkness 1962; The Defector 1966; Tarzan and the Valley of Gold 1966; Enter Laughing 1967; Death of a Gunfighter 1969; Romance of a Horse Thief 1971

Openshaw, Anne Narc 2001; Recipe for Murder 2001; Mary Higgins Clark's We'll Meet Again 2002

Oppenheimer, Alan (1930-) The Groundstar Conspiracy 1972; Westworld 1973; 9 2009

Opper, Don (1949-) Android 1982; Critters 1986; Slam Dance 1987

O'Quinn, Terry aka O'Quinn, Terrance (1952-) Heaven's Gate 1980; Silver Bullet 1985; The Stepfather 1986; Black Widow 1987; Pin 1988; Roe vs Wade 1989; Stepfather II 1989; Blind Fury 1990; Blood Oath 1990; Company Business 1991; Rocketeer 1991; The Cutting Edge 1992; Amityville: a New Generation 1993; Death of a Cheerleader 1994; Don't Talk to Strangers 1994; Hard Evidence 1994; Heart of a Child 1994; Primal Fear 1996; Breast Men 1997; Rated X 2000

Ora, Rita Fifty Shades of Grey 2015; Fifty Shades Darker 2017

Oram, Steve Sightseers 2012; The Canal 2014; Captain Webb 2014; Aaaaaaaah! 2015

O'Rawe, Geraldine Circle of Friends 1995; Resurrection Man 1997; Disco Pigs 2001; Mr In-Between 2001

Orbach, Jerry (1935-2004) Mad Dog Coll 1961; The Gang That Couldn't Shoot Straight 1971; The Sentinel 1977; Prince of the City 1981; Brewster's Millions 1985; FX: Murder by Illusion 1985; Dirty Dancing 1987; Someone to Watch over Me 1987; Last Exit to Brooklyn 1989; Beauty and the Beast 1991; Broadway Bound 1991; Delirious 1991; Out for Justice 1991; Mr Saturday Night 1992; Straight Talk 1992; Universal Soldier 1992; Upworld 1992; Aladdin and the King of Thieves 1996; Beauty and the Beast: the Enchanted Christmas 1997; Belle's Magical World 1997

Orbach, Ron Love Crimes 1991; Erotique 1994

Orbison, Roy (1936-1988) The Fastest Guitar Alive 1966; Hail! Hail! Rock 'n' Roll! 1987

O'Reilly, Cyril (1958-) Porky's 1981; Purple Hearts 1984; Across the Tracks 1990; Spring Thaw 2007

O'Reilly, Kathryn Puppet Master 1989; Zebra Crossing 2013

Orfei, Liana (1937-) Gordon the Black Pirate 1961; Nefertite, Queen of the Nile 1961

Orgolini, Lisa Trick or Treat 1986; Two Deaths 1994

Oriel, Ray Stones for Ibarra 1988; Ticks 1993

O'Riordan, Shaun The Man Who Liked Funerals 1959; Inn for Trouble 1960

Orlamond, William (1867-1957) Flesh and the Devil 1926; Mantrap 1926; The Wind 1928

Orlandi, Felice (1925-2003) Killer's Kiss 1955; The Outside Man 1973; The Driver 1978

Orlando, Orazio (?-1990) Le Bambole 1965; The Masters 1975

Orlando, Silvio (1957-) Il Cielo è Sempre Più Blu 1995; Aprile 1998; The Son's Room 2001; After Midnight 2003; The Caiman 2006

Ormond, Julia (1965-) The Baby of Macon 1993; Nostradamus 1993; Captives 1994; Legends of the Fall 1994; First Knight 1995; Sabrina 1995; Smilla's Feeling for Snow 1996; Animal Farm 1999; The Prime Gig 2000; Varian's War 2000; Iron Jawed Angels 2004; Inland Empire 2006; I Know Who Killed Me 2007; Surveillance 2007; Che Part One 2008; The Curious Case of Benjamin

Button 2008; Temple Grandin 2010; Albatross 2011; My Week with Marilyn 2011; Chained 2012; The East 2013

O'Rorke, Brefni (1889-1946) Don't Take It to Heart 1944; The Root of All Evil 1946

O'Ross, Ed (1949-) Dreams of Gold: the Mel Fisher Story 1986; The Hidden 1987; Red Heat 1988; Another 48 HRS 1990; Universal Soldier 1992

O'Rourke, Heather (1975-1988) Poltergeist 1982; Surviving 1985; Poltergeist II: the Other Side 1986; Poltergeist III 1988

Orr, William T (1917-2002) The Mortal Storm 1940; Unholy Partners 1941

Orser, Leland (1960-) Very Bad Things 1998; The Bone Collector 1999; Resurrection 1999; The Good German 2006; Taken 2 2012; The Guest 2014; Taken 3 2014

Orsi, Leigh Ann (1981-) The Favor 1994; Pet Shop 1995

Orsini, Marina Eddie and the Cruisers II: Eddie Lives! 1989; Agent of Influence 2002

Orsini, Umberto (1934-) Mademoiselle 1966; The Girl and the General 1967; The Sailor from Gibraltar 1967; César and Rosalie 1972; Ludwig 1973; Emmanuelle 2 1975; Love in the Strangest Way 1994

Orth, Frank (1880-1962) Nancy Drew - Detective 1938; Footlight Serenade 1942; The Magnificent Dope 1942; Rings on Her Fingers 1942; The Great Rupert 1950

Orth, Zak (1970-) Spanking the Monkey 1994; When Trumpets Fade 1998; Down to You 2000; Loser 2000; Prime 2005

Ortiz (1), John (1968-) El Cantante 2006; Take the Lead 2006; AVPR: Aliens vs Predator Requiem 2007; American Gangster 2007; Pride and Glory 2007; Jack Goes Boating 2010; The Drop 2014

Osborn, Lyn (1926-1958) The Amazing Colossal Man 1957; The Cosmic Man 1959

Osborne, Holmes (1952-) Bring It On 2000; Waking Up in Reno 2000; Donnie Darko 2001; The Quiet American 2002; The Box 2008

Osborne, John (1929-1994) First Love 1970; Get Carter 1971; Tomorrow Never Comes 1977; Flash Gordon 1980

Osborne, Vivienne (1896-1961) Two Seconds 1932; Supernatural 1933

Osbourne, Ozzy (1948-) Riders of the Storm 1986; Trick or Treat 1986; Private Parts 1997; Gnomeo & Juliet 2011; God Bless Ozzy Osbourne 2011

Oscar, Henry (1891-1969) Seven Sinners 1936; The Return of the Scarlet Pimpernel 1937; The Saint in London 1939; Hatter's Castle 1941; The Greed of William Hart 1948; The Brides of Dracula 1960; Murder Ahoy 1964; City under the Sea 1965

Oscarsson, Per (1927-2010) Hunger 1966; My Sister, My Love 1966; Doctor Glas 1968; The Night Visitor 1970; Endless Night 1971; The Last Valley 1971; The Blockhouse 1973; Victor Frankenstein 1977; Montenegro 1981; House of Angels 1992

Osei-Mansfield, Akai aka Akai StreetDance 2 2012; All Stars 2013

O'Shaughnessy, Brian (1931-2001) Mr Kingstreet's War 1970; Creatures the World Forgot 1971

O'Shea, Kevin (1952-) The Purple Heart 1944; Wing and a Prayer 1944

O'Shea (1), Michael (1906-1973) Lady of Burlesque 1943; The Eve of St Mark 1944; Jack London 1944; Something for the Boys 1944; Circumstantial Evidence 1945; It's a Pleasure 1945; The Big Wheel 1949; The Underworld Story 1950; Fixed Bayonets! 1951; The Model and the Marriage Broker 1951; Bloodhounds of Broadway 1952; It Should Happen to You 1954

O'Shea, Milo (1926-2013) This Other Eden 1959; Carry On Cabby 1963; Barbarella 1967; Ulysses 1967; Romeo and Juliet 1968; The Adding Machine 1969; The Angel Levine 1970; Loot 1970; Digby, the Biggest Dog in the World 1973; Steptoe and Son Ride Again 1973; Arabian Adventure 1979; The Verdict 1982; The Purple Rose of Cairo 1985; The Dream Team 1989; Opportunity Knocks 1990; Only the Lonely 1991; The Playboys 1992; The Butcher Boy 1997; The Matchmaker 1997; Swing Vote 1999

O'Shea, Oscar (1881-1960) Big City 1937; Captains Courageous 1937; Mannequin 1937; Riders of the Purple Sage 1941

O'Shea, Tessie (1917-1995) The Shiralee 1957; Bedknobs and Broomsticks 1971

Osment, Haley Joel (1988-) Bogus 1996; Beauty and the Beast: the

Enchanted Christmas 1997; I'll Remember April 1999; The Sixth Sense 1999; Pay It Forward 2000; AI: Artificial Intelligence 2001; The Country Bears 2002; The Jungle Book 2 2003; Secondhand Lions 2003; Yoga Hosers 2016

Osmond, Cliff (1937-2012) Kiss Me, Stupid 1964; The Fortune Cookie 1966; Shark's Treasure 1975

Osmond, Donny (1957-) Mulan 1998; College Road Trip 2008

Osmond, Hal (1919-1959) To Dorothy, a Son 1954; Dick Turpin - Highwayman 1956; Blood of the Vampire 1958

Ostaszewska, Maja Katyn 2007; In the Name of 2013

Osterloh, Robert (1918-2001) The Dark Past 1948; The Ring 1952; Riot in Cell Block 11 1954

Osugi, Ren (1951-) Hana-Bi 1997; The Twilight Samurai 2002

O'Sullivan, Aisling The Butcher Boy 1997; The One and Only 2001; The Actors 2003

O'Sullivan, Arthur (1912-1981) Girl with Green Eyes 1963; Ryan's Daughter 1970

O'Sullivan, Maureen (1911-1998) Song o' My Heart 1930; A Connecticut Yankee 1931; Payment Deferred 1932; Skyscraper Souls 1932; Strange Interlude 1932; Tarzan, the Ape Man 1932; Tugboat Annie 1933; The Barretts of Wimpole Street 1934; Tarzan and His Mate 1934; The Thin Man 1934; Anna Karenina 1935; Cardinal Richelieu 1935; David Copperfield 1935; Woman Wanted 1935; The Devil-Doll 1936; Tarzan Escapes 1936; A Day at the Races 1937; The Emperor's Candlesticks 1937; The Crowd Roars 1938; Port of Seven Seas 1938; A Yank at Oxford 1938; Tarzan Finds a Son! 1939; Pride and Prejudice 1940; Tarzan's Secret Treasure 1941; Tarzan's New York Adventure 1942; The Big Clock 1948; No Resting Place 1950; Where Danger Lives 1950; All I Desire 1953; The Tall T 1957; Wild Heritage 1958; Never Too Late 1965; Too Scared to Scream 1982; Hannah and Her Sisters 1986; Peggy Sue Got Married 1986

O'Sullivan, Richard (1944-) The Stranger's Hand 1953; Dance Little Lady 1954; The Green Scarf 1954; Dangerous Exile 1957; And Women Shall Weep 1960; Spare the Rod 1961; The Young Ones 1961; Wonderful Life 1964; The Haunted House of Horror 1969; Father Dear Father 1972; Man about the House 1974

Oswald, Patton Ratatouille 2007; Young Adult 2011

Oteri, Cheri (1965-) Inspector Gadget 1999; Lured Innocence 1999; Love & Sex 2000; Dumb and Dumberer: When Harry Met Lloyd 2003; Surveillance 2007

Otis, James One Summer Love 1975; Another Day in Paradise 1998

O'Toole, Annette (1953-) The Entertainer 1975; Smile 1975; Foolin' Around 1980; Cat People 1982; 48 HRS 1982; Superman III 1983; Cross My Heart 1987; Love at Large 1990; Desperate Justice 1993; My Brother's Keeper 1995; Here on Earth 2000

O'Toole, Peter (1932-2013) The Day They Robbed the Bank of England 1960; Kidnapped 1960; The Savage Innocents 1960; Lawrence of Arabia 1962; Becket 1964; Lord Jim 1965; The Sandpiper 1965; What's New, Pussycat? 1965; The Bible... in the Beginning 1966; How to Steal a Million 1966; The Night of the Generals 1966; Casino Royale 1967; Great Catherine 1968; The Lion in Winter 1968; Goodbye, Mr Chips 1969; Country Dance 1970; Murphy's War 1971; Under Milk Wood 1971; Man of La Mancha 1972; The Ruling Class 1972; Man Friday 1975; Rosebud 1975; Power Play 1978; Caligula 1979; Zulu Dawn 1979; The Stunt Man 1980; My Favorite Year 1982; Kim 1984; Supergirl 1984; Creator 1985; Club Paradise 1986; The Last Emperor 1987; High Spirits 1988; The Nutcracker Prince 1990; The Rainbow Thief 1990; Wings of Fame 1990; King Ralph 1991; Rebecca's Daughters 1991; The Seventh Coin 1993; FairyTale: a True Story 1997; Phantoms 1998; The Final Curtain 2002; Bright Young Things 2003; Troy 2004; Lassie 2005; Venus 2006; Ratatouille 2007; Stardust 2007; Dean Spanley 2008

Otowa, Nobuko (1925-1994) Miss Oyu 1951; The Island 1961; Onibaba 1964

Ottiano, Rafaela (1888-1942) As You Desire Me 1932; Curly Top 1935; Maytime 1937

Otto, Barry (1941-) Bliss 1985; The More Things Change 1985; The

Punisher 1989; Strictly Ballroom 1992; The Custodian 1993; Cosi 1996; Dead Letter Office 1998

Otto, Gotz aka Otto, Götz (1967-) Tomorrow Never Dies 1997; The Artist and the Model 2012; Iron Sky 2012

Otto, Miranda (1967-) Emma's War 1985; Daydream Believer 1991; The Last Days of Chez Nous 1992; Doing Time for Patsy Cline 1997; Dead Letter Office 1998; The Jack Bull 1999; Kin 2000; What Lies Beneath 2000; Human Nature 2001; The Lord of the Rings: The Two Towers 2002

Otto, Miranda (1967-) The Lord of the Rings: The Return of the King 2003; Flight of the Phoenix 2004; In My Father's Den 2004; War of the Worlds 2005; I, Frankenstein 2013; Reaching for the Moon 2013; The Turning 2013; The Homesman 2014; The Daughter 2016

Oudrey, Pierre Tout Va Bien 1972; Number Two 1975

Ouedraogo, Adama aka Ouédraogo, Adama Yaaba 1989; The Night of Truth 2004

Ouedraogo, Assita Yam Daabo 1986; La Promesse 1996

Ouedraogo, Rasmane aka Ouédraogo, Rasmané Tilaï 1990; La Promesse 1996; The Night of Truth 2004

Oulton, Brian (1908-1992) The Million Pound Note 1953; The Damned 1961

Oumansky, André (1933-) Sundays and Cybèle 1962; The Love Cage 1964; The Marseille Contract 1974; Othello 1995

Oury, Gérard (1919-2006) Sea Devils 1952; The Heart of the Matter 1953; They Who Dare 1953; Father Brown 1954; The Loves of Three Queens 1954; House of Secrets 1956; The Prize 1963

Ousdal, Sverre Anker (1944-) Kristin Lavransdatter 1995; Hamsun 1996; Insomnia 1997

Ouspenskaya, Maria (1876-1949) Dodsworth 1936; Conquest 1937; Love Affair 1939; Dance, Girl, Dance 1940; Dr Ehrlich's Magic Bullet 1940; The Man I Married 1940; Waterloo Bridge 1940; The Shanghai Gesture 1941; The Wolf Man 1941; Frankenstein Meets the Wolf Man 1943; Tarzan and the Amazons 1945; A Kiss in the Dark 1949

Outerbridge, Peter (1966-) Cool Runnings 1993; Another Woman 1994; For the Moment 1994; Captive Heart 1996; Kissed 1996; Saw VI 2009; Haunter 2013

Outinen, Kati (1961-) Hamlet Goes Business 1987; The Match Factory Girl 1990; Take Care of Your Scarf, Tatjana 1994; Drifting Clouds 1996; Juha 1999; The Man without a Past 2002; Ten Minutes Older: the Trumpet 2002; Le Havre 2011

Overall, Park (1957-) Biloxi Blues 1988; The Vanishing 1993; Taming Andrew 2000

Overman, Lynne (1887-1943) Enter Madame! 1933; Broadway Bill 1934; Little Miss Marker 1934; She Loves Me Not 1934; Rumba 1935; Men with Wings 1938; Spawn of the North 1938; Union Pacific 1939; Edison, the Man 1940; North West Mounted Police 1940; Typhoon 1940; The Forest Rangers 1942; Reap the Wild Wind 1942; Roxie Hart 1942; Dixie 1943; The Desert Song 1944

Overton, Frank (1918-1967) Desire under the Elms 1958; The Last Mile 1959; To Kill a Mockingbird 1962; Fail-Safe 1964

Overton, Kelly Wedding Daze 2004; Desolation Canyon 2006

Overton, Rick (1954-) Eight Legged Freaks 2001; The Informant! 2009

Owe, Baard Gertrud 1964; O'Horten 2007

Owen, Bill (1914-1999) Dancing with Crime 1946; Daybreak 1946; Easy Money 1947; When the Bough Breaks 1947; My Brother's Keeper 1948; Once a Jolly Swagman 1948; Trottie True 1949; Hotel Sahara 1951; The Story of Robin Hood and His Merrie Men 1952; A Day to Remember 1953; The Square Ring 1953; The Rainbow Jacket 1954; The Ship That Died of Shame 1955; Carry On Sergeant 1958; Carve Her Name with Pride 1958; Davy 1958; Carry On Nurse 1959; The Shakedown 1959; Carry On Regardless 1960; The Hellfire Club 1961; Carry On Cabby 1963; Georgy Girl 1966; In Celebration 1974; The Comeback 1977

Owen, Catherine Dale (1900-1965) Born Reckless 1930; The Rogue Song 1930

Owen, Chris (1980-) Angus 1995; October Sky 1999; Dear Wendy 2004; American Pie Presents Band Camp 2005

Owen, Clare Echo of Diana 1963; Shadow of Fear 1963
Owen, Clive (1964-) Vroom 1988; Close My Eyes 1991; Century 1993; Bent 1996; The Rich Man's Wife 1996; Croupier 1998; Greenfingers 2000; Gosford Park 2001; The Bourne Identity 2002; Beyond Borders 2003; I'll Sleep When I'm Dead 2003; Closer 2004; King Arthur 2004; Derailed 2005; Sin City 2005; Children of Men 2006; Inside Man 2006; Elizabeth: the Golden Age 2007; Shoot 'Em Up 2007; The Boys Are Back 2009; Duplicity 2009; The International 2009; Trust 2010; Intruders 2011; Killer Elite 2011; Shadow Dancer 2012; Blood Ties 2013; Words and Pictures 2013; The Last Knights 2015
Owen, Garry (1902-1951) Hold Your Man 1933; Arsenic and Old Lace 1944
Owen, Glyn (1928-2004) Life in Emergency Ward 10 1959; Inn for Trouble 1960; Attack on the Iron Coast 1968
Owen, Lloyd Miss Potter 2006; Apollo 18 2011
Owen, Reginald (1887-1972) The Letter 1929; Platinum Blonde 1931; Sherlock Holmes 1932; Fashions of 1934 1934; The House of Rothschild 1934; Madame Du Barry 1934; Mandalay 1934; Of Human Bondage 1934; Anna Karenina 1935; The Call of the Wild 1935; Enchanted April 1935; Escapade 1935; The Good Fairy 1935; A Tale of Two Cities 1935; The Great Ziegfeld 1936; Love on the Run 1936; Rose Marie 1936; Trouble for Two 1936; The Bride Wore Red 1937; Conquest 1937; Madame X 1937; Personal Property 1937; Rosalie 1937; A Christmas Carol 1938; Everybody Sing 1938; Kidnapped 1938; Paradise for Three 1938; Three Loves Has Nancy 1938; Fast and Loose 1939; The Real Glory 1939; Remember? 1939; The Earl of Chicago 1940; The Ghost Comes Home 1940; Charley's Aunt 1941; Tarzan's Secret Treasure 1941; They Met in Bombay 1941; A Woman's Face 1941; Crossroads 1942; I Married an Angel 1942; Mrs Miniver 1942; Random Harvest 1942; Reunion in France 1942; Somewhere I'll Find You 1942; White Cargo 1942; Woman of the Year 1942; Above Suspicion 1943; Forever and a Day 1943; The Canterville Ghost 1944; National Velvet 1944; Captain Kidd 1945; Kitty 1945; The Sailor Takes a Wife 1945; The Valley of Decision 1945; Cluny Brown 1946; Monsieur Beaucaire 1946; Piccadilly Incident 1946; Bob, Son of Battle 1947; Green Dolphin Street 1947; The Imperfect Lady 1947; Hills of Home 1948; The Pirate 1948; Challenge to Lassie 1949; The Secret Garden 1949; Kim 1950; The Miniver Story 1950; Tammy and the Doctor 1963; The Thrill of It All 1963; Mary Poppins 1964; Bedknobs and Broomsticks 1971
Owen, Rena (1960-) Once Were Warriors 1994; When Love Comes 1998; Mee-Shee: the Water Giant 2005
Owen, Seena (1894-1966) Intolerance 1916; The Fall of Babylon 1919; Queen Kelly 1928
Owen, Tudor (1898-1979) My Cousin Rachel 1952; Back to God's Country 1953; Arrow in the Dust 1954; The King's Thief 1955; The Oklahoma Woman 1956
Owen, Yvonne (1923-1990) The Seventh Veil 1945; Easy Money 1947; Holiday Camp 1947; Miranda 1947; My Brother's Keeper 1948; Third Time Lucky 1949; Someone at the Door 1950
Owens, Chris (1961-) Python 2000; Victor 2008
Owens, Ciaran Agnes Browne 1999; Angela's Ashes 1999
Owens, Patricia (1925-2000) No Down Payment 1957; Sayonara 1957; The Fly 1958; The Gun Runners 1958; The Law and Jake Wade 1958; These Thousand Hills 1959; Hell to Eternity 1960; The Destructors 1968
Owsley, Monroe (1900-1937) Holiday 1930; Honor among Lovers 1931; Indiscreet 1931; This Modern Age 1931; Ex-Lady 1933; Goin' to Town 1935; Remember Last Night? 1935
Oxenberg, Catherine (1961-) The Lair of the White Worm 1988; Treacherous Beauties 1994; Sanctimony 2000
Oxenbould, Ed Alexander and the Terrible, Horrible, No Good, Very Bad Day 2014; Paper Planes 2014; The Visit 2015
Oxley, David (1920-1985) Ill Met by Moonlight 1956; Sea Fury 1958; The Hound of the Baskervilles 1959; Yesterday's Enemy 1959
Oyelowo, David (1976-) Dog Eat Dog 2000; As You Like It 2006; The Last King of Scotland 2006; Rise of the

Planet of the Apes 2011; Jack Reacher 2012; The Paperboy 2012; Red Tails 2012; The Butler 2013; A Most Violent Year 2014; Selma 2014; Captive 2015; A United Kingdom 2017
Oyelowo, Jessica Churchill: the Hollywood Years 2004; Captive 2015
Oyeniran, Femi Kidulthood 2005; Adulthood 2008; It's a Lot 2013
Oz, Frank (1944-) The Muppet Movie 1979; Star Wars Episode V: the Empire Strikes Back 1980; The Great Muppet Caper 1981; Star Wars Episode VI: Return of the Jedi 1983; The Muppets Take Manhattan 1984; Follow That Bird 1985; The Muppet Christmas Carol 1992; Muppet Treasure Island 1996; Muppets from Space 1999; Star Wars Episode I: the Phantom Menace 1999; Monsters, Inc 2001; Star Wars Episode II: Attack of the Clones 2002; Star Wars Episode III: Revenge of the Sith 2005; Zathura: a Space Adventure 2005; I Am Big Bird 2014
Ozawa, Eitaro aka **Ozawa, Sakae** (1909-1988) Record of a Tenement Gentleman 1947; My Love Has Been Burning 1949; Scandal 1950; The Thick-Walled Room 1953; Ugetsu Monogatari 1953; The Crucified Lovers 1954; The H-Man 1954; The Princess Yang Kwei Fei 1955; The Human Condition 1958; The Return of Godzilla 1984; A Taxing Woman 1987
Ozawa, Shoichi (1929-2012) The Ballad of Narayama 1983; Black Rain 1988
Ozdemir, Muzaffer Uzak 2003; Home 2011
Ozeki, Yuya The Grudge: Ju-On 2003; Ju-On: The Grudge 2 2003
Ozeray, Madeleine (1908-1989) Crime and Punishment 1935; The End of the Day 1939
Ozsener, Yigit Times and Winds 2006; The Two Faces of January 2013

P

Paar, Jack (1918-2004) Easy Living 1949; Walk Softly, Stranger 1949; Love Nest 1951
Pace, Judy (1942-) Cotton Comes to Harlem 1970; Up in the Cellar 1970; Brian's Song 1971; Frogs 1972
Pace, Lee (1979-) The Fall 2006; Miss Pettigrew Lives for a Day 2007; Marmaduke 2010; The Resident 2010; Guardians of the Galaxy 2014; The Program 2015
Pacino, Al (1940-) The Panic in Needle Park 1971; The Godfather 1972; Scarecrow 1973; Serpico 1973; The Godfather Part II 1974; Dog Day Afternoon 1975; Bobby Deerfield 1977; ...And Justice for All 1979; Author! Author! 1982; Scarface 1983; Revolution 1985; Sea of Love 1989; Dick Tracy 1990; The Godfather Part III 1990; Frankie & Johnny 1991; Glengarry Glen Ross 1992; Scent of a Woman 1992; Carlito's Way 1993; Heat 1995; Two Bits 1995; City Hall 1996; Looking for Richard 1996; The Devil's Advocate 1997; Donnie Brasco 1997; Any Given Sunday 1999; The Insider 1999; Insomnia 2002; People I Know 2002; The Recruit 2002; SIMØNE 2002; Gigli 2003; William Shakespeare's The Merchant of Venice 2004; Two for the Money 2005; 88 Minutes 2007; Ocean's Thirteen 2007; Righteous Kill 2008; You Don't Know Jack 2010; Jack and Jill 2011; Wilde Salomé 2011; Stand Up Guys 2012; Phil Spector 2013; Salomé 2013; Manglehorn 2014; Danny Collins 2015; Misconduct 2016
Packer, David (1962-) Trust Me 1989; Almost Heroes 1998
Pacôme, Maria (1923-) Up to His Ears 1965; La Crise 1992
Pacula, Joanna (1957-) Gorky Park 1983; Not Quite Jerusalem 1985; Escape from Sobibor 1987; The Kiss 1988; Marked for Death 1990; A Passion for Murder 1992; The Silence of the Hams 1993; Warlock: the Armageddon 1993; The Bomber Boys 1995; Last Gasp 1995; My Giant 1998; Virus 1998; The Art of Murder 1999
Padalecki, Jared (1982-) House of Wax 2004; New York Minute 2004; Cry_Wolf 2005; Friday the 13th 2009
Padden, Sarah (1881-1967) He Was Her Man 1934; Girl Rush 1944; House by the River 1950
Paddick, Hugh (1915-2000) The Killing of Sister George 1968; Up the Chastity Belt 1971
Padilla Jr, Manuel (1956-) Tarzan and the Valley of Gold 1966; Tarzan and the Great River 1967; American Graffiti 1973
Padovani, Lea (1920-1991) Montparnasse 19 1958; The Naked

Maja 1959; The Reluctant Saint 1962; The Empty Canvas 1963
Page, Anita (1910-2008) Our Dancing Daughters 1928; The Broadway Melody 1929; Our Modern Maidens 1929; Free and Easy 1930; Skyscraper Souls 1932
Page, Bradley (1901-1985) Love Affair 1932; This Day and Age 1933; The Affairs of Annabel 1938; Annabel Takes a Tour 1938; The Law West of Tombstone 1938
Page, Diamond Dallas (1956-) First Daughter 1999; Ready to Rumble 2000
Page, Ellen (1987-) Homeless to Harvard: the Liz Murray Story 2003; Hard Candy 2005; Mouth to Mouth 2005; Juno 2007; Smart People 2007; Whip It 2009; Inception 2010; Super 2010; To Rome with Love 2012; The East 2013; Touchy Feely 2013; X-Men: Days of Future Past 2014; Freeheld 2015; Flatliners 2017
Page, Gale (1913-1983) The Amazing Dr Clitterhouse 1938; Four Daughters 1938; Four Wives 1939; Naughty but Nice 1939; You Can't Get Away with Murder 1939; Knute Rockne - All American 1940; They Drive by Night 1940; Four Mothers 1941; Anna Lucasta 1949
Page, Genevieve aka **Page, Geneviève** (1930-) Foreign Intrigue 1956; Song without End 1960; El Cid 1961; Youngblood Hawke 1964; Trois Chambres à Manhattan 1965; Belle de Jour 1967; Decline and Fall... of a Birdwatcher 1968; Mayerling 1968; The Private Life of Sherlock Holmes 1970; Buffet Froid 1979; Aria 1987; Beyond Therapy 1987; Lovers 1999
Page, Geraldine (1924-1987) Hondo 1953; Taxi 1953; Summer and Smoke 1961; Sweet Bird of Youth 1962; Toys in the Attic 1963; Dear Heart 1964; The Three Sisters 1966; You're a Big Boy Now 1966; The Happiest Millionaire 1967; Trilogy 1969; Whatever Happened to Aunt Alice? 1969; The Beguiled 1970; JW Coop 1971; Pete 'n' Tillie 1972; The Day of the Locust 1975; Nasty Habits 1976; The Rescuers 1977; Something for Joey 1977; Interiors 1978; Harry's War 1981; Honky Tonk Freeway 1981; I'm Dancing as Fast as I Can 1982; The Dollmaker 1984; The Parade 1984; The Pope of Greenwich Village 1984; The Bride 1985; The Trip to Bountiful 1985; Walls of Glass 1985; White Nights 1985; My Little Girl 1986; Native Son 1986; Nazi Hunter: the Beate Klarsfeld Story 1986
Page, Haili We Don't Live Here Anymore 2003; Deadly Visions 2004
Page, Harrison Vixen! 1968; AWOL 1990
Page, Jimmy The Song Remains the Same 1976; It Might Get Loud 2008
Page, Joy aka **Page, Joy Ann** (1924-2008) Kismet 1944; The Bullfighter and the Lady 1951; Tonka 1958
Page, Ken Torch Song Trilogy 1988; The Nightmare before Christmas 1993
Page, Patti (1927-2013) Elmer Gantry 1960; Boys' Night Out 1962
Page, Paul (1903-1974) Men without Women 1930; Palmy Days 1931
Page, Rita (1905-1954) Little Nellie Kelly 1940; Vigil in the Night 1940
Paget, Alfred (1880-1925) The Battle of Elderbush 1914; Intolerance 1916; The Fall of Babylon 1919
Paget, Debra (1933-) Cry of the City 1948; Broken Arrow 1950; Anne of the Indies 1951; Bird of Paradise 1951; Fourteen Hours 1951; Belles on Their Toes 1952; Les Misérables 1952; Stars and Stripes Forever 1952; Demetrius and the Gladiators 1954; Prince Valiant 1954; Princess of the Nile 1954; Seven Angry Men 1955; White Feather 1955; The Last Hunt 1956; Love Me Tender 1956; The Ten Commandments 1956; Omar Khayyam 1957; The River's Edge 1957; From the Earth to the Moon 1958; The Indian Tomb 1959; The Tiger of Eschnapur 1959; The Most Dangerous Man Alive 1961; Tales of Terror 1962; The Haunted Palace 1963
Pagett, Nicola (1945-) The Viking Queen 1967; There's a Girl in My Soup 1970; Frankenstein: the True Story 1973; Operation Daybreak 1975; Oliver's Story 1978; Privates on Parade 1982; An Awfully Big Adventure 1994
Paglia, Camille (1947-) The Watermelon Woman 1996; Henry Fool 1997
Pagnol, Jacqueline Topaze 1951; Manon des Sources 1952
Paige, Elaine (1948-) Adventures of a Plumber's Mate 1978; A Closed Book 2009
Paige, Janis (1922-) Hollywood Canteen 1944; Of Human Bondage 1946; Romance on the High Seas 1948; Winter Meeting 1948; The Younger

Brothers 1949; Silk Stockings 1957; Please Don't Eat the Daisies 1960; Bachelor in Paradise 1961; The Caretakers 1963; Follow the Boys 1963
Paige, Mabel (1879-1954) Young and Willing 1942; Happy Go Lucky 1943; True to Life 1943
Paige, Myles Funny Ha Ha 2002; Computer Chess 2013
Paige, Robert aka **Carlyle, David** (1911-1987) Cain and Mabel 1936; Smart Blonde 1936; Hellzapoppin' 1941; Pardon My Sarong 1942; Frontier Badmen 1943; Son of Dracula 1943; Can't Help Singing 1944; Abbott and Costello Go to Mars 1953; Split Second 1953; The Marriage-Go-Round 1960
Paige, Yasmin Tooth 2003; Submarine 2010; Chicken 2015
Pailhas, Géraldine (1971-) IP5 1992; Suite 16 1994; Don Juan DeMarco 1995; 5x2 2004; Jeune & Jolie 2013
Pain, Didier Le Château de Ma Mère 1990; La Gloire de Mon Père 1990; Le Bossu 1997
Pais, Josh (1964-) Teenage Mutant Ninja Turtles 1990; Safe Men 1998; The Station Agent 2003; Teeth 2007; Year of the Dog 2007; Touchy Feely 2013
Paiva, Nestor (1905-1966) Meet Boston Blackie 1941; The Falcon in Mexico 1944; The Southerner 1945; Badman's Territory 1946; Road to Rio 1947; Double Dynamite 1951; A Millionaire for Christy 1951; Prisoners of the Casbah 1953; Creature from the Black Lagoon 1954; Hell on Frisco Bay 1955; Revenge of the Creature 1955; Tarantula 1955; Comanche 1956; The Mole People 1956
Pajala, Turo (1955-2007) Hamlet Goes Business 1987; Ariel 1988
Palance, Holly (1950-) The Comeback 1977; Under Fire 1983; The Best of Times 1986
Palance, Jack aka **Palance, Walter (Jack)** (1919-2006) Halls of Montezuma 1950; Panic in the Streets 1950; Sudden Fear 1952; Arrowhead 1953; Flight to Tangier 1953; Man in the Attic 1953; Second Chance 1953; Shane 1953; Sign of the Pagan 1954; The Silver Chalice 1954; The Big Knife 1955; I Died a Thousand Times 1955; Kiss of Fire 1955; Attack! 1956; House of Numbers 1957; The Lonely Man 1957; The Man Inside 1958; Ten Seconds to Hell 1959; The Battle of Austerlitz 1960; Barabbas 1961; The Mongols 1961; Le Mépris 1963; Once a Thief 1965; The Professionals 1966; The Spy in the Green Hat 1966; Kill a Dragon 1967; Torture Garden 1967; A Professional Gun 1968; They Came to Rob Las Vegas 1968; Che! 1969; Monte Walsh 1970; Chato's Land 1971; The Horsemen 1971; Craze 1973; Oklahoma Crude 1973; Dracula 1974; God's Gun 1977; Hawk the Slayer 1980; Without Warning 1980; Alone in the Dark 1982; Bagdad Café 1987; Gor 1987; Young Guns 1988; Batman 1989; Tango & Cash 1989; Solar Crisis 1990; City Slickers 1991; Cyborg 2: Glass Shadow 1993; City Slickers II: the Legend of Curly's Gold 1994; Cops and Robbersons 1994; The Swan Princess 1994; Treasure Island 1998; Prancer Returns 2001
Palau, Pierre (1885-1966) Devil in the Flesh 1947; Marguerite de la Nuit 1955; Otherworld 2003
Palfrey, Lisa House of America 1996; Otherworld 2003
Palicki, Adrianne Legion 2010; Red Dawn 2012; GI Joe: Retaliation 2013; John Wick 2014
Palin, Michael (1943-) And Now for Something Completely Different 1971; Monty Python and the Holy Grail 1975; Pleasure at Her Majesty's 1976; Jabberwocky 1977; The Rutles - All You Need Is Cash 1978; Monty Python's Life of Brian 1979; Time Bandits 1981; The Missionary 1982; Monty Python Live at the Hollywood Bowl 1982; Monty Python's The Meaning of Life 1983; A Private Function 1984; Brazil 1985; A Fish Called Wanda 1988; American Friends 1991; The Wind in the Willows 1996; Fierce Creatures 1997; Not the Messiah: He's a Very Naughty Boy 2009; A Liar's Autobiography: the Untrue Story of Monty Python's Graham Chapman 2012; Absolutely Anything 2015
Palk, Anna (1941-1990) Play It Cool 1962; The Frozen Dead 1966; Tower of Evil 1972
Palladino, Aleksa (1981-) The Adventures of Sebastian Cole 1998; Wrestling with Alligators 1998; Before the Devil Knows You're Dead 2007
Pallenberg, Anita (1944-) Barbarella 1967; Candy 1968; Performance 1970; Mister Lonely 2007; Chéri 2009

Pallette, Eugene (1889-1954) Terror Island 1920; The Three Musketeers 1921; Mantrap 1926; Lights of New York 1928; The Virginian 1929; Paramount on Parade 1930; It Pays to Advertise 1931; The Half Naked Truth 1932; Shanghai Express 1932; The Kennel Murder Case 1933; Shanghai Madness 1933; Black Sheep 1935; Bordertown 1935; The Ghost Goes West 1935; Steamboat round the Bend 1935; My Man Godfrey 1936; Stowaway 1936; One Hundred Men and a Girl 1937; Topper 1937; The Adventures of Robin Hood 1938; First Love 1939; Mr Smith Goes to Washington 1939; Wife, Husband and Friend 1939; It's a Date 1940; The Mark of Zorro 1940; Young Tom Edison 1940; Appointment for Love 1941; The Bride Came COD 1941; The Lady Eve 1941; Swamp Water 1941; Unfinished Business 1941; The Big Street 1942; The Forest Rangers 1942; Lady in a Jam 1942; The Male Animal 1942; The Gang's All Here 1943; Slightly Dangerous 1943; In the Meantime, Darling 1944; Pin Up Girl 1944; Sensations 1944; Step Lively 1944; The Cheaters 1945
Palma, Andrea (1903-1987) Tarzan and the Mermaids 1948; The Criminal Life of Archibaldo de la Cruz 1955
Palme, Ulf (1920-1993) Miss Julie 1951; Dreams 1955; The Counterfeit Traitor 1962; Doctor Glas 1968
Palmer, Betsy (1926-2015) The Long Gray Line 1955; Mister Roberts 1955; Queen Bee 1955; The Tin Star 1957; The True Story of Lynn Stuart 1957; The Last Angry Man 1959; Friday the 13th 1980
Palmer, Geoffrey (1927-) A Fish Called Wanda 1988; The Madness of King George 1995; Mrs Brown 1997; Tomorrow Never Dies 1997; Rat 2000; Peter Pan 2003
Palmer, Gregg aka **Lee, Palmer** (1927-) Francis Goes to West Point 1952; The All American 1953; Magnificent Obsession 1954; Playgirl 1954; Taza, Son of Cochise 1954; To Hell and Back 1955; The Creature Walks among Us 1956; Hilda Crane 1956; From Hell It Came 1957; The Sad Horse 1959; The Most Dangerous Man Alive 1961
Palmer, Keke (1993-) Knights of the South Bronx 2005; Akeelah and the Bee 2006; Cleaner 2007; Jump In! 2007; Shrink 2009; Joyful Noise 2012
Palmer, Lilli (1914-1986) Secret Agent 1936; Command Performance 1937; Good Morning, Boys 1937; The Great Barrier 1937; Crackerjack 1938; Thunder Rock 1942; The Gentle Sex 1943; English without Tears 1944; The Rake's Progress 1945; Beware of Pity 1946; Cloak and Dagger 1946; Body and Soul 1947; My Girl Tisa 1948; The Long Dark Hall 1951; The Four Poster 1953; Montparnasse 19 1958; But Not for Me 1959; Conspiracy of Hearts 1960; The Pleasure of His Company 1961; The Counterfeit Traitor 1962; Miracle of the White Stallions 1963; The Amorous Adventures of Moll Flanders 1965; Operation Crossbow 1965; Jack of Diamonds 1967; Oedipus the King 1967; Nobody Runs Forever 1968; Sebastian 1968; De Sade 1969; Hard Contract 1969; Murders in the Rue Morgue 1971; The Boys from Brazil 1978; The Holcroft Covenant 1985
Palmer, Maria (1917-1981) Days of Glory 1944; The Web 1947; By the Light of the Silvery Moon 1953
Palmer, Teresa (1986-) December Boys 2007; Bedtime Stories 2008; The Sorcerer's Apprentice 2010; I Am Number Four 2011; Take Me Home Tonight 2011; Warm Bodies 2012; Wish You Were Here 2012; Point Break 2015; The Choice 2016; Lights Out 2016
Palminteri, Chazz (1952-) Oscar 1991; Innocent Blood 1992; A Bronx Tale 1993; Bullets over Broadway 1994; Jade 1995; The Perez Family 1995; The Usual Suspects 1995; Diabolique 1996; Faithful 1996; Mulholland Falls 1996; Hurlyburly 1998; Scarred City 1998; Analyze This 1999; Stuart Little 1999; Lady and the Tramp II: Scamp's Adventure 2000; Down to Earth 2001; Noel 2004; Hoodwinked 2005; In the Mix 2005; Running Scared 2005; A Guide to Recognizing Your Saints 2006; Little Man 2006; Legend 2015
Palomino, Carlos (1949-) Strangers Kiss 1983; Die Watching 1993
Paltrow, Gwyneth (1972-) Hook 1991; Flesh and Bone 1993; Malice 1993; Jefferson in Paris 1995; Moonlight and Valentino 1995; Se7en 1995; Emma 1996; Hard Eight 1996; The Pallbearer 1996; Great Expectations 1997; Sliding Doors 1997; Hush 1998; Shakespeare in

Love 1998; The Talented Mr Ripley 1999; Bounce 2000; Duets 2000; The Anniversary Party 2001; The Royal Tenenbaums 2001; Shallow Hal 2001; Possession 2002; Sylvia 2003; View from the Top 2003; Sky Captain and the World of Tomorrow 2004; The Good Night 2005; Proof 2005; Infamous 2006; Running with Scissors 2006; Iron Man 2008; Two Lovers 2008; Country Strong 2010; Iron Man 2 2010; Contagion 2011; Marvel Avengers Assemble 2012; Thanks for Sharing 2012; Iron Man Three 2013; Mortdecai 2015

Paluzzi, Luciana (1937-) Carlton-Browne of the FO 1958; No Time to Die 1958; Sea Fury 1958; Return to Peyton Place 1961; Muscle Beach Party 1964; Thunderball 1965; To Trap a Spy 1966; The Venetian Affair 1966; A Black Veil for Lisa 1969; Captain Nemo and the Underwater City 1969

Panabaker, Danielle (1987-) Mom at Sixteen 2005; Sky High 2005; Mr Brooks 2007; Friday the 13th 2009; The Crazies 2010; John Carpenter's The Ward 2010; Piranha 3DD 2011

Panabaker, Kay (990-) Fame 2009; Secrets in the Walls 2010

Pandey, Nirmal (1962-2010) Bandit Queen 1994; Train to Pakistan 1997

Panebianco, Richard (1971-) China Girl 1987; Dogfight 1991

Panettiere, Hayden (1989-) A Bug's Life 1998; Joe Somebody 2001; Normal 2002; Lies My Mother Told Me 2004; Racing Stripes 2004; Raising Helen 2004; Ice Princess 2005; Fireflies in the Garden 2007; I Love You, Beth Cooper 2009; Alpha and Omega 2010; Scre4m 2011

Pangborn, Franklin (1893-1958) The Half Naked Truth 1932; Design for Living 1933; My Man Godfrey 1936; All over Town 1937; All over Town 1937; Easy Living 1937; Stage Door 1937; Three Smart Girls 1937; Bluebeard's Eighth Wife 1938; Just around the Corner 1938; Vivacious Lady 1938; Topper Takes a Trip 1939; The Bank Dick 1940; Christmas in July 1940; Call Out the Marines 1941; The Navy Steps Out 1941; Never Give a Sucker an Even Break 1941; Sullivan's Travels 1941; Reveille with Beverly 1943; The Horn Blows at Midnight 1945; I'll Be Yours 1947; Mad Wednesday 1950

Panjabi, Archie (1972-) East Is East 1999; Bend It like Beckham 2001; A Mighty Heart 2007; Traitor 2008; The Infidel 2010; I Origins 2014; San Andreas 2015

Pankin, Stuart (1946-) The Dirt Bike Kid 1986; Fatal Attraction 1987; Love at Stake 1987; Arachnophobia 1990; Life Stinks 1991; Mannequin on the Move 1991; Congo 1995

Pankow, John (1954-) To Live and Die in LA 1985; The Secret of My Success 1987; Monkey Shines 1988; Talk Radio 1988; Mortal Thoughts 1991; Year of the Gun 1991; A Stranger among Us 1992; The Object of My Affection 1998

Panthaki, Ray Bollywood Queen 2002; Provoked: a True Story 2006; City Rats 2008

Pantoliano, Joe (1951-) The Idolmaker 1980; Eddie and the Cruisers 1983; Risky Business 1983; The Goonies 1985; The Mean Season 1985; Running Scared 1986; La Bamba 1987; Empire of the Sun 1987; The Law of the Land 1988; Midnight Run 1988; Nightbreaker 1989; Blue Heat 1990; Downtown 1990; Short Time 1990; Zandalee 1991; Three of Hearts 1992; Calendar Girl 1993; The Fugitive 1993; Me and the Kid 1993; Baby's Day Out 1994; Steal Big, Steal Little 1995; Bound 1996; Top of the World 1997; Hoods 1998; Taxman 1998; US Marshals 1998; The Life before This 1999; The Matrix 1999; A Better Way to Die 2000; Memento 2000; Cats & Dogs 2001; Pluto Nash 2001; Bad Boys II 2003; Daredevil 2003; Racing Stripes 2004; The Moguls 2005; Unknown 2006; Wedding Daze 2006; Cats & Dogs: the Revenge of Kitty Galore 2010

Paolo, Connor Snake Land 2010; Friend Request 2016

Papa, Tom The Informant! 2009; Behind the Candelabra 2013

Papas, Irene (1926-) The Man from Cairo 1953; Tribute to a Bad Man 1956; The Guns of Navarone 1961; The Moon-Spinners 1964; Zorba the Greek 1964; The Desperate Ones 1967; The Brotherhood 1968; Z 1968; Anne of the Thousand Days 1969; A Dream of Kings 1969; The Trojan Women 1971; Moses 1975; Iphigenia 1976; Bloodline 1979; Christ Stopped at Eboli 1979; Lion of the Desert 1981; The Assisi Underground 1985; Chronicle of a Death Foretold 1987; High Season 1987; The Odyssey 1997; Captain

Corelli's Mandolin 2001; Un Filme Falado 2003

Pape, Lionel (1877-1944) The Big Broadcast of 1938 1937; Raffles 1939

Papoulia, Aggeliki Dogtooth 2009; Alps 2011

Paquin, Anna (1982-) The Piano 1993; Fly Away Home 1996; Jane Eyre 1996; Amistad 1997; The Member of the Wedding 1997; Hurlyburly 1998; She's All That 1999; A Walk on the Moon 1999; Almost Famous 2000; Finding Forrester 2000; X-Men 2000; Buffalo Soldiers 2001; Darkness 2002; 25th Hour 2002; Laputa: Castle in the Sky 2003; X2 2003; Steamboy 2004; The Squid and the Whale 2005; X-Men - the Last Stand 2006; Bury My Heart at Wounded Knee 2007; Trick 'r Treat 2007; Margaret 2008; The Courageous Heart of Irena Sendler 2009; Scre4m 2011; X-Men: Days of Future Past 2014

Paradis, Vanessa (1972-) The Girl on the Bridge 1999; Heartbreaker 2010; Café de Flore 2011; A Monster in Paris 2011; Fading Gigolo 2013

Paramore, Kiri The Last Days of Chez Nous 1992; Doing Time for Patsy Cline 1997; Ned Kelly 2003

Paratene, Rawiri Footrot Flats: the Dog's Tale 1986; What Becomes of the Broken Hearted? 1999; Whale Rider 2002; The Insatiable Moon 2010

Pardue, Kip (1976-) Driven 2001; The Rules of Attraction 2002; Thirteen 2003; Imaginary Heroes 2004

Paré, Jessica (1982-) Stardom 2000; Bollywood/Hollywood 2002; Wicker Park 2004

Paré, Michael (1959-) Eddie and the Cruisers 1983; The Philadelphia Experiment 1984; Streets of Fire 1984; World Gone Wild 1988; Eddie and the Cruisers II: Eddie Lives! 1989; Moon 44 1990; Into the Sun 1992; Village of the Damned 1995; Bad Moon 1996; Hope Floats 1998; Sanctimony 2000

Paredes, Marisa (1946-) Dark Habits 1983; High Heels 1991; The Flower of My Secret 1995; Deep Crimson 1996; Three Lives and Only One Death 1996; Life Is Beautiful 1997; Talk of Angels 1998; All about My Mother 1999; No One Writes to the Colonel 1999; The Devil's Backbone 2001; The Skin I Live In 2011

Parely, Mila (1917-2012) La Règle du Jeu 1939; Les Anges du Péché 1943; La Belle et la Bête 1946; Blood Orange 1953

Parfitt, Judy (1935-) Hide and Seek 1963; Hamlet 1969; The Mind of Mr Soames 1970; Champions 1983; The Chain 1984; Maurice 1987; Diamond Skulls 1989; Dolores Claiborne 1995; Wilde 1997; Ever After: a Cinderella Story 1998; Girl with a Pearl Earring 2003; The Aryan Couple 2004; Asylum 2004; Dean Spanley 2008; The Moth Diaries 2011

Parfitt, Rick Status Quo: Hello Quo 2012; Bula Quo! 2013

Parillaud, Anne (1960-) Ecoute Voir... 1978; Nikita 1990; Innocent Blood 1992; Map of the Human Heart 1992; Six Days, Six Nights 1994; Frankie Starlight 1995; The Man in the Iron Mask 1997; Shattered Image 1998; Sex Is Comedy 2002; The Last Mistress 2007

Paris, Jerry (1925-1986) The Glass Wall 1953; Drive a Crooked Road 1954; Good Morning, Miss Dove 1955; Marty 1955; The Naked Street 1955; D-Day the Sixth of June 1956; Zero Hour! 1957; The Female Animal 1958; Sing, Boy, Sing 1958

Parisse, Annie (1975-) Monster-in-Law 2005; Prime 2005

Park In-hwan The Quiet Family 1998; Thirst 2009

Park Joong-Hoon (1964-) American Dragons 1998; Nowhere to Hide 1999; The Truth about Charlie 2002

Park, Megan The Perfect Teacher 2010; What If 2013

Park, Ray (1975-) Star Wars Episode I: The Phantom Menace 1999; X-Men 2000; Ballistic: Ecks vs Sever 2002; GI Joe: the Rise of Cobra 2009

Parke, MacDonald (1891-1960) Summertime 1955; The Mouse That Roared 1959

Parker, Cecil (1897-1971) The Man Who Changed His Mind 1936; Storm in a Teacup 1937; The Citadel 1938; Housemaster 1938; The Lady Vanishes 1938; Sons of the Sea 1939; Under Your Hat 1940; The Saint's Vacation 1941; Caesar and Cleopatra 1945; Hungry Hill 1946; The Magic Bow 1946; Captain Boycott 1947; Quartet 1948; The Weaker Sex 1948; The Chiltern Hundreds 1949; Dear Mr Prohack 1949; Under Capricorn 1949; The Man in the White Suit 1951; His Excellency 1952; I Believe in You 1952; Isn't Life

Wonderful! 1952; Father Brown 1954; For Better, for Worse 1954; The Constant Husband 1955; The Ladykillers 1955; The Court Jester 1956; It's Great to Be Young 1956; True as a Turtle 1956; 23 Paces to Baker Street 1956; The Admirable Crichton 1957; Happy Is the Bride 1957; A Tale of Two Cities 1957; I Was Monty's Double 1958; Indiscreet 1958; The Navy Lark 1959; The Night We Dropped a Clanger 1959; The Wreck of the Mary Deare 1959; A French Mistress 1960; The Pure Hell of St Trinian's 1960; Swiss Family Robinson 1960; Under Ten Flags 1960; On the Fiddle 1961; Petticoat Pirates 1961; The Amorous Prawn 1962; The Brain 1962; Heavens Above! 1963; The Comedy Man 1964; Lady L 1965; A Man Could Get Killed 1966; The Magnificent Two 1967

Parker, Cecilia (1905-1993) Enter Madame! 1933; Riders of Destiny 1933; The Painted Veil 1934; Ah, Wilderness! 1935; A Family Affair 1937; Judge Hardy's Children 1938; Love Finds Andy Hardy 1938; Out West with the Hardys 1938; You're Only Young Once 1938; Andy Hardy Gets Spring Fever 1939; The Hardys Ride High 1939; Judge Hardy and Son 1939; Andy Hardy Meets Debutante 1940; Andy Hardy's Double Life 1942; The Courtship of Andy Hardy 1942; Andy Hardy Comes Home 1958

Parker, Corey (1965-) Biloxi Blues 1988; How I Got Into College 1989; White Palace 1990; Broadway Bound 1991; Mr and Mrs Loving 1993

Parker, Ed (1900-1960) The Star Packer 1934; The Trail Beyond 1934; Abbott and Costello Meet the Mummy 1955

Parker, Eleanor (1922-2013) Mission to Moscow 1943; Between Two Worlds 1944; The Very Thought of You 1944; Pride of the Marines 1945; Never Say Goodbye 1946; Of Human Bondage 1946; Escape Me Never 1947; Voice of the Turtle 1947; The Woman in White 1948; It's a Great Feeling 1949; Caged 1950; Chain Lightning 1950; Three Secrets 1950; Detective Story 1951; A Millionaire for Christy 1951; Valentino 1951; Above and Beyond 1952; Scaramouche 1952; Escape from Fort Bravo 1953; The Naked Jungle 1953; Valley of the Kings 1954; Interrupted Melody 1955; The Man with the Golden Arm 1955; Many Rivers to Cross 1955; Lizzie 1957; Home from the Hill 1960; Return to Peyton Place 1961; Madison Avenue 1962; Panic Button 1964; The Sound of Music 1965; An American Dream 1966; The Oscar 1966; The Tiger and the Pussycat 1967; Warning Shot 1967; How to Steal the World 1968; Eye of the Cat 1969; Sunburn 1979; Once upon a Spy 1980

Parker, Fess (1926-2010) Thunder over the Plains 1953; Davy Crockett, King of the Wild Frontier 1955; Davy Crockett and the River Pirates 1956; The Great Locomotive Chase 1956; Old Yeller 1957; The Light in the Forest 1958; Alias Jesse James 1959; The Hangman 1959; The Jayhawkers 1959; Hell Is for Heroes 1962

Parker, Jameson (1947-) White Dog 1981; Agatha Christie's A Caribbean Mystery 1983; Prince of Darkness 1987

Parker, Jean (1915-2005) Gabriel over the White House 1933; Lady for a Day 1933; Little Women 1933; Caravan 1934; Operator 13 1934; The Ghost Goes West 1935; The Texas Rangers 1936; The Flying Deuces 1939; Zenobia 1939; Bluebeard 1944; Dead Man's Eyes 1944; The Gunfighter 1950; A Lawless Street 1955; Apache Uprising 1965

Parker, Lara (1942-) Hi, Mom! 1970; Night of Dark Shadows 1971; Race with the Devil 1975

Parker, Mary-Louise aka **Parker, Mary Louise** (1964-) Longtime Companion 1990; Fried Green Tomatoes at the Whistle Stop Cafe 1991; Grand Canyon 1991; Mr Wonderful 1992; Bullets over Broadway 1994; The Client 1994; Naked in New York 1994; A Place for Annie 1994; Boys on the Side 1995; Reckless 1995; Murder in Mind 1996; The Portrait of a Lady 1996; Goodbye Lover 1997; The Maker 1997; Legalese 1998; The Five Senses 1999; Let the Devil Wear Black 1999; The Simple Life of Noah Dearborn 1999; Red Dragon 2002; Romance & Cigarettes 2004; The Unexpected Journey 2004; Vinegar Hill 2004; The Assassination of Jesse James by the Coward Robert Ford 2007; The Spiderwick Chronicles 2008; Solitary Man 2009; Howl 2010; Red 2010; R.I.P.D. 2013; Red 2 2013

Parker, Molly (1972-) Kissed 1996; The Five Senses 1999; Sunshine 1999;

Wonderland 1999; Ladies' Room 2000; Suspicious River 2000; Waking the Dead 2000; The Center of the World 2001; The War Bride 2001; Max 2002; Pure 2002; Iron Jawed Angels 2004; Hollywoodland 2006; The Wicker Man 2006; Oliver Sherman 2010

Parker, Nate (1979-) The Great Debaters 2007; Arbitrage 2012; Red Tails 2012; Ain't Them Bodies Saints 2013; Beyond the Lights 2014; Non-Stop 2014

Parker, Nathaniel (1963-) War Requiem 1988; Hamlet 1990; Wide Sargasso Sea 1992; Squanto: the Last Great Warrior 1994; Othello 1995; Beverly Hills Ninja 1997; The Haunted Mansion 2003; Fade to Black 2006; Flawless 2007; The Courageous Heart of Irena Sendler 2009; Malice in Wonderland 2009; Moomins on the Riviera 2014

Parker, Nicole Ari aka Parker, Nicole (1970-) The Incredibly True Adventures of Two Girls in Love 1995; Subway Stories: Tales from the Underground 1997; Blue Streak 1999; Brown Sugar 2002; Imagine That 2009

Parker, Noelle (1969-) Ernest Saves Christmas 1988; Leave of Absence 1994

Parker, Paula Jai (1969-) Friday 1995; Woo 1998; Hustle & Flow 2005

Parker, Sarah Jessica (1965-) My Body, My Child 1982; Firstborn 1984; Footloose 1984; Girls Just Want to Have Fun 1985; Flight of the Navigator 1986; LA Story 1991; Honeymoon in Vegas 1992; Hocus Pocus 1993; Striking Distance 1993; Ed Wood 1994; Miami Rhapsody 1995; Extreme Measures 1996; The First Wives Club 1996; If Lucy Fell 1996; Mars Attacks! 1996; The Substance of Fire 1996; The Sunshine Boys 1997; 'Til There Was You 1997; Dudley Do-Right 1999; Isn't She Great 1999; State and Main 2000; The Family Stone 2005; Failure to Launch 2006; Smart People 2007; Sex and the City: the Movie 2008; Did You Hear about the Morgans? 2009; Sex and the City 2 2010; I Don't Know How She Does It 2011; New Year's Eve 2011; Escape from Planet Earth 2013

Parker, Suzy (1932-2003) Kiss Them for Me 1957; Ten North Frederick 1958; The Best of Everything 1959; Circle of Deception 1960; Flight from Ashiya 1963; Chamber of Horrors 1966

Parker, Trey aka **Schwartz, Juan** (1969-) Cannibal! the Musical 1993; Orgazmo 1997; BASEketball 1998; South Park: Bigger, Longer & Uncut 1999; Team America: World Police 2004; Despicable Me 3 2017

Parker, Willard (1912-1996) A Slight Case of Murder 1938; What a Woman! 1943; Relentless 1948; You Gotta Stay Happy 1948; Calamity Jane and Sam Bass 1949; Slightly French 1949; Apache Drums 1951; The Earth Dies Screaming 1964

Parkes, Shaun Human Traffic 1999; Rage 1999; Offending Angels 2000; Things to Do before You're 30 2004; Clubbed 2008

Parkin, Dean aka Parkin, Duncan "Dean" (1930-) The Cyclops 1957; War of the Colossal Beast 1958

Parkins, Barbara (1942-) Valley of the Dolls 1967; Puppet on a Chain 1970; The Deadly Trap 1971; The Mephisto Waltz 1971; Asylum 1972; Shout at the Devil 1976; Bear Island 1979

Parkinson, Alice Sanctum 2010; The Cup 2011

Parkinson, Craig (1976-) Control 2007; The Other Man 2008; The Unloved 2009; Brighton Rock 2010; When the Lights Went Out 2010; Ghosted 2011

Parkinson, Sacha Awaydays 2009; A Boy Called Dad 2009

Parks, Catherine Friday the 13th Part III 1982; Weekend at Bernie's 1989

Parks, Larry (1914-1975) The Boogie Man Will Get You 1942; Reveille with Beverly 1943; Counter-Attack 1945; The Jolson Story 1946; Down to Earth 1947; Jolson Sings Again 1949; Love Is Better than Ever 1951; Tiger by the Tail 1955; Freud 1962

Parks, Michael (1938-) Bus Riley's Back in Town 1965; The Bible... in the Beginning 1966; The Idol 1966; The Happening 1967; Stranger on the Run 1967; The Last Hard Men 1976; The Private Files of J Edgar Hoover 1977; Breakthrough 1978; Rainbow 1978; The Evictors 1979; North Sea Hijack 1979; Hard Country 1981; Savannah Smiles 1982; The Return of Josey Wales 1986; The Hitman 1991; Storyville 1992; Death Wish V: the Face of Death 1994; Julian Po 1997; Liar 1997; Niagara Niagara 1997; Wicked 1998; From Dusk till

Dawn 3: the Hangman's Daughter 2000; Kill Bill Vol 1 2003

Parks, Michael (1938-) Red State 2011; We Are What We Are 2013; Blood Father 2016

Parkyakarkus (1904-1958) New Faces of 1937 1937; Out of This World 1945

Parlo, Dita (1906-1971) L'Atalante 1934; Mademoiselle Docteur 1936; La Grande Illusion 1937

Parnell, Chris Anchorman: the Legend of Ron Burgundy 2004; Hot Rod 2007; Walk Hard: the Dewey Cox Story 2007

Parnell, Emory (1892-1979) Two o'Clock Courage 1945; Abie's Irish Rose 1946; The Falcon's Alibi 1946; Lost in Alaska 1952; The Rocket Man 1954

Parrish, Helen (1924-1959) Mad about Music 1938; First Love 1939; Three Smart Girls Grow Up 1939; Winter Carnival 1939; You'll Find Out 1940; In Old California 1942

Parrish, Hunter (1987-) RV 2006; Still Alice 2014

Parrish, Julie (1940-2003) Fireball 500 1966; The Doberman Gang 1972

Parrish, Leslie (1935-) Li'l Abner 1959; The Manchurian Candidate 1962; Sex and the Single Girl 1964; Three on a Couch 1966; The Candy Man 1969; The Giant Spider Invasion 1975; The Astral Factor 1976; Crash! 1977

Parrish, Steve Midnight 1989; Scanners III: the Takeover 1992

Parry, Natasha (1930-2015) Dance Hall 1950; Knave of Hearts 1954; Windom's Way 1957; The Rough and the Smooth 1959; Midnight Lace 1960; Girl in the Headlines 1963; Romeo and Juliet 1968; Meetings with Remarkable Men 1979

Parsons, Estelle (1927-) Bonnie and Clyde 1967; Rachel, Rachel 1968; Don't Drink the Water 1969; I Never Sang for My Father 1970; Watermelon Man 1970; Two People 1973; For Pete's Sake 1974; The Lemon Sisters 1989; Dick Tracy 1990; A Private Matter 1992; Arthur Miller's The American Clock 1993; Boys on the Side 1995; Looking for Richard 1996; That Darn Cat 1997; Wilde Salomé 2011

Parsons, Jim (1973-) Home 2014; The Normal Heart 2014; Visions 2014

Parsons, Nancy (1942-2001) Motel Hell 1980; Porky's 1981; Porky's Revenge 1985; Wishman 1991

Parsons, Nicholas (1928-) Brothers in Law 1956; The Long Arm 1956; Happy Is the Bride 1957; Too Many Crooks 1958; Doctor in Love 1960; Murder Ahoy 1964; Don't Raise the Bridge, Lower the River 1968; The Best of Benny Hill 1974; Lady Godiva 2007

Parsons, Percy (1878-1944) The Good Companions 1933; Dangerous Moonlight 1941

Parton, Dolly (1946-) Nine to Five 1980; The Best Little Whorehouse in Texas 1982; Rhinestone 1984; Steel Magnolias 1989; Straight Talk 1992; The Beverly Hillbillies 1993; Blue Valley Songbird 1999; Joyful Noise 2012

Partridge, Ross Amityville: a New Generation 1993; Black and White 1998

Pascal, Christine (1953-1996) The Watchmaker of St Paul 1973; The Young Ladies of Wilko 1979; 'Round Midnight 1986; Le Grand Chemin 1987; See How They Fall 1993

Pascal, Françoise Burke & Hare 1971; Keep It Up Downstairs 1976

Pascal, Pedro Bloodsucking Bosses 2015; Kingsman: The Golden Circle 2017

Pasco, Isabelle (1966-) Roselyne and the Lions 1989; Prospero's Books 1991

Pasco, Richard (1926-) Yesterday's Enemy 1959; Sword of Sherwood Forest 1960; The Gorgon 1964; Rasputin, the Mad Monk 1965; The Watcher in the Woods 1982; Mrs Brown 1997

Pasdar, Adrian (1965-) Streets of Gold 1986; Near Dark 1987; Cookie 1989; Torn Apart 1990; Vital Signs 1990; Just like a Woman 1992; A Mother's Gift 1995

Pasolini, Pier Paolo (1922-1975) Requiescant 1967; Oedipus Rex 1967; The Decameron 1970; The Canterbury Tales 1971

Passante, Mario Gold of Naples 1954; The Mask of Satan 1960

Passgård, Lars (1941-) Through a Glass Darkly 1961; The Pram 1963

Pastell, George (1923-1976) Maniac 1962; Impact 1963; The Curse of the Mummy's Tomb 1964

Pasternak, Reagan A Christmas Visitor 2002; Confessions of an American Bride 2005

Pastor, Rosana The Ages of Lulu 1990; Land and Freedom 1995

Pastore, Vincent (1946-) Serving Sara 2002; American Cousins 2003; Revolver 2005

Pastorelli, Robert (1954-2004) *Dances with Wolves* 1990; *FernGully: the Last Rainforest* 1992; *Folks!* 1992; *Striking Distance* 1993; *The West Side Waltz* 1995; *Eraser* 1996; *Michael* 1996; *A Simple Wish* 1997; *South Pacific* 2001

Patachou (1918-2015) *Wild Target* 1993; *Drôle de Félix* 2000

Pataki, Michael (1938-2010) *Zoltan... Hound of Dracula* 1977; *The Glove* 1978; *Rocky IV* 1985; *Halloween 4: the Return of Michael Myers* 1988

Patch, Wally (1888-1970) *Alf's Button Afloat* 1938; *Bank Holiday* 1938; *Band Waggon* 1939; *Gasbags* 1940; *Gert and Daisy's Weekend* 1941; *George in Ivory Street* 1946; *A Date with a Dream* 1948

Pate, Michael (1920-2008) *Bitter Springs* 1950; *The Strange Door* 1951; *The Black Castle* 1952; *Face to Face* 1952; *Hondo* 1953; *Houdini* 1953; *Julius Caesar* 1953; *The Maze* 1953; *The Revolt of Mamie Stover* 1956; *7th Cavalry* 1956; *The Oklahoman* 1957; *Green Mansions* 1959; *Westbound* 1959; *Beauty and the Beast* 1962; *Tower of London* 1962; *PT 109* 1963; *Mad Dog* 1976; *The Return of Captain Invincible* 1983; *The Wild Duck* 1983

Patekar, Nana (1951-) *Salaam Bombay!* 1988; *Shakti - the Power* 2002; *Bhoot* 2003

Patel, Dev (1990-) *Slumdog Millionaire* 2008; *The Last Airbender* 2010; *The Best Exotic Marigold Hotel* 2011; *Cherry* 2012; *Chappie* 2015; *The Man Who Knew Infinity* 2015; *The Second Best Exotic Marigold Hotel* 2015

Patel, Harish *My Son the Fanatic* 1997; *Run Fatboy Run* 2007; *All in Good Time* 2012; *Jadoo* 2013

Paterson, Bill (1945-) *The Odd Job* 1978; *Comfort and Joy* 1984; *The Killing Fields* 1984; *A Private Function* 1984; *Defence of the Realm* 1985; *The Adventures of Baron Munchausen* 1988; *The Rachel Papers* 1989; *The Witches* 1989; *Truly Madly Deeply* 1990; *The Object of Beauty* 1991; *Victory* 1995; *Heart* 1997; *Hilary and Jackie* 1998; *Complicity* 1999; *Crush* 2001; *Bright Young Things* 2003; *Rag Tale* 2005; *Miss Potter* 2006; *Creation* 2009; *Dad's Army* 2016

Paterson, Caroline *Venus Peter* 1989; *The Hawk* 1992

Paterson, Pat (1911-1978) *Bitter Sweet* 1933; *Charlie Chan in Egypt* 1935; *Spendthrift* 1936

Patil, Smita *aka Smita* (1955-1986) *Nishant* 1975; *In Search of Famine* 1980; *Sadgati* 1981; *Mirch Masala* 1987

Patinkin, Mandy (1952-) *The Big Fix* 1978; *French Postcards* 1979; *Last Embrace* 1979; *Night of the Juggler* 1980; *Ragtime* 1981; *Yentl* 1983; *Maxie* 1985; *The House on Carroll Street* 1987; *The Princess Bride* 1987; *Alien Nation* 1988; *Dick Tracy* 1990; *The Doctor* 1991; *Impromptu* 1991; *True Colors* 1991; *The Music of Chance* 1993; *Squanto: the Last Great Warrior* 1994; *The Hunchback of Notre Dame* 1997; *Men with Guns* 1997; *Lulu on the Bridge* 1998; *The Adventures of Elmo in Grouchland* 1999; *Strange Justice* 1999; *Piñero* 2001; *Choking Man* 2006; *The Wind Rises* 2013; *Wish I Was Here* 2014

Paton, Charles (1874-1970) *Blackmail* 1929; *The Adventurers* 1950

Patric, Jason (1966-) *The Lost Boys* 1987; *The Beast of War* 1988; *After Dark, My Sweet* 1990; *Frankenstein Unbound* 1990; *Rush* 1991; *Geronimo: an American Legend* 1993; *The Journey of August King* 1995; *Sleepers* 1996; *Incognito* 1997; *Speed 2: Cruise Control* 1997; *Your Friends & Neighbors* 1998; *Narc* 2001; *The Alamo* 2004; *Expired* 2007; *In the Valley of Elah* 2007; *My Sister's Keeper* 2009; *The Losers* 2010; *Keyhole* 2011

Patrick, Butch (1953-) *Munster, Go Home!* 1966; *The Phantom Tollbooth* 1969

Patrick, Dennis (1918-2002) *Joe* 1970; *The Air Up There* 1993

Patrick, Dorothy (1922-1987) *Till the Clouds Roll By* 1946; *High Wall* 1947; *Come to the Stable* 1949; *House by the River* 1950; *711 Ocean Drive* 1950; *Torch Song* 1953

Patrick, Gail (1911-1980) *Murders in the Zoo* 1933; *Death Takes a Holiday* 1934; *Mississippi* 1935; *Rumba* 1935; *The Lone Wolf Returns* 1936; *My Man Godfrey* 1936; *Artists and Models* 1937; *Stage Door* 1937; *Mad about Music* 1938; *Wives under Suspicion* 1938; *The Doctor Takes a Wife* 1940; *My Favorite Wife* 1940; *Love Crazy* 1941; *Quiet Please, Murder* 1942; *Change of Heart* 1943; *Up in Mabel's Room* 1944; *Brewster's Millions* 1945; *Claudia and*

David 1946; *Rendezvous with Annie* 1946

Patrick, Lee (1901-1982) *Condemned Women* 1938; *Invisible Stripes* 1939; *Saturday's Children* 1940; *Footsteps in the Dark* 1941; *The Maltese Falcon* 1941; *Million Dollar Baby* 1941; *Dangerously They Live* 1942; *George Washington Slept Here* 1942; *A Night to Remember* 1942; *Somewhere I'll Find You* 1942; *Mrs Parkington* 1944; *Keep Your Powder Dry* 1945; *Mildred Pierce* 1945; *Caged* 1950; *The Lawless* 1950; *Take Me to Town* 1953; *A Girl Named Tamiko* 1962; *7 Faces of Dr Lao* 1963; *The Black Bird* 1975

Patrick, Nigel (1912-1981) *Noose* 1948; *Silent Dust* 1948; *The Perfect Woman* 1949; *Morning Departure* 1950; *Pandora and the Flying Dutchman* 1950; *Trio* 1950; *The Browning Version* 1951; *Encore* 1951; *Young Wives' Tale* 1951; *Meet Me Tonight* 1952; *The Pickwick Papers* 1952; *The Sound Barrier* 1952; *Grand National Night* 1953; *Forbidden Cargo* 1954; *The Sea Shall Not Have Them* 1954; *All for Mary* 1955; *A Prize of Gold* 1955; *Count Five and Die* 1957; *How to Murder a Rich Uncle* 1957; *Raintree County* 1957; *The Man Inside* 1958; *Sapphire* 1959; *The League of Gentlemen* 1960; *The Trials of Oscar Wilde* 1960; *The Informers* 1963; *The Virgin Soldiers* 1969; *The Executioner* 1970; *The Great Waltz* 1972; *Tales from the Crypt* 1972; *The Mackintosh Man* 1973

Patrick, Robert (1958-) *Terminator 2: Judgment Day* 1991; *Fire in the Sky* 1993; *Body Shot* 1994; *Double Dragon* 1994; *Last Gasp* 1995; *Striptease* 1996; *Cop Land* 1997; *The Only Thrill* 1997; *The Faculty* 1998; *Tactical Assault* 1998; *From Dusk till Dawn II: Texas Blood Money* 1999; *All the Pretty Horses* 2000; *SPYkids* 2001; *Texas Rangers* 2001; *Charlie's Angels: Full Throttle* 2003; *Ladder 49* 2004; *Walk the Line* 2005; *Bridge to Terabithia* 2006; *Firewall* 2006; *Flags of Our Fathers* 2006; *Balls of Fury* 2007; *Fly Me to the Moon* 2007; *Strange Wilderness* 2007; *The Men Who Stare at Goatsx* 2009; *Jayne Mansfield's Car* 2012; *Safe House* 2012; *Trouble with the Curve* 2012; *Lovelace* 2013; *Endless Love* 2014

Patricks, Brendan *Heroes and Villains* 2006; *My Last Five Girlfriends* 2009

Patten, Luana (1938-1996) *Song of the South* 1946; *Rock, Pretty Baby* 1956; *Johnny Tremain* 1957; *The Restless Years* 1958; *Home from the Hill* 1960; *Go Naked in the World* 1961; *A Thunder of Drums* 1961

Patterson, Elizabeth (1875-1966) *A Bill of Divorcement* 1932; *No Man of Her Own* 1932; *So Red the Rose* 1935; *Go West, Young Man* 1936; *Small Town Girl* 1936; *High, Wide and Handsome* 1937; *Bluebeard's Eighth Wife* 1938; *Bulldog Drummond's Peril* 1938; *Bulldog Drummond's Bride* 1939; *The Cat and the Canary* 1939; *Anne of Windy Poplars* 1940; *Michael Shayne, Private Detective* 1940; *Remember the Night* 1940; *Belle Starr* 1941; *Kiss the Boys Goodbye* 1941; *Tobacco Road* 1941; *Beyond the Blue Horizon* 1942; *Her Cardboard Lover* 1942; *I Married a Witch* 1942; *The Sky's the Limit* 1943; *Together Again* 1944; *Colonel Effingham's Raid* 1945; *The Secret Heart* 1946; *The Shocking Miss Pilgrim* 1947; *Welcome Stranger* 1947; *Little Women* 1949; *Bright Leaf* 1950; *Pal Joey* 1957

Patterson, James (1932-1972) *Lilith* 1964; *In the Heat of the Night* 1967

Patterson, Jay (1954-) *Nadine* 1987; *Street Smart* 1987; *Teenage Mutant Ninja Turtles* 1990; *American Perfekt* 1997

Patterson, Lee (1929-2007) *Above Us the Waves* 1955; *Dry Rot* 1956; *Reach for the Sky* 1956; *The Flying Scot* 1957; *The Story of Esther Costello* 1957; *Time Lock* 1957; *Cat and Mouse* 1958; *The Golden Disc* 1958; *Jack the Ripper* 1958; *The Three Worlds of Gulliver* 1959; *Bullseye!* 1990

Patterson, Marnette *By Appointment Only* 2007; *Starship Troopers 3: Marauder* 2008

Patterson, Neva (1922-2010) *Taxi* 1953; *The Solid Gold Cadillac* 1956; *An Affair to Remember* 1957; *Desk Set* 1957; *Too Much, Too Soon* 1958; *David and Lisa* 1962; *The Spiral Road* 1962

Patterson, Sarah *The Company of Wolves* 1984; *Do I Love You?* 2003

Patterson, Scott (1958-) *Intent to Kill* 1992; *Saw IV* 2007; *Saw V* 2008; *Concrete Canyons* 2010

Pattinson, Robert (1986-) *Sword of Xanten* 2004; *Harry Potter and the*

Goblet of Fire 2005; *Little Ashes* 2008; *Twilight* 2008; *New Moon* 2009; *Bel Ami* 2010; *Eclipse* 2010; *Remember Me* 2010; *Breaking Dawn Part One* 2011; *Water for Elephants* 2011; *Breaking Dawn Part Two* 2012; *Cosmopolis* 2012; *Maps to the Stars* 2014; *The Rover* 2014; *The Childhood of a Leader* 2015; *Life* 2015; *Queen of the Desert* 2015; *The Lost City of Z* 2016

Patton, Mark (1964-) *Come Back to the Five and Dime, Jimmy Dean, Jimmy Dean* 1982; *A Nightmare on Elm Street 2: Freddy's Revenge* 1985

Patton, Mary (1914-1982) *The Search* 1948; *The Marriage-Go-Round* 1960

Patton, Paula (1975-) *Déjà Vu* 2006; *Idlewild* 2006; *Mirrors* 2008; *Precious (Base on Nol by Saf) (Based on the Novel "Push" by Sapphire)* 2008; *Swing Vote* 2008; *Just Wright* 2010; *Mission: Impossible - Ghost Protocol* 2011; *Disconnect* 2012; *Baggage Claim* 2013; *2 Guns* 2013; *Warcraft: the Beginning* 2016

Patton, Will (1954-) *Belizaire the Cajun* 1985; *Desperately Seeking Susan* 1985; *No Way Out* 1986; *Everybody Wins* 1990; *A Shock to the System* 1990; *The Rapture* 1991; *Cold Heaven* 1992; *In the Soup* 1992; *Romeo Is Bleeding* 1992; *The Client* 1994; *The Puppet Masters* 1994; *Tollbooth* 1994; *Copycat* 1995; *Fled* 1996; *The Spitfire Grill* 1996; *This World, Then the Fireworks* 1996; *Inventing the Abbotts* 1997; *The Postman* 1997; *Armageddon* 1998; *I Woke Up Early the Day I Died* 1998; *Entrapment* 1999; *Jesus' Son* 1999; *Gone in Sixty Seconds* 2000; *Remember the Titans* 2000; *Trixie* 2000; *The Mothman Prophecies* 2001; *Family Sins* 2004; *The Last Ride* 2004; *The Punisher* 2004; *Road House 2* 2006; *Code Name: the Cleaner* 2007; *A Mighty Heart* 2007; *Wendy and Lucy* 2008; *Brooklyn's Finest* 2009; *The Fourth Kind* 2009; *Meek's Cutoff* 2010

Paul, Aaron (1979-) *Whatever It Takes* 2000; *Choking Man* 2006; *The Last House on the Left* 2008; *Smashed* 2012; *Decoding Annie Parker* 2013; *A Long Way Down* 2013; *Exodus: Gods and Kings* 2014; *Hellion* 2014; *Need for Speed* 2014; *Eye in the Sky* 2015; *Fathers and Daughters* 2015; *Triple 9* 2015

Paul, Adrian (1959-) *Dead Men Can't Dance* 1997; *Susan's Plan* 1998; *Highlander: Endgame* 2000; *Merlin the Return* 2000; *The Breed* 2001; *Highlander: the Source* 2007

Paul, Alexandra (1963-) *Christine* 1983; *American Flyers* 1985; *8 Million Ways to Die* 1986; *Dragnet* 1987; *Sunset Grill* 1992; *Death Train* 1993; *Danielle Steel's Mixed Blessings* 1995; *Night Watch* 1995; *Redemption of the Ghost* 2000; *Diary of a Sex Addict* 2001; *A Sister's Secret* 2009; *The Boy She Met Online* 2010

Paul, Don Michael (1963-) *Dangerously Close* 1986; *Aloha Summer* 1988; *Heart of Dixie* 1989; *Robot Wars* 1993

Paul, John (1921-1995) *The Steel Bayonet* 1957; *The Curse of the Mummy's Tomb* 1964; *Doomwatch* 1972

Paulin, Scott (1950-) *Dreams of Gold: the Mel Fisher Story* 1986; *Turner & Hooch* 1989; *Grim Prairie Tales* 1990; *Pump Up the Volume* 1990

Paull, Morgan (1944-2012) *Cahill, United States Marshal* 1973; *Norma Rae* 1979; *Fade to Black* 1980

Paulsen, Albert (1929-2004) *The Three Sisters* 1966; *Mrs Pollifax - Spy* 1970; *The Next Man* 1976

Paulsen, Pat (1927-1997) *Harper Valley PTA* 1978; *Ellie* 1984

Paulsen, Rob (1956-) *A Goofy Movie* 1995; *Cinderella II: Dreams Come True* 2002

Paulson, Jay *Permanent Midnight* 1998; *Black Rock* 2012

Paulson, Sarah (1974-) *The Long Way Home* 1998; *The Other Sister* 1999; *Down with Love* 2003; *The Notorious Bettie Page* 2005; *The Spirit* 2008; *November Christmas* 2010; *Martha Marcy May Marlene* 2011; *Game Change* 2012; *12 Years a Slave* 2013; *Carol* 2015; *The Runner* 2015

Pauly, Rebecca *Near Mrs* 1990; *Road to Ruin* 1992

Pauly, Rodolphe *Merci pour le Chocolat* 2000; *Nathalie...* 2003; *Before Sunset* 2004

Pavan, Marisa (1932-) *Down Three Dark Streets* 1954; *Drum Beat* 1954; *Diane* 1955; *The Rose Tattoo* 1955; *The Man in the Gray Flannel Suit* 1956; *The Midnight Story* 1957; *Solomon and Sheba* 1959

Pávez, Terele (1939-) *Los Santos Inocentes* 1984; *The Day of the Beast* 1995; *La Comunidad* 2000

Pavlow, Muriel (1921-) *Night Boat to Dublin* 1946; *The Shop at Sly Corner* 1946; *It Started in Paradise* 1952; *Conflict of Wings* 1953; *Malta Story* 1953; *The Net* 1953; *Doctor in the House* 1954; *Simon and Laura* 1955; *Eyewitness* 1956; *Reach for the Sky* 1956; *Tiger in the Smoke* 1956; *Doctor at Large* 1957; *Rooney* 1958; *Murder She Said* 1961

Pavlu, Serban *The Death of Mr Lazarescu* 2005; *The Happiest Girl in the World* 2009

Pawar, Lalita (1916-1998) *Mr and Mrs '55* 1955; *Anari* 1959; *Junglee* 1961

Pawle, Lennox (1872-1936) *David Copperfield* 1935; *The Gay Deception* 1935

Pawley, Edward (1901-1988) *"G" Men* 1935; *Smashing the Rackets* 1938

Pawley, William (1905-1952) *Bad Girl* 1931; *Speak Easily* 1932; *Gabriel over the White House* 1933

Pax, James *Kinjite: Forbidden Subjects* 1989; *Bethune: the Making of a Hero* 1990

Paxinou, Katina (1900-1973) *For Whom the Bell Tolls* 1943; *Confidential Agent* 1945; *Mourning Becomes Electra* 1947; *Uncle Silas* 1947; *Confidential Report* 1955; *Rocco and His Brothers* 1960

Paxton, Bill (1955-) *The Lords of Discipline* 1983; *Impulse* 1984; *Streets of Fire* 1984; *Weird Science* 1985; *Aliens* 1986; *Near Dark* 1987; *Next of Kin* 1989; *Slipstream* 1989; *Blue Heat* 1990; *Brain Dead* 1990; *Navy SEALs* 1990; *Predator 2* 1990; *One False Move* 1992; *Trespass* 1992; *The Vagrant* 1992; *Boxing Helena* 1993; *Indian Summer* 1993; *Tombstone* 1993; *True Lies* 1994; *Apollo 13* 1995; *Frank and Jesse* 1995; *The Last Supper* 1995; *The Evening Star* 1996; *Twister* 1996; *Titanic* 1997; *Traveller* 1997; *Mighty Joe Young* 1998; *A Simple Plan* 1998; *U-571* 2000; *Vertical Limit* 2000; *Frailty* 2001; *Broken Lizard's Club Dread* 2004; *Thunderbirds* 2004; *The Colony* 2013; *Nightcrawler* 2013; *2 Guns* 2013; *Edge of Tomorrow* 2014; *Million Dollar Arm* 2014

Paxton, Sara (1988-) *Sleepover* 2004; *Aquamarine* 2006; *Sydney White* 2007; *The Last House on the Left* 2008; *Superhero Movie* 2008; *The Innkeepers* 2011; *Shark Night 3D* 2011; *Cheap Thrills* 2013

Paymer, David (1954-) *Crazy People* 1990; *Mr Saturday Night* 1992; *Heart and Souls* 1993; *Innocent Moves* 1993; *Quiz Show* 1994; *The American President* 1995; *Nixon* 1995; *Carpool* 1996; *City Hall* 1996; *Unforgettable* 1996; *Amistad* 1997; *Gang Related* 1997; *The 6th Man* 1997; *Mighty Joe Young* 1998; *Payback* 1998; *Chill Factor* 1999; *Bartleby* 2000; *For Love or Country: the Arturo Sandoval Story* 2000; *Partners* 2000; *Focus* 2001; *Joe and Max* 2002; *Alex & Emma* 2003; *In Good Company* 2004; *Marilyn Hotchkiss Ballroom Dancing & Charm School* 2005; *Redbelt* 2007; *Resurrecting the Champ* 2007; *Drag Me to Hell* 2009; *Twixt* 2011

Payne, Allen (1968-) *New Jack City* 1991; *CB4* 1993; *Jason's Lyric* 1994; *The Tuskegee Airmen* 1995; *Vampire in Brooklyn* 1995; *A Price above Rubies* 1997; *Double Platinum* 1999

Payne, Bruce *aka* **Payne, Bruce Martyn** (1960-) *For Queen and Country* 1988; *Pyrates* 1991; *Switch* 1991; *Passenger 57* 1992; *Full Eclipse* 1993; *Necronomicon* 1993; *Sweepers* 1999; *Warlock III: the End of Innocence* 1999; *Britannic* 2000; *Highlander: Endgame* 2000; *Steal* 2002; *Dungeons & Dragons: Wrath of the Dragon God* 2005; *Messages* 2007; *Getaway* 2013; *Vendetta* 2013

Payne, Eric *aka* **Payne, Eric A** *DROP Squad* 1994; *Gridlock'd* 1996

Payne, Freda (1945-) *Book of Numbers* 1972; *Nutty Professor 2: the Klumps* 2000

Payne, John *aka* **Payne, John Howard** (1912-1989) *Fair Warning* 1937; *College Swing* 1938; *Maryland* 1940; *Star Dust* 1940; *Tin Pan Alley* 1940; *The Great American Broadcast* 1941; *Remember the Day* 1941; *Sun Valley Serenade* 1941; *Weekend in Havana* 1941; *Footlight Serenade* 1942; *Springtime in the Rockies* 1942; *To the Shores of Tripoli* 1942; *Hello, Frisco, Hello* 1943; *The Dolly Sisters* 1945; *The Razor's Edge* 1946; *Sentimental Journey* 1946; *Miracle on 34th Street* 1947; *The Saxon Charm* 1948; *Kansas City Confidential* 1952; *99 River Street* 1953; *Raiders of the Seven Seas* 1953;

Rails into Laramie 1954; *Silver Lode* 1954; *The Road to Denver* 1955; *Santa Fe Passage* 1955; *Slightly Scarlet* 1956

Payne, Laurence (1919-2009) *Train of Events* 1949; *Ill Met by Moonlight* 1956; *The Trollenberg Terror* 1958; *The Third Alibi* 1961; *Vampire Circus* 1971

Pays, Amanda (1959-) *Oxford Blues* 1984; *The Kindred* 1986; *Saigon* 1988; *Leviathan* 1989; *Solitaire for 2* 1994

Payton-Wright, Pamela (1941-) *Corky* 1972; *Going in Style* 1979; *Resurrection* 1980; *My Little Girl* 1986

Payton, Barbara (1927-1967) *Dallas* 1950; *Kiss Tomorrow Goodbye* 1950; *Only the Valiant* 1950; *Four Sided Triangle* 1953

Peach, Mary (1934-) *Room at the Top* 1958; *No Love for Johnnie* 1960; *A Pair of Briefs* 1961; *Ballad in Blue* 1964

Peacock, Daniel *Party Party* 1983; *I Bought a Vampire Motorcycle* 1989

Peacock, Trevor (1931-) *Hamlet* 1990; *Roseanna's Grave* 1996; *Fred Claus* 2007

Peake, Maxine (1974-) *Clubbed* 2008; *Best Laid Plans* 2011; *Private Peaceful* 2012; *Run and Jump* 2013; *Svengali* 2013; *The Falling* 2014; *Keeping Rosy* 2014; *The Theory of Everything* 2015

Peake, Michael *Mark of the Phoenix* 1957; *The Bay of Saint Michel* 1963

Peaker, E J (1944-) *Hello, Dolly!* 1969; *The All-American Boy* 1973

Pearce, Alice (1913-1966) *On the Town* 1949; *The Belle of New York* 1952; *The Disorderly Orderly* 1964

Pearce, Guy (1967-) *Heaven Tonight* 1990; *Hunting* 1992; *The Adventures of Priscilla, Queen of the Desert* 1994; *Flynn* 1995; *LA Confidential* 1997; *Ravenous* 1999; *Memento* 2000; *Rules of Engagement* 2000; *The Count of Monte Cristo* 2001; *The Hard Word* 2002; *The Time Machine* 2002; *The Proposition* 2004; *Two Brothers* 2004; *Factory Girl* 2006; *Death Defying Acts* 2007; *Bedtime Stories* 2008; *Fragments* 2008; *The Hurt Locker* 2008; *Traitor* 2008; *Animal Kingdom* 2009; *The Road* 2009; *Don't Be Afraid of the Dark* 2010; *The King's Speech* 2010; *Justice* 2011; *Lawless* 2012; *Lockout* 2012; *Prometheus* 2012; *Breathe In* 2013; *Iron Man Three* 2013; *The Rover* 2014; *Genius* 2015; *Holding the Man* 2015; *Results* 2015

Pearce, Jacqueline *The Plague of the Zombies* 1965; *The Reptile* 1966; *Don't Raise the Bridge, Lower the River* 1968; *Guru in Seven* 1997

Pearce, John (1927-2000) *The Great Northfield Minnesota Raid* 1972; *Billy Two Hats* 1973; *Little Treasure* 1985

Pearce, Mary Vivian (1947-) *Mondo Trasho* 1970; *Multiple Maniacs* 1970; *Pink Flamingos* 1972; *Female Trouble* 1974; *Desperate Living* 1977; *Cry-Baby* 1989; *Serial Mom* 1994

Pearl, Aaron *The Accidental Witness* 2006; *Lost Holiday: the Jim and Suzanne Shemwell Story* 2007

Pearl, Barry (1950-) *Grease* 1978; *Avenging Angel* 1985

Pearlman, Stephen (1935-1998) *Rollercoaster* 1977; *Perfect Gentlemen* 1978; *Pi* 1997

Pearson, James Anthony *Control* 2007; *New Town Killers* 2009

Pearson, Neil (1959-) *The Secret Rapture* 1993; *Fever Pitch* 1996; *Bridget Jones: the Edge of Reason* 2004

Pearson (1), Richard (1918-2011) *The Blue Parrot* 1953; *Guns of Darkness* 1962; *Charlie Bubbles* 1967; *The Rise and Rise of Michael Rimmer* 1970; *It Shouldn't Happen to a Vet* 1979; *Tess* 1979

Peary, Harold (1908-1985) *Look Who's Laughing* 1941; *Seven Days' Leave* 1942

Pecheur, Sierra *3 Women* 1977; *Bronco Billy* 1980; *Kalifornia* 1993

Peck, Anthony (1947-1996) *Pirates* 1986; *Die Hard with a Vengeance* 1995

Peck, Bob (1945-1999) *The Kitchen Toto* 1987; *On the Black Hill* 1987; *Slipstream* 1989; *Jurassic Park* 1993; *Smilla's Feeling for Snow* 1996; *Surviving Picasso* 1996; *FairyTale: a True Story* 1997; *The Miracle Maker* 1999

Peck, Cecilia (1958-) *Torn Apart* 1990; *Ambition* 1991

Peck, Gregory (1916-2003) *Days of Glory* 1944; *The Keys of the Kingdom* 1944; *Spellbound* 1945; *The Valley of Decision* 1945; *Duel in the Sun* 1946; *The Yearling* 1946; *Gentleman's Agreement* 1947; *The Macomber Affair* 1947; *The Paradine Case* 1947; *Yellow Sky* 1948; *The Great Sinner* 1949; *Twelve o'Clock High* 1949; *The Gunfighter* 1950; *Only the Valiant* 1950; *Captain Horatio Hornblower RN* 1951; *David and Bathsheba* 1951; *The Snows* of Kilimanjaro 1952; The World in His Arms 1952; The Million Pound Note 1953; Roman Holiday 1953; Night People 1954; The Purple Plain 1954; The Man in the Gray Flannel Suit 1956; Moby Dick 1956; Designing Woman 1957; The Big Country 1958; The Bravados 1958; Beloved Infidel 1959; On the Beach 1959; Pork Chop Hill 1959; The Guns of Navarone 1961; Cape Fear 1962; How the West Was Won 1962; To Kill a Mockingbird 1962; Captain Newman, MD 1963; Behold a Pale Horse 1964; Mirage 1965; Arabesque 1966; The Stalking Moon 1968; The Chairmen 1969; Mackenna's Gold 1969; Marooned 1969; Shoot Out 1971; Billy Two Hats 1973; The Omen 1976; MacArthur 1977; The Boys from Brazil 1978; The Sea Wolves 1980; The Scarlet and the Black 1983; Amazing Grace and Chuck 1987; Old Gringo 1989; Cape Fear 1991; Other People's Money 1991; Moby Dick 1998

Peck, J Eddie (1958-) Dangerously Close 1986; Curse II: The Bite 1989; Lambada 1990

Peck, Josh (1986-) Max Keeble's Big Move 2001; Mean Creek 2004; Ice Age: the Meltdown 2006; Special (PX) - Specioprin Hydrochloride 2006; Drillbit Taylor 2007; The Wackness 2008; Aliens in the Attic 2009; Ice Age 3: Dawn of the Dinosaurs 2009; ATM 2012; Red Dawn 2012; Battle of the Year 2013; Ice Age: Collision Course 2016

Peckinpah, Sam (1925-1984) China 9, Liberty 37 1978; The Visitor 1980

Pecoraro, Susu (1953-) Camila 1984; Sur 1987

Pedersen, Aaron Dead Heart 1996; Mystery Road 2013

Peeples, Nia (1961-) North Shore 1987; DeepStar Six 1989; Improper Conduct 1994; Poodle Springs 1998; Alone with a Stranger 2000; Half Past Dead 2002; Sub Zero 2005

Peers, Joan (1909-1975) Applause 1929; Rain or Shine 1930; Parlor, Bedroom and Bath 1931

Peet, Amanda (1972-) Touch Me 1997; Body Shots 1999; Whipped 1999; Evil Woman 2001; Changing Lanes 2002; High Crimes 2002; Igby Goes Down 2002; Identity 2003; Something's Gotta Give 2003; Melinda and Melinda 2004; The Whole Ten Yards 2004; A Lot like Love 2005; Syriana 2005; Battle for Terra 2007; The X-Files: I Want to Believe 2008; 2012 2009; Gulliver's Travels 2010; Please Give 2010; Identity Thief 2013

Pegg, Simon (1970-) Guest House Paradiso 1999; Shaun of the Dead 2004; George A Romero's Land of the Dead 2005; The Good Night 2005; Big Nothing 2006; Free Jimmy 2006; Mission: Impossible III 2006; Hot Fuzz 2007; Run Fatboy Run 2007; How to Lose Friends & Alienate People 2008; Ice Age 3: Dawn of the Dinosaurs 2009; Star Trek 2009; Burke & Hare 2010; The Chronicles of Narnia: The Voyage of the Dawn Treader 2010; Paul 2010; The Adventures of Tintin: the Secret of the Unicorn 2011; Mission: Impossible - Ghost Protocol 2011; A Fantastic Fear of Everything 2012; Star Trek into Darkness 2013; The World's End 2013; The Boxtrolls 2014; Hector and the Search for Happiness 2014; Absolutely Anything 2015; Man Up 2015; Mission: Impossible - Rogue Nation 2015; Star Wars Episode VII: the Force Awakens 2015; Ice Age: Collision Course 2016; Star Trek Beyond 2016

Peil Sr, Edward aka Peil, Edward aka **Peil Sr, Ed** (1882-1958) Broken Blossoms 1919; Dream Street 1921; Blue Steel 1934; The Man from Utah 1934; The Lone Rider in Ghost Town 1941

Peil, Mary Beth The Odd Couple II 1998; Mirrors 2008

Peirse, Sarah Heavenly Creatures 1994; Rain 2001

Peldon, Ashley (1984-) Deceived 1991; Drop Dead Fred 1991; Cats Don't Dance 1998

Pelé (1940-) Escape to Victory 1981; Hot Shot 1986; Mike Bassett: England Manager 2001; Bo66y 2016

Pelikan, Lisa (1954-) Jennifer 1978; Perfect Gentlemen 1978; Ghoulies 1985; AWOL 1990; Return to the Blue Lagoon 1991

Pellegrin, Raymond (1925-2007) Manon des Sources 1952; Nous Sommes Tous des Assassins 1952; Napoléon 1955; The Light across the Street 1956; Bitter Victory 1957; The Mysteries of Paris 1962; Imperial Venus 1963; Behold a Pale Horse 1964; Le Deuxième Souffle 1966; Beatrice Cenci 1969

Pellegrino, Mark (1965-) Prayer of the Rollerboys 1990; Mulholland Drive

2001; The Hunted 2002; Twisted 2003; Capote 2005; Ellie Parker 2005; The Number 23 2006

Pelletier, Andrée Outrageous! 1977; Bach and Broccoli 1986

Pellicer, Pina (1935-1964) Macario 1960; One-Eyed Jacks 1961

Pellonpaa, Matti (1951-1995) Ariel 1988; Leningrad Cowboys Go America 1989; Take Care of Your Scarf, Tatjana 1994

Peltola, Markku (1956-2007) Drifting Clouds 1996; Juha 1999; The Man without a Past 2002; Ten Minutes Older: the Trumpet 2002

Peltola, Sulevi Frozen Land 2005; Lights in the Dusk 2006

Peltz, Nicola The Last Airbender 2010; Transformers: Age of Extinction 2014

Pemberton, Steve (1967-) Lassie 2005; The League of Gentlemen's Apocalypse 2005; Mr Bean's Holiday 2007

Pempeit, Lilo (1922-1993) Effi Briest 1974; Fear of Fear 1976

Peña, Candela (1973-) All about My Mother 1999; Take My Eyes 2003

Peña, Elizabeth (1961-2014) Down and Out in Beverly Hills 1986; La Bamba 1987; *batteries not included 1987; Vibes 1988; Shannon's Deal 1989; Blue Steel 1990; Jacob's Ladder 1990; The Waterdance 1991; Dead Funny 1995; Lone Star 1995; Aldrich Ames: Traitor Within 1998; Rush Hour 1998; Impostor 2001; Tortilla Soup 2001; Down in the Valley 2004; The Hollywood Mom's Mystery 2004; The Incredibles 2004; Suburban Madness 2004; Transamerica 2005; Goal II: Living the Dream 2007; Racing for Time 2008

Pena, Michael aka Peña, Michael (1976-) The Calcium Kid 2003; World Trade Center 2006; Lions for Lambs 2007; Shooter 2007; My Son, My Son, What Have Ye Done 2009; Observe and Report 2009; Everything Must Go 2010; The Lincoln Lawyer 2011; 30 Minutes or Less 2011; Tower Heist 2011; End of Watch 2012; Turbo 2013; Frontera 2014; Fury 2014; Ant-Man 2015; The Martian 2015; The Vatican Tapes 2015

Peña, Pasqual Garcia The Big Steal 1949; The Black Scorpion 1957

Peña, Vicky (1954-) The House of Bernarda Alba 1987; Secrets of the Heart 1997

Pendergast, Oaklee The Impossible 2011; The Woman in Black: Angel of Death 2014

Pendleton, Austin (1940-) Petulia 1968; Catch-22 1970; Every Little Crook and Nanny 1972; What's Up, Doc? 1972; The Thief Who Came to Dinner 1973; Starting Over 1979; Simon 1980; Short Circuit 1986; Hello Again 1987; The Ballad of the Sad Café 1991; Mr Nanny 1992; My Cousin Vinny 1992; Don't Drink the Water 1994; Guarding Tess 1994; The Associate 1996; The Mirror Has Two Faces 1996; The Proprietor 1996; Trial and Error 1997; Finding Nemo 2003; Uptown Girls 2003

Pendleton, Nat (1895-1967) The Big Pond 1930; Horse Feathers 1932; Lady for a Day 1933; Penthouse 1933; The Cat's Paw 1934; The Gay Bride 1934; Manhattan Melodrama 1934; Sing and Like It 1934; The Thin Man 1934; Reckless 1935; The Great Ziegfeld 1936; Gangway 1937; Life Begins in College 1937; Swing Your Lady 1937; Arsene Lupin Returns 1938; The Crowd Roars 1938; Fast Company 1938; The Shopworn Angel 1938; Young Dr Kildare 1938; Another Thin Man 1939; At the Circus 1939; Calling Dr Kildare 1939; It's a Wonderful World 1939; The Secret of Dr Kildare 1939; Dr Kildare Goes Home 1940; Dr Kildare's Crisis 1940; Northwest Passage 1940; Phantom Raiders 1940; Calling Dr Gillespie 1942; Dr Gillespie's New Assistant 1942; The Mad Doctor of Market Street 1942; Dr Gillespie's Criminal Case 1943; Buck Privates Come Home 1947; Scared to Death 1947

Pendleton, Steve aka Pendleton, Gaylord (1908-1984) Internes Can't Take Money 1937; The Duke of West Point 1938

Penghlis, Thaao (1945-) Slow Dancing in the Big City 1978; Altered States 1980; Les Patterson Saves the World 1987

Penhaligon, Susan (1949-) No Sex Please - We're British 1973; The Land That Time Forgot 1974; House of Mortal Sin 1975; Nasty Habits 1976; Soldier of Orange 1977; The Uncanny 1977; Patrick 1978

Penn, Chris aka Penn, Christopher (1965-2006) All the Right Moves 1983; Rumble Fish 1983; Footloose 1984; The

Wild Life 1984; At Close Range 1985; Pale Rider 1985; Return from the River Kwai 1988; Best of the Best 1989; Leather Jackets 1991; Reservoir Dogs 1991; Best of the Best II 1992; Beethoven's 2nd 1993; Josh and SAM 1993; The Music of Chance 1993; The Pickle 1993; Short Cuts 1993; True Romance 1993; Imaginary Crimes 1994; Fist of the North Star 1995; To Wong Foo, Thanks for Everything, Julie Newmar 1995; Under the Hula Moon 1995; The Funeral 1996; Mulholland Falls 1996; Liar 1997; Rush Hour 1998; Corky Romano 2001; Kiss Kiss (Bang Bang) 2001; Murder by Numbers 2002; Stealing Harvard 2002; After the Sunset 2004; Starsky & Hutch 2004

Penn, Kal (1977-) Van Wilder: Party Liaison 2002; Love Don't Cost a Thing 2003; Harold & Kumar Get the Munchies 2004; A Lot like Love 2005; The Namesake 2006; Epic Movie 2007; Harold & Kumar Escape from Guantanamo Bay 2008; A Very Harold & Kumar 3D Christmas 2011

Penn, Leonard (1907-1975) Man-Proof 1937; The Girl of the Golden West 1938; The Dead Don't Dream 1948

Penn, Sean (1960-) Taps 1981; Fast Times at Ridgemont High 1982; Bad Boys 1983; Racing with the Moon 1984; At Close Range 1985; The Falcon and the Snowman 1985; Shanghai Surprise 1986; Dear America: Letters Home from Vietnam 1987; Colors 1988; Cool Blue 1988; Judgment in Berlin 1988; Casualties of War 1989; We're No Angels 1989; State of Grace 1990; Carlito's Way 1993; Dead Man Walking 1995; Loved 1996; The Game 1997; She's So Lovely 1997; U Turn 1997; Hurlyburly 1998; The Thin Red Line 1998; Up at the Villa 1998; Being John Malkovich 1999; Sweet and Lowdown 1999; Before Night Falls 2000; The Weight of Water 2000; Dogtown and Z-Boys 2001; I Am Sam 2001; It's All about Love 2002; Mystic River 2003; 21 Grams 2003; The Assassination of Richard Nixon 2004; All the King's Men 2005; The Interpreter 2005; Persepolis 2007; What Just Happened? 2007; Milk 2008; Fair Game 2010; The Tree of Life 2010; This Must Be the Place 2011; Gangster Squad 2012; The Secret Life of Walter Mitty 2013; The Gunman 2015

Pennell, Larry Seven Angry Men 1955; The Devil's Hairpin 1957; The FBI Story 1959; The Borrower 1989

Penner, Joe (1904-1941) New Faces of 1937 1937; The Boys from Syracuse 1940

Penner, Jonathan The Last Supper 1995; Let the Devil Wear Black 1999

Pennick, Jack (1895-1964) Lady from Louisiana 1941; Operation Pacific 1951; The Beast from 20,000 Fathoms 1953

Pennock, Christopher Night of Dark Shadows 1971; Frances 1982

Penny, Joe (1956-) The Little Unicorn 1998; The Prophet's Game 1999

Penny, Sydney (1971-) Pale Rider 1985; Hidden Places 2006; The Wish List 2010

Penot, Jacques (1959-) Le Cri du Hibou 1987; The Revolving Doors 1988

Penrose, John (1914-1983) Freedom Radio 1941; Kind Hearts and Coronets 1949; Street of Shadows 1953

Penry-Jones, Rupert (1970-) Hilary and Jackie 1998; Virtual Sexuality 1999; Charlotte Gray 2001; The Four Feathers 2002

Peppard, George (1928-1994) Pork Chop Hill 1959; Home from the Hill 1960; The Subterraneans 1960; Breakfast at Tiffany's 1961; How the West Was Won 1962; The Victors 1963; The Carpetbaggers 1964; Operation Crossbow 1965; The Third Day 1965; The Blue Max 1966; Tobruk 1966; Rough Night in Jericho 1967; House of Cards 1968; What's So Bad about Feeling Good? 1968; Pendulum 1969; Cannon for Cordoba 1970; The Executioner 1970; Banacek: Detour to Nowhere 1972; The Groundstar Conspiracy 1972; Newman's Law 1974; Damnation Alley 1977; From Hell to Victory 1979; Battle beyond the Stars 1980; Race for the Yankee Zephyr 1981; Target Eagle 1982; The A-Team 1983

Pepper, Barbara (1915-1969) Our Daily Bread 1934; Kiss Me, Stupid 1964

Pepper, Barry (1970-) Saving Private Ryan 1998; Battlefield Earth 2000; Knockaround Guys 2001; 61* 2001; 25th Hour 2002; We Were Soldiers 2002; The Three Burials of Melquiades Estrada 2005; Unknown 2006; Seven Pounds 2008; True Grit 2010; Broken City 2013; Snitch 2013; Kill the Messenger 2014; How to Change the World 2015; Monster Trucks 2015

Pêra, Marília (1943-) Pixote 1981; Central Station 1998

Perabo, Piper (1977-) The Adventures of Rocky & Bullwinkle 1999; Whiteboys 1999; Coyote Ugly 2000; Slap Her, She's French! 2001; Cheaper by the Dozen 2003; The I Inside 2003; The Cave 2005; Cheaper by the Dozen 2 2005; Imagine Me and You 2005; The Prestige 2006; Because I Said So 2007; Beverly Hills Chihuahua 2008; Carriers 2008; The Lazarus Project 2008; Looper 2012

Percival, Lance (1933-2015) Carry On Cruising 1962; Twice round the Daffodils 1962; The Big Job 1965; Joey Boy 1965; Yellow Submarine 1968; Darling Lili 1970; Too Late the Hero 1970; Up Pompeii 1971; Up the Chastity Belt 1971; Our Miss Fred 1972; Up the Front 1972

Percy, Esme (1887-1957) Murder 1930; Bitter Sweet 1933; Lord Edgware Dies 1934; Love, Life and Laughter 1934; Nell Gwyn 1934; An Old Spanish Custom 1935; Accused 1936; Land without Music 1936; Song of Freedom 1936; 21 Days 1937

Perego, Didi (1937-1993) Kapo 1959; The Appointment 1968

Perez, Manny Bella 2006; El Cantante 2006

Perez, Marco Amores Perros 2000; Trade 2006

Perez, Rosie (1964-) Do the Right Thing 1989; Night on Earth 1992; White Men Can't Jump 1992; Fearless 1993; Untamed Heart 1993; It Could Happen to You 1994; Somebody to Love 1994; Perdita Durango 1997; Subway Stories: Tales from the Underground 1997; The 24 Hour Woman 1999; The Road to El Dorado 2000; Human Nature 2001; Riding in Cars with Boys 2001; Pineapple Express 2008; Won't Back Down 2012; The Counsellor 2013

Perez, Vincent (1965-) Cyrano de Bergerac 1990; Indochine 1991; La Reine Margot 1994; Beyond the Clouds 1995; The Crow: City of Angels 1996; Amy Foster 1997; Le Bossu 1997; Talk of Angels 1998; Those Who Love Me Can Take the Train 1998; Time Regained 1999; I Dreamed of Africa 2000; Le Libertin 2000; Bride of the Wind 2001; Queen of the Damned 2002; Frankenstein 2004; The Price of Desire 2015

Périer, François (1919-2002) Man about Town 1947; Orphée 1950; Secrets d'Alcove 1954; Gervaise 1956; Nights of Cabiria 1957; Le Samourai 1967; Z 1968; The Red Circle 1970; Juste avant la Nuit 1971; Stavisky 1974; Doctor Françoise Gailland 1975; Soigne Ta Droite 1986

Perkins, Anthony (1932-1992) The Actress 1953; Friendly Persuasion 1956; Fear Strikes Out 1957; The Lonely Man 1957; This Angry Age 1957; The Tin Star 1957; Desire under the Elms 1958; The Matchmaker 1958; Green Mansions 1959; On the Beach 1959; Psycho 1960; Goodbye Again 1961; Phaedra 1962; The Trial 1962; Five Miles to Midnight 1963; A Ravishing Idiot 1964; The Fool Killer 1965; The Champagne Murders 1966; Is Paris Burning? 1966; Pretty Poison 1968; Catch-22 1970; WUSA 1970; Someone behind the Door 1971; Ten Days' Wonder 1971; The Life and Times of Judge Roy Bean 1972; Play It as It Lays 1972; Murder on the Orient Express 1974; Mahogany 1975; Les Misérables 1978; Remember My Name 1978; The Black Hole 1979; North Sea Hijack 1979; Winter Kills 1979; Psycho II 1983; Crimes of Passion 1984; Psycho III 1986; Edge of Sanity 1989; Psycho IV: the Beginning 1990

Perkins, Clare Ladybird Ladybird 1994; Bullet Boy 2004

Perkins, Elizabeth (1960-) About Last Night... 1986; From the Hip 1987; Big 1988; Sweet Hearts Dance 1988; Avalon 1990; Love at Large 1990; Over Her Dead Body 1990; The Doctor 1991; He Said, She Said 1991; For Their Own Good 1993; Indian Summer 1993; The Flintstones 1994; Miracle on 34th Street 1994; Moonlight and Valentino 1995; I'm Losing You 1998; Crazy in Alabama 1999; 28 Days 2000; Cats & Dogs 2001; The Ring Two 2004; Must Love Dogs 2005; Hop 2011

Perkins, Millie (1938-) The Diary of Anne Frank 1959; Wild in the Country 1961; Ensign Pulver 1964; The Shooting 1967; Wild in the Streets 1968; Table for Five 1983; At Close Range 1985; Slam Dance 1987; Two Moon Junction 1988

Perkins, Osgood (1892-1937) Tarnished Lady 1931; Scarface 1932; Madame Du Barry 1934; I Dream Too Much 1935; Gold Diggers of 1937 1936

Perle, Rebecca Tightrope 1984; Not of This Earth 1988

Perlich, Max (1968-) Drugstore Cowboy 1989; The Butcher's Wife 1991; Rush 1991; Born Yesterday 1993; Dead Beat 1994; Shake, Rattle and Rock 1994; Georgia 1995; Sometimes They Come Back... for More 1998

Perlman, Itzhak (1945-) Fantasia 2000 1999; Music of the Heart 1999

Perlman, Rhea (1948-) Over Her Dead Body 1990; We're Back! A Dinosaur's Story 1993; Canadian Bacon 1995; Carpool 1996; Matilda 1996; Sunset Park 1996; Oliver's Ghost 2010; I'll See You in My Dreams 2015

Perlman, Ron (1950-) Quest for Fire 1981; The Ice Pirates 1984; The Name of the Rose 1986; Cronos 1992; Romeo Is Bleeding 1992; Sleepwalkers 1992; The Adventures of Huck Finn 1993; When the Bough Breaks 1993; Police Academy: Mission to Moscow 1994; The City of Lost Children 1995; The Island of Dr Moreau 1996; Alien: Resurrection 1997; Prince Valiant 1997; I Woke Up Early the Day I Died 1998; Happy, Texas 1999; Supreme Sanction 1999; Price of Glory 2000; Titan AE 2000; Enemy at the Gates 2001; Blade II 2002; Star Trek: Nemesis 2002; Hellboy 2004; Tarzan II 2005; Hellboy II: the Golden Army 2008; Mutant Chronicles 2008; Outlander 2008; Bunraku 2010; Season of the Witch 2010; Tangled 2010; Conan the Barbarian 2011; Drive 2011; Pacific Rim 2013; 13 Sins 2013; Book of Life 2014; Stonewall 2015

Pernel, Florence (1966-) Three Colours Blue 1993; The Cow and the President 2000

Perreau, Gigi (1941-) For Heaven's Sake 1950; Never a Dull Moment 1950; The Lady Pays Off 1951; Weekend with Father 1951; Has Anybody Seen My Gal? 1952; Dance with Me Henry 1956; There's Always Tomorrow 1956; The Cool and the Crazy 1958; Wild Heritage 1958; Girls' Town 1959

Perrey, Mireille (1904-1991) Madame de... 1953; The Umbrellas of Cherbourg 1964

Perri, Paul Delta Force 2 1990; Memoirs of an Invisible Man 1992

Perrier, Mireille (1959-) Boy Meets Girl 1984; Chocolat 1988; A World without Pity 1989; Toto Le Héros 1991; Point Blank 2010

Perrier, Olivier (1940-) Les Destinées Sentimentales 2000; Read My Lips 2001; Rivals 2007

Perrin, Jacques (1941-) Z 1968; The Magic Donkey 1970; Blanche 1971; Love Songs 1984; Cinema Paradiso 1988; Winged Migration 2001; L'Enfer 2005

Perrine, Valerie (1944-) Slaughterhouse-Five 1972; The Last American Hero 1973; Lenny 1974; WC Fields and Me 1976; Mr Billion 1977; Superman 1978; The Electric Horseman 1979; The Magician of Lublin 1979; Can't Stop the Music 1980; Superman II 1980; Agency 1981; The Border 1981; Water 1985; Maid to Order 1987; Sweet Bird of Youth 1989; Bright Angel 1990; Boiling Point 1993; Curtain Call 1997

Perrineau, Harold aka Perrineau Jr, Harold (1963-) Smoke 1995; Blood and Wine 1996; William Shakespeare's Romeo + Juliet 1996; The Edge 1997; The Best Man 1999; Woman on Top 2000; 28 Weeks Later 2007; Felon 2008; Justice 2011

Perrins, Leslie (1902-1962) Scotland Yard Mystery 1933; D'Ye Ken John Peel? 1934; Lord Edgware Dies 1934; Tudor Rose 1936; A Run for Your Money 1949

Perrot, François (1924-) Les Innocents aux Mains Sales 1975; Le Choc 1982; Life and Nothing But 1989; Merci la Vie 1991

Perry, Jeff (1955-) Hard Promises 1991; Kingfish: a Story of Huey P Long 1995

Perry, Joan (1911-1996) Meet Nero Wolfe 1936; Blind Alley 1939

Perry, John Bennett (1941-) Lipstick 1976; Fools Rush In 1997

Perry, Katy (1984-) Get Him to the Greek 2010; The Smurfs 2011; Katy Perry: Part of Me 2012; The Smurfs 2 2013; Brand: a Second Coming 2015

Perry, Linda (1912-2001) The Case of the Stuttering Bishop 1937; They Won't Forget 1937

Perry, Luke (1966-) Scorchers 1991; Buffy the Vampire Slayer 1992; 8 Seconds 1994; Normal Life 1996; American Strays 1996; The Fifth Element 1997; Storm 1999; The Enemy 2000; The Gunfighter's Pledge 2008; Goodnight for Justice 2011; The Beat beneath My Feet 2014

Perry, Matthew aka **Perry, Matthew L** (1969-) A Night in the Life of Jimmy Reardon 1988; Getting In 1994; Fools Rush In 1997; Almost Heroes 1998; Three to Tango 1999; The Whole Nine Yards 2000; Serving Sara 2002; The Whole Ten Yards 2004; The Triumph 2006; 17 Again 2009; Misery Loves Comedy 2015

Perry, Roger (1933-) Count Yorga, Vampire 1970; The Return of Count Yorga 1971; The Thing with Two Heads 1972

Perry, Tyler (1969-) Tyler Perry's Why Did I Get Married Too? 2010; Alex Cross 2012; Gone Girl 2014; Teenage Mutant Ninja Turtles - Out of the Shadows 2016

Persbrandt, Mikael (1963-) Dragonflies 2001; Maria Larsson's Everlasting Moments 2008; In a Better World 2010; The Salvation 2014

Perschy, Maria (1938-2004) The Password Is Courage 1962; Man's Favorite Sport? 1964; 633 Squadron 1964; The Desperate Ones 1967; Murders in the Rue Morgue 1971

Persky, Lisa Jane aka **Persky, Lisa** (1955-) The Great Santini 1979; Breathless 1983; The Sure Thing 1985; The Big Easy 1986; When Harry Met Sally... 1989; Coneheads 1993; Pontiac Moon 1994; Dead Funny 1995

Persoff, Nehemiah (1920-) The Wrong Man 1956; Men in War 1957; This Angry Age 1957; The Badlanders 1958; Al Capone 1959; Day of the Outlaw 1959; Green Mansions 1959; Never Steal Anything Small 1959; Some Like It Hot 1959; The Big Show 1961; The Comancheros 1961; The Hook 1962; A Global Affair 1964; The Girl Who Knew Too Much 1969; Mrs Pollifax - Spy 1970; FDR: The Last Year 1980; An American Tail 1986; An American Tail: Fievel Goes West 1991

Personnaz, Raphaël (1981-) The Princess of Montpensier 2010; Special Forces 2011; Marius 2012; Fanny 2013; The New Girlfriend 2014

Pertwee, Jon (1919-1996) Mr Drake's Duck 1950; Will Any Gentleman...? 1953; A Yank in Ermine 1955; Nearly a Nasty Accident 1961; Ladies Who Do 1963; Carry On Cowboy 1965; I've Gotta Horse 1965; Carry On Screaming 1966; The House That Dripped Blood 1970; Adventures of a Private Eye 1977; Wombling Free 1977; The Boys in Blue 1983; Carry On Columbus 1992

Pertwee, Sean (1964-) Dirty Weekend 1992; Leon the Pig Farmer 1992; Shopping 1993; ID 1994; Blue Juice 1995; Event Horizon 1997; Stiff Upper Lips 1997; Talos the Mummy 1997; Soldier 1998; Love, Honour and Obey 2000; 7 Days to Live 2000; Dog Soldiers 2001; The 51st State 2001; Equilibrium 2002; Goal! 2005; Greyfriars Bobby 2005; Wilderness 2006; Botched 2007; Dangerous Parking 2007; Doomsday 2008; Mutant Chronicles 2008; Four 2010; 4.3.2.1 2010; St George's Day 2012; The Seasoning House 2012

Perugorría, Jorge Strawberry and Chocolate 1993; Guantanamera 1995

Pesci, Joe (1943-) Death Collector 1976; Raging Bull 1980; Eureka 1982; I'm Dancing as Fast as I Can 1982; Easy Money 1983; Once upon a Time in America 1984; Man on Fire 1987; Moonwalker 1988; Catchfire 1989; Lethal Weapon 2 1989; Betsy's Wedding 1990; GoodFellas 1990; Home Alone 1990; JFK 1991; The Super 1991; Home Alone 2: Lost in New York 1992; Lethal Weapon 3 1992; My Cousin Vinny 1992; The Public Eye 1992; A Bronx Tale 1993; Jimmy Hollywood 1994; With Honors 1994; Casino 1995; 8 Heads in a Duffel Bag 1997; Gone Fishin' 1997; Lethal Weapon 4 1998; The Good Shepherd 2006

Pescow, Donna (1954-) Saturday Night Fever 1977; Rainbow 1978

Peters, Bernadette (1948-) Ace Eli and Rodger of the Skies 1973; Vigilante Force 1975; Silent Movie 1976; WC Fields and Me 1976; The Jerk 1979; Heartbeeps 1981; Pennies from Heaven 1981; Annie 1982; Pink Cadillac 1989; Slaves of New York 1989; Alice 1990; Impromptu 1991; Anastasia 1997; Beauty and the Beast: the Enchanted Christmas 1997; The Odyssey 1997; Rodgers & Hammerstein's Cinderella 1997; Prince Charming 2001; It Runs in the Family 2002; Living Proof 2008; Legends of Oz: Dorothy's Return 2013

Peters, Brock (1927-2005) Carmen Jones 1954; Porgy and Bess 1959; The L-Shaped Room 1962; To Kill a Mockingbird 1962; Heavens Above! 1963; Major Dundee 1965; The Pawnbroker 1965; The Incident 1967; Ace High 1968; Black Girl 1972;

Slaughter's Big Rip-Off 1973; Soylent Green 1973; Lost in the Stars 1974; Alligator II: the Mutation 1991; The Importance of Being Earnest 1992

Peters, Clarke (1952-) Silver Dream Racer 1980; Outland 1981; Mona Lisa 1986; Death Train 1993; Legacy: Black Ops 2010

Peters, Evan Never Back Down 2008; X-Men: Days of Future Past 2014

Peters, Jean (1926-2000) Captain from Castile 1947; It Happens Every Spring 1949; Anne of the Indies 1951; As Young as You Feel 1951; O Henry's Full House 1952; Viva Zapata! 1952; Wait 'til the Sun Shines, Nellie 1952; Niagara 1953; Pickup on South Street 1953; Apache 1954; Broken Lance 1954; Three Coins in the Fountain 1954; A Man Called Peter 1955

Peters, Kelly Jean Any Wednesday 1966; Little Big Man 1970; Pocket Money 1972; Ace Eli and Rodger of the Skies 1973; Witches' Brew 1979

Peters, Lauri Mr Hobbs Takes a Vacation 1962; Summer Holiday 1963; For Love of Ivy 1968

Peters, Ralph (1902-1959) You Belong to Me 1941; Meeting at Midnight 1944

Peters, Scott (1930-1994) Suicide Battalion 1958; The Girl Hunters 1963

Peters, Susan (1921-1952) The Big Shot 1942; Dr Gillespie's New Assistant 1942; Random Harvest 1942; Keep Your Powder Dry 1945

Peters, Werner (1918-1971) The Thousand Eyes of Dr Mabuse 1960; 36 Hours 1964; Dead Run 1967

Petersen, Colin (1946-) Smiley 1956; A Cry from the Streets 1957; The Scamp 1957

Petersen, William L aka **Petersen, William** (1953-) To Live and Die in LA 1985; Manhunter 1986; Amazing Grace and Chuck 1987; Cousins 1989; Young Guns II 1990; Hard Promises 1991; Passed Away 1992; Fear 1996; 12 Angry Men 1997; The Rat Pack 1998; The Contender 2000; The Skulls 2000; Seeking a Friend for the End of the World 2011

Peterson, Alan C Run 1991; Mary Higgins Clark's The Cradle Will Fall 2004

Peterson, Amanda (1971-2015) Explorers 1985; Can't Buy Me Love 1987; Listen to Me 1989

Peterson, Bob Monsters, Inc 2001; Up 2009

Peterson, Cassandra (1951-) Allan Quatermain and the Lost City of Gold 1987; Elvira, Mistress of the Dark 1988

Peterson, Dorothy (1900-1979) The Beast of the City 1932; Forbidden 1932; Payment Deferred 1932; The Country Doctor 1936; Confession 1937; Lillian Russell 1940; Too Many Husbands 1940

Peterson, Lenka (1925-) The Phenix City Story 1955; Black like Me 1964

Peterson, Marion Lapse of Memory 1992; For Better and for Worse 1993

Peterson, Paul (1945-) The Happiest Millionaire 1967; Journey to Shiloh 1967; A Time for Killing 1967

Peterson, Seth Captured 1998; Hard Ground 2003

Petit-Jacques, Isabelle The Girl on the Bridge 1999; L'Homme du Train 2002

Petit, Aurélia Les Diables 2002; The Science of Sleep 2005

Petrenko, Alexei (1938-) Agony 1975; The Barber of Siberia 1999

Petrie, Alistair Rush 2013; Vendetta 2013

Petrie, Hay (1895-1948) The Wandering Jew 1933; The Old Curiosity Shop 1935; Conquest of the Air 1936; The House of the Spaniard 1936; 21 Days 1937; Crimes at the Dark House 1939; Contraband 1940; Pastor Hall 1940; The Thief of Bagdad 1940; The Ghost of St Michael's 1941; The Great Mr Handel 1942; A Canterbury Tale 1944

Petrie, Howard (1906-1968) Walk Softly, Stranger 1949; Rocky Mountain 1950; Cattle Drive 1951; Pony Soldier 1952; The Wild North 1952; The Bounty Hunter 1954; Seven Brides for Seven Brothers 1954

Petrovitch, Michael Neither the Sea nor the Sand 1972; Turkey Shoot 1981

Petruzzi, Joe Dingo 1991; Paws 1997

Pettet, Joanna (1944-) The Group 1966; The Night of the Generals 1966; Casino Royale 1967; Robbery 1967; The Best House in London 1968; Blue 1968; Welcome to Arrow Beach 1974

Pettiet, Christopher (1976-2000) Horses and Champions 1994; Acts of Love 1995

Pettifer, Brian Heavenly Pursuits 1986; Donkeys 2010

Pettiford, Valarie Glitter 2001; Stomp the Yard 2006

Pettingell, Frank (1891-1966) Sing as We Go 1934; Sailing Along 1938; Busman's Honeymoon 1940; Gaslight 1940; The Goose Steps Out 1942; Gaiety George 1946; Value for Money 1955; Trial and Error 1962

Petty, Lori (1963-) Cadillac Man 1990; Point Break 1991; A League of Their Own 1992; Free Willy 1993; Poetic Justice 1993; In the Army Now 1994; The Glass Shield 1995; Tank Girl 1995; Relax... It's Just Sex 1998; Firetrap 2001

Petty, Tom (1950-) FM 1977; The Postman 1997

Pettyfer, Alex (1990-) Stormbreaker 2006; Wild Child 2008; Tormented 2009; Beastly 2010; I Am Number Four 2011; In Time 2011; Magic Mike 2012; Endless Love 2014; Elvis & Nixon 2016

Pevney, Joseph (1911-2008) Nocturne 1946; Body and Soul 1947; The Street with No Name 1948; Thieves' Highway 1949

Peyser, Penny (1951-) The Frisco Kid 1979; The In-Laws 1979

Pfeiffer, Dedee (1965-) Dangerously Close 1986; Vamp 1986; The Allnighter 1987; House III: The Horror Show 1989; Red Surf 1990; A Row of Crows 1991; Running Cool 1993; Up Close & Personal 1996; Seventeen and Missing 2006; Vickery's Wild Ride 2009

Pfeiffer, Michelle (1958-) Falling in Love Again 1980; Charlie Chan and the Curse of the Dragon Queen 1981; Grease 2 1982; Scarface 1983; Into the Night 1985; Ladyhawke 1985; Sweet Liberty 1986; Amazon Women on the Moon 1987; The Witches of Eastwick 1987; Dangerous Liaisons 1988; Married to the Mob 1988; Tequila Sunrise 1988; The Fabulous Baker Boys 1989; The Russia House 1990; Frankie & Johnny 1991; Batman Returns 1992; Love Field 1992; The Age of Innocence 1993; Wolf 1994; Dangerous Minds 1995; One Fine Day 1996; To Gillian on Her 37th Birthday 1996; Up Close & Personal 1996; A Thousand Acres 1997; The Prince of Egypt 1998; The Deep End of the Ocean 1999; A Midsummer Night's Dream 1999; The Story of Us 1999; What Lies Beneath 2000; I Am Sam 2001; White Oleander 2002; Sinbad: Legend of the Seven Seas 2003; Hairspray 2007; Stardust 2007; Chéri 2009; New Year's Eve 2011; Dark Shadows 2012; People like Us 2012; The Family 2013

Pflug, Jo Ann (1947-) MASH 1969; Catlow 1971; Where Does It Hurt? 1971

Pham, Linh-Dan Indochine 1991; The Beat That My Heart Skipped 2005

Phelan, Brian The Kitchen 1961; Four in the Morning 1965

Phelps, Peter (1960-) The Lighthorsemen 1987; Rough Diamonds 1994; The Square 2008

Pheto, Terry Tsotsi 2005; Catch a Fire 2006; A United Kingdom 2017

Phifer, Mekhi (1975-) Clockers 1995; High School High 1996; Soul Food 1997; I Still Know What You Did Last Summer 1998; A Lesson before Dying 1999; O 2001; 8 Mile 2002; Honey 2003; Slow Burn 2003; Dawn of the Dead 2004; This Christmas 2007

Philbin, John (1965-) Children of the Corn 1984; Return of the Living Dead 1984; North Shore 1987; Shy People 1987; Point Break 1991

Philbin, Mary (1903-1993) The Phantom of the Opera 1925; The Man Who Laughs 1928

Philbrook, James (1924-1982) Son of a Gunfighter 1964; The Thin Red Line 1964

Philipe, Gérard (1922-1959) Devil in the Flesh 1947; La Beauté du Diable 1949; Fanfan la Tulipe 1951; Les Belles de Nuit 1952; The Seven Deadly Sins 1952; The Proud Ones 1953; Royal Affairs in Versailles 1953; Knave of Hearts 1954; Le Rouge et le Noir 1954; Les Grandes Manoeuvres 1955; Montparnasse 19 1958; La Fièvre Monte à el Pao 1959; Les Liaisons Dangereuses 1959

Philippe, Andre (1927-2007) Alex in Wonderland 1970; Black Belt Jones 1974

Philipps, Busy (1979-) White Chicks 2004; Made of Honor 2008

Philips, Gina aka **Phillips, Gina** (1975-) Jeepers Creepers 2001; Stolen Innocence 2007

Philips, Lee (1927-1999) Peyton Place 1957; The Hunters 1958; Tess of the Storm Country 1960

Philips, Mary aka **Phillips, Mary** (1901-1975) A Farewell to Arms 1932; The Bride Wore Red 1937; Mannequin 1937; Capt Eddie 1945; Leave Her to Heaven 1945; Dear Ruth 1947; A Woman's Secret 1949

Philliber, John (1872-1944) It Happened Tomorrow 1944; Summer Storm 1944

Phillippe, Ryan (1974-) White Squall 1996; I Know What You Did Last Summer 1997; 54 1998; Homegrown 1998; Playing by Heart 1998; Cruel Intentions 1999; Antitrust 2000; Company Man 2000; The Way of the Gun 2000; Gosford Park 2001; Igby Goes Down 2002; The Inside 2003; Crash 2004; Breach 2006; Chaos 2006; Flags of Our Fathers 2006; Stop-Loss 2007; Franklyn 2008; MacGruber 2010; The Lincoln Lawyer 2011; Set Up 2011

Phillips, Bijou (1980-) Bully 2001; Octane 2003; The Door in the Floor 2004; Havoc 2005; Hostel: Part II 2007

Phillips, Bobbie (1972-) Back in Action 1993; Carnival of Souls 1999

Phillips, Chris Felix the Cat: the Movie 1989; Doug's 1st Movie 1999

Phillips, Chynna (1968-) Some Kind of Wonderful 1987; The Invisible Kid 1988

Phillips, Conrad (1930-2016) Circus of Horrors 1960; Sons and Lovers 1960; The Shadow of the Cat 1961; Dead Man's Evidence 1962; Don't Talk to Strange Men 1962; Impact 1963

Phillips, Eddie (1899-1969) The Thirteenth Guest 1932; Champagne Charlie 1944

Phillips, Ethan (1955-) Lean on Me 1989; Green Card 1990; The Island 2005

Phillips, Grace All the Vermeers in New York 1990; Truth or Consequences, NM 1997

Phillips, Gregory I Could Go On Singing 1963; I Start Counting 1970

Phillips, Jean (?-1970) Among the Living 1941; Dr Broadway 1942

Phillips (1), John (1915-1995) Floods of Fear 1958; Man in the Moon 1960; Romanoff and Juliet 1961; The Mummy's Shroud 1966

Phillips, Jonathan aka **Phillips, Johnny** (1963-) Killing Dad 1989; One for the Road 2003

Phillips, Julianne (1960-) Seven Hours to Judgment 1988; Fletch Lives 1989; Skin Deep 1989; Big Bully 1996

Phillips, Leslie (1924-) The Sound Barrier 1952; The Big Money 1956; Les Girls 1957; Just My Luck 1957; The Smallest Show on Earth 1957; I Was Monty's Double 1958; The Angry Hills 1959; Carry On Nurse 1959; Carry On Teacher 1959; The Man Who Liked Funerals 1959; The Navy Lark 1959; The Night We Dropped a Clanger 1959; This Other Eden 1959; Carry On Constable 1960; Doctor in Love 1960; Inn for Trouble 1960; No Kidding 1960; Please Turn Over 1960; Watch Your Stern 1960; In the Doghouse 1961; Raising the Wind 1961; Very Important Person 1961; Crooks Anonymous 1962; The Fast Lady 1963; Father Came Too 1963; You Must Be Joking! 1965; Doctor in Clover 1966; Maroc 7 1966; Some Will, Some Won't 1969; Doctor in Trouble 1970; The Magnificent Seven Deadly Sins 1971; Not Now Darling 1972; Don't Just Lie There, Say Something! 1973; Spanish Fly 1975; Not Now, Comrade 1976; Empire of the Sun 1987; Scandal 1988; King Ralph 1991; Carry On Columbus 1992; August 1995; The Canterville Ghost 1996; The Jackal 1997; Saving Grace 2000; Harry Potter and the Philosopher's Stone 2001; Lara Croft: Tomb Raider 2001; Thunderpants 2002; Churchill: the Hollywood Years 2004; Venus 2006; Is Anybody There? 2008

Phillips, Lou Diamond (1962-) La Bamba 1987; Dakota 1988; Stand and Deliver 1988; Young Guns 1988; Disorganized Crime 1989; Renegades 1989; The First Power 1990; A Show of Force 1990; Young Guns II 1990; Ambition 1991; The Dark Wind 1991; Shadow of the Wolf 1992; Sioux City 1994; Courage under Fire 1996; Another Day in Paradise 1998; The Big Hit 1998; Bats 1999; Brokedown Palace 1999; A Better Way to Die 2000; Hangman 2000; Picking Up the Pieces 2000; Supernova 2000; Stark Raving Mad 2002; Hollywood Homicide 2003; The Trail to Hope Rose 2004; Murder at the Presidio 2005; Lone Rider 2008

Phillips, Mackenzie (1959-) American Graffiti 1973; More American Graffiti 1979; Love Child 1982

Phillips, Michelle (1944-) The Last Movie 1971; Dillinger 1973; Valentino 1977; Bloodline 1979; The Man with Bogart's Face 1980; Scissors 1991

Phillips, Nathan (1980-) Wolf Creek 2005; Snakes on a Plane 2006; Chernobyl Diaries 2012; These Final Hours 2013

Phillips, Robin (1942-2015) Decline and Fall... of a Birdwatcher 1968; Two Gentlemen Sharing 1969

Phillips, Sally (1970-) Birthday Girl 2001; Bridget Jones's Diary 2001; Gladiatress 2002; Tooth 2003; Bridget Jones: the Edge of Reason 2004; The Decoy Bride 2011; Set the Thames on Fire 2015; Bridget Jones's Baby 2016

Phillips, Sian (1934-) Becket 1964; Young Cassidy 1965; Goodbye, Mr Chips 1969; Laughter in the Dark 1969; Murphy's War 1971; Under Milk Wood 1971; Clash of the Titans 1981; The Doctor and the Devils 1985; Valmont 1989; The Age of Innocence 1993; House of America 1996; The Gigolos 2006

Phillips, Simon Jack Said 2009; The Last Seven 2010

Phillips, William "Bill" aka **Phillips, William** (1908-1957) Red Light 1949; Cavalry Scout 1951

Philpotts, Ambrosine (1912-1980) Up in the World 1956; The Duke Wore Jeans 1958; Room at the Top 1958; Expresso Bongo 1959; Two and Two Make Six 1961

Phipps, Max (1939-2000) Thirst 1979; Savage Islands 1983; Sky Pirates 1986

Phipps, Nicholas (1913-1980) Elizabeth of Ladymead 1948; Spring in Park Lane 1948; Maytime in Mayfair 1949; Mad about Men 1954; All for Mary 1955; The Navy Lark 1959

Phipps, William (1922-) Crossfire 1947; Belle Starr's Daughter 1948; Cinderella 1950; Five 1951; Rose of Cimarron 1952; The War of the Worlds 1953; Black Gold 1962

Phoenix, Joaquin aka **Phoenix, Leaf** (1974-) SpaceCamp 1986; Russkies 1987; Parenthood 1989; To Die For 1995; Inventing the Abbotts 1997; U Turn 1997; Clay Pigeons 1998; Return to Paradise 1998; 8mm 1999; Gladiator 2000; Quills 2000; The Yards 2000; Buffalo Soldiers 2001; It's All about Love 2003; Signs 2002; Brother Bear 2003; Hotel Rwanda 2004; Ladder 49 2004; The Village 2004; Walk the Line 2005; We Own the Night 2007; Two Lovers 2008; I'm Still Here 2010; The Master 2012; Her 2013; The Immigrant 2013; Inherent Vice 2014; Irrational Man 2015; Unity 2015

Phoenix, Rain (1973-) Even Cowgirls Get the Blues 1993; O 2001; Stranger Inside 2001

Phoenix, River (1970-1993) Explorers 1985; Surviving 1985; The Mosquito Coast 1986; Stand by Me 1986; Little Nikita 1988; A Night in the Life of Jimmy Reardon 1988; Running on Empty 1988; Indiana Jones and the Last Crusade 1989; I Love You to Death 1990; Dogfight 1991; My Own Private Idaho 1991; Sneakers 1992; The Thing Called Love 1993

Phoenix, Summer (1978-) Russkies 1987; SLC Punk! 1999; Dinner Rush 2000; Esther Kahn 2000; The Believer 2001; The Laramie Project 2002; Suzie Gold 2003

Pholdee, Jesdaporn (1977-) The Iron Ladies 2000; The Eye 2 2004

Pialat, Maurice (1925-2003) Que la Bête Meure 1969; To Our Loves 1984; Sous le Soleil de Satan 1987

Piazza, Ben (1934-1991) The Hanging Tree 1959; Tell Me That You Love Me, Junie Moon 1970; The Bad News Bears 1976; I Never Promised You a Rose Garden 1977; Guilty by Suspicion 1990

Piazza, Vincent Rocket Science 2007; Jersey Boys 2014

Pica, Tina (1884-1968) Bread, Love & Dreams 1953; Yesterday, Today and Tomorrow 1963

Picardo, Robert (1953-) The Howling 1981; Legend 1985; Munchies 1987; Jack's Back 1988; Gremlins 2: the New Batch 1990; Motorama 1991; Wagons East! 1994; Star Trek: First Contact 1996

Piccoli, Michel (1925-) French Cancan 1955; Death in the Garden 1956; Le Doulos 1962; Le Mépris 1963; The Diary of a Chambermaid 1964; Lady L 1965; Masquerade 1965; The Sleeping Car Murders 1965; Les Créatures 1966; The Game Is Over 1966; La Guerre Est Finie 1966; Belle de Jour 1967; Danger: Diabolik 1967; La Chamade 1968; The Things of Life 1969; Topaz 1969; Ten Days' Wonder 1971; The Discreet Charm of the Bourgeoisie 1972; La Grande Bouffe 1973; Les Noces Rouges 1973; Le Fantôme de la Liberté 1974; Vincent, François, Paul and the Others 1974; Mado 1976; Atlantic City, USA 1980; A Strange Affair 1981; Passion 1982; La Nuit de Varennes 1983; Dangerous Moves 1984; Success Is the Best Revenge 1984; Death in a French Garden 1985; Mauvais Sang 1986; Le Paltoquet 1986; Milou en Mai 1989;

Martha and I 1990; La Belle Noiseuse 1991; Les Cent et Une Nuits 1995; Beaumarchais l'Insolent 1996; Généalogies d'un Crime 1997; Passion in the Desert 1998. Rien sur Robert 1998; I'm Going Home 2001; Belle Toujours 2006; Gardens in Autumn 2006; We Have a Pope 2011; Holy Motors 2012

Piccolo, Ottavia (1949-) The Widow Couderc 1971; Zorro 1975; Mado 1976

Picerni, Paul (1922-2011) Breakthrough 1950; Force of Arms 1951; Operation Pacific 1951; Mara Maru 1952; House of Wax 1953; Drive a Crooked Road 1954; To Hell and Back 1955; The Big Caper 1957

Pichel, Irving (1851-1954) An American Tragedy 1931; Madame Butterfly 1932; Westward Passage 1932; British Agent 1934; Special Agent 1935; Dracula's Daughter 1936; The Battle of Midway 1942; The Moon Is Down 1943

Pickard, Helena ('900-1959) Nell Gwyn 1934; The Lady with the Lamp 1951

Pickard, John (1913-1993) Hellgate 1952; Black Horse Canyon 1954; The Lone Ranger 1956; Rage 1999

Pickens Jr, James Dead Presidents 1995; Rocketman 1997; Just Wright 2010

Pickens, Slim (1919-1983) Rocky Mountain 1950; The Outcast 1954; Santa Fe Passage 1955; The Great Locomotive Chase 1956; Gunsight Ridge 1957; The Sheepman 1958; Escort West 1959; One-Eyed Jacks 1961; A Thunder of Drums 1961; Dr Strangelove, or How I Learned to Stop Worrying and Love the Bomb 1963; The Glory Guys 1965; In Harm's Way 1965; Up from the Beach 1965; Stagecoach 1966; The Flim-Flam Man 1967; Rough Night in Jericho 1967; Will Penny 1967; Eighty Steps to Jonah 1969; The Ballad of Cable Hogue 1970; The Deserter 1971. The Honkers 1971; The Cowboys 1972; The Getaway 1972; Ginger in the Morning 1973; Pat Garrett and Billy the Kid 1973; The Apple Dumpling Gang 1974; Blazing Saddles 1974; Rancho Deluxe 1975; White Line Fever 1975; Mr Billion 1977; The White Buffalo 1977; Beyond the Poseidon Adventure 1979; 1941 1979; Honeysuckle Rose 1980; Tom Horn 1980; The Howling 1981

Pickering, Adrienne Shutter 2008; The Reef 2010

Pickett, Cindy (1947-) Night Games 1979; Ferris Bueller's Day Off 1986; Hot to Trot 1988; DeepStar Six 1989; Crooked Hearts 1991; Sleepwalkers 1992

Pickford, Mary (1893-1979) The Pride of the Clan 1917; Rebecca of Sunnybrook Farm 1917; A Romance of the Redwoods 1917; Stella Maris 1918; Daddy Long Legs 1919; Pollyanna 1920; Little Lord Fauntleroy 1921; Tess of the Storm Country 1922; Rosita 1923; Little Annie Rooney 1925; Sparrows 1926; The Gaucho 1927; My Best Girl 1927; Coquette 1929; The Taming of the Shrew 1929; Secrets 1933

Pickles, Carolyn Tess 1979; Bonobo 2013

Pickles, Christina (1935-) Seizure 1974; Legends of the Fall 1994

Pickles, Vivian (1933-) Play Dirty 1969; Sunday, Bloody Sunday 1971; Harold and Maude 1972

Pickles, Wilfred (1904-1978) Billy Liar 1963; The Family Way 1966; For the Love of Ada 1972

Pickup, Ronald (1940-) Three Sisters 1970; The Thirty-Nine Steps 1978; Nijinsky 1980; Eleni 1985; The Mission 1986; Testimony 1987; Danny, the Champion of the World 1989; Bethune: the Making of a Hero 1990; Shogun Warrior 1991; Bring Me the Head of Mavis Davis 1997; Greyfriars Bobby 2005; The Best Exotic Marigold Hotel 2011

Picon, Molly (1898-1992) Come Blow Your Horn 1963; Fiddler on the Roof 1971; For Pete's Sake 1974

Piddock, Jim (1956-) She Creature 2001; The Dark Is Rising 2007; The Cold Light of Day 2012

Pidgeon, Rebecca (1963-) The Dawning 1988; Homicide 1991; The Spanish Prisoner 1997; The Winslow Boy 1999; State and Main 2000; Heist 2001; Edmond 2005; Shopgirl 2005; Phil Spector 2013

Pidgeon, Walter (1897-1984) Rockabye 1932; The Kiss before the Mirror 1933; Big Brown Eyes 1936; Fatal Lady 1936; Man-Proof 1937; Saratoga 1937; The Girl of the Golden West 1938; Listen, Darling 1938; The Shopworn Angel 1938; Too Hot to Handle 1938; Nick Carter, Master Detective 1939;

Dark Command 1940; Flight Command 1940; The House across the Bay 1940; It's a Date 1940; Phantom Raiders 1940; Sky Murder 1940; Blossoms in the Dust 1941; Design for Scandal 1941; How Green Was My Valley 1941; Man Hunt 1941; Mrs Miniver 1942; White Cargo 1942; Madame Curie 1943; Mrs Parkington 1944; Week-End at the Waldorf 1945; Holiday in Mexico 1946; The Secret Heart 1946; If Winter Comes 1947; Command Decision 1948; Julia Misbehaves 1948; The Forsyte Saga 1949; The Red Danube 1949; The Miniver Story 1950; Calling Bulldog Drummond 1951; Quo Vadis 1951; Soldiers Three 1951; The Bad and the Beautiful 1952; Million Dollar Mermaid 1952; Dream Wife 1953; Scandal at Scourie 1953; Deep in My Heart 1954; Executive Suite 1954; The Last Time I Saw Paris 1954; Men of the Fighting Lady 1954; Hit the Deck 1955; Forbidden Planet 1956; The Rack 1956; These Wilder Years 1956; Voyage to the Bottom of the Sea 1961; Advise and Consent 1962; Big Red 1962; Cinderella 1965; How I Spent My Summer Vacation 1967; Warning Shot 1967; Funny Girl 1968; Skyjacked 1972; Harry in Your Pocket 1973; The Neptune Factor 1973; The Lindbergh Kidnapping Case 1976; Two-Minute Warning 1976

Piéplu, Claude (1923-) The Discreet Charm of the Bourgeoisie 1972; Les Noces Rouges 1973; Le Paltoquet 1986; Asterix and Obelix Take On Caesar 1999

Piéral, Pierre aka **Piéral** (1923-2003) Eternal Love 1943; That Obscure Object of Desire 1977

Pierce, Bradley aka **Pierce, Bradley Michael** (1982-) Beauty and the Beast 1991; Jumanji 1995; The Borrowers 1997

Pierce, David Hyde aka **Pierce, David** (1959-) The Fisher King 1991; Little Man Tate 1991; Sleepless in Seattle 1993; Wolf 1994; Nixon 1995; A Bug's Life 1998; Isn't She Great 1999; The Mating Habits of the Earthbound Human 1999; Osmosis Jones 2001; Full Frontal 2002; Treasure Planet 2002; Down with Love 2003

Pierce, Justin (1975-2000) kids 1995; Next Friday 1999

Pierce, Maggie (1931-2010) Tales of Terror 1962; The Fastest Guitar Alive 1966

Pierce, Norman The Crimes of Stephen Hawke 1936; Saloon Bar 1940

Pierce, Wendell (1962-) It Could Happen to You 1994; Hackers 1995; The 24 Hour Woman 1999; Stay Alive 2006; Parker 2013; The Runner 2015

Pierlot, Francis (1875-1955) The Affairs of Susan 1945; Bewitched 1945; Anne of the Indies 1951

Pieroni, Ania The House by the Cemetery 1981; Tenebrae 1982

Pierrot, Frédéric (1960-) Land and Freedom 1995; Captains of April 2000; The Girl from Paris 2001; Monsieur N 2003; I've Loved You So Long 2008; Let's Talk about the Rain 2008; Sarah's Key 2010; Jeune & Jolie 2013

Pierson, Geoff Sleeping Dogs Lie. 2006; World's Greatest Dad 2009; Something Borrowed 2011

Pieterse, Sasha Good Luck Chuck 2007; GBF 2013

Pigaut, Roger (1919-1989) The Light across the Street 1956; Une Histoire Simple 1978

Pigg, Alexandra Letter to Brezhnev 1985; A Chorus of Disapproval 1988

Pigott-Smith, Tim (1946-) Sweet William 1980; Clash of the Titans 1981; Escape to Victory 1981; The Hunchback of Notre Dame 1982; Dead Man's Folly 1986; The Remains of the Day 1993; Bloody Sunday 2001; The Four Feathers 2002; Johnny English 2003; V for Vendetta 2005

Pigott, Tempe (1884-1962) The Black Pirate 1926; Dr Jekyll and Mr Hyde 1931; The Devil Is a Woman 1935

Pike, John (1945-) The Cat Gang 1959; Live It Up 1963; Be My Guest 1965

Pike, Rosamund (1979-) Die Another Day 2002; The Libertine 2004; Doom 2005; Pride & Prejudice 2005; Fracture 2007; Fugitive Pieces 2007; An Education 2008; Surrogates 2009; Barney's Version 2010; Jackboots on Whitehall 2010; Made in Dagenham 2010; The Big Year 2011; Johnny English Reborn 2011; Jack Reacher 2012; Wrath of the Titans 2012; A Long Way Down 2013; The World's End 2013; Gone Girl 2014; Hector and the Search for Happiness 2014; What We Did on Our Holiday 2014; Return to Sender 2015; A United Kingdom 2017

Pilavin, Barbara (1923-2005) The Voyage 1974; Frightmare 1981

Pilbeam, Nova (1919-2015) The Man Who Knew Too Much 1934; Young and Innocent 1937; Cheer Boys Cheer 1939; Pastor Hall 1940; Yellow Canary 1943; Counterblast 1948; The Three Weird Sisters 1948

Pileggi, Mitch (1952-) Shocker 1989; The X-Files 1998

Pilger, John The War on Democracy 2007; Utopia 2013

Pilkington, Lorraine (1975-) The Miracle 1990; The Disappearance of Finbar 1996; Last of the High Kings 1996; Human Traffic 1999; My Kingdom 2001; What Richard Did 2012

Pill, Alison (1985-) No Higher Love 1999; Midwives 2001; Pieces of April 2002; Confessions of a Teenage Drama Queen 2004; Dear Wendy 2004; Dan in Real Life 2007; Milk 2008; Scott Pilgrim vs the World 2010; Goon 2011; Cooties 2014

Pillet, Marie Before Sunset 2004; My Best Friend 2006; 2 Days in Paris 2006

Pilmark, Soren (1955-) The Kingdom 1994; King's Game 2004; The Keeper of Lost Causes 2013

Pilon, Daniel (1940-) Malpertuis 1971; Brannigan 1975; Shoot 'Em Up 2007

Pinal, Silvia (1931-) Viridiana 1961; The Exterminating Angel 1962; Simon of the Desert 1965; Shark! 1969

Pinchak, Jimmy "Jax" Hostage 2004; All I Want for Christmas 2007

Pinchot, Bronson (1959-) Risky Business 1983; Beverly Hills Cop 1984; Blame It on the Bellboy 1992; True Romance 1993; Beverly Hills Cop III 1994; Napoleon 1995; Courage under Fire 1996

Pine, Chris (1980-) The Princess Diaries 2: Royal Engagement 2004; Blind Dating 2006; Just My Luck 2006; Surrender Dorothy 2006; Bottle Shock 2008; Carriers 2008; Star Trek 2009; Unstoppable 2010; People like Us 2012; Rise of the Guardians 2012; This Means War 2012; Jack Ryan: Shadow Recruit 2013; Star Trek into Darkness 2013; Horrible Bosses 2 2014; Into the Woods 2014; The Finest Hours 2015; Hell or High Water 2016; Star Trek Beyond 2016; Wonder Woman 2017

Pine, Larry Anna 1987; Plain Clothes 1988; Vanya on 42nd Street 1994; Sunday 1997; The Clearing 2004

Pine, Phillip (1920-2006) Men in War 1957; Murder by Contract 1958

Pine, Robert (1941-) Munster, Go Home! 1966; The Young Warriors 1967; One Little Indian 1973; The Bears and I 1974; Empire of the Ants 1977; The Apple Dumpling Gang Rides Again 1979; Red Eye 2005

Pinette, John (1964-2014) Reckless Kelly 1993; Simon Sez 1999

Pink aka **Moore, Alecia** Get Him to the Greek 2010; Happy Feet Two 2011; Thanks for Sharing 2012

Pinkett Smith, Jada aka **Pinkett, Jada** (1971-) Menace II Society 1993; Jason's Lyric 1994; A Low Down Dirty Shame 1994; Tales from the Crypt: Demon Knight 1995; If These Walls Could Talk 1996; The Nutty Professor 1996; Set It Off 1996; Scream 2 1997; Return to Paradise 1998; Woo 1998; Bamboozled 2000; Ali 2001; The Matrix Reloaded 2003; The Matrix Revolutions 2003; Collateral 2004; Madagascar 2005; Reign over Me 2007; Madagascar: Escape 2 Africa 2008; The Women 2008; Madagascar 3: Europe's Most Wanted 2012; Magic Mike XXL 2015

Pinon, Dominique (1955-) Diva 1981; The Moon in the Gutter 1983; The Legend of the Holy Drinker 1988; Delicatessen 1990; The City of Lost Children 1995; Alien: Resurrection 1997; Amélie 2001; Micmacs 2009; Morris: a Life with Bells On 2009; My Old Lady 2014; The Price of Desire 2015

Pinsent, Gordon (1930-) Colossus: the Forbin Project 1969; Blacula 1972; Newman's Law 1974; Who Has Seen the Wind 1977; Silence of the North 1981; Pippi Longstocking 1997; The Shipping News 2001; Saint Ralph 2004; Ambulance Girl 2005; Away from Her 2006; The Grand Seduction 2013

Pinsent, Leah aka **Pinsent, Leah King** (1968-) Bay Boy 1984; April Fool's Day 1986

Pintea, Adrian Diplomatic Siege 1999; Youth without Youth 2007

Pinter, Harold (1930-2008) The Servant 1963; Accident 1967; The Rise and Rise of Michael Rimmer 1970; Mojo 1998; Mansfield Park 1999; The Tailor of Panama 2000; Wit 2001; Sleuth 2007

Pinto, Freida (1984-) Slumdog Millionaire 2008; Miral 2010; You Will Meet a Tall Dark Stranger 2010; Black

Gold 2011; Immortals 2011; Rise of the Planet of the Apes 2011; Trishna 2011; Desert Dancer 2014; Knight of Cups 2015

Pinza, Ezio (1893-1957) Mr Imperium 1951; Tonight We Sing 1953

Piper, Billie (1982-) The Calcium Kid 2003; Spirit Trap 2004; Things to Do before You're 30 2004; City of Tiny Lights 2016

Piper, Frederick (1902-1979) In Which We Serve 1942; San Demetrio London 1943; Johnny Frenchman 1945; Hue and Cry 1947; The October Man 1947; Brandy for the Parson 1951; Escape Route 1952; Home at Seven 1952; Hunted 1952; The Monster of Highgate Ponds 1961; Only Two Can Play 1961

Piper, Roddy aka **Piper, "Rowdy" Roddy** (1954-2015) Hell Comes to Frogtown 1988; They Live 1988; Back in Action 1993

Pipes, Leah Odd Girl Out 2005; Sorority Row 2009

Pirri, Jim Ring of Steel 1994; And the Beat Goes On: the Sonny and Cher Story 1999

Piscopo, Joe (1951-) Johnny Dangerously 1984; Wise Guys 1986; Dead Heat 1988; Huck and the King of Hearts 1993; The Bomber Boys 1995; Two-Bits and Pepper 1995; Bartleby 2000

Pisier, Marie-France (1944-2011) Love at Twenty 1962; Trans-Europ-Express 1966; Celine and Julie Go Boating 1974; Cousin, Cousine 1975; The Other Side of Midnight 1977; The Brontë Sisters 1979; French Postcards 1979; Love on the Run 1979; Chanel Solitaire 1981; The Hot Touch 1982; Time Regained 1999; Inside Paris 2006

Pistilli, Luigi (1930-1996) Death Rides a Horse 1967; Bay of Blood 1971

Pisu, Mario (1910-1976) 8½ 1963; Juliet of the Spirits 1965; The Looters 1966

Pitagora, Paola (1942-) Fists in the Pocket 1965; The Devil's Advocate 1977

Pitarresi, Maria Ca Commence Aujourd'hui 1999; Laissez-passer 2001

Pithey, Wensley (1914-1993) Kill Me Tomorrow 1957; The Boys 1961; The Knack... and How to Get It 1965

Pitillo, Maria (1965-1993) Bye Bye Love 1995; Frank and Jesse 1995; Dear God 1996; Godzilla 1997; Something to Believe In 1997

Pitoeff, Sacha (1920-1990) Anastasia 1956; Last Year at Marienbad 1961

Pitoniak, Anne aka **Pitoniak, Ann** (1922-2007) The Survivors 1983; Agnes of God 1985; Best Seller 1987; Housekeeping 1987; The Wizard of Loneliness 1988; Where the Money Is 2000

Pitt, Brad (1963-) Cutting Class 1989; Happy Together 1989; Across the Tracks 1990; The Image 1990; He Said, She Said 1991; Johnny Suede 1991; Thelma & Louise 1991; Cool World 1992; A River Runs through It 1992; Kalifornia 1993; True Romance 1993; The Favor 1994; Interview with the Vampire: the Vampire Chronicles 1994; Legends of the Fall 1994; Se7en 1995; Twelve Monkeys 1995; Sleepers 1996; The Devil's Own 1997; Seven Years in Tibet 1997; Meet Joe Black 1998; Being John Malkovich 1999; Fight Club 1999; Snatch 2000; The Mexican 2001; Ocean's Eleven 2001; Spy Game 2001; Sinbad: Legend of the Seven Seas 2003; Ocean's Twelve 2004; Troy 2004; Mr & Mrs Smith 2005; Babel 2006; The Assassination of Jesse James by the Coward Robert Ford 2007; Ocean's Thirteen 2007; Burn after Reading 2008; The Curious Case of Benjamin Button 2008; Inglourious Basterds 2009; Megamind 2010; The Tree of Life 2010; Happy Feet Two 2011; Moneyball 2011; Killing Them Softly 2012; The Counsellor 2013; 12 Years a Slave 2013; World War Z 2013; Fury 2014; The Big Short 2015; By the Sea 2015

Pitt, Chris Lionheart 1986; The Lair of the White Worm 1988

Pitt, Ingrid (1937-2010) Countess Dracula 1970; The House That Dripped Blood 1970; The Vampire Lovers 1970; The Wicker Man 1973

Pitt, Michael (1981-) Finding Forrester 2000; Bully 2001; Hedwig and the Angry Inch 2001; Murder by Numbers 2002; The Dreamers 2003; Last Days 2004; Silk 2007; Funny Games US 2008; I Origins 2014; Ghost in the Shell 2017

Pitts, ZaSu (1894-1963) Rebecca of Sunnybrook Farm 1917; Greed 1925; The Wedding March 1928; Monte Carlo 1930; Bad Sister 1931; Back Street 1932; Blondie of the Follies 1932; Make Me a Star 1932; The Man I Killed 1932; Shopworn 1932; Westward Passage

1932; Hello Sister! 1933; Meet the Baron 1933; Dames 1934; The Gay Bride 1934; Mrs Wiggs of the Cabbage Patch 1934; Sing and Like It 1934; Ruggles of Red Gap 1935; The Plot Thickens 1936; Eternally Yours 1939; Naughty but Nice 1939; Nurse Edith Cavell 1939; It All Came True 1940; No, No, Nanette 1940; Let's Face It 1943; Life with Father 1947; Francis 1949; Denver & Rio Grande 1952; Francis Joins the WACS 1954; The Gazebo 1959; The Thrill of It All 1963

Piven, Jeremy (1965-) Judgment Night 1993; 12:01 1993; PCU 1994; Twogether 1994; Dr Jekyll and Ms Hyde 1995; Don King: Only in America 1997; Music from Another Room 1998; Phoenix 1998; Very Bad Things 1998; The Family Man 2000; Black Hawk Down 2001; Serendipity 2001; Old School 2003; Runaway Jury 2003; Chasing Liberty 2004; Two for the Money 2005; Keeping Up with the Steins 2006; Smokin' Aces 2006; The Kingdom 2007; RocknRolla 2008; The Goods: Live Hard Sell Hard 2009; SPYkids 4: All the Time in the World 2011; The Pirates! in an Adventure with Scientists! 2012; So Undercover 2012; Entourage 2015

Place, Mary Kay (1947-) New York, New York 1977; Starting Over 1979; Act of Love 1980; Modern Problems 1981; The Big Chill 1983; Explorers 1985; Smooth Talk 1985; A New Life 1988; Bright Angel 1990; Crazy from the Heart 1991; Captain Ron 1992; Citizen Ruth 1996; Eye of God 1997; John Grisham's The Rainmaker 1997; Pecker 1998; Being John Malkovich 1999; Human Nature 2001; My First Mister 2001; The Safety of Objects 2001; Sweet Home Alabama 2002; Silver City 2004; Lonesome Jim 2005; City of Ember 2008; Smashed 2012; I'll See You in My Dreams 2015

Placido, Michele (1946-) Three Brothers 1980; Big Business 1988; The Caiman 2006

Placido, Violante Fade to Black 2006; The American 2010; Ghost Rider: Spirit of Vengeance 2012

Plana, Tony (1953-) Salvador 1986; Disorderlies 1987; Romero 1989; Havana 1990; Why Me? 1990; One Good Cop 1991; Live Wire 1992; Half Past Dead 2002

Planer, Nigel (1955-) The Supergrass 1985; Eat the Rich 1987; Carry On Columbus 1992; Clockwork Mice 1994; The Wind in the Willows 1996

Platt, Ben Pitch Perfect 2012; Ricki and the Flash 2015

Platt, Edward aka **Platt, Edward C** (1916-1974) Backlash 1956; Rock, Pretty Baby 1956; House of Numbers 1957; The Gift of Love 1958; The High Cost of Loving 1958; Atlantis, the Lost Continent 1960

Platt, Howard TR Baskin 1971; Three the Hard Way 1974

Platt, Louise (1915-2003) I Met My Love Again 1938; Spawn of the North 1938; Stagecoach 1939; Tell No Tales 1939

Platt, Marc (1913-2014) Tonight and Every Night 1945; Down to Earth 1947; Seven Brides for Seven Brothers 1954

Platt, Oliver (1960-) Working Girl 1988; Flatliners 1990; Beethoven 1992; Midnight Sting 1992; Benny & Joon 1993; Indecent Proposal 1993; The Temp 1993; The Three Musketeers 1993; Funny Bones 1994; Tall Tale 1994; The Infiltrator 1995; Executive Decision 1996; A Time to Kill 1996; Dangerous Beauty 1997; Doctor Dolittle 1998; The Impostors 1998; Simon Birch 1998; Bicentennial Man 1999; Lake Placid 1999; Three to Tango 1999; Gun Shy 2000; Ready to Rumble 2000; Don't Say a Word 2001; Ash Wednesday 2002; Hope Springs 2002; Liberty Stands Still 2002; Pieces of April 2003; Kinsey 2004; Casanova 2005; The Ice Harvest 2005; Frost/Nixon 2008; 2012 2009; Year One 2009; Letters to Juliet 2010; Love & Other Drugs 2010; Please Give 2010; The Oranges 2011; X-Men: First Class 2011; Ginger & Rosa 2012; Lucky Them 2013

Playfair, Nigel (1874-1934) Lady Windermere's Fan 1916; Crime on the Hill 1933

Playten, Alice (1947-2011) Legend 1985; Felix the Cat: the Movie 1989

Plaza, Aubrey (1984-) Safety Not Guaranteed 2012; The To Do List 2013; Life after Beth 2014; Playing It Cool 2014; Dirty Grandpa 2016; Mike and Dave Need Wedding Dates 2016

Plaza, Begona (1966-) Maid to Order 1987; Delta Force 2 1990

Pleasence, Angela (1941-) From beyond the Grave 1973; The Godsend

1980; A Christmas Carol 1984; The Favour, the Watch and the Very Big Fish 1991; The Gigolos 2006

Pleasence, Donald (1919-1995) The Beachcomber 1954; Orders Are Orders 1954; 1984 1955; Value for Money 1955; The Black Tent 1956; The Man in the Sky 1956; Barnacle Bill 1957; Manuela 1957; A Tale of Two Cities 1957; The Man Inside 1958; The Flesh and the Fiends 1959; Hell Is a City 1959; Look Back in Anger 1959; The Shakedown 1959; Circus of Horrors 1960; The Hands of Orlac 1960; Killers of Kilimanjaro 1960; No Love for Johnnie 1960; Sons and Lovers 1960; Suspect 1960; Spare the Rod 1961; What a Carve Up! 1961; The Wind of Change 1961; Dr Crippen 1962; The Inspector 1962; The Caretaker 1963; The Great Escape 1963; The Greatest Story Ever Told 1965; The Hallelujah Trail 1965; Cul-de-Sac 1966; Eye of the Devil 1966; Fantastic Voyage 1966; The Night of the Generals 1966; Will Penny 1967; You Only Live Twice 1967; The Madwoman of Chaillot 1969; Soldier Blue 1970; Wake in Fright 1970; Kidnapped 1971; THX 1138 1971; Death Line 1972; Henry VIII and His Six Wives 1972; The Jerusalem File 1972; From beyond the Grave 1973; Malachi's Cove 1973; The Mutations 1973; Barry McKenzie Holds His Own 1974; The Black Windmill 1974; The Count of Monte Cristo 1974; Escape to Witch Mountain 1975; Hearts of the West 1975; I Don't Want to Be Born 1975; The Eagle Has Landed 1976; The Last Tycoon 1976; Trial by Combat 1976; Blood Relatives 1977; Oh, God! 1977; Telefon 1977; Tomorrow Never Comes 1977; The Uncanny 1977; Halloween 1978; Power Play 1978; Sgt Pepper's Lonely Hearts Club Band 1978; All Quiet on the Western Front 1979; Dracula 1979; Jaguar Lives! 1979; The Monster Club 1980; Escape from New York 1981; Halloween II 1981; Race for the Yankee Zephyr 1981; Witness for the Prosecution 1982; Where Is Parsifal? 1983; The Ambassador 1984; A Breed Apart 1984; Warrior Queen 1986; Ground Zero 1987; Prince of Darkness 1987; Vampire in Venice 1987; Halloween 4: the Return of Michael Myers 1988; Hanna's War 1988; Phantom of Death 1988; Halloween 5: the Revenge of Michael Myers 1989; River of Death 1989; Buried Alive 1990; Shadows and Fog 1991; The Hour of the Pig 1993; Halloween 6: the Curse of Michael Myers 1995

Plemons, Jesse Like Mike 2002; Black Mass 2015

Pleshette, John (1942-) Micki & Maude 1984; Eye of the Stranger 1993

Pleshette, Suzanne (1937-2008) The Geisha Boy 1958; Forty Pounds of Trouble 1962; Rome Adventure 1962; The Birds 1963; A Distant Trumpet 1964; Fate Is the Hunter 1964; Youngblood Hawke 1964; Nevada Smith 1966; The Ugly Dachshund 1966; The Adventures of Bullwhip Griffin 1967; Blackbeard's Ghost 1967; The Power 1968; Suppose They Gave a War and Nobody Came? 1970; Support Your Local Gunfighter 1971; The Shaggy DA 1976; Oh God! Book II 1980; The Lion King II: Simba's Pride 1998; Spirited Away 2001

Plimpton, George (1927-2003) Beyond the Law 1968; Volunteers 1985; Little Man Tate 1991; Just Visiting 2001

Plimpton, Martha (1970-) The River Rat 1984; The Goonies 1985; The Mosquito Coast 1986; Shy People 1987; Another Woman 1988; Running on Empty 1988; Stars and Bars 1988; Parenthood 1989; Stanley & Iris 1989; Josh and SAM 1993; I Shot Andy Warhol 1995; Last Summer in the Hamptons 1995; Beautiful Girls 1996; I'm Not Rappaport 1996; Eye of God 1997; Music from Another Room 1998; Pecker 1998; 200 Cigarettes 1999

Ploszek, Pete Teenage Mutant Ninja Turtles 2014; Teenage Mutant Ninja Turtles - Out of the Shadows 2016

Plotnick, Jack Say It Isn't So 2001; Down with Love 2003; Sleeping Dogs Lie. 2006; Rubber 2010

Plowman, Anna-Louise The Foreigner 2003; Six Bullets 2012

Plowman, Melinda Home Town Story 1951; Billy the Kid vs Dracula 1966

Plowright, Joan (1929-) The Entertainer 1960; Three Sisters 1970; Equus 1977; The Diary of Anne Frank 1980; Brimstone and Treacle 1982; Britannia Hospital 1982; Revolution 1985; The Dressmaker 1988; Drowning by Numbers 1988; Avalon 1990; I Love You to Death 1990; Enchanted April

1991; Dennis 1993; Widows' Peak 1993; Hotel Sorrento 1994; A Pin for the Butterfly 1994; A Place for Annie 1994; A Pyromaniac's Love Story 1995; The Scarlet Letter 1995; Jane Eyre 1996; Mr Wrong 1996; 101 Dalmatians 1996; Surviving Picasso 1996; Aldrich Ames: Traitor Within 1998; Dance with Me 1998; Tea with Mussolini 1998; Tom's Midnight Garden 1998; Back to the Secret Garden 2000; Dinosaur 2000; Callas Forever 2002; Bringing Down the House 2003; Mrs Palfrey at The Claremont 2005; Curious George 2006; The Spiderwick Chronicles 2008

Plummer, Amanda (1957-) Cattle Annie and Little Britches 1980; The Dollmaker 1984; The Hotel New Hampshire 1984; Static 1985; Joe versus the Volcano 1990; The Fisher King 1991; Freejack 1992; Miss Rose White 1992; Last Light 1993; Needful Things 1993; Nostradamus 1993; So I Married an Axe Murderer 1993; Butterfly Kiss 1994; The Prophecy 1994; Pulp Fiction 1994; Under the Piano 1995; Freeway 1996; American Perfekt 1997; A Simple Wish 1997; You Can Thank Me Later 1998; 8½ Women 1999; The Million Dollar Hotel 1999; 7 Days to Live 2000; My Life without Me 2002; Triggermen 2002

Plummer, Christopher (1929-) Stage Struck 1958; Wind across the Everglades 1958; The Fall of the Roman Empire 1964; Inside Daisy Clover 1965; The Sound of Music 1965; Triple Cross 1966; Oedipus the King 1967; Nobody Runs Forever 1968; Battle of Britain 1969; Lock Up Your Daughters! 1969; The Royal Hunt of the Sun 1969; Waterloo 1970; The Return of the Pink Panther 1974; Conduct Unbecoming 1975; The Man Who Would Be King 1975; Aces High 1976; The Disappearance 1977; International Velvet 1978; Murder by Decree 1978; The Silent Partner 1978; Hanover Street 1979; The Shadow Box 1980; Somewhere in Time 1980; The Amateur 1981; Eyewitness 1981; The Scarlet and the Black 1983; Dreamscape 1984; Lily in Love 1985; An American Tail 1986; The Boy in Blue 1986; Dragnet 1987; Vampire in Venice 1987; Light Years 1988; A Ghost in Monte Carlo 1990; Where the Heart Is 1990; Firehead 1991; Star Trek VI: the Undiscovered Country 1991; Wolf 1994; Dolores Claiborne 1995; Twelve Monkeys 1995; Skeletons 1996; The Insider 1996; Madeline: Lost in Paris 1999; Dracula 2001 2000; Possessed 2000; A Beautiful Mind 2001; Lucky Break 2001; Agent of Influence 2002; Ararat 2002; Nicholas Nickleby 2002; Cold Creek Manor 2003; Alexander 2004; National Treasure 2004; Four Minutes 2005; Must Love Dogs 2005; The New World 2005; Syriana 2005; Closing the Ring 2006; Inside Man 2006; The Lake House 2006; Man in the Chair 2006; The Imaginarium of Doctor Parnassus 2009; The Last Station 2009; My Dog Tulip 2009; 9 2009; Up 2009; Beginners 2010; Priest 2010; The Girl with the Dragon Tattoo 2011; Elsa & Fred 2014; Danny Collins 2015; Remember 2015

Plummer, Glenn (1966-) South Central 1992; Trespass 1992; Speed 1994; Showgirls 1995; Strange Days 1995; Pronto 1996; The Substitute 1996; Up Close & Personal 1996; Thursday 1998; History Is Made at Night 1999; The Salton Sea 2002; The Day after Tomorrow 2004; Saw II 2005

Plunkett, Patricia (1926-1974) It Always Rains on Sunday 1947; Bond Street 1948; Landfall 1949; Murder without Crime 1950

Podalydès, Denis (1963-) En Plein Coeur 1998; Laissez-passer 2001; The Officers' Ward 2001; Almost Peaceful 2002; Summer Things 2002; Hidden 2005; An Ordinary Execution 2010

Podemski, Jennifer Dance Me Outside 1994; Take This Waltz 2011

Podesta, Rossana (1934-2013) Ulysses 1954; Helen of Troy 1955; Santiago 1956; Raw Wind in Eden 1958; The Sword and the Cross 1958; Sodom and Gomorrah 1962

Poehler, Amy (1971-) Envy 2003; Mean Girls 2004; Man of the Year 2006; Blades of Glory 2007; Mr Woodcock 2007; Baby Mama 2008; Hamlet 2 2008; Alvin and the Chipmunks: the Squeakquel 2009; Free Birds 2013; They Came Together 2014; Inside Out 2015; Sisters 2015

Poelvoorde, Benoît (1964-) Man Bites Dog 1992; Les Convoyeurs Attendent 1999; Asterix at the Olympic Games 2008; Louise-Michel 2008; Coco avant

Chanel 2009; Romantics Anonymous 2010; The Brand New Testament 2015

Poésy, Clémence (1982-) In Bruges 2008; Heartless 2009; 127 Hours 2011; Mr Morgan's Last Love 2013; The Ones Below 2015

Pogue, Ken (1934-) The Silent Partner 1978; The Grey Fox 1982; Crazy Moon 1986; Keeping Track 1986; Dead of Winter 1987; Welcome Home 1989; The Hitman 1991; Run 1991; The Amy Fisher Story 1993; Sherlock Holmes Returns 1993; The 6th Day 2000

Pohlmann, Eric aka **Pohlman, Eric** (1913-1979) Blackout 1950; Emergency Call 1952; The Gambler and the Lady 1952; Blood Orange 1953; Mogambo 1953; They Who Dare 1953; The Belles of St Trinian's 1954; Break in the Circle 1955; Gentlemen Marry Brunettes 1955; The Glass Cage 1955; Across the Bridge 1957; Mark of the Phoenix 1957; Alive and Kicking 1958; The Duke Wore Jeans 1958; Nor the Moon by Night 1958; Expresso Bongo 1959; The Singer Not the Song 1960; Surprise Package 1960; The Kitchen 1961; Cairo 1962; Shadow of Fear 1963; The Sicilians 1964; Where the Spies Are 1965; Tiffany Jones 1973; The Return of the Pink Panther 1974

Pointer, Priscilla (1924-) Carrie 1976; The Onion Field 1979; Honeysuckle Rose 1980; The Falcon and the Snowman 1985; Rumpelstiltskin 1986; A Nightmare on Elm Street 3: Dream Warriors 1987; Disturbed 1990; The Magic Bubble 1992; Acts of Love 1995

Poiret, Jean (1926-1992) The Last Metro 1980; Cop au Vin 1984; Inspecteur Lavardin 1986

Poitier, Sidney (1927-) No Way Out 1950; Cry, the Beloved Country 1951; Red Ball Express 1952; Go, Man, Go! 1953; Band of Angels 1957; Edge of the City 1957; Something of Value 1957; The Defiant Ones 1958; Virgin Island 1958; Porgy and Bess 1959; All the Young Men 1960; Paris Blues 1961; A Raisin in the Sun 1961; Pressure Point 1962; Lilies of the Field 1963; The Long Ships 1963; The Bedford Incident 1965; The Greatest Story Ever Told 1965; A Patch of Blue 1965; The Slender Thread 1965; Duel at Diablo 1966; Guess Who's Coming to Dinner 1967; In the Heat of the Night 1967; To Sir, with Love 1967; For Love of Ivy 1968; The Lost Man 1969; Brother John 1970; King: a Filmed Record... Montgomery to Memphis 1970; They Call Me Mister Tibbs! 1970; The Organization 1971; Buck and the Preacher 1972; A Warm December 1973; Uptown Saturday Night 1974; Let's Do It Again 1975; The Wilby Conspiracy 1975; A Piece of the Action 1977; Deadly Pursuit 1988; Little Nikita 1988; Sneakers 1992; The Jackal 1997; Mandela and de Klerk 1997; David and Lisa 1998; The Simple Life of Noah Dearborn 1999

Pol, Talitha (1940-1971) Village of Daughters 1961; Return from the Ashes 1965

Polanski, Roman (1933-) A Generation 1954; Repulsion 1965; The Fearless Vampire Killers 1967; The Magic Christian 1969; What? 1973; Blood for Dracula 1974; Chinatown 1974; The Tenant 1976; Back in the USSR 1992; A Pure Formality 1994; Rush Hour 3 2007; Roman Polanski: Wanted and Desired 2008

Poletti, Victor And the Ship Sails On 1983; Meeting Venus 1990

Polish, Mark (1972-) Twin Falls Idaho 1999; Northfork 2002; The Astronaut Farmer 2006

Polito, Jon (1950-) Fire with Fire 1986; The Freshman 1990; Miller's Crossing 1990; Barton Fink 1991; Leather Jackets 1991; Blankman 1994; Bushwhacked 1995; Just Your Luck 1996; Angel's Dance 1999; The Man Who Wasn't There 2001; The Singing Detective 2003; The Honeymooners 2005; Big Nothing 2006

Politoff, Haydée (1949-) La Collectionneuse 1967; The Human Factor 1975

Polivka, Boleslav aka **Polivka, Bolek** Divided We Fall 2000; Bathory 2008

Polk, Brigid aka **Berlin, Brigid** The Chelsea Girls 1966; Bike Boy 1967; Bad 1976; Pecker 1998

Pollack, Sydney (1934-2008) War Hunt 1962; Tootsie 1982; Husbands and Wives 1992; The Player 1992; A Civil Action 1996; Eyes Wide Shut 1999; Random Hearts 1999; Changing Lanes 2002; Charlie: the Life and Art of Charles Chaplin 2003; Michael Clayton 2007; Made of Honor 2008

Pollak, Kevin (1957-) Avalon 1990; Another You 1991; LA Story 1991; Ricochet 1991; A Few Good Men 1992; Grumpy Old Men 1993; Indian Summer

1993; The Opposite Sex and How to Live with Them 1993; Clean Slate 1994; Canadian Bacon 1995; Casino 1995; Miami Rhapsody 1995; The Usual Suspects 1995; Grumpier Old Men 1996; House Arrest 1996; That Thing You Do! 1996; Truth or Consequences, NM 1997; Hoods 1998; Deterrence 1999; End of Days 1999; She's All That 1999; 3000 Miles to Graceland 2000; Dr Dolittle 2 2001; The Santa Clause 2 2002; Stolen Summer 2002; Hostage 2004; The Whole Ten Yards 2004; Niagara Motel 2005; The Staircase Murders 2007; Cop Out 2010

Pollan, Tracy (1960-) Bright Lights, Big City 1988; Promised Land 1988; A Stranger among Us 1992

Pollard, Daphne (1891-1978) Thicker than Water 1935; Our Relations 1936

Pollard, Michael J (1939-) Summer Magic 1963; The Wild Angels 1966; Bonnie and Clyde 1967; Caprice 1967; Enter Laughing 1967; Hannibal Brooks 1968; Dirty Little Billy 1972; Sunday in the Country 1975; Between the Lines 1977; Melvin and Howard 1980; The Patriot 1986; Riders of the Storm 1986; American Gothic 1987; Roxanne 1987; Fast Food 1989; Never Cry Devil 1989; Tango & Cash 1989; Over Her Dead Body 1990; Why Me? 1990; Arizona Dream 1991; Motorama 1991; Split Second 1991; Tumbleweeds 1999

Polley, Sarah (1979-) The Adventures of Baron Munchausen 1988; Exotica 1994; The Hanging Garden 1997; The Sweet Hereafter 1997; Last Night 1998; eXistenZ 1999; Go 1999; Guinevere 1999; The Life before This 1999; The Claim 2000; The Weight of Water 2000; My Life without Me 2002; The I Inside 2003; Dawn of the Dead 2004; Don't Come Knocking 2005; Splice 2009; Stories We Tell 2012

Pollock, Ellen (1903-1997) Sons of the Sea 1939; Something in the City 1950; The Time of His Life 1955; The Hypnotist 1957; Horror Hospital 1973

Pollock, Nancy R (1902-1979) The Last Angry Man 1959; Go Naked in the World 1961

Polo, Teri (1969-) Mystery Date 1991; Aspen Extreme 1993; Quick 1993; Golden Gate 1994; The Arrival 1996; Meet the Parents 2000; Domestic Disturbance 2001; Beyond Borders 2003; Straight from the Heart 2003; Meet the Fockers 2004; The Hole 2009; The Miracle of Dommatina 2009; Little Fockers 2010

Polony, Anna (1939-) Diary for My Children 1982; Diary for My Loves 1987; Diary for My Father and Mother 1990

Polson, John (1965-) Back of Beyond 1995; The Sum of Us 1995; Idiot Box 1996; The Boys 1998; Mission: Impossible 2 1999

Polycarpou, Peter Julie and the Cadillacs 1997; De-Lovely 2004; Cleanskin 2012

Pomeranc, Max (1984-) Innocent Moves 1993; Fluke 1995

Pompeo, Ellen (1969-) Moonlight Mile 2002; Old School 2003

Ponce, Carlos (1972-) Deuce Bigalow: European Gigolo 2005; Just My Luck 2006

Poncela, Eusebio (1947-) The Law of Desire 1987; El Dorado 1988; Intacto 2001

Poncin, Marcel (1953-) So Long at the Fair 1950; Saadia 1953

Pongpass, Jenjira aka **Pongpas Widner, Jenjira** Uncle Boonmee Who Can Recall His Past Lives 2010; Cemetery of Splendour 2015

Pontius, Chris Jackass: the Movie 2002; jackass number two 2006; Jackass 3D 2010; Somewhere 2010

Ponton, Yvan (1945-) Cold Front 1989; Scanners II: the New Order 1991

Pooley, Olaf (1914-2015) Highly Dangerous 1950; The Corpse 1969

Poots, Imogen (1989-) 28 Weeks Later 2007; Cracks 2009; Solitary Man 2009; Chatroom 2010; Jane Eyre 2011; Comes a Bright Day 2012; A Late Quartet 2012; Filth 2013; Jimi: All Is by My Side 2013; A Long Way Down 2013; The Look of Love 2013; That Awkward Moment 2013; Need for Speed 2014; She's Funny That Way 2014; Green Room 2015

Pop, Iggy (1947-) Cry-Baby 1989; Hardware 1990; Dead Man 1995; The Crow: City of Angels 1996; The Rugrats Movie 1998; Snow Day 2000; Coffee and Cigarettes 2003; New York Doll 2005; Persepolis 2007; Blood Orange 2016

Pope, Carly A Cooler Climate 1999; Beneath 2007

Pope, Ryan A Field in England 2013; United We Fall 2014

Poppe, Nils (1908-2000) The Seventh Seal 1957; The Devil's Eye 1960

Poppel, Marc The Boost 1988; Damned River 1989; Separate Lives 1995

Popplewell, Anna (1988-) The Little Vampire 2000; The Chronicles of Narnia: The Lion, the Witch and the Wardrobe 2005; The Chronicles of Narnia: Prince Caspian 2008; Payback Season 2012

Popplewell, Paul Tyrannosaur 2010; The Goob 2014

Popwell, Albert (1926-1999) Cleopatra Jones and the Casino of Gold 1975; The Buddy Holly Story 1978

Porcasi, Paul (1879-1946) Broadway 1929; Devil and the Deep 1932; Enter Madame! 1933

Porizkova, Paulina (1965-) Anna 1987; Her Alibi 1989; Arizona Dream 1991; Female Perversions 1996; Thursday 1998

Poroshina, Maria Night Watch 2004; Day Watch 2006

Portal, Louise (1950-) The Decline of the American Empire 1986; Heading South 2006

Porter, Don aka **Porter, Donald** (1912-1997) Wild Beauty 1946; Buck Privates Come Home 1947; 711 Ocean Drive 1950; Bachelor in Paradise 1961; Live a Little, Love a Little 1968; The Candidate 1972; Mame 1974; White Line Fever 1975

Porter, Eric (1928-1995) The Fall of the Roman Empire 1964; The Pumpkin Eater 1964; The Heroes of Telemark 1965; Kaleidoscope 1966; The Lost Continent 1968; Hands of the Ripper 1971; Antony and Cleopatra 1972; The Belstone Fox 1973; The Day of the Jackal 1973; Hitler: the Last Ten Days 1973; Callan 1974; Hennessy 1975; The Thirty-Nine Steps 1978

Porter, Jean (1925-) Andy Hardy's Blonde Trouble 1944; Bathing Beauty 1944; Abbott and Costello in Hollywood 1945; Till the End of Time 1946; Cry Danger 1951; The Left Hand of God 1955

Porter, Nyree Dawn (1936-2001) Live Now - Pay Later 1962; The Cracksman 1963; Two Left Feet 1963; The House That Dripped Blood 1970; Jane Eyre 1970

Porter, Scott Prom Night 2008; Speed Racer 2008; Bandslam 2009; Dear John 2010

Porter, Susie (1971-) Two Hands 1999; Bootmen 2000; The Monkey's Mask 2000

Portillo, Blanca Volver 2006; Broken Embraces 2009

Portman, Eric (1903-1969) Maria Marten, or the Murder in the Red Barn 1935; The Crimes of Stephen Hawke 1936; Moonlight Sonata 1937; The Prince and the Pauper 1937; 49th Parallel 1941; One of Our Aircraft Is Missing 1942; Uncensored 1942; Millions like Us 1943; We Dive at Dawn 1943; A Canterbury Tale 1944; Great Day 1944; Daybreak 1946; Wanted for Murder 1946; Dear Murderer 1947; The Mark of Cain 1947; The Blind Goddess 1948; The Spider and the Fly 1949; Cairo Road 1950; The Magic Box 1951; His Excellency 1952; South of Algiers 1952; The Colditz Story 1954; The Deep Blue Sea 1955; Child in the House 1956; The Good Companions 1956; The Naked Edge 1961; Freud 1962; The Man Who Finally Died 1962; West 11 1963; The Bedford Incident 1965; The Spy with a Cold Nose 1966; The Whisperers 1967; Deadfall 1968

Portman, Natalie (1981-) Leon 1994; Heat 1995; Beautiful Girls 1996; Everyone I Say I Love You 1996; Anywhere but Here 1999; Star Wars Episode I: the Phantom Menace 1999; Where the Heart Is 2000; Star Wars Episode II: Attack of the Clones 2002; Cold Mountain 2003; Garden State 2003; Closer 2004; Star Wars Episode III: Revenge of the Sith 2005; V for Vendetta 2005; Goya's Ghosts 2006; Mr Magorium's Wonder Emporium 2007; My Blueberry Nights 2007; The Other Boleyn Girl 2008; Brothers 2009; Love and Other Impossible Pursuits 2009; New York, I Love You 2009; Black Swan 2010; Your Highness 2010; No Strings Attached 2011; Thor 2011; Thor: the Dark World 2013; Jane Got a Gun 2015; Knight of Cups 2015

Portnow, Richard (1953-) Aunt Julia and the Scriptwriter 1990; Trial by Jury 1994; Guy 1996; Laughter on the 23rd Floor 2000

Posey, Parker (1968-) Basquiat 1996; subUrbia 1996; Waiting for Guffman 1996; Clockwatchers 1997; Henry Fool 1997; The House of Yes 1997; The Daytrippers 1998; The Misadventures of Margaret 1998; What Rats Won't Do 1998; You've Got Mail 1998; Scream 3

1999; Best in Show 2000; The Anniversary Party 2001; Josie and the Pussycats 2001; Personal Velocity 2001; The Battle of Mary Kay 2002; The Sweetest Thing 2002; Laws of Attraction 2003; A Mighty Wind 2003; Blade: Trinity 2004; Frankenstein 2004; Superman Returns 2006; The Eye 2008; Grace of Monaco 2014; Irrational Man 2015

Post, Markie (1950-) There's Something about Mary 1998; Holiday in Handcuffs 2007; Backyard Wedding 2010

Post Jr, William (1901-1989) Sherlock Holmes and the Secret Weapon 1942; Ship Ahoy 1942

Posta, Adrienne (1948-) Here We Go round the Mulberry Bush 1967; Up the Junction 1967; Up Pompeii 1971; Percy's Progress 1974; Adventures of a Taxi Driver 1975; Adventures of a Private Eye 1977

Postlethwaite, Pete aka **Postlethwaite, Peter** (1946-2011) A Private Function 1988; Distant Voices, Still Lives 1988; The Dressmaker 1988; To Kill a Priest 1988; Split Second 1991; Anchoress 1993; In the Name of the Father 1993; Suite 16 1994; The Usual Suspects 1995; When Saturday Comes 1995; Brassed Off 1996; DragonHeart 1996; James and the Giant Peach 1996; William Shakespeare's Romeo + Juliet 1996; Amistad 1997; The Lost World: Jurassic Park 1997; The Serpent's Kiss 1997; Among Giants 1998; Animal Farm 1999; Rat 2000; When the Sky Falls 2000; The Shipping News 2001; Triggermen 2002; Aeonflux 2005; The Constant Gardener 2005; Dark Water 2005; Closing the Ring 2006; The Omen 2006; The Age of Stupid 2008; Solomon Kane 2009; Inception 2010; Killing Bono 2010; The Town 2010

Poston, Tom (1921-2007) The Old Dark House 1963; Soldier in the Rain 1963; The Happy Hooker 1975

Potel, Victor (1889-1947) The Virginian 1929; Doughboys 1930

Potente, Franka (1974-) Run Lola Run 1998; Anatomy 2000; The Princess & the Warrior 2000; Blow 2001; The Bourne Identity 2002; The Bourne Supremacy 2004; Creep 2004; Che Part Two 2008; The Conjuring 2 2016

Potocean, Alexandru 4 Months, 3 Weeks and 2 Days 2007; Tales from the Golden Age 2009

Potter, Chris (1960-) Arachnid 2001; The Pacifier 2005; The Perfect Assistant 2008

Potter, Madeleine (1963-) The Bostonians 1984; Slaves of New York 1989; Two Evil Eyes 1990; The Golden Bowl 2000

Potter, Martin (1944-) Satyricon 1969; Goodbye Gemini 1970; Satan's Slave 1976

Potter, Monica (1971-) Martha - Meet Frank, Daniel and Laurence 1997; A Cool, Dry Place 1998; Patch Adams 1998; Without Limits 1998; Head over Heels 2000; Along Came a Spider 2001; I'm with Lucy 2002; Saw 2004; The Last House on the Left 2008

Potts, Andrew Lee (1979-) New Year's Day 1999; The Bunker 2001; Red Mist 2008

Potts, Annie (1952-) Corvette Summer 1978; Crimes of Passion 1984; Ghost Busters 1984; Jumpin' Jack Flash 1986; Pretty in Pink 1986; Ghostbusters II 1989; Who's Harry Crumb? 1989; Texasville 1990; Toy Story 1995; Toy Story 2 1999; Defending Our Kids: the Julie Posey Story 2003; Elvis Has Left the Building 2004; The Music Teacher 2012

Potts, Cliff (1942-) Silent Running 1971; Cry for Me Billy 1972; The Groundstar Conspiracy 1972; Snow Job 1972; Sahara 1983

Potts, Jonathan Jason X 2001; Mr Magorium's Wonder Emporium 2007

Potts, Nell (1959-) Rachel, Rachel 1968; The Effect of Gamma Rays on Man-in-the-Moon Marigolds 1972

Potts, Sarah Jane aka **Potts, Sarah-Jane** (1979-) My Son the Fanatic 1997; Barely Legal 2003; Kinky Boots 2005

Pou, José Maria aka **Pou, Josep Maria** Beloved/Friend 1998; Goya in Bordeaux 1999

Pouget, Ely (1961-) Cool Blue 1988; Death Machine 1994; Lawnmower Man 2: Beyond Cyberspace 1995

Poujouly, Georges (1940-2000) Jeux Interdits 1953; And God Created Woman 1956; Lift to the Scaffold 1957

Poulter, Will (1993-) Son of Rambow 2007; The Chronicles of Narnia: The Voyage of the Dawn Treader 2010; Wild Bill 2011; We're the Millers 2013; Glassland 2014; The Maze Runner

2014; Plastic 2014; The Revenant 2015; Kids in Love 2016

Poulton, Mabel (1901-1994) The Constant Nymph 1928; Escape 1930

Pounder, C C H (1952-) As Summers Die 1986; Resting Place 1986; Bagdad Café 1987; Murder in Mississippi 1990; Psycho IV: the Beginning 1990; The Importance of Being Earnest 1992; Benny & Joon 1993; For Their Own Good 1993; RoboCop 3 1993; Sliver 1993; Tales from the Crypt: Demon Knight 1995; If These Walls Could Talk 1996; End of Days 1999; Disappearing Acts 2000; Boycott 2001; Avatar 2009; Orphan 2009

Poupaud, Melvil (1973-) Treasure Island 1986; The Lover 1992; A Summer's Tale 1996; Three Lives and Only One Death 1996; Généalogies d'un Crime 1997; Le Divorce 2003; Time to Leave 2005; The Broken 2008; A Christmas Tale 2008; The Refuge 2009; Laurence Anyways 2012; By the Sea 2015

Poupon, Henri (1882-1953) Angèle 1934; Manon des Sources 1952

Pousse, André (1919-2005) Un Flic 1972; Police Story 1975

Povah, Phyllis (1902-1975) The Women 1939; Let's Face It 1943; The Marrying Kind 1952; Happy Anniversary 1959

Powell, Addison (1921-2010) In the French Style 1963; Three Days of the Condor 1975

Powell, Brittney Airborne 1993; Dragonworld 1994

Powell, Charles (1963-) Screamers 1995; The Call of the Wild 1996; For Hire 1997

Powell, Clifton (1956-) The Pentagon Wars 1998; Phantoms 1998; Bones 2001; Never Die Alone 2004; Ray 2004; Knights of the South Bronx 2005; Norbit 2007

Powell, Dick (1904-1963) Blessed Event 1932; Footlight Parade 1933; 42nd Street 1933; Gold Diggers of 1933 1933; Dames 1934; Flirtation Walk 1934; Wonder Bar 1934; Gold Diggers of 1935 1935; A Midsummer Night's Dream 1935; Page Miss Glory 1935; Shipmates Forever 1935; Thanks a Million 1935; Colleen 1936; Gold Diggers of 1937 1936; Stage Struck 1936; Hollywood Hotel 1937; On the Avenue 1937; Going Places 1938; Hard to Get 1938; Naughty but Nice 1939; Christmas in July 1940; In the Navy 1941; Star Spangled Rhythm 1942; Happy Go Lucky 1943; Riding High 1943; True to Life 1943; Farewell My Lovely 1944; It Happened Tomorrow 1944; Meet the People 1944; Cornered 1945; Johnny o'Clock 1947; Pitfall 1948; Station West 1948; To the Ends of the Earth 1948; Mrs Mike 1949; Right Cross 1950; Cry Danger 1951; The Tall Target 1951; The Bad and the Beautiful 1952; Susan Slept Here 1954

Powell, Eleanor (1912-1982) Broadway Melody of 1936 1935; George White's 1935 Scandals 1935; Born to Dance 1936; Broadway Melody of 1938 1937; Rosalie 1937; Honolulu 1939; Broadway Melody of 1940 1940; Lady Be Good 1941; Ship Ahoy 1942; I Dood It 1943; Sensations 1944; Duchess of Idaho 1950

Powell, Esteban (1977-) Late Bloomers 1995; Hitman's Run 1999

Powell, Jane (1929-) Song of the Open Road 1944; Holiday in Mexico 1946; A Date with Judy 1948; Three Daring Daughters 1948; Nancy Goes to Rio 1950; Rich, Young and Pretty 1951; Royal Wedding 1951; Three Sailors and a Girl 1953; Athena 1954; Seven Brides for Seven Brothers 1954; Hit the Deck 1955; The Girl Most Likely 1957; The Female Animal 1958

Powell, Lovelady I Never Sang for My Father 1970; The Happy Hooker 1975

Powell, Michael (1905-1990) The Edge of the World 1937; Boxcar Bertha 1972

Powell, Robert (1944-) The Asphyx 1972; Asylum 1972; Mahler 1974; Tommy 1975; The Four Feathers 1978; The Thirty-Nine Steps 1978; Harlequin 1980; Jane Austen in Manhattan 1980; The Survivor 1981; The Hunchback of Notre Dame 1982; Imperative 1982; The Jigsaw Man 1984; The Mystery of Edwin Drood 1993

Powell, William (1892-1984) Beau Geste 1926; Beau Sabreur 1928; The Dragnet 1928; The Last Command 1928; The Canary Murder Case 1929; The Four Feathers 1929; Paramount on Parade 1930; Ladies' Man 1931; Man of the World 1931; High Pressure 1932; Jewel Robbery 1932; Lawyer Man 1932; One Way Passage 1932; The Kennel Murder Case 1933; Evelyn Prentice 1934; Fashions of 1934 1934; The Key

1934; Manhattan Melodrama 1934; The Thin Man 1934; Escapade 1935; Reckless 1935; Rendezvous 1935; Star of Midnight 1935; After the Thin Man 1936; The Ex-Mrs Bradford 1936; The Great Ziegfeld 1936; Libeled Lady 1936; My Man Godfrey 1936; Double Wedding 1937; The Emperor's Candlesticks 1937; The Last of Mrs Cheyney 1937; The Baroness and the Butler 1938; Another Thin Man 1939; I Love You Again 1940; Love Crazy 1941; Shadow of the Thin Man 1941; Crossroads 1942; The Heavenly Body 1943; The Thin Man Goes Home 1944; Ziegfeld Follies 1944; The Hoodlum Saint 1946; Life with Father 1947; The Senator Was Indiscreet 1947; Song of the Thin Man 1947; Mr Peabody and the Mermaid 1948; Dancing in the Dark 1949; Treasure of Lost Canyon 1952; The Girl Who Had Everything 1953; How to Marry a Millionaire 1953; Mister Roberts 1955

Power, Chad (1984-) Ruby Cairo 1992; 3 Ninjas 1992

Power, Hartley (1894-1966) Aunt Sally 1933; The Camels Are Coming 1934; Evergreen 1934; Where There's a Will 1936; A Window in London 1939; Return to Yesterday 1940; The Man from Morocco 1944; The Million Pound Note 1953; Roman Holiday 1953; To Dorothy, a Son 1954

Power, Taryn (1953-) Sinbad and the Eye of the Tiger 1977; Tracks 1977

Power, Tyrone aka **Power Jr, Tyrone** aka **Power USMCR, Tyrone** (1914-1958) Fury 1923; Ladies in Love 1936; Lloyd's of London 1936; Café Metropole 1937; In Old Chicago 1937; Love Is News 1937; Thin Ice 1937; Alexander's Ragtime Band 1938; Marie Antoinette 1938; Suez 1938; Jesse James 1939; The Rains Came 1939; Rose of Washington Square 1939; Second Fiddle 1939; Brigham Young 1940; Johnny Apollo 1940; The Mark of Zorro 1940; Blood and Sand 1941; A Yank in the RAF 1941; The Black Swan 1942; Son of Fury 1942; This above All 1942; Crash Dive 1943; The Razor's Edge 1946; Captain from Castile 1947; Nightmare Alley 1947; That Wonderful Urge 1948; Prince of Foxes 1949; An American Guerrilla in the Philippines 1950; The Black Rose 1950; Rawhide 1951; Diplomatic Courier 1952; Pony Soldier 1952; King of the Khyber Rifles 1953; The Mississippi Gambler 1953; The Long Gray Line 1955; Untamed 1955; The Eddy Duchin Story 1956; The Rising of the Moon 1957; Seven Waves Away 1957; The Sun Also Rises 1957; Witness for the Prosecution 1957

Powers, Alexandra (1967-) The Seventh Coin 1993; Last Man Standing 1996

Powers, Mala (1931-2007) Cyrano de Bergerac 1950; Edge of Doom 1950; Rose of Cimarron 1952; City beneath the Sea 1953; City That Never Sleeps 1953; The Yellow Mountain 1954; Bengazi 1955; Rage at Dawn 1955; Tammy and the Bachelor 1957; The Colossus of New York 1958; Daddy's Gone A-Hunting 1969

Powers, Stefanie (1942-) If a Man Answers 1962; McLintock! 1963; Palm Springs Weekend 1963; Die! Die! My Darling 1964; Love Has Many Faces 1965; Stagecoach 1966; Warning Shot 1967; The Boatniks 1970; Crescendo 1970; The Magnificent Seven Ride! 1972; Herbie Rides Again 1974; The Astral Factor 1976; A Death in Canaan 1978; Little Moon & Jud McGraw 1978; Escape to Athena 1979; Rabbit Fever 2005; A Soldier's Love Story 2010

Powers, Tom (1890-1955) Double Indemnity 1944; The Blue Dahlia 1946; Angel and the Badman 1947; They Won't Believe Me 1947; Station West 1948; Up in Central Park 1948; Destination Moon 1950; Right Cross 1950; The Strip 1951; The Well 1951

Powley, Bel The Diary of a Teenage Girl 2015; A Royal Night Out 2015

Powley, Bryan (1871-1962) Conquest of the Air 1936; Love from a Stranger 1936

Prachar, Ilja (1924-2005) All My Good Countrymen 1968; The Cremator 1968

Prada, José Maria (1925-1978) The Hunt 1966; Pancho Villa 1971

Prado, Lilia (1929-2006) Mexican Bus Ride 1951; Wuthering Heights 1953

Praed, Michael (1960-) Staggered 1993; Darkness Falls 1998; 9 Dead Gay Guys 2001

Prager, Stanley aka **Praeger, Stanley** (1917-1972) The Eve of St Mark 1944; In the Meantime, Darling 1944; A Bell for Adano 1945; Do You Love Me? 1946; A Foreign Affair 1948; Gun Crazy 1949

Pran (1920-2013) Madhumati 1958; Bobby 1973; Dharam Veer 1977

Prather, Joan (1950-) Big Bad Mama 1974; The Devil's Rain 1975

Pratt, Chris (1979-) Path of Destruction 2005; Wanted 2008; Moneyball 2011; Take Me Home Tonight 2011; 10 Years 2011; The Five-Year Engagement 2012; Delivery Man 2013; Her 2013; Guardians of the Galaxy 2014; The Lego Movie 2014; Jurassic World 2015; The Magnificent Seven 2016; Passengers 2016; Guardians of the Galaxy Vol 2 2017; Jurassic World 2 2018

Pratt, Judson (1916-2002) The Rise and Fall of Legs Diamond 1960; Sergeant Rutledge 1960; Vigilante Force 1975

Pratt, Kyla (1988-) Barney's Great Adventure 1998; Doctor Dolittle 1998; Dr Dolittle 2 2001; Fat Albert 2004; Dr Dolittle 3 2006; Dr Dolittle: Tail to the Chief 2008; Hotel for Dogs 2008; Dr Dolittle: Million Dollar Mutts 2009

Pratt, Mike (1931-1976) This Is My Street 1963; Goodbye Gemini 1970; Assassin 1973

Pratt, Purnell (1885-1941) The Trespasser 1929; I Cover the Waterfront 1933

Pratt, Susan May (1974-) Drive Me Crazy 1999; 10 Things I Hate about You 1999; Center Stage 2000; Charms for the Easy Life 2001; Adrift 2006

Pratt, Victoria Murder at the Presidio 2005; Her Fatal Flaw 2006

Preboist, Paul (1927-1997) The Two of Us 1967; An Adventure for Two 1979

Preiss, Joana Ma Mère 2004; Inside Paris 2006

Preiss, Wolfgang (1910-2002) The Thousand Eyes of Dr Mabuse 1960; The Train 1964; Von Ryan's Express 1965; Hannibal Brooks 1968; Raid on Rommel 1971; Forget Mozart 1985

Preisser, June (1920-1984) Babes in Arms 1939; Strike Up the Band 1940

Préjean, Albert (1893-1979) Paris Qui Dort 1923; An Italian Straw Hat 1927; Sous les Toits de Paris 1930

Preminger, Otto (1905-1986) The Pied Piper 1942; Margin for Error 1943; They Got Me Covered 1943; Where Do We Go from Here? 1945; Stalag 17 1953

Premnath (1926-1992) Barsaat 1949; Bobby 1973

Prentiss, Ann (1941-) Any Wednesday 1966; The Out of Towners 1970; California Split 1974

Prentiss, Paula (1939-) Where the Boys Are 1960; Bachelor in Paradise 1961; The Horizontal Lieutenant 1962; Follow the Boys 1963; Man's Favorite Sport? 1964; The World of Henry Orient 1964; In Harm's Way 1965; What's New, Pussycat? 1965; Catch-22 1970; Born to Win 1971; The Parallax View 1974; The Stepford Wives 1975; The Black Marble 1980; Buddy Buddy 1981; Saturday the 14th 1981

Prescott, Robert Bachelor Party 1984; Michael Clayton 2007

Presle, Micheline (1922-) La Nuit Fantastique 1942; Devil in the Flesh 1947; An American Guerrilla in the Philippines 1950; Adventures of Captain Fabian 1951; Royal Affairs in Versailles 1953; The Bride Is Too Beautiful 1956; Blind Date 1959; The Seven Deadly Sins 1961; If a Man Answers 1962; Imperial Venus 1963; The Prize 1963; Male Hunt 1964; La Religieuse 1965; The Magic Donkey 1970; The Blood of Others 1984; I Want to Go Home 1989

Presley, Elvis (1935-1977) Love Me Tender 1956; Jailhouse Rock 1957; Loving You 1957; King Creole 1958; Flaming Star 1960; GI Blues 1960; Blue Hawaii 1961; Wild in the Country 1961; Follow That Dream 1962; Girls! Girls! Girls! 1962; It Happened at the World's Fair 1962; Kid Galahad 1962; Fun in Acapulco 1963; Kissin' Cousins 1964; Roustabout 1964; Viva Las Vegas 1964; Girl Happy 1965; Harum Scarum 1965; Tickle Me 1965; Frankie & Johnny 1966; Paradise, Hawaiian Style 1966; Spinout 1966; Clambake 1967; Double Trouble 1967; Easy Come, Easy Go 1967; Live a Little, Love a Little 1968; Speedway 1968; Stay Away, Joe 1968; Change of Habit 1969; Charro! 1969; The Trouble with Girls 1969; Elvis: That's the Way It Is 1970; Elvis on Tour 1972

Presley, Priscilla (1945-) The Naked Gun 1988; The Adventures of Ford Fairlane 1990; The Naked Gun 2½: the Smell of Fear 1991; Naked Gun 33⅓: the Final Insult 1994

Presnell, Harve (1933-2009) The Unsinkable Molly Brown 1964; The Glory Guys 1965; Paint Your Wagon 1969; Fargo 1995; The Whole Wide World 1996; Face/Off 1997; Julian Po 1997; Everything That Rises 1998

Press, Fiona Waiting 1990; Black Water 2007; Disgrace 2008

Press, Natalie (1980-) My Summer of Love 2004; Red Road 2006; Cass 2008; Fifty Dead Men Walking 2008; Donkeys 2010; Island 2011; Ill Manors 2012

Pressly, Jaime (1977-) Ringmaster 1998; Tomcats 2001; Joe Dirt 2001; Not Another Teen Movie 2001; Ticker 2001; Torque 2003; Evel Knievel 2004; DOA: Dead or Alive 2006; Dr Seuss' Horton Hears a Who! 2008; I Love You, Man 2008; A Haunted House 2 2014

Pressman, Lawrence (1939-) The Hellstrom Chronicle 1971; Shaft 1971; Angus 1995; The Maker 1997; Very Bad Things 1998

Presson, Jason (1971-) The Stone Boy 1984; Explorers 1985; Lady in White 1988; Saturday the 14th Strikes Back 1988

Prestia, Jo (1960-) The Dream Life of Angels 1998; Irreversible 2002; Calvaire 2004

Preston, Billy (1946-2006) Sgt Pepper's Lonely Hearts Club Band 1978; Blame It on the Night 1984

Preston, Carrie (1967-) The Journey 1997; My Best Friend's Wedding 1997; Transamerica 2005; Ruth & Alex 2014

Preston, Cyndy Miles to Go 1986; Pin 1988; Whale Music 1994

Preston, J A (1932-) Real Life 1979; Body Heat 1981; Remo - Unarmed and Dangerous 1985; Wings of the Apache 1990; Captain Ron 1992

Preston, Kelly (1962-) Secret Admirer 1985; 52 Pick-Up 1986; SpaceCamp 1986; Love at Stake 1987; A Tiger's Tale 1987; Spellbinder 1988; Twins 1988; The Experts 1989; Run 1991; Only You 1992; Arthur Miller's The American Clock 1993; Citizen Ruth 1996; Jerry Maguire 1996; Addicted to Love 1997; Nothing to Lose 1997; Holy Man 1998; Jack Frost 1998; Daddy and Them 1999; For Love of the Game 1999; Dr Seuss' The Cat in the Hat 2003; View from the Top 2003; What a Girl Wants 2003; Sky High 2005; Broken Bridges 2006; Death Sentence 2007; The Tenth Circle 2008; Old Dogs 2009; The Last Song 2010

Preston, Robert (1918-1987) Beau Geste 1939; Union Pacific 1939; North West Mounted Police 1940; Typhoon 1940; Reap the Wild Wind 1942; This Gun for Hire 1942; Wake Island 1942; The Macomber Affair 1947; Blood on the Moon 1948; Whispering Smith 1948; The Lady Gambles 1949; Tulsa 1949; The Sundowners 1950; Best of the Badmen 1951; Cloudburst 1951; Face to Face 1952; The Last Frontier 1955; The Dark at the Top of the Stairs 1960; How the West Was Won 1962; The Music Man 1962; All the Way Home 1963; Island of Love 1963; Child's Play 1972; Junior Bonner 1972; Mame 1974; Semi-Tough 1977; SOB 1981; Victor/Victoria 1982; The Last Starfighter 1984

Préville, Gisèle Against the Wind 1947; The Dancing Years 1949

Prévost, Daniel (1939-) Le Colonel Chabert 1994; Le Dîner de Cons 1998; Pas sur la Bouche 2003

Prévost, Françoise (1930-1997) Paris Nous Appartient 1960; Payroll 1961

Prevost, Marie (1898-1937) The Marriage Circle 1924; Kiss Me Again 1925; The Godless Girl 1928; The Racket 1928; Ladies of Leisure 1930; Party Girl 1930; The Sin of Madelon Claudet 1931; Sporting Blood 1931; Hell Divers 1932; Three Wise Girls 1932; Only Yesterday 1933; Hands across the Table 1935

Price, Connor Crossed Over 2002; Good Luck Chuck 2007

Price, Dennis (1915-1973) A Canterbury Tale 1944; A Place of One's Own 1944; Caravan 1946; Hungry Hill 1946; The Magic Bow 1946; Dear Murderer 1947; Easy Money 1947; Holiday Camp 1947; Jassy 1947; The Master of Bankdam 1947; Snowbound 1948; The Bad Lord Byron 1949; The Dancing Years 1949; Kind Hearts and Coronets 1949; The Lost People 1949; The Adventurers 1950; Murder without Crime 1950; Lady Godiva Rides Again 1951; The Intruder 1953; For Better, for Worse 1954; Oh, Rosalinda!! 1955; That Lady 1955; Charley Moon 1956; Fortune Is a Woman 1956; Private's Progress 1956; A Touch of the Sun 1956; The Naked Truth 1957; Danger Within 1958; I'm All Right Jack 1959; Oscar Wilde 1959; The Millionairess 1960; No Love for Johnnie 1960; Piccadilly Third Stop 1960; The Pure Hell of St Trinian's 1960; The Rebel 1960; School for Scoundrels 1960; Tunes of Glory 1960; Double Bunk 1961; Go to Blazes 1961; Victim 1961; What a Carve Up! 1961; The Amorous Prawn 1962; Kill or Cure 1962; Play It Cool

1962; The Pot Carriers 1962; The Cracksman 1963; Doctor in Distress 1963; Tamahine 1963; The VIPs 1963; The Comedy Man 1964; The Earth Dies Screaming 1964; A Jolly Bad Fellow 1964; Ten Little Indians 1965; Just like a Woman 1966; Some Will, Some Won't 1969; The Horror of Frankenstein 1970; The Rise and Rise of Michael Rimmer 1970; Vampyros Lesbos 1970; Twins of Evil 1971; The Adventures of Barry McKenzie 1972; Dracula, Prisoner of Frankenstein 1972; Go for a Take 1972; Pulp 1972; That's Your Funeral 1972; Horror Hospital 1973; Theatre of Blood 1973

Price, Lonny The Muppets Take Manhattan 1984; Dirty Dancing 1987
Price, Marc (1968–) Trick or Treat 1986; The Rescue 1988
Price, Molly (1966–) Jersey Girl 1992; Kiss Me, Guido 1997
Price, Nancy (1880–1970) The Stars Look Down 1939; Secret Mission 1942; Madonna of the Seven Moons 1944; I Know Where I'm Going! 1945; I Live in Grosvenor Square 1945; The Master of Bankdam 1947; The Three Weird Sisters 1948; Mandy 1952
Price, Vincent (1911–1993) Green Hell 1939; The Private Lives of Elizabeth and Essex 1939; Tower of London 1939; Brigham Young 1940; The House of the Seven Gables 1940; Hudson's Bay 1940; The Invisible Man Returns 1940; The Song of Bernadette 1943; The Eve of St Mark 1944; The Keys of the Kingdom 1944; Laura 1944; Wilson 1944; Leave Her to Heaven 1945; A Royal Scandal 1945; Dragonwyck 1946; The Long Night 1947; Moss Rose 1947; The Web 1947; The Three Musketeers 1948; Up in Central Park 1948; The Bribe 1949; The Baron of Arizona 1950; Champagne for Caesar 1950; Adventures of Captain Fabian 1951; His Kind of Woman 1951; The Las Vegas Story 1952; House of Wax 1953; Casanova's Big Night 1954; Dangerous Mission 1954; The Mad Magician 1954; Son of Sinbad 1955; Serenade 1956; The Ten Commandments 1956; While the City Sleeps 1956; The Story of Mankind 1957; The Fly 1958; House on Haunted Hill 1958; The Bat 1959; The Big Circus 1959; Return of the Fly 1959; The Tingler 1959; The Fall of the House of Usher 1960; Gordon the Black Pirate 1961; Master of the World 1961; Nefertite, Queen of the Nile 1961; Pit and the Pendulum 1961; Confessions of an Opium Eater 1962; Convicts Four 1962; Tales of Terror 1962; Tower of London 1962; Diary of a Madman 1963; The Haunted Palace 1963; The Raven 1963; Twice Told Tales 1963; The Comedy of Terrors 1964; The Last Man on Earth 1964; The Masque of the Red Death 1964; The Tomb of Ligeia 1964; City under the Sea 1965; Dr Goldfoot and the Bikini Machine 1965; Dr Goldfoot and the Girl Bombs 1966; Histoires Extraordinaires 1967; House of a Thousand Dolls 1967; Witchfinder General 1968; The Oblong Box 1969; Scream and Scream Again 1969; The Trouble with Girls 1969; Cry of the Banshee 1970; The Abominable Dr Phibes 1971; Dr Phibes Rises Again 1972; Theatre of Blood 1973; Madhouse 1974; Percy's Progress 1974; The Monster Club 1980; Bloodbath at the House of Death 1983; House of the Long Shadows 1983; Basil the Great Mouse Detective 1986; The Whales of August 1987; Dead Heat 1988; Catchfire 1989; Edward Scissorhands 1990; The Heart of Justice 1992
Prichard, Robert The Toxic Avenger 1985; Class of Nuke 'Em High 1986
Priestley, Jason (1969–) Calendar Girl 1993; Tombstone 1993; Coldblooded 1995; Love and Death on Long Island 1998; Eye of the Beholder 1999; Lion of Oz 2000; The Fourth Angel 2001; Murder at the Presidio 2005; The Miracle of Dommatina 2009
Prieto, Aurore Thérèse 1986; Docteur Petiot 1990
Prim, Suzy (1895–1991) The Lower Depths 1936; Mayerling 1936
Prima, Louis (1910–1978) Senior Prom 1958; Hey Boy! Hey Girl! 1959; The Jungle Book 1967
Primus, Barry (1938–) Puzzle of a Downfall Child 1970; Boxcar Bertha 1972; New York, New York 1977; Avalanche 1978; Night Games 1979; The Rose 1984; Absence of Malice 1981; The River 1984; SpaceCamp 1986; Big Business 1988; Torn Apart 1990; Night and the City 1992; Flipping 1996; James Dean 2001
Prince (1958–2016) Purple Rain 1984; Under the Cherry Moon 1986; Graffiti Bridge 1990

Prince, Faith (1957–) Dave 1993; My Father the Hero 1994; Big Bully 1996; Picture Perfect 1997
Prince, William (1913–1996) Destination Tokyo 1943; Objective, Burma! 1945; Cinderella Jones 1946; Carnegie Hall 1947; Dead Reckoning 1947; Cyrano de Bergerac 1950; The Vagabond King 1956; Macabre 1958; The Heartbreak Kid 1972; The Gauntlet 1977; Gideon's Trumpet 1980; Kiss Me Goodbye 1982; Spies like Us 1985; Vice Versa 1988
Principal, Victoria (1950–) The Life and Times of Judge Roy Bean 1972; Earthquake 1974; Vigilante Force 1975
Prine, Andrew (1936–) The Miracle Worker 1962; Bandolero! 1968; Generation 1969; Grizzly 1976; Amityville II: the Possession 1982
Pringle, Bryan (1935–2002) Saturday Night and Sunday Morning 1960; French Dressing 1964; The Early Bird 1965; The Boy Friend 1971; Haunted Honeymoon 1986; Drowning by Numbers 1988; The Steal 1994; Darkness Falls 1998
Prinsloo, Sandra The Gods Must Be Crazy 1980; Quest for Love 1988
Prinze Jr, Freddie (1976–) The House of Yes 1997; I Know What You Did Last Summer 1997; I Still Know What You Did Last Summer 1998; She's All That 1999; Wing Commander 1999; Boys and Girls 2000; Down to You 2000; Head over Heels 2000; Summer Catch 2001; Scooby-Doo 2002; Scooby-Doo 2: Monsters Unleashed 2004; Happily N'Ever After 2006; The Reef 2006; Brooklyn Rules 2007
Prip, Henrik (1960–) The Idiots 1998; Minor Mishaps 2002; The Boss of It All 2006
Pritchard, Hilary (1942–1996) Under the Doctor 1976; A Touch of the Sun 1979
Prival, Lucien (1900–1994) Hell's Angels 1930; Party Girl 1930; After Tonight 1933
Privat, Gilles Romuald et Juliette 1989; La Crise 1992
Prochnow, Jürgen (1941–) The Lost Honour of Katharina Blum 1975; The Keep 1983; Beverly Hills Cop II 1987; The Seventh Sign 1988; A Dry White Season 1989; The Fourth War 1990; Robin Hood 1990; Body of Evidence 1992; In the Mouth of Madness 1994; Judge Dredd 1995; The English Patient 1996; Air Force One 1997; Das Boot: the Director's Cut 1997; The Replacement Killers 1998; Wing Commander 1999; The Da Vinci Code 2006; Primeval 2007; Remember 2015
Procopio, Lou (1938–1995) The Wild Angels 1966; Gas-s-s-s, or It Became Necessary to Destroy the World in Order to Save It 1970
Procter, Emily (1968–) Breast Men 1997; Family Plan 1997; Body Shots 1999; Big Momma's House 2 2006
Procter, Philip aka **Procter, Phil** (1940–) A Safe Place 1971; The Rugrats Movie 1998
Procter, Rupert aka **Procter, Rupert** The Low Down 2000; One for the Road 2003
Proietti, Luigi (1940–) Lady Liberty 1971; The Inheritance 1976
Proops, Greg Star Wars Episode I: the Phantom Menace 1999; Asterix and the Vikings 2006
Prophet, Melissa Players 1979; Better Late than Never 1983; Invasion USA 1985
Proske, Jenn Vampires Suck 2010; Shattered Silence 2012
Prosky, Robert (1930–2008) Thief 1981; Hanky Panky 1982; Christine 1983; The Keep 1983; The Lords of Discipline 1983; The Natural 1984; Outrageous Fortune 1987; Things Change 1988; Funny about Love 1990; Green Card 1990; Gremlins 2: the New Batch 1990; Loose Cannons 1990; Age Isn't Everything 1991; Far and Away 1992; Last Action Hero 1993; Dead Man Walking 1995; The Scarlet Letter 1995; The Chamber 1996; Mad City 1997; Dudley Do-Right 1999; Swing Vote 1999
Proud, David Special People 2007; No Fixed Abode 2012
Proulx, Brooklynn aka **Proulx, Brooklyn** Touch the Top of the World 2006; Lost Holiday: the Jim and Suzanne Shemwell Story 2007; The Lazarus Project 2008; The Time Traveler's Wife 2008
Proulx, Danielle (1952–) CRAZY 2005; Monsieur Lazhar 2011
Prouty, Jed (1879–1956) The Broadway Melody 1929; The Devil's Holiday 1930; The Duke of West Point 1938; The Gracie Allen Murder Case 1939; Hollywood Cavalcade 1939; Pot o' Gold 1941

Proval, David (1942–) Mean Streets 1973; Vice Versa 1988; Innocent Blood 1992; Romeo Is Bleeding 1992; Flipping 1996; Murder without Conviction 2004
Provine, Dorothy (1935–2010) Good Neighbor Sam 1964; The Great Race 1965; That Darn Cat! 1965; Kiss the Girls and Make Them Die 1966; One Spy Too Many 1966; Who's Minding the Mint? 1967
Provost, Jon (1950–) Escapade in Japan 1957; Lassie's Great Adventure 1963
Prowse, Dave aka **Prowse, David** (1935–) The Horror of Frankenstein 1970; A Clockwork Orange 1971; Frankenstein and the Monster from Hell 1973; White Cargo 1973; The Best of Benny Hill 1974; Callan 1974; The People That Time Forgot 1977; Star Wars Episode IV: a New Hope 1977; Star Wars Episode V: the Empire Strikes Back 1980; Star Wars Episode VI: Return of the Jedi 1983
Prowse, Juliet (1937–1996) Can-Can 1960; GI Blues 1960; The Fiercest Heart 1961; The Second Time Around 1961
Pryce, Jonathan (1947–) Breaking Glass 1980; Loophole 1980; Agatha Christie's Murder Is Easy 1982; The Ploughman's Lunch 1983; Something Wicked This Way Comes 1983; Brazil 1985; The Doctor and the Devils 1985; Haunted Honeymoon 1986; Man on Fire 1987; The Adventures of Baron Munchausen 1988; Consuming Passions 1988; The Rachel Papers 1989; Freddie as FRO7 1992; Glengarry Glen Ross 1992; Barbarians at the Gate 1993; A Business Affair 1993; Deadly Advice 1993; Shopping 1993; Stanley's Magic Garden 1994; Carrington 1995; Evita 1996; Regeneration 1997; Tomorrow Never Dies 1997; Ronin 1998; Stigmata 1999; The Testimony of Taliesin Jones 2000; Very Annie-Mary 2000; The Affair of the Necklace 2001; Bride of the Wind 2001; Unconditional Love 2001; Pirates of the Caribbean: the Curse of the Black Pearl 2003; What a Girl Wants 2003; De-Lovely 2004; The Brothers Grimm 2005; Pirates of the Caribbean: Dead Man's Chest 2006; Renaissance 2006; Leatherheads 2007; Pirates of the Caribbean: at World's End 2007; Bedtime Stories 2008; GI Joe: the Rise of Cobra 2009; Hysteria 2011; Patience (After Sebald) 2011; Listen Up Philip 2014; Narcopolis 2014; The White King 2016
Pryor, Nicholas (1935–) The Happy Hooker 1975; Smile 1975; Damien – Omen II 1978; Rainbow 1978; Gideon's Trumpet 1980; Risky Business 1983; On Dangerous Ground 1986; Less than Zero 1987; Nightbreaker 1989; Brain Dead 1990
Pryor, Richard (1940–2005) The Busy Body 1967; Wild in the Streets 1968; Dynamite Chicken 1971; Lady Sings the Blues 1972; Hit! 1973; Uptown Saturday Night 1974; The Bingo Long Travelling All-Stars and Motor Kings 1976; Car Wash 1976; Silver Streak 1976; Greased Lightning 1977; Which Way Is Up? 1977; Blue Collar 1978; California Suite 1978; The Wiz 1978; Richard Pryor: Live in Concert 1979; In God We Trust 1980; Stir Crazy 1980; Bustin' Loose 1981; Richard Pryor: Live on the Sunset Strip 1982; The Toy 1982; Superman III 1983; Brewster's Millions 1985; Jo Jo Dancer, Your Life Is Calling 1986; Critical Condition 1987; Moving 1988; Harlem Nights 1989; See No Evil, Hear No Evil 1989; Another You 1991; Lost Highway 1996
Pryor, Roger (1901–1974) Belle of the Nineties 1934; Lady by Choice 1934; The Man They Could Not Hang 1939
Pryse, Hugh (1910–1955) Three Cases of Murder 1953; Valley of Song 1953
Pszoniak, Wojciech aka **Pszoniak, Wojtek** (1942–) Danton 1982; Korczak 1990
Pu Quanxin The Blue Kite 1992; Shower 1999
Pucci, Lou Taylor aka **Pucci, Lou** (1985–) Thumbsucker 2005; Carriers 2008; Horsemen 2009; Brotherhood 2010; Evil Dead 2013; Spring 2014
Pucillo, Filippo Respiro 2002; Golden Door 2006
Pugh, Robert (1950–) Old Scores 1991; Priest 1994; The Englishman Who Went up a Hill, but Came down a Mountain 1995; The Tichborne Claimant 1998; The Testimony of Taliesin Jones 2000; Kinky Boots 2005; Hunky Dory 2011; Love Bite 2012
Pugh, Willard The Color Purple 1985; RoboCop 2 1990; Ambition 1991
Puglia, Frank (1892–1975) Isn't Life Wonderful 1924; Bulldog Drummond's Revenge 1937; Arise, My Love 1940; That Night in Rio 1941; Jungle Book

1942; Ali Baba and the Forty Thieves 1944; Blood on the Sun 1945; Without Reservations 1946; Road to Rio 1947; Colorado Territory 1949; Walk Softly, Stranger 1949; The Black Hand 1950; The Bandits of Corsica 1953; 20 Million Miles to Earth 1957; The Black Orchid 1959; Girls! Girls! Girls! 1962
Pullman, Bill (1953–) Ruthless People 1986; The Serpent and the Rainbow 1987; Spaceballs 1987; The Accidental Tourist 1988; Rocket Gibraltar 1988; Cold Feet 1989; Brain Dead 1990; Bright Angel 1990; Going Under 1990; Sibling Rivalry 1990; Liebestraum 1991; Crazy in Love 1992; Singles 1992; The Last Seduction 1993; Malice 1993; Mr Jones 1993; Sleepless in Seattle 1993; Sommersby 1993; The Favor 1994; Wyatt Earp 1994; Casper 1995; While You Were Sleeping 1995; Independence Day 1996; Lost Highway 1996; Mr Wrong 1996; The End of Violence 1997; Zero Effect 1997; Brokedown Palace 1999; History Is Made at Night 1999; Lake Placid 1999; The Guilty 2000; Titan AE 2000; The Virginian 2000; Igby Goes Down 2002; Dear Wendy 2004; The Grudge 2004; Alien Autopsy 2006; Scary Movie 4 2006; Surveillance 2007; You Kill Me 2007; Bottle Shock 2008; The Killer inside Me 2010; Lola Versus 2012; The Equalizer 2014; Independence Day: Resurgence 2016
Pully, B S (1910–1972) Greenwich Village 1944; Nob Hill 1945; Do You Love Me? 1946; Guys and Dolls 1955
Pulver, Lara A Patch of Fog 2015; Spooks: the Greater Good 2015
Pulver, Liselotte aka **Pulver, Lilo** (1929–) A Time to Love and a Time to Die 1958; One, Two, Three 1961; A Global Affair 1964; La Religieuse 1965
Punch, Lucy (1977–) Being Julia 2004; You Will Meet a Tall Dark Stranger 2010; Bad Teacher 2011; A Little Bit of Heaven 2011; Take Me Home Tonight 2011; Stand Up Guys 2012; The Wedding Video 2012
Punsley, Bernard (1923–2004) Dead End 1937; Angels Wash Their Faces 1939
Pupella, Mario Angela 2002; Salvo 2013
Purcell, Dick aka **Purcell, Richard** (1908–1944) Bullets or Ballots 1936; Arise, My Love 1940; The Bank Dick 1940; New Moon 1940; Reveille with Beverly 1943
Purcell, Dominic (1970–) Equilibrium 2002; Blade: Trinity 2004; Primeval 2007; Blood Creek 2009; Killer Elite 2011; Straw Dogs 2011
Purcell, Irene (1902–1972) The Passionate Plumber 1932; Westward Passage 1932
Purcell, Leah Somersault 2004; Jindabyne 2006
Purcell, Lee (1947–) Adam at 6 AM 1970; Kid Blue 1971; Dirty Little Billy 1972; Mr Majestyk 1974; Almost Summer 1977; Big Wednesday 1978; Eddie Macon's Run 1983; The Incredible Hulk Returns 1988
Purcell, Noel (1900–1985) The Blue Lagoon 1949; No Resting Place 1950; Appointment with Venus 1951; Encore 1951; Father's Doing Fine 1952; Grand National Night 1953; Mad about Men 1954; The Seekers 1954; Jacqueline 1956; Lust for Life 1956; The Rising of the Moon 1957; Ferry to Hong Kong 1958; The Key 1958; Merry Andrew 1958; Rockets Galore 1958; Rooney 1958; No Kidding 1960; Double Bunk 1961; The Iron Maiden 1962; The Violent Enemy 1969; Where's Jack? 1969
Purdell, Reginald (1896–1963) Congress Dances 1931; The Old Curiosity Shop 1935; Variety Jubilee 1942; Bell-Bottom George 1943; We Dive at Dawn 1943; Love Story 1944; Two Thousand Women 1944
Purdom, Edmund (1924–2009) Athena 1954; The Egyptian 1954; The Student Prince 1954; The King's Thief 1955; The Prodigal 1955; Moment of Danger 1960; Nefertite, Queen of the Nile 1961; The Beauty Jungle 1964; The Comedy Man 1964; The Yellow Rolls-Royce 1964; Pieces 1982
Purefoy, James (1964–) Feast of July 1995; Bedrooms and Hallways 1998; Lighthouse 1999; Mansfield Park 1999; Maybe Baby 1999; Women Talking Dirty 1999; Don Quixote 2000; The Wedding Tackle 2000; Resident Evil 2002; Vanity Fair 2004; Solomon Kane 2009; Ironclad 2010; Momentum 2015
Puri, Amrish (1937–2005) Nishant 1975; Indiana Jones and the Temple of Doom 1984; Dilwale Dulhania Le Jayenge 1995; Chachi 420 1997; Pardes 1997; Taal 1999; Zubeidaa 2000; Aitraaz 2004; Dev 2004;

Hulchul 2004; Kisna – the Warrior Poet 2004; Mujhse Shaadi Karogi 2004
Puri, Om (1950–) Sadgati 1981; Mirch Masala 1987; City of Joy 1992; In Custody 1993; Wolf 1994; Brothers in Trouble 1995; The Ghost and the Darkness 1996; Chachi 420 1997; My Son the Fanatic 1997; Such a Long Journey 1998; East Is East 1999; Bollywood Calling 2000; The Mystic Masseur 2001; The Parole Officer 2001; Awara Paagal Deewana 2002; Code 46 2003; Dev 2004; Kisna – the Warrior Poet 2004; Lakshya 2004; Charlie Wilson's War 2007; West Is West 2010; The Reluctant Fundamentalist 2012; The Hundred-Foot Journey 2014
Purl, Linda (1955–) Crazy Mama 1975; The High Country 1981; Man of Miracles 1999
Purviance, Edna (1894–1958) The Tramp 1915; Work 1915; Behind the Screen 1916; The Floorwalker 1916; The Pawnshop 1916; The Rink 1916; The Vagabond 1916; The Cure 1917; The Immigrant 1917; A Dog's Life 1918; Shoulder Arms 1918; A Day's Pleasure 1919; Sunnyside 1919; The Idle Class 1921; The Kid 1921; Pay Day 1922; The Pilgrim 1923; A Woman of Paris 1923
Putzulu, Bruno (1967–) The Bait 1995; Eloge de l'Amour 2001; Monsieur N 2003
Pyle, Denver (1920–1997) Rage at Dawn 1955; 7th Cavalry 1956; Gun Duel in Durango 1957; The Lonely Man 1957; Fort Massacre 1958; Cast a Long Shadow 1959; Geronimo 1962; Mail Order Bride 1963; The Rounders 1965; Gunpoint 1966; Bonnie and Clyde 1967; Welcome to Hard Times 1967; Bandolero! 1968; something big 1971; Winterhawk 1975; Welcome to LA 1976
Pyle, Missi (1972–) Home Alone 4 2002; Charlie and the Chocolate Factory 2005; Just My Luck 2006; Stormbreaker 2006; The Artist 2011; Gone Girl 2014; Captain Fantastic 2015
Pyne, Natasha (1946–) The Idol 1966; The Taming of the Shrew 1967; Father Dear Father 1972; Madhouse 1974; One of Our Dinosaurs Is Missing 1975
Pyper-Ferguson, John aka **Ferguson, John** (1964–) Pin 1988; Hannah's Law 2012; Wolves 2013

Q, Maggie (1979–) Mission: Impossible III 2006; Balls of Fury 2007; Die Hard 4.0 2007; Deception 2008; Priest 2010
Qin Shaobo (1982–) Ocean's Eleven 2001; Ocean's Twelve 2004
Qissi, Michel AWOL 1990; Kickboxer 2: the Road Back 1990
Quaid, Dennis (1954–) Crazy Mama 1975; September 30, 1955 1977; Breaking Away 1979; The Long Riders 1980; All Night Long 1981; Bill 1981; Caveman 1981; The Night the Lights Went Out in Georgia 1981; Tough Enough 1982; Jaws III 1983; The Right Stuff 1983; Dreamscape 1984; Enemy Mine 1985; The Big Easy 1986; Innerspace 1987; Suspect 1987; DOA 1988; Everybody's All-American 1988; Great Balls of Fire! 1989; Come See the Paradise 1990; Postcards from the Edge 1990; Flesh and Bone 1993; Undercover Blues 1993; Wilder Napalm 1993; Wyatt Earp 1994; Something to Talk About 1995; DragonHeart 1996; Gang Related 1997; Savior 1997; Switchback 1997; Everything That Rises 1998; The Parent Trap 1998; Playing by Heart 1998; Any Given Sunday 1999; Frequency 2000; Traffic 2000; Dinner with Friends 2001; Far from Heaven 2002; The Rookie 2002; Cold Creek Manor 2003; The Alamo 2004; The Day after Tomorrow 2004; Flight of the Phoenix 2004; In Good Company 2004; Yours, Mine & Ours 2005; American Dreamz 2006; Battle for Terra 2007; Smart People 2007; The Express 2008; Vantage Point 2008; GI Joe: the Rise of Cobra 2009; Horsemen 2009; Pandorum 2009; Footloose 2011; Soul Surfer 2011; At Any Price 2012; Playing for Keeps 2012; What to Expect When You're Expecting 2012; The Words 2012; Truth 2015
Quaid, Randy aka **Quaid, Randall R "Randy"** (1950–) The Last Picture Show 1971; What's Up, Doc? 1972; The Last Detail 1973; The Lolly-Madonna War 1973; Paper Moon 1973; The Apprenticeship of Duddy Kravitz 1974; Breakout 1975; Bound for Glory 1976; The Missouri Breaks 1976; The Choirboys 1977; Midnight Express 1978; Foxes 1980; The Long Riders 1980; Heartbeeps 1981; National Lampoon's Vacation 1983; The Wild Life 1984; Fool for Love 1985; The Slugger's Wife 1985; The Wraith 1986; No Man's Land

1987; Caddyshack II 1988; Moving 1988; Parents 1988; Bloodhounds of Broadway 1989; Cold Dog Soup 1989; National Lampoon's Christmas Vacation 1989; Days of Thunder 1990; Quick Change 1990; Texasville 1990; Freaked 1993; The Paper 1994; Bye Bye Love 1995; Independence Day 1996; Kingpin 1996 Last Dance 1996; Hard Rain 1997; Vegas Vacation 1997; Last Rites 1998; The Adventures of Rocky & Bullwinkle 1999; Purgatory 1999; The Day the World Ended 2001; Not Another Teen Movie 2001; Pluto Nash 2001; Milwaukee, Minnesota 2002; Home on the Range 2004; Brokeback Mountain 2005; The Ice Harvest 2005; Goya's Ghosts 2006

Qualen, John (1899-1987) Counsellor-at-Law 1933; Our Daily Bread 1934; Black Fury 1935; The Road to Glory 1936; Angels over Broadway 1940; The Grapes of Wrath 1940; The Long Voyage Home 1940; The Devil and Daniel Webster 1941; Out of the Fog 1941; Arabian Nights 1942; Jungle Book 1942; Tortilla Flat 1942; An American Romance 1944; Dark Waters 1944; Adventure 1945; Captain Kidd 1945; Hollow Triumph 1948; The Big Steal 1949; Hans Christian Andersen 1952; Ambush at Tomahawk Gap 1953; At Gunpoint 1955; The Searchers 1956; The Big Land 1957

Qualls, D J (1978-) Road Trip 2000; The Core 2002; Lone Star State of Mind 2002; The New Guy 2002; Hustle & Flow 2005; All about Steve 2009

Quan, Ke Huy (1971-) Indiana Jones and the Temple of Doom 1984; The Goonies 1985

Quarrier, Iain Cul-de-Sac 1966; The Fearless Vampire Killers 1967; Sympathy for the Devil 1968; Wonderwall 1968

Quarry, Robert (1925-2009) Count Yorga, Vampire 1970; The Return of Count Yorga 1971; Dr Phibes Rises Again 1972; Madhouse 1974; Sugar Hill 1974; Haunting Fear 1990

Quarshie, Hugh (1954-) Baby: Secret of the Lost Legend 1985; The Church 1988; Nightbreed 1990; To Walk with Lions 1999; It Was an Accident 2000

Quartermaine, Leon (1876-1967) Escape Me Never 1935; As You Like It 1936

Quast, Philip Clubland 2006; The Devil's Double 2011

Quayle, Anna (1913-169-) A Hard Day's Night 1964; Drop Dead Darling 1966; The Sandwich Man 1966; Smashing Time 1967; Chitty Chitty Bang Bang 1968; Up the Chastity Belt 1971; Adventures of a Private Eye 1977; Adventures of a Plumber's Mate 1978

Quayle, Anthony (1913-1989) Hamlet 1948; Saraband for Dead Lovers 1948; Oh, Rosalinda!! 1955; The Battle of the River Plate 1956; The Wrong Man 1956; The Man Who Wouldn't Talk 1957; No Time for Tears 1957; Woman in a Dressing Gown 1957; Ice Cold in Alex 1958; Serious Charge 1959; Tarzan's Greatest Adventure 1959; The Challenge 1960; The Guns of Navarone 1961; HMS Defiant 1962; Lawrence of Arabia 1962; East of Sudan 1964; The Fall of the Roman Empire 1964; Operation Crossbow 1965; A Study in Terror 1965; The Poppy Is Also a Flower 1966; Before Winter Comes 1968; Anne of the Thousand Days 1969; Mackenna's Gold 1969; Bequest to the Nation 1972; Everything You Always Wanted to Know about Sex … but Were Afraid to Ask 1972; Great Expectations 1974; The Tamarind Seed 1974; Moses 1975; The Eagle Has Landed 1976; Holocaust 2000 1977; Murder by Decree 1978; The Legend of the Holy Drinker 1987; King of the Wind 1989

Quéant, Gilles Odette 1950; Night without Stars 1951

Queen Latifah (1970-) House Party 2 1991; My Life 1993; Set It Off 1996; Living Out Loud 1998; Sphere 1998; The Bone Collector 1999; Brown Sugar 2002; Chicago 2002; Bringing Down the House 2003; Scary Movie 3 2003; Barbershop 2: Back in Business 2004; Taxi 2004; Beauty Shop 2005; The Muppets' Wizard of Oz 2005; Ice Age: the Meltdown 2006; Last Holiday 2006; Stranger than Fiction 2006; Arctic Tale 2007 Hairspray 2007; Mad Money 2008; The Secret Life of Bees 2008; What Happens in Vegas 2008; Ice Age 3: Dawn of the Dinosaurs 2009; Just Wright 2010; The Dilemma 2011; Ice Age 4: Continental Drift 2012; Joyful Noise 2012; Ice Age: Collision Course 2016; Miracles from Heaven 2016

Quennessen, Valérie (1957-1989) French Postcards 1979; Summer Lovers 1982

Quentin, John Blue 1993; Wittgenstein 1993

Questel, Mae (1908-1998) A Majority of One 1961; It'$ Only Money 1962; Funny Girl 1968; New York Stories 1989

Quester, Hugues (1948-) The Flesh of the Orchid 1974; Hôtel du Paradis 1986; A Tale of Springtime 1989

Quick, Diana (1946-) The Duellists 1977; The Odd Job 1978; Nineteen Nineteen 1984; Vroom 1988; Wilt 1989; Nostradamus 1993; The Leading Man 1996; Vigo: Passion for Life 1997; Saving Grace 2000; Revengers Tragedy 2002; Mother's Milk 2012

Quigley, Godfrey (1923-1994) The Siege of Sidney Street 1960; Nothing but the Best 1963; Daleks - Invasion Earth 2150 AD 1966; Barry Lyndon 1975; Educating Rita 1983

Quigley, Juanita aka **Quigley, Baby Jane "Juanita"** (1931-) Riffraff 1936; A Yank at Eton 1942; National Velvet 1944

Quigley, Pearce Millions 2004; Grow Your Own 2007; Breaking the Bank 2014

Quill, Tim Listen to Me 1989; Staying Together 1989

Quillan, Eddie (1907-1990) Broadway to Hollywood 1933; Mutiny on the Bounty 1935; Big City 1937; The Grapes of Wrath 1940; Kid Glove Killer 1942

Quilley, Denis (1927-2003) Evil under the Sun 1982; Privates on Parade 1982; King David 1985; Foreign Body 1986; Mister Johnson 1991

Quilligan, Veronica Malachi's Cove 1973; Lisztomania 1975; Candleshoe 1977; Angel 1982

Quine, Richard (1920-1989) Babes on Broadway 1941; Dr Gillespie's New Assistant 1942; For Me and My Gal 1942; My Sister Eileen 1942; The Clay Pigeon 1949; No Sad Songs for Me 1950

Quinlan, Kathleen (1954-) I Never Promised You a Rose Garden 1977; The Runner Stumbles 1979; Hanky Panky 1982; Independence Day 1983; Warning Sign 1985; Clara's Heart 1988; Sunset 1988; The Doors 1991; Last Light 1993; Perfect Alibi 1994; Trial by Jury 1994; Apollo 13 1995; Breakdown 1997; Event Horizon 1997; Lawn Dogs 1997; Zeus and Roxanne 1997; A Civil Action 1998; My Giant 1998; Perfect Romance 2004; The Riverman 2004; Breach 2006; The Hills Have Eyes 2006; Made of Honor 2008; Cinema Verite 2011

Quinn, Aidan (1959-) Reckless 1984; Desperately Seeking Susan 1985; An Early Frost 1985; The Mission 1986; Stakeout 1987; Crusoe 1988; The Lemon Sisters 1989; Avalon 1990; The Handmaid's Tale 1990; At Play in the Fields of the Lord 1991; The Playboys 1992; A Private Matter 1992; Benny & Joon 1993; Blink 1994; Legends of the Fall 1994; Mary Shelley's Frankenstein 1994; Haunted 1995; The Stars Fell on Henrietta 1995; Commandments 1996; Looking for Richard 1996; Michael Collins 1996; The Assignment 1997; Forbidden Territory: Stanley's Search for Livingstone 1997; In Dreams 1998; Practical Magic 1998; Music of the Heart 1999; Songcatcher 1999; This Is My Father 1999; Two of Us 2000; Evelyn 2002; Song for a Raggy Boy 2002; Stolen Summer 2002; Plainsong 2004; The Unexpected Journey 2004; Bury My Heart at Wounded Knee 2007; Wild Child 2008; Sarah's Key 2010; Unknown 2011; If I Were You 2012

Quinn, Anthony (1915-2001) The Plainsman 1936; Swing High, Swing Low 1937; Waikiki Wedding 1937; The Buccaneer 1938; Bulldog Drummond in Africa 1938; City for Conquest 1940; The Ghost Breakers 1940; Road to Singapore 1940; Blood and Sand 1941; They Died with Their Boots On 1941; The Black Swan 1942; Larceny, Inc 1942; Road to Morocco 1942; Guadalcanal Diary 1943; The Ox-Bow Incident 1943; Buffalo Bill 1944; Irish Eyes Are Smiling 1944; Back to Bataan 1945; China Sky 1945; Where Do We Go from Here? 1945; California 1946; Black Gold 1947; The Imperfect Lady 1947; Sinbad the Sailor 1947; Tycoon 1947; The Brave Bulls 1951; Against All Flags 1952; Viva Zapata! 1952; The World in His Arms 1952; Blowing Wild 1953; City beneath the Sea 1953; East of Sumatra 1953; Ride, Vaquero! 1953; Seminole 1953; La Strada 1954; Ulysses 1954; The Naked Street 1955; The Hunchback of Notre Dame 1956; Lust for Life 1956; The River's Edge 1957; Wild Is the Wind 1957; Hot Spell 1958; The Black Orchid 1959; Last Train from

Gun Hill 1959; Warlock 1959; Heller in Pink Tights 1960; Portrait in Black 1960; The Savage Innocents 1960; Barabbas 1961; The Guns of Navarone 1961; Lawrence of Arabia 1962; Requiem for a Heavyweight 1962; Behold a Pale Horse 1964; The Visit 1964; Zorba the Greek 1964; A High Wind in Jamaica 1965; The Happening 1967; The Rover 1967; The 25th Hour 1967; The Magus 1968; The Shoes of the Fisherman 1968; A Dream of Kings 1969; The Secret of Santa Vittoria 1969; Flap 1970; RPM - Revolutions per Minute 1970; A Walk in the Spring Rain 1970; Across 110th Street 1972; The Marseille Contract 1974; The Con Artists 1976; The Inheritance 1976; The Children of Sanchez 1978; The Greek Tycoon 1978; The Passage 1978; High Risk 1981; Lion of the Desert 1981; The Salamander 1981; Regina 1982; Valentina 1982; 1919 1983; Ghosts Can't Do It 1990; The Old Man and the Sea 1990; Revenge 1990; Jungle Fever 1991; Mobsters 1991; Only the Lonely 1991; Last Action Hero 1993; Somebody to Love 1994; A Walk in the Clouds 1995; Avenging Angelo 2002

Quinn, Colin Grown Ups 2010; Trainwreck 2015

Quinn, Francesco (1962-) Platoon 1986; The Old Man and the Sea 1990; The Gunfighter's Pledge 2008

Quinn, J C (1940-2004) Vision Quest 1985; Barfly 1987; The Abyss 1989; Turner & Hooch 1989; Days of Thunder 1990; Prayer of the Rollerboys 1990; CrissCross 1992

Quinn, Marian Broken Harvest 1994; Heavy 1995

Quinn, Martha (1961-) Eddie and the Cruisers II: Eddie Lives! 1989; Chopper Chicks in Zombietown 1990; Motorama 1991

Quinn, Patricia aka **Quinn, Pat** (1944-) Alice's Restaurant 1969; Shoot Out 1971; The Rocky Horror Picture Show 1975; An Unmarried Woman 1978; The Outsider 1979

Quinn, Tony (1899-1967) Shadow of a Man 1954; Booby Trap 1957; The Rising of the Moon 1957

Quinones, Adolfo "Shabba-Doo" Breakdance 1984; Breakdance 2 - Electric Boogaloo 1984

Quinto, Zachary (1977-) Star Trek 2009; Margin Call 2011; What's Your Number? 2011; Star Trek into Darkness 2013; We'll Never Have Paris 2014; Hitman: Agent 47 2015; Snowden 2016; Star Trek Beyond 2016

Quirke, Pauline (1959-) The Return of the Soldier 1982; Getting It Right 1989; Arthur's Dyke 2001

Quitak, Oscar The Traitor 1957; The Revenge of Frankenstein 1958

Quo, Beulah (1923-2002) The 7th Dawn 1964; Yes, Giorgio 1982

Quon, Marianne China 1943; Charlie Chan in the Secret Service 1944

R

Raab, Ellie (1977-) The Fabulous Baker Boys 1989; Eyes of an Angel 1991

Raab, Kurt (1941-1988) Why Does Herr R Run Amok? 1970; Fear of Fear 1976; Satan's Brew 1976; Bolwieser 1977; Escape from Sobibor 1987

Raaz, Vijay Monsoon Wedding 2001; Mumbai Matinee 2003

Rabagliati, Alberto (1906-1974) Street Angel 1928; Crossed Swords 1954; The Monte Carlo Story 1957

Rabal, Francisco (1926-2001) Nazarín 1958; Viridiana 1961; The Eclipse 1962; La Religieuse 1965; The Witches 1966; Belle de Jour 1967; Los Santos Inocentes 1984; Camorra 1985; A Time of Destiny 1988; Tie Me Up! Tie Me Down! 1990; Goya in Bordeaux 1999

Rabe, Pamela (1959-) Sirens 1994; Cosi 1996

Rabourdin, Olivier Ma Mère 2004; Of Gods and Men 2010; Eastern Boys 2012

Racette, Francine (1947-) The Disappearance 1977; Au Revoir les Enfants 1987

Rachins, Alan (1947-) Always 1985; Heart Condition 1990; Showgirls 1995

Racimo, Victoria (1950-) Journey through Rosebud 1972; Prophecy 1979; On Dangerous Ground 1986; Ernest Goes to Camp 1987; White Fang 2: Myth of the White Wolf 1994

Radcliffe, Daniel (1989-) Harry Potter and the Philosopher's Stone 2001; Harry Potter and the Chamber of Secrets 2002; Harry Potter and the Prisoner of Azkaban 2004; Harry Potter and the Goblet of Fire 2005; December Boys 2007; Harry Potter and the Order of the Phoenix 2007; Harry Potter and the Half-Blood Prince 2009; Harry Potter and the Deathly

Hallows: Part 1 2010; Harry Potter and the Deathly Hallows: Part 2 2011; The Woman in Black 2011; Horns 2013; Kill Your Darlings 2013; What If 2013; Victor Frankenstein 2015; Imperium 2016; Now You See Me 2 2016; Swiss Army Man 2016

Radford, Basil (1897-1952) Young and Innocent 1937; Convict 99 1938; The Lady Vanishes 1938; Just William 1939; Let's Be Famous 1939; Crooks' Tour 1940; Night Train to Munich 1940; Unpublished Story 1942; Millions like Us 1943; A Girl in a Million 1946; It's Not Cricket 1948; Quartet 1948; The Winslow Boy 1948; Passport to Pimlico 1949; Whisky Galore! 1949; Chance of a Lifetime 1950

Radley, Ken Sniper 1992; The Adventures of Priscilla, Queen of the Desert 1994

Radner, Gilda (1946-1989) Animalympics 1979; First Family 1980; Hanky Panky 1982; The Woman in Red 1984; Movers and Shakers 1985; Haunted Honeymoon 1986

Radnor, Josh (1974-) Liberal Arts 2011; Afternoon Delight 2013

Radzin, Elsa aka **Radzinya, Elsa** (1917-) Hamlet 1964; King Lear 1970

Radziwilowicz, Jerzy (1950-) Man of Marble 1977; Man of Iron 1981; Passion 1982; No End 1984; Secret Defense 1997; Histoire de Marie et Julien 2003

Rae, John (1896-1985) The Brave Don't Cry 1952; The Kidnappers 1953; The Big Chance 1957; The Bridal Path 1959

Rae, Paul Daddy Day Camp 2007; The Circuit 2008; True Grit 2010

Rafaelsen, Henrik Happy, Happy 2010; Blind 2014

Raffaelli, Cyril District 13 2004; District 13: Ultimatum 2009

Rafferty, Chips (1909-1971) Forty Thousand Horsemen 1941; The Overlanders 1946; Bush Christmas 1947; The Loves of Joanna Godden 1947; Eureka Stockade 1949; Bitter Springs 1950; Kangaroo 1952; The Desert Rats 1953; Smiley 1956; Smiley Gets a Gun 1959; The Sundowners 1960; The Wackiest Ship in the Army 1961; They're a Weird Mob 1966; Double Trouble 1967; Skullduggery 1969; Wake in Fright 1970

Rafferty, Frances (1922-2004) Barbary Coast Gent 1944; Dragon Seed 1944; Mrs Parkington 1944; Abbott and Costello in Hollywood 1945

Raffin, Deborah (1953-2012) 40 Carats 1973; The Dove 1974; Once Is Not Enough 1975; Maniac 1977; Touched by Love 1979; Agatha Christie's Sparkling Cyanide 1983; Dance of the Dwarfs 1983; Death Wish 3 1985; Scanners II: The New Order 1991; LaVyrle Spencer's Home Song 1996

Raft, George (1895-1980) Palmy Days 1931; Quick Millions 1931; If I Had a Million 1932; Love Is a Racket 1932; Night after Night 1932; Scarface 1932; Taxi! 1932; The Bowery 1933; Bolero 1934; The Glass Key 1935; Rumba 1935; Souls at Sea 1937; Spawn of the North 1938; You and Me 1938; Each Dawn I Die 1939; Invisible Stripes 1939; The House across the Bay 1940; They Drive by Night 1940; Manpower 1941; Broadway 1942; Background to Danger 1943; Stage Door Canteen 1943; Follow the Boys 1944; Johnny Angel 1945; Nob Hill 1945; Nocturne 1946; Whistle Stop 1946; Christmas Eve 1947; Intrigue 1947; A Dangerous Profession 1949; Outpost in Morocco 1949; Red Light 1949; Escape Route 1952; The Man from Cairo 1953; Black Widow 1954; Rogue Cop 1954; A Bullet for Joey 1955; Around the World in 80 Days 1956; Some Like It Hot 1959; The Ladies' Man 1961; Casino Royale 1967; Five Golden Dragons 1967; Skidoo 1968; Deadhead Miles 1972; Sextette 1978; The Man with Bogart's Face 1980

Ragland, Rags (1905-1946) Whistling in the Dark 1941; DuBarry Was a Lady 1943; Girl Crazy 1943; Meet the People 1944; Anchors Aweigh 1945

Ragsdale, William (1961-) Fright Night 1985; Fright Night Part 2 1988; Mannequin on the Move 1991; For One Night 2006; The Reaping 2006

Rahim, Tahar (1981-) A Prophet 2009; The Eagle 2010; Black Gold 2011; Free Men 2011; Our Children 2012; Grand Central 2013; The Informant 2013; The Past 2013; The Cut 2014; Samba 2014

Rai, Aishwarya aka **Rai Bachchan, Aishwarya** (1973-) Hum Dil De Chuke Sanam 1999; Taal 1999; Mohabbatein 2000; Devdas 2002; Shakti - the Power 2002; Chokher Bali 2003; Kuch Naa Kaho 2003; Bride & Prejudice 2004; Dhoom: 2 2006; The Last

Legion 2006; Provoked: a True Story 2006; Guru 2007; Jodhaa Akbar 2008; Sarkar Raj 2008; The Pink Panther 2 2009

Raido, Mel Clubbed 2008; In Our Name 2010

Railsback, Steve (1948-) The Visitors 1972; The Stunt Man 1980; Turkey Shoot 1981; The Golden Seal 1983; Torchlight 1984; Lifeforce 1985; Alligator II: the Mutation 1991; Scissors 1991; Barb Wire 1995; Disturbing Behavior 1998; Made Men 1999; Ed Gein 2000

Raimi, Ted aka **Raimi, Theodore** (1965-) Evil Dead II 1987; Darkman 1990; Lunatics: a Love Story 1991; Candyman 1992; My Name Is Bruce 2008

Raimondi, Ruggero (1941-) Don Giovanni 1979; Life Is a Bed of Roses 1983; Carmen 1984; Tosca 2001

Raimu (1883-1946) Mahlia 1931; Fanny 1932; César 1936; Un Carnet de Bal 1937; The Baker's Wife 1938

Rain, Douglas (1928-) 2001: a Space Odyssey 1968; 2010 1984

Rainer, Luise (1910-2014) Escapade 1935; The Great Ziegfeld 1936; Big City 1937; The Emperor's Candlesticks 1937; The Good Earth 1937; Dramatic School 1938; The Great Waltz 1938; The Toy Wife 1938; The Gambler 1997

Raines, Cristina (1952-) The Duellists 1977; The Sentinel 1977; Touched by Love 1979; Silver Dream Racer 1980; Nightmares 1983; Real Life 1983

Raines, Ella (1920-1988) Corvette K-225 1943; Cry Havoc 1943; Enter Arsene Lupin 1944; Hail the Conquering Hero 1944; Phantom Lady 1944; The Suspect 1944; Tall in the Saddle 1944; The Strange Affair of Uncle Harry 1945; Brute Force 1947; The Senator Was Indiscreet 1947; Time Out of Mind 1947; The Web 1947; A Dangerous Profession 1949; Impact 1949; The Walking Hills 1949; The Man in the Road 1957

Rainey, Ford (1908-2005) The Last Mile 1959; Ada 1961; Bed & Breakfast 1992

Rains, Claude (1889-1967) The Invisible Man 1933; The Clairvoyant 1934; Crime without Passion 1934; The Last Outpost 1935; The Mystery of Edwin Drood 1935; Anthony Adverse 1936; The Prince and the Pauper 1937; They Won't Forget 1937; The Adventures of Robin Hood 1938; Four Daughters 1938; Gold Is Where You Find It 1938; White Banners 1938; Daughters Courageous 1939; Four Wives 1939; Juarez 1939; Mr Smith Goes to Washington 1939; They Made Me a Criminal 1939; Saturday's Children 1940; The Sea Hawk 1940; Four Mothers 1941; Here Comes Mr Jordan 1941; The Wolf Man 1941; Casablanca 1942; Kings Row 1942; Moontide 1942; Now, Voyager 1942; Strange Holiday 1942; Forever and a Day 1943; Phantom of the Opera 1943; Mr Skeffington 1944; Passage to Marseille 1944; Caesar and Cleopatra 1945; This Love of Ours 1945; Angel on My Shoulder 1946; Deception 1946; Notorious 1946; The Unsuspected 1947; The Passionate Friends 1948; Rope of Sand 1949; Where Danger Lives 1950; The White Tower 1950; Sealed Cargo 1951; The Man Who Watched Trains Go By 1952; Lisbon 1956; This Earth Is Mine 1959; The Lost World 1960; Lawrence of Arabia 1962; Twilight of Honor 1963; The Greatest Story Ever Told 1965

Rajot, Pierre-Loup (1958-) La Nouvelle Eve 1998; Drôle de Félix 2000

Rajskub, Mary Lynn (1971-) Punch-Drunk Love 2002; Mysterious Skin 2004; Firewall 2006; Sunshine Cleaning 2008; Julie & Julia 2009

Rall, Tommy aka **Rall, Thomas** (1929-) Kiss Me Kate 1953; Seven Brides for Seven Brothers 1954; My Sister Eileen 1955; Invitation to the Dance 1956; Walk the Proud Land 1956; Merry Andrew 1958; Dancers 1987

Ralli, Giovanna (1935-) General Della Rovere 1959; What Did You Do in the War, Daddy? 1966; Deadfall 1968; A Professional Gun 1968; Cannon for Cordoba 1970; We All Loved Each Other So Much 1974

Ralph, Hanna (1885-1978) The Nibelungen 1924; Faust 1926

Ralph, Jessie (1864-1944) The Affairs of Cellini 1934; One Night of Love 1934; David Copperfield 1935; Enchanted April 1935; I Found Stella Parish 1935; Les Misérables 1935; After the Thin Man 1936; San Francisco 1936; Camille 1937; Double Wedding 1937; The Good Earth 1937; The Last of Mrs Cheyney 1937; Port of Seven Seas 1938; Drums

along the Mohawk 1939; The Bank Dick 1940; They Met in Bombay 1941
Ralph, Michael DROP Squad 1994; Woo 1998

Ralph, Sheryl Lee (1956-) Oliver & Company 1989; The Mighty Quinn 1989; The Distinguished Gentleman 1992; Bogus 1996; Deterrence 1999

Ralston, Esther (1902-1994) The Case of Lena Smith 1929; Rome Express 1932; Black Beauty 1933; By Candlelight 1934; Sadie McKee 1934; Tin Pan Alley 1940

Ralston, Jobyna (1900-1967) Girl Shy 1924; Hot Water 1924; The Freshman 1925; For Heaven's Sake 1926; The Kid Brother 1927; Wings 1927

Ralston, John Mary Higgins Clark's The Cradle Will Fall 2004; Earthstorm 2006; Client Seduction 2014

Ralston, Vera aka Hruba Ralston, Vera (1923-2003) The Lady and the Monster 1944; Dakota 1945; The Fighting Kentuckian 1949; Hoodlum Empire 1952; Fair Wind to Java 1953; Timberjack 1955; Accused of Murder 1956

Ramage, Cecil (1895-1988) Return of a Stranger 1937; Kind Hearts and Coronets 1949

Rambeau, Marjorie (1889-1970) Min and Bill 1930; Inspiration 1931; Laughing Sinners 1931; The Secret Six 1931; Strangers May Kiss 1931; Hell Divers 1932; Man's Castle 1933; Palooka 1934; East of the River 1940; Primrose Path 1940; Tobacco Road 1941; Broadway 1942; War of the Wildcats 1943; Salome, Where She Danced 1945; Forever Female 1953; Torch Song 1953; A Man Called Peter 1955; Man of a Thousand Faces 1957

Ramer, Henry (192?-2009) The Apprenticeship of Duddy Kravitz 1974; Between Friends 1983

Ramírez, Carlos (1914-1986) Bathing Beauty 1944; Where Do We Go from Here? 1945

Ramirez, Dania Quarantine 2008; Premium Rush 2012

Ramirez, Edgar (1977-) Domino 2005; The Bourne Ultimatum 2007; Vantage Point 2008; Carlos 2010; Wrath of the Titans 2012; Deliver Us from Evil 2014; Joy 2015; Point Break 2015; The Girl on the Train 2016; Gold 2016

Ramirez, Efren Napoleon Dynamite 2004; Crank 2006; Employee of the Month 2006; Crank: High Voltage 2009

Ramirez, Frank Smith! 1969; The Snail's Strategy 1993

Ramiro, Andre The Elite Squad 2007; Elite Squad: the Enemy Within 2010

Ramis, Harold (1944-2014) Heavy Metal 1981; Stripes 1981; Ghost Busters 1984; Baby Boom 1987; Stealing Home 1988; Ghostbusters II 1989; Orange County 2001; I'm with Lucy 2002; Walk Hard: the Dewey Cox Story 2007

Ramón, Eulalia (1959-) Outrage 1993; Goya in Bordeaux 1999

Ramos, Nathalia bratz 2007; 31 North 62 East 2009

Ramos, Rudy (1950-) The Driver 1978; Defiance 1979; Quicksilver 1986

Rampling, Charlotte (1946-) Rotten to the Core 1965; Georgy Girl 1966; The Long Duel 1967; The Damned 1969; Three 1969; Asylum 1972; Corky 1972; Henry VIII and His Six Wives 1972; The Night Porter 1973; Zardoz 1973; Caravan to Vaccares 1974; The Flesh of the Orchid 1974; Farewell, My Lovely 1975; Sherlock Holmes in New York 1976; Orca... Killer Whale 1977; The Purple Taxi 1977; Stardust Memories 1980; The Verdict 1982; Max Mon Amour 1986; Angel Heart 1987; Mascara 1987; DOA 1988; Paris by Night 1988; Hammers over the Anvil 1992; The Wings of the Dove 1997; The Cherry Orchard 1998; Aberdeen 2000; Under the Sand 2000; The Fourth Angel 2001; Spy Game 2001; Summer Things 2002; Swimming Pool 2002; I'll Sleep When I'm Dead 2003; The Statement 2003; The Keys to the House 2004; Lemming 2005; Angel 2006; Basic Instinct 2: Risk Addiction 2006; Heading South 2006; Babylon AD 2008; The Duchess 2008; Boogie Woogie 2009; Life during Wartime 2009; Never Let Me Go 2010; StreetDance 2010; The Eye of the Storm 2011; Melancholia 2011; Cleanskin 2012; I, Anna 2012; Jeune & Jolie 2013; The Sea 2013; The Forbidden Room 2015; 45 Years 2015

Ramsay, Bruce (1968-) Alive 1992; Killing Zoe 1993; Dead Beat 1994; Curdled 1995; Hellraiser: Bloodline 1996; Baby for Sale 2004

Ramsay, Remak (1937-) The House on Carroll Street 1987; Addicted to Love 1997

Ramsey, Anne (1929-1988) The Goonies 1985; Deadly Friend 1986; Throw Momma from the Train 1987; Homer and Eddie 1989

Ramsey, Laura (1982-) The Covenant 2006; She's the Man 2006; The Ruins 2008; No One Lives 2012

Ramsey, Logan (1921-2000) The Hoodlum Priest 1961; Head 1968; Busting 1974

Ramsey, Marion Police Academy 2: Their First Assignment 1985; Police Academy 3: Back in Training 1986; Police Academy 6: City under Siege 1989

Rand, Edwin (1911-1993) The Capture 1950; Tarantula 1955

Rand, John (1871-1940) The Pawnshop 1916; The Cure 1917; The Idle Class 1921

Randall, Lexi aka Randall, Lexi Faith (1980-) The Long Walk Home 1990; The War 1994; The Stars Fell on Henrietta 1995

Randall, Meg (1926-) Ma and Pa Kettle 1949; Lover Come Back 1961

Randall, Tony (1920-2004) No Down Payment 1957; Oh, Men! Oh, Women! 1957; Will Success Spoil Rock Hunter? 1957; The Mating Game 1959; Pillow Talk 1959; The Adventures of Huckleberry Finn 1960; Let's Make Love 1960; Lover Come Back 1961; Boys' Night Out 1962; Island of Love 1963; 7 Faces of Dr Lao 1963; The Brass Bottle 1964; Send Me No Flowers 1964; Fluffy 1965; The Alphabet Murders 1966; Our Man in Marrakesh 1966; Hello Down There 1969; Everything You Always Wanted to Know about Sex ... but Were Afraid to Ask 1972; Foolin' Around 1980; The King of Comedy 1983; The Man in the Brown Suit 1989; Gremlins 2: the New Batch 1990; Down with Love 2003

Randle, Frank (1901-1957) Somewhere on Leave 1942; When You Come Home 1947; It's a Grand Life 1953

Randle, Theresa (1967-) Malcolm X 1992; Sugar Hill 1993; Beverly Hills Cop III 1994; Bad Boys 1995; Girl 6 1996; Space Jam 1997; Spawn 1997; Bad Boys II 2003

Randol, Anders (1870-1930) The Black Pirate 1926; The Kiss 1929

Randolph, Donald (1906-1993) Bride of Vengeance 1949; Assignment - Paris 1952; Khyber Patrol 1954; The Mad Magician 1954; Phffft! 1954; The Deadly Mantis 1957

Randolph, Jane (1915-2009) Cat People 1942; The Falcon's Brother 1942; The Falcon Strikes Back 1943; The Curse of the Cat People 1944; Fool's Gold 1946; Railroaded! 1947; T-Men 1947; Abbott and Costello Meet Frankenstein 1948

Randolph, John (1915-2004) Seconds 1966; Pretty Poison 1968; Number One 1969; Smith! 1969; There Was a Crooked Man... 1970; Escape from the Planet of the Apes 1971; Little Murders 1971; Conquest of the Planet of the Apes 1972; Serpico 1973; King Kong 1976; Prizzi's Honor 1985; As Summers Die 1986; The Wizard of Loneliness 1988; National Lampoon's Christmas Vacation 1989; Iron Maze 1991; A Price above Rubies 1997

Randolph, Lillian (1898-1980) The Bachelor and the Bobby-Soxer 1947; Once More, My Darling 1949; Magic 1978

Randone, Salvo (1906-1991) Salvatore Giuliano 1961; Hands over the City 1963; The Tenth Victim 1965; Satyricon 1969; Investigation of a Citizen above Suspicion 1970; The Working Class Goes to Heaven 1971

Ransom, Kenneth aka Ransom, Kenny There Goes My Baby 1994; The Crocodile Hunter: Collision Course 2002

Ransom, Tim (1963-) The Dressmaker 1988; Vital Signs 1990; Vanished without a Trace 1993

Ransome, Prunella (1943-2003) Far from the Madding Crowd 1967; Alfred the Great 1969; Man in the Wilderness 1971

Ransone, James Sinister 2012; Old Boy 2013; Sinister 2 2015

Rao, Dileep Drag Me to Hell 2009; Inception 2010

Rapace, Noomi (1979-) The Girl with the Dragon Tattoo 2009; The Girl Who Played with Fire 2009; The Girl Who Kicked the Hornet's Nest 2009;

Babycall 2011; Passion 2012; Prometheus 2012; Dead Man Down 2013; Child 44 2014; The Drop 2014

Rapaport, Michael (1970-) Zebrahead 1992; Money for Nothing 1993; True Romance 1993; Hand Gun 1994; Kiss of Death 1994; The Scout 1994; Higher Learning 1995; Mighty Aphrodite 1995; Beautiful Girls 1996; illtown 1996; The Pallbearer 1996; Cop Land 1997; Kicked in the Head 1997; Metro 1997; Subway Stories: Tales from the Underground 1997; Palmetto 1998; Deep Blue Sea 1999; Bamboozled 2000; Men of Honor 2000; The 6th Day 2000; Small Time Crooks 2000; Triggermen 2002; Hitch 2005; Special (PX) - Specioprin Hydrochloride 2006; The Heat 2013

Raphael, June Diane aka Raphael, June Year One 2009; Girl Most Likely 2012

Rapp, Anthony (1971-) A Night on the Town 1987; Far from Home 1989; School Ties 1992; Dazed and Confused 1993; A Beautiful Mind 2001; Rent 2005

Rasche, David (1944-) Death Vengeance 1982; An Innocent Man 1989; Wicked Stepmother 1989; Bingo 1991; Delirious 1991; That Old Feeling 1997; Just Married 2003; The Sentinel 2006; The Girl in the Park 2007

Rashad, Phylicia (1948-) David's Mother 1994; Just Wright 2010; Creed 2015

Rasmussen, Rie (1976-) Femme Fatale 2002; Angel-A 2005

Rasp, Fritz (1891-1976) Metropolis 1926; The Love of Jeanne Ney 1927; Diary of a Lost Girl 1929; The Woman in the Moon 1929; The Threepenny Opera 1931

Rasuk, Victor (1984-) Raising Victor Vargas 2002; Lords of Dogtown 2005; Bonneville 2006; Stop-Loss 2007

Rasulala, Thalmus (1939-1991) Blacula 1972; The Autobiography of Miss Jane Pittman 1974; Friday Foster 1975; Mr Ricco 1975; Bulletproof 1987; Mom and Dad Save the World 1992

Rasumny, Mikhail (1890-1956) Road to Morocco 1942; Wake Island 1942; For Whom the Bell Tolls 1943; A Medal for Benny 1945; Anna and the King of Siam 1946; Heartbeat 1946; Her Husband's Affairs 1947; Anything Can Happen 1952; Hot Blood 1956

Ratcliff, Sandy (1950-) Family Life 1971; Radio On 1979; Yesterday's Hero 1979

Rathbone, Basil (1892-1967) The Last of Mrs Cheyney 1929; Anna Karenina 1935; Captain Blood 1935; David Copperfield 1935; The Last Days of Pompeii 1935; A Tale of Two Cities 1935; The Garden of Allah 1936; Love from a Stranger 1936; Romeo and Juliet 1936; Confession 1937; Tovarich 1937; The Adventures of Marco Polo 1938; The Adventures of Robin Hood 1938; The Dawn Patrol 1938; If I Were King 1938; The Adventures of Sherlock Holmes 1939; The Hound of the Baskervilles 1939; Son of Frankenstein 1939; Tower of London 1939; The Mark of Zorro 1940; Rhythm on the River 1940; The Black Cat 1941; Paris Calling 1941; Crossroads 1942; Fingers at the Window 1942; Sherlock Holmes and the Secret Weapon 1942; Sherlock Holmes and the Voice of Terror 1942; Above Suspicion 1943; Sherlock Holmes Faces Death 1943; Sherlock Holmes in Washington 1943; Bathing Beauty 1944; Frenchman's Creek 1944; The House of Fear 1944; The Pearl of Death 1944; The Scarlet Claw 1944; Sherlock Holmes and the Spider Woman 1944; Pursuit to Algiers 1945; The Woman in Green 1945; Dressed to Kill 1946; Heartbeat 1946; Terror by Night 1946; The Adventures of Ichabod and Mr Toad 1949; Casanova's Big Night 1954; We're No Angels 1955; The Black Sleep 1956; The Court Jester 1956; The Last Hurrah 1958; Pontius Pilate 1961; The Magic Sword 1962; Tales of Terror 1962; The Comedy of Terrors 1964; Voyage to the Prehistoric Planet 1965; The Ghost in the Invisible Bikini 1966; Planet of Blood 1966

Rathbone, Jackson Dread 2009; The Last Airbender 2010

Rathebe, Dolly (1928-2004) Mapantsula 1988; Friends 1993; Cry, the Beloved Country 1995

Ratoff, Gregory (1897-1960) Skyscraper Souls 1932; Symphony of Six Million 1932; What Price Hollywood? 1932; Broadway through a Keyhole 1933; I'm No Angel 1933; Sitting Pretty 1933; George White's Scandals 1934; Remember Last Night? 1935; The Road to Glory 1936; Sing, Baby, Sing 1936; Under Two Flags 1936; Café Metropole 1937; Seventh Heaven 1937; Sally, Irene and Mary

1938; All about Eve 1950; O Henry's Full House 1952; The Sun Also Rises 1957; Exodus 1960

Ratray, Devin Home Alone 2: Lost in New York 1992; Blue Ruin 2013

Rattray, Heather (1966-) Across the Great Divide 1977; Basket Case 2 1990

Ratzenberger, John (1947-) Warlords of Atlantis 1978; Arabian Adventure 1979; The Bitch 1979; Hanover Street 1979; Outland 1981; Battletruck 1982; House II: the Second Story 1987; Toy Story 1995; That Darn Cat 1997; Under Pressure 1997; Toy Story 2 1999; Determination of Death 2001; Monsters, Inc 2001; Spirited Away 2001; Finding Nemo 2003; The Incredibles 2004; Cars 2006; Ratatouille 2007; Our First Christmas 2008; WALL-E 2008; Up 2009; Toy Story 3 2010; Cars 2 2011; Monsters University 2013; Planes 2013; Toy Story 4 2017

Rauch, Siegfried (1932-) Le Mans 1971; The Big Red One 1980; Steve McQueen: the Man & Le Mans 2015

Raven-Symoné (1985-) Dr Dolittle 2 2001; For One Night 2006; College Road Trip 2008; Tinker Bell 2008; Good Hair 2009; Revenge of the Bridesmaids 2010; Tinkerbell and the Secret of the Wings 2012; Tinker Bell and the Legend of the NeverBeast 2014; TinkerBell and the Pirate Fairy 2014

Raven, Mike (1924-1997) Crucible of Terror 1971; I, Monster 1971

Ravenscroft, Thurl (1914-2005) The Aristocats 1970; The Brave Little Toaster 1987

Rawal, Paresh (1950-) Awara Paagal Deewana 2002; Aitraaz 2004; Hulchul 2004; Cheeni Kum 2007; Oye Lucky! Lucky Oye! 2008

Rawlings, Margaret (1906-1996) Roman Holiday 1953; Beautiful Stranger 1954; No Road Back 1957; Follow Me 1971

Rawlins, Adrian Mountains of the Moon 1989; Breaking the Waves 1996; My Brother Tom 2001; Wilbur (Wants to Kill Himself) 2002; The Woman in Black: Angel of Death 2014

Rawlinson, Herbert (1885-1953) Confidential 1935; Jail Bait 1954

Rawls, Lou (1933-2006) Angel, Angel Down We Go 1969; Lookin' Italian 1994

Ray, Aldo (1926-1991) The Marrying Kind 1952; Pat and Mike 1952; Let's Do It Again 1953; Miss Sadie Thompson 1953; Battle Cry 1955; We're No Angels 1955; Nightfall 1956; Men in War 1957; God's Little Acre 1958; The Naked and the Dead 1958; The Day They Robbed the Bank of England 1960; Nightmare in the Sun 1964; Sylvia 1964; Dead Heat on a Merry-Go-Round 1966; What Did You Do in the War, Daddy? 1966; Kill a Dragon 1967; The Violent Ones 1967; Welcome to Hard Times 1967; The Green Berets 1968; And Hope to Die 1972; Inside Out 1975; The Glove 1978; Little Moon & Jud McGraw 1978

Ray, Andrew (1939-2003) The Mudlark 1950; The Yellow Balloon 1952; Escape by Night 1953; Woman in a Dressing Gown 1957; Gideon's Day 1958; Serious Charge 1959; Twice round the Daffodils 1962; Paris by Night 1988

Ray, Connie (-) Bobby Jones: Stroke of Genius 2004; Ice Princess 2005

Ray, Lisa Bollywood/Hollywood 2002; Water 2005

Ray, Michel (1944-) The Divided Heart 1954; The Brave One 1956; The Tin Star 1957

Ray, Nicholas (1911-1979) The American Friend 1977; Hair 1979

Ray, René (1911-1993) When London Sleeps 1932; Tiger Bay 1934; The Passing of the Third Floor Back 1935; His Lordship 1936; The Green Cockatoo 1937; Bank Holiday 1938; Housemaster 1938; Old Bill and Son 1940; They Made Me a Fugitive 1947; Women of Twilight 1952; The Good Die Young 1954; The Vicious Circle 1957

Ray, Ted (1906-1977) Meet Me Tonight 1952; Escape by Night 1953; Carry On Teacher 1959; Please Turn Over 1960

Raye, Martha (1916-1994) The Big Broadcast of 1937 1936; Rhythm on the Range 1936; Artists and Models 1937; The Big Broadcast of 1938 1937; Waikiki Wedding 1937; College Swing 1938; Never Say Die 1939; The Boys from Syracuse 1940; Hellzapoppin' 1941; Keep 'Em Flying 1941; Pin Up Girl 1944; Monsieur Verdoux 1947; Jumbo 1962; Pufnstuf 1970

Raymond-James, Michael Black Snake Moan 2006; The Salvation 2014

Raymond, Bill My New Gun 1992; Where the Rivers Flow North 1993

Raymond, Candy (1950-) The Plumber 1979; A Case of Honor 1988

Raymond, Cyril (1897-1973) The Ghost Train 1931; Accused 1936; Come On George 1939; Saloon Bar 1940; Brief Encounter 1945; Angels One Five 1952; Lease of Life 1954; The Safecracker 1958; Don't Talk to Strange Men 1962

Raymond, Gary (1935-) The Moonraker 1957; Look Back in Anger 1959; Suddenly, Last Summer 1959; The Millionairess 1960; El Cid 1961; The Playboy of the Western World 1962; Jason and the Argonauts 1963; The Foreigner 2003

Raymond, Gene (1908-1998) If I Had a Million 1932; Red Dust 1932; Ex-Lady 1933; Flying down to Rio 1933; Zoo in Budapest 1933; Sadie McKee 1934; The Woman in Red 1935; The Bride Walks Out 1936; Mr and Mrs Smith 1941; Smilin' Through 1941; The Locket 1946; Hit the Deck 1955; Plunder Road 1957; The Best Man 1964; I'd Rather Be Rich 1964

Raymond, Paula (1924-2003) Crisis 1950; Devil's Doorway 1950; Duchess of Idaho 1950; The Tall Target 1951; Texas Carnival 1951; The Bandits of Corsica 1953; The Beast from 20,000 Fathoms 1953; City That Never Sleeps 1953; Blood of Dracula's Castle 1967

Raymond, Usher aka Usher (1978-) Light It Up 1999; Texas Rangers 2001; In the Mix 2005; Justin Bieber: Never Say Never 2011

Rea, Peggy (1921-2011) Love Field 1992; Made in America 1993

Rea, Stephen (1946-) Angel 1982; Loose Connections 1983; The Company of Wolves 1984; The Doctor and the Devils 1985; Life Is Sweet 1990; Bad Behaviour 1992; The Crying Game 1992; Angie 1994; Interview with the Vampire: the Vampire Chronicles 1994; Pret-a-Porter 1994; Princess Caraboo 1994; All Men Are Mortal 1995; Citizen X 1995; Crime of the Century 1996; Fever Pitch 1996; Last of the High Kings 1996; Michael Collins 1996; Trojan Eddie 1996; The Butcher Boy 1997; In Dreams 1998; Still Crazy 1998; The End of the Affair 1999; Guinevere 1999; I Could Read the Sky 1999; The Life before This 1999; This Is My Father 1999; The Musketeer 2001; FearDotCom 2002; bl..m 2003; The I Inside 2003; Breakfast on Pluto 2005; River Queen 2005; Tara Road 2005; V for Vendetta 2005; The Reaping 2006; Sixty Six 2006; Stuck 2007; Kisses 2008; The Heavy 2009; Ondine 2009; Blackthorn 2011; Underworld: Awakening 2012; Out of the Dark 2014

Read, Barbara aka Reade, Barbara (1917-1963) Make Way for Tomorrow 1937; Three Smart Girls 1937; Curtain Call 1940; Coroner Creek 1948

Read, James (1953-) The Initiation 1984; Beaches 1988; Love Crimes 1991

Reagan, Ronald (1911-2004) Hollywood Hotel 1937; Swing Your Lady 1937; Boy Meets Girl 1938; Going Places 1938; Angels Wash Their Faces 1939; Dark Victory 1939; Hell's Kitchen 1939; Naughty but Nice 1939; Knute Rockne - All American 1940; Santa Fe Trail 1940; Million Dollar Baby 1941; Desperate Journey 1942; Kings Row 1942; This Is the Army 1943; Voice of the Turtle 1947; The Hasty Heart 1949; It's a Great Feeling 1949; Night unto Night 1949; Storm Warning 1950; Bedtime for Bonzo 1951; She's Working Her Way through College 1952; Law and Order 1953; Cattle Queen of Montana 1954; Prisoner of War 1954; The Killers 1964; Roger & Me 1989

Reaser, Elizabeth (1975-) The Believer 2001; Sweet Land 2005; Twilight 2008; Liberal Arts 2011; Young Adult 2011

Reason, Rex aka Roberts, Bart (1928-2015) Taza, Son of Cochise 1954; Kiss of Fire 1955; Smoke Signal 1955; This Island Earth 1955; The Creature Walks among Us 1956; Raw Edge 1956; Band of Angels 1957; The Sad Horse 1959

Reborn, James (1948-2014) He Knows You're Alone 1981; Scent of a Woman 1992; Carlito's Way 1993; Blank Check 1994; 8 Seconds 1994; Guarding Tess 1994; I Love Trouble 1994; If Lucy Fell 1996; Up Close & Personal 1996; The Game 1997; Snow Falling on Cedars 1999; The Talented Mr Ripley 1999; Meet the Parents 2000; Pluto Nash 2001; Far from Heaven 2002; Head of State 2003; Bernard and Doris 2006; The Box 2008

Recoing, Aurélien (1958-) Time Out 2001; Snuff 2003; 13 (Tzameti) 2005; Intimate Enemies 2007; The Horde 2009; Blue Is the Warmest Colour 2013

Reddick, Lance I Dreamed of Africa 2000; The Guest 2014

Reddin, Keith The Heart of Justice 1992; Lolita 1997

Reddy, Helen (1942-) Airport 1975 1974; Pete's Dragon 1977

Redeker, Quinn (1936-) The Three Stooges Meet Hercules 1962; Spider Baby 1964; The Candidate 1972; At Long Last Love 1975; Coast to Coast 1980

Redfield, William (1927-1976) Conquest of Space 1955; I Married a Woman 1958; Hamlet 1964; Duel at Diablo 1966; Fantastic Voyage 1966; A New Leaf 1971; Death Wish 1974; For Pete's Sake 1974; Fear on Trial 1975; One Flew over the Cuckoo's Nest 1975; Mr Billion 1977

Redford, Robert (1936-) War Hunt 1962; Inside Daisy Clover 1965; Situation Hopeless - but Not Serious 1965; The Chase 1966; This Property Is Condemned 1966; Barefoot in the Park 1967; Butch Cassidy and the Sundance Kid 1969; Downhill Racer 1969; Tell Them Willie Boy Is Here 1969; The Candidate 1972; The Hot Rock 1972; Jeremiah Johnson 1972; The Sting 1973; The Way We Were 1973; The Great Gatsby 1974; The Great Waldo Pepper 1975; Three Days of the Condor 1975; All the President's Men 1976; A Bridge Too Far 1977; The Electric Horseman 1979; Erubaker 1980; The Natural 1984; Out of Africa 1985; Legal Eagles 1986; Havana 1990; Sneakers 1992; Indecent Proposal 1993; Up Close & Personal 1996; The Horse Whisperer 1998; The Last Castle 2001; Spy Game 2001; The Clearing 2004; An Unfinished Life 2005; Charlotte's Web 2006; Lions for Lambs 2007; The Company You Keep 2012; All Is Lost 2013; Captain America: the Winter Soldier 2014; Truth 2015; A Walk in the Woods 2015; Pete's Dragon 2016

Redgrave, Corin (1939-2010) Crooks in Cloisters 1963; A Man for All Seasons 1966; The Charge of the Light Brigade 1968; Oh! What a Lovely War 1969; When Eight Bells Toll 1971; Excalibur 1981; Eureka 1982; In the Name of the Father 1993; Four Weddings and a Funeral 1994; Persuasion 1995; Honest 2000; Enigma 2001; To Kill a King 2003; Enduring Love 2004; The Calling 2009

Redgrave, Jemma (1965-) Dream Demon 1988; Howards End 1992; I'll Be There 2003; Lassie 2005; Love & Friendship 2016

Redgrave, Lynn (1943-2010) Girl with Green Eyes 1963; Tom Jones 1963; The Deadly Affair 1966; Georgy Girl 1966; Smashing Time 1967; The Virgin Soldiers 1969; Last of the Mobile Hot-Shots 1969; Every Little Crook and Nanny 1972; Everything You Always Wanted to Know about Sex ... but Were Afraid to Ask 1972; The National Health 1973; The Happy Hooker 1975; Getting It Right 1989; Midnight 1989; What Ever Happened to...? 1991; Shine 1996; A Father's Betrayal 1997; Gods and Monsters 1998; Strike! 1998; Lion of Oz 2000; The Next Best Thing 2000; The Simian Line 2000; Varian's War 2000; My Kingdom 2001; Unconditional Love 2001; Anita & Me 2002; Spider 2002; Peter Pan 2003; The Wild Thornberrys Movie 2003; The White Countess 2005; The Jane Austen Book Club 2007; My Dog Tulip 2009

Redgrave, Michael (1908-1985) Climbing High 1938; The Lady Vanishes 1938; The Stars Look Down 1939; Stolen Life 1939; A Window in London 1939; Jeannie 1941; Kipps 1941; The Big Blockade 1942; Thunder Rock 1942; Dead of Night 1945; The Way to the Stars 1945; The Captive Heart 1946; The Years Between 1946; Fame Is the Spur 1947; The Man Within 1947; Mourning Becomes Electra 1947; Secret beyond the Door 1948; The Browning Version 1951; The Magic Box 1951; The Importance of Being Earnest 1952; The Dam Busters 1954; The Green Scarf 1954; The Sea Shall Not Have Them 1954; Confidential Report 1955; The Night My Number Came Up 1955; 1984 1955; Oh, Rosalinda!! 1955; The Happy Road 1956; Time without Pity 1957; Behind the Mask 1958; Law and Disorder 1958; The Quiet American 1958; Shake Hands with the Devil 1959; The Wreck of the Mary Deare 1959; The Innocents 1961; No My Darling Daughter 1961; The Loneliness of the Long Distance Runner 1962; The Heroes of Telemark 1965; The Hill 1965; Young Cassidy 1965; The 25th Hour 1967; Battle of Britain 1969; Connecting Rooms 1969; Goodbye, Mr Chips 1969; Oh! What a Lovely War

1969; Goodbye Gemini 1970; The Go-Between 1971

Redgrave, Vanessa (1937-) Behind the Mask 1958; Blowup 1966; A Man for All Seasons 1966; Morgan - a Suitable Case for Treatment 1966; Camelot 1967; The Sailor from Gibraltar 1967; Tonite Let's All Make Love in London 1967; The Charge of the Light Brigade 1968; Isadora 1968; The Sea Gull 1968; Oh! What a Lovely War 1969; The Devils 1971; Mary, Queen of Scots 1971; The Trojan Women 1971; Murder on the Orient Express 1974; Out of Season 1975; Julia 1977; Agatha 1978; Bear Island 1979; Yanks 1979; Playing for Time 1980; My Body, My Child 1982; Wagner 1983; The Bostonians 1984; Steaming 1985; Wetherby 1985; Comrades: a Lanternist's Account of the Tolpuddle Martyrs and What Became of Them 1986; Second Serve 1986; Prick Up Your Ears 1987; Consuming Passions 1988; A Man for All Seasons 1988; The Ballad of the Sad Café 1991; What Ever Happened to...? 1991; Howards End 1992; The House of the Spirits 1993; Mother's Boys 1993; Sparrow 1993; Little Odessa 1994; A Month by the Lake 1994; Mission: Impossible 1996; Smilla's Feeling for Snow 1996; Déjà Vu 1997; Mrs Dalloway 1997; Wilde 1997; Deep Impact 1998; Lulu on the Bridge 1998; Cradle Will Rock 1999; Girl, Interrupted 1999; If These Walls Could Talk 2 2000; The Pledge 2000; A Rumor of Angels 2000; Merci Docteur Rey 2002; Good Boy! 2003; The Thief Lord 2005; The White Countess 2005; Venus 2006; Atonement 2007; Evening 2007; Animals United 2010; Coriolanus 2010; Letters to Juliet 2010; Miral 2010; Robinson in Ruins 2010; The Whistleblower 2010; Anonymous 2011; Song for Marion 2012

Reding, Nick (1962-) Captive 1986; Mister Johnson 1991; In Love and War 2001

Redman Backstage 2000; Seed of Chucky 2004

Redman, Amanda (1959-) For Queen and Country 1988; Sexy Beast 2000; The Wedding Tackle 2000; Mike Bassett: England Manager 2001

Redman, Joyce (1915-2012) Othello 1965; Prudence and the Pill 1968

Redmayne, Eddie (1982-) Like Minds 2006; Savage Grace 2007; Glorious 39 2009; Black Death 2010; My Week with Marilyn 2011; Les Misérables 2012; Jupiter Ascending 2014; The Danish Girl 2015; The Theory of Everything 2015; Thomas & Friends - Sodor's Legend of the Lost Treasure: the Movie 2015; Fantastic Beasts and Where to Find Them 2016; Early Man 2018

Redmond, Liam (1913-1989) I See a Dark Stranger 1946; Daughter of Darkness 1948; The Cruel Sea 1952; Devil on Horseback 1954; The Divided Heart 1954; Final Appointment 1954; The Glass Cage 1955; Jacqueline 1956; 23 Paces to Baker Street 1956; Night of the Demon 1957; Alive and Kicking 1958; Rooney 1958; Scent of Mystery 1960; Under Ten Flags 1960; The Playboy of the Western World 1962; The Luck of Ginger Coffey 1964; The Adventures of Bullwhip Griffin 1967; The Last Safari 1967; Till Death Us Do Part 1968

Redmond, Moira (1928-2006) Pit of Darkness 1961; Jigsaw 1962; Kill or Cure 1962; Nightmare 1963; The Winter's Tale 1966

Redmond, Siobhan (1959-) Captives 1994; Beautiful People 1999

Reece, Brian (1913-1962) A Case for PC 49 1950; Orders are Orders 1954; Carry On Admiral 1957

Reed, Alan aka Openshaw, Falstaff (1907-1977) Days of Glory 1944; Nob Hill 1945; Perfect Strangers 1950; The Redhead and the Cowboy 1950; Viva Zapata! 1952; I, the Jury 1953; The Far Horizons 1955; Kiss of Fire 1955; He Laughed Last 1956; The Tarnished Angels 1957

Reed, Alyson A Chorus Line 1985; Skin Deep 1989; High School Musical 2006; High School Musical 2 2007

Reed, Donna (1921-1986) Shadow of the Thin Man 1941; Apache Trail 1942; Calling Dr Gillespie 1942; The Courtship of Andy Hardy 1942; Eyes in the Night 1942; Dr Gillespie's Criminal Case 1943; The Human Comedy 1943; The Man from Down Under 1943; The Picture of Dorian Gray 1945; They Were Expendable 1945; It's a Wonderful Life 1946; Green Dolphin Street 1947; Hangman's Knot 1952; The Caddy 1953; From Here to Eternity 1953; Gun Fury 1953; Raiders of the Seven Seas 1953; Trouble along the Way 1953; The Last Time I Saw Paris 1954; They Rode

West 1954; The Benny Goodman Story 1955; The Far Horizons 1955; Backlash 1956; Ransom! 1956; The Whole Truth 1958

Reed, Jerry (1937-2008) WW and the Dixie Dancekings 1975; Gator 1976; Smokey and the Bandit 1977; Smokey and the Bandit II 1980; Smokey and the Bandit III 1983; The Survivors 1983; BAT-21 1988; The Waterboy 1998

Reed, Lou (1942-2013) One-Trick Pony 1980; Get Crazy 1983; Faraway, So Close 1993; Blue in the Face 1995; Berlin 2007

Reed, Maxwell (1919-1974) Daybreak 1946; The Brothers 1947; Dear Murderer 1947; Daughter of Darkness 1948; The Lost People 1949; Madness of the Heart 1949; Blackout 1950; The Clouded Yellow 1950; There Is Another Sun 1951; Sea Devils 1952; Marilyn 1953; The Square Ring 1953; The Brain Machine 1954; The Notorious Landlady 1962

Reed, Nikki (1988-) Thirteen 2003; Lords of Dogtown 2005; Twilight 2008; New Moon 2009; Eclipse 2010

Reed, Oliver (1938-1999) The Angry Silence 1960; Beat Girl 1960; The Bulldog Breed 1960; His and Hers 1960; Sword of Sherwood Forest 1960; The Two Faces of Dr Jekyll 1960; The Curse of the Werewolf 1961; The Damned 1961; The Pirates of Blood River 1961; Night Creatures 1962; Paranoiac 1963; The Scarlet Blade 1963; The System 1964; The Party's Over 1965; The Trap 1966; I'll Never Forget What's 'Is Name 1967; The Jokers 1967; The Shuttered Room 1967; Hannibal Brooks 1968; Oliver! 1968; The Assassination Bureau 1969; Women in Love 1969; Take a Girl like You 1970; The Devils 1971; The Hunting Party 1971; ZPG: Zero Population Growth 1971; Sitting Target 1972; The Triple Echo 1972; Blue Blood 1973; The Three Musketeers 1973; And Then There Were None 1974; The Four Musketeers 1974; Royal Flash 1975; The Sellout 1975; Tommy 1975; Burnt Offerings 1976; The Great Scout & Cathouse Thursday 1976; Maniac 1977; The Prince and the Pauper 1977; Tomorrow Never Comes 1977; The Big Sleep 1978; The Class of Miss MacMichael 1978; The Brood 1979; A Touch of the Sun 1979; Dr Heckyl & Mr Hype 1980; Condorman 1981; Lion of the Desert 1981; Venom 1981; Fanny Hill 1983; The Sting II 1983; Two of a Kind 1983; Captive 1986; Castaway 1986; Dragonard 1987; Gor 1987; The Adventures of Baron Munchausen 1988; The House of Usher 1988; The Return of the Musketeers 1989; A Ghost in Monte Carlo 1990; Hired to Kill 1990; Treasure Island 1990; The Pit and the Pendulum 1991; Prisoner of Honor 1991; Funny Bones 1994; The Bruce 1996; Parting Shots 1998; Gladiator 2000

Reed, Pamela (1949-) Eyewitness 1981; The Right Stuff 1983; The Best of Times 1986; The Clan of the Cave Bear 1986; Chattahoochee 1989; Cadillac Man 1990; Caroline? 1990; Kindergarten Cop 1990; Passed Away 1992; Junior 1994; Deadly Whispers 1995; Bean 1997; Proof of Life 2000; Dynasty: the Making of a Guilty Pleasure 2004

Reed, Philip aka **Reed, Phillip** (1908-1996) British Agent 1934; Fashions of 1934 1934; Gambling Lady 1934; Glamour 1934; Jimmy the Gent 1934; Accent on Youth 1935; The Girl from 10th Avenue 1935; The Woman in Red 1935; Klondike Annie 1936; Old Acquaintance 1943; Rendezvous with Annie 1946; Song of Scheherazade 1947; Song of the Thin Man 1947; Bodyguard 1948; Take Me to Town 1953; The Tattered Dress 1957; Harum Scarum 1965

Reed, Ralph (1931-1997) Reform School Girl 1957; The Cry Baby Killer 1958

Reed, Robert (1932-1992) Star! 1968; The Maltese Bippy 1969; The Boy in the Plastic Bubble 1976

Reed, Tracy (1949-) Dr Strangelove, or How I Learned to Stop Worrying and Love the Bomb 1963; Devils of Darkness 1964; A Shot in the Dark 1964; Adam's Woman 1970; A Piece of the Action 1977; The California Dolls 1981

Reed, Walter (1916-2001) Seven Days' Leave 1942; Bombardier 1943; Child of Divorce 1946; Return of the Bad Men 1948; The Clown 1952; Seven Men from Now 1956; Moment to Moment 1965

Reedus, Norman (1969-) Six Ways to Sunday 1997; Dark Harbor 1998; The Boondock Saints 1999; Gossip 1999; Blade II 2002; Octane 2003; Hero Wanted 2008; Triple 9 2015

Reems, Harry (1947-2013) Deep Throat 1972; Deadly Weapons 1974

Reenberg, Jørgen (1927-) The Wolf at the Door 1986; Europa 1991

Rees, Betty Anne The Unholy Rollers 1972; Sugar Hill 1974

Rees, Donogh Constance 1984; Lorca and the Outlaws 1985; Crush 1992

Rees, John (1927-1994) The Long and the Short and the Tall 1960; Passenger 1963

Rees, Roger (1944-2015) Star 80 1983; A Christmas Carol 1984; Teen Agent 1991; Stop! or My Mom Will Shoot 1992; Robin Hood: Men in Tights 1993; The Substance of Fire 1996; Double Platinum 1999; Frida 2002; Return to Never Land 2002; Garfield 2 2006; The Pink Panther 2006

Reese, Della (1932-) Harlem Nights 1989; A Thin Line between Love and Hate 1996; Chasing Secrets 1999; Dinosaur 2000

Reeve, Christopher (1952-2004) Superman 1978; Somewhere in Time 1980; Superman II 1980; Deathtrap 1982; Monsignor 1982; Superman III 1983; The Bostonians 1984; Anna Karenina 1985; The Aviator 1985; Street Smart 1987; Superman IV: the Quest for Peace 1987; Switching Channels 1987; Noises Off 1992; The Remains of the Day 1993; The Sea Wolf 1993; Speechless 1994; Above Suspicion 1995; Village of the Damned 1995; Rear Window 1998

Reeves, George (1914-1959) Argentine Nights 1940; Lydia 1941; So Proudly We Hail 1943; Jungle Jim 1948; Bugles in the Afternoon 1952; Rancho Notorious 1952; The Blue Gardenia 1953

Reeves, Keanu (1964-) Act of Vengeance 1986; Babes in Toyland 1986; Brotherhood of Justice 1986; Youngblood 1986; River's Edge 1987; Bill & Ted's Excellent Adventure 1988; Dangerous Liaisons 1988; The Night Before 1988; Permanent Record 1988; The Prince of Pennsylvania 1988; Parenthood 1989; Aunt Julia and the Scriptwriter 1990; I Love You to Death 1990; Bill & Ted's Bogus Journey 1991; My Own Private Idaho 1991; Point Break 1991; Bram Stoker's Dracula 1992; Even Cowgirls Get the Blues 1993; Freaked 1993; Little Buddha 1993; Much Ado about Nothing 1993; Speed 1994; Johnny Mnemonic 1995; A Walk in the Clouds 1995; Chain Reaction 1996; Feeling Minnesota 1996; The Last Time I Committed Suicide 1996; The Devil's Advocate 1997; The Matrix 1999; The Gift 2000; The Replacements 2000; The Watcher 2000; Hardball 2001; Sweet November 2001; The Matrix Reloaded 2002; The Matrix Revolutions 2003; Something's Gotta Give 2003; Constantine 2005; Thumbsucker 2005; The Lake House 2006; A Scanner Darkly 2006; The Day the Earth Stood Still 2008; Street Kings 2008; The Private Lives of Pippa Lee 2009; Henry's Crime 2010; 47 Ronin 2012; Side by Side 2012; Man of Tai Chi 2013; John Wick 2014; Knock Knock 2015; Exposed 2016; Keanu 2016; The Neon Demon 2016; The Whole Truth 2016

Reeves, Kynaston (1893-1971) Sons of the Sea 1939; Penny Princess 1952; Eight o'Clock Walk 1953; Fiend without a Face 1957

Reeves, Phil Election 1999; 13 Going on 30 2004

Reeves, Saskia (1962-) The Bridge 1990; December Bride 1990; Close My Eyes 1991; Butterfly Kiss 1994; ID 1994; Traps 1994; Different for Girls 1996; Heart 1997; LA without a Map 1998; A Christmas Carol 1999; Mindscape 2013

Reeves, Steve (1926-2000) Athena 1954; Jail Bait 1954; Hercules 1957; Goliath and the Barbarians 1959; The White Warrior 1959; The Giant of Marathon 1960; The Last Days of Pompeii 1960; Morgan the Pirate 1960; Duel of the Titans 1961; The Trojan War 1961; Sandokan the Great 1963

Reeves, Vic (1959-) Once upon a Time in the Midlands 2002; Churchill: the Hollywood Years 2004

Reevis, Steve Geronimo: an American Legend 1993; Last of the Dogmen 1995; The Missing 2003

Regalbuto, Joe (1949-) Six Weeks 1982; The Star Chamber 1983; Lassiter 1984

Regan, Jayne (1909-2000) Thank You, Mr Moto 1937; Mr Moto's Gamble 1938

Regan, Laura My Little Eye 2002; They 2002; Hollow Man II 2006

Regan, Phil (1906-1996) Dames 1934; In Caliente 1935; Sweet Rosie O'Grady 1943

Regan, Vincent (1966-) Hard Men 1996; The Point Men 2000; Black

Knight 2001; 300 2006; Bonded by Blood 2010; Lockout 2012; St George's Day 2012

Regas, George (1890-1940) Bulldog Drummond Strikes Back 1934; Rose Marie 1936; Mr Moto Takes a Chance 1938

Regehr, Duncan (1952-) The Monster Squad 1987; Gore Vidal's Billy the Kid 1989; Danielle Steel's Once in a Lifetime 1994; Blood Surf 2000

Régent, Benoît (1953-1994) Dr M 1989; Three Colours Blue 1993

Reggiani, Serge (1922-2004) Les Portes de la Nuit 1946; La Ronde 1950; The Secret People 1951; Casque d'Or 1952; Napoléon 1955; Paris Blues 1961; Le Doulos 1962; The Leopard 1962; The 25th Hour 1967; Army of Shadows 1969; Vincent, François, Paul and the Others 1974; The Bee Keeper 1986; Mauvais Sang 1986; Henri-Georges Clouzot's Inferno 2009

Regina, Paul (1956-) A Change of Seasons 1980; Adam 1983

Régine (1929-) Marry Me! Marry Me! 1968; The Last Train 1972; Robert et Robert 1978; Le Cop 1985

Regnier, Carola Hôtel du Paradis 1986; Walk on Water 2004

Régnier, Natacha (1974-) The Dream Life of Angels 1998; Criminal Lovers 1999; Comment J'ai Tué Mon Père 2001

Rehak, Frantisek Capricious Summer 1968; Cutting It Short 1980

Rehman, Waheeda (1936-) Pyaasa 1957; Kaagaz Ke Phool 1959; Abhijan 1962

Reicher, Frank (1875-1965) Beau Sabreur 1928; King Kong 1933; Son of Kong 1933; Topaze 1933; Dr Cyclops 1940; The Mummy's Ghost 1944; The Jade Mask 1945

Reichmann, Wolfgang (1932-1991) Signs of Life 1968; Woyzeck 1978; The Second Victory 1986

Reid, Alex (1980-) Arachnid 2001; The Honeymooners 2003; The Descent 2005; Wilderness 2006; The Facility 2012

Reid, Anne (1935-) The Mother 2003; Savage Grace 2007; Faintheart 2008; Believe 2012; Song for Marion 2012

Reid, Audrey Dancehall Queen 1996; Third World Cop 1999

Reid, Beryl (1920-1996) Two Way Stretch 1960; Trial and Error 1962; Inspector Clouseau 1968; The Killing of Sister George 1968; Star! 1968; The Assassination Bureau 1969; Entertaining Mr Sloane 1969; The Beast in the Cellar 1970; Father Dear Father 1972; Psychomania 1972; No Sex Please - We're British 1973; Joseph Andrews 1977; Carry On Emmannuelle 1978; Rosie Dixon: Night Nurse 1978; Yellowbeard 1983; The Doctor and the Devils 1985

Reid, Carl Benton (1893-1973) The Little Foxes 1941; Convicted 1950; The Fuller Brush Girl 1950; In a Lonely Place 1950; Boots Malone 1951; The Great Caruso 1951; Indian Uprising 1951; Lorna Doone 1951; Carbine Williams 1952; Escape from Fort Bravo 1953; The Command 1954; The Spoilers 1955; Wichita 1955; A Day of Fury 1956; The Last Wagon 1956; Time Limit 1957; The Last of the Fast Guns 1958; Tarzan's Fight for Life 1958; The Baited Trap 1959; Pressure Point 1962

Reid, Christopher House Party 1990; House Party 2 1991; Class Act 1992

Reid, Elliott (1920-2013) The Whip Hand 1951; Gentlemen Prefer Blondes 1953; Inherit the Wind 1960; The Absent-Minded Professor 1961; Son of Flubber 1962; Move Over, Darling 1963; The Thrill of It All 1963; Follow Me, Boys! 1966; Blackbeard's Ghost 1967

Reid, Kate (1930-1993) This Property Is Condemned 1966; The Andromeda Strain 1970; A Delicate Balance 1973; Equus 1977; Atlantic City, USA 1980; Circle of Two 1980; Catholic Boys 1985; Death of a Salesman 1985; Fire with Fire 1986; Sweet Hearts Dance 1988; Deceived 1991

Reid, Ric Heart of a Child 1994; Two of Us 2000

Reid, Sam Belle 2013; The Railway Man 2013

Reid, Sheila (1937-) Othello 1965; Three Sisters 1970; The Touch 1971; The Dresser 1983; American Friends 1991; The Winter Guest 1996; Mrs Caldicot's Cabbage War 2000; Containment 2015

Reid, Tara (1975-) The Big Lebowski 1997; American Pie 1999; Body Shots 1999; Murder at Devil's Glen 1999; Dr T & the Women 2000; American Pie 2 2001; Josie and the Pussycats 2001; Just Visiting 2001; Van Wilder: Party Liaison 2002; My Boss's Daughter 2003; The Crow: Wicked Prayer 2005;

American Reunion 2012; Sharknado 2013; Sharknado 2: the Second One 2014

Reilly, John (1936-) The Patricia Neal Story 1981; Touch and Go 1986

Reilly, John C (1965-) Casualties of War 1989; Days of Thunder 1990; State of Grace 1990; Hoffa 1992; Out on a Limb 1992; What's Eating Gilbert Grape 1993; The River Wild 1994; Boys 1995; Dolores Claiborne 1995; Georgia 1995; Hard Eight 1996; Boogie Nights 1997; Chicago Cab 1998; For Love of the Game 1999; Magnolia 1999; Never Been Kissed 1999; The Perfect Storm 2000; The Anniversary Party 2001; The Good Girl 2001; Chicago 2002; Gangs of New York 2002; The Hours 2002; The Aviator 2004; Criminal 2004; Dark Water 2005; A Prairie Home Companion 2006; Talladega Nights: the Ballad of Ricky Bobby 2006; Walk Hard: the Dewey Cox Story 2007; Year of the Dog 2007; Step Brothers 2008; Cirque du Freak: the Vampire's Assistant 2009; 9 2009; Cyrus 2010; Carnage 2011; Cedar Rapids 2011; We Need to Talk about Kevin 2011; The Dictator 2012; Wreck-It Ralph 2012; Life after Beth 2014; When Marnie Was There 2014; Les Cowboys 2015; The Lobster 2015; Tale of Tales 2015; Sing 2016

Reilly, Kelly (1977-) Peaches 2000; Pot Luck 2002; Dead Bodies 2003; The Libertine 2004; Mrs Henderson Presents 2005; Russian Dolls 2005; Puffball 2006; Eden Lake 2008; Sherlock Holmes 2009; Flight 2012; Calvary 2013; Chinese Puzzle 2013; Heaven Is for Real 2014; Bastille Day 2016

Reina, Lucy The Penitent 1988; Romero 1989

Reineke, Gary Why Shoot the Teacher 1976; The Grey Fox 1982; Murder by Phone 1982; George's Island 1991; Spider 2002

Reiner, Carl (1922-) The Gazebo 1959; Happy Anniversary 1959; The Thrill of It All 1963; Art of Love 1965; The Russians Are Coming, the Russians Are Coming 1966; Generation 1969; The Jerk 1979; Skokie 1981; Dead Men Don't Wear Plaid 1982; Slums of Beverly Hills 1998; Ocean's Eleven 2001; Good Boy! 2003; Ocean's Twelve 2004

Reiner, Rob (1945-) Where's Poppa? 1970; Fire Sale 1977; This Is Spinal Tap 1984; Throw Momma from the Train 1987; Postcards from the Edge 1990; Sleepless in Seattle 1993; Bullets over Broadway 1994; Mixed Nuts 1994; Bye Bye Love 1995; For Better or Worse 1995; Primary Colors 1998; Edtv 1999; Alex & Emma 2003; Dickie Roberts: Former Child Star 2003; The Wolf of Wall Street 2013

Reinhold, Judge (1957-) Stripes 1981; Fast Times at Ridgemont High 1982; Pandemonium 1982; The Lords of Discipline 1983; Beverly Hills Cop 1984; Head Office 1986; Off Beat 1986; Ruthless People 1986; Beverly Hills Cop II 1987; Promised a Miracle 1988; A Soldier's Tale 1988; Vice Versa 1988; Rosalie Goes Shopping 1989; Daddy's Dyin'... Who's Got the Will? 1990; Near Mrs 1990; Over Her Dead Body 1990; Zandalee 1991; Baby on Board 1993; Beverly Hills Cop III 1994; The Santa Clause 1994; Family Plan 1997; Runaway Car 1997; Homegrown 1998; My Brother the Pig 1999; Walking across Egypt 1999; Beethoven's 3rd 2000; The Santa Clause 2 2002; Clifford's Really Big Movie 2004; The Santa Clause 3: the Escape Clause 2006; Swing Vote 2008

Reinking, Ann (1949-) All That Jazz 1979; Annie 1982; Micki & Maude 1984

Reis, Michelle (1970-) Fallen Angels 1995; Flowers of Shanghai 1998

Reiser, Paul (1957-) Diner 1982; Aliens 1986; Cross My Heart 1987; Crazy People 1990; Too Hot to Handle 1991; Bye Bye Love 1995; The Story of Us 1999; One Night at McCool's 2001; Life after Beth 2014; Whiplash 2014; Concussion 2015

Reisner, Charles aka **Reisner, Chuck** (1887-1962) A Dog's Life 1918; The Pilgrim 1923

Rekert, Winston (1949-) Agnes of God 1985; Captive Heart 1996; A Cooler Climate 1999; Date with Darkness 2003; The Art of War II: Betrayal 2008

Rekha (1954-) Kama Sutra: a Tale of Love 1996; Zubeidaa 2000; Bhoot 2003; Koi... Mil Gaya 2003

Relph, George (1888-1960) I Believe in You 1952; The Titfield Thunderbolt 1952; The Final Test 1953; Davy 1958

Remar, James (1953-) The Warriors 1979; Windwalker 1980; 48 HRS 1982; The Cotton Club 1984; The Clan of the Cave Bear 1986; Rent-a-Cop 1988; Drugstore Cowboy 1989; Tales from the Darkside: the Movie 1991; White Fang 1991; Fatal Instinct 1993; Blink 1994; Miracle on 34th Street 1994; Renaissance Man 1994; Boys on the Side 1995; One Good Turn 1996; The Phantom 1996; The Quest 1996; Mortal Kombat: Annihilation 1997; Blowback 1999; Rites of Passage 1999; Guardian 2000; What Lies Beneath 2000; Fear X 2002; Our House 2003; 2 Fast 2 Furious 2003; The Girl Next Door 2004; Ike: Countdown to D-Day 2004; Ratatouille 2007; Pineapple Express 2008; The Unborn 2008

Remberg, Erika (1932-) Circus of Horrors 1960; Saturday Night Out 1963

Remick, Lee (1935-1991) A Face in the Crowd 1957; The Long, Hot Summer 1958; Anatomy of a Murder 1959; These Thousand Hills 1959; Wild River 1960; Sanctuary 1961; Days of Wine and Roses 1962; The Running Man 1963; The Wheeler Dealers 1963; Baby the Rain Must Fall 1965; The Hallelujah Trail 1965; The Detective 1968; No Way to Treat a Lady 1968; Hard Contract 1969; Loot 1970; A Severed Head 1970; Sometimes a Great Notion 1971; The Blue Knight 1973; A Delicate Balance 1973; Hennessy 1975; The Omen 1976; Telefon 1977; The Medusa Touch 1978; The Europeans 1979; Tribute 1980; Emma's War 1985

Remsen, Bert (1925-1999) Tess of the Storm Country 1960; McCabe and Mrs Miller 1971; Thieves like Us 1974; Borderline 1980; Code of Silence 1985; Eye of the Tiger 1986; TerrorVision 1986; Three for the Road 1987; Remote Control 1988; Daddy's Dyin'... Who's Got the Will? 1990; Peacemaker 1990; Evil Spirits 1991; Only the Lonely 1991

Remsen, Kerry Dreams of Gold: the Mel Fisher Story 1986; Pumpkinhead 1988

Rémy, Albert (1911-1967) The 400 Blows 1959; Shoot the Pianist 1960; Gigot 1962

Renaldo, Duncan (1904-1980) Trader Horn 1931; Down Mexico Way 1941; The Capture 1950

Renant, Simone (1911-2004) Quai des Orfèvres 1947; Bedevilled 1955; Les Liaisons Dangereuses 1959; That Man from Rio 1964

Renaud (1952-) Germinal 1993; Crime Spree 2002

Renaud, Francis (1967-27/09/1967) 36 Quai des Orfèvres 2004; Anna M. 2007; The Lookout 2012

Renaud, Madeleine (1900-1994) Stormy Waters 1941; Le Plaisir 1951

Renavent, Georges (1894-1969) Rio Rita 1929; Whipsaw 1935

Rendall, Mark Charlie Bartlett 2007; Silk 2007; 30 Days of Night 2007

Renfro, Brad (1982-2008) The Client 1994; The Cure 1995; Tom and Huck 1995; Apt Pupil 1997; Telling Lies in America 1997; Bully 2001; Ghost World 2001; The Jacket 2005

Rénier, Jérémie aka **Renier, Jérémie** (1982-) La Promesse 1996; Criminal Lovers 1999; Brotherhood of the Wolf 2001; The Pornographer 2001; L'Enfant 2005; Private Property 2006; In Bruges 2008; The Silence of Lorna 2008; Summer Hours 2008; Potiche 2010; The Kid with a Bike 2011

Renier, Jérémie (1981-) White Elephant 2012; Saint Laurent 2014

Renier, Yannick Private Property 2006; Born in 68: We'll Love Each Other until Death Do Us Part 2008

Renko, Serge Les Rendez-vous de Paris 1995; Triple Agent 2003

Renna, Patrick (1979-) The Sandlot 1993; The Big Green 1995

Renner, Jeremy (1971-) National Lampoon's Senior Trip 1995; Dahmer 2002; SWAT 2003; North Country 2005; Twelve and Holding 2005; The Assassination of Jesse James by the Coward Robert Ford 2007; 28 Weeks Later 2007; The Hurt Locker 2008; The Town 2010; Mission: Impossible - Ghost Protocol 2011; The Bourne Legacy 2012; Marvel Avengers Assemble 2012; American Hustle 2013; Hansel & Gretel: Witch Hunters 2013; The Immigrant 2013; Kill the Messenger 2014; Mission: Impossible - Rogue Nation 2015

Rennie, Callum Keith (1960-) Last Night 1998; eXistenZ 1999; The Life before This 1999; Memento 2000; Suspicious River 2000; The Butterfly Effect 2004; Code Name: the Cleaner 2007; Case 39 2008; The X-Files: I Want to Believe 2008; The Young and Prodigious TS Spivet 2013; Born to Be Blue 2015; Fifty Shades of Grey 2015

Rennie, Michael (1909-1971) Pimpernel Smith 1941; The Big Blockade 1942; I'll Be Your Sweetheart 1945; The Wicked Lady 1945; The Root of All Evil 1946; The Black Rose 1950; The 13th Letter 1950; Trio 1950; The Day the Earth Stood Still 1951; 5 Fingers 1952; Les Misérables 1952; Phone Call from a Stranger 1952; King of the Khyber Rifles 1953; The Robe 1953; Sailor of the King 1953; Demetrius and the Gladiators 1954; Desiree 1954; Princess of the Nile 1954; The Rains of Ranchipur 1955; Soldier of Fortune 1955; Teenage Rebel 1956; Omar Khayyam 1957; The Battle of the V1 1958; The Lost World 1960; Mary, Mary 1963; Ride beyond Vengeance 1966; The Battle of El Alamein 1968; The Power 1968

Reno, Ginette (1946-) Léolo 1992; Mambo Italiano 2003

Reno, Jean aka **Réno, Jean** (1948-) The Last Battle 1983; Subway 1985; The Big Blue 1988; Nikita 1990; Les Visiteurs 1993; Leon 1994; Beyond the Clouds 1995; French Kiss 1995; Mission: Impossible 1996; Roseanna's Grave 1996; Godzilla 1997; Ronin 1998; Les Visiteurs 2: Les Couloirs du Temps 1998; The Crimson Rivers 2000; Just Visiting 2001; Rollerball 2001; Shut Up! 2003; The Da Vinci Code 2006; Flushed Away 2006; Flyboys 2006; The Pink Panther 2006; Ca$h 2008; Margaret 2008; Armored 2009; Couples Retreat 2009; The Pink Panther 2 2009; The Round Up 2010; 22 Bullets 2010; Hector and the Search for Happiness 2014; The Sweeney: Paris 2015

Reno, Kelly (1966-) The Black Stallion 1979; The Black Stallion Returns 1983

Renoir, Jean (1894-1979) Une Partie de Campagne 1936; La Vie Est à Nous 1936; La Bête Humaine 1938; La Règle du Jeu 1939; The Testament of Dr Cordelier 1959; The Little Theatre of Jean Renoir 1969; The Christian Licorice Store 1971

Renoir, Pierre (1885-1952) La Nuit du Carrefour 1932; Madame Bovary 1933; La Marseillaise 1938; Pièges 1939; Les Enfants du Paradis 1945

Renoir, Sophie Le Beau Mariage 1982; My Girlfriend's Boyfriend 1987

Renucci, Robin (1956-) Entre Nous 1983; Masques 1987; The King's Whore 1990; Les Enfants du Siècle 1999; The Dreamers 2003; Arsène Lupin 2004; A Comedy of Power 2006

Renzi, Eva (1944-2005) Funeral in Berlin 1966; The Pink Jungle 1968; The Bird with the Crystal Plumage 1969

Renzulli, Frank (1958-) Broadway Danny Rose 1984; Wild Hearts Can't Be Broken 1991

Repp, Stafford (1918-1974) Plunder Road 1957; Batman 1966

Resines, Antonio (1954-) How to Be a Woman and Not Die in the Attempt 1991; Acción Mutante 1993; The Girl of Your Dreams 1998; Cell 211 2009

Ressel, Franco (1925-1985) Blood and Black Lace 1964; Sabata 1969

Restorick, Hughie (1990-) My Childhood 1972; My Ain Folk 1973

Rettig, Tommy (1941-1996) For Heaven's Sake 1950; The Jackpot 1950; The Strip 1951; Weekend with Father 1951; The 5,000 Fingers of Dr T 1953; The Raid 1954; River of No Return 1954; At Gunpoint 1955; The Last Wagon 1956

Reuben, Gloria (1964-) Timecop 1994; Nick of Time 1995; Dean Koontz's Sole Survivor 2000; Reasonable Doubt 2014

Reubens, Paul aka **Mall, Paul** aka **Herman, Pee-wee** (1952-) The Blues Brothers 1980; Cheech and Chong's Next Movie 1980; Cheech and Chong's Nice Dreams 1981; Pandemonium 1982; Pee-wee's Big Adventure 1985; Flight of the Navigator 1986; Back to the Beach 1987; Big Top Pee-wee 1988; Buffy the Vampire Slayer 1992; The Nightmare before Christmas 1993; Dunston Checks In 1996; Matilda 1996; Beauty and the Beast: the Enchanted Christmas 1997; Buddy 1997; Mystery Men 1999; South of Heaven, West of Hell 2001; Blow 2001; Overnight 2004; Teacher's Pet 2004

Reuten, Thekla Highlander: the Source 2007; The Silent Army 2008; The American 2010

Revere, Anne (1903-1990) The Devil Commands 1941; Star Spangled Rhythm 1942; The Meanest Man in the World 1943; The Song of Bernadette 1943; National Velvet 1944; Sunday Dinner for a Soldier 1944; The Thin Man Goes Home 1944; Fallen Angel 1945; Dragonwyck 1946; Body and Soul 1947; Forever Amber 1947; Gentleman's Agreement 1947; The Shocking Miss Pilgrim 1947; Secret beyond the Door 1948; You're My Everything 1949; A Place in the Sun 1951; Birch Interval 1976

Revier, Dorothy (1904-1993) The Red Dance 1928; The Iron Mask 1929; By Candlelight 1934

Revill, Clive (1930-) Bunny Lake Is Missing 1965; A Fine Madness 1966; Kaleidoscope 1966; Modesty Blaise 1966; The Double Man 1967; Nobody Runs Forever 1968; The Shoes of the Fisherman 1968; The Assassination Bureau 1969; The Buttercup Chain 1970; The Private Life of Sherlock Holmes 1970; A Severed Head 1970; Avanti! 1972; Ghost in the Noonday Sun 1973; The Legend of Hell House 1973; The Black Windmill 1974; Galileo 1974; The Little Prince 1974; One of Our Dinosaurs Is Missing 1975; Matilda 1978; The Diary of Anne Frank 1980; Zorro, the Gay Blade 1981; Rumpelstiltskin 1986; Mack the Knife 1989; The Sea Wolf 1993

Revolori, Tony The Grand Budapest Hotel 2014; Dope 2015

Rex, Simon (1974-) The Forsaken 2001; Scary Movie 3 2003; Scary Movie 4 2006; Scary Movie V 2013

Rey, Alejandro (1930-1987) Solomon and Sheba 1959; Battle at Bloody Beach 1961; Blindfold 1966; Mr Majestyk 1974; Breakout 1975; High Velocity 1977; Moscow on the Hudson 1984; TerrorVision 1986

Rey, Fernando (1917-1994) The Last Days of Pompeii 1960; Viridiana 1961; The Castilian 1963; Son of a Gunfighter 1964; Chimes at Midnight 1966; Navajo Joe 1966; Return of the Seven 1966; The Desperate Ones 1967; Cervantes 1968; The Immortal Story 1968; Guns of the Magnificent Seven 1969; The Adventurers 1970; Tristana 1970; The French Connection 1971; The Light at the Edge of the World 1971; A Town Called Hell 1971; Antony and Cleopatra 1972; The Discreet Charm of the Bourgeoisie 1972; The Lady with Red Boots 1974; French Connection II 1975; Illustrious Corpses 1976; Seven Beauties 1976; That Obscure Object of Desire 1977; Quintet 1979; Monsignor 1982; The Hit 1984; Rustler's Rhapsody 1985; Saving Grace 1986; Hôtel du Paradis 1986; Moon over Parador 1988; Naked Tango 1990; 1492: Conquest of Paradise 1992

Reyer, Walter (1922-1999) The Indian Tomb 1959; The Tiger of Eschnapur 1959

Reyes Jr, Ernie (1972-) Red Sonja 1985; Teenage Mutant Ninja Turtles II: the Secret of the Ooze 1991; Surf Ninjas 1993; Welcome to the Jungle 2003

Reyes, Judy Our House 2006; Little Girl Lost: the Delimar Vera Story 2008

Reymond, Dominique aka ' (1957-) Will It Snow for Christmas? 1996; The Bridge 1999; Les Destinées Sentimentales 2000; Presque Rien 2000; Demonlover 2002; Ma Mère 2004; Summer Hours 2008

Reynolds, Adeline De Walt (1862-1961) The Tuttles of Tahiti 1942; Pony Soldier 1952

Reynolds, Burt (1936-) Angel Baby 1961; Operation CIA 1965; Navajo Joe 1966; Sam Whiskey 1969; Shark! 1969; Skulduggery 1969; Deliverance 1972; Everything You Always Wanted to Know about Sex ... but Were Afraid to Ask 1972; Fuzz 1972; The Man Who Loved Cat Dancing 1973; Shamus 1973; White Lightning 1973; The Mean Machine 1974; At Long Last Love 1975; Hustle 1975; Lucky Lady 1975; WW and the Dixie Dancekings 1975; Gator 1976; Nickelodeon 1976; Semi-Tough 1977; Smokey and the Bandit 1977; The End 1978; Hooper 1978; Starting Over 1979; Rough Cut 1980; Smokey and the Bandit II 1980; The Cannonball Run 1981; Paternity 1981; Sharky's Machine 1981; Best Friends 1982; The Best Little Whorehouse in Texas 1982; Cannonball Run II 1983; The Man Who Loved Women 1983; Smokey and the Bandit III 1983; Stroker Ace 1983; City Heat 1984; Stick 1985; Heat 1987; Malone 1987; Switching Channels 1987; Physical Evidence 1988; Rent-a-Cop 1988; All Dogs Go to Heaven 1989; Breaking In 1989; Modern Love 1990; Cop and a Half 1993; The Man from Left Field 1993; The Maddening 1995; Citizen Ruth 1996; Striptease 1996; Trigger Happy 1996; Bean 1997; Boogie Nights 1997; Hard Time 1998; Universal Soldier 2: Brothers in Arms 1998; Universal Soldier 3: Unfinished Business 1998; Mystery, Alaska 1999; The Last Producer 2000; Driven 2001; Hotel 2001; Tempted 2001; Gumball 3000: the Movie 2003; Hard Ground 2003; Without a Paddle 2004; The Dukes of Hazzard 2005; The Longest Yard 2005; Broken Bridges 2006; End Game 2006; A Bunch of Amateurs 2008

Reynolds, Craig (1907-1949) The Case of the Black Cat 1936; Smart Blonde 1936; Stage Struck 1936; The Case of the Stuttering Bishop 1937; Nevada 1944

Reynolds, Debbie (1932-) June Bride 1948; The Daughter of Rosie O'Grady 1950; Three Little Words 1950; Mr Imperium 1951; Singin' in the Rain 1952; Skirts Ahoy! 1952; The Affairs of Dobie Gillis 1953; Give a Girl a Break 1953; I Love Melvin 1953; Athena 1954; Susan Slept Here 1954; Hit the Deck 1955; The Tender Trap 1955; Bundle of Joy 1956; The Catered Affair 1956; Tammy and the Bachelor 1957; This Happy Feeling 1958; The Gazebo 1959; It Started with a Kiss 1959; The Mating Game 1959; Say One for Me 1959; Pepe 1960; The Rat Race 1960; The Pleasure of His Company 1961; The Second Time Around 1961; How the West Was Won 1962; My Six Loves 1962; Mary, Mary 1963; Goodbye Charlie 1964; The Unsinkable Molly Brown 1964; The Singing Nun 1966; Divorce American Style 1967; How Sweet It Is! 1968; What's the Matter with Helen? 1971; Charlotte's Web 1973; Heaven and Earth 1993; Mother 1996; In & Out 1997; The Christmas Wish 1998; Kiki's Delivery Service 1998; Rudolph the Red-Nosed Reindeer 1998; Rugrats in Paris: the Movie 2000; These Old Broads 2001; Connie and Carla 2004; One for the Money 2012; Behind the Candelabra 2013

Reynolds, Gene (1925-) Boys Town 1938; They Shall Have Music 1939; The Penalty 1941; The Tuttles of Tahiti 1942; The Country Girl 1954; Down Three Dark Streets 1954

Reynolds, Helene (1914-1990) Confirm or Deny 1941; Moontide 1942; The Bermuda Mystery 1944

Reynolds, Joyce (1925-) George Washington Slept Here 1942; The Constant Nymph 1943

Reynolds, Marjorie (1917-1997) Holiday Inn 1942; Dixie 1943; Up in Mabel's Room 1944; Bring On the Girls 1945; Ministry of Fear 1945; Monsieur Beaucaire 1946; The Time of Their Lives 1946; Heaven Only Knows 1947; Home Town Story 1951

Reynolds, Peter (1926-1975) The Guinea Pig 1948; The Vanquished 1953; The Challenge 1960; Your Money or Your Wife 1960; The Breaking Point 1961; The Painted Smile 1961; Spare the Rod 1961; Gaolbreak 1962

Reynolds, Robert Traps 1994; Tunnel Vision 1994

Reynolds, Ryan (1976-) Ordinary Magic 1993; The Alarmist 1997; Buying the Cow 2000; Van Wilder: Party Liaison 2002; Foolproof 2003; The In-Laws 2003; Blade: Trinity 2004; The Amityville Horror 2005; Just Friends 2005; Waiting... 2005; Smokin' Aces 2006; Fireflies in the Garden 2007; The Nines 2007; Definitely, Maybe 2008; Adventureland 2009; Buried 2009; The Proposal 2009; X-Men Origins: Wolverine 2009; The Change-Up 2011; Green Lantern 2011; Safe House 2012; The Croods 2013; R.I.P.D. 2013; Turbo 2013; The Captive 2014; The Voices 2014; Mississippi Grind 2015; Self/Less 2015; Woman in Gold 2015; Criminal 2016; Deadpool 2016

Reynolds, Simon (1963-) Gate II 1992; P2 2006

Reynolds, William (1931-) Francis Goes to West Point 1952; Has Anybody Seen My Gal? 1952; Son of Ali Baba 1952; Gunsmoke 1953; The Mississippi Gambler 1953; All That Heaven Allows 1955; Away All Boats 1956; There's Always Tomorrow 1956; Mister Cory 1957; A Distant Trumpet 1964

Reynor, Jack What Richard Did 2012; Glassland 2014; A Royal Night Out 2015; Sing Street 2016

Rezaie, Agheleh At Five in the Afternoon 2003; Stray Dogs 2004

Rhames, Ving (1959-) Patty Hearst 1988; Casualties of War 1989; The Long Walk Home 1990; Homicide 1991; The People under the Stairs 1991; Dave 1993; The Saint of Fort Washington 1993; DROP Squad 1994; Kiss of Death 1994; Pulp Fiction 1994; Deadly Whispers 1995; Dangerous Ground 1996; Mission: Impossible 1996; Striptease 1996; Body Count 1997; Con Air 1997; Don King: Only in America 1997; Rosewood 1997; Out of Sight 1998; Bringing Out the Dead 1999; Entrapment 1999; Mission: Impossible 2 1999; Baby Boy 2001; Final Fantasy: the Spirits Within 2001; Dark Blue 2002; Lilo & Stitch 2002; Undisputed 2002; Dawn of the Dead 2004; Mission: Impossible III 2006; I Now

Pronounce You Chuck & Larry 2007; Day of the Dead 2008; The Goods: Live Hard Sell Hard 2009; Surrogates 2009; The Tournament 2009; Piranha 2010; Mission: Impossible - Ghost Protocol 2011; Piranha 3DD 2011; Soldiers of Fortune 2012; Won't Back Down 2012; Mission: Impossible - Rogue Nation 2015; Bastards 2016

Rhee, Phillip (1960-) Silent Assassins 1988; Best of the Best 1989; Best of the Best II 1992

Rheon, Iwan Resistance 2011; The Rise 2012

Rhind-Tutt, Julian (1968-) The Madness of King George 1995; The Trench 1999; Miranda 2001; Rabbit Fever 2005; Lucy 2014

Rhoades, Barbara (1947-) The Shakiest Gun in the West 1967; Don't Just Stand There 1968; The Goodbye Girl 1977

Rhodes, Christopher (1914-1964) The Colditz Story 1954; Tiger in the Smoke 1956; Operation Amsterdam 1958; Gorgo 1961

Rhodes, Cynthia (1957-) Staying Alive 1983; Dirty Dancing 1987

Rhodes, Donnelly (1937-) Gunfight in Abilene 1967; Miracle on the 17th Green 1999

Rhodes, Erik (1906-1990) The Gay Divorce 1934; Charlie Chan in Paris 1935; Top Hat 1935; One Rainy Afternoon 1936; Criminal Lawyer 1937; Woman Chases Man 1937; Mysterious Mr Moto 1938

Rhodes, Grandon (1904-1987) Magnificent Doll 1946; Born Yesterday 1950; On Top of Old Smoky 1953; Revenge of the Creature 1955; Earth vs the Flying Saucers 1956

Rhodes, Hari aka Rhodes, Harry (1932-1992) Shock Corridor 1963; Blindfold 1966; Conquest of the Planet of the Apes 1972; Detroit 9000 1973; Coma 1977

Rhodes, Marjorie (1902-1979) Great Day 1944; The Cure for Love 1949; The Yellow Balloon 1952; Children Galore 1954; Just My Luck 1957; Alive and Kicking 1958; I've Gotta Horse 1965; The Family Way 1966; Hands of the Ripper 1971

Rhue, Madlyn (1934-2003) A Majority of One 1961; Escape from Zahrain 1962; He Rides Tall 1964

Rhys-Davies, John (1944-) Sphinx 1980; Raiders of the Lost Ark 1981; Victor/Victoria 1982; Best Revenge 1983; Sahara 1983; Kim 1984; King Solomon's Mines 1985; Firewalker 1986; The Living Daylights 1987; Waxwork 1988; Young Toscanini 1988; Indiana Jones and the Last Crusade 1989; The Trial of the Incredible Hulk 1989; Shogun Warrior 1991; Sunset Grill 1992; The Unnamable Returns 1992; Cyborg Cop 1993; The Seventh Coin 1993; Aladdin and the King of Thieves 1996; Cats Don't Dance 1998; Britannic 2000; The Lord of the Rings: The Fellowship of the Ring 2001; The Lord of the Rings: The Two Towers 2002; The Jungle Book 2 2003; The Lord of the Rings: The Return of the King 2003; The Medallion 2003; The Princess Diaries 2: Royal Engagement 2004; The Reef 2006; The Ferryman 2007; 31 North 62 East 2009

Rhys Jones, Griff (1953-) Morons from Outer Space 1985; Wilt 1989; As You Like It 1992; Staggered 1993; The Adventures of Pinocchio 1996; Up 'n' Under 1997; The Testimony of Taliesin Jones 2000; Puckoon 2002

Rhys Meyers, Jonathan (1977-) B Monkey 1996; The Disappearance of Finbar 1996; The Governess 1997; The Maker 1997; Velvet Goldmine 1998; The Loss of Sexual Innocence 1999; Ride with the Devil 1999; Titus 1999; Bend It like Beckham 2001; The Magnificent Ambersons 2001; I'll Sleep When I'm Dead 2003; Octane 2003; Vanity Fair 2004; Match Point 2005; Mission: Impossible III 2005; August Rush 2007; Shelter 2008; From Paris with Love 2010; Albert Nobbs 2011; Stonewall 2015

Rhys, Matthew (1974-) House of America 1996; Heart 1997; Titus 1999; Peaches 2000; Shooters 2000; Sorted 2000; The Testimony of Taliesin Jones 2000; Very Annie-Mary 2000; The Abduction Club 2002; Deathwatch 2002; Otherworld 2003; Fakers 2004; The Edge of Love 2008; Patagonia 2010

Rhys, Paul (1963-) Vincent and Theo 1990; Becoming Colette 1991; Rebecca's Daughters 1991; Chaplin 1992; Nina Takes a Lover 1993; Food of Love 2002

Riaboukine, Serge (1957-) Wild Target 1993; Skin of Man, Heart of

Beast 1999; Le Chignon d'Olga 2002; Look at Me 2004; Angel-A 2005

Riach, Ralph Copying Beethoven 2006; Death Defying Acts 2007

Rialson, Candice (1952-) Mama's Dirty Girls 1974; Hollywood Boulevard 1976

Ribeiro, Alfonso Ticks 1993; Love Wrecked 2005

Ribisi, Giovanni aka Ribisi, Vonni (1974-) Promised a Miracle 1988; Lost Highway 1996; subUrbia 1996; Saving Private Ryan 1998; The Mod Squad 1999; The Other Sister 1999; Boiler Room 2000; The Gift 2000; Gone in Sixty Seconds 2000; Heaven 2002; Basic 2003; Cold Mountain 2003; Lost in Translation 2003; Flight of the Phoenix 2004; Sky Captain and the World of Tomorrow 2004; The Big White 2005; Perfect Stranger 2007; Avatar 2009; Public Enemies 2009; The Rum Diary 2011; Contraband 2012; Gangster Squad 2012; Ted 2012; A Million Ways to Die in the West 2014; Selma 2014; Ted 2 2015

Ricci, Christina (1980-) Mermaids 1990; The Addams Family 1991; The Hard Way 1991; Addams Family Values 1993; The Cemetery Club 1993; Casper 1995; Gold Diggers: the Secret of Bear Mountain 1995; Now and Then 1995; Last of the High Kings 1996; The Ice Storm 1997; That Darn Cat 1997; Buffalo '66 1998; Desert Blue 1998; Fear and Loathing in Las Vegas 1998; The Opposite of Sex 1998; Pecker 1998; Small Soldiers 1998; Sleepy Hollow 1999; 200 Cigarettes 1999; Bless the Child 2000; The Man Who Cried 2000; Miranda 2001; The Gathering 2002; The Laramie Project 2002; Anything Else 2003; Monster 2003; Cursed 2005; Black Snake Moan 2006; Home of the Brave 2006; Penelope 2006; Speed Racer 2008; After.Life 2009; Alpha and Omega 2010; Bel Ami 2010; The Smurfs 2 2013

Ricci, Renzo (1898-1978) L'Avventura 1960; Of a Thousand Delights 1965

Riccio, Philip Diary of the Dead 2007; My Family's Secret 2010

Rice, Angourie These Final Hours 2013; The Nice Guys 2016

Rice, Florence (1907-1974) Double Wedding 1937; Navy Blue and Gold 1937; Fast Company 1938; Paradise for Three 1938; Sweethearts 1938; At the Circus 1939; Miracles for Sale 1939; Broadway Melody of 1940 1940; Cherokee Strip 1940; Phantom Raiders 1940

Rice, Joan (1930-1997) Gift Horse 1951; Curtain Up 1952; The Story of Robin Hood and His Merrie Men 1952; A Day to Remember 1953; His Majesty O'Keefe 1953; One Good Turn 1954; Police Dog 1955; Operation Bullshine 1959; The Horror of Frankenstein 1970

Rich, Claude (1929-) The Vanishing Corporal 1962; Male Hunt 1964; The Bride Wore Black 1967; Je T'Aime, Je T'Aime 1968; Stavisky 1974; Maria Chapdelaine 1982; L'Accompagnatrice 1992; D'Artagnan's Daughter 1994; La Bûche 1999; Asterix & Obelix: Mission Cleopatra 2001; Private Fears in Public Places 2006; Looking for Hortense 2012

Rich, Irene (1891-1988) Rosita 1923; Lady Windermere's Fan 1925; They Had to See Paris 1929; Beau Ideal 1931; The Champ 1931; Strangers May Kiss 1931; That Certain Age 1938; The Lady in Question 1940; The Mortal Storm 1940; Angel and the Badman 1947

Richard, Cliff (1940-) Expresso Bongo 1959; Serious Charge 1959; The Young Ones 1961; Summer Holiday 1962; Wonderful Life 1964; Finders Keepers 1966; Two a Penny 1968; Take Me High 1973; Run for Your Wife 2013

Richard, Firmine Romuald et Juliette 1989; 8 Women 2001

Richard, Frida (1873-1946) Faust 1926; The Holy Mountain 1926; Three Loves 1929

Richard, Jean-Louis (1927-) The Last Metro 1980; Jeanne la Pucelle 1994; The Bait 1995; Skin of Man, Heart of Beast 1999

Richard, Nathalie (1962-) Irma Vep 1996; Hidden 2005

Richard, Pierre (1934-) The Tall Blond Man with One Black Shoe 1972; Les Compères 1983; Le Serpent 2006; Paris 36 2008; Paper Souls 2013

Ri'chard, Robert (1983-) Light It Up 1999; House of Wax 2004; Coach Carter 2005

Richard, Wendy (1943-2009) No Blade of Grass 1970; Gumshoe 1971; Bless This House 1972; Carry On Girls 1973; Are You Being Served? 1977

Richards, Addison (1887-1964) Our Daily Bread 1934; Smart Blonde 1936; The Black Legion 1937; Boys Town

1938; The Man from Dakota 1940; Betrayal from the East 1945; Bewitched 1945; The Shanghai Cobra 1945; Criminal Court 1946; Gunsight Ridge 1957

Richards, Ann (1917-2006) An American Romance 1944; Love Letters 1945; Badman's Territory 1946; The Searching Wind 1946; Love from a Stranger 1947; Sorry, Wrong Number 1948

Richards, Ariana (1979-) Tremors 1989; Against Her Will 1992; Jurassic Park 1993; Angus 1995; Tremors 3: Back to Perfection 2001

Richards, Aubrey (1920-2000) The Ipcress File 1965; It! 1966

Richards, Beah (1926-2000) The Miracle Worker 1962; Gone Are the Days 1963; Guess Who's Coming to Dinner 1967; Hurry Sundown 1967; The Biscuit Eater 1972; Mahogany 1975; As Summers Die 1986; Drugstore Cowboy 1989; Homer and Eddie 1989; Out of Darkness 1994; Beloved 1998

Richards, Dakota Blue The Golden Compass 2007; The Secret of Moonacre 2008; The Fold 2013; Chicklit 2016

Richards, Denise (1971-) 919 Fifth Avenue 1995; Starship Troopers 1997; Wild Things 1998; Drop Dead Gorgeous 1999; The World Is Not Enough 1999; Good Advice 2001; Valentine 2001; Empire 2002; Undercover Brother 2002; Elvis Has Left the Building 2004; Edmond 2005; Kambakkht Ishq 2009

Richards, Erin (1986-) The Quiet Ones 2013; That Good Night 2017

Richards, Evan Down and Out in Beverly Hills 1986; Society 1989; Mute Witness 1995

Richards, Jeff (1922-1989) Big Leaguer 1953; Seagulls over Sorrento 1954; Seven Brides for Seven Brothers 1954; Many Rivers to Cross 1955; The Opposite Sex 1956; Born Reckless 1959; The Secret of the Purple Reef 1960

Richards (2), Keith (1943-) Gimme Shelter 1970; Hail! Hail! Rock 'n' Roll! 1987; Pirates of the Caribbean: at World's End 2007; Shine a Light 2007

Richards, Kim (1964-) Escape to Witch Mountain 1975; Assault on Precinct 13 1976; No Deposit No Return 1976; Return from Witch Mountain 1978

Richards, Kyle (1964-) Halloween 1978; The Watcher in the Woods 1982

Richards, Lisa Rolling Thunder 1977; Eating 1990

Richards, Michael (1948-) Transylvania 6-5000 1985; Whoops Apocalypse 1986; UHF 1989; Unstrung Heroes 1995; Trial and Error 1997

Richards, Michele Lamar The Bodyguard 1992; Top Dog 1995

Richardson, Cameron Adrift 2006; Alvin and the Chipmunks 2007

Richardson, Derek Dumb and Dumberer: When Harry Met Lloyd 2003; Hostel 2005; Reeker 2005

Richardson, Haley Lu Escape from Polygamy 2013; Split 2017

Richardson, Ian (1934-2007) Marat/ Sade 1966; A Midsummer Night's Dream 1969; The Darwin Adventure 1972; The Hound of the Baskervilles 1983; The Sign of Four 1983; Brazil 1985; Whoops Apocalypse 1986; Cry Freedom 1987; Burning Secret 1988; King of the Wind 1989; The Plot to Kill Hitler 1990; Rosencrantz and Guildenstern Are Dead 1990; Dirty Weekend 1992; Year of the Comet 1992; M Butterfly 1993; BAPS 1997; Incognito 1997; Dark City 1998; A Knight in Camelot 1998; The King and I 1999; 102 Dalmatians 2000; From Hell 2001; Merry Christmas 2005; Becoming Jane 2006

Richardson, Jake (1985-) Honey, We Shrunk Ourselves 1997; The Dangerous Lives of Altar Boys 2001

Richardson, Joely (1965-) The Hotel New Hampshire 1984; Wetherby 1985; Drowning by Numbers 1988; King Ralph 1991; Rebecca's Daughters 1991; Shining Through 1992; I'll Do Anything 1994; Sister My Sister 1994; Hollow Reed 1995; Loch Ness 1995; 101 Dalmatians 1996; Event Horizon 1997; Wrestling with Alligators 1998; Maybe Baby 1999; The Patriot 2000; Return to Me 2000; The Affair of the Necklace 2001; Lies My Mother Told Me 2004; The Last Mimzy 2007; Anonymous 2011; The Girl with the Dragon Tattoo 2011; Red Lights 2012; Thanks for Sharing 2012; Endless Love 2014; Maggie 2015; The Messenger 2015

Richardson, John (1936-) The Mask of Satan 1960; She 1965; One Million Years BC 1966; On My Way to the Crusades, I Met a Girl Who... 1967; The

Vengeance of She 1968; On a Clear Day You Can See Forever 1970

Richardson, LaTanya (1941-) US Marshals 1998; The Fighting Temptations 2003

Richardson, Lee (1926-1999) Prizzi's Honor 1985; Amazing Grace and Chuck 1987; The Believers 1987; Tiger Warsaw 1988; The Fly II 1989; Q & A 1990; A Stranger among Us 1992

Richardson, Marie (1959-) Eyes Wide Shut 1999; Evil 2003

Richardson, Miranda (1958-) Dance with a Stranger 1984; The Innocent 1984; Eat the Rich 1987; Empire of the Sun 1987; The Bachelor 1990; Enchanted April 1991; The Crying Game 1992; Damage 1992; Century 1993; Tom & Viv 1994; Kansas City 1995; The Evening Star 1996; Swann 1996; The Apostle 1997; The Designated Mourner 1997; Alice in Wonderland 1999; All for Love 1999; Jacob Two Two Meets the Hooded Fang 1999; The King and I 1999; The Miracle Maker 1999; Sleepy Hollow 1999; Chicken Run 2000; Get Carter 2000; Snow White 2001; The Hours 2002; The Rage in Placid Lake 2002; Spider 2002; The Actors 2003; Churchill: the Hollywood Years 2004; The Phantom of the Opera 2004; The Prince & Me 2004; Harry Potter and the Goblet of Fire 2005; Southland Tales 2005; Wah-Wah 2005; Provoked: a True Story 2006; Puffball 2006; Fred Claus 2007; The Young Victoria 2008; Made in Dagenham 2010; Belle 2013

Richardson, Natasha (1963-2009) Gothic 1986; A Month in the Country 1987; Patty Hearst 1988; Shadow Makers 1989; The Handmaid's Tale 1990; The Comfort of Strangers 1991; The Favour, the Watch and the Very Big Fish 1991; Hostages 1993; Widows' Peak 1993; Nell 1994; The Parent Trap 1998; Blow Dry 2000; Waking Up in Reno 2000; Maid in Manhattan 2002; Asylum 2004; The White Countess 2005; Evening 2007; Wild Child 2008; The Wildest Dream 2009

Richardson, Patricia (1951-) The Road Home 1989; Ulee's Gold 1997

Richardson, Peter (1952-) The Supergrass 1985; Carry On Columbus 1992

Richardson, Ralph (1902-1982) Friday the Thirteenth 1933; The Ghoul 1933; Bulldog Jack 1934; The Return of Bulldog Drummond 1934; Java Head 1935; The Man Who Could Work Miracles 1936; Things to Come 1936; Thunder in the City 1937; The Citadel 1938; The Divorce of Lady X 1938; South Riding 1938; The Four Feathers 1939; The Lion Has Wings 1939; Q Planes 1939; The Day Will Dawn 1942; The Silver Fleet 1943; School for Secrets 1946; Anna Karenina 1947; The Fallen Idol 1948; The Heiress 1949; Outcast of the Islands 1951; The Holly and the Ivy 1952; Home at Seven 1952; The Sound Barrier 1952; Richard III 1955; Smiley 1956; The Passionate Stranger 1957; Oscar Wilde 1959; Our Man in Havana 1959; Exodus 1960; Long Day's Journey into Night 1962; The 300 Spartans 1962; Woman of Straw 1964; Doctor Zhivago 1965; Chimes at Midnight 1966; Khartoum 1966; The Wrong Box 1966; Battle of Britain 1969; The Bed Sitting Room 1969; The Looking Glass War 1969; Midas Run 1969; Oh! What a Lovely War 1969; Eagle in a Cage 1971; Who Slew Auntie Roo? 1971; Alice's Adventures in Wonderland 1972; Lady Caroline Lamb 1972; Tales from the Crypt 1972; A Doll's House 1973; Frankenstein: the True Story 1973; O Lucky Man! 1973; Rollerball 1975; The Man in the Iron Mask 1977; Watership Down 1978; Dragonslayer 1981; Time Bandits 1981; Witness for the Prosecution 1982; Invitation to the Wedding 1983; Wagner 1983; Give My Regards to Broad Street 1984; Greystoke: the Legend of Tarzan, Lord of the Apes 1984

Richardson, Salli aka Richardson-Whitfield, Salli (1967-) A Low Down Dirty Shame 1994; Sioux City 1994; Antwone Fisher 2002; Anacondas: the Hunt for the Blood Orchid 2004; I Am Legend 2007

Richardson, Sy (1941-) Repo Man 1984; Cold Steel 1987; Straight to Hell 1987; Walker 1987; Kinjite: Forbidden Subjects 1989; Eye of the Stranger 1993; Searchers 2.0 2007

Richfield, Edwin (1921-1990) The Brain Machine 1954; The Break 1962

Richie, Shane Flushed Away 2006; Risen 2010

Richings, Julian Cube 1997; My Life without Me 2002; Wrong Turn 2003

Richman, Josh Thrashin' 1986; River's Edge 1987

Richman, Peter Mark aka Richman, Mark (1927-) The Black Orchid 1959; The Murder Men 1961; Dark Intruder 1965; Friday the 13th Part VIII: Jason Takes Manhattan 1989

Richmond-Peck, David Family Sins 2004; Mary Higgins Clark's Try to Remember 2004

Richmond, Branscombe (1955-) The Chicken Chronicles 1977; Cage 1989

Richmond, Deon (1978-) Not Another Teen Movie 2001; Hatchet 2006

Richmond, Fiona Exposé 1975; Hardcore 1977; Let's Get Laid 1977; Eat the Rich 1987

Richmond, Kane (1906-1973) Charlie Chan in Reno 1939; The Return of the Cisco Kid 1939; Great Guns 1941; Riders of the Purple Sage 1941; Black Gold 1947

Richter, Andy (1966-) My Boss's Daughter 2003; New York Minute 2004; Madagascar 2005; Semi-Pro 2008

Richter, Deborah (1961-) Square Dance 1987; Promised Land 1988; Cyborg 1989

Richter, Jason James (1980-) Free Willy 1993; Cops and Robbersons 1994; The NeverEnding Story III 1994; Free Willy 2: the Adventure Home 1995; Free Willy 3: the Rescue 1997

Richter, Paul (1887-1961) Dr Mabuse, the Gambler 1922; The Nibelungen 1924

Richter, Sonja (1974-) Open Hearts 2002; The Keeper of Lost Causes 2013; The Homesman 2014

Richwood, Patrick (1962-) Streets 1990; Race to Space 2001

Rickles, Don (1926-) Run Silent Run Deep 1958; The Rat Race 1960; The Man with the X-Ray Eyes 1963; Bikini Beach 1964; Muscle Beach Party 1964; Beach Blanket Bingo 1965; Kelly's Heroes 1970; Innocent Blood 1992; Casino 1995; Toy Story 1995; The Magic Sword: Quest for Camelot 1997; Dennis the Menace Strikes Again 1998; Dirty Work 1998; Toy Story 2 1999; Joan Rivers: a Piece of Work 2010

Rickman, Alan (1946-2016) Die Hard 1988; The January Man 1989; Quigley Down Under 1990; Truly Madly Deeply 1990; Close My Eyes 1991; Closet Land 1991; Robin Hood: Prince of Thieves 1991; Bob Roberts 1992; An Awfully Big Adventure 1994; Sense and Sensibility 1995; Michael Collins 1996; Rasputin 1996; Dark Harbor 1998; Judas Kiss 1998; Dogma 1999; Galaxy Quest 1999; Blow Dry 2000; Help, I'm a Fish! 2000; Harry Potter and the Philosopher's Stone 2001; The Search for John Gissing 2001; Harry Potter and the Chamber of Secrets 2002; Love Actually 2003; Harry Potter and the Prisoner of Azkaban 2004; Harry Potter and the Goblet of Fire 2005; The Hitchhiker's Guide to the Galaxy 2005; Snow Cake 2005; Perfume: the Story of a Murderer 2006; Harry Potter and the Order of the Phoenix 2007; Sweeney Todd: the Demon Barber of Fleet Street 2007; Bottle Shock 2008; Harry Potter and the Half-Blood Prince 2009; The Wildest Dream 2009; Alice in Wonderland 2010; Harry Potter and the Deathly Hallows: Part 1 2010; Harry Potter and the Deathly Hallows: Part 2 2011; Gambit 2012; The Butler 2013; A Promise 2013; A Little Chaos 2014; Eye in the Sky 2015; Alice through the Looking Glass 2016

Ricotta, Vincenzo aka Riotta, Vincent Car Trouble 1985; Leon the Pig Farmer 1992; Under the Tuscan Sun 2003

Rideau, Stéphane (1976-) Les Roseaux Sauvages 1994; Sitcom 1997; Presque Rien 2000; Far Away 2001; Le Clan 2004

Ridgely, John (1909-1968) Dangerously They Live 1942; Air Force 1943; Destination Tokyo 1943; Northern Pursuit 1943; The Doughgirls 1944; Pride of the Marines 1945; The Big Sleep 1946; My Reputation 1946; Cry Wolf 1947; Nora Prentiss 1947; Possessed 1947; Half Angel 1951; Room for One More 1952

Ridgely, Robert (1931-1996) Nightmare in Chicago 1968; Philadelphia 1993

Ridges, Stanley aka Ridges, Stanley C (1891-1951) Crime without Passion 1934; The Scoundrel 1935; Internes Can't Take Money 1937; The Mad Miss Manton 1938; Each Dawn I Die 1939; Nick Carter, Master Detective 1939; The Sea Wolf 1941; Sergeant York 1941; They Died with Their Boots On 1941; The Big Shot 1942; The Lady Is Willing 1942; To Be or Not to Be 1942; Tarzan Triumphs 1943; The Master Race 1944; The Suspect 1944; Because of Him

1946; Possessed 1947; The File on Thelma Jordon 1949; Streets of Laredo 1949; You're My Everything 1949

Ridley, Arnold (1896-1984) The Interrupted Journey 1949; Stolen Face 1952; Dad's Army 1971

Ridley, Daisy (1992-) Star Wars Episode VII: the Force Awakens 2015; Star Wars Episode VIII 2017

Rieck, Billy Avalon: beyond the Abyss 1999; In Hell 2003

Riefenstahl, Leni (1902-2003) The Holy Mountain 1926; The Blue Light 1932; The Wonderful, Horrible Life of Leni Riefenstahl 1993

Riegert, Peter (1947-) National Lampoon's Animal House 1978; Americathon 1979; Chilly Scenes of Winter 1979; National Lampoon's Movie Madness 1981; Local Hero 1983; The City Girl 1984; A Man in Love 1987; Crossing Delancey 1988; A Shock to the System 1990; The Object of Beauty 1991; Oscar 1991; Passed Away 1992; Utz 1992; Barbarians at the Gate 1993; Gypsy 1993; The Mask 1994; Coldblooded 1995; The Infiltrator 1995; Pie in the Sky 1995; Infinity 1996; Hi-Life 1998; Jerry and Tom 1998; Passion of Mind 2000; Surrender Dorothy 2006

Riehle, Richard (1948-) Of Mice and Men 1992; The Public Eye 1992; Lightning Jack 1994; The Odd Couple II 1998; Deuce Bigalow: Male Gigolo 1999; Home on the Range 2004

Riemann, Katja (1963-) The Most Desired Man 1994; Blood and Chocolate 2006

Riemelt, Max The Wave 2008; We Are the Night 2010

Rietty, Robert (1923-2015) Stock Car 1955; The Crooked Road 1964

Rifkin, Ron (1939-) Silent Running 1971; Do You Remember Love 1985; Manhattan Murder Mystery 1993; Wolf 1994; Last Summer in the Hamptons 1995; I'm Not Rappaport 1996; Norma Jean & Marilyn 1996; The Substance of Fire 1996; LA Confidential 1997; The Negotiator 1998; Boiler Room 2000; Flowers for Algernon 2000; Keeping the Faith 2000; Dragonfly 2002; The Sum of All Fears 2002; Tadpole 2002

Rigaud, Georges aka Rigaud, Jorge aka Rigaud, George (1905-1984) Divine 1935; The Castilian 1963; Grand Slam 1967

Rigby, Edward (1879-1951) Lorna Doone 1934; Accused 1936; The Show Goes On 1937; Young and Innocent 1937; A Yank at Oxford 1938; Poison Pen 1939; The Stars Look Down 1939; There Ain't No Justice 1939; Young Man's Fancy 1939; Convoy 1940; The Proud Valley 1940; The Common Touch 1941; Went the Day Well? 1942; They Met in the Dark 1943; Daybreak 1946; The Happiest Days of Your Life 1950; What the Butler Saw 1950

Rigby, Terence (1937-2008) The Homecoming 1973; Watership Down 1978; The Sign of Four 1983; Testimony 1987; The Children 1990; Elizabeth 1998; Essex Boys 1999

Rigg, Carl The Oblong Box 1969; Cry of the Banshee 1970

Rigg, Diana (1938-) The Assassination Bureau 1969; A Midsummer Night's Dream 1969; On Her Majesty's Secret Service 1969; Julius Caesar 1970; The Hospital 1971; Theatre of Blood 1973; A Little Night Music 1977; The Great Muppet Caper 1981; Evil under the Sun 1982; Witness for the Prosecution 1982; Mrs 'arris Goes to Paris 1992; A Good Man in Africa 1993; Danielle Steel's Zoya 1995; Parting Shots 1998; Heidi 2005; The Painted Veil 2006

Rigg, Rebecca (1967-) Spotswood 1991; Hunting 1992; Tunnel Vision 1994; Ellie Parker 2005

Riggle, Rob 21 Jump Street 2012; Dumb and Dumber To 2014; Let's Be Cops 2014

Righetti, Amanda Friday the 13th 2009; Wandering Eye 2011; Dangerous Attraction 2012

Rignault, Alexandre (1901-1985) Crime and Punishment 1935; Volpone 1941; Number Two 1975

Rihanna (1988-) Battleship 2012; Home 2014

Riley, Charlotte Easy Virtue 2008; London Has Fallen 2016

Riley, Jack (1935-) High Anxiety 1977; Attack of the Killer Tomatoes 1978

Riley, Jeannine (1940-) The Big Mouth 1967; Electra Glide in Blue 1973

Riley, Larry (1953-1992) A Soldier's Story 1984; Badge of the Assassin 1985; Unconquered 1989

Riley, Michael (1962-) Perfectly Normal 1990; ...And God Spoke 1993; Homeless to Harvard: the Liz Murray Story 2003; The Tenth Circle 2008

Riley, Sam (1980-) Control 2007; Franklyn 2008; Brighton Rock 2010; 13 2010; Byzantium 2012; Maleficent 2014; Suite Française 2014; Pride and Prejudice and Zombies 2015

Riley, Talulah (1985-) St Trinian's 2007; St Trinian's 2: the Legend of Fritton's Gold 2009; The Knot 2012; The Liability 2012

Riley, Tom A Few Days in September 2006; I Want Candy 2006; Happy Ever Afters 2009

Rilla, Walter (1895-1980) The Scarlet Pimpernel 1934; Victoria the Great 1937; Sixty Glorious Years 1938; The Gang's All Here 1939; The Adventures of Tartu 1943; Candlelight in Algeria 1943; Golden Salamander 1949; State Secret 1950; Venetian Bird 1952; Star of India 1954; The Secret Ways 1961; Cairo 1962; Death Drums along the River 1963; The Face of Fu Manchu 1965

Rimkus, Stevan Cal 1984; Conquest of the South Pole 1989; London Kills Me 1991; American Cousins 2003

Rimmer, Shane (1932-) Thunderbirds Are Go! 1966; Thunderbird 6 1968; The People That Time Forgot 1977; The Spy Who Loved Me 1977; Warlords of Atlantis 1978; Hanover Street 1979; Reunion at Fairborough 1985; A Kiss before Dying 1991; Space Truckers 1996

Rinaldi, Gérard Descent into Hell 1986; For Better and for Worse 1993

Ringer, Noah The Last Airbender 2010; Cowboys & Aliens 2011

Ringwald, Molly (1968-) Tempest 1982; Spacehunter: Adventures in the Forbidden Zone 1983; Sixteen Candles 1984; The Breakfast Club 1985; Surviving 1985; Pretty in Pink 1986; For Keeps 1987; King Lear - Fear and Loathing 1987; The Pick-Up Artist 1987; Fresh Horses 1988; Betsy's Wedding 1990; Loser Takes All 1990; Women and Men: Stories of Seduction 1990; Teaching Mrs Tingle 1999; Cut 2000; Not Another Teen Movie 2001; Jem and the Holograms 2015

Rintoul, David Legend of the Werewolf 1974; Unrelated 2007; Ironclad 2 2014

Riordan, Marjorie (1921-1984) Stage Door Canteen 1943; Mr Skeffington 1944; Pursuit to Algiers 1945; Three Strangers 1946

Rios, Lalo (1927-1973) The Lawless 1950; The Ring 1952; City beneath the Sea 1953

Riotta, Vincent Belly of the Beast 2003; Shadow Man 2006

Ripley, Fay (1967-) Mute Witness 1995; Roseanna's Grave 1996

Ripper, Michael (1913-2000) Eye Witness 1949; Quatermass II 1957; The Steel Bayonet 1957; Woman in a Dressing Gown 1957; The Scarlet Blade 1963; What a Crazy World 1963; The Devil-Ship Pirates 1964; The Plague of the Zombies 1965; The Mummy's Shroud 1966; The Reptile 1966; Where the Bullets Fly 1966; The Deadly Bees 1967; Dracula Has Risen from the Grave 1968; Mumsy, Nanny, Sonny & Girly 1970; The Creeping Flesh 1972; Legend of the Werewolf 1974

Rippy, Leon (30/10/1949-) Track 29 1988; Universal Soldier 1992; Stargate 1994; Eight Legged Freaks 2001; The Life of David Gale 2003; The Alamo 2004; Gridiron Gang 2006

Risdon, Elisabeth (1887-1958) Crime and Punishment 1935; The King Steps Out 1936; Theodora Goes Wild 1936; Make Way for Tomorrow 1937; Mannequin 1937; The Woman I Love 1937; The Affairs of Annabel 1938; The Adventures of Huckleberry Finn 1939; The Girl from Mexico 1939; The Great Man Votes 1939; The Howards of Virginia 1940; Let's Make Music 1940; Mexican Spitfire 1940; Footlight Fever 1941; Higher and Higher 1943; Tall in the Saddle 1944; Weird Woman 1944; Lover Come Back 1946; Bodyguard 1948; Every Girl Should Be Married 1948

Riseborough, Andrea (1981-) Happy-Go-Lucky 2007; Magicians 2007; Brighton Rock 2010; Resistance 2011; W.E. 2011; Disconnect 2012; Shadow Dancer 2012; Welcome to the Punch 2012; Oblivion 2013; Birdman or (The Unexpected Virtue of Ignorance) 2014; The Silent Storm 2014; Battle of the Sexes 2017

Rispoli, Michael (1960-) Household Saints 1993; Angie 1994; While You Were Sleeping 1995; Volcano 1997; Scarred City 1998; Summer of Sam 1999; It Had to Be You 2000; Mr 3000 2004; The Weather Man 2005; Invincible 2006; Kick-Ass 2009; The Rum Diary 2011

Riss, Dan (1910-1970) Panic in the Streets 1950; Wyoming Mail 1950

Risso, Roberto (1925-2010) Bread, Love & Dreams 1953; A Breath of Scandal 1960

Rissone, Checco (1909-1985) Bitter Rice 1949; Eva 1962

Ristovski, Lazar (1952-) Tito and Me 1992; Underground 1995

Ritch, Steven (1921-1995) The Werewolf 1956; Plunder Road 1957; City of Fear 1959

Ritchard, Cyril (1897-1977) Blackmail 1929; Piccadilly 1929; I See Ice 1938; Half a Sixpence 1967

Ritchie, Clint (1938-2009) The St Valentine's Day Massacre 1967; Bandolero! 1968; A Force of One 1979

Ritchie, Jill Breakin' All the Rules 2004; Herbie: Fully Loaded 2005

Ritchie, June (1939-) A Kind of Loving 1962; Live Now - Pay Later 1962; The Mouse on the Moon 1963; This Is My Street 1963; The World Ten Times Over 1963

Ritchie, Reece All in Good Time 2012; Desert Dancer 2014

Ritchson, Alan Teenage Mutant Ninja Turtles 2014; Teenage Mutant Ninja Turtles - Out of the Shadows 2016

Ritt, Martin (1914-1990) End of the Game 1976; The Slugger's Wife 1985

Ritter, Jason (1980-) Swimfan 2002; Freddy vs Jason 2003; Happy Endings 2005; The Education of Charlie Banks 2007; Good Dick 2008

Ritter, John (1948-2003) The Barefoot Executive 1971; Evil Roy Slade 1971; Scandalous John 1971; The Other 1972; Nickelodeon 1976; Americathon 1979; Hero at Large 1980; They All Laughed 1981; Real Men 1987; Skin Deep 1989; Problem Child 1990; Problem Child 2 1991; Noises Off 1992; Stay Tuned 1992; Sling Blade 1995; Montana 1997; Bride of Chucky 1998; Man of Miracles 1999; Panic 2000; Tadpole 2002; Bad Santa 2003; Clifford's Really Big Movie 2004

Ritter, Krysten (1981-) She's out of My League 2008; What Happens in Vegas 2008; Confessions of a Shopaholic 2009; Killing Bono 2010; Vamps 2012; Listen Up Philip 2014; Search Party 2014; Veronica Mars 2014

Ritter, Thelma (1905-1969) City across the River 1949; Father Was a Fullback 1949; All about Eve 1950; Perfect Strangers 1950; As Young as You Feel 1951; The Mating Season 1951; The Model and the Marriage Broker 1951; With a Song in My Heart 1952; The Farmer Takes a Wife 1953; Pickup on South Street 1953; Titanic 1953; Rear Window 1954; Daddy Long Legs 1955; Lucy Gallant 1955; Pillow Talk 1959; The Misfits 1961; The Second Time Around 1961; Birdman of Alcatraz 1962; How the West Was Won 1962; For Love or Money 1963; Move Over, Darling 1963; A New Kind of Love 1963; Boeing Boeing 1965; The Incident 1967; What's So Bad about Feeling Good? 1968

Ritz, Al aka The Ritz Brothers (1901-1965) One in a Million 1936; Sing, Baby, Sing 1936; Life Begins in College 1937; On the Avenue 1937; You Can't Have Everything 1937; The Goldwyn Follies 1938; Kentucky Moonshine 1938; Pack Up Your Troubles 1939; The Three Musketeers 1939; Argentine Nights 1940

Ritz, Harry aka The Ritz Brothers (1907-1986) One in a Million 1936; Sing, Baby, Sing 1936; Life Begins in College 1937; On the Avenue 1937; You Can't Have Everything 1937; The Goldwyn Follies 1938; Kentucky Moonshine 1938; Pack Up Your Troubles 1939; The Three Musketeers 1939; Argentine Nights 1940

Ritz, Jimmy aka The Ritz Brothers (1903-1985) One in a Million 1936; Sing, Baby, Sing 1936; Life Begins in College 1937; On the Avenue 1937; You Can't Have Everything 1937; The Goldwyn Follies 1938; Kentucky Moonshine 1938; Pack Up Your Troubles 1939; The Three Musketeers 1939; Argentine Nights 1940

Riva, Emmanuelle (1927-) Hiroshima, Mon Amour 1959; Kapo 1959; Léon Morin, Priest 1961; Thérèse Desqueyroux 1962; Thomas the Imposter 1964; Amour 2012

Rivas, Carlos (1928-2003) The Beast of Hollow Mountain 1956; The King and I 1956; The Black Scorpion 1957; The Deerslayer 1957

Rivault, Pascale La Bête 1975; Lady Chatterley's Lover 1981

Rivera, Mabel The Sea Inside 2004; Goya's Ghosts 2006; The Orphanage 2006

Rivero, Jorge aka Rivero, George (1938-) Rio Lobo 1970; Soldier Blue

1970; The Last Hard Men 1976; Priest of Love 1981; Target Eagle 1982

Rivers, Joan (1933-2014) Spaceballs 1987; Napoleon 1995; Whispers: an Elephant's Tale 2000; Joan Rivers: a Piece of Work 2010

Rivers, Victor Blood In Blood Out 1992; Two for Texas 1998; What's Cooking? 2000

Rivière, Marie (1956-) The Aviator's Wife 1980; Four Adventures of Reinette and Mirabelle 1986; The Green Ray 1986; An Autumn Tale 1998; Girls Can't Swim 1999; Time to Leave 2005

Rix, Brian (1924-) Dry Rot 1956; Not Wanted on Voyage 1957; The Night We Dropped a Clanger 1959; And the Same to You 1960; The Night We Got the Bird 1960; Don't Just Lie There, Say Something! 1973

Rizzo, Gianni (1925-1992) Face to Face 1967; Adios, Sabata 1970; The Decameron 1970

Röhm, Elisabeth Amber's Story 2006; The Kreutzer Sonata 2008; Desperate Escape 2009

Roach, Alexandra The Iron Lady 2011; Trap for Cinderella 2011; Private Peaceful 2012; One Chance 2013

Roach, Bert (1891-1971) The Crowd 1928; Six Cylinder Love 1931; Bird of Paradise 1932; Murders in the Rue Morgue 1932; The Man in the Iron Mask 1939

Roach, Pat (1937-2004) Clash of the Titans 1981; Willow 1988

Roache, Linus (1964-) Priest 1994; The Wings of the Dove 1997; Best 1999; Siam Sunset 1999; Pandaemonium 2000; Hart's War 2002; Beyond Borders 2003; Blind Flight 2003; The Chronicles of Riddick 2004; The Forgotten 2004; Twelve and Holding 2005; Find Me Guilty 2006; Before the Rains 2007

Roarke, Adam (1937-1996) Hell's Angels on Wheels 1967; Frogs 1972; Play It as It Lays 1972; Sioux City 1994

Robards Sr, Jason aka Robards, Jason (1892-1963) Hills of Kentucky 1927; The Silent Bell 1944; Isle of the Dead 1945; Bedlam 1946; Desperate 1947; Riff-Raff 1947; Thunder Mountain 1947; Trail Street 1947; Guns of Hate 1948

Robards, Jason aka Robards Jr, Jason (1922-2000) By Love Possessed 1961; Tender Is the Night 1961; Wild in the Country 1961; Long Day's Journey into Night 1962; Act One 1963; A Thousand Clowns 1965; Any Wednesday 1966; A Big Hand for a Little Lady 1966; Divorce American Style 1967; Hour of the Gun 1967; The St Valentine's Day Massacre 1967; Isadora 1968; The Night They Raided Minsky's 1968; Once upon a Time in the West 1968; The Ballad of Cable Hogue 1970; Fools 1970; Julius Caesar 1970; Tora! Tora! Tora! 1970; Johnny Got His Gun 1971; Murders in the Rue Morgue 1971; The War between Men and Women 1972; Pat Garrett and Billy the Kid 1973; Mr Sycamore 1974; A Boy and His Dog 1975; All the President's Men 1976; Julia 1977; Comes a Horseman 1978; Hurricane 1979; FDR: the Last Year 1980; Melvin and Howard 1980; Raise the Titanic 1980; The Legend of the Lone Ranger 1981; Max Dugan Returns 1983; Something Wicked This Way Comes 1983; Square Dance 1987; Bright Lights, Big City 1988; Inherit the Wind 1988; The Price of Passion 1988; Black Rainbow 1989; Dream a Little Dream 1989; Parenthood 1989; Reunion 1989; Quick Change 1990; Storyville 1992; The Adventures of Huck Finn 1993; Philadelphia 1993; The Trial 1993; The Enemy Within 1994; Little Big League 1994; The Paper 1994; A Thousand Acres 1997; Enemy of the State 1998; Magnolia 1999

Robards, Sam (1961-) Tempest 1982; Fandango 1985; Not Quite Jerusalem 1985; The Ballad of Little Jo 1993; American Beauty 1999; AI: Artificial Intelligence 2001; Life as a House 2001; Catch That Kid 2004; Awake 2007; The Rebound 2009

Robb, AnnaSophia (1993-) Because of Winn-Dixie 2004; Charlie and the Chocolate Factory 2005; Bridge to Terabithia 2006; The Reaping 2006; Race to Witch Mountain 2009; Soul Surfer 2011; Khumba 2013; The Way Way Back 2013

Robb, David (1947-) The Deceivers 1988; Treasure Island 1998

Robb, R D (1972-) A Christmas Story 1983; Eight Days a Week 1996

Robbie, Margot (1990-) About Time 2013; The Wolf of Wall Street 2013; Suite Française 2014; Focus 2015; The Legend of Tarzan 2016; Suicide Squad

2016; Whiskey Tango Foxtrot 2016; Goodbye Christopher Robin 2017

Robbins, Amy (1971-) Up on the Roof 1997; All the Little Animals 1998

Robbins, Gale (1921-1980) My Girl Tisa 1948; Oh, You Beautiful Doll 1949; The Fuller Brush Girl 1950; Three Little Words 1950; The Belle of New York 1952; Calamity Jane 1953; Quantrill's Raiders 1958

Robbins, James San Quentin 1937; The Barbarian and the Geisha 1958

Robbins, Michael (1930-1992) Lunch Hour 1962; On the Buses 1971; Mutiny on the Buses 1972; Holiday on the Buses 1973

Robbins, Peter (1956-) A Ticklish Affair 1963; Moment to Moment 1966; A Boy Named Charlie Brown 1969

Robbins, Ryan Apollo 18 2011; Reasonable Doubt 2014

Robbins, Tim (1958-) Fraternity Vacation 1985; The Sure Thing 1985; Howard, a New Breed of Hero 1986; Top Gun 1986; Five Corners 1987; Bull Durham 1988; Tapeheads 1988; Erik the Viking 1989; Miss Firecracker 1989; Cadillac Man 1990; Jacob's Ladder 1990; Jungle Fever 1991; Bob Roberts 1992; The Player 1992; Short Cuts 1993; The Hudsucker Proxy 1994; IQ 1994; Pret-a-Porter 1994; The Shawshank Redemption 1994; Nothing to Lose 1997; Arlington Road 1998; Mission to Mars 1999; Antitrust 2000; High Fidelity 2000; Human Nature 2001; The Truth about Charlie 2002; Code 46 2003; Mystic River 2003; War of the Worlds 2005; Zathura: a Space Adventure 2005; Catch a Fire 2006; Tenacious D in The Pick of Destiny 2006; City of Ember 2008; Cinema Verite 2011; Green Lantern 2011; Revenge of the Electric Car 2011; Thanks for Sharing 2012; Life of Crime 2013

Rober, Richard (1910-1952) The File on Thelma Jordon 1949; Port of New York 1949; The Woman on Pier 13 1949; Sierra 1950; Watch the Birdie 1950; Man in the Saddle 1951; The Tall Target 1951; The Well 1951; The Devil Makes Three 1952; The Savage 1953

Robert, Yves (1920-2002) Les Grandes Manoeuvres 1955; Cleo from 5 to 7 1961; La Crise 1992

Roberti, Lyda (1906-1938) The Kid from Spain 1932; Million Dollar Legs 1932; Torch Singer 1933; George White's 1935 Scandals 1935

Roberts, Aled A Feast at Midnight 1994; Back to the Secret Garden 2000

Roberts, Ailene (1928-) The Red House 1947; Knock on Any Door 1949; Union Station 1950

Roberts, Beverly (1914-2009) China Clipper 1936; God's Country and the Woman 1937; The Perfect Specimen 1937

Roberts, Christian (1944-) To Sir, with Love 1967; The Anniversary 1968; The Mind of Mr Soames 1970; The Last Valley 1971

Roberts, Craig (1991-) Submarine 2010; Comes a Bright Day 2012; Benny & Jolene 2014; Premature 2014; The Fundamentals of Caring 2015; Just Jim 2015; Kill Your Friends 2015

Roberts, Dallas (1970-) A Home at the End of the World 2004; Walk the Line 2005; Flicka 2006; Joshua 2007; Shrink 2009; The Factory 2012; The Grey 2012

Roberts (2), David Me Myself I 1999; Gettin' Square 2003; The Square 2008

Roberts, Denise Opal Dream 2005; Razzle Dazzle: a Journey into Dance 2006

Roberts, Doris (1925-2016) A Lovely Way to Go 1968; The Honeymoon Killers 1969; Little Murders 1971; A New Leaf 1971; Such Good Friends 1971; Hester Street 1975; The Diary of Anne Frank 1980; Number One with a Bullet 1986; National Lampoon's Christmas Vacation 1989; Our House 2006; Aliens in the Attic 2009; Mrs Miracle 2009; Call Me Mrs Miracle 2010

Roberts, Emma (1991-) Aquamarine 2006; Nancy Drew 2007; Hotel for Dogs 2008; Lymelife 2008; Wild Child 2008; 4.3.2.1 2010; It's Kind of a Funny Story 2010; The Art of Getting By 2011; Scre4m 2011; Celeste & Jesse Forever 2012; Palo Alto 2013; We're the Millers 2013; Nerve 2016

Roberts, Eric (1956-) King of the Gypsies 1978; Raggedy Man 1981; Star 80 1983; The Pope of Greenwich Village 1984; The Coca-Cola Kid 1985; Runaway Train 1985; Nobody's Fool 1986; Blood Red 1988; Best of the Best 1989; Rude Awakening 1989; The Ambulance 1990; Best of the Best II 1992; By the Sword 1992; Final Analysis 1992; Babyfever 1994; Bad Company 1994; Love, Cheat & Steal 1994; The

Specialist 1994; American Strays 1996; The Cable Guy 1996; The Glass Cage 1996; Heaven's Prisoners 1996; It's My Party 1996; The Odyssey 1997; The Prophecy II 1997; Hitman's Run 1999; Lansky 1999; Purgatory 1999; Luck of the Draw 2000; Sanctimony 2000; National Security 2002; Spun 2002; Graves End 2005; DOA: Dead or Alive 2006; A Guide to Recognizing Your Saints 2006; The Dark Knight 2008; Class 2010; The Expendables 2010; Assumed Killer 2013; The Human Centipede III (Fina. Sequence) 2015

Roberts, Evelyn (1886-1962) Keep Fit 1937; Man of the Moment 1955

Roberts, Ewan (1914-1983) Colonel March Investigates 1953; River Beat 1954; Night of the Demon 1957

Roberts, Florence (1861-1940) Kept Husbands 1931; Make Me a Star 1932; Babes in Toyland 1934; Top Hat 1935

Roberts, J H (1884-1961) The Divorce of Lady X 1938; Charley's (Big Hearted) Aunt 1940

Roberts, Joe (1871-1923) Neighbors 1920; One Week 1920; The Scarecrow 1920; The Paleface 1921; Three Ages 1923

Roberts, Julia (1968-) Blood Red 1988; Mystic Pizza 1988; Satisfaction 1988; Steel Magnolias 1989; Flatliners 1990; Pretty Woman 1990; Dying Young 1991; Hook 1991; Sleeping with the Enemy 1991; The Pelican Brief 1993; I Love Trouble 1994; Pret-a-Porter 1994; Mary Reilly 1995; Something to Talk About 1995; Everyone Says I Love You 1996; Michael Collins 1996; Conspiracy Theory 1997; My Best Friend's Wedding 1997; Stepmom 1998; Notting Hill 1999; Runaway Bride 1999; Erin Brockovich 2000; America's Sweethearts 2001; The Mexican 2001; Ocean's Eleven 2001; Confessions of a Dangerous Mind 2002; Full Frontal 2002; Mona Lisa Smile 2003; Closer 2004; Ocean's Twelve 2004; The Ant Bully 2006; Charlotte's Web 2006; Charlie Wilson's War 2007; Fireflies in the Garden 2007; Duplicity 2009; Eat Pray Love 2010; Valentine's Day 2010; Larry Crowne 2011; Mirror Mirror 2012; August: Osage County 2013; The Normal Heart 2014; Secret in Their Eyes 2015; Money Monster 2016; Mother's Day 2016

Roberts, Leonard aka Drumline 2002; Joe and Max 2002; Red Sands 2009

Roberts, Lynne aka Hart, Mary (1919-1978) Shine On, Harvest Moon 1938; Riders of the Purple Sage 1941; Quiet Please, Murder 1942

Roberts, Michael D The Ice Pirates 1984; Rain Man 1988; Sleepstalker 1995

Roberts, Nita (1882-1962) Cosh Boy 1952; It's a Great Day 1955

Roberts, Nia Solomon and Gaenor 1998; Patagonia 2010; Third Star 2010; The Facility 2012

Roberts, Pascale (1933-) The Sleeping Car Murders 1965; Three 1969; Le Grand Chemin 1987; Marius et Jeannette 1997; La Ville Est Tranquille 2000

Roberts, Pernell (1928-2010) Desire under the Elms 1958; The Sheepman 1958; Ride Lonesome 1959; The Magic of Lassie 1978

Roberts (1), Rachel (1927-1980) Valley of Song 1953; The Good Companions 1956; Saturday Night and Sunday Morning 1960; Girl on Approval 1962; This Sporting Life 1963; A Flea in Her Ear 1968; Doctors' Wives 1970; Alpha Beta 1973; The Belstone Fox 1973; O Lucky Man! 1973; Murder on the Orient Express 1974; Picnic at Hanging Rock 1975; Foul Play 1978; When a Stranger Calls 1979; Yanks 1979; Charlie Chan and the Curse of the Dragon Queen 1981

Roberts, Rick (1965-) Love and Human Remains 1993; Time to Say Goodbye? 1997; As Time Runs Out 1999; Student Seduction 2003; More Sex & the Single Mom 2005; Plague City: Sars in Toronto 2005; Pontypool 2008; The Town Christmas Forgot 2010; Salem Falls 2011

Roberts, Roy (1900-1975) Guadalcanal Diary 1943; Circumstantial Evidence 1945; Smoky 1946; Force of Evil 1948; He Walked by Night 1948; Wyoming Mail 1950; The Enforcer 1951; The Glory Brigade 1953; House of Wax 1953; The Lone Hand 1953; Tumbleweed 1953; Wyoming Renegades 1955

Roberts, Shawn (1984-) Diary of the Dead 2007; Edge of Darkness 2009; I Love You, Beth Cooper 2009; Resident Evil: Afterlife 2010; The Music Teacher 2012; The Girl He Met Online 2014

Roberts, Tanya (1954-) Tourist Trap 1979; The Beastmaster 1982; Sheena

1984; A View to a Kill 1985; Night Eyes 1990

Roberts, Theodore (1861-1928) Male and Female 1919; The Ten Commandments 1923

Roberts, Tony (1939-) The Million Dollar Duck 1971; Play It Again, Sam 1972; Serpico 1973; Call Him Savage 1975; Annie Hall 1977; Just Tell Me What You Want 1980; Stardust Memories 1980; A Midsummer Night's Sex Comedy 1982; Amityville III: the Demon 1983; Hannah and Her Sisters 1986; 18 Again! 1988; Switch 1991; Arthur Miller's The American Clock 1993; The Longest Week 2014

Robertson-Justice, James aka **Robertson Justice, James** (1905-1975) For Those in Peril 1943; Against the Wind 1947; My Brother Jonathan 1947; Vice Versa 1947; Scott of the Antarctic 1948; Whisky Galore! 1949; Pool of London 1950; Anne of the Indies 1951; Captain Horatio Hornblower RN 1951; David and Bathsheba 1951; Les Misérables 1952; Miss Robin Hood 1952; The Story of Robin Hood and His Merrie Men 1952; The Sword and the Rose 1952; Voice of Merrill 1952; Rob Roy, the Highland Rogue 1953; Doctor in the House 1954; Out of the Clouds 1954; Above Us the Waves 1955; An Alligator Named Daisy 1955; Doctor at Sea 1955; Land of the Pharaohs 1955; The Living Idol 1955; Storm over the Nile 1955; Checkpoint 1956; The Iron Petticoat 1956; Moby Dick 1956; Campbell's Kingdom 1957; Doctor at Large 1957; Seven Thunders 1957; Orders to Kill 1958; Upstairs and Downstairs 1959; Doctor in Love 1960; Foxhole in Cairo 1960; A French Mistress 1960; The Guns of Navarone 1961; Murder She Said 1961; A Pair of Briefs 1961; Raising the Wind 1961; Very Important Person 1961; Crooks Anonymous 1962; Dr Crippen 1962; Guns of Darkness 1962; Doctor in Distress 1963; The Fast Lady 1963; Father Came Too 1963; The Face of Fu Manchu 1965; Up from the Beach 1965; You Must Be Joking! 1965; Doctor in Clover 1966; The Trygon Factor 1967; Chitty Chitty Bang Bang 1968; Mayerling 1968; Some Will, Some Won't 1969; Doctor in Trouble 1970

Robertson, Brittany aka **Robertson, Britt** (1990-) The Tenth Circle 2008; Delivery Man 2013; Tomorrowland: a World Beyond 2015; Mother's Day 2016

Robertson, Cliff (1925-2011) Picnic 1955; Autumn Leaves 1956; The Girl Most Likely 1957; The Naked and the Dead 1958; Battle of the Coral Sea 1959; Gidget 1959; All in a Night's Work 1960; The Big Show 1961; Underworld USA 1961; My Six Loves 1962; PT 109 1963; Sunday in New York 1963; The Best Man 1964; 633 Squadron 1964; Love Has Many Faces 1965; Masquerade 1965; Up from the Beach 1965; The Honey Pot 1967; Charly 1968; Too Late the Hero 1970; JW Coop 1971; The Great Northfield Minnesota Raid 1972; Ace Eli and Rodger of the Skies 1973; The Man without a Country 1973; Out of Season 1975; Three Days of the Condor 1975; Battle of Midway 1976; Obsession 1976; Dominique 1978; Brainstorm 1983; Class 1983; Star 80 1983; Dreams of Gold: the Mel Fisher Story 1986; Malone 1987; Wild Hearts Can't Be Broken 1991; Wind 1992; Renaissance Man 1994; Escape from LA 1996; Spider-Man 2002; Spider-Man 3 2007

Robertson, Dale (1923-2013) Fighting Man of the Plains 1949; The Cariboo Trail 1950; Two Flags West 1950; Call Me Mister 1951; Golden Girl 1951; O Henry's Full House 1952; Devil's Canyon 1953; The Farmer Takes a Wife 1953; Sitting Bull 1954; Son of Sinbad 1955; Dakota Incident 1956; A Day of Fury 1956; Coast of Skeletons 1964; The Man from Button Willow 1965

Robertson, Iain (1981-) Small Faces 1995; The Debt Collector 1999; One Last Chance 2003; Acts of Godfrey 2011

Robertson, Kathleen (1973-) Lapse of Memory 1992; Nowhere 1997; Dog Park 1998; Splendor 1999; Beautiful 2000; Scary Movie 2 2001; XX/XY 2001

Robertson, Robbie (1943-) Carny 1980; The Crossing Guard 1995

Robertson, Steven Inside I'm Dancing 2004; Memantine 2005; True North 2006; Straightheads 2007

Robertson, Tim (1944-) Bliss 1985; The Time Guardian 1987; The Big Steal 1990; Holy Smoke 1999

Robertson, Willard (1886-1948) Skippy 1931; Lady Killer 1933; Tugboat Annie 1933; Kentucky 1938; Background to Danger 1943; Deep Valley 1947

Robeson, Paul (1898-1976) The Emperor Jones 1933; Sanders of the River 1935; Show Boat 1936; Song of Freedom 1936; Big Fella 1937; Jericho 1937; King Solomon's Mines 1937; The Proud Valley 1940; Native Land 1942; Tales of Manhattan 1942

Robey, George (1869-1954) Don Quixote 1933; Chu Chin Chow 1934

Robin, Dany aka **Robin, Mme Dany** (1927-1995) Man about Town 1947; Act of Love 1953; The Mysteries of Paris 1962; Waltz of the Toreadors 1962; Follow the Boys 1963; The Best House in London 1968; Topaz 1969

Robin, Michel (1930-) Marquis 1989; Merci pour le Chocolat 2000

Robins, Laila (1959-) An Innocent Man 1989; Welcome Home, Roxy Carmichael 1990; Female Perversions 1996

Robinson, Andrew aka **Robinson, Andy** (1942-) Dirty Harry 1971; Charley Varrick 1973; Cobra 1986; Hellraiser 1987; The Revenge of Pumpkinhead - Blood Wings 1994

Robinson, Ann (1935-) The Glass Wall 1953; The War of the Worlds 1953; Dragnet 1954; Gun Duel in Durango 1957; War of the Worlds 2005

Robinson, Bartlett (1912-1986) The Spirit of St Louis 1957; All Hands on Deck 1961; Sleeper 1973

Robinson, Bill (1878-1949) The Big Broadcast of 1936 1935; In Old Kentucky 1935; The Littlest Rebel 1935; Just around the Corner 1938; Rebecca of Sunnybrook Farm 1938; Stormy Weather 1943

Robinson, Bruce (1946-) The Ballad of Tam Lin 1970; The Story of Adèle H 1975; Still Crazy 1998; For No Good Reason 2012

Robinson, Cardew (1917-1992) The Navy Lark 1959; Light Up the Sky 1960; I Was Happy Here 1966; Come Play with Me 1977

Robinson, Charles Knox aka **Robinson, Charles** aka **Robinson Knox, Charles** (1937-2006) Shenandoah 1965; The Sand Pebbles 1966; Brotherhood of Satan 1970

Robinson, Chris (1938-) Amy 1981; Savannah Smiles 1982

Robinson, Craig Zack and Miri Make a Porno 2008; Miss March 2009; Hot Tub Time Machine 2010; Hot Tub Time Machine 2 2014

Robinson, Edward G (1893-1973) Five Star Final 1931; Little Caesar 1931; Smart Money 1931; The Hatchet Man 1932; Tiger Shark 1932; Two Seconds 1932; The Little Giant 1933; Barbary Coast 1935; The Whole Town's Talking 1935; Bullets or Ballots 1936; Kid Galahad 1937; The Last Gangster 1937; Thunder in the City 1937; The Amazing Dr Clitterhouse 1938; I Am the Law 1938; A Slight Case of Murder 1938; Blackmail 1939; Confessions of a Nazi Spy 1939; Brother Orchid 1940; A Dispatch from Reuters 1940; Dr Ehrlich's Magic Bullet 1940; Manpower 1941; The Sea Wolf 1941; Unholy Partners 1941; Larceny, Inc 1942; Tales of Manhattan 1942; Flesh and Fantasy 1943; Double Indemnity 1944; Journey Together 1944; Mr Winkle Goes to War 1944; Our Vines Have Tender Grapes 1945; Scarlet Street 1945; The Woman in the Window 1945; The Stranger 1946; The Red House 1947; All My Sons 1948; Key Largo 1948; Night Has a Thousand Eyes 1948; House of Strangers 1949; It's a Great Feeling 1949; Actors and Sin 1952; Big Leaguer 1953; The Glass Web 1953; Vice Squad 1953; A Bullet for Joey 1955; Hell on Frisco Bay 1955; Illegal 1955; Tight Spot 1955; The Violent Men 1955; Nightmare 1956; The Ten Commandments 1956; Pepe 1960; Seven Thieves 1960; My Geisha 1962; Two Weeks in Another Town 1962; The Prize 1963; Sammy Going South 1963; Cheyenne Autumn 1964; Good Neighbor Sam 1964; The Outrage 1964; Robin and the 7 Hoods 1964; The Cincinnati Kid 1965; Grand Slam 1967; The Biggest Bundle of Them All 1968; Mackenna's Gold 1969; Song of Norway 1970; Soylent Green 1973

Robinson, Jay (1930-) The Robe 1953; Demetrius and the Gladiators 1954; The Virgin Queen 1955; My Man Godfrey 1957; Bunny O'Hare 1971; Three the Hard Way 1974; Shampoo 1975; Born Again 1978; Partners 1982

Robinson (1), John (1908-1979) Emergency Call 1952; Ghost Ship 1952; The Doctor's Dilemma 1958; Nothing but the Night 1972

Robinson (3), John (1985-) Elephant 2003; Lords of Dogtown 2005; Wendy and Lucy 2008

Robinson, Karen Student Seduction 2003; Lars and the Real Girl 2007

Robinson, Keith Fat Albert 2004; Dreamgirls 2006; Dear John 2010

Robinson, Madeleine (1916-2004) Web of Passion 1959; Une Histoire Simple 1978; Camille Claudel 1988

Robinson, Nick (1995-) The Kings of Summer 2013; The 5th Wave 2016

Robinson, Thomas The Switch 2010; Tomorrowland: a World Beyond 2015

Robinson, Wendy Raquel Ringmaster 1998; Two Can Play That Game 2001; Rebound 2005; Something New 2006

Robinson, Zuleikha aka **Robinson, Zuleika** (1977-) Hidalgo 2003; William Shakespeare's The Merchant of Venice 2004; The Namesake 2006

Robson, Flora (1902-1984) The Rise of Catherine the Great 1934; Fire over England 1937; Invisible Stripes 1939; Poison Pen 1939; We Are Not Alone 1939; Wuthering Heights 1939; The Sea Hawk 1940; Great Day 1944; Two Thousand Women 1944; Caesar and Cleopatra 1945; Saratoga Trunk 1945; The Years Between 1946; Black Narcissus 1947; Frieda 1947; Holiday Camp 1947; Saraband for Dead Lovers 1948; Malta Story 1953; Romeo and Juliet 1954; High Tide at Noon 1957; Innocent Sinners 1957; No Time for Tears 1957; The Gypsy and the Gentleman 1958; 55 Days at Peking 1963; Murder at the Gallop 1963; Guns at Batasi 1964; Those Magnificent Men in Their Flying Machines 1965; Young Cassidy 1965; Eye of the Devil 1966; 7 Women 1966; The Shuttered Room 1967; The Beast in the Cellar 1970; Fragment of Fear 1970; Alice's Adventures in Wonderland 1972; Sin 1972; Dominique 1978; Les Misérables 1978

Robson, May (1858-1942) If I Had a Million 1932; Red-Headed Woman 1932; Strange Interlude 1932; Dancing Lady 1933; Lady for a Day 1933; Reunion in Vienna 1933; The White Sister 1933; Lady by Choice 1934; Anna Karenina 1935; Reckless 1935; Vanessa, Her Love Story 1935; Wife vs Secretary 1936; The Perfect Specimen 1937; A Star Is Born 1937; The Adventures of Tom Sawyer 1938; Bringing Up Baby 1938; Four Daughters 1938; The Texans 1938; Daughters Courageous 1939; Nurse Edith Cavell 1939; That's Right - You're Wrong 1939; They Made Me a Criminal 1939; Four Mothers 1941; Million Dollar Baby 1941; Playmates 1941; Joan of Paris 1942

Robson, Wayne (1946-2011) The Grey Fox 1982; One Magic Christmas 1985; Dead of Winter 1987; Housekeeping 1987; Bye Bye Blues 1989; Stolen Hearts 1996; Cube 1997; Pippi Longstocking 1997; Cool Money 2005

Roc, Patricia (1915-2003) A Window in London 1939; We'll Meet Again 1942; Millions like Us 1943; Love Story 1944; Madonna of the Seven Moons 1944; Two Thousand Women 1944; Johnny Frenchman 1945; The Wicked Lady 1945; Canyon Passage 1946; The Brothers 1947; Jassy 1947; So Well Remembered 1947; When the Bough Breaks 1947; One Night with You 1948; The Man on the Eiffel Tower 1949; The Perfect Woman 1949; Circle of Danger 1950; Black Jack 1952; House in the Woods 1957; The Hypnotist 1957

Rocca, Daniela (1938-1995) The Giant of Marathon 1960; Divorce - Italian Style 1961; Captive City 1962; The Empty Canvas 1963; Behold a Pale Horse 1964

Rocca, Stefania (1971-) Nirvana 1996; Heaven 2002; The Card Player 2004

Rocco, Alex (1936-2015) Motor Psycho 1965; Detroit 9000 1973; The Friends of Eddie Coyle 1973; Hearts of the West 1975; Herbie Goes Bananas 1980; The Stunt Man 1980; Badge of the Assassin 1985; Gotcha! 1985; Return to Horror High 1986; Lady in White 1988; Wired 1989; The Pope Must Die 1991; Goodbye Lover 1997; Dudley Do-Right 1999

Roche, Eugene (1928-2004) Slaughterhouse-Five 1972; Newman's Law 1974; Mr Ricco 1975; The Late Show 1977; Corvette Summer 1978; Oh, God! You Devil 1984

Roche, John (1893-1952) Kiss Me Again 1925; Don Juan 1926

Rochefort, Jean (1930-) Le Masque de Fer 1962; Up to His Ears 1965; The Tall Blond Man with One Black Shoe 1972; The Bit Player 1973; The Watchmaker of St Paul 1973; Les Innocents aux Mains Sales 1975; Pardon Mon Affaire 1976; French Postcards 1979; The Hairdresser's

Husband 1990; Wild Target 1993; Circle of Passion 1996; Ridicule 1996; Wind with the Gone 1998; The Closet 2001; L'Homme du Train 2002; L'Enfer 2005; Tell No One 2006; Mr Bean's Holiday 2007; The Artist and the Model 2012

Rochfort, Spencer (1966-) Operation Delta Force II: Mayday 1998; A Decent Proposal 2006

Rochon, Lela aka **Fuqua, Lela Rochon** (1966-) The Wild Pair 1987; Boomerang 1992; Mr and Mrs Loving 1993; Waiting to Exhale 1995; The Chamber 1996; Gang Related 1997; Knock Off 1998; Why Do Fools Fall in Love? 1998; First Daughter 2004

Rock, Chris (1966-) New Jack City 1991; Boomerang 1992; CB4 1993; Beverly Hills Ninja 1997; Lethal Weapon 4 1998; Dogma 1999; Nurse Betty 2000; Down to Earth 2001; Jay and Silent Bob Strike Back 2001; Osmosis Jones 2001; Bad Company 2002; Head of State 2003; The Aristocrats 2005; The Longest Yard 2005; Madagascar 2005; Bee Movie 2007; Madagascar: Escape 2 Africa 2008; You Don't Mess with the Zohan 2008; Good Hair 2009; Death at a Funeral 2010; Grown Ups 2010; 2 Days in New York 2011; Madagascar 3: Europe's Most Wanted 2012; What to Expect When You're Expecting 2012; Grown Ups 2 2013; Top Five 2014

Rock, Crissy Ladybird Ladybird 1994; A Boy Called Dad 2009

Rocket, Charles (1949-2005) Earth Girls Are Easy 1988; How I Got Into College 1989; Dances with Wolves 1990; Delirious 1991; Brain Smasher... a Love Story 1993; Charlie's Ghost Story 1994; Dumb and Dumber 1994; Tom and Huck 1995

Rockwell, Sam (1968-) Clownhouse 1988; Glory Daze 1995; Box of Moonlight 1996; Lawn Dogs 1997; Jerry and Tom 1998; Safe Men 1998; Galaxy Quest 1999; The Green Mile 1999; Charlie's Angels 2000; Heist 2001; Confessions of a Dangerous Mind 2002; Welcome to Collinwood 2002; Matchstick Men 2003; Piccadilly Jim 2004; The Hitchhiker's Guide to the Galaxy 2005; The Assassination of Jesse James by the Coward Robert Ford 2007; Joshua 2007; Choke 2008; Frost/Nixon 2008; Moon 2008; Everybody's Fine 2009; G-Force 2009; Gentlemen Broncos 2009; Conviction 2010; Iron Man 2 2010; Cowboys & Aliens 2011; The Sitter 2011; Seven Psychopaths 2012; The Way Way Back 2013; Better Living through Chemistry 2014; Say When 2014; Poltergeist 2015

Rodan, Jay Callas Forever 2002; Monsieur N 2003

Rodd, Marcia (1940-) Little Murders 1971; TR Baskin 1971; Citizens Band 1977

Roden, Karel (1962-) 15 Minutes 2001; Bulletproof Monk 2002; Hellboy 2004; Mr Bean's Holiday 2007; Bathory 2008; Orphan 2009; A Lonely Place to Die 2011; Sword of Vengeance 2015

Roderick, Sue Rebecca's Daughters 1991; Hedd Wyn 1992; Under Milk Wood 2015

Rodgers, Anton (1933-2007) Rotten to the Core 1965; The Man Who Haunted Himself 1970; Scrooge 1970; East of Elephant Rock 1976; Agatha Christie's Murder with Mirrors 1985; Dirty Rotten Scoundrels 1988; Impromptu 1991

Rodgers, Ilona (1942-) Salt & Pepper 1968; Utu 1983

Rodman, Dennis (1961-) Double Team 1997; Simon Sez 1999; Cutaway 2000

Rodney, John (1916-) Pursued 1947; Fighter Squadron 1948; Key Largo 1948

Rodrigues, Percy (1918-2007) The Heart Is a Lonely Hunter 1968; Brainwaves 1982

Rodriguez, Freddy (1975-) Dead Presidents 1995; A Walk in the Clouds 1995; Dreamer 2005; Harsh Times 2005; Havoc 2005; Poseidon 2006; Planet Terror 2007; Bottle Shock 2008

Rodriguez, Genesis Casa de Mi Padre 2011; Hours 2013; Big Hero 6 2014

Rodriguez, Marco Disorderlies 1987; Toolbox Murders 2003

Rodriguez, Michelle (1978-) Girlfight 2000; The Fast and the Furious 2001; Blue Crush 2002; Resident Evil 2002; SWAT 2007; The Breed 2006; Battle in Seattle 2007; Avatar 2009; Fast & Furious 2009; Machete 2010; Battle Los Angeles 2011; Resident Evil: Retribution 2012; Fast & Furious 6 2013; Machete Kills 2013; Fast & Furious 7 2014

Rodriguez, Paul (1955-) Miracles 1985; Quicksilver 1986; Born in East LA 1987; Made in America 1993; Rough

Magic 1995; Tortilla Soup 2001; Blood Work 2002; Baadasssss! 2003; The World's Fastest Indian 2005

Rodriguez, Raini Paul Blart: Mall Cop 2009; Paul Blart: Mall Cop 2 2015

Rodriguez, Ramon The Taking of Pelham 123 2009; Transformers: Revenge of the Fallen 2009; Battle Los Angeles 2011; Need for Speed 2014

Rodway, Norman (1929-2001) This Other Eden 1959; Four in the Morning 1965; Chimes at Midnight 1966; The Penthouse 1967

Roe, Paul Adam & Paul 2004; Kisses 2008

Roe, Raymond (1925-2010) The Major and the Minor 1942; The West Point Story 1950

Roebuck, Daniel (1963-) Dudes 1987; River's Edge 1987; The Late Shift 1996; US Marshals 1998; Agent Cody Banks 2: Destination London 2003; Graves End 2005; Flash of Genius 2008

Roel, Gabriela El Dorado 1988; Old Gringo 1989

Roemer, Sarah The Grudge 2 2006; Disturbia 2007; Hachi: a Dog's Tale 2008; Fired Up! 2009

Roëves, Maurice (1937-) Ulysses 1967; Oh! What a Lovely War 1969; When Eight Bells Toll 1971; The Big Man 1990; The Last of the Mohicans 1992; The Acid House 1998; Beautiful Creatures 2000; The Dark 2005; Hallam Foe 2006; Luna 2014

Rogen, Seth (1982-) The 40 Year Old Virgin 2005; You, Me and Dupree 2006; Knocked Up 2007; Superbad 2007; Dr Seuss' Horton Hears a Who! 2008; Fanboys 2008; Kung Fu Panda 2008; Pineapple Express 2008; The Spiderwick Chronicles 2008; Zack and Miri Make a Porno 2008; Funny People 2009; Monsters vs Aliens 2009; Observe and Report 2009; Paper Heart 2009; Paul 2010; 50/50 2011; The Green Hornet 2011; Kung Fu Panda 2 2011; Take This Waltz 2011; For a Good Time, Call... 2012; The Guilt Trip 2013; This Is the End 2013; Bad Neighbours 2014; The Interview 2014; The Night Before 2015; Steve Jobs 2015; Bad Neighbours 2 2016; Sausage Party 2016

Rogers, Charles "Buddy" (1904-1999) My Best Girl 1927; Wings 1927; Old Man Rhythm 1935

Rogers, Ginger (1911-1995) Honor among Lovers 1931; The Thirteenth Guest 1932; Flying down to Rio 1933; 42nd Street 1933; Gold Diggers of 1933 1933; Sitting Pretty 1933; Change of Heart 1934; Finishing School 1934; The Gay Divorce 1934; Romance in Manhattan 1934; Upper World 1934; In Person 1935; Roberta 1935; Star of Midnight 1935; Top Hat 1935; Follow the Fleet 1936; Swing Time 1936; Shall We Dance 1937; Stage Door 1937; Carefree 1938; Having Wonderful Time 1938; Vivacious Lady 1938; Bachelor Mother 1939; 5th Ave Girl 1939; The Story of Vernon and Irene Castle 1939; Kitty Foyle 1940; Lucky Partners 1940; Primrose Path 1940; Tom, Dick and Harry 1941; The Major and the Minor 1942; Once upon a Honeymoon 1942; Roxie Hart 1942; Tales of Manhattan 1942; Tender Comrade 1943; I'll Be Seeing You 1944; Lady in the Dark 1944; Week-End at the Waldorf 1945; Heartbeat 1946; Magnificent Doll 1946; It Had to Be You 1947; The Barkleys of Broadway 1949; Perfect Strangers 1950; Storm Warning 1950; Dreamboat 1952; Monkey Business 1952; We're Not Married 1952; Forever Female 1953; Beautiful Stranger 1954; Black Widow 1954; Tight Spot 1955; The First Travelling Saleslady 1956; Teenage Rebel 1956; Oh, Men! Oh, Women! 1957; Quick, Let's Get Married 1964; Cinderella 1965

Rogers, Jean (1916-1991) Stormy 1935; Flash Gordon 1936; Brigham Young 1940; Let's Make Music 1940; The Man Who Wouldn't Talk 1940; Design for Scandal 1941; Dr Kildare's Victory 1941; The War against Mrs Hadley 1942

Rogers, Kenny (1938-) Six Pack 1982; Wild Horses 1985

Rogers, Mimi (1956-) Gung Ho 1986; Someone to Watch over Me 1987; Street Smart 1987; Hider in the House 1989; The Mighty Quinn 1989; Desperate Hours 1990; The Rapture 1991; Dark Horse 1992; Shooting Elizabeth 1992; White Sands 1992; Far from Home: the Adventures of Yellow Dog 1994; Killer 1994; Monkey Trouble 1994; Reflections on a Crime 1994; The Mirror Has Two Faces 1996; Austin Powers: International Man of Mystery 1997; Lost in Space 1998; The Devil's Arithmetic 1999; Cruel Intentions 2 2000; Ginger Snaps 2000; Charms for the Easy Life 2001; Dumb and

Dumberer: When Harry Met Lloyd 2003; The Door in the Floor 2004; Stone Cold 2005; Big Nothing 2006; For a Good Time, Call... 2012; Hope Springs 2012; Captive 2015

Rogers, Paul (1917-2013) The Beachcomber 1954; Beau Brummell 1954; Circle of Deception 1960; Life for Ruth 1962; The Pot Carriers 1962; The Wild and the Willing 1962; The Third Secret 1964; He Who Rides a Tiger 1965; The Looking Glass War 1969; Three into Two Won't Go 1969; I Want What I Want 1971; The Homecoming 1973; Lost in the Stars 1974; Mister Quilp 1975; The Tenth Man 1988

Rogers, Reg (1962-) Runaway Bride 1999; Analyze That 2002; Stone Cold 2005

Rogers, Roy (1911-1998) Shine On, Harvest Moon 1938; The Arizona Kid 1939; Days of Jesse James 1939; Dark Command 1940; Brazil 1944; Hollywood Canteen 1944; The Yellow Rose of Texas 1944; Bells of Rosarita 1945; My Pal Trigger 1946; Bells of San Angelo 1947; Under California Stars 1948; The Far Frontier 1949; Bells of Coronado 1950; North of the Great Divide 1950; Trail of Robin Hood 1950; Son of Paleface 1952; Alias Jesse James 1959

Rogers, Wayne (1933-2015) Pocket Money 1972; The Hot Touch 1982; The Gig 1985; The Killing Time 1987

Rogers (1), Will (1879-1935) They Had to See Paris 1929; A Connecticut Yankee 1931; Dr Bull 1933; State Fair 1933; Judge Priest 1934; In Old Kentucky 1935; Life Begins at 40 1935; Steamboat round the Bend 1935

Rogers Jr, Will (1911-1993) Look for the Silver Lining 1949; The Boy from Oklahoma 1954; Wild Heritage 1958

Rohde, Armin (1955-) Run Lola Run 1998; Taking Sides 2001

Rohm, Maria (1949-) The Blood of Fu Manchu 1968; The Girl from Rio 1968; The Bloody Judge 1969; Count Dracula 1970; Black Beauty 1971; Treasure Island 1972

Rohner, Clayton (1961-) Private Investigations 1987; BAT-21 1988; The Relic 1996; Sometimes They Come Back... for More 1998

Rohrwacher, Alba My Brother Is an Only Child 2006; I Am Love 2009; The Wonders 2014

Rojo, Gustavo (1926-) It Started with a Kiss 1959; El Condor 1970

Rojo, Ruben (1922-1993) La Hija del Engaño 1951; Cauldron of Blood 1967

Roland, Gilbert (1905-1994) Camille 1927; Life Begins 1932; The Passionate Plumber 1932; After Tonight 1933; Our Betters 1933; She Done Him Wrong 1933; The Last Train from Madrid 1937; My Life with Caroline 1941; Captain Kidd 1945; The Other Love 1947; Malaya 1949; We Were Strangers 1949; Crisis 1950; The Furies 1950; The Bullfighter and the Lady 1951; Ten Tall Men 1951; Glory Alley 1952; The Miracle of Our Lady of Fatima 1952; Beneath the 12-Mile Reef 1953; The Diamond Queen 1953; Thunder Bay 1953; The French Line 1954; The Racers 1955; That Lady 1955; The Treasure of Pancho Villa 1955; Underwater! 1955; Bandido 1956; Three Violent People 1956; The Midnight Story 1957; The Last of the Fast Guns 1958; The Big Circus 1959; The Wild and the Innocent 1959; Guns of the Timberland 1960; Cheyenne Autumn 1964; The Reward 1965; The Poppy Is Also a Flower 1966; The Christian Licorice Store 1971; Running Wild 1973; The Mark of Zorro 1974; Islands in the Stream 1976; Barbarosa 1982

Roland, Jeanne The Curse of the Mummy's Tomb 1964; Salt & Pepper 1968

Rolf, Tutta (1907-1994) Swedenhielms 1935; Dollar 1938

Rolfe, Guy (1915-2003) Broken Journey 1948; Portrait from Life 1948; Fools Rush In 1949; The Spider and the Fly 1949; Prelude to Fame 1950; The Reluctant Widow 1950; Home to Danger 1951; King of the Khyber Rifles 1953; Young Bess 1953; Dance Little Lady 1954; It's Never Too Late 1956; Yesterday's Enemy 1959; Mr Sardonicus 1961; Taras Bulba 1962; The Alphabet Murders 1966; And Now the Screaming Starts! 1973; Dolls 1987

Rolffes, Kirsten (1928-2000) Buster's World 1984; The Kingdom 1994

Rolie, Esther (1920-1998) Summer of My German Soldier 1978; Driving Miss Daisy 1989; The Mighty Quinn 1989; House of Cards 1993; Down in the Delta 1997; Rosewood 1997

Rolleston, James The Dark Horse 2014; The Dead Lands 2014

Rollett, Raymond (1907-1961) Dick Turpin - Highwayman 1956; Blue Murder at St Trinian's 1957

Rollins, Henry (1961-) The Chase 1994; Johnny Mnemonic 1995; Lost Highway 1996; Jack Frost 1998; Time Lapse 2001; Wrong Turn 2: Dead End 2007

Rollins Jr, Howard E (1950-1996) A Doctor's Story 1984; A Soldier's Story 1984

Rolston, Mark (1956-) Lethal Weapon 2 1989; Black Widow Murders 1993; The Shawshank Redemption 1994; The Set Up 1995; Saw V 2008; Saw VI 2009

Romain, Yvonne (1938-) The Curse of the Werewolf 1961; Village of Daughters 1961; Night Creatures 1962; Devil Doll 1964; Smokescreen 1964; Double Trouble 1967

Roman, Candice The Big Bird Cage 1972; The Unholy Rollers 1972

Roman, Leticia aka **Roman, Letitia** (1941-) GI Blues 1960; Pontius Pilate 1961; Fanny Hill: Memoirs of a Woman of Pleasure 1964; The Spy in the Green Hat 1966

Roman, Ric (1916-2000) Appointment in Honduras 1953; Lizzie 1957

Roman, Ruth (1924-1999) Belle Starr's Daughter 1948; Always Leave Them Laughing 1949; Beyond the Forest 1949; Champion 1949; The Window 1949; Barricade 1950; Colt .45 1950; Dallas 1950; Three Secrets 1950; Lightning Strikes Twice 1951; Strangers on a Train 1951; Mara Maru 1952; Young Man with Ideas 1952; Blowing Wild 1953; Down Three Dark Streets 1954; The Far Country 1954; Tanganyika 1954; Joe Macbeth 1955; Beyond the River 1956; Great Day in the Morning 1956; Bitter Victory 1957; Love Has Many Faces 1965; The Baby 1973; The Killing Kind 1973; Impulse 1975

Roman, Susan (1957-) Rabid 1976; Heavy Metal 1981

Romance, Viviane (1912-1991) La Belle Equipe 1936; Mademoiselle Docteur 1936; Any Number Can Win 1963

Romand, Béatrice (1952-) Claire's Knee 1970; Soft Beds, Hard Battles 1973; Le Beau Mariage 1982; Four Adventures of Reinette and Mirabelle 1986; The Green Ray 1986; An Autumn Tale 1998

Romano, Andy (1941-) Over the Edge 1979; Pump Up the Volume 1990; The Gun in Betty Lou's Handbag 1992; Death of a Cheerleader 1994; Two Bits 1995; Under Siege 2 1995; Eraser 1996; Getting Away with Murder 1996

Romano, Larry Lock Up 1989; No Way Home 1996

Romano, Ray (1957-) Ice Age 2002; Welcome to Mooseport 2004; Ice Age: the Meltdown 2006; Ice Age 3: Dawn of the Dinosaurs 2009; Ice Age 4: Continental Drift 2012; Ice Age: Collision Course 2016

Romanus, Richard (1943-) Mean Streets 1973; Sitting Ducks 1979; Heavy Metal 1981; Strangers Kiss 1983; Protocol 1984; Murphy's Law 1986; The Couch Trip 1988; To Protect and Serve 1992; The Assassin 1993

Romay (1), Lina (1919-2010) The Big Wheel 1949; The Man behind the Gun 1953

Rome, Stewart (1886-1965) Dinner at the Ritz 1937; Wings of the Morning 1937

Rome, Sydne (1947-) Some Girls Do 1969; What? 1973; That Lucky Touch 1975; The Twist 1976; Just a Gigolo 1978

Romero, Cesar (1907-1994) British Agent 1934; Cardinal Richelieu 1935; The Devil Is a Woman 1935; The Good Fairy 1935; Rendezvous 1935; Love before Breakfast 1936; Wee Willie Winkie 1937; Always Goodbye 1938; Happy Landing 1938; My Lucky Star 1938; Charlie Chan at Treasure Island 1939; The Cisco Kid and the Lady 1939; Frontier Marshal 1939; The Little Princess 1939; The Return of the Cisco Kid 1939; Wife, Husband and Friend 1939; The Gay Caballero 1940; The Great American Broadcast 1941; Tall, Dark and Handsome 1941; Weekend in Havana 1941; A Gentleman at Heart 1942; Orchestra Wives 1942; Springtime in the Rockies 1942; Tales of Manhattan 1942; Coney Island 1943; Wintertime 1943; Captain from Castile 1947; Julia Misbehaves 1948; That Lady in Ermine 1948; The Beautiful Blonde from Bashful Bend 1949; Happy Go Lovely 1950; Prisoners of the Casbah 1953; Street of Shadows 1953; Vera Cruz 1954; The Americano 1955; Ocean's Eleven 1960; Pepe 1960; If a Man Answers 1962; The Castilian 1963; Donovan's Reef 1963; Two on a

Guillotine 1964; Marriage on the Rocks 1965; Sergeant Deadhead 1965; Batman 1966; Madigan's Millions 1967; Hot Millions 1968; The Computer Wore Tennis Shoes 1969; Crooks and Coronets 1969; Latitude Zero 1969; Midas Run 1969; The Strongest Man in the World 1975; Lust in the Dust 1984

Romero, George A aka **Romero, George** (1940-) Dawn of the Dead 1978; Martin 1978; Midnight Movies: from the Margins to the Mainstream 2005

Romero, Vicente The Hours of the Day 2003; The Night of the Sunflowers 2006

Romijn-Stamos, Rebecca aka **Romijn, Rebecca** (1972-) X-Men 2000; Rollerball 2001; Femme Fatale 2002; Godsend 2003; X2 2003; The Punisher 2004; X-Men - the Last Stand 2006

Ron, Tiny aka **Taylor, Tiny Ron** Seven Hours to Judgment 1988; Rocketeer 1991; Ace Ventura: Pet Detective 1993

Ronan, Saoirse (1994-) Atonement 2007; Death Defying Acts 2007; City of Ember 2008; The Lovely Bones 2009; Arrietty 2010; The Way Back 2010; Hanna 2011; Byzantium 2012; The Host 2013; How I Live Now 2013; Justin and the Knights of Valour 2013; Lost River 2014; Brooklyn 2015; Loving Vincent 2016

Ronane, John (1933-) Doctor Blood's Coffin 1960; That's Your Funeral 1972; A War of Children 1972

Ronay, Edina (1945-) The Black Torment 1964; The Big Job 1965; Praise Marx and Pass the Ammunition 1968; Three 1969

Ronet, Maurice (1927-1983) Lift to the Scaffold 1957; Carve Her Name with Pride 1958; Plein Soleil 1960; Le Feu Follet 1963; The Victors 1963; La Ronde 1964; Trois Chambres à Manhattan 1965; The Champagne Murders 1966; The Road to Corinth 1967; La Femme Infidèle 1968; How Sweet It Is! 1968; The Swimming Pool 1968; Don Juan 73, or If Don Juan Were a Woman 1973; The Marseille Contract 1974; Bloodline 1979; Sphinx 1980; La Balance 1982

Rongione, Fabrizio (1973-) Rosetta 1999; L'Enfant 2005; The Silence of Lorna 2008; The Kid with a Bike 2011; Two Days, One Night 2014

Ronstadt, Linda (1946-) FM 1977; The Pirates of Penzance 1983; Hail! Hail! Rock 'n' Roll! 1987

Rooke, Irene (1878-1958) Lady Windermere's Fan 1916; Hindle Wakes 1927

Rooker, Michael (1955-) Henry: Portrait of a Serial Killer 1986; Mississippi Burning 1988; Sea of Love 1989; Days of Thunder 1990; The Dark Half 1991; JFK 1991; Cliffhanger 1993; American Yakuza 2: Back to Back 1996; The Trigger Effect 1996; Bram Stoker's Shadowbuilder 1997; Liar 1997; Brown's Requiem 1998; The Replacement Killers 1998; The Bone Collector 1999; Here on Earth 2000; The 6th Day 2000; Replicat 2001; Undisputed 2002; Slither 2006; Super 2010; Guardians of the Galaxy 2014

Rooney, Mickey (1920-2014) The Beast of the City 1932; Broadway to Hollywood 1933; Manhattan Melodrama 1934; Upper World 1934; Ah, Wilderness! 1935; A Midsummer Night's Dream 1935; The Devil Is a Sissy 1936; Little Lord Fauntleroy 1936; Riffraff 1936; Captains Courageous 1937; A Family Affair 1937; Live, Love and Learn 1937; Slave Ship 1937; Thoroughbreds Don't Cry 1937; Boys Town 1938; Judge Hardy's Children 1938; Love Finds Andy Hardy 1938; Out West with the Hardys 1938; You're Only Young Once 1938; The Adventures of Huckleberry Finn 1939; Andy Hardy Gets Spring Fever 1939; Babes in Arms 1939; The Hardys Ride High 1939; Judge Hardy and Son 1939; Andy Hardy Meets Debutante 1940; Strike Up the Band 1940; Young Tom Edison 1940; Andy Hardy's Private Secretary 1941; Babes on Broadway 1941; Life Begins for Andy Hardy 1941; Men of Boys Town 1941; Andy Hardy's Double Life 1942; The Courtship of Andy Hardy 1942; A Yank at Eton 1942; Girl Crazy 1943; The Human Comedy 1943; Andy Hardy's Blonde Trouble 1944; National Velvet 1944; Love Laughs at Andy Hardy 1946; Killer McCoy 1947; Summer Holiday 1948; Words and Music 1948; The Big Wheel 1949; The Fireball 1950; Quicksand 1950; The Strip 1951; All Ashore 1953; Military Policeman 1953; The Atomic Kid 1954; The Bridges at Toko-Ri 1954; Drive a Crooked Road 1954; The Twinkle in God's Eye 1955; The Bold

and the Brave 1956; Francis in the Haunted House 1956; Baby Face Nelson 1957; Operation Mad Ball 1957; Andy Hardy Comes Home 1958; A Nice Little Bank That Should Be Robbed 1958; The Big Operator 1959; The Last Mile 1959; The Private Lives of Adam and Eve 1959; Platinum High School 1960; Breakfast at Tiffany's 1961; King of the Roaring 20s - the Story of Arnold Rothstein 1961; Requiem for a Heavyweight 1962; It's a Mad Mad Mad Mad World 1963; Journey back to Oz 1964; The Secret Invasion 1964; How to Fill a Wild Bikini 1966; Ambush Bay 1966; Skidoo 1968; The Comic 1969; Eighty Steps to Jonah 1969; The Extraordinary Seaman 1969; Evil Roy Slade 1971; Pulp 1972; Find the Lady 1976; The Domino Principle 1977; Pete's Dragon 1977; The Magic of Lassie 1978; Arabian Adventure 1979; The Black Stallion 1979; Bill 1981; The Fox and the Hound 1981; Leave 'Em Laughing 1981; The Care Bears Movie 1985; Erik the Viking 1989; My Heroes Have Always Been Cowboys 1991; The Road Home 1995; Babe: Pig in the City 1998; The First of May 1999; Night at the Museum 2006; Night at the Museum: Secret of the Tomb 2014

Rooney, Teddy (1950-) Andy Hardy Comes Home 1958; It Happened to Jane 1959

Roope, Fay (1893-1961) Callaway Went Thataway 1951; The Clown 1952; All Ashore 1953

Rooper, Jemima Kinky Boots 2005; One Chance 2013

Roos, Joanna (1901-1989) Patterns 1956; Two Weeks in Another Town 1962

Root, Amanda (1963-) Persuasion 1995; Whatever Happened to Harold Smith? 1999

Root, Stephen (1951-) Monkey Shines 1988; Bed & Breakfast 1992; A Woman Scorned 1992; Bicentennial Man 1999; Jersey Girl 2003; Dodgeball: a True Underdog Story 2004; Just Friends 2005; Leatherheads 2007; Mad Money 2008; Over Her Dead Body 2008; The Soloist 2008; Unthinkable 2010; Cedar Rapids 2011

Roper, Brian (1929-1994) Just William's Luck 1947; William at the Circus 1948; The Secret Garden 1949

Roquevert, Noël (1892-1973) Fanfan la Tulipe 1951; Les Diaboliques 1954; Une Parisienne 1957; Cartouche 1961; A Monkey in Winter 1962

Rorke, Hayden (1910-1987) The Law and the Lady 1951; Room for One More 1952; The Girl Next Door 1953; South Sea Woman 1953; Lucky Me 1954; A Stranger in My Arms 1959; The Night Walker 1964; The Barefoot Executive 1971

Rory, Rossana (1940-) The Angel Wore Red 1960; Come September 1961; The Eclipse 1962

Rosanova, Rosa (1869-1944) Blood and Sand 1922; The Younger Generation 1929

Rosato, Tony (1954-) Mystery Date 1991; Rent-a-Kid 1992; Kissinger and Nixon 1995

Rosay, Françoise (1891-1974) Carnival in Flanders 1935; Un Carnet de Bal 1937; Drôle de Drame 1937; The Halfway House 1943; Johnny Frenchman 1945; Saraband for Dead Lovers 1948; September Affair 1950; The 13th Letter 1951; La Reine Margot 1954; That Lady 1955; Interlude 1957; Me and the Colonel 1958; The Sound and the Fury 1959; The Full Treatment 1961; Up from the Beach 1965; The Pedestrian 1974

Roscoe, Alan (1888-1933) Long Pants 1927; Flight 1929

Roscoe, Mary Unrelated 2007; Exhibition 2013

Rose Marie (1925-) Top Banana 1953; Dead Heat on a Merry-Go-Round 1966

Rose, Anika Noni (1972-) Dreamgirls 2006; The Princess and the Frog 2009; For Colored Girls 2010; Half of a Yellow Sun 2013

Rose, Clifford (1929-) Marat/Sade 1966; The Girl 1986

Rose, Gabrielle Family Viewing 1987; Speaking Parts 1989; The Adjuster 1991; The Sweet Hereafter 1997

Rose, George (1920-1988) The Square Ring 1953; Barnacle Bill 1957; The Shiralee 1957; Cat and Mouse 1958; Jack the Ripper 1958; The Flesh and the Fiends 1959; A New Leaf 1971; The Hideaways 1973; The Pirates of Penzance 1983

Rose, Jamie (1960-) Heartbreakers 1984; Chopper Chicks in Zombietown 1990

Rose, Jane (1913-1979) Summertime 1955; The Monte Carlo Story 1957; Flipper 1963

Rose, Reva (1940-) *Bunny O'Hare* 1971; *The Nine Lives of Fritz the Cat* 1974
Rose, Veronica (1911-1968) *A Cuckoo in the Nest* 1933; *Fighting Stock* 1935
Rosenbaum, Michael (1972-) *Urban Legend* 1998; *Sorority Boys* 2002
Rosenberg, Alan (1950-) *The Wanderers* 1979; *Promise* 1986; *White of the Eye* 1986; *Impulse* 1990; *The Boys* 1991; *Freaky Friday* 1995
Rosenbloom, Maxie (1903-1976) *Nothing Sacred* 1937; *Louisiana Purchase* 1941; *The Boogie Man Will Get You* 1942; *To the Shores of Tripoli* 1942; *Abbott and Costello Meet the Keystone Cops* 1955; *Hollywood or Bust* 1956
Roshan, Hrithik (1974-) *Kabhi Khushi Kabhie Gham...* 2001; *Yaadein* 2001; *Armaan* 2003; *Koi... Mil Gaya* 2003; *Lakshya* 2004; *Dhoom: 2* 2006; *Jodhaa Akbar* 2008
Rosing, Bodil (1873-1942) *Sunrise* 1927; *The Big Noise* 1928; *Eternal Love* 1929
Rosmer, Milton (1881-1971) *Lady Windermere's Fan* 1916; *The Phantom Light* 1934; *South Riding* 1938; *Goodbye, Mr Chips* 1939; *Return to Yesterday* 1940
Ross, Annie (1930-) *Alfie Darling* 1975; *Superman III* 1983; *Witchcraft* 1989; *Basket Case 2* 1990; *Basket Case 3: the Progeny* 1992; *Short Cuts* 1993
Ross, Anthony (1909-1955) *Kiss of Death* 1947; *The Window* 1949; *The Gunfighter* 1950; *Perfect Strangers* 1950; *On Dangerous Ground* 1951; *The Country Girl* 1954
Ross, Charlotte (1968-) *Foreign Student* 1994; *Fall into Darkness* 1996
Ross, Chelcie (1942-) *The Package* 1989; *The Last Boy Scout* 1991; *Amos & Andrew* 1993; *Chain Reaction* 1996; *A Simple Plan* 1998; *Waking Up in Reno* 2000
Ross, Diana (1944-) *Lady Sings the Blues* 1972; *Mahogany* 1975; *The Wiz* 1978; *Out of Darkness* 1994; *Double Platinum* 1999
Ross, Hugh *Zero Effect* 1997; *Before You Go* 2002; *Extraordinary Rendition* 2007; *Bronson* 2008; *Sunset Song* 2015
Ross, Joe E (1914-1982) *Teaserama* 1955; *Maracaibo* 1958; *All Hands on Deck* 1961
Ross, Katharine (1942-) *Shenandoah* 1965; *The Singing Nun* 1966; *Games* 1967; *The Graduate* 1967; *Butch Cassidy and the Sundance Kid* 1969; *Tell Them Willie Boy Is Here* 1969; *Fools* 1970; *Get to Know Your Rabbit* 1972; *They Only Kill Their Masters* 1972; *The Stepford Wives* 1975; *Voyage of the Damned* 1976; *The Betsy* 1978; *The Legacy* 1978; *The Swarm* 1978; *The Final Countdown* 1980; *The Man with the Deadly Lens* 1982; *A Row of Crows* 1991; *Donnie Darko* 2001
Ross, Lee (1971-) *Buddy's Song* 1990; *Secrets & Lies* 1995; *Hard Men* 1996; *The Island on Bird Street* 1997; *Metroland* 1997; *Virgo: Passion for Life* 1997; *Dreaming of Joseph Lees* 1998; *Goal!* 2005; *Containment* 2015
Ross, Marion (1928-) *The Glenn Miller Story* 1953; *Lizzie* 1957; *Grand Theft Auto* 1977; *Danielle Steel's A Perfect Stranger* 1994; *The Evening Star* 1996; *Superhero Movie* 2008; *Flower Girl* 2009
Ross, Matt *Ed's Next Move* 1996; *Just Visiting* 2001
Ross, Shirley (1913-1975) *The Big Broadcast of 1937* 1936; *San Francisco* 1936; *The Big Broadcast of 1938* 1937; *Waikiki Wedding* 1937; *Paris Honeymoon* 1939; *Some Like It Hot* 1939
Ross, Ted (1934-2002) *The Wiz* 1978; *Arthur* 1981
Ross, Terry Ann *The Three Faces of Eve* 1957; *Cry Terror* 1958
Rossellini, Isabella (1952-) *A Matter of Time* 1976; *White Nights* 1985; *Blue Velvet* 1986; *Siesta* 1987; *Tough Guys Don't Dance* 1987; *Zelly and Me* 1988; *Cousins* 1989; *Wild at Heart* 1990; *Death Becomes Her* 1992; *Fearless* 1993; *The Innocent* 1993; *Immortal Beloved* 1994; *Wyatt Earp* 1994; *Big Night* 1996; *Crime of the Century* 1996; *The Funeral* 1996; *Left Luggage* 1997; *The Odyssey* 1997; *The Impostors* 1998; *Don Quixote* 2000; *Empire* 2002; *Roger Dodger* 2002; *Monte Walsh* 2003; *The Saddest Music in the World* 2003; *Infamous* 2006; *The Accidental Husband* 2008; *Two Lovers* 2008; *My Dog Tulip* 2009; *Keyhole* 2011; *Joy* 2015
Rossi-Drago, Eleonora (1925-2007) *Le Amiche* 1955; *Love at Twenty* 1962; *Let's Talk about Women* 1964

Rossi Stuart, Kim (1969-) *Beyond the Clouds* 1995; *The Keys to the House* 2004; *Romanzo Criminale* 2005; *Angels of Evil* 2010
Rossi, Francis *Status Quo: Hello Quo* 2012; *Bula Quo!* 2013
Rossi, George *Comfort and Joy* 1984; *I Bought a Vampire Motorcycle* 1989
Rossi, Leo (1959-) *Heart like a Wheel* 1983; *The Accused* 1988; *Hit List* 1988; *Relentless* 1989; *Too Much Sun* 1990; *Good Cop, Bad Cop* 1993
Rossi, Theo *CodeBreakers* 2005; *Cloverfield* 2008
Rossington, Norman (1928-1999) *Saturday Night and Sunday Morning* 1960; *Go to Blazes* 1961; *Nurse on Wheels* 1963; *The Comedy Man* 1964; *A Hard Day's Night* 1964; *Tobruk* 1966; *Double Trouble* 1967; *Two Gentlemen Sharing* 1969; *The Adventures of Gerard* 1970; *Simon, Simon* 1970; *Man in the Wilderness* 1971; *Death Line* 1972; *Go for a Take* 1972; *Digby, the Biggest Dog in the World* 1973
Rossiter, Leonard (1926-1984) *Billy Liar* 1963; *A Jolly Bad Fellow* 1964; *King Rat* 1965; *The Witches* 1966; *The Whisperers* 1967; *Deadfall* 1968; *Diamonds for Breakfast* 1968; *Oliver!* 1968; *Otley* 1968; *2001: a Space Odyssey* 1968; *Luther* 1974; *Barry Lyndon* 1975; *The Pink Panther Strikes Again* 1976; *Rising Damp* 1980; *Britannia Hospital* 1982; *Water* 1985
Rossitto, Angelo (1908-1991) *Scared to Death* 1947; *Mad Max beyond Thunderdome* 1985
Rosso, Pablo *[Rec]* 2007; *[Rec]²* 2009
Rossovich, Rick (1957-) *The Lords of Discipline* 1983; *The Terminator* 1984; *Top Gun* 1986; *Roxanne* 1987; *Spellbinder* 1988; *Navy SEALs* 1990
Rossum, Emmy (1986-) *Mystic River* 2003; *The Day after Tomorrow* 2004; *The Phantom of the Opera* 2004; *Poseidon* 2006; *Dragonball Evolution* 2009; *Beautiful Creatures* 2013; *Comet* 2014
Rostill, John (1942-1973) *Wonderful Life* 1964; *Finders Keepers* 1966
Roswell, Maggie *Midnight Madness* 1980; *Fire and Ice* 1983; *Lost in America* 1985
Roth, Andrea (1967-) *Crossworlds* 1996; *Highwaymen* 2003; *Crazy for Christmas* 2005; *War* 2007; *The Collector* 2009
Roth, Cecilia (1958-) *Pepi, Luci, Bom...* 1980; *Labyrinth of Passion* 1982; *All about My Mother* 1999; *Second Skin* 2000; *I'm So Excited* 2013
Roth, Eli (1972-) *Cabin Fever* 2002; *Inglourious Basterds* 2009; *Piranha* 2010; *Aftershock* 2012; *Clown* 2014
Roth, Gene (1903-1976) *Earth vs the Spider* 1958; *Attack of the Giant Leeches* 1960
Roth, Lillian (1910-1980) *The Love Parade* 1929; *Animal Crackers* 1930; *Madam Satan* 1930; *Paramount on Parade* 1930; *Ladies They Talk About* 1933
Roth, Tim (1961-) *The Hit* 1984; *Agatha Christie's Murder with Mirrors* 1985; *A World Apart* 1987; *To Kill a Priest* 1988; *The Cook, the Thief, His Wife and Her Lover* 1989; *Rosencrantz and Guildenstern Are Dead* 1990; *Vincent and Theo* 1990; *Jumpin' at the Boneyard* 1991; *Reservoir Dogs* 1991; *Bodies, Rest & Motion* 1993; *Captives* 1994; *Little Odessa* 1994; *Pulp Fiction* 1994; *Four Rooms* 1995; *Rob Roy* 1995; *Everyone Says I Love You* 1996; *Gridlock'd* 1996; *No Way Home* 1996; *Hoodlum* 1997; *Liar* 1997; *The Legend of 1900* 1999; *The Million Dollar Hotel* 1999; *Vatel* 2000; *Invincible* 2001; *The Musketeer* 2001; *Planet of the Apes* 2001; *To Kill a King* 2003; *Nouvelle-France* 2004; *Silver City* 2004; *Dark Water* 2005; *Don't Come Knocking* 2005; *Youth without Youth* 2007; *Funny Games US* 2008; *The Incredible Hulk* 2008; *Arbitrage* 2012; *Broken* 2012; *The Liability* 2012; *Grace of Monaco* 2014; *Selma* 2014; *Chronic* 2015; *Hardcore Henry* 2015; *The Hateful Eight* 2015
Rotha, Wanda (1910-1982) *Saadia* 1953; *The Magnificent Showman* 1964
Rothery, Teryl (1962-) *The Twelve Days of Christmas Eve* 2004; *Amber's Story* 2006; *White Noise: the Light* 2006; *Battle of the Bulbs* 2010
Rothman, John (1949-) *Stardust Memories* 1980; *The Second Coming* 1980; *The Bonfire of the Vanities* 1990; *Copycat* 1995; *Say It Isn't So* 2001
Rottiers, Vincent *Les Diables* 2002; *Renoir* 2012; *Dheepan* 2015
Roüan, Brigitte *Olivier Olivier* 1991; *Love Songs* 2007; *Les Combattants* 2014

Rouffe, Alida (1874-1949) *Marius* 1931; *Fanny* 1932
Roulien, Raul (1905-2000) *Delicious* 1931; *Flying down to Rio* 1933; *The World Moves On* 1934
Rounds, David (1930-1983) *Child's Play* 1972; *So Fine* 1981
Roundtree, Richard (1942-) *Shaft* 1971; *Shaft's Big Score!* 1972; *Shaft in Africa* 1973; *Earthquake* 1974; *Man Friday* 1975; *Escape to Athena* 1979; *A Game for Vultures* 1979; *An Eye for an Eye* 1981; *Q - the Winged Serpent* 1982; *Young Warriors* 1983; *City Heat* 1984; *Hell Camp* 1986; *Jocks* 1986; *Maniac Cop* 1988; *Bad Jim* 1989; *Crack House* 1989; *Never Cry Devil* 1989; *Christmas in Connecticut* 1992; *Amityville: a New Generation* 1993; *Se7en* 1995; *Theodore Rex* 1995; *Original Gangstas* 1996; *George of the Jungle* 1997; *Steel* 1997; *Antitrust* 2000; *Shaft* 2000; *Corky Romano* 2001; *Boat Trip* 2002; *Joe and Max* 2002; *Brick* 2005; *Ladies of the House* 2008
Rounseville, Robert (1914-1974) *The Tales of Hoffmann* 1951; *Carousel* 1956
Rourke, Mickey (1953-) *1941* 1979; *Act of Love* 1980; *Fade to Black* 1980; *Heaven's Gate* 1980; *Body Heat* 1981; *Diner* 1982; *Eureka* 1982; *Rumble Fish* 1983; *The Pope of Greenwich Village* 1984; *Nine ½ Weeks* 1985; *Year of the Dragon* 1985; *Angel Heart* 1987; *Barfly* 1987; *A Prayer for the Dying* 1987; *Francesco* 1989; *Johnny Handsome* 1989; *Desperate Hours* 1990; *Wild Orchid* 1990; *Harley Davidson and the Marlboro Man* 1991; *White Sands* 1992; *The Last Outlaw* 1993; *FTW* 1994; *Fall Time* 1994; *Bullet* 1995; *Another 9½ Weeks* 1997; *Double Team* 1997; *John Grisham's The Rainmaker* 1997; *Point Blank* 1997; *Buffalo '66* 1998; *Thursday* 1998; *Animal Factory* 2000; *Get Carter* 2000; *The Pledge* 2000; *They Crawl* 2001; *Spun* 2002; *Once upon a Time in Mexico* 2003; *Man on Fire* 2004; *Domino* 2005; *Sin City* 2005; *Stormbreaker* 2006; *The Wrestler* 2008; *The Informers* 2009; *The Expendables* 2010; *Iron Man 2* 2010; *13* 2010; *Immortals* 2011; *I Am Bruce Lee* 2012; *Sin City: a Dame to Kill For* 2014
Rousseau, Stéphane *The Barbarian Invasions* 2003; *Asterix at the Olympic Games* 2008
Roussel, Myriem (1962-) *First Name: Carmen* 1983; *Je Vous Salue, Marie* 1984
Roussel, Nathalie *Le Château de Ma Mère* 1990; *La Gloire de Mon Père* 1990
Roussillon, Jean-Paul (1931-) *The Girl from Paris* 2001; *Kings & Queen* 2004; *A Christmas Tale* 2008
Routh, Brandon *Superman Returns* 2006; *Kambakkht Ishq* 2009; *Scott Pilgrim vs the World* 2010; *Unthinkable* 2010
Routledge, Patricia (1929-) *Pretty Polly* 1967; *To Sir, with Love* 1967; *The Bliss of Mrs Blossom* 1968; *Don't Raise the Bridge, Lower the River* 1968; *30 Is a Dangerous Age, Cynthia* 1968
Rouve, Jean-Paul *La Vie en Rose* 2007; *The Extraordinary Adventures of Adèle Blanc-Sec* 2010
Rouvel, Catherine (1939-) *Lunch on the Grass* 1959; *Borsalino* 1970; *Borsalino and Co* 1974; *The Marseille Contract* 1974; *Black and White in Color* 1976
Rouverol, Jean *It's a Gift* 1934; *The Law West of Tombstone* 1938
Rovena, Marcella (1908-1998) *Friends for Life* 1955; *White Nights* 1957
Rovère, Liliane *The Captive* 2000; *Harry, He's Here to Help* 2000; *The Grocer's Son* 2007
Rowan, Diana *Beyond Reasonable Doubt* 1980; *Battletruck* 1982
Rowan, Kelly (1967-) *The Gate* 1987; *Assassins* 1995; *Candyman: Farewell to the Flesh* 1995; *One Eight Seven* 1997; *Greenmail* 2001
Rowe, Brad (1970-) *Billy's Hollywood Screen Kiss* 1998; *Body Shots* 1999; *Purgatory* 1999; *Though None Go with Me* 2006
Rowe, Nicholas (1966-) *Young Sherlock Holmes* 1985; *Lock, Stock and Two Smoking Barrels* 1998; *Delicious* 2013
Rowell, Victoria (1960-) *Leonard, Part 6* 1987; *Full Eclipse* 1993; *Dumb and Dumber* 1994; *Barb Wire* 1995
Rowland, Henry (1913-1984) *Return to Treasure Island* 1954; *Supervixens* 1975
Rowlands, Gena (1930-) *The High Cost of Loving* 1958; *A Child Is Waiting* 1962; *Lonely Are the Brave* 1962; *The Spiral Road* 1962; *Tony Rome* 1967; *Faces* 1968; *Minnie and Moskowitz* 1971; *A Woman under the Influence* 1974; *Two-Minute Warning* 1976; *Opening Night* 1977; *The Brink's Job* 1978;

Gloria 1980; *Tempest* 1982; *An Early Frost* 1985; *The Betty Ford Story* 1987; *Another Woman* 1988; *Once Around* 1991; *Crazy in Love* 1992; *Night on Earth* 1992; *The Neon Bible* 1995; *Something to Talk About* 1995; *Unhook the Stars* 1996; *She's So Lovely* 1997; *Hope Floats* 1998; *The Mighty* 1998; *Paulie* 1998; *Playing by Heart* 1998; *Charms for the Easy Life* 2001; *Hysterical Blindness* 2002; *The Notebook* 2003; *Taking Lives* 2004; *The Skeleton Key* 2005; *Persepolis* 2007
Rowlands, Lady (1904-1999) *Minnie and Moskowitz* 1971; *A Woman under the Influence* 1974
Rowlands, Patsy (1934-2005) *Carry On Again Doctor* 1969; *Carry On Loving* 1970; *Carry On at Your Convenience* 1971; *Carry On Abroad* 1972; *Carry On Matron* 1972; *Carry On Girls* 1973
Rowley, Peter *Savage Islands* 1983; *Footrot Flats: the Dog's Tale* 1986
Roxburgh, Richard (1962-) *Children of the Revolution* 1996; *Doing Time for Patsy Cline* 1997; *Oscar and Lucinda* 1997; *Thank God He Met Lizzie* 1997; *The Last September* 1999; *Mission: Impossible 2* 1999; *Passion* 1999; *Moulin Rouge!* 2001; *The One and Only* 2001; *Van Helsing* 2004; *Fragile* 2005; *Stealth* 2005; *Like Minds* 2006; *Sanctum* 2010; *The Turning* 2013
Roy, Maxim (1972-) *Hidden Agenda* 2001; *Million Dollar Murder* 2004
Royce, Lionel (1886-1946) *Four Sons* 1940; *Son of Monte Cristo* 1940; *My Favorite Blonde* 1942
Roye, Phillip *The Sergeant* 1968; *Black Caesar* 1973
Royle, Selena (1904-1983) *The Fighting Sullivans* 1944; *Mrs Parkington* 1944; *Courage of Lassie* 1946; *The Green Years* 1946; *You Were Meant for Me* 1948; *The Heiress* 1949; *My Dream Is Yours* 1949; *The Big Hangover* 1950; *Branded* 1950; *The Damned Don't Cry* 1950; *Come Fill the Cup* 1951; *He Ran All the Way* 1951; *Robot Monster* 1953
Ruane, William (1985-) *Sweet Sixteen* 2002; *Tickets* 2005; *The Wind That Shakes the Barley* 2006; *The Angels' Share* 2012; *Honour* 2012; *Kelly + Victor* 2013
Rubes, Jan (1920-2009) *The Amateur* 1981; *One Magic Christmas* 1985; *Witness* 1985; *Dead of Winter* 1987; *The Kiss* 1988; *Courage Mountain* 1989; *The Amityville Curse* 1990; *Class Action* 1991; *On My Own* 1992; *D2: the Mighty Ducks* 1994; *Roommates* 1995; *Never Too Late* 1996
Rubin-Vega, Daphne (1969-) *Wild Things* 1998; *Flawless* 1999; *Jack Goes Boating* 2010
Rubin, Andrew aka Rubin, Andrew A (1946-) *Casey's Shadow* 1978; *Police Academy* 1984
Rubin, Jennifer (1964-) *Permanent Record* 1988; *Bitter Harvest* 1993; *The Crush* 1993; *Screamers* 1995; *Loved* 1996; *Sanctimony* 2000
Rubinek, Saul (1948-) *Agency* 1981; *Ticket to Heaven* 1981; *Against All Odds* 1984; *Sweet Liberty* 1986; *Wall Street* 1987; *The Bonfire of the Vanities* 1990; *Man Trouble* 1992; *Unforgiven* 1992; *True Romance* 1993; *Death Wish V: the Face of Death* 1994; *Getting Even with Dad* 1994; *I Love Trouble* 1994; *Memory Run* 1995; *Open Season* 1995; *Rainbow* 1995; *Bad Manners* 1997; *36 Hours to Die* 1999; *The Bookfair Murders* 2000; *The Contender* 2000; *The Family Man* 2000; *Laughter on the 23rd Floor* 2000; *Triggermen* 2002; *Baadasssss!* 2003; *War* 2007; *Julia* 2008
Rubini, Giulia (1935-) *Goliath and the Barbarians* 1959; *Gordon the Black Pirate* 1961; *The Magnificent Rebel* 1961
Rubini, Sergio (1959-) *Intervista* 1987; *A Pure Formality* 1994; *Nirvana* 1996; *Shooting the Moon* 1998; *The Passion of the Christ* 2004
Rubinoff, David (1897-1986) *Thanks a Million* 1935; *You Can't Have Everything* 1937
Rubinstein, Artur (1887-1982) *Follow the Boys* 1944; *Night Song* 1947
Rubinstein, John (1946-) *The Car* 1977; *The Boys from Brazil* 1978; *Skokie* 1981; *Someone to Watch over Me* 1987; *Norma Jean & Marilyn* 1996
Rubinstein, Zelda (1936-2010) *Poltergeist* 1982; *Anguish* 1986; *Poltergeist II: the Other Side* 1986; *Poltergeist III* 1988
Ruck, Alan (1960-) *Ferris Bueller's Day Off* 1986; *Three for the Road* 1987; *Three Fugitives* 1989; *Young Guns II* 1990; *Speed* 1994; *Twister* 1996; *Ghost Town* 2008
Rudd, Paul (1969-) *Clueless* 1995; *Halloween 6: the Curse of Michael*

Myers 1995; *William Shakespeare's Romeo + Juliet* 1996; *Overnight Delivery* 1997; *A Secret Sin* 1997; *The Object of My Affection* 1998; *The Cider House Rules* 1999; *200 Cigarettes* 1999; *The Great Gatsby* 2000; *The Shape of Things* 2003; *Anchorman: the Legend of Ron Burgundy* 2004; *The 40 Year Old Virgin* 2005; *Knocked Up* 2007; *Walk Hard: the Dewey Cox Story* 2007; *Forgetting Sarah Marshall* 2008; *I Love You, Man* 2008; *Over Her Dead Body* 2008; *Role Models* 2008; *Monsters vs Aliens* 2009; *Dinner for Schmucks* 2010; *How Do You Know* 2010; *Our Idiot Brother* 2011; *Wanderlust* 2011; *The Perks of Being a Wallflower* 2012; *Prince Avalanche* 2012; *This Is 40* 2012; *Admission* 2013; *Anchorman 2: the Legend Continues* 2013; *They Came Together* 2014; *Ant-Man* 2015; *The Fundamentals of Caring* 2015; *Sausage Party* 2016
Rudley, Herbert (1911-2006) *The Seventh Cross* 1944; *Rhapsody in Blue* 1945; *A Walk in the Sun* 1945; *The Black Sleep* 1956; *Raw Edge* 1956; *Beloved Infidel* 1959; *The Jayhawkers* 1959
Rudolph, Lars (1966-) *The Princess & the Warrior* 2000; *Werckmeister Harmonies* 2000
Rudolph, Maya (1972-) *Chuck & Buck* 2000; *Idiocracy* 2006; *A Prairie Home Companion* 2006; *Away We Go* 2009; *Grown Ups* 2010; *MacGruber* 2010; *Shrek Forever After* 2010; *Bridesmaids* 2011; *Friends with Kids* 2011; *Grown Ups 2* 2013; *Turbo* 2013; *The Way Way Back* 2013; *Inherent Vice* 2014; *The Nut Job* 2014; *Sisters* 2015; *The Angry Birds Movie* 2016; *Maggie's Plan* 2016
Rudoy, Joshua (1975-) *Bigfoot and the Hendersons* 1987; *Flatliners* 1990
Rueda, Belén *The Sea Inside* 2004; *The Orphanage* 2006; *Julia's Eyes* 2010
Ruehl, Mercedes (1948-) *The Warriors* 1979; *84 Charing Cross Road* 1986; *The Secret of My Success* 1987; *Big* 1988; *Married to the Mob* 1988; *Slaves of New York* 1989; *Crazy People* 1990; *Another You* 1991; *The Fisher King* 1991; *Last Action Hero* 1993; *Lost in Yonkers* 1993; *Indictment: the McMartin Trial* 1995; *Roseanna's Grave* 1996; *Subway Stories: Tales from the Underground* 1997; *Gia* 1998; *The Minus Man* 1999; *Spooky House* 1999; *What's Cooking?* 2000; *Guilt by Association* 2002; *Mom at Sixteen* 2005; *A Girl like Me* 2006
Ruffalo, Mark (1967-) *Safe Men* 1998; *You Can Count on Me* 1999; *Committed* 2000; *The Last Castle* 2001; *Windtalkers* 2001; *XX/XY* 2001; *My Life without Me* 2002; *Eternal Sunshine of the Spotless Mind* 2003; *In the Cut* 2003; *View from the Top* 2003; *We Don't Live Here Anymore* 2003; *Collateral* 2004; *13 Going on 30* 2004; *All the King's Men* 2005; *Just like Heaven* 2005; *Rumor Has It...* 2005; *Zodiac* 2007; *Blindness* 2008; *The Brothers Bloom* 2008; *Margaret* 2008; *Shutter Island* 2009; *Where the Wild Things Are* 2009; *The Kids Are All Right* 2010; *Marvel Avengers Assemble* 2012; *Thanks for Sharing* 2012; *Begin Again* 2013; *Now You See Me* 2013; *Foxcatcher* 2014; *Infinitely Polar Bear* 2014; *The Normal Heart* 2014; *Avengers: Age of Ultron* 2015; *Spotlight* 2015; *Now You See Me 2* 2016; *Thor: Ragnarok* 2017
Rufus (1942-) *Jonah Who Will Be 25 in the Year 2000* 1976; *Delicatessen* 1990; *Metroland* 1997; *Amélie* 2001
Ruggles, Charles aka Ruggles, Charlie (1886-1970) *Charley's Aunt* 1930; *Her Wedding Night* 1930; *Honor among Lovers* 1931; *The Smiling Lieutenant* 1931; *If I Had a Million* 1932; *Love Me Tonight* 1932; *Madame Butterfly* 1932; *One Hour with You* 1932; *This Is the Night* 1932; *Trouble in Paradise* 1932; *Alice in Wonderland* 1933; *Melody Cruise* 1933; *Murders in the Zoo* 1933; *Six of a Kind* 1934; *Ruggles of Red Gap* 1935; *Anything Goes* 1936; *Bringing Up Baby* 1938; *Invitation to Happiness* 1939; *The Invisible Woman* 1940; *Maryland* 1940; *No Time for Comedy* 1940; *The Doughgirls* 1944; *Incendiary Blonde* 1945; *My Brother Talks to Horses* 1946; *A Stolen Life* 1946; *It Happened on Fifth Avenue* 1947; *Ramrod* 1947; *Give My Regards to Broadway* 1948; *Look for the Silver Lining* 1949; *The Lovable Cheat* 1949; *All in a Night's Work* 1960; *The Parent Trap* 1961; *The Pleasure of His Company* 1961; *Son of Flubber* 1962; *Papa's Delicate Condition* 1963; *I'd Rather Be Rich* 1964; *Follow Me, Boys!* 1966; *The Ugly Dachshund* 1966

Ruginis, Vyto *Clean Slate* 1994; *Last Gasp* 1995

Ruhian, Yayan *The Raid* 2011; *Yakuza Apocalypse* 2015

Ruick, Barbara (1930-1974) *The Affairs of Dobie Gillis* 1953; *Carousel* 1956; *Cinderella* 1965

Rule, Janice (1931-2003) *Goodbye, My Fancy* 1951; *Battle Shock* 1956; *Gun for a Coward* 1957; *The Subterraneans* 1960; *Invitation to a Gunfighter* 1964; *Alvarez Kelly* 1966; *The Chase* 1966; *Welcome to Hard Times* 1967; *The Swimmer* 1968; *Doctors' Wives* 1970; *Gumshoe* 1971; *Kid Blue* 1971; *3 Women* 1977; *American Flyers* 1985

Ruman, Sig *aka* **Rumann, Sig** *aka* **Rumann, Siegfried** *aka* **Rumann, Siegfried "Sig"** (1884-1967) *Marie Galante* 1934; *The World Moves On* 1934; *The Farmer Takes a Wife* 1935; *A Night at the Opera* 1935; *The Wedding Night* 1935; *Heidi* 1937; *Lancer Spy* 1937; *Nothing Sacred* 1937; *Thank You, Mr Moto* 1937; *Think Fast, Mr Moto* 1937; *The Saint in New York* 1938; *Suez* 1938; *Never Say Die* 1939; *Ninotchka* 1939; *Only Angels Have Wings* 1939; *Comrade X* 1940; *Dr Ehrlich's Magic Bullet* 1940; *Victory* 1940; *The Wagons Roll at Night* 1941; *Berlin Correspondent* 1942; *China Girl* 1942; *Desperate Journey* 1942; *To Be or Not to Be* 1942; *Sweet Rosie O'Grady* 1943; *Tarzan Triumphs* 1943; *Summer Storm* 1944; *A Royal Scandal* 1945; *A Night in Casablanca* 1946; *The Emperor Waltz* 1948; *Give My Regards to Broadway* 1948; *On the Riviera* 1951; *O Henry's Full House* 1952; *The World in His Arms* 1952; *Houdini* 1953; *Stalag 17* 1953; *Three Ring Circus* 1954; *White Christmas* 1954; *The Errand Boy* 1961

Runacre, Jenny (1943-) *Husbands* 1970; *The Final Programme* 1973; *The Passenger* 1975; *Jubilee* 1978

Runyon, Jennifer (1960-) *Dreams of Gold: the Mel Fisher Story* 1986; *18 Again!* 1988; *The In Crowd* 1988

RuPaul *aka* **Charles, RuPaul** (1960-) *But I'm a Cheerleader* 1999; *The Eyes of Tammy Faye* 2000

Rupp, Sieghardt *A Fistful of Dollars* 1964; *Dead Pigeon on Beethoven Street* 1972

Rush, Barbara (1927-) *The First Legion* 1951; *When Worlds Collide* 1951; *Flaming Feather* 1952; *It Came from Outer Space* 1953; *The Black Shield of Falworth* 1954; *Magnificent Obsession* 1954; *Taza, Son of Cochise* 1954; *Captain Lightfoot* 1955; *Kiss of Fire* 1955; *Bigger than Life* 1956; *No Down Payment* 1957; *Oh, Men! Oh, Women!* 1957; *Harry Black and the Tiger* 1958; *The Young Lions* 1958; *The Young Philadelphians* 1959; *The Bramble Bush* 1960; *Strangers When We Meet* 1960; *Come Blow Your Horn* 1963; *Robin and the 7 Hoods* 1964; *Hombre* 1967; *The Man* 1972; *Can't Stop the Music* 1980; *Summer Lovers* 1982

Rush, Deborah (1954-) *A Night in Heaven* 1983; *Big Business* 1988; *Parents* 1988; *Family Business* 1989; *My Blue Heaven* 1990; *Three to Tango* 1999

Rush, Geoffrey (1951-) *Dad and Dave: on Our Selection* 1995; *Children of the Revolution* 1996; *Shine* 1996; *Les Misérables* 1997; *Elizabeth* 1998; *Shakespeare in Love* 1998; *House on Haunted Hill* 1999; *The Magic Pudding* 2000; *Quills* 2000; *The Tailor of Panama* 2001; *Lantana* 2001; *The Banger Sisters* 2002; *Frida* 2002; *Finding Nemo* 2003; *Intolerable Cruelty* 2003; *The Life and Death of Peter Sellers* 2003; *Ned Kelly* 2003; *Pirates of the Caribbean: the Curse of the Black Pearl* 2003; *Swimming Upstream* 2003; *Candy* 2005; *Munich* 2005; *Elizabeth: the Golden Age* 2007; *Pirates of the Caribbean: at World's End* 2007; *The King's Speech* 2010; *Legend of the Guardians: the Owls of Ga'Hoole* 2010; *The Warrior's Way* 2010; *The Eye of the Storm* 2011; *Pirates of the Caribbean: on Stranger Tides* 2011; *Deception* 2013; *The Book Thief* 2014; *Holding the Man* 2015; *The Daughter* 2016; *Gods of Egypt* 2016; *Pirates of the Caribbean: Dead Men Tell No Tales* 2017

Rush, Joshua *Parental Guidance* 2012; *Emelie* 2015

Rush, Odeya *The Odd Life of Timothy Green* 2012; *We Are What We Are* 2013; *Goosebumps* 2015

Rushbrook, Claire (1970-) *Secrets & Lies* 1995; *Under the Skin* 1997; *Shiner* 2000

Rushton, Jared (1974-) *Overboard* 1987; *Big* 1988; *Lady in White* 1988; *Honey, I Shrunk the Kids* 1989; *Pet Sematary II* 1992

Rushton, William (1937-1996) *The Best House in London* 1968; *The Bliss of Mrs Blossom* 1968; *Flight of the Doves* 1971; *Keep It Up Downstairs* 1976; *Adventures of a Private Eye* 1977; *Consuming Passions* 1988

Rusler, Robert (1965-) *A Nightmare on Elm Street 2: Freddy's Revenge* 1985; *Weird Science* 1985; *Thrashin'* 1986; *Vamp* 1986; *Shag* 1988; *Sometimes They Come Back* 1991

Ruspoli, Esmeralda (1928-1988) *L'Avventura* 1960; *A Place for Lovers* 1968

Russ, William (1950-) *Beer* 1985; *Second Serve* 1986; *Wanted Dead or Alive* 1986; *Dead of Winter* 1987; *The Unholy* 1988; *Crazy from the Heart* 1991; *Traces of Red* 1992; *Aspen Extreme* 1993; *Breach of Trust* 1999

Russek, Jorge (1932-1998) *The Return of a Man Called Horse* 1976; *Miracles* 1985; *Pure Luck* 1991

Russell, Alex *Chronicle* 2012; *Unbroken* 2014

Russell, Andy (1919-1992) *Make Mine Music* 1946; *Copacabana* 1947

Russell, Betsy (1964-) *Avenging Angel* 1985; *Saw IV* 2007; *Saw V* 2008; *Saw VI* 2009; *Saw: the Final Chapter* 2010

Russell, Bing (1928-2003) *Cattle Empire* 1958; *Suicide Battalion* 1958; *Elvis - the Movie* 1979

Russell, Bryan *A Ticklish Affair* 1963; *Emil and the Detectives* 1964; *The Adventures of Bullwhip Griffin* 1967

Russell, Catherine (1966-) *Soft Top, Hard Shoulder* 1992; *Clockwork Mice* 1994

Russell, Charles (1918-1985) *The Late George Apley* 1947; *Give My Regards to Broadway* 1948

Russell, Clive (1945-) *The Hawk* 1992; *Margaret's Museum* 1995; *Oscar and Lucinda* 1997; *The Emperor's New Clothes* 2001; *Mr In-Between* 2001; *Ladies in Lavender* 2004; *Festival* 2005; *The Wicker Tree* 2010

Russell, Connie (1923-1990) *This Is My Love* 1954; *Nightmare* 1956

Russell, Douglas *Let Us Prey* 2014; *The Survivalist* 2015

Russell, Elizabeth (1916-2002) *Cat People* 1942; *The Curse of the Cat People* 1944

Russell, Gail (1924-1961) *The Uninvited* 1944; *Salty O'Rourke* 1945; *The Unseen* 1945; *Angel and the Badman* 1947; *Calcutta* 1947; *Moonrise* 1948; *Night Has a Thousand Eyes* 1948; *Wake of the Red Witch* 1949; *The Lawless* 1950; *Air Cadet* 1951; *Seven Men from Now* 1956; *The Tattered Dress* 1957

Russell, Jane (1921-2011) *The Outlaw* 1943; *The Paleface* 1948; *Double Dynamite* 1951; *His Kind of Woman* 1951; *The Las Vegas Story* 1952; *Macao* 1952; *Son of Paleface* 1952; *Gentlemen Prefer Blondes* 1953; *The French Line* 1954; *Gentlemen Marry Brunettes* 1955; *The Tall Men* 1955; *Underwater!* 1955; *Hot Blood* 1956; *The Revolt of Mamie Stover* 1956; *The Fuzzy Pink Nightgown* 1957; *Fate Is the Hunter* 1964; *Johnny Reno* 1966; *Waco* 1966; *Born Losers* 1967; *Darker than Amber* 1970

Russell, John (1921-1991) *Yellow Sky* 1948; *The Gal Who Took the West* 1949; *Slattery's Hurricane* 1949; *Undertow* 1949; *Frenchie* 1950; *Saddle Tramp* 1950; *Man in the Saddle* 1951; *Hoodlum Empire* 1952; *Fair Wind to Java* 1953; *The Sun Shines Bright* 1953; *Fort Massacre* 1958; *Rio Bravo* 1959; *Yellowstone Kelly* 1959; *Apache Uprising* 1965; *Buckskin* 1968

Russell, Ken (1927-2011) *Valentino* 1977; *Salome's Last Dance* 1988; *The Russia House* 1990

Russell, Keri (1976-) *Honey, I Blew Up the Kid* 1992; *Eight Days a Week* 1996; *Dead Man's Curve* 1997; *Mad about Mambo* 1999; *We Were Soldiers* 2002; *The Upside of Anger* 2005; *Mission: Impossible III* 2006; *August Rush* 2007; *The Girl in the Park* 2007; *Waitress* 2007; *Bedtime Stories* 2008; *Extraordinary Measures* 2010; *Austenland* 2013; *Dark Skies* 2013; *Dawn of the Planet of the Apes* 2014

Russell, Kimberly *Ghost Dad* 1990; *Hangin' with the Homeboys* 1991

Russell, Kurt (1951-) *It Happened at the World's Fair* 1962; *Follow Me, Boys!* 1966; *The Horse in the Gray Flannel Suit* 1968; *The One and Only, Genuine, Original Family Band* 1968; *The Computer Wore Tennis Shoes* 1969; *Guns in the Heather* 1969; *The Barefoot Executive* 1971; *Dynamite Man from Glory Jail* 1971; *Charley and the Angel* 1973; *The Strongest Man in the World* 1975; *Elvis - the Movie* 1979; *Used Cars* 1980; *Escape from New York* 1981; *The Fox and the Hound* 1981;

The Thing 1982; *Silkwood* 1983; *Swing Shift* 1984; *The Mean Season* 1985; *The Best of Times* 1986; *Big Trouble in Little China* 1986; *Overboard* 1987; *Tequila Sunrise* 1988; *Tango & Cash* 1989; *Backdraft* 1991; *Captain Ron* 1992; *Unlawful Entry* 1992; *Tombstone* 1993; *Stargate* 1994; *Escape from LA* 1996; *Executive Decision* 1996; *Breakdown* 1997; *Soldier* 1998; *3000 Miles to Graceland* 2000; *Vanilla Sky* 2001; *Dark Blue* 2002; *Miracle* 2004; *Dreamer* 2005; *Sky High* 2005; *Poseidon* 2006; *Death Proof* 2007; *The Art of the Steal* 2013; *Bone Tomahawk* 2015; *The Hateful Eight* 2015

Russell, Lucy *Following* 1998; *The Lady & the Duke* 2001; *Angel* 2006

Russell, Nipsey (1924-2005) *The Wiz* 1978; *Wildcats* 1986

Russell, Rebel (1905-1978) *Emma's War* 1985; *Frauds* 1992

Russell, Robert (1936-2008) *Bedazzled* 1967; *Witchfinder General* 1968

Russell, Rosalind (1908-1976) *Evelyn Prentice* 1934; *Forsaking All Others* 1934; *The Casino Murder Case* 1935; *China Seas* 1935; *Reckless* 1935; *Rendezvous* 1935; *Craig's Wife* 1936; *Trouble for Two* 1936; *Under Two Flags* 1936; *Live, Love and Learn* 1937; *Man-Proof* 1937; *Night Must Fall* 1937; *The Citadel* 1938; *Four's a Crowd* 1938; *Fast and Loose* 1939; *His Girl Friday* 1939; *The Women* 1939; *Hired Wife* 1940; *No Time for Comedy* 1940; *This Thing Called Love* 1940; *Design for Scandal* 1941; *The Feminine Touch* 1941; *They Met in Bombay* 1941; *My Sister Eileen* 1942; *Take a Letter, Darling* 1942; *Flight for Freedom* 1943; *What a Woman!* 1943; *Roughly Speaking* 1945; *Sister Kenny* 1946; *The Guilt of Janet Ames* 1947; *Mourning Becomes Electra* 1947; *The Velvet Touch* 1948; *Tell It to the Judge* 1949; *A Woman of Distinction* 1950; *Never Wave at a WAC* 1952; *The Girl Rush* 1955; *Picnic* 1955; *Auntie Mame* 1958; *A Majority of One* 1961; *Five Finger Exercise* 1962; *Gypsy* 1962; *The Trouble with Angels* 1966; *Oh Dad, Poor Dad, Mama's Hung You in the Closet and I'm Feelin' So Sad* 1967; *Rosie!* 1967; *Where Angels Go... Trouble Follows* 1968; *Mrs Pollifax - Spy* 1970

Russell, T E *Trespass* 1992; *Swimming with Sharks* 1994

Russell, Theresa (1957-) *The Last Tycoon* 1976; *Straight Time* 1978; *Bad Timing* 1980; *Eureka* 1982; *The Razor's Edge* 1984; *Insignificance* 1985; *Aria* 1987; *Black Widow* 1987; *Physical Evidence* 1988; *Track 29* 1988; *Impulse* 1990; *Kafka* 1991; *Whore* 1991; *Cold Heaven* 1992; *Being Human* 1994; *The Grotesque* 1995; *The Proposition* 1996; *Wild Things* 1998; *The Believer* 2001; *Earth vs the Spider* 2001; *Spider-Man 3* 2007; *Liz & Dick* 2012

Russell, William (1924-) *One Good Turn* 1954; *Above Us the Waves* 1955; *The Big Chance* 1957

Russo, James (1953-) *Exposed* 1983; *Beverly Hills Cop* 1984; *Extremities* 1986; *China Girl* 1987; *The Blue Iguana* 1988; *We're No Angels* 1989; *A Kiss before Dying* 1991; *My Own Private Idaho* 1991; *Cold Heaven* 1992; *Dangerous Game* 1993; *Trauma* 1993; *Bad Girls* 1994; *The Set Up* 1995; *American Strays* 1996; *No Way Home* 1996; *Donnie Brasco* 1997; *The Postman* 1997; *Too Hard to Die* 1998; *The Ninth Gate* 1999; *Open Range* 2003; *Miss Bala* 2011

Russo, Rene (1954-) *Major League* 1989; *Mr Destiny* 1990; *One Good Cop* 1991; *Freejack* 1992; *Lethal Weapon 3* 1992; *In the Line of Fire* 1993; *Get Shorty* 1995; *Outbreak* 1995; *Ransom* 1996; *Tin Cup* 1996; *Buddy* 1997; *Lethal Weapon 4* 1998; *The Adventures of Rocky & Bullwinkle* 1999; *The Thomas Crown Affair* 1999; *Big Trouble* 2002; *Showtime* 2002; *Two for the Money* 2005; *Yours, Mine & Ours* 2005; *Thor* 2011; *Nightcrawler* 2013; *The Intern* 2015

Rust, Richard (1938-1994) *The Legend of Tom Dooley* 1959; *Comanche Station* 1960; *Homicidal* 1961; *Underworld USA* 1961; *Walk on the Wild Side* 1962

Ruth, Babe *aka* **Ruth, George Herman "Babe"** (1895-1948) *Speedy* 1928; *The Pride of the Yankees* 1942

Rutherford, Amy *Confessions of an American Bride* 2005; *Four Minutes* 2005

Rutherford, Ann (1917-2012) *Dramatic School* 1938; *Judge Hardy's Children* 1938; *Love Finds Andy Hardy* 1938; *Of Human Hearts* 1938; *Out West with the Hardys* 1938; *You're Only Young Once*

1938; *Andy Hardy Gets Spring Fever* 1939; *Dancing Co-Ed* 1939; *The Hardys Ride High* 1939; *Judge Hardy and Son* 1939; *Andy Hardy Meets Debutante* 1940; *The Ghost Comes Home* 1940; *Pride and Prejudice* 1940; *Andy Hardy's Private Secretary* 1941; *Life Begins for Andy Hardy* 1941; *Whistling in the Dark* 1941; *Andy Hardy's Double Life* 1942; *The Courtship of Andy Hardy* 1942; *Orchestra Wives* 1942; *Happy Land* 1943; *The Bermuda Mystery* 1944; *Two o'Clock Courage* 1945; *The Secret Life of Walter Mitty* 1947; *Adventures of Don Juan* 1948; *They Only Kill Their Masters* 1972

Rutherford, Camilla *Stardom* 2000; *The Darjeeling Limited* 2007; *The Edge of Love* 2008

Rutherford, John (1893-1982) *Half Shot at Sunrise* 1930; *Whoopee!* 1930

Rutherford, Kelly (1968-) *I Love Trouble* 1994; *Danielle Steel's No Greater Love* 1996

Rutherford, Margaret (1892-1972) *Dusty Ermine* 1936; *The Demi-Paradise* 1943; *Yellow Canary* 1943; *English without Tears* 1944; *Blithe Spirit* 1945; *Meet Me at Dawn* 1946; *While the Sun Shines* 1946; *Miranda* 1947; *Passport to Pimlico* 1949; *The Happiest Days of Your Life* 1950; *The Magic Box* 1951; *Curtain Up* 1952; *The Importance of Being Earnest* 1952; *Miss Robin Hood* 1952; *Innocents in Paris* 1953; *Trouble in Store* 1953; *Mad about Men* 1954; *The Runaway Bus* 1954; *An Alligator Named Daisy* 1955; *Just My Luck* 1957; *The Smallest Show on Earth* 1957; *I'm All Right Jack* 1959; *Murder She Said* 1961; *On the Double* 1961; *The Mouse on the Moon* 1963; *Murder at the Gallop* 1963; *The VIPs* 1963; *Murder Ahoy* 1964; *Murder Most Foul* 1964; *The Alphabet Murders* 1966; *Chimes at Midnight* 1966; *Arabella* 1967; *A Countess from Hong Kong* 1967

Ruttan, Susan (1950-) *Do You Remember Love* 1985; *Jack Reed: Badge of Honor* 1993; *Without Warning: Terror in the Towers* 1993

Ruysdael, Basil (1888-1960) *Colorado Territory* 1949; *Come to the Stable* 1949; *Pinky* 1949; *Broken Arrow* 1950; *High Lonesome* 1950; *Boots Malone* 1951; *Half Angel* 1951; *Carrie* 1952; *Davy Crockett, King of the Wild Frontier* 1955; *Jubal* 1956; *These Wilder Years* 1956

Ryall, David (1935-2014) *Wilt* 1989; *Truly Madly Deeply* 1990; *Blackball* 2003

Ryan, Amanda *Elizabeth* 1998; *Britannic* 2000; *Sparkle* 2006

Ryan, Amy (1968-) *Keane* 2004; *Capote* 2005; *Before the Devil Knows You're Dead* 2007; *Gone Baby Gone* 2007; *Changeling* 2008; *Green Zone* 2010; *Jack Goes Boating* 2010; *Win Win* 2011; *Breathe In* 2013; *Birdman or (The Unexpected Virtue of Ignorance)* 2014; *Bridge of Spies* 2015; *Goosebumps* 2015; *Monster Trucks* 2016; *Central Intelligence* 2016; *The Infiltrator* 2016

Ryan, Edmon *aka* **Ryan, Edmond** (1905-1984) *Dark Eyes of London* 1939; *The Breaking Point* 1950; *Side Street* 1950; *Undercover Girl* 1950; *Go, Man, Go!* 1953; *Two for the Seesaw* 1962

Ryan, Eileen *At Close Range* 1985; *Anywhere but Here* 1999

Ryan, Ger *The Van* 1996; *interMission* 2003; *Frozen* 2007; *Happy Ever Afters* 2009

Ryan, Irene (1902-1973) *Diary of a Chambermaid* 1946; *The Woman on the Beach* 1947; *Half Angel* 1951; *Blackbeard the Pirate* 1952

Ryan, Jeri (1968-) *Down with Love* 2003; *Secrets in the Walls* 2010

Ryan, John P *aka* **Ryan, John** (1938-2007) *Cops and Robbers* 1973; *Dillinger* 1973; *Shamus* 1973; *It's Alive* 1974; *Futureworld* 1976; *It Lives Again* 1978; *The Postman Always Rings Twice* 1981; *The Escape Artist* 1982; *Breathless* 1983; *Runaway Train* 1985; *Avenging Force* 1986; *Death Wish 4: the Crackdown* 1987; *Three o'Clock High* 1987; *Class of 1999* 1990; *Delta Force 2* 1990; *Bound* 1996

Ryan, Kathleen (1922-1985) *Captain Boycott* 1947; *Odd Man Out* 1947; *Esther Waters* 1948; *Christopher Columbus* 1949; *Prelude to Fame* 1950; *The Sound of Fury* 1950; *The Yellow Balloon* 1952; *Laxdale Hall* 1953; *Captain Lightfoot* 1955; *Jacqueline* 1956

Ryan, Madge (1919-1994) *Tiara Tahiti* 1962; *This Is My Street* 1963

Ryan, Max (1967-) *The Foreigner* 2003; *Death Race* 2008; *Rage* 2014

Ryan, Meg (1961-) *Rich and Famous* 1981; *Amityville III: the Demon* 1983; *Armed and Dangerous* 1986; *Top Gun*

1986; *Innerspace* 1987; *DOA* 1988; *The Presidio* 1988; *Promised Land* 1988; *When Harry Met Sally...* 1989; *Joe versus the Volcano* 1990; *The Doors* 1991; *Prelude to a Kiss* 1992; *Flesh and Bone* 1993; *Sleepless in Seattle* 1993; *IQ* 1994; *When a Man Loves a Woman* 1994; *French Kiss* 1995; *Restoration* 1995; *Courage under Fire* 1996; *Addicted to Love* 1997; *Anastasia* 1997; *City of Angels* 1998; *Hurlyburly* 1998; *You've Got Mail* 1998; *Hanging Up* 2000; *Proof of Life* 2000; *Kate & Leopold* 2002; *Against the Ropes* 2003; *In the Cut* 2003; *My Spy* 2008; *The Women* 2008; *Ithaca* 2015

Ryan, Michelle (1984-) *Cashback* 2005; *I Want Candy* 2006; *Huge* 2009; *4.3.2.1* 2010; *Loves Kitchen* 2010; *Cockneys vs Zombies* 2011; *The Man Inside* 2012

Ryan, Mitchell *aka* **Ryan, Mitch** (1928-) *Monte Walsh* 1970; *Glory Boy* 1971; *The Hunting Party* 1971; *Electra Glide in Blue* 1973; *The Friends of Eddie Coyle* 1973; *High Plains Drifter* 1973; *Magnum Force* 1973; *A Reflection of Fear* 1973; *The Entertainer* 1975; *Lethal Weapon* 1987; *Blue Sky* 1991; *The Opposite Sex and How to Live with Them* 1993; *Halloween 6: the Curse of Michael Myers* 1995; *The Devil's Own* 1997; *Grosse Pointe Blank* 1997; *Liar Liar* 1997

Ryan, Natasha (1970-) *The Amityville Horror* 1979; *The Day Time Ended* 1980

Ryan, Peggy (1924-2004) *Miss Annie Rooney* 1942; *The Merry Monahans* 1944; *Patrick the Great* 1944; *Here Come the Co-Eds* 1945; *All Ashore* 1953

Ryan, R L *Class of Nuke 'Em High* 1986; *Eat and Run* 1986

Ryan, Robert (1909-1973) *Bombardier* 1943; *The Sky's the Limit* 1943; *Tender Comrade* 1943; *Marine Raiders* 1944; *Crossfire* 1947; *Trail Street* 1947; *The Woman on the Beach* 1947; *Berlin Express* 1948; *The Boy with Green Hair* 1948; *Return of the Bad Men* 1948; *Act of Violence* 1949; *Caught* 1949; *The Set-Up* 1949; *The Woman on Pier 13* 1949; *Born to Be Bad* 1950; *Best of the Badmen* 1951; *Flying Leathernecks* 1951; *On Dangerous Ground* 1951; *The Racket* 1951; *Beware, My Lovely* 1952; *Clash by Night* 1952; *Horizons West* 1952; *City beneath the Sea* 1953; *Inferno* 1953; *The Naked Spur* 1953; *About Mrs Leslie* 1954; *Her Twelve Men* 1954; *Bad Day at Black Rock* 1955; *Escape to Burma* 1955; *House of Bamboo* 1955; *The Tall Men* 1955; *Back from Eternity* 1956; *The Proud Ones* 1956; *Men in War* 1957; *God's Little Acre* 1958; *Lonelyhearts* 1958; *Day of the Outlaw* 1959; *Odds against Tomorrow* 1959; *Ice Palace* 1960; *King of Kings* 1961; *Billy Budd* 1962; *The Longest Day* 1962; *The Crooked Road* 1964; *Battle of the Bulge* 1965; *The Dirty Game* 1965; *The Professionals* 1966; *The Busy Body* 1967; *Custer of the West* 1967; *The Dirty Dozen* 1967; *Hour of the Gun* 1967; *Anzio* 1968; *Captain Nemo and the Underwater City* 1969; *The Wild Bunch* 1969; *Lawman* 1971; *The Love Machine* 1971; *And Hope to Die* 1972; *Executive Action* 1973; *The Lolly-Madonna War* 1973; *The Man without a Country* 1973; *The Outfit* 1973

Ryan, Sheila (1921-1975) *The Gay Caballero* 1940; *Great Guns* 1941; *A-Haunting We Will Go* 1942; *Careful, Soft Shoulder* 1942; *Something for the Boys* 1944; *Railroaded!* 1947; *Mule Train* 1950; *On Top of Old Smoky* 1953

Ryan, Thomas Jay (1962-) *Henry Fool* 1997; *The Book of Life* 1998

Ryan, Tim (1899-1956) *Bedtime Story* 1942; *Reveille with Beverly* 1943; *Detour* 1945; *Force of Evil* 1948

Rydall, Derek *Never Cry Devil* 1989; *Popcorn* 1991

Rydeberg, Georg (1907-1983) *Dollar* 1938; *A Woman's Face* 1938

Rydell, Christopher *aka* **Rydell, Chris** (1963-) *On Golden Pond* 1981; *Gotcha!* 1985; *Blood and Sand* 1989; *How I Got Into College* 1989; *For the Boys* 1991; *By the Sword* 1992; *Flesh and Bone* 1993; *Trauma* 1993

Rydell, Mark (1928-) *Crime in the Streets* 1956; *The Long Goodbye* 1973; *Punchline* 1988; *Havana* 1990; *Hollywood Ending* 2002

Ryder, Alfred (1919-1995) *T-Men* 1947; *Invitation to a Gunfighter* 1964

Ryder, Eddie (1923-1997) *The Country Girl* 1954; *Not with My Wife, You Don't!* 1966

Ryder, Winona (1971-) *Lucas* 1986; *Square Dance* 1987; *Beetle Juice* 1988; *1969* 1988; *Great Balls of Fire!* 1989; *Heathers* 1989; *Edward Scissorhands* 1990; *Mermaids* 1990; *Welcome Home, Roxy Carmichael* 1990; *Bram Stoker's*

Dracula 1992; Night on Earth 1992; The Age of Innocence 1993; The House of the Spirits 1993; Little Women 1994; Reality Bites 1994; Boys 1995; How to Make an American Quilt 1995; The Crucible 1996; Looking for Richard 1996; Alien: Resurrection 1997; Celebrity 1998; Girl, Interrupted 1999; Autumn in New York 2000; Lost Souls 2000; Mr Deeds 2002; SIMØNE 2002; A Scanner Darkly 2006; The Informers 2009; The Private Lives of Pippa Lee 2009; Star Trek 2009; Black Swan 2010; The Dilemma 2011; Frankenweenie 2012; The Iceman 2012; Homefront 2013; Experimenter: the Stanley Milgram Story 2014

Rye, Preben Lerdorff (1917-1995) Day of Wrath 1943; Ordet 1955

Rylance, Mark (1960-) Prospero's Books 1991; Angels and Insects 1995; Institute Benjamenta, or This Dream People Call Human Life 1995; Intimacy 2000; The Other Boleyn Girl 2008; We Are Many 2014; Bridge of Spies 2015; The Gunman 2015; The BFG 2016; Dunkirk 2017

Ryu, Chishu (1904-1993) There Was a Father 1942; Record of a Tenement Gentleman 1947; Hen in the Wind 1948; Late Spring 1949; Early Summer 1951; The Flavour of Green Tea over Rice 1952; Tokyo Story 1953; Early Spring 1956; Tokyo Twilight 1957; Floating Weeds 1959; Ohayo 1959; Late Autumn 1960; An Autumn Afternoon 1962; Akira Kurosawa's Dreams 1990

RZA Derailed 2005; American Gangster 2007; The Man with the Iron Fists 2012; Brick Mansions 2014

S

S, Bruno (1932-2010) The Enigma of Kaspar Hauser 1974; Stroszek 1977

Saad, Margit (1929-) The Criminal 1960; The Rebel 1960; The Magnificent Two 1967; The Last Escape 1970

Sabara, Daryl (1992-) SPYkids 2001; SPYkids 2: the Island of Lost Dreams 2002; SPYkids 3-D: Game Over 2003; Murder without Conviction 2004; The Polar Express 2004; Keeping Up with the Steins 2006; World's Greatest Dad 2009; SPYkids 4: All the Time in the World 2011; The Green Inferno 2014

Sabato, Antonio (1943-) Grand Prix 1966; The Good Die First 1967

Sabato Jr, Antonio (1972-) The Big Hit 1998; Fatal Error 1999

Sabri, Hend The Silences of the Palace 1994; La Saison des Hommes 2000

Sabrina (1) (1933-) Blue Murder at St Trinian's 1957; Satan in High Heels 1962

Sabu (1924-1963) Elephant Boy 1937; The Drum 1938; The Thief of Bagdad 1940; Arabian Nights 1942; Jungle Book 1942; White Savage 1943; Cobra Woman 1944; Black Narcissus 1947; The End of the River 1947; A Tiger Walks 1964

Saburi, Shin (1909-1982) There Was a Father 1942; The Flavour of Green Tea over Rice 1952; Equinox Flower 1958

Sachs, Andrew (1930-) Are You Being Served? 1977; Faust 1994; Breaking the Bank 2014

Sachs, Leonard (1909-1990) Men of Sherwood Forest 1954; Man from Tangier 1957; The Siege of Sidney Street 1960; Pit of Darkness 1961; Taste of Fear 1961

Sack, Graham (1931-) A Pig's Tale 1994; Dunston Checks In 1996

Sackhoff, Katee (1980-) Halloween: Resurrection 2002; White Noise: the Light 2006; Oculus 2013; Riddick 2013

Sacks, Michael (1948-) Slaughterhouse-Five 1972; The Sugarland Express 1974; The Private Files of J Edgar Hoover 1977; The Amityville Horror 1979; Hanover Street 1979

Sada, Keiji (1926-1964) Ohayo 1959; Late Autumn 1960; An Autumn Afternoon 1962

Sadler, William aka **Sadler, Bill** (1950-) Project X 1987; Hard to Kill 1989; Die Hard 2: Die Harder 1990; The Hot Spot 1990; Bill & Ted's Bogus Journey 1991; Rush 1991; Trespass 1992; Freaked 1993; Jack Reed: Badge of Honor 1993; Roadracers 1994; The Shawshank Redemption 1994; Tales from the Crypt: Demon Knight 1995; Solo 1996; Rocketman 1997; Disturbing Behavior 1998; Stealth Fighter 1999; Witness Protection 1999; August Rush 2007; The Mist 2007

Sadowski, Jonathan She's the Man 2006; Die Hard 4.0 2007; Chernobyl Diaries 2012

Sadoyan, Isabelle The Return of Martin Guerre 1982; The Eighth Day

1996; Summer Hours 2008; Thérèse Desqueyroux 2012

Safrankova, Libuse (1953-) Elementary School 1991; Kolya 1996

Sagal, Katey (1954-) No Higher Love 1999; Three Wise Guys 2005

Sage, Bill aka **Sage, William** (1962-) Simple Men 1992; Boys 1995; High Art 1998; Boiler Room 2000; The Maldonado Miracle 2003; Mysterious Skin 2004; Electrick Children 2012; We Are What We Are 2013

Sage, Halston Paper Towns 2015; Scouts Guide to the Zombie Apocalypse 2015

Sage, Willard (1922-1974) The Brass Legend 1956; Dirty Little Billy 1972

Sägebrecht, Marianne (1945-) Sugarbaby 1985; Bagdad Café 1987; Rosalie Goes Shopping 1989; The War of the Roses 1989; Martha and I 1990; Dust Devil 1992; Erotique 1994; All Men Are Mortal 1995; Left Luggage 1997; Asterix and Obelix Take On Caesar 1999; The Circle 2014

Sagemiller, Melissa (1974-) Get over It 2001; Soul Survivors 2001; Sorority Boys 2002; The Clearing 2004; The Guardian 2006; Mr Woodcock 2007

Sagnier, Ludivine (1979-) Water Drops on Burning Rocks 1999; 8 Women 2001; Ma Femme Est une Actrice 2001; Petites Coupures 2002; Swimming Pool 2002; Peter Pan 2003; Molière 2006; La Fille Coupée en Deux 2007; Love Songs 2007; A Secret 2007; Love Crime 2010; Beloved 2011; The Devil's Double 2011; Love Is in the Air 2013

Sahara, Kenji (1932-) The H-Man 1954; Rodan 1956; Godzilla's Revenge 1969

Sahl, Mort (1927-) All the Young Men 1960; Don't Make Waves 1967; Nothing Lasts Forever 1984

Saint, Eva Marie (1924-) On the Waterfront 1954; That Certain Feeling 1956; A Hatful of Rain 1957; Raintree County 1957; North by Northwest 1959; Exodus 1960; All Fall Down 1962; 36 Hours 1964; The Sandpiper 1965; Grand Prix 1966; The Russians Are Coming, the Russians Are Coming 1966; The Stalking Moon 1968; Loving 1970; Cancel My Reservation 1972; Nothing in Common 1986; Danielle Steel's Palomino 1991; Time to Say Goodbye? 1997; I Dreamed of Africa 2000; Because of Winn-Dixie 2004; Don't Come Knocking 2005; Superman Returns 2006; A New York Winter's Tale 2014

St Angel, Michael (1916-1984) Bride by Mistake 1944; The Brighton Strangler 1945

St Clement, Pam (1942-) Hedda 1975; Scrubbers 1982

St Cyr, Lili (1918-1999) Son of Sinbad 1955; The Mobster 1958; The Naked and the Dead 1958

Saint-Cyr, Renée (1904-2004) Strange Boarders 1938; Double Dare 1981

St Helier, Ivy (1886-1971) Bitter Sweet 1933; London Belongs to Me 1948

St Hilaire, Soledad Real Women Have Curves 2002; The Maldonado Miracle 2003

St Jacques, Raymond (1930-1990) The Green Berets 1968; Uptight 1968; Cotton Comes to Harlem 1970; Book of Numbers 1972; The Final Comedown 1972; Lost in the Stars 1974; Born Again 1978; The Evil That Men Do 1984; The Wild Pair 1987; They Live 1988

Saint James, Susan (1946-) Jigsaw 1968; Where Angels Go... Trouble Follows 1968; Outlaw Blues 1977; Love at First Bite 1979; SOS Titanic 1979; How to Beat the High Cost of Living 1980; Carbon Copy 1981

St John, Al (1893-1963) The Butcher Boy 1917; Knight of the Plains 1939; The Lone Rider in Ghost Town 1941; Sheriff of Sage Valley 1942

St John, Betta (1929-) All the Brothers Were Valiant 1953; Dream Wife 1953; The Robe 1953; Dangerous Mission 1954; The Student Prince 1954; The Naked Dawn 1955; Tarzan and the Lost Safari 1956; High Tide at Noon 1957; The City of the Dead 1960; Tarzan the Magnificent 1960; Corridors of Blood 1962

St John, Howard (1905-1974) Shockproof 1949; The Undercover Man 1949; Born Yesterday 1950; Mister 880 1950; The Big Night 1951; Close to My Heart 1951; Goodbye, My Fancy 1951; Stop, You're Killing Me 1952; Three Coins in the Fountain 1954; Illegal 1955; The Tender Trap 1955; Li'l Abner 1959; Cry for Happy 1961; One, Two, Three 1961; Sanctuary 1961; Madison Avenue 1962; Strait-Jacket 1963; Strange

Bedfellows 1965; Don't Drink the Water 1969

St John, Jill (1940-) Holiday for Lovers 1959; The Remarkable Mr Pennypacker 1959; The Lost World 1960; The Roman Spring of Mrs Stone 1961; Tender Is the Night 1961; Come Blow Your Horn 1963; Who's Been Sleeping in My Bed? 1963; Who's Minding the Store? 1963; Honeymoon Hotel 1964; The Liquidator 1966; The Oscar 1966; Banning 1967; Eight on the Lam 1967; How I Spent My Summer Vacation 1967; The King's Pirate 1967; Tony Rome 1967; Diamonds Are Forever 1971; Sitting Target 1972; Something to Believe In 1997

St John, Marco (1939-) The Mind Snatchers 1972; The Next Man 1976; Tightrope 1984; Friday the 13th: a New Beginning 1985; Monster 2003

St Polis, John (1873-1946) Coquette 1929; Party Girl 1930

Saint-Simon, Lucile Les Bonnes Femmes 1960; The Hands of Orlac 1960

Saito, James Hot Dog - The Movie 1984; Henry Fool 1997

Sakai, Sachio Godzilla 1954; Godzilla's Revenge 1969

Sakall, S Z aka **Sakall, S Z "Cuddles"** (1884-1955) It's a Date 1940; Ball of Fire 1941; The Devil and Miss Jones 1941; That Night in Rio 1941; Broadway 1942; Casablanca 1942; Yankee Doodle Dandy 1942; Thank Your Lucky Stars 1943; Wintertime 1943; Shine On, Harvest Moon 1944; Christmas in Connecticut 1945; The Dolly Sisters 1945; San Antonio 1945; Wonder Man 1945; Cinderella Jones 1946; Never Say Goodbye 1946; Cynthia 1947; In the Good Old Summertime 1949; My Dream Is Yours 1949; Oh, You Beautiful Doll 1949; The Daughter of Rosie O'Grady 1950; Montana 1950; Tea for Two 1950; Lullaby of Broadway 1951; Sugarfoot 1951; The Student Prince 1954

Sakamoto, Ryuichi (1952-) Merry Christmas Mr Lawrence 1982; The Last Emperor 1987

Sakamoto, Takeshi (1899-1974) I Was Born, but... 1932; There Was a Father 1942; Record of a Tenement Gentleman 1947; Hen in the Wind 1948

Sakasitz, Amy Dennis 1993; A Home of Our Own 1993; Mad Love 1995; House Arrest 1996

Sakata, Harold aka **Sakata "Tosh Togo", Harold** (1920-1982) Goldfinger 1964; The Poppy Is Also a Flower 1966; Impulse 1975

Saks, Gene (1921-2015) A Thousand Clowns 1965; The Prisoner of Second Avenue 1974; The One and Only 1978; Lovesick 1983; IQ 1994; Nobody's Fool 1994

Saldana, Theresa (1954-2016) I Wanna Hold Your Hand 1978; Defiance 1979; Raging Bull 1980; The Evil That Men Do 1984; The Night Before 1988

Saldana, Zoë aka **Saldana, Zoe** (1978-) Center Stage 2000; Crossroads 2002; Drumline 2002; Pirates of the Caribbean: the Curse of the Black Pearl 2003; The Terminal 2004; Guess Who 2005; Avatar 2009; Star Trek 2009; Death at a Funeral 2010; The Losers 2010; Takers 2010; Colombiana 2011; The Words 2012; Blood Ties 2013; Out of the Furnace 2013; Star Trek into Darkness 2013; Book of Life 2014; Guardians of the Galaxy 2014; Infinitely Polar Bear 2014; Live by Night 2016; Star Trek Beyond 2016; Guardians of the Galaxy Vol 2 2017; Avatar 2 2018

Sale, Charles "Chic" (1885-1936) Treasure Island 1934; You Only Live Once 1937

Salée, Catherine Blue Is the Warmest Colour 2013; Two Days, One Night 2014

Salem, Kario (1955-) Triumph of the Spirit 1989; Killing Zoe 1993

Salem, Pamela Never Say Never Again 1983; After Darkness 1985; Gods and Monsters 1998

Salen, Jesper (1978-) The Slingshot 1993; Evil 2003

Salenger, Meredith (1970-) The Journey of Natty Gann 1985; The Kiss 1988; A Night in the Life of Jimmy Reardon 1988; Dream a Little Dream 1989; Dead Beat 1994; Village of the Damned 1995; No Code of Conduct 1998; Out of the Woods 2005

Salerno, Enrico Maria (1926-1994) The Battle of El Alamein 1968; The Bird with the Crystal Plumage 1969

Salew, John (1897-1961) Time Flies 1944; Caravan 1946; Green Grow the Rushes 1951; The Lavender Hill Mob 1951; Three Cases of Murder 1953; Face the Music 1954; It's Great to Be Young 1956; Alive and Kicking 1958; Three on a Spree 1961; The Impersonator 1962

Salim, Dar A Hijacking 2012; A War 2015

Salinger, Diane (1951-) Pee-wee's Big Adventure 1985; The Morning After 1986; The Magic Bubble 1992; Before the Night 1995; Guy 1996

Salinger, Emmanuel Les Cent et Une Nuits 1995; Ma Vie Sexuelle 1996

Salinger, Justin Peaches 2000; Daylight Robbery 2007; We Are Monster 2014

Salinger, Matt (1960-) Captain America 1990; Babyfever 1994

Sallette, Céline House of Tolerance 2011; Rust and Bone 2012; The Connection 2014

Sallis, Peter (1921-) The Doctor's Dilemma 1958; I Thank a Fool 1962; Clash by Night 1963; The Third Secret 1964; Inadmissible Evidence 1968; Scream and Scream Again 1969; Taste the Blood of Dracula 1969; The Road Builder 1971; Witness for the Prosecution 1982; Wallace & Gromit in The Curse of the Were-Rabbit 2005

Salmi, Albert (1928-1990) The Bravados 1958; The Brothers Karamazov 1958; The Unforgiven 1960; Wild River 1960; The Outrage 1964; The Flim-Flam Man 1967; Hour of the Gun 1967; Three Guns for Texas 1968; The Deserter 1971; Escape from the Planet of the Apes 1971; Lawman 1971; something big 1971; Empire of the Ants 1977; Cloud Dancer 1979; Dragonslayer 1981; Love Child 1982; Breaking In 1989

Salminen, Esko (1940-) Flame Top 1980; Hamlet Goes Business 1987

Salmon, Colin (1962-) Captives 1994; All Men Are Mortal 1995; Frantz Fanon: Black Skin White Mask 1996; Tomorrow Never Dies 1997; The Wisdom of Crocodiles 1998; Fanny & Elvis 1999; Resident Evil 2002; Freeze Frame 2003; AVP: Alien vs Predator 2004; Clubbed 2008; Punisher: War Zone 2008; Exam 2009; Shank 2010

Salo, Elina (1936-) Hamlet Goes Business 1987; The Match Factory Girl 1990; Take Care of Your Scarf, Tatjana 1994; Drifting Clouds 1996

Salonga, Lea (1971-) Aladdin 1992; Mulan 1998

Salt, Jennifer (1944-) The Wedding Party 1966; Midnight Cowboy 1969; Hi, Mom! 1970; The Revolutionary 1970; Play It Again, Sam 1972; Sisters 1973; Out of the Darkness 1985

Salter, Ivor (1925-1991) Be My Guest 1965; Tiffany Jones 1973

Salvatori, Renato (1933-1988) Big Deal on Madonna Street 1958; Rocco and His Brothers 1960; Two Women 1960; The Organizer 1963; Burn! 1970; The Burglars 1971; State of Siege 1972; Police Story 1975; La Luna 1979

Salviat, Catherine Romuald et Juliette 1989; The Last Mitterrand 2005

Samberg, Andy (1978-) Hot Rod 2007; I Love You, Man 2008; Space Chimps 2008; Cloudy with a Chance of Meatballs 2009; What's Your Number? 2011; Celeste & Jesse Forever 2012; Hotel Transylvania 2012; That's My Boy 2012; Hotel Transylvania 2 2015; Storks 2016

Sambrell, Aldo aka **Brel Sanchez, Alfredo** (1931-) Navajo Joe 1966; Operation Condor: the Armour of God II 1990

Samel, Udo (1953-) Knife in the Head 1978; The Seventh Continent 1989; 71 Fragments of a Chronology of Chance 1994; The Piano Teacher 2001

Sammel, Richard The Horseman on the Roof 1995; 3 Days to Kill 2014

Samms, Emma (1960-) Arabian Adventure 1979; Agatha Christie's Murder in Three Acts 1986; Delirious 1991; Treacherous Beauties 1994; The Little Unicorn 1998; Mary Higgins Clark's Pretend You Don't See Her 2002; Vendetta 2013

Sampson, Angus Insidious 2010; 100 Bloody Acres 2012; Insidious: Chapter 2 2013; Insidious: Chapter 3 2015

Sampson, George StreetDance 2010; StreetDance 2 2012

Sampson, Robert Hero's Island 1962; Re-Animator 1985; Robot Jox 1989

Sampson, Will (1933-1987) One Flew over the Cuckoo's Nest 1975; Orca... Killer Whale 1977; The White Buffalo 1977; Insignificance 1985; Firewalker 1986; Poltergeist II: the Other Side 1986

Samuel, Joanne (1957-) Mad Max 1979; Nightmaster 1987

Samuel, Xavier The Loved Ones 2009; A Few Best Men 2011; Adore 2013; Frankenstein 2015; Love & Friendship 2016

San Giacomo, Laura (1962-) sex, lies, and videotape 1989; Pretty Woman 1990; Quigley Down Under 1990; Vital Signs 1990; Once Around 1991; Under

Suspicion 1991; For Their Own Good 1993; Nina Takes a Lover 1993; Stuart Saves His Family 1995; Havoc 2005

San Juan, Alberto (1968-) The Other Side of the Bed 2002; Sleep Tight 2011

San Juan, Olga (1927-2009) Blue Skies 1946; Variety Girl 1947; Are You with It? 1948; The Countess of Monte Cristo 1948; One Touch of Venus 1948; The Beautiful Blonde from Bashful Bend 1949

San Martin, Conrado (1921-) The Colossus of Rhodes 1961; The Awful Dr Orlof 1962

Sanada, Hiroyuki (1960-) Ring 1997; Ring 2 1998; The Twilight Samurai 2002; The Last Samurai 2003; The White Countess 2005; 47 Ronin 2012; The Railway Man 2013; The Wolverine 2013

Sanchez-Gijon, Aitana (1968-) Mouth to Mouth 1995; A Walk in the Clouds 1995; Love Walked In 1997; I'm Not Scared 2003; The Machinist 2003

Sanchez, Jaime The Pawnbroker 1965; The Wild Bunch 1969; Bobby Deerfield 1977; Piñero 2001

Sanchez, Kiele A Perfect Getaway 2009; The Purge: Anarchy 2014

Sanchez, Roselyn (1970-) Rush Hour 2 2001; Boat Trip 2002; Underclassman 2004; The Game Plan 2007; Act of Valor 2012

Sancho, José (1944-) El Dorado 1988; Ay, Carmela! 1990; Live Flesh 1997; Arachnid 2001

Sand, Paul (1935-) Every Little Crook and Nanny 1972; The Hot Rock 1972; The Second Coming of Suzanne 1974; The Main Event 1979; Can't Stop the Music 1980; Teen Wolf Too 1987

Sanda, Dominique (1948-) A Gentle Creature 1969; The Conformist 1970; First Love 1970; The Garden of the Finzi-Continis 1971; The Mackintosh Man 1973; Story of a Love Story 1973; Steppenwolf 1974; The Inheritance 1976; 1900 1976; Damnation Alley 1977; I, the Worst of All 1990

Sande, Walter (1906-1971) Corvette K-225 1943; I Love a Soldier 1944; Killer McCoy 1947; The Woman on the Beach 1947; The Duel at Silver Creek 1952; Red Planet Mars 1952; Apache 1954; Texas Lady 1955; Johnny Tremain 1957

Sander, Otto (1941-2013) The Marquise of O 1976; Palermo oder Wolfsburg 1980; Rosa Luxemburg 1986; Wings of Desire 1987; Faraway, So Close 1993

Sanderford, John The Alchemist 1981; My Boyfriend's Back 1989; Leprechaun 1992

Sanders, George (1906-1972) Lloyd's of London 1936; Things to Come 1936; Lancer Spy 1937; Love Is News 1937; Slave Ship 1937; Four Men and a Prayer 1938; Mr Moto's Last Warning 1938; Confessions of a Nazi Spy 1939; The First Rebel 1939; Green Hell 1939; Nurse Edith Cavell 1939; The Saint in London 1939; The Saint Strikes Back 1939; Bitter Sweet 1940; Foreign Correspondent 1940; The House of the Seven Gables 1940; Rebecca 1940; The Saint Takes Over 1940; The Saint's Double Trouble 1940; Son of Monte Cristo 1940; A Date with the Falcon 1941; The Gay Falcon 1941; Man Hunt 1941; Rage in Heaven 1941; The Saint in Palm Springs 1941; Sundown 1941; The Black Swan 1942; The Falcon Takes Over 1942; The Falcon's Brother 1942; Her Cardboard Lover 1942; The Moon and Sixpence 1942; Quiet Please, Murder 1942; Son of Fury 1942; Tales of Manhattan 1942; This Land Is Mine 1943; Action in Arabia 1944; The Lodger 1944; Summer Storm 1944; Hangover Square 1945; The Picture of Dorian Gray 1945; The Strange Affair of Uncle Harry 1945; The Strange Woman 1946; Thieves' Holiday 1946; Forever Amber 1947; The Ghost and Mrs Muir 1947; Lured 1947; The Private Affairs of Bel Ami 1947; The Fan 1949; Samson and Delilah 1949; All about Eve 1950; I Can Get It for You Wholesale 1951; The Light Touch 1951; Assignment – Paris 1952; Black Jack 1952; Ivanhoe 1952; Call Me Madam 1953; Journey to Italy 1953; King Richard and the Crusaders 1954; Witness to Murder 1954; The Big Tip Off 1955; Jupiter's Darling 1955; The King's Thief 1955; Moonfleet 1955; Never Say Goodbye 1955; Death of a Scoundrel 1956; That Certain Feeling 1956; While the City Sleeps 1956; From the Earth to the Moon 1958; The Whole Truth 1958; Solomon and Sheba 1959; That Kind of Woman 1959; A Touch of Larceny 1959; Cone of Silence 1960; The Last Voyage 1960; The Rebel 1960; Village of the Damned 1960; In Search of the Castaways 1961; Cairo 1962; Operation

Snatch 1962; The Cracksman 1963; A Shot in the Dark 1964; The Amorous Adventures of Moll Flanders 1965; The Quiller Memorandum 1966; Good Times 1967; The Jungle Book 1967; Warning Shot 1967; The Best House in London 1968; The Girl from Rio 1968; The Body Stealers 1969; The Candy Man 1969; Endless Night 1971; Doomwatch 1972; Psychomania 1972

Sanders, Hugh (1911-1966) The Damned Don't Cry 1950; Mister 880 1950; Storm Warning 1950; Along the Great Divide 1951; Sugarfoot 1951; That's My Boy 1951; The Pride of St Louis 1952; The Glass Web 1953; The Wild One 1953; Voice in the Mirror 1958

Sanders, Jay O (1953-) Starting Over 1979; The Prince of Pennsylvania 1988; Cold Sassy Tree 1989; Meeting Venus 1990; Mr Destiny 1990; Defenseless 1991; JFK 1991; VI Warshawski 1991; Hostages 1993; My Boyfriend's Back 1993; Angels in the Outfield 1994; The Big Green 1995; Three Wishes 1995; Daylight 1996; For Richer or Poorer 1997; Kiss the Girls 1997; The Matchmaker 1997; Wrestling with Alligators 1998; Earthly Possessions 1999; Tumbleweeds 1999; DC Sniper: 23 Days of Fear 2003; The Day after Tomorrow 2004; Half Nelson 2006; Edge of Darkness 2009

Sanderson, Martyn Beyond Reasonable Doubt 1980; Bad Blood 1982; Sylvia 1984

Sanderson, William (1948-) Coal Miner's Daughter 1980; Death Hunt 1981; Raggedy Man 1981; Blade Runner 1982; Black Moon Rising 1985; Sometimes They Come Back 1991; Wagons East! 1994; Last Man Standing 1996

Sandler, Adam (1966-) Shakes the Clown 1991; Airheads 1994; Mixed Nuts 1994; Billy Madison 1995; Bulletproof 1996; Happy Gilmore 1996; Dirty Work 1998; The Waterboy 1998; The Wedding Singer 1998; Big Daddy 1999; Fortune Hunters 1999; Little Nicky 2000; The Animal 2001; The Hot Chick 2002; Mr Deeds 2002; Punch-Drunk Love 2002; Adam Sandler's Eight Crazy Nights 2003; Anger Management 2003; 50 First Dates 2004; Spanglish 2004; The Longest Yard 2005; Click 2006; I Now Pronounce You Chuck & Larry 2007; Reign over Me 2007; Bedtime Stories 2008; You Don't Mess with the Zohan 2008; Funny People 2009; Grown Ups 2010; Jack and Jill 2011; Just Go with It 2011; Zookeeper 2011; Hotel Transylvania 2012; That's My Boy 2012; Grown Ups 2 2013; Blended 2014; The Cobbler 2014; Men, Women & Children 2014; Top Five 2014; Hotel Transylvania 2 2015; Pixels 2015

Sandoval, Miguel (1951-) Clear and Present Danger 1994; Fair Game 1995; Mrs Winterbourne 1996; Flight of Fancy 2000; Things You Can Tell Just by Looking at Her 2000; Black Point 2001; Ballistic: Ecks vs Sever 2002; Repo Chick 2009

Sandow, Nick No Looking Back 1998; Return to Paradise 1998; The Big Heist 2001

Sandre, Didier The Lie 1992; An Autumn Tale 1998

Sandrelli, Stefania (1946-) Divorce - Italian Style 1961; L'Aíné des Ferchaux 1963; Partner 1968; The Conformist 1970; Alfredo Alfredo 1971; We All Loved Each Other So Much 1974; 1900 1976; The Family 1987; Mignon Has Left 1988; Jamón, Jamón 1992; Of Love and Shadows 1994; Stealing Beauty 1995; Un Filme Falado 2003

Sandri, Anna-Maria (1936-) Le Rouge et le Noir 1954; The Black Tent 1956

Sands, Diana (1934-1973) A Raisin in the Sun 1961; Doctors' Wives 1970; The Landlord 1970

Sands, Johnny aka **Sands, John** (1927-2003) Till the End of Time 1946; The Bachelor and the Bobby-Soxer 1947; Blaze of Noon 1947; Adventure in Baltimore 1949; The Admiral Was a Lady 1950; The Lawless 1950

Sands, Julian (1957-) The Killing Fields 1984; After Darkness 1985; The Doctor and the Devils 1985; A Room with a View 1985; Gothic 1986; Siesta 1987; Vibes 1988; Warlock 1989; Arachnophobia 1990; Night Sun 1990; Impromptu 1991; Naked Lunch 1991; Crazy in Love 1992; Tale of a Vampire 1992; The Turn of the Screw 1992; Boxing Helena 1993; Warlock: the Armageddon 1993; The Browning Version 1994; Leaving Las Vegas 1995; Circle of Passion 1996; The Phantom of the Opera 1998; The Loss of Sexual Innocence 1999; The Million Dollar Hotel 1999; Timecode 1999; Mercy

2000; Vatel 2000; Hotel 2001; The Medallion 2003; Sword of Xanten 2004; Blood and Bone 2009

Sands, Leslie (1921-2001) One More Time 1970; The Ragman's Daughter 1972

Sands, Stark (1978-) Catch That Kid 2004; Pretty Persuasion 2005

Sands, Tommy (1937-) Mardi Gras 1958; Sing, Boy, Sing 1958; Babes in Toyland 1961; Ensign Pulver 1964; None but the Brave 1965; The Violent Ones 1967

Sandweiss, Ellen The Evil Dead 1981; My Name Is Bruce 2008

Sanford, Erskine (1885-1969) Citizen Kane 1941; The Magnificent Ambersons 1942; Ministry of Fear 1945; Angel on My Shoulder 1946; Crack-Up 1946; The Lady from Shanghai 1948; Macbeth 1948

Sanford, Garwin (1955-) Max 1994; The Long Way Home 1998; Life-Size 2000

Sanford, Isabel aka **Sanford, Isabell** (1917-2004) Guess Who's Coming to Dinner 1967; Hickey and Boggs 1972; Love at First Bite 1979; Original Gangstas 1996

Sanford, Ralph (1899-1963) Thunderhead - Son of Flicka 1945; Copacabana 1947; The Glass Menagerie 1950

Sanford, Tiny aka **Stanford, Stanley J** aka **Sanford, Stanley** (1894-1961) The Immigrant 1917; The Circus 1928; Modern Times 1936

Sano, Shiro (1955-) Violent Cop 1989; The Sun 2005

Sano, Shuji (1912-1978) There Was a Father 1942; Hen in the Wind 1948

Sansa, Maya (1975-) Benzina 2001; Good Morning, Night 2003; Female Agents 2007; Villa Amalia 2009; Cycling with Molière 2013

Sansom, Ken (1927-) Winnie the Pooh's Most Grand Adventure 1997; The Tigger Movie 2000; Piglet's Big Movie 2003; Winnie the Pooh: Springtime with Roo 2004; Pooh's Heffalump Movie 2005

Santamaria, Claudio (1974-) Besieged 1998; The Card Player 2004; Romanzo Criminale 2005; BirdWatchers 2008

Santiago-Hudson, Ruben (1957-) Rear Window 1998; Domestic Disturbance 2001; Their Eyes Were Watching God 2005; Mr Brooks 2007

Santiago, Renoly Dangerous Minds 1995; Hackers 1995

Santini, Pierre (1938-) Les Innocents aux Mains Sales 1975; American Dreamer 1984

Santoni, Reni (1939-) Enter Laughing 1967; Anzio 1968; Dirty Harry 1971; I Never Promised You a Rose Garden 1977; Dead Men Don't Wear Plaid 1982; Bad Boys 1983; Brewster's Millions 1985; Cobra 1986

Santoro, Rodrigo (1975-) Behind the Sun 2001; Redbelt 2007; Che Part One 2008; Lion's Den 2008; I Love You Phillip Morris 2009; Post Grad 2009; Rio 2011; The Last Stand 2013; 300: Rise of an Empire 2013; The 33 2014; Focus 2015; Jane Got a Gun 2015

Santos, Bianca aka **Santos, Bianca A** Ouija 2014; The Duff 2015

Santos, Irandhir Elite Squad: the Enemy Within 2010; Neighbouring Sounds 2012

Santos, Joe (1931-2016) The Blue Knight 1973; The Friends of Eddie Coyle 1973; Shamus 1973; Zandy's Bride 1974; Fear City 1984; The Old Man and the Sea 1990; Mo' Money 1992; Auggie Rose 2000

Santschi, Tom (1878-1931) 3 Bad Men 1926; Hills of Kentucky 1927

Sanz, Horatio (1969-) Boat Trip 2002; The Man 2005; Rebound 2005; School for Scoundrels 2006; Lucky You 2007

Sanz, Jorge (1969-) Valentina 1982; Lovers 1991; Belle Epoque 1992; The Girl of Your Dreams 1998

Sapdaru, Ion 12:08 East of Bucharest 2005; Tales from the Golden Age 2009

Sara, Mia (1967-) Legend 1985; Ferris Bueller's Day Off 1986; Apprentice to Murder 1988; A Row of Crows 1991; By the Sword 1992; A Stranger among Us 1992; Timecop 1994; Bullet to Beijing 1995; The Maddening 1995; The Set Up 1995; Hard Time 1998

Sarafian, Barbara 8½ Women 1999; Bullhead 2011

Sarafian, Richard C aka **Sarafian, Richard** (1930-2013) Bugsy 1991; Bound 1996; Dr Dolittle 2 2001

Sarandon, Chris (1942-) Dog Day Afternoon 1975; Lipstick 1976; The Sentinel 1977; Cuba 1979; The Osterman Weekend 1983; Protocol 1984; Fright Night 1985; Collision Course 1987; The Princess Bride 1987;

Child's Play 1988; Forced March 1989; Slaves of New York 1989; Whispers 1990; The Nightmare before Christmas 1993; Danielle Steel's No Greater Love 1996; Desert Gamble 1996; American Perfekt 1997; Safe 2011

Sarandon, Susan (1946-) Joe 1970; Lady Liberty 1971; The Front Page 1974; The Great Waldo Pepper 1975; One Summer Love 1975; The Rocky Horror Picture Show 1975; The Other Side of Midnight 1977; King of the Gypsies 1978; Pretty Baby 1978; Something Short of Paradise 1979; Atlantic City, USA 1980; Loving Couples 1980; Tempest 1982; The Hunger 1983; The Buddy System 1984; Compromising Positions 1985; The Witches of Eastwick 1987; Bull Durham 1988; Sweet Hearts Dance 1988; A Dry White Season 1989; The January Man 1989; White Palace 1990; Light Sleeper 1991; Thelma & Louise 1991; Bob Roberts 1992; Lorenzo's Oil 1992; The Client 1994; Little Women 1994; Safe Passage 1994; The Celluloid Closet 1995; Dead Man Walking 1995; James and the Giant Peach 1996; Stepmom 1998; Twilight 1998; Anywhere but Here 1999; Cradle Will Rock 1999; Earthly Possessions 1999; Cats & Dogs 2001; The Banger Sisters 2002; Igby Goes Down 2002; Moonlight Mile 2002; Ice Bound 2003; Alfie 2004; Noel 2004; Romance & Cigarettes 2004; Shall We Dance 2004; Elizabethtown 2005; Bernard and Doris 2006; Irresistible 2006; Enchanted 2007; In the Valley of Elah 2007; Mr Woodcock 2007; Speed Racer 2008; The Greatest 2009; The Lovely Bones 2009; Solitary Man 2009; Wall Street: Money Never Sleeps 2010; Jeff, Who Lives at Home 2011; Arbitrage 2012; Cloud Atlas 2012; How to Make Money Selling Drugs 2012; Robot & Frank 2012; That's My Boy 2012; Snitch 2013; The Calling 2014; Tammy 2014; The Meddler 2015; The Secret Life of Marilyn Monroe 2015; Unity 2015

Sarda, Rosa Maria (1941-) Actresses 1996; Beloved/Friend 1998; All about My Mother 1999; Take My Eyes 2003

Sardou, Fernand (1910-1976) Marguerite de la Nuit 1955; Une Parisienne 1957; Lunch on the Grass 1959; The Little Theatre of Jean Renoir 1969

Sargent, Dick aka **Sargent, Richard** (1933-1994) The Beast with a Million Eyes 1955; Mardi Gras 1958; Operation Petticoat 1959; Billie 1965; Live a Little, Love a Little 1968; Hardcore 1979

Sarkisyan, Rose Family Viewing 1987; The Adjuster 1991

Sarne, Michael aka **Sarne, Mike** (1939-) A Place to Go 1963; Every Day's a Holiday 1964

Sarrazin, Michael (1940-2011) The Flim-Flam Man 1967; Gunfight in Abilene 1967; Journey to Shiloh 1967; The Sweet Ride 1967; Eye of the Cat 1969; A Man Called Gannon 1969; They Shoot Horses, Don't They? 1969; In Search of Gregory 1970; The Pursuit of Happiness 1971; Sometimes a Great Notion 1971; The Groundstar Conspiracy 1972; Frankenstein: the True Story 1973; Harry in Your Pocket 1973; For Pete's Sake 1974; The Reincarnation of Peter Proud 1975; The Gumball Rally 1976; Death Vengeance 1982; Joshua Then and Now 1985; Keeping Track 1986; Mascara 1987; Lena's Holiday 1990; Bullet to Beijing 1995; Midnight in St Petersburg 1995; The Peacekeeper 1997

Sarsgaard, Peter (1971-) Another Day in Paradise 1998; Boys Don't Cry 1999; The Center of the World 2001; Unconditional Love 2001; Empire 2002; K-19: the Widowmaker 2002; Garden State 2003; Shattered Glass 2003; Kinsey 2004; Flightplan 2005; Jarhead 2005; The Skeleton Key 2005; Rendition 2007; Year of the Dog 2007; An Education 2008; Elegy 2008; In the Electric Mist 2009; Orphan 2009; Knight and Day 2010; Green Lantern 2011; Robot & Frank 2012; Blue Jasmine 2013; Lovelace 2013; Night Moves 2013; Experimenter: the Stanley Milgram Story 2014; The Magnificent Seven 2016

Sartain, Gailard (1946-) Roadie 1980; Hard Country 1981; Ernest Saves Christmas 1988; Mississippi Burning 1988; Blaze 1989; Ernest Goes to Jail 1990; Fried Green Tomatoes at the Whistle Stop Cafe 1991; Stop! or My Mom Will Shoot 1992; The Real McCoy 1993; Getting Even with Dad 1994; Open Season 1995; Murder in Mind 1996

Sartor, Fabio (1954-) Phantom of Death 1988; The Luzhin Defence 2000

Sass, Katrin Good Bye Lenin! 2003; Give Me Your Hand 2008; The Silence 2010

Sassard, Jacqueline (1940-) Accident 1967; Les Biches 1968

Sasso, Will (1974-) Drop Dead Gorgeous 1999; College Road Trip 2008; Finding Mrs Claus 2012; The Three Stooges 2012

Sastre, Inés (1973-) Beyond the Clouds 1995; The Best Man 1998; Druids 2001; Vidocq 2001; The Lost City 2005

Sato, Hitomi Ring 1997; Ring 2 1998

Sato, Kei (1928-2010) Onibaba 1964; Death by Hanging 1968

Sato, Koichi When the Last Sword Is Drawn 2003; Sukiyaki Western Django 2007; Unforgiven 2014

Satton, Lon The Heroes 1968; Hello - Goodbye 1970

Sauer, Gary The Unbelievable Truth 1989; Trust 1990

Saunders, Jennifer (1958-) The Supergrass 1985; Eat the Rich 1987; In the Bleak Midwinter 1995; Muppet Treasure Island 1996; Fanny & Elvis 1999; Shrek 2 2004; Coraline 2008; Absolutely Fabulous: the Movie 2016

Saunders, Mary Jane (1943-) Sorrowful Jones 1949; A Woman of Distinction 1950

Sauvegrain, Didier Sarraouina 1986; Jeanne la Pucelle 1994

Savage, Ann (1921-2008) Passport to Suez 1943; What a Woman! 1943; Detour 1945; My Winnipeg 2007

Savage, Brad (1953-) The Apple Dumpling Gang 1974; Echoes of a Summer 1976; No Deposit No Return 1976; Return from Witch Mountain 1978; Red Dawn 1984

Savage, Fred (1976-) The Boy Who Could Fly 1986; The Princess Bride 1987; Vice Versa 1988; Austin Powers in Goldmember 2002; The Rules of Attraction 2002; Welcome to Mooseport 2004

Savage, John (1949-) Bad Company 1972; The Killing Kind 1973; Steelyard Blues 1973; The Deer Hunter 1978; Hair 1979; The Onion Field 1979; Cattle Annie and Little Britches 1980; Inside Moves: the Guys from Max's Bar 1980; The Amateur 1981; Maria's Lovers 1984; Salvador 1986; Beauty and the Beast 1987; Hotel Colonial 1987; Do the Right Thing 1989; Hunting 1992; Flynn 1995; American Strays 1996; One Good Turn 1996; White Squall 1996; Before Women Had Wings 1997; Message in a Bottle 1998; The Jack Bull 1999; Redemption of the Ghost 2000; The Virginian 2000

Saval, Dany (1942-) Moon Pilot 1962; Boeing Boeing 1965

Savalas, Telly (1922-1994) Mad Dog Coll 1961; The Young Savages 1961; Birdman of Alcatraz 1962; Cape Fear 1962; Johnny Cool 1963; Love Is a Ball 1963; The Man from the Diner's Club 1963; The Greatest Story Ever Told 1965; The Slender Thread 1965; Beau Geste 1966; The Dirty Dozen 1967; The Karate Killers 1967; Buona Sera, Mrs Campbell 1968; The Scalphunters 1968; The Assassination Bureau 1969; Crooks and Coronets 1969; Land Raiders 1969; Mackenna's Gold 1969; On Her Majesty's Secret Service 1969; Kelly's Heroes 1970; Pancho Villa 1971; Pretty Maids All in a Row 1971; A Town Called Hell 1971; Horror Express 1972; A Reason to Live, a Reason to Die 1972; The Marcus-Nelson Murders 1973; Lisa and the Devil 1974; Inside Out 1975; Killer Force 1975; Capricorn One 1978; Beyond the Poseidon Adventure 1979; Escape to Athena 1979; Cannonball Run II 1983; The Cartier Affair 1984

Savané, Souléymane Sy Goodbye Solo 2008; Keep the Lights On 2012

Savant, Doug (1964-) Trick or Treat 1986; Masquerade 1988; Red Surf 1990; A Face to Kill For 1999; First Daughter 1999; First Target 2000; First Shot 2002

Savelyeva, Lyudmila (1942-) War and Peace 1966; Sunflower 1969

Savident, John (1938-) Mountains of the Moon 1989; Brain Donors 1992; Mrs 'arris Goes to Paris 1992

Savin, Eric He Loves Me... He Loves Me Not 2002; Intimate Enemies 2007

Savini, Tom (1946-) Martin 1978; Knightriders 1981; Creepshow 2 1987; Going to Pieces: the Rise and Fall of the Slasher Film 2006

Savoy, Teresa Ann aka **Savoy, Theresa Ann** (1955-) Salon Kitty 1976; Caligula 1979

Savvina, Iya (1936-2011) The Lady with the Little Dog 1960; Asya's Happiness 1967; Private Life 1982

Sawa, Devon (1978-) Little Giants 1994; Wild America 1997; A Cool, Dry Place 1998; Idle Hands 1999; SLC Punk! 1999; Final Destination 2000; The Guilty 2000; Slackers 2001; Extreme Ops 2003

Sawalha, Julia (1968-) In the Bleak Midwinter 1995; The Wind in the Willows 1996; Chicken Run 2000; The Final Curtain 2002; Absolutely Fabulous: the Movie 2016

Sawalha, Nadim (1935-) The Wind and the Lion 1975; Sinbad and the Eye of the Tiger 1977; The Awakening 1980; Sphinx 1980; Half Moon Street 1986; Pascali's Island 1988; The Hawk 1992

Sawyer, Joe aka **Sawyer, Joseph** (1906-1982) I Found Stella Parish 1935; Special Agent 1935; The Petrified Forest 1936; The Black Legion 1937; San Quentin 1937; Down Mexico Way 1941; Hit the Ice 1943; The Outlaw 1943; Tarzan's Desert Mystery 1943; Gilda 1946; Red Skies of Montana 1952; Riding Shotgun 1954

Saxon, John (1935-) Rock, Pretty Baby 1956; The Unguarded Moment 1956; The Reluctant Debutante 1958; The Restless Years 1958; This Happy Feeling 1958; The Big Fisherman 1959; Portrait in Black 1960; The Unforgiven 1960; Mr Hobbs Takes a Vacation 1962; War Hunt 1962; The Night Caller 1965; The Appaloosa 1966; Planet of Blood 1966; Winchester '73 1967; The Intruders 1970; Mr Kingstreet's War 1970; Joe Kidd 1972; Enter the Dragon 1973; Black Christmas 1974; The Swiss Conspiracy 1975; Raid on Entebbe 1977; The Glove 1978; The Electric Horseman 1979; Battle beyond the Stars 1980; Blood Beach 1981; The Man with the Deadly Lens 1982; Tenebrae 1982; A Nightmare on Elm Street 1984; Fever Pitch 1985; Beverly Hills Cop III 1994

Sayer, Philip (?-1991) The Green Horizon 1981; Xtro 1983; Shanghai Surprise 1986

Sayers, Jo Ann (1918-2011) Young Dr Kildare 1938; The Adventures of Huckleberry Finn 1939; Honolulu 1939

Sayle, Alexei (1952-) Gorky Park 1983; The Bride 1985; Whoops Apocalypse 1986; Siesta 1987; Indiana Jones and the Last Crusade 1989; Carry On Columbus 1992; Reckless 1993; Swing 1998; The Thief Lord 2005

Sayles, John (1950-) Return of the Secaucus Seven 1980; Eight Men Out 1988; Little Vegas 1990; Straight Talk 1992; Gridlock'd 1996

Saylor, Syd (1895-1962) Hell Town 1937; The Prince of Thieves 1948; Mule Train 1950

Sbaraglia, Leonardo (1970-) Intacto 2001; The City of No Limits 2002; Carmen 2003; King of the Hill 2007

Sbarge, Raphael (1964-) Risky Business 1983; My Science Project 1985

Sbragia, Mattia (1952-) Year of the Gun 1991; Heaven 2002; The Sin Eater 2002; The Passion of the Christ 2004

Scacchi, Greta (1960-) Heat and Dust 1982; Burke and Wills 1985; The Coca-Cola Kid 1985; Defence of the Realm 1985; Good Morning, Babylon 1987; A Man in Love 1987; White Mischief 1987; Three Sisters 1988; Presumed Innocent 1990; Fires Within 1991; Shattered 1991; The Player 1992; Salt on Our Skin 1992; Turtle Beach 1992; The Browning Version 1994; Country Life 1994; Jefferson in Paris 1995; Emma 1996; Rasputin 1996; The Odyssey 1997; The Serpent's Kiss 1997; The Red Violin 1998; Tom's Midnight Garden 1998; Cotton Mary 1999; Ladies' Room 2000; One of the Hollywood Ten 2000; Festival in Cannes 2001; Beyond the Sea 2004; Flightplan 2005; The Book of Revelation 2006; Brideshead Revisited 2008; The Falling 2014; The White King 2016

Scala, Gia (1934-1972) Don't Go near the Water 1957; The Garment Jungle 1957; Ride a Crooked Trail 1958; The Tunnel of Love 1958; The Angry Hills 1959; Battle of the Coral Sea 1959; I Aim at the Stars 1960; The Guns of Navarone 1961

Scales, Prunella (1932-) Hobson's Choice 1953; Laxdale Hall 1953; Waltz of the Toreadors 1962; The Littlest Horse Thieves 1977; The Boys from Brazil 1978; The Wicked Lady 1983; The Lonely Passion of Judith Hearne 1987; A Chorus of Disapproval 1988; Consuming Passions 1988; Howards End 1992; Second Best 1993; An Awfully Big Adventure 1994; Wolf 1994; Stiff Upper Lips 1997; Mad Cows 1999; The Ghost of Greville Lodge 2000

Scalia, Jack (1951-) Fear City 1984; Amore! 1993; Barbara Taylor Bradford's Everything to Gain 1996; Red Eye 2005; End Game 2006; Honeymoon with Mom 2006

Scamarcio, Riccardo (1979-) Romanzo Criminale 2005; My Brother Is an Only Child 2006; Loose Cannons 2010; The Informer 2013; Pasolini 2014; Burnt 2015

Scanlan, Emmett J Charlie Casanova 2012; Breakdown 2015

Scanlan, Joanna Girl with a Pearl Earring 2003; The Calling 2009; The Invisible Woman 2013

Scarborough, Adrian Love Is the Devil: Study for a Portrait of Francis Bacon 1998; Vera Drake 2004; Delicious 2013

Scardino, Don (1949-) Squirm 1976; He Knows You're Alone 1981

Scardino, Hal (1984-) The Indian in the Cupboard 1995; Marvin's Room 1996

Scarfe, Alan (1946-) Bay Boy 1984; Joshua Then and Now 1985; Keeping Track 1986; Iron Eagle II 1988; Double Impact 1991; Sanctuary 1997

Scarpa, Renato (1939-) Don't Look Now 1973; The Icicle Thief 1989; Il Postino 1994; We Have a Pope 2011

Scarpitta, Carmen (1933-) Casanova 1976; La Cage aux Folles 1978

Scarwid, Diana (1955-) Inside Moves: the Guys from Max's Bar 1980; Mommie Dearest 1981; Rumble Fish 1983; Silkwood 1983; Strange Invaders 1983; Extremities 1986; Psycho III 1986; Heat 1987; Brenda Starr 1989; The Cure 1995; Gold Diggers: the Secret of Bear Mountain 1995; The Neon Bible 1995; Truman 1995; What Lies Beneath 2000; A Guy Thing 2002; Party Monster 2003; The Clearing 2004; Nora Roberts' Tribute 2009

Schaake, Katrin Love Is Colder than Death 1969; Whity 1970; The Bitter Tears of Petra von Kant 1972

Schade, Doris (1924-2012) The German Sisters 1981; Veronika Voss 1982

Schaech, Johnathon (1969-) Sparrow 1993; Doom Generation 1995; Poison Ivy 2 1995; That Thing You Do! 1996; Hush 1998; Finding Graceland 1999; Splendor 1999; The Forsaken 2001; Road House 2 2006; Prom Night 2008; Quarantine 2008; Sex and Lies in Sin City 2008

Schaefer, Joshua aka **Schaefer, Josh** The Bomber Boys ' 1995; Johns 1995; True Crime 1995; Eight Days a Week 1996

Schafer, Natalie (1900-1991) Keep Your Powder Dry 1345; Molly and Me 1945; Secret beyond the Door 1948; Caught 1949; Callaway Went Thataway 1951; The Girl Next Door 1953; Anastasia 1956; Forever, Darling 1956

Schallert, William (1922-2016) The Man from Planet X 1951; The Incredible Shrinking Man 1957; Lonely Are the Brave 1962; In the Heat of the Night 1967; Speedway 1968; Colossus: the Forbin Project 1969; The Computer Wore Tennis Shoes 1969; Mrs Lambert Remembers Love 1991

Schanzer, Karl Tonight for Sure! 1961; Dementia 13 1963

Scheer, Alexander Carlos 2010; When Santa Fell to Earth 2011; West 2013

Scheider, Roy aka **Scheider, Roy R** (1932-2008) The Curse of the Living Corpse 1964; Puzzle of a Downfall Child 1970; The French Connection 1971; Klute 1971; The Outside Man 1973; The Seven-Ups 1973; Jaws 1975; Marathon Man 1976; Jaws 2 1978; All That Jazz 1979; Last Embrace 1979; Still of the Night 1982; Blue Thunder 1983; 2010 1984; 52 Pick-Up 1986; The Men's Club 1986; Cohen and Tate 1988; Listen to Me 1989; The Fourth War 1990; The Russia House 1990; Naked Lunch 1991; Romeo Is Bleeding 1992; Executive Target 1996; The Myth of Fingerprints 1996; John Grisham's The Rainmaker 1997; The Peacekeeper 1997; RKO 281 1999; Time Lapse 2001; King of Texas 2002; The Punisher 2004

Scheine, Raynor (1942-) Ace Ventura: Pet Detective 1993; The Real McCoy 1993; A Stranger's Heart 2007

Scheitz, Clemens Heart of Glass 1976; Stroszek 1977

Schell, Catherine aka **von Schell, Catharina** (1946-) Moon Zero Two 1969; Madame Sin 1972; Callan 1974; The Return of the Pink Panther 1974; Gulliver's Travels 1977

Schell, Maria (1925-2005) The Magic Box 1951; The Heart of the Matter 1953; Napoléon 1955; The Rats 1955; Gervaise 1956; White Nights 1957; The Brothers Karamazov 1958; The Hanging Tree 1959; Cimarron 1960; The Mark 1961; The Bloody Judge 1969;

The Odessa File 1974; Just a Gigolo 1978; Nineteen Nineteen 1984

Schell, Maximilian (1930-2014) The Young Lions 1958; Judgment at Nuremberg 1961; Five Finger Exercise 1962; The Reluctant Saint 1962; Topkapi 1964; Return from the Ashes 1965; The Deadly Affair 1966; Counterpoint 1967; The Desperate Ones 1967; First Love 1970; Pope Joan 1972; The Odessa File 1974; The Pedestrian 1974; St Ives 1976; A Bridge Too Far 1977; Cross of Iron 1977; Julia 1977; Avalanche Express 1979; The Black Hole 1979; Players 1979; The Diary of Anne Frank 1980; The Chosen 1981; Marlene 1984; The Assisi Underground 1985; The Rose Garden 1989; Labyrinth 1991; Miss Rose White 1992; A Far Off Place 1993; Little Odessa 1994; The Eighteenth Angel 1997; Left Luggage 1997; Telling Lies in America 1997; Deep Impact 1998; Vampires 1998; Festival in Cannes 2001; The Brothers Bloom 2008

Schellenberg, August (1936-2013) Kings and Desperate Men 1981; Black Robe 1991; Free Willy 1993; Getting Gotti 1994; Iron Will 1994; Free Willy 2: the Adventure Home 1995; The West Side Waltz 1995; What Love Sees 1996; Free Willy 3: the Rescue 1997; Eight Below 2005; The New World 2005; Bury My Heart at Wounded Knee 2007

Schellhardt, Mary Kate (1978-) What's Eating Gilbert Grape 1993; Apollo 13 1995; Free Willy 2: the Adventure Home 1995

Scherrer, Paul (1968-) Children of the Corn II: the Final Sacrifice 1993; Fall into Darkness 1996

Scheydt, Karl (1940-2009) The American Soldier 1970; Fear Eats the Soul 1973

Schiaffino, Rosanna (1939-2009) Romulus and the Sabines 1961; RoGoPaG 1962; Two Weeks in Another Town 1962; The Long Ships 1963; The Victors 1963; Drop Dead Darling 1966; The Rover 1967

Schiavelli, Vincent (1948-2005) Waiting for the Light 1989; American Yakuza 2: Back to Back 1996; The People vs Larry Flynt 1996; Tomorrow Never Dies 1997; Man on the Moon 1999; Snow White 2001; Hey Arnold! the Movie 2002

Schiff, Richard (1955-) The Arrival 1996; Doctor Dolittle 1998; Heaven 1998; Living Out Loud 1998; The Pentagon Wars 1998; Gun Shy 2000; I Am Sam 2001; People I Know 2002; Last Chance Harvey 2008; The Infidel 2010

Schiffer, Claudia (1970-) The Blackout 1997; Black and White 1999; In Pursuit 2000

Schildkraut, Joseph (1895-1964) Orphans of the Storm 1921; The Road to Yesterday 1925; The King of Kings 1927; Cleopatra 1934; Viva Villa! 1934; The Crusades 1935; The Garden of Allah 1936; Lancer Spy 1937; The Life of Emile Zola 1937; Slave Ship 1937; The Baroness and the Butler 1938; Marie Antoinette 1938; Suez 1938; Idiot's Delight 1939; Lady of the Tropics 1939; The Man in the Iron Mask 1939; Mr Moto Takes a Vacation 1939; Pack Up Your Troubles 1939; The Three Musketeers 1939; Phantom Raiders 1940; The Shop around the Corner 1940; The Cheaters 1945; Flame of the Barbary Coast 1945; Monsieur Beaucaire 1946; The Diary of Anne Frank 1959

Schilling, Gus (1908-1957) Citizen Kane 1941; Hers to Hold 1943; It's a Pleasure 1945; The Lady from Shanghai 1948; Bride for Sale 1949; Our Very Own 1950

Schilling, Taylor The Lucky One 2012; The Overnight 2015

Schilling, William G Ruthless People 1986; White of the Eye 1986

Schirripa, Steve aka **Schirripa, Steven R** (1958-) See Spot Run 2001; My Fake Fiancé 2009

Schlatter, Charlie (1966-) Bright Lights, Big City 1988; 18 Again! 1988; Heartbreak Hotel 1988; The Delinquents 1989

Schmidinger, Walter Hanussen 1988; Requiem 2006

Schmidt, Kevin G (1988-) Cheaper by the Dozen 2003; Cheaper by the Dozen 2 2005

Schmidtner, Christiane (1940-2003) Boeing Boeing 1965; The Giant Spider Invasion 1975

Schmolzer, August Requiem for Dominic 1990; Bride of the Wind 2001

Schnabel, Stefan (1912-1999) The Iron Curtain 1948; Diplomatic Courier 1952; Houdini 1953; The 27th Day 1957; Dracula's Widow 1988

Schnarre, Monika (1971-) Killer 1994; Sanctuary 1997

Schneider, Betty Mon Oncle 1958; Paris Nous Appartient 1960

Schneider, Dan (1966-) Happy Together 1989; Good Burger 1997

Schneider, Gary The Toxic Avenger 1985; Class of Nuke 'Em High 1986

Schneider, John (1960-) Eddie Macon's Run 1983; The Curse 1987; Snow Day 2000; Sydney White 2007; You've Got a Friend 2007

Schneider, Maria (1952-2011) Last Tango in Paris 1972; The Passenger 1975; A Song for Europe 1985; Les Nuits Fauves 1992; Jane Eyre 1996; Something to Believe In 1997

Schneider, Michael Beauty and the Beast 1987; Double Edge 1992

Schneider, Niels Heartbeats 2010; You and the Night 2013

Schneider (2), Paul (1976-) All the Real Girls 2003; Elizabethtown 2005; The Assassination of Jesse James by the Coward Robert Ford 2007; Lars and the Real Girl 2007; Away We Go 2009; Bright Star 2009; Beloved 2011; Water for Elephants 2011; The Flowers of War 2012; Hello Carter 2013; The Daughter 2016

Schneider, Rob (1963-) The Beverly Hillbillies 1993; Surf Ninjas 1993; Judge Dredd 1995; The Adventures of Pinocchio 1996; Down Periscope 1996; Knock Off 1998; Susan's Plan 1998; Big Daddy 1999; Deuce Bigalow: Male Gigolo 1999; The Animal 2001; The Hot Chick 2002; Adam Sandler's Eight Crazy Nights 2003; 50 First Dates 2004; Deuce Bigalow: European Gigolo 2005; The Benchwarmers 2006; The Reef 2006; You Don't Mess with the Zohan 2008; Grown Ups 2010; You May Not Kiss the Bride 2011; Dino Time 2012; Norm of the North 2016

Schnetzer, Ben The Book Thief 2014; Goat 2016

Schöne, Reiner Return of Sabata 1971; Mary Higgins Clark's Pretend You Don't See Her 2002

Schober, Andrea The Merchant of Four Seasons 1971; Chinese Roulette 1976

Schoeffling, Michael (1960-) Sixteen Candles 1984; Belizaire the Cajun 1985; Sylvester 1985; Vision Quest 1985; Mermaids 1990; Wild Hearts Can't Be Broken 1991

Schoelen, Jill (1970-) Chiller 1985; That Was Then... This Is Now 1985; The Stepfather 1986; Curse II: The Bite 1989; Cutting Class 1989; The Phantom of the Opera 1989; Popcorn 1991; There Goes My Baby 1994

Schoenaerts, Matthias (1977-) Bullhead 2011; Rust and Bone 2012; The Drop 2014; A Little Chaos 2014; Suite Française 2014; A Bigger Splash 2015; The Danish Girl 2015; Disorder 2015; Far from the Madding Crowd 2015

Schofield, Andrew Sid and Nancy 1986; Revengers Tragedy 2002; Under the Mud 2006

Schofield, Annabel (1963-) Dragonard 1987; Solar Crisis 1990

Schofield, David (1951-) An American Werewolf in London 1981; Tree of Hands 1988; Gladiator 2000; Chunky Monkey 2001; The Wolfman 2009; F 2010; Ghosted 2011; Last Passenger 2013

Schollin, Christina (1937-) Dear John 1964; Song of Norway 1970; Fanny and Alexander 1982

Scholz, Eva-Ingeborg (1926-) The Lost One 1951; The Devil's General 1955

Schombing, Jason Timecop 1994; Fatal Error 1999; Cool Money 2005

Schorm, Evald (1931-1988) The Party and the Guests 1966; The Joke 1968

Schrader, Maria (1965-) Aimée and Jaguar 1999; In Darkness 2011

Schram, Bitty A League of Their Own 1992; Caught 1996; The Pallbearer 1996

Schram, Jessy American Pie Presents the Naked Mile 2006; Unstoppable 2010

Schrecker, Frederick (1893-1976) Counterspy 1953; The Master Plan 1954

Schreiber, Avery (1934-2002) Swashbuckler 1976; Caveman 1981; Saturday the 14th Strikes Back 1988

Schreiber, Liev (1967-) Mixed Nuts 1994; Denise Calls Up 1995; Ransom 1996; Scream 1996; Walking and Talking 1996; Scream 2 1997; The Sunshine Boys 1997; The Daytrippers 1998; Phantoms 1998; Sphere 1998; Twilight 1998; The Hurricane 1999; Jakob the Liar 1999; RKO 281 1999; Scream 3 1999; A Walk on the Moon 1999; Hamlet 2000; Kate & Leopold 2002; The Sum of All Fears 2002; The Manchurian Candidate 2004; The Omen 2006; The Painted Veil 2006; Love in the Time of Cholera 2007; Defiance 2008; Taking Woodstock 2009; X-Men Origins: Wolverine 2009; Salt 2010; Goon 2011; Mental 2012; The Reluctant Fundamentalist 2012; Fading Gigolo 2013; The Last Days on Mars 2013; Spotlight 2015; The 5th Wave 2016

Schreiber, Pablo Nights in Rodanthe 2008; 13 Hours: the Secret Soldiers of Benghazi 2016

Schrier, Paul (1970-) Mighty Morphin Power Rangers: the Movie 1995; Turbo: a Power Rangers Adventure 1997

Schröder, Ernst aka **Schroeder, Ernst** (1915-1994) The Man Between 1953; The Counterfeit Traitor 1962

Schroder, Rick aka **Schroder, Ricky** (1970-) The Champ 1979; The Earthling 1980; The Last Flight of Noah's Ark 1980; Across the Tracks 1990; There Goes My Baby 1994; Murder at Devil's Glen 1999

Schroeder, Barbet (1941-) The Boulangère de Monceau 1962; Les Carabiniers 1963; Paris Vu Par... 1965; Celine and Julie Go Boating 1974

Schub, Steven Little Noises 1992; Caught 1996; The Thirteenth Floor 1999

Schubert, Karin (1944-) Delusions of Grandeur 1971; Bluebeard 1972

Schuck, John (1940-) Brewster McCloud 1970; McCabe and Mrs Miller 1971; Thieves like Us 1974; Butch and Sundance: the Early Days 1979; Outrageous Fortune 1987; Holy Matrimony 1994

Schull, Amanda Center Stage 2000; Sorority Wars 2009; Imaginary Friend 2012

Schull, Rebecca My Life 1993; Mortal Fear 1994

Schultz, Dwight (1947-) Alone in the Dark 1982; The A-Team 1983; Shadow Makers 1989; The Long Walk Home 1990; The Temp 1993; Star Trek: First Contact 1996; The A-Team 2010

Schulze, Matt (1972-) The Transporter 2002; Torque 2003; Out of Reach 2004; The Flock 2007

Schulze, Paul Laws of Gravity 1992; Hand gun 1994; Rambo 2007

Schumann, Erik (1924-2007) Lili Marleen 1980; Veronika Voss 1982

Schündler, Rudolf (1906-1988) Kings of the Road 1976; Suspiria 1976

Schünzel, Reinhold (1886-1954) The Threepenny Opera 1931; Notorious 1946; Golden Earrings 1947

Schwartz, Scott (1968-) The Toy 1982; A Christmas Story 1983; Fear 1988

Schwartzman, Jason (1980-) Rushmore 1998; Slackers 2001; SIMØNE 2002; Spun 2002; I ❤ Huckabees 2004; Bewitched 2005; Marie Antoinette 2005; Shopgirl 2005; The Darjeeling Limited 2007; Fantastic Mr Fox 2009; Funny People 2009; Scott Pilgrim vs the World 2010; Moonrise Kingdom 2012; Saving Mr Banks 2013; Big Eyes 2014; Listen Up Philip 2014; The Overnight 2015

Schwarz, Jessica The Door 2009; When Santa Fell to Earth 2011

Schwarzenegger, Arnold aka **Strong, Arnold** (1947-) Hercules in New York 1969; Pumping Iron 1976; Stay Hungry 1976; Cactus Jack 1979; The Jayne Mansfield Story 1980; Conan the Barbarian 1982; Conan the Destroyer 1984; The Terminator 1984; Commando 1985; Red Sonja 1985; Raw Deal 1986; Predator 1987; The Running Man 1987; Red Heat 1988; Twins 1988; Kindergarten Cop 1990; Total Recall 1990; Terminator 2: Judgment Day 1991; Last Action Hero 1993; Junior 1994; True Lies 1994; Eraser 1996; Jingle All the Way 1996; Batman and Robin 1997; End of Days 1999; The 6th Day 2000; Collateral Damage 2001; Terminator 3: Rise of the Machines 2003; Around the World in 80 Days 2004; The Expendables 2010; The Expendables 2 2012; Escape Plan 2013; The Last Stand 2013; Sabotage 2013; The Expendables 3 2014; Maggie 2015; Terminator: Genisys 2015

Schweig, Eric (1967-) The Last of the Mohicans 1992; Pontiac Moon 1994; Squanto: the Last Great Warrior 1994; Tom and Huck 1995; Big Eden 2000; The Missing 2003

Schweiger, Til (1963-) The Most Desired Man 1994; Judas Kiss 1998; The Replacement Killers 1998; Driven 2001; Joe and Max 2002; Deuce Bigalow: European Gigolo 2005; The Red Baron 2008; Inglourious Basterds 2009; This Means War 2012

Schwimmer, David (1966-) The Pallbearer 1996; Apt Pupil 1997; Breast Men 1997; Kissing a Fool 1998; Since You've Been Gone 1998; Six Days Seven Nights 1998; Picking Up the Pieces 2000; Hotel 2001; Madagascar 2005; Big Nothing 2006; Madagascar: Escape 2 Africa 2008; The Iceman 2012; Madagascar 3: Europe's Most Wanted 2012

Schwimmer, Rusty Jason Goes to Hell: the Final Friday 1993; A Little Princess 1995; North Country 2005

Schygulla, Hanna (1943-) Gods of the Plague 1969; Love Is Colder than Death 1969; Beware of a Holy Whore 1970; Whity 1970; Why Does Herr R Run Amok? 1970; The Merchant of Four Seasons 1971; The Bitter Tears of Petra von Kant 1972; Effi Briest 1974; The Marriage of Maria Braun 1978; The Third Generation 1979; Berlin Alexanderplatz 1980; Lili Marleen 1980; Circle of Deceit 1981; Passion 1982; La Nuit de Varennes 1983; Storia di Piera 1983; The Delta Force 1986; Forever Lulu 1987; Dead Again 1991; The Girl of Your Dreams 1998; Werckmeister Harmonies 2000; The Edge of Heaven 2007

Scianna, Francesco Baaria 2009; Angels of Evil 2010; The Price of Desire 2015

Sciorra, Annabella (1964-) True Love 1989; Cadillac Man 1990; Reversal of Fortune 1990; The Hard Way 1991; Jungle Fever 1991; The Hand That Rocks the Cradle 1992; Mr Wonderful 1992; Romeo Is Bleeding 1992; Whispers in the Dark 1992; The Night We Never Met 1993; The Addiction 1994; The Cure 1995; The Innocent Sleep 1995; The Funeral 1996; Cop Land 1997; Little City 1997; Mr Jealousy 1997; New Rose Hotel 1998; What Dreams May Come 1998; Above Suspicion 2000; Chasing Liberty 2004; Identity Theft: the Michelle Brown Story 2004; Twelve and Holding 2005; Find Me Guilty 2006

Scob, Edith (1937-) Eyes without a Face 1959; Thérèse Desqueyroux 1962; Judex 1963; The Milky Way 1968; Comédie de l'Innocence 2000; Vidocq 2001; Summer Hours 2008; Holy Motors 2012; Things to Come 2016

Scodelario, Kaya (1992-) Moon 2008; Shank 2010; Wuthering Heights 2011; Now Is Good 2012; Twenty8k 2012; The Maze Runner 2014; Maze Runner: The Scorch Trials 2015; Pirates of the Caribbean: Dead Men Tell No Tales 2017

Scofield, Paul (1922-2008) That Lady 1955; Carve Her Name with Pride 1958; The Train 1964; A Man for All Seasons 1966; Tell Me Lies 1967; King Lear 1970; Bartleby 1971; A Delicate Balance 1973; Scorpio 1973; Nineteen Nineteen 1984; Anna Karenina 1985; Mr Corbett's Ghost 1986; The Attic: the Hiding of Anne Frank 1988; Henry V 1989; When the Whales Came 1989; Hamlet 1990; Utz 1992; London 1994; Quiz Show 1994; The Crucible 1996; The Little Riders 1996; Robinson in Space 1997; Animal Farm 1999; Kurosawa 2001

Scoggins, Tracy (1959-) Timebomb 1991; A Crack in the Floor 2000

Scolari, Peter (1954-) Ticks 1993; The Polar Express 2004

Scorsese, Martin (1942-) Cannonball 1976; Taxi Driver 1976; The King of Comedy 1983; Akira Kurosawa's Dreams 1990; The Grifters 1990; Guilty by Suspicion 1990; Search and Destroy 1995; Bringing Out the Dead 1999; Gangs of New York 2002; Easy Riders, Raging Bulls 2003; Shark Tale 2004; Shine a Light 2007; Cameraman: the Life & Work of Jack Cardiff 2010; Corman's World: Exploits of a Hollywood Rebel 2011; Side by Side 2012; Seduced and Abandoned 2013; Life Itself 2014; Hitchcock Truffaut 2015

Scorupco, Izabella (1970-) GoldenEye 1995; Vertical Limit 2000; Reign of Fire 2001; Exorcist: the Beginning 2004

Scott Thomas, Kristin (1960-) Under the Cherry Moon 1986; A Handful of Dust 1987; The Tenth Man 1988; The Bachelor 1990; Spymaker: the Secret Life of Ian Fleming 1990; Autobus 1991;

Bitter Moon 1992; Four Weddings and a Funeral 1994; An Unforgettable Summer 1994; Angels and Insects 1995; The Confessional 1995; Richard III 1995; The English Patient 1996; Microcosmos 1996; Mission: Impossible 1996; The Revengers' Comedies 1997; The Horse Whisperer 1998; Up at the Villa 1999; Random Hearts 1999; Gosford Park 2001; Life as a House 2001; Petites Coupures 2002; Arsène Lupin 2004; Chromophobia 2005; Keeping Mum 2005; Tell No One 2006; The Walker 2006; Easy Virtue 2008; I've Loved You So Long 2008; Largo Winch 2008; Leaving 2008; The Other Boleyn Girl 2008; Confessions of a Shopaholic 2009; Bel Ami 2010; In Your Hands 2010; Love Crime 2010; Nowhere Boy 2010; Sarah's Key 2010; Salmon Fishing in the Yemen 2011; The Woman in the Fifth 2011; In the House 2012; Only Human 2012; Before the Winter Chill 2013; The Invisible Woman 2013; My Old Lady 2014; Suite Française 2014

Scott Thomas, Serena (1961-) Let Him Have It 1991; Relax... It's Just Sex 1998; Hostage 2004; William & Kate 2011

Scott, Adam (1973-) High Crimes 2002; Torque 2003; The Matador 2005; Monster-in-Law 2005; The Return 2006; Step Brothers 2008; Leap Year 2010; Piranha 2010; Friends with Kids 2011; The Guilt Trip 2013; The Secret Life of Walter Mitty 2013; Hot Tub Time Machine 2 2014; Krampus 2015; The Overnight 2015; Sleeping with Other People 2015

Scott (1), Alex The Sicilians 1964; Darling 1965; Fahrenheit 451 1966; The Abominable Dr Phibes 1971; The Asphyx 1972

Scott (2), Alex Sky Pirates 1986; Romper Stomper 1992

Scott, Andrew (1976-) Nora 1999; Dead Bodies 2003; The Stag 2013; Locke 2014; Pride 2014; Victor Frankenstein 2015; Denial 2016

Scott, Ashley (1977-) Walking Tall 2004; Into the Blue 2005; Lost 2005; 12 Rounds 2008

Scott, Brenda Johnny Tiger 1966; Journey to Shiloh 1967

Scott, Campbell (1962-) Longtime Companion 1990; The Sheltering Sky 1990; Dead Again 1991; Dying Young 1991; Singles 1992; The Innocent 1993; Mrs Parker and the Vicious Circle 1994; Let It Be Me 1995; Big Night 1996; The Spanish Prisoner 1997; The Daytrippers 1998; Hi-Life 1998; The Impostors 1998; Roger Dodger 2002; The Secret Lives of Dentists 2003; Saint Ralph 2004; Duma 2005; The Exorcism of Emily Rose 2005; Music and Lyrics 2007; The Amazing Spider-Man 2 2014

Scott, Donovan (1946-) Zorro, the Gay Blade 1981; Savannah Smiles 1982; Police Academy 1984; Sheena 1984; The Best of Times 1986

Scott, Douglas (1925-1988) And So They Were Married 1936; The Last Gangster 1937; Intermezzo 1939

Scott, Dougray (1965-) Another 9½ Weeks 1997; Regeneration 1997; Twin Town 1997; Ever After: a Cinderella Story 1998; Gregory's Two Girls 1999; Mission: Impossible 2 1999; This Year's Love 1999; Enigma 2001; The Boy David Story 2002; Ripley's Game 2002; One Last Chance 2003; To Kill a King 2003; Things to Do before You're 30 2004; The Truth about Love 2004; Dark Water 2005; Perfect Creature 2005; Hitman 2007; New Town Killers 2009; Loves Kitchen 2010; My Week with Marilyn 2011; A Thousand Kisses Deep 2011; Last Passenger 2013; Taken 3 2014; The Vatican Tapes 2015

Scott, George C (1927-1999) Anatomy of a Murder 1959; The Hanging Tree 1959; The Hustler 1961; Dr Strangelove, or How I Learned to Stop Worrying and Love the Bomb 1963; The List of Adrian Messenger 1963; The Yellow Rolls-Royce 1964; The Bible... in the Beginning 1966; Not with My Wife, You Don't! 1966; The Flim-Flam Man 1967; Petulia 1968; Jane Eyre 1970; Patton 1970; The Hospital 1971; The Last Run 1971; They Might Be Giants 1971; The New Centurions 1972; Rage 1972; The Day of the Dolphin 1973; Oklahoma Crude 1973; Bank Shot 1974; The Savage Is Loose 1974; Fear on Trial 1975; The Hindenburg 1975; Islands in the Stream 1976; The Prince and the Pauper 1977; Movie Movie 1978; Hardcore 1979; The Changeling 1980; The Formula 1980; Taps 1981; Oliver Twist 1982; A Christmas Carol 1984; Firestarter 1984; The Exorcist III 1990; The Rescuers Down Under 1990; Malice 1993; Angus 1995; 12 Angry Men

1997; Gloria 1998; Inherit the Wind 1999

Scott, Gordon (1926-2007) Tarzan and the Lost Safari 1956; Tarzan and the Trappers 1958; Tarzan's Fight for Life 1958; Tarzan's Greatest Adventure 1959; Tarzan the Magnificent 1960; Duel of the Titans 1961

Scott, Jacqueline Macabre 1958; Duel 1971; Charley Varrick 1973; Empire of the Ants 1977

Scott, Janette (1938-) No Place for Jennifer 1949; No Highway 1951; Background 1953; As Long as They're Happy 1955; The Good Companions 1956; Happy Is the Bride 1957; His and Hers 1960; School for Scoundrels 1960; Double Bunk 1961; Two and Two Make Six 1961; The Day of the Triffids 1962; The Old Dark House 1963; Paranoiac 1963; The Siege of the Saxons 1963; The Beauty Jungle 1964; Crack in the World 1964

Scott, Judith My Brother Tom 2001; Guess Who 2005

Scott, Kathryn Leigh (1933-) House of Dark Shadows 1970; Witches' Brew 1979

Scott (1), Ken (1928-1986) Beloved Infidel 1959; Woman Obsessed 1959; Desire in the Dust 1960; The Fiercest Heart 1961; The Second Time Around 1961

Scott, Kimberly The Abyss 1989; Downtown 1990; Flatliners 1990

Scott, Larry B (1961-) A Hero Ain't Nothin' but a Sandwich 1978; Revenge of the Nerds 1984; That Was Then... This Is Now 1985; SpaceCamp 1986; Fear of a Black Hat 1992

Scott, Lizabeth (1922-2015) The Strange Love of Martha Ivers 1946; Dead Reckoning 1947; Desert Fury 1947; I Walk Alone 1947; Pitfall 1948; Easy Living 1949; The Company She Keeps 1950; Dark City 1950; Paid in Full 1950; The Racket 1951; Red Mountain 1951; Stolen Face 1952; Scared Stiff 1953; Bad for Each Other 1954; Silver Lode 1954; Loving You 1957; Pulp 1972

Scott, Margaretta (1912-2005) Things to Come 1936; The Return of the Scarlet Pimpernel 1937; The Girl in the News 1940; Fanny by Gaslight 1944; The Man from Morocco 1944; Calling Paul Temple 1948; Counterblast 1948; The Scamp 1957; Crescendo 1970

Scott, Martha (1914-2003) The Howards of Virginia 1940; Our Town 1940; Cheers for Miss Bishop 1941; One Foot in Heaven 1941; They Dare Not Love 1941; War of the Wildcats 1943; So Well Remembered 1947; The Desperate Hours 1955; Sayonara 1957; Ben-Hur 1959; Charlotte's Web 1973; The Turning Point 1977; Adam 1983

Scott, Pippa (1935-) My Six Loves 1962; Petulia 1968

Scott, Randolph (1898-1987) Island of Lost Souls 1932; Murders in the Zoo 1933; Supernatural 1933; Roberta 1935; She 1935; So Red the Rose 1935; Village Tale 1935; Follow the Fleet 1936; Go West, Young Man 1936; The Last of the Mohicans 1936; High, Wide and Handsome 1937; Rebecca of Sunnybrook Farm 1938; The Texans 1938; Frontier Marshal 1939; Jesse James 1939; Susannah of the Mounties 1939; My Favorite Wife 1940; Virginia City 1940; When the Daltons Rode 1940; Belle Starr 1941; Paris Calling 1941; Western Union 1941; Pittsburgh 1942; The Spoilers 1942; To the Shores of Tripoli 1942; Bombardier 1943; Corvette K-225 1943; The Desperadoes 1943; Gung Ho! 1943; Belle of the Yukon 1944; Follow the Boys 1944; Abilene Town 1945; Captain Kidd 1945; China Sky 1945; Badman's Territory 1946; Home Sweet Homicide 1946; Christmas Eve 1947; Trail Street 1947; Coroner Creek 1948; Return of the Bad Men 1948; Fighting Man of the Plains 1949; The Walking Hills 1949; The Cariboo Trail 1950; Colt .45 1950; Fort Worth 1951; Man in the Saddle 1951; Santa Fe 1951; Sugarfoot 1951; Carson City 1952; Hangman's Knot 1952; The Man behind the Gun 1953; Thunder over the Plains 1953; The Bounty Hunter 1954; Riding Shotgun 1954; A Lawless Street 1955; Rage at Dawn 1955; Tall Man Riding 1955; Ten Wanted Men 1955; Seven Men from Now 1956; 7th Cavalry 1956; Decision at Sundown 1957; Shoot-Out at Medicine Bend 1957; The Tall T 1957; Buchanan Rides Alone 1958; Ride Lonesome 1959; Westbound 1959; Comanche Station 1960; Ride the High Country 1962

Scott, Seann William aka Scott, Seann W (1976-) American Pie 1999; Dude, Where's My Car? 2000; Final Destination 2000; Road Trip 2000; American Pie 2 2001; Evolution 2001;

Jay and Silent Bob Strike Back 2001; Bulletproof Monk 2002; Stark Raving Mad 2002; American Pie: the Wedding 2003; Old School 2003; Welcome to the Jungle 2003; The Dukes of Hazzard 2005; Southland Tales 2005; Ice Age: the Meltdown 2006; Mr Woodcock 2007; Role Models 2008; Ice Age 3: Dawn of the Dinosaurs 2009; Planet 51 2009; Cop Out 2010; Goon 2011; American Reunion 2012; Ice Age: Collision Course 2016

Scott, Terry (1927-1994) The Night We Got the Bird 1960; What a Whopper! 1961; Carry On Up the Khyber 1968; Carry On Camping 1969; Carry On Loving 1970; Carry On Up the Jungle 1970; Carry On Henry 1971; Bless This House 1972; Carry On Matron 1972

Scott, Tom Everett (1970-) That Thing You Do! 1996; An American Werewolf in Paris 1997; Dead Man on Campus 1998; One True Thing 1998; The Love Letter 1999; Attraction 2000; Boiler Room 2000; Surrender Dorothy 2006; Because I Said So 2007; Race to Witch Mountain 2009; The Devil's Teardrop 2010; Parental Guidance 2012; Enemies Closer 2013

Scott, William Lee (1973-) Before Women Had Wings 1997; The Opposite of Sex 1998; October Sky 1999; The Butterfly Effect 2003; Identity 2003

Scott, Zachary (1914-1965) The Mask of Dimitrios 1944; Mildred Pierce 1945; The Southerner 1945; Cass Timberlane 1947; The Unfaithful 1947; Ruthless 1948; Flamingo Road 1949; South of St Louis 1949; Born to Be Bad 1950; Colt .45 1950; Pretty Baby 1950; Let's Make It Legal 1951; Lightning Strikes Twice 1951; The Secret of Convict Lake 1951; Appointment in Honduras 1953; Bandido 1956; The Young One 1960; It'$ Only Money 1962

Scotti, Vito (1918-1996) Master of the World 1961; Cactus Flower 1969; The Aristocats 1970; When the Legends Die 1972

Scoular, Angela (1945-2011) Here We Go round the Mulberry Bush 1967; Doctor in Trouble 1970

Scourby, Alexander (1913-1985) Affair in Trinidad 1952; The Big Heat 1953; The Glory Brigade 1953; The Redhead from Wyoming 1953; The Silver Chalice 1954; Me and the Colonel 1958; The Shaggy Dog 1959; Seven Thieves 1960; The Devil at Four o'Clock 1961

Scrimm, Angus (1926-2016) Phantasm 1978; Phantasm II 1988; Transylvania Twist 1989; Subspecies 1991; Munchie Strikes Back 1994; Wishmaster 1997

Seacat, Sandra The Golden Seal 1983; Country 1984

Seaforth, Susan (1943-) Gunfight at Comanche Creek 1964; Billie 1965

Seagal, Steven (1951-) Nico 1988; Hard to Kill 1989; Marked for Death 1990; Out for Justice 1991; Under Siege 1992; On Deadly Ground 1994; Under Siege 2 1995; Executive Decision 1996; The Glimmer Man 1996; Fire Down Below 1997; Exit Wounds 2001; Ticker 2001; Half Past Dead 2002; Belly of the Beast 2003; The Foreigner 2003; Out for a Kill 2003; Out of Reach 2004; Today You Die 2005; Attack Force 2006; Mercenary for Justice 2006; Shadow Man 2006; Flight of Fury 2007; Renegade Justice 2007; Kill Switch 2008; Pistol Whipped 2008; A Dangerous Man 2009; Driven to Kill 2009; The Keeper 2009; Born to Raise Hell 2010; Machete 2010; A Good Man 2014

Seagrove, Jenny (1958-) Local Hero 1983; Savage Islands 1983; Appointment with Death 1988; A Chorus of Disapproval 1988; The Guardian 1990; Don't Go Breaking My Heart 1999

Seal, Elizabeth (1933-) Town on Trial 1956; Cone of Silence 1960

Seale, Douglas (1913-1999) Ernest Saves Christmas 1988; Almost an Angel 1990; Aladdin 1992

Seales, Franklyn (1952-1990) The Onion Field 1979; Southern Comfort 1981

Sealy-Smith, Alison You Kill Me 2007; Accidental Friendship 2008

Searcy, Nick (1959-) Nell 1994; Cast Away 2000; Head of State 2003; Runaway Jury 2003; Timber Falls 2007

Searle, Jackie aka Searl, Jackie aka Searl, Jack (1921-1991) Huckleberry Finn 1931; Skippy 1931; Topaze 1933; Murder on the Blackboard 1934; No Greater Glory 1934; That Certain Age 1938; The Paleface 1948

Sears, Ann (1933-1992) Cat and Mouse 1958; The Brain 1962

Sears, Heather (1935-1994) Dry Rot 1956; The Story of Esther Costello 1957; Room at the Top 1958; Sons and Lovers 1960; The Phantom of the Opera 1962; Saturday Night Out 1963; The Black Torment 1964

Seay, James (1914-1992) Miracle on 34th Street 1947; Close to My Heart 1951; Return to Treasure Island 1954; The Amazing Colossal Man 1957; Beginning of the End 1957

Sebanek, Josef (1915-1977) A Blonde in Love 1965; The Firemen's Ball 1967

Sebastian, Dorothy (1906-1957) Our Dancing Daughters 1928; The Single Standard 1929; Spite Marriage 1929; The Arizona Kid 1939

Seberg, Jean (1938-1979) Saint Joan 1957; Bonjour Tristesse 1958; A Bout de Souffle 1959; The Mouse That Roared 1959; Let No Man Write My Epitaph 1960; In the French Style 1963; Lilith 1964; A Fine Madness 1966; The Looters 1966; Moment to Moment 1966; The Road to Corinth 1967; Paint Your Wagon 1969; Pendulum 1969; Airport 1970; Kill! 1972

Secombe, Harry (1921-2001) Penny Points to Paradise 1951; Down among the Z-Men 1952; Forces' Sweetheart 1953; Davy 1958; Jet Storm 1959; Oliver! 1968; The Bed Sitting Room 1969; Doctor in Trouble 1970; Song of Norway 1970; The Magnificent Seven Deadly Sins 1971; Sunstruck 1972

Secor, Kyle (1958-) Inherit the Wind 1988; Heart of Dixie 1989; Late for Dinner 1991; Sleeping with the Enemy 1991; Untamed Heart 1993; Drop Zone 1994

Seda, Jon (1970-) Gladiator 1992; I Like It like That 1994; Twelve Monkeys 1995; Dear God 1996; Sunchaser 1996; Selena 1997; Price of Glory 2000; Undisputed 2002

Sedan, Rolfe (1896-1982) The Iron Mask 1929; The Story of Vernon and Irene Castle 1939

Sedaris, Amy (1961-) Commandments 1996; Six Days Seven Nights 1998; Chicken Little 2005; Dance Flick 2009; Jennifer's Body 2009; Puss in Boots 2011

Seddon, Margaret (1872-1968) Smilin' Through 1932; The Worst Woman in Paris? 1933; The Meanest Man in the World 1943

Sedgwick, Edie (1943-1971) Vinyl 1965; The Chelsea Girls 1966; Ciao! Manhattan 1973

Sedgwick, Kyra (1965-) Tai-Pan 1986; Kansas 1988; Born on the Fourth of July 1989; Mr and Mrs Bridge 1990; Pyrates 1991; Miss Rose White 1992; Singles 1992; Heart and Souls 1993; The Low Life 1995; Something to Talk About 1995; Phenomenon 1996; Critical Care 1997; Montana 1997; What's Cooking? 2000; Personal Velocity 2001; Door to Door 2002; Just a Kiss 2002; Secondhand Lions 2003; The Woodsman 2004; The Game Plan 2007; Gamer 2008; Man on a Ledge 2012; The Possession 2012; Time out of Mind 2014; Cop Car 2015

Seely, Tim Please Turn Over 1960; Mutiny on the Bounty 1962

Segado, Alberto I, the Worst of All 1990; We Don't Want to Talk about It 1993

Segal, George (1934-) The Young Doctors 1961; Act One 1963; Invitation to a Gunfighter 1964; King Rat 1965; Ship of Fools 1965; The Quiller Memorandum 1966; Who's Afraid of Virginia Woolf? 1966; The St Valentine's Day Massacre 1967; Bye Bye Braverman 1968; No Way to Treat a Lady 1968; The Bridge at Remagen 1969; The Southern Star 1969; Loving 1970; The Owl and the Pussycat 1970; Where's Poppa? 1970; Born to Win 1971; The Hot Rock 1972; Blume in Love 1973; A Touch of Class 1973; California Split 1974; The Terminal Man 1974; The Black Bird 1975; The Duchess and the Dirtwater Fox 1976; Fun with Dick and Jane 1977; Rollercoaster 1977; Who Is Killing the Great Chefs of Europe? 1978; Lost and Found 1979; The Last Married Couple in America 1980; Carbon Copy 1981; Stick 1985; All's Fair 1989; Look Who's Talking 1989; For the Boys 1991; Look Who's Talking Now! 1993; Seasons of the Heart 1994; The Babysitter 1995; The Cable Guy 1996; Flirting with Disaster 1996; It's My Party 1996; The Mirror Has Two Faces 1996; Fielder's Choice 2005; Love & Other Drugs 2010; The Tale of the Princess Kaguya 2013

Segal, Zohra aka Sehgal, Zohra (1912-2014) Masala 1991; Bhaji on the Beach 1993; Dillagi 1999; Chicken Tikka Masala 2005; Cheeni Kum 2007

Segall, Pamela (1968-) Willy/Milly 1986; After Midnight 1989; Say

Anything... 1989; Gate II 1992; ...At First Sight 1995; Bed of Roses 1995; Recess: School's Out 2001

Segan, Noah Brick 2005; Looper 2012

Segel, Jason (1980-) SLC Punk! 1999; Slackers 2001; Knocked Up 2007; Forgetting Sarah Marshall 2008; I Love You, Man 2008; Despicable Me 2010; Gulliver's Travels 2010; Bad Teacher 2011; Jeff, Who Lives at Home 2011; The Muppets 2011; The Five-Year Engagement 2012; This Is 40 2012; Sex Tape 2014; The End of the Tour 2015

Segura, Santiago (1965-) The Day of the Beast 1995; Perdita Durango 1997; Girl from Rio 2001

Seigner, Emmanuelle (1966-) Detective 1985; Frantic 1988; Bitter Moon 1992; Nirvana 1996; Place Vendôme 1998; Buddy Boy 1999; The Ninth Gate 1999; Berlin 2007; The Diving-Bell and the Butterfly 2007; La Vie en Rose 2007; Essential Killing 2010; In the House 2012; Venus in Fur 2013

Seigner, Françoise L'Enfant Sauvage 1970; Les Misérables 1982

Seigner, Mathilde (1968-) Venus Beauty Institute 1998; Harry, He's Here to Help 2000; Betty Fisher and Other Stories 2001; The Girl from Paris 2001

Seimetz, Amy The Sacrament 2013; Upstream Color 2013

Seiphemo, Rapulana Tarzan and the Lost City 1998; Tsotsi 2005; Gangster's Paradise: Jerusalema 2008

Seitz, John (1937-2005) Call Me 1988; Forced March 1989; Blood and Wine 1996

Sekka, Johnny (1934-2006) Flame in the Streets 1961; East of Sudan 1964; Woman of Straw 1964; Khartoum 1966; The Last Safari 1967; Incense for the Damned 1970; A Warm December 1973

Selby, David (1941-) Night of Dark Shadows 1971; Up the Sandbox 1972; The Super Cops 1973; Rich Kids 1979; Raise the Titanic 1980; Rich and Famous 1981; Dying Young 1991; D3: the Mighty Ducks 1996

Selby, Nicholas (1925-2011) A Midsummer Night's Dream 1969; Macbeth 1971

Selby, Sarah aka Selby, Sara (1905-1980) Beyond the Forest 1949; Tower of London 1962

Selby, Tony (1938-) In Search of Gregory 1970; Adolf Hitler - My Part in His Downfall 1972

Seldes, Marian (1928-2014) Crime and Punishment, USA 1959; Fingers 1978; Tom and Huck 1995; Digging to China 1998; The Haunting 1999; Town & Country 2001; Ballets Russes 2005

Sellars, Elizabeth (1923-) Floodtide 1949; Cloudburst 1951; Night Was Our Friend 1951; The Gentle Gunman 1952; Hunted 1952; The Long Memory 1952; Three Cases of Murder 1953; The Barefoot Contessa 1954; Desiree 1954; Forbidden Cargo 1954; Prince of Players 1955; The Man in the Sky 1956; The Shiralee 1957; Law and Disorder 1958; The Day They Robbed the Bank of England 1960; Never Let Go 1960; The Chalk Garden 1964; The Mummy's Shroud 1966; The Hireling 1973

Selleck, Tom (1945-) Myra Breckinridge 1970; Daughters of Satan 1972; Terminal Island 1973; Coma 1977; The Gypsy Warriors 1978; Divorce Wars 1982; High Road to China 1983; Lassiter 1984; Three Men and a Baby 1987; Her Alibi 1989; An Innocent Man 1989; Quigley Down Under 1990; Three Men and a Little Lady 1990; Christopher Columbus: the Discovery 1992; Folks! 1992; Mr Baseball 1992; Broken Trust 1995; In & Out 1997; The Love Letter 1999; Monte Walsh 2003; Ike: Countdown to D-Day 2004; Stone Cold 2005; Meet the Robinsons 2006; Killers 2010

Sellers, Peter (1925-1980) Penny Points to Paradise 1951; Down among the Z-Men 1952; Orders Are Orders 1954; The Case of the Mukkinese Battle Horn 1955; John and Julie 1955; The Ladykillers 1955; The Naked Truth 1957; The Smallest Show on Earth 1957; Carlton-Browne of the FO 1958; tom thumb 1958; Up the Creek 1958; I'm All Right Jack 1959; The Mouse That Roared 1959; The Running, Jumping and Standing Still Film 1959; The Battle of the Sexes 1960; The Millionairess 1960; Never Let Go 1960; Two Way Stretch 1960; Lolita 1961; Mr Topaze 1961; Only Two Can Play 1961; The Road to Hong Kong 1962; Trial and Error 1962; Waltz of the Toreadors 1962; The Wrong Arm of the Law 1962; Dr Strangelove, or How I Learned to Stop Worrying and Love the Bomb 1963; Heavens Above! 1963; The Pink Panther 1963; A Shot in the Dark 1964; The World of Henry Orient 1964;

What's New, Pussycat? 1965; After the Fox 1966; The Wrong Box 1966; The Bobo 1967; Casino Royale 1967; Woman Times Seven 1967; I Love You, Alice B Toklas 1968; The Party 1968; The Magic Christian 1969; Hoffman 1970; Simon, Simon 1970; There's a Girl in My Soup 1970; Where Does It Hurt? 1971; Alice's Adventures in Wonderland 1972; The Blockhouse 1973; Ghost in the Noonday Sun 1973; The Optimists of Nine Elms 1973; Soft Beds, Hard Battles 1973; The Great McGonagall 1974; The Return of the Pink Panther 1974; Murder by Death 1976; The Pink Panther Strikes Again 1976; Revenge of the Pink Panther 1978; Being There 1979; The Prisoner of Zenda 1979; The Fiendish Plot of Dr Fu Manchu 1980; Trail of the Pink Panther 1982

Sellon, Charles aka **Sellon, Charles A** (1870-1937) The Monster 1925; The Saturday Night Kid 1929; Make Me a Star 1932; Bright Eyes 1934; It's a Gift 1934; In Old Kentucky 1935

Selten, Morton (1850-1939) Moscow Nights 1935; Fire over England 1937; The Divorce of Lady X 1938; Shipyard Sally 1939; The Thief of Bagdad 1940

Selwyn, Ruth (1905-1954) Polly of the Circus 1932; Speak Easily 1932

Selzer, Milton (1918-2006) Marnie 1964; The Legend of Lylah Clare 1968; Miss Rose White 1992

Semmelrogge, Wil y (1923-1984) The Enigma of Kaspar Hauser 1974; Woyzeck 1978

Semon, Larry (1889-1928) The Wizard of Oz 1925; Underworld 1927

Sen, Aparna (1945-) The Guru 1969; Bombay Talkie 1970; The Middleman 1975; Hullabaloo over Georgie and Bonnie's Pictures 1979

Sen, Gita (1930-) And Quiet Rolls the Dawn 1979; In Search of Famine 1980

Sen, Raima Chokher Bali 2003; Parineeta 2005; Manorama Six Feet Under 2007

Sen, Reema Gangs of Wasseypur 2012; Gangs of Wasseypur II 2012

Senda, Koreya (1904-1994) Gate of Hell 1953; The H-Man 1954

Seneca, Joe (1914-1996) Crossroads 1986; School Daze 1988; Mississippi Masala 1991; The Saint of Fort Washington 1993; Freedom Road: the Vernon Johns Story 1994

Sengoku, Noriko (1922-2012) Drunken Angel 1948; Scandal 1950

Sennett, Mack (1880-1960) Abbott and Costello Meet the Keystone Cops 1955; The Great Chase 1961

Serafinowicz, Peter (1972-) Sixty Six 2006; Killing Bono 2010

Serato, Massimo (1916-1989) The Man from Cairo 1953; The Loves of Three Queens 1954; El Cid 1961; Constantine and the Cross 1961; Pontius Pilate 1961; The Tenth Victim 1965; Don't Look Now 1973

Serbedzija, Rade aka **Sherbedgia, Rade** (1946-) Before the Rain 1994; The Saint 1997; The Truce 1997; Mighty Joe Young 1998; Polish Wedding 1998; Eyes Wide Shut 1999; Stigmata 1999; Snatch 2000; South Pacific 2001; The Quiet American 2002; Quicksand 2003; The Eye 2008; Quarantine 2008; Shun Li and the Poet 2011; Taken 2 2012

Serious, Yahoo (1954-) Young Einstein 1988; Reckless Kelly 1993

Serkis, Andy (1964-) Career Girls 1997; Stella Does Tricks 1997; Among Giants 1998; Mojo 1998; Pandaemonium 2000; Shiner 2000; The Lord of the Rings: The Fellowship of the Ring 2001; 24 Hour Party People 2001; Deathwatch 2002; The Escapist 2002; The Lord of the Rings: The Two Towers 2002; The Lord of the Rings: The Return of the King 2003; 13 Going on 30 2004; King Kong 2005; Flushed Away 2006; The Prestige 2006; Extraordinary Rendition 2007; Inkheart 2007; Sugarhouse 2007; The Cottage 2008; Sex & Drugs & Rock & Roll 2009; Animals United 2010; Brighton Rock 2010; Burke & Hare 2010; The Adventures of Tintin: the Secret of the Unicorn 2011; Rise of the Planet of the Apes 2011; Wild Bill 2011; The Hobbit: an Unexpected Journey 2012; Dawn of the Planet of the Apes 2014; Star Wars Episode VII: the Force Awakens 2015; War for the Planet of the Apes 2017; Black Panther 2018; Jungle Book: Origins 2018

Serna, Assumpta (1957-) Lola 1986; Matador 1986; I, the Worst of All 1990; Wild Orchid 1990; Nostradamus 1993; The Shooter 1994

Serna, Pepe (1944-) Shoot Out 1971; Vice Squad 1982; Bad Jim 1989; The Rookie 1990; American Me 1992

Sernas, Jacques aka **Sernas, Jack** (1925-2015) Golden Salamander 1949;

Helen of Troy 1955; Duel of the Titans 1961

Serra, Raymond aka **Serra, Ray** (1931-2003) Alphabet City 1984; Safe Men 1998

Serrano, Julieta (1933-) Dark Habits 1983; Matador 1986; Women on the Verge of a Nervous Breakdown 1988; Tie Me Up! Tie Me Down! 1990

Serrano, Nestor (1957-) Brenda Starr 1989; Hangin' with the Homeboys 1991; Bad Boys 1995; After the Storm 2001; Empire 2002; Act of Valor 2012

Serrault, Michel (1928-2007) Les Diaboliques 1954; King of Hearts 1966; Get Out Your Handkerchiefs 1977; La Cage aux Folles 1978; Buffet Froid 1979; La Cage aux Folles II 1980; Garde à Vue 1981; La Cage aux Folles III: "Elles" Se Marient 1985; Docteur Petiot 1990; The Old Lady Who Walked in the Sea 1991; Le Bonheur Est dans le Pré 1995; Nelly & Monsieur Arnaud 1995; Beaumarchais l'Insolent 1996; Artemisia 1997; Rien Ne Va Plus 1997; The Children of the Marshland 1998; Le Libertin 2000; The Girl from Paris 2001

Servais, Jean (1910-1976) Angèle 1934; Rififi 1955; Celui Qui Doit Mourir 1957; La Fièvre Monte à el Pao 1959; That Man from Rio 1964; Thomas the Imposter 1964; They Came to Rob Las Vegas 1968

Servillo, Toni The Consequences of Love 2004; Il Divo 2008; Gomorrah 2008; The Great Beauty 2013

Sesay, Mo Young Soul Rebels 1991; Bhaji on the Beach 1993

Sessions, John (1953-) The Bounty 1984; Sweet Revenge 1990; The Pope Must Die 1991; Freddie as FRO7 1992; Princess Caraboo 1994; In the Bleak Midwinter 1995; The Adventures of Pinocchio 1996; The Scarlet Tunic 1997; A Midsummer Night's Dream 1999; One of the Hollywood Ten 2000; High Heels and Low Lifes 2001; Five Children and It 2004; Stella Street 2004; William Shakespeare's The Merchant of Venice 2004; Rag Tale 2005; Made in Dagenham 2010; Pudsey the Dog: the Movie 2014; The Silent Storm 2014; Loving Vincent 2016

Seth, Roshan (1942-) Gandhi 1982; Indiana Jones and the Temple of Doom 1984; My Beautiful Launderette 1985; Little Dorrit 1987; Not without My Daughter 1990; London Kills Me 1991; Mississippi Masala 1991; Electric Moon 1992; Solitaire for 2 1994; Street Fighter 1994; The Journey 1997; Bombay Boys 1998; Such a Long Journey 1998; Frozen 2004; Proof 2005; Trishna 2011; City of Tiny Lights 2016

Seton, Bruce (1909-1969) Love from a Stranger 1936; Sweeney Todd, the Demon Barber of Fleet Street 1936; The Green Cockatoo 1937; The Curse of the Wraydons 1946; The Blue Lamp 1949; Whisky Galore! 1949; The Cruel Sea 1952; Eight o'Clock Walk 1953; The Crooked Sky 1957; Undercover Girl 1957; Life in Danger 1959; Gorgo 1961

Settle, Matthew (1969-) Attraction 2000; The In Crowd 2000; The Mystery of Natalie Wood 2004; A Place Called Home 2004; Beneath 2007

Séty, Gérard (1922-1998) Les Espions 1957; Montparnasse 19 1958; Van Gogh 1991

Sevani, Adam G Step Up 2 the Streets 2008; Step Up 3 2010; LOL 2011; Step Up: All In 2014

Severance, Joan (1958-) See No Evil, Hear No Evil 1989; Bird on a Wire 1990; Lake Consequence 1992; The Last Seduction 2 1998

Severn, Christopher (1935-) Mrs Miniver 1942; The Man from Down Under 1943

Severn, Raymond (1932-1994) We Are Not Alone 1939; The Suspect 1944

Sevier, Corey Student Seduction 2003; CodeBreakers 2005; Age of the Dragons 2010

Sevigny, Chloë aka **Sevigny, Chloe** (1974-) kids 1995; Trees Lounge 1996; Gummo 1997; The Last Days of Disco 1998; Palmetto 1998; Boys Don't Cry 1999; julien donkey-boy 1999; A Map of the World 1999; American Psycho 2000; If These Walls Could Talk 2 2000; Demonlover 2002; Ten Minutes Older: the Trumpet 2002; The Brown Bunny 2003; Dogville 2003; Party Monster 2003; Shattered Glass 2003; Melinda and Melinda 2004; Broken Flowers 2005; Zodiac 2007; My Son, My Son, What Have Ye Done 2009; Mr Nice 2010; Love & Friendship 2016

Sevilla, Carmen (1930-) King of Kings 1961; Antony and Cleopatra 1972

Sewell, George (1924-2007) Sparrows Can't Sing 1962; Kaleidoscope 1966; The Vengeance of She 1968

Sewell, Rufus (1967-) Twenty-One 1991; Dirty Weekend 1992; A Man of No Importance 1994; Carrington 1995; Victory 1995; Hamlet 1996; Dangerous Beauty 1997; Martha - Meet Frank, Daniel and Laurence 1997; The Woodlanders 1997; Dark City 1998; Bless the Child 2000; A Knight's Tale 2001; She Creature 2001; Extreme Ops 2003; The Illusionist 2005; The Legend of Zorro 2005; Tristan + Isolde 2005; Amazing Grace 2006; The Holiday 2006; Vinyan 2008; The Tourist 2010; Abraham Lincoln: Vampire Hunter 2012; All Things to All Men 2012; The Sea 2013; Hercules 2014

Sexton III, Brendan aka **Sexton Jr, Brendan** (1980-) Welcome to the Dollhouse 1995; Hurricane Streets 1997; Desert Blue 1998; Pecker 1998; Boys Don't Cry 1999; Session 9 2001

Seydoux, Léa (1985-) Lourdes 2009; Mission: Impossible - Ghost Protocol 2011; Sister 2012; Blue Is the Warmest Colour 2013; Grand Central 2013; Saint Laurent 2014; The Lobster 2015; Spectre 2015

Seyferth, Wilfried aka **Seyfert, Wilfried** (1908-1954) Decision before Dawn 1951; The Devil Makes Three 1952

Seyfried, Amanda (1985-) Mamma Mia! 2008; Boogie Woogie 2009; Chloe 2009; Jennifer's Body 2009; Dear John 2010; Letters to Juliet 2010; In Time 2011; Red Riding Hood 2011; Gone 2012; Les Misérables 2012; The Big Wedding 2013; Epic 2013; Lovelace 2013; A Million Ways to Die in the West 2014; While We're Young 2014; Christmas with the Coopers 2015; Fathers and Daughters 2015; Pan 2015; Ted 2 2015

Seyler, Athene (1889-1990) Blossom Time 1934; Moscow Nights 1935; Quiet Wedding 1940; The Franchise Affair 1950; Young Wives' Tale 1951; Made in Heaven 1952; Treasure Hunt 1952; The Beggar's Opera 1953; Campbell's Kingdom 1957; Happy Is the Bride 1957; How to Murder a Rich Uncle 1957; Night of the Demon 1957; A Tale of Two Cities 1957; The Inn of the Sixth Happiness 1958; Make Mine Mink 1960; Two and Two Make Six 1961; The Girl on the Boat 1962; I Thank a Fool 1962; Satan Never Sleeps 1962; Nurse on Wheels 1963

Seymour, Anne (1909-1988) All the King's Men 1949; The Gift of Love 1958; All the Fine Young Cannibals 1960; The Subterraneans 1960; Good Neighbor Sam 1964; Where Love Has Gone 1964; Blindfold 1966; Triumphs of a Man Called Horse 1983; Trancers 1985

Seymour, Cara (1964-) Silent Grace 2001; Adaptation. 2002; Hotel Rwanda 2004; The Notorious Bettie Page 2005; The Savages 2007; Beyond the Fire 2008; An Education 2008; I Origins 2014

Seymour, Carolyn (1947-) Gumshoe 1971; Unman, Wittering and Zigo 1971; The Ruling Class 1972; Steptoe and Son 1972; The Bitch 1979

Seymour, Dan (1915-1993) A Night in Casablanca 1946; The Searching Wind 1946; Intrigue 1947; Johnny Belinda 1948; Face to Face 1952; Abbott and Costello Meet the Mummy 1955; Return of the Fly 1959

Seymour (1), Jane (1898-1956) Back Door to Heaven 1939; Remember the Day 1941; Tom, Dick and Harry 1941

Seymour (2), Jane (1951-) Frankenstein: the True Story 1973; Live and Let Die 1973; Sinbad and the Eye of the Tiger 1977; Battlestar Galactica 1978; The Four Feathers 1978; Somewhere in Time 1980; The Scarlet Pimpernel 1982; Lassiter 1984; Head Office 1986; Wedding Crashers 2005; Austenland 2013; Fifty Shades of Black 2016

Seymour, Ralph Just before Dawn 1980; Killer Party 1986

Seyrig, Delphine (1932-1990) Pull My Daisy 1959; Last Year at Marienbad 1961; Muriel 1963; Accident 1967; The Milky Way 1968; Stolen Kisses 1968; Daughters of Darkness 1970; The Magic Donkey 1970; The Discreet Charm of the Bourgeoisie 1972; The Day of the Jackal 1973; A Doll's House 1973; The Black Windmill 1974; India Song 1975; Jeanne Dielman, 23 Quai du Commerce, 1080 Bruxelles 1975; Golden Eighties 1986

Seyvecou, Sabrina Secret Things 2002; Cockles & Muscles 2004; Born in 68: We'll Love Each Other until Death Do Us Part 2008

Shadix, Glenn (1952-2010) Heathers 1989; Bingo 1991; Meet the Applegates 1991; Demolition Man 1993; The Nightmare before Christmas 1993; Dunston Checks In 1996

Shadley, Will The Spy Next Door 2009; Love Will Keep Us Together 2010

Shah, Amit The Infidel 2010; The Hundred-Foot Journey 2014

Shah, Naseeruddin (1950-) Nishant 1975; Junoon 1978; Mirch Masala 1987; The Perfect Murder 1988; Electric Moon 1992; Bombay Boys 1998; Such a Long Journey 1998; Monsoon Wedding 2001; The League of Extraordinary Gentlemen 2003; Being Cyrus 2005; Ishqiya 2010

Shah, Satish Saathiya 2002; Kuch Naa Kaho 2003; Mujhse Shaadi Karogi 2004

Shakur, Tupac (1971-1996) Juice 1991; Poetic Justice 1993; Above the Rim 1994; Bullet 1995; Gridlock'd 1996; Gang Related 1997

Shalhoub, Tony (1953-) Barton Fink 1991; IQ 1994; Big Night 1996; Men in Black 1997; A Civil Action 1998; Paulie 1998; The Siege 1998; Galaxy Quest 1999; Impostor 2001; The Man Who Wasn't There 2001; SPYkids 2001; Thir13en Ghosts 2001; Life or Something like It 2002; Men in Black 2 2002; Against the Ropes 2003; The Last Shot 2004; Cars 2006; 1408 2007; How Do You Know 2010; Cars 2 2011; Pain & Gain 2013

Shamata, Chuck aka **Shamata, Charles** Running 1979; Scanners 1980; The Devil and Max Devlin 1981; Between Friends 1983; The Two Mr Kissels 2008

Shandling, Garry (1949-2016) Love Affair 1994; Mixed Nuts 1994; Hurlyburly 1998; What Planet Are You From? 2000; Town & Country 2001; Over the Hedge 2006; Trust the Man 2006; Iron Man 2 2010

Shane, Paul (1940-2013) La Passione 1996; Heartlands 2002

Shankar, Mamata And Quiet Rolls the Dawn 1979; An Enemy of the People 1989; The Stranger 1991

Shanks, Don aka **Shanks, Donald L** (1950-) Halloween 5: the Revenge of Michael Myers 1989; Spirit of the Eagle 1991

Shannon, Frank (1874-1959) Flash Gordon 1936; The Texas Rangers 1936

Shannon, Harry (1890-1964) Once upon a Honeymoon 1942; The Yellow Rose of Texas 1944; The Devil Thumbs a Ride 1947; Mr Blandings Builds His Dream House 1948; Tulsa 1949; Cry of the Hunted 1953; Witness to Murder 1954; The Tall Men 1955; Written on the Wind 1956; Gypsy 1962

Shannon, Michael aka **Shannon, Mike** (1974-) Cecil B Demented 2000; Grand Theft Parsons 2003; Kangaroo Jack 2003; Dead Birds 2004; The Woodsman 2004; Bug 2006; World Trade Center 2006; Shotgun Stories 2007; Revolutionary Road 2008; The Greatest 2009; My Son, My Son, What Have Ye Done 2009; Jonah Hex 2010; The Runaways 2010; 13 2010; Machine Gun Preacher 2011; Return 2011; Take Shelter 2011; The Iceman 2012; Mud 2012; Premium Rush 2012; Man of Steel 2013; Bad Land: Road to Fury 2014; 99 Homes 2014; They Came Together 2014; Freeheld 2015; Midnight Special 2015; Elvis & Nixon 2016; Loving 2016

Shannon, Molly (1964-) Analyze This 1999; Never Been Kissed 1999; Superstar 1999; The Grinch 2000; Serendipity 2001; Good Boy! 2003; The Twelve Days of Christmas Eve 2004; Little Man 2006; Talladega Nights: the Ballad of Ricky Bobby 2006; Year of the Dog 2007; Igor 2008; Life after Beth 2014

Shannon, Peggy (1910-1941) Deluge 1933; The Case of the Lucky Legs 1935; The House across the Bay 1940

Shannon, Polly (1973-) Lie with Me 2005; Victor 2008; Concrete Canyons 2010

Shannon, Richard (1920-1989) Arrowhead 1953; The Bridges at Toko-Ri 1954; Beau James 1957

Shannon, Vicellous Reon (1981-) The Hurricane 1999; Freedom Song 2000

Shapiro, Helen It's Trad, Dad 1961; A Little of What You Fancy 1968

Shaps, Cyril (1923-2003) Passport to Shame 1958; The Pursuers 1961; Operation Daybreak 1975; The Lost Son 1998; The Clandestine Marriage 1999

Sharian, John Death Machine 1994; The Machinist 2004; WAZ 2006

Sharif, Omar (1932-2015) Lawrence of Arabia 1962; Behold a Pale Horse 1964; The Fall of the Roman Empire 1964;

The Yellow Rolls-Royce 1964; Doctor Zhivago 1965; The Night of the Generals 1966; The Poppy Is Also a Flower 1966; More than a Miracle 1967; The Appointment 1968; Funny Girl 1968; Mayerling 1968; Che! 1969; Mackenna's Gold 1969; The Burglars 1971; The Horsemen 1971; The Last Valley 1971; Juggernaut 1974; The Tamarind Seed 1974; Funny Lady 1975; Crime and Passion 1976; Ashanti 1979; Bloodline 1979; The Baltimore Bullet 1980; Green Ice 1981; Top Secret! 1984; The Rainbow Thief 1990; Mrs 'arris Goes to Paris 1992; The 13th Warrior 1999; Hidalgo 2003; Monsieur Ibrahim and the Flowers of the Koran 2003; 10,000 BC 2008

Sharkey, Billy Ray Dudes 1987; After Midnight 1989

Sharkey, Ray (1952-1993) The Lords of Flatbush 1974; Who'll Stop the Rain? 1978; Heart Beat 1979; The Idolmaker 1980; Willie and Phil 1980; Love and Money 1982; Regina 1982; No Mercy 1986; Wise Guys 1986; Private Investigations 1987; Scenes from the Class Struggle In Beverly Hills 1989; Wired 1989; Round Trip to Heaven 1992; Zebrahead 1992; Cop and a Half 1993

Sharma, Romesh Siddhartha 1972; Hum 1991

Sharma, Suraj Life of Pi 2012; Million Dollar Arm 2014

Sharp, Anthony (1915-1984) Gawain and the Green Knight 1973; House of Mortal Sin 1975

Sharp, Lesley Rita, Sue and Bob Too 1986; Close My Eyes 1991; Naked 1993; Priest 1994; The Full Monty 1997

Sharp, Timm Stark Raving Mad 2002; King of the Ants 2003

Sharpe, Albert (1885-1970) Portrait of Jennie 1948; The Return of October 1948; Up in Central Park 1948; Adventure in Baltimore 1949; Royal Wedding 1951; Face to Face 1952; Brigadoon 1954; Darby O'Gill and the Little People 1959; The Day They Robbed the Bank of England 1960

Sharpe, Cornelia (1947-) Serpico 1973; Open Season 1974; The Reincarnation of Peter Proud 1975; The Next Man 1976; Venom 1981

Sharpe, Edith (1870-1968) Old Mother Riley 1937; The Guinea Pig 1948; Landfall 1949; Happy Is the Bride 1957; A French Mistress 1960; Satan Never Sleeps 1962

Sharpe, Karen (1934-) Man with the Gun 1955; The Disorderly Orderly 1964

Sharrett, Michael (1965-) The Magic of Lassie 1978; Deadly Friend 1986

Shatner, William (1931-) The Brothers Karamazov 1958; The Intruder 1961; Judgment at Nuremberg 1961; The Outrage 1964; Incubus 1965; White Comanche 1968; The Hound of the Baskervilles 1972; Big Bad Mama 1974; The Devil's Rain 1975; Impulse 1975; Kingdom of the Spiders 1977; Star Trek: the Motion Picture 1979; The Kidnapping of the President 1980; Airplane II: the Sequel 1982; Star Trek II: the Wrath of Khan 1982; Star Trek III: the Search for Spock 1984; Star Trek IV: the Voyage Home 1986; Star Trek V: the Final Frontier 1989; Star Trek VI: the Undiscovered Country 1991; National Lampoon's Loaded Weapon 1 1993; Star Trek: Generations 1994; Free Enterprise 1998; Miss Congeniality 2000; Osmosis Jones 2001; American Psycho II: All American Girl 2002; Showtime 2002; A Carol Christmas 2003; Miss Congeniality 2: Armed & Fabulous 2005; Over the Hedge 2006; The Wild 2006; Fanboys 2008; Escape from Planet Earth 2013

Shaughnessy, Charles (1955-) Barbara Taylor Bradford's Everything to Gain 1996; The Wishing Well 2009

Shaughnessy, Mickey (1920-1985) Last of the Comanches 1952; Conquest of Space 1955; The Burglar 1956; Designing Woman 1957; Jailhouse Rock 1957; Gunman's Walk 1958; A Nice Little Bank That Should Be Robbed 1958; The Sheepman 1958; Don't Give Up the Ship 1959; Edge of Eternity 1959; The Adventures of Huckleberry Finn 1960; North to Alaska 1960; The Boatniks 1970

Shaver, Helen (1951-) Outrageous! 1977; In Praise of Older Women 1978; The Amityville Horror 1979; The Osterman Weekend 1983; Best Defense 1984; Desert Hearts 1985; The Color of Money 1986; The Believers 1987; The Land before Time 1988; Tree of Hands 1988; Bethune: the Making of a Hero 1990; That Night 1992; Born to Be Wild 1995; Open Season 1995; Tremors II: Aftershocks 1995; DC Sniper: 23 Days of Fear 2003; The Keeper 2003

Shaw, Alonna Double Impact 1991; Cyborg Cop 1993

Shaw, Anabel aka **Shaw, Annabel** (1921-2010) Bulldog Drummond Strikes Back 1947; Dangerous Years 1947; Gun Crazy 1949

Shaw, Denis aka **Shaw, Dennis** (1921-1971) House of Blackmail 1953; Who Done It? 1956; Passport to Shame 1958; Beyond the Curtain 1960

Shaw, Fiona (1958-) Mountains of the Moon 1989; My Left Foot 1989; Three Men and a Little Lady 1990; London Kills Me 1991; Super Mario Bros 1993; Undercover Blues 1993; Persuasion 1995; Jane Eyre 1996; Anna Karenina 1997; The Butcher Boy 1997; The Avengers 1998; The Last September 1999; RKO 281 1999; Harry Potter and the Philosopher's Stone 2001; Harry Potter and the Chamber of Secrets 2002; The Black Dahlia 2006; Catch and Release 2007; Fracture 2007; Harry Potter and the Order of the Phoenix 2007; Dorian Gray 2009; The Tree of Life 2010; The English Teacher 2013

Shaw, Martin (1945-) Macbeth 1971; The Golden Voyage of Sinbad 1973; Operation Daybreak 1975; The Hound of the Baskervilles 1983

Shaw, Oscar (1887-1967) The Cocoanuts 1929; Rhythm on the River 1940

Shaw (1), Peter (1918-2003) Clive of India 1935; Sons of the Sea 1939

Shaw, Reta (1912-1982) The Pajama Game 1957; The Lady Takes a Flyer 1958; Mary Poppins 1964

Shaw, Richard (1920-2010) Booby Trap 1957; Man from Tangier 1957

Shaw, Robert (1927-1978) The Dam Busters 1954; A Hill in Korea 1956; Sea Fury 1958; Tomorrow at Ten 1962; The Caretaker 1963; From Russia with Love 1963; The Luck of Ginger Coffey 1964; Battle of the Bulge 1965; A Man for All Seasons 1966; Custer of the West 1967; The Birthday Party 1968; Battle of Britain 1969; The Royal Hunt of the Sun 1969; Figures in a Landscape 1970; A Town Called Hell 1971; Young Winston 1972; The Hireling 1973; A Reflection of Fear 1973; The Sting 1973; The Taking of Pelham One Two Three 1974; Diamonds 1975; Jaws 1975; Black Sunday 1976; End of the Game 1976; Robin and Marian 1976; Swashbuckler 1976; The Deep 1977; Force 10 from Navarone 1978; Avalanche Express 1979

Shaw, Sebastian (1905-1994) Men Are Not Gods 1936; The Squeaker 1937; The Spy in Black 1939; East of Piccadilly 1940; The Glass Mountain 1949; Landfall 1949; Laxdale Hall 1953; It Happened Here 1963; Star Wars Episode VI: Return of the Jedi 1983; High Season 1987

Shaw, Stan (1952-) The Boys in Company C 1978; The Great Santini 1979; Tough Enough 1982; Harlem Nights 1989; The Court-Martial of Jackie Robinson 1990; Fried Green Tomatoes at the Whistle Stop Cafe 1991; Body of Evidence 1992; Rising Sun 1993; CutThroat Island 1995; Snake Eyes 1998

Shaw, Susan (1929-1978) It Always Rains on Sunday 1947; Here Come the Huggetts 1948; It's Not Cricket 1948; London Belongs to Me 1948; Quartet 1948; Vote for Huggett 1948; The Huggetts Abroad 1949; Train of Events 1949; Pool of London 1950; Waterfront 1950; The Woman in Question 1950; There Is Another Sun 1951; Stock Car 1955; Fire Maidens from Outer Space 1956; Davy 1958

Shaw, Victoria (1935-1988) The Eddy Duchin Story 1956; The Crimson Kimono 1959; Edge of Eternity 1959; Because They're Young 1960; I Aim at the Stars 1960; Alvarez Kelly 1966; Westworld 1973

Shaw, Vinessa (1976-) Ladybugs 1992; Hocus Pocus 1993; LA without a Map 1998; Eyes Wide Shut 1999; Corky Romano 2001; 40 Days and 40 Nights 2002; The Hills Have Eyes 2006; Two Lovers 2008; Big Miracle 2012; Come Out and Play 2012; Side Effects 2013; Cold in July 2014

Shaw, Winifred (1910-1982) Front Page Woman 1935; Gold Diggers of 1935 1935; The Case of the Velvet Claws 1936; Satan Met a Lady 1936; Smart Blonde 1936

Shawkat, Alia (1989-) Deck the Halls 2006; Whip It 2009; The Runaways 2010; Cedar Rapids 2011; Night Moves 2013; The To Do List 2013; Green Room 2015

Shawlee, Joan (1926-1987) Francis Joins the WACS 1954; Some Like It Hot 1959; The Apartment 1960; Buddy Buddy 1981

Shawn, Dick (1923-1987) The Wizard of Baghdad 1960; It's a Mad Mad Mad Mad World 1963; Penelope 1966; What Did You Do in the War, Daddy? 1966; The Producers 1968; Evil Roy Slade 1971; Love at First Bite 1979; Angel 1984; Beer 1985; Water 1985; Maid to Order 1987

Shawn, Wallace (1943-) Manhattan 1979; Simon 1980; My Dinner with Andre 1981; Strange Invaders 1983; The Hotel New Hampshire 1984; Micki & Maude 1984; Catholic Boys 1985; Head Office 1986; The Bedroom Window 1987; Prick Up Your Ears 1987; The Princess Bride 1987; The Moderns 1988; Scenes from the Class Struggle in Beverly Hills 1989; We're No Angels 1989; The Magic Bubble 1992; Mom and Dad Save the World 1992; The Cemetery Club 1993; Vanya on 42nd Street 1994; Clueless 1995; A Goofy Movie 1995; Toy Story 1995; House Arrest 1996; Critical Care 1997; My Favorite Martian 1999; Toy Story 2 1999; The Prime Gig 2000; The Curse of the Jade Scorpion 2001; Personal Velocity 2001; The Haunted Mansion 2003; Our House 2003; The Incredibles 2004; Melinda and Melinda 2004; Chicken Little 2005; Happily N'Ever After 2006; Capitalism: a Love Story 2009; Toy Story 3 2010; Admission 2013; The Double 2013

Shay, John (1915-2010) The Cry Baby Killer 1958; Roadracers 1958

Shaye, Lin (1943-) There's Something about Mary 1998; Contagion 2001; Boat Trip 2002; Dead End 2003; A Cinderella Story 2004; The Hillside Strangler 2004; Insidious 2010; Big Ass Spider 2013; Insidious: Chapter 2 2013; The Signal 2014; Insidious: Chapter 3 2015

Shayne, Konstantin (1888-1974) Till We Meet Again 1944; The Secret Life of Walter Mitty 1947; Vertigo 1958

Shayne, Robert (1900-1992) Mr Skeffington 1944; Christmas in Connecticut 1945; Three Strangers 1946; Let's Live a Little 1948; Indestructible Man 1956

Shayne, Tamara (1902-1983) The Jolson Story 1946; Romanoff and Juliet 1961

Shea, Eric (1960-) Ace Eli and Rodger of the Skies 1973; The Castaway Cowboy 1974

Shea, John (1948-) Missing 1981; Windy City 1984; Light Years 1988; A New Life 1988; Stealing Home 1988; Honey, I Blew Up the Kid 1992; Hard Evidence 1994; Forgotten Sins 1996; The Adventures of Sebastian Cole 1998; The March Sisters at Christmas 2012

Sheard, Michael (1938-2005) England Made Me 1973; The Riddle of the Sands 1978; All Quiet on the Western Front 1979; Green Ice 1981

Shearer, Harry (1943-) Animalympics 1979; This Is Spinal Tap 1984; Pure Luck 1991; Godzilla 1997; Dick 1999; A Mighty Wind 2003; Chicken Little 2005; For Your Consideration 2006; The Simpsons Movie 2007

Shearer, Moira (1926-2006) The Red Shoes 1948; The Tales of Hoffmann 1951; The Story of Three Loves 1953; The Man Who Loved Redheads 1954; Peeping Tom 1960

Shearer, Norma (1900-1983) Way Down East 1920; He Who Gets Slapped 1924; The Student Prince in Old Heidelberg 1927; Hollywood Revue 1929; The Last of Mrs Cheyney 1929; The Divorcee 1930; A Free Soul 1931; Private Lives 1931; Strangers May Kiss 1931; Smilin' Through 1932; Strange Interlude 1932; The Barretts of Wimpole Street 1934; Riptide 1934; Romeo and Juliet 1936; Marie Antoinette 1938; Idiot's Delight 1939; The Women 1939; Escape 1940; Her Cardboard Lover 1942

Shearsmith, Reece The League of Gentlemen's Apocalypse 2005; The Cottage 2008; A Field in England 2013

Sheedy, Ally (1962-) Bad Boys 1983; WarGames 1983; Oxford Blues 1984; The Breakfast Club 1985; St Elmo's Fire 1985; Twice in a Lifetime 1985; Blue City 1986; Short Circuit 1986; Maid to Order 1987; Heart of Dixie 1989; Betsy's Wedding 1990; Only the Lonely 1991; Man's Best Friend 1993; Before the Night 1995; Jailbreak 1997; High Art 1998; Our Guys: Outrage in Glen Ridge 1999; Sugar Town 1999; Life during Wartime 2009; Welcome to the Rileys 2009; Client Seduction 2014

Sheehan, Robert (1988-) Cherrybomb 2008; Killing Bono 2010; Season of the Witch 2010; A Turtle's Tale: Sammy's Adventures 2010; Demons Never Die 2011; The Mortal Instruments: City of Bones 2013; The Messenger 2015; Geostorm 2016

Sheen, Charlie aka **Sheen, Charles** aka **Estevez, Carlos** (1965-) The Execution of Private Slovik 1974; Red Dawn 1984; The Boys Next Door 1985; Out of the Darkness 1985; Ferris Bueller's Day Off 1986; Lucas 1986; Platoon 1986; The Wraith 1986; No Man's Land 1987; Three for the Road 1987; Wall Street 1987; Eight Men Out 1988; Young Guns 1988; Catchfire 1989; Courage Mountain 1989; Major League 1989; Men at Work 1990; Navy SEALs 1990; The Rookie 1990; Hot Shots! 1991; Stockade 1991; Hot Shots! Part Deux 1993; The Three Musketeers 1993; The Chase 1994; Major League II 1994; Terminal Velocity 1994; The Arrival 1996; Shadow Conspiracy 1996; Money Talks 1997; Under Pressure 1997; Free Money 1998; No Code of Conduct 1998; Being John Malkovich 1999; Postmortem 1999; Rated X 2000; Good Advice 2001; Scary Movie 3 2003; The Big Bounce 2004; Scary Movie 4 2006; Machete Kills 2013

Sheen, Martin (1940-) The Incident 1967; The Subject Was Roses 1968; Catch-22 1970; No Drums, No Bugles 1971; Rage 1972; Badlands 1973; The Execution of Private Slovik 1974; The Cassandra Crossing 1976; The Little Girl Who Lives Down the Lane 1976; Eagle's Wing 1978; Apocalypse Now 1979; The Final Countdown 1980; Loophole 1980; Enigma 1982; Gandhi 1982; That Championship Season 1982; The Dead Zone 1983; Man, Woman and Child 1983; Firestarter 1984; Out of the Darkness 1985; The Believers 1987; Siesta 1987; Wall Street 1987; Beyond the Stars 1988; Da 1988; Judgment in Berlin 1988; Cold Front 1989; Nightbreaker 1989; The Maid 1991; Stockade 1991; Running Wild 1992; Gettysburg 1993; Hear No Evil 1993; When the Bough Breaks 1993; Roswell 1994; The American President 1995; The Bomber Boys 1995; Dillinger and Capone 1995; Gospa 1995; Entertaining Angels: the Dorothy Day Story 1996; Hostile Waters 1996; Project ALF 1996; The War at Home 1996; Noose 1997; Spawn 1997; Truth or Consequences, NM 1997; No Code of Conduct 1998; Forget Me Never 1999; Lost & Found 1999; Storm 1999; O 2001; Catch Me If You Can 2002; Bobby 2006; The Departed 2006; Who Killed the Electric Car? 2006; Talk to Me 2007; Imagine That 2009; Love Happens 2009; The Way 2010; The Double 2011; Wrinkles 2011; The Amazing Spider-Man 2012; Salinger 2013; Trash 2014; Rules Don't Apply 2016

Sheen, Michael (1969-) Mary Reilly 1995; Othello 1995; Wilde 1997; The Four Feathers 2002; Heartlands 2002; Bright Young Things 2003; Laws of Attraction 2003; Timeline 2003; Underworld 2003; Kingdom of Heaven 2005; The League of Gentlemen's Apocalypse 2005; Blood Diamond 2006; The Queen 2006; Underworld: Evolution 2006; Frost/Nixon 2008; The Damned United 2009; My Last Five Girlfriends 2009; Underworld: Rise of the Lycans 2009; Alice in Wonderland 2010; Unthinkable 2010; Breaking Dawn Part One 2011; Midnight in Paris 2011; Resistance 2011; Breaking Dawn Part Two 2012; Gospel of Us 2012; Admission 2013; Attacking the Devil: Harold Evans and the Last Nazi War Crime 2014; Kill the Messenger 2014; Far from the Madding Crowd 2015; Alice through the Looking Glass 2016; Passengers 2016

Sheen, Ruth (1952-) High Hopes 1988; The Young Poisoner's Handbook 1994; All or Nothing 2002; Vera Drake 2004; Another Year 2010; Mr Turner 2014; SuperBob 2015

Sheffer, Craig (1960-) That Was Then... This Is Now 1985; Fire with Fire 1986; Some Kind of Wonderful 1987; Nightbreed 1990; A River Runs through It 1992; Fire in the Sky 1993; The Program 1993; Roadflower 1994; Sleep with Me 1994; Head above Water 1996; Bliss 1997; Miss Evers' Boys 1997; Merlin the Return 2000; Turbulence II: Fear of Flying 2000; Without Malice 2000

Sheffield, Jeremy (1966-) Creep 2004; The Wedding Date 2004; The Children 2008

Sheffield, Johnny aka **Sheffield, John** (1931-2010) Tarzan Finds a Son! 1939; Tarzan's Secret Treasure 1941; Tarzan's New York Adventure 1942; Tarzan Triumphs 1943; Tarzan's Desert Mystery 1943; Tarzan and the Amazons 1945; Tarzan and the Leopard Woman 1946; Tarzan and the Huntress 1947

Sheiner, David (1928-) The Odd Couple 1968; A Man Called Gannon 1969; Winning 1969; They Call Me Mister Tibbs! 1970; The Stone Killer 1973; The Big Brawl 1980; Blue Thunder 1983

Sheldon, Gene (1908-1982) Where Do We Go from Here? 1945; Golden Girl 1951; Three Ring Circus 1954; Toby Tyler, or Ten Weeks with a Circus 1960

Shellen, Stephen (1957-) The Stepfather 1986; Casual Sex? 1988; Damned River 1989; A River Runs through It 1992

Shelley, Barbara (1933-) Blood of the Vampire 1958; The Camp on Blood Island 1958; Bobbikins 1959; Village of the Damned 1960; Postman's Knock 1961; The Shadow of the Cat 1961; The Gorgon 1964; Dracula - Prince of Darkness 1965; Rasputin, the Mad Monk 1965; Quatermass and the Pit 1967

Shelley, Carole (1939-) The Odd Couple 1968; Little Noises 1992

Shelley, Norman (1903-1980) The Silver Darlings 1947; The Great Adventure 1953; Gulliver's Travels 1977

Shelley, Paul (1942-) Macbeth 1971; It Shouldn't Happen to a Vet 1979

Shelley, Rachel Lighthouse 1999; Lagaan: Once upon a Time in India 2001; The Children 2008

Shelly, Adrienne (1966-2006) The Unbelievable Truth 1989; Trust 1990; Stepkids 1992; Hexed 1993; Roadflower 1994; Sleep with Me 1994; Wrestling with Alligators 1998; Factotum (A Man Who Preforms Many Jobs) 2005; Waitress 2007

Shelton, Anne (1923-1994) King Arthur Was a Gentleman 1942; Bees in Paradise 1943; Miss London Ltd 1943

Shelton, Deborah (1952-) Body Double 1984; Hunk 1987; Nemesis 1993; Plughead Rewired: Circuitry Man II 1994

Shelton, John (1915-1972) Dr Kildare Goes Home 1940; The Ghost Comes Home 1940; A-Haunting We Will Go 1942; The Time of Their Lives 1946

Shelton, Joy (1922-2000) Bees in Paradise 1943; Millions like Us 1943; Waterloo Road 1944; No Room at the Inn 1948; A Case for PC 49 1950; Emergency Call 1952; Impulse 1955

Shelton, Marley (1974-) Warriors of Virtue 1996; The Bachelor 1999; Lured Innocence 1999; Bubble Boy 2001; Sugar & Spice 2001; Valentine 2001; Just a Kiss 2002; Grand Theft Parsons 2003; Uptown Girls 2003; Planet Terror 2007; A Perfect Getaway 2009

Shen, Parry Better Luck Tomorrow 2001; Hatchet 2006

Shenar, Paul (1936-1989) The Night that Panicked America 1975; The Secret of NIMH 1982; Dream Lover 1986; Raw Deal 1986; The Bedroom Window 1987; Best Seller 1987; Man on Fire 1987; The Big Blue 1988

Shenkman, Ben (1968-) Pi 1997; Roger Dodger 2002; Just like Heaven 2005; Then She Found Me 2007; Breathe In 2013; Concussion 2013

Shepard, Dax (1975-) Without a Paddle 2004; Zathura: a Space Adventure 2005; Employee of the Month 2006; Idiocracy 2006; Baby Mama 2008; Hit & Run 2012

Shepard, Hilary aka **Shepard Turner, Hilary** Peacemaker 1990; Scanner Cop 1994; Turbo: a Power Rangers Adventure 1997

Shepard, Jan King Creole 1958; Attack of the Giant Leeches 1960

Shepard, Jewel (1962-) Hollywood Hot Tubs 1984; Return of the Living Dead 1984

Shepard, Sam (1943-) Days of Heaven 1978; Resurrection 1980; Raggedy Man 1981; Frances 1982; The Right Stuff 1983; Country 1984; Fool for Love 1985; Crimes of the Heart 1986; Baby Boom 1987; Steel Magnolias 1989; Bright Angel 1990; Defenseless 1991; Voyager 1991; Thunderheart 1992; The Pelican Brief 1993; Safe Passage 1994; The Good Old Boys 1995; Curtain Call 1997; The Only Thrill 1997; Purgatory 1999; Snow Falling on Cedars 1999; Hamlet 2000; The Pledge 2000; Black Hawk Down 2001; Kurosawa 2001; Swordfish 2001; Leo 2002; Blind Horizon 2003; The Notebook 2003; Don't Come Knocking 2005; Stealth 2005; Charlotte's Web 2006; The Return 2006; The Assassination of Jesse James by the Coward Robert Ford 2007; Patti Smith: Dream of Life 2007; The Accidental Husband 2008; Felon 2008; Brothers 2009; Fair Game 2010; Blackthorn 2011; Mud 2012; Safe House 2012; Out of the Furnace 2013;

Cold in July 2014; Ithaca 2015; Midnight Special 2015

Shepeard, Jean aka **Shepherd, Jean** (1904-1989) Fame Is the Spur 1947; The Silver Darlings 1947

Shepherd, Cybill (1950-) The Last Picture Show 1971; The Heartbreak Kid 1972; Daisy Miller 1974; At Long Last Love 1975; Special Delivery 1976; Taxi Driver 1976; Silver Bears 1977; The Lady Vanishes 1979; Chances Are 1989; Alice 1990; Texasville 1990; Once upon a Crime 1992; Hard Luck 2006; Nora Roberts' High Noon 2009

Shepherd, Elizabeth (1936-) The Tomb of Ligeia 1964; Hell Boats 1970

Shepherd, Jack (1940-) All Neat in Black Stockings 1969; The Virgin Soldiers 1969; Escape from Sobibor 1987; The Object of Beauty 1991; Twenty-One 1991; Blue Black Permanent 1992; Blue Ice 1992; No Escape 1994; The Scarlet Tunic 1997; Wonderland 1999

Shepherd, John Friday the 13th: a New Beginning 1985; Thunder Run 1986

Shepherd, Sherri Precious (Base on Nol by Saf) (Based on the Novel "Push" by Sapphire) 2008; One for the Money 2012

Shepherd, Simon (1956-) Fire, Ice and Dynamite 1990; Wuthering Heights 1992

Shepherd, Steve John GMT Greenwich Mean Time 1998; Virtual Sexuality 1999; The Best Man 2005

Shepherd, Suzanne The Jerky Boys 1995; Lolita 1997; Living Out Loud 1998; A Dirty Shame 2004

Shepley, Michael (1907-1961) Lord Edgware Dies 1934; Lazybones 1935; Squibs 1935; The Great Mr Handel 1942; A Place of One's Own 1944; Mine Own Executioner 1947; Maytime in Mayfair 1949; Home at Seven 1952; Happy Ever After 1954

Sheppard, Morgan aka **Sheppard, W Morgan** aka **Sheppard, William Morgan** Hawk the Slayer 1980; The Keep 1983; Elvira, Mistress of the Dark 1988; Farewell Mr Kringle 2010

Sheppard, Paula (1957-) Alice, Sweet Alice 1977; Liquid Sky 1982

Sher, Antony (1949-) Shadey 1985; Erik the Viking 1989; The Young Poisoner's Handbook 1994; Alive and Kicking 1996; The Wind in the Willows 1996; Mrs Brown 1997; The Miracle Maker 1999; Churchill: the Hollywood Years 2004; Three and Out 2008; The Wolfman 2009

Sherbedgia, Rade The Fog 2005; Fugitive Pieces 2007

Shergill, Jimmy (1970-) Mohabbatein 2000; Hum Tum 2004; Eklavya: the Royal Guard 2007

Sheridan, Ann aka **Sheridan, Clara Lou** (1915-1967) Kiss and Make-Up 1934; Ladies Should Listen 1934; Mrs Wiggs of the Cabbage Patch 1934; Rumba 1935; The Black Legion 1937; San Quentin 1937; Angels with Dirty Faces 1938; Letter of Introduction 1938; Angels Wash Their Faces 1939; Dodge City 1939; Naughty but Nice 1939; They Made Me a Criminal 1939; Winter Carnival 1939; Castle on the Hudson 1940; City for Conquest 1940; It All Came True 1940; They Drive by Night 1940; Torrid Zone 1940; The Man Who Came to Dinner 1941; George Washington Slept Here 1942; Kings Row 1942; Edge of Darkness 1943; The Doughgirls 1944; Shine On, Harvest Moon 1944; Nora Prentiss 1947; The Unfaithful 1947; Good Sam 1948; Silver River 1948; I Was a Male War Bride 1949; Stella 1950; Appointment in Honduras 1953; Take Me to Town 1953; Come Next Spring 1956; The Opposite Sex 1956; The Woman and the Hunter 1957

Sheridan, Dinah (1920-2012) 29 Acacia Avenue 1945; The Hills of Donegal 1947; Calling Paul Temple 1948; The Huggetts Abroad 1949; Blackout 1950; No Trace 1950; Paul Temple's Triumph 1950; Where No Vultures Fly 1951; Appointment in London 1952; The Sound Barrier 1952; Genevieve 1953; The Story of Gilbert and Sullivan 1953; The Railway Children 1970

Sheridan, Frank (1869-1943) Danger Lights 1930; Washington Merry-Go-Round 1932

Sheridan, Jamey (1951-) Distant Thunder 1988; Shannon's Deal 1989; Stanley & Iris 1989; All I Want for Christmas 1991; Talent for the Game 1991; A Stranger among Us 1992; Whispers in the Dark 1992; Wild America 1997; Let the Devil Wear Black 1999; The Simian Line 2000; Life as a House 2001; Mea Maxima Culpa: Silence in the House of God 2012

Sheridan, Margaret (1926-1982) *The Thing from Another World* 1951; *One Minute to Zero* 1952; *I, the Jury* 1953; *The Diamond* 1954; *Pride of the Blue Grass* 1954

Sheridan, Nicollette (1963-) *The Sure Thing* 1985; *Formula for Death* 1995; *Spy Hard* 1996; *Beverly Hills Ninja* 1997; *Deadly Visions* 2004; *Code Name: the Cleaner* 2007; *Fly Me to the Moon* 2008; *Honeymoon for One* 2011

Sheridan, Tye (1995-) *Mud* 2012; *Joe* 2013; *Scouts Guide to the Zombie Apocalypse* 2015

Sherman, Geraldine (1944-) *Poor Cow* 1967; *Take a Girl like You* 1970; *There's a Girl in My Soup* 1970

Sherman, Hiram (1908-1989) *One Third of a Nation* 1939; *The Solid Gold Cadillac* 1956; *Mary, Mary* 1963

Sherman, Lowell (1885-1934) *Way Down East* 1920; *The Divine Woman* 1928; *Ladies of Leisure* 1930; *Mammy* 1930; *Bachelor Apartment* 1931; *What Price Hollywood?* 1932

Sherrill, David (1962-) *The Wraith* 1986; *Unhook the Stars* 1996

Sherwood, Madeleine (1922-2016) *Cat on a Hot Tin Roof* 1958; *Sweet Bird of Youth* 1962; *Pendulum* 1969

Sherwood, Robin *Tourist Trap* 1979; *Death Wish II* 1981

Shetty, Shefali aka **Shah, Shefali** *Monsoon Wedding* 2001; *WAQT: the Race against Time* 2005

Shetty, Shilpa (1975-) *Baazigar* 1993; *Life in a... METRO* 2007

Shetty, Sunil aka **Shetty, Suniel** (1961-) *Awara Paagal Deewana* 2002; *Hulchul* 2004; *Paheli* 2005

Sheybal, Vladek aka **Sheybal, Wladyslaw** (1923-1992) *Kanal* 1957; *Billion Dollar Brain* 1967; *Women in Love* 1969; *Puppet on a Chain* 1970; *The Boy Friend* 1971; *The Sellout* 1975; *The Wind and the Lion* 1975; *After Midnight* 1990

Shields, Arthur (1896-1970) *The Plough and the Stars* 1936; *Little Nellie Kelly* 1940; *Confirm or Deny* 1941; *The Gay Falcon* 1941; *The Man from Down Under* 1943; *The Corn Is Green* 1945; *Three Strangers* 1946; *The Verdict* 1946; *The Fabulous Dorseys* 1947; *The Fighting O'Flynn* 1948; *She Wore a Yellow Ribbon* 1949; *Tarzan and the Slave Girl* 1950; *Apache Drums* 1951; *The River* 1951; *Scandal at Scourie* 1953; *World for Ransom* 1953; *Pride of the Blue Grass* 1954; *Daughter of Dr Jekyll* 1957; *None but the Brave* 1960

Shields, Brooke (1965-) *Alice, Sweet Alice* 1977; *King of the Gypsies* 1978; *Pretty Baby* 1978; *Just You and Me, Kid* 1979; *Wanda Nevada* 1979; *The Blue Lagoon* 1980; *Endless Love* 1981; *Sahara* 1983; *Brenda Starr* 1989; *Backstreet Dreams* 1990; *Running Wild* 1992; *Freaked* 1993; *Freeway* 1996; *The Misadventures of Margaret* 1998; *The Bachelor* 1999; *Black and White* 1999; *The Midnight Meat Train* 2008; *Chalet Girl* 2010; *Furry Vengeance* 2010; *Mapplethorpe: Look at the Pictures* 2016

Shields, Malcolm *Death Defying Acts* 2007; *Crying with Laughter* 2009

Shiganoya, Benkei *Osaka Elegy* 1936; *Sisters of the Gion* 1936; *Story of the Late Chrysanthemums* 1939

Shigeta, James (1929-2014) *The Crimson Kimono* 1959; *Walk like a Dragon* 1960; *Bridge to the Sun* 1961; *Cry for Happy* 1961; *Flower Drum Song* 1961; *Paradise, Hawaiian Style* 1966; *Lost Horizon* 1973; *The Yakuza* 1975; *Die Hard* 1988; *Cage* 1989; *China Cry* 1990

Shillo, Michael (1920-2007) *Dunkirk* 1958; *The Whole Truth* 1958

Shim, Andrew *A Room for Romeo Brass* 1999; *This Is England* 2006

Shimada, Teru (1905-1988) *Tokyo Joe* 1949; *Battle of the Coral Sea* 1959; *You Only Live Twice* 1957

Shimell, William *Certified Copy* 2009; *Amour* 2012

Shimerman, Armin (1949-) *Single Santa Seeks Mrs Claus* 2004; *What the #$*! Do We Know!?* 2004; *Meet the Santas* 2005; *Ratchet & Clank* 2016

Shimizu, Masao (1908-1975) *The Life of Oharu* 1952; *Sansho the Bailiff* 1954; *Sanjuro* 1962

Shimizu, Misa (1970-) *The Eel* 1997; *Warm Water under a Red Bridge* 2001; *The Sea Is Watching* 2002

Shimkus, Joanna (1943-) *Paris Vu Par...* 1965; *The Adventurers* 1968; *Boom* 1968; *The Lost Man* 1969; *The Virgin and the Gypsy* 1970; *A Time for Loving* 1971

Shimono, Sab (1943-) *Come See the Paradise* 1990; *Teenage Mutant Ninja Turtles III* 1992; *Suture* 1993; *The Shadow* 1994; *The Big Hit* 1998

Shimura, Takashi (1905-1982) *Sanshiro Sugata* 1943; *Drunken Angel* 1948; *Stray Dog* 1949; *Rashomon* 1950; *Scandal* 1950; *The Idiot* 1951; *Ikiru* 1952; *Godzilla* 1954; *Seven Samurai* 1954; *I Live in Fear* 1955; *Throne of Blood* 1957; *The Hidden Fortress* 1958; *The Bad Sleep Well* 1960; *Sanjuro* 1962; *High and Low* 1963; *Ghidrah, the Three-Headed Monster* 1965

Shin Ha-gyun (1960-) *Sympathy for Mr Vengeance* 2002; *Save the Green Planet!* 2003; *Thirst* 2009

Shindo, Eitaro (1899-1977) *Osaka Elegy* 1936; *Sisters of the Gion* 1936; *The Crucified Lovers* 1954; *Sansho the Bailiff* 1954; *Street of Shame* 1955

Shiner, Ronald (1903-1966) *Doctor's Orders* 1934; *Old Bill and Son* 1940; *South American George* 1941; *Bees in Paradise* 1943; *George in Civvy Street* 1946; *The Man Within* 1947; *Innocents in Paris* 1953; *Top of the Form* 1953; *Dry Rot* 1956; *Not Wanted on Voyage* 1957; *The Navy Lark* 1959; *Operation Bullshine* 1959; *The Night We Got the Bird* 1960

Shingler, Helen *Quiet Weekend* 1946; *The Silver Darlings* 1947; *The Lady with the Lamp* 1951

Shioya, Toshi *Blood Oath* 1990; *Mr Baseball* 1992

Shipka, Kiernan *Carriers* 2008; *When Marnie Was There* 2014

Shipp, John Wesley (1956-) *The NeverEnding Story II: the Next Chapter* 1991; *Soft Deceit* 1994

Shirakawa, Yumi (1936-) *The H-Man* 1954; *Rodan* 1956; *The End of Summer* 1961

Shire, Talia aka **Coppola, Talia** (1946-) *The Wild Racers* 1968; *The Dunwich Horror* 1970; *Gas-s-s-s, or It Became Necessary to Destroy the World in Order to Save It* 1970; *The Outside Man* 1973; *The Godfather Part II* 1974; *Rocky* 1976; *Kill Me If You Can* 1977; *Old Boyfriends* 1979; *Prophecy* 1979; *Rocky II* 1979; *Rocky III* 1982; *Rocky IV* 1985; *New York Stories* 1989; *The Godfather Part III* 1990; *Rocky V* 1990; *Bed & Breakfast* 1992; *Cold Heaven* 1992; *Lured Innocence* 1999; *Rocky Balboa* 2006

Shirley, Anne (1918-1993) *Anne of Green Gables* 1934; *Steamboat round the Bend* 1935; *Stella Dallas* 1937; *Boy Slaves* 1938; *Condemned Women* 1938; *Anne of Windy Poplars* 1940; *Saturday's Children* 1940; *Vigil in the Night* 1940; *Bombardier* 1943; *Government Girl* 1943; *Farewell My Lovely* 1944; *Music in Manhattan* 1944

Shirley, Bill (1921-1989) *Abbott and Costello Meet Captain Kidd* 1952; *Sleeping Beauty* 1959

Shishido, Jo (1933-) *Gate of Flesh* 1964; *Branded to Kill* 1967

Shoemaker, Ann (1891-1978) *Alice Adams* 1935; *My Favorite Wife* 1940; *Strike Up the Band* 1940; *Above Suspicion* 1943; *Conflict* 1945; *House by the River* 1950; *Sunrise at Campobello* 1960

Shoop, Pamela aka **Shoop, Pamela Susan** (1948-) *Empire of the Ants* 1977; *Halloween II* 1981

Shor, Dan aka **Shor, Daniel** (1956-) *Wise Blood* 1979; *Back Roads* 1981; *Tron* 1982; *Strangers Kiss* 1983; *Mesmerized* 1984; *Black Moon Rising* 1985; *Bill & Ted's Excellent Adventure* 1988

Shor, Miriam (1971-) *Bedazzled* 2000; *Hedwig and the Angry Inch* 2001

Shore, Dinah (1916-1994) *Thank Your Lucky Stars* 1943; *Belle of the Yukon* 1944; *Follow the Boys* 1944; *Up in Arms* 1944; *Make Mine Music* 1946; *Till the Clouds Roll By* 1946

Shore, Pauly (1968-) *California Man* 1992; *In the Army Now* 1994; *Jury Duty* 1995; *Bio-Dome* 1996; *Casper: a Spirited Beginning* 1997

Short, Clare *Taking Liberties* 2007; *The Killing$* of Tony Blair 2016

Short, Columbus (1982-) *Stomp the Yard* 2006; *This Christmas* 2007; *Cadillac Records* 2008; *Quarantine* 2008; *Armored* 2009; *The Losers* 2010

Short, Martin (1950-) *Lost and Found* 1979; *Three Amigos!* 1986; *Cross My Heart* 1987; *Innerspace* 1987; *The Big Picture* 1989; *Three Fugitives* 1989; *Father of the Bride* 1991; *Pure Luck* 1991; *Captain Ron* 1992; *We're Back! A Dinosaur's Story* 1993; *Father of the Bride Part 2* 1995; *The Pebble and the Penguin* 1995; *Mars Attacks!* 1996; *Jungle 2 Jungle* 1997; *A Simple Wish* 1997; *The Prince of Egypt* 1998; *Alice in Wonderland* 1999; *Mumford* 1999; *Get over It* 2001; *Jimmy Neutron: Boy Genius* 2001; *Prince Charming* 2001; *Treasure Planet* 2002; *The Santa Clause 3: the Escape Clause* 2006; *The*

Spiderwick Chronicles 2008; *Frankenweenie* 2012; *Madagascar 3: Europe's Most Wanted* 2012; *Legends of Oz: Dorothy's Return* 2013; *The Wind Rises* 2013; *Inherent Vice* 2014

Shortt, Pat *Garage* 2007; *SoulBoy* 2010; *Life's a Breeze* 2013

Shotter, Winifred (1904-1996) *Rookery Nook* 1930; *D'Ye Ken John Peel?* 1934

Shou, Robin (1960-) *Beverly Hills Ninja* 1997; *Mortal Kombat: Annihilation* 1997

Showalter, Max aka **Adams, Casey** (1917-2000) *Destination Gobi* 1953; *Niagara* 1953; *Down Three Dark Streets* 1954; *Naked Alibi* 1954; *Bus Stop* 1956; *Dragoon Wells Massacre* 1957; *The Monster That Challenged the World* 1957; *How to Murder Your Wife* 1965; *Racing with the Moon* 1984

Shrapnel, John (1942-) *Testimony* 1987; *How to Get Ahead in Advertising* 1989; *101 Dalmatians* 1996; *The Body* 2000; *Gladiator* 2000; *K-19: the Widowmaker* 2002; *Sparkle* 2006; *Chemical Wedding* 2008; *Mirrors* 2008; *The Awakening* 2011

Shroff, Jackie (1958-) *Yaadein* 2001; *Devdas* 2002; *Hulchul* 2004; *Eklavya: the Royal Guard* 2007

Shu Qi (1976-) *A Man Called Hero* 1999; *So Close* 2002; *The Transporter* 2002; *The Eye 2* 2004; *Three Times* 2005; *Legend of the Fist: the Return of Chen Zhen* 2010; *The Assassin* 2015

Shue, Elisabeth (1963-) *The Karate Kid* 1984; *Link* 1986; *A Night on the Town* 1987; *Cocktail* 1988; *Back to the Future Part II* 1989; *Back to the Future Part III* 1990; *Soapdish* 1991; *Too Hot to Handle* 1991; *Heart and Souls* 1993; *Leaving Las Vegas* 1995; *The Underneath* 1995; *The Trigger Effect* 1996; *Cousin Bette* 1997; *Deconstructing Harry* 1997; *The Saint* 1997; *Palmetto* 1998; *Molly* 1999; *Hollow Man* 2000; *Leo* 2002; *Tuck Everlasting* 2002; *Mysterious Skin* 2004; *Dreamer* 2005; *Hide and Seek* 2005; *Hamlet 2* 2008; *Piranha* 2010; *Chasing Mavericks* 2012; *Hope Springs* 2012; *House at the End of the Street* 2012; *Battle of the Sexes* 2017

Shukla, Saurabh *Bandit Queen* 1994; *Mumbai Matinee* 2003

Shull, Richard B (1929-1999) *Slither* 1973; *The Fortune* 1975; *Hearts of the West* 1975; *The Pack* 1977; *Unfaithfully Yours* 1983; *Splash* 1984; *HouseSitter* 1992

Shum Jr, Harry *Step Up 3* 2010; *Revenge of the Green Dragons* 2013; *Crouching Tiger, Hidden Dragon: Sword of Destiny* 2016

Shyamalan, M Night (1970-) *The Sixth Sense* 1999; *Signs* 2002; *Lady in the Water* 2006

Siao, Josephine (1947-) *The Legend* 1993; *The Legend II* 1993

Siberry, Michael *Biggles* 1986; *Teen Agent* 1991

Siddharth *Baazigar* 1993; *Rang De Basanti* 2006

Siddig, Alexander (1965-) *Reign of Fire* 2001; *Kingdom of Heaven* 2005; *Syriana* 2005; *The Nativity Story* 2006; *Doomsday* 2008; *Miral* 2010

Siddiqui, Nawazuddin *Gangs of Wasseypur II* 2012; *The Lunchbox* 2013

Siddons, Harold (1922-1963) *Genevieve* 1953; *The Purple Plain* 1954; *The Baby and the Battleship* 1956

Sidibe, Gabourey (1983-) *Precious (Base on Nol by Saf) (Based on the Novel "Push" by Sapphire)* 2008; *White Bird in a Blizzard* 2014; *Grimsby* 2016

Sidney (1), George (1876-1945) *For the Love of Mike* 1927; *High Pressure* 1932; *Manhattan Melodrama* 1934

Sidney, Sylvia (1910-1999) *An American Tragedy* 1931; *City Streets* 1931; *Street Scene* 1931; *Madame Butterfly* 1932; *Jennie Gerhardt* 1933; *Thirty-Day Princess* 1934; *Accent on Youth* 1935; *Fury* 1936; *Sabotage* 1936; *The Trail of the Lonesome Pine* 1936; *Dead End* 1937; *You Only Live Once* 1937; *You and Me* 1938; *One Third of a Nation* 1939; *The Wagons Roll at Night* 1941; *Blood on the Sun* 1945; *The Searching Wind* 1946; *Love from a Stranger* 1947; *Les Misérables* 1952; *Violent Saturday* 1955; *Summer Wishes, Winter Dreams* 1973; *Raid on Entebbe* 1977; *Damien - Omen II* 1978; *The Shadow Box* 1980; *Order of Death* 1983; *An Early Frost* 1985; *Beetle Juice* 1988; *Used People* 1992

Siebert, Charles (1938-) *Blue Sunshine* 1977; *White Water Summer* 1987

Siedow, Jim (1920-2003) *The Texas Chain Saw Massacre* 1974; *The Texas Chainsaw Massacre Part 2* 1986

Siegel, Bernard (1868-1940) *Laugh, Clown, Laugh* 1928; *Beau Ideal* 1931

Siegel, Don aka **Siegel, Donald** (1912-1991) *Play Misty for Me* 1971; *Invasion of the Body Snatchers* 1978

Siegmann, George (1882-1928) *The Birth of a Nation* 1915; *The Three Musketeers* 1921; *Oliver Twist* 1922; *Hotel Imperial* 1927

Siemaszko, Casey (1961-) *Secret Admirer* 1985; *Stand by Me* 1986; *Three o'Clock High* 1987; *Biloxi Blues* 1988; *Young Guns* 1988; *Breaking In* 1989; *Near Mrs* 1990; *Of Mice and Men* 1992; *Milk Money* 1994; *Bliss* 1997; *Limbo* 1999; *Killing Kennedy* 2013

Siemaszko, Nina (1970-) *Bed & Breakfast* 1992; *Little Noises* 1992; *Wild Orchid 2: Two Shades of Blue* 1992; *The Saint of Fort Washington* 1993; *Airheads* 1994; *Runaway Car* 1997; *Jakob the Liar* 1999; *A Carol Christmas* 2003

Sierra, Gregory (1941-) *The Thief Who Came to Dinner* 1973; *A Low Down Dirty Shame* 1994; *Vampires* 1998

Silera, Frank (1914-1970) *The Miracle of Our Lady of Fatima* 1952; *White Mane* 1952; *Fear and Desire* 1953; *Killer's Kiss* 1955; *Crime and Punishment, USA* 1959; *Key Witness* 1960; *The Mountain Road* 1960; *The St Valentine's Day Massacre* 1967; *The Stalking Moon* 1968; *Uptight* 1968; *Valdez Is Coming* 1971

Silverheels, Jay (1919-1980) *Broken Arrow* 1950; *The Battle at Apache Pass* 1952; *Drums across the River* 1954; *Saskatchewan* 1954; *The Lone Ranger* 1956; *Walk the Proud Land* 1956; *Alias Jesse James* 1959; *The Man Who Loved Cat Dancing* 1973; *Santee* 1973

Silverman, Jonathan (1966-) *Girls Just Want to Have Fun* 1985; *Brighton Beach Memoirs* 1986; *Caddyshack II* 1988; *Stealing Home* 1988; *Weekend at Bernie's* 1989; *Age Isn't Everything* 1991; *Broadway Bound* 1991; *Class Action* 1991; *Weekend at Bernie's II* 1992; *12:01* 1993; *Little Big League* 1994; *...At First Sight* 1995; *The Odd Couple II* 1998; *Something about Sex* 1998; *These Old Broads* 2001; *Vickery's Wild Ride* 2009; *Swinging with the Finkels* 2010

Silverman, Robert *Head On* 1980; *Prom Night* 1980

Silverman, Sarah (1970-) *The Bachelor* 1999; *The School of Rock* 2003; *Sarah Silverman: Jesus Is Magic* 2005; *School for Scoundrels* 2006; *Take This Waltz* 2011; *Wreck-It Ralph* 2012; *A Million Ways to Die in the West* 2014; *Battle of the Sexes* 2017

Silvers, Phil (1911-1985) *Strike Up the Band* 1940; *Lady Be Good* 1941; *The Penalty* 1941; *Tom, Dick and Harry* 1941; *All through the Night* 1942; *Footlight Serenade* 1942; *My Gal Sal* 1942; *Roxie Hart* 1942; *Coney Island* 1943; *A Lady Takes a Chance* 1943; *Cover Girl* 1944; *Something for the Boys* 1944; *Billy Rose's Diamond Horseshoe* 1945; *A Thousand and One Nights* 1945; *Summer Stock* 1950; *Top Banana* 1953; *Lucky Me* 1954; *Forty Pounds of Trouble* 1962; *It's a Mad Mad Mad Mad World* 1963; *A Funny Thing Happened on the Way to the Forum* 1966; *Carry On Follow That Camel* 1967; *Buona Sera, Mrs Campbell* 1968; *The Boatniks* 1970; *The Strongest Man in the World* 1975; *The Chicken Chronicles* 1977; *The Cheap Detective* 1978; *There Goes the Bride* 1979

Silvers, Sid (1901-1976) *Broadway Melody of 1936* 1935; *Born to Dance* 1936

Silverstone, Alicia (1976-) *The Crush* 1993; *The Babysitter* 1995; *Clueless* 1995; *Hideaway* 1995; *True Crime* 1995; *Batman and Robin* 1997; *Excess Baggage* 1997; *Blast from the Past* 1998; *Love's Labour's Lost* 1999; *Scorched* 2002; *Scooby-Doo 2: Monsters Unleashed* 2004; *Beauty Shop* 2005; *Stormbreaker* 2006; *Vamps* 2012

Silverstone, Ben (1976-) *Apache Drums* 1951; *None but the Brave* 1960; *Kings of the Sun* 1963; *Rage* 1966; *The Scalphunters* 1968; *Two Mules for Sister Sara* 1970

Sim, Alastair (1900-1976) *A Fire Has Been Arranged* 1935; *Keep Your Seats, Please* 1936; *The Man in the Mirror* 1936; *Gangway* 1937; *The Squeaker* 1937; *Alf's Button Afloat* 1938; *Climbing High* 1938; *Sailing Along* 1938; *Cottage to Let* 1941; *Waterloo Road* 1944; *Green for Danger* 1946; *Captain Boycott* 1947; *Hue and Cry* 1947; *London Belongs to Me* 1948; *Stage Fright* 1949; *The Happiest Days of Your Life* 1950; *Lady Godiva Rides Again* 1951; *Laughter in Paradise* 1951; *Scrooge* 1951; *Folly to Be Wise* 1952; *Innocents in Paris* 1953; *The*

Silver, Joe (1922-1989) *The Apprenticeship of Duddy Kravitz* 1974; *Rhinoceros* 1974; *Shivers* 1975; *Rabid* 1976; *You Light Up My Life* 1977; *Boardwalk* 1979; *The Gig* 1985

Silver, Ron (1946-2009) *Semi-Tough* 1977; *The Entity* 1981; *Best Friends* 1982; *Silent Rage* 1982; *Lovesick* 1983; *Silkwood* 1983; *Garbo Talks* 1984; *Oh, God! You Devil* 1984; *Eat and Run* 1986; *Enemies, a Love Story* 1989; *Fellow Traveller* 1989; *Blue Steel* 1990; *Reversal of Fortune* 1990; *Live Wire* 1992; *Mr Saturday Night* 1992; *Timecop* 1994; *Kissinger and Nixon* 1995; *The Arrival* 1996; *Danger Zone* 1996; *Skeletons* 1996; *Black and White* 1998; *In the Company of Spies* 1999; *Cutaway* 2000; *Ali* 2001; *Festival in Cannes* 2001; *When Billie Beat Bobby* 2001; *Jack* 2004; *Find Me Guilty* 2006

Sigman, Stephanie *Miss Bala* 2011; *Pioneer* 2013

Signoret, Simone (1921-1985) *Les Visiteurs du Soir* 1942; *Against the Wind* 1947; *La Ronde* 1950; *Casque d'Or* 1952; *Thérèse Raquin* 1953; *Les Diaboliques* 1954; *Death in the Garden* 1956; *The Witches of Salem* 1957; *Room at the Top* 1958; *Le Joli Mai* 1962; *Term of Trial* 1962; *Ship of Fools* 1965; *The Sleeping Car Murders* 1965; *The Deadly Affair* 1966; *Is Paris Burning?* 1966; *Games* 1967; *The Sea Gull* 1968; *Army of Shadows* 1969; *The Confession* 1970; *The Widow Couderc* 1971; *Burnt Barns* 1973; *The Flesh of the Orchid* 1974; *Madame Rosa* 1977

Sigurdsson, Ingvar E *Falcons* 2002; *Jar City* 2006

Sihol, Caroline aka **Silhol, Caroline** *Confidentially Yours* 1983; *Tenue de Soirée* 1986; *Tous les Matins du Monde* 1991; *Life of Riley* 2014

Sikes, Cynthia (1951-) *Ladies and Gentlemen, the Fabulous Stains* 1981; *The Man Who Loved Women* 1983; *Love Hurts* 1990

Sikking, James B aka **Sikking, James** (1934-) *Point Blank* 1967; *Charro!* 1969; *Daddy's Gone A-Hunting* 1969; *The New Centurions* 1972; *Ordinary People* 1980; *Outland* 1981; *The Star Chamber* 1983; *Star Trek III: the Search for Spock* 1984; *Morons from Outer Space* 1985; *Soul Man* 1986; *Narrow Margin* 1990; *Final Approach* 1991; *The Pelican Brief* 1993; *Nowhere to Land* 2000; *The Perfect Catch* 2005; *Made of Honor* 2008

Siletti, Mario (1897-1977) *The Black Hand* 1950; *Kansas City Confidential* 1952; *Bring Your Smile Along* 1955

Silia, Felix (1937-) *She Freak* 1967; *The Black Bird* 1975; *Buck Rogers in the 25th Century* 1979

Sillas, Karen (1965-) *Simple Men* 1992; *Female Perversions* 1996; *Sour Grapes* 1998; *As Time Runs Out* 1999

Sills, Milton (1882-1930) *The Sea Hawk* 1924; *The Barker* 1928

Silva, David (1917-1976) *El Topo* 1971; *Alucarda* 1975

Silva, Douglas *City of God* 2002; *City of Men* 2007

Silva, Franco (1920-1995) *Hannibal* 1959; *The Mongols* 1961

Silva, Henry (1928-) *A Hatful of Rain* 1957; *The Tall T* 1957; *The Bravados* 1958; *The Law and Jake Wade* 1958; *Ride a Crooked Trail* 1958; *Green Mansions* 1959; *Cinderfella* 1960; *The Manchurian Candidate* 1962; *Sergeants 3* 1962; *Johnny Cool* 1963; *The Secret Invasion* 1964; *The Return of Mr Moto* 1965; *The Reward* 1965; *The Hills Run Red* 1966; *The Plainsman* 1966; *Love and Bullets* 1978; *Buck Rogers in the 25th Century* 1979; *Thirst* 1979; *Alligator* 1980; *Virus* 1980; *Sharky's Machine* 1981; *The Man with the Deadly Lens* 1982; *Chained Heat* 1983; *The Outsider* 1983; *Lust in the Dust* 1984; *Code of Silence* 1985; *Allan Quatermain and the Lost City of Gold* 1987; *Bulletproof* 1987; *Nico* 1988; *The Harvest* 1993; *Ghost Dog: the Way of the Samurai* 1999

Silva, Simone (1928-1957) *Escape by Night* 1953; *Street of Shadows* 1953

Silva, Trinidad (1950-1988) *The Night Before* 1988; *Stones for Ibarra* 1988; *UHF* 1989

Silvani, Aldo (1891-1964) *Four Steps in the Clouds* 1942; *La Strada* 1954; *Nights of Cabiria* 1957

Silveira, Leonor (1970-) *The Divine Comedy* 1992; *Abraham Valley* 1993; *The Convent* 1995; *Journey to the Beginning of the World* 1997; *I'm Going*

Home 2001; *Un Filme Falado* 2003; *Eccentricities of a Blonde-Haired Girl* 2009

Belles of St Trinian's 1954; An Inspector Calls 1954; Geordie 1955; The Green Man 1956; Blue Murder at St Trinian's 1957; The Doctor's Dilemma 1958; Left, Right and Centre 1959; The Millionairess 1960; School for Scoundrels 1960; The Ruling Class 1972; Royal Flash 1975; The Littlest Horse Thieves 1976

Sim, Gerald (1925-2014) Seance on a Wet Afternoon 1964; King Rat 1965; The Whisperers 1967; The Raging Moon 1970; Dr Jekyll & Sister Hyde 1971

Sim, Sheila (1922-2016) A Canterbury Tale 1944; Great Day 1945; Dancing with Crime 1946; The Guinea Pig 1948; Dear Mr Prohack 1949; Pandora and the Flying Dutchman 1950; West of Zanzibar 1954; The Night My Number Came Up 1955

Simcoe, Anthony The Castle 1997; Nim's Island 2008

Simm, John (1970-) Boston Kickout 1995; Diana & Me 1997; Human Traffic 1999; Wonderland 1999; Miranda 2001; Tu£sday 2007; Everyday 2012

Simmons, Dick aka **Simmons, Richard** (1913-2003) Pilot #5 1943; Thousands Cheer 1943; Lady in the Lake 1947; On an Island with You 1948

Simmons, Gene (1949-) Trick or Treat 1986; Wanted Dead or Alive 1986; Red Surf 1990; Detroit Rock City 1999; Extract 2009; Rush: Beyond the Lighted Stage 2010

Simmons, Henry Taxi 2004; World's Greatest Dad 2009; No Good Deed 2014

Simmons, J K (1955-) The Jackal 1997; For Love of the Game 1999; Spider-Man 2002; The Ladykillers 2004; Spider-Man 2 2004; Harsh Times 2005; The Astronaut Farmer 2006; Bury My Heart at Wounded Knee 2007; Juno 2007; I Love You, Man 2008; New in Town 2008; Extract 2009; Jennifer's Body 2009; Red Sands 2009; Contraband 2012; The Words 2012; Dark Skies 2013; Labor Day 2013; The Rewrite 2014; Whiplash 2014; The Meddler 2015; Terminator: Genisys 2015; The Accountant 2016; Bastards 2016; Kung Fu Panda 3 2016; La La Land 2016; Zootropolis 2016

Simmons, Jean (1929-2010) Give Us the Moon 1944; The Way to the Stars 1945; Great Expectations 1946; Hungry Hill 1946; Black Narcissus 1947; Uncle Silas 1947; Hamlet 1948; Adam and Evelyne 1949; The Blue Lagoon 1949; Cage of Gold 1950; The Clouded Yellow 1950; So Long at the Fair 1950; Trio 1950; Androcles and the Lion 1952; The Actress 1953; Affair with a Stranger 1953; Angel Face 1953; The Robe 1953; Young Bess 1953; Beautiful but Dangerous 1954; A Bullet Is Waiting 1954; Desiree 1954; The Egyptian 1954; Footsteps in the Fog 1955; Guys and Dolls 1955; Hilda Crane 1956; This Could Be the Night 1957; Until They Sail 1957; The Big Country 1958; Home before Dark 1958; This Earth Is Mine 1959; Elmer Gantry 1960; The Grass Is Greener 1960; Spartacus 1960; All the Way Home 1963; Life at the Top 1965; Divorce American Style 1967; Rough Night in Jericho 1967; Say Hello to Yesterday 1971; Mr Sycamore 1974; Dominique 1978; Yellow Pages 1984; The Dawning 1988; Inherit the Wind 1988; How to Make an American Quilt 1995; Final Fantasy: the Spirits Within 2001; Howl's Moving Castle 2004; Shadows in the Sun 2008

Simmons, Johnny Evan Almighty 2007; Jennifer's Body 2009; The To Do List 2013

Simms, Ginny (1913-1994) Playmates 1941; Seven Days' Leave 1942; Hit the Ice 1943; Broadway Rhythm 1944; Night and Day 1946

Simms, Larry (1934-2009) Blondie! 1938; The Gay Sisters 1942

Simon, Carly (1945-) Taking Off 1971; No Nukes 1980; Perfect 1985

Simon, Michel (1895-1975) The Passion of Joan of Arc 1928; La Chienne 1931; On Purge Bébé 1931; Boudu, Saved from Drowning 1932; L'Atalante 1934; Drôle de Drame 1937; Le Quai des Brumes 1938; The End of the Day 1939; La Beauté du Diable 1949; Saadia 1953; The Train 1964; The Two of Us 1967; Blanche 1971

Simon, Paul (1941-) Annie Hall 1977; One-Trick Pony 1980; We Are Together 2006

Simon, Robert F aka **Simon, Robert** (1908-1992) The Benny Goodman Story 1955; Bigger than Life 1956; The Catered Affair 1956; Edge of the City 1957; Spring Reunion 1957; Gunman's Walk 1958; Pay or Die 1960; The Wizard of Baghdad 1960

Simon, Simone (1910-2005) Ladies in Love 1936; Seventh Heaven 1937; La Bête Humaine 1938; The Devil and Daniel Webster 1941; Cat People 1942; The Curse of the Cat People 1944; Johnny Doesn't Live Here Anymore 1944; The Silent Bell 1944; Olivia 1950; La Ronde 1950; Le Plaisir 1951; The Extra Day 1956

Simonds, David Amateur 1994; The Book of Life 1998

Simonet, Mathieu Merci pour le Chocolat 2000; Days of Glory 2006

Simons, William Where No Vultures Fly 1951; West of Zanzibar 1954

Simpkins, Ryan Sherrybaby 2006; Surveillance 2007; A Single Man 2009

Simpson, Christopher aka **Simpson, Chris** Brick Lane 2007; Day of the Flowers 2012

Simpson, Ivan (1875-1951) The Man Who Played God 1932; British Agent 1934; Trouble for Two 1936; The Male Animal 1942

Simpson, Jay (1967-) Free Jimmy 2006; Shifty 2008; Acts of Godfrey 2011; The Guvnors 2014

Simpson, Jessica The Dukes of Hazzard 2005; Employee of the Month 2006; Blonde Ambition 2007

Simpson, Jimmi (1975-) Loser 2000; Herbie: Fully Loaded 2005; Stay Alive 2006; Date Night 2010

Simpson, O J (1947-) The Towering Inferno 1974; Killer Force 1975; The Cassandra Crossing 1976; Capricorn One 1978; Firepower 1979; Hambone and Hillie 1984; The Naked Gun 1988; The Naked Gun 2½: the Smell of Fear 1991; No Place to Hide 1992; Naked Gun 33⅓: the Final Insult 1994

Simpson, Russell (1880-1959) Annie Laurie 1927; Billy the Kid 1930; Susan Lenox: Her Fall and Rise 1931; Law and Order 1932; Way Down East 1935; The Grapes of Wrath 1940; Wild Geese Calling 1941; Along Came Jones 1945; Saddle Tramp 1950; The Sun Shines Bright 1953

Sims, Joan (1930-2001) Colonel March Investigates 1953; The Square Ring 1953; Trouble in Store 1953; Will Any Gentleman...? 1953; The Young Lovers 1954; As Long as They're Happy 1955; Dry Rot 1956; Carry On Admiral 1957; Just My Luck 1957; The Naked Truth 1957; No Time for Tears 1957; The Captain's Table 1958; Passport to Shame 1958; Carry On Nurse 1959; Carry On Teacher 1959; Life in Emergency Ward 10 1959; Upstairs and Downstairs 1959; Carry On Constable 1960; Carry On Regardless 1960; Doctor in Love 1960; His and Hers 1960; Please Turn Over 1960; Watch Your Stern 1960; Mr Topaze 1961; No My Darling Daughter 1961; Twice round the Daffodils 1962; Nurse on Wheels 1963; Carry On Cleo 1964; The Big Job 1965; Carry On Cowboy 1965; Carry On - Don't Lose Your Head 1966; Carry On Screaming 1966; Doctor in Clover 1966; Carry On Follow That Camel 1967; Carry On Doctor 1968; Carry On Up the Khyber 1968; Carry On again Doctor 1969; Carry On Camping 1969; Carry On Loving 1970; Carry On Up the Jungle 1970; Doctor in Trouble 1970; Carry On at Your Convenience 1971; Carry On Henry 1971; The Magnificent Seven Deadly Sins 1971; Carry On Abroad 1972; Carry On Matron 1972; Not Now Darling 1972; Carry On Girls 1973; Don't Just Lie There, Say Something! 1973; Carry On Dick 1974; Carry On Behind 1975; Love among the Ruins 1975; One of Our Dinosaurs Is Missing 1975; Carry On England 1976; Carry On Emmannuelle 1978; The Canterville Ghost 1996

Sims, Molly (1973-) The Benchwarmers 2006; Fired Up! 2009

Sims, Warwick He's My Girl 1987; Night Eyes 1990

Sinatra, Frank (1915-1998) Ship Ahoy 1942; Higher and Higher 1943; Reveille with Beverly 1943; Step Lively 1944; Anchors Aweigh 1945; Till the Clouds Roll By 1946; It Happened in Brooklyn 1947; The Miracle of the Bells 1948; The Kissing Bandit 1949; On the Town 1949; Take Me Out to the Ball Game 1949; Double Dynamite 1951; Meet Danny Wilson 1952; From Here to Eternity 1953; Suddenly 1954; Guys and Dolls 1955; The Man with the Golden Arm 1955; Not as a Stranger 1955; The Tender Trap 1955; Young at Heart 1955; Around the World in 80 Days 1956; High Society 1956; Johnny Concho 1956; The Joker Is Wild 1957; Pal Joey 1957; The Pride and the Passion 1957; Some Came Running 1958; Never So Few 1959; Can-Can 1960; Ocean's Eleven 1960; Pepe 1960; The Devil at Four o'Clock 1961; The Manchurian Candidate 1962; The Road

to Hong Kong 1962; Sergeants 3 1962; Come Blow Your Horn 1963; 4 for Texas 1963; The List of Adrian Messenger 1963; Paris When It Sizzles 1964; Robin and the 7 Hoods 1964; Marriage on the Rocks 1965; None but the Brave 1965; Von Ryan's Express 1965; Assault on a Queen 1966; Cast a Giant Shadow 1966; The Oscar 1966; The Naked Runner 1967; Tony Rome 1967; The Detective 1968; Lady in Cement 1968; Dirty Dingus Magee 1970; Cannonball Run II 1983

Sinatra, Nancy (1940-) For Those Who Think Young 1964; Get Yourself a College Girl 1964; Marriage on the Rocks 1965; The Ghost in the Invisible Bikini 1966; The Oscar 1966; The Wild Angels 1966; Speedway 1968

Sinbad (1956-) Coneheads 1993; Houseguest 1995; First Kid 1996; Jingle All the Way 1996; Good Burger 1997

Sinclair Blyth, Stuart Hold Back the Night 1999; 16 Years of Alcohol 2003

Sinclair, Betty (1907-1983) City Streets 1931; Something in the City 1950

Sinclair, Hugh (1903-1962) Our Betters 1933; Escape Me Never 1935; The Four Just Men 1939; The Saint's Vacation 1941; Tomorrow We Live 1942; The Saint Meets the Tiger 1943; They Were Sisters 1945; Don't Ever Leave Me 1949; The Rocking Horse Winner 1949; Trottie True 1949; Circle of Danger 1950; No Trace 1950; Mantrap 1952

Sinclair, Madge (1938-1995) Leadbelly 1976; Convoy 1978; Coming to America 1988; The Lion King 1994

Sinclair, Peter (1900-1994) The Man from Morocco 1944; The Time of His Life 1955; The Heart of a Man 1959

Sinden, Donald (1923-2014) The Cruel Sea 1952; A Day to Remember 1953; Mogambo 1953; The Beachcomber 1954; Doctor in the House 1954; Mad about Men 1954; You Know What Sailors Are 1954; Above Us the Waves 1955; An Alligator Named Daisy 1955; Josephine and Men 1955; Simba 1955; The Black Tent 1956; Eyewitness 1956; Tiger in the Smoke 1956; Doctor at Large 1957; The Captain's Table 1958; Rockets Galore 1958; Operation Bullshine 1959; The Siege of Sidney Street 1960; Your Money or Your Wife 1960; Mix Me a Person 1962; Twice round the Daffodils 1962; Decline and Fall... of a Birdwatcher 1968; Villain 1971; Father Dear Father 1972; Rentadick 1972; The Day of the Jackal 1973; The National Health 1973; The Island at the Top of the World 1974; That Lucky Touch 1975; The Children 1990; The Canterville Ghost 1996

Singer, Campbell (1909-1976) Blackout 1950; Someone at the Door 1950; Conflict of Wings 1953; The Square Peg 1958

Singer, Lori (1962-) Footloose 1984; The Falcon and the Snowman 1985; The Man with One Red Shoe 1985; Trouble in Mind 1985; Warlock 1989; Equinox 1992; Sunset Grill 1992; Short Cuts 1993; FTW 1994

Singer, Marc (1948-) Go Tell the Spartans 1977; Something for Joey 1977; The Beastmaster 1982; The Sea Wolf 1993; Determination of Death 2001; Snowman's Pass 2004

Singer, Ritchie "Crocodile" Dundee 1986; Encounter at Raven's Gate 1988; Dynasty: the Making of a Guilty Pleasure 2004

Singerman, Wesley The Little Polar Bear 2001; Meet the Robinsons 2006

Singh, Gracy Lagaan: Once upon a Time in India 2001; Armaan 2003

Singh, K N (1908-2000) Barsaat 1949; Awara 1951

Singh, Simone Being Cyrus 2005; Marigold 2007

Singleton, Penny (1908-2003) Swing Your Lady 1937; Blondie! 1938; Hard to Get 1938; Racket Busters 1938; Jetsons: the Movie 1990

Sinise, Gary (1955-) My Name Is Bill W 1989; A Midnight Clear 1991; Of Mice and Men 1992; Jack the Bear 1993; Forrest Gump 1994; Apollo 13 1995; The Quick and the Dead 1995; Truman 1995; Albino Alligator 1996; Ransom 1996; Snake Eyes 1998; Mission to Mars 1999; Deception 2000; Impostor 2001; The Human Stain 2003; The Big Bounce 2004; The Forgotten 2004; Open Season 2006

Sirene, Chloe Gypo 2005; The Calling 2009

Sirijanya, Nirut Protégé 2007; Ong-Bak: the Beginning 2008

Sirola, Joseph The Super Cops 1973; Seizure 1974

Sirtis, Marina (1960-) Blind Date 1984; Star Trek: Generations 1994; Star Trek: First Contact 1996; Star Trek:

Insurrection 1998; Star Trek: Nemesis 2002; 31 North 62 East 2009

Sisqo aka **SisQo** (1978-) Get over It 2001; Pieces of April 2002; Snow Dogs 2002

Sisti, Michelan Teenage Mutant Ninja Turtles 1990; Teenage Mutant Ninja Turtles II: the Secret of the Ooze 1991

Sisto, Jeremy (1974-) Grand Canyon 1991; Hideaway 1995; White Squall 1996; Suicide Kings 1997; Without Limits 1998; Angel Eyes 2001; Thirteen 2003; Wrong Turn 2003; A Lot like Love 2005; Unknown 2006; Waitress 2007; The Other Side of the Door 2016

Sivero, Frank Going Ape! 1981; GoodFellas 1990; Cop and a Half 1993

Sives, Jamie (1973-) Wilbur (Wants to Kill Himself) 2002; One Last Chance 2003; Frozen 2004; On a Clear Day 2004; Hallam Foe 2006; Valhalla Rising 2009

Sizemore, Tom (1964-) Lock Up 1989; Blue Steel 1990; Where Sleeping Dogs Lie 1991; Passenger 57 1992; Heart and Souls 1993; Striking Distance 1993; True Romance 1993; Natural Born Killers 1994; Devil in a Blue Dress 1995; Heat 1995; Strange Days 1995; The Relic 1996; Enemy of the State 1998; Saving Private Ryan 1998; Bringing Out the Dead 1999; The Match 1999; Witness Protection 1999; Play It to the Bone 2000; Red Planet 2000; Black Hawk Down 2001; Pearl Harbor 2001; Ticker 2001; Big Trouble 2002; Dreamcatcher 2003; Paparazzi 2004

Sjöberg, Emma (1968-) Taxi 1998; Taxi 2 2000

Sjöberg, Gunnar (1909-1977) The Great Adventure 1953; So Close to Life 1957

Sjöström, Victor aka **Seastrom, Victor** (1879-1960) The Outlaw and His Wife 1917; Karin Ingmarsdotter 1919; A Dangerous Pledge 1920; The Phantom Carriage 1920; Walpurgis Night 1935; To Joy 1950; Wild Strawberries 1957

Skala, Lilia (1896-1994) Lilies of the Field 1963; Caprice 1967; Charly 1968; Roseland 1977; Flashdance 1983; Testament 1983; House of Games 1987

Skarsgård, Alexander (1976-) Ake and His World 1984; Beyond the Pole 2009; 13 2010; Melancholia 2011; Straw Dogs 2011; Battleship 2012; Disconnect 2012; The East 2013; What Maisie Knew 2013; The Giver 2014; The Diary of a Teenage Girl 2015; The Legend of Tarzan 2016

Skarsgård, Gustaf Evil 2003; The Way Back 2010; Kon-Tiki 2012

Skarsgård, Stellan (1951-) The Simple-Minded Murderer 1982; Ake and His World 1984; The Perfect Murder 1988; The Hunt for Red October 1990; The Ox 1991; Wind 1992; The Slingshot 1993; Breaking the Waves 1996; Amistad 1997; Good Will Hunting 1997; Insomnia 1997; My Son the Fanatic 1997; Savior 1997; Ronin 1998; Deep Blue Sea 1999; Timecode 1999; Aberdeen 2000; Passion of Mind 2000; The Glass House 2001; Kiss Kiss (Bang Bang) 2001; Taking Sides 2001; City of Ghosts 2002; No Good Deed 2002; Dogville 2003; Exorcist: the Beginning 2004; King Arthur 2004; Dominion: Prequel to the Exorcist 2005; Goya's Ghosts 2006; Pirates of the Caribbean: Dead Man's Chest 2006; WAZ 2006; Pirates of the Caribbean: at World's End 2007; Mamma Mia! 2008; Angels & Demons 2009; Boogie Woogie 2009; King of Devil's Island 2010; The Girl with the Dragon Tattoo 2011; Melancholia 2011; Thor 2011; Marvel Avengers Assemble 2012; Romeo & Juliet 2012; Nymphomaniac Vol I 2013; The Railway Man 2013; Thor: the Dark World 2013; Hector and the Search for Happiness 2014; In Order of Disappearance 2014; Nymphomaniac Vol II 2014; Cinderella 2015; Our Kind of Traitor 2016

Skarstedt, Georg (1900-1976) To Joy 1950; Summer with Monika 1952

Skellern, Anna The Descent: Part 2 2009; A Night in the Woods 2011; Blood Moon 2014

Skelton, Red aka **Skelton, Richard** (1913-1997) Having Wonderful Time 1938; Flight Command 1940; Dr Kildare's Wedding Day 1941; Lady Be Good 1941; The People vs Dr Kildare 1941; Whistling in the Dark 1941; Ship Ahoy 1942; DuBarry Was a Lady 1943; I Dood It 1943; Bathing Beauty 1944; Merton of the Movies 1947; A Southern Yankee 1948; Neptune's Daughter 1949; The Fuller Brush Girl 1950; Three Little Words 1950; Watch the Birdie 1950; The Yellow Cab Man 1950; Texas Carnival 1951; The Clown 1952; Lovely to Look At 1952

Skerritt, Tom (1933-) War Hunt 1962; Those Calloways 1964; MASH 1969;

Wild Rovers 1971; Fuzz 1972; Big Bad Mama 1974; Thieves like Us 1974; The Devil's Rain 1975; The Turning Point 1977; Cheech & Chong's Up in Smoke 1978; Ice Castles 1978; Alien 1979; Silence of the North 1981; Death Vengeance 1982; The Dead Zone 1983; Calendar Girl Murders 1984; Hell Camp 1986; Miles to Go 1986; SpaceCamp 1986; Top Gun 1986; Wisdom 1986; The Big Town 1987; Maid to Order 1987; Poltergeist III 1988; Steel Magnolias 1989; The Rookie 1990; Knight Moves 1992; Poison Ivy 1992; A River Runs through It 1992; Wild Orchid 2: Two Shades of Blue 1992; Contact 1997; Two for Texas 1998; The Other Sister 1999; High Noon 2000; Greenmail 2001; Path to War 2002; Tears of the Sun 2003; Vinegar Hill 2004; Bonneville 2006; A Hologram for the King 2016

Skilton, Gerry "Crocodile" Dundee II 1988; Crocodile Dundee in Los Angeles 2001

Skinner, Claire (1965-) Life Is Sweet 1990; Naked 1993; Clockwork Mice 1994; ID 1994; The Escort 1999; You're Dead 1999; Strings 2004; And When Did You Last See Your Father? 2007

Skinner, Cornelia Otis (1901-1979) The Uninvited 1944; The Girl in the Red Velvet Swing 1955

Skipper, Pat Femme Fatale 1991; Memoirs of an Invisible Man 1992; Ed Gein 2000

Skipworth, Alison (1863-1952) Raffles 1930; If I Had a Million 1932; Night after Night 1932; Sinners in the Sun 1932; The Song of Songs 1933; Tillie and Gus 1933; The Captain Hates the Sea 1934; Six of a Kind 1934; Becky Sharp 1935; The Casino Murder Case 1935; Dangerous 1935; The Devil Is a Woman 1935; The Girl from 10th Avenue 1935; The Gorgeous Hussy 1936; The Princess Comes Across 1936; Satan Met a Lady 1936

Skjonberg, Espen One Day in the Life of Ivan Denisovich 1971; O'Horten 2007

Skolimowski, Jerzy (1938-) Circle of Deceit 1981; White Nights 1985; Eastern Promises 2007; Marvel Avengers Assemble 2012

Skotnicki, Jan Illumination 1972; The Scar 1976

Skrein, Ed (1983-) Ill Manors 2012; Sword of Vengeance 2015; The Transporter Refuelled 2015; Deadpool 2016

Sky, Jennifer (1977-) My Little Eye 2002; Never Die Alone 2004

Skye, Ione (1971-) River's Edge 1987; A Night in the Life of Jimmy Reardon 1988; The Rachel Papers 1989; Say Anything... 1989; Gas, Food, Lodging 1992; Guncrazy 1992; Dream for an Insomniac 1996

Slade, Demian Better Off Dead 1985; Back to the Beach 1987

Slate, Henry (1910-1996) Bloodhounds of Broadway 1952; Somebody Loves Me 1952; Hey Boy! Hey Girl! 1959

Slate, Jenny (1982-) Alvin and the Chipmunks: Chipwrecked 2011; Obvious Child 2014; The Secret Life of Pets 2016

Slate, Jeremy (1926-2006) Girls! Girls! Girls! 1962; I'll Take Sweden 1965; Born Losers 1967; True Grit 1969; The Lawnmower Man 1992

Slater, Christian (1969-) The Legend of Billie Jean 1985; The Name of the Rose 1986; Beyond the Stars 1988; Gleaming the Cube 1988; Tucker: the Man and His Dream 1988; Heathers 1989; Pump Up the Volume 1990; Young Guns II 1990; Kuffs 1991; Mobsters 1991; Robin Hood: Prince of Thieves 1991; Star Trek VI: the Undiscovered Country 1991; Tales from the Darkside: the Movie 1991; FernGully: the Last Rainforest 1992; True Romance 1993; Untamed Heart 1993; Interview with the Vampire: the Vampire Chronicles 1994; Jimmy Hollywood 1994; Murder in the First 1994; Bed of Roses 1995; Broken Arrow 1996; Hard Rain 1997; Julian Po 1997; Basil 1998; Very Bad Things 1998; The Contender 2000; 3000 Miles to Graceland 2000; Windtalkers 2001; Mindhunters 2003; Churchill: the Hollywood Years 2004; Bobby 2006; Hollow Man II 2006; He Was a Quiet Man 2007; Bullet to the Head 2012; Soldiers of Fortune 2012; Nymphomaniac Vol I 2013; Nymphomaniac Vol II 2014

Slater, Helen (1963-) Supergirl 1984; The Legend of Billie Jean 1985; Ruthless People 1986; The Secret of My Success 1987; Sticky Fingers 1988; Happy Together 1989; City Slickers 1991; 12:01 1993; Lassie: a New Generation 1994; The Steal 1994; No Way Back 1996; Rock the House 2011

Slater, John (1916-1975) Gert and Daisy's Weekend 1941; For Those in Peril 1943; Against the Wind 1947; It Always Rains on Sunday 1947; Passport to Pimlico 1949; The Long Memory 1952; Star of India 1954; Violent Playground 1958; The Night We Got the Bird 1960; Three on a Spree 1961; A Place to Go 1963

Slater, Ryan (1983-) The Amazing Panda Adventure 1995; Home Team 1998

Slattery, John (1963-) Bad Company 2002; Dirty Dancing 2 2003; Mona Lisa Smile 2003; The Brooke Ellison Story 2004; Flags of Our Fathers 2006; The Adjustment Bureau 2010; Return 2011; Mea Maxima Culpa: Silence in the House of God 2012; Spotlight 2015

Slattery, Tony (1959-) Carry On Columbus 1992; The Crying Game 1992; Peter's Friends 1992; To Die For 1994; Up 'n' Under 1997; The Wedding Tackle 2000

Slaughter, Tod (1835-1956) Maria Marten, or the Murder in the Red Barn 1935; The Crimes of Stephen Hawke 1936; Sweeney Todd, the Demon Barber of Fleet Street 1936; It's Never Too Late to Mend 1937; Song of the Road 1937; The Ticket of Leave Man 1937; Sexton Blake and the Hooded Terror 1938; Crimes at the Dark House 1939; The Face at the Window 1939; The Curse of the Wraydons 1946; The Greed of William Hart 1948

Sleep, Wayne (1943-) The Tales of Beatrix Potter 1971; The First Great Train Robbery 1978; Elizabeth 1998

Sleeper, Martha (1907-1983) Penthouse 1933; Spitfire 1934; The Scoundrel 1935; The Bells of St Mary's 1945

Slezak, Victor Beyond Rangoon 1995; The Bridges of Madison County 1995

Slezak, Walter (1902-1983) Once upon a Honeymoon 1942; The Fallen Sparrow 1943; This Land Is Mine 1943; Lifeboat 1944; The Princess and the Pirate 1944; Step Lively 1944; Till We Meet Again 1944; Cornered 1945; Salome, Where She Danced 1945; The Spanish Main 1945; Lady of Deceit 1947; Riff-Raff 1947; Sinbad the Sailor 1947; The Pirate 1948; The Inspector General 1949; Abbott and Costello in the Foreign Legion 1950; The Yellow Cab Man 1950; Bedtime for Bonzo 1951; People Will Talk 1951; Call Me Madam 1953; White Witch Doctor 1953; Ten Thousand Bedrooms 1957; Come September 1961; The Wonderful World of the Brothers Grimm 1962; Emil and the Detectives 1964; Wonderful Life 1964; Black Beauty 1971; Treasure Island 1972

Slinger, Jonathan Still 2014; Bait 2015

Sloane, Everett (1909-1965) Citizen Kane 1941; Journey into Fear 1942; The Lady from Shanghai 1948; Prince of Foxes 1949; The Men 1950; Bird of Paradise 1951; The Desert Fox 1951; The Enforcer 1951; The Prince Who Was a Thief 1951; Sirocco 1951; Way of a Gaucho 1952; Lust for Life 1956; Patterns 1956; Somebody Up There Likes Me 1956; The Gun Runners 1958; Marjorie Morningstar 1958; Home from the Hill 1960; By Love Possessed 1961; The Man from the Diner's Club 1963; The Disorderly Orderly 1964; The Patsy 1964

Sloane, Lindsay (1977-) The In-Laws 2003; Over Her Dead Body 2008; She's out of My League 2008; The Other Guys 2010

Sloane, Olive (1896-1963) Seven Days to Noon 1950; Curtain Up 1952; My Wife's Lodger 1952; The Man in the Road 1957

Sloatman, Lala (1970-) Watchers 1988; Amityville: a New Generation 1993

Slotnick, Joey (1966-) Blast from the Past 1999; Since You've Been Gone 1998; Pirates of Silicon Valley 1999; Hollow Man 2000

Sloyan, James (1940-) The Disappearance of Aimee 1976; Xanadu 1980

Small, Marya aka **Small, Merrya** (1942-) Sleeper 1973; Fade to Black 1980; National Lampoon's Class Reunion 1982; Puppet Master 1989

Small, Sharon (1957-) About a Boy 2002; Dear Frankie 2003

Smalley, Phillips (1875-1939) High Voltage 1929; Charley's Aunt 1930

Smart, Amy (1976-) Road Trip 2000; Rat Race 2001; Barely Legal 2003; Blind Horizon 2003; The Butterfly Effect 2003; Starsky & Hutch 2004; Win a Date with Tad Hamilton! 2004; The Best Man 2005; Just Friends 2005; Crank 2006; Mirrors 2008; Crank: High Voltage 2009; 12 Dates of Christmas 2011

Smart, Jean (1959-) Fire with Fire 1986; Whisper of the Heart 1995; The Odd Couple II 1998; Guinevere 1999; Disney's The Kid 2000; Snow Day 2000; Sweet Home Alabama 2002; Bringing Down the House 2003; Garden State 2003; Balto - Wings of Change 2004; Lucky You 2007; Hero Wanted 2008; Youth in Revolt 2009; Life as We Know It 2010

Smart, Rebecca (1976-) The Shiralee 1986; Celia 1988; Blackrock 1997

Smerczak, Ron aka **Smerczac, Ron** Cyborg Cop 1993; Dangerous Ground 1996; Jackie Chan's Who Am I? 1998

Smet, Laura (1983-) The Bridesmaid 2004; YSL: Yves Saint Laurent 2014

Smethurst, Jack (1932-) A Kind of Loving 1962; For the Love of Ada 1972; Love Thy Neighbour 1973

Smiley, Michael (1963-) Outpost 2007; Down Terrace 2009; Kill List 2011; Shell 2012; A Field in England 2013; For Those in Peril 2013; We Are the Freaks 2013; Glassland 2014; The Hallow 2015; Orthodox 2015

Smith-Cameron, J That Night 1992; Harriet the Spy 1996; The Rage: Carrie 2 1999; You Can Count on Me 1999; Margaret 2008

Smith-Jackson, Jamie The Affair 1973; Breezy 1973; Bug 1975

Smith, Alexis (1921-1993) Affectionately Yours 1941; Dive Bomber 1941; Gentleman Jim 1942; The Constant Nymph 1943; The Adventures of Mark Twain 1944; The Doughgirls 1944; Conflict 1945; The Horn Blows at Midnight 1945; Rhapsody in Blue 1945; San Antonio 1945; The Two Mrs Carrolls 1945; Night and Day 1946; Of Human Bondage 1946; The Woman in White 1948; Any Number Can Play 1949; South of St Louis 1949; Montana 1950; Undercover Girl 1950; Wyoming Mail 1950; Cave of Outlaws 1951; Here Comes the Groom 1951; The Turning Point 1952; Split Second 1953; The Sleeping Tiger 1954; Beau James 1957; This Happy Feeling 1958; The Young Philadelphians 1959; Once Is Not Enough 1975; The Little Girl Who Lives Down the Lane 1976; Casey's Shadow 1978; Tough Guys 1986; The Age of Innocence 1993

Smith, Amber (1972-) Faithful 1996; Dead End 2003

Smith, Anjela Lauren (1978-) Babymother 1998; GMT Greenwich Mean Time 1998; Revolver 2005; Sus 2009

Smith, Art (1899-1973) T-Men 1947; Angel in Exile 1948; Letter from an Unknown Woman 1948; Mr Peabody and the Mermaid 1948; Caught 1949; In a Lonely Place 1950; The Next Voice You Hear 1950; Quicksand 1950

Smith, Billy Underground 1998; The Ghost of Greville Lodge 2000

Smith, Brady Black Widow 2007; Ice Dreams 2009

Smith, Brandon aka **Smith, Brandon Mychal** (1949-) Blaze 1989; Powder 1995; Jeepers Creepers 2001; Slap Her, She's French! 2001; The Triumph 2006

Smith, Britta The Country Girls 1983; In the Name of the Father 1993; The Magdalene Sisters 2002

Smith, Brooke (1967-) Vanya on 42nd Street 1994; Kansas City 1995; Series 7: the Contenders 2001; The Namesake 2006

Smith, Bubba (1945-2011) Stroker Ace 1983; Police Academy 1984; Black Moon Rising 1985; Police Academy 2: Their First Assignment 1985; Police Academy 3: Back in Training 1986; Police Academy 4: Citizens on Patrol 1987; The Wild Pair 1987; Police Academy 5: Assignment Miami Beach 1988; Police Academy 6: City under Siege 1989

Smith, C Aubrey (1863-1948) Birds of Prey 1930; The Bachelor Father 1931; Daybreak 1931; Guilty Hands 1931; Trader Horn 1931; Love Me Tonight 1932; Polly of the Circus 1932; Tarzan, the Ape Man 1932; Trouble in Paradise 1932; The Barbarian 1933; Blonde Bombshell 1933; Morning Glory 1933; Secrets 1933; Bulldog Drummond Strikes Back 1934; Caravan 1934; Cleopatra 1934; Gambling Lady 1934; The House of Rothschild 1934; One More River 1934; The Scarlet Empress 1934; We Live Again 1934; China Seas 1935; The Crusades 1935; The Gilded Lily 1935; The Lives of a Bengal Lancer 1935; The Garden of Allah 1936; Little Lord Fauntleroy 1936; Lloyd's of London 1936; Romeo and Juliet 1936; The Hurricane 1937; The Prisoner of Zenda 1937; Thoroughbreds Don't Cry 1937; Wee Willie Winkie 1937; Four Men and a Prayer 1938; Kidnapped 1938; Sixty Glorious Years 1938; Another Thin Man 1939; East Side of Heaven

1939; Eternally Yours 1939; Five Came Back 1939; The Four Feathers 1939; A Bill of Divorcement 1940; Rebecca 1940; Waterloo Bridge 1940; Dr Jekyll and Mr Hyde 1941; Forever and a Day 1943; Madame Curie 1943; The Adventures of Mark Twain 1944; Sensations 1944; The White Cliffs of Dover 1944; And Then There Were None 1945; Cluny Brown 1946; Rendezvous with Annie 1946; An Ideal Husband 1947; Unconquered 1947; Little Women 1949

Smith, Charles (1920-1988) The General 1927; Three Little Girls in Blue 1946

Smith, Charles Martin aka **Smith, Charlie Martin** (1953-) The Culpepper Cattle Co 1972; American Graffiti 1973; The Spikes Gang 1974; The Buddy Holly Story 1978; More American Graffiti 1979; Herbie Goes Bananas 1980; Never Cry Wolf 1983; Starman 1984; The Untouchables 1987; The Experts 1989; The Hot Spot 1990; Fifty/Fifty 1991; Deep Cover 1992; And the Band Played On 1993; Speechless 1994; Lucky You 2007

Smith, Christie Lynn Backyard Wedding 2010; The Crazies 2010; Assumed Killer 2013

Smith, Constance (1928-2003) Room to Let 1949; The 13th Letter 1950; Red Skies of Montana 1952; Man in the Attic 1953; Taxi 1953; Treasure of the Golden Condor 1953; The Big Tip Off 1955; Impulse 1955; Tiger by the Tail 1955

Smith, Cotter (1949-) The Rape of Richard Beck 1985; Lady Beware 1987; Cameron's Closet 1988; K-9 1989; Run the Wild Fields 2000

Smith, Cynthia Benji 1974; For the Love of Benji 1977

Smith, Cyril (1892-1963) Friday the Thirteenth 1933; The Rocking Horse Winner 1949; Green Grow the Rushes 1951; Sailor Beware! 1956; Light Up the Sky 1960

Smith, Desirée The Delinquents 1989; Almost 1990

Smith, Gerald Oliver (1892-1974) When You're in Love 1937; The Sailor Takes a Wife 1945

Smith, Gregory (1983-) Harriet the Spy 1996; Krippendorf's Tribe 1998; Small Soldiers 1998; Closing the Ring 2006; The Dark Is Rising 2007; Hobo with a Shotgun 2011

Smith, Howard aka **Smith, Howard I** (1893-1968) Kiss of Death 1947; Death of a Salesman 1951; The Caddy 1953; No Time for Sergeants 1958; Wind across the Everglades 1958

Smith, Jaclyn (1945-) The Adventurers 1970; Las Vegas Roundabout 1975; Déjà Vu 1984; Victim of Rage 1994; Ordinary Miracles 2005

Smith, Jacob (1990-) Cheaper by the Dozen 2003; Cheaper by the Dozen 2 2005

Smith, Jaden aka **Smith, Jaden Christopher Syre** (1998-) The Pursuit of Happyness 2006; The Day the Earth Stood Still 2008; The Karate Kid 2010; Justin Bieber: Never Say Never 2011; After Earth 2013

Smith, Jamie Renee (1987-) Dante's Peak 1997; To Live For 1999

Smith, John (1931-1995) Seven Angry Men 1955; Wichita 1955; The Bold and the Brave 1956; The Magnificent Showman 1964; Waco 1966

Smith, Keely (1932-) Senior Prom 1958; Thunder Road 1958; Hey Boy! Hey Girl! 1959

Smith, Kent (1907-1985) Cat People 1942; Hitler's Children 1943; This Land Is Mine 1943; The Curse of the Cat People 1944; The Spiral Staircase 1946; Magic Town 1947; Nora Prentiss 1947; Voice of the Turtle 1947; The Fountainhead 1949; My Foolish Heart 1949; The Damned Don't Cry 1950; Comanche 1956; The Badlanders 1958; Party Girl 1958; This Earth Is Mine 1959; Strangers When We Meet 1960; Games 1967; Death of a Gunfighter 1969

Smith, Kerr (1972-) Final Destination 2000; The Forsaken 2001; My Bloody Valentine 2009

Smith (2), Kevin (1970-) Clerks 1994; Mallrats 1995; Chasing Amy 1996; Dogma 1999; Scream 3 1999; Jay and Silent Bob Strike Back 2001; Daredevil 2003; Southland Tales 2005; Clerks II 2006; This Film Is Not Yet Rated 2006; Catch and Release 2007; Die Hard 4.0 2007; TMNT 2007; Yoga Hosers 2016

Smith, Kurtwood (1943-) RoboCop 1987; Rambo III 1988; Dead Poets Society 1989; True Believer 1989; Company Business 1991; Fortress 1992; Boxing Helena 1993; The Crush 1993; Last of the Dogmen 1995; Under Siege

2 1995; Citizen Ruth 1996; Cedar Rapids 2011

Smith, Lane (1936-2005) On the Yard 1978; Purple Hearts 1984; Prison 1987; Weeds 1987; Air America 1990; The Distinguished Gentleman 1992; The Mighty Ducks 1992; My Cousin Vinny 1992; The Scout 1994; Inherit the Wind 1999

Smith, Lauren Lee (1980-) Lie with Me 1995; Pathology 2007

Smith, Lewis (1958-) Southern Comfort 1981; I Ought to Be in Pictures 1982; The Adventures of Buckaroo Banzai across the 8th Dimension 1984; The Heavenly Kid 1985; The Fulfillment of Mary Gray 1989; Diary of a Hitman 1992

Smith, Liz (1925-) Bleak Moments 1971; It Shouldn't Happen to a Vet 1979; Separate Tables 1983; A Private Function 1984; Apartment Zero 1988; High Spirits 1988; We Think the World of You 1988; Bert Rigby, You're a Fool 1989; The Cook, the Thief, His Wife and Her Lover 1989; Son of the Pink Panther 1993; Haunted 1995; Keep the Aspidistra Flying 1997; The Revengers' Comedies 1997; Tom's Midnight Garden 1998; Keeping Mum 2005; Wallace & Gromit in The Curse of the Were-Rabbit 2005; The Magic Flute 2006

Smith, Lois (1930-) East of Eden 1955; Strange Lady in Town 1955; Five Easy Pieces 1970; Next Stop, Greenwich Village 1976; Foxes 1980; Reuben, Reuben 1983; Reckless 1984; Falling Down 1992; Holy Matrimony 1994; Dead Man Walking 1995; Twister 1996; The Eternal 1998; Minority Report 2002; Sweet Land 2005; Hollywoodland 2006

Smith, Loring (1891-1981) The Clown 1952; Happy Anniversary 1959

Smith, Madeline (1949-) The Vampire Lovers 1970; The Amazing Mr Blunden 1972; Up the Front 1972; Frankenstein and the Monster from Hell 1973; Live and Let Die 1973; Take Me High 1973

Smith, Madolyn aka **Smith Osborne, Madolyn** (1957-) Urban Cowboy 1980; All of Me 1984; 2010 1984; The Caller 1987; Funny Farm 1988; The Plot to Kill Hitler 1990; Final Approach 1991; The Super 1991

Smith, Maggie (1934-) Nowhere to Go 1958; Go to Blazes 1961; The VIPs 1963; The Pumpkin Eater 1964; Othello 1965; Young Cassidy 1965; The Honey Pot 1967; Hot Millions 1968; Oh! What a Lovely War 1969; The Prime of Miss Jean Brodie 1969; Travels with My Aunt 1972; Love and Pain and the Whole Damn Thing 1973; Murder by Death 1976; California Suite 1978; Death on the Nile 1978; Clash of the Titans 1981; Quartet 1981; Evil under the Sun 1982; The Missionary 1982; Better Late than Never 1983; A Private Function 1984; Lily in Love 1985; A Room with a View 1985; The Lonely Passion of Judith Hearne 1987; Hook 1991; Sister Act 1992; The Secret Garden 1993; Sister Act 2: Back in the Habit 1993; Richard III 1995; The First Wives Club 1996; Curtain Call 1997; Washington Square 1997; Tea with Mussolini 1998; The Last September 1999; Gosford Park 2001; Harry Potter and the Philosopher's Stone 2001; Divine Secrets of the Ya-Ya Sisterhood 2002; Harry Potter and the Chamber of Secrets 2002; My House in Umbria 2002; Harry Potter and the Prisoner of Azkaban 2004; Ladies in Lavender 2004; Harry Potter and the Goblet of Fire 2005; Keeping Mum 2005; Becoming Jane 2006; Harry Potter and the Order of the Phoenix 2007; From Time to Time 2009; Harry Potter and the Half-Blood Prince 2009; Nanny McPhee & the Big Bang 2010; The Best Exotic Marigold Hotel 2011; Gnomeo & Juliet 2011; Quartet 2012; My Old Lady 2014; The Lady in the Van 2015; The Second Best Exotic Marigold Hotel 2015

Smith, Matt aka **Smith, Matthew** (1982-) Clone 2010; Lost River 2014; Pride and Prejudice and Zombies 2015; Terminator: Genisys 2015; Mapplethorpe 2016

Smith, Mel (1952-2013) Babylon 1980; Bullshot 1983; Number One 1984; Morons from Outer Space 1985; National Lampoon's European Vacation 1985; Restless Natives 1985; The Princess Bride 1987; The Wolves of Willoughby Chase 1988; Wilt 1989; Brain Donors 1992; Twelfth Night 1996

Smith, Michael Bailey Cyborg 3: The Recycler 1994; In Hell 2003; Monster Man 2003

Smith, Nicholas (1934-2015) Are You Being Served? 1977; Wallace & Gromit in The Curse of the Were-Rabbit 2005

Smith, Oliver Hellraiser 1987; Hellbound: Hellraiser II 1988

Smith, Patricia (1930-) The Bachelor Party 1957; The Spirit of St Louis 1957; The Girl Who Knew Too Much 1969; Save the Tiger 1973

Smith, Patti Patti Smith: Dream of Life 2007; Film Socialisme 2010; Another Day/Another Time 2013; Station to Station 2015

Smith, Paul aka **Smith, Paul L** (1939-) Madron 1970; Midnight Express 1978; Popeye 1980; Pieces 1982; Crimewave 1985; Red Sonja 1985; Haunted Honeymoon 1986; Gor 1987

Smith, Pete The Quiet Earth 1985; Crush 1992; Flight of the Albatross 1995; The Boys 1998; What Becomes of the Broken Hearted? 1999

Smith, Phyllis Bad Teacher 2011; Inside Out 2015

Smith, Queenie (1898-1978) Mississippi 1935; Show Boat 1936; The Long Night 1947; Sleep, My Love 1948; The Great Rupert 1950

Smith, Ray (1936-1991) The Painted Smile 1961; Operation Daybreak 1975

Smith, Rex (1956-) The Pirates of Penzance 1983; The Trial of the Incredible Hulk 1989; Danielle Steel's Once in a Lifetime 1994

Smith, Riley (1978-) Radio 2003; New York Minute 2004; Make It Happen 2008

Smith, Roger (1932-) Auntie Mame 1958; Never Steal Anything Small 1959; Roger & Me 1989

Smith, Roger Guenveur Poetic Justice 1993; Mercenary for Justice 2006; Fighting 2009

Smith, Shawn (1922-1995) It! The Terror from beyond Space 1958; The River Rat 1984

Smith, Shawnee (1970-) Summer School 1987; The Blob 1988; Who's Harry Crumb? 1989; Dead Men Can't Dance 1997; Carnival of Souls 1999; Saw II 2005; Saw III 2006; Saw IV 2007; Secrets of an Undercover Wife 2007; Saw VI 2009

Smith, Sheridan (1981-) Hysteria 2011; Quartet 2012; Tower Block 2012; The Harry Hill Movie 2013; Powder Room 2013

Smith, Will (1968-) Made in America 1993; Six Degrees of Separation 1993; Bad Boys 1995; Independence Day 1996; Men in Black 1997; Enemy of the State 1998; Wild Wild West 1999; The Legend of Bagger Vance 2000; Ali 2001; Men in Black 2 2002; Bad Boys II 2003; Jersey Girl 2003; I, Robot 2004; Shark Tale 2004; Hitch 2005; The Pursuit of Happyness 2006; I Am Legend 2007; Hancock 2008; Seven Pounds 2008; Men in Black 3 2012; After Earth 2013; A New York Winter's Tale 2014; Concussion 2015; Focus 2015; Collateral Beauty 2016; Suicide Squad 2016; Bright 2017

Smith, William aka **Smith, Bill** aka **Smith II, William** (1934-) Atlantis, the Lost Continent 1960; Three Guns for Texas 1968; Backtrack 1969; Hammer 1972; The Deadly Trackers 1973; The Last American Hero 1973; The Rockford Files 1974; The Ultimate Warrior 1975; The Frisco Kid 1979; Seven 1979; Any Which Way You Can 1980; Eye of the Tiger 1986; Hell Comes to Frogtown 1988; Maniac Cop 1988; Spirit of the Eagle 1991

Smith, Wyatt The Gunfighter's Pledge 2008; Never Back Down 2008

Smith, Yeardley (1964-) The Legend of Billie Jean 1985; Maximum Overdrive 1986; As Good as It Gets 1997; The Simpsons Movie 2007; The Wishing Well 2009

Smithers, William (1927-) Attack! 1956; Trouble Man 1972; Deathsport 1978

Smit-McPhee, Kodi (1996-) The Road 2009; Let Me In 2010; Dead Europe 2012; ParaNorman 2012; Bad Land: Road to Fury 2014; Dawn of the Planet of the Apes 2014; Maya the Bee 2014; Slow West 2015

Smitrovich, Bill (1947-) A Killing Affair 1985; Renegades 1989; Crazy People 1990; The Phantom 1996; The Trigger Effect 1996; Futuresport 1998; Mr Murder 1998; While I Was Gone 2004; Seven Pounds 2008; The November Man 2014

Smits, Jimmy (1956-) Hot Shot 1986; Running Scared 1986; Old Gringo 1989; Vital Signs 1990; Fires Within 1991; Switch 1991; My Family 1994; Murder in Mind 1996; The Million Dollar Hotel 1999; Bless the Child 2000; Price of Glory 2000; Star Wars Episode II: Attack of the Clones 2002; The Jane Austen Book Club 2007; Mother and Child 2009

Smits, Sonja (1958-) Videodrome 1982; Owning Mahowny 2002

Smollett, Jurnee (1986-) Eve's Bayou 1997; Beautiful Joe 2000; The Great Debaters 2007

Smoove, J B The Sitter 2011; The Smurfs 2 2013; Search Party 2014; Top Five 2014; Barbershop: a Fresh Cut 2016

Smothers, Tom (1937-) Get to Know Your Rabbit 1972; Silver Bears 1977; There Goes the Bride 1979; Pandemonium 1982

Smulders, Cobie (1982-) Delivery Man 2013; Safe Haven 2013; They Came Together 2014; Results 2015; Jack Reacher: Never Go Back 2016

Smurfit, Victoria (1974-) The Run of the Country 1995; The Wedding Tackle 2000; About a Boy 2002; Bulletproof Monk 2002; The Last Great Wilderness 2002; Bait 2015

Smuts Kennedy, Sarah An Angel at My Table 1990; Jack Be Nimble 1992

Smyrner, Ann (1934-) The Good Die First 1967; House of a Thousand Dolls 1967

Snipes, Wesley (1962-) Streets of Gold 1986; Wildcats 1986; King of New York 1989; Major League 1989; Mo' Better Blues 1990; Jungle Fever 1991; New Jack City 1991; The Waterdance 1991; Passenger 57 1992; White Men Can't Jump 1992; Boiling Point 1993; Demolition Man 1993; Rising Sun 1993; Sugar Hill 1993; Drop Zone 1994; Money Train 1995; To Wong Foo, Thanks for Everything, Julie Newmar 1995; The Fan 1996; Down in the Delta 1997; Murder at 1600 1997; One Night Stand 1997; Blade 1998; Futuresport 1998; US Marshals 1998; The Art of War 2000; Disappearing Acts 2000; Play It to the Bone 2000; Blade II 2002; Liberty Stands Still 2002; Undisputed 2002; Blade: Trinity 2004; Unstoppable 2004; 7 Seconds 2005; Chaos 2006; The Detonator 2006; Hard Luck 2006; The Contractor 2007; The Art of War II: Betrayal 2008; Brooklyn's Finest 2009

Snodgrass, Carrie (1945-2004) Diary of a Mad Housewife 1970; Rabbit, Run 1970; The Fury 1978; A Night in Heaven 1983; Pale Rider 1985; Murphy's Law 1986; Across the Tracks 1990; Blue Sky 1991; The Ballad of Little Jo 1993; 8 Seconds 1994; White Man's Burden 1995; Bartleby 2000; Ed Gein 2000; The Forsaken 2001

Snook, Sarah These Final Hours 2013; Predestination 2014; Oddball and the Penguins 2015

Snoop Dogg aka **Snoop Doggy Dogg** (1971-) Half-Baked 1998; I Got the Hook Up 1998; Ride 1998; Gang Law 1999; Whiteboys 1999; Baby Boy 2001; Bones 2001; Malibu's Most Wanted 2003; Old School 2003; Racing Stripes 2004; Soul Plane 2004; Starsky & Hutch 2004; Boss'n Up 2005; Arthur and the Invisibles 2006; In Prison My Whole Life 2008; Something from Nothing: the Art of Rap 2012; Reincarnated 2013; Turbo 2013

Snow, Brittany (1986-) Whisper of the Heart 1995; The Pacifier 2005; John Tucker Must Die 2006; Hairspray 2007; Prom Night 2008; Pitch Perfect 2012; Pitch Perfect 2 2015; Pitch Perfect 3 2017

Snowden, Leigh (1929-1982) The Square Jungle 1955; The Creature Walks among Us 1956

Snyder, Arlen Dean (1933-) The Night the Lights Went Out in Georgia 1981; Heartbreak Ridge 1986; Kansas 1988; Running Cool 1993

Snyder, Suzanne (1962-) Weird Science 1985; Killer Klowns from Outer Space 1988; The Night Before 1988; Return of the Living Dead Part II 1988; Femme Fatale 1991

Soans, Robin Comrades: a Lanternist's Account of the Tolpuddle Martyrs and What Became of Them 1986; Clockwork Mice 1994

Sobieski, Leelee (1982-) Jungle 2 Jungle 1997; A Soldier's Daughter Never Cries 1998; Never Been Kissed 1999; Here on Earth 2000; The Glass House 2001; My First Mister 2001; Road Kill 2001; Max 2002; The Wicker Man 2006; 88 Minutes 2007; Public Enemies 2009

Socha, Michael Do99ing: a Love Story 2009; Shank 2010

Soderbergh, Steven (1963-) Schizopolis 1996; Waking Life 2001

Sofaer, Abraham (1896-1988) Crooks' Tour 1940; Dual Alibi 1946; Calling Paul Temple 1948; Christopher Columbus 1949; Quo Vadis 1951; His Majesty O'Keefe 1953; Elephant Walk 1954; Bhowani Junction 1956; The First

Texan 1956; Captain Sindbad 1963; Twice Told Tales 1963; Head 1968

Sofer, Rena (1968-) Always and Forever 2008; The Devil's Teardrop 2010

Sohn, Sonja Slam 1998; Step Up 2 the Streets 2008

Söhnker, Hans aka **Sohnker, Hans** (1903-1981) For the First Time 1959; Sherlock Holmes and the Deadly Necklace 1962

Sokol, Marilyn Something Short of Paradise 1979; The Last Married Couple in America 1980

Sokoloff, Marla (1980-) True Crime 1995; Dude, Where's My Car? 2000; Whatever It Takes 2000; Sugar & Spice 2001; Date with Darkness 2003; Flower Girl 2009

Sokoloff, Vladimir aka **Sokoloff, Wladimir** (1889-1962) The Love of Jeanne Ney 1927; The Ship of Lost Men 1929; The Lower Depths 1936; Blockade 1938; Comrade X 1940; Love Crazy 1941; Road to Morocco 1942; For Whom the Bell Tolls 1943; The Conspirators 1944; Till We Meet Again 1944; Cloak and Dagger 1946; To the Ends of the Earth 1948; The Baron of Arizona 1950; Monster from Green Hell 1958; Beyond the Time Barrier 1960; The Magnificent Seven 1960; Mr Sardonicus 1961

Sola, Miguel Angel (1950-) Funny Dirty Little War 1983; Tangos, Exilo de Gardel 1985; Sur 1987

Soler, Andrés (1898-1969) The Great Madcap 1949; El Bruto 1952; La Fièvre Monte à el Pao 1959

Soler, Fernando (1896-1979) The Great Madcap 1949; La Hija del Engaño 1951

Soles, P J (1955-) Halloween 1978; Rock 'n' Roll High School 1979; Stripes 1981; Sweet Dreams 1985; Shake, Rattle and Rock 1994; Little Bigfoot 1995

Soles, Paul The Gunrunner 1984; The Score 2001

Solier, Magaly The Milk of Sorrow 2009; Blackthorn 2011

Solimeno, Cristian Dead Babies 2000; Highlander: the Source 2007; Tu£sday 2007

Solon, Ewen (1917-1985) Behind the Headlines 1956; Account Rendered 1957; Jack the Ripper 1958; The Hound of the Baskervilles 1959; The Sundowners 1960

Solonitsyn, Anatoli aka **Solonitsin, Anatoly** aka **Solonitsin, Anatoli** (1934-1982) Andrei Rublev 1966; Solaris 1972; Stalker 1979

Solovei, Elena (1947-) A Slave of Love 1976; An Unfinished Piece for Mechanical Piano 1976; Oblomov 1980

Somack, Jack (1918-1983) Desperate Characters 1971; Portnoy's Complaint 1972

Somerhalder, Ian The Rules of Attraction 2002; Pulse 2006; The Tournament 2009; The Anomaly 2014

Somers, Julian (1913-1976) The Gambler and the Lady 1952; Hunted 1952

Somers, Suzanne (1946-) Yesterday's Hero 1979; Serial Mom 1994

Somerville, Geraldine Haunted 1995; True Blue 1996

Somerville, Phyllis Little Children 2006; Stoker 2013

Sommars, Julie (1942-) The Harness 1971; Herbie Goes to Monte Carlo 1977

Sommer, Elke (1940-) Don't Bother to Knock 1961; The Prize 1963; The Victors 1963; A Shot in the Dark 1964; Art of Love 1965; Le Bambole 1965; Boy, Did I Get a Wrong Number 1966; The Corrupt Ones 1966; Deadlier than the Male 1966; The Oscar 1966; The Venetian Affair 1966; The Heroes 1968; They Came to Rob Las Vegas 1968; The Wrecking Crew 1969; Percy 1971; Zeppelin 1971; Baron Blood 1972; And Then There Were None 1974; Lisa and the Devil 1974; Percy's Progress 1974; Carry On Behind 1975; The Swiss Conspiracy 1975; The Astral Factor 1976; A Nightingale Sang in Berkeley Square 1979; The Prisoner of Zenda 1979; Lily in Love 1985

Sommer, Josef aka **Somr, Josef** (1934-) Closely Observed Trains 1966; The Joke 1968; Oliver's Story 1978; Hide in Plain Sight 1980; Absence of Malice 1981; Rollover 1981; Hanky Panky 1982; Still of the Night 1982; Agatha Christie's Sparkling Cyanide 1983; Independence Day 1983; Iceman 1984; DARYL 1985; Target 1985; Witness 1985; The Betty Ford Story 1987; The Rosary Murders 1987; Dracula's Widow 1988; Bloodhounds of Broadway 1989; Chances are 1989; Forced March 1989; The Mighty Ducks 1992; Hostages 1993; Don't Drink the Water 1994; The Enemy Within 1994; Nobody's Fool

1994; The Chamber 1996; Patch Adams 1998; The Proposition 1998; The Family Man 2000; The Next Best Thing 2000; The Invasion 2007

Sondergaard, Gale (1899-1985) Anthony Adverse 1936; The Life of Emile Zola 1937; Seventh Heaven 1937; Dramatic School 1938; The Cat and the Canary 1939; Juarez 1939; The Llano Kid 1939; Never Say Die 1939; The Blue Bird 1940; The Letter 1940; The Mark of Zorro 1940; The Black Cat 1941; Paris Calling 1941; My Favorite Blonde 1942; A Night to Remember 1942; Christmas Holiday 1944; Enter Arsene Lupin 1944; The Invisible Man's Revenge 1944; Sherlock Holmes and the Spider Woman 1944; Anna and the King of Siam 1946; The Time of Their Lives 1946; Road to Rio 1947; East Side, West Side 1949; Slaves 1969; The Return of a Man Called Horse 1976

Song Kang-ho (1967-) The Quiet Family 1998; Shiri 1999; Sympathy for Mr Vengeance 2002; Memories of Murder 2003; The Host 2006; The Good the Bad the Weird 2008; Thirst 2009

Song Young-chang Duelist 2005; Thirst 2009

Song, Brenda Like Mike 2002; College Road Trip 2008; The Social Network 2010

Songz, Trey aka **Neverson, Tremaine** aka **Neverson, Tremaine "Trey Songz"** Baggage Claim 2013; Texas Chainsaw 2013

Sonkkila, Paul That Eye, the Sky 1994; Mr Reliable 1996

Soo, Jack (1916-1979) Flower Drum Song 1961; Return from Witch Mountain 1978

Sood, Sonu Jodhaa Akbar 2008; City of Life 2009

Sood, Veena Nina's Heavenly Delights 2006; Secrets of an Undercover Wife 2007

Soral, Agnes (1960-) Un Moment d'Egarement 1977; Three Sisters 1988; Australia 1989

Sorbo, Kevin (1958-) Kull the Conqueror 1997; Avenging Angel 2007; Meet the Spartans 2008; Prairie Fever 2008; Soul Surfer 2011; Shadow on the Mesa 2013

Sordi, Alberto (1920-2003) The White Sheik 1951; I Vitelloni 1953; A Farewell to Arms 1957; The Best of Enemies 1961; Those Magnificent Men in Their Flying Machines 1965; The Witches 1966

Sorel, Jean (1934-) The Four Days of Naples 1962; Le Bambole 1965; Of a Thousand Delights 1965; Belle de Jour 1967; The Short Night of the Glass Dolls 1971

Sorel, Louise (1940-) The Party's Over 1965; Plaza Suite 1971; Every Little Crook and Nanny 1972; The Mark of Zorro 1974

Sorel, Ted (1936-) From Beyond 1986; Basket Case 2 1990

Sorensen, Rickie (1946-1994) Tarzan and the Trappers 1958; Tarzan's Fight for Life 1958; The Sword in the Stone 1963

Sorenson, Linda (1940-) Breaking Point 1976; Joshua Then and Now 1985; Whispers 1990

Sorvino, Mira (1967-) Barcelona 1994; Erotic Tales 1994; Mighty Aphrodite 1995; Sweet Nothing 1995; Beautiful Girls 1996; Norma Jean & Marilyn 1996; Mimic 1997; Romy and Michele's High School Reunion 1997; At First Sight 1998; Free Money 1998; Lulu on the Bridge 1998; The Replacement Killers 1998; Summer of Sam 1999; The Great Gatsby 2000; The Grey Zone 2001; Wiseglrls 2001; Gods and Generals 2002; The Final Cut 2004; Finding Mrs Claus 2012; Exposed 2016

Sorvino, Paul (1939-) Where's Poppa? 1970; The Panic in Needle Park 1971; The Day of the Dolphin 1973; A Touch of Class 1973; The Gambler 1974; Bloodbrothers 1978; The Brink's Job 1978; Slow Dancing in the Big City 1978; Lost and Found 1979; Reds 1981; That Championship Season 1982; Chiller 1985; The Stuff 1985; Surviving 1985; Turk 182! 1985; A Fine Mess 1986; Dick Tracy 1990; GoodFellas 1990; Age Isn't Everything 1991; Rocketeer 1991; Nixon 1995; Love Is All There Is 1996; William Shakespeare's Romeo + Juliet 1996; American Perfekt 1997; Money Talks 1997; Most Wanted 1997; Bulworth 1998; Knock Off 1998; See Spot Run 2001; The Cooler 2002; Hey Arnold! the Movie 2002; Mambo Italiano 2003; Imaginary Friend 2012

Sosa, Roberto Highway Patrolman 1991; How I Spent My Summer Vacation 2012

Sossamon, Shannyn (1978-) A Knight's Tale 2001; 40 Days and 40

Nights 2002; The Rules of Attraction 2002; The Sin Eater 2002; Kiss Kiss Bang Bang 2005; Wristcutters: a Love Story 2006; One Missed Call 2007; Our Family Wedding 2010; Sinister 2 2015

Soter, Paul (1969-) Super Troopers 2001; Broken Lizard's Club Dread 2004; Beerfest 2006

Sothern, Ann (1909-2001) Kid Millions 1934; Folies Bergère 1935; Danger - Love at Work 1937; Trade Winds 1938; Fast and Furious 1939; Maisie 1939; Brother Orchid 1940; Lady Be Good 1941; Cry Havoc 1943; Words and Music 1948; The Judge Steps Out 1949; A Letter to Three Wives 1949; Nancy Goes to Rio 1950; The Blue Gardenia 1953; The Best Man 1964; Lady in a Cage 1964; Sylvia 1964; The Killing Kind 1973; Golden Needles 1974; Crazy Mama 1975; The Manitou 1978; The Whales of August 1987

Sothern, Hugh (1881-1947) The Buccaneer 1938; The Oklahoma Kid 1939

Sotiropoulou, Tonia Berberian Sound Studio 2012; Brotherhood 2016

Soto, Talisa (1967-) Licence to Kill 1989; Hostage 1992; Don Juan DeMarco 1995; Mortal Kombat 1995; Sunchaser 1996; Mortal Kombat: Annihilation 1997; Flight of Fancy 2000; Piñero 2001; Ballistic: Ecks vs Sever 2002

Soualem, Zinedine When the Cat's Away... 1996; JCVD 2008

Souchon, Alain (1944-) Je Vous Aime 1980; One Deadly Summer 1983

Soucie, Kath (1953-) A Christmas Carol 1997; Kiki's Delivery Service 1998; The Rugrats Movie 1998; Rugrats in Paris: the Movie 2000; The Tigger Movie 2000; Return to Never Land 2002; Piglet's Big Movie 2003; Rugrats Go Wild 2003; Winnie the Pooh: Springtime with Roo 2004; Pooh's Heffalump Movie 2005

Soul, David (1943-) Magnum Force 1973; Dogpound Shuffle 1974; Salem's Lot 1979; Appointment with Death 1988; Puritan 2004; Farewell 2010

Soutendijk, Renée (1957-) Spetters 1980; The Girl with Red Hair 1981; The Fourth Man 1983; The Second Victory 1986; Forced March 1989; Eve of Destruction 1991

Souther, J D aka **Souther, John David** My Girl 2 1994; Purgatory 1999

Spaak, Catherine (1945-) The Easy Life 1962; The Empty Canvas 1963; La Ronde 1964; Cat o'Nine Tails 1971; Take a Hard Ride 1975

Space, Arthur (1908-1983) The Big Noise 1944; A Man Alone 1955

Spacek, Sissy (1949-) Prime Cut 1972; Badlands 1973; Ginger in the Morning 1973; Carrie 1976; Welcome to LA 1976; 3 Women 1977; Heart Beat 1979; Coal Miner's Daughter 1980; Missing 1981; Raggedy Man 1981; The Man with Two Brains 1983; The River 1984; Marie: a True Story 1985; Crimes of the Heart 1986; 'Night, Mother 1986; Violets Are Blue 1986; The Long Walk Home 1990; Hard Promises 1991; JFK 1991; A Private Matter 1992; The Mommy Market 1994; A Place for Annie 1994; The Good Old Boys 1995; The Grass Harp 1995; Beyond the Call 1996; If These Walls Could Talk 1996; Affliction 1997; Blast from the Past 1998; The Straight Story 1999; Songs in Ordinary Time 2001; In the Bedroom 2001; Midwives 2001; Tuck Everlasting 2002; A Home at the End of the World 2004; The Ring Two 2004; An American Haunting 2005; North Country 2005; Hot Rod 2007; Four Christmases 2008; Get Low 2009; The Help 2011; Deadfall 2012

Spacey, Kevin (1959-) Rocket Gibraltar 1988; Working Girl 1988; Dad 1989; See No Evil, Hear No Evil 1989; Henry & June 1990; A Show of Force 1990; Consenting Adults 1992; Glengarry Glen Ross 1992; Hostile Hostages 1994; Iron Will 1994; Swimming with Sharks 1994; Outbreak 1995; Se7en 1995; The Usual Suspects 1995; Looking for Richard 1996; A Time to Kill 1996; LA Confidential 1997; Midnight in the Garden of Good and Evil 1997; A Bug's Life 1998; Hurlyburly 1998; The Negotiator 1998; American Beauty 1999; The Big Kahuna 1999; Ordinary Decent Criminal 1999; Pay It Forward 2000; K-PAX 2001; The Shipping News 2001; The United States of Leland 2002; The Life of David Gale 2003; Beyond the Sea 2004; Edison 2005; Superman Returns 2006; Fred Claus 2007; Moon 2008; Recount 2008; Telstar: the Joe Meek Story 2008; 21 2008; The Men Who Stare at Goatsx 2009; Shrink 2009; Horrible Bosses 2011; Margin Call 2011; Horrible Bosses 2 2014; NOW: In the Wings on a

World Stage 2014; Unity 2015; Elvis & Nixon 2016; Nine Lives 2016

Spadaro, Odoardo (1895-1965) The Golden Coach 1953; Divorce - Italian Style 1961

Spade, David (1964-) Coneheads 1993; PCU 1994; Tommy Boy 1995; Black Sheep 1996; 8 Heads in a Duffel Bag 1997; The Rugrats Movie 1998; Senseless 1998; Lost & Found 1999; The Emperor's New Groove 2000; Joe Dirt 2001; Dickie Roberts: Former Child Star 2003; Kronk's New Groove 2005; The Benchwarmers 2006; Grown Ups 2010; Hotel Transylvania 2012; Grown Ups 2 2013

Spader, James (1960-) Endless Love 1981; Pretty in Pink 1986; Baby Boom 1987; Less than Zero 1987; Mannequin 1987; Wall Street 1987; Jack's Back 1988; The Rachel Papers 1989; sex, lies, and videotape 1989; Bad Influence 1990; White Palace 1990; True Colors 1991; Bob Roberts 1992; Storyville 1992; Dream Lover 1993; The Music of Chance 1993; Stargate 1994; Wolf 1994; Crash 1996; Driftwood 1996; Keys to Tulsa 1996; 2 Days in the Valley 1996; Critical Care 1997; Curtain Call 1997; Supernova 2000; The Watcher 2000; Secretary 2001; The Stickup 2001; Alien Hunter 2003; I Witness 2003; Shorts 2009; Lincoln 2012; Avengers: Age of Ultron 2015

Spain, Fay (1932-1983) Dragstrip Girl 1957; God's Little Acre 1958; Al Capone 1959; The Beat Generation 1959; The Private Lives of Adam and Eve 1959; Black Gold 1962; Thunder Island 1963; Flight to Fury 1966; The Gentle Rain 1966; Welcome to Hard Times 1967

Spain, Mark Harlequin 1980; Bush Christmas 1983

Spalding, Kim The True Story of Lynn Stuart 1957; It! The Terror from beyond Space 1958

Spall, Rafe (1983-) The Calcium Kid 2003; Green Street 2004; Kidulthood 2005; Hot Fuzz 2007; The Scouting Book for Boys 2009; Sus 2009; Anonymous 2011; Life of Pi 2012; I Give It a Year 2013; What If 2013; Get Santa 2014; X+Y 2014; The Big Short 2015; The BFG 2016; Swallows and Amazons 2016

Spall, Timothy (1957-) Gothic 1986; Crusoe 1988; Dream Demon 1988; To Kill a Priest 1988; Life Is Sweet 1990; The Sheltering Sky 1990; White Hunter, Black Heart 1990; Secrets & Lies 1995; Hamlet 1996; Still Crazy 1998; The Wisdom of Crocodiles 1998; The Clandestine Marriage 1999; Love's Labour's Lost 1999; Topsy-Turvy 1999; Chicken Run 2000; Intimacy 2000; The Old Man Who Read Love Stories 2000; Vatel 2000; Lucky Break 2001; Rock Star 2001; Vanilla Sky 2001; All or Nothing 2002; My House in Umbria 2002; Nicholas Nickleby 2002; Gettin' Square 2003; The Last Samurai 2003; Harry Potter and the Prisoner of Azkaban 2004; Lemony Snicket's A Series of Unfortunate Events 2004; Pierrepoint 2005; Death Defying Acts 2007; Enchanted 2007; Sweeney Todd: the Demon Barber of Fleet Street 2007; Appaloosa 2008; The Damned United 2009; From Time to Time 2009; Heartless 2009; Alice in Wonderland 2010; Harry Potter and the Deathly Hallows: Part 1 2010; Jackboots on Whitehall 2010; The King's Speech 2010; Reuniting the Rubins 2010; Wake Wood 2010; Comes a Bright Day 2012; Ginger & Rosa 2012; Love Bite 2012; The Rise 2012; The Love Punch 2013; Mr Turner 2014; Away 2016; Denial 2016

Spalla, Ignazio aka **Sanchez, Pedro** (1924-1995) Beatrice Cenci 1969; Sabata 1969; Adios, Sabata 1970; Return of Sabata 1971; Night and the City 1992

Spano, Joe (1946-) Roadie 1980; Terminal Choice 1983; Brotherhood of Justice 1986; Apollo 13 1995; Logan's War: Bound by Honor 1998

Spano, Vincent (1962-) Over the Edge 1979; Baby It's You 1983; The Black Stallion Returns 1983; Rumble Fish 1983; Alphabet City 1984; Creator 1985; Good Morning, Babylon 1987; And God Created Woman 1988; City of Hope 1991; Oscar 1991; Alive 1992; The Ascent 1994; The Tie That Binds 1995; The Prophecy 3: the Ascent 2000; Her Fatal Flaw 2006; Lone Rider 2008

Sparks, Adrian Apprentice to Murder 1988; My Stepmother Is an Alien 1988

Sparks, Jordin Sparkle 2012; Left Behind 2014

Sparks, Ned (1883-1957) The Big Noise 1928; The Devil's Holiday 1930; Kept Husbands 1931; Blessed Event 1932; Gold Diggers of 1933 1933; Lady for a Day 1933; Secrets 1933; Hi, Nellie!

1934; Imitation of Life 1934; Marie Galante 1934; Sing and Like It 1934; George White's 1935 Scandals 1935; Sweet Adeline 1935; The Bride Walks Out 1936; One in a Million 1936; Wake Up and Live 1937; The Star Maker 1939; Magic Town 1947

Sparrow, Walter (1927-2000) The Secret Garden 1993; The Woodlanders 1997; Treasure Island 1998

Sparv, Camilla (1943-) Dead Heat on a Merry-Go-Round 1966; The Trouble with Angels 1966; Nobody Runs Forever 1968; Downhill Racer 1969; Mackenna's Gold 1969

Spearritt, Hannah (1981-) Agent Cody Banks 2: Destination London 2003; Seeing Double 2003; Seed of Chucky 2004; The Goob 2014

Spector, Phil (1940-) Easy Rider 1969; George Harrison: Living in the Material World 2011

Speedman, Scott (1975-) Duets 2000; Dark Blue 2002; My Life without Me 2002; Underworld 2003; xXx: the Next Level 2005; Urderworld: Evolution 2006; Weirdsville 2006; The Strangers 2007; Adoration 2008; Barney's Version 2010; The Moth Diaries 2010; The Vow 2012; The Captive 2014; Out of the Dark 2014

Speer, Hugo (1969-) The Full Monty 1997; Swing 1998; Deathwatch 2002; Nymphomaniac Vol 1 2013

Speleers, Ed Eragon 2006; A Lonely Place to Die 2011; Love Bite 2012; Plastic 2014; Howl 2015; Remainder 2015

Spelling, Tori (1973-) Death of a Cheerleader 1994; The House of Yes 1997; Trick 1999; A Carol Christmas 2003; Family Plan 2005; The Mistle-Tones 2012

Spence, Bruce (1945-) Double Deal 1981; Mad Max 2 1981; Where the Green Ants Dream 1984; Mad Max beyond Thunderdome 1985; Almost 1990; Hercules Returns 1993; Aquamarine 2006; Backtrack 2015

Spence, Sebastian (1969-) First Shot 2002; The Obsession 2006; NYC: Tornado Terror 2008

Spencer, Abigail aka **Spencer, Abigail Leigh** Chasing Mavericks 2012; This Means War 2012

Spencer, Bud (1929-2016) God Forgives... I Don't! 1967; Ace High 1968; Boot Hill 1969; They Call Me Trinity 1970; A Reason to Live, a Reason to Die 1972; Extralarge Moving Target 1990

Spencer, Douglas (1910-1960) The Thing from Another World 1951; The Glass Wall 1953; Shane 1953; River of No Return 1954; Smoke Signal 1955; This Island Earth 1955; The Three Faces of Eve 1957

Spencer, Jesse (1979-) Winning London 2001; Swimming Upstream 2003; Uptown Girls 2003

Spencer, John (1946-2005) Black Rain 1989; Albino Alligator 1996; The Rock 1996; The Negotiator 1998; Ravenous 1999

Spencer, Octavia aka **Spencer, Octavia L** (1970-) Win a Date with Tad Hamilton! 2004; Pulse 2006; Smashed 2012; Fruitvale Station 2013; Snowpiercer 2013

Spengler, Volker Satan's Brew 1976; Bolwieser 1977; Despair 1978; In a Year of 13 Moons 1978; The Third Generation 1979

Spenser, Jeremy (1937-) Portrait of Clare 1950; Prelude to Fame 1950; The Planter's Wife 1952; Background 1953; Devil on Horseback 1954; It's Great to Be Young 1956; The Prince and the Showgirl 1957; Ferry to Hong Kong 1958; The Roman Spring of Mrs Stone 1961; The Brain 1962; He Who Rides a Tiger 1965; Fahrenheit 451 1966

Sperber, Wendie Jo (1958-2005) I Wanna Hold Your Hand 1978; Back to the Future 1985

Speredakos, John Wendigo 2001; The Roost 2005; The Innkeepers 2011

Spevack, Jason (1997-) Crazy for Christmas 2005; The Perfect Catch 2005; Sunshine Cleaning 2008; Ramona and Beezus 2010

Spielberg, David (1939-) Law and Disorder 1974; Act of Love 1980; A Place for Annie 1994

Spielberg, Sasha The Love Letter 1999; The Art of Getting By 2011

Spielberg, Steven (1946-) The Blues Brothers 1980; Ray Harryhausen: Special Effects Titan 2011

Spiesser, Jacques Black and White in Color 1976; Ecoute le Temps 2005; Priceless 2006

Spinell, Joe (1936-1989) Rocky 1976; Rocky II 1979

Spinella, Stephen Virtuosity 1995; Love! Valour! Compassion! 1997; Connie and Carla 2004; Rubber 2010

Spiner, Brent (1949-) Star Trek: Generations 1994; Independence Day 1996; Star Trek: First Contact 1996; Star Trek: Insurrection 1998; Introducing Dorothy Dandridge 1999; South Park: Bigger, Longer & Uncut 1999; Geppetto 2000; The Master of Disguise 2002; Star Trek: Nemesis 2002; Jack 2004; Material Girls 2006; Superhero Movie 2008; Independence Day: Resurgence 2016

Spinetti, Victor (1929-2012) The Wild Affair 1963; A Hard Day's Night 1964; Help! 1965; The Taming of the Shrew 1967; Can Heironymus Merkin Ever Forget Mercy Humppe and Find True Happiness? 1969; Start the Revolution without Me 1970; Under Milk Wood 1971; Digby, the Biggest Dog in the World 1973; The Little Prince 1974; Hardcore 1977; The Attic: the Hiding of Anne Frank 1988; The Krays 1990; The Princess and the Goblin 1992; Julie and the Cadillacs 1997

Sporleder, Gregory Clay Pigeons 1998; G-Men from Hell 2000

Spradlin, G D (1920-2011) Number One 1969; Zabriskie Point 1970; The Hunting Party 1971; Apocalypse Now 1979; The Formula 1980; The Jayne Mansfield Story 1980; The Man with the Deadly Lens 1982; The Lords of Discipline 1983; Resting Place 1986; The War of the Roses 1989; Ed Wood 1994

Spriggs, Elizabeth (1929-2008) Three into Two Won't Go 1969; Lady Chatterley's Lover 1981; An Unsuitable Job for a Woman 1981; Those Glory, Glory Days 1983; Sense and Sensibility 1995; The Secret Agent 1996

Springer, Jerry (1944-) Ringmaster 1998; Domino 2005

Springsteen, Bruce (1949-) No Nukes 1980; Springsteen & I 2013; Twenty Feet from Stardom 2013

Sprouse, Cole (1992-) Big Daddy 1999; I Saw Mommy Kissing Santa Claus 2001

Sprouse, Dylan (1992-) Big Daddy 1999; I Saw Mommy Kissing Santa Claus 2001

Spruell, Sam London to Brighton 2006; Starred Up 2013; Good People 2014; Taken 3 2014

Spurlock, Morgan (1970-) Where in the World Is Osama Bin Laden? 2008; POM Wonderful Presents: The Greatest Movie Ever Sold 2011

Squibb, June (1935-) About Schmidt 2002; Welcome to Mooseport 2004; Nebraska 2013; I'll See You in My Dreams 2015

Squire, Ronald (1886-1958) Dusty Ermine 1936; While the Sun Shines 1946; Woman Hater 1948; The Rocking Horse Winner 1949; Encore 1951; No Highway 1951; It Started in Paradise 1952; My Cousin Rachel 1952; Laxdale Hall 1953; The Million Pound Note 1953; Footsteps in the Fog 1955; Josephine and Men 1955; Raising a Riot 1955; Sea Wife 1957; The Inn of the Sixth Happiness 1958; Law and Disorder 1958; The Sheriff of Fractured Jaw 1958

Squire, William (1916-1989) Anne of the Thousand Days 1969; The Lord of the Rings 1978

St Clair, Jessica She's out of My League 2008; Afternoon Delight 2013; Addicted to Fresno 2015

Stack, Robert (1919-2003) First Love 1939; The Mortal Storm 1940; Nice Girl? 1941; Men of Texas 1942; To Be or Not to Be 1942; A Date with Judy 1948; Fighter Squadron 1948; Miss Tatlock's Millions 1948; Mr Music 1950; The Bullfighter and the Lady 1951; Bwana Devil 1952; War Paint 1953; The High and the Mighty 1954; The Iron Glove 1954; Good Morning, Miss Dove 1955; House of Bamboo 1955; Great Day in the Morning 1956; Written on the Wind 1956; The Tarnished Angels 1957; The Gift of Love 1958; The Last Voyage 1960; The Caretakers 1963; The Corrupt Ones 1966; Is Paris Burning? 1966; 1941 1979; Airplane! 1980; Uncommon Valor 1983; Big Trouble 1985; Transformers - the Movie 1986; Caddyshack II 1988; Plain Clothes 1988; Joe versus the Volcano 1990; Beavis and Butt-head Do America 1996; Mumford 1999; Recess: School's Out 2001

Stack, William (1882-1949) Sarah and Son 1930; Tarzan and His Mate 1934

Stacy, John The Cat Gang 1959; The Agony and the Ecstasy 1965

Stadlober, Robert Summer Storm 2004; Diplomacy 2014

Stadvec, Michael The Dentist 1996; Sometimes They Come Back... for More 1998

Staff, Kathy (1928-2008) Separate Tables 1983; Mary Reilly 1995

Stafford, Frederick (1928-1979) The Looters 1966; The Battle of El Alamein 1968; Topaz 1969

Stafford, Hanley (1899-1968) A Girl in Every Port 1952; The Affairs of Dobie Gillis 1953

Stahl, Nick (1979-) Incident in a Small Town 1993; The Man without a Face 1993; Safe Passage 1994; Tall Tale 1994; Eye of God 1997; Disturbing Behavior 1998; Sunset Strip 2000; Bully 2001; In the Bedroom 2001; Terminator 3: Rise of the Machines 2003; Sin City 2005

Stainton, Philip (1908-1961) Mogambo 1953; The Ladykillers 1955

Staite, Jewel (1982-) Serenity 2005; Widow on the Hill 2005; Call Me Mrs Miracle 2010

Staley, James American Dreamer 1984; Sweet Dreams 1985; Robot Wars 1993

Stallone, Frank (1950-) Barfly 1987; Fear 1988; Heart of Midnight 1988; Midnight Cop 1988

Stallone, Sage (1976-2012) Rocky V 1990; Daylight 1996

Stallone, Sylvester aka **Stallone, Sylvester E** (1946-) Bananas 1971; Rebel 1973; The Lords of Flatbush 1974; The Prisoner of Second Avenue 1974; Capone 1975; Death Race 2000 1975; Farewell, My Lovely 1975; Cannonball 1976; Rocky 1976; FIST 1978; Paradise Alley 1978; Rocky II 1979; Escape to Victory 1981; Nighthawks 1981; First Blood 1982; Rocky III 1982; Rhinestone 1984; Rambo: First Blood, Part II 1985; Rocky IV 1985; Cobra 1986; Over the Top 1987; Rambo III 1988; Lock Up 1989; Tango & Cash 1989; Rocky V 1990; Oscar 1991; Stop! or My Mom Will Shoot 1992; Cliffhanger 1993; Demolition Man 1993; The Specialist 1994; Assassins 1995; Judge Dredd 1995; Daylight 1996; Burn Hollywood Burn 1997; Cop Land 1997; Antz 1998; Get Carter 2000; D-Tox 2001; Driven 2001; Avenging Angelo 2002; SPYkids 3-D: Game Over 2003; Rocky Balboa 2006; Rambo 2007; Kambakkht Ishq 2009; The Expendables 2010; Zookeeper 2011; Bullet to the Head 2012; The Expendables 2 2012; Escape Plan 2013; Grudge Match 2013; The Expendables 3 2014; Creed 2015; Ratchet & Clank 2016

Stalnaker, Charles Custer of the West 1967; Captain Apache 1971

Stamos, John (1963-) Wedding Wars 2006; The Two Mr Kissels 2008

Stamp-Taylor, Enid (1904-1946) Easy Virtue 1927; Take a Chance 1937; Climbing High 1938; Hatter's Castle 1941; South American George 1941; Candlelight in Algeria 1943; The Wicked Lady 1945

Stamp, Terence (1939-) Billy Budd 1962; Term of Trial 1962; The Collector 1965; Modesty Blaise 1966; Far from the Madding Crowd 1967; Histoires Extraordinaires 1967; Poor Cow 1967; Blue 1968; Theorem 1968; The Mind of Mr Soames 1970; Superman 1978; The Thief of Baghdad 1978; Meetings with Remarkable Men 1979; Superman II 1980; The Hit 1984; Legal Eagles 1986; Link 1986; The Sicilian 1987; Wall Street 1987; Alien Nation 1988; Young Guns 1988; The Real McCoy 1993; The Adventures of Priscilla, Queen of the Desert 1994; Bliss 1997; Love Walked In 1997; Bowfinger 1999; The Limey 1999; Star Wars Episode I: the Phantom Menace 1999; Red Planet 2000; Ma Femme Est une Actrice 2001; Revelation 2001; The Haunted Mansion 2003; My Boss's Daughter 2003; Elektra 2005; These Foolish Things 2006; Get Smart 2008; Valkyrie 2008; Wanted 2008; Yes Man 2008; The Adjustment Bureau 2010; Song for Marion 2012; The Art of the Steal 2013; Big Eyes 2014

Stan, Sebastian (1982-) The Covenant 2006; Spread 2008; Captain America: the First Avenger 2011; Gone 2012; Captain America: the Winter Soldier 2014; The Martian 2015; Ricki and the Flash 2015; Captain America: Civil War 2016

Stanbridge, Hanna Outcast 2010; Let Us Prey 2014

Stanczak, Wadeck Rendez-vous 1985; The Scene of the Crime 1986

Standen, Clive Hammer of the Gods 2013; Everest 2015

Stander, Lionel (1908-1994) If You Could Only Cook 1935; Meet Nero Wolfe 1936; The Milky Way 1936; Mr Deeds Goes to Town 1936; The Last Gangster 1937; The League of Frightened Men 1937; A Star Is Born 1937; The Crowd Roars 1938; The Ice Follies of 1939 1939; Guadalcanal Diary 1943; The Kid from Brooklyn 1946;

Specter of the Rose 1946; Unfaithfully Yours 1948; Mad Wednesday 1950; The Loved One 1965; Cul-de-Sac 1966; Promise Her Anything 1966; The Good Die First 1967; The Gang That Couldn't Shoot Straight 1971; Pulp 1972; Treasure Island 1972; The Black Bird 1975; New York, New York 1977; Matilda 1978; Transformers - the Movie 1986; Cookie 1989; Wicked Stepmother 1989

Standing, Guy aka **Standing, Sir Guy** (1873-1937) The Eagle and the Hawk 1933; Death Takes a Holiday 1934; Now and Forever 1934; The Lives of a Bengal Lancer 1935; Lloyd's of London 1936; Bulldog Drummond Escapes 1937

Standing, John (1934-) King Rat 1965; The Psychopath 1966; Walk, Don't Run 1966; Torture Garden 1967; A Touch of Love 1969; Zee and Co 1971; The Eagle Has Landed 1976; The Class of Miss MacMichael 1978; The Legacy 1978; The Man Who Knew Too Little 1997; Mrs Dalloway 1997; 8½ Women 1999; Mad Cows 1999; A Good Woman 2004; Rabbit Fever 2005; Before the Rains 2007

Stanfield, Keith aka **Stanfield, Lakeith** Short Term 12 2013; Miles Ahead 2015

Stanford, Aaron (1977-) Tadpole 2002; The Hills Have Eyes 2006

Stang, Arnold (1918-2009) The Man with the Golden Arm 1955; The Wonderful World of the Brothers Grimm 1962; Hercules in New York 1969

Stanley, Florence (1924-2003) The Prisoner of Second Avenue 1974; The Fortune 1975; Trouble Bound 1993; Trapped in Paradise 1994; A Goofy Movie 1995

Stanley, Helene (1929-1990) The Snows of Kilimanjaro 1952; Wait 'til the Sun Shines, Nellie 1952; Carnival Story 1954; Davy Crockett, King of the Wild Frontier 1955

Stanley, Kim (1925-2001) The Goddess 1958; Seance on a Wet Afternoon 1964; The Three Sisters 1966; Frances 1982; The Right Stuff 1983

Stanley, Margo Career Girls 1997; Girls' Night 1997

Stanley, Paul (1952-) I Heard the Owl Call My Name 1973; Detroit Rock City 1999

Stanley, Phyllis (1914-1992) We'll Smile Again 1942; They Met in the Dark 1943; Take Me to Town 1953

Stansfield, Lisa Swing 1998; The Edge of Love 2008

Stanton, Harry Dean aka **Stanton, Dean** aka **Stanton, H D** (1926-) The Proud Rebel 1958; Pork Chop Hill 1959; The Adventures of Huckleberry Finn 1960; Hero's Island 1962; The Man from the Diner's Club 1963; The Hostage 1966; Rebel Rousers 1967; Day of the Evil Gun 1968; The Intruders 1970; Cisco Pike 1971; Two-Lane Blacktop 1971; Cry for Me Billy 1972; Dillinger 1973; Pat Garrett and Billy the Kid 1973; Where the Lilies Bloom 1974; Zandy's Bride 1974; Farewell, My Lovely 1975; 92 in the Shade 1975; Rancho Deluxe 1975; The Missouri Breaks 1976; Straight Time 1978; Alien 1979; The Rose 1979; Wise Blood 1979; The Black Marble 1980; Death Watch 1980; Private Benjamin 1980; UFOria 1980; Escape from New York 1981; One from the Heart 1982; Young Doctors in Love 1982; Christine 1983; Paris, Texas 1984; Red Dawn 1984; Repo Man 1984; The Care Bears Movie 1985; Fool for Love 1985; One Magic Christmas 1985; Pretty in Pink 1986; Slam Dance 1987; The Last Temptation of Christ 1988; Mr North 1988; Stars and Bars 1988; Dream a Little Dream 1989; The Fourth War 1990; Wild at Heart 1990; Man Trouble 1992; Twin Peaks: Fire Walk with Me 1992; Hostages 1993; Against the Wall 1994; Blue Tiger 1994; Down Periscope 1996; Fire Down Below 1997; She's So Lovely 1997; The Mighty 1998; The Green Mile 1999; The Straight Story 1999; The Man Who Cried 2000; The Pledge 2000; Sonny 2002; The Big Bounce 2004; Alien Autopsy 2006; Inland Empire 2006; Rango 2011; This Must Be the Place 2011; Marvel Avengers Assemble 2012; The Last Stand 2013

Stanton, John (1944-) Dusty 1982; The Naked Country 1985; Tai-Pan 1986; Rent-a-Cop 1988

Stanton, Paul (1884-1955) Red Salute 1935; The Road to Glory 1936; The People vs Dr Kildare 1941

Stanton, Robert (1963-) Bob Roberts 1992; Dennis 1993; Red Corner 1997; Washington Square 1997; Mercury Rising 1998; The Quiet American 2002

Stanton, Will (1885-1969) Sadie Thompson 1928; Devil's Island 1940

Stanwyck, Barbara (1907-1990) Ladies of Leisure 1930; Illicit 1931; The Miracle Woman 1931; Night Nurse 1931; The Bitter Tea of General Yen 1932; Forbidden 1932; The Purchase Price 1932; Shopworn 1932; So Big 1932; Baby Face 1933; Ever in My Heart 1933; Ladies They Talk About 1933; Gambling Lady 1934; The Secret Bride 1934; Annie Oakley 1935; Red Salute 1935; The Woman in Red 1935; Banjo on My Knee 1936; The Bride Walks Out 1936; His Brother's Wife 1936; A Message to Garcia 1936; The Plough and the Stars 1936; Breakfast for Two 1937; Internes Can't Take Money 1937; Stella Dallas 1937; This Is My Affair 1937; Always Goodbye 1938; The Mad Miss Manton 1938; Golden Boy 1939; Union Pacific 1939; Remember the Night 1940; Ball of Fire 1941; The Lady Eve 1941; Meet John Doe 1941; You Belong to Me 1941; The Gay Sisters 1942; The Great Man's Lady 1942; Flesh and Fantasy 1943; Lady of Burlesque 1943; Double Indemnity 1944; Hollywood Canteen 1944; Christmas in Connecticut 1945; The Two Mrs Carrolls 1945; The Bride Wore Boots 1946; California 1946; My Reputation 1946; The Strange Love of Martha Ivers 1946; Cry Wolf 1947; The Other Love 1947; Variety Girl 1947; BF's Daughter 1948; Sorry, Wrong Number 1948; East Side, West Side 1949; The File on Thelma Jordon 1949; The Lady Gambles 1949; The Furies 1950; No Man of Her Own 1950; To Please a Lady 1950; The Man with a Cloak 1951; Clash by Night 1952; All I Desire 1953; Blowing Wild 1953; Jeopardy 1953; The Moonlighter 1953; Titanic 1953; Cattle Queen of Montana 1954; Executive Suite 1954; Witness to Murder 1954; Escape to Burma 1955; The Violent Men 1955; There's Always Tomorrow 1956; These Wilder Years 1956; Crime of Passion 1957; Forty Guns 1957; Trooper Hook 1957; Walk on the Wild Side 1962; The Night Walker 1964; Roustabout 1964; The Love Goddesses 1965

Staples, Mavis Graffiti Bridge 1990; Mavis! 2015

Stapleton, Jean (1923-2013) Damn Yankees 1958; Bells Are Ringing 1960; Up the Down Staircase 1967; The Buddy System 1984; Dead Man's Folly 1986; The Trial 1993; Michael 1996

Stapleton, Maureen (1925-2006) Lonelyhearts 1958; The Fugitive Kind 1960; Bye Bye Birdie 1963; Trilogy 1969; Airport 1970; Plaza Suite 1971; Interiors 1978; Lost and Found 1979; The Runner Stumbles 1979; The Fan 1981; Reds 1981; Johnny Dangerously 1984; Cocoon 1985; The Money Pit 1985; Heartburn 1986; Made in Heaven 1987; Nuts 1987; Cocoon: the Return 1988; Miss Rose White 1992; Passed Away 1992; The Mommy Market 1994; Addicted to Love 1997

Stapleton, Nicola Courage Mountain 1989; Urban Ghost Story 1998; It Was an Accident 2000; Lava 2000; Chunky Monkey 2001

Stapleton, Sullivan (1977-) Darkness Falls 2003; Animal Kingdom 2009; 300: Rise of an Empire 2013

Stapley, Richard (1922-2010) King of the Khyber Rifles 1953; The Iron Glove 1954; D-Day the Sixth of June 1956

Stark, Graham (1922-2013) The Running, Jumping and Standing Still Film 1959; Dentist on the Job 1961; Only Two Can Play 1961; She'll Have to Go 1961; Ladies Who Do 1963; A Shot in the Dark 1964; The Plank 1967; Salt & Pepper 1968; Simon, Simon 1970; The Return of the Pink Panther 1974; Hardcore 1977; Let's Get Laid 1977; Revenge of the Pink Panther 1978; Trail of the Pink Panther 1982; Victor/Victoria 1982; Jane and the Lost City 1987; Son of the Pink Panther 1993

Stark, Jonathan (1952-) Fright Night 1985; House II: the Second Story 1987; Project X 1987

Stark, Koo (1956-) Electric Dreams 1984; Eat the Rich 1987

Starke, Anthony (1963-) Return of the Killer Tomatoes 1988; Repossessed 1990; Nowhere to Run 1992

Starr, Beau (1944-) Halloween 5: the Revenge of Michael Myers 1989; Relentless 1989; Mercy 2000; Mary Higgins Clark's Pretend You Don't See Her 2002; Cheating Fate 2007

Starr, Fredro The Addiction 1994; Sunset Park 1996; Ride 1998; Light It Up 1999; Save the Last Dance 2000

Starr, Martin Good Dick 2008; Adventureland 2009

Starr, Mike (1950-) GoodFellas 1990; Miller's Crossing 1990; The Bodyguard 1992; Mad Dog and Glory 1992; Dumb and Dumber 1994; Ed Wood 1994; Blood and Wine 1996; Flipping 1996; Stolen Hearts 1996; Gloria 1998; The Lady in Question 1999; Murder in a Small Town 1999; Tempted 2001; Jersey Girl 2003; The Ice Harvest 2005; The Black Dahlia 2006; Ca$h! 2010

Starr, Ringo (1940-) A Hard Day's Night 1964; Help! 1965; Candy 1968; The Magic Christian 1969; Blind Man 1971; 200 Motels 1971; Born to Boogie 1972; The Concert for Bangladesh 1972; That'll Be the Day 1973; Lisztomania 1975; The Kids Are Alright 1978; Sextette 1978; Caveman 1981; Give My Regards to Broad Street 1984; George Harrison: Living in the Material World 2011

Starrett, Charles (1903-1986) Fast and Loose 1930; The Royal Family of Broadway 1930; The Mask of Fu Manchu 1932; Our Betters 1933; This Man Is Mine 1934; So Red the Rose 1935

Starrett, Jack (1936-1989) First Blood 1982; The River 1984

Stasey, Caitlin Tomorrow, When the War Began 2010; All Cheerleaders Die 2013

Stassino, Paul (1930-2012) Moment of Danger 1960; Sammy Going South 1963; Where the Spies Are 1965; That Riviera Touch 1966

Statham, Jason (1967-) Lock, Stock and Two Smoking Barrels 1998; Snatch 2000; John Carpenter's Ghosts of Mars 2001; Mean Machine 2001; The One 2001; The Transporter 2002; The Italian Job 2003; Cellular 2004; Revolver 2005; The Transporter 2 2005; Chaos 2006; Crank 2006; War 2007; The Bank Job 2008; Death Race 2008; Transporter 3 2008; Crank: High Voltage 2010; 13 2010; Gnomeo & Juliet 2011; Killer Elite 2011; The Mechanic 2011; Safe 2011; The Expendables 2 2012; Homefront 2013; Hummingbird 2013; Parker 2013; The Expendables 3 2014; Fast & Furious 7 2014; Wild Card 2014; Spy 2015; Mechanic: Resurrection 2016

Staunton, Imelda (1956-) Peter's Friends 1992; Deadly Advice 1993; Much Ado about Nothing 1993; Sense and Sensibility 1995; Remember Me? 1996; Twelfth Night 1996; Shakespeare in Love 1998; Another Life 2000; Chicken Run 2000; Rat 2000; Crush 2001; Blackball 2003; I'll Be There 2003; Vera Drake 2004; Nanny McPhee 2005; Freedom Writers 2006; Shadow Man 2006; Harry Potter and the Order of the Phoenix 2007; A Bunch of Amateurs 2008; Three and Out 2008; Taking Woodstock 2009; Another Year 2010; Arthur Christmas 2011; The Awakening 2011; The Pirates! in an Adventure with Scientists! 2012; Maleficent 2014; Paddington 2014; Pride 2014

Steadman, Alison (1946-) Abigail's Party 1977; P'Tang, Yang, Kipperbang 1982; Champions 1983; Number One 1984; A Private Function 1984; Clockwise 1986; The Adventures of Baron Munchausen 1988; Shirley Valentine 1989; Wilt 1989; Life Is Sweet 1990; Blame It on the Bellboy 1992; Topsy-Turvy 1999; Chunky Monkey 2001; Confetti 2006; Dad's Army 2016

Steadman, John (1909-1993) The Mean Machine 1974; The Hills Have Eyes 1977

Steadman, Ralph Gonzo: the Life and Work of Dr Hunter S Thompson 2008; For No Good Reason 2012

Steafel, Sheila (1935-) The Smashing Bird I Used to Know 1969; Never Too Young to Rock 1975; Bloodbath at the House of Death 1983

Steel, Amy (1963-) Friday the 13th Part 2 1981; Walk like a Man 1987; What Ever Happened to...? 1991

Steel, Anthony (1920-2001) The Mudlark 1950; The Wooden Horse 1950; Another Man's Poison 1951; Laughter in Paradise 1951; Where No Vultures Fly 1951; Emergency Call 1952; The Planter's Wife 1952; Albert, RN 1953; Malta Story 1953; The Master of Ballantrae 1953; Out of the Clouds 1954; The Sea Shall Not Have Them 1954; West of Zanzibar 1954; Passage Home 1955; Storm over the Nile 1955; The Black Tent 1956; Checkpoint 1956; Valerie 1957; Harry Black and the Tiger 1958; Honeymoon 1959; Anzio 1968; The Story of O 1975; Hardcore 1977; Let's Get Laid 1977; The World Is Full of Married Men 1979

Steele, Barbara (1937-) The Mask of Satan 1960; Pit and the Pendulum 1961; 8½ 1963; The She Beast 1965; Curse of the Crimson Altar 1968; Caged Heat

1974; Shivers 1975; Piranha 1978; Pretty Baby 1978; Lost River 2014

Steele, Bob aka **Steele, Robert** (1907-1988) Of Mice and Men 1939; The Big Sleep 1946; Cattle Drive 1951; The Enforcer 1951; Rose of Cimarron 1952; Pork Chop Hill 1959; The Atomic Submarine 1960; Hell Bent for Leather 1960

Steele, Freddie (1912-1984) The Story of GI Joe 1945; Black Angel 1946; Desperate 1947

Steele, Jadrien (1974-) The Mosquito Coast 1986; The Secret Garden 1987

Steele, Karen (1931-1988) Marty 1955; Decision at Sundown 1957; Ride Lonesome 1959; Westbound 1959; The Rise and Fall of Legs Diamond 1960

Steele, Riann Treacle Jr 2010; Sket 2011; Powder Room 2013

Steele, Sarah Spanglish 2004; Please Give 2010

Steele, Tommy (1936-) Kill Me Tomorrow 1957; The Tommy Steele Story 1957; The Duke Wore Jeans 1958; Tommy the Toreador 1959; Light Up the Sky 1960; It's All Happening 1963; Half a Sixpence 1967; The Happiest Millionaire 1967; Finian's Rainbow 1968; Where's Jack? 1969

Steen, Jessica (1965-) Threshold 1981; A Judgement in Stone 1986; Sing 1989; Trial and Error 1997; Chaos 2006; A Nanny's Secret 2008

Steen, Paprika (1964-) Festen 1998; Open Hearts 2002; Skeletons 2010; Love Is All You Need 2012

Steenburgen, Mary (1953-) Goin' South 1978; Time after Time 1979; Melvin and Howard 1980; A Midsummer Night's Sex Comedy 1982; Cross Creek 1983; Romantic Comedy 1983; One Magic Christmas 1985; Dead of Winter 1987; End of the Line 1987; The Attic: the Hiding of Anne Frank 1988; Miss Firecracker 1989; Parenthood 1989; Back to the Future Part III 1990; The Butcher's Wife 1991; Philadelphia 1993; What's Eating Gilbert Grape 1993; It Runs in the Family 1994; Pontiac Moon 1994; The Grass Harp 1995; Nixon 1995; Powder 1995; I Am Sam 2001; Life as a House 2001; Hope Springs 2002; Sunshine State 2002; Casa de los Babys 2003; Elf 2003; Surviving Love 2004; Marilyn Hotchkiss Ballroom Dancing & Charm School 2005; The Brave One 2007; Four Christmases 2008; Step Brothers 2008; Did You Hear about the Morgans? 2009; In the Electric Mist 2009; The Proposal 2009; Last Vegas 2013; The Tale of the Princess Kaguya 2013; A Walk in the Woods 2015

Stefanson, Leslie (1971-) Burn Hollywood Burn 1997; The General's Daughter 1999; Beautiful 2000; The Stickup 2001; The Hunted 2002; Alien Hunter 2003

Stegers, Bernice City of Women 1980; Xtro 1983; The Girl 1986

Stehlé, Jean-Marc Bon Voyage 2003; Film Socialisme 2010

Steiger, Rod (1925-2002) Teresa 1951; On the Waterfront 1954; The Big Knife 1955; The Court-Martial of Billy Mitchell 1955; Oklahoma! 1955; Back from Eternity 1956; The Harder They Fall 1956; Jubal 1956; Across the Bridge 1957; Run of the Arrow 1957; The Unholy Wife 1957; Cry Terror 1958; Al Capone 1959; Seven Thieves 1960; The Mark 1961; Convicts Four 1962; The Longest Day 1962; 13 West Street 1962; Hands over the City 1963; Time of Indifference 1964; Doctor Zhivago 1965; The Loved One 1965; The Pawnbroker 1965; The Girl and the General 1967; In the Heat of the Night 1967; No Way to Treat a Lady 1968; The Sergeant 1968; The Illustrated Man 1969; Three into Two Won't Go 1969; Waterloo 1970; A Fistful of Dynamite 1971; The Lolly-Madonna War 1973; Lucky Luciano 1973; The Last Days of Mussolini 1974; Hennessy 1975; Les Innocents aux Mains Sales 1975; WC Fields and Me 1976; Breakthrough 1978; FIST 1978; Love and Bullets 1978; The Amityville Horror 1979; Wolf Lake 1979; Cattle Annie and Little Britches 1980; The Lucky Star 1980; The Chosen 1981; Lion of the Desert 1981; Cook & Peary: the Race to the Pole 1983; The Naked Face 1984; The Kindred 1986; American Gothic 1987; The January Man 1989; Men of Respect 1990; The Ballad of the Sad Café 1991; Guilty as Charged 1991; The Specialist 1994; The Bomber Boys 1995; Carpool 1996; Mars Attacks! 1996; Shiloh 1996; Incognito 1997; Truth or Consequences, NM 1997; Crazy in Alabama 1999; End of Days 1999; The Hurricane 1999; The Last Producer 2000

Stein, Saul Beer 1985; illtown 1996; Wisegirls 2001; Open Water 2004

Steinberg, David (1942-) The End 1978; Something Short of Paradise 1979

Steiner, Sigfrit (1906-1988) Imperative 1982; Fatherland 1986

Steinfeld, Hailee (1996-) True Grit 2010; Romeo & Juliet 2012; Begin Again 2013; Ender's Game 2013; The Keeping Room 2014; 3 Days to Kill 2014; When Marnie Was There 2014; Barely Lethal 2015; Pitch Perfect 2 2015; Pitch Perfect 3 2017

Steinmiller Jr, Robert J (1978-) Bingo 1991; Jack the Bear 1993; Hostile Hostages 1994

Steinrück, Albert (1872-1929) The Golem 1920; Asphalt 1928

Sten, Anna (1908-1993) Nana 1934; We Live Again 1934; The Wedding Night 1935; The Man I Married 1940; So Ends Our Night 1941; Let's Live a Little 1948

Stepanek, Karel (1899-1980) Tomorrow We Live 1942; State Secret 1950; Walk East on Beacon 1952; City beneath the Sea 1953; Never Let Me Go 1953; Man of the Moment 1955; Anastasia 1956; The Man in the Road 1957; Sink the Bismarck! 1960; Devil Doll 1964; Licensed to Kill 1965; Before Winter Comes 1968

Stéphane, Idwig (1948-) Le Roi Danse 2000; Pauline & Paulette 2001

Stéphane, Nicole (1923-2007) Le Silence de la Mer 1947; Les Enfants Terribles 1949; Le Défroqué 1953

Stephen, Susan (1931-2000) Father's Doing Fine 1952; His Excellency 1952; Stolen Face 1952; Treasure Hunt 1952; The Red Beret 1953; For Better, for Worse 1954; As Long as They're Happy 1955; Value for Money 1955; The Barretts of Wimpole Street 1956; It's Never Too Late 1956

Stephens, Ann (1931-1966) The Upturned Glass 1947; No Room at the Inn 1948; The Franchise Affair 1950

Stephens, Harvey (1901-1986) The Worst Woman in Paris? 1933; Evelyn Prentice 1934; After Office Hours 1935; Let 'Em Have It 1935; Murder Man 1935; Whipsaw 1935; Swing High, Swing Low 1937; The Oklahoma Kid 1939; You Can't Get Away with Murder 1939; Spirit of the People 1940; Joe Smith, American 1942

Stephens, James (1951-) First Monday in October 1981; The Getaway 1994

Stephens, Laraine (1942-) 40 Guns to Apache Pass 1966; The 1,000 Plane Raid 1969

Stephens, Martin (1949-) Harry Black and the Tiger 1958; Count Your Blessings 1959; Village of the Damned 1960; The Innocents 1961; The Battle of the Villa Fiorita 1965

Stephens, Robert (1931-1995) Circle of Deception 1960; The Queen's Guards 1960; A Taste of Honey 1961; The Inspector 1962; Lunch Hour 1962; The Small World of Sammy Lee 1963; Morgan - a Suitable Case for Treatment 1966; The Prime of Miss Jean Brodie 1969; The Private Life of Sherlock Holmes 1970; The Asphyx 1972; Travels with My Aunt 1972; Luther 1974; The Duellists 1977; The Shout 1978; Empire of the Sun 1987; High Season 1987; Henry V 1989; The Children 1990; Afraid of the Dark 1991; The Pope Must Die 1991; Century 1993; Innocent Moves 1993; The Secret Rapture 1993

Stephens, Toby (1969-) Sunset Heights 1996; Twelfth Night 1996; Cousin Bette 1997; Photographing Fairies 1997; Onegin 1999; The Great Gatsby 2000; Die Another Day 2002; Possession 2002; Severance 2006; Terkel in Trouble 2006; All Things to All Men 2012; Believe 2012; The Machine 2013; 13 Hours: the Secret Soldiers of Benghazi 2016

Stephenson, Henry (1871-1956) The Animal Kingdom 1932; A Bill of Divorcement 1932; Cynara 1932; Red-Headed Woman 1932; If I Were Free 1933; Little Women 1933; One More River 1934; The Richest Girl in the World 1934; Thirty-Day Princess 1934; Mutiny on the Bounty 1935; Reckless 1935; Vanessa, Her Love Story 1935; The Charge of the Light Brigade 1936; Little Lord Fauntleroy 1936; Conquest 1937; The Emperor's Candlesticks 1937; The Prince and the Pauper 1937; When You're in Love 1937; The Baroness and the Butler 1938; Dramatic School 1938; Marie Antoinette 1938; Suez 1938; The Adventures of Sherlock Holmes 1939; Tarzan Finds a Son! 1939; Down Argentine Way 1940; It's a Date 1940; Little Old New York 1940; Lady from

Louisiana 1941; Rings on Her Fingers 1942; This above All 1942; Mr Lucky 1943; The Hour before the Dawn 1944; Two Girls and a Sailor 1944; Tarzan and the Amazons 1945; The Locket 1946; Of Human Bondage 1946; Oliver Twist 1948

Stephenson, James (1889-1941) Nancy Drew - Detective 1938; White Banners 1938; King of the Underworld 1939; We Are Not Alone 1939; Devil's Island 1940; The Letter 1940

Stephenson, Mark Kinsey The Unnamable 1988; The Unnamable Returns 1992

Stephenson, Pamela (1950-) The Comeback 1977; Stand Up Virgin Soldiers 1977; History of the World Part 1 1981; Bloodbath at the House of Death 1983; Scandalous 1983; Superman III 1983; Finders Keepers 1984; Les Patterson Saves the World 1987

Sterke, Jeannette The Prisoner 1955; The Safecracker 1958; Live Now - Pay Later 1962; A Stitch in Time 1963

Sterling, Ford (1883-1939) He Who Gets Slapped 1924; Stage Struck 1925; For the Love of Mike 1927; Her Majesty Love 1931

Sterling, Jan (1921-2004) Johnny Belinda 1948; Appointment with Danger 1950; Caged 1950; Mystery Street 1950; Union Station 1950; Ace in the Hole 1951; The Mating Season 1951; Rhubarb 1951; Flesh and Fury 1952; Pony Express 1953; Split Second 1953; The High and the Mighty 1954; Man with the Gun 1955; 1984 1955; Women's Prison 1955; The Harder They Fall 1956; Slaughter on Tenth Avenue 1957; The Female Animal 1958; High School Confidential 1958; First Monday in October 1981

Sterling, Mindy (1953-) Austin Powers: International Man of Mystery 1997; Austin Powers: the Spy Who Shagged Me 1999; Drop Dead Gorgeous 1999; Austin Powers in Goldmember 2002; Mars Needs Moms 2011

Sterling, Robert (1917-2006) The Gay Caballero 1940; Dr Kildare's Victory 1941; Johnny Eager 1941; The Penalty 1941; Two-Faced Woman 1941; Somewhere I'll Find You 1942; The Secret Heart 1946; Roughshod 1949; The Sundowners 1950; Show Boat 1951; Column South 1953; Return to Peyton Place 1961; Voyage to the Bottom of the Sea 1961; A Global Affair 1964

Sterling, Tisha (1944-) Village of the Giants 1965; Coogan's Bluff 1968; The Killer inside Me 1975

Stern, Daniel (1957-) Breaking Away 1979; It's My Turn 1980; Diner 1982; I'm Dancing as Fast as I Can 1982; Blue Thunder 1983; Get Crazy 1983; CHUD 1984; Hannah and Her Sisters 1986; Born in East LA 1987; DOA 1988; Leviathan 1989; Coupe de Ville 1990; The Court-Martial of Jackie Robinson 1990; Home Alone 1990; My Blue Heaven 1990; City Slickers 1991; Home Alone 2: Lost in New York 1992; City Slickers II: the Legend of Curly's Gold 1994; Bushwhacked 1995; Celtic Pride 1996; Very Bad Things 1998; Whip It 2009; Battle of the Bulbs 2010; The Next Three Days 2010

Stern, Isaac (1920-2001) Tonight We Sing 1953; Music of the Heart 1999

Sternhagen, Frances (1930-) Two People 1973; Fedora 1978; Starting Over 1979; Outland 1981; Independence Day 1983; Romantic Comedy 1983; Resting Place 1986; Bright Lights, Big City 1988; Communion 1989; See You in the Morning 1989; Misery 1990; Sibling Rivalry 1990; Doc Hollywood 1991; Raising Cain 1992; Curtain Call 1997; The Con 1998; The Mist 2007

Stevan, Robyn The Stepfather 1986; Bye Bye Blues 1989; Stepping Out 1991

Steve-O (1974-) Jackass: the Movie 2002; jackass number two 2006; Jackass 3D 2010

Stévenin, Jean-François (1944-) Small Change 1976; Olivier Olivier 1991; Le Bossu 1997; L'Homme du Train 2002; My Afternoons with Margueritte 2010; Bright Days Ahead 2013; The Last Diamond 2014

Stevens, Andrew (1955-) The Boys in Company C 1978; The Fury 1978; Death Hunt 1981; 10 to Midnight 1983; Night Eyes 1990; Munchie 1992; Munchie Strikes Back 1994

Stevens, Charles aka **Stevens, Charlie** (1893-1964) The Three Musketeers 1921; The Black Pirate 1926; Mantrap 1926; Aces and Eights 1936; Warpath 1951

Stevens, Connie (1938-) Rock-A-Bye Baby 1958; Susan Slade 1961; Palm Springs Weekend 1963; Two on a Guillotine 1964; Never Too Late 1965; Mister Jerico 1969; Back to the Beach

1987; Tapeheads 1988; Love Is All There Is 1996

Stevens, Craig (1918-2000) The Doughgirls 1944; Night unto Night 1949; Abbott and Costello Meet Dr Jekyll and Mr Hyde 1953; The Deadly Mantis 1957; Buchanan Rides Alone 1958; SOB 1981

Stevens, Dan (1982-) Summer in February 2012; Vamps 2012; The Cobbler 2014; The Guest 2014; Night at the Museum: Secret of the Tomb 2014; A Walk among the Tombstones 2014; Beauty and the Beast 2017

Stevens, Dodie (1946-) Hound Dog Man 1959; Convicts Four 1962

Stevens, Emma Silent Trigger 1996; Summer House 2008

Stevens, Fisher (1963-) The Burning 1981; The Flamingo Kid 1984; My Science Project 1985; Short Circuit 1986; Short Circuit 2 1988; Reversal of Fortune 1990; Mystery Date 1991; Too Hot to Handle 1991; When the Party's Over 1992; Nina Takes a Lover 1993; Super Mario Bros 1993; Cold Fever 1994; Only You 1994; Hackers 1995; Undisputed 2002; Factotum (A Man Who Preforms Many Jobs, 2005; Awake 2007; Henry's Crime 2010

Stevens, Inger (1934-1970) The Buccaneer 1958; Cry Terror 1958; The World, the Flesh and the Devil 1959; A Guide for the Married Man 1967; A Time for Killing 1967; Firecreek 1968; 5 Card Stud 1968; Hang 'Em High 1968; House of Cards 1968; Madigan 1968; A Dream of Kings 1969

Stevens, K T aka **Stevens, Katharine** (1919-1994) The Great Man's Lady 1942; Port of New York 1949; Harriet Craig 1950; Tumbleweed 1953; Vice Squad 1953; Bob & Carol & Ted & Alice 1969

Stevens, Mark (1915-1994) The Dark Corner 1946; From This Day Forward 1946; I Wonder Who's Kissing Her Now 1947; The Snake Pit 1948; The Street with No Name 1948; Dancing in the Dark 1949; Oh, You Beautiful Doll 1949; Please Believe Me 1950; Target Unknown 1951; The Lost Hours 1952; Mutiny 1952; Cry Vengeance 1954; Gunsight Ridge 1957

Stevens, Onslow (1902-1977) Counsellor-at-Law 1933; Peg o' My Heart 1933; The Three Musketeers 1935; Flight from Glory 1937; When Tomorrow Comes 1939; The Man Who Wouldn't Talk 1940; House of Dracula 1945; Angel on My Shoulder 1946; Lorna Doone 1951; Sealed Cargo 1951; The San Francisco Story 1952; Them! 1954; They Rode West 1954; All the Fine Young Cannibals 1960

Stevens, Rachel (1978-) Seeing Double 2003; Deuce Bigalow: European Gigolo 2005

Stevens, Risë (1913-2013) The Chocolate Soldier 1941; Going My Way 1944

Stevens, Ronnie (1925-2006) Dentist in the Chair 1960; Dentist on the Job 1961; Nearly a Nasty Accident 1961; Some Girls Do 1969

Stevens, Stella (1936-) Li'l Abner 1959; Too Late Blues 1961; Girls! Girls! Girls! 1962; The Courtship of Eddie's Father 1963; The Nutty Professor 1963; Advance to the Rear 1964; The Secret of My Success 1965; Rage 1966; The Silencers 1966; Where Angels Go... Trouble Follows 1968; The Ballad of Cable Hogue 1970; A Town Called Hell 1971; The Poseidon Adventure 1972; Cleopatra Jones and the Casino of Gold 1975; Nickelodeon 1976; The Manitou 1978; Wacko 1981; Chained Heat 1983; Monster in the Closet 1983; Eye of the Stranger 1993

Stevens, Warren (1919-2012) The Frogmen 1951; Deadline - USA 1952; Phone Call from a Stranger 1952; Red Skies of Montana 1952; Gorilla at Large 1954; Women's Prison 1955; Accused of Murder 1956; Forbidden Planet 1956; Hot Spell 1958; Intent to Kill 1958; No Name on the Bullet 1959; Forty Pounds of Trouble 1962; Stagecoach to Dancer's Rock 1962; Gunpoint 1966; The Trail to Hope Rose 2004

Stevenson, Charles (1887-1943) Hot Water 1924; The Freshman 1925

Stevenson, Cynthia (1963-) The Player 1992; Forget Paris 1995; Agent Cody Banks 2003; Agent Cody Banks 2: Destination London 2003

Stevenson, Houseley aka **Stevenson, Housley** (1879-1953) Kidnapped 1948; The Lady Gambles 1949; The Wild North 1952

Stevenson, Jessica aka **Hynes, Jessica** (1973-) Bridget Jones: the Edge of Reason 2004; Shaun of the Dead 2004; Confetti 2006; Four Last Songs 2007; Magicians 2007; Son of

Rambow 2007; Faintheart 2008; Burke & Hare 2010; Nativity 2: Danger in the Manger! 2012; Pudsey the Dog: the Movie 2014; Swallows and Amazons 2016

Stevenson, Juliet (1956-) Drowning by Numbers 1988; Truly Madly Deeply 1990; The Secret Rapture 1993; The Trial 1993; Paris Was a Woman 1995; Emma 1996; Bend It like Beckham 2001; Christmas Carol: the Movie 2001; The Search for John Gissing 2001; Food of Love 2002; Nicholas Nickleby 2002; Mona Lisa Smile 2003; Being Julia 2004; Pierrepoint 2005; Breaking and Entering 2006 Infamous 2006; And When Did You Last See Your Father? 2007; The Secret of Moonacre 2008; Diana 2013; Departure 2015.

Stevenson, Parker (1952-) Stroker Ace 1983; Avalon: Beyond the Abyss 1999

Stevenson, Ray (1964-) The Theory of Flight 1998; Outpost 2007; Punisher: War Zone 2008; The Book of Eli 2009; Cirque du Freak: the Vampire's Assistant 2009; Kill the Irishman 2011; The Three Musketeers 2011; Jayne Mansfield's Car 2012; GI Joe: Retaliation 2013; Big Game 2014; The Transporter Refueled 2015

Stevenson, Theo Horrid Henry: the Movie 2011; All Stars 2013

Stevenson, Venetia (1938-) Darby's Rangers 1958; Day of the Outlaw 1959; The City of the Dead 1960; Seven Ways from Sundown 1960

Stewart-Jarrett, Nathan The Comedian 2012; War Book 2014

Stewart, Alexandra (1939-) Tarzan the Magnificent 1960; RoGoPaG 1962; Mickey One 1965; Maroc 7 1966; Only When I Larf 1968; The Man Who Had Power over Women 1970; Zeppelin 1971; Day for Night 1973; Black Moon 1974; The Marseille Contract 1974; The Uncanny 1977; In Praise of Older Women 1978; Phobia 1980; Agency 1981; Sans Soleil 1982; Under the Cherry Moon 1986. Under the Sand 2000

Stewart, Amy Another Woman 1994; My Winnipeg 2007

Stewart, Athole (1879-1940) The Clairvoyant 1934; Accused 1936; Dusty Ermine 1936; Return of a Stranger 1937; The Spy in Black 1939

Stewart, Catherine Mary (1959-) The Apple 1980; The Last Starfighter 1984; Night of the Comet 1984; World Gone Wild 1988; Weekend at Bernie's 1989; The Sea Wolf 1993; Generation Gap 2008; Class 2010

Stewart, Charlotte (1941-) Eraserhead 1976; Human Highway 1982; Tremors 1989; Tremors 3: Back to Perfection 2001

Stewart, Elaine (1929-2011) Take the High Ground 1953; Brigadoon 1954; Night Passage 1957; The Tattered Dress 1957; Escort West 1959; The Rise and Fall of Legs Diamond 1960; The Most Dangerous Man Alive 1961

Stewart, Ewan (1957-) Resurrected 1989; Stella Does Tricks 1997; The Closer You Get 2000; The Last Great Wilderness 2002; One Last Chance 2003; Young Adam 2003; Valhalla Rising 2009

Stewart, French (1964-) Glory Daze 1995; Clockstoppers 2002; Home Alone 4 2002

Stewart, Jack (1913-1966) The Dark Light 1951; Hunted 1952

Stewart (1), Jackie Weekend of a Champion 1971; Leuda: the Untold Story 2014

Stewart, James (1908-1997) Murder Man 1935; After the Thin Man 1936; Born to Dance 1936; The Gorgeous Hussy 1936; Next Time We Love 1936; Rose Marie 1936; Small Town Girl 1936; Speed 1936; Wife vs Secretary 1936; The Last Gangster 1937; Navy Blue and Gold 1937; Seventh Heaven 1937; Of Human Hearts 1938; The Shopworn Angel 1938; Vivacious Lady 1938; You Can't Take It with You 1938; Destry Rides Again 1939; The Ice Follies of 1939 1939; It's a Wonderful World 1939; Made for Each Other 1939; Mr Smith Goes to Washington 1939; The Mortal Storm 1940; No Time for Comedy 1940; The Philadelphia Story 1940; The Shop around the Corner 1940; Come Live with Me 1941; Pot o' Gold 1941; Ziegfeld Girl 1941; It's a Wonderful Life 1946; Magic Town 1947; Call Northside 777 1948; On Our Merry Way 1948; Rope 1948; You Gotta Stay Happy 1948; Malaya 1949; The Stratton Story 1949; Broken Arrow 1950; Harvey 1950; The Jackpot 1950; Winchester '73 1950; No Highway 1951; Bend of the River 1952; Carbine Williams 1952; The Greatest Show on Earth 1952; The Glenn Miller Story 1953; The Naked

Spur 1953; Thunder Bay 1953; The Far Country 1954; Rear Window 1954; The Man from Laramie 1955; Strategic Air Command 1955; The Man Who Knew Too Much 1956; Night Passage 1957; The Spirit of St Louis 1957; Bell, Book and Candle 1958; Vertigo 1958; Anatomy of a Murder 1959; The FBI Story 1959; The Mountain Road 1960; Two Rode Together 1961; X-15 1961; How the West Was Won 1962; The Man Who Shot Liberty Valance 1962; Mr Hobbs Takes a Vacation 1962; Take Her, She's Mine 1963; Cheyenne Autumn 1964; The Flight of the Phoenix 1965; Shenandoah 1965; Dear Brigitte 1965; The Rare Breed 1966; Bandolero! 1968; Firecreek 1968; The Cheyenne Social Club 1970; Dynamite Man from Glory Jail 1971; The Shootist 1976; Airport '77 1977; The Big Sleep 1978; The Magic of Lassie 1978; The Green Horizon 1981; An American Tail: Fievel Goes West 1991

Stewart, Johnny Boots Malone 1951; Last of the Comanches 1952

Stewart, Jon (1962-) Wishful Thinking 1997; Big Daddy 1999; Death to Smoochy 2002

Stewart, Josh The Collector 2009; The Collection 2011

Stewart, Kellee Guess Who 2005; Hot Tub Time Machine 2 2014

Stewart, Kristen (1990-) The Safety of Objects 2001; Panic Room 2002; Cold Creek Manor 2003; Catch That Kid 2004; Zathura: a Space Adventure 2005; Into the Wild 2007; The Messengers 2007; What Just Happened? 2007; Twilight 2008; Adventureland 2009; New Moon 2009; Welcome to the Rileys 2009; Eclipse 2010; The Runaways 2010; Breaking Dawn Part One 2011; On the Road 2011; Breaking Dawn Part Two 2012; Snow White and the Huntsman 2012; Clouds of Sils Maria 2014; Still Alice 2014; American Ultra 2015; Café Society 2016

Stewart, Malcolm (1948-) Fatal Error 1999; Deadlocked 2000; Dr Dolittle: Tail to the Chief 2008; Moon 2008

Stewart, Martha (1922-2012) Daisy Kenyon 1947; I Wonder Who's Kissing Her Now 1947; Are You with It? 1948; In a Lonely Place 1950

Stewart, Patrick (1940-) Hedda 1975; Excalibur 1981; Dune 1984; Code Name: Emerald 1985; The Doctor and the Devils 1985; Lady Jane 1985; Lifeforce 1985; LA Story 1991; Death Train 1993; Robin Hood: Men in Tights 1993; Gunmen 1994; The Pagemaster 1994; Star Trek: Generations 1994; Jeffrey 1995; Let It Be Me 1995; The Canterville Ghost 1996; Star Trek: First Contact 1996; Conspiracy Theory 1997; Dad Savage 1997; Masterminds 1997; Moby Dick 1998; The Prince of Egypt 1998; Star Trek: Insurrection 1998; Animal Farm 1999; A Christmas Carol 1999; X-Men 2000; Jimmy Neutron: Boy Genius 2001; King of Texas 2002; Star Trek: Nemesis 2002; X2 2003; Boo, Zino and the Snurks 2004; Steamboy 2004; Chicken Little 2005; X-Men - the Last Stand 2006; Earth 2007; TMNT 2007; The Invention of Lying 2009; African Cats 2011; Gnomeo & Juliet 2011; Ted 2012; X-Men: Days of Future Past 2014; Green Room 2015; Ted 2 2015; Wolverine 3 2017

Stewart, Paul (1908-1986) Citizen Kane 1941; Government Girl 1943; Mr Lucky 1943; Champion 1949; Easy Living 1949; Twelve o'Clock High 1949; Walk Softly, Stranger 1949; The Window 1949; Appointment with Danger 1950; Edge of Doom 1950; Carbine Williams 1952; Deadline - USA 1952; The Juggler 1953; Deep in My Heart 1954; Hell on Frisco Bay 1955; Kiss Me Deadly 1955; Top Secret Affair 1957; King Creole 1958; A Child Is Waiting 1962; In Cold Blood 1967; Jigsaw 1968; WC Fields and Me 1976; Opening Night 1977; Revenge of the Pink Panther 1978

Stewart, Peggy (1923-) That Certain Age 1938; Back Street 1941

Stewart, Riley Thomas The Beaver 2010; The Lucky One 2012

Stewart, Robin (1946-2015) The Haunted House of Horror 1969; The Legend of the 7 Golden Vampires 1974

Stewart, Rod (1945-) Breaking Glass 1980; Play It to the Bone 2000

Stewart (1), Roy (1883-1933) Sparrows 1926; Zoo in Budapest 1933

Stewart, Sophie (1908-1977) Maria Marten, or the Murder in the Red Barn 1935; As You Like It 1936; The Man Who Could Work Miracles 1936; Things to Come 1936; The Return of the Scarlet Pimpernel 1937; Under the Red Robe 1937; Nurse Edith Cavell 1939; My Son, My Son! 1940; The Lamp Still

Burns 1943; Uncle Silas 1947; Made in Heaven 1952; Yangtse Incident 1956

Stewart, Tonea Leave of Absence 1994; Hood Rat 2001

Stickney, Dorothy (1900-1998) And So They Were Married 1936; The Uninvited 1944; I Never Sang for My Father 1970

Stickney, Phyllis Yvonne Talkin' Dirty after Dark 1991; Tina: What's Love Got to Do with It 1993

Stiers, David Ogden (1942-) Magic 1978; Harry's War 1981; Better Off Dead 1985; Creator 1985; Mrs Delafield Wants to Marry 1986; The Accidental Tourist 1988; Another Woman 1988; Beauty and the Beast 1991; Doc Hollywood 1991; Iron Will 1994; Mighty Aphrodite 1995; Napoleon 1995; Pocahontas 1995; Steal Big, Steal Little 1995; Beauty and the Beast: the Enchanted Christmas 1997; Belle's Magical World 1997; Krippendorf's Tribe 1998; Tomcats 2000; Atlantis: the Lost Empire 2001; The Curse of the Jade Scorpion 2001; The Majestic 2001; Spirited Away 2001; Lilo & Stitch 2002; Teacher's Pet 2004; Winnie the Pooh: Springtime with Roo 2004; Hoodwinked 2005; Pooh's Heffalump Movie 2005; Porco Rosso 2005; Together Again for the First Time 2008

Stiles, Julia (1981-) Before Women Had Wings 1997; Wicked 1998; 10 Things I Hate about You 1999; Down to You 2000; Hamlet 2000; Save the Last Dance 2000; State and Main 2000; The Business of Strangers 2001; O 2001; A Guy Thing 2002; Mona Lisa Smile 2003; The Bourne Supremacy 2004; The Prince & Me 2004; Edmond 2005; The Omen 2006; The Bourne Ultimatum 2007; The Cry of the Owl 2009; Silver Linings Playbook 2012; Out of the Dark 2014; Go with Me 2015; Jason Bourne 2016; Misconduct 2016

Still, Aline A World without Pity 1989; Autobus 1991

Stiller, Ben (1965-) Hot Pursuit 1987; Fresh Horses 1988; Next of Kin 1989; Stella 1990; Highway to Hell 1992; Reality Bites 1994; The Cable Guy 1996; Flirting with Disaster 1996; If Lucy Fell 1996; Zero Effect 1997; Permanent Midnight 1998; There's Something about Mary 1998; Your Friends & Neighbors 1998; Mystery Men 1999; The Suburbans 1999; Keeping the Faith 2000; Meet the Parents 2000; Orange County 2001; The Royal Tenenbaums 2001; Zoolander 2001; Envy 2003; Our House 2003; Along Came Polly 2004; Dodgeball: a True Underdog Story 2004; Meet the Fockers 2004; Starsky & Hutch 2004; Madagascar 2005; Night at the Museum 2006; Tenacious D in The Pick of Destiny 2006; The Heartbreak Kid 2007; Madagascar: Escape 2 Africa 2008; Tropic Thunder 2008; Greenberg 2009; Night at the Museum 2 2009; Little Fockers 2010; Megamind 2010; Tower Heist 2011; Madagascar 3: Europe's Most Wanted 2012; The Watch 2012; The Secret Life of Walter Mitty 2013; Night at the Museum: Secret of the Tomb 2014; While We're Young 2014; Zoolander 2 2016

Stiller, Jerry (1927-) The Taking of Pelham One Two Three 1974; The Ritz 1976; Those Lips, Those Eyes 1980; Hot Pursuit 1987; Nadine 1987; Hairspray 1988; Little Vegas 1990; The Pickle 1993; Subway Stories: Tales from the Underground 1997; On the Line 2001; Zoolander 2001; Serving Sara 2002; Teacher's Pet 2004; The Heartbreak Kid 2007; Ice Dreams 2009; Swinging with the Finkels 2011

Stilley, Margo 9 Songs 2004; Reverb 2006; How to Lose Friends & Alienate People 2008

Stimac, Slavko (1960-) Underground 1995; Life Is a Miracle 2004

Sting (1951-) Quadrophenia 1979; Radio On 1979; Brimstone and Treacle 1982; Dune 1984; The Bride 1985; Bring On the Night 1985; Plenty 1985; Julia and Julia 1987; Stormy Monday 1987; The Adventures of Baron Munchausen 1988; The Grotesque 1995; Lock, Stock and Two Smoking Barrels 1998; Scott Walker: 30 Century Man 2006; Bee Movie 2007; Twenty Feet from Stardom 2013

Stirling, Pamela Candlelight in Algeria 1943; Nor the Moon by Night 1958

Stirling, Rachael (1977-) Complicity 1999; Another Life 2000; Freeze Frame 2003; The Truth 2006; Dangerous Parking 2007; Salmon Fishing in the Yemen 2011; Sixteen 2013

Stirner, Brian All Creatures Great and Small 1945; Overlord 1975

Stock, Nigel (1919-1986) Sons of the Sea 1939; Brighton Rock 1947;

Eyewitness 1956; The Silent Enemy 1958; HMS Defiant 1962; The Password Is Courage 1962; The Lion in Winter 1968; The Lost Continent 1968; Cromwell 1970; Bequest to the Nation 1972; Young Sherlock Holmes 1985

Stockbridge, Sara UFO 1993; The Wedding Tackle 2000; Rag Tale 2005

Stockdale, Carl (1874-1953) The Fall of Babylon 1919; Oliver Twist 1922; Along the Rio Grande 1941

Stockfeld, Betty (1905-1956) The Impassive Footman 1932; The Lad 1935; The Beloved Vagabond 1936; I See Ice 1938

Stockwell, Dean (1936-) Anchors Aweigh 1945; The Green Years 1946; Home Sweet Homicide 1946; Song of the Thin Man 1947; The Boy with Green Hair 1948; Down to the Sea in Ships 1949; The Secret Garden 1949; The Happy Years 1950; Kim 1950; Stars in My Crown 1950; Cattle Drive 1951; The Careless Years 1957; Gun for a Coward 1957; Compulsion 1959; Sons and Lovers 1960; Long Day's Journey into Night 1962; Rapture 1965; The Dunwich Horror 1970; The Last Movie 1971; Werewolf of Washington 1973; Tracks 1977; Alsino and the Condor 1982; Human Highway 1982; Dune 1984; Paris, Texas 1984; The Legend of Billie Jean 1985; To Live and Die in LA 1985; Blue Velvet 1986; Beverly Hills Cop II 1987; Gardens of Stone 1987; The Time Guardian 1987; Married to the Mob 1988; Tucker: the Man and His Dream 1988; Catchfire 1989; The Player 1992; Shame 1992; Chasers 1994; Hard Evidence 1994; Naked Souls 1995; Mr Wrong 1996; Air Force One 1997; John Grisham's The Rainmaker 1997; McHale's Navy 1997; Rites of Passage 1999; In Pursuit 2000; Buffalo Soldiers 2001; The Manchurian Candidate 2004; The Nanny Express 2008

Stockwell, Guy (1934-2002) The War Lord 1965; Beau Geste 1966; Blindfold 1966; The Plainsman 1966; Tobruk 1966; Banning 1967; The King's Pirate 1967; In Enemy Country 1968; It's Alive 1974; Santa Sangre 1989

Stockwell, Harry (1902-1984) All over Town 1937; Snow White and the Seven Dwarfs 1937

Stockwell, John (1961-) Christine 1983; Losin' It 1983; My Science Project 1985; Dangerously Close 1986; Top Gun 1986; Breast Men 1997

Stockwell, Sally The Truth about Demons 2000; The Ferryman 2007

Stoddard, Malcolm (1948-) The Godsend 1980; Tree of Hands 1988

Stojka, Andre Winnie the Pooh's Most Grand Adventure 1997; The Tigger Movie 2000; Piglet's Big Movie 2003

Stoker, Austin (1948-) Battle for the Planet of the Apes 1973; Assault on Precinct 13 1976

Stokes, Barry Ups and Downs of a Handyman 1975; Prey 1977

Stokoe, Matt Hollow 2011; The Dyatlov Pass Incident 2013

Stokowski, Leopold (1882-1977) The Big Broadcast of 1937 1936; One Hundred Men and a Girl 1937

Stole, Mink (1947-) Mondo Trasho 1970; Multiple Maniacs 1970; Pink Flamingos 1972; Female Trouble 1974; Desperate Living 1977; Polyester 1981; Cry-Baby 1989; Serial Mom 1994; Lost Highway 1996; Pecker 1998; But I'm a Cheerleader 1999; A Dirty Shame 2004; I Am Divine 2013

Stoler, Shirley (1929-1999) The Honeymoon Killers 1969; Seven Beauties 1976; The Deer Hunter 1978; Frankenhooker 1990

Stoleru, Josiane Cyrano de Bergerac 1990; Wild Side 2004

Stolhanske, Erik (1968-) Super Troopers 2001; Broken Lizard's Club Dread 2004; Beerfest 2006

Stoll, Corey A Girl like Me 2006; Ant-Man 2015

Stollery, David (1941-) Darling, How Could You! 1951; Jack and the Beanstalk 1952

Stoltz, Eric (1961-) Fast Times at Ridgemont High 1982; The Wild Life 1984; Code Name: Emerald 1985; Mask 1985; Lionheart 1986; Some Kind of Wonderful 1987; Haunted Summer 1988; The Fly II 1989; Say Anything... 1989; Memphis Belle 1990; The Waterdance 1991; The Heart of Justice 1992; Bodies, Rest & Motion 1993; Killing Zoe 1993; Little Women 1994; Naked in New York 1994; The Prophecy 1995; Pulp Fiction 1994; Sleep with Me 1994; Fluke 1995; Rob Roy 1995; Grace of My Heart 1996; Jerry Maguire 1996; Keys to Tulsa 1996; Anaconda 1997; Mr Jealousy 1997; Hi-Life 1998; A Murder of Crows 1998; Our Guys: Outrage in Glen Ridge 1999; The House of Mirth 2000; The

Last Dance 2000; The Simian Line 2000; The Rules of Attraction 2002; The Butterfly Effect 2003; When Zachary Beaver Came to Town 2003; The Honeymooners 2005

Stona, Winston The Harder They Come 1972; The Lunatic 1992; One Love 2003

Stone, Christopher (1940-1995) The Grasshopper 1970; The Howling 1981; Cujo 1983

Stone, Emma (1988-) The House Bunny 2008; The Rocker 2008; Zombieland 2009; Easy A 2010; Marmaduke 2010; Crazy, Stupid, Love 2011; Friends with Benefits 2011; The Help 2011; The Amazing Spider-Man 2012; Gangster Squad 2012; The Croods 2013; Movie 43 2013; The Amazing Spider-Man 2 2014; Birdman or (The Unexpected Virtue of Ignorance) 2014; Magic in the Moonlight 2014; Aloha 2015; Irrational Man 2015; La La Land 2016; Battle of the Sexes 2017

Stone, Fred (1873-1959) Alice Adams 1935; The Trail of the Lonesome Pine 1936; Life Begins in College 1937; The Westerner 1940

Stone, George E aka Stone, George (1903-1967) The Racket 1928; Five Star Final 1931; Little Caesar 1931; Taxi! 1932; The Vampire Bat 1933; Viva Villa! 1934; Frisco Kid 1935; Cherokee Strip 1940; The Face behind the Mask 1941; Road Show 1941; Abie's Irish Rose 1946; Bloodhounds of Broadway 1952

Stone, Harold J (1913-2005) The Harder They Fall 1956; Somebody Up There Likes Me 1956; The Wrong Man 1956; The Garment Jungle 1957; House of Numbers 1957; These Thousand Hills 1959; The Man with the X-Ray Eyes 1963; Showdown 1963; Girl Happy 1965; The Big Mouth 1967

Stone, Leonard (1923-2011) The Big Mouth 1967; Getting Straight 1970; Willy Wonka and the Chocolate Factory 1971; Once upon a Spy 1980

Stone, Lewis (1879-1953) The Prisoner of Zenda 1922; Scaramouche 1923; The Lost World 1925; The Private Life of Helen of Troy 1927; The Patriot 1928; A Woman of Affairs 1928; Madame X 1929; Wild Orchids 1929; The Big House 1930; Romance 1930; Inspiration 1931; Mata Hari 1931; The Secret Six 1931; The Sin of Madelon Claudet 1931; The Mask of Fu Manchu 1932; Red-Headed Woman 1932; The Wet Parade 1932; Bureau of Missing Persons 1933; Queen Christina 1933; The White Sister 1933; The Girl from Missouri 1934; Treasure Island 1934; China Seas 1935; David Copperfield 1935; Shipmates Forever 1935; Vanessa, Her Love Story 1935; Woman Wanted 1935; Small Town Girl 1936; Suzy 1936; Bad Man of Brimstone 1938; Judge Hardy's Children 1938; Love Finds Andy Hardy 1938; Out West with the Hardys 1938; You're Only Young Once 1938; Andy Hardy Gets Spring Fever 1939; The Hardys Ride High 1939; The Ice Follies of 1939 1939; Judge Hardy and Son 1939; Andy Hardy Meets Debutante 1940; Andy Hardy's Private Secretary 1941; Life Begins for Andy Hardy 1941; Andy Hardy's Double Life 1942; The Courtship of Andy Hardy 1942; Andy Hardy's Blonde Trouble 1944; The Hoodlum Saint 1946; Love Laughs at Andy Hardy 1946; State of the Union 1948; Any Number Can Play 1949; Key to the City 1950; Stars in My Crown 1950; Angels in the Outfield 1951; The Prisoner of Zenda 1952; All the Brothers Were Valiant 1953

Stone, Marianne (1922-2009) Passport to Treason 1956; Lolita 1961; Night of the Prowler 1962; The Vault of Horror 1973

Stone, Matt aka Stone, Matthew (1971-) Cannibal! the Musical 1993; Orgazmo 1997; BASEketball 1998; South Park: Bigger, Longer & Uncut 1999; Bowling for Columbine 2002; Team America: World Police 2004; This Film Is Not Yet Rated 2006

Stone, Milburn (1904-1980) The Frozen Ghost 1944; Strange Confession 1945; Branded 1950; Roadblock 1951; Arrowhead 1953; The Siege at Red River 1954; Smoke Signal 1955

Stone, Oliver (1946-) Born on the Fourth of July 1989; Hollywood Banker 2014

Stone, Philip (1924-2003) The Shining 1980; Green Ice 1981; Indiana Jones and the Temple of Doom 1984; The Baby of Macon 1993

Stone, Sharon (1958-) Deadly Blessing 1981; Calendar Girl Murders 1984; Irreconcilable Differences 1984; King Solomon's Mines 1985; Allan

Quatermain and the Lost City of Gold 1987; Cold Steel 1987; Police Academy 4: Citizens on Patrol 1987; Action Jackson 1988; Beyond the Stars 1988; Nico 1988; Blood and Sand 1989; Total Recall 1990; He Said, She Said 1991; Scissors 1991; Where Sleeping Dogs Lie 1991; Year of the Gun 1991; Basic Instinct 1992; Diary of a Hitman 1992; Sliver 1993; Intersection 1994; The Specialist 1994; Casino 1995; The Quick and the Dead 1995; Diabolique 1996; Last Dance 1996; Antz 1998; Gloria 1998; The Mighty 1998; Sphere 1998; The Muse 1999; Simpatico 1999; Beautiful Joe 2000; If These Walls Could Talk 2 2000; Picking Up the Pieces 2000; Cold Creek Manor 2003; Catwoman 2004; Broken Flowers 2005; Alpha Dog 2006; Basic Instinct 2: Risk Addiction 2006; Bobby 2006; Fading Gigolo 2013; Lovelace 2013; Dior and I 2014

Stone, Terry (1971-) Rollin with the Nines 2005; Rise of the Footsoldier 2006; Bronson 2008; Doghouse 2009; Jack Said 2009; Bonded by Blood 2010; Outside Bet 2011

Stoner, Alyson (1993-) Cheaper by the Dozen 2003; Cheaper by the Dozen 2 2005; Camp Rock 2008; Step Up: All In 2014

Stoney, Kevin (1921-2008) Cash on Demand 1961; The Blood Beast Terror 1967

Stoppa, Paolo (1906-1988) La Beauté du Diable 1949; Miracle in Milan 1950; The Miller's Wife 1955; Rocco and His Brothers 1960; The Leopard 1962; Becket 1964; Behold a Pale Horse 1964; The Visit 1964; After the Fox 1966

Stoppard, Ed (1974-) The Pianist 2002; Joy Division 2006; Fugitive Pieces 2007; Papadopoulos & Sons 2012; Blackwood 2013

Storch, Larry (1923-) The Last Blitzkrieg 1958; Who Was That Lady? 1960; Forty Pounds of Trouble 1962; Captain Newman, MD 1963; Sex and the Single Girl 1964; Wild and Wonderful 1964; Bus Riley's Back in Town 1965; That Funny Feeling 1965; The Great Bank Robbery 1969

Storey, Ruth (1913-1997) The Blue Gardenia 1953; Bells Are Ringing 1960; The Subterraneans 1960

Storke, Adam (1962-) Mystic Pizza 1988; Death Becomes Her 1992; Highway to Hell 1992; A Mother's Gift 1995

Storm, Gale (1922-2009) It Happened on Fifth Avenue 1947; The Kid from Texas 1950; The Underworld Story 1950; Al Jennings of Oklahoma 1951

Stormare, Peter (1953-) Damage 1992; Fargo 1995; Playing God 1997; Hamilton 1998; Circus 1999; 8mm 1999; The Million Dollar Hotel 1999; Purgatory 2000; Chocolat 2000; Dancer in the Dark 2000; Windtalkers 2001; Bad Company 2002; Minority Report 2002; Spun 2002; The Tuxedo 2002; Bad Boys II 2003; Birth 2004; The Brothers Grimm 2005; Constantine 2005; Unknown 2006; Premonition 2007; Horsemen 2009; Henry's Crime 2010; Jagarna 2: False Trail 2011; Lockout 2012; Small Apartments 2012; Hansel & Gretel: Witch Hunters 2013; The Last Stand 2013; Clown 2014; Rage 2014; 22 Jump Street 2014

Stossel, Ludwig (1883-1973) The Man I Married 1940; Great Guns 1941; Man Hunt 1941; Hers to Hold 1943; Hitler's Madman 1943; Bluebeard 1944; Dillinger 1945; House of Dracula 1945; The Beginning or the End 1947; Escape Me Never 1947; The Great Sinner 1949; Somebody Loves Me 1952; The Sun Shines Bright 1953; The Blue Angel 1959

Stott, Ken (1955-) Shallow Grave 1994; Fever Pitch 1996; The Boxer 1997; The Debt Collector 1999; Plunkett & Macleane 1999; I'll Sleep When I'm Dead 2003; Casanova 2005; The Mighty Celt 2005; Charlie Wilson's War 2007; Toast 2010; One Day 2011; The Hobbit: an Unexpected Journey 2012

Stowe, Madeleine (1958-) Stakeout 1987; Revenge 1990; The Two Jakes 1990; Closet Land 1991; The Last of the Mohicans 1992; Unlawful Entry 1992; Another Stakeout 1993; Short Cuts 1993; Bad Girls 1994; Blink 1994; China Moon 1994; Twelve Monkeys 1995; Playing by Heart 1998; The Proposition 1998; The General's Daughter 1999; Impostor 2001; The Magnificent Ambersons 2001; Avenging Angelo 2002; We Were Soldiers 2002; Octane 2003

Strachan, Antony The Trench 1999; Sylvia 2003

Stradner, Rose (1913-1958) The Last Gangster 1937; Blind Alley 1939; The Keys of the Kingdom 1944

Strahovski, Yvonne Killer Elite 2011; I, Frankenstein 2013

Straight, Beatrice (1914-2001) Patterns 1956; The Nun's Story 1959; Network 1976; Bloodline 1979; Endless Love 1981; Poltergeist 1982; Two of a Kind 1983; Chiller 1985

Strait, Ralph (1936-1992) The Beastmaster 1982; Halloween III: Season of the Witch 1982

Strait, Steven The Covenant 2006; 10,000 BC 2008; City Island 2009

Strand, Jimmy (1922-1989) Block Busters 1944; Bowery Champs 1944

Strange, Glenn (1899-1973) House of Frankenstein 1944; Knickerbocker Holiday 1944; The Monster Maker 1944; House of Dracula 1945; Abbott and Costello Meet Frankenstein 1948

Strange, Robert (1881-1952) The Walking Dead 1936; The Far Frontier 1949

Strasberg, Lee (1901-1982) The Godfather Part II 1974; The Cassandra Crossing 1976; ...And Justice for All 1979; Boardwalk 1979; Going in Style 1979; Skokie 1981

Strasberg, Susan (1938-1999) The Cobweb 1955; Picnic 1955; Stage Struck 1958; Kapo 1959; Taste of Fear 1961; Hemingway's Adventures of a Young Man 1962; The High Bright Sun 1965; The Trip 1967; The Brotherhood 1968; Sweet Hunters 1969; And Millions Will Die! 1973; Rollercoaster 1977; In Praise of Older Women 1978; The Manitou 1978; The Delta Force 1986; Out of Darkness 1990

Strassman, Marcia (1948-2014) The Aviator 1985; Honey, I Shrunk the Kids 1989; Honey, I Blew Up the Kid 1992; Another Stakeout 1993

Stratas, Teresa (1938-) La Traviata 1982; Under the Piano 1995

Strathairn, David (1949-) Return of the secaucus Seven 1980; Lovesick 1983; Iceman 1984; Call Me 1988; Dominick and Eugene 1988; Eight Men Out 1988; The Feud 1989; Without Warning: the James Brady Story 1991; Passion Fish 1992; Sneakers 1992; Stepkids 1992; Arthur Miller's The American Clock 1993; A Dangerous Woman 1993; The Firm 1993; Lost in Yonkers 1993; The River Wild 1994; Dolores Claiborne 1995; Losing Isaiah 1995; Beyond the Call 1996; Bad Manners 1997; In the Gloaming 1997; LA Confidential 1997; Evidence of Blood 1998; Simon Birch 1998; Limbo 1999; A Map of the World 1999; Harrison's Flowers 2000; Blue Car 2001; Twisted 2003; Good Night, and Good Luck. 2005; The Notorious Bettie Page 2005; The Bourne Ultimatum 2007; Fracture 2007; My Blueberry Nights 2007; Cold Souls 2008; The Spiderwick Chronicles 2008; The Uninvited 2008; Howl 2010; The Tempest 2010; Temple Grandin 2010; The Whistleblower 2010; Lincoln 2012

Stratten, Dorothy (1960-1980) Skateown, USA 1979; They All Laughed 1981

Stratton, Gil aka **Stratton Jr, Gil** (1922-2008) Girl Crazy 1943; Stalag 17 1953

Stratton, John (1925-1991) The Cure for Love 1949; The Cruel Sea 1952; The Happy Family 1952; The Long Arm 1956; The Man in the Sky 1956; Seven Waves Away 1957

Strauss, Peter (1947-) Hail, Hero! 1969; Soldier Blue 1970; The Man without a Country 1973; The Last Tycoon 1976; The Jericho Mile 1979; The Secret of NIMH 1982; Spacehunter: Adventures in the Forbidden Zone 1983; Nick of Time 1995; Keys to Tulsa 1996; Death in the Shadows: the Sam Sheppard Story 1998; Murder on the Orient Express 2001; xXx: the Next Level 2005; Vickery's Wild Ride 2009

Strauss, Robert (1913-1975) Sailor Beware 1951; Jumping Jacks 1952; Act of Love 1953; Here Come the Girls 1953; Money from Home 1953; The Redhead from Wyoming 1953; Stalag 17 1953; The Atomic Kid 1954; The Bridges at Toko-Ri 1954; The Man with the Golden Arm 1955; The Seven Year Itch 1955; Attack! 1956; The Mobster 1958; Girls! Girls! Girls! 1962

Strauss, Ursula Revanche 2008; Michael 2011

Strauss, Zohar Eyes Wide Open 2009; Lebanon 2009

Streep, Meryl (1949-) Julia 1977; The Deer Hunter 1978; Kramer vs Kramer 1979; Manhattan 1979; The Seduction of Joe Tynan 1979; The French Lieutenant's Woman 1981; Sophie's Choice 1982; Still of the Night 1982; Silkwood 1983; Falling in Love 1984;

Out of Africa 1985; Plenty 1985; Heartburn 1986; Ironweed 1987; A Cry in the Dark 1988; She-Devil 1989; Postcards from the Edge 1990; Defending Your Life 1991; Death Becomes Her 1992; The House of the Spirits 1993; The River Wild 1994; The Bridges of Madison County 1995; Before and After 1996; Marvin's Room 1996; First Do No Harm 1997; Dancing at Lughnasa 1998; One True Thing 1998; Music of the Heart 1999; AI: Artificial Intelligence 2001; Adaptation. 2002; The Hours 2002; Lemony Snicket's A Series of Unfortunate Events 2004; The Manchurian Candidate 2004; Prime 2005; The Ant Bully 2006; The Devil Wears Prada 2006; A Prairie Home Companion 2006; Evening 2007; Lions for Lambs 2007; Rendition 2007; Doubt 2008; Mamma Mia! 2008; Fantastic Mr Fox 2009; It's Complicated 2009; Julie & Julia 2009; The Iron Lady 2011; Hope Springs 2012; Radioman 2012; August: Osage County 2013; The Giver 2014; The Homesman 2014; Into the Woods 2014; Ricki and the Flash 2015; Suffragette 2015; Florence Foster Jenkins 2016

Street, Sebastian The Last Seven 2010; Age of Heroes 2011

Streisand, Barbra (1942-) Funny Girl 1968; Hello, Dolly! 1969; On a Clear Day You Can See Forever 1970; The Owl and the Pussycat 1970; Up the Sandbox 1972; What's Up, Doc? 1972; The Way We Were 1973; For Pete's Sake 1974; Funny Lady 1975; A Star Is Born 1976; The Main Event 1979; All Night Long 1981; Yentl 1983; Nuts 1987; The Prince of Tides 1991; The Mirror Has Two Faces 1996; Meet the Fockers 2004; Little Fockers 2010; The Guilt Trip 2013

Stretch, Gary (1968-) Final Combination 1993; Dead Man's Shoes 2004; Freebird 2007; The Heavy 2009

Stribling, Melissa (1927-1992) Dracula 1958; The Safecracker 1958; Only When I Larf 1968

Strickland, Gail (1947-) The Drowning Pool 1975; Bittersweet Love 1976; Bound for Glory 1976; Who'll Stop the Rain? 1978; Norma Rae 1979; My Body, My Child 1982; Starflight One 1983; Oxford Blues 1984; Protocol 1984; The Man in the Moon 1991; Three of Hearts 1992

Strickland, KaDee (1977-) Anything Else 2003; Anacondas: the Hunt for the Blood Orchid 2004; The Grudge 2004; The Flock 2007

Strickland, Robert E aka **Strickland, Robert** Girl Crazy 1943; Good News 1947

Stricklyn, Ray (1928-2002) The Last Wagon 1956; The Return of Dracula 1958; Ten North Frederick 1958; The Big Fisherman 1959; The Remarkable Mr Pennypacker 1959; The Lost World 1960; Arizona Raiders 1965

Stride, John (1936-) Bitter Harvest 1963; Macbeth 1971; Something to Hide 1971; Brannigan 1975; The Omen 1976; Thirteen at Dinner 1985

Striker, Joseph (1898-1974) Annie Laurie 1927; The King of Kings 1927

Stringfield, Sherry (1967-) 54 1998; Autumn in New York 2000; The Stepfather 2009

Stritch, Elaine (1925-2014) Three Violent People 1956; A Farewell to Arms 1957; The Perfect Furlough 1958; Providence 1977; September 1987; Cocoon: the Return 1988; Autumn in New York 2000; Screwed 2000; Small Time Crooks 2000; Monster-in-Law 2005

Strode, Woody (1914-1994) City beneath the Sea 1953; Pork Chop Hill 1959; The Last Voyage 1960; Sergeant Rutledge 1960; The Sins of Rachel Cade 1960; The Man Who Shot Liberty Valance 1962; Tarzan's Three Challenges 1963; The Professionals 1966; 7 Women 1966; Shalako 1968; Boot Hill 1969; Che! 1969; The Deserter 1971; Winterhawk 1975; Keoma 1976; Kingdom of the Spiders 1977; Jaguar Lives! 1979; The Black Stallion Returns 1983; Lust in the Dust 1984; Storyville 1992; Posse 1993

Stroma, Freddie Extraterrestrial 2014; The Inbetweeners 2 2014

Strong, Brenda (1960-) Black Dog 1998; Starship Troopers 2: Hero of the Federation 2004

Strong, Danny (1974-) The Prophecy II 1997; Shriek If You Know What I Did Last Friday the 13th 2000

Strong, Gwyneth Nothing but the Night 1972; Bloody Kids 1979; In Love with Alma Cogan 2011

Strong, Jeremy Robot & Frank 2012; Parkland 2013; Time out of Mind 2014

Strong, Leonard (1908-1980) Blood on the Sun 1945; The Naked Jungle 1953; Jet Attack 1958

Strong, Mark (1963-) Captives 1994; Fever Pitch 1996; If Only 1998; Elephant Juice 1999; To End All Wars 2001; Heartlands 2002; It's All about Love 2002; Oliver Twist 2005; Revolver 2005; Tristan + Isolde 2005; Scenes of a Sexual Nature 2006; Miss Pettigrew Lives for a Day 2007; Stardust 2007; Sunshine 2007; Babylon AD 2008; Body of Lies 2008; Good 2008; RocknRolla 2008; The Young Victoria 2008; Kick-Ass 2009; Sherlock Holmes 2009; Arrietty 2010; The Eagle 2011; Robin Hood 2010; The Way Back 2010; Black Gold 2011; Green Lantern 2011; The Guard 2011; Tinker Tailor Soldier Spy 2011; Blood 2012; John Carter 2012; Welcome to the Punch 2012; Zero Dark Thirty 2012; Justin and the Knights of Valour 2013; Mindscape 2013; Before I Go to Sleep 2014; Closer to the Moon 2014; The Imitation Game 2014; Kingsman: The Secret Service 2015; Grimsby 2016; Kingsman: The Golden Circle 2017

Strong, Michael (1924-1980) Point Blank 1967; Secret Ceremony 1968; Patton 1970

Strong, Rider (1979-) Benefit of the Doubt 1993; Cabin Fever 2002

Strong, Tara Dino Time 2012; Batman: The Killing Joke 2016

Stroud, Don (1937-) Games 1967; Journey to Shiloh 1967; Coogan's Bluff 1968; tick... tick... tick... 1969; Bloody Mama 1970; Joe Kidd 1972; Scalawag 1973; Slaughter's Big Rip-Off 1973; The Killer inside Me 1975; The Choirboys 1977; The Buddy Holly Story 1978; The Amityville Horror 1979; The Night the Lights Went Out in Georgia 1981; Armed and Dangerous 1986; Dillinger and Capone 1995

Stroup, Jessica The Hills Have Eyes II 2007; Prom Night 2008

Strudwick, Shepperd aka **Shepperd, John** (1907-1983) Fast Company 1938; Dr Kildare's Strange Case 1940; Flight Command 1940; Belle Starr 1941; The Men in Her Life 1941; Remember the Day 1941; Rings on Her Fingers 1942; Ten Gentlemen from West Point 1942; Joan of Arc 1948; All the King's Men 1949; The Reckless Moment 1949; The Red Pony 1949; The Kid from Texas 1950; Let's Dance 1950; Autumn Leaves 1956; Beyond a Reasonable Doubt 1956; The Eddy Duchin Story 1956; Cops and Robbers 1973

Strummer, Joe (1952-2002) Candy Mountain 1987; Straight to Hell 1987; Mystery Train 1989; The Future Is Unwritten 2006

Struthers, Sally (1948-) The Getaway 1972; What I Did for Love 2006

Struycken, Carel (1949-) The Witches of Eastwick 1987; The Addams Family 1991; Addams Family Values 1993; Addams Family Reunion 1998; I Woke Up Early the Day I Died 1998

Stryker, Amy A Wedding 1978; Impulse 1984

Stuart, Gloria (1910-2010) Air Mail 1932; The Old Dark House 1932; The Invisible Man 1933; The Kiss before the Mirror 1933; Roman Scandals 1933; Here Comes the Navy 1934; Gold Diggers of 1935 1935; Poor Little Rich Girl 1936; The Prisoner of Shark Island 1936; Life Begins in College 1937; Rebecca of Sunnybrook Farm 1938; The Three Musketeers 1939; The Whistler 1944; Titanic 1997; The Love Letter 1999

Stuart, John (1898-1979) The Pleasure Garden 1925; Hindle Wakes 1927; Kitty 1928; Hindle Wakes 1931; Number Seventeen 1932; D'Ye Ken John Peel? 1934; The Show Goes On 1937; The Big Blockade 1942; Madonna of the Seven Moons 1944; House of Darkness 1948; The Gilded Cage 1954

Stuart, Kathleen (1925-) Just William's Luck 1947; William at the Circus 1948

Stuart, Maxine The Prisoner of Second Avenue 1974; Coast to Coast 1980

Stuart, Randy (1924-1996) Apartment for Peggy 1948; Sitting Pretty 1948; Dancing in the Dark 1949; I Was a Male War Bride 1949; Stella 1950; I Can Get It for You Wholesale 1951; Room for One More 1952; Star in the Dust 1956; The Incredible Shrinking Man 1957

Stubbs, Danny (1874-1950) Alibi 1929; Her Majesty Love 1931

Stubbs, Imogen (1961-) A Summer Story 1987; Erik the Viking 1989; Fellow Traveller 1989; True Colors 1991; A Pin for the Butterfly 1994; Jack & Sarah 1995; Sense and Sensibility 1995; Twelfth Night 1996

Stubbs, Una (1937-) Summer Holiday 1962; Wonderful Life 1964; Three Hats for Lisa 1965; Till Death Us Do Part 1968; Penny Gold 1973; Golden Years 2016

Stuckey, Sophie The Dark 2005; The Woman in Black 2011

Studer, Carl Le Doulos 1962; The Love Cage 1964

Studi, Wes (1947-) The Last of the Mohicans 1992; Geronimo: an American Legend 1993; Street Fighter 1994; Heat 1995; Deep Rising 1998; Mystery Men 1999; Undisputed 2002; The New World 2005; Bury My Heart at Wounded Knee 2007; Avatar 2009

Stuhlbarg, Michael (1968-) Afterschool 2008; A Serious Man 2009; Men in Black 3 2012; Miles Ahead 2015; Steve Jobs 2015

Stuhr, Jerzy (1947-) The Scar 1976; Camera Buff 1979; Three Colours White 1993; We Have a Pope 2011

Stuke, Neil (1966-) Dead Bolt Dead 1999; The Wedding Tackle 2000; Out on a Limb 2005

Sturges, Preston (1898-1959) Sullivan's Travels 1941; Star Spangled Rhythm 1942; Paris Holiday 1958

Sturges, Shannon (1968-) Desire & Hell at Sunset Motel 1991; Tornado! 1996

Sturgess, Jim aka **Sturgess, James** (1978-) The Browning Version 1994; Across the Universe 2007; Crossing Over 2008; Fifty Dead Men Walking 2008; The Other Boleyn Girl 2008; 21 2008; Heartless 2009; Legend of the Guardians: the Owls of Ga'Hoole 2010; The Way Back 2010; One Day 2011; Ashes 2012; Cloud Atlas 2012; Deception 2013; Stonehearst Asylum 2014; Kidnapping Freddy Heineken 2015; Geostorm 2016

Sturridge, Tom (1985-) Like Minds 2006; The Boat That Rocked 2009; Junkhearts 2011; Effie Gray 2014; Far from the Madding Crowd 2015; Remainder 2015

Styler, Trudie (1955-) Bring On the Night 1985; Me without You 2001; Alpha Male 2005

Styles, Edwin (1899-1960) Adam and Evelyne 1949; The Lady with the Lamp 1951; Penny Princess 1952

Styles, Harry (1994-) One Direction: This Is Us 2013; Dunkirk 2017

Suarez, Emma (1964-) 1919 1983; Vacas 1991; The Red Squirrel 1993; Julieta 2016

Suarez, José (1919-1981) Calle Mayor 1956; Texas Adios 1966

Suarez, Miguel Angel aka **Suarez, Miguel** (1939-2009) Bananas 1971; Stir Crazy 1980; Under Suspicion 2000

Subkoff, Tara (1973-) When the Bough Breaks 1993; All over Me 1996

Subor, Michel (1935-) Le Petit Soldat 1960; Topaz 1969; Beau Travail 1999; The Intruder 2004; White Material 2009; Bastards 2013

Suchet, David (1946-) The Hunchback of Notre Dame 1982; The Little Drummer Girl 1984; The Falcon and the Snowman 1985; Iron Eagle 1985; A Song for Europe 1985; Thirteen at Dinner 1985; Bigfoot and the Hendersons 1987; A World Apart 1987; To Kill a Priest 1988; When the Whales Came 1989; Executive Decision 1996; Sunday 1997; RKO 281 1999; Wing Commander 1999; Live from Baghdad 2002; Foolproof 2003; The In-Laws 2003; Flushed Away 2006; The Bank Job 2008; Effie Gray 2014

Sudeikis, Jason (1975-) The Bounty Hunter 2010; Going the Distance 2010; Hall Pass 2011; Horrible Bosses 2011; The Campaign 2012; Drinking Buddies 2013; We're the Millers 2013; Horrible Bosses 2 2014; Masterminds 2015; Sleeping with Other People 2015; The Angry Birds Movie 2016; Mother's Day 2016; Race 2016

Sugai, Ichiro (1907-1973) My Love Has Been Burning 1949; Early Summer 1951; The Life of Oharu 1952; The Crucified Lovers 1954

Sugai, Kin (1926-) Dodes'ka-Den 1970; Death Japanese Style 1988

Sugarman, Sara Those Glory, Glory Days 1983; Dealers 1989

Sugawara, Bunta (1933-2014) The Yakuza Papers 1973; The Burmese Harp 1985

Sugawara, Hideo Tokyo Chorus 1931; I Was Born, but... 1932

Sugimura, Haruko (1905-1997) Late Spring 1949; Early Summer 1951; Tokyo Story 1953; Early Spring 1956; Floating Weeds 1959; Ohayo 1959

Sukhorukov, Viktor (1951-) Brother 1997; Of Freaks and Men 1998; The Island 2006

Sukowa, Barbara (1950-) Berlin Alexanderplatz 1980; The German Sisters 1981; Lola 1982; Rosa

Luxemburg 1986; Europa 1991; Voyager 1991; M Butterfly 1993; The Lady in Question 1999; Thirteen Conversations about One Thing 2001; Hannah Arendt 2012

Suleiman, Elia (1960-) Divine Intervention 2002; Bamako 2006; The Time That Remains: Chronicle of a Present Absentee 2009; 7 Days in Havana 2012

Suliman, Ali Paradise Now 2005; The Kingdom 2007; Lemon Tree 2008

Sulkin, Gregg Sixty Six 2006; Anti-Social 2015

Sullavan, Margaret (1909-1960) Only Yesterday 1933; Little Man, What Now? 1934; The Good Fairy 1935; So Red the Rose 1935; The Moon's Our Home 1936; Next Time We Love 1936; The Shining Hour 1938; The Shopworn Angel 1938; Three Comrades 1938; The Mortal Storm 1940; The Shop around the Corner 1940; Appointment for Love 1941; Back Street 1941; So Ends Our Night 1941; Cry Havoc 1943; No Sad Songs for Me 1950

Sullivan, Barry (1912-1994) And Now Tomorrow 1944; Lady in the Dark 1944; Framed 1947; Any Number Can Play 1949; The Great Gatsby 1949; Tension 1949; A Life of Her Own 1950; Nancy Goes to Rio 1950; The Outriders 1950; Cause for Alarm 1951; Mr Imperium 1951; Payment on Demand 1951; The Bad and the Beautiful 1952; Skirts Ahoy! 1952; Cry of the Hunted 1953; Jeopardy 1953; Her Twelve Men 1954; Playgirl 1954; Queen Bee 1955; Strategic Air Command 1955; Texas Lady 1955; Julie 1956; Dragoon Wells Massacre 1957; Forty Guns 1957; Another Time, Another Place 1958; Seven Ways from Sundown 1960; Light in the Piazza 1961; My Blood Runs Cold 1965; Planet of the Vampires 1965; An American Dream 1966; Buckskin 1968; How to Steal the World 1968; Shark! 1969; Tell Them Willie Boy Is Here 1969; Earthquake 1974; The Human Factor 1975; Take a Hard Ride 1975

Sullivan, Billy L (1980-) Little Big League 1994; The Eig Green 1995

Sullivan, Brad (1931-2008) The Untouchables 1987; Blood Money 1988; Funny Farm 1988; The Prince of Tides 1991; Bushwhacked 1995; The Jerky Boys 1995

Sullivan, Charlotte (1984-) The Cry of the Owl 2009; Unstable 2009; The Colony 2013

Sullivan, Ed (1901-1974) Senior Prom 1958; Bye Bye Birdie 1963; The Singing Nun 1966

Sullivan, Elliott (1907-1974) The Lady Gambles 1949; The Sergeant 1968

Sullivan, Erik Per (1991-) Wendigo 2001; Christmas with the Kranks 2004

Sullivan, Francis L aka **Sullivan, Francis** (1903-1956) When London Sleeps 1932; The Return of Bulldog Drummond 1934; The Mystery of Edwin Drood 1935; Dinner at the Ritz 1937; 21 Days 1937; The Citadel 1938; Climbing High 1938; The Drum 1938; The Ware Case 1938; The Four Just Men 1939; Pimpernel Smith 1941; The Day Will Dawn 1942; Fiddlers Three 1944; Caesar and Cleopatra 1945; Great Expectations 1946; The Man Within 1947; Take My Life 1947; Broken Journey 1948; Joan of Arc 1948; Oliver Twist 1948; The Winslow Boy 1948; Christopher Columbus 1949; The Red Danube 1949; Night and the City 1950; My Favorite Spy 1951

Sullivan, Jean (1923-2003) Uncertain Glory 1944; Roughly Speaking 1945; Squirm 1976

Sullivan, Sean (1921-1985) During One Night 1961; 2001: a Space Odyssey 1968; The Boy in Blue 1986

Sullivan, Susan (1942-) The Incredible Hulk 1977; Danielle Steel's A Perfect Stranger 1994

Sully, Frank (1908-1975) The Doctor Takes a Wife 1940; The Grapes of Wrath 1940; The More the Merrier 1943; Along Came Jones 1945; The Naked Street 1955

Summer, Cree (1969-) The Rugrats Movie 1998; Atlantis: the Lost Empire 2001; Kermit's Swamp Years 2002

Summerfield, Eleanor (1921-2001) Isn't Life Wonderful! 1952; Face the Music 1954; Final Appointment 1954; Lost 1955; Don't Bother to Knock 1961; On the Fiddle 1961; Petticoat Pirates 1961; Spare the Rod 1961; Guns of Darkness 1962; The Running Man 1963

Summerville, Slim aka **Summerville, George "Slim"** (1892-1946) All Quiet on the Western Front 1930; Bad Sister 1931; Air Mail 1932; The Farmer Takes a Wife 1935; Life Begins at 40 1935; Way Down East 1935; Captain January 1936; The Country Doctor 1936; White Fang 1936; Love Is News 1937; Kentucky

Moonshine 1938; Rebecca of Sunnybrook Farm 1938; Submarine Patrol 1938; Charlie Chan in Reno 1939; Anne of Windy Poplars 1940

Sumner, Geoffrey (1908-1989) Traveller's Joy 1949; Band of Thieves 1962; Cul-de-Sac 1966

Sumner, Peter (1942-) Ned Kelly 1970; The Survivor 1981

Sumpter, Donald (1943-) Rosencrantz and Guildenstern Are Dead 1990; K-19: the Widowmaker 2002; The Constant Gardener 2005; Eastern Promises 2007; Way of the Morris 2011; Bypass 2014

Sumpter, Jeremy (1989-) Frailty 2001; Peter Pan 2003; Excision 2012

Sumpter, Tika Ride Along 2014; Ride Along 2 2016

Sun Honglei (1970-) The Road Home 1999; Seven Swords 2005; Mongol 2007; Zhang Yimou's Blood Simple 2009

Sundberg, Clinton (1906-1987) Easter Parade 1948; Good Sam 1948; Mr Peabody and the Mermaid 1948; In the Good Old Summertime 1949; Annie Get Your Gun 1950; Duchess of Idaho 1950; On the Riviera 1951; The Belle of New York 1952; The Caddy 1953; The Girl Next Door 1953; Main Street to Broadway 1953

Sunderland, Matthew Out of the Blue 2006; The Devil's Rock 2011

Sundquist, Bjorn (1948-) Shipwrecked 1990; The Other Side of Sunday 1996

Sung Kang Better Luck Tomorrow 2001; The Fast and the Furious: Tokyo Drift 2006; Ninja Assassin 2009; Bullet to the Head 2012

Sunjata, Daniel Gone 2012; One for the Money 2012

Superstar, Ingrid The Chelsea Girls 1966; Bike Boy 1967

Suplee, Ethan (1976-) Chasing Amy 1996; American History X 1998; Desert Blue 1998; Remember the Titans 2000; Evolution 2001; The Butterfly Effect 2003; Without a Paddle 2004; Mr Woodcock 2007; True Story 2015

Surgère, Hélène (1928-) Salo, or the 120 Days of Sodom 1975; The Brontë Sisters 1979; Australia 1989; Ma Vraie Vie à Rouen 2002; Confidences Trop Intimes 2004

Surovy, Nicolas aka **Surovy, Nicholas** (1944-) 12:01 1993; The Man Who Captured Eichmann 1996

Sussman, Kevin Little Black Book 2004; Killers 2010

Sutcliffe, David (1969-) Million Dollar Murder 2004; Happy Endings 2005; Before You Say "I Do" 2009; The Wish List 2010

Sutera, Paul (1979-) The Brady Bunch Movie 1995; A Very Brady Sequel 1996

Sutherland, Claudette A Little Romance 1979; Man of the Year 1995

Sutherland, Dick (1881-1934) A Sailor-Made Man 1921; Grandma's Boy 1922

Sutherland, Donald (1934-) Die! Die! My Darling 1964; Dr Terror's House of Horrors 1965; The Bedford Incident 1965; Promise Her Anything 1966; The Dirty Dozen 1967; Oedipus the King 1967; Interlude 1968; Sebastian 1968; The Split 1968; MASH 1969; Act of the Heart 1970; Alex in Wonderland 1970; Kelly's Heroes 1970; Start the Revolution without Me 1970; Klute 1971; Little Murders 1971; FTA 1972; Dan Candy's Law 1973; Don't Look Now 1973; Steelyard Blues 1973; The Day of the Locust 1975; Casanova 1976; The Eagle Has Landed 1976; End of the Game 1976; 1900 1976; Blood Relatives 1977; The Disappearance 1977; The Kentucky Fried Movie 1977; The First Great Train Robbery 1978; Invasion of the Body Snatchers 1978; Murder by Decree 1978; Bear Island 1979; A Man, a Woman and a Bank 1979; Ordinary People 1980; Eye of the Needle 1981; Threshold 1981; Max Dugan Returns 1983; Catholic Boys 1985; Revolution 1985; The Wolf at the Door 1986; The Rosary Murders 1987; The Trouble with Spies 1987; Apprentice to Murder 1988; A Dry White Season 1989; Lock Up 1989; The Road Home 1989; Bethune: the Making of a Hero 1990; Backdraft 1991; JFK 1991; Scream of Stone 1991; Buffy the Vampire Slayer 1992; Quicksand: No Escape 1992; Shadow of the Wolf 1992; Benefit of the Doubt 1993; Six Degrees of Separation 1993; Younger and Younger 1993; Disclosure 1994; The Puppet Masters 1994; Citizen X 1995; Outbreak 1995; Hollow Point 1996; Shadow Conspiracy 1996; A Time to Kill 1996; The Assignment 1997; Fallen 1998; Free Money 1998; Virus 1998; Without Limits 1998; Behind the Mask 1999; The Hunley 1999; Instinct 1999; The Art of War 2000; Panic 2000; Space Cowboys 2000; The Big

Heist 2001; Big Shot's Funeral 2001; Final Fantasy: the Spirits Within 2001; Path to War 2002; Cold Mountain 2003; The Italian Job 2003; An American Haunting 2005; Pride & Prejudice 2005; Ask the Dust 2006; Land of the Blind 2006; Puffball 2006; Reign over Me 2007; Fool's Gold 2008; Astro Boy 2009; The Eagle 2010; Horrible Bosses 2011; The Mechanic 2011; The Hunger Games 2012; Deception 2013; The Hunger Games: Catching Fire 2013; The Calling 2014; The Hunger Games: Mockingjay Part 1 2014; Forsaken 2015; The Hunger Games: Mockingjay Part 2 2015

Sutherland, Kiefer (1966-) Max Dugan Returns 1983; Bay Boy 1984; At Close Range 1985; Brotherhood of Justice 1986; Crazy Moon 1986; Stand by Me 1986; The Killing Time 1987; The Lost Boys 1987; Bright Lights, Big City 1988; 1969 1988; Promised Land 1988; Young Guns 1988; Chicago Joe and the Showgirl 1989; Renegades 1989; Flashback 1990; Flatliners 1990; The Nutcracker Prince 1990; Young Guns II 1990; Article 99 1992; A Few Good Men 1992; Last Light 1993; The Three Musketeers 1993; The Vanishing 1993; The Cowboy Way 1994; Eye for an Eye 1995; Freeway 1996; The Last Days of Frankie the Fly 1996; A Time to Kill 1996; Truth or Consequences, NM 1997; Break Up 1998; Dark City 1998; Eye of the Killer 1999; Picking Up the Pieces 2000; To End All Wars 2001; Dead Heat 2002; Phone Booth 2002; Taking Lives 2004; River Queen 2005; The Sentinel 2006; The Wild 2006; Mirrors 2008; Monsters vs Aliens 2009; Marmaduke 2010; Melancholia 2011; The Reluctant Fundamentalist 2012; Pompeii 2014; Forsaken 2015

Sutton, Dudley (1933-) The Boys 1961; The Leather Boys 1963; Rotten to the Core 1965; The Devils 1971; A Town Called Hell 1971; Madame Sin 1972; The Island 1980; The Rainbow 1988; Edward II 1991; Orlando 1992; Up at the Villa 1998; This Filthy Earth 2001; Song for a Raggy Boy 2002; The Football Factory 2004; The Shouting Men 2009; Cockneys vs Zombies 2011

Sutton, Frank (1923-1974) Marty 1955; Town without Pity 1961; The Satan Bug 1965

Sutton, Grady (1908-1995) Pack Up Your Troubles 1932; Alice Adams 1935; Man on the Flying Trapeze 1935; Hard to Get 1938; Vivacious Lady 1938; The Bank Dick 1940; A Lady Takes a Chance 1943; Support Your Local Gunfighter 1971

Sutton, John (1908-1963) Tower of London 1939; Hudson's Bay 1940; The Invisible Man Returns 1940; A Yank in the RAF 1941; My Gal Sal 1942; Ten Gentlemen from West Point 1942; Jane Eyre 1943; The Hour before the Dawn 1944; Claudia and David 1946; Captain from Castile 1947; Bride of Vengeance 1949; The Second Woman 1951; My Cousin Rachel 1952; Thief of Damascus 1952; East of Sumatra 1953; The Bat 1959; Beloved Infidel 1959; Return of the Fly 1959

Sutton, Kay (1915-1988) Carefree 1938; The Saint in New York 1938

Sutton, Michael (1970-) Inventing the Abbotts 1997; Dark Prince - the Legend of Dracula 2000

Sutton, Nick Gummo 1997; Underground 1998

Suvari, Mena (1979-) Nowhere 1997; Slums of Beverly Hills 1998; American Beauty 1999; American Pie 1999; Live Virgin 2000; Loser 2000; American Pie 2 2001; The Musketeer 2001; Sugar & Spice 2001; Sonny 2002; Spun 2002; Trauma 2004; Beauty Shop 2005; Domino 2005; Edmond 2005; Rumor Has It... 2005; Factory Girl 2006; Brooklyn Rules 2007; Stuck 2007; Day of the Dead 2008; Sex and Lies in Sin City 2008; You May Not Kiss the Bride 2011; The Knot 2012

Suzman, Janet (1939-) A Day in the Death of Joe Egg 1971; Nicholas and Alexandra 1971; The Black Windmill 1974; Priest of Love 1981; The Draughtsman's Contract 1982; And the Ship Sails On 1983; A Dry White Season 1989; Nuns on the Run 1990; Leon the Pig Farmer 1992; Max 2002

Suzuki, Anne (1987-) Snow Falling on Cedars 1999; Initial D - Drift Racer 2005

Svennberg, Tore (1858-1941) The Phantom Carriage 1920; A Woman's Face 1938

Svenson, Bo (1941-) The Great Waldo Pepper 1975; Breaking Point 1976; Special Delivery 1976; Inglorious Bastards 1978; North Dallas Forty 1979; The Delta Force 1986; Heartbreak Ridge 1986; On Dangerous Ground

1986; Curse II: The Bite 1989; Kill Bill Vol 2 2004

Sverak, Zdenek (1936-) Elementary School 1991; Kolya 1996

Swain, Dominique (1980-) Face/Off 1997; Lolita 1997; Prairie Fever 2008

Swain, Mack (1876-1935) Tillie's Punctured Romance 1914; The Idle Class 1921; Pay Day 1922; The Pilgrim 1923; The Gold Rush 1925; Hands Up! 1926

Swan, Bob The Dollmaker 1984; Going All the Way 1997

Swanberg, Joe You're Next 2011; V/H/S 2012; The Sacrament 2013

Swank, Hilary (1974-) Buffy the Vampire Slayer 1992; The Next Karate Kid 1994; Victim of Rage 1994; Sometimes They Come Back... Again 1996; Boys Don't Cry 1999; The Gift 2000; The Affair of the Necklace 2001; The Core 2002; Insomnia 2002; 11:14 2003; Iron Jawed Angels 2004; Million Dollar Baby 2004; Red Dust 2004; The Black Dahlia 2006; Freedom Writers 2006; The Reaping 2006; PS I Love You 2007; Amelia 2009; Conviction 2010; The Resident 2010; New Year's Eve 2011; The Homesman 2014

Swann, Robert (1943-2006) if... 1968; Mumsy, Nanny, Sonny & Girly 1970

Swanson, Gary Vice Squad 1982; Convicts 1991

Swanson, Gloria (1897-1983) His New Job 1915; Male and Female 1919; Why Change Your Wife? 1920; Stage Struck 1925; Queen Kelly 1928; Sadie Thompson 1928; The Trespasser 1929; What a Widow! 1930; Indiscreet 1931; Sunset Blvd 1950; The Love Goddesses 1965; Airport 1975 1974

Swanson, Kristy (1969-) Deadly Friend 1986; Flowers in the Attic 1987; Hot Shots! 1991; Mannequin on the Move 1991; Buffy the Vampire Slayer 1992; Highway to Hell 1992; The Program 1993; The Chase 1994; Getting In 1994; Higher Learning 1995; The Phantom 1996; 8 Heads in a Duffel Bag 1997; Big Daddy 1999; Supreme Sanction 1999; Dude, Where's My Car? 2000

Swanson, Maureen (1932-2011) Knights of the Round Table 1953; Valley of Song 1953; Jacqueline 1956; The Spanish Gardener 1956; A Town like Alice 1956; Up in the World 1956; Robbery under Arms 1957

Swanson, Sterling Don't Be Afraid of the Dark 1973; Dogs 1976

Swardson, Nick (1976-) The Benchwarmers 2006; You Don't Mess with the Zohan 2008; Just Go with It 2011; 30 Minutes or Less 2011; A Haunted House 2013

Swart, Rufus (1959-1994) The House of Usher 1988; Dust Devil 1992; Cyborg Cop 1993

Swayze, Don (1958-) Shy People 1987; Eye of the Stranger 1993; Prairie Fever 2008; The Appearing 2014

Swayze, Patrick (1952-2009) Skatetown, USA 1979; The Outsiders 1983; Uncommon Valor 1983; Grandview, USA 1984; Red Dawn 1984; Youngblood 1986; Dirty Dancing 1987; Tiger Warsaw 1988; Next of Kin 1989; Road House 1989; Ghost 1990; Point Break 1991; City of Joy 1992; Father Hood 1993; Tall Tale 1994; Three Wishes 1995; To Wong Foo, Thanks for Everything, Julie Newmar 1995; Black Dog 1998; Waking Up in Reno 2000; Donnie Darko 2001; Dirty Dancing 2 2003; 11:14 2003; Keeping Mum 2005; Christmas in Wonderland 2007; The Fox and the Hound 2 2007

Sweeney, Bob (1918-1992) Toby Tyler, or Ten Weeks with a Circus 1960; Moon Pilot 1962; Marnie 1964

Sweeney, D B (1961-) Gardens of Stone 1987; No Man's Land 1987; Eight Men Out 1988; Sons 1989; Memphis Belle 1990; A Day in October 1991; Leather Jackets 1991; The Cutting Edge 1992; Miss Rose White 1992; Fire in the Sky 1993; Hear No Evil 1993; Roommates 1995; Spawn 1997; Dinosaur 2000; Greenmail 2001; Hardball 2001; Brother Bear 2003; Taken 2 2012

Sweeney, Garry Small Faces 1995; The Acid House 1998

Sweeney, Julia (1961-) Beethoven's 3rd 2000; Whatever It Takes 2000; Clockstoppers 2002

Sweet, Blanche (1895-1986) The Battle of Elderbush 1914; The Escape 1914

Sweet, Gary (1957-) The Lighthorsemen 1987; Gettin' Square 2003; Macbeth 2006; The Chronicles of Narnia: The Voyage of the Dawn Treader 2010; Fatal Honeymoon 2012; Adore 2013

Sweet, Sheila (1927-2003) Conflict of Wings 1953; The Angel Who Pawned Her Harp 1954; It's a Great Day 1955

Swenson, Karl (1908-1978) The Hanging Tree 1959; No Name on the Bullet 1959; Ice Palace 1960; One Foot in Hell 1960; Lonely Are the Brave 1962; Walk on the Wild Side 1962; The Sword in the Stone 1963; Ulzana's Raid 1972

Swift, Clive (1936-) Man at the Top 1973; The National Health 1973

Swift, David (1919-2001) No Sex Please - We're British 1973; Arthur's Hallowed Ground 1985; Jack & Sarah 1995

Swift, Jeremy Oliver Twist 2005; Downhill 2014

Swift, Susan (1964-) Audrey Rose 1977; Harper Valley PTA 1978

Swift, Taylor (1989-) Jonas Brothers: the 3D Concert Experience 2009; Valentine's Day 2010; Dr Seuss' The Lorax 2012; The Giver 2014

Swinburne, Nora (1902-2000) They Flew Alone 1941; The Man in Grey 1943; Fanny by Gaslight 1944; Jassy 1947; The Blind Goddess 1948; Quartet 1948; Christopher Columbus 1949; Fools Rush In 1949; The River 1951; Betrayed 1954; Helen of Troy 1955; Conspiracy of Hearts 1960; Interlude 1968

Swinton, Tilda (1961-) Caravaggio 1986; Aria 1987; The Last of England 1987; War Requiem 1988; The Garden 1990; Edward II 1991; Orlando 1992; Blue 1993; Wittgenstein 1993; Female Perversions 1996; Love Is the Devil: Study for a Portrait of Francis Bacon 1998; The War Zone 1999; The Beach 2000; Possible Worlds 2000; The Deep End 2001; Vanilla Sky 2001; Adaptation. 2002; The Statement 2003; Young Adam 2003; Broken Flowers 2005; The Chronicles of Narnia: The Lion, the Witch and the Wardrobe 2005; Constantine 2005; Thumbsucker 2005; Deep Water 2006; The Man from Uncle 2007; Michael Clayton 2007; Burn after Reading 2008; The Chronicles of Narnia: Prince Caspian 2008; The Curious Case of Benjamin Button 2008; Julia 2008; The Limits of Control 2008; I Am Love 2009; We Need to Talk about Kevin 2011; Moonrise Kingdom 2012; Only Lovers Left Alive 2013; Snowpiercer 2013; The Zero Theorem 2013; The Grand Budapest Hotel 2014; A Bigger Splash 2015; Trainwreck 2015; Doctor Strange 2016; Hail, Caesar! 2016

Swit, Loretta (1937-) Deadhead Miles 1972; Freebie and the Bean 1974; Race with the Devil 1975; Cagney & Lacey 1981; SOB 1981; Beer 1985; Dreams of Gold: the Mel Fisher Story 1986; Whoops Apocalypse 1986

Switzer, Carl "Alfalfa" aka **Switzer, Carl** (1926-1959) There's One Born Every Minute 1942; Track of the Cat 1954; Motorcycle Gang 1957

Swofford, Ken (1932-) Common-Law Cabin 1967; Las Vegas Roundabout 1975; The Domino Principle 1977; Thelma & Louise 1991

Swope, Topo Glory Boy 1971; Tracks 1977

Sy, Omar (1978-) Untouchable 2011; Mood Indigo 2013; Good People 2014; Samba 2014; Burnt 2015; Inferno 2016

Syal, Meera (1961-) Sammy and Rosie Get Laid 1987; Beautiful Thing 1995; Girls' Night 1998; Anita & Me 2002; Mad, Sad & Bad 2009; All in Good Time 2012; Absolutely Anything 2015

Sydney, Basil (1894-1968) Accused 1936; Rhodes of Africa 1936; The Black Sheep of Whitehall 1941; Ships with Wings 1942; Went the Day Well? 1942; Caesar and Cleopatra 1945; Meet Me at Dawn 1946; Jassy 1947; The Man Within 1947; Hamlet 1948; Treasure Island 1950; Salome 1953; The Dam Busters 1954; Hell below Zero 1954; Star of India 1954; Simba 1955; Sea Wife 1957; The Three Worlds of Gulliver 1959; The Hands of Orlac 1960

Sykes, Brenda (1949-) Skin Game 1971; Cleopatra Jones 1973; Mandingo 1975

Sykes, Eric (1923-2012) Orders Are Orders 1954; Tommy the Toreador 1959; Watch Your Stern 1960; Invasion Quartet 1961; Very Important Person 1961; Village of Daughters 1961; Kill or Cure 1962; Heavens Above! 1963; The Bargee 1964; One Way Pendulum 1965; Rotten to the Core 1965; Those Magnificent Men in Their Flying Machines 1965; The Liquidator 1966; The Spy with a Cold Nose 1966; The Plank 1967; Shalako 1968; Monte Carlo or Bust! 1969; The Boys in Blue 1983; Splitting Heirs 1993; The Others 2001; Son of Rambow 2007

Sykes, Wanda (1965-) Monster-in-Law 2005; The Adventures of Brer Rabbit

2006; Barnyard 2006; My Super Ex-Girlfriend 2006; Over the Hedge 2006; Evan Almighty 2007

Sylvester, Harold (1949-) Uncommon Valor 1983; Vision Quest 1985; Corrina, Corrina 1994

Sylvester, William (1922-1995) Appointment in London 1952; The Yellow Balloon 1952; Albert, RN 1953; House of Blackmail 1953; The Stranger Came Home 1954; High Tide at Noon 1957; Dublin Nightmare 1958; Gorgo 1961; Ring of Spies 1963; Devil Doll 1964; Devils of Darkness 1964; The Hand of Night 1966; 2001: a Space Odyssey 1968; Don't Be Afraid of the Dark 1973; Busting 1974

Sylvie (1883-1970) Un Carnet de Bal 1937; The End of the Day 1939; Les Anges du Péché 1943; The Little World of Don Camillo 1951; Thérèse Raquin 1953; Ulysses 1954

Sylwan, Kari Cries and Whispers 1972; Face to Face 1976

Symonds, Amanda Scrubbers 1982; UFO 1993

Syms, Sylvia (1934-) My Teenage Daughter 1956; The Birthday Present 1957; The Moonraker 1957; No Time for Tears 1957; Woman in a Dressing Gown 1957; Bachelor of Hearts 1958; Ferry to Hong Kong 1958; Ice Cold in Alex 1958; No Trees in the Street 1958; Expresso Bongo 1959; Conspiracy of Hearts 1960; The World of Suzie Wong 1960; Flame in the Streets 1961; Victim 1961; The Punch and Judy Man 1962; The Quare Fellow 1962; The World Ten Times Over 1963; East of Sudan 1964; The Big Job 1965; Danger Route 1967; Hostile Witness 1968; Run Wild, Run Free 1969; Born to Win 1971; Asylum 1972; The Tamarind Seed 1974; Give Us Tomorrow 1978; There Goes the Bride 1979; A Chorus of Disapproval 1988; Shirley Valentine 1989; Dirty Weekend 1992; Shining Through 1992; Staggered 1993; Food of Love 1997; I'll Sleep When I'm Dead 2003; What a Girl Wants 2003; The Queen 2006; Is Anybody There? 2008

Szabo, Laszlo (1936-) Le Petit Soldat 1960; Alphaville 1965; Pierrot le Fou 1965; Made in USA 1966; The Confession 1970; Passion 1982; L'Amour par Terre 1984; L'Eau Froide 1994

Szapolowska, Grazyna (1953-) No End 1984; Hanussen 1988; A Short Film about Love 1988

Szarabajka, Keith (1952-) Marie: a True Story 1985; Billy Galvin 1986; A Perfect World 1993

Szekely, Miklos B Damnation 1988; Rothschild's Violin 1996

Szemes, Mari (1932-1988) Diary for My Children 1982; Diary for My Loves 1987

Szeps, Henri (1943-) Travelling North 1986; Les Patterson Saves the World 1987

Szohr, Jessica (1985-) Love Bite 2012; Two Night Stand 2013

Szostak, Stephanie Motherhood 2009; Dinner for Schmucks 2010; R.I.P.D. 2013

Szubanski, Magda (1961-) Babe 1995; Babe: Pig in the City 1998; The Crocodile Hunter: Collision Course 2002; Goddess 2013

T

Tabakov, Oleg (1935-) War and Peace 1966; Oblomov 1980; Taking Sides 2001

Tablian, Vic Sphinx 1980; Raiders of the Lost Ark 1981

Tabori, Kristoffer (1952-) The Glass House 1972; Journey through Rosebud 1972

Tabu (1970-) Chachi 420 1997; Hawa 2003; The Namesake 2006; Cheeni Kum 2007; Life of Pi 2012

Taccone, Jorma Hot Rod 2007; Land of the Lost 2009

Taeger, Ralph (1936-) X-15 1961; The Delta Factor 1970

Tafler, Sydney aka **Tafler, Sidney** (1916-1979) It Always Rains on Sunday 1947; Dance Hall 1950; Hotel Sahara 1951; Scarlet Thread 1951; Emergency Call 1952; The Glass Cage 1955; The Woman for Joe 1955; Fire Maidens from Outer Space 1956; Booby Trap 1957; Bottoms Up 1959; Light Up the Sky 1960; The Birthday Party 1968; The Adventurers 1970

Tagawa, Cary-Hiroyuki (1950-) Spellbinder 1988; Kickboxer 2: the Road Back 1990; Showdown in Little Tokyo 1991; American Me 1992; Nemesis 1993; Rising Sun 1993; Picture Bride 1994; Mortal Kombat 1995; Danger Zone 1996; The Phantom 1996; American Dragons 1997; Top of the

World 1997; Bridge of Dragons 1999; The Art of War 2000; The Ghost 2000; Planet of the Apes 2001; Elektra 2005; Memoirs of a Geisha 2005; Hachi: a Dog's Tale 2008

Taggart, Rita (1947-) Torchlight 1984; Weeds 1987; House III: The Horror Show 1989; Coupe de Ville 1990

Taghmaoui, Saïd (1973-) La Haine 1995; Hideous Kinky 1998; Ali Zaoua 2000; Room to Rent 2000; Crime Spree 2002; The Good Thief 2002; Hidalgo 2003; Spartan 2004; The Kite Runner 2007; Traitor 2008; Vantage Point 2008; My Brother the Devil 2012

Taglioni, Alice Ca$h 2008; Paris-Manhattan 2012; Zaytoun 2012

Tagore, Sharmila (1936-) The World of Apu 1959; Devi 1960; Waqt 1965; Naayak 1966; Company Limited 1971; Mississippi Masala 1991

Taguchi, Tomoroh (1957-) Tetsuo: the Iron Man 1989; Tetsuo II: Body Hammer 1991

Tahan, Charlie (1996-) I Am Legend 2007; Love and Other Impossible Pursuits 2009; Death & Life of Charlie St Cloud 2010; Frankenweenie 2012; Love Is Strange 2014

Tahil, Dalip The Perfect Murder 1988; Baazigar 1993

Tahir, Faran (1963-) ABCD 1999; Anywhere but Here 1999; Iron Man 2008

Taka, Miiko (1932-) Hell to Eternity 1960; Cry for Happy 1961; A Global Affair 1964; Walk, Don't Run 1966; The Challenge 1982

Takaki, Kenji aka **Takagi** (1894-1984) A Town like Alice 1956; The Long and the Short and the Tall 1960

Takakura, Ken (1931-2014) Too Late the Hero 1970; The Yakuza 1975; Black Rain 1989; Mr Baseball 1992; Riding Alone for Thousands of Miles 2005

Takamine, Hideko (1924-2010) Tokyo Chorus 1931; When a Woman Ascends the Stairs 1960

Takanashi, Rin Like Someone in Love 2012; Killers 2014

Takarada, Akira (1934-) Godzilla 1954; Godzilla vs Mothra 1964; Invasion of the Astro-Monster 1965; Ebirah, Horror of the Deep 1966; Latitude Zero 1969

Takashima, Tadao (1930-) King Kong vs Godzilla 1962; Frankenstein Conquers the World 1964; Son of Godzilla 1967

Takeda, Shinji (1972-) Gohatto 1999; The Happiness of the Katakuris 2001; Death Game 2010

Takei, George (1940-) Hell to Eternity 1960; Ice Palace 1960; Red Line 7000 1965; Walk, Don't Run 1966; The Green Berets 1968; Star Trek: the Motion Picture 1979; Star Trek II: the Wrath of Khan 1982; Star Trek III: the Search for Spock 1984; Star Trek IV: the Voyage Home 1986; Return from the River Kwai 1988; Star Trek V: the Final Frontier 1989; Blood Oath 1990; Star Trek VI: the Undiscovered Country 1991; The Curse of the Dragon 1993; Kissinger and Nixon 1995; Mulan 1998; Mulan II 2004; Free Birds 2013; Kubo and the Two Strings 2016

Takenaka, Naoto (1956-) Shall We Dance? 1995; Tokyo Fist 1995; Freezer 2000; The Happiness of the Katakuris 2001; Hara-Kiri: Death of a Samurai 2011

Taktarov, Oleg (1968-) 15 Minutes 2001; Rollerball 2001

Talancón, Ana Claudia El Crimen del Padre Amaro 2002; Love in the Time of Cholera 2007; One Missed Call 2007

Talbot, Lyle (1902-1996) Love Is a Racket 1932; The Purchase Price 1932; The Thirteenth Guest 1932; Three on a Match 1932; Havana Widows 1933; Ladies They Talk About 1933; 20,000 Years in Sing Sing 1933; Fog over Frisco 1934; Mandalay 1934; One Night of Love 1934; The Case of the Lucky Legs 1935; Our Little Girl 1935; Go West, Young Man 1936; The Singing Kid 1936; Second Fiddle 1939; Miracle on Main Street 1940; Sensations 1944; Appointment with Murder 1948; Devil's Cargo 1948; Glen or Glenda 1953; Jail Bait 1954; City of Fear 1959; Plan 9 from Outer Space 1959

Talbot, Nita (1930-) Bundle of Joy 1956; I Married a Woman 1958; Who's Got the Action? 1962; Girl Happy 1965; That Funny Feeling 1965; The Cool Ones 1967; Buck and the Preacher 1972; Serial 1980; Frightmare 1981

Talbott, Gloria (1931-2000) All That Heaven Allows 1955; Crashout 1955; Lucy Gallant 1955; We're No Angels 1955; The Young Guns 1956; The Cyclops 1957; Daughter of Dr Jekyll 1957; The Oklahoman 1957; Cattle Empire 1958; I Married a Monster from

Outer Space 1958; Alias Jesse James 1959; Arizona Raiders 1965

Taliaferro, Michael "Bear" (1961-2006) Half Past Dead 2002; You Got Served 2004

Talley, Steve American Pie Presents the Naked Mile 2006; Beyond the Blackboard 2011

Tallichet, Margaret (1919-1919) Stranger on the Third Floor 1940; It Started with Eve 1941

Tallman, Patricia (1957-) Knightriders 1981; Night of the Living Dead 1990

Talmadge, Constance (1897-1973) Intolerance 1916; The Fall of Babylon 1919

Talman, William (1915-1968) The Woman on Pier 13 1949; Armored Car Robbery 1950; The Racket 1951; One Minute to Zero 1952; City That Never Sleeps 1953; The Hitch-Hiker 1953; Big House, USA 1955; Crashout 1955; Smoke Signal 1955; The Ballad of Josie 1968

Talton, Alix (1919-1992) Rock around the Clock 1956; The Deadly Mantis 1957; Romanoff and Juliet 1961

Tamba, Tetsuro aka **Tanba, Tetsuro** (1922-2006) Bridge to the Sun 1961; The 7th Dawn 1964; You Only Live Twice 1967; Tokyo Pop 1988; The Happiness of the Katakuris 2001

Tamblyn, Amber (1983-) Ten Minutes Older: the Trumpet 2002; The Sisterhood of the Traveling Pants 2005; The Grudge 2 2006; The Sisterhood of the Traveling Pants 2 2008; Beyond a Reasonable Doubt 2009; 127 Hours 2011

Tamblyn, Russ aka **Tamblyn, Russell** aka **Tamblyn, Rusty** (1934-) Samson and Delilah 1949; Retreat, Hell! 1952; Take the High Ground 1953; Seven Brides for Seven Brothers 1954; Hit the Deck 1955; Many Rivers to Cross 1955; The Fastest Gun Alive 1956; The Last Hunt 1956; The Young Guns 1956; Don't Go near the Water 1957; Peyton Place 1957; High School Confidential 1958; tom thumb 1958; Cimarron 1960; West Side Story 1961; The Wonderful World of the Brothers Grimm 1962; Follow the Boys 1963; The Haunting 1963; The Long Ships 1963; Son of a Gunfighter 1964; The Female Bunch 1969; Dracula vs Frankenstein 1970; War of the Gargantuas 1970; The Last Movie 1971; Human Highway 1982

Tambor, Jeffrey (1944-) ...And Justice for All 1979; Saturday the 14th 1981; Three o'Clock High 1987; Brenda Starr 1989; Life Stinks 1991; Big Bully 1996; The Man Who Captured Eichmann 1996; Doctor Dolittle 1998; Meet Joe Black 1998; There's Something about Mary 1998; Girl, Interrupted 1999; Muppets from Space 1999; Teaching Mrs Tingle 1999; The Grinch 2000; Pollock 2000; Get Well Soon 2001; Eloise at the Plaza 2003; Malibu's Most Wanted 2003; My Boss's Daughter 2003; Hellboy 2004; The SpongeBob SquarePants Movie 2004; The Muppets' Wizard of Oz 2005; Hellboy II: the Golden Army 2008; The Hangover 2009; Tangled 2010; Win Win 2011; Phil Spector 2013; The D Train 2015; The Accountant 2016

Tamiroff, Akim aka **The Boss** (1899-1972) The Big Broadcast of 1936 1935; The Gay Deception 1935; The Last Outpost 1935; The Lives of a Bengal Lancer 1935; Anthony Adverse 1936; Desire 1936; The General Died at Dawn 1936; High, Wide and Handsome 1937; The Buccaneer 1938; Spawn of the North 1938; Paris Honeymoon 1939; Union Pacific 1939; The Great McGinty 1940; North West Mounted Police 1940; The Way of All Flesh 1940; The Corsican Brothers 1941; Tortilla Flat 1942; Five Graves to Cairo 1943; For Whom the Bell Tolls 1943; His Butler's Sister 1943; The Miracle of Morgan's Creek 1943; Can't Help Singing 1944; Dragon Seed 1944; Pardon My Past 1945; Thieves' Holiday 1946; Fiesta 1947; My Girl Tisa 1948; Relentless 1948; Black Magic 1949; Outpost in Morocco 1949; Desert Legion 1953; They Who Dare 1953; You Know What Sailors Are 1954; Confidential Report 1955; Anastasia 1956; The Black Sleep 1956; Yangtse Incident 1956; Me and the Colonel 1958; Touch of Evil 1958; Ocean's Eleven 1960; Romanoff and Juliet 1961; The Reluctant Saint 1962; The Trial 1962; The Black Tulip 1963; Panic Button 1964; Topkapi 1964; Alphaville 1965; Le Bambole 1965; Lord Jim 1965; After the Fox 1966; Hotel Paradiso 1966; Lt Robin Crusoe, USN 1966; The Liquidator 1966; Great Catherine 1968; The Great Bank Robbery 1969

Tamm, Mary (1950-2012) The Odessa File 1974; The Likely Lads 1976; Sorted 2000

Tamura, Takahiro (1928-2006) Tora! Tora! Tora! 1970; Muddy River 1981

Tan, Philip (1942-) Vroom 1988; China Cry 1990; Showdown in Little Tokyo 1991; Bloodsport II: The Next Kumite 1996

Tanaka, Haruo (1912-1992) The Crucified Lovers 1954; Ohayo 1959

Tanaka, Kinuyo (1910-1977) Musashi Miyamoto 1944; Five Women around Utamaro 1946; The Victory of Women 1946; The Love of Sumako the Actress 1947; Hen in the Wind 1948; My Love Has Been Burning 1949; The Lady of Musashino 1951; Miss Oyu 1951; The Life of Oharu 1952; Ugetsu Monogatari 1953; Sansho the Bailiff 1954; The Ballad of Narayama 1958; Equinox Flower 1958; Alone on the Pacific 1963

Tanaka, Yoshiko (1956-2011) Black Rain 1988; Ring 0 2000

Tandy, Jessica (1909-1994) The Seventh Cross 1944; The Green Years 1946; Forever Amber 1947; September Affair 1950; The Desert Fox 1951; The Light in the Forest 1958; Hemingway's Adventures of a Young Man 1962; The Birds 1963; Butley 1973; Honky Tonk Freeway 1981; Best Friends 1982; Still of the Night 1982; The World According to Garp 1982; The Bostonians 1984; Cocoon 1985; *batteries not included 1987; Foxfire 1987; The House on Carroll Street 1987; Cocoon: the Return 1988; Driving Miss Daisy 1989; Fried Green Tomatoes at the Whistle Stop Cafe 1991; Used People 1992; Camilla 1993; Nobody's Fool 1994

Tang Wei Lust, Caution 2007; Dragon 2011; Blackhat 2015

Tani, Yoko (1932-1999) The Wind Cannot Read 1958; Piccadilly Third Stop 1960; The Savage Innocents 1960; Invasion 1965

Tannen, Charles (1915-1980) The Return of Frank James 1940; Careful, Soft Shoulder 1942

Tanner, Antwon Never Die Alone 2004; Coach Carter 2005

Tanner, Tony (1932-) The Pleasure Girls 1965; Stop the World, I Want to Get Off 1966

Tanuja (1943-) Saathiya 2002; Bhoot 2003

Tapley, Colin (1907-1995) The Last Outpost 1935; Thank You, Jeeves 1936; Cloudburst 1951; The Dam Busters 1954; Emergency 1962

Tapper, Zoe Stage Beauty 2004; Mrs Palfrey at The Claremont 2005; These Foolish Things 2006

Taracena, Gerardo The Violin 2005; Come Out and Play 2012

Tarantino, Quentin (1963-) Reservoir Dogs 1991; Pulp Fiction 1994; Sleep with Me 1994; Somebody to Love 1994; Desperado 1995; Destiny Turns on the Radio 1995; Four Rooms 1995; From Dusk till Dawn 1995; Little Nicky 2000; The Muppets' Wizard of Oz 2005; Planet Terror 2007; Sukiyaki Western Django 2007; Not Quite Hollywood 2008; Corman's World: Exploits of a Hollywood Rebel 2011; POM Wonderful Presents: The Greatest Movie Ever Sold 2011

Tarbuck, Barbara The Tie That Binds 1995; Walking Tall 2004

Tarbuck, Jimmy (1940-) The Plank 1967; Strictly Sinatra 2000

Tarso, Ignacio Lopez (1925-) Nazarín 1958; Macario 1960; Under the Volcano 1984

Tashman, Lilyan (1899-1934) So This Is Paris 1926; Camille 1927; Bulldog Drummond 1929; Gold Diggers of Broadway 1929; The Marriage Playground 1929; One Heavenly Night 1931; Scarlet Dawn 1932; The Wiser Sex 1932; Riptide 1934

Tate, Catherine (1968-) Scenes of a Sexual Nature 2006; Sixty Six 2006; Starter for 10 2006; Mrs Ratcliffe's Revolution 2007; Gulliver's Travels 2010; Monte Carlo 2011; Khumba 2013; Nativity 3: Dude Where's My Donkey 2014

Tate, Harry (1872-1940) Look Up and Laugh 1935; Midshipman Easy 1935; Keep Your Seats, Please 1936; Wings of the Morning 1937

Tate, Larenz (1975-) Menace II Society 1993; Dead Presidents 1995; Love Jones 1997; The Postman 1997; Why Do Fools Fall in Love? 1998; Biker Boyz 2003; A Man Apart 2003; Ray 2004; Waist Deep 2006

Tate, Nick (1942-) The Devil's Playground 1976; A Cry in the Dark 1988

Tate, Reginald aka **Tate, Sqn/Ldr Reginald** (1896-1955) The Phantom Light 1934; Poison Pen 1939; Next of

Kin 1942; The Man from Morocco 1944; So Well Remembered 1947; Uncle Silas 1947; The Secret People 1951; Escape Route 1952; The Story of Robin Hood and His Merrie Men 1952; Malta Story 1953

Tate, Sharon (1943-1969) Eye of the Devil 1966; Don't Make Waves 1967; The Fearless Vampire Killers 1967; Valley of the Dolls 1967; Twelve plus One 1969; The Wrecking Crew 1969

Tati, Jacques (1908-1982) Devil in the Flesh 1947; Jour de Fête 1947; School for Postmen 1947; Monsieur Hulot's Holiday 1953; Mon Oncle 1958; Cours du Soir 1967; Playtime 1967; Traffic 1970; Parade 1974

Tatum, Channing (1980-) Coach Carter 2005; A Guide to Recognizing Your Saints 2006; She's the Man 2006; Step Up 2006; Stop-Loss 2007; Fighting 2009; GI Joe: the Rise of Cobra 2009; Public Enemies 2009; Dear John 2010; The Eagle 2010; The Dilemma 2011; Haywire 2011; 10 Years 2011; Magic Mike 2012; 21 Jump Street 2012; The Vow 2012; GI Joe: Retaliation 2013; Side Effects 2013; White House Down 2013; Book of Life 2014; Foxcatcher 2014; Jupiter Ascending 2014; 22 Jump Street 2014; The Hateful Eight 2015; Magic Mike XXL 2015; Hail, Caesar! 2016; X-Men: Apocalypse 2016

Taube, Aino aka **Taube-Henrikson, Aino** (1912-1990) One Single Night 1939; Face to Face 1976

Taube, Sven-Bertil (1934-) The Buttercup Chain 1970; Puppet on a Chain 1970; A Game for Vultures 1979; Jerusalem 1996; The Girl with the Dragon Tattoo 2009

Tauber, Richard (1891-1948) Blossom Time 1934; Land without Music 1936

Tautou, Audrey (1978-) Venus Beauty Institute 1998; Amélie 2001; Dirty Pretty Things 2002; He Loves Me... He Loves Me Not 2002; Pot Luck 2002; Pas sur la Bouche 2003; A Very Long Engagement 2004; Russian Dolls 2005; The Da Vinci Code 2006; Priceless 2006; Coco avant Chanel 2009; Beautiful Lies 2010; Delicacy 2011; Thérèse Desqueyroux 2012; Chinese Puzzle 2013; Mood Indigo 2013; Microbe & Gasoline 2015

Tavernier, Nils (1965-) Une Affaire de Femmes 1988; L.627 1992; Mina Tannenbaum 1993; D'Artagnan's Daughter 1994

Tayback, Vic (1930-1990) Door-to-Door Maniac 1961; The Blue Knight 1973; Alice Doesn't Live Here Anymore 1974; The Gambler 1974; Lepke 1975; Dark Victory 1976; Treasure Island 1986; All Dogs Go to Heaven 1989

Taylor-Compton, Scout (1989-) Sleepover 2004; Halloween 2007; April Fool's Day 2008; Halloween II 2009; Obsessed 2009; The Runaways 2010

Taylor-Joy, Anya The Witch 2015; Morgan 2016; Split 2017

Taylor-Smith, Jean (1900-1990) Rob Roy, the Highland Rogue 1953; It's Never Too Late 1956; Ring of Bright Water 1969; My Childhood 1972; My Ain Folk 1973

Taylor-Young, Leigh (1944-) I Love You, Alice B Toklas 1968; The Big Bounce 1969; The Adventurers 1970; The Buttercup Chain 1970; The Gang That Couldn't Shoot Straight 1971; The Horsemen 1971; Soylent Green 1973; Looker 1981; Jagged Edge 1985; Secret Admirer 1985; Slackers 2001

Taylor, Benedict (1960-) Thirteen at Dinner 1985; Every Time We Say Goodbye 1986

Taylor, Buck (1938-) The Wild Angels 1966; Triumphs of a Man Called Horse 1983

Taylor, Chip The Catamount Killing 1974; Melvin and Howard 1980

Taylor, Christine (1971-) The Brady Bunch Movie 1995; The Craft 1996; A Very Brady Sequel 1996; Overnight Delivery 1997; Something about Sex 1998; The Wedding Singer 1998; Zoolander 2001; Dodgeball: a True Underdog Story 2004; License to Wed 2007; Farewell Mr Kringle 2010; Zoolander 2 2016

Taylor, Don (1920-1998) For the Love of Mary 1948; The Naked City 1948; Ambush 1949; Battleground 1949; Father of the Bride 1950; The Blue Veil 1951; Father's Little Dividend 1951; Flying Leathernecks 1951; Submarine Command 1951; Target Unknown 1951; Destination Gobi 1953; Stalag 17 1953; Johnny Dark 1954; Men of Sherwood Forest 1954; I'll Cry Tomorrow 1955; The Bold and the Brave 1956

Taylor, Dub (1907-1994) The Bounty Hunter 1954; Black Gold 1962; Bonnie and Clyde 1967; The Reivers 1969; A

Man Called Horse 1970; Evel Knievel 1971; Burnt Offerings 1976; Gator 1976; Back to the Future Part III 1990; My Heroes Have Always Been Cowboys 1991; Falling from Grace 1992; Maverick 1994

Taylor, Elaine Half a Sixpence 1967; The Anniversary 1968; Diamonds for Breakfast 1968; Lock Up Your Daughters! 1969; The Games 1970

Taylor, Elizabeth (1932-2011) There's One Born Every Minute 1942; Jane Eyre 1943; Lassie Come Home 1943; National Velvet 1944; The White Cliffs of Dover 1944; Courage of Lassie 1946; Cynthia 1947; Life with Father 1947; A Date with Judy 1948; Julia Misbehaves 1948; Conspirator 1949; Little Women 1949; The Big Hangover 1950; Father of the Bride 1950; Callaway Went Thataway 1951; Father's Little Dividend 1951; Love Is Better than Ever 1951; A Place in the Sun 1951; Quo Vadis 1951; Ivanhoe 1952; The Girl Who Had Everything 1953; Beau Brummell 1954; Elephant Walk 1954; The Last Time I Saw Paris 1954; Rhapsody 1954; Giant 1956; Raintree County 1957; Cat on a Hot Tin Roof 1958; Suddenly, Last Summer 1959; Butterfield 8 1960; Scent of Mystery 1960; Cleopatra 1963; The VIPs 1963; The Love Goddesses 1965; The Sandpiper 1965; Who's Afraid of Virginia Woolf? 1966; The Comedians 1967; Doctor Faustus 1967; Reflections in a Golden Eye 1967; The Taming of the Shrew 1967; Boom 1968; Secret Ceremony 1968; Anne of the Thousand Days 1969; The Only Game in Town 1970; Under Milk Wood 1971; Zee and Co 1971; Ash Wednesday 1973; Night Watch 1973; The Driver's Seat 1975; The Blue Bird 1976; Victory at Entebbe 1976; A Little Night Music 1977; Winter Kills 1979; The Mirror Crack'd 1980; Genocide 1981; Between Friends 1983; Young Toscanini 1988; Sweet Bird of Youth 1989; And the Band Played On 1993; The Flintstones 1994; These Old Broads 2001

Taylor, Estelle (1899-1958) The Ten Commandments 1923; Don Juan 1926; Cimarron 1931; Street Scene 1931; The Unholy Garden 1931; The Southerner 1945

Taylor, Holland (1943-) Romancing the Stone 1984; Cop and a Half 1993; Last Summer in the Hamptons 1995; Steal Big, Steal Little 1995; George of the Jungle 1997; The Truman Show 1998; To Live For 1999; Keeping the Faith 2000; Legally Blonde 2001; Cinderella II: Dreams Come True 2002; SPYkids 2: the Island of Lost Dreams 2002; SPYkids 3-D Game Over 2003; The Wedding Date 2004

Taylor, Jack (1936-) Count Dracula 1970; The Female Vampire 1973; The Ninth Gate 1999; Agnosia 2010

Taylor, James Two-Lane Blacktop 1971; No Nukes 1980

Taylor, James Arnold TMNT 2007; Star Wars: The Clone Wars 2008; Ratchet & Clank 2016

Taylor, Joan (1929-2012) Fighting Man of the Plains 1949; The Savage 1953; War Paint 1953; Rose Marie 1954; Apache Woman 1955; Earth vs the Flying Saucers 1956; 20 Million Miles to Earth 1957

Taylor, Joyce (1932-) The FBI Story 1959; Atlantis, the Lost Continent 1960; Ring of Fire 1961; Beauty and the Beast 1962; Twice Told Tales 1963

Taylor, Kent (1907-1987) I'm No Angel 1933; White Woman 1933; Death Takes a Holiday 1934; Mrs Wiggs of the Cabbage Patch 1934; The Gracie Allen Murder Case 1939; I Take This Woman 1940; The Daltons Ride Again 1945; Payment on Demand 1951; Playgirl 1954; Slightly Scarlet 1956; The Iron Sheriff 1957; Gang War 1958

Taylor, Kit (1942-) Long John Silver 1954; Rough Diamonds 1994

Taylor, Lili (1967-) Mystic Pizza 1988; Say Anything... 1989; Bright Angel 1990; Arizona Dream 1991; Dogfight 1991; Household Saints 1993; Rudy 1993; The Addiction 1994; Cold Fever 1994; Pret-a-Porter 1994; I Shot Andy Warhol 1995; Illtown 1996; Ransom 1996; Kicked in the Head 1997; Subway Stories: Tales from the Underground 1997; The Impostors 1998; Pecker 1998; The Haunting 1999; High Fidelity 2000; Live from Baghdad 2002; Casa de los Babys 2003; Factotum (A Man Who Preforms Many Jobs) 2005; The Notorious Bettie Page 2005; Being Flynn 2012; Cherry 2012; The Conjuring 2013

Taylor, Marjorie The Crimes of Stephen Hawke 1936; It's Never Too Late to Mend 1937; The Ticket of Leave Man 1937; The Face at the Window 1939

Taylor, Meshach (1947-2014) Mannequin 1987; Mannequin on the Move 1991; Class Act 1992

Taylor, Noah (1969-) The Year My Voice Broke 1987; Flirting 1989; Dad and Dave: on Our Selection 1995; Shine 1996; Simon Magus 1998; The Escort 1999; Almost Famous 2000; Lara Croft: Tomb Raider 2001; Vanilla Sky 2001; Max 2002; Lara Croft, Tomb Raider: the Cradle of Life 2003; The Life Aquatic with Steve Zissou 2004; The Proposition 2004; The New Daughter 2009; Red White & Blue 2010; Submarine 2010; Red Dog 2011; The Double 2013; Lost in Karastan 2014; Predestination 2014

Taylor, Rachael (1984-) Transformers 2007; Bottle Shock 2008; Shutter 2008; The Darkest Hour 2011; Red Dog 2011

Taylor, Regina (1960-) Clockers 1995; Courage under Fire 1996; A Family Thing 1996; Hostile Waters 1996; Strange Justice 1999

Taylor, Renee (1935-) The Producers 1968; A New Leaf 1971; Lovesick 1983; Love Is All There Is 1996

Taylor (1), Robert (1911-1969) Buried Loot 1934; Broadway Melody of 1936 1935; Magnificent Obsession 1935; The Gorgeous Hussy 1936; His Brother's Wife 1936; Small Town Girl 1936; Broadway Melody of 1938 1937; Camille 1937; Personal Property 1937; This Is My Affair 1937; The Crowd Roars 1938; Three Comrades 1938; A Yank at Oxford 1938; Lady of the Tropics 1939; Remember? 1939; Escape 1940; Flight Command 1940; Waterloo Bridge 1940; Billy the Kid 1941; Johnny Eager 1941; When Ladies Meet 1941; Her Cardboard Lover 1942; Stand by for Action 1942; Bataan 1943; Undercurrent 1946; High Wall 1947; Ambush 1949; The Bribe 1949; Conspirator 1949; Devil's Doorway 1950; Quo Vadis 1951; Westward the Women 1951; Above and Beyond 1952; Ivanhoe 1952; All the Brothers Were Valiant 1953; Knights of the Round Table 1953; Ride, Vaquero! 1953; Rogue Cop 1954; Valley of the Kings 1954; Many Rivers to Cross 1955; Quentin Durward 1955; D-Day the Sixth of June 1956; The Last Hunt 1956; The Power and the Prize 1956; The Law and Jake Wade 1958; Party Girl 1958; Saddle the Wind 1958; The Hangman 1959; The House of the Seven Hawks 1959; Killers of Kilimanjaro 1960; Cattle King 1963; Miracle of the White Stallions 1963; The Night Walker 1964; Johnny Tiger 1966; Where Angels Go... Trouble Follows 1968

Taylor (4), Robert The Hard Word 2002; Long Weekend 2008; Coffin Rock 2009

Taylor, Rod aka **Taylor, Rodney** (1930-2015) Hell on Frisco Bay 1955; World without End 1955; The Catered Affair 1956; Raintree County 1957; Separate Tables 1958; Ask Any Girl 1959; One Hundred and One Dalmatians 1960; The Time Machine 1960; Seven Seas to Calais 1962; The Birds 1963; Sunday in New York 1963; The VIPs 1963; Fate Is the Hunter 1964; 36 Hours 1964; Do Not Disturb 1965; Young Cassidy 1965; The Glass Bottom Boat 1966; The Liquidator 1966; Dark of the Sun 1967; The Hell with Heroes 1968; Nobody Runs Forever 1968; Darker than Amber 1970; The Man Who Had Power over Women 1970; Zabriskie Point 1970; The Deadly Trackers 1973; The Train Robbers 1973; On the Run 1983; Danielle Steel's Palomino 1991; Open Season 1995

Taylor, Russi Duck Tales: the Movie - Treasure of the Lost Lamp 1990; Cinderella II: Dreams Come True 2002

Taylor, Valerie (1902-1988) Berkeley Square 1933; Went the Day Well? 1942; Faces in the Dark 1960; What a Carve Up! 1961

Taylor, Vaughn (1910-1983) Meet Danny Wilson 1952; It Should Happen to You 1954; Jailhouse Rock 1957; Cat on a Hot Tin Roof 1958; The Wizard of Baghdad 1960

Taylor, Wally Shaft's Big Score! 1972; Peacemaker 1990

Tazaki, Jun (1910-1985) Gate of Hell 1953; Ebirah, Horror of the Deep 1966; Destroy All Monsters 1968

Tcherina, Ludmilla (1924-2004) The Red Shoes 1948; The Tales of Hoffmann 1951; Sign of the Pagan 1954; Oh, Rosalinda!! 1955; Honeymoon 1959

Te Wiata, Inia (1915-1971) The Seekers 1954; Man of the Moment 1955

Teagarden, Jack (1905-1964) The Birth of the Blues 1941; Glory Alley 1952

Teakle, Spencer (1916-1999) Cover Girl Killer 1959; The Gentle Trap 1960

Teal, Ray (1902-1976) The Bandit of Sherwood Forest 1946; Ace in the Hole 1951; Along the Great Divide 1951; Distant Drums 1951; The Captive City 1952; Carrie 1952; Ambush at Tomahawk Gap 1953; The Wild One 1953; The Command 1954; Run for Cover 1955; The Burning Hills 1956

Teale, Owen (1961-) War Requiem 1988; Robin Hood 1990; The Hawk 1992; The Cherry Orchard 1998; Conspiracy 2001; Hunky Dory 2011; The Fold 2013

Tearle, Conway (1878-1938) Stella Maris 1918; Gold Diggers of Broadway 1929

Tearle, Godfrey (1884-1953) The 39 Steps 1935; The Last Journey 1936; One of Our Aircraft Is Missing 1942; Tomorrow We Live 1942; The Lamp Still Burns 1943; Undercover 1943; The Rake's Progress 1945; The Beginning or the End 1947; White Corridors 1951; I Believe in You 1952; Mandy 1952; The Titfield Thunderbolt 1952; Decameron Nights 1953

Teasdale, Verree (1904-1987) Payment Deferred 1932; Skyscraper Souls 1932; Roman Scandals 1933; Fashions of 1934 1934; Madame Du Barry 1934; A Midsummer Night's Dream 1935; The Milky Way 1936; 5th Ave Girl 1939; Topper Takes a Trip 1939; I Take This Woman 1940; Come Live with Me 1941

Tedford, Travis The Little Rascals 1994; The Final 2010

Teer, Barbara Ann (1937-) Slaves 1969; The Angel Levine 1970

Teixeira, Virgilio aka **Texera, Virgilio** (1917-2010) The Boy Who Stole a Million 1960; Return of the Seven 1966; The Magnificent Two 1967

Telezynska, Isabella The Music Lovers 1970; Ludwig 1973

Telford, Zoe The Truth 2006; The Waiting Room 2007

Tell, Olive (1894-1951) Delicious 1931; Ladies' Man 1931

Teller (1948-) My Chauffeur 1986; Penn & Teller Get Killed 1989; Fantasia 2000 1999

Teller, Miles (1987-) Rabbit Hole 2010; Footloose 2011; 21 and Over 2012; That Awkward Moment 2013; Two Night Stand 2013; Whiplash 2014; Fantastic Four 2015; Insurgent 2015; The Divergent Series: Allegiant 2016; War Dogs 2016

Temple, Juno (1989-) Cracks 2009; Glorious 39 2009; Greenberg 2009; Year One 2009; Kaboom 2010; Killer Joe 2011; Small Apartments 2012; Afternoon Delight 2013; Horns 2013; Magic Magic 2013; Maleficent 2014; Far from the Madding Crowd 2015; Away 2016

Temple, Shirley (1928-2014) Baby, Take a Bow 1934; Bright Eyes 1934; Change of Heart 1934; Little Miss Marker 1934; Mandalay 1934; Now and Forever 1934; Stand Up and Cheer! 1934; Curly Top 1935; The Little Colonel 1935; The Littlest Rebel 1935; Our Little Girl 1935; Captain January 1936; Dimples 1936; Poor Little Rich Girl 1936; Stowaway 1936; Heidi 1937; Wee Willie Winkie 1937; Just around the Corner 1938; Little Miss Broadway 1938; Rebecca of Sunnybrook Farm 1938; The Little Princess 1939; Susannah of the Mounties 1939; The Blue Bird 1940; Young People 1940; Miss Annie Rooney 1942; I'll Be Seeing You 1944; Since You Went Away 1944; Kiss and Tell 1945; The Bachelor and the Bobby-Soxer 1947; Fort Apache 1948; Adventure in Baltimore 1949; A Kiss for Corliss 1949; Mr Belvedere Goes to College 1949

Tena, Natalia You Instead 2011; SuperBob 2015

Tengroth, Birgit (1915-1983) Dollar 1938; Three Strange Loves 1949

Tennant, David (1971-) LA without a Map 1998; The Last September 1999; Bright Young Things 2003; Harry Potter and the Goblet of Fire 2005; Glorious 39 2009; St Trinian's 2: the Legend of Fritton's Gold 2009; The Decoy Bride 2011; Fright Night 2011; Nativity 2: Danger in the Manger! 2012; The Pirates! in an Adventure with Scientists! 2012; Postman Pat: the Movie 2013; What We Did on Our Holiday 2014

Tennant, Victoria (1950-) The Ragman's Daughter 1972; Strangers Kiss 1983; All of Me 1984; The Holcroft Covenant 1985; Best Seller 1987; Flowers in the Attic 1987; The Handmaid's Tale 1990; Whispers 1990; LA Story 1991; The Plague 1992

Tennberg, Jean-Marc (1924-1971) Fanfan la Tulipe 1951; A Ravishing Idiot 1964

Tenney, Jon (1961-) Lassie: a New Generation 1994; Fools Rush In 1997; Music from Another Room 1998; Buying the Cow 2000; The Stepfather 2009; Rabbit Hole 2010

Tepper, William Drive, He Said 1971; Breathless 1983; Bachelor Party 1984

Ter Steege, Johanna (1961-) The Vanishing 1988; Sweet Emma Dear Böbe 1992; Immortal Beloved 1994

Terajima, Susumu (1963-) Hana-Bi 1997; After Life 1998; Brother 2000; Ichi the Killer 2001

Terao, Akira (1947-) Ran 1985; Akira Kurosawa's Dreams 1990; Casshern 2004

Tergesen, Lee (1965-) Monster 2003; No One Lives 2012

Terhune, Max (1891-1973) Hit the Saddle 1937; Overland Stage Raiders 1938; Red River Range 1938

Terlesky, John (1961-) The Allnighter 1987; Damned River 1989

Terof, Georges La Roue 1923; La Nuit du Carrefour 1932

Terra, Scott (1987-) Redemption of the Ghost 2000; Eight Legged Freaks 2001; Dickie Roberts: Former Child Star 2003

Terranova, Dan (1930-2003) Baby Face Nelson 1957; Young Dillinger 1965

Terraza, Ferran [Rec] 2007; [Rec]² 2009

Terrell, Steven Dragstrip Girl 1957; Invasion of the Saucer Men 1957; Motorcycle Gang 1957

Terry-Thomas (1911-1990) A Date with a Dream 1948; Brothers in Law 1956; The Green Man 1956; Private's Progress 1956; Blue Murder at St Trinian's 1957; Happy Is the Bride 1957; Lucky Jim 1957; The Naked Truth 1957; Carlton-Browne of the FO 1958; tom thumb 1958; Too Many Crooks 1958; I'm All Right Jack 1959; His and Hers 1960; Make Mine Mink 1960; School for Scoundrels 1960; Bachelor Flat 1961; Kill or Cure 1962; Operation Snatch 1962; The Wonderful World of the Brothers Grimm 1962; It's a Mad Mad Mad Mad World 1963; The Mouse on the Moon 1963; The Wild Affair 1963; How to Murder Your Wife 1965; Strange Bedfellows 1965; Those Magnificent Men in Their Flying Machines 1965; You Must Be Joking! 1965; Kiss the Girls and Make Them Die 1966; Munster, Go Home! 1966; Our Man in Marrakesh 1966; The Sandwich Man 1966; Arabella 1967; Danger: Diabolik 1967; Jules Verne's Rocket to the Moon 1967; The Karate Killers 1967; The Perils of Pauline 1967; Don't Raise the Bridge, Lower the River 1968; How Sweet It Is! 1968; Where Were You When the Lights Went Out? 1968; Monte Carlo or Bust! 1969; Twelve plus One 1969; The Abominable Dr Phibes 1971; Robin Hood 1973; The Vault of Horror 1973; Side by Side 1975; Spanish Fly 1975; The Bawdy Adventures of Tom Jones 1976; The Hound of the Baskervilles 1977; The Last Remake of Beau Geste 1977

Terry, Alice (1899-1987) The Four Horsemen of the Apocalypse 1921; The Prisoner of Zenda 1922; Scaramouche 1923; The Arab 1924; Mare Nostrum 1926; The Garden of Allah 1927

Terry, John (1950-) Hawk the Slayer 1980; Evidence of Love 1990; Of Mice and Men 1992; A Dangerous Woman 1993; Reflections on a Crime 1994; The Big Green 1995; Blue Valley Songbird 1999

Terry, Nigel (1945-2015) The Lion in Winter 1968; Excalibur 1981; Déjà Vu 1984; Sylvia 1984; Caravaggio 1986; The Last of England 1987; War Requiem 1988; Edward II 1991; Blue 1993; The Hunchback of Notre Dame 1997; The Emperor's New Clothes 2001; FearDotCom 2002

Terry, Phillip (1909-1993) Music in Manhattan 1944; The Lost Weekend 1945; To Each His Own 1946; Lady of Deceit 1947

Terry, Ruth (1920-) Hold That Co-Ed 1938; Slightly Honorable 1939; Appointment for Love 1941; The Cheaters 1945

Terry, Sheila (1910-1957) Lawyer Man 1932; Scarlet Dawn 1932; The Mayor of Hell 1933; The Sphinx 1933; 'Neath the Arizona Skies 1934; The Lawless Frontier 1935

Terry, William (1914-1962) Stage Door Canteen 1943; Johnny Doesn't Live Here Anymore 1944

Terzieff, Laurent (1935-2010) Les Tricheurs 1958; Kapo 1959; The Milky Way 1968; Medea 1970; Detective 1985; Rouge Baiser 1985; Germinal 1993

Tesco, Nicky Leningrad Cowboys Go America 1989; I Hired a Contract Killer 1990

Tessier, Robert (1934-1990) Born Losers 1967; The Glory Stompers 1967; Hard Times 1975; The Deep 1977

Testa, Karina Frontier(s) 2007; Shadow 2009

Tester, Desmond (1919-2002) The Beloved Vagabond 1936; Sabotage 1936; Tudor Rose 1936; The Drum 1938

Testi, Fabio (1941-) The Garden of the Finzi-Continis 1971; Nada 1974; The Inheritance 1976; China 9, Liberty 37 1978; The Ambassador 1984

Testud, Sylvie (1971-) The Captive 2000; Fear and Trembling 2003; La Vie en Rose 2007; Lourdes 2009; The Round Up 2010

Tetzel, Joan (1921-1977) The File on Thelma Jordon 1949; Hell below Zero 1954

Tewes, Lauren (1954-) Eyes of a Stranger 1980; Doom Generation 1995

Texada, Tia Nurse Betty 2000; Glitter 2001; Thirteen Conversations about One Thing 2001; Spartan 2004

Teynac, Maurice (1915-1992) Night without Stars 1951; Bedevilled 1955; Paris Holiday 1958; Crack in the Mirror 1960; In the French Style 1963; Ash Wednesday 1973

Thaine, Victoria The Night We Called It a Day 2003; Gone 2006; The Loved Ones 2009

Thal, Eric (1965-) The Gun in Betty Lou's Handbag 1992; A Stranger among Us 1992; The Puppet Masters 1994; Wishful Thinking 1997; The Wedding 1998; Mouth to Mouth 2005

Thalbach, Katharina (1954-) The Tin Drum 1979; Mrs Ratcliffe's Revolution 2007; Moon Man 2012

Thames, Byron (1969-) Blame It on the Night 1984; Johnny Dangerously 1984

Thatcher, Heather (1896-1987) If I Were King 1938; Man Hunt 1941; The Undying Monster 1942; Dear Mr Prohack 1949; Father's Doing Fine 1952; Will Any Gentleman...? 1953

Thatcher, Torin (1905-1981) Next of Kin 1942; The End of the River 1947; Affair in Trinidad 1952; Blackbeard the Pirate 1952; The Crimson Pirate 1952; The Snows of Kilimanjaro 1952; The Desert Rats 1953; Houdini 1953; The Robe 1953; The Black Shield of Falworth 1954; Knock on Wood 1954; Diane 1955; Lady Godiva 1955; Love Is a Many-Splendored Thing 1955; Band of Angels 1957; Istanbul 1957; Witness for the Prosecution 1957; Darby's Rangers 1958; The 7th Voyage of Sinbad 1958; Jack the Giant Killer 1962; Hawaii 1966

Thaw, John (1942-2002) The Bofors Gun 1968; Praise Marx and Pass the Ammunition 1968; The Last Grenade 1970; Dr Phibes Rises Again 1972; Sweeney! 1976; Sweeney 2 1978; Business as Usual 1987; Cry Freedom 1987; Chaplin 1992

Thaxter, Phyllis (1919-2012) Thirty Seconds over Tokyo 1944; Bewitched 1945; Week-End at the Waldorf 1945; Living in a Big Way 1947; The Sea of Grass 1947; Blood on the Moon 1948; Act of Violence 1949; The Breaking Point 1950; No Man of Her Own 1950; Come Fill the Cup 1951; Fort Worth 1951; Jim Thorpe - All-American 1951; She's Working Her Way through College 1952; Springfield Rifle 1952; Women's Prison 1955; The World of Henry Orient 1964

Thayer, Lorna (1919-2005) Jennifer 1953; The Beast with a Million Eyes 1955

The Edge U23D 2007; It Might Get Loud 2008

Thelen, Jodi (1963-) The Black Stallion Returns 1983; A Doctor's Story 1984

Theobald, Karl The Truth 2006; Downhill 2014

Theron, Charlize (1975-) That Thing You Do! 1996; 2 Days in the Valley 1996; The Devil's Advocate 1997; Trial and Error 1997; Celebrity 1998; Mighty Joe Young 1998; The Astronaut's Wife 1999; The Cider House Rules 1999; Deception 2000; The Legend of Bagger Vance 2000; Men of Honor 2000; Waking Up in Reno 2000; The Yards 2000; The Curse of the Jade Scorpion 2001; 15 Minutes 2001; Sweet November 2001; Trapped 2002; The Italian Job 2003; The Life and Death of Peter Sellers 2003; Monster 2003; Head in the Clouds 2004; Aeonflux 2005; North Country 2005; Battle in Seattle 2007; In the Valley of Elah 2007; The Burning Plain 2008; Hancock 2008; Astro Boy 2009; The Road 2009; Young Adult 2011; Prometheus 2012; Snow White and the Huntsman 2012; A Million Ways to Die in the West 2014; Dark Places 2015; Mad Max: Fury Road 2015; The

Huntsman: Winter's War 2016; Kubo and the Two Strings 2016; The Coldest City 2017

Theroux, Justin (1971–) Romy and Michele's High School Reunion 1997; American Psycho 2000; The Broken Hearts Club: a Romantic Comedy 2000; Mulholland Drive 2001; Charlie's Angels: Full Throttle 2003; Our House 2003; Inland Empire 2006; Miami Vice 2006; Megamind 2010; Your Highness 2010; Wanderlust 2011; The Girl on the Train 2016

Thesiger, Ernest (1879–1961) The Old Dark House 1932; The Ghoul 1933; Bride of Frankenstein 1935; The Man Who Could Work Miracles 1936; Caesar and Cleopatra 1945; Beware of Pity 1946; The Ghosts of Berkeley Square 1947; The Man Within 1947; The Brass Monkey 1948; The Man in the White Suit 1951; The Robe 1953; Father Brown 1954; Quentin Durward 1955; Value for Money 1955; Who Done It? 1956; The Battle of the Sexes 1960; Sons and Lovers 1960

Thévenet, Virginie Full Moon in Paris 1984; Le Cri du Hibou 1987

Thewlis, David (1963–) Vroom 1988; Resurrected 1989; Life Is Sweet 1990; Naked 1993; Black Beauty 1994; Restoration 1995; Total Eclipse 1995; DragonHeart 1996; The Island of Dr Moreau 1996; James and the Giant Peach 1996; American Perfekt 1997; Seven Years in Tibet 1997; Besieged 1998; Divorcing Jack 1998; The Miracle Maker 1999; Whatever Happened to Harold Smith? 1999; Gangster No 1 2000; Goodbye Charlie Bright 2000; Timeline 2003; Harry Potter and the Prisoner of Azkaban 2004; Kingdom of Heaven 2005; The New World 2005; Basic Instinct 2: Risk Addiction 2006; The Omen 2006; The Boy in the Striped Pyjamas 2008; Harry Potter and the Half-Blood Prince 2009; Harry Potter and the Deathly Hallows: Part 1 2010; London Boulevard 2010; Mr Nice 2010; Anonymous 2011; The Lady 2011; War Horse 2011; The Fifth Estate 2013; Red 2 2013; The Zero Theorem 2013; Queen and Country 2014; Stonehearst Asylum 2014; Anomalisa 2015; Legend 2015; Macbeth 2015; Regression 2015; The Theory of Everything 2015; The Mercy 2016; Wonder Woman 2017

Thibault, Jean-Marc The Lady Cop 1979; Mademoiselle Chambon 2009

Thibeau, Jack Escape from Alcatraz 1979; Action Jackson 1988

Thiele, Hertha (1908-1984) Girls in Uniform 1931; Kühle Wampe 1931

Thieme, Thomas The Lives of Others 2006; The Door 2009

Thieriot, Max (1988–) Catch That Kid 2004; The Pacifier 2005; Nancy Drew 2007; Chloe 2009; My Soul to Take 2010; House at the End of the Street 2012

Thierry, Mélanie (1981–) The Legend of 1900 1999; Babylon AD 2008; Largo Winch 2008; The Princess of Montpensier 2010; The Zero Theorem 2013

Thiess, Ursula (1924-2010) The Iron Glove 1954; The Americano 1955; Bandido 1956

Thiessen, Tiffani-Amber aka **Thiessen, Tiffani** (1974–) From Dusk till Dawn II: Texas Blood Money 1999; ivansxtc. 1999; The Ladies Man 2000; Shriek If You Know What I Did Last Friday the 13th 2000; Hollywood Ending 2002

Thigpen, Lynne (1948-2003) Godspell 1973; Lean on Me 1989; Blankman 1994; The Paper 1994; Novocaine 2001; Anger Management 2003

Thimig, Hermann (1890-1982) The Threepenny Opera 1931; Viktor und Viktoria 1933

Thinnes, Roy (1936–) Journey to the Far Side of the Sun 1969; The Hindenburg 1975

Thirlby, Olivia (1986–) Juno 2007; The Wackness 2008; New York, I Love You 2009; The Darkest Hour 2011; Being Flynn 2012; Dredd 2012

Thomas, Antonia 8 minutes idle 2012; Northern Soul 2014

Thomas, Ashley "Bashy" aka **Thomas, Ashley** (1985–) Shank 2010; Cockneys vs Zombies 2011; The Veteran 2011; The Man Inside 2012; My Brother the Devil 2012

Thomas, Ben aka **Thomas, Benny** Toomorrow 1970; Hotel Sorrento 1994

Thomas, Damien (1942–) Twins of Evil 1971; Tiffany Jones 1973; Pirates 1986

Thomas, Danny (1912-1991) The Unfinished Dance 1947; Call Me Mister 1951; I'll See You in My Dreams 1951; The Jazz Singer 1952; Journey back to Oz 1964

Thomas, Dave (1949–) Love at Stake 1987; Moving 1988; Pippi Longstocking 1997; Brother Bear 2003

Thomas, Eddie Kaye (1980–) American Pie 1999; Freddy Got Fingered 2001; Stolen Summer 2002; American Pie: the Wedding 2003; Harold & Kumar Get the Munchies 2004; Blind Dating 2005

Thomas, Frank M (1889-1989) Behind the Headlines 1937; Criminal Lawyer 1937; Danger Patrol 1937; Smashing the Rackets 1938; Among the Living 1941; The Great Man's Lady 1942

Thomas, Frankie (1921-2006) Nancy Drew - Detective 1938; Angels Wash Their Faces 1939; One Foot in Heaven 1941; Always in My Heart 1942; The Major and the Minor 1942

Thomas, Henry (1971–) Raggedy Man 1981; ET the Extra-Terrestrial 1982; Cloak and Dagger 1984; Valmont 1989; Psycho IV: the Beginning 1990; Fire in the Sky 1993; Legends of the Fall 1994; Indictment: the McMartin Trial 1995; Hijacking Hollywood 1997; Niagara Niagara 1997; Moby Dick 1998; Happy Face Murders 1999; All the Pretty Horses 2000; Gangs of New York 2002; I Capture the Castle 2002; I'm with Lucy 2002; 11:14 2003; Dead Birds 2004; Dear John 2010

Thomas, Jake (1990–) AI: Artificial Intelligence 2001; The Lizzie McGuire Movie 2003; Aces 'n' Eights 2008

Thomas, Jameson (1888-1939) The Farmer's Wife 1928; Piccadilly 1929; Three Wise Girls 1932; It Happened One Night 1934; The Moonstone 1934; Charlie Chan in Egypt 1935; The Last Outpost 1935

Thomas, Jay (1948–) The Gig 1985; Mr Holland's Opus 1995; A Smile like Yours 1997

Thomas (1), Joe The Inbetweeners Movie 2011; The Inbetweeners 2 2014

Thomas, Jonathan Taylor (1981–) The Lion King 1994; Man of the House 1994; Pom Poko 1994; Tom and Huck 1995; The Adventures of Pinocchio 1996; Wild America 1997; I'll Be Home for Christmas 1998; Walking across Egypt 1999

Thomas, Khleo (1989–) Holes 2003; Walking Tall 2004

Thomas, Leonard Bad Lieutenant 1992; Dangerous Game 1993; DROP Squad 1994

Thomas, Marcus Noel 2004; You Kill Me 2007

Thomas, Mario (1938–) Nobody's Child 1986; LOL 2011

Thomas, Philip Michael aka **Thomas, Philip** (1949–) Book of Numbers 1972; Mr Ricco 1975; Extralarge: Moving Target 1990

Thomas, Rachel (1905-1995) The Proud Valley 1940; Undercover 1943; The Captive Heart 1946; Blue Scar 1947; Valley of Song 1953

Thomas, Richard (1951–) Last Summer 1969; Winning 1969; Red Sky at Morning 1971; You'll Like My Mother 1972; September 30, 1955 1977; All Quiet on the Western Front 1979; Battle beyond the Stars 1980; What Love Sees 1996; Fortune Hunters 1999; Wonder Boys 2000; Annie's Point 2005; Wild Hearts 2006; The Music Teacher 2012

Thomas, Robin (1961–) About Last Night... 1986; Summer School 1987; Amityville Dollhouse 1996; Clockstoppers 2002; Ambulance Girl 2005

Thomas, Sean Patrick (1970–) Dracula 2001 2000; Save the Last Dance 2000; Barbershop 2002; Halloween: Resurrection 2002; Barbershop 2: Back in Business 2004

Thomas, Trevor Black Joy 1977; Sheena 1984

Thomas, William Solomon and Gaenor 1998; The Baker 2007

Thomason, Marsha (1976–) Black Knight 2001; Pure 2002; The Haunted Mansion 2003

Thomerson, Tim aka **Thomerson, Timothy** (1945–) Remember My Name 1978; Carny 1980; Fade to Black 1980; Uncommon Valor 1983; Rhinestone 1984; Iron Eagle 1985; Trancers 1985; Volunteers 1985; Near Dark 1987; Cherry 2000 1988; The Incredible Hulk Returns 1988; Who's Harry Crumb? 1989; Trancers II: The Return of Jack Deth 1991; Brain Smasher... a Love Story 1993; Die Watching 1993; The Harvest 1993; Nemesis 1993; American Yakuza 2: Back to Back 1996; Too Hard to Die 1998; Red Team 1999; They Crawl 2001

Thompson, Al A Walk to Remember 2002; Love Don't Cost a Thing 2003

Thompson, Beatrix Dreyfus 1931; The Old Curiosity Shop 1935

Thompson, Bill (1913-1971) Alice in Wonderland 1951; Peter Pan 1953; Lady and the Tramp 1955; Sleeping Beauty 1959

Thompson, Bobb'e J Snow 2004; Role Models 2008

Thompson, Brian (1962–) AWOL 1990; Hired to Kill 1990; Moon 44 1990; Life Stinks 1991; DragonHeart 1996; The Order 2001

Thompson, Carlos (1923-1990) Fort Algiers 1953; Valley of the Kings 1954; Magic Fire 1956; Raw Wind in Eden 1958; La Vie de Château 1965

Thompson, Christopher La Bûche 1999; The Luzhin Defence 2000; Orchestra Seats 2005

Thompson, Derek (1948–) The Long Good Friday 1979; Resurrection Man 1997

Thompson, Don Knight Moves 1992; Slither 2006

Thompson, Emma (1959–) Henry V 1989; The Tall Guy 1989; Dead Again 1991; Impromptu 1991; Howards End 1992; Peter's Friends 1992; In the Name of the Father 1993; Much Ado about Nothing 1993; The Remains of the Day 1993; Junior 1994; Carrington 1995; Sense and Sensibility 1995; The Winter Guest 1996; Judas Kiss 1998; Primary Colors 1998; Maybe Baby 1999; Wit 2001; Treasure Planet 2002; Imagining Argentina 2003; Love Actually 2003; Harry Potter and the Prisoner of Azkaban 2004; Nanny McPhee 2005; Stranger than Fiction 2006; I Am Legend 2007; Brideshead Revisited 2008; An Education 2008; Last Chance Harvey 2008; Nanny McPhee & the Big Bang 2010; Brave 2012; Men in Black 3 2012; Beautiful Creatures 2013; The Love Punch 2013; Saving Mr Banks 2013; Effie Gray 2014; Men, Women & Children 2014; Burnt 2015; The Legend of Barney Thomson 2015; A Walk in the Woods 2015; Beauty and the Beast 2017

Thompson, Eric (1929-1982) Private Potter 1963; Dougal and the Blue Cat 1970; One Day in the Life of Ivan Denisovich 1971

Thompson, Fred Dalton aka **Thompson, Fred** (1942-2015) No Way Out 1986; Feds 1988; Days of Thunder 1990; Curly Sue 1991; Thunderheart 1992; Barbarians at the Gate 1993; In the Line of Fire 1993; Baby's Day Out 1994; Evel Knievel 2004; Bury My Heart at Wounded Knee 2007; Secretariat 2010; Sinister 2012

Thompson, Jack (1940–) Sunday Too Far Away 1974; Caddie 1976; Mad Dog 1976; The Chant of Jimmie Blacksmith 1978; Breaker Morant 1979; The Club 1980; The Earthling 1980; Bad Blood 1982; The Man from Snowy River 1982; Merry Christmas Mr Lawrence 1982; Burke and Wills 1985; Flesh + Blood 1985; Ground Zero 1987; Ruby Cairo 1992; Turtle Beach 1992; Wind 1992; A Far Off Place 1993; Flight of the Albatross 1995; The Sum of Us 1995; Broken Arrow 1996; Last Dance 1996; Excess Baggage 1997; Midnight in the Garden of Good and Evil 1997; The Magic Pudding 2000; Original Sin 2001; The Assassination of Richard Nixon 2004; Feed 2005; The Good German 2006; December Boys 2007; Australia 2008; Don't Be Afraid of the Dark 2010; Mystery Road 2013

Thompson, Kay (1902-1998) Funny Face 1957; Tell Me That You Love Me, Junie Moon 1970

Thompson, Kenan (1978–) Heavyweights 1995; Good Burger 1997; Love Don't Cost a Thing 2003; Fat Albert 2004; Snakes on a Plane 2006

Thompson, Lea (1961–) All the Right Moves 1983; Jaws III 1983; Red Dawn 1984; The Wild Life 1984; Yellow Pages 1984; Back to the Future 1985; Howard, a New Breed of Hero 1986; SpaceCamp 1986; Some Kind of Wonderful 1987; Casual Sex? 1988; The Wizard of Loneliness 1988; Back to the Future Part II 1989; Nightbreaker 1989; Back to the Future Part III 1990; Article 99 1992; The Beverly Hillbillies 1993; Dennis 1993; J Edgar 2011; Left Behind 2014

Thompson, Marshall (1925-1992) The Clock 1945; They Were Expendable 1945; The Secret Heart 1946; Words and Music 1948; Battleground 1949; Devil's Doorway 1950; Mystery Street 1950; The Tall Target 1951; The Caddy 1953; Battle Taxi 1955; Crashout 1955; Cult of the Cobra 1955; Good Morning, Miss Dove 1955; To Hell and Back 1955; Fiend without a Face 1957; First Man into Space 1958; It! The Terror from beyond Space 1958; Clarence, the Cross-Eyed Lion 1965; White Dog 1981

Thompson, Peter M (1920-2001) Santa Fe 1951; A Yank in Ermine 1955

Thompson, Rex (1942–) Her Twelve Men 1954; The Eddy Duchin Story 1956; The King and I 1956; The Day They Gave Babies Away 1957

Thompson, Robert (1916-2010) Patrick 1978; Thirst 1979

Thompson, Sada (1927-2011) Desperate Characters 1971; The Entertainer 1975; Indictment: the McMartin Trial 1995

Thompson, Scott (1959–) Kids in the Hall: Brain Candy 1996; Hijacking Hollywood 1997; The Pacifier 2005

Thompson, Sophie (1962–) Twenty-One 1991; Persuasion 1995; Emma 1996; Dancing at Lughnasa 1998; Relative Values 2000; Fat Slags 2004; Morris: a Life with Bells On 2009

Thompson, Susanna (1958–) Little Giants 1994; Bermuda Triangle 1996; Ghosts of Mississippi 1996; High Noon 2000; Dragonfly 2002

Thompson, Tessa (1983–) When a Stranger Calls 2006; Make It Happen 2008; Dear White People 2014; Creed 2015

Thoms, Tracie Rent 2005; The Devil Wears Prada 2006

Thomsen, Ulrich (1963–) Festen 1998; The Weight of Water 2000; Killing Me Softly 2001; Mike Bassett: England Manager 2001; Max 2002; The Inheritance 2003; The Rocket Post 2003; Brothers 2004; Allegro 2005; Hitman 2007; The Broken 2008; The International 2009; In a Better World 2010; Season of the Witch 2010; The Silence 2010; A Second Chance 2014; The Commune 2016

Thomsett, Sally (1950–) The Railway Children 1970; Baxter 1973; Man about the House 1974

Thomson, Cassi Rock the House 2011; Left Behind 2014

Thomson, Erik (1967–) Somersault 2004; The Boys Are Back 2009

Thomson, Kenneth (1899-1967) The Broadway Melody 1929; Lawyer Man 1932; Movie Crazy 1932; The Little Giant 1933

Thomson, Kim (1960–) Stealing Heaven 1988; The Tall Guy 1989; 1408 2007; Messages 2007

Thomson, R H (1947–) Ticket to Heaven 1981; Max 1994; Bone Daddy 1998; Chloe 2009

Thorburn, June (1931-1967) Children Galore 1954; Orders Are Orders 1954; Touch and Go 1955; True as a Turtle 1956; Rooney 1958; tom thumb 1958; The Three Worlds of Gulliver 1959; Don't Bother to Knock 1961; Fury at Smugglers Bay 1961; The Scarlet Blade 1963; Master Spy 1964

Thordsen, Kelly (1917-1978) The Fearmakers 1958; Boy, Did I Get a Wrong Number 1966; The Ugly Dachshund 1966; The Parallax View 1974

Thorndike, Sybil (1882-1976) Hindle Wakes 1931; Tudor Rose 1936; Major Barbara 1941; Nicholas Nickleby 1947; Britannia Mews 1949; Stage Fright 1949; Gone to Earth 1950; The Prince and the Showgirl 1957; Alive and Kicking 1958; Shake Hands with the Devil 1959; Smiley Gets a Gun 1959

Thorne-Smith, Courtney (1967–) Lucas 1986; Summer School 1987; Sorority Wars 2009

Thorne, Bella (1997–) Alvin and the Chipmunks: the Road Chip 2015; The Duff 2015

Thornton, Billy Bob (1955–) One False Move 1992; Trouble Bound 1993; Floundering 1994; On Deadly Ground 1994; Sling Blade 1995; The Stars Fell on Henrietta 1995; The Winner 1996; The Apostle 1997; U Turn 1997; Armageddon 1998; Homegrown 1998; Primary Colors 1998; A Simple Plan 1998; Daddy and Them 1999; Pushing Tin 1999; South of Heaven, West of Hell 2000; Waking Up in Reno 2000; Bandits 2001; The Man Who Wasn't There 2001; Monster's Ball 2001; Levity 2002; Bad Santa 2003; Intolerable Cruelty 2003; Love Actually 2003; The Alamo 2004; Friday Night Lights 2004; Bad News Bears 2005; The Ice Harvest 2005; The Astronaut Farmer 2006; School for Scoundrels 2006; Mr Woodcock 2007; Eagle Eye 2008; Duplicity 2009; The Informers 2009; Faster 2010; Puss in Boots 2011; The Baytown Outlaws 2012; Jayne Mansfield's Car 2012; Parkland 2013; The Judge 2014; Entourage 2015; London Fields 2015; Our Brand Is Crisis 2015; Whiskey Tango Foxtrot 2016

Thornton, David (1953–) Home Alone 3 1997; High Art 1998; Hush 1998; XX/XY 2001; Swept Away 2002; The Notebook 2003

Thornton, Frank (1921-2013) Side by Side 1975; Spanish Fly 1975; Are You Being Served? 1977

Thornton, Sigrid (1959–) The Man from Snowy River 1982; The Lighthorsemen 1987; Return to Snowy River 1988; Over the Hill 1992

Thorpe, George (1891-1961) Meet Me at Dawn 1946; Quiet Weekend 1946; Daughter of Darkness 1948; The Man on the Eiffel Tower 1949; Father's Doing Fine 1952

Thorson, Linda (1947–) Walls of Glass 1985; The Other Sister 1999

Threlfall, David (1953–) When the Whales Came 1989; The Russia House 1990; Chunky Monkey 2001; Conspiracy 2001; Black Sea 2014

Thring, Frank (1926-1994) The Vikings 1958; Ben-Hur 1959; El Cid 1961; King of Kings 1961; The Man from Hong Kong 1975; Mad Dog 1976; Mad Max beyond Thunderdome 1985

Thuillier, Luc Monsieur Hire 1989; The Old Lady Who Walked in the Sea 1991

Thulin, Ingrid aka **Tulean, Ingrid** (1926-2004) Foreign Intrigue 1956; So Close to Life 1957; Wild Strawberries 1957; The Magician 1958; The Four Horsemen of the Apocalypse 1962; Winter Light 1962; The Silence 1963; Return from the Ashes 1965; La Guerre Est Finie 1966; The Hour of the Wolf 1967; The Damned 1969; The Rite 1969; The Short Night of the Glass Dolls 1971; Cries and Whispers 1972; Moses 1975; The Cassandra Crossing 1976; Salon Kitty 1976; After the Rehearsal 1984

Thundercloud, Chief (1899-1955) Annie Oakley 1935; Colt .45 1950

Thurman, Bill (1920-1995) The Evictors 1979; Alamo Bay 1985

Thurman, Uma (1970–) Kiss Daddy Good Night 1987; The Adventures of Baron Munchausen 1988; Dangerous Liaisons 1988; Johnny Be Good 1988; Henry & June 1990; Robin Hood 1990; Where the Heart Is 1990; Final Analysis 1992; Jennifer Eight 1992; Mad Dog and Glory 1992; Even Cowgirls Get the Blues 1993; A Month by the Lake 1994; Pulp Fiction 1994; Beautiful Girls 1996; The Truth about Cats and Dogs 1996; Batman and Robin 1997; Gattaca 1997; Les Misérables 1997; The Avengers 1998; Sweet and Lowdown 1999; The Golden Bowl 2000; Vatel 2000; Tape 2001; Hysterical Blindness 2002; Kill Bill Vol 1 2003; Paycheck 2003; Kill Bill Vol 2 2004; Be Cool 2005; Prime 2005; The Producers 2005; My Super Ex-Girlfriend 2006; The Life before Her Eyes 2007; The Accidental Husband 2008; Motherhood 2009; Bel Ami 2010; Percy Jackson & the Lightning Thief 2010; Love, Marilyn 2012; Playing for Keeps 2012; Movie 43 2013; Nymphomaniac Vol I 2013; Nymphomaniac Vol II 2014

Thurston, Carol (1923-1969) The Conspirators 1944; The Story of Dr Wassell 1944; China Sky 1945; Flaming Feather 1952

Thwaites, Brenton (1989–) Oculus 2013; Son of a Gun 2013; The Giver 2014; The Signal 2014; Gods of Egypt 2016

Ti Lung (1946–) Shatter 1974; A Better Tomorrow 1986; A Better Tomorrow II 1987; The Warrior's Way 2010

Tian, Valerie The Moth Diaries 2010; Words and Pictures 2013

Ticotin, Rachel (1958–) Fort Apache, the Bronx 1981; Critical Condition 1987; Total Recall 1990; FX 2 1991; One Good Cop 1991; Falling Down 1992; Don Juan DeMarco 1995; Steal Big, Steal Little 1995; Con Air 1997; Turbulence 1997; Something's Gotta Give 2003; Man on Fire 2004; The Sisterhood of the Traveling Pants 2005; The Eye 2008

Tidblad, Inga (1901-1975) Intermezzo 1936; Foreign Intrigue 1956

Tielve, Fernando The Devil's Backbone 2001; Unmade Beds 2009

Tien, James The Big Boss 1971; Fist of Fury 1972

Tiernan, Andrew Edward II 1991; As You Like It 1992; Playing God 1997; The Criminal 1999; Mr In-Between 2001; The Messenger 2015

Tiernan, Tommy Hold Back the Night 1999; About Adam 2000

Tierney, Gene (1920-1991) Hudson's Bay 1940; The Return of Frank James 1940; Belle Starr 1941; The Shanghai Gesture 1941; Sundown 1941; Tobacco Road 1941; China Girl 1942; Rings on Her Fingers 1942; Son of Fury 1942; Heaven Can Wait 1943; Laura 1944; A Bell for Adano 1945; Leave Her to Heaven 1945; Dragonwyck 1946; The Razor's Edge 1946; The Ghost and Mrs Muir 1947; The Iron Curtain 1948; That Wonderful Urge 1948; Whirlpool 1949; Night and the City 1950; Where the Sidewalk Ends 1950; Close to My Heart 1951; The Mating Season 1951; On the Riviera 1951; The Secret of Convict Lake 1951; Plymouth Adventure 1952;

Way of a Gaucho 1952; Never Let Me Go 1953; Personal Affair 1953; Black Widow 1954; The Egyptian 1954; The Left Hand of God 1955; Advise and Consent 1962; Toys in the Attic 1963; The Pleasure Seekers 1964

Tierney, Jacob (1979–) Josh and SAM 1993; The Neon Bible 1995; This Is My Father 1999

Tierney, Lawrence (1919-2002) Dillinger 1945; Badman's Territory 1946; The Devil Thumbs a Ride 1947; Lady of Deceit 1947; Bodyguard 1948; Best of the Badmen 1951; The Greatest Show on Earth 1952; The Female Jungle 1955; Custer of the West 1967; Silver Bullet 1985; Tough Guys Don't Dance 1987; Reservoir Dogs 1991

Tierney, Maura (1965–) Liar Liar 1997; Forces of Nature 1998; Primary Colors 1998; Instinct 1999; Oxygen 1999; Insomnia 2002; Welcome to Mooseport 2004; Baby Mama 2008; Semi-Pro 2008

Tiffany Jetsons: the Movie 1990; Mega Piranha 2010

Tiffin, Pamela (1942–) One, Two, Three 1961; Come Fly with Me 1962; State Fair 1962; For Those Who Think Young 1964; The Pleasure Seekers 1964; The Hallelujah Trail 1965; Harper 1966; Viva Max! 1969

Tigar, Kenneth (1942–) The Gypsy Warriors 1978; Creator 1985; The Betty Ford Story 1987; Snapdragon 1993; Little Bigfoot 1995

Tighe, Kevin (1944–) Matewan 1987; K-9 1989; Road House 1989; Another 48 HRS 1990; School Ties 1992; Geronimo: an American Legend 1993; What's Eating Gilbert Grape 1993; Scorpion Spring 1995; Race the Sun 1996; My Bloody Valentine 2009

Tikaram, Ramon Kama Sutra: a Tale of Love 1996; Mischief Night 2006

Tikhonov, Vyacheslav (1928-2009) War and Peace 1966; Burnt by the Sun 1995

Tilden, Leif (1964–) Teenage Mutant Ninja Turtles 1990; Teenage Mutant Ninja Turtles II: the Secret of the Ooze 1991

Till, Jenny Theatre of Death 1966; A Challenge for Robin Hood 1967

Till, Lucas Hannah Montana: the Movie 2009; Paranoia 2013; Wolves 2013

Tiller, Nadja (1929–) The Rough and the Smooth 1959; The Monk 1972

Tilly, Grant (1937–) Beyond Reasonable Doubt 1980; Race for the Yankee Zephyr 1981; Savage Islands 1983; Warm Nights on a Slow Moving Train 1986

Tilly, Jennifer (1958–) Moving Violations 1985; He's My Girl 1987; High Spirits 1988; Johnny Be Good 1988; Remote Control 1988; The Fabulous Baker Boys 1989; Far from Home 1989; Scorchers 1991; Shadow of the Wolf 1992; Made in America 1993; Bullets over Broadway 1994; Embrace of the Vampire 1994; The Getaway 1994; American Strays 1996; Bound 1996; Desert Gamble 1996; House Arrest 1996; Liar Liar 1997; Bride of Chucky 1998; Hoods 1998; Music from Another Room 1998; Relax... It's Just Sex 1998; Bartok the Magnificent 1999; Stuart Little 1999; Dancing at the Blue Iguana 2000; Hide and Seek 2000; Play It to the Bone 2000; The Cat's Meow 2001; The Magnificent Ambersons 2001; Monsters, Inc 2001; The Haunted Mansion 2003; Home on the Range 2004; Saint Ralph 2004; Seed of Chucky 2004; Tideland 2005; Curse of Chucky 2013

Tilly, Meg (1960–) One Dark Night 1982; Tex 1982; The Big Chill 1983; Psycho II 1983; Impulse 1984; Agnes of God 1985; Off Beat 1986; Masquerade 1988; Valmont 1989; The Two Jakes 1990; Leaving Normal 1992; Body Snatchers 1993; Sleep with Me 1994

Tilton, Charlene (1958–) Border Shootout 1990; Problem Child 2 1991; The Silence of the Hams 1993

Tilvern, Alan (1920-2003) The Bespoke Overcoat 1955; Chase a Crooked Shadow 1957; Danger by My Side 1962; Shadow of Fear 1963; Who Framed Roger Rabbit 1988

Timberlake, Justin (1981–) Edison 2005; Alpha Dog 2006; Black Snake Moan 2006; Shrek the Third 2007; The Love Guru 2008; Shrek Forever After 2010; The Social Network 2010; Yogi Bear 2010; Bad Teacher 2011; Friends with Benefits 2011; In Time 2011; Trouble with the Curve 2012; Inside Llewyn Davis 2013; Runner Runner 2013; Trolls 2016

Timi, Filippo In Memory of Myself 2007; Vincere 2009; Angels of Evil 2010

Timlin, Addison (1991–) Derailed 2005; Odd Thomas 2013

Timothy, Christopher (1940–) Here We Go round the Mulberry Bush 1967; Alfred the Great 1969; The Virgin Soldiers 1969

Tingwell, Charles aka Tingwell, Charles "Bud" aka Tingwell, Bud (1923-2009) Bitter Springs 1950; The Desert Rats 1953; Bobbikins 1959; Life in Emergency Ward 10 1959; Murder She Said 1961; Murder at the Gallop 1963; Murder Ahoy 1964; Murder Most Foul 1964; Dracula - Prince of Darkness 1965; Breaker Morant 1979; Windrider 1986; A Cry in the Dark 1988; Innocence 2000; Irresistible 2006

Tinkerbell Time of Favor 2000; Eyes Wide Open 2009

Tinti, Gabriele (1932-1991) The Legend of Lylah Clare 1968; Delusions of Grandeur 1971

Tipton, Analeigh (1988–) Crazy, Stupid, Love 2011; Damsels in Distress 2011; Warm Bodies 2012; Two Night Stand 2013; Mississippi Grind 2015

Tiran, Itay Beaufort 2007; Lebanon 2009

Tirelli, Jaime Girlfight 2000; Bella 2006

Tisdale, Ashley (1985–) High School Musical 2006; High School Musical 2 2007; High School Musical 3: Senior Year 2008; Aliens in the Attic 2009; Sharpay's Fabulous Adventure 2011; Saving Santa 2013; Scary Movie V 2013

Tissier, Jean (1896-1973) And God Created Woman 1956; The Hunchback of Notre Dame 1956; Dead Run 1967; The Widow Couderc 1971

Tissot, Alice (1895-1971) An Italian Straw Hat 1927; Madame Bovary 1933

To, Chapman (1972–) Infernal Affairs 2002; Infernal Affairs II 2003; Initial D - Drift Racer 2005

Toback, James (1943–) A Fuller Life 2013; Seduced and Abandoned 2013

Tobeck, Joel Little Fish 2005; Eagle vs Shark 2006; The Water Horse 2007

Tobey, Kenneth (1917-2002) The Thing from Another World 1951; Angel Face 1953; The Beast from 20,000 Fathoms 1953; The Bigamist 1953; Down Three Dark Streets 1954; Davy Crockett, King of the Wild Frontier 1955; It Came from beneath the Sea 1955; Davy Crockett and the River Pirates 1956; The Great Locomotive Chase 1956; The Wings of Eagles 1957; Cry Terror 1958; Seven Ways from Sundown 1960; X-15 1961; 40 Guns to Apache Pass 1966; Strange Invaders 1983; Desire & Hell at Sunset Motel 1991

Tobias, George (1901-1980) Maisie 1939; East of the River 1940; Music in My Heart 1940; Saturday's Children 1940; Torrid Zone 1940; Affectionately Yours 1941; The Bride Came COD 1941; Out of the Fog 1941; Sergeant York 1941; The Strawberry Blonde 1941; Captains of the Clouds 1942; My Sister Eileen 1942; Yankee Doodle Dandy 1942; Air Force 1943; Mission to Moscow 1943; This Is the Army 1943; Between Two Worlds 1944; The Mask of Dimitrios 1944; Passage to Marseille 1944; Objective, Burma! 1945; Nobody Lives Forever 1946; My Wild Irish Rose 1947; Sinbad the Sailor 1947; The Judge Steps Out 1949; The Set-Up 1949; Rawhide 1951; Ten Tall Men 1951; The Glenn Miller Story 1953; Seven Little Foys 1955; Silk Stockings 1957; The Tattered Dress 1957; A New Kind of Love 1963; Bullet for a Badman 1964

Tobias, Oliver (1947–) Romance of a Horse Thief 1971; The Stud 1978; Arabian Adventure 1979; A Nightingale Sang in Berkeley Square 1979; The Wicked Lady 1983; Mata Hari 1985; The Brylcreem Boys 1996; Darkness Falls 1998; Grizzly Falls 1999

Tobin, Dan (1910-1982) The Big Clock 1948; The Velvet Touch 1948

Tobin, Genevieve (1899-1995) The Gay Diplomat 1931; One Hour with You 1932; Kiss and Make-Up 1934; The Case of the Lucky Legs 1935; The Woman in Red 1935; The Man in the Mirror 1936; The Petrified Forest 1936; Dramatic School 1938; Zaza 1939; No Time for Comedy 1940

Tobin, Vivian (1904-2002) The Sign of the Cross 1932; If I Were Free 1933

Tobolowsky, Stephen (1951–) Nobody's Fool 1986; Mississippi Burning 1988; Breaking In 1989; Great Balls of Fire! 1989; Roe vs Wade 1989; Bird on a Wire 1990; Funny about Love 1990; Thelma & Louise 1991; Accidental Hero 1992; Memoirs of an Invisible Man 1992; Single White Female 1992; Calendar Girl 1993; Groundhog Day 1993; Josh and SAM 1993; Murder in the First 1994; My Father the Hero 1994; Dr Jekyll and Ms Hyde 1995; The

Glimmer Man 1996; Mr Magoo 1997; The Insider 1999; Memento 2000; The Prime Gig 2000; The Day the World Ended 2001; Freddy Got Fingered 2001; Love Liza 2001; The Country Bears 2002; Freaky Friday 2003; Garfield 2004; Little Black Book 2004; Blind Dating 2005; The Time Traveler's Wife 2008; Buried 2009

Todd, Ann (1909-1993) The Ghost Train 1931; The Return of Bulldog Drummond 1934; Things to Come 1936; The Squeaker 1937; South Riding 1938; Poison Pen 1939; Danny Boy 1941; Ships with Wings 1942; Perfect Strangers 1945; The Seventh Veil 1945; Daybreak 1946; Gaiety George 1946; The Paradine Case 1947; The Passionate Friends 1948; Madeleine 1949; The Sound Barrier 1952; The Green Scarf 1954; Time without Pity 1957; Taste of Fear 1961; The Fiend 1971; The Human Factor 1979

Todd, Ann E aka Todd, Ann (1931–) Intermezzo 1939; Zaza 1939; The Men in Her Life 1941; Remember the Day 1941; Dangerous Years 1947; Three Daring Daughters 1948

Todd, Beverly (1946–) Brother John 1970; Vice Squad 1982; Clara's Heart 1988; Moving 1988; Lean on Me 1989; The Bucket List 2008

Todd, Bob (1921-1992) The Best of Benny Hill 1974; Confessions of a Pop Performer 1975; Ups and Downs of a Handyman 1975

Todd, Hallie (1962–) Sam's Son 1984; The Lizzie McGuire Movie 2003

Todd, James (1908-1968) Riders of the Purple Sage 1931; Torch Song 1953; The Wings of Eagles 1957

Todd, Richard (1919-2009) The Hasty Heart 1949; The Interrupted Journey 1949; Stage Fright 1949; Portrait of Clare 1950; Lightning Strikes Twice 1951; The Story of Robin Hood and His Merrie Men 1952; The Sword and the Rose 1953; Venetian Bird 1952; Rob Roy, the Highland Rogue 1953; The Dam Busters 1954; Secrets d'Alcove 1954; A Man Called Peter 1955; The Virgin Queen 1955; D-Day the Sixth of June 1956; Marie Antoinette 1956; Yangtse Incident 1956; Chase a Crooked Shadow 1957; Saint Joan 1957; Danger Within 1958; Intent to Kill 1958; The Long and the Short and the Tall 1960; Never Let Go 1960; The Boys 1961; Don't Bother to Knock 1961; The Longest Day 1962; The Very Edge 1962; Death Drums along the River 1963; Coast of Skeletons 1964; The Battle of the Villa Fiorita 1965; Asylum 1972; House of the Long Shadows 1983

Todd, Ryan Mrs Lambert Remembers Love 1991; Pontiac Moon 1994

Todd, Thelma (1905-1935) Monkey Business 1931; Horse Feathers 1932; Speak Easily 1932; This Is the Night 1932; Bogus Bandits 1933; Counsellor-at-Law 1933; Sitting Pretty 1933; Palooka 1934; The Bohemian Girl 1936

Todd, Tony (1954–) Night of the Living Dead 1990; Candyman 1992; Excessive Force 1993; Candyman: Farewell to the Flesh 1995; Bram Stoker's Shadowbuilder 1997; Wishmaster 1997; Candyman: Day of the Dead 1999; Le Secret 2000; Hatchet 2006; Final Destination 5 2011; Frankenstein 2015

Todeschini, Bruno (1962–) Those Who Love Me Can Take the Train 1998; Va Savoir 2001; Son Frère 2003; Lourdes 2009; Delicacy 2011; The Connection 2014

Todoroki, Yukiko (1917-1967) Sanshiro Sugata 1943; The Lady of Musashino 1951

Todorovic, Bora (1930-2014) Montenegro 1981; Time of the Gypsies 1988

Todorovic, Srdjan (1965–) Underground 1995; Black Cat, White Cat 1998; A Serbian Film 2010

Tognazzi, Ugo (1922-1990) RoGoPaG 1962; Barbarella 1968; Pigsty 1969; La Grande Bouffe 1973; La Cage aux Folles 1978; Viva Italia! 1978; La Cage aux Folles II 1980; The Tragedy of a Ridiculous Man 1981; La Cage aux Folles III: "Elles" Se Marient 1985

Toibin, Niall (1929–) Eat the Peach 1986; Rawhead Rex 1986; Fools of Fortune 1990; The Nephew 1997

Tokos, Lubor (1923-2003) Invention of Destruction 1958; The Ear 1969

Tokuda, Marilyn Farewell to the King 1988; Cage 1989

Tolan, Michael aka Tolan, Lawrence (1925-2011) The Enforcer 1951; John and Mary 1969; The Lost Man 1969; All That Jazz 1979

Toledo, Guillermo (1970–) The Other Side of the Bed 2002; Only Human 2004

Toler, Sidney (1874-1947) Blonde Venus 1932; Blondie of the Follies 1932;

The Phantom President 1932; Speak Easily 1932; The Call of the Wild 1935; Our Relations 1936; Double Wedding 1937; Charlie Chan at Treasure Island 1939; Charlie Chan in Reno 1939; Charlie Chan in Rio 1941; A Night to Remember 1942; White Savage 1943; Charlie Chan in The Chinese Cat 1944; Charlie Chan in the Secret Service 1944; Meeting at Midnight 1944; The Jade Mask 1945; The Red Dragon 1945; The Scarlet Clue 1945; The Shanghai Cobra 1945; Dangerous Money 1946; Dark Alibi 1946; The Trap 1947

Toles-Bey, John Weeds 1987; A Rage in Harlem 1991; Stockade 1991; Extreme Measures 1996

Tolkan, James (1931–) The River 1984; Opportunity Knocks 1990; Boiling Point 1993

Tolo, Marilu (1944–) Marriage - Italian Style 1964; Bluebeard 1972

Tolubeyev, Yuri (1905-1979) Don Quixote 1957; Hamlet 1964

Tom, David (1978–) Stay Tuned 1992; Swing Kids 1993; Man of Miracles 1999

Tom, Lauren (1961–) Nothing Lasts Forever 1984; The Joy Luck Club 1993; When a Man Loves a Woman 1994; Kidnapped 1995; Bad Santa 2003

Tom, Nicholle (1978–) Beethoven 1992; Beethoven's 2nd 1993; My Family's Secret 2010

Tombes, Andrew (1885-1976) Checkers 1937; Down Mexico Way 1941; They All Kissed the Bride 1942; Can't Help Singing 1944; Frontier Gal 1945; The Devil Thumbs a Ride 1947; Oh, You Beautiful Doll 1949

Tomei, Concetta (1945–) The Betty Ford Story 1987; Don't Tell Mom the Babysitter's Dead 1991

Tomei, Marisa (1964–) The Toxic Avenger 1985; Oscar 1991; Zandalee 1991; Chaplin 1992; Equinox 1992; My Cousin Vinny 1992; Untamed Heart 1993; Only You 1994; The Paper 1994; Four Rooms 1995; The Perez Family 1995; Unhook the Stars 1996; Welcome to Sarajevo 1997; Slums of Beverly Hills 1998; The Watcher 2000; Animal Attraction 2001; In the Bedroom 2001; What Women Want 2001; The Guru 2002; Just a Kiss 2002; Anger Management 2003; The Wild Thornberrys Movie 2003; Alfie 2004; Factotum (A Man Who Preforms Many Jobs) 2005; Marilyn Hotchkiss Ballroom Dancing & Charm School 2005; Before the Devil Knows You're Dead 2007; Wild Hogs 2007; War, Inc 2008; The Wrestler 2008; Cyrus 2010; Crazy, Stupid, Love 2011; The Ides of March 2011; The Lincoln Lawyer 2011; Salvation Boulevard 2011; Parental Guidance 2012; Love Is Strange 2014; The Rewrite 2014; The Big Short 2015; Spider-Man: Homecoming 2017

Tomelty, Frances (1948–) Bullshot 1983; Lamb 1985; Bellman & True 1987; The Field 1990; High Boot Benny 1993; Monk Dawson 1997; Chéri 2009

Tomelty, Joseph (1911-1995) The Gentle Gunman 1952; The Oracle 1952; The Sound Barrier 1952; Hobson's Choice 1953; Meet Mr Lucifer 1953; Happy Ever After 1954; Hell below Zero 1954; The Young Lovers 1954; Bedevilled 1955; Simba 1955; Timeslip 1955; Hell Is a City 1959; Upstairs and Downstairs 1959; The Day They Robbed the Bank of England 1960; The Black Torment 1964

Tomita, Tamlyn (1966–) The Karate Kid Part II 1986; Come See the Paradise 1990; The Joy Luck Club 1993; Picture Bride 1994; The Day after Tomorrow 2004

Tomlin, Lily (1939–) Nashville 1975; The Late Show 1977; Moment by Moment 1978; Nine to Five 1980; The Incredible Shrinking Woman 1981; All of Me 1984; Big Business 1988; The Search for Signs of Intelligent Life in the Universe 1991; Shadows and Fog 1991; And the Band Played On 1993; The Beverly Hillbillies 1993; Short Cuts 1993; Blue in the Face 1995; The Celluloid Closet 1995; Flirting with Disaster 1996; Getting Away with Murder 1996; Krippendorf's Tribe 1998; Tea with Mussolini 1998; Disney's The Kid 2000; Orange County 2001; I ♥ Huckabees 2004; The Ant Bully 2006; A Prairie Home Companion 2006; The Walker 2006; The Pink Panther 2 2009; Grandma 2015

Tomlinson, David (1917-2000) Journey Together 1944; School for Secrets 1946; The Master of Bankdam 1947; Miranda 1947; Here Come the Huggetts 1948; My Brother's Keeper 1948; Sleeping Car to Trieste 1948; Vote for Huggett 1948; The Chiltern Hundreds 1949; So Long at the Fair 1950; The Wooden Horse 1950; Calling

Bulldog Drummond 1951; Hotel Sahara 1951; Made in Heaven 1952; Is Your Honeymoon Really Necessary? 1953; All for Mary 1955; Three Men in a Boat 1956; Carry On Admiral 1957; Further up the Creek 1958; Up the Creek 1958; Mary Poppins 1964; The Truth about Spring 1964; City under the Sea 1965; The Liquidator 1966; The Love Bug 1969; Bedknobs and Broomsticks 1971; Wombling Free 1977; Dominique 1978; The Water Babies 1978; The Fiendish Plot of Dr Fu Manchu 1980

Tomlinson, Eleanor (1992–) Angus, Thongs and Perfect Snogging 2008; Jack the Giant Slayer 2013

Tomlinson, Ricky (1939–) Riff-Raff 1991; Raining Stones 1993; Butterfly Kiss 1994; Bob's Weekend 1996; Preaching to the Perverted 1997; Mojo 1998; Nasty Neighbours 2000; The 51st State 2001; Mike Bassett: England Manager 2001; Once upon a Time in the Midlands 2002; Nativity! 2009

Tommila, Onni Rare Exports from the Land of the Original Santa Claus 2010; Big Game 2014

Tompkins, Angel (1943–) I Love My... Wife 1970; Prime Cut 1972; Crack House 1989; Relentless 1989

Tompkins, Joan (1915-2005) I Love My... Wife 1970; The Harness 1971

Tompkinson, Stephen (1966–) Brassed Off 1996; Hotel Splendide 1999; Harrigan 2013; Hector 2015

Tone, Franchot (1905-1968) The Wiser Sex 1932; Blonde Bombshell 1933; Dancing Lady 1933; Gabriel over the White House 1933; The Stranger's Return 1933; Today We Live 1933; The Girl from Missouri 1934; Sadie McKee 1934; The World Moves On 1934; Dangerous 1935; The Lives of a Bengal Lancer 1935; Mutiny on the Bounty 1935; Reckless 1935; The Gorgeous Hussy 1936; The King Steps Out 1936; Love on the Run 1936; Suzy 1936; The Bride Wore Red 1937; Man-Proof 1937; Quality Street 1937; They Gave Him a Gun 1937; Three Comrades 1938; Three Loves Has Nancy 1938; Fast and Furious 1939; Nice Girl? 1941; Star Spangled Rhythm 1942; Five Graves to Cairo 1943; His Butler's Sister 1943; Pilot #5 1943; True to Life 1943; Dark Waters 1944; The Hour before the Dawn 1944; Phantom Lady 1944; Because of Him 1946; Her Husband's Affairs 1947; Every Girl Should Be Married 1948; Jigsaw 1949; The Man on the Eiffel Tower 1949; Here Comes the Groom 1951; Advise and Consent 1962; Mickey One 1965; Nobody Runs Forever 1968

Tong, Jacqueline How to Get Ahead in Advertising 1989; Angel 2006

Tonge, Philip (1897-1959) Miracle on 34th Street 1947; Hans Christian Andersen 1952; Khyber Patrol 1954; Track of the Cat 1954; Macabre 1958

Tono, Eijiro (1907-1994) The Love of Sumako the Actress 1947; Hen in the Wind 1948; Early Spring 1956; Yojimbo 1961

Tonoyama, Taiji (1915-1989) The Island 1961; In the Realm of the Senses 1976; Tokyo Pop 1988

Toomey, Regis (1898-1991) Alibi 1929; The Finger Points 1931; Other Men's Women 1931; The Crowd Roars 1932; Shopworn 1932; Laughing at Life 1933; Murder on the Blackboard 1934; The Invisible Menace 1938; Arizona 1940; Dive Bomber 1941; They Died with Their Boots On 1941; The Forest Rangers 1942; Tennessee Johnson 1942; Betrayal from the East 1945; The Big Sleep 1946; Child of Divorce 1946; Magic Town 1947; The Boy with Green Hair 1948; Station West 1948; Beyond the Forest 1949; Frenchie 1950; Cry Danger 1951; Drums across the River 1954; Guys and Dolls 1955; Warlock 1959; The Last Sunset 1961; Voyage to the Bottom of the Sea 1961

Toone, Geoffrey (1910-2005) Poison Pen 1939; The Man Between 1953; The King and I 1956; Zero Hour! 1957; Dr Crippen 1962; Echo of Diana 1963; Dr Who and the Daleks 1965

Tootoosis, Gordon (1941-2011) Dan Candy's Law 1973; Legends of the Fall 1994; Alaska 1996; Black Point 2001

Topart, Jean (1922-2012) The Testament of Dr Cordelier 1959; Cop au Vin 1984

Topic, Velibor Second in Command 2006; The All Together 2007

Topol aka Topol, Chaim aka Topol, Haym (1935–) Sallah 1964; Cast a Giant Shadow 1966; Before Winter Comes 1968; Fiddler on the Roof 1971; Follow Me 1971; Galileo 1974; Flash Gordon 1980; For Your Eyes Only 1981; Left Luggage 1997

Toren, Marta (1926-1957) Casbah 1948; Mystery Submarine 1950;

Sirocco 1951; Assignment - Paris 1952; The Man Who Watched Trains Go By 1952

Torena, Juan (1898-1983) A Message to Garcia 1936; An American Guerrilla in the Philippines 1950

Torgov, Sarah Meatballs 1979; American Gothic 1987

Tormé, Mel (1925-1999) Higher and Higher 1943; Good News 1947; Words and Music 1948; Duchess of Idaho 1950; The Fearmakers 1958; The Big Operator 1959; Girls' Town 1959; The Private Lives of Adam and Eve 1959; Walk like a Dragon 1960; A Man Called Adam 1966

Tormey, John Ghost Dog: the Way of the Samurai 1999; Keane 2004

Torn, Rip (1931-) Time Limit 1957; Pork Chop Hill 1959; King of Kings 1961; Hero's Island 1962; Sweet Bird of Youth 1962; Critic's Choice 1963; The Cincinnati Kid 1965; One Spy Too Many 1966; You're a Big Boy Now 1966; Beach Red 1967; Beyond the Law 1968; Payday 1972; Birch Interval 1976; The Man Who Fell to Earth 1976; Coma 1977; The Private Files of J Edgar Hoover 1977; The Seduction of Joe Tynan 1979; One-Trick Pony 1980; The Beastmaster 1982; Jinxed! 1982; Cross Creek 1983; City Heat 1984; Songwriter 1984; Beer 1985; Summer Rental 1985; Extreme Prejudice 1987; Nadine 1987; Hit List 1988; Cold Feet 1989; Sweet Bird of Youth 1989; Beautiful Dreamers 1990; By Dawn's Early Light 1990; Defending Your Life 1991; Hard Promises 1991; RoboCop 3 1993; Where the Rivers Flow North 1993; Fixing the Shadow 1994; Heart of a Child 1994; Canadian Bacon 1995; For Better or Worse 1995; How to Make an American Quilt 1995; Down Periscope 1996; Hercules 1997; Men in Black 1997; Trial and Error 1997; Senseless 1998; The Insider 1999; Wonder Boys 2000; Freddy Got Fingered 2001; Men in Black 2 2002; Dodgeball: a True Underdog Story 2004; Welcome to Mooseport 2004; Marie Antoinette 2005; Yours, Mine & Ours 2005; Zoom 2006; Bee Movie 2007

Torocsik, Mari (1935-) Merry-Go-Round 1956; The Boys of Paul Street 1968; Love 1971; Diary for My Father and Mother 1990; Rothschild's Violin 1996

Torrence, David (1864-1951) Tess of the Storm Country 1922; The Big Noise 1928; Disraeli 1929; The Devil to Pay 1930; Raffles 1930; The Bachelor Father 1931; A Successful Calamity 1932; The Masquerader 1933; What Every Woman Knows 1934; Bonnie Scotland 1935; Rulers of the Sea 1939

Torrence, Ernest (1878-1933) Tol'able David 1921; The Covered Wagon 1923; The Hunchback of Notre Dame 1923; Ruggles of Red Gap 1923; The Pony Express 1925; Mantrap 1926; The King of Kings 1927; Steamboat Bill, Jr 1928; Fighting Caravans 1931; Sporting Blood 1931; Sherlock Holmes 1932; I Cover the Waterfront 1933

Torrens, Pip Valiant 2005; Easy Virtue 2008

Torrent, Ana (1966-) The Spirit of the Beehive 1973; Cría Cuervos 1975; Blood and Sand 1989; Vacas 1991; Tesis 1996; The Other Boleyn Girl 2008

Torres, Fernanda (1965-) Eu Sei Que Vou Te Amar 1986; Four Days in September 1997; Midnight 1998

Torres, Gina (1969-) Bed of Roses 1995; Serenity 2005

Torres (1), José Death Rides a Horse 1967; Django, Prepare a Coffin 1968

Torres, Liz (1947-) Rescue Me 1991; Storm Chasers: Revenge of the Twister 1998

Torres, Raquel (1908-1987) White Shadows in the South Seas 1928; Duck Soup 1933

Torreton, Philippe (1965-) L.627 1992; Ca Commence Aujourd'hui 1999; Monsieur N 2003; District 13: Ultimatum 2009; Rebellion 2011

Torry, Guy Ride 1998; The Animal 2001; Don't Say a Word 2001; Hood Rat 2001

Torvay, José aka **Torvay, Jose** aka **Torvay, José I** (?-1973) The Treasure of the Sierra Madre 1947; Borderline 1950; The Brave Bulls 1951; The Hitch-Hiker 1953; Green Fire 1954; Bandido 1956; Battle Shock 1956

Tosar, Luis (1971-) Mondays in the Sun 2002; Take My Eyes 2003; Miami Vice 2006; The Limits of Control 2008; Cell 211 2009; Even the Rain 2010; Mr Nice 2010; Sleep Tight 2011; ma ma 2015

Toto (1898-1967) Gold of Naples 1954; Big Deal on Madonna Street 1958; Hawks and Sparrows 1966

Tottenham, Merle (1901-1959) Night Must Fall 1937; Bank Holiday 1938; Room to Let 1949

Totter, Audrey (1917-2013) The Sailor Takes a Wife 1945; The Postman Always Rings Twice 1946; The Beginning or the End 1947; High Wall 1947; Lady in the Lake 1947; The Unsuspected 1947; The Saxon Charm 1948; Alias Nick Beal 1949; Any Number Can Play 1949; The Set-Up 1949; Tension 1949; The Blue Veil 1951; Assignment - Paris 1952; The Woman They Almost Lynched 1953; A Bullet for Joey 1955; Women's Prison 1955; Jet Attack 1958

Toub, Shaun The Nativity Story 2006; The Kite Runner 2007; Iron Man 2008; War Dogs 2016

Touliatos, George (1929-) Heavy Metal 1981; Lena: My 100 Children 1987; Avenging Angelo 2002

Toumanova, Tamara (1919-1996) Days of Glory 1944; Tonight We Sing 1953; Deep in My Heart 1954; Invitation to the Dance 1956; Torn Curtain 1966; The Private Life of Sherlock Holmes 1970

Toussaint, Lorraine (1960-) Breaking In 1989; Sad Inheritance 1993

Toussaint, Steve Dog Eat Dog 2000; Shooting Dogs 2005; Flight of Fury 2007

Toutain, Roland (1905-1977) La Règle du Jeu 1939; Eternal Love 1943

Tovey, Roberta (1953-) The Piper's Tune 1962; Dr Who and the Daleks 1965; A High Wind in Jamaica 1965; Daleks - Invasion Earth 2150 AD 1966

Tovey, Russell (1981-) The History Boys 2006; Huge 2009; Grabbers 2012; Tower Block 2012; Blackwood 2013; Moomins on the Riviera 2014

Towb, Harry (1925-2009) The Sleeping Tiger 1954; The Blue Max 1966; All Neat in Black Stockings 1969; Lamb 1985

Towers, Constance (1933-) Bring Your Smile Along 1955; The Horse Soldiers 1959; Sergeant Rutledge 1960; Shock Corridor 1963; The Naked Kiss 1964; Sylvester 1985; The Next Karate Kid 1994

Towles, Tom (1950-2015) Henry: Portrait of a Serial Killer 1986; The Borrower 1989; Night of the Living Dead 1990; Blood In Blood Out 1992; Mad Dog and Glory 1992; Normal Life 1995; Warriors of Virtue 1996

Towne, Robert aka **Wain, Edward** (1936-) The Last Woman on Earth 1960; Creature from the Haunted Sea 1961; Drive, He Said 1971

Townes, Harry (1914-2001) Screaming Mimi 1958; Sanctuary 1961; Fitzwilly 1967; Santee 1973; The Warrior and the Sorceress 1983

Townsend, Colleen (1928-) Chicken Every Sunday 1948; When Willie Comes Marching Home 1950

Townsend, Jill (1945-) Sitting Target 1972; Alfie Darling 1975; The Awakening 1980

Townsend, Patrice Sitting Ducks 1979; Always 1985

Townsend, Robert (1957-) A Soldier's Story 1984; Streets of Fire 1984; American Flyers 1985; Ratboy 1986; Hollywood Shuffle 1987; The Mighty Quinn 1989; The Five Heartbeats 1991; The Meteor Man 1993; Taxman 1998

Townsend, Stanley My Friend Joe 1996; Suzie Gold 2003; Wondrous Oblivion 2003; The Nativity Story 2006

Townsend, Stuart (1972-) Trojan Eddie 1996; Resurrection Man 1997; Shooting Fish 1997; Under the Skin 1997; Simon Magus 1998; The Escort 1999; Wonderland 1999; About Adam 2000; Queen of the Damned 2002; Trapped 2002; The League of Extraordinary Gentlemen 2003; Head in the Clouds 2004; The Best Man 2005

Townshend, Pete (1945-) Jimi Hendrix 1973; The Kids Are Alright 1978; Lambert & Stamp 2014

Toyohara, Kosuke Godzilla vs King Ghidorah 1991; Mr Baseball 1992

Tozzi, Fausto (1921-1978) Constantine and the Cross 1961; The Appointment 1968; The Valachi Papers 1972; The Valdez Horses 1973

Trabaud, Pierre (1922-2005) Le Défroqué 1953; War of the Buttons 1962

Tracey, Ian (1964-) The Keeper 1976; Stakeout 1987; The Last Island 1990; The War between Us 1995; Owning Mahowny 2002; Emile 2003

Trachtenberg, Michelle (1985-) Harriet the Spy 1996; Inspector Gadget 1999; EuroTrip 2004; Mysterious Skin 2004; Ice Princess 2005; Black Christmas 2006; The Circuit 2008; 17

Again 2009; Cop Out 2010; Killing Kennedy 2013

Tracy, Arthur (1899-1997) Limelight 1936; Command Performance 1937

Tracy, Lee (1898-1968) Born Reckless 1930; Blessed Event 1932; Doctor X 1932; The Half Naked Truth 1932; Love Is a Racket 1932; The Strange Love of Molly Louvain 1932; Washington Merry-Go-Round 1932; Blonde Bombshell 1933; Dinner at Eight 1933; The Lemon Drop Kid 1934; Behind the Headlines 1937; Criminal Lawyer 1937; Betrayal from the East 1945; The Best Man 1964

Tracy, Spencer (1900-1967) Up the River 1930; Quick Millions 1931; Six Cylinder Love 1931; Me and My Gal 1932; The Mad Game 1933; Man's Castle 1933; The Power and the Glory 1933; Shanghai Madness 1933; 20,000 Years in Sing Sing 1933; Looking for Trouble 1934; Marie Galante 1934; Dante's Inferno 1935; Murder Man 1935; Whipsaw 1935; Fury 1936; Libeled Lady 1936; Riffraff 1936; San Francisco 1936; Big City 1937; Captains Courageous 1937; Mannequin 1937; They Gave Him a Gun 1937; Boys Town 1938; Test Pilot 1938; Stanley and Livingstone 1939; Boom Town 1940; Edison, the Man 1940; I Take This Woman 1940; Northwest Passage 1940; Dr Jekyll and Mr Hyde 1941; Men of Boys Town 1941; Keeper of the Flame 1942; Tortilla Flat 1942; Woman of the Year 1942; A Guy Named Joe 1944; The Seventh Cross 1944; Thirty Seconds over Tokyo 1944; Without Love 1945; Cass Timberlane 1947; The Sea of Grass 1947; State of the Union 1948; Adam's Rib 1949; Edward, My Son 1949; Malaya 1949; Father of the Bride 1950; Father's Little Dividend 1951; The People against O'Hara 1951; Pat and Mike 1952; The Actress 1953; Broken Lance 1954; Bad Day at Black Rock 1955; The Mountain 1956; Desk Set 1957; The Last Hurrah 1958; The Old Man and the Sea 1958; Inherit the Wind 1960; The Devil at Four o'Clock 1961; Judgment at Nuremberg 1961; How the West Was Won 1962; It's a Mad Mad Mad Mad World 1963; Guess Who's Coming to Dinner 1967

Tracy, William (1917-1967) The Shop around the Corner 1940; Strike Up the Band 1940; Mr and Mrs Smith 1941; Tobacco Road 1941; George Washington Slept Here 1942; To the Shores of Tripoli 1942

Train, Jack (1902-1966) It's That Man Again 1942; King Arthur Was a Gentleman 1942; Miss London Ltd 1943

Trainor, Mary Ellen (1950-2015) Romancing the Stone 1984; Wings of the Apache 1990; Little Giants 1994; Congo 1995

Trammell, Sam Wrestling with Alligators 1998; The Fault in Our Stars 2014

Tran Nu Yen-Khe (1965-) The Scent of Green Papaya 1993; Cyclo 1995; At the Height of Summer 1999

Traubel, Helen (1899-1972) Deep in My Heart 1954; The Ladies' Man 1961

Traue, Antje Pandorum 2009; Despite the Falling Snow 2016

Travanti, Daniel J (1940-) St Ives 1976; Adam 1983; Midnight Crossing 1988; Fellow Traveller 1989; Millennium 1989; Just Cause 1995

Travers, Bill (1922-1994) The Browning Version 1951; Hindle Wakes 1952; Counterspy 1953; The Square Ring 1953; Street of Shadows 1953; Romeo and Juliet 1954; Footsteps in the Fog 1955; Geordie 1955; The Barretts of Wimpole Street 1956; Bhowani Junction 1956; The Smallest Show on Earth 1957; Passionate Summer 1958; The Bridal Path 1959; The Green Helmet 1961; Gorgo 1961; Invasion Quartet 1961; Two Living, One Dead 1961; Born Free 1966; Duel at Diablo 1966; An Elephant Called Slowly 1969; Ring of Bright Water 1969; The Belstone Fox 1973

Travers, Henry (1874-1965) The Invisible Man 1933; Reunion in Vienna 1933; Born to Be Bad 1934; After Office Hours 1935; The Sisters 1938; Dark Victory 1939; Dodge City 1939; Remember? 1939; Stanley and Livingstone 1939; You Can't Get Away with Murder 1939; Anne of Windy Poplars 1940; Edison, the Man 1940; Primrose Path 1940; Ball of Fire 1941; High Sierra 1941; The Navy Steps Out 1941; Mrs Miniver 1942; Random Harvest 1942; Shadow of a Doubt 1942; Madame Curie 1943; The Moon Is Down 1943; None Shall Escape 1944; The Bells of St Mary's 1945; The Naughty Nineties 1945; Thrill of a Romance 1945; It's a Wonderful Life 1946; The Yearling 1946

Travers, Linden (1913-2001) Brief Ecstasy 1937; The Last Adventurers 1937; Bank Holiday 1938; The Lady Vanishes 1938; The Ghost Train 1941; South American George 1941; Beware of Pity 1946; The Master of Bankdam 1947; No Orchids for Miss Blandish 1948; The Bad Lord Byron 1949; Christopher Columbus 1949; Don't Ever Leave Me 1949

Travis, June (1914-2008) Ceiling Zero 1935; The Case of the Black Cat 1936; The Star 1953

Travis, Kylie (1970-) Sanctuary 1997; Gia 1998

Travis, Nancy (1961-) Three Men and a Baby 1987; Air America 1990; Internal Affairs 1990; Loose Cannons 1990; Three Men and a Little Lady 1990; Passed Away 1992; So I Married an Axe Murderer 1993; The Vanishing 1993; Greedy 1994; Destiny Turns on the Radio 1995; Fluke 1995; Bogus 1996; To Live For 1999; Auggie Rose 2000; The Sisterhood of the Traveling Pants 2005; The Jane Austen Book Club 2007; Safe Harbor 2009; Pregnancy Pact 2010

Travis, Randy (1959-) Frank and Jesse 1995; Desert Gamble 1996; Black Dog 1998; Fortune Hunters 1999; Texas Rangers 2001

Travis, Richard aka **Travis, Richard "Dick"** (1913-1989) The Man Who Came to Dinner 1941; The Big Shot 1942; Mission to Moscow 1943

Travis, Stacey Hardware 1990; The Super 1991; Only the Strong 1993; Bandits 2001

Travolta, Joey (1952-) Amazon Women on the Moon 1987; Round Trip to Heaven 1992

Travolta, John (1954-) The Devil's Rain 1975; The Boy in the Plastic Bubble 1976; Carrie 1976; Saturday Night Fever 1977; Grease 1978; Moment by Moment 1978; Urban Cowboy 1980; Blow Out 1981; Staying Alive 1983; Two of a Kind 1983; Perfect 1985; Chains of Gold 1989; The Experts 1989; Look Who's Talking 1989; Look Who's Talking Too 1990; Eyes of an Angel 1991; Shout 1991; Look Who's Talking Now! 1993; Pulp Fiction 1994; Get Shorty 1995; White Man's Burden 1995; Broken Arrow 1996; Michael 1996; Phenomenon 1996; Face/Off 1997; Mad City 1997; She's So Lovely 1997; A Civil Action 1998; Primary Colors 1998; The Thin Red Line 1998; The General's Daughter 1999; Battlefield Earth 2000; Domestic Disturbance 2001; Swordfish 2001; Basic 2003; Ladder 49 2004; A Love Song for Bobby Long 2004; The Punisher 2004; Be Cool 2005; Lonely Hearts 2006; Hairspray 2007; Wild Hogs 2007; Bolt 2008; Old Dogs 2009; The Taking of Pelham 123 2009; From Paris with Love 2010; Savages 2012; Killing Season 2013; In a Valley of Violence 2016

Traylor, Susan Sleep with Me 1994; Greenberg 2009

Treacher, Arthur (1894-1975) Anything Goes 1936; Satan Met a Lady 1936; Stowaway 1936; Thank You, Jeeves 1936; Heidi 1937; Step Lively, Jeeves 1937; Thin Ice 1937; You Can't Have Everything 1937; Mad about Music 1938; My Lucky Star 1938; The Little Princess 1939; Irene 1940; The Amazing Mrs Holliday 1943; Abbott and Costello in Society 1944; National Velvet 1944; Slave Girl 1947; The Countess of Monte Cristo 1948; Mary Poppins 1964

Treacy, Emerson (1900-1967) California Straight Ahead 1937; The Prowler 1951

Treadaway, Harry (1984-) Brothers of the Head 2005; Control 2007; City of Ember 2008; The Disappeared 2008; Fish Tank 2009; Albatross 2011; Cockneys vs Zombies 2011; Honeymoon 2014

Treadaway, Luke (1984-) Brothers of the Head 2005; Do99ing: a Love Story 2009; Heartless 2009; Attack the Block 2010; You Instead 2011; The Rise 2012; Unbroken 2014

Trebor, Robert Out of the Darkness 1985; 52 Pick-Up 1986; My Demon Lover 1987

Tree, David (1915-2009) Knight without Armour 1937; The Return of the Scarlet Pimpernel 1937; The Drum 1938; Pygmalion 1938; French without Tears 1939; Just William 1939; Return to Yesterday 1940; Major Barbara 1941; Don't Look Now 1973

Tree, Dorothy (1906-1992) Here Comes the Navy 1934; The Woman in Red 1935; Sky Murder 1940; Spirit of the People 1940

Treen, Mary aka **Treen, Mary Lou** (1907-1989) They Gave Him a Gun

1937; I Love a Soldier 1944; Let's Live a Little 1948; Room for One More 1952

Tréjan, Guy (1921-2001) Marie Antoinette 1956; La Bête 1975

Trejo, Danny (1944-) From Dusk till Dawn 1995; Anaconda 1997; Point Blank 1997; The Replacement Killers 1998; From Dusk till Dawn II: Texas Blood Money 1999; Animal Factory 2000; From Dusk till Dawn 3: the Hangman's Daughter 2000; Bubble Boy 2001; SPYkids 2001; SPYkids 2: the Island of Lost Dreams 2002; xXx 2002; Once upon a Time in Mexico 2003; The Crow: Wicked Prayer 2005; Lost 2005; Sherrybaby 2006; Renegade Justice 2007; The Line 2008; Machete 2010; Predators 2010; A Very Harold & Kumar 3D Christmas 2011; Machete Kills 2013; Storks 2016

Tremarco, Christine Under the Skin 1997; Hold Back the Night 1999

Tremayne, Les (1913-2003) Francis Goes to West Point 1952; Dream Wife 1953; I Love Melvin 1953; The War of the Worlds 1953; A Man Called Peter 1955; The Unguarded Moment 1956; The Monolith Monsters 1957; The Perfect Furlough 1958; The Angry Red Planet 1959; Say One for Me 1959; The Gallant Hours 1960; Daffy Duck's Movie: Fantastic Island 1983

Tremblay, Jacob (2006-) Before I Wake 2015; Room 2015

Tremblay, Johanne-Marie Jesus of Montreal 1989; Being at Home with Claude 1992; The Barbarian Invasions 2003

Trenker, Luis (1892-1990) The Holy Mountain 1926; The Challenge 1938

Trent, Philip aka **Jones, Clifford** (1907-2001) The Power and the Glory 1933; Tillie and Gus 1933

Trepa, Ricardo (1972-) Belle Toujours 2006; Eccentricities of a Blonde-Haired Girl 2009

Trese, Adam (1969-) Laws of Gravity 1992; Palookaville 1995; The Underneath 1995; illtown 1996; Polish Wedding 1998; Silent House 2011

Treves, Frederick (1925-2012) Paper Mask 1990; Mad Dogs and Englishmen 1994

Treviño, Jorge aka **Trevino, George** Captain Scarlett 1953; The Brave One 1956

Trevor, Austin (1897-1978) Lord Edgware Dies 1934; The Silent Passenger 1935; As You Like It 1936; Dark Journey 1937; Knight without Armour 1937; Under Your Hat 1940; Champagne Charlie 1944; To Paris with Love 1954; Horrors of the Black Museum 1959; Konga 1960; The Day the Earth Caught Fire 1961

Trevor, Claire (1909-2000) The Mad Game 1933; Baby, Take a Bow 1934; Black Sheep 1935; Dante's Inferno 1935; Human Cargo 1936; Dead End 1937; The Amazing Dr Clitterhouse 1938; The First Rebel 1939; Stagecoach 1939; Dark Command 1940; Honky Tonk 1941; Texas 1941; Crossroads 1942; The Desperadoes 1943; Farewell My Lovely 1944; Johnny Angel 1945; Crack-Up 1946; Lady of Deceit 1947; The Babe Ruth Story 1948; Key Largo 1948; Raw Deal 1948; The Velvet Touch 1948; Borderline 1950; Best of the Badmen 1951; Hard, Fast and Beautiful 1951; Hoodlum Empire 1952; Stop, You're Killing Me 1952; The High and the Mighty 1954; Lucy Gallant 1955; Man without a Star 1955; The Mountain 1956; Marjorie Morningstar 1958; Two Weeks in Another Town 1962; The Stripper 1963; How to Murder Your Wife 1965; Kiss Me Goodbye 1982

Trevor, Jack (1893-1976) Secrets of a Soul 1926; Champagne 1928; Crisis 1928

Trevor, Spencer (1875-1945) The Return of Bulldog Drummond 1934; The Life and Death of Colonel Blimp 1943

Trickett, Vicki (1938-) Pepe 1960; The Three Stooges Meet Hercules 1962

Trieste, Leopoldo (1917-2003) The White Sheik 1951; I Vitelloni 1953; Divorce - Italian Style 1961; The Starmaker 1994

Trifunovic, Sergej (1972-) Lovers 1999; A Serbian Film 2010

Trigger, Sarah (1968-) Kid 1990; Bill & Ted's Bogus Journey 1991; PCU 1994

Trinca, Jasmine (1981-) The Son's Room 2001; Romanzo Criminale 2005; The Caiman 2006; House of Tolerance 2011; The Gunman 2015

Trinder, Tommy (1909-1989) Sailors Three 1940; The Foreman Went to France 1941; The Bells Go Down 1943; Champagne Charlie 1944; Fiddlers Three 1944; Bitter Springs 1950; The Beauty Jungle 1964; Barry McKenzie Holds His Own 1974

Trintignant, Jean-Louis (1930-) *And God Created Woman* 1956; *Les Liaisons Dangereuses* 1959; *The Seven Deadly Sins* 1961; *The Easy Life* 1962; *The Sleeping Car Murders* 1965; *Un Homme et une Femme* 1966; *Trans-Europ-Express* 1966; *The Great Silence* 1967; *Les Biches* 1968; *Z* 1968; *My Night with Maud* 1969; *The Conformist* 1970; *And Hope to Live* 1972; *The Last Train* 1972; *The Outside Man* 1973; *Police Story* 1975; *Je Vous Aime* 1980; *Le Grand Pardon* 1981; *Confidentially Yours* 1983; *La Nuit de Varennes* 1983; *Under Fire* 1983; *Rendez-vous* 1985; *A Man and a Woman: 20 Years Later* 1986; *Merci la Vie* 1991; *See How They Fall* 1993; *Three Colours Red* 1994; *A Self-Made Hero* 1995; *Those Who Love Me Can Take the Train* 1998; *Amour* 2012

Trintignant, Marie (1962-2003) *Une Affaire de Femmes* 1988; *Wings of Fame* 1990; *Wild Target* 1993; *Les Apprentis* 1995; *News from the Good Lord* 1996; *Ponette* 1996; *Portraits Chinois* 1996

Tripp, Louis (1974-) *The Gate* 1987; *Gate II* 1992

Tripplehorn, Jeanne (1963-) *Basic Instinct* 1992; *The Firm* 1993; *The Night We Never Met* 1993; *Waterworld* 1995; *Noose* 1997; *Old Man* 1997; *Sliding Doors* 1997; *'Til There Was You* 1997; *Very Bad Things* 1998; *Mickey Blue Eyes* 1999; *Timecode* 1999; *Relative Values* 2000; *Swept Away* 2002; *The Moguls* 2005; *Grey Gardens* 2009

Triska, Jan (1936-) *Elementary School* 1991; *Ronin* 1998; *Lunacy* 2005

Trissenaar, Elisabeth (1944-) *Bolwieser* 1977; *In a Year of 13 Moons* 1978; *Berlin Alexanderplatz* 1980

Tristan, Dorothy (1942-) *End of the Road* 1970; *Klute* 1971; *Scarecrow* 1973; *Fear on Trial* 1975; *Rollercoaster* 1977

Troisi, Massimo (1953-1994) *Hotel Colonial* 1987; *Il Postino* 1994

Troncoso, César *El Baño del Papa* 2007; *XXY* 2007

Troughton, David (1950-) *The Chain* 1984; *Dance with a Stranger* 1984; *Captain Jack* 1998; *Chicklit* 2016

Troughton, Patrick (1920-1987) *Chance of a Lifetime* 1950; *The Black Knight* 1954; *The Moonraker* 1957; *The Black Torment* 1964; *The Gorgon* 1964; *The Viking Queen* 1967; *The Scars of Dracula* 1970; *Frankenstein and the Monster from Hell* 1973; *The Omen* 1976; *Sinbad and the Eye of the Tiger* 1977

Troughton, Sam *Sylvia* 2003; *Spirit Trap* 2004

Trowbridge, Charles (1882-1967) *Nancy Drew - Detective* 1938; *Great Guns* 1941; *The Great Lie* 1941; *Tarzan and the Huntress* 1947; *The Paleface* 1948

Troyer, Verne (1969-) *Austin Powers: the Spy Who Shagged Me* 1999; *Austin Powers in Goldmember* 2002; *The Love Guru* 2008; *The Imaginarium of Doctor Parnassus* 2009; *Keith Lemon: the Film* 2012

Trubshawe, Michael (1905-1985) *They Were Not Divided* 1950; *Brandy for the Parson* 1951; *Operation Snatch* 1962

True, Jim *Singles* 1992; *The Hudsucker Proxy* 1994; *Normal Life* 1995; *Affliction* 1997

True, Rachel (1965-) *The Craft* 1996; *Nowhere* 1997; *Half-Baked* 1998; *Groove* 2000

Trueman, Paula (1900-1994) *Crime without Passion* 1934; *The Outlaw Josey Wales* 1976

Truex, Ernest (1890-1973) *The Adventures of Marco Polo* 1938; *His Girl Friday* 1939; *Christmas in July* 1940; *The Crystal Ball* 1943; *The Girl from Manhattan* 1948; *Fluffy* 1965

Truffaut, François (1932-1984) *L'Enfant Sauvage* 1970; *Anne and Muriel* 1971; *Day for Night* 1973; *Close Encounters of the Third Kind* 1977; *The Green Room* 1978; *Hitchcock Truffaut* 2015

Trujillo, Raoul (1955-) *Scanners II: The New Order* 1991; *Highlander III: the Sorcerer* 1995; *The New World* 2005

Truman, Ralph (1900-1977) *The Saint in London* 1939; *Henry V* 1944; *Mr Perrin and Mr Traill* 1948; *Oliver Twist* 1948; *Eureka Stockade* 1949; *Treasure Island* 1950; *The Golden Coach* 1953; *Malta Story* 1953; *The Night My Number Came Up* 1955; *The Ship That Died of Shame* 1955; *The Black Tent* 1956; *The Long Arm* 1956; *The Man Who Knew Too Much* 1956; *El Cid* 1961

Trump, Donald (1946-) *The Pickle* 1993; *The Little Rascals* 1994; *A Dangerous Game* 2014

Trundy, Natalie (1940-) *The Careless Years* 1957; *Escape from the Planet of the Apes* 1971; *Conquest of the Planet of the Apes* 1972; *Battle for the Planet of the Apes* 1973; *Huckleberry Finn* 1974

Tryon, Tom (1926-1991) *Three Violent People* 1956; *The Unholy Wife* 1957; *I Married a Monster from Outer Space* 1958; *The Story of Ruth* 1960; *The Longest Day* 1962; *Moon Pilot* 1962; *The Cardinal* 1963; *The Glory Guys* 1965; *In Harm's Way* 1965; *Winchester '73* 1967

Tsai Chin (1937-) *The Face of Fu Manchu* 1965; *Invasion* 1965; *The Vengeance of Fu Manchu* 1967; *The Blood of Fu Manchu* 1968; *The Castle of Fu Manchu* 1968; *The Virgin Soldiers* 1969; *The Joy Luck Club* 1993; *Memoirs of a Geisha* 2005

Tsang, Eric aka **Tsang, Eric Chi Wai** (1953-) *Eat a Bowl of Tea* 1989; *The Accidental Spy* 2001; *Infernal Affairs* 2002; *Infernal Affairs II* 2003; *Infernal Affairs 3* 2003

Tsang, Kenneth (1938-) *The Killer* 1989; *The Replacement Killers* 1998; *Die Another Day* 2002; *Memoirs of a Geisha* 2005

Tschechowa, Olga (1897-1980) *Moulin Rouge* 1928; *Liebelei* 1932

Tse, Nicholas (1980-) *A Man Called Hero* 1999; *Time and Tide* 2000; *New Police Story* 2004; *Shaolin* 2011

Tsu, Irene (1910-1989) *Paradise, Hawaiian Style* 1966; *Paper Tiger* 1974; *Snapdragon* 1993

Tsuchiya, Yoshio (1927-) *Red Beard* 1965; *Destroy All Monsters* 1968

Tsuda, Kanji *The Grudge: Ju-On* 2003; *Tokyo Sonata* 2008; *Guilty of Romance* 2011

Tsukamoto, Shinya (1960-) *Tetsuo: the Iron Man* 1989; *Tetsuo II: Body Hammer* 1991; *Tokyo Fist* 1995; *Ichi the Killer* 2001; *A Snake of June* 2002; *Marebito* 2004

Tsukasa, Yoko (1934-) *Late Autumn* 1960; *The End of Summer* 1961; *Rebellion* 1967

Tsumabuki, Satoshi *Villain* 2010; *The Assassin* 2015

Tubb, Barry (1963-) *The Legend of Billie Jean* 1985; *Top Gun* 1986

Tubbs, William (1909-1953) *Paisà* 1946; *The Wages of Fear* 1953

Tucci, Christine *K-911* 1999; *Straight from the Heart* 2003

Tucci, Stanley (1960-) *Monkey Shines* 1988; *Fear, Anxiety, and Depression* 1989; *Slaves of New York* 1989; *Men of Respect* 1990; *Beethoven* 1992; *The Public Eye* 1992; *The Pelican Brief* 1993; *Undercover Blues* 1993; *Kiss of Death* 1994; *Somebody to Love* 1994; *Jury Duty* 1995; *Sex and the Other Man* 1995; *Big Night* 1996; *The Alarmist* 1997; *Deconstructing Harry* 1997; *The Eighteenth Angel* 1997; *Montana* 1997; *The Daytrippers* 1997; *The Impostors* 1998; *In Too Deep* 1999; *A Midsummer Night's Dream* 1999; *Sidewalks of New York* 2000; *America's Sweethearts* 2001; *Conspiracy* 2001; *Big Trouble* 2002; *The Core* 2002; *Maid in Manhattan* 2002; *Road to Perdition* 2002; *The Life and Death of Peter Sellers* 2003; *Shall We Dance* 2004; *The Terminal* 2004; *Robots* 2005; *The Devil Wears Prada* 2006; *The Hoax* 2006; *Lucky Number Slevin* 2006; *Four Last Songs* 2007; *What Just Happened?* 2007; *Space Chimps* 2008; *Swing Vote* 2008; *Julie & Julia* 2009; *The Lovely Bones* 2009; *Space Chimps 2: Zartog Strikes Back* 2009; *Burlesque* 2010; *Easy A* 2010; *Magic Trip: Ken Kesey's Search for a Kool Place* 2011; *Margin Call* 2011; *The Company You Keep* 2012; *Gambit* 2012; *The Hunger Games* 2012; *The Fifth Estate* 2013; *Jack the Giant Slayer* 2013; *Mr Peabody & Sherman* 2013; *The Wind Rises* 2013; *The Hunger Games: Mockingjay Part 1* 2014; *A Little Chaos* 2014; *Transformers: Age of Extinction* 2014; *Wild Card* 2014; *Spotlight* 2015

Tuck, Jessica (1963-) *Secretary* 2001; *A Decent Proposal* 2006

Tucker, Chris (1972-) *Dead Presidents* 1995; *Friday* 1995; *The Fifth Element* 1997; *Money Talks* 1997; *Rush Hour* 1998; *Rush Hour 2* 2001; *Rush Hour 3* 2007; *Silver Linings Playbook* 2012

Tucker, Forrest (1919-1986) *The Westerner* 1940; *Keeper of the Flame* 1942; *Never Say Goodbye* 1946; *The Yearling* 1946; *Coroner Creek* 1948; *The Plunderers* 1948; *Sands of Iwo Jima* 1949; *Warpath* 1951; *Bugles in the Afternoon* 1952; *Flaming Feather* 1952; *Hoodlum Empire* 1952; *Hurricane Smith* 1952; *Pony Express* 1953; *Trouble in the Glen* 1954; *Break in the Circle* 1955; *Rage at Dawn* 1955; *Three Violent People* 1956; *The Abominable Snowman* 1957; *The Deerslayer* 1957; *The Strange World of Planet X* 1957;

Auntie Mame 1958; *Fort Massacre* 1958; *The Trollenberg Terror* 1958; *The Night They Raided Minsky's* 1968; *Barquero* 1970; *Chisum* 1970; *Cancel My Reservation* 1972; *Thunder Run* 1986

Tucker, Joe *Career Girls* 1997; *Lava* 2000; *Outlanders* 2006; *Bronson* 2008

Tucker, Jonathan (1982-) *Stolen Hearts* 1996; *The Deep End* 2001; *The Texas Chainsaw Massacre* 2003; *Criminal* 2004; *Hostage* 2004; *Pulse* 2006; *In the Valley of Elah* 2007; *The Ruins* 2008

Tucker, Michael (1944-) *Eyes of Laura Mars* 1978; *Radio Days* 1987; *Checking Out* 1988; *Day One* 1989; *For Love or Money* 1993; *D2: the Mighty Ducks* 1994; *Taken Away* 1996

Tucker, Richard (1884-1942) *The Jazz Singer* 1927; *The Bat Whispers* 1930; *Manslaughter* 1930; *The Plot Thickens* 1936

Tucker, Sophie (1884-1966) *Broadway Melody of 1938* 1937; *Thoroughbreds Don't Cry* 1937; *Follow the Boys* 1944; *The Joker Is Wild* 1957

Tudor-Pole, Edward *Kull the Conqueror* 1997; *GamerZ* 2005

Tudyk, Alan (1971-) *28 Days* 2000; *A Knight's Tale* 2001; *I, Robot* 2004; *Serenity* 2005; *Death at a Funeral* 2007; *Knocked Up* 2007; *3:10 to Yuma* 2007; *Tucker and Dale vs Evil* 2009; *Wreck-It Ralph* 2012; *42* 2013; *Premature* 2014; *Oddball and the Penguins* 2015; *Trumbo* 2015

Tufts, Sonny (1911-1970) *Government Girl* 1943; *So Proudly We Hail* 1943; *Here Come the Waves* 1944; *I Love a Soldier* 1944; *Bring On the Girls* 1945; *Miss Susie Slagle's* 1945; *The Virginian* 1946; *The Well Groomed Bride* 1946; *Blaze of Noon* 1947; *Variety Girl* 1947; *Easy Living* 1949; *Gift Horse* 1951; *The Seven Year Itch* 1955; *Come Next Spring* 1956

Tukur, Ulrich (1957-) *My Mother's Courage* 1995; *Taking Sides* 2001; *Amen.* 2002; *Solaris* 2002; *The Lives of Others* 2006; *The North Face* 2008; *Séraphine* 2008; *City of War: the Story of John Rabe* 2009; *The White Ribbon* 2009

Tulasne, Patricia *Martyrs* 2008; *I Killed My Mother* 2009

Tully, Tom (1908-1982) *Destination Tokyo* 1943; *Northern Pursuit* 1943; *I'll Be Seeing You* 1944; *Secret Command* 1944; *Adventure* 1945; *Kiss and Tell* 1945; *Till the End of Time* 1946; *Intrigue* 1947; *Killer McCoy* 1947; *Lady in the Lake* 1947; *Blood on the Moon* 1948; *June Bride* 1948; *Rachel and the Stranger* 1948; *A Kiss for Corliss* 1949; *Branded* 1950; *Where the Sidewalk Ends* 1950; *Love Is Better than Ever* 1951; *Tomahawk* 1951; *The Jazz Singer* 1952; *Ruby Gentry* 1952; *The Turning Point* 1952; *The Moon Is Blue* 1953; *Trouble along the Way* 1953; *Arrow in the Dust* 1954; *The Caine Mutiny* 1954; *Love Me or Leave Me* 1955; *Ten North Frederick* 1958; *The Wackiest Ship in the Army* 1961; *The Carpetbaggers* 1964; *Coogan's Bluff* 1968

Tunc, Irène (1938-1972) *Léon Morin, Priest* 1961; *Vivre pour Vivre* 1967; *La Chamade* 1968

Tung, Bill (1934-2006) *Police Story* 1985; *Police Story 2* 1986; *Jackie Chan's First Strike* 1996; *Rumble in the Bronx* 1996

Tunina, Galina *Night Watch* 2004; *Day Watch* 2006

Tunney, Robin (1972-) *California Man* 1992; *Empire Records* 1995; *The Craft* 1996; *Julian Po* 1997; *Montana* 1997; *Niagara Niagara* 1997; *End of Days* 1999; *Supernova* 2000; *Vertical Limit* 2000; *The In-Laws* 2003; *The Secret Lives of Dentists* 2003; *Paparazzi* 2004; *Hollywoodland* 2006; *The Burning Plain* 2008; *The Two Mr Kissels* 2008

Tupou, Manu (1935-2004) *The Extraordinary Seaman* 1969; *A Man Called Horse* 1970; *The Castaway Cowboy* 1974

Turco, Paige (1965-) *Teenage Mutant Ninja Turtles II: the Secret of the Ooze* 1991; *Teenage Mutant Ninja Turtles III* 1992; *Dead Funny* 1995; *The Stepfather* 2009

Turgeon, Peter (1919-2000) *Muscle Beach Party* 1964; *Last Summer* 1969

Turgoose, Thomas *This Is England* 2006; *Eden Lake* 2008; *Somers Town* 2008; *The Scouting Book for Boys* 2009

Turkel, Ann (1942-) *Paper Lion* 1968; *99 and 44/100% Dead* 1974; *The Cassandra Crossing* 1976; *Golden Rendezvous* 1977; *Monster* 1980

Turkel, Joe aka **Turkel, Joseph** (1927-) *Paths of Glory* 1957; *The Shining* 1980

Turman, Glynn (1946-) *A Hero Ain't Nothin' but a Sandwich* 1978; *Buffalo Soldiers* 1997; *Sahara* 2005

Turnbull, John (1880-1956) *Lord Edgware Dies* 1934; *The Passing of the Third Floor Back* 1935; *The Amazing Quest of Ernest Bliss* 1936; *Song of the Road* 1937; *Spare a Copper* 1940; *Daybreak* 1946

Turner, Aidan *The Hobbit: the Desolation of Smaug* 2013; *Loving Vincent* 2016

Turner, Bree *Firehouse Dog* 2006; *Just My Luck* 2006; *The Ugly Truth* 2009

Turner, Fred (1858-1923) *The Escape* 1914; *Intolerance* 1916

Turner, Guinevere (1968-) *Go Fish* 1994; *Chasing Amy* 1996; *The Watermelon Woman* 1996; *Preaching to the Perverted* 1997

Turner, Ike (1931-2007) *Gimme Shelter* 1970; *Taking Off* 1971

Turner, Janine (1963-) *Monkey Shines* 1988; *The Ambulance* 1990; *Cliffhanger* 1993; *Leave It to Beaver* 1997; *Fatal Error* 1999; *A Secret Affair* 1999

Turner, Jim *Shelf Life* 1993; *Joe's Apartment* 1996; *Bewitched* 2005

Turner, John (1932-) *Petticoat Pirates* 1961; *The Black Torment* 1964; *Captain Nemo and the Underwater City* 1969

Turner, Kathleen (1954-) *Body Heat* 1981; *The Man with Two Brains* 1983; *A Breed Apart* 1984; *Crimes of Passion* 1984; *Romancing the Stone* 1984; *The Jewel of the Nile* 1985; *Prizzi's Honor* 1985; *Peggy Sue Got Married* 1986; *Dear America: Letters Home from Vietnam* 1987; *Julia and Julia* 1987; *Switching Channels* 1987; *The Accidental Tourist* 1988; *Who Framed Roger Rabbit* 1988; *The War of the Roses* 1989; *VI Warshawski* 1991; *House of Cards* 1993; *Undercover Blues* 1993; *Naked in New York* 1994; *Serial Mom* 1994; *Moonlight and Valentino* 1995; *The Real Blonde* 1997; *A Simple Wish* 1997; *Legalese* 1998; *Baby Geniuses* 1999; *The Virgin Suicides* 1999; *Beautiful* 2000; *Monster House* 2006; *Marley & Me* 2008; *Dumb and Dumber To* 2014

Turner, Lana (1920-1995) *The Great Garrick* 1937; *They Won't Forget* 1937; *The Adventures of Marco Polo* 1938; *Dramatic School* 1938; *Love Finds Andy Hardy* 1938; *Calling Dr Kildare* 1939; *Dancing Co-Ed* 1939; *Dr Jekyll and Mr Hyde* 1941; *Honky Tonk* 1941; *Johnny Eager* 1941; *Ziegfeld Girl* 1941; *Somewhere I'll Find You* 1942; *Slightly Dangerous* 1943; *Marriage Is a Private Affair* 1944; *Keep Your Powder Dry* 1945; *Week-End at the Waldorf* 1945; *The Postman Always Rings Twice* 1946; *Cass Timberlane* 1947; *Green Dolphin Street* 1947; *Homecoming* 1948; *The Three Musketeers* 1948; *A Life of Her Own* 1950; *Mr Imperium* 1951; *The Bad and the Beautiful* 1952; *The Merry Widow* 1952; *Latin Lovers* 1953; *Betrayed* 1954; *Diane* 1955; *The Prodigal* 1955; *The Rains of Ranchipur* 1955; *The Sea Chase* 1955; *Peyton Place* 1957; *Another Time, Another Place* 1958; *The Lady Takes a Flyer* 1958; *Imitation of Life* 1959; *Portrait in Black* 1960; *Bachelor in Paradise* 1961; *By Love Possessed* 1961; *Who's Got the Action?* 1962; *The Love Goddesses* 1965; *Love Has Many Faces* 1965; *Madame X* 1966; *The Big Cube* 1969; *Persecution* 1974; *Bittersweet Love* 1976; *Witches' Brew* 1979

Turner, Tim (1924-1987) *Police Dog* 1955; *Grip of the Strangler* 1958

Turner, Tina (1939-) *Gimme Shelter* 1970; *Taking Off* 1971; *Tommy* 1975; *Mad Max beyond Thunderdome* 1985

Turner, Tyrin *Menace II Society* 1993; *Panther* 1995; *Belly* 1998

Turpin, Ben (1874-1940) *His New Job* 1915; *Make Me a Star* 1932; *Saps at Sea* 1940

Turturro, Aida (1962-) *True Love* 1989; *Jersey Girl* 1992; *Angie* 1994; *Denise Calls Up* 1995; *Woo* 1998; *Romance & Cigarettes* 2004

Turturro, John (1957-) *Desperately Seeking Susan* 1985; *To Live and Die in LA* 1985; *The Color of Money* 1986; *Gung Ho* 1986; *Off Beat* 1986; *Five Corners* 1987; *The Sicilian* 1987; *Catchfire* 1989; *Do the Right Thing* 1989; *Men of Respect* 1990; *Miller's Crossing* 1990; *State of Grace* 1990; *Barton Fink* 1991; *Jungle Fever* 1991; *Brain Donors* 1992; *Mac* 1992; *Fearless* 1993; *Being Human* 1994; *Erotic Tales* 1994; *Quiz Show* 1994; *Clockers* 1995; *Search and Destroy* 1995; *Unstrung Heroes* 1995; *Box of Moonlight* 1996;

Girl 6 1996; *Grace of My Heart* 1996; *The Big Lebowski* 1997; *The Truce* 1997; *He Got Game* 1998; *Rounders* 1998; *Cradle Will Rock* 1999; *Summer of Sam* 1999; *Company Man* 2000; *The Luzhin Defence* 2000; *The Man Who Cried* 2000; *Monkeybone* 2000; *O Brother, Where Art Thou?* 2000; *Collateral Damage* 2001; *Thirteen Conversations about One Thing* 2001; *Fear X* 2002; *Mr Deeds* 2002; *Anger Management* 2003; *Secret Window* 2004; *She Hate Me* 2004; *A Few Days in September* 2006; *The Good Shepherd* 2006; *Margot at the Wedding* 2007; *Transformers* 2007; *What Just Happened?* 2007; *You Don't Mess with the Zohan* 2008; *The Taking of Pelham 123* 2009; *Transformers: Revenge of the Fallen* 2009; *The Nutcracker in 3D* 2009; *Transformers: Dark of the Moon* 2011; *Fading Gigolo* 2013; *Exodus: Gods and Kings* 2014; *God's Pocket* 2014; *Mia Madre* 2015

Turturro, Nicholas aka **Turturro, Nick** (1962-) *Federal Hill* 1994; *Freefall: Flight 174* 1995; *Shadow Conspiracy* 1996; *Excess Baggage* 1997; *The Hillside Strangler* 2004; *Three Wise Guys* 2005

Tushingham, Rita (1940-) *A Taste of Honey* 1961; *Girl with Green Eyes* 1963; *The Leather Boys* 1963; *A Place to Go* 1963; *Doctor Zhivago* 1965; *The Knack... and How to Get It* 1965; *The Trap* 1966; *Smashing Time* 1967; *Diamonds for Breakfast* 1968; *The Bed Sitting Room* 1969; *The Guru* 1969; *The Human Factor* 1975; *A Judgement in Stone* 1986; *Resurrected* 1989; *Paper Marriage* 1991; *An Awfully Big Adventure* 1994; *The Boy from Mercury* 1996; *Under the Skin* 1997; *Swing* 1998; *Being Julia* 2004; *Puffball* 2006; *The Calling* 2009; *Outside Bet* 2011

Tutin, Dorothy (1930-2001) *The Importance of Being Earnest* 1952; *The Beggar's Opera* 1953; *A Tale of Two Cities* 1957; *Cromwell* 1970; *Savage Messiah* 1972; *The Shooting Party* 1984; *Agatha Christie's Murder with Mirrors* 1985; *Alive and Kicking* 1996

Tuttle, Lurene (1906-1986) *Goodbye, My Fancy* 1951; *The Whip Hand* 1951; *Don't Bother to Knock* 1952; *Never Wave at a WAC* 1952; *Room for One More* 1952; *The Affairs of Dobie Gillis* 1953; *Niagara* 1953; *Sincerely Yours* 1955; *The Fortune Cookie* 1966

Tweddell, Frank (1895-1971) *The Undercover Man* 1949; *The Tattooed Stranger* 1950

Tweed, Shannon (1957-) *Of Unknown Origin* 1983; *Hot Dog - The Movie* 1984; *Cannibal Women in the Avocado Jungle of Death* 1989; *Never Cry Devil* 1989; *Indecent Behavior* 1993; *Forbidden Sins* 1998; *Power Play* 1998; *Detroit Rock City* 1999; *Dead Sexy* 2001

Twelvetrees, Helen (1907-1958) *Bad Company* 1931; *The Painted Desert* 1931

Twiggy (1949-) *The Boy Friend* 1971; *There Goes the Bride* 1979; *The Blues Brothers* 1980; *The Doctor and the Devils* 1985; *Club Paradise* 1986; *Madame Sousatzka* 1988

Twomey, Anne (1951-) *Deadly Friend* 1986; *Last Rites* 1988; *The Scout* 1994; *Picture Perfect* 1997

Tylack, Paul aka **Tylak, Paul** *The Ugly Duckling and Me* 2006; *The Secret of Kells* 2009

Tyler, Aisha *For One Night* 2006; *Death Sentence* 2007

Tyler, Beverly (1928-2005) *The Green Years* 1946; *My Brother Talks to Horses* 1946; *The Beginning or the End* 1947; *The Fireball* 1950; *The Cimarron Kid* 1951; *The Battle at Apache Pass* 1952; *Chicago Confidential* 1957

Tyler, Liv (1977-) *Silent Fall* 1994; *Empire Records* 1995; *Heavy* 1995; *Stealing Beauty* 1995; *That Thing You Do!* 1996; *Inventing the Abbotts* 1997; *U Turn* 1997; *Armageddon* 1998; *Cookie's Fortune* 1999; *Onegin* 1999; *Plunkett & Macleane* 1999; *Dr T & the Women* 2000; *The Lord of the Rings: The Fellowship of the Ring* 2001; *One Night at McCool's* 2001; *The Lord of the Rings: The Two Towers* 2002; *Jersey Girl* 2003; *The Lord of the Rings: The Return of the King* 2003; *Lonesome Jim* 2005; *Reign over Me* 2007; *The Strangers* 2007; *The Incredible Hulk* 2008; *Super* 2010; *Robot & Frank* 2012

Tyler, Steven *The Polar Express* 2004; *Be Cool* 2005

Tyler, Tom (1903-1954) *The Last Outlaw* 1936; *Law and Order* 1936; *The Mummy's Hand* 1940; *Valley of the Sun* 1942; *Badman's Territory* 1946; *Trail of Robin Hood* 1950

Tyne, George (1917-2008) *A Walk in the Sun* 1945; *They Won't Believe Me*

1947; *Not with My Wife, You Don't!* 1966

Tyner, Charles (1925-) *Harold and Maude* 1972; *Jeremiah Johnson* 1972; *Emperor of the North* 1973; *The Mean Machine* 1974; *Pulse* 1988; *Over Her Dead Body* 1990

Tyrrell, Ann (1909-1983) *Bride for Sale* 1949; *The Glass Menagerie* 1950

Tyrrell, Susan (1945-2012) *Shoot Out* 1971; *Fat City* 1972; *Catch My Soul* 1973; *The Killer inside Me* 1975; *Bad* 1976; *Islands in the Stream* 1976; *Another Man, Another Chance* 1977; *I Never Promised You a Rose Garden* 1977; *September 30, 1955* 1977; *Tales of Ordinary Madness* 1981; *Fast-Walking* 1982; *Liar's Moon* 1982; *Fire and Ice* 1983; *Angel* 1984; *Avenging Angel* 1985; *Flesh + Blood* 1985; *Big Top Pee-wee* 1988; *Cry-Baby* 1989; *Far from Home* 1989; *Motorama* 1991; *Powder* 1995; *Relax... It's Just Sex* 1998; *Buddy Boy* 1999

Tyson, Barbara aka Bush, **Barbara** *Between Friends* 1983; *Ernest Goes to Jail* 1990

Tyson, Cathy (1965-) *Mona Lisa* 1986; *Business as Usual* 1987; *The Serpent and the Rainbow* 1987; *Priest* 1994; *The Old Man Who Read Love Stories* 2000; *Ollie Kepler's Expanding Purple World* 2010

Tyson, Cicely (1933-) *A Man Called Adam* 1966; *The Heart Is a Lonely Hunter* 1968; *Sounder* 1972; *The Autobiography of Miss Jane Pittman* 1974; *The Blue Bird* 1976; *A Hero Ain't Nothin' but a Sandwich* 1978; *Airport '79: the Concorde* 1979; *Bustin' Loose* 1981; *Heat Wave* 1990; *Fried Green Tomatoes at the Whistle Stop Cafe* 1991; *The Road to Galveston* 1996; *Hoodlum* 1997; *A Lesson before Dying* 1999; *Because of Winn-Dixie* 2004; *Idlewild* 2006; *Relative Stranger* 2009; *Alex Cross* 2012

Tyson, Mike (1966-) *Black and White* 1999; *Rocky Balboa* 2006; *Tyson* 2008; *The Hangover* 2009; *The Hangover: Part II* 2011; *I Am Ali* 2014; *Mr Calzaghe* 2015

Tyson, Richard (1961-) *Three o'Clock High* 1987; *Two Moon Junction* 1988; *Kindergarten Cop* 1990; *The Glass Cage* 1996; *Kingpin* 1996; *Desert Thunder* 1998; *Battlefield Earth* 2000; *Firetrap* 2001; *The Trail to Hope Rose* 2004

Tyzack, Margaret (1933-2011) *Ring of Spies* 1963; *2001: a Space Odyssey* 1968; *A Touch of Love* 1969; *The Legacy* 1978; *The Quatermass Conclusion* 1979; *The King's Whore* 1990; *Bright Young Things* 2003; *Mother's Milk* 2012

Ubach, Alanna (1977-) *Denise Calls Up* 1995; *Just Your Luck* 1996; *Clockwatchers* 1997

Udenio, Fabiana (1964-) *Bride of Re-Animator* 1991; *Austin Powers: International Man of Mystery* 1997

Udy, Claudia (1960-) *Savage Dawn* 1985; *Dragonard* 1987

Ulliel, Gaspard (1984-) *Strayed* 2003; *A Very Long Engagement* 2004; *Hannibal Rising* 2006; *The Sea Wall* 2008; *The Princess of Montpensier* 2010; *Saint Laurent* 2014

Ullman, Tracey (1959-) *Give My Regards to Broad Street* 1984; *Plenty* 1985; *Jumpin' Jack Flash* 1986; *I Love You to Death* 1990; *Snow White in Happily Ever After* 1990; *Household Saints* 1993; *Robin Hood: Men in Tights* 1993; *I'll Do Anything* 1994; *Pret-a-Porter* 1994; *Panic* 2000; *Small Time Crooks* 2000; *A Dirty Shame* 2004; *Kronk's New Groove* 2005; *Tim Burton's Corpse Bride* 2005; *The Tale of Despereaux* 2008

Ullmann, Liv (1939-) *Persona* 1966; *The Hour of the Wolf* 1967; *Shame* 1968; *A Passion* 1969; *The Night Visitor* 1970; *Cold Sweat* 1971; *The Emigrants* 1971; *Cries and Whispers* 1972; *The New Land* 1972; *Pope Joan* 1972; *40 Carats* 1973; *Lost Horizon* 1973; *Scenes from a Marriage* 1973; *The Abdication* 1974; *Zandy's Bride* 1974; *Face to Face* 1976; *The Serpent's Egg* 1977; *Autumn Sonata* 1978; *The Wild Duck* 1983; *Bay Boy* 1984; *Dangerous Moves* 1984; *Let's Hope It's a Girl* 1985; *Gaby: a True Story* 1987; *La Amiga* 1988; *The Rose Garden* 1989; *The Ox* 1991; *Saraband* 2003

Ulrich, Jennifer *The Wave* 2008; *We Are the Night* 2010

Ulrich, Lars *Mission to Lars* 2012; *Metallica: Through the Never* 2013

Ulrich, Skeet (1969-) *Boys* 1995; *Albino Alligator* 1996; *The Craft* 1996;

Last Dance 1996; *Scream* 1996; *Touch* 1996; *As Good as It Gets* 1997; *The Newton Boys* 1998; *Chill Factor* 1999; *Ride with the Devil* 1999; *Armored* 2009

Ulyanov, Mikhail (1927-2007) *The Theme* 1979; *Private Life* 1982; *A Private Conversation* 1983

Umbach, Martin (1956-) *Witness in the War Zone* 1986; *The NeverEnding Story II: the Next Chapter* 1991

Umbers, Mark (1973-) *A Good Woman* 2004; *These Foolish Things* 2006

Umeki, Miyoshi (1929-2007) *Sayonara* 1957; *Cry for Happy* 1961; *Flower Drum Song* 1961; *A Girl Named Tamiko* 1962; *The Horizontal Lieutenant* 1962

Umemura, Yoko *Osaka Elegy* 1936; *Sisters of the Gion* 1936; *Story of the Late Chrysanthemums* 1939

Underdown, Edward (1908-1989) *The Brass Monkey* 1948; *They Were Not Divided* 1950; *Voice of Merrill* 1952; *Beat the Devil* 1953; *Street of Shadows* 1953; *The Rainbow Jacket* 1954; *The Camp on Blood Island* 1958; *The Third Alibi* 1961; *The Bay of Saint Michel* 1963; *Dr Terror's House of Horrors* 1964; *The Hand of Night* 1966; *Tarka the Otter* 1978

Underwood, Blair (1964-) *Heat Wave* 1990; *Murder in Mississippi* 1990; *Posse* 1993; *Just Cause* 1995; *Set It Off* 1996; *Soul of the Game* 1996; *Rules of Engagement* 2000; *Full Frontal* 2002; *Malibu's Most Wanted* 2003; *Something New* 2006

Underwood, Jay (1968-) *Desert Bloom* 1985; *The Boy Who Could Fly* 1986; *The Invisible Kid* 1988; *Promised Land* 1988; *Uncle Buck* 1989; *Sleepstalker* 1995; *Afterglow* 1997; *And the Beat Goes On: the Sonny and Cher Story* 1999

Underwood, Loyal (1893-1966) *Shoulder Arms* 1918; *The Pilgrim* 1923

Unel, Birol *Head-On* 2003; *Transylvania* 2006

Unger, Deborah Kara aka Unger, **Deborah** (1966-) *Blood Oath* 1990; *Whispers in the Dark* 1992; *Highlander III: the Sorcerer* 1995; *Crash* 1996; *Keys to Tulsa* 1996; *No Way Home* 1996; *The Game* 1997; *Payback* 1998; *The Hurricane* 1999; *Fear X* 2002; *Leo* 2002; *Emile* 2003; *Stander* 2003; *Thirteen* 2003; *A Love Song for Bobby Long* 2004; *White Noise* 2004; *Silent Hill* 2006; *88 Minutes* 2007; *The Way* 2010; *A Dark Truth* 2012; *Fury* 2012

Unger, Joe (1949-) *Go Tell the Spartans* 1977; *Barfly* 1987; *Leatherface: the Texas Chainsaw Massacre III* 1990

Union, Gabrielle (1973-) *Bring It On* 2000; *Two Can Play That Game* 2001; *Welcome to Collinwood* 2002; *Bad Boys II* 2003; *Cradle 2 the Grave* 2003; *Breakin' All the Rules* 2004; *The Honeymooners* 2005; *Cadillac Records* 2008; *Meet Dave* 2008; *Top Five* 2014

Urabe, Kumeko (1902-1989) *Ikiru* 1952; *Street of Shame* 1955

Urban, Karl (1972-) *Heaven* 1998; *The Truth about Demons* 2000; *The Bourne Supremacy* 2004; *The Chronicles of Riddick* 2004; *Doom* 2005; *Out of the Blue* 2006; *Pathfinder* 2007; *Star Trek* 2009; *Priest* 2010; *Red* 2010; *Dredd* 2012; *Riddick* 2013; *Star Trek into Darkness* 2013; *Walking with Dinosaurs: the 3D Movie* 2013; *Pete's Dragon* 2016; *Star Trek Beyond* 2016

Urbaniak, James (1963-) *Henry Fool* 1997; *American Splendor* 2003

Ure, Mary (1933-1975) *Storm over the Nile* 1955; *Windom's Way* 1957; *Look Back in Anger* 1959; *Sons and Lovers* 1960; *The Mind Benders* 1963; *The Luck of Ginger Coffey* 1964; *Custer of the West* 1967; *Where Eagles Dare* 1969; *A Reflection of Fear* 1973

Urecal, Minerva (1894-1966) *Block Busters* 1944; *Good Sam* 1948

Urich, Robert (1946-2002) *Magnum Force* 1973; *The Ice Pirates* 1984; *Turk 182!* 1985; *Danielle Steel's A Perfect Stranger* 1994; *Miracle on the 17th Green* 1999

Urquhart, Molly (1906-1977) *Geordie* 1955; *House of Mystery* 1961

Urquhart, Robert (1922-1995) *Knights of the Round Table* 1953; *Happy Ever After* 1954; *The Dark Avenger* 1955; *Yangtse Incident* 1956; *The Curse of Frankenstein* 1957; *Dunkirk* 1958; *The Bulldog Breed* 1960; *The Break* 1962; *Murder at the Gallop* 1963; *The Looking Glass War* 1969; *Country Dance* 1970; *P'Tang, Yang, Kipperbang* 1982; *Restless Natives* 1985; *Playing Away* 1986; *The Kitchen Toto* 1987

Urzendowsky, Sebastian *The Counterfeiters* 2007; *Goodbye First Love* 2011

Ustinov, Peter (1921-2004) *Odette* 1950; *Hotel Sahara* 1951; *The Magic Box* 1951; *Le Plaisir* 1951; *Quo Vadis* 1951; *Beau Brummell* 1954; *The Egyptian* 1954; *Lola Montès* 1955; *We're No Angels* 1955; *Les Espions* 1957; *Spartacus* 1960; *The Sundowners* 1960; *Romanoff and Juliet* 1961; *Billy Budd* 1962; *John Goldfarb, Please Come Home* 1964; *Topkapi* 1964; *Lady L* 1965; *Blackbeard's Ghost* 1967; *The Comedians* 1967; *Hot Millions* 1968; *Viva Max!* 1969; *Robin Hood* 1973; *One of Our Dinosaurs Is Missing* 1975; *Logan's Run* 1976; *Treasure of Matecumbe* 1976; *The Last Remake of Beau Geste* 1977; *The Mouse and His Child* 1977; *The Purple Taxi* 1977; *Death on the Nile* 1978; *Tarka the Otter* 1978; *The Thief of Baghdad* 1978; *Ashanti* 1979; *Charlie Chan and the Curse of the Dragon Queen* 1981; *The Great Muppet Caper* 1981; *Evil under the Sun* 1982; *Thirteen at Dinner* 1985; *Agatha Christie's Murder in Three Acts* 1986; *Dead Man's Folly* 1986; *Appointment with Death* 1988; *Lorenzo's Oil* 1992; *Stiff Upper Lips* 1997; *Animal Farm* 1999; *The Bachelor* 1999

Uwais, Iko *The Raid* 2011; *The Raid 2* 2013

Uzuner, Muhammet *Home* 2011; *Once upon a Time in Anatolia* 2011

V

Vaananen, Kari (1953-) *Hamlet Goes Business* 1987; *Leningrad Cowboys Go America* 1989; *Drifting Clouds* 1996

Vaccaro, Brenda (1939-) *Midnight Cowboy* 1969; *I Love My... Wife* 1970; *Going Home* 1971; *Summertree* 1971; *Once Is Not Enough* 1975; *Airport '77* 1977; *Capricorn One* 1978; *Zorro, the Gay Blade* 1981; *Supergirl* 1984; *Water* 1985; *Heart of Midnight* 1988; *Cookie* 1989; *Love Affair* 1994; *The Mirror Has Two Faces* 1996; *Sonny* 2002; *You Don't Know Jack* 2010

Vadell, Jaime *Post Mortem* 2010; *The Club* 2015

Vadim, Annette (1936-2005) *Les Liaisons Dangereuses* 1959; *Blood and Roses* 1960

Vadim, David *Little Odessa* 1994; *Staten Island* 2009

Vadim, Roger (1928-2000) *Le Testament d'Orphée* 1960; *Ciao! Manhattan* 1973; *Into the Night* 1985

Vadis, Dan (1938-1987) *The Scalphunters* 1968; *Cahill, United States Marshal* 1973; *Bronco Billy* 1980

Vail, Lester (1900-1959) *Beau Ideal* 1931; *Consolation Marriage* 1931; *Dance, Fools, Dance* 1931

Vaiance, Holly (1983-) *DOA: Dead or Alive* 2006; *Taken* 2007

Valandrey, Charlotte (1968-) *Rouge Baiser* 1985; *Orlando* 1992

Valberg, Birgitta (1916-2014) *Smiles of a Summer Night* 1955; *The Virgin Spring* 1960; *Shame* 1968

Valcke, Serge-Henri (1946-) *Amsterdamned* 1988; *Il Maestro* 1989; *No Man's Land* 2001

Valderrama, Wilmer *Party Monster* 2003; *Grounded* 2006; *Larry Crowne* 2011

Valdivielso, Maru *The Lovers of the Arctic Circle* 1998; *The Christmas Tale* 2005

Valenska, Paula (1922-) *Bond Street* 1948; *The Gay Adventure* 1949

Valenta, Vladimir (1923-2001) *Closely Observed Trains* 1966; *Sunday in the Country* 1975

Valentin, Barbara (1940-2002) *Fear Eats the Soul* 1974; *Martha* 1973

Valentine, Anthony (1939-2015) *Performance* 1970; *Tower of Evil* 1972; *To the Devil a Daughter* 1976; *Les Enfants de Lumière* 1995; *Two Men Went to War* 2002

Valentine, Karen (1947-) *Hot Lead and Cold Feet* 1978; *Hell's Angels* 1979; *Wedding Daze* 2004

Valentine, Nancy -30- 1959; *Tess of the Storm Country* 1960

Valentine, Paul (1919-2006) *Build My Gallows High* 1947; *House of Strangers* 1949; *Love Happy* 1949; *Something to Live For* 1952

Valentini, Mariella *Volere, Volare* 1991; *Benzina* 2001

Valentino, Rudolph (1895-1926) *Camille* 1921; *The Four Horsemen of the Apocalypse* 1921; *The Sheik* 1921; *Blood and Sand* 1922; *The Eagle* 1925; *The Son of the Sheik* 1926

Valenty, Lili (1900-1987) *Wild Is the Wind* 1957; *Tell Me a Riddle* 1980

Valère, Simone (1923-) *La Beauté du Diable* 1949; *The Game Is Over* 1966; *The Assassination of Trotsky* 1972

Valerie, Joan (1911-1983) *Submarine Patrol* 1938; *Michael Shayne, Private Detective* 1940

Valk, Frederick (1895-1956) *Thunder Rock* 1942; *Hotel Reserve* 1944; *Saraband for Dead Lovers* 1948; *Never Let Me Go* 1953; *Magic Fire* 1956; *Zarak* 1956

Vallée, Marcel (1885-1957) *Paris Qui Dort* 1923; *Caravan* 1934; *Topaze* 1951

Vallee, Rudy (1901-1986) *International House* 1933; *George White's Scandals* 1934; *Second Fiddle* 1939; *Time Out for Rhythm* 1941; *The Palm Beach Story* 1942; *Happy Go Lucky* 1943; *The Bachelor and the Bobby-Soxer* 1947; *I Remember Mama* 1948; *My Dear Secretary* 1948; *So This Is New York* 1948; *Unfaithfully Yours* 1948; *The Beautiful Blonde from Bashful Bend* 1949; *Father Was a Fullback* 1949; *Mother Is a Freshman* 1949; *The Admiral Was a Lady* 1950; *Gentlemen Marry Brunettes* 1955; *How to Succeed in Business without Really Trying* 1967; *Live a Little, Love a Little* 1968

Valletta, Amber (1974-) *What Lies Beneath* 2000; *Hitch* 2005; *The Transporter 2* 2005; *Dead Silence* 2007; *Premonition* 2007; *Gamer* 2008; *The Spy Next Door* 2009

Valli, Alida aka Valli (1921-2006) *We the Living* 1942; *The Paradine Case* 1947; *The Miracle of the Bells* 1948; *The Third Man* 1949; *Walk Softly, Stranger* 1949; *The White Tower* 1950; *The Stranger's Hand* 1953; *Senso* 1954; *Les Bijoutiers du Clair de Lune* 1957; *Il Grido* 1957; *This Angry Age* 1957; *Eyes without a Face* 1959; *The Long Absence* 1961; *The Happy Thieves* 1962; *Ophélia* 1962; *The Castilian* 1963; *The Spider's Stratagem* 1970; *The Flesh of the Orchid* 1974; *1900* 1976; *Suspiria* 1976; *Killer Nun* 1978; *La Luna* 1979; *A Month by the Lake* 1994

Valli, Romolo (1925-1980) *The Leopard* 1962; *The Visit* 1964; *Boom* 1968; *A Fistful of Dynamite* 1971; *The Garden of the Finzi-Continis* 1971; *What?* 1973; *Bobby Deerfield* 1977

Vallin, Rick (1919-1977) *Ghosts in the Night* 1943; *Dangerous Money* 1946; *Comanche Territory* 1950

Vallone, Raf (1916-2002) *Bitter Rice* 1949; *Thérèse Raquin* 1953; *Two Women* 1960; *El Cid* 1961; *Phaedra* 1962; *The Cardinal* 1963; *The Secret Invasion* 1964; *Kiss the Girls and Make Them Die* 1966; *Nevada Smith* 1966; *The Desperate Ones* 1967; *The Italian Job* 1969; *Cannon for Cordoba* 1970; *A Gunfight* 1971; *The Human Factor* 1975; *Rosebud* 1975; *That Lucky Touch* 1975; *The Devil's Advocate* 1977; *The Other Side of Midnight* 1977; *The Greek Tycoon* 1978; *Lion of the Desert* 1981; *The Scarlet and the Black* 1983

Valverde, Maria *King of the Hill* 2007; *Cracks* 2009

Vampira aka Nurmi, Maila (1921-2008) *The Beat Generation* 1959; *Night of the Ghouls* 1959; *Plan 9 from Outer Space* 1959

van Ammelrooy, Willeke (1944-) *Antonia's Line* 1995; *The Lake House* 2006

Van Cleef, Lee (1925-1989) *High Noon* 1952; *Kansas City Confidential* 1952; *The Lawless Breed* 1952; *Untamed Frontier* 1952; *Arena* 1953; *The Bandits of Corsica* 1953; *The Beast from 20,000 Fathoms* 1953; *Tumbleweed* 1953; *Vice Squad* 1953; *Arrow in the Dust* 1954; *Dawn at Socorro* 1954; *Rails into Laramie* 1954; *The Big Combo* 1955; *A Man Alone* 1955; *The Road to Denver* 1955; *Ten Wanted Men* 1955; *Accused of Murder* 1956; *The Conqueror* 1956; *It Conquered the World* 1956; *Pardners* 1956; *Tribute to a Bad Man* 1956; *China Gate* 1957; *Gunfight at the OK Corral* 1957; *The Lonely Man* 1957; *The Tin Star* 1957; *The Bravados* 1958; *Day of the Bad Man* 1958; *The Young Lions* 1958; *Ride Lonesome* 1959; *For a Few Dollars More* 1965; *The Good, the Bad and the Ugly* 1966; *Death Rides a Horse* 1967; *The Good Die First* 1967; *Sabata* 1969; *Barquero* 1970; *El Condor* 1970; *Bad Man's River* 1971; *Captain Apache* 1971; *Return of Sabata* 1971; *The Magnificent Seven Ride!* 1972; *Blood Money* 1974; *Take a Hard Ride* 1975; *God's Gun* 1977; *Kid Vengeance* 1977; *The Octagon* 1980; *Escape from New York* 1981; *Codename Wildgeese* 1984; *Cannonball Fever* 1989

Van Dam, José *Don Giovanni* 1979; *The Music Teacher* 1988

Van Damme, Jean-Claude (1960-) *No Retreat, No Surrender* 1985; *Bloodsport* 1987; *Black Eagle* 1988; *Cyborg* 1989; *Kickboxer* 1989; *AWOL* 1990; *Death Warrant* 1990; *Double*

Impact 1991; *Nowhere to Run* 1992; *Universal Soldier* 1992; *Hard Target* 1993; *Street Fighter* 1994; *Timecop* 1994; *Sudden Death* 1995; *Maximum Risk* 1996; *The Quest* 1996; *Double Team* 1997; *Knock Off* 1998; *Legionnaire* 1998; *Desert Heat* 1999; *Universal Soldier - the Return* 1999; *The Order* 2001; *Replicant* 2001; *Derailed* 2002; *In Hell* 2003; *The Hard Corps* 2006; *Second in Command* 2006; *Until Death* 2007; *JCVD* 2008; *The Shepherd* 2008; *Universal Soldier: Regeneration* 2009; *The Expendables 2* 2012; *Six Bullets* 2012; *Enemies Closer* 2013

van de Ven, Monique (1952-) *Turkish Delight* 1973; *Keetje Tippel* 1975; *The Assault* 1986; *Amsterdamned* 1988

Van Den Driessche, Frédéric aka van den Driessche, Frédéric *A Winter's Tale* 1992; *The Exterminating Angels* 2006

Van Der Beek, James (1977-) *I Love You, I Love You Not* 1997; *Varsity Blues* 1999; *Texas Rangers* 2001; *The Rules of Attraction* 2002; *Laputa: Castle in the Sky* 2003; *Mrs Miracle* 2009; *Taken in Broad Daylight* 2009; *Salem Falls* 2011

van der Boom, Claire *The Square* 2008; *Red Hill* 2010; *Ruth & Alex* 2014; *Chronic* 2015

Van Der Velde, Nadine *Critters* 1986; *Munchies* 1987; *After Midnight* 1989

Van Der Vlis, Diana aka Vandervlis, **Diana** (1935-2001) *The Girl in Black Stockings* 1957; *The Man with the X-Ray Eyes* 1963

Van der Wal, Frederique (1967-) *Two Girls and a Guy* 1997; *Wild Wild West* 1999

Van Devere, Trish (1943-) *Where's Poppa?* 1970; *One Is a Lonely Number* 1972; *The Day of the Dolphin* 1973; *Harry in Your Pocket* 1973; *The Savage Is Loose* 1974; *Movie Movie* 1978; *The Changeling* 1980; *Messenger of Death* 1988

Van Dien, Casper (1968-) *Starship Troopers* 1997; *Tarzan and the Lost City* 1998; *Shark Attack* 1999; *Sleepy Hollow* 1999; *Partners* 2000; *Python* 2000; *Sanctimony* 2000; *Aces 'n' Eights* 2008; *Starship Troopers 3: Marauder* 2008; *The Pact* 2011; *Assumed Killer* 2013

Van Doren, Mamie (1931-) *The All American* 1953; *Francis Joins the WACS* 1954; *Ain't Misbehavin'* 1955; *Star in the Dust* 1956; *The Girl in Black Stockings* 1957; *High School Confidential* 1958; *Teacher's Pet* 1958; *The Beat Generation* 1959; *The Big Operator* 1959; *Born Reckless* 1959; *Girls' Town* 1959; *The Private Lives of Adam and Eve* 1959; *The Navy vs the Night Monsters* 1966; *Voyage to the Planet of Prehistoric Women* 1966; *Slackers* 2001

Van Doude *Love in the Afternoon* 1957; *A Bout de Souffle* 1959; *The Sign of Leo* 1959

Van Dreelen, John (1922-1992) *The Wizard of Baghdad* 1960; *Becoming Colette* 1991

Van Dyke, Conny (1945-) *Framed* 1975; *WW and the Dixie Dancekings* 1975

Van Dyke, Dick (1925-) *Bye Bye Birdie* 1963; *Mary Poppins* 1964; *What a Way to Go!* 1964; *Art of Love* 1965; *Lt Robin Crusoe, USN* 1966; *Divorce American Style* 1967; *Fitzwilly* 1967; *Chitty Chitty Bang Bang* 1968; *The Comic* 1969; *The Runner Stumbles* 1979; *Dick Tracy* 1990; *Curious George* 2006; *Murder 101* 2006; *Night at the Museum* 2006; *Alexander and the Terrible, Horrible, No Good, Very Bad Day* 2014

Van Dyke, Jerry (1932-) *The Courtship of Eddie's Father* 1963; *Angel in My Pocket* 1968

Van Eyck, Peter (1911-1969) *Five Graves to Cairo* 1943; *The Moon Is Down* 1943; *The Impostor* 1944; *Sailor of the King* 1953; *The Wages of Fear* 1953; *A Bullet for Joey* 1955; *The Rawhide Years* 1956; *Run for the Sun* 1956; *Foxhole in Cairo* 1960; *The Thousand Eyes of Dr Mabuse* 1960; *The Brain* 1962; *Station Six-Sahara* 1962; *The Dirty Game* 1965; *The Spy Who Came In from the Cold* 1965; *Shalako* 1968; *The Bridge at Remagen* 1969

Van Eyssen, John (1922-1995) *Four Sided Triangle* 1953; *Men of Sherwood Forest* 1954; *The Traitor* 1957; *Dracula* 1958; *Blind Date* 1959

Van Fleet, Jo (1914-1996) *East of Eden* 1955; *I'll Cry Tomorrow* 1955; *The Rose Tattoo* 1955; *Gunfight at the OK Corral* 1957; *This Angry Age* 1957; *Wild River* 1960; *Cinderella* 1965; *Cool Hand Luke* 1967; *I Love You, Alice B Toklas* 1968;

Eighty Steps to Jonah 1969; The Gang That Couldn't Shoot Straight 1971; The Tenant 1976

Van Gorkum, Harry Dragonheart: a New Beginning 1999; Escape under Pressure 2000; Firetrap 2001; Avenging Angelo 2002; The Foreigner 2003

Van Heerden, Marcel Mapantsula 1988; Jobman 1990

Van Hentenryck, Kevin Basket Case 1982; Basket Case 2 1990; Basket Case 3: the Progeny 1992

Van Holt, Brian (1969-) Whipped 1999; Confidence 2002; Basic 2003; SWAT 2003; House of Wax 2004; Man of the House 2005

Van Hool, Roger La Chamade 1968; Conversations with My Gardener 2006

Van Horn, Patrick California Man 1992; Swingers 1995; Free Enterprise 1998

van Houten, Carice (1976-) Black Book 2006; Valkyrie 2008; From Time to Time 2009; Love Life 2009; Black Death 2010; Repo Men 2010; Intruders 2011; Race 2016

Van Huet, Fedja (1973-) Character 1997; The Delivery 1998

Van Lidth, Erland (1953-1987) Alone in the Dark 1982; The Running Man 1987

van Lyck, Henry (1941-) Signs of Life 1968; The Enigma of Kaspar Hauser 1974

Van Nutter, Rik (1930-2005) Thunderball 1965; Pacific Inferno 1979

Van Outen, Denise (1974-) Love, Honour and Obey 2000; Run for Your Wife 2013

Van Pallandt, Nina (1932-) The Long Goodbye 1973; A Wedding 1978; Quintet 1979; American Gigolo 1980; Cutter's Way 1981

Van Patten, Dick (1928-2015) Charly 1968; Westworld 1973; The Strongest Man in the World 1975; Freaky Friday 1976; The Shaggy DA 1976; High Anxiety 1977; Spaceballs 1987; Love Is All There Is 1996

Van Patten, Joyce (1934-) I Love You, Alice B Toklas 1968; something big 1971; Bone 1972; Mame 1974; The Bad News Bears 1976; Billy Galvin 1986; Monkey Shines 1988; Trust Me 1989; Breathing Lessons 1994; Grown Ups 2010

Van Patten, Vincent (1957-) The Valdez Horses 1973; Rock 'n' Roll High School 1979; Hell Night 1981

Van Peebles, Mario (1958-) Rappin' 1985; Heartbreak Ridge 1986; Hot Shot 1986; 3:15 1986; Jaws the Revenge 1987; New Jack City 1991; Full Eclipse 1993; Posse 1993; Gunmen 1994; Highlander III: the Sorcerer 1995; Gang in Blue 1996; Solo 1996; Love Kills 1998; Blowback 1999; Judgment Day 1999; Guardian 2000; Ali 2001; Baadasssss! 2003

Van Peebles, Melvin (1932-) Sweet Sweetback's Baad Asssss Song 1971; Posse 1993; Terminal Velocity 1994; Fist of the North Star 1995; Gang in Blue 1996; Love Kills 1998

Van Rampelberg, Geert The Broken Circle Breakdown 2012; The Treatment 2014

Van Rooten, Luis (1906-1973) City across the River 1949; My Favorite Spy 1951; The Unholy Wife 1957

Van Sloan, Edward (1881-1964) Dracula 1931; Frankenstein 1931; The Mummy 1932; The Death Kiss 1933; Deluge 1933; Dracula's Daughter 1936; Before I Hang 1940

Van Tongeren, Hans (1955-1982) Spetters 1980; Summer Lovers 1982

Van Valkenburgh, Deborah (1952-) Streets of Fire 1984; Rampage 1987; Brain Smasher... a Love Story 1993

Van Vooren, Monique (1933-) Tarzan and the She-Devil 1953; Happy Anniversary 1959 Flesh for Frankenstein 1974

van Wageningen, Yorick (1964-) Beyond Borders 2003; The Chronicles of Riddick 2004; The New World 2005; Winter in Wartime 2008; The Girl with the Dragon Tattoo 2011

Van Wormer, Steve Meet the Deedles 1998; Groove 2000

Van Zandt, Philip (1904-1958) A Thousand and One Nights 1945; Thief of Damascus 1952; Playgirl 1954

Van, Bobby (1930-1980) Skirts Ahoy! 1952; The Affairs of Dobie Gillis 1953; Kiss Me Kate 1953; The Navy vs the Night Monsters 1966; Lost Horizon 1973

Vanbrugh, Irene (1872-1949) The Rise of Catherine the Great 1934; Escape Me Never 1935; Knight without Armour 1937; Wings of the Morning 1937

VanCamp, Emily The Ring Two 2004; Carriers 2008; Beyond the Blackboard 2011

Vance, Courtney B (1960-) The Hunt for Red October 1990; The Adventures of Huck Finn 1993; Fixing the Shadow 1994; Holy Matrimony 1994; Dangerous Minds 1995; The Last Supper 1995; Panther 1995; The Tuskegee Airmen 1995; The Boys Next Door 1996; The Preacher's Wife 1996; 12 Angry Men 1997; Space Cowboys 2000; Extraordinary Measures 2010; The Divide 2011; Final Destination 5 2011

Vander, Musetta (1969-) Under the Hula Moon 1995; Wild Wild West 1999; Kicking & Screaming 2005

Vandernoot, Alexandra (1965-) Le Dîner de Cons 1998; The Closet 2001; The Five Obstructions 2003

Vandis, Titos aka **Wandis, Titos** (1917-2003) Never on Sunday 1960; Topkapi 1964; A Piece of the Action 1977; A Perfect Couple 1979

Vaneck, Pierre (1931-2010) Marianne de Ma Jeunesse 1955; The Science of Sleep 2005

Vanel, Charles (1892-1989) Les Misérables 1934; La Belle Equipe 1936; The Wages of Fear 1953; Les Diaboliques 1954; To Catch a Thief 1955; Death in the Garden 1956; La Vérité 1960; Tintin and the Mystery of the Golden Fleece 1961; L'Aîné des Ferchaux 1963; Three Brothers 1980

Vanilla Ice Cool as Ice 1991; That's My Boy 2012

Vanity (1959-2016) 52 Pick-Up 1986; Action Jackson 1988

Vanni, Renata (1910-2004) Pay or Die 1960; Lady in White 1988; Wait until Spring, Bandini 1989

Vannicola, Joanne (1968-) Love and Human Remains 1993; Iron Eagle IV 1995

Vannucchi, Luigi (1930-1978) The Red Tent 1969; The Assassination of Trotsky 1972; Call Him Savage 1975

Vansittart, Rupert Monk Dawson 1997; Austenland 2013

Varconi, Victor (1891-1976) The Divine Lady 1928; Eternal Love 1929; Roberta 1935; The Plainsman 1936; Big City 1937; The Atomic Submarine 1960

Vardalos, Nia (1962-) My Big Fat Greek Wedding 2002; Connie and Carla 2004; Driving Aphrodite 2008; Larry Crowne 2011; For a Good Time, Call... 2012; My Big Fat Greek Wedding 2 2016

Varden, Evelyn (1893-1958) Stella 1950; When Willie Comes Marching Home 1950; Phone Call from a Stranger 1952; Desiree 1954; The Night of the Hunter 1955; The Bad Seed 1956; Hilda Crane 1956

Varden, Norma (1898-1989) Boys Will Be Boys 1935; Foreign Affaires 1935; Where There's a Will 1936; Windbag the Sailor 1936; Shipyard Sally 1939; The Earl of Chicago 1940; National Velvet 1944; Witness for the Prosecution 1957; Doctor Dolittle 1967

Varela, Gina The Devil's Rock 2011; Breakfast with Jonny Wilkinson 2013

Varela, Leonor (1972-) The Tailor of Panama 2000; Texas Rangers 2001; Blade II 2002; Shut Up! 2003; Goal II: Living the Dream 2007

Varela, Matias Padin aka **Varela, Matias** Easy Money 2010; Easy Money II 2012; Easy Money III: Life Deluxe 2013

Varennes, Jacques (1895-1958) The Eagle Has Two Heads 1948; Orphée 1950

Varga, Veronika The King of Paris 1995; Le Serpent 2006

Vargas, Jacob (1971-) Mi Vida Loca 1993; Selena 1997; Flight of the Phoenix 2004; Jarhead 2005; The Hills Have Eyes II 2007

Vargas, Valentina (1964-) Street of No Return 1989; Hellraiser: Bloodline 1996

Varley, Beatrice (1896-1964) Hatter's Castle 1941; Waterloo Road 1944; Adam and Evelyne 1949; Gone to Earth 1950; The Black Rider 1954; Horrors of the Black Museum 1959

Varma, Indira Kama Sutra: a Tale of Love 1996; Bride & Prejudice 2004

Varney, Jim (1949-2000) Ernest Goes to Camp 1987; Ernest Saves Christmas 1988; Fast Food 1989; Ernest Goes to Jail 1990; Ernest Scared Stupid 1991; The Beverly Hillbillies 1993; Ernest Rides Again 1993; Wilder Napalm 1993; Slam Dunk Ernest 1995; Toy Story 1995; Daddy and Them 1999; Toy Story 2 1999; Atlantis: the Lost Empire 2001

Varney, Reg (1916-2008) Joey Boy 1965; The Great St Trinian's Train Robbery 1966; On the Buses 1971; The Best Pair of Legs in the Business 1972; Go for a Take 1972; Mutiny on the Buses 1972; Holiday on the Buses 1973

Varno, Roland (1908-1996) Three Faces West 1940; The Return of the Vampire 1943; My Name Is Julia Ross 1945; Scared to Death 1947

Varsi, Diane (1938-1992) Peyton Place 1957; From Hell to Texas 1958; Ten North Frederick 1958; Compulsion 1959; Wild in the Streets 1968; Bloody Mama 1970; Johnny Got His Gun 1971

Vartan, Michael (1968-) Fiorile 1993; Dead Man's Curve 1997; Touch Me 1997; Never Been Kissed 1999; It Had to Be You 2000; The Next Best Thing 2000; One Hour Photo 2001; Monster-in-Law 2005; Rogue 2007; Colombiana 2011

Varte, Rosy (1923-2012) Thomas the Imposter 1964; Uncle Benjamin 1969

Vasconcelos, Luiz Carlos Midnight 1998; Me, You, Them 2000; Carandiru 2003

Vassar, Queenie (1870-1960) Primrose Path 1940; Lady in a Jam 1942

Vassilieva, Sofia Eloise at the Plaza 2003; My Sister's Keeper 2009

Vattier, Robert (1906-1982) Fanny 1932; The Baker's Wife 1938; Manon des Sources 1952

Vaughan, Frankie (1928-1999) The Heart of a Man 1959; Let's Make Love 1960

Vaughan, Martin (1931-) We of the Never Never 1982; Phar Lap 1983; Constance 1984

Vaughan, Peter (1923-) Die! Die! My Darling 1965; Smokescreen 1964; The Naked Runner 1967; A Twist of Sand 1967; The Bofors Gun 1968; Hammerhead 1968; Alfred the Great 1969; Eyewitness 1970; Straw Dogs 1971; Savage Messiah 1972; The Blockhouse 1973; The Mackintosh Man 1973; Malachi's Cove 1973; 11 Harrowhouse 1974; Valentino 1977; Porridge 1979; The Razor's Edge 1984; Brazil 1985; Haunted Honeymoon 1986; King of the Wind 1989; Mountains of the Moon 1989; Prisoner of Honor 1991; The Remains of the Day 1993; The Crucible 1996; The Secret Agent 1996; Face 1997; Les Misérables 1997; An Ideal Husband 1999; The Legend of 1900 1999; Kiss Kiss (Bang Bang) 2001; The Life and Death of Peter Sellers 2003; The Mother 2003; Is Anybody There? 2008; Albatross 2011

Vaughn, Hilda (1898-1957) Manslaughter 1930; Susan Lenox: Her Fall and Rise 1931; Today We Live 1933; Anne of Green Gables 1934

Vaughn, Ned (1964-) The Rescue 1988; Gore Vidal's Billy the Kid 1989; Wind 1992

Vaughn (1), Robert (1932-) Teenage Caveman 1958; The Young Philadelphians 1959; The Magnificent Seven 1960; The Big Show 1961; The Caretakers 1963; The Glass Bottom Boat 1966; One of Our Spies Is Missing 1966; One Spy Too Many 1966; The Spy in the Green Hat 1966; The Spy with My Face 1966; To Trap a Spy 1966; The Venetian Affair 1966; The Karate Killers 1967; Bullitt 1968; The Helicopter Spies 1968; How to Steal the World 1968; The Bridge at Remagen 1969; Julius Caesar 1970; The Mind of Mr Soames 1970; The Towering Inferno 1974; Demon Seed 1977; Brass Target 1978; Battle beyond the Stars 1980; Hangar 18 1980; SOB 1981; Superman III 1983; Black Moon Rising 1985; The Delta Force 1986; Hour of the Assassin 1987; Renegade 1987; CHUD II: Bud the Chud 1989; River of Death 1989; Transylvania Twist 1989; Buried Alive 1990; Going under 1990; Joe's Apartment 1996; Motel Blue 1997; BASEketball 1998

Vaughn, Vince (1970-) Just Your Luck 1996; Swingers 1996; The Lost World: Jurassic Park 1997; A Secret Sin 1997; Clay Pigeons 1998; A Cool, Dry Place 1998; Psycho 1998; Return to Paradise 1998; The Cell 2000; The Prime Gig 2000; South of Heaven, West of Hell 2000; Domestic Disturbance 2001; Made 2001; Blackball 2003; Old School 2003; Dodgeball: a True Underdog Story 2004; Starsky & Hutch 2004; Be Cool 2005; Mr & Mrs Smith 2005; Thumbsucker 2005; Wedding Crashers 2005; The Break-Up 2006; Fred Claus 2007; Into the Wild 2007; Four Christmases 2008; Couples Retreat 2009; The Dilemma 2011; Lay the Favorite 2012; The Watch 2012; Delivery Man 2013; The Internship 2013; Unfinished Business 2015

Vaugier, Emmanuelle Secondhand Lions 2003; Reverse Angle 2008; It's Christmas, Carol! 2012

Vavasseur, Sophie (1992-) Evelyn 2002; Resident Evil: Apocalypse 2004

Vavitch, Michael (1885-1930) Hotel Imperial 1927; Two Arabian Knights 1927

Vawter, Ron (1949-1994) sex, lies, and videotape 1989; Swoon 1992; Philadelphia 1993

Veadov, Alex We Own the Night 2007; Act of Valor 2012

Veazie, Carol (1895-1984) A Cry in the Night 1956; Baby the Rain Must Fall 1965

Vega, Alexa (1988-) Run the Wild Fields 2000; SPYkids 2001; SPYkids 2: the Island of Lost Dreams 2002; SPYkids 3-D: Game Over 2003; Sleepover 2004; Odd Girl Out 2005; SPYkids 4: All the Time in the World 2011; Machete Kills 2013; The Remaining 2014

Vega, Isela (1940-) Bring Me the Head of Alfredo Garcia 1974; Drum 1976; Barbarosa 1982

Vega, Paz (1976-) Sex and Lucia 2001; The Other Side of the Bed 2002; Carmen 2003; Spanglish 2004; Fade to Black 2006; The Spirit 2008; Angels of Evil 2010; I'm So Excited 2013; Grace of Monaco 2014

Vegas, Johnny (1971-) Blackball 2003; Sex Lives of the Potato Men 2003; The Libertine 2004; Terkel in Trouble 2006; Grimsby 2016

Veidt, Conrad (1893-1943) The Cabinet of Dr Caligari 1919; Hands of Orlac 1924; Waxworks 1924; The Man Who Laughs 1928; Congress Dances 1931; Rome Express 1932; The Wandering Jew 1933; I Was a Spy 1934; Jew Süss 1934; The Passing of the Third Floor Back 1935; Dark Journey 1937; Under the Red Robe 1937; The Spy in Black 1939; Contraband 1940; Escape 1940; The Thief of Bagdad 1940; The Men in Her Life 1941; Whistling in the Dark 1941; A Woman's Face 1941; All through the Night 1942; Casablanca 1942; Above Suspicion 1943

Velasco, Manuela [Rec] 2007; [Rec]² 2009; [REC] 4: Apocalypse 2014

Velasquez, Patricia (1971-) Committed 2000; The Mummy Returns 2001; Mindhunters 2003; The Twelve Days of Christmas Eve 2004

Velazquez, Nadine The Last Ride 2004; Snitch 2013

Velez, Eddie (1958-) Repo Man 1984; Extremities 1986; Romero 1989

Velez, Lupe (1908-1944) The Gaucho 1927; The Half Naked Truth 1932; Hollywood Party 1934; Palooka 1934; The Girl from Mexico 1939; Mexican Spitfire 1940; Playmates 1941

VelJohnson, Reginald (1952-) Die Hard 1988; Turner & Hooch 1989; Die Hard 2: Die Harder 1990; The Christmas Gift 2009; The Mistle-Tones 2012

Venable, Evelyn (1913-1993) Death Takes a Holiday 1934; Mrs Wiggs of the Cabbage Patch 1934; Alice Adams 1935; The Little Colonel 1935; Pinocchio 1940

Venables, Bruce Daydream Believer 1991; Paperback Hero 1998

Venantini, Venantino (1930-) The Agony and the Ecstasy 1965; The Priest's Wife 1970

Veness, Amy (1876-1960) The Show Goes On 1937; Just William 1939; This Happy Breed 1944; Vote for Huggett 1948; The Astonished Heart 1949

Venito, Lenny Gigli 2003; The Brave One 2007

Vennera, Chick (1952-) Thank God It's Friday 1978; Yanks 1979; High Risk 1981; Last Rites 1988

Venora, Diane (1952-) Wolfen 1981; Cook & Peary: the Race to the Pole 1983; Terminal Choice 1983; FX: Murder by Illusion 1985; Ironweed 1987; Bird 1988; Heat 1995; The Substitute 1996; Surviving Picasso 1996; William Shakespeare's Romeo + Juliet 1996; The Jackal 1997; The Insider 1999; The Joyriders 1999; True Crime 1999; Hamlet 2000

Ventham, Wanda (1939-) The Blood Beast Terror 1967; Mister Ten Per Cent 1967; Captain Kronos: Vampire Hunter 1972; Asylum 2004

Ventimiglia, John The Funeral 1996; Personal Velocity 2001

Ventimiglia, Milo (1977-) Cursed 2005; Rocky Balboa 2006; Pathology 2007; Gamer 2008; Armored 2009; The Divide 2011; Killing Season 2013; Grace of Monaco 2014; Wild Card 2014

Ventresca, Vincent Romy and Michele's High School Reunion 1997; My Neighbor's Secret 2009

Ventura, Jesse (1951-) Predator 1987; The Running Man 1987

Ventura, Lino (1919-1987) Honour among Thieves 1954; Classe Tous Risques 1959; Le Deuxième Souffle 1966; The Adventurers 1968; Army of Shadows 1969; The Sicilian Clan 1969; The Valachi Papers 1972; A Pain in the

A...! 1973; The Silent One 1973; Three Tough Guys 1974; Illustrious Corpses 1976; The Medusa Touch 1978; Garde à Vue 1981; Les Misérables 1982

Ventura, Viviane A High Wind in Jamaica 1965; Battle beneath the Earth 1968

Venture, Richard (1923-) The Effect of Gamma Rays on Man-in-the-Moon Marigolds 1972; The Hunter 1980; Missing 1981; Scent of a Woman 1992; Series 7: the Contenders 2001

Venuta, Benay (1911-1995) Annie Get Your Gun 1950; Call Me Mister 1951; Stars and Stripes Forever 1952

Vera-Ellen (1920-1981) Wonder Man 1945; The Kid from Brooklyn 1946; Three Little Girls in Blue 1946; Words and Music 1948; Love Happy 1949; On the Town 1949; Happy Go Lovely 1950; Three Little Words 1950; The Belle of New York 1952; Big Leaguer 1953; Call Me Madam 1953; White Christmas 1954

Verbeke, Natalia (1975-) Jump Tomorrow 2001; Son of the Bride 2001; The Other Side of the Bed 2002; Dot the i 2003; The Women on the 6th Floor 2010

Verdon, Gwen aka **Verdon, Gwyneth** (1925-2000) On the Riviera 1951; Damn Yankees 1958; The Cotton Club 1984; Cocoon 1985; Nadine 1987; Cocoon: the Return 1988; Alice 1990; Marvin's Room 1996

Verdú, Maribel (1970-) Lovers 1991; Belle Epoque 1992; Golden Balls 1993; Goya in Bordeaux 1999; Y Tu Mamá También 2001; Pan's Labyrinth 2006; La Zona 2007; Tetro 2009; Blancanieves 2011

Verdugo, Elena (1926-) The Frozen Ghost 1944; Little Giant 1946; Thief of Damascus 1952

Vereen, Ben (1946-) Gas-s-s-s, or It Became Necessary to Destroy the World in Order to Save It 1970; Funny Lady 1975; All That Jazz 1979; Buy & Cell 1988; Once upon a Forest 1992; Why Do Fools Fall in Love? 1998; Accidental Friendship 2008; Time out of Mind 2014; Top Five 2014

Vereza, Carlos (1939-) Midnight 1998; The Three Marias 2002

Vergara, Sofia (1972-) Four Brothers 2005; Happy Feet Two 2011; The Three Stooges 2012; Fading Gigolo 2013; Machete Kills 2013; Chef 2014; Wild Card 2014; Hot Pursuit 2015

Verhoeven, Simon (1972-) My Mother's Courage 1995; Bride of the Wind 2001

Verhoeven, Yves La Classe de Neige 1998; A Secret 2007

Verley, Bernard (1939-) The Milky Way 1968; Love in the Afternoon 1972; L'Accompagnatrice 1992; Hélas pour Moi 1993; Six Days, Six Nights 1994; Lady Chatterley 2006

Verlinden, Laura Ben X 2007; The Treatment 2014

Vermilyea, Harold (1889-1958) The Big Clock 1948; The Emperor Waltz 1948; Born to Be Bad 1950

Verne, Kaaren aka **Verne, Karen** (1918-1967) Sky Murder 1940; All through the Night 1942; Sherlock Holmes and the Secret Weapon 1942

Vernier, Pierre (1931-) Les Chiens 1978; The Outsider 1983; Romuald et Juliette 1989; Under the Sand 2000; A Comedy of Power 2006

Verno, Jerry (1895-1975) Broken Blossoms 1936; Sweeney Todd, the Demon Barber of Fleet Street 1936

Vernoff, Kaili No Looking Back 1998; Jump Tomorrow 2001

Vernon, Anne (1924-) The Love Lottery 1953; Terror on a Train 1953; Beautiful but Dangerous 1955; General Della Rovere 1959; The Umbrellas of Cherbourg 1964

Vernon, Glenn (1923-1999) Bedlam 1946; The Devil Thumbs a Ride 1947

Vernon, Howard (1914-1996) Le Silence de la Mer 1947; Bob Le Flambeur 1955; The Thousand Eyes of Dr Mabuse 1960; The Secret Ways 1961; The Awful Dr Orlof 1962; Alphaville 1965; Dracula, Prisoner of Frankenstein 1972

Vernon, John (1932-2005) Point Blank 1967; Tell Them Willie Boy Is Here 1969; Topaz 1969; Dirty Harry 1971; Fear Is the Key 1972; Charley Varrick 1973; The Black Windmill 1974; Brannigan 1975; The Outlaw Josey Wales 1976; Golden Rendezvous 1977; A Special Day 1977; National Lampoon's Animal House 1978; Herbie Goes Bananas 1980; Chained Heat 1983; Savage Streets 1984; Ernest Goes to Camp 1987; Killer Klowns from Outer Space 1988; Sodbusters 1994

Vernon, Kate (1961-) Alphabet City 1984; Malcolm X 1992; Soft Deceit 1994; Family Plan 2005

Vernon, Richard (1925-1997) Cash on Demand 1961; The Servant 1963; A Hard Day's Night 1964; Hot Enough for June 1964; The Tomb of Ligeia 1964; The Early Bird 1965; The Intelligence Men 1965; The Satanic Rites of Dracula 1973; Witness for the Prosecution 1982; A Month in the Country 1987

Vernon, Wally (1905-1970) Happy Landing 1938; Kentucky Moonshine 1938; Broadway Serenade 1939; Bloodhounds of Broadway 1952; Affair with a Stranger 1953

Verrell, Cec Hell Comes to Frogtown 1988; Three of Hearts 1992

Versois, Odile (1930-1980) A Day to Remember 1953; To Paris with Love 1954; The Young Lovers 1954; Checkpoint 1956; Passport to Shame 1958; Cartouche 1961

Verveen, Arie Caught 1996; Running Free 1999; Cabin Fever 2002

Verzhbitsky, Viktor Night Watch 2004; Day Watch 2006

VeSota, Bruno (1922-1976) Rock All Night 1957; Daddy-O 1959; Attack of the Giant Leeches 1960

Vessey, Tricia (1972-) The Alarmist 1997; Ghost Dog: the Way of the Samurai 1999; Trouble Every Day 2000

Vetchy, Ondrej (1962-) Martha and I 1990; Kolya 1996; Dark Blue World 2001

Vetri, Victoria (1944-) Kings of the Sun 1963; When Dinosaurs Ruled the Earth 1969

Viard, Karin (1966-) Delicatessen 1990; La Séparation 1994; La Nouvelle Eve 1998; Les Enfants du Siècle 1999; Time Out 2001; Summer Things 2002; L'Enfer 2005; Potiche 2010; La Famille Bélier 2014

Vibert, Ronan Gladiatress 2002; The Last Seven 2010

Vicius, Nicole Last Days 2004; Sound of My Voice 2011

Vickers, Martha (1925-1971) The Big Sleep 1946; The Man I Love 1946; Ruthless 1948; The Burglar 1956

Vickers, Yvette (1928-2010) Reform School Girl 1957; Short Cut to Hell 1957; Attack of the 50 Foot Woman 1958; The Mobster 1958; Attack of the Giant Leeches 1960

Victor, Charles (1896-1965) My Learned Friend 1943; Rhythm Serenade 1943; The Silver Fleet 1943; Fear in the Night 1947; The Calendar 1948; The Cure for Love 1949; The Woman in Question 1950; Calling Bulldog Drummond 1951; The Frightened Man 1952; Made in Heaven 1952; The Love Lottery 1953; Police Dog 1955; Value for Money 1955; The Extra Day 1956; Home and Away 1956

Victor, Henry (1898-1945) Freaks 1932; Tiger Bay 1934; Conquest of the Air 1936

Vidal, Christina (1981-) Life with Mikey 1993; Welcome to the Dollhouse 1995; Freaky Friday 2003

Vidal, Gore (1925-2012) Fellini's Roma 1972; Gore Vidal's Billy the Kid 1989; Bob Roberts 1992; With Honors 1994; Shadow Conspiracy 1996; Gattaca 1997; Inside Deep Throat 2005; The US vs John Lennon 2006; Salinger 2013; Best of Enemies 2015

Vidal, Henri (1919-1959) Gates of Paris 1957; Une Parisienne 1957

Vidal, Lisa (1965-) Hit and Run 1999; Odd Girl Out 2005

Vidarte, Walter (1931-2011) 1919 1983; Outrage 1993

Vidler, Steven (1960-) The Good Wife 1986; Encounter at Raven's Gate 1988; Two Hands 1999

Vidler, Susan Naked 1993; Trainspotting 1995; The Wedding Tackle 2000; Wilbur (Wants to Kill Himself) 2002

Vidor, Florence (1895-1977) The Marriage Circle 1924; The Patriot 1928

Vidor, King (1894-1982) It's a Great Feeling 1949; Love and Money 1982

Vigoda, Abe (1921-2016) Newman's Law 1974; Plain Clothes 1988; Look Who's Talking 1989; Joe versus the Volcano 1990; Batman: Mask of the Phantasm 1993; Sugar Hill 1993; Jury Duty 1995; Love Is All There Is 1996; Good Burger 1997

Vigran, Herb (1911-1986) Bedtime for Bonzo 1951; Go, Johnny, Go! 1959; Charlotte's Web 1973

Viharo, Robert (1939-) Return to Macon County 1975; Hide in Plain Sight 1980

Vikander, Alicia (1988-) A Royal Affair 2012; Son of a Gun 2013; Ex Machina 2014; Seventh Son 2014; Testament of Youth 2014; The Danish Girl 2015; Jason Bourne 2016

Villagra, Nelson (1937-) The Last Supper 1976; Amnesia 1994

Villalonga, Marthe (1932-) Ma Saison Préférée 1993; Alice et Martin 1998

Villamil, Soledad The Secret in Their Eyes 2009; Everybody Has a Plan 2012

Villard, Tom (1954-1994) Parasite 1982; Popcorn 1991

Villechaize, Herve (1943-1993) The Gang That Couldn't Shoot Straight 1971; The Man with the Golden Gun 1974; Seizure 1974; The One and Only 1978

Villella, Chad V/H/S 2012; Southbound 2015

Villeret, Jacques (1951-2005) Robert et Robert 1978; An Adventure for Two 1979; Les Uns et les Autres 1981; Edith et Marcel 1983; Hold-Up 1985; Soigne Ta Droite 1986; The Favour, the Watch and the Very Big Fish 1991; The Children of the Marshland 1998; Le Dîner de Cons 1998; Strange Gardens 2003

Villiers, James (1933-1998) Eva 1962; Operation Snatch 1962; Father Came Too 1963; Murder at the Gallop 1963; King and Country 1964; The Nanny 1965; Otley 1968; A Nice Girl like Me 1969; Some Girls Do 1969; Blood from the Mummy's Tomb 1971; The Amazing Mr Blunden 1972; The Ruling Class 1972; Ghost in the Noonday Sun 1973; Seven Nights in Japan 1976; Saint Jack 1979; The Scarlet Pimpernel 1982; Under the Volcano 1984; Mountains of the Moon 1989; King Ralph 1991

Vince, Pruitt Taylor (1960-) Shy People 1987; Mississippi Burning 1988; Jacob's Ladder 1990; City Slickers II: the Legend of Curly's Gold 1994; Nobody's Fool 1994; Heavy 1995; Under the Hula Moon 1995; The Legend of 1900 1999; Mumford 1999; Nurse Betty 2000; SIMØNE 2002; Trapped 2002; Identity 2003; Monster 2003; Constantine 2005; Captivity 2006

Vincent, Alex (1981-) Child's Play 1988; Child's Play 2 1990

Vincent, Frank (1940-) Death Collector 1976; Raging Bull 1980; Jungle Fever 1991; Mortal Thoughts 1991; Hand Gun 1994

Vincent, Hélène (1943-) J'Embrasse Pas 1991; Three Colours Blue 1993; Ma Vie en Rose 1997; Attila Marcel 2013

Vincent, Jan-Michael aka **Vincent, Michael** (1944-) Journey to Shiloh 1967; The Undefeated 1969; Going Home 1971; The Mechanic 1972; The World's Greatest Athlete 1973; Buster and Billie 1974; Bite the Bullet 1975; Vigilante Force 1975; White Line Fever 1975; Damnation Alley 1977; Big Wednesday 1978; Hooper 1978; Defiance 1979; Hard Country 1981; Born in East LA 1987; Hit List 1988; Haunting Fear 1990; Raw Nerve 1991; Indecent Behavior 1993; Buffalo '66 1998

Vincent, June (1920-2008) Can't Help Singing 1944; Here Come the Co-Eds 1945; Black Angel 1946; Marry Me Again 1953

Vincent, Virginia (1924-) I Want to Live! 1958; The Return of Dracula 1958; The Black Orchid 1959; The Hills Have Eyes 1977

Ving, Lee Streets of Fire 1984; Black Moon Rising 1985; Dudes 1987

Vinovich, Steve aka **Vinovich, Stephen** Jennifer on My Mind 1971; Mannequin 1987

Vinson, Helen (1907-1999) I Am a Fugitive from a Chain Gang 1932; Lawyer Man 1932; The Kennel Murder Case 1933; The Little Giant 1933; The Power and the Glory 1933; Broadway Bill 1934; The Captain Hates the Sea 1934; Private Worlds 1935; The Wedding Night 1935; Live, Love and Learn 1937; Vogues of 1938 1937; In Name Only 1939; Curtain Call 1940; Torrid Zone 1940; Nothing but the Truth 1941; The Lady and the Monster 1944; The Thin Man Goes Home 1944

Vinson, Sharni Step Up 3 2010; You're Next 2011; Dragon Blade 2015

Vint, Alan (1944-2006) The Panic in Needle Park 1971; The Unholy Rollers 1972; Badlands 1973; Macon County Line 1973; The Ballad of Gregorio Cortez 1983

Vint, Jesse Silent Running 1971; Macon County Line 1973; Bug 1975; Deathsport 1978

Vintas, Gustav Silent Assassins 1988; Midnight 1989

Vinton, Arthur (1896-1963) Washington Merry-Go-Round 1932; Dames 1934

Vinton, Bobby Big Jake 1971; The Train Robbers 1973

Virk, Manjinder The Blue Tower 2008; The Arbor 2010

Visnjic, Goran (1972-) Welcome to Sarajevo 1997; Practical Magic 1998; Committed 2000; The Deep End 2001;

Ice Age 2002; Elektra 2005; The Courageous Heart of Irena Sendler 2009; Beginners 2010

Vitale, Joseph (1901-1994) Road to Rio 1947; The Paleface 1948; Apache Rifles 1964

Vitale, Milly (1932-2006) The Juggler 1953; Seven Little Foys 1955; The Battle of the VI 1958; Hannibal 1959; A Breath of Scandal 1960

Vitali, Leon Barry Lyndon 1975; Victor Frankenstein 1977

Viterelli, Joe (1941-2004) Bullets over Broadway 1994; American Strays 1996; Heaven's Prisoners 1996; Analyze This 1999; Mickey Blue Eyes 1999; See Spot Run 2001; Shallow Hal 2001; Analyze That 2002

Vitez, Antoine (1930-1990) My Night with Maud 1969; Ecoute Voir... 1978; The Green Room 1978

Vitold, Michel (1915-1994) La Nuit Fantastique 1942; The Testament of Dr Cordelier 1959; Judex 1963; Thomas the Imposter 1964; The Confession 1970

Vitti, Monica (1931-) L'Avventura 1960; La Notte 1961; The Eclipse 1962; Red Desert 1964; Le Bambole 1965; Modesty Blaise 1966; On My Way to the Crusades, I Met a Girl Who... 1967; Jealousy, Italian Style 1970; Le Fantôme de la Liberté 1974; Immortal Bachelor 1980; The Oberwald Mystery 1980

Viva (1941-) Bike Boy 1967; Lonesome Cowboys 1968; Sam's Song 1969; Cisco Pike 1971; Play It Again, Sam 1972; Ciao! Manhattan 1973

Vlady, Marina (1938-) Two or Three Things I Know about Her 1966; The Thief of Baghdad 1978; Tangos, Exilo de Gardel 1985

Voda, Clara The Death of Mr Lazarescu 2005; Aurora 2010

Voe, Sandra Breaking the Waves 1996; The Winter Guest 1996; Janice Beard 45 WPM 1999

Vogel, Mike (1979-) The Texas Chainsaw Massacre 2003; Poseidon 2006; Cloverfield 2008; She's out of My League 2008; Blue Valentine 2010; The Help 2011

Vogler, Karl Michael (1928-2009) The Blue Max 1966; How I Won the War 1967; Deep End 1970

Vogler, Rüdiger (1942-) Alice in the Cities 1974; Kings of the Road 1976; The German Sisters 1981; Until the End of the World 1991; Faraway, So Close 1993; Lisbon Story 1994; Anonyma: a Woman in Berlin 2008; OSS 117: Lost in Rio 2009

Vohs, Joan (1927-2001) Cry Vengeance 1954; Sabrina 1954

Voight, Jon (1938-) Hour of the Gun 1967; Midnight Cowboy 1969; Catch-22 1970; The Revolutionary 1970; Deliverance 1972; The All-American Boy 1973; The Odessa File 1974; End of the Game 1976; Coming Home 1978; The Champ 1979; Table for Five 1983; Desert Bloom 1985; Runaway Train 1985; Rainbow Warrior 1992; Heat 1995; Mission: Impossible 1996; Anaconda 1997; John Grisham's The Rainmaker 1997; Most Wanted 1997; Rosewood 1997; U Turn 1997; Enemy of the State 1998; The General 1998; A Dog of Flanders 1999; Varsity Blues 1999; Ali 2001; Lara Croft: Tomb Raider 2001; Pearl Harbor 2001; Zoolander 2001; Holes 2003; The Manchurian Candidate 2004; National Treasure 2004; Glory Road 2006; bratz 2007; National Treasure: Book of Secrets 2007; Pride and Glory 2007; Transformers 2007; Four Christmases 2008; Getaway 2013

Volchek, Galina (1957-) King Lear 1970; The Little Mermaid 1976

Volonté, Gian Maria aka **Wels, Johnny** (1933-1994) The Four Days of Naples 1962; A Fistful of Dollars 1964; For a Few Dollars More 1965; A Bullet for the General 1966; Face to Face 1967; Vent d'Est 1969; Investigation of a Citizen above Suspicion 1970; The Red Circle 1970; The Working Class Goes to Heaven 1971; The Mattei Affair 1972; Lucky Luciano 1973; Christ Stopped at Eboli 1979; The Death of Mario Ricci 1983; Chronicle of a Death Foretold 1987

Volter, Philippe (1959-2005) The Music Teacher 1988; The Double Life of Véronique 1991; Three Colours Blue 1993

Von Bargen, Daniel (1950-2015) Company Business 1991; Lord of Illusions 1995; The Shamrock Conspiracy 1995; Before and After 1996; GI Jane 1997; The Postman 1997; The General's Daughter 1999; Universal Soldier - the Return 1999; Super Troopers 2001

von Borsody, Suzanne (1957-) Flight of the Albatross 1995; Run Lola Run 1998

von Brömssen, Tomas (1943-) My Life as a Dog 1985; All Things Fair 1995

Von Detten, Erik (1982-) Top Dog 1995; Leave It to Beaver 1997; Barely Legal 2003

Von Dohlen, Lenny (1958-) Tender Mercies 1982; Electric Dreams 1984; Billy Galvin 1986; Dracula's Widow 1988; Leaving Normal 1992; Tollbooth 1994; Entertaining Angels: the Dorothy Day Story 1996; One Good Turn 1996; Home Alone 3 1997; Teeth 2007

von Eltz, Theodore (1894-1964) The Four Feathers 1929; Confidential 1935; Beloved Enemy 1936; California Straight Ahead 1937; Devil's Cargo 1948

von Fürstenberg, Ira aka **Furstenberg, Ira** aka **Fürstenberg, Ira** (1940-) Dead Run 1967; The Battle of El Alamein 1968; Hello - Goodbye 1970

Von Leer, Hunter (1944-) Halloween II 1981; Under the Boardwalk 1988

Von Lehndorff, Veruschka aka **Verushka** aka **Veruschka** Blowup 1966; The Bride 1985

von Pfetten, Stefanie (1973-) Date with Darkness 2003; The Twelve Days of Christmas Eve 2004; Too Late to Say Goodbye 2009

von Rezzori, Gregor (1914-1998) A Very Private Affair 1962; Viva Maria! 1965

von Schlettow, Hans Adalbert (1887-1945) Dr Mabuse, the Gambler 1922; Asphalt 1928

von Seyffertitz, Gustav (1863-1943) Sparrows 1926; The Gaucho 1927; The Student Prince in Old Heidelberg 1927; The Docks of New York 1928; The Mysterious Lady 1928; The Canary Murder Case 1929; The Case of Lena Smith 1929; Dishonored 1931; Shanghai Express 1932; Change of Heart 1934; The Moonstone 1934; She 1935

von Stroheim, Erich (1885-1957) Hearts of the World 1918; Blind Husbands 1919; Foolish Wives 1920; The Wedding March 1928; The Great Gabbo 1929; Friends and Lovers 1931; As You Desire Me 1932; The Lost Squadron 1932; La Grande Illusion 1937; Pièges 1939; So Ends Our Night 1941; Five Graves to Cairo 1943; The North Star 1943; The Lady and the Monster 1944; The Great Flamarion 1945; Sunset Blvd 1950; Napoléon 1955

von Sydow, Max (1929-) The Seventh Seal 1957; So Close to Life 1957; The Magician 1958; The Virgin Spring 1960; Through a Glass Darkly 1961; Winter Light 1962; The Greatest Story Ever Told 1965; The Reward 1965; Hawaii 1966; The Quiller Memorandum 1966; The Hour of the Wolf 1967; Shame 1968; A Passion 1969; The Night Visitor 1970; The Emigrants 1971; The Touch 1971; The New Land 1972; The Exorcist 1973; Steppenwolf 1974; Three Days of the Condor 1975; The Ultimate Warrior 1975; Illustrious Corpses 1976; Voyage of the Damned 1976; Exorcist II: The Heretic 1977; March or Die 1977; Brass Target 1978; Hurricane 1979; Death Watch 1980; Flash Gordon 1980; Escape to Victory 1981; She Dances Alone 1981; Conan the Barbarian 1982; Target Eagle 1982; Never Say Never Again 1983; Dreamscape 1984; Dune 1984; Code Name: Emerald 1985; Duet for One 1986; Hannah and Her Sisters 1986; The Second Victory 1986; The Wolf at the Door 1986; Pelle the Conqueror 1987; Awakenings 1990; The Bachelor 1990; Father 1990; Europa 1991; A Kiss before Dying 1991; The Ox 1991; Until the End of the World 1991; Best Intentions 1992; The Silent Touch 1992; Needful Things 1993; Citizen X 1995; Judge Dredd 1995; Hamsun 1996; Hostile Waters 1996; Jerusalem 1996; Private Confessions 1996; What Dreams May Come 1998; Snow Falling on Cedars 1999; Druids 2001; Intacto 2001; Minority Report 2002; Sword of Xanten 2004; Heidi 2005; The Diving-Bell and the Butterfly 2007; Rush Hour 3 2007; Shutter Island 2009; Solomon Kane 2009; Robin Hood 2010; Extremely Loud & Incredibly Close 2012

von Trier, Lars (1956-) The Element of Crime 1984; Side by Side 2012

von Trotta, Margarethe (1942-) Gods of the Plague 1969; The American Soldier 1970; Beware of a Holy Whore 1970

von Twardowski, Hans (1898-1958) The Cabinet of Dr Caligari 1919; The Scarlet Empress 1934

von Walther, Hertha (1903-1987) The Love of Jeanne Ney 1927; Crisis 1928

von Wangenheim, Gustav (1895-1975) Nosferatu, a Symphony of

Horrors 1922; The Woman in the Moon 1929

Von Weitershausen, Gila (1944-) The Pedestrian 1974; Circle of Deceit 1981

Von Zell, Harry (1906-1981) The Guilt of Janet Ames 1947; The Saxon Charm 1948; For Heaven's Sake 1950; Two Flags West 1950; I Can Get It for You Wholesale 1951; Son of Paleface 1952

Von Zerneck, Danielle (1966-) My Science Project 1985; La Bamba 1987; Under the Boardwalk 1988; Living in Oblivion 1995

Voskovec, George (1905-1981) 12 Angry Men 1957; The 27th Day 1957; Wind across the Everglades 1958; Barbarosa 1982

Vosloo, Arnold (1962-) Hard Target 1993; Darkman II: the Return of Durant 1995; Darkman III: Die Darkman Die 1996; Diary of a Serial Killer 1997; Zeus and Roxanne 1997; Progeny 1998; The Mummy 1999; The Mummy Returns 2001; Agent Cody Banks 2003; Blood Diamond 2006

Vosper, Frank (1899-1937) Waltzes from Vienna 1933; Jew Süss 1934; The Man Who Knew Too Much 1934; Königsmark 1935

Vosselli, Judith (1895-1966) The Rogue Song 1930; Inspiration 1931

Votrian, Peter Big House, USA 1955; Crime in the Streets 1956; Fear Strikes Out 1957

Voutsinas, Andreas (1932-2010) The Producers 1968; A Dream of Passion 1978

Voyagis, Yorgo (1945-) The Last Valley 1971; Chronicle of the Burning Years 1975; The Little Drummer Girl 1984; Vampire in Venice 1987; Frantic 1988; Courage Mountain 1989; Swept Away 2002

Vrana, Vlasta (1950-) Scanners II: The New Order 1991; Brainscan 1994; The Assignment 1997; Grey Owl 1999; Vroom, Frederick (1857-1942) The Navigator 1924; The General 1927

Vuco, Olivera (1940-) I Even Met Happy Gypsies 1967; Mark of the Devil 1970

Vuillermoz, Michel News from the Good Lord 1996; Wild Grass 2008; Life of Riley 2014

Vukotic, Milena (1930-) Blood for Dracula 1974; A Good Woman 2004

Vye, Murvyn (1913-1976) Golden Earrings 1947; Whispering Smith 1948; A Connecticut Yankee in King Arthur's Court 1949; Road to Bali 1952; Destination Gobi 1953; Pickup on South Street 1953; Black Horse Canyon 1954; Green Fire 1954; River of No Return 1954; Escape to Burma 1955; Pearl of the South Pacific 1955; The Best Things in Life Are Free 1956; Short Cut to Hell 1957; Al Capone 1959

Vyjayanthimala aka **Vyjayanti Mala** aka **Vyjayantimala** (1936-) Devdas 1955; Madhumati 1958; Sangam 1964

Vyner, Margaret (1914-1993) Climbing High 1938; The Lamp Still Burns 1943

W

Waddell, Justine (1976-) The Misadventures of Margaret 1998; Dracula 2001 2000; The One and Only 2001; The Mystery of Natalie Wood 2004; Chaos 2006; The Fall 2006

Waddington, Steven (1968-) Edward II 1991; The Last of the Mohicans 1992; Prince of Jutland 1994; Carrington 1995; Face 1997; Tarzan and the Lost City 1998; The Hole 2001; The Parole Officer 2001; When the Lights Went Out 2010

Wade, Russell (1917-2006) The Ghost Ship 1943; The Body Snatcher 1945; The Bamboo Blonde 1946

Wadham, Julian (1958-) The Madness of King George 1995; The English Patient 1996; Keep the Aspidistra Flying 1997; Preaching to the Perverted 1997; Exorcist: the Beginning 2004; Dominion: Prequel to the Exorcist 2005; Outpost 2007; Legacy: Black Ops 2010

Wadsworth, Henry (1902-1974) Applause 1929; Fast and Loose 1930; The Thin Man 1934; Ceiling Zero 1935

Wager, Anthony (1932-) Great Expectations 1946; The Hi-Jackers 1963

Wagner, David Thrashin' 1986; Pet Shop 1995

Wagner, Fernando (1973-) Tarzan and the Mermaids 1948; Garden of Evil 1954

Wagner, Lindsay (1949-) The Paper Chase 1973; Two People 1973; The Rockford Files 1974; High Risk 1981; Nighthawks 1981; Martin's Day 1984; Passions 1984; Ricochet 1991; Danielle Steel's Once in a Lifetime 1994; Thicker than Water 2005

Wagner, Lou (1948-) *Planet of the Apes 1967; Conquest of the Planet of the Apes 1972*

Wagner, Robert (1930-) *Halls of Montezuma 1950; The Happy Years 1950; The Frogmen 1951; Let's Make It Legal 1951; Stars and Stripes Forever 1952; What Price Glory? 1952; With a Song in My Heart 1952; Beneath the 12-Mile Reef 1953; Titanic 1953; Broken Lance 1954; Prince Valiant 1954; White Feather 1955; Between Heaven and Hell 1956; A Kiss before Dying 1956; The Mountain 1956; The True Story of Jesse James 1957; The Hunters 1958; In Love and War 1958; Say One for Me 1959; All the Fine Young Cannibals 1960; The Longest Day 1962; The War Lover 1962; The Pink Panther 1963; Harper 1966; Banning 1967; How I Spent My Summer Vacation 1967; The Biggest Bundle of Them All 1968; Don't Just Stand There 1968; Winning 1969; City beneath the Sea 1971; Madame Sin 1972; The Affair 1973; The Towering Inferno 1974; Las Vegas Roundabout 1975; Battle of Midway 1976; Airport '79: the Concorde 1979; The Curse of the Pink Panther 1983; Indiscreet 1988; Delirious 1991; Dragon: the Bruce Lee Story 1993; Austin Powers: International Man of Mystery 1997; Something to Believe In 1997; Wild Things 1998; Austin Powers, the Spy Who Shagged Me 1999; Crazy in Alabama 1999; Fatal Error 1999; Play It to the Bone 2000; Austin Powers in Goldmember 2002; Mystery Woman 2003; Hoot 2006; Man in the Chair 2006*

Wahl, Ken (1957-) *The Wanderers 1979; Fort Apache, the Bronx 1981; Race for the Yankee Zephyr 1981; Jinxed! 1982; Purple Hearts 1984; The Favor 1994*

Wahlberg, Donnie (1969-) *Bullet 1995; Body Count 1997; Purgatory 1999; The Sixth Sense 1999; Triggermen 2002; Dreamcatcher 2003; Annapolis 2005; Marilyn Hotchkiss Ballroom Dancing & Charm School 2005; Saw II 2005; Dead Silence 2007; Saw IV 2007; Righteous Kill 2008*

Wahlberg, Mark aka **Mark, Marky** (1971-) *Renaissance Man 1994; The Basketball Diaries 1995; Fear 1996; Boogie Nights 1997; Traveller 1997; The Big Hit 1998; The Corruptor 1999; Three Kings 1999; The Perfect Storm 2000; The Yards 2000; Planet of the Apes 2001; Rock Star 2001; The Truth about Charlie 2002; The Italian Job 2003; I ♥ Huckabees 2004; Overnight 2004; Four Brothers 2005; The Departed 2006; Invincible 2006; Shooter 2007; We Own the Night 2007; The Happening 2008; Max Payne 2008; The Lovely Bones 2009; Date Night 2010; The Fighter 2010; The Other Guys 2010; Contraband 2012; Ted 2012; Broken City 2013; Lone Survivor 2013; Pain & Gain 2013; 2 Guns 2013; The Gambler 2014; Mojave 2014; Transformers: Age of Extinction 2014; Daddy's Home 2015; Ted 2 2015*

Wainwright, James (1938-1999) *Joe Kidd 1972; Battletruck 1982; The Survivors 1983*

Wainwright III, Loudon aka **Wainwright, Loudon** (1946-) *The Slugger's Wife 1985; Jacknife 1988; Elizabethtown 2005; Knocked Up 2007*

Waite, Ralph (1928-2014) *A Lovely Way to Go 1968; Last Summer 1969; Five Easy Pieces 1970; Chato's Land 1971; Kid Blue 1973; The Magnificent Seven Ride! 1972; Trouble Man 1972; The Stone Killer 1973; The Bodyguard 1992; Sioux City 1994; Homeward Bound II: Lost in San Francisco 1996; The President's Man 2000; Sunshine State 2002; Generation Gap 2008*

Waites, Thomas G aka **Waites, Thomas** aka **Waites, Tom** (1955-) *On the Yard 1978; The Warriors 1979; The Thing 1982; The Clan of the Cave Bear 1986; Blue Jean Cop 1988*

Waits, Tom (1949-) *The Outsiders 1983; Rumble Fish 1983; Down by Law 1986; Candy Mountain 1987; Ironweed 1987; Cold Feet 1989; Mystery Train 1989; At Play in the Fields of the Lord 1991; Queens Logic 1991; Bram Stoker's Dracula 1992; Short Cuts 1993; Coffee and Cigarettes 2003; Wristcutters: a Love Story 2006; The Book of Eli 2009; The Imaginarium of Doctor Parnassus 2009; Twixt 2011; Seven Psychopaths 2012*

Wakabayashi, Akiko (1941-) *What's Up, Tiger Lily? 1966; You Only Live Twice 1967*

Wakao, Ayako (1933-) *Street of Shame 1955; Floating Weeds 1959; An Actor's Revenge 1963*

Wakayama, Tomisaburo (1929-1992) *Sword of Vengeance 1972; Shogun Assassin 1980; Black Rain 1989*

Waked, Amr *Salmon Fishing in the Yemen 2011; Winter of Discontent 2012*

Wakefield, Hugh (1888-1971) *The Fortunate Fool 1933; The Man Who Knew Too Much 1934; Journey Together 1944; Blithe Spirit 1945; One Night with You 1948*

Wakefield, Rhys *Sanctum 2010; The Purge 2013*

Walbrook, Anton aka **Wohlbruck, Adolf** (1900-1967) *Viktor und Viktoria 1933; Victoria the Great 1937; Sixty Glorious Years 1938; Gaslight 1940; Dangerous Moonlight 1941; 49th Parallel 1941; The Life and Death of Colonel Blimp 1943; The Man from Morocco 1944; The Queen of Spades 1948; The Red Shoes 1948; La Ronde 1950; Lola Montès 1955; Oh, Rosalinda!! 1955; Saint Joan 1957; I Accuse! 1958*

Walburn, Raymond (1887-1969) *Broadway Bill 1934; The Count of Monte Cristo 1934; Lady by Choice 1934; She Married Her Boss 1935; Thanks a Million 1935; Born to Dance 1936; The King Steps Out 1936; The Lone Wolf Returns 1936; Mr Deeds Goes to Town 1936; High, Wide and Handsome 1937; Thin Ice 1937; Christmas in July 1940; Third Finger, Left Hand 1940; Confirm or Deny 1941; Kiss the Boys Goodbye 1941; Louisiana Purchase 1941; The Desperadoes 1943; Dixie 1943; And the Angels Sing 1944; Hail the Conquering Hero 1944; Music in Manhattan 1944; The Cheaters 1945; Lover Come Back 1946; Key to the City 1950; Mad Wednesday 1950; Riding High 1950; Golden Girl 1951; Beautiful but Dangerous 1954*

Walcott, Gregory (1928-2015) *Texas Lady 1955; Thunder over Arizona 1956; Jet Attack 1958; Plan 9 from Outer Space 1959; The Outsider 1961; Man of the East 1972; Prime Cut 1972; The Sugarland Express 1974; House 'I: the Second Story 1987*

Walden, Robert (1943-) *Bloody Mama 1970; Blue Sunshine 1977*

Waldis, Otto (1901-1974) *The Exile 1947; Bird of Paradise 1951; Unknown World 1951; The Whip Hand 1951*

Waldman, Marian (1924-1985) *Black Christmas 1974; Deranged 1974*

Waldo, Janet (1920-2016) *Waterloo Bridge 1940; Fantastic Planet 1973*

Waldron, Charles (1874-1946) *Kentucky 1938; Remember the Night 1940; Stranger on the Third Floor 1940; The Big Sleep 1946*

Waldron, Shawna (1982-) *Little Giants 1994; The American President 1995*

Wales, Ethel (1898-1952) *The Covered Wagon 1923; The Saturday Night Kid 1929; Tom Sawyer 1930; Days of Jesse James 1939*

Walken, Christopher (1943-) *The Anderson Tapes 1971; The Mind Snatchers 1972; Next Stop, Greenwich Village 1976; Annie Hall 1977; Roseland 1977; The Sentinel 1977; The Deer Hunter 1978; Last Embrace 1979; The Dogs of War 1980; Heaven's Gate 1980; Pennies from Heaven 1981; Brainstorm 1983; The Dead Zone 1983; At Close Range 1985; A View to a Kill 1985; Witness in the War Zone 1986; Biloxi Blues 1988; The Milagro Beanfield War 1988; Communion 1989; King of New York 1989; The Comfort of Strangers 1991; Batman Returns 1992; Mistress 1992; A Business Affair 1993; True Romance 1993; Wayne's World 2 1993; The Addiction 1994; The Prophecy 1994; Pulp Fiction 1994; Nick of Time 1995; Search and Destroy 1995; Things to Do in Denver When You're Dead 1995; Wild Side 1995; Basquiat 1996; The Funeral 1996; Last Man Standing 1996; Touch 1996; Excess Baggage 1997; Mousehunt 1997; The Prophecy II 1997; Suicide Kings 1997; Antz 1998; Blast from the Past 1998; The Eternal 1998; New Rose Hotel 1998; Sleepy Hollow 1999; The Opportunists 2000; The Prophecy 3: the Ascent 2000; The Affair of the Necklace 2001; America's Sweethearts 2001; Joe Dirt 2001; Catch Me If You Can 2002; The Country Bears 2002; Envy 2003; Gigli 2003; Kangaroo Jack 2003; Welcome to the Jungle 2003; Around the Bend 2004; Man on Fire 2004; Romance & Cigarettes 2004; The Stepford Wives 2004; Domino 2005; Wedding Crashers 2005; Click 2006; Fade to Black 2006; Man of the Year 2006; Balls of Fury 2007; Hairspray 2007; The Heist 2009; Dark Horse 2011; Kill the Irishman 2011; A Late Quartet 2012; Seven Psychopaths 2012; Stand Up Guys 2012; Jersey Boys 2014; Eddie the Eagle 2016; The Jungle Book 2016; Nine Lives 2016*

Walker, Ally (1961-) *Universal Soldier 1992; The Seventh Coin 1993; When the Bough Breaks 1993; Bed of Roses 1995; Steal Big, Steal Little 1995; Kazaam 1996; Happy, Texas 1999; By Appointment Only 2007*

Walker, Amanda (1961-) *Heat and Dust 1982; 7 Days to Live 2000*

Walker, Arnetia (1961-) *Scenes from the Class Struggle In Beverly Hills 1989; Love Crimes 1991*

Walker, Ben *The Magician 2005; The Golden Compass 2007*

Walker, Benjamin (1982-) *Abraham Lincoln: Vampire Hunter 2012; In the Heart of the Sea 2015; The Choice 2016*

Walker, Chris *The Funny Man 1994; When Saturday Comes 1995*

Walker, Clint (1927-) *Yellowstone Kelly 1959; Send Me No Flowers 1964; None but the Brave 1965; The Dirty Dozen 1967; The Great Bank Robbery 1969; Sam Whiskey 1969; Pancho Villa 1971; Baker's Hawk 1976; The White Buffalo 1977; Small Soldiers 1998*

Walker, Dreama *Gran Torino 2008; Compliance 2012*

Walker, Eamonn (1970-) *Tears of the Sun 2003; Duma 2005; Lord of War 2005; Cadillac Records 2008; Blood and Bone 2009; The Messenger 2009; Legacy: Black Ops 2010; A Lonely Place to Die 2011*

Walker, Fiona (1944-) *Far from the Madding Crowd 1967; The Asphyx 1972*

Walker, Helen (1920-1968) *Abroad with Two Yanks 1944; Brewster's Millions 1945; Murder, He Says 1945; Cluny Brown 1946; Nightmare Alley 1947; Call Northside 777 1948; My Dear Secretary 1948; Impact 1949; The Big Combo 1955*

Walker, Jimmie (1947-) *Water 1985; The Guyver 1991*

Walker, Johnny aka **Walker, Johny** (1923-2003) *Mr and Mrs '55 1955; Chori Chori 1956; Pyaasa 1957; Madhumati 1958; Kaagaz Ke Phool 1959*

Walker, Jonathan *American Blue Note 1989; Shooter 2007*

Walker, Kathryn (1943-) *Rich Kids 1979; Neighbors 1981; DARYL 1985*

Walker, Kerry (1948-) *Almost 1990; The Piano 1993*

Walker, Martin (1901-1955) *Sanders of the River 1935; The Vicar of Bray 1937; The Drum 1938; Love on the Dole 1941*

Walker, Matthew (1942-) *Little Women 1994; Intimate Relations 1995; Miracle on the 17th Green 1999*

Walker, Nancy (1922-1992) *Best Foot Forward 1943; Girl Crazy 1943; Broadway Rhythm 1944; Lucky Me 1954; The World's Greatest Athlete 1973*

Walker, Nella (1886-1971) *The Woman in Red 1935; In Name Only 1939; Three Smart Girls Grow Up 1939; When Tomorrow Comes 1939; I Love You Again 1940; Hers to Hold 1943; Sabrina 1954*

Walker, Paul (1973-2013) *Meet the Deedles 1998; She's All That 1999; Varsity Blues 1999; The Skulls 2000; The Fast and the Furious 2001; Road Kill 2001; Joy Ride 2001; 2 Fast 2 Furious 2003; Noel 2004; Eight Below 2005; Into the Blue 2005; Running Scared 2006; Flags of Our Fathers 2006; The Lazarus Project 2008; Fast & Furious 2009; Takers 2010; Fast Five 2011; Fast & Furious 6 2013; Hours 2013; Vehicle 19 2013; Brick Mansions 2014; Fast & Furious 7 2014*

Walker, Polly (1966-) *Enchanted April 1991; Shogun Warrior 1991; Patriot Games 1992; Sliver 1993; The Trial 1993; Restoration 1995; Daniel Defoe's Robinson Crusoe 1996; Emma 1996; Roseanna's Grave 1996; Curtain Call 1997; The Gambler 1997; The Woodlanders 1997; Dark Harbor 1998; Talk of Angels 1998; 8½ Women 1999; Eye of the Killer 1999; D-Tox 2001*

Walker, Ray (1904-1980) *Baby, Take a Bow 1934; Marry Me Again 1953*

Walker, Robert (1918-1951) *Madame Curie 1943; Since You Went Away 1944; Thirty Seconds over Tokyo 1944; The Clock 1945; The Sailor Takes a Wife 1945; Till the Clouds Roll By 1946; The Beginning or the End 1947; The Sea of Grass 1947; Song of Love 1947; One Touch of Venus 1948; Please Believe Me 1950; Strangers on a Train 1951; Vengeance Valley 1951; My Son John 1952*

Walker Jr, Robert aka **Walker, Robert** (1940-) *The Hook 1962; The Ceremony 1963; Ensign Pulver 1964; The Happening 1967; The War Wagon 1967; Easy Rider 1969; Young Billy Young 1969; Beware! The Blob 1971; Don Juan 73, or If Don Juan Were a Woman 1973; Hambone and Hillie 1984*

Walker, Ally (1961-) *Universal Soldier 1992; The Seventh Coin 1993; When the Bough Breaks 1993; Bed of Roses 1995; Steal Big, Steal Little 1995; Kazaam 1996; Happy, Texas 1999; By Appointment Only 2007*

Walker (1), Scott (1944-) *Cahill, United States Marshal 1973; Orca... Killer Whale 1977*

Walker, Syd (1886-1945) *Over She Goes 1937; The Gang's All Here 1939*

Walker, Sydney (1921-1994) *Love Story 1970; Prelude to a Kiss 1992; Getting Even with Dad 1994*

Walker, Tippy (1947-) *The World of Henry Orient 1964; Jennifer on My Mind 1971*

Walker, Zena (1934-2003) *Emergency 1962; Sammy Going South 1963; The Likely Lads 1976; The Dresser 1983*

Wall, Max (1908-1990) *The Hound of the Baskervilles 1977; Jabberwocky 1977; Hanover Street 1979; Little Dorrit 1987; We Think the World of You 1988; Loser Takes All 1990*

Wall, Robert aka **Wall, Bob** (1939-) *Enter the Dragon 1973; The Way of the Dragon 1973; Game of Death 1978*

Wallace Stone, Dee aka **Wallace, Dee** (1948-) *The Hills Have Eyes 1977; 10 1979; The Howling 1981; ET the Extra-Terrestrial 1982; Cujo 1983; Legend of the White Horse 1985; Secret Admirer 1985; Critters 1986; Alligator II: the Mutation 1991; Popcorn 1991; Rescue Me 1991; Huck and the King of Hearts 1993; The Road Home 1995; Temptress 1995; The Frighteners 1996; Skeletons 1996; Swearing Allegiance 1997; Halloween 2007; The House of the Devil 2009; Extraordinary Measures 2010*

Wallace, Anzac (1943-) *Utu 1983; The Quiet Earth 1985*

Wallace, Basil *Marked for Death 1990; Return of the Living Dead III 1993; Road Kill 2001*

Wallace, Bill *A Force of One 1979; Avenging Force 1986*

Wallace, George (1952-) *3 Strikes 2000; The Wash 2001*

Wallace, Jean (1923-1990) *Blaze of Noon 1947; Jigsaw 1949; The Man on the Eiffel Tower 1949; Native Son 1951; Star of India 1954; The Big Combo 1955; The Devil's Hairpin 1957; Maracaibo 1958; Lancelot and Guinevere 1963; Beach Red 1967; No Blade of Grass 1970*

Wallace, Julie T (1961-) *Hawks 1988; The Lunatic 1992*

Wallace, Morgan (1881-1953) *Blonde Venus 1932; Hell's House 1932; Confidential 1935*

Wallace, Paul *Johnny Trouble 1957; Gypsy 1962*

Wallach, Eli (1915-2014) *Baby Doll 1956; The Lineup 1958; The Magnificent Seven 1960; Seven Thieves 1960; The Misfits 1961; Hemingway's Adventures of a Young Man 1962; How the West Was Won 1962; Act One 1963; The Victors 1963; Kisses for My President 1964; The Moon-Spinners 1964; Lord Jim 1965; The Good, the Bad and the Ugly 1966; How to Steal a Million 1966; The Poppy Is Also a Flower 1966; Ace High 1968; A Lovely Way to Go 1968; The Brain 1969; Mackenna's Gold 1969; The Adventures of Gerard 1970; The Angel Levine 1970; Zigzag 1970; Romance of a Horse Thief 1971; Cinderella Liberty 1973; The Deep 1977; The Domino Principle 1977; The Sentinel 1977; Girlfriends 1978; The Silent Flute 1978; Firepower 1979; Winter Kills 1979; The Hunter 1980; The Salamander 1981; Skokie 1981; The Executioner's Song 1982; Sam's Son 1984; Tough Guys 1986; Nuts 1987; The Godfather Part III 1990; The Two Jakes 1990; Article 99 1992; Mistress 1992; Night and the City 1992; Two Much 1995; The Associate 1996; The Bookfair Murders 2000; Keeping the Faith 2000; The Hoax 2006; The Holiday 2006; New York, I Love You 2009; The Ghost 2010; Wall Street: Money Never Sleeps 2010*

Waller, Eddy aka **Waller, Eddy C** (1889-1977) *Indian Uprising 1951; Man without a Star 1955*

Waller, Fats (1904-1943) *King of Burlesque 1936; Stormy Weather 1943*

Walley, Deborah (1943-2001) *Bon Voyage! 1962; Summer Magic 1963; Beach Blanket Bingo 1965; Sergeant Deadhead 1965; Ski Party 1965; The Bubble 1966; The Ghost in the Invisible Bikini 1966; Spinout 1966*

Williams, David (1971-) *A Cock and Bull Story 2005; Marmaduke 2010; The Look of Love 2013; Pudsey the Dog: the Movie 2014*

Wallis, Annabelle *Hello Carter 2013; Annabelle 2014; Sword of Vengeance 2015; The Mummy 2017*

Wallis, Quvenzhané (2003-) *Beasts of the Southern Wild 2012; Annie 2014; Fathers and Daughters 2015*

Wallis, Shani (1933-) *Oliver! 1968; Terror in the Wax Museum 1973; The Pebble and the Penguin 1995*

Wallraff, Diego (1962-) *Of Love and Shadows 1994; The Perez Family 1995; Deadlocked 2000; Mary Higgins Clark's Try to Remember 2004*

Walls, Tom (1883-1949) *Rookery Nook 1930; A Cuckoo in the Nest 1933; Fighting Stock 1935; Foreign Affaires 1935; Crackerjack 1938; Strange Boarders 1938; The Halfway House 1943; They Met in the Dark 1943; Undercover 1943; Love Story 1944; Johnny Frenchman 1945; The Master of Bankdam 1947; While I Live 1947; Spring in Park Lane 1948; The Interrupted Journey 1949; Maytime in Mayfair 1949*

Walsh, Dermot (1924-2002) *Hungry Hill 1946; Jassy 1947; The Mark of Cain 1947; Third Time Lucky 1949; The Frightened Man 1952; Ghost Ship 1952; The Blue Parrot 1953; Counterspy 1953; Sea Fury 1958; The Bandit of Zhobe 1959; The Flesh and the Fiends 1959; Make Mine a Million 1959; The Breaking Point 1961; Emergency 1962*

Walsh, Dylan (1963-) *Nobody's Fool 1994; Congo 1995; Changing Habits 1997; Blood Work 2002; More than Meets the Eye: the Joan Brock Story 2003; Edmond 2005; The Lake House 2006; Lost Holiday: the Jim and Suzanne Shemwell Story 2007; The Stepfather 2009; Secretariat 2010*

Walsh, Eileen (1978-) *Janice Beard 45 WPM 1999; The Magdalene Sisters 2002*

Walsh, George (1889-1981) *Rosita 1923; Me and My Gal 1932; Black Beauty 1933; The Bowery 1933*

Walsh, J T (1943-1998) *Power 1986; Good Morning, Vietnam 1987; House of Games 1987; Tin Men 1987; Tequila Sunrise 1988; The Big Picture 1989; Dad 1989; Wired 1989; Crazy People 1990; The Grifters 1990; Narrow Margin 1990; The Russia House 1990; Why Me? 1990; Backdraft 1991; Defenseless 1991; Iron Maze 1991; True Identity 1991; A Few Good Men 1992; Hoffa 1992; Red Rock West 1992; Sniper 1992; The Last Seduction 1993; Needful Things 1993; Blue Chips 1994; Charlie's Ghost Story 1994; The Client 1994; Miracle on 34th Street 1994; Silent Fall 1994; The Babysitter 1995; The Low Life 1995; Nixon 1995; Sling Blade 1995; Crime of the Century 1996; Gang in Blue 1996; Persons Unknown 1996; Breakdown 1997; The Negotiator 1998; Pleasantville 1998*

Walsh, John (1945-) *The Wild Women of Wongo 1958; Body Parts 1991*

Walsh, Joseph aka **Walsh, Joey** (1937-) *Hans Christian Andersen 1952; The Juggler 1953; Anzio 1968; California Split 1974; The Driver 1978*

Walsh, Kate (1967-) *Henry: Portrait of a Serial Killer, Part II 1996; Kicking & Screaming 2005; The Perks of Being a Wallflower 2012*

Walsh, Kay (1914-2005) *Keep Fit 1937; The Last Adventurers 1937; I See Ice 1938; Sons of the Sea 1939; In Which We Serve 1942; This Happy Breed 1944; The October Man 1947; Vice Versa 1947; Oliver Twist 1948; Stage Fright 1949; Last Holiday 1950; The Magnet 1950; Encore 1951; Hunted 1952; Meet Me Tonight 1952; Young Bess 1953; Lease of Life 1954; The Rainbow Jacket 1954; Cast a Dark Shadow 1957; The Horse's Mouth 1958; Tunes of Glory 1960; Greyfriars Bobby 1961; Lunch Hour 1962; Reach for Glory 1962; Dr Syn, Alias the Scarecrow 1963; 80,000 Suspects 1963; The Beauty Jungle 1964; He Who Rides a Tiger 1965; The Witches 1966; Connecting Rooms 1969; The Virgin and the Gypsy 1970; The Ruling Class 1972*

Walsh, M Emmet (1935-) *Alice's Restaurant 1969; The Prisoner of Second Avenue 1975; At Long Last Love 1975; Straight Time 1978; The Jerk 1979; Ordinary People 1980; Raise the Titanic 1980; Back Roads 1981; Reds 1981; Blade Runner 1982; Cannery Row 1982; The Escape Artist 1982; Fast-Walking 1982; Blood Simple 1983; Scandalous 1983; Grandview, USA 1984; Missing in Action 1984; The Pope of Greenwich Village 1984; Fletch 1985; Back to School 1986; The Best of Times 1986; Critters 1986; Resting Place 1986; Wildcats 1986; Bigfoot and the Hendersons 1987; No Man's Land 1987; Clean and Sober 1988; Sunset 1988; Chattahoochee 1989; The Mighty Quinn 1989; Red Scorpion 1989; Narrow Margin 1990; Equinox 1992; White Sands 1992; Bitter Harvest 1993; The Music of Chance 1993; Wilder Napalm 1993; Free Willy 2: the Adventure Home 1995; From the Mixed-Up Files of Mrs Basil E Frankweiler 1995; Albino Alligator 1996; My Best Friend's Wedding 1997;*

The Iron Giant 1999; Random Hearts 1999; Wild Wild West 1999; Snow Dogs 2002; Christmas with the Kranks 2004; Racing Stripes 2004; Man in the Chair 2006; The Odd Life of Timothy Green 2012
Walsh, Matt Cyrus 2010; Into the Storm 2014
Walsh, Percy (1888-1952) Boys Will Be Boys 1935; Death Drives Through 1935; Pastor Hall 1940
Walsh, Raoul (1887-1980) Sadie Thompson 1928; It's a Great Feeling 1949
Walston, Ray (1914-2001) Kiss Them for Me 1957; Damn Yankees 1958; South Pacific 1958; Say One for Me 1959; The Apartment 1960; Portrait in Black 1960; Convicts Four 1962; Who's Minding the Store? 1963; Kiss Me, Stupid 1964; Caprice 1967; Paint Your Wagon 1969; The Sting 1973; Silver Streak 1976; The Happy Hooker Goes to Washington 1977; Popeye 1980; Johnny Dangerously 1984; Saturday the 14th Strikes Back 1988; Of Mice and Men 1992; Addams Family Reunion 1998; My Favorite Martian 1999; Swing Vote 1999
Walter, Harriet (1950-) Turtle Diary 1985; The Good Father 1986; Milou en Mai 1989; The Hour of the Pig 1993; Sense and Sensibility 1995; The Governess 1997; Keep the Aspidistra Flying 1997; Bedrooms and Hallways 1998; Onegin 1999; Villa des Roses 2002; Bright Young Things 2003; Chromophobia 2005; Atonement 2007; Broken Lines 2008; The Young Victoria 2008; Chéri 2009; Morris: a Life with Bells On 2009; The Wedding Video 2012; Man Up 2015
Walter, Jessica (1940-) Lilith 1964; Grand Prix 1966; The Group 1966; Bye Bye Braverman 1968; Number One 1969; Play Misty for Me 1971; Going Ape! 1981; The Flamingo Kid 1984; Tapeheads 1988; Ghost in the Machine 1993; Leave of Absence 1994; Temptress 1995; Slums of Beverly Hills 1998; Dummy 2002
Walter, Lisa Ann (1963-) Eddie 1996; The Parent Trap 1998; Bruce Almighty 2003; Shall We Dance 2004
Walter, Tracey (1942-) The Hunter 1980; Raggedy Man 1981; Conan the Destroyer 1984; Repo Man 1984; Something Wild 1986; City Slickers 1991; Kidnapped 1995; Wild America 1997
Walters, Ashley (1982-) Bullet Boy 2004; Life & Lyrics 2006; WAZ 2006; Sugarhouse 2007; Tu£sday 2007; Dead Man Running 2009; Demons Never Die 2011; Sket 2011; All Stars 2013
Walters, Jamie aka Walters, James (1969-) Shout 1991; Bed & Breakfast 1992
Walters, Julie (1950-) Educating Rita 1983; She'll Be Wearing Pink Pyjamas 1984; Car Trouble 1985; Personal Services 1987; Prick Up Your Ears 1987; Buster 1988; Killing Dad 1989; Mack the Knife 1989; Stepping Out 1991; Just like a Woman 1992; Wide Eyed and Legless 1993; Sister My Sister 1994; Intimate Relations 1995; Girls' Night 1997; Titanic Town 1998; Billy Elliot 2000; Harry Potter and the Philosopher's Stone 2001; Before You Go 2002; Harry Potter and the Chamber of Secrets 2002; Calendar Girls 2003; Harry Potter and the Prisoner of Azkaban 2004; Wah-Wah 2005; Becoming Jane 2006; Driving Lessons 2006; Mamma Mia! 2008; Gnomeo & Juliet 2011; Brave 2012; The Harry Hill Movie 2013; Justin and the Knights of Valour 2013; One Chance 2013; Effie Gray 2014; Paddington 2014; Brooklyn 2015
Walters, Laurie (1947-) The Harrad Experiment 1973; The Harrad Summer 1974
Walters, Melora (1968-) Magnolia 1999; Wisegirls 2001; The Butterfly Effect 2003
Walters, Nancy (1933-2009) The Green Helmet 1960; Blue Hawaii 1961
Walters, Stephen aka Walters, Stephen Martin Franklyn 2008; Splintered 2008
Walters, Susan (1963-) Russkies 1987; ...At First Sight 1995
Walters, Thorley (1913-1991) Carlton-Browne of the FO 1958; The Pure Hell of St Trinian's 1960; Suspect 1960; Invasion Quartet 1961; Murder She Said 1961; Petticoat Pirates 1961; The Phantom of the Opera 1962; Sherlock Holmes and the Deadly Necklace 1962; Ring of Spies 1963; Dracula - Prince of Darkness 1965; Frankenstein Created Woman 1966; Frankenstein Must Be Destroyed 1969; The Man Who Haunted Himself 1970; Trog 1970; Bartleby 1971; Vampire Circus 1971; The

Adventure of Sherlock Holmes' Smarter Brother 1975; The People That Time Forgot 1977; The Wildcats of St Trinian's 1980; The Sign of Four 1983
Walthall, Henry B (1878-1936) Home, Sweet Home 1914; The Birth of a Nation 1915; The Road to Mandalay 1926; The Scarlet Letter 1926; London after Midnight 1927; The Trespasser 1929; Abraham Lincoln 1930; Chandu the Magician 1932; Me and My Gal 1932; Ride Him, Cowboy 1932; Strange Interlude 1932; Laughing at Life 1933; Judge Priest 1934; The Lemon Drop Kid 1934; Dante's Inferno 1935; A Tale of Two Cities 1935; China Clipper 1936; The Devil-Doll 1936; The Last Outlaw 1936
Walton, Anna Mutant Chronicles 2008; The Seasoning House 2012
Walton, Douglas (1910-1961) The Secret of Madame Blanche 1933; Charlie Chan in London 1934; Bride of Frankenstein 1935; Mary of Scotland 1936; Raffles 1939; Farewell My Lovely 1944; The Picture of Dorian Gray 1945; Dick Tracy vs Cueball 1946
Walton, John (1953-2014) Kangaroo 1986; The Lighthorsemen 1987
Walton, Tasma Virtual Nightmare 2000; Mystery Road 2013
Waltz, Christoph (1956-) Carnage 2011; The Green Hornet 2011; The Three Musketeers 2011; Water for Elephants 2011; Django Unchained 2012; Epic 2013; The Zero Theorem 2013; Big Eyes 2014; Horrible Bosses 2 2014; Muppets Most Wanted 2014; Spectre 2015; The Legend of Tarzan 2016
Waltz, Lisa Brighton Beach Memoirs 1986; The Odd Couple II 1998
Wanamaker, Sam (1919-1993) My Girl Tisa 1948; Mr Denning Drives North 1951; The Criminal 1960; Taras Bulba 1962; The Spy Who Came In from the Cold 1965; Danger Route 1967; The Day the Fish Came Out 1967; Warning Shot 1967; The Sellout 1975; Voyage of the Damned 1976; Death on the Nile 1978; From Hell to Victory 1979; Private Benjamin 1980; Irreconcilable Differences 1984; The Aviator 1985; Raw Deal 1986; Baby Boom 1987; Superman IV: the Quest for Peace 1987; Judgment in Berlin 1988; Guilty by Suspicion 1990; Pure Luck 1991
Wanamaker, Zoë (1949-) The Raggedy Rawney 1987; Amy Foster 1997; Wilde 1997; Harry Potter and the Philosopher's Stone 2001; Five Children and It 2004; It's a Wonderful Afterlife 2010
Wang Baoqiang Blind Shaft 2003; A Touch of Sin 2013; Iceman 2014; Kung Fu Killer 2014
Wang Hong Wei Xiao Wu 1997; Unknown Pleasures 2002
Wang Leehom Lust, Caution 2007; Little Big Soldier 2010
Wang Shuangbao Balzac and the Little Chinese Seamstress 2002; Blind Shaft 2003
Wang Xueqi Yellow Earth 1984; The Big Parade 1986; Reign of Assassins 2010
Wang Yu (1) aka Wang Yu, Jimmy (1944-) One-Armed Swordsman 1967; The Man from Hong Kong 1975; Dragon 2011
Wang Yu-wen Rebels of the Neon God 1992; Eat Drink Man Woman 1994
Wang Zhiwen The Emperor and the Assassin 1999; Together with You 2002
Wang, Peter Chan Is Missing 1982; A Great Wall 1985
Wanninger, Ashley Europa Europa 1991; Romance 1998; Sex Is Comedy 2002
War Eagle, John (1901-1991) The Wild North 1952; The Great Sioux Uprising 1953; When the Legends Die 1972
Waram, Percy (1881-1961) Ministry of Fear 1945; It Had to Be You 1947; The Late George Apley 1947; The Big Hangover 1950; A Face in the Crowd 1957
Warbeck, David (1941-1997) Twins of Evil 1971; The Black Cat 1981
Warburton, John (1887-1981) Nothing but Trouble 1944; Confidential Agent 1945; Saratoga Trunk 1945; Tarzan and the Huntress 1947
Warburton, Patrick (1964-) Dragonard 1987; The Dish 2000; The Emperor's New Groove 2000; Joe Somebody 2001; Men in Black 2 2002; Hoodwinked 2005; Kronk's New Groove 2005; Happily N'Ever After 2006; Open Season 2006; Bee Movie 2007; Underdog 2007; Space Chimps 2008; Space Chimps 2: Zartog Strikes Back 2009
Ward, Amelita The Falcon and the Co-Eds 1943; The Falcon in Danger 1943; Come Out Fighting 1945

Ward, Fred (1942-) Escape from Alcatraz 1979; UFOria 1980; Southern Comfort 1981; The Right Stuff 1983; Silkwood 1983; Uncommon Valor 1983; Swing Shift 1984; Remo - Unarmed and Dangerous 1985; Secret Admirer 1985; Big Business 1988; The Prince of Pennsylvania 1988; Saigon 1988; Catchfire 1989; Tremors 1989; Henry & June 1990; Miami Blues 1990; The Dark Wind 1991; Equinox 1992; The Player 1992; Thunderheart 1992; Short Cuts 1993; The Blue Villa 1994; Naked Gun 33⅓ the Final Insult 1994; Tremors II: Aftershocks 1995; Chain Reaction 1996; Best Men 1997; Dangerous Beauty 1997; First Do No Harm 1997; Circus 1999; Red Team 1999; Corky Romano 2001; Summer Catch 2001; Enough 2002; Sweet Home Alabama 2002; The Last Ride 2004; Feast of Love 2007; Management 2008; Armored 2009; Farewell 2010; 30 Minutes or Less 2011
Ward, James The Night of the Iguana 1964; Red Line 7000 1965; Casper: a Spirited Beginning 1997
Ward, Jonathan (1970-) White Water Summer 1987; Mac and Me 1988; FernGully: the Last Rainforest 1992
Ward, Kelly (1956-) Grease 1978; The Big Red One 1980; A Fuller Life 2013
Ward, Lyman (1941-) Ferris Bueller's Day Off 1986; Guilty as Charged 1991; The Secret Agent Club 1995
Ward, Mackenzie (1903-1976) Sunny 1930; As You Like It 1936; The Girl in the Taxi 1937; Sons of the Sea 1939
Ward, Megan (1969-) Trancers II: The Return of Jack Deth 1991; California Man 1992; Freaked 1993; PCU 1994; Glory Daze 1995; Joe's Apartment 1996; Wes Craven's Don't Look Down 1998; Rated X 2000; Murder without Conviction 2004
Ward, Michael (1909-1997) What the Butler Saw 1950; The Frightened Man 1952
Ward, Polly (1909-1987) The Old Curiosity Shop 1935; It's in the Air 1938
Ward, Rachel (1957-) Sharky's Machine 1981; Dead Men Don't Wear Plaid 1982; Against All Odds 1984; The Good Wife 1986; Hotel Colonial 1987; How to Get Ahead in Advertising 1989; After Dark, My Sweet 1990; Christopher Columbus: the Discovery 1992; Wide Sargasso Sea 1992; The Ascent 1994
Ward, Richard aka Ward, Dick (1915-1979) The Learning Tree 1969; Across 110th Street 1972; Cops and Robbers 1973; Mandingo 1975; The Jerk 1979; Brubaker 1980
Ward, Roger (1936-) Mad Max 1979; Turkey Shoot 1981; Long Weekend 2008
Ward, Ronald (1901-1978) We'll Meet Again 1942; They Met in the Dark 1943
Ward, Sela (1957-) The Man Who Loved Women 1983; Nothing in Common 1986; Hello Again 1987; Bridesmaids 1989; The Fugitive 1993; My Fellow Americans 1996; 54 1998; Dirty Dancing 2 2003; The Day after Tomorrow 2004; Suburban Madness 2004; The Guardian 2006; The Stepfather 2009
Ward, Simon (1941-2012) Frankenstein Must Be Destroyed 1969; I Start Counting 1970; Young Winston 1972; Hitler: the Last Ten Days 1973; All Creatures Great and Small 1974; Dracula 1974; The Four Musketeers 1974; Aces High 1976; Holocaust 2000 1977; Dominique 1978; The Four Feathers 1978; Zulu Dawn 1979; The Monster Club 1980; Supergirl 1984; Leave All Fair 1985; Double X: the Name of the Game 1991
Ward, Skip (1932-2003) Roadracers 1958; Easy Come, Easy Go 1967
Ward, Sophie (1965-) Young Sherlock Holmes 1985; Aria 1987; A Summer Story 1987; Young Toscanini 1988; Wuthering Heights 1992
Ward, Wally aka Langham, Wallace (1965-) Thunder Run 1986; The Chocolate War 1988; The Invisible Kid 1988
Ward, Warwick (1891-1967) Vaudeville 1925; The Wonderful Lie of Nina Petrovna 1929; Birds of Prey 1930
Warde, Harlan (1917-1980) Julie 1956; The Monster That Challenged the World 1957
Warden, Jack (1920-2006) From Here to Eternity 1953; The Bachelor Party 1957; Edge of the City 1957; 12 Angry Men 1957; Darby's Rangers 1958; Run Silent Run Deep 1958; The Sound and the Fury 1959; That Kind of Woman 1959; Escape from Zahrain 1962; Donovan's Reef 1963; The Thin Red Line 1964; Blindfold 1966; Bye Bye Braverman 1968; Brian's Song 1971; The Face of Fear 1971; Summertree

1971; Who Is Harry Kellerman, and Why Is He Saying Those Terrible Things about Me? 1971; Billy Two Hats 1973; The Man Who Loved Cat Dancing 1973; The Apprenticeship of Duddy Kravitz 1974; Shampoo 1975; All the President's Men 1976; Raid on Entebbe 1977; The White Buffalo 1977; Death on the Nile 1978; Heaven Can Wait 1978; ...And Justice for All 1979; Being There 1979; Beyond the Poseidon Adventure 1979; The Champ 1979; Used Cars 1980; Carbon Copy 1981; The Great Muppet Caper 1981; So Fine 1981; The Verdict 1982; The Aviator 1985; September 1987; The Presidio 1988; Everybody Wins 1990; Problem Child 1990; Problem Child 2 1991; Night and the City 1992; Passed Away 1992; Toys 1992; Guilty as Sin 1993; Bullets over Broadway 1994; Things to Do in Denver When You're Dead 1995; While You Were Sleeping 1995; Ed 1996; The Island on Bird Street 1997; Dirty Work 1998; A Dog of Flanders 1999; The Replacements 2000
Wardwell, Geoffrey (1900-1955) The Challenge 1938; Crimes at the Dark House 1939
Ware, Herta (1917-2005) Cocoon 1985; Crazy in Love 1992
Ware, Irene (1911-1993) Chandu the Magician 1932; The Raven 1935
Wareing, Kierston (1976-) It's a Free World... 2007; Fish Tank 2009; Basement 2010; Bonded by Blood 2010; Four 2010; The Fall of the Essex Boys 2012; The Liability 2012; Love Bite 2012; Twenty8k 2012
Warhol, Andy (1928-1987) Dynamite Chicken 1971; The Driver's Seat 1975
Waring, Richard (1925-1994) The Perfect Gentleman 1935; Mr Skeffington 1944
Warlock, Billy (1961-) Hot Shot 1986; Society 1989
Warner, Amelia (1982-) Don Quixote 2000; Quills 2000; Aeonflux 2005; Alpha Male 2005; Stoned 2005; Gone 2006; The Dark Is Rising 2007
Warner, David (1941-) Tom Jones 1963; Morgan - a Suitable Case for Treatment 1966; The Bofors Gun 1968; The Sea Gull 1968; A Midsummer Night's Dream 1969; The Ballad of Cable Hogue 1970; Perfect Friday 1970; A Doll's House 1973; From beyond the Grave 1973; Mister Quilp 1975; The Omen 1976; Cross of Iron 1977; The Disappearance 1977; Providence 1977; Silver Bears 1977; The Thirty-Nine Steps 1978; Airport '79: the Concorde 1979; Nightwing 1979; SOS Titanic 1979; Time after Time 1979; The Island 1980; Tron 1982; The Man with Two Brains 1983; A Christmas Carol 1984; The Company of Wolves 1984; Hanna's War 1988; Mr North 1988; Waxwork 1988; Star Trek V: the Final Frontier 1989; Spymaker: the Secret Life of Ian Fleming 1990; Star Trek VI: the Undiscovered Country 1991; Teenage Mutant Ninja Turtles II: the Secret of the Ooze 1991; The Unnamable Returns 1992; Necronomicon 1993; In the Mouth of Madness 1994; Danielle Steel's Zoya 1995; Naked Souls 1995; The Leading Man 1996; Rasputin 1996; Money Talks 1997; Scream 2 1997; Winnie the Pooh's Most Grand Adventure 1997; The Little Unicorn 1998; Wing Commander 1999; Back to the Secret Garden 2000; Kiss of Life 2003; Ladies in Lavender 2004; The League of Gentlemen's Apocalypse 2005; Black Death 2010; A Thousand Kisses Deep 2011
Warner, H B (1876-1958) The King of Kings 1927; The Divine Lady 1928; The Show of Shows 1929; Five Star Final 1931; Jennie Gerhardt 1933; Supernatural 1933; Mr Deeds Goes to Town 1936; Lost Horizon 1937; Victoria the Great 1937; Bulldog Drummond in Africa 1938; Kidnapped 1938; The Toy Wife 1938; Bulldog Drummond's Bride 1939; Mr Smith Goes to Washington 1939; New Moon 1940; The Corsican Brothers 1941; Topper Returns 1941; Hitler's Children 1943; Action in Arabia 1944; It's a Wonderful Life 1946; High Wall 1947; The Prince of Thieves 1948
Warner, Jack (1895-1981) The Captive Heart 1946; Against the Wind 1947; Dear Murderer 1947; Easy Money 1947; Holiday Camp 1947; Hue and Cry 1947; Here Come the Huggetts 1948; My Brother's Keeper 1948; Vote for Huggett 1948; The Blue Lamp 1949; Boys in Brown 1949; The Huggetts Abroad 1949; Train of Events 1949; Scrooge 1951; Valley of Eagles 1951; Emergency Call 1952; Meet Me Tonight 1952; Albert, RN 1953; The Final Test 1953; The Square Ring 1953; Bang! You're Dead 1954; Forbidden Cargo 1954; The Ladykillers 1955; The

Quatermass Xperiment 1955; Home and Away 1956; Carve Her Name with Pride 1958; Jigsaw 1962; Dominique 1978
Warner, John (1924-2001) The Cruel Sea 1952; A Midsummer Night's Dream 1961
Warner, Julie (1965-) Doc Hollywood 1991; Mr Saturday Night 1992; The Puppet Masters 1994; Tommy Boy 1995; Mr Murder 1998; Stick It 2006; Our First Christmas 2008
Warner, Malcolm-Jamal (1970-) Drop Zone 1994; The Tuskegee Airmen 1995; Fool's Gold 2008
Warren-Markland, Shanika 4.3.2.1 2010; Gone Too Far! 2013
Warren, Barry (1933-1994) Kiss of the Vampire 1962; The Devil-Ship Pirates 1964; Frankenstein Created Woman 1966
Warren, Betty (1905-1990) Variety Jubilee 1942; Champagne Charlie 1944; Passport to Pimlico 1949; So Long at the Fair 1950; Tread Softly Stranger 1958
Warren, C Denier (1889-1971) Good Morning, Boys 1937; Keep Fit 1937; It's in the Air 1938
Warren, E Alyn (1874-1940) Abraham Lincoln 1930; Tarzan the Fearless 1933
Warren, Estella (1978-) Planet of the Apes 2001; The Cooler 2002; Kangaroo Jack 2003
Warren, Gloria (1926-) Always in My Heart 1942; Dangerous Money 1946
Warren, Jennifer (1941-) Sam's Song 1969; Night Moves 1975; Another Man, Another Chance 1977; Slap Shot 1977; Ice Castles 1978; Mutant 1984
Warren, Katherine aka Warren, Katharine (1905-1965) All the King's Men 1949; Tell It to the Judge 1949; Force of Arms 1951; The Prowler 1951; The Star 1953
Warren, Kenneth J (1929-1973) Doctor Blood's Coffin 1960; I, Monster 1971; The Creeping Flesh 1972
Warren, Lesley Ann (1946-) Cinderella 1965; The Happiest Millionaire 1967; The One and Only, Genuine, Original Family Band 1968; Harry and Walter Go to New York 1976; Race for the Yankee Zephyr 1981; Victor/Victoria 1982; A Night in Heaven 1983; Choose Me 1984; Songwriter 1984; Clue 1985; Burglar 1987; Cop 1988; Life Stinks 1991; Pure Country 1992; Desperate Justice 1993; Color of Night 1994; Going All the Way 1997; Love Kills 1998; The Limey 1999; Twin Falls Idaho 1999; Trixie 2000; Secretary 2001; Bound by a Secret 2008
Warren (1), Marc (1967-) Boston Kickout 1995; Dad Savage 1997; The Principles of Lust 2002; Song for a Raggy Boy 2002; Green Street 2004; Do Elephants Pray? 2009
Warren, Marcia (1943-) Unconditional Love 2001; Gladiatress 2002; The Jealous God 2005; Mrs Palfrey at The Claremont 2005
Warren, Michael aka Warren, Mike (1946-) Butterflies Are Free 1972; Storyville 1992; The Wedding 1998
Warren, Ruth Six Cylinder Love 1931; Zoo in Budapest 1933; Bring Your Smile Along 1955
Warrender, Harold (1903-1953) Scott of the Antarctic 1948; Conspirator 1949; Pandora and the Flying Dutchman 1950; Where No Vultures Fly 1951
Warrick, Ruth (1915-2005) Citizen Kane 1941; The Corsican Brothers 1941; Journey into Fear 1942; Guest in the House 1944; Mr Winkle Goes to War 1944; Secret Command 1944; China Sky 1945; Driftwood 1946; Song of the South 1946; Daisy Kenyon 1947; Arch of Triumph 1948; Let's Dance 1950; Ride beyond Vengeance 1966; The Great Bank Robbery 1969
Warrington, Don (1952-) Rising Damp 1980; Bloodbath at the House of Death 1983; Babymother 1998; Lighthouse 1999
Warshofsky, David Suffering Bastards 1989; Personal Velocity 2001; The Future 2011
Warsi, Arshad Hulchul 2004; Ishqiya 2010
Warwick, Dionne (1940-) Slaves 1969; Rent-a-Cop 1988
Warwick, John (1905-1972) The Ticket of Leave Man 1937; The Face at the Window 1939; Flying 55 1939; Spare a Copper 1940; Danny Boy 1941; The Saint's Vacation 1941; Dancing with Crime 1946; While I Live 1947; Escape Route 1952; Contraband Spain 1955; The Square Peg 1958; Horrors of the Black Museum 1959
Warwick, Richard (1945-1997) if... 1968; Sebastiane 1976; The Tempest 1979

Warwick, Robert (1878-1964) Whipsaw 1935; The Bride Walks Out 1936; Blockade 1938; Devil's Island 1940; Sullivan's Travels 1941; I Married a Witch 1942; The Falcon's Adventure 1946; Adventures of Don Juan 1948; A Woman's Secret 1949; In a Lonely Place 1950; Sugarfoot 1951; The Sword of Monte Cristo 1951; Against All Flags 1952; Silver Lode 1954; Chief Crazy Horse 1955; Escape to Burma 1955; Walk the Proud Land 1956

Washbourne, Mona (1903-1988) Once upon a Dream 1948; Adventure in the Hopfields 1954; Child's Play 1954; To Dorothy, a Son 1954; John and Julie 1955; It's Great to Be Young 1956; Cast a Dark Shadow 1957; A Cry from the Streets 1957; The Brides of Dracula 1960; Billy Liar 1963; My Fair Lady 1964; Night Must Fall 1964; The Collector 1965; One Way Pendulum 1965; The Third Day 1965; if.... 1968; The Bed Sitting Room 1969; The Driver's Seat 1975; Mister Quilp 1975; The Blue Bird 1976; Stevie 1978

Washburn, Beverly (1943-) The Juggler 1953; The Lone Ranger 1956; Old Yeller 1957; Spider Baby 1964

Washington, Denzel (1954-) Carbon Copy 1981; A Soldier's Story 1984; Power 1986; Cry Freedom 1987; For Queen and Country 1988; Glory 1989; The Mighty Quinn 1989; Heart Condition 1990; Mo' Better Blues 1990; Mississippi Masala 1991; Ricochet 1991; Malcolm X 1992; Much Ado about Nothing 1993; The Pelican Brief 1993; Philadelphia 1993; Crimson Tide 1995; Devil in a Blue Dress 1995; Virtuosity 1995; Courage under Fire 1996; The Preacher's Wife 1996; Fallen 1998; He Got Game 1998; The Siege 1998; The Bone Collector 1999; The Hurricane 1999; Remember the Titans 2000; John Q 2001; Training Day 2001; Antwone Fisher 2002; Out of Time 2003; Man on Fire 2004; The Manchurian Candidate 2004; Déjà Vu 2006; Inside Man 2006; American Gangster 2007; The Great Debaters 2007; The Book of Eli 2009; The Taking of Pelham 123 2009; Unstoppable 2010; Flight 2012; Safe House 2012; 2 Guns 2013; The Equalizer 2014; The Magnificent Seven 2016

Washington, Fredi (1903-1994) The Emperor Jones 1933; Imitation of Life 1934

Washington, Isaiah (1963-) Mr and Mrs Loving 1993; Clockers 1995; Girl 6 1996; Love Jones 1997; True Crime 1999; Kin 2000; Romeo Must Die 2000; Exit Wounds 2001; Hood Rat 2001; Ghost Ship 2002; Welcome to Collinwood 2002; Hollywood Homicide 2003; Dead Birds 2004; The Moguls 2005

Washington, Jascha Big Momma's House 2000; The Final 2010

Washington, Kerry (1977-) Save the Last Dance 2000; Bad Company 2002; Against the Ropes 2003; Ray 2004; She Hate Me 2004; Fantastic Four 2005; Mr & Mrs Smith 2005; The Last King of Scotland 2006; Little Man 2006; 4: Rise of the Silver Surfer 2007; Lakeview Terrace 2008; Good Hair 2009; Mother and Child 2009; For Colored Girls 2010; Django Unchained 2012

Wasikowska, Mia (1989-) Rogue 2007; Amelia 2009; Alice in Wonderland 2010; The Kids Are All Right 2010; Albert Nobbs 2011; Jane Eyre 2011; Restless 2011; Lawless 2012; The Double 2013; Only Lovers Left Alive 2013; Stoker 2013; Tracks 2013; Madame Bovary 2014; Maps to the Stars 2014; Crimson Peak 2015; Alice through the Looking Glass 2016

Wass, Ted (1952-) The Curse of the Pink Panther 1983; Oh, God! You Devil 1984; Sheena 1984; Danielle Steel's Star 1993

Wasserman, Jerry (1945-) A Cooler Climate 1999; I, Robot 2004; NYC: Tornado Terror 2008

Wasson, Craig (1954-) Go Tell the Spartans 1977; The Boys in Company C 1978; The Outsider 1979; Ghost Story 1981; Body Double 1984; The Men's Club 1986; A Nightmare on Elm Street 3: Dream Warriors 1987; Escape under Pressure 2000

Watanabe, Gedde (1955-) Sixteen Candles 1984; Volunteers 1985; Gung Ho 1986; Vamp 1986

Watanabe, Ken (1959-) Tampopo 1986; The Last Samurai 2003; Memoirs of a Geisha 2005; Letters from Iwo Jima 2006; Cirque du Freak: the Vampire's Assistant 2009; Inception 2010; Godzilla 2014; Unforgiven 2014; The Sea of Trees 2015

Watanabe, Tetsu (1951-) Sonatine 1993; Hana-Bi 1997; Himizu 2011

Waterman, Dennis (1948-) The Pirates of Blood River 1961; Up the Junction 1967; The Smashing Bird I Used to Know 1969; The Scars of Dracula 1970; Fright 1971; Man in the Wilderness 1971; The Belstone Fox 1973; Sweeney! 1976; Sweeney 2 1978; Arthur's Dyke 2001

Waters, Dina (1960-) The Haunted Mansion 2003; Just like Heaven 2005

Waters, Ethel (1896-1977) Tales of Manhattan 1942; Cabin in the Sky 1943; Stage Door Canteen 1943; Pinky 1949; The Member of the Wedding 1952; The Sound and the Fury 1959

Waters (2), John (1946-) Sweet and Lowdown 1999; Seed of Chucky 2004; Inside Deep Throat 2005; Midnight Movies: from the Margins to the Mainstream 2005; This Film Is Not Yet Rated 2006; Excision 2012; I Am Divine 2013

Waters (3), John (1948-) The Getting of Wisdom 1977; Breaker Morant 1979; Attack Force Z 1981; Heaven Tonight 1990; The Mystery of a Hansom Cab 2012

Waters, Russell (1908-1982) Mr Denning Drives North 1951; Adventure in the Hopfields 1954; Yesterday's Enemy 1959; Black Jack 1979

Waterston, Katherine (1980-) Night Moves 2013; Inherent Vice 2014; Queen of Earth 2015; Fantastic Beasts and Where to Find Them 2016

Waterston, Sam (1940-) Fitzwilly 1967; Generation 1969; Three 1969; The Great Gatsby 1974; Rancho Deluxe 1975; Capricorn One 1978; Eagle's Wing 1978; Interiors 1978; Friendly Fire 1979; Heaven's Gate 1980; Hopscotch 1980; Sweet William 1980; The Killing Fields 1984; Warning Sign 1985; Hannah and Her Sisters 1986; Just between Friends 1986; September 1987; Swimming to Cambodia 1987; Crimes and Misdemeanors 1989; Welcome Home 1989; The Man in the Moon 1991; Assault at West Point: the Court Martial of John Whittaker 1994; David's Mother 1994; The Enemy Within 1994; Serial Mom 1994; The Journey of August King 1995; The Proprietor 1996; Shadow Conspiracy 1996; A House Divided 2000; Le Divorce 2003

Watford, Gwen (1927-1994) Never Take Sweets from a Stranger 1960; Taste the Blood of Dracula 1969; The Ghoul 1975

Watkin, Pierre (1889-1960) Dangerous 1935; The Bank Dick 1940; Road to Singapore 1940; Little Giant 1946

Watkins, Jason High Hopes 1988; Confetti 2006; Nativity! 2009

Watkins, Linda (1908-1976) From Hell It Came 1957; Because They're Young 1960

Watkins, Michaela The Back-Up Plan 2010; In a World... 2013

Watling, Dilys (1946-) Calculated Risk 1963; Two Left Feet 1963

Watling, Jack (1923-2001) Journey Together 1944; The Courtneys of Curzon Street 1947; Easy Money 1947; Quartet 1948; The Winslow Boy 1948; Under Capricorn 1949; White Corridors 1951; Meet Mr Lucifer 1953; The Sea Shall Not Have Them 1954; The Admirable Crichton 1957; The Birthday Present 1957; That Woman Opposite 1957; Three on a Spree 1961; The Nanny 1965; Father Dear Father 1972; 11 Harrowhouse 1974

Watling, Leonor (1975-) Talk to Her 2001; My Life without Me 2002; The Baby's Room 2006; The Oxford Murders 2008; If I Were You 2012

Watson, Alberta (1955-2015) In Praise of Older Women 1978; Best Revenge 1983; The Keep 1983; White of the Eye 1986; The Hitman 1991; Spanking the Monkey 1994; The Sweet Hereafter 1997; Hedwig and the Angry Inch 2001; Guilt by Association 2002; The Prince & Me 2004; The Lookout 2007

Watson, Barry (1974-) Teaching Mrs Tingle 1999; Sorority Boys 2002; Boogeyman 2005

Watson, Bobby aka **Watson, Robert** (1888-1965) Going Hollywood 1933; The Paleface 1948

Watson, Bobs (1930-1999) Blackmail 1939; Dr Kildare's Crisis 1940; Men of Boys Town 1941

Watson, Debbie (1949-) Munster, Go Home! 1966; The Cool Ones 1967

Watson, Emily (1967-) Breaking the Waves 1996; The Boxer 1997; Metroland 1997; Hilary and Jackie 1998; Angela's Ashes 1999; Cradle Will Rock 1999; The Luzhin Defence 2000; Trixie 2000; Gosford Park 2001; Equilibrium 2002; Punch-Drunk Love 2002; Red Dragon 2002; The Life and Death of Peter Sellers 2003; Boo, Zino and the Snurks 2004; The Proposition 2004; Separate Lies 2004; Tim Burton's Corpse Bride 2005; Wah-Wah 2005; Miss Potter 2006; Fireflies in the Garden 2007; The Water Horse 2007; The Memory Keeper's Daughter 2008; Synecdoche, New York 2008; Cemetery Junction 2010; Oranges and Sunshine 2010; War Horse 2011; The Book Thief 2014; Testament of Youth 2014; Everest 2015; Molly Moon and the Incredible Book of Hypnotism 2015; A Royal Night Out 2015; The Secret Life of Marilyn Monroe 2015; The Theory of Everything 2015

Watson, Emma (1990-) Harry Potter and the Philosopher's Stone 2001; Harry Potter and the Chamber of Secrets 2002; Harry Potter and the Prisoner of Azkaban 2004; Harry Potter and the Goblet of Fire 2005; Harry Potter and the Order of the Phoenix 2007; The Tale of Despereaux 2008; Harry Potter and the Half-Blood Prince 2009; Harry Potter and the Deathly Hallows: Part 1 2010; Harry Potter and the Deathly Hallows: Part 2 2011; My Week with Marilyn 2011; The Perks of Being a Wallflower 2012; The Bling Ring 2013; This Is the End 2013; Noah 2014; Colonia 2015; Regression 2015; Beauty and the Beast 2017

Watson, Jack (1915-1999) Konga 1960; This Sporting Life 1963; The Gorgon 1964; Master Spy 1964; The Hill 1965; The Night Caller 1965; Tobruk 1966; The Strange Affair 1968; Every Home Should Have One 1970; The McKenzie Break 1970; Tower of Evil 1972; 11 Harrowhouse 1974; Schizo 1976; The Purple Taxi 1977; The Wild Geese 1978; North Sea Hijack 1979

Watson Jr, James A The Organization 1971; Extreme Close-Up 1973; Goldengirl 1979

Watson, Lucile (1879-1962) What Every Woman Knows 1934; Made for Each Other 1939; The Women 1939; Waterloo Bridge 1940; Footsteps in the Dark 1941; The Great Lie 1941; Mr and Mrs Smith 1941; Rage in Heaven 1941; Watch on the Rhine 1943; The Thin Man Goes Home 1944; Till We Meet Again 1944; Uncertain Glory 1944; Tomorrow Is Forever 1945; My Reputation 1946; Never Say Goodbye 1946; Song of the South 1946; The Emperor Waltz 1948; Julia Misbehaves 1948; That Wonderful Urge 1948; Everybody Does It 1949; Little Women 1949; Harriet Craig 1950; Let's Dance 1950; My Forbidden Past 1951

Watson, Mills (1940-) Dirty Little Billy 1972; Yellow Pages 1984

Watson, Minor (1889-1965) The Woman I Love 1937; Boys Town 1938; The Adventures of Huckleberry Finn 1939; The Llano Kid 1939; Spirit of the People 1940; The Big Shot 1942; Gentleman Jim 1942; Woman of the Year 1942; Christmas Holiday 1944; The Falcon Out West 1944; A Southern Yankee 1948; Beyond the Forest 1949; Mister 880 1950; Bright Victory 1951; Face to Face 1952; My Son John 1952; Untamed Frontier 1952; The Star 1953; Trapeze 1956

Watson, Muse (1948-) Assassins 1995; I Know What You Did Last Summer 1997; I Still Know What You Did Last Summer 1998; From Dusk till Dawn II: Texas Blood Money 1999; White Lightnin' 2008

Watson, Tom (1932-2001) Another Time, Another Place 1983; The Slab Boys 1997

Watson, Wylie (1889-1966) The 39 Steps 1935; Jamaica Inn 1939; The Saint Meets the Tiger 1943; Don't Take It to Heart 1944; A Girl in a Million 1946; Brighton Rock 1947; London Belongs to Me 1948; Eye Witness 1949; Whisky Galore! 1949; The Magnet 1950

Wattis, Richard (1912-1975) The Happiest Days of Your Life 1950; Appointment with Venus 1951; Made in Heaven 1952; Blood Orange 1953; Colonel March Investigates 1953; Hobson's Choice 1953; The Intruder 1953; Top of the Form 1953; The Colditz Story 1954; An Alligator Named Daisy 1955; Simon and Laura 1955; The Time of His Life 1955; A Yank in Ermine 1955; The Abominable Snowman 1957; The Prince and the Showgirl 1957; Follow a Star 1959; Left, Right and Centre 1959; Libel 1959; Ten Seconds to Hell 1959; Your Money or Your Wife 1960; Dentist on the Job 1961; Nearly a Nasty Accident 1961; Very Important Person 1961; Come Fly with Me 1962; I Thank a Fool 1962; Play It Cool 1962; Bunny Lake Is Missing 1965; The Great St Trinian's Train Robbery 1966; Wonderwall 1968; The Ballad of Tam Lin 1970; Take Me High 1973

Watts, Charles (1912-1966) An Affair to Remember 1957; The High Cost of Loving 1958; Ada 1961; Jumbo 1962; The Wheeler Dealers 1963; Baby the Rain Must Fall 1965

Watts, Charlie Gimme Shelter 1970; Shine a Light 2007

Watts, Naomi (1968-) Tank Girl 1995; Bermuda Triangle 1996; Persons Unknown 1996; The Christmas Wish 1998; Strange Planet 1999; Mulholland Drive 2001; The Outsider 2001; The Ring 2002; Le Divorce 2003; Ned Kelly 2003; 21 Grams 2003; We Don't Live Here Anymore 2003; The Assassination of Richard Nixon 2004; I ♥ Huckabees 2004; The Ring Two 2004; Ellie Parker 2005; King Kong 2005; Stay 2005; The Painted Veil 2006; Eastern Promises 2007; Funny Games US 2008; The International 2009; Mother and Child 2009; Fair Game 2010; You Will Meet a Tall Dark Stranger 2010; Dream House 2011; The Impossible 2011; J Edgar 2011; Adore 2013; Diana 2013; Movie 43 2013; Birdman or (The Unexpected Virtue of Ignorance) 2014; St Vincent 2014; While We're Young 2014; Demolition 2015; Insurgent 2015; The Sea of Trees 2015; The Divergent Series: Allegiant 2016

Watts, Queenie (1926-1980) Poor Cow 1967; Schizo 1976

Wax, Ruby (1953-) Chariots of Fire 1981; Water 1985; Eat the Rich 1987; The Borrowers 1997; Sir Billi 2012

Waxman, Al (1935-2001) Sunday in the Country 1975; Atlantic City, USA 1980; Cagney & Lacey 1981; Class of 1984 1982; Collision Course 1987; Switching Channels 1987; The Hitman 1991; Live Wire 1992; Iron Eagle IV 1995; Holiday Affair 1996

Way, Ann (1915-1993) Clockwise 1986; Killing Dad 1989

Way, Eileen (1911-1994) Blood Orange 1953; Queen of Hearts 1989

Wayans Jr, Damon Dance Flick 2009; Big Hero 6 2014; Let's Be Cops 2014

Wayans, Craig Don't Be a Menace to South Central while Drinking Your Juice in the Hood 1996; Dance Flick 2009

Wayans, Damon (1960-) Earth Girls Are Easy 1988; Look Who's Talking Too 1990; The Last Boy Scout 1991; Mo' Money 1992; Blankman 1994; Bulletproof 1996; Celtic Pride 1996; The Great White Hype 1996; Bamboozled 2000; Marci X 2003

Wayans, Keenen Ivory (1958-) Hollywood Shuffle 1987; I'm Gonna Git You Sucka 1988; A Low Down Dirty Shame 1994; Don't Be a Menace to South Central while Drinking Your Juice in the Hood 1996; The Glimmer Man 1996; Most Wanted 1997

Wayans, Marlon (1972-) Mo' Money 1992; Above the Rim 1994; Don't Be a Menace to South Central while Drinking Your Juice in the Hood 1996; The 6th Man 1997; Senseless 1998; Dungeons & Dragons 2000; Requiem for a Dream 2000; Scary Movie 2000; Scary Movie 2 2001; The Ladykillers 2004; White Chicks 2004; Little Man 2006; Norbit 2007; Dance Flick 2009; GI Joe: the Rise of Cobra 2009; A Haunted House 2013; The Heat 2013; A Haunted House 2 2014; Fifty Shades of Black 2016

Wayans, Shawn (1971-) Don't Be a Menace to South Central while Drinking Your Juice in the Hood 1996; Scary Movie 2000; Scary Movie 2 2001; White Chicks 2004; Little Man 2006; Dance Flick 2009

Wayne, David (1914-1995) Portrait of Jennie 1948; Adam's Rib 1949; My Blue Heaven 1950; Stella 1950; As Young as You Feel 1951; M 1951; The I Don't Care Girl 1952; Wait 'til the Sun Shines, Nellie 1952; We're Not Married 1952; With a Song in My Heart 1952; How to Marry a Millionaire 1953; Tonight We Sing 1953; Hell and High Water 1954; The Tender Trap 1955; The Sad Sack 1957; The Last Angry Man 1959; The Andromeda Strain 1970; The Apple Dumpling Gang 1974; The Front Page 1974; Huckleberry Finn 1974

Wayne, John (1907-1979) Hangman's House 1928; The Big Trail 1930; Men without Women 1930; The Big Stampede 1932; Ride Him, Cowboy 1932; Baby Face 1933; Riders of Destiny 1933; Blue Steel 1934; The Lucky Texan 1934; The Man from Utah 1934; 'Neath the Arizona Skies 1934; Randy Rides Alone 1934; Sagebrush Trail 1934; The Star Packer 1934; The Trail Beyond 1934; West of the Divide 1934; The Dawn Rider 1935; The Desert Trail 1935; The Lawless Frontier 1935; Paradise Canyon 1935; Texas Terror 1935; Westward Ho 1935; Winds of the Wasteland 1936; California Straight Ahead 1937; Hell Town 1937; Overland Stage Raiders 1938; Red River Range 1938; The First Rebel 1939; Frontier Horizon 1939; Stagecoach 1939; Dark Command 1940; The Long Voyage Home 1940; Seven Sinners 1940; Three Faces West 1940; Lady from Louisiana 1941; A Man Betrayed 1941; The Shepherd of the Hills 1941; Flying Tigers 1942; In Old California 1942; Lady for a Night 1942; Pittsburgh 1942; Reap the Wild Wind 1942; Reunion in France 1942; The Spoilers 1942; A Lady Takes a Chance 1943; War of the Wildcats 1943; The Fighting Seabees 1944; Tall in the Saddle 1944; Back to Bataan 1945; Dakota 1945; Flame of the Barbary Coast 1945; They Were Expendable 1945; Without Reservations 1946; Angel and the Badman 1947; Tycoon 1947; Fort Apache 1948; Red River 1948; Three Godfathers 1948; The Fighting Kentuckian 1949; Sands of Iwo Jima 1949; She Wore a Yellow Ribbon 1949; Wake of the Red Witch 1949; Rio Grande 1950; Flying Leathernecks 1951; Operation Pacific 1951; Big Jim McLain 1952; The Quiet Man 1952; Hondo 1953; Island in the Sky 1953; Trouble along the Way 1953; The High and the Mighty 1954; Blood Alley 1955; The Sea Chase 1955; The Conqueror 1956; The Searchers 1956; Legend of the Lost 1957; The Wings of Eagles 1957; The Barbarian and the Geisha 1958; I Married a Woman 1958; Rio Bravo 1958; The Horse Soldiers 1959; The Alamo 1960; North to Alaska 1960; The Comancheros 1961; Hatari! 1962; How the West Was Won 1962; The Longest Day 1962; The Man Who Shot Liberty Valance 1962; Donovan's Reef 1963; McLintock! 1963; The Magnificent Showman 1964; The Greatest Story Ever Told 1965; In Harm's Way 1965; The Sons of Katie Elder 1965; Cast a Giant Shadow 1966; El Dorado 1967; The War Wagon 1967; The Green Berets 1968; True Grit 1969; The Undefeated 1969; Chisum 1970; Rio Lobo 1970; Big Jake 1971; The Cowboys 1972; Cahill, United States Marshal 1973; The Train Robbers 1973; McQ 1974; Brannigan 1975; Rooster Cogburn 1975; The Shootist 1976

Wayne, Naunton (1901-1970) The Lady Vanishes 1938; Crook's Tour 1940; Night Train to Munich 1940; Millions like Us 1943; A Girl in a Million 1946; It's Not Cricket 1948; Obsession 1948; Passport to Pimlico 1949; Circle of Danger 1950; Highly Dangerous 1950; The Happy Family 1952; The Titfield Thunderbolt 1952; Treasure Hunt 1952; You Know What Sailors Are 1954; Operation Bullshine 1959

Wayne, Nina Dead Heat on a Merry-Go-Round 1966; Luv 1967; The Comic 1969

Wayne, Patrick (1939-) The Long Gray Line 1955; The Young Land 1959; The Alamo 1960; The Comancheros 1961; McLintock! 1963; Shenandoah 1965; Big Jake 1971; The Deserter 1971; The Bears and I 1974; Mustang Country 1976; The People That Time Forgot 1977; Sinbad and the Eye of the Tiger 1977; Her Alibi 1989

Weathers, Carl (1948-) Rocky 1976; Semi-Tough 1977; Force 10 from Navarone 1978; Rocky II 1979; Death Hunt 1981; Rocky III 1982; Rocky IV 1985; Predator 1987; Action Jackson 1988; Happy Gilmore 1996

Weaver, Al Doom 2005; Honeymooner 2010; Powder 2010

Weaver, Dennis (1924-2006) Horizons West 1952; The Lawless Breed 1952; Column South 1953; Law and Order 1953; War Arrow 1953; Seven Angry Men 1955; Touch of Evil 1958; The Gallant Hours 1960; Duel at Diablo 1966; Duel 1971; What's the Matter with Helen? 1971; A Winner Never Quits 1986; Two-Bits and Pepper 1995; High Noon 2000; The Virginian 2000

Weaver, Fritz (1926-) Fail-Safe 1964; The Guns of August 1964; To Trap a Spy 1966; The Maltese Bippy 1969; A Walk in the Spring Rain 1970; The Day of the Dolphin 1973; Black Sunday 1976; Marathon Man 1976; Demon Seed 1977; The Big Fix 1978; Creepshow 1982; My Name Is Bill W 1989; The Thomas Crown Affair 1999

Weaver, Jacki (1947-) Picnic at Hanging Rock 1975; Caddie 1976; Animal Kingdom 2009; Silver Linings Playbook 2012; Stoker 2013; Maya the Bee 2014; The Voices 2014

Weaver, Jason (1979-) The Long Walk Home 1990; Drumline 2002

Weaver, Marjorie (1913-1994) Hold That Co-Ed 1938; Kentucky Moonshine

1938; Sally, Irene and Mary 1938; Three Blind Mice 1938; The Cisco Kid and the Lady 1939; Young Mr Lincoln 1939; Maryland 1940; Michael Shayne, Private Detective 1940

Weaver, Sigourney (1949-) Alien 1979; Eyewitness 1981; The Year of Living Dangerously 1982; Deal of the Century 1983; Ghost Busters 1984; Aliens 1986; Half Moon Street 1986; Gorillas in the Mist 1988; Working Girl 1988; Ghostbusters II 1989; Alien³ 1992; 1492: Conquest of Paradise 1992; Dave 1993; Death and the Maiden 1994; Copycat 1995; Jeffrey 1995; Snow White: a Tale of Terror 1996; Alien: Resurrection 1997; The Ice Storm 1997; Galaxy Quest 1999; A Map of the World 1999; Company Man 2000; Heartbreakers 2001; The Guys 2002; Tadpole 2002; Holes 2003; Imaginary Heroes 2004; The Village 2004; Snow Cake 2006; Happily N'Ever After 2006; Infamous 2006; Be Kind Rewind 2007; The Girl in the Park 2007; Baby Mama 2008; The Tale of Despereaux 2008; Vantage Point 2008; WALL-E 2008; Avatar 2009; Prayers for Bobby 2009; The Cabin in the Woods 2010; Paul 2010; You Again 2010; Abduction 2011; Cedar Rapids 2011; Rampart 2011; The Cold Light of Day 2012; Red Lights 2012; Vamps 2012; Exodus: Gods and Kings 2014; Chappie 2015; A Monster Calls 2016; Avatar 2 2018

Weaving, Hugo (1959-) Almost 1990; Proof 1991; Frauds 1992; The Custodian 1993; Reckless Kelly 1993; The Adventures of Priscilla, Queen of the Desert 1994; Babe 1995; Babe: Pig in the City 1998; Bedrooms and Hallways 1998; The Matrix 1999; Strange Planet 1999; The Magic Pudding 2000; The Old Man Who Read Love Stories 2000; The Lord of the Rings: The Fellowship of the Ring 2001; The Lord of the Rings: The Two Towers 2002; The Matrix Reloaded 2002; The Lord of the Rings: The Return of the King 2003; The Matrix Revolutions 2003; Little Fish 2005; V for Vendetta 2005; Happy Feet 2006; The Wolfman 2009; Oranges and Sunshine 2010; Captain America: the First Avenger 2011; Cloud Atlas 2012; The Hobbit: an Unexpected Journey 2012; Mystery Road 2013; The Turning 2013; The Dressmaker 2015; Strangerland 2015

Webb, Alan (1906-1982) Challenge to Lassie 1949; The Third Secret 1964; King Rat 1965; The Taming of the Shrew 1967; Interlude 1968; Entertaining Mr Sloane 1969; Women in Love 1969; King Lear 1970; The First Great Train Robbery 1978

Webb, Bronson The Lives of the Saints 2005; Pusher 2012; Victor Frankenstein 2015

Webb, Chloe (1960-) Sid and Nancy 1986; The Belly of an Architect 1987; Twins 1988; Heart Condition 1990; Queens Logic 1991; A Dangerous Woman 1993; Love Affair 1994; The Ballad of Lucy Whipple 2001; Repo Chick 2009

Webb, Clifton (1891-1966) Laura 1944; The Dark Corner 1946; The Razor's Edge 1946; Sitting Pretty 1948; Mr Belvedere Goes to College 1949; Cheaper by the Dozen 1950; For Heaven's Sake 1950; Mr Belvedere Rings the Bell 1951; Dreamboat 1952; Stars and Stripes Forever 1952; Titanic 1953; Three Coins in the Fountain 1954; Woman's World 1954; The Man Who Never Was 1955; Boy on a Dolphin 1957; Holiday for Lovers 1959; The Remarkable Mr Pennypacker 1959; Satan Never Sleeps 1962

Webb, Danny aka **Webb, Daniel** (1958-) A Year of the Quiet Sun 1984; Alien³ 1992; Shiner 2000; The Aryan Couple 2004; Attack Force 2006; The Arbor 2010; City of Tiny Lights 2016

Webb, Jack (1920-1982) Appointment with Danger 1950; Dark City 1950; Halls of Montezuma 1950; The Men 1950; Sunset Blvd 1950; Dragnet 1954; Pete Kelly's Blues 1955; -30- 1959

Webb, Richard (1915-1993) Build My Gallows High 1947; Night Has a Thousand Eyes 1948; A Connecticut Yankee in King Arthur's Court 1949; Sands of Iwo Jima 1949; Distant Drums 1951; Carson City 1952; Mara Maru 1952; This Woman Is Dangerous 1952; Beware! The Blob 1971

Webb, Rita (1904-1981) Stranger in the House 1967; Frenzy 1972

Webb, Robert (1972-) Confetti 2006; Magicians 2007; The Wedding Video 2012

Webbe, Simon The Truth about Love 2004; Rollin with the Nines 2004; Everywhere + Nowhere 2011

Webber, Mark (1980-) Whiteboys 1999; Snow Day 2000; Storytelling

2001; Dear Wendy 2004; Broken Flowers 2005; Good Dick 2008; Shrink 2009; Scott Pilgrim vs the World 2010; For a Good Time, Call... 2012; 13 Sins 2013

Webber, Peggy Macbeth 1948; Submarine Command 1951

Webber, Robert (1924-1989) 12 Angry Men 1957; The Stripper 1963; Hysteria 1964; Dead Heat on a Merry-Go-Round 1966; Harper 1966; The Silencers 1966; The Dirty Dozen 1967; Don't Make Waves 1967; The Big Bounce 1969; The Great White Hope 1970; Dollars 1971; Double Indemnity 1973; Bring Me the Head of Alfredo Garcia 1974; The Choirboys 1977; Casey's Shadow 1978; Revenge of the Pink Panther 1978; 10 1979; Private Benjamin 1980; SOB 1981; Who Dares Wins 1982; Wild Geese II 1985; Nuts 1987

Webber, Timothy The Grey Fox 1982; Cypher 2002

Weber, Jacques (1949-) State of Siege 1972; The Lady with Red Boots 1974; Cyrano de Bergerac 1990; Beaumarchais l'insolent 1996

Weber, Jake (1964-) Meet Joe Black 1998; Pushing Tin 1999; Wendigo 2001; Leo 2002; Dawn of the Dead 2004; Learning to Drive 2014

Weber, Kal The Hive 2007; Chemical Wedding 2008

Weber, Stanley Thérèse Desqueyroux 2012; Not Another Happy Ending 2013; Sword of Vengeance 2015

Weber, Steven (1961-) Walls of Glass 1985; Single White Female 1992; The Temp 1993; Dracula: Dead and Loving It 1995; Jeffrey 1995; Leaving Las Vegas 1995; At First Sight 1998; Break Up 1998; Sour Grapes 1998; Love Letters 1999; Joseph: King of Dreams 2000; The Twelve Days of Christmas Eve 2004; Eve of Destruction 2013

Webster, Ben (1864-1947) Downhill 1927; The Old Curiosity Shop 1935

Webster, Hugh (1927-1986) King of the Grizzlies 1969; Never Cry Wolf 1983

Webster, Joy Sailor Beware! 1956; The Woman Eater 1957; The Two Faces of Dr Jekyll 1960; During One Night 1961

Webster, Mary The Delicate Delinquent 1957; The Tin Star 1957; Master of the World 1961

Weddell, Mimi (1915-2009) Student Bodies 1981; Anna 1987

Wedge, Chris Ice Age 4: Continental Drift 2012; Ice Age: Collision Course 2016

Wedgeworth, Ann (1935-) Bang the Drum Slowly 1973; Scarecrow 1973; The Catamount Killing 1974; Law and Disorder 1974; Birch Interval 1976; Citizens Band 1977; Sweet Dreams 1985; Made in Heaven 1987; A Tiger's Tale 1987; Far North 1988; Miss Firecracker 1989; Love and a .45 1994; The Whole Wide World 1996

Weeks, Alan Black Belt Jones 1974; Truck Turner 1974

Weeks, Jimmie Ray aka **Weeks, Jimmy Ray** Frantic 1988; War Party 1988

Weeks, Rollo (1987-) The Little Vampire 2000; The Thief Lord 2005

Wegener, Paul (1874-1948) The Golem 1920; The Living Dead 1932

Wei Heling (1907-1979) Street Angel 1937; Crows and Sparrows 1949

Weidler, Virginia (1926-1968) Peter Ibbetson 1935; Souls at Sea 1937; Men with Wings 1938; Out West with the Hardys 1938; Too Hot to Handle 1938; The Great Man Votes 1939; The Lone Wolf Spy Hunt 1939; The Women 1939; All This, and Heaven Too 1940; The Philadelphia Story 1940; Young Tom Edison 1940; Babes on Broadway 1941; The Affairs of Martha 1942; Best Foot Forward 1943; The Youngest Profession 1943

Weigert, Robin Things We Lost in the Fire 2007; Concussion 2013

Weil, Liza (1980-) Whatever 1998; Stir of Echoes 1999

Weinberg, Mike aka **Weinberg, Michael** Home Alone 4 2002; Stolen Summer 2002

Weingarten, Isabelle Four Nights of a Dreamer 1971; La Maman et la Putain 1973; The State of Things 1982

Weinger, Scott (1975-) Aladdin 1992; Aladdin and the King of Thieves 1996; Metropolis 2001

Weinstein, Harvey (1952-) Burn Hollywood Burn 1997; Overnight 2004

Weiss, Michael T (1962-) Jeffrey 1995; Bones 2001

Weiss, Shaun (1978-) The Mighty Ducks 1992; Heavyweights 1995

Weisser, Morgan (1971-) The Haunted Heart 1995; Murder without Conviction 2004

Weisser, Norbert (1946-) Midnight Express 1978; Android 1982; Adrenalin:

Fear the Rush 1995; Omega Doom 1996; Around the Bend 2004

Weissmuller, Johnny (1904-1984) Tarzan, the Ape Man 1932; Tarzan and His Mate 1934; Tarzan Escapes 1936; Tarzan Finds a Son! 1939; Tarzan's Secret Treasure 1941; Tarzan's New York Adventure 1942; Stage Door Canteen 1943; Tarzan Triumphs 1943; Tarzan's Desert Mystery 1943; Tarzan and the Amazons 1945; Tarzan and the Leopard Woman 1946; Tarzan and the Huntress 1947; Jungle Jim 1948; Tarzan and the Mermaids 1948

Weisz, Rachel (1971-) Death Machine 1994; Stealing Beauty 1995; Chain Reaction 1996; Amy Foster 1997; Going All the Way 1997; The Land Girls 1997; I Want You 1998; The Mummy 1999; Sunshine 1999; Beautiful Creatures 2000; Enemy at the Gates 2001; The Mummy Returns 2001; About a Boy 2002; Confidence 2002; Envy 2003; Runaway Jury 2003; The Shape of Things 2003; The Constant Gardener 2005; Constantine 2005; The Fountain 2005; Eragon 2006; Fred Claus 2007; My Blueberry Nights 2007; The Brothers Bloom 2008; Definitely, Maybe 2008; Agora 2009; The Lovely Bones 2009; The Whistleblower 2010; The Deep Blue Sea 2011; Dream House 2011; 360 2011; The Bourne Legacy 2012; Oz the Great and Powerful 2013; The Lobster 2015; Youth 2015; Denial 2016; The Mercy 2016; My Cousin Rachel 2017

Weitz, Bruce (1943-) No Place to Hide 1992; Danielle Steel's Mixed Blessings 1995; Joe and Max 2002

Weitz, Chris (1970-) Chuck & Buck 2000; Mr & Mrs Smith 2005

Weixler, Jess Teeth 2007; The Face of Love 2013

Welch, Bruce (1941-) The Young Ones 1961; Summer Holiday 1962; Wonderful Life 1964; Finders Keepers 1966

Welch, Christopher Evan (1965-2013) Keane 2004; Vicky Cristina Barcelona 2008

Welch, Elisabeth aka **Welch, Elizabeth** (1904-2003) Song of Freedom 1936; Big Fella 1937; Over the Moon 1937; Fiddlers Three 1944; The Tempest 1979

Welch, Michael (1987-) All the Boys Love Mandy Lane 2006; Day of the Dead 2008

Welch, Raquel (1940-) Roustabout 1964; Fantastic Voyage 1966; One Million Years BC 1966; Bedazzled 1967; Fathom 1967; Bandolero! 1968; The Biggest Bundle of Them All 1968; Lady in Cement 1968; The Magic Christian 1969; Myra Breckinridge 1970; Hannie Caulder 1971; Bluebeard 1972; Fuzz 1972; Kansas City Bomber 1972; Sin 1972; The Last of Sheila 1973; The Three Musketeers 1973; The Four Musketeers 1974; The Wild Party 1975; Mother, Jugs & Speed 1976; The Prince and the Pauper 1977; Legally Blonde 2001; Tortilla Soup 2001

Welch, Sandy Chasing the Deer 1994; The Bruce 1996

Welch, Tahnee (1961-) Cocoon 1985; Night Train to Venice 1993; Improper Conduct 1994; I Shot Andy Warhol 1995

Welchman, Harry (1886-1966) The Common Touch 1941; Eight o'Clock Walk 1953

Weld, Tuesday (1943-) Rock, Rock, Rock! 1956; The Five Pennies 1959; The Private Lives of Adam and Eve 1959; Because They're Young 1960; High Time 1960; Bachelor Flat 1961; Return to Peyton Place 1961; Wild in the Country 1961; Soldier in the Rain 1963; The Cincinnati Kid 1965; I'll Take Sweden 1965; Lord Love a Duck 1966; Pretty Poison 1968; A Safe Place 1971; Play It as It Lays 1972; Looking for Mr Goodbar 1977; Who'll Stop the Rain? 1978; Serial 1980; Thief 1981; Author! Author! 1982; Once upon a Time in America 1984; Heartbreak Hotel 1988; Falling Down 1992; Feeling Minnesota 1996

Welden, Ben (1901-1997) The Avenging Hand 1936; Smashing the Rackets 1938; Search for Danger 1949

Weldon, Charles Stir Crazy 1980; Fast-Walking 1982

Weldon, Joan (1933-) So This Is Love 1953; The Command 1954; Riding Shotgun 1954; Them! 1954; Gunsight Ridge 1957; Day of the Bad Man 1958; Home before Dark 1958

Welker, Frank (1945-) Aladdin 1992; The Pagemaster 1994; A Goofy Movie 1995; Aladdin and the King of Thieves 1996; A Christmas Carol 1997; Doug's 1st Movie 1999; The Road to El Dorado 2000; Curious George 2006; Garfield Gets Real 2007; The Informant! 2009

Welland, Colin (1934-2015) Kes 1969; Straw Dogs 1971; Sweeney! 1976; Dancin' thru the Dark 1989; Spymaker: the Secret Life of Ian Fleming 1990

Weller, Frederick (1969-) Stonewall 1995; The Business of Strangers 2001; The Shape of Things 2003

Weller, Peter (1947-) Butch and Sundance: the Early Days 1979; Just Tell Me What You Want 1980; Shoot the Moon 1982; Of Unknown Origin 1983; The Adventures of Buckaroo Banzai across the 8th Dimension 1984; Firstborn 1984; A Killing Affair 1985; RoboCop 1987; Blue Jean Cop 1988; Cat Chaser 1989; Leviathan 1989; RoboCop 2 1990; Women and Men: Stories of Seduction 1990; Fifty/Fifty 1991; Naked Lunch 1991; Road to Ruin 1992; Sunset Grill 1992; The New Age 1994; Beyond the Clouds 1995; Screamers 1995; Top of the World 1997; Diplomatic Siege 1999; ivansxtc. 1999; Contagion 2000; Dark Prince - the Legend of Dracula 2000; Shadow Hours 2000; Styx 2000; The Sin Eater 2002

Welles, Gwen (1951-1993) A Safe Place 1971; Hit! 1973; California Split 1974; Between the Lines 1977; Desert Hearts 1985; Nobody's Fool 1986; Eating 1990

Welles, Mel (1924-2005) Attack of the Crab Monsters 1957; The Undead 1957; The Little Shop of Horrors 1960; Dr Heckyl & Mr Hype 1980

Welles, Orson (1915-1985) Too Much Johnson 1938; Swiss Family Robinson 1940; Citizen Kane 1941; Journey into Fear 1942; The Magnificent Ambersons 1942; Jane Eyre 1943; Follow the Boys 1944; Tomorrow Is Forever 1945; Duel in the Sun 1946; The Stranger 1946; The Lady from Shanghai 1948; Macbeth 1948; Black Magic 1949; Prince of Foxes 1949; The Third Man 1949; The Black Rose 1950; The Little World of Don Camillo 1951; Return to Glennascaul 1951; Othello 1952; Trent's Last Case 1952; Royal Affairs in Versailles 1953; Three Cases of Murder 1953; Trouble in the Glen 1954; Confidential Report 1955; Napoléon 1955; Moby Dick 1956; Man in the Shadow 1957; Ferry to Hong Kong 1958; The Long, Hot Summer 1958; The Roots of Heaven 1958; Touch of Evil 1958; Compulsion 1959; The Battle of Austerlitz 1960; Crack in the Mirror 1960; King of Kings 1961; RoGoPaG 1962; The Trial 1962; The VIPs 1963; Chimes at Midnight 1966; Is Paris Burning? 1966; A Man for All Seasons 1966; Casino Royale 1967; I'll Never Forget What's 'Is Name 1967; Oedipus the King 1967; The Sailor from Gibraltar 1967; House of Cards 1968; The Immortal Story 1968; The Southern Star 1969; Twelve plus One 1969; Catch-22 1970; Start the Revolution without Me 1970; Waterloo 1970; Malpertuis 1971; A Safe Place 1971; Ten Days' Wonder 1971; Get to Know Your Rabbit 1972; Treasure Island 1972; F for Fake 1973; And Then There Were None 1974; Voyage of the Damned 1976; Hot Money 1979; Genocide 1981; History of the World Part I 1981; Butterfly 1982; Where Is Parsifal? 1983; Transformers - the Movie 1986; Someone to Love 1987; It's All True 1993; Magician: the Astonishing Life and Work of Orson Welles 2014

Welles, Virginia (1925-2002) Kiss and Tell 1945; To Each His Own 1946; Dear Ruth 1947; A Kiss for Corliss 1949; Francis in the Haunted House 1956

Welling, Tom (1977-) Cheaper by the Dozen 2003; Cheaper by the Dozen 2 2005; The Fog 2005; The Choice 2016

Welliver, Titus (1961-) Twisted 2003; The Town 2010

Wells, Carole (1942-) The House of Seven Corpses 1973; Funny Lady 1975

Wells, Dolly Morvern Callar 2001; Benny & Jolene 2014; Black Mountain Poets 2015; 45 Years 2015

Wells, Ingeborg (1917-) House of Blackmail 1953; Child's Play 1954

Wells, John (1936-1998) 30 Is a Dangerous Age, Cynthia 1968; Rentadick 1972; For Your Eyes Only 1981; Greystoke: the Legend of Tarzan, Lord of the Apes 1984; Revolution 1985

Wells, Tico The Five Heartbeats 1991; Universal Soldier 1992

Wells, Vernon (1945-) Mad Max 2 1981; Commando 1985; Innerspace 1987; Circuitry Man 1990; Plughead Rewired: Circuitry Man II 1994

Welsh, Irvine Trainspotting 1995; Upside Down: the Creation Records Story 2010

Welsh, Jane (1905-2001) Just William's Luck 1947; William at the Circus 1948

Welsh, John (1904-1985) Confession 1955; The Birthday Present 1957; The Revenge of Frankenstein 1958; The Night We Dropped a Clanger 1959; Beyond the Curtain 1960; Circle of Deception 1960; Krull 1983

Welsh, Kenneth (1942-) Of Unknown Origin 1983; Physical Evidence 1988; Perfectly Normal 1990; Another Woman 1994; Getting Gotti 1994; Kissinger and Nixon 1995; Margaret's Museum 1995; Eloise at the Plaza 2003; The Day after Tomorrow 2004; Miracle 2004; The Fog 2005; Adoration 2008; George A Romero's Survival of the Dead 2009; The Art of the Steal 2013

Welsh, Margaret Smooth Talk 1985; Mr and Mrs Bridge 1990

Welter, Ariadna (1930-1998) The Criminal Life of Archibaldo de la Cruz 1955; Rage 1966

Wenders, Wim (1945-) Long Shot 1978; Notebook on Cities and Clothes 1989; The Salt of the Earth 2014

Wendt, George (1948-) Dreamscape 1984; Thief of Hearts 1984; Fletch 1985; Gung Ho 1986; House 1986; Plain Clothes 1988; Guilty by Suspicion 1990; Forever Young 1992; The Little Rascals 1994; Man of the House 1995; Space Truckers 1996; Spice World: the Movie 1997; Alice in Wonderland 1999; Outside Providence 1999; The Prime Gig 2000; Wild about Harry 2000; King of the Ants 2003

Wengraf, John (1897-1974) The Lovable Cheat 1949; 5 Fingers 1952; The Pride and the Passion 1957; Valerie 1957; The Return of Dracula 1958; Hitler 1962

Wenham, David (1965-) The Boys 1998; The Bank 2001; Dust 2001; The Crocodile Hunter: Collision Course 2002; Pure 2002; Gettin' Square 2003; The Lord of the Rings: The Return of the King 2003; The Proposition 2004; Van Helsing 2004; 300 2006; Married Life 2007; Australia 2008; Public Enemies 2009; Legend of the Guardians: the Owls of Ga'Hoole 2010; Oranges and Sunshine 2010; 300: Rise of an Empire 2013

Wentworth, Martha (1889-1974) Daughter of Dr Jekyll 1957; One Hundred and One Dalmatians 1960; The Sword in the Stone 1963

Wepper, Fritz (1941-) The Bridge 1959; The Games 1970; Cabaret 1972; The Last Battle 1983

Werle, Barbara (1928-2013) Battle of the Bulge 1965; Gunfight in Abilene 1967; Charro! 1969

Werner, Oskar (1922-1984) Decision before Dawn 1951; Lola Montès 1955; Jules et Jim 1962; Ship of Fools 1965; The Spy Who Came In from the Cold 1965; Fahrenheit 451 1966; Interlude 1968; The Shoes of the Fisherman 1968; Voyage of the Damned 1976

Wernicke, Otto (1893-1965) M 1931; The Testament of Dr Mabuse 1932

Wert, Doug By the Sword 1992; A Murder of Crows 1998

Wesson, Dick (1919-1979) Destination Moon 1950; Force of Arms 1951; Jim Thorpe - All-American 1951; Calamity Jane 1953; The Charge at Feather River 1953; The Desert Song 1953; The Errand Boy 1961

West, Adam (1928-) Geronimo 1962; Soldier in the Rain 1963; Tammy and the Doctor 1963; Robinson Crusoe on Mars 1964; The Outlaws Is Coming 1965; Batman 1966; The Girl Who Knew Too Much 1969; Hooper 1978; One Dark Night 1982; The New Age 1994; Drop Dead Gorgeous 1999; Baadasssss! 2003; Meet the Robinsons 2006

West, Chandra (1970-) Universal Soldier 2: Brothers in Arms 1998; Universal Soldier 3: Unfinished Business 1998; White Noise 2004; My Neighbor's Secret 2009

West, Dominic (1969-) True Blue 1996; Diana & Me 1997; The Gambler 1997; A Midsummer Night's Dream 1999; 28 Days 2000; Rock Star 2001; Chicago 2002; Ten Minutes Older: the Cello 2002; Mona Lisa Smile 2003; The Forgotten 2004; Hannibal Rising 2006; 300 2006; Punisher: War Zone 2008; Centurion 2009; From Time to Time 2009; The Awakening 2011; Johnny English Reborn 2011; Pride 2014; Testament of Youth 2014; Genius 2015; Money Monster 2016

West, Judi The Fortune Cookie 1966; A Man Called Gannon 1969

West, Lockwood (1905-1989) The Birthday Present 1957; The Leather Boys 1963

West, Mae (1892-1980) Night after Night 1932; I'm No Angel 1933; She Done Him Wrong 1933; Belle of the Nineties 1934; Goin' to Town 1935; Go West, Young Man 1936; Klondike Annie

1936; Every Day's a Holiday 1937; My Little Chickadee 1940; The Love Goddesses 1965; Myra Breckinridge 1970; Sextette 1978

West, Martin (1937-) Lord Love a Duck 1966; Sweet November 1968; Assault on Precinct 13 1976; Mac and Me 1988

West, Red (1936-) Road House 1989; Goodbye Solo 2008

West, Samuel aka West, Sam (1966-) Reunion 1989; Howards End 1992; A Feast at Midnight 1994; Carrington 1995; Persuasion 1995; Stiff Upper Lips 1997; Pandaemonium 2000; Iris 2001; Sword of Xanten 2004; Van Helsing 2004; Hyde Park on Hudson 2012; Suffragette 2015

West, Shane (1978-) Whatever It Takes 2000; Get over It 2001; A Walk to Remember 2002; The League of Extraordinary Gentlemen 2003; The Lodger 2009; Red Sands 2009

West, Timothy (1934-) Twisted Nerve 1968; The Day of the Jackal 1973; Hedda 1975; Operation Daybreak 1975; The Devil's Advocate 1977; Agatha 1978; The Thirty-Nine Steps 1978; Rough Cut 1980; Oliver Twist 1982; Cry Freedom 1987; Ever After: a Cinderella Story 1998; Joan of Arc 1999; Iris 2001; Villa des Roses 2002; Beyond Borders 2003; Sinbad: Legend of the Seven Seas 2003

Westbrook, John (1922-1989) Room at the Top 1958; The Tomb of Ligeia 1964

Westcott, Helen (1928-1998) The Gunfighter 1950; With a Song in My Heart 1952; Abbott and Costello Meet Dr Jekyll and Mr Hyde 1953; The Charge at Feather River 1953; Hot Blood 1956; God's Little Acre 1958

Westerfield, James (1913-1971) On the Waterfront 1954; The Proud Rebel 1958; The Gunfight at Dodge City 1959; Wild River 1960; That Funny Feeling 1965; Blue 1968; Hang 'Em High 1968; A Man Called Gannon 1969

Westergren, Håkan (1899-1991) Swedenhielms 1935; Dollar 1938

Westerman, Floyd Red Crow aka Westerman, Floyd (1936-2007) Renegades 1989; Dances with Wolves 1990; Clearcut 1992

Westfeldt, Jennifer (1971-) Kissing Jessica Stein 2001; Before You Say "I Do" 2009; Friends with Kids 2011

Westley, Helen (1875-1942) The Age of Innocence 1934; Anne of Green Gables 1934; Death Takes a Holiday 1934; Roberta 1935; Splendor 1935; Banjo on My Knee 1936; Dimples 1936; Show Boat 1936; Stowaway 1936; Café Metropole 1937; Heidi 1937; I'll Take Romance 1937; Alexander's Ragtime Band 1938; The Baroness and the Butler 1938; Rebecca of Sunnybrook Farm 1938; Zaza 1939; Lillian Russell 1940; Adam Had Four Sons 1941; Lady from Louisiana 1941; Million Dollar Baby 1941; Bedtime Story 1942; My Favorite Spy 1942

Westman, Nydia (1902-1970) Ladies Should Listen 1934; When Tomorrow Comes 1939; The Chocolate Soldier 1941

Weston, Brad Rough Night in Jericho 1967; Barquero 1970

Weston, Celia (1951-) The Road Home 1989; Dead Man Walking 1995; In the Bedroom 2001; Far from Heaven 2002; Junebug 2004; The Invasion 2007; Joshua 2007; After.Life 2009; Observe and Report 2009

Weston, David (1938-) The Beauty Jungle 1964; The Masque of the Red Death 1964; The Heroes of Telemark 1965; The Legend of Young Dick Turpin 1965

Weston, Jack (1924-1996) All in a Night's Work 1960; It'$ Only Money 1962; Palm Springs Weekend 1963; The Cincinnati Kid 1965; Mirage 1965; Wait until Dark 1967; The Counterfeit Killer 1968; The Thomas Crown Affair 1968; The April Fools 1969; Cactus Flower 1969; A New Leaf 1971; Fuzz 1972; Marco 1973; Gator 1976; The Ritz 1976; Cuba 1979; The Four Seasons 1981; High Road to China 1983; Dirty Dancing 1987; Ishtar 1987; Short Circuit 2 1988

Weston, Jonny Chasing Mavericks 2012; Project Almanac 2014; Taken 3 2014; We Are Your Friends 2015

Weston, Michael The Last Kiss 2006; Wedding Daze 2006; Pathology 2007

Westwick, Ed (1937-) Chalet Girl 2010; J Edgar 2011; Romeo & Juliet 2012

Westwood, Patrick The Tommy Steele Story 1957; Guns in the Heather 1969

Wettig, Patricia (1951-) Guilty by Suspicion 1990; City Slickers 1991; City Slickers II: the Legend of Curly's Gold 1994; Dancer, Texas Pop 81 1998

Weyers, Marius (1945-) The Gods Must Be Crazy 1980; Farewell to the

King 1988; DeepStar Six 1989; Happy Together 1989; Windprints 1989; Bopha! 1993; Friends 1993; Charlie 2003; Stander 2003; Red Dust 2004

Whalen, Michael (1902-1974) The Country Doctor 1936; Poor Little Rich Girl 1936; White Fang 1936; Wee Willie Winkie 1937; Ellery Queen Master Detective 1940

Whaley, Frank (1963-) Cold Dog Soup 1989; Field of Dreams 1989; Unconquered 1989; The Freshman 1990; Career Opportunities 1991; The Doors 1991; A Midnight Clear 1991; Back in the USSR 1992; Hoffa 1992; Swing Kids 1993; Swimming with Sharks 1994; Homage 1995; Broken Arrow 1996; The Winner 1996; Curtain Call 1997; When Trumpets Fade 1998; Vacancy 2007

Whalin, Justin (1974-) Child's Play 3 1991; Serial Mom 1994; Dungeons & Dragons 2000

Whalley, Joanne aka Whalley-Kilmer, Joanne (1964-) Dance with a Stranger 1984; No Surrender 1985; The Good Father 1986; Scandal 1988; To Kill a Priest 1988; Willow 1988; Kill Me Again 1989; The Big Man 1990; Navy SEALs 1990; Shattered 1991; Storyville 1992; A Good Man in Africa 1993; Mother's Boys 1993; The Secret Rapture 1993; Trial by Jury 1994; The Man Who Knew Too Little 1997; The Guilty 2000; Run the Wild Fields 2000; Before You Go 2002; 44 Inch Chest 2009; Twixt 2011

Whannell, Leigh (1977-) Saw 2004; Death Sentence 2007; Insidious 2010; Insidious: Chapter 2 2013; Cooties 2014; Insidious: Chapter 3 2015

Whately, Kevin (1951-) The Return of the Soldier 1982; The English Patient 1996; Purely Belter 2000

Wheatley, Alan (1907-1991) Conquest of the Air 1936; Brighton Rock 1947; It's Not Cricket 1948; Home to Danger 1951; Spaceways 1953; The Diamond 1954; The Duke Wore Jeans 1958; Tomorrow at Ten 1962; Clash by Night 1963; Master Spy 1964

Wheatley, Thomas The Living Daylights 1987; Where Angels Fear to Tread 1991

Wheaton, Wil (1972-) The Buddy System 1984; Stand by Me 1986; The Curse 1987; Toy Soldiers 1991; Pie in the Sky 1995; Flubber 1997; The Day Lincoln Was Shot 1998; Python 2000; Star Trek: Nemesis 2002

Wheeler-Nicholson, Dana (1960-) Fletch 1985; Circuitry Man 1990; Denise Calls Up 1995; Frank and Jesse 1995

Wheeler, Bert (1895-1968) Rio Rita 1929; Half Shot at Sunrise 1930

Wheeler, Ira September 1987; Swimming to Cambodia 1987

Whelan, Arleen (1916-1993) Kidnapped 1938; Thanks for Everything 1938; Young Mr Lincoln 1939; Young People 1940; Ramrod 1947; The Senator Was Indiscreet 1947; Suddenly It's Spring 1947; That Wonderful Urge 1948; Flaming Feather 1952; Never Wave at a WAC 1952; The Sun Shines Bright 1953

Whigham, Shea (1969-) Tigerland 2000; All the Real Girls 2003; Wristcutters: a Love Story 2006; Pride and Glory 2007; Take Shelter 2011

Whiley, Manning (1915-1975) Pimpernel Smith 1941; The Saint's Vacation 1941; Bell-Bottom George 1943; The Shop at Sly Corner 1946; Uncle Silas 1947

Whirry, Shannon (1964-) Omega Doom 1996; The Prophet's Game 1999

Whishaw, Ben (1980-) My Brother Tom 2001; Layer Cake 2004; Stoned 2005; Perfume: the Story of a Murderer 2006; I'm Not There. 2007; Brideshead Revisited 2008; Bright Star 2009; The Tempest 2010; Cloud Atlas 2012; Skyfall 2012; Teenage 2013; Lilting 2014; Paddington 2014; The Danish Girl 2015; In the Heart of the Sea 2015; The Lobster 2015; Spectre 2015; Suffragette 2015; Unity 2015; A Hologram for the King 2016

Whitaker, Damon (1970-) Bird 1988; Mr Holland's Opus 1995

Whitaker, Denzel The Great Debaters 2007; My Soul to Take 2010

Whitaker, Forest (1961-) Fast Times at Ridgemont High 1982; Vision Quest 1985; The Color of Money 1986; Platoon 1986; Bloodsport 1987; Good Morning, Vietnam 1987; Stakeout 1987; Bird 1988; Johnny Handsome 1989; Downtown 1990; A Rage in Harlem 1991; Article 99 1992; Consenting Adults 1992; The Crying Game 1992; Diary of a Hitman 1992; Body Snatchers 1993; Last Light 1993; Lush Life 1993; Blown Away 1994; The Enemy Within 1994; Jason's Lyric 1994; Pret-a-Porter 1994; Smoke 1995; Species 1995; Phenomenon 1996; Body Count 1997; Four Dogs Playing Poker 1999; Ghost Dog: the Way of the

Samurai 1999; Light It Up 1999; Witness Protection 1999; Battlefield Earth 2000; The Fourth Angel 2001; Panic Room 2002; Phone Booth 2002; First Daughter 2004; The Last King of Scotland 2006; The Marsh 2006; The Air I Breathe 2007; The Great Debaters 2007; Fragments 2008; Street Kings 2008; Vantage Point 2008; Where the Wild Things Are 2009; Our Family Wedding 2010; Repo Men 2010; A Dark Truth 2012; The Butler 2013; The Last Stand 2013; Out of the Furnace 2013; Zulu 2013; Taken 3 2014; Southpaw 2015; Rogue One: a Star Wars Story 2016

Whitaker, Johnny (1959-) The Biscuit Eater 1972; Napoleon and Samantha 1972; Snowball Express 1972; Something Evil 1972; Tom Sawyer 1973

White, Alice (1904-1983) The Big Noise 1928; Employees' Entrance 1933; Picture Snatcher 1933; Jimmy the Gent 1934

White, Barbara (1923-) Quiet Weekend 1946; While the Sun Shines 1946; Mine Own Executioner 1947

White, Betty (1922-) Hard Rain 1997; Dennis the Menace Strikes Again 1998; Lake Placid 1999; Whispers: an Elephant's Tale 2000; Bringing Down the House 2003; Annie's Point 2005; The Proposal 2009; You Again 2010; Dr Seuss' The Lorax 2012

White, Brian (1975-) Mr 3000 2004; Stomp the Yard 2006; The Game Plan 2007; 12 Rounds 2008; Fighting 2009

White, Carol (1942-1991) Circus Friends 1956; Never Let Go 1960; The Man in the Back Seat 1961; Village of Daughters 1961; Gaolbreak 1962; I'll Never Forget What's 'Is Name 1967; Poor Cow 1967; Daddy's Gone A-Hunting 1969; The Man Who Had Power over Women 1970; Dulcima 1971; something big 1971; The Squeeze 1977; Nutcracker 1982

White, De'Voreaux Die Hard 1988; Trespass 1992

White, Jack It Might Get Loud 2008; Under Great White Northern Lights 2009; Another Day/Another Time 2013

White, Jacqueline (1922-) Crossfire 1947; Night Song 1947; Return of the Bad Men 1948; The Capture 1950; The Narrow Margin 1952

White, Jesse (1917-1997) Harvey 1950; Bedtime for Bonzo 1951; Callaway Went Thataway 1951; Francis Goes to the Races 1951; The Girl in White 1952; Million Dollar Mermaid 1952; Forever Female 1953; Gunsmoke 1953; Witness to Murder 1954; The Bad Seed 1956; The Come On 1956; Designing Woman 1957; Johnny Trouble 1957; The Rise and Fall of Legs Diamond 1960; It'$ Only Money 1962; The Yellow Canary 1963; The Ghost in the Invisible Bikini 1966; The Cat from Outer Space 1978

White, Julianne Sexy Beast 2000; Out on a Limb 2005

White, Julie Slap Her, She's French! 2001; Transformers: Revenge of the Fallen 2009

White, Leo (1882-1948) His New Job 1915; The Tramp 1915; Work 1915; The Vagabond 1916

White, Liz New Town Killers 2009; Wild Bill 2011

White, Marjorie (1908-1935) Sunny Side Up 1929; Possessed 1931

White, Meg Coffee and Cigarettes 2003; Under Great White Northern Lights 2009

White, Michael Jai (1967-) City of Industry 1996; Spawn 1997; Ringmaster 1998; Universal Soldier – the Return 1999; Freedom Song 2000; Exit Wounds 2001; Black Dynamite 2009; Blood and Bone 2009

White, Mike (1970-) Chuck & Buck 2000; The Good Girl 2001; The School of Rock 2003; Gentlemen Broncos 2009

White, Ron (1953-) Guilty as Sin 1993; Kissinger and Nixon 1995; Screamers 1995; Chasing Secrets 1999; Plague City: Sars in Toronto 2005

White, Ruth (1914-1969) Edge of the City 1957; To Kill a Mockingbird 1962; Baby the Rain Must Fall 1965; Up the Down Staircase 1967; Hang 'Em High 1968; Midnight Cowboy 1969; The Reivers 1969; The Pursuit of Happiness 1971

White, Sammy (1894-1960) Show Boat 1936; 711 Ocean Drive 1950; Pat and Mike 1952; About Mrs Leslie 1954

White, Sheila (1950-) Here We Go round the Mulberry Bush 1967; Oliver! 1968; Confessions of a Window Cleaner 1974; Alfie Darling 1975; Confessions of a Pop Performer 1975; Confessions of a Driving Instructor 1976; Confessions from a Holiday Camp 1977; The Spaceman and King Arthur 1979

White, Valerie (1915-1975) Hue and Cry 1947; The Blue Parrot 1953; Travels with My Aunt 1972

Whitehead, O Z (1911-1998) The Grapes of Wrath 1940; Road House 1948; Beware, My Lovely 1952

Whitehead, Paxton (1937-) Back to School 1986; The Adventures of Huck Finn 1993

Whitehouse, Paul (1958-) Kevin & Perry Go Large 2000; Finding Neverland 2004; Tim Burton's Corpse Bride 2005; Alice in Wonderland 2010; Burke & Hare 2010

Whitelaw, Billie (1932-2014) The Sleeping Tiger 1954; Carve Her Name with Pride 1958; Bobbikins 1959; The Flesh and the Fiends 1959; Hell Is a City 1959; Make Mine Mink 1960; No Love for Johnnie 1960; Mr Topaze 1961; Payroll 1961; The Comedy Man 1964; Charlie Bubbles 1967; Twisted Nerve 1968; The Adding Machine 1969; Leo the Last 1970; Start the Revolution without Me 1970; Eagle in a Cage 1971; Gumshoe 1971; Frenzy 1972; Night Watch 1973; The Omen 1976; The Water Babies 1978; An Unsuitable Job for a Woman 1981; The Dark Crystal 1982; The Chain 1984; Shadey 1985; Maurice 1987; The Secret Garden 1987; The Dressmaker 1988; Joyriders 1988; The Krays 1990; Freddie as FRO7 1992; Deadly Advice 1993; Jane Eyre 1996; The Lost Son 1998; Quills 2000; Hot Fuzz 2007

Whiteley, Jon (1945-) Hunted 1952; The Kidnappers 1953; Moonfleet 1955; The Spanish Gardener 1956

Whiteman, Paul (1890-1967) Atlantic City 1944; The Fabulous Dorseys 1947

Whitfield, June (1925-) Bless This House 1972; Carry On Abroad 1972; Carry On Girls 1973; Not Now, Comrade 1976; Carry On Columbus 1992; Jude 1996; Run for Your Wife 2013; Absolutely Fabulous: the Movie 2016

Whitfield, Lynn (1953-) Doctor Detroit 1983; A Thin Line between Love and Hate 1996; Eve's Bayou 1997; Gone Fishin' 1997; Stepmom 1998; The Wedding 1998; Head of State 2003

Whitfield, Mitchell (1968-) Dogfight 1991; My Cousin Vinny 1992; Best Men 1997; Lost & Found 1999; TMNT 2007

Whitford, Bradley aka Whitford, Brad (1959-) Scent of a Woman 1992; My Life 1993; A Perfect World 1993; Billy Madison 1995; Masterminds 1997; Red Corner 1997; Behind the Mask 1999; Kate & Leopold 2002; Little Manhattan 2005; The Sisterhood of the Traveling Pants 2005; Bottle Shock 2008; I Saw the Light 2015; All the Way 2016

Whitford, Peter (1939-) Careful, He Might Hear You 1983; Strictly Ballroom 1992

Whiting, Barbara (1931-2004) Beware, My Lovely 1952; Dangerous When Wet 1953

Whiting, Leonard (1950-) Romeo and Juliet 1968; The Royal Hunt of the Sun 1969; Say Hello to Yesterday 1971; Frankenstein: the True Story 1973

Whiting, Margaret (1924-) The Informers 1963; Sinbad and the Eye of the Tiger 1977

Whitlock Jr, Isiah Jump Tomorrow 2001; Cedar Rapids 2011

Whitman, Mae (1988-) When a Man Loves a Woman 1994; One Fine Day 1996; Hope Floats 1998; Invisible Child 1999; An American Rhapsody 2001; The Jungle Book 2 2003; Nights in Rodanthe 2008; Tinker Bell 2008; Acceptance 2009; The Factory 2012; The Perks of Being a Wallflower 2012; Tinkerbell and the Secret of the Wings 2012; Tinker Bell and the Legend of the NeverBeast 2014; TinkerBell and the Pirate Fairy 2014; The Duff 2015

Whitman, Stuart (1926-) The All American 1953; Rhapsody 1954; Johnny Trouble 1957; Darby's Rangers 1958; The Decks Ran Red 1958; Ten North Frederick 1958; Hound Dog Man 1959; The Sound and the Fury 1959; These Thousand Hills 1959; The Story of Ruth 1960; The Comancheros 1961; The Fiercest Heart 1961; Francis of Assisi 1961; The Mark 1961; Convicts Four 1962; The Longest Day 1962; Rio Conchos 1964; Signpost to Murder 1964; Sands of the Kalahari 1965; Those Magnificent Men in Their Flying Machines 1965; An American Dream 1966; The Heroes 1968; Sweet Hunters 1969; The Last Escape 1970; Captain Apache 1971; City beneath the Sea 1971; Shatter 1974; Welcome to Arrow Beach 1974; Crazy Mama 1975; Eaten Alive 1976; Maniac 1977; Ruby 1977; The White Buffalo 1977; Butterfly 1982; Once upon a Texas Train 1988; Improper Conduct 1994

Whitmire, Steve (1959-) The Muppets Take Manhattan 1984; The Muppet

Christmas Carol 1992; Muppet Treasure Island 1996; Muppets from Space 1999; It's a Very Merry Muppet Christmas Movie 2002; Kermit's Swamp Years 2002; The Muppets' Wizard of Oz 2005; The Muppets 2011; Muppets Most Wanted 2014

Whitmore, James (1921-2009) Battleground 1949; The Undercover Man 1949; The Asphalt Jungle 1950; Mrs O'Malley and Mr Malone 1950; The Next Voice You Hear 1950; The Outriders 1950; Please Believe Me 1950; The Red Badge of Courage 1951; Above and Beyond 1952; Because You're Mine 1952; All the Brothers Were Valiant 1953; The Girl Who Had Everything 1953; Kiss Me Kate 1953; The Command 1954; Them! 1954; Battle Cry 1955; The Last Frontier 1955; The McConnell Story 1955; Oklahoma! 1955; Crime in the Streets 1956; The Eddy Duchin Story 1956; The Deep Six 1958; The Restless Years 1958; Who Was That Lady? 1960; Black like Me 1964; Planet of the Apes 1967; Waterhole #3 1967; Madigan 1968; Guns of the Magnificent Seven 1969; Tora! Tora! Tora! 1970; Chato's Land 1971; The Harrad Experiment 1973; Where the Red Fern Grows 1974; Give 'Em Hell, Harry! 1975; The Serpent's Egg 1977; The Shawshank Redemption 1994; The Relic 1996; Swing Vote 1999; The Majestic 2001

Whitmore Jr, James (1948-) The Boys in Company C 1978; The Gypsy Warriors 1978; A Force of One 1979

Whitney, Claire (1890-1969) A Free Soul 1931; Betrayed 1944

Whitney, Peter (1916-1972) Bring On the Girls 1945; Murder, He Says 1945; The Big Heat 1953; Gorilla at Large 1954; The Last Frontier 1955; Buchanan Rides Alone 1958; The Ballad of Cable Hogue 1970

Whitrow, Benjamin (1937-) Brimstone and Treacle 1982; A Man for All Seasons 1988

Whitsun-Jones, Paul (1923-1974) Stock Car 1955; The Wild Affair 1963; Dr Jekyll & Sister Hyde 1971

Whittaker, Jodie (1982-) Venus 2006; St Trinian's 2007; Good 2008; Perrier's Bounty 2009; St Trinian's 2: the Legend of Fritton's Gold 2009; Attack the Block 2010; Ollie Kepler's Expanding Purple World 2010; One Day 2011; A Thousand Kisses Deep 2011; Ashes 2012; Good Vibrations 2012; Hello Carter 2013; Black Sea 2014; Get Santa 2014; Adult Life Skills 2016

Whittall, Ted Hidden Agenda 2001; Agent of Influence 2002

Whitten, Frank Vigil 1984; Waiting 1990

Whitton, Margaret (1950-) Love Child 1982; Nine ½ Weeks 1985; The Best of Times 1986; The Secret of My Success 1987; Major League 1989; Stepkids 1992; The Man without a Face 1993; Major League II 1994; Trial by Jury 1994

Whitty, Dame May aka Whitty, May (1865-1948) Conquest 1937; Night Must Fall 1937; I Met My Love Again 1938; The Lady Vanishes 1938; Raffles 1939; A Bill of Divorcement 1940; Return to Yesterday 1940; Suspicion 1941; Mrs Miniver 1942; The Constant Nymph 1943; Crash Dive 1943; Forever and a Day 1943; Lassie Come Home 1943; Madame Curie 1943; Slightly Dangerous 1943; Gaslight 1944; My Name Is Julia Ross 1945; Devotion 1946; Green Dolphin Street 1947; If Winter Comes 1947; The Return of October 1948

Whitworth, Johnny (1975-) Empire Records 1995; Limitless 2011; Ghost Rider: Spirit of Vengeance 2012

Whorf, Richard (1906-1966) Midnight 1934; Blues in the Night 1941; Keeper of the Flame 1942; Yankee Doodle Dandy 1942; The Cross of Lorraine 1943; Christmas Holiday 1944; The Impostor 1944; Chain Lightning 1950

Wiazemsky, Anne (1947-) Au Hasard, Balthazar 1966; La Chinoise 1967; Sympathy for the Devil 1968; Theorem 1968; Vent d'Est 1969; Vladimir et Rosa 1970

Wickes, Mary (1910-1995) Too Much Johnson 1938; The Man Who Came to Dinner 1941; Now, Voyager 1942; Who Done It? 1942; Higher and Higher 1943; Anna Lucasta 1949; The Petty Girl 1950; I'll See You in My Dreams 1951; On Moonlight Bay 1951; Young Man with Ideas 1952; The Actress 1953; By the Light of the Silvery Moon 1953; White Christmas 1954; Fate Is the Hunter 1964; Where Angels Go... Trouble Follows 1968; Touched by Love 1979; Postcards from the Edge 1990; Sister Act 1992; Sister Act 2:

Back in the Habit 1993; Little Women 1994

Wickham, Keith Thomas & Friends: Tale of the Brave 2014; Thomas & Friends – Sodor's Legend of the Lost Treasure: the Movie 2015

Wicki, Bernhard (1919–2000) La Notte 1961; Crime and Passion 1976; Despair 1978; Paris, Texas 1984

Widdoes, Kathleen (1939–) Petulia 1968; The Sea Gull 1968; The Mephisto Waltz 1971; Without a Trace 1983

Widerberg, Johan (1974–) All Things Fair 1995; Under the Sun 1998

Widmark, Richard (1914–2008) Kiss of Death 1947; Road House 1948; The Street with No Name 1948; Yellow Sky 1948; Down to the Sea in Ships 1949; Slattery's Hurricane 1949; Halls of Montezuma 1950; Night and the City 1950; No Way Out 1950; Panic in the Streets 1950; The Frogmen 1951; Don't Bother to Knock 1952; O Henry's Full House 1952; Red Skies of Montana 1952; Destination Gobi 1953; Pickup on South Street 1953; Take the High Ground 1953; Broken Lance 1954; Garden of Evil 1954; Hell and High Water 1954; The Cobweb 1955; A Prize of Gold 1955; Backlash 1956; The Last Wagon 1956; Run for the Sun 1956; Saint Joan 1957; Time Limit 1957; The Law and Jake Wade 1958; The Tunnel of Love 1958; The Baited Trap 1959; Warlock 1959; The Alamo 1960; Judgment at Nuremberg 1961; The Secret Ways 1961; Two Rode Together 1961; How the West Was Won 1962; Flight from Ashiya 1963; The Long Ships 1963; Cheyenne Autumn 1964; The Bedford Incident 1965; Alvarez Kelly 1966; The Way West 1967; Madigan 1968; Death of a Gunfighter 1969; When the Legends Die 1972; Murder on the Orient Express 1974; The Sellout 1975; To the Devil a Daughter 1976; Coma 1977; The Domino Principle 1977; Rollercoaster 1977; Twilight's Last Gleaming 1977; The Swarm 1978; Bear Island 1979; National Lampoon's Movie Madness 1981; Hanky Panky 1982; Who Dares Wins 1982; Against All Odds 1984; Once upon a Texas Train 1988; Cold Sassy Tree 1989; True Colors 1991

Wieckiewicz, Robert In Darkness 2011; Walesa: Man of Hope 2013

Wieman, Mathias (1902–1969) Paracelsus 1943; Fear 1954

Wiener, Elisabeth (1946–) Marry Me! Marry Me! 1968; The Monk 1972

Wiest, Dianne (1948–) It's My Turn 1980; I'm Dancing as Fast as I Can 1982; Independence Day 1983; Falling in Love 1984; Footloose 1984; The Purple Rose of Cairo 1985; Hannah and Her Sisters 1986; The Lost Boys 1987; Radio Days 1987; September 1987; Bright Lights, Big City 1988; Cookie 1989; Parenthood 1989; Edward Scissorhands 1990; Little Man Tate 1991; Bullets over Broadway 1994; Cops and Robbersons 1994; The Scout 1994; The Associate 1996; The Birdcage 1996; The Horse Whisperer 1998; Practical Magic 1998; The Simple Life of Noah Dearborn 1999; I Am Sam 2001; Merci Docteur Rey 2002; Robots 2005; A Guide to Recognizing Your Saints 2006; Dan in Real Life 2007; Synecdoche, New York 2008; Rabbit Hole 2010; The Big Year 2011

Wieth, Mogens (1919–1962) The Man Who Knew Too Much 1956; Private Potter 1963

Wifstrand, Naima (1890–1968) Dreams 1955; The Magician 1958

Wiggins, Chris (1931–) King of the Grizzlies 1969; The Neptune Factor 1973; Why Shoot the Teacher 1976; Bay Boy 1984; Evidence of Blood 1998

Wiggins, Wiley (1976–) Dazed and Confused 1993; Boys 1995; Waking Life 2001; Computer Chess 2013

Wight, Peter Naked 1993; Vera Drake 2004; Another Year 2010; Clone 2010

Wight, Stephen Wilderness 2006; Weekender 2011

Wightman, Natasha Revelation 2001; Mouth to Mouth 2005

Wightman, Robert Impulse 1984; Hell Camp 1986

Wiig, Kristen (1973–) The Brothers Solomon 2007; Walk Hard: the Dewey Cox Story 2007; Forgetting Sarah Marshall 2008; Ghost Town 2008; Pretty Bird 2008; Adventureland 2009; Extract 2009; Whip It 2009; All Good Things 2010; Despicable Me 2010; MacGruber 2010; Paul 2010; Bridesmaids 2011; Friends with Kids 2011; Girl Most Likely 2012; Anchorman 2: the Legend Continues 2013; Despicable Me 2 2013; The Secret Life of Walter Mitty 2013; How to Train Your Dragon 2 2014; The Skeleton Twins 2014; Welcome to Me 2014; A

Deadly Adoption 2015; The Diary of a Teenage Girl 2015; The Martian 2015; Masterminds 2015; Ghostbusters 2016; Nasty Baby 2016; Sausage Party 2016; Zoolander 2 2016

Wilbanks, Don Stagecoach to Dancer's Rock 1962; Cry for Me Billy 1972

Wilbur, George P Halloween 4: the Return of Michael Myers 1988; Halloween 6: the Curse of Michael Myers 1995

Wilby, James (1958–) A Handful of Dust 1987; Maurice 1987; A Summer Story 1987; Immaculate Conception 1991; Howards End 1992; Regeneration 1997; Tom's Midnight Garden 1998; Cotton Mary 1999; Jump Tomorrow 2001; De-Lovely 2004; Lady Godiva 2007; Shadows in the Sun 2008

Wilcox, Frank (1907–1974) Conflict 1945; Abbott and Costello Meet the Keystone Cops 1955; Go, Johnny, Go! 1959

Wilcox, Lisa (1964–) A Nightmare on Elm Street 4: The Dream Master 1988; A Nightmare on Elm Street 5: The Dream Child 1989

Wilcox, Paula (1949–) The Lovers! 1972; Man about the House 1974

Wilcox, Robert (1910–1955) The Man They Could Not Hang 1939; Wild Beauty 1946; The Vigilantes Return 1947

Wilcox, Shannon The Border 1981; Six Weeks 1982

Wilcoxon, Henry (1905–1984) Cleopatra 1934; The Crusades 1935; The Last of the Mohicans 1936; Jericho 1937; Souls at Sea 1937; If I Were King 1938; Mysterious Mr Moto 1938; Tarzan Finds a Son! 1939; The Corsican Brothers 1941; That Hamilton Woman 1941; Mrs Miniver 1942; Unconquered 1947; A Connecticut Yankee in King Arthur's Court 1949; Samson and Delilah 1949; The Greatest Show on Earth 1952; Scaramouche 1952; Man in the Wilderness 1971

Wild, Jack (1952–2006) Oliver! 1968; Pufnstuf 1970; Flight of the Doves 1971; Melody 1971; Keep It Up Downstairs 1976; Basil 1998

Wilde, Brian (1927–2008) We Joined the Navy 1962; Rattle of a Simple Man 1964; Porridge 1979

Wilde, Cornel (1915–1989) Life Begins at 8.30 1942; Wintertime 1943; Leave Her to Heaven 1945; A Song to Remember 1945; A Thousand and One Nights 1945; The Bandit of Sherwood Forest 1946; Centennial Summer 1946; Forever Amber 1947; It Had to Be You 1947; Road House 1948; Shockproof 1949; Two Flags West 1950; Sons of the Musketeers 1951; The Greatest Show on Earth 1952; Saadia 1953; Treasure of the Golden Condor 1953; Star of India 1954; Woman's World 1954; The Big Combo 1955; Hot Blood 1956; The Devil's Hairpin 1957; Omar Khayyam 1957; Maracaibo 1958; Edge of Eternity 1959; Constantine and the Cross 1961; Lancelot and Guinevere 1963; The Naked Prey 1966; Beach Red 1967; The Comic 1969; Shark's Treasure 1975; The Norseman 1978; The 5th Musketeer 1979

Wilde, Gabriella Carrie 2013; Endless Love 2014

Wilde, Marty (1939–) What a Crazy World 1963; Stardust 1974

Wilde, Olivia (1984–) Paradise Lost 2006; Year One 2009; The Next Three Days 2010; Tron Legacy 2010; The Change-Up 2011; Cowboys & Aliens 2011; In Time 2011; Deadfall 2012; People like Us 2012; The Words 2012; Drinking Buddies 2013; Her 2013; The Incredible Burt Wonderstone 2013; Rush 2013; Third Person 2013; Better Living through Chemistry 2014; The Longest Week 2014; Christmas with the Coopers 2015

Wilder, Gene (1933–) Bonnie and Clyde 1967; The Producers 1968; Quackser Fortune Has a Cousin in the Bronx 1970; Start the Revolution without Me 1970; Willy Wonka and the Chocolate Factory 1971; Everything You Always Wanted to Know about Sex ... but Were Afraid to Ask 1972; Blazing Saddles 1974; The Little Prince 1974; Rhinoceros 1974; Young Frankenstein 1974; The Adventure of Sherlock Holmes' Smarter Brother 1975; Silver Streak 1976; The Frisco Kid 1979; Stir Crazy 1980; Hanky Panky 1982; The Woman in Red 1984; Haunted Honeymoon 1986; See No Evil, Hear No Evil 1989; Funny about Love 1990; Another You 1991; Alice in Wonderland 1999; The Lady in Question 1999; Murder in a Small Town 1999

Wilder, James (1963–) Zombie High 1987; Scorchers 1991; Tollbooth 1994; The Perfect Marriage 2006

Wilder, John Rock, Pretty Baby 1956; The Unguarded Moment 1956

Wilder, Yvonne The Return of Count Yorga 1971; Bloodbrothers 1978; Seems like Old Times 1980

Wilding, Michael (1912–1979) There Ain't No Justice 1939; Convoy 1940; Sailors Three 1940; Cottage to Let 1941; Kipps 1941; The Big Blockade 1942; In Which We Serve 1942; Secret Mission 1942; Ships with Wings 1942; Undercover 1943; English without Tears 1944; Carnival 1946; Piccadilly Incident 1946; The Courtneys of Curzon Street 1947; An Ideal Husband 1947; Spring in Park Lane 1948; Maytime in Mayfair 1949; Stage Fright 1949; Under Capricorn 1949; The Lady with the Lamp 1951; The Law and the Lady 1951; Derby Day 1952; Trent's Last Case 1952; Torch Song 1953; The Egyptian 1954; The Glass Slipper 1955; Zarak 1956; Danger Within 1958; The World of Suzie Wong 1960; The Best of Enemies 1961; The Naked Edge 1961; A Girl Named Tamiko 1962; The Sweet Ride 1967; Waterloo 1970

Wildman, John (1961–) My American Cousin 1985; American Boyfriends 1989

Wilhoite, Kathleen (1964–) Murphy's Law 1986; Witchboard 1987; Dream Demon 1988; Bad Influence 1990; Everybody Wins 1990; Lorenzo's Oil 1992; Breast Men 1997; The Edge 1997; Quicksand 2003; Family Sins 2004; Ice Dreams 2009

Wilke, Robert J aka Wilke, Robert (1914–1989) 20,000 Leagues under the Sea 1954; The Lone Ranger 1956; Written on the Wind 1956; The Tarnished Angels 1957; Man of the West 1958; Tony Rome 1967; Santee 1973; Days of Heaven 1978

Wilker, José (1946–2014) Medicine Man 1992; The Man of the Year 2002

Wilkin, Jeremy Doppelganger 1969; Battle of Britain 1969; The Thousand Plane Raid 1969; When Dinosaurs Ruled the Earth 1970; Thunderbirds Are Go! 1966; Thunderbird 6 1968

Wilkinson, Tom (1948–) Sylvia 1984; Wetherby 1985; Paper Mask 1990; A Business Affair 1993; Priest 1994; Sense and Sensibility 1995; The Ghost and the Darkness 1996; The Full Monty 1997; The Governess 1997; Oscar and Lucinda 1997; Wilde 1997; Rush Hour 1998; Shakespeare in Love 1998; Essex Boys 1999; Ride with the Devil 1999; The Patriot 2000; Black Knight 2001; In the Bedroom 2001; Before You Go 2002; The Importance of Being Earnest 2002; Normal 2002; Eternal Sunshine of the Spotless Mind 2003; Girl with a Pearl Earring 2003; A Good Woman 2004; If Only 2004; Piccadilly Jim 2004; Separate Lies 2004; Stage Beauty 2004; Batman Begins 2005; The Exorcism of Emily Rose 2005; The Last Kiss 2006; Cassandra's Dream 2007; Michael Clayton 2007; Recount 2008; RocknRolla 2008; Valkyrie 2008; Duplicity 2009; 44 Inch Chest 2009; Burke & Hare 2010; The Conspirator 2010; The Debt 2010; The Ghost 2010; Jackboots on Whitehall 2010; The Best Exotic Marigold Hotel 2011; The Green Hornet 2011; Fury 2012; Belle 2013; Felony 2013; The Lone Ranger 2013; Good People 2014; Selma 2014; Unfinished Business 2015; Denial 2016; Kong: Skull Island 2017

Wilkof, Lee (1951–) Chattahoochee 1989; Addicted to Love 1997

Will i am X-Men Origins: Wolverine 2009; Rio 2011; Rio 2 2014

Willard, Fred (1939–) Americathon 1979; Roxanne 1987; Sodbusters 1994; Waiting for Guffman 1996; Best in Show 2000; American Pie: the Wedding 2003; A Mighty Wind 2003; Anchorman: the Legend of Ron Burgundy 2004; Love Wrecked 2005; Date Movie 2006; For Your Consideration 2006; WALL-E 2008; Youth in Revolt 2009; Fifty Shades of Black 2016

Willcox, Toyah (1958–) Jubilee 1978; Quadrophenia 1979; The Tempest 1979; Anchoress 1993; Julie and the Cadillacs 1997; The Most Fertile Man in Ireland 1999; Aaaaaaaah! 2015

Willes, Jean (1923–1989) Invasion of the Body Snatchers 1956; Desire under the Elms 1958; The FBI Story 1959

William, Warren (1895–1948) Skyscraper Souls 1932; Three on a Match 1932; Employees' Entrance 1933; Gold Diggers of 1933 1933; Lady for a Day 1933; The Mind Reader 1933; The Case of the Howling Dog 1934; Cleopatra 1934; Imitation of Life 1934; The Secret Bride 1934; Upper World 1934; The Case of the Lucky Legs 1935; The Case of the Velvet Claws 1936; Go West, Young Man 1936; Satan Met a Lady 1936; Stage Struck 1936; The Firefly 1937; Madame X 1937; Arsene

Lupin Returns 1938; Wives under Suspicion 1938; The Gracie Allen Murder Case 1939; The Lone Wolf Spy Hunt 1939; The Man in the Iron Mask 1939; Arizona 1940; Lillian Russell 1940; Wild Geese Calling 1941; The Wolf Man 1941; Passport to Suez 1943

Williams, Adam (1922–2006) Vice Squad 1953; Fear Strikes Out 1957; The Badlanders 1958; North by Northwest 1959

Williams (2), Alan Among Giants 1998; Grow Your Own 2007

Williams, Ashley Snow 2004; Something Borrowed 2011

Williams (2), Barbara (1953–) Thief of Hearts 1984; Tiger Warsaw 1988; Watchers 1988; City of Hope 1991; Oh, What a Night 1992; Kidnapped 1995; Bone Daddy 1998

Williams, Bill (1916–1992) Deadline at Dawn 1946; Till the End of Time 1946; The Clay Pigeon 1949; A Dangerous Profession 1949; Fighting Man of the Plains 1949; The Stratton Story 1949; A Woman's Secret 1949; The Cariboo Trail 1950; Rose of Cimarron 1952; Son of Paleface 1952; The Halliday Brand 1957; Space Master X 7 1958; Tickle Me 1965; Buckskin 1968

Williams, Billy Dee (1937–) The Last Angry Man 1959; Brian's Song 1971; The Final Comedown 1972; The Glass House 1972; Lady Sings the Blues 1972; Hit! 1973; Mahogany 1975; The Bingo Long Travelling All-Stars and Motor Kings 1976; Scott Joplin 1977; Star Wars Episode V: the Empire Strikes Back 1980; Nighthawks 1981; Marvin and Tige 1983; Star Wars Episode VI: Return of the Jedi 1983; Fear City 1984; Number One with a Bullet 1986; Batman 1989; Hard Time 1998; The Ladies Man 2000; Undercover Brother 2002; Fanboys 2008; The Lego Movie 2014

Williams, Brook (1938–2005) The Plague of the Zombies 1965; Absolution 1978

Williams, Cara (1925–) Happy Land 1943; Boomerang! 1947; The Saxon Charm 1948; Knock on Any Door 1949; The Girl Next Door 1953; The Helen Morgan Story 1957; Never Steal Anything Small 1959; The Man from the Diner's Club 1963

Williams, Caroline (1957–) The Texas Chainsaw Massacre Part 2 1986; Stepfather II 1989

Williams (1), Charles (1898–1958) Faithless 1932; Convoy 1940

Williams, Chris Dodgeball: a True Underdog Story 2004; The World's Fastest Indian 2005

Williams, Cindy (1947–) Gas-s-s-s, or It Became Necessary to Destroy the World in Order to Save It 1970; Travels with My Aunt 1972; American Graffiti 1973; The Killing Kind 1973; The Conversation 1974; Mr Ricco 1975; More American Graffiti 1979; UForia 1980; Rude Awakening 1989; Bingo 1991

Williams III, Clarence (1939–) The Cool World 1963; King: a Filmed Record... Montgomery to Memphis 1970; Purple Rain 1984; Tough Guys Don't Dance 1987; Maniac Cop 2 1990; My Heroes Have Always Been Cowboys 1991; Deep Cover 1992; Sugar Hill 1993; Against the Wall 1994; Hoodlum 1997; Half-Baked 1998; Last Rites 1998; The General's Daughter 1999; Life 1999; Deception 2000

Williams, Cynda (1966–) Mo' Better Blues 1990; One False Move 1992; Erotic Tales 1994; Gang in Blue 1996; Relax... It's Just Sex 1998; The Wedding 1998; Introducing Dorothy Dandridge 1999

Williams, D J (1868–1949) Maria Marten, or the Murder in the Red Barn 1935; The Crimes of Stephen Hawke 1936; Sweeney Todd, the Demon Barber of Fleet Street 1936; Elephant Boy 1937; It's Never Too Late to Mend 1937

Williams, Dick Anthony aka Williams, Dick (1934–2012) The Anderson Tapes 1971; The Jerk 1979; Gardens of Stone 1987; Tap 1989; Mo' Better Blues 1990

Williams, Don aka **Williams, Don R** (1939–) WW and the Dixie Dancekings 1975; Out of the Woods 2005

Williams, Edy (1942–) Beyond the Valley of the Dolls 1970; Chained Heat 1983; Hollywood Hot Tubs 1984

Williams, Emlyn (1905–1987) Friday the Thirteenth 1933; Evensong 1934; The Dictator 1935; Broken Blossoms 1936; The Citadel 1938; Jamaica Inn 1939; The Stars Look Down 1939; The Girl in the News 1940; Hatter's Castle 1941; Major Barbara 1941; The Last Days of Dolwyn 1949; Another Man's Poison 1951; The Scarf 1951; Ivanhoe 1952; The Deep Blue Sea 1955; I

Accuse! 1958; Beyond This Place 1959; The Wreck of the Mary Deare 1959; The L-Shaped Room 1962; Eye of the Devil 1966; The Walking Stick 1971

Williams, Esther (1921–2013) Andy Hardy's Double Life 1942; Bathing Beauty 1944; A Guy Named Joe 1944; Ziegfeld Follies 1944; Thrill of a Romance 1945; Easy to Wed 1946; The Hoodlum Saint 1946; Fiesta 1947; This Time for Keeps 1947; On an Island with You 1948; Neptune's Daughter 1949; Take Me Out to the Ball Game 1949; Duchess of Idaho 1950; Callaway Went Thataway 1951; Texas Carnival 1951; Million Dollar Mermaid 1952; Skirts Ahoy! 1952; Dangerous When Wet 1953; Easy to Love 1953; Jupiter's Darling 1955; The Unguarded Moment 1956; Raw Wind in Eden 1958; The Big Show 1961

Williams, Finty (1972–) The Mystery of Edwin Drood 1993; Delicious 2013

Williams, Grant (1930–1985) Red Sundown 1956; Showdown at Abilene 1956; Written on the Wind 1956; The Incredible Shrinking Man 1957; The Monolith Monsters 1957; Susan Slade 1961; PT 109 1963

Williams, Guinn "Big Boy" aka **Williams, Guinn** (1899–1962) The Bachelor Father 1931; The Glass Key 1935; The Littlest Rebel 1935; Village Tale 1935; Girls Can Play 1937; Blackmail 1939; Castle on the Hudson 1940; Santa Fe Trail 1940; Virginia City 1940; Billy the Kid 1941; Hoppity Goes to Town 1941; You'll Never Get Rich 1941; The Desperadoes 1943; Belle of the Yukon 1944; Nevada 1944; Station West 1948; Rocky Mountain 1950; Al Jennings of Oklahoma 1951; Southwest Passage 1954

Williams, Guy (1924–1989) Seven Angry Men 1955; Captain Sindbad 1963

Williams, Harcourt (1880–1957) Henry V 1944; Brighton Rock 1947; No Room at the Inn 1948; Eye Witness 1949; Third Time Lucky 1949; Trottie True 1949; The Late Edwina Black 1951; Roman Holiday 1953; Terror on a Train 1953

Williams, Harland (1967–) Rocketman 1997; Half-Baked 1998; Superstar 1999; Sorority Boys 2002; Employee of the Month 2006; Driving Aphrodite 2008

Williams, Heathcote (1941–) The Tempest 1979; Orlando 1992; The Steal 1994; Blue Juice 1995

Williams, Hugh (1904–1969) Charley's Aunt 1930; Rome Express 1932; The Last Journey 1936; Brief Ecstasy 1937; Bank Holiday 1938; Dark Eyes of London 1939; Wuthering Heights 1939; The Day Will Dawn 1942; One of Our Aircraft Is Missing 1942; Secret Mission 1942; A Girl in a Million 1946; An Ideal Husband 1947; Take My Life 1947; The Blind Goddess 1948; Elizabeth of Ladymead 1948; The Romantic Age 1949; Gift Horse 1951; The Holly and the Ivy 1952; The Intruder 1953

Williams, JoBeth (1953–) Kramer vs Kramer 1979; The Dogs of War 1980; Stir Crazy 1980; Poltergeist 1982; Adam 1983; The Big Chill 1983; American Dreamer 1984; Teachers 1984; Desert Bloom 1985; Poltergeist II: the Other Side 1986; Memories of Me 1988; My Name Is Bill W 1989; Welcome Home 1989; Driving Me Crazy 1991; Switch 1991; Victim of Love 1991; Stop! or My Mom Will Shoot 1992; Jungle 2 Jungle 1997; Little City 1997; The Perfect Catch 2005; Uncorked 2008

Williams, John (1903–1983) Kind Lady 1951; Dial M for Murder 1954; Sabrina 1954; The Student Prince 1954; To Catch a Thief 1955; D-Day the Sixth of June 1956; The Solid Gold Cadillac 1956; Will Success Spoil Rock Hunter? 1957; Witness for the Prosecution 1957; Midnight Lace 1960; Dear Brigitte 1966; Double Trouble 1967; A Flea in Her Ear 1968; The Hound of the Baskervilles 1972; Hot Lead and Cold Feet 1978

Williams, Kate Poor Cow 1967; Love Thy Neighbour 1973

Williams, Kathlyn (1888–1960) Our Dancing Daughters 1928; Daddy Long Legs 1931

Williams, Katt Norbit 2007; First Sunday 2008; Cats & Dogs: the Revenge of Kitty Galore 2010

Williams, Kelli (1970–) A Woman Scorned 1992; For Their Own Good 1993; There Goes My Baby 1994; Flowers for Algernon 2000

Williams, Kenneth (1926–1988) Valley of Song 1953; The Seekers 1954; Carry On Sergeant 1958; Carry On Nurse 1959; Carry On Teacher 1959; Tommy the Toreador 1959; Carry On Constable 1960; Carry On Regardless 1960; His and Hers 1960; Make Mine Mink 1960; Raising the Wind 1961; Carry On

Cruising 1962; Twice round the Daffodils 1962; Carry On Jack 1963; Carry On Cleo 1964; Carry On Spying 1964; Carry On Cowboy 1965; Carry On - Don't Lose Your Head 1966; Carry On Screaming 1966; Carry On Follow That Camel 1967; Carry On Doctor 1968; Carry On Up the Khyber 1968; Carry On Again Doctor 1969; Carry On Camping 1969; Carry On Loving 1970; Carry On at Your Convenience 1971; Carry On Henry 1971; Carry On Abroad 1972; Carry On Matron 1972; Carry On Dick 1974; Carry On Behind 1975; The Hound of the Baskervilles 1977; That's Carry On 1977; Carry On Emmannuelle 1978

Williams, Kimberly aka **Williams-Paisley, Kimberly** (1971-) Father of the Bride 1991; Coldblooded 1995; Father of the Bride Part 2 1995; The War at Home 1996 Elephant Juice 1999; Identity Theft: the Michelle Brown Story 2004; Porco Rosso 2005; Amish Grace 2010

Williams, Lia (1964-) Dirty Weekend 1992; Firelight 1997; The King Is Alive 2000; Girl from Rio 2001

Williams, Maisie (1997-) The Falling 2014; Gold 2014

Williams, Malinda (1975-) High School High 1996; A Thin Line between Love and Hate 1996; The Wood 1999; Idlewild 2006; First Sunday 2008

Williams, Mark (1959-) 101 Dalmatians 1996; The Borrowers 1997; High Heels and Low Lifes 2001; Anita & Me 2002; Harry Potter and the Chamber of Secrets 2002

Williams, Michael (1935-2001) Marat/Sade 1966; Dead Cert 1974; Educating Rita 1983; The Blair Witch Project 1998

Williams, Michael Kenneth aka

Williams, Michael K The Road 2009; Snitch 2013; The Gambler 2014; The Purge: Anarchy 2014; Captive 2015

Williams, Michelle (1980-) Halloween H20: 20 Years Later 1998; Dick 1999; Me without You 2001; The United States of Leland 2002; The Station Agent 2003; Imaginary Heroes 2004; Brokeback Mountain 2005; Deception 2008; Incendiary 2008; Synecdoche, New York 2008; Mammoth 2009; Shutter Island 2009; Blue Valentine 2010; Meek's Cutoff 2010; My Week with Marilyn 2011; Take This Waltz 2011; Oz the Great and Powerful 2013; Suite Française 2014

Williams, Olivia (1968-) The Postman 1997; Rushmore 1998; Four Dogs Playing Poker 1999; The Sixth Sense 1999; The Body 2000; Born Romantic 2000; Dead Babies 2000; Lucky Break 2001; The Man from Elysian Fields 2001; Below 2002; The Heart of Me 2002; Peter Pan 2003; To Kill a King 2003; Tara Road 2005; Valiant 2005; Broken Lines 2003; An Education 2008; Flashbacks of a Fool 2008; Sex & Drugs & Rock & Roll 2009; The Ghost 2010; Hanna 2011; Hyde Park on Hudson 2012; Now Is Good 2012; The Last Days on Mars 2013; Sabotage 2013; Maps to the Stars 2014; Seventh Son 2014; Man Up 2015; The White King 2016

Williams, Paul (1940-) Battle for the Planet of the Apes 1973; Phantom of the Paradise 1974 Smokey and the Bandit 1977; Smokey and the Bandit II 1980; Smokey and the Bandit III 1983; A Kind of Hush 1998

Williams, Rex (1917-2004) Tarzan Triumphs 1943; Salty O'Rourke 1945; The Marrying Kind 1952

Williams, Rhoda (1930-2006) Cinderella 1950; Space Master X 7 1958

Williams, Rhys (1897-1969) The Corn Is Green 1945; The Farmer's Daughter 1946; So Goes My Love 1946; The Strange Woman 1946; Hills of Home 1948; Devil's Doorway 1950; Lightning Strikes Twice 1951; The Sword of Monte Cristo 1951; Carbine Williams 1952; Meet Me at the Fair 1952; Mutiny 1952; Man in the Attic 1953; The Black Shield of Falworth 1954; Nightmare 1956; The Restless Breed 1957

Williams, Richard (1933-) The Greengage Summer 1961; Slaughter's Big Rip-Off 1973

Williams, Robert B (1904-1978) Revenge of the Creature 1955; Viva Las Vegas 1964

Williams, Robin aka **Fromage, Marty** (1951-2014) Popeye 1980; The World According to Garp 1982; The Survivors 1983; Moscow on the Hudson 1984; The Best of Times 1986; Club Paradise 1986; Good Morning, Vietnam 1987; The Adventures of Baron Munchausen 1988; Dead Poets Society 1989; Awakenings 1990 Cadillac Man 1990; Dead Again 1991; The Fisher King 1991;

Hook 1991; Shakes the Clown 1991; Aladdin 1992; FernGully: the Last Rainforest 1992; Toys 1992; Mrs Doubtfire 1993; Being Human 1994; Jumanji 1995; Nine Months 1995; Aladdin and the King of Thieves 1996; The Birdcage 1996; Jack 1996; The Secret Agent 1996; Deconstructing Harry 1997; Fathers' Day 1997; Flubber 1997; Good Will Hunting 1997; Patch Adams 1998; What Dreams May Come 1998; Bicentennial Man 1999; Jakob the Liar 1999; AI: Artificial Intelligence 2001; One Hour Photo 2001; Death to Smoochy 2002; Insomnia 2002; The Final Cut 2004; Noel 2004; The Aristocrats 2005; The Big White 2005; Robots 2005; Happy Feet 2006; Man of the Year 2006; Night at the Museum 2006; The Night Listener 2006; RV 2006; August Rush 2007; License to Wed 2007; Night at the Museum 2 2009; Old Dogs 2009; Shrink 2009; World's Greatest Dad 2009; Happy Feet Two 2011; The Butler 2013; The Face of Love 2013; The Angriest Man in Brooklyn 2014; Boulevard 2014; Night at the Museum: Secret of the Tomb 2014

Williams, Samm-Art (1946-) Blood Simple 1983; Cook & Peary: the Race to the Pole 1983

Williams, Saul (1972-) Downtown 81 1981; Slam 1998; K-PAX 2001

Williams, Scot Backbeat 1993; Beyond the Fire 2008; Clubbed 2008; K-Shop 2015

Williams, Simon (1946-) The Odd Job 1978; The Prisoner of Zenda 1979

Williams, Steven (1949-) Missing in Action 2: the Beginning 1985; Jason Goes to Hell: the Final Friday 1993; Graves End 2005

Williams, Treat (1952-) The Ritz 1976; Hair 1979; 1941 1979; Prince of the City 1981; The Pursuit of DB Cooper 1981; Once upon a Time in America 1984; Smooth Talk 1985; The Men's Club 1986; Dead Heat 1988; Heart of Dixie 1989; Where the Rivers Flow North 1993; Hand Gun 1994; Things to Do in Denver When You're Dead 1995; Mulholland Falls 1996; The Phantom 1996; The Devil's Own 1997; Deep Rising 1998; The Deep End of the Ocean 1999; 36 Hours to Die 1999; Hollywood Ending 2002; Miss Congeniality 2: Armed & Fabulous 2005; The Staircase Murders 2007; Chasing a Dream 2009; Safe Harbor 2009; Howl 2010; Beyond the Blackboard 2011; A Little Bit of Heaven 2011; 127 Hours 2011; Deadfall 2012; Eve of Destruction 2013; Reaching for the Moon 2013

Williams, Tyler James Grounded 2006; Dear White People 2014

Williams, Vanessa (1963-) Candyman 1992; DROP Squad 1994; Imagine That 2009

Williams, Vanessa L aka **Williams, Vanessa** (1963-) The Pick-Up Artist 1987; Another You 1991; Harley Davidson and the Marlboro Man 1991; Eraser 1996; Hoodlum 1997; Soul Food 1997; Dance with Me 1998; Futuresport 1998; The Adventures of Elmo in Grouchland 1999; Don Quixote 2000; Shaft 2000; Johnson Family Vacation 2004; Hannah Montana: the Movie 2009

Williams, Wade Andrew Candyman: Day of the Dead 1999; K-911 1999

Williamson, Chase John Dies at the End 2012; The Guest 2014

Williamson, Felix Me Myself I 1999; Strange Planet 1999; Dirty Deeds 2002

Williamson, Fred (1938-) Hammer 1972; Black Caesar 1973; Hell Up in Harlem 1973; Three the Hard Way 1974; Three Tough Guys 1974; Take a Hard Ride 1975; Inglorious Bastards 1978; From Dusk till Dawn 1995; Original Gangstas 1996; Starsky & Hutch 2004

Williamson, Kate (1930-2013) Dream Lover 1993; The Last Time I Committed Suicide 1996; Dahmer 2002

Williamson, Mykelti aka **Williamson, Mykel T** (1960-) Miracle Mile 1989; The First Power 1990; Forrest Gump 1994; Heat 1995; Waiting to Exhale 1995; Soul of the Game 1996; Buffalo Soldiers 1997; Truth or Consequences, NM 1997; 12 Angry Men 1997; Species II 1998; Three Kings 1999; Ali 2001; After the Sunset 2004; The Assassination of Richard Nixon 2004; The Final Destination 2009

Williamson, Nicol (1936-2012) The Bofors Gun 1968; Inadmissible Evidence 1968; Hamlet 1969; Laughter in the Dark 1969; The Reckoning 1969; The Jerusalem File 1972; The Monk 1972; The Wilby Conspiracy 1975; Robin and Marian 1976; The Cheap Detective 1978; The Human Factor 1979;

Excalibur 1981; Venom 1981; I'm Dancing as Fast as I Can 1982; Return to Oz 1985; Black Widow 1987; The Exorcist III 1990; The Hour of the Pig 1993; The Wind in the Willows 1996; Spawn 1997

Willingham, Noble (1930-2004) Big Bad Mama 1974; Aloha, Bobby and Rose 1975; The Boys in Company C 1978; Unconquered 1989; Blind Fury 1990; City Slickers 1991; The Last Boy Scout 1991; The Distinguished Gentleman 1992; Of Mice and Men 1992; Ace Ventura: Pet Detective 1993; Blind Horizon 2003

Willis, Bruce (1955-) Blind Date 1987; Die Hard 1988; Sunset 1988; In Country 1989; Look Who's Talking 1989; The Bonfire of the Vanities 1990; Die Hard 2: Die Harder 1990; Look Who's Talking Too 1990; Billy Bathgate 1991; Hudson Hawk 1991; The Last Boy Scout 1991; Mortal Thoughts 1991; Death Becomes Her 1992; Striking Distance 1993; Color of Night 1994; Nobody's Fool 1994; North 1994; Pulp Fiction 1994; Die Hard with a Vengeance 1995; Four Rooms 1995; Twelve Monkeys 1995; Beavis and Butt-head Do America 1996; Last Man Standing 1996; The Fifth Element 1997; The Jackal 1997; Armageddon 1998; Mercury Rising 1998; The Siege 1998; Breakfast of Champions 1999; The Sixth Sense 1999; The Story of Us 1999; Disney's The Kid 2000; Unbreakable 2000; The Whole Nine Yards 2000; Bandits 2001; Hart's War 2002; Rugrats Go Wild 2003; Tears of the Sun 2003; Hostage 2004; The Whole Ten Yards 2004; Sin City 2005; Alpha Dog 2006; Fast Food Nation 2006; Lucky Number Slevin 2006; Over the Hedge 2006; 16 Blocks 2006; Die Hard 4.0 2007; Nancy Drew 2007; Perfect Stranger 2007; Planet Terror 2007; What Just Happened? 2007; Surrogates 2009; Cop Out 2010; The Expendables 2010; Red 2010; Set Up 2011; The Cold Light of Day 2012; The Expendables 2 2012; Fire with Fire 2012; Lay the Favorite 2012; Looper 2012; Moonrise Kingdom 2012; GI Joe: Retaliation 2013; A Good Day to Die Hard 2013; Red 2 2013; Sin City: a Dame to Kill For 2014; Rock the Kasbah 2015; Precious Cargo 2016

Willis, Jerome The Siege of the Saxons 1963; Winstanley 1975

Willis, Rumer Striptease 1996; The House Bunny 2008; Sorority Row 2009

Willman, Noel (1917-1988) The Net 1953; Across the Bridge 1957; Seven Waves Away 1957; Two Living, One Dead 1961; The Girl on the Boat 1962; Kiss of the Vampire 1962; The Reptile 1966

Willmer, Catherine Women in Love 1969; The Boy Friend 1971

Willock, Dave (1909-1990) Let's Face It 1943; Revenge of the Creature 1955; The Buster Keaton Story 1957; Ten Seconds to Hell 1959

Wills, Chill (1903-1978) Boom Town 1940; The Westerner 1940; Belle Starr 1941; Honky Tonk 1941; Western Union 1941; Apache Trail 1942; Her Cardboard Lover 1942; Tarzan's New York Adventure 1942; Barbary Coast Gent 1944; Sunday Dinner for a Soldier 1944; The Harvey Girls 1946; The Yearling 1946; The Saxon Charm 1948; Francis 1949; Red Canyon 1949; Tulsa 1949; High Lonesome 1950; Rio Grande 1950; The Sundowners 1950; Cattle Drive 1951; Francis Goes to the Races 1951; Francis Goes to West Point 1952; City That Never Sleeps 1953; Francis Covers the Big Town 1953; The Man from the Alamo 1953; Tumbleweed 1953; Francis Joins the WACS 1954; Francis Joins the WACS 1954; Francis in the Navy 1955; Timberjack 1955; Giant 1956; Santiago 1956; Gun for a Coward 1957; Gun Glory 1957; From Hell to Texas 1958; The Sad Horse 1959; The Alamo 1960; Where the Boys Are 1960; The Deadly Companions 1961; Young Guns of Texas 1962; McLintock! 1963; The Wheeler Dealers 1963; The Rounders 1965; Fireball 500 1966; The Liberation of LB Jones 1970; Pat Garrett and Billy the Kid 1973; Mr Billion 1977

Wills, Scott Stickmen 2001; Perfect Creature 2005

Wilmer, Douglas (1920-2016) The Battle of the River Plate 1956; El Cid 1961; The Brides of Fu Manchu 1966; The Vengeance of Fu Manchu 1967; The Vampire Lovers 1970; Unman, Wittering and Zigo 1971; The Golden Voyage of Sinbad 1973; The Adventure of Sherlock Holmes' Smarter Brother 1975

Wilmot, David I Went Down 1997; Rat 2000; interMission 2003; Middletown 2006; The Guard 2011; Gold 2014

Wilmot, Ronan Lamb 1985; Rawhead Rex 1986

Wilms, André (1947-) Monsieur Hire 1989; Europa Europa 1991; L'Enfer 1993; Juha 1999; Le Havre 2011

Wilson-Jones, Anna Mrs Caldicot's Cabbage War 2000; The Mother 2003

Wilson (1), Andrew (1964-) Bottle Rocket 1996; The Big Bounce 2004; Idiocracy 2006

Wilson, Bridgette aka **Wilson, Bridgette L** aka **Wilson-Sampras, Bridgette** (1973-) Billy Madison 1995; Mortal Kombat 1995; I Know What You Did Last Summer 1997; House on Haunted Hill 1999; Beautiful 2000; Buying the Cow 2000; The Wedding Planner 2001; Extreme Ops 2003; Shopgirl 2005

Wilson, Clarence aka **Wilson, Clarence H** (1876-1941) The Penguin Pool Murder 1932; Son of Kong 1933; Tillie and Gus 1933; The Lemon Drop Kid 1934

Wilson, Dana (1949-) A Cry from the Streets 1957; The Shiralee 1957

Wilson, David Eddie and the Cruisers 1983; The Inside Man 1984

Wilson, Don "The Dragon" (1955-) Bloodfist 1989; Ring of Fire 1991

Wilson, Dooley (1886-1953) Casablanca 1942; Stormy Weather 1943; Come to the Stable 1949

Wilson, Dorothy (1909-1998) Lucky Devils 1933; The White Parade 1934; In Old Kentucky 1935; Craig's Wife 1936; The Milky Way 1936

Wilson, Elizabeth (1921-2015) Patterns 1956; The Tunnel of Love 1958; The Graduate 1967; Little Murders 1971; The Prisoner of Second Avenue 1974; The Happy Hooker 1975; Nine to Five 1980; Grace Quigley 1984; The Believers 1987; The Addams Family 1991; Regarding Henry 1991

Wilson, Flip (1933-1998) Uptown Saturday Night 1974; Skatetown, USA 1979

Wilson, Georges (1921-2010) The Long Absence 1961; The Seven Deadly Sins 1961; Tintin and the Mystery of the Golden Fleece 1961; The Empty Canvas 1963; More than a Miracle 1967; The Stranger 1967; Beatrice Cenci 1969; Blanche 1971; Not Here to Be Loved 2005

Wilson, Josephine (1904-1990) We Dive at Dawn 1943; Chance of a Lifetime 1950

Wilson, Kristen (1969-) Bulletproof 1996; Doctor Dolittle 1998; Dungeons & Dragons 2000; Dr Dolittle 2 2001; Confessions of a Dangerous Mind 2002; Walking Tall 2004; Dr Dolittle 3 2006

Wilson, Lambert (1958-) Five Days One Summer 1982; Sahara 1983; The Blood of Others 1984; La Femme Publique 1984; Rendez-vous 1985; Rouge Baiser 1985; The Belly of an Architect 1987; El Dorado 1988; The Leading Man 1996; On Connaît la Chanson 1997; The Last September 1999; Don Quixote 2000; Pas sur la Bouche 2003; Catwoman 2004; Sahara 2005; Private Fears in Public Places 2006; Flawless 2007; Babylon AD 2008; The Lazarus Project 2008; Of Gods and Men 2010; The Princess of Montpensier 2010; Cycling with Molière 2013

Wilson, Lisle (1943-) Sisters 1973; The Incredible Melting Man 1977

Wilson, Lois (1894-1988) The Covered Wagon 1923; Ruggles of Red Gap 1923; Deluge 1933; Female 1933; Laughing at Life 1933; Bright Eyes 1934

Wilson, Luke (1971-) Bottle Rocket 1996; Best Men 1997; Telling Lies in America 1997; Dog Park 1998; Home Fries 1998; Blue Streak 1999; Kill the Man 1999; My Dog Skip 1999; Committed 2000; Legally Blonde 2001; The Royal Tenenbaums 2001; Soul Survivors 2001; Alex & Emma 2003; Legally Blonde 2: Red, White & Blonde 2003; Masked and Anonymous 2003; Old School 2003; Around the World in 80 Days 2004; The Family Stone 2005; Hoot 2006; Idiocracy 2006; My Super Ex-Girlfriend 2006; Battle for Terra 2007; Blonde Ambition 2007; Vacancy 2007; You Kill Me 2007; Death at a Funeral 2010; The Skeleton Twins 2014

Wilson, Mara (1987-) Mrs Doubtfire 1993; Miracle on 34th Street 1994; Matilda 1996; A Simple Wish 1997; Thomas and the Magic Railroad 2000

Wilson, Marie (1916-1972) China Clipper 1936; Satan Met a Lady 1936; The Great Garrick 1937; Boy Meets Girl 1938; Fools for Scandal 1938; The Invisible Menace 1938; My Friend Irma

1949; My Friend Irma Goes West 1950; A Girl in Every Port 1952; Never Wave at a WAC 1952; Marry Me Again 1953; Mr Hobbs Takes a Vacation 1962

Wilson, Niamh The Marsh 2006; They Come Back 2007; The Young and Prodigious TS Spivet 2013

Wilson, Owen aka **Wilson, Owen C** (1968-) Bottle Rocket 1996; Anaconda 1997; Permanent Midnight 1998; Rushmore 1998; The Haunting 1999; The Minus Man 1999; Meet the Parents 2000; Shanghai Noon 2000; Behind Enemy Lines 2001; The Royal Tenenbaums 2001; Zoolander 2001; I Spy 2002; Shanghai Knights 2002; Around the World in 80 Days 2004; The Big Bounce 2004; The Life Aquatic with Steve Zissou 2004; Meet the Fockers 2004; Starsky & Hutch 2004; Wedding Crashers 2005; Cars 2006; Night at the Museum 2006; You, Me and Dupree 2006; The Darjeeling Limited 2007; Drillbit Taylor 2007; Marley & Me 2008; Fantastic Mr Fox 2009; Night at the Museum 2 2009; How Do You Know 2010; Little Fockers 2010; Marmaduke 2010; The Big Year 2011; Cars 2 2011; Hall Pass 2011; Midnight in Paris 2011; Free Birds 2013; The Internship 2013; Inherent Vice 2014; Night at the Museum: Secret of the Tomb 2014; No Escape 2014; She's Funny That Way 2014; Masterminds 2015; Bastards 2016; Zoolander 2 2016

Wilson, Patrick (1973-) The Alamo 2004; The Phantom of the Opera 2004; Hard Candy 2005; Little Children 2006; Evening 2007; Lakeview Terrace 2008; Watchmen 2009; The A-Team 2010; Insidious 2010; Morning Glory 2010; The Switch 2010; Young Adult 2011; The Conjuring 2013; Insidious: Chapter 2 2013; Bone Tomahawk 2015; The Conjuring 2 2016; The Founder 2016

Wilson, Perry (1916-2009) Fear Strikes Out 1957; The Matchmaker 1958

Wilson, Peta (1970-) Mercy 2000; Joe and Max 2002; The League of Extraordinary Gentlemen 2003

Wilson, Rainn (1966-) House of 1000 Corpses 2001; Sahara 2005; My Super Ex-Girlfriend 2006; The Last Mimzy 2007; The Rocker 2008; Monsters vs Aliens 2009; Transformers: Revenge of the Fallen 2009; Super 2010; Cooties 2014

Wilson, Rebel (1980-) Bachelorette 2012; Pain & Gain 2013; Night at the Museum: Secret of the Tomb 2014; Pitch Perfect 2 2015; Grimsby 2016; How to Be Single 2016; Pitch Perfect 3 2017

Wilson, Reno Diary of a Serial Killer 1997; She Creature 2001

Wilson, Richard The Loved Ones 2009; Gnomeo & Juliet 2011

Wilson (3), Richard (1936-) A Passage to India 1984; Fellow Traveller 1989; How to Get Ahead in Advertising 1989; Carry On Columbus 1992; Soft Top, Hard Shoulder 1992; The Man Who Knew Too Little 1997; Women Talking Dirty 1999

Wilson (4), Richard (1984-) The Proposition 2005; Clubland 2006

Wilson, Rita (1958-) Volunteers 1985; Sleepless in Seattle 1993; Mixed Nuts 1994; Now and Then 1995; Jingle All the Way 1996; Invisible Child 1999; Runaway Bride 1999; The Story of Us 1999; Auto Focus 2002; Raise Your Voice 2004; The Chumscrubber 2005; It's Complicated 2009; The Art of Getting By 2011

Wilson, Ruth (1982-) Saving Mr Banks 2013; Locke 2014; Suite Française 2014

Wilson, Scott (1942-) In Cold Blood 1967; The Gypsy Moths 1969; The Grissom Gang 1971; The New Centurions 1972; The Lolly-Madonna War 1973; The Great Gatsby 1974; The Ninth Configuration 1979; A Year of the Quiet Sun 1984; The Aviator 1985; Blue City 1986; Malone 1987; Johnny Handsome 1989; Femme Fatale 1991; Pure Luck 1991; Flesh and Bone 1993; Shiloh 1996; GI Jane 1997; Clay Pigeons 1998; The Way of the Gun 2000; Monster 2003; Junebug 2004; The Heartbreak Kid 2007

Wilson, Sheree J (1958-) Crimewave 1985; Fraternity Vacation 1985

Wilson (1), Stuart (1946-) Dulcima 1971; Lethal Weapon 3 1992; Teenage Mutant Ninja Turtles III 1992; Death and the Maiden 1994; Exit to Eden 1994; No Escape 1994; Crossworlds 1996; Desert Gamble 1996; The Mask of Zorro 1998; The Luzhin Defence 2000; Unstoppable 2004

Wilson (2), Teddy aka **Wilson, Theodore** (1943-1991) Carny 1980; Life Stinks 1991

Wilson, Thomas F aka **Wilson, Tom** (1959-) Back to the Future 1985; Action Jackson 1988; Back to the Future Part II 1989; Back to the Future Part III 1990; The Informant! 2009

Wilson, Tom (1880-1965) A Day's Pleasure 1919; Sunnyside 1919; The Kid 1921; Battling Butler 1926

Wilson, Trey (1948-1989) Raising Arizona 1987; Bull Durham 1988; Twins 1988; Great Balls of Fire! 1989; Welcome Home 1989

Wilton, Penelope (1946-) Clockwise 1986; Cry Freedom 1987; Blame It on the Bellboy 1992; The Secret Rapture 1993; Carrington 1995; Tom's Midnight Garden 1998; Iris 2001; Calendar Girls 2003; Shaun of the Dead 2004; Match Point 2005; Pride & Prejudice 2005; The History Boys 2006; The Best Exotic Marigold Hotel 2011; Belle 2013; The Second Best Exotic Marigold Hotel 2015; The BFG 2016

Wilton, Robb (1882-1957) A Fire Has Been Arranged 1935; It's Love Again 1936; The Love Match 1955

Wimmer, Brian (1959-) Late for Dinner 1991; The Maddening 1995; The Evil beneath Loch Ness 2001; Thicker than Water 2005

Winchell, Paul (1922-2005) The Aristocats 1970; Which Way to the Front? 1970; The Many Adventures of Winnie the Pooh 1977; Winnie the Pooh's Most Grand Adventure 1997

Wincott, Jeff (1957-) Universal Soldier 2: Brothers in Arms 1998; Universal Soldier 3: Unfinished Business 1998

Wincott, Michael (1959-) Circle of Two 1980; Talk Radio 1988; Suffering Bastards 1989; Robin Hood: Prince of Thieves 1991; 1492: Conquest of Paradise 1992; Romeo Is Bleeding 1992; The Three Musketeers 1993; The Crow 1994; Strange Days 1995; Basquiat 1996; Alien: Resurrection 1997; Metro 1997; Before Night Falls 2000; Along Came a Spider 2001; The Count of Monte Cristo 2001; Treasure Planet 2002; The Assassination of Richard Nixon 2004; Seraphim Falls 2006; Forsaken 2015

Windom, William (1923-2012) The Americanization of Emily 1964; One Man's Way 1964; The Detective 1968; Prescription: Murder 1968; The Gypsy Moths 1969; Brewster McCloud 1970; Dynamite Man from Glory Jail 1971; Escape from the Planet of the Apes 1971; The Mephisto Waltz 1971; The Man 1972; Echoes of a Summer 1976; Leave 'Em Laughing 1981; Grandview, USA 1984; She's Having a Baby 1988; Attack of the 50 Ft Woman 1993; Sommersby 1993

Windsor, Barbara (1937-) Too Hot to Handle 1960; Sparrows Can't Sing 1962; Crooks in Cloisters 1963; Carry On Spying 1964; A Study in Terror 1965; Carry On Doctor 1968; Carry On Again Doctor 1969; Carry On Camping 1969; The Boy Friend 1971; Carry On Henry 1971; Carry On Abroad 1972; Carry On Matron 1972; Not Now Darling 1972; Carry On Girls 1973; Carry On Dick 1974; That's Carry On 1977

Windsor, Frank (1927-) Sunday, Bloody Sunday 1971; Assassin 1973

Windsor, Marie (1919-2000) Force of Evil 1948; The Fighting Kentuckian 1949; Outpost in Morocco 1949; Frenchie 1950; The Narrow Margin 1952; The Sniper 1952; City That Never Sleeps 1953; Trouble along the Way 1953; The Bounty Hunter 1954; Abbott and Costello Meet the Mummy 1955; The Killing 1956; The Girl in Black Stockings 1957; The Unholy Wife 1957; Day of the Bad Man 1958; Mail Order Bride 1963; Bedtime Story 1964; Support Your Local Gunfighter 1971; Cahill, United States Marshal 1973; The Outfit 1973

Windsor, Romy aka **Walthall, Romy** The House of Usher 1988; My Brother the Pig 1999

Winfield, Paul (1941-2004) RPM - Revolutions per Minute 1970; Sounder 1972; Trouble Man 1972; Gordon's War 1973; Huckleberry Finn 1974; Hustle 1975; Damnation Alley 1977; High Velocity 1977; Twilight's Last Gleaming 1977; A Hero Ain't Nothin' but a Sandwich 1978; Carbon Copy 1981; White Dog 1981; Star Trek II: The Wrath of Khan 1982; On the Run 1983; Mike's Murder 1984; The Terminator 1984; Blue City 1986; The Serpent and the Rainbow 1987; Presumed Innocent 1990; Cliffhanger 1993; Dennis 1993; Breathing Lessons 1994; Original Gangstas 1996; Relax... It's Just Sex 1998

Winfrey, Oprah (1954-) The Color Purple 1985; Native Son 1986; Throw Momma from the Train 1987; Before

Women Had Wings 1997; Beloved 1998; Charlotte's Web 2006; The Princess and the Frog 2009; The Butler 2013; Selma 2014

Wing, Anna (1914-2013) A Doll's House 1973; Full Circle 1977; Son of Rambow 2007

Wingard, Adam (1982-) V/H/S 2012; V/H/S/2 2013

Winger, Debra (1955-) Slumber Party '57 1976; Thank God It's Friday 1978; French Postcards 1979; Urban Cowboy 1980; Cannery Row 1982; An Officer and a Gentleman 1982; Terms of Endearment 1983; Mike's Murder 1984; Legal Eagles 1986; Black Widow 1987; Betrayed 1988; Everybody Wins 1990; The Sheltering Sky 1990; Leap of Faith 1992; A Dangerous Woman 1993; Shadowlands 1993; Wilder Napalm 1993; Forget Paris 1995; Radio 2003; Dawn Anna 2005; Sometimes in April 2005; Rachel Getting Married 2008; Lola Versus 2012; The Choir 2014

Wingett, Mark (1961-) Quadrophenia 1979; Breaking Glass 1980

Winkler, Angela (1944-) The Lost Honour of Katharina Blum 1975; Knife in the Head 1978; The Tin Drum 1979; Danton 1982; Benny's Video 1992

Winkler, Henry (1945-) The Lords of Flatbush 1974; The One and Only 1978; Night Shift 1982; Scream 1996; The Waterboy 1998; Down to You 2000; Holes 2003; Click 2006; Here Comes the Boom 2012

Winkler, Mel (1941-) Convicts 1991; Doc Hollywood 1991; Devil in a Blue Dress 1995; A Life Less Ordinary 1997

Winn, Kitty (1944-) The Panic in Needle Park 1971; The Exorcist 1973; Exorcist II: The Heretic 1977

Winnick, Katheryn Cold Souls 2008; Killers 2010; The Art of the Steal 2013; Geostorm 2016

Winninger, Charles (1884-1969) Bad Sister 1931; God's Gift to Women 1931; Night Nurse 1931; Show Boat 1936; White Fang 1936; Café Metropole 1937; Every Day's a Holiday 1937; Nothing Sacred 1937; Three Smart Girls 1937; Woman Chases Man 1937; You Can't Have Everything 1937; Hard to Get 1938; Babes in Arms 1939; Destry Rides Again 1939; Three Smart Girls Grow Up 1939; Little Nellie Kelly 1940; My Life with Caroline 1941; Pot o' Gold 1941; Ziegfeld Girl 1941; Coney Island 1943; Hers to Hold 1943; Belle of the Yukon 1944; Broadway Rhythm 1944; Sunday Dinner for a Soldier 1944; State Fair 1945; Lover Come Back 1946; Living in a Big Way 1947; Something in the Wind 1947; Give My Regards to Broadway 1948; The Sun Shines Bright 1953

Winningham, Mare (1959-) One-Trick Pony 1980; Threshold 1981; St Elmo's Fire 1985; Nobody's Fool 1986; A Winner Never Quits 1986; Made in Heaven 1987; Shy People 1987; Miracle Mile 1989; Turner & Hooch 1989; Hard Promises 1991; The War 1994; Wyatt Earp 1994; Georgia 1995; The Boys Next Door 1996; Under Pressure 1997; Everything That Rises 1998; The Maldonado Miracle 2003; Swing Vote 2008; Mirror Mirror 2012; Philomena 2013

Winslet, Kate (1975-) Heavenly Creatures 1994; Sense and Sensibility 1995; Hamlet 1996; Jude 1996; Titanic 1997; Hideous Kinky 1998; Holy Smoke 1999; Quills 2000; Christmas Carol: the Movie 2001; Enigma 2001; Iris 2001; Eternal Sunshine of the Spotless Mind 2003; The Life of David Gale 2003; Finding Neverland 2004; Romance & Cigarettes 2004; All the King's Men 2005; Flushed Away 2006; The Holiday 2006; Little Children 2006; The Fox and the Child 2007; The Reader 2008; Revolutionary Road 2008; Carnage 2011; Contagion 2011; Labor Day 2013; Movie 43 2013; Divergent 2014; A Little Chaos 2014; The Dressmaker 2015; Insurgent 2015; Steve Jobs 2015; Triple 9 2015; Collateral Beauty 2016

Winslow, George aka **Winslow, George "Foghorn"** (1946-2015) Room for One More 1952; Gentlemen Prefer Blondes 1953; The Rocket Man 1954; Artists and Models 1955; Wild Heritage 1958

Winslow, Michael (1960-) Cheech and Chong's Next Movie 1980; Alphabet City 1984; Police Academy 2: Their First Assignment 1985; Police Academy 3: Back in Training 1986; Police Academy 4: Citizens on Patrol 1987; Spaceballs 1987; Buy & Cell 1988; Police Academy 5: Assignment Miami Beach 1988; Police Academy 6: City under Siege 1989; Police Academy 6: Mission to Moscow 1994

Winstead, Mary Elizabeth (1984-) Black Christmas 2006; Final

Destination 3 2006; Death Proof 2007; Die Hard 4.0 2007; Make It Happen 2008; Scott Pilgrim vs the World 2010; The Thing 2011; Abraham Lincoln: Vampire Hunter 2012; Smashed 2012; A Good Day to Die Hard 2013; Swiss Army Man 2016; 10 Cloverfield Lane 2016

Winston, Hattie (1945-) Clara's Heart 1988; Jackie Brown 1997

Winston, Helene (?-2004) What's the Matter with Helen? 1971; A Boy and His Dog 1975

Winstone, Jaime (1985-) Kidulthood 2005; Donkey Punch 2007; Made in Dagenham 2010; Elfie Hopkins 2011; Powder Room 2013; Love, Rosie 2014

Winstone, Lois everything 2004; Fathers of Girls 2010; The Hot Potato 2011

Winstone, Ray aka **Winstone, Raymond** (1957-) Quadrophenia 1979; Scum 1979; Ladies and Gentlemen, the Fabulous Stains 1981; Ladybird Ladybird 1994; Face 1997; Martha - Meet Frank, Daniel and Laurence 1997; Nil by Mouth 1997; Darkness Falls 1998; Final Cut 1998; Agnes Browne 1999; Fanny & Elvis 1999; The War Zone 1999; Love, Honour and Obey 2000; Sexy Beast 2000; There's Only One Jimmy Grimble 2000; Last Orders 2001; The Martins 2001; Ripley's Game 2002; Cold Mountain 2003; everything 2004; King Arthur 2004; The Proposition 2004; The Chronicles of Narnia: The Lion, the Witch and the Wardrobe 2005; The Magic Roundabout 2005; Breaking and Entering 2006; The Departed 2006; Beowulf 2007; Fool's Gold 2008; Indiana Jones and the Kingdom of the Crystal Skull 2008; Edge of Darkness 2009; 44 Inch Chest 2009; Sex & Drugs & Rock & Roll 2009; Fathers of Girls 2010; London Boulevard 2010; 13 2010; Tracker 2010; Elfie Hopkins 2011; The Hot Potato 2011; Hugo 2011; Rango 2011; Ashes 2012; Snow White and the Huntsman 2012; The Sweeney 2012; Noah 2014; 20,000 Days on Earth 2014; The Gunman 2015; The Legend of Barney Thomson 2015; Point Break 2015; Bo66y 2016

Wint, Maurice Dean (1964-) Cube 1997; Hedwig and the Angry Inch 2001; The Circuit 2008

Winter, Alex (1965-) Death Wish 3 1985; Bill & Ted's Excellent Adventure 1988; Haunted Summer 1988; Bill & Ted's Bogus Journey 1991; Freaked 1993

Winter, Ariel Excision 2012; Mr Peabody & Sherman 2013

Winter, Claude Sunday in the Country 1984; Les Nuits Fauves 1992

Winter, Edward aka **Winter, Ed** (1938-2001) A Change of Seasons 1980; The Buddy System 1984

Winter, Vincent (1947-1998) The Kidnappers 1953; Time Lock 1957; Beyond This Place 1959; Gorgo 1961

Winters, Deborah (1955-) Kotch 1971; Class of '44 1973; Blue Sunshine 1977

Winters, Jonathan (1925-2013) It's a Mad Mad Mad Mad World 1963; The Loved One 1965; Penelope 1966; The Russians Are Coming, the Russians Are Coming 1966; Eight on the Lam 1967; Oh Dad, Poor Dad, Mama's Hung You in the Closet and I'm Feelin' So Sad 1967; Viva Max! 1969; Moon over Parador 1988; The Shadow 1994; The Smurfs 2011; The Smurfs 2 2013

Winters, Roland (1904-1989) Cry of the City 1948; Kidnapped 1948; A Dangerous Profession 1949; To Please a Lady 1950; The West Point Story 1950; Follow the Sun: the Ben Hogan Story 1951; She's Working Her Way through College 1952; Bigger than Life 1956; Blue Hawaii 1961

Winters, Shelley aka **Winter, Shelley** (1922-2006) What a Woman! 1943; Knickerbocker Holiday 1944; A Thousand and One Nights 1945; Tonight and Every Night 1945; A Double Life 1947; Cry of the City 1948; Red River 1948; The Great Gatsby 1949; Frenchie 1950; Winchester '73 1950; He Ran All the Way 1951; A Place in the Sun 1951; Meet Danny Wilson 1952; Phone Call from a Stranger 1952; Untamed Frontier 1952; Executive Suite 1954; Playgirl 1954; Saskatchewan 1954; Tennessee Champ 1954; To Dorothy, a Son 1954; The Big Knife 1955; I Am a Camera 1955; I Died a Thousand Times 1955; The Night of the Hunter 1955; The Treasure of Pancho Villa 1955; The Diary of Anne Frank 1959; Odds against Tomorrow 1959; Let No Man Write My Epitaph 1960; Lolita 1961; The Young Savages 1961; The Chapman Report 1962; The Balcony 1963; Time of Indifference 1964; The Greatest Story Ever Told

1965; A Patch of Blue 1965; Alfie 1966; Harper 1966; The Three Sisters 1966; Enter Laughing 1967; Buona Sera, Mrs Campbell 1968; The Scalphunters 1968; Wild in the Streets 1968; Bloody Mama 1970; Flap 1970; How Do I Love Thee? 1970; Something to Hide 1971; What's the Matter with Helen? 1971; Who Slew Auntie Roo? 1971; The Poseidon Adventure 1972; Blume in Love 1973; Cleopatra Jones 1973; Diamonds 1975; That Lucky Touch 1975; Next Stop, Greenwich Village 1976; The Tenant 1976; Pete's Dragon 1977; Tentacles 1977; King of the Gypsies 1978; City on Fire 1979; Elvis - the Movie 1979; The Magician of Lublin 1979; The Visitor 1980; SOB 1981; Fanny Hill 1983; Over the Brooklyn Bridge 1983; Déjà Vu 1984; Ellie 1984; The Delta Force 1986; The Purple People Eater 1988; Stepping Out 1991; The Pickle 1993; The Silence of the Hams 1993; Heavy 1995; The Portrait of a Lady 1996; Gideon 1999

Winton, Jane (1905-1959) Don Juan 1926; The Patsy 1928; Limelight 1936

Wintour, Anna The September Issue 2009; Venus and Serena 2012; Dior and I 2014

Winwood, Estelle (1883-1984) The Glass Slipper 1955; The Swan 1956; 23 Paces to Baker Street 1956; Alive and Kicking 1958; Darby O'Gill and the Little People 1959; The Misfits 1961; The Magic Sword 1962; The Notorious Landlady 1962; Dead Ringer 1964; Camelot 1967; Games 1967; The Producers 1968

Wirth, Billy (1962-) War Party 1988; Body Snatchers 1993; Boys on the Side 1995

Wisden, Robert The War between Us 1995; Taken Away 1996; Excess Baggage 1997; Driven to Kill 2009

Wisdom, Norman (1915-2010) A Date with a Dream 1948; Trouble in Store 1953; One Good Turn 1954; Man of the Moment 1955; Up in the World 1956; Just My Luck 1957; The Square Peg 1958; Follow a Star 1959; The Bulldog Breed 1960; There Was a Crooked Man 1960; The Girl on the Boat 1962; On the Beat 1962; A Stitch in Time 1963 ; The Early Bird 1965; Press for Time 1966; The Sandwich Man 1966; The Night They Raided Minsky's 1968; What's Good for the Goose 1969; Double X: the Name of the Game 1991; Five Children and It 2004

Wisdom, Robert (1953-) Mighty Joe Young 1998; Live from Baghdad 2002; Our House 2003; Barbershop 2: Back in Business 2004; The Forgotten 2004

Wisdom, Tom The Sisterhood of the Traveling Pants 2 2008; Molly Moon and the Incredible Book of Hypnotism 2015

Wise, Ernie (1925-1999) The Intelligence Men 1965; That Riviera Touch 1966; The Magnificent Two 1967; Simon, Simon 1970

Wise, Greg (1966-) Feast of July 1995; Sense and Sensibility 1995; Judas Kiss 1998; Mad Cows 1999; Johnny English 2003; Greyfriars Bobby 2005; The Disappeared 2008; Morris: a Life with Bells On 2009; Honeymoon for One 2011; Blackwood 2013; Effie Gray 2014; Walking on Sunshine 2014

Wise, Ray (1947-) Swamp Thing 1982; The Journey of Natty Gann 1985; RoboCop 1987; Bob Roberts 1992; Twin Peaks: Fire Walk with Me 1992; Rising Sun 1993; Body Shot 1994; Two Can Play That Game 2001; Dead End 2003; Jeepers Creepers 2 2003; Good Night, and Good Luck. 2005; The Flock 2007; One Missed Call 2007; Big Ass Spider 2013; Batman: The Killing Joke 2016

Wise, William TR Baskin 1971; In the Bedroom 2001; Thirteen Conversations about One Thing 2001

Wiseman, Joseph (1918-2009) Detective Story 1951; Viva Zapata! 1952; The Silver Chalice 1954; The Garment Jungle 1957; Dr No 1962; The Happy Thieves 1962; The Night They Braverman 1968; The Counterfeit Killer 1968; The Night They Raided Minsky's 1968; Lawman 1971; The Valachi Papers 1972; The Apprenticeship of Duddy Kravitz 1974; The Betsy 1978; Buck Rogers in the 25th Century 1979; Jaguar Lives! 1979

Wisener, Jayne Sweeney Todd: the Demon Barber of Fleet Street 2007; Life Just Is 2012

Wisniewski, Andreas (1959-) Gothic 1986; Aria 1987; The Living Daylights 1987; Hush 2008

Withers, Bill (1938-) Soul Power 2008; Still Bill: the Bill Withers Story 2009

Withers, Googie (1917-2011) The Love Test 1935; Accused 1936; Convict 99 1938; The Lady Vanishes 1938; Strange

Boarders 1938; The Gang's All Here 1939; Trouble Brewing 1939; Busman's Honeymoon 1940; Jeannie 1941; Back Room Boy 1942; One of Our Aircraft Is Missing 1942; The Silver Fleet 1943; Dead of Night 1945; Pink String and Sealing Wax 1945; It Always Rains on Sunday 1947; The Loves of Joanna Godden 1947; Miranda 1947; Once upon a Dream 1948; Traveller's Joy 1949; Night and the City 1950; White Corridors 1951; Derby Day 1952; Devil on Horseback 1954; Port of Escape 1956; Country Life 1994; Shine 1996

Withers, Grant (1904-1959) College 1927; Other Men's Women 1931; Tennessee Johnson 1942; A Lady Takes a Chance 1943; War of the Wildcats 1943; The Yellow Rose of Texas 1944; Tycoon 1947; Angel in Exile 1948; The Plunderers 1948; Bells of Coronado 1950; Hoodlum Empire 1952; Fair Wind to Java 1953; Run for Cover 1955; The Mobster 1958

Withers, Jane (1926-) Bright Eyes 1934; The Farmer Takes a Wife 1935; Checkers 1937; Pack Up Your Troubles 1939; The North Star 1943; Giant 1956; Captain Newman, MD 1963

Withers, Margaret Car of Dreams 1935; Daybreak 1946; Home at Seven 1952; The Flying Scot 1957; Ferry to Hong Kong 1958

Witherspoon, Cora (1890-1957) Libeled Lady 1936; Piccadilly Jim 1936; On the Avenue 1937; Personal Property 1937; Quality Street 1937; Just around the Corner 1938; Port of Seven Seas 1938; Three Loves Has Nancy 1938; Dark Victory 1939; The Bank Dick 1940; Just for You 1952

Witherspoon, John (1942-) Talkin' Dirty after Dark 1991; Friday 1995; Vampire in Brooklyn 1995; Ride 1998; Next Friday 1999; Little Man 2006

Witherspoon, Reese (1976-) The Man in the Moon 1991; Wildflower 1991; A Far Off Place 1993; SFW 1994; Fear 1996; Freeway 1996; Overnight Delivery 1997; Pleasantville 1998; Twilight 1998; Best Laid Plans 1999; Cruel Intentions 1999; Election 1999; American Psycho 2000; Legally Blonde 2001; The Importance of Being Earnest 2002; Sweet Home Alabama 2002; Legally Blonde 2: Red, White & Blonde 2003; Vanity Fair 2004; Just like Heaven 2005; Walk the Line 2005; Penelope 2006; Rendition 2007; Four Christmases 2008; Monsters vs Aliens 2009; How Do You Know 2010; Water for Elephants 2011; Mud 2012; This Means War 2012; Devil's Knot 2013; The Good Lie 2014; Inherent Vice 2014; Wild 2014; Hot Pursuit 2015; Sing 2016

Withrow, Glenn (1953-) The Lady in Red 1979; The Outsiders 1983; Dudes 1987

Witney, Michael aka **Witney, Mike** (1931-1983) The Way West 1967; Darling Lili 1970; Doc 1971; There Goes the Bride 1979

Witt, Alicia (1975-) Bodies, Rest & Motion 1993; Fun 1994; Mr Holland's Opus 1995; Urban Legend 1998; Cecil B Demented 2000; Vanilla Sky 2001; Two Weeks Notice 2002; Sword of Xanten 2004; The Upside of Anger 2005; Last Holiday 2006; 88 Minutes 2007; Backyard Wedding 2010

Witter, Karen (1961-) Out of the Dark 1988; Midnight 1989; Buried Alive 1990

Witty, Christopher (1950-) Life in Danger 1959; No Kidding 1960

Wokalek, Johanna Aimée and Jaguar 1999; The Baader Meinhof Complex 2008; The North Face 2008

Wolders, Robert (1936-) Beau Geste 1966; Interval 1973

Wolf, Hillary (1977-) Waiting for the Light 1989; Home Alone 2: Lost in New York 1992; Stepkids 1992

Wolf, Kelly Triumph of the Spirit 1989; Graveyard Shift 1990; A Day in October 1991

Wolf, Scott (1968-) Double Dragon 1994; The Evening Star 1996; White Squall 1996; Go 1999; Lady and the Tramp II: Scamp's Adventure 2000

Wolfe, Collette Observe and Report 2009; Hot Tub Time Machine 2010

Wolfe, David (1915-1994) The Undercover Man 1949; Appointment with Danger 1950; Salt of the Earth 1954

Wolfe, Ian (1896-1992) Clive of India 1935; Bedlam 1946; The Falcon's Adventure 1946; They Live by Night 1948; The Magnificent Yankee 1950; The Actress 1953; Houdini 1953; Gaby 1956; Witness for the Prosecution 1957; Games 1967; THX 1138 1971; Reds 1981; Checking Out 1988

Wolfe, Tom Gonzo: the Life and Work of Dr Hunter S Thompson 2008; Salinger 2013

Wolfe, Traci (1961-) Lethal Weapon 1987; Lethal Weapon 2 1989; Lethal Weapon 3 1992; Lethal Weapon 4 1998

Wolfenden, Stuart Dead Man's Shoes 2004; Oranges and Sunshine 2010

Wolff, Frank (1928-1971) Beast from Haunted Cave 1959; Atlas 1960; Salvatore Giuliano 1961; The Four Days of Naples 1962; America, America 1963; Situation Hopeless - but Not Serious 1965; God Forgives... I Don't! 1967; Once upon a Time in the West 1968; Sin 1972

Wolff, Nat (1994-) Stuck in Love 2012; Palo Alto 2013; The Fault in Our Stars 2014; Grandma 2015; Paper Towns 2015

Wolfit, Donald (1902-1968) The Silent Passenger 1935; Calling the Tune 1936; Isn't Life Wonderful! 1952; The Pickwick Papers 1952; A Prize of Gold 1955; Satellite in the Sky 1956; The Man in the Road 1957; The Traitor 1957; Blood of the Vampire 1958; I Accuse! 1958; Room at the Top 1958; The House of the Seven Hawks 1959; The Rough and the Smooth 1959; The Hands of Orlac 1960; The Mark 1961; Dr Crippen 1962; Lawrence of Arabia 1962; Becket 1964; Life at the Top 1965; Decline and Fall... of a Birdwatcher 1968

Wolfman Jack (1938-1995) American Graffiti 1973; Motel Hell 1980

Wolheim, Louis (1880-1931) Dr Jekyll and Mr Hyde 1920; Two Arabian Knights 1927; The Racket 1928; Condemned 1929; All Quiet on the Western Front 1930; Danger Lights 1930

Wolk, Emil Escape from Sobibor 1987; The Tall Guy 1989

Wollter, Sven (1934-) The Sacrifice 1986; House of Angels 1992

Womack, Mark (1961-) Dancin' thru the Dark 1989; Under the Skin 1997; Route Irish 2010; Kelly + Victor 2013

Won Bin Brotherhood 2004; Mother 2009

Wong, Anna May (1907-1961) The Thief of Bagdad 1924; Piccadilly 1929; Shanghai Express 1932; Chu Chin Chow 1934; Tiger Bay 1934; Java Head 1935; Impact 1949; Portrait in Black 1960

Wong (1), Anthony aka Wong Chau-Sang, Anthony (1961-) Full Contact 1992; Hard-Boiled 1992; Beast Cops 1998; Time and Tide 2000; Infernal Affairs 2002; Infernal Affairs II 2003; Infernal Affairs 3 2003; The Medallion 2003; Initial D - Drift Racer 2005; Exiled 2006; The Painted Veil 2006; The Mummy: Tomb of the Dragon Emperor 2008; Legend of the Fist: the Return of Chen Zhen 2010

Wong, B D (1960-) Father of the Bride 1991; Mystery Date 1991; Executive Decision 1996; Seven Years in Tibet 1997; Mulan 1998; Mulan II 2004; Stay 2005; Focus 2015; Jurassic World 2015

Wong, Benedict (1971-) Dirty Pretty Things 2002; On a Clear Day 2004; Grow Your Own 2007; Moon 2008; Hummingbird 2013

Wong, Faye Chung King Express 1994; Chinese Odyssey 2002 2002; 2046 2004

Wong, Michael aka Wong Man-Tak, Michael And Now You're Dead 1998; Beast Cops 1998

Wong, Pauline (1962-) Mr Vampire 1986; Spiritual Love 1987

Wong, Russell (1963-) Tai-Pan 1986; Eat a Bowl of Tea 1989; China Cry 1990; The Prophecy II 1997; Romeo Must Die 2000; Twisted 2003

Wong (2), Victor (1927-2001) Dim Sum: a Little Bit of Heart 1985; Big Trouble in Little China 1986; The Golden Child 1986; The Last Emperor 1987; Prince of Darkness 1987; Eat a Bowl of Tea 1989; Life Is Cheap... but Toilet Paper Is Expensive 1990; 3 Ninjas 1992; Seven Years in Tibet 1997

Wongkamlao, Petchthai Ong-Bak 2003; Warrior King 2005

Wontner, Arthur (1875-1960) Lady Windermere's Fan 1916; The Sign of Four 1932; Thunder in the City 1937

Wood, David (1944-) if... 1968; Sweet William 1980

Wood, Elijah (1981-) Avalon 1990; Paradise 1991; Forever Young 1992; Radio Flyer 1992; The Adventures of Huck Finn 1993; The Good Son 1993; North 1994; The War 1994; Flipper 1996; The Ice Storm 1997; Deep Impact 1998; The Faculty 1998; The Lord of the Rings: The Fellowship of the Ring 2001; The Adventures of Tom Thumb and Thumbelina 2002; Ash Wednesday 2002; The Lord of the Rings: The Two Towers 2002; Eternal Sunshine of the Spotless Mind 2003; The Lord of the Rings: The Return of the King 2003; Green Street 2004; Everything Is Illuminated 2005; Sin City 2005; Bobby 2006; Happy Feet 2006; The

Oxford Murders 2008; 9 2009; Happy Feet Two 2011; Celeste & Jesse Forever 2012; The Hobbit: an Unexpected Journey 2012; Maniac 2012; Grand Piano 2013; Cooties 2014; Set Fire to the Stars 2014; The Last Witch Hunter 2015; The Trust 2016

Wood, Evan Rachel (1987-) Digging to China 1998; The Missing 2003; Thirteen 2003; Down in the Valley 2004; Pretty Persuasion 2005; The Upside of Anger 2005; Asterix and the Vikings 2006; The Reef 2006; Running with Scissors 2007; Battle for Terra 2007; The Life before Her Eyes 2007; The Wrestler 2008; Whatever Works 2009; The Conspirator 2010; The Ides of March 2011; Charlie Countryman 2013; Strange Magic 2015

Wood, G (1920-2000) Harold and Maude 1972; Bank Shot 1974

Wood, Helen (1917-1988) Crack-Up 1936; Give a Girl a Break 1953

Wood, Jake Dad Savage 1997; The Aryan Couple 2004

Wood, Janet Slumber Party '57 1976; Up 1976

Wood (1), John (1909-1965) The Last Days of Pompeii 1935; Over She Goes 1937; Stolen Face 1952

Wood (2), John (1930-2011) Invasion Quartet 1961; Postman's Knock 1961; Just like a Woman 1966; Which Way to the Front? 1970; Somebody Killed Her Husband 1978; WarGames 1983; Lady Jane 1985; Ladyhawke 1985; The Purple Rose of Cairo 1985; Jumpin' Jack Flash 1986; Orlando 1992; Shadowlands 1993; Citizen X 1995; Sabrina 1995; Rasputin 1996; The Gambler 1997; The Revengers' Comedies 1997; An Ideal Husband 1999; The Body 2000; The Little Vampire 2000; Imagining Argentina 2003

Wood, Lana (1946-) Diamonds Are Forever 1971; Grayeagle 1977

Wood, Natalie (1938-1981) Tomorrow Is Forever 1945; The Bride Wore Boots 1946; Driftwood 1946; The Ghost and Mrs Muir 1947; Miracle on 34th Street 1947; Chicken Every Sunday 1948; Father Was a Fullback 1949; The Jackpot 1950; Never a Dull Moment 1950; No Sad Songs for Me 1950; Our Very Own 1950; The Blue Veil 1951; Just for You 1952; The Star 1953; The Silver Chalice 1954; Rebel without a Cause 1955; The Burning Hills 1956; A Cry in the Night 1956; The Girl He Left Behind 1956; The Searchers 1956; Bombers B-52 1957; Marjorie Morningstar 1958; All the Fine Young Cannibals 1960; Cash McCall 1960; Splendor in the Grass 1961; West Side Story 1961; Gypsy 1962; Love with the Proper Stranger 1963; Sex and the Single Girl 1964; The Great Race 1965; Inside Daisy Clover 1965; Penelope 1966; This Property Is Condemned 1966; Bob & Carol & Ted & Alice 1969; The Affair 1973; The Cracker Factory 1979; Meteor 1979; The Last Married Couple in America 1980; Brainstorm 1983

Wood, Peggy (1892-1978) A Star Is Born 1937; The Bride Wore Boots 1946; Magnificent Doll 1946; Dream Girl 1948; The Story of Ruth 1960; The Sound of Music 1965

Wood, Tom (1963-) Bushwhacked 1995; US Marshals 1998

Wood, Victoria (1953-2016) The Wind in the Willows 1996; The League of Gentlemen's Apocalypse 2005

Woodard, Alfre (1952-) Remember My Name 1978; HEALTH 1980; Cross Creek 1983; The Killing Floor 1984; Extremities 1986; Scrooged 1988; Miss Firecracker 1989; Grand Canyon 1991; The Gun in Betty Lou's Handbag 1992; Passion Fish 1992; Bopha! 1993; Heart and Souls 1993; Blue Chips 1994; Crooklyn 1994; How to Make an American Quilt 1995; Primal Fear 1996; Star Trek: First Contact 1996; Down in the Delta 1997; The Member of the Wedding 1997; Miss Evers' Boys 1997; Mumford 1999; Dinosaur 2000; Love & Basketball 2000; What's Cooking? 2000; K-PAX 2001; The Core 2002; Radio 2003; The Forgotten 2004; Beauty Shop 2005; Something New 2006; Take the Lead 2006; 12 Years a Slave 2013; Annabelle 2014; Mississippi Grind 2015

Woodard, Charlayne (1955-) Unbreakable 2000; DC Sniper: 23 Days of Fear 2003

Woodbine, Bokeem (1973-) Jason's Lyric 1994; Panther 1995; Almost Heroes 1998; The Big Hit 1998; Life 1999; The Runner 1999; The Breed 2001; Ray 2004; Total Recall 2012; Riddick 2013

Woodbridge, George (1907-1973) Murder in the Cathedral 1952; Son of Robin Hood 1958

Woodburn, Danny Teenage Mutant Ninja Turtles 2014; Teenage Mutant Ninja Turtles - Out of the Shadows 2016

Woodburn, Eric (1894-1981) The Bridal Path 1959; Trial and Error 1962

Woodbury, Joan (1915-1989) Charlie Chan in The Chinese Cat 1944; The Whistler 1944

Woodlawn, Holly (1946-2015) Trash 1970; Is There Sex after Death? 1971; Women in Revolt 1971; Milwaukee, Minnesota 2002

Woodley, Shailene (1991-) A Place Called Home 2004; The Descendants 2011; Divergent 2014; The Fault in Our Stars 2014; White Bird in a Blizzard 2014; Insurgent 2015; The Divergent Series: Allegiant 2016; Snowden 2016

Woodruff, Largo Bill 1981; The Funhouse 1981

Woods, Aubrey (1928-2013) Loot 1970; The Abominable Dr Phibes 1971; ZPG: Zero Population Growth 1971

Woods, Carol Stepping Out 1991; The Honeymooners 2005

Woods, Donald (1904-1998) Fog over Frisco 1934; Frisco Kid 1935; Sweet Adeline 1935; A Tale of Two Cities 1935; Anthony Adverse 1936; Isle of Fury 1936; The Story of Louis Pasteur 1936; The White Angel 1936; The Case of the Stuttering Bishop 1937; Charlie Chan on Broadway 1937; Beauty for the Asking 1939; The Girl from Mexico 1939; Mexican Spitfire 1940; Watch on the Rhine 1943; Roughly Speaking 1945; Wonder Man 1945; Never Say Goodbye 1946; Scene of the Crime 1949; The Beast from 20,000 Fathoms 1953; 13 Ghosts 1959; Door-to-Door Maniac 1961; Moment to Moment 1966

Woods, Edward (1903-1989) The Public Enemy 1931; Tarzan the Fearless 1933

Woods, Harry (1889-1968) Palmy Days 1931; Law and Order 1932; Days of Jesse James 1939; Thunder Mountain 1947; She Wore a Yellow Ribbon 1949

Woods, James (1947-) Hickey and Boggs 1972; The Visitors 1972; The Way We Were 1973; Night Moves 1975; Alex and the Gypsy 1976; The Disappearance of Aimee 1976; The Choirboys 1977; The Onion Field 1979; The Black Marble 1980; Eyewitness 1981; Fast-Walking 1982; Split Image 1982; Videodrome 1982; Against All Odds 1984; Cat's Eye 1984; Once upon a Time in America 1984; Badge of the Assassin 1985; Joshua Then and Now 1985; Promise 1986; Salvador 1986; Best Seller 1987; The Boost 1988; Cop 1988; Immediate Family 1989; My Name Is Bill W 1989; True Believer 1989; Women and Men: Stories of Seduction 1990; The Boys 1991; The Hard Way 1991; Chaplin 1992; Midnight Sting 1992; Straight Talk 1992; The Getaway 1994; The Specialist 1994; Casino 1995; For Better or Worse 1995; Indictment: the McMartin Trial 1995; Killer: a Journal of Murder 1995; Nixon 1995; Ghosts of Mississippi 1996; The Summer of Ben Tyler 1996; Contact 1997; Hercules 1997; Kicked in the Head 1997; Another Day in Paradise 1998; Vampires 1998; Any Given Sunday 1999; The General's Daughter 1999; True Crime 1999; The Virgin Suicides 1999; Play It to the Bone 2000; Final Fantasy: the Spirits Within 2001; John Q 2001; Race to Space 2001; Recess: School's Out 2001; Riding in Cars with Boys 2001; Scary Movie 2 2001; Northfork 2002; Stuart Little 2 2002; Pretty Persuasion 2005; End Game 2006; Surf's Up 2007; Straw Dogs 2011; jOBS 2013; White House Down 2013

Woods, Michael (1957-) Lady Beware 1987; Secrets of an Undercover Wife 2007

Woodthorpe, Peter (1931-2004) Evil of Frankenstein 1964; The Blue Max 1966

Woodville, Catherine aka Woodville, Kate (1938-2013) The Wild and the Willing 1962; The Informers 1963; The Crooked Road 1964; The Party's Over 1965; Extreme Close-Up 1973

Woodvine, John (1929-) An American Werewolf in London 1981; Danny, the Champion of the World 1989; Leon the Pig Farmer 1992; Dragonworld 1994; Persuasion 1995

Woodward, Edward (1930-2009) The File of the Golden Goose 1969; Incense for the Damned 1970; Sitting Target 1972; The Wicker Man 1973; Callan 1974; Stand Up Virgin Soldiers 1977; Breaker Morant 1979; Who Dares Wins 1982; Champions 1983; A Christmas Carol 1984; King David 1985; The Man in the Brown Suit 1989; Mister Johnson

1991; Deadly Advice 1993; The Shamrock Conspiracy 1995; The Abduction Club 2002; Hot Fuzz 2007

Woodward, Joanne (1930-) Count Three and Pray 1955; A Kiss before Dying 1956; No Down Payment 1957; The Three Faces of Eve 1957; The Long, Hot Summer 1958; The Sound and the Fury 1959; From the Terrace 1960; The Fugitive Kind 1960; Paris Blues 1961; A New Kind of Love 1963; The Stripper 1963; Signpost to Murder 1964; A Big Hand for a Little Lady 1966; A Fine Madness 1966; Rachel, Rachel 1968; Winning 1969; King: a Filmed Record... Montgomery to Memphis 1970; WUSA 1970; They Might Be Giants 1971; The Effect of Gamma Rays on Man-in-the-Moon Marigolds 1972; Summer Wishes, Winter Dreams 1973; The Drowning Pool 1975; The End 1978; The Shadow Box 1980; Harry and Son 1984; Passions 1984; Do You Remember Love 1985; The Glass Menagerie 1987; Mr and Mrs Bridge 1990; The Age of Innocence 1993; Philadelphia 1993; Breathing Lessons 1994

Woodward, Jonathan M aka Woodward, Jonathan (1973-) Wit 2001; The Notorious Bettie Page 2005

Woodward, Morgan (1925-) One Little Indian 1973; Running Wild 1973; The Killing of a Chinese Bookie 1976; Which Way Is Up? 1977; Battle beyond the Stars 1980; Girls Just Want to Have Fun 1985

Woodward, Tim (1953-) Personal Services 1987; B Monkey 1996; Some Mother's Son 1996; K-19: the Widowmaker 2002; Flight of Fury 2007

Woof, Emily (1970-) The Full Monty 1997; Photographing Fairies 1997; The Woodlanders 1997; Fast Food 1998; Velvet Goldmine 1998; Passion 1999; This Year's Love 1999; Pandaemonium 2000; Wondrous Oblivion 2003

Wooland, Norman (1910-1989) Hamlet 1948; Madeleine 1949; Background 1953; The Master Plan 1954; My Teenage Daughter 1956; No Road Back 1957; The Bandit of Zhobe 1959; The Rough and the Smooth 1959; The Fighting Prince of Donegal 1966

Wooldridge, Susan (1952-) Dead Man's Folly 1986; Hope and Glory 1987; How to Get Ahead in Advertising 1989; Twenty-One 1991; Just like a Woman 1992

Woolf King, Walter (1899-1984) Swiss Miss 1938; Go West 1940

Woolf, Henry Figures in a Landscape 1970; The Love Pill 1971

Woolgar, Fenella Bright Young Things 2003; Wah-Wah 2005; Scoop 2006

Woolgar, Jack (1914-1978) Say Hello to Yesterday 1971; Swallows and Amazons 1974

Woolley, Monty (1888-1963) Live, Love and Learn 1937; Arsene Lupin Returns 1938; Everybody Sing 1938; Young Dr Kildare 1938; Dancing Co-Ed 1939; Midnight 1939; The Man Who Came to Dinner 1941; Life Begins at 8.30 1942; The Pied Piper 1942; Holy Matrimony 1943; Irish Eyes Are Smiling 1944; Since You Went Away 1944; Molly and Me 1945; Night and Day 1946; The Bishop's Wife 1947; Miss Tatlock's Millions 1948; As Young as You Feel 1951; Kismet 1955

Woolsey, Robert (1889-1938) Rio Rita 1929; Half Shot at Sunrise 1930

Woolvett, Gordon Michael (1970-) Bordertown Cafe 1991; Bride of Chucky 1998

Woolvett, Jaimz (1967-) Unforgiven 1992; Sanctuary 1997; Rites of Passage 1999; The Guilty 2000

Wootton, Marc Nativity! 2009; Nativity 2: Danger in the Manger! 2012; Nativity 3: Dude Where's My Donkey 2014

Worden, Hank (1901-1992) The Big Sky 1952; UFOria 1980

Wordsworth, Richard (1915-1993) The Quatermass Xperiment 1955; The Revenge of Frankenstein 1958; The Curse of the Werewolf 1961

Workman, Jimmy (1980-) The Addams Family 1991; Christmas in Connecticut 1992; Addams Family Values 1993

Worlock, Frederick aka Worlock, Frederic (1886-1973) Man Hunt 1941; Pursuit to Algiers 1945; Dressed to Kill 1946; One Hundred and One Dalmatians 1960

Wormald, Kenny Footloose 2011; Love & Mercy 2014

Woronov, Mary aka Might, Mary (1943-) The Chelsea Girls 1966; Death Race 2000 1975; Hollywood Boulevard 1976; Jackson County Jail 1976; Rock 'n' Roll High School 1979; Eating Raoul 1982; Get Crazy 1983; Night of the

Comet 1984; TerrorVision 1986; Scenes from the Class Struggle In Beverly Hills 1989; Warlock 1989; Motorama 1991; The Living End 1992; Shake, Rattle and Rock 1994; The House of the Devil 2009

Worth, Brian (1914-1978) The Arsenal Stadium Mystery 1939; Pastor Hall 1940; Cardboard Cavalier 1949; Scrooge 1951; Hindle Wakes 1952; It Started in Paradise 1952; An Inspector Calls 1954; Assignment Redhead 1956; The Square Peg 1958; The Boy Who Turned Yellow 1972

Worth, Constance (1912-1963) Meet Boston Blackie 1941; Crime Doctor 1943

Worth, Irene (1916-2002) The Secret People 1951; Orders to Kill 1958; The Scapegoat 1959; Seven Seas to Calais 1962; To Die in Madrid 1963; King Lear 1970; Eyewitness 1981; Deathtrap 1982; Separate Tables 1983; Lost in Yonkers 1993; Onegin 1999

Worth, Nicholas (1942-) Swamp Thing 1982; Hell Comes to Frogtown 1988; Plughead Rewired: Circuitry Man II 1994

Worthington, Sam (1976-) Bootmen 2000; Dirty Deeds 2002; Gettin' Square 2003; Somersault 2004; Macbeth 2006; Rogue 2007; Avatar 2009; Last Night 2009; Terminator: Salvation 2009; Clash of the Titans 2010; The Debt 2010; Texas Killing Fields 2011; Man on a Ledge 2012; Wrath of the Titans 2012; Sabotage 2013; The Keeping Room 2014; Paper Planes 2014; Cake 2015; Everest 2015; Kidnapping Freddy Heineken 2015; Avatar 2 2018

Wray, Fay (1907-2004) The Wedding March 1928; The Four Feathers 1929; Thunderbolt 1929; Paramount on Parade 1930; The Texan 1930; Dirigible 1931; The Finger Points 1931; The Unholy Garden 1931; Doctor X 1932; The Most Dangerous Game 1932; The Bowery 1933; King Kong 1933; Mystery of the Wax Museum 1933; Shanghai Madness 1933; The Vampire Bat 1933; The Affairs of Cellini 1934; Bulldog Jack 1934; The Clairvoyant 1934; The Richest Girl in the World 1934; Viva Villa! 1934; When Knights Were Bold 1936; Adam Had Four Sons 1941; Treasure of the Golden Condor 1953; Hell on Frisco Bay 1955; Queen Bee 1955; Rock, Pretty Baby 1956; Crime of Passion 1957; Tammy and the Bachelor 1957; Gideon's Trumpet 1980

Wray, John (1887-1940) All Quiet on the Western Front 1930; Quick Millions 1931; Doctor X 1932; The Death Kiss 1933; Blackmail 1939

Wright, Amy (1950-) Girlfriends 1978; Breaking Away 1979; Wise Blood 1979; Inside Moves: the Guys from Max's Bar 1980; Off Beat 1986; The Accidental Tourist 1988; The Telephone 1988; Daddy's Dyin'... Who's Got the Will? 1990; Love Hurts 1990; Deceived 1991; Where the Rivers Flow North 1993; Tom and Huck 1995

Wright (1), Ben (1915-1989) One Hundred and One Dalmatians 1960; The Jungle Book 1967; The Little Mermaid 1989

Wright, Bonnie (1991-) Harry Potter and the Half-Blood Prince 2009; Harry Potter and the Deathly Hallows: Part 1 2010; Harry Potter and the Deathly Hallows: Part 2 2011; The Sea 2013

Wright Jr, Cobina (1921-2011) Charlie Chan in Rio 1941; Moon over Miami 1941; Weekend in Havana 1941; Footlight Serenade 1942

Wright, Dorsey Hair 1979; The Warriors 1979

Wright, Janet (1945-) Bordertown Cafe 1991; Beyond the Call 1996; Emile 2003

Wright, Jeffrey (1965-) Jumpin' at the Boneyard 1991; Basquiat 1996; Ride with the Devil 1999; Crime + Punishment in Suburbia 2000; Shaft 2000; Ali 2001; Boycott 2001; The Manchurian Candidate 2004; Broken Flowers 2005; Syriana 2005; Casino Royale 2006; Lady in the Water 2006; The Invasion 2007; Cadillac Records 2008; Quantum of Solace 2008; W. 2008; The Ides of March 2011; Source Code 2011; Broken City 2013; The Hunger Games: Catching Fire 2013; Only Lovers Left Alive 2013; The Hunger Games: Mockingjay Part 1 2014; The Good Dinosaur 2015

Wright, Jenny (1962-) Pink Floyd - The Wall 1982; The Wild Life 1984; Near Dark 1987; A Shock to the System 1990; The Lawnmower Man 1992

Wright, Jenny Lee (1947-) Husbands 1970; The Triple Echo 1972; The Best of Benny Hill 1974

Wright, Max (1943-) Simon 1980; A Mother's Gift 1995

Wright, Michael (1956-) Streamers 1983; The Principal 1987; The Five Heartbeats 1991; Sugar Hill 1993; Point Blank 1997; Piñero 2001; The Interpreter 2005

Wright, N'Bushe (1970-) Zebrahead 1992; Fresh 1994; Dead Presidents 1995; Blade 1998; 3 Strikes 2000

Wright, Robin aka Wright Penn, Robin (1966-) The Princess Bride 1987; State of Grace 1990; The Playboys 1992; Toys 1992; Forrest Gump 1994; The Crossing Guard 1995; Moll Flanders 1995; Loved 1996; She's So Lovely 1997; Hurlyburly 1998; Message in a Bottle 1998; The Pledge 2000; Unbreakable 2000; White Oleander 2002; The Singing Detective 2003; A Home at the End of the World 2004; Breaking and Entering 2006; Beowulf 2007; What Just Happened? 2007; A Christmas Carol 2009; New York, I Love You 2009; The Private Lives of Pippa Lee 2009; State of Play 2009; The Conspirator 2011; The Girl with the Dragon Tattoo 2011; Moneyball 2011; Rampart 2011; Adore 2013; The Congress 2013; A Most Wanted Man 2013; Everest 2015; Blade Runner 2 2017; Wonder Woman 2017

Wright, Samuel E (1946-) Bird 1988; Thelonious Monk: Straight No Chaser 1988; The Little Mermaid 1989; Dinosaur 2000; The Little Mermaid II: Return to the Sea 2000

Wright, Sarah (1983-) 21 and Over 2012; Mena 2017

Wright, Steven (1955-) Desperately Seeking Susan 1985; The Swan Princess 1994; Canadian Bacon 1995; Babe: Pig in the City 1998; The Muse 1999; Coffee and Cigarettes 2003

Wright, Tandi Black Sheep 2006; Out of the Blue 2006

Wright, Teresa (1918-2005) The Little Foxes 1941; Mrs Miniver 1942; The Pride of the Yankees 1942; Shadow of a Doubt 1942; Casanova Brown 1944; The Best Years of Our Lives 1946; The Imperfect Lady 1947; Pursued 1947; Enchantment 1948; The Capture 1950; The Men 1950; Something to Live For 1952; The Steel Trap 1952; The Actress 1953; Count the Hours 1953; Track of the Cat 1954; Escapade in Japan 1957; The Restless Years 1958; Hail, Hero! 1969; Roseland 1977; Somewhere in Time 1980; The Price of Passion 1988; John Grisham's The Rainmaker 1997

Wright, Tom aka Wright, Thomas (1952-) The Brother from Another Planet 1984; Marked for Death 1990; Weekend at Bernie's II 1992; Palmetto 1998; The Pentagon Wars 1998; Contagion 2001

Wright, Tony (1925-1986) Jumping for Joy 1955; Jacqueline 1956; Tiger in the Smoke 1956; Seven Thunders 1957; The Rough and the Smooth 1959; Faces in the Dark 1960

Wright, Tracy When Night Is Falling 1995; Last Night 1998

Wright, Whittni (1987-) I'll Do Anything 1994; Sudden Death 1995

Wright, Will (1894-1962) Green Grass of Wyoming 1948; They Live by Night 1948; Mrs Mike 1949; A Ticket to Tomahawk 1950; Quantrill's Raiders 1958; Alias Jesse James 1959; The Deadly Companions 1961

Wright, William (1911-1949) A Night to Remember 1942; Reveille with Beverly 1943

Wu Jiang To Live 1994; Shower 1999; Snow Flower and the Secret Fan 2011; A Touch of Sin 2013

Wu Nianzhen (1952-) Taipei Story 1984; A One and a Two 1999

Wu, Daniel (1974-) New Police Story 2004; One Nite in Mongkok 2004; The Banquet 2006; Protégé 2007; Shinjuku Incident 2009

Wu, Tom Belly of the Beast 2003; Mutant Chronicles 2008

Wu, Vivian (1966-) The Guyver 1991; Teenage Mutant Ninja Turtles III 1992; The Pillow Book 1995; 8½ Women 1999; Dinner Rush 2000; Snow Flower and the Secret Fan 2011

Wuhl, Robert (1951-) Good Morning, Vietnam 1987; Bull Durham 1988; Batman 1989; Mistress 1992; Cobb 1994; Open Season 1995

Wuhrer, Kari (1967-) Sex and the Other Man 1995; Anaconda 1997; Touch Me 1997; Kissing a Fool 1998; G-Men from Hell 2000; Eight Legged Freaks 2001; King of the Ants 2003; Tornado Warning 2012; Sharknado 2: the Second One 2014

Wuornos, Aileen Aileen Wuornos: the Selling of a Serial Killer 1992; Aileen: Life and Death of a Serial Killer 2003

Wyatt, Jane (1911-2006) One More River 1934; Lost Horizon 1937; The Navy Comes Through 1942; None but the Lonely Heart 1944; Boomerang!

1947; Gentleman's Agreement 1947; No Minor Vices 1948; Pitfall 1948; Task Force 1949; House by the River 1950; My Blue Heaven 1950; Our Very Own 1950; Never Too Late 1965; Treasure of Matecumbe 1976; Star Trek IV: The Voyage Home 1986; Amityville: the Evil Escapes 1989

Wyatt, Tessa (1948-) The Beast in the Cellar 1970; England Made Me 1973

Wycherley, Don When Brendan Met Trudy 2000; Shrooms 2006; Garage 2007

Wycherly, Margaret (1881-1956) Victory 1940; Sergeant York 1941; Crossroads 1942; Keeper of the Flame 1942; Random Harvest 1942; Hangmen Also Die! 1943; The Moon Is Down 1943; Johnny Angel 1945; The Yearling 1946; Something in the Wind 1947; White Heat 1949; The Man with a Cloak 1951

Wyle, Noah (1971-) Crooked Hearts 1991; There Goes My Baby 1994; The Myth of Fingerprints 1996; Pirates of Silicon Valley 1999; Fail Safe 2000; Donnie Darko 2001; Enough 2002; White Oleander 2002; The Librarian: Quest for the Spear 2004

Wyllie, Dan aka Wyllie, Daniel (1970-) Spotswood 1991; Romper Stomper 1992; Holy Smoke 1999; Chopper 2000; Sanctum 2010; The Water Diviner 2014

Wyman, Bill (1936-) Gimme Shelter 1970; Eat the Rich 1987

Wyman, Jane (1914-2007) Smart Blonde 1936; Slim 1937; The Crowd Roars 1938; Footlight Serenade 1942; Larceny, Inc 1942; My Favorite Spy 1942; Princess O'Rourke 1943; The Doughgirls 1944; Hollywood Canteen 1944; The Lost Weekend 1945; Night and Day 1946; The Yearling 1946; Magic Town 1947; Johnny Belinda 1948; It's a Great Feeling 1949; A Kiss in the Dark 1949; Stage Fright 1949; The Glass Menagerie 1950; The Blue Veil 1951; Here Comes the Groom 1951; Just for You 1952; Let's Do It Again 1953; So Big 1953; Magnificent Obsession 1954; All That Heaven Allows 1955; Lucy Gallant 1955; Miracle in the Rain 1956; Holiday for Lovers 1959; Pollyanna 1960; Bon Voyage! 1962; How to Commit Marriage 1969

Wymark, Patrick (1926-1970) West 11 1963; Repulsion 1965; The Skull 1965; The Psychopath 1966; Tell Me Lies 1967; Witchfinder General 1968; Journey to the Far Side of the Sun 1969; Where Eagles Dare 1969; Blood on Satan's Claw 1970; Cromwell 1970

Wymore, Patrice (1926-2014) Rocky Mountain 1950; Tea for Two 1950; I'll See You in My Dreams 1951; The Big Trees 1952; She's Working Her Way through College 1952; The Man behind the Gun 1953; King's Rhapsody 1955; The Sad Horse 1959; Ocean's Eleven 1960; Chamber of Horrors 1966

Wyn Davies, Geraint (1957-) One of the Hollywood Ten 2000; American Psycho II: All American Girl 2002

Wynant, H M (1927-) Tonka 1958; Marlowe 1969

Wyner, George (1945-) Dogs 1976; Spaceballs 1987; Listen to Me 1989

Wyngarde, Peter (1933-) The Siege of Sidney Street 1960; The Innocents 1961; Night of the Eagle 1961

Wynn, Ed (1886-1966) Alice in Wonderland 1951; The Great Man 1956; Marjorie Morningstar 1958; The Diary of Anne Frank 1959; Cinderfella 1960; Babes in Toyland 1961; Son of Flubber 1962; Mary Poppins 1964; Those Calloways 1964; Dear Brigitte 1966; The Gnome-Mobile 1967

Wynn, Keenan (1916-1986) For Me and My Gal 1942; Somewhere I'll Find You 1942; Lost Angel 1943; Marriage Is a Private Affair 1944; The Clock 1945; Week-End at the Waldorf 1945; Without Love 1945; Easy to Wed 1946; The Hucksters 1947; Song of the Thin Man 1947; B.F.'s Daughter 1948; My Dear Secretary 1948; Neptune's Daughter 1949; That Midnight Kiss 1949; Annie Get Your Gun 1950; Three Little Words 1950; Angels in the Outfield 1951; Kind Lady 1951; Mr Imperium 1951; Royal Wedding 1951; Texas Carnival 1951; The Belle of New York 1952; Desperate Search 1952; Phone Call from a Stranger 1952; All the Brothers Were Valiant 1953; Battle Circus 1953; Kiss Me Kate 1953; The Long, Long Trailer 1954; Men of the Fighting Lady 1954; Tennessee Champ 1954; The Glass Slipper 1955; Shack Out on 101 1955; The Great Man 1956; Johnny Concho 1956; The Man in the Gray Flannel Suit 1956; Don't Go near the Water 1957; The Fuzzy Pink Nightgown 1957; The Deep Six 1958; The Perfect Furlough 1958; A Time to Love and a Time to Die 1958; Touch of Evil 1958; The Crowded

Sky 1960; The Absent-Minded Professor 1961; King of the Roaring 20s - the Story of Arnold Rothstein 1961; Son of Flubber 1962; The Bay of Saint Michel 1963; Dr Strangelove, or How I Learned to Stop Worrying and Love the Bomb 1963; The Americanization of Emily 1964; Bikini Beach 1964; Honeymoon Hotel 1964; Nightmare in the Sun 1964; The Patsy 1964; The Great Race 1965; Promise Her Anything 1966; Stagecoach 1966; Point Blank 1967; The War Wagon 1967; Warning Shot 1967; Welcome to Hard Times 1967; Finian's Rainbow 1968; Once upon a Time in the West 1968; Eighty Steps to Jonah 1969; Mackenna's Gold 1969; Smith! 1969; Viva Max! 1969; Loving 1970; Pretty Maids All in a Row 1971; Black Jack 1972; Cancel My Reservation 1972; The Mechanic 1972; Snowball Express 1972; Herbie Rides Again 1974; The Internecine Project 1974; The Devil's Rain 1975; The Killer inside Me 1975; The Lindbergh Kidnapping Case 1976; The Shaggy DA 1976; High Velocity 1977; Orca... Killer Whale 1977; The Glove 1978; Piranha 1978; Sunburn 1979; A Touch of the Sun 1979; Just Tell Me What You Want 1980; The Last Unicorn 1980; Best Friends 1982; A Piano for Mrs Cimino 1982; Black Moon Rising 1985

Wynn, May (1930-) They Rode West 1954; The Violent Men 1955

Wynne, Christopher Cop 1988; Remote Control 1988

Wynter, Dana (1931-2011) D-Day the Sixth of June 1956; Invasion of the Body Snatchers 1956; Something of Value 1957; In Love and War 1958; Shake Hands with the Devil 1959; Sink the Bismarck! 1960; On the Double 1961; The List of Adrian Messenger 1963; Santee 1973; Call Him Savage 1975; The Return of Ironside 1993

Wynter, Sarah (1973-) Lost Souls 2000; The 6th Day 2000; Bride of the Wind 2001; Abducted 2007

Wynters, Charlotte (1899-1991) The Struggle 1931; Sinners in Paradise 1938; Lulu Belle 1948

Wynyard, Diana (1906-1964) Rasputin and the Empress 1932; Cavalcade 1933; Reunion in Vienna 1933; One More River 1934; Freedom Radio 1940; Gaslight 1940; The Prime Minister 1940; Kipps 1941; An Ideal Husband 1947; Tom Brown's Schooldays 1951; The Feminine Touch 1956

Wyss, Amanda (1960-) A Nightmare on Elm Street 1984; Powwow Highway 1988

X

Xin Shufen Dust in the Wind 1987; A City of Sadness 1989

Xu Jinglei aka Xu Jing Lei The Warlords 2008; Shinjuku Incident 2009

Xuereb, Salvator (1965-) Killing Zoe 1993; Flashpoint 1997

Xzibit aka Joiner, Alvin "Xzibit" (1974-) Derailed 2005; Hoodwinked 2005; xXx: the Next Level 2005; Gridiron Gang 2006; The X-Files: I Want to Believe 2008; The Bad Lieutenant - Port of Call: New Orleans 2009

Y

Yadav, Raghuvir aka Yadav, Raghubir aka Yadav, Raghuveer (1957-) Salaam Bombay! 1988; Electric Moon 1992; Bandit Queen 1994; Lagaan: Once upon a Time in India 2001

Yadav, Rajpal Mujhse Shaadi Karogi 2004; Partner 2007

Yadin, Yossi (1920-2001) Bloomfield 1969; Lies My Father Told Me 1975

Yagher, Jeff (1962-) Dead Man's Folly 1986; Big Bad Mama II 1987

Yagi, James (1923-1997) Bridge to the Sun 1961; King Kong vs Godzilla 1962

Yagira, Yuya Nobody Knows 2003; Unforgiven 2014

Yakovlev, Anton The Beat That My Heart Skipped 2005; The Silence of Lorna 2008

Yakusho, Koji (1956-) Tampopo 1986; Shall We Dance? 1995; The Eel 1997; Eureka 2000; Warm Water under a Red Bridge 2001; Memoirs of a Geisha 2005; Babel 2006; Silk 2007; 13 Assassins 2010; Hara-Kiri: Death of a Samurai 2011

Yam, Simon (1955-) Bullet in the Head 1990; Full Contact 1992; Fulltime Killer 2002; Election 2005; Exiled 2006; Ip Man 2008; Sparrow 2008; Man of Tai Chi 2013

Yamada, Isuzu (1917-2012) The Downfall of Osen 1935; Osaka Elegy 1936; Sisters of the Gion 1936; The Famous Sword 1945; The Lower Depths 1956; Throne of Blood 1957; Tokyo Twilight 1957; Yojimbo 1961

Yamaguchi, Shirley aka Yamaguchi, Yoshiko (1920-2014) Scandal 1950; House of Bamboo 1955

Yamamoto, Reisaburo Drunken Angel 1948; Stray Dog 1949

Yamamura, So aka Yamamura, Soh (1910-2000) The Love of Sumako the Actress 1947; The Lady of Musashino 1951; Tokyo Story 1953; The Princess Yang Kwei Fei 1955; Early Spring 1956; The Barbarian and the Geisha 1958; The Human Condition 1958; Tora! Tora! Tora! 1970; Gung Ho 1986

Yamazaki, Tsutomu (1936-) Kagemusha 1980; Death Japanese Style 1984; Tampopo 1986; A Taxing Woman 1987; Departures 2008

Yang Kuei-Mei (1959-) Eat Drink Man Woman 1994; Vive L'Amour 1994; The Hole 1998; Double Vision 2002

Yankovsky, Oleg (1944-2009) Mirror 1974; Nostalgia 1983; The Kreutzer Sonata 1987; Assassin of the Tsar 1991

Yanne, Jean (1933-2003) Weekend 1967; Le Boucher 1969; Que la Bête Meure 1969; Indochine 1991; Madame Bovary 1991; Pétain 1992; See How They Fall 1993; The Horseman on the Roof 1995; Victory 1995; News from the Good Lord 1996; Brotherhood of the Wolf 2001; Petites Coupures 2002

Yaqub, Atta Ae Fond Kiss... 2004; Nina's Heavenly Delights 2006

Yarde, Margaret (1878-1944) Tiger Bay 1934; Squibs 1935; Crimes at the Dark House 1939

Yasbeck, Amy (1963-) House II: the Second Story 1987; Problem Child 1990; Problem Child 2 1991; Robin Hood: Men in Tights 1993; The Mask 1994; Dracula: Dead and Loving It 1995; Something about Sex 1998

Yates, Cassie (1951-) FM 1977; Agatha Christie's A Caribbean Mystery 1983; Unfaithfully Yours 1983

Yates, Marjorie (1941-) The Optimists of Nine Elms 1973; Legend of the Werewolf 1974; Wetherby 1985; The Long Day Closes 1992

Yazpik, José María Beverly Hills Chihuahua 2008; Abel 2010

Yeh, Sally (1961-) Peking Opera Blues 1986; The Killer 1989

Yelchin, Anton (1989-2016) Hearts in Atlantis 2001; Jack 2004; Alpha Dog 2006; Charlie Bartlett 2007; New York, I Love You 2009; Star Trek 2009; Terminator: Salvation 2009; The Beaver 2010; Fright Night 2011; From Up on Poppy Hill 2011; Like Crazy 2011; Odd Thomas 2013; Only Lovers Left Alive 2013; Star Trek into Darkness 2013; Dying of the Light 2014; Experimenter: the Stanley Milgram Story 2014; Broken Horses 2015; Green Room 2015; Star Trek Beyond 2016

Yen, Donnie aka Yen, Donnie Chi-Tan (1963-) Once upon a Time in China II 1992; Iron Monkey 1993; Highlander: Endgame 2000; Hero 2002; Shanghai Knights 2002; Seven Swords 2005; Flash Point 2007; Ip Man 2008; Legend of the Fist: the Return of Chen Zhen 2010; Dragon 2011; Iceman 2014; Kung Fu Killer 2014; Crouching Tiger, Hidden Dragon: Sword of Destiny 2016

Yennie, Ashlynn The Human Centipede (First Sequence) 2009; The Human Centipede II (Full Sequence) 2011

Yeoh, Michelle (1962-) Drunken Master 1978; Police Story III: Supercop 1992; Twin Warriors 1993; Tomorrow Never Dies 1997; Crouching Tiger, Hidden Dragon 2000; Memoirs of a Geisha 2005; Far North 2007; Sunshine 2007; Babylon AD 2008; The Mummy: Tomb of the Dragon Emperor 2008; Reign of Assassins 2010; The Lady 2011; Crouching Tiger, Hidden Dragon: Sword of Destiny 2016; Mechanic: Resurrection 2016

Yerles, Bernard Les Apprentis 1995; The Cow and the President 2000

Yeung, Charlie aka Young, Charlie (1974-) Fallen Angels 1995; Bangkok Dangerous 2007; Kung Fu Killer 2014

Yiasoumi, George Gold Diggers 1983; King Kong Lives 1986

Yilmaz, Cem Vizontele 2001; The Water Diviner 2014

Yilmaz, Serra Le Fate Ignoranti 2001; Facing Window 2003

Ying Da Farewell My Concubine 1993; Big Shot's Funeral 2001; The White Countess 2005

Ying Ruocheng (1929-2003) The Last Emperor 1987; Little Buddha 1993

Yip, David (1951-) Indiana Jones and the Temple of Doom 1984; A View to a Kill 1985

Yip, Françoise (1972-) Black Mask 1996; Rumble in the Bronx 1996

Yo, Kimiko (1956-) Café Lumière 2003; Departures 2008

Yoakam, Dwight (1956-) Roswell 1994; Sling Blade 1995; The Newton Boys 1998; When Trumpets Fade 1998; The Minus Man 1999; South of Heaven, West of Hell 2000; Panic Room 2002; Hollywood Homicide 2003; The Three Burials of Melquiades Estrada 2005; Crank 2006; Four Christmases 2008; Crank: High Voltage 2009

Yoba, Malik (1967-) Cool Runnings 1993; Ride 1998; Tyler Perry's Why Did I Get Married Too? 2010

Yohn, Erica (1930-) An American Tail 1986; An American Tail: Fievel Goes West 1991; Jack the Bear 1993; Corrina, Corrina 1994

Yoo, Aaron (1979-) Disturbia 2007; Rocket Science 2007; Nick & Norah's Infinite Playlist 2008; 21 2008; The Wackness 2008; Friday the 13th 2009

Yordanoff, Wladimir (1954-) Vincent and Theo 1990; Wild Target 1993; Un Air de Famille 1996; Nathalie... 2003; I Do 2006; Angel of Mine 2008; The Hedgehog 2009

York, Dick aka York, Richard (1928-1992) My Sister Eileen 1955; Operation Mad Ball 1957; Cowboy 1958; The Last Blitzkrieg 1958; Inherit the Wind 1960

York, Jeff (1912-1995) Fear in the Night 1947; Davy Crockett and the River Pirates 1956; The Great Locomotive Chase 1956; Johnny Tremain 1957; Old Yeller 1957

York, Kathleen Checking Out 1988; Cold Feet 1989; Wild Hearts Can't Be Broken 1991; Dream Lover 1993; Sad Inheritance 1993; Dead Men Can't Dance 1997

York, Michael (1942-) Accident 1967; Smashing Time 1967; The Taming of the Shrew 1967; Romeo and Juliet 1968; The Strange Affair 1968; Alfred the Great 1969; The Guru 1969; Justine 1969; Something for Everyone 1970; Zeppelin 1971; Cabaret 1972; England Made Me 1973; Lost Horizon 1973; The Three Musketeers 1973; The Four Musketeers 1974; Great Expectations 1974; Murder on the Orient Express 1974; Conduct Unbecoming 1975; Logan's Run 1976; Seven Nights in Japan 1976; The Island of Dr Moreau 1977; The Last Remake of Beau Geste 1977; Fedora 1978; The Riddle of the Sands 1978; The White Lions 1980; Success Is the Best Revenge 1984; Midnight Cop 1988; Phantom of Death 1988; The Return of the Musketeers 1989; Wide Sargasso Sea 1992; Gospa 1995; Austin Powers: International Man of Mystery 1997; A Christmas Carol 1997; A Knight in Camelot 1998; Wrongfully Accused 1998; Austin Powers: the Spy Who Shagged Me 1999; A Monkey's Tale 1999; Austin Powers in Goldmember 2002

York, Morgan (1993-) Cheaper by the Dozen 2003; The Pacifier 2005

York, Susannah (1939-2011) There Was a Crooked Man 1960; Tunes of Glory 1960; The Greengage Summer 1961; Freud 1962; Tom Jones 1963; The 7th Dawn 1964; Sands of the Kalahari 1965; Kaleidoscope 1966; A Man for All Seasons 1966; Duffy 1968; The Killing of Sister George 1968; Sebastian 1968; Battle of Britain 1969; Lock Up Your Daughters! 1969; Oh! What a Lovely War 1969; They Shoot Horses, Don't They? 1969; Country Dance 1970; Jane Eyre 1970; Zee and Co 1971; Images 1972; Gold 1974; The Maids 1974; Conduct Unbecoming 1975; That Lucky Touch 1975; Long Shot 1978; The Shout 1978; The Silent Partner 1978; Superman 1978; The Awakening 1980; Falling in Love Again 1980; Loophole 1980; Superman II 1980; Yellowbeard 1983; A Christmas Carol 1984; Mio in the Land of Faraway 1987; A Summer Story 1987; Melancholia 1989; The Gigolos 2006; Franklyn 2008; The Calling 2009

Yorker, Jade Gridiron Gang 2006; America 2009

Yost, Herbert (1880-1945) Fast and Loose 1930; The Age of Innocence 1934

Young, Aden (1972-) Black Robe 1991; Sniper 1992; Cosi 1996; Hotel de Love 1996; The War Bride 2001; The Crocodile Hunter: Collision Course 2002; The Tree 2010; Killer Elite 2011; I, Frankenstein 2013; Frontera 2014

Young, Alan (1919-2016) Margie 1946; Chicken Every Sunday 1948; Mr Belvedere Goes to College 1949; Androcles and the Lion 1952; Gentlemen Marry Brunettes 1955; tom thumb 1958; The Time Machine 1960; Baker's Hawk 1976; The Cat from

Outer Space 1978; Duck Tales: the Movie - Treasure of the Lost Lamp 1990

Young (1), Arthur (1898-1959) The Root of All Evil 1946; The Lady with the Lamp 1951; An Inspector Calls 1954; Stranger from Venus 1954

Young, Bill Chopper 2000; Japanese Story 2003

Young, Bruce A aka Young, Bruce (1956-) What Ever Happened to...? 1991; Trespass 1992; Blink 1994; Normal Life 1995; Jurassic Park III 2001

Young, Burt (1940-) Cinderella Liberty 1973; The Gambler 1974; The Killer Elite 1975; Rocky 1976; The Choirboys 1977; Twilight's Last Gleaming 1977; Convoy 1978; Rocky II 1979; Blood Beach 1981; The California Dolls 1981; Amityville II: the Possession 1982; Rocky III 1982; Over the Brooklyn Bridge 1983; Once upon a Time in America 1984; The Pope of Greenwich Village 1984; Rocky IV 1985; Back to School 1986; Blood Red 1988; Last Exit to Brooklyn 1989; Wait until Spring, Bandini 1989; Backstreet Dreams 1990; Bright Angel 1990; Rocky V 1990; Excessive Force 1993; Before Women Had Wings 1997; Kicked in the Head 1997; Mickey Blue Eyes 1999; Transamerica 2005; Rocky Balboa 2006; New York, I Love You 2009; Win Win 2011

Young, Carleton (1907-1971) Reefer Madness 1936; Pride of the Bowery 1941; Thunderhead - Son of Flicka 1945; Smash Up - the Story of a Woman 1947; An American Guerrilla in the Philippines 1950; Herd, Fast and Beautiful 1951; 20,000 Leagues under the Sea 1954; Sergeant Rutledge 1960

Young, Charlie (1974-) New Police Story 2004; Seven Swords 2005

Young, Chris (1971-) The Great Outdoors 1988; Warlock: the Armageddon 1993; PCU 1994

Young, Dan (1899-1970) Off the Dole 1935; Somewhere on Leave 1942; It's a Grand Life 1953

Young, Dey (1955-) Rock 'n' Roll High School 1979; Back in the USSR 1992; No Place to Hide 1992; Pie in the Sky 1995; Tactical Assault 1998

Young, Felicity Cover Girl Killer 1959; The Gentle Trap 1960

Young, Gig aka Barr, Byron (1913-1978) The Gay Sisters 1942; Air Force 1943; Old Acquaintance 1943; Escape Me Never 1947; The Woman in White 1948; Tell It to the Judge 1949; Wake of the Red Witch 1949; Only the Valiant 1950; Come Fill the Cup 1951; Target Unknown 1951; Arena 1953; City That Never Sleeps 1953; The Girl Who Had Everything 1953; Torch Song 1953; The Desperate Hours 1955; Young at Heart 1955; Desk Set 1957; Teacher's Pet 1958; The Tunnel of Love 1958; Ask Any Girl 1959; The Story on Page One 1959; Kid Galanad 1962; That Touch of Mink 1962; Five Miles to Midnight 1963; For Love or Money 1963; A Ticklish Affair 1963; Strange Bedfellows 1965; The Shuttered Room 1967; They Shoot Horses, Don't They? 1969; Lovers and Other Strangers 1970; Bring Me the Head of Alfredo Garcia 1974; The Hindenburg 1975; The Killer Elite 1975; Sherlock Holmes in New York 1976; Game of Death 1978

Young, Gladys (1905-1975) The Courtneys of Curzon Street 1947; The Lady with the Lamp 1951

Young (2), James The Thing from Another World 1951; My Son John 1952

Young, Joan (1903-1984) Easy Money 1947; Vice Versa 1947; The Small Voice 1948; Child's Play 1954; Suddenly, Last Summer 1959

Young, Karen (1958-) Handgun 1983; Almost You 1984; Birdy 1984; Maria's Lovers 1984; Nine 1/2 Weeks 1985; Heat 1987; Jaws the Revenge 1987; Criminal Law 1988; Torch Song Trilogy 1988; The Boy Who Cried Bitch 1991; Daylight 1996; Mercy 2000; Factotum (A Man Who Preforms Mary Jobs) 2005; Heading South 2006

Young, Lee Thompson (1984-2013) Friday Night Lights 2004; Akeelah and the Bee 2006; The Hills Have Eyes II 2007

Young, Loretta (1913-2000) Laugh, Clown, Laugh 1928; The Devil to Pay 1930; Beau Ideal 1931; Platinum Blonde 1931; The Hatchet Man 1932; Life Begins 1932; Taxi! 1932; Employees' Entrance 1933; Heroes for Sale 1933; Man's Castle 1933; Zoo in Budapest 1933; Born to Be Bad 1934; Bulldog Drummond Strikes Back 1934; Caravan 1934; The House of Rothschild 1934; The White Parade 1934; The Call of the Wild 1935; Clive of India 1935; The Crusades 1935; Ladies in Love 1936; Café Metropole 1937; Love Is News

1937; Wife, Doctor and Nurse 1937; Four Men and a Prayer 1938; Kentucky 1938; Suez 1938; Three Blind Mice 1938; Eternally Yours 1939; The Story of Alexander Graham Bell 1939; Wife, Husband and Friend 1939; The Doctor Takes a Wife 1940; The Men in Her Life 1941; Bedtime Story 1942; A Night to Remember 1942; China 1943; And Now Tomorrow 1944; Along Came Jones 1945; The Farmer's Daughter 1946; The Stranger 1946; The Bishop's Wife 1947; Rachel and the Stranger 1948; The Accused 1949; Come to the Stable 1949; Mother Is a Freshman 1949; Key to the City 1950; Cause for Alarm 1951; Half Angel 1951

Young, Nedrick aka Young, Ned (1914-1968) Gun Crazy 1949; Captain Scarlett 1953; Terror in a Texas Town 1958

Young (1), Neil (1945-) Human Highway 1982; Neil Young: Heart of Gold 2006; CSNY/Déjà Vu 2008

Young, Noah (1887-1958) A Sailor-Made Man 1921; Grandma's Boy 1922; Safety Last 1923; For Heaven's Sake 1926

Young, Otis (1932-2001) The Last Detail 1973; Blood Beach 1981

Young, Paul (1944-) Another Time, Another Place 1983; The Girl in the Picture 1985

Young, Polly Ann (1908-1997) The Man from Utah 1934; Invisible Ghost 1941

Young, Ric The Last Emperor 1987; Dragon: the Bruce Lee Story 1993; Booty Call 1997; The Corruptor 1999; Kiss of the Dragon 2001; The Transporter 2002

Young, Richard Friday the 13th: a New Beginning 1985; An Innocent Man 1989

Young (1), Robert (1907-1998) The Sin of Madelon Claudet 1931; Hell Divers 1932; The Kid from Spain 1932; Strange Interlude 1932; The Wet Parade 1932; Today We Live 1933; Tugboat Annie 1933; The House of Rothschild 1934; Spitfire 1934; The Bride Comes Home 1935; Red Salute 1935; Remember Last Night? 1935; The Bride Walks Out 1936; It's Love Again 1936; Secret Agent 1936; Stowaway 1936; The Bride Wore Red 1937; The Emperor's Candlesticks 1937; I Met Him in Paris 1937; Navy Blue and Gold 1937; Paradise for Three 1938; The Shining Hour 1938; Three Comrades 1938; The Toy Wife 1938; Honolulu 1939; Maisie 1939; Miracles for Sale 1939; Dr Kildare's Crisis 1940; The Mortal Storm 1940; Northwest Passage 1940; HM Pulham Esq 1941; Lady Be Good 1941; Western Union 1941; Joe Smith, American 1942; Claudia 1943; Slightly Dangerous 1943; Sweet Rosie O'Grady 1943; The Canterville Ghost 1944; The Enchanted Cottage 1945; Those Endearing Young Charms 1945; Claudia and David 1946; Lady Luck 1946; The Searching Wind 1946; Crossfire 1947; They Won't Believe Me 1947; Relentless 1948; Sitting Pretty 1948; Adventure in Baltimore 1949; And Baby Makes Three 1949; Bride for Sale 1949; The Forsyte Saga 1949; Goodbye, My Fancy 1951; The Second Woman 1951; The Half-Breed 1952; Secret of the Incas 1954

Young, Roland (1887-1953) Madam Satan 1930; One Hour with You 1932; This Is the Night 1932; Wedding Rehearsal 1932; Blind Adventure 1933; His Double Life 1933; David Copperfield 1935; Ruggles of Red Gap 1935; The Man Who Could Work Miracles 1936; One Rainy Afternoon 1936; King Solomon's Mines 1937; Topper 1937; Sailing Along 1938; The Young in Heart 1938; Topper Takes a Trip 1939; Irene 1940; No, No, Nanette 1940; The Philadelphia Story 1940; Star Dust 1940; The Flame of New Orleans 1941; Topper Returns 1941; Two-Faced Woman 1941; They All Kissed the Bride 1942; Standing Room Only 1944; And Then There Were None 1945; Bond Street 1948; You Gotta Stay Happy 1948; The Great Lover 1949; Let's Dance 1950

Young, Sean (1959-) Jane Austen in Manhattan 1980; Stripes 1981; Blade Runner 1982; Young Doctors in Love 1982; Dune 1984; Baby: Secret of the Lost Legend 1985; No Way Out 1986; Wall Street 1987; The Boost 1988; Cousins 1989; Wings of the Apache 1990; A Kiss before Dying 1991; Love Crimes 1991; Blue Ice 1992; Once upon a Crime 1992; Ace Ventura: Pet Detective 1993; Even Cowgirls Get the Blues 1993; Fatal Instinct 1993; Dr Jekyll and Ms Hyde 1995; Barbara Taylor Bradford's Everything to Gain 1996; The Proprietor 1996; Motel Blue 1997; Sugar & Spice 2001; The King and Queen of Moonlight Bay 2003

Young, Stephen (1931-) Patton 1970; Breaking Point 1976; Execution of Justice 1999; Strange Justice 1999

Young, Tammany (1886-1936) The Escape 1914; Tugboat Annie 1933; The Mighty Barnum 1934; The Old-Fashioned Way 1934; The Glass Key 1935

Young, Tony (1938-2002) He Rides Tall 1964; Taggart 1964

Young, William Allen (1953-) Wisdom 1986; The Waterdance 1991; Fear X 2002; Murder 101 2006

Youngman, Henny (1906-1998) The Gore-Gore Girls 1972; National Lampoon's Movie Madness 1981

Youngs, Gail (1953-) The Stone Boy 1984; Belizaire the Cajun 1985

Youngs, Jim (1953-) The Wanderers 1979; Hot Shot 1986; Nobody's Fool 1986

Yu Rong Guang (1958-) Iron Monkey 1993; The Enforcer 1995; Tsui Hark's Vampire Hunters 2002; The Karate Kid 2010; Little Big Soldier 2010

Yuan, Eugenia The Eye 2 2004; Choking Man 2006; Revenge of the Green Dragons 2013

Yue, Shawn (1981-) Infernal Affairs 2002; Infernal Affairs II 2003; Infernal Affairs 3 2003; Initial D - Drift Racer 2005

Yuen Biao (1957-) The Prodigal Son 1983; Project A 1983; Zu Warriors 1983; Wheels on Meals 1984; Once upon a Time in China 1991; A Man Called Hero 1999

Yuen, Anita (1971-) And Now You're Dead 1998; Protégé 2007

Yuen, Simon aka Yuen Hsiao Tian aka Yuen Hsiao-Tien Drunken Master 1978; Snake in the Eagle's Shadow 1978

Yui, Masayuki (1947-) Ran 1985; To End All Wars 2001

Yuill, Jimmy Paper Mask 1990; Extraordinary Rendition 2007; The Raven 2012

Yulin, Harris (1937-) End of the Road 1970; Doc 1971; Night Moves 1975; Victory at Entebbe 1976; The Believers 1987; Candy Mountain 1987; Fatal Beauty 1987; Ghostbusters II 1989; The Heart of Justice 1992; Clear and Present Danger 1994; Loch Ness 1995; Stuart Saves His Family 1995; Hostile Waters 1996; Multiplicity 1996; Bean 1997; American Outlaws 2001; Training Day 2001; Fur: an Imaginary Portrait of Diane Arbus 2006

Yune, Rick (1971-) Snow Falling on Cedars 1999; The Fast and the Furious 2001; Die Another Day 2002; Ninja Assassin 2009; The Man with the Iron Fists 2012

Yung, Elodie District 13: Ultimatum 2009; Narcopolis 2014; Still 2014

Yung, Victor Sen (1915-1980) Charlie Chan at Treasure Island 1939; Charlie Chan in Reno 1939; The Letter 1940; Charlie Chan in Rio 1941; Across the Pacific 1942; China 1943; Dangerous Money 1946; The Trap 1947; Forbidden 1953

Yurka, Blanche (1887-1974) A Tale of Two Cities 1935; Lady for a Night 1942; Cry of the Werewolf 1944; The Southerner 1945; Sons of the Musketeers 1951; Taxi 1953; Thunder in the Sun 1959

Yuro, Robert (1932-) Satan in High Heels 1962; The Ride to Hangman's Tree 1967

Yustman, Odette Cloverfield 2008; The Unborn 2008; You Again 2010

Z

Zabka, William (1965-) The Karate Kid 1984; A Tiger's Tale 1987

Zabou aka Breitman, Zabou (1959-) Dandin 1988; C'est la Vie 1990; La Crise 1992; Almost Peaceful 2002

Zabriskie, Grace (1938-) The Private Eyes 1980; An Officer and a Gentleman 1982; The Burning Bed 1984; Leonard, Part 6 1987; The Boost 1988; My Father, My Son 1988; Drugstore Cowboy 1989; Child's Play 2 1990; Wild at Heart 1990; Ambition 1991; My Own Private Idaho 1991; FernGully: the Last Rainforest 1992; Black Widow Murders 1993; Even Cowgirls Get the Blues 1993; The Passion of Darkly Noon 1995; A Family Thing 1996; Dead Men Can't Dance 1997; They Crawl 2001; No Good Deed 2002; The Grudge 2004; My Son, My Son, What Have Ye Done 2009; Rosemont 2015

Zaccaï, Jonathan (1970-) Ma Vraie Vie à Rouen 2002; The Beat That My Heart Skipped 2005; Paper Souls 2013

Zadok, Arnon (1949-) Beyond the Walls 1984; Witness in the War Zone 1986; Torn Apart 1990

Zadora, Pia (1954-) Butterfly 1982; The Lonely Lady 1983; Hairspray 1988

Zahn, Steve (1967-) Reality Bites 1994; Race the Sun 1996; subUrbia 1996; That Thing You Do! 1996; Subway Stories: Tales from the Underground 1997; Forces of Nature 1998; Safe Men 1998; You've Got Mail 1998; Happy, Texas 1999; Stuart Little 1999; Hamlet 2000; Dr Dolittle 2 2001; Evil Woman 2001; Riding in Cars with Boys 2001; Road Kill 2001; National Security 2002; Stuart Little 2 2002; Daddy Day Care 2003; Shattered Glass 2003; Chicken Little 2005; Sahara 2005; Rescue Dawn 2006; Strange Wilderness 2007; Management 2008; Sunshine Cleaning 2008; A Perfect Getaway 2009; Diary of a Wimpy Kid 2010; Diary of a Wimpy Kid: Rodrick Rules 2011; Diary of a Wimpy Kid 3: Dog Days 2012; Dallas Buyers Club 2013; Captain Fantastic 2015; The Good Dinosaur 2015; War for the Planet of the Apes 2017

Zakir, Wasim Love + Hate 2005; Catch Me Daddy 2014

Zal, Roxana (1969-) Table for Five 1983; Testament 1983; Under the Boardwalk 1988

Zamachowski, Zbigniew Three Colours White 1993; Walesa: Man of Hope 2013

Zamora, Del Repo Man 1984; Straight to Hell 1987; Searchers 2.0 2007; Repo Chick 2009

Zane, Billy (1966-) Brotherhood of Justice 1986; Critters 1986; Dead Calm 1988; Memphis Belle 1990; Femme Fatale 1991; Lake Consequence 1992; Orlando 1992; Sniper 1992; Poetic Justice 1993; Posse 1993; The Silence of the Hams 1993; Only You 1994; Reflections on a Crime 1994; The Set Up 1995; Tales from the Crypt: Demon Knight 1995; Danger Zone 1996; Head above Water 1996; The Phantom 1996; This World, Then the Fireworks 1996; Titanic 1997; I Woke Up Early the Day I Died 1998; Susan's Plan 1998; Dean Koontz's Sole Survivor 2000; The Believer 2001; Three - III 2006; The Roommate 2011; Electrick Children 2012; Hannah's Law 2012

Zane, Lisa (1967-) Bad Influence 1990; Femme Fatale 1991; Freddy's Dead: the Final Nightmare 1991; Monkeybone 2000

Zano, Nick Joy Ride 2: Dead Ahead 2008; The Final Destination 2009

Zapasiewicz, Zbigniew (1934-2009) Camouflage 1977; Blind Chance 1987; 200 Motels 1971

Zappa, Frank (1940-1993) Head 1968; 200 Motels 1971

Zappa, William (1948-) Crush 1992; Bootmen 2000

Zardi, Dominique (1930-2009) Les Biches 1968; Juste avant la Nuit 1971

Zaremba, John (1908-1986) Earth vs the Flying Saucers 1956; 20 Million Miles to Earth 1957

Zayas, David 16 Blocks 2006; The Savages 2007; Skyline 2010

Zbruev, Aleksandr (1938-) Lonely Woman Seeks Lifetime Companion 1987; The Inner Circle 1991

Zegers, Antonia Post Mortem 2010; No 2012; The Club 2015

Zegers, Kevin (1984-) Air Bud 1997; Bram Stoker's Shadowbuilder 1997; Nico the Unicorn 1998; Treasure Island 1998; Four Days 1999; Komodo 1999; Bitter Suite 2000; Wrong Turn 2003; Dawn of the Dead 2004; Transamerica 2005; It's a Boy/Girl Thing 2006; Zoom 2006; The Jane Austen Book Club 2007; Fifty Dead Men Walking 2008; Frozen 2009; The Colony 2013; The Mortal Instruments: City of Bones 2013

Zehetner, Nora Brick 2005; Conversations with Other Women 2005; Beneath 2007; The Brothers Bloom 2008

Zehrfeld, Ronald Barbara 2012; Phoenix 2014

Zellweger, Renée aka Zellweger, Renee (1969-) Love and a .45 1994; Reality Bites 1994; Shake, Rattle and Rock 1994; Texas Chainsaw Massacre: the Next Generation 1994; Empire Records 1995; The Low Life 1995; Jerry Maguire 1996; The Whole Wide World 1996; Liar 1997; A Price above Rubies 1997; One True Thing 1998; The Bachelor 1999; Me, Myself & Irene 2000; Nurse Betty 2000; Bridget Jones's Diary 2001; Chicago 2002; White Oleander 2002; Cold Mountain 2003; Down with Love 2003; Bridget Jones: the Edge of Reason 2004; Shark Tale 2004; Cinderella Man 2005;

Miss Potter 2006; Bee Movie 2007; Leatherheads 2008; Appaloosa 2008; Case 39 2008; New in Town 2008; Bridget Jones's Baby 2016; The Whole Truth 2016

Zelniker, Michael Bird 1988; Naked Lunch 1991

Zem, Roschdy (1965-) Clubbed to Death 1996; Monsieur N 2003; 36 Quai des Orfèvres 2004; Days of Glory 2006; London River 2009; Point Blank 2010

Zenor, Suzanne Get to Know Your Rabbit 1972; The Baby 1973

Zeplichal, Vitus I Only Want You to Love Me 1976; The Third Generation 1979

Zerbe, Anthony (1936-) The Liberation of LB Jones 1970; The Molly Maguires 1970; They Call Me Mister Tibbs! 1970; The Omega Man 1971; The Hound of the Baskervilles 1972; The Strange Vengeance of Rosalie 1972; Papillon 1973; Rooster Cogburn 1975; Who'll Stop the Rain? 1978; The Dead Zone 1983; Hell Camp 1986; Licence to Kill 1989; Listen to Me 1989; See No Evil, Hear No Evil 1989; Star Trek: Insurrection 1998

Zeta-Jones, Catherine (1969-) Christopher Columbus: the Discovery 1992; Splitting Heirs 1993; Blue Juice 1995; The Phantom 1996; The Mask of Zorro 1998; Entrapment 1999; The Haunting 1999; High Fidelity 2000; Traffic 2000; America's Sweethearts 2001; Chicago 2002; Intolerable Cruelty 2003; Sinbad: Legend of the Seven Seas 2003; Ocean's Twelve 2004; The Terminal 2004; The Legend of Zorro 2005; Death Defying Acts 2007; No Reservations 2007; The Rebound 2009; Lay the Favorite 2012; Playing for Keeps 2012; Rock of Ages 2012; Broken City 2013; Red 2 2013; Side Effects 2013; Dad's Army 2016

Zetterling, Mai (1925-1994) Torment 1944; Frieda 1947; Night Is My Future 1948; Portrait from Life 1948; Quartet 1948; The Bad Lord Byron 1949; The Lost People 1949; The Romantic Age 1949; Desperate Moment 1953; Dance Little Lady 1954; Knock on Wood 1954; A Prize of Gold 1955; Seven Waves Away 1957; The Truth about Women 1958; Faces in the Dark 1960; Piccadilly Third Stop 1960; Only Two Can Play 1961; The Main Attraction 1962; The Man Who Finally Died 1962; The Bay of Saint Michel 1963; The Witches 1989; Hidden Agenda 1990

Zhang Fengyi (1956-) Farewell My Concubine 1993; The Emperor and the Assassin 1999; Red Cliff 2008

Zhang Jingchu (1980-) Seven Swords 2005; Protégé 2007; City of War: the Story of John Rabe 2009

Zhang Ziyi aka Zhang, Ziyi (1980-) The Road Home 1999; Crouching Tiger, Hidden Dragon 2000; Rush Hour 2 2001; Hero 2002; House of Flying Daggers 2004; 2046 2004; Memoirs of a Geisha 2005; The Banquet 2006; TMNT 2007; Horsemen 2009

Zhao Dan (1915-1980) Street Angel 1937; Crows and Sparrows 1949

Zhao Tao Platform 2000; Unknown Pleasures 2002; Shun Li and the Poet 2011; A Touch of Sin 2013

Zhao Wei aka Zhao, Vicki aka Zhao Wei, Vicky (1976-) Shaolin Soccer 2001; Chinese Odyssey 2002 2002; So Close 2002; Red Cliff 2008

Zharov, Mikhail (1900-1981) Ivan the Terrible, Part I 1944; Ivan the Terrible, Part II 1946

Zhou Xun (1974-) Suzhou River 2000; Beijing Bicycle 2001; Balzac and the Little Chinese Seamstress 2002; The Banquet 2006; Confucius 2010; Flying Swords of Dragon Gate 2011

Zidane, Zinédine Zidane: a 21st Century Portrait 2006; Goal II: Living the Dream 2007; Asterix at the Olympic Games 2008

Zidi, Malik Water Drops on Burning Rocks 1999; Changing Times 2004; Rebellion 2011

Ziemann, Sonja (1925-) Made in Heaven 1952; The Secret Ways 1961

Ziering, Ian (1966-) Sharknado 2013; Sharknado 2: the Second One 2014

Zima, Madeline (1985-) The Hand That Rocks the Cradle 1992; Mr Nanny 1992; Chasing Secrets 1999; Lucy 2003; A Cinderella Story 2004; The Collector 2009

Zima, Vanessa (1986-) The Baby-Sitter's Club 1995; Wicked 1998

Zima, Yvonne (1989-) The Long Kiss Goodnight 1996; Chasing Secrets 1999; Storm Catcher 1999; The Girl He Met Online 2014

Zimbalist Jr, Efrem (1918-2014) House of Strangers 1949; Band of Angels 1957; Bombers B-52 1957; The Deep Six 1958; Home before Dark

1958; *Too Much, Too Soon* 1958;
Violent Road 1958; *The Crowded Sky*
1960; *By Love Possessed* 1961; *The
Chapman Report* 1962; *The Reward*
1965; *Wait until Dark* 1967; *Airport
1975* 1974; *Hot Shots!* 1991
Zimbalist, Stephanie (1956-) *The
Magic of Lassie* 1978; *The Awakening*
1980; *The Man in the Brown Suit* 1989;
Caroline? 1990; *Incident in a Small
Town* 1993; *The Prophet's Game* 1999;
Malpractice 2001
Zimmer, Constance (1970-) *Mystery
Woman* 2003; *Results* 2015
Zimmerman, Matt *Thunderbirds Are
Go!* 1966; *Thunderbird 6* 1968
Zinta, Preity (1975-) *Armaan* 2003;
Kal Ho Naa Ho 2003; *Koi... Mil Gaya*
2003; *Lakshya* 2004; *Veer-Zaara*
2004
Zirner, August (1959-) *Voyager* 1991;
The Promise 1994; *The Counterfeiters*
2007
Zischler, Hanns (1947-) *Kings of the
Road* 1976; *Dr M* 1989; *Francesco* 1989;
The Cement Garden 1992; *Taking Sides*
2001; *Walk on Water* 2004; *Munich*
2005; *Flame & Citron* 2008
Zivojinovic, Bata *aka* **Zivojinovic,
Velimir Bata** (1933-2016) *I Even Met
Happy Gypsies* 1967; *Pretty Village
Pretty Flame* 1996
Zmed, Adrian (1954-) *Grease 2* 1982;
Bachelor Party 1984; *Storm Chasers:
Revenge of the Twister* 1998
Znaimer, Moses *Atlantic City, USA*
1980; *Best Revenge* 1983
Zolnay, Pal (1928-1995) *Diary for My
Children* 1982; *Diary for My Loves* 1987
Zolotin, Adam *Jack* 1996; *Leave It to
Beaver* 1997
Zolotukhin, Valery *Night Watch* 2004;
Day Watch 2006
Zorich, Louis (1924-) *For Pete's Sake*
1974; *Newman's Law* 1974; *Sunday in
the Country* 1975; *The Muppets Take
Manhattan* 1984; *Death of a Salesman*
1985
Zorina, Vera (1917-2003) *The Goldwyn
Follies* 1938; *Louisiana Purchase* 1941;
Star Spangled Rhythm 1942; *Follow the
Boys* 1944; *Lover Come Back* 1946
Zsoter, Sandor *Rothschild's Violin*
1996; *White God* 2014
Zucco, George (1886-1960) *The Bride
Wore Red* 1937; *London by Night* 1937;
Arsene Lupin Returns 1938; *Three
Comrades* 1938; *The Adventures of
Sherlock Holmes* 1939; *The Cat and the
Canary* 1939; *Arise, My Love* 1940; *The
Mummy's Hand* 1940; *New Moon* 1940;
The Black Swan 1942; *The Mummy's
Tomb* 1942; *My Favorite Blonde* 1942;
Sherlock Holmes in Washington 1943;
The Mummy's Ghost 1944; *Voodoo
Man* 1944; *Fog Island* 1945; *Sudan*
1945; *Desire Me* 1947; *Lured* 1947;
Moss Rose 1947; *Scared to Death* 1947;
Where There's Life 1947; *The Pirate*
1948; *Tarzan and the Mermaids* 1948
Zuckerman, Josh *Surviving Christmas*
2004; *Sex Drive* 2008
Zuniga, Daphne (1963-) *The Initiation*
1984; *The Sure Thing* 1985; *Vision
Quest* 1985; *Spaceballs* 1987; *Last Rites*
1988; *A Cut Above* 1989; *The Fly II*
1989; *800 Leagues down the Amazon*
1993; *Charlie's Ghost Story* 1994; *The
Obsession* 2006
Zuniga, José (1965-) *Fresh* 1994;
Smoke 1995; *Hurricane Streets* 1997;
Gun Shy 2000; *The Opportunists*
2000; *Snow White* 2001; *The Hunted*
2002
Zurer, Ayelet *Munich* 2005; *Fugitive
Pieces* 2007; *Vantage Point* 2008;
Angels & Demons 2009
Zurowski, Desiree *They* 2002;
Butterfly on a Wheel 2007
Zushi, Yoshitaka (1955-) *Dodes'ka-
Den* 1970; *Akira Kurosawa's Dreams*
1990
Zwerling, Darrell (1929-2014)
Chinatown 1974; *Doc Savage: the Man
of Bronze* 1975; *The Ultimate Warrior*
1975
Zylberstein, Elsa (1969-) *Van Gogh*
1991; *Mina Tannenbaum* 1993; *Farinelli
il Castrato* 1994; *Portraits Chinois* 1996;
Metroland 1997; *Monsieur N* 2003; *I've
Loved You So Long* 2008

Alternative titles

A

A Mezzanotte Va la Ronda del Piacere Immortal Bachelor
A Nous Deux An Adventure for Two
Abandon Ship! Seven Waves Away
The ABC Murders The Alphabet Murders
Abe Lincoln in Illinois Spirit of the People
Abismos de Pasion Wuthering Heights
Above the Law Nico
Actors Blood and Woman of Sin Actors and Sin
Adieu au Language Goodbye to Language
Adventures in Babysitting A Night on the Town
The Adventures of a Gnome Named Gnorm Upworld
The Adventures of Don Quixote Don Quixote
The Adventures of Pluto Nash Pluto Nash
The Adventures of Quentin Durward Quentin Durward
The Adventures of Sadie Our Girl Friday
The Adventures of the Flying Pickle The Pickle
The Adventures of Tim Every Day's a Holiday
The Advocate The Hour of the Pig
Affairs of Adelaide Britannia Mews
African Fury Cry, the Beloved Country
After Midnight Captain Carey, USA
Agantuk The Stranger
Agatha Christie's Dead Man's Folly Dead Man's Folly
Agatha Christie's Death on the Nile Death on the Nile
Agatha Christie's Endless Night Endless Night
Agatha Christie's Thirteen at Dinner Thirteen at Dinner
Agent 8¾ Hot Enough for June
Ai No Corrida In the Realm of the Senses
L'Aigle à Deux Têtes The Eagle Has Two Heads
An Alan Smithee Film: Burn, Hollywood, Burn Burn Hollywood Burn
L'Albero degli Zoccoli The Tree of Wooden Clogs
Alferd Packer: the Musical Cannibal! the Musical
The Algonquin Goodbye Silent Trigger
Alias Bulldog Drummond Bulldog Jack
Alien Thunder Dan Candy's Law
Alistair MacLean's Death Train Death Train
Alistair MacLean's Puppet on a Chain Puppet on a Chain
All at Sea Barnacle Bill
All That Money Can Buy The Devil and Daniel Webster
...All the Marbles The California Dolls
All Things Bright and Beautiful It Shouldn't Happen to a Vet
All This and Money Too Love Is a Ball
Allegheny Uprising The First Rebel
Along Came Sally Aunt Sally
Amantes Lovers
The Lovers Les Amants
L'Ami de Mon Amie My Girlfriend's Boyfriend
Amici per la Pelle Friends for Life
The Amorous Adventures of Uncle Benjamin Uncle Benjamin
The Amorous General Waltz of the Toreadors
Un Amour de Swann Swann in Love
L'Amour l'Apres-Midi Love in the Afternoon
The Anatolian Smile America, America
And Nothing but the Truth Giro City
And So They Were Married Johnny Doesn't Live Here Anymore
And Then There Were None Ten Little Indians
Andy Warhol's Bad Bad
Andy Warhol's Dracula Blood for Dracula
Andy Warhol's Flesh Flesh
Andy Warhol's Frankenstein Flesh for Frankenstein
El Angel Exterminador The Exterminating Angel
Angel of Vengeance Ms 45
Angel Street Gaslight
Angels and the Pirates Angels in the Outfield
Die Angst des Tormanns beim Elfmeter The Goalkeeper's Fear of the Penalty Kick
Angst Essen Seele Auf Fear Eats the Soul
Ann Rule's Too Late to Say Goodbye Too Late to Say Goodbye
Anna Karenina Love
L'Année Dernière à Marienbad Last Year at Marienbad
L'Arbre de Noël The Christmas Tree
La Ardilla Roja The Red Squirrel
L'Armée des Ombres Army of Shadows
The Armour of God II Operation Condor: the Armour of God II
Arms and the Dudes War Dogs
Arouse and Beware The Man from Dakota
Arrivederci, Baby! Drop Dead Darling

L'Arrivo di Wang The Arrival of Wang
Arthur Conan Doyle's Sign of Four The Sign of Four
L'Ascenseur pour l'Échafaud Lift to the Scaffold
The Assassin Venetian Bird
L'Assedio Besieged
Assignment Redhead Undercover Girl
At Dawn We Die Tomorrow We Live
At First Sight Entre Nous
Atame Tie Me Up! Tie Me Down!
Atertraffen The Reunion
The Atomic Man Timeslip
Aux Yeux du Monde Autobus
L'Avare Dardin
The Avengers The Day Will Dawn
Avengers 2 Avengers: Age of Ultron
Les Aventuriers du Timbre Perdu Tommy Tricker and the Stamp Traveller
L'Aveu The Confession

B

Bachelor Bait Adventure in Baltimore
Bachelor Girl Apartment Any Wednesday
Bachelor Knight The Bachelor and the Bobby-Soxer
Back to Back: American Yakuza 2 American Yakuza 2: Back to Back
Backtrack Catchfire
Baisers Volés Stolen Kisses
Le Ballon Rouge The Red Balloon
The Battle for Anzio Anzio
Battle of the Brave Nouvelle-France
The Beasts of Marseilles Seven Thunders
A Beating Heart Your Beating Heart
Behind the Iron Mask The 5th Musketeer
Belle's Magical Christmas Beauty and the Beast: the Enchanted Christmas
Best Shot Hoosiers
The Beast La Bête
Beyond Control - The Amy Fisher Story The Amy Fisher Story
Beyond the Law Fixing the Shadow
Beyond the Limit The Honorary Consul
Il Bidone The Swindle
The Big Carnival Ace in the Hole
Big Deal at Dodge City A Big Hand for a Little Lady
Big Girls Don't Cry... They Get Even Stepkids
The Big Heart Miracle on 34th Street
The Big Parade of Comedy MGM's Big Parade of Comedy
Big Stickup at Brink's The Brink's Job
Billy Rose's Jumbo Jumbo
Billy the Kid Gore Vidal's Billy the Kid
Bits and Pieces Il Cielo è Sempre Più Blu
Bizet's Carmen Carmen
Black Ice A Passion for Murder
Black Sky Into the Storm
Der Blaue Engel The Blue Angel
Die Blechtrommel The Tin Drum
Blood Beast from Outer Space The Night Caller
Blood Fiend Theatre of Death
Blood Is My Heritage Blood of Dracula
Blood Simple Zhang Yimou's Blood Simple
Bloom bl,.m
Blow-Out La Grande Bouffe
Blue Three Colours Blue
Blue Jeans Blue Denim
Blue Manhattan Hi, Mom!
Bodas de Sangre Blood Wedding
The Bottom of the Bottle Beyond the River
Bound by Honor Blood In Blood Out
The Bounty Hunters Adios, Sabata
Breakin' Breakdance
Breakin' 2: Electric Boogaloo Breakdance 2 - Electric Boogaloo
Breakout Danger Within
Breathless A Bout de Souffle
The Bride Wasn't Willing Frontier Gal
Brink of Hell Toward the Unknown
Broken Lullaby The Man I Killed
Brotherly Love Country Dance
Un Bruit Qui Rend Fou The Blue Villa
Die Büchse der Pandora Pandora's Box
The Buddy Factor Swimming with Sharks
Bulletproof Heart Killer
Il Buono, Il Brutto, Il Cattivo The Good, the Bad and the Ugly
Burn, Baby, Burn Heat Wave
Burn, Witch, Burn Night of the Eagle
The Butcher Le Boucher
By Hook or by Crook I Dood It

C

Cadaveri Eccellenti Illustrious Corpses
Cadence Stockade
La Caduta degli Dei The Damned
La Cage aux Rossignols A Cage of Nightingales
The Call Girl and the Governor: Client 9 Client-9: the Rise and Fall of Eliot Spitzer
Call Him Mr Shatter Shatter
Call Me a Cab Carry On Cabby
Les Camarades The Organizer

Campanadas a Medianoche Chimes at Midnight
Can a Song Save your Life? Begin Again
Candyman II Candyman: Farewell to the Flesh
Care of the Spitfire Grill The Spitfire Grill
A Caribbean Mystery Agatha Christie's A Caribbean Mystery
Caro Diario Dear Diary
Le Carosse d'Or The Golden Coach
Carried Away Acts of Love
The Carriers Are Waiting Les Convoyeurs Attendent
Carry On Venus Carry On Jack
La Carte du Tendre Map of the Human Heart
La Casa de Bernarda Alba The House of Bernarda Alba
La Casa dell'Esorcismo Lisa and the Devil
Le Casse The Burglars
The Cat in the Hat Dr Seuss' The Cat in the Hat
Catherine the Great The Rise of Catherine the Great
La Caza The Hunt
The Celebration Festen
C'Era una Volta More than a Miracle
Le Cerveau The Brain
C'est Arrivé près de chez Vous Man Bites Dog
Cet Obscur Objet du Désir That Obscure Object of Desire
Chacun Cherche Son Chat When the Cat's Away...
La Chair de l'Orchidée The Flesh of the Orchid
La Chambre Verte The Green Room
Champions The Mighty Ducks
Chance Meeting Blind Date
Charley's American Aunt Charley's Aunt
Charlie Chan and the Red Dragon The Red Dragon
Charlie Chan in Dangerous Money Dangerous Money
Charlie Chan in Dark Alibi Dark Alibi
Charlie Chan in The Trap The Trap
Charlotte, the Lonely Wife Charulata
Le Charme Discret de la Bourgeoisie The Discreet Charm of the Bourgeoisie
Cheatin' Hearts Paper Hearts
Chicago, Chicago Gaily, Gaily
La Chiesa The Church
China Blue Crimes of Passion
The Chinese Connection Fist of Fury
Chippendales: Just Can't Get Enough Just Can't Get Enough
A Choice of Weapons Trial by Combat
Choke Canyon On Dangerous Ground
Les Choses de la Vie The Things of Life
A Christmas Carol Scrooge
A Christmas Carol Christmas Carol: the Movie
A Christmas Carol: the Musical A Christmas Carol
Chuck Berry: Hail! Hail! Rock'n'Roll! Hail! Hail! Rock 'n' Roll!
Le Cinquième Elément The Fifth Element
Circus World The Magnificent Showman
La Città delle Donne City of Women
La Città Prigioniera Captive City
City Unplugged Darkness in Tallinn
A Climate for Killing A Row of Crows
Clinton and Nadine Blood Money
Close to Eden A Stranger among Us
Close to Eden Urga
Clouds over Europe Q Planes
Cobweb Castle Throne of Blood
Un Coeur Qui Bat Your Beating Heart
Cold Cuts Buffet Froid
Cold Water L'Eau Froide
La Collina Degli Stivali Boot Hill
Colonel Blimp The Life and Death of Colonel Blimp
Columbo: Prescription Murder Prescription: Murder
Columbo: Ransom for a Dead Man Ransom for a Dead Man
Common Bonds Chaindance
Como Aqua para Chocolate Like Water for Chocolate
Como Ser Mujer y no Morir en el Intento How to Be a Woman and Not Die in the Attempt
Company of Cowards? Advance to the Rear
Comradeship Kameradschaft
The Concierge For Love or Money
The Concorde - Airport '79 Airport '79: the Concorde
The Concrete Jungle The Criminal
Un condamné à Mort s'est échappé ou le vent souffle où il veut A Man Escaped
Conqueror Worm Witchfinder General
Conte d'Automne An Autumn Tale
Cop Tips Waitress $2 Million It Could Happen to You
The Cosmic Monsters The Strange World of Planet X
Count Dracula and His Vampire Bride The Satanic Rites of Dracula
Clean Slate Coup de Torchon

La Course du Lièvre à travers les Champs And Hope to Die
Court Martial Carrington VC
The Crash of Silence Mandy
Crazy to Kill Dr Gillespie's Criminal Case
The Creeping Unknown The Quatermass Xperiment
Crest of the Wave Seagulls over Sorrento
Cries Unheard: the Donna Yaklich Story Victim of Rage
The Crime of the Century Walk East on Beacon
Crime Wave The City Is Dark
Critical Decision Executive Decision
Crooks in Clover Penthouse
Crossed Swords The Prince and the Pauper
Crossing the Line The Big Man
The Cry of the Owl Le Cri du Hibou
La Curée The Game Is Over
Curse of the Demon Night of the Demon
Cutter and Bone Cutter's Way
Czarina A Royal Scandal
Da Yue Bing The Big Parade

D

Daddy Nostalgie These Foolish Things
Damn the Defiant! HMS Defiant
Dance of Death House of Evil
Dance of the Vampires or Pardon Me, but Your Teeth Are in My Neck The Fearless Vampire Killers
Daniel and the Devil The Devil and Daniel Webster
Dante's Inferno Jacob's Ladder
Dark Obsession Diamond Skulls
The Darkest Hour Hell on Frisco Bay
A Date with a Lonely Girl TR Baskin
The Day the Screaming Stopped The Comeback
De Amor y de Sombras Of Love and Shadows
De Eso no Se habla We Don't Want to Talk about It
Dead Connection Final Combination
Deadline: the New York Times Page One: Inside the New York Times
The Deadly Game All Things to All Men
Deadly Is the Female Gun Crazy
Deadly Roulette How I Spent My Summer Vacation
Debbie Macomber's Call Me Mrs Miracle Call Me Mrs Miracle
Deceiver Liar
Deliverance Sadgati
Dellamorte Dellamore Cemetery Man
Les Demoiselles de Rochefort The Young Girls of Rochefort
The Demon Barber of Fleet Street Sweeney Todd, the Demon Barber of Fleet Street
Dennis Strikes Again Dennis the Menace Strikes Again
La Dentellière The Lacemaker
Derby You've Got a Friend
Le Dernier Métro The Last Metro
Desert Patrol Sea of Sand
Il Deserto Rosso Red Desert
Después de Lucía After Lucia
The Destructors The Marseille Contract
Det Sjunde Inseglet The Seventh Seal
The Detective Father Brown
Detour Too Hard to Die
Detour to Nowhere Banacek: Detour to Nowhere
Les Deux Anglaises et le Continent Anne and Muriel
Deux Billets pour Mexico Dead Run
Deux Hommes dans Manhattan Two Men in Manhattan
Deux Jours, une Nuit Two Days, One Night
The Devil Never Sleeps Satan Never Sleeps
The Devil Takes the Count The Devil Is a Sissy
The Devil within Her I Don't Want to Be Born
The Devil's Backbone The Deserter
The Devils Les Diaboliques
The Devil's Bride The Devil Rides Out
The Devil's Brother Bogus Bandits
The Devil's Own The Witches
El Dia de la Bestia The Day of the Beast
Le Diable au Corps Devil in the Flesh
Le Diable Probablement The Devil, Probably
La Diagonale du Fou Dangerous Moves
Dial Rat for Terror Bone
Diamond Horseshoe Billy Rose's Diamond Horseshoe
Diamond Mercenaries Killer Force
Dick Tracy's Amazing Adventure Dick Tracy Meets Gruesome
Diggstown Midnight Sting
Un Dimanche à la Campagne Sunday in the Country
Dirty Money Un Flic
Disney's First Kid First Kid
The Dividing Line The Lawless
The Dock Brief Trial and Error
The Doctor and the Debutante Dr Kildare's Victory
Dr Bethune Bethune: the Making of a Hero

Laggies Say When
Landru Bluebeard
The Last Adventure The Adventurers
The Last Days of Man on Earth The Final Programme
The Last Great Warrior Squanto: the Last Great Warrior
Last of the Finest Blue Heat
The Last Ride FTW
Les Lèvres Rouges Daughters of Darkness
Legend of the Mummy Bram Stoker's Legend of the Mummy
Len Deighton's Bullet to Beijing Bullet to Beijing
Len Deighton's The Ipcress File The Ipcress File
Leo Tolstoy's Anna Karenina Anna Karenina
Let Me Call You Sweetheart Mary Higgins Clark's Let Me Call You Sweetheart
Les Liens de Sang Blood Relatives
The Life and Adventures of Nicholas Nickleby Nicholas Nickleby
Lights Out Bright Victory
Lionheart AWOL
The Little Death A Funny Kind of Love
The Little Kidnappers The Kidnappers
Live Bait The Bait
Live for Life Vivre pour Vivre
Loco de Amor Two Much
The Locusts A Secret Sin
The Longest Yard The Mean Machine
Look See Ecoute Voir...
Lost Angels The Road Home
The Loudest Whisper The Children's Hour
Love after Love Après l'Amour
Love Eternal Eternal Love
Love Lessons All Things Fair
Love of a Clown Pagliacci
Love, Lies and Lullabies Sad Inheritance
Lovely to Look At Thin Ice
Lovers Must Learn Rome Adventure
Love's Deadly Triangle: The Texas Cadet Murder Swearing Allegiance
Loves of a Blonde A Blonde in Love
The Loves of Count Yorga, Vampire Count Yorga, Vampire
The Loves of Isadora Isadora
La Lune dans le Caniveau The Moon in the Gutter
M Arkadin Confidential Report

M

Ma Nuit chez Maud My Night with Maud
Mädchen in Uniform Girls in Uniform
Madhouse Mansion Ghost Story
Mafia! Jane Austen's Mafia
Mailbag Robbery The Flying Scot
Make Mine a Double The Night We Dropped a Clanger
The Maltese Falcon Dangerous Female
A Man and a Woman Un Homme et une Femme
Man and His Mate One Million BC
Man in a Cocked Hat Carlton-Browne of the FO
A Man Is Ten Feet Tall Edge of the City
Man of Affairs His Lordship
Man of Bronze Jim Thorpe – All-American
Man with a Million The Million Pound Note
The Man with 100 Faces Crackerjack
The Man with the Green Carnation The Trials of Oscar Wilde
The Man with Thirty Sons The Magnificent Yankee
The Manhattan Project The Deadly Game
Manhunt From Hell to Texas
Le Mani Sulla Città Hands over the City
Mania The Flesh and the Fiends
La Mano dello Straniero The Stranger's Hand
March of the Wooden Soldiers Babes in Toyland
Marching Along Stars and Stripes Forever
Le Mari de la Coiffeuse The Hairdresser's Husband
Marianne and Julianne The German Sisters
La Mariée Est Trop Belle The Bride Is Too Beautiful
Mark of the Claw Dick Tracy's Dilemma
The Marrying Man Too Hot to Handle
Marx Brothers Go West Go West
Mary Names the Day Dr Kildare's Wedding Day
Massacre Hill Eureka Stockade
Master of the Islands The Hawaiians
Masters of the Universe II: The Cyborg Cyborg
A Matter of Innocence Pretty Polly
The Night Is Young Mauvais Sang
Me and My Gal For Me and My Gal
Meet Whiplash Willie The Fortune Cookie
Meghe Dhaka Tara The Cloud Capped Star
Melody Inn Riding High
The Memory Expert Man on the Flying Trapeze
Men on Her Mind The Girl from 10th Avenue
Menage Tenue de Soirée

Mensonge The Lie
A Merry War Keep the Aspidistra Flying
Messer im Kopf Knife in the Head
Mi Buenos Aires Querido The Tango Lesson
Mid-August Lunch The Ferragosto Dinner
Midnight at the Wax Museum Midnight at Madame Tussaud's
Midway Battle of Midway
A Midwinter's Tale In the Bleak Midwinter
Miles from Nowhere Chasing a Dream
The Miracle of Fatima The Miracle of Our Lady of Fatima
Mixed Blessings Danielle Steel's Mixed Blessings
The Modern Miracle The Story of Alexander Graham Bell
The Mole El Topo
Mon Oncle Antoine My Uncle Antoine
Un Monde sans Pitié A World without Pity
The Monster I Don't Want to Be Born
Monument Ave Noose
La Mort en Direct Death Watch
The Most Dangerous Man in the World The Chairman
A Mother's Revenge Desperate Justice
La Motocyclette The Girl on a Motorcycle
Moving In Firstborn
The Moving Target Harper
Mrs Loring's Secret The Imperfect Lady
Mujeres al Borde de un Ataque de Nervios Women on the Verge of a Nervous Breakdown
Murder in the Old Red Barn Maria Marten, or the Murder in the Red Barn
The Murder in Thornton Square Gaslight
Murder in Three Acts Agatha Christie's Murder in Three Acts
Murder, Inc The Enforcer
Murder Is Easy Agatha Christie's Murder Is Easy
Murder, My Sweet Farewell My Lovely
Murder Will Out Voice of Merrill
Murder with Mirrors Agatha Christie's Murder with Mirrors
My Father's Glory La Gloire de Mon Père
My Favorite Season Ma Saison Préférée
My Heart Goes Crazy London Town
My Life in Ruins Driving Aphrodite
My Mother's Castle Le Château de Ma Mère
My Sex Life ... or How I got into an Argument Ma Vie Sexuelle
My Summer Story It Runs in the Family
The Mystery of Kaspar Hauser The Enigma of Kaspar Hauser

N

The Nanny The Guardian
The Nature of the Beast Bad Company
Navy Heroes The Blue Peter
Neil Simon's Broadway Bound Broadway Bound
Neil Simon's The Goodbye Girl The Goodbye Girl
Neil Simon's The Sunshine Boys The Sunshine Boys
The Nelson Affair Bequest to the Nation
Never Give an Inch Sometimes a Great Notion
Never to Love A Bill of Divorcement
New Frontier Frontier Horizon
New Tales of the Taira Clan Tales of the Taira Clan
Nicky and Gino Dominick and Eugene
Night Ambush Ill Met by Moonlight
Night and Fog Nuit et Brouillard
Night at the Museum 3 Night at the Museum: Secret of the Tomb
Night of the Cyclone Perfume of the Cyclone
Night of the Demons 3 Demon House
The Night of the Shooting Stars The Night of San Lorenzo
Nightmare on Elm Street 7 Wes Craven's New Nightmare
No Greater Love Danielle Steel's No Greater Love
No Highway in the Sky No Highway
No Secrets A Touch of the Sun
No Sleep till Dawn Bombers B-52
Noi vivi We the Living
Noirs et Blancs en Couleurs Black and White in Color
For the Love of Mike None but the Brave
The North Avenue Irregulars Hill's Angels
Un Nos ola Leuad One Full Moon
Nosferatu a Venezia Vampire in Venice
Notorious Gentleman The Rake's Progress
Novecento 1900
Now about These Women All These Women
La Nuit Américaine Day for Night
Nuit et Jour Night and Day
Les Nuits de la Pleine Lune Full Moon in Paris
Nuke 'em High Class of Nuke 'Em High
Nuovo Cinema Paradiso Cinema Paradiso

O

Occhi senza Volto Eyes without a Face
L'Odeur de la Papaye Verte The Scent of Green Papaya
The Official Version The Official Story
Oh! For a Man Will Success Spoil Rock Hunter?
The Old Curiosity Shop Mister Quilp
Olly, Olly, Oxen Free The Great Balloon Adventure
On Guard Le Bossu
Once in a Lifetime Danielle Steel's Once in a Lifetime
One Hour to Doomsday City beneath the Sea
One Man Mutiny The Court-Martial of Billy Mitchell
One Night Stand Before the Night
One-Piece Bathing Suit Million Dollar Mermaid
One Wild Night Career Opportunities
One Woman's Story The Passionate Friends
Operation Undercover Report to the Commissioner
Opposing Force Hell Camp
Orfeu Negro Black Orpheus
Les Orgueilleux The Proud Ones
L'Oro di Napoli Gold of Naples
Our Man in Marrakesh That Man George
L'Ours The Bear
Out of Rosenheim Bagdad Café
Out of the Past Build My Gallows High
The Outcast Man in the Saddle
The Outsider The Guinea Pig

P

Palomino Danielle Steel's Palomino
Pane, Amore e Fantasia Bread, Love & Dreams
Par-delà les Nuages Beyond the Clouds
Paradise Lagoon The Admirable Crichton
Les Parapluies de Cherbourg The Umbrellas of Cherbourg
Paratrooper The Red Beret
Paris Brûle-t-Il? Is Paris Burning?
Paroles et Musique Love Songs
Pas de Problème No Problem!
Pasqualino Settebellezze Seven Beauties
The Passion of Anna A Passion
Passport to Fame The Whole Town's Talking
Paula Framed
Les Péchés mortels Innocent Lies
The Pearl Necklace Desire
Peppermint Soda Diabolo Menthe
Per Qualche Dollaro in Più For a Few Dollars More
Per un Pugno di Dollari A Fistful of Dollars
Perfect Prey When the Bough Breaks 2: Perfect Prey
Perfect Stranger Danielle Steel's A Perfect Stranger
Péril en la Demeure Death in a French Garden
Personal Column Lured
The Phantom of Liberty Le Fantôme de la Liberté
La Piscine The Swimming Pool
Pistola di Dio God's Gun
Planes 2 Planes: Fire and Rescue
La Planète Sauvage Fantastic Planet
The Pleasure Lovers Naked Fury
Point of No Return The Assassin
Politically Correct Party Animals PCU
Pollux et le Chat Bleu Dougal and the Blue Cat
Polly Fulton BF's Daughter
Porte des Lilas Gates of Paris
Posh The Riot Club
The Postman Il Postino
Poulet au Vinaigre Cop au Vin
Precinct 45: Los Angeles Police The New Centurions
Prénom Carmen First Name: Carmen
Préparez Vos Mouchoirs Get Out Your Handkerchiefs
Pretend You Don't See Her Mary Higgins Clark's Pretend You Don't See Her
Prima della Rivoluzione Before the Revolution
Le Procès The Trial
The Professional Leon
Profundo Carmesi Deep Crimson
The Promoter The Card
The Public Eye Follow Me
I Pugni in Tasca Fists in the Pocket
The Punk and the Princess The Punk
The Purge 2 The Purge: Anarchy
Purple Haze More American Graffiti
Purple Noon Plein Soleil
Pursuit of the Graf Spee The Battle of the River Plate
Pussycat Alley WUSA

Q

Les Quatre Cents Coups The 400 Blows
Quatre Nuits d'un Rêveur Four Nights of a Dreamer
Le Quattro Giornate di Napoli The Four Days of Naples
Queen of Diamonds Popsy-Pop
Queen of the Nile Nefertite, Queen of the Nile

R

RSVP For Better and for Worse
A Race for Life Mask of Dust
The Rainmaker John Grisham's The Rainmaker
Rambo: First Blood First Blood
Rasputin the Mad Monk Rasputin and the Empress
Raw Meat Death Line
Ready to Wear Pret-a-Porter
Re-Animator 2 Bride of Re-Animator
Rebel Highway Shake, Rattle and Rock
Rebel with a Cause The Loneliness of the Long Distance Runner
Red Three Colours Red
Red Dragon: the Pursuit of Hannibal Lecter Manhunter
The Ref Hostile Hostages
Regarde les Hommes Tomber See How They Fall
Reindeer Games Deception
Remembrance Danielle Steel's Remembrance
Remo Williams: the Adventure Begins... Remo – Unarmed and Dangerous
Renegade Girls Caged Heat
A Report on the Party and the Guests The Party and the Guests
Le Retour de Martin Guerre The Return of Martin Guerre
Retribution Hellion
Return of the Corsican Brothers The Bandits of Corsica
The Return of the Dragon The Way of the Dragon
Return of the Magnificent Seven Return of the Seven
The Rich Full Life Cynthia
Riders of Vengeance The Raiders
Ring up the Curtain Broadway to Hollywood
Les Ripoux Le Cop
Riso Amaro Bitter Rice
The Road Warrior Mad Max 2
Robin Cook's Virus Formula for Death
Robinson Crusoe Daniel Defoe's Robinson Crusoe
Rock around the World The Tommy Steele Story
Rocket to the Moon Jules Verne's Rocket to the Moon
Rodgers and Hammerstein's Cinderella Cinderella
Roger Corman's Frankenstein Unbound Frankenstein Unbound
Roma Fellini's Roma
Roma, Città Aperta Rome, Open City
Le Roman de Renard The Tale of the Fox
Romance for Three Paradise for Three
Romeo and Juliet William Shakespeare's Romeo + Juliet
Rommel – Desert Fox The Desert Fox
Rookies Buck Privates
Rookies Come Home Buck Privates Come Home
Room 43 Passport to Shame
Roommates Raising the Wind
Run Rabbit Run Double X: the Name of the Game
The Rundown Welcome to the Jungle
Russ Meyer's Super Vixens Supervixens
Russ Meyer's Common Law Cabin Common-Law Cabin
Russ Meyer's Vixen Vixen!

S

S Club: Seeing Double Seeing Double
The Saboteur: Code Name Morituri Morituri
Sabrina Fair Sabrina
Sacrifices of the Heart Spring Thaw
The Saga of the Viking Women and Their Voyage to the Waters of the Great Sea Serpent Viking Women and the Sea Serpent
Saint Francis God's Jester Francis, God's Jester
Le Salaire de la Peur The Wages of Fear
Les Salauds Bastards
Salut l'Artiste The Bit Player
Sanders Death Drums along the River
Le Sang d'un Poète The Blood of a Poet
Sangre y Arena Blood and Sand
Sarajevo, Mon Amour Esma's Secret
Le Sauvage Call Him Savage
Sauve Qui Peut – la Vie Slow Motion
Savage Nights Les Nuits Fauves

Scandals of Clochemerle Clochemerle
The Scarlet Buccaneer Swashbuckler
Das Schrecklicke Mädchen The Nasty Girl
Scotland Yard Dragnet The Hypnotist
Scream of Fear Taste of Fear
Searching for Bobby Fischer Innocent Moves
Seaside Swingers Every Day's a Holiday
Second Breath Le Deuxième Souffle
The Secret Four Kansas City Confidential
See No Evil Blind Terror
The Seeker: The Dark Is Rising The Dark Is Rising
Separate Beds The Wheeler Dealers
The Shabby Tiger Masquerade
The Shadow Warrior Kagemusha
Shadowbuilder Bram Stoker's Shadowbuilder
Shakedown Blue Jean Cop
Shakespeare's Hamlet Hamlet
Shameless Mad Dogs and Englishmen
She Couldn't Say No Beautiful but Dangerous
Sherlock Holmes and the Scarlet Claw The Scarlet Claw
Sherlock Holmes and the Secret Code Dressed to Kill
Sherlock Holmes and the Woman in Green The Woman in Green
Sherlock Holmes in Dressed to Kill Dressed to Kill
Shoot to Kill Deadly Pursuit
The Shot Title Shot
Sidewalks of London St Martin's Lane
Silent Voice Amazing Grace and Chuck
The Silent Voice The Man Who Played God
Il silenzio dei prosciutti The Silence of the Hams
The Silk Noose Noose
Silken Skin La Peau Douce
A Simple Story Une Histoire Simple
The Sin of Harold Diddlebock Mad Wednesday
Single-Handed Sailor of the King
The Sinister Urge Hellborn
La Sirène du Mississippi Mississippi Mermaid
Sisters Some Girls
The Ski Raiders Snow Job
Slagskämpen The Inside Man
The Sleepers Little Nikita
A Slight Trick of the Mind Mr Holmes
The Small Miracle Never Take No for an Answer
Smilla's Sense of Snow Smilla's Feeling for Snow
The Smugglers The Man Within
Smultronstället Wild Strawberries
Snabba cash II Easy Money II
Snake Eyes Dangerous Game
Snow White Blancanieves
Soldier Love Story A Soldier's Love Story
The Soldiers Les Carabiniers
Il Sole Anche di Notte Night Sun
Soleil Rouge Red Sun
I Soliti Ignoti Big Deal on Madonna Street
Someone like You Animal Attraction
Somewhere in France The Foreman Went to France
Sophie's Place Crooks and Coronets
Sparkling Cyanide Agatha Christie's Sparkling Cyanide
Speed Zone Cannonball Fever
The Spider Earth vs the Spider
The Spider Woman Sherlock Holmes and the Spider Woman
La Spina Dorsale del Diavolo The Deserter
Spitfire The First of the Few
Spoorloos The Vanishing
Spy Busters Guns in the Heather
Spylarks The Intelligence Men
Stacking Season of Dreams
Stairway to Heaven A Matter of Life and Death
Stampeded The Big Land
Stanno Tutti Bene Everybody's Fine
Star Danielle Steel's Star
Star Wars: the Force Awakens Star Wars Episode VII: the Force Awakens
Stephen Hawking: a Brief History of Mine Hawking
Stephen King's Silver Bullet Silver Bullet
Stephen King's Sleepwalkers Sleepwalkers
Stolen Identity The Face on the Milk Carton
The Story of Dr Ehrlich's Magic Bullet Dr Ehrlich's Magic Bullet
Stowaway Girl Manuela
Stranded Valley of Mystery
The Stranger The Intruder
The Stranger and the Gunfighter Blood Money
The Strangler East of Piccadilly
La Strategia del Ragno The Spider's Stratagem
Street Fighters Only the Strong
The Streetfighter Hard Times
Strictly Confidential Broadway Bill
Strike It Rich Loser Takes All
Striptease Lady Lady of Burlesque
Stronger than Fear Edge of Doom
Such Things Happen Love Is a Racket
Sudden Terror Eyewitness

Suicide Squadron Dangerous Moonlight
Sult Hunger
Summer Fling Last of the High Kings
Summer Madness Summertime
Summer of the Seventeenth Doll Season of Passion
Sunless Sans Soleil
Swept from the Sea Amy Foster
The Swindle Rien Ne Va Plus
Swinger's Paradise Wonderful Life
The Swingin' Maiden The Iron Maiden
Sword of Lancelot Lancelot and Guinevere

Tacones Lejanos High Heels
Das Tagebuch einer Verlorenen Diary of a Lost Girl
Take Me Home Again The Lies Boys Tell
Tang Shan Da Xiong The Big Boss
Tartu The Adventures of Tartu
Tarzan and the Jungle Queen Tarzan's Peril
A Taste of Sunshine Sunshine
Tears for Simon Lost
Ted Bundy Bundy
Ten Little Indians And Then There Were None
Ten Little Niggers And Then There Were None
Il Terrore dei Barbari Goliath and the Barbarians
That Forsyte Woman The Forsyte Saga
Their Secret Affair Top Secret Affair
These Are the Damned The Damned
They've Taken Our Children: the Chowchilla Kidnapping Story Vanished without a Trace
Thieves Les Voleurs
The Thing The Thing from Another World
The Third Key The Long Arm
Thirst Three Strange Loves
This Is My Affair I Can Get It for You Wholesale
Those Daring Young Men in Their Jaunty Jalopies Monte Carlo or Bust!
Three Men and a Girl Kentucky Moonshine
Thunder over Tangier Man from Tangier
Tierra y Libertad Land and Freedom
Tiger in the Sky The McConnell Story
Tight Little Island Whisky Galore!
Till Murder Do Us Part A Woman Scorned
Tim Burton's The Nightmare before Christmas The Nightmare before Christmas
Time Is on Our Side Let's Spend the Night Together
Tirez sur le Pianiste Shoot the Pianist
To Catch a Spy Catch Me a Spy
To Reach the Clouds The Walk
To the Victor Owd Bob
Todo Sobre Mi Madre All about My Mother
Tokyo Monogatari Tokyo Story
The Tomahawk and the Cross Pillars of the Sky
Tonight's the Night Happy Ever After
Too Dangerous to Love Perfect Strangers
Toto the Hero Toto Le Héros
A Town Called Bastard A Town Called Hell
Townies Bad Neighbours
The Trap The Baited Trap
37'2 le Matin Betty Blue
The Trial of Joan of Arc Le Procès de Jeanne d'Arc
Triple Deception House of Secrets
Trois Couleurs Blanc Three Colours White
Trois Couleurs Bleu Three Colours Blue
Trois Couleurs Rouge Three Colours Red
Trois Hommes à Abattre Three Men to Destroy
3 Hommes et un Couffin 3 Men and a Cradle
A Troll in Central Park Stanley's Magic Garden
Trouble in the Sky Cone of Silence
The Truth La Vérité
Truth or Dare In Bed with Madonna
La Tulipe Noire The Black Tulip
Tune in Tomorrow Aunt Julia and the Scriptwriter
The Turkish Bath Hamam: the Turkish Bath
Twilight Women Women of Twilight
Two Daughters Teen Kanya
Two English Girls Anne and Muriel
Two If by Sea Stolen Hearts
Tystnaden The Silence

Uccellacci e Uccellini Hawks and Sparrows
Ugly, Dirty and Bad Down and Dirty
La Ultima Cena The Last Supper
The Ultimate Solution of Grace Quigley Grace Quigley
L'Ultimo Tango a Parigi Last Tango in Paris
Under Satan's Sun Sous le Soleil de Satan
Under the Clock The Clock
Die Unendliche Geschichte The NeverEnding Story
The Unidentified Flying Oddball The Spaceman and King Arthur

L'Uomo delle Stelle The Starmaker

Les Vacances de Monsieur Hulot Monsieur Hulot's Holiday
Vacation from Marriage Perfect Strangers
Valley of Fury Chief Crazy Horse
Il Vangelo Secondo Matteo The Gospel According to St Matthew
Vérités et mensonges F for Fake
Vengeance The Brain
A Very Big Weekend A Man, a Woman and a Bank
Victory Escape to Victory
La Vie devant Soi Madame Rosa
La Vie Est un Long Fleuve Tranquille Life Is a Long Quiet River
La Vie Est un Roman Life Is a Bed of Roses
La Vie Rêvée des Anges The Dream Life of Angels
La Vieille Qui Marchait dans la Mer The Old Lady Who Walked in the Sea
The Visitors Les Visiteurs
La Vita E Bella Life Is Beautiful
Viva Las Vegas Meet Me in Las Vegas
A Voice in the Night Freedom Radio
Voices from the Killing Fields Enemies of the People
Vor The Thief
Voyage to Italy Journey to Italy
Voyage to the Beginning of the World Journey to the Beginning of the World

W

Waking Ned Devine Waking Ned
Wall of Death There Is Another Sun
War Gods of the Deep City under the Sea
The War Is Over La Guerre Est Finie
War of the Monsters Godzilla vs Gigan
Warlords of the 21st Century Battletruck
The Warning Without Warning
The Warriors The Dark Avenger
Web of Evidence Beyond This Place
Wedding Bells Royal Wedding
Wedding Breakfast The Catered Affair
Wee Geordie Geordie
Wendy Cracked a Walnut Almost
We're in the Army Now Pack Up Your Troubles
Wes Craven's Chiller Chiller
What a Man Never Give a Sucker an Even Break
What Lola Wants Damn Yankees
What's Love Got to Do with It Tina: What's Love Got to Do with It
When I Fall in Love Everybody's All-American
Where the River Bends Bend of the River
Where There's a Will Good Morning, Boys
Whiskey Down Just Your Luck
White Three Colours White
The Wild Child L'Enfant Sauvage
Wild for Kicks Beat Girl
The Wild Game Jail Bait
The Wild Heart Gone to Earth
The Wild Reeds Les Roseaux Sauvages
William Faulkner's Old Man Old Man
A Window to the Sky The Other Side of the Mountain
The Winged Serpent Q - the Winged Serpent
Wings and the Woman They Flew Alone
Winning Streak Stacy's Knights
A Woman Destroyed Smash Up - the Story of a Woman
The Woman Between The Woman I Love
The Woman in His House The Animal Kingdom
Wonderful to be Young! The Young Ones
The Word Ordet
Wrong Is Right The Man with the Deadly Lens

X

X: the Man with the X-Ray Eyes The Man with the X-Ray Eyes
X, Y and Zee Zee and Co

Y

A Yank in London I Live in Grosvenor Square
Years without Days Castle on the Hudson
The Yellow Winton Flyer The Reivers
Les Yeux sans Visage Eyes without a Face
Yo, la Peor de Todas I, the Worst of All
You Belong to My Heart Mr Imperium
You Can't Sleep Here I Was a Male War Bride
You Can't Take Money Internes Can't Take Money
Young & Beautiful Jeune & Jolie
Young Man of Music Young Man with a Horn
Young Scarface Brighton Rock
Young Sherlock Holmes and the Pyramid of Fear Young Sherlock Holmes
Zemlya Earth

Z

Zentropa Europa
Zero Population Growth ZPG: Zero Population Growth
Zombies: Dawn of the Dead Dawn of the Dead
Zoo A Zed & Two Noughts
Zoya Danielle Steel's Zoya

Awards

1927/28

Academy Awards

OUTSTANDING PICTURE: **Wings** • The Last Command • The Racket • 7th Heaven • The Way of All Flesh
UNIQUE/ARTISTIC PICTURE: **Sunrise** • Chang • The Crowd
DIRECTOR, DRAMA: **Frank Borzage** 7th Heaven • Herbert Brenon Sorrell and Son • King Vidor The Crowd
DIRECTOR, COMEDY: **Lewis Milestone** Two Arabian Knights • Charles Chaplin The Circus • Ted Wilde Speedy
ACTOR: **Emil Jannings** The Last Command; The Way of All Flesh • Richard Barthelmess The Noose; The Patent Leather Kid • Charles Chaplin The Circus
ACTRESS: **Janet Gaynor** 7th Heaven; Street Angel; Sunrise • Louise Dresser A Ship Comes In • Gloria Swanson Sadie Thompson
STORY: **Ben Hecht** Underworld • Lajos Biró The Last Command • Rupert Hughes The Patent Leather Kid
ADAPTATION: **Benjamin Glazer** 7th Heaven • Al Cohn The Jazz Singer • Anthony Coldeway Glorious Betsy
TITLES: **Joseph Farnham** Telling the World • Gerald Duffy The Private Life of Helen of Troy • Joseph Farnham The Fair Co-Ed; Laugh, Clown, Laugh • George Marion Jr Oh Kay!

1928/29

Academy Awards

PICTURE: **The Broadway Melody** • Alibi • Hollywood Revue • In Old Arizona • The Patriot
DIRECTOR: **Frank Lloyd** The Divine Lady • Lionel Barrymore Madame X • Harry Beaumont The Broadway Melody • Irving Cummings In Old Arizona • Frank Lloyd Drag; Weary River • Ernst Lubitsch The Patriot
ACTOR: **Warner Baxter** In Old Arizona • George Bancroft Thunderbolt • Chester Morris Alibi • Paul Muni The Valiant • Lewis Stone The Patriot
ACTRESS: **Mary Pickford** Coquette • Ruth Chatterton Madame X • Betty Compson The Barker • Jeanne Eagels The Letter • Corinne Griffith The Divine Lady • Bessie Love The Broadway Melody
WRITING: **Hans Kräly** The Patriot • Tom Barry In Old Arizona; The Valiant • Elliott Clawson The Cop; The Leatherneck; Sal of Singapore; Skyscraper • Hans Kräly The Last of Mrs Cheyney • Josephine Lovett Our Dancing Daughters • Bess Meredyth A Woman of Affairs; Wonder of Women

1929/30

Academy Awards

PRODUCTION: **All Quiet on the Western Front** • The Big House • Disraeli • The Divorcee • The Love Parade
DIRECTOR: **Lewis Milestone** All Quiet on the Western Front • Clarence Brown Anna Christie; Romance • Robert Z Leonard The Divorcee • Ernst Lubitsch The Love Parade • King Vidor Hallelujah
ACTOR: **George Arliss** Disraeli • George Arliss The Green Goddess • Wallace Beery The Big House • Maurice Chevalier The Big Pond; The Love Parade • Ronald Colman Bulldog Drummond; Condemned • Lawrence Tibbett The Rogue Song
ACTRESS: **Norma Shearer** The Divorcee • Nancy Carroll The Devil's Holiday • Ruth Chatterton Sarah and Son • Greta Garbo Anna Christie; Romance • Norma Shearer Their Own Desire • Gloria Swanson The Trespasser
WRITING: **Frances Marion** The Big House • Maxwell Anderson, George Abbott, Del Andrews All Quiet on the Western Front • Howard Estabrook Street of Chance • Julien Josephson Disraeli • John Meehan The Divorcee

1930/31

Academy Awards

PRODUCTION: **Cimarron** • East Lynne • The Front Page • Skippy • Trader Horn
DIRECTOR: **Norman Taurog** Skippy • Clarence Brown A Free Soul • Lewis Milestone The Front Page • Wesley Ruggles Cimarron • Josef von Sternberg Morocco
ACTOR: **Lionel Barrymore** A Free Soul • Jackie Cooper Skippy • Richard Dix Cimarron • Fredric March The Royal Family of Broadway • Adolphe Menjou The Front Page
ACTRESS: **Marie Dressler** Min and Bill • Marlene Dietrich Morocco • Irene Dunne Cimarron • Ann Harding Holiday • Norma Shearer A Free Soul
STORY: **John Monk Saunders** The Dawn Patrol • Rowland Brown Doorway to Hell • Harry d'Abbadie D'Arrast, Douglas Doty, Donald Ogden Stewart Laughter • Kubec Glasmon, John Bright The Public Enemy • Lucien Hubbard, Joseph Jackson Smart Money
ADAPTATION: **Howard Estabrook** Cimarron • Fred Niblo Jr, Seton I Miller The Criminal Code • Horace Jackson Holiday • Robert N Lee, Francis Edward Faragoh Little Caesar • Joseph L Mankiewicz, Sam Mintz Skippy

1931/32

Academy Awards

PRODUCTION: **Grand Hotel** • Arrowsmith • Bad Girl • The Champ • Five Star Final • One Hour with You • Shanghai Express • The Smiling Lieutenant
DIRECTOR: **Frank Borzage** Bad Girl • King Vidor The Champ • Josef von Sternberg Shanghai Express
ACTOR: **Wallace Beery** The Champ • **Fredric March** Dr Jekyll and Mr Hyde • Alfred Lunt The Guardsman
ACTRESS: **Helen Hayes** The Sin of Madelon Claudet • Marie Dressler Emma • Lynn Fontanne The Guardsman

STORY: **Frances Marion** The Champ • Lucien Hubbard The Star Witness • Grover Jones, William Slavens McNutt Lady and Gent • Jane Murfin, Adela Rogers St John What Price Hollywood?
ADAPTATION: **Edwin Burke** Bad Girl • Percy Heath, Samuel Hoffenstein Dr Jekyll and Mr Hyde • Sidney Howard Arrowsmith

1932/33

Academy Awards

PRODUCTION: **Cavalcade** • A Farewell to Arms • 42nd Street • I Am a Fugitive from a Chain Gang • Lady for a Day • Little Women • The Private Life of Henry VIII • She Done Him Wrong • Smilin' Through • State Fair
DIRECTOR: **Frank Lloyd** Cavalcade • Frank Capra Lady for a Day • George Cukor Little Women
ACTOR: **Charles Laughton** The Private Life of Henry VIII • Leslie Howard Berkeley Square • Paul Muni I Am a Fugitive from a Chain Gang
ACTRESS: **Katharine Hepburn** Morning Glory • May Robson Lady for a Day • Diana Wynyard Cavalcade
STORY: **Robert Lord** One Way Passage • Charles MacArthur Rasputin and the Empress • Frances Marion The Prizefighter and the Lady
ADAPTATION: **Sarah Y Mason, Victor Heerman** Little Women • Paul Green, Sonya Levien State Fair • Robert Riskin Lady for a Day

1934

Academy Awards

PRODUCTION: **It Happened One Night** • The Barretts of Wimpole Street • Cleopatra • Flirtation Walk • The Gay Divorcee • Here Comes the Navy • The House of Rothschild • Imitation of Life • One Night of Love • The Thin Man • Viva Villa! • The White Parade
DIRECTOR: **Frank Capra** It Happened One Night • Victor Schertzinger One Night of Love • W S Van Dyke The Thin Man
ACTOR: **Clark Gable** It Happened One Night • Frank Morgan The Affairs of Cellini • William Powell The Thin Man
ACTRESS: **Claudette Colbert** It Happened One Night • Bette Davis Of Human Bondage • Grace Moore One Night of Love • Norma Shearer The Barretts of Wimpole Street
STORY: **Arthur Caesar** Manhattan Melodrama • Mauri Grashin Hide-Out • Norman Krasna The Richest Girl in the World
ADAPTATION: **Robert Riskin** It Happened One Night • Albert Hackett, Frances Goodrich The Thin Man • Ben Hecht Viva Villa!

1935

Academy Awards

PRODUCTION: **Mutiny on the Bounty** • Alice Adams • Broadway Melody of 1936 • Captain Blood • David Copperfield • The Informer • The Lives of a Bengal Lancer • A Midsummer Night's Dream • Les Misérables • Naughty Marietta • Ruggles of Red Gap • Top Hat
DIRECTOR: **John Ford** The Informer • Michael Curtiz Captain Blood • Henry Hathaway The Lives of a Bengal Lancer • Frank Lloyd Mutiny on the Bounty
ACTOR: **Victor McLaglen** The Informer • Clark Gable, Charles Laughton Mutiny on the Bounty • Paul Muni Black Fury • Franchot Tone Mutiny on the Bounty
ACTRESS: **Bette Davis** Dangerous • Elisabeth Bergner Escape Me Never • Claudette Colbert Private Worlds • Katharine Hepburn Alice Adams • Miriam Hopkins Becky Sharp • Merle Oberon The Dark Angel
SCREENPLAY: **Dudley Nichols** The Informer • Achmed Abdullah, John L Balderston, Grover Jones, William Slavens McNutt, Waldemar Young The Lives of a Bengal Lancer • Jules Furthman, Talbot Jennings, Carey Wilson Mutiny on the Bounty • Casey Robinson Captain Blood
STORY: **Ben Hecht, Charles MacArthur** The Scoundrel • Moss Hart Broadway Melody of 1936 • Stephen Morehouse Avery, Don Hartman The Gay Deception • Gregory Rogers "G" Men

1936

Academy Awards

PRODUCTION: **The Great Ziegfeld** • Anthony Adverse • Dodsworth • Libeled Lady • Mr Deeds Goes to Town • Romeo and Juliet • San Francisco • The Story of Louis Pasteur • A Tale of Two Cities • Three Smart Girls
DIRECTOR: **Frank Capra** Mr Deeds Goes to Town • Gregory La Cava My Man Godfrey • Robert Z Leonard The Great Ziegfeld • W S Van Dyke San Francisco • William Wyler Dodsworth
ACTOR: **Paul Muni** The Story of Louis Pasteur • Gary Cooper Mr Deeds Goes to Town • Walter Huston Dodsworth • William Powell My Man Godfrey • Spencer Tracy San Francisco
ACTRESS: **Luise Rainer** The Great Ziegfeld • Irene Dunne Theodora Goes Wild • Gladys George Valiant Is the Word for Carrie • Carole Lombard My Man Godfrey • Norma Shearer Romeo and Juliet
SUPPORTING ACTOR: **Walter Brennan** Come and Get It • Mischa Auer My Man Godfrey • Stuart Erwin Pigskin Parade • Basil Rathbone Romeo and Juliet • Akim Tamiroff The General Died at Dawn
SUPPORTING ACTRESS: **Gale Sondergaard** Anthony Adverse • Beulah Bondi The Gorgeous Hussy • Alice Brady My Man Godfrey • Bonita Granville These Three • Maria Ouspenskaya Dodsworth
SCREENPLAY: **Sheridan Gibney, Pierre Collings** The Story of Louis Pasteur • Frances Goodrich, Albert Hackett After the

Thin Man • Sidney Howard Dodsworth • Robert Riskin Mr Deeds Goes to Town • Morrie Ryskind, Eric Hatch My Man Godfrey
STORY: **Sheridan Gibney, Pierre Collings** The Story of Louis Pasteur • Adele Comandini Three Smart Girls • Robert Hopkins San Francisco • Norman Krasna Fury • William Anthony McGuire The Great Ziegfeld

1937

Academy Awards

PRODUCTION: **The Life of Emile Zola** • The Awful Truth • Captains Courageous • Dead End • The Good Earth • In Old Chicago • Lost Horizon • One Hundred Men and a Girl • Stage Door • A Star Is Born
DIRECTOR: **Leo McCarey** The Awful Truth • William Dieterle The Life of Emile Zola • Sidney Franklin The Good Earth • Gregory La Cava Stage Door • William A Wellman A Star Is Born
ACTOR: **Spencer Tracy** Captains Courageous • Charles Boyer Conquest • Fredric March A Star Is Born • Robert Montgomery Night Must Fall • Paul Muni The Life of Emile Zola
ACTRESS: **Luise Rainer** The Good Earth • Irene Dunne The Awful Truth • Greta Garbo Camille • Janet Gaynor A Star Is Born • Barbara Stanwyck Stella Dallas
SUPPORTING ACTOR: **Joseph Schildkraut** The Life of Emile Zola • Ralph Bellamy The Awful Truth • Thomas Mitchell The Hurricane • H B Warner Lost Horizon • Roland Young Topper
SUPPORTING ACTRESS: **Alice Brady** In Old Chicago • Andrea Leeds Stage Door • Anne Shirley Stella Dallas • Claire Trevor Dead End • Dame May Whitty Night Must Fall
SCREENPLAY: **Norman Reilly Raine, Heinz Herald, Geza Herczeg** The Life of Emile Zola • Vina Delmar The Awful Truth • Marc Connelly, Dale Van Every, John Lee Mahin Captains Courageous • Morrie Ryskind, Anthony Veiller Stage Door • Alan Campbell, Robert Carson, Dorothy Parker A Star Is Born
STORY: **William A Wellman, Robert Carson** A Star Is Born • Niven Busch In Old Chicago • Heinz Herald, Geza Herczeg The Life of Emile Zola • Hans Kräly One Hundred Men and a Girl • Robert Lord The Black Legion

1938

Academy Awards

PRODUCTION: **You Can't Take It with You** • The Adventures of Robin Hood • Alexander's Ragtime Band • Boys Town • The Citadel • Four Daughters • La Grande Illusion • Jezebel • Pygmalion • Test Pilot
DIRECTOR: **Frank Capra** You Can't Take It with You • Michael Curtiz Angels with Dirty Faces; Four Daughters • Norman Taurog Boys Town • King Vidor The Citadel
ACTOR: **Spencer Tracy** Boys Town • Charles Boyer Algiers • James Cagney Angels with Dirty Faces • Robert Donat The Citadel • Leslie Howard Pygmalion
ACTRESS: **Bette Davis** Jezebel • Fay Bainter White Banners • Wendy Hiller Pygmalion • Norma Shearer Marie Antoinette • Margaret Sullavan Three Comrades
SUPPORTING ACTOR: **Walter Brennan** Kentucky • John Garfield Four Daughters • Gene Lockhart Algiers • Robert Morley Marie Antoinette • Basil Rathbone If I Were King
SUPPORTING ACTRESS: **Fay Bainter** Jezebel • Beulah Bondi Of Human Hearts • Billie Burke Merrily We Live • Spring Byington You Can't Take It with You • Miliza Korjus The Great Waltz
SCREENPLAY: **Ian Dalrymple, Cecil Lewis, WP Lipscomb, George Bernard Shaw** Pygmalion • Ian Dalrymple, Elizabeth Hill, Frank Wead The Citadel • Julius J Epstein, Lenore Coffee Four Daughters • John Meehan, Dore Schary Boys Town • Robert Riskin You Can't Take It with You
STORY: **Dore Schary, Eleanore Griffin** Boys Town • Irving Berlin Alexander's Ragtime Band • Rowland Brown Angels with Dirty Faces • Marcella Burke, Frederick Kohner Mad about Music • John Howard Lawson Blockade • Frank Wead Test Pilot

1939

Academy Awards

PRODUCTION: **Gone with the Wind** • Dark Victory • Goodbye, Mr Chips • Love Affair • Mr Smith Goes to Washington • Ninotchka • Of Mice and Men • Stagecoach • The Wizard of Oz • Wuthering Heights
DIRECTOR: **Victor Fleming** Gone with the Wind • Frank Capra Mr Smith Goes to Washington • John Ford Stagecoach • Sam Wood Goodbye, Mr Chips • William Wyler Wuthering Heights
ACTOR: **Robert Donat** Goodbye, Mr Chips • Clark Gable Gone with the Wind • Laurence Olivier Wuthering Heights • Mickey Rooney Babes in Arms • James Stewart Mr Smith Goes to Washington
ACTRESS: **Vivien Leigh** Gone with the Wind • Bette Davis Dark Victory • Irene Dunne Love Affair • Greta Garbo Ninotchka • Greer Garson Goodbye, Mr Chips
SUPPORTING ACTOR: **Thomas Mitchell** Stagecoach • Brian Aherne Juarez • Harry Carey Mr Smith Goes to Washington • Brian Donlevy Beau Geste • Claude Rains Mr Smith Goes to Washington
SUPPORTING ACTRESS: **Hattie McDaniel** Gone with the Wind • Olivia de Havilland Gone with the Wind • Geraldine Fitzgerald Wuthering Heights • Edna May Oliver Drums along the Mohawk • Maria Ouspenskaya Love Affair
SCREENPLAY: **Sidney Howard** Gone with the Wind • R C Sherriff, Claudine West, Eric Maschwitz Goodbye, Mr Chips • Sidney Buchman Mr Smith Goes to Washington • Charles Brackett, Walter Reisch, Billy Wilder Ninotchka • Ben Hecht, Charles MacArthur Wuthering Heights

STORY: **Sidney Buchman** *Mr Smith Goes to Washington* • Felix Jackson *Bachelor Mother* • Mildred Cram, Leo McCarey *Love Affair* • Melchior Lengyel *Ninotchka* • Lamar Trotti *Young Mr Lincoln*

1940

Academy Awards

PRODUCTION: **Rebecca** • *All This, and Heaven Too* • *Foreign Correspondent* • *The Grapes of Wrath* • *The Great Dictator* • *Kitty Foyle* • *The Letter* • *The Long Voyage Home* • *Our Town* • *The Philadelphia Story*

DIRECTOR: **John Ford** *The Grapes of Wrath* • George Cukor *The Philadelphia Story* • Alfred Hitchcock *Rebecca* • Sam Wood *Kitty Foyle* • William Wyler *The Letter*

ACTOR: **James Stewart** *The Philadelphia Story* • Charles Chaplin *The Great Dictator* • Henry Fonda *The Grapes of Wrath* • Raymond Massey *Spirit of the People* • Laurence Olivier *Rebecca*

ACTRESS: **Ginger Rogers** *Kitty Foyle* • Bette Davis *The Letter* • Joan Fontaine *Rebecca* • Katharine Hepburn *The Philadelphia Story* • Martha Scott *Our Town*

SUPPORTING ACTOR: **Walter Brennan** *The Westerner* • Albert Basserman *Foreign Correspondent* • William Gargan *They Knew What They Wanted* • Jack Oakie *The Great Dictator* • James Stephenson *The Letter*

SUPPORTING ACTRESS: **Jane Darwell** *The Grapes of Wrath* • Judith Anderson *Rebecca* • Ruth Hussey *The Philadelphia Story* • Barbara O'Neil *All This, and Heaven Too* • Marjorie Rambeau *Primrose Path*

SCREENPLAY: **Preston Sturges** *The Great McGinty* • Ben Hecht *Angels over Broadway* • Norman Burnside, Heinz Herald, John Huston *Dr Ehrlich's Magic Bullet* • Charles Bennett, Joan Harrison *Foreign Correspondent* • Charles Chaplin *The Great Dictator*

STORY: **Benjamin Glazer, John S Toldy** *Arise, My Love* • Walter Reisch *Comrade X* • Dore Schary, Hugo Butler *Edison, the Man* • Leo McCarey, Bella Spewack, Sam Spewack *My Favorite Wife* • Stuart N Lake *The Westerner*

ADAPTED SCREENPLAY: **Donald Ogden Stewart** *The Philadelphia Story* • Nunnally Johnson *The Grapes of Wrath* • Dalton Trumbo *Kitty Foyle* • Dudley Nichols *The Long Voyage Home* • Robert E Sherwood, Joan Harrison *Rebecca*

1941

Academy Awards

PICTURE: **How Green Was My Valley** • *Blossoms in the Dust* • *Citizen Kane* • *Here Comes Mr Jordan* • *Hold Back the Dawn* • *The Little Foxes* • *The Maltese Falcon* • *One Foot in Heaven* • *Sergeant York* • *Suspicion*

DIRECTOR: **John Ford** *How Green Was My Valley* • Alexander Hall *Here Comes Mr Jordan* • Howard Hawks *Sergeant York* • Orson Welles *Citizen Kane* • William Wyler *The Little Foxes*

ACTOR: **Gary Cooper** *Sergeant York* • Cary Grant *Penny Serenade* • Walter Huston *Daniel and the Devil* • Robert Montgomery *Here Comes Mr Jordan* • Orson Welles *Citizen Kane*

ACTRESS: **Joan Fontaine** *Suspicion* • Bette Davis *The Little Foxes* • Olivia de Havilland *Hold Back the Dawn* • Greer Garson *Blossoms in the Dust* • Barbara Stanwyck *Ball of Fire*

SUPPORTING ACTOR: **Donald Crisp** *How Green Was My Valley* • Walter Brennan *Sergeant York* • Charles Coburn *The Devil and Miss Jones* • James Gleason *Here Comes Mr Jordan* • Sydney Greenstreet *The Maltese Falcon*

SUPPORTING ACTRESS: **Mary Astor** *The Great Lie* • Sara Allgood *How Green Was My Valley* • Patricia Collinge, Teresa Wright *The Little Foxes* • Margaret Wycherly *Sergeant York*

ORIGINAL SCREENPLAY: **Herman J Mankiewicz, Orson Welles** *Citizen Kane* • Norman Krasna *The Devil and Miss Jones* • Abem Finkel, Harry Chandlee, Howard Koch, John Huston *Sergeant York* • Karl Tunberg, Darrell Ware *Tall, Dark and Handsome* • Paul Jarrico *Tom, Dick and Harry*

STORY: **Harry Segall** *Here Comes Mr Jordan* • Thomas Monroe, Billy Wilder *Ball of Fire* • Monckton Hoffe *The Lady Eve* • Robert Presnell, Richard Connell *Meet John Doe* • Gordon Wellesley *Night Train to Munich*

ADAPTED SCREENPLAY: **Sidney Buchman, Seton I Miller** *Here Comes Mr Jordan* • Charles Brackett, Billy Wilder *Hold Back the Dawn* • Philip Dunne *How Green Was My Valley* • Lillian Hellman *The Little Foxes* • John Huston *The Maltese Falcon*

1942

Academy Awards

PICTURE: **Mrs Miniver** • *49th Parallel* • *Kings Row* • *The Magnificent Ambersons* • *The Pied Piper* • *The Pride of the Yankees* • *Random Harvest* • *The Talk of the Town* • *Wake Island* • *Yankee Doodle Dandy*

DIRECTOR: **William Wyler** *Mrs Miniver* • Michael Curtiz *Yankee Doodle Dandy* • John Farrow *Wake Island* • Mervyn LeRoy *Random Harvest* • Sam Wood *Kings Row*

ACTOR: **James Cagney** *Yankee Doodle Dandy* • Ronald Colman *Random Harvest* • Gary Cooper *The Pride of the Yankees* • Walter Pidgeon *Mrs Miniver* • Monty Woolley *The Pied Piper*

ACTRESS: **Greer Garson** *Mrs Miniver* • Bette Davis *Now, Voyager* • Katharine Hepburn *Woman of the Year* • Rosalind Russell *My Sister Eileen* • Teresa Wright *The Pride of the Yankees*

SUPPORTING ACTOR: **Van Heflin** *Johnny Eager* • William Bendix *Wake Island* • Walter Huston *Yankee Doodle Dandy* • Frank Morgan *Tortilla Flat* • Henry Travers *Mrs Miniver*

SUPPORTING ACTRESS: **Teresa Wright** *Mrs Miniver* • Gladys Cooper *Now, Voyager* • Agnes Moorehead *The Magnificent Ambersons* • Susan Peters *Random Harvest* • Dame May Whitty *Mrs Miniver*

ORIGINAL SCREENPLAY: **Michael Kanin, Ring Lardner Jr** *Woman of the Year* • Michael Powell, Emeric Pressburger *One of Our Aircraft Is Missing* • Don Hartman, Frank Butler *Road to Morocco* • W R Burnett, Frank Butler *Wake Island* • George Oppenheimer *The War against Mrs Hadley*

ADAPTED SCREENPLAY: **Arthur Wimperis, George Froeschel, James Hilton, Claudine West** *Mrs Miniver* • Emeric Pressburger, Rodney Ackland *49th Parallel* • Herman J Mankiewicz, Jo Swerling *The Pride of the Yankees* • George Froeschel, Claudine West, Arthur Wimperis *Random Harvest* • Irwin Shaw, Sidney Buchman *The Talk of the Town*

STORY: **Emeric Pressburger** *49th Parallel* • Irving Berlin *Holiday Inn* • Paul Gallico *The Pride of the Yankees* • Sidney Harmon *The Talk of the Town* • Robert Buckner *Yankee Doodle Dandy*

1943

Academy Awards

PICTURE: **Casablanca** • *Disraeli* • *Heaven Can Wait* • *The Human Comedy* • *In Which We Serve* • *Madame Curie* • *The More the Merrier* • *The Ox-Bow Incident* • *The Song of Bernadette* • *Watch on the Rhine*

DIRECTOR: **Michael Curtiz** *Casablanca* • Clarence Brown *The Human Comedy* • Henry King *The Song of Bernadette* • Ernst Lubitsch *Heaven Can Wait* • George Stevens *The More the Merrier*

ACTOR: **Paul Lukas** *Watch on the Rhine* • Humphrey Bogart *Casablanca* • Gary Cooper *For Whom the Bell Tolls* • Walter Pidgeon *Madame Curie* • Mickey Rooney *The Human Comedy*

ACTRESS: **Jennifer Jones** *The Song of Bernadette* • Jean Arthur *The More the Merrier* • Ingrid Bergman *For Whom the Bell Tolls* • Joan Fontaine *The Constant Nymph* • Greer Garson *Madame Curie*

SUPPORTING ACTOR: **Charles Coburn** *The More the Merrier* • Charles Bickford *The Song of Bernadette* • J Carrol Naish *Sahara* • Claude Rains *Casablanca* • Akim Tamiroff *For Whom the Bell Tolls*

SUPPORTING ACTRESS: **Katina Paxinou** *For Whom the Bell Tolls* • Gladys Cooper *The Song of Bernadette* • Paulette Goddard *So Proudly We Hail* • Anne Revere *The Song of Bernadette* • Lucile Watson *Watch on the Rhine*

ORIGINAL SCREENPLAY: **Norman Krasna** *Princess O'Rourke* • Dudley Nichols *Air Force* • Noël Coward *In Which We Serve* • Lillian Hellman *The North Star* • Allan Scott *So Proudly We Hail*

ADAPTED SCREENPLAY: **Philip G Epstein, Julius J Epstein, Howard Koch** *Casablanca* • Nunnally Johnson *Holy Matrimony* • Robert Russell, Frank Ross, Richard Flournoy, Lewis R Foster *The More the Merrier* • George Seaton *The Song of Bernadette* • Dashiell Hammett *Watch on the Rhine*

STORY: **William Saroyan** *The Human Comedy* • Guy Gilpatric *Action in the North Atlantic* • Delmer Daves *Destination Tokyo* • Robert Russell, Frank Ross *The More the Merrier* • Gordon McDonell *Shadow of a Doubt*

Golden Globe Awards

PICTURE: **The Song of Bernadette**
DIRECTOR: **Henry King** *The Song of Bernadette*
ACTOR: **Paul Lukas** *Watch on the Rhine*
ACTRESS: **Jennifer Jones** *The Song of Bernadette*
SUPPORTING ACTOR: **Akim Tamiroff** *For Whom the Bell Tolls*
SUPPORTING ACTRESS: **Katina Paxinou** *For Whom the Bell Tolls*

1944

Academy Awards

PICTURE: **Going My Way** • *Double Indemnity* • *Gaslight* • *Since You Went Away* • *Wilson*

DIRECTOR: **Leo McCarey** *Going My Way* • Alfred Hitchcock *Lifeboat* • Henry King *Wilson* • Otto Preminger *Laura* • Billy Wilder *Double Indemnity*

ACTOR: **Bing Crosby** *Going My Way* • Charles Boyer *Gaslight* • Barry Fitzgerald *Going My Way* • Cary Grant *None but the Lonely Heart* • Alexander Knox *Wilson*

ACTRESS: **Ingrid Bergman** *Gaslight* • Claudette Colbert *Since You Went Away* • Bette Davis *Mr Skeffington* • Greer Garson *Mrs Parkington* • Barbara Stanwyck *Double Indemnity*

SUPPORTING ACTOR: **Barry Fitzgerald** *Going My Way* • Hume Cronyn *The Seventh Cross* • Claude Rains *Mr Skeffington* • Clifton Webb *Laura* • Monty Woolley *Since You Went Away*

SUPPORTING ACTRESS: **Ethel Barrymore** *None but the Lonely Heart* • Jennifer Jones *Since You Went Away* • Angela Lansbury *Gaslight* • Aline MacMahon *Dragon Seed* • Agnes Moorehead *Mrs Parkington*

ORIGINAL SCREENPLAY: **Lamar Trotti** *Wilson* • Preston Sturges *Hail the Conquering Hero* • Preston Sturges *The Miracle of Morgan's Creek* • Richard Connell, Gladys Lehman *Two Girls and a Sailor* • Jerome Cady *Wing and a Prayer*

ADAPTED SCREENPLAY: **Frank Butler, Frank Cavett** *Going My Way* • Billy Wilder, Raymond Chandler *Double Indemnity* • Walter Reisch, John L Balderston, John Van Druten *Gaslight* • Jay Dratler, Betty Reinhardt, Samuel Hoffenstein *Laura* • Irving Brecher, Fred F Finklehoffe *Meet Me in St Louis*

STORY: **Leo McCarey** *Going My Way* • Chandler Sprague, David Boehm *A Guy Named Joe* • John Steinbeck *Lifeboat* • Alfred Neumann, Joseph Than *None Shall Escape* • Edward Doherty, Jules Schermer *The Fighting Sullivans*

Golden Globe Awards

PICTURE: **Going My Way**
DIRECTOR: **Leo McCarey** *Going My Way*
ACTOR: **Alexander Knox** *Wilson*
ACTRESS: **Ingrid Bergman** *Gaslight*
SUPPORTING ACTOR: **Barry Fitzgerald** *Going My Way*
SUPPORTING ACTRESS: **Agnes Moorehead** *Mrs Parkington*

1945

Academy Awards

PICTURE: **The Lost Weekend** • *Anchors Aweigh* • *The Bells of St Mary's* • *Mildred Pierce* • *Spellbound*

DIRECTOR: **Billy Wilder** *The Lost Weekend* • Clarence Brown *National Velvet* • Alfred Hitchcock *Spellbound* • Leo McCarey *The Bells of St Mary's* • Jean Renoir *The Southerner*

ACTOR: **Ray Milland** *The Lost Weekend* • Bing Crosby *The Bells of St Mary's* • Gene Kelly *Anchors Aweigh* • Gregory Peck *The Keys of the Kingdom* • Cornel Wilde *A Song to Remember*

ACTRESS: **Joan Crawford** *Mildred Pierce* • Ingrid Bergman *The Bells of St Mary's* • Greer Garson *The Valley of Decision* • Jennifer Jones *Love Letters* • Gene Tierney *Leave Her to Heaven*

SUPPORTING ACTOR: **James Dunn** *A Tree Grows in Brooklyn* • Michael Chekhov *Spellbound* • John Dall *The Corn Is Green* • Robert Mitchum *The Story of GI Joe* • J Carrol Naish *A Medal for Benny*

SUPPORTING ACTRESS: **Anne Revere** *National Velvet* • Eve Arden, Ann Blyth *Mildred Pierce* • Angela Lansbury *The Picture of Dorian Gray* • Joan Lorring *The Corn Is Green*

ORIGINAL SCREENPLAY: **Richard Schweizer** *Marie-Louise* • Phil Yordan *Dillinger* • Myles Connolly *Music for Millions* • Milton Holmes *Salty O'Rourke* • Harry Kurnitz *See Here, Private Hargrove*

ADAPTED SCREENPLAY: **Charles Brackett, Billy Wilder** *The Lost Weekend* • Leopold Atlas, Guy Endore, Philip Stevenson *The Story of GI Joe* • Ranald MacDougall *Mildred Pierce* • Albert Maltz *Pride of the Marines* • Frank Davis, Tess Slesinger *A Tree Grows in Brooklyn*

STORY: **Charles G Booth** *The House on 92nd Street* • Thomas Monroe, Laszlo Gorog *The Affairs of Susan* • John Steinbeck, Jack Wagner *A Medal for Benny* • Alvah Bessie *Objective, Burma!* • Ernst Marischka *A Song to Remember*

Golden Globe Awards

PICTURE: **The Lost Weekend**
DIRECTOR: **Billy Wilder** *The Lost Weekend*
ACTOR: **Ray Milland** *The Lost Weekend*
ACTRESS: **Ingrid Bergman** *The Bells of St Mary's*
SUPPORTING ACTOR: **J Carrol Naish** *A Medal for Benny*
SUPPORTING ACTRESS: **Angela Lansbury** *The Picture of Dorian Gray*

1946

Academy Awards

PICTURE: **The Best Years of Our Lives** • *Henry V* • *It's a Wonderful Life* • *The Razor's Edge* • *The Yearling*

DIRECTOR: **William Wyler** *The Best Years of Our Lives* • Clarence Brown *The Yearling* • Frank Capra *It's a Wonderful Life* • David Lean *Brief Encounter* • Robert Siodmak *The Killers*

ACTOR: **Fredric March** *The Best Years of Our Lives* • Laurence Olivier *Henry V* • Larry Parks *The Jolson Story* • Gregory Peck *The Yearling* • James Stewart *It's a Wonderful Life*

ACTRESS: **Olivia de Havilland** *To Each His Own* • Celia Johnson *Brief Encounter* • Jennifer Jones *Duel in the Sun* • Rosalind Russell *Sister Kenny* • Jane Wyman *The Yearling*

SUPPORTING ACTOR: **Harold Russell** *The Best Years of Our Lives* • Charles Coburn *The Green Years* • William Demarest *The Jolson Story* • Claude Rains *Notorious* • Clifton Webb *The Razor's Edge*

SUPPORTING ACTRESS: **Anne Baxter** *The Razor's Edge* • Ethel Barrymore *The Spiral Staircase* • Lillian Gish *Duel in the Sun* • Flora Robson *Saratoga Trunk* • Gale Sondergaard *Anna and the King of Siam*

ORIGINAL SCREENPLAY: **Sydney Box, Muriel Box** *The Seventh Veil* • Raymond Chandler *The Blue Dahlia* • Jacques Prévert *Les Enfants du Paradis* • Ben Hecht *Notorious* • Melvin Frank, Norman Panama *Road to Utopia*

ADAPTED SCREENPLAY: **Robert E Sherwood** *The Best Years of Our Lives* • Talbot Jennings, Sally Benson *Anna and the King of Siam* • David Lean, Anthony Havelock-Allan, Ronald Neame *Brief Encounter* • Anthony Veiller *The Killers* • Sergio Amidei, Federico Fellini *Rome, Open City*

STORY: **Clemence Dane** *Perfect Strangers* • Vladimir Pozner *The Dark Mirror* • Jack Patrick *The Strange Love of Martha Ivers* • Victor Trivas *The Stranger* • Charles Brackett *To Each His Own*

Golden Globe Awards

PICTURE: **The Best Years of Our Lives**
DIRECTOR: **Frank Capra** *It's a Wonderful Life*
ACTOR: **Gregory Peck** *The Yearling*
ACTRESS: **Rosalind Russell** *Sister Kenny*
SUPPORTING ACTOR: **Clifton Webb** *The Razor's Edge*
SUPPORTING ACTRESS: **Anne Baxter** *The Razor's Edge*

Cannes Film Festival

INTERNATIONAL JURY PRIZE: **La Bataille du Rail**
DIRECTOR: **René Clément** *La Bataille du Rail*
ACTOR: **Ray Milland** *The Lost Weekend*
ACTRESS: **Michèle Morgan** *La Symphonie Pastorale*
SCREENPLAY: **Boris Tchirkov** *The Turning Point*

1947

British Film Academy Awards

FILM: **The Best Years of Our Lives**
BRITISH FILM: **Odd Man Out**

Academy Awards

PICTURE: **Gentleman's Agreement** • *The Bishop's Wife* • *Crossfire* • *Great Expectations* • *Miracle on 34th Street*

DIRECTOR: **Elia Kazan** *Gentleman's Agreement* • George Cukor *A Double Life* • Edward Dmytryk *Crossfire* • Henry Koster *The Bishop's Wife* • David Lean *Great Expectations*

ACTOR: **Ronald Colman** *A Double Life* • John Garfield *Body and Soul* • Gregory Peck *Gentleman's Agreement* • William Powell *Life with Father* • Michael Redgrave *Mourning Becomes Electra*

ACTRESS: **Loretta Young** *The Farmer's Daughter* • Joan Crawford *Possessed* • Susan Hayward *Smash Up – the Story of a Woman* • Dorothy McGuire *Gentleman's Agreement* • Rosalind Russell *Mourning Becomes Electra*

SUPPORTING ACTOR: **Edmund Gwenn** *Miracle on 34th Street* • Charles Bickford *The Farmer's Daughter* • Thomas Gomez *Ride the Pink Horse* • Robert Ryan *Crossfire* • Richard Widmark *Kiss of Death*

SUPPORTING ACTRESS: **Celeste Holm** *Gentleman's Agreement* • Ethel Barrymore *The Paradine Case* • Gloria Grahame *Crossfire* • Marjorie Main *The Egg and I* • Anne Revere *Gentleman's Agreement*

ORIGINAL SCREENPLAY: **Sidney Sheldon** *The Bachelor and the Bobby-Soxer* • Abraham Polonsky *Body and Soul* • Ruth Gordon, Garson Kanin *A Double Life* • Charles Chaplin *Monsieur Verdoux* • Cesare Zavattini, Adolfo Franci, Sergio Amidei, Cesare Giulio Viola *Shoeshine*

ADAPTED SCREENPLAY: **George Seaton** *Miracle on 34th Street* • Richard Murphy *Boomerang!* • John Paxton *Crossfire* • Moss Hart *Gentleman's Agreement* • Ronald Neame, Anthony Havelock-Allan, David Lean *Great Expectations*

STORY: **Valentine Davies** *Miracle on 34th Street* • Georges Chaperot, René Wheeler *A Cage of Nightingales* • Herbert Clyde Lewis, Frederick Stephani *It Happened on Fifth Avenue* • Eleazar Lipsky *Kiss of Death* • Frank Cavett, Dorothy Parker *Smash Up – the Story of a Woman*

Golden Globe Awards

PICTURE: **Gentleman's Agreement**
DIRECTOR: **Elia Kazan** *Gentleman's Agreement*
ACTOR: **Ronald Colman** *A Double Life*
ACTRESS: **Rosalind Russell** *Mourning Becomes Electra*
SUPPORTING ACTOR: **Edmund Gwenn** *Miracle on 34th Street*
SUPPORTING ACTRESS: **Celeste Holm** *Gentleman's Agreement*
SCREENPLAY: **George Seaton** *Miracle on 34th Street*

Cannes Film Festival

GRAND PRIX, PSYCHOLOGICAL/ROMANTIC FILMS: **Antoine et Antoinette**
GRAND PRIX, ADVENTURE/CRIME FILMS: **Les Maudits**
GRAND PRIX, SOCIAL FILMS: **Crossfire**
GRAND PRIX, MUSICAL COMEDIES: **Ziegfeld Follies**
GRAND PRIX, ANIMATED FILMS: **Dumbo**
GRAND PRIX, DOCUMENTARIES: **Inondations en Pologne**

1948

British Film Academy Awards

FILM: **Hamlet** • *Crossfire* • *The Fallen Idol* • *Four Steps in the Clouds* • *Monsieur Vincent* • *The Naked City* • *Paisà*
BRITISH FILM: **The Fallen Idol** • *Hamlet* • *Oliver Twist* • *Once a Jolly Swagman* • *The Red Shoes* • *Scott of the Antarctic* • *The Small Voice*

Academy Awards

PICTURE: **Hamlet** • *Johnny Belinda* • *The Red Shoes* • *The Snake Pit* • *The Treasure of the Sierra Madre*
FOREIGN LANGUAGE FILM: **Monsieur Vincent**
DIRECTOR: **John Huston** *The Treasure of the Sierra Madre* • Anatole Litvak *The Snake Pit* • Jean Negulesco *Johnny Belinda* • Laurence Olivier *Hamlet* • Fred Zinnemann *The Search*
ACTOR: **Laurence Olivier** *Hamlet* • Lew Ayres *Johnny Belinda* • Montgomery Clift *The Search* • Dan Dailey *When My Baby Smiles at Me* • Clifton Webb *Sitting Pretty*
ACTRESS: **Jane Wyman** *Johnny Belinda* • Ingrid Bergman *Joan of Arc* • Olivia de Havilland *The Snake Pit* • Irene Dunne *I Remember Mama* • Barbara Stanwyck *Sorry, Wrong Number*
SUPPORTING ACTOR: **Walter Huston** *The Treasure of the Sierra Madre* • Charles Bickford *Johnny Belinda* • José Ferrer *Joan of Arc* • Oscar Homolka *I Remember Mama* • Cecil Kellaway *The Luck of the Irish*
SUPPORTING ACTRESS: **Claire Trevor** *Key Largo* • Barbara Bel Geddes, Ellen Corby *I Remember Mama* • Agnes Moorehead *Johnny Belinda* • Jean Simmons *Hamlet*
SCREENPLAY: **John Huston** *The Treasure of the Sierra Madre* • Charles Brackett, Billy Wilder, Richard L Breen *A Foreign Affair* • Allen Vincent, Irmgard von Cube *Johnny Belinda* • Richard Schweizer, David Wechsler *The Search* • Frank Partos, Millen Brand *The Snake Pit*
STORY: **Richard Schweizer, David Wechsler** *The Search* • Robert Flaherty, Frances Flaherty *Louisiana Story* • Malvin Wald *The Naked City* • Borden Chase *Red River* • Emeric Pressburger *The Red Shoes*

Golden Globe Awards

PICTURE: **Johnny Belinda • The Treasure of the Sierra Madre**
DIRECTOR: **John Huston** *The Treasure of the Sierra Madre*
ACTOR: **Laurence Olivier** *Hamlet*
ACTRESS: **Jane Wyman** *Johnny Belinda*
SUPPORTING ACTOR: **Walter Huston** *The Treasure of the Sierra Madre*
SUPPORTING ACTRESS: **Ellen Corby** *I Remember Mama*
SCREENPLAY: **Richard Schweizer** *The Search*

1949

British Film Academy Awards

FILM: **Bicycle Thieves** • *Berliner Ballade* • *The Last Stage* • *The Set-Up* • *The Third Man* • *The Treasure of the Sierra Madre* • *The Window*

BRITISH FILM: **The Third Man** • *Kind Hearts and Coronets* • *Passport to Pimlico* • *The Queen of Spades* • *A Run for Your Money* • *The Small Back Room* • *Whisky Galore!*

Academy Awards

PICTURE: **All the King's Men** • *Battleground* • *The Heiress* • *A Letter to Three Wives* • *Twelve O'Clock High*
FOREIGN LANGUAGE FILM: **Bicycle Thieves**
DIRECTOR: **Joseph L Mankiewicz** *A Letter to Three Wives* • Carol Reed *The Fallen Idol* • Robert Rossen *All the King's Men* • William A Wellman *Battleground* • William Wyler *The Heiress*
ACTOR: **Broderick Crawford** *All the King's Men* • Kirk Douglas *Champion* • Gregory Peck *Twelve O'Clock High* • Richard Todd *The Hasty Heart* • John Wayne *Sands of Iwo Jima*
ACTRESS: **Olivia de Havilland** *The Heiress* • Jeanne Crain *Pinky* • Susan Hayward *My Foolish Heart* • Deborah Kerr *Edward, My Son* • Loretta Young *Come to the Stable*
SUPPORTING ACTOR: **Dean Jagger** *Twelve O'Clock High* • John Ireland *All the King's Men* • Arthur Kennedy *Champion* • Ralph Richardson *The Heiress* • James Whitmore *Battleground*
SUPPORTING ACTRESS: **Mercedes McCambridge** *All the King's Men* • Ethel Barrymore *Pinky* • Celeste Holm, Elsa Lanchester *Come to the Stable* • Ethel Waters *Pinky*
STORY, SCREENPLAY: **Robert Pirosh** *Battleground* • Sidney Buchman *Jolson Sings Again* • Sergio Amidei, Federico Fellini, Roberto Rossellini, Marcello Pagliero, Alfred Hayes *Paisà* • TEB Clarke *Passport to Pimlico* • Helen Levitt, Janice Loeb, Sidney Meyers *The Quiet One*
SCREENPLAY: **Joseph L Mankiewicz** *A Letter to Three Wives* • Robert Rossen *All the King's Men* • Cesare Zavattini *Bicycle Thieves* • Carl Foreman *Champion* • Graham Greene *The Fallen Idol*
STORY: **Douglas Morrow** *The Stratton Story* • Clare Boothe Luce *Come to the Stable* • Valentine Davies, Shirley W Smith *It Happens Every Spring* • Harry Brown *Sands of Iwo Jima* • Virginia Kellogg *White Heat*

Golden Globe Awards

PICTURE: **All the King's Men**
FOREIGN LANGUAGE FILM: **Bicycle Thieves**
DIRECTOR: **Robert Rossen** *All the King's Men*
ACTOR: **Broderick Crawford** *All the King's Men*
ACTRESS: **Olivia de Havilland** *The Heiress*
SUPPORTING ACTOR: **James Whitmore** *Battleground*
SUPPORTING ACTRESS: **Mercedes McCambridge** *All the King's Men*
SCREENPLAY: **Robert Pirosh** *Battleground*

Cannes Film Festival

GRAND PRIX: **The Third Man**
DIRECTOR: **René Clément** *The Walls of Malapaga*
ACTOR: **Edward G Robinson** *House of Strangers*
ACTRESS: **Isa Miranda** *The Walls of Malapaga*
SCREENPLAY: **Alfred Werker** *Lost Boundaries*

1950

British Film Academy Awards

FILM: **All about Eve** • *The Asphalt Jungle* • *La Beauté du Diable* • *Intruder in the Dust* • *The Men* • *On the Town* • *Orphée*
BRITISH FILM: **The Blue Lamp** • *Chance of a Lifetime* • *Morning Departure* • *Seven Days to Noon* • *State Secret* • *The Wooden Horse*

Academy Awards

PICTURE: **All about Eve** • *Born Yesterday* • *Father of the Bride* • *King Solomon's Mines* • *Sunset Blvd*
FOREIGN LANGUAGE FILM: **The Walls of Malapaga**
DIRECTOR: **Joseph L Mankiewicz** *All about Eve* • George Cukor *Born Yesterday* • John Huston *The Asphalt Jungle* • Carol Reed *The Third Man* • Billy Wilder *Sunset Blvd*
ACTOR: **José Ferrer** *Cyrano de Bergerac* • Louis Calhern *The Magnificent Yankee* • William Holden *Sunset Blvd* • James Stewart *Harvey* • Spencer Tracy *Father of the Bride*
ACTRESS: **Judy Holliday** *Born Yesterday* • Anne Baxter, Bette Davis *All about Eve* • Eleanor Parker *Caged* • Gloria Swanson *Sunset Blvd*
SUPPORTING ACTOR: **George Sanders** *All about Eve* • Jeff Chandler *Broken Arrow* • Edmund Gwenn *Mister 880* • Sam Jaffe *The Asphalt Jungle* • Erich von Stroheim *Sunset Blvd*
SUPPORTING ACTRESS: **Josephine Hull** *Harvey* • Hope Emerson *Caged* • Celeste Holm *All about Eve* • Nancy Olson *Sunset Blvd* • Thelma Ritter *All about Eve*
STORY, SCREENPLAY: **Billy Wilder, Charles Brackett, DM Marshman Jr** *Sunset Blvd* • Ruth Gordon, Garson Kanin *Adam's Rib* • Virginia Kellogg, Bernard C Schoenfeld *Caged* • Carl Foreman *The Men* • Joseph L Mankiewicz, Lesser Samuels *No Way Out*
SCREENPLAY: **Joseph L Mankiewicz** *All about Eve* • Ben Maddow, John Huston *The Asphalt Jungle* • Albert Mannheimer *Born Yesterday* • Albert Maltz *Broken Arrow* • Albert Hackett, Francis Goodrich *Father of the Bride*
STORY: **Edna Anhalt, Edward Anhalt** *Panic in the Streets* • Carlo Lizzani, Giuseppe De Santis *Bitter Rice* • William Bowers, Andre De Toth *The Gunfighter* • Leonard Spigelgass *Mystery Street* • Sy Gomberg *When Willie Comes Marching Home*

Golden Globe Awards

PICTURE: **Sunset Blvd**
DIRECTOR: **Billy Wilder** *Sunset Blvd*
ACTOR, DRAMA: **José Ferrer** *Cyrano de Bergerac*
ACTRESS, DRAMA: **Gloria Swanson** *Sunset Blvd*
ACTOR, COMEDY/MUSICAL: **Fred Astaire** *Three Little Words*
ACTRESS, COMEDY/MUSICAL: **Judy Holliday** *Born Yesterday*

SUPPORTING ACTOR: **Edmund Gwenn** *Mister 880*
SUPPORTING ACTRESS: **Josephine Hull** *Harvey*
SCREENPLAY: **Joseph L Mankiewicz** *All about Eve*

1951

British Film Academy Awards

FILM: **La Ronde** • *An American in Paris* • *The Browning Version* • *Detective Story* • *Edouard et Caroline* • *Fourteen Hours* • *The Lavender Hill Mob* • *The Magic Box* • *The Magic Garden* • *The Man in the White Suit* • *Miss Julie* • *Never Take No for an Answer* • *No Resting Place* • *The Red Badge of Courage* • *The Sound of Fury* • *Sunday in August* • *A Walk in the Sun* • *White Corridors*
BRITISH FILM: **The Lavender Hill Mob** • *The Browning Version* • *The Magic Box* • *The Magic Garden* • *The Man in the White Suit* • *Never Take No for an Answer* • *White Corridors*

Academy Awards

PICTURE: **An American in Paris** • *Decision before Dawn* • *A Place in the Sun* • *Quo Vadis* • *A Streetcar Named Desire*
FOREIGN LANGUAGE FILM: **Rashomon**
DIRECTOR: **George Stevens** *A Place in the Sun* • John Huston *The African Queen* • Elia Kazan *A Streetcar Named Desire* • Vincente Minnelli *An American in Paris* • William Wyler *Detective Story*
ACTOR: **Humphrey Bogart** *The African Queen* • Marlon Brando *A Streetcar Named Desire* • Montgomery Clift *A Place in the Sun* • Arthur Kennedy *Bright Victory* • Fredric March *Death of a Salesman*
ACTRESS: **Vivien Leigh** *A Streetcar Named Desire* • Katharine Hepburn *The African Queen* • Eleanor Parker *Detective Story* • Shelley Winters *A Place in the Sun* • Jane Wyman *The Blue Veil*
SUPPORTING ACTOR: **Karl Malden** *A Streetcar Named Desire* • Leo Genn *Quo Vadis* • Kevin McCarthy *Death of a Salesman* • Peter Ustinov *Quo Vadis* • Gig Young *Come Fill the Cup*
SUPPORTING ACTRESS: **Kim Hunter** *A Streetcar Named Desire* • Joan Blondell *The Blue Veil* • Mildred Dunnock *Death of a Salesman* • Lee Grant *Detective Story* • Thelma Ritter *The Mating Season*
STORY, SCREENPLAY: **Alan Jay Lerner** *An American in Paris* • Billy Wilder, Lesser Samuels, Walter Newman *Ace in the Hole* • Philip Dunne *David and Bathsheba* • Robert Pirosh *Go for Broke!* • Clarence Greene, Russell Rouse *The Well*
SCREENPLAY: **Michael Wilson, Harry Brown** *A Place in the Sun* • John Huston, James Agee *The African Queen* • Philip Yordan, Robert Wyler *Detective Story* • Max Ophüls, Jacques Natanson *La Ronde* • Tennessee Williams *A Streetcar Named Desire*
STORY: **James Bernard, Paul Dehn** *Seven Days to Noon* • Budd Boetticher, Ray Nazarro *The Bullfighter and the Lady* • Oscar Millard *The Frogmen* • Liam O'Brien, Robert Riskin *Here Comes the Groom* • Alfred Hayes, Stewart Stern *Teresa*

Golden Globe Awards

DRAMA: **A Place in the Sun**
COMEDY/MUSICAL: **An American in Paris**
DIRECTOR: **Laslo Benedek** *Death of a Salesman*
ACTOR, DRAMA: **Fredric March** *Death of a Salesman*
ACTRESS, DRAMA: **Jane Wyman** *The Blue Veil*
ACTOR, COMEDY/MUSICAL: **Danny Kaye** *On the Riviera*
ACTRESS, COMEDY/MUSICAL: **June Allyson** *Too Young to Kiss*
SUPPORTING ACTOR: **Peter Ustinov** *Quo Vadis*
SUPPORTING ACTRESS: **Kim Hunter** *A Streetcar Named Desire*
SCREENPLAY: **Robert Buckner** *Bright Victory*

Cannes Film Festival

GRAND PRIX: **Miracle in Milan • Miss Julie**
DIRECTOR: **Luis Buñuel** *Los Olvidados*
ACTOR: **Michael Redgrave** *The Browning Version*
ACTRESS: **Bette Davis** *All about Eve*
SCREENPLAY: **Terence Rattigan** *The Browning Version*

Berlin International Film Festival

GOLDEN BEAR, DRAMA: **Four in a Jeep**
GOLDEN BEAR, CRIME/ADVENTURE: **Justice Est Faite**
GOLDEN BEAR, COMEDY: **Sans Laisser d'Adresse**
GOLDEN BEAR, MUSICAL: **Cinderella**

1952

British Film Academy Awards

FILM: **The Sound Barrier** • *The African Queen* • *Angels One Five* • *The Boy Kumasenu* • *Carrie* • *Casque d'Or* • *Cry, the Beloved Country* • *Death of a Salesman* • *Limelight* • *Los Olvidados* • *Mandy* • *Miracle in Milan* • *Outcast of the Islands* • *Rashomon* • *The River* • *Singin' in the Rain* • *A Streetcar Named Desire* • *Viva Zapata!*
BRITISH FILM: **The Sound Barrier** • *Angels One Five* • *Cry, the Beloved Country* • *Mandy* • *Outcast of the Islands* • *The River*
FOREIGN ACTOR: **Marlon Brando** *Viva Zapata!* • Jean Aurenche *Dieu A Besoin des Hommes* • Humphrey Bogart *The African Queen* • Francesco Golisano *Miracle in Milan* • Fredric March *Death of a Salesman*
FOREIGN ACTRESS: **Simone Signoret** *Casque d'Or* • Colette Audry *Olivia* • Katharine Hepburn *Pat and Mike* • Judy Holliday *The Marrying Kind* • Nicole Stéphane *Les Enfants Terribles*
BRITISH ACTOR: **Ralph Richardson** *The Sound Barrier* • Jack Hawkins *Mandy* • James Hayter *The Pickwick Papers* • Laurence Olivier *Carrie* • Nigel Patrick *The Sound Barrier* • Alastair Sim *Folly to Be Wise*
BRITISH ACTRESS: **Vivien Leigh** *A Streetcar Named Desire* • Phyllis Calvert *Mandy* • Celia Johnson *I Believe in You* • Ann Todd *The Sound Barrier*

Academy Awards

PICTURE: **The Greatest Show on Earth** • High Noon • Ivanhoe • Moulin Rouge • The Quiet Man

FOREIGN LANGUAGE FILM: **Jeux Interdits**

DIRECTOR: **John Ford** The Quiet Man • Cecil B DeMille The Greatest Show on Earth • John Huston Moulin Rouge • Joseph L Mankiewicz 5 Fingers • Fred Zinnemann High Noon

ACTOR: **Gary Cooper** High Noon • Marlon Brando Viva Zapata! • Kirk Douglas The Bad and the Beautiful • José Ferrer Moulin Rouge • Alec Guinness The Lavender Hill Mob

ACTRESS: **Shirley Booth** Come Back, Little Sheba • Joan Crawford Sudden Fear • Bette Davis The Star • Julie Harris The Member of the Wedding • Susan Hayward With a Song in My Heart

SUPPORTING ACTOR: **Anthony Quinn** Viva Zapata! • Richard Burton My Cousin Rachel • Arthur Hunnicutt The Big Sky • Victor McLaglen The Quiet Man • Jack Palance Sudden Fear

SUPPORTING ACTRESS: **Gloria Grahame** The Bad and the Beautiful • Jean Hagen Singin' in the Rain • Colette Marchand Moulin Rouge • Terry Moore Come Back, Little Sheba • Thelma Ritter With a Song in My Heart

STORY, SCREENPLAY: **TEB Clarke** The Lavender Hill Mob • Sydney Boehm The Atomic City • Terence Rattigan The Sound Barrier • Ruth Gordon, Garson Kanin Pat and Mike • John Steinbeck Viva Zapata!

SCREENPLAY: **Charles Schnee** The Bad and the Beautiful • Michael Wilson 5 Fingers • Carl Foreman High Noon • Roger MacDougall, John Dighton, Alexander Mackendrick The Man in the White Suit • Frank S Nugent The Quiet Man

STORY: **Frank Cavett, Fredric M Frank, Theodore St John** The Greatest Show on Earth • Leo McCarey My Son John • Martin Goldsmith, Jack Leonard The Narrow Margin • Guy Trosper The Pride of St Louis • Edward Anhalt, Edna Anhalt The Sniper

Golden Globe Awards

DRAMA: **The Greatest Show on Earth**

COMEDY/MUSICAL: **With a Song in My Heart**

DIRECTOR: **Cecil B DeMille** The Greatest Show on Earth

ACTOR, DRAMA: **Gary Cooper** High Noon

ACTRESS, DRAMA: **Shirley Booth** Come Back, Little Sheba

ACTOR, COMEDY/MUSICAL: **Donald O'Connor** Singin' in the Rain

ACTRESS, COMEDY/MUSICAL: **Susan Hayward** With a Song in My Heart

SUPPORTING ACTOR: **Millard Mitchell** My Six Convicts

SUPPORTING ACTRESS: **Katy Jurado** High Noon

SCREENPLAY: **Michael Wilson** 5 Fingers

Cannes Film Festival

GRAND PRIX: **Two Pennyworth of Hope • Othello**

DIRECTOR: **Christian-Jaque** Fanfan la Tulipe

ACTOR: **Marlon Brando** Viva Zapata!

ACTRESS: **Lee Grant** Detective Story

SCREENPLAY: **Piero Tellini** Guardie e Ladri

Berlin International Film Festival

GOLDEN BEAR: **One Summer of Happiness**

1953

British Film Academy Awards

FILM: **Jeux Interdits** • The Bad and the Beautiful • Come Back, Little Sheba • The Cruel Sea • From Here to Eternity • Genevieve • The Heart of the Matter • Julius Caesar • The Kidnappers • Lili • The Little World of Don Camillo • The Medium • Mogambo • Moulin Rouge • Nous Sommes Tous des Assassins • Roman Holiday • Shane • The Sun Shines Bright • Two Pennyworth of Hope

BRITISH FILM: **Genevieve** • The Cruel Sea • The Heart of the Matter • The Kidnappers • Moulin Rouge

FOREIGN ACTOR: **Marlon Brando** Julius Caesar • Eddie Albert Roman Holiday • Van Heflin Shane • Claude Laydu Diary of a Country Priest • Marcel Mouloudji Nous Sommes Tous des Assassins • Gregory Peck Roman Holiday • Spencer Tracy The Actress

FOREIGN ACTRESS: **Leslie Caron** Lili • Shirley Booth Come Back, Little Sheba • Marie Powers The Medium • Maria Schell The Heart of the Matter

BRITISH ACTOR: **John Gielgud** Julius Caesar • Jack Hawkins The Cruel Sea • Trevor Howard The Heart of the Matter • Duncan Macrae The Kidnappers • Kenneth More Genevieve

BRITISH ACTRESS: **Audrey Hepburn** Roman Holiday • Celia Johnson The Captain's Paradise

Academy Awards

PICTURE: **From Here to Eternity** • Julius Caesar • The Robe • Roman Holiday • Shane

DIRECTOR: **Fred Zinnemann** From Here to Eternity • George Stevens Shane • Charles Walters Lili • Billy Wilder Stalag 17 • William Wyler Roman Holiday

ACTOR: **William Holden** Stalag 17 • Marlon Brando Julius Caesar • Richard Burton The Robe • Montgomery Clift, Burt Lancaster From Here to Eternity

ACTRESS: **Audrey Hepburn** Roman Holiday • Leslie Caron Lili • Ava Gardner Mogambo • Deborah Kerr From Here to Eternity • Maggie McNamara The Moon Is Blue

SUPPORTING ACTOR: **Frank Sinatra** From Here to Eternity • Eddie Albert Roman Holiday • Brandon de Wilde, Jack Palance Shane • Robert Strauss Stalag 17

SUPPORTING ACTRESS: **Donna Reed** From Here to Eternity • Grace Kelly Mogambo • Geraldine Page Hondo • Marjorie Rambeau Torch Song • Thelma Ritter Pickup on South Street

STORY, SCREENPLAY: **Charles Brackett, Walter Reisch, Richard L Breen** Titanic • Betty Comden, Adolph Green The Band Wagon • Richard Murphy The Desert Rats • Harold Jack Bloom, Sam Rolfe The Naked Spur • Millard Kaufman Take the High Ground

---

SCREENPLAY: **Daniel Taradash** From Here to Eternity • Eric Ambler The Cruel Sea • Helen Deutsch Lili • John Dighton, Ian McLellan Hunter Roman Holiday • A B Guthrie Jr Shane

STORY: **Ian McLellan Hunter, Dalton Trumbo** Roman Holiday • Beirne Lay Jr Above and Beyond • Alec Coppel The Captain's Paradise • Louis L'Amour Hondo • Ray Ashley, Morris Engel, Ruth Orkin The Little Fugitive

Golden Globe Awards

DRAMA: **The Robe**

DIRECTOR: **Fred Zinnemann** From Here to Eternity

ACTOR, DRAMA: **Spencer Tracy** The Actress

ACTRESS, DRAMA: **Audrey Hepburn** Roman Holiday

ACTOR, COMEDY/MUSICAL: **David Niven** The Moon Is Blue

ACTRESS, COMEDY/MUSICAL: **Ethel Merman** Call Me Madam

SUPPORTING ACTOR: **Frank Sinatra** From Here to Eternity

SUPPORTING ACTRESS: **Grace Kelly** Mogambo

SCREENPLAY: **Helen Deutsch** Lili

Cannes Film Festival

GRAND PRIX: **The Wages of Fear**

Berlin International Film Festival

GOLDEN BEAR: **The Wages of Fear**

1954

British Film Academy Awards

FILM: **The Wages of Fear** • The Adventures of Robinson Crusoe • Bread, Love and Dreams • The Caine Mutiny • Carrington VC • The Divided Heart • Doctor in the House • Executive Suite • For Better, for Worse • Gate of Hell • Hobson's Choice • How to Marry a Millionaire • The Maggie • The Moon Is Blue • On the Waterfront • The Purple Plain • Rear Window • Riot in Cell Block 11 • Romeo and Juliet • Seven Brides for Seven Brothers

BRITISH FILM: **Hobson's Choice** • Carrington VC • The Divided Heart • Doctor in the House • For Better, for Worse • The Maggie • The Purple Plain • Romeo and Juliet

FOREIGN ACTOR: **Marlon Brando** On the Waterfront • Neville Brand Riot in Cell Block 11 • José Ferrer The Caine Mutiny • Fredric March Executive Suite • James Stewart The Glenn Miller Story

FOREIGN ACTRESS: **Cornell Borchers** The Divided Heart • Shirley Booth About Mrs Leslie • Judy Holliday Phffft! • Grace Kelly Dial M for Murder • Gina Lollobrigida Bread, Love and Dreams

BRITISH ACTOR: **Kenneth More** Doctor in the House • Maurice Denham The Purple Plain • Robert Donat Lease of Life • John Mills Hobson's Choice • David Niven Carrington VC • Donald Wolfit Svengali

BRITISH ACTRESS: **Yvonne Mitchell** The Divided Heart • Brenda de Banzie Hobson's Choice • Audrey Hepburn Sabrina • Margaret Leighton, Noelle Middleton Carrington VC

BRITISH SCREENPLAY: **Robin Estridge, George Tabori** The Young Lovers • Jack Whittingham The Divided Heart • Nicholas Phipps Doctor in the House • David Lean, Norman Spencer, Wynyard Browne Hobson's Choice • Hugh Mills, René Clément Knave of Hearts • William Rose The Maggie • Eric Ambler The Purple Plain • Renato Castellani Romeo and Juliet

Academy Awards

PICTURE: **On the Waterfront** • The Caine Mutiny • The Country Girl • Seven Brides for Seven Brothers • Three Coins in the Fountain

FOREIGN LANGUAGE FILM: **Gate of Hell**

DIRECTOR: **Elia Kazan** On the Waterfront • Alfred Hitchcock Rear Window • George Seaton The Country Girl • William A Wellman The High and the Mighty • Billy Wilder Sabrina

ACTOR: **Marlon Brando** On the Waterfront • Humphrey Bogart The Caine Mutiny • Bing Crosby The Country Girl • James Mason A Star Is Born • Dan O'Herlihy The Adventures of Robinson Crusoe

ACTRESS: **Grace Kelly** The Country Girl • Dorothy Dandridge Carmen Jones • Judy Garland A Star Is Born • Audrey Hepburn Sabrina • Jane Wyman Magnificent Obsession

SUPPORTING ACTOR: **Edmond O'Brien** The Barefoot Contessa • Lee J Cobb, Karl Malden, Rod Steiger On the Waterfront • Tom Tully The Caine Mutiny

SUPPORTING ACTRESS: **Eva Marie Saint** On the Waterfront • Nina Foch Executive Suite • Katy Jurado Broken Lance • Jan Sterling, Claire Trevor The High and the Mighty

STORY, SCREENPLAY: **Budd Schulberg** On the Waterfront • Joseph L Mankiewicz The Barefoot Contessa • William Rose Genevieve • Oscar Brodney, Valentine Davies The Glenn Miller Story • Melvin Frank, Norman Panama Knock on Wood

SCREENPLAY: **George Seaton** The Country Girl • Stanley Roberts The Caine Mutiny • John Michael Hayes Rear Window • Billy Wilder, Ernest Lehman, Samuel Taylor Sabrina • Albert Hackett, Frances Goodrich, Dorothy Kingsley Seven Brides for Seven Brothers

STORY: **Philip Yordan** Broken Lance • Ettore Maria Margadonna Bread, Love and Dreams • Francois Boyer Jeux Interdits • Jed Harris, Thomas Reed Night People • Lamar Trotti There's No Business like Show Business

Golden Globe Awards

DRAMA: **On the Waterfront**

COMEDY/MUSICAL: **Carmen Jones**

FOREIGN LANGUAGE FILM: **Genevieve • La Mujer de las Camelias • No Way Back • Twenty-Four Eyes**

DIRECTOR: **Elia Kazan** On the Waterfront

ACTOR, DRAMA: **Marlon Brando** On the Waterfront

ACTRESS, DRAMA: **Grace Kelly** The Country Girl

ACTOR, COMEDY/MUSICAL: **James Mason** A Star Is Born

ACTRESS, COMEDY/MUSICAL: **Judy Garland** A Star Is Born

SUPPORTING ACTOR: **Edmond O'Brien** The Barefoot Contessa

SUPPORTING ACTRESS: **Jan Sterling** The High and the Mighty

SCREENPLAY: **Billy Wilder, Samuel Taylor, Ernest Lehman** Sabrina

Cannes Film Festival

GRAND PRIX: **Gate of Hell**

Berlin International Film Festival

GOLDEN BEAR: **Hobson's Choice**

1955

British Film Academy Awards

FILM: **Richard III** • Bad Day at Black Rock • Carmen Jones • The Colditz Story • The Dam Busters • East of Eden • The Ladykillers • Marty • The Night My Number Came Up • The Prisoner • Seven Samurai • Simba • La Strada • Summertime

BRITISH FILM: **Richard III** • The Colditz Story • The Dam Busters • The Ladykillers • The Night My Number Came Up • The Prisoner • Simba

FOREIGN ACTOR: **Ernest Borgnine** Marty • James Dean East of Eden • Jack Lemmon Mister Roberts • Toshiro Mifune, Takashi Shimura Seven Samurai • Frank Sinatra Not as a Stranger

FOREIGN ACTRESS: **Betsy Blair** Marty • Dorothy Dandridge Carmen Jones • Judy Garland A Star Is Born • Julie Harris I Am a Camera • Katharine Hepburn Summertime • Grace Kelly The Country Girl • Giulietta Masina La Strada • Marilyn Monroe The Seven Year Itch

BRITISH ACTOR: **Laurence Olivier** Richard III • Alfie Bass The Bespoke Overcoat • Alec Guinness The Ladykillers • The Prisoner • David Kossoff A Kid for Two Farthings • Kenneth More The Deep Blue Sea • Michael Redgrave The Night My Number Came Up

BRITISH ACTRESS: **Katie Johnson** The Ladykillers • Margaret Johnston Touch and Go • Deborah Kerr The End of the Affair • Margaret Lockwood Cast a Dark Shadow

BRITISH SCREENPLAY: **William Rose** The Ladykillers • Sidney Gilliat, Val Valentine The Constant Husband • R C Sherriff The Dam Busters • Terence Rattigan The Deep Blue Sea • Nicholas Phipps, Jack Davies Doctor at Sea • R C Sherriff The Night My Number Came Up • Bridget Boland The Prisoner • John Baines Simba • William Rose Touch and Go

Academy Awards

PICTURE: **Marty** • Love Is a Many-Splendored Thing • Mister Roberts • Picnic • The Rose Tattoo

FOREIGN LANGUAGE FILM: **Samurai**

DIRECTOR: **Delbert Mann** Marty • Elia Kazan East of Eden • David Lean Summertime • Joshua Logan Picnic • John Sturges Bad Day at Black Rock

ACTOR: **Ernest Borgnine** Marty • James Cagney Love Me or Leave Me • James Dean East of Eden • Frank Sinatra The Man with the Golden Arm • Spencer Tracy Bad Day at Black Rock

ACTRESS: **Anna Magnani** The Rose Tattoo • Susan Hayward I'll Cry Tomorrow • Katharine Hepburn Summertime • Jennifer Jones Love Is a Many-Splendored Thing • Eleanor Parker Interrupted Melody

SUPPORTING ACTOR: **Jack Lemmon** Mister Roberts • Arthur Kennedy Trial • Joe Mantell Marty • Sal Mineo Rebel without a Cause • Arthur O'Connell Picnic

SUPPORTING ACTRESS: **Jo Van Fleet** East of Eden • Betsy Blair Marty • Peggy Lee Pete Kelly's Blues • Marisa Pavan The Rose Tattoo • Natalie Wood Rebel without a Cause

STORY, SCREENPLAY: **William Ludwig, Sonya Levien** Interrupted Melody • Milton Sperling, Emmet Lavery The Court-Martial of Billy Mitchell • Betty Comden, Adolph Green It's Always Fair Weather • Jacques Tati, Henri Marquet Monsieur Hulot's Holiday • Jack Rose, Melville Shavelson Seven Little Foys

SCREENPLAY: **Paddy Chayefsky** Marty • Millard Kaufman Bad Day at Black Rock • Richard Brooks The Blackboard Jungle • Paul Osborn East of Eden • Daniel Fuchs, Isobel Lennart Love Me or Leave Me

STORY: **Daniel Fuchs** Love Me or Leave Me • Joe Connelly, Bob Mosher The Private War of Major Benson • Nicholas Ray Rebel without a Cause • Jean Marsan, Jacques Perret, Raoul Ploquin, Henry Troyat, Henri Verneuil The Sheep Has Five Legs • Beirne Lay Jr Strategic Air Command

Golden Globe Awards

DRAMA: **East of Eden • Wichita**

COMEDY/MUSICAL: **Guys and Dolls**

FOREIGN LANGUAGE FILM: **Dangerous Curves • Eyes of Children • Ordet • Sons, Mothers and a General • Stella**

DIRECTOR: **Joshua Logan** Picnic

ACTOR, DRAMA: **Ernest Borgnine** Marty

ACTRESS, DRAMA: **Anna Magnani** The Rose Tattoo

ACTOR, COMEDY/MUSICAL: **Tom Ewell** The Seven Year Itch

ACTRESS, COMEDY/MUSICAL: **Jean Simmons** Guys and Dolls

SUPPORTING ACTOR: **Arthur Kennedy** Trial

SUPPORTING ACTRESS: **Marisa Pavan** The Rose Tattoo

Cannes Film Festival

PALME D'OR: **Marty**

DIRECTOR: **Sergei Vasiliev** Heroes of Shipka • Jules Dassin Rififi

ACTOR: **Spencer Tracy** Bad Day at Black Rock • Male cast A Big Family

ACTRESS: **Female cast** A Big Family

Berlin International Film Festival

GOLDEN BEAR: **The Rats**

1956

British Film Academy Awards

FILM: **Gervaise** • Baby Doll • The Battle of the River Plate • Le Défroqué • Friends for Life • The Grasshopper • Guys and Dolls • The Killing • The Man with the Golden Arm • The Man Who Never Was • Picnic • Reach for the Sky • Rebel without a Cause • The Shadow • Smiles of a Summer Night • A Town like Alice • The Trouble with Harry • War and Peace • Yield to the Night

BRITISH FILM: **Reach for the Sky** • The Battle of the River Plate • The Man Who Never Was • A Town like Alice • Yield to the Night

FOREIGN ACTOR: **François Périer** Gervaise • James Dean Rebel without a Cause • Gunnar Björnstrand Smiles of a Summer Night • Pierre Fresnay Le Défroqué • William Holden Picnic • Karl Malden Baby Doll • Frank Sinatra The Man with the Golden Arm • Spencer Tracy The Mountain

FOREIGN ACTRESS: **Anna Magnani** The Rose Tattoo • Carroll Baker Baby Doll • Eva Dahlbeck Smiles of a Summer Night • Ava Gardner Bhowani Junction • Susan Hayward I'll Cry Tomorrow • Shirley MacLaine The Trouble with Harry • Kim Novak Picnic • Marisa Pavan The Rose Tattoo • Maria Schell Gervaise • Jean Simmons Guys and Dolls

BRITISH ACTOR: **Peter Finch** A Town like Alice • Jack Hawkins The Long Arm • Kenneth More Reach for the Sky

BRITISH ACTRESS: **Virginia McKenna** A Town like Alice • Dorothy Alison Reach for the Sky • Audrey Hepburn War and Peace

BRITISH SCREENPLAY: **Nigel Balchin** The Man Who Never Was • Michael Powell, Emeric Pressburger The Battle of the River Plate • Sidney Gilliat, Frank Launder The Green Man • John Boulting, Frank Harvey Private's Progress • Lewis Gilbert Reach for the Sky • Moore Raymond, Anthony Kimmins Smiley • Hubert Gregg, Vernon Harris Three Men in a Boat • WP Lipscomb, Richard Mason A Town like Alice • Joan Henry, John Cresswell Yield to the Night

Academy Awards

PICTURE: **Around the World in 80 Days** • Friendly Persuasion • Giant • The King and I • The Ten Commandments

FOREIGN LANGUAGE FILM: **La Strada** • The Captain from Kopenick • Gervaise • The Burmese Harp • Qivitoq

DIRECTOR: **George Stevens** Giant • Michael Anderson Around the World in 80 Days • Walter Lang The King and I • King Vidor War and Peace • William Wyler Friendly Persuasion

ACTOR: **Yul Brynner** The King and I • James Dean Giant • Kirk Douglas Lust for Life • Rock Hudson Giant • Laurence Olivier Richard III

ACTRESS: **Ingrid Bergman** Anastasia • Carroll Baker Baby Doll • Katharine Hepburn The Rainmaker • Nancy Kelly The Bad Seed • Deborah Kerr The King and I

SUPPORTING ACTOR: **Anthony Quinn** Lust for Life • Don Murray Bus Stop • Anthony Perkins Friendly Persuasion • Mickey Rooney The Bold and the Brave • Robert Stack Written on the Wind

SUPPORTING ACTRESS: **Dorothy Malone** Written on the Wind • Mildred Dunnock Baby Doll • Eileen Heckart The Bad Seed • Mercedes McCambridge Giant • Patty McCormack The Bad Seed

ORIGINAL SCREENPLAY: **Albert Lamorisse** Red Balloon • Robert Lewin The Bold and the Brave • Andrew L Stone Julie • Federico Fellini, Tullio Pinelli La Strada • William Rose The Ladykillers

ADAPTED SCREENPLAY: **SJ Perelman, James Poe, John Farrow** Around the World in 80 Days • Tennessee Williams Baby Doll • Michael Wilson Friendly Persuasion • Fred Guiol, Ivan Moffat Giant • Norman Corwin Lust for Life

STORY: **Dalton Trumbo** The Brave One • Leo Katcher The Eddy Duchin Story • Edward Bernds, Elwood Ullman High Society • Jean-Paul Sartre The Proud Ones • Cesare Zavattini Umberto D

Golden Globe Awards

DRAMA: **Around the World in 80 Days**

COMEDY/MUSICAL: **The King and I**

FOREIGN LANGUAGE FILM: **Before Sundown • The Girl in Black • Richard III • Roses on the Arm • War and Peace • The White Reindeer**

DIRECTOR: **Elia Kazan** Baby Doll

ACTOR, DRAMA: **Kirk Douglas** Lust for Life

ACTRESS, DRAMA: **Ingrid Bergman** Anastasia

ACTOR, COMEDY/MUSICAL: **Cantinflas** Around the World in 80 Days

ACTRESS, COMEDY/MUSICAL: **Deborah Kerr** The King and I

SUPPORTING ACTOR: **Earl Holliman** The Rainmaker

SUPPORTING ACTRESS: **Eileen Heckart** The Bad Seed

Cannes Film Festival

PALME D'OR: **Le Monde du Silence**

DIRECTOR: **Sergei Yutkevitch** Othello

ACTRESS: **Susan Hayward** I'll Cry Tomorrow

Berlin International Film Festival

GOLDEN BEAR: **Invitation to the Dance**

SILVER BEAR, DIRECTOR: **Robert Aldrich** Autumn Leaves

SILVER BEAR, ACTOR: **Burt Lancaster** Trapeze

SILVER BEAR, ACTRESS: **Elsa Martinelli** Donatella

1957

British Film Academy Awards

FILM: **The Bridge on the River Kwai** • The Bachelor Party • Celui Qui Doit Mourir • Edge of the City • Heaven Knows, Mr Allison • A Man Escaped • Paths of Glory • Pather Panchali • The Prince and the Showgirl • The Shiralee • The Tin Star • That Night • 3:10 to Yuma • 12 Angry Men • Windom's Way

---

BRITISH FILM: **The Bridge on the River Kwai** • The Prince and the Showgirl • The Shiralee • Windom's Way

FOREIGN ACTOR: **Henry Fonda** 12 Angry Men • Richard Basehart Time Limit • Pierre Brasseur Gates of Paris • Tony Curtis Sweet Smell of Success • Jean Gabin La Traversée de Paris • Robert Mitchum Heaven Knows, Mr Allison • Sidney Poitier Edge of the City • Ed Wynn The Great Man

FOREIGN ACTRESS: **Simone Signoret** The Witches of Salem • Augusta Dabney That Night • Katharine Hepburn The Rainmaker • Marilyn Monroe The Prince and the Showgirl • Lilli Palmer Is Anna Anderson Anastasia? • Eva Marie Saint A Hatful of Rain • Joanne Woodward The Three Faces of Eve

BRITISH ACTOR: **Alec Guinness** The Bridge on the River Kwai • Peter Finch Windom's Way • Trevor Howard Manuela • Laurence Olivier The Prince and the Showgirl • Michael Redgrave Time without Pity

BRITISH ACTRESS: **Heather Sears** The Story of Esther Costello • Deborah Kerr Tea and Sympathy • Sylvia Syms Woman in a Dressing Gown

BRITISH SCREENPLAY: **Pierre Boulle** The Bridge on the River Kwai • Arthur Laurents Anastasia • Jack Whittingham The Birthday Present • John Kruse, Cy Endfield Hell Drivers • William Rose, John Eldridge The Man in the Sky • Terence Rattigan The Prince and the Showgirl • William Rose, John Eldridge The Smallest Show on Earth • Charles Kaufman The Story of Esther Costello • Jill Craigie Windom's Way • Ted Willis Woman in a Dressing Gown

Academy Awards

PICTURE: **The Bridge on the River Kwai** • Peyton Place • Sayonara • 12 Angry Men • Witness for the Prosecution

FOREIGN LANGUAGE FILM: **Nights of Cabiria** • The Devil Came at Night • Gates of Paris • Mother India • Nine Lives

DIRECTOR: **David Lean** The Bridge on the River Kwai • Joshua Logan Sayonara • Sidney Lumet 12 Angry Men • Mark Robson Peyton Place • Billy Wilder Witness for the Prosecution

ACTOR: **Alec Guinness** The Bridge on the River Kwai • Marlon Brando Sayonara • Anthony Franciosa A Hatful of Rain • Charles Laughton Witness for the Prosecution • Anthony Quinn Wild Is the Wind

ACTRESS: **Joanne Woodward** The Three Faces of Eve • Deborah Kerr Heaven Knows, Mr Allison • Anna Magnani Wild Is the Wind • Elizabeth Taylor Raintree County • Lana Turner Peyton Place

SUPPORTING ACTOR: **Red Buttons** Sayonara • Vittorio De Sica A Farewell to Arms • Sessue Hayakawa The Bridge on the River Kwai • Arthur Kennedy, Russ Tamblyn Peyton Place

SUPPORTING ACTRESS: **Miyoshi Umeki** Sayonara • Carolyn Jones The Bachelor Party • Elsa Lanchester Witness for the Prosecution • Hope Lange, Diane Varsi Peyton Place

ORIGINAL STORY, SCREENPLAY: **George Wells** Designing Woman • Leonard Gershe Funny Face • R Wright Campbell, Ivan Goff, Ben Roberts, Ralph Wheelwright Man of a Thousand Faces • Joel Kane, Dudley Nichols, Barney Slater The Tin Star • Federico Fellini, Ennio Flaiano, Tullio Pinelli I Vitelloni

ADAPTED SCREENPLAY: **Pierre Boulle, Carl Foreman, Michael Wilson** The Bridge on the River Kwai • Reginald Rose 12 Angry Men • John Huston, John Lee Mahin Heaven Knows, Mr Allison • John Michael Hayes Peyton Place • Paul Osborn Sayonara

Golden Globe Awards

DRAMA: **The Bridge on the River Kwai**

COMEDY/MUSICAL: **Les Girls**

FOREIGN LANGUAGE FILM: **The Confessions of Felix Krull • Tizoc • Woman in a Dressing Gown • Yellow Crow**

DIRECTOR: **David Lean** The Bridge on the River Kwai

ACTOR, DRAMA: **Alec Guinness** The Bridge on the River Kwai

ACTRESS, DRAMA: **Joanne Woodward** The Three Faces of Eve

ACTOR, COMEDY/MUSICAL: **Frank Sinatra** Pal Joey

ACTRESS, COMEDY/MUSICAL: **Kay Kendall** Les Girls

SUPPORTING ACTOR: **Red Buttons** Sayonara

SUPPORTING ACTRESS: **Elsa Lanchester** Witness for the Prosecution

Cannes Film Festival

PALME D'OR: **Friendly Persuasion**

DIRECTOR: **Robert Bresson** A Man Escaped

ACTOR: **John Kitzmiller** Dolina Mira

ACTRESS: **Giulietta Masina** Nights of Cabiria

Berlin International Film Festival

GOLDEN BEAR: **12 Angry Men**

SILVER BEAR, DIRECTOR: **Mario Monicelli** Padri e Figli

SILVER BEAR, ACTOR: **Pedro Infante** Tizoc

SILVER BEAR, ACTRESS: **Yvonne Mitchell** Woman in a Dressing Gown

1958

British Film Academy Awards

FILM: **Room at the Top** • Aparajito • Cat on a Hot Tin Roof • The Cranes Are Flying • The Defiant Ones • Ice Cold in Alex • Indiscreet • Nights of Cabiria • No Down Payment • Orders to Kill • Sea of Sand • The Sheepman • Wild Strawberries • The Young Lions

BRITISH FILM: **Room at the Top** • Ice Cold in Alex • Indiscreet • Orders to Kill • Sea of Sand

FOREIGN ACTOR: **Sidney Poitier** The Defiant Ones • Marlon Brando The Young Lions • Tony Curtis The Defiant Ones • Glenn Ford The Sheepman • Curt Jurgens The Enemy Below • Curt Jurgens The Inn of the Sixth Happiness • Charles Laughton Witness for the Prosecution • Paul Newman Cat on a Hot Tin Roof • Spencer Tracy The Last Hurrah • Victor Sjöström Wild Strawberries

FOREIGN ACTRESS: **Simone Signoret** Room at the Top • Karuna Bannerjee Aparajito • Ingrid Bergman The Inn of the Sixth Happiness • Anna Magnani Wild Is the Wind • Giulietta

---

Masina Nights of Cabiria • Tatyana Samoilova The Cranes Are Flying • Elizabeth Taylor Cat on a Hot Tin Roof • Joanne Woodward No Down Payment

BRITISH ACTOR: **Trevor Howard** The Key • Sydney Boehm Harry Black and the Tiger • Michael Craig Sea of Sand • Laurence Harvey Room at the Top • Anthony Quayle Ice Cold in Alex • Terry-Thomas tom thumb • Donald Wolfit Room at the Top

BRITISH ACTRESS: **Irene Worth** Orders to Kill • Hermione Baddeley Room at the Top • Virginia McKenna Carve Her Name with Pride

BRITISH SCREENPLAY: **Paul Dehn** Orders to Kill

Academy Awards

PICTURE: **Gigi** • Auntie Mame • Cat on a Hot Tin Roof • The Defiant Ones • Separate Tables

FOREIGN LANGUAGE FILM: **Mon Oncle** • Arms and the Man • Big Deal on Madonna Street • The Road a Year Long • La Venganza

DIRECTOR: **Vincente Minnelli** Gigi • Richard Brooks Cat on a Hot Tin Roof • Stanley Kramer The Defiant Ones • Mark Robson The Inn of the Sixth Happiness • Robert Wise I Want to Live!

ACTOR: **David Niven** Separate Tables • Tony Curtis The Defiant Ones • Paul Newman Cat on a Hot Tin Roof • Sidney Poitier The Defiant Ones • Spencer Tracy The Old Man and the Sea

ACTRESS: **Susan Hayward** I Want to Live! • Deborah Kerr Separate Tables • Shirley MacLaine Some Came Running • Rosalind Russell Auntie Mame • Elizabeth Taylor Cat on a Hot Tin Roof

SUPPORTING ACTOR: **Burl Ives** The Big Country • Theodore Bikel The Defiant Ones • Lee J Cobb The Brothers Karamazov • Arthur Kennedy Some Came Running • Gig Young Teacher's Pet

SUPPORTING ACTRESS: **Wendy Hiller** Separate Tables • Peggy Cass Auntie Mame • Martha Hyer Some Came Running • Maureen Stapleton Lonelyhearts • Cara Williams The Defiant Ones

ORIGINAL STORY, SCREENPLAY: **Nedrick Young, Harold Jacob Smith** The Defiant Ones • Paddy Chayefsky The Goddess • Melville Shavelson, Jack Rose Houseboat • William Bowers, James Edward Grant The Sheepman • Fay Kanin, Michael Kanin Teacher's Pet

ADAPTED SCREENPLAY: **Alan Jay Lerner** Gigi • Richard Brooks, James Poe Cat on a Hot Tin Roof • Alec Guinness The Horse's Mouth • Nelson Gidding, Don Mankiewicz I Want to Live! • John Gay, Terence Rattigan Separate Tables

Golden Globe Awards

DRAMA: **The Defiant Ones**

COMEDY: **Auntie Mame**

MUSICAL: **Gigi**

INTERNATIONAL AWARD: **The Girl and the River • The Girl Rosemarie • A Night to Remember • The Road a Year Long**

DIRECTOR: **Vincente Minnelli** Gigi

ACTOR, DRAMA: **David Niven** Separate Tables

ACTRESS, DRAMA: **Susan Hayward** I Want to Live!

ACTOR, COMEDY/MUSICAL: **Danny Kaye** Me and the Colonel

ACTRESS, COMEDY/MUSICAL: **Rosalind Russell** Auntie Mame

SUPPORTING ACTOR: **Burl Ives** The Big Country

SUPPORTING ACTRESS: **Hermione Gingold** Gigi

Cannes Film Festival

PALME D'OR: **The Cranes Are Flying**

DIRECTOR: **Ingmar Bergman** So Close to Life

ACTOR: **Paul Newman** The Long Hot Summer

ACTRESS: **Bibi Andersson, Barbro Hiort Af Ornas, Ingrid Thulin, Eva Dahlbeck** So Close to Life

ORIGINAL SCREENPLAY: **Pier Paolo Pasolini, Massimo Franciosa, Pasquale Festa Campanile** Young Husbands

Berlin International Film Festival

GOLDEN BEAR: **Wild Strawberries**

SILVER BEAR, DIRECTOR: **Tadashi Imai** Jun-Ai Monogatari

SILVER BEAR, ACTOR: **Sidney Poitier** The Defiant Ones

SILVER BEAR, ACTRESS: **Anna Magnani** Wild Is the Wind

1959

British Film Academy Awards

FILM: **Ben-Hur** • Anatomy of a Murder • Ashes and Diamonds • The Big Country • Compulsion • The Magician • Gigi • Look Back in Anger • Maigret Sets a Trap • North West Frontier • The Nun's Story • Sapphire • Some Like It Hot • Tiger Bay • Yesterday's Enemy

BRITISH FILM: **Sapphire** • Look Back in Anger • North West Frontier • Tiger Bay • Yesterday's Enemy

FOREIGN ACTOR: **Jack Lemmon** Some Like It Hot • Zbigniew Cybulski Ashes and Diamonds • Jean Desailly, Jean Gabin Maigret Sets a Trap • Takashi Shimura Ikiru • James Stewart Anatomy of a Murder

FOREIGN ACTRESS: **Shirley MacLaine** Ask Any Girl • Ava Gardner On the Beach • Susan Hayward I Want to Live! • Ellie Lambetti A Matter of Dignity • Rosalind Russell Auntie Mame

BRITISH ACTOR: **Peter Sellers** I'm All Right Jack • Stanley Baker Yesterday's Enemy • Richard Burton Look Back in Anger • Peter Finch The Nun's Story • Laurence Harvey Expresso Bongo • Gordon Jackson Yesterday's Enemy • Laurence Olivier The Devil's Disciple

BRITISH ACTRESS: **Audrey Hepburn** The Nun's Story • Peggy Ashcroft The Nun's Story • Wendy Hiller Separate Tables • Yvonne Mitchell Sapphire • Sylvia Syms No Trees in the Street • Kay Walsh The Horse's Mouth

BRITISH SCREENPLAY: **Frank Harvey, Alan Hackney, John Boulting** I'm All Right Jack • Ben Barzman, Millard Lampbell Blind Date • Wolf Mankowitz Expresso Bongo • Alec Guinness The Horse's Mouth • Nigel Kneale Look Back in Anger •

Robin Estridge *North West Frontier* • Ted Willis *No Trees in the Street* • Janet Green *Sapphire* • John Hawkesworth, Shelley Smith *Tiger Bay*

Academy Awards

PICTURE: **Ben-Hur** • *Anatomy of a Murder* • *The Diary of Anne Frank* • *The Nun's Story* • *Room at the Top*
FOREIGN LANGUAGE FILM: **Black Orpheus** • *The Bridge* • *The Great War* • *Paw* • *The Village on the River*
DIRECTOR: **William Wyler** *Ben-Hur* • Jack Clayton *Room at the Top* • George Stevens *The Diary of Anne Frank* • Billy Wilder *Some Like It Hot* • Fred Zinnemann *The Nun's Story*
ACTOR: **Charlton Heston** *Ben-Hur* • Laurence Harvey *Room at the Top* • Jack Lemmon *Some Like It Hot* • Paul Muni *The Last Angry Man* • James Stewart *Anatomy of a Murder*
ACTRESS: **Simone Signoret** *Room at the Top* • Doris Day *Pillow Talk* • Audrey Hepburn *The Nun's Story* • Katharine Hepburn, Elizabeth Taylor *Suddenly, Last Summer*
SUPPORTING ACTOR: **Hugh Griffith** *Ben-Hur* • Arthur O'Connell, George C Scott *Anatomy of a Murder* • Robert Vaughn *The Young Philadelphians* • Ed Wynn *The Diary of Anne Frank*
SUPPORTING ACTRESS: **Shelley Winters** *The Diary of Anne Frank* • Hermione Baddeley *Room at the Top* • Susan Kohner, Juanita Moore *Imitation of Life* • Thelma Ritter *Pillow Talk*
ORIGINAL STORY, SCREENPLAY: **Stanley Shapiro, Maurice Richlin, Russell Rouse, Clarence Greene** *Pillow Talk* • François Truffaut, Marcel Moussy *The 400 Blows* • Ernest Lehman *North by Northwest* • Stanley Shapiro, Maurice Richlin, Paul King, Joseph Stone *Operation Petticoat* • Ingmar Bergman *Wild Strawberries*
ADAPTED SCREENPLAY: **Neil Paterson** *Room at the Top* • Wendell Mayes *Anatomy of a Murder* • Karl Tunberg *Ben-Hur* • Robert Anderson *The Nun's Story* • Billy Wilder, IAL Diamond *Some Like It Hot*

Golden Globe Awards

DRAMA: **Ben-Hur**
COMEDY: **Some Like It Hot**
MUSICAL: **Porgy and Bess**
INTERNATIONAL AWARD: **Aren't We Wonderful** • **Black Orpheus** • **The Bridge** • **The Key** • **Wild Strawberries**
DIRECTOR: **William Wyler** *Ben-Hur*
ACTOR, DRAMA: **Anthony Franciosa** *Career*
ACTRESS, DRAMA: **Elizabeth Taylor** *Suddenly, Last Summer*
ACTOR, COMEDY/MUSICAL: **Jack Lemmon** *Some Like It Hot*
ACTRESS, COMEDY/MUSICAL: **Marilyn Monroe** *Some Like It Hot*
SUPPORTING ACTOR: **Stephen Boyd** *Ben-Hur*
SUPPORTING ACTRESS: **Susan Kohner** *Imitation of Life*

Cannes Film Festival

PALME D'OR: **Black Orpheus**
DIRECTOR: **François Truffaut** *The 400 Blows*
ACTOR: **Dean Stockwell, Bradford Dillman, Orson Welles** *Compulsion*
ACTRESS: **Simone Signoret** *Room at the Top*

Berlin International Film Festival

GOLDEN BEAR: **Les Cousins**
SILVER BEAR, DIRECTOR: **Akira Kurosawa** *The Hidden Fortress*
SILVER BEAR, ACTOR: **Jean Gabin** *Archimède the Tramp*
SILVER BEAR, ACTRESS: **Shirley MacLaine** *Ask Any Girl*

1960

British Film Academy Awards

FILM: **The Apartment** • *The Angry Silence* • *L'Avventura* • *Black Orpheus* • *La Dolce Vita* • *Elmer Gantry* • *The 400 Blows* • *Hiroshima, Mon Amour* • *Inherit the Wind* • *Let's Make Love* • *Never on Sunday* • *Saturday Night and Sunday Morning* • *Shadows* • *Spartacus* • *Le Testament d'Orphée* • *The Trials of Oscar Wilde* • *Tunes of Glory*
BRITISH FILM: **Saturday Night and Sunday Morning** • *The Angry Silence* • *The Trials of Oscar Wilde* • *Tunes of Glory*
FOREIGN ACTOR: **Jack Lemmon** *The Apartment* • George Hamilton *Crime and Punishment, USA* • Burt Lancaster *Elmer Gantry* • Fredric March *Inherit the Wind* • Yves Montand *Let's Make Love* • Spencer Tracy *Inherit the Wind*
FOREIGN ACTRESS: **Shirley MacLaine** *The Apartment* • Pier Angeli *The Angry Silence* • Melina Mercouri *Never on Sunday* • Emmanuelle Riva *Hiroshima, Mon Amour* • Jean Simmons *Elmer Gantry* • Monica Vitti *L'Avventura*
BRITISH ACTOR: **Peter Finch** *The Trials of Oscar Wilde* • Richard Attenborough *The Angry Silence* • Albert Finney *Saturday Night and Sunday Morning* • John Fraser *The Trials of Oscar Wilde* • Alec Guinness, John Mills *Tunes of Glory* • Laurence Olivier *The Entertainer*
BRITISH ACTRESS: **Rachel Roberts** *Saturday Night and Sunday Morning* • Wendy Hiller *Sons and Lovers* • Hayley Mills *Pollyanna*
BRITISH SCREENPLAY: **Bryan Forbes** *The Angry Silence* • Howard Clewes *The Day They Robbed the Bank of England* • John Osborne, Nigel Kneale *The Entertainer* • Val Guest *Hell Is a City* • Bryan Forbes *The League of Gentlemen* • Wolf Mankowitz *The Millionairess* • Alan Sillitoe *Saturday Night and Sunday Morning* • Roger MacDougall, Guy Hamilton, Ivan Foxwell *A Touch of Larceny* • Ken Hughes *The Trials of Oscar Wilde* • James Kennaway *Tunes of Glory*

Academy Awards

PICTURE: **The Apartment** • *The Alamo* • *Elmer Gantry* • *Sons and Lovers* • *The Sundowners*
FOREIGN LANGUAGE FILM: **The Virgin Spring** • *Kapo* • *Macario* • *The Ninth Circle* • *La Vérité*
DIRECTOR: **Billy Wilder** *The Apartment* • Jack Cardiff *Sons and Lovers* • Jules Dassin *Never on Sunday* • Alfred Hitchcock *Psycho* • Fred Zinnemann *The Sundowners*

ACTOR: **Burt Lancaster** *Elmer Gantry* • Trevor Howard *Sons and Lovers* • Jack Lemmon *The Apartment* • Laurence Olivier *The Entertainer* • Spencer Tracy *Inherit the Wind*
ACTRESS: **Elizabeth Taylor** *Butterfield 8* • Greer Garson *Sunrise at Campobello* • Deborah Kerr *The Sundowners* • Shirley MacLaine *The Apartment* • Melina Mercouri *Never on Sunday*
SUPPORTING ACTOR: **Peter Ustinov** *Spartacus* • Peter Falk *Murder, Inc* • Jack Kruschen *The Apartment* • Sal Mineo *Exodus* • Chill Wills *The Alamo*
SUPPORTING ACTRESS: **Shirley Jones** *Elmer Gantry* • Glynis Johns *The Sundowners* • Shirley Knight *The Dark at the Top of the Stairs* • Janet Leigh *Psycho* • Mary Ure *Sons and Lovers*
ORIGINAL STORY, SCREENPLAY: **Billy Wilder, IAL Diamond** *The Apartment* • Bryan Forbes, Michael Craig, Richard Gregson *The Angry Silence* • Norman Panama, Melvin Frank *The Facts of Life* • Marguerite Duras *Hiroshima, Mon Amour* • Jules Dassin *Never on Sunday*
ADAPTED SCREENPLAY: **Richard Brooks** *Elmer Gantry* • Nedrick Young, Harold Jacob Smith *Inherit the Wind* • TEB Clarke, Gavin Lambert *Sons and Lovers* • Isobel Lennart *The Sundowners* • James Kennaway *Tunes of Glory*

Golden Globe Awards

DRAMA: **Spartacus**
COMEDY: **The Apartment**
MUSICAL: **Song without End**
INTERNATIONAL AWARD: **The Trials of Oscar Wilde** • **La Vérité** • **The Virgin Spring**
DIRECTOR: **Jack Cardiff** *Sons and Lovers*
ACTOR, DRAMA: **Burt Lancaster** *Elmer Gantry*
ACTRESS, DRAMA: **Greer Garson** *Sunrise at Campobello*
ACTOR, COMEDY/MUSICAL: **Jack Lemmon** *The Apartment*
ACTRESS, COMEDY/MUSICAL: **Shirley MacLaine** *The Apartment*
SUPPORTING ACTOR: **Sal Mineo** *Exodus*
SUPPORTING ACTRESS: **Janet Leigh** *Psycho*

Cannes Film Festival

PALME D'OR: **La Dolce Vita**
ACTRESS: **Melina Mercouri** *Never on Sunday* • **Jeanne Moreau** *Moderato Cantabile*

Berlin International Film Festival

GOLDEN BEAR: **Lazarillo**
SILVER BEAR, DIRECTOR: **Jean-Luc Godard** *A Bout de Souffle*
SILVER BEAR, ACTOR: **Fredric March** *Inherit the Wind*
SILVER BEAR, ACTRESS: **Juliette Mayniel** *Kirmes*

1961

British Film Academy Awards

FILM: **Ballad of a Soldier** • **The Hustler** • *The Innocents* • *Judgment at Nuremberg* • *The Long and the Short and the Tall* • *Rocco and His Brothers* • *A Taste of Honey* • *The Sundowners* • *Le Trou* • *Whistle down the Wind* • *The World of Apu*
BRITISH FILM: **A Taste of Honey** • *The Innocents* • *The Long and the Short and the Tall* • *The Sundowners* • *Whistle down the Wind*
FOREIGN ACTOR: **Paul Newman** *The Hustler* • Montgomery Clift *Judgment at Nuremberg* • Vladimir Ivashov *Ballad of a Soldier* • Philippe Leroy *Le Trou* • Sidney Poitier *A Raisin in the Sun* • Maximilian Schell *Judgment at Nuremberg* • Alberto Sordi *The Best of Enemies*
FOREIGN ACTRESS: **Sophia Loren** *Two Women* • Annie Girardot *Rocco and His Brothers* • Piper Laurie *The Hustler* • Claudia McNeil *A Raisin in the Sun* • Jean Seberg *A Bout de Souffle*
BRITISH ACTOR: **Peter Finch** *No Love for Johnnie* • Dirk Bogarde *Victim*
BRITISH ACTRESS: **Dora Bryan** *A Taste of Honey* • Deborah Kerr *The Sundowners* • Hayley Mills *Whistle down the Wind*
BRITISH SCREENPLAY: **Wolf Mankowitz, Val Guest** *The Day the Earth Caught Fire* • **Tony Richardson, Shelagh Delaney** *A Taste of Honey* • Ted Willis *Flame in the Streets* • Carl Foreman *The Guns of Navarone* • Janet Green, John McCormick *Victim* • Keith Waterhouse, Willis Hall *Whistle down the Wind*

Academy Awards

PICTURE: **West Side Story** • *Fanny* • *The Guns of Navarone* • *The Hustler* • *Judgment at Nuremberg*
FOREIGN LANGUAGE FILM: **Through a Glass Darkly** • *Harry and the Butler* • *Immortal Love* • *The Important Man* • *Placido*
DIRECTOR: **Jerome Robbins, Robert Wise** *West Side Story* • Federico Fellini *La Dolce Vita* • Stanley Kramer *Judgment at Nuremberg* • J Lee Thompson *The Guns of Navarone* • Robert Rossen *The Hustler*
ACTOR: **Maximilian Schell** *Judgment at Nuremberg* • Charles Boyer *Fanny* • Paul Newman *The Hustler* • Spencer Tracy *Judgment at Nuremberg* • Stuart Whitman *The Mark*
ACTRESS: **Sophia Loren** *Two Women* • Audrey Hepburn *Breakfast at Tiffany's* • Piper Laurie *The Hustler* • Geraldine Page *Summer and Smoke* • Natalie Wood *Splendor in the Grass*
SUPPORTING ACTOR: **George Chakiris** *West Side Story* • Montgomery Clift *Judgment at Nuremberg* • Peter Falk *Pocketful of Miracles* • Jackie Gleason, George C Scott *The Hustler*
SUPPORTING ACTRESS: **Rita Moreno** *West Side Story* • Fay Bainter *The Children's Hour* • Judy Garland *Judgment at Nuremberg* • Una Merkel *Summer and Smoke* • Jill St John *The Roman Spring of Mrs Stone*
ORIGINAL STORY, SCREENPLAY: **William Inge** *Splendor in the Grass* • Grigori Chukhrai, Valentin Yezhov *Ballad of a Soldier* • Federico Fellini, Ennio Flaiano, Tullio Pinelli, Brunello Rondi *La Dolce Vita* • Indro Montanelli, Sergio Amidei, Diego Fabbri *General Della Rovere* • Stanley Kramer, Paul Henning *Lover Come Back*

ADAPTED SCREENPLAY: **Abby Mann** *Judgment at Nuremberg* • George Axelrod *Breakfast at Tiffany's* • Carl Foreman *The Guns of Navarone* • Sidney Carroll, Robert Rossen *The Hustler* • Ernest Lehman *West Side Story*

Golden Globe Awards

DRAMA: **The Guns of Navarone**
COMEDY: **A Majority of One**
MUSICAL: **West Side Story**
INTERNATIONAL AWARD: **Two Women**
DIRECTOR: **Stanley Kramer** *Judgment at Nuremberg*
ACTOR, DRAMA: **Maximilian Schell** *Judgment at Nuremberg*
ACTRESS, DRAMA: **Geraldine Page** *Summer and Smoke*
ACTOR, COMEDY/MUSICAL: **Glenn Ford** *Pocketful of Miracles*
ACTRESS, COMEDY/MUSICAL: **Rosalind Russell** *A Majority of One*
SUPPORTING ACTOR: **George Chakiris** *West Side Story*
SUPPORTING ACTRESS: **Rita Moreno** *West Side Story*

Cannes Film Festival

PALME D'OR: **Viridiana** • **The Long Absence**
DIRECTOR: **Yulia Solntseva** *The Flaming Years*
ACTOR: **Anthony Perkins** *Goodbye Again*
ACTRESS: **Sophia Loren** *Two Women*

Berlin International Film Festival

GOLDEN BEAR: **La Notte**
SILVER BEAR, DIRECTOR: **Bernhard Wicki** *The Miracle of Malachias*
SILVER BEAR, ACTOR: **Peter Finch** *No Love for Johnnie*
SILVER BEAR, ACTRESS: **Anna Karina** *Une Femme Est une Femme*

1962

British Film Academy Awards

FILM: **Lawrence of Arabia** • *Billy Budd* • *The Island* • *Jules et Jim* • *A Kind of Loving* • *The L-Shaped Room* • *The Lady with the Little Dog* • *Last Year at Marienbad* • *The Long Absence* • *Lola* • *The Manchurian Candidate* • *The Miracle Worker* • *Only Two Can Play* • *Phaedra* • *Thou Shalt Not Kill* • *Through a Glass Darkly* • *The Vanishing Corporal* • *West Side Story*
BRITISH FILM: **Lawrence of Arabia** • *Billy Budd* • *A Kind of Loving* • *The L-Shaped Room* • *Only Two Can Play*
FOREIGN FILM: **Burt Lancaster** *Birdman of Alcatraz* • Jean-Paul Belmondo *Léon Morin, Priest* • Franco Citti *Accattone* • Kirk Douglas *Lonely Are the Brave* • George Hamilton *Light in the Piazza* • Charles Laughton *Advise and Consent* • Anthony Quinn *Lawrence of Arabia* • Robert Ryan *Billy Budd* • Georges Wilson *The Long Absence*
FOREIGN ACTRESS: **Anne Bancroft** *The Miracle Worker* • Harriet Andersson *Through a Glass Darkly* • Anouk Aimée *Lola* • Melina Mercouri *Phaedra* • Jeanne Moreau *Jules et Jim* • Geraldine Page *Sweet Bird of Youth* • Natalie Wood *Splendor in the Grass*
BRITISH ACTOR: **Peter O'Toole** *Lawrence of Arabia* • Richard Attenborough *Trial and Error* • Alan Bates *A Kind of Loving* • James Mason *Lolita* • Laurence Olivier *Term of Trial* • Peter Sellers *Only Two Can Play*
BRITISH ACTRESS: **Leslie Caron** *The L-Shaped Room* • Virginia Maskell *The Wild and the Willing* • Janet Munro *Life for Ruth*
BRITISH SCREENPLAY: **Robert Bolt** *Lawrence of Arabia* • Peter Ustinov, DeWitt Bodeen *Billy Budd* • Willis Hall, Keith Waterhouse *A Kind of Loving* • Bryan Forbes *Only Two Can Play* • Geoffrey Cotterell, Ivan Foxwell *Tiara Tahiti* • Wolf Mankowitz *Waltz of the Toreadors*

Academy Awards

PICTURE: **Lawrence of Arabia** • *The Longest Day* • *The Music Man* • *Mutiny on the Bounty* • *To Kill a Mockingbird*
FOREIGN LANGUAGE FILM: **Sundays and Cybèle** • *Elektra* • *The Four Days of Naples* • *The Given Word* • *Tlayucan*
DIRECTOR: **David Lean** *Lawrence of Arabia* • Pietro Germi *Divorce - Italian Style* • Robert Mulligan *To Kill a Mockingbird* • Arthur Penn *The Miracle Worker* • Frank Perry *David and Lisa*
ACTOR: **Gregory Peck** *To Kill a Mockingbird* • Burt Lancaster *Birdman of Alcatraz* • Jack Lemmon *Days of Wine and Roses* • Marcello Mastroianni *Divorce - Italian Style* • Peter O'Toole *Lawrence of Arabia*
ACTRESS: **Anne Bancroft** *The Miracle Worker* • Bette Davis *What Ever Happened to Baby Jane?* • Katharine Hepburn *Long Day's Journey into Night* • Geraldine Page *Sweet Bird of Youth* • Lee Remick *Days of Wine and Roses*
SUPPORTING ACTOR: **Ed Begley** *Sweet Bird of Youth* • Victor Buono *What Ever Happened to Baby Jane?* • Telly Savalas *Birdman of Alcatraz* • Omar Sharif *Lawrence of Arabia* • Terence Stamp *Billy Budd*
SUPPORTING ACTRESS: **Patty Duke** *The Miracle Worker* • Mary Badham *To Kill a Mockingbird* • Shirley Knight *Sweet Bird of Youth* • Angela Lansbury *The Manchurian Candidate* • Thelma Ritter *Birdman of Alcatraz*
ORIGINAL STORY, SCREENPLAY: **Pietro Germi, Ennio De Concini, Alfredo Giannetti** *Divorce - Italian Style* • Charles Kaufman, Wolfgang Reinhardt *Freud* • Alain Robbe-Grillet *Last Year at Marienbad* • Stanley Shapiro, Nate Monaster *That Touch of Mink* • Ingmar Bergman *Through a Glass Darkly*
ADAPTED SCREENPLAY: **Horton Foote** *To Kill a Mockingbird* • Eleanor Perry *David and Lisa* • Robert Bolt, Michael Wilson *Lawrence of Arabia* • Vladimir Nabokov *Lolita* • William Gibson *The Miracle Worker*

Golden Globe Awards

DRAMA: **Lawrence of Arabia**
COMEDY: **That Touch of Mink**
MUSICAL: **The Music Man**
INTERNATIONAL AWARD: **Divorce - Italian Style**

DIRECTOR: **David Lean** *Lawrence of Arabia*
ACTOR, DRAMA: **Gregory Peck** *To Kill a Mockingbird*
ACTRESS, DRAMA: **Geraldine Page** *Sweet Bird of Youth*
ACTOR, COMEDY/MUSICAL: **Marcello Mastroianni** *Divorce – Italian Style*
ACTRESS, COMEDY/MUSICAL: **Rosalind Russell** *Gypsy*
SUPPORTING ACTOR: **Omar Sharif** *Lawrence of Arabia*
SUPPORTING ACTRESS: **Angela Lansbury** *The Manchurian Candidate*

Cannes Film Festival

PALME D'OR: **The Given Word**
ACTOR: **Ralph Richardson, Jason Robards, Dean Stockwell** *Long Day's Journey into Night* • **Murray Melvin** *A Taste of Honey*
ACTRESS: **Katharine Hepburn** *Long Day's Journey into Night* • **Rita Tushingham** *A Taste of Honey*

Berlin International Film Festival

GOLDEN BEAR: **A Kind of Loving**
SILVER BEAR, DIRECTOR: **Francesco Rosi** *Salvatore Giuliano*
SILVER BEAR, ACTOR: **James Stewart** *Mr Hobbs Takes a Vacation*
SILVER BEAR, ACTRESS: **Rita Gam, Viveca Lindfors** *No Exit*

1963

British Film Academy Awards

FILM: **Tom Jones** • *Billy Liar* • *David and Lisa* • *Days of Wine and Roses* • *Divorce – Italian Style* • *8½* • *The Four Days of Naples* • *Hud* • *Knife in the Water* • *The Servant* • *This Sporting Life* • *To Kill a Mockingbird*
BRITISH FILM: **The Servant** • *Billy Liar* • *This Sporting Life* • *Tom Jones*
FOREIGN ACTOR: **Marcello Mastroianni** *Divorce – Italian Style* • Howard Da Silva *David and Lisa* • Jack Lemmon *Days of Wine and Roses* • Paul Newman *Hud* • Gregory Peck *To Kill a Mockingbird*
FOREIGN ACTRESS: **Patricia Neal** *Hud* • Joan Crawford, Bette Davis *What Ever Happened to Baby Jane?* • Lee Remick *Days of Wine and Roses* • Daniela Rocca *Divorce – Italian Style*
BRITISH ACTOR: **Dirk Bogarde** *The Servant* • Tom Courtenay *Billy Liar* • Albert Finney, Hugh Griffith *Tom Jones* • Richard Harris *This Sporting Life*
BRITISH ACTRESS: **Rachel Roberts** *This Sporting Life* • Julie Christie *Billy Liar* • Edith Evans *Tom Jones* • Sarah Miles *The Servant* • Barbara Windsor *Sparrows Can't Sing*
BRITISH SCREENPLAY: **John Osborne** *Tom Jones* • Keith Waterhouse, Willis Hall *Billy Liar* • Harold Pinter *The Servant* • David Storey *This Sporting Life*

Academy Awards

PICTURE: **Tom Jones** • *America, America* • *Cleopatra* • *How the West Was Won* • *Lilies of the Field*
FOREIGN LANGUAGE FILM: **8½** • *Knife in the Water* • *The Red Lanterns* • *Los Tarantos* • *Twin Sisters of Kyoto*
DIRECTOR: **Tony Richardson** *Tom Jones* • Federico Fellini *8½* • Elia Kazan *America, America* • Otto Preminger *The Cardinal* • Martin Ritt *Hud*
ACTOR: **Sidney Poitier** *Lilies of the Field* • Albert Finney *Tom Jones* • Richard Harris *This Sporting Life* • Rex Harrison *Cleopatra* • Paul Newman *Hud*
ACTRESS: **Patricia Neal** *Hud* • Leslie Caron *The L-Shaped Room* • Shirley MacLaine *Irma la Douce* • Rachel Roberts *This Sporting Life* • Natalie Wood *Love with the Proper Stranger*
SUPPORTING ACTOR: **Melvyn Douglas** *Hud* • Nick Adams *Twilight of Honor* • Bobby Darin *Captain Newman, MD* • Hugh Griffith *Tom Jones* • John Huston *The Cardinal*
SUPPORTING ACTRESS: **Margaret Rutherford** *The VIPs* • Diane Cilento, Edith Evans, Joyce Redman *Tom Jones* • Lilia Skala *Lilies of the Field*
ORIGINAL STORY, SCREENPLAY: **James R Webb** *How the West Was Won* • Elia Kazan *America, America* • Federico Fellini, Tullio Pinelli, Ennio Flajano, Brunello Rondi *8½* • Pasquale Festa Campanile, Massimo Franciosa, Nanni Loy, Carlo Benari, Vasco Pratolini *The Four Days of Naples* • Arnold Schulman *Love with the Proper Stranger*
ADAPTED SCREENPLAY: **John Osborne** *Tom Jones* • Richard L Breen, Phoebe Ephron, Henry Ephron *Captain Newman, MD* • Irving Ravetch, Harriet Frank Jr *Hud* • James Poe *Lilies of the Field* • Serge Bourguignon, Antoine Tudal *Sundays and Cybèle*

Golden Globe Awards

DRAMA: **The Cardinal**
COMEDY/MUSICAL: **Tom Jones**
INTERNATIONAL AWARD: **Tom Jones**
DIRECTOR: **Elia Kazan** *America, America*
ACTOR, DRAMA: **Sidney Poitier** *Lilies of the Field*
ACTRESS, DRAMA: **Leslie Caron** *The L-Shaped Room*
ACTOR, COMEDY/MUSICAL: **Alberto Sordi** *The Devil*
ACTRESS, COMEDY/MUSICAL: **Shirley MacLaine** *Irma la Douce*
SUPPORTING ACTOR: **John Huston** *The Cardinal*
SUPPORTING ACTRESS: **Margaret Rutherford** *The VIPs*

Cannes Film Festival

PALME D'OR: **The Leopard**
ACTOR: **Richard Harris** *This Sporting Life*
ACTRESS: **Marina Vlady** *The Conjugal Bed*
SCREENPLAY: **Henri Colpi** *Codine*

Berlin International Film Festival

GOLDEN BEAR: **The Devil** • *Bushido Zankoku Monogatari*
SILVER BEAR, DIRECTOR: **Nikos Koundouros** *Mikres Aphrodites*
SILVER BEAR, ACTOR: **Sidney Poitier** *Lilies of the Field*
SILVER BEAR, ACTRESS: **Bibi Andersson** *The Swedish Mistress*

1964

British Film Academy Awards

FILM: **Dr Strangelove, or How I Learned to Stop Worrying and Love the Bomb** • *Becket* • *The Pumpkin Eater* • *The Train*
BRITISH FILM: **Dr Strangelove, or How I Learned to Stop Worrying and Love the Bomb** • *Becket* • *King and Country* • *The Pumpkin Eater*
FOREIGN ACTOR: **Marcello Mastroianni** *Yesterday, Today and Tomorrow* • Cary Grant *Charade* • Sterling Hayden *Dr Strangelove, or How I Learned to Stop Worrying and Love the Bomb* • Sidney Poitier *Lilies of the Field*
FOREIGN ACTRESS: **Anne Bancroft** *The Pumpkin Eater* • Ava Gardner *The Night of the Iguana* • Shirley MacLaine *Irma la Douce* • Shirley MacLaine *What a Way to Go!* • Kim Stanley *Seance on a Wet Afternoon*
BRITISH ACTOR: **Richard Attenborough** *Guns at Batasi* • **Richard Attenborough** *Seance on a Wet Afternoon* • Tom Courtenay *King and Country* • Peter O'Toole *Becket* • Peter Sellers *Dr Strangelove, or How I Learned to Stop Worrying and Love the Bomb* • Peter Sellers *The Pink Panther*
BRITISH ACTRESS: **Audrey Hepburn** *Charade* • Edith Evans, Deborah Kerr *The Chalk Garden* • Rita Tushingham *Girl with Green Eyes*
BRITISH SCREENPLAY: **Harold Pinter** *The Pumpkin Eater* • Edward Anhalt *Becket* • Stanley Kubrick, Terry Southern, Peter George *Dr Strangelove, or How I Learned to Stop Worrying and Love the Bomb* • Bryan Forbes *Seance on a Wet Afternoon*

Academy Awards

PICTURE: **My Fair Lady** • *Becket* • *Dr Strangelove, or How I Learned to Stop Worrying and Love the Bomb* • *Mary Poppins* • *Zorba the Greek*
FOREIGN LANGUAGE FILM: **Yesterday, Today and Tomorrow** • *Raven's End* • *Sallah* • *The Umbrellas of Cherbourg* • *Woman in the Dunes*
DIRECTOR: **George Cukor** *My Fair Lady* • Michael Cacoyannis *Zorba the Greek* • Peter Glenville *Becket* • Stanley Kubrick *Dr Strangelove, or How I Learned to Stop Worrying and Love the Bomb* • Robert Stevenson *Mary Poppins*
ACTOR: **Rex Harrison** *My Fair Lady* • Richard Burton, Peter O'Toole *Becket* • Anthony Quinn *Zorba the Greek* • Peter Sellers *Dr Strangelove, or How I Learned to Stop Worrying and Love the Bomb*
ACTRESS: **Julie Andrews** *Mary Poppins* • Anne Bancroft *The Pumpkin Eater* • Sophia Loren *Marriage – Italian Style* • Debbie Reynolds *The Unsinkable Molly Brown* • Kim Stanley *Seance on a Wet Afternoon*
SUPPORTING ACTOR: **Peter Ustinov** *Topkapi* • John Gielgud *Becket* • Stanley Holloway *My Fair Lady* • Edmond O'Brien *Seven Days in May* • Lee Tracy *The Best Man*
SUPPORTING ACTRESS: **Lila Kedrova** *Zorba the Greek* • Gladys Cooper *My Fair Lady* • Edith Evans *The Chalk Garden* • Grayson Hall *The Night of the Iguana* • Agnes Moorehead *Hush... Hush, Sweet Charlotte*
ORIGINAL STORY, SCREENPLAY: **Frank Tarloff, Peter Stone, SH Barnett** *Father Goose* • Alun Owen *A Hard Day's Night* • Raphael Hayes, Orville H Hampton *One Potato, Two Potato* • Mario Monicelli, Scarpelli, Age *The Organizer* • Daniel Boulanger, Ariane Mnouchkine, Jean-Paul Rappeneau, Philippe de Broca *That Man from Rio*
ADAPTED SCREENPLAY: **Edward Anhalt** *Becket* • Stanley Kubrick, Terry Southern, Peter George *Dr Strangelove, or How I Learned to Stop Worrying and Love the Bomb* • Bill Walsh, Don DaGradi *Mary Poppins* • Alan Jay Lerner *My Fair Lady* • Michael Cacoyannis *Zorba the Greek*

Golden Globe Awards

DRAMA: **Becket**
COMEDY/MUSICAL: **My Fair Lady**
INTERNATIONAL AWARD: **Sallah**
DIRECTOR: **George Cukor** *My Fair Lady*
ACTOR, DRAMA: **Peter O'Toole** *Becket*
ACTRESS, DRAMA: **Anne Bancroft** *The Pumpkin Eater*
ACTOR, COMEDY/MUSICAL: **Rex Harrison** *My Fair Lady*
ACTRESS, COMEDY/MUSICAL: **Julie Andrews** *Mary Poppins*
SUPPORTING ACTOR: **Edmond O'Brien** *Seven Days in May*
SUPPORTING ACTRESS: **Agnes Moorehead** *Hush... Hush, Sweet Charlotte*

Cannes Film Festival

GRAND PRIX: **The Umbrellas of Cherbourg**
ACTOR: **Antal Pager** *Pacsirta*
ACTRESS: **Anne Bancroft** *The Pumpkin Eater*

Berlin International Film Festival

GOLDEN BEAR: **Susuz Yaz**
SILVER BEAR, DIRECTOR: **Satyajit Ray** *The Big City*
SILVER BEAR, ACTOR: **Rod Steiger** *The Pawnbroker*
SILVER BEAR, ACTRESS: **Sachiko Hidari** *The Insect Woman* • **Sachiko Hidari** *Kanajo To Kare*

1965

British Film Academy Awards

FILM: **My Fair Lady** • *Hamlet* • *The Hill* • *The Knack... and How to Get It* • *Zorba the Greek*
BRITISH FILM: **The Ipcress File** • *Darling* • *The Hill* • *The Knack... and How to Get It*
FOREIGN ACTOR: **Lee Marvin** *The Killers* • **Lee Marvin** *Cat Ballou* • Jack Lemmon *Good Neighbor Sam* • Jack Lemmon *How to Murder Your Wife* • Anthony Quinn *Zorba the Greek* • Innokenti Smoktunovsky *Hamlet* • Oskar Werner *Ship of Fools*

FOREIGN ACTRESS: **Patricia Neal** *In Harm's Way* • Jane Fonda *Cat Ballou* • Lila Kedrova *Zorba the Greek* • Simone Signoret *Ship of Fools*
BRITISH ACTOR: **Dirk Bogarde** *Darling* • Harry Andrews *The Hill* • Michael Caine *The Ipcress File* • Rex Harrison *My Fair Lady*
BRITISH ACTRESS: **Julie Christie** *Darling* • Julie Andrews *The Americanization of Emily* • Julie Andrews *The Sound of Music* • Maggie Smith *Young Cassidy* • Rita Tushingham *The Knack... and How to Get It*
BRITISH SCREENPLAY: **Frederic Raphael** *Darling* • Ray Rigby *The Hill* • Bill Canaway, James Doran *The Ipcress File* • Charles Wood *The Knack... and How to Get It*

Academy Awards

PICTURE: **The Sound of Music** • *Darling* • *Doctor Zhivago* • *Ship of Fools* • *A Thousand Clowns*
FOREIGN LANGUAGE FILM: **The Shop on the High Street** • *Blood on the Land* • *Dear John* • *Kwaidan* • *Marriage – Italian Style*
DIRECTOR: **Robert Wise** *The Sound of Music* • David Lean *Doctor Zhivago* • John Schlesinger *Darling* • Hiroshi Teshigahara *Woman in the Dunes* • William Wyler *The Collector*
ACTOR: **Lee Marvin** *Cat Ballou* • Richard Burton *The Spy Who Came in from the Cold* • Laurence Olivier *Othello* • Rod Steiger *The Pawnbroker* • Oskar Werner *Ship of Fools*
ACTRESS: **Julie Christie** *Darling* • Julie Andrews *The Sound of Music* • Samantha Eggar *The Collector* • Elizabeth Hartman *A Patch of Blue* • Simone Signoret *Ship of Fools*
SUPPORTING ACTOR: **Martin Balsam** *A Thousand Clowns* • Ian Bannen *The Flight of the Phoenix* • Tom Courtenay *Doctor Zhivago* • Michael Dunn *Ship of Fools* • Frank Finlay *Othello*
SUPPORTING ACTRESS: **Shelley Winters** *A Patch of Blue* • Ruth Gordon *Inside Daisy Clover* • Joyce Redman, Maggie Smith *Othello* • Peggy Wood *The Sound of Music*
ORIGINAL STORY, SCREENPLAY: **Frederic Raphael** *Darling* • Agenore Incrocci, Furio Scarpelli, Suso Cecchi D'Amico, Mario Monicelli, Tonino Guerra, Giorgio Salvioni *Casanova '70* • Jack Davies, Ken Annakin *Those Magnificent Men in Their Flying Machines* • Franklin Coen, Frank Davis *The Train* • Jacques Demy *The Umbrellas of Cherbourg*
ADAPTED SCREENPLAY: **Robert Bolt** *Doctor Zhivago* • Frank Pierson, Walter Newman *Cat Ballou* • Stanley Mann, John Kohn *The Collector* • Abby Mann *Ship of Fools* • Herb Gardner *A Thousand Clowns*

Golden Globe Awards

DRAMA: **Doctor Zhivago**
COMEDY/MUSICAL: **The Sound of Music**
FOREIGN FILM/ENGLISH: **Darling**
FOREIGN FILM/NON-ENGLISH: **Juliet of the Spirits**
DIRECTOR: **David Lean** *Doctor Zhivago*
ACTOR, DRAMA: **Omar Sharif** *Doctor Zhivago*
ACTRESS, DRAMA: **Samantha Eggar** *The Collector*
ACTOR, COMEDY/MUSICAL: **Lee Marvin** *Cat Ballou*
ACTRESS, COMEDY/MUSICAL: **Julie Andrews** *The Sound of Music*
SUPPORTING ACTOR: **Oskar Werner** *The Spy Who Came in from the Cold*
SUPPORTING ACTRESS: **Ruth Gordon** *Inside Daisy Clover*
SCREENPLAY: **Robert Bolt** *Doctor Zhivago*

Cannes Film Festival

GRAND PRIX: **The Knack... and How to Get It**
DIRECTOR: **Liviu Ciulei** *The Lost Forest*
ACTOR: **Terence Stamp** *The Collector*
ACTRESS: **Samantha Eggar** *The Collector*
SCREENPLAY: **RS Allen, Ray Rigby** *The Hill* • Pierre Schoendoerffer *La 317eme Section*

Berlin International Film Festival

GOLDEN BEAR: **Alphaville**
SILVER BEAR, DIRECTOR: **Satyajit Ray** *Charulata*
SILVER BEAR, ACTOR: **Lee Marvin** *Cat Ballou*
SILVER BEAR, ACTRESS: **Madhur Jaffrey** *Shakespeare Wallah*

1966

British Film Academy Awards

FILM: **Who's Afraid of Virginia Woolf?** • *Doctor Zhivago* • *Morgan – a Suitable Case for Treatment* • *The Spy Who Came in from the Cold*
BRITISH FILM: **The Spy Who Came in from the Cold** • *Alfie* • *Georgy Girl* • *Morgan – a Suitable Case for Treatment*
FOREIGN ACTOR: **Rod Steiger** *The Pawnbroker* • Jean-Paul Belmondo *Pierrot le Fou* • Sidney Poitier *A Patch of Blue* • Oskar Werner *The Spy Who Came in from the Cold*
FOREIGN ACTRESS: **Jeanne Moreau** *Viva Maria!* • Brigitte Bardot *Viva Maria!* • Joan Hackett *The Group*
BRITISH ACTOR: **Richard Burton** *The Spy Who Came in from the Cold* • **Richard Burton** *Who's Afraid of Virginia Woolf?* • Michael Caine *Alfie* • Ralph Richardson *The Wrong Box* • Ralph Richardson *Doctor Zhivago* • Ralph Richardson *Khartoum* • David Warner *Morgan – a Suitable Case for Treatment*
BRITISH ACTRESS: **Elizabeth Taylor** *Who's Afraid of Virginia Woolf?* • Julie Christie *Doctor Zhivago* • Julie Christie *Fahrenheit 451* • Lynn Redgrave *Georgy Girl* • Vanessa Redgrave *Morgan – a Suitable Case for Treatment*
BRITISH SCREENPLAY: **David Mercer** *Morgan – a Suitable Case for Treatment* • Bill Naughton *Alfie* • Kevin Brownlow, Andrew Mollo *It Happened Here* • Harold Pinter *The Quiller Memorandum*

Academy Awards

PICTURE: **A Man for All Seasons** • *Alfie* • *The Russians Are Coming, the Russians Are Coming* • *The Sand Pebbles* • *Who's Afraid of Virginia Woolf?*
FOREIGN LANGUAGE FILM: **Un Homme et une Femme** • *The Battle of Algiers* • *A Blonde in Love* • *Pharaoh* • *Three*

DIRECTOR: **Fred Zinnemann** *A Man for All Seasons* • Michelangelo Artonioni *Blowup* • Richard Brooks *The Professionals* • Claude Lelouch *Un Homme et une Femme* • Mike Nichols *Who's Afraid of Virginia Woolf?*

ACTOR: **Paul Scofield** *A Man for All Seasons* • Alan Arkin *The Russians Are Coming, the Russians Are Coming* • Richard Burton *Who's Afraid of Virginia Woolf?* • Michael Caine *Alfie* • Steve McQueen *The Sand Pebbles*

ACTRESS: **Elizabeth Taylor** *Who's Afraid of Virginia Woolf?* • Anouk Aimée *Un Homme et une Femme* • Ida Kaminska *The Shop on the High Street* • Lynn Redgrave *Georgy Girl* • Vanessa Redgrave *Morgan - a Suitable Case for Treatment*

SUPPORTING ACTOR: **Walter Matthau** *The Fortune Cookie* • Mako *The Sand Pebbles* • James Mason *Georgy Girl* • George Segal *Who's Afraid of Virginia Woolf?* • Robert Shaw *A Man for All Seasons*

SUPPORTING ACTRESS: **Sandy Dennis** *Who's Afraid of Virginia Woolf?* • Wendy Hiller *A Man for All Seasons* • Jocelyn La Garde *Hawaii* • Vivien Merchant *Alfie* • Geraldine Page *You're a Big Boy Now*

ORIGINAL STORY, SCREENPLAY: **Claude Lelouch, Pierre Uyttterhoeven** *Un Homme et une Femme* • Michelangelo Antonioni, Tonino Guerra, Edward Bond *Blowup* • Billy Wilder, IAL Diamond *The Fortune Cookie* • Robert Ardrey *Khartoum* • Clint Johnston, Don Peters *The Naked Prey*

ADAPTED SCREENPLAY: **Robert Bolt** *A Man for All Seasons* • Bill Naughton *Alfie* • Richard Brooks *The Professionals* • William Rose *The Russians Are Coming, the Russians Are Coming* • Ernest Lehman *Who's Afraid of Virginia Woolf?*

Golden Globe Awards

DRAMA: *A Man for All Seasons*

COMEDY/MUSICAL: *The Russians Are Coming, the Russians Are Coming*

FOREIGN FILM/ENGLISH: *Alfie*

FOREIGN FILM/NON-ENGLISH: *Un Homme et une Femme*

DIRECTOR: **Fred Zinnemann** *A Man for All Seasons*

ACTOR, DRAMA: **Paul Scofield** *A Man for All Seasons*

ACTRESS, DRAMA: **Anouk Aimée** *Un Homme et une Femme*

ACTOR, COMEDY/MUSICAL: **Alan Arkin** *The Russians Are Coming, the Russians Are Coming*

ACTRESS, COMEDY/MUSICAL: **Lynn Redgrave** *Georgy Girl*

SUPPORTING ACTOR: **Richard Attenborough** *The Sand Pebbles*

SUPPORTING ACTRESS: **Jocelyn La Garde** *Hawaii*

SCREENPLAY: **Robert Bolt** *A Man for All Seasons*

Cannes Film Festival

GRAND PRIX: *Un Homme et une Femme* • **The Birds, the Bees, and the Italians**

DIRECTOR: **Sergei Yutkevitch** *Lenin in Poland*

ACTOR: **Per Oscarsson** *Hunger*

ACTRESS: **Vanessa Redgrave** *Morgan - a Suitable Case for Treatment*

Berlin International Film Festival

GOLDEN BEAR: *Cul-de-Sac*

SILVER BEAR, DIRECTOR: **Carlos Saura** *The Hunt*

SILVER BEAR, ACTOR: **Jean-Pierre Léaud** *Masculine Feminine*

SILVER BEAR, ACTRESS: **Lola Albright** *Lord Love a Duck*

1967

British Film Academy Awards

FILM: *A Man for All Seasons* • *Bonnie and Clyde* • *Un Homme et une Femme* • *In the Heat of the Night*

BRITISH FILM: *A Man for All Seasons* • *Accident* • *Blowup* • *The Deadly Affair*

FOREIGN ACTOR: **Rod Steiger** *In the Heat of the Night* • Warren Beatty *Bonnie and Clyde* • Sidney Poitier *In the Heat of the Night* • Orson Welles *Chimes at Midnight*

FOREIGN ACTRESS: **Anouk Aimée** *Un Homme et une Femme* • Bibi Andersson *My Sister, My Love* • Bibi Andersson *Persona* • Jane Fonda *Barefoot in the Park* • Simone Signoret *The Deadly Affair*

BRITISH ACTOR: **Paul Scofield** *A Man for All Seasons* • Dirk Bogarde *Accident* • Dirk Bogarde *Our Mother's House* • Richard Burton *The Taming of the Shrew* • James Mason *The Deadly Affair*

BRITISH ACTRESS: **Edith Evans** *The Whisperers* • Barbara Jefford *Ulysses* • Elizabeth Taylor *The Taming of the Shrew*

BRITISH SCREENPLAY: **Robert Bolt** *A Man for All Seasons* • Harold Pinter *Accident* • Paul Dehn *The Deadly Affair* • Frederic Raphael *Two for the Road*

Academy Awards

PICTURE: *In the Heat of the Night* • *Bonnie and Clyde* • *Doctor Dolittle* • *The Graduate* • *Guess Who's Coming to Dinner*

FOREIGN LANGUAGE FILM: *Closely Observed Trains* • *El Amor Brujo* • *I Even Met Happy Gypsies* • *Portrait of Chieko* • *Vivre pour Vivre*

DIRECTOR: **Mike Nichols** *The Graduate* • Richard Brooks *In Cold Blood* • Norman Jewison *In the Heat of the Night* • Stanley Kramer *Guess Who's Coming to Dinner* • Arthur Penn *Bonnie and Clyde*

ACTOR: **Rod Steiger** *In the Heat of the Night* • Warren Beatty *Bonnie and Clyde* • Dustin Hoffman *The Graduate* • Paul Newman *Cool Hand Luke* • Spencer Tracy *Guess Who's Coming to Dinner*

ACTRESS: **Katharine Hepburn** *Guess Who's Coming to Dinner* • Anne Bancroft *The Graduate* • Faye Dunaway *Bonnie and Clyde* • Edith Evans *The Whisperers* • Audrey Hepburn *Wait until Dark*

SUPPORTING ACTOR: **George Kennedy** *Cool Hand Luke* • John Cassavetes *The Dirty Dozen* • Gene Hackman *Bonnie and Clyde* • Cecil Kellaway *Guess Who's Coming to Dinner* • Michael J Pollard *Bonnie and Clyde*

SUPPORTING ACTRESS: **Estelle Parsons** *Bonnie and Clyde* • Carol Channing *Thoroughly Modern Millie* • Mildred Natwick

Barefoot in the Park • Beah Richards Guess Who's Coming to Dinner • Katharine Ross The Graduate

ORIGINAL STORY, SCREENPLAY: **William Rose** *Guess Who's Coming to Dinner* • David Newman, Robert Benton *Bonnie and Clyde* • Norman Lear, Robert Kaufman *Divorce American Style* • Jorge Semprun *La Guerre Est Finie* • Frederic Raphael *Two for the Road*

ADAPTED SCREENPLAY: **Stirling Silliphant** *In the Heat of the Night* • Donn Pearce, Frank Pierson *Cool Hand Luke* • Calder Willingham, Buck Henry *The Graduate* • Richard Brooks *In Cold Blood* • Joseph Strick, Fred Haines *Ulysses*

Golden Globe Awards

DRAMA: *In the Heat of the Night*

COMEDY/MUSICAL: *The Graduate*

FOREIGN FILM/ENGLISH: *The Fox*

FOREIGN FILM/NON-ENGLISH: *Vivre pour Vivre*

DIRECTOR: **Mike Nichols** *The Graduate*

ACTOR, DRAMA: **Rod Steiger** *In the Heat of the Night*

ACTRESS, DRAMA: **Edith Evans** *The Whisperers*

ACTOR, COMEDY/MUSICAL: **Richard Harris** *Camelot*

ACTRESS, COMEDY/MUSICAL: **Anne Bancroft** *The Graduate*

SUPPORTING ACTOR: **Richard Attenborough** *Doctor Dolittle*

SUPPORTING ACTRESS: **Carol Channing** *Thoroughly Modern Millie*

SCREENPLAY: **Stirling Silliphant** *In the Heat of the Night*

Cannes Film Festival

GRAND PRIX: *Blowup*

DIRECTOR: **Ferenc Kosa** *Tizezer Nap*

ACTOR: **Uri Zohar** *Three Days and a Child*

ACTRESS: **Pia Degermark** *Elvira Madigan*

SCREENPLAY: **Alain Jessua** *Jeu de Massacre* • **Elio Petri, Ugo Pirro** *We Still Kill the Old Way*

Berlin International Film Festival

GOLDEN BEAR: *Le Départ*

SILVER BEAR, DIRECTOR: **Zivojin Pavlovic** *Budjenje Pacova*

SILVER BEAR, ACTOR: **Michel Simon** *The Two of Us*

SILVER BEAR, ACTRESS: **Edith Evans** *The Whisperers*

1968

British Film Academy Awards

FILM: *The Graduate* • *Closely Observed Trains* • *Oliver!* • *2001: a Space Odyssey*

DIRECTOR: **Mike Nichols** *The Graduate* • Lindsay Anderson *if...* • Carol Reed *Oliver!* • Franco Zeffirelli *Romeo and Juliet*

ACTOR: **Spencer Tracy** *Guess Who's Coming to Dinner* • Trevor Howard *The Charge of the Light Brigade* • Ron Moody *Oliver!* • Nicol Williamson *The Bofors Gun*

ACTRESS: **Katharine Hepburn** *The Lion in Winter* • **Katharine Hepburn** *Guess Who's Coming to Dinner* • Anne Bancroft *The Graduate* • Catherine Deneuve *Belle de Jour* • Joanne Woodward *Rachel, Rachel*

SUPPORTING ACTOR: **Ian Holm** *The Bofors Gun* • Anthony Hopkins *The Lion in Winter* • John McEnery *Romeo and Juliet* • George Segal *No Way to Treat a Lady*

SUPPORTING ACTRESS: **Billie Whitelaw** *Charlie Bubbles* • **Billie Whitelaw** *Twisted Nerve* • Pat Heywood *Romeo and Juliet* • Virginia Maskell *Interlude* • Simone Signoret *Games*

SCREENPLAY: **Calder Willingham, Buck Henry** *The Graduate* • William Rose *Guess Who's Coming to Dinner* • David Sherwin *if...* • James Goldman *The Lion in Winter*

Academy Awards

PICTURE: *Oliver!* • *Funny Girl* • *The Lion in Winter* • *Rachel, Rachel* • *Romeo and Juliet*

FOREIGN LANGUAGE FILM: *War and Peace* • *The Boys of Paul Street* • *The Fireman's Ball* • *The Girl with the Pistol* • *Stolen Kisses*

DIRECTOR: **Carol Reed** *Oliver!* • Anthony Harvey *The Lion in Winter* • Stanley Kubrick *2001: a Space Odyssey* • Gillo Pontecorvo *The Battle of Algiers* • Franco Zeffirelli *Romeo and Juliet*

ACTOR: **Cliff Robertson** *Charly* • Alan Arkin *The Heart Is a Lonely Hunter* • Alan Bates *The Fixer* • Ron Moody *Oliver!* • Peter O'Toole *The Lion in Winter*

ACTRESS: **Katharine Hepburn** *The Lion in Winter* • **Barbra Streisand** *Funny Girl* • Patricia Neal *The Subject Was Roses* • Vanessa Redgrave *Isadora* • Joanne Woodward *Rachel, Rachel*

SUPPORTING ACTOR: **Jack Albertson** *The Subject Was Roses* • Seymour Cassel *Faces* • Daniel Massey *Star!* • Jack Wild *Oliver!* • Gene Wilder *The Producers*

SUPPORTING ACTRESS: **Ruth Gordon** *Rosemary's Baby* • Lynn Carlin *Faces* • Sondra Locke *The Heart Is a Lonely Hunter* • Kay Medford *Funny Girl* • Estelle Parsons *Rachel, Rachel*

ORIGINAL STORY, SCREENPLAY: **Mel Brooks** *The Producers* • Stanley Kubrick, Arthur C Clarke *2001: a Space Odyssey* • Franco Solinas, Gillo Pontecorvo *The Battle of Algiers* • John Cassavetes *Faces* • Ira Wallach, Peter Ustinov *Hot Millions*

ADAPTED SCREENPLAY: **James Goldman** *The Lion in Winter* • Neil Simon *The Odd Couple* • Vernon Harris *Oliver!* • Stewart Stern *Rachel, Rachel* • Roman Polanski *Rosemary's Baby*

Golden Globe Awards

DRAMA: *The Lion in Winter*

COMEDY/MUSICAL: *Funny Girl*

FOREIGN FILM/ENGLISH: *Romeo and Juliet*

FOREIGN FILM/NON-ENGLISH: *War and Peace*

DIRECTOR: **Paul Newman** *Rachel, Rachel*

ACTOR, DRAMA: **Peter O'Toole** *The Lion in Winter*

ACTRESS, DRAMA: **Joanne Woodward** *Rachel, Rachel*

ACTOR, COMEDY/MUSICAL: **Ron Moody** *Oliver!*

ACTRESS, COMEDY/MUSICAL: **Barbra Streisand** *Funny Girl*

SUPPORTING ACTOR: **Daniel Massey** *Star!*

SUPPORTING ACTRESS: **Ruth Gordon** *Rosemary's Baby*

SCREENPLAY: **Stirling Silliphant** *Charly*

Berlin International Film Festival

GOLDEN BEAR: *Who Saw Him Die?*

SILVER BEAR, DIRECTOR: **Carlos Saura** *Peppermint Frappé*

SILVER BEAR, ACTOR: **Jean-Louis Trintignant** *L'Homme Qui Ment*

SILVER BEAR, ACTRESS: **Stéphane Audran** *Les Biches*

1969

British Film Academy Awards

FILM: *Midnight Cowboy* • *Oh! What a Lovely War* • *Women in Love* • *Z*

DIRECTOR: **John Schlesinger** *Midnight Cowboy* • Richard Attenborough *Oh! What a Lovely War* • Ken Russell *Women in Love* • Peter Yates *Bullitt*

ACTOR: **Dustin Hoffman** *Midnight Cowboy* • **Dustin Hoffman** *John and Mary* • Alan Bates *Women in Love* • Walter Matthau *Hello, Dolly!* • Walter Matthau *The Secret Life of an American Wife* • Nicol Williamson *Inadmissible Evidence*

ACTRESS: **Maggie Smith** *The Prime of Miss Jean Brodie* • Mia Farrow *John and Mary* • Mia Farrow *Rosemary's Baby* • Mia Farrow *Secret Ceremony* • Glenda Jackson *Women in Love* • Barbra Streisand *Funny Girl* • Barbra Streisand *Hello, Dolly!*

SUPPORTING ACTOR: **Laurence Olivier** *Oh! What a Lovely War* • Jack Klugman *Goodbye, Columbus* • Jack Nicholson *Easy Rider* • Robert Vaughn *Bullitt*

SUPPORTING ACTRESS: **Celia Johnson** *The Prime of Miss Jean Brodie* • Peggy Ashcroft *Three into Two Won't Go* • Pamela Franklin *The Prime of Miss Jean Brodie* • Mary Wimbush *Oh! What a Lovely War*

SCREENPLAY: **Waldo Salt** *Midnight Cowboy* • Arnold Schulman *Goodbye, Columbus* • Larry Kramer *Women in Love* • Costa-Gavras, Jorge Semprun *Z*

Academy Awards

PICTURE: *Midnight Cowboy* • *Anne of the Thousand Days* • *Butch Cassidy and the Sundance Kid* • *Hello, Dolly!* • *Z*

FOREIGN LANGUAGE FILM: *Z* • *Adalen 31* • *The Battle of Neretva* • *The Brothers Karamazov* • *My Night with Maud*

DIRECTOR: **John Schlesinger** *Midnight Cowboy* • Costa-Gavras *Z* • George Roy Hill *Butch Cassidy and the Sundance Kid* • Arthur Penn *Alice's Restaurant* • Sydney Pollack *They Shoot Horses, Don't They?*

ACTOR: **John Wayne** *True Grit* • Richard Burton *Anne of the Thousand Days* • Dustin Hoffman *Midnight Cowboy* • Peter O'Toole *Goodbye, Mr Chips* • Jon Voight *Midnight Cowboy*

ACTRESS: **Maggie Smith** *The Prime of Miss Jean Brodie* • Geneviève Bujold *Anne of the Thousand Days* • Jane Fonda *They Shoot Horses, Don't They?* • Liza Minnelli *The Sterile Cuckoo* • Jean Simmons *The Happy Ending*

SUPPORTING ACTOR: **Gig Young** *They Shoot Horses, Don't They?* • Rupert Crosse *The Reivers* • Elliott Gould *Bob & Carol & Ted & Alice* • Jack Nicholson *Easy Rider* • Anthony Quayle *Anne of the Thousand Days*

SUPPORTING ACTRESS: **Goldie Hawn** *Cactus Flower* • Catherine Burns *Last Summer* • Dyan Cannon *Bob & Carol & Ted & Alice* • Sylvia Miles *Midnight Cowboy* • Susannah York *They Shoot Horses, Don't They?*

ORIGINAL STORY, SCREENPLAY: **William Goldman** *Butch Cassidy and the Sundance Kid* • Paul Mazursky, Larry Tucker *Bob & Carol & Ted & Alice* • Nicola Badalucco, Enrico Medioli, Luchino Visconti *The Damned* • Peter Fonda, Dennis Hopper, Terry Southern *Easy Rider* • Walon Green, Sam Peckinpah, Roy N Sickner *The Wild Bunch*

ADAPTED SCREENPLAY: **Waldo Salt** *Midnight Cowboy* • Bridget Boland, John Hale, Richard Sokolove *Anne of the Thousand Days* • Arnold Schulman *Goodbye, Columbus* • James Poe, Robert E Thompson *They Shoot Horses, Don't They?* • Costa-Gavras, Jorge Semprun *Z*

Golden Globe Awards

DRAMA: *Anne of the Thousand Days*

COMEDY/MUSICAL: *The Secret of Santa Vittoria*

FOREIGN FILM/ENGLISH: *Oh! What a Lovely War*

FOREIGN FILM/NON-ENGLISH: *Z*

DIRECTOR: **Charles Jarrott** *Anne of the Thousand Days*

ACTOR, DRAMA: **John Wayne** *True Grit*

ACTRESS, DRAMA: **Geneviève Bujold** *Anne of the Thousand Days*

ACTOR, COMEDY/MUSICAL: **Peter O'Toole** *Goodbye, Mr Chips*

ACTRESS, COMEDY/MUSICAL: **Patty Duke** *Me, Natalie*

SUPPORTING ACTOR: **Gig Young** *They Shoot Horses, Don't They?*

SUPPORTING ACTRESS: **Goldie Hawn** *Cactus Flower*

SCREENPLAY: **John Hale, Bridget Boland** *Anne of the Thousand Days*

Cannes Film Festival

GRAND PRIX: *if...*

DIRECTOR: **Glauber Rocha** *Antonio das Mortes* • **Vojtech Jasny** *All My Good Countrymen*

ACTOR: **Jean-Louis Trintignant** *Z*

ACTRESS: **Vanessa Redgrave** *Isadora*

Berlin International Film Festival

GOLDEN BEAR: *Rani Radovi*

1970

British Film Academy Awards

FILM: *Butch Cassidy and the Sundance Kid* • *Kes* • *MASH* • *Ryan's Daughter*

DIRECTOR: **George Roy Hill** *Butch Cassidy and the Sundance Kid* • Robert Altman *MASH* • David Lean *Ryan's Daughter* • Ken Loach *Kes*

ACTOR: **Robert Redford** *Butch Cassidy and the Sundance Kid* • **Robert Redford** *Downhill Racer* • **Robert Redford** *Tell Them Willie Boy Is Here* • Elliott Gould *Bob & Carol & Ted & Alice* •

Elliott Gould *MASH* • Paul Newman *Butch Cassidy and the Sundance Kid* • George C Scott *Patton*

ACTRESS: **Katharine Ross** *Butch Cassidy and the Sundance Kid* • **Katharine Ross** *Tell Them Willie Boy Is Here* • Jane Fonda *They Shoot Horses, Don't They?* • Goldie Hawn *Cactus Flower* • Goldie Hawn *There's a Girl in My Soup* • Sarah Miles *Ryan's Daughter*

SUPPORTING ACTOR: **Colin Welland** *Kes* • Bernard Cribbins *The Railway Children* • John Mills *Ryan's Daughter* • Gig Young *They Shoot Horses, Don't They?*

SUPPORTING ACTRESS: **Susannah York** *They Shoot Horses, Don't They?* • Evin Crowley *Ryan's Daughter* • Estelle Parsons *Watermelon Man* • Maureen Stapleton *Airport*

SCREENPLAY: **William Goldman** *Butch Cassidy and the Sundance Kid* • Paul Mazursky, Larry Tucker *Bob & Carol & Ted & Alice* • Ken Loach, Tony Garnett, Barry Hines *Kes* • James Poe, Robert E Thompson *They Shoot Horses, Don't They?*

Academy Awards

PICTURE: **Patton** • *Airport* • *Five Easy Pieces* • *Love Story* • *MASH*

FOREIGN LANGUAGE FILM: **Investigation of a Citizen above Suspicion** • *First Love* • *Hoa-Binh* • *Paix sur les Champs* • *Tristana*

DIRECTOR: **Franklin J Schaffner** *Patton* • Robert Altman *MASH* • Federico Fellini *Satyricon* • Arthur Hiller *Love Story* • Ken Russell *Women in Love*

ACTOR: **George C Scott** *Patton* • Melvyn Douglas *I Never Sang for My Father* • James Earl Jones *The Great White Hope* • Jack Nicholson *Five Easy Pieces* • Ryan O'Neal *Love Story*

ACTRESS: **Glenda Jackson** *Women in Love* • Jane Alexander *The Great White Hope* • Ali MacGraw *Love Story* • Sarah Miles *Ryan's Daughter* • Carrie Snodgress *Diary of a Mad Housewife*

SUPPORTING ACTOR: **John Mills** *Ryan's Daughter* • Richard Castellano *Lovers and Other Strangers* • Gene Hackman *Little Big Man* • Gene Hackman *I Never Sang for My Father* • John Marley *Love Story*

SUPPORTING ACTRESS: **Helen Hayes** *Airport* • Karen Black *Five Easy Pieces* • Lee Grant *The Landlord* • Sally Kellerman *MASH* • Maureen Stapleton *Airport*

ORIGINAL STORY, SCREENPLAY: **Francis Ford Coppola, Edmund H North** *Patton* • Carole Eastman, Bob Rafelson *Five Easy Pieces* • Norman Wexler *Joe* • Erich Segal *Love Story* • Eric Rohmer *My Night with Maud*

ADAPTED SCREENPLAY: **Ring Lardner Jr** *MASH* • George Seaton *Airport* • Robert W Anderson *I Never Sang for My Father* • Renee Taylor, Joseph Bologna, David Zelag Goodman *Lovers and Other Strangers* • Larry Kramer *Women in Love*

Golden Globe Awards

DRAMA: **Love Story**
COMEDY/MUSICAL: **MASH**
FOREIGN FILM/ENGLISH: **Women in Love**
FOREIGN FILM/NON-ENGLISH: **Rider on the Rain**
DIRECTOR: **Arthur Hiller** *Love Story*
ACTOR, DRAMA: **George C Scott** *Patton*
ACTRESS, DRAMA: **Ali MacGraw** *Love Story*
ACTOR, COMEDY/MUSICAL: **Albert Finney** *Scrooge*
ACTRESS, COMEDY/MUSICAL: **Carrie Snodgress** *Diary of a Mad Housewife*
SUPPORTING ACTOR: **John Mills** *Ryan's Daughter*
SUPPORTING ACTRESS: **Karen Black** *Five Easy Pieces* • **Maureen Stapleton** *Airport*
SCREENPLAY: **Erich Segal** *Love Story*

Cannes Film Festival

GRAND PRIX: **MASH**
DIRECTOR: **John Boorman** *Leo the Last*
ACTOR: **Marcello Mastroianni** *Jealousy, Italian Style*
ACTRESS: **Ottavia Piccolo** *Metello*

1971

British Film Academy Awards

FILM: **Sunday, Bloody Sunday** • *Death in Venice* • *The Go-Between* • *Taking Off*

DIRECTOR: **John Schlesinger** *Sunday, Bloody Sunday* • Milos Forman *Taking Off* • Joseph Losey *The Go-Between* • Luchino Visconti *Death in Venice*

ACTOR: **Peter Finch** *Sunday, Bloody Sunday* • Dirk Bogarde *Death in Venice* • Albert Finney *Gumshoe* • Dustin Hoffman *Little Big Man*

ACTRESS: **Glenda Jackson** *Sunday, Bloody Sunday* • Lynn Carlin *Taking Off* • Julie Christie *The Go-Between* • Jane Fonda *Klute* • Nanette Newman *The Raging Moon*

SUPPORTING ACTOR: **Edward Fox** *The Go-Between* • Michael Gough *The Go-Between* • Ian Hendry *Get Carter* • John Hurt *10 Rillington Place*

SUPPORTING ACTRESS: **Margaret Leighton** *The Go-Between* • Jane Asher *Deep End* • Georgia Brown *The Raging Moon* • Georgia Engel *Taking Off*

SCREENPLAY: **Harold Pinter** *The Go-Between* • Neville Smith *Gumshoe* • Penelope Gilliatt *Sunday, Bloody Sunday* • Milos Forman, John Guare, Jean-Claude Carrière, John Klein *Taking Off*

Academy Awards

PICTURE: **The French Connection** • *A Clockwork Orange* • *Fiddler on the Roof* • *The Last Picture Show* • *Nicholas and Alexandra*

FOREIGN LANGUAGE FILM: **The Garden of the Finzi-Continis** • *Dodes'ka-Den* • *The Emigrants* • *The Policeman* • *Tchaikovsky*

DIRECTOR: **William Friedkin** *The French Connection* • Peter Bogdanovich *The Last Picture Show* • Norman Jewison

Fiddler on the Roof • Stanley Kubrick *A Clockwork Orange* • John Schlesinger *Sunday, Bloody Sunday*

ACTOR: **Gene Hackman** *The French Connection* • Peter Finch *Sunday, Bloody Sunday* • Walter Matthau *Kotch* • George C Scott *The Hospital* • Topol *Fiddler on the Roof*

ACTRESS: **Jane Fonda** *Klute* • Julie Christie *McCabe and Mrs Miller* • Glenda Jackson *Sunday, Bloody Sunday* • Vanessa Redgrave *Mary, Queen of Scots* • Janet Suzman *Nicholas and Alexandra*

SUPPORTING ACTOR: **Ben Johnson** *The Last Picture Show* • Jeff Bridges *The Last Picture Show* • Leonard Frey *Fiddler on the Roof* • Richard Jaeckel *Sometimes a Great Notion* • Roy Scheider *The French Connection*

SUPPORTING ACTRESS: **Cloris Leachman** *The Last Picture Show* • Ann-Margret *Carnal Knowledge* • Ellen Burstyn *The Last Picture Show* • Barbara Harris *Who Is Harry Kellerman, and Why Is He Saying Those Terrible Things about Me?* • Margaret Leighton *The Go-Between*

ORIGINAL STORY, SCREENPLAY: **Paddy Chayefsky** *The Hospital* • Elio Petri, Ugo Pirro *Investigation of a Citizen above Suspicion* • Andy Lewis, Dave Lewis *Klute* • Herman Raucher *Summer of '42* • Penelope Gilliatt *Sunday, Bloody Sunday*

ADAPTED SCREENPLAY: **Ernest Tidyman** *The French Connection* • Stanley Kubrick *A Clockwork Orange* • Bernardo Bertolucci *The Conformist* • Vittorio Bonicelli, Ugo Pirro *The Garden of the Finzi-Continis* • Peter Bogdanovich, Larry McMurtry *The Last Picture Show*

Golden Globe Awards

DRAMA: **The French Connection**
COMEDY/MUSICAL: **Fiddler on the Roof**
FOREIGN FILM/ENGLISH: **Sunday, Bloody Sunday**
FOREIGN FILM/NON-ENGLISH: **The Policeman**
DIRECTOR: **William Friedkin** *The French Connection*
ACTOR, DRAMA: **Gene Hackman** *The French Connection*
ACTRESS, DRAMA: **Jane Fonda** *Klute*
ACTOR, COMEDY/MUSICAL: **Topol** *Fiddler on the Roof*
ACTRESS, COMEDY/MUSICAL: **Twiggy** *The Boy Friend*
SUPPORTING ACTOR: **Ben Johnson** *The Last Picture Show*
SUPPORTING ACTRESS: **Ann-Margret** *Carnal Knowledge*
SCREENPLAY: **Paddy Chayefsky** *The Hospital*

Cannes Film Festival

GRAND PRIX: **The Go-Between**
ACTOR: **Riccardo Cucciolla** *Sacco and Vanzetti*
ACTRESS: **Kitty Winn** *The Panic in Needle Park*

Berlin International Film Festival

GOLDEN BEAR: **The Garden of the Finzi-Continis**
SILVER BEAR, ACTOR: **Jean Gabin** *Le Chat*
SILVER BEAR, ACTRESS: **Shirley MacLaine** *Desperate Characters* • **Simone Signoret** *Le Chat*

1972

British Film Academy Awards

FILM: **Cabaret** • *A Clockwork Orange* • *The French Connection* • *The Last Picture Show*

DIRECTOR: **Bob Fosse** *Cabaret* • Peter Bogdanovich *The Last Picture Show* • William Friedkin *The French Connection* • Stanley Kubrick *A Clockwork Orange*

ACTOR: **Gene Hackman** *The French Connection* • **Gene Hackman** *The Poseidon Adventure* • Marlon Brando *The Godfather* • Marlon Brando *The Nightcomers* • George C Scott *The Hospital* • George C Scott *They Might Be Giants* • Robert Shaw *Young Winston*

ACTRESS: **Liza Minnelli** *Cabaret* • Stéphane Audran *Le Boucher* • Anne Bancroft *Young Winston* • Dorothy Tutin *Savage Messiah*

SUPPORTING ACTOR: **Ben Johnson** *The Last Picture Show* • Max Adrian *The Boy Friend* • Robert Duvall *The Godfather* • Ralph Richardson *Lady Caroline Lamb*

SUPPORTING ACTRESS: **Cloris Leachman** *The Last Picture Show* • Marisa Berenson *Cabaret* • Eileen Brennan *The Last Picture Show* • Shelley Winters *The Poseidon Adventure*

SCREENPLAY: **Paddy Chayefsky** *The Hospital* • **Larry McMurtry, Peter Bogdanovich** *The Last Picture Show* • Jay Presson Allen *Cabaret* • Stanley Kubrick *A Clockwork Orange*

Academy Awards

PICTURE: **The Godfather** • *Cabaret* • *Deliverance* • *The Emigrants* • *Sounder*

FOREIGN LANGUAGE FILM: **The Discreet Charm of the Bourgeoisie** • *The Dawns Here Are Quiet* • *I Love You Rosa* • *My Dearest Señorita* • *The New Land*

DIRECTOR: **Bob Fosse** *Cabaret* • John Boorman *Deliverance* • Francis Ford Coppola *The Godfather* • Joseph L Mankiewicz *Sleuth* • Jan Troell *The Emigrants*

ACTOR: **Marlon Brando** *The Godfather* • Michael Caine, Laurence Olivier *Sleuth* • Peter O'Toole *The Ruling Class* • Paul Winfield *Sounder*

ACTRESS: **Liza Minnelli** *Cabaret* • Diana Ross *Lady Sings the Blues* • Maggie Smith *Travels with My Aunt* • Cicely Tyson *Sounder* • Liv Ullmann *The Emigrants*

SUPPORTING ACTOR: **Joel Grey** *Cabaret* • Eddie Albert *The Heartbreak Kid* • James Caan, Robert Duvall, Al Pacino *The Godfather*

SUPPORTING ACTRESS: **Eileen Heckart** *Butterflies Are Free* • Jeannie Berlin *The Heartbreak Kid* • Geraldine Page *Pete 'n' Tillie* • Susan Tyrrell *Fat City* • Shelley Winters *The Poseidon Adventure*

ORIGINAL STORY, SCREENPLAY: **Jeremy Larner** *The Candidate* • Luis Buñuel, Jean-Claude Carrière *The Discreet Charm of the Bourgeoisie* • Chris Clark, Suzanne De Passe, Terence McCloy *Lady Sings the Blues* • Louis Malle *Le Souffle au Coeur* • Carl Foreman *Young Winston*

ADAPTED SCREENPLAY: **Francis Ford Coppola, Mario Puzo** *The Godfather* • Jay Presson Allen *Cabaret* • Bengt Forslund, Jan Troell *The Emigrants* • Julius J Epstein *Pete 'n' Tillie* • Lonne Elder III *Sounder*

Golden Globe Awards

DRAMA: **The Godfather**
COMEDY/MUSICAL: **Cabaret**
FOREIGN FILM/ENGLISH: **Young Winston**
FOREIGN FILM/NON-ENGLISH: **The Emigrants** • **The New Land**
DIRECTOR: **Francis Ford Coppola** *The Godfather*
ACTOR, DRAMA: **Marlon Brando** *The Godfather*
ACTRESS, DRAMA: **Liv Ullmann** *The Emigrants*
ACTOR, COMEDY/MUSICAL: **Jack Lemmon** *Avanti!*
ACTRESS, COMEDY/MUSICAL: **Liza Minnelli** *Cabaret*
SUPPORTING ACTOR: **Joel Grey** *Cabaret*
SUPPORTING ACTRESS: **Shelley Winters** *The Poseidon Adventure*
SCREENPLAY: **Francis Ford Coppola, Mario Puzo** *The Godfather*

Cannes Film Festival

GRAND PRIX: **The Working Class Goes to Heaven** • **The Mattei Affair**
DIRECTOR: **Miklos Jancso** *Még Kér a Nép*
ACTOR: **Jean Yanne** *Nous Ne Vieillirons Pas Ensemble*
ACTRESS: **Susannah York** *Images*

Berlin International Film Festival

GOLDEN BEAR: **The Canterbury Tales**
SILVER BEAR, DIRECTOR: **Jean-Pierre Blanc** *La Vieille Fille*
SILVER BEAR, ACTOR: **Alberto Sordi** *Detenuto in Attesa di Giudizio*
SILVER BEAR, ACTRESS: **Elizabeth Taylor** *Hammersmith Is Out*

1973

British Film Academy Awards

FILM: **Day for Night** • *The Day of the Jackal* • *The Discreet Charm of the Bourgeoisie* • *Don't Look Now*

DIRECTOR: **François Truffaut** *Day for Night* • Luis Buñuel *The Discreet Charm of the Bourgeoisie* • Nicolas Roeg *Don't Look Now* • Fred Zinnemann *The Day of the Jackal*

ACTOR: **Walter Matthau** *Charley Varrick* • **Walter Matthau** *Pete 'n' Tillie* • Marlon Brando *Last Tango in Paris* • Laurence Olivier *Sleuth* • Donald Sutherland *Don't Look Now* • Donald Sutherland *Steelyard Blues*

ACTRESS: **Stéphane Audran** *The Discreet Charm of the Bourgeoisie* • **Stéphane Audran** *Juste avant la Nuit* • Julie Christie *Don't Look Now* • Glenda Jackson *A Touch of Class* • Diana Ross *Lady Sings the Blues*

SUPPORTING ACTOR: **Arthur Lowe** *O Lucky Man!* • Ian Bannen *The Offence* • Denholm Elliott *A Doll's House* • Michel Lonsdale *The Day of the Jackal*

SUPPORTING ACTRESS: **Valentina Cortese** *Day for Night* • Rosemary Leach *That'll Be the Day* • Delphine Seyrig *The Day of the Jackal* • Ingrid Thulin *Cries and Whispers*

SCREENPLAY: **Luis Buñuel, Jean-Claude Carrière** *The Discreet Charm of the Bourgeoisie* • Kenneth Ross *The Day of the Jackal* • Anthony Shaffer *Sleuth* • Melvin Frank, Jack Rose *A Touch of Class*

Academy Awards

PICTURE: **The Sting** • *American Graffiti* • *Cries and Whispers* • *The Exorcist* • *A Touch of Class*

FOREIGN LANGUAGE FILM: **Day for Night** • *The House on Chelouche Street* • *The Invitation* • *The Pedestrian* • *Turkish Delight*

DIRECTOR: **George Roy Hill** *The Sting* • Ingmar Bergman *Cries and Whispers* • Bernardo Bertolucci *Last Tango in Paris* • William Friedkin *The Exorcist* • George Lucas *American Graffiti*

ACTOR: **Jack Lemmon** *Save the Tiger* • Marlon Brando *Last Tango in Paris* • Jack Nicholson *The Last Detail* • Al Pacino *Serpico* • Robert Redford *The Sting*

ACTRESS: **Glenda Jackson** *A Touch of Class* • Ellen Burstyn *The Exorcist* • Marsha Mason *Cinderella Liberty* • Barbra Streisand *The Way We Were* • Joanne Woodward *Summer Wishes, Winter Dreams*

SUPPORTING ACTOR: **John Houseman** *The Paper Chase* • Vincent Gardenia *Bang the Drum Slowly* • Jack Gilford *Save the Tiger* • Jason Miller *The Exorcist* • Randy Quaid *The Last Detail*

SUPPORTING ACTRESS: **Tatum O'Neal** *Paper Moon* • Linda Blair *The Exorcist* • Candy Clark *American Graffiti* • Madeline Kahn *Paper Moon* • Sylvia Sidney *Summer Wishes, Winter Dreams*

ORIGINAL STORY, SCREENPLAY: **David S Ward** *The Sting* • George Lucas, Gloria Katz, Willard Huyck *American Graffiti* • Ingmar Bergman *Cries and Whispers* • Steve Shagan *Save the Tiger* • Melvin Frank, Jack Rose *A Touch of Class*

ADAPTED SCREENPLAY: **William Peter Blatty** *The Exorcist* • Robert Towne *The Last Detail* • James Bridges *The Paper Chase* • Alvin Sargent *Paper Moon* • Waldo Salt, Norman Wexler *Serpico*

Golden Globe Awards

DRAMA: **The Exorcist**
COMEDY/MUSICAL: **American Graffiti**
FOREIGN LANGUAGE FILM: **The Pedestrian**
DIRECTOR: **William Friedkin** *The Exorcist*
ACTOR, DRAMA: **Al Pacino** *Serpico*
ACTRESS, DRAMA: **Marsha Mason** *Cinderella Liberty*
ACTOR, COMEDY/MUSICAL: **George Segal** *A Touch of Class*
ACTRESS, COMEDY/MUSICAL: **Glenda Jackson** *A Touch of Class*
SUPPORTING ACTOR: **John Houseman** *The Paper Chase*
SUPPORTING ACTRESS: **Linda Blair** *The Exorcist*
SCREENPLAY: **William Peter Blatty** *The Exorcist*

Cannes Film Festival

GRAND PRIX: **Scarecrow • The Hireling**
ACTOR: **Giancarlo Giannini** Love and Anarchy
ACTRESS: **Joanne Woodward** The Effect of Gamma Rays on Man-in-the-Moon Marigolds

Berlin International Film Festival

GOLDEN BEAR: **Distant Thunder**

1974

British Film Academy Awards

FILM: **Lacombe Lucien** • Chinatown • The Last Detail • Murder on the Orient Express
DIRECTOR: **Roman Polanski** Chinatown • Francis Ford Coppola The Conversation • Sidney Lumet Murder on the Orient Express • Louis Malle Lacombe Lucien
ACTOR: **Jack Nicholson** Chinatown • **Jack Nicholson** The Last Detail • Albert Finney Murder on the Orient Express • Gene Hackman The Conversation • Al Pacino Serpico
ACTRESS: **Joanne Woodward** Summer Wishes, Winter Dreams • Faye Dunaway Chinatown • Barbra Streisand The Way We Were • Cicely Tyson The Autobiography of Miss Jane Pittman
SUPPORTING ACTOR: **John Gielgud** Murder on the Orient Express • Adam Faith Stardust • John Huston Chinatown • Randy Quaid The Last Detail
SUPPORTING ACTRESS: **Ingrid Bergman** Murder on the Orient Express • Sylvia Sidney Summer Wishes, Winter Dreams • Sylvia Syms The Tamarind Seed • Cindy Williams American Graffiti
SCREENPLAY: **Robert Towne** Chinatown • **Robert Towne** The Last Detail • Mel Brooks, Norman Steinberg, Andrew Bergman, Richard Pryor, Alan Uger Blazing Saddles • Francis Ford Coppola The Conversation • Louis Malle, Patrick Modiano Lacombe Lucien

Academy Awards

PICTURE: **The Godfather, Part II** • Chinatown • The Conversation • Lenny • The Towering Inferno
FOREIGN LANGUAGE FILM: **Amarcord** • Cats' Play • The Deluge • Lacombe Lucien • The Truce
DIRECTOR: **Francis Ford Coppola** The Godfather, Part II • John Cassavetes A Woman under the Influence • Bob Fosse Lenny • Roman Polanski Chinatown • François Truffaut Day for Night
ACTOR: **Art Carney** Harry and Tonto • Albert Finney Murder on the Orient Express • Dustin Hoffman Lenny • Jack Nicholson Chinatown • Al Pacino The Godfather, Part II
ACTRESS: **Ellen Burstyn** Alice Doesn't Live Here Anymore • Diahann Carroll Claudine • Faye Dunaway Chinatown • Valerie Perrine Lenny • Gena Rowlands A Woman under the Influence
SUPPORTING ACTOR: **Robert De Niro** The Godfather, Part II • Fred Astaire The Towering Inferno • Jeff Bridges Thunderbolt and Lightfoot • Michael V Gazzo, Lee Strasberg The Godfather, Part II
SUPPORTING ACTRESS: **Ingrid Bergman** Murder on the Orient Express • Valentina Cortese Day for Night • Madeline Kahn Blazing Saddles • Diane Ladd Alice Doesn't Live Here Anymore • Talia Shire The Godfather, Part II
ORIGINAL SCREENPLAY: **Robert Towne** Chinatown • Robert Getchell Alice Doesn't Live Here Anymore • Francis Ford Coppola The Conversation • François Truffaut, Suzanne Schiffman, Jean-Louis Richard Day for Night • Paul Mazursky, Josh Greenfeld Harry and Tonto
ADAPTED SCREENPLAY: **Francis Ford Coppola, Mario Puzo** The Godfather, Part II • Mordecai Richler, Lionel Chetwynd The Apprenticeship of Duddy Kravitz • Julian Barry Lenny • Paul Dehn Murder on the Orient Express • Mel Brooks, Gene Wilder Young Frankenstein

Golden Globe Awards

DRAMA: **Chinatown**
COMEDY/MUSICAL: **The Mean Machine**
FOREIGN LANGUAGE FILM: **Scenes from a Marriage**
DIRECTOR: **Roman Polanski** Chinatown
ACTOR, DRAMA: **Jack Nicholson** Chinatown
ACTRESS, DRAMA: **Gena Rowlands** A Woman under the Influence
ACTOR, COMEDY/MUSICAL: **Art Carney** Harry and Tonto
ACTRESS, COMEDY/MUSICAL: **Raquel Welch** The Three Musketeers
SUPPORTING ACTOR: **Fred Astaire** The Towering Inferno
SUPPORTING ACTRESS: **Karen Black** The Great Gatsby
SCREENPLAY: **Robert Towne** Chinatown

Cannes Film Festival

GRAND PRIX: **The Conversation**
ACTOR: **Jack Nicholson** The Last Detail
ACTRESS: **Marie-José Nat** Les Violons du Bal
SCREENPLAY: **Steven Spielberg** The Sugarland Express

Berlin International Film Festival

GOLDEN BEAR: **The Apprenticeship of Duddy Kravitz**

1975

British Film Academy Awards

FILM: **Alice Doesn't Live Here Anymore** • Barry Lyndon • Dog Day Afternoon • Jaws
DIRECTOR: **Stanley Kubrick** Barry Lyndon • Sidney Lumet Dog Day Afternoon • Martin Scorsese Alice Doesn't Live Here Anymore • Steven Spielberg Jaws
ACTOR: **Al Pacino** Dog Day Afternoon • **Al Pacino** The Godfather, Part II • Richard Dreyfuss Jaws • Gene Hackman French Connection II • Gene Hackman Night Moves • Dustin Hoffman Lenny

ACTRESS: **Ellen Burstyn** Alice Doesn't Live Here Anymore • Anne Bancroft The Prisoner of Second Avenue • Valerie Perrine Lenny • Liv Ullmann Scenes from a Marriage
SUPPORTING ACTOR: **Fred Astaire** The Towering Inferno • Martin Balsam The Taking of Pelham One Two Three • Burgess Meredith The Day of the Locust • Jack Warden Shampoo
SUPPORTING ACTRESS: **Diane Ladd** Alice Doesn't Live Here Anymore • Ronee Blakley Nashville • Lelia Goldoni Alice Doesn't Live Here Anymore • Gwen Welles Nashville
SCREENPLAY: **Robert Getchell** Alice Doesn't Live Here Anymore • Frank Pierson Dog Day Afternoon • Peter Benchley, Carl Gottlieb Jaws • Joan Tewkesbury Nashville

Academy Awards

PICTURE: **One Flew over the Cuckoo's Nest** • Barry Lyndon • Dog Day Afternoon • Jaws • Nashville
FOREIGN LANGUAGE FILM: **Dersu Uzala** • Land of Promise • Letters from Marusia • Sandakan No 8 • Scent of a Woman
DIRECTOR: **Milos Forman** One Flew over the Cuckoo's Nest • Robert Altman Nashville • Federico Fellini Amarcord • Stanley Kubrick Barry Lyndon • Sidney Lumet Dog Day Afternoon
ACTOR: **Jack Nicholson** One Flew over the Cuckoo's Nest • Walter Matthau The Sunshine Boys • Al Pacino Dog Day Afternoon • Maximilian Schell The Man in the Glass Booth • James Whitmore Give 'em Hell, Harry!
ACTRESS: **Louise Fletcher** One Flew over the Cuckoo's Nest • Isabelle Adjani The Story of Adèle H • Ann-Margret Tommy • Glenda Jackson Hedda • Carol Kane Hester Street
SUPPORTING ACTOR: **George Burns** The Sunshine Boys • Brad Dourif One Flew over the Cuckoo's Nest • Burgess Meredith The Day of the Locust • Chris Sarandon Dog Day Afternoon • Jack Warden Shampoo
SUPPORTING ACTRESS: **Lee Grant** Shampoo • Ronee Blakley Nashville • Sylvia Miles Farewell, My Lovely • Lily Tomlin Nashville • Brenda Vaccaro Once Is Not Enough
ORIGINAL SCREENPLAY: **Frank Pierson** Dog Day Afternoon • Federico Fellini, Tonino Guerra Amarcord • Claude Lelouch, Pierre Uytterhoeven And Now My Love • Ted Allan Lies My Father Told Me • Warren Beatty, Robert Towne Shampoo
ADAPTED SCREENPLAY: **Bo Goldman, Lawrence Hauben** One Flew over the Cuckoo's Nest • Stanley Kubrick Barry Lyndon • John Huston, Gladys Hill The Man Who Would Be King • Ruggero Maccari, Dino Risi Scent of a Woman • Neil Simon The Sunshine Boys

Golden Globe Awards

DRAMA: **One Flew over the Cuckoo's Nest**
COMEDY/MUSICAL: **The Sunshine Boys**
FOREIGN LANGUAGE FILM: **Lies My Father Told Me**
DIRECTOR: **Milos Forman** One Flew over the Cuckoo's Nest
ACTOR, DRAMA: **Jack Nicholson** One Flew over the Cuckoo's Nest
ACTRESS, DRAMA: **Louise Fletcher** One Flew over the Cuckoo's Nest
ACTOR, COMEDY/MUSICAL: **Walter Matthau** The Sunshine Boys
ACTRESS, COMEDY/MUSICAL: **Ann-Margret** Tommy
SUPPORTING ACTOR: **Richard Benjamin** The Sunshine Boys
SUPPORTING ACTRESS: **Brenda Vaccaro** Once Is Not Enough
SCREENPLAY: **Lawrence Hauben, Bo Goldman** One Flew over the Cuckoo's Nest

Cannes Film Festival

PALME D'OR: **Chronicle of the Burning Years**
DIRECTOR: **Michel Brault** Les Ordres • **Costa-Gavras** Section Spéciale
ACTOR: **Vittorio Gassman** Scent of a Woman
ACTRESS: **Valerie Perrine** Lenny

Berlin International Film Festival

GOLDEN BEAR: **Adoption**
SILVER BEAR, DIRECTOR: **Sergei Solovyov** Sto Dnej Possle Detstwa
SILVER BEAR, ACTOR: **Vlastimil Brodsky** Jacob the Liar
SILVER BEAR, ACTRESS: **Kinuyo Tanaka** Sandakan No 8

1976

British Academy of Film & Television Arts

FILM: **One Flew over the Cuckoo's Nest** • All the President's Men • Bugsy Malone • Taxi Driver
DIRECTOR: **Milos Forman** One Flew over the Cuckoo's Nest • Alan J Pakula All the President's Men • Alan Parker Bugsy Malone • Martin Scorsese Taxi Driver
ACTOR: **Jack Nicholson** One Flew over the Cuckoo's Nest • Robert De Niro Taxi Driver • Dustin Hoffman All the President's Men • Dustin Hoffman Marathon Man • Walter Matthau The Bad News Bears • Walter Matthau The Sunshine Boys
ACTRESS: **Louise Fletcher** One Flew over the Cuckoo's Nest • Lauren Bacall The Shootist • Rita Moreno The Ritz • Liv Ullmann Face to Face
SUPPORTING ACTOR: **Brad Dourif** One Flew over the Cuckoo's Nest • Martin Balsam All the President's Men • Michael Hordern The Slipper and the Rose • Jason Robards All the President's Men
SUPPORTING ACTRESS: **Jodie Foster** Bugsy Malone • **Jodie Foster** Taxi Driver • Annette Crosbie The Slipper and the Rose • Vivien Merchant The Homecoming • Billie Whitelaw The Omen
SCREENPLAY: **Alan Parker** Bugsy Malone • William Goldman All the President's Men • Lawrence Hauben, Bo Goldman One Flew over the Cuckoo's Nest • Neil Simon The Sunshine Boys

Academy Awards

PICTURE: **Rocky** • All the President's Men • Bound for Glory • Network • Taxi Driver

FOREIGN LANGUAGE FILM: **Black and White in Color** • Cousin, Cousine • Jacob the Liar • Nights and Days • Seven Beauties
DIRECTOR: **John G Avildsen** Rocky • Ingmar Bergman Face to Face • Sidney Lumet Network • Alan J Pakula All the President's Men • Lina Wertmuller Seven Beauties
ACTOR: **Peter Finch** Network • Robert De Niro Taxi Driver • Giancarlo Giannini Seven Beauties • William Holden Network • Sylvester Stallone Rocky
ACTRESS: **Faye Dunaway** Network • Marie-Christine Barrault Cousin, Cousine • Talia Shire Rocky • Sissy Spacek Carrie • Liv Ullmann Face to Face
SUPPORTING ACTOR: **Jason Robards** All the President's Men • Ned Beatty Network • Burgess Meredith Rocky • Laurence Olivier Marathon Man • Burt Young Rocky
SUPPORTING ACTRESS: **Beatrice Straight** Network • Jane Alexander All the President's Men • Jodie Foster Taxi Driver • Lee Grant Voyage of the Damned • Piper Laurie Carrie
ORIGINAL SCREENPLAY: **Paddy Chayefsky** Network • Jean-Charles Tacchella, Danièle Thompson Cousin, Cousine • Walter Bernstein The Front • Sylvester Stallone Rocky • Lina Wertmuller Seven Beauties
ADAPTED SCREENPLAY: **William Goldman** All the President's Men • Robert Getchell Bound for Glory • Federico Fellini, Bernardino Zapponi Casanova • Nicholas Meyer The Seven-Per-Cent Solution • David Butler, Steve Shagan Voyage of the Damned

Golden Globe Awards

DRAMA: **Rocky**
COMEDY/MUSICAL: **A Star Is Born**
FOREIGN LANGUAGE FILM: **Face to Face**
DIRECTOR: **Sidney Lumet** Network
ACTOR, DRAMA: **Peter Finch** Network
ACTRESS, DRAMA: **Faye Dunaway** Network
ACTOR, COMEDY/MUSICAL: **Kris Kristofferson** A Star Is Born
ACTRESS, COMEDY/MUSICAL: **Barbra Streisand** A Star Is Born
SUPPORTING ACTOR: **Laurence Olivier** Marathon Man
SUPPORTING ACTRESS: **Katharine Ross** Voyage of the Damned
SCREENPLAY: **Paddy Chayefsky** Network

Cannes Film Festival

PALME D'OR: **Taxi Driver**
DIRECTOR: **Ettore Scola** Down and Dirty
ACTOR: **José Luis Gómez** Pascual Duarte
ACTRESS: **Mari Torocsik** Deryne, Hol Van? • **Dominique Sanda** The Inheritance

Berlin International Film Festival

GOLDEN BEAR: **Buffalo Bill and the Indians, or Sitting Bull's History Lesson**
SILVER BEAR, DIRECTOR: **Mario Monicelli** Caro Michele
SILVER BEAR, ACTOR: **Gerhard Olschewski** Verlorenes Leben
SILVER BEAR, ACTRESS: **Jadwiga Baranska** Nights and Days

1977

British Academy of Film & Television Arts

FILM: **Annie Hall** • A Bridge Too Far • Network • Rocky
DIRECTOR: **Woody Allen** Annie Hall • Richard Attenborough A Bridge Too Far • John G Avildsen Rocky • Sidney Lumet Network
ACTOR: **Peter Finch** Network • Woody Allen Annie Hall • William Holden Network • Sylvester Stallone Rocky
ACTRESS: **Diane Keaton** Annie Hall • Faye Dunaway Network • Shelley Duvall 3 Women • Lily Tomlin The Late Show
SUPPORTING ACTOR: **Edward Fox** A Bridge Too Far • Colin Blakely Equus • Robert Duvall Network • Zero Mostel The Front
SUPPORTING ACTRESS: **Jenny Agutter** Equus • Geraldine Chaplin Welcome to LA • Joan Plowright Equus • Shelley Winters Next Stop, Greenwich Village
SCREENPLAY: **Woody Allen, Marshall Brickman** Annie Hall • Peter Shaffer Equus • Paddy Chayefsky Network • Sylvester Stallone Rocky

Academy Awards

PICTURE: **Annie Hall** • The Goodbye Girl • Julia • Star Wars Episode IV: a New Hope • The Turning Point
FOREIGN LANGUAGE FILM: **Madame Rosa** • Iphigenia • Operation Thunderbolt • A Special Day • That Obscure Object of Desire
DIRECTOR: **Woody Allen** Annie Hall • George Lucas Star Wars Episode IV: a New Hope • Herbert Ross The Turning Point • Steven Spielberg Close Encounters of the Third Kind • Fred Zinnemann Julia
ACTOR: **Richard Dreyfuss** The Goodbye Girl • Woody Allen Annie Hall • Richard Burton Equus • Marcello Mastroianni A Special Day • John Travolta Saturday Night Fever
ACTRESS: **Diane Keaton** Annie Hall • Anne Bancroft The Turning Point • Jane Fonda Julia • Shirley MacLaine The Turning Point • Marsha Mason The Goodbye Girl
SUPPORTING ACTOR: **Jason Robards** Julia • Mikhail Baryshnikov The Turning Point • Peter Firth Equus • Alec Guinness Star Wars Episode IV: a New Hope • Maximilian Schell Julia
SUPPORTING ACTRESS: **Vanessa Redgrave** Julia • Leslie Browne The Turning Point • Quinn Cummings The Goodbye Girl • Melinda Dillon Close Encounters of the Third Kind • Tuesday Weld Looking for Mr Goodbar
ORIGINAL SCREENPLAY: **Woody Allen, Marshall Brickman** Annie Hall • Neil Simon The Goodbye Girl • Robert Benton The Late Show • George Lucas Star Wars Episode IV: a New Hope • Arthur Laurents The Turning Point
ADAPTED SCREENPLAY: **Alvin Sargent** Julia • Peter Shaffer Equus • Lewis John Carlino, Gavin Lambert I Never Promised You a Rose Garden • Larry Gelbart Oh, God! • Luis Buñuel, Jean-Claude Carrière That Obscure Object of Desire

Golden Globe Awards

DRAMA: **The Turning Point**
COMEDY/MUSICAL: **The Goodbye Girl**
FOREIGN LANGUAGE FILM: **A Special Day**
DIRECTOR: **Herbert Ross** The Turning Point
ACTOR, DRAMA: **Richard Burton** Equus
ACTRESS, DRAMA: **Jane Fonda** Julia
ACTOR, COMEDY/MUSICAL: **Richard Dreyfuss** The Goodbye Girl
ACTRESS, COMEDY/MUSICAL: **Marsha Mason** The Goodbye Girl •
Diane Keaton Annie Hall
SUPPORTING ACTOR: **Peter Firth** Equus
SUPPORTING ACTRESS: **Vanessa Redgrave** Julia
SCREENPLAY: **Neil Simon** The Goodbye Girl

Cannes Film Festival

PALME D'OR: **Padre Padrone**
ACTOR: **Fernando Rey** Elisa, Mia Vida
ACTRESS: **Shelley Duvall** 3 Women • **Monique Mercure** JA
Martin Photographe

Berlin International Film Festival

GOLDEN BEAR: **The Ascent**
SILVER BEAR, DIRECTOR: **Manuel Gutierrez Aragon** Camada
Negra
SILVER BEAR, ACTOR: **Fernando Fernán Gómez** El Anacoreta
SILVER BEAR, ACTRESS: **Lily Tomlin** The Late Show

1978

British Academy of Film & Television Arts

FILM: **Julia** • Close Encounters of the Third Kind • Midnight
Express • Star Wars Episode IV: a New Hope
DIRECTOR: **Alan Parker** Midnight Express • Robert Altman A
Wedding • Steven Spielberg Close Encounters of the Third
Kind • Fred Zinnemann Julia
ACTOR: **Richard Dreyfuss** The Goodbye Girl • Brad Davis
Midnight Express • Anthony Hopkins Magic • Peter Ustinov
Death on the Nile
ACTRESS: **Jane Fonda** Julia • Anne Bancroft The Turning Point
• Jill Clayburgh An Unmarried Woman • Marsha Mason The
Goodbye Girl
SUPPORTING ACTOR: **John Hurt** Midnight Express • Gene
Hackman Superman • Jason Robards Julia • François
Truffaut Close Encounters of the Third Kind
SUPPORTING ACTRESS: **Geraldine Page** Interiors • Angela
Lansbury, Maggie Smith Death on the Nile • Mona
Washbourne Stevie
SCREENPLAY: **Alvin Sargent** Julia • Steven Spielberg Close
Encounters of the Third Kind • Neil Simon The Goodbye Girl •
John Considine, Patricia Resnick, Allan Nicholls, Robert
Altman A Wedding

Academy Awards

PICTURE: **The Deer Hunter** • Coming Home • Heaven Can Wait
• Midnight Express • An Unmarried Woman
FOREIGN LANGUAGE FILM: **Get out Your Handkerchiefs** • The
Glass Cell • Hungarians • Viva Italia! • White Bim Black Ear
DIRECTOR: **Michael Cimino** The Deer Hunter • Woody Allen
Interiors • Hal Ashby Coming Home • Warren Beatty, Buck
Henry Heaven Can Wait • Alan Parker Midnight Express
ACTOR: **Jon Voight** Coming Home • Warren Beatty Heaven
Can Wait • Gary Busey The Buddy Holly Story • Robert De
Niro The Deer Hunter • Laurence Olivier The Boys from
Brazil
ACTRESS: **Jane Fonda** Coming Home • Ingrid Bergman
Autumn Sonata • Ellen Burstyn Same Time, Next Year • Jill
Clayburgh An Unmarried Woman • Geraldine Page Interiors
SUPPORTING ACTOR: **Christopher Walken** The Deer Hunter •
Bruce Dern Coming Home • Richard Farnsworth Comes a
Horseman • John Hurt Midnight Express • Jack Warden
Heaven Can Wait
SUPPORTING ACTRESS: **Maggie Smith** California Suite • Dyan
Cannon Heaven Can Wait • Penelope Milford Coming Home •
Maureen Stapleton Interiors • Meryl Streep The Deer Hunter
ORIGINAL SCREENPLAY: **Nancy Dowd, Robert C Jones, Waldo
Salt** Coming Home • Ingmar Bergman Autumn Sonata •
Michael Cimino, Louis Garfinkle, Quinn Redeker, Deric
Washburn The Deer Hunter • Woody Allen Interiors • Paul
Mazursky An Unmarried Woman
ADAPTED SCREENPLAY: **Oliver Stone** Midnight Express • Walter
Newman Bloodbrothers • Neil Simon California Suite •
Warren Beatty, Elaine May Heaven Can Wait • Bernard Slade
Same Time, Next Year

Golden Globe Awards

DRAMA: **Midnight Express**
COMEDY/MUSICAL: **Heaven Can Wait**
FOREIGN LANGUAGE FILM: **Autumn Sonata**
DIRECTOR: **Michael Cimino** The Deer Hunter
ACTOR, DRAMA: **Jon Voight** Coming Home
ACTRESS, DRAMA: **Jane Fonda** Coming Home
ACTOR, COMEDY/MUSICAL: **Warren Beatty** Heaven Can Wait
ACTRESS, COMEDY/MUSICAL: **Ellen Burstyn** Same Time, Next
Year • Maggie Smith California Suite
SUPPORTING ACTOR: **John Hurt** Midnight Express
SUPPORTING ACTRESS: **Dyan Cannon** Heaven Can Wait
SCREENPLAY: **Oliver Stone** Midnight Express

Cannes Film Festival

PALME D'OR: **The Tree of Wooden Clogs**
DIRECTOR: **Nagisa Oshima** Ai No Borei
ACTOR: **Jon Voight** Coming Home
ACTRESS: **Jill Clayburgh** An Unmarried Woman • **Isabelle
Huppert** Violette Nozière

Berlin International Film Festival

GOLDEN BEAR: **Las Truchas • Las Palabras de Max**
SILVER BEAR, DIRECTOR: **Georgi Djulgerov** Avantage
SILVER BEAR, ACTOR: **Craig Russell** Outrageous!
SILVER BEAR, ACTRESS: **Gena Rowlands** Opening Night

1979

British Academy of Film & Television Arts

FILM: **Manhattan** • Apocalypse Now • The China Syndrome •
The Deer Hunter
DIRECTOR: **Francis Ford Coppola** Apocalypse Now • Woody
Allen Manhattan • Michael Cimino The Deer Hunter • John
Schlesinger Yanks
ACTOR: **Jack Lemmon** The China Syndrome • Woody Allen
Manhattan • Robert De Niro The Deer Hunter • Martin Sheen
Apocalypse Now
ACTRESS: **Jane Fonda** The China Syndrome • Diane Keaton
Manhattan • Maggie Smith California Suite • Meryl Streep
The Deer Hunter
SUPPORTING ACTOR: **Robert Duvall** Apocalypse Now • Denholm
Elliott Saint Jack • John Hurt Alien • Christopher Walken The
Deer Hunter
SUPPORTING ACTRESS: **Rachel Roberts** Yanks • Lisa Eichhorn
The Europeans • Mariel Hemingway, Meryl Streep Manhattan
SCREENPLAY: **Woody Allen, Marshall Brickman** Manhattan •
Mike Gray, T S Cook, James Bridges The China Syndrome •
Deric Washburn The Deer Hunter • Colin Welland, Walter
Bernstein Yanks

Academy Awards

PICTURE: **Kramer vs Kramer** • All That Jazz • Apocalypse Now
• Breaking Away • Norma Rae
FOREIGN LANGUAGE FILM: **The Tin Drum** • The Young Ladies of
Wilko • Mama Turns a Hundred • Une Histoire Simple • To
Forget Venice
DIRECTOR: **Robert Benton** Kramer vs Kramer • Francis Ford
Coppola Apocalypse Now • Bob Fosse All That Jazz •
Edouard Molinaro La Cage aux Folles • Peter Yates Breaking
Away
ACTOR: **Dustin Hoffman** Kramer vs Kramer • Jack Lemmon
The China Syndrome • Al Pacino ...And Justice for All • Roy
Scheider All That Jazz • Peter Sellers Being There
ACTRESS: **Sally Field** Norma Rae • Jill Clayburgh Starting Over
• Jane Fonda The China Syndrome • Marsha Mason Chapter
Two • Bette Midler The Rose
SUPPORTING ACTOR: **Melvyn Douglas** Being There • Robert
Duvall Apocalypse Now • Frederic Forrest The Rose • Justin
Henry Kramer vs Kramer • Mickey Rooney The Black Stallion
SUPPORTING ACTRESS: **Meryl Streep** Kramer vs Kramer • Jane
Alexander Kramer vs Kramer • Barbara Barrie Breaking
Away • Candice Bergen Starting Over • Mariel Hemingway
Manhattan
ORIGINAL SCREENPLAY: **Steve Tesich** Breaking Away • Valerie
Curtin, Barry Levinson ...And Justice for All • Robert Alan
Aurthur, Bob Fosse All That Jazz • James Bridges, T S Cook,
Mike Gray The China Syndrome • Woody Allen, Marshall
Brickman Manhattan
ADAPTED SCREENPLAY: **Robert Benton** Kramer vs Kramer •
Francis Ford Coppola, John Milius Apocalypse Now •
Marcello Danon, Edouard Molinaro, Jean Poiret, Francis
Veber La Cage aux Folles • Allan Burns A Little Romance •
Harriet Frank Jr, Irving Ravetch Norma Rae

Golden Globe Awards

DRAMA: **Kramer vs Kramer**
COMEDY/MUSICAL: **Breaking Away**
FOREIGN LANGUAGE FILM: **La Cage aux Folles**
DIRECTOR: **Francis Ford Coppola** Apocalypse Now
ACTOR, DRAMA: **Dustin Hoffman** Kramer vs Kramer
ACTRESS, DRAMA: **Sally Field** Norma Rae
ACTOR, COMEDY/MUSICAL: **Peter Sellers** Being There
ACTRESS, COMEDY/MUSICAL: **Bette Midler** The Rose
SUPPORTING ACTOR: **Robert Duvall** Apocalypse Now • **Melvyn
Douglas** Being There
SUPPORTING ACTRESS: **Meryl Streep** Kramer vs Kramer
SCREENPLAY: **Robert Benton** Kramer vs Kramer

Cannes Film Festival

PALME D'OR: **The Tin Drum • Apocalypse Now**
DIRECTOR: **Terrence Malick** Days of Heaven
ACTOR: **Jack Lemmon** The China Syndrome
ACTRESS: **Sally Field** Norma Rae
SUPPORTING ACTOR: **Stefano Madia** Caro Papà
SUPPORTING ACTRESS: **Eva Mattes** Woyzeck

Berlin International Film Festival

GOLDEN BEAR: **David**
SILVER BEAR, DIRECTOR: **Astrid Henning-Jensen** Vinterborn
SILVER BEAR, ACTOR: **Michele Placido** Ernesto
SILVER BEAR, ACTRESS: **Hanna Schygulla** The Marriage of
Maria Braun

1980

British Academy of Film & Television Arts

FILM: **The Elephant Man** • Being There • Kagemusha • Kramer
vs Kramer
DIRECTOR: **Akira Kurosawa** Kagemusha • Robert Benton
Kramer vs Kramer • David Lynch The Elephant Man • Alan
Parker Fame
ACTOR: **John Hurt** The Elephant Man • Dustin Hoffman
Kramer vs Kramer • Roy Scheider All That Jazz • Peter
Sellers Being There
ACTRESS: **Judy Davis** My Brilliant Career • Shirley MacLaine
Being There • Bette Midler The Rose • Meryl Streep Kramer
vs Kramer

SCREENPLAY: **Jerzy Kosinski** Being There • Jim Abrahams,
David Zucker, Jerry Zucker Airplane! • Christopher de Vore,
Eric Bergren, David Lynch The Elephant Man • Robert
Benton Kramer vs Kramer

Academy Awards

PICTURE: **Ordinary People** • Coal Miner's Daughter • The
Elephant Man • Raging Bull • Tess
FOREIGN LANGUAGE FILM: **Moscow Distrusts Tears** •
Confidence • Kagemusha • The Last Metro • The Nest
DIRECTOR: **Robert Redford** Ordinary People • David Lynch The
Elephant Man • Roman Polanski Tess • Richard Rush The
Stunt Man • Martin Scorsese Raging Bull
ACTOR: **Robert De Niro** Raging Bull • Robert Duvall The Great
Santini • John Hurt The Elephant Man • Jack Lemmon
Tribute • Peter O'Toole The Stunt Man
ACTRESS: **Sissy Spacek** Coal Miner's Daughter • Ellen Burstyn
Resurrection • Goldie Hawn Private Benjamin • Mary Tyler
Moore Ordinary People • Gena Rowlands Gloria
SUPPORTING ACTOR: **Timothy Hutton** Ordinary People • Judd
Hirsch Ordinary People • Michael O'Keefe The Great Santini •
Joe Pesci Raging Bull • Jason Robards Melvin and Howard
SUPPORTING ACTRESS: **Mary Steenburgen** Melvin and Howard
• Eileen Brennan Private Benjamin • Eva Le Gallienne
Resurrection • Cathy Moriarty Raging Bull • Diana Scarwid
Inside Moves: the Guys from Max's Bar
ORIGINAL SCREENPLAY: **Bo Goldman** Melvin and Howard • W D
Richter, Arthur Ross Brubaker • Christopher Gore Fame •
Jean Gruault Mon Oncle d'Amérique • Nancy Myers, Harvey
Miller, Charles Shyer Private Benjamin
ADAPTED SCREENPLAY: **Alvin Sargent** Ordinary People • Bruce
Beresford, Jonathan Hardy, David Stevens Breaker Morant •
Tom Rickman Coal Miner's Daughter • Christopher de Vore,
Eric Bergren, David Lynch The Elephant Man • Richard Rush,
Lawrence B Marcus The Stunt Man

Golden Globe Awards

DRAMA: **Ordinary People**
COMEDY/MUSICAL: **Coal Miner's Daughter**
FOREIGN FILM: **Tess**
DIRECTOR: **Robert Redford** Ordinary People
ACTOR, DRAMA: **Robert De Niro** Raging Bull
ACTRESS, DRAMA: **Mary Tyler Moore** Ordinary People
ACTOR, COMEDY/MUSICAL: **Ray Sharkey** The Idolmaker
ACTRESS, COMEDY/MUSICAL: **Sissy Spacek** Coal Miner's
Daughter
SUPPORTING ACTOR: **Timothy Hutton** Ordinary People
SUPPORTING ACTRESS: **Mary Steenburgen** Melvin and Howard
SCREENPLAY: **William Peter Blatty** The Ninth Configuration

Cannes Film Festival

PALME D'OR: **Kagemusha • All That Jazz**
ACTOR: **Michel Piccoli** Leap into the Void
ACTRESS: **Anouk Aimée** Leap into the Void
SUPPORTING ACTOR: **Jack Thompson** Breaker Morant
SUPPORTING ACTRESS: **Carla Gravina** La Terrazza • **Milena
Dravic** Poseban Tretman
SCREENPLAY: **Agenore Incrocci, Furio Scarpelli, Ettore Scola**
La Terrazza

Berlin International Film Festival

GOLDEN BEAR: **Heartland • Palermo oder Wolfsburg**
SILVER BEAR, DIRECTOR: **István Szabó** Confidence
SILVER BEAR, ACTOR: **Andrzej Seweryn** The Conductor
SILVER BEAR, ACTRESS: **Renate Krössner** Solo Sunny

1981

British Academy of Film & Television Arts

FILM: **Chariots of Fire** • Atlantic City, USA • The French
Lieutenant's Woman • Gregory's Girl • Raiders of the Lost
Ark
DIRECTOR: **Louis Malle** Atlantic City, USA • Bill Forsyth
Gregory's Girl • Hugh Hudson Chariots of Fire • Karel Reisz
The French Lieutenant's Woman
ACTOR: **Burt Lancaster** Atlantic City, USA • Robert De Niro
Raging Bull • Bob Hoskins The Long Good Friday • Jeremy
Irons The French Lieutenant's Woman
ACTRESS: **Meryl Streep** The French Lieutenant's Woman •
Mary Tyler Moore Ordinary People • Maggie Smith Quartet •
Sissy Spacek Coal Miner's Daughter
SUPPORTING ARTIST: **Ian Holm** Chariots of Fire • Denholm
Elliott Raiders of the Lost Ark • John Gielgud Arthur • Nigel
Havers Chariots of Fire
SCREENPLAY: **Bill Forsyth** Gregory's Girl • John Guare Atlantic
City, USA • Colin Welland Chariots of Fire • Harold Pinter The
French Lieutenant's Woman

Academy Awards

PICTURE: **Chariots of Fire** • Atlantic City, USA • On Golden
Pond • Raiders of the Lost Ark • Reds
FOREIGN LANGUAGE FILM: **Mephisto** • The Boat Is Full • Man of
Iron • Muddy River • Three Brothers
DIRECTOR: **Warren Beatty** Reds • Hugh Hudson Chariots of
Fire • Louis Malle Atlantic City, USA • Mark Rydell On Golden
Pond • Steven Spielberg Raiders of the Lost Ark
ACTOR: **Henry Fonda** On Golden Pond • Warren Beatty Reds •
Burt Lancaster Atlantic City, USA • Dudley Moore Arthur •
Paul Newman Absence of Malice
ACTRESS: **Katharine Hepburn** On Golden Pond • Diane Keaton
Reds • Marsha Mason Only When I Laugh • Susan Sarandon
Atlantic City, USA • Meryl Streep The French Lieutenant's
Woman
SUPPORTING ACTOR: **John Gielgud** Arthur • James Coco Only
When I Laugh • Ian Holm Chariots of Fire • Jack Nicholson
Reds • Howard E Rollins Jr Ragtime
SUPPORTING ACTRESS: **Maureen Stapleton** Reds • Melinda
Dillon Absence of Malice • Jane Fonda On Golden Pond •

Joan Hackett *Only When I Laugh* • Elizabeth McGovern *Ragtime*

ORIGINAL SCREENPLAY: **Colin Welland** *Chariots of Fire* • Kurt Luedtke *Absence of Malice* • Steve Gordon *Arthur* • John Guare *Atlantic City, USA* • Warren Beatty, Trevor Griffiths *Reds*

ADAPTED SCREENPLAY: **Ernest Thompson** *On Golden Pond* • Harold Pinter *The French Lieutenant's Woman* • Dennis Potter *Pennies from Heaven* • Jay Presson Allen, Sidney Lumet *Prince of the City* • Michael Weller *Ragtime*

Golden Globe Awards

DRAMA: ***On Golden Pond***
COMEDY/MUSICAL: ***Arthur***
FOREIGN FILM: ***Chariots of Fire***
DIRECTOR: **Warren Beatty** *Reds*
ACTOR, DRAMA: **Henry Fonda** *On Golden Pond*
ACTRESS, DRAMA: **Meryl Streep** *The French Lieutenant's Woman*
ACTOR, COMEDY/MUSICAL: **Dudley Moore** *Arthur*
ACTRESS, COMEDY/MUSICAL: **Bernadette Peters** *Pennies from Heaven*
SUPPORTING ACTOR: **John Gielgud** *Arthur*
SUPPORTING ACTRESS: **Joan Hackett** *Only When I Laugh*
SCREENPLAY: **Ernest Thompson** *On Golden Pond*

Cannes Film Festival

PALME D'OR: ***Man of Iron***
ACTOR: **Ugo Tognazzi** *The Tragedy of a Ridiculous Man*
ACTRESS: **Isabelle Adjani** *Quartet* • **Isabelle Adjani** *Possession*
SUPPORTING ACTOR: **Ian Holm** *Chariots of Fire*
SUPPORTING ACTRESS: **Elena Solovei** *Grouppa Krovi Nol*
SCREENPLAY: **Peter Dobai, István Szabó** *Mephisto*

Berlin International Film Festival

GOLDEN BEAR: ***Deprisa, Deprisa***
SILVER BEAR, ACTOR: **Jack Lemmon** *Tribute* • **Anatoli Solinitsin** *Twenty Six Days in the Life of Dostoevsky*
SILVER BEAR, ACTRESS: **Barbara Grabowska** *Goraczka*

1982

British Academy of Film & Television Arts

FILM: ***Gandhi*** • *ET the Extra-Terrestrial* • *Missing* • *On Golden Pond*
FOREIGN LANGUAGE FILM: ***Christ Stopped at Eboli*** • *Das Boot* • *Diva* • *Fitzcarraldo*
DIRECTOR: **Richard Attenborough** *Gandhi* • Costa-Gavras *Missing* • Mark Rydell *On Golden Pond* • Steven Spielberg *ET the Extra-Terrestrial*
ACTOR: **Ben Kingsley** *Gandhi* • Warren Beatty *Reds* • Albert Finney *Shoot the Moon* • Henry Fonda *On Golden Pond* • Jack Lemmon *Missing*
ACTRESS: **Katharine Hepburn** *On Golden Pond* • Diane Keaton *Reds* • Jennifer Kendal *36 Chowringhee Lane* • Sissy Spacek *Missing*
SUPPORTING ACTOR: **Jack Nicholson** *Reds* • Frank Finlay *The Return of the Soldier* • Edward Fox, Roshan Seth *Gandhi*
SUPPORTING ACTRESS: **Rohini Hattangady** *Gandhi* • Candice Bergen *Gandhi* • Jane Fonda *On Golden Pond* • **Maureen Stapleton** *Reds*
SCREENPLAY: **Costa-Gavras, Donald Stewart** *Missing* • Melissa Mathison *ET the Extra-Terrestrial* • John Briley *Gandhi* • Ernest Thompson *On Golden Pond*

Academy Awards

PICTURE: ***Gandhi*** • *ET the Extra-Terrestrial* • *Missing* • *Tootsie* • *The Verdict*
FOREIGN LANGUAGE FILM: ***Begin the Beguine*** • *Alsino and the Condor* • *Clean Slate* • *The Flight of the Eagle* • *Private Life*
DIRECTOR: **Richard Attenborough** *Gandhi* • Sidney Lumet *The Verdict* • Sydney Pollack *Tootsie* • Wolfgang Petersen *Das Boot* • Steven Spielberg *ET the Extra-Terrestrial*
ACTOR: **Ben Kingsley** *Gandhi* • Dustin Hoffman *Tootsie* • Jack Lemmon *Missing* • Paul Newman *The Verdict* • Peter O'Toole *My Favorite Year*
ACTRESS: **Meryl Streep** *Sophie's Choice* • Julie Andrews *Victor/Victoria* • Jessica Lange *Frances* • Sissy Spacek *Missing* • Debra Winger *An Officer and a Gentleman*
SUPPORTING ACTOR: **Louis Gossett Jr** *An Officer and a Gentleman* • Charles Durning *The Best Little Whorehouse in Texas* • John Lithgow *The World According to Garp* • James Mason *The Verdict* • Robert Preston *Victor/Victoria*
SUPPORTING ACTRESS: **Jessica Lange** *Tootsie* • Glenn Close *The World According to Garp* • Teri Garr *Tootsie* • Kim Stanley *Frances* • Lesley Ann Warren *Victor/Victoria*
ORIGINAL SCREENPLAY: **John Briley** *Gandhi* • Barry Levinson *Diner* • Melissa Mathison *ET the Extra-Terrestrial* • Douglas Day Stewart *An Officer and a Gentleman* • Larry Gelbart, Don McGuire, Murray Schisgal *Tootsie*
ADAPTED SCREENPLAY: **Costa-Gavras, Donald Stewart** *Missing* • Wolfgang Petersen *Das Boot* • Alan J Pakula *Sophie's Choice* • David Mamet *The Verdict* • Blake Edwards *Victor/Victoria*

Golden Globe Awards

DRAMA: ***ET the Extra-Terrestrial***
COMEDY/MUSICAL: ***Tootsie***
FOREIGN FILM: ***Gandhi***
DIRECTOR: **Richard Attenborough** *Gandhi*
ACTOR, DRAMA: **Ben Kingsley** *Gandhi*
ACTRESS, DRAMA: **Meryl Streep** *Sophie's Choice*
ACTOR, COMEDY/MUSICAL: **Dustin Hoffman** *Tootsie*
ACTRESS, COMEDY/MUSICAL: **Julie Andrews** *Victor/Victoria*
SUPPORTING ACTOR: **Louis Gossett Jr** *An Officer and a Gentleman*
SUPPORTING ACTRESS: **Jessica Lange** *Tootsie*
SCREENPLAY: **John Briley** *Gandhi*

Cannes Film Festival

PALME D'OR: ***Missing*** • *Yol*
DIRECTOR: **Werner Herzog** *Fitzcarraldo*
ACTOR: **Jack Lemmon** *Missing*
ACTRESS: **Jadwiga Jankowska-Cieslak** *Another Way*
SCREENPLAY: **Jerzy Skolimowski** *Moonlighting*

Berlin International Film Festival

GOLDEN BEAR: ***Veronika Voss***
SILVER BEAR, DIRECTOR: **Mario Monicelli** *Il Marchese del Grillo*
SILVER BEAR, ACTOR: **Michel Piccoli** *A Strange Affair* • **Stellan Skarsgård** *The Simple-Minded Murderer*
SILVER BEAR, ACTRESS: **Katrin Sass** *Bürgschaft für ein Jahr*

1983

British Academy of Film & Television Arts

FILM: ***Educating Rita*** • *Heat and Dust* • *Local Hero* • *Tootsie*
FOREIGN LANGUAGE FILM: ***Danton*** • *Confidentially Yours* • *Fanny and Alexander* • *La Traviata*
DIRECTOR: **Bill Forsyth** *Local Hero* • James Ivory *Heat and Dust* • Sydney Pollack *Tootsie* • Martin Scorsese *The King of Comedy*
ACTOR: **Michael Caine** *Educating Rita* • Dustin Hoffman *Tootsie* • Michael Caine *The Honorary Consul* • Robert De Niro *The King of Comedy*
ACTRESS: **Julie Walters** *Educating Rita* • Jessica Lange *Tootsie* • Phyllis Logan *Another Time, Another Place* • Meryl Streep *Sophie's Choice*
SUPPORTING ACTOR: **Denholm Elliott** *Trading Places* • Bob Hoskins *The Honorary Consul* • Burt Lancaster *Local Hero* • Jerry Lewis *The King of Comedy*
SUPPORTING ACTRESS: **Jamie Lee Curtis** *Trading Places* • Teri Garr *Tootsie* • Rosemary Harris *The Ploughman's Lunch* • Maureen Lipman *Educating Rita*
ORIGINAL SCREENPLAY: **Paul D Zimmerman** *The King of Comedy* • Bill Forsyth *Local Hero* • Timothy Harris, Herschel Weingrod *Trading Places* • Woody Allen *Zelig*
ADAPTED SCREENPLAY: **Ruth Prawer Jhabvala** *Heat and Dust* • Harold Pinter *Betrayal* • Willy Russell *Educating Rita* • Larry Gelbart, Murray Schisgal *Tootsie*

Academy Awards

PICTURE: ***Terms of Endearment*** • *The Big Chill* • *The Dresser* • *The Right Stuff* • *Tender Mercies*
FOREIGN LANGUAGE FILM: ***Fanny and Alexander*** • *Le Bal* • *Carmen* • *Entre Nous* • *Job's Revolt*
DIRECTOR: **James L Brooks** *Terms of Endearment* • Bruce Beresford *Tender Mercies* • Ingmar Bergman *Fanny and Alexander* • Mike Nichols *Silkwood* • Peter Yates *The Dresser*
ACTOR: **Robert Duvall** *Tender Mercies* • Michael Caine *Educating Rita* • Tom Conti *Reuben, Reuben* • Tom Courtenay, Albert Finney *The Dresser*
ACTRESS: **Shirley MacLaine** *Terms of Endearment* • Jane Alexander *Testament* • Meryl Streep *Silkwood* • Julie Walters *Educating Rita* • Debra Winger *Terms of Endearment*
SUPPORTING ACTOR: **Jack Nicholson** *Terms of Endearment* • Charles Durning *To Be or Not to Be* • John Lithgow *Terms of Endearment* • Sam Shepard *The Right Stuff* • Rip Torn *Cross Creek*
SUPPORTING ACTRESS: **Linda Hunt** *The Year of Living Dangerously* • Cher *Silkwood* • Glenn Close *The Big Chill* • Amy Irving *Yentl* • Alfre Woodard *Cross Creek*
ORIGINAL SCREENPLAY: **Horton Foote** *Tender Mercies* • Lawrence Kasdan, Barbara Benedek *The Big Chill* • Ingmar Bergman *Fanny and Alexander* • Nora Ephron, Alice Arlen *Silkwood* • Lawrence Lasker, Walter F Parkes *WarGames*
ADAPTED SCREENPLAY: **James L Brooks** *Terms of Endearment* • Harold Pinter *Betrayal* • Ronald Harwood *The Dresser* • Willy Russell *Educating Rita* • Julius J Epstein *Reuben, Reuben*

Golden Globe Awards

DRAMA: ***Terms of Endearment***
COMEDY/MUSICAL: ***Yentl***
FOREIGN LANGUAGE FILM: ***Fanny and Alexander***
DIRECTOR: **Barbra Streisand** *Yentl*
ACTOR, DRAMA: **Tom Courtenay** *The Dresser* • **Robert Duvall** *Tender Mercies*
ACTRESS, DRAMA: **Shirley MacLaine** *Terms of Endearment*
ACTOR, COMEDY/MUSICAL: **Michael Caine** *Educating Rita*
ACTRESS, COMEDY/MUSICAL: **Julie Walters** *Educating Rita*
SUPPORTING ACTOR: **Jack Nicholson** *Terms of Endearment*
SUPPORTING ACTRESS: **Cher** *Silkwood*
SCREENPLAY: **James L Brooks** *Terms of Endearment*

Cannes Film Festival

PALME D'OR: ***The Ballad of Narayama***
ACTOR: **Gian Maria Volonté** *The Death of Mario Ricci*
ACTRESS: **Hanna Schygulla** *Storia di Piera*

Berlin International Film Festival

GOLDEN BEAR: ***Ascendancy*** • *La Colmena*
SILVER BEAR, DIRECTOR: **Eric Rohmer** *Pauline at the Beach*
SILVER BEAR, ACTOR: **Bruce Dern** *That Championship Season*
SILVER BEAR, ACTRESS: **Evgenia Glushenko** *Wljubljon Po Sobstvennomu Zhelaniju*

1984

British Academy of Film & Television Arts

FILM: ***The Killing Fields*** • *The Dresser* • *Paris, Texas* • *A Private Function*
FOREIGN LANGUAGE FILM: ***Carmen*** • *The Return of Martin Guerre* • *Swann in Love* • *Sunday in the Country*
DIRECTOR: **Wim Wenders** *Paris, Texas* • Roland Joffé *The Killing Fields* • Sergio Leone *Once upon a Time in America* • Peter Yates *The Dresser*

ACTOR: **Haing S Ngor** *The Killing Fields* • Tom Courtenay, Albert Finney *The Dresser* • Sam Waterston *The Killing Fields*
ACTRESS: **Maggie Smith** *A Private Function* • Shirley MacLaine *Terms of Endearment* • Helen Mirren *Cal* • Meryl Streep *Silkwood*
SUPPORTING ACTOR: **Denholm Elliott** *A Private Function* • Michael Elphick *Gorky Park* • Ian Holm, Ralph Richardson *Greystoke: the Legend of Tarzan, Lord of the Apes*
SUPPORTING ACTRESS: **Liz Smith** *A Private Function* • Eileen Atkins *The Dresser* • Cher *Silkwood* • Tuesday Weld *Once upon a Time in America*
ORIGINAL SCREENPLAY: **Woody Allen** *Broadway Danny Rose* • Lawrence Kasdan, Barbara Benedek *The Big Chill* • Bill Forsyth *Comfort and Joy* • Alan Bennett *A Private Function*
ADAPTED SCREENPLAY: **Bruce Robinson** *The Killing Fields* • Julian Mitchell *Another Country* • Ronald Harwood *The Dresser* • Sam Shepard *Paris, Texas*

Academy Awards

PICTURE: ***Amadeus*** • *The Killing Fields* • *A Passage to India* • *Places in the Heart* • *A Soldier's Story*
FOREIGN LANGUAGE FILM: ***Dangerous Moves*** • *Beyond the Walls* • *Camila* • *Double Feature* • *Wartime Romance*
DIRECTOR: **Milos Forman** *Amadeus* • Woody Allen *Broadway Danny Rose* • Robert Benton *Places in the Heart* • Roland Joffé *The Killing Fields* • David Lean *A Passage to India*
ACTOR: **F Murray Abraham** *Amadeus* • Jeff Bridges *Starman* • Albert Finney *Under the Volcano* • Tom Hulce *Amadeus* • Sam Waterston *The Killing Fields*
ACTRESS: **Sally Field** *Places in the Heart* • Judy Davis *A Passage to India* • Jessica Lange *Country* • Vanessa Redgrave *The Bostonians* • Sissy Spacek *The River*
SUPPORTING ACTOR: **Haing S Ngor** *The Killing Fields* • Adolph Caesar *A Soldier's Story* • John Malkovich *Places in the Heart* • Pat Morita *The Karate Kid* • Ralph Richardson *Greystoke: the Legend of Tarzan, Lord of the Apes*
SUPPORTING ACTRESS: **Peggy Ashcroft** *A Passage to India* • Glenn Close *The Natural* • Lindsay Crouse *Places in the Heart* • Christine Lahti *Swing Shift* • Geraldine Page *The Pope of Greenwich Village*
ORIGINAL SCREENPLAY: **Robert Benton** *Places in the Heart* • Daniel Petrie Jr, Danilo Bach *Beverly Hills Cop* • Woody Allen *Broadway Danny Rose* • Gregory Nava, Anna Thomas *El Norte* • Bruce Jay Friedman, Lowell Ganz, Brian Grazer, Babaloo Mandel *Splash*
ADAPTED SCREENPLAY: **Peter Shaffer** *Amadeus* • Robert Towne, Michael Austin *Greystoke: the Legend of Tarzan, Lord of the Apes* • Bruce Robinson *The Killing Fields* • David Lean *A Passage to India* • Charles Fuller *A Soldier's Story*

Golden Globe Awards

DRAMA: ***Amadeus***
COMEDY/MUSICAL: ***Romancing the Stone***
FOREIGN FILM: ***A Passage to India***
DIRECTOR: **Milos Forman** *Amadeus*
ACTOR, DRAMA: **F Murray Abraham** *Amadeus*
ACTRESS, DRAMA: **Sally Field** *Places in the Heart*
ACTOR, COMEDY/MUSICAL: **Dudley Moore** *Micki & Maude*
ACTRESS, COMEDY/MUSICAL: **Kathleen Turner** *Romancing the Stone*
SUPPORTING ACTOR: **Haing S Ngor** *The Killing Fields*
SUPPORTING ACTRESS: **Peggy Ashcroft** *A Passage to India*
SCREENPLAY: **Peter Shaffer** *Amadeus*

Cannes Film Festival

GRAND PRIX: ***Paris, Texas***
DIRECTOR: **Bertrand Tavernier** *Sunday in the Country*
ACTOR: **Alfredo Landa, Francisco Rabal** *Los Santos Inocentes*
ACTRESS: **Helen Mirren** *Cal*
SCREENPLAY: **Theo Angelopoulos, Tonino Guerra, Thanassis Valtinos** *Voyage to Cythera*

Berlin International Film Festival

GOLDEN BEAR: ***Love Streams***
SILVER BEAR, DIRECTOR: **Ettore Scola** *Le Bal*
SILVER BEAR, ACTOR: **Albert Finney** *The Dresser*
SILVER BEAR, ACTRESS: **Inna Tschurikova** *Wartime Romance*

1985

British Academy of Film & Television Arts

FILM: ***The Purple Rose of Cairo*** • *Amadeus* • *Back to the Future* • *A Passage to India* • *Witness*
FOREIGN LANGUAGE FILM: ***Colonel Redl*** • *Carmen* • *Dim Sum: a Little Bit of Heart* • *Subway*
ACTOR: **William Hurt** *Kiss of the Spider Woman* • Victor Banerjee *A Passage to India* • Harrison Ford *Witness* • F Murray Abraham *Amadeus*
ACTRESS: **Peggy Ashcroft** *A Passage to India* • Mia Farrow *The Purple Rose of Cairo* • Kelly McGillis *Witness* • Alexandra Pigg *Letter to Brezhnev*
SUPPORTING ACTOR: **Denholm Elliott** *Defence of the Realm* • James Fox *A Passage to India* • John Gielgud *Plenty* • Saeed Jaffrey *My Beautiful Laundrette*
SUPPORTING ACTRESS: **Rosanna Arquette** *Desperately Seeking Susan* • Judi Dench *Wetherby* • Anjelica Huston *Prizzi's Honor* • Tracey Ullman *Plenty*
ORIGINAL SCREENPLAY: **Woody Allen** *The Purple Rose of Cairo* • Robert Zemeckis, Bob Gale *Back to the Future* • Hanif Kureishi *My Beautiful Laundrette* • Earl W Wallace, William Kelley *Witness*
ADAPTED SCREENPLAY: **Richard Condon, Janet Roach** *Prizzi's Honor* • Peter Shaffer *Amadeus* • David Lean *A Passage to India* • Julian Bond *The Shooting Party*

Academy Awards

PICTURE: ***Out of Africa*** • *The Color Purple* • *Kiss of the Spider Woman* • *Prizzi's Honor* • *Witness*

FOREIGN LANGUAGE FILM: **The Official Story** • Angry Harvest • Colonel Redl • 3 Men and a Cradle • When Father Was Away on Business

DIRECTOR: **Sydney Pollack** Out of Africa • Hector Babenco Kiss of the Spider Woman • John Huston Prizzi's Honor • Akira Kurosawa Ran • Peter Weir Witness

ACTOR: **William Hurt** Kiss of the Spider Woman • Harrison Ford Witness • James Garner Murphy's Romance • Jack Nicholson Prizzi's Honor • Jon Voight Runaway Train

ACTRESS: **Geraldine Page** The Trip to Bountiful • Anne Bancroft Agnes of God • Whoopi Goldberg The Color Purple • Jessica Lange Sweet Dreams • Meryl Streep Out of Africa

SUPPORTING ACTOR: **Don Ameche** Cocoon • Klaus Maria Brandauer Out of Africa • Robert Loggia Jagged Edge • Joseph L Mankiewicz Forsaking All Others • Eric Roberts Runaway Train

SUPPORTING ACTRESS: **Anjelica Huston** Prizzi's Honor • Margaret Avery The Color Purple • Amy Madigan Twice in a Lifetime • Meg Tilly Agnes of God • Oprah Winfrey The Color Purple

ORIGINAL SCREENPLAY: **William Kelley, Earl W Wallace, Pamela Wallace** Witness • Robert Zemeckis, Bob Gale Back to the Future • Terry Gilliam, Tom Stoppard, Charles McKeown Brazil • Aïda Bortnik, Luis Puenzo The Official Version • Woody Allen The Purple Rose of Cairo

ADAPTED SCREENPLAY: **Kurt Luedtke** Out of Africa • Menno Meyjes The Color Purple • Leonard Schrader Kiss of the Spider Woman • Richard Condon, Janet Roach Prizzi's Honor • Horton Foote The Trip to Bountiful

Golden Globe Awards

DRAMA: **Out of Africa**

COMEDY/MUSICAL: **Prizzi's Honor**

FOREIGN LANGUAGE FILM: **The Official Version**

DIRECTOR: **John Huston** Prizzi's Honor

ACTOR, DRAMA: **Jon Voight** Runaway Train

ACTRESS, DRAMA: **Whoopi Goldberg** The Color Purple

ACTOR, COMEDY/MUSICAL: **Jack Nicholson** Prizzi's Honor

ACTRESS, COMEDY/MUSICAL: **Kathleen Turner** Prizzi's Honor

SUPPORTING ACTOR: **Klaus Maria Brandauer** Out of Africa

SUPPORTING ACTRESS: **Meg Tilly** Agnes of God

SCREENPLAY: **Woody Allen** The Purple Rose of Cairo

Cannes Film Festival

PALME D'OR: **When Father Was Away on Business**

DIRECTOR: **André Téchiné** Rendez-vous

ACTOR: **William Hurt** Kiss of the Spider Woman

ACTRESS: **Norma Aleandro** The Official Version • **Cher** Mask

Berlin International Film Festival

GOLDEN BEAR: **Die Frau und der Fremde** • **Wetherby**

SILVER BEAR, DIRECTOR: **Robert Benton** Places in the Heart

SILVER BEAR, ACTOR: **Fernando Fernán Gómez** Stico

SILVER BEAR, ACTRESS: **Jo Kennedy** Wrong World

1986

British Academy of Film & Television Arts

FILM: **A Room with a View** • Hannah and Her Sisters • The Mission • Mona Lisa

FOREIGN LANGUAGE FILM: **Ran** • Betty Blue • Ginger & Fred • Otello

DIRECTOR: **Woody Allen** Hannah and Her Sisters • Roland Joffé The Mission • Neil Jordan Mona Lisa • James Ivory A Room with a View

ACTOR: **Bob Hoskins** Mona Lisa • Woody Allen, Michael Caine Hannah and Her Sisters • Paul Hogan "Crocodile" Dundee

ACTRESS: **Maggie Smith** A Room with a View • Mia Farrow Hannah and Her Sisters • Meryl Streep Out of Africa • Cathy Tyson Mona Lisa

SUPPORTING ACTOR: **Ray McAnally** The Mission • Klaus Maria Brandauer Out of Africa • Simon Callow, Denholm Elliott A Room with a View

SUPPORTING ACTRESS: **Judi Dench** A Room with a View • Rosanna Arquette After Hours • Barbara Hershey Hannah and Her Sisters • Rosemary Leach A Room with a View

ORIGINAL SCREENPLAY: **Woody Allen** Hannah and Her Sisters • Paul Hogan, Ken Shadie, John Cornell "Crocodile" Dundee • Robert Bolt The Mission • Neil Jordan, David Leland Mona Lisa

ADAPTED SCREENPLAY: **Kurt Luedtke** Out of Africa • Hesper Anderson, Mark Medoff Children of a Lesser God • Menno Meyjes The Color Purple • Akira Kurosawa, Hideo Oguni, Masato Ide Ran • Ruth Prawer Jhabvala A Room with a View

Academy Awards

PICTURE: **Platoon** • Children of a Lesser God • Hannah and Her Sisters • The Mission • A Room with a View

FOREIGN LANGUAGE FILM: **The Assault** • 38 • Betty Blue • The Decline of the American Empire • My Sweet Little Village

DIRECTOR: **Oliver Stone** Platoon • Woody Allen Hannah and Her Sisters • James Ivory A Room with a View • Roland Joffé The Mission • David Lynch Blue Velvet

ACTOR: **Paul Newman** The Color of Money • Dexter Gordon 'Round Midnight • Bob Hoskins Mona Lisa • William Hurt Children of a Lesser God • James Woods Salvador

ACTRESS: **Marlee Matlin** Children of a Lesser God • Jane Fonda The Morning After • Sissy Spacek Crimes of the Heart • Kathleen Turner Peggy Sue Got Married • Sigourney Weaver Aliens

SUPPORTING ACTOR: **Michael Caine** Hannah and Her Sisters • Tom Berenger, Willem Dafoe Platoon • Denholm Elliott A Room with a View • Dennis Hopper Hoosiers

SUPPORTING ACTRESS: **Dianne Wiest** Hannah and Her Sisters • Tess Harper Crimes of the Heart • Piper Laurie Children of a Lesser God • Mary Elizabeth Mastrantonio The Color of Money • Maggie Smith A Room with a View

ORIGINAL SCREENPLAY: **Woody Allen** Hannah and Her Sisters • John Cornell, Paul Hogan, Ken Shadie "Crocodile" Dundee •

Hanif Kureishi My Beautiful Laundrette • Oliver Stone Platoon • Richard Boyle, Oliver Stone Salvador

ADAPTED SCREENPLAY: **Ruth Prawer Jhabvala** A Room with a View • Hesper Anderson, Mark Medoff Children of a Lesser God • Richard Price The Color of Money • Beth Henley Crimes of the Heart • Bruce A Evans, Raynold Gideon Stand by Me

Golden Globe Awards

DRAMA: **Platoon**

COMEDY/MUSICAL: **Hannah and Her Sisters**

FOREIGN LANGUAGE FILM: **The Assault**

DIRECTOR: **Oliver Stone** Platoon

ACTOR, DRAMA: **Bob Hoskins** Mona Lisa

ACTRESS, DRAMA: **Marlee Matlin** Children of a Lesser God

ACTOR, COMEDY/MUSICAL: **Paul Hogan** "Crocodile" Dundee

ACTRESS, COMEDY/MUSICAL: **Sissy Spacek** Crimes of the Heart

SUPPORTING ACTOR: **Tom Berenger** Platoon

SUPPORTING ACTRESS: **Maggie Smith** A Room with a View

SCREENPLAY: **Robert Bolt** The Mission

Cannes Film Festival

PALME D'OR: **The Mission**

DIRECTOR: **Martin Scorsese** After Hours

ACTOR: **Michel Blanc** Tenue de Soirée • **Bob Hoskins** Mona Lisa

ACTRESS: **Barbara Sukowa** Rosa Luxemburg • **Fernanda Torres** Eu Sei Que You Te Amar

Berlin International Film Festival

GOLDEN BEAR: **Stammheim**

SILVER BEAR, DIRECTOR: **Georgi Schengelaja** Achalgazrda Kompozitoris Mogzauroba

SILVER BEAR, ACTOR: **Tuncel Kurtiz** Hiuh Hagdi

SILVER BEAR, ACTRESS: **Marcelia Cartaxo** Hour of the Star • **Charlotte Valandrey** Rouge Baiser

1987

British Academy of Film & Television Arts

FILM: **Jean de Florette** • Cry Freedom • Hope and Glory • Radio Days

FOREIGN LANGUAGE FILM: **The Sacrifice** • Jean de Florette • Manon des Sources • My Life as a Dog

DIRECTOR: **Oliver Stone** Platoon • Richard Attenborough Cry Freedom • Claude Berri Jean de Florette • John Boorman Hope and Glory

ACTOR: **Sean Connery** The Name of the Rose • Gérard Depardieu, Yves Montand Jean de Florette • Gary Oldman Prick Up Your Ears

ACTRESS: **Anne Bancroft** 84 Charing Cross Road • Emily Lloyd Wish You Were Here • Sarah Miles Hope and Glory • Julie Walters Personal Services

SUPPORTING ACTOR: **Daniel Auteuil** Jean de Florette • Ian Bannen Hope and Glory • Sean Connery The Untouchables • John Thaw Cry Freedom

SUPPORTING ACTRESS: **Susan Wooldridge** Hope and Glory • Judi Dench 84 Charing Cross Road • Vanessa Redgrave Prick Up Your Ears • Dianne Wiest Radio Days

ORIGINAL SCREENPLAY: **David Leland** Wish You Were Here • John Boorman Hope and Glory • David Leland Personal Services • Woody Allen Radio Days

ADAPTED SCREENPLAY: **Gérard Brach, Claude Berri** Jean de Florette • Hugh Whitemore 84 Charing Cross Road • Christine Edzard Little Dorrit • Alan Bennett Prick Up Your Ears

Academy Awards

PICTURE: **The Last Emperor** • Broadcast News • Fatal Attraction • Hope and Glory • Moonstruck

FOREIGN LANGUAGE FILM: **Babette's Feast** • Au Revoir les Enfants • Course Completed • The Family • Pathfinder

DIRECTOR: **Bernardo Bertolucci** The Last Emperor • John Boorman Hope and Glory • Lasse Hallström My Life as a Dog • Norman Jewison Moonstruck • Adrian Lyne Fatal Attraction

ACTOR: **Michael Douglas** Wall Street • William Hurt Broadcast News • Marcello Mastroianni Dark Eyes • Jack Nicholson Ironweed • Robin Williams Good Morning, Vietnam

ACTRESS: **Cher** Moonstruck • Glenn Close Fatal Attraction • Holly Hunter Broadcast News • Sally Kirkland Anna • Meryl Streep Ironweed

SUPPORTING ACTOR: **Sean Connery** The Untouchables • Albert Brooks Broadcast News • Morgan Freeman Street Smart • Vincent Gardenia Moonstruck • Denzel Washington Cry Freedom

SUPPORTING ACTRESS: **Olympia Dukakis** Moonstruck • Norma Aleandro Gaby: a True Story • Anne Archer Fatal Attraction • Anne Ramsey Throw Momma from the Train • Ann Sothern The Whales of August

ORIGINAL SCREENPLAY: **John Patrick Shanley** Moonstruck • Louis Malle Au Revoir les Enfants • James L Brooks Broadcast News • John Boorman Hope and Glory • Woody Allen Radio Days

ADAPTED SCREENPLAY: **Bernardo Bertolucci, Mark Peploe** The Last Emperor • Tony Huston The Dead • James Dearden Fatal Attraction • Gustav Hasford, Michael Herr, Stanley Kubrick Full Metal Jacket • Pelle Berglund, Brasse Brännström, Lasse Hallström, Reidar Jonsson My Life as a Dog

Golden Globe Awards

DRAMA: **The Last Emperor**

COMEDY/MUSICAL: **Hope and Glory**

FOREIGN LANGUAGE FILM: **My Life as a Dog**

DIRECTOR: **Bernardo Bertolucci** The Last Emperor

ACTOR, DRAMA: **Michael Douglas** Wall Street

ACTRESS, DRAMA: **Sally Kirkland** Anna

ACTOR, COMEDY/MUSICAL: **Robin Williams** Good Morning, Vietnam

ACTRESS, COMEDY/MUSICAL: **Cher** Moonstruck

SUPPORTING ACTOR: **Sean Connery** The Untouchables

SUPPORTING ACTRESS: **Olympia Dukakis** Moonstruck

SCREENPLAY: **Mark Peploe, Bernardo Bertolucci** The Last Emperor

Cannes Film Festival

PALME D'OR: **Sous le Soleil de Satan**

DIRECTOR: **Wim Wenders** Wings of Desire

ACTOR: **Marcello Mastroianni** Dark Eyes

ACTRESS: **Barbara Hershey** Shy People

Berlin International Film Festival

GOLDEN BEAR: **The Theme**

SILVER BEAR, DIRECTOR: **Oliver Stone** Platoon

SILVER BEAR, ACTOR: **Gian Maria Volonté** Il Caso Moro

SILVER BEAR, ACTRESS: **Ana Beatriz Nogueira** Vera

1988

British Academy of Film & Television Arts

FILM: **The Last Emperor** • Au Revoir les Enfants • Babette's Feast • A Fish Called Wanda

FOREIGN LANGUAGE FILM: **Babette's Feast** • Au Revoir les Enfants • Dark Eyes • Wings of Desire

DIRECTOR: **Louis Malle** Au Revoir les Enfants • Gabriel Axel Babette's Feast • Bernardo Bertolucci The Last Emperor • Charles Crichton A Fish Called Wanda

ACTOR: **John Cleese** A Fish Called Wanda • Michael Douglas Fatal Attraction • Kevin Kline A Fish Called Wanda • Robin Williams Good Morning, Vietnam

ACTRESS: **Maggie Smith** The Lonely Passion of Judith Hearne • Stéphane Audran Babette's Feast • Cher Moonstruck • Jamie Lee Curtis A Fish Called Wanda

SUPPORTING ACTOR: **Michael Palin** A Fish Called Wanda • Joss Ackland White Mischief • Peter O'Toole The Last Emperor • David Suchet A World Apart

SUPPORTING ACTRESS: **Olympia Dukakis** Moonstruck • Maria Aitken A Fish Called Wanda • Anne Archer Fatal Attraction • Judi Dench A Handful of Dust

ORIGINAL SCREENPLAY: **Shawn Slovo** A World Apart • Louis Malle Au Revoir les Enfants • John Cleese A Fish Called Wanda • John Patrick Shanley Moonstruck

ADAPTED SCREENPLAY: **Philip Kaufman, Jean-Claude Carrière** The Unbearable Lightness of Being • Gabriel Axel Babette's Feast • Tom Stoppard Empire of the Sun • Jeffrey Price, Peter S Seaman Who Framed Roger Rabbit

Academy Awards

PICTURE: **Rain Man** • The Accidental Tourist • Dangerous Liaisons • Mississippi Burning • Working Girl

FOREIGN LANGUAGE FILM: **Pelle the Conqueror** • Hanussen • The Music Teacher • Salaam Bombay! • Women on the Verge of a Nervous Breakdown

DIRECTOR: **Barry Levinson** Rain Man • Charles Crichton A Fish Called Wanda • Mike Nichols Working Girl • Alan Parker Mississippi Burning • Martin Scorsese The Last Temptation of Christ

ACTOR: **Dustin Hoffman** Rain Man • Gene Hackman Mississippi Burning • Tom Hanks Big • Edward James Olmos Stand and Deliver • Max von Sydow Pelle the Conqueror

ACTRESS: **Jodie Foster** The Accused • Glenn Close Dangerous Liaisons • Melanie Griffith Working Girl • Meryl Streep A Cry in the Dark • Sigourney Weaver Gorillas in the Mist

SUPPORTING ACTOR: **Kevin Kline** A Fish Called Wanda • Alec Guinness Little Dorrit • Martin Landau Tucker: the Man and His Dream • River Phoenix Running on Empty • Dean Stockwell Married to the Mob

SUPPORTING ACTRESS: **Geena Davis** The Accidental Tourist • Joan Cusack Working Girl • Frances McDormand Mississippi Burning • Michelle Pfeiffer Dangerous Liaisons • Sigourney Weaver Working Girl

ORIGINAL SCREENPLAY: **Ronald Bass, Barry Morrow** Rain Man • Gary Ross, Anne Spielberg Big • Ron Shelton Bull Durham • John Cleese, Charles Crichton A Fish Called Wanda • Naomi Foner Running on Empty

ADAPTED SCREENPLAY: **Christopher Hampton** Dangerous Liaisons • Frank Galati, Lawrence Kasdan The Accidental Tourist • Tab Murphy, Anna Hamilton Phelan Gorillas in the Mist • Christine Edzard Little Dorrit • Jean-Claude Carrière, Philip Kaufman The Unbearable Lightness of Being

Golden Globe Awards

DRAMA: **Rain Man**

COMEDY/MUSICAL: **Working Girl**

FOREIGN LANGUAGE FILM: **Pelle the Conqueror**

DIRECTOR: **Clint Eastwood** Bird

ACTOR, DRAMA: **Dustin Hoffman** Rain Man

ACTRESS, DRAMA: **Shirley MacLaine** Madame Sousatzka • **Jodie Foster** The Accused • **Sigourney Weaver** Gorillas in the Mist

ACTOR, COMEDY/MUSICAL: **Tom Hanks** Big

ACTRESS, COMEDY/MUSICAL: **Melanie Griffith** Working Girl

SUPPORTING ACTOR: **Martin Landau** Tucker: the Man and His Dream

SUPPORTING ACTRESS: **Sigourney Weaver** Working Girl

SCREENPLAY: **Naomi Foner** Running on Empty

Cannes Film Festival

PALME D'OR: **Pelle the Conqueror**

DIRECTOR: **Fernando E Solanas** Sur

ACTOR: **Forest Whitaker** Bird

ACTRESS: **Barbara Hershey, Jodhi May, Linda Mvusi** A World Apart

Berlin International Film Festival

GOLDEN BEAR: **Red Sorghum**
SILVER BEAR, DIRECTOR: **Norman Jewison** Moonstruck
SILVER BEAR, ACTOR: **Manfred Möck, Jörg Pose** Einer Trage des Anderen Last
SILVER BEAR, ACTRESS: **Holly Hunter** Broadcast News

1989

British Academy of Film & Television Arts

FILM: **Dead Poets Society** • My Left Foot • Shirley Valentine • When Harry Met Sally...
FOREIGN LANGUAGE FILM: **Life and Nothing But** • Pelle the Conqueror • Salaam Bombay! • Women on the Verge of a Nervous Breakdown
DIRECTOR: **Kenneth Branagh** Henry V • Stephen Frears Dangerous Liaisons • Alan Parker Mississippi Burning • Peter Weir Dead Poets Society
ACTOR: **Daniel Day-Lewis** My Left Foot • Kenneth Branagh Henry V • Dustin Hoffman Rain Man • Robin Williams Dead Poets Society
ACTRESS: **Pauline Collins** Shirley Valentine • Glenn Close Dangerous Liaisons • Jodie Foster The Accused • Melanie Griffith Working Girl
SUPPORTING ACTOR: **Ray McAnally** My Left Foot • Marlon Brando A Dry White Season • Sean Connery Indiana Jones and the Last Crusade • Jack Nicholson Batman
SUPPORTING ACTRESS: **Michelle Pfeiffer** Dangerous Liaisons • Peggy Ashcroft Madame Sousatzka • Laura San Giacomo sex, lies, and videotape • Sigourney Weaver Working Girl
ORIGINAL SCREENPLAY: **Nora Ephron** When Harry Met Sally... • Tom Schulman Dead Poets Society • Ronald Bass, Barry Morrow Rain Man • Steven Soderbergh sex, lies, and videotape
ADAPTED SCREENPLAY: **Christopher Hampton** Dangerous Liaisons • Frank Galati, Lawrence Kasdan The Accidental Tourist • Shane Connaughton, Jim Sheridan My Left Foot • Willy Russell Shirley Valentine

Academy Awards

PICTURE: **Driving Miss Daisy** • Born on the Fourth of July • Dead Poets Society • Field of Dreams • My Left Foot
FOREIGN LANGUAGE FILM: **Cinema Paradiso** • Camille Claudel • Jesus of Montreal • Waltzing Regitze • What Happened to Santiago
DIRECTOR: **Oliver Stone** Born on the Fourth of July • Woody Allen Crimes and Misdemeanors • Kenneth Branagh Henry V • Jim Sheridan My Left Foot • Peter Weir Dead Poets Society
ACTOR: **Daniel Day-Lewis** My Left Foot • Kenneth Branagh Henry V • Tom Cruise Born on the Fourth of July • Morgan Freeman Driving Miss Daisy • Robin Williams Dead Poets Society
ACTRESS: **Jessica Tandy** Driving Miss Daisy • Isabelle Adjani Camille Claudel • Pauline Collins Shirley Valentine • Jessica Lange Music Box • Michelle Pfeiffer The Fabulous Baker Boys
SUPPORTING ACTOR: **Denzel Washington** Glory • Danny Aiello Do the Right Thing • Dan Aykroyd Driving Miss Daisy • Marlon Brando A Dry White Season • Martin Landau Crimes and Misdemeanors
SUPPORTING ACTRESS: **Brenda Fricker** My Left Foot • Anjelica Huston, Lena Olin Enemies, a Love Story • Julia Roberts Steel Magnolias • Dianne Wiest Parenthood
ORIGINAL SCREENPLAY: **Tom Schulman** Dead Poets Society • Woody Allen Crimes and Misdemeanors • Spike Lee Do the Right Thing • Nora Ephron When Harry Met Sally... • Steven Soderbergh sex, lies, and videotape
ADAPTED SCREENPLAY: **Alfred Uhry** Driving Miss Daisy • Ron Kovic, Oliver Stone Born on the Fourth of July • Paul Mazursky, Roger L Simon Enemies, a Love Story • Phil Alden Robinson Field of Dreams • Shane Connaughton, Jim Sheridan My Left Foot

Golden Globe Awards

DRAMA: **Born on the Fourth of July**
COMEDY/MUSICAL: **Driving Miss Daisy**
FOREIGN LANGUAGE FILM: **Cinema Paradiso**
DIRECTOR: **Oliver Stone** Born on the Fourth of July
ACTOR, DRAMA: **Tom Cruise** Born on the Fourth of July
ACTRESS, DRAMA: **Michelle Pfeiffer** The Fabulous Baker Boys
ACTOR, COMEDY/MUSICAL: **Morgan Freeman** Driving Miss Daisy
ACTRESS, COMEDY/MUSICAL: **Jessica Tandy** Driving Miss Daisy
SUPPORTING ACTOR: **Denzel Washington** Glory
SUPPORTING ACTRESS: **Julia Roberts** Steel Magnolias
SCREENPLAY: **Oliver Stone, Ron Kovic** Born on the Fourth of July

Cannes Film Festival

PALME D'OR: **sex, lies, and videotape**
DIRECTOR: **Emir Kusturica** Time of the Gypsies
ACTOR: **James Spader** sex, lies, and videotape
ACTRESS: **Meryl Streep** A Cry in the Dark

Berlin International Film Festival

GOLDEN BEAR: **Rain Man**
SILVER BEAR, DIRECTOR: **Dusan Hanak** Ja Milujem, Ty Milujes
SILVER BEAR, ACTOR: **Gene Hackman** Mississippi Burning
SILVER BEAR, ACTRESS: **Isabelle Adjani** Camille Claudel • **Kaipo Cohen, Gila Almagor** The Summer of Aviya

1990

British Academy of Film & Television Arts

FILM: **GoodFellas** • Crimes and Misdemeanors • Driving Miss Daisy • Pretty Woman
FOREIGN LANGUAGE FILM: **Cinema Paradiso** • Jesus of Montreal • Milou en Mai • Romuald et Juliette

DIRECTOR: **Martin Scorsese** GoodFellas • Woody Allen Crimes and Misdemeanors • Bruce Beresford Driving Miss Daisy • Giuseppe Tornatore Cinema Paradiso
ACTOR: **Philippe Noiret** Cinema Paradiso • Sean Connery The Hunt for Red October • Tom Cruise Born on the Fourth of July • Robert De Niro GoodFellas
ACTRESS: **Jessica Tandy** Driving Miss Daisy • Shirley MacLaine Postcards from the Edge • Michelle Pfeiffer The Fabulous Baker Boys • Julia Roberts Pretty Woman
SUPPORTING ACTOR: **Salvatore Cascio** Cinema Paradiso • Alan Alda Crimes and Misdemeanors • John Hurt The Field • Al Pacino Dick Tracy
SUPPORTING ACTRESS: **Whoopi Goldberg** Ghost • Anjelica Huston Crimes and Misdemeanors • Shirley MacLaine Steel Magnolias • Billie Whitelaw The Krays
ORIGINAL SCREENPLAY: **Giuseppe Tornatore** Cinema Paradiso • Woody Allen Crimes and Misdemeanors • Bruce Joel Rubin Ghost • J F Lawton Pretty Woman
ADAPTED SCREENPLAY: **Nicholas Pileggi, Martin Scorsese** GoodFellas • Oliver Stone, Ron Kovic Born on the Fourth of July • Alfred Uhry Driving Miss Daisy • Carrie Fisher Postcards from the Edge • Michael Leeson The War of the Roses

Academy Awards

PICTURE: **Dances with Wolves** • Awakenings • Ghost • The Godfather Part III • GoodFellas
FOREIGN LANGUAGE FILM: **Journey of Hope** • Cyrano de Bergerac • Ju Dou • The Nasty Girl • Open Doors
DIRECTOR: **Kevin Costner** Dances with Wolves • Francis Ford Coppola The Godfather Part III • Stephen Frears The Grifters • Barbet Schroeder Reversal of Fortune • Martin Scorsese GoodFellas
ACTOR: **Jeremy Irons** Reversal of Fortune • Kevin Costner Dances with Wolves • Robert De Niro Awakenings • Gérard Depardieu Cyrano de Bergerac • Richard Harris The Field
ACTRESS: **Kathy Bates** Misery • Anjelica Huston The Grifters • Julia Roberts Pretty Woman • Meryl Streep Postcards from the Edge • Joanne Woodward Mr and Mrs Bridge
SUPPORTING ACTOR: **Joe Pesci** GoodFellas • Bruce Davison Longtime Companion • Andy Garcia The Godfather Part III • Graham Greene Dances with Wolves • Al Pacino Dick Tracy
SUPPORTING ACTRESS: **Whoopi Goldberg** Ghost • Annette Bening The Grifters • Lorraine Bracco GoodFellas • Diane Ladd Wild at Heart • Mary McDonnell Dances with Wolves
ORIGINAL SCREENPLAY: **Bruce Joel Rubin** Ghost • Woody Allen Alice • Barry Levinson Avalon • Peter Weir Green Card • Whit Stillman Metropolitan
ADAPTED SCREENPLAY: **Michael Blake** Dances with Wolves • Steven Zaillian Awakenings • Nicholas Pileggi, Martin Scorsese GoodFellas • Donald E Westlake The Grifters • Nicholas Kazan Reversal of Fortune

Golden Globe Awards

DRAMA: **Dances with Wolves**
COMEDY/MUSICAL: **Green Card**
FOREIGN LANGUAGE FILM: **Cyrano de Bergerac**
DIRECTOR: **Kevin Costner** Dances with Wolves
ACTOR, DRAMA: **Jeremy Irons** Reversal of Fortune
ACTRESS, DRAMA: **Kathy Bates** Misery
ACTOR, COMEDY/MUSICAL: **Gérard Depardieu** Green Card
ACTRESS, COMEDY/MUSICAL: **Julia Roberts** Pretty Woman
SUPPORTING ACTOR: **Bruce Davison** Longtime Companion
SUPPORTING ACTRESS: **Whoopi Goldberg** Ghost
SCREENPLAY: **Michael Blake** Dances with Wolves

Cannes Film Festival

PALME D'OR: **Wild at Heart**
DIRECTOR: **Pavel Lounguine** Taxi Blues
ACTOR: **Gérard Depardieu** Cyrano de Bergerac
ACTRESS: **Krystyna Janda** Interrogation

Berlin International Film Festival

GOLDEN BEAR: **Music Box** • **Larks on a String**
SILVER BEAR, DIRECTOR: **Michael Verhoeven** The Nasty Girl
SILVER BEAR, ACTOR: **Iain Glen** Silent Scream
SILVER BEAR, JOINT PERFORMANCE: **Jessica Tandy, Morgan Freeman** Driving Miss Daisy

1991

British Academy of Film & Television Arts

FILM: **The Commitments** • Dances with Wolves • The Silence of the Lambs • Thelma & Louise
FOREIGN LANGUAGE FILM: **The Nasty Girl** • Cyrano de Bergerac • The Hairdresser's Husband • Toto Le Héros
DAVID LEAN AWARD, DIRECTOR: **Alan Parker** The Commitments • Kevin Costner Dances with Wolves • Jonathan Demme The Silence of the Lambs • Ridley Scott Thelma & Louise
ACTOR: **Anthony Hopkins** The Silence of the Lambs • Kevin Costner Dances with Wolves • Gérard Depardieu Cyrano de Bergerac • Alan Rickman Truly Madly Deeply
ACTRESS: **Jodie Foster** The Silence of the Lambs • Geena Davis, Susan Sarandon Thelma & Louise • Juliet Stevenson Truly Madly Deeply
SUPPORTING ACTOR: **Alan Rickman** Robin Hood: Prince of Thieves • Alan Bates Hamlet • Derek Jacobi Dead Again • Andrew Strong The Commitments
SUPPORTING ACTRESS: **Kate Nelligan** Frankie & Johnny • Annette Bening The Grifters • Amanda Plummer The Fisher King • Julie Walters Stepping Out
ORIGINAL SCREENPLAY: **Anthony Minghella** Truly Madly Deeply • Richard LaGravenese The Fisher King • Peter Weir Green Card • Callie Khouri Thelma & Louise
ADAPTED SCREENPLAY: **Dick Clement, Ian La Frenais, Roddy Doyle** The Commitments • Jean-Paul Rappeneau, Jean-Claude Carrière Cyrano de Bergerac • Michael Blake Dances with Wolves • Ted Tally The Silence of the Lambs

Academy Awards

PICTURE: **The Silence of the Lambs** • Beauty and the Beast • Bugsy • JFK • The Prince of Tides
FOREIGN LANGUAGE FILM: **Mediterraneo** • Children of Nature • Elementary School • The Ox • Raise the Red Lantern
DIRECTOR: **Jonathan Demme** The Silence of the Lambs • Barry Levinson Bugsy • Ridley Scott Thelma & Louise • John Singleton Boyz N the Hood • Oliver Stone JFK
ACTOR: **Anthony Hopkins** The Silence of the Lambs • Warren Beatty Bugsy • Robert De Niro Cape Fear • Nick Nolte The Prince of Tides • Robin Williams The Fisher King
ACTRESS: **Jodie Foster** The Silence of the Lambs • Geena Davis Thelma & Louise • Laura Dern Rambling Rose • Bette Midler For the Boys • Susan Sarandon Thelma & Louise
SUPPORTING ACTOR: **Jack Palance** City Slickers • Tommy Lee Jones JFK • Harvey Keitel, Ben Kingsley Bugsy • Michael Lerner Barton Fink
SUPPORTING ACTRESS: **Mercedes Ruehl** The Fisher King • Diane Ladd Rambling Rose • Juliette Lewis Cape Fear • Kate Nelligan The Prince of Tides • Jessica Tandy Fried Green Tomatoes at the Whistle Stop Cafe
ORIGINAL SCREENPLAY: **Callie Khouri** Thelma & Louise • John Singleton Boyz N the Hood • James Toback Bugsy • Richard LaGravenese The Fisher King • Lawrence Kasdan, Meg Kasdan Grand Canyon
ADAPTED SCREENPLAY: **Ted Tally** The Silence of the Lambs • Agnieszka Holland Europa, Europa • Fannie Flagg, Carol Sobieski Fried Green Tomatoes at the Whistle Stop Cafe • Zachary Sklar, Oliver Stone JFK • Pat Conroy, Becky Johnston The Prince of Tides

Golden Globe Awards

DRAMA: **Bugsy**
COMEDY/MUSICAL: **Beauty and the Beast**
FOREIGN LANGUAGE FILM: **Europa, Europa**
DIRECTOR: **Oliver Stone** JFK
ACTOR, DRAMA: **Nick Nolte** The Prince of Tides
ACTRESS, DRAMA: **Jodie Foster** The Silence of the Lambs
ACTOR, COMEDY/MUSICAL: **Robin Williams** The Fisher King
ACTRESS, COMEDY/MUSICAL: **Bette Midler** For the Boys
SUPPORTING ACTOR: **Jack Palance** City Slickers
SUPPORTING ACTRESS: **Mercedes Ruehl** The Fisher King
SCREENPLAY: **Callie Khouri** Thelma & Louise

Cannes Film Festival

PALME D'OR: **Barton Fink**
DIRECTOR: **Joel Coen** Barton Fink
ACTOR: **John Turturro** Barton Fink
ACTRESS: **Irène Jacob** The Double Life of Véronique
SUPPORTING ACTOR: **Samuel L Jackson** Jungle Fever

Berlin International Film Festival

GOLDEN BEAR: **La Casa del Sorriso**
SILVER BEAR, DIRECTOR: **Jonathan Demme** The Silence of the Lambs • **Ricky Tognazzi** Ultrà
SILVER BEAR, ACTOR: **Maynard Eziashi** Mister Johnson
SILVER BEAR, ACTRESS: **Victoria Abril** Lovers

1992

British Academy of Film & Television Arts

FILM: **Howards End** • The Crying Game • The Player • Strictly Ballroom • Unforgiven
FOREIGN LANGUAGE FILM: **Raise the Red Lantern** • Les Amants du Pont-Neuf • Delicatessen • Europa, Europa
DAVID LEAN AWARD, DIRECTOR: **Robert Altman** The Player • Clint Eastwood Unforgiven • James Ivory Howards End • Neil Jordan The Crying Game
ACTOR: **Robert Downey Jr** Chaplin • Daniel Day-Lewis The Last of the Mohicans • Stephen Rea The Crying Game • Tim Robbins The Player
ACTRESS: **Emma Thompson** Howards End • Judy Davis Husbands and Wives • Tara Morice Strictly Ballroom • Jessica Tandy Fried Green Tomatoes at the Whistle Stop Cafe
SUPPORTING ACTOR: **Gene Hackman** Unforgiven • Jaye Davidson The Crying Game • Tommy Lee Jones JFK • Samuel West Howards End
SUPPORTING ACTRESS: **Miranda Richardson** Damage • Kathy Bates Fried Green Tomatoes at the Whistle Stop Cafe • Helena Bonham Carter Howards End • Miranda Richardson The Crying Game
ORIGINAL SCREENPLAY: **Woody Allen** Husbands and Wives • Neil Jordan The Crying Game • Peter Chelsom, Adrian Dunbar Hear My Song • David Webb Peoples Unforgiven
ADAPTED SCREENPLAY: **Michael Tolkin** The Player • Ruth Prawer Jhabvala Howards End • Oliver Stone, Zachary Sklar JFK • Baz Luhrmann, Craig Pearce Strictly Ballroom

Academy Awards

PICTURE: **Unforgiven** • The Crying Game • A Few Good Men • Howards End • Scent of a Woman
FOREIGN LANGUAGE FILM: **Indochine** • Urga • Daens • A Place in the World • Schtonk!
DIRECTOR: **Clint Eastwood** Unforgiven • Robert Altman The Player • Martin Brest Scent of a Woman • James Ivory Howards End • Neil Jordan The Crying Game
ACTOR: **Al Pacino** Scent of a Woman • Robert Downey Jr Chaplin • Clint Eastwood Unforgiven • Stephen Rea The Crying Game • Denzel Washington Malcolm X
ACTRESS: **Emma Thompson** Howards End • Catherine Deneuve Indochine • Mary McDonnell Passion Fish • Michelle Pfeiffer Love Field • Susan Sarandon Lorenzo's Oil
SUPPORTING ACTOR: **Gene Hackman** Unforgiven • Jaye Davidson The Crying Game • Jack Nicholson A Few Good Men • Al Pacino Glengarry Glen Ross • David Paymer Mr Saturday Night
SUPPORTING ACTRESS: **Marisa Tomei** My Cousin Vinny • Judy Davis Husbands and Wives • Joan Plowright Enchanted April

• Vanessa Redgrave *Howards End* • Miranda Richardson *Damage*
ORIGINAL SCREENPLAY: **Neil Jordan** *The Crying Game* • Woody Allen *Husbands and Wives* • Nick Enright, George Miller *Lorenzo's Oil* • John Sayles *Passion Fish* • David Webb Peoples *Unforgiven*
ADAPTED SCREENPLAY: **Ruth Prawer Jhabvala** *Howards End* • Peter Barnes *Enchanted April* • Michael Tolkin *The Player* • Richard Friedenberg *A River Runs through It* • Bo Goldman *Scent of a Woman*

Golden Globe Awards

DRAMA: *Scent of a Woman*
COMEDY/MUSICAL: *The Player*
FOREIGN LANGUAGE FILM: *Indochine*
DIRECTOR: **Clint Eastwood** *Unforgiven*
ACTOR, DRAMA: **Al Pacino** *Scent of a Woman*
ACTRESS, DRAMA: **Emma Thompson** *Howards End*
ACTOR, COMEDY/MUSICAL: **Tim Robbins** *The Player*
ACTRESS, COMEDY/MUSICAL: **Miranda Richardson** *Enchanted April*
SUPPORTING ACTOR: **Gene Hackman** *Unforgiven*
SUPPORTING ACTRESS: **Joan Plowright** *Enchanted April*
SCREENPLAY: **Bo Goldman** *Scent of a Woman*

Cannes Film Festival

PALME D'OR: *Best Intentions*
DIRECTOR: **Robert Altman** *The Player*
ACTOR: **Tim Robbins** *The Player*
ACTRESS: **Pernilla August** *Best Intentions*

Berlin International Film Festival

GOLDEN BEAR: *Grand Canyon*
SILVER BEAR, DIRECTOR: **Jan Troell** *Il Capitano*
SILVER BEAR, ACTOR: **Armin Mueller-Stahl** *Utz*
SILVER BEAR, ACTRESS: **Maggie Cheung** *The Actress*

1993

British Academy of Film & Television Arts

FILM: *Schindler's List* • *The Piano* • *The Remains of the Day* • *Shadowlands*
FOREIGN LANGUAGE FILM: *Farewell My Concubine* • *Un Coeur en Hiver* • *Like Water for Chocolate* • *Indochine*
ALEXANDER KORDA AWARD, BRITISH FILM: *Shadowlands* • *Naked* • *Raining Stones* • *Tom & Viv*
DAVID LEAN AWARD, DIRECTOR: **Steven Spielberg** *Schindler's List* • Richard Attenborough *Shadowlands* • Jane Campion *The Piano* • James Ivory *The Remains of the Day*
ACTOR: **Anthony Hopkins** *The Remains of the Day* • Daniel Day-Lewis *In the Name of the Father* • Anthony Hopkins *Shadowlands* • Liam Neeson *Schindler's List*
ACTRESS: **Holly Hunter** *The Piano* • Miranda Richardson *Tom & Viv* • Emma Thompson *The Remains of the Day* • Debra Winger *Shadowlands*
SUPPORTING ACTOR: **Ralph Fiennes** *Schindler's List* • Tommy Lee Jones *The Fugitive* • Ben Kingsley *Schindler's List* • John Malkovich *In the Line of Fire*
SUPPORTING ACTRESS: **Miriam Margolyes** *The Age of Innocence* • Holly Hunter *The Firm* • Winona Ryder *The Age of Innocence* • Maggie Smith *The Secret Garden*
ORIGINAL SCREENPLAY: **Danny Rubin, Harold Ramis** *Groundhog Day* • Jeff Maguire *In the Line of Fire* • Jane Campion *The Piano* • Nora Ephron, David S Ward *Sleepless in Seattle*
ADAPTED SCREENPLAY: **Steven Zaillian** *Schindler's List* • Terry George, Jim Sheridan *In the Name of the Father* • Ruth Prawer Jhabvala *The Remains of the Day* • Bo Goldman *Scent of a Woman* • William Nicholson *Shadowlands*

Academy Awards

PICTURE: **Schindler's List** • *The Fugitive* • *In the Name of the Father* • *The Piano* • *The Remains of the Day*
FOREIGN LANGUAGE FILM: *Belle Epoque* • *Farewell My Concubine* • *Hedd Wyn* • *The Scent of Green Papaya* • *The Wedding Banquet*
DIRECTOR: **Steven Spielberg** *Schindler's List* • Robert Altman *Short Cuts* • Jane Campion *The Piano* • James Ivory *The Remains of the Day* • Jim Sheridan *In the Name of the Father*
ACTOR: **Tom Hanks** *Philadelphia* • Daniel Day-Lewis *In the Name of the Father* • Laurence Fishburne *Tina: What's Love Got to Do with It* • Anthony Hopkins *The Remains of the Day* • Liam Neeson *Schindler's List*
ACTRESS: **Holly Hunter** *The Piano* • Angela Bassett *Tina: What's Love Got to Do with It* • Stockard Channing *Six Degrees of Separation* • Emma Thompson *The Remains of the Day* • Debra Winger *Shadowlands*
SUPPORTING ACTOR: **Tommy Lee Jones** *The Fugitive* • Leonardo DiCaprio *What's Eating Gilbert Grape* • Ralph Fiennes *Schindler's List* • John Malkovich *In the Line of Fire* • Pete Postlethwaite *In the Name of the Father*
SUPPORTING ACTRESS: **Anna Paquin** *The Piano* • Holly Hunter *The Firm* • Rosie Perez *Fearless* • Winona Ryder *The Age of Innocence* • Emma Thompson *In the Name of the Father*
ORIGINAL SCREENPLAY: **Jane Campion** *The Piano* • Gary Ross *Dave* • Jeff Maguire *In the Line of Fire* • Ron Nyswaner *Philadelphia* • Jeff Arch, Nora Ephron, David S Ward *Sleepless in Seattle*
ADAPTED SCREENPLAY: **Steven Zaillian** *Schindler's List* • Jay Cocks, Martin Scorsese *The Age of Innocence* • Terry George, Jim Sheridan *In the Name of the Father* • Ruth Prawer Jhabvala *The Remains of the Day* • William Nicholson *Shadowlands*

Golden Globe Awards

DRAMA: *Schindler's List*
COMEDY/MUSICAL: *Mrs Doubtfire*
FOREIGN LANGUAGE FILM: *Farewell My Concubine*

DIRECTOR: **Steven Spielberg** *Schindler's List*
ACTOR, DRAMA: **Tom Hanks** *Philadelphia*
ACTRESS, DRAMA: **Holly Hunter** *The Piano*
ACTOR, COMEDY/MUSICAL: **Robin Williams** *Mrs Doubtfire*
ACTRESS, COMEDY/MUSICAL: **Angela Bassett** *Tina: What's Love Got to Do with It*
SUPPORTING ACTOR: **Tommy Lee Jones** *The Fugitive*
SUPPORTING ACTRESS: **Winona Ryder** *The Age of Innocence*
SCREENPLAY: **Steven Zaillian** *Schindler's List*

Cannes Film Festival

PALME D'OR: *The Piano* • *Farewell My Concubine*
DIRECTOR: **Mike Leigh** *Naked*
ACTOR: **David Thewlis** *Naked*
ACTRESS: **Holly Hunter** *The Piano*

Berlin International Film Festival

GOLDEN BEAR: *The Women from the Lake of Scented Souls* • *The Wedding Banquet*
SILVER BEAR, DIRECTOR: **Andrew Birkin** *The Cement Garden*
SILVER BEAR, ACTOR: **Denzel Washington** *Malcolm X*
SILVER BEAR, ACTRESS: **Michelle Pfeiffer** *Love Field*

1994

British Academy of Film & Television Arts

FILM: *Four Weddings and a Funeral* • *Forrest Gump* • *Pulp Fiction* • *Quiz Show*
FOREIGN LANGUAGE FILM: *To Live* • *Belle Epoque* • *Eat Drink Man Woman* • *Three Colours Red*
ALEXANDER KORDA AWARD, BRITISH FILM: *Shallow Grave* • *Backbeat* • *Bhaji on the Beach* • *Priest*
DAVID LEAN AWARD, DIRECTOR: **Mike Newell** *Four Weddings and a Funeral* • Krzysztof Kieslowski *Three Colours Red* • Quentin Tarantino *Pulp Fiction* • Robert Zemeckis *Forrest Gump*
ACTOR: **Hugh Grant** *Four Weddings and a Funeral* • Tom Hanks *Forrest Gump* • Terence Stamp *The Adventures of Priscilla, Queen of the Desert* • John Travolta *Pulp Fiction*
ACTRESS: **Susan Sarandon** *The Client* • Linda Fiorentino *The Last Seduction* • Irène Jacob *Three Colours Red* • Uma Thurman *Pulp Fiction*
SUPPORTING ACTOR: **Samuel L Jackson** *Pulp Fiction* • Simon Callow, John Hannah *Four Weddings and a Funeral* • Paul Scofield *Quiz Show*
SUPPORTING ACTRESS: **Kristin Scott Thomas** *Four Weddings and a Funeral* • Charlotte Coleman *Four Weddings and a Funeral* • Sally Field *Forrest Gump* • Anjelica Huston *Manhattan Murder Mystery*
ORIGINAL SCREENPLAY: **Quentin Tarantino, Roger Avary** *Pulp Fiction* • Stephan Elliott *The Adventures of Priscilla, Queen of the Desert* • Richard Curtis *Four Weddings and a Funeral* • Ron Nyswaner *Philadelphia* • Krzysztof Kieslowski, Krzysztof Piesiewicz *Three Colours Red*
ADAPTED SCREENPLAY: **Paul Attanasio** *Quiz Show* • Ronald Harwood *The Browning Version* • Eric Roth *Forrest Gump* • Amy Tan, Ronald Bass *The Joy Luck Club*

Academy Awards

PICTURE: **Forrest Gump** • *Four Weddings and a Funeral* • *Pulp Fiction* • *Quiz Show* • *The Shawshank Redemption*
FOREIGN LANGUAGE FILM: **Burnt by the Sun** • *Before the Rain* • *Eat Drink Man Woman* • *Farinelli il Castrato* • *Strawberry and Chocolate*
DIRECTOR: **Robert Zemeckis** *Forrest Gump* • Woody Allen *Bullets over Broadway* • Krzysztof Kieslowski *Three Colours Red* • Robert Redford *Quiz Show* • Quentin Tarantino *Pulp Fiction*
ACTOR: **Tom Hanks** *Forrest Gump* • Morgan Freeman *The Shawshank Redemption* • Nigel Hawthorne *The Madness of King George* • Paul Newman *Nobody's Fool* • John Travolta *Pulp Fiction*
ACTRESS: **Jessica Lange** *Blue Sky* • Jodie Foster *Nell* • Miranda Richardson *Tom & Viv* • Winona Ryder *Little Women* • Susan Sarandon *The Client*
SUPPORTING ACTOR: **Martin Landau** *Ed Wood* • Samuel L Jackson *Pulp Fiction* • Chazz Palminteri *Bullets over Broadway* • Paul Scofield *Quiz Show* • Gary Sinise *Forrest Gump*
SUPPORTING ACTRESS: **Dianne Wiest** *Bullets over Broadway* • Rosemary Harris *Tom & Viv* • Helen Mirren *The Madness of King George* • Uma Thurman *Pulp Fiction* • Jennifer Tilly *Bullets over Broadway*
ORIGINAL SCREENPLAY: **Quentin Tarantino, Roger Avary** *Pulp Fiction* • Woody Allen, Douglas McGrath *Bullets over Broadway* • Richard Curtis *Four Weddings and a Funeral* • Peter Jackson, Frances Walsh *Heavenly Creatures* • Krzysztof Kieslowski, Krzysztof Piesiewicz *Three Colours Red*
ADAPTED SCREENPLAY: **Eric Roth** *Forrest Gump* • Alan Bennett *The Madness of King George* • Robert Benton *Nobody's Fool* • Paul Attanasio *Quiz Show* • Frank Darabont *The Shawshank Redemption*

Golden Globe Awards

DRAMA: *Forrest Gump*
COMEDY/MUSICAL: *The Lion King*
FOREIGN LANGUAGE FILM: *Farinelli il Castrato*
DIRECTOR: **Robert Zemeckis** *Forrest Gump*
ACTOR, DRAMA: **Tom Hanks** *Forrest Gump*
ACTRESS, DRAMA: **Jessica Lange** *Blue Sky*
ACTOR, COMEDY/MUSICAL: **Hugh Grant** *Four Weddings and a Funeral*
ACTRESS, COMEDY/MUSICAL: **Jamie Lee Curtis** *True Lies*
SUPPORTING ACTOR: **Martin Landau** *Ed Wood*
SUPPORTING ACTRESS: **Dianne Wiest** *Bullets over Broadway*
SCREENPLAY: **Quentin Tarantino** *Pulp Fiction*

Cannes Film Festival

PALME D'OR: *Pulp Fiction*
DIRECTOR: **Nanni Moretti** *Dear Diary*
ACTOR: **Ge You** *To Live*
ACTRESS: **Virna Lisi** *La Reine Margot*
SCREENPLAY: **Michel Blanc** *Grosse Fatigue*

Berlin International Film Festival

GOLDEN BEAR: *In the Name of the Father*
SILVER BEAR, DIRECTOR: **Krzysztof Kieslowski** *Three Colours Blue*
SILVER BEAR, ACTOR: **Tom Hanks** *Philadelphia*
SILVER BEAR, ACTRESS: **Crissy Rock** *Ladybird Ladybird*

1995

British Academy of Film & Television Arts

FILM: *Sense and Sensibility* • *Babe* • *The Madness of King George* • *The Usual Suspects*
FOREIGN LANGUAGE FILM: *Il Postino* • *Les Misérables* • *La Reine Margot* • *Burnt by the Sun*
ALEXANDER KORDA AWARD, BRITISH FILM: *The Madness of King George* • *Carrington* • *Land and Freedom* • *Trainspotting*
DAVID LEAN AWARD, DIRECTOR: **Michael Radford** *Il Postino* • Mel Gibson *Braveheart* • Nicholas Hytner *The Madness of King George* • Ang Lee *Sense and Sensibility*
ACTOR: **Nigel Hawthorne** *The Madness of King George* • Nicolas Cage *Leaving Las Vegas* • Jonathan Pryce *Carrington* • Massimo Troisi *Il Postino*
ACTRESS: **Emma Thompson** *Sense and Sensibility* • Nicole Kidman *To Die For* • Helen Mirren *The Madness of King George* • Elisabeth Shue *Leaving Las Vegas*
SUPPORTING ACTOR: **Tim Roth** *Rob Roy* • Ian Holm *The Madness of King George* • Martin Landau *Ed Wood* • Alan Rickman *Sense and Sensibility*
SUPPORTING ACTRESS: **Kate Winslet** *Sense and Sensibility* • Joan Allen *Nixon* • Mira Sorvino *Mighty Aphrodite* • Elizabeth Spriggs *Sense and Sensibility*
ORIGINAL SCREENPLAY: **Christopher McQuarrie** *The Usual Suspects* • Woody Allen, Douglas McGrath *Bullets over Broadway* • P J Hogan *Muriel's Wedding* • Andrew Kevin Walker *Se7en*
ADAPTED SCREENPLAY: **John Hodge** *Trainspotting* • George Miller, Chris Noonan *Babe* • Mike Figgis *Leaving Las Vegas* • Alan Bennett *The Madness of King George* • Anna Pavignano, Michael Radford, Furio Scarpelli, Giacomo Scarpelli, Massimo Troisi *Il Postino* • Emma Thompson *Sense and Sensibility*

Academy Awards

PICTURE: **Braveheart** • *Apollo 13* • *Babe* • *Il Postino* • *Sense and Sensibility*
FOREIGN LANGUAGE FILM: **Antonia's Line** • *All Things Fair* • *Dust of Life* • *O Quatrilho* • *The Starmaker*
DIRECTOR: **Mel Gibson** *Braveheart* • Mike Figgis *Leaving Las Vegas* • Chris Noonan *Babe* • Michael Radford *Il Postino* • Tim Robbins *Dead Man Walking*
ACTOR: **Nicolas Cage** *Leaving Las Vegas* • Richard Dreyfuss *Mr Holland's Opus* • Anthony Hopkins *Nixon* • Sean Penn *Dead Man Walking* • Massimo Troisi *Il Postino*
ACTRESS: **Susan Sarandon** *Dead Man Walking* • Elisabeth Shue *Leaving Las Vegas* • Sharon Stone *Casino* • Meryl Streep *The Bridges of Madison County* • Emma Thompson *Sense and Sensibility*
SUPPORTING ACTOR: **Kevin Spacey** *The Usual Suspects* • James Cromwell *Babe* • Ed Harris *Apollo 13* • Brad Pitt *Twelve Monkeys* • Tim Roth *Rob Roy*
SUPPORTING ACTRESS: **Mira Sorvino** *Mighty Aphrodite* • Joan Allen *Nixon* • Kathleen Quinlan *Apollo 13* • Mare Winningham *Georgia* • Kate Winslet *Sense and Sensibility*
ORIGINAL SCREENPLAY: **Christopher McQuarrie** *The Usual Suspects* • Randall Wallace *Braveheart* • Woody Allen *Mighty Aphrodite* • Stephen J Rivele, Oliver Stone, Christopher Wilkinson *Nixon* • Joel Cohen, Pete Docter, John Lasseter, Joe Ranft, Alec Sokolow, Andrew Stanton, Joss Whedon *Toy Story*
ADAPTED SCREENPLAY: **Emma Thompson** *Sense and Sensibility* • William Broyles Jr, Al Reinert *Apollo 13* • George Miller, Chris Noonan *Babe* • Mike Figgis *Leaving Las Vegas* • Anna Pavignano, Michael Radford, Furio Scarpelli, Giacomo Scarpelli, Massimo Troisi *Il Postino*

Golden Globe Awards

DRAMA: *Sense and Sensibility*
COMEDY/MUSICAL: *Babe*
FOREIGN LANGUAGE FILM: *Les Misérables*
DIRECTOR: **Mel Gibson** *Braveheart*
ACTOR, DRAMA: **Nicolas Cage** *Leaving Las Vegas*
ACTRESS, DRAMA: **Sharon Stone** *Casino*
ACTOR, COMEDY/MUSICAL: **John Travolta** *Get Shorty*
ACTRESS, COMEDY/MUSICAL: **Nicole Kidman** *To Die For*
SUPPORTING ACTOR: **Brad Pitt** *Twelve Monkeys*
SUPPORTING ACTRESS: **Mira Sorvino** *Mighty Aphrodite*
SCREENPLAY: **Emma Thompson** *Sense and Sensibility*

Cannes Film Festival

PALME D'OR: *Underground*
DIRECTOR: **Mathieu Kassovitz** *La Haine*
ACTOR: **Jonathan Pryce** *Carrington*
ACTRESS: **Helen Mirren** *The Madness of King George*

Berlin International Film Festival

GOLDEN BEAR: *The Bait*
SILVER BEAR, DIRECTOR: **Richard Linklater** *Before Sunrise*
SILVER BEAR, ACTOR: **Paul Newman** *Nobody's Fool*
SILVER BEAR, ACTRESS: **Josephine Siao** *Xiatian De Xue*

1996

British Academy of Film & Television Arts

FILM: **The English Patient** • Fargo • Secrets & Lies • Shine

FOREIGN LANGUAGE FILM: **Ridicule** • Antonia's Line • Kolya • Nelly & Monsieur Arnaud

ALEXANDER KORDA AWARD, BRITISH FILM: **Secrets & Lies** • Brassed Off • Carla's Song • Richard III

DAVID LEAN AWARD, DIRECTOR: **Joel Coen** Fargo • Scott Hicks Shine • Mike Leigh Secrets & Lies • Anthony Minghella The English Patient

ACTOR: **Geoffrey Rush** Shine • Ralph Fiennes The English Patient • Ian McKellen Richard III • Timothy Spall Secrets & Lies

ACTRESS: **Brenda Blethyn** Secrets & Lies • Frances McDormand Fargo • Kristin Scott Thomas The English Patient • Emily Watson Breaking the Waves

SUPPORTING ACTOR: **Paul Scofield** The Crucible • John Gielgud Shine • Edward Norton Primal Fear • Alan Rickman Michael Collins

SUPPORTING ACTRESS: **Juliette Binoche** The English Patient • Lauren Bacall The Mirror Has Two Faces • Marianne Jean-Baptiste Secrets & Lies • Lynn Redgrave Shine

ORIGINAL SCREENPLAY: **Mike Leigh** Secrets & Lies • Mark Herman Brassed Off • Joel Coen, Ethan Coen Fargo • John Sayles Lone Star • Jan Sardi Shine

ADAPTED SCREENPLAY: **Anthony Minghella** The English Patient • Arthur Miller The Crucible • Alan Parker, Oliver Stone Evita • Ian McKellen, R chard Loncraine Richard III

Academy Awards

PICTURE: **The English Patient** • Fargo • Jerry Maguire • Secrets & Lies • Shine

FOREIGN LANGUAGE FILM: **Kolya** • A Chef in Love • The Other Side of Sunday • Prisoner of the Mountains • Ridicule

DIRECTOR: **Anthony Minghella** The English Patient • Joel Coen Fargo • Milos Forman The People vs Larry Flynt • Scott Hicks Shine • Mike Leigh Secrets & Lies

ACTOR: **Geoffrey Rush** Shine • Tom Cruise Jerry Maguire • Ralph Fiennes The English Patient • Woody Harrelson The People vs Larry Flynt • Billy Bob Thornton Sling Blade

ACTRESS: **Frances McDormand** Fargo • Brenda Blethyn Secrets & Lies • Diane Keaton Marvin's Room • Kristin Scott Thomas The English Patient • Emily Watson Breaking the Waves

SUPPORTING ACTOR: **Cuba Gooding Jr** Jerry Maguire • William H Macy Fargo • Armin Mueller-Stahl Shine • Edward Norton Primal Fear • James Woods Ghosts of Mississippi

SUPPORTING ACTRESS: **Juliette Binoche** The English Patient • Joan Allen The Crucible • Lauren Bacall The Mirror Has Two Faces • Barbara Hershey The Portrait of a Lady • Marianne Jean-Baptiste Secrets & Lies

ORIGINAL SCREENPLAY: **Ethan Coen, Joel Coen** Fargo • Cameron Crowe Jerry Maguire • John Sayles Lone Star • Mike Leigh Secrets & Lies • Scott Hicks, Jan Sardi Shine

ADAPTED SCREENPLAY: **Billy Bob Thornton** Sling Blade • Arthur Miller The Crucible • Anthony Minghella The English Patient • Kenneth Branagh Hamlet • John Hodge Trainspotting

Golden Globe Awards

DRAMA: **The English Patient**

COMEDY/MUSICAL: **Evita**

FOREIGN LANGUAGE FILM: **Kolya**

DIRECTOR: **Milos Forman** The People vs Larry Flynt

ACTOR, DRAMA: **Geoffrey Rush** Shine

ACTRESS, DRAMA: **Brenda Blethyn** Secrets & Lies

ACTOR, COMEDY/MUSICAL: **Tom Cruise** Jerry Maguire

ACTRESS, COMEDY/MUSICAL: **Madonna** Evita

SUPPORTING ACTOR: **Edward Norton** Primal Fear

SUPPORTING ACTRESS: **Lauren Bacall** The Mirror Has Two Faces

SCREENPLAY: **Scott Alexander, Larry Karaszewski** The People vs Larry Flynt

Cannes Film Festival

PALME D'OR: **Secrets & Lies**

DIRECTOR: **Joel Coen** Fargo

ACTOR: **Daniel Auteuil, Pascal Duquenne** The Eighth Day

ACTRESS: **Brenda Blethyn** Secrets & Lies

SCREENPLAY: **Jacques Audiard** A Self-Made Hero

Berlin International Film Festival

GOLDEN BEAR: **Sense and Sensibility**

SILVER BEAR, DIRECTOR: **Ho Yim** The Sun Has Ears • **Richard Loncraine** Richard III

SILVER BEAR, ACTOR: **Sean Penn** Dead Man Walking

SILVER BEAR, ACTRESS: **Anouk Grinberg** Mon Homme

1997

British Academy of Film & Television Arts

FILM: **The Full Monty** • LA Confidential • Mrs Brown • Titanic

FOREIGN LANGUAGE FILM: **L'Appartement** • Lucie Aubrac • Ma Vie en Rose • The Tango Lesson

ALEXANDER KORDA AWARD, BRITISH FILM: **Nil by Mouth** • The Borrowers • The Full Monty • Mrs Brown • Regeneration • TwentyFourSeven

DAVID LEAN AWARD, DIRECTOR: **Baz Luhrmann** William Shakespeare's Romeo + Juliet • James Cameron Titanic • Peter Cattaneo The Full Monty • Curtis Hanson LA Confidential

ACTOR: **Robert Carlyle** The Full Monty • Billy Connolly Mrs Brown • Kevin Spacey LA Confidential • Ray Winstone Nil by Mouth

ACTRESS: **Judi Dench** Mrs Brown • Kim Basinger LA Confidential • Helena Bonham Carter The Wings of the Dove • Kathy Burke Nil by Mouth

SUPPORTING ACTOR: **Tom Wilkinson** The Full Monty • Mark Addy The Full Monty • Rupert Everett My Best Friend's Wedding • Burt Reynolds Boogie Nights

SUPPORTING ACTRESS: **Sigourney Weaver** The Ice Storm • Jennifer Ehle Wilde • Lesley Sharp The Full Monty • Zoë Wanamaker Wilde

ORIGINAL SCREENPLAY: **Gary Oldman** Nil by Mouth • Paul Thomas Anderson Boogie Nights • Simon Beaufoy The Full Monty • Jeremy Brock Mrs Brown

ADAPTED SCREENPLAY: **Craig Pearce, Baz Luhrmann** William Shakespeare's Romeo + Juliet • James Schamus The Ice Storm • Curtis Hanson, Brian Helgeland LA Confidential • Hossein Amini The Wings of the Dove

Academy Awards

PICTURE: **Titanic** • As Good as It Gets • The Full Monty • Good Will Hunting • LA Confidential

FOREIGN LANGUAGE FILM: **Character** • Beyond Silence • Four Days in September • Secrets of the Heart • The Thief

DIRECTOR: **James Cameron** Titanic • Peter Cattaneo The Full Monty • Atom Egoyan The Sweet Hereafter • Curtis Hanson LA Confidential • Gus Van Sant Good Will Hunting

ACTOR: **Jack Nicholson** As Good as It Gets • Matt Damon Good Will Hunting • Robert Duvall The Apostle • Peter Fonda Ulee's Gold • Dustin Hoffman Wag the Dog

ACTRESS: **Helen Hunt** As Good as It Gets • Helena Bonham Carter The Wings of the Dove • Julie Christie Afterglow • Judi Dench Mrs Brown • Kate Winslet Titanic

SUPPORTING ACTOR: **Robin Williams** Good Will Hunting • Robert Forster Jackie Brown • Anthony Hopkins Amistad • Greg Kinnear As Good as It Gets • Burt Reynolds Boogie Nights

SUPPORTING ACTRESS: **Kim Basinger** LA Confidential • Joan Cusack In & Out • Minnie Driver Good Will Hunting • Julianne Moore Boogie Nights • Gloria Stuart Titanic

ORIGINAL SCREENPLAY: **Matt Damon, Ben Affleck** Good Will Hunting • Mark Andrus, James L Brooks As Good as It Gets • Paul Thomas Anderson Boogie Nights • Woody Allen Deconstructing Harry • Simon Beaufoy The Full Monty

ADAPTED SCREENPLAY: **Curtis Hanson, Brian Helgeland** LA Confidential • Paul Attanasio Donnie Brasco • Atom Egoyan The Sweet Hereafter • Hilary Henkin, David Mamet Wag the Dog • Hossein Amini The Wings of the Dove

Golden Globe Awards

DRAMA: **Titanic**

COMEDY/MUSICAL: **As Good as It Gets**

FOREIGN LANGUAGE FILM: **Ma Vie en Rose**

DIRECTOR: **James Cameron** Titanic

ACTOR, DRAMA: **Peter Fonda** Ulee's Gold

ACTRESS, DRAMA: **Judi Dench** Mrs Brown

ACTOR, COMEDY/MUSICAL: **Jack Nicholson** As Good as It Gets

ACTRESS, COMEDY/MUSICAL: **Helen Hunt** As Good as It Gets

SUPPORTING ACTOR: **Burt Reynolds** Boogie Nights

SUPPORTING ACTRESS: **Kim Basinger** LA Confidential

SCREENPLAY: **Matt Damon, Ben Affleck** Good Will Hunting

Cannes Film Festival

PALME D'OR: **The Eel** • A Taste of Cherry

DIRECTOR: **Wong Kar-Wai** Happy Together

ACTOR: **Sean Penn** She's So Lovely

ACTRESS: **Kathy Burke** Nil by Mouth

SCREENPLAY: **James Schamus** The Ice Storm

Berlin International Film Festival

GOLDEN BEAR: **The People vs Larry Flynt**

SILVER BEAR, DIRECTOR: **Eric Heumann** Port Djema

SILVER BEAR, ACTOR: **Leonardo DiCaprio** William Shakespeare's Romeo + Juliet

SILVER BEAR, ACTRESS: **Juliette Binoche** The English Patient

1998

British Academy of Film & Television Arts

FILM: **Shakespeare in Love** • Elizabeth • Saving Private Ryan • The Truman Show

FOREIGN LANGUAGE FILM: **Central Station** • Le Bossu • Life Is Beautiful • Live Flesh

ALEXANDER KORDA AWARD, BRITISH FILM: **Elizabeth** • Hilary and Jackie • Little Voice • Lock, Stock and Two Smoking Barrels • My Name Is Joe • Sliding Doors

DAVID LEAN AWARD, DIRECTOR: **Peter Weir** The Truman Show • Shekhar Kapur Elizabeth • John Madden Shakespeare in Love • Steven Spielberg Saving Private Ryan

ACTOR: **Roberto Benigni** Life Is Beautiful • Michael Caine Little Voice • Joseph Fiennes Shakespeare in Love • Tom Hanks Saving Private Ryan

ACTRESS: **Cate Blanchett** Elizabeth • Jane Horrocks Little Voice • Gwyneth Paltrow Shakespeare in Love • Emily Watson Hilary and Jackie

SUPPORTING ACTOR: **Geoffrey Rush** Shakespeare in Love • Ed Harris The Truman Show • Geoffrey Rush Elizabeth • Tom Wilkinson Shakespeare in Love

SUPPORTING ACTRESS: **Judi Dench** Shakespeare in Love • Kathy Bates Primary Colors • Brenda Blethyn Little Voice • Lynn Redgrave Gods and Monsters

ORIGINAL SCREENPLAY: **Andrew Niccol** The Truman Show • Michael Hirst Elizabeth • Vincenzo Cerami, Roberto Benigni Life Is Beautiful • Marc Norman, Tom Stoppard Shakespeare in Love

ADAPTED SCREENPLAY: **Elaine May** Primary Colors • Frank Cottrell Boyce Hilary and Jackie • Mark Herman Little Voice • David Mamet, Hilary Henkin Wag the Dog

Academy Awards

PICTURE: **Shakespeare in Love** • Elizabeth • Life Is Beautiful • Saving Private Ryan • The Thin Red Line

FOREIGN LANGUAGE FILM: **Life Is Beautiful** • Central Station • The Children of Heaven • The Grandfather • Tango

DIRECTOR: **Steven Spielberg** Saving Private Ryan • Roberto Benigni Life Is Beautiful • John Madden Shakespeare in Love • Terrence Malick The Thin Red Line • Peter Weir The Truman Show

ACTOR: **Roberto Benigni** Life Is Beautiful • Tom Hanks Saving Private Ryan • Ian McKellen Gods and Monsters • Nick Nolte Affliction • Edward Norton American History X

ACTRESS: **Gwyneth Paltrow** Shakespeare in Love • Cate Blanchett Elizabeth • Fernanda Montenegro Central Station • Meryl Streep One True Thing • Emily Watson Hilary and Jackie

SUPPORTING ACTOR: **James Coburn** Affliction • Robert Duvall A Civil Action • Ed Harris The Truman Show • Geoffrey Rush Shakespeare in Love • Billy Bob Thornton A Simple Plan

SUPPORTING ACTRESS: **Judi Dench** Shakespeare in Love • Kathy Bates Primary Colors • Brenda Blethyn Little Voice • Rachel Griffiths Hilary and Jackie • Lynn Redgrave Gods and Monsters

ORIGINAL SCREENPLAY: **Marc Norman, Tom Stoppard** Shakespeare in Love • Warren Beatty, Jeremy Pikser Bulworth • Roberto Benigni, Vincenzo Cerami Life Is Beautiful • Robert Rodat Saving Private Ryan • Andrew Niccol The Truman Show

ADAPTED SCREENPLAY: **Bill Condon** Gods and Monsters • Scott Frank Out of Sight • Elaine May Primary Colors • Scott B Smith A Simple Plan • Terrence Malick The Thin Red Line

Golden Globe Awards

DRAMA: **Saving Private Ryan**

COMEDY/MUSICAL: **Shakespeare in Love**

FOREIGN LANGUAGE FILM: **Central Station**

DIRECTOR: **Steven Spielberg** Saving Private Ryan

ACTOR, DRAMA: **Jim Carrey** The Truman Show

ACTRESS, DRAMA: **Cate Blanchett** Elizabeth

ACTOR, COMEDY/MUSICAL: **Michael Caine** Little Voice

ACTRESS, COMEDY/MUSICAL: **Gwyneth Paltrow** Shakespeare in Love

SUPPORTING ACTOR: **Ed Harris** The Truman Show

SUPPORTING ACTRESS: **Lynn Redgrave** Gods and Monsters

SCREENPLAY: **Marc Norman, Tom Stoppard** Shakespeare in Love

Cannes Film Festival

PALME D'OR: **Eternity and a Day**

DIRECTOR: **John Boorman** The General

ACTOR: **Peter Mullan** My Name Is Joe

ACTRESS: **Élodie Bouchez, Natacha Régnier** The Dream Life of Angels

SCREENPLAY: **Hal Hartley** Henry Fool

Berlin International Film Festival

GOLDEN BEAR: **Central Station**

SILVER BEAR, DIRECTOR: **Neil Jordan** The Butcher Boy

SILVER BEAR, ACTOR: **Samuel L Jackson** Jackie Brown

SILVER BEAR, ACTRESS: **Fernanda Montenegro** Central Station

1999

British Academy Film Awards

FILM: **American Beauty** • East Is East • The End of the Affair • The Sixth Sense • The Talented Mr Ripley

FOREIGN LANGUAGE FILM: **All about My Mother** • Buena Vista Social Club • Festen • Run Lola Run

ALEXANDER KORDA AWARD, BRITISH FILM: **East Is East** • Notting Hill • Onegin • Ratcatcher • Topsy-Turvy • Wonderland

DAVID LEAN AWARD, DIRECTOR: **Pedro Almodóvar** All about My Mother • Neil Jordan The End of the Affair • Sam Mendes American Beauty • Anthony Minghella The Talented Mr Ripley • M Night Shyamalan The Sixth Sense

ACTOR: **Kevin Spacey** American Beauty • Jim Broadbent Topsy-Turvy • Russell Crowe The Insider • Ralph Fiennes The End of the Affair • Om Puri East Is East

ACTRESS: **Annette Bening** American Beauty • Linda Bassett East Is East • Julianne Moore The End of the Affair • Emily Watson Angela's Ashes

SUPPORTING ACTOR: **Jude Law** The Talented Mr Ripley • Wes Bentley American Beauty • Michael Caine The Cider House Rules • Rhys Ifans Notting Hill • Timothy Spall Topsy-Turvy

SUPPORTING ACTRESS: **Maggie Smith** Tea with Mussolini • Thora Birch American Beauty • Cate Blanchett The Talented Mr Ripley • Cameron Diaz Being John Malkovich • Mena Suvari American Beauty

ORIGINAL SCREENPLAY: **Charlie Kaufman** Being John Malkovich • Pedro Almodóvar All about My Mother • Alan Ball American Beauty • M Night Shyamalan The Sixth Sense • Mike Leigh Topsy-Turvy

ADAPTED SCREENPLAY: **Neil Jordan** The End of the Affair • Oliver Parker An Ideal Husband • Ayub Khan-Din East Is East • Anthony Minghella The Talented Mr Ripley

Academy Awards

PICTURE: **American Beauty** • The Cider House Rules • The Green Mile • The Insider • The Sixth Sense

FOREIGN LANGUAGE FILM: **All about My Mother** • Himalaya • East-West • Solomon and Gaenor • Under the Sun

DIRECTOR: **Sam Mendes** American Beauty • Lasse Hallström The Cider House Rules • Spike Jonze Being John Malkovich • Michael Mann The Insider • M Night Shyamalan The Sixth Sense

ACTOR: **Kevin Spacey** American Beauty • Russell Crowe The Insider • Richard Farnsworth The Straight Story • Sean Penn Sweet and Lowdown • Denzel Washington The Hurricane

ACTRESS: **Hilary Swank** Boys Don't Cry • Annette Bening American Beauty • Janet McTeer Tumbleweeds • Julianne Moore The End of the Affair • Meryl Streep Music of the Heart

SUPPORTING ACTOR: **Michael Caine** The Cider House Rules • Tom Cruise Magnolia • Michael Clarke Duncan The Green

Mile • Jude Law *The Talented Mr Ripley* • Haley Joel Osment *The Sixth Sense*
SUPPORTING ACTRESS: **Angelina Jolie** *Girl, Interrupted* • Toni Collette *The Sixth Sense* • Catherine Keener *Being John Malkovich* • Samantha Morton *Sweet and Lowdown* • Chloë Sevigny *Boys Don't Cry*
ORIGINAL SCREENPLAY: **Alan Ball** *American Beauty* • Charlie Kaufman *Being John Malkovich* • Paul Thomas Anderson *Magnolia* • M Night Shyamalan *The Sixth Sense* • Mike Leigh *Topsy-Turvy*
ADAPTED SCREENPLAY: **John Irving** *The Cider House Rules* • Alexander Payne, Jim Taylor *Election* • Frank Darabont *The Green Mile* • Eric Roth, Michael Mann *The Insider* • Anthony Minghella *The Talented Mr Ripley*

Golden Globe Awards

DRAMA: *American Beauty*
COMEDY/MUSICAL: *Toy Story 2*
FOREIGN LANGUAGE FILM: *All about My Mother*
DIRECTOR: **Sam Mendes** *American Beauty*
ACTOR, DRAMA: **Denzel Washington** *The Hurricane*
ACTRESS, DRAMA: **Hilary Swank** *Boys Don't Cry*
ACTOR, COMEDY/MUSICAL: **Jim Carrey** *Man on the Moon*
ACTRESS, COMEDY/MUSICAL: **Janet McTeer** *Tumbleweeds*
SUPPORTING ACTOR: **Tom Cruise** *Magnolia*
SUPPORTING ACTRESS: **Angelina Jolie** *Girl, Interrupted*
SCREENPLAY: **Alan Ball** *American Beauty*

Cannes Film Festival

PALME D'OR: *Rosetta*
DIRECTOR: **Pedro Almodóvar** *All about My Mother*
ACTOR: **Emmanuel Schotté** *L'Humanité*
ACTRESS: **Severine Caneele** *L'Humanité* • **Emilie Dequenne** *Rosetta*
SCREENPLAY: **Yuri Arabov** *Moloch*

Berlin International Film Festival

GOLDEN BEAR: *The Thin Red Line*
SILVER BEAR, DIRECTOR: **Stephen Frears** *The Hi-Lo Country*
SILVER BEAR, ACTOR: **Michael Gwisdek** *Night Shapes*
SILVER BEAR, ACTRESS: **Maria Schrader, Juliane Köhler** *Aimée and Jaguar*

2000

British Academy Film Awards

FILM: *Gladiator* • *Almost Famous* • *Billy Elliot* • *Erin Brockovich*
FOREIGN LANGUAGE FILM: *Crouching Tiger, Hidden Dragon* • *The Girl on the Bridge* • *Harry, un Ami Qui Vous Veut du Bien* • *In the Mood for Love* • *Malena*
ALEXANDER KORDA AWARD, BRITISH FILM: *Billy Elliot* • *Chicken Run* • *The House of Mirth* • *Last Resort* • *Sexy Beast*
DAVID LEAN AWARD, DIRECTOR: **Ang Lee** *Crouching Tiger, Hidden Dragon* • Stephen Daldry *Billy Elliot* • Steven Soderbergh *Erin Brockovich* • Steven Soderbergh *Traffic* • Ridley Scott *Gladiator*
ACTOR: **Jamie Bell** *Billy Elliot* • Russell Crowe *Gladiator* • Michael Douglas *Wonder Boys* • Tom Hanks *Cast Away* • Geoffrey Rush *Quills*
ACTRESS: **Julia Roberts** *Erin Brockovich* • Juliette Binoche *Chocolat* • Kate Hudson *Almost Famous* • Hilary Swank *Boys Don't Cry* • Michelle Yeoh *Crouching Tiger, Hidden Dragon*
SUPPORTING ACTOR: **Benicio Del Toro** *Traffic* • Albert Finney *Erin Brockovich* • Gary Lewis *Billy Elliot* • Joaquin Phoenix, Oliver Reed *Gladiator*
SUPPORTING ACTRESS: **Julie Walters** *Billy Elliot* • Judi Dench *Chocolat* • Frances McDormand *Almost Famous* • Lena Olin *Chocolat* • Zhang Ziyi *Crouching Tiger, Hidden Dragon*
ORIGINAL SCREENPLAY: **Cameron Crowe** *Almost Famous* • Lee Hall *Billy Elliot* • Susannah Grant *Erin Brockovich* • David Franzoni, John Logan, William Nicholson *Gladiator* • Ethan Coen, Joel Coen *O Brother, Where Art Thou?*
ADAPTED SCREENPLAY: **Stephen Gaghan** *Traffic* • Robert Nelson Jacobs *Chocolat* • James Schamus, Wang Hui-Ling, Tsai Kuo-Jung *Crouching Tiger, Hidden Dragon* • D V De Vincentis, Steve Pink, John Cusack, Scott Rosenberg *High Fidelity* • Steve Kloves *Wonder Boys*

Academy Awards

PICTURE: *Gladiator* • *Chocolat* • *Crouching Tiger, Hidden Dragon* • *Erin Brockovich* • *Traffic*
FOREIGN LANGUAGE FILM: *Crouching Tiger, Hidden Dragon* • *Amores Perros* • *Divided We Fall* • *Everybody Famous!* • *Le Goût des Autres*
DIRECTOR: **Steven Soderbergh** *Traffic* • Stephen Daldry *Billy Elliot* • Ang Lee *Crouching Tiger, Hidden Dragon* • Ridley Scott *Gladiator* • Steven Soderbergh *Erin Brockovich*
ACTOR: **Russell Crowe** *Gladiator* • Javier Bardem *Before Night Falls* • Tom Hanks *Cast Away* • Ed Harris *Pollock* • Geoffrey Rush *Quills*
ACTRESS: **Julia Roberts** *Erin Brockovich* • Joan Allen *The Contender* • Juliette Binoche *Chocolat* • Ellen Burstyn *Requiem for a Dream* • Laura Linney *You Can Count on Me*
SUPPORTING ACTOR: **Benicio Del Toro** *Traffic* • Jeff Bridges *The Contender* • Willem Dafoe *Shadow of the Vampire* • Albert Finney *Erin Brockovich* • Joaquin Phoenix *Gladiator*
SUPPORTING ACTRESS: **Marcia Gay Harden** *Pollock* • Judi Dench *Chocolat* • Kate Hudson, Frances McDormand *Almost Famous* • Julie Walters *Billy Elliot*
ORIGINAL SCREENPLAY: **Cameron Crowe** *Almost Famous* • Lee Hall *Billy Elliot* • Susannah Grant *Erin Brockovich* • David Franzoni, John Logan, William Nicholson *Gladiator* • Kenneth Lonergan *You Can Count on Me*
ADAPTED SCREENPLAY: **Stephen Gaghan** *Traffic* • Robert Nelson Jacobs *Chocolat* • James Schamus, Wang Hui-Ling, Tsai Kuo-Jung *Crouching Tiger, Hidden Dragon* • Ethan Coen, Joel Coen *O Brother, Where Art Thou?* • Steve Kloves *Wonder Boys*

Golden Globe Awards

DRAMA: *Gladiator*
COMEDY/MUSICAL: *Almost Famous*
FOREIGN LANGUAGE FILM: *Crouching Tiger, Hidden Dragon*
DIRECTOR: **Ang Lee** *Crouching Tiger, Hidden Dragon*
ACTOR, DRAMA: **Tom Hanks** *Cast Away*
ACTRESS, DRAMA: **Julia Roberts** *Erin Brockovich*
ACTOR, COMEDY/MUSICAL: **George Clooney** *O Brother, Where Art Thou?*
ACTRESS, COMEDY/MUSICAL: **Renee Zellweger** *Nurse Betty*
SUPPORTING ACTOR: **Benicio Del Toro** *Traffic*
SUPPORTING ACTRESS: **Kate Hudson** *Almost Famous*
SCREENPLAY: **Stephen Gaghan** *Traffic*

Cannes Film Festival

PALME D'OR: *Dancer in the Dark*
DIRECTOR: **Edward Yang** *A One and a Two*
ACTOR: **Tony Leung** *In the Mood for Love*
ACTRESS: **Björk** *Dancer in the Dark*
SCREENPLAY: **John C Richards, James Flamberg** *Nurse Betty*

Berlin International Film Festival

GOLDEN BEAR: *Magnolia*
SILVER BEAR, DIRECTOR: **Milos Forman** *Man on the Moon*
SILVER BEAR, ACTOR: **Denzel Washington** *The Hurricane*
SILVER BEAR, ACTRESS: **Bibiana Beglau, Nadja Uhl** *The Legends of Rita*

2001

British Academy Film Awards

FILM: *The Lord of the Rings: The Fellowship of the Ring* • *Amélie* • *A Beautiful Mind* • *Moulin Rouge* • *Shrek*
FOREIGN LANGUAGE FILM: *Amores Perros* • *Amélie* • *Behind the Sun* • *Monsoon Wedding* • *The Piano Teacher*
ALEXANDER KORDA AWARD, BRITISH FILM: *Gosford Park* • *Bridget Jones's Diary* • *Harry Potter and the Philosopher's Stone* • *Iris* • *Me without You*
DAVID LEAN AWARD, DIRECTOR: **Peter Jackson** *The Lord of the Rings: The Fellowship of the Ring* • Robert Altman *Gosford Park* • Ron Howard *A Beautiful Mind* • Jean-Pierre Jeunet *Amélie* • Baz Luhrmann *Moulin Rouge*
ACTOR: **Russell Crowe** *A Beautiful Mind* • Jim Broadbent *Iris* • Ian McKellen *The Lord of the Rings: The Fellowship of the Ring* • Kevin Spacey *The Shipping News* • Tom Wilkinson *In the Bedroom*
ACTRESS: **Judi Dench** *Iris* • Nicole Kidman *The Others* • Sissy Spacek *In the Bedroom* • Audrey Tautou *Amélie* • Renee Zellweger *Bridget Jones's Diary*
SUPPORTING ACTOR: **Jim Broadbent** *Moulin Rouge* • Hugh Bonneville *Iris* • Robbie Coltrane *Harry Potter and the Philosopher's Stone* • Colin Firth *Bridget Jones's Diary* • Eddie Murphy *Shrek*
SUPPORTING ACTRESS: **Jennifer Connelly** *A Beautiful Mind* • Judi Dench *The Shipping News* • Helen Mirren, Maggie Smith *Gosford Park* • Kate Winslet *Iris*
ORIGINAL SCREENPLAY: **Guillaume Laurant, Jean-Pierre Jeunet** *Amélie* • Julian Fellowes *Gosford Park* • Baz Luhrmann, Craig Pearce *Moulin Rouge* • Alejandro Amenábar *The Others* • Wes Anderson, Owen Wilson *The Royal Tenenbaums*
ADAPTED SCREENPLAY: **Joe Stillman, Roger SH Schulman, Ted Elliott, Terry Rossio** *Shrek* • Akiva Goldsman *A Beautiful Mind* • Andrew Davies, Helen Fielding, Richard Curtis *Bridget Jones's Diary* • Charles Wood, Richard Eyre *Iris* • Fran Walsh, Peter Jackson, Philippa Boyens *The Lord of the Rings: The Fellowship of the Ring*

Academy Awards

PICTURE: *A Beautiful Mind* • *Gosford Park* • *In the Bedroom* • *The Lord of the Rings: The Fellowship of the Ring* • *Moulin Rouge*
FOREIGN LANGUAGE FILM: *No Man's Land* • *Amélie* • *Elling* • *Lagaan: Once upon a Time in India* • *Son of the Bride*
DIRECTOR: **Ron Howard** *A Beautiful Mind* • Robert Altman *Gosford Park* • Peter Jackson *The Lord of the Rings: The Fellowship of the Ring* • David Lynch *Mulholland Drive* • Ridley Scott *Black Hawk Down*
ACTOR: **Denzel Washington** *Training Day* • Russell Crowe *A Beautiful Mind* • Sean Penn *I Am Sam* • Will Smith *Ali* • Tom Wilkinson *In the Bedroom*
ACTRESS: **Halle Berry** *Monster's Ball* • Judi Dench *Iris* • Nicole Kidman *Moulin Rouge* • Sissy Spacek *In the Bedroom* • Renee Zellweger *Bridget Jones's Diary*
SUPPORTING ACTOR: **Jim Broadbent** *Iris* • Ethan Hawke *Training Day* • Ben Kingsley *Sexy Beast* • Ian McKellen *The Lord of the Rings: The Fellowship of the Ring* • Jon Voight *Ali*
SUPPORTING ACTRESS: **Jennifer Connelly** *A Beautiful Mind* • Helen Mirren, Maggie Smith *Gosford Park* • Marisa Tomei *In the Bedroom* • Kate Winslet *Iris*
ORIGINAL SCREENPLAY: **Julian Fellowes** *Gosford Park* • Guillaume Laurant, Jean-Pierre Jeunet *Amélie* • Christopher Nolan, Jonathan Nolan *Memento* • Milo Addica, Will Rokos *Monster's Ball* • Owen Wilson, Wes Anderson *The Royal Tenenbaums*
ADAPTED SCREENPLAY: **Akiva Goldsman** *A Beautiful Mind* • Daniel Clowes, Terry Zwigoff *Ghost World* • Rob Festinger, Todd Field *In the Bedroom* • Fran Walsh, Peter Jackson, Philippa Boyens *The Lord of the Rings: The Fellowship of the Ring* • Joe Stillman, Roger SH Schulman, Ted Elliott, Terry Rossio *Shrek*

Golden Globe Awards

DRAMA: *A Beautiful Mind*
COMEDY/MUSICAL: *Moulin Rouge*
FOREIGN LANGUAGE FILM: *No Man's Land*
DIRECTOR: **Robert Altman** *Gosford Park*
ACTOR, DRAMA: **Russell Crowe** *A Beautiful Mind*
ACTRESS, DRAMA: **Sissy Spacek** *In the Bedroom*

ACTOR, COMEDY/MUSICAL: **Gene Hackman** *The Royal Tenenbaums*
ACTRESS, COMEDY/MUSICAL: **Nicole Kidman** *Moulin Rouge*
SUPPORTING ACTOR: **Jim Broadbent** *Iris*
SUPPORTING ACTRESS: **Jennifer Connelly** *A Beautiful Mind*
SCREENPLAY: **Akiva Goldsman** *A Beautiful Mind*

Cannes Film Festival

PALME D'OR: *The Son's Room*
DIRECTOR: **Joel Coen** *The Man Who Wasn't There* • **David Lynch** *Mulholland Drive*
ACTOR: **Benoît Magimel** *The Piano Teacher*
ACTRESS: **Isabelle Huppert** *The Piano Teacher*
SCREENPLAY: **Danis Tanovic** *No Man's Land*

Berlin International Film Festival

GOLDEN BEAR: *Intimacy*
SILVER BEAR, DIRECTOR: **Lin Cheng-sheng** *Betelnut Beauty*
SILVER BEAR, ACTOR: **Benicio Del Toro** *Traffic*
SILVER BEAR, ACTRESS: **Kerry Fox** *Intimacy*

2002

British Academy Film Awards

FILM: *The Pianist* • *Chicago* • *Gangs of New York* • *The Hours* • *The Lord of the Rings: The Two Towers*
FOREIGN LANGUAGE FILM: *Talk to Her* • *City of God* • *Devdas* • *The Warrior* • *Y Tu Mamá También*
ALEXANDER KORDA AWARD, BRITISH FILM: *The Warrior* • *Bend It like Beckham* • *Dirty Pretty Things* • *The Hours* • *The Magdalene Sisters*
DAVID LEAN AWARD, DIRECTOR: **Roman Polanski** *The Pianist* • Stephen Daldry *The Hours* • Peter Jackson *The Lord of the Rings: The Two Towers* • Rob Marshall *Chicago* • Martin Scorsese *Gangs of New York*
ACTOR: **Daniel Day-Lewis** *Gangs of New York* • Adrien Brody *The Pianist* • Nicolas Cage *Adaptation.* • Michael Caine *The Quiet American* • Jack Nicholson *About Schmidt*
ACTRESS: **Nicole Kidman** *The Hours* • Halle Berry *Monster's Ball* • Salma Hayek *Frida* • Meryl Streep *The Hours* • Renee Zellweger *Chicago*
SUPPORTING ACTOR: **Christopher Walken** *Catch Me If You Can* • Chris Cooper *Adaptation.* • Ed Harris *The Hours* • Alfred Molina *Frida* • Paul Newman *Road to Perdition*
SUPPORTING ACTRESS: **Catherine Zeta-Jones** *Chicago* • Toni Collette *About a Boy* • Julianne Moore *The Hours* • Queen Latifah *Chicago* • Meryl Streep *Adaptation.*
ORIGINAL SCREENPLAY: **Pedro Almodóvar** *Talk to Her* • Steven Knight *Dirty Pretty Things* • Jay Cocks, Steve Zaillian, Kenneth Lonergan *Gangs of New York* • Peter Mullan *The Magdalene Sisters* • Carlos Cuarón, Alfonso Cuarón *Y Tu Mamá También*
ADAPTED SCREENPLAY: **Charlie Kaufman, Donald Kaufman** *Adaptation.* • Peter Hedges, Chris Weitz, Paul Weitz *About a Boy* • Jeff Nathanson *Catch Me If You Can* • David Hare *The Hours* • Ronald Harwood *The Pianist*

Academy Awards

PICTURE: *Chicago* • *Gangs of New York* • *The Hours* • *The Lord of the Rings: The Two Towers* • *The Pianist*
FOREIGN LANGUAGE FILM: *Nowhere in Africa* • *El Crimen del Padre Amaro* • *Hero* • *The Man without a Past* • *Zus & Zo*
DIRECTOR: **Roman Polanski** *The Pianist* • Pedro Almodóvar *Talk to Her* • Stephen Daldry *The Hours* • Rob Marshall *Chicago* • Martin Scorsese *Gangs of New York*
ACTOR: **Adrien Brody** *The Pianist* • Nicolas Cage *Adaptation.* • Michael Caine *The Quiet American* • Daniel Day-Lewis *Gangs of New York* • Jack Nicholson *About Schmidt*
ACTRESS: **Nicole Kidman** *The Hours* • Salma Hayek *Frida* • Diane Lane *Unfaithful* • Julianne Moore *Far from Heaven* • Renee Zellweger *Chicago*
SUPPORTING ACTOR: **Chris Cooper** *Adaptation.* • Ed Harris *The Hours* • Paul Newman *Road to Perdition* • John C Reilly *Chicago* • Christopher Walken *Catch Me If You Can*
SUPPORTING ACTRESS: **Catherine Zeta-Jones** *Chicago* • Kathy Bates *About Schmidt* • Julianne Moore *The Hours* • Queen Latifah *Chicago* • Meryl Streep *Adaptation.*
ORIGINAL SCREENPLAY: **Pedro Almodóvar** *Talk to Her* • Todd Haynes *Far from Heaven* • Jay Cocks, Steve Zaillian, Kenneth Lonergan *Gangs of New York* • Nia Vardalos *My Big Fat Greek Wedding* • Alfonso Cuarón, Carlos Cuarón *Y Tu Mamá También*
ADAPTED SCREENPLAY: **Ronald Harwood** *The Pianist* • Peter Hedges, Chris Weitz, Paul Weitz *About a Boy* • Charlie Kaufman, Donald Kaufman *Adaptation.* • Bill Condon *Chicago* • David Hare *The Hours*

Golden Globe Awards

DRAMA: *The Hours*
COMEDY/MUSICAL: *Chicago*
FOREIGN LANGUAGE FILM: *Talk to Her*
DIRECTOR: **Martin Scorsese** *Gangs of New York*
ACTOR, DRAMA: **Jack Nicholson** *About Schmidt*
ACTRESS, DRAMA: **Nicole Kidman** *The Hours*
ACTOR, COMEDY/MUSICAL: **Richard Gere** *Chicago*
ACTRESS, COMEDY/MUSICAL: **Renee Zellweger** *Chicago*
SUPPORTING ACTOR: **Chris Cooper** *Adaptation.*
SUPPORTING ACTRESS: **Meryl Streep** *Adaptation.*
SCREENPLAY: **Alexander Payne, Jim Taylor** *About Schmidt*

Cannes Film Festival

PALME D'OR: *The Pianist*
DIRECTOR: **Paul Thomas Anderson** *Punch-Drunk Love* • Im Kwon-taek *Chihwaseon (Drunk on Women and Poetry)*
ACTOR: **Olivier Gourmet** *The Son*
ACTRESS: **Kati Outinen** *The Man without a Past*
SCREENPLAY: **Paul Laverty** *Sweet Sixteen*

Berlin International Film Festival

GOLDEN BEAR: **Bloody Sunday** • **Spirited Away**
SILVER BEAR, DIRECTOR: **Otar Iosseliani** Monday Morning
SILVER BEAR, ACTOR: **Jacques Gamblin** Laissez-passer
SILVER BEAR, ACTRESS: **Halle Berry** Monster's Ball

2003

British Academy Film Awards

FILM: **The Lord of the Rings: The Return of the King** • Big Fish • Cold Mountain • Lost in Translation • Master and Commander: the Far Side of the World
FOREIGN LANGUAGE FILM: **In This World** • The Barbarian Invasions • Belleville Rendez-vous • Etre et Avoir • Good Bye Lenin! • Spirited Away
ALEXANDER KORDA AWARD, BRITISH FILM: **Touching the Void** • Cold Mountain • Girl with a Pearl Earring • In This World • Love Actually
DAVID LEAN AWARD, DIRECTOR: **Peter Weir** Master and Commander: the Far Side of the World • Tim Burton Big Fish • Sofia Coppola Lost in Translation • Peter Jackson The Lord of the Rings: The Return of the King • Anthony Minghella Cold Mountain
ACTOR: **Bill Murray** Lost in Translation • Benicio Del Toro 21 Grams • Johnny Depp Pirates of the Caribbean: the Curse of the Black Pearl • Jude Law Cold Mountain • Sean Penn Mystic River • Sean Penn 21 Grams
ACTRESS: **Scarlett Johansson** Lost in Translation • Scarlett Johansson Girl with a Pearl Earring • Anne Reid The Mother • Uma Thurman Kill Bill Vol 1 • Naomi Watts 21 Grams
SUPPORTING ACTOR: **Bill Nighy** Love Actually • Paul Bettany Master and Commander: the Far Side of the World • Albert Finney Big Fish • Ian McKellen The Lord of the Rings: The Return of the King • Tim Robbins Mystic River
SUPPORTING ACTRESS: **Renee Zellweger** Cold Mountain • Holly Hunter Thirteen • Laura Linney Mystic River • Judy Parfitt Girl with a Pearl Earring • Emma Thompson Love Actually
ORIGINAL SCREENPLAY: **Thomas McCarthy** The Station Agent • Denys Arcand The Barbarian Invasions • Andrew Stanton, Bob Peterson, David Reynolds Finding Nemo • Sofia Coppola Lost in Translation • Guillermo Arriaga 21 Grams
ADAPTED SCREENPLAY: **Peter Jackson, Fran Walsh, Philippa Boyens** The Lord of the Rings: The Return of the King • John August Big Fish • Anthony Minghella Cold Mountain • Olivia Hetreed Girl with a Pearl Earring • Brian Helgeland Mystic River

Academy Awards

PICTURE: **The Lord of the Rings: The Return of the King** • Lost in Translation • Master and Commander: the Far Side of the World • Mystic River • Seabiscuit
FOREIGN LANGUAGE FILM: **The Barbarian Invasions** • Evil • The Twilight Samurai • Twin Sisters • Zelary
DIRECTOR: **Peter Jackson** The Lord of the Rings: The Return of the King • Sofia Coppola Lost in Translation • Clint Eastwood Mystic River • Fernando Meirelles City of God • Peter Weir Master and Commander: the Far Side of the World
ACTOR: **Sean Penn** Mystic River • Johnny Depp Pirates of the Caribbean: the Curse of the Black Pearl • Ben Kingsley House of Sand and Fog • Jude Law Cold Mountain • Bill Murray Lost in Translation
ACTRESS: **Charlize Theron** Monster • Keisha Castle-Hughes Whale Rider • Diane Keaton Something's Gotta Give • Samantha Morton In America • Naomi Watts 21 Grams
SUPPORTING ACTOR: **Tim Robbins** Mystic River • Alec Baldwin The Cooler • Benicio Del Toro 21 Grams • Djimon Hounsou In America • Ken Watanabe The Last Samurai
SUPPORTING ACTRESS: **Renee Zellweger** Cold Mountain • Shohreh Aghdashloo House of Sand and Fog • Patricia Clarkson Pieces of April • Marcia Gay Harden Mystic River • Holly Hunter Thirteen
ORIGINAL SCREENPLAY: **Sofia Coppola** Lost in Translation • Denys Arcand The Barbarian Invasions • Steven Knight Dirty Pretty Things • Andrew Stanton, Bob Peterson, David Reynolds Finding Nemo • Jim Sheridan, Naomi Sheridan, Kirsten Sheridan In America
ADAPTED SCREENPLAY: **Peter Jackson, Fran Walsh, Philippa Boyens** The Lord of the Rings: The Return of the King • Shari Springer Berman, Robert Pulcini American Splendor • Braulio Mantovani City of God • Brian Helgeland Mystic River • Gary Ross Seabiscuit

Golden Globe Awards

DRAMA: **The Lord of the Rings: The Return of the King**
COMEDY/MUSICAL: **Lost in Translation**
FOREIGN LANGUAGE FILM: **Osama**
DIRECTOR: **Peter Jackson** The Lord of the Rings: The Return of the King
ACTOR, DRAMA: **Sean Penn** Mystic River
ACTRESS, DRAMA: **Charlize Theron** Monster
ACTOR, COMEDY/MUSICAL: **Bill Murray** Lost in Translation
ACTRESS, COMEDY/MUSICAL: **Diane Keaton** Something's Gotta Give
SUPPORTING ACTOR: **Tim Robbins** Mystic River
SUPPORTING ACTRESS: **Renee Zellweger** Cold Mountain
SCREENPLAY: **Sofia Coppola** Lost in Translation

Cannes Film Festival

PALME D'OR: **Elephant**
DIRECTOR: **Gus Van Sant** Elephant
ACTOR: **Muzaffer Ozdemir, Mehmet Emin Toprak** Uzak
ACTRESS: **Marie-Josée Croze** The Barbarian Invasions
SCREENPLAY: **Denys Arcand** The Barbarian Invasions

Berlin International Film Festival

GOLDEN BEAR: **In This World**
SILVER BEAR, DIRECTOR: **Patrice Chéreau** Son Frère

SILVER BEAR, ACTOR: **Sam Rockwell** Confessions of a Dangerous Mind
SILVER BEAR, ACTRESS: **Nicole Kidman, Julianne Moore, Meryl Streep** The Hours

2004

British Academy Film Awards

FILM: **The Aviator** • Eternal Sunshine of the Spotless Mind • Finding Neverland • The Motorcycle Diaries • Vera Drake
FOREIGN LANGUAGE FILM: **The Motorcycle Diaries** • Bad Education • The Chorus • House of Flying Daggers • A Very Long Engagement
ALEXANDER KORDA AWARD, BRITISH FILM: **My Summer of Love** • Dead Man's Shoes • Harry Potter and the Prisoner of Azkaban • Shaun of the Dead • Vera Drake
DAVID LEAN AWARD, DIRECTOR: **Mike Leigh** Vera Drake • Marc Forster Finding Neverland • Michel Gondry Eternal Sunshine of the Spotless Mind • Michael Mann Collateral • Martin Scorsese The Aviator
ACTOR: **Jamie Foxx** Ray • Gael García Bernal The Motorcycle Diaries • Jim Carrey Eternal Sunshine of the Spotless Mind • Johnny Depp Finding Neverland • Leonardo DiCaprio The Aviator
ACTRESS: **Imelda Staunton** Vera Drake • Charlize Theron Monster • Kate Winslet Eternal Sunshine of the Spotless Mind • Kate Winslet Finding Neverland • Zhang Ziyi House of Flying Daggers
SUPPORTING ACTOR: **Clive Owen** Closer • Alan Alda The Aviator • Philip Davis Vera Drake • Rodrigo de la Serna The Motorcycle Diaries • Jamie Foxx Collateral
SUPPORTING ACTRESS: **Cate Blanchett** The Aviator • Julie Christie Finding Neverland • Heather Craney Vera Drake • Natalie Portman Closer • Meryl Streep The Manchurian Candidate
ORIGINAL SCREENPLAY: **Charlie Kaufman** Eternal Sunshine of the Spotless Mind • John Logan The Aviator • Stuart Beattie Collateral • James L White Ray • Mike Leigh Vera Drake
ADAPTED SCREENPLAY: **Alexander Payne, Jim Taylor** Sideways • Christophe Barratier, Philippe Lopes Curval The Chorus • Patrick Marber Closer • David Magee Finding Neverland • José Rivera The Motorcycle Diaries

Academy Awards

PICTURE: **Million Dollar Baby** • The Aviator • Finding Neverland • Ray • Sideways
FOREIGN LANGUAGE FILM: **The Sea Inside** • As It Is in Heaven • The Chorus • Downfall • Yesterday
DIRECTOR: **Clint Eastwood** Million Dollar Baby • Taylor Hackford Ray • Mike Leigh Vera Drake • Alexander Payne Sideways • Martin Scorsese The Aviator
ACTOR: **Jamie Foxx** Ray • Don Cheadle Hotel Rwanda • Johnny Depp Finding Neverland • Leonardo DiCaprio The Aviator • Clint Eastwood Million Dollar Baby
ACTRESS: **Hilary Swank** Million Dollar Baby • Annette Bening Being Julia • Catalina Sandino Moreno Maria Full of Grace • Imelda Staunton Vera Drake • Kate Winslet Eternal Sunshine of the Spotless Mind
SUPPORTING ACTOR: **Morgan Freeman** Million Dollar Baby • Alan Alda The Aviator • Thomas Haden Church Sideways • Jamie Foxx Collateral • Clive Owen Closer
SUPPORTING ACTRESS: **Cate Blanchett** The Aviator • Laura Linney Kinsey • Virginia Madsen Sideways • Sophie Okonedo Hotel Rwanda • Natalie Portman Closer
ORIGINAL SCREENPLAY: **Charlie Kaufman** Eternal Sunshine of the Spotless Mind • Brad Bird The Incredibles • Terry George, Keir Pearson Hotel Rwanda • Mike Leigh Vera Drake • John Logan The Aviator
ADAPTED SCREENPLAY: **Alexander Payne, Jim Taylor** Sideways • Paul Haggis Million Dollar Baby • Richard Linklater, Julie Delpy, Ethan Hawke Before Sunset • David Magee Finding Neverland • José Rivera The Motorcycle Diaries

Golden Globe Awards

DRAMA: **The Aviator**
COMEDY/MUSICAL: **Sideways**
FOREIGN LANGUAGE FILM: **The Sea Inside**
DIRECTOR: **Clint Eastwood** Million Dollar Baby
ACTOR, DRAMA: **Leonardo DiCaprio** The Aviator
ACTRESS, DRAMA: **Hilary Swank** Million Dollar Baby
ACTOR, COMEDY/MUSICAL: **Jamie Foxx** Ray
ACTRESS, COMEDY/MUSICAL: **Annette Bening** Being Julia
SUPPORTING ACTOR: **Clive Owen** Closer
SUPPORTING ACTRESS: **Natalie Portman** Closer
SCREENPLAY: **Alexander Payne, Jim Taylor** Sideways

Cannes Film Festival

PALME D'OR: **Fahrenheit 9/11**
DIRECTOR: **Tony Gatlif** Exiles
ACTOR: **Yuya Yagira** Nobody Knows
ACTRESS: **Maggie Cheung** Clean
SCREENPLAY: **Jean-Pierre Bacri, Agnès Jaoui** Look at Me

Berlin International Film Festival

GOLDEN BEAR: **Head-On**
SILVER BEAR, DIRECTOR: **Kim Ki-Duk** Samaritan Girl
SILVER BEAR, ACTOR: **Daniel Hendler** Lost Embrace
SILVER BEAR, ACTRESS: **Catalina Sandino Moreno** Maria Full of Grace • Charlize Theron Monster

2005

British Academy Film Awards

FILM: **Brokeback Mountain** • Capote • The Constant Gardener • Crash • Good Night, and Good Luck.

FOREIGN LANGUAGE FILM: **The Beat That My Heart Skipped** • Le Grand Voyage • Kung Fu Hustle • Merry Christmas • Tsotsi
ALEXANDER KORDA AWARD, BRITISH FILM: **Wallace & Gromit in The Curse of the Were-Rabbit** • A Cock and Bull Story • The Constant Gardener • Festival • Pride & Prejudice
DAVID LEAN AWARD, DIRECTOR: **Ang Lee** Brokeback Mountain • George Clooney Good Night, and Good Luck. • Paul Haggis Crash • Fernando Meirelles The Constant Gardener • Bennett Miller Capote
ACTOR: **Philip Seymour Hoffman** Capote • Ralph Fiennes The Constant Gardener • Heath Ledger Brokeback Mountain • Joaquin Phoenix Walk the Line • David Strathairn Good Night, and Good Luck.
ACTRESS: **Reese Witherspoon** Walk the Line • Judi Dench Mrs Henderson Presents • Charlize Theron North Country • Rachel Weisz The Constant Gardener • Zhang Ziyi Memoirs of a Geisha
SUPPORTING ACTOR: **Jake Gyllenhaal** Brokeback Mountain • Don Cheadle Crash • George Clooney Good Night, and Good Luck. • George Clooney Syriana • Matt Dillon Crash
SUPPORTING ACTRESS: **Thandie Newton** Crash • Brenda Blethyn Pride & Prejudice • Catherine Keener Capote • Frances McDormand North Country • Michelle Williams Brokeback Mountain
ORIGINAL SCREENPLAY: **Paul Haggis, Bobby Moresco** Crash • Cliff Hollingsworth, Akiva Goldsman Cinderella Man • George Clooney, Grant Heslov Good Night, and Good Luck. • Terry George, Keir Pearson Hotel Rwanda • Martin Sherman Mrs Henderson Presents
ADAPTED SCREENPLAY: **Larry McMurtry, Diana Ossana** Brokeback Mountain • Dan Futterman Capote • Jeffrey Caine The Constant Gardener • Josh Olson A History of Violence • Deborah Moggach Pride & Prejudice

Academy Awards

PICTURE: **Crash** • Brokeback Mountain • Capote • Good Night, and Good Luck. • Munich
FOREIGN LANGUAGE FILM: **Tsotsi** • Don't Tell • Merry Christmas • Paradise Now • Sophie Scholl: the Final Days
DIRECTOR: **Ang Lee** Brokeback Mountain • George Clooney Good Night, and Good Luck. • Paul Haggis Crash • Bennett Miller Capote • Steven Spielberg Munich
ACTOR: **Philip Seymour Hoffman** Capote • Terrence Howard Hustle & Flow • Heath Ledger Brokeback Mountain • Joaquin Phoenix Walk the Line • David Strathairn Good Night, and Good Luck.
ACTRESS: **Reese Witherspoon** Walk the Line • Judi Dench Mrs Henderson Presents • Felicity Huffman Transamerica • Keira Knightley Pride & Prejudice • Charlize Theron North Country
SUPPORTING ACTOR: **George Clooney** Syriana • Matt Dillon Crash • Paul Giamatti Cinderella Man • Jake Gyllenhaal Brokeback Mountain • William Hurt A History of Violence
SUPPORTING ACTRESS: **Rachel Weisz** The Constant Gardener • Amy Adams Junebug • Catherine Keener Capote • Frances McDormand North Country • Michelle Williams Brokeback Mountain
ORIGINAL SCREENPLAY: **Paul Haggis, Bobby Moresco** Crash • George Clooney, Grant Heslov Good Night, and Good Luck. • Woody Allen Match Point • Noah Baumbach The Squid and the Whale
ADAPTED SCREENPLAY: Stephen Gaghan Syriana • **Larry McMurtry, Diana Ossana** Brokeback Mountain • Dan Futterman Capote • Jeffrey Caine The Constant Gardener • Josh Olson A History of Violence • Tony Kushner, Eric Roth Munich

Golden Globe Awards

DRAMA: **Brokeback Mountain**
COMEDY/MUSICAL: **Walk the Line**
FOREIGN LANGUAGE FILM: **Paradise Now**
DIRECTOR: **Ang Lee** Brokeback Mountain
ACTOR, DRAMA: **Philip Seymour Hoffman** Capote
ACTRESS, DRAMA: **Felicity Huffman** Transamerica
ACTOR, COMEDY/MUSICAL: **Joaquin Phoenix** Walk the Line
ACTRESS, COMEDY/MUSICAL: **Reese Witherspoon** Walk the Line
SUPPORTING ACTOR: **George Clooney** Syriana
SUPPORTING ACTRESS: **Rachel Weisz** The Constant Gardener
SCREENPLAY: **Larry McMurtry, Diana Ossana** Brokeback Mountain

Cannes Film Festival

PALME D'OR: **L'Enfant**
DIRECTOR: **Michael Haneke** Hidden
ACTOR: **Tommy Lee Jones** The Three Burials of Melquiades Estrada
ACTRESS: **Hanna Laslo** Free Zone
SCREENPLAY: **Guillermo Arriaga** The Three Burials of Melquiades Estrada

Berlin International Film Festival

GOLDEN BEAR: **U-Carmen e-Khayelitsha**
SILVER BEAR, DIRECTOR: **Marc Rothemund** Sophie Scholl: the Final Days
SILVER BEAR, ACTOR: **Lou Pucci** Thumbsucker
SILVER BEAR, ACTRESS: **Julia Jentsch** Sophie Scholl: the Final Days

2006

British Academy Film Awards

FILM: **The Queen** • Babel • The Departed • The Last King of Scotland • Little Miss Sunshine
FOREIGN LANGUAGE FILM: **Pan's Labyrinth** • Apocalypto • Black Book • Rang De Basanti • Volver
ALEXANDER KORDA AWARD, BRITISH FILM: **The Last King of Scotland** • Casino Royale • Notes on a Scandal • The Queen • United 93

DAVID LEAN AWARD, DIRECTOR: Paul Greengrass *United 93* • Jonathan Dayton, Valerie Faris *Little Miss Sunshine* • Stephen Frears *The Queen* • Alejandro González Iñárritu *Babel* • Martin Scorsese *The Departed*
ACTOR: Forest Whitaker *The Last King of Scotland* • Daniel Craig *Casino Royale* • Leonardo DiCaprio *The Departed* • Richard Griffiths *The History Boys* • Peter O'Toole *Venus*
ACTRESS: Helen Mirren *The Queen* • Penélope Cruz *Volver* • Judi Dench *Notes on a Scandal* • Meryl Streep *The Devil Wears Prada* • Kate Winslet *Little Children*
SUPPORTING ACTOR: Alan Arkin *Little Miss Sunshine* • James McAvoy *The Last King of Scotland* • Jack Nicholson *The Departed* • Leslie Phillips *Venus* • Michael Sheen *The Queen*
SUPPORTING ACTRESS: Jennifer Hudson *Dreamgirls* • Emily Blunt *The Devil Wears Prada* • Abigail Breslin, Toni Collette *Little Miss Sunshine* • Frances de la Tour *The History Boys*
ORIGINAL SCREENPLAY: Michael Arndt *Little Miss Sunshine* • Guillermo Arriaga *Babel* • Guillermo del Toro *Pan's Labyrinth* • Peter Morgan *The Queen* • Paul Greengrass *United 93*
ADAPTED SCREENPLAY: Jeremy Brock, Peter Morgan *The Last King of Scotland* • Neal Purvis, Robert Wade, Paul Haggis *Casino Royale* • William Monahan *The Departed* • Aline Brosh McKenna *The Devil Wears Prada* • Patrick Marber *Notes on a Scandal*

Academy Awards

PICTURE: The Departed • *Babel* • *Letters from Iwo Jima* • *Little Miss Sunshine* • *The Queen*
FOREIGN LANGUAGE FILM: The Lives of Others • *After the Wedding* • *Days of Glory* • *Pan's Labyrinth* • *Water*
DIRECTOR: Martin Scorsese *The Departed* • Clint Eastwood *Letters from Iwo Jima* • Stephen Frears *The Queen* • Paul Greengrass *United 93* • Alejandro González Iñárritu *Babel*
ACTOR: Forest Whitaker *The Last King of Scotland* • Leonardo DiCaprio *Blood Diamond* • Ryan Gosling *Half Nelson* • Peter O'Toole *Venus* • Will Smith *The Pursuit of Happyness*
ACTRESS: Helen Mirren *The Queen* • Penélope Cruz *Volver* • Judi Dench *Notes on a Scandal* • Meryl Streep *The Devil Wears Prada* • Kate Winslet *Little Children*
SUPPORTING ACTOR: Alan Arkin *Little Miss Sunshine* • Jackie Earle Haley *Little Children* • Djimon Hounsou *Blood Diamond* • Eddie Murphy *Dreamgirls* • Mark Wahlberg *The Departed*
SUPPORTING ACTRESS: Jennifer Hudson *Dreamgirls* • Adriana Barraza *Babel* • Cate Blanchett *Notes on a Scandal* • Abigail Breslin *Little Miss Sunshine* • Rinko Kikuchi *Babel*
ORIGINAL SCREENPLAY: Michael Arndt *Little Miss Sunshine* • Guillermo Arriaga *Babel* • Iris Yamashita *Letters from Iwo Jima* • Peter Morgan *The Queen* • Guillermo del Toro *Pan's Labyrinth*
ADAPTED SCREENPLAY: William Monahan *The Departed* • Sacha Baron Cohen, Anthony Hines, Peter Baynham, Dan Mazer *Borat: Cultural Learnings of America for Make Benefit Glorious Nation of Kazakhstan* • Alfonso Cuarón, Timothy J Sexton, David Arata, Mark Fergus, Hawk Ostby *Children of Men* • Todd Field, Tom Perrotta *Little Children* • Patrick Marber *Notes on a Scandal*

Golden Globe Awards

DRAMA: Babel
COMEDY/MUSICAL: Dreamgirls
FOREIGN LANGUAGE FILM: Letters from Iwo Jima
DIRECTOR: Martin Scorsese *The Departed*
ACTOR, DRAMA: Forest Whitaker *The Last King of Scotland*
ACTRESS, DRAMA: Helen Mirren *The Queen*
ACTOR, COMEDY/MUSICAL: Sacha Baron Cohen *Borat: Cultural Learnings of America for Make Benefit Glorious Nation of Kazakhstan*
ACTRESS, COMEDY/MUSICAL: Meryl Streep *The Devil Wears Prada*
SUPPORTING ACTOR: Eddie Murphy *Dreamgirls*
SUPPORTING ACTRESS: Jennifer Hudson *Dreamgirls*
SCREENPLAY: Peter Morgan *The Queen*

Cannes Film Festival

PALME D'OR: The Wind That Shakes the Barley
DIRECTOR: Alejandro González Iñárritu *Babel*
ACTOR: Bernard Blancan, Sami Bouajila, Jamel Debbouze, Samy Naceri, Roschdy Zem *Indigènes*
ACTRESS: Yohana Cobo, Penélope Cruz, Lola Dueñas, Chus Lampreave, Carmen Maura, Blanca Portillo *Volver*
SCREENPLAY: Pedro Almodóvar *Volver*

Berlin International Film Festival

GOLDEN BEAR: Grbavica
SILVER BEAR, DIRECTOR: Mat Whitecross, Michael Winterbottom *The Road to Guantanamo*
SILVER BEAR, ACTOR: Moritz Bleibtreu *Atomised*
SILVER BEAR, ACTRESS: Sandra Hüller *Requiem*

2007

British Academy Film Awards

FILM: Atonement • *American Gangster* • *The Lives of Others* • *No Country for Old Men* • *There Will Be Blood*
FOREIGN LANGUAGE FILM: The Lives of Others • *The Diving-Bell and the Butterfly* • *The Kite Runner* • *Lust, Caution* • *La Vie en Rose*
ALEXANDER KORDA AWARD, BRITISH FILM: This Is England • *Atonement* • *The Bourne Ultimatum* • *Control* • *Eastern Promises*
DAVID LEAN AWARD, DIRECTOR: Ethan Coen, Joel Coen *No Country for Old Men* • Paul Thomas Anderson *There Will Be Blood* • Paul Greengrass *The Bourne Ultimatum* • Florian Henckel von Donnersmarck *The Lives of Others* • Joe Wright *Atonement*
ACTOR: Daniel Day-Lewis *There Will Be Blood* • George Clooney *Michael Clayton* • James McAvoy *Atonement* • Viggo Mortensen *Eastern Promises* • Ulrich Mühe *The Lives of Others*

ACTRESS: Marion Cotillard *La Vie en Rose* • Cate Blanchett *Elizabeth: the Golden Age* • Julie Christie *Away from Her* • Keira Knightley *Atonement* • Ellen Page *Juno*
SUPPORTING ACTOR: Javier Bardem *No Country for Old Men* • Paul Dano *There Will Be Blood* • Tommy Lee Jones *No Country for Old Men* • Philip Seymour Hoffman *Charlie Wilson's War* • Tom Wilkinson *Michael Clayton*
SUPPORTING ACTRESS: Tilda Swinton *Michael Clayton* • Cate Blanchett *I'm Not There.* • Kelly Macdonald *No Country for Old Men* • Samantha Morton *Control* • Saoirse Ronan *Atonement*
ORIGINAL SCREENPLAY: Diablo Cody *Juno* • Steven Zaillian *American Gangster* • Florian Henckel von Donnersmarck *The Lives of Others* • Tony Gilroy *Michael Clayton* • Shane Meadows *This Is England*
ADAPTED SCREENPLAY: Ronald Harwood *The Diving-Bell and the Butterfly* • Christopher Hampton *Atonement* • David Benioff *The Kite Runner* • Ethan Coen, Joel Coen *No Country for Old Men* • Paul Thomas Anderson *There Will Be Blood*

Academy Awards

PICTURE: No Country for Old Men • *Atonement* • *Juno* • *Michael Clayton* • *There Will Be Blood*
FOREIGN LANGUAGE FILM: The Counterfeiters • *Beaufort* • *Mongol* • *Katyn* • *12*
DIRECTOR: Ethan Coen, Joel Coen *No Country for Old Men* • Paul Thomas Anderson *There Will Be Blood* • Tony Gilroy *Michael Clayton* • Jason Reitman *Juno* • Julian Schnabel *The Diving-Bell and the Butterfly*
ACTOR: Daniel Day-Lewis *There Will Be Blood* • George Clooney *Michael Clayton* • Johnny Depp *Sweeney Todd: the Demon Barber of Fleet Street* • Tommy Lee Jones *In the Valley of Elah* • Viggo Mortensen *Eastern Promises*
ACTRESS: Marion Cotillard *La Vie en Rose* • Cate Blanchett *Elizabeth: the Golden Age* • Julie Christie *Away from Her* • Laura Linney *The Savages* • Ellen Page *Juno*
SUPPORTING ACTOR: Javier Bardem *No Country for Old Men* • Casey Affleck *The Assassination of Jesse James by the Coward Robert Ford* • Philip Seymour Hoffman *Charlie Wilson's War* • Hal Holbrook *Into the Wild* • Tom Wilkinson *Michael Clayton*
SUPPORTING ACTRESS: Tilda Swinton *Michael Clayton* • Cate Blanchett *I'm Not There.* • Ruby Dee *American Gangster* • Saoirse Ronan *Atonement* • Amy Ryan *Gone Baby Gone*
ORIGINAL SCREENPLAY: Diablo Cody *Juno* • Nancy Oliver *Lars and the Real Girl* • Tony Gilroy *Michael Clayton* • Brad Bird *Ratatouille* • Tamara Jenkins *The Savages*
ADAPTED SCREENPLAY: Ethan Coen, Joel Coen *No Country for Old Men* • Christopher Hampton *Atonement* • Sarah Polley *Away from Her* • Ronald Harwood *The Diving-Bell and the Butterfly* • Paul Thomas Anderson *There Will Be Blood*

Golden Globe Awards

DRAMA: Atonement
COMEDY/MUSICAL: Sweeney Todd: the Demon Barber of Fleet Street
FOREIGN LANGUAGE FILM: The Diving-Bell and the Butterfly
DIRECTOR: Julian Schnabel *The Diving-Bell and the Butterfly*
ACTOR, DRAMA: Daniel Day-Lewis *There Will Be Blood*
ACTRESS, DRAMA: Julie Christie *Away from Her*
ACTOR, COMEDY/MUSICAL: Johnny Depp *Sweeney Todd: the Demon Barber of Fleet Street*
ACTRESS, COMEDY/MUSICAL: Marion Cotillard *La Vie en Rose*
SUPPORTING ACTOR: Javier Bardem *No Country for Old Men*
SUPPORTING ACTRESS: Cate Blanchett *I'm Not There.*
SCREENPLAY: Ethan Coen, Joel Coen *No Country for Old Men*

Cannes Film Festival

PALME D'OR: 4 Months, 3 Weeks and 2 Days
DIRECTOR: Julian Schnabel *The Diving Bell and the Butterfly*
ACTOR: Konstantin Lavronenko *The Banishment*
ACTRESS: Jeon Do-yeon *Secret Sunshine*
SCREENPLAY: Fatih Akin *The Edge of Heaven*

Berlin International Film Festival

GOLDEN BEAR: Tuya's Marriage
SILVER BEAR, DIRECTOR: Joseph Cedar *Beaufort*
SILVER BEAR, ACTOR: Julio Chávez *The Other*
SILVER BEAR, ACTRESS: Nina Hoss *Yella*

2008

British Academy Film Awards

FILM: Slumdog Millionaire • *The Curious Case of Benjamin Button* • *Frost/Nixon* • *Milk* • *The Reader*
FOREIGN LANGUAGE FILM: I've Loved You So Long • *The Baader Meinhof Complex* • *Gomorrah* • *Persepolis* • *Waltz with Bashir*
ALEXANDER KORDA AWARD, BRITISH FILM: Man on Wire • *Hunger* • *In Bruges* • *Mamma Mia!* • *Slumdog Millionaire*
DAVID LEAN AWARD, DIRECTOR: Danny Boyle *Slumdog Millionaire* • Stephen Daldry *The Reader* • Clint Eastwood *Changeling* • David Fincher *The Curious Case of Benjamin Button* • Ron Howard *Frost/Nixon*
ACTOR: Mickey Rourke *The Wrestler* • Frank Langella *Frost/Nixon* • Dev Patel *Slumdog Millionaire* • Sean Penn *Milk* • Brad Pitt *The Curious Case of Benjamin Button*
ACTRESS: Kate Winslet *The Reader* • Angelina Jolie *Changeling* • Kristin Scott Thomas *I've Loved You So Long* • Meryl Streep *Doubt* • Kate Winslet *Revolutionary Road*
SUPPORTING ACTOR: Heath Ledger *The Dark Knight* • Robert Downey Jr *Tropic Thunder* • Brendan Gleeson *In Bruges* • Philip Seymour Hoffman *Doubt* • Brad Pitt *Burn after Reading*
SUPPORTING ACTRESS: Penélope Cruz *Vicky Cristina Barcelona* • Amy Adams *Doubt* • Freida Pinto *Slumdog Millionaire* • Tilda Swinton *Burn after Reading* • Marisa Tomei *The Wrestler*
ORIGINAL SCREENPLAY: Martin McDonagh *In Bruges* • Ethan Coen, Joel Coen *Burn after Reading* • Philippe Claudel *I've*

Loved You So Long • Dustin Lance Black *Milk* • J Michael Straczynski *Changeling*
ADAPTED SCREENPLAY: Simon Beaufoy *Slumdog Millionaire* • Eric Roth *The Curious Case of Benjamin Button* • Peter Morgan *Frost/Nixon* • David Hare *The Reader* • Justin Haythe *Revolutionary Road*

Academy Awards

PICTURE: Slumdog Millionaire • *The Curious Case of Benjamin Button* • *Frost/Nixon* • *Milk* • *The Reader*
FOREIGN LANGUAGE FILM: Departures • *The Baader Meinhof Complex* • *The Class* • *Revanche* • *Waltz with Bashir*
DIRECTOR: Danny Boyle *Slumdog Millionaire* • Stephen Daldry *The Reader* • David Fincher *The Curious Case of Benjamin Button* • Ron Howard *Frost/Nixon* • Gus Van Sant *Milk*
ACTOR: Sean Penn *Milk* • Richard Jenkins *The Visitor* • Frank Langella *Frost/Nixon* • Brad Pitt *The Curious Case of Benjamin Button* • Mickey Rourke *The Wrestler*
ACTRESS: Kate Winslet *The Reader* • Anne Hathaway *Rachel Getting Married* • Angelina Jolie *Changeling* • Melissa Leo *Frozen River* • Meryl Streep *Doubt*
SUPPORTING ACTOR: Heath Ledger *The Dark Knight* • Josh Brolin *Milk* • Robert Downey Jr *Tropic Thunder* • Philip Seymour Hoffman *Doubt* • Michael Shannon *Revolutionary Road*
SUPPORTING ACTRESS: Penélope Cruz *Vicky Cristina Barcelona* • Amy Adams, Viola Davis *Doubt* • Taraji P Henson *The Curious Case of Benjamin Button* • Marisa Tomei *The Wrestler*
ORIGINAL SCREENPLAY: Dustin Lance Black *Milk* • Courtney Hunt *Frozen River* • Mike Leigh *Happy-Go-Lucky* • Martin McDonagh *In Bruges* • Andrew Stanton, Jim Reardon, Pete Docter *WALL-E*
ADAPTED SCREENPLAY: Simon Beaufoy *Slumdog Millionaire* • Eric Roth, Robin Swicord *The Curious Case of Benjamin Button* • John Patrick Shanley *Doubt* • Peter Morgan *Frost/Nixon* • David Hare *The Reader*

Golden Globe Awards

DRAMA: Slumdog Millionaire
COMEDY/MUSICAL: Vicky Cristina Barcelona
FOREIGN LANGUAGE FILM: Waltz with Bashir
DIRECTOR: Danny Boyle *Slumdog Millionaire*
ACTOR, DRAMA: Mickey Rourke *The Wrestler*
ACTRESS, DRAMA: Kate Winslet *Revolutionary Road*
ACTOR, COMEDY/MUSICAL: Colin Farrell *In Bruges*
ACTRESS, COMEDY/MUSICAL: Sally Hawkins *Happy-Go-Lucky*
SUPPORTING ACTOR: Heath Ledger *The Dark Knight*
SUPPORTING ACTRESS: Kate Winslet *The Reader*
SCREENPLAY: Simon Beaufoy *Slumdog Millionaire*

Cannes Film Festival

PALME D'OR: The Class
DIRECTOR: Nuri Bilge Ceylan *Three Monkeys*
ACTOR: Benicio Del Toro *Che Part One/Che Part Two*
ACTRESS: Sandra Corveloni *Linha de Passe*
SCREENPLAY: Jean-Pierre Dardenne, Luc Dardenne *The Silence of Lorna*

Berlin International Film Festival

GOLDEN BEAR: The Elite Squad
SILVER BEAR, DIRECTOR: Paul Thomas Anderson *There Will Be Blood*
SILVER BEAR, ACTOR: Reza Naji *The Song of Sparrows*
SILVER BEAR, ACTRESS: Sally Hawkins *Happy-Go-Lucky*

2009

British Academy Film Awards

FILM: The Hurt Locker • *Avatar* • *An Education* • *Precious (Base on Nol by Saf)* (Based on the Novel "Push" by Sapphire) • *Up in the Air*
FOREIGN LANGUAGE FILM: A Prophet • *Broken Embraces* • *Coco avant Chanel* • *Let the Right One In* • *The White Ribbon*
ALEXANDER KORDA AWARD, BRITISH FILM: Fish Tank • *An Education* • *In the Loop* • *Moon* • *Nowhere Boy*
DAVID LEAN AWARD, DIRECTOR: Kathryn Bigelow *The Hurt Locker* • Neill Blomkamp *District 9* • James Cameron *Avatar* • Lone Scherfig *An Education* • Quentin Tarantino *Inglourious Basterds*
ACTOR: Colin Firth *A Single Man* • Jeff Bridges *Crazy Heart* • George Clooney *Up in the Air* • Jeremy Renner *The Hurt Locker* • Andy Serkis *Sex & Drugs & Rock & Roll*
ACTRESS: Carey Mulligan *An Education* • Saoirse Ronan *The Lovely Bones* • Gabourey Sidibe *Precious (Base on Nol by Saf)* (Based on the Novel "Push" by Sapphire) • Meryl Streep *Julie & Julia* • Audrey Tautou *Coco avant Chanel*
SUPPORTING ACTOR: Christoph Waltz *Inglourious Basterds* • Alec Baldwin *It's Complicated* • Christian McKay *Me and Orson Welles* • Alfred Molina *An Education* • Stanley Tucci *The Lovely Bones*
SUPPORTING ACTRESS: Mo'Nique *Precious (Base on Nol by Saf)* (Based on the Novel "Push" by Sapphire) • Anne-Marie Duff *Nowhere Boy* • Vera Farmiga, Anna Kendrick *Up in the Air* • Kristin Scott Thomas *Nowhere Boy*
ORIGINAL SCREENPLAY: Mark Boal *The Hurt Locker* • Jon Lucas, Scott Moore *The Hangover* • Quentin Tarantino *Inglourious Basterds* • Ethan Coen, Joel Coen *A Serious Man* • Bob Peterson, Pete Docter *Up*
ADAPTED SCREENPLAY: Jason Reitman, Sheldon Turner *Up in the Air* • Neill Blomkamp, Terri Tatchell *District 9* • Nick Hornby *An Education* • Jesse Armstrong, Simon Blackwell, Armando Iannucci, Tony Roche *In the Loop* • Geoffrey Fletcher *Precious (Base on Nol by Saf)* (Based on the Novel "Push" by Sapphire)

Academy Awards

PICTURE: The Hurt Locker • *Avatar* • *The Blind Side* • *District 9* • *An Education* • *Inglourious Basterds* • *Precious (Base on Nol by Saf)* (Based on the Novel "Push" by Sapphire) • *A Serious Man* • *Up* • *Up in the Air*

FOREIGN LANGUAGE FILM: **Ajami** • *The Milk of Sorrow* • *A Prophet* • *The Secret in Their Eyes* • *The White Ribbon*
DIRECTOR: **Kathryn Bigelow** *The Hurt Locker* • James Cameron *Avatar* • Lee Daniels *Precious (Base on Nol by Saf) (Based on the Novel "Push" by Sapphire)* • Jason Reitman *Up in the Air* • Quentin Tarantino *Inglourious Basterds*
ACTOR: **Jeff Bridges** *Crazy Heart* • George Clooney *Up in the Air* • Colin Firth *A Single Man* • Morgan Freeman *Invictus* • Jeremy Renner *The Hurt Locker*
ACTRESS: **Sandra Bullock** *The Blind Side* • Helen Mirren *The Last Station* • Carey Mulligan *An Education* • Gabourey Sidibe *Precious (Base on Nol by Saf) (Based on the Novel "Push" by Sapphire)* • Meryl Streep *Julie & Julia*
SUPPORTING ACTOR: **Christoph Waltz** *Inglourious Basterds* • Matt Damon *Invictus* • Woody Harrelson *The Messenger* • Christopher Plummer *The Last Station* • Stanley Tucci *The Lovely Bones*
SUPPORTING ACTRESS: **Mo'Nique** *Precious (Base on Nol by Saf) (Based on the Novel "Push" by Sapphire)* • Penélope Cruz *Nine* • Vera Farmiga *Up in the Air* • Maggie Gyllenhaal *Crazy Heart* • Anna Kendrick *Up in the Air*
ORIGINAL SCREENPLAY: **Mark Boal** *The Hurt Locker* • Quentin Tarantino *Inglourious Basterds* • Alessandro Camon, Oren Moverman *The Messenger* • Ethan Coen, Joel Coen *A Serious Man* • Bob Peterson, Pete Docter, Thomas McCarthy *Up*
ADAPTED SCREENPLAY: **Geoffrey Fletcher** *Precious (Base on Nol by Saf) (Based on the Novel "Push" by Sapphire)* • Neill Blomkamp, Terri Tatchell *District 9* • Nick Hornby *An Education* • Jesse Armstrong, Simon Blackwell, Armando Iannucci, Tony Roche *In the Loop* • Jason Reitman, Sheldon Turner *Up in the Air*

Golden Globe Awards

DRAMA: **Avatar**
COMEDY/MUSICAL: **The Hangover**
FOREIGN LANGUAGE FILM: **The White Ribbon**
DIRECTOR: **James Cameron** *Avatar*
ACTOR, DRAMA: **Jeff Bridges** *Crazy Heart*
ACTRESS, DRAMA: **Sandra Bullock** *The Blind Side*
ACTOR, COMEDY/MUSICAL: **Robert Downey Jr** *Sherlock Holmes*
ACTRESS, COMEDY/MUSICAL: **Meryl Streep** *Julie & Julia*
SUPPORTING ACTOR: **Christoph Waltz** *Inglourious Basterds*
SUPPORTING ACTRESS: **Mo'Nique** *Precious (Base on the Novel "Push" by Sapphire)*
SCREENPLAY: **Jason Reitman, Sheldon Turner** *Up in the Air*

Cannes Film Festival

PALME D'OR: **The White Ribbon**
DIRECTOR: **Brillante Mendoza** *Kinatay*
ACTOR: **Christoph Waltz** *Inglourious Basterds*
ACTRESS: **Charlotte Gainsbourg** *Antichrist*
SCREENPLAY: **Lou Ye** *Spring Fever*

Berlin International Film Festival

GOLDEN BEAR: **The Milk of Sorrow**
SILVER BEAR, DIRECTOR: **Asghar Farhadi** *About Elly*
SILVER BEAR, ACTOR: **Sotigui Kouyate** *London River*
SILVER BEAR, ACTRESS: **Birgit Minichmayr** *Everyone Else*

2010

British Academy Film Awards

FILM: **The King's Speech** • *Black Swan* • *Inception* • *The Social Network* • *True Grit*
FOREIGN LANGUAGE FILM: **The Girl with the Dragon Tattoo** • *Biutiful* • *I Am Love* • *Of Gods and Men* • *The Secret in Their Eyes*
ALEXANDER KORDA AWARD, BRITISH FILM: **The King's Speech** • *127 Hours* • *Another Year* • *Four Lions* • *Made in Dagenham*
DAVID LEAN AWARD, DIRECTOR: **David Fincher** *The Social Network* • Darren Aronofsky *Black Swan* • Danny Boyle *127 Hours* • Tom Hooper *The King's Speech* • Christopher Nolan *Inception*
ACTOR: **Colin Firth** *The King's Speech* • Javier Bardem *Biutiful* • Jeff Bridges *True Grit* • Jesse Eisenberg *The Social Network* • James Franco *127 Hours*
ACTRESS: **Natalie Portman** *Black Swan* • Annette Bening, Julianne Moore *The Kids Are All Right* • Noomi Rapace *The Girl with the Dragon Tattoo* • Hailee Steinfeld *True Grit*
SUPPORTING ACTOR: **Geoffrey Rush** *The King's Speech* • Christian Bale *The Fighter* • Andrew Garfield *The Social Network* • Pete Postlethwaite *The Town* • Mark Ruffalo *The Kids Are All Right*
SUPPORTING ACTRESS: **Helena Bonham Carter** *The King's Speech* • Amy Adams *The Fighter* • Barbara Hershey *Black Swan* • Lesley Manville *Another Year* • Miranda Richardson *Made in Dagenham*
ORIGINAL SCREENPLAY: **David Seidler** *The King's Speech* • Mark Heyman, Andres Heinz, John J McLaughlin *Black Swan* • Eric Johnson, Scott Silver, Paul Tamasy *The Fighter* • Christopher No an *Inception* • Lisa Cholodenko, Stuart Blumberg *The Kids Are All Right*
ADAPTED SCREENPLAY: **Aaron Sorkin** *The Social Network* • Danny Boyle, Simon Beaufoy *127 Hours* • Nikolaj Arcel, Rasmus Heisterberg *The Girl with the Dragon Tattoo* • Michael Arndt *Toy Story 3* • Ethan Coen, Joel Coen *True Grit*

Academy Awards

PICTURE: **The King's Speech** • *Black Swan* • *The Fighter* • *Inception* • *The Kids Are All Right* • *127 Hours* • *The Social Network* • *Toy Story 3* • *True Grit* • *Winter's Bone*
FOREIGN LANGUAGE FILM: **In a Better World** • *Biutiful* • *Dogtooth* • *Incendies* • *Outside the Law*
DIRECTOR: **Tom Hooper** *The King's Speech* • Darren Aronofsky *Black Swan* • David O Russell *The Fighter* • David Fincher *The Social Network* • Ethan Coen, Joel Coen *True Grit*
ACTOR: **Colin Firth** *The King's Speech* • Javier Bardem *Biutiful* • Jeff Bridges *True Grit* • Jesse Eisenberg *The Social Network* • James Franco *127 Hours*

ACTRESS: **Natalie Portman** *Black Swan* • Annette Bening *The Kids Are All Right* • Nicole Kidman *Rabbit Hole* • Jennifer Lawrence *Winter's Bone* • Michelle Williams *Blue Valentine*
SUPPORTING ACTOR: **Christian Bale** *The Fighter* • John Hawkes *Winter's Bone* • Jeremy Renner *The Town* • Mark Ruffalo *The Kids Are All Right* • Geoffrey Rush *The King's Speech*
SUPPORTING ACTRESS: **Melissa Leo** *The Fighter* • Amy Adams *The Fighter* • Helena Bonham Carter *The King's Speech* • Hailee Steinfeld *True Grit* • Jacki Weaver *Animal Kingdom*
ORIGINAL SCREENPLAY: **David Seidler** *The King's Speech* • Mike Leigh *Another Year* • Eric Johnson, Scott Silver, Paul Tamasy, Keith Dorrington *The Fighter* • Christopher Nolan *Inception* • Lisa Cholodenko, Stuart Blumberg *The Kids Are All Right*
ADAPTED SCREENPLAY: **Aaron Sorkin** *The Social Network* • Danny Boyle, Simon Beaufoy *127 Hours* • Michael Arndt, John Lasseter, Andrew Stanton, Lee Unkrich *Toy Story 3* • Ethan Coen, Joel Coen *True Grit* • Debra Granik, Anne Rosellini *Winter's Bone*

Golden Globe Awards

DRAMA: **The Social Network**
COMEDY/MUSICAL: **The Kids Are All Right**
FOREIGN LANGUAGE FILM: **In a Better World**
DIRECTOR: **David Fincher** *The Social Network*
ACTOR, DRAMA: **Colin Firth** *The King's Speech*
ACTRESS, DRAMA: **Natalie Portman** *Black Swan*
ACTOR, COMEDY/MUSICAL: **Paul Giamatti** *Barney's Version*
ACTRESS, COMEDY/MUSICAL: **Annette Bening** *The Kids Are All Right*
SUPPORTING ACTOR: **Christian Bale** *The Fighter*
SUPPORTING ACTRESS: **Melissa Leo** *The Fighter*
SCREENPLAY: **Aaron Sorkin** *The Social Network*

Cannes Film Festival

PALME D'OR: **Uncle Boonmee Who Can Recall His Past Lives**
DIRECTOR: **Mathieu Amalric** *On Tour*
ACTOR: **Javier Bardem** *Biutiful* • **Elio Germano** *Our Life*
ACTRESS: **Juliette Binoche** *Certified Copy*
SCREENPLAY: **Lee Chang-dong** *Poetry*

Berlin International Film Festival

GOLDEN BEAR: **Bal**
SILVER BEAR, DIRECTOR: **Roman Polanski** *The Ghost*
SILVER BEAR, ACTOR: **Grigoriy Dobrygin** *How I Ended This Summer*
SILVER BEAR, ACTRESS: **Shinobu Terajima** *Caterpillar*

2011

British Academy Film Awards

FILM: **The Artist** • *The Descendants* • *Drive* • *The Help* • *Tinker Tailor Soldier Spy*
FOREIGN LANGUAGE FILM: **The Skin I Live In** • *Incendies* • *Pina* • *Potiche* • *Nader and Simin, a Separation*
ALEXANDER KORDA AWARD, BRITISH FILM: **Tinker Tailor Soldier Spy** • *My Week with Marilyn* • *Senna* • *Shame* • *We Need to Talk about Kevin*
DAVID LEAN AWARD, DIRECTOR: **Michel Hazanavicius** *The Artist* • Tomas Alfredson *Tinker Tailor Soldier Spy* • Lynne Ramsay *We Need to Talk about Kevin* • Nicolas Winding Refn *Drive* • Martin Scorsese *Hugo*
ACTOR: **Jean Dujardin** *The Artist* • George Clooney *The Descendants* • Michael Fassbender *Shame* • Gary Oldman *Tinker Tailor Soldier Spy* • Brad Pitt *Moneyball*
ACTRESS: **Meryl Streep** *The Iron Lady* • Bérénice Bejo *The Artist* • Viola Davis *The Help* • Tilda Swinton *We Need to Talk about Kevin* • Michelle Williams *My Week with Marilyn*
SUPPORTING ACTOR: **Christopher Plummer** *Beginners* • Kenneth Branagh *My Week with Marilyn* • Jim Broadbent *The Iron Lady* • Jonah Hill *Moneyball* • Philip Seymour Hoffman *The Ides of March*
SUPPORTING ACTRESS: **Octavia Spencer** *The Help* • Jessica Chastain *The Help* • Judi Dench *My Week with Marilyn* • Melissa McCarthy *Bridesmaids* • Carey Mullligan *Drive*
ORIGINAL SCREENPLAY: **Michel Hazanavicius** *The Artist* • Annie Mumolo, Kristen Wiig *Bridesmaids* • John Michael McDonagh *The Guard* • Abi Morgan *The Iron Lady* • Woody Allen *Midnight in Paris*
ADAPTED SCREENPLAY: **Bridget O'Connor, Peter Straughan** *Tinker Tailor Soldier Spy* • Alexander Payne, Nat Faxon, Jim Rash *The Descendants* • Tate Taylor *The Help* • George Clooney, Grant Heslov, Beau Willimon *The Ides of March* • Steven Zaillian, Aaron Sorkin *Moneyball*

Academy Awards

PICTURE: **The Artist** • *The Descendants* • *Extremely Loud & Incredibly Close* • *The Help* • *Hugo* • *Midnight in Paris* • *Moneyball* • *The Tree of Life* • *War Horse*
FOREIGN LANGUAGE FILM: **Nader and Simin, a Separation** • *Bullhead* • *Footnote* • *In Darkness* • *Monsieur Lazhar*
DIRECTOR: **Michel Hazanavicius** *The Artist* • Woody Allen *Midnight in Paris* • Terrence Malick *The Tree of Life* • Alexander Payne *The Descendants* • Martin Scorsese *Hugo*
ACTOR: **Jean Dujardin** *The Artist* • Demian Bichir *A Better Life* • George Clooney *The Descendants* • Gary Oldman *Tinker Tailor Soldier Spy* • Brad Pitt *Moneyball*
ACTRESS: **Meryl Streep** *The Iron Lady* • Glenn Close *Albert Nobbs* • Viola Davis *The Help* • Rooney Mara *The Girl with the Dragon Tattoo* • Michelle Williams *My Week with Marilyn*
SUPPORTING ACTOR: **Christopher Plummer** *Beginners* • Kenneth Branagh *My Week with Marilyn* • Jonah Hill *Moneyball* • Nick Nolte *Warrior* • Max von Sydow *Extremely Loud & Incredibly Close*
SUPPORTING ACTRESS: **Octavia Spencer** *The Help* • Bérénice Bejo *The Artist* • Jessica Chastain *The Help* • Melissa McCarthy *Bridesmaids* • Janet McTeer *Albert Nobbs*
ORIGINAL SCREENPLAY: **Woody Allen** *Midnight in Paris* • Michel Hazanavicius *The Artist* • Annie Mumolo, Kristen Wiig *Bridesmaids* • J C Chandor *Margin Call* • Asghar Farhadi *Nader and Simin, a Separation*

ADAPTED SCREENPLAY: **Alexander Payne, Nat Faxon, Jim Rash** *The Descendants* • John Logan *Hugo* • George Clooney, Grant Heslov, Beau Willimon *The Ides of March* • Steven Zaillian, Aaron Sorkin, Stan Chervin *Moneyball* • Bridget O'Connor, Peter Straughan *Tinker Tailor Soldier Spy*

Golden Globe Awards

DRAMA: **The Descendants**
COMEDY/MUSICAL: **The Artist**
FOREIGN LANGUAGE FILM: **Nader and Simin, a Separation**
DIRECTOR: **Martin Scorsese** *Hugo*
ACTOR, DRAMA: **George Clooney** *The Descendants*
ACTRESS, DRAMA: **Meryl Streep** *The Iron Lady*
ACTOR, COMEDY/MUSICAL: **Jean Dujardin** *The Artist*
ACTRESS, COMEDY/MUSICAL: **Michelle Williams** *My Week with Marilyn*
SUPPORTING ACTOR: **Christopher Plummer** *Beginners*
SUPPORTING ACTRESS: **Octavia Spencer** *The Help*
SCREENPLAY: **Woody Allen** *Midnight in Paris*

Cannes Film Festival

PALME D'OR: **The Tree of Life**
DIRECTOR: **Nicolas Winding Refn** *Drive*
ACTOR: **Jean Dujardin** *The Artist*
ACTRESS: **Kirsten Dunst** *Melancholia*
SCREENPLAY: **Joseph Cedar** *Footnote*

Berlin International Film Festival

GOLDEN BEAR: **Nader and Simin, a Separation**
SILVER BEAR, DIRECTOR: **Ulrich Köhler** *Sleeping Sickness*
SILVER BEAR, ACTOR: **Peyman Moaadi, Ali-Asghar Shabazi, Babak Karimi** *Nader and Simin, a Separation*
SILVER BEAR, ACTRESS: **Leila Hatami, Sareh Bayat, Sarina Farhadi** *Nader and Simin, a Separation*

2012

British Academy Film Awards

FILM: **Argo** • *Life of Pi* • *Lincoln* • *Les Misérables* • *Zero Dark Thirty*
FOREIGN LANGUAGE FILM: **Amour** • *Headhunters* • *The Hunt* • *Rust and Bone* • *Untouchable*
ALEXANDER KORDA AWARD, BRITISH FILM: **Skyfall** • *Anna Karenina* • *The Best Exotic Marigold Hotel* • *Les Misérables* • *Seven Psychopaths*
DAVID LEAN AWARD, DIRECTOR: **Ben Affleck** *Argo* • Kathryn Bigelow *Zero Dark Thirty* • Michael Haneke *Amour* • Ang Lee *Life of Pi* • Quentin Tarantino *Django Unchained*
ACTOR: **Daniel Day-Lewis** *Lincoln* • Ben Affleck *Argo* • Bradley Cooper *Silver Linings Playbook* • Hugh Jackman *Les Misérables* • Joaquin Phoenix *The Master*
ACTRESS: **Emmanuelle Riva** *Amour* • Jessica Chastain *Zero Dark Thirty* • Marion Cotillard *Rust and Bone* • Jennifer Lawrence (2) *Silver Linings Playbook* • Helen Mirren *Hitchcock*
SUPPORTING ACTOR: **Christoph Waltz** *Django Unchained* • Alan Arkin *Argo* • Javier Bardem *Skyfall* • Philip Seymour Hoffman *The Master* • Tommy Lee Jones *Lincoln*
SUPPORTING ACTRESS: **Anne Hathaway** *Les Misérables* • Amy Adams *The Master* • Judi Dench *Skyfall* • Sally Field *Lincoln* • Helen Hunt *The Sessions*
ORIGINAL SCREENPLAY: **Quentin Tarantino** *Django Unchained* • Michael Haneke *Amour* • Paul Thomas Anderson *The Master* • Wes Anderson, Roman Coppola *Moonrise Kingdom* • Mark Boal *Zero Dark Thirty*
ADAPTED SCREENPLAY: **David O Russell** *Silver Linings Playbook* • Chris Terrio *Argo* • Lucy Alibar, Benh Zeitlin *Beasts of the Southern Wild* • David Magee *Life of Pi* • Tony Kushner *Lincoln*

Academy Awards

PICTURE: **Argo** • *Amour* • *Beasts of the Southern Wild* • *Django Unchained* • *Life of Pi* • *Lincoln* • *Les Misérables* • *Silver Linings Playbook* • *Zero Dark Thirty*
FOREIGN LANGUAGE FILM: **Amour** • *Kon-Tiki* • *No* • *A Royal Affair* • *Rebelle*
DIRECTOR: **Ang Lee** *Life of Pi* • Michael Haneke *Amour* • David O Russell *Silver Linings Playbook* • Steven Spielberg *Lincoln* • Benh Zeitlin *Beasts of the Southern Wild*
ACTOR: **Daniel Day-Lewis** *Lincoln* • Bradley Cooper *Silver Linings Playbook* • Hugh Jackman *Les Misérables* • Joaquin Phoenix *The Master* • Denzel Washington *Flight*
ACTRESS: **Jennifer Lawrence (2)** *Silver Linings Playbook* • Jessica Chastain *Zero Dark Thirty* • Emmanuelle Riva *Amour* • Quvenzhané Wallis *Beasts of the Southern Wild* • Naomi Watts *The Impossible*
SUPPORTING ACTOR: **Christoph Waltz** *Django Unchained* • Alan Arkin *Argo* • Robert De Niro *Silver Linings Playbook* • Philip Seymour Hoffman *The Master* • Tommy Lee Jones *Lincoln*
SUPPORTING ACTRESS: **Anne Hathaway** *Les Misérables* • Amy Adams *The Master* • Sally Field *Lincoln* • Helen Hunt *The Sessions* • Jacki Weaver *Silver Linings Playbook*
ORIGINAL SCREENPLAY: **Quentin Tarantino** *Django Unchained* • Michael Haneke *Amour* • John Gatins *Flight* • Wes Anderson, Roman Coppola *Moonrise Kingdom* • Mark Boal *Zero Dark Thirty*
ADAPTED SCREENPLAY: **Chris Terrio** *Argo* • Lucy Alibar, Benh Zeitlin *Beasts of the Southern Wild* • David Magee *Life of Pi* • Tony Kushner *Lincoln* • David O Russell *Silver Linings Playbook*

Golden Globe Awards

DRAMA: **Argo**
COMEDY/MUSICAL: **Les Misérables**
FOREIGN LANGUAGE FILM: **Amour**
DIRECTOR: **Ben Affleck** *Argo*
ACTOR, DRAMA: **Daniel Day-Lewis** *Lincoln*
ACTRESS, DRAMA: **Jessica Chastain** *Zero Dark Thirty*
ACTOR, COMEDY/MUSICAL: **Hugh Jackman** *Les Misérables*
ACTRESS, COMEDY/MUSICAL: **Jennifer Lawrence (2)** *Silver Linings Playbook*

SUPPORTING ACTOR: **Christoph Waltz** *Django Unchained*
SUPPORTING ACTRESS: **Anne Hathaway** *Les Misérables*
SCREENPLAY: **Quentin Tarantino** *Django Unchained*

Cannes Film Festival

PALME D'OR: *Amour*
DIRECTOR: **Carlos Reygadas** *Post Tenebras Lux*
ACTOR: **Mads Mikkelsen** *The Hunt*
ACTRESS: **Cosmina Stratan, Cristina Flutur** *Beyond the Hills*

Berlin International Film Festival

GOLDEN BEAR: **Caesar Must Die**
SILVER BEAR, DIRECTOR: **Christian Petzold** *Barbara*
SILVER BEAR, ACTOR: **Mikkel Følsgaard** *A Royal Affair*
SILVER BEAR, ACTRESS: **Rachel Mwanza** *Rebelle*

2013

British Academy Film Awards

FILM: **12 Years a Slave** • *American Hustle* • *Captain Phillips* • *Gravity* • *Philomena*
FOREIGN LANGUAGE FILM: **The Great Beauty** • *The Act of Killing* • *Blue Is the Warmest Colour* • *Metro Manila* • *Wadjda*
ALEXANDER KORDA AWARD, BRITISH FILM: **Gravity** • *Mandela: Long Walk to Freedom* • *Philomena* • *Rush* • *Saving Mr Banks* • *The Selfish Giant*
DAVID LEAN AWARD, DIRECTOR: **Alfonso Cuarón** *Gravity* • Paul Greengrass *Captain Phillips* • Steve McQueen (2) *12 Years a Slave* • David O Russell *American Hustle* • Martin Scorsese *The Wolf of Wall Street*
ACTOR: **Chiwetel Ejiofor** *12 Years a Slave* • Christian Bale *American Hustle* • Bruce Dern *Nebraska* • Leonardo DiCaprio *The Wolf of Wall Street* • Tom Hanks *Captain Phillips*
ACTRESS: **Cate Blanchett** *Blue Jasmine* • Amy Adams *American Hustle* • Sandra Bullock *Gravity* • Judi Dench *Philomena* • Emma Thompson *Saving Mr Banks*
SUPPORTING ACTOR: **Barkhad Abdi** *Captain Phillips* • Daniel Brühl *Rush* • Bradley Cooper *American Hustle* • Matt Damon *Behind the Candelabra* • Michael Fassbender *12 Years a Slave*
SUPPORTING ACTRESS: **Jennifer Lawrence (2)** *American Hustle* • Sally Hawkins *Blue Jasmine* • Lupita Nyong'o *12 Years a Slave* • Julia Roberts *August: Osage County* • Oprah Winfrey *The Butler*
ORIGINAL SCREENPLAY: **David O Russell, Eric Singer** *American Hustle* • Woody Allen *Blue Jasmine* • Alfonso Cuarón, Jonás Cuarón *Gravity* • Ethan Coen, Joel Coen *Inside Llewyn Davis* • Bob Nelson *Nebraska*
ADAPTED SCREENPLAY: **Steve Coogan, Jeff Pope** *Philomena* • Richard LaGravenese *Behind the Candelabra* • Billy Ray *Captain Phillips* • John Ridley *12 Years a Slave* • Terence Winter *The Wolf of Wall Street*

Academy Awards

PICTURE: **12 Years a Slave** • *American Hustle* • *Captain Phillips* • *Dallas Buyers Club* • *Gravity* • *Her* • *Nebraska* • *Philomena* • *The Wolf of Wall Street*
FOREIGN LANGUAGE FILM: **The Great Beauty** • *The Broken Circle Breakdown* • *The Hunt* • *The Missing Picture* • *Omar*
DIRECTOR: **Alfonso Cuarón** *Gravity* • Steve McQueen (2) *12 Years a Slave* • Alexander Payne *Nebraska* • David O Russell *American Hustle* • Martin Scorsese *The Wolf of Wall Street*
ACTOR: **Matthew McConaughey** *Dallas Buyers Club* • Christian Bale *American Hustle* • Bruce Dern *Nebraska* • Leonardo DiCaprio *The Wolf of Wall Street* • Chiwetel Ejiofor *12 Years a Slave*
ACTRESS: **Cate Blanchett** *Blue Jasmine* • Amy Adams *American Hustle* • Sandra Bullock *Gravity* • Judi Dench *Philomena* • Meryl Streep *August: Osage County*
SUPPORTING ACTOR: **Jared Leto** *Dallas Buyers Club* • Barkhad Abdi *Captain Phillips* • Bradley Cooper *American Hustle* • Michael Fassbender *12 Years a Slave* • Jonah Hill *The Wolf of Wall Street*
SUPPORTING ACTRESS: **Lupita Nyong'o** *12 Years a Slave* • Sally Hawkins *Blue Jasmine* • Jennifer Lawrence (2) *American Hustle* • Julia Roberts *August: Osage County* • June Squibb *Nebraska*
ORIGINAL SCREENPLAY: **Spike Jonze** *Her* • David O Russell, Eric Singer *American Hustle* • Woody Allen *Blue Jasmine* • Craig Borten, Melisa Wallack *Dallas Buyers Club* • Bob Nelson *Nebraska*
ADAPTED SCREENPLAY: **John Ridley** *12 Years a Slave* • Richard Linklater, Julie Delpy, Ethan Hawke *Before Midnight* • Billy Ray *Captain Phillips* • Steve Coogan, Jeff Pope *Philomena* • Terence Winter *The Wolf of Wall Street*

Golden Globe Awards

DRAMA: **12 Years a Slave**
COMEDY/MUSICAL: **American Hustle**
FOREIGN LANGUAGE FILM: **The Great Beauty**
DIRECTOR: **Alfonso Cuarón** *Gravity*
ACTOR, DRAMA: **Matthew McConaughey** *Dallas Buyers Club*
ACTRESS, DRAMA: **Cate Blanchett** *Blue Jasmine*
ACTOR, COMEDY/MUSICAL: **Leonardo DiCaprio** *The Wolf of Wall Street*
ACTRESS, COMEDY/MUSICAL: **Amy Adams** *American Hustle*
SUPPORTING ACTOR: **Jared Leto** *Dallas Buyers Club*
SUPPORTING ACTRESS: **Jennifer Lawrence (2)** *American Hustle*
SCREENPLAY: **Spike Jonze** *Her*

Cannes Film Festival

PALME D'OR: **Blue Is the Warmest Colour**
DIRECTOR: **Amat Escalante** *Heli*
ACTOR: **Bruce Dern** *Nebraska*
ACTRESS: **Bérénice Bejo** *The Past*

Berlin International Film Festival

GOLDEN BEAR: **Child's Pose**
SILVER BEAR, DIRECTOR: **David Gordon Green** *Prince Avalanche*

SILVER BEAR, ACTOR: **Nazif Mujic** *An Episode in the Life of an Iron Picker*
SILVER BEAR, ACTRESS: **Paulina García** *Gloria*

2014

British Academy Film Awards

FILM: **Boyhood** • *Birdman or (The Unexpected Virtue of Ignorance)* • *The Grand Budapest Hotel* • *The Imitation Game* • *The Theory of Everything*
FOREIGN LANGUAGE FILM: **Ida** • *Leviathan* • *The Lunchbox* • *Trash* • *Two Days, One Night*
ALEXANDER KORDA AWARD, BRITISH FILM: **The Theory of Everything** • *The Imitation Game* • *Paddington* • *Pride* • '71 • *Under the Skin*
DAVID LEAN AWARD, DIRECTOR: **Richard Linklater** *Boyhood* • Wes Anderson *The Grand Budapest Hotel* • Damien Chazelle *Whiplash* • Alejandro González Iñárritu *Birdman or (The Unexpected Virtue of Ignorance)* • James Marsh *The Theory of Everything*
ACTOR: **Eddie Redmayne** *The Theory of Everything* • Benedict Cumberbatch *The Imitation Game* • Ralph Fiennes *The Grand Budapest Hotel* • Jake Gyllenhaal *Nightcrawler* • Michael Keaton *Birdman or (The Unexpected Virtue of Ignorance)*
ACTRESS: **Julianne Moore** *Still Alice* • Amy Adams *Big Eyes* • Felicity Jones *The Theory of Everything* • Rosamund Pike *Gone Girl* • Reese Witherspoon *Wild*
SUPPORTING ACTOR: **J K Simmons** *Whiplash* • Steve Carell *Foxcatcher* • Ethan Hawke *Boyhood* • Edward Norton *Birdman or (The Unexpected Virtue of Ignorance)* • Mark Ruffalo *Foxcatcher*
SUPPORTING ACTRESS: **Patricia Arquette** *Boyhood* • Keira Knightley *The Imitation Game* • Rene Russo *Nightcrawler* • Imelda Staunton *Pride* • Emma Stone *Birdman or (The Unexpected Virtue of Ignorance)*
ORIGINAL SCREENPLAY: **Wes Anderson, Hugo Guinness** *The Grand Budapest Hotel* • Alejandro González Iñárritu, Nicolás Giacobone, Alexander Dinelaris, Armando Bo *Birdman or (The Unexpected Virtue of Ignorance)* • Richard Linklater *Boyhood* • Dan Gilroy *Nightcrawler* • Damien Chazelle *Whiplash*
ADAPTED SCREENPLAY: **Anthony McCarten** *The Theory of Everything* • Jason Dean Hall *American Sniper* • Gillian Flynn *Gone Girl* • Graham Moore *The Imitation Game* • Paul King (2) *Paddington*

Academy Awards

PICTURE: **Birdman or (The Unexpected Virtue of Ignorance)** • *American Sniper* • *Boyhood* • *The Grand Budapest Hotel* • *The Imitation Game* • *Selma* • *The Theory of Everything* • *Whiplash*
FOREIGN LANGUAGE FILM: **Ida** • *Leviathan* • *Tangerines* • *Timbuktu* • *Wild Tales*
DIRECTOR: **Alejandro González Iñárritu** *Birdman or (The Unexpected Virtue of Ignorance)* • Wes Anderson *The Grand Budapest Hotel* • Richard Linklater *Boyhood* • Bennett Miller *Foxcatcher* • Morten Tyldum *The Imitation Game*
ACTOR: **Eddie Redmayne** *The Theory of Everything* • Steve Carell *Foxcatcher* • Bradley Cooper *American Sniper* • Benedict Cumberbatch *The Imitation Game* • Michael Keaton *Birdman or (The Unexpected Virtue of Ignorance)*
ACTRESS: **Julianne Moore** *Still Alice* • Marion Cotillard *Two Days, One Night* • Felicity Jones *The Theory of Everything* • Rosamund Pike *Gone Girl* • Reese Witherspoon *Wild*
SUPPORTING ACTOR: **J K Simmons** *Whiplash* • Robert Duvall *The Judge* • Ethan Hawke *Boyhood* • Edward Norton *Birdman or (The Unexpected Virtue of Ignorance)* • Mark Ruffalo *Foxcatcher*
SUPPORTING ACTRESS: **Patricia Arquette** *Boyhood* • Laura Dern *Wild* • Keira Knightley *The Imitation Game* • Emma Stone *Birdman or (The Unexpected Virtue of Ignorance)* • Meryl Streep *Into the Woods*
ORIGINAL SCREENPLAY: **Alejandro González Iñárritu, Nicolás Giacobone, Alexander Dinelaris, Armando Bo** *Birdman or (The Unexpected Virtue of Ignorance)* • Richard Linklater *Boyhood* • E Max Frye, Dan Futterman *Foxcatcher* • Wes Anderson, Hugo Guinness *The Grand Budapest Hotel* • Dan Gilroy *Nightcrawler*
ADAPTED SCREENPLAY: **Graham Moore** *The Imitation Game* • Jason Dean Hall *American Sniper* • Paul Thomas Anderson *Inherent Vice* • Anthony McCarten *The Theory of Everything* • Damien Chazelle *Whiplash*

Golden Globe Awards

DRAMA: **Boyhood**
COMEDY/MUSICAL: **The Grand Budapest Hotel**
FOREIGN LANGUAGE FILM: **Leviathan**
DIRECTOR: **Richard Linklater** *Boyhood*
ACTOR, DRAMA: **Eddie Redmayne** *The Theory of Everything*
ACTRESS, DRAMA: **Julianne Moore** *Still Alice*
ACTOR, COMEDY/MUSICAL: **Michael Keaton** *Birdman or (The Unexpected Virtue of Ignorance)*
ACTRESS, COMEDY/MUSICAL: **Amy Adams** *Big Eyes*
SUPPORTING ACTOR: **J K Simmons** *Whiplash*
SUPPORTING ACTRESS: **Patricia Arquette** *Boyhood*
SCREENPLAY: **Alejandro González Iñárritu, Nicolás Giacobone, Alexander Dinelaris, Armando Bo** *Birdman or (The Unexpected Virtue of Ignorance)*

Cannes Film Festival

PALME D'OR: **Winter Sleep**
DIRECTOR: **Bennett Miller** *Foxcatcher*
ACTOR: **Timothy Spall** *Mr Turner*
ACTRESS: **Julianne Moore** *Maps to the Stars*

Berlin International Film Festival

GOLDEN BEAR: **Black Coal, Thin Ice**
SILVER BEAR, DIRECTOR: **Richard Linklater** *Boyhood*
SILVER BEAR, ACTOR: **Liao Fan** *Black Coal, Thin Ice*
SILVER BEAR, ACTRESS: **Haru Kuroki** *The Little House*

2015

British Academy Film Awards

FILM: **The Revenant** • *The Big Short* • *Bridge of Spies* • *Carol* • *Spotlight*
FOREIGN LANGUAGE FILM: **Wild Tales** • *The Assassin* • *Force Majeure* • *Theeb* • *Timbuktu*
ALEXANDER KORDA AWARD, BRITISH FILM: **Brooklyn** • *45 Years* • *Amy* • *The Danish Girl* • *Ex Machina* • *The Lobster*
DAVID LEAN AWARD, DIRECTOR: **Alejandro González Iñárritu** *The Revenant* • Todd Haynes *Carol* • Adam McKay *The Big Short* • Ridley Scott *The Martian* • Steven Spielberg *Bridge of Spies*
ACTOR: **Leonardo DiCaprio** *The Revenant* • Bryan Cranston *Trumbo* • Matt Damon *The Martian* • Michael Fassbender *Steve Jobs* • Eddie Redmayne *The Danish Girl*
ACTRESS: **Brie Larson** *Room* • Cate Blanchett *Carol* • Saoirse Ronan *Brooklyn* • Maggie Smith *The Lady in the Van* • Alicia Vikander *The Danish Girl*
SUPPORTING ACTOR: **Mark Rylance** *Bridge of Spies* • Christian Bale *The Big Short* • Benicio Del Toro *Sicario* • Idris Elba *Beasts of No Nation* • Mark Ruffalo *Spotlight*
SUPPORTING ACTRESS: **Kate Winslet** *Steve Jobs* • Jennifer Jason Leigh *The Hateful Eight* • Rooney Mara *Carol* • Alicia Vikander *Ex Machina* • Julie Walters *Brooklyn*
ORIGINAL SCREENPLAY: **Thomas McCarthy, Josh Singer** *Spotlight* • Matt Charman, Ethan Coen, Joel Coen *Bridge of Spies* • Alex Garland *Ex Machina* • Quentin Tarantino *The Hateful Eight* • Pete Docter, Josh Cooley, Meg LeFauve *Inside Out*
ADAPTED SCREENPLAY: **Adam McKay, Charles Randolph** *The Big Short* • Nick Hornby *Brooklyn* • Phyllis Nagy *Carol* • Emma Donoghue *Room* • Aaron Sorkin *Steve Jobs*

Academy Awards

PICTURE: **Spotlight** • *The Big Short* • *Brooklyn* • *Bridge of Spies* • *Mad Max: Fury Road* • *The Martian* • *The Revenant* • *Room*
FOREIGN LANGUAGE FILM: **Son of Saul** • *Embrace of the Serpent* • *Mustang* • *Theeb* • *A War*
DIRECTOR: **Alejandro González Iñárritu** *The Revenant* • Lenny Abrahamson *Room* • Thomas McCarthy *Spotlight* • George Miller (2) *Mad Max: Fury Road* • Adam McKay *The Big Short*
ACTOR: **Leonardo DiCaprio** *The Revenant* • Bryan Cranston *Trumbo* • Matt Damon *The Martian* • Michael Fassbender *Steve Jobs* • Eddie Redmayne *The Danish Girl*
ACTRESS: **Brie Larson** *Room* • Cate Blanchett *Carol* • Jennifer Lawrence (2) *Joy* • Charlotte Rampling *45 Years* • Saoirse Ronan *Brooklyn*
SUPPORTING ACTOR: **Mark Rylance** *Bridge of Spies* • Christian Bale *The Big Short* • Tom Hardy *The Revenant* • Mark Ruffalo *Spotlight* • Sylvester Stallone *Creed*
SUPPORTING ACTRESS: **Alicia Vikander** *The Danish Girl* • Jennifer Jason Leigh *The Hateful Eight* • Rooney Mara *Carol* • Rachel McAdams *Spotlight* • Kate Winslet *Steve Jobs*
ORIGINAL SCREENPLAY: **Thomas McCarthy, Josh Singer** *Spotlight* • Matt Charman, Ethan Coen, Joel Coen *Bridge of Spies* • Alex Garland *Ex Machina* • Pete Docter, Josh Cooley, Meg LeFauve, Ronaldo Del Carmen *Inside Out* • Andrea Berloff, Jonathan Herman, S Leigh Savidge, Alan Wenkus *Straight Outta Compton*
ADAPTED SCREENPLAY: **Adam McKay, Charles Randolph** *The Big Short* • Nick Hornby *Brooklyn* • Phyllis Nagy *Carol* • Drew Goddard *The Martian* • Emma Donoghue *Room*

Golden Globe Awards

DRAMA: **The Revenant**
COMEDY/MUSICAL: **The Martian**
FOREIGN LANGUAGE FILM: **Son of Saul**
DIRECTOR: **Alejandro González Iñárritu** *The Revenant*
ACTOR, DRAMA: **Leonardo DiCaprio** *The Revenant*
ACTRESS, DRAMA: **Brie Larson** *Room*
ACTOR, COMEDY/MUSICAL: **Matt Damon** *The Martian*
ACTRESS, COMEDY/MUSICAL: **Jennifer Lawrence (2)** *Joy*
SUPPORTING ACTOR: **Sylvester Stallone** *Creed*
SUPPORTING ACTRESS: **Kate Winslet** *Steve Jobs*
SCREENPLAY: **Aaron Sorkin** *Steve Jobs*

Cannes Film Festival

PALME D'OR: **Dheepan**
DIRECTOR: **Hou Hsiao-Hsien** *The Assassin*
ACTOR: **Vincent Lindon** *The Measure of a Man*
ACTRESS: **Emmanuelle Bercot** *Mon Roi* • **Rooney Mara** *Carol*

Berlin International Film Festival

GOLDEN BEAR: **Taxi**
SILVER BEAR, DIRECTOR: **Radu Jude** *Aferim!* • Malgorzata Szumowska *Body*
SILVER BEAR, ACTOR: **Tom Courtenay** *45 Years*
SILVER BEAR, ACTRESS: **Charlotte Rampling** *45 Years*

2016

Cannes Film Festival

PALME D'OR: **I, Daniel Blake**
DIRECTOR: **Cristian Mungiu** *Graduation* • Olivier Assayas *Personal Shopper*
ACTOR: **Shahab Hosseini** *The Salesman*
ACTRESS: **Jaclyn Jose** *Ma' Rosa*

Berlin International Film Festival

GOLDEN BEAR: **Fire at Sea**
SILVER BEAR, DIRECTOR: **Mia Hansen-Løve** *Things to Come*
SILVER BEAR, ACTOR: **Majd Mastoura** *Hedi*
SILVER BEAR, ACTRESS: **Trine Dyrholm** *The Commune*

Five-star and four-star films

ACTION ★★★★★

The Adventures of Robin Hood 1938...DVD
Aliens 1986...DVD Blu-ray
The Bourne Ultimatum 2007...DVD Blu-ray
Crouching Tiger, Hidden Dragon 2000...DVD Blu-ray
The Dark Knight 2008...DVD Blu-ray
Die Hard 1988...DVD Blu-ray
Hero 2002...DVD Blu-ray
The Hunger Games: Catching Fire 2013...DVD Blu-ray
Indiana Jones and the Last Crusade 1989...DVD Blu-ray
Looper 2012...DVD Blu-ray
Mad Max 1979...DVD Blu-ray
Marvel Avengers Assemble 2012...DVD Blu-ray
The Matrix 1999...DVD Blu-ray
Only Angels Have Wings 1939...DVD Blu-ray
The Prisoner of Zenda 1937...DVD
The Raid 2 2013...DVD Blu-ray
Raiders of the Lost Ark 1981...DVD Blu-ray
Seven Samurai 1954...DVD Blu-ray
Sicario 2015...DVD Blu-ray
Speed 1994...DVD Blu-ray
Star Wars Episode VII: the Force Awakens 2015...Blu-ray
The Terminator 1984...DVD Blu-ray
Terminator 2: Judgment Day 1991...DVD Blu-ray
Yojimbo 1961...DVD Blu-ray

ACTION ★★★★

Air Force One 1997...DVD Blu-ray
Alien: Resurrection 1997...DVD Blu-ray
American Sniper 2014...DVD Blu-ray
Anthony Adverse 1936...
Apocalypto 2006...DVD Blu-ray
Ashes of Time 1994...
Attack the Block 2010...DVD Blu-ray
Avengers: Age of Ultron 2015...DVD Blu-ray
Backdraft 1991...DVD Blu-ray
Bad Boys 1995...DVD Blu-ray
Batman 1966...DVD Blu-ray
Batman 1989...DVD Blu-ray
Batman Returns 1992...DVD Blu-ray
Batman Forever 1995...DVD Blu-ray
Batman: Mask of the Phantasm 1993...DVD
Batman Begins 2005...DVD Blu-ray
Battle of the Bulge 1965...DVD
Battle Royale 2000...DVD Blu-ray
A Better Tomorrow 1986...DVD
Beverly Hills Cop 1984...DVD Blu-ray
Big Hero 6 2014...DVD Blu-ray
Black Mask 1996...DVD
The Black Pirate 1926...DVD
The Black Swan 1942...DVD
Das Boot: the Director's Cut 1981/1997...DVD Blu-ray
The Bourne Identity 2002...DVD Blu-ray
The Bourne Supremacy 2004...DVD Blu-ray
The Bride with White Hair 1993...DVD
Captain America: the Winter Soldier 2014...DVD Blu-ray
Captain America: Civil War 2016...
Captain Blood 1935...DVD
A Chinese Ghost Story 1987...DVD
Chocolate 2008...DVD Blu-ray
The Chronicles of Narnia: The Voyage of the Dawn Treader 2010...DVD Blu-ray
City on Fire 1987...DVD
Cliffhanger 1993...DVD Blu-ray
Collateral 2004...DVD Blu-ray
Con Air 1997...DVD Blu-ray
The Crimson Pirate 1952...DVD
Crimson Tide 1995...DVD Blu-ray
The Crow 1994...DVD
The Dark Knight Rises 2012...DVD Blu-ray
Dawn of the Planet of the Apes 2014...DVD Blu-ray
The Dead Lands 2014...DVD
Desperado 1995...DVD
Detective Dee and the Mystery of the Phantom Flame 2010...DVD Blu-ray
Die Hard 2: Die Harder 1990...DVD Blu-ray
Die Hard with a Vengeance 1995...DVD Blu-ray
Die Hard 4.0 2007...DVD Blu-ray
The Dirty Dozen 1967...DVD
District 9 2009...DVD Blu-ray
Drunken Master 1978...DVD
Eagle Eye 2008...DVD Blu-ray
Eklavya: the Royal Guard 2007...DVD
Emperor of the North 1973...DVD
Enter the Dragon 1973...DVD Blu-ray
Excalibur 1981...DVD Blu-ray
Exiled 2006...DVD
Face/Off 1997...DVD
The Fast and the Furious 2001...DVD Blu-ray
Fast Five 2011...DVD Blu-ray
Fast & Furious 7 2014...DVD Blu-ray
The Fifth Element 1997...DVD Blu-ray
48 HRS 1982...DVD Blu-ray
From Dusk till Dawn 1995...DVD Blu-ray
Full Contact 1992...DVD
GI Joe: the Rise of Cobra 2009...DVD Blu-ray
Green Zone 2010...DVD Blu-ray

Guadalcanal Diary 1943...DVD
Guardians of the Galaxy 2014...DVD Blu-ray
Hanna 2011...DVD Blu-ray
Hard-Boiled 1992...DVD
Hard Times 1975...DVD
The Hard Way 1991...DVD
Hooper 1978...DVD
Hot Fuzz 2007...DVD Blu-ray
House of Flying Daggers 2004...DVD Blu-ray
The Hunger Games 2012...DVD Blu-ray
The Hunger Games: Mockingjay Part 1 2014...DVD Blu-ray
The Hunger Games: Mockingjay Part 2 2015...DVD Blu-ray
The Hurt Locker 2008...DVD Blu-ray
I, Robot 2004...DVD Blu-ray
In Harm's Way 1965...DVD
Inception 2010...DVD Blu-ray
The Incredible Hulk 2008...DVD Blu-ray
Indiana Jones and the Temple of Doom 1984...DVD Blu-ray
Indiana Jones and the Kingdom of the Crystal Skull 2008...DVD Blu-ray
Iron Man 2008...DVD Blu-ray
Iron Man Three 2013...DVD Blu-ray
Ivanhoe 1952...DVD
Jackie Chan's Who Am I? 1998...DVD
Jason Bourne 2016...
The Jewel of the Nile 1985...DVD Blu-ray
John Wick 2014...DVD Blu-ray
Kick-Ass 2009...DVD Blu-ray
Kill Bill Vol 1 2003...DVD Blu-ray
The Killer 1989...DVD
King Boxer 1972...DVD
Kingsman: The Secret Service 2015...DVD Blu-ray
Kiss Kiss Bang Bang 2005...DVD Blu-ray
Kiss of the Dragon 2001...DVD Blu-ray
Kon-Tiki 2012...DVD Blu-ray
Kung Fu Hustle 2004...DVD Blu-ray
Last Action Hero 1993...DVD Blu-ray
The Last Legion 2006...DVD
The Last Samurai 2003...DVD Blu-ray
Lethal Weapon 1987...DVD Blu-ray
The Lives of a Bengal Lancer 1935...
The Lone Ranger 2013...DVD Blu-ray
The Long Kiss Goodnight 1996...DVD Blu-ray
Mad Dog 1976...DVD
Mad Max 2 1981...DVD Blu-ray
Mad Max: Fury Road 2015...DVD Blu-ray
The Mark of Zorro 1940...DVD
The Mask of Zorro 1998...DVD Blu-ray
Minority Report 2002...DVD Blu-ray
Miss Congeniality 2000...DVD
Mission: Impossible 1996...DVD Blu-ray
Mission: Impossible 2 1999...DVD Blu-ray
Mission: Impossible - Ghost Protocol 2011...DVD Blu-ray
Mission: Impossible - Rogue Nation 2015...DVD Blu-ray
Momentum 2015...DVD Blu-ray
The Negotiator 1998...DVD Blu-ray
New Jack City 1991...DVD
Ocean's Eleven 2001...DVD Blu-ray
Oldboy 2003...DVD Blu-ray
Once upon a Time in China 1991...DVD
Ong-Bak 2003...DVD
Operation Condor: the Armour of God II 1990...
Peking Opera Blues 1986...
Pirates of the Caribbean: the Curse of the Black Pearl 2003...DVD Blu-ray
Point Break 1991...DVD Blu-ray
Predator 1987...DVD Blu-ray
Pride and Prejudice and Zombies 2015...DVD Blu-ray
Princess Mononoke 1997/2001...DVD Blu-ray
The Prisoner of Zenda 1952...
The Raid 2011...DVD Blu-ray
Rebellion 1967...
Red Cliff 2008...DVD Blu-ray
Redbelt 2007...DVD Blu-ray
The Rink 1916...DVD
Rise of the Planet of the Apes 2011...DVD Blu-ray
Robin Hood: Prince of Thieves 1991...DVD Blu-ray
RoboCop 2014...DVD Blu-ray
The Rock 1996...DVD Blu-ray
Ronin 1998...DVD Blu-ray
The Rover 2014...DVD Blu-ray
Runaway Train 1985...DVD Blu-ray
Rush Hour 1998...DVD Blu-ray
Scaramouche 1923...
Scaramouche 1952...
The Sea Hawk 1924...
The Sea Hawk 1940...
Serenity 2005...DVD Blu-ray
The 6th Day 2000...DVD Blu-ray
Snake in the Eagle's Shadow 1978...
Snowpiercer 2013...
Southern Comfort 1981...DVD Blu-ray
Speed Racer 2008...DVD Blu-ray
Spider-Man 2002...DVD Blu-ray
Spider-Man 2 2004...DVD Blu-ray
SPYkids 2001...DVD
SPYkids 2: the Island of Lost Dreams 2002...DVD Blu-ray
Strange Days 1995...DVD
Sudden Death 1995...DVD Blu-ray

Sweet Sweetback's Baad Asssss Song 1971...DVD
Sympathy for Mr Vengeance 2002...DVD Blu-ray
Taken 2007...DVD Blu-ray
13 Assassins 2010...DVD Blu-ray
Thor: the Dark World 2013...DVD Blu-ray
300 2006...DVD Blu-ray
300: Rise of an Empire 2013...DVD Blu-ray
Three Kings 1999...DVD Blu-ray
The Three Musketeers 1921...
The Three Musketeers 1973...DVD Blu-ray
Time and Tide 2000...DVD
Tokyo Drifter 1966...DVD
Tokyo Fist 1995...DVD
A Touch of Zen 1969...DVD Blu-ray
Transformers 2007...DVD Blu-ray
Transformers: Dark of the Moon 2011...DVD Blu-ray
Tropic Thunder 2008...DVD Blu-ray
True Lies 1994...DVD
Turbo Kid 2014...DVD Blu-ray
21 Jump Street 2012...DVD Blu-ray
22 Jump Street 2014...DVD Blu-ray
2 Guns 2013...DVD Blu-ray
Under Siege 1992...DVD Blu-ray
Uzumasa Limelight 2014...Blu-ray
Warrior 2011...DVD Blu-ray
The Warriors 1979...DVD Blu-ray
Watchmen 2009...DVD Blu-ray
When the Last Sword Is Drawn 2003...DVD
Where Eagles Dare 1969...DVD Blu-ray
The Wild Angels 1966...DVD
X2 2003...DVD Blu-ray
X-Men: First Class 2011...DVD Blu-ray
X-Men: Days of Future Past 2014...DVD Blu-ray
Zatoichi 2003...DVD Blu-ray
Zero Dark Thirty 2012...DVD Blu-ray

ADVENTURE ★★★★★

The Adventures of Robin Hood 1938...DVD
The African Queen 1951...DVD Blu-ray
Aladdin 1992...DVD Blu-ray
Back to the Future 1985...DVD Blu-ray
Beau Geste 1939...
The Black Stallion 1979...DVD
Dr No 1962...DVD Blu-ray
Don Quixote 1957...
ET the Extra-Terrestrial 1982...DVD Blu-ray
Finding Dory 2016...
Finding Nemo 2003...DVD Blu-ray
The 5,000 Fingers of Dr T 1953...
Forbidden Planet 1956...DVD Blu-ray
The Four Feathers 1939...DVD
From Russia with Love 1963...DVD Blu-ray
Goldfinger 1964...DVD Blu-ray
Gravity 2013...DVD Blu-ray
The Great Escape 1963...DVD Blu-ray
Gunga Din 1939...
Harry Potter and the Deathly Hallows: Part 2 2011...DVD Blu-ray
The Hidden Fortress 1958...DVD Blu-ray
The Hunger Games: Catching Fire 2013...DVD Blu-ray
The Incredibles 2004...DVD Blu-ray
Indiana Jones and the Last Crusade 1989...DVD Blu-ray
Inside Out 2015...DVD Blu-ray
Jaws 1975...DVD Blu-ray
The Jungle Book 1967...DVD Blu-ray
Jurassic Park 1993...DVD Blu-ray
King Kong 1933...DVD
Lady and the Tramp 1955...DVD Blu-ray
Lassie Come Home 1943...DVD
The Last of the Mohicans 1920...
Lawrence of Arabia 1962...DVD Blu-ray
The Little Mermaid 1989...DVD
The Lord of the Rings: The Fellowship of the Ring 2001...DVD Blu-ray
The Lord of the Rings: The Two Towers 2002...DVD Blu-ray
The Lord of the Rings: The Return of the King 2003...DVD Blu-ray
Lost Horizon 1937...DVD
Mad Max 1979...DVD Blu-ray
The Man Who Would Be King 1975...DVD
Marvel Avengers Assemble 2012...DVD Blu-ray
Monsters, Inc 2001...DVD Blu-ray
One Hundred and One Dalmatians 1960...DVD Blu-ray
Only Angels Have Wings 1939...DVD Blu-ray
Planet of the Apes 1967...DVD Blu-ray
The Prisoner of Zenda 1937...DVD
Raiders of the Lost Ark 1981...DVD Blu-ray
The Revenant 2015...DVD Blu-ray
Skyfall 2012...DVD Blu-ray
Star Trek: First Contact 1996...DVD Blu-ray
Star Wars Episode IV: a New Hope 1977...DVD Blu-ray
Star Wars Episode V: the Empire Strikes Back 1980...DVD Blu-ray
Star Wars Episode VII: the Force Awakens 2015...Blu-ray
Superman 1978...DVD Blu-ray
The Thief of Bagdad 1940...DVD
Toy Story 1995...DVD Blu-ray

Toy Story 2 1999...DVD Blu-ray
Toy Story 3 2010...DVD Blu-ray
The Treasure of the Sierra Madre 1947...DVD Blu-ray
Up 2009...DVD Blu-ray
The Vikings 1958...DVD
The Wages of Fear 1953...DVD Blu-ray
You Only Live Twice 1967...DVD Blu-ray

ADVENTURE ★★★★

The Adventures of Baron Munchausen 1988...DVD Blu-ray
The Adventures of Robinson Crusoe 1952...
The Adventures of Tom Sawyer 1938...DVD
Aladdin and the King of Thieves 1996...DVD
Alone on the Pacific 1963...
An American Tail 1986...DVD
Antz 1998...DVD
Apocalypto 2006...DVD Blu-ray
Apollo 13 1995...DVD Blu-ray
The Arabian Nights 1974...DVD
The Aristocats 1970...DVD Blu-ray
Around the World in 80 Days 1956...DVD
Atlantis: the Lost Empire 2001...DVD
Avengers: Age of Ultron 2015...DVD Blu-ray
Azur & Asmar: the Princes' Quest 2006...
Back to the Future Part III 1990...DVD Blu-ray
The Beach 2000...DVD Blu-ray
The Bear 1988...
The Beast from 20,000 Fathoms 1953...DVD
Beau Geste 1926...
The Bedford Incident 1965...DVD
Belleville Rendez-vous 2003...DVD Blu-ray
Beowulf 2007...DVD Blu-ray
The Big Blue 1988...DVD
Big Hero 6 2014...DVD Blu-ray
The Big Sky 1952...DVD
The Black Pirate 1926...DVD
Black Sea 2014...DVD Blu-ray
The Black Swan 1942...DVD
Bolt 2008...DVD Blu-ray
Boom Town 1940...
Born Free 1966...DVD
The Brave Little Toaster 1987...DVD
Bridge to Terabithia 2006...DVD Blu-ray
A Bug's Life 1998...DVD
Captain America: the Winter Soldier 2014...DVD Blu-ray
Captain America: Civil War 2016...
Captain Blood 1935...DVD
Casino Royale 2006...DVD Blu-ray
The Castle of Cagliostro 1979...DVD Blu-ray
Chicken Run 2000...DVD
China Seas 1935...
The Chronicles of Narnia: The Voyage of the Dawn Treader 2010...DVD Blu-ray
The City of Lost Children 1995...DVD Blu-ray
The Count of Monte Cristo 1934...
Cowboys & Aliens 2011...DVD Blu-ray
The Crimson Pirate 1952...
"Crocodile" Dundee 1986...DVD
The Darjeeling Limited 2007...DVD Blu-ray
The Dark Crystal 1982...DVD Blu-ray
Dawn of the Planet of the Apes 2014...DVD Blu-ray
Desperado 1995...DVD
Detective Dee and the Mystery of the Phantom Flame 2010...DVD Blu-ray
Dick Tracy 1990...DVD
The Dirty Dozen 1967...DVD
Dr Seuss' Horton Hears a Who! 2008...DVD Blu-ray
Dredd 2012...DVD Blu-ray
The Drum 1938...
Drums along the Mohawk 1939...DVD
The Eagle 1925...DVD
Eklavya: the Royal Guard 2007...DVD
Embrace of the Serpent 2015...DVD Blu-ray
Emperor of the North 1973...DVD
Enter the Dragon 1973...DVD
Escape from the Planet of the Apes 1971...DVD Blu-ray
Fantastic Mr Fox 2009...DVD Blu-ray
Fantastic Voyage 1966...DVD Blu-ray
The Fifth Element 1997...DVD Blu-ray
Fire over England 1937...
The Flight of the Phoenix 1965...DVD Blu-ray
Fort Saganne 1984...
Frozen 2013...DVD Blu-ray
GI Joe: the Rise of Cobra 2009...DVD Blu-ray
GoldenEye 1995...DVD
The Good Dinosaur 2015...
Guardians of the Galaxy 2014...DVD Blu-ray
The Guns of Navarone 1961...DVD Blu-ray
Happy Feet 2006...DVD Blu-ray
Harry Potter and the Philosopher's Stone 2001...DVD Blu-ray
Harry Potter and the Chamber of Secrets 2002...DVD Blu-ray
Harry Potter and the Prisoner of Azkaban 2004...DVD Blu-ray
Harry Potter and the Goblet of Fire 2005...DVD Blu-ray
Harry Potter and the Order of the Phoenix 2007...DVD Blu-ray

Harry Potter and the Half-Blood Prince 2009 ... DVD BD
Hatari! 1962 ... DVD
Hellboy II: the Golden Army 2008 ... DVD BD
The Hobbit: the Battle of the Five Armies 2014 ... DVD BD
The House of Magic 2013 ... DVD BD
How to Train Your Dragon 2010 ... DVD BD
How to Train Your Dragon 2 2014 ... DVD BD
The Hunger Games: Mockingjay Part 1 2014 ... DVD BD
The Hunger Games: Mockingjay Part 2 2015 ... DVD BD
If I Were King 1938 ...
The Incredible Hulk 2008 ... DVD BD
The Incredible Journey 1963 ... DVD
Independence Day 1996 ... DVD BD
The Indian in the Cupboard 1995 ... DVD
Indiana Jones and the Temple of Doom 1984 ... DVD BD
Indiana Jones and the Kingdom of the Crystal Skull 2008 ... DVD BD
Interstellar 2014 ... DVD BD
Into the Wild 2007 ... DVD BD
The Iron Giant 1999 ... DVD
Iron Man 2008 ... DVD BD
Iron Man Three 2013 ... DVD BD
Ivanhoe 1952 ... DVD
James and the Giant Peach 1996 ... DVD
Jason and the Argonauts 1963 ... DVD
The Jewel of the Nile 1985 ... DVD BD
Journey to the Center of the Earth 1959 ... DVD
Judex 1963 ... DVD
Jumanji 1995 ... DVD BD
The Jungle Book 2016 ... DVD BD
Jurassic World 2015 ... DVD BD
King Boxer 1972 ... DVD
King Kong 2005 ... DVD BD
Kingsman: The Secret Service 2015 ... DVD BD
Kirikou and the Sorceress 1998 ... DVD
A Knight's Tale 2001 ... DVD BD
Kon-Tiki 2012 ... DVD BD
Ladyhawke 1985 ... DVD BD
The Land before Time 1988 ... DVD
Lassie 2005 ...
Last Action Hero 1993 ... DVD BD
The Last Legion 2006 ... DVD
The Last Mimzy 2007 ... DVD
The Last of the Mohicans 1992 ... DVD BD
The Lego Movie 2014 ... DVD BD
The Lion King 1994 ... DVD BD
Lion of the Desert 1981 ... DVD
Live and Let Die 1973 ... DVD BD
The Lives of a Bengal Lancer 1935 ...
The Lone Ranger 2013 ... DVD BD
Lord Jim 1965 ... DVD
The Lost Squadron 1932 ...
Mad Max 2 198? ... DVD BD
Mad Max: Fury Road 2015 ... DVD BD
The Many Adventures of Winnie the Pooh 1977 ... DVD
The Mark of Zorro 1940 ... DVD
The Mask of Zorro 1998 ... DVD BD
Master and Commander: the Far Side of the World 2003 ... DVD BD
Megamind 2010 ... DVD BD
Mission: Impossible - Rogue Nation 2015 ... DVD BD
Mr Peabody & Sherman 2013 ... DVD BD
Mulan 1998 ... DVD BD
The Muppet Movie 1979 ... DVD
Muppet Treasure Island 1996 ... DVD
Muppets from Space 1999 ... DVD
Mutiny on the Bounty 1935 ... DVD
Mutiny on the Bounty 1962 ... DVD
My Neighbour Totoro 1988 ... DVD BD
The Naked Jungle 1953 ... DVD
Nanny McPhee & the Big Bang 2010 ... DVD BD
The Navigator - a Medieval Odyssey 1988 ...
The NeverEnding Story 1984 ... DVD BD
The New Land 1972 ... DVD BD
The New World 2005 ... DVD BD
North to Alaska 1960 ... DVD
Old Yeller 1957 ... DVD
On Her Majesty's Secret Service 1969 ... DVD BD
Ong-Bak 2003 ... DVD
Operation Condor: the Armour of God II 1990 ... DVD BD
Pan 2015 ... DVD BD
Pathfinder 1987 ...
Peking Opera Blues 1986 ...
Perceval le Gallois 1978 ...
Peter Pan 1953 ... DVD BD
The Pirates! in an Adventure with Scientists! 2012 ...
Pirates of the Caribbean: the Curse of the Black Pearl 2003 ... DVD BD
Ponyo 2008 ... DVD
The Pride and the Passion 1957 ... DVD
The Princess Bride 1987 ... DVD BD
The Prisoner of Zenda 1952 ...
Puss in Boots 2011 ... DVD BD
The Rescuers 1977 ... DVD
Rio 2011 ... DVD BD

Rise of the Guardians 2012 ... DVD BD
Rise of the Planet of the Apes 2011 ... DVD BD
The River Wild 1994 ... DVD BD
Rob Roy 1995 ... DVD BD
Robin and Marian 1976 ... DVD
Robin Hood 1922 ... DVD
Robin Hood 1973 ... DVD
Robin Hood 1990 ... DVD
Robin Hood: Prince of Thieves 1991 ... DVD BD
Rocketeer 1991 ... DVD
Romancing the Stone 1984 ... DVD BD
Runaway Train 1985 ... DVD BD
Scaramouche 1952 ... DVD
The Scarlet Pimpernel 1982 ... DVD
Scott of the Antarctic 1948 ... DVD
The Sea Hawk 1924 ...
The Sea Hawk 1940 ... DVD
The Sea Wolf 1941 ... DVD
Serenity 2005 ... DVD BD
The 7th Voyage of Sinbad 1958 ... DVD
The Shamer's Daughter 2015 ... DVD
Shaun the Sheep Movie 2015 ... DVD
The Sheik 1921 ... DVD
The Shiralee 1986 ...
Sholay 1975 ... DVD
The Silver Brumby 1992 ...
Sky High 2005 ... DVD BD
Snoopy and Charlie Brown: the Peanuts Movie 2015 ...
The Son of the Sheik 1926 ...
Speed Racer 2008 ... DVD BD
Spider-Man 2002 ... DVD BD
Spider-Man 2 2004 ... DVD BD
The Spiders 1919 ... DVD
The Spiderwick Chronicles 2008 ... DVD BD
Spirited Away 2001 ... DVD BD
The SpongeBob SquarePants Movie 2004 ... DVD
The SpongeBob Movie: Sponge out of Water 2015 ... DVD BD
SPYkids 2001 ... DVD BD
SPYkids 2: the Island of Lost Dreams 2002 ... DVD BD
The Spy Who Loved Me 1977 ... DVD BD
Stanley and Livingstone 1939 ...
Star Trek II: the Wrath of Khan 1982 ... DVD BD
Star Trek IV: the Voyage Home 1986 ... DVD BD
Star Trek VI: the Undiscovered Country 1991 ... DVD BD
Star Trek: Generations 1994 ... DVD BD
Star Trek 2009 ... DVD BD
Star Trek into Darkness 2013 ... DVD BD
Star Trek Beyond 2016 ...
Star Wars Episode VI: Return of the Jedi 1983 ... DVD BD
Stardust 2007 ... DVD BD
Stargate 1994 ... DVD BD
Starship Troopers 1997 ... DVD BD
The Sundowners 1960 ...
Super 8 2011 ... DVD BD
Superman II 1980 ... DVD BD
Superman Returns 2006 ... DVD BD
Swiss Family Robinson 1960 ... DVD
Tangled 2010 ... DVD BD
The Tarnished Angels 1957 ... DVD BD
Tarzan and His Mate 1934 ... DVD
Tarzan, the Ape Man 1932 ... DVD
Ten Canoes 2006 ... DVD
That Man from Rio 1964 ... DVD
The Thief of Bagdad 1924 ... DVD BD
13 Assassins 2010 ... DVD BD
This Island Earth 1955 ...
Thomas & Friends - Sodor's Legend of the Lost Treasure: the Movie 2015 ... DVD
Thor: the Dark World 2013 ... DVD BD
300 2006 ... DVD BD
300: Rise of an Empire 2013 ... DVD BD
Three Kings 1999 ... DVD BD
The Three Musketeers 1921 ...
The Three Musketeers 1973 ... DVD BD
The Time Machine 1960 ... DVD
Titan AE 2000 ... DVD
Tom Jones 1963 ... DVD
Tom Sawyer 1973 ...
Tomorrow Never Dies 1997 ... DVD BD
Too Hot to Handle 1938 ...
A Town Called Panic 2009 ... DVD
Trader Horn 1931 ...
Transformers 2007 ... DVD BD
Transformers: Dark of the Moon 2011 ... DVD BD
The Trap 1966 ...
Tropic Thunder 2008 ... DVD BD
Turbo 2013 ... DVD BD
Turbo Kid 2014 ... DVD BD
The 12 Tasks of Asterix 1975 ... DVD
20,000 Leagues under the Sea 1954 ... DVD
Under Siege 1992 ... DVD BD
A Walk in the Woods 2015 ... DVD BD
Wallace & Gromit in The Curse of the Were-Rabbit 2005 ... DVD BD
The War of the Worlds 1953 ... DVD
The Water Horse 2007 ... DVD BD
Waterworld 1995 ... DVD BD
Where No Vultures Fly 1951 ...

The White Dawn 1974 ...
White Hunter, Black Heart 1990 ...
White Mane 1952 ...
The Wind and the Lion 1975 ... DVD
The Wings of Honneamise 1987 ...
The World Is Not Enough 1999 ... DVD BD
The World's Fastest Indian 2005 ... DVD BD
X2 2003 ... DVD BD
X-Men: First Class 2011 ... DVD BD
X-Men: Days of Future Past 2014 ... DVD BD
Zathura: a Space Adventure 2005 ... DVD
Zatoichi 2003 ... DVD BD

ANIMATION ★★★★★

Aladdin 1992 ... DVD BD
Anomalisa 2015 ... DVD BD
Bambi 1942 ... DVD
Beauty and the Beast 1991 ... DVD BD
The Cat Concerto 1947 ...
The Dot and the Line 1965 ...
Duck Dodgers in the 24½ Century 1953 ...
Dumbo 1941 ... DVD BD
Fantasia 1940 ... DVD BD
Faust 1994 ...
Finding Dory 2016 ...
Finding Nemo 2003 ... DVD BD
Gertie the Dinosaur 1914 ...
The Incredibles 2004 ... DVD BD
Inside Out 2015 ... DVD BD
The Jungle Book 1967 ... DVD BD
King-Size Canary 1947 ...
Lady and the Tramp 1955 ... DVD BD
The Little Mermaid 1989 ... DVD BD
Monsters, Inc 2001 ... DVD BD
The Nightmare before Christmas 1993 ... DVD BD
The Old Mill 1937 ...
One Froggy Evening 1955 ...
One Hundred and One Dalmatians 1960 ... DVD BD
Pinocchio 1940 ... DVD BD
Snow White and the Seven Dwarfs 1937 ... DVD BD
Steamboat Willie 1928 ...
The Three Little Pigs 1933 ... DVD
The Tortoise and the Hare 1935 ...
Toy Story 1995 ... DVD BD
Toy Story 2 1999 ... DVD BD
Toy Story 3 2010 ... DVD BD
Up 2009 ... DVD BD
WALL-E 2008 ... DVD BD
What's Opera, Doc? 1957 ...
Who Framed Roger Rabbit 1988 ... DVD BD
Zootropolis 2016 ... DVD BD

ANIMATION ★★★★

Akira 1988 ... DVD BD
Aladdin and the King of Thieves 1996 ... DVD
Alice 1988 ... DVD BD
An American Tail 1986 ... DVD BD
Animal Farm 1954 ... DVD BD
Antz 1998 ... DVD
The Aristocats 1970 ... DVD BD
Atlantis: the Lost Empire 2001 ... DVD
Azur & Asmar: the Princes' Quest 2006 ... DVD
Batman: Mask of the Phantasm 1993 ... DVD
Bee Movie 2007 ... DVD BD
Belleville Rendez-vous 2003 ... DVD
Beowulf 2007 ... DVD BD
Big Hero 6 2014 ... DVD BD
Birds Anonymous 1957 ...
Bolt 2008 ... DVD BD
Book of Life 2014 ... DVD BD
Brave 2012 ... DVD BD
The Brave Little Toaster 1987 ... DVD
The Bugs Bunny/Road Runner Movie 1979 ...
A Bug's Life 1998 ... DVD BD
The Castle of Cagliostro 1979 ... DVD BD
Chicken Run 2000 ... DVD
Cinderella 1950 ... DVD BD
Cloudy with a Chance of Meatballs 2009 ... DVD BD
Cobain: Montage of Heck 2015 ... DVD BD
Coraline 2008 ... DVD BD
Despicable Me 2010 ... DVD BD
Despicable Me 2 2013 ... DVD BD
Dr Seuss' Horton Hears a Who! 2008 ... DVD BD
The Emperor's New Groove 2000 ... DVD BD
Enchanted 2007 ... DVD BD
Fantastic Mr Fox 2009 ... DVD BD
Fantastic Planet 1973 ... DVD
The Five Obstructions 2003 ... DVD
The Flaw 2011 ...
Flowers and Trees 1932 ...
Frankenweenie 2012 ... DVD BD
Frozen 2013 ... DVD BD
Ghost in the Shell 1995 ... DVD BD
The Good Dinosaur 2015 ... DVD BD
Grave of the Fireflies 1988 ... DVD BD
The Halloween Tree 1993 ...
Happy Feet 2006 ... DVD BD
The House of Magic 2013 ... DVD BD

How to Train Your Dragon 2010 ... DVD BD
How to Train Your Dragon 2 2014 ... DVD BD
The Hunchback of Notre Dame 1996 ... DVD BD
The Illusionist 2010 ... DVD
Invention of Destruction 1958 ...
The Iron Giant 1999 ... DVD
James and the Giant Peach 1996 ... DVD
Kill Bill Vol 1 2003 ... DVD BD
The King and the Mockingbird 1980 ... DVD
Kirikou and the Sorceress 1998 ... DVD
The Land before Time 1988 ... DVD
The Lego Movie 2014 ... DVD BD
Lilo & Stitch 2002 ... DVD BD
The Lion King 1994 ... DVD BD
Little Otik 2000 ... DVD
Lunacy 2005 ... DVD
Make Mine Music 1946 ... DVD
The Many Adventures of Winnie the Pooh 1977 ... DVD
Mary and Max 2008 ... DVD
Megamind 2010 ... DVD BD
A Midsummer Night's Dream 1961 ...
Mr Peabody & Sherman 2013 ... DVD BD
Monster House 2006 ... DVD BD
Monsters University 2013 ... DVD BD
Monsters vs Aliens 2009 ... DVD BD
Mulan 1998 ... DVD BD
My Neighbour Totoro 1988 ... DVD BD
The New Gulliver 1935 ...
Paprika 2006 ... DVD
ParaNorman 2012 ... DVD BD
Persepolis 2007 ... DVD BD
Peter Pan 1953 ... DVD BD
The Phantom Tollbooth 1969 ... DVD
The Pirates! in an Adventure with Scientists! 2012 ... DVD BD
Ponyo 2008 ... DVD
The Prince of Egypt 1998 ... DVD
Princess Mononoke 1997/2001 ... DVD BD
Puss in Boots 2011 ... DVD BD
Ratatouille 2007 ... DVD BD
The Rescuers 1977 ... DVD
Rio 2011 ... DVD BD
Rise of the Guardians 2012 ... DVD BD
Robin Hood 1973 ... DVD
Roujin Z 1991 ... DVD
Shaun the Sheep Movie 2015 ... DVD
Shrek 2001 ... DVD BD
Shrek 2 2004 ... DVD BD
The Simpsons Movie 2007 ... DVD BD
Sleeping Beauty 1959 ... DVD BD
Smash & Grab: the Story of the Pink Panthers 2012 ... DVD
Snoopy and Charlie Brown: the Peanuts Movie 2015 ... DVD BD
Song of the Sea 2014 ... DVD BD
South Park: Bigger, Longer & Uncut 1999 ... DVD
Spirited Away 2001 ... DVD BD
The SpongeBob SquarePants Movie 2004 ... DVD
The SpongeBob Movie: Sponge out of Water 2015 ... DVD
Strings 2004 ... DVD
Surviving Life 2010 ... DVD
Tangled 2010 ... DVD BD
Thomas & Friends - Sodor's Legend of the Lost Treasure: the Movie 2015 ... DVD
Tim Burton's Corpse Bride 2005 ... DVD BD
Titan AE 2000 ... DVD
A Town Called Panic 2009 ... DVD
Town Rat, Country Rat 1923 ...
Tuck Everlasting 1980 ...
Turbo 2013 ... DVD BD
The 12 Tasks of Asterix 1975 ...
Volere, Volare 1991 ...
Wallace & Gromit in The Curse of the Were-Rabbit 2005 ... DVD
Waltz with Bashir 2008 ... DVD BD
When Magoo Flew 1955 ...
When the Wind Blows 1986 ... DVD
A Wild Hare 1940 ...
The Wings of Honneamise 1987 ...
Yellow Submarine 1968 ... DVD BD

BIOGRAPHY ★★★★★

Amadeus 1984 ... DVD BD
Andrei Rublev 1966 ... DVD BD
An Angel at My Table 1990 ... DVD BD
Born on the Fourth of July 1989 ... DVD BD
Chopper 2000 ... DVD
The Colour of Pomegranates 1969 ... DVD
Dear Diary 1994 ...
The Diary of Anne Frank 1959 ... DVD
Ed Wood 1994 ... DVD BD
The Elephant Man 1980 ... DVD BD
The Fighter 2010 ... DVD BD
Florence Foster Jenkins 2016 ...
Gandhi 1982 ... DVD BD
The General 1998 ... DVD
Gods and Monsters 1998 ... DVD
Heavenly Creatures 1994 ... DVD BD
Jacquot de Nantes 1991 ... DVD
Jeanne la Pucelle 1994 ...
The Jolson Story 1946 ... DVD BD
The Killing Fields 1984 ... DVD BD

The Long Day Closes 1992 .... DVD
The Madness of King George 1995 ...... DVD
Midnight Express 1978 .... DVD BD
Milk 2008 .... DVD BD
The Miracle Worker 1962 .... DVD
Mr Turner 2014 .... DVD
The Motorcycle Diaries 2004 ..... DVD BD
My Left Foot 1989 .... DVD BD
Patton 1970 .... DVD BD
Prick Up Your Ears 1987 .... DVD
Quills 2000 .... DVD
Raging Bull 1980 .... DVD BD
Reds 1981 .... DVD
Schindler's List 1993 .... DVD BD
The Sea Inside 2004 .... DVD
Shadowlands 1993 .... DVD
Shine 1996 .... DVD
The Straight Story 1999 .... DVD
10 Rillington Place 1970 .... DVD
Thirty Two Short Films about Glenn Gould 1993 .... DVD
Topsy-Turvy 1999 .... DVD

BIOGRAPHY ★★★★

The Actress 1953
Adam 1983
Al Capone 1959
All the Way 2016
American Splendor 2003 .... DVD
And When Did You Last See Your Father? 2007
Angels of Evil 2010 .... DVD BD
Anna Boleyn 1920
The Apple 1998 .... DVD
At Close Range 1985 .... DVD
The Attic: the Hiding of Anne Frank 1988
Auto Focus 2002 .... DVD
The Aviator 2004 .... DVD BD
Awakenings 1990 .... DVD
Bad Blood 1982 .... DVD
Bandit Queen 1994 .... DVD
The Barretts of Wimpole Street 1934
Beau James 1957
Before Night Falls 2000 .... DVD
Behind the Candelabra 2013 ...... DVD BD
The Believer 2001 .... DVD
The Best Things in Life Are Free 1956
The Betty Ford Story 1987
Bill 1981
Bird 1988 .... DVD
Birdman of Alcatraz 1962 .... DVD
Blind Flight 2003 .... DVD
Born Free 1966 .... DVD
Born to Be Blue 2015 .... DVD BD
The Boston Strangler 1968 .... DVD
Bound for Glory 1976 .... DVD
Brian's Song 1971
The Buddy Holly Story 1978 ...... DVD BD
Bully 2001 .... DVD
The Burning Bed 1984
The Burning Season 1994
Calendar Girls 2003 .... DVD
Camille Claudel 1915 2013 .... DVD
Capote 2005 .... DVD BD
Captive of the Desert 1990
Caravaggio 1986 .... DVD
Carrington 1995 .... DVD
Carve Her Name with Pride 1958 ..... DVD
Catch Me If You Can 2002 .... DVD
Chameleon Street 1989
Charlie Wilson's War 2007 ...... DVD BD
Che Part One 2008 .... DVD BD
Chihwaseon (Drunk on Women and Poetry) 2002
Cinderella Man 2005 .... DVD BD
Coal Miner's Daughter 1980 .... DVD
Cobb 1994
Coco avant Chanel 2009 .... DVD BD
Confessions of a Dangerous Mind 2002 .... DVD
Control 2007 .... DVD
The Court-Martial of Billy Mitchell 1955
The Court-Martial of Jackie Robinson 1990
Cry Freedom 1987 .... DVD
A Cry in the Dark 1988 .... DVD
Daens 1992
The Dance of Reality 2013
Dance with a Stranger 1984 .... DVD
The Danish Girl 2015 .... DVD BD
Dead Man Walking 1995 .... DVD
Diary for My Children 1982 .... DVD
Diary for My Loves 1987
Dillinger 1945 .... DVD
Dillinger 1973
The Diving-Bell and the Butterfly 2007 .... DVD
Docteur Petiot 1990
Dragon: the Bruce Lee Story 1993 ..... DVD
The Eddy Duchin Story 1956 .... DVD
84 Charing Cross Road 1986 .... DVD
Elvis - the Movie 1979
The Enigma of Kaspar Hauser 1974 ... DVD BD
Erin Brockovich 2000 .... DVD BD
Europa Europa 1991 .... DVD
Evidence of Love 1990 .... DVD
Farinelli il Castrato 1994 .... DVD
Fear on Trial 1975
Fear Strikes Out 1957

The Fighting Sullivans 1944 .... DVD
Finding Neverland 2004 .... DVD BD
The Five Pennies 1959 .... DVD
Fly Away Home 1996 .... DVD
Four Days in September 1997
Frances 1982 .... DVD
Francis, God's Jester 1950 .... DVD
Frida 2002 .... DVD BD
Friendly Fire 1979 .... DVD
Funny Girl 1968 .... DVD
The Future Is Unwritten 2006 .... DVD
The Glenn Miller Story 1953 .... DVD
Good Vibrations 2012 .... DVD BD
Gorillas in the Mist 1988 .... DVD
Goya in Bordeaux 1999
The Great Caruso 1951 .... DVD
The Great Moment 1944 .... DVD
The Great Waltz 1938 .... DVD
The Great Ziegfeld 1936 .... DVD
Gypsy 1962 .... DVD
Hannah Arendt 2012
Hilary and Jackie 1998 .... DVD
Hors la Vie 1991
The Hurricane 1999 .... DVD
I Shot Andy Warhol 1995 .... DVD
I Want to Live! 1958 .... DVD
I'll Cry Tomorrow 1955
Immortal Beloved 1994 .... DVD
In the Name of the Father 1993 .... DVD BD
The Inn of the Sixth Happiness 1958 ... DVD
Innocent Moves 1993 .... DVD
Interrupted Melody 1955 .... DVD
Intervista 1987
Into the Wild 2007 .... DVD BD
Invictus 2009 .... DVD BD
The Invisible Woman 2013 .... DVD BD
Iris 2001 .... DVD
Isadora 1968 .... DVD
Jimi: All Is by My Side 2013 ...... DVD BD
Julie & Julia 2009 .... DVD BD
Kinsey 2004 .... DVD
The Krays 1990 .... DVD
Lady Sings the Blues 1972
The Last American Hero 1973 .... DVD
The Last Emperor 1987 .... DVD BD
Leave 'Em Laughing 1981
Let Him Have It 1991 .... DVD
The Libertine 2004 .... DVD
The Life of Emile Zola 1937 .... DVD
Lincoln 2012 .... DVD BD
The Look of Love 2013 .... DVD BD
Love Me or Leave Me 1955 .... DVD
Lucky Luciano 1973 .... DVD
Lust for Life 1956 .... DVD
Mad Dog 1976 .... DVD
The Magic Box 1951 .... DVD
Man on the Moon 1999 .... DVD
Mandela 1987 .... DVD
Marie Antoinette 1938 .... DVD
Mask 1985 .... DVD
Mesrine: Killer Instinct 2008 ...... DVD BD
Mesrine: Public Enemy No 1 2008 .... DVD BD
Michael Collins 1996 .... DVD BD
A Mighty Heart 2007 .... DVD BD
Mirror 1974 .... DVD
Mishima: a Life in Four Chapters 1985
Mommie Dearest 1981 .... DVD
Monarch 1996
Monsieur Vincent 1947 .... DVD
Moulin Rouge 1952 .... DVD
Mrs Parker and the Vicious Circle 1994 .... DVD
My Ain Folk 1973
My Mother's Courage 1995
My Way Home 1978
Napoléon 1955
Nijinsky 1980
Nixon 1995 .... DVD
Nowhere Boy 2010 .... DVD BD
Les Nuits Fauves 1992
Out of Africa 1985 .... DVD BD
Papillon 1973 .... DVD
The People vs Larry Flynt 1996 .... DVD
The Pianist 2002 .... DVD BD
Pollock 2000 .... DVD
The Pride of the Yankees 1942 .... DVD
Private Parts 1997 .... DVD
Public Enemies 2009 .... DVD BD
Rasputin 1996 .... DVD
Ray 2004 .... DVD BD
Reach for the Sky 1956 .... DVD
Reversal of Fortune 1990 .... DVD
The Rise and Fall of Legs Diamond 1960 ....
A Room and a Half or a Sentimental Journey Back Home 2009 .... DVD
Rosa Luxemburg 1986
Salvador 1986 .... DVD
Second Serve 1986
Secret Honor 1984 .... DVD
Séraphine 2008 .... DVD
Sergeant York 1941 .... DVD
Sid and Nancy 1986 .... DVD BD
Silkwood 1983 .... DVD
Sister Kenny 1946
Somebody Up There Likes Me 1956 ...... DVD
The Song of Bernadette 1943 .... DVD
Sophie Scholl: the Final Days 2005 .... DVD BD
Star 80 1983

Steve Jobs 2015
The Story of GI Joe 1945 .... DVD
The Story of Vernon and Irene Castle 1939
Straight Outta Compton 2015 ..... DVD BD
Superstar: the Karen Carpenter Story 1987
Surviving Picasso 1996
Talk to Me 2007 .... DVD BD
Temple Grandin 2010
Testament of Youth 2014 .... DVD BD
The Theory of Everything 2015 ... DVD BD
They Died with Their Boots On 1941 .....
This Boy's Life 1993 .... DVD
Three Little Words 1950 .... DVD
Till the Clouds Roll By 1946 .... DVD
Tina: What's Love Got to Do with It 1993
To Walk with Lions 1999 .... DVD
Tracks 2013 .... DVD BD
Truman 1995 .... DVD
Van Gogh 1991 .... DVD BD
Veronica Guerin 2003 .... DVD
Violette 2013
Walesa: Man of Hope 2013 .... DVD
Walk the Line 2005 .... DVD BD
Wilde 1997 .... DVD BD
With a Song in My Heart 1952 .... DVD
The Wonderful, Horrible Life of Leni Riefenstahl 1993 .... DVD
Yankee Doodle Dandy 1942 .... DVD
Young Mr Lincoln 1939 .... DVD
The Young Mr Pitt 1942

COMEDY ★★★★★

Abigail's Party 1977 .... DVD
Adam's Rib 1949 .... DVD
Airplane! 1980 .... DVD BD
All about My Mother 1999 .... DVD
Amarcord 1973 .... DVD BD
Amélie 2001 .... DVD BD
American Beauty 1999 .... DVD BD
American Graffiti 1973 .... DVD BD
Annie Hall 1977 .... DVD BD
Anomalisa 2015 .... DVD BD
The Apartment 1960 .... DVD BD
Arsenic and Old Lace 1944 .... DVD
The Awful Truth 1937 .... DVD
Back to the Future 1985 .... DVD BD
Being John Malkovich 1999 .... DVD BD
Big Business 1929 .... DVD
Billy Liar 1963 .... DVD
Birdman or (The Unexpected Virtue of Ignorance) 2014 .... DVD BD
Born Yesterday 1950 .... DVD
Braindead 1992 .... DVD
Bridesmaids 2011 .... DVD BD
Bringing Up Baby 1938 .... DVD
Butch Cassidy and the Sundance Kid 1969 .... DVD BD
Calamity Jane 1953 .... DVD
The Cameraman 1928 .... DVD
Capricious Summer 1968 .... DVD
The Cat Concerto 1947
Charade 1963 .... DVD BD
City Lights 1931 .... DVD BD
College 1927 .... DVD
Crimes and Misdemeanors 1989 .... DVD
Day Dreams 1922 .... DVD
Dear Diary 1994 .... DVD
Destry Rides Again 1939 .... DVD
The Discreet Charm of the Bourgeoisie 1972 .... DVD BD
Dr Strangelove, or How I Learned to Stop Worrying and Love the Bomb 1963 .... DVD BD
The Dot and the Line 1965
Duck Dodgers in the 24½ Century 1953
Duck Soup 1933 .... DVD
Fargo 1995 .... DVD BD
Finding Nemo 2003 .... DVD BD
A Fish Called Wanda 1988 .... DVD BD
Flirting 1989
Florence Foster Jenkins 2016 .... DVD
4 Clowns 1970
Four Weddings and a Funeral 1994 .... DVD BD
Frances Ha 2012 .... DVD
The Freshman 1925 .... DVD
The Full Monty 1997 .... DVD BD
Galaxy Quest 1999 .... DVD BD
The General 1927 .... DVD
Ginger & Fred 1986 .... DVD
Girl Shy 1924
The Gold Rush 1925 .... DVD BD
The Graduate 1967 .... DVD BD
The Great Dictator 1940 .... DVD
Groundhog Day 1993 .... DVD BD
Hail the Conquering Hero 1944 .... DVD
Hannah and Her Sisters 1986 .... DVD
Happiness 1998 .... DVD
A Hard Day's Night 1964 .... DVD BD
Harvey 1950 .... DVD
Heathers 1989 .... DVD
Heaven Can Wait 1943 .... DVD
His Girl Friday 1939 .... DVD
Holiday 1938 .... DVD
Horse Feathers 1932 .... DVD
The House on Trubnaya Square 1928 ......

Husbands and Wives 1992 .... DVD
I Know Where I'm Going! 1945 .... DVD
I Was a Male War Bride 1949 .... DVD
I Was Born, but... 1932 .... DVD
I'm All Right Jack 1959 .... DVD BD
The Immigrant 1917 .... DVD
In the Company of Men 1997
The Incredibles 2004 .... DVD BD
Inside Llewyn Davis 2013 .... DVD BD
Inside Out 2015 .... DVD BD
It Happened One Night 1934 .... DVD BD
An Italian Straw Hat 1927
It's a Gift 1934 .... DVD
Jour de Fête 1947 .... DVD BD
The Kid Brother 1927
Kikujiro 1999 .... DVD BD
Kind Hearts and Coronets 1949 ..... DVD BD
The King of Comedy 1983 .... DVD
King-Size Canary 1947
The Lady Eve 1941 .... DVD
The Ladykillers 1955 .... DVD BD
The Lavender Hill Mob 1951 ..... DVD BD
Let's Talk about the Rain 2008 .... DVD BD
Life Is Sweet 1990 .... DVD BD
Lola 1960
Lolita 1961 .... DVD
Lost in Translation 2003 .... DVD BD
Love Affair 1939
Love in the Afternoon 1957 .... DVD
Love Me Tonight 1932
The Man with Two Brains 1983 .... DVD
Manhattan 1979 .... DVD BD
The Marriage Circle 1924
MASH 1969 .... DVD
The Mask 1994 .... DVD BD
Micmacs 2009 .... DVD
Midnight 1939
A Million Ways to Die in the West 2014 .... DVD BD
The Miracle of Morgan's Creek 1943 ....
Miracle on 34th Street 1947 .... DVD
Mister Roberts 1955
Mr Smith Goes to Washington 1939 .... DVD
Mistress America 2015
Modern Times 1936 .... DVD BD
Mon Oncle 1958 .... DVD BD
Monkey Business 1952 .... DVD
Monsieur Hulot's Holiday 1953 .... DVD BD
Monsters, Inc 2001 .... DVD BD
The Music Box 1932 .... DVD
The Naked Gun 1988 .... DVD BD
Nashville 1975 .... DVD BD
Nebraska 2013 .... DVD BD
A Night at the Opera 1935 .... DVD
Ninotchka 1939 .... DVD
One Froggy Evening 1955
One Hundred and One Dalmatians 1960 .... DVD BD
Our Hospitality 1923 .... DVD
Pack Up Your Troubles 1932 .... DVD
The Paleface 1922 .... DVD
Perfect Day 1929 .... DVD
The Philadelphia Story 1940 .... DVD
Playtime 1967 .... DVD BD
The Producers 1968 .... DVD
Pygmalion 1938 .... DVD
The Quiet Man 1952 .... DVD
La Règle du Jeu 1939 .... DVD
Roman Holiday 1953 .... DVD
The Royal Tenenbaums 2001 .... DVD
Ruggles of Red Gap 1935 ...... DVD BD
Sabrina 1954 .... DVD
Safety Last 1923 .... DVD
Scream 1996 .... DVD BD
Shakespeare in Love 1998 .... DVD BD
Shallow Grave 1994 .... DVD BD
Shaun of the Dead 2004 .... DVD BD
Sherlock Junior 1924 .... DVD
Show People 1928
Sideways 2004 .... DVD BD
Sightseers 2012 .... DVD BD
Smiles of a Summer Night 1955 .... DVD
The Smiling Lieutenant 1931
Some Like It Hot 1959 .... DVD BD
Sons of the Desert 1933 .... DVD
Steamboat Bill, Jr 1928 .... DVD
Stolen Kisses 1968 .... DVD BD
The Story of a Cheat 1936 .... DVD
Strictly Ballroom 1992 .... DVD BD
Sullivan's Travels 1941 .... DVD BD
Swing Time 1936 .... DVD
This Is Spinal Tap 1984 .... DVD
The Three Little Pigs 1933 .... DVD
Top Hat 1935 .... DVD
Topsy-Turvy 1999 .... DVD
The Tortoise and the Hare 1935 ......
A Touch of Class 1973
Toy Story 1995 .... DVD BD
Toy Story 2 1999 .... DVD BD
Toy Story 3 2010 .... DVD BD
Tremors 1989 .... DVD BD
Trouble in Paradise 1932 .... DVD
The Trouble with Harry 1954 ...... DVD BD
The Truman Show 1998 .... DVD BD
Twentieth Century 1934
The Two Tars 1928 .... DVD
Volver 2006 .... DVD
WALL-E 2008 .... DVD BD
Way Out West 1937 .... DVD
What's Up, Doc? 1972 .... DVD

When Harry Met Sally... 1989......*DVD* 🅑
Whisky Galore! 1949.................*DVD* 🅑
Who Framed Roger Rabbit 1988 ..*DVD* 🅑
The Wolf of Wall Street 2013.......*DVD* 🅑
Women on the Verge of a Nervous
Breakdown 1988 ....*DVD*
You Can't Take It with You 1938.......*DVD*
Young Frankenstein 1974 ....*DVD* 🅑
Zéro de Conduite 1933 ....*DVD*
Zootropolis 2016.........................*DVD* 🅑

COMEDY ★★★★

About a Boy 2002.......................*DVD* 🅑
About Schmidt 2002.......................*DVD*
About Time 2013.........................*DVD* 🅑
Accidental Hero 1992 ....*DVD*
The Accidental Tourist 1988 ....*DVD*
Ace Ventura: Pet Detective 1993.....*DVD*
Adaptation. 2002.........................*DVD*
The Addams Family 1991 ....*DVD* 🅑
Addams Family Values 1993..........*DVD*
Adventureland 2009 ....*DVD* 🅑
The Adventures of Priscilla, Queen of the
Desert 1994 ....*DVD* 🅑
After Hours 1985 ....*DVD* 🅑
Un Air de Famille 1996....................
Alan Partridge: Alpha Papa
2013 ....*DVD* 🅑
Alfie 1966.................................*DVD* 🅑
Alice Adams 1935.........................
Almost Famous 2000 ....*DVD* 🅑
The Ambulance 1990.......................
American Honey 2016.......................
American Pie 1999.....................*DVD* 🅑
The American President 1995...........*DVD*
American Psycho 2000 ....*DVD*
An American Werewolf in London
1981 ....*DVD* 🅑
The Americanization of Emily 1964 ....
Analyze This 1999.........................*DVD*
And Now for Something Completely
Different 1971 ....*DVD*
Angus, Thongs and Perfect Snogging
2008 ....*DVD*
Animal Crackers 1930.....................*DVD*
Another Year 2010.........................*DVD*
Appropriate Behaviour 2014....................
Arachnophobia 1990 ....*DVD*
Ariel 1988 ....
Arise, My Love 1940 ....
Arthur 1981..................................*DVD*
Artists and Models 1955....................
As Good as It Gets 1997 ....*DVD*
The Assassination Bureau 1969 ....
Attack the Block 2010 ....*DVD* 🅑
Auntie Mame 1958.........................
Austin Powers: International Man of
Mystery 1997 ....*DVD*
Austin Powers: the Spy Who Shagged Me
1999 ....*DVD* 🅑
An Autumn Tale 1998...................*DVD*
Avanti! 1972 ....*DVD*
The Aviator's Wife 1980...................*DVD*
Babe 1995 ....*DVD* 🅑
The Bachelor and the Bobby-Soxer
1947 ....*DVD*
Back to the Future Part III 1990..*DVD* 🅑
Bad 1976.....................................
Bad Boys 1995 ....*DVD* 🅑
Bad Neighbours 2 2016.....................
Bad Taste 1987.............................*DVD*
Bagdad Café 1987.........................*DVD*
The Baker's Wife 1938 ....
Ball of Fire 1941...........................*DVD*
The Ballad of Cable Hogue 1970........*DVD*
The Bank Dick 1940 ....*DVD*
The Barbarian Invasions 2003 ....*DVD*
The Barber Shop 1933.....................*DVD*
Barcelona 1994 ....
Barefoot in the Park 1967 ....*DVD*
Basket Case 1982.........................*DVD*
The Be All and End All 2009..........*DVD*
Be Kind Rewind 2007 ....*DVD* 🅑
Bean 1997 ....*DVD* 🅑
Le Beau Mariage 1982......................*DVD*
The Beautiful Blonde from Bashful Bend
1949 ....*DVD*
Bedtime Story 1964.......................*DVD*
Bee Movie 2007 ....*DVD* 🅑
Beethoven 1992.............................*DVD*
Beetle Juice 1988..........................*DVD* 🅑
Begin Again 2013 ....*DVD* 🅑
Being There 1979 ....*DVD* 🅑
Belle Epoque 1992......................*DVD*
The Best Exotic Marigold Hotel
2011 ....*DVD* 🅑
Between the Lines 1977 ....
Beverly Hills Cop 1984.................*DVD* 🅑
Bienvenido Mr Marshall 1953.............*DVD*
Big 1988.................................*DVD* 🅑
The Big Broadcast 1932 ....
Big Daddy 1999 ....*DVD*
Big Deal on Madonna Street 1958 ....
The Big Lebowski 1997..................*DVD* 🅑
Big Night 1996.............................
The Big Store 1941.........................*DVD*
Bill & Ted's Excellent Adventure
1988 ....*DVD* 🅑
Bill & Ted's Bogus Journey 1991 ......*DVD*

Biloxi Blues 1988 ....*DVD*
The Bingo Long Travelling All-Stars and
Motor Kings 1976 ....*DVD*
Birds Anonymous 1957 ....
Black Cat, White Cat 1998 ....*DVD*
Black Pond 2011 ....*DVD*
Black Sheep 2006 ....*DVD* 🅑
The Black Sheep of Whitehall 1941......*DVD*
Blazing Saddles 1974..................*DVD* 🅑
Bliss 1985 ....
Blithe Spirit 1945 ....*DVD*
Blockheads 1938 ....*DVD*
A Blonde in Love 1965 ....*DVD*
The Blues Brothers 1980................*DVD* 🅑
Blume in Love 1973.........................
Bob Le Flambeur 1955 ....*DVD*
Bob Roberts 1992 ....*DVD*
Bolt 2008 ....*DVD* 🅑
Bon Voyage 2003..........................*DVD*
Bonne Chance 1935.......................
Bonnie Scotland 1935 ....*DVD*
The Book of Life 1998 ....
Book of Life 2014 ....*DVD* 🅑
Borat: Cultural Learnings of America for
Make Benefit Glorious Nation of
Kazakhstan 2006 ....*DVD* 🅑
Boudu, Saved from Drowning 1932 .....*DVD*
Bowfinger 1999..............................*DVD*
Box of Moonlight 1996 ....*DVD*
A Boy and His Dog 1975 ....*DVD*
Brain Damage 1988.........................
Breaking Away 1979.......................*DVD*
Bridget Jones's Diary 2001........*DVD* 🅑
Broadcast News 1987......................*DVD*
Broadway Danny Rose 1984............*DVD*
Broadway Melody of 1936 1935.........*DVD*
Broken Flowers 2005....................*DVD*
Brooklyn 2015 ....*DVD* 🅑
The Brothers Bloom 2008 ....*DVD* 🅑
Brothers in Law 1956 ....*DVD*
Buffalo Soldiers 2001 ....*DVD*
Bugsy Malone 1976...................*DVD* 🅑
Bull Durham 1988.........................*DVD*
Bullets over Broadway 1994..............*DVD*
Bulworth 1998..............................*DVD*
The 'Burbs 1989.........................*DVD* 🅑
Burn after Reading 2008...........*DVD* 🅑
Bus Stop 1956..............................*DVD*
The Butcher Boy 1917 ....
The Butcher Boy 1997 ....
Bye Bye Birdie 1963.......................
Bye Bye Braverman 1968..................
La Cage aux Folles 1978 ....*DVD*
Calendar Girls 2003.......................*DVD*
California Dreamin' 2007..................*DVD*
California Suite 1978 ....*DVD*
Call Me Madam 1953.......................*DVD*
The Campaign 2012 ....*DVD* 🅑
Can She Bake a Cherry Pie? 1983 ....
Car Wash 1976..............................*DVD*
Caramel 2007 ....*DVD*
Career Girls 1997..........................*DVD*
Careful 1992.................................
Careful, Soft Shoulder 1942..............*DVD*
The Carer 2015 ....
Carnage 2011 ....*DVD* 🅑
Carry On Again Doctor 1969..............*DVD*
Carry On Cleo 1964.....................*DVD* 🅑
Carry On - Don't Lose Your Head
1966 ....*DVD*
Carry On Screaming 1966..............*DVD* 🅑
Carry On Up the Khyber 1968...........*DVD*
The Cars That Ate Paris 1974..........*DVD*
Casper 1995.................................*DVD*
The Castle 1997...........................*DVD*
The Cat and the Canary 1939..........*DVD*
Cat Ballou 1965............................*DVD*
Catch Me If You Can 2002 ....*DVD*
Cedar Rapids 2011.....................*DVD* 🅑
Chameleon Street 1989....................
The Change-Up 2011...................*DVD* 🅑
Charlie Wilson's War 2007............*DVD* 🅑
Chasing Amy 1996......................*DVD* 🅑
Chef 2014.................................*DVD* 🅑
Chicago 2002.............................*DVD* 🅑
Chicken Run 2000.........................*DVD*
Le Chignon d'Olga 2002 ....*DVD*
The Children of Heaven 1997 ....*DVD*
The Children of the Marshland 1998........*DVD*
Children of the Revolution 1996.............
Chimes at Midnight 1966 ....*DVD* 🅑
Chocolat 2000.........................*DVD* 🅑
Choose Me 1984............................*DVD*
Chori Chori 1956 ....
A Christmas Story 1983..................*DVD*
A Christmas Tale 2008....................*DVD*
Chuck & Buck 2000.......................*DVD*
Chung King Express 1994..................*DVD*
The Circus 1928.......................*DVD* 🅑
Citizens Band 1977 ....
City Island 2009..........................*DVD*
City Slickers 1991 ....*DVD*
Claire's Knee 1970.........................*DVD*
Claudia 1943 ....
Clerks 1994.............................*DVD* 🅑
Closely Observed Trains 1966............*DVD*
Cloudy with a Chance of Meatballs
2009 ....*DVD* 🅑
Club de Femmes 1936......................

Clueless 1995 ....*DVD*
A Cock and Bull Story 2005.............*DVD*
Come as You Are 2011.................*DVD* 🅑
Come Live with Me 1941...................
Comfort and Joy 1984 ....*DVD* 🅑
The Comic 1969 ....
Les Compères 1983.........................
Confessions of a Dangerous Mind
2002 ....*DVD*
Confidences Trop Intimes 2004 ....*DVD*
Conspirators of Pleasure 1996 ....*DVD*
The Constant Husband 1955................
Conversations with My Gardener 2006 .....
Les Convoyeurs Attendent 1999 ....
The Cook, the Thief, His Wife and Her Lover
1989 ....*DVD* 🅑
Cool Runnings 1993........................*DVD*
Le Cop 1985..................................
Cotton Comes to Harlem 1970 ....
The Court Jester 1956.....................*DVD*
The Courtship of Eddie's Father 1963........
Cover Girl 1944............................*DVD*
Crazy from the Heart 1991 ....
Crazy, Stupid, Love 2011............*DVD* 🅑
The Cremator 1968.........................
Le Cri du Hibou 1987......................
Le Crime de Monsieur Lange 1935........*DVD*
Crimes of the Heart 1986 ....*DVD*
La Crise 1992...............................*DVD*
"Crocodile" Dundee 1986.................*DVD*
Cross My Heart 1990.......................
Crossing Delancey 1988....................
The Cup 1999...............................*DVD*
The Cure 1917.............................*DVD*
Cycling with Molière 2013 ....
Cyrus 2010.............................*DVD* 🅑
Daddy Long Legs 1919.....................
Daddy Long Legs 1955.....................*DVD*
Daisies 1966...............................*DVD*
Dan in Real Life 2007 ....*DVD* 🅑
Dandin 1987.................................
The Darjeeling Limited 2007 ....*DVD* 🅑
Date Night 2010.......................*DVD* 🅑
Dave 1993..................................*DVD*
A Day in the Death of Joe Egg 1971 ....*DVD*
The Day of the Beast 1995 ....*DVD*
The Daytrippers 1998......................*DVD*
Dazed and Confused 1993............*DVD* 🅑
The Dead and the Deadly 1983 ....
Dead Man's Curve 1997...................*DVD*
Dead Men Don't Wear Plaid 1982 ......*DVD*
Dean Spanley 2008 ....*DVD* 🅑
Dear Heart 1964 ....
Dear White People 2014 ....*DVD*
Death Becomes Her 1992 ....*DVD*
Death by Hanging 1968.....................
Death in Brunswick 1990 ....
Death Japanese Style 1984................
Death of a Bureaucrat 1966 ....
The Death of Mr Lazarescu 2005 ......*DVD*
The Decline of the American Empire
1986 ....*DVD*
Delicacy 2011.........................*DVD* 🅑
Delicatessen 1990 ....*DVD* 🅑
The Dentist 1932.........................*DVD*
The Descendants 2011 ....*DVD* 🅑
Designing Woman 1957 ....
Desire 1936..................................*DVD*
Desk Set 1957 ....*DVD*
Desperately Seeking Susan 1985........*DVD*
Despicable Me 2010 ....*DVD* 🅑
Despicable Me 2 2013 ....*DVD* 🅑
Devils on the Doorstep 2000..............*DVD*
Dim Sum: a Little Bit of Heart 1985....*DVD*
Diner 1982.................................*DVD*
Le Dîner de Cons 1998 ....*DVD*
Dinner at Eight 1933.......................*DVD*
Dinner Rush 2000.........................*DVD*
The Dish 2000..............................*DVD*
Divorce - Italian Style 1961..............*DVD*
Doctor in the House 1954 ....*DVD*
Dom Hemingway 2013 ....*DVD* 🅑
Don Jon 2013 ....*DVD*
Doña Herlinda and Her Son 1986 ....
Le Donk & Scor-Zay-Zee 2009 ....*DVD*
Don's Party 1976...........................
Dope 2015.................................*DVD*
Down by Law 1986......................*DVD* 🅑
The Dream Team 1989.....................*DVD*
The Dressmaker 2015..................*DVD* 🅑
Drinking Buddies 2013 ....*DVD*
Drôle de Drame 1937......................
Drowning by Numbers 1988 ....*DVD* 🅑
Drunken Master 1978 ....*DVD*
Dumb and Dumber 1994.............*DVD* 🅑
East Is East 1999 ....*DVD* 🅑
Easy A 2010............................*DVD* 🅑
Easy Living 1937.........................*DVD*
Eat Drink Man Woman 1994 ....
Eating Raoul 1982 ....*DVD*
Edtv 1999...................................*DVD*
Educating Rita 1983 ....*DVD*
El 1953......................................*DVD*
Election 1999.........................*DVD* 🅑
Elf 2003..................................*DVD* 🅑
Elling 2001.................................*DVD*
The Emperor's New Groove
2000 ....*DVD* 🅑
Enemies, a Love Story 1989 ....*DVD*
Enough Said 2013 ....*DVD*

Eternal Sunshine of the Spotless Mind
2003 ....*DVD* 🅑
An Everlasting Piece 2000................*DVD*
Everybody Wants Some!! 2016...............
Everyone Says I Love You 1996 ....
Everything Must Go 2010 ....*DVD* 🅑
Evil Roy Slade 1971.......................
Factotum (A Man Who Preforms Many
Jobs) 2005 ....*DVD*
The Fairy 2011 ....*DVD*
Fallen Angels 1995 ....*DVD* 🅑
La Famille Bélier 2014 ....*DVD*
Family Plot 1976.......................*DVD* 🅑
The Family Way 1966 ....*DVD*
Fantastic Mr Fox 2009 ....*DVD* 🅑
Fast Times at Ridgemont High
1982 ....*DVD* 🅑
Father Brown 1954 ....*DVD*
Father of the Bride 1950 ....*DVD*
Father of the Bride 1991 ....*DVD*
Fear and Trembling 2003 ....*DVD*
The Fearless Vampire Killers 1967 ....*DVD*
The Ferragosto Dinner 2008 ....*DVD*
Ferris Bueller's Day Off 1986......*DVD* 🅑
Fever Pitch 1996..........................*DVD*
Fiddler on the Roof 1971................*DVD* 🅑
50/50 2011.............................*DVD* 🅑
Filth 2013.................................*DVD* 🅑
The First Wives Club 1996 ....*DVD*
The Five-Year Engagement
2012 ....*DVD* 🅑
The Flim-Flam Man 1967 ....
The Floorwalker 1916 ....*DVD*
Flowers and Trees 1932....................
Follow the Boys 1944 ....*DVD*
Follow the Fleet 1936 ....*DVD*
For Heaven's Sake 1926 ....
For Your Consideration 2006 ....*DVD*
A Foreign Affair 1948 ....*DVD*
Forrest Gump 1994 ....*DVD* 🅑
The Fortune Cookie 1966 ....*DVD*
Four Lions 2010.......................*DVD* 🅑
Four Steps in the Clouds 1942 ....
The Fourth Man 1983......................*DVD*
Frank 2013...............................*DVD* 🅑
The Freshman 1990 ....*DVD*
Fright Night 1985 ....*DVD*
The Frighteners 1996 ....*DVD* 🅑
From Dusk till Dawn 1995 ....*DVD* 🅑
The Front Page 1974 ....*DVD*
Full Moon in Paris 1984 ....*DVD*
Funny Bones 1994.........................*DVD*
Funny Dirty Little War 1983 ....
Funny Face 1957 ....*DVD* 🅑
Garden State 2003 ....*DVD* 🅑
Gardens in Autumn 2006 ....
The Gay Divorce 1934.....................*DVD*
Genevieve 1953 ....*DVD*
Gentlemen Prefer Blondes 1953...*DVD* 🅑
Georgy Girl 1966 ....*DVD*
Get Him to the Greek 2010..........*DVD* 🅑
Get Santa 2014..........................*DVD*
Get Shorty 1995.......................*DVD* 🅑
The Ghost Breakers 1940 ....*DVD*
The Ghost of St Michael's 1941 ....*DVD*
Ghost Busters 1984...................*DVD* 🅑
Gidget 1959 ....*DVD*
Gimme the Loot 2012 ....*DVD*
The Girl Can't Help It 1956 ....*DVD*
Girl 6 1996.................................*DVD*
Girlfriends 1978 ....*DVD*
Girls' Night 1997 ....*DVD*
Go 1999...................................*DVD* 🅑
Go West 1925 ....*DVD*
God Bless America 2011 ....*DVD*
Gold of Naples 1954 ....*DVD*
The Good Companions 1933..............*DVD*
The Good Dinosaur 2015 ....*DVD* 🅑
The Good Fairy 1935 ....*DVD*
Good Morning, Boys 1937.................*DVD*
Good News 1947...........................*DVD*
Good Vibrations 2012 ....*DVD* 🅑
The Goodbye Girl 1977 ....*DVD*
The Goose Steps Out 1942 ....*DVD*
Le Goût des Autres 1999 ....*DVD*
Grabbers 2012.........................*DVD* 🅑
The Grand Budapest Hotel 2014...*DVD* 🅑
Grand Theft Parsons 2003 ....*DVD*
Les Grandes Manoeuvres 1955.........*DVD*
Grandma 2015 ....*DVD*
Grandma's Boy 1922 ....*DVD*
The Great Beauty 2013 ....*DVD* 🅑
The Great McGinty 1940 ....*DVD*
The Great Race 1965 ....*DVD*
The Green Butchers 2003 ....*DVD*
Green for Danger 1946 ....*DVD*
The Green Man 1956.......................*DVD*
The Green Ray 1986.......................*DVD*
Gregory's Girl 1980....................*DVD* 🅑
Gremlins 1984.........................*DVD* 🅑
The Grinch 2000.......................*DVD* 🅑
Grosse Pointe Blank 1997 ....*DVD*
Grow Your Own 2007 ....*DVD*
The Guard 2011 ....*DVD* 🅑
Guess Who's Coming to Dinner 1967...*DVD*
Gumshoe 1971.............................*DVD*
Guys and Dolls 1955 ....*DVD*
Hail, Caesar! 2016....................*DVD* 🅑
Hairspray 1988 ....*DVD*
Hairspray 2007 ....*DVD* 🅑

The Half Naked Truth 1932....................
Hamlet Goes Business 1987 ....*DVD*
Hands across the Table 1935..................
Hangin' with the Homeboys 1991 ......*DVD*
The Hangover 2009 ....*DVD* *BD*
The Happiest Days of Your Life 1950..*DVD*
The Happiness of the Katakuris
2001..*DVD*
Happy, Texas 1999 ....*DVD*
The Hard Way 1991 ....*DVD*
Harold and Maude 1972 ......*DVD* *BD*
Harry and Tonto 1974..........................
Le Havre 2011 ....*DVD* *BD*
Head 1968 ....
Hear My Song 1991..........................*DVD*
Heartbreaker 2010..................*DVD* *BD*
Hearts of the West 1975....................
The Heat 2013 ....*DVD*
Heaven Can Wait 1978........................
Hellzapoppin' 1941 ....
Help! 1965 ....*DVD* *BD*
Henry Fool 1997................................
Here Comes Mr Jordan 1941 ......*DVD* *BD*
Hi, Mom! 1970 ....
High Fidelity 2000 ....*DVD*
High Hopes 1988 ....*DVD* *BD*
High Society 1956 ....
Historias Mínimas 2002....................*DVD*
Hobson's Choice 1953..............*DVD* *BD*
Hold Back the Dawn 1941....................
Holiday Inn 1942 ....*DVD* *BD*
Hollywood or Bust 1956......................
Holy Matrimony 1943..........................
Home Alone 1990 ....*DVD* *BD*
L'Homme du Train 2002 ....*DVD*
Honey, I Shrunk the Kids 1989..........*DVD*
Honeymoon in Vegas 1992 ......*DVD* *BD*
The Honeymooners 2003 ....*DVD*
Hooper 1978 ....
Hot Fuzz 2007 ....*DVD* *BD*
House of Angels 1992 ....
House Party 1990 ....
Houseboat 1958..............................
Housekeeping 1987 ....
How I Won the War 1967....................
How to Marry a Millionaire 1953...*DVD* *BD*
How to Murder Your Wife 1965..........*DVD*
How to Succeed in Business without Really
Trying 1967 ....
How to Train Your Dragon 2010...*DVD* *BD*
How to Train Your Dragon 2
2014 ....*DVD* *BD*
The Howling 1981..............................*DVD*
The Hudsucker Proxy 1994 ....*DVD*
Hue and Cry 1947 ....*DVD* *BD*
Humpday 2009 ....*DVD*
I ♥ Huckabees 2004..........................*DVD*
I Love You Again 1940......................
I Married a Witch 1942......................*DVD*
I Ought to Be in Pictures 1982............
IQ 1994..*DVD*
An Ideal Husband 1999 ....*DVD*
The Idiots 1998................................*DVD*
If You Could Only Cook 1935..............
I'm Going Home 2001........................*DVD*
I'm No Angel 1933..............................
The Importance of Being Earnest
1952 ....*DVD*
In a World... 2013............................*DVD*
In & Out 1997..................................*DVD*
In Bruges 2008 ....*DVD* *BD*
In Her Shoes 2005............................*DVD*
In Search of a Midnight Kiss 2008 .....*DVD*
In the Loop 2009 ....*DVD* *BD*
Indian Summer 1993..........................*DVD*
Infinitely Polar Bear 2014..................*DVD*
Insignificance 1985..........................*DVD*
Irma la Douce 1963..........................*DVD*
Irma Vep 1996..................................*DVD*
The Iron Petticoat 1956......................*DVD*
Irreconcilable Differences 1984 ....
It Should Happen to You 1954............*DVD*
Italian for Beginners 2000..................*DVD*
It's a Wonderful World 1939................
It's Always Fair Weather 1955............
It's Complicated 2009................*DVD* *BD*
It's Great to Be Young 1956................
It's Kind of a Funny Story 2010...*DVD* *BD*
Jackie Chan's Who Am I? 1998 ....*DVD*
Jamón, Jamón 2002..........................*DVD*
Janice Beard 45 WPM 1999 ....*DVD*
Jealousy, Italian Style 1970 ....
Jeffrey 1995 ....*DVD*
The Jerk 1979 ....*DVD* *BD*
Jerry Maguire 1996..........................*DVD*
Johnny Suede 1991..........................*DVD*
Jonah Who Will Be 25 in the Year 2000
1976..
Judy Berlin 1999................................
Jumbo 1962 ....*DVD*
Junebug 2004........................*DVD* *BD*
Juno 2007 ....*DVD* *BD*
Keep Cool 1997..................................
Kenny 2006 ....*DVD*
Kick-Ass 2009 ....*DVD* *BD*
The Kid 1921......................................*BD*
The Kid from Spain 1932....................
The Kidnapping of Michel Houellebecq
2014 ....*DVD* *BD*
The Kids Are All Right 2010 ......*DVD* *BD*

King of Hearts 1966 ....
King, Queen, Knave 1972 ....
The Kingdom 1994..........................*DVD*
Kings & Queen 2004..........................*DVD*
Kiss Kiss Bang Bang 2005 ......*DVD* *BD*
Kiss Me Kate 1953............................*DVD*
Kitchen Stories 2003........................*DVD*
Knocked Up 2007 ....*DVD* *BD*
Kolya 1996 ....*DVD*
Kung Fu Hustle 2004..............*DVD* *BD*
LA Story 1991..................................*DVD*
The Ladies' Man 1961........................*DVD*
Lady for a Day 1933..........................*DVD*
Lady Killer 1933................................
Lady L 1965 ....
Lady with a Past 1932........................
The Landlord 1970............................*DVD*
Last Action Hero 1993............*DVD* *BD*
Last Life in the Universe 2003............*DVD*
The Last of the Good Old Days 1989......
The Late Shift 1996 ....
Laughter in Paradise 1951..................
Laurel and Hardy's Laughing 20s 1965 ......
La Lectrice 1988 ....*DVD*
Legally Blonde 2001..............*DVD* *BD*
The Lego Movie 2014..............*DVD* *BD*
Leningrad Cowboys Go America 1989 ......
Léolo 1992..
Let's Make Love 1960........................*DVD*
Letter to Brezhnev 1985....................*DVD*
Liar Liar 1997........................*DVD* *BD*
Libeled Lady 1936............................*DVD*
Liberal Arts 2011..............................*DVD*
Life Is a Long Quiet River 1988 ....
Life of Riley 2014 ....*DVD*
Life with Father 1947........................*DVD*
Li'l Abner 1959 ....
Lilo & Stitch 2002 ....*DVD* *BD*
Limelight 1952......................*DVD* *BD*
Little Manhattan 2005......................
Little Miss Sunshine 2006..........*DVD* *BD*
Little Murders 1971 ....
Little Otik 2000................................*DVD*
Little Shop of Horrors 1986......*DVD* *BD*
Little Vegas 1990 ....
Little Voice 1998..............................*DVD*
Live Flesh 1997................................*DVD*
Live Now – Pay Later 1962..................
Living in Oblivion 1995......................*DVD*
Local Hero 1983................................*DVD*
Lock, Stock and Two Smoking Barrels
1998 ....*DVD* *BD*
Lola 1982 ....
Lonely Hearts 1981..........................
Long Live the Lady! 1987....................
Long Pants 1927 ....
Look at Me 2004................................*DVD*
The Look of Love 2013..............*DVD* *BD*
Looking for Eric 2009................*DVD* *BD*
Loot 1970..
Love among the Ruins 1975................
Love and Death 1975..............*DVD* *BD*
Love & Friendship 2016......................
Love at First Bite 1979......................
The Love Bug 1969............................*DVD*
Love Exposure 2008..........................*DVD*
Love in the Afternoon 1972................*DVD*
Love Is Colder than Death 1969..........
The Love Parade 1929........................
The Love Punch 2013................*DVD* *BD*
Love with the Proper Stranger 1963 ......
Lovers and Other Strangers 1970 ......
Lucas 1986..
Lucky Break 2001..............................*DVD*
Lucky Jim 1957................................*DVD*
Made in Dagenham 2010..........*DVD* *BD*
The Maggie 1953................................*DVD*
Major Barbara 1941 ....
Make Way for Tomorrow 1937......*BD*
The Male Animal 1942........................
Mamma Mia! 2008 ....*DVD* *BD*
Man about Town 1947........................
Man Bites Dog 1992..........................*DVD*
Man on the Moon 1999......................*DVD*
Man Up 2015 ....*DVD* *BD*
The Man Who Came to Dinner 1941 ......
The Man without a Past 2002............*DVD*
Manhattan Murder Mystery 1993.......*DVD*
Man's Favorite Sport? 1964 ....*DVD*
Margie 1946......................................
Marius et Jeannette 1997..................
Married to the Mob 1988 ....*DVD*
Mars Attacks! 1996................*DVD* *BD*
Mary and Max 2008..........................*DVD*
Matilda 1996........................*DVD* *BD*
Matinee 1993........................*DVD* *BD*
The Mating Game 1959......................
Me and You and Everyone We Know
2005..*DVD*
Me Myself I 1999..............................
Me without You 2001........................*DVD*
The Mean Machine 1974....................*DVD*
The Meddler 2015 ....
Mediterraneo 1991............................
Meet the Parents 2000..............*DVD* *BD*
Megamind 2010....................*DVD* *BD*
Melvin and Howard 1980....................
Men in Black 1997 ....*DVD* *BD*

Men in Black 3 2012 ....*DVD* *BD*
Men o' War 1929................................
Mermaids 1990..................................*DVD*
The Merry Widow 1934......................
Mexican Bus Ride 1951......................*DVD*
Midnight in Paris 2011......................*DVD*
Midnight Run 1988..................*DVD* *BD*
A Midsummer Night's Dream 1935......
A Midsummer Night's Sex Comedy
1982 ....*DVD*
A Mighty Wind 2003..........................*DVD*
The Milky Way 1936..........................*DVD*
Le Million 1931..................................
The Million Pound Note 1953..............*DVD*
A Millionaire for Christy 1951............
Millions 2004....................................*DVD*
Mischief Night 2006..........................*DVD*
Miss Congeniality 2000......................*DVD*
Miss Tatlock's Millions 1948..............
Miss You Already 2015..............*DVD* *BD*
Mr and Mrs '55 1955........................*DVD*
Mr Blandings Builds His Dream House
1948..
Mr Deeds Goes to Town 1936............*DVD*
Mr Reliable 1996..............................
Mr Vampire 1986................................
Mitsuko Delivers 2011 ....*DVD*
Mon Père Ce Héros 1991....................*DVD*
Monday Morning 2002........................*DVD*
Monkey Business 1931......................*DVD*
Monsieur Verdoux 1947......................*DVD*
Monsoon Wedding 2001....................*DVD*
Monster House 2006 ....*DVD* *BD*
Monsters University 2013..........*DVD* *BD*
Monsters vs Aliens 2009..........*DVD* *BD*
Monty Python and the Holy Grail
1975 ....*DVD* *BD*
Monty Python's Life of Brian
1979 ....*DVD* *BD*
Moonstruck 1987................................*BD*
The More the Merrier 1943..................
Motorama 1991 ....
Mousehunt 1997................................*DVD*
Move Over, Darling 1963....................*DVD*
Mrs Delafield Wants to Marry 1986 ......
Mrs Doubtfire 1993................*DVD* *BD*
Much Ado about Nothing 1993 ...*DVD* *BD*
The Muppet Movie 1979......................*DVD*
The Muppet Christmas Carol 1992 ......*DVD*
Muppet Treasure Island 1996.............*DVD*
Muppets from Space 1999..................*DVD*
The Muppets 2011..................*DVD* *BD*
Muriel's Wedding 1994......................*DVD*
The Music Man 1962..........................*DVD*
My Best Friend's Wedding 1997...*DVD* *BD*
My Boyfriend's Back 1989..................
My Cousin Vinny 1992........................*DVD*
My Favorite Blonde 1942....................*DVD*
My Favorite Wife 1940........................*DVD*
My Favorite Year 1982........................
My Girlfriend's Boyfriend 1987............*DVD*
My Learned Friend 1943......................*DVD*
My Life as a Dog 1985........................*DVD*
My Man Godfrey 1936........................*DVD*
Mystery Train 1989................*DVD* *BD*
Mystic Pizza 1988............................*DVD*
The Naked Gun 2½: the Smell of Fear
1991 ....*DVD* *BD*
Naked Gun 33⅓: the Final Insult
1994 ....*DVD* *BD*
The Naked Truth 1957........................*DVD*
National Lampoon's Animal House
1978 ....*DVD* *BD*
Nationale 7 1999..............................
The Navigator 1924..........................*DVD*
Neighbors 1920..................................
Never Give a Sucker an Even Break
1941..*DVD*
A New Leaf 1971....................*DVD* *BD*
Next Stop Wonderland 1998................
The Nice Guys 2016..........................
Night Shift 1984................................
The Night We Never Met 1993............*DVD*
No Way to Treat a Lady 1968 ....
North to Alaska 1960........................*DVD*
The Northerners 1992........................
Not Here to Be Loved 2005................
Not One Less 1999............................
Nothing but the Best 1963..................
Notting Hill 1999....................*DVD* *BD*
La Nuit Fantastique 1942....................
The Nutty Professor 1963....................*DVD*
The Nutty Professor 1996....................*DVD*
O Brother, Where Art Thou? 2000.....*DVD*
O Henry's Full House 1952..................
OSS 117: Lost in Rio 2009..................
Obvious Child 2014............................*DVD*
The Odd Couple 1968........................*DVD*
Offside 2006....................................*DVD*
Oh, God! 1977..................................
Oh, Mr Porter! 1937..........................*DVD*
Ohayo 1959..........................*DVD* *BD*
The Old Dark House 1932....................*DVD*
The Old-Fashioned Way 1934..............
One, Two, Three 1961........................*DVD*
One Week 1920..................................
Only Two Can Play 1961......................
Only You 1994..................................*DVD*
Operation Petticoat 1959....................*DVD*
The Opposite of Sex 1998..................*DVD*

The Original Kings of Comedy 2000 ......
Orphans 1998........................*DVD* *BD*
Our Betters 1933................................
Our Brand Is Crisis 2015....................
The Out of Towners 1970..................*DVD*
Overboard 1987......................*DVD* *BD*
Paddington 2014....................*DVD* *BD*
A Pain in the A...! 1973......................
The Palm Beach Story 1942 ....*DVD*
Palooka 1934....................................
Palookaville 1995..............................*DVD*
Pan 2015 ....*DVD* *BD*
Papa's Delicate Condition 1963..........
The Paper 1994................................*DVD*
The Paper Chase 1973......................*DVD*
Paper Moon 1973 ....*DVD* *BD*
ParaNorman 2012..................*DVD* *BD*
Parenthood 1989....................*DVD* *BD*
Parents 1988 ....
Pas sur la Bouche 2003......................*DVD*
Passport to Pimlico 1949..........*DVD* *BD*
Pat and Mike 1952............................*DVD*
Pauline & Paulette 2001....................*DVD*
Pauline at the Beach 1983..................*DVD*
The Pawnshop 1916............................*BD*
The Pentagon Wars 1998....................
Period of Adjustment 1962..................*DVD*
Les Petites Vacances 2006................*DVD*
A Pigeon Sat on a Branch Reflecting on
Existence 2014......................*DVD* *BD*
Pillow Talk 1959....................*DVD* *BD*
Ping Pong 2002................................*DVD*
The Pink Panther 1963........................*DVD*
The Pirates! in an Adventure with
Scientists! 2012....................*DVD* *BD*
Planes, Trains and Automobiles
1987 ....*DVD* *BD*
Play It Again, Sam 1972....................*DVD*
Playing by Heart 1998........................*DVD*
Pleasantville 1998............................*DVD*
Please Don't Eat the Daisies 1960......*DVD*
Pleasure at Her Majesty's 1976..........*DVD*
Poppy 1936..
Postcards from the Edge 1990............*DVD*
Il Posto 1961....................................*DVD*
A Prairie Home Companion 2006........*DVD*
Pretty Woman 1990................*DVD* *BD*
Pride 2014............................*DVD* *BD*
Primary Colors 1998..........................
Private Fears in Public Places 2006...*DVD*
A Private Function 1984......................*DVD*
Private Parts 1997............................*DVD*
Private's Progress 1956......................*DVD*
Prizzi's Honor 1985............................*DVD*
The Projectionist 1970........................
P'Tang, Yang, Kipperbang 1982........*DVD*
Punch-Drunk Love 2002............*DVD* *BD*
The Purple Rose of Cairo 1985 ....*DVD*
Puss in Boots 2011................*DVD* *BD*
Quartet 2012..........................*DVD* *BD*
Radio Days 1987..............................*DVD*
The Railrodder 1965..........................*DVD*
Raining Stones 1993..........................
Raising Arizona 1987........................*DVD*
Rang De Basanti 2006........................*DVD*
Ratatouille 2007....................*DVD* *BD*
The Raven 1963................................*DVD*
Ravenous 1999..................................
Re-Animator 1985................*DVD* *BD*
Red Rock West 1992..........................*DVD*
The Red Squirrel 1993........................*DVD*
The Reivers 1969..............................*DVD*
Remember the Night 1940..................
Results 2015....................................*DVD*
Ride 'Em Cowboy 1942......................
Rien Ne Va Plus 1997........................*DVD*
The Rink 1916....................................*BD*
Rio 2011................................*DVD* *BD*
Risky Business 1983................*DVD* *BD*
Rita, Sue and Bob Too 1986................*DVD*
Road to Morocco 1942........................*DVD*
Road to Rio 1947................................*DVD*
Road to Utopia 1945..........................*DVD*
Robin and the 7 Hoods 1964..........*BD*
Robot & Frank 2012................*DVD* *BD*
Rocket Science 2007..........................*DVD*
Roger Dodger 2002............................*DVD*
Role Models 2008 ....*DVD* *BD*
Romancing the Stone 1984........*DVD* *BD*
Romantics Anonymous 1986..............
A Room for Romeo Brass 1999............*DVD*
Rose Marie 1936................................*DVD*
Roxanne 1987..................................*DVD*
Roxie Hart 1942................................
Rush Hour 1998....................*DVD* *BD*
Rushmore 1998................................*DVD*
The Russians Are Coming, the Russians
Are Coming 1966..............................*DVD*
Ruthless People 1986........................*DVD*
The Rutles – All You Need Is Cash
1978..*DVD*
Safety Not Guaranteed 2012 ....*DVD* *BD*
A Sailor-Made Man 1921....................
St Vincent 2014....................*DVD* *BD*
Salty O'Rourke 1945..........................
Samaritan Girl 2004..........................*DVD*
Samba 2014......................................
Same Time, Next Year 1978................
The Sapphires 2012............................*DVD*
The Scarecrow 1920............................*BD*

Scenes from the Class Struggle In Beverly Hills 1989 .... *DVD*
School for Postmen 1947 ....
The School of Rock 2003 ....*DVD*
The Scout 1994 ....
Scram! 1932 ....*DVD*
The Second Best Exotic Marigold Hotel 2015 .... *DVD* 🔵
Secret Ballot 2001 ....*DVD*
The Secret Life of Walter Mitty 1947 ......
The Secret Lives of Dentists 2003 .....*DVD*
The Secret of Santa Vittoria 1969 ....
The Secret Policeman's Ball 1980 ...*DVD*
Seeking a Friend for the End of the World 2011 .... *DVD* 🔵
Send Me No Flowers 1964 ....*DVD* 🔵
A Serious Man 2009 ....*DVD* 🔵
The Seven Year Itch 1955 ....*DVD* 🔵
Shall We Dance? 1995 ....*DVD*
Shaun the Sheep Movie 2015 ....*DVD*
She Done Him Wrong 1933 ....*DVD*
The Sheepman 1958 ....
The Sheriff of Fractured Jaw 1958 ....
She's Gotta Have It 1986 ....*DVD*
Shirley Valentine 1989 ....
The Shop around the Corner 1940 ....
A Shot in the Dark 1964 ....
Shrek 2001 .... *DVD* 🔵
Shrek 2 2004 .... *DVD* 🔵
Silver Linings Playbook 2012 ......*DVD* 🔵
Silver Streak 1976 ....*DVD*
Simple Men 1992 ....*DVD*
The Simpsons Movie 2007 ...*DVD* 🔵
Sing, Baby, Sing 1936 ....
Singles 1992 ....*DVD*
Sister Act 1992 .... *DVD* 🔵
Sitcom 1997 ....*DVD*
Sitting Ducks 1979 ....
Six of a Kind 1934 ....
Sky High 2005 .... *DVD* 🔵
Slacker 1989 ....*DVD*
Sleeper 1973 .... *DVD* 🔵
Sleepless in Seattle 1993 ....*DVD*
Slums of Beverly Hills 1998 ....*DVD*
The Smallest Show on Earth 1957 ....*DVD*
Smokey and the Bandit 1977 ......*DVD* 🔵
Snake in the Eagle's Shadow 1978 ....
Sneakers 1992 ....*DVD*
Snoopy and Charlie Brown: the Peanuts Movie 2015 .... *DVD* 🔵
Snow Cake 2005 ....*DVD*
Soapdish 1991 ....*DVD*
Soldier in the Rain 1963 ....
Something Wild 1986 ....*DVD*
Son of Paleface 1952 ....
Son of Rambow 2007 ....*DVD* 🔵
South Park: Bigger, Longer & Uncut 1999 ....*DVD*
Spanglish 2004 ....*DVD*
Sparkle 2006 ....
Speak Easily 1932 ....*DVD*
Special People 2007 ....
Splash 1984 ....*DVD*
The SpongeBob SquarePants Movie 2004 ....*DVD*
The SpongeBob Movie: Sponge out of Water 2015 .... *DVD* 🔵
Spy 2015 .... *DVD* 🔵
The Squid and the Whale 2005 ....*DVD*
Stage Door 1937 ....
Stage Fright 1949 ....*DVD*
Stand Up Guys 2012 .... *DVD* 🔵
Stardust Memories 1980 ....*DVD*
Start the Revolution without Me 1970 ....
Starter for 10 2006 ....*DVD* 🔵
State and Main 2000 ....*DVD*
The Station Agent 2003 ....*DVD*
Steel Magnolias 1989 ....*DVD*
Still Crazy 1998 ....*DVD*
Stowaway 1936 ....*DVD*
Straight Talk 1992 ....*DVD*
Stranger than Fiction 2006 ......*DVD* 🔵
The Strawberry Blonde 1941 ....
The Strong Man 1926 ....*DVD*
Such Good Friends 1971 ....
Sugarbaby 1985 ....
Summer Things 2002 ....*DVD*
A Summer's Tale 1996 ....*DVD*
The Sunshine Boys 1975 ....
Superbad 2007 .... *DVD* 🔵
Support Your Local Gunfighter 1971 ....
Support Your Local Sheriff! 1969 ......*DVD*
The Sure Thing 1985 ....*DVD*
Surviving Life 2010 ....
Sweet and Lowdown 1999 ....*DVD*
Sweetie 1989 ....
Swingers 1996 .... *DVD* 🔵
Take Care of Your Scarf, Tatjana 1994 ....
Taking Off 1971 .... 🔵
The Talk of the Town 1942 ....*DVD*
The Taming of the Shrew 1967 ....*DVD*
Tangerine 2015 ....*DVD*
Tangled 2010 .... *DVD* 🔵
Taxi zum Klo 1980 ....
A Taxing Woman 1987 ....
Teacher's Pet 1958 ....*DVD*
Ted 2012 .... 🔵
10 1979 ....*DVD*
Ten Canoes 2006 ....*DVD*

10 Things I Hate about You 1999 .... *DVD* 🔵
The Tender Trap 1955 ....*DVD*
Thank You for Smoking 2005 ....*DVD*
That Man from Rio 1964 ....
That Thing You Do! 1996 ....*DVD*
Theatre of Blood 1973 .... *DVD* 🔵
Their First Mistake 1932 ....*DVD*
Them Thar Hills! 1934 ....*DVD*
Theodora Goes Wild 1936 ....
There Was a Crooked Man 1960 ....
There's Something about Mary 1998 .... *DVD* 🔵
They All Laughed 1981 ....
The Thief of Paris 1967 ....
The Thin Man 1934 ....*DVD*
Things Change 1988 ....
Things You Can Tell Just by Looking at Her 2000 ....
This Is the End 2013 .... *DVD* 🔵
Those Lips, Those Eyes 1980 ....
Those Magnificent Men in Their Flying Machines 1965 ....*DVD*
Three Ages 1923 ....*DVD*
Three Coins in the Fountain 1954 ....*DVD*
Three Colours White 1993 .... *DVD* 🔵
Three Lives and Only One Death 1996 ......
Three Men and a Baby 1987 ....*DVD*
3 Men and a Cradle 1985 ....*DVD*
Three Men in a Boat 1956 ....*DVD*
The Three Musketeers 1973 ....*DVD* 🔵
Three Smart Girls 1937 ....*DVD*
The Threepenny Opera 1931 ....*DVD*
Throw Momma from the Train 1987 ....*DVD*
Thursday 1998 ....
Tickets 2005 ....*DVD*
Time Bandits 1981 .... *DVD* 🔵
The Time of Your Life 1948 ....*DVD*
The Time That Remains: Chronicle of a Present Absentee 2009 ....*DVD*
Tin Men 1987 ....*DVD*
Tiny Furniture 2010 ....*DVD*
Tit for Tat 1934 ....*DVD*
Tito and Me 1992 ....*DVD*
Toast 2010 ....*DVD*
Tokyo Chorus 1931 ....*DVD*
Tollbooth 1994 ....*DVD*
Tom Jones 1963 ....*DVD*
Too Hot to Handle 1938 ....*DVD*
Tootsie 1982 .... *DVD* 🔵
Topaze 1933 ....*DVD*
Topkapi 1964 ....*DVD*
Topper 1937 ....*DVD*
Towed in a Hole 1932 ....*DVD*
Trading Places 1983 ....*DVD*
Traffic 1970 .... *DVD* 🔵
Trainwreck 2015 .... *DVD* 🔵
The Tramp 1915 ....*DVD*
Tramp, Tramp, Tramp 1926 ....*DVD*
Transamerica 2005 ....*DVD*
Travelling North 1986 ....
Trees Lounge 1996 ....*DVD*
Tricks 2007 ....*DVD*
Trigger Happy 1996 ....
Triple Bogey on a Par Five Hole 1991 .....
Trop Belle pour Toi 1989 ....*DVD*
Tropic Thunder 2008 .... *DVD* 🔵
True Lies 1994 ....*DVD*
True Love 1989 ....
True Romance 1993 .... *DVD* 🔵
The Truth about Cats and Dogs 1996 ..*DVD*
Tucker and Dale vs Evil 2009 .....*DVD* 🔵
Tulpan 2008 ....*DVD*
Turbo 2013 .... *DVD* 🔵
Turtles Can Fly 2004 ....*DVD*
12:08 East of Bucharest 2005 ....*DVD*
24 Hour Party People 2001 ....*DVD*
21 Jump Street 2012 .... *DVD* 🔵
22 Jump Street 2014 .... *DVD* 🔵
Twins 1988 ....*DVD*
Two for the Road 1967 .... *DVD* 🔵
Two Girls and a Guy 1997 ....
The Two of Us 1967 ....
Two Way Stretch 1960 ....*DVD*
U Turn 1997 ....*DVD*
Unfaithfully Yours 1948 ....*DVD*
An Unmarried Woman 1978 ....
Unstrung Heroes 1995 ....*DVD*
Untouchable 2011 .... *DVD* 🔵
Up in the Air 2009 .... *DVD* 🔵
Up in the Cellar 1970 ....
Used Cars 1980 ....*DVD*
Va Savoir 2001 ....*DVD*
Valley Girl 1983 ....
The Vanishing Corporal 1962 ....*DVD*
Very Bad Things 1998 ....
Vessel of Wrath 1938 ....
Vicky Cristina Barcelona 2008 ...*DVD* 🔵
La Vie de Château 1965 ....*DVD*
Les Visiteurs 1993 ....*DVD*
Vodka Lemon 2003 ....*DVD*
The Voices 2014 .... *DVD* 🔵
The Wackness 2008 .... *DVD* 🔵
Wag the Dog 1997 ....*DVD*
Waitress 2007 ....*DVD*
Walk Hard: the Dewey Cox Story 2007 ....*DVD*
Wallace & Gromit in The Curse of the Were-Rabbit 2005 ....*DVD*
Waltz of the Toreadors 1962 ....*DVD*

The War of the Roses 1989 ....*DVD*
waydowntown 2000 ....
Wayne's World 1992 ....*DVD*
A Wedding 1978 ....
The Wedding Banquet 1993 ....*DVD*
The Wedding Singer 1998 ....*DVD* 🔵
Welcome to the Dollhouse 1995 ....*DVD*
What about Bob? 1991 ....*DVD*
What We Did on Our Holiday 2014 .... *DVD* 🔵
What We Do in the Shadows 2014 .... *DVD* 🔵
What Women Want 2001 .... *DVD* 🔵
What's Your Number? 2011 .... *DVD* 🔵
When Ladies Meet 1933 ....
When Magoo Flew 1955 ....
When the Cat's Away... 1996 ....
Where There's Life 1947 ....
Where's Poppa? 1970 ....
While We're Young 2014 .... *DVD* 🔵
While You Were Sleeping 1995 ....*DVD*
Whisky 2004 ....
White Men Can't Jump 1992 ......*DVD* 🔵
The Whole Town's Talking 1935 ....
Wiener-Dog 2016 ....
Wife vs Secretary 1936 ....
Wilbur (Wants to Kill Himself) 2002 ...*DVD*
Wild about Harry 2000 ....
A Wild Hare 1940 ....
Wild Target 1993 ....
Wind with the Gone 1998 ....
Wish You Were Here 1987 ....*DVD*
The Witches of Eastwick 1987 ....*DVD*
Withnail & I 1986 .... *DVD* 🔵
Woman of the Year 1942 ....*DVD*
The Women 1939 ....
Wonder Boys 2000 ....*DVD*
Working Girl 1988 ....
The World of Henry Orient 1964 ....*DVD*
The Wrong Arm of the Law 1962 ....*DVD*
Xala 1974 ....
You, the Living 2007 ....*DVD*
The Young in Heart 1938 ....
The Young Poisoner's Handbook 1994 .....
Zelig 1983 ....
Zero Effect 1997 ....
Zoolander 2001 .... *DVD* 🔵

CRIME ★★★★★

Anatomy of a Murder 1959 ....*DVD*
Angels with Dirty Faces 1938 ....*DVD*
Animal Kingdom 2009 .... *DVD* 🔵
L'Argent 1983 ....*DVD*
The Asphalt Jungle 1950 ....*DVD*
Atlantic City, USA 1980 ....*DVD*
La Bête Humaine 1938 ....*DVD*
The Big Sleep 1946 ....*DVD*
Bonnie and Clyde 1967 .... *DVD* 🔵
Chopper 2000 ....*DVD*
City of God 2002 .... *DVD* 🔵
Cyclo 1995 ....*DVD*
Dirty Harry 1971 .... *DVD* 🔵
The French Connection 1971 ...... *DVD* 🔵
The Godfather 1972 .... *DVD* 🔵
The Godfather Part II 1974 .... *DVD* 🔵
GoodFellas 1990 .... *DVD* 🔵
Heavenly Creatures 1994 .... *DVD* 🔵
The Hill 1965 ....*DVD*
In the Heat of the Night 1967 ..... *DVD* 🔵
LA Confidential 1997 .... *DVD* 🔵
The Lavender Hill Mob 1951 .... *DVD* 🔵
The Long Goodbye 1973 .... *DVD* 🔵
M 1931 .... *DVD* 🔵
A Man Escaped 1956 ....*DVD*
Micmacs 2009 .... *DVD* 🔵
Miller's Crossing 1990 .... *DVD* 🔵
Nightcrawler 2013 .... *DVD* 🔵
No Country for Old Men 2007 ...... *DVD* 🔵
Los Olvidados 1950 ....*DVD*
On the Waterfront 1954 .... *DVD* 🔵
Once upon a Time in America 1984 .... *DVD* 🔵
The Public Enemy 1931 ....*DVD*
Pulp Fiction 1994 .... *DVD* 🔵
Reservoir Dogs 1991 .... *DVD* 🔵
Scarface 1932 ....
Se7en 1995 .... *DVD* 🔵
The Shawshank Redemption 1994 .... *DVD* 🔵
Shoot the Pianist 1960 .... *DVD* 🔵
A Short Film about Killing 1988 ....*DVD*
Sicario 2015 .... *DVD* 🔵
Sonatine 1993 ....*DVD*
The Sting 1973 .... *DVD* 🔵
10 Rillington Place 1970 ....*DVD*
To Die For 1995 ....*DVD*
Touch of Evil 1958 .... *DVD* 🔵
12 Angry Men 1957 ....*DVD*
The Untouchables 1987 .... *DVD* 🔵
The Usual Suspects 1995 .... *DVD* 🔵
White Heat 1949 ....*DVD*
Who Framed Roger Rabbit 1988 ..*DVD* 🔵
Witness for the Prosecution 1957 .....*DVD*
You Only Live Once 1937 ....*DVD*

CRIME ★★★★

After Dark, My Sweet 1990 ....
Al Capone 1959 ....
Alphaville 1965 ....*DVD*
The American Friend 1977 ....*DVD*
American Gangster 2007 ....*DVD* 🔵
American Hustle 2013 .... *DVD* 🔵
The American Soldier 1970 ....*DVD*
Analyze This 1999 ....*DVD*
And Then There Were None 1945 ....*DVD*
Angel 1982 ....*DVD*
Angel Face 1953 ....*DVD*
Angels of Evil 2010 .... *DVD* 🔵
Antibodies 2005 ....
Aurora 2010 ....
Bad Blood 1982 ....
Bad Lieutenant 1992 .... *DVD* 🔵
The Bad Lieutenant – Port of Call: New Orleans 2009 .... *DVD* 🔵
Badlands 1973 ....*DVD*
The Bait 1995 ....
La Balance 1982 ....*DVD*
Bande à Part 1964 ....*DVD*
The Beat That My Heart Skipped 2005 ....*DVD*
Before the Devil Knows You're Dead 2007 .... *DVD* 🔵
Big Deal on Madonna Street 1958 ....
The Big Easy 1986 ....*DVD*
The Big House 1930 ....
The Black Bird 1926 ....
Black Butler 2014 ....
Black Coal, Thin Ice 2014 ....
Black Souls 2014 ....
Black Sunday 1976 ....
The Bling Ring 2013 .... 🔵
Blood Oath 1990 ....
The Blue Lamp 1949 ....*DVD*
Blue Ruin 2013 .... *DVD* 🔵
Bob Le Flambeur 1955 ....*DVD*
Boomerang! 1947 .... *DVD* 🔵
Borsalino 1970 ....
The Boston Strangler 1968 ....*DVD*
Bound 1996 ....*DVD*
Brighton Rock 1947 .... *DVD* 🔵
Bring Me the Head of Alfredo Garcia 1974 ....*DVD*
A Bronx Tale 1993 .... *DVD* 🔵
Brother 1997 ....*DVD*
Brubaker 1980 ....*DVD*
Brute Force 1947 ....*DVD*
Bugsy 1991 ....*DVD*
Bugsy Malone 1976 .... *DVD* 🔵
Bullets over Broadway 1994 ....*DVD*
Bullitt 1968 .... *DVD* 🔵
Bully 2001 ....*DVD*
Burn after Reading 2008 ....*DVD* 🔵
Bus 174 2002 ....*DVD*
Cagney & Lacey 1981 ....
Call Northside 777 1948 ....*DVD*
Carandiru 2003 ....*DVD*
Carlito's Way 1993 .... *DVD* 🔵
Cash on Demand 1961 ....
Casino 1995 .... *DVD* 🔵
Chaos 1999 ....*DVD*
Charley Varrick 1973 ....*DVD*
The Cheap Detective 1978 ....
Choice of Arms 1981 ....
The Clan 2015 ....*DVD*
Collateral 2004 .... *DVD* 🔵
Compulsion 1959 ....
Confessions of a Serial Killer 1987 ....*DVD*
Cool Hand Luke 1967 .... *DVD* 🔵
Cop 1988 ....
Cop Land 1997 .... *DVD* 🔵
Cotton Comes to Harlem 1970 ....
The Court-Martial of Billy Mitchell 1955 ....
Crime and Punishment 1935 ....
Crime and Punishment 1935 ....
Crime in the Streets 1956 ....
Cutter's Way 1981 ....*DVD*
DOA 1988 ....*DVD*
Dangerous Female 1931 ....
Darkness in Tallinn 1993 ....
Dead End 1937 ....*DVD*
Dead Man Walking 1995 ....*DVD*
Dead Men Don't Wear Plaid 1982 ....*DVD*
Deep Cover 1992 ....*DVD*
The Defiant Ones 1958 ....*DVD*
The Departed 2006 ....*DVD* 🔵
Detective Story 1951 ....*DVD*
Devil in a Blue Dress 1995 ....*DVD*
Dick Tracy 1990 ....*DVD*
Dillinger 1945 ....*DVD*
Dillinger 1973 ....*DVD*
Diva 1981 ....*DVD*
Dobermann 1997 ....*DVD*
Dr Mabuse, the Gambler 1922 ...*DVD* 🔵
Dog Day Afternoon 1975 .... *DVD* 🔵
Dom Hemingway 2013 .... *DVD* 🔵
Donnie Brasco 1997 ....*DVD*
Drive 2011 .... *DVD* 🔵
The Driver 1978 .... *DVD* 🔵
Drunken Angel 1948 ....*DVD*
Easy Money 2010 .... *DVD* 🔵
Easy Money II 2012 .... *DVD* 🔵
Easy Money III: Life Deluxe 2013 .... *DVD* 🔵
Election 2005 ....*DVD*

FIVE- AND FOUR-STAR FILMS

The Element of Crime 1984 ..... *DVD*
The Enforcer 1951 ..... *DVD*
Escape from Alcatraz 1979 ..... *DVD*
Evidence of Love 1990 ..... *DVD*
Exiled 2006 ..... *DVD*
The FBI Story 1959 .....
FX: Murder by Illusion 1985 ..... *DVD*
Farewell, My Lovely 1975 ..... *DVD*
La Femme Publique 1984 .....
A Few Good Men 1992 ..... *DVD*
Fort Apache, the Bronx 1981 .....
The Friends of Eddie Coyle 1973 ..*DVD*
Fury 1936 .....
Gang Related 1997 ..... *DVD*
Gangs of Wasseypur 2012 .....
Gangs of Wasseypur II 2012 .....
Gangster Squad 2012 ..... *DVD*
Gangster's Paradise: Jerusalema 2008 ..... *DVD*
Garde à Vue 1981 .....
Get Carter 1971 ..... *DVD*
Get Shorty 1995 ..... *DVD*
The Getaway 1972 ..... *DVD*
Ghosts... of the Civil Dead 1988 .....
Gideon's Day 1958 .....
Gideon's Trumpet 1980 .....
Gimme the Loot 2012 .....
The Girl with the Dragon Tattoo 2009 ..... *DVD*
The Girl with the Dragon Tattoo 2011 ..... *DVD*
The Glass House 1972 ..... *DVD*
Go 1999 ..... *DVD*
Godmoney 1997 .....
Gomorrah 2008 ..... *DVD*
Good Morning, Night 2003 .....
The Grifters 1990 .....
Gumshoe 1971 ..... *DVD*
Hana-Bi 1997 ..... *DVD*
Hard-Boiled 1992 ..... *DVD*
Harper 1966 .....
Headhunters 2011 ..... *DVD*
Heat 1995 ..... *DVD*
Heist 2001 .....
Hell or High Water 2016 .....
Hide in Plain Sight 1980 .....
High and Low 1963 ..... *DVD*
Hobo with a Shotgun 2011 ..... *DVD*
Homicide 1991 ..... *DVD*
The Honeymoon Killers 1969 ..... *DVD*
Honour among Thieves 1954 .....
The Horseman 2008 ..... *DVD*
Hot Fuzz 2007 ..... *DVD*
I Want to Live! 1958 ..... *DVD*
In Cold Blood 1967 ..... *DVD*
In the Valley of Elah 2007 ..... *DVD*
Indictment: the McMartin Trial 1995 .....
Infernal Affairs 2002 ..... *DVD*
Inherent Vice 2014 ..... *DVD*
Inherit the Wind 1960 ..... *DVD*
Inherit the Wind 1999 .....
Inside Man 2006 ..... *DVD*
Insomnia 2002 ..... *DVD*
Internal Affairs 1990 .....
It Always Rains on Sunday 1947 ..*DVD*
Jackie Brown 1997 ..... *DVD*
Jackson County Jail 1976 .....
The Jericho Mile 1979 .....
John Grisham's The Rainmaker 1997 ..*DVD*
Johnny Angel 1945 .....
Le Jour Se Lève 1939 ..... *DVD*
Katalin Varga 2008 ..... *DVD*
The Killers 1964 ..... *DVD*
The Killing of a Chinese Bookie 1976 ..... *DVD*
The King of Marvin Gardens 1972 ..... *DVD*
King of New York 1989 ..... *DVD*
King Rat 1965 ..... *DVD*
Kiss Tomorrow Goodbye 1950 ..... *DVD*
The Krays 1990 ..... *DVD*
L.627 1992 ..... *DVD*
The Lady from Shanghai 1948 ..... *DVD*
The Lady in Red 1979 .....
The Last Run 1971 .....
Laws of Gravity 1992 .....
The League of Gentlemen 1960 ..... *DVD*
Leave Her to Heaven 1945 ..... *DVD*
Let Him Have It 1991 ..... *DVD*
Lift to the Scaffold 1957 ..... *DVD*
Little Caesar 1931 ..... *DVD*
Lock, Stock and Two Smoking Barrels 1998 ..... *DVD*
London to Brighton 2006 ..... *DVD*
The Long Good Friday 1979 ..... *DVD*
Love Is Colder than Death 1969 .....
Lucky Break 2001 ..... *DVD*
Lucky Luciano 1973 ..... *DVD*
Mad City 1997 ..... *DVD*
Made in Hong Kong 1997 .....
Madigan 1968 .....
The Man Who Wasn't There 2001 ..... *DVD*
Mapantsula 1988 .....
Marked Woman 1937 .....
Marshland 2014 ..... *DVD*
The Mattei Affair 1972 .....
The Mean Machine 1974 ..... *DVD*
Mesrine: Killer Instinct 2008 ..... *DVD*
Mesrine: Public Enemy No 1 2008 ..... *DVD*
Miami Blues 1990 ..... *DVD*

Midnight in the Garden of Good and Evil 1997 ..... *DVD*
Miss Bala 2011 ..... *DVD*
Mr Holmes 2014 ..... *DVD*
Mona Lisa 1986 ..... *DVD*
Monster 2003 ..... *DVD*
Monster's Ball 2001 ..... *DVD*
A Most Violent Year 2014 ..... *DVD*
Mother 2009 ..... *DVD*
The Naked City 1948 ..... *DVD*
The Narrow Margin 1952 .....
Natural Born Killers 1994 ..... *DVD*
Never Steal Anything Small 1959 .....
The New Centurions 1972 .....
The Nice Guys 2016 .....
Night and the City 1950 ..... *DVD*
The Night of the Sunflowers 2006 ..*DVD*
Nightmare 1956 .....
Nightmare in Chicago 1968 .....
Nine Queens 2000 ..... *DVD*
Northwest 2013 ..... *DVD*
Ocean's Eleven 1960 ..... *DVD*
Ocean's Eleven 2001 ..... *DVD*
Odds against Tomorrow 1959 ..... *DVD*
Once upon a Time in Anatolia 2011 ..... *DVD*
One False Move 1992 ..... *DVD*
One Nite in Mongkok 2004 ..... *DVD*
Only God Forgives 2012 ..... *DVD*
The Organization 1971 .....
Out of Sight 1998 ..... *DVD*
Out of the Darkness 1985 .....
A Pain in the A...! 1973 .....
Palookaville 1995 ..... *DVD*
Le Paltoquet 1986 ..... *DVD*
Papillon 1973 ..... *DVD*
Pickpocket 1959 ..... *DVD*
Pitfall 1962 ..... *DVD*
The Place beyond the Pines 2012 ..... *DVD*
The Pledge 2000 ..... *DVD*
Plein Soleil 1960 ..... *DVD*
Police 1985 .....
Police, Adjective 2009 ..... *DVD*
Prescription: Murder 1968 ..... *DVD*
Primal Fear 1996 ..... *DVD*
The Prime Gig 2000 ..... *DVD*
Prisoners 2013 ..... *DVD*
A Prophet 2009 ..... *DVD*
The Proposition 2004 ..... *DVD*
Public Enemies 2009 ..... *DVD*
Pusher II 2004 .....
A Question of Silence 1982 .....
A Rage in Harlem 1991 ..... *DVD*
Rampart 2011 ..... *DVD*
Rapt 2009 ..... *DVD*
Revanche 2008 ..... *DVD*
Rififi 1955 ..... *DVD*
Riot in Cell Block 11 1954 .....
The Rise and Fall of Legs Diamond 1960 .....
Road to Perdition 2002 ..... *DVD*
The Roaring Twenties 1939 ..... *DVD*
Roberto Succo 2000 ..... *DVD*
Rome Express 1932 ..... *DVD*
Roxie Hart 1942 .....
Ruby 1992 .....
Run Lola Run 1998 ..... *DVD*
The Running Man 1963 .....
Salvatore Giuliano 1961 ..... *DVD*
Sarkar 2005 ..... *DVD*
Scarface 1983 ..... *DVD*
Scum 1979 ..... *DVD*
The Secret in Their Eyes 2009 ..... *DVD*
Serpico 1973 ..... *DVD*
Sexy Beast 2000 ..... *DVD*
Shaft 2000 ..... *DVD*
Shifty 2008 ..... *DVD*
Shotgun Stories 2007 ..... *DVD*
Sin City 2005 ..... *DVD*
The Sleeping Tiger 1954 ..... *DVD*
The Sniper 1952 .....
Snow Falling on Cedars 1999 ..... *DVD*
The Sound of Fury 1950 .....
The Spider and the Fly 1949 .....
Spring Breakers 2012 ..... *DVD*
Stand Up Guys 2012 ..... *DVD*
The Stanford Prison Experiment 2015 .....
Starred Up 2013 ..... *DVD*
State of Grace 1990 ..... *DVD*
State of Play 2009 ..... *DVD*
The Stoker 2010 .....
The Street with No Name 1948 ..... *DVD*
Suburban Mayhem 2006 ..... *DVD*
Suburra 2015 .....
The Talented Mr Ripley 1999 ..... *DVD*
Targets 1968 .....
That Man from Rio 1964 .....
Thérèse Raquin 1953 ..... *DVD*
Thief 1981 ..... *DVD*
Thieves like Us 1974 ..... *DVD*
The Thin Man 1934 ..... *DVD*
Things Change 1988 .....
Things to Do in Denver When You're Dead 1995 ..... *DVD*
Thunderbolt 1929 .....
Thunderbolt and Lightfoot 1974 ..*DVD*
Thursday 1998 .....
Time after Time 1979 .....
Time and Tide 2000 ..... *DVD*
Toni 1935 ..... *DVD*

Topkapi 1964 ..... *DVD*
The Town 2010 ..... *DVD*
Traffic 2000 ..... *DVD*
Training Day 2001 ..... *DVD*
The Treatment 2014 .....
36 Quai des Orfèvres 2004 ..... *DVD*
Trigger Happy 1996 .....
Le Trou 1959 ..... *DVD*
Trouble in Mind 1985 ..... *DVD*
Tsotsi 2005 ..... *DVD*
12 Angry Men 1997 .....
Two against the Law 1973 .....
2 Guns 2013 ..... *DVD*
Two Way Stretch 1960 ..... *DVD*
Underground 1998 ..... *DVD*
Underworld 1927 .....
Underworld USA 1961 .....
The Unholy Three 1925 .....
The Unsuspected 1947 .....
Victoria 2015 ..... *DVD*
Violent Saturday 1955 ..... *DVD*
The Voices 2014 ..... *DVD*
Wanda 1971 .....
The Watchmaker of St Paul 1973 ..... *DVD*
Welcome to the Punch 2012 ..... *DVD*
The Whole Town's Talking 1935 .....
Who'll Stop the Rain? 1978 ..... *DVD*
The Wrong Arm of the Law 1962 ..... *DVD*
The Wrong Man 1956 ..... *DVD*
The Yakuza Papers 1973 ..... *DVD*
Zero Effect 1997 .....
Zodiac 2007 ..... *DVD*

DISASTER ★★★★★

Airplane! 1980 ..... *DVD*
Testament 1983 .....

DISASTER ★★★★

The Day after Tomorrow 2004 ..... *DVD*
Earthquake 1974 ..... *DVD*
The Impossible 2011 ..... *DVD*
A Night to Remember 1958 ..... *DVD*
The Poseidon Adventure 1972 ..... *DVD*
San Francisco 1936 .....
Titanic 1997 ..... *DVD*
The Towering Inferno 1974 ..... *DVD*

DOCUMENTARY ★★★★★

The Act of Killing 2012 ..... *DVD*
Armadillo 2010 ..... *DVD*
Berlin: Symphony of a Great City 1927 .....
The Blues, a Musical Journey: Feel like Going Home 2003 ..... *DVD*
Bowling for Columbine 2002 ..... *DVD*
The Celluloid Closet 1995 .....
The Ecstasy of Wilko Johnson 2015 .....
Exit through the Gift Shop 2010 ..*DVD*
The Gatekeepers 2012 ..... *DVD*
A Great Day in Harlem 1994 .....
Grizzly Man 2005 ..... *DVD*
Hawking 2013 ..... *DVD*
Hearts of Darkness: a Film-Maker's Apocalypse 1991 ..... *DVD*
Henri-Georges Clouzot's Inferno 2009 ..... *DVD*
Hoop Dreams 1994 ..... *DVD*
Hotel Terminus: the Life and Times of Klaus Barbie 1987 .....
Kandahar 2001 ..... *DVD*
Land without Bread 1933 .....
The Last Waltz 1978 ..... *DVD*
Man on Wire 2007 ..... *DVD*
Man with a Movie Camera 1928 ..*DVD*
Marcello Mastroianni: I Remember 1997 .....
Night Mail 1936 .....
Nuit et Brouillard 1955 ..... *DVD*
People on Sunday 1929 ..... *DVD*
The River 1937 .....
Roger & Me 1989 ..... *DVD*
Senna 2010 ..... *DVD*
Shoah 1985 ..... *DVD*
Sing Your Song 2011 ..... *DVD*
Song of Ceylon 1934 .....
The Sorrow and the Pity 1969 ..... *DVD*
Stories We Tell 2012 ..... *DVD*
The TAMI Show 1964 .....
The Thin Blue Line 1988 ..... *DVD*
This Is Spinal Tap 1984 ..... *DVD*
20,000 Days on Earth 2014 ..... *DVD*
Undefeated 2011 ..... *DVD*
When We Were Kings 1996 ..... *DVD*
Woodstock 1970 ..... *DVD*

DOCUMENTARY ★★★★

ABC Africa 2001 .....
A Propos de Nice 1930 .....
Addicted to Sheep 2015 .....
After the Apocalypse 2010 .....
Alexandria Encore 1990 .....
Amy 2015 ..... *DVD*
Anne Frank Remembered 1995 .....
Anvil: the Story of Anvil 2008 ..*DVD*
The Armstrong Lie 2013 ..... *DVD*
At Berkeley 2013 .....
Attacking the Devil: Harold Evans and the Last Nazi War Crime 2014 .....

Awesome; I F***in' Shot That! 2006 ..*DVD*
Ballets Russes 2005 ..... *DVD*
The Battle of Midway 1942 .....
The Battles of Coronel and Falkland Islands 1927 ..... *DVD*
The Beaches of Agnès 2008 .....
Benda Bilili! 2010 ..... *DVD*
Berlin 2007 .....
Best Boy 1979 .....
Best of Enemies 2015 ..... *DVD*
Beware of Mr Baker 2012 ..... *DVD*
Beyond the Mat 1999 ..... *DVD*
The Big One 1997 ..... *DVD*
The Big TNT Show 1966 .....
Bill Cunningham New York 2010 .....
The Black Power Mixtape 1967-1975 2011 ..... *DVD*
Blackfish 2013 ..... *DVD*
The Blues, a Musical Journey: Godfathers and Sons 2003 ..... *DVD*
The Blues, a Musical Journey: The Road to Memphis 2003 ..... *DVD*
The Blues, a Musical Journey: The Soul of a Man 2003 ..... *DVD*
Bob Roberts 1992 ..... *DVD*
Bo66y 2016 ..... *DVD*
Bodysong 2002 ..... *DVD*
The Boy Mir: Ten Years in Afghanistan 2011 .....
Brand: a Second Coming 2015 ..... *DVD*
Bright Leaves 2003 .....
The British Guide to Showing Off 2011 ..... *DVD*
Buena Vista Social Club 1998 ..... *DVD*
Burden of Dreams 1982 ..... *DVD*
Bus 174 2002 ..... *DVD*
CSNY/Déjà Vu 2008 .....
Cameraman: the Life & Work of Jack Cardiff 2010 .....
Capturing the Friedmans 2003 ..... *DVD*
Carmen Miranda: Bananas Is My Business 1994 .....
Catfish 2010 ..... *DVD*
Cave of Forgotten Dreams 2010 ..*DVD*
Chang 1927 .....
Charlie: the Life and Art of Charles Chaplin 2003 .....
Ciao, Federico! 1970 .....
Citizenfour 2014 .....
The Class of '92 2013 .....
Close-Up 1989 ..... *DVD*
The Clowns 1970 ..... *DVD*
Cobain: Montage of Heck 2015 ..*DVD*
Common Threads: Stories from the Quilt 1989 .....
Concerning Violence 2014 .....
The Confessions of Thomas Quick 2015 .....
The Conquest of Everest 1953 ..... *DVD*
Cool and Crazy 2000 ..... *DVD*
Corman's World: Exploits of a Hollywood Rebel 2011 ..... *DVD*
The Corporation 2003 ..... *DVD*
The Cove 2009 .....
The Crash Reel 2013 .....
A Crude Awakening: the Oil Crash 2006 ..... *DVD*
Crumb 1995 ..... *DVD*
Dancing in Jaffa 2013 .....
Dear America: Letters Home from Vietnam 1987 .....
Death of a Gentleman 2015 ..... *DVD*
The Decline of Western Civilization 1980 ..... *DVD*
Deep Blue 2003 ..... *DVD*
Deep Water 2006 ..... *DVD*
Dirty Wars 2013 .....
Le Donk & Scor-Zay-Zee 2009 ..... *DVD*
Don't Look Back 1967 ..... *DVD*
Double Take 2009 .....
Dreamcatcher 2015 .....
Dreams of a Life 2011 ..... *DVD*
Earth 2007 .....
Electric Boogaloo: the Wild, Untold Story of Cannon Films 2014 ..... *DVD*
Elvis: That's the Way It Is 1970 ..... *DVD*
Enemies of the People 2009 .....
Etre et Avoir 2002 ..... *DVD*
Everything or Nothing: the Untold Story of 007 2012 ..... *DVD*
Fahrenheit 9/11 2004 ..... *DVD*
The Fall 2016 .....
The Fear of 13 2015 .....
Festival Express 2003 ..... *DVD*
Filmed in Supermarionation 2014 ..... *DVD*
Finding Vivian Maier 2014 ..... *DVD*
Fire at Sea 2016 .....
Fire in the Blood 2012 ..... *DVD*
Fire in the Night 2013 .....
Fires Were Started 1943 ..... *DVD*
First 2012 ..... *DVD*
The First Film 2015 .....
The Five Obstructions 2003 ..... *DVD*
The Flaw 2011 .....
The Fog of War: Eleven Lessons from the Life of Robert S McNamara 2003 ..... *DVD*
Four Days in November 1964 .....
Four Days inside Guantanamo 2010 ..*DVD*
4 Little Girls 1997 ..... *DVD*
Frank Lloyd Wright 1997 .....

From Mao to Mozart: Isaac Stern in China 1980 .....
The Future Is Unwritten 2006 .... *DVD*
Future Shock! The Story of 2000AD 2015 ..... *DVD*
Gabbeh 1995 .....
Gallivant 1996 ..... *DVD*
Genocide 1981 .....
George Harrison: Living in the Material World 2011 ..... *DVD* ⬡
Ghosts of Cité Soleil 2005 .....
Gimme Shelter 1970 ..... *DVD*
Glastonbury 2006 ..... *DVD*
The Gleaners and I 2000 ..... *DVD*
God Bless Ozzy Osbourne 2011 .... *DVD* ⬡
God's Country 1985 .....
Grass 1999 ..... *DVD*
Grass: a Nation's Battle for Life 1925 ....
The Great Hip Hop Hoax 2013 .....
The Great Museum 2014 .....
The Great Rock 'n' Roll Swindle 1979 .. *DVD*
The Great White Silence 1924 ..... *DVD* ⬡
Grey Gardens 1975 ..... *DVD* ⬡
Hail! Hail! Rock 'n' Roll! 1987 .....
Häxan 1921 ..... *DVD*
He Named Me Malala 2015 .....
Heart of a Dog 2015 .....
Hearts and Minds 1974 ..... *DVD*
Her Name Is Sabine 2007 .....
Hockney 2014 .....
Homework 1989 .....
Hostages 1993 .....
The House on 92nd Street 1945 .... *DVD*
How to Re-Establish a Vodka Empire 2011 ..
How We Used to Live 2013 .....
I Am Breathing 2012 .....
I Am Bruce Lee 2012 ..... *DVD* ⬡
I Have Never Forgotten You: the Life and Legacy of Simon Wiesenthal 2007 ..... *DVD*
If a Tree Falls: a Story of the Earth Liberation Front 2011 .....
The Imposter 2012 ..... *DVD* ⬡
In the Hands of the Gods 2007 ..... *DVD*
In This World 2002 ..... *DVD*
Inside Job 2010 ..... *DVD*
The Internet's Own Boy 2014 .....
The Interrupters 2011 ..... *DVD*
Intervista 1987 .....
Into Great Silence 2005 ..... *DVD*
Into the Abyss: a Tale of Death, a Tale of Life 2011 ..... *DVD* ⬡
Iris 2014 .....
The Island President 2011 ..... *DVD*
It's All True 1993 .....
Janis: Little Girl Blue 2015 .....
Jason Becker: Not Dead Yet 2012 ..... *DVD*
Jimi Hendrix 1973 .....
Jiro Dreams of Sushi 2011 .....
Joan Rivers: a Piece of Work 2010 ..... *DVD*
Le Joli Mai 1962 .....
Joy Division 2008 ..... *DVD*
Joy of Madness 2003 ..... *DVD*
Jungle Cat 1959 .....
Katy Perry: Part of Me 2012 ..... *DVD* ⬡
The King of Kong: a Fistful of Quarters 2007 .....
Land of Silence and Darkness 1971 .....
The Last Days 1998 .....
Last Days in Vietnam 2014 .....
The Last Man on the Moon 2015 .....
The Last of the Unjust 2013 .....
Latcho Drom 1993 .....
Let It Be 1970 .....
Let the Good Times Roll 1973 .....
Life in a Day 2011 .....
Life Itself 2014 .....
The Life of Riley 2012 ..... *DVD* ⬡
Listen to Me Marlon 2015 ..... *DVD* ⬡
The Living Desert 1953 .....
London 1994 ..... *DVD*
London – Babylon 2012 ..... *DVD*
The Long Way Home 1996 .....
The Look of Silence 2014 .....
Looking for Richard 1996 ..... *DVD*
Lost in La Mancha 2002 ..... *DVD*
McCullin 2012 ..... *DVD* ⬡
Made of Stone 2013 ..... *DVD* ⬡
Magician: the Astonishing Life and Work of Orson Welles 2014 ..... *DVD*
Maidan 2014 .....
Mandela 1995 .....
March of the Penguins 2005 ..... *DVD* ⬡
Memphis Belle 1943 .....
Microcosmos 1996 ..... *DVD*
Milius 2013 .....
Mission to Lars 2012 ..... *DVD* ⬡
Mistaken for Strangers 2013 .....
Mr Death: the Rise and Fall of Fred A Leuchter Jr 1999 .....
Moana 1926 .....
Modern Life 2008 ..... *DVD*
Le Monde du Silence 1956 ..... *DVD* ⬡
Mondovino 2004 ..... *DVD*
Monterey Pop 1968 .....
The Moo Man 2013 .....
More than Honey 2012 ..... *DVD* ⬡
The Most Dangerous Man in America: Daniel Ellsberg and the Pentagon Papers 2009 .....
Muhammad Ali, the Greatest 1974 ..... *DVD*

Murderball 2005 ..... *DVD*
Muscle Shoals 2013 ..... *DVD*
My Architect 2003 ..... *DVD*
My Name Is Salt 2013 .....
My Voyage to Italy 1999 ..... *DVD*
My Winnipeg 2007 ..... *DVD*
Le Mystère Picasso 1956 .....
Neil Young: Heart of Gold 2006 ..... *DVD*
New York Doll 2005 ..... *DVD*
Night Will Fall 2014 .....
The Nine Muses 2010 .....
9.79* 2012 .....
1971 2014 .....
No Greater Love 2009 .....
No Home Movie 2015 .....
Nostalgia for the Light 2010 .... *DVD* ⬡
Notes on Blindness 2016 .....
The Notorious Mr Bout 2014 .....
Olympiad 1938 .....
On Any Sunday 1971 ..... *DVD*
One Day in September 1999 .....
One Life 2011 ..... *DVD* ⬡
Only When I Dance 2008 .....
Orion: the Man Who Would Be King 2015 ..
Over Your Cities Grass Will Grow 2010 ..... *DVD*
Pandora's Promise 2013 .....
Paragraph 175 1999 .....
Paris Is Burning 1990 ..... *DVD*
Patience (After Sebald) 2011 .....
Patti Smith: Dream of Life 2007 ..... *DVD*
The Pearl Button 2015 .....
Phantom India 1968 .....
Pina 2011 .....
Pleasure at Her Majesty's 1976 .... *DVD*
The Plow That Broke the Plains 1934 .....
The Posters Come from the Wall 2008 .....
Project Nim 2011 ..... *DVD* ⬡
Pumping Iron 1976 ..... *DVD*
Pumping Iron II: the Women 1984 .....
The Queen of Versailles 2012 ..... *DVD*
The Quince Tree Sun 1991 .....
Ray Harryhausen: Special Effects Titan 2011 .....
Recount 2008 .....
Return to Homs 2013 .....
Riding Giants 2004 .....
Robert Altman's Jazz '34: Remembrances of Kansas City Swing 1996 .....
Robinson in Space 1997 ..... *DVD*
Robinson in Ruins 2010 .....
The Rocky Road to Dublin 1968 ..... *DVD*
The Rutles – All You Need Is Cash 1978 ..... *DVD*
Sans Soleil 1982 .....
The September Issue 2009 ..... *DVD* ⬡
Sherpa 2015 .....
Shut Up & Sing: Dixie Chicks 2006 .... *DVD*
Sick: the Life and Death of Bob Flanagan, Supermasochist 1997 ..... *DVD*
Sicko 2007 ..... *DVD*
Side by Side 2012 ..... *DVD*
sleep furiously 2007 .....
Smash & Grab: the Story of the Pink Panthers 2012 .....
Something from Nothing: the Art of Rap 2012 ..... *DVD* ⬡
Soul in the Hole 1995 ..... *DVD*
Southpaw 1998 .....
Spellbound 2002 .....
Springsteen & I 2013 .....
Status Quo: Hello Quo 2012 .... *DVD* ⬡
Stop Making Sense 1984 ..... *DVD*
A Story of Children and Film 2013 .....
The Story of the Weeping Camel 2003 ..... *DVD*
Super 8 Stories 2001 .....
Super Size Me 2004 ..... *DVD*
Superstar: the Life and Times of Andy Warhol 1991 ..... *DVD*
A Syrian Love Story 2015 .....
A Tale of Two Thieves 2014 ..... *DVD*
Tales of the Grim Sleeper 2014 .....
Taxi to the Dark Side 2007 ..... *DVD*
This Film Is Not Yet Rated 2006 .... *DVD*
The Times of Harvey Milk 1983 .....
Titicut Follies 1967 .....
Tokyo Olympiad 1965 .....
Toryboy the Movie 2010 ..... *DVD*
Touching the Void 2003 ..... *DVD* ⬡
Tupac: Resurrection 2003 ..... *DVD*
Twenty Feet from Stardom 2013 ..... *DVD* ⬡
Tyson 2008 ..... *DVD*
Uncovered: the War on Iraq 2004 ..... *DVD*
The Undeclared War 1992 .....
Universal Horror 1998 .....
The Unknown Known 2013 ..... *DVD*
Unzipped 1995 .....
Utopia 2013 ..... *DVD*
Versus: The Life and Films of Ken Loach 2016 .....
Village at the End of the World 2012 .....
Visions of Light 1992 ..... *DVD*
Wall 2004 ..... *DVD*
Waltz with Bashir 2008 ..... *DVD* ⬡
The War Game 1965 ..... *DVD*
War Requiem 1988 ..... *DVD*
The War Room 1993 .....
Waste Land 2009 ..... *DVD*

We Are Many 2014 ..... *DVD*
We Are the Giant 2014 .....
We Are Together 2006 .....
We Steal Secrets: the Story of WikiLeaks 2013 .....
We Went to War 2012 .....
Weekend of a Champion 1971 .....
Welcome to Leith 2015 .....
West of Memphis 2012 ..... *DVD*
Who Is Dayani Cristal? 2013 .....
Wild Man Blues 1997 ..... *DVD*
Will & Testament 2014 .....
Winged Migration 2001 ..... *DVD* ⬡
Wisecracks 1991 .....
The Wonderful, Horrible Life of Leni Riefenstahl 1993 .....
World without Sun 1964 ..... *DVD* ⬡
Zelig 1983 ..... *DVD*
Zidane: a 21st Century Portrait 2006 ..... *DVD* ⬡

DRAMA ★★★★★

A Bout de Souffle 1959 ..... *DVD* ⬡
Abigail's Party 1977 ..... *DVD*
Las Acacias 2011 ..... *DVD* ⬡
Accident 1967 ..... *DVD*
Ace in the Hole 1951 ..... *DVD*
Aguirre, Wrath of God 1972 ..... *DVD*
All about Eve 1950 ..... *DVD* ⬡
All about My Mother 1999 ..... *DVD*
All Quiet on the Western Front 1930 ..... *DVD* ⬡
Amadeus 1984 ..... *DVD* ⬡
Amarcord 1973 ..... *DVD*
Amélie 2001 ..... *DVD* ⬡
American Graffiti 1973 ..... *DVD*
Amores Perros 2000 ..... *DVD*
Amour 2012 ..... *DVD* ⬡
Anatomy of a Murder 1959 ..... *DVD*
Andrei Rublev 1966 ..... *DVD* ⬡
An Angel at My Table 1990 ..... *DVD*
Angels with Dirty Faces 1938 ..... *DVD*
Les Anges du Péché 1943 .....
Animal Kingdom 2009 ..... *DVD* ⬡
Anomalisa 2015 ..... *DVD* ⬡
The Apartment 1960 ..... *DVD* ⬡
Apocalypse Now 1979 ..... *DVD* ⬡
L'Argent 1983 ..... *DVD*
Army of Shadows 1969 ..... *DVD* ⬡
The Artist 2011 ..... *DVD* ⬡
Ashes and Diamonds 1958 ..... *DVD*
Asya's Happiness 1967 .....
L'Atalante 1934 ..... *DVD*
Atlantic City, USA 1980 ..... *DVD*
Atonement 2007 ..... *DVD* ⬡
Au Hasard, Balthazar 1966 ..... *DVD*
The Autobiography of Miss Jane Pittman 1974 ..... *DVD*
An Autumn Afternoon 1962 ..... *DVD*
L'Avventura 1960 ..... *DVD* ⬡
Baaria 2009 ..... *DVD*
Babette's Feast 1987 ..... *DVD* ⬡
Bad Day at Black Rock 1955 ..... *DVD* ⬡
Barry Lyndon 1975 ..... *DVD* ⬡
The Battle of Algiers 1965 ..... *DVD* ⬡
The Battleship Potemkin 1925 ..... *DVD*
Belle de Jour 1967 ..... *DVD* ⬡
La Belle Noiseuse 1991 ..... *DVD*
Berlin Alexanderplatz 1980 ..... *DVD*
The Best Years of Our Lives 1946 ..... *DVD*
La Bête Humaine 1938 ..... *DVD*
Betty Blue 1986 ..... *DVD*
Bicycle Thieves 1948 ..... *DVD* ⬡
The Big Parade 1925 ..... *DVD*
The Big Sleep 1946 ..... *DVD*
Billy Liar 1963 ..... *DVD* ⬡
Birdman or (The Unexpected Virtue of Ignorance) 2014 ..... *DVD* ⬡
Black Narcissus 1947 ..... *DVD* ⬡
Blonde Venus 1932 .....
Body and Soul 1947 ..... *DVD*
Bonnie and Clyde 1967 ..... *DVD* ⬡
Boogie Nights 1997 ..... *DVD*
Born on the Fourth of July 1989 .. *DVD* ⬡
Boyhood 2014 ..... *DVD* ⬡
Boyz N the Hood 1991 ..... *DVD*
Breakfast at Tiffany's 1961 ..... *DVD* ⬡
Breaking the Waves 1996 ..... *DVD*
Brief Encounter 1945 ..... *DVD* ⬡
Brokeback Mountain 2005 ..... *DVD* ⬡
Burnt by the Sun 1995 ..... *DVD*
Butch Cassidy and the Sundance Kid 1969 ..... *DVD* ⬡
Cabaret 1972 ..... *DVD* ⬡
Café de Flore 2011 ..... *DVD*
Capricious Summer 1968 .....
Captain Phillips 2013 ..... *DVD* ⬡
Carol 2015 ..... *DVD* ⬡
Casablanca 1942 ..... *DVD* ⬡
Celine and Julie Go Boating 1974 .... *DVD*
The Charge of the Light Brigade 1968 ..... *DVD*
Chariots of Fire 1981 ..... *DVD* ⬡
Chopper 2000 ..... *DVD*
The Cider House Rules 1999 ..... *DVD* ⬡
Cinema Paradiso 1988 ..... *DVD* ⬡
Citizen Kane 1941 ..... *DVD* ⬡
City of Hope 1991 .....
Cleo from 5 to 7 1961 ..... *DVD*

Close Encounters of the Third Kind 1977 ..... *DVD* ⬡
The Colour of Pomegranates 1969 ..... *DVD*
The Conformist 1970 ..... *DVD* ⬡
Crash 1996 ..... *DVD*
Cries and Whispers 1972 ..... *DVD*
Crimes and Misdemeanors 1989 ..... *DVD*
The Crowd 1928 .....
Cyclo 1995 .....
Cyrano de Bergerac 1990 ..... *DVD*
The Dam Busters 1954 ..... *DVD* ⬡
Les Dames du Bois de Boulogne 1946 ..... *DVD*
David Copperfield 1935 .....
Day for Night 1973 ..... *DVD* ⬡
Day of Wrath 1943 ..... *DVD*
The Day the Earth Stood Still 1951 ..... *DVD* ⬡
Dear Diary 1994 ..... *DVD*
Death in Venice 1971 ..... *DVD*
The Deer Hunter 1978 ..... *DVD* ⬡
Destry Rides Again 1939 ..... *DVD*
The Devil Is a Woman 1935 ..... *DVD*
Diary of a Country Priest 1950 ..... *DVD*
Diary of a Lost Girl 1929 ..... *DVD* ⬡
The Diary of Anne Frank 1959 ..... *DVD*
The Discreet Charm of the Bourgeoisie 1972 ..... *DVD* ⬡
Dishonored 1931 ..... *DVD*
Distant Voices, Still Lives 1988 ..... *DVD*
La Dolce Vita 1960 ..... *DVD*
The Draughtsman's Contract 1982 ..... *DVD*
The Duke of Burgundy 2014 ..... *DVD* ⬡
Earth 1930 ..... *DVD*
Ed Wood 1994 ..... *DVD*
Eddie the Eagle 2016 ..... *DVD* ⬡
An Education 2008 ..... *DVD*
8½ 1963 ..... *DVD* ⬡
The Elephant Man 1980 ..... *DVD* ⬡
Elmer Gantry 1960 ..... *DVD*
Eloge de l'Amour 2001 ..... *DVD*
The End of Summer 1961 ..... *DVD*
Les Enfants du Paradis 1945 ..... *DVD* ⬡
The English Patient 1996 ..... *DVD* ⬡
Fanny and Alexander 1982 ..... *DVD*
Far from Heaven 2002 ..... *DVD*
Farewell My Concubine 1993 ..... ⬡
Fight Club 1999 ..... *DVD*
The Fighter 2010 ..... *DVD* ⬡
Fires on the Plain 1959 ..... *DVD*
The Fisher King 1991 ..... *DVD*
Fitzcarraldo 1982 .....
Five Easy Pieces 1970 ..... *DVD*
Flirting 1989 .....
Florence Foster Jenkins 2016 ..... *DVD* ⬡
45 Years 2015 ..... *DVD* ⬡
The Fountain 2005 ..... *DVD* ⬡
The 400 Blows 1959 ..... *DVD* ⬡
4 Months, 3 Weeks and 2 Days 2007 ..... *DVD*
Foxcatcher 2014 ..... *DVD* ⬡
Frances Ha 2012 .....
The French Connection 1971 ..... *DVD* ⬡
From Here to Eternity 1953 ..... *DVD* ⬡
Full Metal Jacket 1987 ..... *DVD* ⬡
The Full Monty 1997 ..... *DVD* ⬡
Gandhi 1982 ..... *DVD* ⬡
The Garden of the Finzi-Continis 1971 ..... *DVD*
Gate of Hell 1953 ..... *DVD*
The General 1998 ..... *DVD*
Gertrud 1964 ..... *DVD*
Glengarry Glen Ross 1992 ..... *DVD* ⬡
The Godfather 1972 ..... *DVD* ⬡
The Godfather Part II 1974 ..... *DVD* ⬡
Gods and Monsters 1998 ..... *DVD*
Gone with the Wind 1939 ..... *DVD* ⬡
Goodbye, Mr Chips 1939 ..... *DVD*
GoodFellas 1990 ..... *DVD* ⬡
The Gospel According to St Matthew 1964 ..... *DVD* ⬡
The Graduate 1967 ..... *DVD* ⬡
Grand Hotel 1932 ..... *DVD*
La Grande Illusion 1937 ..... *DVD* ⬡
The Grapes of Wrath 1940 ..... *DVD* ⬡
Great Expectations 1946 ..... *DVD* ⬡
Greed 1925 .....
Hamlet 1948 ..... *DVD* ⬡
Hannah and Her Sisters 1986 ..... *DVD*
Happiness 1998 ..... *DVD*
He Who Gets Slapped 1924 .....
Heavenly Creatures 1994 ..... *DVD* ⬡
Heimat 1984 ..... *DVD*
Heimat 2 1992 ..... *DVD*
Heimat 3: a Chronicle of Endings and Beginnings 2004 ..... *DVD*
The Heiress 1949 ..... *DVD*
Henry V 1944 ..... *DVD* ⬡
The Hill 1965 .....
Hope and Glory 1987 ..... *DVD*
How Green Was My Valley 1941 ... *DVD* ⬡
Howards End 1992 ..... *DVD*
Hud 1963 ..... *DVD*
The Human Condition 1958 ..... *DVD*
The Hunchback of Notre Dame 1939 ... *DVD*
Hunger 2008 ..... *DVD*
The Hunt 1966 .....
Husbands and Wives 1992 ..... *DVD*
The Hustler 1961 ..... *DVD* ⬡
I Was Born, but... 1932 ..... *DVD*

The Ice Storm 1997 .... *DVD*
Ikiru 1952 .... *DVD*
Imitation of Life 1934 .... *DVD*
Imitation of Life 1959 .... *DVD*
The Immigrant 1917 .... *DVD*
In the Company of Men 1997 ....
In the Heat of the Night 1967 ..... *DVD BD*
In Which We Serve 1942 .... *DVD BD*
Inside Llewyn Davis 2013 .... *DVD BD*
The Insider 1999 .... *DVD*
Intolerance 1916 .... *DVD BD*
It's a Wonderful Life 1946 .... *DVD BD*
Ivan the Terrible, Part I 1944 ..... *DVD*
Ivan the Terrible, Part II 1946 .... *DVD*
Ivan's Childhood 1962 .... *DVD*
Jacquot de Nantes 1991 .... *DVD*
Jean de Florette 1986 .... *DVD*
Jeanne la Pucelle 1994 ....
Jeux Interdits 1953 .... *DVD*
The Joyless Street 1925 ....
Ju Dou 1990 ....
Jules et Jim 1962 .... *DVD BD*
Julius Caesar 1953 ....
Kameradschaft 1931 ....
Kandahar 2001 .... *DVD*
Kes 1969 .... *DVD BD*
Kikujiro 1999 .... *DVD BD*
The Killing Fields 1984 .... *DVD BD*
The King of Comedy 1983 .... *DVD BD*
The Kreutzer Sonata 1987 ....
LA Confidential 1997 .... *DVD BD*
The Last Command 1928 .... *DVD BD*
The Last Laugh 1924 .... *DVD BD*
The Last Picture Show 1971 .... *DVD*
Last Tango in Paris 1972 .... *DVD BD*
Last Year at Marienbad 1961 .... *DVD BD*
The Leopard 1962 .... *DVD BD*
Let's Talk about the Rain 2008 .... *DVD*
Leviathan 2014 ....
The Life and Death of Colonel Blimp
1943 .... *DVD BD*
The Life of Oharu 1952 ....
The Lion in Winter 1968 .... *DVD*
Little Dorrit 1987 ....
A Little Princess 1995 .... *DVD*
The Lives of Others 2006 .... *DVD BD*
Lola 1960 .... *DVD*
Lola Montès 1955 .... *DVD*
Lolita 1961 .... *DVD BD*
Lone Star 1995 .... *DVD*
The Loneliness of the Long Distance
Runner 1962 .... *DVD BD*
The Long Day Closes 1992 .... *DVD*
The Long Goodbye 1973 .... *DVD BD*
Lost in Translation 2003 .... *DVD BD*
Love Affair 1939 ....
M 1931 .... *DVD BD*
Macbeth 2015 .... *DVD BD*
The Madness of King George 1995 ..... *DVD*
The Magnificent Ambersons 1942 ... *DVD*
Magnolia 1999 .... *DVD*
La Maman et la Putain 1973 ....
A Man Escaped 1956 .... *DVD*
Man on Wire 2007 .... *DVD BD*
Maria Larsson's Everlasting Moments
2008 .... *DVD*
Marty 1955 .... *DVD*
Master of the House 1925 .... *DVD*
Medium Cool 1969 .... *DVD BD*
Men with Guns 1997 ....
Mephisto 1981 .... *DVD*
Midnight Cowboy 1969 .... *DVD BD*
Midnight Express 1978 .... *DVD BD*
Mildred Pierce 1945 .... *DVD*
Milk 2008 .... *DVD BD*
The Milky Way 1968 .... *DVD*
Miller's Crossing 1990 .... *DVD BD*
Million Dollar Baby 2004 .... *DVD BD*
The Miracle Worker 1962 .... *DVD*
Mister Roberts 1955 ....
Mr Smith Goes to Washington 1939 ... *DVD*
Mr Turner 2014 .... *DVD BD*
Mommy 2014 .... *DVD*
Mother 1926 ....
The Motorcycle Diaries 2004 ..... *DVD BD*
Mouchette 1966 .... *DVD BD*
Mrs Brown 1997 .... *DVD*
Mrs Miniver 1942 .... *DVD*
My Beautiful Laundrette 1985 .... *DVD*
My Left Foot 1989 .... *DVD BD*
My Name Is Joe 1998 .... *DVD*
Mysteries of Lisbon 2010 .... *DVD*
Napoléon 1927 .... *DVD*
Nashville 1975 .... *DVD BD*
Nightcrawler 2013 .... *DVD BD*
Nights of Cabiria 1957 .... *DVD*
Nil by Mouth 1997 ....
La Notte 1961 .... *DVD BD*
Now, Voyager 1942 .... *DVD*
The Nun's Story 1959 .... *DVD*
Odd Man Out 1947 .... *DVD BD*
Oliver Twist 1948 .... *DVD*
Los Olvidados 1950 .... *DVD*
On the Waterfront 1954 .... *DVD BD*
Once upon a Time in America
1984 .... *DVD BD*
One Flew over the Cuckoo's Nest
1975 .... *DVD BD*
Ordet 1955 .... *DVD*
Osaka Elegy 1936 .... *DVD BD*

Othello 1952 .... *DVD*
The Ox-Bow Incident 1943 .... *DVD BD*
A Page of Madness 1926 ....
Pandora's Box 1929 .... *DVD*
Les Parents Terribles 1948 ....
Paris, Texas 1984 .... *DVD BD*
Une Partie de Campagne 1936 ..... *DVD*
A Passage to India 1984 .... *DVD*
The Passion of Joan of Arc
1928 .... *DVD BD*
Pather Panchali 1955 .... *DVD BD*
Paths of Glory 1957 .... *DVD BD*
Patton 1970 .... *DVD BD*
The Pawnbroker 1965 ....
People on Sunday 1929 .... *DVD*
Pépé le Moko 1937 .... *DVD*
Performance 1970 .... *DVD*
Persona 1966 .... *DVD*
Philadelphia 1993 .... *DVD BD*
The Piano 1993 .... *DVD BD*
Pierrot le Fou 1965 .... *DVD BD*
Pink Flamingos 1972 ....
Pixote 1981 ....
Le Plaisir 1951 ....
Platoon 1986 .... *DVD BD*
Il Postino 1994 .... *DVD*
Prick Up Your Ears 1987 .... *DVD*
The Prime of Miss Jean Brodie 1969 ....
Providence 1977 ....
The Public Enemy 1931 .... *DVD*
Pulp Fiction 1994 .... *DVD BD*
Le Quai des Brumes 1938 .... *DVD BD*
Le Quattro Volte 2010 .... *DVD*
The Queen 2006 .... *DVD BD*
The Quiet Man 1952 .... *DVD BD*
Quills 2000 .... *DVD*
Raging Bull 1980 .... *DVD BD*
The Railway Children 1970 .... *DVD BD*
Rain Man 1988 .... *DVD BD*
Raise the Red Lantern 1991 ....
Ran 1985 .... *DVD BD*
Rashomon 1950 .... *DVD BD*
Rebel without a Cause 1955 .... *DVD BD*
The Red Shoes 1948 .... *DVD BD*
Red Sorghum 1987 .... *DVD*
Reds 1981 .... *DVD*
La Règle du Jeu 1939 .... *DVD*
The Remains of the Day 1993 ..... *DVD BD*
Reservoir Dogs 1991 .... *DVD BD*
Ride with the Devil 1999 ....
Rome, Open City 1945 .... *DVD*
La Ronde 1950 .... *DVD*
Room at the Top 1958 .... *DVD*
La Roue 1923 ....
The Round-Up 1966 .... *DVD*
The Royal Tenenbaums 2001 .... *DVD*
Russian Ark 2002 .... *DVD*
Salt of the Earth 1954 ....
Sansho the Bailiff 1954 .... *DVD*
The Saragossa Manuscript 1964 ......
Saturday Night and Sunday Morning
1960 .... *DVD BD*
Saturday Night Fever 1977 .... *DVD BD*
Saving Mr Banks 2013 .... *DVD BD*
Scarface 1932 ....
The Scarlet Empress 1934 ....
The Scent of Green Papaya 1993 ...... *DVD*
Schindler's List 1993 .... *DVD BD*
Scrooge 1951 .... *DVD*
The Sea Inside 2004 .... *DVD*
Secrets & Lies 1995 .... *DVD BD*
Sense and Sensibility 1995 .... *DVD BD*
Seven Samurai 1954 .... *DVD BD*
The Seventh Seal 1957 .... *DVD BD*
Shadowlands 1993 .... *DVD*
Shadows of Our Forgotten Ancestors
1964 .... *DVD BD*
Shallow Grave 1994 .... *DVD BD*
The Shanghai Gesture 1941 .... *DVD*
The Shawshank Redemption
1994 .... *DVD BD*
Shine 1996 .... *DVD BD*
Shoeshine 1946 ....
Shoot the Pianist 1960 .... *DVD BD*
Short Cuts 1993 .... *DVD*
A Short Film about Killing 1988 ...... *DVD*
Sideways 2004 .... *DVD BD*
Le Silence de la Mer 1947 .... *DVD BD*
Sisters of the Gion 1936 .... *DVD BD*
The Sixth Sense 1999 .... *DVD BD*
The Social Network 2010 .... *DVD BD*
Son of Saul 2015 .... *DVD BD*
Sonatine 1993 .... *DVD*
The Son's Room 2001 .... *DVD*
The Southerner 1945 ....
The Spider's Stratagem 1970 ....
The Spirit of the Beehive 1973 .... *DVD*
Spotlight 2015 .... *DVD BD*
Spring, Summer, Autumn, Winter ... and
Spring 2003 ....
Stand by Me 1986 .... *DVD BD*
A Star Is Born 1954 .... *DVD*
Storm over Asia 1928 .... *DVD*
The Story of a Cheat 1936 ....
The Story of Qiu Ju 1992 ....
Story of the Late Chrysanthemums 1939 ...
A Streetcar Named Desire 1951 ... *DVD BD*
Strictly Ballroom 1992 .... *DVD BD*
Sullivan's Travels 1941 .... *DVD BD*
Summer of My German Soldier 1978 ......

Summer with Monika 1952 .... *DVD*
Sunrise 1927 .... *DVD BD*
Sunset Blvd 1950 .... *DVD BD*
Sweet Smell of Success 1957 ..... *DVD BD*
La Symphonie Pastorale 1946 ....
A Tale of Two Cities 1935 ....
A Taste of Honey 1961 ....
Taxi Driver 1976 .... *DVD BD*
10 Rillington Place 1970 .... *DVD BD*
Testament 1983 ....
That Obscure Object of Desire
1977 .... *DVD BD*
There Will Be Blood 2007 .... *DVD BD*
The Thin Red Line 1998 .... *DVD BD*
Thirty Two Short Films about Glenn Gould
1993 ....
This Happy Breed 1944 .... *DVD BD*
This Sporting Life 1963 .... *DVD BD*
Three Colours Blue 1993 .... *DVD BD*
Three Colours Red 1994 .... *DVD BD*
Throne of Blood 1957 .... *DVD BD*
Time of the Gypsies 1988 ....
To Die For 1995 .... *DVD BD*
To Have and Have Not 1944 .... *DVD*
Tokyo Story 1953 .... *DVD BD*
Tokyo Twilight 1957 .... *DVD*
Topsy-Turvy 1999 .... *DVD*
Trainspotting 1995 .... *DVD BD*
Tristana 1970 .... *DVD*
The Truman Show 1998 .... *DVD BD*
12 Angry Men 1957 .... *DVD BD*
12 Years a Slave 2013 .... *DVD BD*
Two Stage Sisters 1964 ....
Tyrannosaur 2010 .... *DVD BD*
Ugetsu Monogatari 1953 .... *DVD BD*
Umberto D 1952 .... *DVD*
The Untouchables 1987 .... *DVD BD*
Viridiana 1961 .... *DVD*
Vivre Sa Vie 1962 .... *DVD BD*
Volver 2006 .... *DVD*
Walkabout 1970 .... *DVD BD*
Watch on the Rhine 1943 ....
Way Down East 1920 .... *DVD*
The Wedding March 1928 ....
Weekend 1967 .... *DVD*
Went the Day Well? 1942 .... *DVD BD*
West Side Story 1961 .... *DVD BD*
What Ever Happened to Baby Jane?
1962 .... *DVD*
Whiplash 2014 .... *DVD BD*
White Heat 1949 .... *DVD*
Wild Strawberries 1957 .... *DVD*
The Wind 1928 .... *DVD*
Winter Sleep 2014 .... *DVD BD*
Witness for the Prosecution 1957 ...... *DVD*
The Wolf of Wall Street 2013 ..... *DVD BD*
Woman of the Dunes 1963 .... *DVD*
Women in Love 1969 .... *DVD*
The World of Apu 1959 .... *DVD*
The Wrestler 2008 .... *DVD BD*
Wuthering Heights 1939 .... *DVD*
Yellow Earth 1984 ....
Yojimbo 1961 .... *DVD BD*
Yol 1982 ....
You Only Live Once 1937 .... *DVD*
Zéro de Conduite 1933 .... *DVD*
Zulu 1963 .... *DVD BD*

DRAMA ★★★★

AI: Artificial Intelligence 2001 ..... *DVD BD*
Abel 2010 .... *DVD*
About a Boy 2002 .... *DVD BD*
About Elly 2009 .... *DVD*
About Schmidt 2002 .... *DVD*
Above Suspicion 1943 ....
Accattone 1961 .... *DVD BD*
Accidental Hero 1992 ....
The Accidental Tourist 1988 .... *DVD*
L'Accompagnatrice 1992 ....
The Accused 1988 .... *DVD*
An Actor's Revenge 1963 .... *DVD*
The Actress 1953 ....
Adam 1983 ....
Adaptation. 2002 .... *DVD*
Adventureland 2009 .... *DVD*
The Adventures of Priscilla, Queen of the
Desert 1994 .... *DVD BD*
Advise and Consent 1962 ....
An Affair to Remember 1957 ...... *DVD BD*
After Life 1998 .... *DVD*
Afterglow 1997 ....
The Age of Innocence 1993 .... *DVD*
Un Air de Famille 1996 ....
Air Force 1943 .... *DVD*
Ake and His World 1984 ....
Al Capone 1959 ....
The Alamo 1960 .... *DVD*
Alexandra 2007 .... *DVD*
Alexandria Encore 1990 ....
Alexandria Why? 1979 ....
Alfie 1966 .... *DVD*
Alice Adams 1935 ....
Alice Doesn't Live Here Anymore
1974 ....
All Fall Down 1962 ....
All Is Lost 2013 .... *DVD*
All My Good Countrymen 1968 ....
All or Nothing 2002 .... *DVD*
All over Me 1996 .... *DVD*

All That Heaven Allows 1955 ...... *DVD BD*
All That Jazz 1979 .... *DVD*
All the King's Men 1949 .... *DVD*
All the Vermeers in New York 1990 ......
All the Way 2016 ....
All the Way Home 1963 ....
All This, and Heaven Too 1940 ....
Almost Famous 2000 .... *DVD BD*
Alphaville 1965 .... *DVD BD*
Alps 2011 ....
Les Amants 1958 .... *DVD*
Amateur 1994 .... *DVD BD*
The American Friend 1977 .... *DVD*
American Gangster 2007 .... *DVD BD*
American History X 1998 .... *DVD BD*
American Honey 2016 ....
American Psycho 2000 .... *DVD*
American Sniper 2014 .... *DVD BD*
The American Soldier 1970 .... *DVD*
American Splendor 2003 .... *DVD*
The Americanization of Emily 1964 ......
Le Amiche 1955 .... *DVD BD*
L'Amour Fou 1968 ....
Anastasia 1956 .... *DVD*
And Quiet Flows the Don 1957 ....
And Quiet Rolls the Dawn 1979 ....
And When Did You Last See Your Father?
2007 .... *DVD*
Andaz 1949 .... *DVD*
Angel and Tony 2010 ....
Angel Face 1953 ....
Angèle 1934 ....
Angels of Evil 2010 .... *DVD BD*
Angi Vera 1980 ....
Angus, Thongs and Perfect Snogging
2008 .... *DVD*
Aniki-Bobó 1942 ....
The Animal Kingdom 1932 .... *DVD*
Ankur 1974 ....
Anna Boleyn 1920 ....
Anna Karenina 1935 .... *DVD*
Anne and Muriel 1971 .... *DVD BD*
The Anniversary Party 2001 .... *DVD*
Anonymous 2011 .... *DVD BD*
Another Country 1984 ....
Another Day in Paradise 1998 .... *DVD*
Another Time, Another Place 1983 ...... *DVD*
Another Woman 1988 .... *DVD*
Another Year 2010 .... *DVD*
La Antena 2007 .... *DVD*
Anthony Adverse 1936 ....
Antonio das Mortes 1969 .... *DVD*
Any Given Sunday 1999 .... *DVD*
Apa 1966 .... *DVD*
Aparajito 1956 ....
Apollo 13 1995 .... *DVD BD*
The Apostle 1997 ....
L'Appartement 1996 .... *DVD*
Applause 1929 ....
The Apple 1998 .... *DVD*
The Apprenticeship of Duddy Kravitz
1974 ....
The April Fools 1969 ....
Apt Pupil 1997 .... *DVD*
Ariel 1988 ....
Arise, My Love 1940 ....
The Army of Crime 2009 .... *DVD BD*
The Artist and the Model 2012 ....
As Good as It Gets 1997 .... *DVD*
The Ascent 1976 ....
Ashes of Time 1994 ....
Ashik Kerib 1988 ....
Asphalt 1928 .... *DVD*
The Assassin 2015 .... *DVD*
The Assassination of Jesse James by the
Coward Robert Ford 2007 ...... *DVD BD*
The Asthenic Syndrome 1989 ....
At Any Price 2012 ....
At Close Range 1985 .... *DVD*
At Five in the Afternoon 2003 .... *DVD*
Atanarjuat: the Fast Runner 2001 ...... *DVD*
Attack! 1956 ....
The Attic: the Hiding of Anne Frank 1988 ..
Au Revoir les Enfants 1987 .... *DVD*
Aurora 2010 ....
Auto Focus 2002 .... *DVD*
Autumn Moon 1992 ....
An Autumn Tale 1998 .... *DVD*
The Aviator 2004 .... *DVD BD*
Awakenings 1990 .... *DVD*
Awara 1951 ....
Away from Her 2006 .... *DVD*
Baadasssss! 2003 .... *DVD*
The Baader Meinhof Complex 2008 .... *DVD*
The Bachelor Party 1957 ....
Back Street 1941 ....
Back Street 1961 ....
Backdraft 1991 .... *DVD BD*
The Bad and the Beautiful 1952 .... *DVD*
Bad Blood 1973 ....
Bad Lieutenant 1992 .... *DVD BD*
The Bad Lieutenant - Port of Call: New
Orleans 2009 .... *DVD BD*
Bad Timing 1980 .... *DVD BD*
Badlands 1973 .... *DVD*
Bagdad Café 1987 ....
The Bait 1995 ....
Bal 2010 ....
Ballad of a Soldier 1959 .... *DVD*
The Ballad of Narayama 1983 ..... *DVD BD*

The Man Who Wasn't There 2001......DVD
The Man with the Golden Arm 1955......DVD BD
The Man without a Past 2002......DVD
Mandingo 1975......
Mandy 1952......
Manon des Sources 1986......DVD
Man's Hope 1945......
Mansfield Park 1999......DVD
Map of the Human Heart 1992......DVD
A Map of the World 1999......DVD
Mapantsula 1988......
Maps to the Stars 2014......DVD BD
Margin Call 2011......DVD BD
Maria do Mar 1930......
Marius 1931......
Marius 2012......
Marius et Jeannette 1997......
Marked Woman 1937......
Marnie 1964......DVD BD
The Marquise of O 1976......DVD
The Marriage of Maria Braun 1978......DVD
The Married Woman 1964......
The Marrying Kind 1952......
Martha and I 1990......
Martha Marcy May Marlene 2011...DVD BD
Marvin's Room 1996......DVD
Mary and Max 2008......DVD
Mary, Queen of Scots 1971......DVD
Mask 1985......DVD
The Mask of Dimitrios 1944......
The Master 2012......DVD BD
Master and Commander: the Far Side of the World 2003......DVD BD
Mata Hari 1931......DVD
Matewan 1987......DVD
Matinee 1993......DVD BD
The Mattei Affair 1972......
Me and Earl and the Dying Girl 2015...DVD
Me and You and Everyone We Know 2005......DVD
Me without You 2001......DVD
Mean Creek 2004......DVD
Mean Streets 1973......DVD BD
The Meddler 2015......
Mediterraneo 1991......DVD
Melancholia 2011......DVD BD
Mélo 1986......DVD
Melvin and Howard 1980......
Memoirs of a Geisha 2005......DVD
Memories of Underdevelopment 1968......DVD
The Men 1950......DVD
Men Don't Leave 1990......
Men on the Bridge 2009......DVD
The Merchant of Four Seasons 1971...DVD
Merrill's Marauders 1962......
Merry Christmas Mr Lawrence 1982......DVD BD
The Merry Widow 1925......
Mesrine: Killer Instinct 2008......DVD BD
Mesrine: Public Enemy No 1 2008......DVD BD
The Messenger 2009......DVD BD
Mexican Bus Ride 1951......DVD
Michael Collins 1996......DVD BD
The Middleman 1975......
A Midnight Clear 1991......DVD BD
Midnight in the Garden of Good and Evil 1997......DVD
Midnight Special 2015......
The Mighty 1998......DVD
A Mighty Heart 2007......DVD BD
The Milagro Beanfield War 1988...DVD
The Milk of Sorrow 2009......
Millions 2004......DVD
Millions like Us 1943......DVD
Mina Tannenbaum 1993......DVD
Minor Mishaps 2002......DVD
The Miracle 1990......
The Miracle of Bern 2003......DVD
Mirror 1974......DVD
Mischief Night 2006......DVD
The Misfits 1961......DVD BD
Mishima: a Life in Four Chapters 1985......
Miss Bala 2011......DVD
Miss Evers' Boys 1997......
Miss Julie 1951......
Miss Rose White 1992......
Miss You Already 2015......DVD BD
Missing 1981......DVD
Mission to Moscow 1943......
Mississippi Burning 1988......DVD BD
Mississippi Grind 2015......
Mississippi Masala 1991......
Mr and Mrs '55 1955......DVD
Mr Holland's Opus 1995......DVD
Mister John 2013......DVD
Mr Reliable 1996......
Mr Skeffington 1944......DVD
Moebius 2013......
The Moment of Truth 1964......
Mommie Dearest 1981......DVD
Mona Lisa 1986......DVD BD
Monarch 1996......DVD
Monday Morning 2002......DVD
Moneyball 2011......DVD BD
Monsieur Lazhar 2011......DVD BD
Monsieur Vincent 1947......
Monsoon Wedding 2001......DVD

Monster 2003......DVD
Monsters 2010......DVD BD
Monster's Ball 2001......DVD
A Month in the Country 1987...DVD BD
Mood Indigo 2013......DVD BD
Moolaadé 2004......DVD
Moon 2008......DVD BD
Moonlighting 1982......
Morituri 1965......DVD
Morvern Callar 2001......DVD
The Mosquito Coast 1986......DVD
The Mother 2003......DVD
Mother and Son 1997......DVD
Mother India 1957......DVD
Mother Küsters Goes to Heaven 1975......
Moulin Rouge 1952......DVD
Moulin Rouge! 2001......DVD BD
The Mouth Agape 1974......DVD
Mrs Doubtfire 1993......DVD BD
Mrs Parker and the Vicious Circle 1994...DVD
Much Ado about Nothing 1993...DVD BD
Mud 2012......DVD BD
Muddy River 1981......
Mudhoney 1965......DVD
Munich 2005......DVD
Murder in Mississippi 1990......DVD
Murder in the First 1994......DVD
Muriel 1963......DVD
Muriel's Wedding 1994......DVD
Museum Hours 2012......DVD
Music Box 1989......DVD
The Musketeers of Pig Alley 1912......
Mustang 2015......DVD BD
My Ain Folk 1973......DVD
My Boyfriend's Back 1989......DVD
My Brilliant Career 1979......DVD
My Family 1994......
My First Wife 1984......
My Friend Flicka 1943......DVD
My Friend Ivan Lapshin 1982......DVD
My Girlfriend's Boyfriend 1987...DVD
My Life as a Dog 1985......DVD
My Life without Me 2003......DVD
My Love Has Been Burning 1949......
My Mother's Courage 1995......
My Name Is Bill W 1989......
My Night with Maud 1969......DVD
My Own Private Idaho 1991......DVD
My Son, My Son! 1940......
My Summer of Love 2004......DVD
My Way Home 1978......DVD
My Week with Marilyn 2011......DVD BD
Mystery Train 1989......DVD BD
Mystic River 2003......DVD BD
Nader and Simin, a Separation 2011......DVD BD
Naked 1993......DVD
The Naked City 1948......DVD BD
The Naked Jungle 1953......DVD
The Naked Kiss 1964......DVD
Napoléon 1955......
Nasty Baby 2016......
National Velvet 1944......DVD
Nationale 7 1999......
The Natural 1984......DVD
Natural Born Killers 1994......DVD BD
Nazarín 1958......
Nazi Hunter: the Beate Klarsfeld Story 1986......
The Negotiator 1998......DVD BD
Neighbouring Sounds 2012......
Nelly & Monsieur Arnaud 1995......
Network 1976......DVD BD
Never Steal Anything Small 1959......
The New Centurions 1972......
New Jack City 1991......DVD
The New Land 1972......DVD
New York, New York 1977......DVD BD
Newsfront 1978......
Next of Kin 1942......DVD
Next to Her 2014......
Nicholas Nickleby 1947......DVD
Nicholas Nickleby 2002......DVD
Night and Day 1991......
Night and the City 1950......DVD BD
'Night, Mother 1986......DVD
The Night of Counting the Years 1969......
The Night of San Lorenzo 1981...DVD BD
A Night to Remember 1958......DVD BD
Nightmare 1956......
Nightmare in Chicago 1968......DVD
Nijinsky 1980......
Nine Queens 2000......DVD
Nineteen Eighty-Four 1984......DVD
1900 1976......DVD BD
Nixon 1995......DVD
No Love for Johnnie 1960......DVD
No Regrets for Our Youth 1946...DVD
Nobody Knows 2003......DVD
Nobody's Child 1986......
Nobody's Fool 1994......DVD
Norma Rae 1979......DVD
The Normal Heart 2014......
El Norte 1983......
Northern Soul 2012......DVD BD
The Northerners 1992......
Northwest 2013......DVD
Nostalgia 1983......DVD
Not One Less 1999......DVD
Notes on a Scandal 2006......DVD BD

Notes on Blindness 2016......
Nowhere Boy 2010......DVD BD
Nowhere in Africa 2001......DVD
Les Nuits Fauves 1992......
Nymphomaniac Vol I 2013......DVD
Nymphomaniac Vol II 2014......DVD
O 2001......DVD
O Henry's Full House 1952......
October Sky 1999......DVD
Odds against Tomorrow 1959......DVD
Ode to Billy Joe 1976......
Of Gods and Men 2010......DVD BD
Of Human Bondage 1934......DVD
Of Mice and Men 1939......DVD
Of Mice and Men 1992......DVD
The Offence 1972......DVD BD
The Officers' Ward 2001......DVD
The Official Story 1985......DVD
Offside 2006......DVD
Ohayo 1959......DVD BD
Old Joy 2005......DVD
The Old Maid 1939......DVD
Old Man 1997......DVD
Old Yeller 1957......DVD
Olivia 1950......DVD
Olivier Olivier 1991......DVD
On Golden Pond 1981......DVD
Once 2006......DVD BD
Once upon a Time in Anatolia 2011......DVD BD
Once upon a Time in China 1991...DVD
Once Were Warriors 1994......DVD
One against the Wind 1991......
A One and a Two 1999......DVD
One False Move 1992......DVD
127 Hours 2011......DVD BD
One More Kiss 1999......DVD
One of Us 1989......
One Way Passage 1932......DVD
The Only Son 1936......
Only Yesterday 1933......DVD
Open Hearts 2002......DVD
Opening Night 1977......DVD BD
Orders to Kill 1958......DVD
Ordinary People 1980......DVD
The Organization 1971......DVD
The Organizer 1963......
Orphans 1998......DVD BD
Orphans of the Storm 1921......DVD
Osama 2003......DVD
Oslo, August 31st 2011......DVD
Ossessione 1942......DVD
Othello 1955......DVD
Othello 1965......DVD
Other Men's Women 1931......
Our Brand Is Crisis 2015......
Our Children 2012......DVD BD
Our Little Sister 2015......
Our Vines Have Tender Grapes 1945......
Out of Africa 1985......DVD BD
Out of Sight 1998......DVD BD
Over the Edge 1979......
The Oyster Princess 1919......
Padre Padrone 1977......DVD BD
Palookaville 1995......DVD
Le Paltoquet 1986......DVD
Pandora and the Flying Dutchman 1950......DVD BD
The Panic in Needle Park 1971...DVD
Panic in the Streets 1950......DVD
Panic in Year Zero 1962......DVD
The Paper 1994......DVD
The Paper Chase 1973......
Paper Moon 1973......DVD BD
Papillon 1973......DVD
The Parade 1984......DVD
Paradise Now 2005......DVD
Parineeta 1953......DVD
Parineeta 2005......DVD
Paris Blues 1961......DVD
Paris Nous Appartient 1960......DVD
Paris 36 2008......DVD
Paris Trout 1991......
Park Row 1952......DVD
Parkland 2013......DVD BD
The Party and the Guests 1966...DVD
Pascali's Island 1988......
Passenger 1963......
The Passenger 1975......DVD
A Passion 1969......DVD
Passion 1996......
Passion Fish 1992......DVD
The Past 2013......DVD BD
Pastor Hall 1940......
A Patch of Fog 2015......
Path to War 2002......DVD
Pathfinder 1987......
The Patience Stone 2012......DVD
The Patricia Neal Story 1981......
Pauline & Paulette 2001......DVD
Pauline at the Beach 1983......DVD
Payday 1972......
La Peau Douce 1964......DVD BD
Pelle the Conqueror 1987......DVD
Pelo Malo 2013......
Penny Serenade 1941......DVD BD
The People vs Larry Flynt 1996...DVD
A Perfect World 1993......DVD
Period of Adjustment 1962......DVD
Persepolis 2007......DVD BD

Pétain 1992......
Pete Kelly's Blues 1955......
Peter and Pavla 1964......
Peter Ibbetson 1935......
Le Petit Prince A Dit 1992......
Le Petit Soldat 1960......DVD
Les Petites Vacances 2006......DVD
The Petrified Forest 1936......DVD
Petulia 1968......DVD
Peyton Place 1957......DVD
The Phantom Carriage 1920......DVD
Phar Lap 1983......
Phil Spector 2013......
Philomena 2013......DVD BD
The Pianist 2002......DVD BD
Pickpocket 1959......DVD
The Picture of Dorian Gray 1945......
A Pigeon Sat on a Branch Reflecting on Existence 2014......DVD BD
The Pillow Book 1995......DVD BD
Pimpernel Smith 1941......
Ping Pong 2002......DVD
Pitfall 1962......DVD
The Place beyond the Pines 2012......DVD BD
A Place for Annie 1994......DVD
A Place in the Sun 1951......DVD
Places in the Heart 1984......DVD
Platform 2000......DVD
Playing by Heart 1998......DVD
Playing for Time 1980......
Pleasantville 1998......DVD
The Pledge 2000......DVD
Plein Soleil 1960......DVD BD
The Ploughman's Lunch 1983......DVD
Poetry 2010......DVD BD
Poil de Carotte 1932......
Police, Adjective 2009......DVD
The Polish Bride 1998......
Pollock 2000......DVD
Pollyanna 1920......
Pollyanna 1960......DVD
Polyester 1981......
Pork Chop Hill 1959......DVD BD
Les Portes de la Nuit 1946......
A Portrait of the Artist as a Young Man 1977......DVD
The Portuguese Nun 2009......DVD
Postcards from the Edge 1990......DVD
Il Posto 1961......DVD
Powder 1995......DVD
Precious (Base on Noi by Saf) (Based on the Novel "Push" by Sapphire) 2008......DVD BD
Pressure Point 1962......DVD
Pretty Baby 1978......DVD
Pretty Village Pretty Flame 1996...DVD
Pride 2014......DVD BD
Pride and Prejudice 1940......DVD
Pride & Prejudice 2005......DVD BD
Priest 1994......DVD
Primary Colors 1998......DVD
The Prime Gig 2000......DVD
The Prince of Egypt 1998......DVD
The Prince of Tides 1991......DVD
Prisoner of Honor 1991......
Prisoner of the Mountains 1996......DVD
Private 2004......DVD
The Private Affairs of Bel Ami 1947......
Private Fears in Public Places 2006...DVD
The Private Life of Henry VIII 1933...DVD
A Private Matter 1992......
Private Property 2006......DVD
Le Procès de Jeanne d'Arc 1962...DVD
The Profound Desire of the Gods 1968......DVD BD
Project Nim 2011......DVD BD
La Promesse 1996......DVD
Promise 1986......
Promised a Miracle 1988......
Proof 1991......DVD
A Prophet 2009......DVD BD
The Proposition 2004......DVD BD
Prospero's Books 1991......
Public Enemies 2009......DVD BD
Pull My Daisy 1959......
The Pumpkin Eater 1964......DVD
Punch-Drunk Love 2002......DVD BD
Punishment Park 1971......DVD
Pure 2002......DVD
Pusher II 2004......DVD
Pyaasa 1957......DVD
Quadrophenia 1979......DVD BD
Quartet 2012......DVD BD
Queen Christina 1933......DVD
Queen of Hearts 1989......
The Queen of Spades 1948......DVD
Quentin Durward 1955......
A Question of Silence 1982......
The Quiet American 2002......DVD BD
Quiz Show 1994......DVD
RKO 281 1999......DVD
Rabbit Hole 2010......DVD
Rachel, Rachel 1968......
Rain 2001......DVD
Raining Stones 1993......DVD
Raintree County 1957......
Rampart 2011......DVD BD
Rang De Basanti 2006......DVD
The Rape of Richard Beck 1985......

Time out of Mind 2014 .... *DVD*
Time Regained 1999 .... *DVD*
The Time That Remains: Chronicle of a
Present Absentee 2009 ....
The Time to Live and the Time to Die 1985
Timecode 1999 .... *DVD*
Times and Winds 2006 .... *DVD*
The Tin Drum 1979 .... *DVD* *BD*
Tin Men 1987 .... *DVD*
Tina: What's Love Got to Do with It
1993 .... *DVD*
Tito and Me 1992 ....
To Each His Own 1946 ....
To Kill a Mockingbird 1962 ...... *DVD* *BD*
To Live 1994 ....
To Our Loves 1984 ....
To Sleep with Anger 1990 .... *DVD*
To the Starry Island 1994 .... *DVD*
To Walk with Lions 1999 .... *DVD*
Toast 2010 ....
Tokyo Chorus 1931 ....
Tokyo Fist 1995 .... *DVD* *BD*
Tokyo Sonata 2008 .... *DVD* *BD*
Tokyo Tribe 2014 .... *DVD* *BD*
Tol'able David 1921 .... *DVD*
Tollbooth 1994 ....
Tomboy 2011 .... *DVD* *BD*
Tomorrow 1972 ....
Toni 1935 .... *DVD*
Tony Takitani 2004 .... *DVD*
Topaze 1933 ....
Torch Song Trilogy 1988 ....
The Torrent 1926 ....
Toto Le Héros 1991 .... *DVD*
A Touch of Sin 2013 .... *DVD* *BD*
A Touch of Zen 1969 .... *DVD* *BD*
Touching the Void 2003 .... *DVD* *BD*
Tous les Matins du Monde 1991... *DVD*
Tracks 2013 .... *DVD* *BD*
Traffic 2000 .... *DVD*
Traffic in Souls 1913 ....
The Train 1964 .... *DVD*
Training Day 2001 .... *DVD* *BD*
Transamerica 2005 ....
The Traveller 1974 ....
Travelling North 1986 ....
The Travelling Players 1975 ....
A Tree Grows in Brooklyn 1945 ...... *DVD*
The Tree of Life 2010 .... *DVD* *BD*
The Tree of Wooden Clogs 1978... *DVD*
Treeless Mountain 2008 ....
Trees Lounge 1996 .... *DVD*
36 Quai des Orfèvres 2004 .... *DVD*
Trial 1955 ....
The Trial 1962 .... *DVD*
The Trials of Oscar Wilde 1960 ....
Tricks 2007 ....
The Trip to Bountiful 1985 ....
Trishna 2011 .... *DVD* *BD*
Le Trou 1959 ....
True Love 1989 ....
True North 2006 ....
Truly Madly Deeply 1990 .... *DVD*
Truman 1995 .... *DVD*
Tsotsi 2005 .... *DVD*
Tuesdays with Morrie 1999 .... *DVD*
Tulpan 2008 .... *DVD*
Tunes of Glory 1960 ....
The Turin Horse 2011 .... *DVD* *BD*
Turkish Delight 1973 .... *DVD*
Turtles Can Fly 2004 .... *DVD*
The Tuskegee Airmen 1995 ....
12 Angry Men 1997 ....
12:08 East of Bucharest 2005.... *DVD*
Twelve o'Clock High 1949 .... *DVD*
24 Hour Party People 2001............ *DVD*
21 Grams 2003 .... *DVD* *BD*
Twice in a Lifetime 1985 ....
The Twilight Samurai 2002 .... *DVD*
Twin Peaks: Fire Walk with Me
1992 .... *DVD* *BD*
Twin Sisters of Kyoto 1963 ....
Two against the Law 1973 ....
Two Days, One Night 2014 .... *DVD* *BD*
Two for the Road 1967 .... *DVD* *BD*
Two Girls and a Guy 1997 ....
2 Guns 2013 .... *DVD* *BD*
The Two of Us 1967 ....
Two or Three Things I Know about Her
1966 ....
Two Weeks in Another Town 1962 ......
Ulee's Gold 1997 .... *DVD*
Ulysses' Gaze 1995 ....
Unbreakable 2000 .... *DVD* *BD*
Unbroken 2014 .... *DVD* *BD*
The Uncle 1964 .... *DVD*
Unconquered 1989 ....
Under Fire 1983 ....
Under the Sand 2000 ....
Under the Skin 1997 ....
Under the Skin 2013 .... *DVD* *BD*
Underground 1928 .... *DVD* *BD*
Underworld 1927 ....
Underworld USA 1961 ....
An Unfinished Piece for Mechanical Piano
1976 ....
An Unforgettable Summer 1994 ....
The Unholy Three 1925 ....
United 93 2006 .... *DVD* *BD*
The Unknown 1927 .... *DVD*

Unstrung Heroes 1995 .... *DVD*
The Unsuspected 1947 ....
Untouchable 2011 .... *DVD* *BD*
Untouchable 1947 ....
Up in the Air 2009 .... *DVD* *BD*
Urga 1990 ....
A Useful Life 2010 .... *DVD*
Uzak 2003 ....
Uzumasa Limelight 2014 .... *BD*
Va Savoir 2001 .... *DVD*
Vagabond 1985 ....
Valley of the Dolls 1967 .... *DVD*
Valmont 1989 ....
Les Valseuses 1974 .... *DVD*
Van Gogh 1991 .... *DVD* *BD*
The Vanishing Corporal 1962 .... *DVD*
Vassa 1983 ....
Vaudeville 1925 ....
Veer-Zaara 2004 .... *DVD*
Vendredi Soir 2002 .... *DVD*
Vera Drake 2004 .... *DVD*
Veronica Guerin 2003 .... *DVD*
A Very Long Engagement 2004 .... *DVD*
Vessel of Wrath 1938 ....
Vicky Cristina Barcelona 2008 .. *DVD* *BD*
La Vie de Château 1965 .... *DVD*
Villa Amalia 2009 ....
La Ville Est Tranquille 2000 .... *DVD*
Violent Saturday 1955 .... *DVD* *BD*
Violette 2013 ....
The Violin 2005 .... *DVD*
The Virgin Spring 1960 .... *DVD*
The Virgin Suicides 1999 .... *DVD*
The Visitor 2007 .... *DVD*
I Vitelloni 1953 ....
Vive L'Amour 1994 ....
Vodka Lemon 2003 ....
Voyage to Cythera 1984 ....
WUSA 1970 ....
The Wackness 2008 .... *DVD* *BD*
Wadjda 2012 .... *DVD* *BD*
Waiting for Happiness 2002 .... *DVD*
Wake Island 1942 ....
Walesa: Man of Hope 2013 .... *DVD*
A Walk in the Sun 1945 ....
Walk the Line 2005 .... *DVD* *BD*
The Walking Stick 1970 ....
Wall Street 1987 .... *DVD* *BD*
Walpurgis Night 1935 ....
Wanda 1971 ....
Waqt 1965 .... *DVD*
A War 2015 ....
The War Game 1965 ....
War Horse 2011 .... *DVD* *BD*
A War of Children 1972 ....
War Requiem 1988 ....
The War Zone 1999 .... *DVD*
Warrior 2011 .... *DVD* *BD*
The Warriors 1979 .... *DVD* *BD*
The Watchmaker of St Paul 1973 ..... *DVD*
Water Lilies 2007 ....
Waterloo Bridge 1940 ....
The Wave 2008 .... *DVD*
The Way Ahead 1944 .... *DVD*
The Way of All Flesh 1927 ....
The Way to the Stars 1945 .... *DVD*
The Way We Were 1973 .... *DVD*
We All Loved Each Other So Much 1974.....
We Are the Best! 2013 .... *DVD*
We Are What We Are 2010 .... *DVD* *BD*
We Are What We Are 2013 ....
We Don't Live Here Anymore 2003.... *DVD*
We Don't Want to Talk about It 1993........
We Need to Talk about Kevin
2011 .... *DVD* *BD*
We the Living 1942 ....
A Wedding 1978 ....
Weekend 2011 .... *DVD* *BD*
Welcome to New York 2014........ *DVD* *BD*
Welcome to the Dollhouse 1995........ *DVD*
The Well Digger's Daughter 2010 ...... *DVD*
Wendy and Lucy 2008 .... *DVD*
Werckmeister Harmonies 2000 .... *DVD*
West Beirut 1998 ....
Westfront 1918 1930 ....
Wetherby 1985 .... *DVD*
The Whales of August 1987 ....
What Maisie Knew 2013 .... *DVD* *BD*
What Price Hollywood? 1932 ....
What Richard Did 2012 .... *DVD* *BD*
What We Did on Our Holiday
2014 .... *DVD* *BD*
When a Woman Ascends the Stairs 1960 ...
When Father Was Away on Business
1985 .... *DVD*
When Ladies Meet 1933 ....
When the Last Sword Is Drawn 2003... *DVD*
When the Legends Die 1972 ....
When Trumpets Fade 1998 .... *DVD*
Where Is My Friend's House? 1987 ......
While We're Young 2014 .... *DVD* *BD*
Whisky 2004 .... *DVD*
The Whisperers 1967 ....
Whistle down the Wind 1961 .... *DVD*
The White Balloon 1995 ....
The White Dawn 1974 ....
White Dog 1981 .... *DVD* *BD*
White God 2014 .... *DVD* *BD*
White Hunter, Black Heart 1990 ....
White Mane 1952 ....
White Men Can't Jump 1992 ...... *DVD* *BD*

White Palace 1990 .... *DVD*
The White Ribbon 2009 .... *DVD* *BD*
Who'll Stop the Rain? 1978 .... *DVD*
Who's Afraid of Virginia Woolf? 1966 .. *DVD*
The Wicked Lady 1945 .... *DVD*
Wide Eyed and Legless 1993 ....
The Widow Couderc 1971 ....
Wife vs Secretary 1936 ....
Wilbur (Wants to Kill Himself) 2002 ... *DVD*
The Wild Angels 1966 ....
Wild at Heart 1990 .... *DVD* *BD*
The Wild One 1953 ....
Wild River 1960 .... *DVD*
Wilde 1997 .... *DVD* *BD*
William Shakespeare's Romeo + Juliet
1996 .... *DVD* *BD*
The Wind Will Carry Us 1999........... *DVD*
Wind with the Gone 1998 ....
Windom's Way 1957 .... *DVD*
Wings of Desire 1987 .... *DVD* *BD*
The Wings of the Dove 1997 ..... *DVD* *BD*
The Winslow Boy 1948 .... *DVD*
The Winslow Boy 1999 .... *DVD*
Winstanley 1975 .... *DVD*
A Winter's Tale 1992 .... *DVD*
Wish You Were Here 1987 .... *DVD*
Wit 2001 .... *DVD*
The Witches of Eastwick 1987........ *DVD*
With a Song in My Heart 1952 ....
Without Warning: the James Brady Story
1991 ....
Woman in a Dressing Gown 1957... *DVD*
A Woman of Paris 1923 .... *DVD*
A Woman's Face 1938 ....
A Woman's Face 1941 ....
Wonder Boys 2000 .... *DVD*
The Wonderful Lie of Nina Petrovna 1929...
Wonderland 1999 ....
The Woodsman 2004 .... *DVD*
A World Apart 1987 ....
The World Changes 1933 ....
Woyzeck 1978 .... *DVD*
Written on the Wind 1956 .... *DVD*
The Wrong Man 1956 .... *DVD*
Wyatt Earp 1994 .... *DVD* *BD*
XXY 2007 .... *DVD*
Xala 1974 ....
The Yakuza Papers 1973 .... *DVD*
The Year My Voice Broke 1987..........
A Year of the Quiet Sun 1984 ....
The Yearling 1946 ....
You & Me Forever 2012 ....
You Can Count on Me 1999 .... *DVD*
You, the Living 2007 .... *DVD*
You Will Be My Son 2012 .... *DVD*
Young Adam 2003 .... *DVD*
The Young in Heart 1938 ....
The Young Ladies of Wilko 1979 ....
Young Man with a Horn 1950 .... *DVD*
Young Mr Lincoln 1939 .... *DVD*
The Young Mr Pitt 1942 ....
Youth 2015 .... *DVD* *BD*
Z 1968 ....
Zodiac 2007 .... *DVD* *BD*
Zorba the Greek 1964 .... *DVD*

EPIC ★★★★★

Apocalypse Now 1979 .... *DVD* *BD*
Ben-Hur 1959 ....
Ben-Hur: a Tale of the Christ 1925 ......
The Bridge on the River Kwai
1957 .... *DVD* *BD*
El Cid 1961 .... *DVD* *BD*
Dances with Wolves 1990 .... *DVD* *BD*
Doctor Zhivago 1965 .... *DVD* *BD*
Farewell My Concubine 1993....... *BD*
Gandhi 1982 .... *DVD* *BD*
Gladiator 2000 .... *DVD* *BD*
Heimat 1984 .... *DVD*
Heimat 2 1992 .... *DVD*
Heimat 3: a Chronicle of Endings and
Beginnings 2004 .... *DVD*
The Human Condition 1958 .... *DVD* *BD*
The Iron Horse 1924 ....
Lawrence of Arabia 1962 .... *DVD* *BD*
Les Misérables 1934 .... *DVD* *BD*
Once upon a Time in America
1984 .... *DVD* *BD*
Ran 1985 .... *DVD* *BD*
Reds 1981 .... *DVD*
Ryan's Daughter 1970 .... *DVD*
Sansho the Bailiff 1954 .... *DVD*
Spartacus 1960 .... *BD*
2001: a Space Odyssey 1968 ..... *DVD* *BD*
The Vikings 1958 .... *DVD*

EPIC ★★★★

Alexander Nevsky 1938 .... *DVD*
Battle of Britain 1969 .... *DVD* *BD*
The Birth of a Nation 1915 .... *DVD* *BD*
Cabiria 1914 ....
Cheyenne Autumn 1964 ....
Cimarron 1931 ....
Come and See 1985 .... *DVD*
The Dead Lands 2014 .... *DVD*
Exodus 1960 .... *DVD*
The Fall of the Roman Empire
1964 .... *DVD* *BD*

Giant 1956 .... *DVD* *BD*
The Greatest Show on Earth 1952 ..... *DVD*
How the West Was Won 1962 ..... *DVD* *BD*
Ivanhoe 1952 .... *DVD*
Junoon 1978 ....
King of Kings 1961 ....
Kingdom of Heaven 2005 .... *DVD* *BD*
The Last Emperor 1987............ *DVD* *BD*
The Legend of 1900 1999 .... *DVD*
Legends of the Fall 1994 .... *DVD*
Little Big Man 1970 .... *DVD*
Lloyd's of London 1936 ....
The Loyal 47 Ronin 1941 .... *DVD*
Marie Antoinette 1938 ....
Les Misérables 1935 ....
Les Misérables 1995 ....
Mughal-e-Azam 1960 .... *DVD*
The Nibelungen 1924 ....
1900 1976 .... *DVD* *BD*
October 1928 .... *DVD*
The Pride and the Passion 1957 .... *DVD*
The Sign of the Cross 1932 ....
Star Wars Episode VI: Return of the Jedi
1983 .... *DVD* *BD*
Sunshine 1999 .... *DVD*
The Ten Commandments 1923 ....
The Ten Commandments 1956.... *DVD* *BD*
Things to Come 1936 .... *DVD* *BD*
Titanic 1997 .... *DVD* *BD*
To Live 1994 ....
The Travelling Players 1975 ....
Ulysses' Gaze 1995 ....
Veer-Zaara 2004 .... *DVD*
War and Peace 1966 .... *DVD*
The War Lord 1965 .... *DVD* *BD*
Waterloo 1970 .... *DVD* *BD*
Wyatt Earp 1994 .... *DVD* *BD*

EXPERIMENTAL ★★★★★

Berlin: Symphony of a Great City 1927 ......
Celine and Julie Go Boating 1974... *DVD*
Un Chien Andalou 1928 .... *DVD*
Eloge de l'Amour 2001 ....
Man with a Movie Camera 1928 ... *DVD* *BD*
Russian Ark 2002 .... *DVD*

EXPERIMENTAL ★★★★

A Propos de Nice 1930 ....
Bike Boy 1967 ....
Blue 1993 .... *DVD*
Bodysong 2002 .... *DVD*
The Chelsea Girls 1966 ....
La Chinoise 1967 .... *DVD*
Close-Up 1989 .... *DVD*
Conspirators of Pleasure 1996 .... *DVD*
Cremaster 3 2002 .... *DVD*
Daughters of the Dust 1991 ....
Dog Star Man 1964 ....
Dreams That Money Can Buy 1946 ......
Eaux d'Artifice 1953 ....
Eraserhead 1976 .... *DVD* *BD*
Le Fantôme de la Liberté 1974 ... *DVD*
The Forbidden Room 2015 .... *DVD* *BD*
The Holy Mountain 1973 .... *DVD*
India Song 1975 ....
Mirror 1974 .... *DVD*
The Northerners 1992 ....
Pink Narcissus 1971 ....
Pull My Daisy 1959 ....
The Seashell and the Clergyman 1928 ......
The Seventh Continent 1989 .... *DVD*
Superstar: the Karen Carpenter Story
1987 ....
Le Testament d'Orphée 1960...... *DVD*
Timecode 1999 .... *DVD*
Two or Three Things I Know about Her
1966 ....
War Requiem 1988 .... *DVD*
Wind with the Gone 1998 ....

FANTASY ★★★★★

Bambi 1942 .... *DVD* *BD*
Beauty and the Beast 1991........ *DVD* *BD*
Being John Malkovich 1999 ...... *DVD* *BD*
La Belle et la Bête 1946 .... *DVD*
Brazil 1985 .... *DVD* *BD*
Celine and Julie Go Boating 1974 ... *DVD*
The Dark Knight 2008 .... *DVD* *BD*
Don't Look Now 1973 .... *DVD* *BD*
Dumbo 1941 .... *DVD* *BD*
Edward Scissorhands 1990 .... *DVD* *BD*
Faust 1926 .... *DVD* *BD*
Faust 1994 ....
The Fisher King 1991 .... *DVD*
The 5,000 Fingers of Dr T 1953.........
Groundhog Day 1993 .... *DVD* *BD*
Harry Potter and the Deathly Hallows: Part
2 2011 .... *DVD* *BD*
Harvey 1950 .... *DVD* *BD*
The Haunting 1963 .... *DVD*
Heaven Can Wait 1943 .... *DVD*
Hero 2002 .... *DVD* *BD*
It's a Wonderful Life 1946 .... *DVD* *BD*
King Kong 1933 .... *DVD*
A Little Princess 1995 .... *DVD*
The Lord of the Rings: The Fellowship of
the Ring 2001 .... *DVD* *BD*

The Lord of the Rings: The Two Towers 2002
The Lord of the Rings: The Return of the King 2003 .... *DVD* 🔵
Lost Horizon 1937 .... *DVD*
Marvel Avengers Assemble 2012 .... *DVD* 🔵
Mary Poppins 1964 .... *DVD* 🔵
The Mask 1994 .... *DVD* 🔵
A Matter of Life and Death 1946.... *DVD*
Metropolis 1926 .... *DVD* 🔵
Miracle on 34th Street 1947............ *DVD*
The Nightmare before Christmas 1993 .... *DVD* 🔵
Orphée 1950 .... *DVD* 🔵
Pan's Labyrinth 2006 .... *DVD* 🔵
Pinocchio 1940 .... *DVD* 🔵
The Saragossa Manuscript 1964....
The Sixth Sense 1999 .... *DVD* 🔵
Snow White and the Seven Dwarfs 1937 .... *DVD* 🔵
Star Wars Episode VII: the Force Awakens 2015 .... 🔵
Superman 1978................. *DVD* 🔵
The Thief of Bagdad 1940 ....*DVD*
Time of the Gypsies 1988 ....
Up 2009 .... *DVD* 🔵
The Wizard of Oz 1939 .... *DVD* 🔵

FANTASY ★★★★

AI: Artificial Intelligence 2001.....*DVD* 🔵
The Adventures of Baron Munchausen 1988 .... *DVD* 🔵
After Life 1998 .... *DVD*
Akira 1988 .... *DVD* 🔵
Alice 1988 .... *DVD* 🔵
La Antena 2007..................... *DVD*
Antz 1998 .... *DVD*
The Arabian Nights 1974 ....*DVD*
Ashik Kerib 1988.................... *DVD*
The Asphyx 1972.................... *DVD*
Atlantis: the Lost Empire 2001 ....*DVD*
Azur & Asmar: the Princes' Quest 2006 ....
Babe 1995 .... *DVD* 🔵
Babes in Toyland 1934 .... *DVD*
The Baby's Room 2006 ....
Batman 1966 .... *DVD* 🔵
Batman 1989 .... *DVD* 🔵
Batman Returns 1992.......... *DVD* 🔵
Batman Forever 1995.......... *DVD* 🔵
Batman: Mask of the Phantasm 1993 ....
Batman Begins 2005 .... *DVD* 🔵
Beautiful Creatures 2013............ *DVD* 🔵
Before I Wake 2015 ....
Les Belles de Nuit 1952 ....
Beowulf 2007 .... *DVD* 🔵
Berkeley Square 1933 ....
Black Rainbow 1989 .... *DVD*
The Blair Witch Project 1998 .....*DVD* 🔵
Blancanieves 2011......................
Blithe Spirit 1945 .... *DVD*
Bluebeard 2009 ....
Brave 2012 .... *DVD* 🔵
The Bride with White Hair 1993 ....*DVD*
Bridge to Terabithia 2006 .... *DVD* 🔵
Brigadoon 1954.................... *DVD*
Casper 1995......................
Cemetery of Splendour 2015........
Chitty Chitty Bang Bang 1968 ....*DVD* 🔵
The Chronicles of Narnia: The Voyage of the Dawn Treader 2010 .... *DVD* 🔵
Cinderella 1950.................... *DVD* 🔵
Cinderella 2015.................... 🔵
The City of Lost Children 1995....*DVD* 🔵
City of Women 1980.................... 🔵
Cloudy with a Chance of Meatballs 2009 .... *DVD* 🔵
Cocoon 1985 .... *DVD* 🔵
Conspirators of Pleasure 1996 ....*DVD*
Coraline 2008 .... *DVD* 🔵
Cremaster 3 2002.................... *DVD*
The Crow 1994..................... *DVD* 🔵
The Curious Case of Benjamin Button 2008 .... *DVD* 🔵
The Curse of the Cat People 1944 ....
Dark City 1998 .... *DVD*
The Dark Crystal 1982 .... *DVD* 🔵
The Dark Knight Rises 2012 .....*DVD* 🔵
Dark Water 2002 .... *DVD* 🔵
Darkman 1990.................... *DVD*
The Dead and the Deadly 1983 ....
Delicatessen 1990 .... *DVD* 🔵
Destiny 1921......................
The Devil's Backbone 2001 ....*DVD* 🔵
Dodes'ka-Den 1970.................... *DVD*
Donnie Darko 2001.................... 🔵
Double Take 2009 ....
Drag Me to Hell 2009 .... *DVD* 🔵
Dredd 2012 .... *DVD* 🔵
Eaux d'Artifice 1953......................
Eclipse 2010 .... *DVD* 🔵
The Element of Crime 1984 ....*DVD*
Elf 2003 .... *DVD* 🔵
Enchanted 2007 .... *DVD* 🔵
Enemy Mine 1985 .... *DVD* 🔵
Ever After: a Cinderella Story 1998 .... *DVD* 🔵

Excalibur 1981 .... *DVD* 🔵
Fantastic Planet 1973.................... *DVD* 🔵
Faust 2011......................
Field of Dreams 1989.................... *DVD* 🔵
Fireworks 1947......................
Frankenweenie 2012.................... *DVD* 🔵
Frequency 2000 .... *DVD*
The Frighteners 1996 ....
Gabbeh 1995......................
Get Santa 2014.................... *DVD* 🔵
The Ghost and Mrs Muir 1947 ....*DVD*
Ghost Busters 1984.................... *DVD*
Goto, l'Ile d'Amour 1968.................... *DVD*
The Grinch 2000 .... *DVD* 🔵
The Halloween Tree 1993......................
Harry Potter and the Philosopher's Stone 2001 .... *DVD* 🔵
Harry Potter and the Chamber of Secrets 2002 ....
Harry Potter and the Prisoner of Azkaban 2004 ....
Harry Potter and the Goblet of Fire 2005 ....
Harry Potter and the Order of the Phoenix 2007 ....
Harry Potter and the Half-Blood Prince 2009 ....
Hawks and Sparrows 1966.......... *DVD* 🔵
Heartless 2009 .... *DVD* 🔵
Heaven Can Wait 1978 .... *DVD*
Hellboy II: the Golden Army 2008 .... *DVD* 🔵
Here Comes Mr Jordan 1941 ....*DVD* 🔵
The Hobbit: the Battle of the Five Armies 2014 .... *DVD* 🔵
Honey, I Shrunk the Kids 1989 ....*DVD*
Horns 2013......................
I Married a Witch 1942 .... *DVD*
Iceman 1984......................
India Song 1975......................
The Indian in the Cupboard 1995.........*DVD*
Invention of Destruction 1958................
Iron Man 2008 .... *DVD* 🔵
Iron Man Three 2013.................... *DVD* 🔵
It Happened Tomorrow 1944 ....*DVD*
James and the Giant Peach 1996.......*DVD*
Jason and the Argonauts 1963..........*DVD*
Johnny Suede 1991......................
Jumanji 1995 .... *DVD* 🔵
The King and the Mockingbird 1980....*DVD*
King Kong 2005 .... *DVD* 🔵
Kirikou and the Sorceress 1998..........*DVD*
Lady in White 1988 .... *DVD*
Ladyhawke 1985 .... *DVD*
The Last Mimzy 2007 .... *DVD*
The Last Wave 1977......................
Life Is a Bed of Roses 1983 ....*DVD*
Like Water for Chocolate 1993 ....*DVD*
Little Otik 2000.................... *DVD*
The Living Dead 1932......................
Lunacy 2005 .... *DVD*
Macario 1960......................
Malpertuis 1971......................
Matilda 1996 .... *DVD* 🔵
Me Myself I 1999......................
Meet the Applegates 1991......................
A Midsummer Night's Dream 1935........
A Midsummer Night's Dream 1961........
The Mighty 1998 .... *DVD*
Mood Indigo 2013.................... 🔵
Motorama 1991......................
The Muppet Christmas Carol 1992 .....*DVD*
My Neighbour Totoro 1988.......... *DVD* 🔵
My Winnipeg 2007.................... *DVD*
Nanny McPhee & the Big Bang 2010 .... *DVD* 🔵
The Navigator – a Medieval Odyssey 1988..
The NeverEnding Story 1984.......*DVD* 🔵
The New Gulliver 1935......................
The Nibelungen 1924.................... *DVD*
La Nuit Fantastique 1942......................
Opera do Malandro 1986......................
Pan 2015 .... *DVD* 🔵
Pandora and the Flying Dutchman 1950 .... *DVD* 🔵
Paranormal Activity 2007.........*DVD* 🔵
Peter Ibbetson 1935......................
Peter Pan 1953 .... *DVD* 🔵
The Phantom Carriage 1920 ....*DVD*
The Phantom Tollbooth 1969......................
Pink Narcissus 1971......................
Pirates of the Caribbean: the Curse of the Black Pearl 2003 .... *DVD* 🔵
Pleasantville 1998 .... *DVD* 🔵
Ponyo 2008 .... *DVD* 🔵
Powder 1995 .... *DVD*
The Princess Bride 1987.................... *DVD*
Princess Mononoke 1997/2001 ...*DVD* 🔵
The Projectionist 1970......................
The Purple Rose of Cairo 1985 ....*DVD*
Q – the Winged Serpent 1982 ....*DVD*
The Queen of Spades 1948.................... *DVD*
The Red Balloon 1956 .... *DVD* 🔵
The Rite 2011 .... *DVD* 🔵
Rocketeer 1991 .... *DVD*
Rouge 1987......................
Satyricon 1969 .... *DVD*
The Secret Lives of Dentists 2003.....*DVD*
The Secret of Roan Inish 1993......................
The 7th Voyage of Sinbad 1958 ....*DVD*

The Shamer's Daughter 2015.................
Shrek 2001 .... *DVD* 🔵
Shrek 2 2004 .... *DVD* 🔵
Sitcom 1997.................... *DVD*
Sky High 2005 .... *DVD* 🔵
Sleeping Beauty 1959 .... *DVD* 🔵
Sleepy Hollow 1999......................
Song of the Sea 2014.................... *DVD* 🔵
Speed Racer 2008.................... *DVD* 🔵
Spider-Man 2002 .... *DVD* 🔵
Spider-Man 2 2004.................... *DVD* 🔵
The Spiderwick Chronicles 2008 .... *DVD* 🔵
Spirited Away 2001......... *DVD* 🔵
Splash 1984 .... *DVD*
SPYkids 2001 .... *DVD* 🔵
SPYkids 2: the Island of Lost Dreams 2002 .... *DVD* 🔵
Stardust 2007 .... *DVD* 🔵
Stranger than Fiction 2006 .... *DVD* 🔵
Strings 2004 .... *DVD*
Superman II 1980 .... *DVD* 🔵
Superman Returns 2006.................... *DVD* 🔵
Superstar: the Karen Carpenter Story 1987 ....
Surviving Life 2010.................... 🔵
Suspiria 1976 .... *DVD* 🔵
Tale of Tales 2015.................... 🔵
The Tale of the Fox 1931 ....
The Tempest 1979 .... *DVD*
The Thief of Bagdad 1924 ....*DVD* 🔵
Thomas the Imposter 1964 ....
Three Lives and Only One Death 1996.......
Thunder Rock 1942.................... *DVD*
Tim Burton's Corpse Bride 2005 .... *DVD* 🔵
Time Bandits 1981 .... *DVD* 🔵
The Time Machine 1960 .... *DVD*
tom thumb 1958......................
Topper 1937......................
The Tree of Life 2010.......... *DVD* 🔵
Tuck Everlasting 1980......................
Unbreakable 2000.................... 🔵
Les Visiteurs 1993.................... *DVD*
Les Visiteurs du Soir 1942......................
Volere, Volare 1991......................
Watchmen 2009 .... 🔵
The Water Horse 2007 .... *DVD* 🔵
Willy Wonka and the Chocolate Factory 1971 .... *DVD* 🔵
Wings of Desire 1987.................... 🔵
The Witch 2015 .... *DVD* 🔵
X2 2003 .... 🔵
X-Men: First Class 2011 .... *DVD* 🔵
X-Men: Days of Future Past 2014 .... *DVD* 🔵
Yeelen 1987......................
Yellow Submarine 1968 .... *DVD* 🔵
Zathura: a Space Adventure 2005.....*DVD*
Zu Warriors 1983 .... *DVD*

FILM NOIR ★★★★★

Build My Gallows High 1947.................
Double Indemnity 1944 .... *DVD* 🔵
Farewell My Lovely 1944 .... *DVD*
Gilda 1946 .... *DVD* 🔵
In a Lonely Place 1950 .... *DVD* 🔵
The Killers 1946 .... *DVD* 🔵
Kiss Me Deadly 1955 .... *DVD*
Laura 1944 .... *DVD*
The Maltese Falcon 1941......... *DVD* 🔵
Mildred Pierce 1945 .... *DVD*
The Postman Always Rings Twice 1946 .... *DVD*
The Strange Love of Martha Ivers 1946 ....

FILM NOIR ★★★★

Beyond a Reasonable Doubt 1956 ......*DVD*
The Big Combo 1955......................
The Big Heat 1953 .... *DVD*
The Blue Dahlia 1946.......... *DVD* 🔵
The Chase 1946 .... *DVD*
Crime of Passion 1957......................
Criss Cross 1949......................
Crossfire 1947......................
Cry of the City 1948.................... *DVD*
Dead Reckoning 1947 .... *DVD*
Desperate 1947......................
Fallen Angel 1945 .... *DVD* 🔵
Fear in the Night 1947 .... *DVD*
Force of Evil 1948......................
The Glass Key 1942 .... *DVD* 🔵
Gun Crazy 1949......................
The Hitch-Hiker 1953 .... *DVD*
I Wake Up Screaming 1941 ....
Kiss of Death 1947 .... *DVD* 🔵
Lady in the Lake 1947......................
Moonrise 1948......................
Phantom Lady 1944......................
Pitfall 1948......................
Raw Deal 1948......................
T-Men 1947......................
They Live by Night 1948 ....
Where the Sidewalk Ends 1950.....*DVD*
The Woman in the Window 1945 ....
The Woman on the Beach 1947.................

HISTORICAL ★★★★★

Argo 2012 .... *DVD* 🔵
The Battleship Potemkin 1925 ....*DVD*
Captain Phillips 2013 .... *DVD* 🔵
Changeling 2008 .... *DVD* 🔵
The Charge of the Light Brigade 1968 ....
Chariots of Fire 1981.......... *DVD* 🔵
El Cid 1961 .... 🔵
Eddie the Eagle 2016 .... *DVD* 🔵
Foxcatcher 2014 .... 🔵
Henry V 1944 .... 🔵
The Insider 1999.................... *DVD*
Ivan the Terrible, Part I 1944 ....*DVD*
Ivan the Terrible, Part II 1946 ....*DVD*
Jeanne la Pucelle 1994 ....
Julius Caesar 1953 ....
Lawrence of Arabia 1962 .... *DVD* 🔵
The Lion in Winter 1968 .... *DVD*
Lola Montès 1955.................... *DVD*
The Madness of King George 1995......*DVD*
Maria Larsson's Everlasting Moments 2008 .... *DVD*
Mrs Brown 1997.................... *DVD*
Napoléon 1927......................
The Queen 2006 .... *DVD* 🔵
The Revenant 2015.................... 🔵
The Round-Up 1966.................... 🔵
Saving Mr Banks 2013 .... *DVD* 🔵
The Scarlet Empress 1934 ....
The Social Network 2010.................... 🔵
Spartacus 1960......................
Spotlight 2015 .... *DVD* 🔵
12 Years a Slave 2013.......... *DVD* 🔵
The Wolf of Wall Street 2013.......... 🔵
Zulu 1963 .... *DVD* 🔵

HISTORICAL ★★★★

The Alamo 1960.................... *DVD*
Alexander Nevsky 1938 .... *DVD*
American Gangster 2007 .... *DVD* 🔵
American Hustle 2013 .... 🔵
American Sniper 2014 .... 🔵
Apollo 13 1995 ....
The Baader Meinhof Complex 2008....*DVD*
Barbarians at the Gate 1993......................
Becket 1964.................... *DVD*
Belle 2013 .... *DVD* 🔵
The Birth of a Nation 1915.......... *DVD* 🔵
The Blind Side 2009.......... *DVD* 🔵
The Bling Ring 2013 .... 🔵
Bloody Sunday 2001.................... *DVD*
Boomerang! 1947.................... *DVD*
The Bounty 1984.................... *DVD*
Boycott 2001......................
Braveheart 1995 .... *DVD* 🔵
Breach 2006.................... *DVD*
Breaker Morant 1979.................... *DVD*
Bridge of Spies 2015.......... *DVD* 🔵
Call Northside 777 1948.................... *DVD*
Carandiru 2003......................
The Charge of the Light Brigade 1936 ....
The Chess Players 1977 ....
Chimes at Midnight 1966.......... *DVD* 🔵
Cinema Verite 2011 ....
City of Life and Death 2009.........*DVD* 🔵
The Clan 2015......................
Comrades: a Lanternist's Account of the Tolpuddle Martyrs and What Became of Them 1986 .... *DVD*
Conquest 1937......................
Cool Runnings 1993......................
The Counterfeiters 2007.................... *DVD*
Cromwell 1970.................... *DVD*
Dallas Buyers Club 2013.......... *DVD* 🔵
Danton 1982......................
The Dark Horse 2014......................
The Day the Sun Turned Cold 1994.......
Death by Hanging 1968......................
The Deep 2012 .... *DVD*
The Devil and the Nun 1960.................... *DVD*
The Devils 1971 .... *DVD*
Il Divo 2008......................
Downfall 2004.................... *DVD*
Eagle in a Cage 1971......................
Effie Gray 2014 .... *DVD* 🔵
Eisenstein in Guanajuato 2014 ....
Elizabeth 1998.................... 🔵
Elizabeth: the Golden Age 2007 ..*DVD* 🔵
L'Enfant Sauvage 1970 .... *DVD*
Escape from Alcatraz 1979 .... *DVD* 🔵
Escape from Sobibor 1987 ....
The Execution of Private Slovik 1974....*DVD*
FairyTale: a True Story 1997 .... 🔵
The Fall of the Roman Empire 1964 .... *DVD*
Fanfan la Tulipe 1951 .... *DVD*
Farewell 2010......................
The Fifth Estate 2013......................
55 Days at Peking 1963 .... *DVD* 🔵
Fire over England 1937......................
Fort Saganne 1984......................
Fourteen Hours 1951......................
1492: Conquest of Paradise 1992....*DVD*
Friday Night Lights 2004.................... *DVD*
Frost/Nixon 2008 .... *DVD* 🔵
Fruitvale Station 2013 .... *DVD* 🔵

Ghosts 2006 ... DVD
Gideon's Trumpet 1980
Glory 1989 ... DVD BD
Gohatto 1999 ... DVD
Good Morning, Night 2003 ... DVD
Good Night, and Good Luck. 2005 ... DVD BD
Grand Theft Parsons 2003 ... DVD
The Great Debaters 2007
Greyfriars Bobby 1961 ... DVD
Heat Wave 1990
Henry V 1989 ... DVD
The Hoax 2006 ... DVD
Holding the Man 2015 ... DVD
The Honeymoon Killers 1969 ... DVD
Hotel Rwanda 2004 ... DVD
I Saw Ben Barka Get Killed 2005 ... DVD
I, the Worst of All 1990 ... DVD
The Imitation Game 2014 ... DVD BD
The Impossible 2011 ... DVD BD
In Cold Blood 1967 ... DVD BD
In the Realm of the Senses 1976 ... DVD BD
Indictment: the McMartin Trial 1995 ... DVD
JFK 1991 ... DVD BD
Journey of Hope 1990 ... DVD
Joy 2015 ... DVD BD
Judgment at Nuremberg 1961 ... DVD
Kajaki: The True Story 2014 ... DVD BD
Katyn 2007 ... DVD BD
Kill Me If You Can 1977
The Killing of John Lennon 2006 ... DVD
The King's Speech 2010 ... DVD BD
Kon-Tiki 2012 ... DVD
Labyrinth of Lies 2014 ... DVD
The Lady & the Duke 2001 ... DVD
The Last King of Scotland 2006 ... DVD BD
The Last Stage 1947
The Late Shift 1996
Lena: My 100 Children 1987 ... DVD
Lloyd's of London 1936
London Road 2014 ... DVD
Loving 2016
The Loyal 47 Ronin 1941
Made in Dagenham 2010 ... DVD
A Man for All Seasons 1966 ... DVD
The Man Who Captured Eichmann 1996 ... DVD
Mary, Queen of Scots 1971 ... DVD
Matewan 1987 ... DVD
The Mattei Affair 1972 ... DVD
Mayerling 1936
The Miracle of Bern 2003 ... DVD
Miss Evers' Boys 1997
Missing 1981 ... DVD
Mississippi Burning 1988 ... DVD BD
Mr Reliable 1996
Moneyball 2011 ... DVD BD
Monsieur N 2003
Monster 2003 ... DVD
Munich 2005 ... DVD
Murder in Mississippi 1990
Murder in the First 1994 ... DVD
Mutiny on the Bounty 1935 ... DVD
Mutiny on the Bounty 1962 ... DVD
My Name Is Bill W 1989
My Week with Marilyn 2011 ... DVD BD
The Nasty Girl 1990 ... DVD
Nazi Hunter: the Beate Klarsfeld Story 1986
The New World 2005 ... DVD BD
The Night of Counting the Years 1969 ...
A Night to Remember 1958 ... DVD
No Regrets for Our Youth 1946 ... DVD
Nobody's Child 1986
Norma Rae 1979 ... DVD
The Normal Heart 2014 ... DVD
October 1928 ... DVD
October Sky 1999 ... DVD
One against the Wind 1991 ...
127 Hours 2011 ... DVD BD
Our Brand Is Crisis 2015 ... DVD
Our Children 2012 ... DVD BD
Out of the Darkness 1985
Padre Padrone 1977 ... DVD BD
Parkland 2013 ... DVD BD
Path to War 2002 ... DVD
The Patricia Neal Story 1981 ...
Pétain 1992
Phil Spector 2013
Philomena 2013 ... DVD BD
Playing for Time 1980
Pride 2014 ... DVD BD
Prisoner of Honor 1991
A Private Matter 1992
Promised a Miracle 1988
Queen Christina 1933 ... DVD
Quiz Show 1994 ... DVD
RKO 281 1999 ... DVD
Red Cliff 2008 ... DVD BD
Reign of Terror 1949
The Return of Martin Guerre 1982 ... DVD
Richard III 1955 ... DVD BD
Richard III 1995 ... DVD
Ridicule 1996 ... DVD
The Right Stuff 1983 ... DVD
The Rise to Power of Louis XIV 1966 ...
The Rite 2011 ... DVD BD
Rob Roy 1995 ... DVD BD
Roberto Succo 2000 ... DVD
Rosewater 2014 ... DVD BD
Rush 2013 ... DVD BD

The Saga of Anatahan 1953
Salvatore Giuliano 1961 ... DVD BD
The Sapphires 2012 ... DVD
Sarraouina 1986
Satyricon 1969 ... DVD BD
Scott of the Antarctic 1948 ... DVD
Selma 2014 ... DVD BD
Serpico 1973 ... DVD BD
The Sign of the Cross 1932 ... DVD
Skokie 1981 ... DVD
Something for Joey 1977
Soul of the Game 1996
The Spirit of St Louis 1957
Stand and Deliver 1988
The Stanford Prison Experiment 2015 ...
Stanley and Livingstone 1939
Stavisky 1974 ... DVD
Suffragette 2015 ... DVD BD
The Sun 2005 ... DVD
The Switch 1993 ... DVD
Thirteen Days 2000 ... DVD
Three Came Home 1950 ... DVD
300 2006 ... DVD BD
300: Rise of an Empire 2013 ... DVD BD
Tous les Matins du Monde 1991 ... DVD
The Trials of Oscar Wilde 1960 ... DVD
Tuesdays with Morrie 1999 ... DVD
The Tuskegee Airmen 1995
24 Hour Party People 2001 ... DVD
Unbroken 2014 ... DVD BD
Unconquered 1989
United 93 2006 ... DVD BD
Unstrung Heroes 1995 ... DVD
Untouchable 2011 ... DVD BD
A Walk in the Woods 2015 ... DVD BD
War and Peace 1966 ... DVD
Waterloo 1970 ... DVD
Welcome to New York 2014 ... DVD BD
What Richard Did 2012 ... DVD BD
Winstanley 1975 ... DVD
Without Warning: the James Brady Story 1991
A World Apart 1987 ... DVD
The World's Fastest Indian 2005 ... DVD
The Wrong Man 1956 ... DVD
Zero Dark Thirty 2012 ... DVD BD
Zodiac 2007 ... DVD BD

HORROR ★★★★★

Alien 1979 ... DVD BD
The Birds 1963 ... DVD BD
The Black Cat 1934 ... DVD
Blood and Black Lace 1964 ... DVD BD
The Body Snatcher 1945 ... DVD
Braindead 1992 ... DVD
Bride of Frankenstein 1935 ... DVD BD
The Cabinet of Dr Caligari 1919 ... DVD BD
Carrie 1976 ... DVD BD
Dawn of the Dead 1978 ... DVD BD
Dead of Night 1945 ... DVD BD
Dracula 1958 ... DVD BD
The Exorcist 1973 ... DVD BD
Eyes without a Face 1959 ... DVD BD
Frankenstein 1931 ... DVD BD
Halloween 1978 ... DVD BD
The Haunting 1963 ... DVD
Henry: Portrait of a Serial Killer 1986 ... DVD BD
The Hunchback of Notre Dame 1939 ... DVD
The Innocents 1961 ... DVD BD
The Invisible Man 1933 ... DVD BD
Island of Lost Souls 1932 ... DVD BD
Night of the Living Dead 1968 ... DVD BD
Nosferatu, a Symphony of Horrors 1922 ... DVD
Pan's Labyrinth 2006 ... DVD BD
Psycho 1960 ... DVD BD
Rosemary's Baby 1968 ... DVD BD
Scream 1996 ... DVD BD
Shaun of the Dead 2004 ... DVD BD
The Shining 1980 ... DVD BD
The Texas Chain Saw Massacre 1974 ... DVD BD
Tremors 1989 ... DVD BD
The Uninvited 1944 ... DVD
Vampyr 1932 ... DVD
What Ever Happened to Baby Jane? 1962 ... DVD
The Wicker Man 1973/2002 ... DVD BD
Witchfinder General 1968 ... DVD BD
Young Frankenstein 1974 ... DVD BD

HORROR ★★★★

The Abominable Dr Phibes 1971 ... DVD BD
Abraham Lincoln: Vampire Hunter 2012 ... DVD BD
The Addams Family 1991 ... DVD BD
Addams Family Values 1993 ... DVD
Alice, Sweet Alice 1977
Alligator 1980 ... DVD
American Mary 2012 ... DVD BD
An American Werewolf in London 1981 ... DVD BD
Anatomy 2000 ... DVD
Anguish 1986
Antiviral 2012 ... DVD
Arachnophobia 1990 ... DVD
The Asphyx 1972 ... DVD

Audition 1999 ... DVD BD
The Babadook 2013 ... DVD BD
The Baby's Room 2006
The Bad Seed 1956
Bad Taste 1987 ... DVD
Bait 2015
Basket Case 1982 ... DVD
The Bay 2012 ... DVD BD
Bay of Blood 1971 ... DVD BD
The Beast with Five Fingers 1946 ... DVD
Beetle Juice 1988 ... DVD BD
Before Dawn 2012 ... DVD
Before I Wake 2015
Berberian Sound Studio 2012 ... DVD BD
Black Christmas 1974 ... DVD
Black Death 2010 ... DVD
Black Sabbath 1963 ... DVD
Black Sheep 2006 ... DVD
The Blair Witch Project 1998 ... DVD BD
The Blob 1988 ... DVD
Blue Sunshine 1977 ... DVD
Body Snatchers 1993 ... DVD
Bone Tomahawk 2015 ... DVD BD
Brain Damage 1988
Bram Stoker's Dracula 1992 ... DVD BD
The Brides of Dracula 1960 ... DVD
The Brood 1979 ... DVD BD
Byzantium 2012 ... DVD BD
The Cabin in the Woods 2010 ... DVD BD
Candyman 1992 ... DVD
Carnival of Souls 1962 ... DVD
Cat People 1942 ... DVD BD
Cemetery Man 1994 ... DVD
Chamber of Horrors 1966 ... DVD
A Chinese Ghost Story 1987 ... DVD
The Conjuring 2 2016 ... DVD BD
The Corpse 1969 ... DVD
The Crazies 2010 ... DVD BD
Creature from the Black Lagoon 1954 ... DVD BD
Cronos 1992 ... DVD
The Curse of Frankenstein 1957 ... DVD BD
The Curse of the Cat People 1944 ... DVD
Dark Water 2002 ... DVD BD
Darkman 1990 ... DVD
Daughters of Darkness 1970 ... DVD
The Day of the Beast 1995 ... DVD
Day of the Dead 1985 ... DVD BD
The Dead Zone 1983 ... DVD
Death Line 1972
Demon Seed 1977 ... DVD
The Descent 2005 ... DVD BD
The Devils 1971 ... DVD
The Devil's Backbone 2001 ... DVD BD
Diary of the Dead 2007 ... DVD BD
The Disappeared 2008 ... DVD
The Divide 2011 ... DVD BD
Dr Jekyll and Mr Hyde 1931 ... DVD
Dog Soldiers 2001 ... DVD
Dracula 1931 ... DVD BD
Dracula 1979 ... DVD BD
Dracula - Prince of Darkness 1965 ... DVD BD
Drag Me to Hell 2009 ... DVD BD
Dust Devil 1992 ... DVD
Eclipse 2010 ... DVD BD
Eraserhead 1976 ... DVD BD
The Evil Dead 1981 ... DVD BD
Evil Dead 2013 ... DVD BD
The Eye 2002 ... DVD BD
F 2010 ... DVD BD
The Face behind the Mask 1941 ... DVD
The Fall of the House of Usher 1960 ... DVD BD
The Fearless Vampire Killers 1967 ... DVD
The Flesh Eaters 1964
The Fly 1986 ... DVD BD
Frankenstein: the True Story 1973 ... DVD
Freaks 1932 ... DVD BD
Freezer 2000 ... DVD
Fright Night 1985 ... DVD
From Dusk till Dawn 1995 ... DVD BD
From Hell 2001 ... DVD BD
The Fury 1978 ... DVD
The Ghost Breakers 1940 ... DVD
The Ghoul 1933 ... DVD
Ginger Snaps 2000 ... DVD
A Girl Walks Home Alone at Night 2014 ... DVD BD
The Girl with All the Gifts 2016 ... DVD
Godzilla 1954 ... DVD BD
The Golem 1920 ... DVD
Grabbers 2012 ... DVD BD
Gremlins 1984 ... DVD BD
The Hallow 2015 ... DVD
The Hands of Orlac 1960 ... DVD
The Happiness of the Katakuris 2001 ... DVD
Hardware 1990 ... DVD
Häxan 1921 ... DVD
Heartless 2009 ... DVD
Hellboy II: the Golden Army 2008 ... DVD BD
The Hidden 1987 ... DVD
The Hills Have Eyes 1977 ... DVD
The Hills Have Eyes 2006 ... DVD BD
Histoires Extraordinaires 1967 ... DVD
Horns 2013 ... DVD BD
The Host 2006 ... DVD BD
House of Dark Shadows 1970 ... DVD

House of Wax 1953 ... DVD
The Howling 1981 ... DVD BD
The Hunchback of Notre Dame 1982 ... DVD
I Saw the Devil 2010 ... DVD BD
I Walked with a Zombie 1943 ... DVD
In Fear 2012 ... DVD BD
It Follows 2014 ... DVD BD
Jeepers Creepers 2001 ... DVD
Kill List 2011 ... DVD BD
Killers 2014 ... DVD
The Kingdom 1994 ... DVD
Let the Right One In 2008 ... DVD BD
Little Shop of Horrors 1986 ... DVD BD
The Living Dead 1932 ... DVD
Love at First Bite 1979
The Loved Ones 2009 ... DVD BD
Lunacy 2005 ... DVD
Lust of the Vampire 1956 ... DVD
Mad Love 1935
Maggie 2015 ... DVD BD
Malpertuis 1971 ... DVD
Martin 1978 ... DVD
Martyrs 2008 ... DVD BD
The Mask of Satan 1960 ... DVD BD
The Masque of the Red Death 1964 ... DVD
Mr Vampire 1986 ... DVD
Monkey Shines 1988 ... DVD
Monster House 2006 ... DVD BD
The Most Dangerous Game 1932 ... DVD
Mother's Day 2010 ... DVD BD
Mystery of the Wax Museum 1933 ... DVD
Nadja 1995
Near Dark 1987 ... DVD BD
Night of the Demon 1957 ... DVD
Night of the Living Dead 1990 ... DVD
A Nightmare on Elm Street 1984 ... DVD BD
No One Lives 2012 ... DVD
Oculus 2013 ... DVD BD
Of Unknown Origin 1983 ... DVD
The Old Dark House 1932 ... DVD
The Omen 1976 ... DVD BD
The Other 1972 ... DVD BD
Paranormal Activity 2007 ... DVD BD
ParaNorman 2012 ... DVD BD
Parents 1988
The Phantom of the Opera 1925 ... DVD BD
The Picture of Dorian Gray 1945 ... DVD
Pit and the Pendulum 1961 ... DVD BD
The Plague of the Zombies 1965 ... DVD BD
Poltergeist 1982 ... DVD BD
Pride and Prejudice and Zombies 2015 ... DVD BD
Prometheus 2012 ... DVD BD
Q - the Winged Serpent 1982 ... DVD
Rabid 1976 ... DVD
The Raven 1935 ... DVD
The Raven 1963 ... DVD
Ravenous 1999 ... DVD
Re-Animator 1985 ... DVD BD
[Rec] 2007 ... DVD BD
[Rec]3 Génesis 2012 ... DVD BD
A Reflection of Fear 1973 ... DVD
Ring 1997 ... DVD
Saw 2004 ... DVD BD
Saw II 2005 ... DVD BD
Saw: the Final Chapter 2010 ... DVD BD
Scanners 1980 ... DVD
The Seasoning House 2012 ... DVD BD
Session 9 2001 ... DVD
Shivers 1975 ... DVD BD
Sinister 2012 ... DVD BD
Sitcom 1997 ... DVD
Sleep Tight 2011 ... DVD
Sleepy Hollow 1999 ... DVD BD
Son of Frankenstein 1939 ... DVD
The Stepfather 1986 ... DVD
Storage 24 2012 ... DVD BD
Suspiria 1976 ... DVD BD
Sweeney Todd: the Demon Barber of Fleet Street 2007 ... DVD BD
Switchblade Romance 2003 ... DVD BD
Tales from the Crypt 1972 ... DVD
The Testament of Dr Cordelier 1959 ... DVD
The Testament of Dr Mabuse 1932 ... DVD BD
The Texas Chainsaw Massacre Part 2 1986 ... DVD BD
Theatre of Blood 1973 ... DVD BD
Them 2006 ... DVD
The Thing 1982 ... DVD BD
The Thing 2011 ... DVD BD
The Thing from Another World 1951 ...
The Tingler 1959 ... DVD
Tokyo Fist 1995 ... DVD
The Tomb of Ligeia 1964 ... DVD BD
Triangle 2009 ... DVD BD
Trick 'r Treat 2007 ... DVD
The Troll Hunter 2010 ... DVD BD
Tucker and Dale vs Evil 2009 ... DVD BD
28 Days Later... 2002 ... DVD BD
28 Weeks Later 2007 ... DVD BD
V/H/S 2012 ... DVD
V/H/S/2 2013 ... DVD BD
Vacancy 2007 ... DVD
Videodrome 1982 ... DVD BD
Village of the Damned 1960 ... DVD
Waxworks 1924 ... DVD
We Are What We Are 2010 ... DVD BD
We Are What We Are 2013 ... DVD

12 Years a Slave 2013............DVD BD
Two Stage Sisters 1964...........DVD BD
Ugetsu Monogatari 1953 ....DVD BD
Women in Love 1969 ....DVD
Yellow Earth 1984..................DVD
Yojimbo 1961 ....DVD BD

PERIOD ★★★★

The Age of Innocence 1993 ....DVD
All the Way Home 1963............
Anastasia 1956.....................DVD
Anna Karenina 1935...............DVD
Anonymous 2011 ....DVD BD
Anthony Adverse 1936 ....
Apocalypto 2006 ....DVD
Ashes of Time 1994 ....
The Assassin 2015..................DVD BD
The Assassination Bureau 1969 ....
Bang the Drum Slowly 1973........
Barton Fink 1991 ....DVD BD
Becky Sharp 1935...................
Belle 2013 ....DVD BD
Berkeley Square 1933 ....
Big Night 1996......................
The Bingo Long Travelling All-Stars and Motor Kings 1976 ....
Blanche 1971 ....DVD BD
Bobby 2006..........................DVD
Bullets over Broadway 1994........DVD
Burn! 1970 ....DVD
Camelot 1967 ....DVD
Careful 1992.........................
Celia 1988 ....
C'est la Vie 1990 ....
Chamber of Horrors 1966 ....
The Chant of Jimmie Blacksmith 1978 .....
Character 1997 ....
Charulata 1964 ....DVD BD
The Chess Player 1927 ....
The Children of the Marshland 1998.......
The Claim 2000......................DVD
Colonel Redl 1984...................DVD
The Color Purple 1985.............DVD BD
Compulsion 1959....................DVD BD
The Count of Monte Cristo 1934 ...
Country Life 1994...................
The Crimson Curtain 1952 ....
The Crucible 1996...................DVD
The Crucified Lovers 1954 ....DVD
Cuba 1979 ....DVD
Curse of the Golden Flower 2006 ....DVD BD
Daens 1992..........................
The Damned 1969....................DVD
Dangerous Liaisons 1988...........DVD
Daughters of the Dust 1991 ....
The Dawning 1988 ....
The Day of the Locust 1975........DVD
Days of Heaven 1978................DVD
The Dead 1987.......................BD
Dead Poets Society 1989...........DVD BD
Dean Spanley 2008 ....
The Decameron 1970.................
Desert Bloom 1985 ....
Les Destinées Sentimentales 2000....DVD
Detective Dee and the Mystery of the Phantom Flame 2010 ....DVD BD
Devil in a Blue Dress 1995.........DVD
The Devil's Backbone 2001 ....DVD BD
Don't Move, Die and Rise Again 1989 .....
Don't Touch the Axe 2006..........DVD
The Dreamers 2003..................DVD
Drôle de Drame 1937 ....
The Drum 1938 ....
The Duellists 1977 ....
Effi Briest 1974.....................DVD BD
Effie Gray 2014......................DVD BD
Eklavya: the Royal Guard 2007 .....DVD
Emma 1996 ....DVD
L'Enfant Sauvage 1970 ....DVD
England Made Me 1973...............
The Enigma of Kaspar Hauser 1974 ....DVD
The Europeans 1979.................DVD
FairyTale: a True Story 1997 ....BD
Far from the Madding Crowd 1967 ...DVD BD
Finding Neverland 2004.............DVD BD
The First Teacher 1965 ....
Five Women around Utamaro 1946 ....DVD BD
Flowers of Shanghai 1998..........
Forever and a Day 1943 ....
Friendly Persuasion 1956 ....
From Hell 2001 ....DVD BD
Gaslight 1944 ....DVD
Gate of Flesh 1964..................DVD
Girl with a Pearl Earring 2003.....DVD
Glorious 39 2009 ....DVD
The Go-Between 1971................DVD BD
The Golden Bowl 2000...............DVD
The Golden Coach 1953 ....
Gone to Earth 1950.................
Good Morning, Babylon 1987.......
Good Night, and Good Luck. 2005 ....DVD BD
Gosford Park 2001..................DVD
Greyfriars Bobby 1961...............DVD
A Handful of Dust 1987..............DVD
Hara-Kiri: Death of a Samurai 2011 ...DVD

Harakiri 1962 ....DVD BD
Hard Times 1975 ....DVD
Heart of Glass 1976.................DVD
Hester Street 1975 ....DVD
The History of Mr Polly 1948 ....DVD
The Home and the World 1984 ......DVD
Honour of the Knights 2006..........DVD
House of Flying Daggers 2004....DVD BD
House of Wax 1953 ....
Humanity and Paper Balloons 1937 ....DVD
I Capture the Castle 2002 ....DVD
I Remember Mama 1948..............
An Ideal Husband 1999 ....DVD
If I Were King 1938..................
The Illusionist 2005.................DVD
The Immigrant 2013.................
The Importance of Being Earnest 1952 ....DVD
Indiana Jones and the Temple of Doom 1984 ....DVD BD
Indiana Jones and the Kingdom of the Crystal Skull 2008 ....DVD BD
Indochine 1991 ....DVD
L'Innocente 1976...................
The Invisible Woman 2013 ....DVD BD
The Irishman 1978..................DVD
Jane Eyre 1943......................DVD
Jauja 2014 ....DVD
Jude 1996 ....DVD
Junoon 1978 ....DVD
Kagemusha 1980 ....DVD
Kaos 1984 ....DVD BD
The King and I 1956.................DVD BD
King Kong 2005......................DVD BD
The King of Kings 1927 ....DVD
King of Kings 1961..................DVD
Kingdom of Heaven 2005...........DVD BD
Kitchen Stories 2003................DVD
Kitty 1945 ....
A Knight's Tale 2001.................DVD BD
Kung Fu Hustle 2004...............DVD BD
Lady Chatterley 2006 ....DVD
The Lady in Red 1979 ....
Lady L 1965 ....
Lassie 2005 ....DVD
The Last Legion 2006...............DVD
The Last of the Mohicans 1992.....DVD BD
The Last Samurai 2003.............DVD BD
The Last Tycoon 1976 ....DVD
The Last Valley 1971.................DVD
The Legend of 1900 1999...........DVD
The Libertine 2004..................DVD
Liberty Heights 1999................DVD
The Little Foxes 1941................DVD
Little Women 1933..................DVD
Lord Jim 1965 ....DVD
Love & Friendship 2016.............DVD
The Lower Depths 1956..............DVD
Macario 1960 ....DVD
Madame Bovary 1933 ....DVD
The Magdalene Sisters 2002 ....DVD
Man about Town 1947...............
The Man Who Laughs 1928..........
The Man Who Wasn't There 2001...DVD
Mandingo 1975......................DVD
Manon des Sources 1986............DVD
Mansfield Park 1999.................DVD
The Marquise of O 1976.............DVD
Martha and I 1990 ....DVD
Master and Commander: the Far Side of the World 2003...............DVD BD
Memoirs of a Geisha 2005 ....DVD
Les Misérables 1935.................DVD
Les Misérables 1995.................DVD
Miss Evers' Boys 1997 ....
Miss Julie 1951......................
Mughal-e-Azam 1960 ....DVD
My Brilliant Career 1979............DVD
My Friend Ivan Lapshin 1982 ....
My Life as a Dog 1985...............DVD
The Name of the Rose 1986.........DVD
Nanny McPhee & the Big Bang 2010 ....DVD BD
Nicholas Nickleby 1947.............DVD
Nicholas Nickleby 2002.............DVD
1900 1976 ....DVD BD
Nowhere in Africa 2001.............DVD
The Old Maid 1939..................DVD
Old Man 1997 ....DVD
Olivia 1950 ....DVD
The Organizer 1963.................DVD
Orphans of the Storm 1921.........DVD
Papa's Delicate Condition 1963 ....DVD
Paper Moon 1973..................DVD BD
Paris 36 2008........................DVD
Paris Trout 1991....................
Park Row 1952.......................DVD
Pascali's Island 1988................
Peking Opera Blues 1986............
Pelle the Conqueror 1987...........DVD
Perceval le Gallois 1978.............
Persuasion 1995 ....DVD BD
Picnic at Hanging Rock 1975 ......DVD BD
The Picture of Dorian Gray 1945....DVD
Places in the Sun 1984 ....DVD
Pollyanna 1960......................DVD
The Prestige 2006 ....DVD BD
Pretty Baby 1978 ....DVD
Pride and Prejudice 1940 ....
Pride & Prejudice 2005..............DVD BD

Pride and Prejudice and Zombies 2015 ....DVD BD
The Pride and the Passion 1957......DVD
The Prince of Egypt 1998 ....
The Private Affairs of Bel Ami 1947.........
The Proposition 2004...............DVD BD
Quentin Durward 1955 ....
RKO 281 1999 ....DVD
Radio Days 1987....................DVD
Raintree County 1957...............
Ravenous 1999......................DVD
Rebellion 1967 ....
Red Beard 1965 ....DVD
The Reivers 1969 ....DVD
Restoration 1995 ....
A River Runs through It 1992 ....DVD
The Road Home 1999................DVD
Road to Perdition 2002..............DVD BD
A Room with a View 1985 ....DVD BD
Rue Cases Nègres 1983..............
The Scarlet Pimpernel 1982 ....DVD
The Secret Garden 1993 ....DVD
The Secret of Roan Inish 1993......
Séraphine 2008 ....
7 Women 1966.......................
Sherlock Holmes 2009 ....DVD BD
The Shooting Party 1984 ....DVD
Sophie's Choice 1982...............DVD BD
Splendor in the Grass 1961 ....BD
Springtime in a Small Town 2002 ...DVD
Start the Revolution without Me 1970.......
Starter for 10 2006 ....DVD BD
Stavisky 1974 ....DVD
Stiff Upper Lips 1998 ....
The Summer of Ben Tyler 1996 ....
A Summer Story 1987 ....
Sunday in the Country 1984.........
Sweet and Lowdown 1999............DVD
Swiss Family Robinson 1960 ....DVD
Tale of Tales 2015...................
The Tall Target 1951.................
The Ten Commandments 1923 ......
The Ten Commandments 1956....DVD BD
Tess 1979...........................DVD BD
They Came to Cordura 1959 ....DVD
The Thief of Paris 1967 ....
Thieves like Us 1974................DVD
13 Assassins 2010 ....DVD BD
Those Magnificent Men in Their Flying Machines 1965.......................DVD
The Time to Live and the Time to Die 1985 .....
Tito and Me 1992...................
Tom Jones 1963.....................DVD
Tom Sawyer 1973 ....
A Tree Grows in Brooklyn 1945 .....DVD
The Tree of Wooden Clogs 1978 ....DVD
Triple Agent 2003 ....DVD
The Twilight Samurai 2002 ....DVD
An Unfinished Piece for Mechanical Piano 1976 .....
An Unforgettable Summer 1994 .....
Up at the Villa 1998 ....
Valmont 1989........................
Vera Drake 2004 ....DVD
A Very Long Engagement 2004 .....DVD
The Virgin Spring 1960 ....DVD
The War Lord 1965..................DVD BD
We Don't Want to Talk about It 1993.......
The Well Digger's Daughter 2010 ...DVD
When Father Was Away on Business 1985 .....
When the Last Sword Is Drawn 2003...DVD
The White Dawn 1974 ....
The White Ribbon 2009 ....DVD BD
The Wicked Lady 1945 ....DVD
Wilde 1997..........................DVD BD
The Wind and the Lion 1975.........DVD
The Wings of the Dove 1997 ......DVD BD
The Winslow Boy 1999...............DVD
The Witch 2015 ....DVD BD
Young Adam 2003 ....DVD
Zatoichi 2003 ....DVD BD

ROAD MOVIE ★★★★★

Las Acacias 2011.................DVD BD
Easy Rider 1969...................DVD BD
The Motorcycle Diaries 2004 ....DVD BD
Nebraska 2013.....................DVD BD
The Straight Story 1999.............DVD
Thelma & Louise 1991 ....DVD BD

ROAD MOVIE ★★★★

Alice in the Cities 1974 ....DVD
Eureka 2000.........................DVD
Grand Theft Parsons 2003 ....DVD
Heaven's Burning 1997 ....
Jump Tomorrow 2001...............DVD
Kings of the Road 1976 ....DVD
Leningrad Cowboys Go America 1989 ....
Little Miss Sunshine 2006...........DVD BD
Motorama 1991 ....
Stranger than Paradise 1984......DVD BD
Trans 1998 ....
Transamerica 2005 ....DVD

ROMANCE ★★★★

The African Queen 1951............DVD BD
Amélie 2001.........................DVD BD
Annie Hall 1977 ....DVD BD
The Artist 2011 ....DVD BD
L'Atalante 1934 ....DVD
Atonement 2007 ....DVD BD
Born Yesterday 1950 ....DVD
Breakfast at Tiffany's 1961.........DVD BD
Brief Encounter 1945 ....DVD
Brokeback Mountain 2005..........DVD BD
Café de Flore 2011 ....DVD
Carol 2015 ....DVD BD
Casablanca 1942 ....DVD BD
Charade 1963 ....DVD BD
City Lights 1931 ....DVD
College 1927.........................DVD
Crouching Tiger, Hidden Dragon 2000 ....DVD BD
Cyrano de Bergerac 1990 ....DVD
The Devil Is a Woman 1935.........DVD
Doctor Zhivago 1965 ....DVD BD
The Dot and the Line 1965 ....
The English Patient 1996............DVD BD
Far from Heaven 2002 ....DVD
The Fountain 2005 ....DVD BD
Four Weddings and a Funeral 1994 ....DVD BD
Gone with the Wind 1939 ....DVD BD
Groundhog Day 1993 ....DVD BD
Holiday 1938 ....DVD
I Know Where I'm Going! 1945.......DVD
It Happened One Night 1934 ....DVD BD
Lola 2000...........................DVD BD
Lola Montès 1955 ....DVD
Lost in Translation 2003...........DVD BD
Love Affair 1939 ....
Love in the Afternoon 1957 ....
Manhattan 1979 ....DVD BD
Marty 1955 ....DVD
Master of the House 1925 ....DVD
A Matter of Life and Death 1946....DVD
Morocco 1930........................DVD
Notorious 1946.......................DVD
Now, Voyager 1942 ....DVD
Une Partie de Campagne 1936 .....DVD
Pépé le Moko 1937 ....DVD
The Philadelphia Story 1940........DVD
Il Postino 1994 ....DVD
Le Quai des Brumes 1938 ....DVD BD
The Quiet Man 1952 ....DVD BD
Rebecca 1940........................DVD
The Red Shoes 1948.................DVD BD
Roman Holiday 1953 ....DVD
Ryan's Daughter 1970 ....DVD
Sabrina 1954.........................DVD
Sense and Sensibility 1995 ....DVD BD
Shadowlands 1993 ....DVD
Shakespeare in Love 1998 ....DVD BD
Sideways 2004.....................DVD BD
Smiles of a Summer Night 1955 ....DVD
Stolen Kisses 1968 ....DVD BD
Strictly Ballroom 1992...............DVD
Summer of My German Soldier 1978 .....
Summer with Monika 1952 ....DVD
Sunrise 1927 ....DVD
To Have and Have Not 1944 ....DVD
A Touch of Class 1973 ....
Trouble in Paradise 1932 ....DVD
West Side Story 1961................DVD BD
When Harry Met Sally... 1989.......DVD BD
Witness 1985 ....DVD
Wuthering Heights 1939 ....DVD

ROMANCE ★★★★

About a Boy 2002 ....DVD BD
About Time 2013...................DVD BD
Adventureland 2009 ....DVD BD
An Affair to Remember 1957 ......DVD BD
The Age of Innocence 1993 ....DVD
All the Vermeers in New York 1990 ....
All This, and Heaven Too 1940 .....
The American President 1995........DVD
Anna Karenina 1935 ....DVD
Anne and Muriel 1971 ....DVD BD
L'Appartement 1996 ....DVD
The April Fools 1969 ....
Arise, My Love 1940 ....
As Good as It Gets 1997 ....DVD
An Autumn Tale 1998...............DVD
Avanti! 1972 ....
Back Street 1941 ....
Back Street 1961 ....
Barefoot in the Park 1967 ....DVD
Before Sunrise 1995................DVD BD
Before Midnight 2013...............DVD BD
Begin Again 2013 ....DVD BD
Berkeley Square 1933 ....
Betrayal 1982........................
The Big Blue 1988 ....DVD BD
A Blonde in Love 1965 ....DVD
Blood and Sand 1941................
The Blue Veil 1951...................
Le Bonheur 1965 ....
The Bride with White Hair 1993 .....DVD
The Bridges of Madison County 1995 ..DVD
Bridget Jones's Diary 2001.........DVD BD
Brigadoon 1954......................DVD

SATIRE ★★★★★

SATIRE ★★★★

Hollywood Shuffle 1987 ....
I Served the King of England 2006 ....
if... 1968 .... DVD BD
Irma Vep 1996 .... DVD
Jesus of Montreal 1989 .... DVD
Larks on a String 1969 .... DVD
Life Is a Long Quiet River 1988 ....
Love and Death 1975 .... DVD BD
Major Barbara 1941 .... DVD
Male and Female 1919 ....
Man Bites Dog 1992 .... DVD
Mars Attacks! 1996 .... DVD BD
Meet the Applegates 1991 ....
The Middleman 1975 ....
A Mighty Wind 2003 .... DVD
The Million Pound Note 1953 .... DVD
Moebius 2013 ....
The Nasty Girl 1990 .... DVD
Nothing but the Best 1963 ....
Oblomov 1980 ....
Oh! What a Lovely War 1969 .... DVD
Phantom of the Paradise 1974 .... DVD BD
Polyester 1981 ....
The President's Analyst 1967 ....
The Rocky Horror Picture Show
1975 .... DVD BD
Scorpio Rising 1963 ....
Secret Ballot 2001 .... DVD
Seven Beauties 1976 ....
Slaughterhouse-Five 1972 .... DVD
Smile 1975 ....
Starship Troopers 1997 .... DVD BD
Stiff Upper Lips 1997 ....
Supervixens 1975 .... DVD
The Tale of the Fox 1931 ....
Tampopo 1986 ....
Thank You for Smoking 2005 .... DVD
This Is the End 2013 .... DVD BD
Vixen! 1968 .... DVD
Wag the Dog 1997 .... DVD
Xala 1974 ....
Zoolander 2001 .... DVD BD

SCI-FI ★★★★★

Alien 1979 .... DVD BD
Aliens 1986 .... DVD BD
Back to the Future 1985 .... DVD BD
Blade Runner 1982 .... DVD BD
Brazil 1985 .... DVD BD
Close Encounters of the Third Kind
1977 .... DVD BD
The Day the Earth Stood Still
1951 ....
Duck Dodgers in the 24½ Century 1953 ......
ET the Extra-Terrestrial 1982 .. DVD BD
Forbidden Planet 1956 .... DVD BD
The Fountain 2005 .... DVD BD
Galaxy Quest 1999 .... DVD BD
The Hunger Games: Catching Fire
2013 .... DVD BD
The Incredible Shrinking Man 1957 ..... DVD
Invasion of the Body Snatchers
1956 ....
The Invisible Man 1933 .... DVD BD
Island of Lost Souls 1932 .... DVD BD
La Jetée 1962 .... DVD
Jurassic Park 1993 .... DVD BD
Looper 2012 .... DVD BD
Mad Max 1979 .... DVD BD
The Matrix 1999 .... DVD BD
Metropolis 1926 .... DVD BD
Planet of the Apes 1967 .... DVD BD
RoboCop 1987 .... DVD BD
Star Trek: First Contact 1996 .... DVD BD
Star Wars Episode IV: a New Hope
1977 .... DVD BD
Star Wars Episode V: the Empire Strikes
Back 1980 ....
The Terminator 1984 .... DVD BD
Terminator 2: Judgment Day
1991 .... DVD BD
Them! 1954 .... DVD
2001: a Space Odyssey 1968 .... DVD BD
Le Voyage dans la Lune 1902 ...... DVD
WALL-E 2008 .... DVD BD

SCI-FI ★★★★

AI: Artificial Intelligence 2001 ..... DVD BD
About Time 2013 .... DVD BD
Akira 1988 .... DVD BD
Alien: Resurrection 1997 .... DVD BD
Alien Nation 1988 .... DVD
Alphaville 1965 .... DVD
The Andromeda Strain 1970 ...... DVD
Antiviral 2012 .... DVD
Attack the Block 2010 .... DVD BD
Back to the Future Part III 1990 .. DVD BD
Battle Royale 2000 .... DVD BD
The Beast from 20,000 Fathoms
1953 .... DVD
The Blob 1988 .... DVD BD
Body Snatchers 1993 .... DVD
A Boy and His Dog 1975 .... DVD
Brainstorm 1983 ....
Children of Men 2006 .... DVD BD
Chronicle 2012 .... DVD BD
A Clockwork Orange 1971 .... DVD BD
Cocoon 1985 .... DVD BD

Comet 2014 ....
Cowboys & Aliens 2011 .... DVD BD
Cube 1997 .... DVD BD
Dark City 1998 .... DVD
Dark Star 1973 .... DVD BD
Dawn of the Planet of the Apes
2014 .... DVD BD
Deep Impact 1998 .... DVD
Demolition Man 1993 .... DVD BD
Demon Seed 1977 .... DVD
District 9 2009 .... DVD BD
Dredd 2012 .... DVD BD
Encounter at Raven's Gate 1988 ......
Enemy Mine 1985 .... DVD BD
Escape from the Planet of the Apes
1971 .... DVD BD
Ex Machina 2014 .... DVD BD
eXistenZ 1999 .... DVD
The Falls 1980 .... DVD
Fantastic Planet 1973 .... DVD BD
Fantastic Voyage 1966 .... DVD BD
The Fifth Element 1997 .... DVD BD
Gattaca 1997 .... DVD BD
Ghost in the Shell 1995 .... DVD BD
The Girl with All the Gifts 2016 ......
Grabbers 2012 .... DVD BD
Guardians of the Galaxy 2014 .... DVD BD
Hard to Be a God 2013 .... DVD BD
Hardware 1990 .... DVD BD
The Hidden 1987 ....
The Host 2006 .... DVD BD
The Hunger Games 2012 .... DVD BD
I Origins 2014 ....
I, Robot 2004 .... DVD BD
In Time 2011 .... DVD BD
Inception 2010 .... DVD BD
The Incredible Hulk 2008 .... DVD BD
Independence Day 1996 .... DVD BD
Interstellar 2014 .... DVD BD
Invaders from Mars 1953 .... DVD
The Iron Giant 1999 .... DVD
It Came from Outer Space 1953 .... DVD
Journey to the Center of the Earth
1959 ....
Jurassic World 2015 .... DVD BD
The Last Battle 1983 .... DVD
The Last Mimzy 2007 .... DVD
Lilo & Stitch 2002 .... DVD BD
Limitless 2011 .... DVD BD
Looker 1981 ....
Mad Max 2 1981 .... DVD BD
Mad Max: Fury Road 2015 .... DVD BD
The Man Who Fell to Earth 1976 .. DVD BD
The Man with the X-Ray Eyes 1963 .... DVD
Mars Attacks! 1996 .... DVD BD
The Maze Runner 2014 .... DVD BD
Melancholia 2011 .... DVD BD
Men in Black 1997 .... DVD BD
Men in Black 3 2012 .... DVD BD
Midnight Special 2015 ....
The Mind of Mr Soames 1970 ......
Minority Report 2002 .... DVD BD
Mr Peabody & Sherman 2013 .... DVD BD
Monsters 2010 .... DVD BD
Monsters: Dark Continent 2014 ... DVD BD
Monsters vs Aliens 2009 .... DVD BD
Moon 2008 .... DVD BD
Muppets from Space 1999 .... DVD
Nineteen Eighty-Four 1984 ...... DVD
Nirvana 1996 ....
The Omega Man 1971 .... DVD BD
Panic in Year Zero 1962 .... DVD
Paprika 2006 ....
Pitch Black 1999 .... DVD BD
Planeta Burg 1962 ....
Predator 1987 .... DVD BD
Prometheus 2012 .... DVD BD
Quatermass II 1957 ....
Repo Man 1984 .... DVD BD
Rise of the Planet of the Apes
2011 .... DVD BD
The Road 2009 .... DVD BD
Robinson Crusoe on Mars 1964 .. DVD BD
RoboCop 2014 .... DVD BD
Robot & Frank 2012 .... DVD BD
Roswell 1994 .... DVD
The Rover 2014 .... DVD BD
Scanners 1980 .... DVD BD
Seconds 1966 .... DVD BD
Seeking a Friend for the End of the World
2011 .... DVD BD
Serenity 2005 .... DVD BD
Silent Running 1971 .... DVD BD
The 6th Day 2000 .... DVD BD
Slaughterhouse-Five 1972 ...... DVD
Sleeper 1973 .... DVD BD
Snowpiercer 2013 ....
Solaris 1972 .... DVD
Source Code 2011 .... DVD BD
Stalker 1979 .... DVD
Star Trek II: the Wrath of Khan
1982 .... DVD BD
Star Trek IV: the Voyage Home
1986 .... DVD BD
Star Trek VI: the Undiscovered Country
1991 .... DVD BD
Star Trek: Generations 1994 ...... DVD BD
Star Trek 2009 .... DVD BD
Star Trek into Darkness 2013 .... DVD BD
Star Trek Beyond 2016 ....

Star Wars Episode VI: Return of the Jedi
1983 .... DVD BD
Stargate 1994 .... DVD BD
Starman 1984 .... DVD
Starship Troopers 1997 .... DVD BD
The Stepford Wives 1975 .... DVD
Storage 24 2012 .... DVD BD
Strange Days 1995 .... DVD
Strange Invaders 1983 ....
Super 8 2011 .... DVD BD
The Survivalist 2015 .... DVD BD
THX 1138 1971 .... DVD BD
10 Cloverfield Lane 2016 .... DVD BD
The Terminal Man 1974 ....
The Thing 1982 .... DVD BD
The Thing 2011 .... DVD BD
The Thing from Another World 1951 ......
Things to Come 1936 .... DVD
This Island Earth 1955 ....
Time after Time 1979 ....
The Time Machine 1960 .... DVD
Titan AE 2000 ....
Tokyo Tribe 2014 .... DVD BD
Tomorrowland: a World Beyond
2015 .... DVD BD
Total Recall 1990 .... DVD BD
Transformers 2007 .... DVD BD
Transformers: Dark of the Moon
2011 .... DVD BD
Trouble in Mind 1985 .... DVD
Turbo Kid 2014 .... DVD BD
Twelve Monkeys 1995 .... DVD BD
12:01 1993 ....
The Ultimate Warrior 1975 ...... DVD
Under the Skin 2013 .... DVD BD
Village of the Damned 1960 ...... DVD
The War of the Worlds 1953 ...... DVD
War of the Worlds 2005 .... DVD BD
Waterworld 1995 .... DVD
Westworld 1973 .... DVD BD
The X-Files 1998 .... DVD

SPORTS ★★★★★

Body and Soul 1947 .... DVD
Chariots of Fire 1981 .... DVD BD
Eddie the Eagle 2016 .... DVD BD
The Fighter 2010 .... DVD BD
Foxcatcher 2014 .... DVD BD
Hoop Dreams 1994 .... DVD
The Hustler 1961 .... DVD BD
Million Dollar Baby 2004 .... DVD BD
Raging Bull 1980 .... DVD BD
The Red Shoes 1948 .... DVD BD
Saturday Night Fever 1977 ...... DVD BD
Senna 2010 .... DVD BD
Undefeated 2011 .... DVD
When We Were Kings 1996 ...... DVD
The Wrestler 2008 .... DVD BD

SPORTS ★★★★

Any Given Sunday 1999 .... DVD
Bang the Drum Slowly 1973 ......
Beyond the Mat 1999 .... DVD
Big Wednesday 1978 .... DVD
The Bingo Long Travelling All-Stars and
Motor Kings 1976 ....
The Blind Side 2009 .... DVD BD
Blood Wedding 1981 .... DVD
Breaking Away 1979 .... DVD
Brian's Song 1971 ....
Bull Durham 1988 .... DVD
Carmen 1983 .... DVD
The Champ 1931 .... DVD
Champion 1949 .... DVD
Cinderella Man 2005 .... DVD BD
Cobb 1994 ....
The Color of Money 1986 .... DVD
The Company 2003 .... DVD
Cool Runnings 1993 ....
Cooperstown 1993 ....
Creed 2015 .... DVD BD
The Damned United 2009 .... DVD BD
Dancing in Jaffa 2013 ....
Death of a Gentleman 2015 ...... DVD
Fat City 1972 ....
Fear Strikes Out 1957 ....
Fever Pitch 1996 .... DVD BD
First 2012 .... DVD BD
Friday Night Lights 2004 .... DVD BD
Girlfight 2000 .... DVD
He Got Game 1998 .... DVD
Hoosiers 1986 .... DVD
Invictus 2009 .... DVD BD
Kid Galahad 1937 ....
The Mean Machine 1974 .... DVD
The Milky Way 1936 .... DVD
The Miracle of Bern 2003 .... DVD
Moneyball 2011 .... DVD BD
Murderball 2005 .... DVD
National Velvet 1944 .... DVD
The Natural 1984 .... DVD
Only When I Dance 2008 .... DVD
Pat and Mike 1952 .... DVD
Pina 2011 .... DVD
Ping Pong 2002 .... DVD
The Pride of the Yankees 1942 ......
Rocky 1976 .... DVD BD
Roseland 1977 .... DVD

Rush 2013 .... DVD BD
Salty O'Rourke 1945 ....
The Scout 1994 ....
The Set-Up 1949 ....
Somebody Up There Likes Me 1956 ......
Soul in the Hole 1995 .... DVD
Soul of the Game 1996 .... DVD
Southpaw 1998 ....
StreetDance 2010 .... DVD BD
StreetDance 2 2012 .... DVD BD
That's Dancing! 1985 ....
Tyson 2008 .... DVD
White Men Can't Jump 1992 .... DVD BD
Zidane: a 21st Century Portrait
2006 .... DVD BD

SPY ★★★★★

The Bourne Ultimatum 2007 ...... DVD BD
Dishonored 1931 .... DVD
Dr No 1962 .... DVD BD
From Russia with Love 1963 ...... DVD BD
Goldfinger 1964 .... DVD BD
North by Northwest 1959 .... DVD BD
Skyfall 2012 .... DVD BD
The 39 Steps 1935 .... DVD
You Only Live Twice 1967 ...... DVD BD

SPY ★★★★

Above Suspicion 1943 ....
Austin Powers: International Man of
Mystery 1997 .... DVD
Austin Powers: the Spy Who Shagged Me
1999 .... DVD BD
The Bourne Identity 2002 .... DVD BD
The Bourne Supremacy 2004 .... DVD BD
Breach 2006 .... DVD
Bridge of Spies 2015 .... DVD BD
Casino Royale 2006 .... DVD BD
The Deadly Affair 1966 ....
Enemy of the State 1998 .... DVD BD
Foreign Correspondent 1940 .... DVD
GoldenEye 1995 .... DVD BD
The House on 92nd Street 1945 .. DVD
The Ipcress File 1965 .... DVD BD
Journey into Fear 1942 .... DVD
Kingsman: The Secret Service
2015 .... DVD BD
Live and Let Die 1973 .... DVD BD
Mademoiselle Docteur 1936 ......
The Mask of Dimitrios 1944 ......
Mata Hari 1931 .... DVD
Michael Clayton 2007 .... DVD BD
Mission: Impossible 1996 .... DVD BD
Mission: Impossible 2 1999 ...... DVD BD
Mission: Impossible - Ghost Protocol
2011 .... DVD BD
Mission: Impossible - Rogue Nation
2015 .... DVD BD
Morituri 1965 .... DVD
Night Train to Munich 1940 ......
OSS 117: Lost in Rio 2009 ......
On Her Majesty's Secret Service
1969 .... DVD BD
Le Petit Soldat 1960 .... DVD
Pimpernel Smith 1941 ....
The Quiller Memorandum 1966 .. DVD BD
The Russia House 1990 .... DVD
Saboteur 1942 .... DVD BD
Secret Agent 1936 .... DVD
Spies 1928 ....
The Spy Who Came In from the Cold 1965 ..
The Spy Who Loved Me 1977 ...... DVD BD
36 Hours 1964 ....
Tinker Tailor Soldier Spy 2011 .... DVD BD
Tomorrow Never Dies 1997 ...... DVD BD
The World Is Not Enough 1999 .... DVD BD

THRILLER ★★★★★

Alien 1979 .... DVD BD
Aliens 1986 .... DVD BD
All the President's Men 1976 .... DVD
Argo 2012 .... DVD BD
The Asphalt Jungle 1950 .... DVD
Assault on Precinct 13 1976 .... DVD
Bad Day at Black Rock 1955 ......
Blade Runner 1982 .... DVD BD
Blood and Black Lace 1964 ...... DVD BD
Blue Velvet 1986 .... DVD BD
The Bourne Ultimatum 2007 ...... DVD BD
Changeling 2008 .... DVD BD
Charade 1963 .... DVD BD
Chinatown 1974 .... DVD BD
City of God 2002 .... DVD BD
The Conversation 1974 .... DVD BD
The Day of the Jackal 1973 ...... DVD
Deliverance 1972 .... DVD
Les Diaboliques 1954 .... DVD BD
Die Hard 1988 .... DVD BD
Dirty Harry 1971 .... DVD BD
Don't Look Now 1973 .... DVD BD
Duel 1971 .... DVD BD
Fargo 1995 .... DVD BD
Gravity 2013 .... DVD BD
Illustrious Corpses 1976 ....
The Incredible Shrinking Man 1957 .... DVD
Invasion of the Body Snatchers
1956 .... DVD

Jaws 1975 — DVD Blu-ray
Klute 1971 — DVD Blu-ray
The Lady Vanishes 1938 — DVD Blu-ray
Leon 1994 — DVD Blu-ray
Looper 2012 — DVD Blu-ray
The Manchurian Candidate 1962 — DVD Blu-ray
The Matrix 1999 — DVD Blu-ray
Memento 2000 — DVD Blu-ray
Monsieur Hire 1989 — DVD
Mulholland Drive 2001 — DVD Blu-ray
The Night of the Hunter 1955 — DVD Blu-ray
No Country for Old Men 2007 — DVD Blu-ray
North by Northwest 1959 — DVD Blu-ray
Notorious 1946 — DVD
The Parallax View 1974 — DVD
Peeping Tom 1960 — DVD Blu-ray
Point Blank 1967 — DVD
Psycho 1960 — DVD Blu-ray
The Raid 2 2013 — DVD Blu-ray
Rear Window 1954 — DVD Blu-ray
Rebecca 1940 — DVD
Repulsion 1965 — DVD
RoboCop 1987 — DVD Blu-ray
Le Samouraï 1967 — DVD Blu-ray
Se7en 1995 — DVD Blu-ray
Shadow of a Doubt 1942 — DVD Blu-ray
Sicario 2015 — DVD Blu-ray
The Silence of the Lambs 1991 — DVD Blu-ray
Speed 1994 — DVD Blu-ray
Strangers on a Train 1951 — DVD
The Terminator 1984 — DVD Blu-ray
Terminator 2: Judgment Day 1991 — DVD Blu-ray
The Third Man 1949 — DVD Blu-ray
The 39 Steps 1935 — DVD Blu-ray
Touch of Evil 1958 — DVD Blu-ray
Twilight's Last Gleaming 1977
The Usual Suspects 1995 — DVD Blu-ray
Vertigo 1958 — DVD Blu-ray
The Wages of Fear 1953 — DVD Blu-ray
Wake in Fright 1970 — DVD Blu-ray
Witness 1985 — DVD

THRILLER ★★★★

Abraham Lincoln: Vampire Hunter 2012 — DVD Blu-ray
Across the Bridge 1957 — DVD
After Dark, My Sweet 1990 — DVD
Air Force One 1997 — DVD Blu-ray
Alice, Sweet Alice 1977 — DVD
Alien: Resurrection 1997 — DVD Blu-ray
Alien Nation 1988 — DVD
Alleluia 2014
The Ambulance 1990 — DVD
Amnesia 1994 — DVD
The Andromeda Strain 1970 — DVD
Angel 1982 — DVD
Antibodies 2005 — DVD
Antiviral 2012 — DVD
Arbitrage 2012 — DVD Blu-ray
Arlington Road 1998 — DVD
Autobus 1991
Bad Boys 1995 — DVD Blu-ray
La Balance 1982 — DVD
The Bank 2001
Battle Royale 2000 — DVD Blu-ray
The Bay 2012 — DVD Blu-ray
The Beach 2000 — DVD Blu-ray
Before I Go to Sleep 2014 — DVD Blu-ray
Before the Devil Knows You're Dead 2007 — DVD Blu-ray
Best Seller 1987 — DVD
Betrayed 1988 — DVD
A Better Tomorrow 1986 — DVD
The Big Easy 1986 — DVD
The Bird with the Crystal Plumage 1969 — DVD Blu-ray
Black Christmas 1974 — DVD
Black Coal, Thin Ice 2014 — DVD
Black Mask 1996 — DVD
Black Rainbow 1989 — DVD
Black Sea 2014 — DVD Blu-ray
Black Sunday 1976 — DVD
Black Swan 2010 — DVD Blu-ray
Blood Simple 1983 — DVD Blu-ray
Blow Out 1981 — DVD Blu-ray
Blue Ruin 2013 — DVD Blu-ray
Blue Steel 1990 — DVD
Blue Sunshine 1977 — DVD
Body Double 1984 — DVD
Body Heat 1981 — DVD
Boiling Point 1990 — DVD
Boiling Point 1993 — DVD
Borsalino 1970 — DVD
Bound 1996 — DVD Blu-ray
The Bourne Identity 2002 — DVD Blu-ray
The Bourne Supremacy 2004 — DVD Blu-ray
Brainstorm 1983
Branded to Kill 1967 — DVD Blu-ray
Breakdown 1997 — DVD
Bridge of Spies 2015 — DVD Blu-ray
Bullitt 1968 — DVD Blu-ray
Buried 2009 — DVD Blu-ray
Byzantium 2012 — DVD Blu-ray
The Cabin in the Woods 2010 — DVD Blu-ray
Cal 1984 — DVD
Cape Fear 1962 — DVD Blu-ray
Cape Fear 1991 — DVD Blu-ray
Capricorn One 1978 — DVD Blu-ray

Cash on Demand 1961 — DVD
La Cérémonie 1995 — DVD
Chaos 1999 — DVD
Children of Men 2006 — DVD Blu-ray
City on Fire 1987 — DVD
The Client 1994 — DVD
Cliffhanger 1993 — DVD Blu-ray
Cold in July 2014 — DVD Blu-ray
Collateral 2004 — DVD Blu-ray
The Collector 1965 — DVD
The Colour of Lies 1999 — DVD
Coma 1977 — DVD
Con Air 1997 — DVD Blu-ray
The Confessional 1995 — DVD
Confessions 2010 — DVD Blu-ray
The Constant Gardener 2005 — DVD Blu-ray
Cop 1988 — DVD
Cop Car 2015 — DVD
Copycat 1995 — DVD
Cotton Comes to Harlem 1970 — DVD
Le Cri du Hibou 1987 — DVD
Crimson Tide 1995 — DVD Blu-ray
Cube 1997 — DVD
DOA 1988 — DVD
Dark City 1998 — DVD
The Dark Mirror 1946 — DVD
Darkness in Tallinn 1993 — DVD
Dead Calm 1988 — DVD
Dead Ringers 1988 — DVD
Death in a French Garden 1985 — DVD
Deep Cover 1992 — DVD
Defence of the Realm 1985 — DVD
Demolition Man 1993 — DVD Blu-ray
The Desperate Hours 1955 — DVD
Desperately Seeking Susan 1985 — DVD
Detour 1945 — DVD
Devil in a Blue Dress 1995 — DVD
Dial M for Murder 1954 — DVD
Die Hard 2: Die Harder 1990 — DVD Blu-ray
Die Hard with a Vengeance 1995 — DVD Blu-ray
Die Hard 4.0 2007 — DVD Blu-ray
Disorder 2015 — DVD Blu-ray
The Divide 2011 — DVD Blu-ray
Dobermann 1997 — DVD
Dr Mabuse, the Gambler 1922 — DVD Blu-ray
Donkey Punch 2008 — DVD Blu-ray
Drag Me to Hell 2009 — DVD Blu-ray
Dressed to Kill 1980 — DVD Blu-ray
Drive 2011 — DVD Blu-ray
The Driver 1978 — DVD Blu-ray
Dust Devil 1992 — DVD
Eagle Eye 2008 — DVD Blu-ray
The Ear 1969 — DVD
Eastern Promises 2007 — DVD Blu-ray
Easy Money 2010 — DVD Blu-ray
Easy Money II 2012 — DVD Blu-ray
Easy Money III: Life Deluxe 2013 — DVD Blu-ray
Encounter at Raven's Gate 1988
Enemy 2013 — DVD Blu-ray
Enemy of the State 1998 — DVD Blu-ray
Europa 1991 — DVD
Ex Machina 2014 — DVD Blu-ray
Executive Action 1973 — DVD
eXistenZ 1999 — DVD
The Eye 2002 — DVD
Eye in the Sky 2015 — DVD Blu-ray
F 2010 — DVD Blu-ray
FX: Murder by Illusion 1985 — DVD
Face/Off 1997 — DVD Blu-ray
The Fallen Idol 1948 — DVD Blu-ray
The Falling 2014 — DVD
Falling Down 1992 — DVD Blu-ray
Family Plot 1976 — DVD Blu-ray
Farewell 2009 — DVD
The Fast and the Furious 2001 — DVD Blu-ray
Fast Five 2011 — DVD Blu-ray
Fast & Furious 7 2014 — DVD Blu-ray
Fatal Attraction 1987 — DVD
Father Brown 1954 — DVD
Felicia's Journey 1999 — DVD
La Femme Infidèle 1968 — DVD
The Firm 1993 — DVD Blu-ray
Foreign Correspondent 1940 — DVD
48 HRS 1982 — DVD
Fourteen Hours 1951 — DVD
The Fourth Man 1983 — DVD
Frantic 1988 — DVD
Freeway 1996 — DVD
French Connection II 1975 — DVD Blu-ray
Frenzy 1972 — DVD Blu-ray
Frequency 2000 — DVD
The Frighteners 1996 — DVD Blu-ray
The Fugitive 1993 — DVD Blu-ray
Full Contact 1992 — DVD
Gattaca 1997 — DVD Blu-ray
Get Carter 1971 — DVD Blu-ray
The Getaway 1972 — DVD Blu-ray
The Ghost 2010 — DVD Blu-ray
The Ghost of St Michael's 1941 — DVD
A Girl Walks Home Alone at Night 2014 — DVD Blu-ray
The Girl with All the Gifts 2016
The Girl with the Dragon Tattoo 2009 — DVD Blu-ray
The Girl with the Dragon Tattoo 2011 — DVD Blu-ray
Gloria 1980 — DVD
Glorious 39 2009 — DVD

Gone Girl 2014 — DVD Blu-ray
Green for Danger 1946 — DVD
Green Room 2015
Green Zone 2010 — DVD Blu-ray
The Guard 2011 — DVD Blu-ray
The Guest 2014 — DVD Blu-ray
Guilty Conscience 1985 — DVD
The Hand That Rocks the Cradle 1992 — DVD
Handgun 1983 — DVD
Hanna 2011 — DVD Blu-ray
Harper 1966 — DVD
The Heart of Justice 1992 — DVD
Heat 1995 — DVD Blu-ray
Heaven's Burning 1997 — DVD
Hell Drivers 1957 — DVD
Hennessy 1975 — DVD
Hidden 2005 — DVD Blu-ray
High Boot Benny 1993 — DVD
A Hijacking 2012 — DVD Blu-ray
A History of Violence 2005 — DVD Blu-ray
The Hit 1984 — DVD
The Hitcher 1986 — DVD
Homicide 1991 — DVD
Horns 2013 — DVD
The Horseman 2008 — DVD
House of Games 1987 — DVD
The House on Telegraph Hill 1951 — DVD
The Hunger Games 2012 — DVD Blu-ray
The Hunt for Red October 1990 — DVD Blu-ray
The Hurt Locker 2008 — DVD Blu-ray
Hustle 1975 — DVD
I Origins 2014 — DVD
I, Robot 2004 — DVD Blu-ray
I Saw the Devil 2010 — DVD Blu-ray
The Imitation Game 2014 — DVD Blu-ray
In the Line of Fire 1993 — DVD Blu-ray
In Time 2011 — DVD Blu-ray
Inception 2010 — DVD Blu-ray
Inside Man 2006 — DVD Blu-ray
Insomnia 2002 — DVD
Internal Affairs 1990 — DVD
The Ipcress File 1965 — DVD Blu-ray
JFK 1991 — DVD Blu-ray
Jackie Brown 1997 — DVD Blu-ray
Jagged Edge 1985 — DVD
Jason Bourne 2016 — DVD Blu-ray
John Wick 2014 — DVD Blu-ray
Juste avant la Nuit 1971 — DVD
Keep Cool 1997 — DVD
The Killer 1989 — DVD
The Killers 1964 — DVD Blu-ray
Killers 2014 — DVD
The Killing 1956 — DVD Blu-ray
The Killing of a Chinese Bookie 1976 — DVD Blu-ray
King of New York 1989 — DVD Blu-ray
The Kingdom 1994 — DVD
Kiss Kiss Bang Bang 2005 — DVD Blu-ray
Kiss of the Dragon 2001 — DVD Blu-ray
Knife in the Head 1978 — DVD
Lady in White 1988 — DVD
Lady Killer 1933 — DVD
Lantana 2001 — DVD
Last Embrace 1979 — Blu-ray
The Last King of Scotland 2006 — DVD Blu-ray
The Last Seduction 1993 — DVD Blu-ray
The Leopard Man 1943 — DVD
Lethal Weapon 1987 — DVD Blu-ray
Lift to the Scaffold 1957 — DVD Blu-ray
The Limey 1999 — DVD
Limitless 2011 — DVD Blu-ray
Live Flesh 1997 — DVD
The Lodger 1926 — DVD Blu-ray
The Lodger 1944 — DVD
The Long Kiss Goodnight 1996 — DVD Blu-ray
Looker 1981 — DVD
Lost Highway 1996 — DVD Blu-ray
The Lost Honour of Katharina Blum 1975 — DVD Blu-ray
Love and a .45 1994 — DVD
The Loved Ones 2009 — DVD Blu-ray
Lust, Caution 2007 — DVD
La Madre Muerta 1993 — DVD
Maggie 2015 — DVD Blu-ray
Mahal 1949 — DVD
The Man Who Knew Too Much 1934 — DVD Blu-ray
The Man with the X-Ray Eyes 1963 — DVD
The Manchurian Candidate 2004 — DVD Blu-ray
Manhattan Murder Mystery 1993 — DVD
Manhunter 1986 — DVD Blu-ray
Marathon Man 1976 — DVD Blu-ray
Married to the Mob 1988 — DVD
Marshland 2014 — DVD
Masques 1987 — DVD
Match Point 2005 — DVD Blu-ray
The Maze Runner 2014 — DVD Blu-ray
Melancholia 1989 — DVD
Miami Blues 1990 — DVD
Michael Clayton 2007 — DVD Blu-ray
Midnight Run 1988 — DVD Blu-ray
The Mind of Mr Soames 1970 — DVD
Minority Report 2002 — DVD Blu-ray
The Minus Man 1999 — DVD
Mirage 1965 — DVD
Misery 1990 — DVD Blu-ray
Mission: Impossible 1996 — DVD Blu-ray

Mission: Impossible 2 1999 — DVD Blu-ray
Mission: Impossible - Ghost Protocol 2011 — DVD Blu-ray
Mr Klein 1976 — DVD
Momentum 2015 — DVD
Monsieur N 2003 — DVD
Monsters: Dark Continent 2014 — DVD Blu-ray
A Most Violent Year 2014 — DVD Blu-ray
Mother 2009 — DVD Blu-ray
Mother's Day 2010 — DVD Blu-ray
Mute Witness 1995 — DVD
The Narrow Margin 1952 —
Niagara 1953 — DVD
The Nice Guys 2016 — DVD Blu-ray
Night Moves 1975 — DVD
Night Moves 2013 — DVD Blu-ray
Night Must Fall 1937 — DVD
The Night of the Sunflowers 2006 — DVD
Night Train to Munich 1940 — DVD
Nightwatch 1994 — DVD
Nikita 1990 — DVD Blu-ray
Nirvana 1996 — DVD
No One Lives 2012 — DVD
No Way Out 1986 — DVD
Oldboy 2003 — DVD Blu-ray
Omar 2013 — DVD Blu-ray
The Omega Man 1971 — DVD Blu-ray
[One] Cavale 2002 — DVD
One Deadly Summer 1983 — DVD
One Hour Photo 2001 — DVD Blu-ray
One Nite in Mongkok 2004 — DVD
Only God Forgives 2012 — DVD Blu-ray
Open Your Eyes 1997 — DVD
Out of the Darkness 1985
Outbreak 1995 — DVD Blu-ray
The Outfit 1973 — DVD
The Page Turner 2006 — DVD
Paprika 2006 — DVD Blu-ray
The Pelican Brief 1993 — DVD Blu-ray
Pièges 1939 — DVD
Pin 1988 — DVD
Pitch Black 1999 — DVD Blu-ray
Play Misty for Me 1971 — DVD Blu-ray
Pluto 2012 — DVD
Point Blank 2010 — DVD Blu-ray
Point Break 1991 — DVD Blu-ray
Police 1985 — DVD
Predator 1987 — DVD Blu-ray
The Prestige 2006 — DVD Blu-ray
Presumed Innocent 1990 — DVD
Primal Fear 1996 — DVD
Prisoners 2013 — DVD Blu-ray
Public Access 1993 — DVD
Quai des Orfèvres 1947 — DVD
Quatermass II 1957 — DVD
Que la Bête Meure 1969 — DVD
The Quiller Memorandum 1966 — DVD Blu-ray
A Rage in Harlem 1991 — DVD
The Raid 2011 — DVD Blu-ray
Raising Cain 1992 — DVD Blu-ray
The Raven 1943 — DVD Blu-ray
[Rec]³ Génesis 2012 — DVD Blu-ray
The Red Circle 1970 — DVD Blu-ray
Red Lights 2003 — DVD
Red Rock West 1992 — DVD Blu-ray
Redbelt 2007 — DVD Blu-ray
Repo Man 1984 — DVD Blu-ray
Revanche 2008 — DVD
Rien Ne Va Plus 1997 — DVD
The Rite 2011 — DVD Blu-ray
The River Wild 1994 — DVD Blu-ray
RoboCop 2014 — DVD Blu-ray
The Rock 1996 — DVD Blu-ray
Romeo Is Bleeding 1992 — DVD
Ronin 1998 — DVD Blu-ray
Roujin Z 1991 — Blu-ray
La Rupture 1970 — DVD
Sabotage 1936 — DVD Blu-ray
Saboteur 1942 — DVD Blu-ray
Saw 2004 — DVD Blu-ray
Saw II 2005 — DVD Blu-ray
Sea of Love 1989 — DVD Blu-ray
The Seasoning House 2012 — DVD Blu-ray
Seconds 1966 — DVD Blu-ray
Secret Agent 1936 — DVD
Serpico 1973 — DVD Blu-ray
Session 9 2001 — DVD
The Set Up 1995 — DVD
Seven Days in May 1964 — DVD
Seven Days to Noon 1950 — DVD
Seven Minutes 1989 — DVD
'71 2014 — DVD Blu-ray
Shadow Dancer 2012 — DVD Blu-ray
Shaft 2000 — DVD
Sherlock Holmes 2009 — DVD Blu-ray
The Short Night of the Glass Dolls 1971 — DVD
Silver Streak 1976 — DVD
A Simple Plan 1998 — DVD
Single White Female 1992 — DVD
Sisters 1973 — DVD Blu-ray
The 6th Day 2000 — DVD Blu-ray
Sleep Tight 2011 — DVD
Sneakers 1992 — DVD
Someone to Watch over Me 1987 — DVD
Sorry, Wrong Number 1948 — DVD
Source Code 2011 — DVD Blu-ray
The Spanish Prisoner 1997 — DVD
Spies 1928 — DVD Blu-ray
The Spiral Staircase 1946 — DVD Blu-ray
Stage Fright 1949 — DVD

State of Grace 1990 .... *DVD* ⓑ
State of Play 2009 .... *DVD* ⓑ
The Stepfather 1986 .... *DVD*
The Stepford Wives 1975 .... *DVD*
Still of the Night 1982 ....
Stoker 2013 .... *DVD* ⓑ
Strange Days 1995 .... *DVD* ⓑ
Straw Dogs 1971 .... *DVD* ⓑ
The Street with No Name 1948 .... *DVD* ⓑ
Subway 1985 .... *DVD* ⓑ
Sudden Death 1995 .... *DVD*
Supervixens 1975 .... *DVD*
The Survivalist 2015 .... *DVD*
Suspicion 1941 .... *DVD*
Switchblade Romance 2003 .... *DVD* ⓑ
Sympathy for Mr Vengeance
2002 .... *DVD* ⓑ
Syriana 2005 .... *DVD* ⓑ
The Taking of Pelham One Two Three
1974 .... *DVD* ⓑ
The Talented Mr Ripley 1999 ...... *DVD* ⓑ
The Tall Target 1951 ....
Targets 1968 .... *DVD*
Taste of Fear 1961 .... *DVD*
Tell No One 2006 .... *DVD* ⓑ
10 Cloverfield Lane 2016 .... *DVD* ⓑ
The Terminal Man 1974 ....
Them 2006 .... *DVD* ⓑ
These Final Hours 2013 ....
Thieves' Highway 1949 ....
The Third Voice 1960 ....
13 (Tzameti) 2005 .... *DVD*
36 Hours 1964 ....
Three Days of the Condor 1975 ... *DVD* ⓑ
Thunderheart 1992 .... *DVD*
Tightrope 1984 .... *DVD* ⓑ
Time after Time 1979 ....
Time and Tide 2000 .... *DVD*
A Time to Kill 1996 .... *DVD*
Tinker Tailor Soldier Spy 2011 ..... *DVD* ⓑ
Tokyo Drifter 1966 .... *DVD*
Tony Manero 2008 .... *DVD*
Total Recall 1990 .... *DVD* ⓑ
Tower Block 2012 .... *DVD* ⓑ
The Town 2010 .... *DVD* ⓑ
The Treatment 2014 ....
Triangle 2009 .... *DVD* ⓑ
Triple Agent 2003 .... *DVD*
The Troll Hunter 2010 .... *DVD* ⓑ
Trouble in Mind 1985 .... *DVD*
True Romance 1993 .... *DVD* ⓑ
Twelve Monkeys 1995 .... *DVD* ⓑ
12:01 1993 ....
28 Weeks Later 2007 .... *DVD* ⓑ
23 Paces to Baker Street 1956 ...... *DVD*
The Two Faces of January 2013 ... *DVD* ⓑ
U Turn 1997 ....
The Ultimate Warrior 1975 .... *DVD*
Underground 1995 .... *DVD*
Up at the Villa 1998 ....
Vacancy 2007 .... *DVD* ⓑ
The Vanishing 1988 .... *DVD* ⓑ
Victoria 2015 .... *DVD* ⓑ
Videodrome 1982 .... *DVD* ⓑ
Violent Cop 1989 .... *DVD*
The Voices 2014 .... *DVD* ⓑ
Wait until Dark 1967 .... *DVD* ⓑ
War of the Worlds 2005 .... *DVD* ⓑ
WarGames 1983 .... *DVD*
Watchmen 2009 .... *DVD* ⓑ
Welcome to the Punch 2012 ...... *DVD* ⓑ
Westworld 1973 ....
Whatever Happened to Aunt Alice?
1969 .... *DVD*
Where Eagles Dare 1969 .... *DVD* ⓑ
Wild Target 1993 ....
The Window 1949 ....
Winter's Bone 2010 .... *DVD* ⓑ
The X-Files 1998 .... *DVD*
The Yakuza 1975 .... *DVD*
The Year of Living Dangerously 1982 ....
Zero Dark Thirty 2012 .... *DVD* ⓑ
Zero Effect 1997 ....

WAR ★★★★★

All Quiet on the Western Front
1930 ....
Army of Shadows 1969 .... *DVD* ⓑ
The Bridge on the River Kwai
1957 ....
The Dam Busters 1954 .... *DVD* ⓑ
Dishonored 1931 ....
The English Patient 1996 .... *DVD*
Fires on the Plain 1959 ....
From Here to Eternity 1953 .... *DVD* ⓑ
The Garden of the Finzi-Continis
1971 .... *DVD*
La Grande Illusion 1937 .... *DVD*
The Great Escape 1963 .... *DVD* ⓑ
Hail the Conquering Hero 1944 ....
Hope and Glory 1987 .... *DVD*
In Which We Serve 1942 .... *DVD*
Ivan's Childhood 1962 .... *DVD*
MASH 1969 .... *DVD*
Mrs Miniver 1942 .... *DVD*
Paths of Glory 1957 .... *DVD* ⓑ
Rome, Open City 1945 .... *DVD*
Schindler's List 1993 .... *DVD* ⓑ
Son of Saul 2015 .... *DVD* ⓑ

Summer of My German Soldier 1978 ....
The Thin Red Line 1998 .... *DVD* ⓑ
To Be or Not to Be 1942 ....
To Have and Have Not 1944 .... *DVD*
Went the Day Well? 1942 .... *DVD* ⓑ

WAR ★★★★

L'Accompagnatrice 1992 ....
Air Force 1943 .... *DVD*
Alexandria Why? 1979 ....
Another Time, Another Place 1983 ..... *DVD*
Arise, My Love 1940 ....
The Army of Crime 2009 .... *DVD* ⓑ
The Ascent 1976 ....
Attack! 1956 .... *DVD*
Au Revoir les Enfants 1987 .... *DVD*
Battle Cry 1955 .... *DVD*
Battle of Britain 1969 .... *DVD* ⓑ
The Battle of Midway 1942 ....
Battle of the Bulge 1965 .... *DVD*
Battleground 1949 .... *DVD*
Beach Red 1967 ....
The Big Red One 1980 .... *DVD*
Biloxi Blues 1988 .... *DVD*
The Blue Max 1966 .... *DVD*
Bon Voyage 2003 .... *DVD*
Das Boot: the Director's Cut 1981/
1997 .... *DVD* ⓑ
The Bridge 1959 .... *DVD*
A Canterbury Tale 1944 .... *DVD*
The Captive Heart 1946 .... *DVD* ⓑ
Careful, Soft Shoulder 1942 ....
Carve Her Name with Pride 1958 ..... *DVD*
Closely Observed Trains 1966 .... *DVD*
The Cockleshell Heroes 1955 .... *DVD*
The Colditz Story 1954 .... *DVD* ⓑ
Come and See 1985 .... *DVD*
Command Decision 1948 .... *DVD*
Conspiracy of Hearts 1960 .... *DVD*
The Counterfeiters 2007 .... *DVD*
Cross of Iron 1977 .... *DVD* ⓑ
The Cruel Sea 1952 .... *DVD* ⓑ
The Dawn Patrol 1938 ....
Day One 1989 ....
Days of Glory 2006 .... *DVD* ⓑ
Destiny of a Man 1959 ....
Devils on the Doorstep 2000 ....
Diplomacy 2014 .... *DVD*
The Dirty Dozen 1967 .... *DVD*
Divided We Fall 2000 .... *DVD*
Downfall 2004 .... *DVD* ⓑ
The Dressmaker 1988 ....
The End of the Affair 1954 ....
The End of the Affair 1999 .... *DVD*
The Enemy Below 1957 .... *DVD*
Escape from Sobibor 1987 ....
Europa Europa 1991 ....
The Execution of Private Slovik 1974 .. *DVD*
Fires Were Started 1943 ....
Five Graves to Cairo 1943 .... *DVD*
For Freedom 1940 ....
49th Parallel 1941 .... *DVD* ⓑ
The Four Days of Naples 1962 ....
Four Sons 1928 ....
Friendly Fire 1979 .... *DVD*
Fury 2014 .... *DVD* ⓑ
Gallipoli 1981 .... *DVD*
General Della Rovere 1959 .... *DVD*
A Generation 1954 ....
The Goose Steps Out 1942 .... *DVD*
Grave of the Fireflies 1988 .... *DVD* ⓑ
Guadalcanal Diary 1943 ....
The Guns of Navarone 1961 .... *DVD* ⓑ
Heaven Knows, Mr Allison 1957 ..... *DVD*
Hell in the Pacific 1968 ....
The Human Comedy 1943 ....
I Was Monty's Double 1958 .... *DVD*
Ice Cold in Alex 1958 .... *DVD* ⓑ
Ill Met by Moonlight 1956 ....
The Imitation Game 2014 .... *DVD* ⓑ
In Harm's Way 1965 .... *DVD*
In the Fog 2012 ....
It Happened Here 1963 .... *DVD*
Kanal 1957 ....
Katyn 2007 .... *DVD* ⓑ
King of Hearts 1966 ....
King Rat 1965 .... *DVD*
Lacombe Lucien 1974 .... *DVD*
Land and Freedom 1995 .... *DVD*
Landscape after Battle 1970 ....
The Last Days of Mussolini 1974 ...... *DVD*
The Last Stage 1947 ....
Léon Morin, Priest 1961 .... *DVD*
Lifeboat 1944 .... *DVD* ⓑ
The Long Voyage Home 1940 ....
The Longest Day 1962 .... *DVD* ⓑ
Lust, Caution 2007 .... *DVD*
The McKenzie Break 1970 .... *DVD*
Mademoiselle Docteur 1936 ....
The Man I Married 1940 ....
Memphis Belle 1943 ....
Merrill's Marauders 1962 ....
Merry Christmas Mr Lawrence
1982 .... *DVD* ⓑ
The Messenger 2009 .... *DVD* ⓑ
A Midnight Clear 1991 .... *DVD* ⓑ
Millions like Us 1943 .... *DVD*
Mr Klein 1976 ....
My Mother's Courage 1995 ....
My Son, My Son! 1940 ....
Next of Kin 1942 ....

The Night of San Lorenzo 1981 .... *DVD* ⓑ
La Nuit Fantastique 1942 ....
The Officers' Ward 2001 .... *DVD*
Oh! What a Lovely War 1969 .... *DVD*
Operation Petticoat 1959 .... *DVD*
Orders to Kill 1958 .... *DVD*
Pastor Hall 1940 ....
The Pianist 2002 .... *DVD* ⓑ
Pimpernel Smith 1941 ....
Private's Progress 1956 ....
Reach for the Sky 1956 .... *DVD*
Regeneration 1997 .... *DVD*
Reunion in France 1942 ....
Run Silent Run Deep 1958 .... *DVD*
Saving Private Ryan 1998 .... *DVD* ⓑ
The Scarlet and the Black 1983 .... *DVD*
The Secret of Santa Vittoria 1969 ....
Seven Minutes 1989 ....
The Shop on the High Street 1965 .... *DVD*
The Shopworn Angel 1938 ....
Sink the Bismarck! 1960 .... *DVD*
So Well Remembered 1947 ....
Soldier of Orange 1977 .... *DVD*
A Song for Beko 1992 ....
Sophie Scholl: the Final Days
2005 .... *DVD* ⓑ
Stalag 17 1953 .... *DVD* ⓑ
The Story of GI Joe 1945 .... *DVD*
Suite Française 2014 ....
36 Hours 1964 ....
Thomas the Imposter 1964 ....
Three Came Home 1950 .... *DVD*
Three Kings 1999 .... *DVD* ⓑ
The Tin Drum 1979 .... *DVD* ⓑ
The Train 1964 .... *DVD*
The Tuskegee Airmen 1995 ....
Twelve o'Clock High 1949 .... *DVD*
The Two of Us 1967 ....
The Vanishing Corporal 1962 .... *DVD*
La Vie de Château 1965 .... *DVD*
Wake Island 1942 ....
A Walk in the Sun 1945 .... *DVD*
War Horse 2011 .... *DVD* ⓑ
The Way Ahead 1944 .... *DVD*
The Way to the Stars 1945 ....
Westfront 1918 1930 ....
When Trumpets Fade 1998 .... *DVD*
Where Eagles Dare 1969 .... *DVD* ⓑ

WESTERN ★★★★★

Annie Get Your Gun 1950 ....
The Big Country 1958 .... *DVD*
Brokeback Mountain 2005 .... *DVD* ⓑ
Butch Cassidy and the Sundance Kid
1969 .... *DVD* ⓑ
Calamity Jane 1953 .... *DVD*
The Covered Wagon 1923 ....
Dances with Wolves 1990 .... *DVD* ⓑ
Destry Rides Again 1939 .... *DVD*
El Dorado 1967 .... *DVD*
A Fistful of Dollars 1964 .... *DVD* ⓑ
For a Few Dollars More 1965 ...... *DVD* ⓑ
Fort Apache 1948 .... *DVD*
The Good, the Bad and the Ugly
1966 .... *DVD* ⓑ
High Noon 1952 .... *DVD*
The Iron Horse 1924 .... *DVD*
The Magnificent Seven 1960 .... *DVD* ⓑ
The Man Who Shot Liberty Valance
1962 .... *DVD* ⓑ
A Million Ways to Die in the West
2014 .... *DVD* ⓑ
My Darling Clementine 1946 .... *DVD* ⓑ
Once upon a Time in the West
1968 .... *DVD* ⓑ
The Ox-Bow Incident 1943 .... *DVD* ⓑ
Red River 1948 .... *DVD*
Rio Bravo 1958 .... *DVD* ⓑ
Rio Grande 1950 .... *DVD*
The Searchers 1956 .... *DVD* ⓑ
Shane 1953 .... *DVD* ⓑ
She Wore a Yellow Ribbon 1949 .... *DVD*
Stagecoach 1939 .... *DVD*
3:10 to Yuma 1957 .... *DVD*
The Tin Star 1957 ....
The Treasure of the Sierra Madre
1947 .... *DVD* ⓑ
Unforgiven 1992 .... *DVD* ⓑ
Way Out West 1937 .... *DVD*
The Wild Bunch 1969 .... *DVD* ⓑ

WESTERN ★★★★

Apache 1954 .... *DVD*
Appaloosa 2008 .... *DVD*
The Assassination of Jesse James by the
Coward Robert Ford 2007 ...... *DVD* ⓑ
Bad Company 1972 .... *DVD*
The Ballad of Cable Hogue 1970 .... *DVD*
The Beautiful Blonde from Bashful Bend
1949 ....
Bend of the River 1952 .... *DVD*
The Big Sky 1952 .... *DVD*
The Big Trail 1930 .... *DVD*
Billy the Kid 1941 ....
Black God, White Devil 1964 .... *DVD*
Blazing Saddles 1974 .... *DVD* ⓑ
Bone Tomahawk 2015 .... *DVD* ⓑ
Broken Arrow 1950 .... *DVD*
Broken Lance 1954 .... *DVD*
Canyon Passage 1946 ....

Cat Ballou 1965 .... *DVD*
Cheyenne Autumn 1964 ....
Cimarron 1931 ....
City Slickers 1991 .... *DVD*
Comanche Station 1960 ....
The Comancheros 1961 .... *DVD*
Cowboys & Aliens 2011 .... *DVD* ⓑ
The Culpepper Cattle Co 1972 ....
A Distant Trumpet 1964 ....
Django 1966 .... *DVD*
Django Unchained 2012 .... *DVD* ⓑ
Doc 1971 ....
Dodge City 1939 ....
Drums along the Mohawk 1939 .... *DVD*
Duel in the Sun 1946 .... *DVD*
Everything That Rises 1998 ....
Evil Roy Slade 1971 ....
Flaming Star 1960 .... *DVD*
The Furies 1950 ....
Geronimo: an American Legend 1993 ... *DVD*
The Grey Fox 1982 ....
Gunfight at the OK Corral 1957 .... *DVD*
The Gunfighter 1950 .... *DVD*
The Hanging Tree 1959 ....
The Hateful Eight 2015 .... *DVD* ⓑ
High Plains Drifter 1973 .... *DVD* ⓑ
High, Wide and Handsome 1937 ....
The Hired Hand 1971 .... *DVD*
Hombre 1967 ....
The Homesman 2014 .... *DVD* ⓑ
Hour of the Gun 1967 ....
How the West Was Won 1962 ...... *DVD* ⓑ
Invitation to a Gunfighter 1964 .... *DVD*
The Jack Bull 1999 .... *DVD*
Jesse James 1939 ....
Johnny Guitar 1954 .... *DVD*
Jubal 1956 .... *DVD*
The Last Hunt 1956 ....
Last Train from Gun Hill 1959 .... *DVD*
The Last Wagon 1956 .... *DVD*
The Law and Jake Wade 1958 .... *DVD*
Law and Order 1932 ....
The Left Handed Gun 1958 .... *DVD*
Little Big Man 1970 ....
The Lone Ranger 2013 .... *DVD* ⓑ
Lonely Are the Brave 1962 .... *DVD*
The Long Riders 1980 .... *DVD* ⓑ
McCabe and Mrs Miller 1971 ....
The Man from Laramie 1955 .... *DVD*
Man in the Saddle 1951 ....
Man of the West 1958 .... *DVD* ⓑ
Man without a Star 1955 .... *DVD*
Meek's Cutoff 2010 ....
The Missouri Breaks 1976 .... *DVD*
The Naked Spur 1953 ....
No Name on the Bullet 1959 ....
One-Eyed Jacks 1961 .... *DVD*
Open Range 2003 ....
The Outlaw Josey Wales 1976 .... *DVD*
Pat Garrett and Billy the Kid 1973 ..... *DVD*
The Plainsman 1936 ....
The Professionals 1966 .... *DVD* ⓑ
The Proud Rebel 1958 ....
Pursued 1947 ....
Ride Lonesome 1959 .... *DVD*
Ride the High Country 1962 .... *DVD*
Riders of the Purple Sage 1925 ....
Run of the Arrow 1957 ....
The Salvation 2014 .... *DVD* ⓑ
Seven Men from Now 1956 .... *DVD*
The Sheepman 1958 ....
Shenandoah 1965 .... *DVD*
The Sheriff of Fractured Jaw 1958 ....
The Shootist 1976 .... *DVD*
Silverado 1985 .... *DVD* ⓑ
Slow West 2015 .... *DVD* ⓑ
Son of Paleface 1952 ....
The Sons of Katie Elder 1965 .... *DVD*
Star in the Dust 1956 ....
Support Your Local Gunfighter 1971.... *DVD*
Support Your Local Sheriff! 1969 ..... *DVD*
The Tall Men 1955 .... *DVD*
The Tall T 1957 .... *DVD*
The Texas Rangers 1936 .... *DVD*
They Died with Their Boots On 1941 ....
3 Bad Men 1926 ....
The Three Burials of Melquiades Estrada
2005 .... *DVD* ⓑ
3:10 to Yuma 2007 .... *DVD* ⓑ
Tombstone 1993 .... *DVD* ⓑ
Tribute to a Bad Man 1956 ....
True Grit 1969 .... *DVD* ⓑ
True Grit 2010 .... *DVD* ⓑ
Two Mules for Sister Sara 1970 .... *DVD* ⓑ
Ulzana's Raid 1972 ....
The Unforgiven 1960 .... *DVD*
Vera Cruz 1954 .... *DVD* ⓑ
The Virginian 1929 ....
Wagonmaster 1950 ....
Warlock 1959 .... *DVD*
The Way West 1967 ....
The Westerner 1940 ....
When the Legends Die 1972 ....
Wild Bill 1995 .... *DVD*
Wild Rovers 1971 ....
Will Penny 1967 .... *DVD*
Winchester '73 1950 .... *DVD*
Windwalker 1980 ....
The Winning of Barbara Worth 1926 ....
The Wonderful Country 1959 ....
Wyatt Earp 1994 .... *DVD* ⓑ